50th Edition

ULRICH'S™

PERIODICALS DIRECTORY

2012

International Periodicals Information Since 1932

Ulrich's Periodicals Directory
was prepared by ProQuest Serials Editorial Department

Editorial
Laurie Kaplan, Director, Serials
Martha David, Quality Control/Technical Manager
Ewa Kowalska, Managing Editor
Valerie A. Mahon, Manager, Technical Content
Christopher King, Senior Editor
Shawn Chen, Pappaparvathi Patham, Senior Associate Editors
Halyna Testerman, Filippo Valli, and Michael Weingardner, Associate Editors
Debra James, Margit Linforth, Maria R. Mucino, Anne Picker, and Leo Weinstock, Contributing Editors

Data Acquisition
O'Sheila Delgado, Provider Relations Analyst

50th Edition

ULRICH'S™

PERIODICALS DIRECTORY

2012

International Periodicals Information Since 1932

Including

Irregular Serials & Annuals

Volume 3

Classified List of Serials
Med-G – Z

5489-8278

ProQuest®
Start here.

Published by ProQuest
630 Central Avenue, New Providence, NJ 07974

Ulrich's Hotline (U.S. only): 1-800-346-6049
Editorial (Canada only, call collect): 1-908-219-0286
ProQuest Fax (overseas users): (+1) 908-219-0182
ProQuest E-mail: ulrichs@proquest.com
URL: http://www.ulrichsweb.com

International Standard Book Number
ISBN 13: 978-1-60030-632-7 (4-Volume set)
ISBN 13: 978-1-60030-628-0 (Volume 1)
ISBN 13: 978-1-60030-629-7 (Volume 2)
ISBN 13: 978-1-60030-630-3 (Volume 3)
ISBN 13: 978-1-60030-631-0 (Volume 4)

International Standard Serial Number
0000-2100

Library of Congress Control Number
32-16320

Printed and bound in the United States of America

ISBN 978-1-60030-632-7
90000
9 781600 306327

Contents

Ulrich's Serials Librarianship Award

Presented by the Serials Section
Association for Library Collections and Technical Services (ALCTS)
Division of the American Library Association (ALA)

Sponsored by ProQuest

Formerly sponsored by R.R. Bowker LLC

This annual award is given in recognition of distinguished and ongoing contributions to serials librarianship. Qualified individuals demonstrate leadership in serials-related activities through their participation in professional associations, groups, and/or library education programs; make significant contributions to serials literature; and, in general, strive to enhance our comprehension of the serials world.

AWARD RECIPIENTS

1985 Marcia Tuttle

1986 Ruth C. Carter

1987 James P. Danky

1988 Marjorie E. Bloss

1989 John E. Merriman

1990 Jean S. Cook

1991 Deana L. Astle/Charles A. Hamaker

1992 Linda K. Bartley

1993 Ann L. Okerson

1994 Tina Feick

1995 Peter Gellatly

1996 Jean L. Hirons

1997 Cindy Hepfer

1998 Crystal Graham

1999 Regina Romano Reynolds

2000 Trisha L. Davis

2001 not awarded

2002 Eric Lease Morgan

2003 Frieda Rosenberg

2004 Pamela Bluh

2005 Dan Tonkery

2006 Karen Hunter

2007 Julia Blixrud

2008 Vicky Reich

2009 Brian Green

2010 Steve C. Shadle

2011 Peter McCracken

Preface

In the 80 years since **Ulrich's™ Periodicals Directory** was first published, technology has substantially transformed both the methods and mission of the library and research center. Access, rather than ownership, has become a key consideration. Resource sharing and networking have become common practices in the effort to maintain the flow of quality information. As promising as these changes in collections and services may be, they generate a new set of questions in nearly every sphere of serials management: acquisition; bibliographic control; conservation and preservation; access; standards; and education and training.

At ProQuest, we have set ourselves the task of addressing these transitions by developing and expanding **Ulrich's™ Periodicals Directory** in a variety of ways. Now in its 50th edition, **Ulrich's** has established itself as the premier serials reference source in the world, providing serials users with essential bibliographic and access information that ranges from subscription rates to the latest web sites. For complete details on these changes, please see the User's Guide on pages ix-xv of the prefatory material of Volumes 1-4.

As libraries, institutions, and researchers shift focus from physical ownership of materials to acquiring individual articles on demand, our coverage of document delivery services now includes 12 different services offering the full text of articles from 43,626 serials listed in **Ulrich's**. For a brief explanation of such services, please refer to the "Document Suppliers" section in the User's Guide, page xiii of the prefatory material. For contact information for these services, please see the company listings section on page xxvi of the prefatory material.

Though the printed serial is by no means on the wane, the use of electronic research tools, whether online or on CD-ROM, continues unabated. There has been a dramatic increase in the use of the Internet as a publishing medium, resulting in new breeds of serials. Electronic publications, such as e-journals and e-zines, emerge every day and are reflected in **Ulrich's**. This edition includes 83,549 serials available exclusively online or in addition to other media. 7,420 serials are indicated as available on CD-ROM. These serials are indicated by a notation in the main entry and a bullet (•) in the TITLE INDEX.

Regardless of the publication medium, serials remain the key tools for scholarship and the primary source of current information and topical news in all fields of endeavor. In toto, the 50th edition of **Ulrich's** contains information on 220,562 serials published throughout the world, classified and cross-referenced under 903 subject headings. Additionally, each entry is assigned at minimum one Dewey Decimal Classification number from the 22nd edition. Included are serials that are currently available, issued more frequently than once a year and usually published at regular intervals, as well as publications issued annually or less frequently than once a year, or irregularly. While aiming for maximum title coverage, we have established certain criteria for inclusion. We report all publications that meet the definition of a serial except administrative publications of governmental agencies below state level that can be easily found elsewhere. A limited selection of membership directories, comic books, and puzzle and game books is included.

Entries have been updated to reflect the most current information available and 11,454 serials have been added this year, some of which may have since ceased or suspended publication. Included in this edition is cessation or suspension information that has been recorded in our database during the past year for 3,481 titles. The ceased or suspended titles are preceded by a dagger (†) in the TITLE INDEX for instant identification.

Users can identify 9,388 newer serials, which are known to have begun publication since January 1, 2009, by an inverted solid triangle (▼) in both the CLASSIFIED LIST OF SERIALS and the TITLE INDEX. This symbol is also used to highlight the 509 forthcoming serial launches announced for publication in the years 2011-2012. In addition, 30,329 refereed serials notations, 98,972 brief descriptions, 56,455 LC Classification Numbers, and 17,781 CODEN appear in this edition.

Further facilitating access to serials are indicators found in 70,788 titles denoting coverage by 1,006 abstracting and indexing services, 20,845 notations of reprint availability, 60,179 e-mail addresses and 63,805 company URLs (Uniform Resource Locators on the World Wide Web).

There are many copyright implications associated with the distribution of published material from the Internet and the delivery and sharing of other documents. We therefore provide Copyright Clearance Center notations for 31,278 registered titles along with 12,174 entries with Rights & Permissions contact names. When available, we include telephone contact information as well. These data elements make it easy to comply with the law without interrupting the flow of information.

Beginning with the 34th edition, the publication date of **Ulrich's** moved from August to November. Publication in November enables us to provide thousands of updated prices for 2012 since many publishers establish prices for the upcoming year between May and October. Prices set and received by us later than mid-September were not updated for this print edition. However, data are entered as received, so price changes and other information, such as title changes, cessations, and new releases, received after mid-September will appear in issues of the electronic versions of **Ulrich's**. These include **ulrichsweb.com™**, updated weekly on the Internet at http://www.ulrichsweb.com, providing article-level content and linking to journal full-text; Ulrich's Serials Analysis System™, the collection evaluation and reporting tool for library professionals at http://www.ulrichsweb.com/analysis.

Your purchase and use of **Ulrich's** is complemented by access to the **Ulrich's Hotline**, a toll-free number that subscribers may phone for help in solving particular research problems and questions. Canadian users are asked to call a special number collect, and our overseas users are asked to use a designated fax number. (Please refer to page iv for our mailing address, telephone/fax numbers, and e-mail address.) Publishers are encouraged to e-mail updates as changes to their titles occur, using the e-mail address ulrichs@proquest.com.

As we continue to research, plan, and implement enhancements to the **Ulrich's** database and our database maintenance system, we consider feedback from our users to be essential. Please contact us to let us know your thoughts and suggestions.

Gratitude is extended to the entire staff of **Ulrich's** for their unflagging dedication and diligent work in updating and maintaining the serials database in preparation of the 50th edition of **Ulrich's**. Appreciation is also extended to all vendors and service suppliers for working with us to produce this directory. Finally, we thank the various information specialists, serialists, national libraries, and serials publishers throughout the world who have aided us in updating **Ulrich's**. We consider their participation and interest in the dissemination of accurate and comprehensive serials information to be of tremendous value to **Ulrich's** and its users.

User's Guide

This directory offers two primary access methods for locating periodicals: by subject in the CLASSIFIED LIST OF SERIALS (Volumes 1-3), and alphabetically in the TITLE INDEX (Volume 4). Ceased serials are listed in a separate CESSATIONS section (Volume 4) and are also accessible by means of the TITLE INDEX. In addition, Volume 4 provides an ISSN INDEX, the CROSS-INDEX TO SUBJECTS and the U.S. Newspapers Indexes. See the User's Guide in Volume 4 for a content description and use instructions for the U.S. NEWSPAPERS section.

Separate subheadings for "Abstracting, Bibliographies and Statistics" under major subject headings provide convenient access to these types of publications.

The "User's Guide" is separated into three divisions for ease of use: (I) Section Descriptions, (II) Full Entry Content Description, and (III) Cataloging Rules for Main Entry Title.

Section Descriptions

CLASSIFIED LIST OF SERIALS

This is the main section of the book, containing bibliographic information for currently published serials classified by subject. Entries are arranged alphabetically by title within each subject heading. Subject cross-references in the text direct the user to the location of subheadings.

Volume 1 contains subjects A - Edu-C, from "Abstracting and Indexing" through "Education-Computer Applications." Volume 2 contains subjects Edu-G - Med-F, "Education - Guides to Schools and Colleges" through "Medical Sciences - Forensic Sciences." Volume 3 contains subjects Med-G - Z, from "Medical Sciences - Gastroenterology" through "Zoology."

A complete listing of the "Subjects" used in the CLASSIFIED LIST OF SERIALS appears on p. liii. To aid international users, this list is translated into four languages. For additional guidance on the subject classification scheme, the user should also consult the CROSS-INDEX TO SUBJECTS in Volume 4, which contains additional key word references.

Each serial is listed with full bibliographic information only once. If a serial covers several subjects, title cross-references appear under the related headings, directing the user to the heading where the full entry is listed.

New serials beginning publication in the past three years, as well as titles announced for publication in the coming year are highlighted by an inverted triangle symbol ▼ in front of the title.

The "Cataloging Rules for Main Entry Title" section of this "User's Guide" explains the title cataloging rules followed in compiling **Ulrich's**.

CESSATIONS

In this section, entries for serials for which cessation was noted in the past year are listed alphabetically by title. The cessation entry includes: title, Dewey Decimal Classification number, former frequency of publication, publisher name and address, country-of-publication code, and, if available, other information such as ISSN, subtitle, corporate author, year of first issue, and year ceased. Titles which were originally planned as continuing series but which have closed are included in the CESSATIONS section although back issues may still be available.

If a title has "ceased" because a new title is being used, there will not be an entry in the CESSATIONS section. Instead, the entry is maintained in the CLASSIFIED LIST OF SERIALS under the new title, with a **"Formerly"** or **"Former titles"** indication.

ISSN INDEX

The ISSN INDEX lists serials in order by ISSN number. It includes all serials contained in the **Ulrich's** database, whether current, ceased, or inactive, to which an ISSN has been assigned in our file. A dagger symbol (†) indicates that the title is ceased. If an ISSN appears twice, it usually indicates that the serial has split into two or more parts. Titles that have changed and for which new ISSNs have been assigned will show cross-references from one ISSN to the new ISSN. If no new ISSN has been assigned, the cross-reference is from ISSN to new title. Entries for inactive titles do not appear in the book.

Boldface type indicates the page number where a complete entry can be found for active titles. ISSNs of inactive titles do not have page references. A full description of the ISSN and its use is provided on p.xvi.

TITLE INDEX

The TITLE INDEX is the second major access point for serials. To locate a serial by its title, the user should be familiar with title cataloging rules as described in the "Cataloging Rules for Main Entry Titles" paragraphs of this "User's Guide."

The TITLE INDEX lists all current and ceased serials included in this directory. **Boldface** type indicates the page number where the complete entry will be found.

For serials with identical titles published within a country, the city of publication is added in parentheses, and sometimes the year of first publication is given to further distinguish the titles.

If a serial title consists of or contains an acronym, a cross-reference is provided from the full name to the acronym form of the title.

Cross-references are provided from former titles and variant titles, and from the alternate language titles of multi-language publications. Recent title changes are noted, with a reference to the current title. The TITLE INDEX also lists the country code for all serials, along with the ISSN, if known.

The inverted triangle symbol (▼) used in the "Classified List of Serials" to indicate new serials also appears in this index, preceding the title. A dagger (†) appears preceding the title if the publication has ceased. The bullet symbol (•) indicates that the title is available in one or more electronic formats, including online, CD-ROM or e-mail, either exclusively or in addition to printed formats. The arrow symbol (➤) indicates that a title is refereed or peer-reviewed by an editorial board. These symbols appear in a new footer at the bottom of every right-hand page.

CROSS-INDEX TO SUBJECTS

This index lists alphabetically all main subject headings in the **Ulrich's** Subject Authority Database, as well as keyword references that direct users to main or subheadings where publications on those topics are likely to be found. The number following each subject term directs users to the page on which the subject begins within the CLASSIFIED LIST OF SERIALS.

A keyword may refer the user to more than one subject category. In this case, the subject references are listed in alphabetical order and are not necessarily listed in hierarchical order.

Main subject headings appear in uppercase, e.g. AGRICULTURE. Subheadings contain the main subject term in uppercase and the specific subheading term in mixed case, e.g. AGRICULTURE—Agricultural Economics. The keywords, except for acronyms, are displayed entirely in mixed case.

Full Entry Content Description

Basic Information

The following elements are mandatory for listing and appear in all entries: main entry title, frequency of publication, publisher address, country code, and Dewey Decimal Classification number.

Certain electronic journals may not have a physical mailing address; the URL and/or e-mail address provide a means of contacting the publication.

Dewey Decimal Classification Number

The Dewey Decimal number is printed at the top left of each entry. More than one Dewey number may have been assigned if a serial covers several subjects.

LC Classification Number

The Library of Congress classification number, if known, appears directly below the Dewey Decimal number. Shelf numbers are not included.

Country Code

The ISO Country Code is printed at the top center of each entry following the Dewey Decimal number. A complete list of country codes used will be found beginning on page xxii.

ISSN

The ISSN for the main entry title is printed to the right of the country code. Not all publications have been assigned an ISSN, and lack of a number does not render a publication ineligible for listing.

CODEN

The CODEN designation, if known, is printed directly below the country code and ISSN. The CODEN is an alphanumeric code, applied uniquely to a specific publication. Devised by the American Society for Testing and Materials, it is used primarily for scientific and technical titles. New CODEN are assigned by Chemical Abstracts Service.

Title Information

The main title is printed in **boldface** and uppercase as the first item in the entry. Titles are catalogued according to rules described below in the "Cataloging Rules for Main Entry Title" section. For multi-language publications, the parallel language title is also printed in uppercase, immediately following the main entry title, and is separated from it by a slash.

An inverted triangle symbol (▼) printed before the title indicates that the title began publishing within the past three years. This symbol also appears before titles announced for publication in the coming year. An asterisk (*) printed after the title indicates that the address in the entry was not verified by the publisher for this edition.

The subtitle is printed in lowercase after the title. Variant titles are given within the entry and are labeled as such. The Key Title, which is assigned at the time of ISSN assignment by the responsible center of the International Serials Data System, is given only if it is different from the main entry title. Former titles are given at the end of the bibliographic data. See the paragraph below.

Language

The language or languages is given, even if a serial is written in the main language of the country of publication. The order of languages is generally alphabetical and does not represent prominence. If a serial includes abstracts, summaries or sections in additional language(s), that information will be provided as well.

Year First Published

The year first published is given if provided by the publisher. If a title has been suspended and later resumed publication, these dates may be provided as well. If volume numbering was restarted, the notation "N.S." denoting new series precedes the date. If information is lacking, a volume number and specific year may be provided to indicate the approximate age of the publication.

Frequency

The frequency of publication is given in abbreviated form, such as "a." for annual, "irreg." for irregular, "m." for monthly, "3/yr." for three times per year. All abbreviations used are listed in the "General Abbreviations and Special Symbols" on page xix.

Price

Unless otherwise indicated, the price given is the annual price for an individual subscription in the currency of the country of origin. The price in U.S. dollars may also be given if it is provided by the publisher. No attempt is made to convert foreign currency to U.S. dollars. Separate postage information is not given, since postal rates vary widely. A complete list of ISO currency codes used will be found beginning on page xx.

Special Features

A listing of special features may include such items as book or other types of reviews, advertising (usually meaning commercial, not classified advertising), charts, illustrations, bibliography section, article abstracts, and an annual index to the periodical's contents.

Reprint Services

If a serial is known to be available from a reprint service, a code referring to the service appears in the entry. More than one code may be listed. For a list of reprint services and a translation of the codes, please refer to page xxx.

Pages Per Issue; Columns Per Page

When known, the number of pages per issue (p./no.:) and/or columns per page (cols./p.:) is/are noted.

Refereed Serial

The manuscript peer review and evaluation system is utilized to protect, maintain and raise the quality of scholarly material published in serials. The arrow symbol (➤) appears before the title if a serial is known to be refereed or juried. This information is generally provided by the serial publisher.

Document Type

Notations are included to indicate type of publication, e.g. Academic/Scholarly, Trade, Newsletter, or Abstract/Index. The words "**Document type**" appear in boldface, followed by the document type description, in entries where this information is known. More than one document type may be listed for a single publication, if applicable.

Brief Description

A brief description of the contents and editorial focus of the publication may be provided, preceded by the word "**Description:**" at the end of the bibliographic data.

These descriptions were submitted by the publisher or were written by editorial staff after examination of sample copies or publisher catalogs.

Former Titles

Title changes are common phenomena in serials publishing. Many entries contain extensive former title information, providing a history of changes which may be useful for bibliographic record-keeping. Previous titles for the serial are given, along with their ISSN, if known. ISSN are assigned to specific titles and therefore change with the title. The former titles are preceded by a description of the type of title change. Simple title changes are noted by the words "Formerly" or "Former titles." Other types may include mergers, incorporations or supersessions. Dates provided are generally the date that the change became effective. For mergers and incorporations, date ranges indicate the years of publication for that previous title.

Media

The primary medium is specified for other than the traditional print on paper, with the exception of the notation "Duplicated." Common media listed include Online, CD-ROM, Diskette,

Microfilm and Microfiche. Online - full text denotes that the entire text of all the articles of a serial is available online, while Online - full content denotes that the entire content including graphics is available. If a serial is primarily available in Braille or Large Type, that notation will be found here.

Related Titles

This section provides information on all available formats, editions and related publications. Often the title and ISSN are provided. The diamond symbol (◆) indicates that there is a complete listing elsewhere in the CLASSIFIED LIST OF SERIALS. Please refer to the TITLE INDEX for the page number of that listing. When no complete record is available, data such as start year, frequency, or price may be provided.

Information on alternate media editions, such as online, CD-ROM or microform editions, is provided here. For publications available in microform, a three-letter code for the vendor or micropublisher is provided. A list of names, addresses, and contact information begins on page xxviii.

Abstracting and Indexing

The notation "**Indexed**" precedes a list of abbreviations for all abstracting and indexing services known to cover the serial on a regular basis. The complete names of the abstracting and indexing services are listed with their abbreviations on page xxxiii. This section also includes status information and related titles. Consult the TITLE INDEX for page references to entries in the CLASSIFIED LIST OF SERIALS for active services.

SAMPLE ENTRY

1 641.337 **2** USA **3** ISSN 1234-5678
4 HD9199.A1 **5** CODEN: COCIEO

6 ➤ **7** **CHINESE JOURNAL OF COFFEE RESEARCH;** **8** short articles on coffee research. **9** Key title: Coffee Research **10** (In 3 sections.) **11** Text in Chinese, English. **12** 1987. **13** 24/yr. (in 2 vols.) **14** USD 136 in US and Canada; USD 148 elsewhere (effective 2001) **15** bk.rev. abstr. illus. cum. index: 1987-1997; **16** back issues avail.; reprint service avail. from SWZ,UMI **17** 8 cols./p., 20 p./no. **18** **Document type**: *Academic/scholarly.* **19** **Description:** Offers articles, coffee news and data analyses to scientists, engineers and research managers.

20 **Supersedes in part** (in 1989): Acta Scientifica Cafe **21** (0000-8888); Which was formerly: Coffee Research Techniques

22 **Media:** Online - full text (from Grinder, Inc.) **23** **Related titles:** CD-ROM ed.: Coffee Research on Disc. 1992. q. USD 32. (from Cafe Institute (File no.42), Platter Corp.); Microfilm ed. (from SMI); Japanese ed.: ISSN 2345-6789. Supplement: Annual Coffee Review. ISSN 6789-1234.

24 **Indexed:** Food Sci.& Tech.Abstr.

25 --- BLDSC (1234.567890), CISTI, GNLM **26** **CCC.**

27 **Published by:** (Coffee Research Institute), **28** Chinese Coffee Inc., **29** 140 US Rte 400, Parsippany, NJ 07974. **30** TEL 908-665-2800, **31** FAX 908-771-7725, **32** Telex 9735 PARV TH, **33** usinfo@coffee.com, **34** http://www.coffeeresearch.com. **35** Eds. Shawn King, Jane Weiner. **36** Pub. Richard Stocker. **37** R&P Ewa Picker TEL 908-665-2875. **38** Adv. contact Sankar Lara **39** adv.: B&W page USD 2,300, color page USD 3,500; trim 7 x 10. **40** circ. 5,000 (paid); 3,200 (controlled) **41** Wire service: SP **42** **Subscr. in the Americas to:** Science Research Centre, Regional Sales Office, PO Box 435, New York, NY 10159-0945. TEL 212-465-7645, FAX 212-576-4785; **43** **Dist. by:** Cafe Distributors, 23 Chen Lu, Beijing 100031, People's Republic of China. TEL 86-10-12345, FAX 86-10-34567. **44** **Co-sponsors:** Chinese Coffee Organization; Chinese Science Society. **Affiliate:** United States Coffee Research Society.

KEY

1 Dewey Decimal Classification
2 ISO Country Code
3 ISSN
4 LC Classification
5 CODEN
6 Refereed Symbol
7 Main Entry Title
8 Subtitle
9 Key Title
10 Bibliographic Note
11 Language
12 First Published
13 Frequency
14 Price
15 Special Features
16 Back Issues & Reprint
17 Page Format
18 Document Type
19 Brief Description
20 Title Changes
21 Former ISSN
22 Media
23 Related Editions
24 Abstracting & Indexing
25 Document Suppliers
26 Copyright Clearance Center
27 Corporate Author
28 Publishing Company
29 Address
30 Telephone
31 Fax
32 Telex
33 E-mail
34 URL
35 Editor
36 Publisher
37 Rights & Permissions Contact
38 Advertising Contact
39 Advertising Rates
40 Circulation
41 Wire Service
42 Subscription
43 Distributor
44 Co-sponsors and other bodies

Document Suppliers

These notations are preceded by an em-dash (—). The presence of a notation indicates the availability of articles from that serial through the specified service, by permission from the copyright holder. Such permissions are subject to change without notice. Articles may be available in paper and/or electronic format, depending on the service. The full names and complete address and contact information for these companies are listed beginning on page xxvi.

The British Library Document Supply Centre shelfmark number, a unique identifier of each serial, appears in parentheses after that organization's code, ex. "BLDSC (0000.000000)." The format of the shelf mark is four digits, a decimal point, then six digits.

The **Ulrich's** database and the individual databases of document suppliers were matched on the presence of ISSNs. When a match was successful, the appropriate document supplier code was noted. Not all serials titles in general or in these individual databases, have ISSNs. Therefore, the absence of one or any document supplier codes in an **Ulrich's** listing does not necessarily mean the title is not available from one or any of these suppliers.

Copyright Clearance Center, Inc.

Copyright Clearance Center, Inc. (CCC), the largest licenser of text reproduction rights in the world, was formed in 1978 to facilitate compliance with U.S. Copyright law. CCC provides licensing systems for reproduction and distribution of copyrighted materials in print and electronic formats. CCC manages rights for over 1.75 million works and represents over 9,600 publishers and hundreds of thousands of authors and other creators, directly or through their representatives. CCC-licensed customers in the U.S. number over 10,000 corporations and subsidiaries, and thousands of government agencies, law firms, document suppliers, libraries, academic institutions, copy shops and bookstores.

The boldfaced CCC notation appears in the entries of titles for which the CCC has been authorized by the publisher to grant photocopy permissions on any of their works.
Contact them at 222 Rosewood Dr., Danvers, MA 01923, USA; tel: 978-750-8400; fax: 978-750-4470;
URL: http://www.copyright.com.

Publishing Company Information

This section begins with the bold phrase "**Published by**" or "***Address***" if the company name is the same as the title.

Many serials are editorially controlled by a sponsoring organization or corporate author and published by a commercial publisher. In these instances, the commercial publishing company's name and address are given, and the name of the corporate author is given in parentheses immediately preceding. In other instances, either a sponsoring organization or a commercial publishing company has sole responsibility, and only one name is given. We avoid listing printers as publishing companies, preferring the name and address of someone with editorial responsibility. For the same reason, we avoid listing distributors as publishing companies.

Telephone, Fax, Telex Numbers, E-mail, and Web Site Addresses

Telephone, fax, telex numbers and e-mail as well as web site addresses (URLs) are given when provided by the publisher. U.S. and Canadian numbers are given in standard North American format. Toll-free numbers within U.S. and Canada are also included, when available. Numbers in other countries are provided in the same format as supplied by the publisher, resulting in some inconsistencies (e.g. sometimes with a country and/or city code, sometimes without). Users are advised to consult an international operator before placing calls.

Editor

Only one or two names are given when known, preceded by the notation "Ed." or "Eds." Advanced degrees and titles are omitted, except for medical, military and religious titles; absence of a title does not mean that the editor has none.

Publisher

Only one or two names are given when known, preceded by the notation "Pub." or "Pubs." Advanced degrees and titles are omitted, except for medical, military and religious titles; absence of a title does not mean that the publisher has none.

If the publisher is also the editor, and no publishing company name is available, the person's name is given in place of company name with the notation "Ed. & Pub."

Rights and Permissions Contact

A name is given when supplied, preceded by the notation "R&P contact." The telephone number information follows, when known and different from the main number.

Advertising Rates and Contact

When provided by the publisher, the name of the advertising contact, as well as full-page advertising rates and sizes are indicated. Most dimensions are listed in millimeters, except for U.S. publications, the dimensions of which are usually in inches.

Circulation

All circulation figures used are approximate. Circulation is given only if provided by the publisher. The notation "controlled" indicates that the publication is available only to qualified persons, usually members of a particular trade or profession. The notation "paid" indicates that subscribers pay to receive the publication, while the notation "free" indicates that the title is freely distributed.

Wire Services

If a newspaper is known to use one or more news or photo wire services, abbreviations or names of the services used are listed in the entry. Such information is preceded by the words "Wire Service(s)." Abbreviations for wire services used are listed on page xxxi of this volume.

Subscription or Distribution Information

A second address is given only if the address for ordering subscriptions is different from the publishing company's address. Distributors are listed only if we have been informed that a particular organization is the exclusive distributor. Additional subscription and/or distribution offices of international publishers are listed, if known. Telephone and fax numbers and e-mail and URL addresses for subscription and/or distribution offices appear if provided by the publisher.

Other related organizations and companies such as co-sponsors, affiliates, or co-publishers may be noted here.

Newspaper Ownership

The name of the owner(s) of a newspaper is listed, usually accompanied by the owner(s) address, and telephone and fax numbers. The owner address may differ from the newspaper location address. Owner information is preceded by the notation "Owner(s):."

Cataloging Rules for Main Entry Title

The majority of titles in the Ulrich's database were cataloged according to *Anglo-American Cataloging Rules* prior to 1978, the date of the new edition of *Anglo-American Cataloging Rules. The new AACR II* reflects a trend toward the Key Title concept of cataloging as used by the International Serials Data System (ISDS) and published in its *International Standard Bibliographic Description for Serials* (1974).

Because recataloging such a database was not feasible, our cataloging rules were modified but not radically changed. Cross-references are provided in the TITLE INDEX from variant forms of title, such as Key Title, to aid users searching by other methods.

Whenever possible, main entry title cataloging is done from a sample of the title page of the most recent issue, according to the following rules:

Articles at the beginning of titles are omitted, or are bypassed in filing.

Serials with distinctive titles are usually entered under title. For example:

Annual Bulletin of Historical Literature
Business Week
Milton Studies

If a title consists only of a generic term followed by the name of the issuing body, or if the name of the issuing body clarifies the content of the publication, entry is under the name of the issuing body. For example:

Newsetter of the American Theological Library Association

is entered as

American Theological Library Association. Newsletter

Economic Performance and Prospects, issued by the Private Development Corporation of the Philippines

is entered as

Private Development Corporation of the Philippines. Economic Performance and Prospects

A title which consists of a subject modified generic term followed by the name of the issuing body is considered nondistinctive and is entered under the name of the isssuing body. For example:

Annual Meeting Scientific Proceedings of the American Animal Hospital Association

is entered as

American Animal Hospital Association. Annual Meeting Scientific Proceedings

Government publications with nondistinctive titles are entered under the name of the government jurisdiction of the issuing body, although distinctive titles of government organizations may be entered directly under title. For example:

Great Britain. Economic and Social Research Council. Annual Report

but

Statistical Abstract of Iceland

Titles which begin with the initials of the issuing body are entered under the initials. Cross-references from the full name are provided in the TITLE INDEX.

If a geographic name is part of the name of the issuing body, entry will be under the common form of the name of the body.

For example:

University of the West Indies. Vice-Chancellor's Report

not

West Indies. University. Vice-Chancellor's Report

Note, however, that government publications retain similar cataloging as government jurisdiction.

Canada. Statistics Canada. Field Crop Reporting Series

Multilingual titles are entered under the first title given on the title page, or the first title reported by the publisher if the title page is not available. Titles in other languages are entered directly after the main entry title. Cross-references are provided in the TITLE INDEX for each language title.

FILING RULES

Due to the restrictions imposed by computer filing of titles, the following special filing rules should be noted. The majority of punctuation marks are treated as spaces. A combination of punctuation and spaces is treated as one space.

Acronyms and initials are treated as such and are listed at the beginning of each letter of the alphabet.

D H Lawrence Review
D.L.A.N.Y. Newsletter
D N R
Dade County Teacher

Hyphenated words are treated as separate words:

Pre-Text

precedes

Preaching

Initial articles may be provided for a title, but do not affect their alphabetization. Articles and prepositions within titles are alphabetized as words:

Journal of the West

precedes

Journal of Theological Studies

Diacritical marks have been omitted. The German and Scandinavian umlaut has been replaced by the letter "e" following the vowels a, e, o, and u. In Danish, Norwegian, and Swedish, the letter å is sequenced as "aa" and the letter Ø as "oe."

International Standard Serial Number (ISSN)

1. What is the ISSN?

An internationally accepted, concise, unique, and unambiguous code for the identification of serial publications. One ISSN represents one serial title.

The ISSN consists of seven numbers with an eighth check digit calculated according to Modulus 11 and used to verify the number in computer processing. A hyphen is printed after the fourth digit, as a visual aid, and the acronym, ISSN, precedes the number.

2. How did the ISSN evolve as an international system?

The International Organization for Standardization Technical Committee 46 (ISO/TC 46) is the agency responsible for the development of the ISSN as an international standard. The organization responsible for the administration and coordination of ISSN assignments worldwide is the ISSN International Centre in Paris, which is supported by the French government and UNESCO.

ISSNs are assigned by over 50 national centers worldwide. The National Serials Data Program (NSDP) is the U.S. national center. The centers form a network that is coordinated by the ISSN International Centre located in Paris.

The implementation of the ISSN system started with the numbering of 70,000 titles in the serials database of R.R. Bowker (*Ulrich's International Periodicals Directory and Irregular Serials and Annuals*). The next serials database numbering was the *New Serials Titles 1950-70* cumulation listing 220,000 titles, cumulated, converted to magnetic tape, and published by R.R. Bowker in collaboration with the Serials Record Division of the Library of Congress. These two databases were used as the starting base for the implementation of the ISSN.

3. What types of publications are assigned ISSNs?

For assignment of an ISSN, a serial is defined as a publication in print or non-print form, issued in successive parts, usually having numerical or chronological designations, and intended to be continued indefinitely.

4. How is the ISSN used?

The ISSN is employed as a component of bar codes and as a tool for the communication of basic information about a serial title and for such processes as ordering, billing, inventory control, abstracting, and indexing. In library processes, the ISSN is used in operations such as acquisitions, claiming, binding, accessioning, shelving, cooperative cataloging, circulation, interlibrary loans, and retrieval of requests.

5. Can a publication have an International Standard Book Number (ISBN) and an ISSN?

Yes! Monographic series (separate works issued indefinitely under a common title, generally in a uniform format with numeric designations) and annuals or titles planned to be issued indefinitely under the same title may be defined as serials. The ISSN is assigned to the serial title, while an ISBN is assigned to each individual title or monograph in the series.

A new ISBN is assigned to each volume or edition by the publisher, while the ISSN, which is assigned by the ISSN International Centre or national ISSN centers, remains the same for each issue. Both numbers should be printed on the copyright page or other appropriate page of each volume, with their acronyms or words preceding each number for immediate identification. With the availability of both an ISSN and ISBN, the problem of defining the overlap of serials and monographs has been resolved.

SAMPLE TITLE

Advances in the Biosciences
ISSN 0065-3446

Vol. 1 Proceedings: Berlin. Schering
Symposium of Endocrinology, Berlin. Ed.
by Gerhard Raspe. 1969. 40.00
(ISBN 0-08-013395-9). Pergamon.

Vol. 2 Proceedings. Schering
Symposium on Biodynamics & Mechanisms
of Action of Steroid Hormones, Berlin. Ed.
by Gerhard Raspe. 1969. 41.25
(ISBN 0-08-006942-8). Pergamon.

Vol. 3 Proceedings. Schering Workshop on Steroid Metabolism "in Vitro Versus in Vivo," Berlin. Ed. by Gerhard Raspe. 1969. 41.25 (ISBN 0-08-017544-9). Pergamon.

Vol. 4 Proceedings. Schering Symposium on Mechanisms Involved in Conception. Berlin. Ed. by Gerhard Raspe. 1970. Text ed. 41.25 (ISBN 0-08-017546-5). Pergamon.

Vol. 25 Development of Responsiveness to Steroid Hormones. Alvin M. Kaye & Myra Kaye et al. LC 79-42938. 1980. 66.00 (ISBN 0-08-024949-X). Pergamon.

6. Where should the ISSN appear on the serial?

In a prominent position on or in each issue of the serial, such as the front cover, back cover, masthead, title, or copyright pages. The international standard recommendation is that the ISSN of a periodical be printed, whenever possible, in the upper right corner of the front cover. Promotional and descriptive materials about the serial should include the ISSN.

7. When a title changes, is a new ISSN assigned?

In most instances, a new ISSN is assigned when a title changes. However, the determination is made by the ISSN International Centre or the appropriate national ISSN centers. Publishers should report all the title changes to their respective centers.

8. How does a publisher apply for an ISSN?

The publisher should contact the appropriate national ISSN center or the ISSN International Centre. Centers require bibliographic evidence of a serial, including a copy of the title page and cover. There is no charge to publishers for the assignment of ISSNs.

For full information, publishers should contact the national library or bibliographic center in the country where they are publishing. The address of the ISSN International Centre is:

ISSN International Centre
45, rue de Turbigo
75003 Paris
France
Tel: +33 (0) 1 44 88 22 20
Fax:+33 (0) 1 40 26 32 43
E-mail: issnicissn.org
URL: http://www.issn.org

The address for the U.S. national ISSN center is:

National Serials Data Program (NSDP)
Library of Congress
Washington, DC 20540-4160
Tel: 202-707-6452
Fax: 202-707-6333
E-mail: ISSNloc.gov
URL: http://lcweb.loc.gov/issn

9. What is SISAC?

SISAC stands for the Serials Industry Systems Advisory Committee. SISAC is an industry group formed to develop voluntary standardized formats for electronically transmitting serials business transaction information. SISAC provides a forum where serial (particularly journal) publishers, library system vendors, and librarians discuss mutual concerns regarding the electronic transmission of serial information and develop cooperative solutions, in the form of standardized formats, to efficiently address these concerns. (*Reprinted permission from SISAC.*)

10. What is the SISAC Symbol (SICI) and its relationship to the ISSN?

The Serial Item and Contribution Identifier (SICI) is a serial identification code that follows the ISSN and is a string letters and/or numbers that uniquely identify a particular issue of a serial. Encoded in the SICI are chronological and enumeration data that identify serials by date volume/issue numbers. According to SISAC, "the ANSI* standard extends the code down to the article level adding location number and necessary title information, plus a record validation character. Code 128 is the code symbology selected by SISAC for displaying number string in scannable form. When displayed in Code 128 symbology, the SICI is called the SISAC symbol." The SICI is the ANSI standard; the SISAC symbol is the bar code. (*Reprinted with permission SISAC.*)

*ANSI American National Standards Institute. Organization coordinates the voluntary standards system in the United States. member of the International Standards Organization (ISO).

Abbreviations

General Abbreviations and Special Symbols

a.	annual
abstr.	abstracts
adv.	advertising
approx.	approximately
avail.	available
B&W	Black & White
bi-m.	bimonthly (every two months)
bi-w.	biweekly (every two weeks)
bibl.	bibliographies
bk.rev.	book reviews
CCC	Copyright Clearance Center
c/o	care of
circ.	circulation
cols./p.	columns per page
cum.index	cumulative index
Cy.	County
d.	daily
dance rev.	dance reviews
Dir.	Director
dist.	distributed
ed., eds.	edition(s)
Ed., Eds.	Editor(s)
film rev.	film reviews
fortn.	fortnightly (every two weeks)
ISSN	International Standard Serial Number
illus.	illustrations
irreg.	irregular
m.	monthly, month
mkt.	market prices
mos.	months
music rev.	music reviews
N.S.	New Series
no., nos.	number(s)
pat.	patents
play rev.	play reviews (theater reviews)
p./no.	pages per issue/number
Prof.	Professor
pt.	point type
Pub., Pubs.	Publisher(s)
q.	quarterly
R&P	Rights & Permissions
rec.rev.	record reviews
rev.	reviews
s-a.	semiannually (twice annually)
s-m.	semimonthly (twice monthly)
s-w.	semiweekly (twice weekly)
software rev.	software reviews
stat.	statistics
subscr.	subscription
tel.rev.	television program reviews
3/m.	3 times a month
3/w.	3 times a week
3/yr.	3 times a year
tr.lit.	trade literature (manufacturers' catalogs, reader response cards)
tr.mk.	trade marks
video rev.	video reviews
vol., vols.	volume(s)
w.	weekly, week
yr., yrs.	year(s)
●	electronic serial
▼	new serial
†	ceased
•	complete listing available
➤	refereed xix

Currency Codes

This list of world currencies and their codes is the International Standards Organization (ISO) set of three-letter currency abbreviations. This is the complete list of ISO codes, though not all currencies may be present in **Ulrich's**. The codes are mnemonic in most cases, with the first two letters representing the country name and the third representing the currency name.

CODE	CURRENCY
ADP	Andorran Peseta
AED	United Arab Emirates Dirham
AFA	Afghanistan Afghani
ALL	Albanian Lek
AMD	Armenian Dram
ANG	Netherlands Antillian Guilder
AON	Angolan New Kwanza
ARS	Argentinean Peso
ATS	Austrian Schilling
AUD	Australian Dollars
AWG	Aruban Florin
AZM	Azerbaijan Manat
BAD	Bosnian Dinar
BAM	Bosnia & Herzegovina Convertible Mark
BBD	Barbados Dollar
BDT	Bangladeshi Taka
BEF	Belgian Franc
BGL	Bulgarian Lev
BHD	Bahraini Dinar
BIF	Burundi Franc
BMD	Bermudan Dollar
BND	Brunei Dollar
BOB	Bolivian Boliviano
BPS	British Pounds Sterling
BRL	Brazilian Real
BSD	Bahamian Dollar
BTN	Bhutan Ngultrum
BWP	Botswanan Pula
BYB	Belarus Ruble
BZD	Belize Dollar
CHF	Swiss Franc
CLP	Chilean Peso
CND	Canadian Dollars
CNY	Yuan (Chinese) Renminbi
COP	Colombian Peso
CRC	Costa Rican Colon
CSD	Serbian Dinar
CUP	Cuban Peso
CVE	Cape Verde Escudo
CYP	Cyprus Pound
CZK	Czech Koruna
DEM	Deutsche Mark
DJF	Djibouti Franc

CODE	CURRENCY
DKK	Danish Krone
DOP	Dominican Peso
DZD	Algerian Dinar
ECS	Ecuador Sucre
EEK	Estonian Kroon
EGP	Egyptian Pound
ERB	Eritrean Birr
ESP	Spanish Peseta
ETB	Ethiopian Birr
EUR	Euro
FIM	Finnish Markka
FJD	Fiji Dollar
FKP	Falkland Islands Pound
FRF	French Franc
GBP	British Pound
GEL	Georgian Lari
GHC	Ghanaian Cedi
GIP	Gibraltar Pound
GMD	Gambian Dalasi
GNF	Guinea Franc
GNS	Guinea Syli
GRD	Greek Drachma
GTQ	Guatemalan Quetzal
GWP	Guinea-Bissau Peso
GYD	Guyanan Dollar
HKD	Hong Kong Dollar
HNL	Honduran Lempira
HRK	Croatian Kuna
HTG	Haitian Gourde
HUF	Hungarian Forint
IDR	Indonesian Rupiah
IEP	Irish Punt
ILS	Israeli Shekel
INR	Indian Rupee
IQD	Iraqi Dinar
IRR	Iranian Rial
ISK	Iceland Krona
ITL	Italian Lira
JMD	Jamaican Dollar
JOD	Jordanian Dinar
JPY	Japanese Yen
KES	Kenyan Schilling
KGS	Kyrgyzstan Som
KHR	Cambodian New Riel

KMF	Comoros Franc
KPW	North Korean Won
KRW	South Korean Won
KWD	Kuwaiti Dinar
KYD	Cayman Islands Dollar
KZT	Kazakhstani Tenge
LAK	Lao Kip
LBP	Lebanese Pound
LKR	Sri Lanka Rupee
LRD	Liberian Dollar
LSL	Lesotho Loti
LTL	Lithuanian Litas
LUF	Luxembourg Franc
LVL	Latvian Lat
LYD	Libyan Dinar
MAD	Moroccan Dirham
MDL	Moldova Leu
MGF	Malagasy Franc
MKD	Macedonian Denar
MLF	Mali Franc
MMK	Myanmar Kyat
MNT	Mongolian Tugrik
MOP	Macao Pataca
MRK	German Marks
MRO	Mauritanian Ouguiya
MTL	Maltese Lira
MUR	Mauritius Rupee
MVR	Maldive Rufiyaa
MWK	Malawi Kwacha
MXN	Mexican New Peso
MYR	Malaysian Ringgit
MZM	Mozambique Metical
NAD	Namibian Dollar
NGN	Nigerian Naira
NIC	Nicaraguan Gold Cordoba
NLG	Dutch Guilder
NOK	Norwegian Kroner
NPR	Nepalese Rupee
NZD	New Zealand Dollar
OMR	Omani Rial
PAB	Panamanian Balboa
PEN	Peruvian New Sol
PGK	Papua New Guinea Kina
PHP	Philippine Peso
PKR	Pakistan Rupee
PLZ	Polish Zloty
PTE	Portuguese Escudo
PYG	Paraguay Guarani
QAR	Qatari Rial
ROL	Romanian Leu
RUR	Russian Ruble
RWF	Rwanda Franc
SAR	Saudi Arabian Riyal
SBD	Solomon Islands Dollar
SCR	Seychelles Rupee
SDP	Sudanese Pound
SEK	Swedish Krona
SGD	Singapore Dollar
SHP	St. Helena Pound
SIT	Slovenian Tolar
SKK	Slovakian Koruna
SLL	Sierra Leone Leone
SOS	Somali Schilling
SRG	Suriname Guilder
SSP	South Sudanese Pound
STD	Sao Tome and Principe Dobra
SVC	El Salvador Colon
SYP	Syrian Pound
SZL	Swaziland Lilangeni
THB	Thai Bhat
TJR	Tajikistan Rubl
TMM	Turkemenistan Manat
TND	Tunisian Dinar
TOP	Tongan Pa'anga
TPE	East Timor Escudo
TRL	Turkish Lira
TTD	Trinidad and Tobago Dollar
TWD	Taiwan Dollar
TZS	Tanzanian Schilling
UAK	Ukraine Hryvnia
UGX	Uganda Shilling
USD	US Dollars
UYP	Peso Uruguayo
UZS	Uzbek Som
VEB	Venezuelan Bolivar
VND	Vietnamese Dong
VUV	Vanuatu Vatu
WST	Somoan Tala
XAF	CFA Franc BEAC
XDR	Special Drawing Rights
XEC	Eastern Caribbean Dollar
XOF	CFA Franc BCEAO
XPF	French Polynesian Franc
YER	Yemeni Rial
YUN	Yugoslavian New Dinar
ZAR	South African Rand
ZMK	Zambian Kwacha
ZWD	Zimbabwe Dollar

Country of Publication Codes

Foreign Publishers are listed with the three letter International Standards Organization (ISO) code for their country of domicile. This is the complete list of ISO codes though not all countries may be represented. The codes are mnemonic in most cases. The country names here may be shortened to a more common usage form.

Code Sequence

ABW	ARUBA
AFG	AFGHANISTAN
AGO	ANGOLA
AIA	ANGUILLA
ALB	ALBANIA
AND	ANDORRA
ANT	NETHERLANDS ANTILLES
ARG	ARGENTINA
ARM	ARMENIA
ASM	AMERICAN SAMOA
ATA	ANTARCTICA
ATF	FRENCH SOUTHERN TERRITORIES
ATG	ANTIGUA & BARBUDA
AUS	AUSTRALIA
AUT	AUSTRIA
AZE	AZERBAIJAN
BDI	BURUNDI
BEL	BELGIUM
BEN	BENIN
BFA	BURKINA FASO
BGD	BANGLADESH
BGR	BULGARIA
BHR	BAHRAIN
BHS	BAHAMAS
BIH	BOSNIA & HERZEGOVINA
BLR	BELARUS
BLZ	BELIZE
BMU	BERMUDA
BOL	BOLIVIA
BRA	BRAZIL
BRB	BARBADOS
BRD	WEST GERMANY
BRN	BRUNEI DARUSSALAM
BTN	BHUTAN
BVT	BOUVET ISLAND
BWA	BOTSWANA
BWI	BRITISH WEST INDIES
CAF	CENTRAL AFRICAN REPUBLIC
CAN	CANADA
CCK	COCOS (KEELING) ISLANDS
CHE	SWITZERLAND
CHL	CHILE
CHN	CHINA
CIV	COTE' D' IVOIRE
CMR	CAMEROON
COD	CONGO, THE DEMOCRATIC REPUBLIC OF
COG	CONGO
COK	COOK ISLANDS
COL	COLOMBIA
COM	COMOROS
CPV	CAPE VERDE
CRI	COSTA RICA
CSK	CZECHOSLOVAKIA
CUB	CUBA
CXR	CHRISTMAS ISLAND
CYM	CAYMAN ISLANDS
CYP	CYPRUS
CZE	CZECH REPUBLIC
DDR	EAST GERMANY
DEU	GERMANY
DJI	DJIBOUTI
DMA	DOMINICA
DNK	DENMARK
DOM	DOMINICAN REPUBLIC
DZA	ALGERIA
ECU	ECUADOR
EGY	EGYPT (ARAB REPUBLIC OF EGYPT)
ERI	ERITREA
ESH	WESTERN SAHARA
ESP	SPAIN
EST	ESTONIA
ETH	ETHIOPIA
FIN	FINLAND
FJI	FIJI
FLK	FALKLAND ISLANDS
FRA	FRANCE
FRO	FAROE ISLANDS
FSM	FEDERATED STATES OF MICRONESIA
GAB	GABON
GBR	UNITED KINGDOM
GEO	GEORGIA
GHA	GHANA
GIB	GIBRALTAR
GIN	GUINEA
GLP	GUADELOUPE
GMB	GAMBIA
GNB	GUINEA-BISSAU
GNQ	EQUATORIAL GUINEA
GRC	GREECE
GRD	GRENADA
GRL	GREENLAND
GTM	GUATEMALA
GUF	FRENCH GUIANA
GUM	GUAM
GUY	GUYANA
HKG	HONG KONG
HMD	HEARD ISLAND & MCDONALD ISLANDS
HND	HONDURAS
HRV	CROATIA
HTI	HAITI
HUN	HUNGARY
IDN	INDONESIA
IND	INDIA
IOT	BRITISH INDIAN OCEAN TERRITORY
IRL	IRELAND
IRN	IRAN, ISLAMIC REPUBLIC OF
IRQ	IRAQ
ISL	ICELAND
ISR	ISRAEL
ITA	ITALY
JAM	JAMAICA
JOR	JORDAN
JPN	JAPAN
KAZ	KAZAKSTAN
KEN	KENYA
KGZ	KYRGYZSTAN
KHM	CAMBODIA
KIR	KIRIBATI
KNA	SAINT KITTS & NEVIS
KOR	KOREA, REPUBLIC OF
KOS	KOSOVA
KWT	KUWAIT
LAO	LAO PEOPLE'S DEMOCRATIC
LBN	LEBANON
LBR	LIBERIA
LBY	LIBYAN ARAB JAMAHIRIYA
LCA	ST. LUCIA
LIE	LIECHTENSTEIN
LKA	SRI LANKA
LSO	LESOTHO
LTU	LITHUANIA
LUX	LUXEMBOURG
LVA	LATVIA
MAC	MACAU
MAR	MOROCCO
MCO	MONACO
MDA	MOLDOVA, REPUBLIC OF
MDG	MADAGASCAR
MDV	MALDIVE ISLANDS
MEX	MEXICO
MHL	MARSHALL ISLANDS
MKD	MACEDONIA
MLI	MALI
MLT	MALTA
MMR	MYANMAR
MNE	MONTENEGRO
MNG	MONGOLIA
MNP	NORTHERN MARIANA ISLANDS
MOZ	MOZAMBIQUE

MRT	MAURITANIA
MSR	MONTSERRAT
MTQ	MARTINIQUE
MUS	MAURITIUS
MWI	MALAWI
MYS	MALAYSIA
MYT	MAYOTTE
NAM	NAMIBIA
NCL	NEW CALEDONIA
NER	NIGER
NFK	NORFOLK ISLAND
NGA	NIGERIA
NIC	NICARAGUA
NIU	NIUE
NLD	NETHERLANDS
NOR	NORWAY
NPL	NEPAL
NRU	NAURU
NZL	NEW ZEALAND
OMN	OMAN
PAK	PAKISTAN
PAN	PANAMA
PCN	PITCAIRN
PER	PERU
PHL	PHILIPPINES
PLW	PALAU
PNG	PAPUA NEW GUINEA
POL	POLAND
PRI	PUERTO RICO
PRK	KOREA, DEMOCRATIC PEOPLE'S REPUBLIC OF
PRT	PORTUGAL
PRY	PARAGUAY
PSE	OCCUPIED PALESTINIAN TERRITORY
PYF	FRENCH POLYNESIA
QAT	QATAR
REU	REUNION
ROM	ROMANIA
RUS	RUSSIAN FEDERATION
RWA	RWANDA
SAU	SAUDI ARABIA
SCG	SERBIA & MONTENEGRO
SDN	SUDAN
SEN	SENEGAL
SGP	SINGAPORE
SGS	SOUTH GEORGIA & THE SANDWICH ISLANDS
SHN	SAINT HELENA
SJM	SVALBARD & JAN MAYEN
SLB	SOLOMON ISLANDS
SLE	SIERRA LEONE
SLV	EL SALVADOR
SMR	SAN MARINO
SOM	SOMALIA
SPM	SAINT PIERRE & MIQUELON
SRB	SERBIA
SSD	SOUTH SUDAN, REPUBLIC OF
STP	SAO TOME E PRINCIPE
SUN	U.S.S.R.
SUR	SURINAME
SVK	SLOVAKIA
SVN	SLOVENIA
SWE	SWEDEN
SWZ	SWAZILAND
SYC	SEYCHELLES
SYR	SYRIAN ARAB REPUBLIC
TCA	TURKS & CAICOS ISLANDS
TCD	CHAD
TGO	TOGO
THA	THAILAND
TJK	TAJIKISTAN
TKL	TOKELAU
TKM	TURKMENISTAN
TMP	EAST TIMOR
TON	TONGA
TTO	TRINIDAD & TOBAGO
TUN	TUNISIA
TUR	TURKEY
TUV	TUVALU
TWN	TAIWAN, REPUBLIC OF CHINA
TZA	TANZANIA, UNITED REPUBLIC
UAE	UNITED ARAB EMIRATES
UGA	UGANDA
UKR	UKRAINE
UMI	UNITED STATES MINOR OUTLYING ISLANDS
URY	URUGUAY
USA	UNITED STATES
UZB	UZBEKISTAN
VAT	VATICAN CITY STATE (HOLY SEE)
VCT	SAINT VINCENT & THE GRENADINES
VEN	VENEZUELA
VGB	VIRGIN ISLANDS, BRITISH
VIR	VIRGIN ISLANDS, U. S.
VNM	VIET NAM
VUT	VANUATU
WLF	WALLIS & FUTUNA
WSM	SAMOA
YEM	YEMEN
YUG	YUGOSLAVIA
ZAF	SOUTH AFRICA
ZAR	ZAIRE
ZMB	ZAMBIA
ZWE	ZIMBABWE

Country Sequence

AFGHANISTAN	AFG
ALBANIA	ALB
ALGERIA	DZA
AMERICAN SAMOA	ASM
ANDORRA	AND
ANGOLA	AGO
ANGUILLA	AIA
ANTARCTICA	ATA
ANTIGUA & BARBUDA	ATG
ARGENTINA	ARG
ARMENIA	ARM
ARUBA	ABW
AUSTRALIA	AUS
AUSTRIA	AUT
AZERBAIJAN	AZE
BAHAMAS	BHS
BAHRAIN	BHR
BANGLADESH	BGD
BARBADOS	BRB
BELARUS	BLR
BELGIUM	BEL
BELIZE	BLZ
BENIN	BEN
BERMUDA	BMU
BHUTAN	BTN
BOLIVIA	BOL
BOSNIA & HERZEGOVINA	BIH
BOTSWANA	BWA
BOUVET ISLAND	BVT
BRAZIL	BRA
BRITISH INDIAN OCEAN TERRITORY	IOT
BRITISH WEST INDIES	BWI
BRUNEI DARUSSALAM	BRN
BULGARIA	BGR
BURKINA FASO	BFA
BURUNDI	BDI
CAMBODIA	KHM
CAMEROON	CMR
CANADA	CAN
CAPE VERDE	CPV
CAYMAN ISLANDS	CYM
CENTRAL AFRICAN REPUBLIC	CAF
CHAD	TCD
CHILE	CHL
CHINA	CHN
CHRISTMAS ISLAND	CXR
COCOS (KEELING) ISLANDS	CCK
COLOMBIA	COL
COMOROS	COM
CONGO	COG
CONGO, THE DEMOCRATIC REPUBLIC OF	COD
COOK ISLANDS	COK
COSTA RICA	CRI
COTE' D' IVOIRE	CIV
CROATIA	HRV
CUBA	CUB
CYPRUS	CYP
CZECH REPUBLIC	CZE
CZECHOSLOVAKIA	CSK
DENMARK	DNK
DJIBOUTI	DJI
DOMINICA	DMA
DOMINICAN REPUBLIC	DOM
EAST GERMANY	DDR
EAST TIMOR	TMP
ECUADOR	ECU
EGYPT (ARAB REPUBLIC OF EGYPT)	EGY
EL SALVADOR	SLV
EQUATORIAL GUINEA	GNQ
ERITREA	ERI
ESTONIA	EST
ETHIOPIA	ETH
FALKLAND ISLANDS	FLK
FAROE ISLANDS	FRO
FEDERATED STATES OF MICRONESIA	FSM
FIJI	FJI
FINLAND	FIN
FRANCE	FRA
FRENCH GUIANA	GUF
FRENCH POLYNESIA	PYF
FRENCH SOUTHERN TERRITORIES	ATF
GABON	GAB
GAMBIA	GMB
GEORGIA	GEO
GERMANY	DEU
GHANA	GHA
GIBRALTAR	GIB
GREECE	GRC
GREENLAND	GRL
GRENADA	GRD
GUADELOUPE	GLP
GUAM	GUM
GUATEMALA	GTM
GUINEA	GIN
GUINEA-BISSAU	GNB
GUYANA	GUY
HAITI	HTI
HEARD ISLAND & MCDONALD ISLANDS	HMD
HONDURAS	HND
HONG KONG	HKG
HUNGARY	HUN
ICELAND	ISL
INDIA	IND
INDONESIA	IDN
IRAN, ISLAMIC REPUBLIC OF	IRN
IRAQ	IRQ
IRELAND	IRL
ISRAEL	ISR
ITALY	ITA
JAMAICA	JAM
JAPAN	JPN
JORDAN	JOR
KAZAKSTAN	KAZ
KENYA	KEN
KIRIBATI	KIR
KOREA, DEMOCRATIC PEOPLE'S REPUBLIC OF	PRK
KOREA, REPUBLIC OF	KOR
KOSOVA	KOS
KUWAIT	KWT
KYRGYZSTAN	KGZ
LAO PEOPLE'S DEMOCRATIC	LAO
LATVIA	LVA
LEBANON	LBN
LESOTHO	LSO
LIBERIA	LBR
LIBYAN ARAB JAMAHIRIYA	LBY
LIECHTENSTEIN	LIE
LITHUANIA	LTU
LUXEMBOURG	LUX
MACAU	MAC
MACEDONIA	MKD
MADAGASCAR	MDG
MALAWI	MWI
MALAYSIA	MYS
MALDIVE ISLANDS	MDV
MALI	MLI
MALTA	MLT
MARSHALL ISLANDS	MHL
MARTINIQUE	MTQ
MAURITANIA	MRT
MAURITIUS	MUS
MAYOTTE	MYT
MEXICO	MEX
MOLDOVA, REPUBLIC OF	MDA
MONACO	MCO
MONGOLIA	MNG
MONTENEGRO	MNE
MONTSERRAT	MSR

MOROCCO	MAR
MOZAMBIQUE	MOZ
MYANMAR	MMR
NAMIBIA	NAM
NAURU	NRU
NEPAL	NPL
NETHERLANDS	NLD
NETHERLANDS ANTILLES	ANT
NEW CALEDONIA	NCL
NEW ZEALAND	NZL
NICARAGUA	NIC
NIGER	NER
NIGERIA	NGA
NIUE	NIU
NORFOLK ISLAND	NFK
NORTHERN MARIANA ISLANDS	MNP
NORWAY	NOR
OCCUPIED PALESTINIAN TERRITORY	PSE
OMAN	OMN
PAKISTAN	PAK
PALAU	PLW
PANAMA	PAN
PAPUA NEW GUINEA	PNG
PARAGUAY	PRY
PERU	PER
PHILIPPINES	PHL
PITCAIRN	PCN
POLAND	POL
PORTUGAL	PRT
PUERTO RICO	PRI
QATAR	QAT
REUNION	REU
ROMANIA	ROM
RUSSIAN FEDERATION	RUS
RWANDA	RWA

SAINT HELENA	SHN
SAINT KITTS & NEVIS	KNA
SAINT PIERRE & MIQUELON	SPM
SAINT VINCENT & THE GRENADINES	VCT
SAMOA	WSM
SAN MARINO	SMR
SAO TOME E PRINCIPE	STP
SAUDI ARABIA	SAU
SENEGAL	SEN
SERBIA	SRB
SERBIA & MONTENEGRO	SCG
SEYCHELLES	SYC
SIERRA LEONE	SLE
SINGAPORE	SGP
SLOVAKIA	SVK
SLOVENIA	SVN
SOLOMON ISLANDS	SLB
SOMALIA	SOM
SOUTH AFRICA	ZAF
SOUTH GEORGIA & THE SANDWICH ISLANDS	SGS
SOUTH SUDAN, REPUBLIC OF	SSD
SPAIN	ESP
SRI LANKA	LKA
ST. LUCIA	LCA
SUDAN	SDN
SURINAME	SUR
SVALBARD & JAN MAYEN	SJM
SWAZILAND	SWZ
SWEDEN	SWE
SWITZERLAND	CHE
SYRIAN ARAB REPUBLIC	SYR
TAIWAN, REPUBLIC OF CHINA	TWN
TAJIKISTAN	TJK

TANZANIA, UNITED REPUBLIC	TZA
THAILAND	THA
TOGO	TGO
TOKELAU	TKL
TONGA	TON
TRINIDAD & TOBAGO	TTO
TUNISIA	TUN
TURKEY	TUR
TURKMENISTAN	TKM
TURKS & CAICOS ISLANDS	TCA
TUVALU	TUV
U.S.S.R.	SUN
UGANDA	UGA
UKRAINE	UKR
UNITED ARAB EMIRATES	UAE
UNITED KINGDOM	GBR
UNITED STATES	USA
UNITED STATES MINOR OUTLYING ISLANDS	UMI
URUGUAY	URY
UZBEKISTAN	UZB
VANUATU	VUT
VATICAN CITY STATE (HOLY SEE)	VAT
VENEZUELA	VEN
VIET NAM	VNM
VIRGIN ISLANDS, BRITISH	VGB
VIRGIN ISLANDS, U.S.	VIR
WALLIS & FUTUNA	WLF
WEST GERMANY	BRD
WESTERN SAHARA	ESH
YEMEN	YEM
YUGOSLAVIA	YUG
ZAIRE	ZAR
ZAMBIA	ZMB
ZIMBABWE	ZWE

Document Suppliers

AskIEEE — **AskIEEE**
20 Westport, Ste 105, Wilton, CT 06897
TEL 800-422-4633
E-mail askieee@ieee.org
URL http://ieee.org/portal/pages/services/askieee/index.html

BLDSC — **British Library Document Supply Centre**
Boston Spa, Wetherby, West Yorkshire LS23 7BQ, United Kingdom
TEL 44-1937-546060,
FAX 44-1937-546333
E-mail customer-services@bl.uk
URL http://www.bl.uk/articles

CASDDS — **Chemical Abstracts Service Document Detective Service**
Service discontinued effective March, 2011

CIS — **ProQuest Congressional**
(Subsidiary of: ProQuest)
789 E. Eisenhawer Pkwy, PO Box 1346, Ann Arbor, MI 48106-1346
TEL 800-521-0600
FAX 888-241-5612
E-mail academicinfo@proquest.com
URL http://proquest.com

East View — **East View Information Services**
10601 Wayzata Blvd, Minneapolis, MN 55305
TEL 952-252-1201, 800-477-1005,
FAX 952-252-1202
E-mail info@eastview.com
URL http://www.eastview.com

GNLM — **German National Library of Medicine /Deutsche Zentralbibliothek fuer Medizin**
Gleueler Str 60, Cologne 50931, Germany
TEL 49-221-4787109,
FAX 49-221-4787451
E-mail dokulieferung@zbmed.de
URL http://www.zbmed.de/en/search-and-order/lieferdienste/document-delivery.html

IE — **Information Express**
565 Middlefield Rd, 2nd, Menlo Park, CA 94025-3443
TEL 650-812-3588,
FAX 650-812-3570
E-mail orders@ieonline.com
URL http://www.ieonline.com

Infotrieve — **Infotrieve**
20 Westport Rd, Ste 105, PO Box 7102, Wilton, CT 06897
TEL 203-423-2175, 800-422-4633,
FAX 203-423-2155
E-mail service@infotrieve.com
URL http://www4.infotrieve.com/docdelivery.asp

ingenta — **IngentaConnect**
(Subsidiary of: Publishing Technology Plc.)
875 Massachusetts Ave., 7th Fl., Cambridge, MA 02139
TEL 617-497-6514, 800-772-4570
FAX 617-354-6875
E-mail help@ingentaconnect.com
URL http://www.ingentaconnect.com/

INIST — **Centre National de la Recherche Scientifique, Institut de l'Information Scientifique et Technique**
8, rue Jean Calvin, Paris 75005, France
TEL 33-1-45350177,
FAX 33-1-43370019
2, Allee du Parc de Brabois, CS 10310, Vandoeuve-les-Nancy 54519, France
TEL 33-3-83504600,
FAX 33-3-83504650
URL http://www.inist.fr, http://www.inist.fr/spip.php?article63

Linda Hall **Linda Hall Library of Science, Engineering & Technology, Document Delivery Services**
5109 Cherry St, Kansas City, MO 64110-2498
TEL 816-363-4600, 800-662-1545,
FAX 816-926-8785
E-mail requests@lindahall.org
URL http://www.lindahall.org/services/document_delivery/

PADDS **Petroleum Abstracts Document Delivery System**
Univeristy of Tulsa - McFarlin Library, 2933 E 6th St, Tulsa, OK 74104-3123
TEL 918-631-2231, 800-247-8678,
FAX 918-613-3823
URL http://www.pa.utulsa.edu/padds.mhtml

Micropublishers and Distributors

AJP **American Jewish Periodical Center**
No Longer a Micropublisher

ALP **Alpha Com**
Sportallee 6, Hamburg 22335, Germany
TEL 49-40-51302-0,
FAX 49-40-51302111
E-mail info-hamburg@alpha-com.de
URL http://www.alpha-com.de

BHP **Brookhaven Press**
(Division of: N M T Corporation)
PO Box 2287, La Crosse, WI 54602-2287
TEL 608-781-0850,
FAX 608-781-3883
E-mail brookhaven@nmt.com
URL http://www.brookhavenpress.com

BNQ **Bibliotheque et Archives Nationales du Quebec**
2275, rue Holt, Montreal, PQ H2G 3H1, Canada
TEL 514-873-1100, 800-363-9028,
FAX 514-873-9312
URL http://www.banq.qc.ca/

CIS **ProQuest Congressional**
(Subsidiary of: ProQuest)
789 E. Eisenhawer Pkwy, PO Box 1346, Ann Arbor, MI 48106-1346
TEL 800-521-0600
FAX 888-241-5612
E-mail academicinfo@proquest.com
URL http://proquest.com

CML **Commonwealth Imaging**
200, 1601-9th Ave SE, Calgary, AB T2G 0H4, Canada
TEL 403-245-2555, 800-267-2555,
FAX 403-228-5712
URL http://www.commonwealthimaging.com/

EVP **East View Information Services**
10601 Wayzata Blvd, Minneapolis, MN 55305
TEL 952-252-1201, 800-477-1005,
FAX 952-252-1202
E-mail info@eastview.com
URL http://www.eastview.com

IDC **I D C Publishers**
(Subsidiary of: Brill)
PO Box 9000, Leiden 2300, Netherlands
TEL 31-71-5353500,
FAX 31-71-5317532
E-mail info@idc.nl
URL http://www.idc.nl

LCP **The Library of Congress Duplication Service**
101 Independence Ave SE, Washington, DC 20540-4917
TEL 202-707-5640,
FAX 202-707-1771
E-mail duplication@loc.gov
URL http://www.loc.gov/duplicationservices/

LIB **B M I Imaging Systems**
1115 E Arques Ave, Sunnyvale, CA 94805
TEL 800-359-3456,
FAX 408-736-4397
E-mail info@bmiimaging.com
URL http://www.bmiimaging.com

MIM **Elsevier**
No Longer a Micropublisher

MML **Micromedia ProQuest**
(Subsidiary of: ProQuest)
789 E Eisenhower Pkwy, PO Box 1346, Anne Arbor, MI 48106-1346
TEL 734-761-4700, 800-521-0600
URL http://www.proquest.com

MMP **McLaren Micropublishing**
37 Hocken Ave, Toronto, ON M6G 2K1, Canada
TEL 416-651-1610
E-mail mmicro@interlog.com
URL http://home.interlog.com/~mmicro/home.htm

NBI **Newsbank, Inc.**
5801 Pelican Bay Blvd., Ste. 600, Naples, FL 34108
TEL 802-875-2910, 800-762-8182,
FAX 239-263-3004
E-mail sales@newsbank.com
URL http://www.newsbank.com

NTI **U.S. Department of Commerce, National Technical Information Service**
5301 Shawnee Rd, Alexandria, VA 22312
TEL 703-605-6050, 888-584-8332,
FAX 703-605-6900
E-mail customerservice@ntis.gov
URL http://www.ntis.gov

PMC **Princeton Microfilm Corp.**
43 Princeton Hightstown Rd #C, Princeton Jct, NJ 08550-1118
TEL 609-452-2066, 800-257-9502,
FAX 609-275-6201

PQC **ProQuest**
(Subsidiary of: Cambridge Information Group)
789 E Eisenhower Pky, PO Box 1346, Ann Arbor, MI 48106
TEL 734-761-4700, 800-521-0600,
FAX 734-997-4040, 888-241-5612
E-mail info@proquest.com
URL http://www.proquest.com

RPI **Primary Source Media**
(Subsidiary of: Gale)
12 Lunar Dr, Woodbridge, CT 06525-2398
TEL 203-397-2600, 800-444-0799,
FAX 203-397-3893
E-mail gale.sales@cengage.com
URL http://www.gale.cengage.com/psm/

SOC **Societe Canadienne du Microfilm Inc. /Canadian Microfilming Company Limited**
464, rue Saint-Jean, Ste 110, Montreal, PQ H2Y 2S1, Canada
TEL 514-288-5404,
FAX 514-843-4690
E-mail info@socami.qc.ca
URL http://www.socami.qc.ca

SWZ **Nashuatec Farrington**
No Longer a Micropublisher

WMP **World Microfilms**
PO Box 35488, St John's Wood, London NW8 6WD, United Kingdom
TEL 44-20-75864499,
FAX 44-20-77221068
E-mail microworld@ndirect.co.uk
URL http://www.microworld.uk.com/

WSH **William S. Hein & Co., Inc.**
1285 Main St, Buffalo, NY 14209
TEL 716-882-2600, 800-828-7571,
FAX 716-883-8100
E-mail order@wshein.com
URL http://www.wshein.com

Reprint Services

IRC **International Reprint Corp.**
287 E H St, Benicia, CA 94510
TEL 707-746-8740,
FAX 707-746-1643
E-mail irc@intlreprints.com
URL http://www.intlreprints.com

PSC **Periodicals Service Co.**
11 Main St, Germantown, NY 12526
TEL 518-537-4700,
FAX 518-537-5899
E-mail psc@periodicals.com
URL http://www.periodicals.com

SCH **Schmidt Periodicals GmbH**
Dettendorf Roemerring 12, Bad Feilnbach D
83075, Germany
TEL 49-8064221,
FAX 49-8064557
E-mail schmidt@periodicals.com
URL http://www.periodicals.com

WSH **William S. Hein & Co., Inc.**
1285 Main St, Buffalo, NY 14209-1987
TEL 716-882-2600, 800-828-7571
FAX 716-883-8100
E-mail order@wshein.com
URL http://www.wshein.com

Wire Services

AAP **Australian Associated Press**
3 Rider Blvd, Rhodes Waterside, Rhodes, NSW 2138, Australia
TEL 61-2-93228000
URL http://aap.com.au

AFP **Agence France-Presse**
11-15 Place de la Bourse, Paris 75002, France
TEL 33-1-40414646
E-mail contact@afp.com
URL http://www.afp.com

AP **Associated Press**
450 W 33rd St, New York, NY 10001
TEL 212-621-1500
E-mail info@ap.org
URL http://www.ap.org

APP **Associated Press of Pakistan**
18, Mauve Area, G-7/1, Islamabad, Pakistan
TEL 92-51-2203064,
FAX 92-51-2203069
E-mail news@app.com.pk
URL http://www.app.com.pk

BNS **Baltic News Service**
(Subsidiary of: Alma Media Group)
Toompuiestee 35, Tallinn 15043, Estonia
TEL 372-6108800,
FAX 372-6108811
E-mail bns@bns.ee
URL http://www.bns.ee

CNS **Creators Syndicate**
5777 West Century Blvd, Ste 700, PO Box 120190, Los Angeles, CA 90045
TEL 310-337-7003,
FAX 310-337-7625
E-mail info@creators.com
URL http://www.creators.com

CaNS **Catholic News Service**
3211 Fourth St, NE, Washington, DC 20017
TEL 202-541-3250,
FAX 202-541-3255
E-mail cns@catholicnews.com
URL http://www.catholicnews.com

CanP **The Canadian Press**
36 King St East, Toronto, ON M5C 2L9, Canada
TEL 416-364-0321
FAX 416-364-0207
E-mail info@cp.org
URL http://www.thecanadianpress.com

CiNS **City News Service**
11400 W Olympic Blvd, Ste 780, Los Angeles, CA 90064
TEL 310-481-0404,
FAX 310-481-0416
E-mail news@socalnews.com
URL http://www.socalnews.com

DJNS **Dow Jones Newswires**
(Subsidiary of: Dow Jones & Company)
1155 Avenue of the Americas, 7th Fl, New York, NY 10036
TEL 800-223-2274
E-mail newswires@dowjones.com
URL http://dowjones.com/product-djnewswires.asp

EFE **Agencia EFE**
C/Espronceda, 32, Madrid 28003, Spain
TEL 34-91-3467400, 34-91-3467100
E-mail comunicacion@efe.es
URL http://www.efe.com/

GNS **Gannett News Service**
7950 Jones Branch Dr, McLean, VA 22107
TEL 703-854-5800,
FAX 703-854-2152
URL http://www.gannett.com

JTA **Jewish Telegraphic Agency**
330 Seventh Ave, 17th Fl, New York, NY 10001
TEL 212-643-1890,
FAX 212-643-8499
E-mail newsdesk@jta.org
URL http://www.jta.org

LAT-WAT **Los Angeles Times-Washington Post News Service**
Service discontinued effective January 2010

MCT **McClatchy-Tribune Information Services**
700 12th St, NW, Ste 1000, Washington, DC 20005
TEL 202-383-6095, 800-435-7578
URL http://www.mctdirect.com

NYT **New York Times News Service**
620 Eight Ave, 9th Fl, New York, NY 10018
TEL 212-556-1927
E-mail nytimes@nytimes.com
URL http://www.nytsyn.com

PR **PR Newswire Association LLC**
350 Hudson St, Ste 300, New York, NY 10014
TEL 800-776-8090,
FAX 800-793-9313
URL http://www.prnewswire.com

RN **Reuters**
(Subsidiary of: Thomson Reuters Corp.)
The Thomson Reuters Building, 30 South Colonnade, Canary Wharf, London E14 5EP, United Kingdom
TEL 44-20-72501122
URL http://www.reuters.com

SAPA **South African Press Association**
Cotswold House, Greenacres Office Park, Cnr. Victory & Rustenburg Rds, Victory Park, PO Box 7766, Johannesburg 2000, South Africa
TEL 27-11-7821600,
FAX 27-11-7821587
E-mail comms@sapa.org.za
URL http://www.sapa.org.za

SH **Scripps Howard News Service**
1090 Vermont Ave., N.W., Ste. 1000, Washington, DC 20005
TEL 202-408-1484,
FAX 202-408-2062
E-mail copelandp@shns.com
URL http://www.shns.com

UPI **United Press International**
1133 19th St NW, Washington, DC 20036
TEL 202-898-8000,
FAX 202-898-8048
E-mail jugo@upi.com
URL http://www.upi.com

Abstracting and Indexing Services

This list contains the full names of all abstracting and indexing services whose abbreviations are used in entries in the CLASSIFIED LIST OF SERIALS. For all currently published abstracting and indexing services, please consult the TITLE INDEX for page references to full entries in the CLASSIFIED LIST OF SERIALS. (Bibliographic information on titles for which cessations were noted more than one year ago are not listed in this book. To view information on such titles, one must refer to ulrichsweb.com

A

A&AAb †Astronomy and Astrophysics Abstracts (Supersedes (in 1969): Astronomischer Jahresbericht)

A&ATA A A T A Online (Art and Archaeology Technical Abstracts) (Former titles (until 2002): Art and Archaeology Technical Abstracts (Print Edition); (until 1966): I I C Abstracts)

A01 Academic Search Complete

A02 Academic Search Elite

A03 Academic Search Premier

A04 Alt HealthWatch

A05 Applied Science & Technology Full Text

A06 Art Index Retrospective: 1929-1984

A07 Art Full Text

A08 Academic Search Alumni Edition

A09 Associates Program Source

A10 Associates Program Source Plus

A11 Australia/New Zealand Reference Centre

A12 ABI/INFORM Global (American Business Information)

A13 ABI/INFORM Research (American Business Information)

A14 ABI/INFORM Select (American Business Information)

A15 ABI/INFORM Trade & Industry (American Business Information)

A16 ABI/INFORM Dateline (American Business Information)

A17 ABI/INFORM (American Business Information)

A18 ABI/INFORM Archive Complete (American Business Information)

A20 Arts and Humanities Search

A21 ATLA Religion (American Theological Library Association)

A22 ArticleFirst

A23 Applied Science & Business Periodicals Retrospective: 1913-1983

A24 Applied Science & Technology Index Retrospective: 1913-1983

A25 Academic ASAP

A26 Academic OneFile

A27 Arts Module

A28 Aerospace & High Technology Database

A29 Algology Mycology and Protozoology Abstracts (Microbiology C)

A30 Art & Architecture Index

A31 Art & Architecture Complete

A32 Aqualine

A33 Arctic & Antarctic Regions (AAR)

A34 Animal Science Database

A35 AgBiotechNet

A36 Abstracts on Hygiene and Communicable Diseases

A37 Agricultural Engineering Abstracts

A38 Animal Breeding Abstracts

A39 Academic Papers Database

AA Art Abstracts

AAR Accounting Articles (Formerly: C C H Accounting Articles)

ABC †BioCommerce Abstracts (Formerly (until 1997): Abstracts in Biocommerce)

ABCPolSci C S A Political Science & Government (Cambridge Scientific Abstracts) (Formerly (until vol. 32, no. 6, 2000): A B C Pol Sci)

ABCT †ARTbibliographies Current Titles (Email Edition) (Formerly (until 2003): ARTbibliographies Current Titles (Print Edition))

ABSTRACTING AND INDEXING SERVICES

ABIPC	Abstract Bulletin of Paper Science and Technology (Former titles (until 1998): Institute of Paper Science and Technology. Abstract Bulletin; (until Jul.1989): Institute of Paper Chemistry. Abstract Bulletin; (until 1958): Institute of Paper Chemistry. Bulletin)
ABIX	†A B I X: Australasian Business Intelligence (Former titles: A B I X; (until 1995): Australian Business Index)
ABIn	ABI/INFORM Complete
ABM	ARTbibliographies Modern
ABRCLP	†Abstracts of Book Reviews in Current Legal Periodicals
ABS&EES	American Bibliography of Slavic and East European Studies (Formerly (until 1966): American Bibliography of Russian and East European Studies)
ABSML	†Abstracts of Bulgarian Scientific Medical Literature (Online Edition) (Former titles (until 1996): Abstracts of Bulgarian Scientific Medical Literature (Print Edition); (until 1968): Abstracts of Bulgarian Scientific Literature. Medicine; (until 1966): Abstracts of Bulgarian Scientific Literature. Medicine and Physical Culture; (until 1963): Abstracts of Bulgarian Scientific Literature. Biology and Medicine)
ABTICS	†Abstracts and Book Title Index Card Service (ABTICS)
AC&P	†Criminology, Penology & Police Science Abstracts (Formed by the merger of: Police Science Abstracts; Which was formerly: Abstracts on Police Science; Criminology and Penology Abstracts; Abstracts on Criminology and Penology; Excerpta Criminologica)
AD&D	†Alcohol, Drugs and Driving (Formerly: Alcohol, Drugs and Driving: Abstracts and Reviews)
ADPA	†Accounting & Finance Abstracts (Former titles (until 2001): Anbar Accounting & Finance Abstracts; (until 1991): Accounting & Data Processing Abstracts; Which superseded in part: Anbar Management Services Abstracts)
AEBA	Agricultural & Environmental Biotechnology Abstracts (Online)
AEI	Australian Education Index (Online)
AES	†Abstracts of English Studies
AESIS	†A M F Alert (Australian Mineral Foundation) (Formed by the merger of (1976-1998): A E S I S Quarterly; (1995-1998): A M F Reviews; Which was formerly (1973-1995): Earth Science and Related Information)
AFA	†American Fisheries Abstracts
AFS	†Abstracts of Folklore Studies
AGBP	†Guide to Botanical Periodicals (Formerly: Asher's Guide to Botanical Periodicals)
AHCI	†Abstracts in Human - Computer Interaction (Formerly: H C I Abstracts)
AHCMS	†Abstracts of Health Care Management Studies (Formerly: Abstracts of Hospital Management Studies)
AIA	†Artificial Intelligence Abstracts (US)
AIAP	Avery Index to Architectural Periodicals
AICP	Anthropological Index Online
AIDS Ab	†AIDS Abstracts (Formerly (until 1993): AIDS Information)
AIDS&CR	†AIDS & Cancer Research
AIIM	†Abstracts in Medicine and Key Word Index (Formerly: Abstracts in Internal Medicine)
AIM	†Abridged Index Medicus *consists of:* †Cumulated Abridged Index Medicus
AIPP	†Roth's American Poetry Annual (Incorporates (1985-1986): Annual Survey of American Poetry; (1983-1986): American Poetry Index; (1984-1986): Annual Index to Poetry in Periodicals)
AIT	†A I T Reports and Publications on Energy. Abstracts (Asian Institute of Technology) (Formerly: A I T Reports and Publications on Renewable Energy Resources. Abstracts)
AJEE	†Abstract Journal in Earthquake Engineering
ALISA	†A L I S A (Online) (Australian Library and Information Science Abstracts) (Formerly (until 1996): A L I S A (Print))
ALMD	Australian Legal Monthly Digest (Formerly (until 1967): Legal Monthly Digest)
AMB	Abstracts of Military Bibliography (Former titles (until 1976): Resumenes Analiticos sobre Defensa y Seguridad Nacional; (until 1970): Resumenes Analiticos de Bibliografia Militar)
AMED	A M E D (Allied and Complementary Medicine Database)
AMHA	†Adolescent Mental Health Abstracts
AMR	†European Muslims and Christian-Muslim Relations. Abstracts
ANAG	†Abstracts of North American Geology
APA	Advanced Polymers Abstracts
APC	†Abstracts of Popular Culture
APD	†Acid Precipitation Digest
APEL	Asian - Pacific Economic Literature
API	Architectural Publications Index (Formerly (until 1995): Architectural Periodicals Index; Supersedes: R I B A Library Bulletin)
APIAb	EnCompassLit (Formerly: A P I Lit)
APICat	Technical Literature Abstracts: Catalysts - Zeolites (Online)

APIH&E Technical Literature Abstracts: Health & Environment (Online)
APIOC Technical Literature Abstracts: Oilfield Chemicals (Online)
APIPR Technical Literature Abstracts: Petroleum Refining & Petrochemicals (Online)
APIPS Technical Literature Abstracts: Petroleum Substitutes (Online)
APITS Technical Literature Abstracts: Transportation & Storage (Online)
APW Alt-PressWatch
ARDT †Abstracts on Rural Development in the Tropics
ARG Abridged Readers' Guide to Periodical Literature
ARI †Australian Road Index
AS&TA Applied Science & Technology Abstracts
AS&TI Applied Science & Technology Index
ASA †Australian Speleo Abstracts
ASCA Personal Alert (E-mail) (Former titles: Research Alert (Print); (until 1989): Automatic Subject Citation Alert; A S C A Topics)
ASD †African Studies Abstracts (Formerly (until 1994): Afrika Studiecentrum. Documentatieblad)
ASEANManA A S E A N Management Abstracts (Association of Southeast Asian Nations) (Formerly (until 1982): Management Abstracts of Singapore)
ASFA Aquatic Sciences & Fisheries Abstracts
consists of:
A S F A Aquaculture Abstracts (Online)
A S F A Marine Biotechnology Abstracts (Online)
Aquatic Sciences & Fisheries Abstracts. Part 1: Biological Sciences and Living Resources
Aquatic Sciences & Fisheries Abstracts. Part 2: Ocean Technology, Policy and Non-living Resources
Aquatic Sciences & Fisheries Abstracts. Part 3: Aquatic Pollution and Environmental Quality
ASG Abstracts in Social Gerontology
ASI †Australian Science Index
ASIP Access: The Supplementary Index to Periodicals (Incorporates (1978-1979): Monthly Periodical Index)
ASLHA †American Speech - Language - Hearing Abstracts
ASSIA A S S I A (Online) (Applied Social Sciences Index & Abstracts) (Supersedes (in 1999): A S S I A (Print))
ASTIS †A S T I S Bibliography (Arctic Science & Technology Information System) (Supersedes (in 1995): A S T I S Bibliography (Microfiche))
ATA †Agriculture and Environment for Developing Regions (Former titles (until 1996): Abstracts on Tropical Agriculture; (until 1975): Tropical Abstracts)
ATI ProQuest Accounting & Tax Database (Formerly: Accounting & Tax Database)
AUNI Air University Library Index to Military Periodicals
AbAn Abstracts in Anthropology
Acal †Academic Index
AcoustA †Acoustics Abstracts (Formerly (until 1967): Acoustics and Ultrasonics Abstracts)
AddicA †Addiction Abstracts
AgBio AgBiotech News and Information
AgeL AgeLine
Agr AGRICOLA (AGRIcultural OnLine Access)
AgrAg Agro-Agen
AgrForAb Agroforestry Abstracts (Online)
AgrLib Agro-Librex
Agrind †Agrindex
AltPI Alternative Press Index
AmH&L America: History and Life
AmHI Humanities International Index (Formerly (until 2005): American Humanities Index (Online Edition))
AmStI American Statistics Index
AnBeAb Animal Behavior Abstracts (Formerly (until 1974): Behavioural Biology Abstracts, Section A: Animal Behaviour)
AnthLit Anthropological Literature (Online)
ApMecR Applied Mechanics Reviews
ApicAb †Apicultural Abstracts
ArcBib †Arctic Bibliography
ArchI Architectural Index
ArtHuCI Arts & Humanities Citation Index
ArtIAb †Artificial Intelligence Abstracts (UK)
ArtInd Art Index
Artemisa Artemisa
AusPAIS A P A I S: Australian Public Affairs Information Service (Online)

B

B&AI Biological & Agricultural Index Plus
B&BAb Biotechnology & Bioengineering Abstracts
consists of:
†A S F A Marine Biotechnology Abstracts (Print)
Agricultural & Environmental Biotechnology Abstracts (Online)
BioEngineering Abstracts (Online)
Genetics Abstracts
Medical & Pharmaceutical Biotechnology Abstracts (Online)
Microbiology Abstracts: Section A. Industrial & Applied Microbiology

B01 Business Source Complete
B02 Business & Company ProFile ASAP
B03 Business & Industry (Formerly (until 199?): Business & Industry (CD-ROM))
B04 Biography Index
B05 Book Review Digest
B06 Business Source Alumni Edition
B07 Business Source Corporate
B08 Business Source Elite
B09 Business Source Premier
B10 Biological & Agricultural Index
B11 Business and Management Practices
B12 Business Dateline
B13 Business Periodicals Index Retrospective
B14 Book Review Index Online Plus
B15 Business & Company Resource Center
B16 Business Module
B17 Business ASAP
B18 Business ASAP International
B19 Biotechnology Research Abstracts (Formed by the merger of (1993-2007): Agricultural and Environmental Biotechnology Abstracts; (1993-2007): BioEngineering Abstracts; (1993-2007): Medical and Pharmaceutical Biotechnology Abstracts; All of which superseded in part (1983-1993): Biotechnology Research Abstracts)
B21 Biological Sciences
B22 BazTech
B23 Biocontrol News and Information
B24 B H A Bibliography of the History of Art (Online)
B25 Biological Abstracts (Online)
B26 Biotechnology Citation Index (Online)
B27 Biochemistry and Biophysics Citation Index (Online)
B28 British Nursing Index Database
B29 British Education Index (Online)
BA Biofuels Abstracts
BAS Bibliography of Asian Studies (Online)
BBO Bibliografia Brasileira de Odontologia (Online)
BCIRA †B C I R A Abstracts of International Literature on Metal Castings Production (British Cast Iron Research Association) (Former titles: B C I R A Abstracts of International Foundry Literature; (until 1978): B C I R A Abstracts of Foundry Literature)
BDM&CN †Bibliography of Developmental Medicine and Child Neurology. Books and Articles Received
BEL&L Annual Bibliography of English Language and Literature (Formerly (until 1924): Bibliography of English Language and Literature)
BIOBASE BIOBASE
consists of:
Current Advances in Applied Microbiology & Biotechnology
Current Advances in Cancer Research
Current Advances in Cell & Developmental Biology
Current Advances in Clinical Chemistry
Current Advances in Ecological & Environmental Sciences
Current Advances in Endocrinology & Metabolism
Current Advances in Genetics & Molecular Biology
Current Advances in Immunology & Infectious Diseases
Current Advances in Neuroscience
Current Advances in Plant Science
Current Advances in Protein Biochemistry
Current Advances in Toxicology
BIOSIS Prev BIOSIS Previews
BLI Banking Information Source (Online) (Former titles (until 2000): Banking Information Index (Print); (until 1994): American Bankers Association Banking Literature Index)
BMT B M T Abstracts (British Maritime Technology Ltd.) (Former titles (until 1986): B S R A. Journal of Abstracts; (until 1970): British Ship Research Association. Journal of Abstracts; (until 1968): British Ship Research Association. Journal; (until 1962): British Shipbuilding Research Association. Journal)
BNI †B N I (British Newspaper Index)
BNNA Bibliography of Native North Americans
BP Botanical Pesticides Abstracts
BPI Business Periodicals Index
BPIA †Business Publications Index and Abstracts
BPRC&P †Biweekly List of Papers on Radiation Chemistry and Photochemistry (Former titles (until 1978): Biweekly List of Papers on Radiation Chemistry; Weekly List of Papers on Radiation Chemistry; Which incorporated: Index and Cumulative List of Papers on Radiation Chemistry)
BRD Book Review Digest Plus
BRI Book Review Index
BRM †Book Reviews of the Month
BSLBiol †Abstracts of Bulgarian Scientific Literature. Biology (Formerly: Abstracts of Bulgarian Scientific Literature. Biology and Biochemistry)

BSLEcon †Abstracts of Bulgarian Scientific Literature. Economics and Law

BSLGeo †Abstracts of Bulgarian Scientific Literature. Geosciences (Formerly: Abstracts of Bulgarian Scientific Literature. Geology and Geography)

BSLIndus †Abstracts of Bulgarian Scientific Literature. Industry, Building and Transport

BSLMath †Abstracts of Bulgarian Scientific Literature. Mathematical and Physical Sciences (Formerly: Abstracts of Bulgarian Scientific Literature. Mathematics, Physics, Astronomy, Geophysics, Geodesy)

BehAb †Behavioural Abstracts

BibAg †Bibliography of Agriculture
consists of:
†Bibliography of Agriculture. Annual Cumulative Index

BibCart Bibliographia Cartographica (Formerly (until 1972): Bibliotheca Cartographica)

BibInd Bibliographic Index

BibLing Linguistic Bibliography

BibRep Human Reproduction Update (Incorporates (1963-1994): Bibliography of Reproduction)

BioDAb †Biodeterioration Abstracts

BioEngAb BioEngineering Abstracts (Online)

BiolDig Biology Digest

Biostat Biostatistica

BldManAb Construction Research and Innovation (Former titles (until 2010): Chartered Institute of Building. Construction Information Quarterly; Which incorporated (1976-19??): Building Management Abstracts; (until 1999): Construction Information File - C I F; (until 1992): Technical Information Service - T I S; Which was formed by the merger of (1971-1982): Chartered Institute of Building. Estimating Information Service; (1971-1982): Chartered Institute of Building. Site Management Information Service; (1977-1982): Chartered Institute of Building. Maintenance Information Service; (1979-1982): Chartered Institute of Building. Surveying Information Service)

BrArAb British and Irish Archaeological Bibliography (Online)

BrCerAb World Ceramics Abstracts (Online) (Former titles (until 2002): World Ceramics Abstracts (Print); (until 1989): British Ceramic Abstracts)

BrGeoL †British Geological Literature

BrHumI British Humanities Index

BrRB †British Railways Board. Monthly Review of Technical Literature

BrTechI Abstracts in New Technologies and Engineering (Former titles (until 1997): Current Technology Index; British Technology Index)

BullT&T †Bulletin of Chemical Thermodynamics (Former titles (until 1976): Bulletin of Thermodynamics and Thermochemistry; (until 1961): Bulletin of Chemical Thermodynamics; Which superseded: Thermochemical Bulletin and Bulletin of Unpublished Thermal Material)

BusEdI †Business Education Index

BusI †Business Index

C

C&CR Catalysts & Catalysed Reactions

C&CSA Computer & Communications Security Abstracts (Formerly (until 1999): Computer & Communications Security Reviews)

C&ISA Computer and Information Systems Abstracts Journal (Former titles (until 1978): Computer and Information Systems; (until 1969): Information Processing Journal)

C01 Clase and Periodica

C02 Canadian Newsstand

C03 C B C A Complete (Canadian Business and Current Affairs)

C04 Canadian Points of View Reference Centre

C05 Canadian Reference Centre

C06 CINAHL Plus

C07 CINAHL Plus with Full Text

C08 CINAHL with Full Text

C10 Computers & Applied Sciences Complete

C11 Consumer Health Complete

C12 Corporate ResourceNet

C13 Chemical Abstracts Student Edition

C14 Canadian Newsstand Atlantic

C15 Canadian Newsstand Black Press

C16 Canadian Newsstand Major Dailies

C17 Canadian Newsstand Ontario

C18 Canadian Newsstand Pacific

C19 Canadian Newsstand Prairies

C20 Canadian Newsstand Quebec

C21 Canadian Newsstand Torstar

C22 Children's Module

C23 Computer Source

C24 Chimica

C25 Crop Science Database

C26 CAB Abstracts Archive

C27 Contemporary Research Index

C28 Child Development & Adolescent Studies

C29 Current Index to Scholarly Journals

C30 Crop Physiology Abstracts
C31 ChemInform
C32 Caribbean Search
C33 Chemical Abstracts (Online)
CA Current Abstracts
CA&I †Children's Authors and Illustrators
CA/WCA Ceramic Abstracts / World Ceramic Abstracts
CABA CAB Abstracts
CADCAM †C A D - C A M Abstracts (Computer Aided Design - Computer Aided Manufacturing)
CALL †C A L L (Current Awareness - Library Literature)
CANZLLI †Current Australian and New Zealand Legal Literature Index
CBA †Conservation Biology Abstracts
CBCABus C B C A Business (Canadian Business and Current Affairs) (Supersedes in part (in 1998): C B C A Fulltext; Which was formerly (until 1997): Canadian Business and Current Affairs Fulltext (CD-ROM))
CBCARef C B C A Reference (Canadian Business and Current Affairs) (Supersedes in part (in 1998): C B C A Fulltext; Which was formerly (until 1997): Canadian Business and Current Affairs - Fulltext (CD-ROM))
CBCuEv C B C A Current Events (Canadian Business and Current Affairs)
CBNB Chemical Business NewsBase
CBPI †Canadian Index (Formed by the merger of: Canadian Magazine Index; Canadian News Index; Which was formerly: Canadian Newspaper Index; Canadian Business Index; Which was formerly: Canadian Business Periodicals Index)
CBRC †Current Book Review Citations
CBRI Children's Book Review Index
CBTA †Current Biotechnology (Incorporates (1985-2000): Biotechnology: Apparatus, Plant, and Equipment; Which was formerly (until 1991): Biotechnologie; Formerly (until 1990): Current Biotechnology Abstracts)
CCA †Current Contents Africa (Formerly (until 1978): C C A (Current Contents Africa))
CCI Chemistry Citation Index
CCIOG Combined Cumulative Index to Obstetrics and Gynecology
CCIP Combined Cumulative Index to Pediatrics
CCME Electronic Current Contents of Periodicals on the Middle East (Formerly: Current Contents of Periodicals on the Middle East)
CCMJ Current Mathematical Publications (Formed by the merger of (1964-1975): American Mathematical Society. New Publications; (1969-1975): Contents of Contemporary Mathematical Journals)
CCR †Current Thoughts & Trends (Formerly: Current Christian Abstracts)
CDA †Child Development Abstracts and Bibliography
CDSP Current Digest of the Russian Press (Former titles (until 2011): Current Digest of the Post-Soviet Press; (until 1992): Current Digest of the Soviet Press; Which incorporated (1968-1970): Current Abstracts of the Soviet Press)
CEA Process and Chemical Engineering (Formerly (until 1991): Chemical Engineering Abstracts)
CEABA Chemical Engineering and Biotechnology Abstracts (Online) *consists of:*
†Current Biotechnology
†Environmental and Safety Technology
Process and Chemical Engineering
Theoretical Chemical Engineering
CEI C B C A Education (Canadian Business and Current Affairs) (Formerly (until 1998): Canadian Education Index (CD-ROM))
CERDIC †Universite de Strasbourg. Centre de Recherche et de Documentation des Institutions Chretiennes. Bulletin du CERDIC
CFA †Canadian Fisheries Abstracts
CHNI †Consumer Health and Nutrition Index
CIA Composites Industry Abstracts
CIN †Chemical Industry Notes
CINAHL CINAHL (Cumulative Index to Nursing & Allied Health Literature)
CIRFAb †T & D Abstracts (Training & Development) (Supersedes: C I R F Abstracts)
CIS Current Index to Statistics (Online) (Formerly (until 2001): Current Index to Statistics (Print))
CISA †Safety and Health at Work (Former titles: C I S Abstracts; Occupational Safety and Health Abstracts)
CISI C I S Index to Publications of the United States Congress (Congressional Information Service, Inc.)
CJA †Criminal Justice Abstracts (Print) (Former titles: Abstracts on Crime and Juvenile Delinquency; Crime and Delinquency Literature; Formed by the merger of: Information Review on Crime and Delinquency; Selected Highlights of Crime and Delinquency)
CJA Criminal Justice Abstracts

CJPI	ProQuest Criminal Justice (Formerly (until 200?): Criminal Justice Periodicals Index)
CLA	Canon Law Abstracts
CLFP	†Current Literature in Family Planning
CLI	Current Law Index
CLL	Leather Science Abstracts (Formerly (until 1988): Current Leather Literature)
CLOSS	†Current Literature on Science of Science (Formerly (until 1973): Index to Literature on Science of Science)
CLT&T	†Current Literature in Traffic and Transportation
CLitI	†Canadian Literature Index
CMCI	†Compumath Citation Index
CMHR	Journal of Prevention and Intervention in the Community (Former titles (until 1996): Prevention in Human Services; (until 1981): Community Mental Health Review)
CMM	Communication & Mass Media Complete (Formed by the 2003 merger of: CommSearch; Mass Media Articles Index)
CMPI	Canadian Music Periodical Index
CPE	Contents Pages in Education
CPEI	Compendex (COMPuterized ENgineering InDEX)
CPI	†Current Physics Index
CPL	The Catholic Periodical and Literature Index (Formerly (until 1968): Catholic Periodical Index; Incorporates (1888-1967): Guide to Catholic Literature)
CPLI	†Chicago Psychoanalytic Literature Index
CPM	Contents Pages in Management (Formerly (until 1974): Current Contents in Management)
CPerI	CPI.Q (Canadian Periodical Index)
CRCL	†Canadian Review of Comparative Literature
CREJ	†Contents of Recent Economics Journals
CRFR	†Current References in Fish Research
CRIA	N C B Abstracts (National Council for Cement and Building Materials) (Formerly (until 2000): C R I Abstracts)
CRICC	N C B Current Contents (National Council for Cement and Building Materials) (Formerly (until 2000): C R I Current Contents)
CSI	†Directory of Statistics in Canada (Formerly: Canadian Statistics Index)
CSNB	Chemical Safety NewsBase *consists of:* Chemical Hazards in Industry; Laboratory Hazards Bulletin; †Managing Safety & Health at Work
CTA	Calcium and Calcified Tissue Abstracts (Online)
CTD	†Current Titles in Dentistry
CTE	†Current Titles in Electrochemistry (Incorporates: Electrochemical News)
CTFA	†Cotton and Tropical Fibres (Formerly (until 1991): Cotton and Tropical Fibres Abstracts)
CTO	†Current Titles in Ocean, Coastal, Lake & Waterway Sciences
CWI	Contemporary Women's Issues
CWPI	†Canadian Women's Periodicals Index (Former titles: Canadian Women's Periodicals: Title Word Index; Canadian Women's Periodicals: K W I C Index)
CZA	†Canadian Zoology Abstracts
Cadscan	Cadscan (Formerly (until Oct. 1986): Cadmium Abstracts)
CalPI	California Periodicals Index
CerAb	Ceramic Abstracts (Supersedes in part (in 1922): American Ceramic Society. Journal; Which was formerly (until 1917): American Ceramic Society. Transactions)
ChLitAb	†Children's Literature Abstracts
ChPerI	†Chicano Index (Formerly (until 1989): Chicano Periodical Index)
ChemAb	†Chemical Abstracts (Print) (Supersedes: American Chemical Research. Review) *consists of:* †Chemical Abstracts - Applied Chemistry and Chemical Engineering Sections; †Chemical Abstracts - Biochemistry Sections; †Chemical Abstracts - Macromolecular Sections; †Chemical Abstracts - Organic Chemistry Sections; †Chemical Abstracts - Physical, Inorganic and Analytical Chemistry Sections; †Chemical Abstracts - Section Groupings; †Chemical Abstracts Service Source Index
ChemTitl	†Chemical Titles
ChemoAb	Chemoreception Abstracts (Online)
Chicano	Chicano Database (Consists of: Chicano Index; Arte Chicano; Chicano Anthology Index; Chicana Studies Index; Hispanic Mental Health Research; Spanish Speaking Mental Health Database)
ChrPI	Christian Periodical Index
ChromAb	Chromatography Abstracts (Former titles (until 1986): Gas and Liquid Chromatography Abstracts; (until 1970): Gas Chromatography Abstracts)

CivEngAb C S A Civil Engineering Abstracts (Cambridge Scientific Abstracts)

CommAb Communication Abstracts Online

CompAb Computer Abstracts (Incorporates (1960-1980): Computer News; Former titles (until 1960): Computer Bibliography; (until 1959): Bibliography Series. Computers; I O T A Services Ltd. Monthly Bibliographical Series. Computors)

CompB †Computer Business

CompC †Computer Contents

CompD Computer Database

CompI †Computer Index

CompIU †Computer Industry Update

CompLI Computer Science Index (Former titles (until 2002): Computer Literature Index (Print); (until 1980): Quarterly Bibliography of Computers and Data Processing)

CompR Computing Reviews

ConcrAb †Concrete Abstracts

ConsI †Consumers Index

Copeia †Copeia Abstracts (Formerly: ABSEARCH Ichthyology and Herpetology)

CoppAb †International Copper Information Bulletin (Supersedes: Copper Abstracts; Incorporates: Kupfer - Mitteilungen; Cuivre, Laitons, Alliages - Bibliographie; Rame - Schede Bibliografiche; Cobre - Resumenes Bibliograficos)

CorrAb Corrosion Abstracts (Incorporates: Corrosion Prevetion Technology; Which was formerly (1978-1995): Corrosion Prevention - Inhibition Digest)

CurCR Current Chemical Reactions Database

CurCont Current Contents
consists of:
Current Contents: Agriculture, Biology & Environmental Sciences
Current Contents: Arts & Humanities
Current Contents: Clinical Medicine
Current Contents: Engineering, Computing & Technology
†Current Contents: Health Services Administration
Current Contents: Life Sciences
Current Contents: Physical, Chemical & Earth Sciences
Current Contents: Social & Behavioral Sciences

CurPA †Current Packaging Abstracts (Formerly (until 1973): Packaging Bulletin)

CybAb †Cybernetics Abstracts (Formerly (until 1965): Theoretical Cybernetics Abstracts)

D

D01 Dairy Science Abstracts

D02 Dentistry & Oral Sciences Source

D03 Digital Journals Database

D04 Directory of Academic Resources

D05 Design and Applied Arts Index (Online)

DBA Derwent Biotechnology Abstracts

DIP Dietrich's Index Philosophicus

DM&T †Aerospace Defense Markets & Technology (Formerly: Defense Markets and Technology)

DNP Digest of Neurology & Psychiatry (Online)

DPD †Data Processing Digest

DRIE Database of Research on International Education

DSHAb †D S H Abstracts (Deafness, Speech and Hearing)

DYW †Diversity Your World

DentAb Dental Abstracts

DentInd †Index to Dental Literature

DiabCont †Diabetes Contents

Djerelo Djerelo

DoGi DoGi Database - Legal Literature

DokArb †Arbeitsmedizin (Former titles: Beruf und Gesundheit - Occupational Health; (until 1985): Dokumentation Arbeitsmedizin - Documentation Occupational Health)

DokStr Dokumentation Strasse

E

E&CAJ Electronics and Communications Abstracts Journal (Former titles (until 1993): Electronics and Communications Abstracts; (until 1992): Electronics and Communications Abstracts Journal; (until 1972): Electronics Abstracts Journal)

E&PHSE E & P Health, Safety and Environment (Exploration and Production)

E-psyche †E-psyche

E01 Electronic Collections Online

E02 Education Full Text

E03 Education Research Complete

E04 Environment Complete

E05 Environment Index (Former titles (until 2006): Environmental Issues & Policy Index; (until Dec. 2002): Environmental Policy Index; (until 2002): Environmental Knowledge Base (Online); (until 2000): Environmental Periodicals Bibliography (Print); (until 1973): Environmental Periodicals)

E06 Education Index Retrospective

E07 Educator's Reference Complete

E08 Expanded Academic ASAP

E09 Education Module

E10 European Business ASAP

E11 C S A Engineering Research Database

E12 Environmental Impact
E13 Elite Scientific Journals Archive
E14 Energy & Power Source
E15 Educational Management Abstracts (Online)
E16 Educational Technology Abstracts (Online)
E17 Ecology Abstracts (Online)
EA †Ecology Abstracts (Moscow) (Formerly: ABSEARCH Ecology & Plant Science)
EAA Educational Administration Abstracts
ECER †Exceptional Child Education Resources (Online) (Former titles (until 2004): Exceptional Child Education Resources (Print); (until 1977): Exceptional Child Education Abstracts)
ECI †E C Index (European Communities)
EEA Earthquake Engineering Abstracts
EFA †Essential Fisheries Abstracts
EI E I (Online) (Excerpta Indonesica) (Formerly (until 2002): E I (Print))
EIA †Energy Information Abstracts
EIP Ekistic Index of Periodicals
ELJI †European Legal Journals Index
ELLIS †E L L I S (European Legal Literature Information Service)
EMA Engineered Materials Abstracts
consists of:
Advanced Polymers Abstracts
Composites Industry Abstracts
EMBASE EMBASE
ENW Ethnic NewsWatch (Online) (Formerly (until 200?): Ethnic NewsWatch (CD-ROM))
ERA Educational Research Abstracts Online
ERI †Education Research Index
ERIC ERIC (Education Resources Information Center)
ERO EdResearch Online
ESPM Environmental Sciences and Pollution Management
EZ&PSA †Essential Ecology, Zoology & Plant Science Abstracts
EconLit EconLit
EdA Education Abstracts
EdI Education Index
EmerIntel E M X 95 (Former titles (until 2008): Emerald Fulltext; (until 200?): Emerald Intelligence & Fulltext; (until 1999): Emerald)
Emerald Emerald Management Reviews (Online) (Former titles (until 2002): Emerald Reviews (Online); (until 2001): Anbar International Management Database; (until 1999): Anbar Management Intelligence (CD-ROM))
consists of:
†Accounting & Finance Abstracts
†Human Resource Management Abstracts
†Information Management and Technology Abstracts
†Management Books and Resources
†Management Development Abstracts
†Management of Quality Abstracts
†Marketing & Logistics Abstracts
†Operations & Production Management Abstracts
†Top Management Abstracts
EnerInd †Energy Information Abstracts Annual (Formed by the 1988 merger of: Energy Index; Energy Information Abstracts Annual)
EnerRA †Energy Research Abstracts (Formerly (until 1977): E R D A Energy Research Abstracts; (until 1976): E R D A Reports Abstracts)
EnerRev †Energy Review (Santa Barbara)
EngInd The Engineering Index Monthly (Former titles (until 1984): Engineering Index Monthly and Author Index; (until 1971): Engineering Index Monthly)
EntAb Entomology Abstracts
EnvAb †Environment Abstracts (Print) (Incorporates (1985-1991): Acid Rain Abstracts; Formerly (until 1974): Environment Information Access)
EnvEAb Environmental Engineering Abstracts
EnvInd †Environment Abstracts Annual (Incorporates (1971-1987): Environment Index; (1988-1990): Acid Rain Abstracts Annual; Which incorporated (19??-1988): Acid Rain Annual Index)
ErgAb Ergonomics Abstracts Online
ExcerpMed Excerpta Medica. Abstract Journals
consists of:
Excerpta Medica. Section 1: Anatomy, Anthropology, Embryology & Histology
Excerpta Medica. Section 2: Physiology
Excerpta Medica. Section 3: Endocrinology
Excerpta Medica. Section 4: Microbiology: Bacteriology, Mycology, Parasitology and Virology

Excerpta Medica. Section 5: General Pathology and Pathological Anatomy
Excerpta Medica. Section 6: Internal Medicine
Excerpta Medica. Section 7: Pediatrics and Pediatric Surgery
Excerpta Medica. Section 8: Neurology and Neurosurgery
Excerpta Medica. Section 9: Surgery
Excerpta Medica. Section 10: Obstetrics and Gynecology
Excerpta Medica. Section 11: Otorhinolaryngology
Excerpta Medica. Section 12: Ophthalmology
Excerpta Medica. Section 13: Dermatology and Venereology
Excerpta Medica. Section 14: Radiology
Excerpta Medica. Section 15: Chest Diseases, Thoracic Surgery and Tuberculosis
Excerpta Medica. Section 16: Cancer
Excerpta Medica. Section 17: Public Health, Social Medicine and Epidemiology
Excerpta Medica. Section 18: Cardiovascular Diseases and Cardiovascular Surgery
Excerpta Medica. Section 19: Rehabilitation and Physical Medicine
Excerpta Medica. Section 20: Gerontology and Geriatrics
Excerpta Medica. Section 21: Developmental Biology and Teratology
Excerpta Medica. Section 22: Human Genetics
Excerpta Medica. Section 23: Nuclear Medicine
Excerpta Medica. Section 24: Anesthesiology
Excerpta Medica. Section 25: Hematology
Excerpta Medica. Section 26: Immunology, Serology and Transplantation
Excerpta Medica. Section 27: Biophysics, Bio-Engineering and Medical Instrumentation
Excerpta Medica. Section 28: Urology and Nephrology
Excerpta Medica. Section 29: Clinical and Experimental Biochemistry
Excerpta Medica. Section 30: Clinical and Experimental Pharmacology
Excerpta Medica. Section 31: Arthritis and Rheumatism
Excerpta Medica. Section 32: Psychiatry
Excerpta Medica. Section 33: Orthopedic Surgery
†Excerpta Medica. Section 34: Plastic Surgery
Excerpta Medica. Section 35: Occupational Health and Industrial Medicine
Excerpta Medica. Section 36: Health Policy, Economics and Management
†Excerpta Medica. Section 37: Drug Literature Index
Excerpta Medica. Section 38: Adverse Reactions Titles
Excerpta Medica. Section 40: Drug Dependence, Alcohol Abuse and Alcoholism
Excerpta Medica. Section 46: Environmental Health and Pollution Control
Excerpta Medica. Section 48: Gastroenterology
Excerpta Medica. Section 49: Forensic Science Abstracts
Excerpta Medica. Section 50: Epilepsy Abstracts
†Excerpta Medica. Section 51: Mycobacterial Diseases: Leprosy, Tuberculosis and Related Subjects
Excerpta Medica. Section 52: Toxicology
†Excerpta Medica. Section 54: AIDS
†Excerpta Medica. Section 130: Clinical Pharmacology

ExtraMED ExtraMED

F

F&EA Fuel and Energy Abstracts (Former titles (until 1978): Fuel Abstracts and Current Titles; (until 1960): Fuel Abstracts)

F&GI †Farm and Garden Index

F&WA †Essential Forestry & Wildfire Abstracts

F01 Film & Television Literature Index (Formerly (until 2006): Film Literature Index (Online))

F02 Film & Television Literature Index with Full Text

F03 Fuente Academica

F04 Fuente Academica Premier

F05 Foodline Market

F06 Foodline Science

F07 Foodline News

F08 Forest Science Database

F09 Family & Society Studies Worldwide

F10 Food Science Source

F11 Forest Products Abstracts

F12 Forestry Abstracts

FAMLI †F A M L I (Family Medicine Literature Index)

FCA Field Crop Abstracts

FLP Index to Foreign Legal Periodicals

FLUIDEX FLUIDEX
consists of:
†Current Fluid Engineering Titles
Fluid Abstracts: Civil Engineering
Fluid Abstracts: Process Engineering
†Industrial Jetting Report
†Pumps and Turbines
†River and Flood Control Abstracts
†Tribology & Corrosion Abstracts
†World Ports and Harbours News

FPRD	†H T F S Digest (Incorporates (1979-1992): Fouling Prevention Research Digest; Former titles (until 1986): Heat Transfer and Fluid Flow Digest; (until 1976): H T F S Digest)
FR	F R A N C I S
FS&TA	Food Science and Technology Abstracts
FaBeAb	†Faba Bean Abstracts
FamI	†Family Index
FemPer	Feminist Periodicals (Online) (Formerly (until 2008): Feminist Periodicals (Print))
FiP	Fed in Print (Online) (Formerly (until 2000): Fed in Print (Print); Which incorporated (1962-1976): Federal Reserve Bank Reviews Selected Subjects)
FoMM	†Focus On: Molecular Medicine
FoP	†Focus On: Psychopharmacology
FoSS&M	†Focus On: Sports Science and Medicine
FoVS&M	†Focus On: Veterinary Science and Medicine
FutSurv	Future Survey (Formerly: Public Policy Book Forecast)

G

G01	General Science Collection
G02	GreenFILE
G03	General Science Full Text
G04	General Business File ASAP
G05	General Reference Center
G06	General Reference Center Gold
G07	General Reference Centre International
G08	General OneFile
G09	General Interest Module
G10	Gender Studies Database
G11	Grasslands and Forage Abstracts (Online)
GALA	†Institute of Paper Science and Technology. Graphic Arts Bulletin (Former titles (until 1992): Graphic Arts Literature Abstracts; (until 1953): Graphic Arts Progress; Which incorporated (1951-1953): Graphic Arts Index; Which superseded: P I A Management Reports)
GEOBASE	GEOBASE *consists of:* Ecological Abstracts; Geographical Abstracts: Human Geography; Geographical Abstracts: Physical Geography; Geological Abstracts; Geomechanics Abstracts; International Development Abstracts; Oceanographic Literature Review
GH	Global Health
GIPL	Guide to Indian Periodical Literature
GJP	European Psychologist (Formerly (until 1995): German Journal of Psychology)
GP&P	†Gas Processing and Pipelining
GPAA	†General Physics Advance Abstracts
GPAI	†Genealogical Periodical Annual Index
GSA	General Science Abstracts
GSI	General Science Index
GSS&RPL	Guide to Social Science and Religion (Former titles (until 1988): Guide to Social Science and Religion in Periodical Literature; (until 1970): Guide to Religious and Semi-religious Periodicals)
GSW	GeoScienceWorld
GW	GenderWatch (Online) (Former titles (until 200?): GenderWatch (CD-ROM); (until 1998): Women 'R')
GardL	Garden, Landscape & Horticulture Index (Former titles (until 2006): Garden Literature Index (Online); (until 2001): Garden Literature (Print))
GasAb	†Gas Abstracts
GdIns	†Guidelines
GenetAb	Genetics Abstracts
GeoRef	GeoRef
GeophysAb	†Geophysical Abstracts
GeosDoc	Geoscience Documentation
GeotechAb	†Geotechnical Abstracts

H

H&SSA	Health and Safety Science Abstracts (Online)
H&TI	Hospitality & Tourism Index (Incorporates (1998-2003): Articles in Hospitality and Tourism; Former titles (until 2003): Lodging, Restaurant and Tourism Index; (until 1995): Lodging and Restaurant Index)
H01	Health Business Elite
H02	Health Business FullTEXT
H03	Health Source: Consumer Edition
H04	Health Source: Nursing/Academic Edition
H05	History Reference Center
H06	Hospitality & Tourism Complete
H07	Humanities International Complete
H08	Humanities Full Text
H09	Humanities & Social Sciences Index Retrospective
H10	Humanities Index Retrospective
H11	Health & Wellness Resource Center
H12	Health Reference Center Academic
H13	Health Module
H14	Humanities Module
H15	C S A High Technology Research Database with Aerospace
H16	Horticultural Science Database

H17 Helminthological Abstracts (Online)
H19 Home Improvement Reference Center
H20 Hobbies & Crafts Reference Center
H21 Hispanic American Periodicals Index (Online)
HAb Humanities Abstracts
HBB †Hungarian Building Bulletin
HEA Higher Education Abstracts (Formerly (until 1984): College Student Personnel Abstracts)
HECAB †Higher Education Current Awareness Bulletin (Formerly (until 1973): Higher Education)
HGA †Human Genome Abstracts
HL&ISA Hungarian Library and Information Science Abstracts
HPNRM C S A Human Population & Natural Resource Management
HRA Human Resources Abstracts
HRIR †Human Rights Internet Reporter (Formerly: Human Rights Internet Newsletter)
HRIS T R I S Electronic Bibliographic Data Base (Transportation Research Information Services) (Incorporates (in 1996): Highway Research Abstracts; Which was formerly (1968-1990): H R I S Abstracts)
HistAb Historical Abstracts (Online)
HlthInd †Health Index
HongKongiana †HongKongiana
HospAb †Health & Social Care Abstracts (Formerly (until 2003): Health Service Abstracts; Incorporates (1961-1985): Hospital Abstracts; (1974-1985): Current Literature on Health Services; Current Literature on General Medical Practice)
HospI †International Hospitality and Tourism Database CD-ROM (Formerly (until 1995): Hospitality Index)
HospLI †Hospital and Health Administration Index (Former titles (until 1995): Hospital Literature Index; Hospital Periodical Literature Index)
HumInd Humanities Index (Online)

I

I-WA †Ibis - Wildfowl Abstracts
I01 Index to Legal Periodicals Full Text
I02 International Security & Counter Terrorism Reference Center
I03 Index to Legal Periodicals Retrospective
I04 Informe Revistas en Espanol
I05 InfoTrac Custom
I06 InfoTrac Junior Edition
I07 InfoTrac Student Edition
I08 International Module
I09 InfoTrac Kids Edition
I11 Irrigation and Drainage Abstracts
I12 International Pharmaceutical Abstracts
I13 International Political Science Abstracts Database
I14 Index Islamicus Database
IAALC †Indice Agricola de America Latina y el Caribe (Formerly: Bibliografia Agricola Latinoamericana y del Caribe)
IAB †Humans & Other Species (Former titles (until 1997): InterActions Bibliography; (until vol.3, 1992): Interactions of Man and Animals)
IABS Current Awareness in Biological Sciences (Former titles (until 1983): International Abstracts of Biological Sciences; (until 1956): British Abstracts of Medical Sciences; (until 1954): British Abstracts. A3: Physiology, Biochemistry, Anatomy, Pharmacology, Experimental Medicine; (until 1945): British Chemical and Physiological Abstracts. A3: Physiology and Biochemistry; (until 1937): British Chemical Abstracts. AIII: Biochemistry; Which superseded in part (in 1936): British Chemical Abstracts. A: Pure Chemistry; Which was formerly (until 1926): Journal of the Chemical Society. Abstracts; Which superseded in part (in 1877): Journal of the Chemical Society)
IAJS Index of Articles on Jewish Studies (Online) (Formerly (until 2000): Index of Articles on Jewish Studies (Print))
IAOP International Abstracts in Operations Research
IAPV †Index of American Periodical Verse
IBR Internationale Bibliographie der Rezensionen Geistes- und Sozialwissenschaftlicher Literatur
IBRH †Index to Book Reviews in the Humanities
IBSS International Bibliography of the Social Sciences *consists of:* International Bibliography of Political Science; International Bibliography of the Social Sciences. Anthropology; International Bibliography of the Social Sciences. Economics; International Bibliography of the Social Sciences. Sociology
IBT&D International Bibliography of Theatre & Dance with Full Text (Formerly (until 1999): International Bibliography of Theatre (Print))
IBibSS †International Bibliography of the Social Sciences: Anthropology, Political Science, Economics, Sociology
IBuildSA International Building Services Abstracts (E-Mail Edition)

ICEA International Civil Engineering Abstracts (Former titles (until 1982): I C E Abstracts; (until 1975): European Civil Engineering Abstracts)

ICLPL Index to Canadian Legal Periodical Literature

ICM Children's Magazine Guide (Formerly (until 1981): Subject Index to Children's Magazines)

ICUIS †I C U I S Justice Ministries (Institute on the Church in Urban-Industrial Society) (Supersedes (1970-1978): I C U I S Abstract Service)

IDIS IDIS (Iowa Drug Information Service)

IDP †Index to Dance Periodicals

IECT Bibliografia Espanola de Revistas Cientificas de Ciencia y Tecnologia (Formerly (until 1998): Indice Espanol de Ciencia y Tecnologia)

IFP †Index to Free Periodicals

IGCS †International Guide to Classical Studies

IHD †Industrial Hygiene Digest

IHP Mapfte'ah L'khit've 'Et B'ivrit

IHTDI Index to How to Do It Information (Online)

IIBP International Index to Black Periodicals

IIFP International Index to Film Periodicals

IIL †R S N A Index to Imaging Literature (Radiological Society of North America)

IIMP International Index to Music Periodicals

IIPA International Index to the Performing Arts

IIPL †Index to Indian Periodical Literature

IIS Index to International Statistics

IITV †International Index to Television Periodicals

IJCS †Index to Journals in Communication Studies

IJP Index to Jewish Periodicals

ILD †International Labour Documentation

ILM †Index to Little Magazines

ILP Index to Legal Periodicals & Books

ILSA Indian Library Science Abstracts

IME †Indice Medico Espanol (Online)

IMI †International Management Information Business Digest

IMMAb I M M Abstracts (Institution of Mining and Metallurgy)

INI †International Nursing Index

INIS AtomInd I N I S Atomindex (Online) (International Nuclear Information System) (Formerly (until 1997): I N I S Atomindex (Print); (until 1968): List of References on Nuclear Energy; I N I S Atomindex (Print) incorporates (1948-1976): United States. Energy Research and Development Administration. Nuclear Science Abstracts; Which was formed by the 1948 merger of: Abstracts of Declassified Documents; Guide to Published Research on Atomic Energy)

INZP †Te Puna CD-ROM (Former titles: Index New Zealand; (until 1986): Index to New Zealand Periodicals)

IPARL †Index to Periodical Articles Related to Law

IPB Repertoire Bibliographique de la Philosophie (Former titles (until 1949): Revue Philosophique de Louvain. Supplement. Repertoire Bibliographique; (until 1946): Revue Neoscolastique de Philosophie. Repertoire Bibliographique)

IPI Insurance Periodicals Index

IPP Index to Philippine Periodicals (Formerly (until 1960): Index to Philippine Periodical Literature)

IPackAb Packaging Month (Formerly (until 2001): International Packaging Abstracts; Which was formed by the merger of (1944-1981): Packaging Abstracts; (1976-1981): Referatedienst Verpackung)

IPsyAb †Indian Psychological Abstracts and Reviews (Formerly (until 1994): Indian Psychological Abstracts)

ISA Indian Science Abstracts (Former titles (until 1965): Bibliography of Scientific Publications of South & South-East Asia; (until 1955): Bibliography of Scientific Publications of South Asia)

ISAP Index to South African Periodicals

ISMEC Mechanical Engineering Abstracts (Former titles (until 1993): I S M E C - Mechanical Engineering Abstracts; (until 1988): I S M E C Bulletin)

ISR Index to Scientific Reviews

ISRS †International Science Review Series

ISTA Information Science & Technology Abstracts (Online)

IUSGP U.S. Government Periodicals Index (Online)

IZBG International Review of Biblical Studies

ImmunAb Immunology Abstracts (Online)

IndBusRep †Index to Business Reports

IndChem Index Chemicus (Online)

IndIndia †Index India

IndMed †Index Medicus

IndVet Index Veterinarius

Inpharma †Inpharma Weekly (Formerly (until 1990): Inpharma)

Inspec Inspec
consists of:
Computer & Control Abstracts
†Current Papers in Electrical & Electronics Engineering
Current Papers in Physics
†Current Papers on Computers & Control
Electrical & Electronics Abstracts
Key Abstracts - Advanced Materials
Key Abstracts - Antennas & Propagation
Key Abstracts - Artificial Intelligence
Key Abstracts - Business Automation
Key Abstracts - Computer Communications and Storage
Key Abstracts - Computing in Electronics & Power
Key Abstracts - Electronic Circuits
Key Abstracts - Electronic Instrumentation
Key Abstracts - Factory Automation
Key Abstracts - High-Temperature Superconductors
Key Abstracts - Human-Computer Interaction
Key Abstracts - Machine Vision
Key Abstracts - Measurements in Physics
Key Abstracts - Microelectronics & Printed Circuits
Key Abstracts - Microwave Technology
Key Abstracts - Neural Networks
Key Abstracts - Optoelectronics
Key Abstracts - Power Systems & Applications
Key Abstracts - Robotics & Control
Key Abstracts - Semiconductor Devices
Key Abstracts - Software Engineering
Key Abstracts - Telecommunications
Physics Abstracts

J

J01 Jewish Studies Source

JAIE †Journal of Abstracts in International Education

JCLA †Journal of Current Laser Abstracts

JCQM †Journal Contents in Quantitative Methods

JCR-S J C R Web Science Edition

JCR-SS J C R Web Social Science Edition

JCT †Japan Computer Technology and Applications Abstracts

JEL Journal of Economic Literature (Formerly (until 1968): Journal of Economic Abstracts)

JHMA †Junior High Magazine Abstracts

JOF Journal of Ferrocement (Former titles: N Z F C M A Bulletin; N Z F C M A Newsletter)

JPI Kokuritsu Kokkai Toshokan Zasshi Kiji Sakuin CD-ROM Karento-Ban (Formerly (until 2002): N D L CD-ROM - Line Zasshi Kiji Sakuin. Karento-Ban; Which was formed by the merger of (1948-1996): Zasshi Kiji Sakuin. Jinbun Shakai-Hen - Japanese Periodicals Index. Humanities and Social Science; (1950-1996): Zasshi Kiji Sakuin. Gijutsu-Hen - Japanese Periodicals Index. Science and Technology)

JTA †Japan Technology Series (Formerly (until 1988): Japanese Technical Abstracts)

JW Journal Watch General Medicine (Formerly (until 2009): Journal Watch)

JW-C Journal Watch Cardiology

JW-D Journal Watch Dermatology

JW-EM Journal Watch Emergency Medicine

JW-G Journal Watch Gastroenterology

JW-ID Journal Watch Infectious Diseases

JW-N Journal Watch Neurology

JW-P Journal Watch Psychiatry

JW-WH Journal Watch Women's Health

JewAb †Jewish Abstracts

K

KES †Key to Economic Science (Formerly: Economic Abstracts)

KWIWR †Key Word Index of Wildlife Research

Kidney Kidney

L

L&LBA C S A Linguistics and Language Behavior Abstracts

L01 LGBT Life (Lesbian, Gay, Bisexual and Transgender)

L02 LGBT Life with Full Text (Lesbian, Gay, Bisexual and Transgender)

L03 Legal Collection

L04 Library, Information Science & Technology Abstracts (LISTA) with Full Text

L05 Literary Reference Center

L06 Literary Reference Center Plus

L07 Library Literature

L08 Library Literature & Information Science Full Text

L09 Library Literature & Information Science Retrospective

L10 Law Module

L11 Linguistics Abstracts (Online)

L13 L I S A: Library & Information Science Abstracts

LAMP L A M P (Literature Analysis of Microcomputer Publications)

LCR †Literary Criticism Register

LHTB †Library Hi Tech Bibliography

LID&ISL Lancaster Index to Defence & International Security Literature

LIFT	Literary Journals Index Full Text
LII	†Life Insurance Index
LIMI	Legal Information Management Index
LISTA	Library, Information Science & Technology Abstracts (LISTA)
LJI	†Legal Journals Index
LOIS	Law Office Information Service
LRI	LegalTrac (Formely: Legal Resource Index (Online))
LT&LA	Language Teaching (Former titles (until 1982): Language Teaching and Linguistics Abstracts; (until 1975): Language-Teaching Abstracts; (until 1968): English Teaching Abstracts)
LeadAb	†Leadscan (Formerly: Lead Abstracts)
LeftInd	Left Index (Online)
LegCont	†Legal Contents (Former titles (until 1980): C C L P: Contents of Current Legal Periodicals; (until 1976: Contents of Current Legal Periodicals; Incorporates: Survey of Law Reviews)
LibLit	Library Literature & Information Science Index
LogistBibl	Online Logistics Bibliography (Formerly: Bibliography of Logistics Management. Supplement)

M

M&GPA	Meteorological and Geoastrophysical Abstracts (Formerly (until 1960): Meteorological Abstracts and Bibliography)
M&MA	†Management and Marketing Abstracts (Formerly (until 1976): Marketing Abstracts)
M&PBA	Medical & Pharmaceutical Biotechnology Abstracts (Online)
M&TEA	C S A Mechanical & Transportation Engineering Abstracts (Cambridge Scientific Abstracts)
M01	MasterFILE Elite
M02	MasterFILE Premier
M04	Middle Search Plus
M05	Military & Government Collection
M06	Military and Intelligence
M07	Military Module
M08	Multicultural Module
M09	C S A Materials Research Database with METADEX
M10	Middle Eastern & Central Asian Studies
M11	Music Index (Online)
M12	Multicultural Education Abstracts (Online)
MA	†Mammalogy Abstracts
MAB	†Marine Affairs Bibliography
MAG	†Music Article Guide
MASUSE	M A S Ultra - School Edition (Magazine Article Summaries)
MBF	Materials Business File *consists of:* †Nonferrous Metals Alert †Polymers, Ceramics, Composites Alert †Steels Alert
MCIU	†Microcomputer Industry Update
MCR	Medical Care Research and Review (Former titles (until Mar. 1995): Medical Care Review; Public Health Economics and Medical Care Abstracts)
MEA&I	Middle East: Abstracts and Index
MEDLINE	MEDLINE
MEDOC	†Medoc: Index to U S Government Publications in the Medical and Health Sciences
MEDSOC	†Medical Socioeconomic Research Sources (Formerly: Index to the Literature of Medical Socioeconomics)
MELSA	†M E L S A Messenger (Metropolitan Library Service Agency)
METADEX	METADEX *consists of:* Alloys Index Metals Abstracts Metals Abstracts Index
MFA	Surface Finishing Abstracts (Online)
MLA	†M L A Abstracts of Articles in Scholarly Journals
MLA-IB	M L A International Bibliography (Modern Language Association)
MMI	†Michigan Magazine Index
MOS	Methods in Organic Synthesis
MPI	†United Methodist Periodical Index (Formerly: Methodist Periodical Index)
MRD	†Media Review Digest (Formerly (until 1974): Multi Media Reviews Index)
MRefA	†Developmental Disabilities Abstracts (Former titles: Mental Retardation and Developmental Disabilities Abstracts; Mental Retardation Abstracts)
MResA	†Market Research Abstracts (Online) (Formerly (until 2000): Market Research Abstracts (Print))
MS&D	Medical & Surgical Dermatology
MSB	Mass Spectrometry Bulletin
MSCI	Materials Science Citation Index
MSCT	†Marine Science Contents Tables
MSF	Mystery Short Fiction
MSN	MathSciNet *consists of:* Current Mathematical Publications Mathematical Reviews
MagInd	†Magazine Index Plus (Formerly: Magazine Index)
MaizeAb	Maize Abstracts (Online)

ABSTRACTING AND INDEXING SERVICES

ManagAb	Indian Management Abstracts (Incorporates (1972-1989): Management Abstracts)
ManagCont	†Management Contents
MathR	Mathematical Reviews
MedAb	†Medical Abstract Service
MicrocompInd	Internet & Personal Computing Abstracts (Online)
MinerAb	†MinAbs Online (Formerly (until 2004): Mineralogical Abstracts (Print))
MusicInd	†The Music Index (Print)
MycolAb	†Abstracts of Mycology

N

N01	National Newspaper Index
N02	Nutrition and Food Sciences Database
N03	Nutrition Abstracts and Reviews Series A: Human and Experimental
N04	Nutrition Abstracts and Reviews Series B: Livestock Feeds and Feeding
N06	Nonprofit Organization Reference Center
NAA	†Nordic Archaeological Abstracts
NAmW	†North American Wildlife & Natural Resources Abstracts
NBA	†Notiziario Bibliografico di Audiologia O R L e Foniatria (Formerly: Notiziario Bibliografico di Audiologia)
NPI	†New Periodicals Index
NPPA	†Noise Pollution Publications Abstracts
NPU	Natural Product Updates
NRN	Nutrition Research Newsletter (Incorporates (1990-1998): Food Safety Notebook)
NSA	C S A Neurosciences Abstracts (Online) (Cambridge Scientific Abstracts)
NSCI	Neuroscience Citation Index
NTA	New Testament Abstracts (Online)
NewsAb	Newspaper Abstracts
NucAcAb	Nucleic Acids Abstracts (Online)
NumL	Numismatic Literature
NurAb	†Nursing Abstracts

O

OGFA	C S A Oncogenes and Growth Factors Abstracts (Cambridge Scientific Abstracts)
OR	Organic Research Database
ORA	†Oral Research Abstracts
ORMS	Operations Research - Management Science
OTA	Old Testament Abstracts
OceAb	Oceanic Abstracts (Former titles (until 1984): Oceanic Abstracts with Indexes; (until 1972): Oceanic Index; Oceanic Citation Index)
OffTech	†Offshore Technology
OphLit	†Ophthalmic Literature
OrnA	†Ornithology Abstracts
OrnithAb	†Essential Ornithological Abstracts

P

P&BA	Paperbase Abstracts (Incorporates (1989-2001): Nonwovens Abstracts; Formerly (until 1995): Paper and Board Abstracts)
P01	Primary Search
P02	Periodical Abstracts
P03	PsycFIRST
P04	Professional Development Collection
P05	Points of View Reference Centre
P06	P A I S Archive
P07	Professional Collection
P08	PRISMA (Publicaciones y Revistas Sociales y Humanisticas)
P09	PCI Espanol
P10	ProQuest Research Library
P11	ProQuest Agriculture Journals
P12	Psychology Module
P13	ProQuest Research Library Core
P14	ProQuest Asian Business
P15	ProQuest Biology Journals
P16	ProQuest Career and Technical Education
P17	ProQuest Computing
P18	ProQuest Education Journals
P19	ProQuest Family Health
P20	ProQuest Health and Medical Complete
P21	ProQuest Health Management
P22	ProQuest Medical Library
P23	ProQuest Newsstand (Complete)
P24	ProQuest Nursing and Allied Health Source
P25	ProQuest Psychology Journals
P26	ProQuest Science Journals
P27	ProQuest Social Science Journals
P28	ProQuest Religion
P29	ProQuest Telecommunications
P30	PubMed
P32	Plant Genetics and Breeding Database
P33	Parasitology Database
P34	Public Affairs Index
P36	Pakistan Psychological Abstracts (Online)
P41	ProQuest Entrepreneurship
P42	Political Science Complete
P43	Psychology & Behavioral Sciences Collection
P44	Petroleum Abstracts (Online)
P45	ProQuest Political Science
P46	ProQuest Sociology
P47	ProQuest Military Collection
P48	Professional ProQuest Central

P49	ProQuest Computer Science Collection
P50	ProQuest Public Health
P51	Professional ABI/INFORM Complete
P52	ProQuest SciTech Journals
P53	ProQuest 5000
P54	ProQuest 5000 International
P55	ProQuest Professional Education
P56	ProQuest Natural Science Journals
PAA&I	Documentation in Public Administration (Supersedes: Public Administration Abstracts and Index of Articles)
PABMI	†Performing Arts Biography Master Index (Formerly: Theatre, Film, and Television Biographies Master Index)
PADDI	Planning Architecture Design Database Ireland
PAIS	P A I S International (Public Affairs Information Service)
PC&CA	†Abstracts of Research in Pastoral Care and Counseling (Formerly: Pastoral Care and Counseling Abstracts)
PCAb	†P C Abstracts
PCI	PIO - Periodicals Index Online (Formerly (until 2006): Periodicals Contents Index)
PCR2	P C R 2 (Personal Computer Review - Squared)
PEBNI	†Petroleum - Energy Business News Index
PEI	Physical Education Index
PGegResA	Plant Genetic Resources Abstracts
PGrRegA	Plant Growth Regulator Abstracts
PHN&I	Postharvest News and Information
PLESA	Quarterly Index to Africana Periodical Literature (Formerly (until 2000): Quarterly Index to Periodical Literature, Eastern and Southern Africa)
PLII	†Property & Liability Insurance Index
PMA	International Abstracts of Human Resources (Formerly (until 2003): Personnel Management Abstracts)
PMI	†Photography Magazine Index
PMPI	†Popular Music Periodicals Index
PMR	†Magazine Article Summaries (Formerly (until 1987): Popular Magazine Review)
PN&I	Pig News & Information
PNI	Pharmaceutical News Index
PPI	†Popular Periodical Index
PQC	ProQuest Central
PRA	Peace Research Abstracts
PROMT	PROMT (Predicasts Overview of Markets and Technology)
PSA	C S A Worldwide Political Science Abstracts (Cambridge Scientific Abstracts) (Formed by the 2000 merger of: A B C Pol Sci (Online); (1984-2000): Political Science Abstracts (Online); Which superseded (in 1997): Political Science Abstracts. Annual Supplement (Print); (1967-1980): Political Science, Government, and Public Policy Series. Annual Supplement)
PSI	†Philanthropic Studies Index
PST	†Packaging Science and Technology Abstracts
PdeR	Repere (Online) (Former titles: Repere (Print); (until 1993): Point de Repere; Which was formed by the merger of (1972-1983): Periodex; (1972-1983): Radar (Montreal))
PerIslam	†Periodica Islamica
PersLit	†Personnel Literature
PetrolAb	†Petroleum Abstracts (Print)
PhilInd	The Philosopher's Index
PhilipAb	Philippine Science and Technology Abstracts (Formerly: Philippine Science and Technology Abstracts Bibliography; Formed by the merger of: Philippine Abstracts; Philippine Science Index)
PhotoAb	Imaging Abstracts (Formerly (until 1988): Photographic Abstracts)
PhotoInd	Photography Index
PhysBer	†Physics Briefs - Physikalische Berichte (Formerly (until 1980): Physikalische Berichte; Which was formed by the merger of (1877-1920): Beiblaetter zu den Annalen der Physik; (1845-1920): Halbmonatliches Literaturverzeichnis der Fortschritte der Physik)
Pinpoint	†Pinpointer
PlantSci	†Plant Science
PollutAb	Pollution Abstracts (Incorporates (1970-2009): E I S)
PopulInd	†Population Index (Formerly (until 1937): Population Literature)
Press	Press (Formed by the merger of (1946-2001): Printing Abstracts; (1991-2001): World Publishing Monitor; Which was formerly (1983-1991): Electronic Publishing Abstracts)
PsycInfo	PsycINFO
PsycholAb	†Psychological Abstracts
PsycholRG	†Psychological Reader's Guide
PsychopharAb	†Psychopharmacology Abstracts

Q

QAb	†Quality Abstracts
QC&AS	Quality Control and Applied Statistics

R

R&TA	Religious & Theological Abstracts
R01	Regional Business News

R02	Risk Management Reference Center
R03	Readers' Guide Full Text Mega Edition
R04	Readers' Guide Retrospective
R05	Religion and Philosophy Collection
R06	Resource/One
R07	Review of Agricultural Entomology
R08	Review of Medical and Veterinary Entomology
R09	Rehabilitation & Sports Medicine Source
R14	Recent Science Index
R15	Referencia Latina
R16	Reaction Citation Index (Online)
R17	Research into Higher Education Abstracts (Online)
R18	Rapra Abstracts Database
RA&MP	Review of Aromatic and Medicinal Plants
RASB	Russian Academy of Sciences Bibliographies
REE&TA	†Rural Extension, Education and Training Abstracts
RGAb	Readers' Guide Abstracts
RGPR	Readers' Guide to Periodical Literature (Online)
RGYP	†Reader's Guide for Young People
RI-1	†Religion Index One: Periodicals (Formerly: Index to Religious Periodical Literature)
RI-2	†Religion Index Two: Multi-Author Works
RICS	Isurv Knowledge Alert (Formed by the merger of (1965-2005): R I C S Abstracts and Reviews; (1965-2005): R I C S Weekly Briefing)
RILM	RILM Abstracts of Music Literature (Repertoire International de Litterature Musicale)
RM&VM	Review of Medical and Veterinary Mycology (Formerly (until 1951): An Annotated Bibliography of Medical Mycology)
RPFIA	Reference Point: Food Industry Abstracts (Former titles (until 1980): F M I Monthly Index Service; (until 1976): S M I Monthly Index Service (Super Market Institute))
RRTA	Leisure, Recreation and Tourism Abstracts (Formerly (until 1981): Rural Recreation and Tourism Abstracts)
Reac	Reactions Weekly (Print) (Formerly (until 1990): Reactions)
RefSour	†Reference Sources (Supersedes (in 1979): Reference Book Review Index)
RefZh	Referativnyi Zhurnal
RefugAb	Refugee Survey Quarterly (Formerly (until 1994): Refugee Abstracts)
RehabLit	†Rehabilitation Literature (Formerly (until 195?): Bulletin on Current Literature)
Repind	Repindex
ResCtrInd	Resource Center Index (Formerly: Micrographics Index)
RiskAb	Risk Abstracts (Online)
RoboAb	†Robotics Abstracts (Formerly (until 1989): Robomatix Reporter)

S

S&MA	†Sorghum and Millets (Supersedes (in 1994): Sorghum and Millets Abstracts)
S&VD	Shock & Vibration Digest
S01	Science and Technology
S02	SocINDEX
S03	SocINDEX with Full Text
S04	Science Full Text Select
S05	Social Sciences Index Retrospective
S06	Science in Context (Formerly: Science Resource Center)
S07	Shakespeare Collection
S08	Student Resource Center College (w/Academic ASAP)
S09	Student Resource Center College (w/ Expanded Academic ASAP)
S10	Sciences Module
S11	Social Sciences Module
S12	Sugar Industry Abstracts
S13	Soil Science Database
S14	Scientific Publications Index
S15	Scholarly Journals Index
S18	Scientific Resources Database
S19	Sociology of Education Abstracts (Online)
S20	Special Educational Needs Abstracts (Online)
S21	Studies on Women and Gender Abstracts (Online)
S22	Small Business Reference Center
S23	Student Resources in Context (Formed by the 2010 merger of: Student Resource Center College (w/ Expanded Academic ASAP); Student Resource Center College (w/ Academic ASAP))
SAA	†Small Animals (Formerly (until 1991): Small Animal Abstracts)
SASA	State Academies of Science Abstracts
SBPI	Southern Baptist Periodical Index
SCI	Science Citation Index Expanded
SCIMP	†S C I M P (Selective Cooperative Index of Management Periodicals)
SCOPUS	Scopus
SD	SPORTDiscus with Full Text
SEJI	State Education Journal Index and Educators' Guide to Periodicals Research Strategies (Formerly (until 1985): State Education Journal Index)
SFSA	Family Studies Abstracts
SJI	Stamp Journals Index
SJW	†Selected Journals on Water

SLSI	†Sri Lanka Science Index
SOPODA	†Social Planning - Policy & Development Abstracts (Formerly: Social Welfare, Social Planning, Policy and Social Development)
SPAA	Public Administration Abstracts (Formerly (until 2008): Sage Public Administration Abstracts (Online))
SPI	†Sports Periodicals Index
SPPI	South Pacific Periodicals Index (Formerly (until 1978): Bibliography of Periodical Articles Relating to the South Pacific)
SRI	Statistical Reference Index
SRRA	Race Relations Abstracts (Formerly (until 2008): Sage Race Relations Abstracts (Online))
SSA	Social Services Abstracts
SSAI	Social Sciences Full Text *consists of:* Social Sciences Abstracts; Social Sciences Index
SSAb	Social Sciences Abstracts
SSCI	Social Sciences Citation Index
SSI	Social Sciences Index
SSciA	C S A Sustainability Science Abstracts (Cambridge Scientific Abstracts)
ST&MA	†Statistical Theory and Method Abstracts (CD-ROM) (Former titles (until vol.42, 2002): Statistical Theory and Method Abstracts (Print); (until 1964): International Journal of Abstracts)
SUSA	Urban Studies Abstracts (Formerly (until 2008): Sage Urban Studies Abstracts (Online))
SWR&A	Social Work Abstracts (Supersedes in part (in 1994): Social Work Research and Abstracts; Which was formerly (until 1977): Abstracts for Social Workers)
SWRA	Water Resources Abstracts (Online)
Search	†Search (Devon)
SociolAb	Sociological Abstracts (Online)
SoftAbEng	†Software Abstracts for Engineers
SoftBase	SoftBase
SolStAb	Solid State and Superconductivity Abstracts (Former titles: Solid State Abstracts Journal; Solid State Abstracts; Incorporates: Science Research Abstracts Journal. Laser and Electro-Optic Reviews, Quantum Electronics, Unconventional Energy Sources; Science Research Abstracts Journal. Superconductivity, Magnetohydrodynamics and Plasma, Theoretical Physics; Which was formerly: Science Research Abstracts, Part A. MHD and Plasma, Superconductivity and Research, and Theoretical Physics; Which incorporated: Theoretical Physics Journal)
SoyAb	Soybean Abstracts (Online)
SpeleolAb	Speleological Abstracts
SportS	†SportSearch (Former titles (until 1985): Sport and Fitness Index; (until 1984): Sport and Recreation Index - Index de la Litterature des Sports et des Loisirs; (until 1977): Sport Articles)

T

T&DA	†Training and Development Alert
T&II	†Trade & Industry Index
T01	Textile Technology Complete
T02	TOC Premier (Table of Contents)
T03	TableBase
T04	C S A Technology Research Database
T05	Tropical Diseases Bulletin
TAR	TropAg & Rural
TCEA	Theoretical Chemical Engineering (Formerly (until 1991): Theoretical Chemical Engineering Abstracts)
THA	†Tobacco & Health Abstracts (Formerly: Tobacco and Health)
TM	TEMA - Technology and Management
TMA	†Top Management Abstracts (Supersedes in part: Anbar Management Services Abstracts)
TOM	†T O M (Text on Microfilm)
TOSA	†Tropical Oil Seeds (Formerly (until 1991): Tropical Oil Seeds Abstracts)
TRA	†Transportation Research Abstracts (Formerly: Highway Research Abstracts)
TTI	Textile Technology Index (Formerly (until 2002): Textile Technology Digest (Online))
TelAb	†Telecommunications Abstracts
Telegen	†Telegen Abstracts (Formerly: Telegen Reporter)
TobAb	Tobacco Abstracts
ToxAb	Toxicology Abstracts
TriticAb	Wheat, Barley and Triticale Abstracts (Formerly (until 1984): Triticale Abstracts)

U

U01	UK/EIRE Reference Centre

V

UAA	†Urban Affairs Abstracts
V&AA	Violence & Abuse Abstracts
V01	Vente et Gestion (Formerly: French Business Source)
V02	Vocational & Career Collection
V03	Vocational Studies Complete
V04	Vocational Studies Premier

V05 Vocational Education & Training Abstracts (Online) (Formerly (until 2009): Technical Education & Training Abstracts (Online))

VITIS Vitis - Viticulture and Oenology Abstracts (Online) (Formerly (until 2003): Vitis - Viticulture and Oenology Abstracts (Print))

VirolAbstr Virology and AIDS Abstracts (Formerly (until 1988): Virology Abstracts)

W

W&CBA †Essential Wildlife & Conservation Biology Abstracts

W01 Wilson Business Abstracts

W02 Wilson Business Full Text

W03 Wilson OmniFile: Full Text Mega Edition

W04 World History Collection

W05 Wilson OmniFile: Full Text Select

W06 Women's Interests Module

W07 Web of Science

W08 Wildlife & Ecology Studies Worldwide (Incorporates: Wildlife Review Abstracts)

W09 Women's Studies International

W10 Weed Abstracts

W11 World Agricultural Economics and Rural Sociology Abstracts

WAA Aluminum Industry Abstracts (Formerly (until 1991): World Aluminum Abstracts)

WBA World Banking Abstracts

WBSS †World Bibliography of Social Security

WLA †Wildlife Abstracts

WLR †Wildlife Review

WMB †World Magazine Bank

WSA Women Studies Abstracts

WSCA World Surface Coating Abstracts (Formerly (until 1969): Review of Current Literature on the Paint and Allied Industries)

WSI †G. K. Hall's Women's Studies Index (Formerly (until 1999): Women's Studies Index (Year))

WTA World Textile Abstracts (Online)

WasteInfo WasteInfo

WatResAb Hydro-Abstracts (Formerly (until 1980): Water Resources Abstracts)

Weldasearch Weldasearch Select (Formerly: Weldalert)

WildRev Wildlife Review Abstracts (Formerly (until 1996): Wildlife Review (Print))

WorkRelAb †Work Related Abstracts (Formerly: Employment Relations Abstracts)

Y

YAE&RB †Association for Education and Rehabilitation of the Blind and Visually Impaired. Yearbook (Incorporates (in 1982): Blindness, Visual Impairment, Deaf-Blindness; Which was formerly: Blindness)

Z

Z01 Zoological Record Online

Z02 Zentralblatt MATH (Online)

Zincscan Zincscan (Former titles (until 1986): Zinc Abstracts; (until 1961): Z D A Abstracts)

Subjects

English	Francais	Deutsch	Español
Abstracting and Indexing Services	Services d'Analyse et d'Indexage	Referate- und Indexdienste	Servicio de Análisis e Indización
Advertising and Public Relations	Publicité et Relations Publiques	Reklamewesen und Public Relations	Relaciones Públicas y Publicidad
Aeronautics and Space Flight	Aéronautique et Astronautique	Luft- und Raumfahrt	Aeronáutica y Vuelo Espacial
Computer Applications	Applications Informatiques	Computer Anwendung	Aplicaciones para Computadoras
Agriculture	Agriculture	Landwirtschaft	Agricultura
Agricultural Economics	Agriculture Economique	Agrarökonomie	Economía Agrícola
Agricultural Equipment	Outillage Agricole	Landwirtschaftsgeräte	Equipo para la Agricultura
Computer Applications	Applications Informatiques	Computer Anwendung	Aplicaciones para Computadoras
Crop Production and Soil	Production Végétale et Terrain	Ernte und Acker	Producción de Cosecha, Tierra
Dairying and Dairy Products	Production Laitière	Milchwirtschaft	Lechería y Productos Lácteos
Feed, Flour and Grain	Pature, Farine et Grain	Futter, Mehl und Getreide	Forraje, Granos y Harina
Poultry and Livestock	Elevage	Geflügel- und Viehwirtschaft	Aves de Corral y Ganadería
Alternative Medicine	Médecine Alternative	Alternative Heilkunde	Medicina Alternativa
Animal Welfare	Protection des Animaux	Tierschutz	Protección a los Animales
Anthropology	Anthropologie	Anthropologie	Antropología
Antiques	Antiquités	Antiquitäten	Antigüedades
Archaeology	Archeologie	Archaeologie	Arqueología
Computer Applications	Applications Informatiques	Computer Anwendung	Aplicaciones para Computadoras
Architecture	Architecture	Architektur	Arquitectura
Computer Applications	Applications Informatiques	Computer Anwendung	Aplicaciones para Computadoras
Art	Art	Kunst	Arte
Computer Applications	Applications Informatiques	Computer Anwendung	Aplicaciones para Computadoras
Arts and Handicrafts	Arts et Métiers	Kunst und Handwerk	Artesanías y Obras Manuales
Asian Studies	Etudes Asiatiques	Asiatische Studien	Asiatische Studien
Astrology	Astrologie	Astrologie	Astrología
Astronomy	Astronomie	Astronomie	Astronomía
Computer Applications	Applications Informatiques	Computer Anwendung	Aplicaciones para Computadoras
Beauty Culture	Soins de Beauté	Schönheitspflege	Belleza Personal
Perfumes and Cosmetics	Parfums et Cosmétiques	Kosmetik und Parfüme	Perfumes y Cosméticos
Beverages	Boissons	Getränke	Bebidas
Bibliographies	Bibliographies	Bibliographien	Bibliografías
Biography	Biographie	Biographie	Biografía
Biology	Biologie	Biologie	Biología
Biochemistry	Biochimie	Biochemie	Bio-química
Bioengineering	Biogénie	Bioingenieurwesen	Bio-ingeniería
Biophysics	Biophysique	Biophysik	Biofísica
Biotechnology	Biotechnologie	Biotechnologie	Biotecnología
Botany	Botanique	Botanik	Botánica
Computer Applications	Applications Informatiques	Computer Anwendung	Aplicaciones para Computadoras
Cytology and Histology	Cytologie et Histologie	Zytologie und Histologie	Citología e Histología
Entomology	Entomologie	Entomologie	Entomología
Genetics	Génétique	Genetik	Genética
Microbiology	Microbiologie	Mikrobiologie	Microbiología
Microscopy	Microscopie	Mikroskopie	Microscopía
Ornithology	Ornithologie	Ornithologie	Ornitología
Physiology	Physiologie	Physiologie	Fisiología
Zoology	Zoologie	Zoologie	Zoología
Birth Control	Limitation des Naissances	Geburtenregelung	Control de Natalidad
Building and Construction	Bâtiment et Construction	Bauwesen	Edificios y Construcción
Carpentry and Woodwork	Charpenterie et Menuiserie	Zimmerhandwerk und Holzbau	Carpintería y Ebanistería
Hardware	Quincaillerie	Metallbaustoffe	Ferretería
Business and Economics	Affaires et Economie	Wirtschaft und Handel	Economía y Negocios
Accounting	Comptabilité	Rechnungswesen	Contabilidad
Banking and Finance	Banque et Finance	Bank- und Finanzwesen	Bancos y Finanzas
Banking and Finance-Computer Applications	Banque et Finance-Applications Informatiques	Bank- und Finanzwesen-Computer Anwendung	Bancos y Finanzas-Aplicaciones para Computadoras
Chamber of Commerce Publications	Publications des Chambres de Commerce	Veröffentlichungen von Handelskammern	Publicaciones de las Cámaras de Comercio
Computer Applications	Applications Informatiques	Computer Anwendung	Aplicaciones para Computadoras
Cooperatives	Coopératives	Genossenschaften	Cooperativas
Domestic Commerce	Commerce Interieur	Binnenhandel	Comercio Interno
Economic Situation and Conditions	Situations et Conditions Economiques	Wirtschaftliche Situation und Verhältnisse	Condiciones y Situaciones Económicas
Economic Systems and Theories, Economic History	Systèmes et Théories Economiques, Histoire Economique	Okonomische Systeme und Theorien, Wirtschafts-geschichte	Sistemas y Teorías Economicos, Historia de la Economia
International Commerce	Commerce International	Aussenhandel	Comercio Internacional
International Development and Assistance	Aide et Développement Internationaux	Internationale Entwicklungshilfe	Desarrollo y Asistencia Internacional
Investments	Investissements	Investitionen	Inversiones
Labor and Industrial Relations	Travail et Relations Industrielles	Arbeits und Industrielle Beziehungen	Trabajo y Relaciones Industriales
Macroeconomics	Macroéconomie	Makroökonomie	Macroeconomía
Management	Gestion	Betriebsführung	Gerencia
Marketing and Purchasing	Marketing et Achats	Marketing und Kauf	Ventas y Mercadeo
Office Equipment and Services	Matériel et Entretien de Bureaux	Büroeinrichtung und Service	Equipo y Servicios de Oficinas
Personnel Management	Gestion du Personnel	Personal Führung	Administración de Personal
Production of Goods and Services	Production de Biens et Services	Produktion	Producción de Bienes y Servicios
Public Finance, Taxation	Tresor Publique, Fiscalité	Staatsfinanzen, Steuerwesen	Finanzas Públicas e Impuestos
Small Business	Petites et Moyennes Entreprises	Kleinbetrieb	Pequeños Negocios
Trade and Industrial Directories	Annuaires de Commerce et d'Industrie	Firmenverzeichnisse	Directorios de la Industria y el Comercio
Ceramics, Glass and Pottery	Céramique, Verrerie et Poterie	Keramik, Glas und Töpferei	Cerámica, Vidrio y Porcelana

SUBJECTS

- Chemistry
  - Analytical Chemistry
  - Computer Applications
  - Crystallography
  - Electrochemistry
  - Inorganic Chemistry
  - Organic Chemistry
  - Physical Chemistry
- Children and Youth
  - About
  - For
- Civil Defense
- Classical Studies
- Cleaning and Dyeing
- Clothing Trade
  - Fashions
- Clubs
- College and Alumni
- Communications
  - Computer Applications
  - Postal Affairs
  - Radio
  - Telephone and Telegraph
  - Television and Cable
  - Video
- Computers
  - Artificial Intelligence
  - Automation
  - Calculating Machines
  - Circuits
  - Computer Architecture
  - Computer-Assisted Instruction
  - Computer Engineering
  - Computer Games
  - Computer Graphics
  - Computer Industry
  - Computer Industry Directories
  - Computer Industry, Vocational Guidance
  - Computer Music
  - Computer Networks
  - Computer Programming
  - Computer Sales
  - Computer Security
  - Computer Simulation
  - Computer Systems
  - Cybernetics
  - Data Base Management
  - Data Communications, Data Transmission Systems
  - Electronic Data Processing
  - Hardware
  - Information Science, Information Theory
  - Internet
  - Machine Theory
  - Microcomputers
  - Minicomputers
  - Personal Computers
  - Robotics
  - Software
  - Theory of Computing
  - Word Processing
- Conservation
- Consumer Education and Protection
- Criminology and Law Enforcement
  - Computer Applications
  - Security
- Dance
- Drug Abuse and Alcoholism
- Earth Sciences
  - Computer Applications
  - Geology
  - Geophysics
  - Hydrology
  - Oceanography
- Education
  - Adult Education
  - Computer Applications
  - Guides to Schools and Colleges
  - Higher Education
  - International Education Programs
  - School Organization and Administration
  - Special Education and Rehabilitation
  - Teaching Methods and Curriculum

- Chimie
  - Chimie Analytique
  - Applications Informatiques
  - Cristallographie
  - Electrochimie
  - Chimie Inorganique
  - Chimie Organique
  - Physicochimie
- Enfants et Adolescents
  - Au Sujet des
  - Pour
- Defense Civile
- Etudes Classiques
- Nettoyage et Teinturerie
- Vêtement
  - Mode
- Clubs
- Université et Diplomés
- Communications
  - Applications Informatiques
  - Courrier
  - Radio
  - Téléphone et Télégraphe
  - Télévision
  - Vidéo
- Ordinateurs
  - Intelligence Artificielle
  - Automation
  - Calculateurs
  - Circuits
  - Architecture de la Machine
  - Enseignement Assisté par Ordinateur
  - Technique Informatique
  - Jeux sur Ordinateurs
  - Conception Assistée par Ordinateur
  - Industrie Informatique
  - Annuaire de l'Industrie Informatique
  - Industrie Informatique, Orientation Professionnelle
  - Musique sur Ordinateur
  - Réseaux d'Ordinateurs
  - Programmation Informatique
  - Ventes d'Ordinateurs
  - Sécurité Informatique
  - Simulation sur Ordinateurs
  - Systèmes Informatiques
  - Cybernétique
  - Gestion de Base de Données
  - Communication de Données
  - Traitement de l'Information Electronique
  - Matériel
  - Théorie de l'Information
  - Internet
  - Théorie de Machine
  - Micro-Ordinateurs
  - Mini-Ordinateurs
  - Ordinateurs Personnels
  - Robotique
  - Logiciel
  - Théorie de Traitement
  - Traitement de Textes
- Conservation
- Protection du Consommateur
- Criminologie et Police
  - Applications Informatiques
  - Securité
- Danse
- Toxicomanie et Alcoolisme
- Sciences Géologiques
  - Applications Informatiques
  - Géologie
  - Géophysique
  - Hydrologie
  - Océanographie
- Education
  - Enseignement des Adultes
  - Applications Informatiques
  - Guides des Ecoles et Colleges
  - Enseignement Supérieur
  - Programmes d'Education Internationale
  - Organisation et Administration de l'Ecole
  - Enseignement Special et Réhabilitation
  - Méthodes Pédagogiques et Programmes Scolaires

- Chemie
  - Analytische Chemie
  - Computer Anwendung
  - Kristallographie
  - Elektrochemie
  - Anorganische Chemie
  - Organische Chemie
  - Physikalische Chemie
- Kinder und Jugend
  - Uber
  - Für
- Ziviler Bevölkerungsschutz
- Klassische Studien
- Reinigen und Färben
- Bekleidungsgewerbe
  - Moden
- Klubs
- Universitäten und Hochschulabsolventen
- Nachrichtentechnik
  - Computer Anwendung
  - Postwesen
  - Rundfunk
  - Telephon und Telegraph
  - Fernsehen und Bildfrequenzkanal
  - Video
- Computer
  - Künstliche Intelligenz
  - Automatisierung
  - Rechenmaschine
  - Schaltungen
  - Computer Architektur
  - Computerunterstützter Unterricht
  - Computerentwicklung
  - Computer Spiele
  - Computergraphik
  - Computerbetrieb
  - Computerbetriebverzeichnisse
  - Computerbetrieb Berufsberatung
  - Computer Musik
  - Rechnernetz
  - Computerprogrammierung
  - Computervertrieb
  - Computersicherheit
  - Computersimulation
  - Computersystemen
  - Kybernetik
  - Datenbankverwaltung
  - Datenübertragung, Datenübertragungssystem
  - Elektronische Datenverarbeitung
  - Hardware
  - Informationstheorie
  - Internet
  - Maschinetheorie
  - Mikrocomputer
  - Minicomputer
  - Persönlichecomputer
  - Robotersysteme
  - Software
  - Computertheorie
  - Textverarbeitung
- Landschaftsschutz
- Verbraucherswirtschaftsschutz
- Kriminologie und Strafvollzug
  - Computer Anwendung
  - Sicherheit
- Tanz
- Rauschgiftsucht und Alkoholismus
- Wissenschaften der Erde
  - Computer Anwendung
  - Geologie
  - Geophysik
  - Hydrologie
  - Ozeanographie
- Bildungswesen
  - Erwachsenenbildung
  - Computer Anwendung
  - Führer zur Schulen und Universitäten
  - Hochschulwesen
  - Internazionale Erziehungsprogramme
  - Organisation und Verwaltung von dem Schule
  - Fachunterricht und Rehabilitierung
  - Lehrmethoden und Lehrplan

- Química
- Química Analítica
  - Aplicaciones para Computadoras
  - Cristalografía
  - Electroquímica
  - Química Inorgánica
  - Química Orgánica
  - Química Física
- Niños y Jóvenes
  - Acerca
  - Para
- Defensa Civil
- Estudios Clásicos
- Limpieza y Tintura
- Industria del Vestido
  - Modas
- Clubes
- Universidades y Exalumnos
- Comunicaciones
  - Aplicaciones para Computadoras
  - Correo
  - Radio
  - Teléfono y Telégrafo
  - Cable y Televisión
  - Video
- Computadoras
  - Inteligencia Artificial
  - Automatización
  - Calculadoras
  - Circuitos
  - Arquitectura de las Computadoras
  - Enseñanza con la Ayuda de las Computadoras
  - Ingeniería de las Computadoras
  - Juegos para Computadoras
  - Diseño a través de Computadoras
  - Industria de las Computadoras
  - Directorios de la Industria de las Computadoras
  - Guía para la Industria de las Computadoras
  - Música a través de Computadoras
  - Redes de Computadoras
  - Programación de Computadoras
  - Ventas de Computadoras
  - Seguridad en Computadoras
  - Simulación a través de Computadoras
  - Sistemas de Computadoras
  - Cibernética
  - Bases de Datos
  - Comunicación y Transmisión de Datos
  - Procesamiento Electrónico de Datos
  - Equipo Físico
  - Ciencia y Teoría de la Información
  - Internet
  - Teoría de las Máquinas
  - Microcomputadoras
  - Minicomputadoras
  - Computadoras Personales
  - Robótica
  - Aplicaciones de Computadora
  - Teoría de Cálculo
  - Procesador de Textos
- Conservación
- Protección al Consumidor
- Criminología y Acción Policial
  - Aplicaciones para Computadoras
  - Seguridad
- Baile
- Alcoholismo y Drogadicción
- Ciencias Geológicas
  - Aplicaciones para Computadoras
  - Geología
  - Geofísica
  - Hidrología
  - Oceanografía
- Educación
  - Educación para Adultos
  - Aplicaciones para Computadoras
  - Guías de Escuelas y Colegios
  - Educación Superior
  - Programas Internacionales de Educación
  - Administración y Dirección de Escuelas
  - Educación Especial y Rehabilitación
  - Métodos y Planes de Estudio

- Electronics
  - Computer Applications
- Encyclopedias and General Almanacs
- Energy
  - Computer Applications
  - Electrical Energy
  - Geothermal Energy
  - Hydroelectrical Energy
  - Nuclear Energy
  - Solar Energy
  - Wind Energy
- Engineering
  - Chemical Engineering
  - Civil Engineering
  - Computer Applications
  - Electrical Engineering
  - Engineering Mechanics and Materials
  - Hydraulic Engineering
  - Industrial Engineering
  - Mechanical Engineering
- Environmental Studies
  - Computer Applications
  - Pollution
  - Toxicology and Environmental Safety
  - Waste Management
- Ethnic Interests
- Fire Prevention
- Fish and Fisheries
- Folklore
- Food and Food Industries
  - Bakers and Confectioners
  - Grocery Trade
- Forest and Forestry
  - Lumber and Wood
- Funerals
- Gardening and Horticulture
  - Florist Trade
- Genealogy and Heraldry
  - Computer Applications
- General Interest Periodicals (Subdivided by country)
- Geography
  - Computer Applications
- Gerontology and Geriatrics
- Giftware and Toys
- Handicapped
  - Computer Applications
  - Hearing Impaired
  - Physically Impaired
  - Visually Impaired
- Health Facilities and Administration
- Heating, Plumbing, and Refrigeration
- History
  - Computer Applications
  - History of Africa
  - History of Asia
  - History of Australasia and Other Areas
  - History of Europe
  - History of North and South America
  - History of Near East
- Hobbies
- Home Economics
- Homosexuality
- Hotels and Restaurants
  - Computer Applications
- Housing and Urban Planning
  - Computer Applications
- How-To and Do-It-Yourself
- Humanities: Comprehensive Works
  - Computer Applications
- Instruments
- Insurance
  - Computer Applications
- Interior Design and Decoration
  - Furniture and House Furnishings
- Jewelry, Clocks and Watches
- Journalism
- Labor Unions
- Law
  - Civil Law
  - Computer Applications
  - Constitutional Law
  - Corporate Law
  - Criminal Law

- Electronique
  - Applications Informatiques
- Encyclopédies et Almanachs Générales
- Energie
  - Applications Informatiques
  - Energie Electrique
  - Energie Géothermique
  - Energie Hydraulique
  - Energie Nucléaire
  - Energie Solaire
  - Energie Eolienne
- Ingénierie
  - Génie Chimique
  - Génie Civil
  - Applications Informatiques
  - Génie Electrique
  - Méchanique et Materiels
  - Génie Hydraulique
  - Génie Industriel
  - Génie Mécanique
- Science de l'Environnement
  - Applications Informatiques
  - Pollution
  - Toxicologie et Sécurité de l'Environnement
  - Gestion de Déchets
- Ethnologie
- Prévention d'Incendie
- Poisson et Pêche
- Folklore
- Alimentation et Industries Alimentaires
  - Boulangerie et Confiserie
  - Epicerie
- Forêts et Exploitation Forestière
  - Bois
- Funérailles
- Jardinage et Horticulture
  - Commerce des Fleurs
- Généalogie et Science Héraldique
  - Applications Informatiques
- Publications d'Intérêt Général (Selon pays)
- Géographie
  - Applications Informatiques
- Gérontologie
- Cadeaux et Jouets
- Handicapés
  - Applications Informatiques
  - Sourds
  - Handicapés Physiques
  - Aveugles
- Etablissements de Santé et Administration
- Chauffage, Plomberie et Réfrigeration
- Histoire
  - Applications Informatiques
  - Histoire de l'Afrique
  - Histoire de l'Asie
  - Histoire de l'Australasie et Autres Pays
  - Histoire de l'Europe
  - Histoire de l'Amérique du Nord et du Sud
  - Histoire du Proche-Orient
- Passe-Temps
- Gestion Domestique
- Homosexualité
- Hôtels et Restaurants
  - Applications Informatiques
- Logement et Urbanisme
  - Applications Informatiques
- Bricolage
- Humanités: Oeuvres d'Ensemble
  - Applications Informatiques
- Instruments
- Assurances
  - Applications Informatiques
- Agencements Intérieurs et Décoration
  - Meubles et Articles pour la Maison
- Bijouterie et Horlogerie
- Journalisme
- Syndicalisme
- Droit
  - Droit Civil
  - Applications Informatiques
  - Droit Constitutionel
  - Droit Commercial
  - Droit Pénal

- Elektronik
  - Computer Anwendung
- Enzyklopädien und Allgemeine Nachschlagewerke
- Energie
  - Computer Anwendung
  - Elektrizitätsenergie
  - Thermalenergie
  - Hydroelektroenergie
  - Kernenergie
  - Sonnenenergie
  - Windenergie
- Ingenieurwesen
  - Chemieingenieurwesen
  - Bauingenieurwesen
  - Computer Anwendung
  - Elektrotechnik
  - Ingenieurwesen Mechanik und Materialien
  - Wasserbau
  - Industrieingenieurwesen
  - Maschinenbau
- Umweltschutz
  - Computer Anwendung
  - Umweltverschmutzung
  - Toxokologie und Umweltsicherheit
  - Abfallwirtschaft
- Allgemeine Völkerkunde
- Brandbekämpfung
- Fische und Fischerei
- Volkskunde
- Nahrungsmittel und Lebensmittelindustrie
  - Bäcker- und Konditorgewerbe
  - Kolonialwarenhandel
- Forstwesen und Waldwirtschaft
  - Holz
- Beerdigungen
- Gartenpflege und Gartenbau
  - Blumenhandel
- Genealogie und Wappenkunde
  - Computer Anwendung
- Allgemeine Zeitschriften (nach Land)
- Geographie
  - Computer Anwendung
- Gerontologie
- Geschenkartikel und Spielwaren
- Behinderung
  - Computer Anwendung
  - Schwerhörigkeit
  - Körperbehinderung
  - Blindheit
- Gesundheitsanlagen und -verwaltung
- Heizung, Kühlung und Installation
- Geschichte
  - Computer Anwendung
  - Geschichte-Afrika
  - Geschichte-Asien
  - Geschichte-Australasien und Andere Gebieten
  - Geschichte-Europa
  - Geschichte-Nord- und Südamerika
  - Geschichte-Nahe Osten
- Hobbies
- Hauswirtschaft
- Homosexualität
- Hotels und Restaurants
  - Computer Anwendung
- Wohnungswesen und Stadtplanung
  - Computer Anwendung
- Selbstanfertigung
- Klassische Philologie
  - Computer Anwendung
- Instrumente
- Versicherungswesen
  - Computer Anwendung
- Innenarchitektur und Innenausstattung
  - Möbel und Wohnungseinrichtung
- Schmuck und Uhren
- Journalismus
- Gewerkschaften
- Rechtswissenschaft
  - Zivilrecht
  - Computer Anwendung
  - Verfassungsrecht
  - Handelsrecht
  - Strafrecht

- Electrónica
  - Aplicaciones para Computadoras
- Enciclopedias y Almanaques Generales
- Energía
  - Aplicaciones para Computadoras
  - Energía Eléctrica
  - Energía Geotérmica
  - Energía Hidroeléctrica
  - Energía Nuclear
  - Energía Solar
  - Energía de Viento
- Ingeniería
  - Ingeniería Química
  - Ingeniería Civil
  - Aplicaciones para Computadoras
  - Ingeniería Eléctrica
  - Ingeniería Mecanica y de Materiales
  - Ingeniería Hidráulica
  - Ingeniería Industrial
  - Ingeniería Mecánica
- Estudios Ambientales
  - Aplicaciones para Computadoras
  - Contaminación
  - Toxicología y Seguridad Ambiental
  - Administración de Desperdicios
- Publicaciones de Temas Etnicos
- Prevención del Fuego
- Pesca y Pesquerías
- Folklore
- Alimentos e Industrias de Alimentos
  - Panaderías y Dulcerías
  - Abacerías
- Bosques y Selvicultura
  - Maderas
- Funerales
- Jardinería y Horticultura
  - Comercio de Flores
- Genealogía y Heráldica
  - Aplicaciones para Computadoras
- Periódicos de Interés General (por país)
- Geografía
  - Aplicaciones para Computadoras
- Gerontología y Geriátrica
- Juguetes y Regalos
- Minusválido
  - Aplicaciones para Computadoras
  - Discapacitado del Oído
  - Discapacitado Físicamente
  - Discapacitado Visualmente
- Salud Pública y Administración
- Calefacción, Plomería y Refrigeración
- Historia
  - Aplicaciones para Computadoras
  - Historia de Africa
  - Historia de Asia
  - Historia de Australasia y Otras Areas
  - Historia de la Europa
  - Historia de América del Norte y del Sur
  - Historia del Cercano Oriente
- Pasatiempos
- Economía Doméstica
- Homosexualidad
- Restaurantes y Hoteles
  - Aplicaciones para Computadoras
- Planificación Urbana y Vivienda
  - Aplicaciones para Computadoras
- Cómo Hacerlo Usted Mismo
- Humanidades: Obras Completas
  - Aplicaciones para Computadoras
- Instrumentos
- Seguros
  - Aplicaciones para Computadoras
- Diseño Interior y Ornamentación
  - Muebles y Articulos para el Hogar
- Joyería y Relojería
- Periodismo
- Sindicatos
- Derecho
  - Derecho Civil
  - Aplicaciones para Computadoras
  - Derecho Constitucional
  - Derecho Corporativo
  - Derecho Criminal

SUBJECTS

Estate Planning
Family and Matrimonial Law
International Law
Judicial Systems
Legal Aid
Maritime Law
Military Law
Leather and Fur Industries
Leisure and Recreation
Library and Information Science
Computer Applications
Lifestyle
Linguistics
Computer Applications
Literary and Political Reviews

Literature
Adventure and Romance
Mystery and Detective
Poetry
Science Fiction, Fantasy, Horror

Machinery
Computer Applications
Mathematics
Computer Applications
Matrimony
Computer Applications
Medical Sciences
Allergology and Immunology
Anaesthesiology
Cardiovascular Diseases
Chiropractic, Homeopathy, Osteopathy
Communicable Diseases
Computer Applications
Dentistry
Dermatology and Venereology

Endocrinology
Experimental Medicine Laboratory Technique
Forensic Sciences
Gastroenterology
Hematology
Hypnosis
Internal Medicine
Nurses and Nursing
Obstetrics and Gynecology
Oncology
Ophthalmology and Optometry
Orthopedics and Traumatology
Otorhinolaryngology
Pediatrics
Physical Medicine and Rehabilitation
Psychiatry and Neurology
Radiology and Nuclear Medicine
Respiratory Diseases
Rheumatology
Sports Medicine
Surgery
Urology and Nephrology
Meetings and Congresses
Men's Health
Men's Interests
Men's Studies
Metallurgy
Computer Applications
Welding
Meteorology
Computer Applications
Metrology and Standardization
Computer Applications
Military
Mines and Mining Industry
Computer Applications
Motion Pictures
Museums and Art Galleries
Music
Computer Applications
Native American Studies

Needlework
New Age
Numismatics
Nutrition and Dietetics
Occupational Health and Safety

Occupations and Careers
Packaging
Computer Applications
Paints and Protective Coatings
Paleontology
Computer Applications

Succession
Droit Familial et Matrimonial
Droit International
Système Judiciaire
Assistance Judiciaire
Droit Maritime
Droit Militaire
Maroquinerie et Fourrure
Loisirs et Récréation
Bibliothéconomie et Informatique

Applications Informatiques
Divertissement
Linguistique
Applications Informatiques
Revues Littéraires et Politiques

Littérature
Aventure et Romance
Mystère et Policier
Poésie
Science-Fiction, Fantastisque, Horreur
Machines
Applications Informatiques
Mathématiques
Applications Informatiques
Mariage
Applications Informatiques
Médecine
Allergologie et Immunologie
Anesthésiologie
Maladies Cardiovasculaires
Chiropraxie, Homéopathie, Ostéopathie
Maladies Contagieuses
Applications Informatiques
Dentisterie
Dermatologie et Maladies Vénériennes
Endocrinologie
Médecine Expérimentale, Techniques de Laboratoire
Médecine Légale
Gastroentérologie
Hématologie
Hypnose
Médecine Interne
Personnel et Soins Infirmiers
Obstétrique et Gynécologie
Cancer
Ophtalmologie et Optométrie
Orthopédie et Traumatologie
Otorhinolaryngologie
Pédiatrie
Médecine Physique et Réhabilitation
Psychiatrie et Neurologie
Radiologie et Médecine Nucléaire
Maladies Respiratoires
Rhumatologie
Médecine du Sport
Chirurgie
Urologie et Néphrologie
Réunions et Congrès
Santé de l'Homme
Publications d'Intérêt Masculin
Etudes de l'Homme
Métallurgie
Applications Informatiques
Soudure
Météorologie
Applications Informatiques
Métrologie et Standardisation
Applications Informatiques
Militaires
Mines et Resources Minières
Applications Informatiques
Cinéma
Musées et Galleries
Musique
Applications Informatiques
Etudes des Amérindiens

Travaux de Couture
New Age
Numismatique
Nutrition et Diététique
Médecine du Travail et Prévention

Emplois et Carrières
Emballage
Applications Informatiques
Couleurs et Peintures
Paléontologie
Applications Informatiques

Mobiliarvermögensrecht
Ehegesetz und Familienrecht
Völkerrecht
Gerichtswesen
Rechtshilfe
Seerecht
Kriegsrecht
Leder und Pelz
Freizeit und Unterhaltung
Bibliothek- und Informationswissenschaft
Computer Anwendung
Lebensstil
Sprachwissenschaft
Computer Anwendung
Literarische und Politische Zeitschriften
Literatur
Abenteuer und Romantik
Geheimnis und Detektivroman
Poesie
Zukunftsroman, Phantasiegebilde, Grausen
Maschinenwesen
Computer Anwendung
Mathematik
Computer Anwendung
Ehestand
Computer Anwendung
Medizinische Wissenschaften
Allergie und Immunologie
Anaesthesiologie
Kreislauferkrankungen
Chiropraktik, Homöopathie, Osteopathie
Infektiöse Krankheiten
Computer Anwendung
Zahnmedizin
Dermatologie und Geschlechtskrankheiten
Endokrinologie
Versuchsmedizin, Laboratoriumstechnik
Gerichtliche Medizin
Gastroenterologie
Hämatologie
Hypnose
Innere Medizin
Krankenpflege
Gynäkologie und Geburtshilfe
Onkologie
Opthalmologie und Optometrie
Orthopädie und Traumatologie
Otorhinolaryngologie
Pädiatrie
Physikalische Heilkunde und Rehabilitation
Psychiatrie und Neurologie
Radiologie und Nuklearmedizin
Atmungskrankheiten
Rheumatologie
Sportmedizin
Chirurgie
Urologie und Nephrologie
Tagungen und Kongresse
Gesundheit von Männern
Männer Interessen
Männerstudien
Metallurgie
Computer Anwendung
Schweissen
Meteorologie
Computer Anwendung
Mass- und Gewichtskunde, Normung
Computer Anwendung
Militärwesen
Bergwesen und Bergbauindustrie
Computer Anwendung
Film und Kino
Museen und Kunstgalerien
Musik
Computer Anwendung
Studienfach Eingeborenen Amerikaner
Näherei
New Age
Numismatik
Ernährung und Diätetik
Berufsgesundheitspflege und Sicherheit
Berufe
Verpackung
Computer Anwendung
Farben und Beläge
Paleontologie
Computer Anwendung

Planificación de Bienes Raíces
Derecho Familial y Matrimonial
Derecho Internacional
Sistemas Judiciales
Ayuda Legal
Derecho Marítimo
Derecho Militar
Pieles y Cuero
Tiempo Libre y Recreación
Bibliotecología y Ciencias de la Información
Aplicaciones para Computadoras
Entretenimiento
Lingüística
Aplicaciones para Computadoras
Revistas Literarias y Políticas

Literatura
Aventura y Romance
Misterio y Novela Policiaca
Poesía
Ciencia Ficción, Fantasía, Horror

Maquinaria
Aplicaciones para Computadoras
Matemáticas
Aplicaciones para Computadoras
Matrimonio
Aplicaciones para Computadoras
Ciencias Médicas
Alergología e Imunología
Anestesiología
Enfermedades Cardiovasculares
Quiropráctica, Homeopatía, Osteopatía
Enfermedades Contagiosas
Aplicaciones para Computadoras
Odontología
Dermatología y Venereología

Endocrinología
Medicina Experimental, Técnicas del Laboratorio
Ciencias Forenses
Gastroenterología
Hematología
Hipnotismo
Medicina Interna
Enfermeros y Enfermería
Obstetricia y Ginecología
Oncología
Oftalmología y Optometría
Ortopedia y Traumatología
Otorinolaringología
Pediatría
Medicina Física y de Rehabilitación
Psiquiatría y Neurología
Radiología y Medicina Nuclear
Enfermedades Respiratorias
Reumatología
Medicina del Deporte
Cirugía
Urología y Nefrología
Conferencias y Congresos
Salud de los Hombres
Intereses Masculinos
Estudios de los Hombres
Metalurgia
Aplicaciones para Computadoras
Soldadura
Meteorología
Aplicaciones para Computadoras
Metrología y Normalización
Aplicaciones para Computadoras
Militares
Minas e Industria Minera
Aplicaciones para Computadoras
Películas
Museos y Galerías del Arte
Música
Aplicaciones para Computadoras
Estudios de los Americanos Nativos

Bordado
Nueva Epoca
Numismática
Dietas y Nutrición
Sanidad y Seguridad en el Trabajo

Empleos y Ocupaciones
Empaque
Aplicaciones para Computadoras
Pinturas y Revestimientos Protectores
Paleontología
Aplicaciones para Computadoras

Paper and Pulp	Papier et Pulpe	Papier und Papierstoff	Papel y Pulpa
Parapsychology and Occultism	Parapsychologie et Occultisme	Parapsychologie und Okkultismus	Parapsicología y Ocultismo
Patents, Trademarks and Copyrights	Brevets, Marques Commerciales et Droits d'Auteur	Patente, Schutzmarken und Urheberrechte	Patentes, Marcas Registradas y Derechos de Autor
Petroleum and Gas	Pétrole et Gas Naturel	Petroleum und Gas	Petróleo y Gas Natural
Computer Applications	Applications Informatiques	Computer Anwendung	Aplicaciones para Computadoras
Pets	Animaux Familiers	Haustiere	Mascotas
Pharmacy and Pharmacology	Pharmacie et Pharmacologie	Pharmazie und Pharmakologie	Farmacia y Farmacología
Computer Applications	Applications Informatiques	Computer Anwendung	Aplicaciones para Computadoras
Philately	Philatélie	Briefmarkenkunde	Filatelia
Philosophy	Philosophie	Philosophie	Filosofía
Photography	Photographie	Photographie	Fotografía
Computer Applications	Applications Informatiques	Computer Anwendung	Aplicaciones para Computadoras
Physical Fitness and Hygiene	Santé Physique et Hygiène	Gesundheitszustand und Hygiene	Salud Física e Higiene
Physics	Physique	Physik	Física
Computer Applications	Applications Informatiques	Computer Anwendung	Aplicaciones para Computadoras
Electricity	Electricité	Elektrizität	Electricidad
Heat	Chaleur	Wärme	Calor
Mechanics	Mécanique	Mechanik	Mecánica
Nuclear Physics	Physique Nucléaire	Kernphysik	Física Nuclear
Optics	Optique	Optik	Optica
Sound	Son	Schall	Sonido
Plastics	Plastiques	Kunststoffe	Plásticos
Computer Applications	Applications Informatiques	Computer Anwendung	Aplicaciones para Computadoras
Political Science	Sciences Politiques	Politische Wissenschafte	Ciencias Políticas
Civil Rights	Droits Civiques	Bürgerrechte	Derechos Civiles
International Relations	Relations Internationales	Internationale Beziehungen	Relaciones Internacionales
Population Studies	Démographie	Bevölkerungswissenschaft	Demografía
Printing	Imprimerie	Druck	Imprenta
Computer Applications	Applications Informatiques	Computer Anwendung	Aplicaciones para Computadoras
Psychology	Psychologie	Psychologie	Psicología
Public Administration	Administration Publique	Offentliche Verwaltung	Administración Pública
Computer Applications	Applications Informatiques	Computer Anwendung	Aplicaciones para Computadoras
Municipal Government	Gouvernement Municipal	Kommunalverwaltung	Gobierno Municipal
Public Health and Safety	Santé Publique et Prévention	Offentliche Gesundheitspflege	Salud y Seguridad Pública
Publishing and Book Trade	Edition et Commerce du Livre	Verlagswesen und Buchhandel	Editoriales y Ferias de Libros
Computer Applications	Applications Informatiques	Computer Anwendung	Aplicaciones para Computadoras
Real Estate	Immobiliers	Grundbesitz und Immobilien	Bienes Raíces
Computer Applications	Applications Informatiques	Computer Anwendung	Aplicaciones para Computadoras
Religions and Theology	Religions et Théologie	Religion und Theologie	Religión y Teología
Buddhist	Bouddhisme	Buddhist	Budismo
Eastern Orthodox	Eglises Orthodoxes	Orthodox	Inglesias Ortodoxas
Hindu	Hindouisme	Hindu	Hinduísmo
Islamic	Islam	Islamische	Islamísmo
Judaic	Judaisme	Jüdäistische	Judaísmo
Protestant	Protestantisme	Evangelische	Iglesia Protestante
Roman Catholic	Catholicisme Romain	Römisch-katholische	Católico Romano
Other Denominations and Sects	Autres	Andere Bekenntnisse und Sekte	Otras Denominaciones y Sectas
Rubber	Caoutchouc	Gummi	Caucho
Computer Applications	Applications Informatiques	Computer Anwendung	Aplicaciones para Computadoras
Sciences: Comprehensive Works	Sciences: Oeuvres d'Ensemble	Wissenschaften: Umfassende Werke	Ciencias: Obras Completas
Computer Applications	Applications Informatiques	Computer Anwendung	Aplicaciones para Computadoras
Shoes and Boots	Chaussures et Bottes	Schuhe und Stiefel	Zapatos y Botas
Singles' Interests and Lifestyles	Intérêts et Style de Vie Célibataire	Ledigenstandinteressen	Intereses y Estilos de Vida de Solteros
Social Sciences: Comprehensive Works	Sciences Sociales: Oeuvres d'Ensemble	Sozialwissenschaften: Umfassende Werke	Ciencias Sociales: Obras Completas
Social Service and Welfare	Service Social et Protection Sociale	Sozialpflege und Fürsorge	Asistencia y Bienestar Social
Sociology	Sociologie	Soziologie	Sociología
Computer Applications	Applications Informatiques	Computer Anwendung	Aplicaciones para Computadoras
Sound Recording and Reproduction	Enregistrement et Reproduction du Son	Tonaufnahme und Tonwiedergabe	Grabaciones y Reproducciones Sonoras
Computer Applications	Applications Informatiques	Computer Anwendung	Aplicaciones para Computadoras
Sports and Games	Sports et Jeux	Sport und Spiele	Deportes y Juegos
Ball Games	Jeux de Balle	Ballspiele	Juegos de Pelota
Bicycles and Motorcycles	Bicyclettes et Motocyclettes	Fahrräder und Motorräder	Bicicletas y Motocicletas
Boats and Boating	Bateaux et Canotage	Boote und Bootfahren	Barcos y Canotaje
Horses and Horsemanship	Equitation	Pferde und Reitsport	Caballos y Equitación
Outdoor Life	Vie en Plein Air	Im Freien	Vida de Campo
Statistics	Statistiques	Statistik	Estadísticas
Technology: Comprehensive Works	Technologie: Oeuvres d'Ensemble	Technologie: Umfassende Werke	Tecnología: Obras Completas
Textile Industries and Fabrics	Textiles	Textil	Telas e Industria Textil
Computer Applications	Applications Informatiques	Computer Anwendung	Aplicaciones para Computadoras
Theater	Théâtre	Theater	Teatro
Tobacco	Tabac	Tabak	Tabaco
Transportation	Transports	Transport	Transporte
Air Transport	Transport Aérien	Luftverkehr	Transporte Aéreo
Automobiles	Automobiles	Kraftfahrzeugen	Automóviles
Computer Applications	Applications Informatiques	Computer Anwendung	Aplicaciones para Computadoras
Railroads	Chemins de Fer	Eisenbahnen	Ferrocarriles
Roads and Traffic	Routes et Circulation	Strassen und Strassenverkehr	Caminos y Tráfico
Ships and Shipping	Navires et Transport Maritimes	Schiffe und Schiffahrt	Barcos y Embarques
Trucks and Trucking	Transports Routiers	Lastkraftwagen	Camiones
Travel and Tourism	Voyages et Tourisme	Reisen und Tourismus	Viaje y Turismo
Airline Inflight and Hotel Inroom	Revues pour Vol de Lignes Aériennes et pour Chambres d'Hôtels	Fluggesellschaft und Hotel Veröffentlichungen	Vuelo en Aerolínea y Cuarto de Hotel
Veterinary Sciences	Science Vétérinaire	Tierheilkunde	Veterinaria
Computer Applications	Applications Informatiques	Computer Anwendung	Aplicaciones para Computadoras
Water Resources	Ressources en Eau	Wasserwirtschaft	Recursos del Agua
Computer Applications	Applications Informatiques	Computer Anwendung	Aplicaciones de los Computadoras
Women's Health	Santé de la Femme	Gesundheit von Frauen	Salud de las Mujeres
Women's Interests	Publications d'Intérêt Féminin	Fraueninteresse	Intereses Femininos
Women's Studies	Etudes de la Femme	Frauenstudien	Estudios de las Mujeres

Classified List of Serials
Subjects Med-G - Z

This section contains bibliographic information for currently published serials, classified by subject. Publisher, address and contact data are provided. See the User's Guide for more information on the many fields included in complete entries.

MEDICAL SCIENCES—Gastroenterology

616.33 USA
A G A EDIGEST. Text in English. 19??. w. free to members (effective 2010). back issues avail. **Document type:** *Newsletter, Academic/Scholarly.*
Formerly: A G A News (Print) (1064-8097)
Media: E-mail. **Related titles:** Online - full content ed.
Published by: American Gastroenterological Association, 4930 Del Ray Ave, Bethesda, MD 20814. TEL 301-654-2055, FAX 301-654-5920, info@gastro.org. Eds. Eugene Chang, F Taylor Wootton.

616.3 USA ISSN 1554-3366
A G A PERPECTIVES. Text in English. 2005 (Feb./Mar.). bi-m. free to members (effective 2010). back issues avail. **Document type:** *Magazine, Trade.* **Description:** Provides an opinion forum for noted gastroenterologists to debate today's most controversial topics and provides brief updates on other topics relevant to academic and practicing physicians and scientists.
Related titles: Online - full text ed.: ISSN 1555-7502. free (effective 2010).
Published by: American Gastroenterological Association, 4930 Del Ray Ave, Bethesda, MD 20814. TEL 301-654-2055, FAX 301-654-5920, info@gastro.org. Ed. Sheila E Crowe.

616.3 616.07 USA ISSN 0942-8925
RC804.D52 CODEN: ABIMEL
➤ **ABDOMINAL IMAGING.** Text in English. 1976. bi-m. (in 1 vol., 6 nos./vol.). EUR 964, USD 1,020 combined subscription to institutions (print & online eds.) (effective 2012). adv. back issues avail.; reprint service avail. from PSC. **Document type:** *Journal, Academic/Scholarly.* **Description:** Brings together previously disparate information of value to radiologists, internists, and surgeons involved in diagnostic imaging of the alimentary tract and the genitourinary system.
Formerly: Gastrointestinal Radiology (0364-2356); Incorporates (in 1993): Urologic Radiology (0171-1091)
Related titles: Microform ed.: (from PQC); Online - full text ed.: ISSN 1432-0509 (from IngentaConnect).
Indexed: A01, A03, A08, A22, A26, ASCA, B&BAb, B19, B25, BIOSIS Prev, CA, CurCont, E01, EMBASE, ExcerpMed, H12, IIL, ISR, IndMed, Inpharma, JW-G, MEDLINE, MycolAb, P20, P22, P24, P30, P48, P54, PQC, R10, Reac, SCI, SCOPUS, T02, W07.
—BLDSC (0537.809800), GNLM, IE, Infotrieve, Ingenta, INIST. **CCC.**
Published by: Springer New York LLC (Subsidiary of: Springer Science+Business Media), 233 Spring St, New York, NY 10013. TEL 212-460-1500, 800-777-4643, journals@springer-ny.com. Ed. Morton A Meyers TEL 631-444-2480. **Subscr. outside the Americas to:** Springer Distribution Center, Kundenservice Zeitschriften, Haberstr 7, Heidelberg 69126, Germany. TEL 49-6221-3454303, FAX 49-6221-3454229, subscriptions@springer.com; **Subscr. to:** Journal Fulfillment, PO Box 2485, Secaucus, NJ 07096. TEL 201-348-4033, FAX 201-348-4505.

616.4 616.3 FRA ISSN 0240-642X
RC78.7.E5 CODEN: AENDD5
ACTA ENDOSCOPICA. Text in English, French. 1971. 5/yr. EUR 278, USD 295 combined subscription to institutions (print & online eds.) (effective 2012). adv. bk.rev. reprint service avail. from PSC. **Document type:** *Journal, Academic/Scholarly.*
Formerly (until 1978): Acta Endoscopica et Radiocinematographica (0397-9164)
Related titles: Online - full text ed.: ISSN 1765-3134 (from IngentaConnect); ♦ Supplement(s): Acta Endoscopica. Supplement. ISSN 1242-1383.
Indexed: A22, E01, EMBASE, ExcerpMed, FR, P30, R10, Reac, SCI, SCOPUS, W07.
—BLDSC (0614.620000), GNLM, IE, Infotrieve, Ingenta, INIST. **CCC.**
Published by: Springer France (Subsidiary of: Springer Science+Business Media), 22 Rue de Palestro, Paris, 75002, France. TEL 33-1-53009860, FAX 33-1-53009861, sylvie.kamara@springer.com. Ed. Denis Heresbach. Circ: 4,500. **Subscr. in Americas to:** Springer New York LLC, Journal Fulfillment, PO Box 2485, Secaucus, NJ 07096. TEL 800-777-4643, 201-348-4033, FAX 201-348-4505, journals-ny@springer.com, http://www.springer.com; **Subscr. to:** Springer Distribution Center, Kundenservice Zeitschriften, Haberstr 7, Heidelberg 69126, Germany. TEL 49-6221-3454303, FAX 49-6221-3454229, subscriptions@springer.com, http://link.springer.de. **Co-sponsors:** Interamerican Society for Digestive Endoscopy; Societe Medicale d'Imagerie, Enseignement et Recherche.

616.4 616.3 FRA ISSN 1242-1383
ACTA ENDOSCOPICA. SUPPLEMENT. Text in French. 1987. irreg., latest 2002.
Related titles: ♦ Supplement to: Acta Endoscopica. ISSN 0240-642X.
—INIST.
Published by: Springer France (Subsidiary of: Springer Science+Business Media), 22 Rue de Palestro, Paris, 75002, France. TEL 33-1-53009860, FAX 33-1-53009861, sylvie.kamara@springer.com, http://www.springer.com.

616.3 BEL ISSN 1784-3227
CODEN: AGEBAX
➤ **ACTA GASTRO-ENTEROLOGICA BELGICA.** Text in English. 1933. q. free domestic; EUR 34.80 in Europe; EUR 51.80 elsewhere (effective 2007). adv. bk.rev. abstr.; bibl.; charts; illus. index. Supplement avail. **Document type:** *Journal, Academic/Scholarly.*
Formerly (until 1996): Acta Gastro-Enterologica Belgica (Multilingual Edition) (0001-5644)
Related titles: Online - full text ed.
Indexed: A22, ASCA, ChemAb, CurCont, EMBASE, ExcerpMed, IndMed, Inpharma, MEDLINE, P30, P35, R10, Reac, SCI, SCOPUS, W07.
—BLDSC (0616.700000), CASDDS, GNLM, IE, Infotrieve, Ingenta, INIST. **CCC.**
Published by: (Societe Royale Belge de Gastro-Enterologie), Universa Press, Rue Hoender 24, Wetteren, 9230, Belgium. TEL 32-9-3691563, info@universa.be. Ed. Pierre Deprez. Circ: 1,000.

616.3 ARG ISSN 0300-9033
RC799 CODEN: AGLTBL
➤ **ACTA GASTROENTEROLOGICA LATINOAMERICANA.** Text in Spanish. 1969. 5/yr. ARS 50 domestic; USD 70 foreign (effective 2010). adv. bk.rev. **Document type:** *Academic/Scholarly.* **Description:** Contains original research in clinical or basic gastroenterology.
Related titles: CD-ROM ed.
Indexed: A22, B25, BIOSIS Prev, C01, ChemAb, EMBASE, ExcerpMed, IndMed, MEDLINE, MycolAb, P30, R10, Reac, SCOPUS.
—BLDSC (0616.730000), CASDDS, GNLM, IE, Infotrieve, Ingenta.
Published by: Sociedad Argentina de Gastroenterologia, Marcelo T de Alvear 1381, 9o Piso, Buenos Aires, Argentina. TEL 54-11-4816 9391, FAX 54-11-4812 6568, secretaria@sage.org.ar, http://www.sage.org.ar. Circ: 3,500 (controlled).

616.3 ITA ISSN 1721-2596
ACTA VULNOLOGICA; a journal on physiopathology and therapy of chronic cutaneous ulcers. Text in Multiple languages. 2002. q. EUR 240 combined subscription in the European Union to institutions print & online eds.; EUR 265 combined subscription elsewhere to institutions print & online eds. (effective 2011). **Document type:** *Journal, Academic/Scholarly.* **Description:** Covers the pathophysiology and clinical medicine of chronic cutaneous ulcers.
Related titles: Online - full text ed.: ISSN 1827-1774. 2005.
—BLDSC (0672.130000).
Published by: (Associazione Italiana Ulcere Cutanee), Edizioni Minerva Medica, Corso Bramante 83-85, Turin, 10126, Italy. TEL 39-011-678282, FAX 39-011-674502, journals.dept@minervamedica.it, http://www.minervamedica.it.

616.35 FRA ISSN 1622-4191
LES ACTUALITES EN GASTROENTEROLOGIE. Variant title: Actualites Medicales Internationales. Gastroenterologie. Text in French. 1987. m. adv. Supplement avail. **Document type:** *Journal, Academic/Scholarly.* **Description:** Covers clinical and applied research in the field.
Formerly (until 2000): Gastroenterologie (0989-263X)
—**CCC.**
Published by: Medica-Press International, 62-64 rue Jean-Jaures, Puteaux, 92800, France. TEL 33-1-41458000, FAX 33-1-41458025, contact@edimark.fr, http://www.edimark.fr.

616.3 616.994 GBR ISSN 1479-9995
QP151
ADVANCES IN GASTROINTESTINAL CANCERS. Text in English. 2003. q. GBP 88 domestic to individuals; GBP 100 in Europe to individuals; GBP 120 elsewhere to individuals; GBP 150 domestic to institutions; GBP 160 in Europe to institutions; GBP 170 elsewhere to institutions (effective 2010). **Document type:** *Journal, Academic/Scholarly.* **Description:** Provide educational and academic information that is current, topical and generally of a high reference value.
Indexed: A01, A26, EMBASE, ExcerpMed, H12, I05, SCOPUS.
—BLDSC (0707.670000), IE, Ingenta. **CCC.**
Published by: Mediscript Ltd., 1 Mountview Ct, 310 Friern Barnet Ln, London, N20 0LD, United Kingdom. TEL 44-20-84468898, FAX 44-20-84469194, info@mediscript.ltd.uk, http://www.mediscript.ltd.uk/.

616.3 FRA ISSN 2106-9085
AFAMAGAZINE. Text in French. 199?. s-a. **Document type:** *Magazine, Consumer.*
Published by: Association Francois Aupetit, La Maison des MICI, 78 Quai de Jemmapes, Paris, 75010, France. TEL 31-1-42000040, info-accueil@afa.asso.fr, http://www.afa.asso.fr.

616.3 GBR ISSN 0269-2813
CODEN: APTHEN
➤ **ALIMENTARY PHARMACOLOGY AND THERAPEUTICS.** Variant title: A P & T. Text in English. 1987. s-m. GBP 1,694 in United Kingdom to institutions; EUR 2,151 in Europe to institutions; USD 3,132 in the Americas to institutions; USD 3,652 elsewhere to institutions; GBP 1,949 combined subscription in United Kingdom to institutions (print & online eds.); EUR 2,475 combined subscription in Europe to institutions (print & online eds.); USD 3,602 combined subscription in the Americas to institutions (print & online eds.); USD 4,200 combined subscription elsewhere to institutions (print & online eds.) (effective 2012). adv. bk.rev. illus. index. back issues avail.; reprint service avail. from PSC. **Document type:** *Journal, Academic/Scholarly.* **Description:** Provides specialising in clinical aspects of gastroenterology.
Related titles: Microform ed.: (from PQC); Online - full text ed.: ISSN 1365-2036. GBP 1,694 in United Kingdom to institutions; EUR 2,151 in Europe to institutions; USD 3,132 in the Americas to institutions; USD 3,652 elsewhere to institutions (effective 2012) (from IngentaConnect); ♦ Supplement(s): Alimentary Pharmacology and Therapeutics. Supplement. ISSN 0953-0673.

Indexed: A01, A02, A03, A08, A22, A26, A29, A36, A37, ASCA, AgrForAb, B20, B21, B25, BIOSIS Prev, C11, CA, CABA, CIN, ChemAb, ChemTitl, CurCont, D01, DBA, E01, E12, EMBASE, ESPM, ExcerpMed, F08, F12, FR, GH, H04, H12, I10, ISR, ImmunAb, IndMed, Inpharma, JW-G, LT, MEDLINE, MycolAb, N02, N03, NSA, P30, P33, P35, P39, PHN&I, PN&I, R07, R10, R12, RA&MP, RM&VM, RRTA, Reac, S01, S12, SCI, SCOPUS, SoyAb, T02, T05, TriticAb, VS, VirolAbstr, W07, W10.
—BLDSC (0787.886000), CASDDS, GNLM, IE, Infotrieve, Ingenta, INIST. **CCC.**
Published by: Wiley-Blackwell Publishing Ltd. (Subsidiary of: John Wiley & Sons, Inc.), 9600 Garsington Rd, Oxford, OX4 2DQ, United Kingdom. TEL 44-1865-776868, FAX 44-1865-714591, customerservices@blackwellpublishing.com. Eds. R E Pounder, W L Peterson. Pub. Allen Stevens. R&P Sophie Savage. Adv. contact Jenny Applin. Circ: 1,920.

616.3 GBR ISSN 0953-0673
ALIMENTARY PHARMACOLOGY AND THERAPEUTICS. SUPPLEMENT. Text in English. 1987. s-m. USD 3,066 (effective 2009). adv. **Document type:** *Journal, Academic/Scholarly.*
Related titles: Online - full text ed.: USD 3,066 (effective 2009) (from IngentaConnect); ◆ Supplement to: Alimentary Pharmacology and Therapeutics. ISSN 0269-2813.
Indexed: SCOPUS.
—Ingenta, INIST. **CCC.**
Published by: Wiley-Blackwell Publishing Ltd. (Subsidiary of: John Wiley & Sons, Inc.), 9600 Garsington Rd, Oxford, OX4 2DQ, United Kingdom. TEL 44-1865-776868, FAX 44-1865-714591, customerservices@blackwellpublishing.com, http://www.wiley.com/. Ed. Anne-Marie Cannon.

616.3 ESP
AMERICAN JOURNAL OF GASTROENTEROLOGIA (SPANISH EDITION). Text in Spanish. 6/yr. EUR 75 (effective 2005). back issues avail. **Document type:** *Journal, Academic/Scholarly.*
Related titles: ◆ English ed.: American Journal of Gastroenterology. ISSN 0002-9270.
Published by: Grupo Saned, Capitan Haya 60, 1o, Madrid, 28028, Spain. TEL 34-91-7499500, FAX 34-91-7499501, saned@medynet.com, http://www.gruposaned.com. Ed. Juan Ramon Malagelada.

616.3 USA ISSN 0002-9270
RC799 CODEN: AJGAAR
➤ **AMERICAN JOURNAL OF GASTROENTEROLOGY.** Abbreviated title: A J G. Text in English. 1934. m. EUR 936 in Europe to institutions; GBP 605 to institutions in UK & elsewhere;; USD 1,177 in the Americas to institutions; JPY 160,200 in Japan to institutions (effective 2011). bk.rev. abstr.; bibl.; illus.; stat. index. back issues avail.; reprints avail. **Document type:** *Journal, Academic/Scholarly.* **Description:** Contains articles and reviews of current topics for gastroenterologists and internists.
Formerly (until 1954): Review of Gastroenterology (0096-2929)
Related titles: Microform ed.; Online - full text ed.: ISSN 1572-0241 (from IngentaConnect); ◆ Spanish ed.: American Journal of Gastroenterologia (Spanish Edition); ◆ Supplement(s): American Journal of Gastroenterology Supplements. ISSN 1948-9498.
Indexed: A01, A03, A08, A20, A22, A26, A29, A36, AIDS Ab, ASCA, B20, B21, B25, BIOBASE, BIOSIS Prev, CA, CABA, CIN, ChemAb, ChemTitl, Chicano, CurCont, D01, DBA, DentInd, E01, E12, EMBASE, ESPM, ExcerpMed, F08, FR, GH, H12, H16, H17, I10, IABS, IDIS, INI, ISR, IndMed, Inpharma, JW, JW-G, JW-ID, LT, MEDLINE, MycolAb, N02, N03, NRN, NSA, P30, P32, P33, P35, P37, P38, PN&I, R08, R10, R11, R12, RA&MP, RM&VM, RRTA, Reac, S01, S13, S16, SCI, SCOPUS, SoyAb, T02, T05, THA, TriticAb, VITIS, VS, VirolAbstr, W07.
—CASDDS, GNLM, IE, Infotrieve, Ingenta, INIST. **CCC.**
Published by: (American College of Gastroenterology, Inc.), Nature Publishing Group (Subsidiary of: Macmillan Publishers Ltd.), 75 Varick St, 9th Fl, New York, NY 10013. TEL 212-726-9200, FAX 212-696-9006, subscriptions@nature.com. Eds. Paul Moayyedi, William D Chey.

616.3 USA ISSN 1948-9498
▼ ➤ **AMERICAN JOURNAL OF GASTROENTEROLOGY SUPPLEMENTS.** Text in English. 2010. s-a. **Document type:** *Journal, Academic/Scholarly.* **Description:** A supplement series for American Journal of Gastroenterology, featuring research on all aspects of gastroenterology and hepatology.
Related titles: Online - full text ed.: ISSN 1948-9501; ◆ Supplement to: American Journal of Gastroenterology. ISSN 0002-9270.
—CCC.
Published by: Nature Publishing Group (Subsidiary of: Macmillan Publishers Ltd.), 75 Varick St, 9th Fl, New York, NY 10013. TEL 212-726-9200, FAX 212-696-9006, nature@natureny.com.

➤ **AMERICAN JOURNAL OF PHYSIOLOGY: GASTROINTESTINAL AND LIVER PHYSIOLOGY.** *see* BIOLOGY—Physiology

616.3 GRC ISSN 1108-7471
➤ **ANNALS OF GASTROENTEROLOGY.** Text in English. 1988. q. adv. bk.rev. **Document type:** *Journal, Academic/Scholarly.*
Formerly (until 2000): Ellenike Gastroenterologia / Hellenic Journal of Gastroenterology (1012-0424)
Related titles: Online - full text ed.: ISSN 1792-7463. free (effective 2011).
Indexed: EMBASE, ExcerpMed, R10, Reac, SCOPUS.
—BLDSC (1040.660000), GNLM, IE, Infotrieve, Ingenta.
Published by: (Hellenike Gastroenterologike Etaireia/Hellenic Society of Gastroenterology), Beta Medical Publishers Ltd., 3 Adrianiou St, Athens, 115 25, Greece. TEL 30-210-671-4371, FAX 30-210-671-5015, BetaMedArts@hol.gr.

616.3 GBR ISSN 2043-0221
▼ ➤ **THE ANNALS OF GASTROENTEROLOGY & HEPATOLOGY.** Abbreviated title: A G H. Text in English. 2010 (Jun.). s-a. free (effective 2011). back issues avail.; reprints avail. **Document type:** *Journal, Academic/Scholarly.*
Related titles: Online - full text ed.: ISSN 2043-023X.
Published by: San Lucas Medical Ltd., 11-12 Freetrade House, Lowther Rd, Stanmore, Middlesex HA7 1EP, United Kingdom. TEL 44-20-88167950, http://www.slm-oncology.com/.

616.3 NLD ISSN 1687-1979
RC799
➤ **ARAB JOURNAL OF GASTROENTEROLOGY.** Text in English. 2000. q. EUR 283 in Europe to institutions; JPY 47,200 in Japan to institutions; USD 449 elsewhere to institutions (effective 2012). **Document type:** *Journal, Academic/Scholarly.* **Description:** Publishes different studies related to the digestive system. It encompasses diverse studies related to the digestive system and its disorders, and serving the Pan-Arab and wider community working on gastrointestinal disorders.
Related titles: Online - full text ed.: ISSN 2090-2387 (from ScienceDirect).
Indexed: A26, CA, EMBASE, I05, P30, SCOPUS, T02.
—CCC.
Published by: (The Pan-Arab Association of Gastroenterology EGY), Elsevier BV, North-Holland (Subsidiary of: Elsevier Science & Technology), Sara Burgerhartstraat 25, Amsterdam, 1055 KV, Netherlands. TEL 31-20-4853911, FAX 31-20-4852457, JournalsCustomerServiceEMEA@elsevier.com. Ed. Abdel Meguid Kassem.

616.3 SRB ISSN 0354-2440
CODEN: ARGAEJ
ARCHIVES OF GASTROENTEROHEPATOLOGY; international quarterly journal devoted to clinical and basic studies of the digestive tract and liver. Text and summaries in English, Serbo-Croatian. 1982. q. free (effective 2007). adv. abstr.; bibl.; charts; illus.; pat.; stat. **Document type:** *Journal, Academic/Scholarly.* **Description:** Concerned with the practice and research of gastroenterology and hepatology.
Formerly: Gastroenterohepatoloski Arhiv (0352-082X)
Related titles: Online - full text ed.; ◆ Supplement(s): Archives of Gastroenterohepatology. Supplement. ISSN 0354-5644.
Indexed: EMBASE, ExcerpMed, R10, Reac, SCOPUS.
—BLDSC (1634.335000), GNLM, IE, Ingenta.
Published by: Srpsko Lekarsko Drustvo, Gastroenteroloska Sekcija, c/o Prof Goran Jankovic, Clinic for Gastroenterology and Hepatology, Clinical Center of Serbia, K Todorovica 6, Belgrade, 11000. gorjan@eunet.yu. Ed. Goran Jankovic. Circ: 800.

616.3 SRB ISSN 0354-5644
➤ **ARCHIVES OF GASTROENTEROHEPATOLOGY. SUPPLEMENT.** Text in English, Serbo-Croatian. 1994. a. **Document type:** *Journal, Academic/Scholarly.* **Description:** Devoted to clinical and basic studies of digestive tract and liver.
Related titles: ◆ Supplement to: Archives of Gastroenterohepatology. ISSN 0354-2440.
Published by: Srpsko Lekarsko Drustvo, Gastroenteroloska Sekcija, c/o Prof Goran Jankovic, Clinic for Gastroenterology and Hepatology, Clinical Center of Serbia, K Todorovica 6, Belgrade, 11000. gorjan@eunet.yu. Ed. Goran Jankovic.

616.3 ARG ISSN 0004-0517
ARCHIVOS ARGENTINOS DE ENFERMEDADES DEL APARATO DIGESTIVO. Text in Spanish. 1925. bi-m. adv. bk.rev.
Formerly (until 1947): Archivos Argentinos de Enfermedades del Aparato Digestivo y de la Nutricion (0301-5122)
Published by: Sociedad Argentina de Gastroenterologia, Marcelo T de Alvear 1381, 9o Piso, Buenos Aires, Argentina. TEL 54-11-4816 9391, FAX 54-11-4812 6568. Ed. Dr. Leonardo Pinchuck. Circ: 1,350.

ARCHIVOS DE ODONTOESTOMATOLOGIA. *see* MEDICAL SCIENCES—Dentistry

616.3 ITA ISSN 1120-8651
ARGOMENTI DI GASTROENTEROLOGIA CLINICA. Text in Italian. 1988. q. EUR 66 per issue (effective 2009). adv. **Document type:** *Journal, Academic/Scholarly.*
Indexed: A22, EMBASE, ExcerpMed, Inpharma, R10, Reac, SCOPUS.
—BLDSC (1664.344950), GNLM, IE, Ingenta. **CCC.**
Published by: Elsevier Masson (Subsidiary of: Elsevier Health Sciences), Via Paleocapa 7, Milan, 20121, Italy. TEL 39-02-881841, FAX 39-02-88184302, info@masson.it, http://www.masson.it. Ed. Gabriele Bianchi Porro. Circ: 6,000.

617.43 BRA ISSN 0102-6720
➤ **ARQUIVOS BRASILEIROS DE CIRURGIA DIGESTIVA.** Abbreviated title: A B C D. Text in English; Summaries in Portuguese. 1985. q. adv. bk.rev. cum.index. back issues avail. **Document type:** *Journal, Academic/Scholarly.*
Related titles: Online - full text ed.
Indexed: C01.
—GNLM.
Published by: (Universidade de Sao Paulo, Faculdade de Medicina), Lemos Editorial & Graficos Ltda., Rua Rui Barbosa, 70, B Vista, Sao Paulo, SP 01326-010, Brazil. TEL 55-11-251-4300, FAX 55-11-251-4300.

616.3 BRA ISSN 0004-2803
CODEN: ARQGAF
➤ **ARQUIVOS DE GASTROENTEROLOGIA.** Text in English, French, Portuguese, Spanish; Summaries in English, Portuguese. 1964. q. adv. bk.rev. charts; illus. index. reprint service avail. from IRC. **Document type:** *Journal, Academic/Scholarly.* **Description:** Publishes original papers, review articles, and case reports concerning all aspects of the digestive tract, including the liver.
Related titles: Microfilm ed.: (from PQC); Online - full text ed.: ISSN 1678-4219. 1999. free (effective 2011).
Indexed: A22, A36, B25, BIOSIS Prev, C01, CABA, ChemAb, E12, EMBASE, ExcerpMed, GH, H17, IndMed, MEDLINE, MycolAb, N02, N03, P30, P33, P39, R10, R12, RM&VM, Reac, SCOPUS, T05, VS, W11.
—BLDSC (1695.430000), CASDDS, GNLM, IE, Infotrieve, Ingenta, INIST.
Published by: Instituto Brasileiro de Estudos e Pesquisas de Gastroenterologia/Brazilian Institute for Studies and Research in Gastroenterology, Rua Dr Seng, 320, B Vista, Sao Paulo, SP 01331-020, Brazil. TEL 55-11-2882119, FAX 55-11-2892768. Ed. Nelson Henrique Michelsohn. Circ: 5,000 (controlled). **Co-sponsor:** Brazilian Society of Digestive Motility.

616.3005 AUS ISSN 1445-0232
ASIA PACIFIC DIGESTIVE NEWS. Abbreviated title: A P D. Text in English. 1999 (Dec.). irreg. **Document type:** *Newsletter, Consumer.*
Formerly (until 2000): Asian Pacific Gastroenterology News (1443-1386)
Related titles: Online - full text ed.: ISSN 1445-1425.
—CCC.
Published by: Wiley-Blackwell Publishing Asia (Subsidiary of: Wiley-Blackwell Publishing Ltd.), 155 Cremorne St, Richmond, VIC 3121, Australia. TEL 61-3-92743100, FAX 61-3-92743101, melbourne@wiley.com, http://www.wiley.com/WileyCDA/.

616.3 USA ISSN 0892-9386
➤ **AUDIO-DIGEST GASTROENTEROLOGY.** Text in English. 1987. s-m. USD 449.81 domestic; USD 479.72 in Canada; USD 527.72 elsewhere (effective 2010). back issues avail. **Document type:** *Journal, Academic/Scholarly.*
Media: Audio cassette/tape. **Related titles:** Audio CD ed.: USD 399.89 domestic; USD 431.72 in Canada; USD 479.72 elsewhere (effective 2010); Online - full text ed.: USD 359.72 (effective 2010).
Published by: Audio-Digest Foundation (Subsidiary of: California Medical Association), 1577 E Chevy Chase Dr, Glendale, CA 91206. TEL 818-240-7500, 800-423-2308, FAX 818-240-7379.

663 GBR ISSN 1471-230X
CODEN: BGMABE
➤ **B M C GASTROENTEROLOGY.** (BioMed Central) Text in English. 2001 (Jan.). irreg. free (effective 2011). adv. back issues avail.; reprints avail. **Document type:** *Journal, Academic/Scholarly.* **Description:** Features original research articles on all aspects of the prevention, diagnosis and management of gastrointestinal and hepatobiliary disorders, as well as related molecular genetics, pathophysiology, and epidemiology.
Media: Online - full text.
Indexed: A01, A02, A03, A08, A26, A34, A36, C06, C07, CA, CABA, CurCont, D01, E12, EMBASE, ExcerpMed, GH, H16, H17, I05, IndVet, Inpharma, MEDLINE, N02, N03, P20, P22, P30, P33, P35, P39, R08, R10, R12, RM&VM, Reac, S12, SCI, SCOPUS, SoyAb, T02, T05, VS, W07.
—Infotrieve. **CCC.**
Published by: BioMed Central Ltd. (Subsidiary of: Springer Science+Business Media), 236 Gray's Inn Rd, London, WC1X 8HB, United Kingdom. TEL 44-20-31922000, FAX 44-20-31922010, info@biomedcentral.com. Ed. Dr. Melissa Norton. Adv. contact Natasha Bailey TEL 44-20-31922231.

616.3 USA ISSN 1938-0127
B M I, BODY, MIND, INSPIRATION. Text in English. 2007. bi-m. **Document type:** *Newsletter, Consumer.*
Media: Online - full text.
Published by: Matrix Medical Communications, LLC, 1595 Paoli Pike, Ste 103, West Chester, PA 19380. TEL 484-266-0702, 866-325-9907, FAX 484-266-0726, editorial@matrixmedcom.com, http://www.matrixmedcom.com.

616.3 DEU
B V G D INFO. (Bundesverband Gastroenterologie Deutschland) Text in German. 2006. 4/yr. adv. **Document type:** *Magazine, Trade.*
Published by: Bundesverband Gastroenterologie Deutschland e.V., Olivaer Platz 7, Berlin, 10707, Germany. TEL 49-30-88729523, FAX 49-30-88774786, info@bvgd-online.de, http://www.bvgd-online.de. adv.: B&W page EUR 2,490, color page EUR 3,660. Circ: 3,700 (controlled).

616.3 GBR
RC799 CODEN: BBPGFG
➤ **BEST PRACTICE & RESEARCH: CLINICAL GASTROENTEROLOGY.** Text in English. 1987. bi-m. EUR 655 in Europe to institutions; JPY 70,600 in Japan to institutions; USD 580 elsewhere to institutions (effective 2012). back issues avail. **Document type:** *Journal, Academic/Scholarly.* **Description:** Provides a comprehensive review of current clinical practice and thinking within the specialty of gastroenterology.
Former titles (until 2001): Bailliere's Best Practice & Research: Clinical Gastroenterology (1521-6918); (until 1999): Bailliere's Clinical Gastroenterology (0950-3528); Which superseded in part (in 1987): Clinics in Gastroenterology (0300-5089)
Related titles: Online - full text ed.: ISSN 1532-1916 (from ScienceDirect).
Indexed: A22, A26, A35, A36, ASCA, AgBio, B19, CA, CABA, CurCont, D01, E01, E12, EMBASE, ExcerpMed, GH, H17, I05, ISR, IndMed, Inpharma, MEDLINE, N02, N03, P30, P33, P39, R10, R13, RM&VM, Reac, SCI, SCOPUS, T02, T05, TriticAb, W07.
—GNLM, IE, Infotrieve, Ingenta, INIST. **CCC.**
Published by: Bailliere Tindall (Subsidiary of: Elsevier Health Sciences), The Blvd, Langford Ln, Kidlington, Oxford OX5 1GB, United Kingdom. TEL 44-1865-843000, FAX 44-1865-843010, directenquiries@elsevier.com. Ed. E J Kuipers.

616.3 USA
C C F A COMMUNIQUE. (Crohn's and Colitis Foundation of America, Inc.) Text in English. q. membership. **Document type:** *Newsletter.*
Published by: Crohn's and Colitis Foundation of America, Inc., Philadelphia - Delaware Valley Chapter, 367 East Street Rd, Trevose, PA 19053. TEL 215-396-9100, FAX 215-396-1170. Ed. Barbara Berman.

616.3 GBR ISSN 1367-9015
CODEN: CJGHF7
C M E JOURNAL. GASTROENTEROLOGY, HEPATOLOGY, AND NUTRITION. Text in English. 1997. 3/yr. GBP 45 per vol. domestic to individuals; GBP 60 per vol. foreign to individuals; GBP 60 per vol. domestic to institutions; GBP 90 per vol. foreign to institutions (effective 2009). back issues avail. **Document type:** *Journal, Academic/Scholarly.* **Description:** Contains significant review articles on gastroenterology, hepatology, and nutrition.
Related titles: Online - full content ed.: GBP 30 per vol. (effective 2009).
Indexed: EMBASE, ExcerpMed, R10, Reac, SCOPUS.
—CCC.
Published by: Rila Publications Ltd., 73 Newman St, London, W1A 4PG, United Kingdom. TEL 44-20-76311299, FAX 44-20-75807166, admin@rila.co.uk. Ed. Dr. Marios Panos.

617.5 CAN ISSN 1701-2473
➤ **CANADIAN ASSOCIATION FOR ENTEROSTOMAL THERAPY. THE LINK.** Text in English, French. 1988. q. free to members. adv. **Document type:** *Newsletter.*
Formerly (until 2000): C A E T Journal (1192-0890)
Related titles: Online - full text ed.
Indexed: C06, C07, C08, CINAHL.
—BLDSC (5221.472650), Ingenta. **CCC.**

Published by: Canadian Association for Enterostomal Therapy/ Association Canadienne des Stomotherapeutes, c/o Harvey Schwartz, Ed., 1720 chemin Norway, Montreal, PQ H4P 1Y2, Canada. TEL 888-739-3035, FAX 514-739-3035. Ed. Harvey Schwartz. Circ: 200.

616.3 CAN ISSN 0835-7900
RC799

➤ **CANADIAN JOURNAL OF GASTROENTEROLOGY.** Text in English. 1987. 9/yr. CAD 220 domestic to individuals; USD 220 in United States to individuals; USD 270 elsewhere to individuals; CAD 270 domestic to institutions; USD 270 in United States to institutions; USD 320 elsewhere to institutions (effective 2006). adv. bk.rev. **Document type:** *Journal, Academic/Scholarly.* **Description:** Original papers, case reports and reviews pertaining to gastroenterology and hepatology.
Related titles: Online - full text ed.
Indexed: A22, A34, A36, ASCA, CABA, CurCont, D01, E12, EMBASE, ExcerpMed, GH, H17, IndMed, IndVet, Inpharma, MEDLINE, N02, N03, NRN, P30, P33, P35, P39, PHN&I, R10, RA&MP, RM&VM, Reac, SCI, SCOPUS, T05, VS, W07.
—BLDSC (3031.550000), GNLM, IE, Infotrieve, Ingenta, INIST. **CCC.**
Published by: (The Canadian Association of Gastroenterology), Pulsus Group Inc., 2902 S Sheridan Way, Oakville, ON L6J 7L6, Canada. TEL 905-829-4770, FAX 905-829-4799, pulsus@pulsus.com. Ed. Dr. L Sutherland. Adv. contact Lisa Robb. B&W page CAD 2,445; 8.125 x 10.875. Circ: 15,500 (controlled).

➤ **CANCERO DIGEST.** *see* MEDICAL SCIENCES—Oncology

616.3 CHE ISSN 1662-0631
RC816

➤ **CASE REPORTS IN GASTROENTEROLOGY.** Text in English. 2007. irreg. free (effective 2011). **Document type:** *Journal, Academic/ Scholarly.* **Description:** Publishes original case reports covering the entire spectrum of gastroenterology.
Media: Online - full text.
Indexed: A22, E01, P30, SCOPUS.
—IE.
Published by: S. Karger AG, Allschwilerstr 10, Basel, 4055, Switzerland. TEL 41-61-3061111, FAX 41-61-3061234, karger@karger.ch, http://www.karger.ch. Ed. Raul Urrutia.

616.3 USA ISSN 2090-6528

▼ ➤ **CASE REPORTS IN GASTROINTESTINAL MEDICINE.** Text in English. 2011. **Document type:** *Journal, Academic/Scholarly.* **Description:** Publishes case reports in all areas of gastrointestinal medicine.
Related titles: Online - full text ed.: ISSN 2090-6536. 2011. free (effective 2011).
Published by: Hindawi Publishing Corporation, 410 Park Ave, 15th Fl, PMB 287, New York, NY 10022. FAX 215-893-4392, 866-446-3294, info@hindawi.com.

616.362 USA ISSN 2090-6587

▼ ➤ **CASE REPORTS IN HEPATOLOGY.** Text in English. 2011. **Document type:** *Journal, Academic/Scholarly.* **Description:** Publishes case reports in all areas of hepatology.
Related titles: Online - full text ed.: ISSN 2090-6595. 2011. free (effective 2011).
Published by: Hindawi Publishing Corporation, 410 Park Ave, 15th Fl, PMB 287, New York, NY 10022. FAX 215-893-4392, 866-446-3294, info@hindawi.com.

616.3 CZE ISSN 1213-323X
CODEN: CSGAEE

➤ **CESKA A SLOVENSKA GASTROENTEROLOGIE A HEPATOLOGIE/ CZECH AND SLOVAK GASTROENTEROLOGY AND HEPATOLOGY.** Text in Czech, Slovak; Summaries in Czech, English. 1947. 6/yr. CZK 600 domestic; EUR 24 foreign (effective 2010). adv. bk.rev. abstr.; charts; illus. index. **Document type:** *Journal, Academic/Scholarly.* **Description:** Publishes original papers on the digestive system including liver, gastrointestinal endoscopy, gastroenterosurgery, clinical nutrition and allied disorders, as well as articles serving postgraduate education of gastroenterologists in practice.
Former titles (until 2001): Ceska a Slovenska Gastroenterologie (1210-7824); (until Aug. 1994): Cesko-Slovenska Gastroenterologie a Vyziva (0009-0565)
Related titles: Online - full text ed.
Indexed: CIN, CISA, ChemAb, ChemTitl, EMBASE, ExcerpMed, FS&TA, IndMed, P30, R10, Reac, SCOPUS.
—BLDSC (3120.258420), CASDDS, GNLM, IE, Ingenta, INIST. **CCC.**
Published by: (Ceska Lekarska Spolecnost J.E. Purkyne, Ceska Gastroenterologicka Spolecnost/Czech Medical Association of J.E. Purkyne, Czech Gastroenterological Society, Ceska Hepatologicka Spolecnost C L S J.E. Purkyne), Medica Healthworld a.s., Bidlaky 20, Brno, 63900, Czech Republic. TEL 420-533-337311, FAX 420-533-337312, info@mhw.cz, http://www.mhw.cz. Ed. Milan Kment. adv.: B&W page CZK 27,500, color page CZK 39,800; 244 x 167. Circ: 900.

➤ **CIRUGEST ARCHIVOS DE CIRUGIA GENERAL Y DIGESTIVA.** *see* MEDICAL SCIENCES—Surgery

616.3 GBR ISSN 1178-7023
RC799

➤ **CLINICAL AND EXPERIMENTAL GASTROENTEROLOGY.** Text in English. 2008. irreg. free (effective 2011). **Document type:** *Journal, Academic/Scholarly.* **Description:** Covers all aspects of gastroenterology.
Media: Online - full text.
Indexed: A01, EMBASE, SCOPUS.
—**CCC.**
Published by: Dove Medical Press Ltd., Beechfield House, Winterton Way, Macclesfield, SK11 0JL, United Kingdom. TEL 44-1625-509130, FAX 44-1625-617933. Ed. Ronnie Fass.

616.3 USA ISSN 2155-384X

▼ ➤ **CLINICAL AND TRANSLATIONAL GASTROENTEROLOGY.** Text in English. 2010 (Jul.). m. free (effective 2010). **Document type:** *Journal, Academic/Scholarly.*
Media: Online - full text.
Indexed: A22, E01.
Published by: Nature Publishing Group (Subsidiary of: Macmillan Publishers Ltd.), 75 Varick St, 9th Fl, New York, NY 10013. TEL 212-726-9200, FAX 212-696-9006, nature@natureny.com.

663 USA

➤ **CLINICAL GASTROENTEROLOGY.** Text in English. 2001. irreg., latest 2009. price varies. illus. 300 p./no.; back issues avail. **Document type:** *Monographic series, Academic/Scholarly.* **Description:** Covers all aspects of gastroenterology, including related diseases and general medicine.
Related titles: Online - full text ed.
Published by: Humana Press, Inc. (Subsidiary of: Springer Science+Business Media), 233 Spring St, New York, NY 10013. TEL 212-460-1500, FAX 212-460-1575, service-ny@springer.com. Ed. George Y Wu.

616.33 USA ISSN 1542-3565
CODEN: CGHLAW

➤ **CLINICAL GASTROENTEROLOGY AND HEPATOLOGY.** Abbreviated title: C G H. Text in English. 2003. m. USD 477 in United States to institutions; USD 546 elsewhere to institutions (effective 2012). adv. back issues avail.; reprints avail. **Document type:** *Journal, Academic/Scholarly.* **Description:** Provides readers with a broad spectrum of themes in clinical gastroenterology and hepatology, including the diagnostic, endoscopic, interventional and therapeutic advances in cancer, inflammatory diseases, functional gastrointestinal disorders, nutrition, absorption, and secretion.
Formerly (until 2003): Clinical Perspectives in Gastroenterology (1098-8351)
Related titles: Online - full text ed.: ISSN 1542-7714 (from ScienceDirect).
Indexed: A26, CA, CurCont, EMBASE, ExcerpMed, I05, JW-G, MEDLINE, P30, R10, Reac, SCI, SCOPUS, T02, W07.
—BLDSC (3286.286600), IE, Ingenta. **CCC.**
Published by: (American Gastroenterological Association), W.B. Saunders Co. (Subsidiary of: Elsevier Health Sciences), Elsevier, Health Sciences Division, Order Fulfillment, 3251 Riverport Ln, Maryland Heights, MO 63043. TEL 314-872-8370, 800-325-4177, FAX 314-432-1380, JournalCustomerService-usa@elsevier.com, http://www.us.elsevierhealth.com. Ed. C Mel Wilcox. Pub. Theresa Monturano. Adv. contact Jim Pattis TEL 201-767-4170. Circ: 18,150.

616.3 JPN ISSN 1865-7257

➤ **CLINICAL JOURNAL OF GASTROENTEROLOGY.** Text in English. 2008. q. EUR 150, USD 225 combined subscription to institutions (print & online eds.) (effective 2012). reprint service avail. from PSC. **Document type:** *Journal, Academic/Scholarly.* **Description:** Contains research on all aspects of the digestive tract, liver, biliary tract, and pancreas.
Related titles: Online - full text ed.: ISSN 1865-7265. 2008 (from IngentaConnect).
Indexed: A22, A26, E01, E08, EMBASE, ExcerpMed, R10, Reac, S09, SCOPUS.
—IE. **CCC.**
Published by: Springer Japan KK (Subsidiary of: Springer Science+Business Media), No 2 Funato Bldg, 1-11-11 Kudan-kita, Chiyoda-ku, Tokyo, 102-0073, Japan. TEL 81-3-68317000, FAX 81-3-68317001, orders@springer.jp, http://www.springer.jp. Ed. Yutaka Kogo.

616.3 NZL ISSN 1179-5522

➤ **CLINICAL MEDICINE INSIGHTS: GASTROENTEROLOGY.** Text in English. 2007. irreg. free (effective 2011). **Document type:** *Journal, Academic/Scholarly.* **Description:** Covers all aspects of the diagnosis, management and prevention of gastroenterological disorders, in addition to related genetic, pathophysiological and epidemiological topics.
Formerly (until 2010): Clinical Medicine: Gastroenterology (1178-119X)
Media: Online - full text.
Indexed: A01, C06, C07, EMBASE, ExcerpMed, P30, SCOPUS, T02.
—**CCC.**
Published by: Libertas Academica Ltd., PO Box 300-874, Mairangi Bay, Auckland, 0751, New Zealand. TEL 64-9-4763930, FAX 64-9-3531397, enquiries@la-press.com. Ed. Tushar Patel.

➤ **CLINICAL NUTRITION.** *see* NUTRITION AND DIETETICS

616.3 FRA ISSN 2210-7401
RC799 CODEN: GCBIDC

➤ **CLINICS AND RESEARCH IN HEPATOLOGY AND GASTROENTEROLOGY.** Text in English. 1976. 10/yr. EUR 594 in Europe to institutions; EUR 431.93 in France to institutions; JPY 92,300 in Japan to institutions; USD 772 elsewhere to institutions (effective 2012). adv. bk.rev. illus. index. reprints avail. **Document type:** *Journal, Academic/Scholarly.* **Description:** Publishes original work, clinical radiological laboratory and pathological documents related to gastroenterology, laboratory or experimental research on the digestive tract and related glands.
Former titles (until 2011): Gastroenterologie Clinique et Biologique (0399-8320); Which was formed by the merger of (1968-1976): Biologie et Gastro - Enterologie (0006-3258); (1966-1976): Archives Francaises des Maladies de l'Appareil Digestif (0003-9772); Which was formerly (until 1966): Archives des Maladies de l'Appareil Digestif et des Maladies de la Nutrition (0365-4117); (1907-1925): Archives des Maladies de l'Appareil Digestif et de la Nutrition (0150-9691)
Related titles: Online - full text ed.: ISSN 2210-741X (from ScienceDirect).
Indexed: A22, A34, A35, A36, A38, AgBio, B25, BIOSIS Prev, CABA, CIN, ChemAb, ChemTitl, CurCont, D01, DentInd, E12, EMBASE, ExcerpMed, FR, GH, H17, IBR, IBZ, ISR, IndMed, IndVet, Inpharma, LT, MEDLINE, MycolAb, N02, N03, P30, P33, P35, P39, PN&I, R08, R10, R12, RM&VM, RRTA, Reac, SCI, SCOPUS, T05, VS, W07, W11.
—BLDSC (3286.540955), CASDDS, GNLM, IE, Infotrieve, Ingenta, INIST. **CCC.**
Published by: (Societe Nationale Francaise de Gastro-Enterologie), Elsevier Masson (Subsidiary of: Elsevier Health Sciences), 62 Rue Camille Desmoulins, Issy les Moulineaux, Cedex 92442, France. TEL 33-1-71165500, infos@elsevier-masson.fr, http://www.elsevier-masson.fr. Ed. R Poupon. Circ: 4,500. **Subscr. to:** Societe de Periodiques Specialises, BP 22, Vineuil Cedex 41354, France. TEL 33-2-54504612, FAX 33-1-54504611.

➤ **CLINICS IN COLON & RECTAL SURGERY.** *see* MEDICAL SCIENCES—Surgery

616.362 USA ISSN 1089-3261
RC845

CLINICS IN LIVER DISEASE. Text in English. 1997. q. USD 343 in United States to institutions; USD 413 elsewhere to institutions (effective 2012). adv. back issues avail.; reprints avail. **Document type:** *Journal, Academic/Scholarly.* **Description:** Provides current, practical information on the diagnosis and treatment of conditions affecting the liver and biliary tract.
Related titles: Online - full text ed.: ISSN 1557-8224 (from ScienceDirect).
Indexed: CurCont, EMBASE, ExcerpMed, IndMed, MEDLINE, P30, R10, Reac, SCI, SCOPUS, W07.
—BLDSC (3286.576000), IE, Infotrieve, Ingenta, INIST. **CCC.**
Published by: (American Association for the Study of Liver Diseases), W.B. Saunders Co. (Subsidiary of: Elsevier Health Sciences), Elsevier, Health Sciences Division, Order Fulfillment, 3251 Riverport Ln, Maryland Heights, MO 63043. TEL 314-872-8370, 800-325-4177, FAX 314-432-1380, JournalCustomerService-usa@elsevier.com, http://www.us.elsevierhealth.com. Adv. contact John Marmero TEL 212-633-3657.

616.3 FRA ISSN 1261-7458

CLUB DE REFLEXION DES CABINETS ET GROUPES D'HEPATO-GASTROENTEROLOGIE. LETTRE. Variant title: La Lettre du C R E G G. Text in French. 199?. irreg. back issues avail. **Document type:** *Journal, Academic/Scholarly.*
Published by: (Club de Reflexion des Cabinets et Groupes d'Hepato-Gastroenterologie (C R E G G)), A L N Editions, 127 Rue Saint-Dizier, Nancy, 54000, France.

616.3 ARG ISSN 1667-9083

COLECCION TRABAJOS DISTINGUIDOS. SERIE GASTROENTEROLOGIA. Text in Spanish. 1999. 6/yr. back issues avail. **Document type:** *Journal, Academic/Scholarly.*
Media: Online - full text.
Published by: Sociedad Iberoamericana de Informacion Cientifica (S I I C), Ave Belgrano 430, Buenos Aires, C1092AAR, Argentina. TEL 54-11-43424901, FAX 54-11-43313305, atencionallector@siicsalud.com, http://www.siicsalud.com. Ed. Rafael Bernal Castro.

616.3 FRA ISSN 2107-1527

▼ **COLLECTION S N F C P.** (Societe Nationale Francaise de Colo-Proctologie) Text in French. 2009. irreg. EUR 28.50 per issue (effective 2011). **Document type:** *Monographic series.*
Published by: Springer France (Subsidiary of: Springer Science+Business Media), 22 Rue de Palestro, Paris, 75002, France. TEL 33-1-53009860, FAX 33-1-53009861, http://www.springer.com.

616.3 DEU ISSN 0174-2442

➤ **COLO-PROCTOLOGY.** Text in German. 1979. bi-m. EUR 210, USD 270 combined subscription to institutions (print & online eds.) (effective 2012). adv. bk.rev. index. back issues avail.; reprint service avail. from PSC. **Document type:** *Journal, Academic/Scholarly.* **Description:** Covers case reports and techniques in proctology. Includes new product information, calendar of events and reviews of journal articles.
Formerly (until 1980): Proktologie (0174-240X)
Related titles: Online - full text ed.: ISSN 1615-6730 (from IngentaConnect).
Indexed: A22, A26, CA, E01, EMBASE, ExcerpMed, R10, Reac, SCOPUS, T02.
—BLDSC (3320.408750), GNLM, IE, Infotrieve, Ingenta. **CCC.**
Published by: (Berufsverband der Koloproktologen Deutschland e.V.), Urban und Vogel Medien und Medizin Verlagsgesellschaft mbH (Subsidiary of: Springer Science+Business Media), Neumarkter Str 43, Munich, 81673, Germany. TEL 49-89-4372-1411, FAX 49-89-4372-1410, verlag@urban-vogel.de. Ed. Daniela Oesterle. Adv. contact Renate Senfft. B&W page EUR 2,400, color page EUR 3,650; trim 174 x 240. Circ: 4,000 (paid and controlled). **Co-sponsor:** Deutsche Gesellschaft fuer Koloproktologie.

616.3 GBR ISSN 1462-8910
RC860 CODEN: CODIFU

➤ **COLORECTAL DISEASE.** Text in English. 1999. 9/yr. GBP 736 in United Kingdom to institutions; EUR 933 in Europe to institutions; USD 1,356 in the Americas to institutions; USD 1,587 elsewhere to institutions; GBP 847 combined subscription in United Kingdom to institutions (print & online eds.); EUR 1,073 combined subscription in Europe to institutions (print & online eds.); USD 1,560 combined subscription in the Americas to institutions (print & online eds.); USD 1,826 combined subscription elsewhere to institutions (print & online eds.) (effective 2012). adv. back issues avail.; reprint service avail. from PSC. **Document type:** *Journal, Academic/Scholarly.* **Description:** Provides original research relating to the demanding, rapidly expanding field of colorectal diseases.
Related titles: ◆ Online - full text ed.: Colorectal Disease Online. ISSN 1463-1318; Supplement(s): ISSN 1455-8998.
Indexed: A01, A02, A03, A08, A22, A26, B21, C11, CA, CurCont, E01, EMBASE, ExcerpMed, H04, H12, ImmunAb, MEDLINE, P30, R10, Reac, SCI, SCOPUS, T02, W07.
—BLDSC (3322.110000), IE, Infotrieve, Ingenta. **CCC.**
Published by: (European Association of Coloproctology, Association of Coloproctology of Great Britain and Ireland), Wiley-Blackwell Publishing Ltd. (Subsidiary of: John Wiley & Sons, Inc.), 9600 Garsington Rd, Oxford, OX4 2DQ, United Kingdom. TEL 44-1865-776868, FAX 44-1865-714591, customerservices@blackwellpublishing.com. Ed. R J Nicholls. Pub. Allen Stevens. Adv. contact Jenny Applin. Circ: 1,000.

616.3 GBR ISSN 1463-1318

➤ **COLORECTAL DISEASE ONLINE.** Text in English. 1999. bi-m. GBP 736 in United Kingdom to institutions; EUR 933 in Europe to institutions; USD 1,356 in the Americas to institutions; USD 1,587 elsewhere to institutions (effective 2012). back issues avail.; reprints avail. **Document type:** *Journal, Academic/Scholarly.* **Description:** Provides original research relating to the demanding, rapidly expanding field of colorectal diseases.
Media: Online - full text (from IngentaConnect). **Related titles:** ◆ Print ed.: Colorectal Disease. ISSN 1462-8910.
—**CCC.**

M

Published by: (European Association of Coloproctology, Association of Coloproctology of Great Britain and Ireland), Wiley-Blackwell Publishing Ltd. (Subsidiary of: John Wiley & Sons, Inc.), 9600 Garsington Rd, Oxford, OX4 2DQ, United Kingdom. TEL 44-1865-776868, FAX 44-1865-714591, customerservices@blackwellpublishing.com, http://www.wiley.com/. Ed. R J Nicholls.

616.362 GBR ISSN 1476-5926
QM1
➤ **COMPARATIVE HEPATOLOGY.** Text in English. 2002 (Aug.). irreg. free (effective 2011). adv. back issues avail. **Document type:** *Journal, Academic/Scholarly.* **Description:** Provides a reference forum for the publication of high quality original research on the normal or disrupted anatomy and physiology of the liver, including any of its supracellular, cellular or subcellular components.
Media: Online - full text.
Indexed: A01, A26, CA, EMBASE, ExcerpMed, I05, P20, P22, P30, PQC, R10, Reac, SCOPUS, T02.
—CCC.
Published by: BioMed Central Ltd. (Subsidiary of: Springer Science+Business Media), 236 Gray's Inn Rd, London, WC1X 8HB, United Kingdom. TEL 44-20-31922000, FAX 44-20-31922010, info@biomedcentral.com, http://www.biomedcentral.com. Ed. Eduardo Rocha TEL 351-22-2062254. Adv. contact Natasha Bailey TEL 44-20-31922231.

616.33 GBR ISSN 0960-6289
CONSPECTUS GASTROENTEROLOGY. Text in English. 1990. q. **Document type:** *Journal, Academic/Scholarly.*
—CCC.
Published by: Wells Medical Ltd., Speldhurst Pl, Speldhurst Rd, Royal Tunbridge Wells, Kent TN4 0JB, United Kingdom. TEL 44-1892-511600, FAX 44-1892-511400, info@wellsmed.co.uk.

CORE JOURNALS IN GASTROENTEROLOGY. *see* MEDICAL SCIENCES—Abstracting, Bibliographies, Statistics

616.3 CAN ISSN 1197-4982
CROHN'S AND COLITIS FOUNDATION OF CANADA. JOURNAL. Text in English. 1979. q. CAD 30 (effective 2006). **Document type:** *Magazine, Consumer.*
Formerly (until 1993): Canadian Foundation for Ileitis and Colitis. Journal (0827-4681)
Published by: Crohn's & Colitis Foundation of Canada, 600-60 St Clair Ave E, Toronto, ON M4T 1N5, Canada. TEL 416-920-5035, 800-387-1479, FAX 416-929-0364, ccfc@ccfc.ca.

CURRENT COLORECTAL CANCER REPORTS. *see* MEDICAL SCIENCES—Oncology

616.3 USA ISSN 1946-3030
RC799
▼ **CURRENT DIAGNOSIS & TREATMENT: GASTROENTEROLOGY, HEPATOLOGY, & ENDOSCOPY.** Text in English. 2009. triennial. USD 69.95 per issue (effective 2009). **Document type:** *Monographic series, Academic/Scholarly.* **Description:** For the diagnosis and medical management of digestive and liver diseases.
Published by: McGraw-Hill Professional (Subsidiary of: McGraw-Hill Companies, Inc.), Two Penn Plz, 23rd Fl, New York, NY 10121. TEL 212-904-2000, FAX 212-904-6030, customer.service@mcgraw-hill.com, http://www.mhprofessional.com/index.php.

616.13 USA ISSN 1534-312X
RC799
➤ **CURRENT GASTROENTEROLOGY REPORTS (ONLINE).** Text in English. 1999. bi-m. EUR 954, USD 1,270 to institutions (effective 2012). back issues avail.; reprints avail. **Document type:** *Journal, Academic/Scholarly.*
Media: Online - full text.
—CCC.
Published by: Current Medicine Group LLC (Subsidiary of: Springer Science+Business Media), 400 Market St, Ste 700, Philadelphia, PA 19106. TEL 215-574-2266, FAX 215-574-2225, service-ny@springer.com, http://www.current-medicine.com/. Ed. Dr. Joel Richter.

616.3623 USA ISSN 1540-3416
CURRENT HEPATITIS REPORTS. Text in English. 2002 (Nov.). q. reprint service avail. from PSC. **Document type:** *Journal, Academic/Scholarly.* **Description:** Provides insightful reviews of recent literature in hepatitis.
Related titles: Online - full text ed.: ISSN 1541-0706. USD 1,158 to institutions (effective 2010).
Indexed: A22, A26, A36, CABA, E01, E08, E12, EMBASE, ExcerpMed, GH, H12, N02, P30, R10, R12, Reac, S09, SCOPUS, T05, W11.
—BLDSC (3497.393000), IE, Ingenta. **CCC.**
Published by: Current Medicine Group LLC (Subsidiary of: Springer Science+Business Media), 400 Market St, Ste 700, Philadelphia, PA 19106. TEL 215-574-2266, 800-427-1796, FAX 215-574-2225, info@phl.cursci.com, http://www.current-medicine.com. Ed. Bruce Bacon.

CURRENT MEDICAL LITERATURE. COLORECTAL CANCER. *see* MEDICAL SCIENCES—Oncology

016.3 GBR ISSN 0263-2659
RC799 CODEN: CMLGDE
➤ **CURRENT MEDICAL LITERATURE. GASTROENTEROLOGY.** Text in English. 1982. q. GBP 60 to individuals; GBP 130 to institutions; free to qualified personnel (effective 2009). back issues avail. **Document type:** *Journal, Academic/Scholarly.* **Description:** Aims to provide physicians and allied healthcare professionals with rapid access to expert commentary and analysis on key topics in gastroenterology.
Related titles: Online - full text ed.: ISSN 1759-8109.
Indexed: A01, A03, A08, CA, T02.
—CCC.
Published by: Remedica Medical Education and Publishing Ltd., Commonwealth House, 1 New Oxford St, London, WC1A 1NU, United Kingdom. TEL 44-20-77592999, FAX 44-20-77592951, info@remedica.com, http://www.remedica.com. Ed. Lesley Ezekiel.

616.3 USA ISSN 0267-1379
RC799 CODEN: COGAEK
➤ **CURRENT OPINION IN GASTROENTEROLOGY.** Text in English. 1985. bi-m. USD 1,112 domestic to institutions; USD 1,198 foreign to institutions (effective 2011). adv. bibl.; illus. back issues avail.; reprints avail. **Document type:** *Journal, Academic/Scholarly.* **Description:** Covers key subjects, spanning topics such as nutrition, large intestine, small intestine, liver, biliary tract, esophagus, stomach and duodenum, pancreas and immunology.
Related titles: Online - full text ed.: ISSN 1531-7056. USD 257 to individuals (effective 2011); Optical Disk - DVD ed.: Current Opinion in Gastroenterology, with Evaluated MEDLINE. ISSN 1080-8167. 1995.
Indexed: A22, A34, A35, A36, A38, ASCA, AgBio, BIOBASE, BP, C06, C07, C08, CABA, CIN, CINAHL, ChemAb, ChemTitl, CurCont, D01, E01, E12, EMBASE, ExcerpMed, GH, H16, H17, IABS, IndVet, Inpharma, MEDLINE, MaizeAb, N02, N03, N04, P30, P33, P39, R10, RA&MP, RM&VM, Reac, S12, SCI, SCOPUS, SoyAb, T05, TriticAb, VS, W07.
—BLDSC (3500.775000), CASDDS, GNLM, IE, Infotrieve, Ingenta, INIST. **CCC.**
Published by: Lippincott Williams & Wilkins (Subsidiary of: Wolters Kluwer N.V.), 530 Walnut St, Philadelphia, PA 19106. TEL 215-521-8300, FAX 215-521-8902, customerservice@lww.com, http://www.lww.com. Ed. Daniel K Podolsky. Pub. Ian Burgess. Circ: 3,919.

616.33 USA ISSN 1534-309X
➤ **CURRENT TREATMENT OPTIONS IN GASTROENTEROLOGY (ONLINE).** Text in English. 1998. bi-m. EUR 825, USD 1,098 to institutions (effective 2009). **Document type:** *Journal, Academic/Scholarly.*
Media: Online - full content.
—CCC.
Published by: Current Science Inc. (Subsidiary of: Current Medicine Group LLC), 400 Market St, Ste 700, Philadelphia, PA 19106-2514. TEL 215-574-2266, info@current-reports.com, http://www.current-science.com.

616.3 NLD ISSN 0167-935X
➤ **DEVELOPMENTS IN GASTROENTEROLOGY.** Text in English. 1981. irreg., latest vol.15, 1997. price varies. **Document type:** *Monographic series, Academic/Scholarly.*
—BLDSC (3579.071870). **CCC.**
Published by: Springer Netherlands (Subsidiary of: Springer Science+Business Media), Van Godewijckstraat 30, Dordrecht, 3311 GX, Netherlands. TEL 31-78-6576050, FAX 31-78-6576474.

➤ **DIABETIC MEDICINE**; journal of diabetes UK. *see* MEDICAL SCIENCES—Endocrinology

➤ **DIABETIC MEDICINE ONLINE.** *see* MEDICAL SCIENCES—Endocrinology

616.3 CHE ISSN 0012-2823
QP141.A1 CODEN: DIGEBW
➤ **DIGESTION**; international journal of gastroenterology. Text in English. 1896. 8/yr. CHF 2,872, EUR 2,296, USD 2,816 to institutions; CHF 3,152, EUR 2,520, USD 3,088 combined subscription to institutions (print & online eds.) (effective 2012). adv. bibl.; illus. back issues avail. **Document type:** *Journal, Academic/Scholarly.* **Description:** Publishes research reports on diseases and pathophysiology of the gastrointestinal tract, liver and pancreas and on gastrointestinal endocrinology.
Former titles (until 1968): Gastroenterologia (0301-164X); (until 1939): Archiv fuer Verdauungskrankheiten, Stoffwechselpathologie und Diaetetik (0365-8325); (until 1931): Archiv fuer Verdauungskrankheiten (0365-8228)
Related titles: Microform ed.; Online - full text ed.: ISSN 1421-9867. CHF 2,804, EUR 2,244, USD 2,722 to institutions (effective 2012).
Indexed: A01, A03, A08, A20, A22, A34, A36, ASCA, AgrForAb, B25, BIOBASE, BIOSIS Prev, BP, CA, CABA, CIN, ChemAb, ChemTitl, CurCont, D01, DentInd, E01, E12, EMBASE, ExcerpMed, F08, F11, F12, GH, IABS, IBR, IBZ, ISR, IndMed, Inpharma, JW-G, LT, MEDLINE, MycolAb, N02, N03, NRN, P20, P22, P30, P33, P35, P39, P48, P54, PQC, R07, R10, R11, R12, RA&MP, RM&VM, RRTA, Reac, S12, SCI, SCOPUS, T02, T05, VS, W07.
—BLDSC (3588.345000), CASDDS, GNLM, IE, Infotrieve, Ingenta, INIST. **CCC.**
Published by: S. Karger AG, Allschwilerstr 10, Basel, 4055, Switzerland. TEL 41-61-3061111, FAX 41-61-3061234, karger@karger.ch, http://www.karger.ch. Eds. B Goeke, C Beglinger. adv.: page CHF 1,730; trim 210 x 280. Circ: 3,600.

616.3 GBR ISSN 1590-8658
CODEN: ITJGDH
➤ **DIGESTIVE AND LIVER DISEASE.** Text in English; Summaries in English, Italian. 1969. m. EUR 513 in Europe to institutions; JPY 68,600 in Japan to institutions; USD 512 elsewhere to institutions (effective 2012). adv. bk.rev. index, cum.index. back issues avail.; reprints avail. **Document type:** *Journal, Academic/Scholarly.* **Description:** Publishes original articles concerning basic and clinical research, case reports, editorials, articles discussing hypotheses and interpretations, and the proceedings of the national congresses on gastroenterology and hepatology.
Former titles (until 2000): Italian Journal of Gastroenterology and Hepatology (1125-8055); (until 1997): Italian Journal of Gastroenterology (0392-0623); (until 1978): Rendiconti di Gastro-Enterologia (0300-0877); (until 1972): Rendiconti Romani di Gastro-Enterologia (0300-0524); (until 1970): Rendiconti delle Riunioni Romane di Gastro-Enterology (0390-4857)
Related titles: Microform ed.: (from PQC); Online - full text ed.: ISSN 1878-3562. USD 414 to institutions (effective 2009) (from ScienceDirect); Supplement(s): Digestive and Liver Disease. Supplement. ISSN 1594-5804. 2000.
Indexed: A22, A26, ASCA, B25, BIOSIS Prev, CA, CIN, ChemAb, ChemTitl, CurCont, EMBASE, ExcerpMed, FR, I05, ISR, IndMed, Inpharma, MEDLINE, MycolAb, P30, P35, R10, Reac, SCI, SCOPUS, T02, W07.
—BLDSC (3588.345600), CASDDS, GNLM, IE, Ingenta, INIST. **CCC.**
Published by: (Italian Society of Pediatric Gastroenterology and Hepatology ITA, Italian Association for the Study of the Pancreas ITA, Italian Society of Gastroenterology ITA), W.B. Saunders Co. Ltd. (Subsidiary of: Elsevier Health Sciences), 32 Jamestown Rd, Camden, London, NW1 7BY, United Kingdom. TEL 44-20-74244200, FAX 44-20-74832293, elsols@elsevier.com. Ed. Mario Angelico.
Co-sponsor: Italian Association for the Study of the Liver.

616.3 CHE ISSN 0257-2753
RC799 CODEN: DIDIEW
➤ **DIGESTIVE DISEASES**; clinical reviews. Text in English. 1983. q. CHF 2,346, EUR 1,875, USD 2,298.50 to institutions; CHF 2,576, EUR 2,059, USD 2,521.50 combined subscription to institutions (print & online eds.) (effective 2012). adv. illus. index. back issues avail. **Document type:** *Journal, Academic/Scholarly.* **Description:** Covers both clinical and basic science topics in gastrointestinal function and disorders, including medicine, liver disease, surgery, nutrition, pathology and the basic sciences.
Formerly: Survey of Digestive Diseases (0253-4398)
Related titles: Online - full text ed.: ISSN 1421-9875. CHF 2,295, EUR 1,836, USD 2,228 to institutions (effective 2012).
Indexed: A20, A22, A36, ASCA, B21, BIOSIS Prev, CA, CABA, ChemAb, E01, EMBASE, ExcerpMed, GH, H17, ImmunAb, IndMed, Inpharma, LT, MEDLINE, MycolAb, N02, N03, NRN, P30, P33, P39, R10, RM&VM, RRTA, Reac, SCI, SCOPUS, T02, T05, TriticAb, VS, W07.
—BLDSC (3588.346000), CASDDS, GNLM, IE, Infotrieve, Ingenta, INIST. **CCC.**
Published by: S. Karger AG, Allschwilerstr 10, Basel, 4055, Switzerland. TEL 41-61-3061111, FAX 41-61-3061234, karger@karger.ch, http://www.karger.ch. Ed. P. Malfertheiner. adv.: page CHF 1,730; trim 210 x 280. Circ: 800.

616.3 USA ISSN 0163-2116
RC799 CODEN: DDSCDJ
➤ **DIGESTIVE DISEASES AND SCIENCES.** Text in English. 1934. m. EUR 1,790, USD 1,842 combined subscription to institutions (print & online eds.) (effective 2012). adv. bk.rev. illus. back issues avail.; reprint service avail. from PSC. **Document type:** *Journal, Academic/Scholarly.* **Description:** Disseminates articles on basic research and clinical practice in gastroenterology and related fields.
Former titles (until 1979): American Journal of Digestive Diseases (0002-9211); (until 1938): American Journal of Digestive Diseases and Nutrition (0092-5640)
Related titles: Microfilm ed.: (from PQC); Online - full text ed.: ISSN 1573-2568 (from IngentaConnect).
Indexed: A01, A03, A08, A22, A26, A34, A35, A36, A38, AIIM, AIM, ASCA, AgBio, Agr, AgrForAb, B20, B21, B25, BIOBASE, BIOSIS Prev, BP, BibLing, C13, C25, CA, CABA, CIN, ChPerl, ChemAb, ChemTitl, CurCont, D01, DBA, DentInd, E01, E12, EMBASE, ESPM, ExcerpMed, F08, F11, F12, FR, FaBeAb, G08, GH, H11, H12, H16, H17, IABS, IBR, IBZ, IDIS, INI, ISR, ImmunAb, IndMed, Inpharma, JW-G, LT, MEDLINE, MaizeAb, MycolAb, N02, N03, N04, NRN, P19, P20, P22, P24, P30, P33, P35, P38, P39, P48, P54, PN&I, PQC, R08, R10, R11, R12, RA&MP, RM&VM, RRTA, Reac, RefZh, S12, SAA, SCI, SCOPUS, SoyAb, T02, T05, THA, TriticAb, VS, W07, W10, W11.
—BLDSC (3588.346100), CASDDS, GNLM, IE, Infotrieve, Ingenta, INIST. **CCC.**
Published by: Springer New York LLC (Subsidiary of: Springer Science+Business Media), 233 Spring St, New York, NY 10013. TEL 212-460-1500, FAX 212-460-1575, service-ny@springer.com. Ed. Emmet B Keeffe. adv.: B&W page USD 1,225, color page USD 2,730. Circ: 6,500 (paid).

616.3 USA ISSN 1542-1902
RC799
DIGESTIVE DISORDERS. Text in English. 2002. a. USD 19.95 per issue (effective 2010). **Document type:** *Monographic series, Academic/Scholarly.*
Published by: (Johns Hopkins Medical Institutions), Medletter Associates, 6 Trowbridge Dr, Bethel, CT 06801. Ed. Simeon Margolis.

616.3 AUS ISSN 0915-5635
RC804.E6 CODEN: BIRSE8
➤ **DIGESTIVE ENDOSCOPY.** Text in English. 1989. q. GBP 562 in United Kingdom to institutions; EUR 715 in Europe to institutions; USD 909 in the Americas to institutions; USD 1,102 elsewhere to institutions; GBP 647 combined subscription in United Kingdom to institutions (print & online eds.); EUR 823 combined subscription in Europe to institutions (print & online eds.); USD 1,046 combined subscription in the Americas to institutions (print & online eds.); USD 1,267 combined subscription elsewhere to institutions (print & online eds.) (effective 2012). adv. bk.rev. abstr. back issues avail.; reprint service avail. from PSC. **Document type:** *Journal, Academic/Scholarly.* **Description:** Covers the study and investigation relating to the various endoscopic techniques used in diagnosis and treatment of digestive disease.
Related titles: Online - full text ed.: ISSN 1443-1661. GBP 562 in United Kingdom to institutions; EUR 715 in Europe to institutions; USD 909 in the Americas to institutions; USD 1,102 elsewhere to institutions (effective 2012) (from IngentaConnect).
Indexed: A01, A03, A08, A22, A26, CA, E01, EMBASE, ExcerpMed, INIS AtomInd, MEDLINE, P30, R10, Reac, RefZh, SCI, SCOPUS, T02, W07.
—BLDSC (3588.346200), GNLM, IE, Infotrieve, Ingenta. **CCC.**
Published by: (Japan Gastroenterological Endoscopy Society JPN), Wiley-Blackwell Publishing Asia (Subsidiary of: Wiley-Blackwell Publishing Ltd.), 155 Cremorne St, Richmond, VIC 3121, Australia. TEL 61-3-92743100, FAX 61-3-92743101, subs@blackwellpublishingasia.com, http://www.wiley.com/WileyCDA/. Ed. Hiromitsu Saisho. Circ: 1,000. **Subscr. to:** Wiley-Blackwell Publishing Ltd.

➤ **DIGESTIVE SURGERY.** *see* MEDICAL SCIENCES—Surgery

616.3 616.994 NLD ISSN 2212-019X
DOORGANG. Text in Dutch. 199?. q. EUR 16 membership (effective 2011). **Document type:** *Magazine, Consumer.*
Formerly (until 2010): Stichting Doorgang. Nieuwsbrief (1879-7121)
Published by: Stichting voor Patienten met Kanker aan het Spijsverteringskanaal, c/o Nederlandse Federatie van Kankerpatientenorganisaties, Postbus 8152, Utrecht, 3503 RD, Netherlands. TEL 31-30-2616090, FAX 31-30-6046101, secretariaat@spks.nl.

616.3 SWE ISSN 1653-9214
E C C O NEWS. (European Crohn's and Colitis Organization) Text in English. 2006. q. **Document type:** *Newsletter, Academic/Scholarly.*
Related titles: Online - full text ed.: ISSN 2223-4330. 2007.
Published by: (European Crohn's and Colitis Organisation AUT), Mediahuset i Goeteborg AB, Marieholmsgatan 10 C, Goeteborg, 41502, Sweden. TEL 46-31-7071930, FAX 46-31-848642. Eds. Peter Lakatos, Tom Oeresland. Adv. contact Dan Johansson TEL 46-31-7072448.

616.3 EGY ISSN 0304-4831
THE EGYPTIAN JOURNAL OF GASTROENTEROLOGY. Text in English. 1964. s-a. **Document type:** *Journal, Academic/Scholarly.*
Published by: Egyptian Society of Gastroenterology, Dar El-Hekma, 42 Qasr El-Aini Str, Cairo, Egypt. TEL 20-2-7943406. Ed. Dr. Muhammad Awadh-Allah Sallam.

616.3 RUS ISSN 1682-8658
➤ **EKSPERIMENTAL'NAYA I KLINICHESKAYA GASTROENTEROLOGIYA.** Text in Russian. 1993. 3/yr. **Document type:** *Journal, Academic/Scholarly.*
Formerly (until 2002): Rossiiskii Gastroenterologicheskii Zhurnal (1560-408X)
Indexed: EMBASE, ExcerpMed, MEDLINE, P30, R10, Reac, RefZh, SCOPUS.
—BLDSC (0397.983000), East View.
Published by: (Komitet Zdravookhraneniya goroda Moskvy, Tsentral'nyi Nauchno-Issledovatel'skii Institut Gastroenterologii/Moscow Committee for Public Health, Central Scientific Research Institute of Gastroenterology, Nauchnoe Obshchestvo Gastroenterologov Rossii/Russian Scientific Society of Gastroenterologists), Izdatel'stvo Anakharsis, M Mogil'tsevskii per, dom 4A, kv 2, ofis 1, Moscow, 119002, Russian Federation. TEL 7-095-2415925, http://www.anakharsis.ru. Ed. Leonid Lazebnik.

616.3 BRA
➤ **THE ELECTRONIC JOURNAL OF PEDIATRIC GASTROENTEROLOGY, NUTRITION, AND LIVER DISEASES.** Text in English, Portuguese, Spanish. 1997. q. **Document type:** *Journal, Academic/Scholarly.*
Media: Online - full content.
Published by: Instituto Brasileiro de Assuntos de Cultura, Saude e Meio Ambiente, Rua Pedro de Toledo 441, Vila Clementino, Sao Paulo, 04039-031, Brazil. ulyneto@osite.com.br. Ed. Ulysses Fagundes Neto.

616.3 FRA ISSN 1155-1968
➤ **ENCYCLOPEDIE MEDICO-CHIRURGICALE. GASTRO-ENTEROLOGIE.** Cover title: Traite de Gastro-Enterologie. Variant title: Encyclopedie Medico-Chirurgicale, Instantanes Medicaux. Gastro-Enterologie. Text in French. 1936. 4 base vols. plus q. updates. EUR 749.62 (effective 2003). bibl.; charts; illus. **Document type:** *Academic/Scholarly.* **Description:** Provides gastroenterologists with a comprehensive, up-to-date reference for diagnosing and treating various conditions and disorders.
Formerly (until 1991): Encyclopedie Medico-Chirurgicale. Estomac - Intestin (0246-0327)
Related titles: Online - full text ed.
—INIST. **CCC.**
Published by: Elsevier Masson (Subsidiary of: Elsevier Health Sciences), 62 Rue Camille Desmoulins, Issy les Moulineaux, Cedex 92442, France. TEL 33-1-71165500, FAX 33-1-71165600, infos@elsevier-masson.fr.

616.3 FRA ISSN 1155-1976
➤ **ENCYCLOPEDIE MEDICO-CHIRURGICALE. HEPATOLOGIE.** Cover title: Traite d'Hepatologie. Variant title: Encyclopedie Medico-Chirurgicale, Instantanes Medicaux. Hepatologie. Text in French. 1935. 3 base vols. plus q. updates. EUR 676 (effective 2006). bibl.; charts; illus. **Document type:** *Academic/Scholarly.* **Description:** Offers hepatologists a comprehensive, up-to-date reference for diagnosing and treating disorders and conditions of the liver.
Former titles (until 1991): Encyclopedie Medico-Chirurgicale. Foie - Pancreas (0246-053X); (until 1960): Encyclopedie Medico-Chirurgicale. Foie (0246-0688)
Related titles: Online - full text ed.
—INIST. **CCC.**
Published by: Elsevier Masson (Subsidiary of: Elsevier Health Sciences), 62 Rue Camille Desmoulins, Issy les Moulineaux, Cedex 92442, France. TEL 33-1-71165500, FAX 33-1-71165600, infos@elsevier-masson.fr.

➤ **ENCYCLOPEDIE MEDICO-CHIRURGICALE. RADIOLOGIE ET IMAGERIE MEDICALE. ABDOMINALE - DIGESTIVE.** *see* MEDICAL SCIENCES—Radiology And Nuclear Medicine

➤ **ENCYCLOPEDIE MEDICO-CHIRURGICALE. TECHNIQUES CHIRURGICALES. APPAREIL DIGESTIF.** *see* MEDICAL SCIENCES—Surgery

➤ **ENCYCLOPEDIE MEDICO-CHIRURGICALE. TECNICAS QUIRURGICAS. APARATO DIGESTIVO.** *see* MEDICAL SCIENCES—Surgery

➤ **ENCYCLOPEDIE MEDICO-CHIRURGICALE. TECNICHE CHIRURGICHE. CHIRURGIA ADDOMINALE.** *see* MEDICAL SCIENCES—Surgery

616.3 DEU ISSN 0177-4077
➤ **ENDOPRAXIS.** Text in German. 1987. q. EUR 36 to institutions; EUR 102 combined subscription to institutions (print & online eds.); EUR 15 newsstand/cover (effective 2011). adv. **Document type:** *Journal, Academic/Scholarly.*
Related titles: Online - full text ed.: ISSN 1611-6429. 2006. EUR 102 to institutions (effective 2011).
Indexed: A22.
—IE. **CCC.**
Published by: Georg Thieme Verlag, Ruedigerstr 14, Stuttgart, 70469, Germany. TEL 49-711-8931421, FAX 49-711-8931410, kunden.service@thieme.de. Adv. contact Andreas Schweiger TEL 49-711-8931245. Circ: 3,850 (paid).

616.3 DEU ISSN 0013-726X
RC804.E6 CODEN: ENDCAM
➤ **ENDOSCOPY.** Text in English. 1969. m. EUR 628 to institutions; EUR 819 combined subscription to institutions (print & online eds.); EUR 58 newsstand/cover (effective 2011). adv. bk.rev. abstr.; illus. index. reprints avail. **Document type:** *Journal, Academic/Scholarly.*
Related titles: Microform ed.: (from PQC); Online - full text ed.: ISSN 1438-8812. EUR 789 to institutions (effective 2011).
Indexed: A01, A03, A08, A20, A22, A36, ASCA, C06, C07, CA, CABA, CurCont, DentInd, E12, EMBASE, ExcerpMed, FR, GH, H17, ISR, IndMed, Inpharma, JW-G, MEDLINE, N02, N03, P30, P33, P35, P39, PN&I, R10, RM&VM, Reac, RefZh, SCI, SCOPUS, T02, T05, TM, W07.
—BLDSC (3743.600000), GNLM, IE, Infotrieve, Ingenta, INIST. **CCC.**
Published by: (European Society of Gastronintestinal Endoscopy), Georg Thieme Verlag, Ruedigerstr 14, Stuttgart, 70469, Germany. TEL 49-711-8931421, FAX 49-711-8931410, leser.service@thieme.de. Ed. Thomas T Roesch. adv.: B&W page EUR 1,990, color page EUR 3,190. Circ: 6,800 (paid and controlled). **Subscr. to:** Thieme Medical Publishers, 333 Seventh Ave, New York, NY 10001. TEL 212-760-0888, 800-782-3488, FAX 212-947-1112, custserv@thieme.com, http://www.thieme.com/journals.

616.3 DEU ISSN 0933-811X
CODEN: ENDHE7
ENDOSKOPIE HEUTE. Text in German. 1988. q. EUR 134 to institutions; EUR 178 combined subscription to institutions (print & online eds.); EUR 44 newsstand/cover (effective 2011). adv. **Document type:** *Journal, Academic/Scholarly.*
Related titles: Online - full text ed.: ISSN 1439-2577. EUR 170 to institutions (effective 2011).
Indexed: A22, SCI, SCOPUS, W07.
—BLDSC (3743.630000), GNLM, IE, Infotrieve, Ingenta, INIST. **CCC.**
Published by: Georg Thieme Verlag, Ruedigerstr 14, Stuttgart, 70469, Germany. TEL 49-711-8931421, FAX 49-711-8931410, kunden.service@thieme.de. Ed. H-J Schulz. Adv. contact Ulrike Bradler. Circ: 1,680 (paid).

616.35 NLD ISSN 2210-4178
ERVARING. Text in Dutch. 1985. q.
Published by: Vereniging Anusatresie, Postbus 78, Huizen, 1270 AB, Netherlands. TEL 31-35-5233782, info@anusatresie.nl, http://www.anusatresie.nl. Circ: 425.

616.3 JPN ISSN 1612-9059
➤ **ESOPHAGUS.** Text in English. 2003 (Dec). q. EUR 266, USD 333 combined subscription to institutions (print & online eds.) (effective 2012). reprint service avail. from PSC. **Document type:** *Journal, Academic/Scholarly.* **Description:** Contains research in the fields of benign and malignant diseases of the esophagus.
Related titles: Online - full text ed.: ISSN 1612-9067 (from IngentaConnect).
Indexed: A22, A26, BIOBASE, E01, EMBASE, ExcerpMed, IABS, JW-G, R10, Reac, SCI, SCOPUS, W07.
—BLDSC (3811.300500), IE, Ingenta. **CCC.**
Published by: (Japan Esophageal Society), Springer Japan KK (Subsidiary of: Springer Science+Business Media), No 2 Funato Bldg, 1-11-11 Kudan-kita, Chiyoda-ku, Tokyo, 102-0073, Japan. TEL 81-3-68317000, FAX 81-3-68317001, http://www.springer.jp. Ed. Nobutoshi Ando. **Subscr. to:** Springer Distribution Center, Kundenservice Zeitschriften, Haberstr 7, Heidelberg 69126, Germany. TEL 49-6221-3454303, FAX 49-6221-3454229, subscriptions@springer.com; Springer New York LLC, Journal Fulfillment, PO Box 2485, Secaucus, NJ 07096. TEL 201-348-4033, 800-777-4643, FAX 201-348-4505, journals-ny@springer.com.

616.3 USA ISSN 0954-691X
RC799 CODEN: EJGHES
➤ **EUROPEAN JOURNAL OF GASTROENTEROLOGY AND HEPATOLOGY.** Text in English. 1989. m. USD 1,559 domestic to institutions; USD 1,653 foreign to institutions (effective 2011). adv. bibl.; illus. index. back issues avail.; reprints avail. **Document type:** *Journal, Academic/Scholarly.* **Description:** Brings out papers reporting clinical and scientific research which are of a high standard and which contribute to the advancement of knowledge in the field of gastroenterology and hepatology.
Related titles: CD-ROM ed.; Online - full text ed.: ISSN 1473-5687. 2001; Hungarian ed.; Supplement(s): ISSN 0969-9163.
Indexed: A20, A22, A34, A36, ASCA, AgrForAb, BIOBASE, C06, C07, C08, C25, CABA, CINAHL, CurCont, D01, E01, E12, EMBASE, ExcerpMed, F08, F11, F12, GH, H17, IABS, IndMed, IndVet, Inpharma, JW-G, LT, MEDLINE, N02, N03, N04, P30, P32, P33, P35, P39, PHN&I, PN&I, R10, R11, R12, RA&MP, RM&VM, RRTA, Reac, SCI, SCOPUS, T05, TriticAb, VS, W07.
—BLDSC (3829.729400), GNLM, IE, Infotrieve, Ingenta, INIST. **CCC.**
Published by: Lippincott Williams & Wilkins (Subsidiary of: Wolters Kluwer N.V.), 530 Walnut St, Philadelphia, PA 19106. TEL 215-521-8300, FAX 215-521-8902, customerservice@lww.com, http://www.lww.com. Eds. Didier Lebrec, Reinhold W Stockbrugger. Pub. Phil Daly. Circ: 177.

➤ **EXCERPTA MEDICA. SECTION 48: GASTROENTEROLOGY.** *see* MEDICAL SCIENCES—Abstracting, Bibliographies, Statistics

616.3 POL ISSN 1734-3038
➤ **EXPERIMENTAL & CLINICAL HEPATOLOGY.** Text and summaries in English. 2005. q. PLZ 300 domestic; EUR 149 in Europe; USD 199 elsewhere (effective 2011). abstr.; illus. back issues avail. **Document type:** *Journal, Academic/Scholarly.* **Description:** Addressed to all scientists and clinicians interested in liver disease.
Related titles: Online - full text ed.
Indexed: A01, EMBASE, ExcerpMed, R10, Reac, SCOPUS.
—BLDSC (3838.637250), IE.
Published by: (Polskie Towarzystwo Hepatologiczne/Polish Association for the Study of the Liver), Index Copernicus International S.A., Al. Jerozolimskie 146 C, Warsaw, 02-305, Poland. TEL 48-22-3475077, FAX 48-22-3475086, j.lewczuk@indexcopernicus.com, http://indexcopernicus.com/pages/view/id/32. Ed. Anna Boron-Kaczmarska. Pub., R&P Joanna Lewczuk. Circ: 500 (paid).

616.33 GBR ISSN 1747-4124
➤ **EXPERT REVIEW OF GASTROENTEROLOGY & HEPATOLOGY.** Text in English. 2007 (Oct.). bi-m. GBP 695 combined subscription domestic (print & online eds.); USD 1,220 combined subscription in North America (print & online eds.); JPY 129,000 combined subscription in Japan (print & online eds.); EUR 975 combined subscription elsewhere (print & online eds.) (effective 2011). adv. back issues avail.; reprints avail. **Document type:** *Journal, Academic/Scholarly.* **Description:** Addresses scientific, commercial and policy issues in gastrointestinal and hepatic medicine including news and views, concise commentary and analysis, reports from the conference circuit, as well as full review articles.
Related titles: Online - full text ed.: ISSN 1747-4132. GBP 615 domestic to institutions; USD 1,080 in North America to institutions; JPY 115,500 in Japan to institutions; EUR 865 elsewhere to institutions (effective 2011) (from IngentaConnect).
Indexed: A22, E08, EMBASE, ExcerpMed, H11, H12, I05, MEDLINE, P20, P22, P30, P48, P54, PQC, R10, Reac, SCOPUS, T02.
—BLDSC (9830.067000), IE. **CCC.**
Published by: Expert Reviews Ltd. (Subsidiary of: Future Science Ltd.), Unitec House, 2 Albert Pl, London, N3 1QB, United Kingdom. TEL 44-20-83716080, FAX 44-20-83716099, info@expert-reviews.com. Ed. Elisa Manzotti TEL 44-20-83716090. Pub. David Hughes. Adv. contact Simon Boisseau. Circ: 320.

616.3 ESP ISSN 2171-2107
▼ **FLASH EN GASTROENTEROLOGIA.** Text in Spanish. 2009. s-a. **Document type:** *Journal, Academic/Scholarly.*
Published by: Jarpyo Editores S.A., Ave de la Concha Espina, No. 9 Dcha., Madrid, 28016, Spain. TEL 34-91-3144338, editorial@jarpyo.es, http://www.jarpyo.es. Ed. Enrique Rey. Circ: 2,000.

616.3 USA ISSN 1869-1978
QP141.A1
▼ ➤ **FOOD DIGESTION.** Text in English. 2010. 2/yr. EUR 311, USD 420 combined subscription to institutions (print & online eds.) (effective 2012). **Document type:** *Journal, Academic/Scholarly.* **Description:** Publishes original papers and reviews that describe interrelationships between foods and all aspects of the physiological, biophysical, microbial and neuro-humoral components of digestion, acquisition and assimilation.
Related titles: Online - full text ed.: ISSN 1869-1986. 2010 (from IngentaConnect).
Indexed: SCOPUS.
—**CCC.**
Published by: Springer New York LLC (Subsidiary of: Springer Science+Business Media), 233 Spring St, New York, NY 10013. TEL 212-460-1500, FAX 212-460-1575, journals-ny@springer.com. Eds. Peter Wilde, Roger Lentle.

➤ **FOODBORNE PATHOGENS AND DISEASE.** *see* MEDICAL SCIENCES—Communicable Diseases

▼ ➤ **FRONTIERS IN ENTERIC NEUROSCIENCE.** *see* MEDICAL SCIENCES—Psychiatry And Neurology

616.3 JPN ISSN 1342-1484
FRONTIERS IN GASTROENTEROLOGY. Text in Japanese. 1996. q. JPY 8,820 (effective 2005). **Document type:** *Journal, Academic/Scholarly.*
—BLDSC (4042.021000).
Published by: Medikaru Rebyusha/Medical Review Co., Ltd., 1-7-3 Hirano-Machi, Chuo-ku, Yoshida Bldg., Osaka-shi, 541-0046, Japan. TEL 81-6-62231468, FAX 81-6-62231245.

616.3 CHE ISSN 0302-0665
CODEN: FGREDT
➤ **FRONTIERS OF GASTROINTESTINAL RESEARCH.** Text in English. 1960. irreg., latest vol.29, 2010. price varies. reprints avail. **Document type:** *Monographic series, Academic/Scholarly.* **Description:** Covers pathological, pharmacological, diagnostic and therapeutic considerations relating to the digestive system, as well as the latest techniques and instrumentation used in the management of gastrointestinal disorders.
Formerly (until 1975): Bibliotheca Gastroenterologica (0067-7949)
Related titles: Online - full text ed.: ISSN 1662-3754.
Indexed: A22, ASCA, CIN, ChemAb, ChemTitl, EMBASE, ExcerpMed, IndMed, P30, SCOPUS.
—BLDSC (4042.022000), CASDDS, GNLM, Infotrieve, Ingenta, INIST. **CCC.**
Published by: S. Karger AG, Allschwilerstr 10, Basel, 4055, Switzerland. TEL 41-61-3061111, FAX 41-61-3061234, karger@karger.ch, http://www.karger.ch. Ed. M M Lerch.

616.33 GBR ISSN 2041-4137
▼ ➤ **FRONTLINE GASTROENTEROLOGY.** Abbreviated title: F G. Text in English. 2010. q. USD 170 combined subscription in United States to non-members (print & online eds.); GBP 87 combined subscription elsewhere to non-members (print & online eds.); free to members (effective 2010). adv. back issues avail.; reprints avail. **Document type:** *Journal, Academic/Scholarly.* **Description:** Aims to accelerate the adoption of best practice in the fields of gastroenterology and hepatology.
Related titles: Online - full text ed.: ISSN 2041-4145. GBP 88.13 domestic; USD 146 in United States; GBP 75 elsewhere (effective 2010).
—**CCC.**
Published by: (British Society of Gastroenterology), B M J Group, BMA House, Tavistock Sq, London, WC1H 9JR, United Kingdom. TEL 44-20-73836373, FAX 44-20-73836668, http://group.bmj.com. Ed. Roland Valori. Pub. Julie Soloman TEL 44-20-73836263. Adv. contact Nick Gray TEL 44-20-73836386.

616.3 BRA ISSN 0101-7772
G E D. (Gastroenterologia e Endoscopia Digestiva) Text in Portuguese; Summaries in English, Portuguese. 1982. bi-m. abstr.; bibl.; illus. **Document type:** *Journal, Academic/Scholarly.*
Indexed: C01, EMBASE, ExcerpMed, R10, Reac, SCOPUS.
—BLDSC (4088.500000).
Published by: (Sociedade Brasileira de Endoscopia Digestiva (S O B E D)), Redprint Editora Ltda., Rua Domingos de Morais 2777 - 13o, Sao Paulo, SP, 04035-001, Brazil. TEL 55-11-5724813, FAX 55-11-5711719.

616.3 VEN ISSN 0016-3503
G E N. (Gastroenterologia, Endocrinologia y Nutricion) Variant title: Sociedad Venezolana de Gastroenterologia. Revista. Text in Spanish; Summaries in English, Spanish. 1946. q. VEB 100 domestic; USD 60 foreign (effective 2009). adv. bk.rev. abstr.; bibl.; charts; illus. **Document type:** *Journal, Academic/Scholarly.*
Indexed: A22, C01, IBR, IBZ, IndMed, P30, SCOPUS.
—BLDSC (4096.385000), GNLM, IE, Ingenta.
Published by: Sociedad Venezolana de Gastroenterologia/Venezuelan Society of Gastroenterology, Paseo Enrique Eraso, Torre La Noria, Piso 5o, Of 3B-3, Urbanizacion Las Mercedes, Seccion San Roman, Caracas, DF 1061, Venezuela. TEL 58-212-9912660, FAX 58-212-9927879, 58-2-9799380, gastrove@cantv.net. Ed. Dr. Mercedes Alvarado. Circ: 1,200.

616.3 USA ISSN 1934-3450
RC799
G I & HEPATOLOGY NEWS. Text in English. 2007 (Jan.). m. USD 209 in US & Canada to institutions; USD 209 elsewhere to institutions (effective 2012). adv. back issues avail. **Document type:** *Newspaper, Academic/Scholarly.* **Description:** Provides the gastroenterologist with relevant news and commentary about clinical developments and about the impact of health-care policy.
Related titles: Online - full text ed.: free (effective 2010).

—CCC.
Published by: (American Gastroenterological Association), Elsevier Society News Group (Subsidiary of: Elsevier Inc.), 5635 Fishers Ln, Ste 6000, Rockville, MD 20852. TEL 240-221-4500, FAX 240-221-4400, m.branca@elsevier.com, http://www.esng-meded.com. Ed. Charles J Lightdale.

G I G NEWSLETTER. *see* NUTRITION AND DIETETICS

G I ONCOLOGY REVIEW & OUTLOOK. (Gastrointestinal) *see* MEDICAL SCIENCES—Oncology

616.3 JPN ISSN 0918-9408
CODEN: GIREFM

G.I. RESEARCH. (Gastrointestinal) Variant title: Journal of Gastrointestinal Research. Text in Japanese. 1994. bi-m. **Document type:** *Journal, Academic/Scholarly.*
Published by: Sentan Igaku-sha, 1-9-7 Higashi-Nihonbashi, Chuo-ku, Tokyo, 103-0004, Japan. TEL 81-3-58202100, FAX 81-3-58202501, book@sentan.com, http://www.sentan.com/.

617.5562 CHN ISSN 1006-4761

GANDAN WAIKE ZAZHI/JOURNAL OF HEPATOBILIARY SURGERY. Text in Chinese. 1993. bi-m. USD 21.60 (effective 2009). **Document type:** *Journal, Academic/Scholarly.*
Related titles: Online - full text ed.
—East View.
Published by: Anhui Yike Daxue/Anhui Medical University, 218, Jiqi Lu, Hefei, 230022, China. TEL 86-551-3633411 ext 2335, FAX 86-551-3633411 ext 2299. **Dist. by:** China International Book Trading Corp, 35 Chegongzhuang Xilu, Haidian District, PO Box 399, Beijing 100044, China. TEL 86-10-68412045, FAX 86-10-68412023, cibtc@mail.cibtc.com.cn, http://www.cibtc.com.cn.

616.3 CHN ISSN 1007-1954

GANDANYI WAIKE ZAZHI/JOURNAL OF HEPATOPANCREATOBILIARY SURGERY. Text in Chinese. 1989. q. USD 24.60 (effective 2009). **Document type:** *Journal, Academic/Scholarly.*
Related titles: Online - full text ed.
—East View.
Published by: Wenzhou Yixueyuan/Wenzhou Institute of Medical Sciences, 82, Xueyuan Xilu, Wenzhou, 325027, China. TEL 86-577-88833805, FAX 86-577-88831892. **Dist. by:** China International Book Trading Corp, 35 Chegongzhuang Xilu, Haidian District, PO Box 399, Beijing 100044, China. TEL 86-10-68412045, FAX 86-10-68412023, cibtc@mail.cibtc.com.cn, http://www.cibtc.com.cn.

616.3 CHN ISSN 1008-1704

GANZANG/CHINESE HEPATOLOGY. Text in Chinese. 1992. q. USD 31.20 (effective 2009). **Document type:** *Journal, Academic/Scholarly.*
Related titles: Online - full text ed.
—East View.
Published by: Shanghai-shi Yixuehui/Shanghai Medical Association, 9585, Huamin Lu, Shanghai, 200235, China. TEL 86-21-54483359, FAX 86-21-64829943. **Dist. by:** China International Book Trading Corp, 35 Chegongzhuang Xilu, Haidian District, PO Box 399, Beijing 100044, China. TEL 86-10-68412045, FAX 86-10-68412023, cibtc@mail.cibtc.com.cn, http://www.cibtc.com.cn.

GASTRIC CANCER. *see* MEDICAL SCIENCES—Oncology

616.3 DEU ISSN 1861-9681

DER GASTROENTEROLOGE; Zeitschrift fuer Gastroenterologie und Hepatologie. Text in German. 2006. 4/yr. EUR 274, USD 337 combined subscription to institutions (print & online eds.) (effective 2012). adv. reprint service avail. from PSC. **Document type:** *Journal, Academic/Scholarly.*
Related titles: Online - full text ed.: ISSN 1861-969X (from IngentaConnect).
Indexed: A22, A26, E01, EMBASE, SCOPUS.
—IE, Ingenta. **CCC.**
Published by: Springer (Subsidiary of: Springer Science+Business Media), Tiergartenstr 17, Heidelberg, 69121, Germany. TEL 49-6221-4870, FAX 49-6221-345229, orders-hd-individuals@springer.com, http://www.springer.com. Ed. H E Blum. Circ: 3,000 (paid and controlled).

616.3 ESP ISSN 1576-0839

GASTROENTEROLOGIA INTEGRADA. Text in Multiple languages. 2000. bi-m. EUR 68.12 domestic to individuals print & online eds.; EUR 106.44 domestic to institutions print & online eds.; EUR 134.95 in the European Union print & online eds.; EUR 116.34 elsewhere print & online eds. (effective 2004). back issues avail. **Document type:** *Journal, Academic/Scholarly.*
Related titles: Online - full text ed.: ISSN 1578-1615. 2000.
Published by: Elsevier Doyma (Subsidiary of: Elsevier Health Sciences), Traversa de Gracia 17-21, Barcelona, 08021, Spain. TEL 34-932-418800, FAX 34-932-419020, doyma@doyma.es, http://www.doyma.es.

616.3 ESP ISSN 1888-3605

GASTROENTEROLOGIA INTERNACIONAL. Text in Spanish. 2008. 3/yr.
Published by: Luzan 5 S.A. de Ediciones, Pasaje Virgen de la Alegria 14, Madrid, 28027, Spain. TEL 34-91-4057260, FAX 34-91-4034907, luzan@luzan5.es, http://www.luzan5.es.

616.3 POL ISSN 2081-1020

▼ ➤ **GASTROENTEROLOGIA KLINICZNA.** Text in Polish. 2009. q. PLZ 57 to individuals; PLZ 114 to institutions (effective 2011). **Document type:** *Journal, Academic/Scholarly.*
Related titles: Online - full text ed.: ISSN 2081-5115.
Published by: (Polska Fundacja Gastroenterologii), Wydawnictwo Via Medica, ul Swietokrzyska 73, Gdansk, 80180, Poland. TEL 48-58-3209494, FAX 48-58-3209460, redakcja@viamedica.pl, http://www.viamedica.pl. Ed. Jaroslaw Regula.

616.3 CHL ISSN 0716-8594

GASTROENTEROLOGIA LATINOAMERICANA. Text in Spanish. 1990. q. **Document type:** *Journal, Academic/Scholarly.*
Published by: Sociedad Chilena de Gastroenterologia, El Trovador 4280, Of.615, Las Condes, Santiago, Chile. TEL 56-2-3425004, FAX 56-2-3425005, schgastr@netline.cl, http://www.socgastro.cl.

616.3 POL ISSN 1232-9886

GASTROENTEROLOGIA POLSKA/POLISH GASTROENTEROLOGY. Text in Polish. 1994. q. **Document type:** *Journal, Academic/Scholarly.*
Related titles: Online - full text ed.: free (effective 2011).
Indexed: A01, CA, EMBASE, ExcerpMed, R10, Reac, SCOPUS, T02.
—BLDSC (4088.961000), IE, Ingenta.
Published by: (Polskie Towarzystwo Gastroenterologii), Wydawnictwo Cornetis, ul Dlugosza 2-6, Wroclaw, 51162, Poland. TEL 48-71-3252808, FAX 48-71-3252803, sekretariat@cornetis.com.pl. Ed. Zbigniew Knapik. **Dist. by:** Ars Polona, Obroncow 25, Warsaw 03933, Poland. TEL 48-22-5098609, FAX 48-22-5098610, arspolona@arspolona.com.pl, http://www.arspolona.com.pl.

616.3 ESP ISSN 1130-9431

GASTROENTEROLOGIA PRACTICA. Text in Spanish. 1991. bi-m. EUR 51.50 domestic (effective 2009). **Document type:** *Journal, Trade.*
Published by: Ediciones Mayo S.A., Calle Aribau 185-187, 2a Planta, Barcelona, 08021, Spain. TEL 34-93-2090255, FAX 34-93-2020643, edmayo@ediciones.mayo.es, http://www.edicionesmayo.es. Ed. Ramon Planas Vila. Circ: 2,500.

616.3 SVK ISSN 1336-1473

➤ **GASTROENTEROLOGIA PRE PRAX.** Text in Slovak. 2002. q. EUR 11.98 (effective 2009). **Document type:** *Journal, Academic/Scholarly.*
Published by: Samedi s.r.o., Racianska 20, Bratislava, 839 27, Slovakia. TEL 421-2-55645901, FAX 421-2-55645902, samedi@samedi.sk. Ed. Danica Paulenova.

616.3 ESP ISSN 0210-5705
CODEN: GHEPDF

GASTROENTEROLOGIA Y HEPATOLOGIA. Text in Spanish; Summaries in English. 1978. m. (10/yr.). EUR 138.21 combined subscription to individuals print & online eds.; EUR 349.88 combined subscription to institutions print & online eds. (effective 2009). back issues avail.; reprints avail. **Document type:** *Journal, Academic/Scholarly.* **Description:** Covers gastroenterology, hepatology and pathology of the digestive tract, liver, pancreas and biliary paths.
Related titles: Online - full text ed.: ISSN 1578-9519. 1998. EUR 115.12 (effective 2009) (from ScienceDirect); Supplement(s): Gastroenterologia y Hepatologia. Monografias. ISSN 1885-6136. 2003.
Indexed: A22, EMBASE, ExcerpMed, IME, IndMed, MEDLINE, P30, R10, Reac, SCI, SCOPUS, W07.
—BLDSC (4088.955000), GNLM, IE, Infotrieve, Ingenta, INIST. **CCC.**
Published by: Elsevier Doyma (Subsidiary of: Elsevier Health Sciences), Traversa de Gracia 17-21, Barcelona, 08021, Spain. TEL 34-932-418800, FAX 34-932-419020, editorial@elsevier.com. Ed. J. Rodes Teixidor. Adv. contact Eulalia Valls. Circ: 2,500.

616.3 ESP ISSN 1578-1550

GASTROENTEROLOGIA Y HEPATOLOGIA CONTINUADA. Text in Spanish. 2001. bi-m. EUR 434.40 combined subscription domestic print & online eds.; EUR 801.78 combined subscription foreign print & online eds. (effective 2009). back issues avail. **Document type:** *Journal, Academic/Scholarly.*
Related titles: Online - full text ed.: ISSN 1578-7575. 2001. EUR 147.20 (effective 2009) (from ScienceDirect).
Indexed: EMBASE, ExcerpMed, SCOPUS.
—CCC.
Published by: Asociacion Espanola de Gastroenterologia, Travessera de Gracia, 17 2o Piso, Barcelona, 08021, Spain. TEL 34-93-2000711, FAX 34-93-091136, secretaria@aegastro.es, http://www.aegastro.es/. Ed. Josep M Pique.

616.3 PRT ISSN 1646-4656

GASTROENTEROLOGIA Y HEPATOLOGIA CONTINUADA (PORTUGUESE EDITION). Text in Portuguese. 2006. bi-m. **Document type:** *Journal, Academic/Scholarly.*
Published by: Medicografica Edicoes Medicas, Rua Camilo Castelo Branco 23-5, Lisbon, 1150-083, Portugal. geral@medicografica.pt, http://www.medicografica.pt.

616.3 JPN ISSN 0387-1207

➤ **GASTROENTEROLOGICAL ENDOSCOPY.** Text in Japanese. 1958. m. JPY 12,000 membership (effective 2005). adv. charts; illus.; abstr. 10 p./no.; back issues avail. **Document type:** *Journal, Academic/Scholarly.* **Description:** Serves as a medium for presenting original articles that offer significant contributions to knowledge in the broad field of endoscopy; also includes case reports, informal editorial opinions, abstracts, and news items that maybe of interest to endoscopists.
Indexed: EMBASE, ExcerpMed, INIS AtomInd, R10, Reac, SCOPUS.
—BLDSC (4088.965000), GNLM.
Published by: Nihon Shokaki Naishikyo Gakkai/Japan Gastroenterological Endoscopy Society, Taimei Bldg, 3-22, Kanda Ogawa-machi, Chiyoda-ku, Tokyo, 101-0052, Japan. TEL 81-3-32914111, FAX 81-3-32915568, info@jges.or.jp, http://www.jges.net. Ed. Takashi Nakamura. adv.: page JPY 78,000; 182 x 256. Circ: 28,500.

663 DEU ISSN 1616-9670

GASTROENTEROLOGIE UP2DATE. Text in German. 2005. q. EUR 140 to institutions; EUR 192 combined subscription to institutions (print & online eds.); EUR 46 newsstand/cover (effective 2011). adv. **Document type:** *Journal, Academic/Scholarly.*
Related titles: Online - full text ed.: ISSN 1616-9727. EUR 185 to institutions (effective 2011).
—IE. **CCC.**
Published by: Georg Thieme Verlag, Ruedigerstr 14, Stuttgart, 70469, Germany. TEL 49-711-8931421, FAX 49-711-8931410, leser.service@thieme.de. Ed. Dr. Guido Adler. Adv. contact Ulrike Bradler. Circ: 2,200 (paid and controlled).

616.3 ITA ISSN 0391-8939

IL GASTROENTEROLOGO. Text in Italian; Summaries in Italian, English. 1979. q. USD 15 domestic; USD 30 foreign (effective 2008). adv. **Document type:** *Journal, Academic/Scholarly.*
Published by: C I C Edizioni Internazionali, Corso Trieste 42, Rome, 00198, Italy. TEL 39-06-8412673, FAX 39-06-8412688, info@gruppocic.it, http://www.gruppocic.it.

616.3 USA ISSN 0016-5085
RC799 CODEN: GASTAB

➤ **GASTROENTEROLOGY.** Text in English. 1943. 13/yr. USD 1,072 in United States to institutions; USD 1,354 elsewhere to institutions (effective 2012). bk.rev. abstr.; charts; illus. cum.index. Supplement avail.; back issues avail.; reprints avail. **Document type:** *Journal, Academic/Scholarly.* **Description:** Provides clinical coverage of all areas of the digestive tract, including the liver.
Related titles: Microform ed.: (from PQC); Online - full text ed.: ISSN 1528-0012 (from ScienceDirect).
Indexed: A22, A26, A34, A35, A36, AIIM, AIM, ASCA, AgBio, AgrForAb, B25, BIOBASE, BIOSIS Prev, BP, C13, CA, CABA, CIN, CISA, ChemAb, ChemTitl, CurCont, D01, DBA, DentInd, E01, E12, EMBASE, ExcerpMed, F08, FR, FS&TA, GH, H16, H17, I12, IABS, IDIS, INI, ISR, IndMed, IndVet, Inpharma, JW, JW-G, JW-ID, Kidney, MEDLINE, MS&D, MycolAb, N02, N03, N04, NRN, P30, P32, P33, P35, P39, P40, PGegResA, PN&I, R10, RA&MP, RM&VM, Reac, S12, SAA, SCI, SCOPUS, SoyAb, T02, T05, THA, TriticAb, VS, W07.
—BLDSC (4089.000000), CASDDS, GNLM, IE, Infotrieve, Ingenta, INIST. **CCC.**
Published by: (American Gastroenterological Association), W.B. Saunders Co. (Subsidiary of: Elsevier Health Sciences), Elsevier, Health Sciences Division, Order Fulfillment, 3251 Riverport Ln, Maryland Heights, MO 63043. TEL 314-872-8370, 800-325-4177, FAX 314-432-1380, JournalCustomerService-usa@elsevier.com, http://www.us.elsevierhealth.com. Ed. Dr. Anil A. Rustgi. Pub. Theresa Monturano. Adv. contact Jim Pattis TEL 201-767-4170. Circ: 14,850.

616.35 USA ISSN 0883-8348
RC864.A1

GASTROENTEROLOGY AND ENDOSCOPY NEWS. Text in English. 1950. m. USD 70 domestic; USD 90 foreign; USD 7 per issue domestic; USD 10 per issue foreign; free to qualified personnel (effective 2010). adv. bk.rev. bibl.; illus. index. back issues avail. **Document type:** *Newspaper, Trade.* **Description:** Provides comprehensive and objective news and reviews to gastroenterologists, colon and rectal surgeons, and hepatologists.
Former titles (until 1985): American Journal of Proctology, Gastroenterology and Colon and Rectal Surgery (0162-6566); (until 1978): American Journal of Proctology (0002-9521)
Related titles: Microform ed.: (from PQC); Online - full text ed.
Indexed: IndMed, P30, SCOPUS.
—GNLM, INIST. **CCC.**
Published by: McMahon Group, 545 W 45th St, 8th Fl, New York, NY 10036. TEL 212-957-5300, FAX 212-957-7230, info@mcmahongroup.com, http://www.mcmahongroup.com. Pub. Raymond E McMahon. Circ: 15,233.

616.3 USA ISSN 1554-7914

➤ **GASTROENTEROLOGY & HEPATOLOGY.** Text in English. 2005. bi-m. free to qualified personnel (effective 2010). adv. back issues avail. **Document type:** *Journal, Academic/Scholarly.*
Related titles: Online - full text ed.
Indexed: C06, C07, EMBASE, ExcerpMed, P30, R10, Reac, SCOPUS.
—BLDSC (4089.026500), IE.
Published by: Millennium Medical Publishing, Inc., 611 Broadway, Ste 310, New York, NY 10012. TEL 212-995-2211, FAX 212-995-5572, info@clinicaladvances.com. Ed. Gary R Lichtenstein. Adv. contact Paul McDaniel TEL 212-995-5552. Circ: 16,731.

616.3 IRN ISSN 2008-2258

GASTROENTEROLOGY AND HEPATOLOGY FROM BED TO BENCH. Text in English. 2008. q. **Document type:** *Journal, Academic/Scholarly.*
Formerly (until 2009): Iranian Journal of Gastroenterology and Hepatology (2008-1685)
Related titles: Online - full text ed.: ISSN 2008-4234. free (effective 2011).
Indexed: A01, A34, A36, C06, CABA, GH, N02, N03, P33, T02, T05.
Published by: Shaheed Beheshti Medical University, Research Institute for Gastroenterology and Liver Diseases, PO Box 19835-178, Tehran, Iran. TEL 98-21-22432515, FAX 98-21-22432517. Ed. Mohammad Reza Zali.

616.3 USA ISSN 0889-8553
RC799 CODEN: GCNAEF

➤ **GASTROENTEROLOGY CLINICS OF NORTH AMERICA.** Text in English. 1972. q. USD 458 in United States to institutions; USD 558 elsewhere to institutions (effective 2012). adv. back issues avail.; reprints avail. **Document type:** *Journal, Academic/Scholarly.* **Description:** Focuses on a single topic relevant to gastroenterology or internal medicine practice, from medical therapy of irritable bowel disease to the clinical implications of genetic and molecular medicine in GI diseases.
Supersedes in part (in 1987): Clinics in Gastroenterology (0300-5089)
Related titles: Online - full text ed.: ISSN 1558-1942 (from ScienceDirect).
Indexed: A22, ASCA, C06, C07, C08, CINAHL, ChemAb, CurCont, DentInd, EMBASE, ExcerpMed, FR, ISR, IndMed, Inpharma, MEDLINE, P30, R10, Reac, SCI, SCOPUS, W07.
—BLDSC (4089.031500), CASDDS, GNLM, IE, Infotrieve, Ingenta, INIST. **CCC.**
Published by: (American College of Gastroenterology, Inc.), W.B. Saunders Co. (Subsidiary of: Elsevier Health Sciences), Elsevier, Health Sciences Division, Order Fulfillment, 3251 Riverport Ln, Maryland Heights, MO 63043. TEL 314-872-8370, 800-325-4177, FAX 314-432-1380, JournalCustomerService-usa@elsevier.com, http://www.us.elsevierhealth.com. Adv. contact John Marmero TEL 212-633-3657.

➤ **GASTROENTEROLOGY CODING ALERT;** your practical adviser for ethically optimizing coding, payment, and efficiency for gastroenterology practices. *see* INSURANCE

616.3 GBR ISSN 1752-8763

GASTROENTEROLOGY IN PRIMARY CARE. Text in English. 1987. q. adv. back issues avail. **Document type:** *Journal, Academic/Scholarly.*
Formerly (until 2006): Gastroenterology in Perspective (0952-7958)
Related titles: Online - full text ed.: ISSN 2041-5516. free (effective 2010).
Published by: Primay Care Society for Gastroenterology, 21 Tower St, Covent Garden, London, WC2H 9NS, United Kingdom. TEL 44-20-78360088, secretariat@pcsg.org.uk. Ed. Jamie Dalrymple.

616.3 ITA ISSN 2036-7414

▼ ➤ **GASTROENTEROLOGY INSIGHTS.** Text in English. 2009. irreg. **Document type:** *Journal, Academic/Scholarly.*
Related titles: Online - full text ed.: ISSN 2036-7422. free (effective 2011).
Indexed: A01, T02.
Published by: Pagepress, Via Giuseppe Belli 4, Pavia, 27100, Italy. TEL 39-0382-1751762, FAX 39-0382-1750481. Ed. Qiang Cai.

616.3 USA ISSN 1042-895X
CODEN: GANUER

➤ **GASTROENTEROLOGY NURSING.** Text in English. 1977. bi-m. USD 340.51 domestic to institutions; USD 446 foreign to institutions (effective 2011). adv. bk.rev. back issues avail.; reprints avail. **Document type:** *Journal, Academic/Scholarly.* **Description:** Provides a resource for current SGNA guidelines, new GI procedures, pharmacology, career development, and certification review.
Former titles (until 1989): S G A Journal (0744-1126); (until 198?): Society of Gastrointestinal Assistants. Journal (0149-6212)
Related titles: Online - full text ed.: ISSN 1538-9766.
Indexed: A22, C06, C07, C08, CINAHL, CurCont, EMBASE, ExcerpMed, INI, MEDLINE, P30, R10, Reac, SCI, SCOPUS, SSCI, W07.
—BLDSC (4089.032300), GNLM, IE, Infotrieve, Ingenta. **CCC.**
Published by: (Society of Gastroenterology Nurses and Associates), Lippincott Williams & Wilkins (Subsidiary of: Wolters Kluwer N.V.), Two Commerce Sq, 2001 Market St, Philadelphia, PA 19103. TEL 215-521-8300, FAX 215-521-8902, customerservice@lww.com, http://www.lww.com. Ed. Kathy A Baker. Pub. Sandy Kasko. Adv. contact Gregg Willinger TEL 203-801-9696. Circ: 8,397.

616.3 CAN ISSN 1918-2805

➤ **GASTROENTEROLOGY RESEARCH.** Text in English. 2008. bi-m. **Document type:** *Journal, Academic/Scholarly.*
Related titles: Online - full text ed.: ISSN 1918-2813. free (effective 2011).
Published by: Elmer Press, 8485 Rue Outaouais, Brossard, Montreal, PQ J4Y 3E2, Canada. TEL 514-467-3868, FAX 450-812-3126.

616.3 USA ISSN 1687-6121

➤ **GASTROENTEROLOGY RESEARCH AND PRACTICE.** Text in English. 2007. irreg. USD 395 (effective 2011). **Document type:** *Journal, Academic/Scholarly.* **Description:** Publishes articles and research results related to basic science relevant to gastroenterology including immunology, molecular biology and genetics.
Related titles: Online - full text ed.: ISSN 1687-630X. free (effective 2011).
Indexed: A01, A26, B21, C06, C07, CA, CurCont, EMBASE, ExcerpMed, ImmunAb, P30, SCI, SCOPUS, T02, W07.
—IE.
Published by: Hindawi Publishing Corporation, 410 Park Ave, 15th Fl, PMB 287, New York, NY 10022. FAX 215-893-4392, 866-446-3294, hindawi@hindawi.com.

616.3 IND

GASTROENTEROLOGY TODAY. Text in English. 19??. q. **Document type:** *Journal, Academic/Scholarly.*
Published by: C M P Medica (Subsidiary of: C M P Medica Ltd.), Sagar Tech Plz A 615-617, 6th Fl, Andheri Kurla Rd, Saki Naka Jct, Andheri E, Mumbai, 400 072, India. TEL 91-22-66122600, FAX 91-22-66122626, info.india@ubm.com, http://www.ubmindia.in/cmp-medica.asp.

616.3 GBR ISSN 0969-0131

GASTROENTEROLOGY TODAY. Text in English. 1991. q. GBP 24 domestic to individuals; GBP 48 foreign to individuals; GBP 40 domestic to institutions; GBP 72 foreign to institutions; free to members (effective 2010). adv. **Document type:** *Journal, Trade.* **Description:** Provides information about the field of Gastroenterology and it's related areas.
—**CCC.**
Published by: Media Publishing Company, Media House, 48 High St, Swanley, Kent BR8 8BQ, United Kingdom. TEL 44-1322-660434, FAX 44-1322-666539, mediajournals@aol.com. adv.: B&W page GBP 800, color page GBP 1,200; trim 210 x 297.

616.3 USA ISSN 1543-6756

GASTROENTEROLOGY WEEK. Text in English. 2003. w. USD 2,295 in US & Canada; USD 2,495 elsewhere; USD 2,525 combined subscription in US & Canada (print & online eds.); USD 2,755 combined subscription elsewhere (print & online eds.) (effective 2008). back issues avail. **Document type:** *Newsletter, Trade.* **Description:** Covers drug development, therapies, risk factors, and pathology for diseases and conditions affecting the gastro-intestinal tract.
Related titles: E-mail ed.; Online - full text ed.: ISSN 1543-6748. USD 2,295 combined subscription (online & email eds.); single user (effective 2008).
Indexed: A26, E08, G08, H11, H12, I05, S09.
—CIS.
Published by: NewsRx, 2727 Paces Ferry Rd SE, Ste 2-440, Atlanta, GA 30339. TEL 770-435-8286, 800-726-4550, FAX 770-435-6800, pressrelease@newsrx.com, http://www.newsrx.com. Pub. Susan Hasty TEL 770-507-7777.

616.3 SRB

GASTROENTEROPATOLOSKI ARHIV. Text in Serbian. s-a. **Document type:** *Journal, Academic/Scholarly.*
Published by: Srpsko Lekarsko Drustvo/Serbian Medical Association, George Washington St, 19, Belgrade, 11000. TEL 381-11-3234450, FAX 381-11-3246090, sld@eunet.yu, http://www.sld.org.yu. Ed. Goran Jankovic.

616.3 GBR ISSN 1478-1239

GASTROHEP; the global online resource for gastroenterology, hepatology & endoscopy. Text in English. 2003. irreg. **Document type:** *Journal, Academic/Scholarly.* **Description:** Education and information resource in gastroenterology, hepatology and endoscopy, for health-care professionals working in these areas. Provides quick and comprehensive access to all the latest information for clinical practice and trainee education.
Media: Online - full text.
Published by: Wiley-Blackwell Publishing Ltd. (Subsidiary of: John Wiley & Sons, Inc.), 9600 Garsington Rd, Oxford, OX4 2DQ, United Kingdom. TEL 44-1865-776868, FAX 44-1865-714591, customerservices@blackwellpublishing.com, http://www.wiley.com/. Ed. Roy Pounder.

GASTROINTESTINAL CANCER RESEARCH. *see* MEDICAL SCIENCES—Oncology

▼ **GASTROINTESTINAL CANCER: TARGETS AND THERAPY.** *see* MEDICAL SCIENCES—Oncology

616.3 USA ISSN 0016-5107
RC804.E6 CODEN: GAENBQ

➤ **GASTROINTESTINAL ENDOSCOPY.** Text in English. 1954. 13/yr. USD 511 in United States to institutions; USD 649 elsewhere to institutions (effective 2012). adv. bk.rev. abstr. index. back issues avail.; reprints avail. **Document type:** *Journal, Academic/Scholarly.* **Description:** Contains current papers in endoscopy for gastroenterologists and general surgeons.
Former titles (until 1965): Gastrointestinal Endoscopy. Bulletin (1051-7472); (until 1961): Gastroscopy and Esophagoscopy. Bulletin
Related titles: CD-ROM ed.: ISSN 1085-8741; Online - full text ed.: ISSN 1097-6779 (from ScienceDirect).
Indexed: A22, A26, A34, A36, A37, AMED, ASCA, AgrForAb, C06, C07, C08, CABA, CINAHL, CurCont, E12, EMBASE, ExcerpMed, F08, FR, GH, H12, H17, I05, INI, ISR, IndMed, IndVet, Inpharma, JW-G, MEDLINE, N02, N03, P30, P33, P35, P39, PN&I, R10, R12, RA&MP, RM&VM, Reac, S12, SCI, SCOPUS, T02, T05, VS, W07, W11.
—BLDSC (4089.050000), GNLM, IE, Infotrieve, Ingenta, INIST. **CCC.**
Published by: (American Society for Gastrointestinal Endoscopy), Mosby, Inc. (Subsidiary of: Elsevier Health Sciences), 1600 John F. Kennedy Blvd, Ste 1800, Philadelphia, PA 19103. TEL 215-239-3900, 800-523-1649, FAX 215-239-3990, elspcs@elsevier.com, http://www.us.elsevierhealth.com. Ed. Glenn M Eisen.

616.3 USA ISSN 1052-5157
CODEN: GECNED

GASTROINTESTINAL ENDOSCOPY CLINICS OF NORTH AMERICA. Text in English. 1991. q. USD 414 in United States to institutions; USD 505 elsewhere to institutions (effective 2012). adv. back issues avail.; reprints avail. **Document type:** *Journal, Academic/Scholarly.* **Description:** Each issue focuses on the treatment or diagnosis of a condition or disease of the digestive tract.
Related titles: Microform ed.: (from PQC); Online - full text ed.: ISSN 1558-1950 (from ScienceDirect).
Indexed: A22, C06, C07, C08, CINAHL, EMBASE, ExcerpMed, IndMed, MEDLINE, P30, R10, Reac, SCOPUS.
—BLDSC (4089.052000), GNLM, IE, Infotrieve, Ingenta, INIST. **CCC.**
Published by: W.B. Saunders Co. (Subsidiary of: Elsevier Health Sciences), Elsevier, Health Sciences Division, Order Fulfillment, 3251 Riverport Ln, Maryland Heights, MO 63043. TEL 314-872-8370, 800-325-4177, FAX 314-432-1380, JournalCustomerService-usa@elsevier.com, http://www.us.elsevierhealth.com. Ed. Dr. Charles J Lightdale. Adv. contact John Marmero TEL 212-633-3657.

616.8 610.736 GBR ISSN 1479-5248

GASTROINTESTINAL NURSING. Text in English. 2003 (Feb.). m. GBP 69 to individuals (in UK & Eire); EUR 120 in Europe to individuals; USD 177 elsewhere to individuals (effective 2009). adv. back issues avail. **Document type:** *Journal, Academic/Scholarly.* **Description:** Covers issues pertaining to all aspects of gastroenteology, from chronic diseases to acute episodes, from new methods of diagnosis to treatment of all forms of gut disorder.
Indexed: B28, C06, C07, C08, CA, CINAHL, SCOPUS, T02.
—BLDSC (4089.066000), IE, Ingenta. **CCC.**
Published by: M A Healthcare Ltd., St Jude's Church, Dulwich Rd, London, SE24 0PB, United Kingdom. TEL 44-20-7738545, subscriptions@markallengroup.com, http://www.mahealthcareevents.co.uk. Ed. Alice Hall. Adv. contact Kirtsy Medlock.

616.3 USA ISSN 1556-1267

GASTROINTESTINAL PHYSIOLOGY. Text in English. 2005. irreg., latest 2005, 1st ed. USD 36.95 1st ed. (effective 2008). **Document type:** *Journal, Academic/Scholarly.* **Description:** Summarizes and explains gastointestinal physiology and diagnosis of GI disorders.
Published by: McGraw-Hill Companies, Inc., 1221 Ave of the Americas, 43rd fl, New York, NY 10020. TEL 212-512-2000, customer.service@mcgraw-hill.com, http://www.mcgraw-hill.com.

611.3 SWE ISSN 1651-0453

GASTROKURIREN. Text in Swedish. 1996. 5/yr. adv. **Document type:** *Magazine, Trade.*
Related titles: Online - full text ed.
Published by: (Svensk Gastroenterologisk Foerening), Mediahuset i Goeteborg AB, Marieholmsgatan 10 C, Goeteborg, 41502, Sweden. TEL 46-31-7071930, FAX 46-31-848642, http://www.mediahuset.se. Ed. Charlotte Hoeoeg. Adv. contact Olla Lundblad.

616.3 DEU ISSN 1869-1005

▼ **GASTRONEWS.** Text in German. 2009. bi-m. EUR 73 (effective 2011). **Document type:** *Journal, Academic/Scholarly.*
Published by: Urban und Vogel Medien und Medizin Verlagsgesellschaft mbH (Subsidiary of: Springer Science+Business Media), Neumarkter Str 43, Munich, 81673, Germany. TEL 49-89-4372-1411, FAX 49-89-4372-1410, verlag@urban-vogel.de, http://www.urban-vogel.de.

616.3 ESP ISSN 0211-058X

GASTRUM; patologia del aparato digestivo. Text in Spanish. 1977. s-a. adv. **Document type:** *Monographic series, Academic/Scholarly.*
Published by: Jarpyo Editores S.A., Antonio Lopez Aguado 4, Madrid, 28029, Spain. TEL 34-91-3144338, FAX 34-91-3144499, editorial@jarpyo.es, http://www.jarpyo.es. Circ: 3,000.

616.3 ITA ISSN 0394-0225

GIORNALE ITALIANO DI ENDOSCOPIA DIGESTIVA. Text in Italian; Summaries in English. 1978. 4/yr. adv. 80 p./no.; reprints avail. **Document type:** *Journal, Academic/Scholarly.*
Formerly (until 1980): Giornale di Gastroenterologia ed Endoscopia (0394-0489)
Indexed: EMBASE, ExcerpMed, R10, Reac, SCOPUS.
—BLDSC (4178.214600), GNLM, IE, Ingenta. **CCC.**
Published by: Societa Italiana di Endoscopia Digestiva (S I E D), Via Francesco Ferrara 40, Rome, 00191, Italy. TEL 39-06-3290250, FAX 39-06-36306897, sied@scstudiocongressi.it, http://sied.it. Circ: 2,000.

616.3 CHN ISSN 1001-1188

GUOWAI YIXUE (KOUQIANG YIXUE FENCE)/FOREIGN MEDICAL SCIENCE (STOMATOLOGY). Text in Chinese. 1974. bi-m. CNY 48 domestic; USD 20.40 foreign (effective 2005). **Document type:** *Journal, Academic/Scholarly.*
Related titles: Online - full text ed.
—East View.
Published by: Huaxi Yike Daxue/West China University of Medical Sciences, Section 3, no.17, Renmin Nanlu, Chengdu, Sichuan 610041, China. TEL 86-28-85502414, FAX 86-28-85503479. **Dist. by:** China International Book Trading Corp, 35 Chegongzhuang Xilu, Haidian District, PO Box 399, Beijing 100044, China. TEL 86-10-68412045, FAX 86-10-68412023, cibtc@mail.cibtc.com.cn, http://www.cibtc.com.cn.

616.3 CHN ISSN 1001-1153

GUOWAI YIXUE (XIAOHUAXI JIBING FENCE)/FOREIGN MEDICAL SCIENCES (DIGESTIVE SYSTEM DISEASES). Text in Chinese. 1963. bi-m. USD 28.20 (effective 2009). **Document type:** *Journal, Academic/Scholarly.*
Related titles: Online - full content ed.; Online - full text ed.
—East View.
Published by: Shanghai Shi Yixue Kexue Jishu Qingbao Yanjiusuo, 602, Jianquo Xilu, Shanghai, 200031, China. TEL 86-21-64159094. **Dist. by:** China International Book Trading Corp, 35 Chegongzhuang Xilu, Haidian District, PO Box 399, Beijing 100044, China. TEL 86-10-68412045, FAX 86-10-68412023, cibtc@mail.cibtc.com.cn, http://www.cibtc.com.cn.

616.3 GBR ISSN 0017-5749
RC799 CODEN: GUTTAK

➤ **GUT**; an international journal of gastroenterology & hepatology. Text in English. 1960. m. GBP 600 to institutions; GBP 748 combined subscription to institutions small FTE (print & online eds.) (effective 2011); subscr. includes Frontline Gastroenterology. adv. bk.rev. charts; illus. index. back issues avail.; reprints avail. **Document type:** *Journal, Academic/Scholarly.* **Description:** Covers all diseases of the alimentary tract, liver, biliary tree, and pancreas.
Related titles: CD-ROM ed.; Microform ed.: (from PQC); Online - full text ed.: Gut Online. ISSN 1468-3288. GBP 629 to institutions small FTE (effective 2011); Japanese ed.: ISSN 1883-5821; Spanish ed.: ISSN 1886-9831. 2006. EUR 101.89 to individuals; EUR 152.83 to institutions (effective 2009).
Indexed: A01, A03, A08, A22, A26, A34, A35, A36, AIM, AgBio, B21, B25, BIOBASE, BIOSIS Prev, CA, CABA, CIN, ChemAb, ChemTitl, CurCont, D01, DBA, DentInd, E01, E08, E12, EMBASE, ExcerpMed, F08, FR, G08, GH, H11, H12, H17, I05, IABS, IBR, IBZ, IDIS, INI, ISR, ImmunAb, IndMed, IndVet, Inpharma, JW-G, MEDLINE, MaizeAb, MycolAb, N02, N03, N04, NRN, P20, P22, P26, P30, P33, P35, P39, P48, P54, PN&I, PQC, R10, RM&VM, Reac, S09, SCI, SCOPUS, T02, T05, TriticAb, VS, W07.
—BLDSC (4232.400000), CASDDS, GNLM, IE, Infotrieve, Ingenta, INIST. **CCC.**
Published by: (British Society of Gastroenterology), B M J Group, BMA House, Tavistock Sq, London, WC1H 9JR, United Kingdom. TEL 44-20-73836373, FAX 44-20-73836668, membership@bma.org.uk, http://group.bmj.com. Ed. Emad El-Omar. Pub. Allison Lang TEL 44-20-73836212. Adv. contact Nick Gray TEL 44-20-73836386. Circ: 4,210. **Subscr. to:** PO Box 299, London WC1H 9TD, United Kingdom. TEL 44-20-73836270, FAX 44-20-73836402, support@bmjgroup.com.

573.38 KOR ISSN 1976-2283

GUT AND LIVER. Text in English. 2007. q. KRW 30,000 (effective 2008). **Document type:** *Journal, Academic/Scholarly.* **Description:** Publishes original articles, case reports, brief communications, letters to the editor, and invited review articles in the field of gastroenterology.
Indexed: EMBASE, ExcerpMed, P30, SCI, SCOPUS, W07.
—BLDSC (4232.420000), IE.
Published by: Gut and Liver, Editorial Office, 305 Lotte Gold Rose II, 890-59 Daechi-dong, Gangnam-gu, Seoul, 135-839, Korea, S. TEL 82-2-5380627, FAX 82-2-5380635. Ed. Young S. Kim TEL 415-750-2095. **Co-sponsors:** Korean College of Helicobacter and Upper Gastrointestinal Research; Korean Society of Gastroenterology/Daehan Sohwa'gi'byeong Haghoe; Korean Society of Gastrointestinal Endoscopy/Daehan Sohwa'gi Naesi'gyeong Haghoe; Korean Society of Pancreatobiliary Disease; Korean Association for the Study of Intestinal Diseases/Daehan Jang Yeon'gu Haghoe; Korean Association for the Study of the Liver/Daehan gan Haghoe; Korean Society of Neurogastroenterology and Motility.

616.3 579 USA ISSN 1949-0976
QR171.G29

▼ **GUT MICROBES.** Text in English. 2010 (Jan.). q. USD 1,400 combined subscription in US & Canada (print & online eds.); USD 1,460 combined subscription elsewhere (print & online eds.) (effective 2011). **Document type:** *Journal, Academic/Scholarly.* **Description:** Publishes original research articles and commentaries covering the latest aspects of molecular, biological, biomedical and clinical studies on gut microorganisms and their host, focusing on microorganisms such as fungi, parasites, bacteria and viruses populating the gastrointestinal tract, both commensals and pathogens.
Related titles: Online - full text ed.: ISSN 1949-0984. forthcoming.
Indexed: P30, SCOPUS.
—**CCC.**
Published by: Landes Bioscience, 1002 W Ave, Austin, TX 78701. TEL 512-637-6050, FAX 512-637-6079, info@landesbioscience.com. Ed. Gail Hecht.

616.3 GBR ISSN 1757-4749

▼ ➤ **GUT PATHOGENS.** Text in English. 2009. irreg. free (effective 2009). **Document type:** *Journal, Academic/Scholarly.* **Description:** Covers all aspects of the biology and pathogenesis of bacterial, parasitic and viral infections of the gut, including their diagnosis and clinical management.
Media: Online - full text.
Indexed: A01, A26, CA, E08, G06, G07, G08, H12, I05, P30, S09, T02.
Published by: (The International Society for Genomic and Evolutionary Microbiology ITA), BioMed Central Ltd. (Subsidiary of: Springer Science+Business Media), 236 Gray's Inn Rd, London, WC1X 8HB, United Kingdom. TEL 44-20-31922000, FAX 44-20-31922010, info@biomedcentral.com, http://www.biomedcentral.com. Eds. Francis Megraud, Leonardo Sechi, Niyaz Ahmed.

616.3 616.994 NLD ISSN 2210-3465

HET H N P C C-LYNCH JOURNAAL. (Hereditary Nonpolyposis Colorectal Cancer) Text in Dutch. 200?. q. **Document type:** *Journal, Consumer.*
Published by: Vereniging H N P C C - Lynch, Postbus 8152, Utrecht, 3503 RD, Netherlands. TEL 31-30-2916090, secretariaat@vereniginghnpcc.nl, http://www.hnpcc.nfk.nl.

616.36 GBR ISSN 1365-182X
H P B. (Hepato Pancreato Biliary) Variant title: H P B Surgery. Text in English. 1997. 8/yr. GBP 653 in United Kingdom to institutions; EUR 824 in Europe to institutions; USD 1,278 elsewhere to institutions; GBP 752 combined subscription in United Kingdom to institutions (print & online eds.); EUR 948 combined subscription in Europe to institutions (print & online eds.); USD 1,470 combined subscription elsewhere to institutions (print & online eds.) (effective 2012). back issues avail.; reprint service avail. from PSC. **Document type:** *Journal, Academic/Scholarly.* **Description:** Contains articles, expert reviews, original articles, images, editorials, and reader correspondence encompassing all aspects of benign and malignant hepatobiliary disease and its management.
Related titles: Online - full text ed.: ISSN 1477-2574. 2000. GBP 653 in United Kingdom to institutions; EUR 824 in Europe to institutions; USD 1,278 elsewhere to institutions (effective 2012) (from IngentaConnect).
Indexed: A01, A03, A08, A22, CA, E01, EMBASE, ExcerpMed, MEDLINE, P30, R10, Reac, SCI, SCOPUS, T02, W07.
—IE, Infotrieve, Ingenta. **CCC.**
Published by: (American Hepato-Pancreato-Biliary Association USA, European Hepato-Pancreato-Biliary Association USA, International Hepato Pancreato Biliary Association), Wiley-Blackwell Publishing Ltd. (Subsidiary of: John Wiley & Sons, Inc.), 9600 Garsington Rd, Oxford, OX4 2DQ, United Kingdom. TEL 44-1865-776868, FAX 44-1865-714591, customerservices@blackwellpublishing.com. Ed. James Garden.

HELICOBACTER (OXFORD). see BIOLOGY—Microbiology

616.3 GBR ISSN 1478-4041
HELICOBACTER. SUPPLEMENT. Text in English. 1994. a. **Document type:** *Journal, Academic/Scholarly.*
Formerly (until 2002): The Year In Helicobacter Pylori (1358-7269)
Related titles: Online - full text ed.; ◆ Supplement to: Helicobacter (Oxford). ISSN 1083-4389.
Indexed: SCOPUS.
—Infotrieve, INIST. **CCC.**
Published by: (European Helicobacter Pylori Study Group), Wiley-Blackwell Publishing Ltd. (Subsidiary of: John Wiley & Sons, Inc.), 9600 Garsington Rd, Oxford, OX4 2DQ, United Kingdom. TEL 44-1865-776868, FAX 44-1865-714591, customer@wiley.co.uk, http://www.wiley.com/.

616.3 GBR ISSN 1179-1535
▼ **HEPATIC MEDICINE**; evidence and research. Text in English. 2009. a. free (effective 2011). **Document type:** *Journal, Academic/Scholarly.*
Media: Online - full text.
Indexed: P30.
—**CCC.**
Published by: Dove Medical Press Ltd., Beechfield House, Winterton Way, Macclesfield, SK11 0JL, United Kingdom. TEL 44-1625-509130, FAX 44-1625-617933. Ed. Gerond V Lake-Bakaar.

616.3 IRN ISSN 1735-143X
➤ **HEPATITIS MONTHLY.** Text in English. 2004. m. **Document type:** *Journal, Academic/Scholarly.* **Description:** Serves as a forum for exchange of scientific information in the field of liver diseases with special attention to hepatitis.
Related titles: Online - full text ed.: ISSN 1735-3408. free (effective 2011).
Indexed: A01, A34, A36, C06, C07, CA, CABA, D01, E12, EMBASE, ExcerpMed, GH, H17, N02, N03, P10, P20, P33, P48, P53, P54, PN&I, PQC, R10, R12, RA&MP, Reac, SCI, SCOPUS, T02, T05, VS, W07.
—IE.
Published by: Tehran Hepatitis Center, 92 Vesal St, Keshavarz Blvd, 3d Fl, Tehran, Iran. TEL 98-21-8967923, FAX 98-21-8958048. Ed. Seyed-Moayed Alavian.

616.36230072 NZL ISSN 1170-3202
HEPATITIS RESEARCH REVIEW. Variant title: N Z Hepatitis Research Review. Text in English. 2008. q. free to qualified personnel (effective 2009). back issues avail. **Document type:** *Journal, Academic/Scholarly.*
Media: Online - full content.
Published by: Research Review Ltd., N Shore Mail Centre, PO Box 100116, Auckland, New Zealand. TEL 64-9-4102277, info@researchreview.co.nz.

616.3 616.992 FRA CODEN: HEGAF6
HEPATO - GASTRO & ONCOLOGIE DIGESTIVE. Text in French. 1994. bi-m. EUR 384 combined subscription domestic to institutions (print & online eds.); EUR 408 combined subscription in the European Union to institutions (print & online eds.); EUR 420 combined subscription elsewhere to institutions (print & online eds.) (effective 2011). **Document type:** *Journal, Academic/Scholarly.* **Description:** Used as a training and updating tool in digestive pathology. Includes bibliographical synopses, mini-reviews and annotated clinical cases.
Formerly (until 2009): Hepato - Gastro (1253-7020)
Related titles: CD-ROM ed.; Online - full text ed.: ISSN 1952-4048.
Indexed: A22, EMBASE, ExcerpMed, Inpharma, R10, Reac, SCOPUS.
—BLDSC (4295.833700), GNLM, IE, Ingenta, INIST. **CCC.**
Published by: John Libbey Eurotext, 127 Av. de la Republique, Montrouge, 92120, France. TEL 33-1-46730660, FAX 33-1-40840999, contact@jle.com, http://www.john-libbey-eurotext.fr. Circ: 1,000.

616.3 GRC ISSN 0172-6390 CODEN: HEGAD4
➤ **HEPATO-GASTROENTEROLOGY**; current medical and surgical trends. Text in English; Summaries in English, German. 1954. 8/yr. EUR 620 to institutions (effective 2011). adv. bk.rev. abstr.; bibl.; charts; illus.; stat. index. back issues avail.; reprints avail. **Document type:** *Journal, Academic/Scholarly.*
Former titles: Acta Hepato-Gastroenterologica (0300-970X); Acta Hepato- Splenologica (0001-5822)
Related titles: Microform ed.: (from PQC).
Indexed: A20, A22, A34, A36, ASCA, AgrForAb, B25, BIOBASE, BIOSIS Prev, CABA, ChemAb, CurCont, D01, E01, E12, EMBASE, ExcerpMed, F08, GH, H17, IABS, IBR, IBZ, INI, ISR, IndMed, Inpharma, JW-G, MEDLINE, MycolAb, N02, N03, P30, P33, P35, P39, R10, R12, RA&MP, RM&VM, Reac, SCI, SCOPUS, T05, VS, W07, W10.
—BLDSC (4295.835000), CASDDS, GNLM, IE, Infotrieve, Ingenta, INIST. **CCC.**
Address: PO Box 17160, Athens, 100 24, Greece. TEL 30-1-3623333, FAX 30-1-7245988. Ed. Dr. N J Lygidakis. Circ: 2,700. **Subscr. to:** Georg Thieme Verlag, Postfach 301120, Stuttgart 70451, Germany. http://www.thieme.de.

616.3 CHN ISSN 1499-3872
RC845 CODEN: HPDIAJ
➤ **HEPATOBILIARY & PANCREATIC DISEASES INTERNATIONAL.** Text in English. 2002. q. back issues avail. **Document type:** *Journal, Academic/Scholarly.* **Description:** Publishes original papers, reviews and editorials concerned with clinical practice and research in the fields of hepatobiliary and pancreatic diseases.
Indexed: EMBASE, ExcerpMed, MEDLINE, P30, R10, Reac, SCI, SCOPUS, W07.
—BLDSC (4295.832200), IE, Ingenta.
Published by: The First Affiliated Hospital, Zhejiang University School of Medicine, 79 Qingchun Rd, Hangzhou, 310003, China. TEL 86-571-87236559, FAX 86-571-87236600. Ed. Shu-Sen Zheng.

616.3 POL ISSN 1232-9878
HEPATOLOGIA POLSKA. Text in Polish. 1994. q.
Indexed: EMBASE, ExcerpMed, R10, Reac, SCOPUS.
—BLDSC (4295.835500), Ingenta.
Published by: Wydawnictwo Volumed Sp. z. o. o., Ul Olsztynska 3, Wroclaw, 51423, Poland. TEL 48-71-3253561.

616.362 USA ISSN 0270-9139
RC845 CODEN: HPTLD9
➤ **HEPATOLOGY.** Text in English. 1981. m. USD 1,922 domestic to institutions; USD 2,258 in Canada & Mexico to institutions; USD 2,426 elsewhere to institutions; GBP 1,238 in United Kingdom to institutions; EUR 1,566 in Europe to institutions; USD 2,115 combined subscription domestic to institutions (print & online eds.); USD 2,451 combined subscription in Canada & Mexico to institutions (print & online eds.); USD 2,619 combined subscription elsewhere to institutions (print & online eds.); GBP 1,336 combined subscription in United Kingdom to institutions (print & online eds.); EUR 1,690 combined subscription in Europe to institutions (print & online eds.) (effective 2010); subscr. includes Liver Transplantation & Hepatology. bk.rev. back issues avail.; reprint service avail. from PSC. **Document type:** *Journal, Academic/Scholarly.* **Description:** Examines hepatitis, gallstone formation, drug injury, liver physiology and disease. For gastroenterologists and internists.
Related titles: Online - full text ed.: ISSN 1527-3350. USD 1,922, GBP 981, EUR 1,241 to institutions (effective 2010); subscr. includes Liver Transplantation & Hepatology.
Indexed: A22, A26, A34, A35, A36, A37, A38, ASCA, AgBio, B25, BIOBASE, BIOSIS Prev, BP, CABA, CIN, ChemAb, ChemTitl, CurCont, D01, E01, E12, EMBASE, ExcerpMed, F08, F11, F12, FR, GH, H16, H17, I05, I12, IABS, IBR, IBZ, ISR, IndMed, Inpharma, JW, JW-G, Kidney, LT, MEDLINE, MycolAb, N02, N03, N04, P30, P33, P35, PN&I, R07, R08, R10, R12, RA&MP, RRTA, Reac, S12, SCI, SCOPUS, SoyAb, T05, VITIS, VS, W07.
—BLDSC (4295.836000), CASDDS, GNLM, IE, Infotrieve, Ingenta, INIST. **CCC.**
Published by: (American Association for the Study of Liver Diseases), John Wiley & Sons, Inc., 111 River St, Hoboken, NJ 07030. TEL 201-748-6000, FAX 201-748-6088, info@wiley.com, http://www.wiley.com/WileyCDA/. Ed. Keith D Lindor TEL 703-299-9766.

616.362 GBR ISSN 1386-6346
RC845 CODEN: HPRSFM
➤ **HEPATOLOGY RESEARCH.** Text in English. 1993. m. GBP 915 in United Kingdom to institutions; EUR 1,161 in Europe to institutions; USD 1,693 in the Americas to institutions; USD 1,792 elsewhere to institutions; GBP 1,053 combined subscription in United Kingdom to institutions (print & online eds.); EUR 1,336 combined subscription in Europe to institutions (print & online eds.); USD 1,948 combined subscription in the Americas to institutions (print & online eds.); USD 2,061 combined subscription elsewhere to institutions (print & online eds.) (effective 2012). adv. back issues avail.; reprint service avail. from PSC. **Document type:** *Journal, Academic/Scholarly.* **Description:** Provides original articles, reviews and short comunications dealing with hepatology.
Formerly (until 1997): International Hepatology Communications (0928-4346); Which was previously announced as: Hepatology Letters
Related titles: Microform ed.: (from PQC); Online - full text ed.: ISSN 1872-034X. GBP 915 in United Kingdom to institutions; EUR 1,161 in Europe to institutions; USD 1,693 in the Americas to institutions; USD 1,792 elsewhere to institutions (effective 2012) (from IngentaConnect).
Indexed: A01, A03, A08, A22, A26, A34, A35, A36, ASCA, AgBio, B21, B25, BIOSIS Prev, BP, CA, CABA, CurCont, D01, E01, E12, EMBASE, ExcerpMed, GH, H16, H17, I05, ImmunAb, IndVet, Inpharma, MycolAb, N02, N03, P30, P33, P35, P39, PN&I, R08, R10, RA&MP, RM&VM, Reac, SCI, SCOPUS, SoyAb, T02, T05, VS, VirolAbstr, W07.
—BLDSC (4295.845000), GNLM, IE, Infotrieve, Ingenta, INIST. **CCC.**
Published by: (Japan Society of Hepatology JPN), Wiley-Blackwell Publishing Ltd. (Subsidiary of: John Wiley & Sons, Inc.), 9600 Garsington Rd, Oxford, OX4 2DQ, United Kingdom. TEL 44-1865-776868, FAX 44-1865-714591, customerservices@blackwellpublishing.com. Ed. Hirohito Tsubouchi TEL 81-99-2755323.

616.3623 ITA ISSN 1973-9648
HOT TOPICS IN VIRAL HEPATITIS. Text in Multiple languages. 2005. 3/yr. **Document type:** *Monographic series, Academic/Scholarly.*
Related titles: Online - full text ed.: ISSN 2036-0932.
Indexed: A01, EMBASE, SCOPUS.
Published by: F B Communication, Via Mascherella 19, Modena, 41121, Italy. TEL 39-059-4270122, FAX 39-059-4279368, info@fbcommunication.org. Eds. Chritopher P Cannon, Sergio Dalla Volta.

616.3 NZL ISSN 1172-4137
I B D RESEARCH REVIEW. (Inflammatory Bowel Disease) Variant title: N Z Inflammatory Bowel Disease Research Review. Text in English. 2008. q. free to qualified personnel (effective 2009). back issues avail. **Document type:** *Journal, Academic/Scholarly.*
Media: Online - full text.
Published by: Research Review Ltd., N Shore Mail Centre, PO Box 100116, Auckland, New Zealand. TEL 64-9-4102277, info@researchreview.co.nz.

616.3 USA ISSN 2090-4398
▼ ➤ **I S R N GASTROENTEROLOGY.** (International Scholarly Research Network) Text in English. 2011. irreg. **Document type:** *Journal, Academic/Scholarly.*
Related titles: Online - full text ed.: ISSN 2090-4401. free (effective 2011).
Published by: Hindawi Publishing Corporation, 410 Park Ave, 15th Fl, PMB 287, New York, NY 10022. FAX 215-893-4392, 866-446-3294, info@hindawi.com.

616.3 JPN ISSN 0536-2180
I TO CHO/STOMACH AND INTESTINE. Text in Japanese; Summaries in English. 1966. m. JPY 40,850; JPY 53,200 combined subscription (print & online eds.) (effective 2010).
Related titles: Online - full text ed.
Indexed: A22, INIS AtomInd, MycolAb, SCOPUS.
—BLDSC (8465.870000), GNLM, IE, Ingenta.
Published by: Igaku Shoin Ltd., 1-28-36 Hongo, Bunkyo-ku, Tokyo, 113-8719, Japan. TEL 81-3-3817-5600, FAX 81-3-3815-7791, info@igaku-shoin.co.jp. Circ: 15,000.

616.3 IND ISSN 0254-8860
RC799 CODEN: IJOGD
➤ **INDIAN JOURNAL OF GASTROENTEROLOGY.** Text in English. 1982. bi-m. EUR 270, USD 366 combined subscription to institutions (print & online eds.) (effective 2012). adv. bk.rev. abstr.; bibl. back issues avail. **Document type:** *Proceedings, Academic/Scholarly.* **Description:** Publishes the latest research related to the digestive tract and allied diseases.
Related titles: Online - full text ed.: ISSN 0975-0711 (from IngentaConnect); ◆ Supplement(s): Indian Society of Gastroenterology. Proceedings of the Annual Conference.
Indexed: A22, A34, A36, CABA, D01, E01, E12, EMBASE, ExcerpMed, F08, GH, H17, IndMed, MEDLINE, N02, N03, P30, P33, P39, R08, R10, R12, RA&MP, RM&VM, Reac, SCOPUS, T05, VS, W10.
—BLDSC (4412.760000), GNLM, IE, Infotrieve, Ingenta. **CCC.**
Published by: (Indian Society of Gastroenterology), Springer (India) Private Ltd. (Subsidiary of: Springer Science+Business Media), 212, Deen Dayal Upadhyaya Marg, 3rd Fl, Gandharva Mahavidyalaya, New Delhi, 110 002, India. Ed. Shobna Bhatia. Circ: 1,200.

616.3 IND
INDIAN SOCIETY OF GASTROENTEROLOGY. PROCEEDINGS OF THE ANNUAL CONFERENCE. Text in English. 1962. a. bk.rev. **Document type:** *Proceedings, Academic/Scholarly.*
Related titles: ◆ Supplement to: Indian Journal of Gastroenterology. ISSN 0254-8860.
Indexed: IndMed.
Published by: Indian Society of Gastroenterology, Moti Lal Nehru Medical College, Allahabad, 211001, India. TEL 91-532-2256087, FAX 91-532-256878, drspmisra@gmail.com, http://www.isg.org.in/.

616.344 GBR ISSN 1466-7401
RC862.I53
➤ **INFLAMMATORY BOWEL DISEASE MONITOR.** Text in English. 1999. q. GBP 100 to individuals; GBP 200 to institutions; free to qualified personnel (effective 2009). **Document type:** *Journal, Academic/Scholarly.* **Description:** Features in-depth review articles, written by practicing specialists in gastroenterology and related disciplines, discussing current and emerging topics of clinical interest.
Related titles: Online - full text ed.: ISSN 2040-3909.
Indexed: A01, T02.
—BLDSC (4478.845380). **CCC.**
Published by: Remedica Medical Education and Publishing Ltd., Commonwealth House, 1 New Oxford St, London, WC1A 1NU, United Kingdom. TEL 44-20-77592999, FAX 44-20-77592951, info@remedica.com, http://www.remedica.com. Ed. Stephen Hanauer. Pub. Simon Kirsch.

616.344 USA ISSN 1078-0998 CODEN: IBDNBG
➤ **INFLAMMATORY BOWEL DISEASES.** Text in English. 1976. m. GBP 520 in United Kingdom to institutions; EUR 657 in Europe to institutions; USD 765 in United States to institutions; USD 933 in Canada & Mexico to institutions; USD 1,017 elsewhere to institutions; GBP 599 combined subscription in United Kingdom to institutions (print & online eds.); EUR 758 combined subscription in Europe to institutions (print & online eds.); USD 880 combined subscription in United States to institutions (print & online eds.); USD 1,048 combined subscription in Canada & Mexico to institutions (print & online eds.); USD 1,132 combined subscription elsewhere to institutions (print & online eds.) (effective 2012). adv. bk.rev. abstr.; bibl. back issues avail.; reprint service avail. from PSC. **Document type:** *Journal, Academic/Scholarly.* **Description:** Articles on basic research and clinical studies related to Crohn's disease and ulcerative colitis, also known as inflammatory bowel disease.
Former titles (until 1995): Progress in Inflammatory Bowel Disease; (until 1990): I B D News
Related titles: Microfiche ed.: (from PQC); Online - full text ed.: ISSN 1536-4844. GBP 391 in United Kingdom to institutions; EUR 494 in Europe to institutions; USD 765 elsewhere to institutions (effective 2012).
Indexed: A20, B21, CTA, CurCont, EMBASE, ExcerpMed, INI, ISR, ImmunAb, IndMed, Inpharma, JW-G, MEDLINE, P30, P35, R10, Reac, SCI, SCOPUS, W07.
—BLDSC (4478.845400), GNLM, IE, Infotrieve, Ingenta, INIST. **CCC.**
Published by: (Crohn's & Colitis Foundation of America, Inc.), John Wiley & Sons, Inc., 111 River St, Hoboken, NJ 07030. TEL 201-748-6000, FAX 201-748-6088, info@wiley.com, http://www.wiley.com/WileyCDA/. Eds. Richard P MacDermott, Robert Burakoff. Adv. contact Randi Fischer TEL 201-767-4170. Circ: 4,938.

616.3 USA ISSN 1047-5028 CODEN: IDITE8
INFLAMMATORY DISEASE AND THERAPY. Text in English. 1989. irreg. price varies. **Document type:** *Monographic series.*
Related titles: Online - full text ed.
Indexed: CIN, ChemAb, ChemTitl.
—CASDDS. **CCC.**
Published by: C R C Press, LLC (Subsidiary of: Taylor & Francis Group), 6000 Broken Sound Pky, NW, Ste 300, Boca Raton, FL 33487. TEL 800-272-7737, FAX 800-374-3401, orders@crcpress.com.

616.3 USA ISSN 2090-3456
▼ ➤ **INTERNATIONAL JOURNAL OF HEPATOLOGY.** Text in English. 2011. free (effective 2011). **Document type:** *Journal, Academic/Scholarly.*

Media: Online - full text.
Published by: Sage - Hindawi Access to Research, 410 Park Ave, 15th Fl, 287 PMB, New York, NY 10022. FAX 866-446-3294.

616.3 CAN ISSN 1188-4525
INTERNATIONAL SEMINARS IN PAEDIATRIC GASTROENTEROLOGY AND NUTRITION. Text in English. 1990. q. CAD 129.60 domestic to individuals; USD 88.15 foreign to individuals; CAD 155.60 combined subscription domestic to individuals print & online eds.; USD 105.80 combined subscription foreign to individuals print & online eds.; CAD 186.55 domestic to institutions; USD 126.85 foreign to institutions (effective 2008). back issues avail. **Document type:** *Newsletter, Academic/Scholarly.* **Description:** Offers a review of current investigation and clinical practice in the nutritional management of children.
Formerly (until 1992): Seminars in Paediatric Gastroenterology and Nutrition (1188-0244)
Related titles: Online - full text ed.: CAD 142.65 domestic to individuals; USD 97 foreign to individuals (effective 2008).
Indexed: A01, A03, A08, C03, CA, CBCARef, F10, P48, PQC, T02.
—CCC.
Published by: B.C. Decker Inc., 50 King St E, 2nd Fl, Hamilton, ON L8N 2A1, Canada. TEL 905-522-7017, 800-568-7281, FAX 905-522-7839, 888-311-4987, info@bcdecker.com. Ed. W Allan Walker.

616.3 USA ISSN 1528-8323
RC799
➤ **THE INTERNET JOURNAL OF GASTROENTEROLOGY.** Text in English. 2000. s-a. free (effective 2011). adv. bk.rev. back issues avail. **Document type:** *Journal, Academic/Scholarly.* **Description:** Provides information from the field of gastroenterology and digestive diseases; contains original articles, reviews, case reports, streaming slide shows, streaming videos, letters to the editor, press releases, and meeting information.
Media: Online - full text.
Indexed: A01, A02, A03, A08, A26, C06, C07, CA, G08, H11, H12, I05, T02.
Published by: Internet Scientific Publications, Llc., 23 Rippling Creek Dr, Sugar Land, TX 77479. TEL 832-443-1193, FAX 281-240-1533, wenker@ispub.com. Ed. Dr. Praveen K. Roy.

616.3 KOR ISSN 1598-9100
INTESTINAL RESEARCH. Text in Korean. 2003. s-a. **Document type:** *Journal, Academic/Scholarly.*
Published by: Korean Association for the Study of Intestinal Diseases/ Daehan Jang Yeon'gu Haghoe, Lottegoldrose 2/F, Rm 305, 890-59, Daechi-dong, Gangnam-gu, Seoul, 135-280, Korea, S. TEL 86-2-9576145, thekasid@kornet.net, http://www.gut.or.kr/.

616.3 IRQ ISSN 1998-1678
IRAQI JOURNAL OF GASTROENTEROLOGY. Text in English. 2001 (Oct). irreg. **Document type:** *Journal, Academic/Scholarly.*
Published by: Iraqi Society of Gastroenterology and Hepatology, PO Box 61103, Baghdad-Medical City-Bab-Almuaddam, Iraq. TEL 9641-4141052, FAX 9641-4154642, society@iraq-git.com, http://www.iraq-git.com/isgh. Ed. Dr. Makki H Fayadh.

616.330994 AUS
J G E N C A. (Journal of the Gastroenterlogical Nurses College of Australia) Text in English. q. AUD 165 (effective 2010). adv. **Document type:** *Journal, Academic/Scholarly.*
—BLDSC (4597.101000).
Published by: Gastroenterological Nurses College of Australia, Inc., PO Box 483, Boronia, VIC 3155, Australia. FAX 61-3-97625165, http://www.genca.org/. Ed. Di Jones.

616.3 BRA ISSN 1678-5436
JORNAL BRASILEIRO DE GASTROENTEROLOGIA. Text in Portuguese. 2001. q. **Document type:** *Journal, Academic/Scholarly.*
Published by: Sociedade de Gastroenterologia do Rio de Janeiro, Rua Siqueira Campos 93/802, Copacabana, Rio de Janeiro, 22031-070, Brazil. TEL 55-21-22364510, FAX 55-21-22558282.

616.3 PRT ISSN 0872-8178
JORNAL PORTUGUES DE GASTRENTEROLOGIA. Abbreviated title: G E. Text in Multiple languages. 1994. q. **Document type:** *Journal, Academic/Scholarly.*
Related titles: Online - full text ed.: free (effective 2011).
Published by: (Sociedade Portuguesa de Gastrenterologia), Cortex - Publicacoes Tecnicas e Cientificas, Rua Diogo Silves 4 B, Lisbon, 1400-107, Portugal. TEL 351-21-3020706, FAX 351-21-3020707.

616.3 FRA ISSN 1954-3204
JOURNAL AFRICAIN D'HEPATO-GASTROENTEROLOGIE. Text in French. 2007. q. EUR 134, USD 159 combined subscription to institutions (print & online eds.) (effective 2011). reprint service avail. from PSC. **Document type:** *Journal, Academic/Scholarly.*
Related titles: Online - full text ed.: ISSN 1954-3212 (from IngentaConnect).
Indexed: A22, A26, E01, E08, EMBASE, ExcerpMed, H12, R10, Reac, SCOPUS.
—IE, INIST. **CCC.**
Published by: Springer France (Subsidiary of: Springer Science+Business Media), 22 Rue de Palestro, Paris, 75002, France. TEL 33-1-53009860, FAX 33-1-53009861, sylvie.kamara@springer.com. Eds. F Klotz, J-C Debongnie.

616.3 AUT ISSN 1728-6263
RC799
JOURNAL FUER GASTROENTEROLOGISCHE UND HEPATOLOGISCHE ERKRANKUNGEN. Text in German. 2003. 4/yr. EUR 36; EUR 10 newsstand/cover (effective 2005). **Document type:** *Journal, Academic/Scholarly.*
Related titles: Online - full text ed.: ISSN 1728-6271. free (effective 2011).
Indexed: EMBASE, ExcerpMed, R10, Reac, SCOPUS.
—CCC.
Published by: Krause & Pachernegg GmbH, Mozartgasse 10, Gablitz, 3003, Austria. TEL 43-2231-612580, FAX 43-2231-6125810, k_u_p@eunet.at, http://www.kup.at/verlag.htm. Ed. Arnulf Ferlitsch.

616.3 USA ISSN 0192-0790
RC799
➤ **JOURNAL OF CLINICAL GASTROENTEROLOGY.** Text in English. 1979. 10/yr. USD 999 domestic to institutions; USD 1,099 foreign to institutions (effective 2011). adv. bk.rev. charts; illus.; stat. index. back issues avail.; reprints avail. **Document type:** *Journal, Academic/Scholarly.* **Description:** Covers relevant clinical studies and reviews, case reports, and technical expertise in a single source. Features include articles and clinical reviews that put the research and development into the context of practice.
Related titles: Online - full text ed.: ISSN 1539-2031. USD 637 domestic academic site license; USD 646 foreign academic site license; USD 710.50 domestic corporate site license; USD 719.50 foreign corporate site license (effective 2002).
Indexed: A20, A22, A34, A35, A36, ASCA, AgBio, B23, BIOBASE, C06, C07, CABA, CurCont, D01, E12, EMBASE, ExcerpMed, FR, GH, H16, H17, IABS, IBR, IBZ, INI, ISR, IndMed, IndVet, Inpharma, JW-G, MEDLINE, N02, N03, NRN, P30, P33, P35, P39, R08, R10, RA&MP, RM&VM, Reac, S12, SCI, SCOPUS, SoyAb, T05, THA, TriticAb, VS, W07, W11.
—BLDSC (4958.470000), GNLM, IE, Infotrieve, Ingenta, INIST. **CCC.**
Published by: Lippincott Williams & Wilkins (Subsidiary of: Wolters Kluwer N.V.), Two Commerce Sq, 2001 Market St, Philadelphia, PA 19103. TEL 215-521-8300, FAX 215-521-8902, customerservice@lww.com, http://www.lww.com. Ed. Dr. Martin H Floch TEL 203-855-0620. Pub. Paul Gee. Adv. contact Renee Artuso TEL 516-741-1772. Circ: 543.

616.3 NLD ISSN 1873-9946
RC862.I53
➤ **JOURNAL OF CROHN'S AND COLITIS.** Text in English. 2008. 4/yr. EUR 668 in Europe to institutions; JPY 109,500 in Japan to institutions; USD 901 elsewhere to institutions (effective 2012). **Document type:** *Journal, Academic/Scholarly.*
Related titles: Online - full text ed.: ISSN 1876-4479 (from ScienceDirect); ◆ Supplement(s): Journal of Crohn's and Colitis Supplements. ISSN 1873-9954.
Indexed: CA, CurCont, EMBASE, ExcerpMed, MEDLINE, P30, R10, Reac, SCI, SCOPUS, T02, W07.
—BLDSC (4965.651500), IE. **CCC.**
Published by: Elsevier BV (Subsidiary of: Elsevier Science & Technology), Radarweg 29, PO Box 211, Amsterdam, 1000 AE, Netherlands. TEL 31-20-4853911, FAX 31-20-4852457, JournalsCustomerServiceEMEA@elsevier.com. Ed. Miquel A Gassull.

616.3 NLD ISSN 1873-9954
RC862.I53
JOURNAL OF CROHN'S AND COLITIS SUPPLEMENTS. Text in English. 2007. irreg.
Related titles: Online - full text ed.: ISSN 1876-4460 (from ScienceDirect); ◆ Supplement to: Journal of Crohn's and Colitis. ISSN 1873-9946.
Indexed: CA, EMBASE, ExcerpMed, SCOPUS, T02.
—IE. **CCC.**
Published by: Elsevier BV (Subsidiary of: Elsevier Science & Technology), Radarweg 29, PO Box 211, Amsterdam, 1000 AE, Netherlands. TEL 31-20-4853911, FAX 31-20-4852457, http://www.elsevier.com.

616.37 NLD ISSN 1569-1993
➤ **JOURNAL OF CYSTIC FIBROSIS.** Text in English. 2002. 6/yr. EUR 439 in Europe to institutions; JPY 50,700 in Japan to institutions; USD 453 elsewhere to institutions (effective 2012). **Document type:** *Journal, Academic/Scholarly.* **Description:** Devoted to promoting the research and treatment of cystic fibrosis.
Related titles: Online - full text ed.: ISSN 1873-5010 (from IngentaConnect, ScienceDirect).
Indexed: A01, A03, A08, A26, CA, CurCont, EMBASE, ExcerpMed, I05, MEDLINE, P30, R10, Reac, SCI, SCOPUS, T02, W07.
—BLDSC (4965.977000), IE, Ingenta. **CCC.**
Published by: Elsevier BV (Subsidiary of: Elsevier Science & Technology), Radarweg 29, PO Box 211, Amsterdam, 1000 AE, Netherlands. TEL 31-20-4853911, FAX 31-20-4852457, JournalsCustomerServiceEMEA@elsevier.com, http://www.elsevier.nl. Ed. G Doering. **Co-publisher:** European Cystic Fibrosis Society.

616.3 AUS ISSN 1751-2980
➤ **JOURNAL OF DIGESTIVE DISEASES (ONLINE).** Text in English. 2000. q. GBP 264 in United Kingdom to institutions; EUR 334 in Europe to institutions; USD 427 in the Americas to institutions; USD 516 elsewhere to institutions (effective 2012). **Document type:** *Journal, Academic/Scholarly.*
Formerly (until 2007): Chinese Journal of Digestive Diseases Online (1443-9573)
Media: Online - full text (from IngentaConnect). **Related titles:** ◆ Print ed.: Journal of Digestive Diseases (Print). ISSN 1751-2972.
—CCC.
Published by: Wiley-Blackwell Publishing Asia (Subsidiary of: Wiley-Blackwell Publishing Ltd.), 155 Cremorne St, Richmond, VIC 3121, Australia. TEL 61-3-92743100, FAX 61-3-92743101, subs@blackwellpublishingasia.com, http://www.wiley.com/WileyCDA/

616.3 AUS ISSN 1751-2972
RC799 CODEN: CJDDA9
➤ **JOURNAL OF DIGESTIVE DISEASES (PRINT).** Text in English. 2000. q. GBP 264 in United Kingdom to institutions; EUR 334 in Europe to institutions; USD 427 in the Americas to institutions; USD 516 elsewhere to institutions; GBP 305 combined subscription in United Kingdom to institutions (print & online eds.); EUR 385 combined subscription in Europe to institutions (print & online eds.); USD 491 combined subscription in the Americas to institutions (print & online eds.); USD 593 combined subscription elsewhere to institutions (print & online eds.) (effective 2012). adv. back issues avail.; reprint service avail. from PSC. **Document type:** *Journal, Academic/Scholarly.* **Description:** Publishes original papers, review articles and editorials concerned with research relating to the esophagus, stomach, small intestine, colon, liver, biliary tract and pancreas.
Formerly (until 2006): Chinese Journal of Digestive Diseases (1443-9611)
Related titles: ◆ Online - full text ed.: Journal of Digestive Diseases (Online). ISSN 1751-2980.
Indexed: A01, A03, A08, A22, A26, A34, A36, BP, CA, CABA, D01, E01, EMBASE, ExcerpMed, F08, F11, F12, GH, H16, MEDLINE, N02, N03, P30, P33, R10, RA&MP, Reac, SCI, SCOPUS, T02, T05, W07.
—BLDSC (4969.606000), IE, Infotrieve, Ingenta. **CCC.**
Published by: (Chinese Society of Gastroenterology CHN), Wiley-Blackwell Publishing Asia (Subsidiary of: Wiley-Blackwell Publishing Ltd.), 155 Cremorne St, Richmond, VIC 3121, Australia. TEL 61-3-92743100, FAX 61-3-92743101, melbourne@wiley.com, http://www.wiley.com/WileyCDA/. Ed. Shu Dong Xiao. **Subscr. to:** Wiley-Blackwell Publishing Ltd., Journal Customer Services, 9600 Garsington Rd, PO Box 1354, Oxford OX4 2XG, United Kingdom. TEL 44-1865-778315, FAX 44-1865-471775. **Co-sponsor:** Zhonghua Yixuehui, Shanghai Fenhui/Chinese Medical Association, Shanghai Branch.

616.3 IND ISSN 0976-5042
▼ **JOURNAL OF DIGESTIVE ENDOSCOPY.** Text and summaries in English. 2010. q. **Document type:** *Journal, Academic/Scholarly.*
Related titles: Online - full text ed.: ISSN 0976-5050.
—CCC.
Published by: (Sheri-i-Kashmir Institute of Medical Sciences), Medknow Publications and Media Pvt. Ltd., B-9, Kanara Business Ctr, Off Link Rd, Ghatkopar (E), Mumbai, Maharastra 400 075, India. TEL 91-22-66491818, FAX 91-22-66491817, publishing@medknow.com, journals@medknow.com, http://www.medknow.com. Ed., R&P Showkat Ali Zargar. Pub. Hemant Manjrekar.

616.3 JPN ISSN 0944-1174
RC799 CODEN: JOGAET
➤ **JOURNAL OF GASTROENTEROLOGY.** Text in English. 1966. m. EUR 600, USD 695 combined subscription to institutions (print & online eds.) (effective 2012). adv. abstr. Index. back issues avail.; reprint service avail. from PSC. **Document type:** *Journal, Academic/Scholarly.* **Description:** Publishes original papers, case reports, reports of multi-center trials, and review articles on all aspects of the field of gastroenterology.
Formerly (until 1993): Gastroenterologia Japonica (0435-1339)
Related titles: Online - full text ed.: ISSN 1435-5922 (from IngentaConnect).
Indexed: A01, A02, A03, A08, A22, A26, A34, A35, A36, ASCA, Agr, B25, BIOSIS Prev, BP, C06, C07, C08, C11, CA, CABA, CIN, CINAHL, ChemAb, ChemTitl, CurCont, D01, E01, E12, EMBASE, ExcerpMed, F08, F11, F12, GH, H04, H12, H17, INIS AtomInd, IndMed, IndVet, Inpharma, LT, MEDLINE, MaizeAb, MycolAb, N02, N03, N04, OR, P19, P20, P22, P24, P30, P33, P35, P39, P48, P54, PN&I, PQC, R10, R11, RA&MP, RRTA, Reac, SCI, SCOPUS, SoyAb, T02, T05, VS, W07.
—BLDSC (4987.610000), CASDDS, GNLM, IE, Infotrieve, Ingenta, INIST. **CCC.**
Published by: (Nihon Shokakibyo Gakkai/Japanese Society of Gastroenterology), Springer Japan KK (Subsidiary of: Springer Science+Business Media), No 2 Funato Bldg, 1-11-11 Kudan-kita, Chiyoda-ku, Tokyo, 102-0073, Japan. TEL 81-3-68317000, FAX 81-3-68317001, http://www.springer.jp. Ed. Mamoru Watanabe. Circ: 4,500. **Subscr. in the Americas to:** Springer New York LLC, Journal Fulfillment, PO Box 2485, Secaucus, NJ 07096. TEL 800-777-4643, 201-348-4033, FAX 201-348-4505, journals-ny@springer.com, http://www.springer.com; **Subscr. to:** Springer Distribution Center, Kundenservice Zeitschriften, Haberstr 7, Heidelberg 69126, Germany. TEL 49-6221-3454303, FAX 49-6221-3454229, subscriptions@springer.com.

616.3 AUS ISSN 0815-9319
RC799 CODEN: JGHEEO
➤ **JOURNAL OF GASTROENTEROLOGY AND HEPATOLOGY.** Text in English. 1986. m. GBP 958 in United Kingdom to institutions; EUR 1,215 in Europe to institutions; USD 1,544 in the Americas to institutions; USD 1,875 elsewhere to institutions; GBP 1,102 combined subscription in United Kingdom to institutions (print & online eds.); EUR 1,398 combined subscription in Europe to institutions (print & online eds.); USD 1,776 combined subscription in the Americas to institutions (print & online eds.); USD 2,157 combined subscription elsewhere to institutions (print & online eds.) (effective 2012). adv. illus. Index. back issues avail.; reprint service avail. from PSC. **Document type:** *Journal, Academic/Scholarly.* **Description:** Covers original contributions concerned with clinical practice and research in the fields of gastroenterology and hepatology.
Related titles: Microform ed.: (from PQC); Online - full text ed.: ISSN 1440-1746. GBP 958 in United Kingdom to institutions; EUR 1,215 in Europe to institutions; USD 1,544 in the Americas to institutions; USD 1,875 elsewhere to institutions (effective 2012) (from IngentaConnect).
Indexed: A01, A03, A08, A20, A22, A26, A34, A35, A36, ASCA, AgBio, B21, B25, BA, BIOBASE, BIOSIS Prev, BP, CA, CABA, CIN, ChemAb, ChemTitl, CurCont, D01, E01, E12, EMBASE, ExcerpMed, GH, H12, H16, H17, IABS, ISR, ImmunAb, IndMed, IndVet, Inpharma, MEDLINE, MaizeAb, MycolAb, N02, N03, N04, P30, P32, P33, P35, P39, P40, PGegResA, PHN&I, PN&I, R08, R10, R12, RA&MP, RM&VM, Reac, S12, S17, SCI, SCOPUS, SoyAb, T02, T05, TriticAb, VS, VirolAbstr, W07, W10, W11.
—BLDSC (4987.615000), CASDDS, GNLM, IE, Infotrieve, Ingenta, INIST. **CCC.**
Published by: (Gastroenterological Society of Australia, Asian Pacific Association for the Study of the Liver JPN, Asian Pacific Association of Gastroenterology HKG), Wiley-Blackwell Publishing Asia (Subsidiary of: Wiley-Blackwell Publishing Ltd.), 155 Cremorne St, Richmond, VIC 3121, Australia. TEL 61-3-92743100, FAX 61-3-92743101, subs@blackwellpublishingasia.com, http://www.wiley.com/WileyCDA/. Eds. Geoffrey Farrell, S Miura, T Chiba. adv.: B&W page AUD 1,375, color page AUD 2,585; trim 210 x 275. Circ: 3,000. **Co-sponsor:** The Hong Kong Society of Gastroenterology.

616.3 ROM ISSN 1841-8724
JOURNAL OF GASTROINTESTINAL AND LIVER DISEASES. Text in Multiple languages. 1992. q. **Document type:** *Journal, Academic/Scholarly.*
Formerly (until 2006): Romanian Journal of Gastroenterology (1221-4167)
Related titles: Online - full text ed.: ISSN 1842-1121. 2005.
Indexed: A01, CA, EMBASE, MEDLINE, P30, R10, SCI, SCOPUS, T02, W07.
—BLDSC (4987.618500), IE.

Published by: (Romanian Society of Gastroenterology and Hepatology), Universitatea de Medicina si Farmacie "Iuliu Hatieganu", 13 Emil Isac, Cluj-Napoca, 400023, Romania. TEL 40-264-597256, FAX 40-264-597257, http://www.umfcluj.ro. Ed. Monica Acalovschi.

JOURNAL OF GASTROINTESTINAL CANCER. *see* MEDICAL SCIENCES—Endocrinology

616.3 616.992 HKG ISSN 2078-6891
▼ **JOURNAL OF GASTROINTESTINAL ONCOLOGY.** Text in English. 2010. q. **Document type:** *Journal, Academic/Scholarly.*
Related titles: Online - full text ed.: ISSN 2219-679X. free (effective 2011).
Published by: Pioneer Bioscience Publishing Company, 8F, CNT Comm Bldg, 302 Queen's Rd Central, Hong Kong, Hong Kong. TEL 852-21393077, FAX 852-21393217. Ed. Gary Yang.

JOURNAL OF HEALTH POPULATION AND NUTRITION. *see* MEDICAL SCIENCES—Abstracting, Bibliographies, Statistics

616.3 NLD ISSN 0168-8278
RC845 CODEN: JOHEEC
➤ **JOURNAL OF HEPATOLOGY.** Text and summaries in English. 1985. 12/yr. EUR 1,212 in Europe to institutions; JPY 108,600 in Japan to institutions; USD 1,270 elsewhere to institutions (effective 2012). adv. bk.rev. illus. index. back issues avail.; reprints avail. **Document type:** *Journal, Academic/Scholarly.* **Description:** Publishes original papers and reviews concerned with practice and research in the field of hepatology.
Related titles: Online - full text ed.: ISSN 1600-0641. DKK 1,710 to individuals; DKK 4,860 to institutions (effective 2001) (from IngentaConnect, ScienceDirect); ◆ Supplement(s): Journal of Hepatology. Supplement. ISSN 0169-5185.
Indexed: A01, A03, A08, A22, A26, A35, A36, ASCA, AddicA, AgBio, B25, BIOBASE, BIOSIS Prev, CA, CABA, CIN, ChemAb, ChemTitl, CurCont, D01, E12, EMBASE, ExcerpMed, GH, H16, H17, I05, IABS, INI, ISR, IndMed, Inpharma, JW-G, MEDLINE, MaizeAb, MycolAb, N02, N03, P30, P33, P35, PHN&I, PN&I, R10, R12, RA&MP, RM&VM, Reac, S12, SCI, SCOPUS, SoyAb, T02, T05, VS, W07, W11.
—BLDSC (4997.700000), CASDDS, GNLM, IE, Infotrieve, Ingenta, INIST. **CCC.**
Published by: (European Association for the Study of the Liver DNK), Elsevier BV (Subsidiary of: Elsevier Science & Technology), Radarweg 29, PO Box 211, Amsterdam, 1000 AE, Netherlands. TEL 31-20-4853911, FAX 31-20-4852457, JournalsCustomerServiceEMEA@elsevier.com, http://www.elsevier.nl. Ed. M Colombo.

616.3 NLD ISSN 0169-5185
JOURNAL OF HEPATOLOGY. SUPPLEMENT. Text in English. 1985. irreg. price varies. **Document type:** *Monographic series, Academic/Scholarly.*
Related titles: Online - full text ed.; ◆ Supplement to: Journal of Hepatology. ISSN 0168-8278.
Indexed: P30, SCOPUS.
—Infotrieve, INIST. **CCC.**
Published by: Elsevier BV (Subsidiary of: Elsevier Science & Technology), Radarweg 29, PO Box 211, Amsterdam, 1000 AE, Netherlands. TEL 31-20-4853911, FAX 31-20-4852457, JournalsCustomerServiceEMEA@elsevier.com, http://www.elsevier.nl.

616.3 USA ISSN 2154-1280
▼ ➤ **JOURNAL OF INTERVENTIONAL GASTROENTEROLOGY.** Text in English. 2010 (July). q. **Description:** Focuses on interventional procedures, including endoscopy, radiology and ultrasonography, used in the study, diagnosis, and treatment of digestive diseases.
Related titles: Online - full text ed.: ISSN 2154-1299. 2010 (July).
Published by: Landes Bioscience, 1002 W Ave, Austin, TX 78701. info@landesbioscience.com.

➤ **JOURNAL OF PEDIATRIC GASTROENTEROLOGY AND NUTRITION.** *see* NUTRITION AND DIETETICS

➤ **JOURNAL OF PEPTIDE SCIENCE.** *see* CHEMISTRY—Organic Chemistry

616.3 ITA ISSN 1590-8577
➤ **JOURNAL OF THE PANCREAS.** Abbreviated title: J O P. Text in English. 2000. bi-m. free (effective 2011). abstr.; illus. back issues avail. **Document type:** *Journal, Academic/Scholarly.* **Description:** Focuses on the entire spectrum of the pancreatic gland aspects: normal function, etiology, epidemiology, prevention, genetics, pathophysiology, diagnosis, surgical and medical management of pancreatic diseases including cancer, inflammatory diseases, diabetes mellitus, cystic fibrosis and other congenital disorders. JOP also publishes: case reports, state-of-the-art reviews, book reviews, hypotheses and letters to the Editors. Comments on controversial issues and reviews of articles are also considered.
Media: Online - full text.
Indexed: EMBASE, ExcerpMed, MEDLINE, P30, R10, Reac, SCOPUS.
Published by: E S Burioni Ricerche Bibliografiche, Corso Firenze 41/2, Genova, 16136, Italy. TEL 39-010-2722178, FAX 39-010-2722913. Eds. Generoso Uomo, Raffaele Pezzilli.

616.3 GBR ISSN 1352-0504
RC848.H43 CODEN: JVHEER
➤ **JOURNAL OF VIRAL HEPATITIS.** Abbreviated title: J V H. Text in English. 1994. m. GBP 1,479 in United Kingdom to institutions; EUR 1,880 in Europe to institutions; USD 2,736 in the Americas to institutions; USD 3,191 elsewhere to institutions; GBP 1,702 combined subscription in United Kingdom to institutions (print & online eds.); EUR 2,162 combined subscription in Europe to institutions (print & online eds.); USD 3,148 combined subscription in the Americas to institutions (print & online eds.); USD 3,670 combined subscription elsewhere to institutions (print & online eds.) (effective 2012). adv. back issues avail.; reprint service avail. from PSC. **Document type:** *Journal, Academic/Scholarly.* **Description:** Publishes reviews, original research, and short rapid communications in the area of viral hepatitis.
Related titles: Microform ed.: (from PQC); Online - full text ed.: ISSN 1365-2893. 1999. GBP 1,479 in United Kingdom to institutions; EUR 1,880 in Europe to institutions; USD 2,736 in the Americas to institutions; USD 3,191 elsewhere to institutions (effective 2012) (from IngentaConnect); Japanese Translation: ISSN 1345-2533; Supplement(s): Journal of Viral Hepatitis. Supplement. ISSN 1366-3992.
Indexed: A01, A02, A03, A08, A22, A26, A34, A35, A36, AIDS&CR, ASCA, AgBio, AgrForAb, B21, B25, BIOSIS Prev, BP, C11, CA, CABA, CurCont, D01, E01, E12, EMBASE, ESPM, ExcerpMed, F08, GH, H&SSA, H04, H12, H17, ISR, IndMed, IndVet, Inpharma, LT, MEDLINE, MycolAb, N02, P30, P33, P35, P37, PN&I, R10, R12, RA&MP, Reac, RefZh, SCI, SCOPUS, SoyAb, T02, T05, VS, VirolAbstr, W07.
—BLDSC (5072.485500), GNLM, IE, Infotrieve, Ingenta. **CCC.**
Published by: Wiley-Blackwell Publishing Ltd. (Subsidiary of: John Wiley & Sons, Inc.), 9600 Garsington Rd, Oxford, OX4 2DQ, United Kingdom. TEL 44-1865-776868, FAX 44-1865-714591, customerservices@blackwellpublishing.com. Ed. Howard Thomas.

➤ **JOURNAL WATCH GASTROENTEROLOGY.** *see* MEDICAL SCIENCES—Abstracting, Bibliographies, Statistics

616.362 JPN ISSN 0451-4203
CODEN: KNZOA
➤ **KANZO/ACTA HEPATOLOGICA JAPONICA.** Text in Japanese; Summaries in English, Japanese. 1960. m. 50 p./no.; **Document type:** *Journal, Academic/Scholarly.*
Indexed: CIN, ChemAb, ChemTitl, EMBASE, ExcerpMed, INIS AtomInd, R10, Reac, SCOPUS.
—CASDDS, GNLM.
Published by: Nihon Kanzo Gakkai/Japanese Society of Hepatology, 28-10 Hongo 3-chome, Bunkyo-ku, Tokyo, 113-0033, Japan. TEL 81-3-38121567, FAX 81-3-38126620, jsh@sepia.ocn.ne.jp, http://www.jsh.or.jp/.

616.3 JPN ISSN 0300-9149
CODEN: KOGZA9
KOKUBYO GAKKAI ZASSHI/JAPAN STOMATOLOGICAL SOCIETY. JOURNAL. Text in Japanese. 1927. q. JPY 7,000 membership (effective 2005). **Document type:** *Journal, Academic/Scholarly.*
Indexed: EMBASE, ExcerpMed, MEDLINE, P30, R10, Reac, SCOPUS.
—BLDSC (4904.020000). **CCC.**
Published by: Kokubyo Gakkai/Stomatological Society, Japan, 1-43-9, Komagome, Toshima-ku, Tokyo, 170-0003, Japan. TEL 81-3-39478891, FAX 81-3-39478873, http://wwwsoc.nii.ac.jp/koubyou/.

616.3 DEU
KOMPAKT GASTROENTEROLOGIE. Text in German. 2003. 6/yr. adv. **Document type:** *Journal, Trade.*
Published by: Biermann Verlag GmbH, Otto-Hahn-Str 7, Cologne, 50997, Germany. TEL 49-2236-3760, FAX 49-2236-376999, info@biermann.net, http://www.biermann-verlag.de. Ed. Britta Achenbach. Adv. contact Michael Kesten. Circ: 3,200 (paid and controlled).

616.34 KOR ISSN 1598-9992
➤ **KOREAN JOURNAL OF GASTROENTEROLOGY.** Text in Korean. 1968. m. KRW 5,000 domestic to individuals; KRW 60,000 foreign to individuals; KRW 7,000 domestic to institutions; KRW 84,000 foreign to institutions (effective 2009). **Document type:** *Journal, Academic/Scholarly.* **Description:** Contains articles on clinical and basic studies pertaining to physiology, epidemiology, pathophysiology or treatment of the diseases which are originated from the digestive system such as esophagus, stomach, small bowel, colon, pancreas and hepatobiliary system.
Formerly (until 2003): Daehan Sohwa'gi'byeong Haghoe Jabji (0301-2883)
Related titles: Online - full text ed.
Indexed: A22, EMBASE, ExcerpMed, MEDLINE, P30, R10, Reac, SCOPUS.
—BLDSC (5113.550600), IE, Ingenta.
Published by: Korean Society of Gastroenterology/Daehan Sohwa'gi'byeong Haghoe, 305 Lotte Gold Rose II, 890-59 Daechi-dong, Gangnam-gu, Seoul, 140-031, Korea, S. TEL 82-2-5380627, FAX 82-2-5380635, gastrokorea@kams.or.kr, http://www.gastrokorea.or.kr/. Ed. Dr. Byung-Ho Kim.

616.362 KOR ISSN 1738-222X
RC845
KOREAN JOURNAL OF HEPATOLOGY. Text in Korean; Abstracts and contents page in English. 1995. q. back issues avail. **Document type:** *Journal, Academic/Scholarly.*
Formerly (until 2004): Daehan gan Hag'hoeji (1226-0479)
Related titles: Online - full content ed.: 1996. free (effective 2011).
Indexed: A22, EMBASE, ExcerpMed, MEDLINE, P30, R10, Reac, SCOPUS.
—BLDSC (5113.554100), IE, Ingenta.
Published by: Korean Association for the Study of the Liver/Daehan gan Haghoe, A402, Shinyoung G-Well Officetel, 461 Gongdeok-dong, Mapo-gu, Seoul, 121-805, Korea, S. TEL 82-2-21239047, FAX 82-2-21239048, kasl@kams.or.kr.

616.3 FRA ISSN 1286-580X
➤ **LA LETTRE DE L'HEPATO-GASTROENTEROLOGUE.** Text in French. 1998. bi-m. EUR 96 in Europe to individuals; EUR 108 elsewhere to individuals (effective 2009). **Document type:** *Newsletter, Academic/Scholarly.*
—INIST.
Published by: Edimark S.A.S., 2 Rue Sainte-Marie, Courbevoie, Cedex 92418, France. TEL 33-1-41458000, FAX 33-1-41458025, contact@edimark.fr. Ed. M A Bigard.

616.3 NLD ISSN 1574-7867
LEVER. Text in Dutch. q.
Formerly (until 2005): Nederlandse Vereniging voor Hepatologie. Nieuwsbrief (1385-5948)
Published by: Nederlandse Vereniging voor Hepatologie, Postbus 657, Haarlem, 2003 RR, Netherlands. TEL 31-23-5513016, FAX 31-23-5513087, secretariaat@nvh.nl. Eds. L C Baak, M J van Gijtenbeek, S W C van Mil.

LIFELINELETTER. *see* NUTRITION AND DIETETICS

616.362 CHN ISSN 1001-5256
LINCHUANG GANDANBING ZAZHI/CHINESE JOURNAL OF CLINICAL HEPATOLOGY. Text in Chinese. 1985. bi-m. USD 31.20 (effective 2009). **Document type:** *Journal, Academic/Scholarly.*
Related titles: Online - full text ed.
—East View.
Published by: Jilin Daxue Baiqiuen Yixuebu, 71, Xinmin Dajie, Changchun, 130021, China. **Dist. by:** China International Book Trading Corp, 35 Chegongzhuang Xilu, Haidian District, PO Box 399, Beijing 100044, China. TEL 86-10-68412045, FAX 86-10-68412023, cibtc@mail.cibtc.com.cn, http://www.cibtc.com.cn.

616.3 CHN ISSN 1003-1634
LINCHUANG KOUQIANG YIXUE/JOURNAL OF CLINICAL STOMATOLOGY. Text in Chinese. 1985. m. USD 39.60 (effective 2009). **Document type:** *Journal, Academic/Scholarly.*
Related titles: Online - full text ed.
—East View.
Published by: Zhonghua Yixuehui, Wuhan Fenhui, 1095, Jiefang Dadao, Tongji Yiyuan, Wuhan, 430030, China. TEL 86-27-83662018. **Dist. by:** China International Book Trading Corp, 35 Chegongzhuang Xilu, Haidian District, PO Box 399, Beijing 100044, China. TEL 86-10-68412045, FAX 86-10-68412023, cibtc@mail.cibtc.com.cn, http://www.cibtc.com.cn.

616.3 CHN ISSN 1005-541X
LINCHUANG XIAOHUABING ZAZHI/CLINICAL DIGESTION. Variant title: Chinese Journal of Clinical Gastroenterology. Text in Chinese. bi-m. **Document type:** *Journal, Academic/Scholarly.*
Related titles: Online - full text ed.: (from WanFang Data Corp.).
—BLDSC (3180.301700), East View.
Published by: Huazhong Keji Daxue Tongji Yixueyuan Fushu Xiehe Yiyuan/Tongji Medical University, Union Hospital, 1277, Jiefang Dadao, Wuhan, 430022, China. TEL 86-27-85726447, http://www.whuh.com/. **Dist. by:** China International Book Trading Corp, 35 Chegongzhuang Xilu, Haidian District, PO Box 399, Beijing 100044, China. TEL 86-10-68412045, FAX 86-10-68412023, cibtc@mail.cibtc.com.cn, http://www.cibtc.com.cn.

616.3 USA ISSN 1478-3223
CODEN: LIINCM
➤ **LIVER INTERNATIONAL.** Text in English. 1981. 10/yr. GBP 662 in United Kingdom to institutions; EUR 840 in Europe to institutions; USD 1,109 in the Americas to institutions; USD 1,296 elsewhere to institutions; GBP 762 combined subscription in United Kingdom to institutions (print & online eds.); EUR 966 combined subscription in Europe to institutions (print & online eds.); USD 1,276 combined subscription in the Americas to institutions (print & online eds.); USD 1,491 combined subscription elsewhere to institutions (print & online eds.) (effective 2012). bk.rev. illus.; stat. index. back issues avail.; reprint service avail. from PSC. **Document type:** *Journal, Academic/Scholarly.*
Formerly (until 2002): Liver (0106-9543)
Related titles: Online - full text ed.: ISSN 1478-3231. GBP 662 in United Kingdom to institutions; EUR 840 in Europe to institutions; USD 1,109 in the Americas to institutions; USD 1,296 elsewhere to institutions (effective 2012) (from IngentaConnect); Supplement(s): Liver. Supplement. ISSN 1399-1698. 1999.
Indexed: A01, A03, A08, A22, A26, A34, A35, A36, ASCA, AgBio, B&BAb, B19, B21, B25, BIOBASE, BIOSIS Prev, BP, CA, CABA, CurCont, D01, E01, E12, EMBASE, ExcerpMed, F08, F11, F12, GH, GenetAb, H12, H16, H17, IABS, ISR, IndMed, IndVet, Inpharma, MEDLINE, MycolAb, N02, N03, P30, P33, P35, PN&I, R08, R10, R12, RA&MP, RM&VM, Reac, S12, SCI, SCOPUS, SoyAb, T02, T05, VS, VirolAbstr, W07.
—BLDSC (5280.514000), CASDDS, GNLM, IE, Ingenta, INIST. **CCC.**
Published by: (International Association for the Study of the Liver DEU), Wiley-Blackwell Publishing, Inc. (Subsidiary of: Wiley-Blackwell Publishing Ltd.), Commerce Pl, 350 Main St, Malden, MA 02148. TEL 781-388-8200, FAX 781-388-8210, info@wiley.com, http://www.wiley.com/WileyCDA/. Ed. Samuel S Lee.

617 616.362 USA ISSN 1527-6465
RD545 CODEN: LITRFO
➤ **LIVER TRANSPLANTATION.** Text in English. 1995. m. USD 1,922 domestic to institutions; USD 2,258 in Canada & Mexico to institutions; USD 2,426 elsewhere to institutions; GBP 1,238 in United Kingdom to institutions; EUR 1,566 in Europe to institutions; USD 2,115 combined subscription domestic to institutions (print & online eds.); USD 2,451 combined subscription in Canada & Mexico to institutions (print & online eds.); USD 2,619 combined subscription elsewhere to institutions (print & online eds.); GBP 1,336 combined subscription in United Kingdom to institutions (print & online eds.); EUR 1,690 combined subscription in Europe to institutions (print & online eds.) (effective 2010); subscr. includes Hepatology. adv. back issues avail.; reprint service avail. from PSC. **Document type:** *Journal, Academic/Scholarly.* **Description:** Discusses surgical techniques, clinical investigations, and drug research in the subspecialties of liver transplantation and surgery.
Formerly (until 2000): Liver Transplantation and Surgery (1074-3022)
Related titles: Online - full text ed.: ISSN 1527-6473. USD 1,922, GBP 981, EUR 1,241 to institutions (effective 2010); subscr. includes Hepatology.
Indexed: A22, A26, B&BAb, B19, B21, CurCont, E01, EMBASE, ExcerpMed, I05, INI, ISR, ImmunAb, IndMed, Inpharma, MEDLINE, P30, P35, R10, Reac, SCI, SCOPUS, VirolAbstr, W07.
—BLDSC (5280.522000), GNLM, IE, Infotrieve, Ingenta, INIST. **CCC.**
Published by: (American Association for the Study of Liver Diseases), John Wiley & Sons, Inc., 111 River St, Hoboken, NJ 07030. TEL 201-748-6000, FAX 201-748-6088, info@wiley.com, http://www.wiley.com/WileyCDA/. Eds. John Fung TEL 703-299-9766, Jorge Rakela. **Co-sponsor:** International Liver Transplantation Society.

➤ **LIVING WITHOUT;** a lifestyle guide for people with allergies and food sensitivities. *see* LIFESTYLE

616.3 FRA ISSN 1952-8442
MALADIES INFLAMMATOIRES CHRONIQUES DE L'INTESTIN DIGEST. Variant title: M I C I Digest. Text in French. 2004. a. back issues avail. **Document type:** *Journal, Academic/Scholarly.*
Published by: (Club de Reflexion des Cabinets et Groupes d'Hepato-Gastroenterologie (C R E G G)), A L N Editions, 127 Rue Saint-Dizier, Nancy, 54000, France.

616.3 BGR ISSN 1311-5030
➤ **MEDITSINSKI PREGLED. GASTROENTEROLOGIIA.** Text in Bulgarian; Summaries in Bulgarian, English. 1970. q. BGL 14 domestic; USD 40 foreign (effective 2005). adv. bk.rev. abstr.; bibl. index. back issues avail. **Document type:** *Journal, Academic/Scholarly.* **Description:** Presents original articles and abstracts of foreign publications in the field of gastroenterology, including methods and techniques of diagnosis, drug therapy, risk factors.
Former titles: Gastroenterologiia; Gastroenterologichni Zaboliavaniia (0324-1513); (until 1974): Zabolavania na Stomasno-Crevnia Trakt i Cernia Drob (0324-1777)

Published by: Meditsinski Universitet - Sofia, Tsentralna Meditsinska Biblioteka, Tsentur za Informatsiia po Meditsina/Medical University - Sofia, Central Medical Library, Medical Information Center, 1 Sv Georgi Sofiiski ul, Sofia, 1431, Bulgaria. TEL 359-2-9522342, FAX 359-2-9522393, lydia@medun.acad.bg, http://www.medun.acad.bg/cmb_htm/cmb1_home_bg.htm. Ed. S Stoinov. R&P, Adv. contact Lydia Tacheva. B&W page USD 50, color page USD 150; 12 x 18. Circ: 300.

616.3 USA ISSN 1532-0413
MEDSCAPE GASTROENTEROLOGY. Text in English. 1999. bi-m. free to members (effective 2010). **Document type:** *Journal, Consumer.* **Description:** Provides information about gastro related disease and treatment.
Media: Online - full text.
Published by: WebMD Medscape Health Network, 370 Seventh Ave, Ste 1101, New York, NY 10001. TEL 212-301-6700, 888-506-6098, medscapecustomersupport@webmd.net. Ed. Geoffrey Braden.

616.3 IRN ISSN 2008-5230
▼ ➤ **MIDDLE EAST JOURNAL OF DIGESTIVE DISEASES.** Text in English. 2009. s-a. **Document type:** *Journal, Academic/Scholarly.*
Related titles: E-mail ed.: ISSN 2008-8205; Online - full text ed.: ISSN 2008-5249. free (effective 2011).
Indexed: A36, C06, CABA, GH, N02, N03, P33, T05.
Published by: (Iranian Association of Gastroenterology and Hepatology), Shiraz University of Medical Sciences, Nemazee Hospital, Shiraz, 71934, Iran. TEL 98-71-660134, FAX 98-71-661001, vessalk@pearl.sums.ac.ir. Ed. Reza Malekzadeh.

616.3 ITA ISSN 1121-421X
RC799 CODEN: MDGADI
➤ **MINERVA GASTROENTEROLOGICA E DIETOLOGICA**; a journal on gastroenterology, nutrition and dietetics. Text in Italian; Summaries in English, Italian. 1960. q. EUR 240 combined subscription in the European Union to institutions (print & online eds.); EUR 265 combined subscription elsewhere to institutions (print & online eds.) (effective 2011). adv. bk.rev. bibl.; charts; illus. index. **Document type:** *Journal, Academic/Scholarly.* **Description:** A journal on the diseases of the gastrointestinal system, of the liver, of the pancreas and of the biliary tract and on dietetic nutrition.
Formerly (until 1990): Minerva Dietologica e Gastroenterologica (0391-1993); Which was formed by the merger of: Minerva Dietologica (0026-475X); Minerva Gastroenterologica (0026-4776)
Related titles: Microform ed.: (from PQC); Online - full text ed.: ISSN 1827-1642.
Indexed: A22, A34, A36, CABA, ChemAb, D01, DentInd, EMBASE, ExcerpMed, GH, IndMed, LT, MEDLINE, N02, N03, N04, P30, P33, P39, R10, RA&MP, RM&VM, RRTA, Reac, S12, SCOPUS, T05, VS.
—BLDSC (5794.178000), CASDDS, GNLM, IE, Infotrieve, Ingenta, INIST. **CCC.**
Published by: Edizioni Minerva Medica, Corso Bramante 83-85, Turin, 10126, Italy. TEL 39-011-678282, FAX 39-011-674502, journals.dept@minervamedica.it, http://www.minervamedica.it. Ed. M Rizzetto. Pub. A Oliaro. Circ: 3,000 (paid).

616.3 GBR ISSN 0969-935X
N A C C NEWS. Text in English. 1980. q. free to members (effective 2009). bk.rev. **Document type:** *Newsletter, Trade.* **Description:** Provides a forum for members to exchange ideas, practical suggestions and personal experiences as well as gives medical and practical information based on individual problems that members have experienced.
Formerly (until 1991): N A C C Newsletter (0144-6967)
Published by: National Association for Colitis and Crohn's Disease, 4 Beaumont House, Sutton Rd, St Albans, Herts AL1 5HH, United Kingdom. TEL 44-845-1302233, FAX 44-1727-862550, info@nacc.org.uk.

616.3 GBR ISSN 1759-5045
➤ **NATURE REVIEWS. GASTROENTEROLOGY & HEPATOLOGY.** Text in English. 2004 (Nov.). m. EUR 1,224 in Europe to institutions; USD 1,257 in the Americas to institutions; GBP 741 to institutions in the UK & elsewhere (effective 2011). adv. back issues avail.; reprints avail. **Document type:** *Journal, Academic/Scholarly.* **Description:** Provides physicians with authoritative and timely interpretations of key developments in the field, translating the latest findings into clinical practice.
Formerly (until 2009): Nature Clinical Practice Gastroenterology & Hepatology (1743-4378)
Related titles: Online - full text ed.: ISSN 1759-5053.
Indexed: A26, B21, C06, C07, CA, CurCont, EMBASE, ExcerpMed, H12, I05, ImmunAb, Inpharma, MEDLINE, P30, P35, R10, Reac, SCI, SCOPUS, W07.
—BLDSC (6046.280150), IE, Ingenta. **CCC.**
Published by: Nature Publishing Group (Subsidiary of: Macmillan Publishers Ltd.), The MacMillan Bldg, 4 Crinan St, London, N1 9XW, United Kingdom. TEL 44-20-78334000, FAX 44-20-78334640, NatureReviews@nature.com. Eds. Natalie Wood, Dr. Philip Campbell. Adv. contact Andy Douglas TEL 44-22-78434975. **Subscr. to:** Brunel Rd, Houndmills, Basingstoke, Hamps RG21 6XS, United Kingdom. TEL 44-1256-329242, FAX 44-1256-812358, subscriptions@nature.com.

616.3 NLD ISSN 1879-985X
NEDERLANDSE VERENIGING VOOR GASTRO-ENTEROLOGIE. NIEUWSBULLETIN. Text in Dutch. 198?. q. EUR 35 membership (effective 2010).
Published by: Nederlandse Vereniging voor Gastro-enterologie, Postbus 657, Haarlem, 2003 RR, Netherlands. TEL 31-23-5513016, FAX 31-23-5513087, secretariaat@nvge.nl, http://www.nvge.nl.

616.3 CHE ISSN 1660-2854
RC347
NEURODEGENERATIVE DISEASES. Text in English. 2004 (Apr.). bi-m. CHF 1,718, EUR 1,372, USD 1,696 to institutions; CHF 1,884, EUR 1,504, USD 1,858 combined subscription to institutions (print & online eds.) (effective 2012). adv. **Document type:** *Journal, Academic/Scholarly.* **Description:** Publishes results from basic and clinical scientific research programs designed to better understand the normal functions of genes and proteins involved in neurodegenerative diseases, to characterize their role in pathogenic disease mechanisms, to model their functions in animals and to explore their roles in the diagnosis, treatment and prevention of neurodegenerative diseases.
Related titles: Online - full text ed.: ISSN 1660-2862. CHF 1,650, EUR 1,320, USD 1,602 to institutions (effective 2012).
Indexed: A22, B21, B25, BIOBASE, BIOSIS Prev, CA, E01, EMBASE, ExcerpMed, IABS, MEDLINE, MycolAb, NSA, NSCI, P30, R10, Reac, SCI, SCOPUS, T02, W07.
—BLDSC (6081.365550), IE, Ingenta. **CCC.**
Published by: S. Karger AG, Allschwilerstr 10, Basel, 4055, Switzerland. TEL 41-61-3061111, FAX 41-61-3061234, karger@karger.ch, http://www.karger.ch. Eds. C Hock, R M Nitsch. adv.: page CHF 1,730; trim 210 x 280. Circ: 800 (controlled).

616.3 GBR ISSN 1350-1925
QP180 CODEN: NMOTEK
➤ **NEUROGASTROENTEROLOGY AND MOTILITY.** Text in English. 1989. m. GBP 1,314 in United Kingdom to institutions; EUR 1,667 in Europe to institutions; USD 2,420 in the Americas to institutions; USD 2,824 elsewhere to institutions; GBP 1,511 combined subscription in United Kingdom to institutions (print & online eds.); EUR 1,917 combined subscription in Europe to institutions (print & online eds.); USD 2,784 combined subscription in the Americas to institutions (print & online eds.); USD 3,248 combined subscription elsewhere to institutions (print & online eds.) (effective 2012). adv. bk.rev. abstr.; bibl.; illus. index. back issues avail.; reprint service avail. from PSC. **Document type:** *Journal, Academic/Scholarly.* **Description:** Contains papers on all basic and clinical aspects of gastrointestinal motility and its control by myogenic, neural and chemical mechanisms.
Formerly (until 1994): Journal of Gastrointestinal Motility (1043-4518)
Related titles: Microform ed.: (from PQC); ◆ Online - full text ed.: Neurogastroenterology and Motility Online. ISSN 1365-2982; Supplement(s): Neurogastroenterology and Motility. Supplement. ISSN 1743-3150.
Indexed: A01, A02, A03, A08, A22, A26, ASCA, B21, BIOBASE, C11, CA, CurCont, E01, EMBASE, ExcerpMed, H04, H12, IABS, ISR, IndMed, Inpharma, MEDLINE, NSA, NSCI, P30, P35, R10, Reac, SCI, SCOPUS, T02, W07.
—BLDSC (6081.371450), GNLM, IE, Infotrieve, Ingenta. **CCC.**
Published by: (European Society of Neurogastroenterology and Motility, American Neurogastroenterology & Motility Society USA), Wiley-Blackwell Publishing Ltd. (Subsidiary of: John Wiley & Sons, Inc.), 9600 Garsington Rd, Oxford, OX4 2DQ, United Kingdom. TEL 44-1865-776868, FAX 44-1865-714591, customerservices@blackwellpublishing.com. Eds. Jan Tack, Joseph Szurszewski TEL 507-284-2568, Keith Sharkey.

616.3 GBR ISSN 1365-2982
➤ **NEUROGASTROENTEROLOGY AND MOTILITY ONLINE.** Text in English. 1999. m. GBP 1,314 in United Kingdom to institutions; EUR 1,667 in Europe to institutions; USD 2,420 in the Americas to institutions; USD 2,824 elsewhere to institutions (effective 2012). adv. back issues avail. **Document type:** *Journal, Academic/Scholarly.* **Description:** Provides a forum where current issues and advances relating to the motor function of the GI tract can be presented and discussed.
Media: Online - full text (from IngentaConnect). **Related titles:** Microform ed.: (from PQC); ◆ Print ed.: Neurogastroenterology and Motility. ISSN 1350-1925; Supplement(s): ISSN 1743-3169.
—**CCC.**
Published by: (European Society of Neurogastroenterology and Motility, American Neurogastroenterology & Motility Society USA), Wiley-Blackwell Publishing Ltd. (Subsidiary of: John Wiley & Sons, Inc.), 9600 Garsington Rd, Oxford, OX4 2DQ, United Kingdom. TEL 44-1865-776868, FAX 44-1865-714591, customerservices@blackwellpublishing.com, http://www.wiley.com/. Eds. Jan Tack, Joseph Szurszewski TEL 507-284-2568, Keith Sharkey.

➤ **NIHON KIKAN SHOKUDOKA GAKKAI KAIHO/JAPAN BRONCHO-ESOPHAGOLOGICAL SOCIETY. JOURNAL.** *see* MEDICAL SCIENCES—Respiratory Diseases

616.3 JPN ISSN 0386-9768
NIHON SHOKAKI GEKA GAKKAI ZASSHI/JAPANESE JOURNAL OF GASTROENTEROLOGICAL SURGERY. Text in Japanese; Summaries in English, Japanese. 1969. m. JPY 1,000 per issue. **Document type:** *Journal, Academic/Scholarly.*
Related titles: Online - full text ed.: ISSN 1348-9372.
Indexed: INIS AtomInd, SCOPUS.
—BLDSC (4651.970000).
Published by: Nihon Shokaki Geka Gakkai/Japanese Society of Gastroenterological Surgery, Yusenkayabacho Bldg. 7F, 2-9-8, Nihonbashi kayabacho, Chuo-ku, Tokyo, 103-0025, Japan. TEL 81-3-56413500, FAX 81-3-56413588.

616.3 JPN ISSN 0912-0505
CODEN: EFDDE7
NIHON SHOKAKI NAISHIKYO GAKKAI KOSHIN'ETSU CHIHOKAI ZASSHI/ENDOSCOPIC FORUM FOR DIGESTIVE DISEASE. Text in Japanese; Summaries in English. 1986. s-a. JPY 8,000 (effective 2003). adv. bk.rev. back issues avail. **Document type:** *Journal, Academic/Scholarly.*
Indexed: A22, EMBASE, ExcerpMed, R10, Reac, SCOPUS.
—BLDSC (3743.560000), GNLM, IE, Ingenta.
Published by: Japanese Journal of Cancer and Chemotherapy Publishers Inc., Risshu Bldg. 2/F, 2-2-3 Nihonbashi, Chuo-ku, Tokyo, 103-0027, Japan. TEL 81-3-32780052, FAX 81-3-32810435. Ed., Pub. Masayuki A Fujino. Adv. contact Hachiro Sato.

616.3 JPN ISSN 1345-4110
NIHON SHOKAKI SHUDAN KENSHIN GAKKAI ZASSHI/JOURNAL OF GASTROENTEROLOGICAL MASS SURVEY. Text in Japanese. 1963. bi-m. **Document type:** *Journal, Academic/Scholarly.*
Former titles (until 1999): Shokaki Shudan Kenshin (0287-6132); (until 1982): Igan to Shudan Kenshin (0386-9652)
—Infotrieve.
Published by: Nihon Shokaki Shudan Kenshin Gakkai/Japanese Society of Gastroenterological Mass Survey, Tohoedogawabashi Bldg, 2F, 1-4-7, Sekiguchi, Bunkyo-ku, Tokyo, 112-0014, Japan. TEL 81-3-3235-6754, FAX 81-3-3235-7647, info@jsgms.or.jp, http://www.jsgms.or.jp/index.html.

616.3 JPN ISSN 0446-6586
CODEN: NIPAA4
NIHON SHOKABIYO GAKKAI ZASSHI/JAPANESE JOURNAL OF GASTROENTEROLOGY. Text in Japanese. 1902. m. subscr. incld. with membership. **Document type:** *Journal, Academic/Scholarly.*
Related titles: Online - full text ed.: ISSN 1349-7693.
Indexed: EMBASE, ExcerpMed, INIS AtomInd, MEDLINE, MycolAb, P30, R10, Reac, SCOPUS.
—BLDSC (4651.980000). **CCC.**
Published by: Nihon Shokakibyo Gakkai/Japanese Society of Gastroenterology, Ginza Orient Bldg 8F, 8-9-13 Ginza, Chuo-ku, Tokyo, 104-0061, Japan. TEL 81-3-35734297, FAX 81-3-32892359, info@jsge.or.jp, http://www.jsge.or.jp/.

616.6 JPN ISSN 1882-0115
NIHON SUTOMA HAISETSU RIHABIRITESHON GAKKAISHI/JAPANESE SOCIETY OF STOMA AND CONTINENCE REHABILITATION. JOURNAL. Text in Japanese. 1985. s-a. membership. **Document type:** *Journal, Academic/Scholarly.*
Former titles (until 2007): Nihon Sutoma Rihabiriteshon Gakkaishi (0916-6440); (until 1989): Nihon Sutoma Rihabiriteshon Kenkyukaishi (0912-0408)
Indexed: P30.
—BLDSC (6113.116100). **CCC.**
Published by: Nihon Sutoma Haisetsu Rihabiriteshon Gakkai/Japanese Society of Stoma and Continence Rehabilitation, 1-1 Aichi Cancer Center, Chikusa-ku, Nagoya, 464-8681, Japan. TEL 81-52-7642939, FAX 81-52-7635233, shouge@aichi-cc.jp, http://www.jsscr.jp.

616.3 JPN ISSN 0047-1801
CODEN: NDKGAU
NIPPON DAICHO KOMONBYO GAKKAI ZASSHI/JAPAN SOCIETY OF COLO-PROCTOLOGY. JOURNAL. Text in Japanese. 1940. 10/yr. JPY 10,000 membership (effective 2005). **Document type:** *Journal, Academic/Scholarly.*
Indexed: A22, INIS AtomInd, MycolAb, P30, SCOPUS.
—BLDSC (4807.030000), GNLM, IE, Infotrieve, Ingenta. **CCC.**
Published by: Nippon Daicho Komonbyo Gakkai/Japan Society of Colo-Proctology, Department of General & Gastrointestinal Surgery, Toho University School of Medicine, 6-11-1, Omorinishi Ota-ku, Tokyo, 143-8541, Japan. TEL 81-3-37624151, FAX 81-3-37667121, http://www.coloproctology.gr.jp/.

ODONTOESTOMATOLOGIA. *see* MEDICAL SCIENCES—Dentistry

616.3 DEU ISSN 1431-6579
OLD HERBORN UNIVERSITY SEMINAR MONOGRAPH. Text in English. 1990. irreg., latest vol.22, 2008. price varies. **Document type:** *Monographic series, Academic/Scholarly.* **Description:** Provides coverage of a series of seminars dedicated to the microbial ecology of the digestive tract, related areas, epithelial and other surfaces and its relevance to the medical field.
—BLDSC (6253.813500), IE, Ingenta.
Published by: Old Herborn University, Am Kornmarkt 2, Herborn-Dill, 35745, Germany. TEL 49-2772-921100, FAX 49-2772-921101, info@old-herborn-university.de, http://www.old-herborn-university.de.

616.3 NLD ISSN 1874-2599
RC799
➤ **THE OPEN GASTROENTEROLOGY JOURNAL.** Text in English. 2007. irreg. free (effective 2011). **Document type:** *Journal, Academic/Scholarly.*
Media: Online - full text.
Indexed: A01, NSA.
Published by: Bentham Open (Subsidiary of: Bentham Science Publishers Ltd.), PO Box 294, Bussum, AG 1400, Netherlands. TEL 31-35-6923800, FAX 31-35-6980150, subscriptions@bentham.org. Ed. George Sachs.

616.3 NLD ISSN 1876-5173
➤ **THE OPEN HEPATOLOGY JOURNAL.** Text in English. 2008. irreg. free (effective 2009). **Document type:** *Journal, Academic/Scholarly.*
Media: Online - full text.
Published by: Bentham Open (Subsidiary of: Bentham Science Publishers Ltd.), PO Box 294, Bussum, AG 1400, Netherlands. TEL 31-35-6923800, FAX 31-35-6980150, subscriptions@bentham.org.

➤ **PANCREAS.** *see* MEDICAL SCIENCES—Endocrinology

616.3 USA ISSN 0277-4208
CODEN: PRGAEE
PRACTICAL GASTROENTEROLOGY; for the busy gastroenterologist. Text in English. 1977. 12/yr. USD 125 domestic; USD 180 foreign (effective 2005). adv. bk.rev. abstr.; bibl.; charts; illus.; tr.lit. index. back issues avail.; reprints avail. **Document type:** *Magazine, Trade.* **Description:** For the gastroenterologist on the diagnosis, therapy and management of digestive disorders. Includes articles on topics that the practitioner encounters in daily practice.
Former titles (until 1980): Primary Care Physician's Guide to Practical Gastroenterology (0163-7894); (until 1978): Physician's Guide to Practical Gastroenterology (0149-9912)
Related titles: Microfilm ed.: (from PQC); Online - full text ed.
Indexed: A22, EMBASE, ExcerpMed, P30, R10, Reac, SCOPUS.
—BLDSC (6594.062000), GNLM, IE, Infotrieve, Ingenta. **CCC.**
Published by: Shugar Publishing, Inc., 99b Main St., Westhampton Beach, NY 11978-2607. TEL 631-288-4404, FAX 631-288-4435. Ed. Dorine Kitay. Pub., R&P, Adv. contact Vivian Mahl. B&W page USD 3,580, color page USD 4,360.50. Circ: 19,000 (controlled).

616.3 FRA ISSN 1953-7816
PROCTO DIGEST. Text in French. 2005. irreg. back issues avail. **Document type:** *Newsletter, Trade.*
Published by: (Club de Reflexion des Cabinets et Groupes d'Hepato-Gastroenterologie (C R E G G)), A L N Editions, 127 Rue Saint-Dizier, Nancy, 54000, France.

616.3 JPN ISSN 1348-9844
PROGRESS OF DIGESTIVE ENDOSCOPY. Text in Japanese; Summaries in English. 1972. s-a. JPY 5,000 to members (effective 2007). charts; illus. back issues avail. **Document type:** *Journal, Academic/Scholarly.*
Formerly (until 2001): Shokaki Naishikyo no Shinpo (0389-9403)
—BLDSC (6868.155000).
Published by: Nihon Shokaki Naishikyo Gakkai, Kanto Bukai/Japan Gastroenterological Endoscopy Society, Kanto Chapter, c/o National Center Center, Central Hospital, Department of Endoscopy, 5-1-1 Tsukiji, Chuo-ku, Tokyo, 105-0004, Japan. TEL 81-3-35422511 ext 5312, FAX 81-3-35423815, jgeskanto@nifty.com, http://www.metaco.co.jp/jges-kanto/. Circ: 2,000.

616.3 POL ISSN 1895-5770
➤ **PRZEGLAD GASTROENTEROLOGICZNY.** Text in Polish. 2006. q. PLZ 69 domestic (effective 2010). **Document type:** *Journal, Academic/Scholarly.*
Related titles: Online - full text ed.: ISSN 1897-4317.
Indexed: EMBASE, SCI, SCOPUS, W07.

Published by: Termedia sp. z o.o./Termedia Publishing House, ul Wenedow 9/1, Poznan, 61614, Poland. TEL 48-61-8227781, FAX 48-61-8227781, termedia@termedia.pl. Ed. Grazyna M Rydzewska. Circ: 2,500.

616.3 ESP ISSN 1988-317X
REVISTA ANDALUZA DE PATOLOGIA DIGESTIVA. Text in Spanish. 1978. s-a. back issues avail. **Document type:** *Journal, Academic/ Scholarly.*
Former titles (unil 2006): Revista Andaluza de Patologia Digestiva (Print edition) (1134-7821); (until 1993): Sociedad Andaluza de Patologia Digestiva. Revista (0211-5573)
Media: Online - full text.
Published by: Sociedad Andaluza de Patologia Digestiva, Colegio de Medicos de Sevilla, Ave. de la Barbolla, 47, Sevilla, 41013, Spain. TEL 34-95-5008801, FAX 34-95-5008805, sapd@sapd.es. Ed. Pedro Herguea Delgado.

616.3 ARG ISSN 0326-9620
REVISTA ARGENTINA DE COLOPROCTOLOGIA. Text in Spanish. 1987. 3/yr. USD 40 domestic; USD 50 foreign (effective 2005). **Document type:** *Journal, Academic/Scholarly.*
Published by: Sociedad Argentina de Coloproctologia, Tucuman 1545, 4o"C", Buenos Aires, C1050AAE, Argentina. http://www.sacp.org.ar. Ed. Jorge Ruiz Martin.

616.3 COL ISSN 0120-9957
➤ **REVISTA COLOMBIANA DE GASTROENTEROLOGIA.** Text in Spanish. 1987. q. **Document type:** *Journal, Academic/Scholarly.*
Related titles: Online - full text ed.: free (effective 2011) (from SciELO).
Indexed: CA, SCOPUS, T02.
Published by: Asociacion Colombiana de Gastroenterologia, Carrera 22 No 85-94, Of 203, Bogota, Colombia. TEL 57-1-6169950, FAX 57-1-6162376. Ed. Mario Humberto Rey Tovar.

616.3 MEX ISSN 0375-0906
CODEN: RGMXA
➤ **REVISTA DE GASTROENTEROLOGIA DE MEXICO.** Text in Spanish; Summaries in English. 1935. q. MXN 420 domestic; MXN 110 foreign (effective 2005). back issues avail. **Document type:** *Journal, Academic/Scholarly.* **Description:** Contains original articles, research reports, review articles, clinical cases, and notices related to gastroenterology.
Related titles: CD-ROM ed.; Online - full text ed.
Indexed: A22, C01, EMBASE, ExcerpMed, IBR, IBZ, IndMed, MEDLINE, P30, R10, Reac, SCOPUS.
—GNLM, IE, Infotrieve, Ingenta.
Published by: Asociacion Mexicana de Gastroenterologia, Nicolas San Juan No 233, Col. del Valle, Mexico, D.F., 03100, Mexico. TEL 52-55-5639-8757, FAX 52-55-5639-9971, amg@gastro.org.mx, http://www.gastro.org.mx/sitio.html. Eds. Mario Arturo Ballesteros Amozurrutia, Ricardo Mondragon Sanchez. Circ: 2,400. **Dist. by:** Distribuidora Editorial de Mexico SA de CV, P.O. Box 76-026, Mexico City, DF 04201, Mexico. TEL 52-5-544-7953, FAX 52-5-689-6545.

616.3 PER ISSN 1022-5129
REVISTA DE GASTROENTEROLOGIA DEL PERU. Text in Spanish, English, Portuguese. 1981. 3/yr. adv. Supplement avail. **Document type:** *Journal, Academic/Scholarly.* **Description:** Contains gastroenterology articles, reviews and case reports.
Related titles: Online - full text ed.: ISSN 1609-722X. 2001. free (effective 2011) (from SciELO).
Indexed: EMBASE, ExcerpMed, INIS AtomInd, MEDLINE, P30, R10, Reac, SCOPUS.
—BLDSC (7856.550000), IE, Infotrieve, Ingenta.
Published by: Sociedad de Gastroenterologia del Peru, Juan de Aliaga 204, Magdalena del Mar, Lima, 17, Peru. TEL 51-1-2640157, FAX 51-1-2641400, abussalleu@upch.edu.pe. Ed. Dr. Herman Vildosola G.

616.3 ESP ISSN 1576-0545
➤ **REVISTA ESPANOLA DE ECOGRAFIA DIGESTIVA.** Text in Spanish. 1998. 3/yr. USD 50 to qualified personnel; USD 77 to institutions; USD 38 to students (effective 2007). adv. illus.; stat.; bibl. back issues avail. **Document type:** *Journal, Academic/Scholarly.*
Formerly (until 1998): Ecografia Digestiva (1139-8884)
Published by: Aran Ediciones, Castello 128, 1o, Madrid, 28006, Spain. TEL 34-91-7820030, FAX 34-91-5615787, edita@grupoaran.com, http://www.grupoaran.com. Ed. L. Martin Herrera. Pub. Jose Jimenez Marquez. R&P Maria Dolores Linares TEL 34-91-7820035. Circ: 3,000.

616.3 ESP ISSN 1130-0108
CODEN: REDIE
➤ **REVISTA ESPANOLA DE ENFERMEDADES DIGESTIVAS.** Text in Spanish; Summaries in English, Spanish. 1918. m. EUR 110 to qualified personnel; EUR 193 to institutions; EUR 78 to students (effective 2007). adv. bk.rev. abstr.; bibl.; charts; illus.; stat. back issues avail.; reprints avail. **Document type:** *Journal, Academic/ Scholarly.*
Former titles (until 1989): Revista Espanola de las Enfermedades del Aparato Digestivo (0034-9437); (until 1967): Revista Espanola de las Enfermedades del Aparato Digestivo y de la Nutricion (0370-4343); (until 1934): Archivos Espanoles de las Enfermedades del Aparato Digestivo y de la Nutrition (0210-1556)
Related titles: Microform ed.: (from PQC); Online - full text ed.: free (effective 2011); Supplement(s): Revista Espanola de Enfermedades Digestivas. Suplemento. ISSN 1130-4588. 1990.
Indexed: A22, A35, A36, AIDS&CR, AgBio, B21, B25, BIOSIS Prev, C06, C07, C08, CABA, CINAHL, CTA, ChemAb, ChemTitl, CurCont, D01, E12, EMBASE, ExcerpMed, F08, GH, H17, IME, IndMed, Inpharma, MEDLINE, MycolAb, N02, N03, P30, P33, P35, P39, R10, R12, RA&MP, RM&VM, Reac, SCI, SCOPUS, T05, VS, W07.
—BLDSC (7853.970000), CASDDS, GNLM, IE, Infotrieve, Ingenta, INIST. **CCC.**
Published by: (Sociedad Espanola de Patologia Digestiva), Aran Ediciones, Castello 128, 1o, Madrid, 28006, Spain. TEL 34-91-7820030, FAX 34-91-5615787, edita@grupoaran.com, http://www.grupoaran.com. Ed. J.A Solis-Herruzo. Pub. Jose Jimenez Marquez. R&P Maria Dolores Linares TEL 34-91-7820035. Circ: 3,500.

616.3 610.73 BRA ISSN 1806-3144
➤ **REVISTA ESTIMA.** Text in Portuguese; Summaries in English, Portuguese, Spanish. 2003. q. free to members (effective 2011). adv. abstr. back issues avail. **Document type:** *Journal, Academic/ Scholarly.* **Description:** Covers scientific research on enterostomal therapy, includes studies conducted by nursing professionals and articles from fields such as medicine, nutrition, and physical therapy, etc.
Related titles: Online - full text ed.
Indexed: C06.
Published by: Associacao Brasileira de Estomaterapia, Rua Antonio de Godoi, N.35, Conj.102, Centro, S. Paulo, SP 01034-001, Brazil. TEL 55-11-30810659, FAX 55-11-30810659, sobest@sobest.org.br. Eds. Dr. Maria Angela Boccara de Paula, Dr. Vera Lucia C Gouveia Santos. Pub., R&P Dr. Vera Lucia C Gouveia Santos.

616.34 MEX
REVISTA MEXICANA DE COLOPROCTOLOGIA. Text in Spanish. 1995. s-a. **Document type:** *Journal, Academic/Scholarly.*
Formerly (until 2002): Sociedad Mexicana de Cirujanos de Recto y Colon. Revista
Published by: Asociacion Mexicana de Cirujanos de Recto y Colon, Durgndo 290-309, Col. Roma, Mexico, D.F., 06700, Mexico. smcrc@smcrc.org.mx, http://www.smcrc.org.mx/.

616.3 JPN ISSN 0911-601X
RINSHO SHOKAKI NAIKA/CLINICAL GASTROENTEROLOGY. Text in Japanese. 1986. m. (13/yr.). JPY 33,000 (effective 2007). **Document type:** *Journal, Academic/Scholarly.*
Published by: Nihon Medikaru Senta/Nihon Medical Center, Inc., Kyowa Bldg., 1-64, Kanda-jinbo-cho, Chiyoda-ku, Tokyo, 101-0051, Japan. TEL 81-3-32913901, FAX 81-3-32913377, http://www.nmckk.co.jp/.

616.3 IND ISSN 1319-3767
➤ **THE SAUDI JOURNAL OF GASTROENTEROLOGY.** Text in English. 1994. q. INR 2,400 domestic; USD 200 foreign (effective 2011). adv. **Document type:** *Journal, Academic/Scholarly.* **Description:** Publishes clinical and experimental research in diseases and conditions of the digestive tract.
Related titles: Online - full text ed.: ISSN 1998-4049. INR 2,000 domestic; USD 160 foreign (effective 2011).
Indexed: A01, A26, A36, C06, C07, CA, CABA, E12, EMBASE, ExcerpMed, GH, H17, I05, MEDLINE, N02, N03, P10, P20, P22, P30, P33, P39, P48, P53, P54, PQC, R07, R08, RA&MP, RM&VM, SCOPUS, T02, T05, VS.
—IE. **CCC.**
Published by: (Saudi Gastroenterology Association SAU), Medknow Publications and Media Pvt. Ltd., B-9, Kanara Business Ctr, Off Link Rd, Ghatkopar (E), Mumbai, Maharastra 400 075, India. TEL 91-22-66491816, http://www.medknow.com. Eds. Ibrahim A Al Mofleh, Mohammed I Al Mouzan.

616.3 GBR ISSN 0036-5521
RC799 CODEN: SJGRA4
➤ **SCANDINAVIAN JOURNAL OF GASTROENTEROLOGY.** Text in English. 1966. m. GBP 850, EUR 1,120, USD 1,400 combined subscription to institutions (print & online eds.); GBP 1,695, EUR 2,235, USD 2,800 combined subscription to corporations (print & online eds.) (effective 2010). adv. bk.rev. charts; illus. index. back issues avail.; reprint service avail. from PSC. **Document type:** *Journal, Academic/Scholarly.* **Description:** Membership journal for the gastroenterologic societies of Denmark, Finland, Iceland, Norway and Sweden.
Related titles: Microform ed.: (from PQC); Online - full text ed.: ISSN 1502-7708. 1998 (from IngentaConnect); Chinese ed.; Spanish ed.; ◆ Supplement(s): Scandinavian Journal of Gastroenterology. Supplement. ISSN 0085-5928.
Indexed: A01, A03, A08, A20, A22, A34, A36, A38, B25, BIOBASE, BIOSIS Prev, CA, CABA, CIN, ChemAb, ChemTitl, CurCont, D01, DBA, DentInd, E01, E12, EMBASE, ExcerpMed, FR, GH, H16, H17, IABS, IDIS, ISR, IndMed, IndVet, Inpharma, JW-G, MEDLINE, MycolAb, N02, N03, N04, NRN, P30, P33, P35, P37, P38, P39, PHN&I, PN&I, R08, R10, R11, R12, RA&MP, RM&VM, Reac, RefZh, S12, SCI, SCOPUS, SoyAb, T02, T05, TriticAb, VS, W07.
—BLDSC (8087.507000), CASDDS, GNLM, IE, Infotrieve, Ingenta, INIST. **CCC.**
Published by: Informa Healthcare (Subsidiary of: T & F Informa plc), Telephone House, 69-77 Paul St, London, EC2A 4LQ, United Kingdom. TEL 44-20-70175000, FAX 44-20-70176792, healthcare.enquiries@informa.com. Ed. Kristian Bjoro. **Subscr. in N. America to:** Taylor & Francis Inc., Customer Services Dept, 325 Chestnut St, 8th Fl, Philadelphia, PA 19106. TEL 215-625-8900, 800-354-1420, FAX 215-625-8914, customerservice@taylorandfrancis.com; **Subscr. outside N. America to:** Taylor & Francis Ltd., Journals Customer Service, Sheepen Pl, Colchester, Essex CO3 3LP, United Kingdom. TEL 44-20-70175544, FAX 44-20-70175198, tf.enquiries@tfinforma.com.

616.3 NOR ISSN 0085-5928
RC799 CODEN: SJGSB8
SCANDINAVIAN JOURNAL OF GASTROENTEROLOGY. SUPPLEMENT. Text in English. 1968. irreg. price varies. back issues avail.; reprint service avail. from PSC. **Document type:** *Monographic series, Academic/Scholarly.*
Related titles: Microform ed.: (from PQC); Online - full text ed.: ISSN 1751-1895; ◆ Supplement to: Scandinavian Journal of Gastroenterology. ISSN 0036-5521.
Indexed: A01, A03, A08, A22, B21, CTA, ChemAb, ChemTitl, ChemoAb, DentInd, EMBASE, ExcerpMed, IndMed, Inpharma, MEDLINE, NSA, P30, P35, R10, Reac, SCOPUS, T02, THA, ViroIAbstr.
—BLDSC (8087.508000), CASDDS, IE, Infotrieve, Ingenta, INIST. **CCC.**
Published by: Taylor & Francis A S (Subsidiary of: Taylor & Francis Group), Biskop Gunnerusgate 14A, PO Box 12 Posthuset, Oslo, 0051, Norway. TEL 47-23-103460, FAX 47-23-103461, journals@tandf.no, http://www.tandf.co.uk.

SEMINARS IN COLON AND RECTAL SURGERY. *see* MEDICAL SCIENCES—Surgery

616.344 CAN ISSN 1496-8290
RC862.I53
SEMINARS IN INFLAMMATORY BOWEL DISEASE. Text in English. 2001. q. CAD 129.60 domestic to individuals; USD 88.15 foreign to individuals; CAD 155.58 combined subscription domestic to individuals print & online eds.; USD 105.80 combined subscription foreign to individuals print & online eds.; CAD 186.55 domestic to institutions; USD 126.85 foreign to institutions (effective 2008). **Description:** Intends to familiarize gastroenterologists and primary care physicians with the presentations, courses, complications, and management of ulcerative colitis and Crohn's disease.
Related titles: Online - full text ed.: CAD 142.65 domestic to individuals; USD 97 foreign to individuals (effective 2008).
Indexed: A01, CA, T02.
—IE. **CCC.**
Published by: (Crohn's & Colitis Foundation of America, Inc. USA), B.C. Decker Inc., 50 King St E, 2nd Fl, Hamilton, ON L8N 2A1, Canada. TEL 905-522-7017, 800-568-7281, FAX 905-522-7839, 888-311-4987, info@bcdecker.com. Ed. Theodore M Bayless.

616.3 USA ISSN 0272-8087
CODEN: SLDIEE
➤ **SEMINARS IN LIVER DISEASE.** Text in English. 1981. q. USD 761 domestic to institutions; USD 673 foreign to institutions; USD 798 combined subscription domestic to institutions (print & online eds.); USD 824 combined subscription foreign to institutions (print & online eds.) (effective 2011). adv. abstr. reprints avail. **Document type:** *Journal, Academic/Scholarly.* **Description:** Provides in-depth coverage with articles and issues focusing on topics such as cirrhosis, transplantation, vascular and coagulation disorders, cytokines, hepatitis b & v, nonalcoholic steatosis syndromes, pediatric liver diseases, hepatic stem cells, porphyrias as well as a myriad of other diseases related to the liver.
Related titles: Microform ed.: (from PQC); Online - full text ed.: ISSN 1098-8971. USD 778 domestic to institutions; USD 792 foreign to institutions (effective 2011).
Indexed: A01, A03, A08, A22, ASCA, BIOSIS Prev, CA, CurCont, E01, EMBASE, ExcerpMed, ISR, IndMed, Inpharma, MEDLINE, MycolAb, P30, R10, Reac, SCI, SCOPUS, T02, W07.
—BLDSC (8239.454000), CASDDS, GNLM, IE, Infotrieve, Ingenta, INIST. **CCC.**
Published by: Thieme Medical Publishers (Subsidiary of: Georg Thieme Verlag), 333 Seventh Ave, New York, NY 10001. TEL 212-760-0888, 800-782-3488, FAX 212-947-1112, info@thieme.com. Ed. Dr. Paul D Berk TEL 212-851-5166. Adv. contact James C Cunningham TEL 201-767-4170. Circ: 2,485.

616.3 CHN ISSN 1006-7248
SHANGHAI KOUQIANG YIXUE/SHANGHAI JOURNAL OF STOMATOLOGY. Text in Chinese. 1992. bi-m. USD 31.20 (effective 2009). **Document type:** *Journal, Academic/Scholarly.*
Related titles: Online - full text ed.
Indexed: CA, EMBASE, ExcerpMed, MEDLINE, P30, R10, Reac, SCOPUS, T02.
—BLDSC (8254.589797), East View.
Published by: Shanghai Di-2 Yike Daxue, 639, Zhizaoju Lu, Shanghai, 200011, China. TEL 86-21-33083812, FAX 86-21-63121780. **Dist. by:** China International Book Trading Corp, 35 Chegongzhuang Xilu, Haidian District, PO Box 399, Beijing 100044, China. TEL 86-10-68412045, FAX 86-10-68412023, cibtc@mail.cibtc.com.cn, http://www.cibtc.com.cn.

616.3 CHN
SHIJIE HEXIN YIXUE QIKAN WENZHAI (WEICHANGBINGXUE FENCE)/DIGEST OF THE WORLD CORE MEDICAL JOURNALS (GASTROENTEROLOGY). Text in Chinese. 2004. bi-m. **Document type:** *Journal, Academic/Scholarly.*
Supersedes in part (in 2005): Shijie Zuixin Yixue Xinxi Wenzhai/Digest of the World Latest Medical Information (1671-3141)
Related titles: Online - full text ed.
—East View.
Published by: Shijie Tushu Chuban Xi'an Gongsi, 17, Nandajie, Xi'an, 710001, China. TEL 86-29-87265319, FAX 86-29-87265318, wzg1995@163.com, http://wuzhigang.bookonline.com.cn/. **Dist. by:** China International Book Trading Corp, 35 Chegongzhuang Xilu, Haidian District, PO Box 399, Beijing 100044, China. TEL 86-10-68412045, FAX 86-10-68412023, cibtc@mail.cibtc.com.cn, http://www.cibtc.com.cn.

616.3 CHN ISSN 1009-3079
CODEN: WJGAF2
SHIJIE HUAREN XIAOHUA ZAZHI/WORLD CHINESE JOURNAL OF DIGESTOLOGY. Text in Chinese; Summaries in English. 1993. s-m. USD 385.20 (effective 2009). adv. bk.rev. abstr.; bibl.; illus.; mkt.; stat. back issues avail. **Document type:** *Journal, Academic/Scholarly.* **Description:** Covers all aspects of gastroenterology, including hepatology, oncology, and radiology, in basic and clinical medicine. Publishes mainly original research articles and clinical trials, case reports, reviews, comments, and news.
Former titles (until 1998): Huaren Xiaohua Zazhi - Chinese Digestology Journal (1007-9319); (until 1997): Xin Xiaohuabingxueazhi - China National Journal of New Gastroenterology (1005-2631)
Related titles: Diskette ed.; E-mail ed.; Fax ed.; Online - full text ed.; ◆ English ed.: World Journal of Gastroenterology. ISSN 1007-9327.
Indexed: A22, EMBASE, ExcerpMed, R10, Reac, SCOPUS.
—BLDSC (9353.206000), CASDDS, IE, Ingenta.
Published by: W J G Press, PO Box 2345, Beijing, 100023, China. FAX 86-10-85381893. Circ: 9,000. **Dist. by:** China International Book Trading Corp, 35 Chegongzhuang Xilu, Haidian District, PO Box 399, Beijing 100044, China. TEL 86-10-68412045, FAX 86-10-68412023, cibtc@mail.cibtc.com.cn, http://www.cibtc.com.cn.

616.3 CHN ISSN 1001-3733
CODEN: SKYZFS
SHIYONG KOUQIANG YIXUE ZAZHI/JOURNAL OF PRACTICAL STOMATOLOGY. Text in Chinese. 1985. bi-m. USD 37.20 (effective 2009). **Document type:** *Journal, Academic/Scholarly.*
Related titles: Online - full text ed.
—BLDSC (5041.750000), East View.
Published by: Di-4 Junyi Daxue, Kouqiang Yixueyuan, 7, Kangfu Lu, Xi'an, 710032, China. **Dist. by:** China International Book Trading Corp, 35 Chegongzhuang Xilu, Haidian District, PO Box 399, Beijing 100044, China. TEL 86-10-68412045, FAX 86-10-68412023, cibtc@mail.cibtc.com.cn, http://www.cibtc.com.cn.

616.3 JPN ISSN 0389-3626
CODEN: SHKYEZ
SHOKA TO KYUSHU/DIGESTION & ABSORPTION. Text in English, Japanese. 1978. s-a. free to members (effective 2005). **Document type:** *Journal, Academic/Scholarly.*
—CCC.
Published by: Nihon Shoka Kyushu Gakkai/Japanese Society of Digestion and Absorption, 30-1 Ohyaguchi-kamimachi, I tabashi-ku, Nihon University, School of Medicine, Tokyo, 173-8610, Japan. TEL 86-3-39729373, FAX 86-3-39729373, http://www.js-d-and-a.org/.

616.3 JPN ISSN 0387-2645
SHOKAKI GEKA/GASTROENTEROLOGICAL SURGERY. Text in Japanese; Contents page in English. 1978. m. JPY 36,750 (effective 2007). **Document type:** *Journal, Academic/Scholarly.*
Indexed: A22, INIS AtomInd.
—BLDSC (4088.966000), IE, Ingenta.
Published by: Herusu Shuppan/Herusu Publishing Co. Inc., 2-2-3 Nakano, Nakano-ku, Tokyo, 164-0001, Japan. TEL 81-3-33848035, info@herusu-shuppan.co.jp, http://www.herusu-shuppan.co.jp/.

SHOKAKI GEKA NURSING/GASTROENTEROLOGICAL SURGERY NURSING. *see* MEDICAL SCIENCES—Nurses And Nursing

616.3 JPN ISSN 0915-3217
SHOKAKI NAISHIKYO/ENDOSCOPIA DIGESTIVA. Text in Japanese; Summaries in English. 1989. m. JPY 38,800 (effective 2005). **Document type:** *Journal, Academic/Scholarly.*
—BLDSC (3743.550000).
Published by: Tokyo Igakusha Ltd., 35-4 Hongo 3-chome, Bunkyo-ku, Tokyo, 113-0033, Japan. TEL 81-3-38114119, FAX 81-3-38116135, shoge@tokyo-igakusha.co.jp.

616.3 JPN ISSN 0289-8756
CODEN: SHOKCB
SHOKAKIKA/DIGESTIVE MEDICINE. Text in Japanese. 1984. m. JPY 2,625 (effective 2003). **Document type:** *Journal, Academic/Scholarly.*
—BLDSC (4089.015000).
Published by: Kagaku-Hyoronsha Co. Ltd., 2-10-8, Kana Tomiyama-cho, Chiyoda-ku, Tokyo, 101-8531, Japan. TEL 81-3-32527741, FAX 81-3-32525952, http://www.kahyo.com/index.html.

616.3 RUS
➤ **SIBIRSKII ZHURNAL GASTROENTEROLOGII I GEPATOLOGII.** Text in Russian. 1995. a. USD 93 foreign (effective 2007). **Document type:** *Journal, Academic/Scholarly.*
Published by: Sibirskii Gosudarstvennyi Meditsinskii Institut/Sibir State Medical University, ul Lenina 107, Tomsk, 63405, Russian Federation. TEL 7-3822-514153. **Dist. by:** East View Information Services, 10601 Wayzata Blvd, Minneapolis, MN 55305. TEL 952-252-1201, 800-477-1005, FAX 952-252-1202, info@eastview.com, http://www.eastview.com.

➤ **SOKI DAICHOGAN/EARLY COLORECTAL CANCER.** *see* MEDICAL SCIENCES—Oncology

616.3 ZAF ISSN 1812-1659
SOUTH AFRICAN GASTROENTEROLOGY REVIEW. Text in English. 2003. q. **Document type:** *Journal, Academic/Scholarly.* **Description:** Publishes articles pertinent to the practicing of gastroenterology in South Africa.
Related titles: Online - full text ed.
Indexed: A01, A36, CABA, EMBASE, ExcerpMed, GH, LT, N02, N03, R12, RRTA, SCOPUS, T02, T05, TAR.
—BLDSC (8337.825000), IE.
Published by: In House Publications, PO Box 412748, Craighall, Johannesburg 2024, South Africa. TEL 27-11-7889139, FAX 27-11-7889136, inhouse@iafrica.com, http://www.inhousepub.co.za. Eds. Herbie Schneider, Keith Petterngell.

SURGICAL LAPAROSCOPY, ENDOSCOPY AND PERCUTANEOUS TECHNIQUES. *see* MEDICAL SCIENCES—Surgery

616.3 CAN ISSN 1913-4533
SURVEILLANCE DES DIARRHEES ASSOCIEES A CLOSTRIDIUM DIFFICILE AU QUEBEC. Text in French. 2005. 3/yr. **Document type:** *Journal, Government.*
Published by: Institut National de Sante Publique du Quebec, 945 Av Wolfe, Quebec, PQ G1V 5B3, Canada. TEL 418-650-5115 ext 5336, FAX 418-646-9328.

616.3 TWN
CODEN: CMHCE
TAIWAN XIAOHUA XIYI XUEHUI ZAZHI/GASTROENTEROLOGICAL SOCIETY OF TAIWAN. JOURNAL. Text in Chinese. 1982. q. free to members. **Document type:** *Trade.*
Formerly: Zhonghua Minguo Xiaohua Xiyi Xuehui Zazhi (1013-7696)
Indexed: SCOPUS.
—BLDSC (3180.330000).
Published by: Taiwan Xiaohua Xiyi Xuehui/Gastroenterological Society of Taiwan, no. 1, Changde Road, 2nd Fl, Jingfuguan, Taipei, Taiwan. TEL 886-2-23119062, FAX 886-2-23114181, gest@ha.mc.ntu.edu.tw, http://www.gest.org.tw/.

616.3 USA
TAKE CHARGE (EMAIL). Text in English. 1977. 3/yr. free (effective 2007). adv. bk.rev. back issues avail. **Document type:** *Newsletter, Consumer.* **Description:** Features stories about coping with Crohn's disease (ileitis) and ulcerative colitis; articles on CCFA-sponsored research and education programs; medical news and profiles of individuals.
Former titles: Take Charge (Print); (until 2006): Foundation Focus (0897-6759)
Media: E-mail.
Published by: Crohn's & Colitis Foundation of America, Inc., 386 Park Ave S, 17th Fl, New York, NY 10016. TEL 212-685-3440, 800-932-2423, FAX 212-779-4098, info@ccfa.org, http://www.ccfa.org. R&P Rosemary Bimculli. Circ: 65,000.

616.3 ITA ISSN 1123-6337
RD544 CODEN: TECOFO
➤ **TECHNIQUES IN COLOPROCTOLOGY.** Variant title: U C P News. Text in English. 1995. 3/yr. EUR 334, USD 427 combined subscription to institutions (print & online eds.) (effective 2012). reprint service avail. from PSC. **Document type:** *Journal, Academic/Scholarly.*
Related titles: ◆ Online - full text ed.: Techniques in Coloproctology (Online). ISSN 1128-045X.
Indexed: A01, A03, A08, A22, A26, CA, CurCont, E01, EMBASE, ExcerpMed, H12, MEDLINE, P20, P22, P30, P48, P54, PQC, R10, Reac, SCI, SCOPUS, T02, W07.
—BLDSC (8743.875000), IE, Infotrieve, Ingenta. **CCC.**
Published by: (Italian Association of Coloproctology Units, U C P Club), Springer Italia Srl (Subsidiary of: Springer Science+Business Media), Via Decembrio 28, Milan, 20137, Italy. TEL 39-02-54259722, FAX 39-02-55193360, springer@springer.it. Ed. Mario Pescatori. **Subscr. in the Americas to:** Springer New York LLC, Journal Fulfillment, PO Box 2485, Secaucus, NJ 07096. TEL 201-348-4033, 800-777-4643, FAX 201-348-4505, journals-ny@springer.com, http://www.springer.com; **Subscr. to:** Springer Distribution Center, Kundenservice Zeitschriften, Haberstr 7, Heidelberg 69126, Germany. TEL 49-6221-3454303, FAX 49-6221-3454229, subscriptions@springer.com.

616.3 ITA ISSN 1128-045X
➤ **TECHNIQUES IN COLOPROCTOLOGY (ONLINE).** Text in English. 3/yr. 64 p./no.; **Document type:** *Journal, Academic/Scholarly.*
Media: Online - full text (from IngentaConnect). **Related titles:** ◆ Print ed.: Techniques in Coloproctology. ISSN 1123-6337.
—CCC.
Published by: Springer Italia Srl (Subsidiary of: Springer Science+Business Media), Via Decembrio 28, Milan, 20137, Italy. TEL 39-02-54259722, FAX 39-02-55193360, springer@springer.it, http://www.springer.com. Ed. Mario Pescatori. Adv. contact F Polverosi.

663 USA ISSN 1096-2883
RC804.E6 CODEN: TGEEAD
➤ **TECHNIQUES IN GASTROINTESTINAL ENDOSCOPY.** Text in English. 1999. q. USD 363 in United States to institutions; USD 442 elsewhere to institutions (effective 2012). illus. back issues avail.; reprints avail. **Document type:** *Journal, Academic/Scholarly.* **Description:** Provides a comprehensive, current overview of a clinical condition or surgical procedure in gastrointestinal endoscopy, combining the effectiveness of an atlas with the timeliness of a journal.
Related titles: Online - full text ed.: ISSN 1558-5050 (from ScienceDirect).
Indexed: A26, CA, EMBASE, ExcerpMed, I05, P30, R10, Reac, SCOPUS, T02.
—BLDSC (8745.055000), IE, Ingenta. **CCC.**
Published by: W.B. Saunders Co. (Subsidiary of: Elsevier Health Sciences), Elsevier, Health Sciences Division, Order Fulfillment, 3251 Riverport Ln, Maryland Heights, MO 63043. TEL 314-872-8370, 800-325-4177, FAX 314-432-1380, JournalCustomerService-usa@elsevier.com, http://www.us.elsevierhealth.com. Ed. Michael Kochman. Pub. Joan Anuels. Adv. contact John Marmero TEL 212-633-3657.

616.3 GBR ISSN 1756-283X
RC799
➤ **THERAPEUTIC ADVANCES IN GASTROENTEROLOGY.** Text in English. 2008. bi-m. USD 1,071, GBP 579 combined subscription to institutions (print & online eds.); USD 1,050, GBP 567 to institutions (effective 2011). back issues avail.; reprint service avail. from PSC. **Document type:** *Journal, Academic/Scholarly.* **Description:** Contains research relating to medicine and pharmacology in the field of gastroenterology and hepatology.
Related titles: Online - full text ed.: ISSN 1756-2848. 2008. USD 964, GBP 521 to institutions (effective 2011).
Indexed: A22, E01, EMBASE, ExcerpMed, P30, SCOPUS.
—CCC.
Published by: Sage Publications Ltd. (Subsidiary of: Sage Publications, Inc.), 1 Oliver's Yard, 55 City Rd, London, EC1Y 1SP, United Kingdom. TEL 44-20-73248500, FAX 44-20-73248600, info@sagepub.co.uk, http://www.uk.sagepub.com/home.nav. Eds. Alessandro Baliani, Timothy Cragin Wang.

616.3 AUS
➤ **THERAPEUTIC GUIDELINES. GASTROINTESTINAL.** Text in English. 1994. irreg. (every 3-4 yrs.), latest 2006, version 4. AUD 39 newsstand/cover; AUD 30 newsstand/cover to students (effective 2008). **Document type:** *Handbook/Manual/Guide, Academic/Scholarly.* **Description:** Provides recommendations for rational therapy of gastrointestinal disease and where necessary justifies the choice of therapy.
Formerly (until 1995): Gastrointestinal Drug Guidelines (1329-4962)
Related titles: CD-ROM ed.; Online - full text ed.; ◆ Series of: e T G Complete. ISSN 1447-1868.
Published by: Therapeutic Guidelines Ltd., Ground Flr, 23-47 Villiers St, North Melbourne, VIC 3051, Australia. TEL 61-3-93291566, 800-061-260, FAX 61-3-93265632, sales@tg.com.au, http://www.tg.com.au. Eds. Dr. Alice Glover, Dr. Michael Kingsford. Circ: 20,000.

616.3 USA ISSN 0307-6598
RC799 CODEN: TOGAD2
➤ **TOPICS IN GASTROENTEROLOGY.** Text in English. 1973. irreg., latest vol.3, 1992. USD 205 per vol. (effective 2010). back issues avail. **Document type:** *Monographic series, Academic/Scholarly.*
—CCC.
Published by: Springer New York LLC (Subsidiary of: Springer Science+Business Media), 233 Spring St, New York, NY 10013. TEL 212-460-1500, FAX 212-460-1575, service-ny@springer.com.

616.3 IND ISSN 0250-636X
TROPICAL GASTROENTEROLOGY. Text in English. 1980. q. INR 600, USD 40 to individuals; INR 700, USD 80 to institutions; INR 200, USD 10 per issue (effective 2011). adv. back issues avail. **Document type:** *Journal, Academic/Scholarly.* **Description:** Comprising literature and original work in the fields of gastroenterology, hepatology, gastrointestinal surgery and paediatric gastroenterology.
Related titles: Online - full text ed.: free (effective 2011).
Indexed: A22, EMBASE, ExcerpMed, MEDLINE, P30, R10, Reac, SCOPUS.
—BLDSC (9056.166000), IE, Ingenta.
Published by: Digestive Diseases Foundation, Rm No 3066, All India Institute of Medical Sciences, Ansari Nagar, New Delhi, 110 029, India. TEL 91-11-26593627, FAX 91-11-26589130, http://www.ddfindia.org/. Eds. S K Acharya, Vineet Ahuja. Adv. contact Vineet Ahuja.

616.33 TUR ISSN 1300-4948
RC799 CODEN: TJGAF
➤ **THE TURKISH JOURNAL OF GASTROENTEROLOGY/TURK GASTROENTEROLOJI DERGISI.** Text in English, Turkish. 1990. q. **Document type:** *Journal, Academic/Scholarly.* **Description:** Publishes original papers, case reports, and letters to the editor on all aspects of gastroenterology and hepatology.
Formerly (until 1995): Gastroenteroloji (1300-2856)
Related titles: Online - full text ed.: free (effective 2010).
Indexed: EMBASE, ExcerpMed, MEDLINE, P30, R10, Reac, SCI, SCOPUS, W07.
—BLDSC (9072.468760), GNLM, IE, Ingenta.
Published by: Turkish Society of Gastroenterology, Turk Gastroenteroloji Vakfi, Gaziler Sokak 22/1, Abidinpasa Ankara, 06620, Turkey. TEL 90-312-362-2145, FAX 90-312-362-5948, bilgi@tgv.org.tr. Ed. Cihan Yurdaydin.

616.300 GBR ISSN 1758-3934
➤ **U S GASTROENTEROLOGY AND HEPATOLOGY REVIEW.** (United States) Text in English. 2005. s-a. EUR 80 combined subscription in Europe to individuals (print & online eds.); USD 100 combined subscription in United States to individuals (print & online eds.); EUR 180 combined subscription in Europe to institutions (print & online eds.); USD 225 combined subscription in United States to institutions (print & online eds.) (effective 2009). back issues avail. **Document type:** *Journal, Academic/Scholarly.* **Description:** Features balanced and comprehensive articles written by leading authorities, addressing the most important and salient developments inthe field of oncologists.
Formerly (until 2008): U S Gastroenterology Review (1754-5056)
Related titles: Online - full text ed.: ISSN 1758-3942. 2005. EUR 70 in Europe to individuals; USD 85 in United States to individuals; EUR 170 in Europe to institutions; USD 210 in United States to institutions (effective 2009).
—CCC.
Published by: Touch Briefings (Subsidiary of: Touch Group plc), Saffron House, 6-10 Kirby St, London, EC1N 8TS, United Kingdom. TEL 44-20-74525600, FAX 44-20-74525606, info@touchbriefings.com, http://www.touchbriefings.com/.

616.33 USA ISSN 2090-1526
▼ ➤ **ULCERS.** Text in English. 2009. irreg. USD 195 (effective 2011). **Document type:** *Journal, Academic/Scholarly.* **Description:** Publishes original research articles, review articles, case reports, and clinical studies related to all aspects of ulcers.
Related titles: Online - full text ed.: ISSN 2090-1534. free (effective 2011).
Indexed: A01, T02.
Published by: Hindawi Publishing Corporation, 410 Park Ave, 15th Fl, PMB 287, New York, NY 10022. FAX 215-893-4392, 866-446-3294, info@hindawi.com.

➤ **VAN GISTEREN NAAR MORGEN.** *see* MEDICAL SCIENCES—Oncology

616.3 GBR ISSN 2041-1162
▼ **VIRAL HEPATITIS IN PRACTICE.** Abbreviated title: V H I P. Text in English. 2009. q. adv. **Document type:** *Journal, Academic/Scholarly.* **Description:** Provides updates, guidance and practical advice in the field of Hepatology.
Related titles: Online - full text ed.: ISSN 2045-7863. GBP 60, EUR 80 to individuals; GBP 250, EUR 375 to institutions (effective 2010).
Published by: Hayward Medical Communications Ltd. (Subsidiary of: Hayward Group plc), 8-10 Dryden St, Covent Garden, London, WC2E 9NA, United Kingdom. TEL 44-20-72404493, FAX 44-20-72404479, edit@hayward.co.uk, http://www.hayward.co.uk. Ed. Alastair Miller.

616.3 CHE ISSN 1662-6664
CODEN: CHGAF6
➤ **VISZERALMEDIZIN**; gastrointestinal medicine and surgery. Text in English, German. 1985. q. CHF 337, EUR 213, USD 366.50 to institutions; CHF 409, EUR 263, USD 441.50 combined subscription to institutions (print & online eds.) (effective 2012). adv. **Document type:** *Journal, Academic/Scholarly.*
Formerly (until 2009): Chirurgische Gastroenterologie (0177-9990)
Related titles: Microform ed.: (from PQC); Online - full text ed.: ISSN 1662-6672. CHF 286, EUR 197, USD 296 to institutions (effective 2012).
Indexed: A22, ASCA, E01, EMBASE, R10, Reac, SCOPUS, T02.
—BLDSC (9241.575000), GNLM, IE, Infotrieve, Ingenta. **CCC.**
Published by: S. Karger AG, Allschwilerstr 10, Basel, 4055, Switzerland. TEL 41-61-3061111, FAX 41-61-3061234, karger@karger.ch, http://www.karger.ch. Eds. E Klar, J Moessner. R&P Tatjana Sepin. adv.: B&W page EUR 2,500; trim 180 x 242. Circ: 4,000 (paid and controlled).

616.3 SVK ISSN 1337-9879
▼ **VITA GASTRO MAGAZIN.** Text in Slovak. 2009. q. **Document type:** *Magazine, Trade.*
Published by: MedMedia, s.r.o. herda@medmedia.sk, http://www.medmedia.sk.

616.3 NLD ISSN 1874-0278
VITALIA. Text in Dutch. 2004. s-a.
Formerly (until 2006): Maag Lever Darm Stichting. Nieuws (1574-7670); Which was formed by the merger of (2002-2003): M L D S Newz (1570-5218); Which was formerly (until 2002): Organiek (1385-495X); (until 1997): Nederlandse Lever Darm Stichting. Actueel (0925-1448); (1998-2003): M L D S Report (1571-6333); Which was formerly (until 2002): Digesto (1388-7297)
Published by: Maag Lever Darm Stichting, Postbus 430, Nieuwegein, 3430 AK, Netherlands. TEL 31-30-6055881, FAX 31-30-6049871, info@mlds.nl, http://www.mlds.nl.

616.3 CHN ISSN 1008-7125
WEICHANGBINGXUE/CHINESE JOURNAL OF GASTROENTEROLOGY. Text in Chinese. 1996. bi-m. USD 46.80 (effective 2009). **Document type:** *Journal, Academic/Scholarly.*
Related titles: Online - full text ed.
Indexed: A22, EMBASE, ExcerpMed, R10, Reac, SCOPUS.
—BLDSC (3180.329000), East View, IE, Ingenta.
Published by: Shanghai Di-2 Yike Daxue, 145, Shandong Zhonglu, Shanghai, 200001, China. TEL 86-21-63286942, FAX 86-21-33070444. **Dist. by:** China International Book Trading Corp, 35 Chegongzhuang Xilu, Haidian District, PO Box 399, Beijing 100044, China. TEL 86-10-68412045, FAX 86-10-68412023, cibtc@mail.cibtc.com.cn, http://www.cibtc.com.cn.

616.33 CHN ISSN 1006-5709
WEICHANGBINGXUE HE GANBINGXUE ZAZHI/CHINESE JOURNAL OF GASTROENTEROLOGY AND HEPATOLOGY. Text in Chinese. 1992. q. USD 74.40 (effective 2009). **Document type:** *Journal, Academic/Scholarly.*
Related titles: Online - full text ed.
—BLDSC (3180.331000), East View, IE, Ingenta.
Address: 2 Jingba Road, Zhengzhou, 450003, China. TEL 86-371-3921444, FAX 86-371-6960571. **Dist. by:** China International Book Trading Corp, 35 Chegongzhuang Xilu, Haidian District, PO Box 399, Beijing 100044, China. TEL 86-10-68412045, FAX 86-10-68412023, cibtc@mail.cibtc.com.cn, http://www.cibtc.com.cn.

616.3 AUS ISSN 0819-4610
➤ **WORLD COUNCIL OF ENTEROSTOMAL THERAPISTS JOURNAL.** Text in English. 1986. q. USD 60 to individuals; USD 120 to institutions; USD 15 per issue (effective 2008). adv. bk.rev. back issues avail. **Document type:** *Journal, Academic/Scholarly.*
Description: Specializes in the care of patients who have had their bowel or bladder removed and are given an alternative method of elimination. Covers draining wounds and fistulae.
Indexed: C06, C07, C08, CINAHL.
Published by: (World Council of Enterostomal Therapists CAN), Cambridge Publishing (Subsidiary of: Cambridge Media), 128 Northwood St, West Leederville, W.A. 6007, Australia. TEL 61-8-93823911, FAX 61-8-93823187, mail@cambridgmedia.com.au. Ed. Elizabeth A Ayello. Circ: 6,000.

616.3 NLD ISSN 1567-7753
WORLD GASTROENTEROLOGY NEWS. Text in English. 2000. s-a. **Document type:** *Newsletter, Trade.*
Published by: Marathon International, Noorderstr 46, Hoorn, 1621 HV, Netherlands. TEL 31-229-211980, FAX 31-229-211241, http://www.marathonmultimedia.com. Ed. John Baillie. Pub. K Foley. Circ: 50,000 (controlled).

616.3 CHN ISSN 1007-9327
CODEN: WJGAF2
WORLD JOURNAL OF GASTROENTEROLOGY. Text in English. 1995 (Oct). w. **Document type:** *Journal, Academic/Scholarly.* **Description:** Aims to strengthen international exchanges of modern and traditional gastroenterology, to promote the development of gastroenterology, and to make contributions to human health.
Formerly: China National Journal of New Gastroenterology
Related titles: Online - full text ed.: ISSN 2219-2840. free (effective 2011); ◆ Chinese ed.: Shijie Huaren Xiaohua Zazhi. ISSN 1009-3079,
Indexed: A20, A34, A35, A36, AgBio, AgrForAb, BP, C25, C30, CA, CABA, CurCont, D01, E12, EMBASE, ExcerpMed, F08, F11, F12, GH, H16, H17, IndVet, Inpharma, LT, MEDLINE, N02, N03, N04, P30, P32, P33, P37, P38, P39, P40, PGegResA, PGrRegA, PHN&I, PN&I, R07, R08, R10, R11, R12, RA&MP, RM&VM, RRTA, Reac, S12, S17, SCI, SCOPUS, SoyAb, T02, T05, TriticAb, VS, W07, W10.
—BLDSC (9356.073300), IE, Infotrieve, Ingenta. **CCC.**
Published by: (Chinese Association of the Integrated Traditional Chinese and Western Medicine), Beijing Baishideng BioMed Scientific Co., Ltd (Subsidiary of: Baishideng Publishing Group Co., Limited), Rm 903, Bldg D, Ocean International Center, 62 Dongsihuan Zhonglu, Chaoyang District, Beijing, 100025, China. TEL 86-10-85381892, FAX 86-10-85381893, baishideng@wjgnet.com. **Subscr. to:** Maney Publishing, China Journal Distribution Services, Hudson Rd, Leeds LS9 7DI, United Kingdom. TEL 44-113-2497481, FAX 44-113-2486983, subscriptions@maney.co.uk. **Dist. by:** China International Book Trading Corp, 35 Chegongzhuang Xilu, Haidian District, PO Box 399, Beijing 100044, China. TEL 86-10-68412045, FAX 86-10-68412023, cibtc@mail.cibtc.com.cn, http://www.cibtc.com.cn.

616.3 CHN ISSN 1948-5190
▼ **WORLD JOURNAL OF GASTROINTESTINAL ENDOSCOPY.** Text in English. 2009. m. free (effective 2011). **Document type:** *Journal, Academic/Scholarly.* **Description:** Features medical research on gastrointestinal endoscopy.
Media: Online - full text.
Indexed: P30.
Published by: Beijing Baishideng BioMed Scientific Co., Ltd (Subsidiary of: Baishideng Publishing Group Co., Limited), Rm 903, Bldg D, Ocean International Center, 62 Dongsihuan Zhonglu, Chaoyang District, Beijing, 100025, China. TEL 86-10-85381892, FAX 86-10-85381893, baishideng@wjgnet.com.

616.3 CHN ISSN 2150-5330
▼ **WORLD JOURNAL OF GASTROINTESTINAL PATHOPHYSIOLOGY.** Text in English. 2010. m. free (effective 2011). **Document type:** *Journal, Academic/Scholarly.* **Description:** Features medical research on gastrointestinal pathophysiology.
Media: Online - full text.
Published by: Beijing Baishideng BioMed Scientific Co., Ltd (Subsidiary of: Baishideng Publishing Group Co., Limited), Rm 903, Bldg D, Ocean International Center, 62 Dongsihuan Zhonglu, Chaoyang District, Beijing, 100025, China. TEL 86-10-85381892, FAX 86-10-85381893, baishideng@wjgnet.com.

616.3 615 CHN ISSN 2150-5349
▼ **WORLD JOURNAL OF GASTROINTESTINAL PHARMACOLOGY AND THERAPEUTICS.** Text in English. 2009. m. free (effective 2011). **Document type:** *Journal, Academic/Scholarly.* **Description:** Features medical research in gastrointestinal pharmacology and therapeutics.
Media: Online - full text.
Published by: Beijing Baishideng BioMed Scientific Co., Ltd (Subsidiary of: Baishideng Publishing Group Co., Limited), Rm 903, Bldg D, Ocean International Center, 62 Dongsihuan Zhonglu, Chaoyang District, Beijing, 100025, China. TEL 86-10-85381892, FAX 86-10-85381893, baishideng@wjgnet.com.

616.3 617 CHN ISSN 1948-9366
▼ **WORLD JOURNAL OF GASTROINTESTINAL SURGERY.** Text in English. 2009. m. free (effective 2011). **Document type:** *Journal, Academic/Scholarly.* **Description:** Features medical research on gastrointestinal surgery.
Media: Online - full text.
Indexed: P30.
Published by: Beijing Baishideng BioMed Scientific Co., Ltd (Subsidiary of: Baishideng Publishing Group Co., Limited), Rm 903, Bldg D, Ocean International Center, 62 Dongsihuan Zhonglu, Chaoyang District, Beijing, 100025, China. TEL 86-10-85381892, FAX 86-10-85381893, baishideng@wjgnet.com.

616.3 CHN ISSN 1003-7632
XIANDAI KOUQIANG YIXUE ZAZHI/JOURNAL OF MODERN STOMATOLOGY. Text in Chinese. 1987. bi-m. USD 31.20 (effective 2009). **Document type:** *Journal, Academic/Scholarly.*
Related titles: Online - full text ed.
—East View.
Address: 361, Zhongshan Donglu, Shijiazhuang, 050017, China. **Dist. by:** China International Book Trading Corp, 35 Chegongzhuang Xilu, Haidian District, PO Box 399, Beijing 100044, China. TEL 86-10-68412045, FAX 86-10-68412023, cibtc@mail.cibtc.com.cn, http://www.cibtc.com.cn.

616.3 USA
RC799
YEAR BOOK OF GASTROENTEROLOGY. Text in English. 1984. a. USD 217 in United States to institutions; USD 235 elsewhere to institutions (effective 2012). adv. illus. **Document type:** *Yearbook, Academic/Scholarly.* **Description:** Presents abstracts of pertinent literature with commentary by leading experts in the field.
Formerly (until 19??): Year Book of Digestive Diseases (0739-5930)
Related titles: CD-ROM ed.; Online - full text ed.
—GNLM, INIST. **CCC.**
Published by: Mosby, Inc. (Subsidiary of: Elsevier Health Sciences), 11830 Westline Industrial Dr, St Louis, MO 63146-3318. elspcs@elsevier.com, http://www.us.elsevierhealth.com. Ed. Dr. Gary Lichtenstein.

616.3 GBR ISSN 1745-8498
THE YEAR IN GASTROENTEROLOGY AND HEPATOLOGY. Text in English. 2005 (Jan.). a., latest vol.2, 2006. USD 99.95 per issue in US & Canada; GBP 59.99 per issue elsewhere (effective 2009). **Document type:** *Journal, Academic/Scholarly.* **Description:** Provides information on the latest advances in diagnostics, pharmacological therapy and surgery.
Related titles: Online - full text ed.
Indexed: P20, P22, P48, P54, PQC.
—BLDSC (9371.628365). **CCC.**
Published by: Clinical Publishing (Subsidiary of: Atlas Medical Publishing Ltd), Oxford Centre for Innovation, Mill St, Oxford, OX2 0JX, United Kingdom. TEL 44-1865-811116, FAX 44-1865-251550, info@clinicalpublishing.co.uk. Eds. B Lashner, N Zein. **Dist. by:** Marston Book Services Ltd., Unit 160, Milton Park, Abingdon, Oxfordshire OX14 4SD, United Kingdom. TEL 44-1235-465500, FAX 44-1235-465555, trade.orders@marston.co.uk, http://www.marston.co.uk/.

616 DEU ISSN 0044-2771
RC799 CODEN: ZGASAX
➤ **ZEITSCHRIFT FUER GASTROENTEROLOGIE.** Text in German. 1963. m. EUR 274 to institutions; EUR 374 combined subscription to institutions (print & online eds.); EUR 46 newsstand/cover (effective 2011). adv. bk.rev. abstr.; charts; illus.; stat.; tr.lit. **Document type:** *Journal, Academic/Scholarly.*
Related titles: Online - full text ed.: ISSN 1439-7803. EUR 360 to institutions (effective 2011).
Indexed: A20, A22, A34, A36, ASCA, B25, BIOSIS Prev, C25, CABA, CIN, ChemAb, ChemTitl, CurCont, E12, EMBASE, ExcerpMed, FR, GH, H17, IBR, IBZ, INI, ISR, IndMed, Inpharma, MEDLINE, MycolAb, N02, N03, N04, P30, P33, P35, P39, R10, RM&VM, Reac, SCI, SCOPUS, T05, W07.
—BLDSC (9462.350000), CASDDS, GNLM, IE, Infotrieve, Ingenta, INIST. **CCC.**
Published by: (Deutsche Gesellschaft fuer Verdauungs- und Stoffwechselkrankheiten), Georg Thieme Verlag, Ruedigerstr 14, Stuttgart, 70469, Germany. TEL 49-711-8931421, FAX 49-711-8931410, kunden.service@thieme.de. Eds. Dr. Guido Adler, Dr. T Seufferlein. Adv. contact Ulrike Bradler. Circ: 5,900 (paid and controlled). **Co-sponsors:** Oesterreichische Gesellschaft fuer Gastroenterologie; Deutsche Gesellschaft fuer Gastroenterologische Endoskopie.

616.3 CHN ISSN 1000-1174
➤ **ZHONGGUO GANGCHANGBING ZAZHI/CHINESE JOURNAL OF COLO-PROCTOLOGY.** Text in Chinese; Abstracts in Chinese, English. 1981. m. USD 36 (effective 2009). adv. **Document type:** *Journal, Academic/Scholarly.* **Description:** Covers the latest achievements in scientific research on the prevention, diagnosis and treatment of anorectal diseases in China.
Published by: Zhongguo Gangchangbing Zazhi Bianjibu, 42, Wenhua Xilu, Jinan, Shandong, 250011, China. TEL 86-531-2963276. Circ: 15,000 (paid).

616.3 CHN ISSN 1671-038X
ZHONGGUO ZHONG-XIYI JIEHE XIAOHUA ZAZHI/CHINESE JOURNAL OF INTEGRATED TRADITIONAL AND WESTERN MEDICINE ON DIGESTION. Text in Chinese. 1993. bi-m. USD 24 (effective 2009). **Document type:** *Journal, Academic/Scholarly.*
Formerly: Zhongguo Zhongxiyi Jiehe Piwei Zazhi (1006-3153)
Related titles: Online - full text ed.
—East View.
Address: 1277, Jiefang Dadao, Wuhan, 430022, China. TEL 86-27-85726835. **Dist. by:** China International Book Trading Corp, 35 Chegongzhuang Xilu, Haidian District, PO Box 399, Beijing 100044, China. TEL 86-10-68412045, FAX 86-10-68412023, cibtc@mail.cibtc.com.cn, http://www.cibtc.com.cn.

617.6 CHN ISSN 1002-0098
CODEN: ZKYZE2
ZHONGHUA KOUQIANG YIXUE ZAZHI/CHINESE JOURNAL OF STOMATOLOGY. Text in Chinese. 1953-1959; resumed 1987. bi-m. USD 87.60 (effective 2009). **Document type:** *Journal, Academic/Scholarly.*
Formerly (1953-1959): Chung-Hua K'ou Ch'iang K'o Tsa Chih (0412-4014)
Related titles: Online - full content ed.; Online - full text ed.
Indexed: A22, EMBASE, ExcerpMed, IndMed, MEDLINE, P30, R10, Reac, SCOPUS.
—BLDSC (3180.677000), East View, IE, Ingenta.
Published by: Zhonghua Yixuehui Zazhishe/Chinese Medical Association Publishing House, 42 Dongsi Xidajie, Beijing, 100710, China. TEL 86-1-65251918. **Dist. by:** China International Book Trading Corp, 35 Chegongzhuang Xilu, Haidian District, PO Box 399, Beijing 100044, China. TEL 86-10-68412045, FAX 86-10-68412023, cibtc@mail.cibtc.com.cn, http://www.cibtc.com.cn.

ZHONGHUA WEI-CHANG WAIKE ZAZHI/CHINESE JOURNAL OF GASTROINTESTINAL SURGERY. *see* MEDICAL SCIENCES—Surgery

616.3 CHN ISSN 1673-9752
CODEN: ZXWZBC
➤ **ZHONGHUA XIAOHUA WAIKE ZAZHI/CHINESE JOURNAL OF DIGESTIVE SURGERY.** Text in Chinese; Abstracts in Chinese, English. 2002. bi-m. CNY 90, USD 38 (effective 2009). **Document type:** *Journal, Academic/Scholarly.* **Description:** Covers the latest developments of theoretical and applied researches in the fields of digestive surgery in China.
Formerly (until 2006): Xiaohua Waike/Journal of Digestive Surgery (1671-4555)
Related titles: Online - full text ed.
Indexed: A29, A34, A35, A36, AgBio, B&BAb, B19, B20, B21, CABA, E12, ESPM, F08, GH, H16, H17, ImmunAb, N02, N03, NucAcAb, OGFA, P33, PN&I, R12, RA&MP, RM&VM, S12, T05, VS, ViroIAbstr.
—East View.
Published by: Xiaohua Waike, 29, Gaotanyan, Chongqing, 400038, China. TEL 86-23-68754655, FAX 86-23-65317637. Ed. Jia-hong Dong. Circ: 2,000. **Dist. by:** China International Book Trading Corp, 35 Chegongzhuang Xilu, Haidian District, PO Box 399, Beijing 100044, China. TEL 86-10-68412045, FAX 86-10-68412023, cibtc@mail.cibtc.com.cn, http://www.cibtc.com.cn.

616.3 CHN ISSN 0254-1432
ZHONGHUA XIAOHUA ZAZHI/CHINESE JOURNAL OF DIGESTION. Text in Chinese; Abstracts in Chinese, English. bi-m. USD 74.40 (effective 2009). reprints avail.
Related titles: CD-ROM ed.; Online - full content ed.; Online - full text ed.
Indexed: ExtraMED.
—East View.
Published by: Zhonghua Yixuehui, Shanghai Fenhui/Chinese Medical Association, Shanghai Branch, 1623 Beijing Xilu, Shanghai, 200040, China. TEL 86-21-62531885, FAX 86-21-62550842, cma-sb@online.sh.cn. Ed. Shu-Dong Xiao. Circ: 13,000. **Dist. by:** China International Book Trading Corp, 35 Chegongzhuang Xilu, Haidian District, PO Box 399, Beijing 100044, China. TEL 86-10-68412045, FAX 86-10-68412023, cibtc@mail.cibtc.com.cn, http://www.cibtc.com.cn.

ZHONGHUA YIXIANBING ZAZHI/CHINESE JOURNAL OF PANCREATOLOGY. *see* MEDICAL SCIENCES—Endocrinology

MEDICAL SCIENCES—Hematology

613.7 616.15 USA ISSN 1092-0412
A B C NEWSLETTER. Text in English. 1978. w. USD 264 in North America; USD 288 elsewhere (effective 2000). adv. bk.rev. index. back issues avail. **Document type:** *Newsletter.* **Description:** Current events and trends in community blood services and transfusion medicine.
Formerly: C C B C Newsletter (1083-3811)
Related titles: E-mail ed.: USD 216 (effective 2000).
Published by: America's Blood Centers, 725 15th St, N W, Ste 700, Washington, DC 20005-2109. TEL 202-393-5725, 888-872-5663, FAX 202-393-1282. Ed. Jane M Starkey. Circ: 580 (paid).

616.15 PRT ISSN 0874-2731
A B O; revista de medicina transfusional. Text in Portuguese. 2000. q. **Document type:** *Journal, Academic/Scholarly.*
Related titles: Online - full text ed.
Published by: Ministerio da Saude, Instituto Portugues do Sangue/Ministry of Health, Portuguese Institute of Blood, Parque de Saude de Lisboa, Av. do Brasil, no. 53 - Pav. 17, Lisboa, 1749-005, Portugal. TEL 351-213-154947, FAX 351-213-154952, dirips@ips.min-saude.pt.

616.15 CHE ISSN 0001-5792
QP91 CODEN: ACHAAH
➤ **ACTA HAEMATOLOGICA.** Text in English. 1948. 8/yr. (2 vols. per yr.). CHF 2,848, EUR 2,276, USD 2,794 to institutions; CHF 3,126, EUR 2,498, USD 3,062 combined subscription to institutions (print & online eds.) (effective 2012). adv. bk.rev. abstr.; illus. index. back issues avail. **Document type:** *Journal, Academic/Scholarly.* **Description:** Features balanced, wide-ranging coverage of current hematology research.
Related titles: Online - full text ed.: ISSN 1421-9662. CHF 2,780, EUR 2,224, USD 2,700 to institutions (effective 2012).
Indexed: A01, A03, A08, A22, ASCA, B&BAb, B19, B21, B25, BIOSIS Prev, CA, CIN, ChemAb, ChemTitl, CurCont, E01, EMBASE, ExcerpMed, IBR, IBZ, ISR, IndMed, Inpharma, MEDLINE, MycolAb, P30, P35, R10, Reac, SCI, SCOPUS, SPPI, T02, Telegen, ViroIAbstr, W07.
—BLDSC (0623.000000), CASDDS, GNLM, IE, Infotrieve, Ingenta, INIST. **CCC.**
Published by: S. Karger AG, Allschwilerstr 10, Basel, 4055, Switzerland. TEL 41-61-3061111, FAX 41-61-3061234, karger@karger.ch, http://www.karger.ch. Ed. I. Ben-Bassat. adv.: page CHF 1,730; trim 210 x 280. Circ: 800 (paid).

616.15 POL ISSN 0001-5814
CODEN: AHPLBO
➤ **ACTA HAEMATOLOGICA POLONICA.** Text and summaries in Polish, English. 1970. 4/yr. EUR 61 foreign (effective 2006). adv. bk.rev. index. 140 p./no. 1 cols./p.; reprints avail. **Document type:** *Journal, Academic/Scholarly.* **Description:** Features case reports on hematology, transfusion and immunology.
Indexed: A22, B25, BIOSIS Prev, ChemAb, EMBASE, ExcerpMed, INIS AtomInd, IndMed, MycolAb, P30, R10, Reac, SCOPUS.
—BLDSC (0623.200000), CASDDS, GNLM, IE, Infotrieve, Ingenta, INIST.
Published by: Polskie Towarzystwo Hematologow i Transfuzjologow/Polish Society of Hematology and Transfusiology, c/o Klinika Hematologii Akademii Medycznej, Ul Pabianicka 62, Lodz, 93513, Poland. TEL 48-42-6895191, FAX 48-42-6895192, korycka@cks.am.lodz.pl. Ed. Tadeusz Robak. Adv. contact Anna Korycka TEL 48-42-6895198. B&W page PLZ 1,500, B&W page USD 30, color page PLZ 3,000, color page USD 50. Circ: 1,150. **Dist. by:** Ars Polona, Obroncow 25, Warsaw 03933, Poland. TEL 48-22-5098609, FAX 48-22-5098610, arspolona@arspolona.com.pl, http://www.arspolona.com.pl. **Co-sponsor:** Instytut Hematologii i Transfuzjologii.

616.15 ITA ISSN 1593-232X
ACTA PHLEBOLOGICA; a journal on plebology. Text in Multiple languages. 2000. 3/yr. EUR 240 combined subscription in the European Union to institutions print & online eds.; EUR 265 combined subscription elsewhere to institutions print & online eds. (effective 2011). **Document type:** *Journal, Academic/Scholarly.*

Related titles: Online - full text ed.: ISSN 1827-1766. 2005.
Indexed: RefZh.
—BLDSC (0648.550000).
Published by: Edizioni Minerva Medica, Corso Bramante 83-85, Turin, 10126, Italy. TEL 39-011-678282, FAX 39-011-674502, journals.dept@minervamedica.it, http://www.minervamedica.it.

616.15 616.99419 AUS ISSN 1833-055X
ACUTE MYELOID LEUKEMIA RESEARCH TODAY. Text in English. 2004. m. free (effective 2008). adv. back issues avail. **Document type:** *Journal, Consumer.* **Description:** Contains information about research on acute myeloid leukemia, including details on aml, symptoms, treatment, information.
Media: Online - full text.
Published by: Research Today Publications ad@researchtoday.net, http://www.researchtoday.net.

616.13 USA ISSN 1687-9104
➤ **ADVANCES IN HEMATOLOGY.** Text in English. 2008. irreg. USD 395 (effective 2011). **Document type:** *Journal, Academic/Scholarly.* **Description:** Publishes original research articles as well as review articles in all areas of hematology.
Related titles: Online - full text ed.: ISSN 1687-9112. 2008. free (effective 2011).
Indexed: A01, A26, A34, A36, B21, C06, C07, CA, CABA, E08, E12, EMBASE, GH, H11, H12, I05, ImmunAb, N02, N03, P30, P33, P39, SCOPUS, T02, T05.
Published by: Hindawi Publishing Corporation, 410 Park Ave, 15th Fl, PMB 287, New York, NY 10022. FAX 866-446-3294, orders@hindawi.com.

616.992 DEU ISSN 1866-296X
AERZTE ZEITUNG FUER ONKOLOGEN - HAEMATOLOGEN. Text in German. 2007. m. EUR 21.40 (effective 2008). adv. **Document type:** *Journal, Trade.*
Published by: Aerzte Zeitung Verlagsgesellschaft mbH (Subsidiary of: Springer Science+Business Media), Am Forsthaus Gravenbruch 5, Neu-Isenburg, 63263, Germany. TEL 49-6102-506157, FAX 49-6102-506123, info@aerztezeitung.de, http://www.aerztezeitung.de. adv.: B&W page EUR 2,900, color page EUR 4,130. Circ: 5,900 (controlled).

616.15 USA ISSN 2160-1992
▼ ➤ **AMERICAN JOURNAL OF BLOOD RESEARCH.** Text in English. 2011. free (effective 2011). **Document type:** *Journal, Academic/Scholarly.*
Media: Online - full text.
Published by: E-Century Publishing Corporation, 40 White Oaks Ln, Madison, WI 53711. TEL 608-230-6435, FAX 608-230-6435, info@e-century.org, http://www.e-century.org/. Ed. Larry W Kwak.

616.1 USA ISSN 0361-8609
QP91 CODEN: AJHEDD
➤ **AMERICAN JOURNAL OF HEMATOLOGY.** Text in English. 1976. m. GBP 2,906 in United Kingdom to institutions; EUR 3,674 in Europe to institutions; USD 5,441 in United States to institutions; USD 5,609 in Canada & Mexico to institutions; USD 5,693 elsewhere to institutions; GBP 3,343 combined subscription in United Kingdom to institutions (print & online eds.); EUR 4,228 combined subscription in Europe to institutions (print & online eds.); USD 6,258 combined subscription in United States to institutions (print & online eds.); USD 6,426 combined subscription in Canada & Mexico to institutions (print & online eds.); USD 6,510 combined subscription elsewhere to institutions (print & online eds.) (effective 2012). adv. bibl.; illus. back issues avail.; reprint service avail. from PSC. **Document type:** *Journal, Academic/Scholarly.* **Description:** Provides coverage of experimental and clinical features of blood diseases in humans and in animal models of human disease.
Related titles: Microform ed.: (from PQC); Online - full text ed.: ISSN 1096-8652. GBP 2,777 in United Kingdom to institutions; EUR 3,511 in Europe to institutions; USD 5,441 elsewhere to institutions (effective 2012).
Indexed: A22, A34, A36, AIIM, ASCA, B25, BIOBASE, BIOSIS Prev, CABA, CIN, ChemAb, ChemTitl, CurCont, DentInd, E12, EMBASE, ExcerpMed, FR, GH, H17, IABS, ISR, IndMed, Inpharma, LT, MEDLINE, MycolAb, N02, N03, P30, P33, P35, P39, R08, R10, RA&MP, RM&VM, RRTA, Reac, RefZh, SCI, SCOPUS, T05, VS, W07, W10.
—BLDSC (0824.800000), CASDDS, GNLM, IE, Infotrieve, Ingenta, INIST. **CCC.**
Published by: John Wiley & Sons, Inc., 111 River St, Hoboken, NJ 07030. TEL 201-748-6000, FAX 201-748-6088, info@wiley.com, http://www.wiley.com/WileyCDA/. Ed. Carlo Brugnara. Pub. Kim Thompkins TEL 212-850-6921. **Subscr. outside the Americas to:** John Wiley & Sons Ltd., The Atrium, Southern Gate, Chichester, West Sussex PO19 8SQ, United Kingdom. TEL 44-1243-779777, 800-243407, FAX 44-1243-775878, cs-journals@wiley.com.

➤ **AMERICAN JOURNAL OF KIDNEY DISEASES.** *see* MEDICAL SCIENCES—Urology And Nephrology

616 USA ISSN 1559-7237
AMERICAN SOCIETY OF HEMATOLOGY IMAGE BANK. Text in English. 2001. irreg. free (effective 2010). **Document type:** *Monographic series, Academic/Scholarly.* **Description:** Serves as a comprehensive reference and teaching tool that is widely accessible to physicians and hematology students around the world.
Media: Online - full text.
—CCC.
Published by: American Society of Hematology, 1900 M St, NW, Ste 200, Washington, DC 20036. TEL 202-776-0544, FAX 202-776-0545, ash@hematology.org, http://www.hematology.org. Eds. John Lazarchick, Peter Maslak.

616.15 USA ISSN 2090-1267
▼ ➤ **ANEMIA.** Text in English. 2009. irreg. USD 195 (effective 2011). **Document type:** *Journal, Academic/Scholarly.* **Description:** Publishes original research articles, review articles, case reports, and clinical studies related to all aspects of anemia.
Related titles: Online - full text ed.: ISSN 2090-1275. 2009. free (effective 2011).
Indexed: A01, P30, T02.
Published by: Hindawi Publishing Corporation, 410 Park Ave, 15th Fl, PMB 287, New York, NY 10022. FAX 866-446-3294, hindawi@hindawi.com.

616.15 DEU ISSN 0939-5555
RC633.A1 CODEN: ANHEE8
➤ **ANNALS OF HEMATOLOGY.** Text in English. 1950. m. EUR 2,511, USD 3,036 combined subscription to institutions (print & online eds.) (effective 2012). adv. bk.rev. abstr.; bibl.; charts; illus. index. back issues avail.; reprint service avail. from PSC. **Document type:** *Journal, Academic/Scholarly.* **Description:** Covers the entire spectrum of clinical and experimental hematology, hemostasiology, immunohematology and blood transfusion, including the diagnosis and treatment of hematopoietic and lymphatic neoplasia and of bone marrow transplantation.
Formerly (until 1991): Blut (0006-5242); Incorporates (1996-2000): Hematology and Cell Therapy (1269-3286)
Related titles: Microform ed.: (from PQC); Online - full text ed.: ISSN 1432-0584 (from IngentaConnect); Supplement(s): Annals of Hematology. Supplement. ISSN 0945-8077.
Indexed: A01, A03, A08, A22, A26, A36, ASCA, Agr, B21, B25, BIOSIS Prev, CA, CABA, CIN, ChemAb, ChemTitl, CurCont, E01, E12, EMBASE, ExcerpMed, GH, H12, H17, IBR, IBZ, ISR, IndMed, Inpharma, Kidney, LT, MEDLINE, MycolAb, N02, N03, P20, P22, P24, P30, P33, P35, P39, P48, P54, PQC, R10, RM&VM, RRTA, Reac, SCI, SCOPUS, T02, T05, VS, W07.
—BLDSC (1040.855000), CASDDS, GNLM, IE, Infotrieve, Ingenta, INIST. **CCC.**
Published by: (Gesellschaft fuer Thrombose und Haemostaseforschung), Springer (Subsidiary of: Springer Science+Business Media), Tiergartenstr 17, Heidelberg, 69121, Germany. TEL 49-6221-4870, FAX 49-6221-345229. Ed. Arnold Ganser. adv.: B&W page EUR 790, color page EUR 1,830. Circ: 650 (paid and controlled). **Subscr. in the Americas to:** Springer New York LLC, Journal Fulfillment, PO Box 2485, Secaucus, NJ 07096. TEL 201-348-4033, 800-777-4643, FAX 201-348-4505, journals-ny@springer.com, http://www.springer.com; **Subscr. to:** Springer Distribution Center, Kundenservice Zeitschriften, Haberstr 7, Heidelberg 69126, Germany. TEL 49-6221-3454303, FAX 49-6221-3454229, subscriptions@springer.com. **Co-sponsors:** Deutsche Gesellschaft fuer Transfusionsmedizin und Immunhaematologie; Deutsche Gesellschaft fuer Haematologie und Onkologie.

618.92 MEX ISSN 1665-2681
ANNALS OF HEPATOLOGY. Text in Spanish. 2002. a. back issues avail. **Document type:** *Journal, Academic/Scholarly.*
Related titles: Online - full text ed.
Indexed: B&BAb, B21, C01, CurCont, EMBASE, MEDLINE, P30, R10, Reac, SCI, SCOPUS, VirolAbstr, W07.
Published by: Sociedad Mexicana de Hepatologia, Puente de Piedra No 150, Col. Toriello Guerra, Mexico, D.F., 14040, Mexico. TEL 52-55-56066222, FAX 52-55-56664031. Ed. Nahum Mendez Sanchez.

616.15 JPN
ANNUAL REVIEW KETSUEKI/ANNUAL REVIEW. BLOOD. Text in Japanese. 1988. a. JPY 9,200 per issue (effective 2007). adv. **Document type:** *Academic/Scholarly.*
Published by: Chugai Igakusha, 62 Yarai-cho, Shinjuku-ku, Tokyo, 162-0805, Japan. TEL 81-3-32682701, FAX 81-3-32682722, http://www.chugaiigaku.jp/.

616.15 USA
APLASTIC ANEMIA & M D S INTERNATIONAL FOUNDATION. NEWSLETTER. Text in English. 1987. q. free. back issues avail. **Document type:** *Newsletter.*
Formerly: Aplastic Anemia Foundation of America. Newsletter
Published by: Aplastic Anemia & M D S International Foundation, Inc., PO Box 613, Annapolis, MD 21404-0613. TEL 410-867-0242, 800-747-2820, FAX 410-867-0240. Ed., R&P Marilyn Baker. Circ: 15,000.

▼ **ASIA PACIFIC JOURNAL OF ONCOLOGY & HEMATOLOGY.** *see* MEDICAL SCIENCES—Oncology

▼ **ASIA-PACIFIC ONCOLOGY AND HAEMATOLOGY.** *see* MEDICAL SCIENCES—Oncology

615.39 IND ISSN 0973-6247
➤ **ASIAN JOURNAL OF TRANSFUSION SCIENCE.** Text in English. 1980. s-a. INR 1,200 domestic; USD 120 foreign to individuals; USD 250 foreign to institutions; INR 1,500 combined subscription domestic (print & online eds.); USD 145 combined subscription foreign to individuals (print & online eds.); USD 300 combined subscription foreign to institutions (print & online eds.) (effective 2011). adv. **Document type:** *Journal, Academic/Scholarly.* **Description:** Disseminates the knowledge of transfusion science to all members. It is a special window particularly for the Asian scientists to put forward their scientific materials to the world community.
Formerly (until 2006): Transfusion Bulletin (0973-1326)
Related titles: Online - full text ed.: ISSN 1998-3565. INR 1,000 domestic; USD 95 foreign to individuals; USD 200 foreign to institutions (effective 2011).
Indexed: A01, A26, A36, C06, C07, CA, CABA, D01, GH, H17, I05, N02, N03, P10, P30, P33, P39, P48, P53, P54, PQC, R08, R12, T02, T05.
—IE. **CCC.**
Published by: (Indian Society of Blood Transfusion and Immunohematology), Medknow Publications and Media Pvt. Ltd., B-9, Kanara Business Ctr, Off Link Rd, Ghatkopar (E), Mumbai, Maharastra 400 075, India. TEL 91-22-66491816, FAX 91-22-66491817, http://www.medknow.com. Ed. Dr. N Choudhury.

616.15 GBR ISSN 1471-2326
RC1 CODEN: BBDMB4
➤ **B M C BLOOD DISORDERS.** (BioMed Central) Text in English. 2000. irreg. free (effective 2011). adv. back issues avail.; reprints avail. **Document type:** *Journal, Academic/Scholarly.* **Description:** Covers original research articles in all aspects of the prevention, diagnosis and management of blood disorders, as well as related molecular genetics, pathophysiology, and epidemiology.
Media: Online - full text.
Indexed: A01, A26, A36, C06, C07, CA, CABA, EMBASE, ExcerpMed, GH, I05, N02, N03, P20, P22, P30, PQC, R10, Reac, SCOPUS, T02, T05.
—Infotrieve. **CCC.**
Published by: BioMed Central Ltd. (Subsidiary of: Springer Science+Business Media), 236 Gray's Inn Rd, London, WC1X 8HB, United Kingdom. TEL 44-20-31922000, FAX 44-20-31922010, info@biomedcentral.com. Ed. Dr. Melissa Norton. Adv. contact Natasha Bailey TEL 44-20-31922231.

616.15 GBR ISSN 1472-6890
RB1 CODEN: BCPMB3
➤ **B M C CLINICAL PATHOLOGY.** (BioMed Central) Text in English. 2000. irreg. free (effective 2011). adv. back issues avail.; reprints avail. **Document type:** *Journal, Academic/Scholarly.* **Description:** Covers original research articles in all aspects of histopathology, haematology, clinical biochemistry, and medical microbiology, including virology, parasitology and infection control.
Media: Online - full text.
Indexed: A01, A26, B19, B20, CA, EMBASE, ESPM, ExcerpMed, GenetAb, I05, P20, P22, P30, PQC, R10, Reac, SCOPUS, T02, VirolAbstr.
—Infotrieve. **CCC.**
Published by: BioMed Central Ltd. (Subsidiary of: Springer Science+Business Media), 236 Gray's Inn Rd, London, WC1X 8HB, United Kingdom. TEL 44-20-31922000, FAX 44-20-31922010, info@biomedcentral.com. Ed. Dr. Melissa Norton. Adv. contact Natasha Bailey TEL 44-20-31922231.

362.19699419 CHN ISSN 1009-9921
BAIXUEBING. LINBABING/JOURNAL OF LEUKEMIA & LYMPHOPATHY. Text in Chinese. 1992. m. CNY 72; CNY 6 per issue (effective 2011). back issues avail. **Document type:** *Journal, Academic/Scholarly.*
Former titles (until 2001): Baixuebing/Journal of Leukemia (1006-6934); (until 1995): Shanxi Baixuebing (1004-3683)
Related titles: Online - full text ed.
Indexed: B21, EMBASE, ExcerpMed, GenetAb, ImmunAb, OGFA, R10, Reac, SCOPUS.
—BLDSC (1857.245000), IE.
Published by: Shanxi Sheng Zhongliu Yiyuan, Shanxi Sheng Zhongliu Yanjiusuo/Shanxi Cancer Hospital, Shanxi Cancer Institute, 3, Zigong Xinjie, Taiyuan, Shanxi 030013, China. TEL 86-351-4650389, FAX 86-351-4651415. Ed. Yu-luan Wang. **Dist. by:** China International Book Trading Corp, 35 Chegongzhuang Xilu, Haidian District, PO Box 399, Beijing 100044, China. TEL 86-10-68412045, FAX 86-10-68412023, cibtc@mail.cibtc.com.cn, http://www.cibtc.com.cn. **Co-sponsor:** Chinese Medical Association.

616.5 GBR
➤ **BEST PRACTICE & RESEARCH: CLINICAL HAEMATOLOGY.** Text in English. 1972. q. EUR 485 in Europe to institutions; JPY 52,600 in Japan to institutions; USD 432 elsewhere to institutions (effective 2012). adv. back issues avail. **Document type:** *Journal, Academic/Scholarly.* **Description:** Provides a comprehensive review of current clinical practice and thinking within the specialty of haematology.
Former titles (until 2001): Bailliere's Best Practice & Research: Clinical Haematology (1521-6926); (until 1999): Bailliere's Clinical Haematology (0950-3536); (until 1987): Clinics in Haematology (0308-2261)
Related titles: Online - full text ed.: ISSN 1532-1924 (from ScienceDirect).
Indexed: A22, A26, ASCA, CA, CurCont, E01, EMBASE, ExcerpMed, I05, ISR, IndMed, Inpharma, MEDLINE, P30, R10, Reac, SCI, SCOPUS, T02, W07.
—BLDSC (1942.327828), GNLM, IE, Infotrieve, Ingenta, INIST. **CCC.**
Published by: Bailliere Tindall (Subsidiary of: Elsevier Health Sciences), The Blvd, Langford Ln, Kidlington, Oxford OX5 1GB, United Kingdom. TEL 44-1865-843000, FAX 44-1865-843010, directenquiries@elsevier.com. Ed. Dr. Jacob M Rowe.

616.15 SRB ISSN 0354-4494
➤ **BILTEN ZA TRANSFUZIOLOGIJU.** Text in Serbian; Summaries in English. 1954. s-a. adv. bk.rev. back issues avail. **Document type:** *Journal, Academic/Scholarly.* **Description:** Covers current topics, original and professional papers in the transfusion medicine and hematology fields.
Former titles (until 1994): Bilten za Hematologiju i Transfuziologiju (0354-1142); (until 1991): Bilten za Hematologiju i Transfuziju (0350-2023); (until 1973): Bilten za Transfuzije (0523-6150)
Related titles: Diskette ed.; Fax ed.
Indexed: IndMed, P30.
—GNLM.
Published by: Zavod za Transfuziju Krvi Srbije/Institute for Blood Transfusion of Serbia, Svetog Save 39, Belgrade, 11000. TEL 381-11-4318861, FAX 381-11-458328. Ed. Baklaja Radmila. Pub. Vukman Gligorovic. Adv. contact Antuljeskov Gordana TEL 381-1-431886. B&W page USD 50. Circ: 300.

616.15 USA ISSN 1083-8791
RD123.5 CODEN: BBMTF6
➤ **BIOLOGY OF BLOOD AND MARROW TRANSPLANTATION.** Abbreviated title: B B & M T. Text in English. 1995. m. USD 618 in United States to institutions; USD 729 elsewhere to institutions (effective 2012). adv. back issues avail.; reprints avail. **Document type:** *Journal, Academic/Scholarly.* **Description:** Describes blood and marrow transplantation processes for the medical profession.
Related titles: Online - full text ed.: ISSN 1523-6536 (from IngentaConnect, ScienceDirect).
Indexed: A01, A03, A08, A20, A26, BIOBASE, CA, CurCont, EMBASE, ExcerpMed, I05, IABS, ISR, IndMed, Inpharma, MEDLINE, P30, P35, R10, Reac, SCI, SCOPUS, T02, W07.
—BLDSC (2087.013000), CASDDS, IE, Infotrieve, Ingenta. **CCC.**
Published by: (American Society for Blood and Marrow Transplantation), Elsevier Inc. (Subsidiary of: Elsevier Science & Technology), 1600 John F Kennedy Blvd, Philadelphia, PA 19103. TEL 215-239-3900, FAX 215-238-7883, JournalCustomerService-usa@elsevier.com, http://www.elsevier.com. Ed. Robert Korngold TEL 201-336-8664. Adv. contact Kevin Dunn TEL 201-767-4170. Circ: 1,425.

616.15 DEU ISSN 0934-0734
➤ **BIOMEDICAL PROGRESS;** clinical trends in coagulation and fibrinolysis. Text in English. 1988. q. USD 32 (effective 2001). **Document type:** *Journal, Academic/Scholarly.*
—GNLM. **CCC.**
Published by: Die Medizinische Verlagsgesellschaft Umwelt & Medizin mbH, Scharderhohlweg 35, Koenigstein, 61462, Germany. TEL 49-69-638204, FAX 49-69-637109. Ed. Dr. Eberhard Mammen. Circ: 14,000 (paid).

616.15 USA ISSN 0006-4971
RB145 CODEN: BLOOAW

➤ **BLOOD.** Text in English. 1945. w. USD 1,290 combined subscription domestic to institutions for a single-site two-year colleges & small hospitals (print & online eds.); USD 1,510 combined subscription foreign to institutions for a single-site two-year colleges & small hospitals (print & online eds.); USD 1,350 combined subscription domestic to institutions for a single site masters colleges, charitable org. & large hospitals (print & online eds.); USD 1,570 combined subscription foreign to institutions for a single site masters colleges, charitable org. & large hospitals (print & online eds.); free to members (effective 2009). adv. bk.rev. abstr.; bibl.; charts; illus. index.
Document type: *Journal, Academic/Scholarly.* **Description:** Publishes original articles relating to all phases of hematology.
Formerly: Blood: The Journal of Hematology
Related titles: Online - full text ed.: ISSN 1528-0020. USD 2,400 domestic multiple sites - 2 geographic locations; USD 4,500 foreign multiple sites - 4 geographic locations (effective 2009).
Indexed: A20, A22, A34, A35, A36, AIDS Ab, AIIM, AIM, ASCA, AgBio, B21, B25, BIOBASE, BIOSIS Prev, C13, C30, C33, CABA, CIN, CTA, ChemAb, ChemTitl, CurCont, D01, DBA, DentInd, E12, EMBASE, ExcerpMed, F08, F11, F12, GH, H16, H17, I12, IABS, IBR, IBZ, IDIS, INIS AtomInd, ISR, IndMed, IndVet, Inpharma, JW, MEDLINE, MycolAb, N02, N03, P30, P32, P33, P35, P37, P39, R07, R08, R10, R12, R13, RA&MP, RM&VM, Reac, S12, SAA, SCI, SCOPUS, T05, Telegen, VS, W07.
—BLDSC (2112.000000), CASDDS, GNLM, IE, Infotrieve, Ingenta, INIST. **CCC.**
Published by: American Society of Hematology, 1900 M St, NW, Ste 200, Washington, DC 20036. TEL 202-776-0544, FAX 202-776-0551, ash@hematology.org, http://www.hematology.org. Ed. Dr. Sanford J. Shattil. adv.: B&W page USD 1,840, color page USD 3,290; trim 7 x 10. Circ: 13,835. **Subscr. to:** Elsevier, Subscription Customer Service, 6277 Sea Harbor Dr, Orlando, FL 32887-4800. TEL 407-345-4000, 800-654-2452, FAX 407-363-9661, usjcs@elsevier.com.

▼ ➤ **BLOOD AND LYMPHATIC CANCER: TARGETS AND THERAPY.** *see* MEDICAL SCIENCES—Oncology

➤ **BLOOD CELL BIOCHEMISTRY.** *see* BIOLOGY—Biochemistry

616.1 USA ISSN 1079-9796
QP94 CODEN: BCMDFX

➤ **BLOOD CELLS, MOLECULES AND DISEASES.** Text in English. 1975. 8/yr. EUR 1,277 in Europe to institutions; JPY 133,200 in Japan to institutions; USD 1,072 elsewhere to institutions (effective 2012). adv. back issues avail.; reprints avail. **Document type:** *Journal, Academic/Scholarly.* **Description:** Covers all aspects of molecular basis of hematologic disease and studies of the diseases themselves.
Formerly (until 1995): Blood Cells (0340-4684)
Related titles: Microform ed.: (from PQC); Online - full text ed.: ISSN 1096-0961 (from IngentaConnect, ScienceDirect).
Indexed: A01, A03, A08, A20, A22, A26, ASCA, B25, BIOSIS Prev, CA, CIN, ChemAb, ChemTitl, CurCont, E01, EMBASE, ExcerpMed, I05, ISR, IndMed, Inpharma, MEDLINE, MycolAb, P30, P35, P48, PQC, R10, Reac, SCI, SCOPUS, T02, W07.
—BLDSC (2112.300000), CASDDS, GNLM, IE, Infotrieve, Ingenta, INIST. **CCC.**
Published by: (Blood Cells Foundation), Academic Press (Subsidiary of: Elsevier Science & Technology), 3251 Riverport Ln, Maryland Heights, MO 63043. TEL 314-447-8010, FAX 314-447-8030, JournalCustomerService-usa@elsevier.com, http://www.elsevierdirect.com/imprint.jsp?iid=5. Ed. Dr. M A Lichtman TEL 585 275-2205. Adv. contact Tino DeCarlo TEL 212-633-3815.

616.15 USA ISSN 0957-5235
QP93.5 CODEN: BLFIE7

➤ **BLOOD COAGULATION AND FIBRINOLYSIS.** Text in English. 1990. 8/yr. USD 2,331 domestic to institutions; USD 2,506 foreign to institutions (effective 2011). adv. bk.rev. back issues avail.; reprints avail. **Document type:** *Journal, Academic/Scholarly.* **Description:** Features review and research articles on all clinical, laboratory and experimental aspects of haemostasis and thrombosis.
Related titles: Online - full text ed.: ISSN 1473-5733.
Indexed: A22, ASCA, B25, BIOBASE, BIOSIS Prev, CIN, ChemAb, ChemTitl, CurCont, E01, EMBASE, ExcerpMed, IABS, ISR, IndMed, Inpharma, MEDLINE, MycolAb, P30, P35, R10, Reac, SCI, SCOPUS, VITIS, W07.
—BLDSC (2112.650000), CASDDS, GNLM, IE, Infotrieve, Ingenta, INIST. **CCC.**
Published by: Lippincott Williams & Wilkins (Subsidiary of: Wolters Kluwer N.V.), 530 Walnut St, Philadelphia, PA 19106. TEL 215-521-8300, FAX 215-521-8902, customerservice@lww.com, http://www.lww.com. Eds. Evgueni L Saenko TEL 410-706-8226, Richard Marlar TEL 405-270-0501 ext 5261. Pub. Phil Daly. Circ: 201.

➤ **BLOOD PRESSURE MONITORING.** *see* MEDICAL SCIENCES—Cardiovascular Diseases

616.15 CHE ISSN 0253-5068
RC901.7.H45 CODEN: BLPUDO

➤ **BLOOD PURIFICATION.** Text and summaries in English. 1983. bi-m. CHF 3,036, EUR 2,426, USD 2,976 to institutions; CHF 3,332, EUR 2,664, USD 3,262 combined subscription to institutions (print & online eds.) (effective 2012). adv. illus. index. back issues avail. **Document type:** *Journal, Academic/Scholarly.* **Description:** Includes practical information on hemodialysis, hemofiltration, peritoneal dialysis and plasma filtration.
Related titles: Microform ed.: (from PQC); Online - full text ed.: ISSN 1421-9735. CHF 2,968, EUR 2,374, USD 2,882 to institutions (effective 2012).
Indexed: A01, A03, A08, A22, ASCA, B25, BIOSIS Prev, CA, CIN, ChemAb, ChemTitl, CurCont, E01, EMBASE, ExcerpMed, ISR, IndMed, Inpharma, MEDLINE, MycolAb, P30, P35, R10, Reac, SCI, SCOPUS, T02, W07.
—BLDSC (2113.037000), CASDDS, GNLM, IE, Infotrieve, Ingenta, INIST. **CCC.**
Published by: S. Karger AG, Allschwilerstr 10, Basel, 4055, Switzerland. TEL 41-61-3061111, FAX 41-61-3061234, karger@karger.ch, http://www.karger.ch. Ed. Claudio Ronco. adv.: page CHF 1,815; trim 210 x 280. Circ: 1,000.

616.15 GBR ISSN 0268-960X
CODEN: BLOREB

➤ **BLOOD REVIEWS.** Text in English. 1987. bi-m. EUR 692 in Europe to institutions; JPY 74,500 in Japan to institutions; USD 628 elsewhere to institutions (effective 2012). adv. back issues avail.; reprints avail. **Document type:** *Journal, Academic/Scholarly.* **Description:** Covers all aspects of hematology. Presents current ideas in clinical and laboratory practice.
Related titles: Online - full text ed.: ISSN 1532-1681 (from ScienceDirect).
Indexed: A22, A26, ASCA, BIOBASE, BIOSIS Prev, CA, CurCont, E01, EMBASE, ExcerpMed, I05, IABS, ISR, IndMed, Inpharma, MEDLINE, MycolAb, P30, R10, Reac, RefZh, SCI, SCOPUS, T02, W07.
—BLDSC (2113.038000), GNLM, IE, Infotrieve, Ingenta, INIST. **CCC.**
Published by: Churchill Livingstone (Subsidiary of: Elsevier Health Sciences), The Blvd, Langford Ln, Kidlington, OX5 1GB, United Kingdom. TEL 44-1865-843434, FAX 44-1865-843970, directenquiries@elsevier.com, http://www.elsevierhealth.com/imprint.jsp?iid=9. Eds. Dr. Jacob M Rowe TEL 972-4854-2541, Trevor Baglin TEL 44-1223-216748. Adv. contact Emma Steel TEL 44-207-4244221. Circ: 324.

616.15 ITA ISSN 1723-2007
CODEN: TRSABD

BLOOD TRANSFUSION. Text mainly in English. 1956. q. EUR 150 to institutions (effective 2009). adv. bk.rev. abstr.; bibl.; charts; illus. index. **Document type:** *Journal, Academic/Scholarly.*
Formerly (until Jan. 2003): La Trasfusione del Sangue (0041-1787)
Related titles: Online - full text ed.: free (effective 2011).
Indexed: EMBASE, ExcerpMed, MEDLINE, P30, R10, Reac, SCI, SCOPUS, W07.
—BLDSC (2113.055800), CASDDS, GNLM, IE, INIST.
Published by: (Societa Italiana di Medicina Trasfusionale e Immunoematologia), S I M T I Servizi srl, Viale Beatrice d'Este 5, Milan, 20122, Italy. TEL 39-02-58316525, FAX 39-02-58316353, editoria@simtiservizi.com. Ed. Claudio Velati.

616.6 USA ISSN 1065-6073
RC633.A1

BLOOD WEEKLY. Text in English. 1986. w. (43/yr.). USD 2,295 in US & Canada; USD 2,495 elsewhere; USD 2,525 combined subscription in US & Canada (print & online eds.); USD 2,755 combined subscription elsewhere (print & online eds.) (effective 2008). back issues avail. **Document type:** *Newsletter, Trade.* **Description:** Concentrates on blood-related news and research worldwide, with original reporting, reviews of periodicals and journal articles and calendars of forthcoming professional meetings.
Related titles: E-mail ed.; Online - full text ed.: ISSN 1532-4559. USD 2,295 combined subscription (online & email eds.); single user (effective 2008).
Indexed: A26, B02, B03, B15, B17, B18, CWI, G04, G06, G07, G08, H11, H12, H13, I05, P10, P19, P20, P24, P48, P53, P54, PQC.
—CIS. **CCC.**
Published by: NewsRx, 2727 Paces Ferry Rd SE, Ste 2-440, Atlanta, GA 30339. TEL 770-435-8286, 800-726-4550, FAX 770-435-6800, pressrelease@newsrx.com. Pub. Susan Hasty TEL 770-507-7777.

616.15 GBR ISSN 1478-1247

➤ **BLOODMED**; the global source for hematology education, practice and research. Text in English. 2003. irreg. GBP 747 in United Kingdom to institutions; EUR 949 in Europe to institutions; USD 1,207 in the Americas to institutions; USD 1,465 elsewhere to institutions (effective 2009). reprints avail. **Document type:** *Journal, Academic/Scholarly.* **Description:** Provides high quality hematological resources to the broadest global community.
Media: Online - full content.
Published by: Wiley-Blackwell Publishing Ltd. (Subsidiary of: John Wiley & Sons, Inc.), 9600 Garsington Rd, Oxford, OX4 2DQ, United Kingdom. TEL 44-1865-776868, FAX 44-1865-714591, customerservices@blackwellpublishing.com, http://www.wiley.com/. Eds. Cheryl Willman, Dr. Finbarr Cotter. **Co-sponsor:** British Society for Haematology.

616.15 USA ISSN 2090-2999

▼ ➤ **BONE MARROW RESEARCH.** Text in English. 2011. irreg. USD 195 (effective 2011). **Document type:** *Journal, Academic/Scholarly.* **Description:** Publishes original research articles, review articles, and clinical studies related to all aspects of bone marrow.
Related titles: Online - full text ed.: ISSN 2090-3006. 2011. free (effective 2011).
Indexed: A01.
Published by: Hindawi Publishing Corporation, 410 Park Ave, 15th Fl, PMB 287, New York, NY 10022. FAX 215-893-4392, 866-446-3294, info@hindawi.com.

616.15 GBR ISSN 0007-1048
RC633.A1 CODEN: BJHEAL

➤ **BRITISH JOURNAL OF HAEMATOLOGY.** Abbreviated title: B J H. Text in English. 1955. s-m. GBP 1,320 in United Kingdom to institutions; EUR 1,676 in Europe to institutions; USD 2,443 in the Americas to institutions; USD 2,849 elsewhere to institutions; GBP 1,518 combined subscription in United Kingdom to institutions (print & online eds.); EUR 1,929 combined subscription in Europe to institutions (print & online eds.); USD 2,809 combined subscription in the Americas to institutions (print & online eds.); USD 3,277 combined subscription elsewhere to institutions (print & online eds.) (effective 2012). adv. bk.rev. bibl.; charts; illus. index. back issues avail.; reprint service avail. from PSC. **Document type:** *Journal, Academic/Scholarly.* **Description:** Provides original research papers in clinical, laboratory and experimental haematology.
Related titles: CD-ROM ed.; Microform ed.: (from PQC); Online - full text ed.: ISSN 1365-2141. 1997. GBP 1,320 in United Kingdom to institutions; EUR 1,676 in Europe to institutions; USD 2,443 in the Americas to institutions; USD 2,849 elsewhere to institutions (effective 2012) (from IngentaConnect); ◆ Supplement(s): British Journal of Haematology. Supplement. ISSN 0963-1860.
Indexed: A01, A02, A03, A08, A22, A26, A34, A35, A36, A38, ASCA, AgBio, B20, B21, B25, BIOBASE, BIOSIS Prev, C11, CA, CABA, CIN, ChemAb, ChemTitl, CurCont, DBA, DentInd, E01, E12, EMBASE, ESPM, ExcerpMed, GH, H04, H12, H17, IABS, INI, ISR, ImmunAb, IndMed, IndVet, Inpharma, LT, MEDLINE, MycolAb, N02, N03, P30, P33, P35, P39, R08, R10, RA&MP, RM&VM, RRTA, Reac, RefZh, SCI, SCOPUS, T02, T05, Telegen, VS, W07.
—BLDSC (2309.000000), CASDDS, GNLM, IE, Infotrieve, Ingenta, INIST. **CCC.**
Published by: Wiley-Blackwell Publishing Ltd. (Subsidiary of: John Wiley & Sons, Inc.), 9600 Garsington Rd, Oxford, OX4 2DQ, United Kingdom. TEL 44-1865-776868, FAX 44-1865-714591, customerservices@blackwellpublishing.com. Eds. Deborah Rund, Dr. Finbarr Cotter. Pub. Allen Stevens. R&P Sophie Savage. Adv. contact Jenny Applin. Circ: 3,430. **Co-sponsors:** European Haematology Association; British Society for Haematology.

616.15 GBR ISSN 0963-1860

BRITISH JOURNAL OF HAEMATOLOGY. SUPPLEMENT. Text in English. 1967. irreg. includes with subscr. to British Journal of Haematology. adv. **Document type:** *Journal, Academic/Scholarly.*
Related titles: Online - full text ed.; ◆ Supplement to: British Journal of Haematology. ISSN 0007-1048.
Indexed: SCOPUS.
—Infotrieve, INIST. **CCC.**
Published by: Wiley-Blackwell Publishing Ltd. (Subsidiary of: John Wiley & Sons, Inc.), 9600 Garsington Rd, Oxford, OX4 2DQ, United Kingdom. TEL 44-1865-776868, FAX 44-1865-714591, customerservices@blackwellpublishing.com, http://www.wiley.com/. Pub. Allen Stevens. R&P Sophie Savage. Adv. contact Jenny Applin.

CALCIFIED TISSUE INTERNATIONAL. *see* MEDICAL SCIENCES—Endocrinology

616.15 CAN ISSN 0840-5360

CANADIAN RED CROSS SOCIETY. BLOOD SERVICES. ANNUAL REPORT. Text in English, French. 1946. a. free.
Formerly (until 1986): Canadian Red Cross Blood Transfusion Service. Annual Report (0708-7047)
Related titles: French ed.: Societe Canadienne de la Croix-Rouge. Services Transfusionnels. Rapport Annuel. ISSN 0840-6103.
Published by: Canadian Red Cross Society, National Headquarters, 5700 Cancross Court, Mississauga, ON L5R 3E9, Canada. TEL 416-890-1000. Circ: 6,000.

616.15 CAN ISSN 1912-3620

CANADIAN SOCIETY FOR TRANSFUSION MEDICINE. BULLETIN. Text in English. 1989. q. **Document type:** *Bulletin, Trade.*
Supersedes in part (1989-2004): Canadian Society for Transfusion Medicine. Bulletin (1180-0461)
Media: Online - full text. **Related titles:** French ed.: Societe Canadienne de Medecine Transfusionnelle. Bulletin. ISSN 1912-3639.
Published by: Canadian Society for Transfusion Medicine (C S T M)/Societe Canadienne de Medecine Transfusionnelle (S C M T), 774 Promenade Echo Dr, Ottawa, ON K1S 5N8, Canada. TEL 613-260-6198, FAX 613-730-1116, office@transfusion.ca, http://www.transfusion.ca/new/index.html.

CANCER DRUG DISCOVERY AND DEVELOPMENT. *see* MEDICAL SCIENCES—Oncology

CARDIOVASCULAR & HEMATOLOGICAL AGENTS IN MEDICINAL CHEMISTRY. *see* MEDICAL SCIENCES—Cardiovascular Diseases

CARDIOVASCULAR & HEMATOLOGICAL DISORDERS - DRUG TARGETS. *see* MEDICAL SCIENCES—Cardiovascular Diseases

616.15 USA ISSN 2090-6560

▼ ➤ **CASE REPORTS IN HEMATOLOGY.** Text in English. 2011. **Document type:** *Journal, Academic/Scholarly.* **Description:** Publishes case reports in all areas of hematology.
Related titles: Online - full text ed.: ISSN 2090-6579. 2011. free (effective 2011).
Published by: Hindawi Publishing Corporation, 410 Park Ave, 15th Fl, PMB 287, New York, NY 10022. FAX 215-893-4392, 866-446-3294, info@hindawi.com.

➤ **CEREBROVASCULAR DISEASES.** *see* MEDICAL SCIENCES—Psychiatry And Neurology

616.15 616.992 USA ISSN 1543-0790

➤ **CLINICAL ADVANCES IN HEMATOLOGY & ONCOLOGY.** Text in English. 2003. m. free (effective 2010). adv. back issues avail. **Document type:** *Journal, Academic/Scholarly.* **Description:** Aims to contribute to the advancement of these interrelated fields by providing indispensable editorial content to oncology, oncology/hematology, and pure hematology clinicians. Editorial content encompasses a wide array of topics relevant to the fields of oncology and hematology.
Indexed: EMBASE, ExcerpMed, MEDLINE, P30, R10, Reac, SCOPUS.
—BLDSC (3286.244800), IE, Ingenta. **CCC.**
Published by: Millennium Medical Publishing, Inc., 611 Broadway, Ste 310, New York, NY 10012. TEL 212-995-2211, FAX 212-995-5572, info@clinicaladvances.com. Ed. Dr. Bruce D Cheson. Adv. contact Paul McDaniel TEL 212-995-5552. Circ: 32,929.

616.15 USA ISSN 1076-0296
CODEN: CATHF9

➤ **CLINICAL AND APPLIED THROMBOSIS / HEMOSTASIS.** Text in English. 1995. bi-m. USD 1,091, GBP 642 combined subscription to institutions (print & online eds.); USD 1,069, GBP 629 to institutions (effective 2011). adv. back issues avail.; reprint service avail. from PSC. **Document type:** *Journal, Academic/Scholarly.* **Description:** Publishes the latest results of new clinical trials and studies, discussions of new pharmacologic methodologies, and new management strategies.
Related titles: Microform ed.: (from PQC); Online - full text ed.: ISSN 1938-2723. USD 982, GBP 578 to institutions (effective 2011).
Indexed: A22, ASCA, CA, CurCont, E01, EMBASE, ExcerpMed, IndMed, Inpharma, MEDLINE, P30, P35, R10, Reac, SCI, SCOPUS, T02, W07.
—BLDSC (3286.247800), CASDDS, GNLM, IE, Infotrieve, Ingenta, INIST. **CCC.**
Published by: (Academy of Clinical and Applied Thrombosis - Hemostasis), Sage Publications, Inc., 2455 Teller Rd, Thousand Oaks, CA 91320. TEL 805-499-9774, 800-818-7243, FAX 805-499-0871, 800-583-2665, info@sagepub.com, http://www.sagepub.com. Ed. Russell D Hull. adv.: B&W page USD 620, color page USD 1,555. Circ: 684.

616.15 NLD ISSN 1386-0291
QP105.15 CODEN: CHMIFQ

➤ **CLINICAL HEMORHEOLOGY AND MICROCIRCULATION**; an international journal on blood flow, vessel wall, interstitium, transport and interactions. Text in English. 1981. m. (in 2 vols.). USD 1,938 combined subscription in North America (print & online eds.); EUR 1,385 combined subscription elsewhere (print & online eds.) (effective 2012). adv. **Document type:** *Journal, Academic/Scholarly.* **Description:** Topics covered include pathogenesis, symptomatology, and diagnostic, prophylactic and therapeutic methods.

Formerly (until 1997): Clinical Hemorheology (0271-5198)
Related titles: Microfilm ed.: (from PQC); Online - full text ed.: ISSN 1875-8622 (from IngentaConnect).
Indexed: A01, A03, A08, A20, A22, A34, A36, ASCA, B25, BIOSIS Prev, CA, CABA, ChemAb, CurCont, E01, E12, EMBASE, ExcerpMed, F08, GH, IBR, IBZ, ISR, IndMed, IndVet, Inpharma, MEDLINE, MycolAb, N02, N03, P30, P33, P35, R08, R10, RA&MP, Reac, SCI, SCOPUS, T02, T05, VS, W07.
—BLDSC (3286.290050), CASDDS, GNLM, IE, Infotrieve, Ingenta, INIST. **CCC.**
Published by: I O S Press, Nieuwe Hemweg 6B, Amsterdam, 1013 BG, Netherlands. TEL 31-20-6883355, FAX 31-20-6870019, info@iospress.nl. Eds. Dr. F Jung, H Niimi, J.-F. Stoltz, S Forconi. Circ: 300. **Subscr. to:** Globe Publication Pvt. Ltd., C-62 Inderpuri, New Delhi 100 012, India. TEL 91-11-579-3212, 91-11-579-3211, FAX 91-11-579-8876, custserve@globepub.com, http://www.globepub.com; I O S Press, Inc, 4502 Rachael Manor Dr, Fairfax, VA 22032-3631. iosbooks@iospress.com; Kinokuniya Co Ltd., Shinjuku 3-chome, Shinjuku-ku, Tokyo 160-0022, Japan. FAX 81-3-3439-1094, journal@kinokuniya.co.jp, http://www.kinokuniya.co.jp.

➤ **CLINICAL LABORATORY**; journal for clinical laboratories and laboratories related to blood transfusion. *see* MEDICAL SCIENCES—Endocrinology

➤ **CLINICAL LEUKEMIA (ONLINE).** *see* MEDICAL SCIENCES—Oncology

➤ **CLINICAL LYMPHOMA, MYELOMA & LEUKEMIA.** *see* MEDICAL SCIENCES—Oncology

616.15 NZL ISSN 1179-545X
RC633.A1
▼ **CLINICAL MEDICINE INSIGHTS: BLOOD DISORDERS.** Text in English. 2010. irreg. free (effective 2011). **Document type:** *Journal, Academic/Scholarly.*
Media: Online - full text.
Indexed: A01, C06, C07, T02.
—CCC.
Published by: Libertas Academica Ltd., PO Box 302-624, North Harbour, Auckland, 1330, New Zealand. TEL 64-21-662617, FAX 64-21-740006, editorial@la-press.com. Ed. Robert E Richard.

616.15 GBR ISSN 1618-5641
QP91 CODEN: CCPOAJ
➤ **COMPARATIVE CLINICAL PATHOLOGY.** Text in English. 1991. q. EUR 748, USD 746 combined subscription to institutions (print & online eds.) (effective 2011). back issues avail.; reprint service avail. from PSC. **Document type:** *Journal, Academic/Scholarly.* **Description:** Publishes papers encompassing the entire spectrum of comparative haematology, including immunological, toxicological and cellular aspects, data from human, veterinary and zoological studies, as well as experimental and diagnostic studies.
Formerly (until 2002): Comparative Haematology International (0938-7714)
Related titles: Online - full text ed.: ISSN 1618-565X (from IngentaConnect).
Indexed: A01, A03, A08, A22, A26, A34, A35, A36, A38, ASCA, AgBio, Agr, AgrForAb, CA, CABA, CIN, ChemAb, ChemTitl, D01, E01, E12, F08, F11, F12, G11, GH, H16, H17, ISR, IndVet, Inpharma, MaizeAb, N02, N03, N04, P30, P33, P37, P39, R08, R12, R13, RA&MP, RM&VM, SCOPUS, T02, T05, TAR, TriticAb, VS, W10, W11, Z01.
—BLDSC (3363.752705), CASDDS, GNLM, IE, Infotrieve, Ingenta. **CCC.**
Published by: Springer U K (Subsidiary of: Springer Science+Business Media), Ashbourne House, The Guildway, Old Portsmouth Rd, Guildford, Surrey GU3 1LP, United Kingdom. TEL 44-1483-734433, FAX 44-1483-734411, postmaster@svl.co.uk. Ed. Dr. Paul Sibbons TEL 44-181-869-3266. Adv. contact Clare Colwell. **Subscr. in the Americas to:** Springer New York LLC, Journal Fulfillment, PO Box 2485, Secaucus, NJ 07096. TEL 800-777-4643, 201-348-4033, FAX 201-348-4505, journals-ny@springer.com, http://www.springer.com; **Subscr. to:** Springer Distribution Center, Kundenservice Zeitschriften, Haberstr 7, Heidelberg 69126, Germany. TEL 49-6221-3454303, FAX 49-6221-3454229, subscriptions@springer.com.

616.15 USA ISSN 1931-2482
➤ **CONTEMPORARY HEMATOLOGY.** Text in English. 1977-1984; resumed 1998. irreg. price varies. illus. Index. 350 p./no.; back issues avail.; reprints avail. **Document type:** *Monographic series, Academic/Scholarly.* **Description:** Includes myeloma, infectious diseases, the newest therapies for lymphoma, and epigenetic modulation.
Former titles: Contemporary Hematology - Oncology (0197-3649); (until 1980): Year in Hematology (0160-7014)
Related titles: Online - full text ed.
—CASDDS, GNLM.
Published by: Humana Press, Inc. (Subsidiary of: Springer Science+Business Media), 233 Spring St, New York, NY 10013. TEL 212-460-1500, FAX 212-460-1575, service-ny@springer.com. Ed. Judith E karp.

➤ **CORRESPONDANCES EN ONCO-HEMATOLOGIE.** *see* MEDICAL SCIENCES—Oncology

➤ **CRITICAL REVIEWS IN ONCOLOGY / HEMATOLOGY.** *see* MEDICAL SCIENCES—Oncology

➤ **CURRENT CLINICAL ONCOLOGY.** *see* MEDICAL SCIENCES—Oncology

616.15 USA ISSN 1558-8211
CURRENT HEMATOLOGIC MALIGNANCY REPORTS. Text in English. 2006 (Jan.). q. reprint service avail. from PSC. **Document type:** *Journal, Academic/Scholarly.*
Related titles: Online - full text ed.: ISSN 1558-822X. EUR 870, USD 1,158 to institutions (effective 2010).
Indexed: A22, A26, E01, E08, EMBASE, ExcerpMed, H12, MEDLINE, P30, R10, Reac, S09, SCOPUS.
—BLDSC (3497.340000), IE. **CCC.**
Published by: Current Medicine Group LLC (Subsidiary of: Springer Science+Business Media), 400 Market St, Ste 700, Philadelphia, PA 19106. TEL 215-574-2266, 800-427-1796, FAX 215-574-2225, info@phl.cursci.com, http://www.current-medicine.com. Ed. Jorge Cortes.

616.15 USA ISSN 1065-6251
RC633.A1 CODEN: COHEF4
CURRENT OPINION IN HEMATOLOGY. Text in English. 1993. bi-m. USD 1,254 domestic to institutions; USD 1,346 foreign to institutions (effective 2011). adv. back issues avail.; reprints avail. **Document type:** *Journal, Academic/Scholarly.* **Description:** Covers key subjects such as myeloid biology, myeloid disease, vascular biology, lymphoid biology and diseases etc.
Related titles: Online - full text ed.: ISSN 1531-7048. USD 273 to individuals (effective 2011); Optical Disk - DVD ed.: Current Opinion in Hematology, with Evaluated MEDLINE. ISSN 1080-8213.
Indexed: A22, C06, C07, C08, CINAHL, CurCont, E01, EMBASE, ExcerpMed, IndMed, Inpharma, MEDLINE, P30, P35, R10, Reac, SCI, SCOPUS, W07.
—BLDSC (3500.775200), GNLM, IE, Infotrieve, Ingenta, INIST. **CCC.**
Published by: Lippincott Williams & Wilkins (Subsidiary of: Wolters Kluwer N.V.), 530 Walnut St, Philadelphia, PA 19106. TEL 215-521-8300, FAX 215-521-8902, customerservice@lww.com, http://www.lww.com. Ed. Thomas P Stossel. Pub. Ian Burgess. Circ: 616.

616.1 CHE ISSN 0258-0330
CODEN: CSHTE8
➤ **CURRENT STUDIES IN HEMATOLOGY AND BLOOD TRANSFUSION.** Text in English. 1955. irreg., latest vol.62, 1998. price varies. back issues avail.; reprints avail. **Document type:** *Monographic series, Academic/Scholarly.* **Description:** Presents current data in areas of hematology and transfusion medicine where problems are far from solved.
Formerly (until 1985): Bibliotheca Haematologica (0067-7957)
Related titles: Online - full text ed.: ISSN 1662-2952; ♦ Supplement to: Vox Sanguinis. ISSN 0042-9007.
Indexed: A22, CIN, ChemAb, ChemTitl, EMBASE, ExcerpMed, IndMed, MEDLINE, P30, SCOPUS.
—CASDDS, GNLM, Infotrieve, Ingenta, INIST. **CCC.**
Published by: (European Society of Hematology), S. Karger AG, Allschwilerstr 10, Basel, 4055, Switzerland. TEL 41-61-3061111, FAX 41-61-3061234, karger@karger.ch, http://www.karger.ch. Ed. H W Reesink.

615.505 GBR ISSN 1465-3249
➤ **CYTOTHERAPY.** Text in English. 1999. 8/yr. GBP 780, EUR 1,035, USD 1,295 combined subscription to institutions (print & online eds.); GBP 1,570, EUR 2,070, USD 2,590 combined subscription to corporations (print & online eds.) (effective 2010). adv. back issues avail.; reprint service avail. from PSC. **Document type:** *Journal, Academic/Scholarly.* **Description:** Covers new therapies emerging from the manipulation of cytokines and cells, also bringing readers the news and opinion in the fast-moving field of vaccines, cytokine and cellular therapy.
Incorporates (1997-2004): Cytokines, Cellular & Molecular Therapy (1368-4736); Which was formerly (1995-1997): Cytokines and Molecular Therapy (1355-6568)
Related titles: Online - full text ed.: ISSN 1477-2566. 2000 (from IngentaConnect).
Indexed: A01, A03, A08, A22, B&BAb, B19, B21, B25, B26, BIOBASE, BIOSIS Prev, CA, CurCont, E01, EMBASE, ExcerpMed, IABS, ImmunAb, Inpharma, M&PBA, MEDLINE, MycolAb, P30, P35, R10, Reac, SCI, SCOPUS, T02, W07.
—BLDSC (3506.883500), IE, Infotrieve, Ingenta. **CCC.**
Published by: (International Society for Cellular Therapy CAN), Informa Healthcare (Subsidiary of: T & F Informa plc), Telephone House, 69-77 Paul St, London, EC2A 4LQ, United Kingdom. TEL 44-20-70175000, FAX 44-20-70176792, healthcare.enquiries@informa.com. Eds. Edwin M Horwitz, Gunnar Kvalheim, Jedd Wolchok. **Subscr. in N. America:** Taylor & Francis Inc., Customer Services Dept, 325 Chestnut St, 8th Fl, Philadelphia, PA 19106. TEL 215-625-8900, 800-354-1420, FAX 215-625-8914, customerservice@taylorandfrancis.com; **Subscr. to:** Taylor & Francis Ltd., Journals Customer Service, Sheepen Pl, Colchester, Essex CO3 3LP, United Kingdom. TEL 44-20-70175544, FAX 44-20-70175198, tf.enquiries@tfinforma.com.

616.15 NLD ISSN 0167-9201
CODEN: DHIMDR
➤ **DEVELOPMENTS IN HEMATOLOGY AND IMMUNOLOGY.** Text in English. 1980. irreg., latest vol.39, 2005. price varies. **Document type:** *Monographic series, Academic/Scholarly.*
Formerly (until 1982): Developments in Hematology (0167-448X)
Indexed: CIN, ChemAb, ChemTitl.
—BLDSC (3579.075400), CASDDS, IE, Ingenta, INIST. **CCC.**
Published by: Springer Netherlands (Subsidiary of: Springer Science+Business Media), Van Godewijckstraat 30, Dordrecht, 3311 GX, Netherlands. TEL 31-78-6576050, FAX 31-78-6576474.

616.15 NLD ISSN 1361-4606
E H A NEWSLETTER. Text in English. 1995. s-a.
Published by: European Hematology Association, Westblaak 71, Rotterdam, 3012 KE, Netherlands. TEL 31-10-4361760, info@ehaweb.org. Eds. Catherine Lacombe, Shaun McCann.

616.15 EGY ISSN 1110-1067
THE EGYPTIAN JOURNAL OF HAEMATOLOGY. Text in English. 1976. q. **Document type:** *Magazine, Academic/Scholarly.*
Published by: The Egyptian Society of Haematology, 35 Ismaail Ramzy St, Heliopolis, Cairo, Egypt. TEL 202-2267-8336, FAX 202-2267-8338, esh@esh-egypt.org. Ed. Dr. Tarif Hamza Sallam.

616.15 FRA ISSN 1155-1984
➤ **ENCYCLOPEDIE MEDICO-CHIRURGICALE. HEMATOLOGIE.** Cover title: Traite d'Hematologie. Text in French. 1937. 3 base vols. plus q. updates. EUR 676 (effective 2006). bibl.; charts; illus. **Document type:** *Academic/Scholarly.* **Description:** Provides a comprehensive, up-to-date reference for diagnosing conditions in hematology.
Former titles (until 1990): Encyclopedie Medico-Chirurgicale, Instantanes Medicaux. Sang, Organes Hematopoietiques (0246-0556); (until 1959): Encyclopedie Medico-Chirurgicale. Sang, Organes Hematopoietiques, Systeme Vegetatif (0246-0696); (until 1951): Encyclopedie Medico-Chirurgicale. Sang, Systeme Vegetatif (0246-070X)
Related titles: Online - full text ed.
—INIST.
Published by: Elsevier Masson (Subsidiary of: Elsevier Health Sciences), 62 Rue Camille Desmoulins, Issy les Moulineaux, Cedex 92442, France. TEL 33-1-71165500, FAX 33-1-71165600, infos@elsevier-masson.fr.

616.15 USA ISSN 0902-4441
RC633.A1 CODEN: EJHAEC
➤ **EUROPEAN JOURNAL OF HAEMATOLOGY.** Text in English. 1964. m. GBP 922 in United Kingdom to institutions; EUR 1,170 in Europe to institutions; USD 1,548 in the Americas to institutions; USD 1,805 elsewhere to institutions; GBP 1,060 combined subscription in United Kingdom to institutions (print & online eds.); EUR 1,346 combined subscription in Europe to institutions (print & online eds.); USD 1,780 combined subscription in the Americas to institutions (print & online eds.); USD 2,076 combined subscription elsewhere to institutions (print & online eds.) (effective 2012). adv. bk.rev. bibl.; charts; illus. back issues avail.; reprint service avail. from PSC. **Document type:** *Journal, Academic/Scholarly.* **Description:** Reports basic and clinical research in haematology including molecular, cellular and clinical research on diseases of the blood, vascular and lymphatic tissue, and on basic molecular and cellular research related to normal development and function of the blood, vascular and lymphatic tissue.
Formerly (until 1987): Scandinavian Journal of Haematology (0036-553X)
Related titles: Online - full text ed.: ISSN 1600-0609. GBP 922 in United Kingdom to institutions; EUR 1,170 in Europe to institutions; USD 1,548 in the Americas to institutions; USD 1,805 elsewhere to institutions (effective 2012) (from IngentaConnect).
Indexed: A01, A02, A03, A08, A22, A26, A36, ASCA, AgrForAb, B25, BIOBASE, BIOSIS Prev, C11, CA, CABA, CIN, ChemAb, ChemTitl, CurCont, DentInd, E01, E12, EMBASE, ExcerpMed, F08, GH, H04, H12, IABS, ISR, IndMed, Inpharma, LT, MEDLINE, MycolAb, N02, N03, P30, P33, P35, P39, R07, R08, R10, RA&MP, RM&VM, RRTA, Reac, SCI, SCOPUS, T02, T05, W07.
—BLDSC (3829.729700), CASDDS, GNLM, IE, Infotrieve, Ingenta, INIST, Linda Hall. **CCC.**
Published by: Wiley-Blackwell Publishing, Inc. (Subsidiary of: Wiley-Blackwell Publishing Ltd.), Commerce Pl, 350 Main St, Malden, MA 02148. TEL 781-388-8200, FAX 781-388-8210, info@wiley.com, http://www.wiley.com/WileyCDA/. Ed. Niels Borregaard. Adv. contact Claire Rogers.

➤ **EXCERPTA MEDICA. SECTION 25: HEMATOLOGY.** *see* MEDICAL SCIENCES—Abstracting, Bibliographies, Statistics

616.15 USA ISSN 0301-472X
RB145 CODEN: EXHMA6
➤ **EXPERIMENTAL HEMATOLOGY.** Text in English. 1973. m. USD 916 in United States to institutions; USD 963 elsewhere to institutions (effective 2012). adv. back issues avail.; reprints avail. **Document type:** *Journal, Academic/Scholarly.* **Description:** Brings out research reports, reviews, letters to the editor, and abstracts of the annual meeting of the International Society for Experimental Hematology.
Related titles: Online - full text ed.: ISSN 1873-2399 (from IngentaConnect, ScienceDirect); ♦ Supplement(s): Experimental Hematology. Supplement. ISSN 0256-9280.
Indexed: A01, A03, A08, A22, A26, ASCA, B25, BIOSIS Prev, CA, CIN, ChemAb, ChemTitl, CurCont, DentInd, EMBASE, ExcerpMed, I05, INIS AtomInd, ISR, IndMed, Inpharma, MEDLINE, MycolAb, P30, P35, R10, Reac, SCI, SCOPUS, T02, W07.
—BLDSC (3839.360000), CASDDS, GNLM, IE, Infotrieve, Ingenta, INIST. **CCC.**
Published by: (International Society for Experimental Hematology), Elsevier Inc. (Subsidiary of: Elsevier Science & Technology), 1600 John F Kennedy Blvd, Philadelphia, PA 19103. TEL 215-239-3900, FAX 215-238-7883, JournalCustomerService-usa@elsevier.com, http://www.elsevier.com. Ed. Dr. Esmail D Zanjani. Adv. contact John Marmero Jr. TEL 212-633-3657.

615.15 GBR ISSN 1747-4086
➤ **EXPERT REVIEW OF HEMATOLOGY.** Text in English. 2008. bi-m. GBP 695 combined subscription domestic (print & online eds.); USD 1,220 combined subscription in North America (print & online eds.); JPY 129,000 combined subscription in Japan (print & online eds.); EUR 975 combined subscription elsewhere (print & online eds.) (effective 2011). adv. back issues avail.; reprints avail. **Document type:** *Journal, Academic/Scholarly.* **Description:** Provides commentary and analysis to elucidate best clinical practice in hematology today and helps to transform advances in research - in areas such as immunology, stem cell research, and cell and gene therapy - into the clinical context.
Related titles: Online - full text ed.: ISSN 1747-4094. GBP 615 domestic to institutions; USD 1,080 in North America to institutions; JPY 115,500 in Japan to institutions; EUR 865 elsewhere to institutions (effective 2011) (from IngentaConnect).
Indexed: A26, E08, EMBASE, H11, H12, I05, MEDLINE, P20, P30, P48, P54, PQC, SCI, SCOPUS, W07.
—BLDSC (9830.227000), IE. **CCC.**
Published by: Expert Reviews Ltd. (Subsidiary of: Future Science Ltd.), Unitec House, 2 Albert Pl, London, N3 1QB, United Kingdom. TEL 44-20-83716080, FAX 44-20-83716099, info@expert-reviews.com. Ed. Elisa Manzotti TEL 44-20-83716090. Pub. David Hughes. Adv. contact Simon Boisseau. Circ: 200.

616.15 RUS ISSN 1997-6976
FLEBOLOGIYA. Text in Russian. 2007. q. **Document type:** *Journal, Academic/Scholarly.*
Related titles: Online - full text ed.
Indexed: RefZh.
Published by: (Assotsiatsiya Flebologov Rossii), Media Sfera, Dmitrovskoe shosse 46, korp 2, etazh 4, P.O. Box 54, Moscow, 127238, Russian Federation. TEL 7-095-4824329, FAX 7-095-4824312, podpiska@mediasphera.ru, http://mediasphera.ru. Ed. A I Kirienko.

616.15 RUS ISSN 0234-5730
CODEN: GETRE8
➤ **GEMATOLOGIYA I TRANSFUSIOLOGIYA/HEMATOLOGY AND TRANSFUSIOLOGY.** Text in Russian; Summaries in English. 1956. bi-m. USD 242 foreign (effective 2005). adv. Website rev. **Document type:** *Journal, Academic/Scholarly.* **Description:** Publishes original theoretical and clinical investigations, reviews and clinical notes concerning different problems of hematology and blood transfusion.
Formerly (until 1983): Problemy Gematologii i Perelivaniya Krovi (0552-2080)
Indexed: ASCA, B25, BIOSIS Prev, CIN, ChemAb, ChemTitl, CurCont, IndMed, Inpharma, MycolAb, P30, P35, R10, Reac, RefZh, SCI, SCOPUS, W07.
—BLDSC (0047.072000), CASDDS, East View, GNLM, IE, Ingenta, INIST. **CCC.**

Published by: Izdatel'stvo Meditsina/Meditsina Publishers, ul B Pirogovskaya, d 2, str 5, Moscow, 119435, Russian Federation. TEL 7-095-2483324, meditsina@mtu-net.ru, http://www.medlit.ru. Ed. Andrei I Vorob'ev. Pub. A M Stochik. R&P L Kosmodemyanskaya. Adv. contact O A Fadeeva TEL 7-095-923-51-40. Circ: 1,100. **Dist. by:** M K - Periodica, ul Gilyarovskogo 39, Moscow 129110, Russian Federation. TEL 7-095-2845008, FAX 7-095-2813798, info@periodicals.ru, http://www.mkniga.ru.

616.15 CHN ISSN 1001-1013
GUOWAI YIXUE (SHUXUE YU XUEYEXUE FENCE)/FOREIGN MEDICAL SCIENCES (BLOOD TRANSFUSION AND HEMATOLOGY). Text in Chinese. 1979. bi-m. USD 37.20 (effective 2009). **Document type:** *Journal, Academic/Scholarly.*
Related titles: Online - full text ed.
—East View.
Published by: Zhonghua Yixue Kexueyuan, Shuxie Yanjiusuo/Chinese Academy of Medical Sciences, Blood Transfusion Research Institute, Sec.3, no.20, Renmin Nanlu, Sichuan Daxue, Huaxi De-2 Yiyuan, Chengdu, Sichuan 610041, China. TEL 86-28-85501759, FAX 86-28-85501764. **Dist. by:** China International Book Trading Corp, 35 Chegongzhuang Xilu, Haidian District, PO Box 399, Beijing 100044, China. TEL 86-10-68412045, FAX 86-10-68412023, cibtc@mail.cibtc.com.cn, http://www.cibtc.com.cn.

616.15 GRC ISSN 1108-2682 CODEN: HAGAB8
HAEMA. Text in English. 1998. q. EUR 75 to individuals; EUR 100 to institutions (effective 2007). **Document type:** *Journal, Academic/Scholarly.*
Related titles: Online - full text ed.
Indexed: EMBASE, ExcerpMed, R10, Reac, SCOPUS.
—BLDSC (4237.775000), IE.
Published by: Haema Journal, Epsilon, 20 Potamianou St., Athens, 11528, Greece. TEL 30-1-7487587, FAX 30-1-7487588.

616.15 DEU
HAEMATO-ONKOLOGISCHE NACHRICHTEN. Text in German. 2005. 6/yr. adv. **Document type:** *Journal, Academic/Scholarly.*
Formerly (until 2007): Kompakt Onkologie
Published by: Biermann Verlag GmbH, Otto-Hahn-Str 7, Cologne, 50997, Germany. TEL 49-2236-3760, FAX 49-2236-376999, info@biermann.net, http://www.biermann-verlag.de. Circ: 3,500 (controlled).

616.1 ITA ISSN 0390-6078
QP91 CODEN: HAEMAX
➤ **HAEMATOLOGICA**; the hematology journal. Text and summaries in English. 1914. m. EUR 400 combined subscription (print & online eds.) (effective 2009). adv. bk.rev. abstr.; bibl.; charts; illus. index. back issues avail.; reprints avail. **Document type:** *Journal, Academic/Scholarly.*
Formerly (until 1973): Haematologica Prima, Archivio (0390-606X); Which superseded in part (1020-1929): Haematologica. Archivio Italiano di Ematologia e Sierologia (0017-6567)
Related titles: Online - full text ed.: ISSN 1592-8721. free (effective 2011).
Indexed: A22, A29, ASCA, B&BAb, B20, B21, B25, BIOSIS Prev, CIN, ChemAb, ChemTitl, CurCont, EMBASE, ESPM, ExcerpMed, INI, ISR, IndMed, Inpharma, MEDLINE, MycolAb, P30, P35, R10, Reac, SCI, SCOPUS, VirolAbstr, W07.
—BLDSC (4238.000000), CASDDS, GNLM, IE, Infotrieve, Ingenta, INIST.
Published by: Fondazione Ferrata Storti, Strada Nuova 134, Pavia, PV 27100, Italy. TEL 39-0382-531182, FAX 39-0382-27721, http://www.haematologica.it. Circ: 2,000.

616.1 ITA ISSN 1970-7339
HAEMATOLOGY MEETING REPORTS. Text in Multiple languages. 2005. m. **Document type:** *Journal, Academic/Scholarly.*
Formerly (until 2006): Haematologica Reports (1824-9337)
Related titles: Online - full text ed.: free (effective 2006).
Indexed: A01, EMBASE, ExcerpMed, P30, SCOPUS, T02.
—BLDSC (4291.607500).
Published by: Fondazione Ferrata Storti, Strada Nuova 134, Pavia, PV 27100, Italy. TEL 39-0382-531182, FAX 39-0382-27721, http://www.haematologica.it.

616.1572 GBR ISSN 1351-8216
RC642
➤ **HAEMOPHILIA.** Text in English. 1994. bi-m. GBP 721 in United Kingdom to institutions; EUR 915 in Europe to institutions; USD 1,330 in the Americas to institutions; USD 1,552 elsewhere to institutions; GBP 829 combined subscription in United Kingdom to institutions (print & online eds.); EUR 1,053 combined subscription in Europe to institutions (print & online eds.); USD 1,530 combined subscription in the Americas to institutions (print & online eds.); USD 1,786 combined subscription elsewhere to institutions (print & online eds.) (effective 2012). adv. back issues avail.; reprint service avail. from PSC. **Document type:** *Journal, Academic/Scholarly.* **Description:** Contains review articles, original scientific papers and case reports related to haemophilia care, with frequent supplements.
Related titles: ◆ Online - full text ed.: Haemophilia Online. ISSN 1365-2516; ◆ Supplement(s): Haemophilia. Supplement. ISSN 1355-0691.
Indexed: A01, A02, A03, A08, A20, A22, A26, ASCA, B21, C11, CA, CurCont, E01, EMBASE, ExcerpMed, GenetAb, H04, H12, IndMed, Inpharma, MEDLINE, P30, P35, R10, Reac, SCI, SCOPUS, T02, W07.
—BLDSC (4238.086500), GNLM, IE, Infotrieve, Ingenta, INIST. **CCC.**
Published by: (World Federation of Haemophilia CAN), Wiley-Blackwell Publishing Ltd. (Subsidiary of: John Wiley & Sons, Inc.), 9600 Garsington Rd, Oxford, OX4 2DQ, United Kingdom. TEL 44-1865-776868, FAX 44-1865-714591, customerservices@blackwellpublishing.com. Eds. Christine A Lee, Craig Kessler.

616.15 AUS
HAEMOPHILIA FOUNDATION, VICTORIA. NEWSLETTER. Abbreviated title: H F V Newsletter(Haemophilia Foundation Victoria. Newsletter). Text in English. 1976. q. free to members (effective 2009). bk.rev. back issues avail. **Document type:** *Newsletter.* **Description:** Information for people with haemophilia and related bleeding disorders on their families and careers.
Formerly (until 1993): Haemophilia Society of Victoria. Newsletter
Related titles: Online - full text ed.
Published by: Haemophilia Foundation Victoria, 13 Keith St, Hampton East, VIC 3187, Australia. TEL 61-3-95557595, FAX 61-3-95557375, info@hfv.org.au, http://www.hfv.org.au.

616.1572 GBR ISSN 1365-2516
RC642
➤ **HAEMOPHILIA ONLINE.** Text in English. 1998. bi-m. GBP 721 in United Kingdom to institutions; EUR 915 in Europe to institutions; USD 1,330 in the Americas to institutions; USD 1,552 elsewhere to institutions (effective 2012). adv. back issues avail. **Document type:** *Journal, Academic/Scholarly.* **Description:** Contains review articles, original scientific papers and case reports related to haemophilia care, with frequent supplements.
Media: Online - full text (from IngentaConnect). **Related titles:** ◆ Print ed.: Haemophilia. ISSN 1351-8216.
—**CCC.**
Published by: (World Federation of Haemophilia CAN), Wiley-Blackwell Publishing Ltd. (Subsidiary of: John Wiley & Sons, Inc.), 9600 Garsington Rd, Oxford, OX4 2DQ, United Kingdom. TEL 44-1865-776868, FAX 44-1865-714591, customerservices@blackwellpublishing.com, http://www.wiley.com/.

615.1572 GBR ISSN 1355-0691
HAEMOPHILIA. SUPPLEMENT. Text in English. 1994. irreg. includes with subscr. to Haemophilia. adv. back issues avail.; reprints avail. **Document type:** *Monographic series, Academic/Scholarly.*
Related titles: Online - full text ed.; ◆ Supplement to: Haemophilia. ISSN 1351-8216.
Indexed: SCOPUS.
—INIST. **CCC.**
Published by: (World Federation of Haemophilia CAN), Wiley-Blackwell Publishing Ltd. (Subsidiary of: John Wiley & Sons, Inc.), 9600 Garsington Rd, Oxford, OX4 2DQ, United Kingdom. TEL 44-1865-776868, FAX 44-1865-714591, customerservices@blackwellpublishing.com, http://www.wiley.com/.

616.15 DEU ISSN 0720-9355 CODEN: HAEMD2
➤ **HAEMOSTASEOLOGIE**; Diagnostik, Therapie und Grundlagenforschung von Haemorrhagien und Thromboembolien. Text in German. 1981. 4/yr. EUR 140 to individuals; EUR 263 to institutions; EUR 70 to students; EUR 44 newsstand/cover (effective 2011). adv. **Document type:** *Journal, Academic/Scholarly.*
Related titles: Online - full text ed.
Indexed: A22, CIN, ChemAb, ChemTitl, EMBASE, ExcerpMed, MEDLINE, P30, R10, Reac, SCI, SCOPUS, W07.
—BLDSC (4241.515000), CASDDS, GNLM, IE. **CCC.**
Published by: Schattauer GmbH, Hoelderlinstr 3, Stuttgart, 70174, Germany. TEL 49-711-229870, FAX 49-711-2298750, info@schattauer.de, http://www.schattauer.com. Ed. Barbara Tshisuaka. Adv. contact Christian Matthe. Circ: 3,100 (paid and controlled).

616.15 DEU
HAMOTHERAPIE, BEITRAGE ZUR TRANSFUSIONSMEDIZIN. Text in German. 2003. irreg., latest vol.12, 2009. **Document type:** *Magazine, Trade.*
Formed by the merger of (1987-2003): Beitrage zur Transfusionsmedizin (0943-5476); (1983-2003): Hamotherapie (0936-8132); Which was formerly (until 1984): Hamo-Journal (0724-9608)
Related titles: Regional ed(s).: Hamotherapie, Beitrage zur Transfusionsmedizin (Sachsen Edition). ISSN 1612-5657; Hamotherapie, Beitrage zur Transfusionsmedizin (Bayern Edition). ISSN 1612-5584; Hamotherapie, Beitrage zur Transfusionsmedizin (Nordrhein-Westfalen, Rheinland-Pfalz, Saarland Edition). ISSN 1612-5606; Hamotherapie, Beitrage zur Transfusionsmedizin (Berlin, Brandenburg Edition). ISSN 1612-5649; Hamotherapie, Beitrage zur Transfusionsmedizin (Hamburg, Schleswig-Holstein Edition). ISSN 1612-5622; Hamotherapie, Beitrage zur Transfusionsmedizin (Mecklenburg-Vorpommern Edition). ISSN 1612-5630; Hamotherapie, Beitrage zur Transfusionsmedizin (Baden-Wurttemberg, Hessen Edition). ISSN 1612-5592; Hamotherapie, Beitrage zur Transfusionsmedizin (Bremen, Niedersachsen, Sachsen-Anhalt, Thuringen Edition). ISSN 1612-5614.
Published by: Deutsches Rotes Kreuz, D R K - Blutspendedienste, Feithstr 182, Hagen, 58097, Germany. TEL 49-2331-8070, FAX 49-2331-881326, https://www.drk-blutspende.de. Ed. Detlev Nagl.

616.15 USA ISSN 1088-7008
HEM AWARE. Text in English. 1996. bi-m. free to members. adv. illus. **Document type:** *Magazine, Consumer.* **Description:** Offers treatment news about bleeding disorders, highlights new programs and new resources in the field of hemophiliac research.
Published by: National Hemophilia Foundation, 116 W 32nd St, 11th Fl, New York, NY 10001. TEL 212-328-3700, 800-42-HANDI, FAX 212-328-3799. Ed. Blake Zeff. Pub., R&P Jodie Landes Corngold. Adv. contact Jacqueline Cortez.

616.15 616.992 USA ISSN 2150-5632
▼ ➤ **HEM-ONC.** Text in English. 2010 (July). q. USD 900 combined subscription in US & Canada to institutions (print & online eds.); USD 950 combined subscription elsewhere to institutions (print & online eds.) (effective 2010). **Document type:** *Journal, Academic/Scholarly.* **Description:** Provides cutting-edge information on basic and applied clinical research in leukemias, lymphomas, multiple myeloma and other hematologic malignancies.
Related titles: Online - full text ed.: ISSN 2150-5640. 2010 (July). USD 750 combined subscription to institutions (effective 2010).
Published by: Landes Bioscience, 1002 W Ave, Austin, TX 78701. TEL 512-637-6050, FAX 512-637-6079, info@landesbioscience.com.

616.15 616.99 USA ISSN 1526-0488
RC633.A1
➤ **HEM/ONC TODAY**; clinical news in hematology and oncology. Text in English. 1999. m. USD 429 to individuals; USD 549 to institutions; USD 39 per issue (effective 2010). adv. reprints avail. **Document type:** *Journal, Academic/Scholarly.* **Description:** Reports news and feature articles about clinical developments for the hematologists, the oncologists as well as hem/onc (the combined specialist).
Related titles: Online - full text ed.
Indexed: A01, P20, P34, P48, P54, PQC.
—**CCC.**
Published by: Slack, Inc., 6900 Grove Rd, Thorofare, NJ 08086. TEL 856-848-1000, FAX 856-848-6091, customerservice@slackinc.com, http://www.slackinc.com. Ed. Harry Jacob. Adv. contact Robin Geller TEL 877-307-5255 ext 267.

616.15 POL ISSN 2081-0768
▼ **HEMATOLOGIA.** Text in Polish. 2010. q. PLZ 84 to individuals; PLZ 167 to institutions (effective 2011). **Document type:** *Journal, Academic/Scholarly.*
Related titles: Online - full text ed.: ISSN 2081-3287.
Published by: (Instytut Hematologii i Transfuzjologii), Wydawnictwo Via Medica, ul Swietokrzyska 73, Gdansk, 80180, Poland. TEL 48-58-3209494, FAX 48-58-3209460, redakcja@viamedica.pl, http://www.viamedica.pl. Ed. Krzystof Warzocha.

616.15 616.07 ESP ISSN 1138-6029 CODEN: HEMABW
➤ **HEMATOLOGIA, CITOQUINAS, INMUNOTERAPIA Y TERAPIA CELULAR.** Text in Spanish; Abstracts in Spanish, English. 1998. q. EUR 50 to qualified personnel; EUR 76 to institutions; EUR 38 to students (effective 2005). adv. abstr.; bibl.; illus.; stat. back issues avail. **Document type:** *Journal, Academic/Scholarly.*
Related titles: CD-ROM ed.
Indexed: SCOPUS.
—**CCC.**
Published by: Aran Ediciones, Castello 128, 1o, Madrid, 28006, Spain. TEL 34-91-7820030, FAX 34-91-5615787, edita@grupoaran.com, http://www.grupoaran.com. Ed. J. Garcia Conde. Pub. Jose Jimenez Marquez. R&P Maria Dolores Linares TEL 34-91-7820035. Circ: 3,000.

616.15 ESP ISSN 1886-4325
HEMATOLOGIA PRACTICA. Text in Spanish. 2006. 3/yr. **Document type:** *Journal, Trade.*
Published by: Ediciones Mayo S.A., Calle Aribau 185-187, 2a Planta, Barcelona, 08021, Spain. TEL 34-93-2090255, FAX 34-93-2020643, edmayo@ediciones.mayo.es, http://www.edicionesmayo.es. Circ: 1,000.

616.15 GBR ISSN 0278-0232
RC280.H47 CODEN: HAONDL
➤ **HEMATOLOGICAL ONCOLOGY.** Text in English. 1983. q. GBP 880 in United Kingdom to institutions; EUR 1,112 in Europe to institutions; USD 1,724 elsewhere to institutions; GBP 968 combined subscription in United Kingdom to institutions (print & online eds.); EUR 1,224 combined subscription in Europe to institutions (print & online eds.); USD 1,897 combined subscription elsewhere to institutions (print & online eds.) (effective 2010). adv. bk.rev. charts; illus. index. back issues avail.; reprint service avail. from PSC. **Document type:** *Journal, Academic/Scholarly.* **Description:** Presents a variety of clinical and scientific specialties concerned with neoplastic disease of the hemopoietic system, and any neoplastic or related process that may directly or indirectly involve the hemopoietic system.
Related titles: Microform ed.: (from PQC); Online - full text ed.: ISSN 1099-1069. GBP 880 in United Kingdom to institutions; EUR 1,112 in Europe to institutions; USD 1,724 elsewhere to institutions (effective 2010).
Indexed: A22, A29, ASCA, B20, B21, B25, BIOBASE, BIOSIS Prev, C06, C07, C08, CINAHL, CTA, ChemAb, CurCont, EMBASE, ESPM, ExcerpMed, I10, IABS, ISR, IndMed, Inpharma, MEDLINE, MycolAb, NSA, P30, P35, R10, Reac, SCI, SCOPUS, T02, Telegen, VirolAbstr, W07.
—CASDDS, GNLM, IE, Infotrieve, Ingenta, INIST. **CCC.**
Published by: John Wiley & Sons Ltd. (Subsidiary of: John Wiley & Sons, Inc.), 1-7 Oldlands Way, PO Box 808, Bognor Regis, West Sussex PO21 9FF, United Kingdom. TEL 44-1865-778315, FAX 44-1243-843232, cs-journals@wiley.com, http://eu.wiley.com/WileyCDA/. Ed. Francesco Bertoni. **Subscr. to:** John Wiley & Sons, Inc., 111 River St, Hoboken, NJ 07030. TEL 201-748-6645, subinfo@wiley.com

616.1 FRA ISSN 1264-7527
➤ **HEMATOLOGIE.** Text in French. 1995. bi-m. EUR 384 domestic to institutions (print & online eds.); EUR 408 in the European Union to institutions (print & online eds.); EUR 420 elsewhere to institutions (print & online eds.) (effective 2011). **Document type:** *Journal, Academic/Scholarly.*
Related titles: CD-ROM ed.: ISSN 1766-0327; Online - full text ed.: ISSN 1950-6368.
Indexed: EMBASE, ExcerpMed, Inpharma, R10, Reac, SCOPUS.
—BLDSC (4291.552000), IE, Ingenta, INIST. **CCC.**
Published by: John Libbey Eurotext, 127 Av. de la Republique, Montrouge, 92120, France. TEL 33-1-46730660, FAX 33-1-40840999, contact@jle.com, http://www.john-libbey-eurotext.fr. Ed. Francois Sigaux.

616 USA ISSN 1520-4391
RC633.A2
HEMATOLOGY. Text in English. 1969. a. free to members (effective 2010). back issues avail. **Document type:** *Journal, Academic/Scholarly.*
Formerly (until 1980): Education Program
Related titles: Online - full text ed.: ISSN 1520-4383. 2000. free (effective 2011).
Indexed: EMBASE, ExcerpMed, MEDLINE, P30, R10, Reac, SCOPUS.
—**CCC.**
Published by: American Society of Hematology, 1900 M St, NW, Ste 200, Washington, DC 20036. TEL 202-776-0544, FAX 202-776-0545, ash@hematology.org, http://www.hematology.org. Eds. Alan M Gewirtz, Alexis A Thompson, Armand Keating.

616.15 GBR ISSN 1024-5332 CODEN: HMATFL
➤ **HEMATOLOGY.** Text in French. 1985. bi-m. GBP 647 combined subscription to institutions (print & online eds.); USD 1,099 combined subscription in United States to institutions (print & online eds.) (effective 2012). reprint service avail. from PSC. **Document type:** *Journal, Academic/Scholarly.* **Description:** Aims to bridge the interests and practices of both those carrying out laboratory work and those whose main inclination is towards patient care.
Supersedes (with vol.9): Hematology Reviews and Communications (0882-8083)
Related titles: CD-ROM ed.; Microform ed.; Online - full text ed.: ISSN 1607-8454. GBP 582 to institutions; USD 989 in United States to institutions (effective 2012) (from IngentaConnect).
Indexed: A01, A03, A08, A22, ASCA, CA, CurCont, E01, EMBASE, ExcerpMed, MEDLINE, P30, R10, Reac, SCI, SCOPUS, T02, W07.
—BLDSC (4291.565000), GNLM, IE, Infotrieve, Ingenta. **CCC.**

Published by: (International Society of Hematology INT), Maney Publishing, Ste 1C, Joseph's Well, Hanover Walk, Leeds, W Yorks LS3 1AB, United Kingdom. TEL 44-113-2432800, FAX 44-113-3868178, maney@maney.co.uk, http://www.maney.co.uk. Ed. Adrian Newland. **Subscr. in N. America to:** Maney Publishing, 875 Massachusetts Ave, 7th Fl, Cambridge, MA 02139. TEL 866-297-5154, FAX 617-354-6875, maney@maneyusa.com.

616.15 NLD ISSN 1872-5503
HEMATOLOGY EDUCATION. Text in English. 2005. a.
Formerly (until 2006): Hematology (1872-2202)
Published by: European Hematology Association, Westblaak 71, Rotterdam, 3012 KE, Netherlands. TEL 31-10-4361760, FAX 31-10-4361817, info@ehaweb.org, http://www.ehaweb.org.

616.15 616.992 616.02774 SAU ISSN 1658-3876
RC633.A1
➤ **HEMATOLOGY - ONCOLOGY AND STEM CELL THERAPY.** Text in English. 2008. irreg. **Document type:** *Journal, Academic/Scholarly.*
Description: Covers clinical and basic research in hematology and oncology and reflects the growing importance of stem cell therapy in treating hematological and other malignancies.
Related titles: Online - full text ed.
Indexed: EMBASE, ExcerpMed, MEDLINE, P30, R10, Reac, SCOPUS.
Published by: King Faisal Specialist Hospital and Research Centre, Publication Office (MBC 36), P O Box 3354, Riyadh, 11211, Saudi Arabia. TEL 966-1-4647272, web_annals@kfshrc.edu.sa, http://www.kfshrc.edu.sa. Ed. Mahmoud Aljurf.

616.15 PAK ISSN 1728-9467
HEMATOLOGY. PROCEEDINGS. Text in English. 1985. m. GBP 300 (effective 2005). **Document type:** *Proceedings, Academic/Scholarly.*
Description: Study of hematology and hemoparasitic diseases.
Published by: (International Society of Hematological Research), International Press, P O Box 17700, Karachi, 75300, Pakistan. TEL 92-21-4947486, FAX 92-21-4989257, light_68@hotmail.com. Ed. Dr. C H Badar.

616.15 ITA ISSN 2038-8322
➤ **HEMATOLOGY REPORTS.** Text in Multiple languages. 2007. q. **Document type:** *Journal, Academic/Scholarly.*
Formerly (until 2009): Hematology Reviews (1970-6804)
Related titles: Online - full text ed.: ISSN 2038-8330. free (effective 2011).
Indexed: A01, EMBASE, SCOPUS, T02.
Published by: Pagepress, Via Giuseppe Belli 4, Pavia, 27100, Italy. TEL 39-0382-1751762, FAX 39-0382-1750481. Ed. Giovanni Martinelli.

616.15 USA ISSN 1543-673X
HEMATOLOGY WEEK. Text in English. 2003. w. USD 2,295 in US & Canada; USD 2,495 elsewhere; USD 2,525 combined subscription in US & Canada (print & online eds.); USD 2,755 combined subscription elsewhere (print & online eds.) (effective 2008). back issues avail. **Document type:** *Newsletter, Trade.* **Description:** Covers current research, drug development, clinical trials, therapies and technologies impacting diseases and conditions of the blood; includes stem cell research.
Related titles: E-mail ed.; Online - full text ed.: ISSN 1543-6721. USD 2,295 combined subscription (online & email eds.); single user (effective 2008).
Indexed: A26, E08, G08, H11, H12, I05, S09.
—CIS.
Published by: NewsRx, 2727 Paces Ferry Rd SE, Ste 2-440, Atlanta, GA 30339. TEL 770-435-8286, 800-726-4550, FAX 770-435-6800, pressrelease@newsrx.com, http://www.newsrx.com. Pub. Susan Hasty TEL 770-507-7777.

616.15 USA ISSN 1492-7535
RC901.7.H45
HEMODIALYSIS INTERNATIONAL. Text in English. 1997. q. GBP 241 in United Kingdom to institutions; EUR 306 in Europe to institutions; USD 306 in the Americas to institutions; USD 471 elsewhere to institutions; GBP 278 combined subscription in United Kingdom to institutions (print & online eds.); EUR 352 combined subscription in Europe to institutions (print & online eds.); USD 352 combined subscription in the Americas to institutions (print & online eds.); USD 542 combined subscription elsewhere to institutions (print & online eds.) (effective 2012). adv. back issues avail.; reprint service avail. from PSC. **Document type:** *Journal, Academic/Scholarly.*
Description: Contains original articles, review articles, commentary and latest news to keep readers completely updated in the field of hemodialysis.
Formerly (until 2000): Home Hemodialysis International (1480-0225)
Related titles: Online - full text ed.: ISSN 1542-4758. GBP 241 in United Kingdom to institutions; EUR 306 in Europe to institutions; USD 306 in the Americas to institutions; USD 471 elsewhere to institutions (effective 2012) (from IngentaConnect).
Indexed: A01, A03, A08, A22, A26, A36, CA, CABA, CurCont, E01, E12, EMBASE, ExcerpMed, GH, MEDLINE, N02, N03, P30, P33, P39, R10, R12, RA&MP, RM&VM, Reac, SCI, SCOPUS, T02, T05, W07.
—BLDSC (4295.038000), IE, Ingenta. **CCC.**
Published by: (International Society for Hemodialysis), Wiley-Blackwell Publishing, Inc. (Subsidiary of: Wiley-Blackwell Publishing Ltd.), 111 River St, Hoboken, NJ 07030. TEL 201-748-6000, FAX 201-748-6088, info@wiley.com. Ed. Christopher R Blagg. Adv. contact Stephen Donohue TEL 781-388-8511.

616.15 GBR ISSN 0363-0269
RC641.7.H35 CODEN: HEMOD8
➤ **HEMOGLOBIN**; international journal for hemoglobin research. Text in English. 1976. bi-m. GBP 1,840, EUR 2,590, USD 3,240 combined subscription to institutions (print & online eds.); GBP 3,685, EUR 5,180, USD 6,475 combined subscription to corporations (print & online eds.) (effective 2010). adv. back issues avail.; reprint service avail. from PSC. **Document type:** *Journal, Academic/Scholarly.*
Description: Emphasizes several topic areas concerning normal, modified, and abnormal human hemoglobins.
Related titles: Microform ed.: (from RPI); Online - full text ed.: ISSN 1532-432X (from IngentaConnect).
Indexed: A01, A03, A08, A22, A36, ASCA, B21, B25, B27, BIOBASE, BIOSIS Prev, C33, CA, CABA, CIN, ChemAb, ChemTitl, E01, EMBASE, ExcerpMed, GH, GenetAb, IABS, ISR, IndMed, Inpharma, MEDLINE, MycolAb, N02, N03, P30, P33, P39, R10, R12, RA&MP, Reac, RefZh, SCI, SCOPUS, T02, T05, THA, W07.
—BLDSC (4295.040000), CASDDS, GNLM, IE, Infotrieve, Ingenta, INIST. **CCC.**

Published by: Informa Healthcare (Subsidiary of: T & F Informa plc), Telephone House, 69-77 Paul St, London, EC2A 4LQ, United Kingdom. TEL 44-20-70175000, FAX 44-20-70176792, healthcare.enquiries@informa.com. Ed. Dr. Henri Wajcman TEL 33-1-49813578. Adv. contact Per Sonnerfeldt. **Subscr. in N. America to:** Taylor & Francis Inc., Customer Services Dept, 325 Chestnut St, 8th Fl, Philadelphia, PA 19106. TEL 215-625-8900, 800-354-1420, FAX 215-625-8914, customerservice@taylorandfrancis.com; **Subscr. to:** Taylor & Francis Ltd., Journals Customer Service, Sheepen Pl, Colchester, Essex CO3 3LP, United Kingdom. TEL 44-20-70175544, FAX 44-20-70175198, tf.enquiries@tfinforma.com.

616.15 DEU
HEMOPHILIA SYMPOSIUM. Text in English. irreg., latest vol.37, 2006. price varies. **Document type:** *Monographic series, Academic/Scholarly.* **Description:** Covers epidemiolgy, treatment of inhibitors in hemophiliacs, hemophilic arthropathy and synovitis, relevant hemophilia treatment, and pediatric hemostasiology.
Related titles: Online - full text ed.
Published by: Springer (Subsidiary of: Springer Science+Business Media), Tiergartenstr 17, Heidelberg, 69121, Germany. TEL 49-6221-4870, FAX 49-6221-345229, subscriptions@springer.com, http://www.springer.com. Eds. I Scharrer, W Schramm.

616.15 CAN ISSN 0046-7251
HEMOPHILIA TODAY. Text in English. 1964. 3/yr. free. **Document type:** *Magazine, Academic/Scholarly.* **Description:** Strives to improve health and quality of life for all people with inherited bleeding disorders and find a cure.
Related titles: Online - full content ed.; French ed.: L' Hemophilie de Nos Jours. 1964.
Published by: Canadian Hemophilia Society, 625 President Kennedy Ave, Ste 505, Montreal, PQ H3A 1K2, Canada. TEL 514-848-0503, 800-668-2686, FAX 514-848-9661, chs@hemophilia.ca. Ed. Francois Laroche. Circ: 6,000.

616.15 USA ISSN 1941-8493
RB144
HEMOSTASIS LABORATORY. Text in English. 2008. q. USD 295 to institutions; USD 442 combined subscription to institutions (print & online eds.) (effective 2012). **Document type:** *Journal, Academic/Scholarly.* **Description:** Aims to increase the clinical and academic importance of hemostasis diagnostic.
Related titles: Online - full text ed.: USD 295 to institutions (effective 2012).
Published by: Nova Science Publishers, Inc., 400 Oser Ave, Ste 1600, Hauppauge, NY 11788. TEL 631-231-7269, FAX 631-231-8175, main@novapublishers.com. Ed. Thomas W Stief.

616.15 FRA ISSN 1630-7399
L'HEMOVIGILANCE. Text in French. 2000. irreg. **Document type:** *Bulletin, Trade.*
Media: Online - full text.
Published by: Agence Francaise de Securite Sanitaire des produits de Sante (A F S S A P S), 143, 147 Bd Anatole France, Saint-Denis, Cedex 93285, France. TEL 33-1-55873000.

616.15 NLD ISSN 2210-8580
HOOFDPUNTEN T R I P RAPPORT HEMO- EN WEEFSELLVIGILANTIE. (Transfusie Reacties in Patienten) Text in Dutch. 2008. a.
Published by: Stichting T R I P, Postbus 40551, The Hague, 2504 LN, Netherlands. TEL 31-70-3083120, FAX 31-70-3682626, info@tripnet.nl.

615.39 GBR ISSN 1751-2816
I S B T SCIENCE SERIES. Text in English. 2006 (Sep.). a. back issues avail.; reprint service avail. from PSC. **Document type:** *Monographic series, Academic/Scholarly.*
Related titles: Online - full text ed.: ISSN 1751-2824 (from IngentaConnect); ◆ Supplement to: Vox Sanguinis. ISSN 0042-9007.
Indexed: A01, A22, CA, E01, T02.
—BLDSC (4582.773100), IE, Ingenta, INIST. **CCC.**
Published by: (Societe Internationale de Transfusion Sanguine (S I T S)/International Society of Blood Transfusion (I S B T) NLD), Wiley-Blackwell Publishing Ltd. (Subsidiary of: John Wiley & Sons, Inc.), 9600 Garsington Rd, Oxford, OX4 2DQ, United Kingdom. TEL 44-1865-776868, FAX 44-1865-714591, customerservices@blackwellpublishing.com, http://www.wiley.com/.

616.15 USA ISSN 2090-441X
▼ ➤ **I S R N HEMATOLOGY.** (International Scholarly Research Network) Text in English. 2011. irreg. **Document type:** *Journal, Academic/Scholarly.*
Related titles: Online - full text ed.: ISSN 2090-4428. free (effective 2011).
Published by: Hindawi Publishing Corporation, 410 Park Ave, 15th Fl, PMB 287, New York, NY 10022. FAX 215-893-4392, 866-446-3294, info@hindawi.com.

616.15 USA ISSN 0894-203X
CODEN: IMMUEQ
IMMUNOHEMATOLOGY. Text in English. 1984. q.
Related titles: Online - full text ed.: ISSN 1930-3955.
Indexed: BIOBASE, EMBASE, ExcerpMed, IABS, MEDLINE, P30, R10, Reac, SCOPUS.
—BLDSC (4369.674500), IE, Ingenta.
Published by: American Red Cross, 2025 E St, NW, Washington, DC 20006. TEL 202-303-4498, info@usa.redcross.org.

INFORMATSIONNYI SBORNIK. SERDECHNO-SOSUDISTAYA KHIRURGIYA. NOVOSTI NAUKI I TEKHNIKI. *see* MEDICAL SCIENCES—Abstracting, Bibliographies, Statistics

616.15 BRA ISSN 0103-3263
CODEN: RIECF4
INSTITUTO ESTADUAL DE HEMATOLOGIA ARTHUR DE SIQUEIRA CAVALCANTI. REVISTA. Text in Portuguese; Summaries in English. 1971. s-a. bk.rev. bibl.; charts. reprint service avail. from IRC. **Document type:** *Journal, Academic/Scholarly.*
Formerly (until vol.4, no.2, 1976): Instituto Estadual de Hematologia Arthur de Siqueira Cavalcanti. Boletim (0046-9963)
Published by: Instituto Estadual de Hematologia Arthur de Siqueira Cavalcanti, Rua Frei Caneca 08, Rio de Janiero, RJ 20211-030, Brazil. TEL 55-21-22999442, http://www.hemorio.rj.gov.br.

INTERNATIONAL ANGIOLOGY; a journal on angiology. *see* MEDICAL SCIENCES—Cardiovascular Diseases

616.15 PAK ISSN 1021-0113
THE INTERNATIONAL JOURNAL OF HEMATOLOGICAL RESEARCH. Abbreviated title: I J H R. Text in English. 1985. m. GBP 300 (effective 2005). **Document type:** *Journal, Academic/Scholarly.* **Description:** Study of hematological research and hemoparasitic diseases over wide variety of species serves as a unifying discipline for veterinarians, clinical physicians and research scientists.
Published by: (International Society of Hematological Research), International Press, P O Box 17700, Karachi, 75300, Pakistan. TEL 92-21-4947486, FAX 92-21-4989257, light_68@hotmail.com. Ed. Dr. G A Gondal.

616.15 JPN ISSN 0925-5710
RB145 CODEN: IJHEEY
➤ **INTERNATIONAL JOURNAL OF HEMATOLOGY.** Text in English. 1938. 10/yr. EUR 273, USD 363 combined subscription to institutions (print & online eds.) (effective 2012). adv. bk.rev. reprint service avail. from PSC. **Document type:** *Journal, Academic/Scholarly.*
Description: Publishes original papers and reviews of international origin in basic and clinical hematology.
Formerly (until 1991): Acta Haematologica Japonica (0001-5806)
Related titles: Microform ed.: (from PQC); Online - full text ed.: ISSN 1865-3774. 2001 (from IngentaConnect).
Indexed: A20, A22, A29, A34, A35, A36, ASCA, ASFA, AgBio, B20, B21, B25, BIOBASE, BIOSIS Prev, BP, CABA, CIN, ChemAb, ChemTitl, CurCont, D01, DentInd, E01, E12, EMBASE, ESPM, ExcerpMed, GH, I10, IABS, IndMed, IndVet, Inpharma, MEDLINE, MycolAb, N02, N03, P20, P22, P24, P30, P33, P35, P39, P48, P54, PQC, R07, R08, R10, RA&MP, RM&VM, Reac, SCI, SCOPUS, T05, VS, VirolAbstr, W07.
—BLDSC (4542.280400), CASDDS, GNLM, IE, Infotrieve, Ingenta, INIST. **CCC.**
Published by: (Japanese Society of Hematology), Springer Japan KK (Subsidiary of: Springer Science+Business Media), No 2 Funato Bldg, 1-11-11 Kudan-kita, Chiyoda-ku, Tokyo, 102-0073, Japan. TEL 81-3-68317000, FAX 81-3-68317001, orders@springer.jp, http://www.springer.jp. Ed. Toshio Suda. Circ: 5,000.

616.15 IRN ISSN 1735-1243
INTERNATIONAL JOURNAL OF HEMATOLOGY-ONCOLOGY AND BONE MARROW TRANSPLANTATION. Text in English. 2004. q. IRR 2,400,000 domestic; USD 40 foreign (effective 2007). **Document type:** *Journal, Academic/Scholarly.*
Related titles: Online - full text ed.
Indexed: EMBASE, ExcerpMed.
Published by: Tehran University of Medical Sciences Publications, Central Library & Documents Center, Poursina St, Tehran, 14174, Iran. TEL 98-21-6112743, FAX 98-21-6404377, http://diglib.tums.ac.ir/pub/journals.asp. Ed. Ghavamzadeh A.

616.15 GBR ISSN 1751-553X
INTERNATIONAL JOURNAL OF LABORATORY HEMATOLOGY (ONLINE). Text in English. bi-m. GBP 971 in United Kingdom to institutions; EUR 1,234 in Europe to institutions; USD 1,798 in the Americas to institutions; USD 2,097 elsewhere to institutions (effective 2012). **Document type:** *Journal, Academic/Scholarly.*
Formerly (until 2007): Clinical and Laboratory Haematology (Online) (1365-2257)
Media: Online - full text (from IngentaConnect). **Related titles:** Microform ed.: (from PQC); ◆ Print ed.: International Journal of Laboratory Hematology (Print). ISSN 1751-5521.
—**CCC.**
Published by: Wiley-Blackwell Publishing Ltd. (Subsidiary of: John Wiley & Sons, Inc.), 9600 Garsington Rd, Oxford, OX4 2DQ, United Kingdom. TEL 44-1865-776868, FAX 44-1865-714591, customerservices@blackwellpublishing.com, http://www.wiley.com/WileyCDA/.

616.15 GBR ISSN 1751-5521
RC633.A1 CODEN: CLHAD3
➤ **INTERNATIONAL JOURNAL OF LABORATORY HEMATOLOGY (PRINT).** Text in English. 1979. bi-m. GBP 971 in United Kingdom to institutions; EUR 1,234 in Europe to institutions; USD 1,798 in the Americas to institutions; USD 2,097 elsewhere to institutions; GBP 1,118 combined subscription in United Kingdom to institutions (print & online eds.); EUR 1,420 combined subscription in Europe to institutions (print & online eds.); USD 2,069 combined subscription in the Americas to institutions (print & online eds.); USD 2,412 combined subscription elsewhere to institutions (print & online eds.) (effective 2012). adv. bk.rev. abstr.; bibl.; charts; illus. index. back issues avail.; reprint service avail. from PSC. **Document type:** *Journal, Academic/Scholarly.* **Description:** Provides a forum for the communication of new developments, research topics and the practice of clinical and laboratory haematology.
Formerly (until 2007): Clinical and Laboratory Haematology (Print) (0141-9854)
Related titles: Microform ed.: (from PQC); ◆ Online - full text ed.: International Journal of Laboratory Hematology (Online). ISSN 1751-553X.
Indexed: A01, A02, A03, A08, A22, A26, A36, ASCA, B21, C06, C07, C08, C11, CA, CABA, CINAHL, CurCont, E01, EMBASE, ExcerpMed, FR, GH, H04, H12, H17, IBR, IBZ, ISR, ImmunAb, IndMed, Inpharma, LT, MEDLINE, N02, N03, P30, P33, P39, R08, R10, RA&MP, RM&VM, RRTA, Reac, SCI, SCOPUS, T02, T05, W07.
—BLDSC (4542.312220), CASDDS, GNLM, IE, Infotrieve, Ingenta, INIST. **CCC.**
Published by: (International Society for Laboratory Hematology USA), Wiley-Blackwell Publishing Ltd. (Subsidiary of: John Wiley & Sons, Inc.), 9600 Garsington Rd, Oxford, OX4 2DQ, United Kingdom. TEL 44-1865-776868, FAX 44-1865-714591, customerservices@blackwellpublishing.com. Eds. Dr. Steve Kitchen, William G Finn.

616.15 USA ISSN 1540-2649
RB1
➤ **THE INTERNET JOURNAL OF HEMATOLOGY.** Text in English. 2003. s-a. free (effective 2011). adv. **Document type:** *Journal, Academic/Scholarly.*
Media: Online - full text.
Indexed: A01, A02, A03, A08, A26, C06, C07, CA, EMBASE, ExcerpMed, G08, H11, H12, I05, R10, Reac, SCOPUS, T02, T05.
Published by: Internet Scientific Publications, Llc., 23 Rippling Creek Dr, Sugar Land, TX 77479. TEL 832-443-1193, FAX 281-240-1533, wenker@ispub.com. Ed. Peter Horn.

➤ **IRONIC BLOOD**; information on iron overload. *see* MEDICAL SCIENCES—Endocrinology

612.1 AUT ISSN 1605-718X
JATROS HAEMATOLOGIE UND ONKOLOGIE. Text in German. 2000. 4/yr. EUR 18 (effective 2007). adv. **Document type:** *Journal, Academic/Scholarly.*
Related titles: Online - full text ed.: ISSN 1991-9131.
Published by: Universimed Verlags- und Service GmbH, Markgraf-Ruediger-Str 8, Vienna, 1150, Austria. TEL 43-1-87679560, FAX 43-1-876795620, office@universimed.com, http://www.universimed.com. Ed. Alice Kment. Adv. contact Karin Duderstadt. Circ: 4,200 (paid).

616.15 JPN ISSN 1341-1594
CODEN: JIKEFK
JINKO KETSUEKI/ARTIFICIAL BLOOD. Text in Japanese. 1993. q. JPY 10,000 membership (effective 2005). **Document type:** *Journal, Academic/Scholarly.*
—BLDSC (4669.040700).
Published by: Nihon Ketsueki Daitaibutsu Gakkai/Society of Blood Substitutes, Japan, Division of General Thoracic Surgery, Department of Surgery, Keio University, School of Medicine, 35 Shinanomachi,Shinjuku-ku, Tokyo, 160-8582, Japan. TEL 81-3-53633493, FAX 81-3-53633499, amorjsbs@sc.itc.keio.ac.jp, http://www.blood-sub.jp/home/.

616.15 CAN ISSN 0715-8602
JOURNAL: NEWS OF THE BLOOD PROGRAMME IN CANADA. Text in English, French. 1983. q. free.
Published by: Canadian Red Cross Society, National Headquarters, 5700 Cancross Court, Mississauga, ON L5R 3E9, Canada. TEL 416-890-1000. Circ: 4,000.

616.15 USA ISSN 2155-9864
▼ ➤ **JOURNAL OF BLOOD DISORDERS & TRANSFUSION.** Text in English. 2010 (Oct.). bi-m. free (effective 2011). **Document type:** *Journal, Trade.* **Description:** Covers all aspects of hematology, including disorders of platelets, leukocytes, erythrocytes, haemostatic mechanisms, immunology, vascular biology, immunology, and haematologic oncology.
Media: Online - full text.
Published by: Omics Publishing Group, 5716 Corse Ave, Ste 110, Westlake, Los Angeles, CA 91362. TEL 650-268-9744, 800-216-6499, info@omicsonline.com, http://www.omicsonline.com.

616.15 GBR ISSN 1179-2736
▼ ➤ **JOURNAL OF BLOOD MEDICINE.** Text in English. 2010. irreg. free (effective 2011). **Document type:** *Journal, Academic/Scholarly.*
Media: Online - full text.
—**CCC.**
Published by: Dove Medical Press Ltd., Beechfield House, Winterton Way, Macclesfield, SK11 0JL, United Kingdom. TEL 44-1625-509130, FAX 44-1625-617933. Ed. Martin H Bluth.

616.15 JPN ISSN 1346-4280
RC633.A1
JOURNAL OF CLINICAL AND EXPERIMENTAL HEMATOPATHOLOGY. Text in English. 2001. s-a. **Document type:** *Journal, Academic/Scholarly.*
Supersedes in part (in 2001): Nihon Rimpa Monaikei Gakkai Kaishi/Japanese Society of Lymphoreticular Tissue. Journal (1342-9248); Which was formerly (until 1997): Nihon Monaikei Gakkai Kaishi/Japan Society of the Reticuloendothelial System. Journal (0386-9725)
Related titles: Online - full text ed.: ISSN 1880-9952. free (effective 2011).
Indexed: EMBASE, ExcerpMed, MEDLINE, P30, R10, Reac, SCOPUS.
—BLDSC (4958.369970). **CCC.**
Published by: Japanese Society for Lymphoreticular Tissue Research/Nihon Rimpa Monaikei Gakkai, Nagoya University Graduate School of Medicine, High-Technology Application of Medicine, Clinical Pathophysi, 65 Tsurumai, Showa-ku, Nagoya, 466-8550, Japan. TEL 81-52-7442085, FAX 81-52-7442897, http://www.jsltr.org/. Ed. Dr. Mitsunori Yamakawa.

616.15 USA ISSN 0733-2459
RM173 CODEN: JCAPES
➤ **JOURNAL OF CLINICAL APHERESIS.** Text in English. 1982. bi-m. GBP 912 in United Kingdom to institutions; EUR 1,152 in Europe to institutions; USD 1,660 in United States to institutions; USD 1,744 in Canada & Mexico to institutions; USD 1,786 elsewhere to institutions; GBP 1,050 combined subscription in United Kingdom to institutions (print & online eds.); EUR 1,326 combined subscription in Europe to institutions (print & online eds.); USD 1,910 combined subscription in United States to institutions (print & online eds.); USD 1,994 combined subscription in Canada & Mexico to institutions (print & online eds.); USD 2,036 combined subscription elsewhere to institutions (print & online eds.) (effective 2012). adv. back issues avail.; reprint service avail. from PSC. **Document type:** *Journal, Academic/Scholarly.* **Description:** Examines research articles on all topics relating to apheresis: plasmapheresis, lymphoplasmapheresis, and ctyapheresis, including experimental and technical developments.
Related titles: Microform ed.: (from PQC); Online - full text ed.: ISSN 1098-1101. GBP 848 in United Kingdom to institutions; EUR 1,071 in Europe to institutions; USD 1,660 elsewhere to institutions (effective 2012).
Indexed: A22, ASCA, CurCont, EMBASE, ExcerpMed, INI, ISR, IndMed, Inpharma, MEDLINE, P30, R10, Reac, SCI, SCOPUS, W07.
—BLDSC (4958.381500), GNLM, IE, Infotrieve, Ingenta, INIST. **CCC.**
Published by: (American Society for Apheresis CAN), John Wiley & Sons, Inc., 111 River St, Hoboken, NJ 07030. TEL 201-748-6000, FAX 201-748-6088, info@wiley.com, http://www.wiley.com/WileyCDA/. Ed. Robert Weinstein. Pub., Adv. contact Kim Thompkins TEL 212-850-6921. **Subscr. outside the Americas to:** John Wiley & Sons Ltd.

616.15 GBR ISSN 2041-7969
▼ ➤ **THE JOURNAL OF COAGULATION DISORDERS.** Text in English. 2009 (Oct.). s-a. free (effective 2010). adv. back issues avail.; reprints avail. **Document type:** *Journal, Academic/Scholarly.*
Related titles: E-mail ed.; Online - full text ed.: free (effective 2011).
Indexed: A01, P20, P30, P48, P54, PQC, T02.
Published by: San Lucas Medical Ltd., 11-12 Freetrade House, Lowther Rd, Stanmore, Middlesex HA7 1EP, United Kingdom. TEL 44-20-70840330, FAX 44-20-70840330, http://www.slm-oncology.com/. Ed. Jim Jones. Pub. Stephen Davidson. Adv. contact Ryan Joshi TEL 44-20-71930673. B&W page GBP 7,000, color page GBP 10,000. Circ: 8,000.

616.15 PAK ISSN 1728-9475
JOURNAL OF HEMATOLOGICAL RESEARCH. Text in English. 1985. m. GBP 300 (effective 2005). **Document type:** *Journal, Academic/Scholarly.* **Description:** Study of clinical and hemoparasitic diseases.
Published by: (International Society of Hematological Research), International Press, P O Box 17700, Karachi, 75300, Pakistan. TEL 92-21-4947486, FAX 92-21-4989257, light_68@hotmail.com. Ed. Dr. M Bilal.

616.15 PAK ISSN 1728-9483
THE JOURNAL OF HEMATOLOGY AND HEMOPARASITIC DISEASES RESEARCH. Text in English. 1985. m. GBP 300 (effective 2005). **Document type:** *Journal, Academic/Scholarly.* **Description:** Study of clinical and veterinary blood and blood parasitic diseases.
Published by: (International Society of Hematological Research), International Press, P O Box 17700, Karachi, 75300, Pakistan. TEL 92-21-4947486, FAX 92-21-4989257, light_68@hotmail.com. Ed. Dr. G Sabir.

616.15 GBR ISSN 1756-8722
RB145
➤ **JOURNAL OF HEMATOLOGY & ONCOLOGY.** Text in English. 2008. irreg. free (effective 2011). adv. back issues avail. **Document type:** *Journal, Academic/Scholarly.* **Description:** Aims to provide an international platform for sharing laboratory and clinical findings in an open access format among laboratory scientists, physician scientists, hematologists and oncologists.
Media: Online - full text.
Indexed: A01, A26, CA, CurCont, E08, EMBASE, ExcerpMed, H12, I05, MEDLINE, P30, R10, Reac, S09, SCI, SCOPUS, T02, W07.
—**CCC.**
Published by: BioMed Central Ltd. (Subsidiary of: Springer Science+Business Media), 236 Gray's Inn Rd, London, WC1X 8HB, United Kingdom. TEL 44-20-31922000, FAX 44-20-31922010, info@biomedcentral.com, http://www.biomedcentral.com. Ed. Delong Liu. Adv. contact Natasha Bailey TEL 44-20-31922231.

616.15 DEU ISSN 1865-5785
RC633.A1
➤ **JOURNAL OF HEMATOPATHOLOGY.** Text in English. 2008. 4/yr. EUR 383, USD 517 to institutions (effective 2012). reprint service avail. from PSC. **Document type:** *Journal, Academic/Scholarly.*
Media: Online - full content. **Related titles:** Online - full text ed.: (from IngentaConnect).
Indexed: A22, E01, P30, SCOPUS.
—IE, Linda Hall. **CCC.**
Published by: Springer (Subsidiary of: Springer Science+Business Media), Tiergartenstr 17, Heidelberg, 69121, Germany. TEL 49-6221-4870, FAX 49-6221-345229, orders-hd-individuals@springer.com. Ed. J H van Krieken.

➤ **JOURNAL OF PEDIATRIC HEMATOLOGY / ONCOLOGY.** *see* MEDICAL SCIENCES—Oncology

616.15 ITA ISSN 2038-1298
▼ **JOURNAL OF PLATELETS.** Text in Italian. 2010. q. **Document type:** *Journal, Trade.*
Published by: Wolters Kluwer Health Italy (Subsidiary of: Wolters Kluwer N.V.), Via B Lanino 5, Milan, 20144, Italy. http://www.wkhealth.it.

616.35 GBR ISSN 1538-7933
RC694.3 CODEN: JTHOA5
➤ **JOURNAL OF THROMBOSIS AND HAEMOSTASIS.** Abbreviated title: J T H. Text in English. 2003 (Jan.). m. GBP 801 in United Kingdom to institutions; EUR 1,017 in Europe to institutions; USD 1,068 in the Americas to institutions; USD 1,568 elsewhere to institutions; GBP 922 combined subscription in United Kingdom to institutions (print & online eds.); EUR 1,170 combined subscription in Europe to institutions (print & online eds.); USD 1,229 combined subscription in the Americas to institutions (print & online eds.); USD 1,804 combined subscription elsewhere to institutions (print & online eds.) (effective 2012). adv. back issues avail.; reprint service avail. from PSC. **Document type:** *Journal, Academic/Scholarly.* **Description:** Aims to advance science related to the important medical problems of thrombosis, bleeding disorders and vascular biology through the diffusion and exchange of information and ideas within the international research community.
Related titles: Online - full text ed.: ISSN 1538-7836. 2003. GBP 798 in United Kingdom to institutions; EUR 1,012 in Europe to institutions; USD 1,064 in the Americas to institutions; USD 1,562 elsewhere to institutions (effective 2012) (from IngentaConnect); ◆ Supplement(s): Journal of Thrombosis and Haemostasis. Supplement. ISSN 1740-3332.
Indexed: A01, A03, A08, A22, A26, CA, CurCont, E01, EMBASE, ESPM, ExcerpMed, H12, ISR, Inpharma, MEDLINE, P30, P35, R10, Reac, RefZh, RiskAb, SCI, SCOPUS, T02, VITIS, W07.
—BLDSC (5069.345000), IE, Ingenta, INIST. **CCC.**
Published by: (International Society on Thrombosis and Haemostasis USA), Wiley-Blackwell Publishing Ltd. (Subsidiary of: John Wiley & Sons, Inc.), 9600 Garsington Rd, Oxford, OX4 2DQ, United Kingdom. TEL 44-1865-776868, FAX 44-1865-714591, customerservices@blackwellpublishing.com, http://www.wiley.com/. Eds. David Lane TEL 44-20-83832295, Mike Greaves TEL 44-1224-553015. Pub. Shawn Morton. Adv. contact Steve Jezzard. B&W page USD 1,405, color page USD 2,655; trim 8.25 x 10.875. Circ: 3,326 (paid).

616.35 GBR ISSN 1740-3332
JOURNAL OF THROMBOSIS AND HAEMOSTASIS. SUPPLEMENT. Text in English. 2003. irreg. includes with subscr. to Journal of Thrombosis and Haemostasis. **Document type:** *Journal, Academic/Scholarly.*
Media: Online - full text. **Related titles:** CD-ROM ed.: ISSN 1740-3340; ◆ Supplement to: Journal of Thrombosis and Haemostasis. ISSN 1538-7933.
Published by: (International Society on Thrombosis and Haemostasis USA), Wiley-Blackwell Publishing Ltd. (Subsidiary of: John Wiley & Sons, Inc.), 9600 Garsington Rd, Oxford, OX4 2DQ, United Kingdom. TEL 44-1865-776868, FAX 44-1865-714591, customerservices@blackwellpublishing.com, http://www.wiley.com/.

616.15 POL ISSN 1689-6017
JOURNAL OF TRANSFUSION MEDICINE. Text in Polish. 2008. q. PLZ 84 domestic to individuals; PLZ 167 domestic to institutions (effective 2011). **Document type:** *Journal, Academic/Scholarly.*
Related titles: Online - full text ed.: ISSN 2080-1505.
Published by: (Instytut Hematologii i Transfuzjologii), Wydawnictwo Via Medica, ul Swietokrzyska 73, Gdansk, 80180, Poland. TEL 48-58-3209494, FAX 48-58-3209460, redakcja@viamedica.pl, http://www.viamedica.pl. Ed. Magdalena Letowska.

JOURNAL WATCH ONCOLOGY AND HEMATOLOGY. *see* MEDICAL SCIENCES—Oncology

616.15 JPN ISSN 1344-6940
KETSUEKI FURONTIA/HEMATOLOGY FRONTIER. Text in Japanese. 1991. m. JPY 27,720; JPY 2,310 newsstand/cover (effective 2005). adv. **Document type:** *Academic/Scholarly.*
Formerly: Nichijo Shinryo to Ketsueki/Practical Hematology (0917-5776)
—BLDSC (4291.602000).
Published by: Iyaku Journal-sha/Medicine & Drug Journal Co., Ltd., Highness Awajimachi Bldg. 21/F, 3-1-5 Awajimachih, Chuo-Ku, Osaka, 541-0047, Japan. TEL 81-6-62027280, FAX 81-6-62025295, ij-main@iyaku-j.com, http://www.iyaku-j.com/. R&P, Adv. contact Kiriko Numata.

616.15 JPN ISSN 0917-7833
KETSUEKI JIGYO/BLOOD PROGRAMME. Variant title: Society for Japanese Blood Programme. Journal. Text in Japanese. q. JPY 1,000 per issue. **Document type:** *Journal, Academic/Scholarly.*
Published by: Nihon Ketsueki Jigyo Gakkai/Japanese Red Cross Society Blood Programme, 1-1-3 Shiba Daimon, Minato-ku, Tokyo, 105-8521, Japan. TEL 81-3-34381311, FAX 81-3-34358509, info@jrc.or.jp, http://www.jrc.or.jp/.

616 JPN ISSN 0915-8529
CODEN: KETSBI
KETSUEKI SHUYOKA/HEMATOLOGY & ONCOLOGY. Text in Japanese. 1970. m. JPY 2,625 per issue (effective 2003).
Formerly (until 1989): Ketsueki to Myakukan (0386-9717)
Indexed: INIS AtomInd.
—GNLM.
Published by: Kagaku-Hyoronsha Co. Ltd., 2-10-8, Kana Tomiyama-cho, Chiyoda-ku, Tokyo, 101-8531, Japan. TEL 81-3-32527741, FAX 81-3-32525952, http://www.kahyo.com/index.html.

616.15 BGR ISSN 0861-7880
➤ **KLINICHNA I TRANSFUZIONNA HEMATOLOGIIA/CLINICAL AND TRANSFUSION HAEMATOLOGY.** Text in Bulgarian; Summaries in Bulgarian, English. 1965. q. free (effective 2005). adv. bk.rev. abstr.; bibl. index. 48 p./no.; back issues avail. **Document type:** *Journal, Academic/Scholarly.* **Description:** Presents original articles of Bulgarian medical researchers and practitioners and abstracts of foreign publications in the field of hematology and blood transfusion.
Indexed: ABSML, EMBASE, ExcerpMed, R10, Reac, SCOPUS.
Published by: Meditsinski Universitet - Sofia, Tsentralna Meditsinska Biblioteka, Tsentur za Informatsiia po Meditsina/Medical University - Sofia, Central Medical Library, Medical Information Center, 1 Sv Georgi Sofiiski ul, Sofia, 1431, Bulgaria. TEL 359-2-9522342, FAX 359-2-9522393, pslavova@medun.acad.bg, http://www.medun.acad.bg/cmb_htm/cmb1_home_bg.htm. Ed. Dr. Georgi Balacenko. R&P, Adv. contact Lydia Tacheva. B&W page USD 50, color page USD 200; 12 x 18. Circ: 250.

616.15 USA ISSN 1080-2924
CODEN: LHAEAE
LABORATORY HEMATOLOGY. Text in English. 1995. q. adv. back issues avail. **Document type:** *Journal, Academic/Scholarly.* **Description:** Publishes high-quality reports of original research, reviews, editorials and letters to the editor in all fields of laboratory hematology.
Related titles: Online - full text ed.: ISSN 1523-6528. USD 175 to individuals; USD 250 to institutions (effective 2010).
Indexed: EMBASE, ExcerpMed, MEDLINE, P30, R10, Reac, SCOPUS.
—GNLM, IE, Infotrieve, Ingenta. **CCC.**
Published by: (International Society for Laboratory Hematology), Carden Jennings Publishing Co., Ltd., 375 Greenbrier Dr, Ste 100, Charlottesville, VA 22901. TEL 434-817-2010, FAX 434-817-2020, ijh@cjp.com, http://www.cjp.com. Ed. Kenneth A. Ault. Adv. contact Marcus Weathersby.

616 AUT ISSN 1991-2838
LEADING OPINIONS. HAEMATOLOGIE UND ONKOLOGIE. Text in German. 2004. 5/yr. adv. **Document type:** *Journal, Academic/Scholarly.*
Related titles: Online - full text ed.: ISSN 1991-2846. 2005.
Published by: Universimed Verlags- und Service GmbH, Markgraf-Ruediger-Str 8, Vienna, 1150, Austria. TEL 43-1-87679560, FAX 43-1-876795620, office@universimed.com, http://www.universimed.com. Ed. Hannelore Noebauer. Adv. contact Sabine Baeckert. Circ: 2,650 (controlled).

616.15 GBR ISSN 0887-6924
RC643 CODEN: LEUKED
➤ **LEUKEMIA.** Text in English. 1987. m. EUR 2,323 in Europe to institutions; USD 2,922 in the Americas to institutions; JPY 397,100 in Japan to institutions; GBP 1,499 to institutions in the UK & elsewhere (effective 2011). adv. inde. back issues avail.; reprints avail. **Document type:** *Journal, Academic/Scholarly.* **Description:** Covers all aspects of the research and treatment of leukemia and allied diseases.
Related titles: Online - full text ed.: ISSN 1476-5551.
Indexed: A01, A02, A03, A08, A22, A26, A29, A34, A36, AIDS&CR, ASCA, B20, B21, B25, BIOBASE, BIOSIS Prev, CA, CABA, CurCont, E01, E12, EMBASE, ESPM, ExcerpMed, FR, GH, GenetAb, H12, HGA, I05, I10, IABS, ISR, ImmunAb, IndMed, IndVet, Inpharma, MEDLINE, MycolAb, N02, N03, NucAcAb, OGFA, P20, P22, P24, P30, P33, P35, P48, P50, P54, PQC, R10, RM&VM, Reac, SCI, SCOPUS, T02, Telegen, VS, VirolAbstr, W07.
—BLDSC (5185.249000), CASDDS, GNLM, IE, Infotrieve, Ingenta, INIST. **CCC.**
Published by: Nature Publishing Group (Subsidiary of: Macmillan Publishers Ltd.), The MacMillan Bldg, 4 Crinan St, London, N1 9XW, United Kingdom. TEL 44-20-78334000, FAX 44-20-78334640. Ed. Dr. Nicole Muller-Berat Killman TEL 33-1-40036769. Adv. contact Ben Harkinson TEL 617-475-9222. **Subscr. to:** Brunel Rd, Houndmills, Basingstoke, Hamps RG21 6XS, United Kingdom. TEL 44-1256-329242, FAX 44-1256-812358, subscriptions@nature.com.
Co-sponsor: Leukemia Research Fund.

616.15 GBR ISSN 1042-8194
RC643 CODEN: LELYEA
➤ **LEUKEMIA AND LYMPHOMA.** Text in English. 1989. m. GBP 3,210, EUR 3,630, USD 4,540 combined subscription to institutions (print & online eds.); GBP 6,415, EUR 7,260, USD 9,075 combined subscription to corporations (print & online eds.) (effective 2010). adv. back issues avail.; reprint service avail. from PSC. **Document type:** *Journal, Academic/Scholarly.* **Description:** Offers clinical-pathologic correlation and brings together clinical and laboratory data on lymphomas, leukemias, and allied disorders, including myeloma and myelodysplastic syndromes.
Related titles: CD-ROM ed.: ISSN 1026-8022. 1995; Microform ed.; Online - full text ed.: ISSN 1029-2403 (from IngentaConnect).
Indexed: A01, A03, A08, A22, A35, A36, AIDS Ab, AIDS&CR, ASCA, AgBio, B21, BIOBASE, CA, CABA, CurCont, D01, E01, E12, EMBASE, ExcerpMed, F08, FamI, GH, H16, IABS, ImmunAb, IndMed, Inpharma, MEDLINE, N02, N03, OGFA, P30, P33, P35, P39, R08, R10, RA&MP, RM&VM, Reac, SCI, SCOPUS, T02, T05, VS, VirolAbstr, W07.
—GNLM, IE, Infotrieve, Ingenta, INIST. **CCC.**
Published by: Informa Healthcare (Subsidiary of: T & F Informa plc), Telephone House, 69-77 Paul St, London, EC2A 4LQ, United Kingdom. TEL 44-20-70175000, FAX 44-20-70176792, healthcare.enquiries@informa.com. Eds. Aaron Polliack, John Seymour, Koen Van Besien. **Subscr. in N. America to:** Taylor & Francis Inc., Customer Services Dept, 325 Chestnut St, 8th Fl, Philadelphia, PA 19106. TEL 215-625-8900, 800-354-1420, FAX 215-625-8914, customerservice@taylorandfrancis.com; **Subscr. outside N. America to:** Taylor & Francis Ltd., Journals Customer Service, Sheepen Pl, Colchester, Essex CO3 3LP, United Kingdom. TEL 44-20-70175544, FAX 44-20-70175198, tf.enquiries@tfinforma.com.

➤ **LEUKEMIA INSIGHTS.** see MEDICAL SCIENCES—Oncology

616 GBR ISSN 0145-2126
RC643 CODEN: LEREDD
➤ **LEUKEMIA RESEARCH**; clinical and laboratory studies. Text in English. 1977. 12/yr. EUR 3,070 in Europe to institutions; JPY 407,500 in Japan to institutions; USD 3,433 elsewhere to institutions (effective 2012). adv. bk.rev. abstr.; bibl.; charts; illus. index. back issues avail. **Document type:** *Journal, Academic/Scholarly.* **Description:** Covers comprehensive and current information to all health care professionals involved in basic and (or) applied clinical research in leukemias, lymphomas, multiple myeloma and other hematologic malignancies.
Related titles: Microfilm ed.: (from PQC); Online - full text ed.: ISSN 1873-5835 (from IngentaConnect, ScienceDirect).
Indexed: A01, A03, A08, A22, A26, A29, A34, A36, AIDS&CR, ASCA, B20, B21, B25, BIOBASE, BIOSIS Prev, CA, CABA, CIN, ChemAb, ChemTitl, CurCont, D01, E12, EMBASE, ESPM, ExcerpMed, F08, F11, F12, GH, H16, I05, I10, IABS, IBR, IBZ, ISR, ImmunAb, IndMed, IndVet, Inpharma, MEDLINE, MycolAb, N02, N03, OGFA, P30, P33, P35, P37, R08, R10, RA&MP, RM&VM, Reac, SCI, SCOPUS, SoyAb, T02, T05, Telegen, VS, VirolAbstr, W07.
—BLDSC (5185.270000), CASDDS, GNLM, IE, Infotrieve, Ingenta, INIST. **CCC.**
Published by: Pergamon (Subsidiary of: Elsevier Science & Technology), The Blvd, Langford Ln, East Park, Kidlington, Oxford OX5 1GB, United Kingdom. TEL 44-1865-843000, FAX 44-1865-843010, JournalsCustomerServiceEMEA@elsevier.com. Eds. Dr. John M Bennett TEL 585-275-4915, Terry J Hamblin TEL 44-1202-704783. **Subscr. to:** Elsevier BV, Radarweg 29, PO Box 211, Amsterdam 1000 AE, Netherlands. TEL 31-20-4853757, FAX 31-20-4853432, http://www.elsevier.nl.

➤ **LEUKONIEUWS.** see MEDICAL SCIENCES—Oncology

➤ **LINCHUANG SHUXUE YU JIANYAN/JOURNAL OF CLINICAL TRANSFUSION AND LABORATORY MEDICINE.** see MEDICAL SCIENCES—Experimental Medicine, Laboratory Technique

616.15 CHN ISSN 1004-2806
LINCHUANG XUEYEXUE ZAZHI/CLINICAL HEMATOLOGY. Text in Chinese. 1988. bi-m. **Document type:** *Journal, Academic/Scholarly.*
Related titles: Online - full text ed.: (from WanFang Data Corp.).
—East View.
Published by: Huazhong Keji Daxue Tongji Yixueyuan Fushu Xiehe Yiyuan/Tongji Medical University, Union Hospital, 1277, Jiefang Dadao, Wuhan, 430022, China. TEL 86-27-85726342 ext 8806, FAX 86-27-85727988, http://www.whuh.com/. **Dist. by:** China International Book Trading Corp, 35 Chegongzhuang Xilu, Haidian District, PO Box 399, Beijing 100044, China. TEL 86-10-68412045, FAX 86-10-68412023, cibtc@mail.cibtc.com.cn, http://www.cibtc.com.cn.

▼ **LYMPHOMA AND CHRONIC LYMPHOCYTIC LEUKEMIAS.** see MEDICAL SCIENCES—Oncology

616.994190072 NZL ISSN 1170-3105
LYMPHOMA / LEUKAEMIA REVIEW. Variant title: N Z Lymphoma / Leukaemia Review. Text in English. 2008. q. back issues avail. **Document type:** *Journal, Academic/Scholarly.*
Media: Online - full content.
Published by: Research Review Ltd., N Shore Mail Centre, PO Box 100116, Auckland, New Zealand. TEL 64-9-4102277, info@researchreview.co.nz.

M.D. ANDERSON CLINICAL PERSPECTIVES. LYMPHOMA & MYELOMA. see MEDICAL SCIENCES—Oncology

M P R (HEMATOLOGY/ONCOLOGY EDITION). (Monthly Prescribing Reference) see PHARMACY AND PHARMACOLOGY

MEDICAL TRIBUNE ONKOLOGIE - HAEMATOLOGIE. see MEDICAL SCIENCES—Oncology

616.15 ITA ISSN 2035-3006
▼ **MEDITERRANEAN JOURNAL OF HEMATOLOGY AND INFECTIOUS DISEASES.** Text in English. 2009. q. free (effective 2011). **Document type:** *Journal, Academic/Scholarly.*
Media: Online - full text.
Indexed: P30.
Published by: Universita Cattolica del Sacro Cuore, Istituto di Ematologia, Policlinico Gemelli, Largo Gemelli 8, Rome, 00168, Italy. TEL 39-06-30154180, FAX 39-06-35503777. Ed. Giuseppe Leone.

616.15 616.992 USA ISSN 1535-6701
MEDSCAPE HEMATOLOGY-ONCOLOGY. Text in English. 1997. irreg., latest 2002. free to members (effective 2011). **Document type:** *Journal, Academic/Scholarly.*
Formerly (until 2000): Medscape Oncology
Media: Online - full text.
Published by: Medscape, Llc., 825 Eighth Ave, 11th Fl, New York, NY 10019. TEL 212-301-6700, MedscapeMemberServices@webmd.net.

616.41005 GBR ISSN 1754-0542
MYELOPROLIFERATIVE DISORDERS IN PRACTICE. Text in English. 2007. q. adv. **Document type:** *Journal, Academic/Scholarly.* **Description:** Provides review-based articles of interest to all members of the secondary care team working in the therapeutic area.
Related titles: Online - full text ed.: ISSN 2045-7871. GBP 60, EUR 80 to individuals; GBP 250, EUR 375 to institutions (effective 2010).
—BLDSC (5995.763500), IE. **CCC.**
Published by: Hayward Medical Communications Ltd. (Subsidiary of: Hayward Group plc), 8-10 Dryden St, Covent Garden, London, WC2E 9NA, United Kingdom. TEL 44-20-72404493, FAX 44-20-72404479, edit@hayward.co.uk, http://www.hayward.co.uk. Ed. John Reilly.

616.15 USA ISSN 1941-2576
NANOGRAMS; small bits of information for people interested in iron levels in the body. Text in English. 2007. bi-m. **Document type:** *Newsletter, Consumer.*
Related titles: Online - full text ed.: ISSN 1941-2584.
Published by: Iron Disorders Institute, 2722 Wade Hampton Blvd, Ste A, Greenville, SC 29615. TEL 864-292-1175, 888-565-4766, FAX 864-292-1878, PatientServices@irondisorders.org.

616.15 AUS ISSN 1832-1909
NATIONAL BLOOD AUTHORITY. ANNUAL REPORT. Abbreviated title: N B A Annual Report. Text in English. 2004. a. free (effective 2009). back issues avail. **Document type:** *Government.*
Related titles: Online - full text ed.
Published by: National Blood Authority, Locked Bag 8430, Canberra, ACT 2601, Australia. TEL 612-62118300, FAX 612-62118330, nationalbloodauthority@nba.gov.au.

616.15 NLD ISSN 1572-1590
➤ **NEDERLANDS TIJDSCHRIFT VOOR HEMATOLOGIE/DUTCH JOURNAL OF HEMATOLOGY.** Text in Dutch. 2004. 8/yr. **Document type:** *Journal, Trade.*
Published by: Ariez Medical Publishing, Kruislaan 419, Amsterdam, 1098 VA, Netherlands. TEL 31-20-5612070, FAX 31-20-5612051, info@ariezmp.nl, http://www.ariezmp.nl.

616.15 JPN ISSN 1340-5888
NIHON AFERESHISU GAKKAI ZASSHI/JAPANESE JOURNAL OF APHERESIS. Text in Japanese. 198?. 3/yr.
Related titles: English ed.: Therapeutic Plasmapheresis. ISSN 1341-786X.
—BLDSC (4650.848000).
Published by: Nihon Afereshisu Gakkai/Japanese Society for Apheresis, 3-1-3 Hongo, Bunko-ku, Tokyo, 113-8431, Japan. TEL 81-3-38133111, FAX 81-3-56844722.

616.15 JPN ISSN 0915-7441
CODEN: NKSGEL
NIHON KESSEN SHIKETSU GAKKAISHI/JAPANESE SOCIETY ON THROMBOSIS AND HEMOSTASIS. JOURNAL. Text in Japanese. 1990. bi-m. **Document type:** *Journal, Academic/Scholarly.*
Indexed: A22, INIS AtomInd.
—BLDSC (4658.901000), IE, Ingenta.
Published by: Nihon Kessen Shiketsu Gakkai/Japanese Society on Thrombosis and Hemostasis, 572, Waseda-Tsurumakicho, Shinjuku-ku, Tokyo, 162-0041, Japan. TEL 81-3-32609730, FAX 81-3-32609750.

616.15 618.92 JPN ISSN 0913-8706
CODEN: NSKZEQ
NIHON SHONI KETSUEKI GAKKAI ZASSHI/JAPANESE JOURNAL OF PEDIATRIC HEMATOLOGY. Text in Japanese. 1987. q. JPY 10,000 membership (effective 2005). **Document type:** *Journal, Academic/Scholarly.*
Related titles: Online - full text ed.
Indexed: INIS AtomInd.
—BLDSC (4656.935000). **CCC.**
Published by: Nihon Shoni Ketsueki Gakkai/Japanese Society of Pediatric Hematology, Shinanomachi-Rengakan Bldg., Shinanomachi 35, Shinjuku-Ku, Tokyo, 160-0016, Japan. TEL 81-3-53617107, FAX 81-3-53617091, http://www.med.hokudai.ac.jp/~ped-w/JSPH.htm.

362.1784 JPN ISSN 0546-1448
CODEN: NYGZAA
NIPPON YUKETSU GAKKAI ZASSHI/JAPAN SOCIETY OF BLOOD TRANSFUSION. JOURNAL. Text in Japanese. 1958. bi-m. **Document type:** *Journal, Academic/Scholarly.*
Formerly: Ketsueki To Yuketsu
Indexed: INIS AtomInd.
—**CCC.**
Published by: Nippon Yuketsu Gakkai/Japan Society of Blood Transfusion, 4-1-31 Hiroo, Shibuya-ku, Tokyo, 150-0012, Japan. TEL 81-3-54856020, FAX 81-3-54663111.

NOU TO JONKAN/BRAIN AND CIRCULATION. see MEDICAL SCIENCES—Psychiatry And Neurology

▼ **ONCOLOG-HEMATOLOG.RO.** see MEDICAL SCIENCES—Oncology

THE ONCOLOGIST. see MEDICAL SCIENCES—Oncology

616.15 NLD ISSN 1874-2769
RC633.A1
➤ **THE OPEN HEMATOLOGY JOURNAL.** Text in English. 2007. irreg. free (effective 2011). **Document type:** *Journal, Academic/Scholarly.* **Description:** Covers all areas of clinical, laboratory and experimental hematology including stem cells and blood disorders.
Media: Online - full text.
Indexed: A01, EMBASE, ExcerpMed, SCOPUS.
Published by: Bentham Open (Subsidiary of: Bentham Science Publishers Ltd.), PO Box 294, Bussum, AG 1400, Netherlands. TEL 31-35-6923800, FAX 31-35-6980150, subscriptions@bentham.org.

616.15 PAK ISSN 2075-907X
▼ **OPEN JOURNAL OF HEMATOLOGY.** Text in English. 2009. irreg. free (effective 2011). **Document type:** *Journal, Academic/Scholarly.*
Media: Online - full text.
Published by: Ross Science Publishers

PEDIATRIC HEMATOLOGY & ONCOLOGY. see MEDICAL SCIENCES—Pediatrics

PEDIATRIC HEMATOLOGY - ONCOLOGY SERIES. see MEDICAL SCIENCES—Oncology

PERFUSION: Kreislauferkrankungen in Klinik und Praxis. see MEDICAL SCIENCES—Cardiovascular Diseases

616.15 USA ISSN 1947-5764
▼ ➤ **PLASMA MEDICINE.** Text in English. 2009. q. USD 595; USD 150 per issue (effective 2009). **Document type:** *Journal, Academic/Scholarly.* **Description:** Research on plasma medicine and technology.
Related titles: Online - full text ed.: ISSN 1947-5772.
Indexed: CPEI, SCOPUS.
Published by: Begell House Inc., 50 Cross Hwy, Redding, CT 06896. TEL 203-938-1300, FAX 203-938-1304, orders@begellhouse.com.

573.159 GBR ISSN 0953-7104
QP97 CODEN: PLTEEF
➤ **PLATELETS (LONDON).** Text in English. 1990. 8/yr. GBP 1,130, EUR 1,625, USD 2,040 combined subscription to institutions (print & online eds.); GBP 2,265, EUR 3,260, USD 4,075 combined subscription to corporations (print & online eds.) (effective 2010). adv. 64 p./no.; back issues avail.; reprint service avail. from PSC. **Document type:** *Journal, Academic/Scholarly.* **Description:** Covers all aspects of platelet-related research, including vascular disease, cerebral and myocardial ischaemia, asthma, inflammation, growth factors, pathology and morphology of platelets, and comparison with other cells and clinical trials of anti-platelet agents.
Related titles: Online - full text ed.: ISSN 1369-1635 (from IngentaConnect).
Indexed: A01, A03, A08, A22, A34, A35, A36, AgBio, AgrForAb, B21, B25, BIOSIS Prev, C30, C33, CA, CABA, CTA, ChemAb, CurCont, E01, EMBASE, ExcerpMed, F08, F11, F12, GH, H16, IBR, IBZ, ISR, ImmunAb, IndMed, IndVet, Inpharma, MEDLINE, MycolAb, N02, N03, P30, P33, P35, P39, PGrRegA, PHN&I, PN&I, R08, R10, RA&MP, Reac, RefZh, SCI, SCOPUS, T02, T05, VS, W07.
—CASDDS, GNLM, IE, Infotrieve, Ingenta. **CCC.**
Published by: Informa Healthcare (Subsidiary of: T & F Informa plc), Telephone House, 69-77 Paul St, London, EC2A 4LQ, United Kingdom. TEL 44-20-70175000, FAX 44-20-70176792, healthcare.enquiries@informa.com. Ed. S Heptinstall TEL 44-115-8231013. Adv. contact Per Sonnerfeldt. **Subscr. in N. America to:** Taylor & Francis Inc., Customer Services Dept, 325 Chestnut St, 8th Fl, Philadelphia, PA 19106. TEL 215-625-8900, 800-354-1420, FAX 215-625-8914, customerservice@taylorandfrancis.com; **Subscr. outside N. America to:** Taylor & Francis Ltd., Journals Customer Service, Sheepen Pl, Colchester, Essex CO3 3LP, United Kingdom. TEL 44-20-70175544, FAX 44-20-70175198, tf.enquiries@tfinforma.com.

➤ **PROGRESS IN CARDIOVASCULAR DISEASES.** see MEDICAL SCIENCES—Cardiovascular Diseases

➤ **PROPRAXIS ONKOLOGIE - HAEMATOLOGIE.** see MEDICAL SCIENCES—Oncology

616.15 POL ISSN 1232-7174
PRZEGLAD FLEBOLOGICZNY. Text in Polish. 1993. q. **Document type:** *Journal, Academic/Scholarly.*
Related titles: Online - full text ed.: ISSN 1509-5738.
Indexed: C06, C07.
Published by: (Polskie Towarzystwo Flebologiczne), Blackhorse Scientific Publishers, Ltd., Zeganska 16, Warsaw, 04713, Poland. TEL 48-22-4999099, FAX 48-22-4995081, blackhorse@blackhorse.pl, http://blackhorse.pl/blackhorse.

616.15 CAN ISSN 1719-6612
RECOMMANDATIONS ET GUIDES DE PRATIQUE EN MEDECINE TRANSFUSIONNELLE. Text in French. 2002. irreg. **Document type:** *Handbook/Manual/Guide, Consumer.*
Published by: Quebec, Department of Health and Social Services/ Quebec, Sante et Services Sociaux, 1075, chemin Sainte-Foy, 16e etage, Quebec, PQ G1S 2M1, Canada. TEL 418-266-8900, 800-707-3380, http://www.msss.gouv.qc.ca/index.php.

616.15 RUS ISSN 1682-6655
➤ **REGIONARNOE KROVOOBRASHCHENIE I MIKROTSIRKULYATSIYA/REGIONAL BLOOD CIRCULATION AND MICROCIRCULATION.** Text in Russian. 2002. q. looseleaf. RUR 250, USD 37 per issue (effective 2008). abstr.; bibl.; charts; illus. back issues avail. **Document type:** *Journal, Academic/Scholarly.* **Description:** Designed for surgeons, therapists, cardiologists and neurologists. Publishes articles, reviews, brief communications about microcirculation, and blood disorders, new methods of diagnostics and treatment of vessels.
Indexed: RefZh.
—BLDSC (0140.586720), East View, IE.
Published by: Izdatel'stvo SP Minimaks, ul L'va Tolstogo, 7, Sankt-Peterburg, 197376, Russian Federation. TEL 7-812-2349546, FAX 7-812-2343877, minimax7@lek.ru, http://www.minimax.ru. Ed. Nikolai N Petrishchev. Circ: 1,000.

616.15 ARG ISSN 0325-6030
REVISTA ARGENTINA DE TRANSFUSION. Text in Spanish. 1941. q. **Document type:** *Journal, Academic/Scholarly.*
Formerly (until 1961): Sociedad Argentina de Hematologia y Hemoterapia. Revista (0326-1506)
Published by: Asociacion Argentina de Hemoterapia y Inmunohematologia, Lavalleja 1214, Buenos Aires, Argentina.

616.15 BRA ISSN 1516-8484
REVISTA BRASILEIRA DE HEMATOLOGIA E HEMOTERAPIA. Text in Multiple languages. 1999. 3/yr. free (effective 2005). **Document type:** *Journal, Academic/Scholarly.* **Description:** Publishes original articles with origins in researches, revisions, debates, commentaries and other scientifical contributions related to the areas of hemathology and hemotherapy.
Related titles: Online - full text ed.: free (effective 2011).
Indexed: SCOPUS.
Published by: Sociedade Brasileira de Hematologia e Hemoterapia, Av Brigadeiro Faria Lima 5416, Unidade TMO HB/FUNFARME/ FAMERP, Sao Jose do Rio Preto, SP 15090-000, Brazil. sbhh@terra.com.br, milruiz@yahoo.com.br, http://www.sbhh.com.br/.

REVISTA CHILENA DE CANCEROLOGIA Y HEMATOLOGIA. see MEDICAL SCIENCES—Oncology

616.15 CUB ISSN 0864-0289
REVISTA CUBANA DE HEMATOLOGIA, INMUNOLOGIA Y HEMATERAPIA. Text in Spanish; Summaries in English, Spanish. s-a. USD 30 in North America; USD 32 in South America; USD 34 elsewhere (effective 2005). adv. charts; illus.; stat. index. **Document type:** *Journal, Academic/Scholarly.* **Description:** Covers immunology, hematologic and hematopoietic system diseases, AIDS research and the application of hemotherapy techniques.
Related titles: Online - full text ed.: ISSN 1561-2996. 1995. free (effective 2011).
Indexed: C01, CA, EMBASE, ExcerpMed, SCOPUS, SociolAb, T02.
Published by: (Centro Nacional de Informacion de Ciencias Medicas (C N I C M), Cuba. Ministerio de Salud Publica), Editorial Ciencias Medicas, Linea Esq 1, 10o, Vedado, Havana, 10400, Cuba. TEL 53-7-8323863. Ed. Ivette Cabrera. Circ: 1,200. **Co-sponsors:** Instituto Nacional Hematologia e Inmunologia; sociedad Cubana de Hematologia.

616.4 JPN ISSN 0485-1439
RINSHO KETSUEKI/JAPANESE JOURNAL OF CLINICAL HEMATOLOGY. Text in Japanese. 1960. m. **Document type:** *Journal, Academic/Scholarly.*
Related titles: Online - full text ed.: ISSN 1882-0824.
Indexed: A22, EMBASE, ExcerpMed, INIS AtomInd, MEDLINE, P30, R10, Reac, SCOPUS.
—BLDSC (4651.374000), IE, Ingenta, INIST. **CCC.**
Published by: Nihon Rinsho Ketsueki Gakkai/Japan Society of Clinical Hematology, 35 Shinanomachi, Shinjuku-ku, Tokyo, 160-0016, Japan. TEL 81-3-32265746, FAX 81-3-32265748, rinketsu@imic.or.jp, http://www.rinketsu.jp/.

616.15 FRA ISSN 0999-7385
CODEN: STVAEY
SANG THROMBOSE VAISSEAUX. Abbreviated title: S T V. Text in French. 10/yr. EUR 384 combined subscription domestic to institutions (print & online eds.); EUR 424 combined subscription in the European Union to institutions (print & online eds.); EUR 444 combined subscription elsewhere to institutions (print & online eds.) (effective 2011). **Document type:** *Journal, Academic/Scholarly.* **Description:** Studies fundamental and practical aspects of blood and vascular problems.
Related titles: Online - full text ed.: ISSN 1950-6104. FRF 630 to individuals; FRF 1,120 to institutions; FRF 430 to students (effective 2001).
Indexed: A22, EMBASE, ExcerpMed, Inpharma, R10, Reac, RefZh, SCI, SCOPUS, W07.
—BLDSC (8073.160000), GNLM, IE, Ingenta, INIST. **CCC.**
Published by: John Libbey Eurotext, 127 Av. de la Republique, Montrouge, 92120, France. TEL 33-1-46730660, FAX 33-1-40840999, contact@jle.com, http://www.john-libbey-eurotext.fr. Ed. Bernard Levy.

616.15 NLD ISSN 1574-1664
SANQUIN. SCIENTIFIC REPORT. Text in English. 2000. a.
Formerly (until 2002): C L B Scientific Report (1574-1656)
Published by: Sanquin, Postbus 9892, Amsterdam, 1006 AN, Netherlands. TEL 31-20-5123000, FAX 31-20-5123303, research@sanquin.nl, http://www.sanquin.nl.

616.15 NLD ISSN 1875-9734
SCRIPT HEMATOLOGIE. Text in Dutch. 2008. q. adv.
Published by: Van Zuiden Communications B.V., Postbus 2122, Alphen aan den Rijn, 2400 CC, Netherlands. TEL 31-172-476191, FAX 31-172-471882, zuiden@zuidencomm.nl, http://www.zuidencomm.nl. Circ: 600 (controlled).

616.15 USA ISSN 0037-1963
RC633.A1 CODEN: SEHEA3
➤ **SEMINARS IN HEMATOLOGY.** Text in English. 1964. q. USD 374 in United States to institutions; USD 488 elsewhere to institutions (effective 2012). adv. bibl.; charts; illus. index. back issues avail.; reprints avail. **Document type:** *Journal, Academic/Scholarly.* **Description:** Presents review articles of current importance in clinical hematology and related fields.
Related titles: Microform ed.: (from SWZ); Online - full text ed.: ISSN 1532-8686 (from ScienceDirect).
Indexed: A22, A36, B&BAb, B19, B21, BIOBASE, BIOSIS Prev, CABA, ChemAb, ChemTitl, CurCont, EMBASE, ExcerpMed, GH, H17, IABS, ISR, ImmunAb, IndMed, Inpharma, MEDLINE, MycolAb, N02, N03, P30, P33, P39, R08, R10, RM&VM, Reac, SCI, SCOPUS, T05, VS, W07.
—BLDSC (8239.450000), CASDDS, GNLM, IE, Infotrieve, Ingenta, INIST. **CCC.**
Published by: W.B. Saunders Co. (Subsidiary of: Elsevier Health Sciences), Elsevier, Health Sciences Division, Order Fulfillment, 3251 Riverport Ln, Maryland Heights, MO 63043. TEL 314-872-8370, 800-325-4177, FAX 314-432-1380, JournalCustomerService-usa@elsevier.com, http://www.us.elsevierhealth.com. Eds. Dr. Neal S. Young, Dr. Photis Beris. Pub. Kate Williamson. Circ: 2,000.

616.15 USA ISSN 0094-6176
RC633.A1 CODEN: STHMBV
➤ **SEMINARS IN THROMBOSIS AND HEMOSTASIS.** Text in English. 1975. 8/yr. USD 863 domestic to institutions; USD 883 foreign to institutions; USD 1,055 combined subscription domestic to institutions (print & online eds.); USD 1,090 combined subscription foreign to institutions (print & online eds.) (effective 2011). reprints avail. **Document type:** *Journal, Academic/Scholarly.* **Description:** Focuses on all issues relating to hemostatic and thrombotic disorder and offers an informed perspective on today's pivotal issues, including hemophilia A & B, thrombophilia, gene therapy, venous and arterial thrombosis, von willebrand disease, vascular disorders and thromboembolic diseases.
Incorporates (2001-2005): Seminars in Vascular Medicine (1528-9648)
Related titles: Microform ed.: (from PQC); Online - full text ed.: ISSN 1098-9064. USD 1,015 domestic to institutions; USD 1,026 foreign to institutions (effective 2011).
Indexed: A01, A03, A08, A22, ASCA, BIOSIS Prev, CA, ChemAb, CurCont, E01, E12, EMBASE, ExcerpMed, ISR, IndMed, Inpharma, MEDLINE, MycolAb, P30, R10, Reac, SCI, SCOPUS, T02, W07.
—BLDSC (8239.480000), CASDDS, GNLM, IE, Infotrieve, Ingenta, INIST. **CCC.**
Published by: Thieme Medical Publishers (Subsidiary of: Georg Thieme Verlag), 333 Seventh Ave, New York, NY 10001. TEL 212-760-0888, 800-782-3488, FAX 212-947-1112, info@thieme.com. Ed. Emmanuel J Favaloro TEL 61-2-98456618. Adv. contact James C Cunningham TEL 201-767-4170. Circ: 1,265.

616.15 BRA ISSN 1516-2451
SOCIEDADE BRASILEIRA DE HEMATOLOGIA E HEMOTERAPIA. BOLETIM. Text in Portuguese. 1984. 3/yr. **Document type:** *Bulletin, Academic/Scholarly.*
Media: Online - full text.
Published by: Sociedade Brasileira de Hematologia e Hemoterapia, Rua da Assembleia, No 10, Grupo 1700 Centro, Rio de Janeiro, 20011-901, Brazil. TEL 55-21-22210950, FAX 55-21-22210941, sbhh@terra.com.br, http://www.sbhh.com.br/.

615.39 USA ISSN 0730-6865
RM172
STANDARDS FOR BLOOD BANKS AND TRANSFUSION SERVICES. Text in English. 1958. irreg., latest vol.23, 2004. price varies. **Document type:** *Journal, Trade.*
Formerly (until 1966): Standards for a Blood Transfusion Service (0272-2038)
Published by: American Association of Blood Banks, Committee on Standards, 8101 Glenbrook Rd, Bethesda, MD 20814. TEL 301-907-6977, FAX 301-907-6895, standards@aabb.org, http://www.aabb.org.

616.15 NLD ISSN 1873-8869
T R I P RAPPORT. (Transfusie Reacties in Patienten) Text in Dutch. 2003. a.
Published by: Stichting T R I P, Postbus 40551, The Hague, 2504 LN, Netherlands. TEL 31-70-3083120, FAX 31-70-3682626, info@tripnet.nl.

616.15 NLD ISSN 2210-8564
▼ **T R I P RAPPORT HEMOVIGILANTIE.** (Transfusie Reacties in Patienten) Text in Dutch. 2009. a.
Published by: Stichting T R I P, Postbus 40551, The Hague, 2504 LN, Netherlands. TEL 31-70-3083120, FAX 31-70-3682626, info@tripnet.nl.

616.15 NLD ISSN 2210-8572
▼ **T R I P RAPPORT WEEFSELVIGILANTIE.** (Transfusie Reacties in Patienten) Text in Dutch. 2009. a.
Published by: Stichting T R I P, Postbus 40551, The Hague, 2504 LN, Netherlands. TEL 31-70-3083120, FAX 31-70-3682626, info@tripnet.nl.

TETSU TAISHA KENKYUKAI PUROGURAMU SHOROKUSHU/ CONFERENCE ON CURRENT TOPICS FOR IRON METABOLISM. PROGRAM AND ABSTRACTS. *see* BIOLOGY—Biochemistry

616.15 GBR ISSN 2040-6207
▼ **THERAPEUTIC ADVANCES IN HEMATOLOGY.** Text in English. 2010 (Dec.). bi-m. USD 1,071, GBP 579 combined subscription to institutions (print & online eds.); USD 1,050, GBP 567 to institutions (effective 2011). **Document type:** *Journal, Academic/Scholarly.*
Related titles: Online - full text ed.: ISSN 2040-6215. USD 964, GBP 521 to institutions (effective 2011).
—**CCC.**
Published by: Sage Publications Ltd. (Subsidiary of: Sage Publications, Inc.), 1 Oliver's Yard, 55 City Rd, London, EC1Y 1SP, United Kingdom. TEL 44-20-73248500, FAX 44-20-73248600, info@sagepub.co.uk, http://www.uk.sagepub.com/home.nav. Ed. Michael Mauro.

616.15 NLD ISSN 1875-9424
➤ **TIJDSCHRIFT VOOR BLOEDTRANSFUSIE/JOURNAL OF BLOOD TRANSFUSION.** Text in Dutch. 2008. q. **Document type:** *Journal, Trade.*
Published by: Ariez Medical Publishing, Kruislaan 419, Amsterdam, 1098 VA, Netherlands. TEL 31-20-5612070, FAX 31-20-5612051, info@ariezmp.nl, http://www.ariezmp.nl.

616.15 GBR ISSN 1295-9022
➤ **TRANSFUSION ALTERNATIVES IN TRANSFUSION MEDICINE.** Abbreviated title: T A T M. Text in English. 1999. q. GBP 168 combined subscription in United Kingdom to institutions (print & online eds.); EUR 215 combined subscription in Europe to institutions (print & online eds.); USD 426 combined subscription in the Americas to institutions (print & online eds.); USD 466 combined subscription elsewhere to institutions (print & online eds.) (effective 2011). adv. back issues avail.; reprint service avail. from PSC. **Document type:** *Journal, Academic/Scholarly.* **Description:** Provides network of medical practitioners, researchers, and opinion leaders from a wide variety of medical and scientific disciplines who are dedicated to helping their peers learn more about recent advances in blood conservation and transfusion alternatives.
Related titles: Online - full text ed.: ISSN 1778-428X. GBP 153 in United Kingdom to institutions; EUR 194 in Europe to institutions; USD 387 in the Americas to institutions; USD 424 elsewhere to institutions (effective 2011) (from IngentaConnect).
Indexed: A01, A22, A26, A36, CA, CABA, E01, EMBASE, ExcerpMed, GH, H17, MaizeAb, N02, N03, P30, P33, P38, P39, RefZh, SCOPUS, T02, T05.
—BLDSC (9020.704300), IE, Ingenta. **CCC.**
Published by: (Network for Advancement of Transfusion Alternatives FRA), Wiley-Blackwell Publishing Ltd. (Subsidiary of: John Wiley & Sons, Inc.), 9600 Garsington Rd, Oxford, OX4 2DQ, United Kingdom. TEL 44-1865-776868, FAX 44-1865-714591, customerservices@blackwellpublishing.com. Ed. Konrad Messmer.

616.15 GBR ISSN 1473-0502
RM171 CODEN: TASRCE
➤ **TRANSFUSION AND APHERESIS SCIENCE.** Text in English. 6/yr. EUR 1,280 in Europe to institutions; JPY 170,100 in Japan to institutions; USD 1,431 elsewhere to institutions (effective 2012). back issues avail. **Document type:** *Journal, Academic/Scholarly.* **Description:** Presents scientific and clinical studies in the areas of immunohematology, transfusion practice and apheresis.
Former titles (until 2001): Transfusion Science (0955-3886); (until 1989): Plasma Therapy and Transfusion Technology (0278-6222); (until 1981): Plasma Therapy (0196-4267)
Related titles: Microfilm ed.: (from PQC); Online - full text ed.: ISSN 1878-1683 (from IngentaConnect, ScienceDirect).
Indexed: A01, A03, A08, A20, A22, A26, ASCA, B&BAb, B19, B21, B25, BIOBASE, BIOSIS Prev, BioEngAb, CA, CurCont, EMBASE, ExcerpMed, I05, IABS, Inpharma, MEDLINE, MycolAb, P30, R10, Reac, SCI, SCOPUS, T02, VirolAbstr, W07.
—BLDSC (9020.704500), GNLM, IE, Ingenta, INIST. **CCC.**
Published by: (Societa Italiana di Emaferesi e Manipolazione Cellulare ITA, World Apheresis Association, Interdisciplinary European Society for Haemapheresis and Haemotherapy AUT), Pergamon (Subsidiary of: Elsevier Science & Technology), The Blvd, Langford Ln, East Park, Kidlington, Oxford OX5 1GB, United Kingdom. TEL 44-1865-843000, FAX 44-1865-843010, JournalsCustomerServiceEMEA@elsevier.com. Ed. Gail A Rock TEL 613-748-9613. **Subscr. to:** Elsevier BV, Radarweg 29, PO Box 211, Amsterdam 1000 AE, Netherlands. TEL 31-20-4853757, FAX 31-20-4853432, http://www.elsevier.nl.

616.1 FRA ISSN 1246-7820
RM171 CODEN: TCBIFL
➤ **TRANSFUSION CLINIQUE ET BIOLOGIQUE.** Text mainly in French; Text occasionally in English; Abstracts in English, French. 1958. 6/yr. EUR 320 in Europe to institutions; EUR 308.52 in France to institutions; JPY 42,500 in Japan to institutions; USD 451 elsewhere to institutions (effective 2012). bk.rev. index. reprints avail. **Document type:** *Journal, Academic/Scholarly.* **Description:** Bridges the gap between fundamental research and everyday applications in blood transfusion.
Former titles (until 1994): Revue Francaise de Transfusion et d'Hemobiologie (1140-4639); (until 1989): Revue Francaise de Transfusion et Immuno-Hematologie (0338-4535); (until 1975): Revue Francaise de Transfusion (0035-2977); (until 1968): Transfusion (0372-1248)
Related titles: Microform ed.: (from PQC); Online - full text ed.: ISSN 1953-8022. 1999 (from IngentaConnect, ScienceDirect).
Indexed: A01, A03, A08, A20, A22, A26, ASCA, CA, ChemAb, CurCont, DentInd, EMBASE, ExcerpMed, FR, I05, INI, ISR, IndMed, Inpharma, MEDLINE, P30, R10, Reac, SCI, SCOPUS, T02, W07.
—BLDSC (9020.705000), CASDDS, GNLM, IE, Infotrieve, Ingenta, INIST. **CCC.**
Published by: (Societe Francaise de Transfusion Sanguine), Elsevier Masson (Subsidiary of: Elsevier Health Sciences), 62 Rue Camille Desmoulins, Issy les Moulineaux, Cedex 92442, France. TEL 33-1-71165500, FAX 33-1-71165600, infos@elsevier-masson.fr. Ed. Philippe Rouger. Circ: 1,000.

616.15 GBR ISSN 0958-7578
CODEN: TRMDET
➤ **TRANSFUSION MEDICINE.** Text in English. 1991. bi-m. GBP 560 in United Kingdom to institutions; EUR 711 in Europe to institutions; USD 1,037 in the Americas to institutions; USD 1,211 elsewhere to institutions; GBP 645 combined subscription in United Kingdom to institutions (print & online eds.); EUR 818 combined subscription in Europe to institutions (print & online eds.); USD 1,193 combined subscription in the Americas to institutions (print & online eds.); USD 1,393 combined subscription elsewhere to institutions (print & online eds.) (effective 2012). adv. bk.rev. illus. index. back issues avail.; reprint service avail. from PSC. **Document type:** *Journal, Academic/Scholarly.* **Description:** Reflects the interest of clinicians, scientists and other professionals working in the broad field of blood transfusion medicine.
Related titles: Microform ed.: (from PQC); Online - full text ed.: ISSN 1365-3148. 1999. GBP 560 in United Kingdom to institutions; EUR 711 in Europe to institutions; USD 1,037 in the Americas to institutions; USD 1,211 elsewhere to institutions (effective 2012) (from IngentaConnect); Supplement(s): Transfusion Medicine. Supplement. ISSN 0960-5592.
Indexed: A01, A02, A03, A08, A22, A26, A36, ASCA, BIOBASE, C11, CA, CABA, CurCont, E01, E12, EMBASE, ExcerpMed, GH, H04, H12, IABS, INI, ISR, IndMed, Inpharma, LT, MEDLINE, N02, N03, P30, P33, P35, P39, R08, R10, R12, RRTA, Reac, S13, S16, SCI, SCOPUS, T02, T05, W07, W11.
—BLDSC (9020.706000), IE, Infotrieve, Ingenta. **CCC.**
Published by: (British Blood Transfusion Society), Wiley-Blackwell Publishing Ltd. (Subsidiary of: John Wiley & Sons, Inc.), 9600 Garsington Rd, Oxford, OX4 2DQ, United Kingdom. TEL 44-1865-776868, FAX 44-1865-714591, customerservices@blackwellpublishing.com. Ed. Jean-Pierre Allain TEL 44-1223-568050.

616.15 USA ISSN 0887-7963
RM171 CODEN: TMEREU
➤ **TRANSFUSION MEDICINE REVIEWS.** Text in English. 1987 (Apr.). q. USD 350 in United States to institutions; USD 474 elsewhere to institutions (effective 2012). abstr.; bibl.; charts; illus. index. back issues avail.; reprints avail. **Document type:** *Journal, Academic/Scholarly.* **Description:** Delivers authoritative reviews of important advances in the basic science and clinical aspects of transfusion medicine ranging from blood products to blood banking and laboratory medicine.
Related titles: Online - full text ed.: ISSN 1532-9496 (from ScienceDirect).
Indexed: A22, A26, ASCA, BIOSIS Prev, C06, C07, C08, CINAHL, CurCont, EMBASE, ExcerpMed, H12, I05, ISR, IndMed, Inpharma, MEDLINE, MycolAb, P30, R10, Reac, SCI, SCOPUS, T02, W07.
—BLDSC (9020.707000), GNLM, IE, Infotrieve, Ingenta. **CCC.**
Published by: W.B. Saunders Co. (Subsidiary of: Elsevier Health Sciences), Elsevier, Health Sciences Division, Order Fulfillment, 3251 Riverport Ln, Maryland Heights, MO 63043. TEL 314-872-8370, 800-325-4177, FAX 314-432-1380, JournalCustomerService-usa@elsevier.com, http://www.us.elsevierhealth.com. Ed. Dr. Morris A Blajchman TEL 905-525-9140 ext 26276. Pub. Rachel Garland. Adv. contact John Marmero TEL 212-633-3657. Circ: 500.

616.15 NLD ISSN 1015-3276
TRANSFUSION TODAY (ENGLISH EDITION). Text in English. 1989. q. adv. bk.rev. **Document type:** *Magazine, Trade.* **Description:** Articles on blood transfusion and related topics.
Related titles: Spanish ed.: Transfusion Today (Spanish Edition). ISSN 1015-3292; French ed.: Transfusion Today (French Edition). ISSN 1015-3284.
—BLDSC (9020.711000), IE, Infotrieve, Ingenta. **CCC.**
Published by: Societe Internationale de Transfusion Sanguine (S I T S)/International Society of Blood Transfusion (I S B T), Jan van Goyenkade 11, Amsterdam, 1075 HP, Netherlands. TEL 31-20-5709636, FAX 31-20-6737306, info@isbt-web.org. Ed. Claudine Hossenlopp. adv.: color page EUR 2,500; trim 210 x 297.

616.15 TUR ISSN 1300-7777
➤ **TURKISH JOURNAL OF HEMATOLOGY.** Text in English. 1951. q. back issues avail. **Document type:** *Journal, Academic/Scholarly.* **Description:** Covers review articles, research articles, brief reports, case reports, letter to the editor, images in haematology.
Former titles (1954-1983): New Istanbul Contribution of Clinical Science (0028-5447); (until 1952): Istanbul Contribution to Clinical Science (0367-7273)
Related titles: Online - full text ed.: free (effective 2011).
Indexed: A01, A26, C06, C07, CA, EMBASE, ExcerpMed, H12, I05, P20, P22, P30, P48, P54, PQC, R10, Reac, SCI, SCOPUS, T02, W07.
—BLDSC (9072.468761).
Published by: Turk Hematoloji Dernegi, Turan Gunes Bulv., Sancak Mah. 613. Sok. No.8, Cankaya, Ankara, Turkey. TEL 90-312-4909897, FAX 90-312-4909868, info@ijh.com.tr. Ed. Aytemiz Gurgey.

➤ **U H O D/INTERNATIONAL JOURNAL OF HEMATOLOGY AND ONCOLOGY**; uluslararasi hematoloji-onkoloji dergisi. *see* MEDICAL SCIENCES—Oncology

616.15 USA
VEIN THERAPY NEWS. Text in English. bi-m. USD 45 (effective 2011). **Document type:** *Newsletter, Trade.* **Description:** Serves the entire vein therapy industry. Addresses topics such as new procedures, marketing strategies, and developments in technology.
Published by: Publications & Communications, Inc., 13581 Pond Springs Rd, Ste 450, Austin, TX 78729. TEL 512-250-9023, 800-678-9724, FAX 512-331-3950, pci@pcinews.com, http://www.pcinews.com/. Ed. Larry Storer TEL 254-399-6484. Adv. contact Gary Pittman.

616.1 CAN ISSN 0084-1765
WORLD FEDERATION OF HEMOPHILIA. PROCEEDINGS OF CONGRESS. Text in English. irreg., latest 1975, 11th, Helsinki. **Document type:** *Proceedings.*
Published by: World Federation of Hemophilia, 1425 Rene Levesque Blvd. W., Suite 1010, Montreal, PQ H3G 1T7, Canada. TEL 514-875-7944, FAX 514-875-8916, wfh@wfh.org, http://www.wfh.org.

616.15 CHN ISSN 1009-6213
XUESHUAN YU ZHIXUEXUE/CHINESE JOURNAL OF THROMBOSIS AND HEMOSTASIS. Variant title: Xueshuan yu Xuexue. Text in English. 1994. bi-m. CNY 12 per issue (effective 2009). **Document type:** *Journal, Academic/Scholarly.*
Related titles: Online - full text ed.
—BLDSC (9367.111000), East View.
Published by: Xueshuan yu Zhixuexue Jikanshe, 250, Dong Lu, Guangzhou, 510260, China. TEL 86-20-34152578. **Dist. by:** China International Book Trading Corp, 35 Chegongzhuang Xilu, Haidian District, PO Box 399, Beijing 100044, China. TEL 86-10-68412045, FAX 86-10-68412023, cibtc@mail.cibtc.com.cn, http://www.cibtc.com.cn.

616.15 CHN ISSN 1009-2137
ZHONGGUO SHIYAN XUEYEXUE ZAZHI/JOURNAL OF EXPERIMENTAL HEMATOLOGY. Text in Chinese. 1993. bi-m. USD 53.40 (effective 2009). **Document type:** *Journal, Academic/Scholarly.*
Related titles: Online - full text ed.
Indexed: A22, EMBASE, ExcerpMed, MEDLINE, P30, R10, Reac, SCOPUS.
—BLDSC (4981.550000), East View, IE, Ingenta.
Address: Haidian-qu, 27, Taiping Lu, Beijing, 100850, China. TEL 86-10-66930873, FAX 86-10-68215932. **Dist. by:** China International Book Trading Corp, 35 Chegongzhuang Xilu, Haidian District, PO Box 399, Beijing 100044, China. TEL 86-10-68412045, FAX 86-10-68412023, cibtc@mail.cibtc.com.cn, http://www.cibtc.com.cn.

616.15 CHN ISSN 1671-4091
ZHONGGUO XUEYE JINGHUA/CHINESE JOURNAL OF BLOOD PURIFICATION. Text in Chinese. 2002. m. USD 60 (effective 2009). **Document type:** *Journal, Academic/Scholarly.*
Related titles: Online - full text ed.
—East View.
Published by: Zhonghua Yiyuan Guanli Xuehui, 11, Nan Dajie, Xizhimen, Xicheng-qu, Beijing, 100044, China. **Dist. by:** China International Book Trading Corp, 35 Chegongzhuang Xilu, Haidian District, PO Box 399, Beijing 100044, China. TEL 86-10-68412045, FAX 86-10-68412023, cibtc@mail.cibtc.com.cn, http://www.cibtc.com.cn.

616.15 CHN ISSN 1009-881X
ZHONGGUO XUEYE-LIUBIANXUE ZAZHI/CHINESE JOURNAL OF HEMORHEOLOGY. Text in Chinese. 1991. q. **Document type:** *Journal, Academic/Scholarly.*
Formerly (until 1992): Xueye-liubianxue Zazhi
Related titles: Online - full text ed.: (from WanFang Data Corp.).
—BLDSC (9512.827500).
Published by: (Zhongguo Shengwu Yixue Gongcheng Xuehui/Chinese Society of Biomedical Engineering), Suzhou Daxue/Soochow University, 708, Renmin Lu, Su-Da Nan-xiao Qu, Suzhou, 215007, China. TEL 86-512-67780961, http://www.suda.edu.cn/.

616.15 CHN ISSN 0253-2727
CODEN: CHTCD7
ZHONGHUA XUEYEXUE ZAZHI/CHINESE JOURNAL OF HEMATOLOGY. Text in Chinese; Abstracts in Chinese, English. 1980. m. USD 74.40 (effective 2009). adv. **Document type:** *Journal, Academic/Scholarly.* **Description:** Covers the latest development on hematology in China. Contains original articles, case reports and laboratory techniques.
Related titles: CD-ROM ed.; Online - full text ed.
Indexed: ChemAb, EMBASE, ExcerpMed, ExtraMED, IndMed, MEDLINE, P30, R10, Reac, SCOPUS.
—BLDSC (3180.350000), CASDDS, East View.
Published by: Zhongguo Yixue Kexueyuan, Xueye Yanjiusuo/Chinese Academy of Medical Sciences, Institute of Hematology, 288 Nanjing Lu, Tianjin 300020, China. TEL 86-22-2730-4167, FAX 86-22-2730-4167, cnblood@shell.tjvan.net.cn. Ed. Jiazeng Li. R&P Zhifang Zhang. Adv. contact Rurui Wang. B&W page USD 1,400, color page USD 3,000. Circ: 10,000. **Dist. by:** China International Book Trading Corp, 35 Chegongzhuang Xilu, Haidian District, PO Box 399, Beijing 100044, China. TEL 86-10-68412045, FAX 86-10-68412023, cibtc@mail.cibtc.com.cn, http://www.cibtc.com.cn.

MEDICAL SCIENCES—Hypnosis

154.7 616.891 USA ISSN 0002-9157
CODEN: AJHNA3
➤ **AMERICAN JOURNAL OF CLINICAL HYPNOSIS.** Abbreviated title: A J C H. Text in English. 1958. q. GBP 278 combined subscription in United Kingdom to institutions (print & online eds.); EUR 366, USD 458 combined subscription to institutions (print & online eds.) (effective 2012). adv. bk.rev. abstr.; illus. index, cum.index. 88 p./no. 1 cols./p.; back issues avail. **Document type:** *Journal, Academic/Scholarly.* **Description:** Provides peer reviewed research and case reports on clinical hypnosis.
Related titles: Microform ed.: 1958 (from PQC); Online - full text ed.: GBP 250 in United Kingdom to institutions; EUR 330, USD 412 to institutions (effective 2012).
Indexed: A20, A22, AMED, AMHA, BRI, BibInd, CurCont, E-psyche, EMBASE, ExcerpMed, F09, FamI, IBR, IBZ, IndMed, MEA&I, MEDLINE, P03, P20, P22, P25, P30, P48, P54, PQC, PsycInfo, PsycholAb, R10, RILM, Reac, SCOPUS, SSCI, W07.
—BLDSC (0822.800000), GNLM, IE, Infotrieve, Ingenta, INIST. **CCC.**
Published by: American Society of Clinical Hypnosis, 140 N Bloomingdale Rd, Bloomingdale, IL 60108. TEL 630-986-4740, FAX 630-351-8490, info@asch.net. Ed. Stephen Lankton.

➤ **ANESTEZIOLOGIIA I INTENSIVNO LECHENIE.** *see* MEDICAL SCIENCES—Anaesthesiology

➤ **ARCHIVES OF PSYCHIATRY AND PSYCHOTHERAPY.** *see* MEDICAL SCIENCES—Psychiatry And Neurology

616.891 AUS ISSN 0156-0417
CODEN: AJCHDV
AUSTRALIAN JOURNAL OF CLINICAL AND EXPERIMENTAL HYPNOSIS. Abbreviated title: A J C E H. Text in English. 1973. s-a. AUD 44 domestic to individuals; AUD 45 foreign to individuals; AUD 55 to institutions; free to members (effective 2008). adv. bk.rev. back issues avail. **Document type:** *Journal, Academic/Scholarly.* **Description:** Contains research and clinical reports, with a focus on the clinical applications of hypnosis across the domains of medicine, psychology, and dentistry.
Former titles (until 1977): Australian Journal of Clinical Hypnosis (0311-7111); (until 1974): Australian Journal of Medical Sophrology and Hypnotherapy (0311-0508)
Indexed: A01, A11, A22, C06, C07, CA, E-psyche, IndMed, P03, P25, P48, PQC, PsycInfo, PsycholAb, RILM, SCOPUS, T02.
—BLDSC (1806.200000), GNLM, IE, Ingenta. **CCC.**
Published by: Australian Society of Hypnosis Ltd., PO Box 3009, Willoughby North, NSW 2068, Australia. TEL 61-2-94170091, FAX 61-2-94170091, ashltd@optusnet.com.au. Ed. Kathryn M Gow. Circ: 1,100.

616.891 AUS ISSN 0810-0713
➤ **AUSTRALIAN JOURNAL OF CLINICAL HYPNOTHERAPY AND HYPNOSIS.** Text in English. 1980. s-a. free to members (effective 2008). bk.rev. abstr.; stat. Index. 70 p./no.; back issues avail. **Document type:** *Journal, Academic/Scholarly.* **Description:** Covers clinical research, reviews and theoretical and historical reports dealing with the professional application of hypnosis and hypnotherapy.
Formerly (until 1981): Australian Journal of Clinical Hypnotherapy (0159-7175)
Related titles: Online - full text ed.
Indexed: A11, A22, A26, AMED, C06, C07, CA, E-psyche, H11, H12, I05, P03, P25, P30, P48, PQC, PsycInfo, PsycholAb, SCOPUS, T02.
—BLDSC (1806.353000), GNLM, IE, Ingenta.
Published by: Australian Society of Clinical Hypnotherapists, 65 Hume St, Crows Nest, NSW 2065, Australia. TEL 300-851-176, admin@asch.com.au, http://www.asch.com.au. Ed. Lindsay Duncan TEL 61-2-92642292.

154.7 CAN ISSN 1715-8486
CLOSE-UP HYPNOSIS. Text in English. 2006 (Sum.). a. USD 39.95 per issue (effective 2006). **Document type:** *Journal, Academic/Scholarly.* **Description:** Contains a number of hypnotic experiments, achievable by anyone in realworld inpromptu conditions.
Published by: Underwords, 207-1425 Marine Dr, West Vancouver, BC V7T 1B9, Canada. TEL 866-308-3388, FAX 604-677-7476. Ed., Pub., R&P Dr. Fabio Tabbo'. Circ: 1,000 (paid).

COMPREHENSIVE PSYCHIATRY. *see* MEDICAL SCIENCES—Psychiatry And Neurology

616.89 GBR ISSN 0960-5290
RC490 CODEN: COHYET
➤ **CONTEMPORARY HYPNOSIS.** Text in English. 1978. q. GBP 217 in United Kingdom to institutions; EUR 274 in Europe to institutions; USD 425 in the Americas to institutions; USD 425 elsewhere to institutions; GBP 239 combined subscription in United Kingdom to institutions (print & online eds.); EUR 302 combined subscription in Europe to institutions (print & online eds.); USD 468 combined subscription in the Americas to institutions (print & online eds.); USD 468 combined subscription elsewhere to institutions (print & online eds.) (effective 2009). adv. bk.rev. index. back issues avail.; reprint service avail. from PSC. **Document type:** *Journal, Academic/Scholarly.* **Description:** Covers all aspects of theory, research and practice of hypnosis.
Former titles (until 1991): British Journal of Experimental and Clinical Hypnosis (0265-1033); (until 1983): British Society of Experimental and Clinical Hypnosis. Bulletin (0263-046X); (until 1982): Hypnosis (0266-4364)
Related titles: Online - full text ed.: ISSN 1557-0711. GBP 217 in United Kingdom to institutions; EUR 274 in Europe to institutions; USD 425 in the Americas to institutions; USD 425 elsewhere to institutions (effective 2009).
Indexed: A01, A02, A03, A08, AMED, ASSIA, C06, C07, C08, C11, CA, CINAHL, E-psyche, H04, P03, P24, P25, P30, P43, P48, PQC, PsycInfo, PsycholAb, S02, S03, SCOPUS, T02.
—BLDSC (3425.182900), GNLM, IE, Infotrieve, Ingenta. **CCC.**
Published by: (British Society of Experimental and Clinical Hypnosis), John Wiley & Sons Ltd. (Subsidiary of: John Wiley & Sons, Inc.), 1-7 Oldlands Way, PO Box 808, Bognor Regis, West Sussex PO21 9FF, United Kingdom. TEL 44-1865-778315, FAX 44-1243-843232, cs-journals@wiley.com, http://eu.wiley.com/WileyCDA/. Ed. John H Gruzelier. **Subscr. to:** 1-7 Oldlands Way, PO Box 809, Bognor Regis, West Sussex PO21 9FG, United Kingdom. TEL 44-1865-778054, cs-agency@wiley.com. **Dist. by:** Turpin Distribution Services Ltd.

➤ **DTH.** *see* PSYCHOLOGY

615.8512 154.7 GBR ISSN 1351-1297
➤ **EUROPEAN JOURNAL OF CLINICAL HYPNOSIS.** Text in English. 1993. q. GBP 65 domestic to individuals; GBP 70 in Europe to individuals; GBP 75 elsewhere to individuals; GBP 75 combined subscription domestic to individuals (print & online eds.); GBP 80 combined subscription in Europe to individuals (print & online eds.); GBP 85 combined subscription elsewhere to individuals (print & online eds.); GBP 250 combined subscription to institutions (print & online eds.) (effective 2009). back issues avail. **Document type:** *Journal, Academic/Scholarly.* **Description:** Provides a platform for the publication of evidence-based research into clinical hypnosis.
Related titles: Online - full text ed.: GBP 55 (effective 2009).
Indexed: A01, A02, A03, A04, A08, C11, CA, P03, PsycInfo, T02.
—BLDSC (3829.727000).
Published by: (British Association of Medical Hypnosis), European Journal of Clinical Hypnosis Ltd, 27 Gloucester Pl, London, W1U 8HU, United Kingdom. TEL 44-207-4863939. Ed. Rumi Peynovska.

616.89 ESP ISSN 1989-9866
▼ **HIPNOLOGICA**; revista de hipnosis clinica y experimental. Text in Spanish. 2009. s-a. **Document type:** *Magazine, Academic/Scholarly.*
Media: Online - full text.
Published by: Grupo Hipnologica Ed. Isidro Perez Hidalgo.

615.8 DEU ISSN 1862-4731
HYPNOSE. Text in German. 2005. a. EUR 15 (effective 2006). **Document type:** *Journal, Academic/Scholarly.*
Formed by the merger of (1983-2005): Experimentelle und Klinische Hypnose (0933-1093); (1984-2005): Hypnose und Kognition (0178-093X)
Published by: M E G - Stiftung, Hauptstr 39, Wilhelmsthal-Hesselbach, 96352, Germany. TEL 49-9260-964780, FAX 49-9260-964781, Burkhard-Peter@t-online.de, http://meg-stiftung.de.

615.8512 FRA ISSN 1951-2376
HYPNOSE & THERAPIES BREVES. Text in French. 2006. q. EUR 39 domestic; EUR 42 elsewhere (effective 2009). back issues avail. **Document type:** *Journal, Trade.*
Published by: Editions Metawalk, 45 Av. Franklin Roosevelt, Avon, 77210, France. TEL 33-1-60964778, metawalk@wanadoo.fr. Ed. Patrick Bellet.

615.8512 154.7 SWE ISSN 1653-6290
HYPNOSNYTT. Text in English. 1978. q. SEK 550 in Europe to non-members (effective 2010). back issues avail. **Document type:** *Journal, Academic/Scholarly.*
Former titles (until 2006): Hypnos (0282-5090); (until 1985): Svensk Tidskrift for Hypnos (0349-7550); Incorporates (1986-2002): Hypnos-Nytt (Nykoeping) (1100-7052)
Indexed: AMED.
—IE, Ingenta.
Published by: Svenska Foereningen foer Klinisk och Experimentell Hypnos/Swedish Society of Clinical and Experimental Hypnosis, Erik Dahlbergsgatan 9, Goeteborg, 41126, Sweden. TEL 46-31-7117118, FAX 46-31-137978, kansli@hypnosforeningen.se. Ed. Stefan Fransson.

616.891 370.15 USA ISSN 0882-8652
HYPNOTHERAPY TODAY. Text in English. 1980. q. membership. bk.rev. tr.lit. **Document type:** *Newsletter, Trade.* **Description:** Studies the therapeutic uses of hypnosis for the body, mind and spiritual needs.
Related titles: E-mail ed.; Online - full text ed.
Indexed: E-psyche.
Published by: American Association of Professional Hypnotherapists, 4149 El Camino Way No A, Palo Alto, CA 94306-4036. TEL 650-323-3224. Ed. Mary Horngren. Pub. Josie Hadley. Circ: 1,000.

154.7 616.891 GBR ISSN 0020-7144
RC490 CODEN: IJEHAO
➤ **INTERNATIONAL JOURNAL OF CLINICAL AND EXPERIMENTAL HYPNOSIS.** Abbreviated title: I J C E H. Text in English; Summaries in French, German, Spanish. 1953. q. GBP 355 combined subscription in United Kingdom to institutions (print & online eds.); EUR 471, USD 592 combined subscription to institutions (print & online eds.) (effective 2012). adv. bk.rev. illus. cum.index. back issues avail.; reprint service avail. from PSC. **Document type:** *Journal, Academic/Scholarly.* **Description:** Publishes research papers dealing with hypnosis in psychology, psychiatry, the medical and dental specialties, and related studies.
Formerly (until 1959): Journal of Clinical and Experimental Hypnosis (0095-988X)
Related titles: Microfilm ed.: (from PQC); Online - full text ed.: ISSN 1744-5183. GBP 319 in United Kingdom to institutions; EUR 424, USD 532 to institutions (effective 2012) (from IngentaConnect).
Indexed: A20, A22, AMED, AMHA, ASCA, C06, C07, C08, CA, CINAHL, CurCont, DIP, E-psyche, E01, EMBASE, ExcerpMed, FR, IBR, IBZ, ISR, IndMed, MEA&I, MEDLINE, P03, P24, P25, P30, P50, PQC, PsycInfo, PsycholAb, R10, Reac, RefZh, S02, S03, SCOPUS, SSCI, SWR&A, T02, V&AA, W07.
—BLDSC (4542.170000), GNLM, IE, Infotrieve, Ingenta, INIST. **CCC.**
Published by: (Society for Clinical and Experimental Hypnosis USA), Routledge (Subsidiary of: Taylor & Francis Group), 4 Park Square, Milton Park, Abingdon, Oxon OX14 4RN, United Kingdom. subscriptions@tandf.co.uk, http://www.routledge.com. Ed. Arreed Barabasz TEL 509-335-8166. Adv. contact Linda Hann TEL 44-1344-779945. Circ: 2,500. **Subscr. in Europe to:** Taylor & Francis Ltd., Journals Customer Service, Sheepen Pl, Colchester, Essex CO3 3LP, United Kingdom. TEL 44-20-70175544, FAX 44-20-70175198; **Subscr. in N. America to:** Taylor & Francis Inc., Customer Services Dept, 325 Chestnut St, 8th Fl, Philadelphia, PA 19106. TEL 215-625-8900, 800-354-1420, FAX 215-625-2940, orders@taylorandfrancis.com.

615.8512 IRN ISSN 1735-9104
R97
IRANIAN JOURNAL OF MEDICAL HYPOTHESIS & IDEAS. Text in Persian, Modern, English. s-a. **Document type:** *Journal, Academic/Scholarly.*
Related titles: Online - full text ed.: free (effective 2011).
Indexed: A01, EMBASE, ExcerpMed, P20, P54, SCOPUS, T02.
Published by: Tehran University of Medical Sciences Publications, Central Library & Documents Center, Poursina St, Tehran, 14174, Iran. TEL 98-21-6112743, FAX 98-21-6404377, http://diglib.tums.ac.ir/pub/journals.asp.

PSYCHOTERAPIA. *see* MEDICAL SCIENCES—Psychiatry And Neurology

154.7 BRA ISSN 1516-232X
REVISTA BRASILEIRA DE HIPNOSE. Text in Portuguese. 1973. s-a.
Document type: *Journal, Academic/Scholarly.*
Formerly (until 1993): Revista Brasileira de Hipnologia (0100-2325)
Published by: Sociedade Brasileira de Hipnose, Rua Desembargador Jorge Fontana 408, Sala 502 Belvedere, Belo Horizonte, MG 30320-670, Brazil. TEL 55-31-32868339, FAX 55-31-32865235, http://www.sbhip.org.

154.7 616.891 USA
S C E H FOCUS. (Society for Clinical and Experimental Hypnosis) Variant title: Focus. Text in English. 1955. q. free to members. bk.rev.
Document type: *Newsletter.*
Formerly: S C E H Newsletter (0583-8975)
Related titles: Online - full content ed.
Published by: Society for Clinical and Experimental Hypnosis, Massachusetts School of Professional Psychology, 221 Rivermoor St, Boston, MA 02132. TEL 617-469-1981, FAX 617-469-1889, sceh@mspp.edu, http://www.sceh.us. Ed. Grant Benham. Circ: 1,200.

MEDICAL SCIENCES—Internal Medicine

see also MEDICAL SCIENCES—Cardiovascular Diseases ; MEDICAL SCIENCES—Communicable Diseases ; MEDICAL SCIENCES—Endocrinology ; MEDICAL SCIENCES—Gastroenterology ; MEDICAL SCIENCES—Hematology ; MEDICAL SCIENCES—Oncology ; MEDICAL SCIENCES—Respiratory Diseases ; MEDICAL SCIENCES—Rheumatology ; MEDICAL SCIENCES—Urology And Nephrology

616 USA ISSN 1548-9345
A C P MEDICINE. (American College of Physician) Text in English. 2004. m. **Document type:** *Magazine, Trade.*
Related titles: ◆ Print ed.: A C P Medicine. ISSN 1547-1632.
Indexed: A22.
Published by: WebMD Inc., 669 River Dr, Center 2, Elmwood Park, NJ 07407. TEL 201-703-3400, FAX 201-703-3401, http://www.webmd.com.

616 CAN ISSN 1547-1632
RC55
A C P MEDICINE. (American College of Physicians) Text in English. 2004. 2 base vols. plus m. updates. USD 169 base vol(s).; USD 199 (effective 2009). **Document type:** *Magazine, Trade.*
Related titles: CD-ROM ed.: ISSN 1547-1640. USD 329 (effective 2009); Online - full text ed.: ISSN 1547-1659. USD 179 (effective 2009); ◆ Print ed.: A C P Medicine. ISSN 1548-9345.
Published by: (American College of Physicians USA), B.C. Decker Inc., 50 King St E, 2nd Fl, Hamilton, ON L8N 2A1, Canada. TEL 905-522-7017, 800-568-7281, FAX 905-522-7839, 888-311-4987, info@bcdecker.com, http://www.bcdecker.com. Ed. Dr. Elizabeth G Nabel.

616 BRA ISSN 0104-4885
ACADEMIA NACIONAL DE MEDICINA. ANAIS. Text in Portuguese; Summaries in English, Portuguese. 1841. q. adv. charts; bibl.; illus. back issues avail. **Document type:** *Journal, Academic/Scholarly.* **Description:** Presents studies in clinical medicine.
Former titles (until 1991): Academia Nacional de Medicina. Boletim (0001-3838); (until 1918): Academia Nacional de Medicina de Rio de Janeiro. Annals (0102-1451); (until 1915): Academia de Medicina de Rio de Janeiro. Annals (0102-1435); (until 1885): Annals Brazilienses de Medicina (0102-1443)
Indexed: ChemAb, P30.
—GNLM.
Published by: Academia Nacional de Medicina, Av General Justo 365, 7o Andar, Centro, Rio de Janeiro, 20021-130, Brazil. TEL 55-21-25242164, FAX 55-21-22408673, http://www.anm.org.br.

616 COL ISSN 0120-2448
R21 CODEN: AAMCD3
ACTA MEDICA COLOMBIANA. Text in Spanish. 1976. q. **Document type:** *Journal, Academic/Scholarly.*
Related titles: Online - full text ed.: free (effective 2011) (from SciELO).
Indexed: A26, FR, I04, I05, P30.
—INIST.
Published by: Asociacion Colombiana de Medicina Interna (A C M I), Carrera 16A, No 77-11, oficina 204, Bogota, Colombia. TEL 57-1-2368994, FAX 57-1-2187860, http://www.linemed.co. Ed. Paulo Emilio Archila.

616 GBR ISSN 1747-4884
➤ **ACUTE MEDICINE.** Text in English. 1999. 3/yr. GBP 45 per vol. domestic to individuals; GBP 60 per vol. foreign to individuals; GBP 60 per vol. domestic to institutions; GBP 90 per vol. foreign to institutions (effective 2009). back issues avail. **Document type:** *Journal, Academic/Scholarly.* **Description:** Contains significant review articles on acute medicine.
Former titles (until 2005): C P D Journal. Acute Medicine (1476-5063); (until 2002): C P D Journal. Internal Medicine (1466-2914)
Related titles: ◆ Online - full text ed.: Acute Medicine (Online). ISSN 1747-4892.
Indexed: EMBASE, ExcerpMed, R10, Reac, SCOPUS.
—BLDSC (0678.077500), IE, Ingenta. **CCC.**
Published by: Rila Publications Ltd., 73 Newman St, London, W1A 4PG, United Kingdom. TEL 44-20-76311299, FAX 44-20-75807166, admin@rila.co.uk. Ed. Dr. Chris D Roseveare TEL 44-2380-794716.

616 GBR ISSN 1747-4892
➤ **ACUTE MEDICINE (ONLINE).** Text in English. 2005. 3/yr. GBP 30 per vol. (effective 2009). **Document type:** *Journal, Academic/Scholarly.* **Description:** Contains significant review articles on acute medicine.
Media: Online - full text. **Related titles:** ◆ Print ed.: Acute Medicine. ISSN 1747-4884.
Published by: Rila Publications Ltd., 73 Newman St, London, W1A 4PG, United Kingdom. TEL 44-20-76311299, FAX 44-20-75807166, admin@rila.co.uk.

610 USA
AMERICAN SOCIETY FOR ARTIFICIAL INTERNAL ORGANS. ABSTRACTS, ANNUAL MEETING. Text in English. 1972. a. **Document type:** *Proceedings, Trade.*
—**CCC.**
Published by: American Society for Artificial Internal Organs, Inc., 980 N Federal Hwy, Ste 212, Boca Raton, FL 33432-2711. TEL 561-391-8589, FAX 561-368-9153, info@asaio.com, http://www.asaio.com.

616 USA
AMERICAN SOCIETY OF BARIATRIC PHYSICIANS. NEWS. Short title: News from A S B P. Text in English. 1986. bi-m. free to members (effective 2010). adv. **Document type:** *Newsletter, Consumer.*
Published by: The American Society of Bariatric Physicians, 2821 S Parker Rd, Ste 625, Aurora, CO 80014. info@asbp.org, http://www.asbp.org. Adv. contact Nicola Grun.

616.02 ESP ISSN 0212-7199
➤ **ANALES DE MEDICINA INTERNA.** Text in Spanish; Abstracts in Spanish, English. 1983. m. EUR 88 to qualified personnel; EUR 149 to institutions; EUR 66 to students (effective 2008). adv. abstr.; bibl.; illus.; stat. back issues avail. **Document type:** *Journal, Academic/Scholarly.*
Related titles: Online - full text ed.: free (effective 2011).
Indexed: A22, A36, AIDS&CR, CABA, E12, EMBASE, ExcerpMed, F08, GH, H17, INI, IndMed, LT, MEDLINE, N02, N03, P30, P33, P39, R10, R12, RA&MP, RM&VM, RRTA, Reac, S12, SCI, SCOPUS, T05, W07.
—BLDSC (0890.018000), GNLM, IE, Infotrieve, Ingenta, INIST. **CCC.**
Published by: (Sociedad Espanola de Medicina Interna), Aran Ediciones, Castello 128, 1o, Madrid, 28006, Spain. TEL 34-91-7820030, FAX 34-91-5615787, edita@grupoaran.com, http://www.grupoaran.com. Ed. Dr. J De Portugal. Pub. Jose Jimenez Marquez. R&P Maria Dolores Linares TEL 34-91-7820035. Circ: 5,000.

616 TUR ISSN 1301-3114
ANKEM DERGISI/JOURNAL OF ANKEM. Text in Turkish. 1987. q. **Document type:** *Journal, Academic/Scholarly.*
Related titles: Online - full text ed.: free (effective 2009).
Published by: Ankem Merkezi, Rumeli Cad. Ipek Ap. No. 70 K.7, Osmanbey - Istanbul, 80220, Turkey. TEL 90-212-2199339, FAX 90-212-2199341.

616.026 USA ISSN 0003-4819
R11 CODEN: AIMEAS
➤ **ANNALS OF INTERNAL MEDICINE.** Text in English. 1920. s-m. USD 260 in US & Canada to individuals; USD 411 elsewhere to individuals (effective 2009). adv. bk.rev. charts; illus. cum.index. back issues avail. **Document type:** *Journal, Academic/Scholarly.* **Description:** Contains reports of original clinical research, reviews, and commentaries.
Incorporates (1991-2008): A C P Journal Club (1056-8751); Former titles (until 1927): Annals of Clinical Medicine (0095-9944); (until 1922): Annals of Medicine (0099-7137)
Related titles: CD-ROM ed.; Microform ed.: (from PMC, PQC); Online - full text ed.: ISSN 1539-3704; Supplement(s): Annals of Internal Medicine. Supplement. ISSN 0570-183X.
Indexed: A01, A02, A03, A08, A20, A22, A26, A34, A36, AHCMS, AIDS Ab, AIIM, AIM, AMED, ASCA, AbAn, AddicA, B21, B25, BIOSIS Prev, C06, C07, C08, C11, CA, CABA, CIN, CINAHL, CIS, CISA, CTA, ChemAb, ChemTitl, ChemoAb, CurCont, D01, DBA, DentInd, DiabCont, DokArb, E08, E12, EMBASE, ExcerpMed, F08, F11, F12, FAMLI, FR, G08, G10, GH, H04, H11, H12, H13, H17, HospLI, I05, I12, IDIS, INI, ISR, ImmunAb, IndMed, IndVet, Inpharma, JW, JW-C, JW-D, JW-EM, JW-G, JW-ID, JW-N, JW-P, JW-WH, Kidney, LT, MCR, MEDLINE, MS&D, MycolAb, N02, N03, NRN, NSA, P10, P19, P20, P21, P22, P24, P30, P33, P34, P35, P37, P38, P39, P50, P53, P54, PHN&I, PN&I, PQC, R08, R10, R11, R12, RA&MP, RM&VM, RRTA, Reac, S02, S03, S09, S21, SCI, SCOPUS, SoyAb, T02, T05, THA, TriticAb, VS, W07, W11.
—BLDSC (1041.200000), CASDDS, GNLM, IE, Infotrieve, Ingenta, INIST. **CCC.**
Published by: American College of Physicians, 190 N Independence Mall W, Philadelphia, PA 19106. TEL 215-351-2400, 800-523-1546, FAX 215-351-2799, custserv@mail.acponline.org, http://www.annalsonline.org. Ed. Dr. Christine Laine. Adv. contact Brian S Barker. B&W page USD 6,645, color page USD 8,740; trim 8.25 x 10.8125. Circ: 101,613. **Subscr. to:** Allen Press Inc., 810 E 10th St, PO Box 368, Lawrence, KS 66044. TEL 785-843-1234, 800-627-0326, FAX 785-843-1226, http://www.allenpress.com.

616 IND ISSN 1817-1737
ANNALS OF THORACIC MEDICINE. Text in English. 2006. q. INR 2,500 domestic; USD 75 foreign to individuals; USD 150 foreign to institutions (effective 2011). adv. **Document type:** *Journal, Academic/Scholarly.* **Description:** Features clinical investigations in the multidisciplinary specialties of chest medicine, such as pulmonology, cardiology, thoracic surgery, transplantation, sleep and breathing and airways disease.
Related titles: Online - full text ed.: ISSN 1998-3557. INR 2,000 domestic; USD 60 foreign to individuals; USD 120 foreign to institutions (effective 2011).
Indexed: A01, A26, A34, A36, C06, C07, CA, CABA, E08, EMBASE, ExcerpMed, G08, GH, H11, H12, H17, I05, IndVet, N02, N03, P10, P30, P32, P33, P37, P48, P53, P54, PN&I, PQC, R10, R12, RA&MP, RM&VM, Reac, S09, S12, SCI, SCOPUS, T02, T05, VS, W07.
—**CCC.**
Published by: (Saudi Thoracic Society SAU), Medknow Publications and Media Pvt. Ltd., B-9, Kanara Business Ctr, Off Link Rd, Ghatkopar (E), Mumbai, Maharastra 400 075, India. TEL 91-22-66491818, 91-22-66491816, journals@medknow.com, http://www.medknow.com.

616 USA ISSN 0003-9926
R11 CODEN: AIMDAP
➤ **ARCHIVES OF INTERNAL MEDICINE.** Text in English. 1908. 22/yr. USD 645 domestic to institutions; USD 806 in the Americas to institutions; EUR 652 in Europe to institutions; GBP 553 elsewhere to institutions (effective 2012). adv. charts; illus. index. back issues avail.; reprints avail. **Document type:** *Journal, Academic/Scholarly.* **Description:** Features manuscripts relevant to internists practicing as generalists or as medical sub-specialists.
Former titles (until 1960): A M A Archives of Internal Medicine (0888-2479); (until 1950): Archives of Internal Medicine (0730-188X)
Related titles: Microform ed.: (from PMC, PQC); Online - full text ed.: ISSN 1538-3679. free to members (effective 2012); Translation: Archives of Internal Medicine (Spanish Edition). ISSN 1667-4901.
Indexed: A01, A02, A03, A08, A20, A22, A26, A34, A36, AHCMS, AIDS Ab, AIIM, AIM, AMED, ASCA, ASG, AddicA, AgeL, B04, B25, BIOBASE, BIOSIS Prev, BRD, BiolDig, C06, C07, C08, CA, CABA, CIN, CINAHL, CIS, CISA, CLFP, ChemAb, ChemTitl, Chicano, CurCont, D01, DBA, DentInd, DiabCont, DokArb, E08, E12, EMBASE, ExcerpMed, F08, F11, F12, FR, FamI, G03, G08, G10, GH, GSA, GSI, H11, H12, H13, H17, HospLI, I05, I12, IABS, IBR, IBZ, IDIS, INI, ISR, IndMed, IndVet, Inpharma, JW, JW-C, JW-D, JW-EM, JW-G, JW-ID, JW-N, JW-P, JW-WH, Kidney, LT, MEDLINE, MLA-IB, MS&D, MycolAb, N02, N03, NRN, P02, P10, P20, P21, P22, P24, P30, P33, P34, P35, P37, P39, P48, P50, P53, P54, PQC, R08, R10, R12, RA&MP, RILM, RM&VM, RRTA, Reac, S02, S03, S09, S12, SCI, SCOPUS, SoyAb, T02, T05, THA, VITIS, VS, W03, W07, W09, W11.
—BLDSC (1634.850000), CASDDS, GNLM, IE, Infotrieve, Ingenta, INIST. **CCC.**
Published by: American Medical Association, 515 N State St, Chicago, IL 60654. TEL 312-464-4200, 800-621-8335, FAX 312-464-4142, journalsales@ama-assn.org, http://www.ama-assn.org. Eds. Rita F Redberg TEL 312-464-5984, Dr. Catherine D DeAngelis. **Subscr. in the Americas to:** PO Box 10946, Chicago, IL 60654. TEL 312-670-7827, 800-262-2350, ama-subs@ama-assn.org; **Subscr. outside the Americas to:** American Medical Association, J A M A and Archive Journals.

616 URY ISSN 0250-3816
ARCHIVOS DE MEDICINA INTERNA. Text in Spanish. 1979. q. USD 80 (effective 2005).
Indexed: C01, INIS AtomInd, P30.
Published by: (Sociedad de Medicia de Montevideo), Prensa Medica Latinoamericana Ltda., Guayabo 1790, Esq 504, Montevideo, 11200, Uruguay. TEL 598-2-4092933, FAX 598-2-4000916, prensmed@chasque.apc.org.

616 BRA ISSN 0365-0723
R21 CODEN: ABMEAD
ARQUIVOS BRASILEIROS DE MEDICINA. Text in Portuguese; Summaries in English, Portuguese. 1911. bi-m. BRL 54 domestic; USD 72 foreign (effective 2000). adv. bk.rev. index, cum.index. back issues avail. **Document type:** *Academic/Scholarly.* **Description:** Presents studies in internal medicine.
Indexed: A22, C01, IBR, IBZ, IndMed, P30, R10, Reac, SCOPUS.
—GNLM, Infotrieve, INIST.
Published by: (Universidade Federal Fluminense), Editora Cientifica Nacional Ltda. (E C N), Rua da Gloria 366, 3o Andar, Gloria, Rio de Janeiro, RJ 20241-180, Brazil. Ed. Antonio Alves de Couto. R&P, Adv. contact Maria Luiza Carvalho. Circ: 10,000.

610 BRA ISSN 0571-1320
➤ **ARS CURANDI. CLINICA MEDICA.** Text in Portuguese. 1968. m. adv. back issues avail. **Document type:** *Journal, Academic/Scholarly.* **Description:** Publishes a variety of research and clinical articles in general-practice medicine.
Indexed: C01.
Published by: Elea Ciencia Editorial Ltda., Rua Barao de Uba 48, Rio de Janeiro, RJ 20260-050, Brazil. TEL 55-21-2932112, FAX 55-21-2937818. Ed. Luiz Augusto Rodrigues. Adv. contact Alexandre Augusto Rodrigues.

616.028 MEX ISSN 0187-8433
ASOCIACION MEXICANA DE MEDICINA CRITICA Y TERAPIA INTENSIVA. REVISTA. Text in Spanish. 1996. bi-m. MXN 400 domestic; USD 80 in Latin America; USD 90 in US & Canada; USD 100 elsewhere (effective 2007). back issues avail. **Document type:** *Journal, Trade.*
Related titles: Online - full text ed.
Indexed: C01.
Published by: Asociacion Mexicana de Medicina Critica y Terapia Intensiva, Cleveland No 33-101, Col. Nochebuena, Mexico, D.F., 03720, Mexico. TEL 52-55-55981684, FAX 52-55-56112585, amimcti@prodigy.net.mx. Ed. Alejandro Arroliga.

ATKINS: A PASSION FOR HEALTHY LIVING. *see* NUTRITION AND DIETETICS

616 016 USA ISSN 0271-1303
➤ **AUDIO-DIGEST INTERNAL MEDICINE.** Variant title: Internal Medicine. Text in English. 1954. s-m. USD 449.81 domestic; USD 479.72 in Canada; USD 527.72 elsewhere (effective 2010). index. back issues avail. **Document type:** *Journal, Academic/Scholarly.*
Media: Audio cassette/tape. **Related titles:** Audio CD ed.: USD 399.89 domestic; USD 431.72 in Canada; USD 479.72 elsewhere (effective 2010); Online - full text ed.: USD 359.72 (effective 2010).
Published by: Audio-Digest Foundation (Subsidiary of: California Medical Association), 1577 E Chevy Chase Dr, Glendale, CA 91206. TEL 818-240-7500, 800-423-2308, FAX 818-240-7379.

616 DEU
B D I AKTUELL. (Berufsverband Deutscher Internisten) Text in German. 1998. m. adv. **Document type:** *Journal, Trade.*
Formerly (until 2001): B D I Rundschreiben
Published by: Berufsverband Deutscher Internisten e.V., Schoene Aussicht 5, Wiesbaden, 65193, Germany. TEL 49-611-181330, FAX 49-611-1813350, info@bdi.de. adv.: B&W page EUR 2,910, color page EUR 4,010. Circ: 22,400 (controlled).

616 USA ISSN 1099-4521
➤ **BARIATRICIAN.** Variant title: American Journal of Bariatric Medicine. Text in English. 1988. s-a. free to qualified personnel (effective 2010). adv. illus.; stat.; tr.lit. reprints avail. **Document type:** *Journal, Consumer.* **Description:** Covers various aspects of the medical treatment of overweight, obesity and associated conditions, and with administrative aspects of operating a bariatrics practice.
Published by: The American Society of Bariatric Physicians, 2821 S Parker Rd, Ste 625, Aurora, CO 80014. info@asbp.org, http://www.asbp.org. Adv. contact Nicola Grun.

616 CZE ISSN 1803-5701
BIOLOGICKA LECBA. Text in Czech. 2008. 3/yr. **Document type:** *Journal, Academic/Scholarly.*
Published by: Medica Healthworld a.s., Bidlaky 20, Brno, 63900, Czech Republic. TEL 420-533-337311, FAX 420-533-337312, info@mhw.cz, http://www.mhw.cz. Circ: 3,000.

616 ESP ISSN 2013-7419
BUTLETI DE LA MEDICINA DE FAMILIA A CATALUNYA. Text in Catalan, Spanish. 2008. q. **Document type:** *Bulletin, Consumer.*
Media: Online - full text.

Published by: Societat Catalana de Medicina Familiar i Comunitaria, C Portaferrissa, No. 8 Pral., Barcelona, 08002, Spain. TEL 34-93-3011777, FAX 34-93-3181001, http://www.camfit.cat/.

616 ESP ISSN 2013-2263
▼ **EL CAPCALERA.** Text in Catalan. 2009. m. back issues avail. **Document type:** *Bulletin, Consumer.*
Media: Online - full text.
Published by: Societat Catalana de Medicina Familiar i Comunitaria, C Portaferrissa, No. 8 Pral., Barcelona, 08002, Spain. TEL 34-93-3011777, FAX 34-93-3181001, http://www.camfit.cat/.

616.044 CAN ISSN 0228-8699
RA644.8.C2 CODEN: CDSCFA
➤ **CHRONIC DISEASES IN CANADA.** Text in English. 1980. q. free. **Document type:** *Journal, Academic/Scholarly.* **Description:** Focuses on current evidence relevant to the control and prevention of chronic diseases and injuries in Canada.
Related titles: Online - full text ed.: ISSN 1481-8523. free (effective 2011); ◆ French ed.: Maladies Chroniques au Canada. ISSN 0228-8702.
Indexed: A36, A37, C03, CABA, CBCARef, D01, E12, EMBASE, ExcerpMed, GH, LT, MEDLINE, N02, N03, P30, P48, PAIS, PQC, R10, R12, RRTA, Reac, S13, SCI, SCOPUS, T05, W07, W11.
—**CCC.**
Published by: (Canada. Public Works and Government Services Canada/Travaux Publics et Services Gouvernementaux Canada), Public Health Agency of Canada/Agence de Sante Publique du Canada, 0904A, Buock Claxton Bldg, Tunney's Pasture, Ottawa, ON K1A OK9, Canada. TEL 613-957-2991, FAX 613-941-5366, info@hc-sc.gc.ca, http://www.hc-sc.gc.ca. Ed. Debby Baker.

616 NZL ISSN 1178-1149
➤ **CLINICAL MEDICINE: ARTHRITIS AND MUSCULOSKELETAL DISORDERS.** Text in English. 2008. irreg. free (effective 2011). **Document type:** *Journal, Academic/Scholarly.* **Description:** Covers all aspects of the prevention, diagnosis and management of all associated disorders in addition to related genetic, pathophysiological and epidemiological topics.
Media: Online - full text.
Indexed: A01, EMBASE, ExcerpMed, SCOPUS, T02.
Published by: Libertas Academica Ltd., PO Box 302-624, North Harbour, Auckland, 1330, New Zealand. TEL 64-21-662617, FAX 64-21-740006, editorial@la-press.com, http://www.la-press.com. Ed. Tariq M Haqqi.

616 NZL ISSN 1178-2269
➤ **CLINICAL MEDICINE: BLOOD DISORDERS.** Text in English. 2008. irreg. free (effective 2011). **Document type:** *Journal, Academic/Scholarly.* **Description:** Covers all aspects of the diagnosis, management and prevention of blood disorders in addition to related genetic, pathophysiological and epidemiological topics.
Media: Online - full text.
Indexed: A01, EMBASE, ExcerpMed, SCOPUS, T02.
Published by: Libertas Academica Ltd., PO Box 302-624, North Harbour, Auckland, 1330, New Zealand. TEL 64-21-662617, FAX 64-21-740006, editorial@la-press.com, http://www.la-press.com. Ed. Robert E Richard.

➤ **COCUK ENFEKSIYON DERGISI/JOURNAL OF PEDIATRIC INFECTIONS.** *see* MEDICAL SCIENCES—Pediatrics

➤ **COMMUNITY REFERENCE LABORATORY FOR SALMONELLA. NEWSLETTER (ONLINE).** *see* BIOLOGY—Microbiology

616 JPN ISSN 1342-4904
CODEN: CTKEFK
COMPLICATION/TONYOBYO TO KEKKAN. Text in Japanese. 1996. s-a. JPY 4,572 per issue (effective 2005). **Document type:** *Journal, Academic/Scholarly.*
—CASDDS.
Published by: Medikaru Rebyusha/Medical Review Co., Ltd., 1-7-3 Hirano-Machi, Chuo-ku, Yoshida Bldg., Osaka-shi, 541-0046, Japan. TEL 81-6-62231468, FAX 81-6-62231245.

616 USA ISSN 1051-1040
➤ **CONTEMPORARY INTERNAL MEDICINE.** Text in English. 1988. irreg., latest vol.8, 1996. price varies. **Document type:** *Monographic series, Academic/Scholarly.* **Description:** Provides clinically practical information in areas of high interest to internists and specialist physicians.
—**CCC.**
Published by: Springer New York LLC (Subsidiary of: Springer Science+Business Media), 233 Spring St, New York, NY 10013. TEL 212-460-1500, FAX 212-460-1575, service-ny@springer.com.

616 USA ISSN 1930-4765
RB127
CURRENT DIAGNOSIS & TREATMENT OF PAIN. Text in English. 2006. triennial. USD 72.95 per issue (effective 2010). **Document type:** *Journal, Trade.* **Description:** A clinical and management oriented journal on pain medicine.
Published by: McGraw-Hill Companies, Inc., McGraw-Hill Professional, PO Box 182604, Columbus, OH 43272. TEL 877-833-5524, FAX 614-759-3749, customer.service@mcgraw-hill.com, http://www.mcgraw-hill.com.

616 USA ISSN 1550-0705
CURRENT ESSENTIALS OF CRITICAL CARE. Text in English. 2004. biennial. USD 36.95 per issue (effective 2008). 250 p./no.; **Document type:** *Journal, Trade.*
Published by: McGraw-Hill Professional (Subsidiary of: McGraw-Hill Companies, Inc.), 1221 Ave of the Americas, New York, NY 10020. TEL 212-904-2000, FAX 212-512-2000, customer.service@mcgraw-hill.com, http://www.mhprofessional.com/index.php. Ed. Darryl Y Sue.

616 NLD ISSN 0272-1465
➤ **CURRENT HISTOPATHOLOGY.** Text in English. 1980. irreg., latest vol.24, 1994. price varies. **Document type:** *Monographic series, Academic/Scholarly.*
—**CCC.**
Published by: Springer Netherlands (Subsidiary of: Springer Science+Business Media), Van Godewijckstraat 30, Dordrecht, 3311 GX, Netherlands. TEL 31-78-6576050, FAX 31-78-6576474.

616 GBR ISSN 1756-2317
CODEN: CDPAFN
DIAGNOSTIC HISTOPATHOLOGY (OXFORD). Text in English. 1994. m. EUR 762 in Europe to institutions; JPY 82,400 in Japan to institutions; USD 679 elsewhere to institutions (effective 2012). bk.rev. back issues avail. **Document type:** *Journal, Academic/Scholarly.* **Description:** Publishes reviews in histopathology and cytology for the diagnostic pathologist.
Formerly (until 2008): Current Diagnostic Pathology (0968-6053)
Related titles: Online - full text ed.: ISSN 1876-7621 (from ScienceDirect).
Indexed: A22, A26, CA, E01, EMBASE, ExcerpMed, I05, P30, SCOPUS, T02.
—BLDSC (3579.657700), GNLM, IE, Infotrieve, Ingenta. **CCC.**
Published by: The Medicine Publishing Company (Subsidiary of: Elsevier Ltd), The Boulevard, Langford Ln, Kidlington, Oxford, OX5 1GB, United Kingdom. TEL 44-1865-843154, FAX 44-1865-843965, JournalsCustomerServiceEMEA@elsevier.com, http://www.medicinepublishing.co.uk. Ed. Dr. Simon Cross. Pub. Melanie Burton.

616.026 BRA ISSN 1413-9979
➤ **DIAGNOSTICO & TRATAMENTO.** Text in English; Summaries in Portuguese. 1996. q. adv. bk.rev. back issues avail. **Document type:** *Journal, Academic/Scholarly.*
Related titles: Online - full text ed.
Published by: (Associacao Paulista de Medicina), Lemos Editorial & Graficos Ltda., Rua Rui Barbosa, 70, B Vista, Sao Paulo, SP 01326-010, Brazil. TEL 55-11-251-4300, FAX 55-11-251-4300, lemospl@netpoint.com.br, http://www.lemos.com.br.

➤ **DIRECTORY OF PARTICIPATING DIALYSIS CENTRES, TRANSPLANT CENTRES AND ORGAN PROCUREMENT ORGANIZATIONS IN CANADA/REPERTOIRE DES CENTRES DE DIALYSE PARTICIPANTS AU CANADA.** *see* MEDICAL SCIENCES—Urology And Nephrology

616 EGY ISSN 1110-7782
THE EGYPTIAN JOURNAL OF INTERNAL MEDICINE. Text in English. 1992. q. **Document type:** *Journal, Academic/Scholarly.*
Published by: The Egyptian Society of Internal Medicine, 5 El-Gomhria St, Abdeen, Cairo, Egypt. TEL 202-396-0960, FAX 202-391-4575, info@esim.org.eg, http://www.esim.org.eg. Ed. Dr. El-Sawi Habib.

616 NLD ISSN 0953-6205
R5 CODEN: EJIMEJ
➤ **EUROPEAN JOURNAL OF INTERNAL MEDICINE.** Text in English; Summaries in French. 1990. 8/yr. EUR 395 in Europe to institutions; JPY 49,600 in Japan to institutions; USD 442 elsewhere to institutions (effective 2012). **Document type:** *Journal, Academic/Scholarly.* **Description:** Covers all aspects of internal medicine.
Related titles: Online - full text ed.: ISSN 1879-0828 (from IngentaConnect, ScienceDirect).
Indexed: A01, A03, A08, A20, A22, A26, CA, CurCont, EMBASE, ExcerpMed, I05, MEDLINE, P30, R10, Reac, SCI, SCOPUS, T02, W07.
—BLDSC (3829.730700), GNLM, IE, Infotrieve, Ingenta. **CCC.**
Published by: Elsevier BV (Subsidiary of: Elsevier Science & Technology), Radarweg 29, PO Box 211, Amsterdam, 1000 AE, Netherlands. TEL 31-20-4853911, FAX 31-20-4852457, JournalsCustomerServiceEMEA@elsevier.com, http://www.elsevier.nl. Ed. P W de Leeuw.

616 GBR ISSN 1352-2779
EUROPEAN JOURNAL OF PALLIATIVE CARE. Text in English. 1994. bi-m. GBP 90 in Europe to individuals; GBP 135 elsewhere to individuals; GBP 255 in Europe to institutions; GBP 345 elsewhere to institutions; GBP 145 combined subscription in Europe to individuals (print & online eds.); GBP 190 combined subscription elsewhere to individuals (print & online eds.); GBP 415 combined subscription in Europe to institutions (print & online eds.); GBP 455 combined subscription elsewhere to institutions (print & online eds.) (effective 2009). illus. back issues avail. **Document type:** *Journal, Academic/Scholarly.* **Description:** Covers clinical and social aspects of palliative care.
Related titles: Online - full text ed.: ISSN 1479-0793. GBP 45, EUR 60, USD 80 to individuals; GBP 120, EUR 180, USD 220 to institutions (effective 2009); French ed.
Indexed: AMED, B28, C06, C07, C08, CINAHL, SCOPUS.
—BLDSC (3829.733390), IE, Ingenta. **CCC.**
Published by: (European Association for Palliative Care), Hayward Medical Communications Ltd. (Subsidiary of: Hayward Group plc), 8-10 Dryden St, Covent Garden, London, WC2E 9NA, United Kingdom. TEL 44-20-72404493, FAX 44-20-72404479, edit@hayward.co.uk, http://www.hayward.co.uk. Eds. Julia Riley, Elaine Bennett. Pub. Douglas Wright.

EXCERPTA MEDICA. SECTION 6: INTERNAL MEDICINE. *see* MEDICAL SCIENCES—Abstracting, Bibliographies, Statistics

616.042 GBR ISSN 1462-3994
QH506 CODEN: ERMMFS
EXPERT REVIEWS IN MOLECULAR MEDICINE. Text in English. 1997. irreg. (electronic journal constantly updated). GBP 250, USD 435 to institutions (effective 2012). adv. bk.rev. back issues avail. **Document type:** *Journal, Academic/Scholarly.* **Description:** Comprises an expanding collection of review articles in the area of molecular medicine.
Media: Online - full text.
Indexed: A22, B19, B25, B26, BIOSIS Prev, D01, E01, EMBASE, ExcerpMed, H17, MEDLINE, MycolAb, P20, P22, P30, P48, P54, PQC, R10, Reac, SCI, SCOPUS, W07.
—**CCC.**
Published by: (University of Cambridge, Centre for Applied Research in Educational Technologies, University of Cambridge, School of Clinical Medicine), Cambridge University Press, The Edinburgh Bldg, Shaftesbury Rd, Cambridge, CB2 8RU, United Kingdom. TEL 44-1223-312393, FAX 44-1223-315052, journals@cambridge.org, http://www.cambridge.org/uk. Eds. Andrea Bowden, Carolyn Elliss. **Subscr. to:** Cambridge University Press, 32 Ave of the Americas, New York, NY 10013. TEL 212-337-5000, FAX 212-691-3239, journals_subscriptions@cup.org.

616 USA ISSN 2159-3000
F P ESSENTIALS. (Family Physicians) Text in English. 19??. m. USD 79 combined subscription (print & online eds.) (effective 2011). back issues avail. **Document type:** *Monographic series, Academic/Scholarly.* **Description:** Covers all aspects of clinical information. Helps to enhance clinical knowledge, CME credit, and prepare for the ABFM exam.
Formerly (until 2003): Home Study Monograph
Related titles: Online - full text ed.: ISSN 2161-9344.
Published by: American Academy of Family Physicians, PO Box 11210, Shawnee Mission, KS 66207. TEL 913-906-6000, 800-274-2237, FAX 913-906-6075, contactcenter@aafp.org.

FAMILY PRACTICE CODING ALERT; the practical adviser for ethically optimizing coding, payment, and efficiency in family practices. *see* INSURANCE

616 POL ISSN 1897-3590
➤ **FORUM MEDYCYNY RODZINNEJ.** Text in Polish. 2007. bi-m. **Document type:** *Journal, Academic/Scholarly.*
Related titles: Online - full text ed.: ISSN 1897-7839.
Published by: (Polskie Towarzystwo Medycyny Rodzinnej), Wydawnictwo Via Medica, ul Swietokrzyska 73, Gdansk, 80180, Poland. TEL 48-58-3209494, FAX 48-58-3209460, redakcja@viamedica.pl, http://www.viamedica.pl. Ed. Janusz Siebert.

➤ **GELBE LISTE PHARMINDEX. INTERNISTEN.** *see* PHARMACY AND PHARMACOLOGY

616 ESP ISSN 1576-1487
GUIA PUNTEX. ANUARIO ESPANOL DE ANALITICA. Text in Spanish. 1977. a. EUR 84 domestic; EUR 111 in Europe; EUR 140 elsewhere (effective 2008). adv. back issues avail. **Document type:** *Yearbook, Consumer.*
Former titles (until 1995): Guia Puntex. Anuario Espanol Portugues de Analitica (1576-253X); (until 1989): Guia Puntex. Anuario Espanol de Diagnostica Analitica (1576-1568); (until 1986): Guia Puntex. Anuario Espanol de Diagnostica (1576-155X); (until 1983): Guia Puntex de Proveedores para Analisis e Investigacion Clinica (1576-1541)
Published by: Publicaciones Nacionales Tecnicas y Extranjeras (PUNTEX), Padilla 323, Barcelona, 08025, Spain. TEL 34-934-462820, FAX 34-934-462064, puntex@puntex.es, http://www.puntex.es. Ed. Martin Yolanda. adv.: B&W page EUR 1,575; trim 170 x 240. Circ: 10,000.

616 CHN ISSN 2095-2058
GUOJI NEIKEXUE ZAZHI/INTERNATIONAL JOURNAL OF INTERNAL MEDICINE. Text in Chinese. 1974. m. **Document type:** *Journal, Academic/Scholarly.*
Formerly (until 2007): Guowai Yixue (Neikexue Fence)/Foreign Medical Sciences (Internal Medicine) (1004-2369)
Related titles: Online - full text ed.
—East View.
Published by: Zhongshan Daxue Fushu Di-3 Yiyuan/The Third Affiliated Hospital of Sun Yat-Sen University, 74, Zhongshan Erlu, Guangzhou, 510080, China. TEL 86-20-87331647, http://www.zssy.com.cn/. **Dist. by:** China International Book Trading Corp, 35 Chegongzhuang Xilu, Haidian District, PO Box 399, Beijing 100044, China. TEL 86-10-68412045, FAX 86-10-68412023, cibtc@mail.cibtc.com.cn, http://www.cibtc.com.cn.

GUT REACTION. *see* MEDICAL SCIENCES

616 USA
HARRISON'S PRINCIPLES OF INTERNAL MEDICINE. Text in English. 1966. irreg., latest 17th ed. USD 199 17th ed. (effective 2008).
Formerly: Principles of Internal Medicine
Related titles: Online - full text ed.: ISSN 1096-7133. USD 125 to individuals (effective 2004); Optical Disk - DVD ed.
Published by: McGraw-Hill Companies, Inc., 1221 Ave of the Americas, 43rd fl, New York, NY 10020. TEL 212-512-2000, customer.service@mcgraw-hill.com, http://www.mcgraw-hill.com.

616 USA
I M ADVANTAGE (ONLINE). (Internal Medicine) Text in English. 197?. m. membership only. **Document type:** *Newsletter.* **Description:** Covers the socioeconomics of internal medicine practice.
Former titles: I M Advantage (Print) (1093-0655); (until 1997): Internist's Intercom (0164-6419)
Media: Online - full text.
Published by: American Society of Internal Medicine, American College of Physicians, 190 N. Independence Mall West, Philadelphia, PA 19106-1572. TEL 800-523-1546, FAX 215-351-2799, custserv@acponline.org, http://www.acponline.org. Ed. Barbara Lauter. R&P Stacy Rosenberg. Circ: 20,000.

616.1 IND ISSN 0377-9343
RC941
➤ **THE INDIAN JOURNAL OF CHEST DISEASES AND ALLIED SCIENCES.** Text in English. 1959. q. USD 75 (effective 2011). bk.rev. abstr.; illus. 60 p./no. 2 cols./p.; **Document type:** *Journal, Academic/Scholarly.* **Description:** Covers the clinical and experimental work dealing with all aspects of Chest Diseases and Allied Sciences. It publishes original articles, review Articles, radiology forum, case reports, short communications, book reviews and letter to the editor.
Formerly (until 1976): Indian Journal of Chest Diseases (0019-5111)
Related titles: CD-ROM ed.; Online - full text ed.: free (effective 2011).
Indexed: A22, A36, CABA, ChemAb, DentInd, DokArb, E12, EMBASE, ExcerpMed, ExtraMED, FR, GH, H17, IndMed, MEDLINE, N02, N03, P30, P33, R08, R10, R12, RM&VM, Reac, SCOPUS, T05.
—BLDSC (4410.710000), GNLM, IE, Infotrieve, Ingenta, INIST. **CCC.**
Published by: University of Delhi, Vallabhbhai Patel Chest Institute, Publication Division, New Delhi, 110 007, India. TEL 91-11-27667102, FAX 91-11-27666549, ijcdas@yahoo.co.in. Ed., Pub. V K Vijayan. **Co-sponsor:** National College of Chest Physicians.

616 IND ISSN 0253-7184
RC201.A1
➤ **INDIAN JOURNAL OF SEXUALLY TRANSMITTED DISEASES AND A I D S.** Text in English. 1980. s-a. INR 1,000 domestic; USD 100 foreign; INR 1,200 combined subscription domestic (print & online eds.); USD 120 combined subscription foreign (print & online eds.) (effective 2011). adv. **Document type:** *Journal, Academic/Scholarly.*
Related titles: Online - full text ed.: ISSN 1998-3816. 2004. INR 800 domestic; USD 80 foreign (effective 2011).
Indexed: A01, A26, A36, CA, CABA, D01, E08, E12, EMBASE, ExcerpMed, FR, GH, H12, H17, I05, N02, N03, P30, P33, P39, R08, R12, RM&VM, S09, SCOPUS, T02, T05.
—BLDSC (4421.160000), IE, Ingenta, INIST.

Published by: (Indian Association for the Study of Sexually Transmitted Diseases and AIDS), Medknow Publications and Media Pvt. Ltd., B-9, Kanara Business Ctr, Off Link Rd, Ghatkopar (E), Mumbai, Maharastra 400 075, India. TEL 91-22-66491816, FAX 91-22-66491817, http://www.medknow.com. Ed. Dr. Y S Marfatia.

616 NLD ISSN 1871-2916
INFO SOURCE. Text in English. 2002. q. EUR 12.95 (effective 2010).
Document type: *Newsletter.*
Published by: Transplant Creations, PO Box 51342, Amsterdam, 1007 EH, Netherlands. TEL 31-6-12433616, http://www.transplantcreations.com.

INSIDE OUT. *see* MEDICAL SCIENCES

616 AUT ISSN 0936-8507
➤ **INTENSIVMEDIZINISCHES SEMINAR.** Text in German. 1989. irreg., latest vol.8, 1995. price varies. **Document type:** *Monographic series, Academic/Scholarly.*
—CCC.
Published by: Springer Wien (Subsidiary of: Springer Science+Business Media), Sachsenplatz 4-6, Vienna, W 1201, Austria. TEL 43-1-330-2415, FAX 43-1-330-2426, journals@springer.at, http://www.springer.at. Eds. A N Laggner, K Lenz.

616 SVK ISSN 1335-8359
➤ **INTERNA MEDICINA.** Text in Slovak. 2001. 11/yr. EUR 25.29 (effective 2009). **Document type:** *Journal, Academic/Scholarly.*
Published by: Samedi s.r.o., Racianska 20, Bratislava, 839 27, Slovakia. TEL 421-2-55645901, FAX 421-2-55645902, samedi@samedi.sk. Ed. Maria Mercegova.

616.02 ITA ISSN 1828-0447
R61 CODEN: AIMIEA
➤ **INTERNAL AND EMERGENCY MEDICINE.** Text in Italian. 1986. q. EUR 336, USD 405 combined subscription to institutions (print & online eds.) (effective 2012). adv. bk.rev. reprint service avail. from PSC. **Document type:** *Journal, Academic/Scholarly.* **Description:** Designed for internists and emergency care physicians.
Formerly (until 2006): Annali Italiani di Medicina Interna (0393-9340)
Related titles: Online - full text ed.: ISSN 1970-9366. 2006 (from IngentaConnect); Supplement(s): Annali Italiani di Medicina Interna. Supplement. 1992.
Indexed: A22, A26, C06, C07, E01, E08, EMBASE, ExcerpMed, H12, IndMed, MEDLINE, P20, P22, P30, P48, P54, PQC, R10, Reac, S09, SCI, SCOPUS, W07.
—BLDSC (4534.676200), GNLM, IE, Infotrieve, Ingenta. **CCC.**
Published by: Springer Italia Srl (Subsidiary of: Springer Science+Business Media), Via Decembrio 28, Milan, 20137, Italy. TEL 39-02-54259722, FAX 39-02-55193360, springer@springer.it. Ed. D Prisco.

616 JPN ISSN 0918-2918
CODEN: IEDIEP
➤ **INTERNAL MEDICINE (TOKYO, 1992).** Text in English. 1962. m. abstr.; charts; illus. back issues avail. **Document type:** *Journal, Academic/Scholarly.* **Description:** Contains original articles devoted to internal medicine and its subspecialities.
Formerly (until 1992): Japanese Journal of Medicine (0021-5120)
Related titles: Online - full text ed.: Internal Medicine (Online). ISSN 1349-7235. 2004. free (effective 2011).
Indexed: A22, A36, B25, BIOSIS Prev, CABA, CIN, ChemAb, ChemTitl, CurCont, E12, EMBASE, ExcerpMed, FR, GH, H17, INIS AtomInd, IndMed, Inpharma, LT, MEDLINE, MycolAb, N02, N03, P30, P33, R08, R10, RM&VM, RRTA, Reac, SCI, SCOPUS, T05, W07.
—CASDDS, GNLM, IE, Infotrieve, Ingenta, INIST. **CCC.**
Published by: Nihon Naika Gakkai/Japanese Society of Internal Medicine, 28-8, 3-chome, Hongo, Bunkyo-ku, Tokyo, 113-8433, Japan. TEL 81-3-38135991, FAX 81-3-38181556, naika@mb.infoweb.ne.jp, http://www.naika.or.jp/. Ed. Hidehiko Saito. Pub. Satoshi Kimura. Circ: 6,500 (paid). **Dist. overseas by:** Japan Publications Trading Co., Ltd., Book Export II Dept, PO Box 5030, Tokyo International, Tokyo 101-3191, Japan. TEL 81-3-32923753, FAX 81-3-32920410.

616 USA ISSN 0195-315X
INTERNAL MEDICINE ALERT. Text in English. 1979. s-m. USD 319 combined subscription (print & online eds.); USD 53 per issue (effective 2010). index. 8 p./no.; reprints avail. **Document type:** *Newsletter, Trade.*
Incorporates (1985-1991): Diagnostic Testing Alert (8756-7474)
Related titles: Audio cassette/tape ed.; Online - full text ed.
Indexed: A01, A26, E08, G08, H11, H12, I05, P20, P48, P54, PQC, S09.
—CCC.
Published by: A H C Media LLC (Subsidiary of: Thomson Corporation, Healthcare Information Group), 3525 Piedmont Rd, NE, Bldg 6, Ste 400, Atlanta, GA 30305. TEL 404-262-7436, 800-688-2421, FAX 404-262-7837, 800-284-3291, customerservice@ahcmedia.com, http://www.ahcmedia.com/. Ed. Stephen A Brunton. Pub. Brenda L Mooney TEL 404-262-5403. **Subscr. to:** PO Box 105109, Atlanta, GA 30348. TEL 404-262-5476, FAX 404-262-5560.

616 ITA ISSN 1590-9271
INTERNAL MEDICINE. CLINICAL AND LABORATORY. Text in Italian. 1993. 3/yr. EUR 46 domestic; EUR 56 foreign (effective 2009). **Document type:** *Journal, Academic/Scholarly.*
Indexed: EMBASE, ExcerpMed, R10, Reac, SCOPUS.
Published by: Pacini Editore SpA, Via A Gherardesca 1, Ospedaletto, PI 56121, Italy. TEL 39-050-313011, FAX 39-050-3130300, pacini.editore@pacinieditore.it, http://www.pacinimedicina.it. Ed. Angelo Carpi.

INTERNAL MEDICINE CODING ALERT; the practical adviser for ethically optimizing coding reimbursement and efficiency for internal medicine practices. *see* INSURANCE

616 AUS ISSN 1445-5994
R99
➤ **INTERNAL MEDICINE JOURNAL (ONLINE).** Text in English. bi-m. GBP 751 in United Kingdom to institutions; EUR 952 in Europe to institutions; USD 1,215 in the Americas to institutions; USD 1,470 elsewhere to institutions (effective 2012). **Document type:** *Journal, Academic/Scholarly.*
Media: Online - full text (from IngentaConnect). **Related titles:** ◆ Print ed.: Internal Medicine Journal (Print). ISSN 1444-0903.
—CCC.
Published by: Wiley-Blackwell Publishing Asia (Subsidiary of: Wiley-Blackwell Publishing Ltd.), 155 Cremorne St, Richmond, VIC 3121, Australia. TEL 61-3-92743100, FAX 61-3-92743101, subs@blackwellpublishingasia.com, http://www.wiley.com/WileyCDA/.

616 AUS ISSN 1444-0903
R99 CODEN: IMJNAK
➤ **INTERNAL MEDICINE JOURNAL (PRINT).** Abbreviated title: I M J. Text in English. 1946. m. GBP 751 in United Kingdom to institutions; EUR 952 in Europe to institutions; USD 1,215 in the Americas to institutions; USD 1,470 elsewhere to institutions; GBP 864 combined subscription in United Kingdom to institutions (print & online eds.); EUR 1,095 combined subscription in Europe to institutions (print & online eds.); USD 1,398 combined subscription in the Americas to institutions (print & online eds.); USD 1,690 combined subscription elsewhere to institutions (print & online eds.) (effective 2012). adv. back issues avail.; reprint service avail. from PSC. **Document type:** *Journal, Academic/Scholarly.* **Description:** Provides original medical research, both laboratory and clinical, relating to the study and research of human disease from all over the world.
Former titles (until 2000): Australian and New Zealand Journal of Medicine (0004-8291); (until 1970): Australasian Annals of Medicine (0571-9283); (until 1951): Australasian College of Physicians. Proceedings of the Royal Australasian College of Physicians
Related titles: ◆ Online - full text ed.: Internal Medicine Journal (Online). ISSN 1445-5994.
Indexed: A01, A03, A08, A20, A22, A26, A29, A36, ASG, B20, B21, BIOBASE, C06, C07, C08, CA, CABA, CINAHL, CurCont, D01, DBA, E01, E12, EMBASE, ESPM, ExcerpMed, FR, GH, GeoRef, H&SSA, H12, H17, I10, I12, IABS, ISR, Inpharma, LT, MEDLINE, N02, N03, P30, P33, P35, P39, R07, R08, R10, R12, RA&MP, RM&VM, RRTA, Reac, S13, S16, SCI, SCOPUS, T02, T05, VITIS, VirolAbstr, W07, W10, W11.
—BLDSC (4534.905200), IE, Infotrieve, Ingenta, INIST. **CCC.**
Published by: (The Royal Australasian College of Physicians, Adult Medicine Division), Wiley-Blackwell Publishing Asia (Subsidiary of: Wiley-Blackwell Publishing Ltd.), 155 Cremorne St, Richmond, VIC 3121, Australia. TEL 61-3-92743100, FAX 61-3-92743101, melbourne@wiley.com, http://www.wiley.com/WileyCDA/. Ed. Dr. Jeff Szer.

616 USA ISSN 1097-8690
INTERNAL MEDICINE NEWS. Text in English. 1968. s-m. USD 146 in United States to institutions; USD 293 elsewhere to institutions (effective 2012). adv. bk.rev. back issues avail.; reprints avail. **Document type:** *Newspaper, Trade.* **Description:** Covers internal medicine and associated specialties.
Former titles (until 1995): Internal Medicine News and Cardiology News (0274-5542); (until 1980): Internal Medicine News (0099-152X); (until 1975): Internal Medicine News and Diagnosis News (0099-1538); (until 1971): Internal Medicine and Diagnosis News (0012-1908); (until 1968): Diagnosis News
Related titles: Microform ed.: (from PQC); Online - full text ed.
Indexed: A26, G08, H11, H12, I05.
—CCC.
Published by: International Medical News Group (Subsidiary of: Elsevier Health Sciences), 5635 Fishers Ln, Ste 6000, Rockville, MD 20852. TEL 877-524-9332, FAX 240-221-4400, m.altier@elsevier.com, http://www.imng.com. Pub. Alan J Imhoff TEL 973-290-8216. Circ: 120,076. **Subscr. to:** Elsevier, Subscription Customer Service, 60 Columbia Rd, Bldg B, Morristown, NJ 07960. TEL 973-290-8200, FAX 973-290-8250, http://www.elsevier.com/.

616 NZL ISSN 1178-6140
INTERNAL MEDICINE RESEARCH REVIEW. Text in English. 2007. bi-m. free to qualified personnel (effective 2009). back issues avail. **Document type:** *Journal, Academic/Scholarly.*
Media: Online - full text.
Published by: Research Review Ltd., N Shore Mail Centre, PO Box 100116, Auckland, New Zealand. TEL 64-9-4102277, info@researchreview.co.nz.

616 IND ISSN 0975-3702
▼ ➤ **INTERNATIONAL JOURNAL OF PARASITOLOGY RESEARCH.** Text in English. 2009. s-a. USD 425 (effective 2011). **Document type:** *Journal, Academic/Scholarly.* **Description:** Publishes all the latest research articles, reviews and letters in all areas of parasitology.
Related titles: Online - full text ed.: ISSN 0975-9182. free (effective 2011).
Indexed: A01, A34, A35, AgrForAb, C25, CABA, E12, F08, GH, MaizeAb, P32, P33, R07, R08, S13, T02, T05.
Published by: Bioinfo Publications, 49/F-72, Vighnahar Complex, Front of Overseas Bank, Sector 12, Kharghar, Navi Mumbai, 410 210, India. TEL 91-22-27743967, FAX 91-22-66736413, editor@bioinfo.in. Eds. Somnath Waghmare, Dr. Virendra S Gomase, Wej Choochote.

616 NLD ISSN 2211-100X
INTERNE GENEESKUNDE. Text in Dutch. 197?. q. EUR 47.50 (effective 2011). adv. **Document type:** *Magazine, Trade.*
Formerly (until 2010): Nederlandsche Internisten Vereniging. Nieuwsbrief (1381-379X)
Published by: (Nederlandse Internisten Vereniging), Van Zuiden Communications B.V., Postbus 2122, Alphen aan den Rijn, 2400 CC, Netherlands. TEL 31-172-476191, FAX 31-172-471882, zuiden@zuidencomm.nl, http://www.zuidencomm.nl. Ed. N Oudenaarden. Circ: 2,950.

616 USA ISSN 1528-8358
R5
➤ **THE INTERNET JOURNAL OF FAMILY PRACTICE.** Text in English. 2000. s-a. free (effective 2011). adv. bk.rev. back issues avail. **Document type:** *Journal, Academic/Scholarly.* **Description:** Provides information from the field of family practice medicine; contains original articles, reviews, case reports, streaming slide shows, streaming videos, letters to the editor, press releases and meeting information.
Media: Online - full text.
Indexed: A01, A02, A03, A08, A26, A39, C06, C07, C27, C29, CA, D03, D04, E13, G08, H11, H12, I05, R14, S14, S15, S18, T02.
Published by: Internet Scientific Publications, Llc., 23 Rippling Creek Dr, Sugar Land, TX 77479. TEL 832-443-1193, FAX 281-240-1533, wenker@ispub.com. Ed. Dr. Sanjay Kalra. R&P Olivier Wenker TEL 832-754-0335.

616 USA ISSN 1528-8382
RC11
➤ **THE INTERNET JOURNAL OF INTERNAL MEDICINE.** Text in English. 2000. s-a. free (effective 2011). bk.rev. back issues avail. **Document type:** *Journal, Academic/Scholarly.* **Description:** Provides information from the field of general and internal medicine; contains original articles, reviews, case reports, streaming slide shows, streaming videos, letters to the editor, press releases and meeting information.
Media: Online - full text.
Indexed: A01, A02, A03, A08, A26, C06, C07, CA, EMBASE, G08, H11, H12, I05, SCOPUS, T02.
Published by: Internet Scientific Publications, Llc., 23 Rippling Creek Dr, Sugar Land, TX 77479. TEL 832-443-1193, FAX 281-240-1533, wenker@ispub.com. Ed. Deepak Asudani.

616 CZE ISSN 1212-7299
➤ **INTERNI MEDICINA PRO PRAXI.** Text in Czech. 1999. m. CZK 840; CZK 70 per issue (effective 2010). **Document type:** *Journal, Academic/Scholarly.*
Related titles: Online - full text ed.: ISSN 1803-5256.
Published by: Solen s.r.o., Lazecka 297/51, Olomouc 51, 779 00, Czech Republic. TEL 420-582-396038, FAX 420-582-396099, solen@solen.cz, http://www.solen.cz. Ed. Dr. Hana Sarapatkova. Circ: 5,000.

616 DEU ISSN 0020-9554
RC46 CODEN: INTEAG
➤ **DER INTERNIST.** Text in German. 1946. m. EUR 565, USD 630 combined subscription to institutions (print & online eds.) (effective 2012). adv. bk.rev. charts; illus. index, cum.index. back issues avail.; reprint service avail. from PSC. **Document type:** *Journal, Academic/Scholarly.* **Description:** Contains research articles and papers of interest to internists and general practitioners.
Formerly (until 1960): Aerztliche Wochenschrift (0365-6403)
Related titles: Microform ed.: (from PQC); Online - full text ed.: ISSN 1432-1289 (from IngentaConnect).
Indexed: A20, A22, A26, A34, A36, ASCA, BP, CABA, CurCont, D01, DBA, E01, E08, E12, EMBASE, ExcerpMed, GH, H17, I05, INI, ISR, IndMed, IndVet, Inpharma, LT, MEDLINE, N02, N03, P30, P33, P35, P39, R08, R10, RM&VM, RRTA, Reac, S02, S03, S09, SCI, SCOPUS, T05, VS, W07.
—BLDSC (4557.200000), CASDDS, GNLM, IE, Infotrieve, Ingenta, INIST. **CCC.**
Published by: (Berufsverband Deutscher Internisten e.V.), Springer (Subsidiary of: Springer Science+Business Media), Tiergartenstr 17, Heidelberg, 69121, Germany. TEL 49-6221-4870, FAX 49-6221-345229. Ed. W Hiddemann. Adv. contact Stephan Kroeck TEL 49-30-827875739. Circ: 37,807 (paid and controlled). **Subscr. in the Americas to:** Springer New York LLC, Journal Fulfillment, PO Box 2485, Secaucus, NJ 07096. TEL 201-348-4033, 800-777-4643, FAX 201-348-4505, journals-ny@springer.com, http://www.springer.com; **Subscr. to:** Springer Distribution Center, Kundenservice Zeitschriften, Haberstr 7, Heidelberg 69126, Germany. TEL 49-6221-3454303, FAX 49-6221-3454229, subscriptions@springer.com. **Co-sponsor:** Deutsche Gesellschaft fuer Innere Medizin.

616 ITA ISSN 1121-9017
CODEN: IRNIE
➤ **L'INTERNISTA**; giornale di medicina interna e specialistica. Text and summaries in English, Italian. 1993. s-a. EUR 68 in Europe to institutions; EUR 77 elsewhere to institutions (effective 2008). bk.rev. index. **Document type:** *Journal, Academic/Scholarly.* **Description:** Provides editorials, reviews, original clinical works and case reports, news, scientific notes, and letters to the editor.
Indexed: A22, R10, Reac, SCOPUS.
—BLDSC (4557.208000), GNLM, IE, Ingenta.
Published by: (Ospedale Niguarda - Ca Grande), Mattioli 1885 SpA, Via Coduro 1, Fidenza, PR 43036, Italy. TEL 39-0524-84547, FAX 39-0524-84751, http://www.mattioli1885.com. Ed. Gianfranco Rizzato. Circ: 5,000.

616 DEU ISSN 0020-9570
CODEN: INPXAJ
INTERNISTISCHE PRAXIS; Zeitschrift fuer die gesamte Innere Medizin. Text in German. 1961. 4/yr. EUR 175 (effective 2010). bk.rev. abstr.; bibl.; charts; illus. index, cum.index every 5 yrs. reprints avail. **Document type:** *Journal, Academic/Scholarly.* **Description:** Practical information of interest to specialists in internal medicine. Features the latest research in the field. Includes questions and answers.
Related titles: Microfilm ed.: (from PQC).
Indexed: A22, AMED, EMBASE, ExcerpMed, IndMed, P30, R10, Reac, SCOPUS.
—BLDSC (4557.220000), GNLM, IE, Infotrieve, Ingenta. **CCC.**
Published by: Hans Marseille Verlag GmbH, Buerkleinstr 12, Munich, 80538, Germany. TEL 49-89-227988, FAX 49-89-2904643, marseille-verlag@t-online.de. Ed. Dr. M Ritter. Circ: 4,800 (controlled).

616 IRN ISSN 1735-5303
IRANIAN JOURNAL OF PATHOLOGY/MAJALLAH-I ASIB/SHINASI-I IRAN. Text in English. 2006. q. IRR 80,000 domestic; USD 60 foreign (effective 2008). **Document type:** *Journal, Academic/Scholarly.*
Related titles: Online - full text ed.: free (effective 2011).
Indexed: A36, CABA, D01, GH, H17, N02, N03, P33, T05.
Published by: Iranian Society of Pathology, No: 1 Shaheed Tousi (Shabahang) St, Tehran, Iran. TEL 98-21-88951899, FAX 98-21-88970015, http://ijp.iranpath.org. Ed. Mohammad Reza Jalali Nadoushan.

616 QAT ISSN 1999-7086
➤ **J E M T A C.** (Journal of Emergency Medicine Trauma & Acute Care) Text in English. 2000. 3/yr. **Document type:** *Journal, Academic/Scholarly.*
Formerly (until 2008): Middle East Journal of Emergency Medicine (1729-6455)
Related titles: Online - full text ed.: ISSN 1999-7094.
Indexed: EMBASE, ExcerpMed, R10, Reac, SCOPUS.
—BLDSC (4663.540000).
Published by: Hamad International Trianing Center, PO Box 3050, Doha, Qatar. TEL 974-439-7396, FAX 974-439-7763, jemtac@hmc.org.qa, http://www.hmc.org.qa. Ed. Dr. Abdul Wahab Al Musleh.

616 CAN ISSN 1910-7595
JOURNAL OF GAMBLING ISSUES. Text in English. 2000. 3/yr. free (effective 2011). **Document type:** *Journal, Academic/Scholarly.*
Formerly (until 2004): EGambling (1494-5185)
Media: Online - full text.
Indexed: CA, P03, PsycInfo, S02, S03, T02.
—CCC.
Published by: Centre for Addiction and Mental Health (C A M H), 33 Russell St, Toronto, ON M5S 2S1, Canada. TEL 416-595-6111, 800-463-6273, public_affairs@camh.net.

616 USA ISSN 0884-8734
R11 CODEN: JGIMEJ
➤ **JOURNAL OF GENERAL INTERNAL MEDICINE.** Short title: J G I M. Text in English. 1986. m. EUR 504, USD 614 combined subscription to institutions (print & online eds.) (effective 2012). adv. back issues avail.; reprint service avail. from PSC. **Document type:** *Journal, Academic/Scholarly.* **Description:** Focuses on the training and practice of the general internist.
Related titles: Online - full text ed.: ISSN 1525-1497 (from IngentaConnect); ◆ Supplement(s): S G I M Forum. ISSN 1940-2899.
Indexed: A01, A02, A03, A08, A20, A22, A26, A29, A34, A36, AIDS Ab, ASCA, B20, B21, B25, BIOSIS Prev, C11, CA, CABA, CurCont, D01, E01, E12, EMBASE, ESPM, ExcerpMed, F08, F11, F12, FR, GH, GenetAb, H04, H12, H13, INI, ISR, IndMed, IndVet, Inpharma, JW-P, JW-WH, LT, MEDLINE, MycolAb, N02, N03, NRN, P02, P03, P10, P20, P21, P22, P24, P30, P33, P34, P35, P39, P48, P53, P54, PQC, PsycInfo, PsycholAb, R08, R10, R12, RA&MP, RM&VM, RRTA, Reac, S13, S16, SCI, SCOPUS, SoyAb, T02, T05, THA, VS, ViroIAbstr, W07, W11.
—BLDSC (4987.827000), GNLM, IE, Infotrieve, Ingenta, INIST. **CCC.**
Published by: (American College of Physicians, Society of General Internal Medicine), Springer New York LLC (Subsidiary of: Springer Science+Business Media), 233 Spring St, New York, NY 10013. TEL 212-460-1500, FAX 212-460-1575, service-ny@springer.com. Eds. Mitchell D Feldman, Richard L Kravitz. Adv. contact Scott L Marshall TEL 212-620-8405.

610 GBR ISSN 0954-6820
R81 CODEN: JINMEO
➤ **JOURNAL OF INTERNAL MEDICINE;** from genes and molecules to patients. Abbreviated title: J I M. Text in English. 18??. m. GBP 823 in United Kingdom to institutions; EUR 1,046 in Europe to institutions; USD 1,383 in the Americas to institutions; USD 1,614 elsewhere to institutions; GBP 947 combined subscription in United Kingdom to institutions (print & online eds.); EUR 1,203 combined subscription in Europe to institutions (print & online eds.); USD 1,590 combined subscription in the Americas to institutions (print & online eds.); USD 1,857 combined subscription elsewhere to institutions (print & online eds.) (effective 2012). adv. abstr.; bibl.; charts; illus. index. cum.index: vols.52-140. back issues avail.; reprint service avail. from PSC. **Document type:** *Journal, Academic/Scholarly.* **Description:** Aims are to serve clinical and pre-clinical researchers with a forum for publication of original articles concerning the broad panorama of diseases within internal medicine.
Formerly (until 1989): Acta Medica Scandinavica (0001-6101); (until 1919): Nordiskt Medicinskt Arkiv. Avd. 2, Arkiv foer Inre Medicin (0365-3250); Supersedes in part (in 1909): Nordiskt Medicinskt Arkiv (0369-4879)
Related titles: Microform ed.: (from PQC); Online - full text ed.: ISSN 1365-2796. GBP 823 in United Kingdom to institutions; EUR 1,046 in Europe to institutions; USD 1,383 in the Americas to institutions; USD 1,614 elsewhere to institutions (effective 2012) (from IngentaConnect); ◆ Supplement(s): Journal of Internal Medicine. Supplement. ISSN 0955-7873.
Indexed: A01, A02, A03, A08, A22, A26, A34, A36, AIIM, ASCA, B20, B21, B25, BIOBASE, BIOSIS Prev, C06, C07, C08, C11, CA, CABA, CINAHL, CISA, ChemAb, ChemTitl, CurCont, DBA, DentInd, E01, E12, EIA, EMBASE, ESPM, EnerInd, ExcerpMed, FR, FamI, GH, H04, H12, IABS, IBR, IBZ, IDIS, ISR, IndMed, IndVet, Inpharma, Kidney, LT, MEDLINE, MS&D, MycolAb, N02, N03, NRN, P30, P33, P35, P37, P39, PN&I, R08, R10, R12, RM&VM, RRTA, Reac, SCI, SCOPUS, T02, T05, THA, VS, W07.
—BLDSC (5007.548700), CASDDS, GNLM, IE, Infotrieve, Ingenta, INIST. **CCC.**
Published by: Wiley-Blackwell Publishing Ltd. (Subsidiary of: John Wiley & Sons, Inc.), 9600 Garsington Rd, Oxford, OX4 2DQ, United Kingdom. TEL 44-1865-776868, FAX 44-1865-714591, customerservices@blackwellpublishing.com. Ed. Ulf de Faire.

616 IND ISSN 0972-1096
JOURNAL OF INTERNAL MEDICINE OF INDIA. Text in English. 1998. 3/yr. **Document type:** *Journal, Academic/Scholarly.*
Indexed: EMBASE, ExcerpMed, R10, Reac, SCOPUS.
—BLDSC (5007.548830), IE, Ingenta.
Published by: Association of Physicians of India, Turf Estate, #6 & 7, Ground Fl, Opp. Shakti Mills Compound, Dr. E. Moses Road, Opp. Mahalaxmi Station (West), Mumbai, Maharashtra 400 011, India. TEL 91-22 56663224, FAX 91-22 24920263, srjoshi@vsnl.com, http://www.apiindia.org.

616 GBR ISSN 0955-7873
CODEN: JIMSE3
JOURNAL OF INTERNAL MEDICINE. SUPPLEMENT. Text in English. 1922. q. includes with subscr. to Journal of Internal Medicine. adv. **Document type:** *Journal, Academic/Scholarly.*
Formerly (until 1988): Acta Medica Scandinavica. Supplementum (0365-463X)
Related titles: Online - full text ed.; ◆ Supplement to: Journal of Internal Medicine. ISSN 0954-6820.
Indexed: A22, CIN, ChemAb, ChemTitl, EMBASE, ExcerpMed, IndMed, Inpharma, MEDLINE, P30, P35, SCOPUS.
—CASDDS, IE, Infotrieve, INIST. **CCC.**
Published by: Wiley-Blackwell Publishing Ltd. (Subsidiary of: John Wiley & Sons, Inc.), 9600 Garsington Rd, Oxford, OX4 2DQ, United Kingdom. TEL 44-1865-776868, FAX 44-1865-714591, customerservices@blackwellpublishing.com, http://www.wiley.com/, http://www.wiley.com/WileyCDA/.

612.67 FRA ISSN 1279-7707
QP86
JOURNAL OF NUTRITION, HEALTH AND AGING. Text in English. 1997. 10/yr. EUR 428, USD 515 combined subscription to institutions (print & online eds.) (effective 2011). reprint service avail. from PSC. **Document type:** *Journal, Academic/Scholarly.* **Description:** Features studies about nutrition's effect on the elderly, includes reports on research funding, international conferences and literature abstracts of interest to professionals in gerontology, geridrics, medicine, community health, public health, biology, social medicine, epidemiology and biostatistics.
Related titles: Online - full text ed.: ISSN 1760-4788 (from IngentaConnect).
Indexed: A22, A34, A35, A36, ASG, AgBio, AgeL, BIOBASE, C06, C07, C25, CA, CABA, CurCont, D01, E01, E12, EMBASE, ExcerpMed, F05, F06, F07, F08, F10, FS&TA, GH, H16, IABS, IndMed, LT, MEDLINE, N02, N03, N04, P03, P20, P22, P25, P30, P37, P38, P48, P50, P54, PHN&I, PN&I, PQC, PsycholAb, R10, R12, RA&MP, RRTA, Reac, SCI, SCOPUS, SoyAb, T02, T05, VS, W07, W11.
—BLDSC (5024.716000), IE, Infotrieve, Ingenta, INIST. **CCC.**
Published by: Editions S E R D I, 320 Rue Saint-Honore, Paris, 75001, France. TEL 33-5-61757912, FAX 33-5-61751128, serdi@serdi-fr.com. Ed. Bruno Vellas.

616 JPN ISSN 0913-2384
CODEN: KRRYEI
KAGAKU RYOHO NO RYOIKI/ANTIBIOTICS AND CHEMOTHERAPY. Text in Japanese. 1985. m. JPY 32,865; JPY 2,415 newsstand/cover (effective 2005). **Document type:** *Academic/Scholarly.*
Indexed: CIN, ChemAb, ChemTitl.
—BLDSC (1546.995500), CASDDS, GNLM.
Published by: (Kagaku Ryoho Kenkyukai/Committee of Chemotherapy), Iyaku Journal-sha/Medicine & Drug Journal Co., Ltd., Highness Awajimachi Bldg. 21/F, 3-1-5 Awajimachih, Chuo-Ku, Osaka, 541-0047, Japan. TEL 81-6-62027280, FAX 81-6-62025295, ij-main@iyaku-j.com, http://www.iyaku-j.com/.

368.382 USA ISSN 1542-2488
KEEP UP TO DATE ON INTERNAL MEDICINE CODING & REIMBURSEMENT. Text in English. 2002 (Oct.). m. USD 198 (effective 2008). 8 p./no.; **Document type:** *Newsletter, Trade.* **Description:** Designed to help coding professionals stay informed of the latest coding changes and claim procedures to ethically ensure maximum reimbursement.
Published by: Progressive Business Publications, 370 Technology Dr, Malvern, PA 19355. TEL 610-695-8600, 800-220-5000, FAX 610-647-8089, customer_service@pbp.com. Ed. Renee Cocchi.

616 KOR ISSN 1738-9364
R97.7.K6 CODEN: TNHCA3
➤ **THE KOREAN JOURNAL OF MEDICINE.** Text in Korean; Abstracts in English. 1958. m. membership. Supplement avail. **Document type:** *Journal, Academic/Scholarly.* **Description:** Publishes editorials, original articles and case reports in all areas of medical science.
Former titles (until 2005): Daehan Nae'gwa Haghoeji (1226-329X); (until 1993): Daihan Naigwa Haghoi Jabji/Korean Journal of Internal Medicine (0494-4712)
Related titles: Online - full text ed.
Indexed: IndMed, P30, R10, Reac, SCOPUS.
—CASDDS, GNLM.
Published by: Daihan Naigwa Haghoi/Korean Association of Internal Medicine, Korean Medical Association Bldg., 302-75, Dongbu Ichon-dong, Yongsan-Ku, PO Box 2062, Seoul, 140-721, Korea, S. TEL 82-2-7934364, FAX 82-2-7900993, kaim@users.unitel.co.kr. Ed. Dr. Dong Hoo Lee.

616 CAN ISSN 1910-6165
LUPUS LINK NOTES. Text in English. 2006. s-a. **Document type:** *Newsletter, Consumer.*
Published by: Lupus Ontario, 211 - 590 Alden Rd, Markham, ON L3R 8N2, Canada. TEL 905-415-1099, 877-240-1099, FAX 905-415-9874, lupusontario@bellnet.ca.

616 POL
MAGAZYN LEKARZA RODZINNEGO. Text in Polish. q. PLZ 72 domestic (effective 2005). **Document type:** *Journal.*
Published by: Agencja Wydawniczo-Reklamowa, ul Wadowicka 8a, Krakow, 30415, Poland. medicus@medicus.com.pl, http://www.medicus.com.pl.

616.044 CAN ISSN 0228-8702
➤ **MALADIES CHRONIQUES AU CANADA.** Text in French. 1980. q. **Document type:** *Journal, Academic/Scholarly.*
Related titles: Online - full text ed.: ISSN 1481-854X. free (effective 2011); ◆ English ed.: Chronic Diseases in Canada. ISSN 0228-8699.
Published by: Public Health Agency of Canada/Agence de Sante Publique du Canada, 0904A, Buock Claxton Bldg, Tunney's Pasture, Ottawa, ON K1A OK9, Canada. TEL 613-957-2991, FAX 613-941-5366, info@hc-sc.gc.ca, http://www.hc-sc.gc.ca. Ed. Sylvie Stachenko.

616 TUR ISSN 1306-617X
MEDICAL NETWORK DAHILI TIP BILIMLERI DERGISI/JOURNAL OF INTERNAL MEDICINE/M N INTERNAL MEDICINE JOURNAL OF SCIENCE. Text in Turkish; Summaries in English. 2006. 6/yr. TRY 15 to individuals; TRY 60 to institutions; TRY 50 doctors; TRY 40 to students (effective 2010). **Document type:** *Journal, Academic/Scholarly.*
Related titles: Online - full text ed.: free (effective 2010).
Published by: Medical Network, Public Sokak No.4/2, Ankara, 06420, Turkey. info@medicalnetwork.com.tr.

616 JPN ISSN 0025-7699
CODEN: MDCHBH
MEDICINA; journal of internal medicine. Text in Japanese. 1964. m. JPY 36,740; JPY 47,800 combined subscription (print & online eds.) (effective 2010). adv. charts; illus. Index. back issues avail. **Document type:** *Journal, Academic/Scholarly.*
Related titles: Online - full text ed.: ISSN 1882-1189.
Indexed: CIN, ChemAb, ChemTitl.
—BLDSC (5532.400000), CASDDS.
Published by: Igaku Shoin Ltd., 1-28-36 Hongo, Bunkyo-ku, Tokyo, 113-8719, Japan. TEL 81-3-3817-5600, FAX 81-3-3815-7791, info@igaku-shoin.co.jp. Circ: 19,000.

616 PRT ISSN 0872-671X
MEDICINA INTERNA. Text in Multiple languages. 1994. q. **Document type:** *Journal, Academic/Scholarly.*
Published by: Sociedade Portuguesa de Medicina Interna, Rua da Tobis Portuguesa 8, 2o Sala 7, Lisbon, 1750-292, Portugal. TEL 351-21-7520570, FAX 351-21-7520579, secretariado@spmi.webside.pt, http://www.spmi.pt.

616.026 ROM ISSN 1220-5818
MEDICINA INTERNA. Text in Romanian; Summaries in English, French, German, Russian. 1905. q. adv. bk.rev. abstr.; bibl.; charts; illus. **Document type:** *Journal, Academic/Scholarly.*
Former titles (until 1991): Revista de Medicina Interna, Neurologie, Psihiatrie, Neuro-Chirurgie, Dermato-Venerologie. Series Medicina Interna (1220-0905); (until 1974): Medicina Interna (0025-7869); (until 1954): Revista Stiintelor Medicale (1013-414X)
Indexed: ChemAb, DentInd, INIS AtomInd, IndMed, P30, SCOPUS.
—GNLM, INIST.
Published by: Societatea Romana de Medicina Interna, Str Domnita Anastasia 13, Sector 5, Bucharest, 707, Romania. **Subscr. to:** ILEXIM, Str. 13 Decembrie 3, PO Box 136-137, Bucharest 70116, Romania.

616 MEX ISSN 0186-4866
➤ **MEDICINA INTERNA DE MEXICO.** Text in Spanish; Summaries in English, Spanish. 1985. bi-m. MXN 210, USD 40 (effective 2005). back issues avail. **Document type:** *Journal, Academic/Scholarly.* **Description:** Contains original articles, research reports, review articles, clinical cases and notices related to internal medicine.
Related titles: Online - full text ed.
Indexed: A01, C01, CA, EMBASE, ExcerpMed, Inpharma, P35, R10, Reac, SCOPUS, T02.
Published by: Colegio de Medicina Interna de Mexico, Insurgentes Sur No 569 Piso 6, Col. Napoles, Mexico, D.F., 03810, Mexico. TEL 52-55-55366067, FAX 52-55-55431265, amim96@data.net.mx, http://www.amim.org.mx/. Eds. Asisclo Villagomez, Manuel Ramiro. Circ: 3,000. **Dist. by:** Distribuidora Editorial de Mexico SA de CV, P.O. Box 76-026, Mexico City, DF 04201, Mexico. TEL 52-5-544-7953, FAX 52-5-689-6545.

613 ESP ISSN 1135-2841
MEDICINA PREVENTIVA. Text in Spanish. 1995. q. **Document type:** *Journal, Academic/Scholarly.*
Indexed: SCOPUS.
Published by: (Sociedad Espanola de Higiene y Medicina Preventiva), Editores Medicos, S.A., Alsasua 16, Madrid, 28013, Spain. TEL 34-91-3768140, FAX 34-91-3769907, edimsa@edimsa.es, http://www.edimsa.es. Ed. Pastor Aldeguer.

616 VEN ISSN 1690-8686
R61
MEDICRIT. REVISTA DE MEDICINA INTERNA Y MEDICINA CRITICA. Text in Spanish. 2004. m. free (effective 2011). back issues avail. **Document type:** *Journal, Academic/Scholarly.*
Media: Online - full text.
Indexed: C01.
Published by: Medicrit, Apdo Postal 869, Merida, 5101, Venezuela. gamal@medicrit.com, http://www.medicrit.com/.

616.042 USA ISSN 1543-1894
CODEN: MMMEFN
➤ **METHODS IN MOLECULAR MEDICINE.** Text and summaries in English. 1996. irreg., latest 2008. price varies. adv. bk.rev. back issues avail. **Document type:** *Monographic series, Academic/Scholarly.* **Description:** Contains protocols essential to the study of the molecular basis of disease processes.
Related titles: Online - full text ed.: ISSN 1940-6037.
Indexed: A29, B20, B21, CTA, ChemoAb, EMBASE, ESPM, ExcerpMed, GenetAb, I10, MEDLINE, NSA, NucAcAb, P30, R10, Reac, SCOPUS, ViroIAbstr.
—BLDSC (5748.202250). **CCC.**
Published by: Humana Press, Inc. (Subsidiary of: Springer Science+Business Media), 233 Spring St, New York, NY 10013. TEL 212-460-1500, FAX 212-460-1575, service-ny@springer.com. Ed. John M Walker.

➤ **MICROBE MAGIC.** *see* MEDICAL SCIENCES

616 AUS ISSN 1837-9052
➤ **MIDDLE EAST JOURNAL OF INTERNAL MEDICINE.** Text in English. 2008. bi-m. adv. back issues avail. **Document type:** *Journal, Academic/Scholarly.* **Description:** Features clinical and educational research of interest to the medical field, practicing internists, internist in training and others involved in the internal medicine field and medical education.
Related titles: Online - full text ed.: ISSN 1837-9060. free (effective 2010).
Published by: Medi+World International, 11 Colston Ave, Sherbrooke, VIC 3789, Australia. TEL 61-3-90059847, FAX 61-3-90125857, admin@mediworld.com.au, http://www.mediworld.com.au. Eds. Abdul Abyad, Ahmad Husari TEL 61-3-98191224. Pub. Lesley Pocock.

616 ITA ISSN 0026-4806
R61 CODEN: MIMEAO
➤ **MINERVA MEDICA;** a journal on internal medicine. Text in Italian; Summaries in English, Italian. 1909. bi-m. (in 10 vols.). EUR 255 combined subscription in the European Union to institutions (print & online eds.); EUR 280 combined subscription elsewhere to institutions (print & online eds.) (effective 2011). adv. bibl.; illus. **Document type:** *Journal, Academic/Scholarly.* **Description:** Covers internal medicine.
Supersedes (1963-1969): Minerva Medica Siciliana (0026-4822); Which was formerly (1869-1963): Gazzetta Medica Siciliana (0540-1585)
Related titles: Microform ed.: (from PQC); Online - full text ed.: ISSN 1827-1669.
Indexed: A22, CISA, ChemAb, CurCont, DBA, DentInd, DokArb, EMBASE, ExcerpMed, F09, IndMed, Inpharma, MEDLINE, P30, R10, Reac, RefZh, SCI, SCOPUS, W07.
—BLDSC (5794.250000), CASDDS, GNLM, IE, Infotrieve, Ingenta, INIST. **CCC.**
Published by: Edizioni Minerva Medica, Corso Bramante 83-85, Turin, 10126, Italy. TEL 39-011-678282, FAX 39-011-674502, journals.dept@minervamedica.it, http://www.minervamedica.it. Ed. M L Benzo. Pub. Alberto Oliaro. Circ: 5,000 (paid).

616 JPN ISSN 0022-1961
NAIKA/INTERNAL MEDICINE (TOKYO, 1958). Text in Japanese. 1958. m. JPY 36,225 domestic; JPY 48,000 foreign; JPY 4,200 newsstand/cover (effective 2007). adv. charts; illus. s-a. index. **Document type:** *Journal, Academic/Scholarly.* **Description:** Covers internal medicine.

Indexed: INIS AtomInd, P30, SPPI.
—BLDSC (4534.890000), GNLM, INIST.
Published by: Nankodo Co. Ltd., 3-42-6 Hongo, Bunkyo-ku, Tokyo, 113-8410, Japan. TEL 81-3-38117140, FAX 81-3-38117265, http://www.nankodo.co.jp/. Circ: 13,000.

616 CHN ISSN 1007-1024
NEIKE JIWEI ZHONGZHENG ZAZHI/JOURNAL OF INTERNAL INTENSIVE MEDICINE. Text in Chinese. 1995. bi-m. **Document type:** *Journal, Academic/Scholarly.*
Related titles: Online - full text ed.: (from WanFang Data Corp.).
—East View.
Published by: Huazhong Keji Daxue Tongji Yixueyuan/Huazhong University of Science and Technology, Tongji Medical College, 1095 Jiefang Dadao, Wuhan, 430030, China. TEL 86-27-83663644, FAX 86-27-83663644, http://www.tjmu.edu.cn/. **Dist. by:** China International Book Trading Corp, 35 Chegongzhuang Xilu, Haidian District, PO Box 399, Beijing 100044, China. TEL 86-10-68412045, FAX 86-10-68412023, cibtc@mail.cibtc.com.cn, http://www.cibtc.com.cn.

616 TWN ISSN 1016-7390
R97.7.C5
NEIKE XUEZHI/JOURNAL OF INTERNAL MEDICINE R O C. Text in Chinese. 1990. q. free to members. **Document type:** *Journal, Academic/Scholarly.*
Indexed: EMBASE, ExcerpMed, R10, Reac, SCOPUS.
Published by: Zhonghua Minguo Neike Yixuehui/Society of Internal Medicine of Taiwan, Sec.26, no.50, 22nd Fl., Zhong Xiao West Road, Taipei, Taiwan. TEL 886-2-23758068, FAX 886-2-23758072, tsim@seed.net.tw, http://www.sim.org.tw/. Ed. Ding-Shinn Chen. Pub. Yaun-Teh Lee.

616 NLD ISSN 0300-2977
CODEN: NLJMAV
➤ **NETHERLANDS JOURNAL OF MEDICINE.** Text in English. 1958. m. EUR 670 in Europe (print & online eds.); EUR 609 in North America (print & online eds.); EUR 803 elsewhere (print & online eds.) (effective 2009). adv. bk.rev. bibl.; charts; illus. back issues avail. **Document type:** *Journal, Academic/Scholarly.* **Description:** Publishes original articles and reviews in all relevant fields of internal medicine.
Formerly (until 1973): Folia Medica Neerlandica (0015-5624)
Related titles: Microform ed.: (from PQC); Online - full text ed.: ISSN 1872-9061 (from IngentaConnect).
Indexed: A22, A36, ASCA, B25, BIOBASE, BIOSIS Prev, CABA, CIN, ChemAb, ChemTitl, CurCont, DBA, E12, EMBASE, ExcerpMed, FR, GH, H16, H17, IABS, INI, ISR, IndMed, Inpharma, LT, MEDLINE, MycolAb, N02, N03, NRN, P30, P33, P35, P39, R08, R10, R12, RM&VM, RRTA, Reac, SCI, SCOPUS, T05, W07.
—BLDSC (6077.003000), CASDDS, GNLM, IE, Ingenta, INIST. **CCC.**
Published by: (Nederlandse Internisten Vereniging), Van Zuiden Communications B.V., Postbus 2122, Alphen aan den Rijn, 2400 CC, Netherlands. TEL 31-172-476191, FAX 31-172-471882, zuiden@zuidencomm.nl, http://www.zuidencomm.nl. Ed. Marcel Levi. adv.: color page EUR 2,935; trim 210 x 297. Circ: 2,800.

616 USA
NEW MEDICAL THERAPIES BRIEFS. OSTEOPOROSIS. Text in English. 200?. irreg. free (effective 2009). **Document type:** *Newsletter, Trade.*
Media: Online - full content.
Published by: CenterWatch (Subsidiary of: Jobson Medical Information LLC.), 100 N Washington St, Ste 301, Boston, MA 02114. TEL 617-948-5100, 866-219-3440, customerservice@centerwatch.com.

616.8583005 USA
NEW MEDICAL THERAPIES BRIEFS. SEXUAL DYSFUNCTION. Text in English. 200?. irreg. free (effective 2009). **Document type:** *Newsletter, Trade.*
Media: Online - full content.
Published by: CenterWatch (Subsidiary of: Jobson Medical Information LLC.), 100 N Washington St, Ste 301, Boston, MA 02114. TEL 617-948-5100, 866-219-3440, customerservice@centerwatch.com.

616 NGA ISSN 0794-859X
QP1
NIGERIAN JOURNAL OF PHYSIOLOGICAL SCIENCES. Text in English. 1983. q. **Document type:** *Journal, Academic/Scholarly.*
Related titles: Online - full text ed.: free (effective 2011).
Indexed: EMBASE, ExcerpMed, MEDLINE, P30, R10, Reac, SCOPUS.
Published by: University of Calabar, College of Medical Sciences, Eta Agbo Rd, PO Box 1115, Calabar, Nigeria. TEL 234-87-222790, FAX 234-87-65103, gcejezie@netscape.net. Ed. E E Osim.

NIHON KOKYUKI GAKKAI ZASSHI/JAPANESE RESPIRATORY SOCIETY. JOURNAL. *see* MEDICAL SCIENCES—Respiratory Diseases

616 JPN ISSN 0915-924X
NIHON KYUKYU IGAKKAI ZASSHI/JAPANESE ASSOCIATION FOR ACUTE MEDICINE. JOURNAL. Text in English, Japanese. 1990. bi-m. JPY 10,000 membership (effective 2005). **Document type:** *Journal, Academic/Scholarly.* **Description:** Aims to contribute to progress in the establishment of acute medicine as a specialty.
Indexed: A22, INIS AtomInd.
—BLDSC (4808.579000), IE, Ingenta. **CCC.**
Published by: Nihon Kyukyu Igakkai/Japanese Association for Acute Medicine, K's Bldg, 3F, Hongo 3-3-12, Bunkyo-ku, Tokyo, 113-0033, Japan. TEL 81-3-58409870, FAX 81-3-58409876, http://www.jaam.jp/.

616 JPN ISSN 0021-5384
R97.7.J3 CODEN: NNGAAS
NIHON NAIKA GAKKAI ZASSHI/JAPANESE SOCIETY OF INTERNAL MEDICINE. JOURNAL. Text in Japanese. 1913. m. adv. charts; illus. cum.index. **Document type:** *Journal, Academic/Scholarly.* **Description:** Covers internal medicine.
Related titles: Online - full text ed.: ISSN 1883-2083.
Indexed: DentInd, EMBASE, ExcerpMed, INI, INIS AtomInd, IndMed, MEDLINE, P30, R10, Reac, SCOPUS.
—CASDDS, GNLM, INIST. **CCC.**
Published by: Nihon Naika Gakkai/Japanese Society of Internal Medicine, 28-8, 3-chome, Hongo, Bunkyo-ku, Tokyo, 113-8433, Japan. TEL 81-3-38135991, FAX 81-3-38181556, naika@mb.infoweb.ne.jp. Ed. Hidehiko Saito. Circ: 77,000.

NIHON SHOKAKI NAISHIKYO GAKKAI KOSHIN'ETSU CHIHOKAI ZASSHI/ENDOSCOPIC FORUM FOR DIGESTIVE DISEASE. *see* MEDICAL SCIENCES—Gastroenterology

612.3 MEX ISSN 1665-5125
NUTRICION CLINICA. Text in Spanish. 1995. q. back issues avail. **Document type:** *Journal, Academic/Scholarly.*
Indexed: CA, T02.
Published by: Nieto Editores, Ave de las Tzinnias 10, Col Jardines de Coyoacan, Mexico, D.F., 04890, Mexico. TEL 52-55-56782811, FAX 52-55-56796591, anieto@nietoeditores.com.mx. Ed. Consuelo Velasquez Alva. Circ: 3,000.

616.02 DEU ISSN 1869-0874
➤ **ONKOLOGISCHE WELT.** Text in German. 1978. 6/yr. EUR 72 to individuals; EUR 96 to institutions; EUR 48 to students; EUR 16 newsstand/cover (effective 2011). adv. **Document type:** *Journal, Academic/Scholarly.*
Former titles (until 2009): Die Internistische Welt Onkologie (1866-8720); (until 2007): Die Internistische Welt (0344-4201)
—BLDSC (4557.220200), GNLM, IE, Infotrieve, INIST. **CCC.**
Published by: Schattauer GmbH, Hoelderlinstr 3, Stuttgart, 70174, Germany. TEL 49-711-229870, FAX 49-711-2298750, info@schattauer.de, http://www.schattauer.com. Adv. contact Christoph Brocker. B&W page EUR 1,900, color page EUR 3,015; trim 183 x 255. Circ: 9,800 (controlled).

616 NLD ISSN 1876-8237
RC628
▼ ➤ **OPEN OBESITY JOURNAL.** Text in English. 2009. irreg. free (effective 2011). **Document type:** *Journal, Academic/Scholarly.*
Media: Online - full text.
Indexed: A01, ESPM, NSA, RiskAb.
Published by: Bentham Open (Subsidiary of: Bentham Science Publishers Ltd.), PO Box 294, Bussum, AG 1400, Netherlands. TEL 31-35-6923800, FAX 31-35-6980150, subscriptions@bentham.org.

➤ **THE ORIGINAL INTERNIST**; a scientific publication on natural health care. *see* MEDICAL SCIENCES—Chiropractic, Homeopathy, Osteopathy

616 GBR ISSN 1750-1172
RC48.8
➤ **ORPHANET JOURNAL OF RARE DISEASES.** Text in English. 2006. irreg. free (effective 2011). adv. back issues avail. **Document type:** *Journal, Academic/Scholarly.* **Description:** Covers all aspects of rare diseases and orphan drugs.
Media: Online - full text.
Indexed: A01, A26, BIOSIS Prev, C06, C07, CA, EMBASE, ExcerpMed, I05, MEDLINE, MycolAb, P30, R10, Reac, S06, SCI, SCOPUS, T02, W07.
—CCC.
Published by: BioMed Central Ltd. (Subsidiary of: Springer Science+Business Media), 236 Gray's Inn Rd, London, WC1X 8HB, United Kingdom. TEL 44-20-31922000, FAX 44-20-31922010, info@biomedcentral.com, http://www.biomedcentral.com. Eds. Bruno Dallapiccola, Dian Donna, Segolene Ayme.

616 ITA ISSN 1127-4867
OSPEDALI SAN CAMILLO E FORLANINI. ANNALI. Text in Italian; Summaries in English. 1999. q. USD 100 domestic to institutions; USD 200 foreign to institutions (effective 2009). **Document type:** *Journal, Academic/Scholarly.*
Formed by the merger of (1937-1997): Istituto Carlo Forlanini. Annali (0021-2431); (1991-1997): Ospedale San Camillo (1590-8151)
Indexed: SCOPUS.
Published by: (Azienda Ospedaliera San Camillo - Forlanini), Societa Editrice Universo, Via Giovanni Battista Morgagni 1, Rome, RM 00161, Italy. TEL 39-06-44231171, FAX 39-06-4402033, amministrazione@seu-roma.it, http://www.seuroma.com.

616 ITA
CODEN: PMMDAE
➤ **PANMINERVA MEDICA**; a journal on internal medicine. Text in English. 1959. q. EUR 260 combined subscription in the European Union to institutions (print & online eds.); EUR 285 combined subscription elsewhere to institutions (print & online eds.) (effective 2011). bk.rev. abstr.; bibl.; charts; illus. reprints avail. **Document type:** *Journal, Academic/Scholarly.* **Description:** Covers clinical and experimental medicine and surgery.
Formerly: Panminerva Medica - Europa Medica; Which was formed by the merger of: Panminerva Medica (0031-0808); Europa Medica (0014-2557)
Related titles: Microfilm ed.: (from PQC); Online - full text ed.: ISSN 1827-1898. 2005.
Indexed: A22, A36, ASCA, B25, BIOSIS Prev, CABA, ChemAb, CurCont, D01, DentInd, EMBASE, ExcerpMed, F08, F11, F12, GH, IndMed, Inpharma, MEDLINE, MycolAb, N02, N03, P30, P35, RA&MP, RefZh, SCI, SCOPUS, SoyAb, T05, VS, W07.
—BLDSC (6357.380000), CASDDS, GNLM, IE, Ingenta, INIST. **CCC.**
Published by: Edizioni Minerva Medica, Corso Bramante 83-85, Turin, 10126, Italy. TEL 39-011-678282, FAX 39-011-674502, journals.dept@minervamedica.it, http://www.minervamedica.it. Ed. M L Benzo. Pub. Alberto Oliaro. Circ: 5,000 (paid).

616 578.65 GBR ISSN 1756-3305
QL757
➤ **PARASITES & VECTORS.** Text in English. 2007. irreg. free (effective 2011). adv. back issues avail. **Document type:** *Journal, Academic/Scholarly.* **Description:** Contains dealing with the biology of parasites, parasitic diseases, intermediate hosts, vectors and vector-borne pathogens.
Formed by the merger of (2002-2007): Filaria Journal (1475-2883); (2002-2007): Kinetoplastid Biology and Disease (1475-9292)
Media: Online - full text.
Indexed: A01, A26, A34, A35, A36, A38, AgBio, AgrForAb, B23, BP, C25, CA, CABA, D01, E12, E17, EMBASE, EntAb, ExcerpMed, F08, F12, FCA, GH, H16, H17, I05, IndVet, LT, N02, OR, P30, P32, P33, P39, PN&I, R07, R08, R12, RA&MP, RM&VM, S13, S16, SCI, SCOPUS, T02, T05, TAR, VS, W07.
—CCC.
Published by: BioMed Central Ltd. (Subsidiary of: Springer Science+Business Media), 236 Gray's Inn Rd, London, WC1X 8HB, United Kingdom. TEL 44-20-31922000, FAX 44-20-31922010, info@biomedcentral.com, http://www.biomedcentral.com. Ed. Chris Arme. Adv. contact Natasha Bailey TEL 44-20-31922231.

➤ **PELVIPERINEOLOGY.** *see* MEDICAL SCIENCES—Obstetrics And Gynecology

616 PHL ISSN 0556-0071
R97 CODEN: APPYEK
PHILIPPINE JOURNAL OF INTERNAL MEDICINE. Text in English. 1963. bi-m. **Document type:** *Journal, Academic/Scholarly.*
Related titles: CD-ROM ed.
Indexed: A22, ExtraMED, P30, SCOPUS.
—GNLM, Infotrieve.
Published by: Philippine College of Physicians, Units 2201-2203, 22 Fl. One San Miguel Ave. Bldg., San Miguel Ave. cor. Shaw Blvd. Ortigas Center, Pasig City, Philippines. TEL 632-910-2250, FAX 632-910-2251, secretariat@pcp.org.ph.

616.026 POL ISSN 0032-3772
CODEN: PAMWAL
➤ **POLSKIE ARCHIWUM MEDYCYNY WEWNETRZNEJ/POLISH ARCHIVES OF INTERNAL MEDICINE.** Text in Polish; Summaries in English. 1923. m. adv. bk.rev. charts; illus. index. back issues avail. **Document type:** *Journal, Academic/Scholarly.* **Description:** Publishes original papers, clinical papers, case reports, review papers.
Related titles: Online - full text ed.: ISSN 1897-9483. free (effective 2011).
Indexed: A22, ChemAb, DentInd, EMBASE, ExcerpMed, IndMed, MEDLINE, P30, R10, Reac, SCI, SCOPUS, W07.
—BLDSC (6546.500000), CASDDS, GNLM, IE, Infotrieve, Ingenta, INIST.
Published by: (Towarzystwo Internistow Polskich/Polish Society of Internal Medicine), Wydawnictwo Medyczne Urban i Partner, ul Marii Sklodowskiej-Curie 55-61, Wroclaw, 50950, Poland. TEL 48-71-3285487, FAX 48-71-3284391, http://www.urbanpartner.pl. Ed. Anetta Undas.

616 USA ISSN 2090-2867
▼ ➤ **REHABILITATION RESEARCH AND PRACTICE.** Text in English. 2010. q. USD 195 (effective 2011). **Document type:** *Journal, Academic/Scholarly.* **Description:** Publishes original research articles, review articles, and clinical studies in all areas of rehabilitation.
Related titles: Online - full text ed.: ISSN 2090-2875. free (effective 2011).
Indexed: A01, T02.
Published by: Hindawi Publishing Corporation, 410 Park Ave, 15th Fl, PMB 287, New York, NY 10022. FAX 866-446-3294, hindawi@hindawi.com.

616 GBR ISSN 1179-7282
▼ ➤ **RESEARCH AND REPORTS IN TROPICAL MEDICINE.** Text in English. 2010. irreg. free (effective 2011). **Document type:** *Journal, Academic/Scholarly.*
Media: Online - full text.
Indexed: A34, AgrForAb, CABA, E12, F08, GH, P33, R07, R08, T05.
—CCC.
Published by: Dove Medical Press Ltd., Beechfield House, Winterton Way, Macclesfield, SK11 0JL, United Kingdom. TEL 44-1625-509130, FAX 44-1625-617933. Ed. Tom Unnasch.

616 CHL ISSN 0718-4743
REVISTA LATINOAMERICANA DE ACTUALIDADES BIOMEDICAS. Text in Spanish. 2007. m.
Media: Online - full content.
Published by: Centro de Diagnostico Oncoinmunologico, Ltda., Cardenio Avello 36, Concepcion, Chile. axelyoy@gmail.com.

616 FRA ISSN 0248-8663
R41 CODEN: RMEIDE
➤ **LA REVUE DE MEDECINE INTERNE.** Text in French; Summaries in English, French. 1962; N.S. 1980. 12/yr. EUR 502 in Europe to institutions; EUR 477.96 in France to institutions; JPY 63,000 in Japan to institutions; USD 663 elsewhere to institutions (effective 2012). adv. bk.rev. illus. index. **Document type:** *Journal, Academic/Scholarly.* **Description:** Covers internal medicine.
Formerly (until 1980): Coeur et Medecine Interne (0010-0234)
Related titles: Microform ed.: N.S. (from PQC); Online - full text ed.: ISSN 1768-3122 (from IngentaConnect, ScienceDirect).
Indexed: A01, A03, A08, A22, A26, A34, A36, ASCA, BIOBASE, CA, CABA, CISA, ChemAb, CurCont, D01, E12, EMBASE, ExcerpMed, FR, GH, H17, I05, IABS, INI, IndMed, IndVet, Inpharma, LT, MEDLINE, N02, N03, P30, P32, P33, P35, P39, P40, R08, R10, R13, RM&VM, RRTA, Reac, SCI, SCOPUS, T02, T05, VS, W07.
—BLDSC (7930.940000), GNLM, IE, Infotrieve, Ingenta, INIST. **CCC.**
Published by: (Societe Nationale Francaise de Medecine Interne), Elsevier Masson (Subsidiary of: Elsevier Health Sciences), 62 Rue Camille Desmoulins, Issy les Moulineaux, Cedex 92442, France. TEL 33-1-71165500, FAX 33-1-71165600, infos@elsevier-masson.fr.

616.026 ROM ISSN 1582-3296
CODEN: RRINEH
ROMANIAN JOURNAL OF INTERNAL MEDICINE/REVUE ROUMAINE DE MEDECINE INTERNE. Text in English, French, German, Russian. 1974. 4/yr. bk.rev. charts; illus. index. reprints avail. **Document type:** *Journal, Academic/Scholarly.* **Description:** Contains reviews, articles, results of experimental studies and new book information.
Former titles (until 1998): Revue Roumaine de Medecine Interne (1220-4749); (until 1990): Revue Roumaine de Medecine. Serie Medecine Interne (0377-1202); Which superseded in part (in 1975): Revue Roumaine de Medecine (0303-822X); Which was formed by the merger of (1953-1974): Revue Roumaine de Neurologie et de Psychiatrie (0301-7303); Which was formerly (until 1974): Revue Roumaine de Neurologie (0035-3981); (1953-1974): Revue Roumaine d'Endocrinologie (0035-4015); (1953-1974): Revue Roumaine de Medecine Interne (0035-3973); All of which superseded in part (in 1964): Revue de Sciences Medicales (0484-8632); Which superseded in part (in 1954): La Science dans la Republique Populaire Roumaine (1220-4757)
Related titles: Online - full text ed.: (from PQC).
Indexed: A22, ChemAb, EMBASE, ExcerpMed, IndMed, MEDLINE, P30, R10, Reac, SCOPUS.
—BLDSC (8019.632000), CASDDS, GNLM, IE, Infotrieve, Ingenta, INIST, Linda Hall.

Published by: (Academia de Stiinte Medicale), Editura Academiei Romane/Publishing House of the Romanian Academy, Calea 13 Septembrie 13, Sector 5, Bucharest, 050711, Romania. TEL 40-21-3188146, FAX 40-21-3182444, edacad@ear.ro, http://www.ear.ro. Ed. S Purice. Circ: 1,500. **Dist. by:** Rodipet S.A., Piata Presei Libere 1, sector 1, PO Box 33-57, Bucharest 3, Romania. TEL 40-21-2224126, 40-21-2226407, rodipet@rodipet.ro.

616 USA ISSN 1940-2899
S G I M FORUM. Text in English. m. free. **Document type:** *Newsletter.* **Description:** Seeks to provide a forum for information and opinions of interest to SGIM members and to general internists and those engaged in the study, teaching or operation of general internal medicine.
Related titles: Online - full text ed.: ISSN 1940-2902; ♦ Supplement to: Journal of General Internal Medicine. ISSN 0884-8734.
Published by: Society of General Internal Medicine, 2501 M St NW, Ste 575, Washington, DC 20037. TEL 202-887-5150, 800-822-3060. Ed. Rich Kravitz.

616 NLD ISSN 2211-6036
SARCOSCOOP. Text in Dutch. 198?. q. EUR 21 membership (effective 2011). **Document type:** *Magazine, Trade.*
Formerly (until 2011): Sarcoidose Nieuws (1568-4326)
Published by: Sarcoidose Belangenvereniging Nederland, Postbus 18, Nijkerk, 3860 AA, Netherlands. TEL 31-33-2471467, info@sarcoidose.nl. Circ: 2,500.

616 CHN ISSN 1671-7813
SHIYONG ZHONGYI NEIKE ZAZHI/JOURNAL OF PRACTICAL TRADITIONAL CHINESE INTERNAL MEDICINE. Text in Chinese. 1987. m.
Related titles: Online - full text ed.: (from WanFang Data Corp.).
—BLDSC (8267.297967).
Published by: Liaoning Sheng Zhongyiyao Yanjiuyuan, 60, Huanghe Bei Dajie, Huanggu-qu, Shenyang, 110034, China. TEL 86-24-86803478, FAX 86-24-86803478. **Co-sponsors:** Liaoning Sheng Zhongyiyao Xuehui; Zhonghua Zhongyiyao Xuehui.

616 PER ISSN 1681-9721
SOCIEDAD PERUANA DE MEDICINA INTERNA. REVISTA. Text in Spanish. 1987. q. **Document type:** *Journal, Academic/Scholarly.*
Formerly (until 2001): Sociedad Peruana de Medicina Interna. Boletin (1019-309X)
Related titles: Online - full text ed.: ISSN 1609-7173. 1991.
Published by: Sociedad Peruana de Medicina Interna, Av Jose Pardo 139, Of 401, Miraflores, Lima, Peru. TEL 51-1-4455158, FAX 51-1-4455396, casilla@spmi.net, http://www.spmi.net.

616 CZE ISSN 1213-7790
SOUCASNA KLINICKA PRAXE (CZECH EDITION). Text in Czech. 2002. 3/yr. **Document type:** *Journal, Academic/Scholarly.*
Published by: Medica Healthworld a.s., Bidlaky 20, Brno, 63900, Czech Republic. TEL 420-533-337311, FAX 420-533-337312, info@mhw.cz, http://www.mhw.cz.

616 CZE ISSN 1214-7036
SOUCASNA KLINICKA PRAXE (SLOVAK EDITION). Text in Slovak. 3/yr. **Document type:** *Journal, Academic/Scholarly.*
Published by: Medica Healthworld a.s., Bidlaky 20, Brno, 63900, Czech Republic. TEL 420-533-337311, FAX 420-533-337312, info@mhw.cz, http://www.mhw.cz.

616.3 NLD ISSN 2210-2019
SPREEKUUR INTERNE GENEESKUNDE. Text in Dutch. 1996. q. free (effective 2010). adv. **Document type:** *Journal, Trade.*
Formerly (until 2010): Internisten Vademecum (1384-6620)
Published by: Bohn Stafleu van Loghum B.V. (Subsidiary of: Springer Science+Business Media), Postbus 246, Houten, 3990 GA, Netherlands. TEL 31-30-6383872, FAX 31-30-6383991, boekhandels@bsl.nl, http://www.bsl.nl. adv.: color page EUR 3,941; trim 210 x 297. Circ: 1,708.

616 NLD ISSN 1871-4005
STAM CEL TRANSPLANTATIES CONTACT. Key Title: S C T Contact. Text in Dutch. 1999. q. EUR 16 (effective 2009).
Formerly (until 2005): Been Merg Transplantaties Contact (1572-0888)
Published by: Contactgroep Stamceltransplantaties (SCT), c/o IKA, Postbus 9236, Amsterdam, 1066 AE, Netherlands. info@sct.nfkpv.nl, http://www.kankerpatient.nl/sct. Eds. Gerard Bruin, Leo van Holten, Melanie Blaauw.

616.37 JPN ISSN 0913-0071
SUIZO/JAPAN PANCREAS SOCIETY. JOURNAL. Text in Japanese. 1986. q. **Document type:** *Journal, Academic/Scholarly.*
Indexed: INIS AtomInd.
—BLDSC (4805.677000). **CCC.**
Published by: Nihon Suizo Gakkai/Japan Pancreas Society, Tohoku University Graduate School of Medical Science, Department of Surgery, 1-1, Seiryo-machi, Aoba-ku, Sendai, 980-8574, Japan. jps@surg1.med.tohoku.ac.jp, http://www.kojin.or.jp/suizou/.

616 DEU ISSN 1616-9654
THIEME REFRESHER INNERE MEDIZIN. Text in German. 2007. irreg. **Document type:** *Monographic series, Academic/Scholarly.*
—BLDSC (8820.102957).
Published by: Georg Thieme Verlag, Ruedigerstr 14, Stuttgart, 70469, Germany. TEL 49-711-8931421, FAX 49-711-8931410, leser.service@thieme.de, http://www.thieme.de.

616 USA ISSN 1090-4964
TRANSPLANT NEWS. Text in English. 1990. s-m. USD 324 (effective 2006). **Document type:** *Newsletter, Consumer.*
Related titles: Online - full text ed.
Indexed: A26, C06, C07, G05, G06, G07, G08, H11, H12, I05, PROMT.
Published by: Transplant Communications, Inc., 3500 Boston St., Ste. 317, Baltimore, MD 21224. TEL 410-732-4477, 800-689-4262, FAX 410-732-4499, http://www.trannews.com. Ed. Jim Warren.

616 TUR ISSN 0494-1373
RC306 CODEN: TBZTAQ
➤ **TUBERKULOZ VE TORAKS/TURKISH JOURNAL OF TUBERCULOSIS & THORAX.** Text in Turkish, English. 2004. q. USD 50 (effective 2011). **Document type:** *Journal, Academic/Scholarly.* **Description:** Covers research of thorax diseases, manuscripts and case reports.
Related titles: Online - full text ed.: 2003. free (effective 2011).
Indexed: A34, A36, CABA, E12, EMBASE, ExcerpMed, GH, H17, IndVet, MEDLINE, N02, N03, P30, P33, R10, R12, RM&VM, Reac, SCOPUS, T05, VS.
Published by: Turkish Association of Tuberculosis & Torax, c/o Dr Doganay Alper, Ankara University, Faculty of Medicine Pulmonary Diseases, Cebeci Ankara, 06100, Turkey. TEL 90-312-3190027, FAX 90-312-3190046, akaya@medicine.ankara.edu.tr. Eds. Dr. Doganay Alper, Ozlem Ozdemir Kumbasar.

616 TUR ISSN 1302-7808
➤ **TURKS TORAKS DERGISI/TURKISH THORACIC JOURNAL.** Text in Turkish. 2000. q. free to qualified personnel (effective 2011). **Document type:** *Journal, Academic/Scholarly.* **Description:** Publishes article related to respiratory disease, clinical, experimental and epidemiological studies. Target audience of chest diseases and chest surgery, physicians, internal medicine physicians and general practitioners who are interested in respiratory diseases.
Related titles: Online - full text ed.: ISSN 1308-5387. free (effective 2011); English ed.
Indexed: A01, A26, C06, C07, CA, EMBASE, ExcerpMed, H12, I05, P20, P22, P48, P54, PQC, SCOPUS, T02.
Published by: (Turkish Thoracic Society), Aves Yayincilik, Kizilelma Cad 5/3, Findikazade, Istanbul, 34096, Turkey. TEL 90-212-5890053, FAX 90-212-5890094, info@avesyayincilik.com, http://www.avesyayincilik.com. Eds. Bartu Saryal, Sema Umut.

616 CAN ISSN 1920-7425
▼ ➤ **U B C FACULTY OF MEDICINE MEDICAL JOURNAL.** Abbreviated title: U B C M J. Variant title: U B C Medical Journal. Text in English. 2009. s-a. free to members (effective 2010). adv. back issues avail. **Document type:** *Journal, Academic/Scholarly.* **Description:** Features research and review articles in medicine to medical trends, clinical reports, elective reports and commentaries in the principles and practice of medicine.
Related titles: Online - full text ed.: free (effective 2010).
Published by: University of British Columbia, Faculty of Medicine, 2750 Heather St, Vancouver, BC V5Z 4M2, Canada. abuchan@medd.med.ubc.ca, http://www.med.ubc.ca. Ed. Pamela Verma. Adv. contact Kevin Lowe.

616 ITA ISSN 1125-0747
UNIVERSITA DI FERRARA. ANNALI. SEZIONE 12: MEDICINA INTERNA. Text in Italian. 1936. a. price varies. **Document type:** *Journal, Academic/Scholarly.*
Supersedes in part (in 1951): Universita di Ferrara. Annali (0365-7833)
Published by: Universita degli Studi di Ferrara, Via Savonarola 9, Ferrara, 44100, Italy. TEL 39-0532-293111, FAX 39-0532-293031, http://www.unife.it.

616 USA ISSN 1559-4017
VISIBLE HUMAN JOURNAL OF ENDOSCOPY. Abbreviated title: V H J O E. Text in English. 2002. q. free (effective 2010). **Document type:** *Journal, Academic/Scholarly.*
Formerly (until 2003): Visible Human Journal of Endosonography (1536-5840)
Media: Online - full text.
Published by: University of Colorado Health Sciences Center, Center for Human Simulation, PO Box 6508, Aurora, CO 80045. TEL 303-724-0500, http://www.uchsc.edu/sm/chs/open.html. Ed. John Deutsch. Pub. Victor Spitzer.

616 CHN ISSN 1948-5182
▼ **WORLD JOURNAL OF HEPATOLOGY.** Text in English. 2009. m. free (effective 2011). **Document type:** *Journal, Academic/Scholarly.* **Description:** Features medical research on hepatology.
Media: Online - full text.
Indexed: P30.
Published by: Beijing Baishideng BioMed Scientific Co., Ltd (Subsidiary of: Baishideng Publishing Group Co., Limited), Rm 903, Bldg D, Ocean International Center, 62 Dongsihuan Zhonglu, Chaoyang District, Beijing, 100025, China. TEL 86-10-85381892, FAX 86-10-85381893, baishideng@wjgnet.com.

616 AUT ISSN 1812-9501
RC691
ZEITSCHRIFT FUER GEFAESSMEDIZIN. Text in German. 4/yr. EUR 36 (effective 2005). **Document type:** *Journal, Academic/Scholarly.*
Related titles: Online - full text ed.: ISSN 1812-951X. 2004. free (effective 2011).
Indexed: EMBASE, ExcerpMed, R10, Reac, SCOPUS.
—CCC.
Published by: Krause & Pachernegg GmbH, Mozartgasse 10, Gablitz, 3003, Austria. TEL 43-2231-612580, FAX 43-2231-6125810, k_u_p@eunet.at, http://www.kup.at/verlag.htm. Eds. E Minar, M Schillinger.

616 CHN ISSN 1005-2194
➤ **ZHONGGUO SHIYONG NEIKE ZAZHI/CHINESE JOURNAL OF PRACTICAL INTERNAL MEDICINE.** Text in Chinese; Abstracts in English. 1981. s-m. USD 49.20 (effective 2009). adv. **Document type:** *Journal, Academic/Scholarly.* **Description:** Features new developments and methods of practical diagnosis, treatment and prevention of internal diseases.
Formerly: Shiyong Neike Zazhi - Journal of Practical Internal Medicine (1001-084X)
Related titles: Online - full text ed.
Indexed: A29, A34, A35, A36, AgBio, B20, B21, B23, C30, CABA, D01, E12, ESPM, GH, GenetAb, H16, H17, ImmunAb, LT, N02, N03, N04, NSA, P32, P33, P39, P40, R08, R12, R13, RA&MP, RM&VM, RRTA, S12, SoyAb, T05, VS, VirolAbstr, W10.
—BLDSC (3180.560000).
Published by: Zhongguo Shiyong Yixue Zazhishe, 9, Nanjing Nan Jie, 5th Fl., Heping-qu, Shenyang, Liaoning 110001, China. TEL 86-24-23866520, FAX 86-24-23866530. Eds. Jian Kang, Yangang Ren. R&P Guohua Du. adv.: page USD 2,000. Circ: 60,000. **Dist. by:** China International Book Trading Corp, 35 Chegongzhuang Xilu, Haidian District, PO Box 399, Beijing 100044, China. TEL 86-10-68412045, FAX 86-10-68412023, cibtc@mail.cibtc.com.cn, http://www.cibtc.com.cn.

➤ **ZHONGGUO YIXUE WENZHAI (NEIKE XUE)/CHINESE MEDICAL DIGEST (INTERNAL MEDICINE).** *see* MEDICAL SCIENCES—Abstracting, Bibliographies, Statistics

616.362 CHN ISSN 1007-3418
ZHONGHUA GANZANGBING ZAZHI/CHINESE JOURNAL OF HEPATOLOGY. Text in Chinese. 1996. bi-m. USD 80.40 (effective 2009). **Document type:** *Academic/Scholarly.*
Related titles: Online - full text ed.
Indexed: A22, EMBASE, ExcerpMed, IndMed, MEDLINE, P30, R10, Reac, SCOPUS.
—BLDSC (3180.350500), East View, IE, Ingenta.
Published by: Zhonghua Yixuehui Zazhishe/Chinese Medical Association Publishing House, 42 Dongsi Xidajie, Beijing, 100710, China. **Dist. by:** China International Book Trading Corp, 35 Chegongzhuang Xilu, Haidian District, PO Box 399, Beijing 100044, China. TEL 86-10-68412045, FAX 86-10-68412023, cibtc@mail.cibtc.com.cn, http://www.cibtc.com.cn.

616.02 CHN ISSN 0578-1426
R97.7.C5 CODEN: CHHNAB
ZHONGHUA NEIKE ZAZHI/CHINESE JOURNAL OF INTERNAL MEDICINE. Key Title: Chung-Hua Nei K'o Tsa Chih. Text in Chinese. 1953. m. USD 80.40 (effective 2009). **Document type:** *Journal, Academic/Scholarly.*
Related titles: CD-ROM ed.; Online - full text ed.
Indexed: A22, ChemAb, EMBASE, ExcerpMed, ExtraMED, IndMed, MEDLINE, P30, R10, Reac, SCOPUS, ToxAb, VirolAbstr.
—BLDSC (3180.360000), East View, IE, Infotrieve, Ingenta.
Published by: Zhonghua Yixuehui Zazhishe/Chinese Medical Association Publishing House, 42 Dongsi Xidajie, Beijing, 100710, China. http://www.medline.org.cn/. **Dist. by:** China International Book Trading Corp, 35 Chegongzhuang Xilu, Haidian District, PO Box 399, Beijing 100044, China. TEL 86-10-68412045, FAX 86-10-68412023, cibtc@mail.cibtc.com.cn, http://www.cibtc.com.cn.

MEDICAL SCIENCES—Nurses And Nursing

see also GERONTOLOGY AND GERIATRICS ; HEALTH FACILITIES AND ADMINISTRATION

610.73 USA
A A N N SYNAPSE. Text in English. bi-m. membership only. **Document type:** *Newsletter.*
Published by: American Association of Neuroscience Nurses, 4700 W Lake Ave, Glenview, IL 60025. TEL 847-375-4733, 888-557-2266, FAX 847-375-6333, bsimmons@amctec.com, http://www.aann.org. R&P Barbara Simmons. Circ: 4,000.

610.7346 USA ISSN 0746-620X
A A O H N NEWS. (American Association of Occupational Health Nurses) Text in English. 198?. m. free to members (effective 2005). **Document type:** *Newsletter.*
Formerly (until 198?): A A O H N Newsletter (0745-4376)
Indexed: C06, C07, C08, CINAHL.
—CCC.
Published by: American Association of Occupational Health Nurses, Inc., 7794 Grow Dr, Pensacola, FL 32514. TEL 854-474-6963, FAX 854-484-8762, aaohn@aaohn.org.

610.73 USA ISSN 1046-7041
➤ **A B N F JOURNAL.** Text in English. 1990. q. USD 150 domestic to individuals; USD 325 domestic to institutions; USD 400 foreign; free to members (effective 2010). bk.rev. back issues avail.; reprints avail. **Document type:** *Journal, Academic/Scholarly.* **Description:** Documents the distinct nature and health-care needs of the Black patient with original research and health-related manuscripts, material, reviews.
Related titles: Online - full text ed.
Indexed: A01, A02, A03, A08, A26, C06, C07, C08, C11, CA, CINAHL, E08, EMBASE, ExcerpMed, G08, H04, H11, H12, I05, IIBP, INI, MEDLINE, P20, P22, P24, P30, P48, P54, PQC, S03, S09, SCOPUS, T02.
—BLDSC (0549.610000), IE, Infotrieve, Ingenta. **CCC.**
Published by: (Association of Black Nursing Faculty, Inc.), Tucker Publications, Inc., PO Box 580, Lisle, IL 60532. TEL 630-969-3895, FAX 630-969-3895, info@tuckerpub.com, http://www.tuckerpub.com. Ed. Gloria J McNeal TEL 609-747-1536. Pub. Dr. Sallie Tucker-Allen.

➤ **A C O R N**; the journal of perioperative nursing in Australia. *see* HEALTH FACILITIES AND ADMINISTRATION

610.73 GBR
A F P P NEWSLETTER. (Association for Perioperative Practice) Text in English. 19??. m. free to members (effective 2009). **Document type:** *Newsletter, Trade.*
Former titles (until 2005): N A T N Newsletter; (until 2000): N A T Newsletter
Published by: Association for Perioperative Practice, Daisy Ayris House, 6 Grove Park Ct, Harrogate, Yorks HG1 4DP, United Kingdom. TEL 44-1423-508079, FAX 44-1423-531613, hq@afpp.org.uk, http://www.afpp.org.uk.

610.73 COL ISSN 0120-1832
A N E C. Text in Spanish. 1966. irreg. COP 15,000; COP 5,000 per issue (effective 2005). adv. bk.rev. illus.
Formerly: Asociacion Nacional de Enfermeras de Colombia. A N E C. Revista
Indexed: INI.
Published by: Asociacion Nacional de Enfermeras de Colombia, Cra 27, No 46-21Piso 2, Bogota, 05987, Colombia. TEL 57-1-2683535, FAX 57-1-2692095. Eds. Beatriz Carballo, Esperanza Morales. Circ: 1,500,811.

610.73 ESP ISSN 2171-4274
▼ **A N E C O R M PRESS.** Text in Spanish. 2009. s-a. back issues avail. **Document type:** *Journal, Academic/Scholarly.*
Published by: Asociacion Nacional de Enfermeria Cordinadora de Recursos Materiales, C Orenze, 85, Madrid, 28020, Spain. TEL 34-902-190848, FAX 34-902-190850.

610.73 GBR ISSN 1754-3185
➤ **A N P JOURNAL.** Text in English. 2007. q. free to members (effective 2009). back issues avail. **Document type:** *Journal, Academic/Scholarly.* **Description:** Contains news and provides opinion and analysis on important issues. Includes clinical features which keep you up to date on the latest management of chronic conditions.
Published by: (Association for Nurse Prescribing), Haymarket Medical Publications Ltd. (Subsidiary of: Haymarket Media Group), 174 Hammersmith Rd, London, W6 7JP, United Kingdom. TEL 44-20-82675000, healthcare.republic@haymarket.com, http://www.healthcarerepublic.com.

610.73 USA ISSN 0001-2092
RD99.A1 CODEN: AOJOEL
A O R N JOURNAL. Text in English. 1963. m. USD 317 in United States to institutions; USD 375 elsewhere to institutions (effective 2012). adv. bk.rev. abstr.; bibl.; charts; illus.; stat. cum.index. 200 p./no.; back issues avail.; reprints avail. **Document type:** *Journal, Academic/ Scholarly.* **Description:** Contains clinical information, research articles, and perioperative nursing standards of practice.
Supersedes (1960-1963): O R Nursing
Related titles: CD-ROM ed.; Microfilm ed.: (from PQC); Online - full text ed.: ISSN 1878-0369 (from ScienceDirect).
Indexed: A20, A22, A25, A26, AHCMS, AMED, B28, C06, C07, C08, CA, CINAHL, E08, EMBASE, ExcerpMed, F09, FamI, G08, H11, H12, H13, HospLI, I05, INI, IndMed, M06, MEDLINE, NurAb, P10, P20, P22, P24, P30, P48, P53, P54, PQC, R10, Reac, S08, S09, SCOPUS, T02.
—BLDSC (1567.727000), GNLM, IE, Infotrieve, Ingenta. **CCC.**
Published by: (Association of periOperative Registered Nurses, Inc.), Elsevier Inc. (Subsidiary of: Elsevier Science & Technology), 1600 John F Kennedy Blvd, Philadelphia, PA 19103. TEL 215-239-3900, FAX 215-238-7883, JournalCustomerService-usa@elsevier.com. Ed. Patricia C Seifert.

610.73 NLD ISSN 1877-6868
▼ **A O R N OR PRODUCT DIRECTORY.** Text in English. 2009. a. adv. **Document type:** *Directory, Trade.*
Published by: (Association of periOperative Registered Nurses, Inc. USA), Elsevier BV (Subsidiary of: Elsevier Science & Technology), Radarweg 29, PO Box 211, Amsterdam, 1000 AE, Netherlands. TEL 31-20-4853911, FAX 31-20-4852457, http://www.elsevier.com.

610.73 USA ISSN 1050-5237
A P N A NEWS. Text in English. 1989. bi-m. free to members (effective 2009). **Document type:** *Newsletter, Trade.*
—**CCC.**
Published by: American Psychiatric Nurses Association, 1555 Wilson Blvd, Ste 530, Arlington, VA 22209. TEL 703-243-2443, 866-243-2443, FAX 703-243-3390, klewis@apna.org. Ed. Michele Valentino.

610.73 CAN
A R N N L ACCESS. Text in English. 1981. 3/yr. CAD 25 (effective 2010). adv. **Document type:** *Newsletter, Trade.* **Description:** Deals with issues affecting nurses in the province. It is sent to all practicing nurses in the province.
Former titles: A R N N Access (1182-8897); (until 1990): A R N N News News News (0822-7160); (until 1981): News! News! News! (0319-7611)
Related titles: Online - full text ed.
Published by: Association of Registered Nurses of Newfoundland and Labrador, 55 Military Rd, St. John's, NF A1C 2C5, Canada. TEL 709-753-6040, 800-563-3200, FAX 709-753-4940, info@arnnl.nf.ca. Ed. Janice Lockyer. adv.: B&W page USD 425, color page USD 450. Circ: 6,300.

610.73 USA
A R N NETWORK. Text in English. 1976. bi-m. free to members (effective 2010). adv. back issues avail. **Document type:** *Newsletter, Trade.* **Description:** Provides information about the latest professional and organizational news to its members, including information about upcoming educational events, new educational resources, and approaching deadlines for grant applications and award submissions etc.
Formerly: A R N News (1075-5764)
Indexed: C06, CINAHL.
Published by: Association of Rehabilitation Nurses, 4700 W Lake Ave, Glenview, IL 60025. TEL 847-375-4710, 800-229-7530, FAX 847-375-6481, info@rehabnurse.org. Adv. contact Terri Berkowitz TEL 847-375-4763.

610.73 USA
A S B N UPDATE. Text in English. 1997. bi-m. adv. back issues avail. **Document type:** *Newsletter, Trade.*
Related titles: Online - full text ed.: free (effective 2009).
Published by: (Arkansas State Board of Nursing), Publishing Concepts, Inc., 14109 Taylor Loop Rd, Little Rock, AR 72223. TEL 501-221-9986, 800-561-4686, FAX 501-225-3735, vrobertson@pcipublishing.com, http://www.pcipublishing.com/. Eds. LouAnn Walker, Vicky Morris. Adv. contact David Brown. color page USD 3,200; trim 8.375 x 10.875. Circ: 48,000.

616.0472 610.73 USA
A S P M N PATHWAYS. Text in English. 3/yr. **Document type:** *Newsletter.* **Description:** Features news, clinical topics, job opportunities, literature review, and a calendar of events.
Published by: American Society of Pain Management Nursing, 7794 Grow Drive, Pensacola, FL 32514. TEL 850-473-0233, 888-34-ASPMN, FAX 850-484-8762, aspmn@puetzamc.com, http://www.aspmn.org.

610.73 CAN ISSN 1196-0914
ABORIGINAL NURSE/INFIRMIERE AUTOCHTONE. Text in English, French. 1985. s-a. CAD 25 (effective 2002). **Document type:** *Newsletter, Academic/Scholarly.*
Former titles (until 1992): Native Nurse (1188-5548); (until 1989): Indian and Inuit Nurses of Canada. Newsletter (1193-3364)
Related titles: Online - full text ed.
Indexed: C03, C06, C07, C08, CBCARef, CINAHL, P24, P48, PQC.
Published by: Aboriginal Nurses Association of Canada, 56 Sparks St, Ste 502, Ottawa, ON K1P 5A, Canada. TEL 613-724-4677, FAX 613-724-4718, info@anac.on.ca, http://www.anac.on.ca/.

610.73 USA ISSN 1062-0249
THE ACADEMIC NURSE. Text in English. 19??. s-a. back issues avail. **Document type:** *Magazine, Consumer.* **Description:** Contains news of the school of nursing, including faculty research and accomplishments, school events, and alumni news and notes.
Formerly (until 1987): S N C
Related titles: Online - full text ed.: free (effective 2010).
Indexed: C06, C07, C08, CINAHL, P30, SCOPUS.
—BLDSC (0570.513970).
Published by: Columbia University, School of Nursing, 630 W 168th St, PO Box 6, New York, NY 10032. TEL 212-305-3742, FAX 212-342-1909, nursingalumni@columbia.edu.

610.73 FIN ISSN 1455-8203
ACTA CARITATIS ACADEMIAE ABOENSIS. Text in English, Swedish. 1998. irreg., latest 2007. price varies. back issues avail. **Document type:** *Monographic series, Academic/Scholarly.*
Published by: Aabo Akademi, Institionen foer Vaardvetenskap/Aabo Akademi University. Department of Caring Science, PO Box 311, Vasa, 65101, Finland. TEL 358-6-3247502, FAX 358-6-3247503, caring@abo.fi, http://www.vasa.abo.fi/svf/vv.

610.73 BRA ISSN 0103-2100
RT8.B6
ACTA PAULISTA DE ENFERMAGEM. Text in Portuguese. 1988. q. **Document type:** *Journal, Academic/Scholarly.*
Related titles: Online - full text ed.: free (effective 2011).
Indexed: C06, C07, C08, CINAHL, SCI, SCOPUS, SSCI, SociolAb, W07.
—BLDSC (0644.295000).
Published by: Escola Paulista de Medicina, Departamento de Enfermagem, Rua Napoleao de Barros, no 754 - Vila Clementino, Sao Paulo, 04024-002, Brazil.

610.73 CAN ISSN 1482-4590
ACTUALITES PROFESSIONNELLES. Text in French. 197?. 3/yr. CAD 15 (effective 2006).
Former titles (until 1996): Nursing Montreal (0710-6157); (until 1976): Format XI (0710-6149)
Indexed: C06, C07, C08, CINAHL, P30.
Published by: Ordre Regional des Infirmieres et Infirmiers de Montreal/ Laval, 3850 rue Jean-Talon Ouest, Bureau 149, Montreal, PQ H3R 2G8, Canada. TEL 514-343-3707, FAX 514-343-9070, oriiml@bellnet.ca, http://www.oriiml.org.

610.73 COL ISSN 0123-5583
ACTUALIZACIONES EN ENFERMERIA. Text in Spanish. 1997. q. **Document type:** *Journal, Academic/Scholarly.*
Published by: Fundacion Santa Fe de Bogota, Calle 116 No 9-02, Cundinamarca, Bogota, 110246, Colombia. TEL 57-1-6030303, FAX 57-1-6196317, enfermeria@fsfb.org.co, http://www.fundacionsantafe.com/cms. Ed. Sonia Echeverri de Pimiento.

610.73 618.92 KOR ISSN 1226-1815
ADONG GANHO HAGHOEJI/KOREAN ACADEMY OF CHILD HEALTH NURSING. JOURNAL. Text in Korean. q. **Document type:** *Journal, Academic/Scholarly.*
Formerly (until 2005): Adong Kanho Hakhoe Chi/Korean Journal of Child Health Nursing
Related titles: Online - full text ed.
—BLDSC (0696.591235).
Published by: Korean Academy of Child Health Nursing, Yonsei University College of Nursing, 134 Sinchon-dong, Seodaemun-gu, Seoul, 120-752, Korea, S. TEL 82-2-22283274, FAX 82-2-3645027.

610.73 USA ISSN 1096-6293
ADVANCE FOR NURSE PRACTITIONERS. Text in English. 1993. m. free to qualified personnel (effective 2008). adv. back issues avail.; reprints avail. **Document type:** *Magazine, Trade.* **Description:** Contains peer-reviewed clinical articles, as well as professional news and practice guidance, for today's nurse practitioners.
Related titles: Online - full text ed.: free to qualified personnel (effective 2008).
Indexed: C06, EMBASE, ExcerpMed, F09, INI, MEDLINE, P30, R10, Reac, SCOPUS, W09.
Published by: Merion Publications, Inc., 2900 Horizon Dr, PO Box 61556, King of Prussia, PA 19406. TEL 610-278-1400, 800-355-5627, FAX 610-278-1421, advance@merion.com, http://www.advanceweb.com. Ed. Michelle Pronsati. Pub. Ann Kielinski. Adv. contact Cynthia Caramanico. B&W page USD 3,881, color page USD 4,931; trim 8.375 x 10.5. Circ: 64,180.

610.73 USA ISSN 2159-6220
ADVANCE FOR NURSES MID-ATLANTIC & LOWER GREAT LAKES. Text in English. 199?. bi-w. free to qualified personnel (effective 2011). adv. **Document type:** *Magazine, Trade.*
Formed by the merger of (200?-2011): Advance for Nurses Serving R Ns in Areas of Maryland, Washington DC and Virginia; (200?-2011): Advance for Nurses, Serving R Ns in the Areas of PA, NJ and DE (1941-3750); Which was formerly (until 200?): Advance for Nurses, Serving the Greater Philadelphia/Tri-State Metro Area (1541-4892)
Related titles: Online - full text ed.: ISSN 2159-6328. free (effective 2011).
Published by: Merion Publications, Inc., 2900 Horizon Dr, PO Box 61556, King of Prussia, PA 19406. TEL 610-278-1400, 800-355-5627, FAX 610-278-1421, advance@merion.com, http://www.advanceweb.com.

610.73 USA ISSN 2159-6042
ADVANCE FOR NURSES NORTHEAST. Text in English. 19??. bi-w. free to qualified personnel (effective 2011). adv. **Document type:** *Magazine, Trade.* **Description:** Provides concise, practical information on clinical, management, professional and career development issues for nurses practicing in all areas of the profession.
Formerly (until 2011): Advance for Nurses, Serving R Ns in the Greater NY/NJ Metro Areas (1548-9779)
Related titles: Online - full text ed.: ISSN 2159-6050. free (effective 2011).
Published by: Merion Publications, Inc., 2900 Horizon Dr, King of Prussia, PA 19406. TEL 800-355-5627, FAX 610-278-1425, advance@merion.com, http://www.advanceweb.com. Ed. Richard Krisher TEL 800-355-5627 ext 1391.

610.73 USA ISSN 1934-2373
ADVANCE FOR NURSES, SERVING R NS IN GREATER CHICAGO & METRO AREAS OF WISCONSIN & INDIANA. Text in English. 200?. bi-w. free to qualified personnel (effective 2009). adv. reprints avail. **Document type:** *Magazine, Trade.* **Description:** Covers clinical and management issues for nurses of all specialties.
Related titles: Online - full content ed.
Indexed: C06.
Published by: Merion Publications, Inc., 2900 Horizon Dr, PO Box 61556, King of Prussia, PA 19406. TEL 610-278-1400, 800-355-5627, FAX 610-278-1421, http://www.advanceweb.com. Eds. Donna Jones Pelkie, Pamela Tarapchak TEL 610-278-1400 ext 1360, Robin Hocevar. adv.: B&W page USD 19,964, color page USD 25,564; trim 10.5 x 16.75. Circ: 85,100.

610.73 USA ISSN 2159-6123
▼ **ADVANCE FOR NURSES SOUTH.** Text in English. 2011. bi-w. free to qualified personnel (effective 2011). adv. back issues avail. **Document type:** *Magazine, Trade.* **Description:** Provides concise, practical information on clinical, management, professional and career development issues for nurses practicing in all areas of the profession.
Formed by the merger of (200?-2011): Advance for Nurses Serving R Ns in the State of Florida (1542-572X); (200?-2011): Advance for Nurses Serving R Ns in Metro Areas of Texas and Louisiana; (200?-2011): Advance for Nurses, Serving R Ns in the Southeastern States (2159-6085); Which was formerly (until 200?): Advance for Nurses, Serving the Metro Areas of the Carolinas and Georgia (1541-4884)
Related titles: Online - full text ed.: ISSN 2159-614X. free (effective 2011).
Published by: Merion Publications, Inc., 2900 Horizon Dr, PO Box 61556, King of Prussia, PA 19406. TEL 610-278-1400, 800-355-5627, FAX 610-278-1421, advance@merion.com, http://www.advanceweb.com. Ed. Lisa A Brzezicki. Adv. contact Christina Allmer.

610.7361 USA
ADVANCE FOR PROVIDERS OF POST-ACUTE CARE. Text in English. m. Free to qualified subscribers. adv. **Document type:** *Magazine, Trade.* **Description:** Covers both business and clinical information for providers of long-term care, home care and subacute care.
Related titles: Online - full content ed.
Published by: Merion Publications, Inc., 2900 Horizon Dr, PO Box 61556, King of Prussia, PA 19406. TEL 610-278-1400, 800-355-5627, FAX 610-278-1421, advance@merion.com, http://www.advanceweb.com.

ADVANCED EMERGENCY NURSING JOURNAL. *see* MEDICAL SCIENCES—Orthopedics And Traumatology

610.73 USA ISSN 1558-0172
ADVANCED STUDIES IN NURSING. Text in English. 2003 (Oct.). irreg. USD 150 per issue domestic; USD 200 per issue foreign (effective 2010). **Document type:** *Journal, Academic/Scholarly.* **Description:** Aims to provide a forum for continuing education activities in nursing and related fields.
Related titles: Online - full text ed.: ISSN 1558-0180.
Indexed: C06, C07, C08, CINAHL, EMBASE, ExcerpMed, R10, Reac, SCOPUS.
—BLDSC (0696.929800), IE. **CCC.**
Published by: (Institute for Johns Hopkins Nursing), Galen Publishing, LLC, 166 W Main St, PO Box 340, Somerville, NJ 08876. TEL 908-253-9001, FAX 908-253-9002, info@asimcme.com, http://www.galenpublishing.com. Pub. Jack M Ciattarelli.

610.73 AUS ISSN 1832-9861
➤ **ADVANCES IN CONTEMPORARY NURSING.** Text in English. 2006 (Jan.). q. AUD 495 in Australia & New Zealand to individuals includes Pacific, China, South & South-East Asia, South America & Africa; USD 495 elsewhere to institutions (effective 2007). adv. back issues avail. **Document type:** *Journal, Academic/Scholarly.*
Related titles: Online - full text ed.: free to qualified personnel (effective 2007).
Published by: eContent Management Pty Ltd, PO Box 1027, Maleny, QLD 4552, Australia. TEL 61-7-54352900, FAX 61-7-54352911, info@e-contentmanagement.com, http://www.e-contentmanagement.com. Ed. Debra Jackson.

➤ **ADVANCES IN NEONATAL CARE.** *see* MEDICAL SCIENCES—Pediatrics

610.73 USA ISSN 0161-9268
RT1
➤ **ADVANCES IN NURSING SCIENCE.** Abbreviated title: A N S. Text in English. 1978. q. USD 426.51 domestic to institutions; USD 550 foreign to institutions (effective 2011). adv. Index. back issues avail.; reprints avail. **Document type:** *Journal, Academic/Scholarly.* **Description:** Features a single timely research topic with implications for patient care.
Related titles: CD-ROM ed.; Online - full text ed.: ISSN 1550-5014.
Indexed: A20, A22, A26, ASCA, B28, C06, C07, C08, CA, CINAHL, CMCI, CurCont, E-psyche, E08, EMBASE, ExcerpMed, F09, FamI, G08, G10, H11, H12, I05, INI, IndMed, MEDLINE, NurAb, P03, P16, P20, P22, P24, P25, P30, P48, P50, P53, P54, PQC, PsycInfo, PsycholAb, R10, RILM, Reac, S02, S03, S08, S09, SCI, SCOPUS, SSCI, T02, W07, W09.
—BLDSC (0709.508000), GNLM, IE, Infotrieve, Ingenta. **CCC.**
Published by: Lippincott Williams & Wilkins (Subsidiary of: Wolters Kluwer N.V.), Two Commerce Sq, 2001 Market St, Philadelphia, PA 19103. TEL 215-521-8300, FAX 215-521-8902, customerservice@lww.com, http://www.lww.com. Ed. Peggy L Chinn. Pub. Sandra Kasko. Adv. contact Pat Wendelken. Circ: 1,079.

610.7365 AUS ISSN 1834-9706
AGED CARE ACTION. Text in English. q. **Document type:** *Newsletter, Trade.*
—**CCC.**
Published by: New South Wales Nurses' Association, 43 Australia St, Camperdown, NSW 2050, Australia. TEL 61-2-85951234, FAX 61-2-95503667, gensec@nswnurses.asn.au, http://www.nswnurses.asn.au.

610.73 FRA ISSN 1166-3413
L'AIDE SOIGNANTE. Text in French. 10/yr. EUR 117 in Europe to institutions; EUR 109.70 in France to institutions; JPY 14,900 in Japan to institutions; USD 156 elsewhere to institutions (effective 2012). **Document type:** *Journal, Academic/Scholarly.* **Description:** Deals with day-to-day auxilliary nursing practice, providing the profession with the information it needs to enhance professionnal skills. Publishes news in the therapeutic, economic and public health fields.
Formerly (until 1992): L' Ami de la Petite Camargue Alsacienne (0987-8947)
Related titles: Online - full text ed.
Indexed: FR, SCOPUS.
—**CCC.**
Published by: Elsevier Masson (Subsidiary of: Elsevier Health Sciences), 62 Rue Camille Desmoulins, Issy les Moulineaux, Cedex 92442, France. TEL 33-1-71165500, FAX 33-1-71165600, infos@elsevier-masson.fr. Circ: 20,000.

362.12 USA ISSN 1067-991X
➤ **AIR MEDICAL JOURNAL.** Text in English. 1989. bi-m. USD 180 in United States to institutions; USD 233 elsewhere to institutions (effective 2012). **Document type:** *Journal, Academic/Scholarly.* **Description:** Provides information for the medical transport industry, addressing the unique concerns of medical transport physicians, nurses, pilots, paramedics, emergency medical technicians, communication specialists, and program administrators. The journal contains practical how-to articles, debates on controversial industry issues, legislative updates, case studies, and original research articles covering all aspects of the medical transport profession.
Incorporates (1995-2000): AirMed (1079-6134); Formerly (until 1993): The Journal of Air Medical Transport (1046-9095); Which was formed by the merger of (1982-1989): Hospital Aviation (0740-8315); (1986-1989): AeroMedical Journal (0894-8321)
Related titles: Online - full text ed.: ISSN 1532-6497 (from ScienceDirect).
Indexed: A26, B21, C06, C07, C08, CINAHL, EMBASE, ESPM, H&SSA, H12, I05, MEDLINE, P30, SCOPUS, T02.
—IE. **CCC.**
Published by: (Air & Surface Transport Nurses Association, International Association of Flight Paramedics, National E M S Pilots Association, Air Medical Physician Association, Association of Air Medical Services), Mosby, Inc. (Subsidiary of: Elsevier Health Sciences), 1600 John F. Kennedy Blvd, Ste 1800, Philadelphia, PA 19103. TEL 215-239-3900, 800-523-1649, FAX 215-239-3990, periodical.service@mosby.com, http://www.us.elsevierhealth.com. Eds. Eric R Swanson, Jacqueline C Stocking.

610.73 USA ISSN 0002-4317
ALABAMA NURSE. Text in English. 19??. q. looseleaf. Free to qualified subscribers. adv. 24 p./no.; **Document type:** *Newsletter, Trade.* **Description:** Covers issues and employment opportunities of interest to licensed nursing professionals.
Supersedes: Alabama State Nurses' Association. Bulletin
Related titles: Online - full text ed.
Indexed: C06, C07, C08, CINAHL, EMBASE, ExcerpMed, MEDLINE, P20, P22, P24, P30, P48, P54, PQC, R10, Reac, SCOPUS.
Published by: (Alabama State Nurses' Association), Arthur L. Davis Publishing Agency, Inc., 517 Washington St, PO Box 216, Cedar Falls, IA 50613. TEL 319-277-2414, 800-626-4081, FAX 319-277-4055, sales@aldpub.com, http://www.nursingald.com. Ed. Mark Miller. R&P Karen Pakkala. Adv. contact Jim Larson. Circ: 75,000.

610.73 USA ISSN 0002-4546
ALASKA NURSE. Text in English. 1951. q. USD 15 domestic to non-members; USD 20 foreign to non-members (effective 2000). adv. bk.rev. illus.
Related titles: Online - full text ed.
Indexed: C06, C07, C08, CINAHL, INI, P30.
—GNLM.
Published by: Alaska Nurses Association, 2207 E. Tudor Rd., Ste. 34, Anchorage, AK 99507-1069. TEL 907-274-0827, FAX 907-272-0292. Ed. Kathy North. R&P, Adv. contact Wanda Katinscky. Circ: 650 (paid).

610.73 CAN ISSN 1481-9988
ALBERTA R N. (Registered Nurses) Text in English. 1948. 6/yr. CAD 35 domestic; CAD 40 foreign (effective 2005). adv. bk.rev. illus.; stat. **Document type:** *Journal, Trade.* **Description:** Provides information on current trends and issues in nursing in Alberta. Lists educational and career opportunities and a calendar of events.
Formerly (until 1998): A A R N Newsletter (0001-0197)
Related titles: Online - full text ed.
Indexed: A22, C03, C06, C07, C08, CA, CBCARef, CINAHL, EMBASE, ExcerpMed, INI, MEDLINE, P20, P22, P24, P30, P48, P54, PQC, R10, Reac, SCOPUS, T02.
—BLDSC (0786.588700), GNLM. **CCC.**
Published by: Alberta Association of Registered Nurses, 11620 168 St, Edmonton, AB T5M 4A6, Canada. TEL 780-451-0043, 800-252-9392, FAX 780-452-3276, aarn@nurses.ab.ca, http://www.nurses.ab.ca. Ed. Michaleen Elabdi. Adv. contact Jan Henry. B&W page CAD 1,300, color page CAD 1,750; trim 10 x 7.75. Circ: 24,000 (controlled).

610.7 IRL ISSN 1471-0854
ALL IRELAND JOURNAL OF NURSING AND MIDWIFERY. Text in English. 1982. m. adv. **Document type:** *Journal, Trade.*
Formerly (until 2000): Nursing Review (0790-0368)
Indexed: B28, C06, C07, C08, CINAHL.
—BLDSC (0788.832000), IE.
Published by: Smurfit Communications, 2 Clanwilliam Ct., Lower Mount St., Dublin, 2, Ireland. TEL 353-1-2405300, FAX 353-1-6619757, info@smurfit-comms.ie, http://www.smurfit.ie/comms. adv.: B&W page EUR 1,150, color page EUR 1,900; trim 210 x 297. Circ: 20,000 (paid and controlled).

610.73 DEU ISSN 0002-6573
ALTENHEIM; Zeitschrift fuer das Altenhilfe Management. Text in German. 1962. m. EUR 118 foreign (effective 2010). adv. bk.rev. charts; illus.; stat. index. **Document type:** *Magazine, Trade.*
Indexed: DokArb.
—GNLM. **CCC.**
Published by: Vincentz Verlag, Plathnerstr 4c, Hannover, 30175, Germany. TEL 49-511-9910000, FAX 49-511-9910099, info@vincentz.de, http://www.vincentz.de. Ed. Monika Gaier. adv.: B&W page EUR 2,400, color page EUR 4,140. Circ: 9,158 (paid).

ALTENHEIM ADRESSBUCH. *see* GERONTOLOGY AND GERIATRICS

ALTENHEIM EINKAUFSFUEHRER. *see* GERONTOLOGY AND GERIATRICS

610.73 DEU ISSN 0341-0455
ALTENPFLEGE; Fachmagazin fuer ambulante und stationaere Altenpflege. Text in German. 1976. m. EUR 75 foreign (effective 2010). adv. bk.rev. charts; illus.; stat. index. **Document type:** *Journal, Trade.*
—GNLM. **CCC.**
Published by: Vincentz Verlag, Plathnerstr 4c, Hannover, 30175, Germany. TEL 49-511-9910000, FAX 49-511-9910099, info@vincentz.de, http://www.vincentz.de. Ed. Holger Jenrich. adv.: B&W page EUR 2,500, color page EUR 4,360. Circ: 20,380 (paid).

610.73 USA ISSN 1041-2972
RT82.8 CODEN: JANPEB
➤ **AMERICAN ACADEMY OF NURSE PRACTITIONERS. JOURNAL.** Abbreviated title: J A A N P. Text in English. 1988. m. GBP 288 in United Kingdom to institutions; EUR 344 in Europe to institutions; USD 288 in the Americas to institutions; USD 561 elsewhere to institutions; GBP 331 combined subscription in United Kingdom to institutions (print & online eds.); EUR 396 combined subscription in Europe to institutions (print & online eds.); USD 331 combined subscription in the Americas to institutions (print & online eds.); USD 646 combined subscription elsewhere to institutions (print & online eds.) (effective 2012). reprint service avail. from PSC. **Document type:** *Journal, Academic/Scholarly.* **Description:** Captures what's happening in clinical practice, management, education, research and legislation.
Related titles: Online - full text ed.: ISSN 1745-7599. GBP 288 in United Kingdom to institutions; EUR 344 in Europe to institutions; USD 288 in the Americas to institutions; USD 561 elsewhere to institutions (effective 2012) (from IngentaConnect).
Indexed: A01, A02, A03, A08, A20, A22, A26, C06, C07, C08, C11, CA, CINAHL, CurCont, E01, EMBASE, ExcerpMed, FamI, H04, H12, INI, MEDLINE, P03, P20, P22, P24, P30, P48, P50, P54, PQC, PsycInfo, R10, Reac, SCI, SCOPUS, SSCI, T02, W07, W09.
—BLDSC (4683.731500), GNLM, IE, Infotrieve, Ingenta. **CCC.**
Published by: (American Academy of Nurse Practitioners), Wiley-Blackwell Publishing, Inc. (Subsidiary of: Wiley-Blackwell Publishing Ltd.), 111 River St, Hoboken, NJ 07030. TEL 201-748-6000, FAX 201-748-6088, info@wiley.com, http://www.wiley.com/WileyCDA/. Ed. Charon Pierson. Adv. contact Matthew Difilippo TEL 856-768-9360.

610.73 USA ISSN 0898-6622
AMERICAN ASSOCIATION FOR THE HISTORY OF NURSING. BULLETIN. Text in English. 1982. q. **Document type:** *Newsletter.*
Indexed: P30, SCOPUS.
Published by: American Association for the History of Nursing, PO Box 175, Lanoka Harbor, NJ 08734. TEL 609-693-7250, FAX 609-693-1037, http://www.aahn.org/.

610.73 USA ISSN 0891-0162
RC966
➤ **AMERICAN ASSOCIATION OF OCCUPATIONAL HEALTH NURSES JOURNAL.** Abbreviated title: A A O H N Journal. Text in English. 1953. m. USD 109 to individuals; USD 246 to institutions; USD 28 per issue (effective 2010). adv. bk.rev. charts; illus. index. **Document type:** *Journal, Academic/Scholarly.* **Description:** Offers original articles of professional interest to the occupational health nurses.
Former titles (until 1986): Occupational Health Nursing (0029-7933); (until 1969): American Association of Industrial Nurses Journal (0098-6097)
Related titles: Microfilm ed.; Online - full text ed.: ISSN 1938-2448. free to members (effective 2010).
Indexed: A22, C06, C07, C08, CINAHL, CISA, CSNB, CurCont, EMBASE, ESPM, ExcerpMed, F09, FamI, H&SSA, IHD, INI, L12, MEDLINE, NPPA, NurAb, P20, P22, P24, P30, P48, P50, P54, PQC, RILM, SCI, SCOPUS, SSCI, W07, W09.
—BLDSC (0537.501300), GNLM, IE, Infotrieve, Ingenta. **CCC.**
Published by: (American Association of Occupational Health Nurses, Inc.), Slack, Inc., 6900 Grove Rd, Thorofare, NJ 08086. TEL 856-848-1000, FAX 856-848-6091, customerservice@slackinc.com, http://www.slackinc.com. Ed. Joy E Wachs. Adv. contact Kara Datz TEL 856-848-1000 ext 549.

610.73 USA ISSN 1522-1431
AMERICAN JOURNAL FOR NURSE PRACTITIONERS. Text in English. 1997. 10/yr. USD 59 to non-members (effective 2010). **Document type:** *Journal, Trade.*
Related titles: Online - full text ed.: ISSN 2155-8701. USD 25 (effective 2010).
Indexed: C06, C07, C08, CINAHL.
—BLDSC (0828.460000).
Published by: (American College of Nurse Practitioners), N P Communications, LLC, 109 S Main St, Cranbury, NJ 08512 . TEL 609-371-5085, npcdawn@aol.com.

610.73 616 USA ISSN 1062-3264
➤ **AMERICAN JOURNAL OF CRITICAL CARE.** Abbreviated title: A J C C. Text in English. 1992. bi-m. USD 59 domestic to individuals; USD 83 foreign to individuals; USD 270 domestic to institutions (print or online ed.); USD 335 foreign to institutions; USD 380 combined subscription domestic to institutions (print & online eds.); USD 445 combined subscription foreign to institutions (print & online eds.); free to members (effective 2010). adv. back issues avail. **Document type:** *Journal, Academic/Scholarly.* **Description:** Communicates important advances in clinical science and research in critical care.
Related titles: CD-ROM ed.; Online - full text ed.: ISSN 1937-710X.
Indexed: A20, A22, A26, C06, C07, C08, C11, CA, CINAHL, CurCont, E08, EMBASE, ExcerpMed, G08, H11, H12, I05, INI, IndMed, MEDLINE, P03, P16, P20, P22, P24, P25, P26, P30, P48, P53, P54, PQC, PsycInfo, PsycholAb, R10, Reac, S09, SCI, SCOPUS, T02, W07.
—BLDSC (0824.210000), GNLM, IE, Infotrieve, Ingenta. **CCC.**
Published by: American Association of Critical Care Nurses, 101 Columbia, Ste 100, Aliso Viejo, CA 92656. TEL 949-362-2000, 800-899-2226, FAX 949-362-2020, info@aacn.org, http://www.aacn.org. Ed. Cindy L Munro. Adv. contact Kathy Huntley TEL 800-257-8290 ext 249.

610.73 USA ISSN 0002-936X
RT1
➤ **AMERICAN JOURNAL OF NURSING.** Abbreviated title: A J N. Text in English. 1900. m. USD 387 domestic to institutions; USD 429 foreign to institutions (effective 2011). adv. bk.rev. bibl.; charts; illus.; tr.lit. cum.index: 1961-65, 1966-70, 1971-75. back issues avail.; reprints avail. **Document type:** *Journal, Academic/Scholarly.* **Description:** Aims to promote excellence in nursing and health care through the dissemination of evidence-based, clinical information and research, discussion of relevant and controversial professional issues.
Related titles: CD-ROM ed.; Microform ed.: (from PMC, PQC); Online - full text ed.: ISSN 1538-7488.
Indexed: A01, A02, A03, A08, A20, A22, A25, A26, AHCMS, AIM, AMED, AMHA, ASCA, ASSIA, Acal, AgeL, B04, B14, B28, BRD, BRI, C06, C07, C08, CA, CBRI, CINAHL, CLFP, ChemAb, Chicano, CurCont, DentInd, DokArb, E-psyche, E06, E08, ECER, EMBASE, ExcerpMed, F09, FamI, G03, G08, G10, GSA, GSI, H04, H09, H10, H11, H12, H13, HlthInd, HospLI, I05, I12, INI, ISR, IndMed, L09, M01, M02, M06, MCR, MEDLINE, NRN, NurAb, P02, P06, P10, P13, P16, P20, P24, P26, P30, P34, P48, P50, P53, P54, PAIS, PQC, PsycholAb, R10, Reac, S02, S03, S05, S08, S09, S21, SCI, SCOPUS, SSCI, SWR&A, T&II, T02, V02, W03, W07, W09.
—BLDSC (0828.500000), GNLM, IE, Infotrieve, Ingenta, INIST. **CCC.**
Published by: (American Nurses Association), Lippincott Williams & Wilkins (Subsidiary of: Wolters Kluwer N.V.), 333 7th Ave, 19th Fl, New York, NY 10001. TEL 646-674-6530, FAX 646-674-6500, customerservice@lww.com, http://www.lww.com. Ed. Diana J Mason TEL 646-674-6604. Pub. Anne Dabrow Woods TEL 215-628-6579. Adv. contact Paula Gould TEL 570-223-6640.

610.73 USA ISSN 0098-1486
RT1
THE AMERICAN NURSE. Abbreviated title: T A N. Text in English. 1967. bi-m. USD 20 to qualified personnel; USD 10 to students; free to members (effective 2010). adv. back issues avail.; reprints avail. **Document type:** *Newspaper, Trade.* **Description:** Covers trends and issues affecting staff nurses.
Formerly (until 1972): A N A in Action (0587-3053)
Related titles: Microform ed.: (from PQC); Online - full text ed.
Indexed: A01, A02, A03, A08, A22, C06, C07, C08, C11, CA, CINAHL, EMBASE, ExcerpMed, H04, HospLI, INI, MEDLINE, NurAb, P19, P20, P22, P24, P30, P34, P48, P54, PQC, R10, Reac, SCOPUS, T02, W09.
—GNLM.
Published by: American Nurses Association, 8515 Georgia Ave, Ste 400, Silver Spring, MD 20910. TEL 301-628-5000, 800-274-4262, FAX 301-628-5001, memberinfo@ana.org.

610.73 USA ISSN 1930-5583
RT1
➤ **AMERICAN NURSE TODAY.** Text in English. 2006 (Oct.). m. USD 29.90 domestic to individuals; USD 40.95 foreign to individuals; USD 89.95 combined subscription domestic to institutions (print & online eds.); USD 138.95 combined subscription foreign to institutions (print & online eds.) (effective 2010). adv. back issues avail. **Document type:** *Journal, Academic/Scholarly.* **Description:** Covers issues in nursing practice and keeps nurses abreast of ANA's advocacy on behalf of the profession. Provides clinical, and career management information that nurses can use to stay on practices, enhance patient outcomes, and advance their professional careers.
Related titles: Online - full text ed.: USD 14.95 to individuals (effective 2010).
Indexed: C06, C07, C08, CINAHL.
—BLDSC (0847.125000), IE.
Published by: (American Nurses Association), HealthCom Media, 259 Veterans Ln, Fl 3, Doylestown, PA 18901. TEL 215-489-7000, FAX 215-489-7007, jkenny@healthcommedia.com, http://www.healthcommedia.com/. Ed. Pamela F Cipriano. Adv. contact Judy Smith TEL 404-816-9882.

610.73 USA ISSN 1940-5634
TR4
AMERICAN NURSING REVIEW. Text in English. 2007 (Nov.). q. free to members (effective 2009). back issues avail. **Document type:** *Journal, Trade.* **Description:** Features articles on the latest scientific and medical findings that affect nursing.
Media: Online - full content.
Published by: American Society of Registered Nurses, 1001 Bridgeway, Ste 411, Sausalito, CA 94965. TEL 415-331-2700, 800-331-1206, FAX 415-476-4558, office@asrn.org. Ed. Alison Palmer.

610.73 USA ISSN 1536-3929
AMERICAN NURSING STUDENT. Abbreviated title: A N S. Variant title: Nursing (Year): A N S. Text in English. 1995. q. free to qualified personnel (effective 2010). back issues avail. **Document type:** *Newsletter, Academic/Scholarly.* **Description:** Provides advice and insights on what to expect both in and out of the nursing classroom.
Related titles: Online - full text ed.
—**CCC.**
Published by: Lippincott Williams & Wilkins (Subsidiary of: Wolters Kluwer N.V.), 351 W Camden St, Baltimore, MD 21201. TEL 410-528-4000, FAX 410-528-4312, customerservice@lww.com.

610.73 616.89 USA ISSN 1078-3903
➤ **AMERICAN PSYCHIATRIC NURSES ASSOCIATION. JOURNAL.** Text in English. 1995. bi-m. USD 502, GBP 296 combined subscription to institutions (print & online eds.); USD 492, GBP 290 to institutions (effective 2011). adv. index. Supplement avail.; back issues avail.; reprint service avail. from PSC. **Document type:** *Journal, Academic/Scholarly.* **Description:** Covers a blend of clinical and research topics, practice challenges, and changes occurring in this ever-changing field.
Related titles: Online - full text ed.: ISSN 1532-5725. USD 452, GBP 266 to institutions (effective 2011).
Indexed: A22, A26, B21, C06, C07, C08, CA, CINAHL, E-psyche, E01, E08, ESPM, FamI, G08, H&SSA, H11, H12, I05, NurAb, P03, P30, PsycInfo, PsycholAb, S09, SCOPUS, T02.
—BLDSC (4692.068000), IE, Infotrieve, Ingenta. **CCC.**
Published by: (American Psychiatric Nurses Association), Sage Publications, Inc., 2455 Teller Rd, Thousand Oaks, CA 91320. TEL 805-499-9774, FAX 805-499-0871, info@sagepub.com. Ed. Karen Farchaus Stein. adv.: B&W page USD 1,090, color page USD 1,710; trim 8.125 x 10.875. Circ: 5,085 (paid). **Subscr. overseas to:** Sage Publications Ltd., 1 Oliver's Yard, 55 City Rd, London EC1Y 1SP, United Kingdom. TEL 44-207-3248701, FAX 44-207-3248733, subscription@sagepub.co.uk.

610.73 TUR ISSN 1309-5471
ANADOLOU HEMSIRELIK VE SAGLIK BILIMLERI DERGISI/JOURNAL OF ANATOLIA NURSING AND HEALTH SCIENCES. Text in Turkish. 1998. irreg. free (effective 2011). **Document type:** *Journal, Academic/Scholarly.*
Media: Online - full text.
Published by: Ataturk Universitesi, Tip Fakultesi/Ataturk University, Faculty of Medicine, Erzurum, Turkey. TEL 90-0442-2311111, FAX 90-0442-2361014, ata@atauni.edu.tr, http://beta.atauni.edu.tr.

610.73 USA ISSN 0739-6686
RT81.5
ANNUAL REVIEW OF NURSING RESEARCH. Text in English. 1983. a., latest vol.26, 2008. USD 85 per issue (effective 2009). back issues avail. **Document type:** *Monographic series, Academic/Scholarly.* **Description:** Focuses on Complementary Health and Pain Management.
Related titles: Online - full text ed.: ISSN 1944-4028. USD 300 (effective 2009) (from IngentaConnect).
Indexed: A22, C06, C07, C08, CINAHL, EMBASE, ExcerpMed, F09, INI, IndMed, MEDLINE, P20, P22, P24, P30, P48, P54, PQC, R10, Reac, SCOPUS.
—BLDSC (1524.200000), GNLM, IE, Infotrieve, Ingenta, INIST. **CCC.**
Published by: Springer Publishing Company, 11 W 42nd St, 15th Fl, New York, NY 10036. TEL 212-431-4370, FAX 212-941-7842, contactus@springerpub.com. Ed. Christine Kasper. Circ: 1,500.

610.73 CAN ISSN 1918-1345
▼ **APORIA;** the nursing journal. Text in English, French. 2009. irreg. free (effective 2011). **Document type:** *Journal, Academic/Scholarly.* **Description:** Dedicated to scholarly debates in nursing and the health sciences.
Media: Online - full text.
Indexed: C06, T02.
Published by: University of Ottawa, 550 Cumberland, Ottawa, ON K1N 6N5, Canada. TEL 613-562-5700, http://www.uottawa.ca. Ed. Dave Holmes.

610.73 616 USA ISSN 0897-1897
RT1 CODEN: ANUREA
➤ **APPLIED NURSING RESEARCH.** Abbreviated title: A N R. Text in English. 1988. q. USD 319 in United States to institutions; USD 397 elsewhere to institutions (effective 2012). adv. back issues avail.; reprints avail. **Document type:** *Journal, Academic/Scholarly.* **Description:** Devoted to advancing nursing as a research-based profession and bridging the gap between research and practice in nursing.
Related titles: Online - full text ed.: ISSN 1532-8201 (from ScienceDirect).
Indexed: A20, A22, A26, ASCA, ASSIA, C06, C07, C08, CA, CINAHL, CurCont, E-psyche, E01, EMBASE, ExcerpMed, F09, FamI, H12, I05, INI, IndMed, MEDLINE, P24, P30, P48, PQC, R10, Reac, SCI, SCOPUS, SSCI, T02, W07.
—BLDSC (1576.236000), GNLM, IE, Infotrieve, Ingenta. **CCC.**
Published by: W.B. Saunders Co. (Subsidiary of: Elsevier Health Sciences), Elsevier, Health Sciences Division, Order Fulfillment, 3251 Riverport Ln, Maryland Heights, MO 63043. TEL 314-872-8370, 800-325-4177, FAX 314-432-1380, JournalCustomerService-usa@elsevier.com, http://www.us.elsevierhealth.com. Ed. Dr. Joyce J Fitzpatrick. Pub. Jami Walker. Adv. contact Barbara Blum TEL 215-239-3156. Circ: 525.

610.73 616.8 USA ISSN 0883-9417
RC440
➤ **ARCHIVES OF PSYCHIATRIC NURSING.** Abbreviated title: A P N. Text in English. 1987. bi-m. USD 233 in United States to institutions; USD 324 elsewhere to institutions (effective 2012). adv. bk.rev. abstr.; bibl.; charts; illus. index. back issues avail.; reprints avail. **Document type:** *Journal, Academic/Scholarly.* **Description:** Approaches the field from the broadest possible perspective through articles and case reports relating to theories, practices, and research applications.
Related titles: Online - full text ed.: ISSN 1532-8228 (from ScienceDirect).
Indexed: A20, A22, A26, ASCA, ASSIA, B28, C06, C07, C08, CINAHL, ChPerI, CurCont, E-psyche, E01, EMBASE, ExcerpMed, FamI, H12, I05, INI, IndMed, MEDLINE, NurAb, P03, P24, P30, P48, PQC, PsycInfo, PsycholAb, R10, RILM, Reac, SCI, SCOPUS, SSCI, T02, W07.
—BLDSC (1640.410000), GNLM, IE, Infotrieve, Ingenta, INIST. **CCC.**
Published by: (International Society of Psychiatric-Mental Health Nurses, SERPN Division), W.B. Saunders Co. (Subsidiary of: Elsevier Health Sciences), Elsevier, Health Sciences Division, Order Fulfillment, 3251 Riverport Ln, Maryland Heights, MO 63043. TEL 314-872-8370, 800-325-4177, FAX 314-432-1380, JournalCustomerService-usa@elsevier.com, http://www.us.elsevierhealth.com. Ed. Dr. Joyce J Fitzpatrick. Adv. contact Jeffrey S Berman TEL 215-249-3060. Circ: 860.

610.73 ESP ISSN 1699-602X
ARCHIVOS DE LA MEMORIA. Text in Spanish. 2004. a. **Document type:** *Journal, Trade.*
Media: Online - full text.
Published by: Fundacion Index, Calle Horno de Marina 2, Granada, 18001, Spain. http://www.index-f.com/fundacion.php.

610.73 USA ISSN 0004-1599
ARIZONA NURSE. Text in English. 1947. bi-m. USD 30 (effective 2007). adv. bk.rev. illus. reprints avail. **Document type:** *Newsletter, Trade.* **Description:** Provides coverage and analysis of the nursing profession in the state.
Related titles: Microfilm ed.: (from PQC); Online - full text ed.
Indexed: A26, C06, C07, C08, CINAHL, E08, H12, I05, INI, P24, P30, P48, PQC, S09.
—GNLM, Infotrieve.
Published by: Arizona Nurses Association, 1850 E Southern Ave, Ste 1, Tempe, AZ 85282. TEL 480-831-0404, FAX 480-839-4780, info@aznurse.org, http://www.aznurse.org. Ed. Ela Joy Lehrman. R&P Lyndall Eddy. Adv. contact Jennifer McAfee. Circ: 2,000.

610.73 USA
ARIZONA STATE BOARD OF NURSING. NEWSLETTER. Text in English. 19??. q. looseleaf. Free to qualified subscribers. adv. 28 p./no.; back issues avail. **Document type:** *Newsletter, Trade.* **Description:** Covers issues and employment opportunities of interest to licensed nursing professionals.
Published by: (Arizona State Board of Nursing), Arthur L. Davis Publishing Agency, Inc., 517 Washington St, PO Box 216, Cedar Falls, IA 50613. TEL 319-277-2414, 800-626-4081, FAX 319-277-4055, sales@aldpub.com, http://www.nursingald.com. Ed. Mark Miller. R&P Joey Ridenour. Adv. contact Jim Larson. Circ: 90,000.

610.73 USA ISSN 1539-8528
ARKANSAS NURSING NEWS. Text in English. 1984. q. free to members (effective 2009). **Document type:** *Magazine, Trade.*
Published by: (Arkansas Nurses Association), Publishing Concepts, Inc., 14109 Taylor Loop Rd, Little Rock, AR 72223. TEL 501-221-9986, 800-561-4686, FAX 501-225-3735, http://www.pcipublishing.com/.

ASIAN JOURNAL OF CARDIOVASCULAR NURSING. *see* MEDICAL SCIENCES—Cardiovascular Diseases

610.73 IND ISSN 2231-1149
▼ ➤ **ASIAN JOURNAL OF NURSING EDUCATION AND RESEARCH.** Abbreviated title: A J N E R. Text in English. 2011. q. INR 1,000 domestic; USD 200 foreign (effective 2011). **Document type:** *Journal, Academic/Scholarly.* **Description:** Publishes original research articles, short communications, review articles in all areas of nursing sciences.
Published by: A & V Publications, E-282 Saikripa Sector-4, Pt. Deendayal Upadhya Nagar, Raipur, Chattisgarh 492 010, India. TEL 91-9406051618, avpublications@gmail.com. Ed. Daharwal S Monika.

610.73 HKG ISSN 1022-2464
➤ **ASIAN JOURNAL OF NURSING STUDIES.** Text in English. 1993. q. USD 35 to individuals; USD 50 to institutions (effective 2006). **Document type:** *Journal, Academic/Scholarly.*
Indexed: C06, C07, C08, CINAHL.
—BLDSC (1742.520000).
Published by: Hong Kong Polytechnic University, School of Nursing, Ste. C, 10/F Wo On Bldg., 10 Wo On Ln., Central, Hong Kong. TEL 852-28689171, FAX 852-28689269, http://nhs.polyu.edu.hk/nhs/. Ed. David G. Arthur.

610.73 GBR ISSN 1976-1317
➤ **ASIAN NURSING RESEARCH.** Text in English. 2007. s-a. EUR 143 in Europe to institutions; JPY 18,600 in Japan to institutions; USD 200 elsewhere to institutions (effective 2012). **Document type:** *Journal, Academic/Scholarly.* **Description:** Publishes English articles on the 4th and 8th issues of Daehan Ganho Haghoeji.
Related titles: Online - full text ed.: (from ScienceDirect); ◆ Issued with: Korean Academy of Nursing. Journal. ISSN 2005-3673.
Indexed: A26, C06, C07, CurCont, I05, P30, SCI, SCOPUS, SSCI, W07.
—IE. **CCC.**
Published by: (Korean Society of Nursing Science/han-gug Ganho Gwahaghoe KOR), Elsevier Ltd (Subsidiary of: Elsevier Science & Technology), The Blvd, Langford Ln, Kidlington, Oxford, OX5 1GB, United Kingdom. TEL 44-1865-843434, FAX 44-1865-843970, customerserviceau@elsevier.com. Ed. Susie Kim.

610.73 ITA ISSN 1592-5986
ASSISTENZA INFERMIERISTICA E RICERCA. Text in Italian. q. EUR 120 domestic to institutions; EUR 150 foreign to institutions (effective 2009). adv. 64 p./no.; **Document type:** *Journal, Academic/Scholarly.*
Formerly (until 1999): Rivista dell'Infermiere (1120-3803)
Related titles: Online - full text ed.: ISSN 2038-1778.
Indexed: C06, C07, C08, CINAHL, EMBASE, ExcerpMed, INI, MEDLINE, P30, R10, Reac, SCI, SCOPUS, SSCI, W07.
—BLDSC (1746.661970), GNLM.
Published by: Il Pensiero Scientifico Editore, Via Bradano 3-C, Rome, 00199, Italy. TEL 39-06-862821, FAX 39-06-86282250, pensiero@pensiero.it, http://www.pensiero.it.

ASSOCIATION OF NURSES IN AIDS CARE. JOURNAL. *see* MEDICAL SCIENCES—Communicable Diseases

610.73 GBR ISSN 1467-5625
ASSOCIATION OF NURSES IN SUBSTANCE ABUSE. JOURNAL BULLETIN. Text in English. 1988. 3/yr. free to members. adv. bk.rev. **Document type:** *Journal, Academic/Scholarly.* **Description:** Carries information about the activities of the association; provides features and abstracts about substance misuse and conference course information.
Formerly (until 1997): A N S A Journal (0960-8508)
—BLDSC (1541.844720).
Published by: Association of Nurses in Substance Abuse, 37 Star St, Ware, Herts SG12 7AA, United Kingdom. TEL 44-870-2413503, FAX 44-192-0462730, info@ansauk.org, http://www.ansa.uk.net. Ed. Alan Staff. Circ: 400 (controlled).

610.73 TUR ISSN 1301-9899
ATATURK UNIVERSITESI HEMSIRELIK YUKSEKOKULU. Text in Turkish. 1998. s-a. **Document type:** *Journal, Academic/Scholarly.*
Published by: Ataturk Universitesi, Hemsirelik Yuksekokulu, c/o Dr. Ayse Okanli, Erzurum, 25240, Turkey. TEL 90-442-2360983, FAX 90-442-2360984, hyodergi@atauni.edu.tr.

610.73 616.025 GBR ISSN 1574-6267
RT1
➤ **AUSTRALASIAN EMERGENCY NURSING JOURNAL.** Abbreviated title: A E N J. Text in English. 1996. 4/yr. EUR 278 in Europe to institutions; JPY 32,900 in Japan to institutions; USD 277 elsewhere to institutions (effective 2012). back issues avail. **Document type:** *Journal, Academic/Scholarly.* **Description:** Provides contemporary information relevant to emergency nurses in Australia today.
Formerly (until 2005): Australian Emergency Nursing Journal (1328-2743)
Related titles: Online - full text ed.: (from ScienceDirect).
Indexed: A26, ASSIA, C06, C07, C08, CA, CINAHL, H12, I05, SCOPUS, T02.
—BLDSC (1793.999000), IE, Ingenta. **CCC.**
Published by: (College of Emergency Nursing Australasia AUS), Elsevier Ltd (Subsidiary of: Elsevier Science & Technology), The Blvd, Langford Ln, Kidlington, Oxford, OX5 1GB, United Kingdom. TEL 44-1865-843000, FAX 44-1865-843010, journalscustomerserviceemea@elsevier.com. Ed. Ramon Shaban TEL 61-2-97459615.

610.73 USA ISSN 1036-7314
RC86
➤ **AUSTRALIAN CRITICAL CARE.** Abbreviated title: A C C. Text in English. 1988. q. EUR 184 in Europe to institutions; JPY 24,500 in Japan to institutions; USD 206 elsewhere to institutions (effective 2012). adv. bk.rev. abstr. back issues avail.; reprints avail. **Document type:** *Journal, Academic/Scholarly.* **Description:** For critical care nurses, universities, hospital libraries, agencies.
Formerly (until 1991): Confederation of Australian Critical Care Nurses. Journal (1033-3355); Which was formed by the merger of (19??-1988): Pulse (0813-4928); (1986-1988): C N S A Journal (0818-8157)
Related titles: Online - full text ed.: ISSN 1878-1721 (from ScienceDirect).
Indexed: C06, C07, C08, CA, CINAHL, CurCont, EMBASE, ExcerpMed, INI, MEDLINE, P20, P22, P24, P30, P48, P54, PQC, R10, Reac, SCI, SCOPUS, SSCI, W07.
—BLDSC (1798.264300), GNLM, IE, Infotrieve, Ingenta. **CCC.**
Published by: (Australian College of Critical Care Nurses Ltd. AUS), Elsevier Inc. (Subsidiary of: Elsevier Science & Technology), 1600 John F Kennedy Blvd, Philadelphia, PA 19103. TEL 215-239-3900, FAX 215-238-7883, JournalCustomerService-usa@elsevier.com, http://www.elsevier.com. Ed. Gavin Leslie TEL 61-8-92242498. Circ: 2,610.

610.73 AUS ISSN 1447-4328
➤ **THE AUSTRALIAN JOURNAL OF ADVANCED NURSING (ONLINE).** Variant title: A J A N. Text in English. 1983. q. free (effective 2008). back issues avail. **Document type:** *Journal, Academic/Scholarly.* **Description:** Covers nursing research and allied philosophical study.
Formerly (until 2007): Australian Journal of Advanced Nursing (Print) (0813-0531)
Media: Online - full text.
Indexed: A01, A02, A03, A08, A22, A26, AEI, B28, C06, C07, C08, CA, CINAHL, CurCont, EMBASE, ExcerpMed, H12, I05, INI, MEDLINE, P20, P22, P24, P30, P48, P54, PQC, R10, Reac, SCI, SCOPUS, SSCI, T02, VirolAbstr, W07.
—BLDSC (1801.830000), GNLM, IE, Infotrieve, Ingenta. **CCC.**
Published by: Australian Nursing Federation, Level 2, 21 Victoria St, Melbourne, VIC 3000, Australia. TEL 6-13-96395211, FAX 6-13-96520567, journals@anf.org.au, http://www.anf.org.au. Ed. Jill Iliffe. Circ: 1,000.

➤ **AUSTRALIAN JOURNAL OF RURAL HEALTH.** *see* PUBLIC HEALTH AND SAFETY

610.73 AUS
AUSTRALIAN NURSING AND MIDWIFERY COUNCIL. ANNUAL REPORT. Abbreviated title: A N M C Annual Report. Text in English. 1993. a. free (effective 2008). back issues avail. **Document type:** *Report, Trade.* **Description:** Includes the purposes and objects of the council, program structure and goals, organizational structure, professional activities, staff and financial statements.
Formerly (until 2005): Australian Nursing Council. Annual Report
Related titles: Online - full text ed.: free (effective 2008).
Published by: Australian Nursing and Midwifery Council Inc., 20 Challis St, PO Box 873, Dickson, ACT 2602, Australia. TEL 61-2-62577960, FAX 61-2-62577955, anmc@anmc.org.au. Ed. Jan Duke. Circ: 300.

610.73 AUS
AUSTRALIAN NURSING AND MIDWIFERY COUNCIL. NEWSLETTER (ONLINE). Abbreviated title: A N M C Newsletter. Text in English. 1993. s-a. free (effective 2008). adv. back issues avail. **Document type:** *Newsletter, Trade.* **Description:** Contains news on current activities of the organization and other issues on nursing nationally and internationally.
Former titles (until 2008): Australian Nursing and Midwifery Council. Newsletter (Print); (until 2004): Australian Nursing Council Newsletter (1321-117X)
Media: Online - full text.
Published by: Australian Nursing and Midwifery Council Inc., 20 Challis St, PO Box 873, Dickson, ACT 2602, Australia. TEL 61-2-62577960, FAX 61-2-62577955, anmc@anmc.org.au. Circ: 750.

610.73 AUS ISSN 1320-3185
RT15
AUSTRALIAN NURSING JOURNAL. Variant title: A N J. Text in English. 1935. m. AUD 66 domestic to individuals; AUD 99 domestic to institutions; AUD 130 foreign; AUD 33 to students & members (effective 2008). adv. bk.rev. back issues avail. **Document type:** *Journal, Academic/Scholarly.* **Description:** Multi-purpose professional and trade union nursing journal.
Former titles (until 1993): Australian Nurses' Journal (0045-0758); (until 1976): Journal of West Australian Nurses; (until 1971): Journal of the West Australian Nurses
Related titles: Online - full text ed.
Indexed: A01, A02, A03, A08, A11, A22, A26, AMED, B28, C06, C07, C08, C11, CA, CINAHL, E08, EMBASE, ExcerpMed, G08, H04, H11, H12, H13, I05, INI, M01, M02, MEDLINE, NRN, P10, P20, P22, P24, P30, P34, P48, P53, P54, PQC, R10, Reac, S09, SCOPUS, T02, WBA, WMB.
—BLDSC (1815.830000), GNLM, IE, Infotrieve, Ingenta. **CCC.**
Published by: Australian Nursing Federation, Level 2, 21 Victoria St, Melbourne, VIC 3000, Australia. TEL 61-3-96395211, FAX 61-3-96520567, journals@anf.org.au, http://www.anf.org.au. Ed. Catherine Beadnell. Adv. contact Joe Korac TEL 61-2-98727708. Circ: 56,000.

610.73 COL ISSN 0121-4500
RT81.C7
AVANCES EN ENFERMERIA. Text in Spanish. 1982. s-a. USD 40 (effective 2010). back issues avail. **Document type:** *Journal, Academic/Scholarly.*
Indexed: C06, C07, F04.
Published by: Universidad Nacional de Colombia, Facultad de Enfermeria, Tore de Enfermeria Ofic 202, Ciudad Universitaria, Bogota, Colombia. TEL 57-1-3165000, FAX 57-1-3165314, correo_febog@unal.edu.co. Ed. Gloria Lucia Arango. Circ: 500.

610.73 GBR ISSN 1472-6955
RT1 CODEN: BNMUAK
➤ **B M C NURSING.** (BioMed Central) Text in English. 2000. irreg. free (effective 2011). adv. back issues avail.; reprints avail. **Document type:** *Journal, Academic/Scholarly.* **Description:** Publishes original research articles in all aspects of nursing research, training, education, and practice.
Media: Online - full text.
Indexed: A01, A26, B28, C06, C07, C08, CA, CINAHL, H12, I05, P20, P22, P30, PQC, R10, Reac, SCOPUS, T02.
—**CCC.**
Published by: BioMed Central Ltd. (Subsidiary of: Springer Science+Business Media), 236 Gray's Inn Rd, London, WC1X 8HB, United Kingdom. TEL 44-20-31922000, FAX 44-20-31922010, info@biomedcentral.com. Ed. Dr. Melissa Norton. Adv. contact Natasha Bailey TEL 44-20-31922231.

610.73 USA
B R N REPORT. (Board of Registered Nursing) Text in English. a. **Document type:** *Newsletter, Trade.*
Published by: California Board of Registered Nursing, 400 R St, Ste 4030, PO Box 944210, Sacramento, CA 94244-2100. TEL 916-322-3350, FAX 916-327-4402, http://www.rn.ca.gov/.

610.73 GBR
BAILLIERE'S NURSES' DICTIONARY; for nurses and healthcare workers. Text in English. 1912. irreg., latest 2009, 25th ed. GBP 8.99 per issue (effective 2009). back issues avail. **Document type:** *Monographic series, Academic/Scholarly.* **Description:** Provides essential information for those involved in nursing and healthcare.
Published by: Bailliere Tindall (Subsidiary of: Elsevier Health Sciences), The Blvd, Langford Ln, Kidlington, Oxford OX5 1GB, United Kingdom. TEL 44-1865-474010, directenquiries@elsevier.com. Ed. Barbara F Weller.

BALANCE (ALEXANDRIA). *see* GERONTOLOGY AND GERIATRICS

610.73677 USA ISSN 1557-1459
➤ **BARIATRIC NURSING AND SURGICAL PATIENT CARE.** Text in English. 2006 (Mar.). q. USD 315 domestic to institutions; USD 365 foreign to institutions; USD 370 combined subscription domestic to institutions (print & online eds.); USD 432 combined subscription foreign to institutions (print & online eds.) (effective 2012). adv. reprint service avail. from PSC. **Document type:** *Journal, Academic/ Scholarly.* **Description:** Provides the cutting-edge research, clinical protocols, and practical tools to provide optimal care for all bariatric patients whose health is seriously compromised by their high BMI and comorbid conditions. The Journal includes original articles, clinical reviews, profiles of successful bariatric surgical programs, roundtable discussions, interviews, Q and A, resources, and much more.
Related titles: Online - full text ed.: ISSN 1557-1467. USD 312 to institutions (effective 2012).
Indexed: A20, A22, A26, C06, C07, C08, CINAHL, CurCont, E01, E07, H12, I05, P03, P24, P48, PQC, PsycInfo, SCI, SCOPUS, SSCI, W07.
—BLDSC (1863.628830), IE. **CCC.**
Published by: Mary Ann Liebert, Inc. Publishers, 140 Huguenot St, 3rd Fl, New Rochelle, NY 10801. TEL 914-740-2100, FAX 914-740-2101, 800-654-3237, info@liebertpub.com. Ed. Kristin L Seidl TEL 410-328-5492. Adv. contact Harriet I Matysko TEL 914-740-2182.

➤ **BARNBLADET**; tidskrift foer Sveriges barnsjukskoeterskor. *see* MEDICAL SCIENCES—Pediatrics

610.73 USA ISSN 1071-2984
BEGINNINGS (FLAGSTAFF); the official newsletter of the American holistic nurses' association. Text in English. 1981. m. (10/yr.). USD 34 domestic to non-members; USD 39 in Canada to non-members; USD 48 elsewhere to non-members; free to members (effective 2011). adv. bk.rev. tr.lit. **Document type:** *Newsletter, Trade.* **Description:** Promotes the education of nurses and the public in the concepts and practice of health of the whole person.
Indexed: C06, C07, C08, CINAHL, EMBASE, ExcerpMed, INI, MEDLINE, P30, R10, Reac, SCOPUS.
—BLDSC (1876.607000).
Published by: American Holistic Nurses' Association, PO Box 2130, Flagstaff, AZ 86003. TEL 520-526-2196, 800-278-AHNA, FAX 520-526-2752, ahna-flag@flaglink.com. Ed. Lynne Nemeth.

610.73 NLD ISSN 1871-7268
BIJZIJN. Text in Dutch. 1987. m. EUR 88, USD 132 to institutions (effective 2009). adv. **Document type:** *Journal, Trade.*
Former titles (until 2005): V P N (1386-4491); (until 1997): Verpleegkunde Nieuws (0920-8941); Which incorporated (1994-1994): Verpleegkunde Professioneel (1381-415X)
Related titles: ◆ Supplement(s): Bijzijn XL. ISSN 2211-6524; ◆ Bijzijn. Ziekenhuizen. ISSN 1871-7276.
—IE.
Published by: Bohn Stafleu van Loghum B.V. (Subsidiary of: Springer Science+Business Media), Postbus 246, Houten, 3990 GA, Netherlands. TEL 31-30-6383838, FAX 31-30-6383839, boekhandels@bsl.nl, http://www.bsl.nl. Ed. Paulien Spieker. adv.: page EUR 2,500; trim 210 x 297. Circ: 21,134.

610.73 NLD ISSN 2211-6524
BIJZIJN XL. Text in Dutch. 2008. 4/yr.
Related titles: ◆ Supplement to: Bijzijn. ISSN 1871-7268.
Published by: Bohn Stafleu van Loghum B.V. (Subsidiary of: Springer Science+Business Media), Postbus 246, Houten, 3990 GA, Netherlands. TEL 31-30-6383872, FAX 31-30-6383991, boekhandels@bsl.nl, http://www.bsl.nl.

610.73 USA ISSN 1099-8004
➤ **BIOLOGICAL RESEARCH FOR NURSING.** Text in English. 1999. q. USD 690, GBP 406 combined subscription to institutions (print & online eds.); USD 676, GBP 398 to institutions (effective 2011). adv. 88 p./no.; back issues avail.; reprint service avail. from PSC. **Document type:** *Journal, Academic/Scholarly.* **Description:** Provides nurses with a forum for dialogue concerning substantive, theoretical, and methodological research related to normal and abnormal function.
Formerly (until 1999): Biological Nursing Research
Related titles: Online - full text ed.: ISSN 1552-4175. USD 621, GBP 365 to institutions (effective 2011).
Indexed: A01, A02, A03, A08, A22, B07, C06, C07, C08, CA, CINAHL, E01, EMBASE, ExcerpMed, FamI, H04, IndMed, MEDLINE, P30, R10, Reac, S01, SCI, SCOPUS, T02, V02, W07.
—BLDSC (2077.679000), IE, Infotrieve, Ingenta. **CCC.**
Published by: Sage Publications, Inc., 2455 Teller Rd, Thousand Oaks, CA 91320. TEL 805-499-9774, FAX 805-499-0871, info@sagepub.com. Ed. Carolyn Yucha. adv.: color page USD 775, B&W page USD 385; 7 x 10. Circ: 200 (paid). **Subscr. overseas to:** Sage Publications Ltd., 1 Oliver's Yard, 55 City Rd, London EC1Y 1SP, United Kingdom. TEL 44-207-3248701, FAX 44-207-3248733, subscription@sagepub.co.uk.

➤ **BIRTH**; issues in perinatal care. *see* MEDICAL SCIENCES—Obstetrics And Gynecology

610.73 616.8 JPN ISSN 0910-8459
BRAIN NURSING/BUREIN NASHINGU. Text in Japanese. 1984. m. JPY 20,412; JPY 1,890 newsstand/cover (effective 2007). **Document type:** *Journal, Academic/Scholarly.*
Published by: Medicus Shuppan/Medicus Publishing Inc., 18-24 Hiroshiba-cho, Suita-shi, Osaka-fu 564-8580, Japan. TEL 81-6-63856911, FAX 81-6-63856873, http://www.medica.co.jp/.

610.736 GBR ISSN 1742-6456
BRITISH JOURNAL OF ANAESTHETIC & RECOVERY NURSING. Short title: B J A R N. Text in English. 1991. q. GBP 192, USD 350 to institutions; GBP 199, USD 360 combined subscription to institutions (print & online eds.) (effective 2012). adv. back issues avail.; reprint service avail. from PSC. **Document type:** *Journal, Academic/ Scholarly.* **Description:** Contains original articles from the specialty of anaesthetic & recovery nursing and remains one of the only UK based journals representing this area.
Formerly (until 1999): Anaesthetic & Recovery Nurse (1363-1861)
Related titles: Online - full text ed.: ISSN 1744-2192. GBP 160, USD 291 to institutions (effective 2012).
Indexed: A22, B21, B28, C06, C07, C08, CINAHL, E01, ESPM, P24, PQC.
—BLDSC (2303.950000), IE. **CCC.**
Published by: (British Anaesthetic & Recovery Nurses Association), Cambridge University Press, The Edinburgh Bldg, Shaftesbury Rd, Cambridge, CB2 8RU, United Kingdom. TEL 44-1223-312393, FAX 44-1223-315052, journals@cambridge.org, http://www.cambridge.org/uk. Ed. Jessica Inch. Adv. contact Rebecca Roberts TEL 44-1223-325083. B&W page GBP 240, B&W page USD 455, color page GBP 610, color page USD 1,160. **Subscr. to:** Cambridge University Press, 32 Ave of the Americas, New York, NY 10013. TEL 212-337-5000, FAX 212-691-3239, journals_subscriptions@cup.org.

610.73 GBR ISSN 1462-4753
RT98
➤ **BRITISH JOURNAL OF COMMUNITY NURSING.** Abbreviated title: B J C N. Text in English. 1996. m. GBP 116 domestic to individuals; EUR 175 in Europe to individuals; USD 261 elsewhere to individuals; GBP 82 to students (effective 2010). adv. back issues avail.; reprints avail. **Document type:** *Journal, Academic/Scholarly.* **Description:** Promotes excellence in primary care.
Formerly (until 1998): British Journal of Community Health Nursing (1362-4407); Incorporates (200?-2003): Wound Care (1748-8710)
Related titles: Online - full text ed.
Indexed: A01, A02, A03, A08, AMED, B28, C06, C07, C08, C11, CA, CINAHL, EMBASE, ExcerpMed, H04, MEDLINE, P30, P34, R10, Reac, SCOPUS, T02.
—BLDSC (2307.280000), IE, Infotrieve, Ingenta. **CCC.**
Published by: Mark Allen Publishing Ltd., St Jude's Church, Dulwich Rd, London, SE24 0PB, United Kingdom. TEL 44-20-77385454, FAX 44-20-79798316, subscriptions@markallengroup.com, http://www.markallengroup.com. Ed. Julie Smith. Adv. contact Farhad Buffery.

610.73 GBR ISSN 1753-1586
➤ **BRITISH JOURNAL OF HEALTHCARE ASSISTANTS.** Text in English. 2007. m. GBP 64.80 to individuals in UK & Ireland; EUR 103.50 in Europe to individuals; USD 172.80 elsewhere to individuals; GBP 47.70 to students in UK & Ireland; EUR 81 in Europe to students; USD 139.50 elsewhere to students (effective 2008). **Document type:** *Journal, Trade.* **Description:** Contains a wide range of evidence-based reviews providing positive examples of good practice.
Related titles: Online - full text ed.
Indexed: B28, C06, C07, CA, T02.
—BLDSC (2309.090000), IE. **CCC.**
Published by: M A Healthcare Ltd. (Subsidiary of: Mark Allen Publishing Ltd.), St. Jude's Church, Dulwich Rd, London, SE24 0PB, United Kingdom. TEL 44-20-77385454, FAX 44-20-77332325. Ed. Julie Smith TEL 44-20-77385454.

➤ **BRITISH JOURNAL OF NEUROSCIENCE NURSING.** *see* MEDICAL SCIENCES—Psychiatry And Neurology

610.73 GBR ISSN 0966-0461
RT1
➤ **BRITISH JOURNAL OF NURSING.** Text in English. 1979. fortn. GBP 117.90 to individuals in UK & Ireland; EUR 169.20 in Europe to individuals; USD 217.80 elsewhere to individuals; GBP 87.30 to students in UK & Ireland; EUR 129.60 in Europe to students; USD 171 elsewhere to students (effective 2008). adv. **Document type:** *Journal, Academic/Scholarly.* **Description:** Covers educational, ethical, legal and professional issues and provides a forum for serious professional debate and discussion.
Formerly: Nursing (0142-0372)
Related titles: Online - full text ed.
Indexed: A01, A02, A03, A08, A22, AMED, ASSIA, B28, C06, C07, C08, CA, CINAHL, DiabCont, EMBASE, ExcerpMed, F09, FamI, H04, INI, MEDLINE, NurAb, P24, P30, P34, P48, PQC, R10, Reac, SCOPUS, T&II, T02.
—BLDSC (2311.980100), GNLM, IE, Infotrieve, Ingenta, INIST. **CCC.**
Published by: M A Healthcare Ltd. (Subsidiary of: Mark Allen Publishing Ltd.), St. Jude's Church, Dulwich Rd, London, SE24 0PB, United Kingdom. TEL 44-20-77385454, FAX 44-20-77332325, healthcare/index.html. Ed. Asa Bailey. Pub. Mark Allen. Adv. contact Anthony Kerr TEL 44-20-75016726.

610.736 GBR ISSN 2040-7475
➤ **THE BRITISH JOURNAL OF PRIMARY CARE NURSING - CARDIOVASCULAR DISEASE, DIABETES AND KIDNEY CARE.** Text in English. 2004 (Mar.). q. GBP 110 combined subscription in Europe to individuals (print & online eds.); GBP 176 combined subscription elsewhere to individuals (print & online eds.); GBP 170 combined subscription in Europe to institutions (print & online eds.); GBP 242 combined subscription foreign to institutions (print & online eds.) (effective 2009). adv. back issues avail. **Document type:** *Journal, Academic/Scholarly.* **Description:** Aims to provide guidance for the practical application of evidence-based medicine in diagnosing and managing patients with established cardiovascular disease and diabetes, through pragmatic interpretation of research and guidelines.
Formerly (until 2009): The British Journal of Primary Care Nursing - Cardiovascular Disease and Diabetes (1741-430X)
Related titles: Online - full text ed.: ISSN 1752-4377.
Indexed: B28, C06, CINAHL.
—BLDSC (2320.100500). **CCC.**
Published by: (Primary Care Training Centre Ltd), Sherborne Gibbs Ltd., Edgbaston House, 3 Duchess Pl, Birmingham, B16 8NH, United Kingdom. TEL 44-121-4544114, FAX 44-121-4541190, info@sherbornegibbs.com, http://www.sherbornegibbs.co.uk/. Ed. Jan Procter-King. Pub. Michael W Gibbs. adv.: page GBP 1,300; trim 216 x 280. Circ: 10,000.

616.240231 GBR ISSN 1752-4385
THE BRITISH JOURNAL OF PRIMARY CARE NURSING. RESPIRATORY DISEASES AND ALLERGY. Text in English. 2006. q. GBP 110 combined subscription in Europe to individuals (print & online eds.); GBP 176 combined subscription elsewhere to individuals (print & online eds.); GBP 170 combined subscription in Europe to institutions (print & online eds.); GBP 242 combined subscription elsewhere to institutions (print & online eds.) (effective 2009). adv. back issues avail. **Document type:** *Journal, Academic/Scholarly.* **Description:** Provides practice nurses with up-to-date news and reviews about COPD, asthma, smoking cessation and other respiratory diseases as well as allergy.
Related titles: Online - full text ed.: ISSN 1752-4393.
Indexed: B28.
—BLDSC (2320.120000), IE. **CCC.**
Published by: (Education for Health), Sherborne Gibbs Ltd., Edgbaston House, 3 Duchess Pl, Birmingham, B16 8NH, United Kingdom. TEL 44-121-4544114, FAX 44-121-4541190, info@sherbornegibbs.com, http://www.sherbornegibbs.co.uk/. Ed. Monica Fletcher. Pub. Michael W Gibbs. adv.: page GBP 1,500; trim 216 x 280. Circ: 7,000.

BRITISH NURSING INDEX; index of journal articles of interest to nurses, midwives and community staff. *see* MEDICAL SCIENCES—Abstracting, Bibliographies, Statistics

BRITISH NURSING INDEX DATABASE. *see* MEDICAL SCIENCES—Abstracting, Bibliographies, Statistics

610.73 330 USA ISSN 1934-7502
THE BUSINESS OF CARING. Text in English. 2006. 10/yr. USD 85 to non-members; USD 70 to members (effective 2008). adv. back issues avail.; reprints avail. **Document type:** *Newsletter, Trade.* **Description:** Assists nurses with understanding the business side of the health care industry, including core healthcare business concepts and practical issues such as communicating with staff and business terminology.
Related titles: Online - full text ed.
—**CCC.**
Published by: Healthcare Financial Management Association, 2 Westbrook Corporate Ctr, Ste 700, Westchester, IL 60154. TEL 708-531-9600, 800-252-4362, FAX 708-531-0032. Eds. Lauren Phillips, Margaret Veach, Robert Fromberg. adv.: B&W page USD 2,675, color page USD 3,725; 7 x 9.5.

610.736 USA
C A N A NEWS. Text in English. 2001. irreg. adv.
Formerly (until 2004): C A N A, Inc. (Online Edition)
Media: Online - full text.
Published by: California Association of Nurse Anesthetists, 224 W Maple Ave, Orange, CA 92866-1322. TEL 714-744-0155. adv.: page USD 350; 7.25 x 9.1875.

610.7369 616.6 CAN ISSN 1498-5136
C A N N T JOURNAL. Text in English, French. 1990. q. CAD 40 in North America to libraries; CAD 75 elsewhere to libraries; CAD 7.50 newsstand/cover (effective 2007). adv. **Document type:** *Journal, Trade.*
Formerly (until 1996): Journal C A N N T (1483-698X)
Related titles: Online - full text ed.
Indexed: A26, C06, C07, C08, CINAHL, CPerI, EMBASE, ExcerpMed, H11, H12, I05, INI, MEDLINE, P20, P22, P24, P30, P48, P54, PQC, R10, Reac, SCOPUS.
—IE, Ingenta. **CCC.**
Published by: (Canadian Association of Nephrology Nurses and Technologists), Pappin Communications, The Victoria Centre, 84 Isabella St, Pembroke, ON K8A 5S5, Canada. TEL 613-735-0952, FAX 613-735-7983, info@pappin.com, http://www.pappin.com. Ed. Gillian Brunier. Pub. Bruce Pappin. Adv. contact Heather Coughlin. page CAD 440; trim 8.5 x 11.

610.73 370.285 USA ISSN 1551-9104
C A R I N G. Text in English. q. free to members. **Document type:** *Newsletter.* **Description:** Covers issues, trends, research, and technology related to nursing informatics.
Indexed: A26, C06, C07, C08, CA, CINAHL, H12, I05, T02.
Published by: Capital Area Roundtable on Informatics in Nursing, c/o Dr Susan K Newbold, 429 Woodcrest LN, Franklin, TN 37067-8533. TEL 866-552-6404. Ed. Liberty Rovira.

610.73 CAN ISSN 1205-5611
C I N A. Text in English. 1975. a. adv. **Document type:** *Yearbook, Trade.*
Indexed: C06, C07, C08, CINAHL.
—BLDSC (3198.496830), IE, Ingenta.
Published by: (Canadian Intravenous Nurses Association), Pappin Communications, The Victoria Centre, 84 Isabella St, Pembroke, ON K8A 5S5, Canada. TEL 613-735-0952, FAX 613-735-7983, info@pappin.com, http://www.pappin.com. Ed. Bonnie Kennedy. Pub. Bruce Pappin. Adv. contact Heather Coughlin. B&W page CAD 510, color page CAD 1,060. Circ: 700.

610.73 USA ISSN 1543-2998
R728.8
C M A TODAY. (Certified Medical Assistant) Text in English. 1956. bi-m. USD 30 to non-members; free to members (effective 2005). adv. bk.rev. illus. index. **Document type:** *Magazine, Trade.* **Description:** Educational articles of interest to medical assistants in the office, hospital, clinic or school setting.
Former titles (until 2003): Professional Medical Assistant (0033-0140); (until 1968): A A M A Bulletin
Related titles: Microform ed.: (from PQC); Online - full text ed.
Indexed: A22, C06, C07, C08, CINAHL, P24, P48, PQC.
—BLDSC (3287.181000), IE, Ingenta.
Published by: American Association of Medical Assistants, Inc., 20 N Wacker Dr, Ste 1575, Chicago, IL 60606-2903. TEL 312-899-1500, 800-228-2262, FAX 312-899-1259. Adv. contact Sylvia Edstrom. B&W page USD 940, color page USD 1,828; trim 10.88 x 8.25. Circ: 23,000 (paid).

610.73 USA ISSN 1545-7028
C N A TRAINING ADVISOR. (Certified Nursing Assistant) Text in English. 198?. m. USD 149 combined subscription (print & online eds.) (effective 2011). **Document type:** *Newsletter, Trade.* **Description:** Assists nursing homes, hospitals, home health agencies, and assisted living facilities in training nursing aides.
Formerly (until 2003): Program Plans. Nursing Basic Series (0734-1431)
Related titles: Online - full text ed.: ISSN 1937-7487. USD 99 (effective 2004).
Indexed: A26, C06, C07, C08, CINAHL, H11, I05, P21, P24, P48, PQC.

—CCC.
Published by: H C Pro, Inc., 200 Hoods Ln, PO Box 1168, Marblehead, MA 01945. TEL 781-639-1872, 800-650-6787, FAX 781-639-7857, 800-639-8511, customerservice@hcpro.com, http://www.hcpro.com. Ed. Justin Veiga. Pub. Emily Sheahan.

610.73 GBR ISSN 1361-021X
C T I CENTRE FOR NURSING AND MIDWIFERY. NEWSLETTER. Variant title: Nursing and Midwifery Newsletter. Text in English. 1995. q. **Document type:** *Newsletter, Academic/Scholarly.*
Published by: University of Sheffield, C T I Centre for Nursing and Midwifery, 301 Glossop Rd, Sheffield, S10 2HL, United Kingdom. TEL 44-114-2229889, FAX 44-114-2229856.

610.73 CAN ISSN 0843-6096
➤ **CANADIAN JOURNAL OF CARDIOVASCULAR NURSING.** Text in English, French. 1973. q. CAD 43 domestic to individuals; CAD 70 domestic to institutions; CAD 75 foreign to institutions; CAD 27 domestic to students (effective 2007). adv. bk.rev. **Document type:** *Journal, Academic/Scholarly.* **Description:** Concerned with health care issues related to cardiovascular health and illness.
Supersedes (in Apr. 1989): Canadian Bulletin of Cardiovascular Nursing (0831-4462)
Indexed: A22, C06, C07, C08, CA, CINAHL, EMBASE, ExcerpMed, FamI, INI, MEDLINE, P30, R10, Reac, SCOPUS, T02.
—BLDSC (3030.600000), GNLM, IE, Infotrieve, Ingenta. **CCC.**
Published by: Canadian Council of Cardiovascular Nurses, 222 Queen St, Ste 1402, Ottawa, ON K1P 5V9, Canada. TEL 613-569-4361, FAX 613-569-3278, info@cardiovascularnurse.com. Ed. Kirsten Woodend. Circ: 1,200.

610.7368 CAN ISSN 1913-7176
➤ **CANADIAN JOURNAL OF NEUROSCIENCE NURSING.** Text in French, English. 1979. q. CAD 65 domestic; USD 65 foreign (effective 2009). adv. **Document type:** *Journal, Academic/Scholarly.*
Formerly (until 2007): Axon (0834-7824)
Indexed: A20, C06, C07, C08, CINAHL, EMBASE, ExcerpMed, MEDLINE, P30, R10, Reac, SCOPUS.
—BLDSC (3033.320000), IE, Infotrieve, Ingenta. **CCC.**
Published by: (Canadian Association of Neuroscience Nurses), Pappin Communications, The Victoria Centre, 84 Isabella St, Pembroke, ON K8A 5S5, Canada. TEL 613-735-0952, FAX 613-735-7983, info@pappin.com, http://www.pappin.com. Ed. Dr. Sonia Poochikian-Sarkissian. Adv. contact Heather Coughlin. B&W page CAD 425, color page CAD 975. Circ: 400.

610.73 CAN ISSN 0844-5621
CODEN: CJNRE3
➤ **THE CANADIAN JOURNAL OF NURSING RESEARCH/REVUE CANADIENNE DE RECHERCHE EN SCIENCES INFIRMIERES.** Text in English, French. 1969. q. CAD 400 combined subscription domestic to institutions (print & online eds.); USD 400 combined subscription foreign to institutions (print & online eds.) (effective 2010). adv. **Document type:** *Journal, Academic/Scholarly.* **Description:** Provides a forum for research and articles relevant to nursing and health. Covers clinical research, methodological issues, education research, and theory.
Formerly: Nursing Papers - Perspectives en Nursing (0318-1006)
Related titles: Online - full text ed.: ISSN 1705-7051 (from IngentaConnect).
Indexed: A22, AHCMS, B28, C03, C06, C07, C08, CBCARef, CINAHL, E-psyche, EMBASE, ExcerpMed, F09, FamI, HospAb, INI, MEDLINE, NurAb, P03, P30, P48, PQC, PdeR, PsycInfo, PsycholAb, R10, Reac, SCOPUS, SOPODA, SocioIAb, W09.
—BLDSC (3033.400000), GNLM, IE, Infotrieve, Ingenta. **CCC.**
Published by: McGill University, School of Nursing, 3506 University St, Montreal, PQ H3A 2A7, Canada. TEL 514-398-4160, FAX 514-398-8455. Ed. Dr. Laurie N Gottleib. R&P Joanna Toti.

610.73 CAN ISSN 0008-4581
➤ **CANADIAN NURSE.** Text in English. 1905. 9/yr. (m. except. Jul., Aug. and Dec.). CAD 46.49 domestic; CAD 75.08 in United States; CAD 92.40 elsewhere (effective 2010). adv. bk.rev.; film rev. bibl.; charts; illus.; stat.; tr.lit. Index. back issues avail.; reprints avail. **Document type:** *Journal, Academic/Scholarly.*
Incorporates (1959-1985): Infirmiere Canadienne (0019-9605); Former titles (until 1924): Canadian Nurse and Hospital Review (0315-1018); (until 1910): Canadian Nurse (0836-9771)
Related titles: Microfilm ed.: (from PMC, PQC); Online - full text ed.; French ed.: Infirmiere Canadienne. ISSN 1492-5494.
Indexed: A22, A26, A33, AMED, B28, C03, C06, C07, C08, CA, CBCARef, CBPI, CINAHL, CPerI, EMBASE, ExcerpMed, F09, FR, FamI, G08, H12, HospAb, INI, MEDLINE, NurAb, P20, P22, P24, P30, P48, P54, PQC, PdeR, R10, Reac, SCOPUS, T02, W09.
—BLDSC (3043.110000), GNLM, IE, Ingenta. **CCC.**
Published by: Canadian Nurses Association/Association des Infirmieres et Infirmiers du Canada, 50 Driveway, Ottawa, ON K2P 1E2, Canada. TEL 613-237-2133, 800-361-8404, FAX 613-237-3520, info@canadian-nurse.com, http://www.cna-nurses.ca. Eds. Joan Salton, Lisa Brazeau. adv.: B&W page CAD 4,155, color page CAD 5,730; trim 10.875 x 16.25. Circ: 112,000.

610.73 CAN
CANADIAN NURSING MANAGEMENT. Text in English. 1987. 10/yr. CAD 109. **Document type:** *Newsletter.*
Published by: M P L Communications Inc., 133 Richmond St W, Ste 700, Toronto, ON M5H 3M8, Canada. TEL 416-869-1177, FAX 416-869-0456. Ed. John Hobel. Circ: 800.

610.73 616.99 CAN ISSN 1181-912X
CANADIAN ONCOLOGY NURSING JOURNAL/REVUE CANADIENNE DE NURSING ONCOLOGIQUE. Abbreviated title: C O N J. Text and summaries in English, French. 1991. 3/yr. CAD 104.81 domestic to individuals NS/NB/NFLD; CAD 117.14 domestic to institutions NS/NB/NFLD; CAD 97.46 domestic to individuals elsewhere in Canada; CAD 108.92 domestic to institutions elsewhere in Canada; CAD 131.84 foreign (effective 2007). adv. back issues avail. **Document type:** *Newsletter, Trade.* **Description:** Covers clinical oncology nursing practice, education and research. Also serves as newsletter and networking vehicle for nurses.
Indexed: C06, C07, C08, CINAHL, EMBASE, ExcerpMed, INI, MEDLINE, P30, R10, Reac, SCOPUS.
—BLDSC (3043.176000), IE, Infotrieve, Ingenta. **CCC.**
Published by: (Canadian Association of Nurses in Oncology), Pappin Communications, The Victoria Centre, 84 Isabella St, Pembroke, ON K8A 5S5, Canada. TEL 613-735-0952, FAX 613-735-7983, http://www.pappin.com. Ed. Heather B Porter. Pub. Bruce Pappin. Adv. contact Heather Coughlin. B&W page CAD 950, color page CAD 1,550; trim 11 x 8.5. Circ: 1,100.

610.73 CAN ISSN 0712-6778
➤ **CANADIAN OPERATING ROOM NURSING JOURNAL.** Text in English. 1983. q. CAD 30 domestic; CAD 52 foreign (effective 2007). **Document type:** *Journal, Academic/Scholarly.*
Related titles: Online - full text ed.
Indexed: A22, C03, C06, C07, C08, CBCARef, CINAHL, EMBASE, ExcerpMed, INI, MEDLINE, P20, P22, P24, P30, P48, P54, PQC, R10, Reac, SCOPUS.
—BLDSC (3043.177000), GNLM, IE, Infotrieve, Ingenta. **CCC.**
Published by: (Operating Room Nurses Association of Canada), Clockwork Communications, P O Box 33145, Halifax, NS, Canada. TEL 902-497-1598, FAX 902-444-0694, info@clockworkcanada.com, http://www.clockworkcanada.com/index.html. Ed. Deborah Murphy. Circ: 4,020.

610.73 616.99 USA ISSN 0162-220X
RC266
➤ **CANCER NURSING**; an international journal for cancer care. Text in English. 1978. bi-m. USD 372.51 domestic to institutions; USD 504 foreign to institutions (effective 2011). adv. bk.rev. charts; illus.; stat.; tr.lit. back issues avail.; reprints avail. **Document type:** *Journal, Academic/Scholarly.* **Description:** Addresses the whole spectrum of problems arising in the care and support of cancer patients.
Related titles: CD-ROM ed.; Microform ed.; Online - full text ed.: ISSN 1538-9804. USD 219.70 domestic academic site license; USD 245.70 foreign academic site license; USD 245.05 domestic corporate site license; USD 271.05 foreign corporate site license (effective 2002).
Indexed: A20, A22, AMED, ASCA, B28, C06, C07, C08, CINAHL, CurCont, DentInd, E-psyche, EMBASE, ExcerpMed, F09, FamI, H13, INI, IndMed, MEDLINE, NurAb, P02, P03, P10, P20, P24, P30, P48, P53, P54, PQC, PsycInfo, R10, Reac, SCI, SCOPUS, SSCI, THA, W07.
—BLDSC (3046.491000), GNLM, IE, Infotrieve, Ingenta, INIST. **CCC.**
Published by: Lippincott Williams & Wilkins (Subsidiary of: Wolters Kluwer N.V.), Two Commerce Sq, 2001 Market St, Philadelphia, PA 19103. TEL 215-521-8300, FAX 215-521-8902, customerservice@lww.com, http://www.lww.com. Ed. Pamela S Hinds TEL 202-476-4432. Pub. Kathleen M Phelan. Adv. contact Diane Shapiro TEL 215-628-6538. Circ: 1,135.

610.736 616.994 GBR ISSN 1475-4266
RC266
CANCER NURSING PRACTICE. Text in English. 2002 (Feb). 10/yr. GBP 200 in Europe to institutions; GBP 225 elsewhere to institutions (effective 2011). adv. back issues avail. **Document type:** *Journal, Academic/Scholarly.* **Description:** Provides clinical articles, cutting edge research, comprehensive news round up and Continuing Professional Development articles.
Related titles: Online - full text ed.: GBP 200 to institutions (effective 2011).
Indexed: A26, B28, C06, C07, C08, CA, CINAHL, E08, G08, H11, H12, I05, P20, P24, P48, P54, PQC, S09, T02.
—BLDSC (3046.491300), IE, Ingenta. **CCC.**
Published by: R C N Publishing Co. (Subsidiary of: B M J Group), The Heights, 59-65 Lowlands Rd, Harrow, Middx HA1 3AW, United Kingdom. TEL 44-20-84231066, FAX 44-20-84239196, advertising@rcnpublishing.co.uk, http://www.rcnpublishing.co.uk. Eds. Lisa Berry, Jean Gray. Adv. contact Neil Hobson TEL 44-20-88723123. page GBP 1,705; trim 216 x 279. Circ: 4,808.

610.73 USA
CAPITAL NURSING. Text in English. 1984. q. adv. index. back issues avail. **Description:** Covers news and activities of the Association.
Published by: District of Columbia Nurses Association, 5100 Wisconsin Ave, N W, Ste 306, Washington, DC 20016. TEL 202-244-2705, FAX 202-362-8285, ejones@dcna.org, http://www.dcna.org. Ed. Evelyn Sommers. Adv. contact Nancy Kofie. page USD 1,000. Circ: 15,000 (controlled).

610.73 CAN ISSN 0843-9966
CARE CONNECTION. Text in English. 1985. q. CAD 23.50; CAD 29 foreign. adv. bk.rev. illus.; tr.lit. back issues avail. **Document type:** *Newsletter, Trade.* **Description:** Contains educational articles and health care issue updates.
Former titles: Bedside Specialist (0835-6203); Green Band
Indexed: C06, C07, C08, CINAHL.
Published by: Registered Nurses' Association of Ontario, 5025 Orbitor Dr, Ste 200, Bldg 4, Mississauga, ON L4W 4Y5, Canada. TEL 905-602-4664, FAX 905-602-4666. Ed., R&P Barbara Thornber. Adv. contact Bonnie Krakenberg. B&W page CAD 450; trim 11 x 8.5. Circ: 5,500.

CARE INVEST. *see* GERONTOLOGY AND GERIATRICS

610.73 USA ISSN 1521-0987
RA645.3 CODEN: CMJOFU
➤ **CARE MANAGEMENT JOURNALS**; journal of case management and the journal of long term home health care. Text in English. 1999. q. USD 90 to individuals; USD 135 to institutions (effective 2009). adv. bk.rev.; software rev.; video rev. 80 p./no.; back issues avail.; reprints avail. **Document type:** *Journal, Academic/Scholarly.* **Description:** Comprehensive resource for professional care givers, nurses, nursing home administrators and case managers.
Formed by the merger of (1992-1998): Journal of Case Management (1061-3706); (1994-1998): Journal of Long Term Home Health Care (1072-4281); Which was formerly (1982-1994): Pride Institute Journal of Long Term Home Health Care (0743-5088)
Related titles: Online - full text ed.: ISSN 1938-9019 (from IngentaConnect).
Indexed: A22, ASG, AgeL, C06, C07, C08, CA, CINAHL, EMBASE, ExcerpMed, FamI, HospI, INI, IndMed, MEDLINE, P20, P22, P24, P30, P48, P54, PAIS, PQC, PsycholAb, R10, Reac, S02, S03, SCOPUS, SOPODA, SSA, SWR&A, SocioIAb, T02.
—BLDSC (3051.572000), GNLM, IE, Infotrieve, Ingenta. **CCC.**
Published by: (St. Vincent's Hospital, Pride Institute), Springer Publishing Company, 11 W 42nd St, 15th Fl, New York, NY 10036. TEL 212-431-4370, FAX 212-941-7842, contactus@springerpub.com. Eds. F Russell Kellogg, Joan Quinn. R&Ps Dorothy Kouwenberg, Jessica Perl. Adv. contact Jessica Perl. B&W page USD 400; trim 8.5 x 11. Circ: 236 (paid).

610.73 CAN ISSN 1492-7802
CAREGIVER. Text in English. 1988. q. **Document type:** *Newsletter, Trade.*
Formerly (until 1989): At Home (0840-6812)
Indexed: C11.
Published by: Caregiver Network Inc., 2 Oaklawn Gardens, Unit C, Toronto, ON M4V 2C6, Canada. TEL 416-323-1090, FAX 416-323-9422, karenh@caregiver.on.ca, http://www.caregiver.on.ca/.

CARELINK; popular trade publication. *see* HEALTH FACILITIES AND ADMINISTRATION

610.73 GBR
CAREWEEK. Text in English. 1997. w. free (effective 2009). adv. bk.rev. tr.lit. back issues avail. **Document type:** *Magazine, Trade.* **Description:** Covers nursing home training, finances, medical information, health, and safety management for proprietors and managers.
Former titles (until 200?): Nursing & Care Home Business (Print); Nursing Home Business
Media: Online - full text.
Published by: Park View Publishing Ltd., Park View House, 19 The Ave, Eastbourne, E Sussex BN21 3YD, United Kingdom. TEL 44-1323-433705, FAX 44-1323-411654, rob@parkview-publishing.co.uk, http://www.parkview-publishing.co.uk/. Ed. Laura Knight TEL 44-1323-433701. Pub. Lee Mansfield TEL 44-1323-411601. Adv. contact Rob Collyer.

610.73 CAN
CARING. Text in English. 1945. 3/yr. free to members (effective 2005). adv. **Document type:** *Newsletter.*
Formerly (until 1990): Nurses News
Related titles: Online - full content ed.
Published by: College of Licensed Practical Nurses of Manitoba, 463 St. Anne's Rd, Winnipeg, MB R2M 3C9, Canada. TEL 204-663-1212, FAX 204-663-1207, info@clpnm.ca, http://www.clpnm.ca. Ed., R&P, Adv. contact Verna Holgate.

658 610 USA ISSN 0738-467X
RA645.35 CODEN: CARGET
CARING (WASHINGTON). Text in English. 1982. m. USD 49 domestic to individuals; USD 75 in Canada & Mexico to individuals; USD 90 elsewhere to individuals; USD 120 domestic to institutions; USD 155 in Canada & Mexico to institutions; USD 170 elsewhere to institutions; free to members (effective 2010). adv. bk.rev. charts; stat.; illus. index. back issues avail.; reprints avail. **Document type:** *Magazine, Trade.* **Description:** Contains articles, special sections and departments covering national and international aspects of the home health care and hospice fields.
Supersedes: Home Health Review (0193-2683)
Related titles: Online - full text ed.: free (effective 2010).
Indexed: A22, AHCMS, AgeL, C06, C07, C08, CINAHL, EMBASE, ExcerpMed, F09, FamI, HospLI, INI, MEDLINE, P30, R10, Reac, SCOPUS.
—BLDSC (3053.222000), GNLM, IE, Infotrieve, Ingenta.
Published by: National Association for Home Care & Hospice, 228 Seventh St, SE, Washington, DC 20003. TEL 202-547-7424, FAX 202-547-3540, pubs@nahc.org. Eds. Gary L Thietten, Val J Halamandaris. Pub. Val J Halamandaris.

CARING TODAY; practical advice for the family caregiver. *see* HOME ECONOMICS

610.73 CAN ISSN 1719-9697
CENTRE POINTS. Text in English. 2005. 3/yr. **Document type:** *Newsletter, Trade.* **Description:** Published to inform about the RNAO Centre for Professional Nursing Excellence.
Published by: Registered Nurses' Association of Ontario, 158 Pearl St., Toronto, ON M5H-1L3, Canada. TEL 416-599-1925, 800-268-7199, FAX 416-599-1926, info@rnao.org.

610.73 CAN ISSN 1912-5976
CERTIFICATION. BULLETIN. Text in French. 1997. a. **Document type:** *Newsletter, Trade.*
Formerly (until 2004): Nouvelles de la Certification (1206-3908)
Related titles: English ed.: Certification Bulletin. ISSN 1912-5968. 1997.
Published by: Canadian Nurses Association/Association des Infirmieres et Infirmiers du Canada, 50 Driveway, Ottawa, ON K2P 1E2, Canada. TEL 613-237-2133, 800-361-8404, FAX 613-237-3520, pubs@cna-nurses.ca, http://www.cna-nurses.ca.

610.73 USA ISSN 0069-2778
RT5.I3
CHART. Text in English. 1904. bi-m. free to members. adv. **Document type:** *Newsletter, Trade.* **Description:** Covers health care and professional issues of importance to all nurses.
Related titles: Microfilm ed.: (from PQC); Online - full text ed.
Indexed: C06, C07, C08, CINAHL, CPerI, INI, P24, P30, P48, PQC, SCOPUS.
—BLDSC (3129.960000), GNLM, Infotrieve.
Published by: Illinois Nurses Association, 105 W Adams St, Ste 2101, Chicago, IL 60603. TEL 312-419-2900, FAX 312-419-2920, http://www.illinoisnurses.org. Circ: 8,000.

610.73 USA ISSN 1049-2259
THE CHRONICLE (PHILADELPHIA). Text in English. 1990. s-a. **Document type:** *Newsletter.*
Indexed: C06, C07, C08, CINAHL, P30, PRA.
Published by: University of Pennsylvania, School of Nursing & Center for the Study of the History of Nursing, 370 Nursing Education Bldg, 420 Guardian Dr, Philadelphia, PA 19104-6096. TEL 215-898-4502, FAX 215-573-2168, nhistory@nursing.upenn.edu, http://www.nursing.upenn.edu/history/default.htm.

610.73 USA ISSN 1940-5642
RT4
CHRONICLE OF NURSING. Abbreviated title: C N. Text in English. 2007 (Nov.). m. free to members (effective 2009). back issues avail. **Document type:** *Journal, Trade.* **Description:** Features articles that will advance the reader's knowledge of medical research and science.
Media: Online - full content.

Published by: American Society of Registered Nurses, 1001 Bridgeway, Ste 411, Sausalito, CA 94965. TEL 415-331-2700, 800-331-1206, FAX 415-476-4558, office@asrn.org. Ed. Alison Palmer.

610.73 ESP ISSN 1579-5527
CIBER REVISTA ENFERMERIADEURGENCIAS.COM. Text in Spanish. 2000. q. back issues avail. **Document type:** *Journal, Academic/Scholarly.*
Media: Online - full text.
Published by: Sociedad Espanola de Enfermeria de Urgencias y Emergencias, C Capitan Haya, 60, Madrid, 28020, Spain. TEL 34-91-5701284, FAX 34-91-5708911. Ed. Sixto Agustin Prieto Flores.

610.73 CHL ISSN 0717-2079
RT8.C5
CIENCIA Y ENFERMERIA. Text in Spanish. 1995. s-a. CLP 20 for 2 yrs. domestic; USD 60 for 2 yrs. foreign (effective 2010). back issues avail. **Document type:** *Journal, Academic/Scholarly.* **Description:** Includes news and in-depth articles on nursing and general well being.
Related titles: Online - full text ed.: ISSN 0717-9553. 2002. free (effective 2011).
Indexed: SCOPUS.
Published by: Universidad de Concepcion, Departamento de Enfermeria, Casilla 160-C, Concepcion, Chile. TEL 56-41-228353, rev-enf@udec.cl, http://www.udec.cl/. Ed. Jasna Stiepovich Bertoni.

610.73 TWN ISSN 1683-1624
CIJI HULI ZAZHI/TZU CHI NURSING JOURNAL. Text in Chinese; Abstracts in Chinese, English. 2002. bi-m. TWD 720 (effective 2010). **Document type:** *Magazine, Trade.*
Related titles: Online - full text ed.
Indexed: C06, C07, C08, CINAHL.
—BLDSC (9512.696700).
Published by: Caituan Faren Fojiao Ciji Zhonghe Yiyuan/Buddhist Tzu Chi General Hospital, no.707, sec.3, Chung Yang Rd., Hualien, 970, Taiwan. TEL 886-3-8561825 ext 2120, FAX 886-3-8562021, nursing@tzuchi.com.tw. Ed. Hui-Ling Lai.

CINAHL. (Cumulative Index to Nursing & Allied Health Literature) *see* MEDICAL SCIENCES—Abstracting, Bibliographies, Statistics

CINAHL PLUS. *see* MEDICAL SCIENCES—Abstracting, Bibliographies, Statistics

CINAHL PLUS WITH FULL TEXT. *see* MEDICAL SCIENCES—Abstracting, Bibliographies, Statistics

CINAHL WITH FULL TEXT. *see* MEDICAL SCIENCES—Abstracting, Bibliographies, Statistics

610.73 USA ISSN 1524-7317
RT82.8
THE CLINICAL ADVISOR. Variant title: Clinical Advisor for Nurse Practitioners. Text in English. 1998. m. USD 75 domestic; USD 85 in Canada; USD 110 elsewhere; free to qualified personnel (effective 2009). adv. back issues avail.; reprints avail. **Document type:** *Magazine, Trade.* **Description:** Provides practitioners with the latest information about diagnosing, treating, managing, and preventing conditions seen in a typical office-based primary-care setting.
Related titles: Online - full text ed.
Indexed: A26, C06, C07, C08, CINAHL, E08, G08, H11, H12, I05, P24, P48, PQC.
—BLDSC (3286.245500). **CCC.**
Published by: Haymarket Media Inc. (Subsidiary of: Haymarket Group Ltd.), 114 W 26th St, 4th Fl, New York, NY 10001. TEL 646-638-6000, FAX 646-638-6117, custserv@haymarketmedia.com, http://www.haymarket.com. Ed. Joe Kopcha TEL 646-638-6076. adv.: B&W page USD 5,110, color page USD 7,320; trim 7.675 x 10.5. Circ: 125,000.

610.73 616.99 USA ISSN 1092-1095
RC266
➤ **CLINICAL JOURNAL OF ONCOLOGY NURSING.** Abbreviated title: C J O N. Text in English. 1997. bi-m. USD 175 domestic to institutions; USD 195 foreign to institutions; free to members (effective 2010). 56 p./no. 3 cols./p.; back issues avail.; reprints avail. **Document type:** *Journal, Academic/Scholarly.* **Description:** Provides practical information for direct care of patients and their families across the cancer continuum.
Related titles: Online - full text ed.: ISSN 1538-067X.
Indexed: A01, A02, A03, A08, A20, A22, A26, C06, C07, C08, C11, CA, CINAHL, CurCont, EMBASE, ExcerpMed, H04, H12, I05, INI, MEDLINE, P03, P20, P22, P24, P30, P48, P54, PQC, PsycInfo, R10, Reac, SCI, SCOPUS, SSCI, T02, W07.
—BLDSC (3286.294100), IE, Infotrieve, Ingenta. **CCC.**
Published by: Oncology Nursing Society, 125 Enterprise Dr, Pittsburgh, PA 15275. TEL 412-859-6100, 866-257-4667, FAX 412-859-6165, 877-369-5497, customer.service@ons.org. Ed. Deborah K Mayer. Pub. Leonard Mafrica. Adv. contact Anthony J Jannetti TEL 856-256-2300. Circ: 36,000.

610.73 USA ISSN 0887-6274
RT82.8
➤ **CLINICAL NURSE SPECIALIST**; a journal for advanced nursing practice. Abbreviated title: C N S. Text in English. 1987. bi-m. USD 350.51 domestic to institutions; USD 521 foreign to institutions (effective 2011). adv. back issues avail.; reprints avail. **Document type:** *Journal, Academic/Scholarly.* **Description:** Brings out scholarly works by clinical nurse specialists and other practice nurses whose manuscripts advance the practice of nursing.
Related titles: Online - full text ed.: ISSN 1538-9782. USD 204.10 domestic academic site license; USD 227.65 domestic corporate site license; USD 244.10 foreign academic site license; USD 267.65 foreign corporate site license (effective 2002).
Indexed: A20, A22, C06, C07, C08, CINAHL, CurCont, EMBASE, ExcerpMed, F09, Faml, INI, MEDLINE, NurAb, P24, P30, P48, PQC, R10, Reac, SCI, SCOPUS, SSCI, T02, W07.
—BLDSC (3286.314100), GNLM, IE, Infotrieve, Ingenta, INIST. **CCC.**
Published by: (National Association of Clinical Nurse Specialists), Lippincott Williams & Wilkins (Subsidiary of: Wolters Kluwer N.V.), Two Commerce Sq, 2001 Market St, Philadelphia, PA 19103. TEL 215-521-8300, FAX 215-521-8902, customerservice@lww.com, http://www.lww.com. Ed. Janet S Fulton TEL 317-274-2421. Pub. Kathleen M Phelan. Adv. contact Pat Wendelken. Circ: 3,258.

610.73 USA ISSN 1054-7738
RT81.5 CODEN: CNREFD
➤ **CLINICAL NURSING RESEARCH.** Text in English. 1992. q. USD 671, GBP 394 combined subscription to institutions (print & online eds.); USD 658, GBP 386 to institutions (effective 2011). adv. back issues avail.; reprint service avail. from PSC. **Document type:** *Journal, Academic/Scholarly.* **Description:** Provides an international forum for scholarly research focusing on clinical nursing practice, including the clinical application of research findings.
Related titles: Online - full text ed.: ISSN 1552-3799. USD 604, GBP 355 to institutions (effective 2011).
Indexed: A01, A02, A03, A08, A22, A25, A26, AMED, ASG, ASSIA, B07, B21, C06, C07, C08, CA, CINAHL, CurCont, E-psyche, E01, E08, EMBASE, ExcerpMed, Faml, G08, H04, H11, H12, H13, I05, INI, MEDLINE, NSA, P02, P03, P10, P20, P24, P25, P30, P48, P53, P54, PQC, PsycInfo, PsycholAb, R10, Reac, S08, S09, SCI, SCOPUS, SFSA, SOPODA, SSCI, SociolAb, T02, V02, W07.
—BLDSC (3286.314150), GNLM, IE, Infotrieve, Ingenta. **CCC.**
Published by: (University of Alberta CAN), Sage Publications, Inc., 2455 Teller Rd, Thousand Oaks, CA 91320. TEL 805-499-9774, 800-818-7243, FAX 805-499-0871, 800-583-2665, info@sagepub.com. Ed. Pamela Z Cacchione. Circ: 600 (paid). **Subscr. outside the Americas to:** Sage Publications Ltd., 1 Oliver's Yard, 55 City Rd, London EC1Y 1SP, United Kingdom. TEL 44-20-73248701, FAX 44-20-73248733, subscription@sagepub.co.uk.

610.73 USA ISSN 1939-2095
RT1
➤ **CLINICAL SCHOLARS REVIEW.** Text in English. 2008. s-a. USD 55 domestic to individuals; USD 150 domestic to institutions; USD 75 foreign to individuals; USD 170 foreign to institutions (effective 2008). **Document type:** *Journal, Academic/Scholarly.*
Related titles: Online - full text ed.: ISSN 1939-2109 (from IngentaConnect).
Indexed: ASSIA, C06, C07, CA, T02.
—**CCC.**
Published by: Springer Publishing Company, 11 W 42nd St, 15th Fl, New York, NY 10036. TEL 212-431-4370, FAX 212-941-7842, contactus@springerpub.com. Ed. Jennifer Smith.

610.73 USA ISSN 1876-1399
➤ **CLINICAL SIMULATION IN NURSING.** Text in English. 2005. bi-m. USD 336 in United States to institutions; USD 336 elsewhere to institutions (effective 2012). adv. back issues avail.; reprints avail. **Document type:** *Journal, Academic/Scholarly.* **Description:** Provides information about the collaborating, mentoring, and networking for the advancement of nursing and health care education and practice through simulation and technology.
Related titles: Online - full text ed.: ISSN 1876-1402 (from ScienceDirect).
Indexed: C06, C07, C08, CA, CINAHL, SCOPUS, T02.
—IE. **CCC.**
Published by: (International Nursing Association for Clinical Simulation and Learning), Elsevier Inc. (Subsidiary of: Elsevier Science & Technology), 1600 John F Kennedy Blvd, Philadelphia, PA 19103. TEL 215-239-3900, FAX 215-238-7883, JournalCustomerService-usa@elsevier.com, http://www.elsevier.com. Ed. Suzie Kardong-Edgren. Pub. Jami Walker TEL 314-447-8987. Adv. contact Hank Blaney TEL 212-633-3648.

610.73 USA ISSN 1935-9365
CLINICIAN'S DIGEST. Text in English. 2007 (Mar.). q. **Document type:** *Journal, Trade.*
Related titles: Online - full text ed.: free (effective 2011).
Published by: Brandofino Communications, LLC, 12 Spruce Park, Syosset, NY 11791. TEL 516-364-2575, http://brandofinocommunications.com/. Ed. Paula S Katz. Pub. Jeanette Brandofino.

610.73 CAN
THE COLLEGE CONNECTION. Text in English. 1957. q. free to members. **Document type:** *Newsletter.*
Formerly: L P N Association of British Columbia Newsletter
Published by: College of Licensed Practical Nurses of British Columbia, 3823 Henning Dr, Ste 217, Burnaby, BC V5C 6P3, Canada. TEL 604-775-0412, 888-440-6900, FAX 604-660-2899, http://www.clpnbc.org. Ed. Pamela Clarke.

610.73 310 CAN ISSN 1719-4318
COLLEGE OF NURSES OF ONTARIO. MEMBERSHIP STATISTICS REPORT. Text in English. 2004. a., latest 2005. **Document type:** *Report, Trade.*
Published by: College of Nurses of Ontario, 101 Davenport Rd, Toronto, ON M5R 3P1, Canada. TEL 416-928-0900, FAX 416-928-6507, http://www.cno.org/index.html.

610.73 NLD ISSN 1322-7696
RT1
➤ **COLLEGIAN.** Text in English. 1994. q. EUR 192 in Europe to institutions; JPY 30,500 in Japan to institutions; USD 261 elsewhere to institutions (effective 2012). adv. 44 p./no.; back issues avail. **Document type:** *Journal, Academic/Scholarly.* **Description:** Seeks to educate, inform and stimulate the nursing profession with articles broad in scope. Discusses topical issues, focusing on practice and professional and policy issues. Aimed primarily at nurse practicioners and educators.
Related titles: Online - full text ed.: ISSN 1876-7575 (from ScienceDirect).
Indexed: ASSIA, C06, C07, C08, CINAHL, EMBASE, ExcerpMed, MEDLINE, P30, R10, Reac, SCI, SCOPUS, SSCI, W07.
—BLDSC (3311.326300), IE, Ingenta. **CCC.**
Published by: (Royal College of Nursing Australia AUS), Elsevier BV (Subsidiary of: Elsevier Science & Technology), Radarweg 29, PO Box 211, Amsterdam, 1000 AE, Netherlands. TEL 31-20-4853911, FAX 31-20-4852457, JournalsCustomerServiceEMEA@elsevier.com, http://www.elsevier.nl. Ed. John Daly.

610.73 USA ISSN 8750-846X
COLORADO NURSE. Text in English. 1947 (vol.73). q. looseleaf. USD 20 domestic; USD 25 foreign (effective 2008); Free to qualified subscribers. adv. 28 p./no.; back issues avail. **Document type:** *Newsletter, Trade.* **Description:** Covers issues and employment opportunities of interest to licensed nursing professionals.
Former titles (until 1985): Colorado Nurse Update (8750-8451); (until 1984): Colorado Nurse (0010-1680)
Indexed: A26, C06, C07, C08, CA, CINAHL, EMBASE, ExcerpMed, H12, I05, INI, MEDLINE, P30, SCOPUS, T02.
—GNLM.
Published by: (Colorado Nurses Association), Arthur L. Davis Publishing Agency, Inc., 517 Washington St, PO Box 216, Cedar Falls, IA 50613. TEL 319-277-2414, 800-626-4081, FAX 319-277-4055, sales@aldpub.com, http://www.aldpub.com. Eds. Fran Ricker, Mark Miller. R&P Linda Metzner. Adv. contact Jim Larson. Circ: 63,000.

610.73 USA ISSN 0898-4093
COLUMBIA UNIVERSITY-PRESBYTERIAN HOSPITAL. SCHOOL OF NURSING ALUMNI ASSOCIATION. ALUMNI MAGAZINE. Variant title: The Alumni Magazine. Text in English. 1906. 3/yr.
Formerly (until 1985): Columbia University-Presbyterian Hospital. School of Nursing Alumnae Association. Alumnae Magazine (0069-634X)
Indexed: C06, C07, C08, CINAHL, P30, SCOPUS.
Published by: Columbia University-Presbyterian Hospital, School of Nursing Alumni Association, Inc., 6 Xavier Dr, Yonkers, NY 10704-1309. TEL 914-966-3699, 800-435-3856, FAX 914-966-3693, cuphsonaa@aol.com, http://www.cuphsonaa.com.

610.73 GBR ISSN 2047-170X
COMMONWEALTH NURSE. Text in English. 1985. s-a. free to qualified personnel (effective 2011). back issues avail. **Document type:** *Journal, Trade.*
Formerly (until 2009): Commonwealth Nurses Federation. Newsletter (0268-4063)
Related titles: Online - full text ed.
Published by: Commonwealth Nurses Federation, c/o Royal College of Nursing, 20 Cavendish Sq, London, W1G 0RN, United Kingdom. TEL 44-20-76473593, FAX 44-20-76473413, cnf@commonwealthnurses.org.

610.73 USA ISSN 0160-1652
RT73
COMMUNICATING NURSING RESEARCH. Text in English. 1968. irreg. **Document type:** *Monographic series.*
Indexed: C06, C07, C08, CINAHL, EMBASE, ExcerpMed, MEDLINE, P30, R10, Reac, SCOPUS.
—BLDSC (3341.380000), GNLM.
Published by: Western Institute of Nursing, SN-4S, 3455 SW Veterans Hospital Rd, Portland, OR 97239-2941. TEL 503-494-6772, FAX 503-494-3691, mcneilp@ohsu.edu, http://www.winursing.org.

610.73 USA ISSN 0887-4557
THE COMMUNIQUE (MILWAUKEE). Text in English. 1979. q. **Document type:** *Newsletter.*
Indexed: P30.
Published by: Wisconsin League for Nursing, 2121 E Newport Ave, Milwaukee, WI 53211. http://www.cuw.edu/AdultEd_Graduate/programs/nursing/wln/.

610.73 GBR ISSN 1462-2815
RT97
➤ **COMMUNITY PRACTITIONER.** Text in English. 1927. m. free to members (effective 2009). bk.rev.; film rev. illus. index. reprints avail. **Document type:** *Journal, Academic/Scholarly.* **Description:** Provides topical news, in-depth news features, policy analysis, practice updates, and professional and clinical papers.
Former titles (until 1998): Health Visitor (0017-9140); (until 1964): Woman Health Officer
Related titles: Microfilm ed.: (from PQC); Online - full text ed.: (from IngentaConnect); Supplement(s): Health Visitor Opportunities.
Indexed: A22, A26, ASSIA, B28, C06, C07, C08, CA, CINAHL, DentInd, EMBASE, ExcerpMed, F09, Faml, H12, I05, INI, MEDLINE, P20, P22, P24, P30, P48, P50, P54, PQC, R10, Reac, SCOPUS, T02.
—BLDSC (3363.648420), GNLM, IE, Ingenta. **CCC.**
Published by: (Community Practitioners' and Health Visitors' Association), Ten Alps Publishing (Subsidiary of: Ten Alps Group), 9 Savoy St, London, WC2E 7HR, United Kingdom. TEL 44-20-78782404, FAX 44-20-73797155, info@tenalpspublishing.com, http://www.tenalpspublishing.com.

616.834 GBR
COMPASS (WOKINGHAM); the global MS nurse journal. Text in English. 2006. 3/yr. free to qualified personnel (effective 2008). **Document type:** *Journal, Trade.* **Description:** Specifically written for nurses and other healthcare professionals providing care and support for people with Multiple Sclerosis. Creates a platform that allows nurses in different countries, who provide care for people with MS, to learn from each other, share ideas and exchange information.
Published by: Plexus, Resource House, 20 Denmark St, Wokingham, Berkshire RG40 2BB, United Kingdom. TEL 44-1189-369109, FAX 44-1189-794670. Ed. Louise Rath. Circ: 4,500.

610.73 618.202 GBR ISSN 1744-3881
RT41
➤ **COMPLEMENTARY THERAPIES IN CLINICAL PRACTICE.** Text in English. 1995. q. EUR 502 in Europe to institutions; JPY 54,200 in Japan to institutions; USD 460 elsewhere to institutions (effective 2012). adv. bk.rev. 56 p./no. 2 cols./p.; back issues avail.; reprints avail. **Document type:** *Journal, Academic/Scholarly.* **Description:** Publishes articles on all aspects of individual therapies and includes original research in nursing practice.
Formerly (until 2005): Complementary Therapies in Nursing & Midwifery (1353-6117)
Related titles: Online - full text ed.: ISSN 1873-6947 (from ScienceDirect).
Indexed: A22, A26, AMED, ASSIA, B28, C06, C07, C08, CA, CINAHL, E01, EMBASE, ExcerpMed, H12, I05, INI, MEDLINE, P30, R10, Reac, SCOPUS, SociolAb, T02.
—BLDSC (3364.203747), GNLM, IE, Infotrieve, Ingenta. **CCC.**
Published by: Churchill Livingstone (Subsidiary of: Elsevier Health Sciences), The Blvd, Langford Ln, Kidlington, OX5 1GB, United Kingdom. TEL 44-1865-843434, FAX 44-1865-843970, directenquiries@elsevier.com, http://www.elsevierhealth.com/imprint.jsp?iid=9. Ed. Denise Rankin-Box. Adv. contact Emma Steel TEL 44-207-4244221.

➤ **COMPUTERS, INFORMATICS, NURSING.** *see* MEDICAL SCIENCES—Computer Applications

610.73 CAN
CONCERN. Text in English. 1968. 6/yr. adv.
Published by: ProWest Publications, 208, 438 Victoria Ave E, Regina, SK S4N 0N7, Canada. TEL 306-352-3400, FAX 306-525-0960. Circ: 9,700.

610.73 USA ISSN 0278-4092
CONNECTICUT NURSING NEWS. Text in English. 1921. q. looseleaf. USD 30; free to qualified personnel (effective 2008). adv. 24 p./no.; back issues avail. **Document type:** *Newspaper, Trade.* **Description:** Covers issues and employment opportunities of interest to licensed nursing professionals.
Former titles (until 1980): Nursing News (0029-652X); (until 1953): Connecticut Nursing News
Related titles: Online - full text ed.
Indexed: C06, C07, C08, CINAHL, INI, P24, P30, P48, PQC, SCOPUS.
—GNLM.
Published by: (Connecticut Nurses Association), Arthur L. Davis Publishing Agency, Inc., 517 Washington St, PO Box 216, Cedar Falls, IA 50613. TEL 319-277-2414, 800-626-4081, FAX 319-277-4055, sales@aldpub.com, http://www.aldpub.com. Ed. Mark Miller. R&P Polly Barey. Adv. contact Jim Larson. Circ: 53,000.

610.730994 AUS ISSN 1037-6178
RT15
➤ **CONTEMPORARY NURSE**; health care across the lifespan. Text in English. 1992. bi-m. AUD 299 in Australia & New Zealand to individuals includes Pacific, China, South and South-East Asia, South America, Africa; USD 299 elsewhere to individuals; AUD 825 in Australia & New Zealand to institutions includes Pacific, China, South and South-East Asia, South America, Africa; USD 825 elsewhere to institutions; AUD 1,250 combined subscription in Australia & New Zealand (print & online eds.) ; includes Pacific, China, South and South-East Asia, South America, Africa; USD 1,250 combined subscription elsewhere (print & online eds.) (effective 2009). adv. bk.rev. back issues avail. **Document type:** *Journal, Academic/Scholarly.* **Description:** Designed to increase nursing skills, knowledge, research and communication, assist in professional development and enhance educational standards by publishing stimulating and useful educational articles on a range of issues influencing professional nursing.
Related titles: Online - full text ed.
Indexed: A01, A02, A03, A08, A26, B21, C06, C07, C08, CA, CINAHL, EMBASE, ESPM, ExcerpMed, H&SSA, H12, I05, INI, MEDLINE, P03, P20, P22, P24, P30, P48, P54, PQC, PsycInfo, R10, Reac, SCI, SCOPUS, SSCI, T02, W07, W09.
—BLDSC (3425.195500), IE, Infotrieve, Ingenta. **CCC.**
Published by: eContent Management Pty Ltd, PO Box 1027, Maleny, QLD 4552, Australia. TEL 61-7-54352900, FAX 61-7-54352911, info@e-contentmanagement.com, http://www.e-contentmanagement.com. Ed. Jenny Gibson. Pub., R&P James Davidson. Adv. contact Heather H Richmond TEL 61-7-54352900. Circ: 1,000 (controlled).

610.73 NGA ISSN 2141-4173
➤ **CONTINENTAL JOURNAL OF NURSING SCIENCE.** Text in English. 2008. a. NGN 2,500 domestic to individuals; USD 120 foreign to individuals; NGN 5,000 domestic to institutions; USD 200 foreign to institutions (effective 2010). Index. back issues avail.; reprints avail. **Document type:** *Journal, Academic/Scholarly.* **Description:** Contributes to the advancement of evidence-based nursing, midwifery and healthcare by disseminating high quality research and scholarship of contemporary relevance and with potential to advance knowledge for practice, education, management or policy.
Related titles: Online - full text ed.
Published by: Wilolud Journals, 2 Church Ave, Oke Eri qrt, Oba Ile, Ondo State 340001, Nigeria. TEL 234-803-4458674, managingeditor.olawale71@gmail.com. Ed. Idongesit I Akpabio.

610.73 USA
CONVENIENT CARE. Text in English. 2008. bi-m. **Document type:** *Magazine, Trade.* **Description:** Provides clinical content addressing the needs of nurse practitioners and physician assistants who practice in the retail/convenient care clinic environment.
Published by: Quadrant HealthCom, 7 Century Dr, Ste 302, Parsippany, NJ 07054. TEL 973-206-3434, FAX 973-206-9251, http://www.qhc.com. Circ: 10,000.

610.73 USA ISSN 1078-4535
RT1
➤ **CREATIVE NURSING**; a journal of values, issues, experience & collaboration. Text in English. 1982. q. USD 220 domestic to institutions; USD 260 foreign to institutions; USD 250 combined subscription domestic to institutions (print & online eds.); USD 325 combined subscription foreign to institutions (print & online eds.) (effective 2009). bk.rev. 16 p./no. 2 cols./p.; back issues avail.; reprints avail. **Document type:** *Journal, Academic/Scholarly.* **Description:** Features interviews with nursing leaders, cutting edge information and analysis from a national and international perspective.
Formerly (until Sep.1994): Primarily Nursing (0739-4446)
Related titles: Online - full text ed.: ISSN 1946-1895. USD 200 domestic to institutions; USD 240 foreign to institutions (effective 2009) (from IngentaConnect).
Indexed: A01, A02, A03, A08, ASSIA, C06, C07, C08, C11, C12, CA, CINAHL, EMBASE, ExcerpMed, H04, INI, M01, M02, MEDLINE, P20, P22, P24, P30, P48, P54, PQC, R10, Reac, SCOPUS, T02.
—BLDSC (3487.240500), GNLM, IE, Infotrieve, Ingenta. **CCC.**
Published by: (Creative Health Care Management, Inc.), Springer Publishing Company, 11 W 42nd St, 15th Fl, New York, NY 10036. TEL 212-431-4370, FAX 212-941-7842, contactus@springerpub.com. Ed. Marie Manthey.

610.73 USA ISSN 0279-5442
RT120.I5 CODEN: CCNUEV
➤ **CRITICAL CARE NURSE**; the journal for high acuity, progressive, and critical care. Abbreviated title: C C N. Text in English. 1980. bi-m. USD 39 domestic to individuals; USD 60 foreign to individuals; USD 205 domestic to institutions (print or online ed.); USD 270 foreign to institutions; USD 292 combined subscription domestic to institutions (print & online eds.); USD 358 combined subscription foreign to institutions (print & online eds.); free to members (effective 2010). adv. 96 p./no. 3 cols./p.; back issues avail.; reprints avail. **Document type:** *Journal, Academic/Scholarly.* **Description:** Provides current information and perspectives on a wide range of topics in critical care nursing.
Related titles: Online - full text ed.: ISSN 1940-8250.
Indexed: A01, A02, A03, A08, A20, A22, A26, C06, C07, C08, C11, CA, CINAHL, CurCont, E08, EMBASE, ExcerpMed, FamI, G08, H04, H11, H12, I05, INI, MEDLINE, NurAb, P16, P20, P22, P24, P30, P48, P53, P54, PQC, R10, Reac, S09, SCI, SCOPUS, SSCI, T02, W07.
—BLDSC (3487.451100), GNLM, IE, Infotrieve, Ingenta, INIST. **CCC.**
Published by: American Association of Critical Care Nurses, 101 Columbia, Ste 100, Aliso Viejo, CA 92656. TEL 949-362-2000, 800-899-2226, FAX 949-362-2020, info@aacn.org, http://www.aacn.org. Ed. JoAnn Grif Alspach. Adv. contact Kathy Huntley TEL 800-257-8290 ext 249. **Subscr. to:** PO Box 15055, North Hollywood, CA 91615. TEL 818-487-2075, 800-336-6348, FAX 818-487-4550.

610.7 USA ISSN 0899-5885
RT120.I5
CRITICAL CARE NURSING CLINICS OF NORTH AMERICA. Text in English. 1989. q. USD 282 in United States to institutions; USD 353 elsewhere to institutions (effective 2012). adv. Index. back issues avail.; reprints avail. **Document type:** *Journal, Academic/Scholarly.* **Description:** Focuses on a single topic relevant to critical care and intensive care unit nursing practice, including pain management, palliative care, wound care, burns, heart failure, pharmacology, respiratory care, error reduction, and rehabilitation.
Related titles: Microform ed.: (from PQC); Online - full text ed.: ISSN 1558-3481 (from IngentaConnect, ScienceDirect); Supplement(s): Critical Care Nursing Clinics of North America. Continuing Education Supplement. ISSN 1557-7880. 2004. USD 99 per issue (effective 2006).
Indexed: A22, C06, C07, C08, CINAHL, EMBASE, ExcerpMed, F09, FamI, INI, MEDLINE, P30, R10, Reac, SCOPUS.
—BLDSC (3487.451150), GNLM, IE, Infotrieve, Ingenta. **CCC.**
Published by: W.B. Saunders Co. (Subsidiary of: Elsevier Health Sciences), Elsevier, Health Sciences Division, Order Fulfillment, 3251 Riverport Ln, Maryland Heights, MO 63043. TEL 314-872-8370, 800-325-4177, FAX 314-432-1380, JournalCustomerService-usa@elsevier.com, http://www.us.elsevierhealth.com. Adv. contact John Marmero TEL 212-633-3657.

610 USA ISSN 0887-9303
CODEN: CCNQEJ
➤ **CRITICAL CARE NURSING QUARTERLY.** Abbreviated title: C C N Q. Text in English. 1978. q. USD 339 domestic to institutions; USD 507 foreign to institutions (effective 2011). adv. back issues avail.; reprints avail. **Document type:** *Journal, Academic/Scholarly.* **Description:** Provides practice-oriented information for the continuing education and improved clinical practice of critical care professionals, including nurses, physicians, and allied health care professionals.
Formerly (until 1987): Critical Care Quarterly (0160-2551)
Related titles: Microform ed.: (from PQC); Online - full text ed.: ISSN 1550-5111.
Indexed: A22, A26, C06, C07, C08, CA, CINAHL, E08, EMBASE, ExcerpMed, F09, FamI, G08, H11, H12, H13, I05, INI, MEDLINE, NurAb, P10, P16, P20, P22, P24, P30, P48, P53, P54, PQC, PsycholAb, R10, Reac, S08, S09, SCOPUS, T02.
—BLDSC (3487.451200), GNLM, IE, Infotrieve, Ingenta, INIST. **CCC.**
Published by: Lippincott Williams & Wilkins (Subsidiary of: Wolters Kluwer N.V.), Two Commerce Sq, 2001 Market St, Philadelphia, PA 19103. TEL 215-521-8300, FAX 215-521-8902, customerservice@lww.com, http://www.lww.com. Ed. Janet M Barber. Pub. Theresa M Steltzer. Adv. contact Diane Shapiro TEL 215-628-6538. Circ: 831.

➤ **CRITICAL TIMES.** *see* MEDICAL SCIENCES—Orthopedics And Traumatology

610.73 618.202 ZAF ISSN 0379-8577
RT14 CODEN: ASENEL
➤ **CURATIONIS**; accredited research journal of the Democratic Nursing Organisation of South Africa. Text in Afrikaans, English. 1977. q. adv. bk.rev. charts; illus. 88 p./no.; back issues avail. **Document type:** *Journal, Academic/Scholarly.* **Description:** Publishes accredited research articles.
Indexed: A22, C06, C07, C08, CINAHL, EMBASE, ExcerpMed, F09, INI, ISAP, MEDLINE, P30, R10, Reac, SCOPUS.
—BLDSC (3493.458000), GNLM, IE, Infotrieve, Ingenta.
Published by: Democratic Nursing Organisation of South Africa, PO Box 1280, Pretoria, 0001, South Africa. TEL 27-12-3432315, FAX 27-12-3445750, http://www.denosa.org.za. Eds. Bhungani ka Mzolo, Nelouise Geyer. Adv. contact Bhungani ka Mzolo. Circ: 600 (paid).

➤ **CURRENT NURSING IN GERIATRIC CARE.** *see* GERONTOLOGY AND GERIATRICS

➤ **CURRENT REVIEWS FOR PERIANESTHESIA NURSES.** *see* MEDICAL SCIENCES—Anaesthesiology

610.73 USA ISSN 1534-2778
CURTINCALLS. Text in English. 199?. m.
Published by: Metier Publications, 5932 Rapid Run Rd, Cincinnati, OH 45233. TEL 513-941-2888, 888-377-5828, FAX 513-941-3208. Ed., Pub. Leah Curtin.

610.73 USA
D N A REPORTER. (Delaware Nurses' Association) Text in English. 1968. q. looseleaf. USD 20 domestic; USD 30 foreign (effective 2008). adv. bk.rev. 24 p./no.; back issues avail.; reprints avail. **Document type:** *Newsletter, Trade.* **Description:** Covers issues and employment opportunities of interest to licensed nursing professionals.
Formerly (until 19??): Delaware Nurses' Association Reporter (0418-5412); Which superseded (in 1972): Delaware Nurse (0070-3281)
Related titles: Online - full text ed.
Indexed: C06, C07, C08, CINAHL, P30.
Published by: (Delaware Nurses Association), Arthur L. Davis Publishing Agency, Inc., 517 Washington St, PO Box 216, Cedar Falls, IA 50613. TEL 319-277-2414, 800-626-4081, FAX 319-277-4055, sales@aldpub.com, http://www.aldpub.com. Ed. Mark Miller. R&P Ruth Bashford. Adv. contact Jim Larson. B&W page USD 150; trim 7.25 x 9.5. Circ: 13,300.

DAGENS MEDICIN. *see* MEDICAL SCIENCES

610.73 USA
DAKOTA NURSE CONNECTION. Abbreviated title: D N C. Text in English. 19??. q. free to members (effective 2009). adv. **Document type:** *Magazine, Trade.* **Description:** Provides updated information on clinical practices, government affairs initiatives and helps to discover what best practices are being implemented, and provides insight into how healthcare providers are facing today's challenges.
Formerly (until 2002): South Dakota Board of Nursing. Newsletter
Related titles: Online - full text ed.: free (effective 2009).
Published by: (South Dakota Board of Nursing, North Dakota Board of Nursing), Publishing Concepts, Inc., 14109 Taylor Loop Rd, Little Rock, AR 72223. TEL 501-221-9986, 800-561-4686, FAX 501-225-3735, http://www.pcipublishing.com/. Adv. contact Randall Eden TEL 800-561-4686 ext 109. color page USD 2,370; trim 8.375 x 10.875. Circ: 52,000 (paid).

610.73 CHN ISSN 1006-6411
DANGDAI HUSHI/TODAY NURSE. Text in Chinese. 1993. m. USD 36 (effective 2009). **Document type:** *Journal, Academic/Scholarly.*
Related titles: Online - full text ed.
—East View.
Address: 30, Xiangya Lu, Changsha, 410006, China. TEL 86-731-4822290, FAX 86-731-4494236. **Dist. by:** China International Book Trading Corp, 35 Chegongzhuang Xilu, Haidian District, PO Box 399, Beijing 100044, China. TEL 86-10-68412045, FAX 86-10-68412023, cibtc@mail.cibtc.com.cn, http://www.cibtc.com.cn.

610.73 USA
DEAN'S NOTES. Text in English. 1984. 5/yr. back issues avail. **Document type:** *Newsletter, Trade.*
Related titles: Online - full text ed.: free (effective 2010).
Indexed: P24.
Published by: (National Student Nurses' Association), Jannetti Publications, Inc., E Holly Ave, PO Box 56, Pitman, NJ 08071. TEL 856-256-2300, contact@ajj.com. Ed. Carol A Fetters Andersen. Pub. Anthony J Jannetti.

610.73 USA ISSN 1944-0804
RM301.12
DELMAR NURSE'S DRUG HANDBOOK. Text in English. 1996. a. USD 41.95 per issue (effective 2010). **Document type:** *Handbook/Manual/Guide, Trade.* **Description:** Highlights prevention of medication errors and clinical accountability like no other drug resource, making it a trusted product for nursing students, practicing nurses, and other health care professionals.
Former titles (until 2009): P D R Nurse's Drug Handbook (1535-4601); (until 2000): P D R Nurse's Handbook (1094-4141)
Published by: Delmar Cengage Learning (Subsidiary of: Cengage Learning), 5 Maxwell Dr, Clifton Park, NY 12065-2919. TEL 518-348-2300.

610.73 616.5 USA ISSN 1945-760X
▼ ➤ **DERMATOLOGY NURSES' ASSOCIATION. JOURNAL.** Abbreviated title: J D N A. Text in English. 2009 (Jan.). bi-m. USD 273.51 domestic to institutions; USD 299 foreign to institutions (effective 2011). adv. back issues avail.; reprints avail. **Document type:** *Journal, Academic/Scholarly.* **Description:** Addresses dermatology professionals' needs and will focus on the key areas of interest and development touching all nursing and practice professionals working in the dermatology field.
Related titles: Online - full text ed.: ISSN 1945-7618.
Indexed: CA, T02.
—CCC.
Published by: (Dermatology Nurses' Association), Lippincott Williams & Wilkins (Subsidiary of: Wolters Kluwer N.V.), 530 Walnut St, Philadelphia, PA 19106. TEL 215-521-8300, FAX 215-521-8902, customerservice@lww.com, http://www.lww.com. Ed. Barbara Starr. Pub. Kathleen Gaffney. Adv. contact Paula Gould TEL 570-223-6640.

➤ **DIABETIC MEDICINE**; journal of diabetes UK. *see* MEDICAL SCIENCES—Endocrinology

➤ **DIABETIC MEDICINE ONLINE.** *see* MEDICAL SCIENCES—Endocrinology

➤ **DIALAESEN**; tidningen foer personal inom transplantation & njursjukvaard i Norden. *see* MEDICAL SCIENCES—Urology And Nephrology

610.736 616.12 ITA ISSN 1722-6759
DIBATTITO; giornale italiano di infermieristica cardiologica. Text in Multiple languages. 2003. 3/yr. **Document type:** *Journal, Academic/Scholarly.*
Published by: Societa Editrice Universo, Via Giovanni Battista Morgagni 1, Rome, RM 00161, Italy. TEL 39-06-44231171, FAX 39-06-4402033, amministrazione@seu-roma.it, http://www.seuroma.com.

610.73 DEU
DIE ROTKREUZSCHWESTER. Text in German. 1989. q. EUR 16; EUR 4 per issue (effective 2011). adv. **Document type:** *Magazine, Trade.*
Formerly (until 2007): Die Schwester
Published by: Verlag W. Waechter GmbH, Elsasser Str 41, Bremen, 28211, Germany. TEL 49-421-348420, FAX 49-421-3476766, info@waechter.de. Adv. contact James Huebner. Circ: 22,000.

610.73 USA ISSN 0730-4625
RT120.I5
DIMENSIONS OF CRITICAL CARE NURSING. Abbreviated title: D C C N. Text in English. 1982. bi-m. USD 295 domestic to institutions; USD 472 foreign to institutions (effective 2011). adv. illus. Index. back issues avail.; reprints avail. **Document type:** *Journal, Academic/Scholarly.* **Description:** Provides nurses relevant information and services to excel in critical care practice.
Related titles: Online - full text ed.: ISSN 1538-8646.
Indexed: A01, A02, A03, A08, A22, C06, C07, C08, C11, CA, CINAHL, EMBASE, ExcerpMed, FamI, H04, INI, MEDLINE, NurAb, P16, P20, P22, P24, P30, P48, P53, P54, PQC, R10, Reac, SCOPUS, T02.
—BLDSC (3588.471200), GNLM, IE, Infotrieve, Ingenta. **CCC.**
Published by: Lippincott Williams & Wilkins (Subsidiary of: Wolters Kluwer N.V.), Two Commerce Sq, 2001 Market St, Philadelphia, PA 19103. TEL 215-521-8300, FAX 215-521-8902, customerservice@lww.com, http://www.lww.com. Ed. Dr. Vickie A Miracle. Pub. Theresa M Steltzer. Adv. contact Sue Ryan. Circ: 919.

610.73 658.3 USA ISSN 1551-8418
THE DIRECTOR (CINCINNATI). Text in English. 199?. q. USD 35 to non-members; USD 10 per issue to non-members; free to members (effective 2011). adv. back issues avail. **Document type:** *Journal, Academic/Scholarly.* **Description:** Provides articles within selected topics and disease states.
Related titles: Online - full text ed.: free (effective 2011).
Indexed: EMBASE, ExcerpMed, MEDLINE, P30, SCOPUS.
—BLDSC (3590.390000).
Published by: National Association Directors of Nursing Administration in Long Term Care, 10101 Alliance Rd, #140, Cincinnati, OH 45242. TEL 800-222-0539, FAX 513-791-3699. Circ: 20,000.

362.102541 GBR ISSN 1755-490X
DIRECTORY OF COMMUNITY HEALTH SERVICES (YEARS). Text in English. 1980. a. GBP 75 per issue (effective 2010). adv. **Document type:** *Directory, Trade.* **Description:** Provides district nurses, health visitors, school health visitors, and midwives with information on all aspects of healthcare including contact details to make a referral, transfer or discharge.
Former titles (until 200?): Directory of Community Nursing (Years) (1747-2652); (until 2000): Handbook and Directory of Community Nursing
Published by: Pavilion Publishing, PO Box 100, Chichester, W Sussex PO18 8HD, United Kingdom. TEL 44-1243-576444, FAX 44-1243-576456, info@pavpub.com, http://www.pavpub.com/. Ed. Angharad Truelove.

DIRECTORY OF FUNDING SOURCES (COMPUTER FILE). *see* EDUCATION—Higher Education

610.73 USA ISSN 1062-8835
RG950
DIRECTORY OF NURSE-MIDWIFERY PRACTICES (YEAR). Text in English. a. free to members (effective 2007). adv. **Document type:** *Directory.* **Description:** Lists nurse-midwifery practices.
Formerly: Registry of Nurse-Midwifery Services and Practices
Published by: American College of Nurse-Midwives, 8403 Colesville Rd, Ste 1550, Silver Spring, MD 20910. TEL 240-485-1800, FAX 240-485-1818, http://www.amcbmidwife.org. Ed. John Boggess. Circ: 6,000.

610.73 617.1 USA ISSN 1540-2487
➤ **DISASTER MANAGEMENT & RESPONSE.** Abbreviated title: D M R. Text in English. 1995. q. adv. back issues avail. **Document type:** *Journal, Academic/Scholarly.* **Description:** Focuses on topics of key interest to readers and are clinically relevant to trauma nurses.
Formerly (until 2002): International Journal of Trauma Nursing (1075-4210)
Related titles: Online - full text ed.: ISSN 1540-2495.
Indexed: A22, A26, C06, C07, C08, CA, CINAHL, E01, H12, I05, INI, P30, SCOPUS, T02.
—BLDSC (3595.459700), IE, Ingenta. **CCC.**
Published by: (Emergency Nurses Association, Trauma Nursing Coalition), Mosby, Inc. (Subsidiary of: Elsevier Health Sciences), 1600 John F. Kennedy Blvd, Ste 1800, Philadelphia, PA 19103. TEL 215-239-3900, 800-523-1649, FAX 215-239-3990, elspcs@elsevier.com, http://www.us.elsevierhealth.com.
Co-sponsors: Association of Rehabilitation Nurses; American Association of Critical Care Nurses; Air and Surface Transport Nurses Association; American Association of Nurse Anesthetists; Emergency Nurses Association; Association of periOperative Registered Nurses, Inc.

610.73 NZL ISSN 1174-7579
THE DISSECTOR. Variant title: New Zealand Nurses Organisation. Perioperative Nurses College. Journal. Text in English. 1974. q. free to members (effective 2008). **Document type:** *Journal, Academic/Scholarly.*
Indexed: C06, C07, C08, CINAHL.
—BLDSC (3598.865550).
Published by: (Perioperative Nurses College of New Zealand Nurses Organisation), AdVantage Publishing Ltd., PO Box 299, Kumeu, New Zealand. TEL 64-9-4165013, FAX 64-9-4165308. Ed. Kathryn Fraser. Pub. Michael Esdaile.

610.73 USA
DISTRICT OF COLUMBIA NURSE. Text in English. 2003. q. free to members (effective 2009). **Document type:** *Journal, Trade.*
Published by: (District of Columbia Board of Nursing), Publishing Concepts, Inc., 14109 Taylor Loop Rd, Little Rock, AR 72223. TEL 501-221-9986, 800-561-4686, FAX 501-225-3735, http://www.thinkaboutitnursing.com/, http://www.pcipublishing.com/.

610.73 ESP ISSN 1136-2243
DOCUMENTOS ENFERMERIA. Text in Spanish. 1996. q. **Document type:** *Journal, Academic/Scholarly.*
Published by: Ilustre Colegio Oficial de Enfermeria de Huelva, Calle Berdigon 35, 1o, Huelva, Spain. TEL 34-959-540904, FAX 34-959-256270, coleg21@enfermundi.com, http://www.colegiooficialdeenfermeriadehuelva.es/.

610.73 CAN
THE DOGWOOD NEWS. Text in English. 1957. q. free to members. **Description:** Includes information for the association general membership, as well as, pertinent articles relating to Licensed Practical Nurses practicing in the health care field, provincially and nationally.
Published by: Licenced Practical Nurses Association of British Columbia, 3302 McIver Rd, Westbank, BC V4T 1G2, Canada. TEL 604-768-2482. Ed. Barry E Phillips.

DRUG INFORMATION HANDBOOK FOR NURSING. *see* PHARMACY AND PHARMACOLOGY

610.7361 CAN ISSN 1497-3715
DYNAMICS. Text in English. 1990. q. CAD 64.20 membership (effective 2005). adv. **Document type:** *Journal, Trade.* **Description:** Represents nurses in clinical practice, education, research and administration within adult, neonatal and pediatric critical care in Canada.
Formerly (until 2000): Canadian Association of Critical Care Nurses. Official Journal (1201-2580)
Indexed: A26, C06, C07, C08, CINAHL, CPerl, EMBASE, ExcerpMed, H12, I05, INI, MEDLINE, P30, R10, Reac, SCOPUS.
—BLDSC (3637.143083), IE, Ingenta. **CCC.**
Published by: (Canadian Association of Critical Care Nurses), Pappin Communications, The Victoria Centre, 84 Isabella St, Pembroke, ON K8A 5S5, Canada. TEL 613-735-0952, FAX 613-735-7983, info@pappin.com, http://www.pappin.com. Ed. Paula Price. Pub. Bruce Pappin. Adv. contact Heather Coughlin. B&W page CAD 870, color page CAD 1,420. Circ: 1,000. **Subscr. to:** CACCN, P O Box 22006, London, ON N6C 4N0, Canada. TEL 519-649-5284.

610.736 USA ISSN 1096-4304
E D NURSING. (Emergency Department) Text in English. 1997. m. USD 299 combined subscription (print & online eds.); USD 50 per issue (effective 2010). **Document type:** *Newsletter, Trade.* **Description:** Provides emergency department nurses with solutions for difficult procedures, uncooperative patients, and other tough clinical situations they face on a daily basis.
Related titles: Online - full text ed.: ISSN 1945-0761.
Indexed: A26, C06, C07, C08, CINAHL, G08, H11, H12, I05, P20, P24, P48, P54, PQC, SCOPUS.
—BLDSC (3659.744950). **CCC.**
Published by: A H C Media LLC (Subsidiary of: Thomson Corporation, Healthcare Information Group), 3525 Piedmont Rd, NE, Bldg 6, Ste 400, Atlanta, GA 30305. TEL 404-262-7436, 800-688-2421, FAX 404-262-7837, 800-284-3291, customerservice@ahcmedia.com, http://www.ahcmedia.com/. Pub. Brenda L Mooney TEL 404-262-5403. **Subscr. to:** PO Box 105109, Atlanta, GA 30348. TEL 404-262-5476, FAX 404-262-5560.

610.73 ESP
E-DUCARE 21. Text in Spanish. 2003. m. back issues avail. **Document type:** *Magazine, Academic/Scholarly.*
Media: Online - full text.
Published by: Difusion Avances de Enfermeria, Poligono Industrial Olivral, Parcela 1o., Bloque A, Nave 3 Carretera III Km. 330, Ribarroja, Valencia, 46394, Spain. TEL 34-96-1667384, correo-metas@enfermeria21.com, http://www.enfermeria21.com/index.php.

610.73 FRA ISSN 1877-7848
▼ **E M C - SAVOIRS ET SOINS INFIRMIERS.** (Encyclopedie Medico Chirurgicale) Text in French. 2009. q. **Document type:** *Journal, Academic/Scholarly.*
—**CCC.**
Published by: Elsevier Masson (Subsidiary of: Elsevier Health Sciences), 62 Rue Camille Desmoulins, Issy les Moulineaux, Cedex 92442, France. TEL 33-1-71165500, FAX 33-1-71165600, infos@elsevier-masson.fr.

L'ECHO DU R I I R. (Regroupement des Infirmieres et Infirmiers Retraitees) *see* SOCIAL SERVICES AND WELFARE

ELI'S HOSPICE INSIDER. *see* HEALTH FACILITIES AND ADMINISTRATION

610.73 GBR ISSN 1354-5752
EMERGENCY NURSE. Text in English. 1993. 10/yr. GBP 200 in Europe to institutions; GBP 225 elsewhere to institutions (effective 2011). adv. back issues avail. **Document type:** *Journal, Trade.* **Description:** Contains articles on clinical innovations and practice guidelines, as well as coverage of management and education issues.
Related titles: Online - full text ed.: GBP 200 to institutions (effective 2011).
Indexed: A01, A02, A03, A08, A26, B28, C06, C07, C08, C11, CA, CINAHL, E08, EMBASE, ExcerpMed, G08, H04, H11, H12, I05, INI, MEDLINE, P16, P20, P22, P24, P30, P48, P53, P54, PQC, R10, Reac, S09, SCOPUS, T02.
—BLDSC (3733.192900), IE, Infotrieve, Ingenta. **CCC.**
Published by: (R C N Accident & Emergency Nursing Association), R C N Publishing Co. (Subsidiary of: B M J Group), The Heights, 59-65 Lowlands Rd, Harrow, Middx HA1 3AW, United Kingdom. TEL 44-20-84231066, FAX 44-20-84239196, advertising@rcnpublishing.co.uk, http://www.rcnpublishing.co.uk. Ed. Jean Gray. Adv. contact Neil Hobson TEL 44-20-88723123. page GBP 1,705; trim 216 x 279. Circ: 5,629.

ENDONURSE; the authority for the continuing advancement of endoscopic nursing. *see* MEDICAL SCIENCES—Endocrinology

610.73 ESP ISSN 1988-348X
ENE; revista de enfermeria. Variant title: Revista Ene de Enfermeria. Text in Spanish. 2007. s-a. free (effective 2011). **Document type:** *Journal, Academic/Scholarly.*
Media: Online - full text.
Published by: Enfermeros.org Ed. Cristina Toledo Rosell.

610.73 MEX
ENFERMERAS. Text in Spanish. 1953. 3/yr. charts; illus.; stat. back issues avail. **Document type:** *Journal, Trade.* **Description:** Covers nursing research, practice and news on events of interest to nurses. Presents scientific and technical advances in the Mexican nursing field.
Former titles: Colegio Nacional de Enfermeras. Revista (0045-7329); Asociacion Mexicana de Enfermeras. Revista
Indexed: INI, P30.
Published by: Colegio Nacional de Enfermeras, Obrero Mundial 229, Mexico City, DF 03100, Mexico. TEL 52-55-369955, http://www.cnemex.org. Ed. Ezequiel Canela. Pub., Adv. contact Bertha Delgado. R&P Josefina Reyes Gonzalez.

610.73 CHL ISSN 0378-6285
ENFERMERIA. Text in Spanish. 1965. q. back issues avail. **Document type:** *Journal, Academic/Scholarly.*
Related titles: Online - full text ed.
Indexed: P30.
Published by: Colegio de Enfermeras de Chile, A.G., Miraflores, 563, Santiago, Chile. TEL 56-2-6398556, FAX 56-2-6380218.

610.73 CRI ISSN 1409-4568
RT7.C7
ENFERMERIA ACTUAL EN COSTA RICA. Text in Spanish. s-a. free (effective 2011). back issues avail. **Document type:** *Journal, Academic/Scholarly.*
Media: Online - full text.
Published by: Universidad de Costa Rica, Escuela de Enfermeria, San Pedro de Monste de Oca, San Jose, Costa Rica. TEL 506-2074445, FAX 506-2565360, revenf@cariari.ucr.ac.cr, http://www.revenf.ucr.ac.cr/. Ed. Ana Guzman Aguilar.

610.73 ESP ISSN 1130-8621
ENFERMERIA CLINICA. Text in Spanish. 1990. bi-m. EUR 84.68 combined subscription to individuals print & online eds.; EUR 214.36 combined subscription to institutions print & online eds. (effective 2009). **Document type:** *Journal, Academic/Scholarly.* **Description:** Studies clinical nursing to promote a solution to the health problems of individuals, families and communities. Contributes to the theoretical and practical development of the profession in Spain.
Related titles: Online - full text ed.: ISSN 1579-2013. 1998. EUR 70.54 (effective 2009) (from ScienceDirect).
Indexed: A22, C06, C07, C08, CINAHL, EMBASE, ExcerpMed, MEDLINE, P30, R10, Reac, SCOPUS.
—BLDSC (3747.900700), IE. **CCC.**
Published by: Elsevier Doyma (Subsidiary of: Elsevier Health Sciences), Traversa de Gracia 17-21, Barcelona, 08021, Spain. TEL 34-932-418800, FAX 34-932-419020, editorial@elsevier.com. Ed. T. Moreno Casbas. Adv. contact Anna Pahissa. Circ: 2,500.

610.73 ESP ISSN 1698-4242
ENFERMERIA COMUNITARIA. Text in Multiple languages. 2005. s-a. **Document type:** *Journal, Trade.*
Related titles: Online - full text ed.: ISSN 1699-0641.
Published by: Fundacion Index, Calle Horno de Marina 2, Granada, 18001, Spain. http://www.index-f.com/fundacion.php.

610.73 616.12 ESP ISSN 1575-4146
ENFERMERIA EN CARDIOLOGIA. Text in Spanish. 1994. 3/yr. back issues avail. **Document type:** *Journal, Academic/Scholarly.*
Formerly (until 1999): Asociacion Espanola de Enfermeria en Cardiologia. Boletin Informativo (1134-8054)
Related titles: Online - full text ed.
Published by: Asociacion Espanola de Enfermeria en Cardiologia, Casa del Corazon, C/ Nuestra Senora de Guadalupe 5-7, Madrid, 28028, Spain. TEL 34-91-7242375, FAX 34-91-7242371, secre@enfermeriaencardiologia.com, http://www.enfermeriaencardiologia.com. Circ: 1,200.

610.73 ESP ISSN 1695-6141
R71
ENFERMERIA GLOBAL; revista electronica semestral de enfermeria. Text in Spanish. 2002. 3/yr. free (effective 2011). **Document type:** *Journal, Academic/Scholarly.*
Media: Online - full text.
Published by: Universidad de Murcia, Servicio de Publicaciones, Edificio Saavedra Fajardo, C/ Actor Isidoro Maiquez 9, Murcia, 30007, Spain. TEL 34-968-363887, FAX 34-968-363414, vgm@um.es, http://www.um.es/publicaciones/.

610.73 ESP ISSN 0214-0128
ENFERMERIA INTEGRAL. Text in Spanish. 1977. q. **Document type:** *Journal, Academic/Scholarly.*
Former titles (until 1985): Blanc (0214-011X); (until 1982): Inquietudes Profesionales (0214-0101); (until 1982): Objectivos Profesionales (0214-0098); (until 1981): Objectivos (0214-008X)
Published by: Colegio Enfermeria de Valencia, Av Blasco Ibanez 64, Valencia, 46021, Spain. TEL 34-96-3937015, FAX 34-96-3930428, info@enfervalencia.org, http://www.enfervalencia.org.

610.73 ESP ISSN 1130-2399
➤ **ENFERMERIA INTENSIVA.** Text in Spanish. 1988. q. EUR 65.81 combined subscription to individuals print & online eds.; EUR 166.61 combined subscription to institutions print & online eds. (effective 2009). bk.rev. index. back issues avail.; reprints avail. **Document type:** *Journal, Academic/Scholarly.*
Related titles: Online - full text ed.: ISSN 1578-1291. 1996. EUR 54.82 (effective 2009) (from ScienceDirect).
Indexed: A22, C06, C07, C08, CINAHL, EMBASE, ExcerpMed, IME, INI, MEDLINE, P30, R10, Reac, SCOPUS.
—BLDSC (3747.900800), IE, Infotrieve, Ingenta. **CCC.**
Published by: (Sociedad Espanola de Enfermeria Intensiva y Unidades Coronarias), Elsevier Doyma (Subsidiary of: Elsevier Health Sciences), Traversa de Gracia 17-21, Barcelona, 08021, Spain. TEL 34-932-418800, FAX 34-932-419020, editorial@elsevier.com. Ed. J.C. Munos Camargo. R&P Monica Barnes. Adv. contact Jose Antonio Hernandez. Circ: 1,800.

610.73 ESP ISSN 1576-5520
ENFERMERIA ONCOLOGICA. Variant title: Revista de Enfermeria Oncologica. Text in Spanish; Abstracts in English, Spanish. 1986. q. free to members (effective 2009). abstr. back issues avail. **Document type:** *Journal, Academic/Scholarly.*
Related titles: E-mail ed.
Published by: Sociedad Espanola de Enfermeria Oncologica, Apdo Postal 46-351, Madrid, Spain. info@seeo.org.

610.73 PRT ISSN 1646-9607
ENFORMACAO. Text in Portuguese. 2008. 3/yr. **Document type:** *Newsletter, Trade.*
Published by: Associacao Cientifica dos Enfermeiros, Centro Hospitalar de Lisboa Central, Hospital S Jose Lisboa-Pena, Rua Jose Antonio Serrano, Lisbon, 1150-199, Portugal. TEL 351-218-841000, FAX 351-218-841023, http://www.acenfermeiros.pt.

610.73 BRA ISSN 1414-8145
ESCOLA ANNA NERY REVISTA DE ENFERMAGEM/ANNA NERY SCHOOL JOURNAL OF NURSING/ESCUELA ANNA NERY REVISTA DE ENFERMERIA. Text in Portuguese, Spanish. 1997. q. **Document type:** *Journal, Academic/Scholarly.*
Related titles: Online - full text ed.: ISSN 2177-9465. free (effective 2011).
Indexed: C06, C07, C08, CINAHL.
Published by: Universidade Federal do Rio de Janeiro, Escola Anna Nery, Rua Alfonso Cavalcanti 275, Cidade Nova, Rio de Janeiro, 20211-110, Brazil. Ed. Antonio Jose de Almeida Filho.

610.73 ESP ISSN 1139-837X
ESCUELA UNIVERSITARIA DE ENFERMERIA "LA FE". REVISTA. Text in Spanish. 1998. a. back issues avail. **Document type:** *Journal, Academic/Scholarly.*
Published by: (Universitat de Valencia, Escuela Universitaria de Enfermeria "La Fe"), Generalitat Valenciana, Conselleria de Sanitat, Avda Blasco Ibanez 17, Valencia, 46010, Spain.

610.73 CAN ISSN 1910-7838
ETUDE SUR LES PERMIS D'EXERCICE DE LA PROFESSION D'INFIRMIERE DELIVRES. Text in French. 1999. a. CAD 15 per issue to members; CAD 18 per issue to non-members (effective 2006). **Document type:** *Journal, Trade.*
Published by: Ordre des Infirmieres et Infirmiers du Quebec/Order of Nurses of Quebec, 4200 Dorchester Blvd W, Montreal, PQ H3Z 1V4, Canada. TEL 514-935-2501, 800-363-6048, FAX 514-935-1799, http://www.oiiq.org.

610.73 FRA ISSN 1285-6959
ETUDIANTS I F S I. (Institut de Formation en Soins Infirmiers) Text in French. 1997. irreg. **Document type:** *Monographic series, Academic/Scholarly.*
Related titles: Series: Processus Physiopathologiques. ISSN 2109-7208. 2010.
Published by: Editions Lamarre (Subsidiary of: Wolters Kluwer France), 1 Rue Eugene et Armand Peugeot, Rueil Malmaison, 92500, France. TEL 33-1-76733000, FAX 33-1-76734857, contact@espaceinfirmier.com, http://www.espaceinfirmier.com.

610.73 616.462 GBR ISSN 1551-7853
➤ **EUROPEAN DIABETES NURSING.** Abbreviated title: E D N. Text in English. 2004 (Fall). 3/yr. GBP 93 in United Kingdom to institutions; EUR 109 in Europe to institutions; USD 182 elsewhere to institutions; GBP 108 combined subscription in United Kingdom to institutions (print & online eds.); EUR 126 combined subscription in Europe to institutions (print & online eds.); USD 209 combined subscription elsewhere to institutions (print & online eds.) (effective 2012). adv. back issues avail.; reprint service avail. from PSC. **Document type:** *Journal, Academic/Scholarly.* **Description:** Aims to embrace clinical practice, policy, research and systems of care specifically for nurses who work in diabetes across Europe.
Related titles: Online - full text ed.: ISSN 1551-7861. GBP 93 in United Kingdom to institutions; EUR 109 in Europe to institutions; USD 182 elsewhere to institutions (effective 2012).
Indexed: B28, C06, C07, C08, CA, CINAHL, P03, PsycInfo, SCOPUS, T02.
—BLDSC (3829.689223), IE. **CCC.**
Published by: (Federation of European Nurses in Diabetes), John Wiley & Sons Ltd. (Subsidiary of: John Wiley & Sons, Inc.), 1-7 Oldlands Way, PO Box 808, Bognor Regis, West Sussex PO21 9FF, United Kingdom. TEL 44-1865-778315, FAX 44-1243-843232, cs-journals@wiley.com, http://eu.wiley.com/WileyCDA/. **Subscr. to:** 1-7 Oldlands Way, PO Box 809, Bognor Regis, West Sussex PO21 9FG, United Kingdom. TEL 44-1865-778054, cs-agency@wiley.com.

610.736 616.1 NLD ISSN 1474-5151
RC674 CODEN: EJCNAM
➤ **EUROPEAN JOURNAL OF CARDIOVASCULAR NURSING.** Text in English. 2002. 4/yr. EUR 308 in Europe to institutions; JPY 40,800 in Japan to institutions; USD 345 elsewhere to institutions (effective 2012). **Document type:** *Journal, Academic/Scholarly.* **Description:** Covers the broad field of cardiovascular nursing in chronic and acute care, pediatric cardiology, congenital heart disease, cardiac rehabilitation, primary and secondary prevention, heart failure, acute coronary syndromes, interventional cardiology, and cardiac care.
Related titles: Online - full text ed.: ISSN 1873-1953 (from IngentaConnect, ScienceDirect).
Indexed: A01, A03, A08, A26, B28, C06, C07, C08, CA, CINAHL, EMBASE, ExcerpMed, H12, I05, MEDLINE, P30, R10, Reac, SCI, SCOPUS, SSCI, T02, W07.
—BLDSC (3829.725660), IE, Ingenta. **CCC.**
Published by: (European Society of Cardiology FRA), Elsevier BV (Subsidiary of: Elsevier Science & Technology), Radarweg 29, PO Box 211, Amsterdam, 1000 AE, Netherlands. TEL 31-20-4853911, FAX 31-20-4852457, JournalsCustomerServiceEMEA@elsevier.com, http://www.elsevier.nl. Ed. T Jaarsma.

610.73 616.9 GBR ISSN 1462-3889
RC266
➤ **EUROPEAN JOURNAL OF ONCOLOGY NURSING.** Abbreviated title: E J O N. Text in English. 1997. 5/yr. EUR 557 in Europe to institutions; JPY 59,900 in Japan to institutions; USD 494 elsewhere to institutions (effective 2012). adv. bk.rev. abstr.; bibl. 72 p./no. 2 cols./p.; back issues avail.; reprints avail. **Document type:** *Journal, Academic/Scholarly.* **Description:** Discusses clinical and experimental trends and techniques in nursing for cancer-care patients.
Formerly (until 1998): Journal of Cancer Nursing (1364-9825)
Related titles: Online - full text ed.: ISSN 1532-2122 (from ScienceDirect).
Indexed: A22, A26, ASSIA, B21, B28, C06, C07, C08, CA, CINAHL, CurCont, E01, EMBASE, ExcerpMed, H12, I05, MEDLINE, OGFA, P03, P30, PsycInfo, R10, Reac, SCI, SCOPUS, SSCI, T02, W07.
—BLDSC (3829.733100), IE, Infotrieve, Ingenta. **CCC.**
Published by: (European Oncology Nursing Society BEL), Churchill Livingstone (Subsidiary of: Elsevier Health Sciences), The Blvd, Langford Ln, Kidlington, OX5 1GB, United Kingdom. TEL 44-1865-843434, FAX 44-1865-843970, directenquiries@elsevier.com, http://www.elsevierhealth.com/imprint.jsp?iid=9. Ed. Alexander Molassiotis. Adv. contact Sarah Jane Cahill TEL 44-20-74244538. Circ: 293.

610.73 GBR ISSN 1367-6539
RT1
EVIDENCE - BASED NURSING; an international digest of the evidence for nursing practice. Abbreviated title: E B N. Text in English. 1997. q. GBP 206 to institutions; GBP 258 combined subscription to institutions small FTE (print & online eds.) (effective 2011). adv. back issues avail.; reprints avail. **Document type:** *Journal, Academic/Scholarly.* **Description:** Designed to help nurses take their clinical decisions on the best current clinical evidence.
Related titles: E-mail ed.; Online - full text ed.: ISSN 1468-9618. 1998. GBP 212 to institutions small FTE (effective 2011).
Indexed: A01, A03, A08, A22, A26, B28, C06, C07, C08, CA, CINAHL, E08, EMBASE, ExcerpMed, G08, H11, H12, I05, MEDLINE, P20, P22, P24, P30, P48, P54, PQC, R10, Reac, S09, SCOPUS, T02.
—BLDSC (3831.037300), IE, Infotrieve, Ingenta. **CCC.**
Published by: B M J Group, BMA House, Tavistock Sq, London, WC1H 9JR, United Kingdom. TEL 44-20-73836373, FAX 44-20-73836668, http://group.bmj.com. Ed. Alison Twycross. Pub. Allison Lang TEL 44-20-73836212. Adv. contact Nick Gray TEL 44-20-73836386. Circ: 10,900. **Co-publisher:** R C N Publishing Co.

610.73 ESP ISSN 1697-638X
EVIDENTIA; revista de enfermeria basada en la evidencia. Text in Spanish. 2004. 3/yr. **Document type:** *Magazine, Trade.*
Media: Online - full text.
Published by: Fundacion Index, Calle Horno de Marina 2, Granada, 18001, Spain. http://www.index-f.com/fundacion.php.

610.7 JPN ISSN 0911-0194
EXPERT NURSE/EKISUPATO NASU. Text in Japanese. 1985. m. **Document type:** *Magazine, Trade.*
Published by: Shogakukan Inc., 3-1 Hitotsubashi 2-chome, Chiyoda-ku, Tokyo, 101-8001, Japan. TEL 81-3-3230-5211, FAX 81-3-3264-8471, http://www.shogakukan.co.jp.

610.73 CAN ISSN 1911-5288
F I I Q WOMEN'S NETWORK. LE RESEAU. Text in English. 2005. irreg. **Document type:** *Monographic series, Trade.*
Related titles: French ed.: Reseau des Femmes de la F I I Q. Le Reseau. ISSN 1710-9841.
Published by: Federation Interprofessionnelle de la Sante du Quebec, 1260 Blvd. Lebourgneuf, Bureau 300, Quebec, PQ G2K 2G2, Canada. TEL 418-626-2226, 800-463-6770, FAX 418-626-2111, info@fiqsante.qc.ca, http://www.fiqsante.qc.ca.

610.73 CAN ISSN 1914-2609
F I Q EN ACTION (ENGLISH EDITION). (Federation Interprofessionnelle de la Sante du Quebec) Variant title: En Action. Text in English. 1988. irreg. **Document type:** *Newsletter, Trade.*
Formerly (until 2006): F I I Q en Action (0838-4207)
Related titles: ◆ French ed.: F I Q en Action (French Edition). ISSN 1914-2595.
Published by: Federation Interprofessionnelle de la Sante du Quebec, 1260 Blvd. Lebourgneuf, Bureau 300, Quebec, PQ G2K 2G2, Canada. TEL 418-626-2226, 800-463-6770, FAX 418-626-2111, info@fiqsante.qc.ca.

610.73 CAN ISSN 1914-2595
F I Q EN ACTION (FRENCH EDITION). Variant title: En Action. Text in French. 1988. irreg. **Document type:** *Newsletter, Trade.*
Formerly (until 2006): F I I Q en Action (0838-4207)
Related titles: ◆ English ed.: F I Q en Action (English Edition). ISSN 1914-2609.
Published by: Federation Interprofessionnelle de la Sante du Quebec, 1260 Blvd. Lebourgneuf, Bureau 300, Quebec, PQ G2K 2G2, Canada. TEL 418-626-2226, 800-463-6770, FAX 418-626-2111, info@fiqsante.qc.ca.

610.73 BEL ISSN 1379-7476
F N I B FLASH-INFO. (Federation Nationale des Infirmieres de Belgique) Text in French. 1921. bi-m. adv. illus.
Former titles (until 2000): F N I B - Info (0774-935X); (until 1987): Flash-informations (0771-8187); (until 1983): F N I B - N VB V (0301-0813); (until 1971): Infirmiere (0019-9591)
Indexed: EMBASE, ExcerpMed, MEDLINE, P30, R10, Reac, SCOPUS.
—GNLM.
Published by: Federation Nationale des Infirmieres de Belgique, Rue de la Source 18, Brussels, 1060, Belgium. TEL 32-75-365153, FAX 32-75-365153, http://www.fnib.be. Ed. Yves Mengal.

610.73 NOR ISSN 1502-4946
F O U - RAPPORT. (Forsknings- og Utviklingsarbeid) Text in Norwegian. 1996. irreg., latest vol.13, 2006. back issues avail. **Document type:** *Monographic series, Academic/Scholarly.*
Formerly (until 2000): Diakonissehjemmets Hoegskole. Publikasjon (1501-2328)
Related titles: Online - full text ed.: ISSN 0809-7062. 2004.
Published by: Diakonissehjemmets Hoegskole/Bergen Deaconess University College, Ulriksdal 10, Bergen, 5009, Norway. TEL 47-55-979630, dsh@bergendsh.no.

610.73 362.23 USA ISSN 1559-9981
FAMILIES OF LOVED ONES. Text in English. 2005 (Win.). q. USD 12 (effective 2005). adv. **Document type:** *Magazine, Consumer.* **Description:** Aims to engage the families, friends, professionals and all of those who care and interact with long term care residents to the fullest extent possible.
Published by: Cantwell Media, LLC, 310 Grant Ave, Dumont, NJ 07628. TEL 201-694-1860, http://www.cantwellmedia.com. Ed. Rene Cantwell. adv.: color page USD 2,455; trim 7.5 x 10.

610.73 NLD ISSN 1573-9651
FEITEN OVER VERPLEEGKUNDIGE EN VERZORGENDE BEROEPEN IN NEDERLAND. Text in Dutch. 1997. a. price varies.
Formerly (until 2001): Feiten over Verpleging en Verzorging in Nederland (1567-3235)
Published by: Landelijk Expertisecentrum Verpleging en Verzorging, Bernadottelaan 11, Postbus 3135, Utrecht, 3502 GC, Netherlands. TEL 31-30-2919039.

610.73 615.82 ESP ISSN 0211-5638
➤ **FISIOTERAPIA**; revista de salud, discapacidad y terapeutica fisica. Text in Spanish; Summaries in English. 1969. q. EUR 89.94 combined subscription domestic print & online eds.; EUR 227.70 combined subscription foreign print & online eds. (effective 2009). bk.rev. index. back issues avail.; reprints avail. **Document type:** *Journal, Academic/Scholarly.*
Related titles: Online - full text ed.: ISSN 1578-2107. 1996. EUR 74.92 (effective 2009) (from ScienceDirect); ◆ Supplement(s): Fisioterapia. Monografico. ISSN 1578-2069.
Indexed: C06, C07, C08, CINAHL, SCOPUS.
—BLDSC (3945.580000), IE. **CCC.**
Published by: (Sociedad Espanola de Fisioterapia), Elsevier Doyma (Subsidiary of: Elsevier Health Sciences), Traversa de Gracia 17-21, Barcelona, 08021, Spain. TEL 34-932-418800, FAX 34-932-419020, editorial@elsevier.com. Ed. R. Fernandez Cervantes. Circ: 9,300.

610.73 615.82 ESP ISSN 1578-2069
FISIOTERAPIA. MONOGRAFICO. Text in Spanish. 199?. s-a. back issues avail. **Document type:** *Monographic series, Academic/Scholarly.*
Related titles: Print ed.: ISSN 1578-2050. 2000; ◆ Supplement to: Fisioterapia. ISSN 0211-5638.
Published by: Elsevier Doyma (Subsidiary of: Elsevier Health Sciences), Traversa de Gracia 17-21, Barcelona, 08021, Spain. TEL 34-932-418800, FAX 34-932-419020, editorial@elsevier.com, http://www.elsevier.es/.

610.73 USA
FITNE HEALTHNET. (Fuld Institute for Technology in Nursing Education) Text in English. irreg.
Media: Online - full text.
Published by: FITNE, Inc., 5 Depot St, Athens, OH 45701. TEL 740-592-2511, 800-691-8480, FAX 740-592-2650, info@FITNE.net, http://www.FITNE.net.

610.73 USA ISSN 0015-4199
CODEN: STALDT
FLORIDA NURSE. Text in English. 1952. q. looseleaf. USD 20; free to members (effective 2008). adv. bk.rev. illus. 36 p./no.; Supplement avail.; back issues avail.; reprints avail. **Document type:** *Newsletter, Trade.* **Description:** Covers issues and employment opportunities of interest to licensed nursing professionals.
Related titles: Online - full text ed.
Indexed: A01, A02, A03, A08, AMED, C06, C07, C08, C11, CA, CINAHL, EMBASE, ExcerpMed, H04, INI, MEDLINE, P20, P22, P24, P30, P34, P48, P54, PQC, R10, Reac, SCOPUS, T02.
—BLDSC (3956.080000), GNLM.
Published by: (Florida Nurses Association), Arthur L. Davis Publishing Agency, Inc., 517 Washington St, PO Box 216, Cedar Falls, IA 50613. TEL 319-277-2414, 800-626-4081, FAX 319-277-4055, sales@aldpub.com, http://www.aldpub.com. Eds. Leah Nash, Mark Miller. R&P Paula Massey. Adv. contact Jim Larson. Circ: 185,000 (free).

610.73 SWE ISSN 0283-913X
FOERETAGSSKOETERSKAN. Text in Swedish. 1957. q. SEK 250 (effective 2000). adv. **Document type:** *Newsletter, Trade.*
Supersedes: Industriskoeterskan
Published by: Riksfoereningen foer Foeretagsskoeterskor, c/o Birgitta Langlet Soederholm, Loevdalsvaegen 5A, Saltsjoe-Boo, 13241, Sweden. Ed., Pub., R&P Birgitta Langlet Soederholm TEL 46-8-7158530.

610.73 GBR ISSN 1474-9408
FOUNDATION OF NURSING STUDIES NEWSLETTER. Text in English. bi-m. free.
Media: Online - full content.
Indexed: C06, C07, C08, CINAHL.
Published by: Foundation of Nursing Studies, 32 Buckingham Palace Rd, London, SW1W 0RE, United Kingdom. TEL 44-20-72335750, FAX 44-20-72335759, kate.sanders@fons.org, http://www.fons.org.

610.73 CAN ISSN 1922-9232
FRONT LINES. Text in English. 2001. bi-m. free to members (effective 2010). back issues avail. **Document type:** *Newsletter, Trade.*
Related titles: Online - full text ed.: free (effective 2010).
Published by: Ontario Nurses' Association, 85 Grenville St, Ste 400, Toronto, ON M5S 3A2, Canada. TEL 416-964-8833, 800-387-5580, FAX 416-964-8864, 866-964-8864, onamail@ona.org. Ed. Ruth Featherstone.

610.73 USA ISSN 0016-2116
F452
FRONTIER NURSING SERVICE QUARTERLY BULLETIN. Text in English. 1925. q. USD 6 to individuals; USD 10 to institutions (effective 2000). adv. illus. back issues avail. **Document type:** *Newsletter.* **Description:** Provides an overview of the Frontier Nursing Service of Eastern Kentucky.
Related titles: Microform ed.: (from PQC); Online - full text ed.
Indexed: A22, C06, C07, C08, CA, CINAHL, INI, P24, P30, P48, PQC, SCOPUS, T02.
—BLDSC (4041.200000), GNLM.
Published by: Frontier Nursing Service, Inc., 132 FNS Dr, Wendover, KY 41775. TEL 606-672-2317, FAX 606-672-3022, fnstours@yahoo.com, http://www.frontiernursing.org. Ed., R&P Barb Gibson. Circ: 8,000.

610.73 GHA ISSN 0855-0948
G R M A NEWS. (Ghana Registered Midwives Association) Text in English. 1988. q. **Document type:** *Newsletter, Trade.*
Indexed: P30.
Published by: Ghana Registered Midwives Association (G R M A), PO Box 147, Accra, Ghana. TEL 233-21-779348.

GASTROINTESTINAL NURSING. *see* MEDICAL SCIENCES—Gastroenterology

610.73 JPN ISSN 0389-8326
GEKKAN NASHINGU/JAPANESE JOURNAL OF NURSING. Text in Japanese. 1981. m. JPY 17,400; JPY 1,200 newsstand/cover (effective 2007).
Indexed: DentInd.
Published by: Gakken Co. Ltd., 1-17-15, Nakaikegami, Otaku, Tokyo, 145-0064, Japan. TEL 81-3-37268124, FAX 81-3-37268122, http://www.gakken.co.jp/.

610.73 USA ISSN 0016-8335
RT5.G4
GEORGIA NURSING. Text in English. 1945. q. looseleaf. free to qualified personnel. adv. 36 p./no.; back issues avail. **Document type:** *Newsletter, Trade.* **Description:** Covers issues and employment opportunities of interest to licensed nursing professionals.
Related titles: Online - full text ed.
Indexed: A26, C06, C07, C08, CINAHL, H12, I05, INI, P24, P30, P48, PQC.
—BLDSC (4158.457000), GNLM.
Published by: (Georgia Nurses Association), Arthur L. Davis Publishing Agency, Inc., 517 Washington St, PO Box 216, Cedar Falls, IA 50613. TEL 319-277-2414, 800-626-4081, FAX 319-277-4055, sales@aldpub.com, http://www.aldpub.com. Ed. Mark Miller. Adv. contact Jim Larson. Circ: 101,000.

GERIATRIC NURSING. *see* GERONTOLOGY AND GERIATRICS

GEROKOMOS. *see* GERONTOLOGY AND GERIATRICS

610.73 RUS
GLAVNAYA MEDITSINSKAYA SESTRA. Text in Russian. 2000. m. USD 298 foreign (effective 2007). **Document type:** *Journal, Trade.*
Published by: Mezhdunarodnyi Tsentr Finansovo-Ekonomicheskogo Razvitiya, ul Yaroslavskaya, dom 8, k 5, Moscow, 126106, Russian Federation. TEL 7-495-9379080, FAX 7-495-9379087, ap@mcfr.ru, http://www.zdrav.ru. **Dist. by:** East View Information Services, 10601 Wayzata Blvd, Minneapolis, MN 55305. TEL 952-252-1201, 800-477-1005, FAX 952-252-1202, info@eastview.com, http://www.eastview.com.

610.73072 USA ISSN 1527-0009
RT75
GRADUATE RESEARCH IN NURSING EDUCATION. Text in English. 1999. bi-m. USD 24 (effective 2004). adv. **Description:** Publishes research and other scholarly writings of nursing graduate students.
Media: Online - full content.
Indexed: C06, C07, C08, CINAHL.
Published by: Graduate Research, LLC, 2917 E Manchester Dr, Tucson, AZ 85716. TEL 520-318-9946, FAX 520-318-3022. Ed., Pub. Naja McKenzie.

610.73 USA ISSN 1060-4162
➤ **THE GROWING LAMP.** Variant title: J O C E P S. Journal of Chi Eta Phi Sorority. Text in English. 1949. a. USD 15 to individuals; USD 30 to institutions; USD 15 to students (effective 2005). **Description:** Serves as a medium of communication for the members of the sorority, for the nursing community, and other health care professionals.
Indexed: C06, C07, C08, CINAHL.
Published by: Chi Eta Phi Sorority, 3029 13th St., N W, Washington, DC 20009. TEL 202-232-3858, FAX 202-232-3460.

610.73 ESP ISSN 1576-1584
GUIA PUNTEX. ANUARIO ESPANOL DE ENFERMERIA. Text in Spanish. 1994. a. EUR 54 domestic; EUR 84 in Europe; EUR 110 elsewhere (effective 2008). adv. back issues avail. **Document type:** *Monographic series, Consumer.*
Published by: Publicaciones Nacionales Tecnicas y Extranjeras (PUNTEX), Padilla 323, Barcelona, 08025, Spain. TEL 34-934-462820, FAX 34-934-462064, puntex@puntex.es, http://www.puntex.es. Ed. Martin Yolanda. adv.: B&W page EUR 1,005; 170 x 240. Circ: 5,000.

GUIDE TO SUCCESSFUL GRANT APPLICATIONS. *see* EDUCATION—Higher Education

610.73 CHN ISSN 1001-1099
GUOWAI YIXUE (HULIXUE FENCE)/FOREIGN MEDICAL SCIENCES (NURSING). Text in Chinese. 1980. m. CNY 42 domestic; USD 20.40 foreign (effective 2005). **Document type:** *Journal, Academic/Scholarly.*
Related titles: Online - full text ed.
—East View.
Published by: Weishengbu, Yixue Xinxi Guanli Weiyuanhui, 971, Jianzhen Lu, Changchun, 130061, China. **Dist. by:** China International Book Trading Corp, 35 Chegongzhuang Xilu, Haidian District, PO Box 399, Beijing 100044, China. TEL 86-10-68412045, FAX 86-10-68412023, cibtc@mail.cibtc.com.cn, http://www.cibtc.com.cn.

610.73 USA ISSN 1939-5671
H C PRO'S ADVISOR TO THE A N C C MAGNET RECOGNITION PROGRAM. Text in English. 2005. m. USD 399 (effective 2011). back issues avail. **Document type:** *Newsletter, Trade.* **Description:** Provides the information needed to ease the application and reapplication processes.
Formerly (until 2007): Magnet Status Advisor (1554-4753)
Related titles: Online - full text ed.: ISSN 1937-7533.
Indexed: A26, H11, I05, P21, P24, P48, PQC.
—**CCC.**
Published by: H C Pro, Inc., 200 Hoods Ln, PO Box 1168, Marblehead, MA 01945. TEL 781-639-1872, 800-650-6787, FAX 781-639-7857, customerservice@hcpro.com. Pub. Matt Cann TEL 888-834-4678.

610.73 CAN
HAND IN HAND. Text in English. 3/yr. membership. **Document type:** *Newspaper.*
Formerly: S N A A Newsletter
Published by: Saskatchewan Association of Licensed Practical Nurses, 2310 Smith, Regina, SK S4P 2P6, Canada. TEL 306-525-1436, FAX 306-347-7784. Ed., R&P, Adv. contact Ede Leeson. Circ: 2,600.

610.73 USA ISSN 1559-5366
HANDBOOK OF NURSING DIAGNOSIS. Text in English. 1982. biennial, latest 13th ed. USD 39.95 per issue (effective 2010). **Document type:** *Handbook/Manual/Guide, Academic/Scholarly.* **Description:** Contains listings of associated Nursing Interventions Classifications (NIC) and Nursing Outcomes Classifications (NOC).
Published by: Lippincott Williams & Wilkins (Subsidiary of: Wolters Kluwer N.V.), 530 Walnut St, Philadelphia, PA 19106. TEL 215-521-8300, FAX 215-521-8902, customerservice@lww.com.

610.73 618.202 IRN ISSN 1735-2215
➤ **HAYAT.** Text in Persian, Modern; Abstracts in English, Persian, Modern. 1991. q. **Document type:** *Journal, Academic/Scholarly.* **Description:** Publishes orginal or reviews manuscripts related to new issues in Nursing and Midwifery education, research or health care.
Related titles: Online - full text ed.: ISSN 2008-188X.
Indexed: A34, A36, A38, B21, C06, C07, C08, CA, CABA, CINAHL, D01, E12, ESPM, F08, GH, H&SSA, LT, N02, N03, N04, P33, P38, R08, R12, RA&MP, RRTA, S13, S16, T02, T05, V5, W.
Published by: Danishgah-i Ulum-i Pizishki-i Tihran, Danishkadah-'i Parastari va Mamayi/Tehran University of Medical Sciences, Faculty of Nursing & Midwifery, PO Box 6459, Tehran, Iran. TEL 98-21-66591888. Ed. Negarandeh R.

➤ **THE HEALTH CARE MANAGER.** *see* HEALTH FACILITIES AND ADMINISTRATION

➤ **HEALTH CAREER POST.** *see* HEALTH FACILITIES AND ADMINISTRATION

➤ **HEALTH INFORMATICS JOURNAL.** *see* MEDICAL SCIENCES—Computer Applications

610.736 GRC ISSN 1791-809X
RT120.I5
➤ **HEALTH SCIENCE JOURNAL.** Text in English. 2000. q. free to qualified personnel (effective 2010). adv. Index. back issues avail. **Document type:** *Journal, Academic/Scholarly.* **Description:** Dedicated to the dissemination of information, scholarship and experience in education, practice and investigation within medicine, nursing and all related areas of health care.
Formerly (until 2007): I C U s and Nursing Web Journal (1108-7366)
Media: Online - full text.
Indexed: C06, C07, C08, CA, CINAHL, P24, P48, PQC, SCOPUS, T02.
Published by: Technological Educational Institute of Athens, Ag Spyridonos, Egaleo, 12210, Greece. TEL 30-210-5385613, http://www.teiath.gr. Ed. Christina Marvaki. R&P Georgios Vasilopoulos.

➤ **HEALTH SOURCE: NURSING/ACADEMIC EDITION.** *see* MEDICAL SCIENCES—Abstracting, Bibliographies, Statistics

610.73 USA ISSN 0199-8552
HEALTHWIRE. Text in English. 1980. bi-m. membership. 8 p./no. 4 cols./p.; **Document type:** *Newsletter, Trade.* **Description:** Describes membership and local union activities, provides readers with national union news and an update on activities organized at the national level. Covers topics of interest to healthcare professionals and provides information on professional development workshops, conferences and publications.
Published by: (American Federation of Teachers), AFT Healthcare (Subsidiary of: American Federation of Teachers), 555 New Jersey Ave, N W, Washington, DC 20001. TEL 202-879-4491, healthcare@aft.org, http://www.afthealthcare.org. Ed., R&P Adrienne Coles TEL 202-434-4688. Circ: 63,000 (paid).

616.12 USA ISSN 0147-9563
RC681.A1 CODEN: HELUAI
➤ **HEART & LUNG;** the journal of acute and critical care. Text in English. 1972. bi-m. USD 400 in United States to institutions; USD 471 elsewhere to institutions (effective 2012). adv. bk.rev. charts; illus. index. reprints avail. **Document type:** *Journal, Academic/Scholarly.* **Description:** Publishes practical articles on critical care.
Related titles: CD-ROM ed.; Microfilm ed.: (from PQC); Online - full text ed.: ISSN 1527-3288 (from ScienceDirect).
Indexed: A20, A22, A26, AHCMS, AIM, ASCA, B21, C06, C07, C08, CA, CINAHL, ChemAb, CurCont, E01, EMBASE, ESPM, ExcerpMed, F09, FR, Faml, G08, H&SSA, H11, H12, HospLI, INI, ISR, IndMed, Inpharma, MEDLINE, NurAb, P24, P30, P35, P48, PQC, R10, Reac, SCI, SCOPUS, T02, THA, W07.
—BLDSC (4275.295000), CASDDS, GNLM, IE, Infotrieve, Ingenta, INIST. **CCC.**
Published by: Mosby, Inc. (Subsidiary of: Elsevier Health Sciences), 1600 John F. Kennedy Blvd, Ste 1800, Philadelphia, PA 19103. TEL 215-239-3900, 800-523-1649, FAX 215-239-3990, elspcs@elsevier.com, http://www.us.elsevierhealth.com. Ed. Dr. Kathleen S Stone. Pub. Jami Walker.

610.73 616.1 JPN ISSN 0914-2819
HEART NURSING/HATO NASHINGU. Text in Japanese. 1987. m. JPY 20,412; JPY 1,890 newsstand/cover (effective 2007). Supplement avail. **Document type:** *Journal, Academic/Scholarly.*
Published by: Medicus Shuppan/Medicus Publishing Inc., 18-24 Hiroshiba-cho, Suita-shi, Osaka-fu 564-8580, Japan. TEL 81-6-63856911, FAX 81-6-63856873, http://www.medica.co.jp/.

610.73 CHE
HEBAMME.CH. Text in French, German. 1903. m. CHF 105 domestic; CHF 140 foreign; CHF 12 newsstand/cover (effective 2007). adv. bk.rev. **Document type:** *Magazine, Trade.*
Formerly (until 2005): Die Schweizer Hebamme (1422-4526)
Indexed: P30.
Published by: Schweizerischer Hebammenverband, Rosenweg 25 C, Bern 23, 3000, Switzerland. TEL 41-31-3326340, FAX 41-31-3327619, info@hebamme.ch. Ed. Gerlinde Michel. Circ: 2,900.

HELEN K. MUSSALLEM LIBRARY SELECTED ACQUISITIONS. *see* MEDICAL SCIENCES—Abstracting, Bibliographies, Statistics

610.73 ESP ISSN 1134-5160
HIADES. Text and summaries in Spanish. 1994. a. EUR 36 (effective 2008). back issues avail. **Document type:** *Journal, Academic/Scholarly.*
Related titles: CD-ROM ed.: ISSN 1576-852X; Online - full text ed.: ISSN 1576-8570.
Published by: Asociacion Cultural Qabat Chabir, C/ Bailen 88, Alcala de Guadaira, Sevilla, 41500, Spain. TEL 34-954-627886199, hiades@arrakis.es.

610.73 305.898 USA ISSN 1540-4153
RA448.5.H57
➤ **HISPANIC HEALTH CARE INTERNATIONAL.** Text in English. 2003. q. USD 210 domestic to institutions; USD 250 foreign to institutions; USD 315 combined subscription domestic to institutions (print & online eds.); USD 375 combined subscription foreign to institutions (print & online eds.) (effective 2009). adv. **Document type:** *Journal, Academic/Scholarly.* **Description:** Serves as an interdisciplinary forum of information for clinical practice, education, research, and policy on issues concerning Hispanic/Latino populations in the United States.
Related titles: Online - full text ed.: ISSN 1938-8993 (from IngentaConnect).
Indexed: ASSIA, C06, C07, C08, CINAHL, EMBASE, ExcerpMed, P20, P21, P24, P30, P48, P54, PAIS, PQC, SCOPUS.
—BLDSC (4315.772300), IE, Ingenta. **CCC.**
Published by: (National Association of Hispanic Nurses), Springer Publishing Company, 11 W 42nd St, 15th Fl, New York, NY 10036. TEL 212-431-4370, FAX 212-941-7842, contactus@springerpub.com, http://www.springerjournals.com. Eds. Elias Provencio-Vaskuez, Nilda Peragallo. adv.: B&W page USD 1,000, color page USD 2,500; trim 8.5 x 11. Circ: 1,405 (paid and free).

610.73699 GBR ISSN 1474-7359
HIV NURSING; caring for people affected by HIV. (Human Immunodeficiency Virus) Text in English. 2001 (Jun.). q. GBP 60 domestic to individuals; GBP 70 in Europe to individuals; GBP 75 elsewhere to individuals; GBP 90 domestic to institutions; GBP 100 in Europe to institutions; GBP 115 elsewhere to institutions (effective 2010). **Document type:** *Journal, Academic/Scholarly.* **Description:** Provides a medium for communication on issues relating to HIV care.
Indexed: A26, B28, C06, C07, C08, CINAHL, H12, I05, SCOPUS.
—BLDSC (4319.045950), IE. **CCC.**
Published by: Mediscript Ltd., 1 Mountview Ct, 310 Friern Barnet Ln, London, N20 0LD, United Kingdom. TEL 44-20-84468898, FAX 44-20-84469194, info@mediscript.ltd.uk, http://www.mediscript.ltd.uk/.

610.73 616 FIN ISSN 0786-5686
➤ **HOITOTIEDE/NURSING SCIENCE;** journal of nursing science. Text in Finnish. 1958. bi-m. EUR 38 in Scandinavia; EUR 38 domestic; EUR 55 elsewhere; EUR 28 domestic to students (effective 2005). **Document type:** *Journal, Academic/Scholarly.* **Description:** Reports about the results of nursing research and provides a discussion forum for nurse researches.
Formerly (until 1989): Sairaanhoidon Vuosikirja (0301-0651)
Indexed: A22, C06, C07, C08, CINAHL, INI, P30, SCOPUS.
—BLDSC (4322.216500), IE, Infotrieve, Ingenta.
Published by: Hoitotieteiden Tutkimusseura/Finnish Association of Nursing Science, Department of Nursing Science, University of Kuopio, PO Box1627, Kuopio, 70211, Finland. TEL 358-17-162618, FAX 358-17-162632. Ed. Pirkko Routasalo TEL 358-2-3338403.

610.73 JPN ISSN 0018-3369
HOKENFU NO KEKKAKU TENBO/REVIEW OF TUBERCULOSIS FOR PUBLIC HEALTH NURSE. Text in Japanese. 1963. s-a. JPY 1,700 (effective 2001). adv. bk.rev. charts; illus.; stat. 100 p./no.; **Document type:** *Academic/Scholarly.*
Published by: Japan Anti-Tuberculosis Association/Kekkaku Yobokai, 1-3-12 Misaki-cho, Chiyoda-ku, Tokyo, 101-0061, Japan. TEL 81-3-3292-0211, FAX 81-3-3292-9208, jata@jatahq.org, http://www.jatahq.org. Pub. Toru Mori. Circ: 1,700.

610.73 USA ISSN 0887-9311
RT1
➤ **HOLISTIC NURSING PRACTICE;** the science of health and healing. Abbreviated title: H N P. Text in English. 1979. bi-m. USD 345.51 domestic to institutions; USD 483 foreign to institutions (effective 2011). adv. back issues avail.; reprints avail. **Document type:** *Journal, Academic/Scholarly.* **Description:** Explores holistic models of nursing practice. Content emphasizes traditional and holistic nursing and healthcare practices.
Formerly (until 1986): Topics in Clinical Nursing (0164-0534)
Related titles: Online - full text ed.: ISSN 1550-5138.
Indexed: A22, A26, AMED, C06, C07, C08, CA, CINAHL, E08, EMBASE, ExcerpMed, F09, Faml, G08, H11, H12, H13, I05, INI, MEDLINE, NurAb, P10, P20, P22, P24, P30, P48, P53, P54, PQC, S09, SCOPUS, T02, W09.
—BLDSC (4322.302600), GNLM, IE, Infotrieve, Ingenta, INIST. **CCC.**
Published by: Lippincott Williams & Wilkins (Subsidiary of: Wolters Kluwer N.V.), Two Commerce Sq, 2001 Market St, Philadelphia, PA 19103. TEL 215-521-8300, FAX 215-521-8902, customerservice@lww.com, http://www.lww.com. Ed. Gloria F Donnelly. Pub. Kathleen M Phelan. Adv. contact Pat Wendelken. Circ: 837.

610.73 USA ISSN 1527-6821
HOME CARE AND HOSPICE UPDATE. Text in English. 1994. m. **Description:** Provides timely and useful information to clinician and managers practicing or managing in home care and hospice.
Formerly (until 1999): Home Care Nurse News (1077-2251)
Indexed: C06, C07, C08, CINAHL.
Address: Box 629, Boca Grande, FL 33921-0629. FAX 941-697-2901, 800-993-6397, news@marrelli.com.

HOME CARE SALARY & BENEFITS REPORT. *see* OCCUPATIONS AND CAREERS

610.73 362.13 USA ISSN 1541-2490
HOMECARE ADMINISTRATOR. Text in English. 1994. m. USD 347 (effective 2009). **Document type:** *Newsletter, Trade.* **Description:** Provides guidance on how to handle a broad range of homecare management challenges.
Formerly (until 2002): Homecare Administrative Horizons (1079-0225)
Indexed: G08, I05.
—**CCC.**
Published by: Beacon Health, 12308 N Corporate Pkwy, Ste 100, Mequon, WI 53092-3380. TEL 800-553-2041, FAX 800-639-8511, info@beaconhealth.org.

610.73 USA ISSN 1069-4560
HOMECARE DIRECTION. Text in English. 1993. m. USD 337 (effective 2009). **Document type:** *Newsletter, Trade.* **Description:** Contains information and advice on compliance, care delivery, training, and documentation involving home health care.
Indexed: G08, H11, I05.
—**CCC.**
Published by: Beacon Health, 12308 N Corporate Pkwy, Ste 100, Mequon, WI 53092-3380. TEL 800-553-2041, FAX 800-639-8511, info@beaconhealth.org.

362.14 330 USA ISSN 1529-1715
HD9995.H56
HOMECARE MAGAZINE. Text in English. 1978. m. USD 59 domestic; USD 67 in Canada; USD 84 elsewhere; free domestic to qualified personnel (effective 2011). adv. **Document type:** *Magazine, Trade.* **Description:** Provides comprehensive coverage of the home health care industry, including trends, issues, acquisitions, products and legislation.
Former titles (until 199?): Homecare (0882-2700); (until 1984): Homecare Rental - Sales (0192-1673)
Related titles: Online - full text ed.
Indexed: A09, A10, A15, ABIn, B02, B07, B15, B17, B18, BPI, BRD, G04, G06, G07, G08, H01, I05, P19, P21, PQC, T02, V03, V04, W01, W02, W03, W05.
—**CCC.**
Published by: Penton Media, Inc., 6151 Powers Ferry Rd, Ste 200, Atlanta, GA 30339. TEL 770-955-2500, FAX 770-618-0204, information@penton.com, http://www.penton.com. Ed. Gail Walker. Circ: 17,020 (controlled).

362.14 USA ISSN 1525-982X
HOMECARE MONDAY. Text in English. 1997. w. free. adv. **Document type:** *Newsletter.* **Description:** Provides the latest industry and financial news, including legislation, products, and trends.
Media: E-mail. **Related titles:** Fax ed.
Published by: Penton Media, Inc., 249 W 17th St, New York, NY 10011. TEL 212-204-4200, FAX 212-206-3622, information@penton.com, http://www.penton.com.

610.73 USA ISSN 1045-1242
HOMECARE NEWS. Text in English. q. USD 20 (effective 2000). **Document type:** *Newspaper.*
Published by: National Association for Home Care & Hospice, 228 Seventh St, SE, Washington, DC 20003. FAX 202-547-3540, pubs@nahc.org. Ed., R&P Janet Neigh. Pub. Val J Halamandaris. Adv. contact Cathrine Wolden. Circ: 28,000.

610.73 JPN ISSN 1341-7045
HOMON KANGO TO KAIGO/JAPANESE JOURNAL OF HOME CARE NURSING. Text in English. 1996. m. JPY 13,200; JPY 18,200 combined subscription (print & online eds.) (effective 2010). **Document type:** *Journal, Academic/Scholarly.*
Related titles: Online - full text ed.: ISSN 1882-143X.
—BLDSC (4326.344250).
Published by: Igaku Shoin Ltd., 1-28-36 Hongo, Bunkyo-ku, Tokyo, 113-8719, Japan. TEL 81-3-3817-5600, FAX 81-3-3815-7791, info@igaku-shoin.co.jp.

610.73 HKG ISSN 0073-3253
BQ3
➤ **HONG KONG NURSING JOURNAL/HSIANG KANG HU LI TSA CHIH.** Key Title: Xianggang Huli Zazhi. Text in Chinese, English. 1965. q. adv. bk.rev. **Document type:** *Journal, Academic/Scholarly.* **Description:** Contains articles on all issues relating to nursing.
Related titles: Online - full text ed.
Indexed: A22, C06, C07, C08, CINAHL, HongKongiana, P30, SCOPUS.
—BLDSC (4326.402000), IE, Infotrieve, Ingenta.

Published by: (Hong Kong College of Nursing), Medcom Limited, Rm 808, Two Chinachem Exchange Sq, 338 King's Rd, North Point, Hong Kong. TEL 852-25783833, FAX 852-25783929, mcl@medcom.com.hk, http://www.medcom.com.hk. Ed. Dr. C Y Leung. Circ: 4,500.

610.73 CHL ISSN 0716-8861
HORIZONTE DE ENFERMERIA. Text in Spanish. 1990. s-a. CLP 7 domestic to individuals; CLP 16 domestic to institutions; CLP 5 domestic to students; USD 20 in Latin America to individuals; USD 25 in Latin America to institutions; USD 15 in Latin America to students; USD 25 elsewhere to individuals; USD 30 elsewhere to institutions; USD 20 elsewhere to students. back issues avail. **Document type:** *Journal, Academic/Scholarly.*
Indexed: P30.
Published by: Pontificia Universidad Catolica de Chile, Escuela de Enfermeria, Ave Vicuna Mackenna, 4860, Macul, Santiago, Chile. TEL 56-2-3545831, FAX 56-2-3547025, revistahorizonte@uc.cl.

HOSPICE INFORMATION BULLETIN. *see* HEALTH FACILITIES AND ADMINISTRATION

HOSPITAL & NURSING HOME WEEK. *see* HEALTH FACILITIES AND ADMINISTRATION

610.73 CAN
HOSPITAL AUXILIARIES ASSOCIATION OF ONTARIO. VOLUNTEER. Text in English. q. CAD 10 (effective 2003). **Document type:** *Newsletter.*
Formerly: Hospital Auxiliaries Association of Ontario. Quarterly Newsletter
Published by: Hospital Auxiliaries Association of Ontario, c/o Marilyn Slater, Editor, 305 Southgate Crt, RR#15, Thunder Bay, ON P7A 7Z5, Canada. FAX 807-767-6890, kenmar@tbaytel.net, http://www.haao.com.

610.73 CHN ISSN 1671-315X
HULI GUANLI ZAZHI/JOURNAL OF NURSING ADMINISTRATION. Text in Chinese. 1999. m. USD 36 (effective 2009). **Document type:** *Journal, Academic/Scholarly.*
Related titles: Online - full text ed.
—East View.
Published by: Zhongguo Renmin Jiefangjun, Beijing Junqu Zongyiyuan, 5, Nanmencang, Dongcheng-qu, Beijing, 100700, China. TEL 86-10-66721461, FAX 86-10-66721265. **Dist. by:** China International Book Trading Corp, 35 Chegongzhuang Xilu, Haidian District, PO Box 399, Beijing 100044, China. TEL 86-10-68412045, FAX 86-10-68412023, cibtc@mail.cibtc.com.cn, http://www.cibtc.com.cn.

610.73 TWN ISSN 2072-9235
HULI JI JIANKANG ZHAOHU YANJIU/JOURNAL OF NURSING AND HEALTHCARE RESEARCH. Text in Chinese. 2005. q. **Document type:** *Journal, Academic/Scholarly.*
Formerly (until 2009): Shizheng Hulu Jikan/Journal of Evidence-Based Nursing (1814-2869)
Indexed: C06, C07, C08, CINAHL.
—BLDSC (4335.915300), IE.
Published by: Taiwan Huli Xuehui/Taiwan Nurses Association, 4F, 281 Sec 4, Hsin-Yi Rd, Taipei, 10681, Taiwan. TEL 886-2-27552291, FAX 886-2-27019817, twna@twna.org.tw, http://www.twna.org.tw.

610.73 CHN
HULI XUEBAO/JOURNAL OF NURSING (CHINA). Text in Chinese. 1995. m. USD 49.20 (effective 2009). **Document type:** *Journal, Academic/Scholarly.*
Formerly: Nanfang Huli Xuebao/Nanfang Journal of Nursing (1008-9969)
Related titles: Online - full text ed.
—East View.
Published by: Nanfang Huli Xuebao, 1838, Guangzhou Dadao Bei, Guangzhou, 510515, China. **Dist. by:** China International Book Trading Corp, 35 Chegongzhuang Xilu, Haidian District, PO Box 399, Beijing 100044, China. TEL 86-10-68412045, FAX 86-10-68412023, cibtc@mail.cibtc.com.cn, http://www.cibtc.com.cn.

610.73 CHN ISSN 1009-6493
HULI YANJIU/CHINESE NURSING RESEARCH. Text in Chinese. 1987. every 3 mos. (10th, 20th, & 30th of each mo.). CNY 84 (effective 2009). **Document type:** *Journal, Academic/Scholarly.*
Formerly (until 1999): Shanxi Huli Zazhi/Shanxi Journal of Nursing (1006-1584)
Related titles: Online - full text ed.
Indexed: C06, C07, C08, CINAHL.
—BLDSC (3181.030900), East View.
Address: 85, Jiefang Nanlu, Taiyuan, 030001, China. TEL 86-351-4044111ext 25772, FAX 86-351-8825007. **Dist. by:** China International Book Trading Corp, 35 Chegongzhuang Xilu, Haidian District, PO Box 399, Beijing 100044, China. TEL 86-10-68412045, FAX 86-10-68412023, cibtc@mail.cibtc.com.cn, http://www.cibtc.com.cn.

610.73 615.82 CHN ISSN 1671-9875
HULI YU KANGFU/NURSING AND REHABILITATION JOURNAL. Text in Chinese. 2002. bi-m. CNY 6 newsstand/cover (effective 2006). **Document type:** *Journal, Academic/Scholarly.*
Related titles: Online - full text ed.
—BLDSC (4335.919000).
Published by: Zhejiang Huli Xuehui, 108, Yuancheng Dong Lu, Hanglin Huayuan, 1-Chuang 1-Danyuan, 203-Shi, Hangzhou, 310009, China.

610.73 TWN ISSN 0047-262X
➤ **HULI ZAZHI/JOURNAL OF NURSING.** Text in Chinese. 1954. bi-m. USD 70 (effective 2008). adv. bk.rev. illus. cum.index: 1954-1997. back issues avail. **Document type:** *Journal, Academic/Scholarly.*
Indexed: A22, C06, C07, C08, CINAHL, EMBASE, ExcerpMed, F09, INI, MEDLINE, P30, R10, Reac, SCOPUS.
—BLDSC (5023.690000), IE, Infotrieve, Ingenta.
Published by: Taiwan Huli Xuehui/Taiwan Nurses Association, 4F, 281 Sec 4, Hsin-Yi Rd, Taipei, 10681, Taiwan. TEL 886-2-27552291, FAX 886-2-27019817, twna@twna.org.tw, http://www.twna.org.tw. adv.: B&W page USD 250, color page USD 720; trim 210 x 150. Circ: 28,300.

610.73 CHN ISSN 1001-4152
HULIXUE ZAZHI/JOURNAL OF NURSING SCIENCE. Text in Chinese; Contents page in English. 1986. m. CNY 9 per issue. **Document type:** *Journal, Academic/Scholarly.*
Related titles: Online - full text ed.
—BLDSC (4335.922000), East View.
Published by: Huazhong Keji Daxue Tongji Yixueyuan/Huazhong University of Science and Technology, Tongji Medical College, 1095 Jiefang Dadao, Wuhan, 430030, China. TEL 86-27-83662666, FAX 86-27-83662666, http://www.tjmu.edu.cn/. **Dist. by:** China International Book Trading Corp, 35 Chegongzhuang Xilu, Haidian District, PO Box 399, Beijing 100044, China. TEL 86-10-68412045, FAX 86-10-68412023, cibtc@mail.cibtc.com.cn, http://www.cibtc.com.cn.

610.73 CHN ISSN 1002-6975
HUSHI JINXIU ZAZHI/JOURNAL OF NURSES TRAINING. Text in Chinese. 1986. m. USD 98.40 (effective 2009). **Document type:** *Journal, Academic/Scholarly.*
Related titles: Online - full text ed.
—East View.
Published by: Guizhou Sheng Yiyao Weisheng Xuehui Bangongsi, 11, Beilu, Guiyang, 550004, China. TEL 86-851-6854912, FAX 86-851-6824371. **Dist. by:** China International Book Trading Corp, 35 Chegongzhuang Xilu, Haidian District, PO Box 399, Beijing 100044, China. TEL 86-10-68412045, FAX 86-10-68412023, cibtc@mail.cibtc.com.cn, http://www.cibtc.com.cn.

610.73 ESP ISSN 1576-3056
HYGIA DE ENFERMERIA. Text in Spanish. 1987. 3/yr. **Document type:** *Magazine, Trade.*
Formerly (until 1997): Hygia (1137-7178)
Published by: Ilustre Colegio Oficial de Enfermeria de Sevilla, Avenida Ramon y Cajal 20, Seville, Spain. TEL 34-954-933800, FAX 34-954-933803, colegio@icoe.es.

610.73 IRL
I N O JOURNAL OF NURSING RESEARCH. Text in English. 2001. a. **Document type:** *Journal, Academic/Scholarly.*
Published by: (Irish Nurses' Organisation), MedMedia Ltd., 25 Adelaide St, Dun Laoghaire, Co. Dublin, Ireland. TEL 353-1-2803967, FAX 353-1-2807076, niamh@medmedia.ie, http://www.ijpm.org.

610.73 USA
I N S NEWSLINE. Text in English. 1973. bi-m. membership. adv. bk.rev. stat. **Document type:** *Newsletter, Trade.* **Description:** Offers timely coverage on clinical issues, product developments, IV drug safety, legislative and entrepreneurial topics affecting IV nurse specialists, and opportunities for continuing education and professional advancement.
Former titles: I N S Update; N I T A Update
Published by: Infusion Nurses Society, 220 Norwood Park S, Norwood, MA 02062. FAX 781-440-9409. Ed. Kate Kate Callahan TEL 781-440-9408 ext 311. Adv. contact Danielle R Petrella. Circ: 8,000.

610.73 USA ISSN 1550-6304
I S M P MEDICATION SAFETY ALERT!. NURSE ADVISE - E R R. Text in English. 2003. m. free (effective 2010). **Document type:** *Newsletter, Academic/Scholarly.* **Description:** Designed to meet the medication safety information needs of nurses who transcribe orders, administer medications, and monitor the effects of medications on patients.
Media: E-mail.
Published by: Institute for Safe Medication Practices, 200 Lakeside Dr, Ste 200, Horsham, PA 19044. TEL 215-947-7797, FAX 215-914-1492. Ed. Judy Smetzer.

610.73 USA
I S N A BULLETIN. (Indiana State Nursing Association) Text in English. 1903. q. looseleaf. Free to qualified subscribers. adv. back issues avail. **Document type:** *Newsletter, Trade.* **Description:** Covers issues and employment opportunities of interest to licensed nursing professionals.
Formerly (until 1971): Indiana Nurse
Related titles: Online - full text ed.
Published by: (Indiana State Nurses Association), Arthur L. Davis Publishing Agency, Inc., 517 Washington St, PO Box 216, Cedar Falls, IA 50613. TEL 319-277-2414, 800-626-4081, FAX 319-277-4055, sales@aldpub.com, http://www.nursingald.com. Eds. Ernest C Klein Jr., Mark Miller. Adv. contact Jim Larson. Circ: 108,600.

610.73 USA ISSN 2090-5483
▼ ➤ **I S R N NURSING.** (International Scholarly Research Network) Text in English. 2011. **Document type:** *Journal, Academic/Scholarly.* **Description:** Publishes original research articles, review articles, and clinical studies in all areas of nursing.
Related titles: Online - full text ed.: ISSN 2090-5491. 2011. free (effective 2011).
Published by: Hindawi Publishing Corporation, 410 Park Ave, 15th Fl, PMB 287, New York, NY 10022. FAX 215-893-4392, 866-446-3294, info@hindawi.com.

610.73 USA ISSN 0019-3062
RT1
IMPRINT (NEW YORK). Text in English. 1954. 5/yr. USD 18 in US & Canada to individuals; USD 30 elsewhere to individuals; USD 36 to institutions; USD 5 per issue to non-members; USD 3 per issue to members (effective 2010). adv. illus. index. 3 cols./p.; back issues avail.; reprints avail. **Document type:** *Magazine, Trade.* **Description:** Contains in-depth news section informing members of association news.
Former titles (until 1968): N S N A Newsletter; (until 1965): National Student Nurses' Association. Newsletter
Related titles: Online - full text ed.: free (effective 2010).
Indexed: A22, C06, C07, C08, CINAHL, EMBASE, ExcerpMed, F09, INI, MEDLINE, P30, SCOPUS.
—BLDSC (4371.486500), IE, Infotrieve, Ingenta.
Published by: National Student Nurses' Association, 45 Main St, Ste 606, Brooklyn, NY 11201. TEL 718-210-0705, FAX 718-797-1186, nsna@nsna.org. Ed. Alison Faust. Pub. Diane J Mancino. adv.: B&W page USD 3,550, color page USD 4,350; trim 7.875 x 10.5. Circ: 51,000.

610.73 GBR ISSN 1747-9800
INDEPENDENT NURSE. Text in English. 2005. fortn. GBP 65 to non-members; free to members (effective 2009). adv. back issues avail. **Document type:** *Magazine, Trade.* **Description:** Provides practice information for primary care and community nurses.
Indexed: B28, C06, C07, C08, CINAHL.
—CCC.
Published by: (Association for Nurse Prescribing), Haymarket Medical Publications Ltd. (Subsidiary of: Haymarket Media Group), 174 Hammersmith Rd, London, W6 7JP, United Kingdom. TEL 44-20-82675000, healthcare.republic@haymarket.com. Eds. Emma Bower TEL 44-20-82674857, Colin Cooper TEL 44-20-82674802. Adv. contact Dave Saunders TEL 44-20-82674869. Circ: 11,724. **Subscr. to:** 12-13 Cranleigh Gardens Industrial Estate, Southall UB1 2DB, United Kingdom. TEL 44-8451-557355, FAX 44-8451-948840, subscriptions@haymarket.com, http://www.haymarketbusinesssubs.com.

610.73 USA
INDIANA NURSING FOCUS. Text in English. 2005. q. free to members (effective 2009). back issues avail. **Document type:** *Magazine, Trade.* **Description:** Provide an expedient licensing process for regulated professionals by maintaining a climate that fosters the growth of commerce while ensuring the health, safety and welfare of the citizens of our great state.
Related titles: Online - full text ed.: free (effective 2009).
Published by: (Indiana State Board of Nursing), Publishing Concepts, Inc., 14109 Taylor Loop Rd, Little Rock, AR 72223. TEL 501-221-9986, 800-561-4686, FAX 501-225-3735, http://www.pcipublishing.com/. Pub. Virginia Robertson. Adv. contact Tom kennedy TEL 501-221-9986.

610.73 ITA ISSN 2037-4364
INFERMIERE OGGI. Text in Italian. 1990. q. **Document type:** *Magazine, Trade.*
Related titles: Online - full text ed.
Published by: Collegio IPASVI di Roma, Viale Giulio Cesare 78, Rome, 00192, Italy. TEL 39-06-37511597, http://www.ipasvi.roma.it.

610.73 618.92 ITA ISSN 2036-2218
▼ **GLI INFERMIERI DEI BAMBINI. GIORNALE ITALIANO DI SCIENZE INFERMIERISTICHE PEDIATRICHE.** Text in Italian. 2009. q. free to members (effective 2011). **Document type:** *Journal, Trade.*
Published by: Societa Italiana di Scienze Infermieristiche Pediatriche (S I S I P), Via Borgognoni 7C, Pistoia, 51100, Italy. Ed. Filippo Festini.

610.73 USA ISSN 2153-6538
▼ **THE INFERTILITY NURSE.** Text in English. 2009. bi-m. adv. **Document type:** *Journal, Academic/Scholarly.* **Description:** Provides information on the physiologic, medical, and psychological aspects of human reproduction, focusing on the role of the OB/GYN, infertility, and urology nurse in patient care.
Supersedes in part (in 2009): The O B / G Y N and Infertility Nurse (2151-8394)
Related titles: Online - full text ed.: free to qualified personnel (effective 2009).
Published by: (American Academy of OB/GYN and Infertility Nurses), Greenhill Healthcare Communications, 241 Forsgate Dr, Ste 205D, Monroe Township, NJ 08831. TEL 732-656-7935, FAX 732-656-7938, editorial@greenhillhc.com. Eds. Debra Moynihan, Sue Jasulaitis.

610.73 CAN ISSN 1923-5577
L'INFIRMIERE CLINICIENNE. Text in French. 2004. a. **Document type:** *Journal, Academic/Scholarly.*
Media: Online - full text.
Published by: Universite du Quebec a Rimouski, 300 Allee des Ursulines, Rimouski, PQ G5L 3A1, Canada. http://www.uqar.qc.ca/campusRimouski/index.asp.

610.736 FRA ISSN 1633-339X
L'INFIRMIERE ET LA DOULEUR. LA LETTRE. Text in French. 2002. 2/yr. **Document type:** *Newsletter, Academic/Scholarly.* **Description:** Advises nurses on pain management.
Related titles: Online - full text ed.: free.
Published by: Institut UPSA de la Douleur, 3 rue Joseph Monier, B P 325, Rueil Malmaison Cedex, 92506, France. TEL 33-1-58838994, FAX 33-1-58838901, institut.upsa@bms.com.

610.73 FRA ISSN 1267-9925
L'INFIRMIERE LIBERALE MAGAZINE. Text in French. 199?. 11/yr. EUR 105.78 domestic; EUR 126.88 DOM-TOM; EUR 157 elsewhere (effective 2009). **Document type:** *Magazine, Trade.*
Formerly (until 1995): L' Infirmiere Liberale
Published by: Editions Lamarre (Subsidiary of: Wolters Kluwer France), 1 Rue Eugene et Armand Peugeot, Rueil Malmaison, 92500, France. TEL 33-1-76733000, FAX 33-1-76734857, contact@espaceinfirmier.com, http://www.espaceinfirmier.com. Circ: 55,000.

610.73 BEL
INFO-NURSING. Text in English. 1929. 8/yr. adv. **Document type:** *Bulletin, Trade.*
Published by: Association Nationale Catholique du Nursing, Av Hippocrate 91, Brussels, 1200, Belgium. TEL 32-2-762-5618, FAX 32-2-772-5219, acn@infirmieres.be, http://www.infirmieres.be/index.htm. Ed., Pub., R&P, Adv. contact Hans Sabine TEL 32-21762-5618.

610.73 CAN ISSN 0846-524X
INFO NURSING. Text in English, French. 1967. 4/yr. CAD 25 domestic; USD 30 foreign (effective 2000). adv. bk.rev. illus. **Document type:** *Newsletter.*
Former titles (until 1989): Info - Nurses Association of New Brunswick (0842-3210); (until 1984): Info - New Brunswick Association of Registered Nurses (0382-5574); (until 1975): N B A R N News (0382-5566)
Indexed: A26, C06, C07, C08, CINAHL, H12, I05.
—BLDSC (4478.876830). **CCC.**
Published by: Nurses Association of New Brunswick/Association des Infirmieres et Infirmiers du Nouveau-Brunswick, 165 Regent St, Fredericton, NB E3B 7B4, Canada. TEL 506-458-8731, FAX 506-459-2838. Ed., Adv. contact George Bergeron. Circ: 8,900.

610.73 USA ISSN 1942-7425
RT4
INFORMATION DIGEST FOR THE SKILLED NURSING INDUSTRY. Text in English. 2008 (Jun.). q. USD 495 print ed.; USD 695 online ed. (effective 2008). **Document type:** *Handbook/Manual/Guide, Trade.*
Related titles: CD-ROM ed.: ISSN 2154-8994; Online - full text ed.: ISSN 1942-7433.
Published by: Valuation & Information Group, 6167 Bristol Pkwy, Ste 430, Culver City, CA 90230. TEL 310-342-0123, 800-259-4216, FAX 310-342-0147, http://valinfo.com.

INSIGHT (SAINT LOUIS). *see* MEDICAL SCIENCES—Ophthalmology And Optometry

INSTITUT FORMATION SOINS INFIRMIERS. REUSSIR LE DIPLOME D'ETAT. *see* EDUCATION—Higher Education

610.73 MEX ISSN 0188-431X
RT1

INSTITUTO MEXICANO DEL SEGURO SOCIAL. REVISTA DE ENFERMERIA. Text in Multiple languages. 1988. 3/yr. **Document type:** *Journal, Trade.*
Related titles: Online - full text ed.
Indexed: A36, CABA, D01, E12, GH, LT, N02, N03, P33, R08, R12, RM&VM, T05, TAR, W11.
Published by: Instituto Mexicano del Seguro Social, Avenida Paseo de la Reforma 476, Col Juarez, Mexico City, DF 06600, Mexico. TEL 52-55-52382700, http://www.imss.gob.mx.

610.73 615.5 USA ISSN 1542-3344

INTEGRATIVE NURSING. Text in English. 2002 (Sept./Oct.). bi-m. USD 39.99 (effective 2003). **Document type:** *Journal, Trade.*
Indexed: C06, C07, C08, CINAHL.
Published by: Harren Publishing, 4134 E. Hawthorne St., Tucson, AZ 85711. TEL 888-815-5961. Ed. Mary Jo Kreitzer, PhD, RN. Pub. Catherine E. Harold.

610.73 USA ISSN 1940-7009
RA1

INTELLIGENCE REPORTS. Text in English. 2007. q. free (effective 2008). back issues avail. **Document type:** *Newsletter, Trade.* **Description:** Provides information about American Society of Registered Nurses.
Media: Online - full content.
Published by: American Society of Registered Nurses, 1001 Bridgeway, Ste 411, Sausalito, CA 94965. TEL 415-331-2700, 800-331-1206, FAX 415-476-4558, office@asrn.org.

610.73 GBR ISSN 0964-3397
RT120.I5 CODEN: GGRUEL

➤ **INTENSIVE AND CRITICAL CARE NURSING.** Text in English. 1985. bi-m. EUR 565 in Europe to institutions; JPY 61,000 in Japan to institutions; USD 501 elsewhere to institutions (effective 2012). adv. bk.rev. abstr. 64 p./no. 2 cols./p.; back issues avail.; reprints avail. **Document type:** *Journal, Academic/Scholarly.* **Description:** Provides international and interdisciplinary forum for specialist nurses.
Formerly (until 1992): Intensive Care Nursing (0266-612X)
Related titles: Online - full text ed.: ISSN 1532-4036 (from ScienceDirect).
Indexed: A22, A26, ASSIA, B28, C06, C07, C08, CINAHL, E01, E08, EMBASE, ExcerpMed, FamI, H11, H12, INI, MEDLINE, P03, P30, PsycInfo, R10, Reac, S09, SCOPUS, T02.
—BLDSC (4531.836000), GNLM, IE, Infotrieve, Ingenta. **CCC.**
Published by: (British Association of Critical Care Nurses), Churchill Livingstone (Subsidiary of: Elsevier Health Sciences), The Blvd, Langford Ln, Kidlington, OX5 1GB, United Kingdom. TEL 44-1865-843434, FAX 44-1865-843970, directenquiries@elsevier.com, http://www.elsevierhealth.com/imprint.jsp?iid=9. Ed. Deborah Dawson. Adv. contact Emma Steel TEL 44-207-4244221. Circ: 449.

610.73 FRA ISSN 0242-3960

INTER BLOC; la revue de reference infirmiere du bloc operatoire et de la chirurgie. Text in French. 1980. 4/yr. EUR 128 in Europe to institutions; EUR 109.70 in France to institutions; JPY 18,500 in Japan to institutions; USD 163 elsewhere to institutions (effective 2012). **Document type:** *Journal, Academic/Scholarly.* **Description:** Topics covered include hygiene, surgical technique and technology, and legal and professional aspects.
Incorporates (1981-1997): Soins. Chirurgie (0249-6429)
Related titles: Online - full text ed.
Indexed: A22, FR, SCOPUS.
—BLDSC (4531.850200), IE, Ingenta, INIST. **CCC.**
Published by: (Association des Enseignants des Ecoles d'Infirmieres de Bloc Operatoire), Elsevier Masson (Subsidiary of: Elsevier Health Sciences), 62 Rue Camille Desmoulins, Issy les Moulineaux, Cedex 92442, France. TEL 33-1-71165500, infos@elsevier-masson.fr. Circ: 2,500. **Subscr. to:** Societe de Periodiques Specialises, BP 22, Vineuil Cedex 41354, France. TEL 33-2-54504612, FAX 33-2-54504611.

610.73 USA ISSN 1066-1441
RT83

INTERACTION (WASHINGTON D.C). Text in English. 1982. q.
Indexed: A26, C06, C07, C08, CINAHL, CPerI, H12, I05.
Published by: American Assembly for Men in Nursing, 11 Cornell Rd, Latham, NY 12110-1499, NY 12110-1499. TEL 518-782-9400, FAX 518-782-9530, aamn@aamn.org, http://aamn.org/.

610.73 GBR ISSN 1755-599X
RT120.E4

➤ **INTERNATIONAL EMERGENCY NURSING.** Text in English. 1993. q. EUR 482 in Europe to institutions; JPY 51,900 in Japan to institutions; USD 428 elsewhere to institutions (effective 2012). adv. bk.rev. 64 p./no. 2 cols./p.; back issues avail.; reprints avail. **Document type:** *Journal, Academic/Scholarly.* **Description:** Covers various topics in emergency-care nursing.
Formerly (until 2008): Accident and Emergency Nursing (0965-2302)
Related titles: Online - full text ed.: ISSN 1878-013X (from ScienceDirect).
Indexed: A22, A26, A28, APA, ASSIA, B28, BrCerAb, C&ISA, C06, C07, C08, CA, CA/WCA, CIA, CINAHL, CerAb, CivEngAb, CorrAb, E&CAJ, E01, E08, E11, EEA, EMA, EMBASE, ESPM, EnvEAb, ExcerpMed, F09, FamI, H11, H12, H15, INI, M&TEA, M09, MBF, MEDLINE, METADEX, P30, R10, Reac, S09, SCOPUS, SolStAb, T02, T04, WAA.
—BLDSC (4539.929500), GNLM, IE, Infotrieve, Ingenta. **CCC.**
Published by: Elsevier Ltd (Subsidiary of: Elsevier Science & Technology), The Blvd, Langford Ln, Kidlington, Oxford, OX5 1GB, United Kingdom. TEL 44-1865-843434, FAX 44-1865-843970. Ed. Heather McClelland. **Subscr. to:** Harcourt Publishers Ltd., Foots Cray High St, Sidcup, Kent DA14 5HP, United Kingdom. TEL 44-20-83085700, FAX 44-20-8309-0807; **Subscr. to:** Elsevier, Subscription Customer Service, 6277 Sea Harbor Dr, Orlando, FL 32887-4800. TEL 800-654-2452, http://www.elsevier.com/.

610.73 USA ISSN 1091-5710
RT86

➤ **INTERNATIONAL JOURNAL FOR HUMAN CARING.** Abbreviated title: I J H C. Text in English. 1997. q. USD 80 domestic to individuals; USD 90 in Canada to individuals; USD 96 elsewhere to individuals; USD 130 domestic to institutions; USD 140 in Canada to institutions; USD 146 elsewhere to institutions; free to members (effective 2011). back issues avail. **Document type:** *Journal, Academic/Scholarly.* **Description:** Serves as a scholarly forum for nurses to advance knowledge of care and caring within the discipline of nursing.
Indexed: C06, C07, C08, CINAHL, P03, PsycInfo, S02, S03.
—BLDSC (4542.286000), IE, Ingenta.
Published by: International Association for Human Caring, 801 E Park Dr, Ste 100, Harrisburg, PA 17111. TEL 717-703-0033, FAX 717-234-6798, ruth@pronursingresources.com.

➤ **INTERNATIONAL JOURNAL OF MENTAL HEALTH NURSING.** *see* MEDICAL SCIENCES—Psychiatry And Neurology

▼ ➤ **INTERNATIONAL JOURNAL OF NURSING AND MIDWIFERY.** *see* MEDICAL SCIENCES—Obstetrics And Gynecology

610.73 USA ISSN 1548-923X

➤ **INTERNATIONAL JOURNAL OF NURSING EDUCATION SCHOLARSHIP.** Abbreviated title: I J N E S. Text in English. 2004. a. USD 175 per issue to institutions; USD 525 per issue to corporations (effective 2011). back issues avail. **Document type:** *Journal, Academic/Scholarly.* **Description:** Presents papers that advance nursing education, to enhance and advance nursing education globally, and to provide a forum for the dissemination of international perspectives and scholarship in nursing education.
Media: Online - full text.
Indexed: A28, APA, ASSIA, BrCerAb, C&ISA, C06, C07, C08, CA, CA/WCA, CIA, CINAHL, CerAb, CivEngAb, CorrAb, E&CAJ, E03, E11, EEA, EMA, EMBASE, ERI, ESPM, EnvEAb, ExcerpMed, H15, M&TEA, M09, MBF, MEDLINE, METADEX, P03, P30, PsycInfo, R10, Reac, SCOPUS, SD, SolStAb, T02, T04, WAA.
—**CCC.**
Published by: Berkeley Electronic Press, 2809 Telegraph Ave, Ste 202, Berkeley, CA 94705. TEL 510-665-1200, FAX 510-665-1201, info@bepress.com. Eds. Betty Cragg, David M Gregory.

610.73 USA ISSN 1941-2800
RC569.7

➤ **INTERNATIONAL JOURNAL OF NURSING IN INTELLECTUAL AND DEVELOPMENTAL DISABILITIES.** Abbreviated title: I J N I D D. Text in English. 2004. irreg., latest vol.5, no.1, 2009. free (effective 2009). back issues avail. **Document type:** *Journal, Academic/Scholarly.* **Description:** Provides information and resources on a wide range of topics and addresses clinical, non-clinical and research issues.
Media: Online - full content.
Indexed: CA, T02.
Published by: Developmental Disabilities Nurses Association, PO Box 536489, Orlando, FL 32853. TEL 407-835-0642, 800-888-6733, FAX 407-426-7440, http://www.ddna.org. Ed. Ann Smith TEL 508-478-2631 ext 502.

610.73 AUS ISSN 1322-7114

➤ **INTERNATIONAL JOURNAL OF NURSING PRACTICE.** Text in English. 1995. bi-m. GBP 600 in United Kingdom to institutions; EUR 763 in Europe to institutions; USD 971 in the Americas to institutions; USD 1,176 elsewhere to institutions; GBP 691 combined subscription in United Kingdom to institutions (print & online eds.); EUR 876 combined subscription in Europe to institutions (print & online eds.); USD 1,117 combined subscription in the Americas to institutions (print & online eds.); USD 1,352 combined subscription elsewhere to institutions (print & online eds.) (effective 2012). adv. back issues avail.; reprint service avail. from PSC. **Document type:** *Journal, Academic/Scholarly.* **Description:** Explores and promotes nursing as both a profession and an academic discipline.
Related titles: Online - full text ed.: ISSN 1440-172X. GBP 600 in United Kingdom to institutions; EUR 763 in Europe to institutions; USD 971 in the Americas to institutions; USD 1,176 elsewhere to institutions (effective 2012) (from IngentaConnect).
Indexed: A01, A02, A03, A08, A20, A22, A26, ASSIA, B21, B28, C06, C07, C08, C11, CA, CINAHL, CurCont, E01, EMBASE, ESPM, ExcerpMed, H&SSA, H04, H12, INI, MEDLINE, P02, P03, P30, P48, PQC, PsycInfo, PsycholAb, R10, Reac, SCI, SCOPUS, SSCI, T02, W07.
—BLDSC (4542.406800), GNLM, IE, Infotrieve, Ingenta, INIST. **CCC.**
Published by: Wiley-Blackwell Publishing Asia (Subsidiary of: Wiley-Blackwell Publishing Ltd.), 155 Cremorne St, Richmond, VIC 3121, Australia. TEL 61-3-92743100, FAX 61-3-92743101, subs@blackwellpublishingasia.com, http://www.wiley.com/WileyCDA/. Ed. Alan Pearson. Adv. contact Daniel Nash TEL 61-3-83591071. B&W page AUD 935, color page AUD 1,950; trim 210 x 275.

610.730 GBR ISSN 0020-7489
RT1

➤ **INTERNATIONAL JOURNAL OF NURSING STUDIES.** Abbreviated title: I J N S. Text in English. 1963. 12/yr. EUR 1,498 in Europe to institutions; JPY 188,600 in Japan to institutions; USD 1,676 elsewhere to institutions (effective 2012). adv. bk.rev. charts; illus. index. back issues avail.; reprints avail. **Document type:** *Journal, Academic/Scholarly.* **Description:** Aims to contribute to the advancement of the science and practice of nursing and interrelated disciplines worldwide by the international dissemination of sound information based on rigorous methods of research and scholarship.
Related titles: Microfilm ed.: (from PQC); Online - full text ed.: ISSN 1873-491X. 199? (from IngentaConnect, ScienceDirect).
Indexed: A01, A03, A08, A20, A22, A26, AHCMS, ASCA, ASSIA, B21, B28, C06, C07, C08, CA, CINAHL, CurCont, E-psyche, E08, EMBASE, ESPM, ExcerpMed, F09, FR, FamI, H&SSA, H11, H12, HospAb, INI, IndMed, MEDLINE, P03, P24, P30, P48, PQC, PsycInfo, PsycholAb, R10, Reac, S02, S03, S09, S21, SCI, SCOPUS, SSCI, T02, W07, W09.
—BLDSC (4542.407000), GNLM, IE, Infotrieve, Ingenta, INIST. **CCC.**
Published by: Elsevier Ltd (Subsidiary of: Elsevier Science & Technology), 54 Siward Rd, Bromley, BR2 9JZ, United Kingdom. TEL 44-20-84640304. Ed. Ian Norman.

610.73 USA ISSN 1541-5147
RT48.6

➤ **THE INTERNATIONAL JOURNAL OF NURSING TERMINOLOGIES AND CLASSIFICATIONS.** Abbreviated title: I J N T C. Text in English. 1974. q. GBP 141 in United Kingdom to institutions; EUR 179 in Europe to institutions; USD 215 in the Americas to institutions; USD 274 elsewhere to institutions; GBP 163 combined subscription in United Kingdom to institutions (print & online eds.); EUR 206 combined subscription in Europe to institutions (print & online eds.); USD 247 combined subscription in the Americas to institutions (print & online eds.); USD 315 combined subscription elsewhere to institutions (print & online eds.) (effective 2012). adv. back issues avail.; reprint service avail. from PSC. **Document type:** *Journal, Academic/Scholarly.* **Description:** Promotes the development, refinement, and utilization of nursing language and classification.
Former titles (until 2002): Nursing Diagnosis (1046-7459); (until 1990): Nursing Diagnosis Newsletter (0890-7188)
Related titles: Microform ed.: (from PQC); Online - full text ed.: ISSN 1744-618X. GBP 141 in United Kingdom to institutions; EUR 179 in Europe to institutions; USD 215 in the Americas to institutions; USD 274 elsewhere to institutions (effective 2012) (from IngentaConnect).
Indexed: A01, A02, A03, A08, A22, A25, A26, ASSIA, C06, C07, C08, C11, CA, CINAHL, E01, E08, EMBASE, ExcerpMed, FR, FamI, G08, H04, H11, H12, H13, I05, INI, MEDLINE, P10, P20, P22, P24, P30, P48, P53, P54, PQC, R10, Reac, S08, S09, SCOPUS, T02.
—BLDSC (4542.408000), GNLM, IE, Ingenta. **CCC.**
Published by: (North American Nursing Diagnosis Association), Wiley-Blackwell Publishing, Inc. (Subsidiary of: Wiley-Blackwell Publishing Ltd.), 111 River St, Hoboken, NJ 07030. TEL 201-748-6000, FAX 201-748-6088, info@wiley.com. Ed. Jane Flanagan.

610.7365 GBR ISSN 1748-3735
RC954

➤ **INTERNATIONAL JOURNAL OF OLDER PEOPLE NURSING.** Text in English. 2004. q. GBP 224 in United Kingdom to institutions; EUR 286 in Europe to institutions; USD 415 in the Americas to institutions; USD 481 elsewhere to institutions; GBP 258 combined subscription in United Kingdom to institutions (print & online eds.); EUR 329 combined subscription in Europe to institutions (print & online eds.); USD 478 combined subscription in the Americas to institutions (print & online eds.); USD 554 combined subscription elsewhere to institutions (print & online eds.) (effective 2011). adv. back issues avail.; reprint service avail. from PSC. **Document type:** *Journal, Academic/Scholarly.* **Description:** Provides scholarly and accessible material that challenges assumptions and provokes new ideas, helping nurses develop and inform their practice and engage in the debates about the health and social care services for older people.
Related titles: Online - full text ed.: ISSN 1748-3743. GBP 224 in United Kingdom to institutions; EUR 286 in Europe to institutions; USD 415 in the Americas to institutions; USD 481 elsewhere to institutions (effective 2011) (from IngentaConnect).
Indexed: A22, A26, ASSIA, B28, C06, C07, C08, CA, CINAHL, E01, ESPM, H12, MEDLINE, P03, P30, PsycInfo, RiskAb, T02.
—BLDSC (4542.424500), IE, Ingenta. **CCC.**
Published by: Wiley-Blackwell Publishing Ltd. (Subsidiary of: John Wiley & Sons, Inc.), 9600 Garsington Rd, Oxford, OX4 2DQ, United Kingdom. TEL 44-1865-776868, FAX 44-1865-714591, customerservices@blackwellpublishing.com. Eds. Brendan McCormack, Jan Reed. Adv. contact Joanna Baker TEL 44-1865-476271.

610.73 617 GBR ISSN 1878-1241
RD753

➤ **INTERNATIONAL JOURNAL OF ORTHOPAEDIC AND TRAUMA NURSING.** Text in English. 1997. q. EUR 432 in Europe to institutions; JPY 46,500 in Japan to institutions; USD 384 elsewhere to institutions (effective 2012). adv. bk.rev. abstr. back issues avail.; reprints avail. **Document type:** *Journal, Academic/Scholarly.* **Description:** Seeks to promote the development and exchange of specialist knowledge within orthopaedic and trauma practice.
Formerly (until 2010): Journal of Orthopaedic Nursing (1361-3111)
Related titles: Online - full text ed.: (from ScienceDirect).
Indexed: A22, A26, B28, C06, C07, C08, CA, CINAHL, E01, E08, H11, H12, I05, S09, SCOPUS, T02.
—BLDSC (5027.663000), IE, Infotrieve, Ingenta. **CCC.**
Published by: (Canadian Orthopaedic Nurses Association CAN), Elsevier Ltd (Subsidiary of: Elsevier Science & Technology), 54 Siward Rd, Bromley, BR2 9JZ, United Kingdom. TEL 44-20-84640304, customerserviceau@elsevier.com. Eds. Bryan Smith, Julie Santy-Tomlinson.

610.73 GBR ISSN 1357-6321
RT87.T45

➤ **INTERNATIONAL JOURNAL OF PALLIATIVE NURSING.** Abbreviated title: I J P N. Text in English. 1995. s-m. GBP 161 domestic to individuals; EUR 223 in Europe to individuals; USD 322 elsewhere to individuals; GBP 114 to students (effective 2010). adv. back issues avail.; reprints avail. **Document type:** *Journal, Academic/Scholarly.* **Description:** Provides information on palliative care for nurses with an international focus.
Related titles: Online - full text ed.
Indexed: A01, A02, A03, A08, A22, AMED, B28, C06, C07, C08, C11, CA, CINAHL, EMBASE, ExcerpMed, F09, H04, MEDLINE, P30, R10, Reac, SCOPUS, T02.
—BLDSC (4542.440900), IE, Infotrieve, Ingenta. **CCC.**
Published by: Mark Allen Publishing Ltd., St Jude's Church, Dulwich Rd, London, SE24 0PB, United Kingdom. TEL 44-20-77385454, FAX 44-20-79788316, subscriptions@markallengroup.com, http://www.markallengroup.com. Ed. Laura Dean-Osgood. Adv. contact Roger Allen.

610.73 616.6 GBR ISSN 1749-7701
RC874.7
➤ **INTERNATIONAL JOURNAL OF UROLOGICAL NURSING.** Text in English. 2007 (Mar.). 3/yr. GBP 191 in United Kingdom to institutions; EUR 242 in Europe to institutions; USD 351 in the Americas to institutions; USD 410 elsewhere to institutions; GBP 220 combined subscription in United Kingdom to institutions (print & online eds.); EUR 279 combined subscription in Europe to institutions (print & online eds.); USD 404 combined subscription in the Americas to institutions (print & online eds.); USD 471 combined subscription elsewhere to institutions (print & online eds.) (effective 2012). adv. back issues avail.; reprint service avail. from PSC. **Document type:** *Journal, Academic/Scholarly.* **Description:** Covers general urology, continence care, oncology, andrology, stoma care, pediatric urology, men's health, reconstructive surgery, clinical audit, clinical governance, nurse-led services, reflective analysis, education, management, research, and leadership.
Related titles: Online - full text ed.: ISSN 1749-771X. GBP 191 in United Kingdom to institutions; EUR 242 in Europe to institutions; USD 351 in the Americas to institutions; USD 410 elsewhere to institutions (effective 2012) (from IngentaConnect).
Indexed: A22, B21, C06, C07, CA, CurCont, E01, NSA, SCI, SCOPUS, SSCI, T02, W07.
—IE. **CCC.**
Published by: (British Association of Urological Nurses), Wiley-Blackwell Publishing Ltd. (Subsidiary of: John Wiley & Sons, Inc.), 9600 Garsington Rd, Oxford, OX4 2DQ, United Kingdom. TEL 44-1865-776868, FAX 44-1865-714591, customerservices@blackwellpublishing.com. Ed. Oliver Slevin. Adv. contact Joanna Baker TEL 44-1865-476271.

610.73 ITA ISSN 1592-6478
INTERNATIONAL NURSING PERSPECTIVES. Text in Multiple languages. 2001. 3/yr. EUR 39.91 (effective 2008). **Document type:** *Journal, Academic/Scholarly.*
Indexed: C06, C07, C08, CINAHL, SCOPUS.
—BLDSC (4544.454000), IE, Ingenta.
Published by: Societa Editrice Universo, Via Giovanni Battista Morgagni 1, Rome, RM 00161, Italy. TEL 39-06-44231171, FAX 39-06-4402033, amministrazione@seu-roma.it, http://www.seuroma.com.

610.73 GBR ISSN 0020-8132
RT1
➤ **INTERNATIONAL NURSING REVIEW.** Abbreviated title: I N R. Text in English. 1926. q. GBP 215 in United Kingdom to institutions; EUR 272 in Europe to institutions; USD 397 in the Americas to institutions; USD 464 elsewhere to institutions; GBP 247 combined subscription in United Kingdom to institutions (print & online eds.); EUR 313 combined subscription in Europe to institutions (print & online eds.); USD 457 combined subscription in the Americas to institutions (print & online eds.); USD 534 combined subscription elsewhere to institutions (print & online eds.) (effective 2012). adv. bk.rev. illus. index. back issues avail.; reprint service avail. from PSC. **Document type:** *Journal, Academic/Scholarly.* **Description:** Focuses on original articles that help to forward the International Council of Nurses mission world-wide by representing nursing, advancing the profession and shaping health policy.
Incorporates (1968-1971): I C N Calling (0538-690X); Former titles (until 1954): International Nursing Bulletin (0141-5557); (until 1945): International Nursing Review (0142-5412); (until 1930): I C N. International Council of Nurses
Related titles: Microform ed.: (from PQC); ◆ Online - full text ed.: International Nursing Review Online. ISSN 1466-7657; Spanish ed.: International Nursing Review en Espanol. ISSN 1577-9378. 2001.
Indexed: A01, A02, A03, A08, A20, A22, A26, AHCMS, ASSIA, B21, B28, C06, C07, C08, C11, CA, CINAHL, CurCont, E01, EMBASE, ESPM, ExcerpMed, Faml, H&SSA, H04, H12, INI, IndMed, MEDLINE, P03, P06, P30, P34, PsycInfo, PsycholAb, R10, Reac, S02, S03, SCI, SCOPUS, SSCI, T02, W07, W09.
—BLDSC (4544.500000), GNLM, IE, Infotrieve, Ingenta, INIST. **CCC.**
Published by: (International Council of Nurses CHE), Wiley-Blackwell Publishing Ltd. (Subsidiary of: John Wiley & Sons, Inc.), 9600 Garsington Rd, Oxford, OX4 2DQ, United Kingdom. TEL 44-1865-776868, FAX 44-1865-714591, customerservices@blackwellpublishing.com. Ed. Dr. Jane Robinson. Adv. contact Joanna Baker TEL 44-1865-476271.

610.73 GBR ISSN 1466-7657
RT1
➤ **INTERNATIONAL NURSING REVIEW ONLINE.** Text in English. 1954. q. GBP 215 in United Kingdom to institutions; EUR 272 in Europe to institutions; USD 397 in the Americas to institutions; USD 464 elsewhere to institutions (effective 2012). adv. back issues avail. **Document type:** *Journal, Academic/Scholarly.* **Description:** Focuses on original articles that help to forward the International Council of Nurses mission world-wide by representing nursing, advancing the profession and shaping health policy.
Media: Online - full text (from IngentaConnect). **Related titles:** Microform ed.: (from PQC); ◆ Print ed.: International Nursing Review. ISSN 0020-8132.
—**CCC.**
Published by: (International Council of Nurses CHE), Wiley-Blackwell Publishing Ltd. (Subsidiary of: John Wiley & Sons, Inc.), 9600 Garsington Rd, Oxford, OX4 2DQ, United Kingdom. TEL 44-1865-776868, FAX 44-1865-714591, customerservices@blackwellpublishing.com, http://www.wiley.com/. Adv. contact Joanna Baker TEL 44-1865-476271.

610.73 USA ISSN 1523-6064
RT1
➤ **THE INTERNET JOURNAL OF ADVANCED NURSING PRACTICE.** Text in English. 1997. s-a. free (effective 2011). bk.rev. back issues avail. **Document type:** *Journal, Academic/Scholarly.* **Description:** Contains information from the field of nursing, including original articles, reviews, case reports, streaming slide shows, streaming videos, letters to the editor, press releases, and meeting information.
Media: Online - full text.
Indexed: A01, A02, A03, A08, A26, C06, C07, C08, C11, CA, CINAHL, G08, H04, H11, H12, I05, SCOPUS, T02.
Published by: Internet Scientific Publications, Llc., 23 Rippling Creek Dr, Sugar Land, TX 77479. TEL 832-443-1193, FAX 281-240-1533, wenker@ispub.com. Ed. Susan Ruppert. R&P Olivier Wenker TEL 832-754-0335.

610.73 COL ISSN 0120-5307
RT81.C7
INVESTIGACION Y EDUCACION EN ENFERMERIA. Text in Spanish; Summaries in English, Spanish. 1983. s-a. adv. bk.rev. bibl. **Document type:** *Journal, Academic/Scholarly.* **Description:** Publishes works from Latin American institutions that are of importance to health and social science workers.
Related titles: Online - full text ed.: ISSN 2216-0280. 2010. free (effective 2011) (from SciELO).
Indexed: A26, C01, C06, C07, C08, CINAHL, H12, I04, I05.
—GNLM.
Published by: Universidad de Antioquia, Facultad de Enfermeria, Carrera 53 no. 62-65, Apartado Aereo 1226, Medellin, ANT, Colombia. TEL 57-4-510-6335, FAX 57-4-211-0058, meruiz@catios.udea.edu.co. Ed. Bertha Ligia Diez Mejia. adv.: page USD 300. Circ: 500 (controlled).

610.73 USA
IOWA BOARD OF NURSING. NEWSLETTER. Text in English. 1982. q. looseleaf. Free to qualified subscribers. adv. 32 p./no.; back issues avail. **Document type:** *Newsletter, Trade.* **Description:** Covers issues and employment opportunities of interest to licensed nursing professionals.
Formerly (until 1987): Nursing Newsletter & Continuing Education Calendar
Published by: (Iowa Board of Nursing), Arthur L. Davis Publishing Agency, Inc., 517 Washington St, PO Box 216, Cedar Falls, IA 50613. TEL 319-277-2414, 800-626-4081, FAX 319-277-4055, sales@aldpub.com, http://www.nursingald.com. Ed. Mark Miller. R&P Lorinda Inman. Adv. contact Jim Larson. Circ: 51,900.

610.73 IRL ISSN 0790-7257
IRISH NURSING FORUM & HEALTH SERVICES. Text in English. 1983. 6/yr.
Formerly (until 1986): Irish Nursing Forum (0790-0678)
Address: 127 Lower Baggot St., Dublin, 2, Ireland. TEL 789318, FAX 767072. Ed. Eivlin Roden.

610.7 IRL ISSN 1649-4571
IRISH PRACTICE NURSE. Text in English. 1999. m. EUR 66 (effective 2005). adv. **Document type:** *Journal, Academic/Scholarly.* **Description:** Contains clinical articles reflecting on patient care areas where practice nurses have an important role to play.
Published by: (Irish Practice Nurses Association), Eireann Healthcare Publications, 25-26 Windsor Pl., Dublin, 2, Ireland. TEL 353-1-4753300, FAX 353-1-4753311, mhenderson@eireannpublications.ie, http://www.eireannpublications.ie. Ed. Ann-Marie Hardiman. Adv. contact Sharon Magee. B&W page EUR 1,672; trim 204 x 288. Circ: 1,379 (paid and controlled).

610.73 USA ISSN 0885-0046
ISSUES (CHICAGO). Text in English. 1980. q.
Indexed: C06, C07, C08, CINAHL, EMBASE, ExcerpMed, MEDLINE, P30, SCOPUS.
Published by: National Council of State Boards of Nursing, 111 East Wacker Dr, Ste 2900, Chicago, IL 60601. TEL 312-525-3600, 866-293-9600, FAX 312-279-1032, info@ncsbn.org, http://www.ncsbn.org.

610.73 GBR ISSN 0146-0862
CODEN: ICNUDS
➤ **ISSUES IN COMPREHENSIVE PEDIATRIC NURSING.** Text in English. 1976. q. GBP 230, EUR 300, USD 380 combined subscription to institutions (print & online eds.); GBP 460, EUR 600, USD 750 combined subscription to corporations (print & online eds.) (effective 2010). adv. bk.rev. bibl.; charts; illus. index. back issues avail.; reprint service avail. from PSC. **Document type:** *Journal, Academic/Scholarly.* **Description:** Features articles pertinent to the critical aspects of pediatric nursing.
Related titles: Online - full text ed.: ISSN 1521-043X (from IngentaConnect).
Indexed: A01, A02, A03, A08, A22, ASSIA, C06, C07, C08, C11, CA, CINAHL, E-psyche, E01, EMBASE, ExcerpMed, F09, Faml, H04, INI, JAIE, MEDLINE, P03, P30, P43, PsycInfo, PsycholAb, R10, Reac, SCOPUS, SFSA, SOPODA, SociolAb, T02.
—GNLM, IE, Infotrieve, Ingenta. **CCC.**
Published by: Informa Healthcare (Subsidiary of: T & F Informa plc), Telephone House, 69-77 Paul St, London, EC2A 4LQ, United Kingdom. TEL 44-20-70175000, FAX 44-20-70176792, healthcare.enquiries@informa.com. Ed. Jane Bliss-Holtz TEL 732-776-2495. Adv. contact Per Sonnerfeldt. **Subscr. in N. America to:** Taylor & Francis Inc., Customer Services Dept, 325 Chestnut St, 8th Fl, Philadelphia, PA 19106. TEL 215-625-8900, 800-354-1420, FAX 215-625-8914, customerservice@taylorandfrancis.com; **Subscr. outside N. America to:** Taylor & Francis Ltd., Journals Customer Service, Sheepen Pl, Colchester, Essex CO3 3LP, United Kingdom. TEL 44-20-70175544, FAX 44-20-70175198, tf.enquiries@tfinforma.com.

616.8 USA ISSN 0161-2840
CODEN: IHNUDT
➤ **ISSUES IN MENTAL HEALTH NURSING.** Text in English. 1978. m. GBP 670, EUR 870, USD 1,090 combined subscription to institutions (print & online eds.); GBP 1,330, EUR 1,745, USD 2,180 combined subscription to corporations (print & online eds.) (effective 2010). adv. bk.rev.; film rev. bibl.; charts; illus. index. back issues avail.; reprint service avail. from PSC. **Document type:** *Journal, Academic/Scholarly.* **Description:** Presents practical information about psychosocial and mental health issues in nursing.
Related titles: Online - full text ed.: ISSN 1096-4673 (from IngentaConnect).
Indexed: A01, A02, A03, A08, A22, ASG, ASSIA, C06, C07, C08, C11, CA, CINAHL, E-psyche, E01, EMBASE, ExcerpMed, F09, Faml, G10, H04, INI, JAIE, MEDLINE, NurAb, P03, P30, P34, P43, PsycInfo, PsycholAb, R10, Reac, S02, S03, SCOPUS, SFSA, SOPODA, SociolAb, T02, V&AA, W09.
—GNLM, IE, Infotrieve, Ingenta. **CCC.**
Published by: Informa Healthcare (Subsidiary of: T & F Informa plc), 52 Vanderbilt Ave, New York, NY 10017. TEL 212-262-8230, FAX 212-262-8234, healthcare.enquiries@informa.com, http://www.informahealthcare.com. Ed. Sandra P Thomas. Adv. contact Daniel Wallen. **Subscr. outside N. America to:** Informa Healthcare.

➤ **J G E N C A.** (Journal of the Gastroenterological Nurses College of Australia) *see* MEDICAL SCIENCES—Gastroenterology

610.73 JPN ISSN 0912-3741
J J N SUPESHARU/JAPANESE JOURNAL OF NURSING SPECIAL. Text in Japanese. 1986. irreg. price varies. **Document type:** *Monographic series, Academic/Scholarly.*
Published by: Igaku Shoin Ltd., 1-28-36 Hongo, Bunkyo-ku, Tokyo, 113-8719, Japan. TEL 81-3-3817-5600, FAX 81-3-3815-7791, info@igaku-shoin.co.jp. Circ: 30,000.

616.98023 USA ISSN 1070-4329
J M N R. (Journal of Military Nursing & Research) Text in English. 1993. q. USD 29.95 to individuals; USD 49.95 to institutions; USD 9 newsstand/cover (effective 2005). adv. bk.rev.; software rev.; video rev. illus. **Document type:** *Journal, Trade.* **Description:** Covers nursing and medical research for military, veteran administration and US Public Health Service professionals.
Indexed: C06, C07, C08, CINAHL, IndMed.
Published by: E.J. Gossett Publishing, Inc, 7145 S Maplewood Ave, Chicago, IL 60629-2045. TEL 312-476-5978, 800-779-JMNR, FAX 312-476-3259. Ed., Pub. Evalyn J Gossett. Circ: 2,000.

344.032 USA ISSN 1520-9229
KF3821.A15
J O N A'S HEALTHCARE LAW, ETHICS, AND REGULATION. (Journal of Nursing Administration) Text in English. 1999. q. USD 95.65 domestic to institutions; USD 160.97 foreign to institutions (effective 2011). adv. back issues avail.; reprints avail. **Document type:** *Journal, Academic/Scholarly.* **Description:** Provides valuable information on the changing regulations affecting healthcare will keep readers up-to-date on this dynamic and critical aspect of the profession.
Related titles: Online - full text ed.: ISSN 1539-073X.
Indexed: A22, C06, C07, C08, CINAHL, EMBASE, ExcerpMed, MEDLINE, P03, P30, PsycInfo, R10, Reac, SCOPUS.
—BLDSC (4673.259250), IE, INIST. **CCC.**
Published by: Lippincott Williams & Wilkins (Subsidiary of: Wolters Kluwer N.V.), 530 Walnut St, Philadelphia, PA 19106. TEL 215-521-8300, FAX 215-521-8492, customerservice@lww.com, http://www.lww.com. Ed. Rebecca F Cady TEL 401-835-0686. Pub. Beth Guthy.

610.73 JAM ISSN 0021-4140
RT1
JAMAICAN NURSE. Text in English. 1961. 3/yr. USD 25 (effective 1998). adv. bk.rev. charts; illus. cum.index. **Document type:** *Journal, Academic/Scholarly.*
Indexed: C06, C07, C08, CINAHL, INI, P30.
—GNLM.
Published by: Nurses Association of Jamaica, Mary Seacole Annex, 4 Trevennion Park Rd, PO Box 277, Kingston, 5, Jamaica. TEL 876-929-5213. Ed. Cyringa Marshall Burnett. Circ: 2,500.

610.73 JPN ISSN 1742-7932
JAPAN JOURNAL OF NURSING SCIENCE. Text in English. 2004. s-a. GBP 172 in United Kingdom to institutions; EUR 219 in Europe to institutions; USD 282 in the Americas to institutions; USD 338 elsewhere to institutions; GBP 198 combined subscription in United Kingdom to institutions (print & online eds.); EUR 252 combined subscription in Europe to institutions (print & online eds.); USD 325 combined subscription in the Americas to institutions (print & online eds.); USD 388 combined subscription elsewhere to institutions (print & online eds.) (effective 2012). reprint service avail. from PSC. **Document type:** *Journal, Academic/Scholarly.* **Description:** Contains original articles on the science of nursing.
Related titles: Online - full text ed.: ISSN 1742-7924. GBP 172 in United Kingdom to institutions; EUR 219 in Europe to institutions; USD 282 in the Americas to institutions; USD 338 elsewhere to institutions (effective 2012) (from IngentaConnect).
Indexed: A22, A26, B21, C06, C07, C08, CINAHL, E01, EMBASE, ESPM, ExcerpMed, H&SSA, H12, MEDLINE, P03, P30, PsycInfo, SCI, SCOPUS, SSCI, W07.
—BLDSC (4648.330400), IE, Ingenta. **CCC.**
Published by: (Japan Academy of Nursing Science), Wiley-Blackwell Publishing Japan (Subsidiary of: Wiley-Blackwell Publishing Ltd.), GS Chiyoda Bldg, 5F 3-11-14 Iidabashi, Chiyoda-ku, Tokyo, 102-0072, Japan. TEL 81-3-52153051, FAX 81-3-52153052, tokyo@blackwellpublishingasia.com. Ed. William L. Holzemer.

610.73 JPN ISSN 1348-8333
THE JAPANESE JOURNAL FOR PUBLIC HEALTH NURSE. Text in Japanese. 1951. m. JPY 15,000; JPY 20,000 combined subscription (print & online eds.) (effective 2010).
Formerly (until 2003): Hokenfu Zasshi (0047-1844)
Related titles: Online - full text ed.: ISSN 1882-1413.
Indexed: P30.
—BLDSC (4658.420000), GNLM.
Published by: Igaku Shoin Ltd., 1-28-36 Hongo, Bunkyo-ku, Tokyo, 113-8719, Japan. TEL 81-3-3817-5600, FAX 81-3-3815-7791, info@igaku-shoin.co.jp. Circ: 8,500.

610.73 371.42 JPN ISSN 0911-0844
JAPANESE NURSING ASSOCIATION RESEARCH REPORT. Text in Japanese; Summaries in English. 1975. irreg. JPY 1,500 (effective 2003). abstr. **Document type:** *Bulletin, Academic/Scholarly.* **Description:** Reports on status of nursing personnel.
Published by: Japanese Nursing Association, 5-8-2 Jingu-Mae, Shibuya-ku, Tokyo, 150-0001, Japan. Ed. Kazuo Fujita.

610.73 CHN ISSN 1008-9993
JIEFANGJUN HULI ZAZHI/NURSING JOURNAL OF CHINESE PEOPLE'S LIBERATION ARMY. Text in Chinese. 1984. m. USD 98.40 (effective 2009). **Document type:** *Journal, Academic/Scholarly.*
Related titles: Online - full text ed.
Published by: Di-2 Jun-Yi Daxue/Second Military Medical University, 800, Xiangyin Lu, Shanghai, 200433, China. TEL 86-21-25074487.

610.73 USA
CODEN: ICCPDQ
JOHNS HOPKINS NURSING. Text in English. 1956. q. free. adv. illus. **Document type:** *Magazine, Trade.*
Former titles: Johns Hopkins Nurses' Alumni Magazine; (until 1987): Johns Hopkins Hospital School of Nursing. Alumni Association. Alumni Magazine (0149-2608); (until 1972): Johns Hopkins Hospital School of Nursing. Alumnae Association. Alumnae Magazine (0002-6700)
Related titles: Online - full content ed.
Indexed: P30, SCOPUS.

Published by: The Johns Hopkins' Nurses Alumni Association, 525 N Wolfe St, Baltimore, MD 21205. TEL 410-614-4695, FAX 410-614-9704, communications@son.jhmi.edu. Ed. Kelly Brooks-Staub.

JOSAN ZASSHI/JAPANESE JOURNAL FOR MIDWIVES. *see* MEDICAL SCIENCES—Obstetrics And Gynecology

610.73 USA ISSN 1555-4155
➤ **JOURNAL FOR NURSE PRACTITIONERS.** Abbreviated title: J N P. Text in English. 2005 (Jul.). 10/yr. USD 153 in United States to institutions; USD 203 elsewhere to institutions (effective 2012). adv. back issues avail.; reprints avail. **Document type:** *Journal, Academic/Scholarly.* **Description:** Provides a resource for nurse practitioners stay current with the clinical and policy concerns affecting their day-to-day practice.
Related titles: Online - full text ed.: ISSN 1878-058X (from ScienceDirect).
Indexed: A26, ASSIA, C06, C07, C08, CA, CINAHL, H12, I05, P30, SCOPUS, T02.
—IE, Ingenta. **CCC.**
Published by: (American College of Nurse Practitioners), Elsevier Inc. (Subsidiary of: Elsevier Science & Technology), 1600 John F Kennedy Blvd, Philadelphia, PA 19103. TEL 215-239-3900, FAX 215-238-7883, JournalCustomerService-usa@elsevier.com, http://www.elsevier.com. Ed. Marilyn Winterton Edmunds. Pub. Nina Lander McElroy. Circ: 50,050.

658 USA ISSN 1098-7886
RT76
➤ **JOURNAL FOR NURSES IN STAFF DEVELOPMENT.** Abbreviated title: J N S D. Text in English. 1985. bi-m. USD 443.51 domestic to institutions; USD 569.78 foreign to institutions (effective 2011). adv. illus. Index. back issues avail.; reprints avail. **Document type:** *Journal, Academic/Scholarly.* **Description:** Designed for staff development and patient educators in all healthcare settings. Provides educators with information on planning, implementing, and evaluating educational activities.
Formerly (until 1998): Journal of Nursing Staff Development (0882-0627)
Related titles: CD-ROM ed.; Microform ed.: (from PQC); Online - full text ed.: ISSN 1538-9049. USD 308.10 domestic academic site license; USD 358.10 foreign academic site license; USD 343.65 domestic corporate site license; USD 393.65 foreign corporate site license (effective 2002).
Indexed: A22, C06, C07, C08, CINAHL, EMBASE, ExcerpMed, FamI, INI, MEDLINE, P30, SCOPUS.
—BLDSC (5023.660000), GNLM, IE, Infotrieve, Ingenta. **CCC.**
Published by: (National Nursing Staff Development Organization), Lippincott Williams & Wilkins (Subsidiary of: Wolters Kluwer N.V.), Two Commerce Sq, 2001 Market St, Philadelphia, PA 19103. TEL 215-521-8300, FAX 215-521-8902, customerservice@lww.com, http://www.lww.com. Ed. Belinda Puetz TEL 850-501-2860. Pub. Beth Guthy. Adv. contact Pat Wendelken. Circ: 4,575.

610.73 USA ISSN 1539-0136
RJ245 CODEN: MCNJA2
➤ **JOURNAL FOR SPECIALISTS IN PEDIATRIC NURSING.** Variant title: J S P N. Text in English. 1972. q. GBP 143 in United Kingdom to institutions; EUR 180 in Europe to institutions; USD 204 in the Americas to institutions; USD 276 elsewhere to institutions; GBP 165 combined subscription in United Kingdom to institutions (print & online eds.); EUR 207 combined subscription in Europe to institutions (print & online eds.); USD 235 combined subscription in the Americas to institutions (print & online eds.); USD 317 combined subscription elsewhere to institutions (print & online eds.) (effective 2012). adv. bk.rev. back issues avail.; reprint service avail. from PSC. **Document type:** *Journal, Academic/Scholarly.* **Description:** Publishes articles on the professional care of mothers and children for the expert nurse practitioner.
Former titles (until 2002): Society of Pediatric Nurses. Journal (1088-145X); (until 1996): Maternal - Child Nursing Journal (0090-0702)
Related titles: Microform ed.: (from PQC); Online - full text ed.: ISSN 1744-6155. GBP 143 in United Kingdom to institutions; EUR 180 in Europe to institutions; USD 204 in the Americas to institutions; USD 276 elsewhere to institutions (effective 2012) (from IngentaConnect).
Indexed: A01, A02, A03, A08, A22, A26, C06, C07, C08, C11, CA, CINAHL, CurCont, E-psyche, E01, E08, EMBASE, ExcerpMed, FamI, G06, G07, G08, H04, H11, H12, I05, INI, IndMed, MEDLINE, NurAb, P03, P16, P20, P22, P24, P25, P30, P43, P48, P53, P54, PQC, PsycInfo, PsycholAb, R10, Reac, S09, SCI, SCOPUS, SFSA, SSCI, T02, V02, W07.
—BLDSC (5066.139000), GNLM, IE, Ingenta, INIST. **CCC.**
Published by: (Society of Pediatric Nurses), Wiley-Blackwell Publishing, Inc. (Subsidiary of: Wiley-Blackwell Publishing Ltd.), 111 River St, Hoboken, NJ 07030. TEL 201-748-6000, FAX 201-748-6088, info@wiley.com. Ed. Roxie L Foster. Adv. contact Karl Franz TEL 781-388-8470.

610.73 362.29 GBR ISSN 1088-4602
CODEN: ADNUFH
➤ **JOURNAL OF ADDICTIONS NURSING.** Text in English. 1989. q. GBP 320, EUR 415, USD 520 combined subscription to institutions (print & online eds.); GBP 630, EUR 830, USD 1,035 combined subscription to corporations (print & online eds.) (effective 2010). adv. back issues avail.; reprint service avail. from PSC. **Document type:** *Journal, Academic/Scholarly.* **Description:** Brings out articles on current research, issues, practices and innovations as they relate to the field of addictions. Also offers continuing education credits for nursing addiction professionals.
Former titles (until 1996): Addictions Nursing (1073-886X); (until 1994): Addictions Nursing Network (0899-9112)
Related titles: Online - full text ed.: ISSN 1548-7148 (from IngentaConnect).
Indexed: A20, A22, ASSIA, AddicA, C06, C07, C08, CINAHL, CurCont, E01, FamI, P03, P30, PsycInfo, PsycholAb, S02, S03, SCI, SCOPUS, SSCI, THA, W07.
—BLDSC (4918.934030), IE, Ingenta. **CCC.**
Published by: (International Nurses Society on Addictions USA), Informa Healthcare (Subsidiary of: T & F Informa plc), Telephone House, 69-77 Paul St, London, EC2A 4LQ, United Kingdom. TEL 44-20-70175000, FAX 44-20-70176792, healthcare.enquiries@informa.com. Ed. Christine Vourakis TEL 916-278-4663. Adv. contact Per Sonnerfeldt. **Subscr. in N. America to:** Taylor & Francis Inc., Customer Services Dept, 325 Chestnut St, 8th Fl, Philadelphia, PA 19106. TEL 215-625-8900, 800-354-1420, FAX 215-625-8914, customerservice@taylorandfrancis.com; **Subscr. outside N. America to:** Taylor & Francis Ltd., Journals Customer Service, Sheepen Pl, Colchester, Essex CO3 3LP, United Kingdom. TEL 44-20-70175544, FAX 44-20-70175198, tf.enquiries@tfinforma.com.

610.73 GBR ISSN 0309-2402
RT1
➤ **JOURNAL OF ADVANCED NURSING.** Abbreviated title: J A N. Text in English. 1976. m. GBP 1,498 in United Kingdom to institutions; EUR 1,903 in Europe to institutions; USD 2,771 in the Americas to institutions; USD 3,233 elsewhere to institutions; GBP 1,723 combined subscription in United Kingdom to institutions (print & online eds.); EUR 2,189 combined subscription in Europe to institutions (print & online eds.); USD 3,188 combined subscription in the Americas to institutions (print & online eds.); USD 3,719 combined subscription elsewhere to institutions (print & online eds.) (effective 2012). adv. bk.rev. bibl.; illus. index. back issues avail.; reprint service avail. from PSC. **Document type:** *Journal, Academic/Scholarly.* **Description:** Promotes diversity of research and scholarship in terms of culture, paradigm and healthcare context.
Related titles: CD-ROM ed.; Microform ed.: (from PQC); Online - full text ed.: ISSN 1365-2648. GBP 1,498 in United Kingdom to institutions; EUR 1,903 in Europe to institutions; USD 2,771 in the Americas to institutions; USD 3,233 elsewhere to institutions (effective 2012) (from IngentaConnect).
Indexed: A01, A02, A03, A08, A20, A22, A26, AHCMS, AMED, ASCA, ASG, AgeL, B28, C06, C07, C08, C11, CA, CINAHL, CurCont, DiabCont, E01, EMBASE, ExcerpMed, F09, FR, FamI, G10, H04, H12, INI, IndMed, MEDLINE, P02, P03, P24, P30, P34, P48, P50, PQC, PsycInfo, PsycholAb, R10, Reac, S02, S03, S21, SCI, SCOPUS, SSCI, T02, W07, W09.
—BLDSC (4918.947000), GNLM, IE, Infotrieve, Ingenta, INIST. **CCC.**
Published by: Wiley-Blackwell Publishing Ltd. (Subsidiary of: John Wiley & Sons, Inc.), 9600 Garsington Rd, Oxford, OX4 2DQ, United Kingdom. TEL 44-1865-776868, FAX 44-1865-714591, customerservices@blackwellpublishing.com, http://www.wiley.com/. Ed. Alison Tierney. Adv. contact Joanna Baker TEL 44-1865-476271.

610.73 USA ISSN 1940-5626
RT4
JOURNAL OF ADVANCED PRACTICE NURSING. Text in English. 2007 (Nov.). q. free to members (effective 2009). back issues avail. **Document type:** *Journal, Trade.* **Description:** Features important research that serves the needs of advanced practice nurses.
Media: Online - full content.
Published by: American Society of Registered Nurses, 1001 Bridgeway, Ste 411, Sausalito, CA 94965. TEL 415-331-2700, 800-331-1206, FAX 415-476-4558, office@asrn.org. Ed. Alison Palmer.

THE JOURNAL OF CARDIOVASCULAR NURSING. *see* MEDICAL SCIENCES—Cardiovascular Diseases

616.89 155.4 USA ISSN 1073-6077
RJ499.A1
➤ **JOURNAL OF CHILD AND ADOLESCENT PSYCHIATRIC NURSING.** Abbreviated title: J C A P N. Text in English. 1987-1991; resumed 1994. q. GBP 159 in United Kingdom to institutions; EUR 203 in Europe to institutions; USD 243 in the Americas to institutions; USD 312 elsewhere to institutions; GBP 184 combined subscription in United Kingdom to institutions (print & online eds.); EUR 234 combined subscription in Europe to institutions (print & online eds.); USD 280 combined subscription in the Americas to institutions (print & online eds.); USD 360 combined subscription elsewhere to institutions (print & online eds.) (effective 2012). adv. bk.rev. back issues avail.; reprint service avail. from PSC. **Document type:** *Journal, Academic/Scholarly.* **Description:** Provides a professional forum for nurses involved in promoting the mental health of children and adolescents and caring for emotionally disturbed youth and their families.
Formerly (until 1994): Journal of Child and Adolescent Psychiatric and Mental Health Nursing (0897-9685)
Related titles: Online - full text ed.: ISSN 1744-6171. GBP 159 in United Kingdom to institutions; EUR 203 in Europe to institutions; USD 243 in the Americas to institutions; USD 312 elsewhere to institutions (effective 2012) (from IngentaConnect).
Indexed: A01, A02, A03, A08, A22, A26, B21, C06, C07, C08, C11, CA, CINAHL, E-psyche, E01, E03, E07, E08, EMBASE, ERI, ExcerpMed, F09, FamI, G08, H04, H11, H12, I05, INI, MEDLINE, NSA, P03, P04, P10, P12, P18, P20, P22, P24, P30, P48, P53, P54, P55, PQC, PsycInfo, PsycholAb, R10, Reac, S09, SCOPUS, T02.
—BLDSC (4957.423500), GNLM, IE, Infotrieve, Ingenta. **CCC.**
Published by: (Association of Child & Adolescent Psychiatric Nurses), Wiley-Blackwell Publishing, Inc. (Subsidiary of: Wiley-Blackwell Publishing Ltd.), 111 River St, Hoboken, NJ 07030. TEL 201-748-6000, FAX 201-748-6088, info@wiley.com. Ed. Dr. Elizabeth C Poster TEL 817-272-2776. Adv. contact Karl Franz TEL 781-388-8470.

610.73 USA ISSN 0743-2550
RT85
➤ **JOURNAL OF CHRISTIAN NURSING.** Abbreviated title: J C N. Text in English. 1950. q. USD 228 domestic to institutions; USD 344 foreign to institutions (effective 2011). adv. bk.rev.; film rev.; video rev. abstr. cum.index. back issues avail.; reprints avail. **Document type:** *Journal, Academic/Scholarly.* **Description:** Aims to help nurses and nursing students practice from a biblically-based, Christian perspective.
Formerly (until 1984): Nurses Lamp (0885-5854)
Related titles: Microform ed.: (from PQC); Online - full text ed.: ISSN 1931-7662.
Indexed: A22, C06, C07, C08, CA, CINAHL, ChrPI, EMBASE, ExcerpMed, FamI, INI, MEDLINE, NurAb, P30, R10, Reac, SCOPUS, T02.
—BLDSC (4958.275000), GNLM, IE, Infotrieve, Ingenta. **CCC.**
Published by: (InterVarsity Christian Fellowship, Nurses Christian Fellowship), Lippincott Williams & Wilkins (Subsidiary of: Wolters Kluwer N.V.), Two Commerce Sq, 2001 Market St, Philadelphia, PA 19103. TEL 215-521-8300, FAX 215-521-8902, customerservice@lww.com, http://www.lww.com. Ed. Kathy Schoonover-Shoffner. Pub. Terry Materese. Adv. contact Pat Wendelken. Circ: 5,452.

610.73 GBR ISSN 0962-1067
RT41 CODEN: JCCNEW
➤ **JOURNAL OF CLINICAL NURSING.** Abbreviated title: J C N. Text in English. 1992. m. (1 combined). GBP 1,212 in United Kingdom to institutions; EUR 1,540 in Europe to institutions; USD 2,238 in the Americas to institutions; USD 2,611 elsewhere to institutions; GBP 1,394 combined subscription in United Kingdom to institutions (print & online eds.); EUR 1,771 combined subscription in Europe to institutions (print & online eds.); USD 2,574 combined subscription in the Americas to institutions (print & online eds.); USD 3,003 combined subscription elsewhere to institutions (print & online eds.) (effective 2012). adv. bk.rev. bibl. index. back issues avail.; reprint service avail. from PSC. **Document type:** *Journal, Academic/Scholarly.* **Description:** Seeks to enhance nurses practice, focusing directly on the theory and practice of nursing and highlighting matters of concern to practicing nurses.
Related titles: CD-ROM ed.; Microform ed.: (from PQC); Online - full text ed.: ISSN 1365-2702. GBP 1,212 in United Kingdom to institutions; EUR 1,540 in Europe to institutions; USD 2,238 in the Americas to institutions; USD 2,611 elsewhere to institutions (effective 2012) (from IngentaConnect); ◆ Supplement(s): Journal of Nursing and Healthcare of Chronic Illness. ISSN 1752-9816.
Indexed: A01, A02, A03, A08, A20, A22, A26, ASCA, ASG, AgeL, B21, B28, C06, C07, C08, C11, CA, CINAHL, CurCont, DiabCont, E01, EMBASE, ESPM, ExcerpMed, F09, FR, FamI, H&SSA, H04, H12, INI, MEDLINE, P03, P24, P30, P34, P48, PQC, PsycInfo, R10, Reac, SCI, SCOPUS, SSCI, T02, W07, W09.
—BLDSC (4958.595000), GNLM, IE, Infotrieve, Ingenta, INIST. **CCC.**
Published by: Wiley-Blackwell Publishing Ltd. (Subsidiary of: John Wiley & Sons, Inc.), 9600 Garsington Rd, Oxford, OX4 2DQ, United Kingdom. TEL 44-1865-776868, FAX 44-1865-714591, customerservices@blackwellpublishing.com. Eds. Carol Haigh, Debra Jackson, Roger Watson. Adv. contact Joanna Baker TEL 44-1865-476271.

610.73 USA ISSN 0737-0016
RT98
➤ **JOURNAL OF COMMUNITY HEALTH NURSING.** Text in English. 1984. q. GBP 394 combined subscription in United Kingdom to institutions (print & online eds.); EUR 526, USD 661 combined subscription to institutions (print & online eds.) (effective 2012). adv. bk.rev. abstr.; charts; illus. back issues avail.; reprint service avail. from PSC. **Document type:** *Journal, Academic/Scholarly.* **Description:** Focuses on health care issues relevant to all aspects of community practice - schools, homes, visiting nursing services, clinics, hospices, education, and public health administration.
Related titles: Online - full text ed.: ISSN 1532-7655. GBP 355 in United Kingdom to institutions; EUR 473, USD 595 to institutions (effective 2012).
Indexed: A01, A02, A03, A08, A22, A29, ASSIA, B20, B21, C06, C07, C08, C11, CA, CINAHL, CurCont, E-psyche, E01, EMBASE, ESPM, ExcerpMed, F09, FamI, H&SSA, H04, I10, INI, IndMed, MEDLINE, P03, P20, P24, P25, P30, P34, P43, P48, P50, P54, PQC, PsycInfo, PsycholAb, R10, Reac, S02, S03, SCI, SCOPUS, SSCI, T02, THA, ViroIAbstr, W07.
—BLDSC (4961.722000), GNLM, IE, Infotrieve, Ingenta, INIST. **CCC.**
Published by: Routledge (Subsidiary of: Taylor & Francis Group), 325 Chestnut St, Ste 800, Philadelphia, PA 19106. TEL 800-354-1420, FAX 215-625-2940, journals@routledge.com, http://www.routledge.com. Adv. contact Linda Hann TEL 44-1344-779945.

610.73 GBR
JOURNAL OF COMMUNITY NURSING. Abbreviated title: J C N. Text in English. 1977. m. GBP 65 domestic; GBP 114 foreign; free to qualified personnel (effective 2009). adv. bk.rev. back issues avail. **Document type:** *Journal, Trade.* **Description:** Promotes excellence in primary care practice and nurse prescribing.
Former titles (until 1992): Journal of District Nursing (0263-4465); (until 1982): Journal of Community Nursing (0140-0908)
Related titles: Online - full text ed.
Indexed: A26, B28, C06, C07, C08, CINAHL, H12, H13, I05, P10, P20, P24, P48, P50, P53, P54, PQC, SCOPUS.
—IE, Ingenta. **CCC.**
Published by: P T M Publishers Ltd., 282 High St, Sutton, Surrey SM1 1PQ, United Kingdom. TEL 44-20-8642-0162, FAX 44-20-8642-2275. Ed. Fiona Meehan. Pub. Stephen Mell. Adv. contact Joanna Issa. Circ: 23,500.

610.73 USA ISSN 0022-0124
RT90
➤ **THE JOURNAL OF CONTINUING EDUCATION IN NURSING.** Text in English. 1970. m. USD 124 combined subscription to individuals (print & online eds.); USD 345 combined subscription to institutions (print & online eds.); USD 28 per issue (effective 2010). adv. bk.rev. reprints avail. **Document type:** *Journal, Academic/Scholarly.* **Description:** Provides articles on continued career comnpetence through education and staff development.
Related titles: Microform ed.: (from PQC); Online - full text ed.: ISSN 1938-2472.
Indexed: A22, AMED, B04, BRD, C06, C07, C08, CA, CINAHL, CPE, CurCont, E02, E03, EMBASE, ERI, EdA, EdI, ExcerpMed, FamI, INI, MEDLINE, NurAb, P03, P18, P20, P22, P24, P30, P48, P53, P54, P55, PQC, PsycInfo, R10, Reac, S04, S21, SCI, SCOPUS, SSCI, T02, W03, W05, W07.
—BLDSC (4965.246000), GNLM, IE, Infotrieve, Ingenta. **CCC.**
Published by: Slack, Inc., 6900 Grove Rd, Thorofare, NJ 08086. TEL 856-848-1000, FAX 856-848-6091, customerservice@slackinc.com, http://www.slackinc.com. Ed. Patricia S Yoder Wise. Adv. contact Kara Datz TEL 856-848-1000 ext 549.

306 USA ISSN 1071-5568
RT86.54
➤ **JOURNAL OF CULTURAL DIVERSITY;** an interdisciplinary journal. Abbreviated title: J C D. Text in English. 1994. q. USD 150 domestic to individuals; USD 350 domestic to institutions; USD 425 foreign (effective 2010). bk.rev.; software rev.; video rev. abstr.; charts; illus. index. back issues avail.; reprints avail. **Document type:** *Journal, Academic/Scholarly.* **Description:** Documents the distinct nature and health-care needs of the multi-cultural patient with original research and health-related manuscripts, materials, and reviews.
Related titles: Online - full text ed.
Indexed: A01, A02, A03, A08, A22, A26, ABS&EES, C06, C07, C08, CA, CINAHL, E07, E08, EMBASE, ExcerpMed, FamI, G08, H04, H11, H12, I05, INI, MEDLINE, P10, P20, P22, P24, P30, P48, P50, P53, P54, PQC, R10, Reac, S02, S03, S09, SCOPUS, T02.

—BLDSC (4965.842000), GNLM, IE, Infotrieve, Ingenta. **CCC.**
Published by: Tucker Publications, Inc., PO Box 580, Lisle, IL 60532. TEL 630-969-3895, FAX 630-969-3895, info@tuckerpub.com, http://www.tuckerpub.com. Eds. Dr. Barbara Broome, Dr. Kay Edwards. Pub. Dr. Sallie Tucker-Allen.

610.736 616.462 GBR ISSN 1368-1109
RT1
JOURNAL OF DIABETES NURSING; the journal for professionals working in the field of diabetes nursing. Text in English. 1997. 10/yr. free to qualified personnel (effective 2010). adv. back issues avail. **Document type:** *Journal, Trade.* **Description:** Features articles covering clinical, professional issues, education, research, and primary and secondary care interface, along with diabetes nursing.
Related titles: Online - full text ed.
Indexed: A26, B28, C06, C07, C08, CINAHL, E08, G08, H11, H12, I05, S09, SCOPUS.
—BLDSC (4969.408000), IE, Ingenta. **CCC.**
Published by: S B Communications Group (Subsidiary of: Schofield Publishing), 3.05 Enterprise House, 1-2 Hatfields, London, SE1 9PG, United Kingdom. TEL 44-20-76271510, FAX 44-20-76271570, info@sbcommunicationsgroup.com, http://www.sbcommunicationsgroup.com. Ed. Debbie Hicks. Pub. Simon Breed. adv.: page GBP 1,339; trim 210 x 297.

610.73 USA ISSN 0099-1767
RT120.E4
➤ **JOURNAL OF EMERGENCY NURSING.** Key Title: JEN, Journal of Emergency Nursing. Variant title: J E N. Text in English. 1975. bi-m. USD 362 in United States to institutions; USD 389 elsewhere to institutions (effective 2012). adv. bk.rev. illus. index. Supplement avail.; back issues avail.; reprints avail. **Document type:** *Journal, Academic/Scholarly.* **Description:** Provides information on emergency care, with articles written and reviewed by emergency nurses.
Related titles: CD-ROM ed.; Microfilm ed.: (from PQC); Online - full text ed.: ISSN 1527-2966 (from ScienceDirect).
Indexed: A20, A22, A26, ASSIA, B28, C06, C07, C08, CA, CINAHL, CurCont, E01, EMBASE, ExcerpMed, F09, FamI, H12, I05, INI, MEDLINE, NurAb, P24, P30, P48, P50, PQC, R10, Reac, SCI, SCOPUS, SSCI, T02, W07.
—BLDSC (4977.300000), GNLM, IE, Infotrieve, Ingenta. **CCC.**
Published by: (Emergency Nurses Association), Mosby, Inc. (Subsidiary of: Elsevier Health Sciences), 1600 John F. Kennedy Blvd, Ste 1800, Philadelphia, PA 19103. TEL 215-239-3900, 800-523-1649, FAX 215-239-3990, elspcs@elsevier.com, http://www.us.elsevierhealth.com. Ed. Renee Semonin Holleran. Pub. Jami Walker.

614 GBR ISSN 1474-9114
THE JOURNAL OF FAMILY HEALTH CARE. Abbreviated title: J F H C. Text in English. 1965. bi-m. GBP 30 domestic to individuals; GBP 42 in Europe to individuals; GBP 50 elsewhere to individuals; GBP 55 domestic to libraries; GBP 70 in Europe to libraries; GBP 77 elsewhere to libraries (effective 2009); subscr. includes School Health Journal. adv. bk.rev. index. **Document type:** *Journal, Academic/Scholarly.* **Description:** Covers a wide range of clinical, nutritional and social issues affecting families.
Former titles (until 2002): Professional Care of Mother & Child (0964-4156); (until 1991): Midwife Health Visitor & Community Nurse (0306-9699); (until 1975): Midwife and Health Visitor (0026-3516)
Indexed: A22, A26, B28, C06, C07, C08, CINAHL, DentInd, E07, EMBASE, ExcerpMed, F09, FamI, I05, INI, MEDLINE, P30, R10, Reac, SCOPUS.
—BLDSC (4983.665000), GNLM, IE, Ingenta. **CCC.**
Published by: Pavilion Publishing, PO Box 100, Chichester, W Sussex PO18 8HD, United Kingdom. TEL 44-1243-576444, FAX 44-1243-576456, info@pavpub.com, http://www.pavpub.com/. Ed. Pat Scowen TEL 44-1243-816689. Adv. contact Sarah Monger.

610.73 USA ISSN 1074-8407
RT120.F34 CODEN: JFNUFS
➤ **JOURNAL OF FAMILY NURSING.** Text in English. 1995. q. USD 831, GBP 489 combined subscription to institutions (print & online eds.); USD 814, GBP 479 to institutions (effective 2011). adv. bk.rev. back issues avail.; reprint service avail. from PSC. **Document type:** *Journal, Academic/Scholarly.* **Description:** Publishes empirical and theoretical analyses and scholarly work on nursing research, education, and policy issues pertaining to family health and illness.
Related titles: Online - full text ed.: ISSN 1552-549X. USD 748, GBP 440 to institutions (effective 2011).
Indexed: A01, A02, A03, A08, A20, A22, ASG, ASSIA, B07, C06, C07, C08, CA, CINAHL, CurCont, E-psyche, E01, EMBASE, ExcerpMed, F09, FamI, H04, H13, MEDLINE, P02, P03, P10, P20, P24, P25, P30, P48, P50, P53, P54, PQC, PsycInfo, PsycholAb, R10, Reac, S02, S03, SCI, SCOPUS, SFSA, SOPODA, SSCI, SociolAb, T02, V02, W07.
—BLDSC (4983.720000), IE, Infotrieve, Ingenta. **CCC.**
Published by: (University of Calgary CAN, Faculty of Nursing CAN), Sage Publications, Inc., 2455 Teller Rd, Thousand Oaks, CA 91320. TEL 805-499-9774, 800-818-7243, FAX 805-499-0871, 800-583-2665, info@sagepub.com. Ed. Janice M Bell. Circ: 600 (paid). **Subscr. to:** Sage Publications Ltd., 1 Oliver's Yard, 55 City Rd, London EC1Y 1SP, United Kingdom. TEL 44-207-3248701, FAX 44-207-3248733, subscription@sagepub.co.uk.

610.73 USA ISSN 1556-3693
RA1155
➤ **JOURNAL OF FORENSIC NURSING.** Abbreviated title: J F N. Text in English. 2005. q. GBP 115 in United Kingdom to institutions; EUR 146 in Europe to institutions; USD 229 in the Americas to institutions; USD 223 elsewhere to institutions; GBP 133 combined subscription in United Kingdom to institutions (print & online eds.); EUR 168 combined subscription in Europe to institutions (print & online eds.); USD 264 combined subscription in the Americas to institutions (print & online eds.); USD 257 combined subscription elsewhere to institutions (print & online eds.) (effective 2012). adv. back issues avail.; reprint service avail. from PSC. **Document type:** *Journal, Academic/Scholarly.* **Description:** Contains articles on advances in forensic nursing practice, research, administration, and education.
Related titles: Online - full text ed.: ISSN 1939-3938. GBP 115 in United Kingdom to institutions; EUR 146 in Europe to institutions; USD 229 in the Americas to institutions; USD 223 elsewhere to institutions (effective 2012) (from IngentaConnect).
Indexed: A22, A26, C06, C07, C08, CINAHL, E01, E08, EMBASE, ExcerpMed, G08, H11, H12, I05, MEDLINE, P03, P24, P30, P48, P52, PQC, PsycInfo, R10, Reac, SCOPUS.
—BLDSC (4984.592700), IE, Ingenta. **CCC.**
Published by: (International Association of Forensic Nurses), Wiley-Blackwell Publishing, Inc. (Subsidiary of: Wiley-Blackwell Publishing Ltd.), 111 River St, Hoboken, NJ 07030. TEL 201-748-6000, FAX 201-748-6088, info@wiley.com. Ed. Cindy Peternelj-Taylor. Adv. contact Karl Franz TEL 781-388-8470.

➤ **JOURNAL OF GERONTOLOGICAL NURSING**; for nursing care of older adults. *see* GERONTOLOGY AND GERIATRICS

➤ **JOURNAL OF GYNECOLOGIC ONCOLOGY NURSING.** *see* MEDICAL SCIENCES—Oncology

610.73 USA ISSN 0898-0101
RT42 CODEN: JHNUF8
➤ **JOURNAL OF HOLISTIC NURSING.** Text in English. 1983. q. USD 519, GBP 305 combined subscription to institutions (print & online eds.); USD 509, GBP 299 to institutions (effective 2011). adv. index. back issues avail.; reprint service avail. from PSC. **Document type:** *Journal, Academic/Scholarly.* **Description:** Offers a holistic nursing foundation for practitioners and educators through shared research and clinical experience; publishes original work and disseminates the ideals of holistic nursing to the health care community.
Related titles: Online - full text ed.: ISSN 1552-5724. USD 467, GBP 275 to institutions (effective 2011).
Indexed: A22, AMED, ASSIA, C06, C07, C08, CINAHL, E-psyche, E01, EMBASE, ExcerpMed, F09, FamI, H13, INI, MEDLINE, P02, P10, P20, P24, P30, P48, P53, P54, PQC, R10, Reac, SCOPUS, SOPODA, SociolAb.
—BLDSC (5002.710000), GNLM, IE, Infotrieve, Ingenta. **CCC.**
Published by: (American Holistic Nurses' Association), Sage Publications, Inc., 2455 Teller Rd, Thousand Oaks, CA 91320. TEL 805-499-9774, 800-818-7243, FAX 805-499-0871, 800-583-2665, info@sagepub.com. Ed. W Richard Cowling III. Circ: 3,226 (paid). **Subscr. outside the Americas to:** Sage Publications Ltd., 1 Oliver's Yard, 55 City Rd, London EC1Y 1SP, United Kingdom. TEL 44-20-73248701, FAX 44-20-73248733, subscription@sagepub.co.uk.

610.73 USA ISSN 1522-2179
RT87.T45
➤ **JOURNAL OF HOSPICE AND PALLIATIVE NURSING.** Abbreviated title: J H P N. Text in English. 1999. bi-m. USD 244.51 domestic to institutions; USD 365 foreign to institutions (effective 2011). adv. back issues avail.; reprints avail. **Document type:** *Journal, Academic/Scholarly.* **Description:** Focuses on clinical articles of interest to nurses caring for patients enrolled in hospice programs and nurses providing palliative care in a variety of settings.
Related titles: Online - full text ed.: ISSN 1539-0705.
Indexed: ASG, B28, C06, C07, C08, CA, CINAHL, CurCont, P30, P34, SCI, SCOPUS, SSCI, T02, W07.
—BLDSC (5003.230000), IE. **CCC.**
Published by: (Hospice and Palliative Nurses Association), Lippincott Williams & Wilkins (Subsidiary of: Wolters Kluwer N.V.), 530 Walnut St, Philadelphia, PA 19106. TEL 215-521-8300, FAX 215-521-8902, customerservice@lww.com, http://www.lww.com. Ed. Dr. Betty Rolling Ferrell. Pub. Kathleen M Phelan. Adv. contact Robert Reed TEL 630-845-1285. color page USD 3,030, B&W page USD 1,585; trim 7.75 x 10.75. Circ: 9,057.

658 USA ISSN 1533-1458
CODEN: JINOCS
➤ **JOURNAL OF INFUSION NURSING.** Text in English. 1978. bi-m. USD 335.51 domestic to institutions; USD 451 foreign to institutions (effective 2011). adv. abstr.; bibl.; charts; illus. Index. back issues avail.; reprints avail. **Document type:** *Journal, Academic/Scholarly.* **Description:** Aims to promote excellence in infusion nursing by presenting new research, clinical reviews, case studies, and professional development information relevant to the practice of infusion therapy.
Former titles (until 2001): Journal of Intravenous Nursing (0896-5846); (until 1988): N I T A (0160-3930)
Related titles: CD-ROM ed.; Microform ed.: (from PQC); Online - full text ed.: ISSN 1539-0667.
Indexed: A22, C06, C07, C08, CINAHL, EMBASE, ExcerpMed, I12, INI, MEDLINE, NurAb, P30, R10, Reac, SCOPUS.
—BLDSC (5006.865000), GNLM, IE, Ingenta. **CCC.**
Published by: (Infusion Nurses Society), Lippincott Williams & Wilkins (Subsidiary of: Wolters Kluwer N.V.), Two Commerce Sq, 2001 Market St, Philadelphia, PA 19103. TEL 215-521-8300, FAX 215-521-8902, customerservice@lww.com, http://www.lww.com. Ed. Mary Alexander. Pub. Sandra Kasko. Circ: 7,000.

➤ **JOURNAL OF INTELLECTUAL DISABILITIES.** *see* EDUCATION—Special Education And Rehabilitation

610.73 340 USA ISSN 1080-3297
K10
THE JOURNAL OF LEGAL NURSE CONSULTING. Text in English. 1990. q. USD 145 membership (effective 2005). adv. bk.rev. back issues avail. **Document type:** *Newsletter.* **Description:** Provides a forum for continuing education, facilities and exchange of information; establishes a communication network for its members; it also functions as a resource to other professional organizations of similar interest.
Formerly (until vol.6, 1995): American Association of Legal Nurse Consultants Network (1065-3449)
Indexed: C06, C07, C08, CINAHL.
—BLDSC (5010.271500).
Published by: American Association of Legal Nurse Consultants, 4700 W Lake Ave, Glenview, IL 60025-1485. TEL 847-375-4713, FAX 847-375-4777, JLNC@aalnc.org. Ed. S Fandray. Adv. contact Pat Delaney. page USD 470. Circ: 1,800 (paid).

JOURNAL OF MIDWIFERY & WOMEN'S HEALTH. *see* MEDICAL SCIENCES—Obstetrics And Gynecology

612.652 GBR ISSN 1355-1841
RJ253
➤ **JOURNAL OF NEONATAL NURSING.** Text in English. 1994. 6/yr. EUR 376 in Europe to institutions; JPY 51,300 in Japan to institutions; USD 473 elsewhere to institutions (effective 2012). adv. bk.rev. abstr.; charts; illus. back issues avail. **Document type:** *Journal, Academic/Scholarly.* **Description:** Guides for nurses, midwives and all other professionals concerned with the care of preterm infants and small, vulnerable term infants and their families.
Related titles: Online - full text ed.: ISSN 1878-089X (from ScienceDirect).
Indexed: A26, ASSIA, B28, C06, C07, C08, CINAHL, H12, I05, P03, P30, PsycInfo, SCOPUS.
—BLDSC (5021.399200), IE, Ingenta. **CCC.**
Published by: (Neonatal Nurses Association), Elsevier Ltd (Subsidiary of: Elsevier Science & Technology), The Blvd, Langford Ln, Kidlington, Oxford, OX5 1GB, United Kingdom. TEL 44-1865-843000, FAX 44-1865-843010, journalscustomerserviceemea@elsevier.com. Ed. Dee Beresford. adv.: B&W page GBP 830, color page GBP 1,260; trim 210 x 297. Circ: 3,750 (paid); 500 (controlled).

610.73 USA ISSN 0888-0395
RC350.5 CODEN: JNNUEF
➤ **JOURNAL OF NEUROSCIENCE NURSING.** Abbreviated title: J N N. Text in English. 1969. bi-m. USD 274.37 domestic to institutions; USD 311.78 foreign to institutions (effective 2011). adv. bk.rev. illus. back issues avail.; reprints avail. **Document type:** *Journal, Academic/Scholarly.* **Description:** Contains original articles on advances in neurosurgical and neurological techniques as they affect nursing procedures and commentary on the role of the neuroscience nurse in the health care team.
Formerly (until 1986): Journal of Neurosurgical Nursing (0047-2603)
Related titles: Microform ed.: (from PQC); Online - full text ed.: ISSN 1945-2810.
Indexed: A22, A25, A26, C06, C07, C08, CINAHL, CurCont, E08, EMBASE, ExcerpMed, F09, FamI, G06, G07, G08, H11, H12, HospLI, I05, INI, IndMed, MEDLINE, NurAb, P20, P22, P24, P30, P48, P54, PQC, PsycInfo, R10, Reac, S08, S09, SCI, SCOPUS, SSCI, W07.
—BLDSC (5022.085000), GNLM, IE, Infotrieve, Ingenta, INIST. **CCC.**
Published by: (American Association of Neuroscience Nurses), Lippincott Williams & Wilkins (Subsidiary of: Wolters Kluwer N.V.), 333 7th Ave, 19th Fl, New York, NY 10001. TEL 212-886-1200, FAX 212-886-1205, customerservice@lww.com, http://www.lww.com. Ed. V Susan Carroll. Pub. Beth Guthy. Adv. contact Mark Harling. Circ: 6,379.

610.736 USA ISSN 1942-4469
JOURNAL OF NURSE LIFE CARE PLANNING. Variant title: A A N L C P Journal of Nurse Life Care Planning. Text in English. 1998. q. **Document type:** *Journal, Trade.*
Indexed: C06, C07.
Published by: American Association of Nurse Life Care Planners, 3267 E 3300 S #309, Salt Lake City, UT 84109. TEL 801-274-1184, 888-575-4047, FAX 801-274-1535, http://www.aanlcp.org.

610.73 USA ISSN 1940-6967
RT4
JOURNAL OF NURSING. Text in English. 2007. m. free to members (effective 2009). back issues avail. **Document type:** *Journal, Trade.* **Description:** Features important research that serves the needs of advanced practice nurses.
Media: Online - full content.
Published by: American Society of Registered Nurses, 1001 Bridgeway, Ste 411, Sausalito, CA 94965. TEL 415-331-2700, 800-331-1206, FAX 415-476-4558, office@asrn.org. Ed. Alison Palmer.

610.73 USA ISSN 0002-0443
RT89 CODEN: JNUAA
➤ **THE JOURNAL OF NURSING ADMINISTRATION.** Abbreviated title: J O N A. Text in English. 1971. 11/yr. USD 533.01 domestic to institutions; USD 661 foreign to institutions (effective 2011). adv. illus. Index. back issues avail.; reprints avail. **Document type:** *Journal, Academic/Scholarly.* **Description:** Provides information on developments and advances in patient care leadership.
Related titles: CD-ROM ed.; Microform ed.: (from PQC); Online - full text ed.: ISSN 1539-0721.
Indexed: A01, A03, A08, A20, A22, AHCMS, AIM, ASCA, C06, C07, C08, CA, CINAHL, CurCont, EMBASE, ExcerpMed, FamI, H13, HospLI, INI, IndMed, MEDLINE, NurAb, P10, P20, P21, P24, P30, P48, P50, P53, P54, PQC, R10, Reac, SCI, SCOPUS, SSCI, T02, W07.
—BLDSC (5023.700000), GNLM, IE, Infotrieve, Ingenta, INIST. **CCC.**
Published by: Lippincott Williams & Wilkins (Subsidiary of: Wolters Kluwer N.V.), 530 Walnut St, Philadelphia, PA 19106. TEL 215-521-8300, FAX 215-521-8902, customerservice@lww.com, http://www.lww.com. Ed. Suzanne P Smith. Pub. Beth Guthy. Adv. contact Diane Shapiro TEL 215-628-6538. B&W page USD 2,295, color page USD 3,775; trim 7.75 x 10.75. Circ: 4,394.

610.73 USA ISSN 1948-5816
RT1
JOURNAL OF NURSING, ALLIED HEALTH & HEALTH EDUCATION. Text in English. 2007. s-a. free (effective 2009). **Document type:** *Journal, Academic/Scholarly.*
Media: Online - full content.
Published by: Scientific Journals International (Subsidiary of: Global Commerce & Communication, Inc), 1407 33rd St S, Saint Cloud, MN 56301. TEL 320-217-6019, info@scientificjournals.org.

610.73 GBR ISSN 1752-9816
RT120.C45
➤ **JOURNAL OF NURSING AND HEALTHCARE OF CHRONIC ILLNESS**; an international interdisciplinary journal. Text in English. 2007. q. GBP 311 in United Kingdom to institutions; EUR 395 in Europe to institutions; USD 610 in the Americas to institutions; USD 773 elsewhere to institutions; GBP 358 combined subscription in United Kingdom to institutions (print & online eds.); EUR 455 combined subscription in Europe to institutions (print & online eds.); USD 702 combined subscription in the Americas to institutions (print & online eds.); USD 889 combined subscription elsewhere to institutions (print & online eds.) (effective 2011). adv. back issues avail. **Document type:** *Journal, Academic/Scholarly.* **Description:** Publishes original research articles, literature reviews, policy reports and analyses, case reports, and descriptions of professional practice initiatives in the area of chronic illness.

Related titles: Online - full text ed.: ISSN 1752-9824. GBP 311 in United Kingdom to institutions; EUR 395 in Europe to institutions; USD 610 in the Americas to institutions; USD 773 elsewhere to institutions (effective 2011); ◆ Supplement to: Journal of Clinical Nursing. ISSN 0962-1067.
Indexed: A22, C06, C07, C08, CA, CINAHL, E01, T02.
—IE. **CCC.**
Published by: Wiley-Blackwell Publishing Ltd. (Subsidiary of: John Wiley & Sons, Inc.), 9600 Garsington Rd, Oxford, OX4 2DQ, United Kingdom. TEL 44-1865-776868, FAX 44-1865-714591, customerservices@blackwellpublishing.com. Ed. Debbie Kralik.

610.73 USA ISSN 1057-3631
RT85.5
➤ **JOURNAL OF NURSING CARE QUALITY.** Abbreviated title: J N C Q. Text in English. 1986. q. USD 350.51 domestic to institutions; USD 485 foreign to institutions (effective 2011). adv. back issues avail.; reprints avail. **Document type:** *Journal, Academic/Scholarly.* **Description:** Provides practicing nurses as well as nurses who have leadership roles in nursing care quality programs with useful information regarding the application of quality principles and concepts in the practice setting.
Formerly (until 1991): Journal of Nursing Quality Assurance (0889-4647)
Related titles: Microfiche ed.; Online - full text ed.: ISSN 1550-5065.
Indexed: A22, A26, ASG, B21, C06, C07, C08, CA, CINAHL, CurCont, E08, EMBASE, ESPM, ExcerpMed, F09, FamI, G08, H&SSA, H11, H12, I05, INI, IndMed, MEDLINE, NurAb, P16, P20, P22, P24, P30, P48, P53, P54, PQC, R10, Reac, RiskAb, S09, SCI, SCOPUS, SSCI, T02, W07.
—BLDSC (5023.770000), GNLM, IE, Infotrieve, Ingenta, INIST. **CCC.**
Published by: Lippincott Williams & Wilkins (Subsidiary of: Wolters Kluwer N.V.), Two Commerce Sq, 2001 Market St, Philadelphia, PA 19103. TEL 215-521-8300, FAX 215-521-8902, customerservice@lww.com, http://www.lww.com. Ed. Dr. Marilyn H Oermann. Pub. Sandy Kasko. Adv. contact Pat Wendelken. Circ: 1,074.

610.73 USA ISSN 0148-4834
➤ **JOURNAL OF NURSING EDUCATION.** Text in English. 1962. m. USD 124 combined subscription to individuals (print & online eds.); USD 359 combined subscription to institutions (print & online eds.); USD 28 per issue (effective 2010). adv. illus. index. 48 p./no.; reprints avail. **Document type:** *Journal, Academic/Scholarly.* **Description:** Provides a forum for original articles and new ideas for nursing educators in various types and levels of nursing programs.
Formerly (until 1983): J N E: Journal of Nursing Education
Related titles: Microform ed.: (from PQC); Online - full text ed.: ISSN 1938-2421.
Indexed: A20, A22, ASCA, AgeL, B04, BRD, C06, C07, C08, CA, CINAHL, CPE, CurCont, E02, E03, E06, E09, EMBASE, ERI, EdA, EdI, ExcerpMed, FamI, H13, HospLI, INI, ISR, IndMed, MEDLINE, NurAb, P02, P10, P16, P18, P20, P22, P24, P30, P48, P53, P54, PQC, R10, Reac, S04, S21, SCI, SCOPUS, SSCI, T02, W03, W05, W07, W09.
—BLDSC (5023.800000), GNLM, IE, Ingenta, INIST. **CCC.**
Published by: Slack, Inc., 6900 Grove Rd, Thorofare, NJ 08086. TEL 856-848-1000, FAX 856-848-6091, customerservice@slackinc.com, http://www.slackinc.com. Ed. Christine Tanner.

610.73 340 USA ISSN 1073-7472
K10
➤ **JOURNAL OF NURSING LAW.** Text in English. 1993. q. USD 105 domestic to individuals; USD 145 foreign to individuals; USD 275 domestic to institutions; USD 310 foreign to institutions; USD 158 combined subscription domestic to individuals (print & online eds.); USD 220 combined subscription foreign to individuals (print & online eds.); USD 415 combined subscription domestic to institutions (print & online eds.); USD 475 combined subscription foreign to institutions (print & online eds.) (effective 2009). adv. abstr. back issues avail. **Document type:** *Journal, Academic/Scholarly.* **Description:** Addresses issues of concern to lawyers, nurses, policy makers, and ethicists. It analyzes nursing law relating to nursing practice, education, and administration.
Related titles: Microform ed.; Online - full text ed.: ISSN 1938-2995. USD 95 domestic to individuals; USD 135 foreign to individuals; USD 250 domestic to institutions; USD 290 foreign to institutions (effective 2009) (from IngentaConnect).
Indexed: ASSIA, C06, C07, C08, CINAHL, FamI, P20, P21, P22, P24, P30, P48, P54, PQC, R10, Reac, SCOPUS.
—BLDSC (5023.828000), IE, Infotrieve, Ingenta. **CCC.**
Published by: Springer Publishing Company, 11 W 42nd St, 15th Fl, New York, NY 10036. TEL 212-431-4370, FAX 212-941-7842, contactus@springerpub.com, http://www.springerjournals.com. Ed. Diane K Kjervik. adv.: B&W page USD 400; trim 8.5 x 11. Circ: 669 (paid).

610.73 658 GBR ISSN 0966-0429
RT89 CODEN: JNMNEN
➤ **JOURNAL OF NURSING MANAGEMENT.** Text in English. 1993. 8/yr. GBP 576 in United Kingdom to institutions; EUR 731 in Europe to institutions; USD 1,065 in the Americas to institutions; USD 1,242 elsewhere to institutions; GBP 663 combined subscription in United Kingdom to institutions (print & online eds.); EUR 841 combined subscription in Europe to institutions (print & online eds.); USD 1,225 combined subscription in the Americas to institutions (print & online eds.); USD 1,428 combined subscription elsewhere to institutions (print & online eds.) (effective 2012). adv. bk.rev. bibl.; illus. index. back issues avail.; reprint service avail. from PSC. **Document type:** *Journal, Academic/Scholarly.* **Description:** Disseminates scholarly papers on all aspects of nursing management, that is, management practice, education, and research.
Related titles: Microform ed.: (from PQC); Online - full text ed.: ISSN 1365-2834. GBP 576 in United Kingdom to institutions; EUR 731 in Europe to institutions; USD 1,065 in the Americas to institutions; USD 1,242 elsewhere to institutions (effective 2012) (from IngentaConnect); Supplement(s): Journal of Nursing Management. Supplement. ISSN 0969-9473.
Indexed: A01, A02, A03, A08, A22, A26, B21, B28, C06, C07, C08, C11, CA, CINAHL, CurCont, E01, EMBASE, ESPM, ExcerpMed, FamI, H&SSA, H04, H12, INI, MEDLINE, P03, P30, P34, P48, PQC, PsycInfo, PsycholAb, R10, Reac, SCI, SCOPUS, SSCI, T02, W07.
—BLDSC (5023.830000), GNLM, IE, Infotrieve, Ingenta. **CCC.**
Published by: Wiley-Blackwell Publishing Ltd. (Subsidiary of: John Wiley & Sons, Inc.), 9600 Garsington Rd, Oxford, OX4 2DQ, United Kingdom. TEL 44-1865-776868, FAX 44-1865-714591, customerservices@blackwellpublishing.com. Ed. Melanie Jasper TEL 44-1227-782298. Adv. contact Joanna Baker TEL 44-1865-476271.

610.73 USA ISSN 1061-3749
RT81.5
➤ **JOURNAL OF NURSING MEASUREMENT.** Text in English. 1993. 3/yr. USD 80 domestic to individuals; USD 110 foreign to individuals; USD 220 domestic to institutions; USD 250 foreign to institutions; USD 120 combined subscription domestic to individuals; USD 165 combined subscription foreign to individuals; USD 330 combined subscription domestic to institutions; USD 375 combined subscription foreign to institutions (effective 2009). adv. bk.rev. abstr.; charts; stat. 100 p./no.; back issues avail.; reprints avail. **Document type:** *Journal, Academic/Scholarly.* **Description:** Provides a forum for disseminating information on instruments, tools, approaches, and procedures developed or used to measure variables in nursing, spanning practice, education, and research.
Related titles: Online - full text ed.: ISSN 1945-7049. USD 70 domestic to individuals; USD 100 foreign to individuals; USD 200 domestic to institutions; USD 230 foreign to institutions (effective 2009) (from IngentaConnect).
Indexed: A22, ASSIA, C06, C07, C08, CINAHL, E-psyche, EMBASE, ExcerpMed, FamI, INI, IndMed, MEDLINE, P03, P20, P21, P22, P24, P25, P30, P48, P54, PQC, PsycInfo, PsycholAb, R10, Reac, SCOPUS, SOPODA.
—BLDSC (5023.832000), GNLM, IE, Infotrieve, Ingenta. **CCC.**
Published by: Springer Publishing Company, 11 W 42nd St, 15th Fl, New York, NY 10036. TEL 212-431-4370, FAX 212-941-7842, contactus@springerpub.com, http://www.springerjournals.com. Eds. Ada Sue Hinshaw, Ora L Strickland. R&P, Adv. contact Jessica Perl. B&W page USD 300; 6 x 9. Circ: 300 (paid); 50 (controlled).

610.73 USA ISSN 1940-7068
JOURNAL OF NURSING PRACTICE. Text in English. 2007 (Dec.). q. **Document type:** *Journal, Academic/Scholarly.*
Media: Online - full content.
Published by: American Society of Registered Nurses, 1001 Bridgeway, Ste 411, Sausalito, CA 94965. TEL 415-331-2700, 800-331-1206, FAX 415-476-4558, office@asrn.org, http://www.asrn.org.

610.73 USA ISSN 2155-8256
RT4
▼ ➤ **JOURNAL OF NURSING REGULATION.** Text in English. 2010. q. USD 245 domestic to institutions; USD 32 elsewhere to institutions (effective 2010). **Document type:** *Journal, Trade.* **Description:** Dedicated to advancing regulatory excellence for the public's protection related to nursing regulation and practice.
Related titles: Online - full text ed.: ISSN 2155-8264.
Indexed: C06.
Published by: National Council of State Boards of Nursing, 111 East Wacker Dr, Ste 2900, Chicago, IL 60601. TEL 312-525-3600, FAX 312-279-1032, info@ncsbn.org, http://www.ncsbn.org.

610.73 USA ISSN 1682-3141
➤ **JOURNAL OF NURSING RESEARCH.** Abbreviated title: J N R. Text in English. 1993. q. (Bi-m. until Jun., 2001). USD 154 domestic to institutions; USD 154 foreign to institutions (effective 2011). bk.rev. cum.index: 1993-1997. back issues avail. **Document type:** *Journal, Academic/Scholarly.*
Formerly (until 2001): Huli Yanjiu Jikan (1022-6265)
Related titles: Online - full text ed.: ISSN 1948-965X.
Indexed: A01, A02, A03, A08, ASG, C06, C07, C08, CA, CINAHL, EMBASE, ExcerpMed, MEDLINE, P30, R10, Reac, SCOPUS, T02.
—BLDSC (5023.845000), IE, Ingenta. **CCC.**
Published by: (Taiwan Huli Xuehui/Taiwan Nurses Association TWN), Lippincott Williams & Wilkins (Subsidiary of: Wolters Kluwer N.V.), 530 Walnut St, Philadelphia, PA 19106. TEL 215-238-4200, FAX 215-238-4227, customerservice@lww.com, http://www.lww.com. Ed. Rung-Chuang Feng.

610.73 USA ISSN 1527-6546
CODEN: IMNSEP
➤ **JOURNAL OF NURSING SCHOLARSHIP.** Text in English. 1967. q. GBP 176 in United Kingdom to institutions; EUR 224 in Europe to institutions; USD 242 in the Americas to institutions; USD 345 elsewhere to institutions; GBP 203 combined subscription in United Kingdom to institutions (print & online eds.); EUR 258 combined subscription in Europe to institutions (print & online eds.); USD 279 combined subscription in the Americas to institutions (print & online eds.); USD 397 combined subscription elsewhere to institutions (print & online eds.) (effective 2012). adv. back issues avail.; reprint service avail. from PSC. **Document type:** *Journal, Academic/Scholarly.* **Description:** Presents cutting-edge thinking from top writers and researchers in nursing.
Former titles (until 2000): Image: Journal of Nursing Scholarship (0743-5150); (until 1983): Image (0363-2792)
Related titles: CD-ROM ed.; Microfiche ed.; Online - full text ed.: ISSN 1547-5069. GBP 176 in United Kingdom to institutions; EUR 224 in Europe to institutions; USD 242 in the Americas to institutions; USD 345 elsewhere to institutions (effective 2012) (from IngentaConnect).
Indexed: A01, A02, A03, A08, A20, A22, A25, A26, ASSIA, B21, B28, C06, C07, C08, C11, CA, CINAHL, CurCont, E-psyche, E01, E08, EMBASE, ESPM, ExcerpMed, FamI, G06, G07, G08, H&SSA, H04, H11, H12, I05, INI, IndMed, MEDLINE, NurAb, P03, P10, P20, P21, P22, P24, P25, P30, P48, P50, P53, P54, PQC, PsycInfo, PsycholAb, R10, Reac, S02, S03, S08, S09, SCI, SCOPUS, SSCI, T02, W07.
—BLDSC (5023.850000), GNLM, IE, Infotrieve, Ingenta. **CCC.**
Published by: (Sigma Theta Tau International Honor Society of Nursing), Wiley-Blackwell Publishing, Inc. (Subsidiary of: Wiley-Blackwell Publishing Ltd.), 111 River St, Hoboken, NJ 07030. TEL 201-748-6000, FAX 201-748-6088, info@wiley.com. Ed. Susan Gennaro. Adv. contact Karl Franz TEL 781-388-8470.

618 USA ISSN 0884-2175
RG951 CODEN: JOGNEY
➤ **JOURNAL OF OBSTETRIC, GYNECOLOGIC, AND NEONATAL NURSING.** Abbreviated title: J O G N N. Text in English. 1972. bi-m. GBP 573 in United Kingdom to institutions; EUR 727 in Europe to institutions; USD 1,030 in the Americas to institutions; USD 1,121 elsewhere to institutions; GBP 659 combined subscription in United Kingdom to institutions (print & online eds.); EUR 836 combined subscription in Europe to institutions (print & online eds.); USD 1,185 combined subscription in the Americas to institutions (print & online eds.); USD 1,289 combined subscription elsewhere to institutions (print & online eds.) (effective 2012). adv. bk.rev. illus. 120 p./no. 2 cols./p.; back issues avail.; reprint service avail. from PSC. **Document type:** *Journal, Academic/Scholarly.*
Incorporates (in 1993): A W H O N N's Clinical Issues in Perinatal and Women's Health Nursing (1066-3614); Which was formerly (1990-1992): N A A C O G's Clinical Issues Perinatal and Women's Health Nursing (1046-7475); Former titles (until 1985): J O G N Nursing (0090-0311); Nurses Association of the American College of Obstetricians and Gynecologists. Bulletin News (0044-7641); Nurses Association of A.C.O.G. Bulletin (0095-2982)
Related titles: CD-ROM ed.; Microform ed.: (from PQC); Online - full text ed.: ISSN 1552-6909. GBP 573 in United Kingdom to institutions; EUR 727 in Europe to institutions; USD 1,030 in the Americas to institutions; USD 1,121 elsewhere to institutions (effective 2012) (from IngentaConnect).
Indexed: A20, A22, A26, A36, B07, B20, B21, B28, C06, C07, C08, C28, CA, CABA, CINAHL, ChPerI, CurCont, D01, E01, E12, EMBASE, ESPM, ExcerpMed, F09, FamI, G10, GH, H04, H12, INI, IndMed, LT, MEDLINE, N02, N03, NurAb, OR, P02, P03, P10, P24, P30, P33, P39, P48, P50, P53, P54, PQC, PsycInfo, R07, R10, R12, RA&MP, RRTA, Reac, S02, S03, S10, SCI, SCOPUS, SFSA, SSCI, SoyAb, T02, T05, TAR, V02, W07, W09, W11.
—BLDSC (4670.352000), GNLM, IE, Infotrieve, Ingenta, INIST. **CCC.**
Published by: (Association of Women's Health, Obstetric, and Neonatal Nurses), Wiley-Blackwell Publishing, Inc. (Subsidiary of: Wiley-Blackwell Publishing Ltd.), 111 River St, Hoboken, NJ 07030. TEL 201-748-6000, FAX 201-748-6088, info@wiley.com. Ed. Nancy K Lowe. Adv. contact Greg Pessagno TEL 443-512-8899 ext 109.

610.73 USA ISSN 0882-5963
RJ245 CODEN: JLPNEO
➤ **JOURNAL OF PEDIATRIC NURSING;** nursing care of children and families. Abbreviated title: J P N. Text in English. 1986. bi-m. USD 287 in United States to institutions; USD 397 elsewhere to institutions (effective 2012). bk.rev. bibl.; charts; illus. index. back issues avail.; reprints avail. **Document type:** *Journal, Academic/Scholarly.* **Description:** Provides research that is based on the philosophy that pediatric nursing incorporates a family-centered approach. Topics include pharmacology, nutrition, pain management, diabetes, endocrinology, asthma, special needs.
Related titles: Online - full text ed.: ISSN 1532-8449 (from ScienceDirect).
Indexed: A22, A26, ASSIA, C06, C07, C08, CA, CINAHL, E01, EMBASE, ExcerpMed, F09, FamI, H12, I05, INI, IndMed, MEDLINE, P24, P30, P48, P50, PQC, R10, Reac, SCOPUS, T02, THA.
—BLDSC (5030.190000), GNLM, IE, Infotrieve, Ingenta. **CCC.**
Published by: (Society of Pediatric Nurses), W.B. Saunders Co. (Subsidiary of: Elsevier Health Sciences), Elsevier, Health Sciences Division, Order Fulfillment, 3251 Riverport Ln, Maryland Heights, MO 63043. TEL 314-872-8370, 800-325-4177, FAX 314-432-1380, JournalCustomerService-usa@elsevier.com, http://www.us.elsevierhealth.com. Ed. Dr. Cecily Lynn Betz. Pub. Jami Walker. Adv. contact Matt DiFilippo TEL 856-768-9360. Circ: 4,410.

➤ **JOURNAL OF PEDIATRIC ONCOLOGY NURSING.** *see* MEDICAL SCIENCES—Oncology

610.73 617.96 USA ISSN 1089-9472
➤ **JOURNAL OF PERIANESTHESIA NURSING.** Text in English. 1986. bi-m. USD 328 in United States to institutions; USD 454 elsewhere to institutions (effective 2012). adv. bibl.; charts; illus. cum.index. back issues avail.; reprints avail. **Document type:** *Journal, Academic/Scholarly.* **Description:** Provides a forum for sharing professional knowledge and experience relating to management, ethics, legislation, research, and other aspects of perianesthesia nursing.
Formerly (until 1996): Journal of Post Anasthesia Nursing (0883-9433)
Related titles: Online - full text ed.: ISSN 1532-8473 (from ScienceDirect).
Indexed: A22, A26, B28, C06, C07, C08, CA, CINAHL, CurCont, E01, EMBASE, ExcerpMed, H12, I05, INI, MEDLINE, P30, R10, Reac, SCI, SCOPUS, SSCI, T02, W07.
—BLDSC (5030.546000), IE, Infotrieve, Ingenta. **CCC.**
Published by: (American Society of PeriAnesthesia Nurses), W.B. Saunders Co. (Subsidiary of: Elsevier Health Sciences), Elsevier, Health Sciences Division, Order Fulfillment, 3251 Riverport Ln, Maryland Heights, MO 63043. TEL 314-872-8370, 800-325-4177, FAX 314-432-1380, JournalCustomerService-usa@elsevier.com, http://www.us.elsevierhealth.com. Eds. Jan Odom-Forren, Vallire D Hooper. Pub. Shannon Magee TEL 215-239-3730. Circ: 13,900.

610.73 618.2 USA ISSN 0893-2190
RG951 CODEN: JPNNE8
➤ **JOURNAL OF PERINATAL AND NEONATAL NURSING.** Abbreviated title: J P N N. Text in English. 1987. q. USD 318.51 domestic to institutions; USD 474 foreign to institutions (effective 2011). adv. back issues avail.; reprints avail. **Document type:** *Journal, Academic/Scholarly.* **Description:** Covers topics in critical care, obstetrics, neonatal intensive care, intervention outcomes, home care, professional development, and state-of-the-art technological advances.
Related titles: Online - full text ed.: ISSN 1550-5073.
Indexed: A22, A26, ASCA, C06, C07, C08, CA, CINAHL, CurCont, E08, EMBASE, ExcerpMed, F09, FamI, G08, H11, H12, H13, I05, INI, MEDLINE, NurAb, P03, P10, P20, P22, P24, P30, P48, P53, P54, PQC, PsycInfo, R10, Reac, S09, SCI, SCOPUS, SSCI, T02, W07.
—BLDSC (5030.548000), GNLM, IE, Infotrieve, Ingenta, INIST. **CCC.**
Published by: Lippincott Williams & Wilkins (Subsidiary of: Wolters Kluwer N.V.), Two Commerce Sq, 2001 Market St, Philadelphia, PA 19103. TEL 215-521-8300, FAX 215-521-8902, customerservice@lww.com, http://www.lww.com. Eds. Diane J Angelini, Susan Bakewell-Sachs. Pub. Beth L Guthy. Circ: 1,480.

M

610.73 GBR ISSN 1750-4589
➤ **JOURNAL OF PERIOPERATIVE PRACTICE.** Abbreviated title: J P P. Text in English. 19??. m. free to members (effective 2009). adv. bk.rev. back issues avail. **Document type:** *Journal, Academic/Scholarly.* **Description:** News and research articles on the professional, technological, administrative, and procedural aspects of providing care and services to patients in the operating room, with announcements of the educational activities and membership of the association.
Former titles (until 2006): British Journal of Perioperative Nursing (1467-1026); (until 2000): British Journal of Theatre Nursing (1353-0224); (until 1991): N A T News (0027-6049); (until 1965): Midland N A T News
Related titles: Online - full text ed.
Indexed: A22, A26, B28, C06, C07, C08, CA, CINAHL, EMBASE, ExcerpMed, H12, I05, INI, MEDLINE, P20, P22, P24, P30, P48, PQC, R10, Reac, SCOPUS, T02.
—BLDSC (5030.760000), GNLM, IE, Infotrieve, Ingenta. **CCC.**
Published by: Association for Perioperative Practice, Daisy Ayris House, 6 Grove Park Ct, Harrogate, Yorks HG1 4DP, United Kingdom. TEL 44-1423-508079, FAX 44-1423-531613, hq@afpp.org.uk.

610.73 USA ISSN 0022-3867
RT1
➤ **JOURNAL OF PRACTICAL NURSING.** Added title page title: J P N. Text in English. 1951. q. USD 25 domestic to non-members; USD 75 foreign to non-members; free to members (effective 2011). bk.rev. abstr.; bibl.; charts; illus.; stat. index, cum.index. reprints avail. **Document type:** *Journal, Academic/Scholarly.*
Formerly (until 1963): Practical Nursing
Related titles: Microform ed.: (from PQC); Online - full text ed.: USD 10 domestic; USD 25 foreign (effective 2011).
Indexed: A22, C06, C07, C08, CINAHL, DentInd, EMBASE, ExcerpMed, F09, HospLI, INI, MEDLINE, P20, P22, P24, P30, P48, P54, PQC, R10, Reac, RehabLit, SCOPUS.
—BLDSC (5041.600000), GNLM, IE, Infotrieve, Ingenta.
Published by: National Association for Practical Nurse Education and Service, Inc., 1940 Duke St, Ste 200, PO Box 25647, Alexandria, VA 22314. TEL 703-933-1003, FAX 703-940-4089, napnes@bellatlantic.ne.

➤ **JOURNAL OF PRACTICE TEACHING IN HEALTH & SOCIAL WORK.** *see* SOCIAL SERVICES AND WELFARE

610.73 USA ISSN 8755-7223
RT1 CODEN: JPNUET
➤ **JOURNAL OF PROFESSIONAL NURSING.** Text in English. 1985. 6/yr. USD 330 in United States to institutions; USD 427 elsewhere to institutions (effective 2012). adv. bk.rev. back issues avail. **Document type:** *Journal, Academic/Scholarly.* **Description:** Addresses the practice, research, and policy roles of nurses through general articles, research articles, reviews, and editorials.
Related titles: Online - full text ed.: ISSN 1532-8481 (from ScienceDirect).
Indexed: A20, A22, A26, AMED, ASCA, ASSIA, C06, C07, C08, CA, CINAHL, CurCont, E01, E03, EMBASE, ERI, ExcerpMed, FR, FamI, H12, I05, INI, IndMed, MEDLINE, NurAb, P03, P24, P30, P48, PQC, PsycInfo, R10, Reac, SCI, SCOPUS, SSCI, T02, W07.
—BLDSC (5042.697000), GNLM, IE, Infotrieve, Ingenta, INIST. **CCC.**
Published by: W.B. Saunders Co. (Subsidiary of: Elsevier Health Sciences), Independence Sq W, Ste 300, The Curtis Center, Philadelphia, PA 19106-3399. TEL 215-238-5667, FAX 215-238-8772, hhspcs@wbsaunders.com, http://www.us.elsevierhealth.com. Ed. Ellen Olshansky. adv.: B&W page USD 720, color page USD 1,670; trim 10 x 7. Circ: 2,396.

610.736 616.8 USA ISSN 0279-3695
RC440
➤ **JOURNAL OF PSYCHOSOCIAL NURSING AND MENTAL HEALTH SERVICES.** Text in English. 1963. m. USD 89 combined subscription to individuals (print & online eds.); USD 303 to institutions (print & online eds.); USD 28 per issue (effective 2010). adv. bk.rev. charts; illus. index. 56 p./no.; reprints avail. **Document type:** *Journal, Academic/Scholarly.* **Description:** Provides up-to-date practical information for today's psychosocial nurse.
Former titles (until 1981): Journal of Psychiatric Nursing and Mental Health Services (0360-5973); (until 1967): Journal of Psychiatric Nursing (0277-2973)
Related titles: Microform ed.: (from PQC); Online - full text ed.: ISSN 1938-2413.
Indexed: A20, A22, AMHA, B28, C06, C07, C08, CINAHL, ChPerI, CurCont, E-psyche, EMBASE, ExcerpMed, F09, FR, FamI, INI, IndMed, MEA&I, MEDLINE, NurAb, P02, P03, P10, P12, P20, P22, P24, P25, P30, P48, P50, P53, P54, PQC, PsycInfo, PsycholAb, R10, Reac, S02, S03, SCI, SCOPUS, SSCI, W07, W09.
—BLDSC (5043.475000), GNLM, IE, Infotrieve, Ingenta, INIST. **CCC.**
Published by: (Alliance for Psychosocial Nursing), Slack, Inc., 6900 Grove Rd, Thorofare, NJ 08086. TEL 856-848-1000, FAX 856-848-6091, customerservice@slackinc.com, http://www.slackinc.com. Ed. Shirley Smoyak. Adv. contact Kara Datz TEL 856-848-1000 ext 549. Circ: 4,220 (paid).

610.73 USA ISSN 1546-0843
➤ **JOURNAL OF RADIOLOGY NURSING.** Text in English. 198?. q. USD 152 in United States to institutions; USD 202 elsewhere to institutions (effective 2012). adv. back issues avail.; reprints avail. **Document type:** *Journal, Academic/Scholarly.* **Description:** Promotes the quality patient care in the diagnostic and therapeutic imaging environments.
Formerly (until 2004): Images (1055-1476)
Related titles: Online - full text ed.: ISSN 1555-9912 (from ScienceDirect).
Indexed: A26, ASSIA, AmHI, C06, C07, C08, CA, CINAHL, EMBASE, ExcerpMed, H12, I05, R10, Reac, SCOPUS, T02.
—BLDSC (5044.350000), IE, Ingenta. **CCC.**
Published by: (Association for Radiologic and Imaging Nursing), Elsevier Inc. (Subsidiary of: Elsevier Science & Technology), 1600 John F Kennedy Blvd, Philadelphia, PA 19103. TEL 215-239-3900, FAX 215-238-7883, JournalCustomerService-usa@elsevier.com, http://www.elsevier.com. Ed. Kathleen Gross TEL 443-849-2714. Pub. Jami Walker TEL 314-447-8987. Adv. contact Michael Targowski TEL 212-633-3693. Circ: 2,105.

➤ **JOURNAL OF RENAL CARE.** *see* MEDICAL SCIENCES—Urology And Nephrology

610.73 GBR ISSN 1744-9871
➤ **JOURNAL OF RESEARCH IN NURSING.** Abbreviated title: J R N. Text in English. 1995. bi-m. USD 655, GBP 354 combined subscription to institutions (print & online eds.); USD 642, GBP 347 to institutions (effective 2011). adv. back issues avail.; reprint service avail. from PSC. **Document type:** *Journal, Academic/Scholarly.* **Description:** Contains papers covering a wide range of policy, management and education issues from an international perspective.
Formerly (until 2005): N T Research (1361-4096)
Related titles: Online - full text ed.: ISSN 1744-988X. USD 590, GBP 319 to institutions (effective 2011).
Indexed: A22, B21, B28, C06, C07, C08, CA, CINAHL, E01, ESPM, H&SSA, P03, PsycInfo, PsycholAb, RiskAb, SCOPUS, T02.
—BLDSC (5052.024000), IE, Infotrieve, Ingenta. **CCC.**
Published by: Sage Publications Ltd. (Subsidiary of: Sage Publications, Inc.), 1 Oliver's Yard, 55 City Rd, London, EC1Y 1SP, United Kingdom. TEL 44-20-73248500, FAX 44-20-73248600, info@sagepub.co.uk, http://www.uk.sagepub.com/home.nav. Ed. Veronica Bishop. adv.: B&W page GBP 450; 140 x 210. **Subscr. in the Americas to:** Sage Publications, Inc., 2455 Teller Rd, Thousand Oaks, CA 91320. TEL 805-499-9774, FAX 805-499-0871, journals@sagepub.com.

610.73 371.7 USA ISSN 1059-8405
➤ **THE JOURNAL OF SCHOOL NURSING.** Text in English. 1970; N.S. 1985. bi-m. USD 209, GBP 123 combined subscription to institutions (print & online eds.); USD 205, GBP 121 to institutions (effective 2011). adv. 64 p./no.; back issues avail.; reprint service avail. from PSC. **Document type:** *Journal, Academic/Scholarly.* **Description:** Professional journal for school nurses. Contains articles on the practice of school nursing, pertinent research projects, and legal issues which will affect school nurses.
Formerly (until vol.7, no.3, 1991): School Nurse (0048-945X)
Related titles: Online - full text ed.: ISSN 1546-8364. USD 188, GBP 111 to institutions (effective 2011).
Indexed: A22, B28, C06, C07, C08, CA, CINAHL, CurCont, E01, E03, EMBASE, ERI, ERIC, ExcerpMed, F09, FR, INI, MEDLINE, P03, P20, P22, P24, P30, P48, P50, P54, PQC, PsycInfo, PsycholAb, R10, Reac, SCI, SCOPUS, SSCI, T02, W07.
—BLDSC (5052.665000), GNLM, IE, Infotrieve, Ingenta, INIST. **CCC.**
Published by: (National Association of School Nurses Inc.), Sage Publications, Inc., 2455 Teller Rd, Thousand Oaks, CA 91320. TEL 805-499-9774, 800-818-7243, FAX 805-499-0871, 800-583-2665, info@sagepub.com, http://www.sagepub.com. Ed. Julia Muennich Cowell. adv.: B&W page USD 1,635, color page USD 2,530; bleed 11.25 x 8.75. Circ: 9,500 (paid). **Subscr. outside the Americas to:** Sage Publications Ltd., 1 Oliver's Yard, 55 City Rd, London EC1Y 1SP, United Kingdom. TEL 44-20-73248701, 44-207-3248701, subscription@sagepub.co.uk.

➤ **JOURNAL OF SUBSTANCE USE.** *see* DRUG ABUSE AND ALCOHOLISM

610.736 616.992 USA ISSN 2150-0878
▼ **THE JOURNAL OF THE ADVANCED PRACTITIONER IN ONCOLOGY.** Text in English. 2010 (May). 6/yr. adv. **Document type:** *Journal, Academic/Scholarly.* **Description:** Aims to improve the quality of care for patients with cancer, support critical issues in advanced practice in oncology, and recognize the expanding contributions of advanced practitioners in oncology.
Related titles: Online - full text ed.: ISSN 2150-0886. 2010 (May).
Published by: Harborside Press, 37 Main St, Cold Spring Harbor, NY 11724. TEL 631-692-0800, FAX 631-692-0805, info@harborsidepress.com, http://www.harborsidepress.com. Ed. Pamela Hallquist Viale.

610.73 USA ISSN 1086-4431
RT84.5
➤ **JOURNAL OF THEORY CONSTRUCTION AND TESTING.** Abbreviated title: J T C T. Text in English. 1997. s-a. USD 90 domestic to individuals; USD 150 domestic to institutions; USD 225 foreign (effective 2010). reprints avail. **Document type:** *Journal, Academic/Scholarly.* **Description:** Committed to the advancement and development of the scientific base of nursing as a practice discipline.
Related titles: Online - full text ed.
Indexed: A01, A02, A03, A08, A20, A26, C06, C07, C08, C11, CA, CINAHL, E08, G08, H04, H11, H12, I05, P16, P24, P30, P48, P53, P54, PQC, S09, T02.
—BLDSC (5069.075890), IE, Ingenta. **CCC.**
Published by: Tucker Publications, Inc., PO Box 580, Lisle, IL 60532. TEL 630-969-3895, FAX 630-969-3895, info@tuckerpub.com, http://www.tuckerpub.com. Ed. Dr. Charles T Walker.

610.73 USA ISSN 1043-6596
➤ **JOURNAL OF TRANSCULTURAL NURSING.** Text in English. 1989. q. USD 639, GBP 376 to institutions; USD 652, GBP 384 combined subscription to institutions (print & online eds.) (effective 2012). bk.rev. back issues avail.; reprint service avail. from PSC. **Document type:** *Journal, Academic/Scholarly.* **Description:** Serves as an international forum for researchers who desire to share their ideas culturally congruent health care delivery.
Related titles: Online - full text ed.: ISSN 1552-7832. USD 587, GBP 346 to institutions (effective 2012).
Indexed: A01, A02, A03, A08, A20, A22, B07, B28, C06, C07, C08, CA, CINAHL, CurCont, E01, EMBASE, ExcerpMed, FamI, H04, INI, MEDLINE, P03, P24, P25, P30, P48, PQC, PsycInfo, PsycholAb, S02, S03, SCI, SCOPUS, SSCI, SociolAb, T02, V02, W07, W09.
—BLDSC (5069.795000), GNLM, IE, Infotrieve, Ingenta. **CCC.**
Published by: Sage Publications, Inc., 2455 Teller Rd, Thousand Oaks, CA 91320. TEL 800-818-7243, FAX 800-583-2665, info@sagepub.com, http://www.sagepub.com. Ed. Marilyn Marty Douglas.

610.73 USA ISSN 1078-7496
RT120.E4
➤ **JOURNAL OF TRAUMA NURSING.** Abbreviated title: J T N. Text in English. 1994. q. USD 293.17 domestic to institutions; USD 383 foreign to institutions (effective 2011). adv. bk.rev.; software rev.; video rev. abstr. back issues avail.; reprints avail. **Document type:** *Journal, Academic/Scholarly.* **Description:** Aims to provide articles and information that reflect the practice of trauma nursing in the areas of clinical practice, education, health policy and administration, and research.
Formerly: S T N's Journal of Trauma Nursing (1076-4747)
Related titles: Online - full text ed.: ISSN 1932-3883.
Indexed: A26, C06, C07, C08, CA, CINAHL, E08, EMBASE, ExcerpMed, G08, H11, H12, I05, INI, MEDLINE, P16, P20, P22, P24, P30, P48, P53, P54, PQC, R10, Reac, S09, SCOPUS, T02.
—BLDSC (5070.515000), GNLM, IE, Infotrieve, Ingenta. **CCC.**
Published by: (Society of Trauma Nurses), Lippincott Williams & Wilkins (Subsidiary of: Wolters Kluwer N.V.), Two Commerce Sq, 2001 Market St, Philadelphia, PA 19103. TEL 215-521-8300, FAX 215-521-8902, customerservice@lww.com, http://www.lww.com. Ed. Kathryn Schroeter. Pub. Kathleen M Phelan. Adv. contact Sue Ryan. Circ: 1,565.

610.73 USA ISSN 1522-8223
RT71
JOURNAL OF UNDERGRADUATE NURSING SCHOLARSHIP. Text in English. 1999. a. free (effective 2010). **Document type:** *Journal, Academic/Scholarly.* **Description:** A platform for undergraduate nursing students to publish their papers.
Media: Online - full text.
Indexed: C06, C07, C08, CINAHL.
Published by: University of Arizona, College of Nursing, 1305 N Martin St, Tucson, AZ 85721. TEL 520-626-6154, FAX 520-626-6424, http://www.nursing.arizona.edu/. Eds. Amy Davis, Judith A Effken, Mary Koithan.

610.736 616.1 USA ISSN 1062-0303
RC691
➤ **JOURNAL OF VASCULAR NURSING.** Text in English. 1982. q. USD 191 in United States to institutions; USD 227 elsewhere to institutions (effective 2012). adv. **Document type:** *Journal, Academic/Scholarly.* **Description:** Provides coverage of state-of-the-art nursing techniques in the care of vascular patients, valuable insights on surgical implications, and product information.
Formerly (until 19??): S P V N
Related titles: Online - full text ed.: ISSN 1532-6578 (from ScienceDirect).
Indexed: A22, A26, ASSIA, C06, C07, C08, CA, CINAHL, E01, EMBASE, ExcerpMed, H12, I05, INI, MEDLINE, P30, R10, Reac, SCOPUS, T02.
—BLDSC (5072.268500), GNLM, IE, Infotrieve, Ingenta. **CCC.**
Published by: (Society for Vascular Nursing, Inc.), Mosby, Inc. (Subsidiary of: Elsevier Health Sciences), 1600 John F. Kennedy Blvd, Ste 1800, Philadelphia, PA 19103. TEL 215-239-3900, 800-523-1649, FAX 215-239-3990, elspcs@elsevier.com, http://www.us.elsevierhealth.com. Ed. Cindy Lewis.

610.73 USA
K B NURSING CONNECTION. (Kentucky Board) Text in English. 2004. q. free to members (effective 2009). adv. back issues avail. **Document type:** *Journal, Trade.*
Related titles: Online - full text ed.: free (effective 2009).
Published by: (Kentucky State Board of Nursing), Publishing Concepts, Inc., 14109 Taylor Loop Rd, Little Rock, AR 72223. TEL 501-221-9986, 800-561-4686, FAX 501-225-3735, http://www.pcipublishing.com/. Ed. Carrie Driscoll TEL 502-429-3343. Pub. Virginia Robertson. Adv. contact Michele Forinash TEL 501-221-9986.

610.73 DEU ISSN 1868-3169
K M A PFLEGE. (Klinik Management aktuell) Text in German. 1990. q. EUR 63 to institutions; EUR 18 newsstand/cover (effective 2011). adv. **Document type:** *Magazine, Trade.*
Former titles (until 2008): Pflege & Management (1613-5695); (until 2002): B A L K Info (1434-9574)
Related titles: Online - full text ed.
Published by: (Bundesarbeitsgemeinschaft Leitender Krankenpflegepersonen e.V.), Georg Thieme Verlag, Ruedigerstr 14, Stuttgart, 70469, Germany. TEL 49-711-8931421, FAX 49-711-8931410, leser.service@thieme.de, http://www.thieme.de.

610.73 NZL ISSN 1173-2032
RT16.N4
➤ **KAI TIAKI: NURSING NEW ZEALAND.** Text in English. 1993; N.S. 1995. m. NZD 130 foreign to individuals; NZD 175 domestic to institutions; NZD 190 foreign to institutions; free to members (effective 2008). adv. bk.rev. charts; illus.; stat. 48 p./no.; back issues avail. **Document type:** *Journal, Academic/Scholarly.* **Description:** Contains information on professional issues and issues concerning nurses' pay and conditions. Includes clinical and research articles, news and events and reports from staff around the country.
Formerly (until Feb.1995): Nursing New Zealand (1172-1979); Which was formed by the merger of (1909-1993): New Zealand Nursing Journal (0028-8535); Which was formerly: Kai Tiaki; (1982-1993): N Z N U News (0111-865X); Which was formed by the merger of (1979-1982): N.Z. Nurses News (0111-297X); New Zealand Nurses Union News
Related titles: Online - full text ed.
Indexed: A22, A26, C06, C07, C08, CINAHL, E08, EMBASE, ExcerpMed, F09, FamI, G08, H11, H12, I05, INI, INZP, MEDLINE, P30, R10, Reac, S09, SCOPUS.
—BLDSC (5081.173000), GNLM, IE, Infotrieve, Ingenta. **CCC.**
Published by: New Zealand Nurses Organisation, PO Box 2128, Wellington, New Zealand. TEL 64-4-3850847, FAX 64-4-3829993, teresao@nzno.org.nz. Eds. Anne Manchester, Teresa O'Connor TEL 64-3-548-0018. R&P Teresa O'Connor TEL 64-3-548-0018. Adv. contact Evelyn Nelson TEL 64-4-384-4952. B&W page NZD 1,500, color page NZD 2,100; trim 210 x 285. Circ: 27,000 (controlled).

610.73 362 658 JPN
KAIGO BIJON/CARE VISION. Text in Japanese. m. JPY 14,400 (effective 2007). **Document type:** *Magazine, Trade.*
Published by: Nihon Iryo Kikaku/Japan Medical Planning, 4-14 Kanda-Iwamoto-cho, Chiyoda-ku, Tokyo, 101-0033, Japan. TEL 81-3-32562861, FAX 81-3-32562865.

610.73 JPN
KAIGO NO GAKKOU. Text in Japanese. 2004. m. JPY 6,000 (effective 2007). **Document type:** *Journal, Academic/Scholarly.*
Published by: Nihon Iryo Kikaku/Japan Medical Planning, 4-14 Kanda-Iwamoto-cho, Chiyoda-ku, Tokyo, 101-0033, Japan. TEL 81-3-32562861, FAX 81-3-32562865.

610.73 JPN ISSN 1344-8404
KAIGO SHIEN SEMMON'IN/CARE MANAGER. Text in English. 1999. bi-m. JPY 9,450 (effective 2005). **Document type:** *Journal, Academic/Scholarly.*
Published by: Medikaru Rebyusha/Medical Review Co., Ltd., 1-7-3 Hirano-Machi, Chuo-ku, Yoshida Bldg., Osaka-shi, 541-0046, Japan. TEL 81-6-62231468, FAX 81-6-62231245.

610.73 SWE
KANALEN. Variant title: Vaardfoerbundet Kanalen. Text in Swedish. 11/yr.
Document type: *Magazine, Trade.*
Published by: Vaardfoerbundet/The Swedish Association of Health Professionals, Adolf Fredriks Kyrkogatan 11, PO Box 3260, Stockholm, 10365, Sweden. TEL 46-8-14-77-00, FAX 46-8-411-19-93, http://www.vardforbundet.se.

610.73 JPN ISSN 0022-8362
KANGO/JAPANESE JOURNAL OF NURSING. Text in Japanese. 1949. m. membership. adv. bk.rev.; film rev.; play rev. abstr.; bibl.; charts; illus.; stat. cum.index. **Document type:** *Journal, Trade.*
Indexed: INI, P30.
—BLDSC (5085.356000), GNLM.
Published by: Japanese Nursing Association, 5-8-2 Jingu-Mae, Shibuya-ku, Tokyo, 150-0001, Japan. TEL 81-3-57788831, http://www.nurse.or.jp. Circ: 50,000.

610.73 JPN ISSN 0385-5988
KANGO GAKUSEI/NURSE STUDENT. Text in Japanese. 1951. m. JPY 13,230 (effective 2007). Supplement avail.; back issues avail. **Document type:** *Journal, Academic/Scholarly.* **Description:** Learning guide and drills for student nurses.
Formed by the merger of: Kango Gakushu Ichi-nen; Shikaku Shiken Juken Kosu
Published by: Medical Friend Co. Ltd./Mejikaru Furendo Sha, 3-2-4 Kudan-Kita, Chiyoda-ku, Tokyo, 102-0073, Japan. TEL 81-3-32646611, http://www.medical-friend.co.jp/. Circ: 30,000.

610.7 JPN ISSN 0449-752X
KANGO GIJUTSU/JAPANESE JOURNAL OF NURSING ARTS. Text in Japanese. 1950. m. JPY 18,900; JPY 1,155 newsstand/cover (effective 2007). bk.rev. Supplement avail.; back issues avail. **Document type:** *Journal, Academic/Scholarly.* **Description:** Case studies in clinical nursing.
Indexed: DentInd, INI, P30.
—BLDSC (4656.740500), GNLM.
Published by: Medical Friend Co. Ltd./Mejikaru Furendo Sha, 3-2-4 Kudan-Kita, Chiyoda-ku, Tokyo, 102-0073, Japan. TEL 81-3-32646611, http://www.medical-friend.co.jp/. Circ: 100,000.

610.73 JPN ISSN 0917-1355
KANGO KANRI/JAPANESE JOURNAL OF NURSING ADMINISTRATION. Text in Japanese. 1991. m. JPY 18,450; JPY 23,500 combined subscription (effective 2010). back issues avail. **Document type:** *Journal, Academic/Scholarly.*
Related titles: Online - full text ed.
—BLDSC (5085.387000).
Published by: Igaku Shoin Ltd., 1-28-36 Hongo, Bunkyo-ku, Tokyo, 113-8719, Japan. TEL 81-3-3817-5600, FAX 81-3-3815-7791, info@igaku-shoin.co.jp.

610.73 JPN ISSN 0022-8370
KANGO KENKYU/JAPANESE JOURNAL OF NURSING RESEARCH. Text in Japanese. 1968. q. JPY 12,600; JPY 17,600 combined subscription (print & online eds.) (effective 2010).
Related titles: Online - full text ed.: ISSN 1882-1405.
Indexed: A22, INI, P30, SCOPUS.
—BLDSC (4656.745000), GNLM, IE, Infotrieve, Ingenta.
Published by: Igaku Shoin Ltd., 1-28-36 Hongo, Bunkyo-ku, Tokyo, 113-8719, Japan. TEL 81-3-3817-5600, FAX 81-3-3815-7791, info@igaku-shoin.co.jp. Circ: 8,000.

610.73 JPN ISSN 0047-1895
KANGO KYOIKU/JAPANESE JOURNAL OF NURSING EDUCATION. Text in Japanese. 1960. m. JPY 16,250; JPY 21,300 combined subscription (print & online eds.) (effective 2010). illus. **Document type:** *Journal, Academic/Scholarly.*
Related titles: Online - full text ed.: ISSN 1882-1391.
Indexed: INI, P30.
—GNLM.
Published by: Igaku Shoin Ltd., 1-28-36 Hongo, Bunkyo-ku, Tokyo, 113-8719, Japan. TEL 81-3-3817-5600, FAX 81-3-3815-7791, info@igaku-shoin.co.jp. Circ: 10,000.

610.73 JPN ISSN 0385-549X
KANGO TENBO/JAPANESE JOURNAL OF NURSING SCIENCE. Text in Japanese. 1976. m. JPY 18,900 (effective 2007). Index. Supplement avail.; back issues avail. **Document type:** *Journal, Academic/Scholarly.* **Description:** Covers the administrative issues of nursing and contains various discussions on nursing education.
Indexed: INI, P30.
—GNLM.
Published by: Medical Friend Co. Ltd./Mejikaru Furendo Sha, 3-2-4 Kudan-Kita, Chiyoda-ku, Tokyo, 102-0073, Japan. TEL 81-3-32646611, http://www.medical-friend.co.jp/. Circ: 30,000.

610.73 JPN ISSN 0386-9830
KANGOGAKU ZASSHI/JAPANESE JOURNAL OF NURSING. Text in Japanese. 1946. m. JPY 13,200; JPY 18,200 combined subscription (print & online eds.) (effective 2010). **Document type:** *Journal, Academic/Scholarly.*
Related titles: Online - full content ed.: ISSN 1345-2746.
Indexed: F09, P30.
—BLDSC (4656.700000).
Published by: Igaku Shoin Ltd., 1-28-36 Hongo, Bunkyo-ku, Tokyo, 113-8719, Japan. TEL 81-3-3817-5600, FAX 81-3-3815-7791, info@igaku-shoin.co.jp.

610.73 USA ISSN 0022-8710
RT1
➤ **KANSAS NURSE.** Text in English. 1941. 10/yr. USD 30 domestic to non-members; USD 45 foreign to non-members; USD 12 to members (effective 2011). adv. bk.rev. illus. reprints avail. **Document type:** *Journal, Academic/Scholarly.* **Description:** Features articles and up-to-date information affecting nurses and the nursing profession.
Related titles: Microform ed.: (from PQC); Online - full text ed.
Indexed: A22, C06, C07, C08, CINAHL, EMBASE, ExcerpMed, F09, INI, MEDLINE, P20, P22, P24, P30, P48, P54, PQC, R10, Reac, SCOPUS.
—BLDSC (5085.648000), GNLM, IE, Infotrieve, Ingenta.
Published by: Kansas State Nurses Association, 1109 SW Topeka Blvd, Topeka, KS 66612. TEL 785-233-8638, FAX 785-233-5222, ksna@ksna.net, http://www.ksnurses.com/index.html.

610.73 USA ISSN 0742-8367
RT1
KENTUCKY NURSE. Text in English. 1952. q. looseleaf. USD 18 to non-members; USD 6 to members (effective 2008). adv. bk.rev. 32 p./no.; back issues avail.; reprints avail. **Document type:** *Newsletter, Trade.* **Description:** Covers issues and employment opportunities of interest to licensed nursing professionals.
Former titles (until 1982): Kentucky Nurse Association. Newsletter (0023-0316); (until 1978): Kentucky Nurses' Association. Newsletter; (until 197?): Kentucky Nurses' Association. Newsletter
Related titles: Online - full text ed.
Indexed: C06, C07, C08, CA, CINAHL, EMBASE, ExcerpMed, MEDLINE, P20, P22, P24, P30, P48, P54, PQC, R10, Reac, SCOPUS, T02.
—BLDSC (5089.653500).
Published by: (Kentucky Nurses Association), Arthur L. Davis Publishing Agency, Inc., 517 Washington St, PO Box 216, Cedar Falls, IA 50613. TEL 319-277-2414, 800-626-4081, FAX 319-277-4055, sales@aldpub.com, http://www.aldpub.com. Eds. Ida Slusher, Mark Miller. R&P Anne Powell. Adv. contact Jim Larson. Circ: 68,000.

610.73 KEN ISSN 0301-0333
KENYA NURSING JOURNAL. Text in English. 1972. s-a. KES 100 (effective 2007). adv. bk.rev. back issues avail. **Document type:** *Journal, Academic/Scholarly.*
Indexed: INI, P30.
Published by: National Nurses Association of Kenya, Professional Centre, Lowerground Fl, Parliament Rd, P O Box 49422, Nairobi, Kenya. TEL 254-20-229083, FAX 254-20-341883, nnak@nursesassociationke.org. Ed. J B Khachina. Circ: 2,750.

610.73 618.92 DEU ISSN 0723-2276
KINDERKRANKENSCHWESTER. Text in German. 1982. m. EUR 29.50; EUR 2.95 newsstand/cover (effective 2011). adv. bk.rev. back issues avail. **Document type:** *Journal, Trade.*
Indexed: A22, EMBASE, ExcerpMed, F09, INI, MEDLINE, P30, R10, Reac, SCOPUS.
—BLDSC (5095.637000), GNLM, IE, Infotrieve, Ingenta. **CCC.**
Published by: Max Schmidt-Roemhild KG, Mengstr 16, Luebeck, 23552, Germany. TEL 49-451-703101, FAX 49-451-7031253, info@schmidt-roemhild.de, http://www.beleke.de/unternehmen/verlage/schmidtroemhild/index.html.

610.73 JPN ISSN 1344-168X
KITA NIHON KANGO GAKKAISHI/NORTH JAPAN ACADEMY OF NURSING SCIENCE. JOURNAL. Text in Japanese. irreg. (1-2/yr.). **Document type:** *Journal, Academic/Scholarly.*
—**CCC.**
Published by: Kita Nihon Kango Gakkai/North Japan Academy of Nursing Science, Yamagata University School of Medicine, Department of Nursing, 2-2-2, Iida-nishi, Yamagata, 990-9585, Japan. TEL 81-90-84240830, njans@njans.zive.net, http://njans.zive.net/.

610.73 DNK ISSN 0902-2767
KLINISK SYGEPLEJE. Text in Danish. 1987. 4/yr. DKK 520 combined subscription to individuals; DKK 420 to individuals print edition; DKK 380 to individuals online edition; DKK 190 to students online edition; DKK 2,500 combined subscription to institutions (effective 2009). index. back issues avail. **Document type:** *Journal, Academic/Scholarly.*
Related titles: Online - full text ed.: ISSN 1903-2285. 2002.
Indexed: C06, C07, C08, CINAHL, P30.
—BLDSC (5099.510000), Infotrieve. **CCC.**
Published by: Munksgaard Danmark A/S (Subsidiary of: Gyldendal Akademisk A/S), Sjaeleboderne 2, Copenhagen K, 1122, Denmark. TEL 45-33-755900, FAX 45-33-755901, forlaget@munksgaarddanmark.dk, http://www.munksgaarddanmark.dk. Ed. Ingrid Poulsen.

610.73 KOR ISSN 2005-3673
➤ **KOREAN ACADEMY OF NURSING. JOURNAL.** Text in Korean. 1998. q. membership. **Document type:** *Journal, Academic/Scholarly.*
Former titles (until 2008): Daehan Ganho Haghoeji/Korean Society of Nursing Science. Journal (1598-2874); (until 1997): Gan'ho Hag'hoeji/Nurses Academic Society. Journal (0378-004X)
Related titles: ◆ Includes: Asian Nursing Research. ISSN 1976-1317.
Indexed: F09, P30, R10, Reac, SCOPUS.
—BLDSC (4811.370000).
Published by: Korean Society of Nursing Science/han-gug Ganho Gwahaghoe, Korea Science & Technology Center, 635-4 Yeoksam-dong, Kangnam-gu, Seoul, 135-703, Korea, S. TEL 82-2-5677236, FAX 82-2-5640249, kan@kan.or.kr, http://www.kan.or.kr/.

➤ **KRANKENDIENST**; Zeitschrift fuer kath. Krankenhaeuser, Sozialstationen und Pflegeberufe. *see* HEALTH FACILITIES AND ADMINISTRATION

610.73 DEU
KRANKENPFLEGE JOURNAL (ONLINE); Krankenhaus Magazin. Text in German. 1963. irreg. illus. **Document type:** *Magazine, Trade.*
Former titles (until 2005): Krankenpflege Journal (Print) (0174-108X); (until 1980): Schwestern Revue (0048-9549)
Media: Online - full content.
Indexed: A22, EMBASE, ExcerpMed, INI, MEDLINE, P30, R10, Reac, SCOPUS.
—BLDSC (5118.146600), GNLM, IE, Infotrieve, Ingenta. **CCC.**
Published by: Die Schwestern Revue GmbH, Postfach 1003, Illertissen, 89251, Germany. TEL 49-7303-910030, FAX 49-7303-5299. Ed. Knut Wenzel Backe.

610.73 JPN ISSN 0388-5585
KURINIKARU SUTADI/CLINICAL STUDY. Text in Japanese. 1980. m. JPY 15,750 (effective 2007). Supplement avail.; back issues avail. **Document type:** *Journal, Academic/Scholarly.* **Description:** Case studies in nursing process and miscellanies for student nurses.
Indexed: INI, P30.
Published by: Medical Friend Co. Ltd./Mejikaru Furendo Sha, 3-2-4 Kudan-Kita, Chiyoda-ku, Tokyo, 102-0073, Japan. TEL 81-3-32646611, http://www.medical-friend.co.jp/. Circ: 60,000.

610.73 GBR ISSN 1354-1412
L F N BULLETIN. (Libraries for Nursing) Text in English. 1981. q. free membership. adv. bk.rev. **Document type:** *Bulletin, Academic/Scholarly.* **Description:** Includes news, articles, reviews, and reports relevant to the provision of library services to nurses and the nursing profession.
Former titles: Libraries for Nursing Bulletin (0968-817X); (until 1993): N I S G Newsletter (0263-4945)
Indexed: B28, C06, C07, CA, P24, P48, PQC, T02.
—BLDSC (5186.094000). **CCC.**
Published by: Library Association Health Libraries Group, Libraries for Nursing, c/o Lori Havard, Membership Secretary, School of Health Sciences & Clinical School Librarian, University of Wales Swansea, Singleton Park, Swansea, SA2 8PP, United Kingdom. TEL 44-1792-295038, l.d.havard@swan.ac.uk, http://www.cilip.org.uk/get-involved/special-interest-groups/health/subject-groups/libraries-for-nursing/pages/default.aspx. Ed. Jane Shelley. Circ: 150 (paid).

610.73 USA ISSN 1550-6541
L N C RESOURCE. (Legal Nurse Consultants) Text in English. 2004. m. USD 149.95 (effective 2004). adv. **Document type:** *Newspaper, Trade.* **Description:** Brings you the most up to date information on litigation issues, LNC services, LNC spotlight, technology, expert witnesses, medical records, references and resources, marketing, and more.
Related titles: Online - full text ed.: ISSN 1550-655X.
Published by: L N C Resource, Inc., 6567 Towne Woods Dr, Ste 9700, St Louis, MO 63129-4521. TEL 877-562-1200. Ed., Pub. Cindy G Banes. Adv. contact Bill Potthoff. B&W page USD 1,800; trim 11 x 17. Circ: 8,500 (controlled).

610.73 USA ISSN 1553-0582
➤ **L P N (YEAR)**; the journal for excellence in practical nursing. (Licensed Practical Nurse) Text in English. 2005. bi-m. USD 146.86 domestic to institutions; USD 190.37 foreign to institutions (effective 2009). illus. **Document type:** *Journal, Academic/Scholarly.* **Description:** Targets the growth challenges, clinical responsibilities, and career objective unique to LPNs. Also includes authoritative guidance on medical treatments, drug administration, assessment, patient education and more.
Related titles: Online - full text ed.: ISSN 1553-0590.
Indexed: SCOPUS.
—**CCC.**
Published by: Lippincott Williams & Wilkins (Subsidiary of: Wolters Kluwer N.V.), 530 Walnut St, Philadelphia, PA 19106. TEL 215-521-8300, FAX 215-521-8902, customerservice@lww.com. Ed. Richard R Gibbs.

610.73 USA ISSN 1542-2194
THE L T C NURSE'S COMPANION. (Long Term Care) Text in English. 2002 (Aug.). 10/yr. USD 129 (effective 2002).
Published by: Frontline Publishing, P. O. Box 441002, Somerville, MA 02144. TEL 800-348-0605, FAX 617-625-7446, info@frontlinepub.com, http://www.frontlinepub.com. Ed. Rhoda Meador.

L T C NURSING ASSISTANT TRAINER. (Long Term Care) *see* HEALTH FACILITIES AND ADMINISTRATION

610.7 AUS ISSN 0047-3936
THE LAMP. Text in English. 1943. m. AUD 70 domestic to individuals; AUD 106 domestic to institutions; AUD 116 foreign; free to members (effective 2009). adv. bk.rev. back issues avail. **Document type:** *Magazine, Consumer.* **Description:** Features industrial and professional news and development of interest to nurses.
Related titles: Microfiche ed.; Online - full text ed.
Indexed: A11, A22, A26, C06, C07, C08, CA, CINAHL, H11, H12, HRIS, I05, INI, P20, P24, P30, P48, P54, PQC, SCOPUS, T02.
—BLDSC (5145.050000), GNLM, IE, Infotrieve, Ingenta. **CCC.**
Published by: New South Wales Nurses' Association, PO Box 40, Camperdown, NSW 2050, Australia. TEL 61-2-85951234, 300-367-962, FAX 61-2-95503667, gensec@nswnurses.asn.au, http://www.nswnurses.asn.au. Adv. contact Patricia Purcell TEL 61-2-85952139.

610.7365 AUT ISSN 1024-6908
LAZARUS; Oesterreichs Zeitschrift fuer Kranken- und Altenpflege. Text in German. 1986. m. bk.rev. **Document type:** *Journal, Trade.*
Published by: PflegeNetzWerk Lazarus, Doppel 29, Kirchstetten, N 3062, Austria. TEL 43-2743-8797, FAX 43-2743-8797, office@lazarus.at, http://www.lazarus.at. Ed., R&P, Adv. contact Erich Hofer. Circ: 24,000.

610.73 344.0414 USA ISSN 1085-4924
KF2915.N8
LEGAL EAGLE EYE NEWSLETTER FOR THE NURSING PROFESSION. Text in English. 1992. m. USD 155 (effective 2004). **Document type:** *Newsletter, Trade.* **Description:** Focuses on nurses' professional negligence, employment, discrimination, and licensing issues.
Formerly: Legal Eagle Eye Newsletter for Nursing Management
Indexed: A26, C06, C07, C08, CINAHL, H12, I05.
—BLDSC (5181.315000). **CCC.**
Published by: Legal Eagle Eye Newsletter, PO Box 4592, Seattle, WA 98104-0592. TEL 206-440-5860, 877-985-0977, FAX 206-440-5862, info@nursinglaw.com. Ed., Pub. Kenneth Snyder.

610.73 340 USA ISSN 8756-0054
KF2915.N8
LEGISLATIVE NETWORK FOR NURSES; policy and politics for the nursing profession. Text in English. 1984. bi-w. looseleaf. USD 245 (effective 2007). back issues avail.; reprints avail. **Document type:** *Newsletter.* **Description:** Covers regulations and how they affect the nursing profession - salaries, training, recruiting, and unionizing.
Incorporates (in 2003): Emergency Department Law (1042-2978)
Related titles: CD-ROM ed.; Online - full text ed.: ISSN 1545-7427. USD 247 (effective 2005).
Indexed: A26, C06, C07, C08, CINAHL, G05, G06, G07, G08, H11, H12, I05.
—**CCC.**
Published by: Business Publishers, Inc. (Subsidiary of: Eli Research, Inc.), PO Box 17592, Baltimore, MD 21297. TEL 800-274-6737, custserv@bpinews.com, http://www.bpinews.com/. Eds. Sarah Spencer, Ami Dodson. Pub. Adam P Goldstein.

LINK INTERNATIONAL. *see* RELIGIONS AND THEOLOGY—Roman Catholic

LIPPINCOTT'S NURSING DRUG GUIDE. *see* PHARMACY AND PHARMACOLOGY

LIST OF CANADIAN NURSING-RELATED PERIODICALS. *see* MEDICAL SCIENCES—Abstracting, Bibliographies, Statistics

LONG TERM CARE. *see* GERONTOLOGY AND GERIATRICS

649.8 USA ISSN 1940-9958
LONG-TERM LIVING. Text in English. 1950. m. USD 125 domestic; USD 165 foreign (effective 2010). adv. illus.; stat. back issues avail.; reprints avail. **Document type:** *Magazine, Trade.* **Description:** For professionals in planning, directing, organizing and delivering quality long-term care in the proprietary nursing home field.
Former titles (until 2008): Nursing Homes (1061-4753); (until 1991): Nursing Homes and Senior Citizen Care (0896-6915); (until 1986): Nursing Homes (0029-649X)
Related titles: Microform ed.: (from PQC); Online - full text ed.
Indexed: A01, A02, A03, A08, A12, A13, A14, A17, A22, A23, A26, ABIn, AgeL, B01, B02, B04, B06, B07, B08, B09, B13, B15, B16, B17, B18, BPI, BRD, BusI, C06, C07, C08, C11, C12, CINAHL, G04, G06, G07, G08, H01, H02, H03, H04, H05, H11, H12, H13, HospLI, I05, INI, M01, M02, P02, P10, P16, P19, P20, P21, P24, P27, P30, P34, P48, P51, P53, P54, PQC, RehabLit, S23, SCOPUS, T&II, T02, V02, W01, W02, W03.
—BLDSC (5294225330), GNLM, IE, Ingenta. **CCC.**
Published by: Vendome Group, LLC, 149 5th Ave, New York, NY 10010. TEL 212-812-8420, 800-519-3692, FAX 212-473-8786, customerservice@Vendomegrpsubs.com, http://www.vendomegrp.com/. Ed. Richard L Peck TEL 216-373-1212. Circ: 45,000.

610.73 USA
LOUISIANA STATE BOARD OF NURSING. ANNUAL REPORT TO THE GOVERNOR OF THE STATE OF LOUISIANA. Text in English. 1973. a. free. **Document type:** *Government.*
Former titles (until 1986): Louisiana. State Board of Nursing. Report (Calendar Year); (until 1976): Louisiana. State Board of Nurse Examiners. Report (0095-5884)
Related titles: Online - full text ed.
Published by: Louisiana State Board of Nursing, 5207 Essen Ln, Ste 6, Baton Rouge, LA 70809. TEL 225-763-3570, FAX 225-763-3580, lsbn@lsbn.state.la.us, http://www.lsbn.state.la.us. Ed. Barbara L Morvant. R&P Barbara Morvant. Circ: 150.

610.73 USA ISSN 0361-929X
RG951 CODEN: MCNNEI
M C N: THE AMERICAN JOURNAL OF MATERNAL CHILD NURSING. (Maternal Child Nursing) Text in English. 1976. bi-m. USD 294.51 domestic to institutions; USD 407 foreign to institutions (effective 2011). adv. bk.rev. bibl.; charts; illus. Index. back issues avail.; reprints avail. **Document type:** *Journal, Academic/Scholarly.*
Related titles: CD-ROM ed.; Microform ed.: (from PQC); Online - full text ed.: ISSN 1539-0683. USD 113.10 domestic academic site license; USD 133.10 foreign academic site license; USD 126.15 domestic corporate site license; USD 146.15 foreign corporate site license (effective 2002).
Indexed: A22, B28, C06, C07, C08, CA, CINAHL, CurCont, EMBASE, ExcerpMed, F09, FamI, INI, IndMed, MEDLINE, NurAb, P03, P24, P30, P48, P50, PQC, PsycInfo, PsycholAb, R10, Reac, SCI, SCOPUS, SSCI, T02, W07, W09.
—BLDSC (5413.499800), GNLM, IE, Infotrieve, Ingenta, INIST. **CCC.**
Published by: Lippincott Williams & Wilkins (Subsidiary of: Wolters Kluwer N.V.), Two Commerce Sq, 2001 Market St, Philadelphia, PA 19103. TEL 215-521-8300, FAX 215-521-8902, customerservice@lww.com, http://www.lww.com. Ed. Margaret Comerford Freda. Pub. Sandy Kasko.

M D S 3.0 UPDATE. (Minimum Data Set) *see* HEALTH FACILITIES AND ADMINISTRATION

610.73 GBR
M I M S FOR NURSES. (Monthly Index of Medical Specialties) Text in English. 2000. s-a. GBP 40; free to qualified personnel (effective 2009). adv. **Document type:** *Magazine, Trade.* **Description:** Provides news on the latest changes to the industry, individual titles also offer a wide range of advice for nurses.
Published by: Haymarket Medical Publications Ltd. (Subsidiary of: Haymarket Media Group), 174 Hammersmith Rd, London, W6 7JP, United Kingdom. TEL 44-20-82675000, healthcare.republic@haymarket.com, http://www.healthcarerepublic.com. Ed. Jenny Gowans TEL 44-20-82674614. Adv. contact Rob Nuzzaci TEL 44-20-82674884. Circ: 11,455. **Subscr. to:** 12-13 Cranleigh Gardens Industrial Estate, Southall UB1 2DB, United Kingdom. TEL 44-8451-557355, FAX 44-8451-948840, subscriptions@haymarket.com, http://www.haymarketbusinesssubs.com.

610.736 GBR ISSN 1361-9020
MACMILLAN NURSE. Text in English. 1996. q. **Document type:** *Journal, Trade.*
—**CCC.**
Published by: Macmillan Cancer Support, 89 Albert Embankment, London, SE1 7UQ, United Kingdom. TEL 44-20-78407840, FAX 44-20-78407841, webmanager@macmillan.org.uk, http://www.macmillan.org.uk.

610.73 618 POL ISSN 1425-6789
MAGAZYN PIELEGNIARKI I POLOZNEJ. Text in Polish. 1995. m. PLZ 78 domestic; EUR 75 foreign (effective 2006). adv. illus. reprints avail. **Document type:** *Journal, Academic/Scholarly.* **Description:** Covers all fields of nursing and midwifery.
Published by: (Naczelna Rada Pielegniarek i Poloznych), Wydawnictwo Czelej Sp. z o.o., ul Czeremchowa 21, Lublin, 20807, Poland. TEL 48-81-7437766, FAX 48-81-5347788, wydawnictwo@czelej.com.pl, http://www.czelej.com.pl. Ed. Maria Karpiuk-Domagala. adv.: color page USD 850. Circ: 10,000 (controlled). **Dist. by:** Ars Polona, Obroncow 25, Warsaw 03933, Poland. TEL 48-22-5098609, FAX 48-22-5098610, arspolona@arspolona.com.pl, http://www.arspolona.com.pl.

610.73 USA ISSN 0025-0767
THE MAINE NURSE. Text in English. 1969. 6/yr. **Description:** Covers issues and employment opportunities of interest to licensed nursing professionals.
Related titles: Online - full text ed.
Indexed: C06, C07, C08, CINAHL, P24, P30, P48, PQC.
Published by: Maine State Nurses Association, 160 Capital St Ste 1, Augusta, ME 34330. TEL 207-622-1057, mainenurse@verizon.net, http://www.mainenurse.org/.

610.73 USA
➤ **MARYLAND NURSE.** Text in English. 1970. q. looseleaf. USD 20 (effective 2008); Free to qualified subscribers. adv. 32 p./no.; back issues avail.; reprints avail. **Document type:** *Newsletter, Trade.* **Description:** Covers issues and employment opportunities of interest to licensed nursing professionals.
Supersedes: Maryland Nurses News; Formerly (until 1999): The Maryland Nurse (0047-6080)
Related titles: Online - full text ed.
Indexed: A22, A26, C06, C07, C08, CINAHL, H12, I05, INI, P30.
—BLDSC (5383.518000), GNLM.
Published by: (Maryland Nurses Association), Arthur L. Davis Publishing Agency, Inc., 517 Washington St, PO Box 216, Cedar Falls, IA 50613. TEL 319-277-2414, 800-626-4081, FAX 319-277-4055, sales@aldpub.com, http://www.aldpub.com. Ed. Mark Miller. R&P Kathryn V Hall. Adv. contact Jim Larson. Circ: 76,000.

610.73 USA ISSN 1941-367X
RT5.M4
THE MASSACHUSETTS NURSE ADVOCATE. Text in English. 1932. q. looseleaf. USD 20 domestic; USD 28 foreign (effective 2008); Free to qualified subscribers. adv. 36 p./no.; back issues avail. **Document type:** *Newsletter, Trade.* **Description:** Covers issues and employment opportunities of interest to licensed nursing professionals.
Former titles (until 2007): Massachusetts Nurse (0163-0784); (until vol.44, 1975): Massachusetts Nurses Association. Bulletin (0025-4843)
Related titles: Online - full text ed.
Indexed: A01, A02, A03, A08, C06, C07, C08, C11, CA, CINAHL, H04, INI, P30, P34, SCOPUS, T02.
—GNLM.
Published by: Massachusetts Nurses Association, 340 Turnpike St, Canton, MA 02021-2700. TEL 781-821-4625, FAX 781-821-4445, http://www.massnurses.org. Ed. Jen Johnson. Circ: 107,000 (free).

MEDICARE SKILLED NURSING FACILITY MANUAL. *see* INSURANCE

610.73 RUS ISSN 0869-7760
RA421 CODEN: MESEAQ
MEDITSINSKAYA POMOSHCH/MEDICAL CARE. Text in Russian; Summaries in English. 1942. bi-m. USD 88 foreign (effective 2005). adv. bk.rev.; Website rev. index. **Document type:** *Journal, Academic/Scholarly.* **Description:** Publishes articles on the care of patients, medical technique, medical advances, and sanitary education.
Formerly (until 1993): Meditsinskaya Sestra (0025-8342)
Indexed: ChemAb, DentInd, INI, ISR, P30.
—BLDSC (0104.700000), East View, GNLM. **CCC.**
Published by: Izdatel'stvo Meditsina/Meditsina Publishers, ul B Pirogovskaya, d 2, str 5, Moscow, 119435, Russian Federation. TEL 7-095-2483324, meditsina@mtu-net.ru, http://www.medlit.ru. Ed. Khasan A Musalatov. Pub. A M Stochik. R&P L Vecherkina. Adv. contact O A Fadeeva TEL 7-095-923-51-40. Circ: 12,000. **Dist. by:** M K - Periodica, ul Gilyarovskogo 39, Moscow 129110, Russian Federation. TEL 7-095-2845008, FAX 7-095-2813798, info@periodicals.ru, http://www.mkniga.ru.

610.73 RUS
MEDITSINSKAYA SESTRA; nauchno-prakticheskii i publitsisticheskii zhurnal. Text in Russian. bi-m. 48 p./no.; **Document type:** *Journal.*
Published by: Izdatel'skii Dom Russkii Vrach, ul Bol'shaya Pirogovskaya, dom 2, str. 3, Moscow, Russian Federation. rvrach@mmascience.ru, http://www.rusvrach.ru. Ed. G M Perfilieva.

610.73 BGR ISSN 1310-7496
➤ **MEDITSINSKI PREGLED. SESTRINSKO DELO.** Text in Bulgarian; Summaries in Bulgarian, English. 1969. q. BGL 14 domestic; USD 40 foreign (effective 2005). adv. bk.rev. back issues avail. **Document type:** *Journal, Academic/Scholarly.* **Description:** Presents original articles and abstracts of foreign publications in the fields of nursing care, education, nursing services, nurse-patient relations, hospital nursing staff.
Formerly: Za Srednite Meditsinski Kadri (0324-1726)
Indexed: A36, CABA, D01, E12, GH, LT, N02, N03, R12, RA&MP, RRTA, S12, SoyAb, T05, W11.
Published by: Meditsinski Universitet - Sofia, Tsentralna Meditsinska Biblioteka, Tsentur za Informatsiia po Meditsina/Medical University - Sofia, Central Medical Library, Medical Information Center, 1 Sv Georgi Sofiiski ul, Sofia, 1431, Bulgaria. TEL 359-2-9522342, FAX 359-2-9522393, lydia@medun.acad.bg, http://www.medun.acad.bg/cmb_htm/cmb1_home_bg.htm. Ed. Dr. M Mitova. R&P, Adv. contact Lydia Tacheva. B&W page USD 50, color page USD 150; trim 160 x 110. Circ: 300.

610.73 DEU ISSN 1864-1938
DIE MEDIZINISCHE FACHANGESTELLTE. Text in German. 1963. m. EUR 55.80; EUR 46.80 to students (effective 2010). adv. bk.rev. index. **Document type:** *Magazine, Trade.*
Formerly (until 2007): Die Arzthelferin (0931-5853); Which incorporated (1966-1989): Helferin des Arztes (0017-9949)
—**CCC.**
Published by: Friedrich Kiehl Verlag GmbH (Subsidiary of: Verlag Neue Wirtschafts-Briefe GmbH & Co. KG), Eschstr 22, Herne, 44629, Germany. TEL 49-2323-141700, FAX 49-2323-141123, service@kiehl.de, http://www.kiehl.de.

MEDSURG NURSING; the journal of adult health. *see* MEDICAL SCIENCES—Surgery

MENTAL HEALTH NURSING (ONLINE). *see* MEDICAL SCIENCES—Psychiatry And Neurology

MENTAL HEALTH PRACTICE. *see* MEDICAL SCIENCES—Psychiatry And Neurology

610.73 ESP ISSN 1138-7262
METAS DE ENFERMERIA. Text in Spanish. 1998. m. EUR 87 domestic to individuals; EUR 118 in Portugal to individuals; EUR 150 in Europe to individuals; EUR 170 elsewhere to individuals; EUR 180 domestic to institutions; EUR 230 in Portugal to institutions; EUR 270 in Europe to institutions; EUR 280 elsewhere to institutions (effective 2009). back issues avail. **Document type:** *Magazine, Consumer.*
Related titles: Online - full text ed.: EUR 72 to individuals; EUR 139 to institutions (effective 2005); Supplement(s): Metas de Enfermeria. Suplemento. ISSN 1575-8516. 1999.
Indexed: C06, C07, C08, CINAHL.
Published by: Difusion Avances de Enfermeria, Poligono Industrial Olivral, Parcela 1o., Bloque A, Nave 3 Carretera III Km. 330, Ribarroja, Valencia, 46394, Spain. TEL 34-96-1667384, correo-metas@enfermeria21.com, http://www.enfermeria21.com/index.php. Ed. Elena Acebes Seisdedos.

610.73 USA ISSN 0026-2366
RT5.M5
MICHIGAN NURSE. Text in English. 1924. 11/yr. USD 33 domestic; USD 50 foreign (effective 2005). adv. illus. index. back issues avail. **Document type:** *Magazine, Trade.* **Description:** Publishes information of interest to nurses, including topics related to the profession, announcements of continuing education opportunities, and convention reports. Reports on Michigan Nurses Association programs, elections, and committee activities.
Related titles: Microform ed.: (from PQC).
Indexed: C06, C07, C08, CINAHL, EMBASE, ExcerpMed, INI, MEDLINE, MMI, P30, R10, Reac, SCOPUS.
—BLDSC (5755.540000), GNLM. **CCC.**
Published by: Michigan Nurses Association, 2310 Jolly Oak Rd, Okemos, MI 48864-4599. TEL 517-349-5640, 800-832-2051, FAX 517-349-5818, minurses@minurses.org. Ed., R&P Ann Kettering Sincox. Adv. contacts Ann Kettering Sincox, Lisa Gottlieb-Kinnaird. Circ: 10,000.

MIDWIFERY. *see* MEDICAL SCIENCES—Obstetrics And Gynecology

610.736 GBR ISSN 0961-1479
MIDWIFERY MATTERS. Text in English. 1978. q. free to members (effective 2009). adv. bk.rev. back issues avail. **Document type:** *Journal, Trade.* **Description:** Disseminates ideas, skills and information with colleagues and clients. Helps midwives develop their role as advocates for women's active participation in maternity care.
Former titles (until 1989): Association of Radical Midwives Magazine (0951-5488); (until 1987): Association of Radical Midwives. Newsletter (0142-4610)
Related titles: Online - full text ed.
Indexed: A04, A22, B28, C06, C07, C08, C11, CA, CINAHL, GW, P48, PQC, T02.
—BLDSC (5761.449232), IE, Ingenta. **CCC.**
Published by: Association of Radical Midwives, 62 Greetby Hill, Ormskirk, Lancs L39 2DT, United Kingdom. ikargar@tiscali.co.uk.

610.73 USA ISSN 0026-5586
MINNESOTA NURSING ACCENT. Variant title: M N A Accent. Text in English. 1927. 10/yr. USD 25 domestic to non-members; USD 45 foreign to non-members (effective 2001). adv. bk.rev. illus. **Document type:** *Journal, Trade.*
Indexed: C06, C07, C08, CINAHL, INI, P30.
—GNLM.
Published by: Minnesota Nurses Association, 1625 Energy Park Dr, St. Paul, MN 55108. TEL 651-646-4807, 800-536-4662, FAX 651-647-5301, mnnurses@mnnurses.org, http://www.mnnurses.org. Ed., R&P, Adv. contact Jan Rabbers TEL 612-646-4807 ext 161. Pub. Marilyn Cunningham. Circ: 14,000.

MINORITY NURSE; the career and education resource for minority nursing professionals, students and faculty. *see* OCCUPATIONS AND CAREERS

610.73 USA ISSN 0026-6388
MISSISSIPPI R N. (Registered Nurse) Text in English. 1939. bi-m. USD 18 domestic; USD 25 foreign (effective 2000). adv. bk.rev. illus. **Document type:** *Journal, Trade.*
Related titles: Online - full text ed.
Indexed: C06, C07, C08, CINAHL, EMBASE, ExcerpMed, INI, MEDLINE, P30, R10, Reac, SCOPUS.
—GNLM.
Published by: Mississippi Nurses' Association, 31 Woodgreen Pl, Madison, MS 39110-9531. TEL 601-898-0670, FAX 601-898-0190. Ed. Betty Dickson. Adv. contact Clay Cazier. Circ: 2,000.

610.73 USA ISSN 0026-6655
RT1
MISSOURI NURSE. Text in English. 1932. bi-m. USD 25 to non-members; USD 30 foreign to non-members (effective 1999). adv. charts; illus.; tr.lit. back issues avail. **Document type:** *Newsletter.* **Description:** Disseminates information regarding policies, positions and activities of the Association; strives to provide a forum for discussion of nursing issues relevant to Association members.
Indexed: A26, C06, C07, C08, CINAHL, EMBASE, ExcerpMed, H12, I05, INI, MEDLINE, P30, R10, Reac, SCOPUS.
—GNLM.
Published by: Missouri Nurses Association, 1904 Bubba Ln, Jefferson City, MO 65110-5228. TEL 573-636-4623, FAX 573-636-9576, klbmona@aol.com, http://www.missourinurses.org. Ed., R&P, Adv. contact Karen Backus. B&W page USD 350; trim 7.3333 x 9.5. Circ: 2,100.

610.73 USA
MISSOURI STATE BOARD OF NURSING. NEWSLETTER. Text in English. 19??. q. looseleaf. Free to qualified subscribers. adv. 24 p./no.; back issues avail. **Document type:** *Newsletter, Trade.* **Description:** Covers issues and employment opportunities of interest to licensed nursing professionals.
Related titles: Online - full text ed.
Published by: (Missouri State Board of Nursing), Arthur L. Davis Publishing Agency, Inc., 517 Washington St, PO Box 216, Cedar Falls, IA 50613. TEL 319-277-2414, 800-626-4081, FAX 319-277-4055, sales@aldpub.com, http://www.aldpub.com. Ed. Mark Miller. R&P Calvina Thomas. Adv. contact Jim Larson. Circ: 111,000.

610.73 USA
MOMENTUM (LITTLE ROCK). Text in English. 2003. q. free to members (effective 2009). back issues avail. **Document type:** *Journal, Trade.*
Related titles: Online - full text ed.: free (effective 2009).
Published by: (Ohio Board of Nursing), Publishing Concepts, Inc., 14109 Taylor Loop Rd, Little Rock, AR 72223. TEL 501-221-9986, 800-561-4686, FAX 501-225-3735, http://www.thinkaboutitnursing.com/, http://www.pcipublishing.com/. Adv. contact Greg Jones TEL 501-221-9986.

610.73 USA ISSN 1044-8470
RM301.12
MOSBY'S NURSING DRUG REFERENCE. Text in English. 1988. a. price varies. **Document type:** *Directory, Trade.* **Description:** Provides the most complete drug information for each drug, including uses, side effects, and interactions.
—**CCC.**

Published by: Mosby, Inc. (Subsidiary of: Elsevier Health Sciences), 1600 John F. Kennedy Blvd, Ste 1800, Philadelphia, PA 19103. TEL 215-239-3900, 800-523-1649, FAX 215-239-3990, elspcs@elsevier.com, http://www.us.elsevierhealth.com.

612.652 USA ISSN 1554-3382
N A N N CENTRAL. Text in English. 198?. q. free to members (effective 2005). **Document type:** *Newsletter, Trade.* **Description:** Announces news and events of interest to nurses working with neonatal patients.
Former titles: N A N N Central Lines (1080-3807); N A N N News (1070-0277)
Indexed: C06, C07, C08, CINAHL.
Published by: National Association of Neonatal Nurses, 4700 W Lake Ave, Glenview, IL 60025. TEL 847-299-NANN, 847-375-3660, 800-451-3795, FAX 888-477-6266.

610.73 USA ISSN 1942-602X
LB3405
N A S N SCHOOL NURSE. Text in English. 1986. bi-m. USD 209, GBP 123 combined subscription to institutions (print & online eds.); USD 205, GBP 121 to institutions (effective 2011). adv. **Document type:** *Newsletter, Trade.* **Description:** Covers news, issues, conferences and resources of interest to school nurses.
Formerly (until 2008): N A S N Newsletter (1047-4757)
Related titles: Online - full text ed.: ISSN 1942-6038. USD 188, GBP 111 to institutions (effective 2011).
Indexed: A22, C06, C07, C08, CINAHL, E01, EMBASE, ExcerpMed, MEDLINE, P20, P22, P24, P30, P48, P54, PQC, R10, Reac, SCOPUS.
—IE. **CCC.**
Published by: (National Association of School Nurses Inc.), Sage Publications, Inc., 2455 Teller Rd, Thousand Oaks, CA 91320. TEL 805-499-9774, FAX 805-499-0871, info@sagepub.com, http://www.sagepub.com/. Ed. Devin Dinkel. adv.: B&W page USD 1,075, color page USD 1,925; bleed 11.25 x 8.5. Circ: 9,000 (paid).

610.73 AUS ISSN 1832-4800
N M B UPDATE. (Nurses and Midwives Board) Text in English. 1997. 3/yr. back issues avail. **Document type:** *Newsletter, Trade.*
Formerly (until 2005): Board Works (1444-0350)
Related titles: Online - full text ed.: free (effective 2009).
Published by: Nurses and Midwives Board of New South Wales, Haymarket, PO Box K599, Sydney, NSW 1238, Australia. TEL 61-2-92190222, FAX 61-2-92812030, mail@nmb.nsw.gov.au.

610.73 618 GBR ISSN 1478-1832
N M C NEWS. Text in English. 1987. q. free to qualified personnel (effective 2009). adv. back issues avail. **Document type:** *Magazine, Trade.* **Description:** Aims to keep nurses, midwives, students and the general public informed about the NMC's work.
Formerly (until 2002): Register - United Kingdom Central Council for Nursing Midwifery and Health Visiting (0951-788X)
Related titles: Online - full text ed.: free (effective 2009).
Published by: Nursing and Midwifery Council, 23 Portland Pl, London, W1B 1PZ, United Kingdom. TEL 44-20-73339333, communications@nmc-uk.org. Ed. Andrew Bence. Adv. contacts Ian Lydon-James TEL 44-20-78782361, Katy Eggleton TEL 44-20-78782344. page GBP 13,000. Circ: 571,136.

610.73 618 IRN ISSN 2008-5923
➤ **NASHRIYYAH-I PARASTARI-I IRAN/IRAN JOURNAL OF NURSING.** Text in Persian, Modern; Summaries in English. 1987. bi-m. IRR 6,000, USD 6 (effective 2011). abstr.; bibl.; charts. back issues avail. **Document type:** *Journal, Academic/Scholarly.* **Description:** Publishes original articles, review articles, case reports, and brief research reports contributing to nursing care, research, practice, education, and management.
Formerly (until 2009): Faslnamah-i Parastari va Mamayi-i Iran/Quarterly Nursing and Midwifery Journal of Iran (1025-0581)
Related titles: Online - full text ed.: ISSN 2008-5931.
Published by: (Anjuman-i Ilmi-i Parastari-i Iran/Iranian Nursing Scientific Association), Danishgah-i Ulum-i Pizishki-i Tihran, Danishkadah-'i Parastari va Mamayi/Tehran University of Medical Sciences, Faculty of Nursing & Midwifery, Rashid Yasami St. Valiasr Ave., PO Box 19395-4798, Tehran, 19964, Iran. TEL 98-21-82471170, FAX 98-21-88794300. Ed. Forough Rafii. R&P Seyede Fatemeh Haghdoost Oskouie TEL 98-21-82471106. Circ: 700.

610.73 JPN
NASU BINZU SMART NURSE. Text in Japanese. 1999. m. JPY 11,340; JPY 1,050 newsstand/cover (effective 2007). Supplement avail. **Document type:** *Journal, Academic/Scholarly.*
Former titles (until 2006): Nasu Binzu (1345-952X); (until 2000): Nasu, Magu (1344-4417)
Published by: Medicus Shuppan/Medicus Publishing Inc., 18-24 Hiroshiba-cho, Suita-shi, Osaka-fu 564-8580, Japan. TEL 81-6-63856911, FAX 81-6-63856873, http://www.medica.co.jp/.

612.652 USA
NATIONAL ASSOCIATION OF NEONATAL NURSES. POSITION STATEMENT. Text in English. irreg. USD 15 per issue to members; USD 25 per issue to non-members (effective 2000). back issues avail. **Document type:** *Monographic series.* **Description:** Discusses important issues in neonatal and pediatric nursing.
Published by: National Association of Neonatal Nurses, 4700 W Lake Ave, Glenview, IL 60025. TEL 847-375-3660, 847-299-NANN, 800-451-3795, FAX 888-477-6266.

610.73 USA ISSN 0885-6028
RT1
➤ **NATIONAL BLACK NURSES' ASSOCIATION. JOURNAL.** Abbreviated title: J N B N A. Text in English. 1986. s-a. USD 150 to non-members; free to members (effective 2011). adv. **Document type:** *Journal, Academic/Scholarly.* **Description:** Publishes scholarly papers, research reports, critical essays, resource listings, documents and reviews focusing on issues related to factors affecting health care in Black communities and nurses.
Indexed: A22, Agr, C06, C07, C08, CA, CINAHL, EMBASE, ExcerpMed, MEDLINE, P30, R10, Reac, S02, S03, SCOPUS, SWR&A, T02, W09.
—BLDSC (4829.350000), IE, Infotrieve, Ingenta.
Published by: National Black Nurses' Association, 8630 Fenton St, Ste 330, Silver Spring, MD 20910. TEL 301-589-3200, 800-575-6298, FAX 301-589-3223, contact@nbna.org. Ed. Joyce Newman Giger.

610.73 USA ISSN 2153-0386
NATIONAL NURSE. Text in English. 1904. 10/yr. USD 40 domestic; USD 45 foreign; USD 100 to institutions (effective 2010). adv. bk.rev. back issues avail.; reprints avail. **Document type:** *Magazine, Trade.* **Description:** Provides news of the California Nurses Association's activities reports on developments of concern to all RNs in the state. Also carries general coverage and commentory on matters of nursing practice, community health and healthcare policy.
Former titles (until 2010): Registered Nurse (1932-8966); (until 2006): California Nurse (0008-1310); (until 1969): C N A Bulletin
Related titles: Microfilm ed.: 1904 (from PQC); Online - full text ed.: ISSN 2153-0394. free (effective 2007).
Indexed: A01, A02, A03, A08, A22, C06, C07, C08, C11, CA, CINAHL, CalPI, H04, INI, M02, P30, P34, T02.
—BLDSC (7344.145000), GNLM, Infotrieve.
Published by: California Nurses' Association, 2000 Franklin St., Ste. 300, Oakland, CA 94612. TEL 510-273-2251, FAX 510-663-0629, cbloice@calnurses.org, http://www.calnurse.org. Ed. Lucia Hwang. Adv. contact Felicia Mello TEL 510-273-2251. page USD 1,300; 8.75 x 10. Circ: 30,200 (controlled and free).

610.73 USA ISSN 0028-1921
RT1
NEBRASKA NURSE. Text in English. 1947. q. looseleaf. free to members (effective 2009); Free to qualified subscribers. adv. 36 p./no.; back issues avail. **Document type:** *Newsletter, Trade.* **Description:** Covers issues and employment opportunities of interest to licensed nursing professionals.
Related titles: Online - full text ed.
Indexed: C06, C07, C08, CINAHL, EMBASE, ExcerpMed, INI, MEDLINE, P30, R10, Reac, SCOPUS.
—GNLM.
Published by: (Nebraska Nurses' Association), Arthur L. Davis Publishing Agency, Inc., 517 Washington St, PO Box 216, Cedar Falls, IA 50613. TEL 319-277-2414, 800-626-4081, FAX 319-277-4055, sales@aldpub.com, http://www.aldpub.com. Adv. contacts Jim Larson, Mark Miller. Circ: 30,000.

610.73 USA ISSN 0730-0832
CODEN: NEONEE
➤ **NEONATAL NETWORK**; the journal of neonatal nursing. Text in English. 1981. bi-m. USD 65 combined subscription domestic to individuals (print & online eds.); USD 70 combined subscription in Canada to individuals (print & online eds.); USD 100 combined subscription elsewhere to individuals (print & online eds.); USD 225 combined subscription domestic to institutions (print & online eds.); USD 260 combined subscription in Canada to institutions (print & online eds.); USD 300 combined subscription elsewhere to institutions (print & online eds.) (effective 2011). adv. bk.rev. illus. index. back issues avail. **Document type:** *Journal, Academic/Scholarly.* **Description:** Dedicated to assist neonatal nurses and related healthcare professionals to remain current in their fields.
Related titles: Online - full text ed.: ISSN 1539-2880.
Indexed: A22, B28, C06, C07, C08, CA, CINAHL, EMBASE, ExcerpMed, F09, FamI, INI, IndMed, MEDLINE, P30, R10, Reac, SCOPUS, T02.
—BLDSC (6075.624000), GNLM, IE, Infotrieve, Ingenta. **CCC.**
Published by: (National Association of Neonatal Nurses), Neonatal Network, 1425 N McDowell Blvd, Ste 105, Petaluma, CA 94954. TEL 707-795-1421, FAX 707-795-0786, http://www.neonatalnetwork.com/. Circ: 10,000.

610.7362 AUS ISSN 1441-6638
RJ245
➤ **NEONATAL, PAEDIATRIC AND CHILD HEALTH NURSING.** Abbreviated title: N P C H N Journal. Text in English. 1986. 3/yr. AUD 180 (effective 2008). adv. bk.rev. illus. back issues avail. **Document type:** *Journal, Academic/Scholarly.* **Description:** Presents a broad range of content in the specialties of neonatal, pediatric and child health nursing, including original research, discussion papers, and case studies.
Formerly (until 1998): Paediatric Nursing Review (1038-5029)
Related titles: Online - full text ed.
Indexed: B28, C06, C07, C08, CINAHL, SCOPUS.
—BLDSC (6075.624200), IE, Ingenta.
Published by: (Australian College of Neonatal Nurses Inc., Australian Confederation of Paediatric and Child Health Nurses), Cambridge Publishing (Subsidiary of: Cambridge Media), 128 Northwood St, West Leederville, W.A. 6007, Australia. TEL 61-8-93823911, FAX 61-8-93823187, mail@cambridgemedia.com.au, http://www.cambridgemedia.com.au. Ed. Kaye Spence. Adv. contact Simon Henriques TEL 61-8-93823911. color page AUD 1,890, page AUD 1,520; 210 x 297. Circ: 2,000. **Co-sponsor:** Australian Neonatal Nurses Association.

616.083 BRA ISSN 1676-4293
NEP ENESEN. BOLETIM ELECTRONICO. (Nucleo de Estudos e Pesquisas sobre Atividades de Efermagen. Boletim Electronico) Text in Portuguese. 2001. bi-w. back issues avail. **Document type:** *Bulletin, Academic/Scholarly.*
Media: Online - full text.
Published by: Nucleo de Estudos e Pesquisas sobre Atividades de Efermagen, Dr Celestino, 74, Centro, Niteroi, RJ 2402-091, Brazil. TEL 55-21-26299468, FAX 55-21-9589948. Ed. Isabel Cristina Fonseca Cruz.

610.73 616.1 USA ISSN 1526-744X
RC902.A1
➤ **NEPHROLOGY NURSING JOURNAL.** Text in English. 1974. bi-m. USD 42 domestic to individuals; USD 72 foreign to individuals; USD 69 domestic to institutions; USD 99 foreign to institutions; USD 15 per issue domestic; USD 20 per issue foreign (effective 2010). adv. bk.rev. back issues avail. **Document type:** *Journal, Academic/Scholarly.* **Description:** Provides current information on wide variety of subjects to facilitate the practice of professional nephrology nursing. Its purpose is to disseminate information on the latest advances in research, practice, and education to nephrology nurses to positively influence the quality of care they provide.
Former titles (until 2000): A N N A Journal (8750-0779); (until 1984): A A N N T Journal (0744-1479); (until 1981): American Association of Nephrology Nurses and Technicians (0360-7615)
Related titles: Online - full text ed.
Indexed: A01, A02, A03, A08, A20, A22, A25, A26, C06, C07, C08, C11, CA, CINAHL, CurCont, E08, EMBASE, ExcerpMed, G08, H04, H11, H12, H13, I05, INI, IndMed, MEDLINE, NurAb, P10, P20, P22, P24, P30, P48, P53, P54, PQC, R10, Reac, S08, S09, SCI, SCOPUS, SSCI, T02, W07.
—BLDSC (6075.686500), GNLM, IE, Infotrieve, Ingenta, INIST. **CCC.**
Published by: (American Nephrology Nurses' Association), Jannetti Publications, Inc., E Holly Ave, PO Box 56, Pitman, NJ 08071. TEL 856-256-2300, FAX 856-589-7463, contact@ajj.com, http://www.ajj.com/. Ed. Beth Ulrich. Pub. Anthony J Jannetti. Circ: 15,500 (paid).

610.736 ITA ISSN 1723-2538
NEU. Text in Italian. 1976. q. free to members. **Document type:** *Magazine, Trade.* **Description:** NEU is the training and information tool of the Associazione Nazionale Infermieri Neuroscienze.
Formerly (until 1992): Infermieristica Neurochirurgica (0391-4445)
Published by: Associazione Nazionale Infermieri Neuroscienze (A N I N), Via Robecchi Brichetti 14, Pavia, 2700, Italy. TEL 39-0382-423200, segreteria@anin.it, http://www.anin.it.

610.73 USA ISSN 0273-4117
RT5.N3
NEVADA R N FORMATION. Key Title: Nevada RNformation. Variant title: Nevada Registered Nurse Information. Text in English. 1931. q. looseleaf. free to qualified personnel (effective 2008). adv. 36 p./no.; back issues avail.; reprints avail. **Document type:** *Newsletter, Trade.* **Description:** Reports information on topics of concern to registered nurses in Nevada, as well as association business.
Related titles: Online - full text ed.
Indexed: A26, C06, C07, C08, CINAHL, H12, I05, INI, P24, P30, P48, PQC, SCOPUS.
Published by: (Nevada Nurses Association), Arthur L. Davis Publishing Agency, Inc., 517 Washington St, PO Box 216, Cedar Falls, IA 50613. TEL 319-277-2414, 800-626-4081, FAX 319-277-4055, sales@aldpub.com, http://www.aldpub.com. Eds. Beatrice Razor, Mark Miller. R&P Richard Schlegel. Adv. contact Jim Larson. Circ: 25,000.

610.73 USA ISSN 0196-4895
RT5.N4
NEW JERSEY NURSE. Text in English. 1970 (vol.26). bi-m. USD 22 domestic; USD 32 foreign; USD 3.50 per issue (effective 2005). adv. bk.rev. **Document type:** *Newsletter.* **Description:** News and information of interest to association members.
Formerly: N J S N A Newsletter (0028-5870)
Related titles: Online - full text ed.
Indexed: C06, C07, C08, CINAHL, EMBASE, ExcerpMed, INI, MEDLINE, P20, P22, P24, P30, P48, P54, PQC, R10, Reac, SCOPUS.
Published by: New Jersey State Nurses' Association, 1479 Pennington Rd, Trenton, NJ 08618-2661. TEL 609-883-5335, 888-876-5762, FAX 609-883-5343. Ed. Andrea Aughenbaugh. R&P Sandra Kerr. Adv. contact Julia Schneider. Circ: 6,000.

610.73 USA ISSN 1934-7588
NEW YORK NURSE. Text in English. 1969. 10/yr. USD 33 to non-members; free to members (effective 2010). adv. back issues avail. **Document type:** *Newsletter, Trade.* **Description:** Brings out research studies and other scholarly articles of interested nurses.
Formerly (until 2007): New York State Nurses Association. Report (0028-7652)
Related titles: Online - full text ed.: ISSN 1934-7596.
—**CCC.**
Published by: New York State Nurses Association, 11 Cornell Rd, Latham, NY 12110. TEL 518-782-9400, FAX 518-782-9533, info@nysna.org.

610.73 USA
NEW YORK STATE ASSOCIATION OF SCHOOL NURSES COMMUNICATOR. Text in English. 3/yr. free to members (effective 2006). **Document type:** *Newsletter, Trade.*
Published by: New York State Association of School Nurses, 3138 East River Rd, Grand Island, NY 14072. nysasnsecretary@yahoo.com, http://www.nysasn.org. Ed. Cynthia Kaiser.

610.73 USA ISSN 0028-7644
RT5.N5 CODEN: JNYNA
➤ **NEW YORK STATE NURSES ASSOCIATION. JOURNAL.** Text in English. 1970. s-a. USD 17 to non-members; free to members (effective 2010). bk.rev. abstr.; bibl.; charts; illus.; stat. back issues avail. **Document type:** *Journal, Academic/Scholarly.* **Description:** Publishes research reports and scholarly articles on nurses and nursing.
Formerly (until 200?): New York State Nurse
Related titles: Online - full text ed.: (from PQC).
Indexed: A22, A26, C06, C07, C08, CINAHL, EMBASE, ExcerpMed, H12, I05, INI, MEDLINE, P30, R10, Reac, SCOPUS, SWR&A.
—BLDSC (4832.940000), GNLM, IE, Infotrieve, Ingenta. **CCC.**
Published by: New York State Nurses Association, 11 Cornell Rd, Latham, NY 12110. TEL 518-782-9400, FAX 518-782-9533, info@nysna.org.

610.73 NZL ISSN 1175-2904
NEW ZEALAND NURSING REVIEW. Text in English. 2000. m. NZD 48 domestic; NZD 78 foreign (effective 2008). adv. **Document type:** *Newspaper, Trade.* **Description:** Essential reading for anyone involved in the healthcare sector in New Zealand and provides nurses with the latest news and developments in the health industry.
Incorporates: New Zealand Health Review (1176-5542)
Related titles: Online - full text ed.
Published by: A P N Educational Media (NZ) Ltd., Level 1, Saatchi & Saatchi Bldg, Wellington, New Zealand. TEL 64-4-4711600, FAX 64-4-4711080. adv.: B&W page NZD 4,000, color page NZD 5,000.

610.7362 USA ISSN 1527-3369
RJ101
➤ **NEWBORN AND INFANT NURSING REVIEWS.** Text in English. 2001. q. USD 200 in United States to institutions; USD 256 elsewhere to institutions (effective 2012). **Document type:** *Journal, Academic/Scholarly.* **Description:** Providing in-depth discussions of diagnosis, treatment, nursing implications/applications, new developments, clinical/evidence-based research, and controversies in the field.
Related titles: Online - full text ed.: ISSN 1558-352X (from ScienceDirect).
Indexed: A26, C06, C07, C08, CINAHL, H12, I05, P30, SCOPUS, T02.
—BLDSC (6100.357000), IE, Ingenta. **CCC.**

Published by: W.B. Saunders Co. (Subsidiary of: Elsevier Health Sciences), Elsevier, Health Sciences Division, Order Fulfillment, 3251 Riverport Ln, Maryland Heights, MO 63043. TEL 314-872-8370, 800-325-4177, FAX 314-432-1380, JournalCustomerService-usa@elsevier.com, http://www.us.elsevierhealth.com. Ed. Leslie Altimier. Pub. Shannon Magee TEL 215-239-3730. Adv. contact Carol Clark TEL 212-633-3719.

➤ **NIEUWSBRIEF ZORGVISIE.** *see* HEALTH FACILITIES AND ADMINISTRATION

610.73 NGA ISSN 0331-4448
NIGERIAN NURSE. Text in English. 1973. bi-m. USD 13.50 (effective 2000). bibl.; illus. **Document type:** *Journal, Academic/Scholarly.*
Indexed: C06, C07, P30.
Published by: (National Association of Nigeria Nurses and Midwives), Literamed Publications Nigeria Ltd, PMB 21068, Ikeja, Oregun Village, Lagos, Nigeria. TEL 234-64-962512, FAX 234-64-961037. Ed. Anu Adegoroye. Pub. O M Lawal Solarin. Circ: 10,000.

610.73 USA ISSN 0894-5780
NIGHTINGALE. Text in English. 1973. q. USD 15 (effective 2005). stat.; tr.lit. back issues avail.
Related titles: Microform ed.: (from PQC).
Published by: National Association of Physician Nurses, 900 S Washington St, Ste G 13, Falls Church, VA 22046. TEL 703-237-8616. Ed. Adrianne Avillion.

610.73 JPN ISSN 0917-513X
NIHON KANGO GAKKAISHI/JAPANESE SOCIETY OF NURSING. JOURNAL. Text in Japanese. 1991. s-a. **Document type:** *Journal, Academic/Scholarly.* **Description:** Publishes selected papers presented at the JNA department research conferences.
Indexed: INI.
Published by: J N A Publishing Company, Japanese Nursing Association, Nursing Education & Research Center, Koubun-Kousan Bldg, 2-4-3 Hitotsubashi, Chiyoda-ku, Tokyo, 101-0003, Japan. TEL 81-3-5275-5871, http://www.nurse.or.jp/. Ed. Kayoko Matsumoto. Adv. contact Toshiaki Okuno.

610.73 JPN ISSN 1349-5429
NIHON KANGO GIJUTSU GAKKAISHI/JAPANESE JOURNAL OF NURSING ART AND SCIENCE. Text in Japanese. irreg. membership. **Document type:** *Journal, Academic/Scholarly.*
—BLDSC (6112.736600), IE. **CCC.**
Published by: Nihon Kango Gijutsu Gakkai/Japanese Society of Nursing Art and Science, Gunma University Graduate School of Medicine, Division of Health Sciences, 3-39-22, Showa-machi, Maebashi, Gunma 371-8511, Japan. TEL 81-27-2208907, FAX 81-27-2208907, jsnas@health.gunma-u.ac.jp.

610.7 JPN ISSN 0287-5330
NIHON KANGO KAGAKKAISHI/JAPAN ACADEMY OF NURSING SCIENCE. JOURNAL. Text in Japanese. 1981. s-a. JPY 10,000 membership (effective 2005). **Document type:** *Journal, Academic/Scholarly.*
Indexed: C06, C07, C08, CINAHL, P30, SCOPUS.
—BLDSC (4804.145000). **CCC.**
Published by: Nihon Kango Kagaku Gakkai/Japan Academy of Nursing Science, 201 Fujimi Bldg, 3-37-3 Hongo, Bunkyo-Ku, Tokyo, 113-0033, Japan. TEL 81-3-58051280, FAX 81-3-58051281, jans-office@umin.ac.jp, http://plaza.umin.ac.jp/~jans/.

610.73 NOR ISSN 1892-2678
▼ **NORDISK SYGEPLEJEFORSKNING.** Text in Norwegian, Danish, Swedish. 2011. 4/yr. NOK 1,000 to institutions (effective 2011). **Document type:** *Journal, Academic/Scholarly.*
Formed by the merger of (1985-2011): Tidsskrift for Sygeplejeforskning (0900-3002); (1985-2011): Norsk Tidsskrift for Sykepleieforskning (1501-4754); Which was formerly (until 1999): Tidsskrift for Norsk Sykepleieforskning (0801-1923)
—CCC.
Published by: Universitetsforlaget AS/Scandinavian University Press (Subsidiary of: Aschehoug & Co.), Sehesteds Gate 3, P O Box 508, Sentrum, Oslo, 0105, Norway. TEL 47-24-147500, FAX 47-24-147501, post@universitetsforlaget.no. Ed. Olle Soederhamn.

610.73 ESP ISSN 1136-8985
NOSOCOMIO; revista para el tecnico en cuidados de enfermeria. Text in Spanish. 1996. q. EUR 25 (effective 2009). back issues avail. **Document type:** *Journal, Academic/Scholarly.*
Published by: Elsevier Doyma (Subsidiary of: Elsevier Health Sciences), Traversa de Gracia 17-21, Barcelona, 08021, Spain. TEL 34-932-418800, FAX 34-932-419020, editorial@elsevier.com, http://www.elsevier.es/, http://www.doyma.es. Ed. Dolores Martinez Marquez.

610.73 CHE ISSN 1422-4178
NOVA. Text in French, German, Italian. 11/yr. CHF 92 (effective 2001). adv. **Document type:** *Magazine, Trade.*
Published by: Schweizer Berufs- und Fachverband der Geriatrie-, Rehabilitations- und Langzeitpflege, Obergrundstr 44, Luzern, 6003, Switzerland. TEL 41-41-2407822, FAX 41-41-2407820, info@sbgrl.ch, http://www.sbgrl.ch. Circ: 6,000.

610.73 HUN ISSN 0864-7003
➤ **NOVER**; az apolas elmelete es gyakorlata/a Hungarian journal of nursing theory and practice. Text in Hungarian; Summaries in English. 1988. bi-m. adv. bk.rev. index. **Document type:** *Journal, Academic/Scholarly.* **Description:** Directed at the continuing education of nurses, nursing theory and practice.
Indexed: C06, C07, C08, CINAHL.
—BLDSC (6180.365000).
Published by: Egeszsegugyi Strategiai Kutatointezet/National Institute for Strategic Health Research, POB 278, Budapest, 1444, Hungary. TEL 36-1-3545316, FAX 36-1-3545317. Ed. Maria Bauko. Pub. Gyula Kincses. adv.: B&W page HUF 30,000, color page HUF 45,000. Circ: 3,500.

610.73 ESP ISSN 1697-218X
RT1
NURE INVESTIGACION. Text in Spanish. 2003. m. free (effective 2011). **Document type:** *Journal, Academic/Scholarly.*
Media: Online - full text.
Indexed: C06, C07, C08, CINAHL.
—IE. **CCC.**
Published by: Fundacion para el Desarrollo de la Enfermeria, Costa de Santo Domingo 6, Madrid, 28013, Spain. TEL 34-91-5416581, http://www.fuden.es. Ed. Ana Belen Salamanca.

610.73 AUS ISSN 1440-1541
RT15
➤ **NURITINGA**; an electronic journal of nursing. Text in English. 1998. irreg., latest 2008. free (effective 2009). bk.rev. back issues avail. **Document type:** *Journal, Academic/Scholarly.* **Description:** Aims to showcase the excellent nursing student work including essays, articles or seminar presentations from student nurses.
Media: Online - full text. **Related titles:** E-mail ed.
Indexed: C06, C07, C08, CINAHL.
Published by: University of Tasmania, School of Nursing & Midwifery, Locked Bag 1322, Launceston, TAS 7250, Australia. TEL 61-3-63243318, FAX 61-3-63243952, Leanne.Costello@utas.edu.au.

610.73 CAN ISSN 0382-8476
NURSCENE. Text in English. 1967. 4/yr. CAD 30; CAD 40 foreign. bk.rev. **Document type:** *Journal, Trade.* **Description:** Includes articles on healthcare, profiles of nurses, updates on education, seminars, meetings and forums dealing with the provision and administration of healthcare in Manitoba and elsewhere.
Formerly: Marnews
Published by: Manitoba Association of Registered Nurses, 647 Broadway, Winnipeg, MB R3C 0X2, Canada. TEL 204-774-3477, 800-665-2027, FAX 204-775-6052. Ed., R&P Linda Neyedly. adv.: B&W page CAD 825. Circ: 12,000 (controlled).

610.73 GBR ISSN 1473-2114
NURSE 2 NURSE. Variant title: Nurse to Nurse. Text in English. 2000. m. GBP 30 domestic; EUR 45 in Europe; EUR 55 elsewhere (effective 2005). **Document type:** *Magazine, Trade.*
Indexed: B28, C06, C07, C08, CA, CINAHL.
—BLDSC (6187.028735), IE, Ingenta.
Published by: N 2 N Publications Ltd., Lilford House, St Helens Rd, Leigh, WN7 4HG, United Kingdom. TEL 44-1942-737050, FAX 44-1942-201141, enquiries@n2nmagazine.co.uk. Ed. Maureen Benbow. Pub. Karen Hargreaves.

610.73 NLD ISSN 1878-7150
▼ **NURSE ACADEMY**; nascholingstijdschrift voor verpleegkundigen. Text in Dutch. 2009. q. EUR 99 (effective 2010). **Document type:** *Journal, Trade.*
Related titles: Online - full text ed.: ISSN 1878-7193.
Published by: Prelum Uitgevers, Postbus 545, Houten, 3990 GH, Netherlands. TEL 31-30-6355060, FAX 31-30-6355069, info@prelum.nl, http://www.prelum.nl. Ed. Paulien Spieker.

NURSE AIDE - V I P; published especially for those very important people who care for the elderly. *see* GERONTOLOGY AND GERIATRICS

NURSE AUTHOR AND EDITOR (ONLINE); a newsletter for nurse authors, editors, and editorial board members. *see* JOURNALISM

610.73 USA ISSN 2162-0407
NURSE.COM NURSING SPECTRUM (GREATER CHICAGO EDITION). Text in English. 1989. bi-w. free to qualified personnel (effective 2011). adv. back issues avail. **Document type:** *Magazine, Trade.* **Description:** Provides specialty-related news and information, such as what's happening in the world of critical care, emergency, medical/surgical, pediatrics, perioperative and oncology nursing.
Formerly (until 2011): Nursing Spectrum (Greater Chicago Edition) (2150-9999)
Related titles: Online - full text ed.
Indexed: C06, C07, C08, CINAHL.
—CCC.
Published by: Gannett Healthcare Group, 1721 Moon Lake Blvd, Ste 540, Hoffman Estates, IL 60169. TEL 800-770-0866, OnlineSupport@GannettHG.com.

610.73 USA ISSN 2162-0342
NURSE.COM NURSING SPECTRUM (NEW ENGLAND EDITION). Text in English. 1997. bi-w. free to qualified personnel (effective 2011). adv. **Document type:** *Magazine, Trade.* **Description:** Features local and national nursing news, as well as highly regarded continuing education modules and job opportunities.
Formerly (until 2011): Nursing Spectrum (New England Edition) (1557-8038)
—CCC.
Published by: Gannett Healthcare Group, 1721 Moon Lake Blvd, Ste 540, Hoffman Estates, IL 60169. TEL 800-770-0866, OnlineSupport@GannettHG.com.

610.73 USA ISSN 2162-0350
RT1
NURSE.COM NURSING SPECTRUM (NEW YORK/NEW JERSEY METRO EDITION). Text in English. 1989. bi-w. free to qualified personnel (effective 2011). **Document type:** *Magazine, Trade.* **Description:** Features local and national nursing news, as well as highly regarded continuing education modules and job opportunities.
Formerly (until 2011): Nursing Spectrum (Greater New York/New Jersey Metro Edition) (1081-3101)
Related titles: Online - full text ed.
Indexed: C06, C07, C08, CINAHL.
—CCC.
Published by: Gannett Healthcare Group, 1721 Moon Lake Blvd, Ste 540, Hoffman Estates, IL 60169. TEL 800-770-0866, OnlineSupport@GannettHG.com.

610.73 GBR ISSN 1471-5953
➤ **NURSE EDUCATION IN PRACTICE.** Text in English. 2001 (Mar). bi-m. EUR 420 in Europe to institutions; JPY 45,400 in Japan to institutions; USD 375 elsewhere to institutions (effective 2012). adv. bk.rev. abstr. back issues avail.; reprints avail. **Document type:** *Journal, Academic/Scholarly.* **Description:** Features articles on using research evidence in teaching and learning, developing practice through education and collaborative education development.
Related titles: Online - full text ed.: ISSN 1873-5223 (from ScienceDirect).
Indexed: A22, A26, ASSIA, B28, C06, C07, C08, CA, CINAHL, CPE, E01, E16, EMBASE, ERA, ExcerpMed, H12, I05, MEDLINE, P30, S21, SCOPUS, T02, V05, W03.
—BLDSC (6187.028370), IE, Ingenta. **CCC.**
Published by: Churchill Livingstone (Subsidiary of: Elsevier Health Sciences), The Blvd, Langford Ln, Kidlington, OX5 1GB, United Kingdom. TEL 44-1865-843434, FAX 44-1865-843970, directenquiries@elsevier.com, http://www.elsevierhealth.com/imprint.jsp?iid=9. Ed. Karen Holland. Adv. contact Emma Steel TEL 44-207-4244221. Circ: 331.

610.73 GBR ISSN 0260-6917
➤ **NURSE EDUCATION TODAY.** Text in English. 1981. 8/yr. EUR 900 in Europe to institutions; JPY 96,800 in Japan to institutions; USD 796 elsewhere to institutions (effective 2012). adv. bk.rev. illus.; abstr. 88 p./no. 2 cols./p.; back issues avail.; reprints avail. **Document type:** *Journal, Academic/Scholarly.* **Description:** Features articles on aspects of nurse education worldwide as well as covers a broad range of disciplines.
Related titles: Microform ed.: (from PQC); Online - full text ed.: ISSN 1532-2793 (from IngentaConnect, ScienceDirect).
Indexed: A20, A22, A26, ASCA, ASSIA, B28, C06, C07, C08, CA, CINAHL, CPE, CurCont, DIP, E01, E03, E07, E08, E16, EMBASE, ERA, ERI, ExcerpMed, FamI, H11, H12, HospAb, IBR, IBZ, INI, MEDLINE, P24, P30, P48, PQC, R10, R17, Reac, S09, S19, S21, SCI, SCOPUS, SSCI, T02, V05, W03, W07.
—BLDSC (6187.028400), GNLM, IE, Infotrieve, Ingenta. **CCC.**
Published by: Churchill Livingstone (Subsidiary of: Elsevier Health Sciences), The Blvd, Langford Ln, Kidlington, OX5 1GB, United Kingdom. TEL 44-1865-843434, FAX 44-1865-843970, directenquiries@elsevier.com, http://www.elsevierhealth.com/imprint.jsp?iid=9. Ed. William Lauder. Adv. contact Emma Steel TEL 44-207-4244221. Circ: 402.

610.73 USA ISSN 0363-3624
RT71 CODEN: NUEDEC
➤ **NURSE EDUCATOR.** Text in English. 1976. bi-m. USD 448.51 domestic to institutions; USD 580 foreign to institutions (effective 2011). adv. bk.rev. back issues avail.; reprints avail. **Document type:** *Journal, Academic/Scholarly.* **Description:** Provides practical and applied information on both the theories and practice of academic nursing education, including educational philosophy, policies, and procedures, organizational, program, curriculum, course, and faculty development etc.
Related titles: CD-ROM ed.; Microform ed.: (from PQC); Online - full text ed.: ISSN 1538-9855.
Indexed: A20, A22, BRD, C06, C07, C08, CA, CINAHL, CurCont, E02, E03, EMBASE, ERI, EdA, EdI, ExcerpMed, F09, INI, MEDLINE, NurAb, P24, P30, P48, PQC, R10, Reac, SCI, SCOPUS, SSCI, T02, W03, W07.
—BLDSC (6187.028500), GNLM, IE, Infotrieve, Ingenta. **CCC.**
Published by: Lippincott Williams & Wilkins (Subsidiary of: Wolters Kluwer N.V.), 530 Walnut St, Philadelphia, PA 19106. TEL 215-521-8300, FAX 215-521-8902, customerservice@lww.com, http://www.lww.com. Ed. Suzanne P Smith. Pub. Beth Guthy. Adv. contact Pat Wendelken. Circ: 2,688.

610.73 USA ISSN 1541-4612
NURSE LEADER. Text in English. 1993. bi-m. USD 185 in United States to institutions; USD 297 elsewhere to institutions (effective 2012). adv. back issues avail.; reprints avail. **Document type:** *Journal, Academic/Scholarly.* **Description:** Offers insight from a broad spectrum of successful management and leadership perspectives, tailoring the information to the specific needs of nurses.
Formerly (until 2003): Seminars for Nurse Managers (1066-3851)
Related titles: Online - full text ed.: ISSN 1541-4620 (from ScienceDirect).
Indexed: A26, ASSIA, C06, C07, C08, CA, CINAHL, H12, I05, P30, SCOPUS, T02.
—BLDSC (6187.028560), IE, Ingenta. **CCC.**
Published by: (American Organization of Nurse Executives), Mosby, Inc. (Subsidiary of: Elsevier Health Sciences), 1600 John F. Kennedy Blvd, Ste 1800, Philadelphia, PA 19103. TEL 215-239-3900, 800-523-1649, FAX 215-239-3990, elspcs@elsevier.com, http://www.us.elsevierhealth.com. Ed. Roxane B Spitzer. Pub. Shannon Magee.

610.73 USA ISSN 1543-7353
NURSE MANAGER WEEKLY. Text in English. 2001 (Dec.). w. free. **Document type:** *Newsletter, Trade.* **Description:** Delivers helpful tips and advice for nursing professionals.
Media: Online - full text.
Published by: H C Pro, Inc., 200 Hoods Ln, PO Box 1168, Marblehead, MA 01945. TEL 781-639-1872, FAX 781-639-7857, customerservice@hcpro.com.

610.73 USA ISSN 0361-1817
RT1 CODEN: NRPRDJ
➤ **THE NURSE PRACTITIONER**; the American journal of primary healthcare. Abbreviated title: N P. Text in English. 1975. m. USD 394 domestic to institutions; USD 599 foreign to institutions (effective 2011). adv. charts; illus.; stat. Index. back issues avail.; reprints avail. **Document type:** *Journal, Academic/Scholarly.* **Description:** Provides clinical and professional information for nurse practitioners.
Related titles: Microform ed.: (from PQC); Online - full text ed.: ISSN 1538-8662.
Indexed: A01, A02, A03, A08, A22, A26, B28, C06, C07, C08, C11, CA, CINAHL, CLFP, E08, EMBASE, ExcerpMed, F09, FAMLI, FamI, G06, G07, G08, H04, H11, H12, H13, HospLI, I05, I12, INI, IndMed, MEDLINE, NurAb, P10, P20, P22, P24, P30, P48, P53, P54, PQC, R10, Reac, S09, SCOPUS, T02, W09.
—BLDSC (6187.028700), GNLM, IE, Infotrieve, Ingenta, INIST. **CCC.**
Published by: Lippincott Williams & Wilkins (Subsidiary of: Wolters Kluwer N.V.), 323 Norristown Rd, Ste 200, Ambler, PA 19002. TEL 215-628-7789, FAX 215-367-2157, customerservice@lww.com, http://www.lww.com. Ed. Jamesetta A Newland. Pub. Theresa M Steltzer. Adv. contact Diane Shapiro TEL 215-628-6538. Circ: 20,490.

610.73 USA ISSN 1520-8737
NURSE PRACTITIONER WORLD NEWS. Abbreviated title: N P W N. Text in English. 199?. bi-m. USD 20 (effective 2011). back issues avail.; reprints avail. **Document type:** *Journal, Academic/Scholarly.* **Description:** Publishes articles and updates on the professional activities and thoughts of ACNP members.
Indexed: C06, C07, C08, CINAHL.
Published by: (American College of Nurse Practitioners), N P Communications, LLC, 109 S Main St, Cranbury, NJ 08512 . TEL 609-371-5085, FAX 609-371-5086, subscriptions@npcommunications.com. Eds. Laurie Lewis, Charlene M Hanson. Pub. Louise K Young.

NURSE PRACTITIONERS' PRESCRIBING REFERENCE. *see* PHARMACY AND PHARMACOLOGY

610.73 616 GBR ISSN 1351-5578
➤ **NURSE RESEARCHER.** Text in English. 1993. q. GBP 74.14 in Europe to non-members; GBP 121 elsewhere to non-members; GBP 70.40 in Europe to members; GBP 88.66 elsewhere to members; GBP 160 in Europe to institutions; GBP 185 elsewhere to institutions (effective 2009). back issues avail. **Document type:** *Journal, Academic/Scholarly.* **Description:** Contains authoritative papers on the appropriate application and relevance of research methods to nursing.
Related titles: CD-ROM ed.; Online - full text ed.
Indexed: A01, A02, A03, A08, A26, B28, C06, C07, C08, C11, CA, CINAHL, E08, EMBASE, ExcerpMed, G08, H04, H11, H12, I05, MEDLINE, P20, P22, P24, P30, P48, P54, PQC, R10, Reac, S09, SCOPUS, T02.
—BLDSC (6187.028730), GNLM, IE, Infotrieve, Ingenta. **CCC.**
Published by: R C N Publishing Co. (Subsidiary of: B M J Group), R C N Direct, Copse Walk, Cardiff Gate Business Park, Cardiff, CF23 8XG, United Kingdom. TEL 44-29-2054-6450, FAX 44-29-2054-6401, directjournalsteam@rcn.org.uk, http://www.rcn.org.uk/. Ed. Stephen Black.

610.73 USA
NURSE-ZINE. Variant title: Nursing Electronic Newsletter. Text in English. 1997. bi-w. adv. back issues avail. **Document type:** *Newsletter, Trade.*
Media: Online - full text.
Published by: Allnurses.com Ed. Brian Short. Circ: 21,000.

610.73 USA ISSN 1557-3184
RT41
NURSELINE. Text in English. 2002 (Jan.). w. **Document type:** *Newsletter, Trade.*
Media: Online - full content.
Published by: Michigan Nurses Association, 2310 Jolly Oak Rd, Okemos, MI 48864-4599. TEL 517-349-5640, 800-832-2051, FAX 517-349-5818, minurses@minurses.org.

610.73 USA
NURSELINX. Text in English. d. adv. **Document type:** *Newsletter.* **Description:** Includes current nursing news and medical information for nurses and healthcare professionals.
Media: Online - full text. **Related titles:** E-mail ed.
Published by: MDLinx.com Inc, 1232 22nd St NW, Washington, DC 20037-1202. info@mdlinx.com. Ed. Dave Rothenberg.

NURSERY MANAGEMENT TODAY. *see* MEDICAL SCIENCES—Pediatrics

610.73 USA ISSN 1548-5269
NURSES-DIGEST. Text in English. 2004. m. **Document type:** *Magazine, Trade.*
Related titles: Online - full text ed.
Published by: Audio-Digest Foundation, 1577 E Chevy Chase Dr, Glendale, CA 91206. TEL 818-240-7500, FAX 818-240-7379, http://www.nursesdigest.org/pages/htmlos/03318.2.157384895435285518O/ndo/home.html.

610.73 USA
NURSES WORLD. Text in English. 2003. bi-m. USD 39 to individuals; USD 20 to students; free to qualified personnel (effective 2007). adv. back issues avail. **Document type:** *Magazine, Trade.*
Published by: Nurses World Magazine, 6167 Bristol Pkwy, Ste 325, Culver City, CA 90230. TEL 310-216-9172, FAX 310-216-0391. Ed. Sean O'Meara. Pub. Camillus Ehigie. Adv. contacts Peter D Scott, Peter Scott Jr. B&W page USD 9,325; trim 8 x 10.875. Circ: 10,000 (controlled).

610.73 USA ISSN 2153-3571
NURSEWEEK (WEST). Text in English. 1996. m. adv. **Document type:** *Magazine, Trade.* **Description:** Covers reports on news and issues about nursing.
Former titles (until 2010): Nurseweek California (1534-2204); (until 200?): Nurseweek (1533-368X); (until 19??): Nursing & Allied Healthweek (1088-436X); Which was formed by the merger of (1989-1996): NurseWeek (1063-2859); (1987-1996): Allied HealthWeek
Related titles: Regional ed(s).: NurseWeek (South Central Edition). ISSN 1547-5131. 1994; NurseWeek (Great Lakes Edition); NurseWeek (Midwest Edition); NurseWeek (Mountain West Edition). ISSN 1547-0571. 2000.
Indexed: C06, C07, C08, CINAHL.
—**CCC.**
Published by: Gannett Healthcare Group, 1721 Moon Lake Blvd, Ste 540, Hoffman Estates, IL 60169. TEL 800-770-0866, http://www.gannetthg.com. Ed. Judith Mitiguy. Pub. Steve Hauber. Adv. contact Ray Riordan.

610.73 BRA
NURSING. Text in Multiple languages. 200?. m. 52 p./no.; **Document type:** *Magazine, Trade.*
Related titles: CD-ROM ed.: ISSN 1806-4477. 2004; Online - full text ed.
Published by: Editorial Bolina Brasil (Subsidiary of: Grupo Editorial Bolina), Alameda Pucurui 51-59 B, Tamporere - Barueri, Sao Paulo, 06460-100, Brazil. Ed. Fernando Gaio. Circ: 15,000.

610.73 NLD ISSN 1381-5911
NURSING. Text in Dutch. 1994. m. (11/yr.). EUR 64.50 to individuals; EUR 130.75 to institutions; EUR 32.25 to students; EUR 11.25 newsstand/cover to students (effective 2008). adv. illus. **Document type:** *Journal, Trade.* **Description:** Offers nurses in all areas of medical care practical professional and clinical advice.
Incorporates (1944-1996): Verpleegkundigen en Gemeenschapszorg
—IE, Infotrieve.
Published by: Elsevier Gezondheidszorg bv (Subsidiary of: Reed Business bv), Planetenbaan 80-99, Maarssen, 3606 AK, Netherlands. TEL 31-346-577577, http://www.elseviergezondheidszorg.nl. Ed. Yolanda Stil. Pub. Ben Konings. adv.: B&W page EUR 3,873, color page EUR 5,266; trim 215 x 285. Circ: 25,116. **Subscr. to:** Elsevier Den Haag, Postbus 16500, The Hague 2500 BM, Netherlands. TEL 31-70-381-9900, FAX 31-70-333-8399.

610.73 PRT ISSN 0871-6196
NURSING; revista de formacao continua em enfermagem. Variant title: Revista Tecnica de Enfermagem. Text in Portuguese. 1988. m. EUR 44 domestic; EUR 80 in Europe; EUR 90 elsewhere (effective 2005). **Document type:** *Magazine, Trade.*
Related titles: Online - full text ed.
Indexed: C06, C07, C08, CINAHL.
Published by: Serra Pinto - Edicoes e Publicacoes de Revistas, Unipessoal, Lda., Rua Gomes Freire 135, 3o Esq, Lisbon, 1150-180, Portugal. TEL 351-21-3584300, FAX 351-21-3584309. Ed., Pub., R&P Pedro Serra Pinto. Adv. contact Bruno Miguel Chaves TEL 351-21-3584307. Circ: 15,000.

610.73 ESP ISSN 0212-5382
NURSING (SPANISH EDITION). Text in Spanish. 1983. m. (10/yr.). EUR 95.64 combined subscription to individuals print & online eds.; EUR 142.13 combined subscription to institutions print & online eds. (effective 2009). back issues avail.; reprints avail. **Document type:** *Journal, Academic/Scholarly.* **Description:** Covers nursing within and outside of the hospital environment. Serves the continuing education needs of nurses on a scientific and technical level.
Related titles: Online - full text ed.: ISSN 1988-6780. EUR 79.67 (effective 2009); ◆ English ed.: Nursing (Year). ISSN 0360-4039.
—**CCC.**
Published by: Elsevier Doyma (Subsidiary of: Elsevier Health Sciences), Traversa de Gracia 17-21, Barcelona, 08021, Spain. TEL 34-932-418800, FAX 34-932-419020, editorial@elsevier.com. Ed. Margarita Peya Gascon. Adv. contact Juan Esteva de Sagrera. Circ: 8,300.

610.73 USA ISSN 0360-4039
NURSING (YEAR); the voice and vision of nursing. Text in English. 1971. m. USD 339 domestic to institutions; USD 429 foreign to institutions (effective 2011). bibl.; charts; illus. Index. back issues avail.; reprints avail. **Document type:** *Journal, Trade.* **Description:** Addresses the practical needs of nurses who are direct caregivers, focusing on clinical, legal, ethical, career and professional issues. Includes special sections for hospital, critical care and home health nurses.
Incorporates (1981-1988): Nursing Life (0279-3091); (1970-1976): Nursing Update
Related titles: Diskette ed.; Magnetic Tape ed.; Microform ed.: (from PQC); Online - full text ed.: ISSN 1538-8689; ◆ Spanish ed.: Nursing (Spanish Edition). ISSN 0212-5382; Supplement(s): A Guide to Women's Health.
Indexed: A01, A02, A03, A08, A22, A25, A26, AMED, B02, B04, B15, B17, B18, B28, BRD, C06, C07, C08, C11, C28, CA, CINAHL, CLFP, E08, EMBASE, ExcerpMed, F09, FamI, G03, G04, G06, G07, G08, G10, GSA, GSI, H04, H11, H12, H13, HospLI, I05, I12, INI, IndMed, M01, M02, M06, MEDLINE, NurAb, P02, P07, P10, P16, P20, P22, P24, P26, P30, P34, P48, P50, P53, P54, PQC, R10, Reac, S02, S03, S08, S09, S23, SCOPUS, T&II, T02, V02, W03, W09.
—BLDSC (6187.037500), GNLM, IE, Infotrieve, Ingenta, INIST. **CCC.**
Published by: Lippincott Williams & Wilkins (Subsidiary of: Wolters Kluwer N.V.), 323 Norristown Rd, Ste 200, Ambler, PA 19002. TEL 215-628-7760, FAX 215-367-2157, http://www.lww.com, http://lww.custhelp.com. Eds. Katherine W Carey, Linda Laskowski-Jones.

610.73025 USA ISSN 0192-2394
RT82
NURSING (YEAR) CAREER DIRECTORY. Text in English. 1979. a. charts; illus.; tr.lit. **Document type:** *Directory, Trade.* **Description:** Directed to Registered Nurses and nursing graduate students seeking employment in American hospitals.
Indexed: C06, C07, C08, CINAHL.
—**CCC.**
Published by: Springhouse Corporation (Subsidiary of: Lippincott Williams & Wilkins), 323 Norristown Rd, Ste 200, Ambler, PA 19002. TEL 215-646-8700, FAX 215-367-2157, http://www.lww.com.

610.73 USA ISSN 1558-447X
NURSING (YEAR) CRITICAL CARE; the journal of critical care excellence. Text in English. 2006 (Jan./Feb.). bi-m. USD 289 domestic to institutions; USD 285 foreign to institutions (effective 2011). adv. back issues avail.; reprints avail. **Document type:** *Journal, Academic/Scholarly.* **Description:** Addresses the information needs of the busy critical care nurse with digests of clinical practice developments, research findings and assessments that reflect the latest critical care standards.
Related titles: Online - full text ed.: ISSN 1558-450X.
—BLDSC (6187.042100), IE. **CCC.**
Published by: Lippincott Williams & Wilkins (Subsidiary of: Wolters Kluwer N.V.), 323 Norristown Rd, Ste 200, Ambler, PA 19002. TEL 215-628-7789, customerservice@lww.com, http://www.lww.com. Ed. AnneMarie Palatnik. Adv. contact Pat Wendelken.

610.73 USA ISSN 0273-320X
RM301.12
NURSING (YEAR) DRUG HANDBOOK. Text in English. 1979. a. **Document type:** *Handbook/Manual/Guide, Trade.*
Formerly (until 1981): Nurse's Guide to Drugs
Related titles: CD-ROM ed.: ISSN 1526-1697.
Published by: Springhouse Corporation (Subsidiary of: Lippincott Williams & Wilkins), 323 Norristown Rd, Ste 200, Ambler, PA 19002. TEL 215-646-8700, FAX 215-367-2157.

610.73 USA ISSN 0363-9568
RT89
➤ **NURSING ADMINISTRATION QUARTERLY.** Abbreviated title: N A Q. Text in English. 1976. q. USD 388.51 domestic to institutions; USD 530 foreign to institutions (effective 2011). adv. bk.rev. illus. back issues avail.; reprints avail. **Document type:** *Journal, Academic/Scholarly.* **Description:** Focuses on a selected aspect of nursing administration that offers new opportunities for patient-care and institutional leadership in today's fast-evolving health care industry.
Related titles: Microform ed.: (from PQC); Online - full text ed.: ISSN 1550-5103.
Indexed: A22, A25, A26, AHCMS, C06, C07, C08, CA, CINAHL, E08, EMBASE, ExcerpMed, F09, G08, H11, H12, H13, I05, INI, MEDLINE, NurAb, P10, P20, P21, P22, P24, P30, P34, P48, P53, P54, PQC, R10, Reac, S08, S09, SCOPUS, T02.
—BLDSC (6187.038400), GNLM, IE, Infotrieve, Ingenta. **CCC.**
Published by: Lippincott Williams & Wilkins (Subsidiary of: Wolters Kluwer N.V.), 530 Walnut St, Philadelphia, PA 19106. TEL 215-521-8300, FAX 215-521-8902, customerservice@lww.com, http://www.lww.com. Ed. Barbara J Brown. Pub. Beth Guthy. Adv. contact Pat Wendelken. B&W page USD 1,100, color page USD 2,385; trim 6.875 x 10. Circ: 1,800.

610.73 AUS ISSN 1033-6303
➤ **NURSING AND HEALTH SCIENCE EDUCATION.** Text in English. 2000. s-a. AUD 429 domestic to institutions; AUD 390 in New Zealand to institutions; GBP 148 in Europe to institutions; USD 218 elsewhere to institutions (effective 2003). adv. bk.rev. index. **Document type:** *Journal, Academic/Scholarly.* **Description:** Provides nursing practitioners, nursing educators, hospital administrators and health science educators with current and innovative theory and practice in various major areas of nursing and health science education.
Published by: James Nicholas Publishers, Pty. Ltd., PO Box 5179, South Melbourne, VIC 3205, Australia. TEL 61-3-96905955, FAX 61-3-96992040, custservice@jnponline.com, http://www.jamesnicholaspublishers.com.au. Ed. Joseph Zajda. Pub. Rea Zajda. R&P Mary Berchmans. Adv. contact Irene Schevchenko.

M

610.736 AUS ISSN 1441-0745
RT1 CODEN: NHSUA4
➤ **NURSING AND HEALTH SCIENCES.** Text in English. 1999. q. GBP 454 in United Kingdom to institutions; EUR 578 in Europe to institutions; USD 734 in the Americas to institutions; USD 891 elsewhere to institutions; GBP 522 combined subscription in United Kingdom to institutions (print & online eds.); EUR 665 combined subscription in Europe to institutions (print & online eds.); USD 844 combined subscription in the Americas to institutions (print & online eds.); USD 1,023 combined subscription elsewhere to institutions (print & online eds.) (effective 2012). adv. back issues avail.; reprint service avail. from PSC. **Document type:** *Journal, Academic/Scholarly.* **Description:** Publishes research in all areas of nursing and related fields.
Related titles: Online - full text ed.: ISSN 1442-2018. GBP 454 in United Kingdom to institutions; EUR 578 in Europe to institutions; USD 734 in the Americas to institutions; USD 891 elsewhere to institutions (effective 2012) (from IngentaConnect).
Indexed: A01, A02, A03, A08, A22, A26, ASSIA, B28, C06, C07, C08, C11, CA, CINAHL, E01, EMBASE, ExcerpMed, F09, H04, H12, H13, MEDLINE, P02, P03, P10, P20, P30, P34, P48, P53, P54, PQC, PsycInfo, PsycholAb, R10, Reac, SCI, SCOPUS, SSCI, T02, W07.
—BLDSC (6187.038820), IE, Infotrieve, Ingenta. **CCC.**
Published by: Wiley-Blackwell Publishing Asia (Subsidiary of: Wiley-Blackwell Publishing Ltd.), 155 Cremorne St, Richmond, VIC 3121, Australia. TEL 61-3-92743100, FAX 61-3-92743101, melbourne@wiley.com, http://www.wiley.com/WileyCDA/. Eds. Masato Tsukahara, Sue Turale. Adv. contact Amanda Munce TEL 61-3-83591071. **Subscr. to:** PO Box 378, Carlton South, VIC 3053, Australia.

610.73 GBR ISSN 1465-9301
RT120.H65
➤ **NURSING & RESIDENTIAL CARE.** Abbreviated title: N R C. Text in English. 1999. m. GBP 139 domestic to individuals; EUR 225 in Europe to individuals; USD 323 elsewhere to individuals; GBP 101 to students (effective 2010). adv. back issues avail.; reprints avail. **Document type:** *Journal, Academic/Scholarly.* **Description:** Provides up-to-date clinical reviews, self directed learning, professional issues, regular product focuses, and job courses.
Related titles: Online - full text ed.
Indexed: AMED, B28, C06, C07, C08, CINAHL.
—BLDSC (6187.038840), IE, Ingenta. **CCC.**
Published by: Mark Allen Publishing Ltd., St Jude's Church, Dulwich Rd, London, SE24 0PB, United Kingdom. TEL 44-20-77385454, FAX 44-20-77878316, subscriptions@markallengroup.com, http://www.markallengroup.com. Ed. Laura Dean-Osgood. Adv. contact Chloe Moffat.

610.73 USA ISSN 1542-2178
NURSING ASSISTANT MONTHLY; continuing education for nursing assistants. Text in English. 1994. 10/yr. USD 119 (effective 2007). **Document type:** *Journal, Trade.* **Description:** Aims to develop the professional skills of nursing assistants.
Related titles: Online - full text ed.: ISSN 1936-6736.
Published by: Frontline Publishing, P. O. Box 441002, Somerville, MA 02144. TEL 800-348-0605, FAX 617-625-7446, info@frontlinepub.com. Ed. Richard Hoffman.

610.73 CAN ISSN 1185-3638
NURSING B C. (British Columbia) Text in English. 1968. 5/yr. CAD 55 to non-members (effective 2000). adv. bk.rev. illus. reprints avail. **Document type:** *Report, Trade.* **Description:** Official publication of the Registered Nurses Association of British Columbia; reports on significant issues affecting nurses' ability to practice safely and competently.
Formerly: R N A B C News (0048-7104)
Related titles: Microform ed.: (from PQC); Online - full text ed.
Indexed: A26, C03, C06, C07, C08, CBCARef, CINAHL, EMBASE, ExcerpMed, H12, I05, INI, MEDLINE, P20, P22, P24, P30, P48, P54, PQC, R10, Reac, SCOPUS.
—BLDSC (6187.038950), GNLM. **CCC.**
Published by: Registered Nurses Association of British Columbia, 2855 Arbutus St, Vancouver, BC V6J 3Y8, Canada. TEL 604-736-7331, 800-565-6505, FAX 604-738-2272. Ed., R&P Bruce Wells. Adv. contact Gord Smart. Circ: 35,000 (controlled).

610.73 USA
NURSING BULLETIN. Text in English. 19??. 3/yr. USD 12 per issue to non-members; free to members (effective 2009). back issues avail.; reprints avail. **Document type:** *Bulletin, Trade.*
Related titles: Online - full text ed.: free (effective 2009).
Published by: (North Carolina Board of Nursing), Publishing Concepts, Inc., 14109 Taylor Loop Rd, Little Rock, AR 72223. TEL 501-221-9986, 800-561-4686, FAX 501-225-3735, http://www.pcipublishing.com/. Ed. David Kalbacker. Adv. contact Greg Jones TEL 501-221-9986.

610.73 330 JPN ISSN 1881-5766
NURSING BUSINESS/NASHINGU BIJINESU. Text in Japanese. 2007. m. JPY 22,680 (effective 2007). **Document type:** *Journal, Academic/Scholarly.*
Published by: Medicus Shuppan/Medicus Publishing Inc., 18-24 Hiroshiba-cho, Suita-shi, Osaka-fu 564-8580, Japan. TEL 81-6-63856911, FAX 81-6-63856873, http://www.medica.co.jp/.

610.7362 GBR ISSN 2046-2336
NURSING CHILDREN AND YOUNG PEOPLE. Abbreviated title: N C Y P. Text in English. 1988. 10/yr. GBP 89.60 in Europe to non-members; GBP 130 elsewhere to non-members; GBP 75.70 in Europe to members; GBP 111 elsewhere to members; GBP 174.70 combined subscription in Europe to non-members (print & online eds.); GBP 215.10 combined subscription elsewhere to non-members (print & online eds.); GBP 147.60 combined subscription in Europe to members (print & online eds.); GBP 182.90 combined subscription elsewhere to members (print & online eds.) (effective 2011). adv. back issues avail. **Document type:** *Journal, Trade.* **Description:** Presents news, practice guidelines and clinical research on the latest treatments and techniques, expert commentary and the latest news.
Formerly (until 2011): Paediatric Nursing (0962-9513)
Related titles: Online - full text ed.: ISSN 2046-2344. GBP 85.10 to non-members; GBP 71.90 to members (effective 2011).
Indexed: A01, A02, A03, A08, A22, A26, B28, C06, C07, C08, C11, CA, CINAHL, E08, EMBASE, ExcerpMed, F09, G08, H04, H11, H12, I05, INI, MEDLINE, P20, P22, P24, P30, PQC, R10, Reac, S09, SCOPUS, T02.
—BLDSC (6333.399760), IE, Infotrieve, Ingenta. **CCC.**
Published by: (Royal College of Nursing), R C N Publishing Co. (Subsidiary of: B M J Group), The Heights, 59-65 Lowlands Rd, Harrow, Middx HA1 3AW, United Kingdom. TEL 44-20-84231066, http://www.rcnpublishing.co.uk. Ed. Christine Walker. Adv. contact Neil Hobson TEL 44-20-88723123.

610.73 USA ISSN 0029-6465
RT1 CODEN: NCNAAK
NURSING CLINICS OF NORTH AMERICA. Text in English. 1966. q. USD 343 in United States to institutions; USD 419 elsewhere to institutions (effective 2012). adv. index. back issues avail.; reprints avail. **Document type:** *Journal, Trade.* **Description:** Aimed at students and graduate nurses.
Related titles: Microform ed.: (from PQC); Online - full text ed.: ISSN 1558-1357 (from ScienceDirect).
Indexed: A20, A22, AHCMS, AIM, AMED, ASCA, ASSIA, AgeL, B28, C06, C07, C08, CINAHL, ChemAb, Chicano, CurCont, EMBASE, ExcerpMed, F09, FR, FamI, HospLI, INI, IndMed, MEDLINE, NurAb, P24, P30, P48, PQC, R10, Reac, SCI, SCOPUS, SSCI, W07, W09.
—BLDSC (6187.040000), GNLM, IE, Infotrieve, Ingenta, INIST. **CCC.**
Published by: W.B. Saunders Co. (Subsidiary of: Elsevier Health Sciences), Elsevier, Health Sciences Division, Order Fulfillment, 3251 Riverport Ln, Maryland Heights, MO 63043. TEL 314-872-8370, 800-325-4177, FAX 314-432-1380, JournalCustomerService-usa@elsevier.com, http://www.us.elsevierhealth.com. Adv. contact John Marmero TEL 212-633-3657.

610.73 USA ISSN 0746-1739
RT86.73
➤ **NURSING ECONOMICS**; the journal for health care leaders. Text in English. 1983. bi-m. USD 69 domestic to individuals; USD 99 foreign to individuals; USD 85 domestic to institutions; USD 115 foreign to institutions (effective 2010). adv. illus. Index. back issues avail.; reprints avail. **Document type:** *Journal, Academic/Scholarly.* **Description:** Provides information and thoughtful analyses of current and emerging best practices in health care management, economics, and policymaking.
Related titles: Online - full text ed.
Indexed: A01, A02, A03, A08, A15, A22, A25, A26, ABIn, ASCA, B07, C06, C07, C08, C11, CA, CINAHL, CurCont, E08, EMBASE, ExcerpMed, FamI, G08, H01, H02, H04, H05, H11, H12, H13, I05, INI, MEDLINE, NurAb, P10, P20, P21, P22, P24, P30, P34, P48, P51, P53, P54, PQC, R10, Reac, S08, S09, SCI, SCOPUS, SSCI, T02, W07.
—BLDSC (6187.046800), GNLM, IE, Infotrieve, Ingenta. **CCC.**
Published by: Jannetti Publications, Inc., E Holly Ave, PO Box 56, Pitman, NJ 08071. TEL 856-256-2300, FAX 856-589-7463, http://www.ajj.com/jpi. Ed. Donna M Nickitas. Adv. contact Rick Gabler TEL 856-256-2300. color page USD 2,025, B&W page USD 1,550; 7 x 10. Circ: 5,500.

610.73 USA ISSN 1536-5026
RT1
➤ **NURSING EDUCATION PERSPECTIVES.** Text in English. 1952. bi-m. USD 90 domestic to non-members; USD 110 in Canada to non-members; USD 120 elsewhere to non-members; USD 40 domestic to members; USD 60 in Canada to members; USD 68 elsewhere to members; USD 152 domestic to libraries; USD 172 in Canada to libraries; USD 182 elsewhere to libraries (effective 2011). bk.rev. illus. reprints avail. **Document type:** *Journal, Academic/Scholarly.* **Description:** Features news and articles on interdisciplinary, community-based health care delivery, education and research, as well as social and economic issues that affect health care and higher education.
Former titles (until 2002): Nursing and Health Care Perspectives (1094-2831); (until 1997): N and H C Perspectives on Community (1081-8731); (until 1995): Nursing and Health Care (0276-5284); (until 1980): N L N News (0027-6804)
Related titles: CD-ROM ed.; Microfiche ed.: 1952 (from CIS); Microform ed.: 1952 (from PQC); Online - full text ed.: 1952.
Indexed: A01, A02, A03, A08, A20, A22, A26, AMED, C06, C07, C08, C11, CA, CINAHL, E03, E07, E08, EMBASE, ERI, ExcerpMed, FamI, G06, G07, G08, H04, H11, H12, I05, INI, MCR, MEDLINE, MLA-IB, NurAb, P07, P18, P20, P22, P24, P30, P34, P48, P53, P54, PQC, R10, Reac, S09, SCOPUS, SRI, T02.
—BLDSC (6187.046830), GNLM, IE, Ingenta. **CCC.**
Published by: National League for Nursing, 61 Broadway, 33rd Fl, New York, NY 10006. TEL 212-363-5555, 800-669-1656, FAX 212-812-0391, generalinfo@nln.org. Ed. Joyce Fitzpatrick.

610.73 GBR ISSN 0969-7330
RT85
➤ **NURSING ETHICS**; an international journal for health care professionals. Text in English. 1994. bi-m. USD 802, GBP 434 combined subscription to institutions (print & online eds.); USD 786, GBP 425 to institutions (effective 2011). adv. back issues avail.; reprint service avail. from PSC. **Document type:** *Journal, Academic/Scholarly.* **Description:** Examines ethical issues as an integral part of nursing practice, education and research.
Related titles: Online - full text ed.: ISSN 1477-0989. USD 722, GBP 391 to institutions (effective 2011).
Indexed: A01, A02, A03, A08, A20, A22, ASCA, ASG, ASSIA, B28, C06, C07, C08, C11, CA, CINAHL, CurCont, E01, EMBASE, ESPM, ExcerpMed, FamI, H01, H04, H13, INI, L03, MEDLINE, P03, P10, P19, P20, P21, P22, P24, P30, P34, P48, P53, P54, PQC, PhilInd, PsycInfo, R10, Reac, RiskAb, S02, S03, SCI, SCOPUS, SSCI, T02, W07.
—BLDSC (6187.046970), GNLM, IE, Infotrieve, Ingenta. **CCC.**
Published by: Sage Publications Ltd. (Subsidiary of: Sage Publications, Inc.), 1 Oliver's Yard, 55 City Rd, London, EC1Y 1SP, United Kingdom. TEL 44-20-73248500, 44-20-73248701, FAX 44-20-73248600, info@sagepub.co.uk, http://www.uk.sagepub.com/home.nav. Ed. Ann Gallagher. adv.: B&W page GBP 450; 160 x 215.

➤ **NURSING FOR WOMEN'S HEALTH.** *see* WOMEN'S HEALTH

610.73 USA ISSN 0029-6473
RT1 CODEN: NUFOA
➤ **NURSING FORUM**; an independent voice for nursing. Text in English. 1961. q. GBP 158 in United Kingdom to institutions; EUR 202 in Europe to institutions; USD 233 in the Americas to institutions; USD 310 elsewhere to institutions; GBP 183 combined subscription in United Kingdom to institutions (print & online eds.); EUR 233 combined subscription in Europe to institutions (print & online eds.); USD 268 combined subscription in the Americas to institutions (print & online eds.); USD 357 combined subscription elsewhere to institutions (print & online eds.) (effective 2012). adv. bk.rev. charts; illus. index. back issues avail.; reprint service avail. from PSC. **Document type:** *Magazine, Academic/Scholarly.* **Description:** Presents innovative ideas and emerging issues in nursing.
Related titles: Microfilm ed.: (from PQC); Online - full text ed.: ISSN 1744-6198. GBP 158 in United Kingdom to institutions; EUR 202 in Europe to institutions; USD 233 in the Americas to institutions; USD 310 elsewhere to institutions (effective 2012) (from IngentaConnect).
Indexed: A01, A02, A03, A08, A22, A25, A26, ASSIA, B28, C06, C07, C08, C11, CA, CINAHL, E01, E08, EMBASE, ExcerpMed, FamI, G08, H04, H11, H12, H13, HospLI, I05, INI, IndMed, MEDLINE, P10, P20, P22, P24, P30, P48, P53, P54, PQC, R10, Reac, S08, S09, SCOPUS, T02.
—BLDSC (6187.050000), GNLM, IE, Infotrieve, Ingenta, INIST. **CCC.**
Published by: Wiley-Blackwell Publishing, Inc. (Subsidiary of: Wiley-Blackwell Publishing Ltd.), 111 River St, Hoboken, NJ 07030. TEL 201-748-6000, FAX 201-748-6088, info@wiley.com. Ed. Patricia S Yoder-Wise. Adv. contact Karl Franz TEL 781-388-8470.

610.73 USA ISSN 1062-8061
RT31
➤ **NURSING HISTORY REVIEW.** Text in English. 1993. a. USD 85 (effective 2009). adv. bk.rev. **Document type:** *Journal, Academic/Scholarly.* **Description:** Traces new and developing work in the fields of nursing and health care history. Includes coverage of national and international activities in health care history.
Related titles: Online - full text ed.: ISSN 1938-1913 (from IngentaConnect).
Indexed: A20, A22, ASCA, AmH&L, C06, C07, C08, CINAHL, CurCont, EMBASE, ExcerpMed, H13, HistAb, INI, IndMed, MEDLINE, P10, P20, P22, P24, P30, P48, P53, P54, PQC, SCOPUS, SSCI, T02, W07.
—BLDSC (6187.051000), GNLM, IE, Infotrieve, Ingenta. **CCC.**
Published by: (American Association for the History of Nursing), Springer Publishing Company, 11 W 42nd St, 15th Fl, New York, NY 10036. TEL 212-431-4370, FAX 212-941-7842, contactus@springerpub.com, http://www.springerpub.com. Ed. Patricia D'Antonio. Adv. contact Jessica Perl. B&W page USD 300.

330 610.73 USA ISSN 1552-2563
NURSING HOME & ELDER BUSINESS WEEK. Text in English. 2004. w. USD 2,295 in US & Canada; USD 2,495 elsewhere; USD 2,525 combined subscription in US & Canada (print & online eds.); USD 2,755 combined subscription elsewhere (print & online eds.) (effective 2008). back issues avail. **Document type:** *Newsletter, Trade.* **Description:** Provides latest news and developments in business trends and state and federal regulatory changes, including fiscal reports, mergers, acquisitions and joint ventures, expansions, Medicare and Medicaid changes, and state and federal compliance issues.
Related titles: E-mail ed.; Online - full text ed.: ISSN 1552-2571. USD 2,295 combined subscription (online & email eds.); single user (effective 2008).
Indexed: A15, ABIn, B16, H13, P10, P20, P21, P27, P48, P51, P53, P54, PQC.
Published by: NewsRx, 2727 Paces Ferry Rd SE, Ste 2-440, Atlanta, GA 30339. TEL 770-435-8286, 800-726-4550, FAX 770-435-6800, pressrelease@newsrx.com. Pub. Susan Hasty TEL 770-507-7777.

NURSING HOME LEGAL INSIDER. *see* LAW

649.8 USA ISSN 1085-0309
RA997.A1
NURSING HOME STATISTICAL YEARBOOK. Text in English. 1995. a.
Published by: Cowles Research Group, Inc, 20300 Swallow Point Rd, Montgomery Village, MD 20866. TEL 301-990-1986, FAX 301-987-0857, mickcowles@aol.com.

610.73 GBR ISSN 1362-1017
RT120.I5
➤ **NURSING IN CRITICAL CARE.** Text in English. 1996. bi-m. GBP 298 in United Kingdom to institutions; EUR 381 in Europe to institutions; USD 551 in the Americas to institutions; USD 644 elsewhere to institutions; GBP 344 combined subscription in United Kingdom to institutions (print & online eds.); EUR 438 combined subscription in Europe to institutions (print & online eds.); USD 633 combined subscription in the Americas to institutions (print & online eds.); USD 741 combined subscription elsewhere to institutions (print & online eds.) (effective 2012). adv. back issues avail.; reprint service avail. from PSC. **Document type:** *Journal, Academic/Scholarly.* **Description:** Focuses on topics of particular interest to specialist nurses working in accident and emergency, coronary care, renal care, and adult, pediatric and neonatal intensive care.
Related titles: Online - full text ed.: ISSN 1478-5153. GBP 298 in United Kingdom to institutions; EUR 381 in Europe to institutions; USD 551 in the Americas to institutions; USD 644 elsewhere to institutions (effective 2012) (from IngentaConnect).
Indexed: A01, A03, A08, A22, A26, B28, C06, C07, C08, CA, CINAHL, E01, EMBASE, ExcerpMed, H12, INI, MEDLINE, P03, P30, PsycInfo, R10, Reac, SCOPUS, T02.
—BLDSC (6187.042200), IE, Infotrieve, Ingenta. **CCC.**
Published by: (British Association of Critical Care Nurses), Wiley-Blackwell Publishing Ltd. (Subsidiary of: John Wiley & Sons, Inc.), 9600 Garsington Rd, Oxford, OX4 2DQ, United Kingdom. TEL 44-1865-776868, FAX 44-1865-714591, customerservices@blackwellpublishing.com. Eds. John Albarran, Julie Scholes.

610.73 CAN ISSN 1492-2878
NURSING IN FOCUS. Text in English. 1961. 3/yr. adv. bk.rev. **Document type:** *Journal, Trade.*
Former titles (until 2000): Nurse to Nurse (0849-3383); (until 1990): R N A N S Bulletin (0319-4604)
Indexed: C06, C07, C08, CINAHL.
—BLDSC (6187.047700).
Published by: Registered Nurses Association of Nova Scotia, Ste 600, Barrington Tower, Scotia Square, 1849 Barrington St, Halifax, NS B3J 2A8, Canada. TEL 902-491-9744, 800-565-9744, FAX 902-491-9510, info@crnns.ca, http://www.crnns.ca. Ed. Marie Dauphinee Booth. Adv. contact Colleen Burke. Circ: 10,000.

610.73 GBR ISSN 1473-9445
NURSING IN PRACTICE; the journal for today's primary care nurse. Abbreviated title: N I P. Text in English. 2001. bi-m. GBP 70 domestic to individuals; GBP 85 foreign to individuals; free to qualified personnel (effective 2009). adv. back issues avail. **Document type:** *Journal, Academic/Scholarly.* **Description:** Provides a wide range of information critical to the clinical practice of today's primary care nurse.
Related titles: Online - full text ed.
Indexed: B28, C06, C07, C08, CINAHL.
—BLDSC (6187.109202), IE, Ingenta. **CCC.**
Published by: Campden Publishing Ltd., 1 St John's Sq, London, EC1M 4PN, United Kingdom. TEL 44-20-72140500, FAX 44-20-72140501, enquiries@campden.com, http://www.campden.com. Ed. Elaine Linnane TEL 44-20-72140514. Adv. contact Edward Burkle TEL 44-20-72140526.

610.73 IRL ISSN 1649-0657
NURSING IN THE COMMUNITY; clinical guide for Irish nurses. Text in English. 1999. bi-m. **Document type:** *Journal, Academic/Scholarly.*
Indexed: B28, C06, C07, C08, CINAHL.
—BLDSC (6187.041000), IE, Ingenta.
Published by: MedMedia Ltd., 25 Adelaide St, Dun Laoghaire, Co. Dublin, Ireland. TEL 353-1-2803967, FAX 353-1-2807076. Ed. Moira Cassidy. Pub. Geradine Meagan. **Dist. addr.:** Turpin Distribution Services Ltd., Pegasus Dr, Stratton Business Park, Biggleswade, Bedfordshire SG18 8QB, United Kingdom. TEL 44-1767-604800, FAX 44-1767-601640, custserv@turpin-distribution.com, http://www.turpin-distribution.com/.

610.73 GBR ISSN 1320-7881
➤ **NURSING INQUIRY.** Text in English. 1994. q. GBP 387 in United Kingdom to institutions; EUR 491 in Europe to institutions; USD 718 in the Americas to institutions; USD 833 elsewhere to institutions; GBP 446 combined subscription in United Kingdom to institutions (print & online eds.); EUR 565 combined subscription in Europe to institutions (print & online eds.); USD 826 combined subscription in the Americas to institutions (print & online eds.); USD 958 combined subscription elsewhere to institutions (print & online eds.) (effective 2012). adv. bk.rev. illus. back issues avail.; reprint service avail. from PSC. **Document type:** *Journal, Academic/Scholarly.* **Description:** Discusses the practical, methodological, ethical, and philosophical issues in nursing from a variety of perspectives.
Related titles: Online - full text ed.: ISSN 1440-1800. GBP 387 in United Kingdom to institutions; EUR 491 in Europe to institutions; USD 718 in the Americas to institutions; USD 833 elsewhere to institutions (effective 2012) (from IngentaConnect).
Indexed: A01, A02, A03, A08, A20, A22, A26, B28, C06, C07, C08, C11, CA, CINAHL, CurCont, E-psyche, E01, EMBASE, ExcerpMed, FamI, H04, H12, INI, MEDLINE, P03, P30, PsycInfo, PsycholAb, R10, Reac, SCI, SCOPUS, SSCI, T02, W07, W09.
—BLDSC (6187.072000), IE, Infotrieve, Ingenta. **CCC.**
Published by: Wiley-Blackwell Publishing Ltd. (Subsidiary of: John Wiley & Sons, Inc.), 9600 Garsington Rd, Oxford, OX4 2DQ, United Kingdom. TEL 44-1865-776868, FAX 44-1865-714591, customerservices@blackwellpublishing.com. Ed. Sioban Nelson. Adv. contact Joanna Baker TEL 44-1865-476271.

610.73 USA ISSN 1040-2373
RM301
NURSING IV DRUG HANDBOOK. Text in English. 1989. irreg., latest vol.9, 2005. back issues avail. **Document type:** *Handbook/Manual/Guide, Trade.*
Published by: Springhouse Corporation (Subsidiary of: Lippincott Williams & Wilkins), 323 Norristown Rd, Ste 200, Ambler, PA 19002. TEL 215-646-8700, FAX 215-367-2157.

610.73 IND ISSN 0029-6503
RT13
➤ **THE NURSING JOURNAL OF INDIA.** Text in English, Hindi. 1910. m. INR 1,100 domestic; USD 60 foreign (effective 2011). bk.rev. charts; illus. index. back issues avail.; reprints avail. **Document type:** *Journal, Academic/Scholarly.* **Description:** For members of the Trained Nurses' Association of India. Keeps them informed of the latest developments in the field of Nursing and allied subjects.
Related titles: Microfilm ed.: (from PQC); Online - full text ed.
Indexed: A22, C06, C07, C08, CINAHL, EMBASE, ExcerpMed, F09, INI, MEDLINE, P20, P22, P24, P30, P48, P54, PQC, R10, Reac, SCOPUS, W09.
—BLDSC (6187.080000), GNLM, IE, Infotrieve, Ingenta.
Published by: Trained Nurses Association of India, Florence Nightingale Ln, L-17 Green Park (Main), New Delhi, 110 016, India. TEL 91-11-26566665, FAX 91-11-26858304, tnai_2003@yahoo.com.

610.73 344.01 USA ISSN 1528-848X
NURSING LAW'S REGAN REPORT. Variant title: N L R R. Regan Report. Text in English. 1960. m. USD 52 domestic; USD 64 foreign (effective 2000). stat. reprints avail. **Description:** Reports the latest appellate court decisions on nursing law in a case and comment format.
Formerly (until 2000): Regan Report on Nursing Law (0034-3196)
Related titles: Microform ed.: (from PQC); Online - full content ed.; Online - full text ed.
Indexed: A25, A26, C06, C07, C08, CA, CINAHL, E08, EMBASE, ExcerpMed, G08, H11, H12, I05, INI, MEDLINE, P30, R10, Reac, S08, S09, SCOPUS, T02.
—BLDSC (6187.091200), GNLM. **CCC.**

Published by: Medica Press Inc., 500 Westminster Sq Bldg, Providence, RI 02903. TEL 401-421-4747. Ed., R&P, Adv. contact A David Tammelleo. Circ: 10,000.

610.73 658 CAN ISSN 1910-622X
➤ **NURSING LEADERSHIP.** Text in English. 1988. q. CAD 95 domestic to individuals; USD 95 foreign to individuals; CAD 355 domestic to institutions; USD 355 foreign to institutions (effective 2006). adv. **Document type:** *Journal, Academic/Scholarly.* **Description:** For Canadian nurse administrators, managers and educators.
Formerly (until 2003): Canadian Journal of Nursing Leadership (1481-9643); Which superseded (in 1999): Canadian Journal of Nursing Administration (0838-2948)
Related titles: Online - full text ed.
Indexed: A22, ASSIA, C06, C07, C08, CINAHL, EMBASE, ExcerpMed, INI, MEDLINE, NurAb, P30, SCOPUS.
—GNLM, IE, Ingenta. **CCC.**
Published by: (Academy of Canadian Executive Nurses), Longwoods Publishing Corp., 260 Adelaide St East, P.O. Box 8, Toronto, ON M5A 1N1, Canada. TEL 416-864-9667, FAX 416-368-6292, subscribe@longwoods.com, http://www.longwoods.com. Ed. Dorothy Pringle. Pub. Anton Hart. Adv. contact Susan Hale.

610.73 USA ISSN 1544-5186
NURSING MADE INCREDIBLY EASY!. Text in English. 2003 (Sept./Oct.). bi-m. USD 240 domestic to institutions; USD 285 foreign to institutions (effective 2011). back issues avail.; reprints avail. **Document type:** *Journal, Academic/Scholarly.*
Related titles: Online - full text ed.: ISSN 1552-2032.
Indexed: C06, C07, C08, CA, CINAHL, SCOPUS, T02.
—**CCC.**
Published by: Lippincott Williams & Wilkins (Subsidiary of: Wolters Kluwer N.V.), 323 Norristown Rd, Ste 200, Ambler, PA 19002. TEL 215-628-7789, FAX 215-367-2157, customerservice@lww.com, http://www.lww.com. Pub. Theresa M Steltzer. Adv. contact Diane Shapiro TEL 215-628-6538. Circ: 47,164.

610.73 GBR ISSN 1354-5760
NURSING MANAGEMENT. Text in English. 1979. 10/yr. GBP 70.40 in Europe to members; GBP 103.40 elsewhere to members; GBP 83.38 in Europe to non-members; GBP 121 elsewhere to non-members; GBP 160 combined subscription in Europe to institutions (print & online eds.); GBP 185 combined subscription elsewhere to institutions (print & online eds.); GBP 162.58 combined subscription in Europe to non-members (print & online eds.); GBP 200.20 combined subscription elsewhere to non-members (print & online eds.); GBP 137.28 combined subscription in Europe to members (print & online eds.); GBP 170.28 combined subscription elsewhere to members (print & online eds.) (effective 2009). adv. back issues avail. **Document type:** *Journal, Trade.* **Description:** Designed for senior clinical nurses and administrative nurse managers.
Former titles (until 1994): Senior Nurse (0265-9999); (until 1984): Nursing Focus (0144-4069)
Related titles: CD-ROM ed.; Microform ed.: (from PQC); Online - full text ed.: GBP 79.20 to non-members; GBP 66.88 to members (effective 2009).
Indexed: A01, A02, A03, A08, A15, A22, A26, ABIn, ASSIA, B01, B06, B07, B09, B28, C06, C07, C08, C11, CA, CINAHL, E08, EMBASE, ExcerpMed, G08, H01, H04, H11, H12, I05, MEDLINE, P20, P21, P22, P24, P30, P48, P51, P54, PQC, R10, Reac, S09, SCOPUS, SociolAb, T02.
—BLDSC (6187.093500), GNLM, IE, Infotrieve, Ingenta. **CCC.**
Published by: (Royal College of Nursing), R C N Publishing Co. (Subsidiary of: B M J Group), The Heights, 59-65 Lowlands Rd, Harrow, Middx HA1 3AW, United Kingdom. TEL 44-20-84231066, FAX 44-20-84239196, advertising@rcnpublishing.co.uk, http://www.rcnpublishing.co.uk. Eds. Nick Lipley, Jean Gray. Adv. contact Neil Hobson TEL 44-20-88723123. page GBP 1,705; trim 216 x 279. Circ: 4,413.

610.73 USA ISSN 0744-6314
RT89
NURSING MANAGEMENT. Text in English. 1970. m. USD 63.23 domestic to individuals; USD 139.77 foreign to individuals; USD 333.24 domestic to institutions; USD 459.76 foreign to institutions (effective 2010). adv. bk.rev. illus. 5060 p./no. 2 cols./p.; back issues avail.; reprints avail. **Document type:** *Journal, Academic/Scholarly.* **Description:** Addresses aspects of nursing management and related medical, legal, economic, personnel and ethical issues. Emphasizes new skills required in today's health care arena.
Formerly (until 1981): Supervisor Nurse (0039-5870); Incorporates (1994-1999): Recruitment, Retention & Restructuring Report; Which was formerly (1988-1994): Recruitment & Retention Report (1044-0666)
Related titles: Microform ed.: (from PQC); Online - full text ed.: ISSN 1538-8670; Supplement(s): Critical Care Choices. ISSN 1043-2205. 1988.
Indexed: A01, A02, A03, A08, A12, A13, A14, A15, A17, A22, A26, ABIn, AMED, B01, B06, B07, B08, B09, B28, C06, C07, C08, C11, C12, CA, CINAHL, E08, EMBASE, ExcerpMed, FamI, G06, G07, G08, H01, H04, H11, H12, H13, HospLI, I05, INI, MEDLINE, NurAb, P10, P13, P20, P21, P22, P24, P30, P34, P48, P51, P53, P54, PQC, R10, Reac, S09, SCOPUS, T02.
—BLDSC (6187.094000), GNLM, IE, Infotrieve, Ingenta. **CCC.**
Published by: Lippincott Williams & Wilkins (Subsidiary of: Wolters Kluwer N.V.), 323 Norristown Rd, Ste 200, Ambler, PA 19002. TEL 215-646-8700, FAX 215-367-2157, customerservice@lww.com, http://www.lww.com. Ed. Richard Hader. Circ: 110,000 (paid).

610.73 USA ISSN 0029-6538
NURSING NEWS (CONCORD). Text in English. 1949. q. looseleaf. USD 24 (effective 2008). adv. 28 p./no.; back issues avail. **Document type:** *Newsletter, Trade.* **Description:** Covers issues and employment opportunities of interest to licensed nursing professionals.
Formerly: New Hampshire State Nurses Association. Newsletter
Related titles: Online - full text ed.
Indexed: C06, C07, C08, CINAHL, INI, P30.
—BLDSC (6187.104000).
Published by: (New Hampshire Nurses' Association), Arthur L. Davis Publishing Agency, Inc., 517 Washington St, PO Box 216, Cedar Falls, IA 50613. TEL 319-277-2414, 800-626-4081, FAX 319-277-4055, sales@aldpub.com, http://www.aldpub.com. Ed. Mark Miller. R&P Robert Best. Adv. contact Jim Larson. Circ: 25,000.

610.73 USA ISSN 0029-6546
NURSING NEWS (FLORAL PARK). Text in English. 1944. q. USD 25 to non-members (effective 2000). adv. bk.rev. illus. **Document type:** *Newsletter, Trade.* **Description:** Provides updates on current affairs in the nursing profession and healthcare in general. Aims for the education and motivation of people in the nursing profession.
Published by: Nurses Association of the Counties of Long Island, 99 Tulip Ave, 404, Floral Park, NY 11001-1959. TEL 516-352-0717, FAX 516-352-4993. Ed., Adv. contact Anne J Quashen. Circ: 3,500.

610.73 USA ISSN 0029-6554
RT1
➤ **NURSING OUTLOOK.** Text in English. 1909. bi-m. USD 201 in United States to institutions; USD 264 elsewhere to institutions (effective 2012). adv. bk.rev. charts; illus.; tr.lit. index. back issues avail.; reprints avail. **Document type:** *Journal, Academic/Scholarly.* **Description:** Examines current issues and trends in nursing practice, education, and research.
Supersedes (in 1953): Public Health Nursing; Which was formerly (until 1931): Public Health Nurse; (until 1918): Public Health Nurse Quarterly; (until 1913): Visiting Nurse Quarterly of Cleveland
Related titles: Microform ed.: (from PQC); Online - full text ed.: ISSN 1528-3968 (from ScienceDirect).
Indexed: A20, A22, A26, AHCMS, AIM, ASCA, ASSIA, B28, C06, C07, C08, CA, CINAHL, CISA, CLFP, Chicano, CurCont, E01, ECER, EMBASE, ExcerpMed, FamI, H09, H12, I05, INI, IndMed, MCR, MEDLINE, NurAb, P24, P30, P48, P50, PQC, PsycholAb, R10, Reac, RehabLit, S05, SCI, SCOPUS, SSCI, SWR&A, T02, W07, W09.
—BLDSC (6187.108000), GNLM, IE, Ingenta, INIST. **CCC.**
Published by: (American Academy of Nursing), Mosby, Inc. (Subsidiary of: Elsevier Health Sciences), 1600 John F. Kennedy Blvd, Ste 1800, Philadelphia, PA 19103. TEL 215-239-3900, 800-523-1649, FAX 215-239-3990, http://www.us.elsevierhealth.com. Ed. Marion E Broome. Pub. J Walker.

610.73 100 GBR ISSN 1466-7681
RT84.5
➤ **NURSING PHILOSOPHY**; an international journal for healthcare professionals. Text in English. 2000. q. GBP 297 in United Kingdom to institutions; EUR 378 in Europe to institutions; USD 552 in the Americas to institutions; USD 644 elsewhere to institutions; GBP 342 combined subscription in United Kingdom to institutions (print & online eds.); EUR 435 combined subscription in Europe to institutions (print & online eds.); USD 634 combined subscription in the Americas to institutions (print & online eds.); USD 741 combined subscription elsewhere to institutions (print & online eds.) (effective 2012). adv. back issues avail.; reprint service avail. from PSC. **Document type:** *Journal, Academic/Scholarly.* **Description:** Provides a forum for discussion of philosophical issues in nursing.
Related titles: Online - full text ed.: ISSN 1466-769X. 2000. GBP 297 in United Kingdom to institutions; EUR 378 in Europe to institutions; USD 552 in the Americas to institutions; USD 644 elsewhere to institutions (effective 2012) (from IngentaConnect).
Indexed: A01, A02, A03, A08, A20, A22, A26, B28, C06, C07, C08, C11, CA, CINAHL, CurCont, E-psyche, E01, EMBASE, ExcerpMed, H04, H12, MEDLINE, P30, PhilInd, SCI, SCOPUS, SSCI, T02, W07.
—BLDSC (6187.109020), IE, Infotrieve, Ingenta. **CCC.**
Published by: (International Philosophy of Nursing Society), Wiley-Blackwell Publishing Ltd. (Subsidiary of: John Wiley & Sons, Inc.), 9600 Garsington Rd, Oxford, OX4 2DQ, United Kingdom. TEL 44-1865-776868, FAX 44-1865-714591, customerservices@blackwellpublishing.com. Ed. Derek Sellman TEL 44-1173-288771. Adv. contact Craig Pickett TEL 44-1865-476267.

610.73 NZL ISSN 0112-7438
RT16
➤ **NURSING PRAXIS IN NEW ZEALAND.** Text in English. 1985. 3/yr. NZD 45 domestic to individuals; NZD 54 foreign to individuals; NZD 90 domestic to institutions; NZD 99 foreign to institutions (effective 2009). bk.rev. back issues avail. **Document type:** *Journal, Academic/Scholarly.* **Description:** Presents articles of interest to the international nursing community. Focuses on publishing New Zealand nurses writing about issues relevant to New Zealand nursing.
Related titles: Online - full text ed.
Indexed: A11, A26, C06, C07, C08, CA, CINAHL, EMBASE, ExcerpMed, H12, I05, INI, INZP, MEDLINE, P30, R10, Reac, SCOPUS, T02.
—BLDSC (6187.109210), GNLM, IE, Infotrieve, Ingenta. **CCC.**
Published by: Nursing Praxis in N.Z., PO Box 1984, Palmerston North, New Zealand. admin@nursingpraxisnz.org.nz. Ed. Tina Smith. Circ: 750.

610.73025 USA ISSN 1552-7743
RT79
NURSING PROGRAMS. Variant title: Peterson's Nursing Programs. Text in English. 1994. a. USD 18.48 (effective 2009). **Document type:** *Directory, Academic/Scholarly.* **Description:** Contains profiles of more than 3,600 undergraduate, graduate and postdoctoral options at more than 700 institutions.
Formerly (until 2003): Peterson's Guide to Nursing Programs (1073-7820)
Published by: (American Association of Colleges of Nursing), Thomson Peterson's (Subsidiary of: Thomson Reuters Corp.), Princeton Pike Corporate Center, 2000 Lenox Dr, 3rd Fl, PO Box 67005, Lawrenceville, NJ 08648. TEL 609-896-1800, 800-338-3282 ext 54229, FAX 609-896-4531, custsvc@petersons.com, http://www.petersons.com.

610.73 378 USA
NURSING PROGRESS. Text in English. 1988. 3/yr. adv. back issues avail. **Document type:** *Magazine, Academic/Scholarly.* **Description:** Covers information on nursing research, new educational programs and upcoming School events.
Published by: Oregon Health Sciences University, School of Nursing Alumni Association, 3181 S W Sam Jackson Park Rd, Portland, OR 97239-3098. TEL 503-494-8311, sonnews@ohsu.edu. Ed., Adv. contact Todd Schwartz. page USD 650; trim 11 x 8.5. Circ: 8,000.

610.73 ITA ISSN 2039-4403
▼ ➤ **NURSING REPORTS.** Text in English. 2010. irreg. **Document type:** *Journal, Academic/Scholarly.*
Media: Online - full text.
Published by: Pagepress, Via Giuseppe Belli 4, Pavia, 27100, Italy. TEL 39-0382-1751762, FAX 39-0382-1750481, http://www.pagepress.org. Ed. Marilyn Kirshbaum.

610.73 USA ISSN 0029-6562
RT1 CODEN: NURNA
➤ **NURSING RESEARCH.** Text in English. 1952. bi-m. USD 477.51 domestic to institutions; USD 570 foreign to institutions (effective 2011). adv. bk.rev. abstr.; charts; stat. cum.index: 1952-1963. back issues avail.; reprints avail. **Document type:** *Journal, Academic/Scholarly.* **Description:** Covers key issues in nursing research, including health promotion, human responses to illness, acute care nursing research, symptom management, cost-effectiveness, vulnerable populations, health services, and community-based nursing studies.
Related titles: CD-ROM ed.; Microform ed.: (from PQC); Online - full text ed.: ISSN 1538-9847.
Indexed: A01, A03, A08, A20, A22, AHCMS, AIM, AMED, ASCA, ASSIA, AgeL, B04, B28, BRD, C06, C07, C08, CA, CDA, CINAHL, CIS, CurCont, DentInd, E-psyche, EMBASE, ExcerpMed, F09, FR, FamI, G03, G10, GSA, GSI, H04, HospLI, INI, ISR, IndMed, MCR, MEA&I, MEDLINE, MEDSOC, MRefA, NurAb, P03, P24, P30, P48, P50, PQC, PsycInfo, PsycholAb, R10, RILM, Reac, S02, S03, S21, SCI, SCOPUS, SSCI, SWR&A, T02, W03, W07, W09.
—BLDSC (6187.110000), GNLM, IE, Infotrieve, Ingenta, INIST. **CCC.**
Published by: Lippincott Williams & Wilkins (Subsidiary of: Wolters Kluwer N.V.), 530 Walnut St, Philadelphia, PA 19106. TEL 215-521-8300, FAX 215-521-8902, customerservice@lww.com, http://www.lww.com. Ed. Molly C Dougherty. Pub. Sandra Kasko. Adv. contact Pat Wendelken. Circ: 3,652.

610.73 USA ISSN 2090-1429
▼ ➤ **NURSING RESEARCH AND PRACTICE.** Text in English. 2009. irreg. USD 195 (effective 2011). **Document type:** *Journal, Academic/Scholarly.*
Related titles: Online - full text ed.: ISSN 2090-1437. 2009. free (effective 2011).
Indexed: A01, T02.
Published by: Hindawi Publishing Corporation, 410 Park Ave, 15th Fl, PMB 287, New York, NY 10022. FAX 215-893-4392, 866-446-3294, info@hindawi.com.

610.73 AUS ISSN 1326-0472
NURSING REVIEW. Text in English. m. AUD 55 domestic to non-members; AUD 87 foreign to non-members (effective 2007). adv. **Document type:** *Newspaper, Trade.* **Description:** Deals with practice, research, education, policy and more.
Indexed: C06, C07.
Published by: (Royal College of Nursing Australia), A P N Educational Media Pty. Ltd., 100 William St, Level 4, North Sydney, NSW 2011, Australia. TEL 61-2-93334999, FAX 61-2-93334900, info@apn.com.au, http://www.apn.com.au. **Co-sponsor:** Australian Provincial Newspapers.

610.73 USA ISSN 0894-3184
RT1
➤ **NURSING SCIENCE QUARTERLY**; theory, research and practice. Text in English. 1988. q. USD 590, GBP 348 combined subscription to institutions (print & online eds.); USD 578, GBP 341 to institutions (effective 2011). bk.rev. abstr.; bibl.; charts; illus.; stat. index. back issues avail.; reprint service avail. from PSC. **Document type:** *Journal, Academic/Scholarly.* **Description:** Covers key aspects of nursing science, such as theoretical dilemmas, research issues, and practice applications.
Related titles: Online - full text ed.: ISSN 1552-7409. USD 531, GBP 313 to institutions (effective 2011).
Indexed: A01, A02, A03, A08, A20, A22, ASCA, B07, C06, C07, C08, CA, CINAHL, CurCont, E01, EMBASE, ExcerpMed, FamI, H04, INI, MEDLINE, NurAb, P24, P30, P48, PQC, R10, Reac, SCI, SCOPUS, SSCI, T02, V02, W07.
—BLDSC (6187.116340), GNLM, IE, Infotrieve, Ingenta. **CCC.**
Published by: Sage Publications, Inc., 2455 Teller Rd, Thousand Oaks, CA 91320. TEL 805-499-9774, 800-818-7243, FAX 805-499-0871, 800-583-2665, info@sagepub.com. Ed. Rosemarie Rizzo Parse. Circ: 1,000 (paid). **Subscr. outside the Americas to:** Sage Publications Ltd., 1 Oliver's Yard, 55 City Rd, London EC1Y 1SP, United Kingdom. TEL 44-20-73248701, FAX 44-20-73248733, subscription@sagepub.co.uk.

610.73 USA ISSN 1940-6983
RT86.73
NURSING SHORTAGE UPDATE. Text in English. 2007. q. free to members (effective 2009). back issues avail. **Document type:** *Journal, Trade.* **Description:** Covers the nursing supply and demand, trending, models and forecasts.
Media: Online - full content.
Published by: American Society of Registered Nurses, 1001 Bridgeway, Ste 411, Sausalito, CA 94965. TEL 415-331-2700, 800-331-1206, FAX 415-476-4558, office@asrn.org. Ed. Kirsten Nicole.

610.73 USA ISSN 1559-4653
NURSING SPECTRUM - D.C. - MARYLAND - VIRGINIA EDITION. Text in English. 1990. bi-w. free to qualified personnel (effective 2011). adv. **Document type:** *Magazine, Trade.* **Description:** Features local and national nursing news, as well as highly regarded continuing education modules and job opportunities.
Formerly (until 2004): Nursing Spectrum - Washington DC - Baltimore Metro Edition (1098-9153)
Indexed: C06, C07, C08, CINAHL, P30, SCOPUS.
—**CCC.**
Published by: Gannett Healthcare Group, 1721 Moon Lake Blvd, Ste 540, Hoffman Estates, IL 60169. TEL 800-770-0866, OnlineSupport@GannettHG.com. Pub. Steve Hauber. Adv. contact Ray Riordan.

NURSING SPECTRUM DRUG HANDBOOK. *see* PHARMACY AND PHARMACOLOGY

610.73 USA ISSN 1077-7946
RT1
NURSING SPECTRUM - FLORIDA EDITION. Text in English. 1991. m. free to qualified personnel. adv. **Document type:** *Newspaper, Trade.* **Description:** Designed for people interested in registered nursing as a career.
Related titles: Online - full text ed.
Indexed: C06, C07, C08, CINAHL, P30.
—**CCC.**

Published by: Gannett Healthcare Group, 1001 W Cypress Creed Rd, Ste 300, Fort Lauderdale, FL 33309. TEL 954-776-1455, FAX 954-776-1456, pclass@nursingspectrum.com. Ed. Phyllis Class. Pub. Patti Rager. adv.: color page USD 9,100; trim 8 x 10.5. Circ: 43,000.

610.73 USA ISSN 1074-858X
RT1
NURSING SPECTRUM - GREATER PHILADELPHIA - TRI-STATE EDITION. Text in English. 1992. bi-w. free to qualified personnel (effective 2011). adv. **Document type:** *Magazine, Trade.* **Description:** Features local and national nursing news, as well as highly regarded continuing education modules and job opportunities.
Indexed: C06, C07, C08, CINAHL, P30.
—CCC.
Published by: Gannett Healthcare Group, 1721 Moon Lake Blvd, Ste 540, Hoffman Estates, IL 60169. TEL 800-770-0866, OnlineSupport@GannettHG.com. Pub. Steve Hauber. Adv. contact Ray Riordan.

610.73 GBR ISSN 0029-6570
RT11 CODEN: NSTAEU
NURSING STANDARD. Text in English. 1968. w. GBP 96.80 in Europe to non-members; GBP 225.50 elsewhere to non-members; GBP 88 in Europe to members; GBP 212.85 elsewhere to members; GBP 190 combined subscription in Europe to institutions (print & online eds.); GBP 265 combined subscription elsewhere to institutions (print & online eds.); GBP 188.76 combined subscription in Europe to non-members (print & online eds.); GBP 317.46 combined subscription elsewhere to non-members (print & online eds.); GBP 171.60 combined subscription in Europe to members (print & online eds.); GBP 296.45 combined subscription elsewhere to members (print & online eds.) (effective 2009). adv. bk.rev. illus. back issues avail.; reprint service avail. from IRC. **Document type:** *Journal, Academic/Scholarly.*
Related titles: CD-ROM ed.; Online - full text ed.: GBP 91.96 to non-members; GBP 83.60 to members (effective 2009); Supplement(s): Nursing Standard. Special Supplement. ISSN 0963-522X. 1988.
Indexed: A01, A02, A03, A08, A22, A26, AMED, B28, C06, C07, C08, CA, CINAHL, E08, EMBASE, ExcerpMed, F09, FamI, G08, G10, H11, H12, I05, INI, MEDLINE, P16, P20, P22, P24, P30, P34, P48, P50, P53, P54, PQC, R10, Reac, S09, SCOPUS, T02, W09.
—BLDSC (6187.116700), GNLM, IE, Infotrieve, Ingenta, INIST. **CCC.**
Published by: (Royal College of Nursing), R C N Publishing Co. (Subsidiary of: B M J Group), The Heights, 59-65 Lowlands Rd, Harrow, Middx HA1 3AW, United Kingdom. TEL 44-20-84231066, FAX 44-20-84239196, advertising@rcnpublishing.co.uk, http://www.rcnpublishing.co.uk. Eds. Graham Scott, Jean Gray. Adv. contact Neil Hobson TEL 44-20-88723123. page GBP 2,495; trim 185 x 260. Circ: 70,214.

610.73 GBR ISSN 0954-7762
NURSING TIMES; the independent voice of nursing. Text in English. 1985. w. GBP 70 (effective 2009). adv. bk.rev. illus. index. reprints avail. **Document type:** *Journal, Trade.* **Description:** Aims to inform, inspire and entertain as it campaigns for a better deal for patients and for the nurses, midwives and health visitors who care for them.
Incorporates (1985-2005): Professional Nurse (0266-8130); Formerly (until 1987): Nursing Times, Nursing Mirror (0269-7289); Which was formed by the merger of (1905-1985): Nursing Times (0029-6589); (1977-1985): Nursing Mirror (0029-6511); Which was formerly (until 1977): Nursing Mirror and Midwives Journal (0143-2524); Which incorporated (1973-1977): Queen's Nursing Journal (0301-0821); Which was formerly (until 1973): District Nursing (0012-4044)
Related titles: Microfilm ed.: (from BHP); Microform ed.: (from PQC); Online - full text ed.
Indexed: A22, A26, AHCMS, AMED, B28, C06, C07, C08, CINAHL, CISA, DentInd, EMBASE, ExcerpMed, F09, FamI, G08, G10, H11, H12, HospAb, HospLI, I05, INI, IndMed, MEDLINE, P20, P22, P24, P30, P48, P50, P54, PQC, R10, Reac, S02, S03, SCOPUS, W09.
—BLDSC (6187.120000), GNLM, IE, Infotrieve, Ingenta, INIST. **CCC.**
Published by: Emap Healthcare Ltd. (Subsidiary of: Emap Communications Ltd.), Greater London House, Hampstead Rd, London, NW1 7EJ, United Kingdom. TEL 44-20-77283703, http://www.emap.com. Ed. Alastair McLellan TEL 44-20-77283701. **Subscr. to:** CDS Global, Tower House, Sovereign Park, Market Harborough, Leics LE16 9EF, United Kingdom. TEL 44-1858-468811, FAX 44-1858-432164.

610.73 USA ISSN 1940-6975
RT1
NURSING TODAY. Text in English. 2007. m. free to members (effective 2009). back issues avail. **Document type:** *Journal, Trade.* **Description:** Features articles written for nurses.
Media: Online - full content.
Published by: American Society of Registered Nurses, 1001 Bridgeway, Ste 411, Sausalito, CA 94965. TEL 415-331-2700, 800-331-1206, FAX 415-476-4558, office@asrn.org. Ed. Laura Fitzgerald.

610.73 618.202 ZAF
➤ **NURSING UPDATE.** Text in English. 1935. m. ZAR 300, USD 80 (effective 2001). adv. bk.rev. illus. back issues avail. **Document type:** *Magazine, Academic/Scholarly.* **Description:** Nursing magazine including news and educational articles.
Formerly: Nursing News (1018-9238); Supersedes in 1978: South African Nursing Journal (0038-2507)
Indexed: C06, C07, P30, SCOPUS.
—GNLM.
Published by: Democratic Nursing Organisation of South Africa, PO Box 1280, Pretoria, 0001, South Africa. TEL 27-12-3432315, FAX 27-12-3440750, info@denosa.org.za, http://www.denosa.org.za. Eds., R&Ps, Adv. contacts Bhungani ka Mzolo, Darryl Egnal. B&W page ZAR 3,864, color page ZAR 5,620; bleed 273 x 210. Circ: 92,000 (paid).

610.73 USA
NURSINGMATTERS: WISCONSIN EDITION; envisioning a future for nursing. Text in English. 1997 (vol.8, no.12). m. free to qualified personnel. adv. **Document type:** *Newspaper, Trade.* **Description:** Provides news and information about professional nursing in Wisconsin, including career opportunities and continuing education information.
Related titles: Online - full text ed.
Published by: Capital Newspapers, Inc., 1901 Fish Hatchery Rd, Madison, WI 53713. TEL 608-252-6200, FAX 608-250-4155, customerservice@capitalnewspapers.com, http://www.capitalnewspapers.com.

610.73 USA
NURSING'S SOCIAL POLICY STATEMENT; the essence of the profession. Text in English. 19??. irreg., latest 2010. USD 19.95 per issue to members (effective 2010). back issues avail. **Document type:** *Trade.* **Description:** Contains description of the nursing profession and its essential elements.
Published by: American Nurses Association, 8515 Georgia Ave, Ste 400, Silver Spring, MD 20910. TEL 301-628-5000, 800-274-4262, FAX 301-628-5001, memberinfo@ana.org, http://www.nursingworld.org.

O N S CONNECT. *see* MEDICAL SCIENCES—Oncology

610.7362 USA ISSN 1931-6321
O N S FOUNDATION NEWS. (Oncology Nursing Society) Text in English. 1994. s-a. **Document type:** *Newsletter, Consumer.*
Published by: Oncology Nursing Society Foundation, 125 Enterprise Dr, Pittsburgh, PA 15275-1214. TEL 412-859-6100, FAX 412-859-6163.

613.62 610.73 CAN ISSN 0828-542X
➤ **O O H N A JOURNAL.** Text in English. 1980. 3/yr. CAD 25 domestic; CAD 30 in United States; CAD 35 elsewhere; CAD 9 newsstand/cover domestic; CAD 10.50 newsstand/cover in United States; CAD 12 newsstand/cover elsewhere (effective 2004). adv. Website rev.; bk.rev. bibl.; charts; illus.; stat. 32 p./no. 3 cols./p.; **Document type:** *Journal, Academic/Scholarly.*
Indexed: C06, C07, C08, CINAHL.
Published by: Ontario Occupational Health Nurses Association, Ste 605, 302 The East Mall, Etobicoke, ON M9B 6C7, Canada. TEL 416-239-6462, FAX 416-239-5462, http://www.oohna.on.ca. Ed., Adv. contact Frances MacCusworth. R&P Brian Verrall. B&W page CAD 980; trim 8.5 x 11. Circ: 1,200 (paid).

610.73 617 JPN ISSN 0913-5014
O P E NURSING/OPE NASHINGU. (Operating Room) Text in Japanese. 1986. m. JPY 20,412; JPY 1,890 newsstand/cover (effective 2007). Supplement avail. **Document type:** *Journal, Academic/Scholarly.*
Published by: Medicus Shuppan/Medicus Publishing Inc., 18-24 Hiroshiba-cho, Suita-shi, Osaka-fu 564-8580, Japan. TEL 81-6-63856911, FAX 81-6-63856873, http://www.medica.co.jp/.

610.73 USA ISSN 1933-3145
➤ **O R NURSE.** (Operating Room) Text in English. 2007. 10/yr. USD 245 domestic to institutions; USD 353 foreign to institutions (effective 2011). adv. back issues avail.; reprints avail. **Document type:** *Magazine, Trade.* **Description:** Presents clinical and practical information, technological and product advances, for perioperative nurses, managers, and directors working in hospitals and ambulatory surgery settings.
Related titles: Online - full text ed.: ISSN 1933-3161.
Indexed: C06, C07.
—CCC.
Published by: Lippincott Williams & Wilkins (Subsidiary of: Wolters Kluwer N.V.), 530 Walnut St, Philadelphia, PA 19106. TEL 215-521-8300, customerservice@lww.com. Ed. Elizabeth Thompson.

610.73 USA ISSN 2153-6562
▼ **THE OB-GYN NURSE.** Text in English. 2009. bi-m. adv. back issues avail. **Document type:** *Journal, Academic/Scholarly.* **Description:** Focuses on the role of the OB/GYN, infertility, and urology nurse in patient care.
Supersedes in part (in 2009): The O B / G Y N and Infertility Nurse (2151-8394)
Related titles: Online - full text ed.: ISSN 2153-6546.
Published by: (American Academy of OB/GYN and Infertility Nurses), Greenhill Healthcare Communications, 241 Forsgate Dr, Ste 205D, Monroe Township, NJ 08831. TEL 732-656-7935, FAX 732-656-7938, editorial@greenhillhc.com. Eds. Debra Moynihan, Sue Jasulaitis, Dalia Buffery TEL 732-992-1889.

610.73 FRA ISSN 1163-4634
OBJECTIF SOINS; la revue de management des cadres de sante. Text in French. 1992. m. (10/yr.). EUR 114.60 domestic to individuals; EUR 135.78 DOM-TOM to individuals; EUR 185 elsewhere to individuals; EUR 134.19 domestic to institutions; EUR 202 foreign to institutions (effective 2009). adv. **Document type:** *Magazine, Trade.*
Indexed: FR.
Published by: Editions Lamarre (Subsidiary of: Wolters Kluwer France), 1 Rue Eugene et Armand Peugeot, Rueil Malmaison, 92500, France. TEL 33-1-76733000, FAX 33-1-76734857, contact@espaceinfirmier.com, http://www.espaceinfirmier.com. Circ: 7,696.

610.73 SVN ISSN 1318-2951
CODEN: OZNEF5
➤ **OBZORNIK ZDRAVSTVENE NEGE/SLOVENIAN NURSING REVIEW.** Summaries in English, Slovenian; Text in Slovenian. 1966. q. EUR 62 to institutions (effective 2011). adv. bk.rev. index. back issues avail. **Document type:** *Journal, Academic/Scholarly.* **Description:** Publishes interdisciplinary oriented articles, which contribute toward the professional development of nursing and midwifery practice in Slovenia.
Formerly (until 1993): Zdravstveni Obzornik (0350-9516)
Indexed: C06, C07, C08, CINAHL.
—BLDSC (6208.490000).
Published by: Zbornica Zdravstvene in Babiske Nege Slovenije/Nurses and Midwives Association of Slovenia, Ob zeleznici 30A, Ljubljana, 1000, Slovenia. TEL 386-1-5445480, narocnina.racuni@zbornica-zveza.si, http://www.zbornica-zveza.si. Ed. Andreja Mihelic Zajec. Circ: 2,400.

610.73 GBR ISSN 0029-7917
➤ **OCCUPATIONAL HEALTH**; a journal for the occupational health team. Text in English. 1949. m. GBP 128 domestic; USD 324 foreign (effective 2009). adv. bk.rev. illus. index. **Document type:** *Magazine, Trade.* **Description:** Provides expert advice on how to develop and implement workable health and safety policies for your organization.
Incorporates (1986-2008): Occupational Health Review (0951-4600)
Related titles: Microform ed.: (from PQC); Online - full text ed.
Indexed: A01, A02, A03, A08, A12, A13, A15, A17, A22, A26, ABIn, B01, B02, B06, B07, B09, B15, B17, B18, B28, BPI, BRD, BrTechI, C06, C07, C08, C11, CA, CINAHL, CISA, CSNB, E08, E11, FamI, G04, G08, H01, H04, H11, H12, I05, INI, L12, P19, P21, P24, P30, P34, P48, P51, P53, P54, PQC, R09, R10, Reac, S09, SCOPUS, SD, T02, T04, W01, W02, W03, W05.
—BLDSC (6228.849000), GNLM, IE, Infotrieve, Ingenta. **CCC.**
Published by: Reed Business Information Ltd. (Subsidiary of: Reed Business), Quadrant House, The Quadrant, Sutton, Surrey SM2 5AS, United Kingdom. TEL 44-20-86523500, FAX 44-20-86528932, rbi.subscriptions@qss-uk.com, http://www.reedbusiness.co.uk/. Ed. Noel O'Reillly TEL 44-20-86524669. Pub. Susan Downey. Adv. contact Peter Collis TEL 44-20-86524668. Circ: 4,638 (paid). **Subscr. to:** Quadrant Subscription Services, PO Box 302, Haywards Heath, W Sussex RH16 3YY, United Kingdom. TEL 44-1444-445566, FAX 44-1444-445447.

610.73 AUT
OESTERREICHISCHE PFLEGEZEITSCHRIFT. Text in German. 1948. 10/yr. EUR 25 domestic; EUR 31 foreign (effective 2003). adv. bk.rev. abstr.; illus. 52 p./no.; **Document type:** *Journal, Trade.*
Former titles (until 200?): Oesterreichische Krankenpflegezeitschrift (0303-4461); (until 1974): Oesterreichische Schwesternzeitung (0029-9480); (until 1966): Krankenschwester (0303-500X)
Indexed: INI, P30, SCOPUS.
—GNLM, Ingenta. **CCC.**
Published by: Oesterreichischer Gesundheits- und Krankenpflegeverband, Mollgasse 3 a, Vienna, W 1180, Austria. TEL 43-1-4782710. Ed. Elisabeth Marcher. Adv. contact Ulrike Galuska. B&W page EUR 1,600; trim 180 x 260. Circ: 10,000 (paid and controlled).

610.73 AUT
OESTERREICHISCHER KRANKENPFLEGEVERBAND. FORTBILDUNGSPROGRAMM. Text in German. 1969. a. free. adv. **Document type:** *Academic/Scholarly.*
Published by: Oesterreichischer Gesundheits- und Krankenpflegeverband, Mollgasse 3 a, Vienna, W 1180, Austria. TEL 43-1-4782710. Ed. Harald Verworner. Adv. contact Ulrike Galuska. Circ: 15,000.

610.73 USA ISSN 0030-0993
RT5.O47
OHIO NURSES REVIEW. Text in English. 1926. m. (10/yr.). free to members (effective 2004). adv. index. **Document type:** *Magazine, Trade.* **Description:** Official publication of the ONA, publishes independent study abstracts, updates/registration forms for ONA events and articles including economic and general welfare, health policy, nursing practice and continuing education.
Indexed: C06, C07, C08, CINAHL, EMBASE, ExcerpMed, INI, MEDLINE, P30, R10, Reac, SCOPUS.
—BLDSC (6247.150000).
Published by: Ohio Nurses Association, 4000 E Main St, Columbus, OH 43213-2983. TEL 614-237-5414, FAX 614-237-6074. Ed. Carol A Jenkins. adv.: B&W page USD 580; 10 x 7. Circ: 10,000 (controlled).

OK OPERATIONEEL. (OperatieKamer) *see* MEDICAL SCIENCES—Surgery

610.73 USA ISSN 0030-1787
RT5.O5
OKLAHOMA NURSE. Text in English. 1926. q. looseleaf. USD 20 (effective 2008). adv. 24 p./no.; back issues avail.; reprints avail. **Document type:** *Newsletter, Trade.* **Description:** Covers issues and employment opportunities of interest to licensed nursing professionals.
Related titles: Online - full text ed.
Indexed: A22, A26, C06, C07, C08, CINAHL, EMBASE, ExcerpMed, H11, H12, I05, INI, MEDLINE, P30, R10, Reac, SCOPUS.
Published by: (Oklahoma Nurses Association), Arthur L. Davis Publishing Agency, Inc., 517 Washington St, PO Box 216, Cedar Falls, IA 50613. TEL 319-277-2414, 800-626-4081, FAX 319-277-4055, sales@aldpub.com, http://www.aldpub.com. Ed. Mark Miller. R&P Audra Aldridge. Adv. contact Jim Larson. Circ: 56,000.

OMSORG; nordisk tidsskrift for palliativ medicin. *see* SOCIAL SERVICES AND WELFARE

610.73 SWE ISSN 1652-0858
OMVAARDNADSMAGASINET. Text in Swedish. 1979. bi-m. SEK 200 (effective 2006). adv. back issues avail. **Document type:** *Magazine, Trade.*
Former titles (until 2003): S S F - Nytt (1401-0437); (until 1995): Sjukskoeterskan (0280-3526)
Indexed: P30.
Published by: Svensk Sjukskoeterskefoerening/Swedish Society of Nursing, Baldersgatan 1, Stockholm, 11427, Sweden. TEL 46-8-4122400, FAX 46-8-4122424, ssf@swenurse.se. Ed. Rolf Maansson TEL 46-8-308703. Adv. contact Elva Bengtsson. page SEK 33,000; 182 x 237. Circ: 95,000.

610.73 616.992 USA ISSN 1944-9801
THE ONCOLOGY NURSE. Text in English. 2008. 7/yr. free to qualified personnel. adv. **Document type:** *Newspaper, Trade.* **Description:** Provides timely and relevant information to oncology nurses on the front line of patient care and provides CE credit offerings.
Related titles: Online - full text ed.: ISSN 1944-9798.
Published by: Greenhill Healthcare Communications, 241 Forsgate Dr, Ste 205D, Monroe Township, NJ 08831. TEL 732-656-7935, FAX 732-656-7938, editorial@greenhillhc.com, http://www.greenhillhc.com. Ed. Beth Faiman. Pub. Phil Pawelko TEL 732-992-1887. adv.: B&W page USD 4,070; trim 10.875 x 13.875. Circ: 31,790.

610.73 616.992 USA ISSN 2154-350X
▼ **ONCOLOGY NURSE ADVISOR.** Text in English. 2010 (May). bi-m. **Document type:** *Journal, Trade.* **Description:** Offers clinical updates and evidence-based guidance to the oncology nurse community.
Related titles: Online - full text ed.: ISSN 2157-6602.
Indexed: A26, H12, I05.
—CCC.
Published by: Haymarket Media Inc. (Subsidiary of: Haymarket Group Ltd.), 114 W 26th St, 4th Fl, New York, NY 10001. TEL 646-638-6000, FAX 646-638-6114, custserv@haymarketmedia.com, http://www.haymarket.com.

610.73 616.99 USA ISSN 0190-535X
RC266
➤ **ONCOLOGY NURSING FORUM.** Abbreviated title: O N F. Text in English. 1974. bi-m. USD 175 domestic to institutions; USD 195 foreign to institutions; free to members (effective 2010). adv. bk.rev.; video rev.; Website rev. index. 170 p./no. 3 cols./p.; Supplement avail.; back issues avail.; reprints avail. **Document type:** *Journal, Academic/Scholarly.* **Description:** Brings out articles related to developments in oncology nursing practice, technology, and research. Focuses on promoting a positive image of professional specialized nursing.
Formerly (until 1977): Oncology Nursing Society. Newsletter
Related titles: Microfilm ed.: (from PQC); Online - full text ed.: ISSN 1538-0688. USD 150 (effective 2001).
Indexed: A01, A02, A03, A08, A20, A22, A26, AMED, B28, C06, C07, C08, C11, CA, CINAHL, ChPerl, CurCont, EMBASE, ExcerpMed, F09, Faml, H04, H11, H12, I05, INI, IndMed, MEDLINE, NurAb, P03, P20, P22, P24, P30, P34, P48, P54, PQC, PsycInfo, R10, Reac, SCI, SCOPUS, SSCI, T02, W07.
—BLDSC (6256.980000), GNLM, IE, Infotrieve, Ingenta, INIST. **CCC.**
Published by: Oncology Nursing Society, 125 Enterprise Dr, Pittsburgh, PA 15275. TEL 412-859-6100, 866-257-4667, FAX 412-859-6165, 877-369-5497, customer.service@ons.org. Ed. Rose Mary Carroll Johnson. Pub. Leonard Mafrica. Adv. contact Anthony J Jannetti TEL 856-256-2300. Circ: 36,000.

610.73 616.992 USA ISSN 1936-4385
ONCOLOGY NURSING NEWS. Abbreviated title: O N N. Text in English. 2007. bi-m. **Document type:** *Journal, Trade.* **Description:** Provides clinical news and practical guidance to nurses, nurse practitioners and physician assistants across all settings of cancer care and supportive services.
Related titles: Online - full text ed.
Indexed: B02, B15, B17, B18, G04, I05, P24, P48, PQC.
—CCC.
Published by: Haymarket Media Inc. (Subsidiary of: Haymarket Group Ltd.), 114 W 26th St, 4th Fl, New York, NY 10001. TEL 646-638-6000, custserv@haymarketmedia.com, http://www.haymarket.com. Ed. Sara Elan TEL 212-755-4296 ext 404. Pub. Charles Benaiah TEL 212-755-4296 ext 212.

610.73 BRA ISSN 1676-4285
➤ **ONLINE BRAZILIAN JOURNAL OF NURSING.** Text in English, Spanish, Portuguese. 2002. q. free (effective 2011). **Document type:** *Journal, Academic/Scholarly.*
Media: Online - full content.
Indexed: C06, C07, C08, CA, CINAHL, SCOPUS, T02.
Published by: Universidade Federal Fluminense, Nursing Activities Interest Group, Rua Dr. Celestino, 74, Niteroi, RJ 24020-091, Brazil. TEL 51-21-27194411, FAX 51-21-27198073. Ed. Dr. Isabel da Cruz.

610.73 USA ISSN 2160-2824
▼ **ONLINE JOURNAL OF CULTURAL COMPETENCE IN NURSING AND HEALTHCARE.** Text in English. 2011. q. free (effective 2011). **Document type:** *Journal, Trade.* **Description:** Seeks to disseminate scholarly work among nurses and other health care professionals through publication of articles on culturally competent and congruent care-based research, theory, education, practice, administration, and policy.
Media: Online - full text.
Indexed: C06.
Published by: University of Michigan - Flint, Department of Nursing, 303 E Kearsley St, 2180 William S White Bldg, Flint, MI 48502. TEL 810-424-5650, FAX 810-766-6851, hallca@umflint.edu, http://www.umflint.edu/nursing/. Ed. Margaret M Andrews TEL 810-762-3422.

610.73 USA ISSN 1091-3734
RT1
➤ **ONLINE JOURNAL OF ISSUES IN NURSING.** Text in English. 1996. 3/yr. free (effective 2011); free. back issues avail. **Document type:** *Journal, Academic/Scholarly.* **Description:** Provides a forum for discussion of pertinent issues in nursing along with different views on topics that affect nursing research, education and practice. The interactive format encourages dialogue with readers, resulting in a comprehensive discussion of topics.
Media: Online - full text.
Indexed: A01, A03, A08, C06, C07, C08, C11, CA, CINAHL, EMBASE, ExcerpMed, H04, IndMed, MEDLINE, P20, P22, P24, P30, P34, P48, P54, PQC, R10, Reac, SCOPUS, T02.
Published by: American Nurses Association, 8515 Georgia Ave, Ste 400, Silver Spring, MD 20910. TEL 301-628-5000, 800-274-4262, FAX 202-651-7005. Ed. Harrcet Coeling.

610.73 USA ISSN 1089-9758
➤ **ONLINE JOURNAL OF NURSING INFORMATICS.** Abbreviated title: O J N I. Text in English. 1996. 3/yr. free (effective 2011). back issues avail. **Document type:** *Journal, Academic/Scholarly.* **Description:** Addresses the theoretical and practical aspects of nursing informatics as it relates to the art of nursing.
Media: Online - full text.
Indexed: C06, C07, C08, CINAHL, SCOPUS.
Published by: Online Journal of Nursing Informatics Corporation, 100 Serenity Ln, Kittanning, PA 16201. Ed. Dr. Dee McGonigle.

610.73 USA ISSN 1539-3399
➤ **ONLINE JOURNAL OF RURAL NURSING AND HEALTH CARE.** Text in English. 2000. s-a. free (effective 2011). back issues avail. **Document type:** *Journal, Academic/Scholarly.* **Description:** Features research and practice-related features for rural nurses and other health professionals.
Media: Online - full text.
Indexed: A26, C06, C07, C08, CA, CINAHL, H12, I05, P30, T02.
Published by: Rural Nurse Organization, PO Box 870358, Tuscaloosa, AL 35487. rno@bama.ua.edu. Ed. Dr. Jeri Dunkin TEL 205-348-9877.

610.73 NLD ISSN 1874-4346
RT1
➤ **THE OPEN NURSING JOURNAL.** Text in English. 2007. irreg. free (effective 2011). **Document type:** *Journal, Academic/Scholarly.*
Media: Online - full text.
Indexed: C06, C07, P30, T02.
Published by: Bentham Open (Subsidiary of: Bentham Science Publishers Ltd.), PO Box 294, Bussum, AG 1400, Netherlands. TEL 31-35-6923800, FAX 31-35-6980150, subscriptions@bentham.org. Ed. Julie Scholes.

610.73 GBR ISSN 1368-1249
➤ **OPHTHALMIC NURSING;** international journal of ophthalmic nursing. Text in English. 1997. q. GBP 16 domestic to individuals; GBP 25 in the European Union to individuals; GBP 45 elsewhere to individuals; GBP 50 domestic to institutions; GBP 60 in the European Union to institutions; GBP 75 elsewhere to institutions (effective 2000). adv. back issues avail. **Document type:** *Journal, Academic/Scholarly.* **Description:** Contains research papers, clinical articles, news features, letters page, noticeboard of events, and book review page.
Indexed: B28, C06, C07, C08, CINAHL.
—IE, Ingenta. **CCC.**
Published by: T M & D Press Ltd., Omnibus House, 41 North Rd, London, N7 9DP, United Kingdom. TEL 44-20-7700-3479, FAX 44-20-7700-2049, tmd.press@btinternet.com. Ed. Heather Waterman. Pub. Kevin Kibble. R&P Penny Stephens. Adv. contact Mike Brearley. B&W page GBP 795, color page GBP 1,020; trim 210 x 297. Circ: 3,500 (paid).

610.73 617 GBR ISSN 0961-1258
OPPORTUNITIES FOR THEATRE STAFF & OTHER SPECIALISTS. Text in English. 1980. fortn. adv. bk.rev. **Document type:** *Newsletter.*
Published by: Newton Mann Ltd., The Derwent Business Centre, Clarke Street, Derby, DE1 2BU, United Kingdom. TEL 44-1629-583941, FAX 44-1629-580479, admin@newtonmann.co.uk, http://www.opps.co.uk. Ed. Mark Moore. Pub. Charles Mann. Adv. contact John Eaton TEL 0207-878-2317. Circ: 7,000 (controlled).

610.73 USA ISSN 0030-4751
RT1
OREGON NURSE. Text in English. 1932. 4/yr. adv. bk.rev. illus. **Document type:** *Newsletter, Trade.* **Description:** Provides articles about nursing issues, health care trends, collective bargaining for nurses; legislative health care issues.
Related titles: Online - full text ed.
Indexed: C06, C07, C08, CINAHL, EMBASE, ExcerpMed, INI, MEDLINE, P30, R10, Reac, SCOPUS.
—BLDSC (6281.600000), IE, Infotrieve, Ingenta.
Published by: Oregon Nurses Association, 18765 SW Boones Ferry Rd., Ste. 200, Tualatin, OR 97062-8498. TEL 503-293-0011, FAX 503-293-0013. Ed., R&P Sandy Marron. Adv. contact Debra Feammelli. B&W page USD 735; trim 11 x 17. Circ: 6,000. **Subscr. to:** ONA, 9600 SW Oak St, Ste 550, Portland, OR 97223.

610.73 617.3 USA ISSN 0744-6020
RD701 CODEN: CLATDP
➤ **ORTHOPAEDIC NURSING JOURNAL.** Text in English. 1981. bi-m. USD 251.51 domestic to institutions; USD 356 foreign to institutions (effective 2011). adv. bk.rev. back issues avail.; reprints avail. **Document type:** *Journal, Academic/Scholarly.* **Description:** Provides departmental sections on current events, organizational activities, research, product and drug information, and literature findings.
Related titles: Online - full text ed.: ISSN 1542-538X.
Indexed: A22, A26, B28, C06, C07, C08, CA, CINAHL, CurCont, E08, EMBASE, ExcerpMed, F09, G06, G07, G08, H11, H12, H13, I05, MEDLINE, NurAb, P03, P10, P20, P22, P24, P30, P34, P48, P53, P54, PQC, PsycInfo, R10, Reac, S09, SCI, SCOPUS, SSCI, T02, W07.
—BLDSC (6296.125300), GNLM, IE, Infotrieve, Ingenta. **CCC.**
Published by: (National Association of Orthopaedic Nurses), Lippincott Williams & Wilkins (Subsidiary of: Wolters Kluwer N.V.), Two Commerce Sq, 2001 Market St, Philadelphia, PA 19103. TEL 215-521-8300, FAX 215-521-8902, customerservice@lww.com, http://www.lww.com. Ed. Mary Faut Rodts. Pub. Sandra Kasko. Adv. contact Robert Reed TEL 630-845-1285. Circ: 6,601.

➤ **ORTHOSCOPE.** see MEDICAL SCIENCES—Orthopedics And Traumatology

610.7361 CAN ISSN 1499-3627
RT120.E4
OUTLOOK (PEMBROKE). Text in English. s-a. adv.
Indexed: C06, C07, C08, CINAHL.
Published by: (National Emergency Nurses Affiliation Inc.), Pappin Communications, The Victoria Centre, 84 Isabella St, Pembroke, ON K8A 5S5, Canada. TEL 613-735-0952, FAX 613-735-7983, info@pappin.com, http://www.pappin.com. Ed. Valerie Eden. Adv. contact Heather Coughlin. B&W page CAD 870, color page CAD 1,420. Circ: 1,300.

610.73 THA ISSN 1906-8107
➤ **PACIFIC RIM INTERNATIONAL JOURNAL OF NURSING RESEARCH.** Text in English. q. USD 100 to individuals; THB 300 to members; THB 400 domestic to non-members; USD 50 foreign to non-members; USD 200 to students (effective 2011). **Document type:** *Journal, Academic/Scholarly.*
Formerly (until 2010): Thai Journal of Nursing Research (0859-7685)
Related titles: Online - full text ed.: free.
Indexed: C06, C07, C08, CINAHL.
—BLDSC (6330.879530), IE, Ingenta.
Published by: Thailand Nursing Council, Nagarindrasri Bldg., Ministry of Public Health, Tiwanon Rd., Amphur Muang, Nonthaburi, 11000, Thailand. TEL 66-2-9510145 ext 51, nursec@ji-net.com, http://www.tnc.or.th/index.php. Eds. Clinton E. Lambert, Somchi Hanucharurnkul, Vickie A. Lambert.

610.73 ESP ISSN 1989-2829
PAGINASENFERURG.COM. Text in Spanish. 2008. q. free (effective 2011). **Document type:** *Journal, Academic/Scholarly.*
Media: Online - full text.
Published by: Plataforma Enferurg

PAIN MANAGEMENT NURSING. see MEDICAL SCIENCES—Anaesthesiology

610.73 NZL ISSN 1178-2242
R726.8
➤ **PALLIATIVE CARE: RESEARCH AND TREATMENT.** Text in English. 2008. irreg. free (effective 2011). **Document type:** *Journal, Academic/Scholarly.* **Description:** Covers clinical, scientific and policy issues in palliative care.
Media: Online - full text.
Indexed: A01, C06, C07, T02.
—CCC.
Published by: Libertas Academica Ltd., PO Box 302-624, North Harbour, Auckland, 1330, New Zealand. TEL 64-21-662617, FAX 64-21-740006, editorial@la-press.com. Ed. Parag Bharadwaj.

610.73 AUS ISSN 1031-3443
PATRICIA CHOMLEY ORATIONS; nursing and human service. Text in English. a. back issues avail. **Document type:** *Journal, Trade.* **Description:** Publishes historical speeches on nursing.
Published by: Royal College of Nursing Australia, 1 Napier Close, PO Box 219, Deakin, ACT 2600, Australia. TEL 61-2-62833400, FAX 61-2-62823565, canberra@rcna.org.au, http://www.rcna.org.au.

610.73 618.92 USA ISSN 2155-1529
▼ **PEDIATRIC N P / P A.** Variant title: Pediatric Nurse Practitioner & Physician Assistant. Text in English. 2010 (Oct.). bi-m. **Document type:** *Newspaper, Trade.* **Description:** News and information for pediatric nurses and advanced practitioners.
Related titles: Online - full text ed.: ISSN 2155-1553. 2010 (Oct.).
Published by: Novellus Healthcare Communications, LLC, 241 Forsgate Dr, Ste 205D, Monroe Township, NJ 08831. blanche@engagehc.com.

610.73 USA ISSN 0886-9006
PEDIATRIC NURSE PRACTITIONER. Text in English. bi-m. USD 130 to individual members; USD 65 to students (effective 2007). **Document type:** *Newsletter.*
Published by: National Association of Pediatric Nurse Association and Practitioners, 20 Brace Rd, Ste 200, Cherry Hill, NJ 08034-2634. TEL 856-857-9700, FAX 856-857-1600, info@napnap.org, http://www.napnap.org/. Ed. Timothy W Gordon. R&P Joe Casey. Circ: 4,000.

610.73 USA ISSN 0097-9805
RJ245 CODEN: PENUEI
➤ **PEDIATRIC NURSING.** Text in English. 1975. bi-m. USD 45 domestic to individuals; USD 75 foreign to individuals; USD 69 domestic to institutions; USD 99 foreign to institutions; USD 15 per issue (effective 2010). adv. bk.rev. illus. back issues avail.; reprints avail. **Document type:** *Journal, Academic/Scholarly.* **Description:** Provides information related to health care for normal, sick, or disabled children and their families; pediatric clients in the hospital, clinic or office, school, community, or home.
Related titles: Microfilm ed.: (from PQC); Online - full text ed.
Indexed: A01, A02, A03, A08, A22, A25, A26, B16, C06, C07, C08, C11, CA, CINAHL, CWI, DentInd, E03, E07, E08, EMBASE, ERI, ExcerpMed, F09, Faml, G06, G07, G08, H04, H11, H12, I05, INI, MEDLINE, NurAb, P04, P07, P10, P16, P18, P20, P22, P24, P30, P48, P53, P54, PQC, R10, Reac, S08, S09, SCOPUS, T02, V02.
—BLDSC (6417.605300), GNLM, IE, Infotrieve, Ingenta, INIST. **CCC.**
Published by: Jannetti Publications, Inc., E Holly Ave, PO Box 56, Pitman, NJ 08071. TEL 856-256-2300, FAX 856-589-7463, contact@ajj.com. Ed. Judy A Rollins. Pub. Anthony J Jannetti.

610.73 USA ISSN 0031-4161
RT1
PELICAN NEWS. Text in English. 1970 (vol.26). q. looseleaf. free to members (effective 2005). adv. 20 p./no.; back issues avail. **Document type:** *Newsletter, Trade.* **Description:** Covers issues and employment opportunities of interest to licensed nursing professionals.
Related titles: Online - full text ed.
Indexed: C06, C07, C08, CINAHL, P30.
Published by: Louisiana State Nurses Association, 5800 One Perkins Place Dr., Ste. 2B, Baton Rouge, LA 70808-9114. Circ: 61,000 (free).

610.73 USA ISSN 0031-4617
RT1
THE PENNSYLVANIA NURSE. Text in English. 1946. bi-m. free to members (effective 2004). adv. bk.rev. illus. back issues avail. **Document type:** *Magazine, Trade.* **Description:** Keeps Pennsylvania nurses informed of events affecting nursing, with timely reporting of professional, practice, economic, legislative, legal, ethical and education issues.
Related titles: Online - full text ed.
Indexed: C06, C07, C08, CINAHL, EMBASE, ExcerpMed, F09, INI, MEDLINE, P30, R10, Reac, SCOPUS.
—BLDSC (6421.747000), GNLM, Infotrieve.
Published by: Pennsylvania State Nurses Association, Editorial Board, PO Box 68525, Harrisburg, PA 17106-8525. TEL 717-657-1222, FAX 717-657-3796. Ed. Lori Anne Artz. adv.: B&W page USD 449; trim 15 x 11.5. Circ: 3,000.

610.73 PRT ISSN 0873-8904
PENSAR ENFERMAGEM. Text in Spanish. 1997. s-a. EUR 15 domestic; EUR 20 foreign (effective 2006). back issues avail. **Document type:** *Journal, Academic/Scholarly.*
Published by: Escola Supeior de Enfermagen de Maria Fernanda Resende, Ave do Brasil 53B, Lisbon, 1700-063, Portugal. TEL 351-21-7024100, FAX 351-21-7924127, uide@esenfcgl.pt. Ed. Marta Lima Basto.

610.73 USA ISSN 1556-7931
PERIOPERATIVE NURSING CLINICS. Text in English. 2006 (Mar.). q. USD 213 in United States to institutions; USD 245 elsewhere to institutions (effective 2012). adv. back issues avail.; reprints avail. **Document type:** *Journal, Trade.* **Description:** Includes information on both clinical nursing and skills in surgical procedures, including bariatric, pediatric, orthopedic and thoracic surgery, as well as such topics as patient positioning, infection and minimally invasive procedures.
Related titles: Online - full text ed.: (from ScienceDirect).
Indexed: ASSIA, C06, C07, SCOPUS.
—CCC.
Published by: W.B. Saunders Co. (Subsidiary of: Elsevier Health Sciences), Elsevier, Health Sciences Division, Order Fulfillment, 3251 Riverport Ln, Maryland Heights, MO 63043. TEL 314-872-8370, 800-325-4177, FAX 314-432-1380, JournalCustomerService-usa@elsevier.com, http://www.us.elsevierhealth.com. Adv. contact John Marmero TEL 212-633-3657.

610.73 VEN ISSN 0379-8208
PERSPECTIVAS. Text in Spanish. 1972. q. **Document type:** *Journal, Academic/Scholarly.*
Indexed: P30.
Published by: Universidad del Zulia, Facultad de Medicina, Calle 65 Esq Ave 19, Apdo 15165, Maracaibo, Venezuela. http://www.luz.edu.ve/.

610.73 CAN ISSN 1708-1890
PERSPECTIVE INFIRMIERE. Text in French. 1974. bi-m. CAD 15.95 domestic; USD 73 foreign (effective 2008). adv. bk.rev. illus. 64 p./no. 2 cols./p.; **Document type:** *Journal, Trade.*

M

Former titles (until 2003): Infirmiere du Quebec (1195-2695); (until Sep. 1993): Nursing Quebec (0381-6419); (until 1976): Order of Nurses of Quebec. News and Notes (0319-2636)
Indexed: C06, C07, C08, CINAHL, CPerI, EMBASE, ExcerpMed, FR, I05, INI, MEDLINE, P30, PdeR, R10, Reac, SCOPUS.
—BLDSC (6428.135805), GNLM, Infotrieve. **CCC.**
Published by: Ordre des Infirmieres et Infirmiers du Quebec/Order of Nurses of Quebec, 4200 Dorchester Blvd W, Montreal, PQ H3Z 1V4, Canada. TEL 514-935-2501, 800-363-6048, FAX 514-935-1799. Ed. Colette Pilon-Bergman. R&P Marlene Lavoie. Adv. contact Julie Diamond TEL 514-762-1667. B&W page CAD 1,865, color page CAD 3,235; trim 10.88 x 8.13. Circ: 61,803 (controlled).

PERSPECTIVES (TORONTO, 1977)). *see* GERONTOLOGY AND GERIATRICS

610.736 USA ISSN 0031-5990
RC475 CODEN: PEPYA2
➤ **PERSPECTIVES IN PSYCHIATRIC CARE**; journal for advanced practice psychiatric nurses. Text in English. 1963. q. GBP 171 in United Kingdom to institutions; EUR 216 in Europe to institutions; USD 252 in the Americas to institutions; USD 332 elsewhere to institutions; GBP 198 combined subscription in United Kingdom to institutions (print & online eds.); EUR 249 combined subscription in Europe to institutions (print & online eds.); USD 290 combined subscription in the Americas to institutions (print & online eds.); USD 382 combined subscription elsewhere to institutions (print & online eds.) (effective 2012). bk.rev. Index. back issues avail.; reprint service avail. from PSC. **Document type:** *Journal, Academic/Scholarly.* **Description:** Focuses on research, clinical practice, trends and innovations in psychiatric and mental-health nursing.
Related titles: Microfilm ed.: (from PQC); Online - full text ed.: ISSN 1744-6163. GBP 171 in United Kingdom to institutions; EUR 216 in Europe to institutions; USD 252 in the Americas to institutions; USD 332 elsewhere to institutions (effective 2012) (from IngentaConnect).
Indexed: A01, A02, A03, A08, A20, A22, A26, ASCA, C06, C07, C08, C11, CA, CINAHL, CurCont, E-psyche, E01, E08, EMBASE, ExcerpMed, F09, FamI, G08, H04, H11, H12, H13, HospLI, I05, I07, INI, IndMed, MEDLINE, NurAb, P03, P10, P20, P22, P24, P25, P26, P30, P43, P48, P53, P54, PQC, PsycInfo, PsycholAb, R10, Reac, S09, S23, SCI, SCOPUS, SSCI, T02, W07.
—BLDSC (6428.160000), GNLM, IE, Infotrieve, Ingenta, INIST. **CCC.**
Published by: (International Society of Psychiatric-Mental Health Nurses, Adult and Geropsychiatric Division), Wiley-Blackwell Publishing, Inc. (Subsidiary of: Wiley-Blackwell Publishing Ltd.), 111 River St, Hoboken, NJ 07030. TEL 201-748-6000, FAX 201-748-6088, info@wiley.com. Ed. Geraldine S Pearson. Adv. contact Karl Franz TEL 781-388-8470.

610.73 CHE ISSN 1012-5302
➤ **PFLEGE**; die wissenschaftliche Zeitschrift fuer Pflegeberufe. Text in German. 1988. bi-m. CHF 194, EUR 129 to institutions (effective 2011). adv. 64 p./no.; **Document type:** *Journal, Academic/Scholarly.*
Related titles: Online - full text ed.: ISSN 1664-283X.
Indexed: C06, C07, C08, CINAHL, EMBASE, ExcerpMed, INI, MEDLINE, P30, R10, Reac, SCI, SCOPUS, SSCI, W07.
—BLDSC (6440.710000), GNLM, IE, Infotrieve, Ingenta.
Published by: Verlag Hans Huber AG (Subsidiary of: Hogrefe Verlag GmbH & Co. KG), Laenggassstr 76, Bern 9, 3000, Switzerland. TEL 41-31-3004500, FAX 41-31-3004590, verlag@hanshuber.com, http://www.hanshuber.com. Eds. Berta Schrems, Eva-Maria Panfil, Rebecca Spirig. Circ: 2,700 (controlled).

➤ **PFLEGE UND GESELLSCHAFT**; Zeitschrift fuer Pflegewissenschaft. *see* PUBLIC HEALTH AND SAFETY

610.73 DEU ISSN 1433-2795
DER PFLEGEBRIEF; das Online-Magazin fuer die Pflege. Text in German. 1995. bi-m. free (effective 2010). adv. abstr.; illus. back issues avail. **Document type:** *Newsletter, Academic/Scholarly.* **Description:** Contains topics on nursing care.
Media: Online - full content. **Related titles:** E-mail ed.: ISSN 1433-1985. 1995; Fax ed.: ISSN 1433-1993.
Published by: Schluetersche Verlagsgesellschaft mbH und Co. KG, Hans-Boeckler-Allee 7, Hannover, 30173, Germany. TEL 49-511-85500, FAX 49-511-85501100, info@schluetersche.de, http://www.schluetersche.de. Ed., Adv. contact Henrik Crone-Muenzebrock. Circ: 8,050 (controlled).

PFLEGEIMPULS; Zeitschrift fuer Recht und Praxis im Pflegemanagement. *see* SOCIAL SERVICES AND WELFARE

610 DEU ISSN 1612-8664
PFLEGEN INTENSIV; Die Fachzeitschrift fuer Intensivpflege und Anaesthesie. Text in German. 2004. q. EUR 36; EUR 10 newsstand/cover (effective 2010). adv. **Document type:** *Magazine, Trade.*
Published by: Bibliomed - Medizinische Verlagsgesellschaft mbH, Postfach 1150, Melsungen, 34201, Germany. TEL 49-5661-73440, FAX 49-5661-8360, info@bibliomed.de. Circ: 2,200 (paid and controlled).

681 CHE ISSN 1662-3029
➤ **PFLEGEWISSENSCHAFT.** Text in German. 1998. m. EUR 118 combined subscription to individuals (print & online eds.); EUR 168 combined subscription to institutions (print & online eds.); EUR 78 combined subscription to students (print & online eds.) (effective 2009). adv. **Document type:** *Journal, Academic/Scholarly.*
Formerly (until 2008): www.PrInterNet.info (1422-8629); Which incorporated (1992-1999): Pflege-Management (1019-8393); (1991-1999): PflegePaedagogik (1019-0651); Which was formerly (1988-1991): Recom-Monitor (0935-9788)
Related titles: CD-ROM ed.: ISSN 1424-6627. 2000; Online - full text ed.: ISSN 1422-8610.
Indexed: C06, C07, C08, CINAHL.
—CCC.
Published by: H P S Media GmbH, Usterstr 25, Moenchaltorf, 8617, Switzerland. TEL 41-44-9480474, FAX 41-44-9480277, service@printernet.info. Ed. Andreas Lauterbach. Adv. contact Sonja Mehr. page EUR 1,980; trim 210 x 297. Circ: 3,000 (paid and controlled).

610.73 DEU ISSN 0945-1129
PFLEGEZEITSCHRIFT. Text in German. 1948. m. EUR 52.30; EUR 29.50 to students; EUR 9.10 per issue (effective 2010). adv. bk.rev. **Document type:** *Journal, Academic/Scholarly.*
Former titles (until 1994): Deutsche Krankenpflege-Zeitschrift (0012-074X); (until 1971): Deutsche Schwesternzeitung
Media: Large Type.
Indexed: A22, DokArb, EMBASE, ExcerpMed, F09, INI, MEDLINE, P30, R10, Reac, SCOPUS.
—BLDSC (6440.715000), GNLM, IE, Infotrieve, Ingenta. **CCC.**
Published by: W. Kohlhammer GmbH, Hessbruehlstr 69, Stuttgart, 70565, Germany. TEL 49-711-78630, FAX 49-711-78638204, kohlhammerkontakt@kohlhammer.de, http://www.kohlhammer.de. Ed. Ivonne Rommoser. adv.: B&W page EUR 1,550, color page EUR 2,945. Circ: 7,596 (paid and controlled).

610.73 PHL ISSN 0048-3818
➤ **PHILIPPINE JOURNAL OF NURSING.** Text in English. 1926. q. PHP 100 domestic; USD 35 foreign (effective 2003). adv. bk.rev. illus.; abstr. 56 p./no. 2 cols./p.; back issues avail. **Document type:** *Magazine, Academic/Scholarly.*
Formerly (until 1953): Filipino Nurse
Indexed: A22, C06, C07, C08, CINAHL, INI, IPP, P30, SCOPUS.
—BLDSC (6455.629000), GNLM, IE, Infotrieve, Ingenta.
Published by: Philippine Nurses Association, 1663 F Tirona Benitez St, Malate, Manila, 1004, Philippines. TEL 63-2-536-1888, FAX 63-2-525-1596, pna@thenet.ph. Eds. Shirley V Pena, Victoria L Vidal, Marilyn D Yap. Adv. contacts Lily Ann Baldago, Mrs. Rosie S de Leon. Circ: 13,000.

617.3 305.895 USA ISSN 1939-3776
PHILIPPINE NURSES MONITOR. Text in English. 2006. m. free (effective 2007). adv. **Document type:** *Magazine, Trade.* **Description:** Addresses economic, social and healthcare issues of concern to nurses, with a particular emphasis on Philippine nurses worldwide.
Published by: Cagayan River Development Corp, 3550 Wilshire Blvd, Ste 1755-D, Los Angeles, CA 90010. TEL 213-385-6308, editor@philippinenursesmonitor.com. Ed. E M Wagner. adv.: page USD 3,000; 7.5 x 9.75.

PHYSICIAN ASSISTANTS' PRESCRIBING REFERENCE. *see* PHARMACY AND PHARMACOLOGY

610.73 POL ISSN 1730-1912
PIELEGNIARSTWO XXI WIEKU. Variant title: Pielegniarstwo Dwudziestego Pierwszego Wieku. Text in Polish. 2002. q. PLZ 32 (effective 2005). **Document type:** *Journal, Academic/Scholarly.*
Published by: Wydawnictwo Czelej Sp. z o.o., ul Czeremchowa 21, Lublin, 20807, Poland. TEL 48-81-7437766, FAX 48-81-5347788, wydawnictwo@czelej.com.pl, http://www.czelej.com.pl.

610.73 POL ISSN 1897-3116
PIELEGNIARSTWO CHIRURGICZNE I ANGIOLOGICZNE/SURGICAL AND VASCULAR NURSING. Text in Polish. 2007. q. PLZ 29 domestic (effective 2010). **Document type:** *Journal, Academic/Scholarly.*
Related titles: Online - full text ed.
Published by: (Polskie Towarzystwo Pielegniarstwa Angiologicznego), Termedia sp. z o.o./Termedia Publishing House, ul Wenedow 9/1, Poznan, 61614, Poland. TEL 48-61-8227781, FAX 48-61-8227781, termedia@termedia.pl. Ed. Arkadiusz Jawien.

610.73 POL ISSN 0860-8466
PIELEGNIARSTWO POLSKIE. Text and summaries in English, Polish. 1989. q. **Document type:** *Journal, Academic/Scholarly.*
Published by: (Uniwersytet Medyczny im. Karola Marcinkowskiego w Poznaniu), Wydawnictwo Naukowe Uniwersytetu Medycznego im. Karola Marcinkowskiego w Poznaniu, ul. Bukowska 70, Poznan, 60812, Poland. TEL 48-61-8547152, FAX 48-61-8547151, http://www.wydawnictwo.ump.edu.pl. Ed. Maria D Glowacka.

610.73 617.95 USA ISSN 0741-5206
CODEN: PSNUEE
PLASTIC SURGICAL NURSING. Text in English. 1981. q. USD 335.51 domestic to institutions; USD 434 foreign to institutions (effective 2011). adv. back issues avail.; reprints avail. **Document type:** *Journal, Academic/Scholarly.* **Description:** Presents the advances in plastic and reconstructive surgical nursing practice.
Formerly (until 1983): The Journal of Plastic and Reconstructive Surgical Nursing (0273-3285)
Related titles: Online - full text ed.: ISSN 1550-1841.
Indexed: A22, A26, B28, C06, C07, C08, CA, CINAHL, E08, EMBASE, ExcerpMed, G08, H11, H12, H13, I05, INI, MEDLINE, NurAb, P10, P20, P22, P24, P26, P30, P48, P53, P54, PQC, R10, Reac, S09, SCOPUS, T02.
—BLDSC (6528.938100), GNLM, IE, Infotrieve, Ingenta. **CCC.**
Published by: (American Society of Plastic Surgical Nurses), Lippincott Williams & Wilkins (Subsidiary of: Wolters Kluwer N.V.), 530 Walnut St, Philadelphia, PA 19106. TEL 215-521-8300, FAX 215-521-8902, customerservice@lww.com, http://www.lww.com. Ed. Candise Flippin. Pub. Kathleen M Phelan. Adv. contact Sue Ryan. Circ: 1,384.

610.73 USA ISSN 0098-4345
RT1
POINT OF VIEW (SOMERVILLE). Text in English. 196?. 3/yr.
Indexed: A22, C06, C07, C08, CINAHL.
—IE, Ingenta.
Published by: Ethicon, Inc., PO Box 151, Somerville, NJ 08876-0151. Ed. Patricia A Jones.

610.73 USA ISSN 1527-1544
RT86.7
➤ **POLICY, POLITICS & NURSING PRACTICE.** Text in English. 2000. q. USD 518, GBP 305 combined subscription to institutions (print & online eds.); USD 508, GBP 299 to institutions (effective 2011). adv. back issues avail.; reprint service avail. from PSC. **Document type:** *Journal, Academic/Scholarly.* **Description:** Serves as a forum for examining policies, political activities and health services research that affect nursing practice across all venues of care delivery. Topics including legislation affecting nursing practice and health care, case studies involving policy and political action, interviews with government and other policy makers and health professionals, international health policy issues, related conferences and media reviews.
Related titles: Online - full text ed.: ISSN 1552-7468. USD 466, GBP 275 to institutions (effective 2011).
Indexed: A01, A02, A03, A08, A22, ASSIA, B07, C06, C07, C08, CA, CINAHL, E01, EMBASE, ExcerpMed, H04, H05, MEDLINE, P03, P30, P34, P42, PsycInfo, SCOPUS, T02, V02.
—BLDSC (6543.327388), IE, Ingenta. **CCC.**
Published by: Sage Publications, Inc., 2455 Teller Rd, Thousand Oaks, CA 91320. TEL 805-499-9774, 800-818-7243, FAX 805-499-0871, 800-583-2665, info@sagepub.com. Ed. David M Keepnews. **Subscr. outside the Americas to:** Sage Publications Ltd., 1 Oliver's Yard, 55 City Rd, London EC1Y 1SP, United Kingdom. TEL 44-20-73248701, FAX 44-20-73248733, subscription@sagepub.co.uk.

610.7365 USA ISSN 1090-3909
POST ACUTE CARE STRATEGY REPORT; the newsletter for integrating post acute services. Text in English. 1996. m. USD 297 (effective 2000). charts; stat. back issues avail. **Document type:** *Newsletter.* **Description:** Provides strategic advice and case studies to hospital and nursing home administrators, nursing staff and company recruiters on how to integrate post acute services such as rehab, home health, skilled nursing into a network. Contains regulatory and medical reimbursement news.
—CCC.
Published by: Harling Communications, Inc., 25575 W. Timberlake Rd., Barrington, IL 60010-1444. TEL 847-304-1011, 800-894-8786, FAX 847-304-1035. Eds. Harriet Gill, Matthew Hay. Pub., R&P Mark Harling TEL 516-379-7097.

610.73 GBR ISSN 0953-6612
PRACTICE NURSE. Text in English. 1988. 22/yr. EUR 520 in Europe to institutions; JPY 71,000 in Japan to institutions; USD 657 elsewhere to institutions (effective 2012). adv. index. back issues avail.; reprints avail. **Document type:** *Journal, Academic/Scholarly.* **Description:** Covers news, clinical features, self-assessment tests and research.
Related titles: Online - full text ed.
Indexed: A01, A02, A03, A08, A15, A26, ABIn, B01, B06, B07, B09, B28, BRD, C06, C07, C08, C11, CA, CINAHL, E08, G03, G06, G07, G08, GSA, GSI, H01, H04, H11, H12, I05, P24, P34, P48, P51, PQC, S04, S09, SCOPUS, T02, W03, W05.
—BLDSC (6597.170000), IE, Ingenta. **CCC.**
Published by: Elsevier Ltd (Subsidiary of: Elsevier Science & Technology), The Blvd, Langford Ln, Kidlington, Oxford, OX5 1GB, United Kingdom. TEL 44-1865-843434, FAX 44-1865-843970, journalscustomerserviceemea@elsevier.com. Circ: 6,500.

610.73 GBR ISSN 0964-9271
RT1
➤ **PRACTICE NURSING.** Text in English. 1990. m. GBP 140 domestic to individuals; EUR 200 in Europe to individuals; USD 289 elsewhere to individuals; GBP 114 to students (effective 2010). adv. back issues avail.; reprints avail. **Document type:** *Journal, Academic/Scholarly.* **Description:** Features clinical, professional and educational articles of the highest quality, together with clinics on travel health, immunization and vaccination, and dermatology.
Related titles: Online - full text ed.
Indexed: AMED, B28, C06, C07, C08, CA, CINAHL, T02.
—BLDSC (6597.175000), IE, Ingenta. **CCC.**
Published by: Mark Allen Publishing Ltd., St Jude's Church, Dulwich Rd, London, SE24 0PB, United Kingdom. TEL 44-20-77385454, FAX 44-20-79788316, subscriptions@markallengroup.com, http://www.markallengroup.com. Eds. Liam Benison TEL 44-20-75016709, Jeannett Martin. Adv. contact Stacy Schwarz.

➤ **THE PRACTISING MIDWIFE.** *see* MEDICAL SCIENCES—Obstetrics And Gynecology

610.73 USA ISSN 0032-6666
RT1
PRAIRIE ROSE. Text in English. 1931. q. looseleaf. free to members (effective 2005). adv. bk.rev. 32 p./no.; back issues avail. **Document type:** *Newsletter, Trade.* **Description:** Covers issues and employment opportunities of interest to licensed nursing professionals.
Indexed: C06, C07, C08, CINAHL, EMBASE, ExcerpMed, INI, MEDLINE, P30, R10, Reac, SCOPUS.
Published by: North Dakota Nurses Association, 531 Airport Road, Ste D, Bismarck, ND 58504. TEL 701-223-1385, FAX 701-223-0575, info@ndna.org, http://www.ndna.org. Circ: 12,000.

610.73 610 NLD ISSN 1876-2573
DE PRAKTIJK (ALPHEN AAN DEN RIJN). Text in Dutch. 2008. q. EUR 37 (effective 2010). adv. **Document type:** *Magazine, Trade.*
Published by: Van Zuiden Communications B.V., Postbus 2122, Alphen aan den Rijn, 2400 CC, Netherlands. TEL 31-172-476191, FAX 31-172-471882, zuiden@zuidencomm.nl, http://www.zuidencomm.nl. adv.: color page EUR 2,025; trim 210 x 297. Circ: 2,000.

610.73 CAN ISSN 1197-2297
PRE & POST NATAL NEWS. Text in English. 1987. 3/yr. adv. **Document type:** *Newsletter.* **Description:** Covers the latest medical and social research affecting pregnancy, birth and infant care.
Formerly: Canadian Childbirth Educator (0835-586X)
Published by: (Today's Parent Group), Professional Publishing Associates, 269 Richmond St W, Toronto, ON M5V 1X1, Canada. TEL 416-596-8680, FAX 416-596-1991. Ed. Jennifer Elliott. Circ: 7,000 (controlled).

610.73 AUS ISSN 1838-0840
PRIMARY TIMES. Text in English. 2007. q. free to members (effective 2011). **Document type:** *Magazine, Trade.* **Description:** Features all aspects of practice nursing and provides the latest tips, techniques and practical applications for your day to day working lives.
Published by: Australian Practice Nurses Association, 149 Drummond St, PO Box 55, Carlton, VIC 3053, Australia. TEL 61-3-96697400, FAX 61-3-96697499, admin@apna.asn.au.

610.73 AUS ISSN 1834-9714
PRIVATE & CONFIDENTIAL. Text in English. 2006. irreg. **Document type:** *Newsletter, Trade.*
—CCC.
Published by: New South Wales Nurses' Association, 43 Australia St, Camperdown, NSW 2050, Australia. TEL 61-2-85951234, FAX 61-2-95503667, gensec@nswnurses.asn.au, http://www.nswnurses.asn.au.

610.73 POL ISSN 1233-9989
➤ **PROBLEMY PIELEGNIARSTWA/NURSING TOPICS.** Text in Polish. 1993. s-a. PLZ 132 domestic to institutions; EUR 30 foreign to institutions (effective 2011). bk.rev. **Document type:** *Journal, Academic/Scholarly.* **Description:** Presents review articles, original experimental investigations in the field of nursing and similar domains, reports, comments and official statements of international trade unions.
Related titles: Online - full text ed.

Published by: (Polskie Towarzystwo Pielegniarskie/Polish Nurses Association), Wydawnictwo Via Medica, ul Swietokrzyska 73, Gdansk, 80180, Poland. TEL 48-58-3209494, FAX 48-58-3209460, redakcja@viamedica.pl, http://www.viamedica.pl. Ed. Aleksandra Gaworska-Krzeminska.

610.73 AUT ISSN 0949-7323
➤ **PROCARE;** Aktuelle Information, Fort- und Weiterbildung fuer die Mitarbeiter der Gesundheits- und Krankenpflege. Text in German. 1996. m. EUR 98, USD 120 combined subscription to institutions (print & online eds.) (effective 2012). adv. **Document type:** *Journal, Academic/Scholarly.* **Description:** Contains articles of interest to health care aides.
Related titles: Online - full text ed.: ISSN 1613-7574.
Indexed: A22, A26, E01.
—IE. **CCC.**
Published by: Springer Wien (Subsidiary of: Springer Science+Business Media), Sachsenplatz 4-6, Vienna, W 1201, Austria. TEL 43-1-33024150, FAX 43-1-3302426, journals@springer.at, http://www.springer.at. Adv. contact Margit Hauser. color page EUR 3,130; 210 x 297. Circ: 8,000 (paid). **Subscr. in the Americas to:** Springer New York LLC, Journal Fulfillment, PO Box 2485, Secaucus, NJ 07096. TEL 800-777-4643, 201-348-4033, FAX 201-348-4505, journals-ny@springer.com, http://www.springer.com; **Subscr. to:** Springer Distribution Center, Kundenservice Zeitschriften, Haberstr 7, Heidelberg 69126, Germany. TEL 49-6221-3454303, FAX 49-6221-3454229, subscriptions@springer.com.

➤ **PROFESSION SAGE-FEMME.** *see* MEDICAL SCIENCES—Obstetrics And Gynecology

610.73 USA ISSN 1932-8087
➤ **PROFESSIONAL CASE MANAGEMENT.** Abbreviated title: P C M. Text in English. 1996. bi-m. USD 286.51 domestic to institutions; USD 429 foreign to institutions (effective 2011). adv. back issues avail.; reprints avail. **Document type:** *Journal, Academic/Scholarly.* **Description:** Features practices and industry benchmarks for the professional case manager and also features hands-on information for case managers new to the specialty.
Former titles (until 2007): Lippincott's Case Management (1529-7764); Which incorporated (1994-2003): Inside Case Management (1073-6514); (until 2000): Nursing Case Management (1084-3647)
Related titles: CD-ROM ed.; Online - full text ed.: ISSN 1932-8095. USD 149.50 domestic academic site license; USD 173.50 foreign academic site license; USD 166.75 domestic corporate site license; USD 190.75 foreign corporate site license (effective 2002).
Indexed: A22, C06, C07, C08, CINAHL, EMBASE, ExcerpMed, INI, MEDLINE, P30, R10, Reac, SCOPUS.
—IE, Infotrieve, Ingenta, INIST. **CCC.**
Published by: (Case Management Society of America), Lippincott Williams & Wilkins (Subsidiary of: Wolters Kluwer N.V.), 530 Walnut St, Philadelphia, PA 19106. TEL 215-521-8300, FAX 215-521-8902, customerservice@lww.com, http://www.lww.com. Ed. Suzanne K Powell TEL 623-465-0684. Pub. Sandy Kasko. Adv. contact Robert Reed TEL 630-845-1285. Circ: 13,217.

610.73 AUS ISSN 1325-7706
PROFESSIONAL DEVELOPMENT SERIES. Text in English. 1995. irreg., latest vol.9. price varies. adv. **Document type:** *Monographic series, Trade.* **Description:** Publishes several perspectives on a topic of immediate concern for the nursing profession and other health disciplines.
Published by: Royal College of Nursing Australia, 1 Napier Close, PO Box 219, Deakin, ACT 2600, Australia. TEL 61-2-62833400, FAX 61-2-62823565, canberra@rcna.org.au, http://www.rcna.org.au. Adv. contact Joanne Ramadge.

610.73 ZAF ISSN 1607-6672
➤ **PROFESSIONAL NURSING TODAY.** Text in English. 1997. bi-m. **Document type:** *Journal, Academic/Scholarly.* **Description:** Focuses on clinical nursing and midwifery disciplines and related topics inside and outside the hospital and private practice.
Related titles: Online - full text ed.: ISSN 2220-1076.
Indexed: A36, CABA, GH, N02, N03, R12, T05.
Published by: Medpharm Publications (Pty) Ltd, PO Box 14804, Lyttelton, 0140, South Africa. TEL 27-12-6647460, FAX 27-12-6646276, reception@medpharm.co.za, http://www.medpharm.co.za.

610.73 ITA ISSN 0033-0205
PROFESSIONI INFERMIERISTICHE. Text in Italian. 1947. q. EUR 60 domestic to individuals; EUR 100 domestic to institutions; EUR 120 foreign (effective 2007). reprints avail. **Document type:** *Journal, Trade.*
Indexed: C06, C07, C08, CINAHL, EMBASE, ExcerpMed, INI, MEDLINE, P30, SCOPUS.
—BLDSC (6864.230000), GNLM, IE, Infotrieve, Ingenta.
Published by: Consociazione Nazionale Associazione Infermieri (C N A I), Via Trebbia 9, Milan, 20139, Italy. TEL 39-02-58306892, FAX 39-02-58308892, segreteria@cnai.info, http://www.cnai.info. Ed. Julita Sansoni.

PROQUEST NURSING AND ALLIED HEALTH SOURCE. *see* MEDICAL SCIENCES—Abstracting, Bibliographies, Statistics

610.73 USA ISSN 0737-1209
CODEN: BICODM
➤ **PUBLIC HEALTH NURSING.** Text in English. 1984. bi-m. GBP 535 in United Kingdom to institutions; EUR 679 in Europe to institutions; USD 674 in Canada & Mexico to institutions; USD 699 in the Americas to institutions; USD 1,045 elsewhere to institutions; GBP 615 combined subscription in United Kingdom to institutions (print & online eds.); EUR 781 combined subscription in Europe to institutions (print & online eds.); USD 775 combined subscription in Canada & Mexico to institutions (print & online eds.); USD 804 combined subscription in the Americas to institutions (print & online eds.); USD 1,201 combined subscription elsewhere to institutions (print & online eds.) (effective 2012). adv. back issues avail.; reprint service avail. from PSC. **Document type:** *Journal, Academic/Scholarly.* **Description:** Publishes theoretical and practical discussions, reviews, and clinical reports in the field of public-health nursing.
Related titles: Online - full text ed.: ISSN 1525-1446. GBP 535 in United Kingdom to institutions; EUR 679 in Europe to institutions; USD 674 in Canada & Mexico to institutions; USD 699 in the Americas to institutions; USD 1,045 elsewhere to institutions (effective 2012) (from IngentaConnect).
Indexed: A01, A02, A03, A08, A20, A22, A26, A34, A36, ASCA, AgeL, B21, B28, C06, C07, C08, C11, CA, CABA, CINAHL, Chicano, CurCont, D01, E-psyche, E01, E12, EMBASE, ESPM, ExcerpMed, F09, FR, FamI, GH, H&SSA, H04, H05, H12, INI, IndMed, IndVet, LT, MEDLINE, N02, N03, NurAb, P03, P24, P30, P33, P34, P37, P48, P50, PEI, PQC, PsycInfo, PsycholAb, R08, R10, R12, RM&VM, RRTA, Reac, RiskAb, S02, S03, S13, S16, SCI, SCOPUS, SSCI, T02, T05, THA, VS, W07, W09, W11.
—BLDSC (6964.760000), GNLM, IE, Infotrieve, Ingenta, INIST. **CCC.**
Published by: Wiley-Blackwell Publishing, Inc. (Subsidiary of: Wiley-Blackwell Publishing Ltd.), 111 River St, Hoboken, NJ 07030. TEL 201-748-6000, FAX 201-748-6088, info@wiley.com. Eds. Dr. Judith C Hays, Dr. Sarah E Abrams. Adv. contact Karl Franz TEL 781-388-8470.

610.73 USA ISSN 0033-4189
THE PULSE (CEDAR FALLS). Text in English. 1938. q. looseleaf. free to qualified personnel (effective 2004). adv. 20 p./no.; back issues avail.; reprints avail. **Document type:** *Newsletter, Trade.* **Description:** Covers issues and employment opportunities of interest to licensed nursing professionals.
Formerly (until 1956): Montana State Nurses Association. Bulletin
Indexed: C06, C07, C08, CINAHL, P30, SCOPUS.
Published by: (Montana Nurses' Association), Arthur L. Davis Publishing Agency, Inc., 517 Washington St, PO Box 216, Cedar Falls, IA 50613. TEL 319-277-2414, 800-626-4081, FAX 319-277-4055, sales@aldpub.com, http://www.aldpub.com. Ed. Claudia Clifford. Circ: 17,000.

610.73 USA ISSN 1946-7257
THE PULSE MAGAZINE. Text in English. 2008. irreg. (1-2/yr). free to qualified personnel (effective 2009). back issues avail. **Document type:** *Magazine, Trade.* **Description:** Provides the alumni, staff and friends of Oakland University's School of Nursing and select school of nursing deans with informative medical articles.
Related titles: Online - full text ed.: free (effective 2009).
Published by: Oakland University, School of Nursing, 2200 N Squirrel Rd, Rochester, MI 48309. TEL 248-370-2100, nrsinfo@oakland.edu, http://www4.oakland.edu/?id=4597&sid=166. Ed. Claudette Zolkowski.

CHN ISSN 1674-4748
QUANKE HULI/CHINESE GENERAL NURSING. Text in Chinese. 2003 (Feb.). every 3 mos. (10th, 20th & 30th of every mo.). CNY 10 per issue (effective 2009). **Document type:** *Journal, Academic/Scholarly.*
Formerly: Jiating Hushi/Family Nurse (1672-1888)
Related titles: Online - full text ed.
—East View.
Published by: (Zhonghua Huli Xuehui Shanxi Fenhui/Chinese Nursing Association Shanxi Branch), Quanke Huli Zazhishe, PO Box 1, Guangchang Shoutou Fenju, Taiyuan, 030001, China. TEL 86-351-7230748. **Dist. by:** China International Book Trading Corp, 35 Chegongzhuang Xilu, Haidian District, PO Box 399, Beijing 100044, China. TEL 86-10-68412045, FAX 86-10-68412023, cibtc@mail.cibtc.com.cn, http://www.cibtc.com.cn.

610.73 AUS ISSN 0815-936X
RT15
QUEENSLAND NURSE. Variant title: Q N U Journal. Text in English. 1959. bi-m. free to members (effective 2009). adv. **Document type:** *Journal, Trade.* **Description:** Contains up to date information about wages and working conditions for nurses as well as information on the latest professional developments in nursing.
Former titles (until 1982): R A N F Review; (until 1970): Queensland Nurses Journal (0033-6211)
Indexed: A22, C06, C07, C08, CINAHL, EMBASE, ExcerpMed, MEDLINE, P20, P22, P24, P30, P48, P54, PQC, R10, Reac, SCOPUS.
—BLDSC (7216.004000), IE, Infotrieve, Ingenta. **CCC.**
Published by: Queensland Nurses' Union, GPO Box 1289, Brisbane, QLD 4001, Australia. TEL 61-7-38401444, 800-177-273, FAX 61-7-38449387, qnu@qnu.org.au. Ed., Adv. contact Gay Hawksworth. B&W page AUD 1,872, color page AUD 2,398; trim 180 x 245.

QUEENSLAND NURSES' UNION. UNION UPDATE. *see* LABOR UNIONS

610.73 USA ISSN 0196-3805
QUICKENING. Text in English. bi-m. free to members (effective 2007); Includes Journal of Midwifery. **Document type:** *Newsletter.*
Published by: American College of Nurse-Midwives, 8403 Colesville Rd, Ste 1550, Silver Spring, MD 20910. TEL 240-485-1800, FAX 240-485-1818, http://www.acnm.org. Ed. Gina Harps. Circ: 5,000.

610.73 USA ISSN 1946-7249
R A A REVIEW. (Roy Adaptation Association) Text in English. 19??. s-a. free to members (effective 2009). **Document type:** *Newsletter, Trade.*
Related titles: Online - full text ed.: free (effective 2009).
Published by: Roy Adaptation Association, c/o Boston College, 140 Commonwealth Ave, Connell School of Nursing, Chestnut Hill, MA 02467. TEL 617-552-3100, 800-360-2522, FAX 617-552-0798, http://www.bc.edu/schools/son/faculty/theorist/Roy_Adaptation_Association.html.

610.73 BRA ISSN 1677-7271
R E C E N F. REVISTA TECNICO CIENTIFICA DE ENFERMAGEM. Text in Portuguese. 2004. bi-m. BRL 68.75 (effective 2006). back issues avail. **Document type:** *Journal, Academic/Scholarly.*
Published by: Bioeditora, Rua Tenente Francisco Ferreira de Souza, 3636, Boqueirao, Curitiba, PR 81670-010, Brazil. TEL 55-41-32767000, FAX 55-41-32785166, bioeditora@bioeditora.com.br, http://www.bioeditora.com.br/.

610.73 USA ISSN 0192-298X
R.N. IDAHO. (Registered Nurse) Text in English. 1942. q. free to members. adv. **Document type:** *Newsletter, Trade.*
Former titles: Gem State R N Newsletter; Gem State R N (0072-0569); Idaho State Bulletin
Indexed: P30.
Published by: Idaho Nurses Association, 2417 Bank Dr., Ste. 111, Boise, ID 83705-2572. TEL 208-345-0500, FAX 208-385-0166. Ed. Myrl Wheeler. Circ: 600.

A REASON FOR HOPE. *see* MEDICAL SCIENCES—Psychiatry And Neurology

610.73 PRT ISSN 0874-0283
REFERENCIA. Text in Spanish, Portuguese. 1998. s-a. **Document type:** *Journal, Academic/Scholarly.*
Indexed: A01, C06, C07, C08, CA, CINAHL, F03, F04, T02.
Published by: Escola Superior de Enfermagem de Coimbra, Ave Bissaya Barreto, Apdo. 55, Coimbra, 3001-901, Portugal. TEL 351-239-802850, FAX 351-239-442648, http://www.esenfc.pt/.

610.73 367 USA
REFLECTIONS ON NURSING LEADERSHIP (ONLINE). Abbreviated title: R N L. Text in English. 1975. d. free to members (effective 2011). adv. back issues avail. **Document type:** *Magazine, Trade.* **Description:** Highlights the meetings, conferences, seminars, and national and international events of the organization.
Former titles (until 2005): Reflections on Nursing Leadership (Print) (1527-6538); (until 2000): Reflections (0885-8144)
Media: Online - full text.
Indexed: C06, C07, C08, CINAHL, INI, P30, SCOPUS.
—**CCC.**
Published by: Sigma Theta Tau International Honor Society of Nursing, 550 W N St, Indianapolis, IN 46202. TEL 317-634-8171, 888-634-7575, FAX 317-634-8188, stti@stti.iupui.edu, http://www.nursingsociety.org. Ed. James E Mattson. Pub. Renee Wilmeth. Adv. contact Rachael McLaughlin.

610.73 CAN ISSN 1484-0863
REGISTERED NURSE. Short title: R N. Text in English. 6/yr. CAD 36 domestic; CAD 42 foreign (effective 1999). adv. **Document type:** *Magazine, Trade.* **Description:** Acts as a forum between the association and its members, discussing ethical, legal, moral, professional and economic issues within the profession.
Former titles (until 1996): Registered Nurse Journal (1203-9659); Registered Nurse (0840-8831)
Indexed: C06, C07, C08, CINAHL, P30.
—BLDSC (7344.161000), IE. **CCC.**
Published by: Registered Nurses' Association of Ontario, 438 University Ave, Ste 1600, Toronto, ON M5G 2K8, Canada. TEL 416-599-1925, 800-268-7199, FAX 416-599-1926. Ed., R&P Lesley Frey. Pub. Sine MacKinnon. Adv. contact Kimberley Kearsey. B&W page CAD 1,215, color page CAD 2,015; trim 10.75 x 8.13. Circ: 16,000.

610.73 CAN ISSN 1719-6892
REGISTERED NURSES ASSOCIATION OF ONTARIO. ANNUAL REPORT (ONLINE). Text in English. a. **Document type:** *Report, Trade.*
Formerly (until 1994): Registered Nurses' Association of Ontario. Annual Report (Print) (1180-9744)
Media: Online - full text.
Published by: Registered Nurses' Association of Ontario, 158 Pearl St., Toronto, ON M5H-1L3, Canada. TEL 416-599-1925, 800-268-7199, FAX 416-599-1926, info@rnao.org, http://www.rnao.org.

610.73 CAN
REGISTERED PSYCHIATRIC NURSES' ASSOCIATION OF SASKATCHEWAN. R P NEWS. Text in English. q. CAD 10. adv. **Document type:** *Newsletter.*
Formerly: Saskatchewan Psychiatric Nurses' Association. Newsletter
Published by: Registered Psychiatric Nurses Association of Saskatchewan, 2055 Lorne St, Regina, SK S4P 2M4, Canada. TEL 306-586-4617, FAX 306-586-6000. Ed., R&P, Adv. contact Marion Rieger. Circ: 1,400.

610.73 615.82 USA ISSN 0278-4807
RT120.R4
➤ **REHABILITATION NURSING.** Text in English. 1975. bi-m. USD 120 combined subscription domestic to individuals; USD 195 combined subscription foreign to individuals; USD 175 combined subscription domestic to institutions; USD 195 combined subscription foreign to institutions; free to members (effective 2010). adv. bk.rev. charts; illus. index. back issues avail.; reprints avail. **Document type:** *Journal, Academic/Scholarly.* **Description:** Provides information on a spectrum of rehabilitation nursing topics.
Formerly (until 1981): A R N Journal (0362-3505)
Related titles: Microform ed.: (from PQC); Online - full text ed.: USD 120 domestic to individuals; USD 195 foreign to individuals; USD 175 domestic to institutions; USD 195 foreign to institutions (effective 2010).
Indexed: A20, A22, AMED, B28, C06, C07, C08, CINAHL, CurCont, EMBASE, ExcerpMed, F09, FamI, INI, MEDLINE, NurAb, P20, P22, P24, P30, P48, P54, PQC, R10, Reac, SCI, SCOPUS, SSCI, W07.
—BLDSC (7350.285000), GNLM, IE, Infotrieve, Ingenta. **CCC.**
Published by: Association of Rehabilitation Nurses, 4700 W Lake Ave, Glenview, IL 60025. TEL 847-375-4710, 800-229-7530, FAX 847-375-6481, info@rehabnurse.org, http://www.rehabnurse.org. Ed. Elaine Tilka Miller.

610.73 USA ISSN 1541-6577
CODEN: SINPFV
➤ **RESEARCH AND THEORY FOR NURSING PRACTICE;** an international journal. Text in English. 1986. q. USD 95 domestic to individuals; USD 135 foreign to individuals; USD 280 domestic to institutions; USD 320 foreign to institutions; USD 145 combined subscription domestic to individuals (print & online eds.); USD 205 combined subscription foreign to individuals (print & online eds.); USD 420, USD 480 combined subscription foreign to institutions (print & online eds.) (effective 2009). adv. 80 p./no.; back issues avail.; reprints avail. **Document type:** *Journal, Academic/Scholarly.* **Description:** Publishes original manuscripts concerned with the development and testing of theory relevant to nursing practice to facilitate the integration of theory, research and practice.
Formerly (until vol.16, 2002): Scholarly Inquiry for Nursing Practice (0889-7182)
Related titles: Online - full text ed.: ISSN 1945-7286. USD 80 domestic to individuals; USD 120 foreign to individuals; USD 235 domestic to institutions; USD 275 foreign to institutions (effective 2009) (from IngentaConnect).
Indexed: A22, C06, C07, C08, CINAHL, CurCont, E-psyche, EMBASE, ExcerpMed, FamI, INI, IndMed, MEDLINE, P03, P20, P21, P22, P24, P30, P48, P54, PQC, PsycInfo, PsycholAb, R10, RILM, Reac, SCI, SCOPUS, SOPODA, SSCI, W07.
—BLDSC (7716.206500), GNLM, IE, Ingenta. **CCC.**
Published by: Springer Publishing Company, 11 W 42nd St, 15th Fl, New York, NY 10036. TEL 212-431-4370, FAX 212-941-7842, contactus@springerpub.com. Ed. Dr. Donna Algase. R&P Jessica Perl. Adv. contact Bob Friel. B&W page USD 300; trim 6.75 x 10. Circ: 478 (paid).

M

610.73072 USA ISSN 1526-999X
RT81.5
RESEARCH FOR NURSING PRACTICE. Text in English. 1999. bi-m. USD 24 (effective 2004). adv. **Description:** Publishes research, case studies and other practice-based work developed by nurses in the practice setting.
Media: Online - full content.
Indexed: C06, C07, C08, CINAHL.
Published by: Graduate Research, LLC, 2917 E Manchester Dr, Tucson, AZ 85716. TEL 520-318-9946, FAX 520-318-3022. Ed., Pub. Naja McKenzie.

610.73 USA ISSN 0160-6891
RT81.5
➤ **RESEARCH IN NURSING & HEALTH.** Text in English. 1978. bi-m. GBP 867 in United Kingdom to institutions; EUR 1,097 in Europe to institutions; USD 1,572 in United States to institutions; USD 1,656 in Canada & Mexico to institutions; USD 1,698 elsewhere to institutions; GBP 998 combined subscription in United Kingdom to institutions (print & online eds.); EUR 1,262 combined subscription in Europe to institutions (print & online eds.); USD 1,809 combined subscription in United States to institutions (print & online eds.); USD 1,893 combined subscription in Canada & Mexico to institutions (print & online eds.); USD 1,935 combined subscription elsewhere to institutions (print & online eds.) (effective 2012). adv. back issues avail.; reprint service avail. from PSC. **Document type:** *Journal, Academic/Scholarly.* **Description:** Covers nursing practice, education and administration.
Related titles: Microform ed.: (from PQC); Online - full text ed.: ISSN 1098-240X. 1996. GBP 803 in United Kingdom to institutions; EUR 1,016 in Europe to institutions; USD 1,572 elsewhere to institutions (effective 2012).
Indexed: A20, A22, ASCA, ASSIA, AgeL, B28, C06, C07, C08, CINAHL, CurCont, E-psyche, EMBASE, ExcerpMed, F09, FR, FamI, H13, INI, IndMed, MEDLINE, NurAb, P02, P03, P10, P20, P24, P30, P48, P50, P53, P54, PQC, PsycInfo, PsycholAb, R10, Reac, SCI, SCOPUS, SOPODA, SSCI, SociolAb, THA, W07, W09.
—BLDSC (7750.150000), GNLM, IE, Infotrieve, Ingenta, INIST. **CCC.**
Published by: John Wiley & Sons, Inc., 111 River St, Hoboken, NJ 07030. TEL 201-748-6000, FAX 201-748-6088, info@wiley.com, http://www.wiley.com/WileyCDA/. Ed. Judith G Baggs TEL 503-494-1043. **Subscr. outside the Americas to:** John Wiley & Sons Ltd., The Atrium, Southern Gate, Chichester, West Sussex PO19 8SQ, United Kingdom. TEL 44-1243-779777, 800-243407, FAX 44-1243-775878, cs-journals@wiley.com.

610.73 CAN ISSN 1922-3129
LE RESEAU. Text in English, French. 2006. s-a. **Document type:** *Bulletin, Trade.*
Related titles: Online - full text ed.: free (effective 2010).
Published by: Interprofessional Federation of Quebec's Health, 1234, Papineau Ave, Montreal, PQ H2K 0A4, Canada. TEL 514-987-1141, 800-363-6541, info@fiqsante.qc.ca, http://www.fiqsante.qc.ca. Ed. Sylvie Charbonneau.

610.73 CAN ISSN 1920-6070
▼ **LE RESEAU DES JEUNES (ENGLISH EDITION).** Text in English. 2009. irreg. **Document type:** *Bulletin, Trade.*
Related titles: Online - full text ed.: ISSN 1920-6089. free (effective 2010).
Published by: Federation Interprofessionnelle de la Sante du Quebec, 1260 Blvd. Lebourgneuf, Bureau 300, Quebec, PQ G2K 2G2, Canada. TEL 418-626-2226, 800-463-6770, FAX 418-626-2111, info@fiqsante.qc.ca.

610.7365 USA ISSN 1542-2186
THE RESIDENT ASSISTANT; bi-monthly education for resident assistants in assisted living. Text in English. 1999 (Sept.). bi-m. USD 49 (effective 2002).
Published by: Frontline Publishing, P. O. Box 441002, Somerville, MA 02144. TEL 800-348-0605, FAX 617-625-7446, info@frontlinepub.com, http://www.frontlinepub.com. Ed. Martin Schumacher.

610.73 GBR
RESOURCES FOR NURSING RESEARCH; an annotated bibliography. Text in English. irreg., latest 2005, 4th ed. USD 67 per issue (effective 2010). **Document type:** *Directory, Bibliography.* **Description:** Provides a comprehensive bibliography of sources on nursing research, and includes references for books, journal papers and Internet resources.
Related titles: Online - full text ed.
Published by: (Chartered Institute of Library and Information Professionals (C I L I P)), Sage Publications Ltd. (Subsidiary of: Sage Publications, Inc.), 1 Oliver's Yard, 55 City Rd, London, EC1Y 1SP, United Kingdom. TEL 44-20-73248500, FAX 44-20-73248600, info@sagepub.co.uk, http://www.uk.sagepub.com/home.nav.

610.73 BRA ISSN 0034-7167
RT8.B6
➤ **REVISTA BRASILEIRA DE ENFERMAGEM.** Text in Portuguese; Abstracts in English. 1932. q. bk.rev. abstr.; bibl.; charts; illus.; stat. back issues avail. **Document type:** *Journal, Academic/Scholarly.* **Description:** Provides nurses and health professionals with information from different knowledge areas of nursing, aimed at scientific, technical and cultural development.
Formerly (until 1954): Anais de Enfermagen (0100-6843)
Related titles: Online - full text ed.: free (effective 2011).
Indexed: C01, C06, C07, C08, CINAHL, EMBASE, ExcerpMed, F09, IBR, IBZ, INI, MEDLINE, P30, R10, Reac, SCOPUS.
—BLDSC (7844.400000), GNLM. **CCC.**
Published by: Associacao Brasileira de Enfermagem, Av. L2 Norte Q. 603, Modulo B, Brasilia, DF, Brazil. TEL 55-61-2260653, FAX 55-61-2254473, reben@persocom.com.br, http://www.persocom.com.br/aben. Ed. Maria Therezinha Nobrega da Silva.

610.73 CUB ISSN 0864-0319
RT7.C9
REVISTA CUBANA DE ENFERMERIA. Text in Spanish; Summaries in English, French, Spanish. 1985. 3/yr. USD 26 in North America; USD 28 in South America; USD 30 elsewhere (effective 2005). bibl.; charts; illus. index. back issues avail. **Document type:** *Journal, Academic/Scholarly.*
Related titles: Online - full text ed.: ISSN 1561-2961. 1995. free (effective 2011).
Indexed: A01, C01, CA, INI, P30, SCOPUS, T02.
—BLDSC (7852.104000), GNLM.
Published by: (Centro Nacional de Informacion de Ciencias Medicas (C N I C M), Cuba. Ministerio de Salud Publica), Editorial Ciencias Medicas, Linea Esq 1, 10o, Vedado, Havana, 10400, Cuba. TEL 53-7-8323863, ecimed@infomed.sld.cu. Ed. Dania Silva Hernandez. Circ: 2,500. **Co-sponsor:** Sociedad Cubana de Enfermeria.

610.73 COL ISSN 1794-5232
REVISTA CULTURAL DEL CUIDADO ENFERMERIA. Key Title: Cultura del Cuidado Enfermeria. Text in Spanish. 2005. s-a. **Document type:** *Journal, Academic/Scholarly.*
Published by: Universidad Libre, Facultad de Ciencias de la Salud, Campus Universitario Belmonte, Ave. Sur, Pereira, Colombia. TEL 57-6-3155600, FAX 57-6-3155619. Ed. Maria Teresa Rodriguez.

610.73 ESP ISSN 1131-7957
REVISTA DE ENFERMERIA. Text in Spanish. 1990. s-a. **Document type:** *Journal, Academic/Scholarly.*
Published by: Universidad de Castilla-La Mancha, Escuela Universitaria de Enfermeria de Albacete, Campus de Albacete, Albacete, Spain.

610.73 BRA ISSN 2175-5361
➤ **REVISTA DE PESQUISA: CUIDADO E FUNDAMENTAL (ONLINE).** Text in Portuguese; Summaries in English. 1997-2006; resumed 2009. 3/yr. free (effective 2011). abstr.; bibl.; charts; illus.; maps; pat.; stat.; tr.mk.; tr.lit. back issues avail. **Document type:** *Journal, Academic/Scholarly.*
Former titles (until 2009): Revista de Pesquisa: Cuidado e Fundamental (Print) (1809-6107); (until 2001): Caderno de Pesquisa (1415-4285)
Media: Online - full text.
Indexed: C06, C07, T02.
Published by: Universidade Federal do Estado do Rio de Janeiro, Programa de Pos-Graduacao em Enfermagem, c/o Fernando Ramos Porto, Av. Pasteu 296, Urca, Rio de Janeiro, Brazil. TEL 51-21-25424517, FAX 51-21-25424517, http://www.unirio.br/propg/posgrad/stricto_paginas/site%20Enfermagem/SiteENFv3/index.htm. Eds. Carlos Roberto Lyra da Silva, Fernando Porto.

610.73 BRA ISSN 1518-1944
RT8.B6
REVISTA ELETRONICA DE ENFERMAGEM. Text in Multiple languages. 1999. s-a. free (effective 2011). **Document type:** *Journal, Academic/Scholarly.*
Media: Online - full text.
Indexed: C06, C07, C08, CA, CINAHL, F04, T02.
—IE. **CCC.**
Published by: Universidade Federal de Goias, Faculdade de Enfermagem, Rua 227 Qd 68 s/n, Setor Leste Universitario, Goiana, Goias 74605-080, Brazil. TEL 55-62-32096136, FAX 55-62-35211807.

610.73 BRA ISSN 0104-3552
REVISTA ENFERMAGEM. Text in Portuguese. 1993. s-a. BRL 100 to individuals; BRL 200 to institutions; BRL 50 to students (effective 2006). back issues avail. **Document type:** *Journal, Academic/Scholarly.*
Related titles: Online - full text ed.
Indexed: C01, C06, C07, C08, CINAHL.
Published by: Universidade do Estado do Rio de Janeiro, Faculdade de Enfermagem, Blvd. 28 de Setembro 157, 7o Andar, Sala 710, Vila Isabel, Rio de Janeiro, 20551-030, Brazil. TEL 55-21-25876335, FAX 55-21-25678177, revenf@uerj.br, http://www.uerj.br/modulos/kernel/index.php?pagina=54.

REVISTA ESTIMA. *see* MEDICAL SCIENCES—Gastroenterology

610.73 BRA ISSN 0102-6933
REVISTA GAUCHA DE ENFERMAGEM. Text in Burmese. 1976. s-a. abstr.; bibl. cum.index: 1976-1986, 1987-1990, 1991-1995. back issues avail. **Document type:** *Journal, Academic/Scholarly.* **Description:** Presents articles, research, and monographs done by nurses throughout Brazil.
Related titles: Online - full text ed.: free (effective 2011).
Indexed: C06, C07, C08, CINAHL, EMBASE, ExcerpMed, F09, INI, IndMed, MEDLINE, P30, R10, Reac, SCOPUS.
Published by: Universidade Federal do Rio Grande do Sul, Escola de Enfermagem, Rua Sao Manoel, 963, Campus da Saude, Porto Alegre, RGS 90620-110, Brazil. TEL 55-51-3165242, FAX 55-51-3321601, revista@enf.ufrgs.br, http://www.ufrgs.br/eenf/revist.htm. Ed. Maria da Graca Crossetti.

610.73 PRT ISSN 0874-7695
REVISTA INVESTIGACAO EM ENFERMAGEM. Text in Portuguese. 2000. bi-m. EUR 31 domestic to individuals; EUR 45 domestic to institutions; EUR 58 in Europe; EUR 87 elsewhere (effective 2006). back issues avail. **Document type:** *Journal, Academic/Scholarly.*
Published by: Formasau, Formacao e Saude, Ltda, Apdo 7067, Vale Gemil, Coimbra, 3041-801, Portugal. TEL 351-239-801020, http://www.sinaisvitais.pt/index.php?option=com_frontpage&Itemid=1.

610.73 BRA ISSN 0104-1169
➤ **REVISTA LATINO-AMERICANA DE ENFERMAGEM.** Text in English, Portuguese, Spanish. 1993. bi-m. BRL 60 domestic to individuals; BRL 100 domestic to institutions; USD 70 (effective 2003). abstr. **Document type:** *Journal, Academic/Scholarly.* **Description:** Covers issues about all areas of nursing: practice, education, research, policies, etc.
Related titles: Online - full text ed.: free (effective 2011).
Indexed: A01, A35, A36, A37, AgBio, C01, C06, C07, C08, CA, CABA, CINAHL, D01, E12, EMBASE, ExcerpMed, F04, F08, F09, GH, LT, MEDLINE, N02, N03, P03, P30, P33, PsycInfo, PsycholAb, R10, R12, RA&MP, RM&VM, RRTA, Reac, S12, SCI, SCOPUS, SSCI, T02, T05, TAR, W07, W11.
—BLDSC (7863.410000), IE, Infotrieve, Ingenta.
Published by: Universidade de Sao Paulo, Ribeirao Preto College of Nursing, Escola de Enfermagem de Ribeirao Preto, Av. Bandeirantes, 3900, Ribeirao Preto, Sao Paulo, 14040-902, Brazil. TEL 55-16-6023451, FAX 55-16-6333271. Ed. Dr. Maria Helena Palucci-Marziale.

610.73 PRY ISSN 1816-9260
REVISTA PARAGUAYA DE ENFERMERIA. Text in Spanish. 2005. s-a. **Document type:** *Magazine, Trade.*
Published by: Asociacion Paraguaya de Enfermeria, Eligio Ayala 1191 Esq Constitucion, 1er Piso, Asuncion, Paraguay. TEL 595-21-212350, FAX 595-21-211284, ape@ape.org.py, http://www.ape.org.py.

610.73 BRA ISSN 0100-8889
REVISTA PAULISTA DE ENFERMAGEM. Text in Portuguese. 1981. q. BRL 100 domestic to individuals; USD 100 foreign to individuals; BRL 200 domestic to institutions; USD 200 foreign to institutions (effective 2006). back issues avail. **Document type:** *Journal, Academic/Scholarly.*
Indexed: C06, C07, C08, CINAHL, P30.
—BLDSC (7869.564000).
Published by: Associacao Brasileira de Enfermagem, Secao Sao Paulo, Rua napoleao de Barros, 275, Vila Clementino, Sao Paulo, 04024-000, Brazil. TEL 55-11-55752288, abensp@netpoint.com.br. Ed. Leila Maria Rissi. Circ: 750.

REVISTA PERUANA DE OBSTETRICIA Y ENFERMERIA. *see* MEDICAL SCIENCES—Obstetrics And Gynecology

610.73 616.8 PRT ISSN 1647-2160
▼ **REVISTA PORTUGUESA DE ENFERMAGEM DE SAUDE MENTAL.** Text in Portuguese. 2009. s-a. **Document type:** *Magazine, Trade.*
Published by: Sociedade Portuguesa de Enfermagem de Saude Mental (S P E S M), Escola Superior de Enfermagem do Porto, Rua Dr. Antonio Bernardino de Almeida s/n, Porto, 4200, Portugal. secretariado@spesm.org.

658 ESP ISSN 0210-5020
REVISTA ROL DE ENFERMERIA. Text in Spanish. 1978. m. EUR 91.20 to individuals; EUR 182.40 to institutions (effective 2009). adv. back issues avail. **Document type:** *Newsletter, Consumer.* **Description:** Updates, developments, and research in nursing in hospitals, first aid, teaching, public health, health administration and management.
Related titles: Supplement(s): Revista Rol de Enfermeria. Formacion Permanente. ISSN 0212-8934. 1980.
Indexed: A22, C06, C07, C08, CINAHL, EMBASE, ExcerpMed, F09, MEDLINE, P30, R10, Reac, SCOPUS.
—BLDSC (7870.510000), GNLM, IE, Infotrieve, Ingenta. **CCC.**
Published by: Ediciones Rol S.A., Sepulveda 45-47, Esc. B Entrlo 2o, Barcelona, 08015, Spain. TEL 34-93-2008033, FAX 34-93-2002762, rol@e-rol.es. Ed. Julia Martinez Saavedra. Adv. contact Jose Garcia Rey. page EUR 1,370.31. Circ: 25,000.

610.73 URY ISSN 0797-6194
REVISTA URUGUAYA DE ENFERMERIA. Text in Spanish. 1989. 3/yr. charts; illus. back issues avail. **Document type:** *Journal, Academic/Scholarly.* **Description:** Its objective is to spread scientific and technical information on advances in the field of health, especially nursing. It also aims at building theories, revise methodologies and procedures and investigate unexplored issues.
Published by: (Universidad de la Republica, Instituto Nacional de Enfermeria, Universidad de la Republica, Colegio de Enfermeras del Uruguay), Ediciones Sciencias Biologicas, Nicaragua 2037, Montevideo, 11800, Uruguay. TEL 598-2-401 5159, FAX 598-2-401 5159. Pub. Pablo Anzalone.

610.73 FRA ISSN 1293-8505
➤ **REVUE DE L'INFIRMIERE.** Text in French. 1951. 10/yr. EUR 174 in Europe to institutions; EUR 154.75 in France to institutions; JPY 19,500 in Japan to institutions; USD 226 elsewhere to institutions (effective 2012). adv. bk.rev. charts; illus. index. back issues avail. **Document type:** *Journal, Academic/Scholarly.* **Description:** Offers practical, up-to-date information on all aspects of nursing.
Formerly (until 1971): Revue de l'Infirmiere et de l'Assistante Sociale (0397-7900)
Related titles: Online - full text ed.; Supplement(s): Revue de l'Infirmiere. Informations. ISSN 0397-7897. 1974.
Indexed: A22, AMED, C06, C07, DentInd, EMBASE, ExcerpMed, F09, FR, INI, MEDLINE, P30, PdeR, R10, Reac, S02, S03, SCOPUS.
—BLDSC (7924.170000), GNLM, IE, Ingenta, INIST. **CCC.**
Published by: Elsevier Masson (Subsidiary of: Elsevier Health Sciences), 62 Rue Camille Desmoulins, Issy les Moulineaux, Cedex 92442, France. TEL 33-1-71165500, FAX 33-1-71165600, infos@elsevier-masson.fr. Circ: 60,000.

610.73 FRA ISSN 1879-3991
▼ **REVUE DE SANTE SCOLAIRE ET UNIVERSITAIRE.** Text in French. 2010. bi-m. EUR 102 domestic to institutions; EUR 128 in Europe to institutions (except France); JPY 15,400 in Japan to institutions; USD 166 elsewhere to institutions (effective 2011). **Document type:** *Journal, Academic/Scholarly.*
—**CCC.**
Published by: Elsevier Masson (Subsidiary of: Elsevier Health Sciences), 62 Rue Camille Desmoulins, Issy les Moulineaux, Cedex 92442, France. TEL 33-1-71165500, FAX 33-1-71165600, infos@elsevier-masson.fr, http://www.elsevier-masson.fr. Ed. Yasmina Oouharzoune.

610.73 200 USA ISSN 1932-6998
RIGHTEOUS NURSE MAGAZINE. Text in English. 2006. q. USD 22 (effective 2007). adv. **Document type:** *Magazine, Trade.* **Description:** Presents current nursing practices and Christian faith for nurses and other healthcare professionals to share through stories, poems, devotionals and the latest in news in nursing education and health care.
Published by: Righteous Nurse, PO Box 7031, Sherwood, AR 72124. TEL 501-772-2556, righteousnursemag@righteousnurse.com. Circ: 5,000.

610.73 JPN ISSN 0386-7722
RINSHO KANGO/JAPANESE JOURNAL OF CLINICAL NURSING, MONTHLY. Text in Japanese. 1975. m. JPY 18,480; JPY 1,155 newsstand/cover (effective 2007). **Document type:** *Journal, Academic/Scholarly.*
Published by: Herusu Shuppan/Herusu Publishing Co. Inc., 2-2-3 Nakano, Nakano-ku, Tokyo, 164-0001, Japan. TEL 81-3-33848035, info@herusu-shuppan.co.jp.

610.73 ESP ISSN 1577-242X
S E M A P. REVISTA. (Sociedad de Enfermeria Madrilena de Atencion Primaria) Text in Spanish. 2000. 3/yr. back issues avail. **Document type:** *Magazine, Trade.*
Published by: Sociedad de Enfermeria Madrilena de Atencion Primaria (S E M A P), Apartado de Correos 202067, Madrid, 28080, Spain. TEL 34-91-646383440, SEMAP@SEMAP.ORG.

610.73 BRA ISSN 1414-4425
S O B E C C. REVISTA. (Sociedade Brasileira de Enfermeiros de Centro Cirurgico) Text in Portuguese. 1996. q. **Document type:** *Magazine, Trade.*
Indexed: C06, C07.

Published by: Sociedade Brasileira de Enfermeiros de Centro Cirurgico (S O B E C C), Rua Vergueiro 875, Conj 21, Liberdade, Sao Paulo, SP 01504-001, Brazil. TEL 55-11-33414044, FAX 55-11-32081285, sobecc@sobecc.org.br, http://www.sobecc.org.br.

SABIOS - REVISTA DE SAUDE E BIOLOGIA. *see* BIOLOGY

610.73 FIN ISSN 0785-7527
SAIRAANHOITAJA. Text in Finnish. 1984. m. EUR 80 (effective 2005). adv. **Document type:** *Magazine, Trade.*
Supersedes in part (in 1984): Tehy (0358-4038)
Related titles: Online - full text ed.
Indexed: C06, C07, C08, CINAHL, P30, SCOPUS.
Published by: Suomen Sairaanhoitajaliitto ry, Asemamiehenkatu 4, Helsinki, 00520, Finland. TEL 358-9-2290020, http://www.sairaanhoitajaliitto.fi. Ed. Kaarina Wilskman TEL 358-9-22900233. Adv. contact Rita Valtakari. B&W page EUR 1,310, color page EUR 2,030. Circ: 44,000.

610.73 CAN ISSN 1180-3983
SANTE QUEBEC. Text in French, English. 1990. q. CAD 20; CAD 0.25 foreign (effective 1999). adv. bk.rev. back issues avail. **Document type:** *Bulletin.* **Description:** Contains information for nursing assistants.
Indexed: P30.
Published by: Ordre des Infirmieres et Infirmiers Auxiliaires du Quebec, 531 Sherbrooke E, Montreal, PQ H2L 1K2, Canada. TEL 514-282-9511, FAX 514-282-0631. R&P Francine Saucier TEL 514-282-8511. Adv. contact Francine Soucier. B&W page CAD 1,000, color page CAD 1,300; 10.5 x 8.

610.73 CAN ISSN 1494-7668
SASKATCHEWAN REGISTERED NURSES' ASSOCIATION. NEWSBULLETIN. Variant title: S R N A Newsbulletin. Text in English. 1948. bi-m. CAD 20; USD 30 foreign (effective 1999). adv. bk.rev. **Document type:** *Bulletin, Academic/Scholarly.* **Description:** Information about the association's activities in nursing education.
Former titles (until 1999): Saskatchewan ConceRN (0836-7310); (until 1987): Saskatchewan Registered Nurses' Association. News Bulletin (0319-8499)
Related titles: Online - full text ed.
Indexed: C03, C06, C07, C08, CBCARef, CINAHL, P24, P30, P48, PQC, SCOPUS.
Published by: Saskatchewan Registered Nurses' Association, 2066 Retallack St, Regina, SK S4T 7X5, Canada. TEL 306-359-4245, FAX 306-525-0849. Ed. Joy Johnson. Adv. contact Linda Laxdal. Circ: 10,000.

SCANDINAVIAN JOURNAL OF PRIMARY HEALTH CARE. *see* MEDICAL SCIENCES

SCANDINAVIAN JOURNAL OF PRIMARY HEALTH CARE. SUPPLEMENT. *see* MEDICAL SCIENCES

SCHOOL HEALTH. *see* EDUCATION—School Organization And Administration

610.73 USA ISSN 1048-3896
SCHOOL HEALTH ALERT. Text in English. 1986. m. (10/yr.). USD 39 domestic (effective 2005). adv. bk.rev. **Document type:** *Newsletter.* **Description:** Addresses the needs of school nurses, health educators, and special education teachers and administrators to remain current with professional, and clinical matters.
Address: P.O. Box 150127, Nashville, TN 37215. TEL 615-370-7899, FAX 615-370-9993. Eds. Dr. Jan Ozias, Richard M. Adams. Pub. Robert Andrews. Circ: 9,500 (paid).

610.73 USA ISSN 1080-7543
SCHOOL NURSE NEWS; the independent voice of all school nurses. Text in English. 1994 (vol.11). 5/yr. USD 16 (effective 2007). adv. illus. **Document type:** *Journal, Trade.* **Description:** Aims to present readers with an unbiased overview of current and relevant information for school nurses to evaluate and incorporate in their school nurse practice, as they promote optimal health care and facilitate educational endeavors for students, their families, faculty and staff.
Formerly: Community Nurse Forum
Indexed: C06, C07, C08, CA, CINAHL, EMBASE, ExcerpMed, MEDLINE, P30, R10, Reac, SCOPUS, T02.
—**CCC.**
Published by: Franklin Communications, Inc., 53 Stickle Ave, Ste 1, Rockaway, NJ 07866. TEL 973-625-8811, FAX 973-625-7914. Ed. Deb Ilardi. adv.: B&W page USD 1,950; trim 8.125 x 10.875. Circ: 10,000 (paid).

610.73 DEU ISSN 1612-2631
SCHRIFTEN ZUR PFLEGEWISSENSCHAFT. Text in German. 2003. irreg., latest vol.3, 2006. price varies. **Document type:** *Monographic series, Academic/Scholarly.*
Published by: Verlag Dr. Kovac, Leverkusenstr 13, Hamburg, 22761, Germany. TEL 49-40-3988800, FAX 49-40-39888055, info@verlagdrkovac.de.

610.73 DEU ISSN 0340-5303
DIE SCHWESTER - DER PFLEGER; die Fachzeitschrift fuer Pflegeberufe. Text in German. 1962. m. EUR 45 domestic; EUR 52.20 foreign; EUR 7 newsstand/cover (effective 2010). adv. bk.rev. **Document type:** *Journal, Academic/Scholarly.*
Incorporates (in 2006): Pflege Aktuell (0944-8918); Which was formerly (until 1993): Krankenpflege (0944-9183); (until 1972): Die Agnes-Karll-Schwester, Der Krankenpfleger (0944-9175); (until 1967): Die Agnes-Karll-Schwester (0944-9167)
Related titles: Online - full text ed.; ◆ Supplement(s): Die Schwester - Der Pfleger Plus. ISSN 1866-9611.
Indexed: DokArb.
—GNLM, IE, Infotrieve.
Published by: Bibliomed - Medizinische Verlagsgesellschaft mbH, Postfach 1150, Melsungen, 34201, Germany. TEL 49-5661-73440, FAX 49-5661-8360, info@bibliomed.de. Ed. Markus Boucsein. Adv. contact Waltraud Zemke TEL 49-5661-734481. Circ: 53,383 (paid and controlled).

610.73 JPN ISSN 1344-1922
SEI ROKA KANGO GAKKAISHI/ST. LUKE'S SOCIETY FOR NURSING RESEARCH. JOURNAL. Text in Japanese. 1998. s-a. free to members. **Document type:** *Journal, Academic/Scholarly.*
Indexed: C06, C07, C08, CINAHL.
—BLDSC (4903.250000). **CCC.**
Published by: Sei Roka Kango Gakkai/Luke's Society for Nursing Research, St. Luke's College of Nursing, 10-1 Akashi-cho, Chuoku, Tokyo, 104-0044, Japan. TEL 81-3-35436391, FAX 81-3-55651626, http://slnr.umin.jp/.

610.73 616.7 JPN ISSN 1342-4718
SEIKEI-GEKA KANGO/JAPANESE JOURNAL OF ORTHOPEDIC NURSING. Text in Japanese. 1996. m. JPY 20,412; JPY 1,890 newsstand/cover (effective 2007). Supplement avail. **Document type:** *Journal, Academic/Scholarly.*
Published by: Medicus Shuppan/Medicus Publishing Inc., 18-24 Hiroshiba-cho, Suita-shi, Osaka-fu 564-8580, Japan. TEL 81-6-63856911, FAX 81-6-63856873, http://www.medica.co.jp/.

SEISHIN KANGO/PSYCHIATRIC MENTAL HEALTH NURSING. *see* MEDICAL SCIENCES—Psychiatry And Neurology

610.73 USA
➤ **SELF-CARE, DEPENDENT-CARE & NURSING.** Text in English. 1994. 3/yr. back issues avail. **Document type:** *Journal, Academic/Scholarly.*
Formerly (until 2002): The International Orem Society Newsletter (1081-7700)
Related titles: Online - full text ed.
Indexed: C06, C07, C08, CINAHL.
Published by: International Orem Society for Nursing Science and Scholarship, S28 School of Nursing, University of Missouri, Columbia, MO 65211. Ed. Violeta Berbiglia.

610.736 616.992 USA ISSN 0749-2081
SEMINARS IN ONCOLOGY NURSING. Text in English. 1985. q. USD 298 in United States to institutions; USD 402 elsewhere to institutions (effective 2012). adv. bibl.; charts; illus. index. back issues avail.; reprints avail. **Document type:** *Journal, Academic/Scholarly.* **Description:** Focuses on a single topic and keeps readers abreast of the latest innovations, research findings, applications, and methods in the field.
Related titles: Online - full text ed.: ISSN 1878-3449 (from ScienceDirect).
Indexed: A22, A26, AMED, ASSIA, C06, C07, C08, CINAHL, EMBASE, ExcerpMed, FR, H12, I05, INI, IndMed, MEDLINE, NurAb, P30, R10, Reac, SCOPUS, T02.
—BLDSC (8239.456600), GNLM, IE, Infotrieve, Ingenta, INIST. **CCC.**
Published by: W.B. Saunders Co. (Subsidiary of: Elsevier Health Sciences), Elsevier, Health Sciences Division, Order Fulfillment, 3251 Riverport Ln, Maryland Heights, MO 63043. TEL 314-872-8370, 800-325-4177, FAX 314-432-1380, JournalCustomerService-usa@elsevier.com, http://www.us.elsevierhealth.com. Ed. Connie H Yarbro. Pub. Shannon Magee TEL 215-239-3730. Adv. contact Barbara Blum TEL 215-239-3156.

610.73 CAN ISSN 1192-5299
SERVO. Text in English, French. 1967. 2/yr. CAD 5. adv. back issues avail. **Document type:** *Newsletter.* **Description:** For hospital auxiliary volunteers.
Published by: Association of Hospital Auxiliaries of the Province of Quebec, 505 Maisonneuve W, Ste 400, Montreal, PQ H3A 3C2, Canada. TEL 514-282-4264, FAX 514-282-4289. Adv. contact Andree Quinn. Circ: 300.

610.73 CZE ISSN 1210-0404
SESTRA. Text in Czech. 1951. 10/yr. CZK 600 (effective 2011). adv. illus. Supplement avail. **Document type:** *Magazine, Trade.*
Formerly (until 1991): Zdravotnicka Pracovnice (0049-8572)
Related titles: Online - full content ed.: CZK 300 (effective 2007).
Indexed: INI, P30.
Published by: (Ceska Lekarska Spolecnost J.E. Purkyne/Czech Medical Association), Mlada Fronta, Mezi Vodami 1952/9, Prague 4, 14300, Czech Republic. TEL 420-2-25276201, FAX 420-2-25276222, online@mf.cz, http://www.mf.cz. Ed. Martina Pelikanova TEL 420-2-25276355. Adv. contact Lenka Mihulkova.

610.73 SVK ISSN 1335-9444
SESTRA. Text in Slovak. 2002. 6/yr. EUR 13.54; EUR 2.06 newsstand/cover (effective 2009). adv. **Document type:** *Magazine, Trade.*
Published by: Sanoma Magazines Slovakia s.r.o., Kutlikova 17, Bratislava, 851 02, Slovakia. TEL 421-2-32150111, FAX 421-2-63830093, info@sanomaslovakia.sk. Ed. Vlasta Husarova. Adv. contact Milos Inger. color page EUR 1,710; trim 210 x 280. Circ: 6,000 (paid and controlled).

610.73 616.3 JPN ISSN 1341-7819
SHOKAKI GEKA NURSING/GASTROENTEROLOGICAL SURGERY NURSING. Text in Japanese. 1995. bi-m. JPY 20,412; JPY 1,890 newsstand/cover (effective 2007). Supplement avail. **Document type:** *Journal, Academic/Scholarly.*
Published by: Medicus Shuppan/Medicus Publishing Inc., 18-24 Hiroshiba-cho, Suita-shi, Osaka-fu 564-8580, Japan. TEL 81-6-63856911, FAX 81-6-63856873, http://www.medica.co.jp/.

610.7362 JPN ISSN 0386-6289
SHONI KANGO/JAPANESE JOURNAL OF CHILD NURSING, MONTHLY. Text in Japanese. 1978. m. JPY 17,640; JPY 1,260 newsstand/cover (effective 2007). **Document type:** *Journal, Academic/Scholarly.*
Published by: Herusu Shuppan/Herusu Publishing Co. Inc., 2-2-3 Nakano, Nakano-ku, Tokyo, 164-0001, Japan. TEL 81-3-33848035, info@herusu-shuppan.co.jp.

610.73 SGP
SINGAPORE NURSING JOURNAL. Text in English. 1972. q. SGD 40 domestic; SGD 80 foreign (effective 2007). adv. **Document type:** *Magazine, Trade.* **Description:** Contains president's message, from the editor's desk, clinical focus, research education, words of wisdom, occasional papers, local and international news and reports.
Former titles (until 1998): Professional Nurse (0218-0995); (until 1987): Nursing Journal of Singapore - Berita Jururawat (0067-5814); S T N A Newsletter
Indexed: C06, C07, C08, CINAHL, DiabCont, INI, P30, SCOPUS.
Published by: Singapore Nurses' Association, 77 Maude Rd, Singapore, 208353, Singapore. TEL 65-63920770, sna@sna.org.sg. Circ: 4,000.

610.73 SWE
SKANDINAVIEN DIREKT. Text in Swedish. 1999. 13/yr. free to qualified personnel; SEK 35 newsstand/cover. adv. **Document type:** *Magazine, Trade.*
Published by: Florence Kompetensutveckling AB, Box 3348, Stockholm, 10367, Sweden. TEL 46-8-10-66-00, FAX 46-8-10-25-04, http://www.florence.se. Ed. Anna-Karin Andersson. Adv. contact Magnus Sjoeberg. page SEK 39,000; trim 250 x 370. Circ: 12,000 (controlled).

610.7309411 GBR
SKILLS4NURSES. Text in English. 2008. m. GBP 2 per issue (effective 2009). back issues avail. **Document type:** *Magazine, Trade.* **Description:** Contains information on all aspects of nursing and midwifery as well as other areas in the health and caring professions.
Formed by the merger of (1998-2007): Irish Nurse (1463-3817); (1995-2007): Scottish Nurse (1361-4177)
Related titles: Online - full text ed.
Indexed: B28, C06, C07, C08, CINAHL.
—BLDSC (4574.390000), IE. **CCC.**
Published by: Strathayr Publishing Ltd., Gibbs Yard, Auchincruive, Ayr, Scotland KA8 8BG, United Kingdom. TEL 44-1292-525970, FAX 44-1292-525979, strathayrltd@btclick.com, http://www.scottishirishhealthcare.com. Ed. Shona McMahon TEL 44-1292-525978. Adv. contact Elaine Patterson TEL 44-1292-525973. Circ: 60,000.

610.73 SWE ISSN 0284-284X
SKOLHAELSAN. Text in Swedish. 1993. q. SEK 150; SEK 50 newsstand/cover (effective 2000 & 2001). **Document type:** *Trade.*
Published by: (Riksfoereningen foer Skolskoeterskor), Via Media, PO Box 640, Landskrona, 26125, Sweden. TEL 46-418-10780, FAX 46-418-12394. Ed. Kaerstin Loeoef. Circ: 2,300 (paid).

610.73 SWE ISSN 1653-6533
SKRIFTSERIE I VAARDVETENSKAP. Text in Swedish. 1997. irreg. price varies. back issues avail. **Document type:** *Monographic series, Academic/Scholarly.*
Formerly (until 2006): Oerebro Universitet. Institutionen foer Vaardvetenskap. Skrift (1402-1439)
Published by: (Oerebro Universitet, Haelsovetenskapliga Institutionen/University of Oerebro. Department of Health Sciences), Oerebro Universitet, Universitetsbiblioteket/University of Oerebro. University Library, Fakultetsgatan 1, Oerebro, 70182, Sweden. TEL 46-19-303240, FAX 46-19-331217, biblioteket@ub.oru.se. Ed. Joanna Jansdotter.

610.736 SWE ISSN 1402-1048
SMAERTA. Text in Swedish. 1996. q. SEK 250; SEK 70 newsstand/cover (effective 2000 & 2001). **Document type:** *Trade.*
Published by: (Riksfoereningen mot Smaerta), Via Media, PO Box 640, Landskrona, 26125, Sweden. TEL 46-418-10780, FAX 46-418-12394. Ed. Leena Sundberg. Circ: 2,500 (paid).

SOCIEDAD ESPANOLA DE ENFERMERIA NEFROLOGICA. REVISTA. *see* MEDICAL SCIENCES—Urology And Nephrology

610.73 BRA ISSN 1676-3793
SOCIEDADE BRASILEIRA DE INFERMEIROS PEDIATRAS. REVISTA. Text in Portuguese. 2001. s-a. BRL 40 domestic to individuals; BRL 60 domestic to institutions; USD 50 foreign (effective 2006). **Document type:** *Magazine, Trade.*
Published by: Sociedade Brasileira de Infermeiros Pediatras, c/o Escola de Enfermagem Anna Nary/UFRJ, Rua Afonso Cavalcanti 275, Cidade Nova, Rio de Janeiro, 20211-110, Brazil. http://www.ellusaude.com.br/sociedades/sobep/. Circ: 1,000.

610.73 JPN ISSN 0038-0660
SOGO KANGO; comprehensive nursing quarterly. Text in Japanese. 1966. q. JPY 4,800 (effective 2007). adv. bk.rev. **Document type:** *Journal, Academic/Scholarly.*
Indexed: INI, P30, SCOPUS.
Published by: Gendaisha/Gendaisha Publishing Co. Ltd., 514, Waseda-Tsurumakicho, Shinjukuku, Tokyo, 162, Japan. TEL 81-3-32035061, FAX 81-3-32035217, eigyou@gendaisha.co.jp, http://www.gendaisha.co.jp/. Circ: 12,000.

610.73 FRA ISSN 0038-0814
SOINS; la revue de reference infirmiere. Text in French. 1956. 10/yr. EUR 263 in Europe to institutions; EUR 198.82 in France to institutions; JPY 37,700 in Japan to institutions; USD 336 elsewhere to institutions (effective 2012). bk.rev. **Document type:** *Journal, Academic/Scholarly.* **Description:** Covers management, communication, health, psychology, education as they relate to nursing and nurses.
Related titles: Online - full text ed.
Indexed: AMED, C06, C07, EMBASE, ExcerpMed, F09, FR, INI, MEDLINE, P30, PdeR, R10, Reac, S02, S03, SCOPUS.
—BLDSC (8327.117000), GNLM, IE, Infotrieve, Ingenta, INIST. **CCC.**
Published by: Elsevier Masson (Subsidiary of: Elsevier Health Sciences), 62 Rue Camille Desmoulins, Issy les Moulineaux, Cedex 92442, France. TEL 33-1-71165500, infos@elsevier-masson.fr. Circ: 30,000.

610.73 FRA ISSN 1770-9857
SOINS AIDES SOIGNANTES. Text in French. 2004. bi-m. EUR 104 in Europe to institutions; EUR 81.29 in France to institutions; JPY 16,200 in Japan to institutions; USD 135 elsewhere to institutions (effective 2012). **Document type:** *Journal, Academic/Scholarly.*
Indexed: SCOPUS.
—**CCC.**
Published by: Elsevier Masson (Subsidiary of: Elsevier Health Sciences), 62 Rue Camille Desmoulins, Issy les Moulineaux, Cedex 92442, France. TEL 33-1-71165500, infos@elsevier-masson.fr.

610.73 FRA ISSN 1961-3989
SOINS & PREUVES; relier la recherche aux pratiques. Text in French. 2007. irreg. **Document type:** *Journal, Trade.*
Published by: RanD, 212 Av. Paul Doumer, Rueil-Malamaison, Cedex 92508, France. TEL 33-1-41422020, cschoen@gtnholding.com.

610.736 FRA ISSN 1268-6034
SOINS GERONTOLOGIE; la revue de tous les acteurs du soin a la personne agee. Text in French. 1996. 5/yr. EUR 202 in Europe to institutions; EUR 160.63 in France to institutions; JPY 29,000 in Japan to institutions; USD 260 elsewhere to institutions (effective 2012). **Document type:** *Journal, Academic/Scholarly.*
Incorporates (2003-2006): Revue du Soignant en Geriatrie (1760-2882)
Related titles: Online - full text ed.
Indexed: A22, C06, EMBASE, ExcerpMed, F09, INI, MEDLINE, P30, R10, Reac, SCOPUS.
—BLDSC (8327.117270), INIST. **CCC.**
Published by: Elsevier Masson (Subsidiary of: Elsevier Health Sciences), 62 Rue Camille Desmoulins, Issy les Moulineaux, Cedex 92442, France. TEL 33-1-71165500, infos@elsevier-masson.fr.

610.73 FRA ISSN 1259-4792
SOINS PEDIATRIE - PUERICULTURE; la revue de tous les acteurs du soin a l'enfant. Text in French. 1980. 6/yr. EUR 202 in Europe to institutions; EUR 160.63 in France to institutions; JPY 29,700 in Japan to institutions; USD 263 elsewhere to institutions (effective 2012). **Document type:** *Journal, Academic/Scholarly.* **Description:** Each issue covers a clinical case.
Former titles (until 1995): Soins - Gynecologie, Obstetrique, Puericulture, Pediatrie (0766-1193); (until 1981): Soins - Gynecologie, Obstetrique, Puericulture (0151-6655)
Related titles: Online - full text ed.
Indexed: A22, C06, EMBASE, ExcerpMed, F09, INI, MEDLINE, P30, R10, Reac, SCOPUS.
—BLDSC (8327.117550), GNLM, IE, Infotrieve, Ingenta, INIST. **CCC.**
Published by: Elsevier Masson (Subsidiary of: Elsevier Health Sciences), 62 Rue Camille Desmoulins, Issy les Moulineaux, Cedex 92442, France. TEL 33-1-71165500, infos@elsevier-masson.fr. Circ: 5,000.

610.73 616.8 FRA ISSN 0241-6972
SOINS PSYCHIATRIE; la revue de tous les acteurs du soin et sante mentale. Text in French. 1980. 6/yr. EUR 202 in Europe to institutions; EUR 152.79 in France to institutions; JPY 29,000 in Japan to institutions; USD 260 elsewhere to institutions (effective 2012). **Document type:** *Journal, Academic/Scholarly.* **Description:** Specializes in the training of psychiatric nurses.
Related titles: Online - full text ed.
Indexed: A22, C06, C07, E-psyche, EMBASE, ExcerpMed, F09, MEDLINE, P30, R10, Reac, SCOPUS.
—BLDSC (8327.117600), GNLM, IE, Infotrieve, Ingenta, INIST. **CCC.**
Published by: Elsevier Masson (Subsidiary of: Elsevier Health Sciences), 62 Rue Camille Desmoulins, Issy les Moulineaux, Cedex 92442, France. TEL 33-1-71165500, infos@elsevier-masson.fr. Circ: 5,000.

610.73 USA ISSN 0038-335X
SOUTH DAKOTA NURSE. Text in English. m. USD 247 membership (effective 2005).
Indexed: C06, C07, C08, CINAHL, P30.
—BLDSC (8351.300000).
Published by: South Dakota Nurses Association, P O Box 1015, Pierre, SD 57501-1015. TEL 605-945-4265, FAX 605-945-4266, sdnurse@midco.net, http://www.nursingworld.org.

610.73 USA ISSN 1538-0696
RT81.5
SOUTHERN ONLINE JOURNAL OF NURSING RESEARCH. Text in English. 1999. 8/yr.
Media: Online - full text.
Indexed: C06, C07, C08, CINAHL, P30.
Published by: Southern Nursing Research Society, PO Box 870388, Tuscaloosa, AL 35487-0388. TEL 877-314-7677, info@snrs.org.

610.73 USA ISSN 0272-1473
SPRINGER SERIES ON THE TEACHING OF NURSING. Text in English. 1977. irreg., latest 2001. price varies. back issues avail. **Document type:** *Monographic series, Academic/Scholarly.* **Description:** Deals with various aspects of professional training in nursing.
Published by: Springer Publishing Company, 11 W 42nd St, 15th Fl, New York, NY 10036. TEL 212-431-4370, FAX 212-941-7842, contactus@springerpub.com, http://www.springerpub.com. Ed. Patricia Moccia. R&P Dorothy Kouwenberg.

610.73 USA ISSN 1520-3107
➤ **STANFORD NURSE.** Text in English. 1984. s-a. free to qualified personnel. illus. **Document type:** *Newsletter, Trade.* **Description:** Discusses ways in which nurses can and have enhanced their profession and their own fulfillment.
Related titles: Online - full content ed.
Indexed: C06, C07, C08, CINAHL.
—BLDSC (8432.590000), IE.
Published by: Stanford Hospital and Clinics, Division of Patient Care Services, Center for Education and Professional Development, 300 Pasteur Dr, MC 5534, Stanford, CA 94305. Ed. Suzanne Taylor. Pub. Cindy Day.

610.73 USA ISSN 0038-9986
STAT (MADISON). Text in English. 1941. m. free to members. illus. **Document type:** *Bulletin, Trade.*
Indexed: A26, C06, C07, C08, CINAHL, H12, I05, INI, P30, SCOPUS.
Published by: Wisconsin Nurses Association, 6117 Monona Dr, Madison, WI 53716-3932. TEL 608-221-0383, FAX 608-221-2788, info@wisconsinnurses.org, http://www.wisconsinnurses.org/. Circ: 2,700.

610.73 USA ISSN 1535-847X
STRATEGIES FOR NURSE MANAGERS. Text in English. 2001. m. USD 129 combined subscription (print or online eds.) (effective 2011). adv. 12 p./no.; **Document type:** *Newsletter, Trade.* **Description:** Provides nurse leaders like you with field-tested ideas, tips, and how-to's on managing effectively, gaining the respect of your peers and employees, recruiting and retaining the best staff, making the best of employee relations, and avoiding the number one pitfall of nurse managers - burnout.
Related titles: Online - full content ed.: ISSN 1937-7673. USD 99 (effective 2008).
Indexed: A26, H11, I05, P21, P24, P48, PQC.
—CCC.
Published by: H C Pro, Inc., 200 Hoods Ln, PO Box 1168, Marblehead, MA 01945. TEL 781-639-1872, 800-650-6787, FAX 781-639-7857, 800-639-8511, customerservice@hcpro.com, http://www.hcpro.com. Ed. Debbie Blumberg. Pub. Emily Sheahan.

STREIFLICHT. *see* HEALTH FACILITIES AND ADMINISTRATION

610.73 USA ISSN 1947-8968
STRESSED OUT NURSES WEEKLY. Text in English. 2006. w. free. back issues avail. **Document type:** *Newsletter, Trade.* **Description:** Provides nurses-aspiring, new, and experienced-with some respite from the fast-paced and demanding routines of daily life by offering a collection of humor, news, and other fun tidbits.
Media: Online - full content.
Published by: H C Pro, Inc., 200 Hoods Ln, PO Box 1168, Marblehead, MA 01945. TEL 781-639-1872, 800-650-6787, FAX 781-639-7857, 800-639-8511, customerservice@hcpro.com.

610.7365 USA
SUNRISE MAGAZINE; for you and your loved ones. Text in English. 2006 (Sum./Spr.). s-a. free (effective 2009); Dist. free to Sunrise Senior Living communities. back issues avail.; reprints avail. **Document type:** *Magazine, Consumer.* **Description:** Designed for family caregivers and their loved ones.
Published by: (Sunrise Senior Living Inc.), Haymarket Media Inc. (Subsidiary of: Haymarket Group Ltd.), 114 W 26th St, 4th Fl, New York, NY 10001. TEL 646-638-6000, FAX 646-638-6117, custserv@haymarketmedia.com, http://www.haymarket.com. Circ: 500,000.

610.73 DNK ISSN 0106-8350
SYGEPLEJERSKEN. Text in Danish. 1901. 22/yr. DKK 1,375; DKK 62.50 per issue (effective 2009). adv. bk.rev. illus. **Document type:** *Magazine, Academic/Scholarly.*
Former titles (until 1972): Tidsskrift for Sygeplejersker (0049-3856); (until 1950): Tidsskrift for Sygepleje (0909-4032)
Related titles: Online - full text ed.: ISSN 1601-7617. 1997.
Indexed: A22, C06, C07, C08, CINAHL, DentInd, F09, INI, IndMed, P30, SCOPUS.
—BLDSC (8579.400000), IE, Infotrieve, Ingenta. **CCC.**
Published by: Dansk Sygeplejeraad/Danish Nurses Organization, Sankt Annae Plads 30, PO Box 1084, Copenhagen K, 1250, Denmark. TEL 45-33-151555, FAX 45-33-152455, dsr@dsr.dk, www.dsr.dk. Ed. Sigurd Nissen-Petersen TEL 45-46-954193. Circ: 78,000.

610.7306 332.88 NOR ISSN 0806-7511
SYKEPLEIEN. Key Title: Tidsskriftet Sykepleien. Variant title: Sykepleienjobb. Text in Norwegian. 1995. 14/yr. NOK 798 (effective 2011). adv. bk.rev. **Document type:** *Journal, Trade.*
Formed by the merger of (1990-1995): Sykepleien. Journalen (0802-9776); Which was formerly (1912-1990): Sykepleien (0039-7628); (1992-1995): Sykepleien Fag (0804-1342); Which was formerly (1990-1992): Sykepleien Fagtidsskrift (0802-9768)
Related titles: Online - full text ed.; ◆ Includes: Sykepleien Forskning. ISSN 1890-2936.
Indexed: DentInd, INI, P30, SCOPUS.
—CCC.
Published by: Norsk Sykepleierforbund/Norwegian Nurses Association, Tollbugata 22, PO Box 456, Sentrum, Oslo, 0104, Norway. TEL 47-22-043200, FAX 47-22-043375, post@sykepleierforbundet.no, http://www.sykepleierforbundet.no. Ed. Ingunn Roald.

610.73 NOR ISSN 1890-2936
➤ **SYKEPLEIEN FORSKNING.** Text in Norwegian. 2006. q. **Document type:** *Magazine, Academic/Scholarly.*
Related titles: ◆ Issued with: Sykepleien. ISSN 0806-7511.
Indexed: T02.
Published by: Norsk Sykepleierforbund/Norwegian Nurses Association, Tollbugata 22, PO Box 456, Sentrum, Oslo, 0104, Norway. TEL 47-22-043200, FAX 47-22-043375, post@sykepleierforbundet.no, http://www.sykepleierforbundet.no. Circ: 80,000.

610.73 NLD ISSN 1380-3425
T V Z: TIJDSCHRIFT VOOR VERPLEEGKUNDIGEN. Text in Dutch. 1891. 10/yr. EUR 103.50 to individuals; EUR 169.25 to institutions; EUR 51.75 to students (effective 2008). adv. bk.rev. charts; illus. index. **Document type:** *Journal, Academic/Scholarly.* **Description:** Reports on issues of concern to nurses and other nursing professionals.
Former titles (until 1994): Tijdschrift voor Ziekenverpleging (0303-6456); (until 1914): Maandblad voor Ziekenverpleging (0926-342X)
Indexed: CISA, DentInd, INI, P30, S02, S03, SCOPUS.
—GNLM, IE, Infotrieve.
Published by: (Stichting Publikaties voor Verpleegkundigen en Verzorgenden), Elsevier Gezondheidszorg bv (Subsidiary of: Reed Business bv), Planetenbaan 80-99, Maarssen, 3606 AK, Netherlands. TEL 31-346-577577, marketing.gezondheidszorg@reedbusiness.nl, http://www.elseviergezondheidszorg.nl. Ed. Tonny van de Pasch. Pub. Ben Konings. adv.: B&W page EUR 1,589, color page EUR 2,868; trim 215 x 285. Circ: 4,450. **Subscr. to:** Elsevier Den Haag, Postbus 16500, The Hague 2500 BM, Netherlands. TEL 31-70-381-9900, FAX 31-70-333-8399.

610.73 KOR ISSN 0047-3618
RT1
TAEHAN KANHO/KOREAN NURSE. Text in Korean. 1961. bi-m. membership. adv. bk.rev. illus. **Document type:** *Journal, Academic/Scholarly.*
Related titles: CD-ROM ed.
Indexed: C06, C07, C08, CINAHL, ExtraMED, INI, P30, SCOPUS.
—Infotrieve.
Published by: Taehan Kanho Hyophoe/Korean Nurses' Association, 88-7 Sanglim-Dong, Choong Ku, Seoul, 100-400, Korea, S. TEL 82-2-22602511, FAX 82-2-22602519, edpsm@koreanurse.or.kr, http://www.koreanurse.or.kr/. Ed. San Cho Chun.

610.73 USA ISSN 0039-9620
TAR HEEL NURSE. Text in English. 1939. bi-m. free to members. adv. charts; illus. reprints avail. **Document type:** *Newsletter, Trade.*
Related titles: Microform ed.: (from PQC).
Indexed: A22, C06, C07, C08, CINAHL, EMBASE, ExcerpMed, INI, MEDLINE, P30, R10, Reac, SCOPUS.
Published by: North Carolina Nurses Association, PO Box 12025, Raleigh, NC 27605. TEL 919-821-4250, 800-626-2153, FAX 919-829-5807, rns@ncnurses.org, http://www.ncnurses.org. Ed., R&P Sindy Barker. Adv. contact Beth Holder. Circ: 3,500.

610.73 378 USA ISSN 1557-3087
RT1
➤ **TEACHING AND LEARNING IN NURSING.** Abbreviated title: T L N. Text in English. 2006 (Jun.). q. USD 152 in United States to institutions; USD 221 elsewhere to institutions (effective 2012). adv. back issues avail.; reprints avail. **Document type:** *Journal, Academic/Scholarly.* **Description:** Focuses on the advancement of associate degree nursing education and practice, and promotes collaboration in charting the future of health care education and delivery.
Related titles: Online - full text ed.: ISSN 1557-2013. 2006 (Jun.) (from ScienceDirect).
Indexed: A26, ASSIA, C06, C07, C08, CA, CINAHL, E03, H12, I05, SCOPUS, T02.
—BLDSC (8614.004200), IE. **CCC.**
Published by: (National Organization of Associate Degree Nursing), Elsevier Inc. (Subsidiary of: Elsevier Science & Technology), 1600 John F Kennedy Blvd, Philadelphia, PA 19103. TEL 215-239-3900, FAX 215-238-7883, JournalCustomerService-usa@elsevier.com, http://www.elsevier.com. Ed. Maris Lown TEL 732-224-2418. Pub. Jami Walker TEL 314-447-8987. Adv. contact Barbara Blum TEL 215-239-3156. Circ: 1,305.

610.73 FIN ISSN 0358-4038
TEHY. Text in Finnish, Swedish. 1981. 20/yr. adv. bk.rev.; film rev. bibl.; charts; illus. **Document type:** *Magazine, Trade.*
Formed by the merger of (1967-1981): Laboratoriohoitaja (0788-2777); (1961-1981): Lastenhoitajalehti (0355-5089); (1966-1981): Sairaanhoitaja (0036-3278); Which was formed by the merger of (1925-1966): Sairaanhoitajalehti (0788-3420); (1908-1966): Epione (0788-3412)
Indexed: P30, SCOPUS.
Published by: Tehy ry/Union of Health and Social Care Services, TEHY, P O Box 40, Tehy, 00060, Finland. TEL 358-9-1552700, FAX 358-9-1483038. Ed. Satu Vasantola. adv.: B&W page EUR 1,880, color page EUR 3,170; 217 x 280. Circ: 110,000.

610.73 CAN ISSN 1912-0265
TENDANCES DE LA MAIN-D'OEUVRE DES INFIRMIERES ET INFIRMIERS AUTORISES AU CANADA (ONLINE). Text in French. 1999. a. **Document type:** *Journal, Trade.*
Formerly (until 2002): Nombre et Repartition des Infirmieres et Infirmiers Autorises au Canada (1912-0249)
Media: Online - full text. **Related titles:** ◆ Print ed.: Tendances de la Main-d'Oeuvre des Infirmieres et Infirmiers Autorises au Canada (Print). ISSN 1709-7525; English ed.: Workforce Trends of Licensed Practical Nurses in Canada (Online). ISSN 1910-8850.
Published by: Canadian Institute for Health Information/Institut Canadien d'Information sur la Sante, 377 Dalhousie St, Ste 200, Ottawa, ON K1N 9N8, Canada. TEL 613-241-7860, FAX 613-241-8120, nursing@cihi.ca, http://www.cihi.ca.

610.73 CAN ISSN 1709-7525
CA1H115-18
TENDANCES DE LA MAIN-D'OEUVRE DES INFIRMIERES ET INFIRMIERS AUTORISES AU CANADA (PRINT). Text in French. 1999. a. **Document type:** *Journal, Trade.* **Description:** A reference document that can be used to support registered nursing research and planning.
Formerly (until 2002): Nombre et Repartition des Infirmierseres Autorisesees au Canada (1497-0589)
Related titles: ◆ Online - full text ed.: Tendances de la Main-d'Oeuvre des Infirmieres et Infirmiers Autorises au Canada (Online). ISSN 1912-0265; English ed.: Workforce Trends of Licensed Practical Nurses in Canada. ISSN 1711-0688.
Published by: Canadian Institute for Health Information/Institut Canadien d'Information sur la Sante, 377 Dalhousie St, Ste 200, Ottawa, ON K1N 9N8, Canada. TEL 613-241-7860, FAX 613-241-8120, http://www.cihi.ca.

610.736 331.1 CAN ISSN 1711-0459
CA1H115-20
TENDANCES DE LA MAIN-D'OEUVRE DES INFIRMIERES ET INFIRMIERS PSYCHIATRIQUES AUTORISES AU CANADA. Text in French. 2002. a. **Document type:** *Journal, Trade.*
Related titles: Online - full text ed.: ISSN 1910-9695. 2003; ◆ English ed.: Workforce Trends of Registered Psychiatric Nurses in Canada. ISSN 1711-2613.
Published by: Canadian Institute for Health Information/Institut Canadien d'Information sur la Sante, 377 Dalhousie St, Ste 200, Ottawa, ON K1N 9N8, Canada. TEL 613-241-7860, FAX 613-241-8120, nursing@cihi.ca, http://www.cihi.ca.

610.73 USA ISSN 1055-3134
➤ **TENNESSEE NURSE.** Text in English. 1934. bi-m. free to qualified personnel (effective 2010). adv. bk.rev. illus. back issues avail. **Document type:** *Journal, Academic/Scholarly.* **Description:** Contains reports on current developments and trends in nursing and health care.
Former titles (until 1990): Tennessee Nurses Association. Bulletin (0040-3342); (until 19??): Tennessee State Nurses Association. Bulletin
Related titles: Microform ed.: (from PQC).
Indexed: A22, A26, C06, C07, C08, CINAHL, EMBASE, ExcerpMed, H12, I05, INI, MEDLINE, P30, R10, Reac, SCOPUS.
—BLDSC (8790.733500), GNLM.
Published by: Tennessee Nurses Association, 545 Mainstream Dr, Ste 405, Nashville, TN 37228. TEL 615-254-0350, 800-467-1350, FAX 615-254-0303, tna@tnaonline.org. Adv. contact Arthur Davis.

610.73 USA ISSN 0095-036X
TEXAS NURSING. Text in English. 1925. m. free to members; USD 30 to non-members (effective 2005). adv. bk.rev. back issues avail. **Document type:** *Magazine, Trade.*
Former titles (until 1973): Texas Nurses Association. Bulletin (0040-4500); (until 1964): Texas Graduate Nurses' Association. Bulletin
Related titles: Microform ed.
Indexed: C06, C07, C08, CINAHL, EMBASE, ExcerpMed, INI, MEDLINE, P30, R10, Reac, SCOPUS.
—BLDSC (8799.560000), GNLM, IE, Infotrieve, Ingenta.
Published by: Texas Nurses Association, 7600 Burnet Rd, Ste 440, Austin, TX 78757. TEL 512-452-0645, FAX 512-452-0648. Ed., Adv. contact Joyce Cunningham. Circ: 6,500 (paid).

610.73 USA
TEXAS NURSING VOICE. Text in English. q. free to qualified personnel. **Document type:** *Newsletter.* **Description:** Strives to cover continuing nursing education and other topic areas that can be of interest to a general nursing audience.
—BLDSC (8799.560050).
Published by: Texas Nurses Association, 7600 Burnet Rd, Ste 440, Austin, TX 78757. TEL 512-452-0645, 800-862-2022, FAX 512-452-0648. Ed. Clair B Jordan.

610.73 BRA ISSN 0104-0707
TEXTO & CONTEXTO-ENFERMAGEM. Variant title: Revista Texto & Contexto-Enfermagem. Text in Portuguese, Spanish, English. 1992. s-a. **Document type:** *Journal, Academic/Scholarly.*
Related titles: Online - full text ed.: ISSN 1980-265X. free (effective 2011).
Indexed: C06, C07, C08, CINAHL, SCI, SCOPUS, SSCI, W07.
—IE.

Published by: Universidade Federal de Santa Catarina, Departamento de Enfermagem, Programa de Pos-Graduacao de Enfermagem, Bairro Trindade, Florianopolis, 88040-970, Brazil. TEL 55-48-3319480, FAX 55-48-3319787.

610.73 NLD ISSN 0921-5832
HET TIJDSCHRIFT VOOR VERZORGENDEN. Text in Dutch. 1968. 10/yr. EUR 57.50 to individuals; EUR 130.75 to institutions; EUR 28.75 to students (effective 2008). adv. bk.rev. tr.lit. index. **Document type:** *Trade.* **Description:** Offers clinical and professional advice to nurses and caregivers for ailing persons in every sector.
Former titles (until 1988): B K Z (0169-7765); (until 1983): Tijdschrift voor Bejaarden-, Kraam- en Ziekenverzorging (0049-3880); Incorporates (1980-1995): Thuiszorg (0926-3217); Which was formerly (until 1991): Tijdschrift voor Gezinsverzorging (0920-7678)
Indexed: A22, INI, P30.
—IE, Infotrieve.
Published by: Elsevier Gezondheidszorg bv (Subsidiary of: Reed Business bv), Planetenbaan 80-99, Maarssen, 3606 AK, Netherlands. TEL 31-346-577577, http://www.elseviergezondheidszorg.nl. Ed. Yolanda Stil. Pub. Ben Konings. adv.: B&W page EUR 1,350, color page EUR 2,020; trim 215 x 285. Circ: 10,082. **Subscr. to:** Elsevier Den Haag, Postbus 16500, The Hague 2500 BM, Netherlands. TEL 31-70-381-9900, FAX 31-70-333-8399.

610.73 ISL ISSN 1022-2278
TIMARIT HJUKRUNARFRAEDINGA. Text in Icelandic. 1925. 5/yr. adv. bk.rev. illus. back issues avail. **Document type:** *Magazine, Trade.* **Description:** Publishes a wide variety of articles and news relevant to nursing as a profession and trade.
Former titles (until 1993): Hjukrun (0250-4731); (until 1978): Timarit Hjukrunarfelags Islands (0046-7634); (until 1960): Hjukrunarkvennabladid (0258-3798); (until 1935): Timarit Fjelags Islenskra Hjukrunarkvenna (1670-6218)
Indexed: INI, P30.
Published by: Felag Islenskra Hjukrunarfraedinga/Icelandic Nurses' Association, Sudurlandsbraut 22, Reykjavik, 108, Iceland. TEL 354-540-6400, FAX 354-540-6401. Eds. Sigridur Halldorsdottir, Sigrudur Ingimundardottier. Circ: 3,500.

610.73 USA ISSN 1535-2250
➤ **TOPICS IN ADVANCED PRACTICE NURSING.** Text in English. 2001. q. free (effective 2011). back issues avail. **Document type:** *Journal, Academic/Scholarly.* **Description:** Publishes original clinical articles with the depth credibility needed to improve the science and art of medicine.
Media: Online - full text.
Indexed: C06, C07, C08, CINAHL, SCOPUS.
Published by: WebMD Medscape Health Network, 370 Seventh Ave, Ste 1101, New York, NY 10001. TEL 212-301-6700, 888-506-6098, medscapecustomersupport@webmd.net. Ed. Susan Yox.

610.73 617 AUS ISSN 1323-5109
TRANSPLANT NURSES JOURNAL. Abbreviated title: T N J. Text in English. 1992. 3/yr. free (effective 2009); c/w membership. **Document type:** *Journal, Trade.* **Description:** Provides significant information to the nurses and allied health professionals involved in the transplant field and associated areas.
Indexed: C06, C07, C08, CINAHL, SCOPUS.
Published by: Transplant Nurses' Association, Missenden Rd, PO Box M94, Camperdown, NSW 2050, Australia. TEL 61-8-82931276, FAX 61-8-82046959, william1@bigpond.net.au. Ed. Myra Sgorbini.

610.73 BRA ISSN 1981-8963
U F P E. REVISTA DE ENFERMAGEM ON LINE. (Universidade Federal de Pernambuco) Text in Portuguese. 2007. q. free (effective 2011). **Document type:** *Journal, Academic/Scholarly.*
Media: Online - full text.
Indexed: C06, C07, T02.
Published by: Universidade Federal de Pernambuco, Departamanto de Enfermagem, Av Prof Moraes Rego 1235, Cidade Universitaria, Recife, PE 50670-901, Brazil. reuol.ufpe@gmail.com. Ed. Ednaldo Cavalcante de Araujo.

610.73 BRA ISSN 0080-6234
UNIVERSIDADE DE SAO PAULO. ESCOLA DE ENFERMAGEM. REVISTA. Text in Portuguese. 1967. 4/yr. adv. index, cum.index. **Document type:** *Journal, Academic/Scholarly.*
Related titles: Online - full text ed.: ISSN 1980-220X. free (effective 2011).
Indexed: A22, C01, C06, C07, C08, CINAHL, EMBASE, ExcerpMed, F09, FR, INI, IndMed, MEDLINE, P30, R10, Reac, S21, SCI, SCOPUS, SSCI, W07.
—BLDSC (7805.530000), IE, Infotrieve, Ingenta, INIST.
Published by: Universidade de Sao Paulo, Escola de Enfermagem, Av Dr Eneas Carvalho de Aguiar, 419, C Cesar, Sao Paulo, SP 05403-000, Brazil. TEL 55-11-30667524, FAX 55-11-30667524.

610.73 GBR ISSN 1367-3602
UNIVERSITY OF SHEFFIELD. SCHOOL OF NURSING AND MIDWIFERY. RESEARCH REPORT. Text in English. 1996. irreg. **Document type:** *Monographic series, Academic/Scholarly.*
—BLDSC (7769.086200).
Published by: University of Sheffield, School of Nursing and Midwifery, Samuel Fox House, Northern General Hospital, Herries Rd, Sheffield, S5 7AU, United Kingdom. TEL 44-114-2269778, FAX 44-114-2269790, snm.enquiries@sheffield.ac.uk, http://www.shef.ac.uk/snm/. Ed. University Of Sheffield.

UROLOGIC NURSING. *see* MEDICAL SCIENCES—Urology And Nephrology

610.73 USA ISSN 0049-5727
UTAH NURSE. Text in English. 1975. q. looseleaf. USD 25 out of state; USD 241 to members (effective 2008). adv. 24 p./no.; back issues avail. **Document type:** *Newsletter, Trade.* **Description:** Covers issues and employment opportunities of interest to licensed nursing professionals.
Former titles: Pro Re Nata (1044-4025); (until 1987): One on One (0270-6628); U N A Communique; Utah Nurse
Related titles: Online - full text ed.
Indexed: C06, C07, C08, CINAHL, P30.
Published by: (Utah Nurses Association), Arthur L. Davis Publishing Agency, Inc., 517 Washington St, PO Box 216, Cedar Falls, IA 50613. TEL 319-277-2414, 800-626-4081, FAX 319-277-4055, sales@aldpub.com, http://www.aldpub.com. Eds. Carol Roberts, Karen Dewey. R&P Karen Dewey. Circ: 26,000.

610.73 USA
V N A B NEWSLETTER. (Visiting Nurse Association of Brooklyn) Text in English. 1970. s-a. free. charts; illus. **Document type:** *Newsletter.* **Description:** Covers news and services of the Visiting Nurse Association of Brooklyn.
Former titles: V N A Newsletter; In Step with the Visiting Nurse Association of Brooklyn (0046-8770)
Published by: Visiting Nurse Association of Brooklyn, 111 Livingston St, Brooklyn, NY 11201. TEL 718-923-7100, FAX 718-636-7572. Ed. Jane Gould. R&P Glynis McBean TEL 718-230-6921. Circ: 5,000.

610.73 CAN
V O N CANADA ANNUAL REPORT (YEAR). (Victorian Order of Nurses) Text in English. a. adv. **Document type:** *Corporate.*
Published by: Victorian Order of Nurses for Canada, 5 Blackburn Ave, Ottawa, ON K1N 8A2, Canada. TEL 613-233-5694. Ed. Richard Marritt. R&P, Adv. contact Marie Belanger.

610.73 CAN ISSN 0846-135X
V O N CANADA REPORT. (Victorian Order of Nurses) Text in English. q. **Document type:** *Newsletter.* **Description:** Reports on VON's commitment to innovative community based nursing and other health care and support services.
Published by: Victorian Order of Nurses for Canada, 5 Blackburn Ave, Ottawa, ON K1N 8A2, Canada. TEL 613-233-5694. Ed. Richard Marritt. R&P Marie Belanger.

610.73 NOR ISSN 0107-4083
RT12.D4
➤ **VAARD I NORDEN/NURSING SCIENCE AND RESEARCH IN THE NORDIC COUNTRIES**; sykepleievitenskap, omvaardnadsforskning og utvikling. Text in Danish, English, Norwegian, Swedish; Abstracts in English. 1981. q. NOK 280; NOK 70 per issue (effective 2003). bk.rev. charts; illus.; abstr. back issues avail. **Document type:** *Journal, Academic/Scholarly.* **Description:** Focuses on development and research in nursing in the Nordic countries.
Related titles: CD-ROM ed.; E-mail ed.; Fax ed.; Online - full text ed.
Indexed: A22, A26, C06, C07, C08, CINAHL, H12, I05, P24, P30, P48, PQC, SCOPUS.
—IE, Infotrieve, Ingenta. **CCC.**
Published by: Sykepleiernes Samarbeid i Norden/Northern Nurses Federation, Postboks 456, Sentrum, Oslo, N-0104, Norway. TEL 47-22-043304, FAX 47-22-414868, http://www.ssn-nnf.org/ssn. Ed. Martha Quivey. Circ: 1,500.

610.73 USA ISSN 1529-4609
RT5.V4
VERMONT NURSE CONNECTION. Text in English. 199?. q. looseleaf. USD 18 to libraries (effective 2009). adv. 20 p./no.; back issues avail. **Document type:** *Newsletter, Trade.* **Description:** Covers issues and employment opportunities of interest to licensed nursing professionals.
Incorporates (1934-1999): Vermont Registered Nurse (0191-1880)
Related titles: Online - full text ed.
Indexed: A26, C06, C07, C08, CINAHL, H12, I05.
—BLDSC (9172.570000).
Published by: (Vermont State Nurses' Association), Arthur L. Davis Publishing Agency, Inc., 517 Washington St, PO Box 216, Cedar Falls, IA 50613. TEL 319-277-2414, 800-626-4081, FAX 319-277-4055, sales@aldpub.com, http://www.aldpub.com. Eds. Eileen Girling, Jean E Graham TEL 802-651-8886, Mark Miller. R&P Fran Keeler. Adv. contact Jim Larson. Circ: 20,000.

610.73 NLD ISSN 0920-3273
VERPLEEGKUNDE; Nederlandse-Vlaams wetenschappelijk tijdschrift voor verpleegkundigen. Text in Dutch, Flemish. 1986. q. EUR 69.50 to individuals; EUR 99.50 to institutions; EUR 49.50 to students (effective 2008). adv. bk.rev. **Document type:** *Academic/Scholarly.* **Description:** Covers case studies, research and items of interest to nursing leaders and teachers.
Indexed: A22, P30, SCOPUS.
—GNLM, IE, Infotrieve.
Published by: Y-Publicaties, Postbus 10208, Amsterdam, 1001 EE, Netherlands. TEL 31-20-5206060, FAX 31-20-5206061, info@y-publicaties.nl, http://www.y-publicaties.nl. Pub. Ralf Beekveldt. adv.: B&W page EUR 550, color page EUR 1,490; trim 170 x 240. Circ: 800.

610.73 USA ISSN 1084-4740
VIRGINIA NURSES TODAY. Text in English. 1976. q. looseleaf. free to qualified personnel (effective 2005). adv. bk.rev. 28 p./no.; back issues avail.; reprints avail. **Document type:** *Newsletter, Trade.* **Description:** Covers issues and employment opportunities of interest to licensed nursing professionals.
Former titles (until 1992): Virginia Nurse (0270-7780); Virginia Nurse Quarterly (0042-6695)
Related titles: Online - full text ed.
Indexed: C06, C07, C08, CINAHL, INI, P30, SCOPUS.
Published by: (West Virginia Nurses Association), Arthur L. Davis Publishing Agency, Inc., 517 Washington St, PO Box 216, Cedar Falls, IA 50613. TEL 319-277-2414, 800-626-4081, FAX 319-277-4055, sales@aldpub.com, http://www.aldpub.com. Ed. Nellie Lucas. Circ: 83,000 (free).

610.73 USA ISSN 1072-4532
RT1
VISIONS: THE JOURNAL OF ROGERIAN NURSING SCIENCE. Text in English. 1993. a. free to members (effective 2010). back issues avail. **Document type:** *Journal, Academic/Scholarly.*
Related titles: Online - full text ed.: free (effective 2010).
Indexed: A01, A03, A08, A26, C06, C07, C08, C11, CA, CINAHL, H04, H12, I05, T02.
—BLDSC (9240.952700).
Published by: Society of Rogerian Scholars, College of Nursing, New York University, 246 Greene St, 8th Fl, New York, NY 10003. info@societyofrogerianscholars.org. Eds. Martha Bramlett TEL 704-932-5876, Sonya Hardin TEL 704-687-7970.

610.73 USA
VITAL SIGNS (PUEBLO). Text in English.
Published by: Colorado Student Nurses' Association, 2200 Bonforte Blvd, Pueblo, CO 81001-4901. TEL 719- 549-2461, FAX 719-549-2419, http://www.colostate-pueblo.edu.

610.73 FRO ISSN 0904-504X
VOEKA. Text in Faroese. 1976. 3/yr. **Document type:** *Magazine, Trade.*
Published by: Foeroyskir Sjukraroektaefroedingar/Faroese Nurses Association, Lucas Debesargoeta 14, Torshavn, 100, Faeroe Islands. TEL 298-311309, FAX 298-316272, sff@sff.fo, http://www.sff.fo. Ed. Brynhild Danielsen.

610.73 USA ISSN 0734-5666
RT1
THE WASHINGTON NURSE. Text in English. 1929. q. USD 26 domestic; USD 28 foreign (effective 2006). adv. bk.rev. 35 p./no.; back issues avail. **Document type:** *Magazine, Trade.* **Description:** Provides information about professional, educational, ethical, legal, economic, and legislative issues affecting the practice of nursing.
Supersedes (in 1977): W S N A Mini Journal
Related titles: Online - full text ed.
Indexed: C06, C07, C08, CINAHL, INI, P30.
—BLDSC (9263.210000).
Published by: Washington State Nurses Association, 575 Andover Park W, Ste 101, Seattle, WA 98188-3348. TEL 206-575-7979, FAX 206-575-1908, wsna@wsna.org. Ed. Judy Huntington. Adv. contact Debra Weston. page USD 549; 6.5 x 9. Circ: 9,000 (paid).

610.73 NGA ISSN 1117-9686
➤ **WEST AFRICAN JOURNAL OF NURSING.** Text in English. 1993. s-a. NGN 600 domestic; USD 4 in West Africa; GBP 5 in United Kingdom; USD 10 elsewhere to individuals; USD 20 elsewhere to institutions (effective 2010). adv. charts; illus.; bibl.; abstr. **Document type:** *Journal, Academic/Scholarly.*
Indexed: C06, C07, C08, CA, CINAHL, T02.
Published by: West African College of Nursing, 6, Taylor Dr, Yaba, P.M.B. 2023, Lagos, Nigeria. TEL 234-1-4729865. Ed. Valerie M Nylender.

610.73 USA ISSN 1074-8091
RT5.W4
WEST VIRGINIA NURSE. Text in English. 1927. q. looseleaf. Free to qualified subscribers. adv. 20 p./no.; back issues avail.; reprints avail. **Document type:** *Newsletter, Trade.* **Description:** Covers issues and employment opportunities of interest to licensed nursing professionals.
Formerly (until 1992): The Weather Vane (0043-1664)
Related titles: Online - full text ed.
Indexed: C06, C07, C08, CINAHL, INI, P30.
Published by: (West Virginia Nurses Association), Arthur L. Davis Publishing Agency, Inc., 517 Washington St, PO Box 216, Cedar Falls, IA 50613. TEL 319-277-2414, 800-626-4081, FAX 319-277-4055, sales@aldpub.com, http://www.nursingald.com. Eds. Mark Miller, Nellie Lucas. Adv. contact Jim Larson. Circ: 32,900.

610.73 USA ISSN 0193-9459
➤ **WESTERN JOURNAL OF NURSING RESEARCH**; an international forum for communicating nursing research. Text in English. 1979. 8/yr. USD 1,307, GBP 769 combined subscription to institutions (print & online eds.); USD 1,281, GBP 754 to institutions (effective 2011). adv. bk.rev.; film rev. abstr.; bibl.; charts; illus.; stat. cum.index. back issues avail.; reprint service avail. from PSC. **Document type:** *Journal, Academic/Scholarly.* **Description:** Provides a forum for scholarly debate and for research and theoretical papers. Clinical studies have commentaries and rebuttals.
Related titles: Online - full text ed.: ISSN 1552-8456. USD 1,176, GBP 692 to institutions (effective 2011).
Indexed: A01, A02, A03, A08, A20, A22, A26, ASCA, ASSIA, B07, B21, C06, C07, C08, CA, CINAHL, ChPerl, CurCont, E-psyche, E01, E08, EMBASE, ESPM, ExcerpMed, F09, FamI, G06, G07, G08, G10, H&SSA, H04, H11, H12, H13, HRA, I05, INI, IndMed, MEDLINE, P02, P03, P10, P20, P24, P25, P30, P34, P48, P53, P54, PQC, PsycInfo, PsycholAb, R10, Reac, RiskAb, S02, S03, S09, SCI, SCOPUS, SSCI, T02, THA, V&AA, V02, W07, W09.
—BLDSC (9300.835000), GNLM, IE, Infotrieve, Ingenta, INIST. **CCC.**
Published by: Sage Publications, Inc., 2455 Teller Rd, Thousand Oaks, CA 91320. TEL 805-499-9774, 800-818-7243, FAX 805-499-0871, 800-583-2665, info@sagepub.com. Ed. Vicki Conn. Circ: 1,000 (paid). **Subscr. overseas to:** Sage Publications Ltd., 1 Oliver's Yard, 55 City Rd, London EC1Y 1SP, United Kingdom. TEL 44-207-3248701, FAX 44-207-3248733, subscription@sagepub.co.uk.

610.7365 USA ISSN 2155-7276
KF3826.N8
WESTLAW JOURNAL. NURSING HOME. Text in English. 1998. bi-w. back issues avail. **Document type:** *Newsletter, Trade.* **Description:** Covers the latest legal developments affecting nursing homes, other long-term care facilities and their patients.
Former titles (until 200?): Andrews Litigation Reporter: Nursing Home (1556-9993); (until 2004): Nursing Home Litigation Reporter (1522-628X)
Related titles: Online - full text ed.
—**CCC.**
Published by: Andrews Publications (Subsidiary of: Thomson West), 175 Strafford Ave, Bldg 4, Ste 140, Wayne, PA 19087. TEL 800-328-4880, FAX 800-220-1640, west.customer.service@thomson.com, http://www.andrewsonline.com. Pub. Mary Ellen Fox.

610.73 NZL ISSN 1173-1966
WHITIREIA NURSING JOURNAL. Text in English. 1994. a. **Document type:** *Journal, Academic/Scholarly.*
Related titles: Online - full text ed.
Indexed: A26, C06, C07, C08, CINAHL, H11, H12, I05, P24, P48, PQC.
Published by: Whitireia Community Polytechnic, Nursing Centre of Learning, Private Bag 50910, Porirua, New Zealand. TEL 64-4-2373100, FAX 64-4-2373101, info@whitireia.ac.nz, http://www.whitireia.ac.nz.

610.73 USA
WINDOWS IN TIME. Text in English. s-a. **Description:** Publishes news of recent nursing history programs and conferences, announcements of events, updates on the Center's activities, and articles on nursing history.
Published by: Center for Nursing Historical Inquiry, School of Nursing, McLeod Hall, PO Box 800782, Charlottesville, VA 22908-0782. TEL 434-924-0083, FAX 434-982-1809, nurs-hxc@virginia.edu, http://www.nursing.virginia.edu/centers/cnhi/index.html.

610.73 331.1 CAN ISSN 1709-7541
RT6.A1
WORKFORCE TRENDS OF REGISTERED NURSES IN CANADA. Text in English. 1999. a.
Formerly (until 2002): Supply and Distribution of Registered Nurses in Canada (1497-0597)
Related titles: Online - full text ed.: ISSN 1912-0257.

Published by: Canadian Institute for Health Information/Institut Canadien d'Information sur la Sante, 377 Dalhousie St, Ste 200, Ottawa, ON K1N 9N8, Canada. TEL 613-241-7860, FAX 613-241-8120, nursing@cihi.ca, http://www.cihi.ca.

610.736 331.1 CAN ISSN 1711-2613
RC440
WORKFORCE TRENDS OF REGISTERED PSYCHIATRIC NURSES IN CANADA. Text in English. 2002. a. **Document type:** *Journal, Trade.*
Related titles: Online - full text ed.: ISSN 1910-9687; ◆ French ed.: Tendances de la Main-d'Oeuvre des Infirmieres et Infirmiers Psychiatriques Autorises au Canada. ISSN 1711-0459.
Published by: Canadian Institute for Health Information/Institut Canadien d'Information sur la Sante, 377 Dalhousie St, Ste 200, Ottawa, ON K1N 9N8, Canada. TEL 613-241-7860, FAX 613-241-8120, nursing@cihi.ca, http://www.cihi.ca.

610.73 USA ISSN 1940-6991
RA1
WORLD NEWS & NURSING REPORT. Text in English. 2007. q. free to members (effective 2009). back issues avail. **Document type:** *Journal, Trade.* **Description:** Features current news and global events.
Media: Online - full content.
Published by: American Society of Registered Nurses, 1001 Bridgeway, Ste 411, Sausalito, CA 94965. TEL 415-331-2700, 800-331-1206, FAX 415-476-4558, office@asrn.org. Ed. Stan Kenyon.

610.73 IRL
THE WORLD OF IRISH NURSING & MIDWIFERY. Short title: W I N. Text in English. 1936. m. EUR 132 to institutions (effective 2006). adv. **Document type:** *Journal, Trade.*
Former titles (until 2005): The World of Irish Nursing (1393-8088); (until 1995): The New World of Irish Nursing (1393-807X); (until 1993): World of Irish Nursing (0332-3056); (until 1971): Irish Nurses' Journal (0021-1346); Which incorporated (1931-1968): Irish Nursing and Hospital World (0790-7702); (until 1968): Irish Nurse (0578-7513); (until 1963): Irish Nurses' Magazine (0332-3005); (until 1939): Irish Nurses' Journal (0332-2955)
Indexed: B28, C06, C07, C08, CINAHL, INI, P30, SCOPUS.
—IE, Ingenta. **CCC.**
Published by: (Irish Nurses Organisation), MedMedia Ltd., 25 Adelaide St, Dun Laoghaire, Co. Dublin, Ireland. TEL 353-1-2803967, FAX 353-1-2807076, http://www.ijpm.org. adv.: color page EUR 2,200. Circ: 25,000. **Dist. addr.:** Turpin Distribution Services Ltd., Pegasus Dr, Stratton Business Park, Biggleswade, Bedfordshire SG18 8QB, United Kingdom. TEL 44-1767-604800, FAX 44-1767-601640, custserv@turpin-distribution.com, http://www.turpin-distribution.com/.

610.73 USA ISSN 1741-6787
➤ **WORLDVIEWS ON EVIDENCE-BASED NURSING.** Text in English. 1993. q. GBP 284 in United Kingdom to institutions; EUR 360 in Europe to institutions; USD 391 in the Americas to institutions; USD 554 elsewhere to institutions; GBP 327 combined subscription in United Kingdom to institutions (print & online eds.); EUR 414 combined subscription in Europe to institutions (print & online eds.); USD 450 combined subscription in the Americas to institutions (print & online eds.); USD 638 combined subscription elsewhere to institutions (print & online eds.) (effective 2011). adv. back issues avail.; reprints avail. **Document type:** *Journal, Academic/Scholarly.* **Description:** Provides a source of information for using evidence-based nursing practice to improve patient care.
Formerly (until 2003): Online Journal of Knowledge Synthesis for Nursing (1072-7639)
Media: Online - full text (from IngentaConnect). **Related titles:** Print ed.: ISSN 1545-102X. GBP 284 in United Kingdom to institutions; EUR 360 in Europe to institutions; USD 391 in the Americas to institutions; USD 554 elsewhere to institutions (effective 2011).
Indexed: A22, A26, C06, C07, C08, CINAHL, CurCont, E01, EMBASE, ExcerpMed, H12, MEDLINE, P03, P30, Reac, SCI, SCOPUS, SSCI.
—IE. **CCC.**
Published by: (Sigma Theta Tau International Honor Society of Nursing), Wiley-Blackwell Publishing, Inc. (Subsidiary of: Wiley-Blackwell Publishing Ltd.), 111 River St, Hoboken, NJ 07030. TEL 201-748-6000, FAX 201-748-6088, info@wiley.com. Ed. Dr. Jo Rycroft-Malone. Adv. contact Karl Franz TEL 781-388-8470.

610.73 USA
WYOMING NURSE. Text in English. 1926. q. looseleaf. Free to qualified subscribers. adv. 24 p./no.; back issues avail. **Document type:** *Newsletter, Trade.* **Description:** Covers issues and employment opportunities of interest to licensed nursing professionals.
Formerly: Wyoming Nurses Newsletter (0084-3164)
Related titles: Online - full text ed.
Published by: (Wyoming Nurses Association), Arthur L. Davis Publishing Agency, Inc., 517 Washington St, PO Box 216, Cedar Falls, IA 50613. TEL 319-277-2414, 800-626-4081, FAX 319-277-4055, sales@aldpub.com, http://www.nursingald.com. Ed. Mark Miller. R&P Beverly J McDermott. Adv. contact Jim Larson. Circ: 7,500.

610.73 CHN ISSN 1671-8283
XIANDAI LINCHUANG HULI/MODERN CLINICAL NURSING. Text in Chinese. 2002. q. CNY 6 newsstand/cover (effective 2006). **Document type:** *Journal, Academic/Scholarly.*
Related titles: Online - full text ed.
Published by: Zhongshan Daxue Fushu Di-1 Yiyuan/Sun Yat-sen University, 58, Zhongshan Er-Lu, Guangzhou, 510080, China. TEL 86-20-87755766 ext 8050, FAX 86-20-87330961.

YANKE XIN JINZHAN/RECENT ADVANCES IN OPHTHALMOLOGY. *see* MEDICAL SCIENCES—Ophthalmology And Optometry

616 USA ISSN 1536-0024
RC271.C5
(YEAR) ONCOLOGY NURSING DRUG HANDBOOK. Text in English. 19??. a. USD 90.95 per issue (effective 2010). back issues avail. **Document type:** *Handbook/Manual/Guide, Trade.* **Description:** Provides valuable information on effective symptom management, patient education, and chemotherapy administration.
Formerly (until 1998): Oncology Nursing Drug Reference
—BLDSC (6256.979000). **CCC.**
Published by: Jones & Bartlett Learning, 40 Tall Pine Dr, Sudbury, MA 01776. TEL 978-443-5000, 800-832-0034, FAX 978-443-8000, info@jblearning.com.

610.73 KOR ISSN 1225-9543
YEOSEONG GEON-GANG GANHO HAG-HOEJI/KOREAN WOMEN'S HEALTH NURSING ACADEMIC SOCIETY. JOURNAL. Text in Korean. 1995. s-a. **Document type:** *Journal, Academic/Scholarly.*
Indexed: C06, C07, CA, T02.
—BLDSC (9418.328000), IE.
Published by: Yosong Kon'gang Kanho Hakhoe/Korean Academy of Women's Health Nursing, Chonnam National University, College of Nursing, 5 Hak-dong, Gwangju, 501-746, Korea, S. TEL 82-62-2204344, FAX 82-62-2253307, http://women-health-nursing.or.kr/.

610.73 TWN ISSN 1990-7680
YUANYUAN HULI/YUAN-YUAN NURSING. Text in Chinese. 2006. s-a. TWD 250 domestic to individuals; USD 30 foreign to individuals; TWD 150 newsstand/cover (effective 2007).
Published by: Guofang Yixueyuan Huli Xuexi Xiyou Lianyihui/National Defense Medical Center, School of Nursing Alumni Association, PO Box 810, Taibei, Taiwan. TEL 86-2-87923124, FAX 86-2-87922911, health_cheng@yahoo.com.tw, http://www.ndmcnd.url.tw/.

610.73 CHN ISSN 1674-3768
ZHONGGUO LINCHUANG HULI/CHINESE CLINICAL NURSING. Text in Chinese. 1986. bi-m. **Document type:** *Journal, Academic/Scholarly.*
Formerly (until 2009): Zhongguo Yixue Wenzhai (Hulixue) (1001-1331)
Related titles: Online - full text ed.
Published by: Wuhan Shi Yixue Kexue Yanjiusuo, 47, Hankou Lihuangpi, Wuhan, 430014, China. TEL 86-10-86871650. **Co-sponsor:** Zhongguo Yiyao Xuehui.

610.73 CHN ISSN 0254-1769
RT1 CODEN: ZHZAED
ZHONGHUA HULI ZAZHI/CHINESE JOURNAL OF NURSING. Text in Chinese. 1954. m. USD 49.20 (effective 2009). **Document type:** *Journal, Academic/Scholarly.*
Related titles: Online - full text ed.
Indexed: A22, P30, SCOPUS.
—BLDSC (3180.439000), East View, IE, Infotrieve, Ingenta.
Published by: Zhonghua Huli Xuehui, Shilipu Ganlu Xi Yuan, no.1 Bldg., Rm. 314, Beijing, 100025, China. TEL 86-10-65561480. **Dist. by:** China International Book Trading Corp, 35 Chegongzhuang Xilu, Haidian District, PO Box 399, Beijing 100044, China. TEL 86-10-68412045, FAX 86-10-68412023, cibtc@mail.cibtc.com.cn, http://www.cibtc.com.cn.

610.73 CHN ISSN 1674-2907
ZHONGHUA XIANDAI HULI ZAZHI/CHINESE JOURNAL OF MODERN NURSING. Text in Chinese. 1995. every 10 days. CNY 360; CNY 10 per issue (effective 2010). **Document type:** *Journal, Academic/Scholarly.*
Former titles (until 2008): Xiandai Huli/Modern Nursing (1009-9689); (until 2000): Heilongjiang Huli Zazhi/Heilongjiang Nursing Journal (1007-8436)
Related titles: Online - full text ed.
—BLDSC (9512.840560), East View.
Published by: Xiandai Huli Zazahishe, Xuanwumen Wai Dajie, no.2, 1-7-301, Xiangluying Dong Xiang, Xuanwu, 100052, China. TEL 86-10-83191170, FAX 86-10-83191171. **Dist. by:** China International Book Trading Corp, 35 Chegongzhuang Xilu, Haidian District, PO Box 399, Beijing 100044, China. TEL 86-10-68412045, FAX 86-10-68412023, cibtc@mail.cibtc.com.cn, http://www.cibtc.com.cn.

610.73 614 NLD ISSN 2211-4793
ZORG ANNO N U. (Nieuwe Unie) Text in Dutch. 1972. bi-m. adv. **Document type:** *Magazine, Trade.*
Former titles (until 2011): Verpleging N U! (0927-4774); (until 1991): Nederlandse Maatschappij voor Verpleegkunde Visie (0923-5663); (until 1989): Beterschap (0923-5655); (until 1979): Transfusie (0166-5235)
Published by: Nieuwe Unie 91, Postbus 6001, Utrecht, 3503 PA, Netherlands. TEL 31-30-2964144, FAX 31-30-2963904, communicatie@nu91.nl. Ed. Yvonne Sturkenboom.

ZORGVISIE. *see* HEALTH FACILITIES AND ADMINISTRATION

MEDICAL SCIENCES—Obstetrics And Gynecology

see also WOMEN'S HEALTH

A C O G CLINICAL REVIEW. *see* MEDICAL SCIENCES—Abstracting, Bibliographies, Statistics

618 USA ISSN 1074-861X
RG14
A C O G COMMITTEE OPINIONS. Text in English. 1978. irreg., latest vol.460, 2010. back issues avail. **Document type:** *Monographic series, Academic/Scholarly.* **Description:** Provides timely information on crucial issues, ethical concerns, and emerging approaches to clinical management.
Indexed: P30, SCOPUS.
—CCC.
Published by: American College of Obstetricians and Gynecologists, PO Box 96920, Washington, DC 20090. TEL 202-638-5577, publication@acog.org.

618 USA
A C O G EDUCATIONAL BULLETIN. Text in English. 1965. m. free to members (effective 2010). **Document type:** *Journal, Academic/Scholarly.*
Formerly (until 1996): A C O G Technical Bulletin (1074-8628)
Related titles: Online - full text ed.
Indexed: P30.
—CCC.
Published by: American College of Obstetricians and Gynecologists, PO Box 96920, Washington, DC 20090. TEL 202-638-5577, publication@acog.org.

618 USA ISSN 1074-8601
A C O G PATIENT EDUCATION. Text in English. 1964. s-m. back issues avail. **Document type:** *Bulletin, Academic/Scholarly.*
—CCC.
Published by: American College of Obstetricians and Gynecologists, PO Box 96920, Washington, DC 20090. TEL 202-638-5577, publication@acog.org.

618 USA ISSN 1099-3630
A C O G PRACTICE BULLETIN. Text in English. 1998. irreg. free to members (effective 2010). **Document type:** *Monographic series, Academic/Scholarly.*
—CCC.
Published by: American College of Obstetricians and Gynecologists, PO Box 96920, Washington, DC 20090. TEL 202-638-5577, publication@acog.org.

618 ITA ISSN 1720-0296
A G U I NEWS. (Associazione Ginecologi Universitari Italiani) Text in Italian. 2002. q. adv. **Document type:** *Newsletter, Trade.* **Description:** This official organ of the Associazione Ginecologi Universitari Italiani provides information on the association itself as well as medical subjects with a focus on gynecology.
Related titles: Online - full text ed.
Published by: (Associazione Ginecologi Universitari Italiani), C I C Edizioni Internazionali, Corso Trieste 42, Rome, 00198, Italy. TEL 39-06-8412673, FAX 39-06-8412688, info@gruppocic.it, http://www.gruppocic.it. adv.: B&W page EUR 1,681.07, color page EUR 2,114.89; 210 x 290.

618.12 613 GBR ISSN 1357-9657
A I M S JOURNAL. Text in English. 1960. q. GBP 25 to non-members; free to members (effective 2009). back issues avail. **Document type:** *Journal, Academic/Scholarly.*
Former titles (until 1994): A I M S Quarterly Journal (0265-5004); (until 1982): Association for Improvements in the Maternity Services. Quarterly Newsletter (0308-0307)
Related titles: Online - full text ed.
Indexed: B28, C06, C07, C08, CINAHL, GW, P48, PQC, SCOPUS.
—BLDSC (0773.265000), IE, Ingenta. **CCC.**
Published by: Association for Improvements in Maternity Services, c/o Beverley Lawrence Beech, 5 Ann's Ct, Grove Rd, Surbiton, Surrey KT6 4BE, United Kingdom. TEL 44-20-83909534, FAX 44-20-83904381, chair@aims.org.uk. Ed. Vicki Williams.

A I U M SOUND WAVES; news from the association for medical ultrasound. *see* MEDICAL SCIENCES—Radiology And Nuclear Medicine

618 CAN ISSN 1719-9182
A L A R M COURSE MANUAL. (Advances in Labour and Risk Management) Text in English. irreg. **Document type:** *Monographic series, Trade.*
Formerly (until 2011): A L A R M Course Syllabus (1719-9182)
Related titles: French ed.: Manuel du cours Gesta. ISSN 1926-139X.
Published by: Society of Obstetricians and Gynaecologists of Canada, 780 Echo Drive, Ottawa, ON K1S 5R7, Canada. TEL 613-730-4192, 800-561-2416, FAX 613-730-4314, helpdesk@sogc.com, http://www.sogc.org.

A P P P A H NEWSLETTER. *see* PSYCHOLOGY

ACTA CHIRURGICA MEDITERRANEA. *see* MEDICAL SCIENCES—Surgery

618 ESP ISSN 0001-5776
CODEN: ACGLA
ACTA GINECOLOGICA. Text in Spanish; Summaries in English. 1950. 6/yr. adv. bk.rev. illus. index. **Document type:** *Magazine, Academic/Scholarly.*
Related titles: Translation of: Journal of Gynaecology & Obstetrics.
Indexed: A22, ChemAb, EMBASE, ExcerpMed, IME, IndMed, P30, R10, Reac, SCOPUS.
—BLDSC (0622.600000), GNLM, IE, Infotrieve, Ingenta. **CCC.**
Published by: Editores Medicos, S.A., Alsasua 16, Madrid, 28013, Spain. TEL 34-91-3768140, FAX 34-91-3769907, edimsa@edimsa.es, http://www.edimsa.es. Circ: 2,000.

618 PRT ISSN 1646-5830
ACTA OBSTETRICA E GINECOLOGICA PORTUGUESA. Text in Portuguese, English. 2007. q. **Document type:** *Journal, Academic/Scholarly.*
Related titles: Online - full text ed.: free (effective 2011).
Published by: (Sociedade Portuguesa de Obstetricia e Ginecologia), Momento Medico, Praca de Alvalade 9, 3 B, Lisbon, 1700-037, Portugal. TEL 351-21-7828060, FAX 351-21-7828069, geral@momentomedico.com.pt, http://www.momentomedico.pt. Ed. Diogo Ayres-de-Campos.

618 GBR ISSN 0001-6349
RG1 CODEN: AOGSAE
➤ **ACTA OBSTETRICIA ET GYNECOLOGICA SCANDINAVICA.** Text in English. 1922. m. GBP 809 in United Kingdom to institutions; EUR 1,071 in Europe to institutions; USD 1,340 elsewhere to institutions; GBP 930 combined subscription in United Kingdom to institutions (print & online eds.); EUR 1,232 combined subscription in Europe to institutions (print & online eds.); USD 1,542 combined subscription elsewhere to institutions (print & online eds.) (effective 2012). adv. bk.rev. bibl.; charts; illus. cum.index: 1922-1952; 1953-1962. back issues avail.; reprint service avail. from PSC. **Document type:** *Journal, Academic/Scholarly.* **Description:** Reports advances in clinical and experimental research with topical discussions.
Formerly (until 1925): Acta Gynecologica Scandinavica (0786-4981)
Related titles: Microfiche ed.; Online - full text ed.: ISSN 1600-0412. GBP 809 in United Kingdom to institutions; EUR 1,071 in Europe to institutions; USD 1,340 elsewhere to institutions (effective 2012) (from IngentaConnect); ◆ Spanish ed.: Acta Obstetrica et Gynecologica.
Indexed: A01, A03, A08, A20, A22, A36, ASCA, CA, CABA, CLFP, ChemAb, CurCont, D01, DBA, E01, E12, EMBASE, ExcerpMed, F08, F11, F12, FR, G10, GH, H16, H17, ISR, IndMed, Inpharma, LT, MEDLINE, N02, N03, NRN, P30, P33, P35, P39, R08, R10, R12, RA&MP, RM&VM, RRTA, Reac, S02, S03, SCI, SCOPUS, SoyAb, T02, T05, W07, W09.
—BLDSC (0641.600000), CASDDS, GNLM, IE, Infotrieve, Ingenta, INIST. **CCC.**
Published by: (Nordic Federation of Societies of Obstetrics and Gynecology ISL), John Wiley & Sons Ltd. (Subsidiary of: John Wiley & Sons, Inc.), 9600 Garsington Rd, Oxford, OX4 2DQ, United Kingdom. TEL 44-1865-776868, FAX 44-1865-714591, cs-journals@wiley.com. Ed. Reynir Thomas Geirsson. Circ: 4,600.

618 616.6 NLD
➤ **ADVANCES IN REPRODUCTIVE HEALTH CARE.** Text in English. 1984. irreg., latest vol.6, 1985. price varies. back issues avail. **Document type:** *Monographic series, Academic/Scholarly.*

Published by: Springer Netherlands (Subsidiary of: Springer Science+Business Media), Van Godewijckstraat 30, Dordrecht, 3311 GX, Netherlands. TEL 31-78-6576050, FAX 31-78-6576474.

618 DEU ISSN 1436-2627 CODEN: TWGYE
AERZTLICHE PRAXIS. GYNAEKOLOGIE. Short title: Ae P Gynaekologie. Text in German. 1988. bi-m. adv. **Document type:** *Journal, Trade.*
Former titles (until 1998): T und E Gynaekologie (1435-7739); (until 1997): T W Gynaekologie (0935-3208)
Indexed: SCOPUS.
—BLDSC (1738.516000), GNLM, IE, Ingenta. **CCC.**
Published by: Biermann Verlag GmbH, Otto-Hahn-Str 7, Cologne, 50997, Germany. TEL 49-2236-3760, FAX 49-2236-376999, info@biermann.net, http://www.biermann-verlag.de. Ed. Ulrike Roll. Adv. contact Isabelle Becker. Circ: 11,118 (paid and controlled).

618.2 DEU ISSN 0935-0810
AERZTLICHER RATGEBER FUER WERDENDE UND JUNGE ELTERN; die Schwangerschaft, Geburt und Babyzeit. Text in German. 1964. 3/yr. free (effective 2010). adv. **Document type:** *Magazine, Consumer.* **Description:** Supplies useful information to expectant mothers as well as single mothers and fathers.
Related titles: Online - full text ed.
Published by: (Deutsches Gruenes Kreuz e.V.), Wort und Bild Verlag Konradshoehe GmbH, Konradshoehe, Baierbrunn, 82065, Germany. TEL 49-89-744330, FAX 49-89-74433150, info@wortundbildverlag.de, http://www.wortundbild.de. Ed. Stefanie Becker. adv.: B&W page EUR 15,900, color page EUR 21,400; trim 185 x 258. Circ: 250,682 (controlled).

618 ZAF ISSN 1682-5055
AFRICAN JOURNAL OF NURSING AND MIDWIFERY. Text in English. 1999. s-a. **Document type:** *Journal, Academic/Scholarly.*
Indexed: C06, C07, C08, CINAHL, ISAP, P30, SCOPUS.
—BLDSC (0732.160737). **CCC.**
Published by: University of South Africa, Department of Health Studies, Preller St, Muckleneuk, Pretoria, South Africa. TEL 27-12-4296783, FAX 27-12-4296688, kistas@unisa.ac.za, http://unisa.ac.za.

649 PRI
AGENDA PARA MAMA. Text in Spanish. 1994. a., latest 2003. USD 12.95 (effective 2003). adv. **Description:** Written by physicians and specialists in an easy-to-understand language, this publication is for future parents and other family members. It is a month-by-month guide to pregnancy and baby's first year.
Published by: Casiano Communications Inc., 1700 Fernandez Juncos Ave, San Juan, 00909-2999, Puerto Rico. TEL 787-728-3000, FAX 787-268-5058, cservice@casiano.com. Ed. Elena Menendez. R&P Dianne Pacheco. Adv. contact Ivonne Lizardi. B&W page USD 6,837, color page USD 9,850; 8.125 x 10.75. Circ: 40,000.

618.1 USA ISSN 1945-4589
RC952.A1
AGING. Text in English. 2008. bi-m. free (effective 2009). back issues avail. **Document type:** *Journal, Academic/Scholarly.* **Description:** Publishes high-impact research papers of general interest and biological significance in all fields of aging research.
Media: Online - full content.
Indexed: B25, BIOSIS Prev, EMBASE, MEDLINE, P30, SCI, W07.
Published by: Impact Journals LLC publisher@impactjournals.com, http://impactjournals.com/. Eds. Judith Campisi, Mikhail V Blagosklonny.

618 JPN ISSN 0917-0162
AICHI BOSEI EISEI GAKKAISHI/AICHI JOURNAL OF MATERNAL HEALTH. Text in Japanese. 1985. a. JPY 2,000. adv. bk.rev.; film rev.; software rev. bibl.; illus. **Document type:** *Journal, Academic/Scholarly.*
Published by: Aichi Bosei Eisei Gakkai/Aichi Society of Maternal Health, c/o Yamada Kiyomi, Nagoya City University, School of Nursing, 1 Kawasumi, Mizuho-cho, Mizuho-ku, Nagoya, 467-8601, Japan. TEL 81-52-8538055. Ed. Miyoko Ogiso. Circ: 300.

618 RUS ISSN 0300-9092
AKUSHERSTVO I GINEKOLOGIYA/OBSTETRICS AND GYNECOLOGY. Text in Russian; Summaries in English. 1922. bi-m. USD 93 foreign (effective 2005). adv. bk.rev.; Website rev. illus. index. **Document type:** *Journal, Academic/Scholarly.* **Description:** Publishes original and survey papers dealing with modern scientific achievements in the field of obstetrics and gynecology. Covers physiology and pathology of the fetus and the newborn, scientific and practical problems of diagnosis, treatment of complications in pregnancy, labor and gynecologic diseases.
Indexed: ABSML, CIN, ChemAb, ChemTitl, ISR, IndMed, RefZh.
—East View, GNLM. **CCC.**
Published by: Izdatel'stvo Meditsina/Meditsina Publishers, ul B Pirogovskaya, d 2, str 5, Moscow, 119435, Russian Federation. TEL 7-095-2483324, meditsina@mtu-net.ru, http://www.medlit.ru. Ed. Dr. Vladimir I Kulakov. R&P N Biyatova. Circ: 6,000. **Dist. by:** M K - Periodica, ul Gilyarovskogo 39, Moscow 129110, Russian Federation. TEL 7-095-2845008, FAX 7-095-2813798, info@periodicals.ru, http://www.mkniga.ru; **US dist. addr.:** East View Information Services, 10601 Wayzata Blvd, Minneapolis, MN 55305. TEL 952-252-1201, 800-477-1005, FAX 952-252-1202, info@eastview.com, http://www.eastview.com.

618 CAN ISSN 1712-0780
ALBERTA REPRODUCTIVE HEALTH, PREGNANCIES AND BIRTHS. Text in English. 1996. a. **Document type:** *Government.*
Former titles (until 2002): Alberta Reproductive Health, Pregnancy Outcomes (1493-8707); (until 1997): Reproductive Health, Pregnancy Outcomes, Alberta (1480-1876)
Published by: Alberta Health and Wellness, PO Box 1360, Station Main, Edmonton, AB T5J 2N3, Canada. TEL 780-427-1432, FAX 780-422-0102, http://www.health.gov.ab.ca.

AMERICAN BABY. THE FIRST YEAR OF LIFE; a guide to your baby's growth and development month by month. *see* CHILDREN AND YOUTH—About

618 USA ISSN 0002-9378
RG1 CODEN: AJOGAH
➤ **AMERICAN JOURNAL OF OBSTETRICS & GYNECOLOGY.** Text in English. 1868. m. USD 744 in United States to institutions; USD 850 elsewhere to institutions (effective 2012). adv. illus. s-a. index. back issues avail.; reprints avail. **Document type:** *Journal, Academic/Scholarly.* **Description:** Devoted to obstetrics, gynecology, fetuses, the placenta and the newborn.
Formerly (until 1920): The American Journal of Obstetrics and Diseases of Women and Children (0894-5543)
Related titles: CD-ROM ed.: ISSN 1085-8709; Microform ed.: (from PMC, PQC); Online - full text ed.: ISSN 1097-6868 (from ScienceDirect).
Indexed: A20, A21, A22, A26, A34, A35, A36, A38, AIDS Ab, AIM, ASCA, AbAn, AgBio, B25, B28, BDM&CN, BIOBASE, BIOSIS Prev, BP, C06, C07, C08, C13, CA, CABA, CCIOG, CIN, CINAHL, CLFP, ChemAb, ChemTitl, CurCont, D01, DBA, DiabCont, DokArb, E01, E08, E12, EMBASE, ExcerpMed, F08, F09, FAMLI, FR, Faml, G08, GH, H04, H11, H12, H17, I05, I12, IABS, IDIS, INI, ISR, IndMed, IndVet, Inpharma, JW, JW-WH, Kidney, LT, M01, M02, MEDLINE, MS&D, MycolAb, N02, N03, NRN, P30, P32, P33, P35, P39, P40, PRA, R08, R10, R12, RI-1, RI-2, RRTA, Reac, S09, SCI, SCOPUS, SoyAb, T02, T05, THA, TM, VS, W07, W09, W11.
—BLDSC (0828.700000), CASDDS, GNLM, IE, Infotrieve, Ingenta, INIST. **CCC.**
Published by: (American Gynecological and Obstetrical Society), Mosby, Inc. (Subsidiary of: Elsevier Health Sciences), 1600 John F. Kennedy Blvd, Ste 1800, Philadelphia, PA 19103. TEL 215-239-3900, 800-523-1649, FAX 215-239-3990, elspcs@elsevier.com, http://www.us.elsevierhealth.com. Eds. Dr. Moon H Kim, Dr. Thomas J Garite. **Co-sponsor:** American Board of Obstetrics and Gynecology, Society of Gynecologic Surgeons, Society of Perinatal Obstetricians.

618.3 USA ISSN 0735-1631
RG600
➤ **AMERICAN JOURNAL OF PERINATOLOGY;** neonatal and maternal-fetal medicine. Text in English. 1983. 10/yr. USD 809 domestic to institutions; USD 839 foreign to institutions; USD 1,012 combined subscription domestic to institutions (print & online eds.); USD 1,063 combined subscription foreign to institutions (print & online eds.) (effective 2011). adv. bk.rev. reprints avail. **Document type:** *Journal, Academic/Scholarly.* **Description:** Focuses on clinical and translational research, clinical and technical advances in diagnosis, monitoring, and treatment as well as evidence-based reviews. Includes the epidemiology, diagnosis, prevention, and management of maternal, fetal, and neonatal diseases.
Related titles: Online - full text ed.: ISSN 1098-8785. USD 962 domestic to institutions; USD 983 foreign to institutions (effective 2011).
Indexed: A01, A03, A08, A22, A34, A36, A38, ASCA, B25, BDM&CN, BIOSIS Prev, C06, C07, C08, CA, CABA, CINAHL, CurCont, D01, E01, E12, EMBASE, ExcerpMed, FR, GH, INI, IndMed, Inpharma, MEDLINE, MycolAb, N02, N03, P30, P33, P35, P39, R08, R10, R12, RA&MP, RM&VM, Reac, SCI, SCOPUS, T02, T05, VS, W07, W10.
—BLDSC (0829.900000), GNLM, IE, Infotrieve, Ingenta, INIST. **CCC.**
Published by: Thieme Medical Publishers (Subsidiary of: Georg Thieme Verlag), 333 Seventh Ave, New York, NY 10001. TEL 212-760-0888, 800-782-3488, FAX 212-947-1112, info@thieme.com. Eds. George R Saade TEL 409-747-0476, Rosemary D Higgins TEL 301-435-7909. Adv. contact James C Cunningham TEL 201-767-4170. Circ: 1,045.

➤ **AMERICAN JOURNAL OF REPRODUCTIVE IMMUNOLOGY (ONLINE).** *see* MEDICAL SCIENCES—Allergology And Immunology

➤ **AMERICAN JOURNAL OF REPRODUCTIVE IMMUNOLOGY (PRINT).** *see* MEDICAL SCIENCES—Allergology And Immunology

➤ **AMERICAN JOURNAL OF REPRODUCTIVE IMMUNOLOGY. SUPPLEMENT.** *see* MEDICAL SCIENCES—Allergology And Immunology

618 SWE ISSN 1102-7207
AMNINGSNYTT. Text in Swedish. 1974. q. SEK 250 (effective 2007). adv. bk.rev. **Document type:** *Magazine, Consumer.* **Description:** For nursing mothers.
Published by: Amningshjaelpen, Jutvik Krosfall, Rimforsa, 59041, Sweden. Ed. Marit Olanders TEL 46-410-29442. adv.: page SEK 2,250. Circ: 2,000.

618 TUR ISSN 1308-8254
➤ **ANATOLIAN JOURNAL OF OBSTETRICS & GYNECOLOGY.** Text in Multiple languages. 1991. irreg. free (effective 2011). **Document type:** *Journal, Academic/Scholarly.*
Formerly (until 2009): Turkiye Klinikleri Jinekoloji Obstetrik (1300-0306)
Media: Online - full text.
Indexed: A01, A36, CABA, D01, E12, EMBASE, GH, H17, N02, N03, P33, R12, SCOPUS, T05.
—BLDSC (9073.785000), IE.
Published by: Alkim Basin Yayin Ltd., Gundogdu Mah. Fidan Sok. 26A, Cebeci, Ankara, 06230, Turkey. Eds. Ernest I Kohorn, Roy M Pitkin, Thinus F Kruger.

➤ **ANNALES CHIRURGIAE ET GYNAECOLOGIAE. SUPPLEMENTUM.** *see* MEDICAL SCIENCES—Surgery

618 JPN ISSN 0913-8307
AOMORIKEN RINSHO SANFUJINKA IKAISHI/AOMORI SOCIETY OF OBSTETRICIANS AND GYNECOLOGISTS. JOURNAL. Text in English, Japanese; Summaries in English. 1986. s-a. **Document type:** *Journal, Academic/Scholarly.*
Published by: Aomoriken Rinsho Sanfujinka Ikai/Aomori Society of Obstetricians and Gynecologists, c/o Hirosaki University, School of Medicine, Department of Obstetrics & Gynecology, 5 Zaifu, Hirosaki, Aomori 036-8562, Japan.

618.92 GBR ISSN 1359-2998
➤ **ARCHIVES OF DISEASE IN CHILDHOOD. FETAL AND NEONATAL EDITION;** an international peer-reviewed journal for health professionals and researchers covering neonatal and perinatal medicine. Text in English. 1988. bi-m. Included with subscr. to Archives of Disease in Childhood. adv. bk.rev. abstr.; charts; illus. Index. back issues avail.; reprints avail. **Document type:** *Journal, Academic/Scholarly.* **Description:** Focuses on research in neonatology, genetics, fetal medicine, neurodevelopmental medicine, fetal physiology, and perinatal epidemiology.
Related titles: Microfilm ed.: (from PQC); Online - full text ed.: e A D C - F & N. ISSN 1468-2052. 1997; ◆ Supplement to: Archives of Disease in Childhood. ISSN 0003-9888.
Indexed: A01, A03, A08, A20, A22, A26, B21, B28, C06, C07, C08, CA, CINAHL, CurCont, E01, E08, EMBASE, G08, H11, H12, I05, INI, IndMed, Inpharma, MEDLINE, P20, P22, P30, P35, P48, P54, PQC, R10, Reac, S09, SCI, SCOPUS, T02, THA, ViroIAbstr, W07.
—BLDSC (1634.200500), IE, Infotrieve, Ingenta, INIST. **CCC.**
Published by: (Royal College of Paediatrics and Child Health), B M J Group, BMA House, Tavistock Sq, London, WC1H 9JR, United Kingdom. TEL 44-20-73836373, FAX 44-20-73836668, membership@bma.org.uk, http://group.bmj.com. Ed. Howard Bauchner. Pub. Janet O'Flaherty TEL 44-20-73836154. Adv. contact Nick Gray TEL 44-20-73836386. **Subscr. to:** PO Box 299, London WC1H 9TD, United Kingdom. TEL 44-20-73836270, FAX 44-20-73836402.

618.1 DEU ISSN 0932-0067
RG1 CODEN: AGOBEJ
➤ **ARCHIVES OF GYNECOLOGY AND OBSTETRICS.** Text in English. 1870. 8/yr. EUR 2,512, USD 3,029 combined subscription to institutions (print & online eds.) (effective 2012). adv. bibl.; charts; illus. index. back issues avail.; reprint service avail. from PSC. **Document type:** *Journal, Academic/Scholarly.* **Description:** Informs about the latest advances in gynecology and allied fields.
Former titles: Archives of Gynecology (0170-9925); Archiv fuer Gynaekologie (0003-9128)
Related titles: Microfiche ed.: (from BHP); Microform ed.: (from PQC); Online - full text ed.: ISSN 1432-0711 (from IngentaConnect).
Indexed: A01, A03, A08, A22, A26, ASCA, B25, BIOSIS Prev, CA, CIN, ChemAb, ChemTitl, CurCont, E01, EMBASE, ExcerpMed, H12, IBR, IBZ, ISR, IndMed, Inpharma, MEDLINE, MycolAb, NRN, P30, R10, Reac, S02, S03, SCI, SCOPUS, T02, W07.
—BLDSC (1634.404000), CASDDS, GNLM, IE, Infotrieve, Ingenta, INIST. **CCC.**
Published by: (Deutschen Gesellschaft fuer Gynaekologie und Geburtshilfe), Springer (Subsidiary of: Springer Science+Business Media), Tiergartenstr 17, Heidelberg, 69121, Germany. TEL 49-6221-4870, FAX 49-6221-345229. Eds. Hans Ludwig, Dr. Klaus Diedrich. adv.: B&W page EUR 700, color page EUR 1,740. Circ: 200 (paid and controlled). **Subscr. in the Americas to:** Springer New York LLC, Journal Fulfillment, PO Box 2485, Secaucus, NJ 07096. TEL 800-777-4643, 201-348-4033, FAX 201-348-4505, journals-ny@springer.com, http://www.springer.com; **Subscr. to:** Springer Distribution Center, Kundenservice Zeitschriften, Haberstr 7, Heidelberg 69126, Germany. TEL 49-6221-3454303, FAX 49-6221-3454229, subscriptions@springer.com.

618 POL ISSN 1505-0580
ARCHIVES OF PERINATAL MEDICINE. Text in English. 1996. q. EUR 147 foreign (effective 2006). **Document type:** *Journal, Academic/Scholarly.*
Related titles: Online - full text ed.: ISSN 1508-4868; Supplement(s): Archives of Perinatal Medicine. Supplement. ISSN 1505-0610. 1997.
—BLDSC (1638.967000).
Published by: (Polskie Towarzystwo Medycyny Perinatalnej/Polish Society of Perinatal Medicine), Blackhorse Scientific Publishers, Ltd., Zeganska 16, Warsaw, 04713, Poland. TEL 48-22-4999099, FAX 48-22-4995081, blackhorse@blackhorse.pl, http://blackhorse.pl/blackhorse. Ed. Grzegorz Breborowicz. **Dist. by:** Ars Polona, Obroncow 25, Warsaw 03933, Poland. TEL 48-22-5098609, FAX 48-22-5098610, arspolona@arspolona.com.pl, http://www.arspolona.com.pl.

618 URY ISSN 0797-0803
ARCHIVOS DE GINECOLOGIA Y OBSTETRICIA. Text in Spanish. 1942. 3/yr. free (effective 2005). back issues avail. **Document type:** *Journal, Academic/Scholarly.*
Formerly (until 1942): Hospital Pereira Rossell. Seccional de Ginecologia y Obstetricia. Archivos
Related titles: Online - full text ed.
Indexed: INIS AtomInd, P30.
Published by: Sociedad Ginecotocologica del Uruguay, H Pereira Rossell, Bvar Artigas 1550, 2o Piso, Montevideo, 11600, Uruguay. squbib@chasque.apc.org. Ed. Ricardo Topolanski.

ASIAN AND PACIFIC WOMEN'S RESOURCE AND ACTION SERIES. *see* WOMEN'S INTERESTS

618 612.167 613.04244 ARG ISSN 1666-0056
ASOCIACION ARGENTINA PARA EL ESTUDIO DEL CLIMATERIO. REVISTA. Text in Spanish. 2001. 3/yr. **Document type:** *Journal, Academic/Scholarly.*
Published by: Asociacion Argentina para el Estudio del Climaterio (A A P E C), Azcuenaga 1049, Buenos Aires, C1115AAE, Argentina. http://www.aapec.org.

ASSISTED HUMAN REPRODUCTION AGENCY OF CANADA. ESTIMATES. PART III. REPORT ON PLANS AND PRIORITIES/ BUDGET DES DEPENSES. PARTIE III. RAPPORT SUR LES PLANS ET LES PRIORITES. *see* BUSINESS AND ECONOMICS—Public Finance, Taxation

618 USA ISSN 0271-129X
➤ **AUDIO-DIGEST OBSTETRICS - GYNECOLOGY.** Text in English. 1954. s-m. USD 449.81 domestic; USD 479.72 in Canada; USD 527.72 elsewhere (effective 2010). back issues avail. **Document type:** *Journal, Academic/Scholarly.*
Media: Audio cassette/tape. **Related titles:** Audio CD ed.: USD 399.89 domestic; USD 431.72 in Canada; USD 479.72 elsewhere (effective 2010); Online - full text ed.: USD 359.72 (effective 2010).
—Ingenta.
Published by: Audio-Digest Foundation (Subsidiary of: California Medical Association), 1577 E Chevy Chase Dr, Glendale, CA 91206. TEL 818-240-7500, 800-423-2308, FAX 818-240-7379.

▼ ➤ **AUSTIN PREGNANCY MAGAZINE.** *see* WOMEN'S INTERESTS

618 AUS ISSN 0004-8666
RG1 CODEN: AZOGBS
➤ **THE AUSTRALIAN AND NEW ZEALAND JOURNAL OF OBSTETRICS AND GYNAECOLOGY.** Abbreviated title: A N Z J O G. Text in English. 1961. bi-m. GBP 305 in United Kingdom to institutions; EUR 386 in Europe to institutions; USD 491 in the Americas to institutions; USD 594 elsewhere to institutions; GBP 351 combined subscription in United Kingdom to institutions (print & online eds.); EUR 445 combined subscription in Europe to institutions (print & online eds.); USD 565 combined subscription in the Americas to institutions (print & online eds.); USD 683 combined subscription elsewhere to institutions (print & online eds.) (effective 2012). adv. bk.rev. charts; illus. Index. back issues avail.; reprint service avail. from PSC. **Document type:** *Journal, Academic/Scholarly.* **Description:** Covers clinical obstetrics and gynaecology and related research.
Related titles: Online - full text ed.: ISSN 1479-828X. GBP 305 in United Kingdom to institutions; EUR 386 in Europe to institutions; USD 491 in the Americas to institutions; USD 594 elsewhere to institutions (effective 2012) (from IngentaConnect).
Indexed: A01, A02, A03, A08, A20, A22, A26, A36, ASCA, B21, BDM&CN, C06, C07, C08, CA, CABA, CINAHL, CTA, CurCont, D01, E01, E12, EMBASE, ExcerpMed, F08, F09, F11, F12, FamI, G10, GH, H12, IndMed, Inpharma, MEDLINE, N02, N03, NRN, P30, P33, P35, P39, R10, R12, RA&MP, RM&VM, Reac, RefZh, SCI, SCOPUS, SPPI, SoyAb, T02, T05, THA, W07, W09.
—BLDSC (1796.890000), CASDDS, GNLM, IE, Infotrieve, Ingenta, INIST. **CCC.**
Published by: (Royal Australian & New Zealand College of Obstetricians & Gynecologists, Research Foundation, Royal Australian & New Zealand College of Obstetricians & Gynecologists), Wiley-Blackwell Publishing Asia (Subsidiary of: Wiley-Blackwell Publishing Ltd.), 155 Cremorne St, Richmond, VIC 3121, Australia. TEL 61-3-92743100, FAX 61-3-92743101, melbourne@wiley.com, http://www.wiley.com/WileyCDA/. Ed. Jan Dickinson. Circ: 5,300 (paid and controlled).

618.202 AUS ISSN 1446-5612
AUSTRALIAN MIDWIFERY NEWS. Text in English. 2001. q. free to members (effective 2009). adv. **Document type:** *Magazine, Trade.*
Indexed: C06, C07, C08, CINAHL.
—BLDSC (1814.375000).
Published by: (Australian College of Midwives Inc.), Minnis Communications, 4/16 Maple Grove, Toorak, VIC 3142, Australia. TEL 61-3-98245241, FAX 61-3-98245247, info@minniscomms.com.au. adv.: page AUD 2,300; trim 210 x 297.

618 GBR ISSN 1470-0328
CODEN: BJOGAS
➤ **B J O G**; an international journal of obstetrics and gynaecology. Text in English. 1902. m. GBP 405 in United Kingdom to institutions; EUR 515 in Europe to institutions; USD 678 in the Americas to institutions; USD 873 elsewhere to institutions; GBP 467 combined subscription in United Kingdom to institutions (print & online eds.); EUR 592 combined subscription in Europe to institutions (print & online eds.); USD 780 combined subscription in the Americas to institutions (print & online eds.); USD 1,004 combined subscription elsewhere to institutions (print & online eds.) (effective 2012). adv. bk.rev. abstr.; bibl.; charts; illus. index. back issues avail.; reprint service avail. from PSC. **Document type:** *Journal, Academic/Scholarly.* **Description:** Aims to publish the highest quality medical research in women's health, worldwide.
Former titles (until 2000): British Journal of Obstetrics & Gynaecology (0306-5456); (until 1975): Journal of Obstetrics and Gynaecology of the British Commonwealth (0022-3204); (until 1961): Journal of Obstetrics and Gynaecology of the British Empire (0307-1871)
Related titles: Online - full text ed.: ISSN 1471-0528. GBP 405 in United Kingdom to institutions; EUR 515 in Europe to institutions; USD 678 in the Americas to institutions; USD 873 elsewhere to institutions (effective 2012) (from IngentaConnect); ◆ Supplement(s): British Journal of Obstetrics & Gynaecology. Supplement. ISSN 0140-7686.
Indexed: A01, A03, A08, A20, A22, A26, A34, A35, A36, A38, AIM, ASCA, AgBio, B21, B28, BDM&CN, C06, C07, C08, CA, CABA, CIN, CINAHL, CLFP, CTA, ChemAb, ChemTitl, CurCont, D01, DBA, DentInd, DiabCont, E01, E12, EMBASE, ExcerpMed, F09, FR, FamI, G08, G10, GH, H11, H12, H13, H17, IBR, IBZ, IDIS, INI, ISR, IndMed, Inpharma, JW-WH, Kidney, LT, MEDLINE, MS&D, N02, N03, NRN, OR, P02, P10, P20, P30, P33, P34, P35, P39, P48, P50, P53, P54, PQC, R08, R10, R12, RA&MP, RM&VM, RRTA, Reac, RefZh, S02, S03, SCI, SCOPUS, SoyAb, T02, T05, THA, VS, W07, W09, W11.
—BLDSC (2105.748000), CASDDS, GNLM, IE, Ingenta, INIST. **CCC.**
Published by: (Royal College of Obstetricians and Gynaecologists), Wiley-Blackwell Publishing Ltd. (Subsidiary of: John Wiley & Sons, Inc.), 9600 Garsington Rd, Oxford, OX4 2DQ, United Kingdom. TEL 44-1865-776868, FAX 44-1865-714591, customerservices@blackwellpublishing.com, http://www.wiley.com/. Ed. Philip J Steer. Adv. contact Neil Chesher TEL 44-1865-476383. Circ: 6,400.

618.2 GBR ISSN 1471-2393
RG551 CODEN: BPCMBT
➤ **B M C PREGNANCY AND CHILDBIRTH.** (BioMed Central) Text in English. 2000. irreg. free (effective 2011). adv. back issues avail.; reprints avail. **Document type:** *Journal, Academic/Scholarly.* **Description:** Publishes original research articles on all aspects of pregnancy and childbirth.
Media: Online - full text.
Indexed: A01, A26, A36, C06, C07, CA, CABA, D01, E12, EMBASE, ESPM, ExcerpMed, GH, H17, I05, MEDLINE, N02, N03, P20, P22, P30, P33, P39, PQC, R08, R10, R12, RA&MP, Reac, RiskAb, SCOPUS, T02, T05, VS.
—Infotrieve. **CCC.**
Published by: BioMed Central Ltd. (Subsidiary of: Springer Science+Business Media), 236 Gray's Inn Rd, London, WC1X 8HB, United Kingdom. TEL 44-20-31922000, FAX 44-20-31922010, info@biomedcentral.com. Ed. Dr. Melissa Norton. Adv. contact Natasha Bailey TEL 44-20-31922231.

➤ **BABY CENTER.** *see* HOME ECONOMICS

618.2 GBR
BAILLIERE'S MIDWIVES' DICTIONARY. Text in English. 1951. irreg., latest 2008, 11th ed. GBP 10.99 per issue (effective 2009). back issues avail. **Document type:** *Monographic series, Academic/Scholarly.*
Published by: Bailliere Tindall (Subsidiary of: Elsevier Health Sciences), The Blvd, Langford Ln, Kidlington, Oxford OX5 1GB, United Kingdom. TEL 44-1865-474010, directenquiries@elsevier.com.

618 BGD ISSN 1018-4287
BANGLADESH JOURNAL OF OBSTETRICS AND GYNECOLOGY. Text in English. 1986. s-a. **Document type:** *Journal, Academic/Scholarly.*
Indexed: EMBASE, ExcerpMed, R10, Reac, SCOPUS.
—BLDSC (1861.676600).
Published by: Obstetrical & Gynaecological Society of Bangladesh, House 14/1 D, 2nd Fl, Road 4, Dhanmondi R/A, Dhaka, 1205, Bangladesh.

618 GBR
CODEN: BPRGFM
➤ **BEST PRACTICE & RESEARCH: CLINICAL OBSTETRICS & GYNAECOLOGY.** Text in English. 1974. bi-m. EUR 681 in Europe to institutions; JPY 90,000 in Japan to institutions; USD 818 elsewhere to institutions (effective 2012). adv. back issues avail. **Document type:** *Journal, Academic/Scholarly.* **Description:** Provides a comprehensive review of current clinical practice and thinking within the specialties of obstetrics and gynecology.
Former titles (until 2001): Bailliere's Best Practice & Research: Clinical Obstetrics & Gynaecology (1521-6934); (until 1999): Bailliere's Clinical Obstetrics and Gynaecology (0950-3552); (until 1987): Clinics in Obstetrics and Gynaecology (0306-3356)
Related titles: Online - full text ed.: ISSN 1878-156X (from ScienceDirect).
Indexed: A20, A22, A26, ASCA, B28, C06, C07, C08, CINAHL, CurCont, E01, EMBASE, ExcerpMed, I05, ISR, IndMed, Inpharma, MEDLINE, P30, R10, Reac, SCI, SCOPUS, W07.
—GNLM, IE, Infotrieve, Ingenta, INIST. **CCC.**
Published by: Bailliere Tindall (Subsidiary of: Elsevier Health Sciences), The Blvd, Langford Ln, Kidlington, Oxford OX5 1GB, United Kingdom. TEL 44-1865-843000, FAX 44-1865-843010, directenquiries@elsevier.com. Eds. K Hayes, Dr. S Arulkumaran TEL 44-20-87255956.

301.4 618 USA ISSN 0730-7659
RG651 CODEN: BRTHDD
➤ **BIRTH**; issues in perinatal care. Text in English. 1973. q. GBP 403 in United Kingdom to institutions; EUR 511 in Europe to institutions; USD 551 in Canada & Mexico to institutions; USD 522 in the Americas to institutions; USD 789 elsewhere to institutions; GBP 464 combined subscription in United Kingdom to institutions (print & online eds.); EUR 589 combined subscription in Europe to institutions (print & online eds.); USD 633 combined subscription in Canada & Mexico to institutions (print & online eds.); USD 600 combined subscription in the Americas to institutions (print & online eds.); USD 908 combined subscription elsewhere to institutions (print & online eds.) (effective 2012). adv. bk.rev. illus. Index. back issues avail.; reprint service avail. from PSC. **Document type:** *Journal, Academic/Scholarly.* **Description:** Covers education and technology regarding childbirth for childbirth educators, midwives and physicians.
Formerly (until 1982): Birth and the Family Journal (0098-860X)
Related titles: Microform ed.: (from PQC); Online - full text ed.: ISSN 1523-536X. GBP 403 in United Kingdom to institutions; EUR 511 in Europe to institutions; USD 551 in Canada & Mexico to institutions; USD 522 in the Americas to institutions; USD 789 elsewhere to institutions (effective 2012) (from IngentaConnect).
Indexed: A01, A03, A08, A20, A22, A26, A36, ASSIA, B28, C06, C07, C08, C28, CA, CABA, CINAHL, CurCont, D01, DokArb, E01, E12, EMBASE, ESPM, ExcerpMed, F09, FamI, G10, GH, H12, INI, IndMed, Inpharma, MEDLINE, N02, N03, NRN, P03, P24, P30, P35, P48, P50, PQC, PsycInfo, PsycholAb, R10, R12, Reac, RiskAb, S02, S03, SCI, SCOPUS, SSCI, T02, T05, W07, W09, W11.
—BLDSC (2094.081000), GNLM, IE, Infotrieve, Ingenta, INIST. **CCC.**
Published by: Wiley-Blackwell Publishing, Inc. (Subsidiary of: Wiley-Blackwell Publishing Ltd.), 111 River St, Hoboken, NJ 07030. TEL 201-748-6000, FAX 201-748-6088, info@wiley.com, http://www.wiley.com/WileyCDA/. Ed. Diony Young. Adv. contact Karl Franz TEL 781-388-8470.

618 USA ISSN 0890-3255
THE BIRTH GAZETTE. Text in English. 1977; N.S. 1985. q. USD 59.50 (effective 2004). adv. bk.rev. illus.; stat. reprints avail. **Document type:** *Bulletin, Consumer.* **Description:** Covers midwifery, childbirth issues, and access to maternity care.
Formerly (until vol.11, no.4, 1985): Practicing Midwife (0733-8317)
Related titles: Microform ed.: N.S. (from PQC); Online - full text ed.
Indexed: A04, C06, C07, C08, CINAHL, FamI, GW, INI, P30, P48, PQC, SCOPUS.
—GNLM, Infotrieve. **CCC.**
Published by: Second Foundation, 42 The Farm, Summertown, TN 38483. TEL 615-964-2519, brthgzt@usit.net. Ed., Pub. Ina May Gaskin. Adv. contact Kim Trainor. B&W page USD 650, color page USD 1,200. Circ: 3,000.

BIRTH PSYCHOLOGY BULLETIN. *see* PSYCHOLOGY

618.202 USA ISSN 1075-4733
THE BIRTHKIT. Text in English. 1994. q. USD 20 domestic; USD 23 in Canada & Mexico; USD 25 elsewhere (effective 2007). adv. bk.rev. illus.; tr.lit. back issues avail. **Document type:** *Newsletter, Consumer.* **Description:** Carries news, articles reviews and information for midwives, doulas, birth educators and other birth practitioners.
Related titles: Online - full text ed.
Indexed: A04, C06, C07, C08, C11, CINAHL, CWI, GW, P48, PQC, T02.
Published by: Midwifery Today Association, PO Box 2672, Eugene, OR 97402. TEL 541-344-7438, 800-743-0974, FAX 541-344-1422, admin@midwiferytoday.com. Ed., Pub., R&P Jan Tritten. Adv. contact Heather Maurer. Circ: 500.

618.92 ARG ISSN 1851-3298
BOLETIN DE LA MATERNIDAD. Text in Spanish. 2007. 3/yr.
Related titles: Online - full text ed.: ISSN 1851-3395.
Published by: Observatorio de la Maternidad, Ave Scalabrini Ortiz 2019 8o. E, Buenos Aires, C1425DBB, Argentina. TEL 54-11-48325047, info@0-maternidad.org.ar, http://www.o-maternidad.org.ar/observatoriodelaMaternidad.aspx. Ed. Carina Lupica.

618 616.4 ITA ISSN 2038-8489
BOLLETTINO DI GINECOLOGIA ENDOCRINOLOGICA. Text in Italian. 2007. bi-m. **Document type:** *Bulletin, Trade.*
Media: Online - full text.
Published by: Biomedical Technologies, Via Pasquale Cugia 1, Cagliari, 09129, Italy. TEL 39-070-340293, http://www.biomedicaltechnologies.com.

618 IRL
THE BOUNTY PREGNANCY GUIDE. Text in English. 1991. a. adv. **Document type:** *Journal, Consumer.*
Published by: Bounty Services (Ireland) Ltd., Bromhill Rd, Unit 66, Tallaght, Dublin, 24, Ireland. TEL 353-1-4596066, FAX 353-1-4596082.

618 GBR
BOUNTY YOUR PREGNANCY. Text in English. 1982. a. free (effective 2010). adv. **Document type:** *Journal, Consumer.*
Formerly (until 19??): The Bounty Pregnancy Guide
Related titles: Online - full text ed.
Published by: Bounty Publications Ltd., 29 Broadwater Rd, Welwyn Garden City, Herts, AL7 3BQ, United Kingdom.

618.1 GBR ISSN 0960-9776
CODEN: BREAEK
➤ **THE BREAST.** Text in English. 1992. q. EUR 1,111 in Europe to institutions; JPY 120,000 in Japan to institutions; USD 985 elsewhere to institutions (effective 2012). adv. abstr.; bibl. back issues avail.; reprints avail. **Document type:** *Journal, Academic/Scholarly.* **Description:** Covers the physiology of the normal breast and the etiology, biology, investigation, medical and surgical treatment and management of benign and malignant breast diseases.
Related titles: Online - full text ed.: ISSN 1532-3080 (from ScienceDirect).
Indexed: A20, A22, A26, A36, B25, BIOBASE, BIOSIS Prev, CA, CABA, CurCont, D01, E01, E12, EMBASE, ExcerpMed, G10, GH, H17, I05, IABS, Inpharma, MEDLINE, MycolAb, N02, N03, P30, P33, R10, R12, RM&VM, Reac, SCI, SCOPUS, T02, T05, W07.
—BLDSC (2277.492700), GNLM, IE, Infotrieve, Ingenta. **CCC.**
Published by: (Australasian Society for Breast Disease AUS, German Society for Senology DEU, European Society of Breast Cancer Specialists), Churchill Livingstone (Subsidiary of: Elsevier Health Sciences), The Blvd, Langford Ln, Kidlington, OX5 1GB, United Kingdom. TEL 44-1865-843434, FAX 44-1865-843970, directenquiries@elsevier.com, http://www.elsevierhealth.com/imprint.jsp?iid=9. Eds. Alberto Costa, Fatima Cardoso. Adv. contact Sarah Jane Cahill TEL 44-20-74244538. Circ: 852.

➤ **BREAST CANCER WEEKLY.** *see* MEDICAL SCIENCES—Oncology

618.1 CHE ISSN 1661-3791
RC942
➤ **BREAST CARE**; multidisciplinary journal for research, diagnosis and therapy. Text in English. 2006. bi-m. CHF 305, EUR 195, USD 333.50 to institutions; CHF 377, EUR 245, USD 408.50 combined subscription to institutions (print & online eds.) (effective 2012). adv. **Document type:** *Journal, Academic/Scholarly.*
Related titles: Online - full text ed.: ISSN 1661-3805. 2006. CHF 254, EUR 175, USD 263 to institutions (effective 2012).
Indexed: A20, A22, C06, C07, C08, CA, CINAHL, E01, EMBASE, ExcerpMed, P30, R10, Reac, SCI, SCOPUS, T02, W07.
—IE, Ingenta. **CCC.**
Published by: S. Karger AG, Allschwilerstr 10, Basel, 4055, Switzerland. TEL 41-61-3061111, FAX 41-61-3061234, karger@karger.ch, http://www.karger.ch. Ed. N Harbeck. adv.: page EUR 2,900; trim 210 x 297. Circ: 4,000 (paid).

618.1 616.99 NLD ISSN 0888-6008
RC280.B8 CODEN: BRDIE5
➤ **BREAST DISEASE.** Text in English. 1987. 4/yr. USD 646 combined subscription in North America (print & online eds.); EUR 460 combined subscription elsewhere (print & online eds.) (effective 2012). back issues avail. **Document type:** *Journal, Academic/Scholarly.* **Description:** Provides information on all aspects of human breast disease - benign and malignant - to help improve the health care and management of patients.
Related titles: Online - full text ed.: ISSN 1558-1551 (from IngentaConnect).
Indexed: A01, A03, A08, A22, BIOBASE, CA, E01, EMBASE, ExcerpMed, IABS, MEDLINE, NRN, P30, R10, Reac, SCOPUS, T02.
—BLDSC (2277.494070), CASDDS, GNLM, IE, Infotrieve, Ingenta, INIST. **CCC.**
Published by: I O S Press, Nieuwe Hemweg 6B, Amsterdam, 1013 BG, Netherlands. TEL 31-20-6883355, FAX 31-20-6870019, info@iospress.nl. Ed. Jeffrey E Green. **Subscr. to:** I O S Press, Inc, 4502 Rachael Manor Dr, Fairfax, VA 22032-3631. sales@iospress.com.

618.1 616.994 NLD
BREAST DISEASE SERIES. Text in English. irreg., latest vol.29, 2008. price varies. **Document type:** *Monographic series, Academic/Scholarly.*
Published by: I O S Press, Nieuwe Hemweg 6B, Amsterdam, 1013 BG, Netherlands. TEL 31-20-6883355, FAX 31-20-6870039, info@iospress.nl. **Subscr. to:** I O S Press, Inc, 4502 Rachael Manor Dr, Fairfax, VA 22032-3631. sales@iospress.com.

016.61819 USA ISSN 1043-321X
CODEN: TMGIDC
BREAST DISEASES: A YEAR BOOK QUARTERLY. Text in English. 1990. q. USD 301 in United States to institutions; USD 349 elsewhere to institutions (effective 2012). adv. back issues avail.; reprints avail. **Document type:** *Journal, Academic/Scholarly.* **Description:** Provides an interdisciplinary perspective on advances in prevention, diagnosis, and management of breast diseases.
Related titles: Microfilm ed.: (from PQC); Online - full text ed.: ISSN 1878-1918 (from ScienceDirect).
Indexed: A26, CA, EMBASE, ExcerpMed, I05, SCOPUS, T02.
—IE, Ingenta. **CCC.**
Published by: Mosby, Inc. (Subsidiary of: Elsevier Health Sciences), 1600 John F. Kennedy Blvd, Ste 1800, Philadelphia, PA 19103. TEL 215-239-3900, 800-523-1649, FAX 215-239-3990, elspcs@elsevier.com, http://www.us.elsevierhealth.com. Ed. Thomas A Buchholz.

618.19 USA ISSN 1075-122X
RG491 CODEN: BRJOFK
➤ **THE BREAST JOURNAL.** Text in English. 1995. bi-m. GBP 543 in United Kingdom to institutions; EUR 689 in Europe to institutions; USD 671 in the Americas to institutions; USD 1,064 elsewhere to institutions; GBP 625 combined subscription in United Kingdom to institutions (print & online eds.); EUR 793 combined subscription in Europe to institutions (print & online eds.); USD 772 combined subscription in the Americas to institutions (print & online eds.); USD 1,224 combined subscription elsewhere to institutions (print & online eds.) (effective 2012). adv. back issues avail.; reprints avail. **Document type:** *Journal, Academic/Scholarly.* **Description:** Encompasses the latest news and technologies from the many medical specialties concerned with breast disease care in order to address the disease within the context of an integrated breast health care.
Related titles: Online - full text ed.: ISSN 1524-4741. GBP 543 in United Kingdom to institutions; EUR 689 in Europe to institutions; USD 671 in the Americas to institutions; USD 1,064 elsewhere to institutions (effective 2012) (from IngentaConnect).
Indexed: A01, A02, A03, A08, A20, A22, A26, B&BAb, B19, B21, C06, C07, C08, C11, CA, CINAHL, CurCont, E01, EMBASE, ExcerpMed, G10, H04, H12, MEDLINE, OGFA, P30, R10, Reac, SCI, SCOPUS, T02, W07, W09.
—BLDSC (2277.494100), GNLM, IE, Infotrieve, Ingenta. **CCC.**
Published by: (American Society of Breast), Wiley-Blackwell Publishing, Inc. (Subsidiary of: Wiley-Blackwell Publishing Ltd.), 111 River St, Hoboken, NJ 07030. TEL 201-748-6000, FAX 201-748-6088, info@wiley.com. Ed. Dr. Shahla Masood. Adv. contact Stephen Donohue TEL 781-388-8511.

➤ **BREAST NEWS.** *see* MEDICAL SCIENCES—Oncology

618.1 AUS ISSN 1833-0177
BREASTSCREEN VICTORIA. ANNUAL REPORT (YEAR). Text in English. 1992. a., latest 2004. free upon request (effective 2008). back issues avail. **Document type:** *Report, Consumer.*
Former titles (until 2002): BreastScreen Victoria. Financial and Executive Report; (until 1995): BreastScreen. Annual Report (Year)
Related titles: Online - full text ed.: free (effective 2008).
Published by: BreastScreen Victoria, Level 1, 31 Pelham St, Carlton South, VIC 3053, Australia. TEL 61-3-96606888, FAX 61-3-96623881, info@breastscreen.org.au.

618.3 USA ISSN 0897-6112
RG627.6.D79
BRIGGS UPDATE: DRUGS IN PREGNANCY AND LACTATION. Key Title: Drugs in Pregnancy and Lactation. Text in English. 1983. q. USD 220 domestic to institutions; USD 319 foreign to institutions (effective 2011). adv. back issues avail. **Document type:** *Newsletter, Academic/Scholarly.* **Description:** Brings out news on prescription and nonprescription drugs.
—**CCC.**
Published by: Lippincott Williams & Wilkins (Subsidiary of: Wolters Kluwer N.V.), 530 Walnut St, Philadelphia, PA 19106. TEL 215-521-8300, FAX 215-521-8902, customerservice@lww.com. Eds. Gerald G Briggs, Dr. Roger K Freeman, Dr. Sumner J Yaffe.

618 GBR ISSN 0969-4900
RG950.A1
➤ **BRITISH JOURNAL OF MIDWIFERY.** Abbreviated title: B J M. Text in English. 1993. m. GBP 140 domestic to individuals; EUR 211 per issue in Europe to individuals; USD 312 per issue elsewhere to individuals; GBP 115 per issue to students (effective 2010). adv. back issues avail.; reprints avail. **Document type:** *Journal, Academic/Scholarly.* **Description:** Contains clinical reviews, original research and evidence-based articles available, and ensures that midwives are kept fully up-to-date with the latest developments taking place in clinical practice.
Related titles: Online - full text ed.
Indexed: A01, A02, A03, A08, AMED, B28, C06, C07, C08, C11, CA, CINAHL, F09, FamI, H04, SCOPUS, T02.
—BLDSC (2311.885000), IE, Infotrieve, Ingenta. **CCC.**
Published by: Mark Allen Publishing Ltd., St Jude's Church, Dulwich Rd, London, SE24 0PB, United Kingdom. TEL 44-20-77385454, FAX 44-20-79788316, subscriptions@markallengroup.com, http://www.markallengroup.com. Eds. Victoria Clift-Matthews, Tina Lavender, Yana Richens.

618 016 GBR ISSN 0140-7686
BRITISH JOURNAL OF OBSTETRICS & GYNAECOLOGY. SUPPLEMENT. Text in English. 1977. irreg. includes with subscr. to British Journal of Obstetrics & Gynecology. adv. **Document type:** *Journal, Academic/Scholarly.*
Related titles: Online - full text ed.; ◆ Supplement to: B J O G. ISSN 1470-0328.
Indexed: A22, SCOPUS.
—BLDSC (2312.310000), IE, Ingenta, INIST. **CCC.**
Published by: (Royal College of Obstetricians and Gynaecologists), Wiley-Blackwell Publishing Ltd. (Subsidiary of: John Wiley & Sons, Inc.), 9600 Garsington Rd, Oxford, OX4 2DQ, United Kingdom. TEL 44-1865-776868, FAX 44-1865-714591, customerservices@blackwellpublishing.com, http://www.wiley.com/. Pub. Allen Stevens. R&P Sarah Pollard. Adv. contact Jenny Applin.

618.2 617.96 JPN ISSN 0387-2653
BUNBEN TO MASUI/JOURNAL OF OBSTETRICS AND ANESTHESIA. Text in Japanese; Summaries in English. 1961. irreg.
Published by: (Bunben to Masui Kenkyukai), Kokuseido Shuppan K.K./Kokuseido Publishing Co. Ltd., 23-5-202 Hongo 3-chome, Bunkyo-ku, Tokyo, 113-0033, Japan. TEL 81-3-38110995, FAX 81-3-38131866.

618.19 GBR ISSN 1475-3480
➤ **C M E BREAST.** (Continuing Medical Education) Text in English. 2001. irreg., latest 2007. GBP 45 per vol. domestic to individuals; GBP 60 per vol. foreign to individuals; GBP 60 per vol. domestic to institutions; GBP 90 per vol. foreign to institutions (effective 2010). back issues avail. **Document type:** *Journal, Academic/Scholarly.*
Related titles: Online - full text ed.: GBP 30 per vol. (effective 2010).
Published by: Rila Publications Ltd., 73 Newman St, London, W1A 4PG, United Kingdom. TEL 44-20-76311299, FAX 44-20-75807166, admin@rila.co.uk. Eds. Gerald Gui, Hemant Singhai TEL 44-20-88692076.

618 HUN ISSN 1219-9087
CODEN: CJGOFS
C M E JOURNAL. GYNECOLOGIC ONCOLOGY; an international journal for continuing medical education on basic and clinical gynecologic oncology. (Continuing Medical Education) Text in English. 1996. 3/yr. EUR 190 to individuals; EUR 330 to institutions (effective 2003 - 2004). **Document type:** *Journal, Academic/Scholarly.* **Description:** Focuses on controversial issues and new developments in gynecologic oncology with the aim of providing a unique opportunity for those interested in postgraduate education in gynecologic oncology.
Indexed: EMBASE, ExcerpMed, R10, Reac, SCOPUS.
—BLDSC (3287.223046), IE, Ingenta.
Published by: Primed -X Press Publishing Ltd., PO Box 46, Budapest, 1301, Hungary. mail@primed-x.hu. Ed. Peter Bosze.

618.202 CAN ISSN 1703-2121
➤ **CANADIAN JOURNAL OF MIDWIFERY RESEARCH AND PRACTICE.** Text in English. 2002. 3/yr. USD 60 domestic to individuals; USD 80 foreign to individuals; USD 100 domestic to institutions; USD 120 foreign to institutions; USD 30 per issue (effective 2008). back issues avail.; reprints avail. **Document type:** *Journal, Academic/Scholarly.* **Description:** Publishes midwifery research, abstracts, case reports, clinical management strategies and news and information articles.
Related titles: Online - full content ed.
Indexed: C06, C07.
Published by: (Canadian Association of Midwives/Association Canadieene des Sages-Femmes), Log Cabin Press, 62 Mary St, Guelph, ON N1G 2B1, Canada. TEL 519-824-9000, FAX 519-824-9000, http://www.piper.ca/lcphome.html. Circ: 750.

➤ **CARING NOTES**; a professional newsletter by S H A R E. *see* PSYCHOLOGY

618 USA ISSN 2090-6684
▼ ➤ **CASE REPORTS IN OBSTETRICS AND GYNECOLOGY.** Text in English. 2011. **Document type:** *Journal, Academic/Scholarly.* **Description:** Publishes case reports in all areas of obstetrics and gynecology.
Related titles: Online - full text ed.: ISSN 2090-6692. 2011. free (effective 2011).
Published by: Hindawi Publishing Corporation, 410 Park Ave, 15th Fl, PMB 287, New York, NY 10022. FAX 215-893-4392, 866-446-3294, info@hindawi.com.

618 CZE ISSN 1210-7832
➤ **CESKA GYNEKOLOGIE/CZECH GYNAECOLOGY.** Text in Czech, Slovak; Summaries in English, Russian. 1936. 6/yr. CZK 660, EUR 39.60 (effective 2010). adv. bk.rev. **Document type:** *Journal, Academic/Scholarly.* **Description:** Publishes original papers from clinical practice, as well as information on the activities of professional societies.
Formerly (until 1993): Ceskoslovenska Gynekologie (0374-6852)
Related titles: Online - full text ed.
Indexed: A22, EMBASE, ExcerpMed, IndMed, MEDLINE, P30, R10, Reac, SCOPUS.
—GNLM, Infotrieve, INIST. **CCC.**
Published by: (Ceska Lekarska Spolecnost J.E. Purkyne/Czech Medical Association), Nakladatelske Stredisko C L S J.E. Purkyne, Sokolska 31, Prague, 12026, Czech Republic. nts@cls.cz. Ed. Dr. Radovan Pilka. adv.: B&W page CZK 27,300, color page CZK 39,700; 244 x 167. Circ: 2,400. **Co-sponsor:** Ceska Spolecnost Gynekologicka a Porodnicka.

618 USA ISSN 1076-1721
CHILDBIRTH (YEAR); your guide to the last trimester. Text in English. 1984. 3/yr. Dist. with The American Baby Basket for Expectant Parents through participating childbirth educators only. adv. illus. **Document type:** *Magazine, Consumer.* **Description:** Answers the questions of couples approaching the birth of their child. The magazine's four sections include: your pregnant body, getting ready for baby, labor and birth, and baby's early weeks.
Indexed: C06, C07, C08, CINAHL.
Published by: Meredith Corporation, 1716 Locust St, Des Moines, IA 50309. TEL 515-284-3000, 800-678-8091, FAX 515-284-3058, patrick.taylor@meredith.com, http://www.meredith.com. Ed., Adv. contact Maria Jakubek. B&W page USD 65,700, color page USD 90,900; trim 7.875 x 10.5. Circ: 2,300,000.

CLIMACTERIC. *see* WOMEN'S HEALTH

618 ESP ISSN 0210-573X
CODEN: CIGODJ
CLINICA E INVESTIGACION EN GINECOLOGIA Y OBSTETRICIA. Text in Spanish; Summaries in English. 1974. m. (10/yr.). EUR 146.56 combined subscription to individuals print & online eds.; EUR 431.05 combined subscription to institutions print & online eds. (effective 2009). reprints avail. **Document type:** *Journal, Academic/Scholarly.* **Description:** Covers the early detection of gynecological diseases and conditions, the improvement of family planning methods, the treatment of sterility and infertility, and the mother-child relationship during pregnancy.
Related titles: Online - full text ed.: ISSN 1578-9349. 1998. EUR 112.98 (effective 2009) (from ScienceDirect).
Indexed: A22, EMBASE, ExcerpMed, IME, P30, R10, Reac, SCOPUS.
—BLDSC (3286.202000), GNLM, IE, Infotrieve, Ingenta, INIST. **CCC.**
Published by: Elsevier Doyma (Subsidiary of: Elsevier Health Sciences), Traversa de Gracia 17-21, Barcelona, 08021, Spain. TEL 34-932-418800, FAX 34-932-419020, editorial@elsevier.com. Ed. Esteban Altirriba. Adv. contact Olga Gomez. Circ: 1,500.

618 CAN ISSN 0390-6663
CODEN: CEOGA4
➤ **CLINICAL AND EXPERIMENTAL OBSTETRICS AND GYNECOLOGY.** Text and summaries in English. 1974. q. USD 170 to individuals; USD 280 to institutions (effective 2005). adv. back issues avail. **Document type:** *Journal, Academic/Scholarly.*
Indexed: A22, ChemAb, CurCont, EMBASE, ExcerpMed, IndMed, MEDLINE, P30, R10, Reac, SCI, SCOPUS, W07.
—BLDSC (3286.251900), CASDDS, GNLM, IE, Infotrieve, Ingenta, INIST. **CCC.**
Published by: I R O G Canada, Inc., 4900 Cote St Luc, # 212, Montreal, PQ H3W 2H3, Canada. TEL 514-489-3242, FAX 514-485-4513, canlux@qc.aira.com. Ed. Antonio Onnis. Adv. contact Moriuz Morsoui.

618.1 GBR ISSN 1745-0837
➤ **CLINICAL FOCUS: OBSTETRICS & GYNAECOLOGY.** Text in English. 2004. irreg., latest 2007. GBP 45 per vol. domestic to individuals; GBP 60 per vol. foreign to individuals; GBP 60 per vol. domestic to institutions; GBP 90 per vol. foreign to institutions (effective 2010). back issues avail. **Document type:** *Journal, Academic/Scholarly.*
Related titles: Online - full text ed.: GBP 30 per vol. (effective 2010).
Published by: Rila Publications Ltd., 73 Newman St, London, W1A 4PG, United Kingdom. TEL 44-20-76311299, FAX 44-20-75807166, admin@rila.co.uk. Ed. Farook Al-Azzawi TEL 44-116-2523165.

618 USA ISSN 0009-9201
RG101 CODEN: COGYAK
➤ **CLINICAL OBSTETRICS AND GYNECOLOGY.** Text in English. 1958. q. USD 814 domestic to institutions; USD 1,033 foreign to institutions (effective 2011). adv. back issues avail.; reprints avail. **Document type:** *Journal, Academic/Scholarly.* **Description:** Focuses on one or two timely topics of interest in obstetrics and gynecology.
Related titles: Microform ed.: (from PQC); Online - full text ed.: ISSN 1532-5520. USD 295 to individuals (effective 2010).
Indexed: A01, A03, A08, A20, A22, A36, BDM&CN, C06, C07, C08, CA, CABA, CCIOG, CINAHL, ChemAb, CurCont, D01, DokArb, E12, EMBASE, ExcerpMed, FR, FamI, G10, GH, HospLI, ISR, IndMed, Inpharma, MEDLINE, N02, N03, P30, P33, P35, P39, R10, R12, Reac, SCI, SCOPUS, T02, T05, W07, W09.
—BLDSC (3286.316000), CASDDS, GNLM, IE, Infotrieve, Ingenta, INIST. **CCC.**
Published by: Lippincott Williams & Wilkins (Subsidiary of: Wolters Kluwer N.V.), Two Commerce Sq, 2001 Market St, Philadelphia, PA 19103. TEL 215-521-8300, FAX 215-521-8902, customerservice@lww.com, http://www.lww.com. Eds. Dr. James R Scott, Steven Gabbe. Pub. Matthew Jozwiak.

616.992 618.1 USA ISSN 1941-4390
➤ **CLINICAL OVARIAN CANCER AND OTHER GYNECOLOGIC MALIGNANCIES.** Text in English. 2008 (Jun.). s-a. USD 420 in United States to institutions; USD 470 elsewhere to institutions (effective 2012). **Document type:** *Journal, Academic/Scholarly.* **Description:** Publishes original articles describing various aspects of clinical and translational research in ovarian cancer, including detection, diagnosis, prevention, and treatment of ovarian and other gynecologic cancers. The main emphasis is on recent scientific developments in all areas related to gynecologic malignancies.
Related titles: Online - full text ed.: ISSN 1941-4404. 2008 (Jun.). USD 380 (effective 2009).
Indexed: A22, C06, C07, CA, E01, EMBASE, ExcerpMed, SCOPUS, T02.
—**CCC.**
Published by: C I G Media Group, L.P., 3500 Maple Ave, Ste 750, Dallas, TX 75219. TEL 214-367-3348, FAX 214-367-3301, http://www.cigjournals.com/. Ed. Tate Thigpen.

618 USA ISSN 0178-0328
CLINICAL PERSPECTIVES IN OBSTETRICS AND GYNECOLOGY. Text in English. 1983. irreg., latest vol.19, 1996. price varies. back issues avail. **Document type:** *Monographic series, Academic/Scholarly.*
Published by: Springer New York LLC (Subsidiary of: Springer Science+Business Media), 233 Spring St, New York, NY 10013. TEL 212-460-1500, FAX 212-460-1575, service-ny@springer.com. Ed. I Schiff.

618.92 618.12 CMR ISSN 1812-5840
➤ **CLINICS IN MOTHER AND CHILD HEALTH.** Text in English. 2003. 3/yr. USD 120 foreign (effective 2007). **Document type:** *Journal, Academic/Scholarly.* **Description:** Publishes original and review articles, case reports, editorials, reports from seminars and congresses relating to mother and child health issues.
Related titles: Online - full text ed.
Indexed: A01, A36, CABA, D01, GH, N02, N03, T05.
Published by: Yaounde Gyneco-Obstetric and Pediatric Hospital, PO Box 4362, Yaounde, Cameroon. tandersondoh@yahoo.com. Ed. Dr. Doh Anderson TEL 237-2212431.

618 USA ISSN 0095-5108
CODEN: CLPEDL
➤ **CLINICS IN PERINATOLOGY.** Text in English. 1974. q. USD 382 in United States to institutions; USD 485 elsewhere to institutions (effective 2012). adv. back issues avail.; reprints avail. **Document type:** *Journal, Academic/Scholarly.* **Description:** Provides updates on the latest trends in patient management; keeps up to date on the newest advances; and provides a sound basis for choosing treatment options.
Related titles: Online - full text ed.: ISSN 1557-9840 (from ScienceDirect); ◆ Spanish Translation: Clinicas de Perinatologia de Norteamerica; Supplement(s): Clinics in Perinatology: Continuing Medical Education Supplement. ISSN 1557-7864. USD 138 (effective 2000).
Indexed: A20, A22, A36, ASCA, BDM&CN, BIOSIS Prev, C06, C07, C08, CABA, CIN, CINAHL, ChemAb, ChemTitl, CurCont, D01, DentInd, EMBASE, ExcerpMed, F09, FR, GH, ISR, IndMed, Inpharma, MEDLINE, MycolAb, N02, N03, P30, P33, P39, R10, R12, RM&VM, Reac, SCI, SCOPUS, T05, W07.
—BLDSC (3286.585000), CASDDS, GNLM, IE, Infotrieve, Ingenta, INIST. **CCC.**
Published by: W.B. Saunders Co. (Subsidiary of: Elsevier Health Sciences), Elsevier, Health Sciences Division, Order Fulfillment, 3251 Riverport Ln, Maryland Heights, MO 63043. TEL 314-872-8370, 800-325-4177, FAX 314-432-1380, JournalCustomerService-usa@elsevier.com, http://www.us.elsevierhealth.com. Adv. contact John Marmero TEL 212-633-3657.

➤ **CLIO**; die Zeitschrift fuer Frauengesundheit. *see* WOMEN'S HEALTH

618 ARG ISSN 1667-913X
COLECCION TRABAJOS DISTINGUIDOS. SERIE OBSTETRICIA Y GINECOLOGIA. Text in Spanish. 1987. 6/yr. back issues avail. **Document type:** *Journal, Academic/Scholarly.*
Media: Online - full text.
Published by: Sociedad Iberoamericana de Informacion Cientifica (S I I C), Ave Belgrano 430, Buenos Aires, C1092AAR, Argentina. TEL 54-11-43424901, FAX 54-11-43313305, atencionallector@siicsalud.com, http://www.siicsalud.com. Ed. Rafael Bernal Castro.

618 USA ISSN 1559-4300
COMPENDIUM OF SELECTED PUBLICATIONS. Text in English. 1999. a. (in 2 vols.). USD 226 per issue to non-members; USD 99 per issue to members (effective 2010). **Document type:** *Journal, Academic/ Scholarly.*
Related titles: CD-ROM ed.: USD 104 per issue to non-members; USD 59 per issue to members (effective 2010).
Published by: American College of Obstetricians and Gynecologists, PO Box 96920, Washington, DC 20090. TEL 202-638-5577, publication@acog.org.

618 649 USA ISSN 0829-8564
HQ759
THE COMPLEAT MOTHER; the magazine of pregnancy, birth and breastfeeding. Text in English. 1985. q. USD 12 domestic (effective 2010). adv. bk.rev. illus. Index. back issues avail.; reprints avail. **Document type:** *Magazine, Consumer.*
Related titles: Online - full text ed.: USD 9 (effective 2010).
Published by: Compleat Mother, c/o Jody McLaughlin, P O Box 209, Minot, ND 58702. TEL 701-852-2822. Ed. Jody McLaughlin. Adv. contact Gail Gallant TEL 818-244-2941. B&W page USD 390; 6.75 x 9.25. **Subscr. in Canada to:** c/o Lonnie Gustafson, PO Box 2170, Fort St. James, BC V0J 1P0, Canada. TEL 250-996-7128, lonawas@yahoo.ca.

COMPLEMENTARY THERAPIES IN CLINICAL PRACTICE. *see* MEDICAL SCIENCES—Nurses And Nursing

618 FRA ISSN 2108-2340
▼ **CONSULTATION HYGIENE INTIME.** Text in French. 2010. irreg.
Published by: Help Medical, 211 b, Av Charles de Gaulle, Neuilly-sur Seine, 92200, France.

618 USA ISSN 0090-3159
RG1
➤ **CONTEMPORARY O B / G Y N.** (Obstetrics / Gynaecology) Text in English. 1973. m. USD 110 domestic; USD 140 foreign; USD 17 newsstand/cover domestic; USD 22 newsstand/cover in Canada & Mexico; USD 23 newsstand/cover elsewhere (effective 2011). adv. charts; illus.; stat. index. back issues avail. **Document type:** *Journal, Trade.* **Description:** Features practical advice by leading authorities in the ob-gyn field emphasizing clinical problems.
Related titles: Microfilm ed.: (from PQC); Online - full text ed.: ISSN 2150-6264.
Indexed: A22, A26, C06, C07, C08, CA, CINAHL, CLFP, E08, Faml, G08, H11, H12, I05, P30, P34, S02, S03, S09, SCOPUS, T02, W09.
—BLDSC (3425.196000), GNLM, IE, Infotrieve, Ingenta, INIST. **CCC.**
Published by: Advanstar Communications, Inc., 6200 Canoga Ave, 2nd Fl, Woodland Hills, CA 91367. TEL 818-593-5000, FAX 818-593-5020, info@advanstar.com, http://www.advanstar.com. Ed. Charles J Lockwood. Adv. contact Bill Smith TEL 440-891-2718. B&W page USD 5,645, color page USD 8,960.

➤ **CONTRACEPTION.** *see* BIRTH CONTROL

618 FRA ISSN 2107-514X
▼ **CONTRACEPTION PRATIQUE & GYNECOLOGIE.** Text in French. 2010. q.
Published by: L E N Medical - Axis Sante, 15 Rue des Sablons, Paris, 75116, France. TEL 33-1-47553131, FAX 33-1-47553132, info@len-medical.fr, http://www.len-medical.fr.

618.1 618.2 CHE ISSN 0304-4246
CODEN: CGOBD6
➤ **CONTRIBUTIONS TO GYNECOLOGY AND OBSTETRICS.** Text in English. 1950. irreg., latest vol.20, 2000. price varies. back issues avail.; reprints avail. **Document type:** *Monographic series, Academic/ Scholarly.* **Description:** Devoted to current problems in all fields of gynecology including endocrinology, reproduction biology, oncology, and perinatal medicine.
Formerly (until 1976): Advances in Obstetrics and Gynaecology (0065-2997)
Related titles: Online - full text ed.: ISSN 1662-2901.
Indexed: A22, ASCA, CIN, ChemAb, ChemTitl, EMBASE, ExcerpMed, IndMed, MEDLINE, P30, R10, Reac, SCOPUS.
—BLDSC (3458.610000), CASDDS, GNLM, Infotrieve, Ingenta, INIST. **CCC.**
Published by: S. Karger AG, Allschwilerstr 10, Basel, 4055, Switzerland. TEL 41-61-3061111, FAX 41-61-3061234, karger@karger.ch, http://www.karger.ch. Ed. O R Kochli.

618.202 AUS
COSMOPOLITAN PREGNANCY. Text in English. 2000. biennial. AUD 11.95 newsstand/cover (effective 2008). adv. **Document type:** *Magazine, Consumer.* **Description:** Provides information possible to pregnant women about pregnancy, birth and motherhood.
Related titles: ◆ Supplement to: Cosmopolitan (Australian Edition). ISSN 0310-2076.
Published by: A C P Magazines Ltd. (Subsidiary of: P B L Media Pty Ltd.), 54-58 Park St, Sydney, NSW 2000, Australia. TEL 61-2-92828000, FAX 61-2-91263769, research@acpaction.com.au. Ed. Franki Hobson. Adv. contact Cameron Jones TEL 61-2-92889123. color page AUD 6,800; trim 220 x 297.

COST SURVEY FOR OBSTETRICS AND GYNECOLOGY PRACTICES. *see* HEALTH FACILITIES AND ADMINISTRATION

CREATING FAMILIES/TRAVAIL EN COURS; the Canadian journal of reproductive health. *see* MEDICAL SCIENCES—Endocrinology

CURATIONIS; accredited research journal of the Democratic Nursing Organisation of South Africa. *see* MEDICAL SCIENCES—Nurses And Nursing

618 GBR ISSN 1759-8117
CURRENT MEDICAL LITERATURE. GYNECOLOGY & OBSTETRICS (ONLINE). Text in English. 2004. q. free to qualified personnel (effective 2009). back issues avail. **Document type:** *Journal, Academic/Scholarly.*
Media: Online - full text.
Published by: Remedica Medical Education and Publishing Ltd., Commonwealth House, 1 New Oxford St, London, WC1A 1NU, United Kingdom. TEL 44-20-77592999, FAX 44-20-77592951, info@remedica.com, http://www.remedica.com. Ed. Natalie Nkwor.

618 USA ISSN 1040-872X
RG1 CODEN: COOGEA
➤ **CURRENT OPINION IN OBSTETRICS & GYNECOLOGY.** Text in English. 1989. bi-m. USD 1,157 domestic to institutions; USD 1,245 foreign to institutions (effective 2011). adv. bibl.; illus. index. back issues avail.; reprints avail. **Document type:** *Journal, Academic/ Scholarly.* **Description:** Covers key subjects such as gynecologic oncology and pathology, maternal-fetal medicine, prenatal diagnosis, fertility, reproductive endocrinology, endoscopic surgery, adult and pediatric gynecology, urogynecology, and women's health.
Related titles: Diskette ed.; Online - full text ed.: ISSN 1473-656X. USD 275 to individuals (effective 2011); Optical Disk - DVD ed.: Current Opinion in Obstetrics & Gynecology, with Evaluated MEDLINE. ISSN 1080-8256.
Indexed: A20, A22, ASCA, BIOBASE, C06, C07, C08, CINAHL, CurCont, E01, EMBASE, ExcerpMed, IABS, IndMed, Inpharma, MEDLINE, P30, R10, Reac, SCI, SCOPUS, W07.
—BLDSC (3500.776200), GNLM, IE, Infotrieve, Ingenta, INIST. **CCC.**
Published by: Lippincott Williams & Wilkins (Subsidiary of: Wolters Kluwer N.V.), 530 Walnut St, Philadelphia, PA 19106. TEL 215-521-8300, FAX 215-521-8902, customerservice@lww.com, http://www.lww.com. Ed. Jonathan S Berek. Pub. Ian Burgess. Circ: 559.

618 NLD ISSN 1573-4048
RG1
➤ **CURRENT WOMEN'S HEALTH REVIEWS.** Text in English. 2005 (Jan.). q. USD 480 to institutions (print or online ed.) (effective 2012). adv. back issues avail.; reprints avail. **Document type:** *Journal, Academic/Scholarly.* **Description:** Publishes frontier reviews on all the latest advances on obstetrics and gynecology.
Related titles: Online - full text ed.: ISSN 1875-6581 (from IngentaConnect).
Indexed: A01, C06, C07, CA, EMBASE, ExcerpMed, P30, R10, Reac, SCOPUS, T02.
—IE, Ingenta. **CCC.**
Published by: Bentham Science Publishers Ltd., PO Box 294, Bussum, 1400 AG, Netherlands. TEL 31-35-6923800, FAX 31-35-6980150, sales@bentham.org, http://www.bentham.org. Ed. Jose M Belizan. **Subscr. to:** Bentham Science Publishers Ltd., c/o Richard E Morrissy, PO Box 446, Oak Park, IL 60301. TEL 312-413-5867, FAX 312-996-7107, subscriptions@bentham.org.

618 DEU ISSN 0723-8029
DEUTSCHE GESELLSCHAFT FUER GYNAEKOLOGIE UND GEBURTSHILFE. MITTEILUNGEN. Text in German. 1977. q. **Document type:** *Journal, Academic/Scholarly.*
Published by: Deutsche Gesellschaft fuer Gynaekologie und Geburtshilfe, Robert-Koch-Platz 7, Berlin, 10115, Germany. TEL 49-30-5148833, FAX 49-30-51488344, info@dggg.de, http://www.dggg.de. Circ: 3,000.

618 DEU ISSN 0012-026X
DEUTSCHE HEBAMMEN-ZEITSCHRIFT; Fachblatt fuer Hebammen und Entbildungspfleger. Text in German. 1886. m. EUR 68; EUR 28 to students; EUR 6 newsstand/cover (effective 2009). adv. bk.rev. charts; illus.; stat. index. **Document type:** *Magazine, Trade.*
Incorporates (1948-1969): Sueddeutsche Hebammen-Zeitung (0176-0807)
—GNLM. **CCC.**
Published by: (Bund Deutscher Hebammen), Elwin Staude Verlag GmbH, Postfach 510660, Hannover, 30636, Germany. TEL 49-511-651003, FAX 49-511-651788, info@staudeverlag.de. Ed. Katja Baumgarten. Pub. Britta Zickfeldt. adv.: B&W page EUR 1,550, color page EUR 2,350; trim 185 x 265. Circ: 9,029 (paid and controlled).

DIRECTORY OF FETAL ALCOHOL SPECTRUM DISORDER (F A S D) INFORMATION AND SUPPORT SERVICES IN CANADA/ REPERTOIRE CANADIEN DES SERVICES D'INFORMATION ET DE SOUTIEN SUR L'ENSEMBLE DES TROUBLES CAUSES PAR L'ALCOOLISME FOETALE (E T C A F). *see* SOCIAL SERVICES AND WELFARE

DISABILITY, PREGNANCY & PARENTHOOD INTERNATIONAL; journal for disabled parents and professionals to exchange information and experience. *see* HANDICAPPED

DONALD SCHOOL JOURNAL OF ULTRASOUND IN OBSTETRICS AND GYNECOLOGY. *see* MEDICAL SCIENCES—Radiology And Nuclear Medicine

618 FRA ISSN 0767-8193
LES DOSSIERS DE L'OBSTETRIQUE. Text in French. 1974. 11/yr. EUR 7.50 newsstand/cover (effective 2008). **Document type:** *Magazine, Trade.*
—BLDSC (3619.780500), IE.
Published by: E L P E A, 62 Rue du Faubourg-Poissonniere, Paris, 75010, France. TEL 33-1-42466996, FAX 33-1-47703702, info.do@elpea.fr, http://www.elpea.fr.

618 EGY ISSN 1687-8388
E L C A SCIENTIFIC JOURNAL/MAGALLAT AL-'ILMIYYAT LI-L-GAM'IYYAT AL-MISRIYYAT LI-ISTSHARI AL-RIDHA'AT AL-TABI'IYYAT/MAJALLAT AL-'ILMIYYAT LI-L-JAM'IYYAT AL-MISRIYYAT LI-ISTSHARI AL-RIDHA'AT AL-TABI'IYYAT. (Egyptian Lactation Consultant Association) Text in English. 2006. q. **Document type:** *Journal, Academic/Scholarly.*
Published by: Egyptian Lactation Consultant Association, 2 Aly Ibrahim St, El-Muniera, Cairo, Egypt. TEL 202-3362-4681, FAX 202-3362-4689, azfadl@yahoo.com. Ed. Dr. Muhammad Emad El-Din Salem.

618.2 IRL ISSN 0378-3782
RG600 CODEN: EHDEDN
➤ **EARLY HUMAN DEVELOPMENT.** Text in English. 1977. 12/yr. EUR 2,027 in Europe to institutions; JPY 268,500 in Japan to institutions; USD 2,265 elsewhere to institutions (effective 2012). adv. bk.rev. back issues avail. **Document type:** *Journal, Academic/Scholarly.* **Description:** Publishes original research papers with particular emphasis on the continuum between fetal life and the perinatal period; aspects of postnatal growth influenced by early events; and the safeguarding of the quality of human survival.
Incorporates (1992-1996): Screening (0925-6164); Which was previously announced as: International Journal of Neonatal and Later Screening
Related titles: Microform ed.: (from PQC); Online - full text ed.: ISSN 1872-6232 (from IngentaConnect, ScienceDirect).
Indexed: A01, A03, A08, A22, A26, A34, A36, A38, B21, B25, BDM&CN, BIOSIS Prev, C06, C07, CA, CABA, CIN, CTA, ChemAb, ChemTitl, CurCont, D01, E-psyche, E07, E08, E12, EMBASE, ExcerpMed, F09, FR, Faml, GH, H11, H12, H16, INI, ISR, IndMed, Inpharma, MEDLINE, MycolAb, N02, N03, N04, NRN, NSA, P03, P30, P33, P35, P39, PHN&I, PsycInfo, PsycholAb, R10, R12, RA&MP, RM&VM, Reac, S09, S12, SCI, SCOPUS, SoyAb, T02, T05, THA, VS, W07.
—BLDSC (3642.983000), CASDDS, GNLM, IE, Infotrieve, Ingenta, INIST. **CCC.**
Published by: Elsevier Ireland Ltd (Subsidiary of: Elsevier Science & Technology), Elsevier House, Brookvale Plaza, E. Park, Shannon, Co. Clare, Ireland. TEL 353-61-709600, FAX 353-61-709100. Ed. E F Maalouf. R&P Annette Moloney. **Subscr. to:** Elsevier BV, Radarweg 29, PO Box 211, Amsterdam 1000 AE, Netherlands. TEL 31-20-4853757, FAX 31-20-4853432, JournalsCustomerServiceEMEA@elsevier.com, http://www.elsevier.nl.

618 USA ISSN 1930-2657
EDOULA. Text in English. 2005. m. **Document type:** *Newsletter, Consumer.*
Media: Online - full text.
Published by: Creatonomy, 1661 N Water St, Ste 200, Milwaukee, WI 53202. TEL 414-223-7500, FAX 414-223-7501, http://www.creatonomy.com.

618 EGY ISSN 0258-3216
CODEN: JESGD2
EGYPTIAN SOCIETY OF OBSTETRICS & GYNECOLOGY. JOURNAL. Text in English. 1975. 3/yr. **Document type:** *Journal, Academic/ Scholarly.*
Indexed: P30.
Published by: The Egyptian Society of Obstetrics and Gynecology, Dar El-Hekma, 42 Qasr el-Aini St, Cairo, Egypt. TEL 20-2-7943406. Ed. Dr. Muhammad B Sammour.

618.202 DEU
ELTERN SPECIAL GEBURT. Text in German. 1986. a. EUR 3.90 newsstand/cover (effective 2010). adv. **Document type:** *Magazine, Consumer.*
Formerly (until 2006): Eltern Sonderheft Geburt
Published by: Gruner + Jahr AG & Co, Weihenstephaner Str 7, Munich, 81673, Germany. TEL 49-89-41520, FAX 49-89-4152651, guj-redaktion@guj.de, http://www.guj.de. Adv. contact Nicole Schostak. Circ: 110,000 (controlled).

618.2 DEU
ELTERN SPECIAL SCHWANGERSCHAFT. Text in German. 1979. a. EUR 3.80 newsstand/cover (effective 2010). adv. **Document type:** *Magazine, Consumer.*
Formerly (until 2006): Eltern Sonderheft Schwangerschaft
Published by: Gruner + Jahr AG & Co, Weihenstephaner Str 7, Munich, 81673, Germany. TEL 49-89-41520, FAX 49-89-4152651, guj-redaktion@guj.de, http://www.guj.de. Adv. contact Nicole Schostak. Circ: 130,000 (controlled).

618.2 ESP ISSN 1575-1694
EMBARAZO SANO. Text in Spanish. 1999. 6/yr. EUR 12.60 domestic; EUR 38 in Europe; EUR 47 elsewhere (effective 2009). adv. **Document type:** *Magazine, Consumer.* **Description:** Contains articles on health issues, hygiene, nutrition and recommended exercises for pregnant women and their newborns.
Related titles: ◆ Supplement(s): Embarazo Sano Extra. ISSN 1576-8945.
Published by: Globus Comunicacion (Subsidiary of: Bonnier AB), Covarrubias 1, Madrid, 28010, Spain. TEL 34-91-4471202, FAX 34-91-4471043, txhdez@globuscom.es, http://www.globuscom.es. Ed. Pilar Marcos Arango. adv.: color page EUR 3,845; trim 19.5 x 27. Circ: 19,919.

618.2 ESP ISSN 1576-8945
EMBARAZO SANO EXTRA. Text in Spanish. 2000. bi-m. adv. **Document type:** *Monographic series, Consumer.*
Related titles: ◆ Supplement to: Embarazo Sano. ISSN 1575-1694.
Published by: Globus Comunicacion (Subsidiary of: Bonnier AB), Covarrubias 1, Madrid, 28010, Spain. TEL 34-91-4471202, FAX 34-91-4471043, txhdez@globuscom.es, http://www.globuscom.es. Eds. Nuria Penalva, Terry Grajera.

618 GBR
EMMA'S DIARY. Text in English. 1992. 2/yr. free. adv. **Document type:** *Magazine, Consumer.* **Description:** Designed to provide pregnant mothers with an up-to-date guide to pregnancy.
Published by: (Royal College of General Practitioners), Lifecycle Marketing (Mother & Baby) Ltd., 1 Globeside Business Park, Fieldhouse Lane, Morrow, Bucks SL7 1HY, United Kingdom.

ENCEINTE & ACCOUCHER. *see* WOMEN'S HEALTH

618 FRA ISSN 1283-081X
ENCYCLOPEDIE MEDICO-CHIRURGICALE. GINECOLOGIA - OBSTETRICIA. Cover title: Tratado de Ginecologia - Obstetricia. Text in Spanish. 1998. 5 base vols. plus q. updates. EUR 937.02 (effective 2003). bibl.; charts; illus. **Document type:** *Academic/Scholarly.* **Description:** Provides a comprehensive, up-to-date reference for topics in gynecology and obstetrics.
Related titles: ◆ French ed.: Encyclopedie Medico-Chirurgicale. Gynecologie. ISSN 0246-1064; ◆ Italian ed.: Encyclopedie Medico-Chirurgicale. Ginecologia - Ostetricia. ISSN 1293-2639.
Published by: Elsevier Masson (Subsidiary of: Elsevier Health Sciences), 62 Rue Camille Desmoulins, Issy les Moulineaux, Cedex 92442, France. TEL 33-1-71165500, FAX 33-1-71165600, infos@elsevier-masson.fr, http://www.elsevier-masson.fr.

618 FRA ISSN 1293-2639
ENCYCLOPEDIE MEDICO-CHIRURGICALE. GINECOLOGIA - OSTETRICIA; la collana della donna, dalla prevenzione alla condotta terapeutica. Cover title: Trattato di Ginecologia - Ostetricia. Text in Italian. 1998. 5 base vols. plus q. updates. EUR 937.02 (effective 2003). bibl.; charts; illus. **Document type:** *Academic/Scholarly.* **Description:** Provides up-to-date reference topics in gynecology and obstetrics.
Related titles: ◆ French ed.: Encyclopedie Medico-Chirurgicale. Gynecologie. ISSN 0246-1064; ◆ Spanish ed.: Encyclopedie Medico-Chirurgicale. Ginecologia - Obstetricia. ISSN 1283-081X.
Published by: Elsevier Masson (Subsidiary of: Elsevier Health Sciences), 62 Rue Camille Desmoulins, Issy les Moulineaux, Cedex 92442, France. TEL 33-1-71165500, FAX 33-1-71165600, infos@elsevier-masson.fr, http://www.elsevier-masson.fr.

618 FRA ISSN 0246-1064
➤ **ENCYCLOPEDIE MEDICO-CHIRURGICALE. GYNECOLOGIE.** Cover title: Traite de Gynecologie. Variant title: Encyclopedie Medico-Chirurgicale, Instantanes Medicaux. Gynecologie. Receuil Periodique de l'Encyclopedie Medico-Chirurgicale. Gynecologie. Text in French. 1930. 4 base vols. plus q. updates. EUR 902 to individuals (effective 2006). bibl.; charts; illus. **Document type:** *Academic/Scholarly.* **Description:** Offers gynecologists and obstetricians a comprehensive, up-to-date reference for diagnosing and treating gynecologic conditions and disorders.
Formerly: Encyclopedie Medico-Chirurgicale. Gynecologie - Mamelle (0246-067X)
Related titles: Online - full text ed.; ◆ Italian ed.: Encyclopedie Medico-Chirurgicale. Ginecologia - Ostetricia. ISSN 1293-2639; ◆ Spanish ed.: Encyclopedie Medico-Chirurgicale. Ginecologia - Obstetricia. ISSN 1283-081X.
—INIST. **CCC.**
Published by: Elsevier Masson (Subsidiary of: Elsevier Health Sciences), 62 Rue Camille Desmoulins, Issy les Moulineaux, Cedex 92442, France. TEL 33-1-71165500, FAX 33-1-71165600, infos@elsevier-masson.fr.

618.2 FRA ISSN 0246-0335
➤ **ENCYCLOPEDIE MEDICO-CHIRURGICALE. OBSTETRIQUE.** Cover title: Traite d'Obstetrique. Variant title: Encyclopedie Medico-Chirurgicale, Instantanes Medicaux. Obstetrique. Text in French. 4 base vols. plus q. updates. EUR 749.62 (effective 2003). bibl.; charts; illus. **Document type:** *Academic/Scholarly.* **Description:** Provides a comprehensive, up-to-date reference for diagnosing and treating obstetric conditions and disorders.
Related titles: Online - full text ed.
—INIST. **CCC.**
Published by: Elsevier Masson (Subsidiary of: Elsevier Health Sciences), 62 Rue Camille Desmoulins, Issy les Moulineaux, Cedex 92442, France. TEL 33-1-71165500, FAX 33-1-71165600, infos@elsevier-masson.fr.

➤ **ENCYCLOPEDIE MEDICO-CHIRURGICALE. RADIOLOGIE ET IMAGERIE MEDICALE. GENITO-URINAIRE - GYNECO-OBSTETRICALE - MAMMAIRE.** *see* MEDICAL SCIENCES—Radiology And Nuclear Medicine

➤ **ENCYCLOPEDIE MEDICO-CHIRURGICALE. TECHNIQUES CHIRURGICALES. GYNECOLOGIE.** *see* MEDICAL SCIENCES—Surgery

618 USA ISSN 0897-1870
ENDOMETRIOSIS ASSOCIATION NEWSLETTER. Text in English. 1980. bi-m. USD 35 membership; USD 40 to non-members (effective 2003). bk.rev. abstr.; bibl.; charts; illus.; stat. Index. 2 cols./p.; reprints avail. **Document type:** *Newsletter, Consumer.* **Description:** Offers information about endometriosis, a chronic disease affecting women and girls primarily in their reproductive years. Includes medical research and patient news and information.
Formerly (until 1988): Endometriosis Association (0899-2967)
Published by: Endometriosis Association, Inc., 8585 N 76th Pl, Milwaukee, WI 53223. TEL 414-355-2200, 800-992-3636, FAX 414-355-6065. Ed. Mary Lou Ballweg. R&P Sheila Schmidt. Circ: 10,000.

618 USA ISSN 1554-1894
EPREGNANCY. Text in English. 2002 (Jun.). m. USD 10; USD 4.99 newsstand/cover (effective 2005). adv. **Document type:** *Magazine, Consumer.* **Description:** Contains informative articles, helpful tools and interactive resources about everything related to pregnancy.
Published by: Myria Media, Inc., 3606 E. Monona Dr., Phoenix, AZ 85050-4847. feedback@myria.com, http://myriamedia.com. adv.: color page USD 23,000.

618.12 USA
ESPERA. Text in Spanish. s-a. free avail. through participating Ob/Gyn offices (effective 2008). adv. **Document type:** *Magazine, Consumer.* **Description:** Prepares Hispanic mothers-to-be for all phases of their pregnancy and delivery.
Published by: Meredith Corporation, 1716 Locust St, Des Moines, IA 50309. TEL 515-284-3000, 800-678-8091, FAX 515-284-3058, patrick.taylor@meredith.com. Pub. Emedina Vega-Amaez TEL 212-499-2106. adv.: color page AUD 32,100, B&W page AUD 23,600; trim 7.875 x 10.5. Circ: 375,000.

618.2 DEU ISSN 1435-6945
EUROPAEISCHER ARBEITSKREIS FUER PRAE- UND POSTNATALE ENTWICKLUNGSFORSCHUNG. SCHRIFTENREIHE. Text in German. 1995. irreg., latest vol.4, 1995. price varies. **Document type:** *Monographic series, Academic/Scholarly.*
Published by: Verlag Dr. Kovac, Leverkusenstr 13, Hamburg, 22761, Germany. TEL 49-40-3988800, FAX 49-40-39888055, info@verlagdrkovac.de.

618.2 POL ISSN 0071-2698
EUROPEAN CONGRESS OF PERINATAL MEDICINE. PROCEEDINGS. Text in German. biennial, latest 2008, 21st, Istanbul. **Document type:** *Proceedings, Academic/Scholarly.*
Published by: European Association of Perinatal Medicine, c/o Grzegorz Breborowicz, ul Polna, 33, Poznan, 60 535, Poland. TEL 48-61-8419283, FAX 48-61-8419204, gbrebor@sk3.usoms.poznan.pl, http://www.eapm.pl.

THE EUROPEAN JOURNAL OF CONTRACEPTION AND REPRODUCTIVE HEALTH CARE. *see* BIRTH CONTROL

EUROPEAN JOURNAL OF GYNECOLOGICAL ONCOLOGY. *see* MEDICAL SCIENCES—Oncology

618 IRL ISSN 0301-2115
CODEN: EOGRAL
➤ **EUROPEAN JOURNAL OF OBSTETRICS & GYNECOLOGY AND REPRODUCTIVE BIOLOGY.** Text in English. 1889. 12/yr. EUR 3,421 in Europe to institutions; JPY 454,500 in Japan to institutions; USD 3,829 elsewhere to institutions (effective 2012). adv. bk.rev. bibl.; charts. back issues avail. **Document type:** *Journal, Academic/Scholarly.* **Description:** Serves both the clinical practitioner and researcher by publishing studies, case reports and reviews of developments, as well as basic biochemical, physiological, embryological and genetic research related to human reproduction.
Former titles (until 1973): European Journal of Obstetrics and Gynecology (0028-2243); (until 1971): Nederlandsch Tijdschrift voor Verloskunde en Gynaecologie (0301-2247)
Related titles: Microform ed.: (from PQC); Online - full text ed.: ISSN 1872-7654 (from IngentaConnect, ScienceDirect); ◆ Spanish ed.: European Journal of Obstetrics and Gynecology and Reproductive Biology (Spanish Edition). ISSN 1576-7965; ◆ Supplement(s): European Journal of Obstetrics, Gynaecology and Reproductive Biology. Supplement. ISSN 0921-8750.
Indexed: A01, A03, A08, A20, A22, A26, A29, A34, A35, A36, A38, ASCA, AgBio, B20, B21, BIOBASE, CA, CABA, CIN, CTA, ChemAb, ChemTitl, CurCont, D01, DentInd, E12, EMBASE, ESPM, ExcerpMed, F09, FR, GH, H16, H17, I05, I10, IABS, INI, ISR, IndMed, Inpharma, MEDLINE, N02, N03, N04, NRN, P30, P33, P35, P39, R08, R10, R12, RA&MP, RM&VM, Reac, SCI, SCOPUS, SoyAb, T02, T05, VS, W07, W09.
—BLDSC (3829.733000), CASDDS, GNLM, IE, Infotrieve, Ingenta, INIST. **CCC.**
Published by: (European Association of Gynaecologists and Obstetricians), Elsevier Ireland Ltd (Subsidiary of: Elsevier Science & Technology), Elsevier House, Brookvale Plaza, E. Park, Shannon, Co. Clare, Ireland. TEL 353-61-709600, FAX 353-61-709100. Ed. J O Drife. R&P Annette Moloney. **Subscr. to:** Elsevier BV, Radarweg 29, PO Box 211, Amsterdam 1000 AE, Netherlands. TEL 31-20-4853757, FAX 31-20-4853432, JournalsCustomerServiceEMEA@elsevier.com, http://www.elsevier.nl.

618 ESP ISSN 1576-7965
EUROPEAN JOURNAL OF OBSTETRICS AND GYNECOLOGY AND REPRODUCTIVE BIOLOGY (SPANISH EDITION). Text in Spanish. 2000. bi-m. EUR 75. back issues avail. **Document type:** *Journal, Academic/Scholarly.*
Related titles: ◆ English ed.: European Journal of Obstetrics & Gynecology and Reproductive Biology. ISSN 0301-2115.
—**CCC.**
Published by: Grupo Saned, Capitan Haya 60, 1o, Madrid, 28028, Spain. TEL 34-91-7499500, FAX 34-91-7499501, saned@medynet.com, http://www.gruposaned.com. Ed. Luis Cabero. Circ: 3,000.

618 IRL ISSN 0921-8750
EUROPEAN JOURNAL OF OBSTETRICS, GYNAECOLOGY AND REPRODUCTIVE BIOLOGY. SUPPLEMENT. Text in English. 1988. irreg.
Related titles: ◆ Supplement to: European Journal of Obstetrics & Gynecology and Reproductive Biology. ISSN 0301-2115.
Published by: Elsevier Ireland Ltd (Subsidiary of: Elsevier Science & Technology), Elsevier House, Brookvale Plaza, E. Park, Shannon, Co. Clare, Ireland. TEL 353-61-709600, FAX 353-61-709100, nlinfo@elsevier.nl, http://www.elsevier.nl. **Subscr. to:** Elsevier BV, Radarweg 29, PO Box 211, Amsterdam 1000 AE, Netherlands. TEL 31-20-4853757, FAX 31-20-4853432, http://www.elsevier.nl.

618 NLD ISSN 1625-1180
EUROPEAN PRACTICE IN GYNAECOLOGY AND OBSTETRICS. Text in English. 2002. irreg., latest vol.9, 2006. price varies. **Document type:** *Monographic series, Academic/Scholarly.* **Description:** Reviews basic science, recent concepts in pathophysiology, clinical aspects, imaging, treatment, and unresolved problems or controversies in gynecology and obstetrics.
Published by: Elsevier BV (Subsidiary of: Elsevier Science & Technology), Radarweg 29, PO Box 211, Amsterdam, 1000 AE, Netherlands. JournalsCustomerServiceEMEA@elsevier.com, http://www.elsevier.com.

618.202 GBR ISSN 1479-4489
EVIDENCE - BASED MIDWIFERY. Text in English. 2003. s-a.
Related titles: ◆ Supplement to: Midwives.
Indexed: A26, B28, C06, C07, C08, CINAHL, H12, I05, SCOPUS.
—BLDSC (3831.037250), IE.
Published by: Ten Alps Publishing (Subsidiary of: Ten Alps Group), Bridgewater House, Whitworth St, Manchester, M1 6LT, United Kingdom. TEL 44-161-8326000, FAX 44-161-8324176, http://www.tenalps.com.

EXCERPTA MEDICA. SECTION 10: OBSTETRICS AND GYNECOLOGY. *see* MEDICAL SCIENCES—Abstracting, Bibliographies, Statistics

EXCERPTA MEDICA. SECTION 21: DEVELOPMENTAL BIOLOGY AND TERATOLOGY. *see* BIOLOGY—Abstracting, Bibliographies, Statistics

618.05 GBR ISSN 1747-4108
RG1
➤ **EXPERT REVIEW OF OBSTETRICS & GYNECOLOGY.** Text in English. 2006 (Sep.). bi-m. GBP 695 combined subscription domestic (print & online eds.); USD 1,220 combined subscription in North America (print & online eds.); JPY 129,000 combined subscription in Japan (print & online eds.); EUR 975 combined subscription elsewhere (print & online eds.) (effective 2011). adv. back issues avail.; reprints avail. **Document type:** *Journal, Academic/Scholarly.* **Description:** Provides evaluated, structured commentary from international leaders in the key field of obstetrics and gynecology.
Related titles: Online - full text ed.: ISSN 1747-4116. GBP 615 domestic to institutions; USD 1,080 in North America to institutions; JPY 115,500 in Japan to institutions; EUR 865 elsewhere to institutions (effective 2011) (from IngentaConnect).
Indexed: A26, CA, E08, EMBASE, ExcerpMed, H11, H12, I05, P20, P30, P48, P54, PQC, SCOPUS.
—BLDSC (9830.006000), IE, Ingenta. **CCC.**
Published by: Expert Reviews Ltd. (Subsidiary of: Future Science Ltd.), Unitec House, 2 Albert Pl, London, N3 1QB, United Kingdom. TEL 44-20-83716080, FAX 44-20-83716099, info@expert-reviews.com. Ed. Elisa Manzotti TEL 44-20-83716090. Pub. David Hughes. Adv. contact Simon Boisseau. Circ: 375.

618.1 DEU ISSN 0342-2801
➤ **EXTRACTA GYNAECOLOGICA.** Text in German. 1977-1993; N.S. 2008. bi-m. EUR 278, USD 421 to institutions (effective 2012). adv. bk.rev. bibl.; charts; illus. back issues avail. **Document type:** *Journal, Academic/Scholarly.*
—GNLM. **CCC.**
Published by: Springer (Subsidiary of: Springer Science+Business Media), Tiergartenstr 17, Heidelberg, 69121, Germany. TEL 49-6221-4870, FAX 49-6221-345229, orders-hd-individuals@springer.com, http://www.springer.com. Ed. Dr. Sonja Kempinski. Adv. contact Kathrin Koelling. Circ: 6,900.

618 ARG
F A S G O CIENCIA. (Federacion Argentina de Sociedades de Ginecologia y Obstetrica) Text in Spanish. 2001. s-a.
Media: Online - full text.
Published by: Federacion Argentina de Sociedades de Ginecologia y Obstetrica (F A S G O), Ave. Cordoba 1646, 5o. Of. 201, Buenos Aires, Argentina. TEL 54-11-48123656, FAX 54-11-48128860, fasgo@abaconet.com.ar, http://www.fasgo.org.ar.

618 ARG
F A S G O INFORMA. (Federacion Argentina de Sociedades de Ginecologia y Obstetrica) Text in Spanish. 1998. irreg. back issues avail.
Media: Online - full text.
Published by: Federacion Argentina de Sociedades de Ginecologia y Obstetrica (F A S G O), Ave. Cordoba 1646, 5o. Of. 201, Buenos Aires, Argentina. TEL 54-11-48123656, FAX 54-11-48128860, fasgo@abaconet.com.ar, http://www.fasgo.org.ar.

618 USA
FAMILY BUILDING. Text in English. 2001. q. **Description:** Covers infertility issues from medical options, treatments, psychological issues, adoption, and other related topics.
Published by: RESOLVE: The National Infertility Association, 1310 Broadway, Somerville, MA 02144. TEL 617-623-0744, FAX 617-623-0252, resolveinc@aol.com, http://www.resolve.org/.

618.1780599 IRN ISSN 1726-7536
➤ **FASLNAMAH-I PIZISHKI-I BARVARI VA NABARVARI/MEDICAL JOURNAL OF REPRODUCTION AND INFERTILITY.** Text in Arabic; Abstracts in English. 2000. q. IRR 60,000 domestic Members of Iran's Medical Council; IRR 70,000 domestic to institutions; IRR 40,000 domestic to students; USD 100 foreign (effective 2010). back issues avail. **Document type:** *Journal, Academic/Scholarly.* **Description:** Publishes original research articles, clinical trials, review articles, case reports, letters to the editor, editorials, commentaries, latest related news and views on life sciences with focus on research articles on reproduction, fertility and infertility. Includes research on reproductive gynecology, reproductive medicine, gynecologic oncology affecting fertility, reproductive endocrinology, reproductive physiology, immunology, genetic and pathology, andrology, prenatal and preimplantation genetic diagnosis, sexually transmitted infections, reproductive law and bioethics, epidemiological and psychological studies concerning reproduction and infertility.
Related titles: Online - full text ed.: ISSN 1735-8507. 2005. free (effective 2011).
Indexed: A01, A26, A34, A36, A38, C06, C07, CABA, D01, E08, E12, GH, H11, H12, I05, N02, N03, P10, P20, P48, P53, P54, PQC, R12, RA&MP, T02, T05.
Published by: Avicenna Research Institute/Pizhuhishkadah-i Ibn-i Sina, No.2 & 3, Shabo Alley, St. No.18, Velenjak Ave., Yemen St., Shaheed Chamran Expwy., Tehran, 19615-1177, Iran. TEL 98-21-22403100, FAX 98-21-22404144, journal@avicenna.ac.ir, http://www.avicenna.ac.ir/. Ed. Sadeghi M. R.

618 BRA
FEMINA (ONLINE EDITION). Text in Portuguese. 1972. bi-m. **Document type:** *Magazine, Consumer.*
Formerly (until 2001): Femina (Print Edition) (0100-7254)
Media: Online - full text.
Indexed: C01, P30.
Published by: Federacao Brasileira das Sociedades de Ginecologia e Obstetricia (F E B R A S G O), Av das Americas 8445, Sala 711, Barra da Tijuca, Rio de Janeiro, 22793-081, Brazil. TEL 55-21-24876336, FAX 55-21-24295133, publicacoes@febrasgo.org.br.

618.178 USA ISSN 0015-0282
RC889 CODEN: FESTAS
➤ **FERTILITY AND STERILITY.** Text in English. 1950. m. USD 636 in United States to institutions; USD 890 elsewhere to institutions (effective 2012). adv. bk.rev. bibl.; charts; illus. index, cum.index: vols.1-50. back issues avail.; reprints avail. **Document type:** *Journal, Academic/Scholarly.* **Description:** Brings out scientific articles in clinical and laboratory research relevant to reproductive endocrinology, urology, andrology, physiology, immunology, genetics, contraception, and menopause.
Related titles: CD-ROM ed.; Online - full text ed.: ISSN 1556-5653 (from IngentaConnect, ScienceDirect); ◆ Supplement(s): Sexuality, Reproduction & Menopause. ISSN 1546-2501.
Indexed: A01, A03, A08, A20, A22, A26, A34, A35, A36, A38, ASCA, AbAn, AgBio, B25, BIOSIS Prev, CA, CABA, CCIOG, CLFP, ChemAb, CurCont, D01, DBA, DentInd, E12, EMBASE, ExcerpMed, F08, F09, F11, F12, FR, FamI, G10, GH, H16, H17, I05, I12, IDIS, ISR, IndMed, IndVet, Inpharma, JW, JW-WH, LT, MEDLINE, MS&D, MycolAb, N02, N03, P30, P33, P35, P38, P39, R07, R08, R10, R12, R13, RA&MP, RM&VM, RRTA, Reac, S02, S03, SCI, SCOPUS, SoyAb, T02, T05, TAR, THA, VS, W07, W09, W10.
—BLDSC (3909.750000), CASDDS, GNLM, IE, Infotrieve, Ingenta, INIST. **CCC.**
Published by: (American Society for Reproductive Medicine), Elsevier Inc. (Subsidiary of: Elsevier Science & Technology), 1600 John F Kennedy Blvd, Philadelphia, PA 19103. TEL 215-239-3900, FAX 215-238-7883, JournalCustomerService-usa@elsevier.com, http://www.elsevier.com. Ed. Dr. Alan H DeCherney. Adv. contact Carol Clark TEL 212-633-3719. Circ: 7,920. **Co-sponsor:** Pacific Coast Fertility Society, Canadian Fertility Society.

618 USA
FERTILITY, REPRODUCTION AND SEXUALITY. Text in English. 2001. irreg., latest vol.18, 2009. price varies. back issues avail. **Document type:** *Monographic series, Academic/Scholarly.* **Description:** Addresses current debates and issues of global relevance on the changing dynamics of fertility, human reproduction and sexuality.
Published by: Berghahn Books Inc., 150 Broadway, Ste 812, New York, NY 10038. TEL 212-233-6004, FAX 212-233-6007, journals@berghahnbooks.com. Eds. David Parkin, Marcia C Inhorn, Soraya Tremayne. Pub. Marion Berghahn.

618.1780599 USA ISSN 1559-8888
RC889
FERTILITY TODAY. Text in English. 2005. bi-m. USD 27.80 domestic; USD 34 in Canada; USD 42 elsewhere (effective 2010). adv. back issues avail. **Document type:** *Magazine, Consumer.* **Description:** Covers all aspects of fertility and infertility.
Related titles: Online - full content ed.: ISSN 1559-8896. USD 29.95 (effective 2005).
Indexed: C11, P05, P19, P20, P48, P54, PQC.
Address: PO Box 117, Laurel, MD 20725. TEL 410-715-8559. adv.: B&W page USD 2,980, color page USD 4,250; 8.125 x 10.75. Circ: 2,250,000.

618 USA ISSN 1086-1068
QP251
FERTILITY WEEKLY. Text in English. 1995. w. (48/yr.). USD 759 in North America; USD 859 elsewhere (effective 2005). **Document type:** *Newsletter, Consumer.* **Description:** Covers research, discoveries, news and conferences on fertility and human reproductive science, including such areas as infertility, assisted reproductive techniques, sterility, reproductive law, andrology, and more.
Related titles: Online - full text ed.
Indexed: A01, A02, A03, A08, C11, CA, H04, M02, T02.
Address: 109 Pine Crest Dr, Atlanta, GA 30040. TEL 770-889-6970, FAX 770-889-6969, kkey@atl.mindspring.com. Ed., Pub., R&P Keith K Key. Adv. contact Mike Chrisptopher.

618 GBR ISSN 0965-5395
CODEN: FMMREI
➤ **FETAL AND MATERNAL MEDICINE REVIEW.** Text in English. 1989. q. adv. back issues avail.; reprint service avail. from PSC. **Document type:** *Journal, Academic/Scholarly.* **Description:** Aims to bring together all multidisciplinary interests and approaches appropriate to the advancement of knowledge and clinical practice in obstetrics.
Formerly (until 1992): Fetal Medicine Review (0953-8267)
Related titles: Online - full text ed.: ISSN 1469-5065. GBP 250, USD 425 to institutions (effective 2012).
Indexed: A01, A03, A08, A22, A36, B21, BIOBASE, CA, CABA, CTA, E01, EMBASE, ExcerpMed, GH, IABS, N02, N03, NSA, P20, P24, P48, P50, P54, PQC, R10, Reac, SCOPUS, T02, T05, VS.
—BLDSC (3910.846000), GNLM, IE, Infotrieve, Ingenta. **CCC.**
Published by: Cambridge University Press, The Edinburgh Bldg, Shaftesbury Rd, Cambridge, CB2 8RU, United Kingdom. TEL 44-1223-312393, FAX 44-1223-315052, journals@cambridge.org, http://www.cambridge.org/uk. Ed. Stephen Robson. R&P Linda Nicol TEL 44-1223-325702. Adv. contact Rebecca Roberts TEL 44-1223-325083. **Subscr. to:** Cambridge University Press, 32 Ave of the Americas, New York, NY 10013. TEL 212-337-5000, FAX 212-691-3239, journals_subscriptions@cup.org.

618 CHE ISSN 1015-3837
RG628 CODEN: FDTHES
➤ **FETAL DIAGNOSIS AND THERAPY**; clinical advances and basic research. Text in English. 1986. 8/yr. CHF 2,626, EUR 2,098, USD 2,578 to institutions; CHF 2,882, EUR 2,304, USD 2,826 combined subscription to institutions (print & online eds.) (effective 2012). adv. back issues avail. **Document type:** *Journal, Academic/Scholarly.* **Description:** Focuses on the fetus as a patient. Provides a wide range of biomedical specialists with a unique single source of reports aimed at ameliorating and/or preventing congenital abnormalities.
Formerly: Fetal Therapy (0257-2788)
Related titles: Microform ed.: (from PQC); Online - full text ed.: ISSN 1421-9964. CHF 2,558, EUR 2,046, USD 2,484 to institutions (effective 2012).
Indexed: A01, A03, A08, A22, ASCA, B21, B25, BIOSIS Prev, C06, C07, CA, CTA, CurCont, E01, EMBASE, ExcerpMed, FR, H13, IndMed, Inpharma, MEDLINE, MycolAb, NSA, P10, P20, P22, P30, P35, P48, P53, P54, PQC, R10, Reac, SCI, SCOPUS, T02, W07.
—BLDSC (3910.848000), GNLM, IE, Infotrieve, Ingenta, INIST. **CCC.**
Published by: (International Fetal Medicine and Surgery Society), S. Karger AG, Allschwilerstr 10, Basel, 4055, Switzerland. TEL 41-61-3061111, FAX 41-61-3061234, karger@karger.ch, http://www.karger.ch. Ed. W Holzgreve. adv.: page CHF 1,730; trim 210 x 280. Circ: 950.

618 613.7 USA ISSN 1079-3615
FIT PREGNANCY. Variant title: Shape Presents Fit Pregnancy. Text in English. 1995. bi-m. USD 11.97 domestic; USD 22.97 foreign (effective 2008). adv. illus. back issues avail. **Document type:** *Magazine, Consumer.* **Description:** Contains all the necessary information and advice about having babies and taking care of babies.
Related titles: Online - full text ed.
Indexed: A11, C05, C11, CPerI, G05, G06, G07, G08, H03, H11, H12, I05, M02, SD, T02, U01.
Published by: A M I - Weider Publications (Subsidiary of: American Media, Inc.), 1 Park Ave, 3d Fl, New York, NY 10016. TEL 212-545-4800, FAX 212-448-9890, http://www.amilink.com. Ed. Peg Moline. Pub. Kevin Walsh. Adv. contact Aaron Woloff TEL 212-743-6614. color page USD 49,625, B&W page USD 39,710. **Dist. in UK by:** Comag, Tavistock Rd, W Drayton, Middlesex UB7 7QE, United Kingdom. TEL 44-1895-433600, FAX 44-189-543-3606.

618.12 613.7 ZAF ISSN 1812-3058
FIT PREGNANCY. Text in English. 2004. q. ZAR 88; ZAR 21.95 newsstand/cover (effective 2006). adv. **Document type:** *Magazine, Consumer.*
Published by: Touchline Media, PO Box 16368, Vlaeberg, Cape Town 8018, South Africa. TEL 27-21-4083800, FAX 27-21-4083811. Ed. Robyn von Geusau TEL 27-21-4083930. Pub. Elsa Carpenter-Frank. Adv. contact Paul Goddard TEL 27-21-4083992. color page ZAR 18,500; trim 210 x 276.

FITT MAMA; healthy mother, healthy baby. *see* WOMEN'S HEALTH

618.2 649 SWE ISSN 1400-268X
FOEDSEL & FOERAELDRASKAP. Text in Swedish. 1981. q. SEK 275 domestic; SEK 375 in Europe; SEK 427 elsewhere (effective 2004). adv. bk.rev. back issues avail. **Document type:** *Newsletter, Consumer.*
Formerly (until 1994): Foeda Hemma (0282-4272)
Published by: Foereningen Foeda Hemma, c/o Katerina Janouch, Roerstrandsgatan 3, Stockholm, 11340, Sweden. Eds. Katerina Janouch, Helena Lindgren. Circ: 3,600.

618 ESP ISSN 1137-2990
FOLIA CLINICA EN OBSTETRICIA Y GINECOLOGIA. Text in Spanish. 1996. bi-m. EUR 46.30 domestic; EUR 72.50 foreign (effective 2009). **Document type:** *Journal, Academic/Scholarly.*
Indexed: P02, P20, P48, P54, PQC.
Published by: Ediciones Mayo S.A., Calle Aribau 185-187, 2a Planta, Barcelona, 08021, Spain. TEL 34-93-2090255, FAX 34-93-2020643, edmayo@ediciones.mayo.es, http://www.edicionesmayo.es. Circ: 5,000.

618 DEU
FRAUENAERZTLICHE TASCHENBUECHER. Text in German. 1999. irreg., latest 2011. price varies. **Document type:** *Monographic series, Academic/Scholarly.*
Published by: Walter de Gruyter GmbH & Co. KG, Genthiner Str 13, Berlin, 10785, Germany. TEL 49-30-26005220, FAX 49-30-26005251, info@degruyter.com, http://www.degruyter.de. Eds. Andreas Ebert, Thomas Roemer.

618.1 DEU ISSN 0016-0237
DER FRAUENARZT. Text in German. 1951. m. adv. bk.rev. bibl.; illus. **Document type:** *Journal, Academic/Scholarly.*
—GNLM, IE, Infotrieve. **CCC.**
Published by: (Berufsverband der Frauenaerzte e.V.), Publimed Medizin und Medien GmbH, Paul-Heyse-Str 31a, Munich, 80336, Germany. TEL 49-89-51616171, FAX 49-89-51616199, schreiber@publimed.de. Pub. Uwe Schreiber. Adv. contact Monika Fuerst-Ladner. B&W page EUR 3,930, color page EUR 5,490; trim 174 x 232. Circ: 18,858 (paid and controlled).

A FRIEND INDEED; for women in the prime of life. *see* WOMEN'S INTERESTS

618 DEU ISSN 0016-5751
RG1 CODEN: GEFRA2
➤ **GEBURTSHILFE UND FRAUENHEILKUNDE.** Text in German; Summaries in English, German. 1940. m. EUR 296 to institutions; EUR 413 combined subscription to institutions (print & online eds.); EUR 46 newsstand/cover (effective 2011). adv. bk.rev. abstr.; bibl.; stat. index. reprints avail. **Document type:** *Journal, Academic/Scholarly.*
Incorporates (2001-2008): GebFra Refresher (1611-6410)
Related titles: Online - full text ed.: ISSN 1438-8804. EUR 397 to institutions (effective 2011).
Indexed: A20, A22, ASCA, CIN, ChemAb, ChemTitl, CurCont, DBA, EMBASE, ExcerpMed, FR, ISR, IndMed, Inpharma, P30, P35, R10, Reac, S02, S03, SCI, SCOPUS, W07.
—BLDSC (4095.650000), CASDDS, GNLM, IE, Infotrieve, Ingenta, INIST. **CCC.**
Published by: (Deutsche Gesellschaft fuer Gynaekologie und Geburtshilfe), Georg Thieme Verlag, Ruedigerstr 14, Stuttgart, 70469, Germany. TEL 49-711-8931421, FAX 49-711-8931410, leser.service@thieme.de. Ed. J Baltzer. Adv. contact Ulrike Bradler. Circ: 4,100 (paid and controlled).

➤ **GELBE LISTE PHARMINDEX. GYNAEKOLOGEN.** *see* PHARMACY AND PHARMACOLOGY

➤ **GENEESMIDDELEN, ZWANGERSCHAP EN BORSTVOEDING.** *see* PHARMACY AND PHARMACOLOGY

618.1 ROM ISSN 1841-4435
GINECO.RO. Text in Romanian. 2005. m. ROL 90 (effective 2011). adv. **Document type:** *Magazine, Trade.*
Related titles: Online - full text ed.: ISSN 2065-250X. 2008.
Indexed: SCI, SCOPUS, W07.
Published by: Versa Puls Media, s.r.l., Calea Rahovei 266-268, corp 1, etaj 2, Bucharest, 050912, Romania. TEL 40-31-4254040, FAX 40-31-4254041, office@pulsmedia.ro. Ed. Jan Andi Marin. Adv. contact George Pavel.

618 ITA ISSN 0393-5337
GINECOLOGIA DELL'INFANZIA E DELL'ADOLESCENZA. Text in Italian; Summaries in English. 1985-1992; resumed 2001. q. free to qualified personnel. adv. **Document type:** *Newspaper, Trade.*
Published by: (Societa Italiana di Ginecologia dell'Infanzia e dell'Adolescenza (S I G I A)), C I C Edizioni Internazionali, Corso Trieste 42, Rome, 00198, Italy. TEL 39-06-8412673, FAX 39-06-8412688, info@gruppocic.it, http://www.gruppocic.it.

618 PER ISSN 1015-3047
GINECOLOGIA Y OBSTETRICIA. Text in Spanish. 1947. 3/yr. **Document type:** *Journal, Academic/Scholarly.*
Related titles: Online - full text ed.: ISSN 1609-7246. 1991.
Indexed: P30.
Published by: Sociedad Peruana de Obstetricia y Ginecologia, Ave Aramburr, 321 Ofi. 4, San Isidro, Lima, Peru. TEL 51-1-4214251, FAX 51-1-4224573, spog@terra.com.pe, http://www.spog.org.pe/saludodelpresidente_p.html.

618 ESP ISSN 1695-3827
GINECOLOGIA Y OBSTETRICIA CLINICA. Text in Spanish. 1970. q. EUR 70 to institutions (effective 2009). back issues avail. **Document type:** *Journal, Academic/Scholarly.*
Former titles (until 2002): Ginecologia Clinica y Quirurgica (1576-3560); (until 1999): Gine-Dips (0211-6901)
Indexed: A22, EMBASE, ExcerpMed, R10, Reac, SCI, SCOPUS, W07.
—BLDSC (4176.377500), IE, Ingenta. **CCC.**
Published by: Nexus Medica Editores, C/ Passeig d'Amunt 38, Barcelona, 08024, Spain. TEL 34-93-5510260, FAX 34-93-2136672, redaccion@nexusmedica.com.

618 MEX ISSN 0300-9041
CODEN: GOMEAY
GINECOLOGIA Y OBSTETRICIA DE MEXICO. Text in Spanish. 1946. m. MXN 600 domestic; USD 140 foreign (effective 2005). back issues avail. **Document type:** *Journal, Academic/Scholarly.*
Related titles: CD-ROM ed.; Online - full text ed.
Indexed: A22, Artemisa, C01, CA, EMBASE, ExcerpMed, IBR, IBZ, IndMed, MEDLINE, P30, R10, Reac, S02, S03, SCOPUS, T02, W09.
—BLDSC (4176.400000), CASDDS, GNLM, IE, Infotrieve, Ingenta, INIST.
Published by: Asociacion Mexicana de Ginecologia y Obstetricia, Torrw WTC Montecito No. 38, Piso 29 Ofic 21, Col. Napoles, Mexico, D.F., 03810, Mexico. http://www.amgo.org.mx/. Ed. Carlos Fernandez del Castillo.

618 ITA ISSN 1827-7152
IL GINECOLOGO; rivista di ostetricia e ginecologia. Text in Italian. 2006. q. EUR 70 combined subscription to individuals (print & online eds.); EUR 130 combined subscription to institutions (print & online eds.) (effective 2010). **Document type:** *Journal, Academic/Scholarly.*
Related titles: Online - full text ed.: ISSN 1827-7144.
Published by: Editrice Kurtis s.r.l., Via Luigi Zoja 30, Milan, 20153, Italy. TEL 39-02-48202740, FAX 39-02-48201219, info@kurtis.it, http://www.kurtis.it. Ed. Felice Petraglia.

618.1 ITA ISSN 0391-8920
GINECORAMA. Text in Italian. 1979. 10/yr. adv. **Document type:** *Journal, Trade.*
Formerly (until 1982): Il Ginecologo Ospedaliero (1971-6400)
Related titles: Online - full text ed.: ISSN 1971-3762. 2007.
Published by: C I C Edizioni Internazionali, Corso Trieste 42, Rome, 00198, Italy. TEL 39-06-8412673, FAX 39-06-8412688, info@gruppocic.it, http://www.gruppocic.it. Ed. Andrea Salvati.

618.1 POL ISSN 0017-0011
CODEN: GIPOA3
GINEKOLOGIA POLSKA. Text in Polish; Summaries in English, Russian. 1922. m. EUR 172 foreign (effective 2006). adv. bk.rev. abstr.; bibl.; charts; illus. index; cum.index. **Document type:** *Journal, Academic/Scholarly.*
Indexed: ChemAb, DokArb, EMBASE, ExcerpMed, F09, G10, IndMed, MEDLINE, P30, R10, Reac, S02, S03, SCI, SCOPUS, W07, W09.
—BLDSC (4176.500000), CASDDS, GNLM, IE, Infotrieve, Ingenta, INIST.
Published by: Polskie Towarzystwo Ginekologiczne/Polish Society of Gynaecology, Klinika Onkologii Ginekologicznej, Malgorzata Skowronska, ul Polna 33, Poznan, 60535, Poland. TEL 48-61-8419265, FAX 48-61-8419465, ptgzg@gpsk.am.poznan.pl, http://www.gpsk.am.poznan.pl/ptg. Ed. Z Slomko. Circ: 2,600. **Dist. by:** Ars Polona, Obroncow 25, Warsaw 03933, Poland. TEL 48-22-5098609, FAX 48-22-5098610, arspolona@arspolona.com.pl, http://www.arspolona.com.pl.

618 POL ISSN 1231-6407
GINEKOLOGIA PRAKTYCZNA. Text in Polish. 1993. q. PLZ 60 domestic (effective 2010). **Document type:** *Journal, Academic/Scholarly.*
Related titles: Online - full text ed.
Indexed: EMBASE, R10, SCOPUS.
Published by: (Fundacja Edukacja w Poloznictwie i Ginekologii), Termedia sp. z o.o./Termedia Publishing House, ul Wenedow 9/1, Poznan, 61614, Poland. TEL 48-61-8227781, FAX 48-61-8227781, termedia@termedia.pl. Ed. Tadeusz Pisarski.

618.1 RUS
GINEKOLOGIYA; zhurnal dlya praktticheskikh vrachei. Text in Russian. 2000. bi-m. USD 175 in United States (effective 2007). **Document type:** *Journal.*
Published by: Izdatel'skii Holding Media Medika, a/ya 37, Moscow, 125047, Russian Federation. TEL 7-095-2343784, media@consilium-medicum.com. Ed. V I Prilepskaya. **Dist. by:** East View Information Services, 10601 Wayzata Blvd, Minneapolis, MN 55305. TEL 952-252-1201, 800-477-1005, FAX 952-252-1202, info@eastview.com, http://www.eastview.com.

618 SRB
GINEKOLOSKO AKUSERSKI GLASNIK. Text in Serbian. s-a. **Document type:** *Journal, Academic/Scholarly.*
Published by: Srpsko Lekarsko Drustvo/Serbian Medical Association, George Washington St, 19, Belgrade, 11000. TEL 381-11-3234450, FAX 381-11-3246090, sld@eunet.yu, http://www.sld.org.yu. Ed. Paja Momcilov.

618 ITA ISSN 0391-9013
GIORNALE ITALIANO DI OSTETRICIA E GINECOLOGIA. Text in Italian; Summaries in English. 1979. m. EUR 80 domestic; EUR 110 foreign (effective 2008). adv. **Document type:** *Journal, Academic/Scholarly.*
Incorporates (1971-1982): Rivista d'Ostetricia e Ginecologis Pratica e di Medicina Perinatale (0391-0970); Which was formerly (1919-1971): Rivista d'Ostetricia e Ginecologia Pratica (0370-6591)
Related titles: Online - full text ed.: ISSN 1971-1433.
Indexed: A22, EMBASE, ExcerpMed, P30, R10, Reac, RefZh, SCOPUS.
—BLDSC (4178.237000), GNLM, IE, Ingenta, INIST. **CCC.**
Published by: C I C Edizioni Internazionali, Corso Trieste 42, Rome, 00198, Italy. TEL 39-06-8412673, FAX 39-06-8412688, info@gruppocic.it, http://www.gruppocic.it. adv.: B&W page EUR 1,239.50, color page EUR 1,704.31; 210 x 280. **Co-sponsors:** Gruppo Operativo per la Ricerca Clinica in Ostetricia e Ginecologia; Gruppo di Ricerca ed Applicazioni Tecnologiche in Ostetricia e Ginecologia.

618.2 618.1 BRA ISSN 1414-3534
GO ATUAL. Text in Portuguese. 1992. 10/yr. USD 450 (effective 2000 - 2001). abstr.; bibl. Index.
Published by: Editora de Publicacoes Cientificas Ltda., Rua Major Suckow 30, Rocha, Rio de Janeiro, RJ 20911-160, Brazil. TEL 55-21-2013722, 55-21-5010057, FAX 55-21-2613749. Eds. Paulo Belfort, J M Melo. R&P, Adv. contact Ana Paula. Circ: 14,500.

618 USA ISSN 1559-6982
GRACE REPORT. Text in English. 2005. irreg. USD 13.65 per week domestic; USD 13.90 per week in Canada; USD 14.35 per week elsewhere (effective 2007). **Document type:** *Report, Trade.* **Description:** A business intelligence service prepared exclusively for CEO's, CFO's, COO's, partners, practice managers, administrators, and other senior executives working in OB-Gyn practices and women's healthcare.
Published by: The Grace Report Intelligence Service, 21806 Briarcliff Dr, Spicewood, TX 78669. TEL 512-264-7103, 877-636-3634, FAX 512-264-0969, http://www.gracereport.com/index.htm. Pub. Robert L Michel.

618 DNK ISSN 1398-5604
GRAVID; alt om dig i de 9 maaneder. Variant title: Alt om Baby. Text in Danish. 1997. q. DKK 219 (effective 2009). adv. **Document type:** *Magazine, Consumer.* **Description:** Information for the expecting mother.
Published by: Egmont Magasiner A/S, Hellerupvej 51, Hellerup, 2900, Denmark. TEL 45-39-457500, FAX 45-39-457404, abo@egmontmagasiner.dk, http://www.egmont-magasiner.dk. Ed. Mille Collin Flaherty TEL 45-39-457409. Adv. contact Pia Kensoe larsen TEL 45-39-457505. page DKK 25,500; 185 x 262.

618.2 NOR ISSN 1500-2144
GRAVID. Text in Norwegian. 1997. q. NOK 189 (effective 2009). adv. **Document type:** *Magazine, Consumer.*
Published by: Hjemmet Mortensen AS, Gullhaugveien 1, Nydalen, Oslo, 0441, Norway. TEL 47-22-585000, FAX 47-22-585959, firmapost@hm-media.no, http://www.hm-media.no. adv.: color page NOK 36,900.

GREAT BRITAIN. GOVERNMENT STATISTICAL SERVICE. ABORTION STATISTICS, ENGLAND AND WALES (YEAR) (ONLINE). *see* BIRTH CONTROL—Abstracting, Bibliographies, Statistics

618.4 ESP ISSN 1138-8412
GUIA DE EMBARAZO Y PARTO. Text in Spanish. 1996. s-a. free to qualified personnel. **Description:** Presents information on childbirth for pregnant women.
Formerly (until 1998): Enhorabuena Futura Mama (1136-3320)
Published by: Sfera Editores S.L., Pol. Mas Blau Ed. Muntadas, C. Solsones, 2-B, El Prat de Llobregat, Barcelona, 08820, Spain. TEL 34-93-3708585, FAX 34-93-3705060, info@sfera.es, http://www.sfera.es/. Ed. Juan Turu. Circ: 104,076.

618 USA
GUIDELINES FOR PERINATAL CARE. Text in English. 1983. irreg., latest 2008, 6th ed. USD 79.95 to non-members 6th ed.; USD 74.95 to members 6th ed. (effective 2008). **Document type:** *Monographic series, Trade.* **Description:** Guidelines for care of pregnant women, fetuses, and neonates including discussion of preconceptional and antenatal screening, adoption, perinatal infections, and fetal monitoring.
Published by: American Academy of Pediatrics, 141 NW Pt Blvd, Elk Grove Village, IL 60007. TEL 847-434-4000, FAX 847-434-8000, journals@aap.org, http://www.aap.org. Pub. Robert Perelman. **Co-sponsor:** American College of Obstetricians and Gynecologists.

618 CHN ISSN 1674-1870
➤ **GUOJI FUCHAN KEXUE ZAZHI/JOURNAL OF INTERNATIONAL OBSTETRICS AND GYNECOLOGY.** Text in Chinese. 1973. bi-m. CNY 48; CNY 8 per issue (effective 2009). **Document type:** *Journal, Academic/Scholarly.*
Formerly (until 2008): Guowai Yixue (Fuchan Kexue Fence)/Foreign Medical Sciences (Gynecology & Obstetrics) (1003-479X)
Related titles: Online - full text ed.
—East View.
Published by: Tianjin Yixue Keji Qingbao Yanjiusuo/Tianjin Medical Science and Technology Information Institute, 96-D, Guizhou Lu, Heping-qu, Tianjin, 300070, China. TEL 86-22-23337521, http://www.tjmic.ac.cn/. **Dist. by:** China International Book Trading Corp, 35 Chegongzhuang Xilu, Haidian District, PO Box 399, Beijing 100044, China. TEL 86-10-68412045, FAX 86-10-68412023, cibtc@mail.cibtc.com.cn, http://www.cibtc.com.cn.

618 CHN ISSN 1008-2514
GUOWAI YIXUE (FU-YOU BAOJIAN FENCE)/FOREIGN MEDICAL SCIENCES (WOMEN & CHILDREN HEALTH CARE). Text in Chinese. bi-m. CNY 41.40 domestic; USD 19.80 foreign (effective 2005). **Document type:** *Journal, Academic/Scholarly.*
Related titles: Online - full text ed.
Published by: Xi'an Jiaotong Daxue, 76, Yanta Xilu, Xi'an, 710061, China. TEL 86-29-88546568, FAX 86-29-82655049. **Dist. by:** China International Book Trading Corp, 35 Chegongzhuang Xilu, Haidian District, PO Box 399, Beijing 100044, China. TEL 86-10-68412045, FAX 86-10-68412023, cibtc@mail.cibtc.com.cn, http://www.cibtc.com.cn.

618.1 DEU ISSN 1432-2870
GYN; praktische Gynaekologie. Text in German. 1996. bi-m. EUR 50; EUR 15 newsstand/cover (effective 2010). adv. **Document type:** *Magazine, Trade.*
—BLDSC (4233.496000).
Published by: OmniMed Verlagsgesellschaft mbH, Borsteler Chaussee 85-99a, Haus 16, Hamburg, 22453, Germany. TEL 49-40-232334, FAX 49-40-230292, info@omnimedonline.de, http://www.omnimedonline.de. Ed. Dr. A. Salfelder. Adv. contact Vanessa Baack. Circ: 14,881 (paid and controlled).

618.1 DEU ISSN 1435-5507
GYN-DEPESCHE; Schnellinformationen fuer niedergelassenen Gynaekologen. Text in German. 1998. 6/yr. EUR 36 (effective 2010). adv. **Document type:** *Magazine, Trade.*
Published by: Gesellschaft fuer Medizinische Information, Paul-Wassermann-Str 15, Munich, 81829, Germany. TEL 49-89-4366300, FAX 49-89-436630210, info@gfi.online.de. Ed. Wilfried Ehnert.

618 HRV ISSN 1330-0091
CODEN: GYPREQ
➤ **GYNAECOLOGIA ET PERINATOLOGIA**; journal for gynaecology, perinatology, reproductive medicine, and ultrasonic diagnostics. Text in Croatian, English; Summaries in English. 1960. q. USD 30. adv. bk.rev. bibl.; charts; illus. index. 60 p./no.; back issues avail.; reprints avail. **Document type:** *Journal, Academic/Scholarly.*
Former titles (until 1992): Jugoslavenska Ginekologija i Perinatologija (0352-5562); (until 1985): Jugoslavenska Ginekologija i Opstetricija (0017-002X); Ginekologija i Opstetricija
Related titles: Supplement(s): Gynaecologia et Perinatologia. Supplement. ISSN 1331-0151. 1992.
Indexed: DentInd, EMBASE, ExcerpMed, IndMed, P30, R10, Reac, SCOPUS.
—GNLM.
Published by: Hrvatsko Drustvo Ginekologa i Opstetricara/Croatian Society of Gynecology & Obstetrics, Petrova 13, Zagreb, 10000, Croatia. TEL 385-1-4604616, FAX 385-1-4633512. Eds. Dr. Ante Drazancic, Dr. Asim Kurjak, Dr. Zdravko Pavlic. Circ: 1,350.

618.1 NLD ISSN 1384-5454
GYNAECOLOGY FORUM. Text in English. 1996. q. EUR 150 to individuals; EUR 175 to institutions (effective 2009). **Document type:** *Journal, Academic/Scholarly.*
—BLDSC (4233.515000), IE, Infotrieve, Ingenta.
Published by: Medical Forum International BV, PO Box 1663, Amersfoort, 3800 BR, Netherlands. FAX 31-30-6930162, info@medforum.nl. Circ: 20,000.

618.1 DEU ISSN 0017-5994
RG1 CODEN: GYNKAP
➤ **DER GYNAEKOLOGE.** Text in German. 1968. m. EUR 489, USD 524 combined subscription to institutions (print & online eds.) (effective 2012). adv. back issues avail.; reprint service avail. from PSC. **Document type:** *Journal, Academic/Scholarly.* **Description:** Covers all aspects of gynecology and women's health.
Related titles: Microform ed.: (from PQC); Online - full text ed.: ISSN 1433-0393 (from IngentaConnect).
Indexed: A20, A22, A26, ASCA, E01, EMBASE, ExcerpMed, IndMed, Inpharma, P30, R10, Reac, SCOPUS.
—BLDSC (4233.550000), GNLM, IE, Infotrieve, Ingenta, INIST. **CCC.**
Published by: Springer (Subsidiary of: Springer Science+Business Media), Tiergartenstr 17, Heidelberg, 69121, Germany. TEL 49-6221-4870, FAX 49-6221-345229. Ed. H G Bender. Adv. contact Stephan Kroeck TEL 49-30-827875739. Circ: 5,400 (paid and controlled). **Subscr. in the Americas to:** Springer New York LLC, Journal Fulfillment, PO Box 2485, Secaucus, NJ 07096. TEL 800-777-4643, 201-348-4033, FAX 201-348-4505, journals-ny@springer.com, http://www.springer.com; **Subscr. to:** Springer Distribution Center, Kundenservice Zeitschriften, Haberstr 7, Heidelberg 69126, Germany. FAX 49-6221-345-4229, subscriptions@springer.com.

618.1 CHE ISSN 1420-6811
GYNAEKOLOGIE FUER HAUSAERZTE. Text in German. 1996. q. CHF 36; CHF 46 in Europe; CHF 62 elsewhere (effective 2000). adv. **Document type:** *Magazine, Academic/Scholarly.*
Related titles: ◆ Supplement to: Ars Medici. ISSN 0004-2897.
Indexed: EMBASE, ExcerpMed, SCOPUS.
—BLDSC (4233.550500), GNLM.
Published by: Rosenfluh Publikationen, Schaffhauserstr 13, Neuhausen, 8212, Switzerland. info@rosenfluh.ch, http://www.rosenfluh.ch. Ed. Dr. Barbel Hirrle. **Subscr. to:** EDP Services, Ebenaustr, Horw 6048, Switzerland. TEL 41-41-3491760, FAX 41-41-3491718.

618 CHE ISSN 1661-9390
GYNAEKOLOGIE-PRAXIS. Text in German. 2006. irreg. **Document type:** *Journal, Academic/Scholarly.*
Published by: Springer Medizin Verlag Schweiz AG (Subsidiary of: Springer Science+Business Media), Nordstr 31, Zurich, 8006, Switzerland. TEL 41-44-2502800, FAX 41-44-2502803, verlag@springer-medizin.ch, http://www.springer-medizin.ch.

618 DEU ISSN 1439-3557
GYNAEKOLOGIE UND GEBURTSHILFE. Text in German. 1996. bi-m. EUR 122, USD 143 to institutions (effective 2012). adv. **Document type:** *Journal, Academic/Scholarly.*
Formerly (until 1998): Hautnah Gynaekologie und Geburtshilfe (1431-5688)
Indexed: A26.
—BLDSC (4233.551000), IE. **CCC.**
Published by: Urban und Vogel Medien und Medizin Verlagsgesellschaft mbH (Subsidiary of: Springer Science+Business Media), Neumarkter Str 43, Munich, 81673, Germany. TEL 49-89-4372-1411, FAX 49-89-4372-1410, verlag@urban-vogel.de, http://www.urban-vogel.de. Ed. Markus Seidl. Adv. contact Ines Spankau. B&W page EUR 2,750, color page EUR 4,250; trim 174 x 237. Circ: 11,000 (paid). **Subscr. to:** Springer Distribution Center, Kundenservice Zeitschriften, Haberstr 7, Heidelberg 69126, Germany. TEL 49-6221-3454303, FAX 49-6221-3454229, subscriptions@springer.com.

618.1 616.4 DEU ISSN 1610-2894
RG1
➤ **GYNAEKOLOGISCHE ENDOKRINOLOGIE.** Text in German. 2003. q. EUR 298, USD 336 combined subscription to institutions (print & online eds.) (effective 2012). adv. reprint service avail. from PSC. **Document type:** *Journal, Academic/Scholarly.*
Related titles: Online - full text ed.: ISSN 1610-2908 (from IngentaConnect).
Indexed: A22, A26, E01, EMBASE, ExcerpMed, R10, Reac, SCOPUS.
—BLDSC (4233.567000), IE, Ingenta. **CCC.**
Published by: Springer (Subsidiary of: Springer Science+Business Media), Tiergartenstr 17, Heidelberg, 69121, Germany. TEL 49-6221-4870, FAX 49-6221-345229. Eds. Dr. Klaus Diedrich, Thomas Strowitzki. Adv. contact Stephan Kroeck TEL 49-30-827875739. Circ: 1,400 (paid and controlled). **Subscr. in the Americas to:** Springer New York LLC, Journal Fulfillment, PO Box 2485, Secaucus, NJ 07096. TEL 800-777-4643, 201-348-4033, FAX 201-348-4505, journals-ny@springer.com, http://www.springer.com; **Subscr. to:** Springer Distribution Center, Kundenservice Zeitschriften, Haberstr 7, Heidelberg 69126, Germany. TEL 49-6221-3454303, FAX 49-6221-3454229, subscriptions@springer.com.

618.1 DEU ISSN 1439-4898
GYNAEKOLOGISCHE NACHRICHTEN. Text in German. 1997. 14/yr. adv. **Document type:** *Journal, Trade.*
Published by: Biermann Verlag GmbH, Otto-Hahn-Str 7, Cologne, 50997, Germany. TEL 49-2236-3760, FAX 49-2236-376999, info@biermann.net, http://www.biermann-verlag.de. Ed. Dieter Kaulard. Adv. contact Katrin Groos TEL 49-2236-376504. Circ: 8,000 (paid and controlled).

618 DEU ISSN 0341-8677
GYNAEKOLOGISCHE PRAXIS; Zeitschrift fuer Frauenheilkunde und Geburtshilfe. Text in German. 1977. 4/yr. EUR 175 (effective 2010). **Document type:** *Journal, Academic/Scholarly.*
Indexed: EMBASE, ExcerpMed, P30, R10, Reac, SCOPUS.
—BLDSC (4233.570000), GNLM, IE, Infotrieve. **CCC.**
Published by: Hans Marseille Verlag GmbH, Buerkleinstr 12, Munich, 80538, Germany. TEL 49-89-227988, FAX 49-89-2904643, marseille-verlag@t-online.de. Ed. W Siebert.

618 DEU ISSN 0179-9185
GYNE. Text in German. 1980. m. EUR 30; EUR 3 newsstand/cover (effective 2007). adv. index. back issues avail. **Document type:** *Journal, Academic/Scholarly.*
Related titles: ◆ Supplement(s): Horme. ISSN 0935-2880; ◆ Ikon. ISSN 0941-911X; ◆ Korasion. ISSN 0932-0601.
Indexed: A22.
—BLDSC (4233.630000), GNLM, IE, Infotrieve. **CCC.**
Published by: Medizinische Medien Informations GmbH, Am Forsthaus Gravenbruch 7, Neu-Isenburg, 63263, Germany. TEL 49-6102-5020, FAX 49-6102-502243, info@mmi.de, http://www.mmi.de. adv.: page EUR 2,150. Circ: 8,700 (paid).

618 CHE ISSN 0378-7346
RG1 CODEN: GOBIDS
➤ **GYNECOLOGIC AND OBSTETRIC INVESTIGATION.** Text in English. 1895. 8/yr. (in 2 vols.). CHF 3,158, EUR 2,524, USD 3,094 to institutions; CHF 3,468, EUR 2,772, USD 3,394 combined subscription to institutions (print & online eds.) (effective 2012). adv. bibl.; illus. index. back issues avail. **Document type:** *Journal, Academic/Scholarly.* **Description:** Covers the most active and promising areas of current research in gynecology and obstetrics. Original papers report selected experimental and clinical investigations in all fields related to gynecology, obstetrics and reproduction.
Former titles (until 1978): Gynecologic Investigation (0017-5986); (until 1970): Gynaecologia (0367-5513); (until 1946): Monatsschrift fuer Geburtshilfe und Gynaekologie (0368-9867); (until 1939): Monatsschrift fuer Geburtshuelfe und Gynaekologie (1421-573X)
Related titles: Microform ed.; Online - full text ed.: ISSN 1423-002X. CHF 3,090, EUR 2,472, USD 3,000 to institutions (effective 2012).
Indexed: A01, A03, A08, A21, A22, A36, ASCA, B25, BIOSIS Prev, CA, CABA, CIN, ChemAb, ChemTitl, CurCont, D01, E01, E12, EMBASE, ExcerpMed, FR, FamI, GH, IBR, IBZ, ISR, IndMed, Inpharma, MEDLINE, MycolAb, N02, N03, NRN, P20, P22, P30, P32, P33, P35, P39, P48, P54, PQC, R10, R12, R13, RI-1, RM&VM, Reac, SCI, SCOPUS, SoyAb, T02, T05, THA, W07.
—BLDSC (4233.650000), CASDDS, GNLM, IE, Infotrieve, Ingenta, INIST. **CCC.**
Published by: S. Karger AG, Allschwilerstr 10, Basel, 4055, Switzerland. TEL 41-61-3061111, FAX 41-61-3061234, karger@karger.ch, http://www.karger.ch. Ed. T. D'Hooghe. adv.: page CHF 1,815; trim 210 x 280. Circ: 800.

618.1 USA ISSN 0090-8258
RC280.G5 CODEN: GYNOA3
➤ **GYNECOLOGIC ONCOLOGY.** Text in English. 1972. m. EUR 4,084 in Europe to institutions; JPY 426,500 in Japan to institutions; USD 3,120 elsewhere to institutions (effective 2012). adv. index. back issues avail.; reprints avail. **Document type:** *Journal, Academic/Scholarly.* **Description:** Serves as an archive devoted to the publication of clinical and investigative articles that concern tumors of the female reproductive tract.
Related titles: Online - full text ed.: ISSN 1095-6859 (from IngentaConnect, ScienceDirect).
Indexed: A01, A03, A08, A20, A22, A26, A34, A36, A38, ASCA, ApicAb, B25, BIOBASE, BIOSIS Prev, CA, CABA, CIN, ChemAb, ChemTitl, CurCont, D01, E01, EMBASE, ExcerpMed, F08, FR, GH, H17, I05, IABS, INIS AtomInd, ISR, IndMed, IndVet, Inpharma, MEDLINE, MycolAb, N02, N03, NRN, P30, P33, P35, P37, R08, R10, R12, RA&MP, RM&VM, Reac, SCI, SCOPUS, SoyAb, T02, T05, THA, VS, W07.
—BLDSC (4233.710000), CASDDS, GNLM, IE, Infotrieve, Ingenta, INIST. **CCC.**
Published by: Academic Press (Subsidiary of: Elsevier Science & Technology), 3251 Riverport Ln, Maryland Heights, MO 63043. TEL 314-447-8010, FAX 314-447-8030, JournalCustomerService-usa@elsevier.com, http://www.elsevierdirect.com/imprint.jsp?iid=5. Ed. Dr. Beth Y Karlan. Adv. contact Tino DeCarlo TEL 212-633-3815.

➤ **GYNECOLOGICAL ENDOCRINOLOGY.** *see* MEDICAL SCIENCES—Endocrinology

➤ **GYNECOLOGICAL SURGERY**; endoscopy, imaging, and allied techniques. *see* MEDICAL SCIENCES—Surgery

618 301.426 FRA ISSN 1297-9589
RG1 CODEN: GOFEF4
GYNECOLOGIE OBSTETRIQUE ET FERTILITE. Text in French. 1968. 12/yr. EUR 407 in Europe to institutions; EUR 281.10 in France to institutions; JPY 37,200 in Japan to institutions; USD 529 elsewhere to institutions (effective 2012). adv. bk.rev. **Document type:** *Journal, Academic/Scholarly.* **Description:** Explores various planned parenthood issues.
Former titles (until 2000): Contraception - Fertilite - Sexualite (1165-1083); (until 1992): Fertilite, Contraception, Sexualite (1164-7418); (until 1992): Contraception Fertilite Sexualite (1157-8181); (until 1991): Fertilite Contraception Sexualite (0980-3904); (until 1986): Contraception Fertilite Sexualite (0301-861X); (until 1973): Fertilite Orthogenie (0991-8841)
Related titles: Online - full text ed.: ISSN 1769-6682. 2001 (from IngentaConnect, ScienceDirect).
Indexed: A01, A03, A08, A22, A26, A35, A36, ASCA, AgBio, CA, CABA, D01, E12, EMBASE, ExcerpMed, FR, GH, I05, IndMed, Inpharma, MEDLINE, N02, N03, P30, P33, P39, R07, R10, Reac, S02, S03, S13, S16, SCI, SCOPUS, T02, T05, VS, W07, W09.
—BLDSC (4233.765000), GNLM, IE, Infotrieve, Ingenta, INIST. **CCC.**
Published by: Elsevier Masson (Subsidiary of: Elsevier Health Sciences), 62 Rue Camille Desmoulins, Issy les Moulineaux, Cedex 92442, France. TEL 33-1-71165500, FAX 33-1-71165600, infos@elsevier-masson.fr. Ed. Patrick Madelenat. Circ: 5,000.

618 FRA ISSN 0988-6990
GYNECOLOGIE - OBSTETRIQUE PRATIQUE. Text in French. 1988. m. (10/yr.). **Document type:** *Newspaper, Trade.*
Published by: L E N Medical - Axis Sante, 15 Rue des Sablons, Paris, 75116, France. TEL 33-1-47553131, FAX 33-1-47553132, info@len-medical.fr, http://www.len-medical.fr.

618 TUR ISSN 1300-4751
GYNECOLOGY OBSTETRICS & REPRODUCTIVE MEDICINE. Abbreviated title: G O R M. Text in English. 1995. 3/yr. TRY 15 to individuals; TRY 45 to institutions; TRY 35 doctors; TRY 30 to students (effective 2009). **Document type:** *Journal, Academic/Scholarly.*
Published by: (The Society of Maternal-Fetal Medicine and Perinatology, The Southeast European Society of Perinatal Medicine), Medical Network, Public Sokak No.4/2, Ankara, 06420, Turkey. info@medicalnetwork.com.tr.

618.1 SVK ISSN 1338-0958
▼ **GYNEKO MAGAZIN.** Text in Slovak. 2009. bi-m. adv. **Document type:** *Magazine, Trade.*
Published by: Medikapharm s.r.o., Racianska 81, Bratislava, 83102, Slovakia. Circ: 40,000 (controlled).

618 CZE ISSN 1210-1133
GYNEKOLOG. Text in Czech. 1992. bi-m. CZK 396 domestic; CZK 66 per issue domestic (effective 2010). **Document type:** *Journal, Trade.*
Published by: Medexart s.r.o., Borska 1135, Trebechovice pod Orebem, 50346, Czech Republic. TEL 420-495-833381, FAX 420-495-592625. Ed. Jindrich Tohner.

618 SVK ISSN 1336-3425
➤ **GYNEKOLOGIA PRE PRAX.** Text in Slovak. 2003. q. EUR 11.98 (effective 2009). **Document type:** *Journal, Academic/Scholarly.*
Published by: Samedi s.r.o., Racianska 20, Bratislava, 839 27, Slovakia. TEL 421-2-55645901, FAX 421-2-55645902, samedi@samedi.sk. Ed. Maria Mercegova.

618 CZE ISSN 1213-2578
➤ **GYNEKOLOGIE PO PROMOCI.** Text in Czech. 2000. bi-m. free. **Document type:** *Journal, Academic/Scholarly.*
Related titles: Online - full text ed.
Published by: Medical Tribune CZ, s.r.o., Na Morani 5, Prague 2, 12800, Czech Republic. TEL 420-224-916916, FAX 420-224-922436, info@medical-tribune.cz. Ed. Tomas Novotny.

618.1 301.5 USA ISSN 0892-628X
H E R S NEWSLETTER. Text in English. 1982. q. bk.rev. abstr.; stat. cum.index. back issues avail. **Document type:** *Newsletter, Consumer.* **Description:** Presents medical and scientific reviews discussing alternatives and consequences of hysterectomies.
Published by: (Hysterectomy Educational Resources & Services), H E R S Foundation, 422 Bryn Mawr Ave, Bala Cynwyd, PA 19004. TEL 610-667-7757, FAX 610-667-8096, hersfdn@aol.com, http://www.hersfoundation.com/. Ed. Joanne West. R&P Nora W Coffey. Circ: 15,000.

HAYAT. *see* MEDICAL SCIENCES—Nurses And Nursing

HEALTH CARE FOR WOMEN INTERNATIONAL. *see* WOMEN'S HEALTH

618.202 DEU ISSN 0932-8122
DIE HEBAMME; Fortbildungszeitschrift fuer Hebammen und Entbildungspfleger. Text in German. 1988. q. EUR 54 to institutions; EUR 102 combined subscription to institutions (print & online eds.); EUR 18.10 newsstand/cover (effective 2011). adv. reprint service avail. from IRC. **Document type:** *Journal, Academic/Scholarly.*
Related titles: Online - full text ed.: ISSN 1439-4197. EUR 102 to institutions (effective 2011).
Indexed: A22.
—GNLM, IE. **CCC.**
Published by: Hippokrates Verlag in MVS Medizinverlage Stuttgart GmbH & Co.KG (Subsidiary of: Georg Thieme Verlag), Oswald-Hesse-Str 50, Stuttgart, 70469, Germany. TEL 49-711-89310, FAX 49-711-8931706, kunden.service@thieme.de. Ed. Dr. Renate Reutter. Adv. contact Achim Wienert. B&W page EUR 1,198, color page EUR 2,200; trim 210 x 280. Circ: 4,400 (paid and controlled).

618 DEU ISSN 1611-4566
HEBAMMEN-FORUM. Text in German. 2000. m. adv. **Document type:** *Magazine, Trade.*
Published by: Bund Deutscher Hebammen, Gartenstr 26, Karlsruhe, 76133, Germany. TEL 49-721-981890, FAX 49-721-9818920, info@bdh.de. Ed. Katharina Kerlen-Petri. adv.: B&W page EUR 1,200, color page EUR 1,950; trim 184 x 269. Circ: 11,884 (paid and controlled).

618 618.202 HKG ISSN 1608-9367
➤ **HONG KONG JOURNAL OF GYNAECOLOGY, OBSTETRICS AND MIDWIFERY.** Text in English. 2000. a. (Jul.). HKD 200 domestic; USD 50 foreign (effective 2010); free to members. **Document type:** *Journal, Academic/Scholarly.*
Related titles: Online - full text ed.
Published by: (Obstetrics & Gynaecology Society of Hong Kong, Hong Kong Midwives Association), Hong Kong Academy of Medicine Press, Rm.901, 9/F, HKAM Bldg., 99 Wong Hunk Hang Rd., Aberdeen, Hong Kong. TEL 852-28718822, FAX 852-25159061, hkampress@hkam.org.hk. Ed. KY Leung.

618 DEU ISSN 0935-2880
HORME. Text in German. 1988. 3/yr. **Document type:** *Journal, Academic/Scholarly.*
Related titles: ◆ Supplement to: Gyne. ISSN 0179-9185.
—GNLM.
Published by: H U F Verlag, Lindenhof 47, Muehlheim, 45481, Germany. TEL 49-208-480027, FAX 49-208-485899, huf-verlag@ob.kamp.net.

618 616.4 JPN ISSN 1340-220X
CODEN: HFGYFH
HORMONE FRONTIER IN GYNECOLOGY. Text in Japanese. 1994. q. JPY 9,660 (effective 2005). **Document type:** *Journal, Academic/Scholarly.*
Indexed: CIN, ChemAb, ChemTitl.
—BLDSC (4327.350000), CASDDS.
Published by: Medikaru Rebyusha/Medical Review Co., Ltd., 1-7-3 Hirano-Machi, Chuo-ku, Yoshida Bldg., Osaka-shi, 541-0046, Japan. TEL 81-6-62231468, FAX 81-6-62231245.

618 618.92 ARG ISSN 1514-9838
HOSPITAL MATERNO INFANTIL RAMON SARDA. REVISTA. Text in Spanish. 1970. q. **Document type:** *Journal, Academic/Scholarly.*
Formerly (until 1988): Hospital Municipal Materno Infantil Ramon Sarda. Revista (1515-9205)
Related titles: Online - full text ed.: free (effective 2011).
Published by: Hospital Materno Infantil Ramon Sarda, Asociacion de Profesionales, Esteban e Luca 2151, Buenos Aires, CP 1259, Argentina. Ed. Carlos Grandi.

618 CHL ISSN 0718-3127
HOSPITAL SANTIAGO ORIENTE DR. LUIS TISNE BROUSSE. REVISTA DE OBSTETRICA Y GINECOLOGIA. Text in Spanish. 2006. q. **Document type:** *Journal, Academic/Scholarly.*
Published by: Hospital Santiago Oriente Dr. Luis Tisne Brousse, Reconciled Torres 4150, Penalolen, Santiago, Chile. TEL 56-2-4725293.

618 GBR
HUMAN CONCERN NEWSPAPER. Text in English. 1968. q. membership. adv. bk.rev. stat. **Document type:** *Newspaper.*
Formerly: Society for the Protection of Unborn Children. Bulletin (0307-448X)
Published by: Society for the Protection of Unborn Children, 3 Whitacre Mews, Stannary St, London, SE11 4AB, United Kingdom. TEL 44-20-70917091, FAX 44-20-78203131, information@spuc.org.uk, http://www.spuc.org.uk/. Ed. Phyllis Bowman. Circ: 65,000.

618 GBR ISSN 1464-7273
QP251
➤ **HUMAN FERTILITY**; an international, multidisciplinary journal dedicated to furthering research and promoting good practice. Text in English. 1996. q. GBP 400, EUR 540, USD 680 combined subscription to institutions (print & online eds.); GBP 810, EUR 1,120, USD 1,395 combined subscription to corporations (print & online eds.) (effective 2010). adv. back issues avail.; reprint service avail. from PSC. **Document type:** *Journal, Academic/Scholarly.* **Description:** Provides research into all aspects of human fertility and reproduction.
Formerly (until 1998): British Fertility Society. Journal (1363-9579)
Related titles: Online - full text ed.: ISSN 1742-8149 (from IngentaConnect).
Indexed: A01, A22, B&BAb, B21, B28, C06, C07, C08, CA, CINAHL, E01, EMBASE, ESPM, ExcerpMed, HPNRM, MEDLINE, P30, R10, Reac, RiskAb, SCOPUS, SSciA, T02.
—BLDSC (4336.086000), IE, Infotrieve, Ingenta, INIST. **CCC.**
Published by: (British Fertility Society), Informa Healthcare (Subsidiary of: T & F Informa plc), Telephone House, 69-77 Paul St, London, EC2A 4LQ, United Kingdom. TEL 44-20-70175000, FAX 44-20-70176792, healthcare.enquiries@informa.com. Ed. Henry Leese. Adv. contact Per Sonnerfeldt. **Subscr. in N. America to:** Taylor & Francis Inc., Customer Services Dept, 325 Chestnut St, 8th Fl, Philadelphia, PA 19106. TEL 215-625-8900, 800-354-1420, FAX 215-625-8914, customerservice@taylorandfrancis.com; **Subscr. outside N. America to:** Taylor & Francis Ltd., Journals Customer Service, Sheepen Pl, Colchester, Essex CO3 3LP, United Kingdom. TEL 44-20-70175544, FAX 44-20-70175198, tf.enquiries@tfinforma.com.

618 616.4 GBR ISSN 0268-1161
QP251 CODEN: HUREEE
➤ **HUMAN REPRODUCTION.** Text in English. 1986. m. GBP 1,003 in United Kingdom to institutions; EUR 1,503 in Europe to institutions; USD 2,005 in US & Canada to institutions; GBP 1,003 elsewhere to institutions; GBP 1,094 combined subscription in United Kingdom to institutions (print & online eds.); EUR 1,640 combined subscription in Europe to institutions (print & online eds.); USD 2,188 combined subscription in US & Canada to institutions (print & online eds.); GBP 1,094 combined subscription elsewhere to institutions (print & online eds.) (effective 2012). adv. illus. index. back issues avail.; reprint service avail. from PSC. **Document type:** *Journal, Academic/Scholarly.* **Description:** For scientists and clinicians working in international human reproduction research and practice.
Related titles: Online - full text ed.: ISSN 1460-2350. 1997. GBP 823 in United Kingdom to institutions; EUR 1,235 in Europe to institutions; USD 1,646 in US & Canada to institutions; GBP 823 elsewhere to institutions (effective 2012) (from IngentaConnect); Supplement(s): Human Reproduction. Supplement. ISSN 1359-5911. 1986.
Indexed: A01, A03, A08, A20, A22, A34, A35, A36, A38, ASCA, AgBio, B21, B25, BIOSIS Prev, BP, CA, CABA, CIN, ChemAb, ChemTitl, CurCont, D01, E01, E12, EMBASE, ESPM, ExcerpMed, F08, F09, F11, F12, FR, Faml, G10, GH, GenetAb, H13, H16, HPNRM, ISR, IndMed, IndVet, Inpharma, JW-WH, LT, MEDLINE, MycolAb, N02, N03, N04, NucAcAb, O01, P10, P20, P22, P30, P32, P33, P35, P39, P48, P50, P53, P54, PGegResA, PQC, R07, R08, R10, R12, RA&MP, RM&VM, RRTA, Reac, RiskAb, S02, S03, S12, SCI, SCOPUS, SSciA, SoyAb, T02, T05, THA, VS, W07, W09.
—BLDSC (4336.431000), CASDDS, GNLM, IE, Infotrieve, Ingenta, INIST. **CCC.**
Published by: (European Society of Human Reproduction and Embryology BEL), Oxford University Press, Great Clarendon St, Oxford, OX2 6DP, United Kingdom. TEL 44-1865-556767, FAX 44-1865-556646, enquiry@oup.co.uk, http://www.oxfordjournals.org. Ed. A Van Steirteghem.

618.2 DEU
HURRA, ICH BIN SCHWANGER. Variant title: Leben und Erziehen - Hurra, Ich Bin Schwanger. Text in German. 2005. a. adv. **Document type:** *Magazine, Consumer.*
Published by: Bayard Media GmbH & Co. KG, Boeheimstr 8, Augsburg, 86153, Germany. TEL 49-821-45548181, FAX 49-821-45548110, redaktion@bayard-media.de, http://www.bayard-media.de. Adv. contact Armin Baier. page EUR 8,250; trim 210 x 280. Circ: 95,000 (paid).

HYPERTENSION IN PREGNANCY. *see* MEDICAL SCIENCES—Cardiovascular Diseases

618.71 USA
I L C A GLOBE. Text in English.
Published by: International Lactation Consultant Association, 1500 Sunday Dr, Suite 102, Raleigh, NC 27607. TEL 919-787-5181, FAX 919-787-4916, info@ilca.org, http://www.ilca.org. Ed. Beverleye Rae.

618 USA ISSN 2090-4436
▼ ➤ **I S R N OBSTETRICS AND GYNECOLOGY.** (International Scholarly Research Network) Text in English. 2011. irreg. **Document type:** *Journal, Academic/Scholarly.*
Related titles: Online - full text ed.: ISSN 2090-4444. free (effective 2011).
Published by: Hindawi Publishing Corporation, 410 Park Ave, 15th Fl, PMB 287, New York, NY 10022. FAX 215-893-4392, 866-446-3294, info@hindawi.com.

618 DEU ISSN 0941-911X
IKON. Text in German. 1991. s-a. **Document type:** *Magazine, Academic/Scholarly.*
Related titles: ◆ Supplement to: Gyne. ISSN 0179-9185.
Published by: H U F Verlag, Lindenhof 47, Muehlheim, 45481, Germany. TEL 49-208-480027, FAX 49-208-485899, huf-verlag@ob.kamp.net.

IN VERWACHTING. *see* CHILDREN AND YOUTH—About

618.1 IND ISSN 0974-0724
INDIAN JOURNAL OF GYNAECOLOGICAL ENDOSCOPY. Text in English. 1999. s-a. INR 300 to non-members; free to members (effective 2011). **Document type:** *Journal, Academic/Scholarly.* **Description:** Focuses on minimal access surgery in gynaenecology including endoscopists and vaginal surgery, and related subjects.
Published by: Delhi Gynaecological Endoscopists Society, C-557 Defence Colony, New Delhi, 110 024, India. TEL 91-11-24333026, secretary@endogyne.org. Ed. Renu Misra.

618 USA ISSN 1064-7449
RG218 CODEN: IDOGEX
➤ **INFECTIOUS DISEASES IN OBSTETRICS AND GYNECOLOGY.** Text in English. 1993. irreg. USD 195 (effective 2011). back issues avail. **Document type:** *Journal, Academic/Scholarly.* **Description:** Publishes original papers focusing on the study or treatment of infectious disease in the obstetric patient or the female reproductive organs. Provides detailed coverage of such areas as viral, microbial, and bacterial infections; sexually transmitted disease and HIV; ante-partum infections, opportunistic infection in chemotherapy patients; and new developments in antibiotics and other therapeutic measures.
Related titles: Online - full text ed.: ISSN 1098-0997. 1996. free (effective 2011) (from IngentaConnect).
Indexed: A01, A03, A08, A22, A26, A29, A36, APA, B20, B21, B23, C&ISA, C06, C07, CA, CABA, CorrAb, D01, E&CAJ, E01, E04, E05, EEA, EMBASE, ESPM, EnvEAb, ExcerpMed, Faml, GH, H11, H12, H13, H17, I05, I10, IndMed, MEDLINE, N02, P02, P10, P20, P22, P30, P33, P39, P48, P50, P53, P54, PQC, R08, R10, R13, RM&VM, Reac, SCOPUS, SolStAb, T02, T05, ViroIAbstr, WAA.
—GNLM, IE, Infotrieve, Ingenta, INIST. **CCC.**
Published by: Hindawi Publishing Corporation, 410 Park Ave, 15th Fl, PMB 287, New York, NY 10022. FAX 215-893-4392, 866-446-3294, hindawi@hindawi.com.

▼ ➤ **THE INFERTILITY NURSE.** *see* MEDICAL SCIENCES—Nurses And Nursing

618.1 CHE ISSN 1664-8382
▼ **INFO@GYNAEKOLOGIE.** Text in German. 2011. bi-m. CHF 80 (effective 2011). **Document type:** *Journal, Trade.*
Published by: Aerzteverlag Medinfo AG, Seestr 141, Erlenbach, 8703, Switzerland. TEL 41-44-9157080, FAX 41-44-9157089, info@medinfo-verlag.ch. Circ: 3,000 (controlled).

618 649 NLD ISSN 1871-1057
INFORMATIEBLAD VOOR ZORGVERLENERS. Text in Dutch. 2005. irreg., latest vol.3, 2007.
Published by: Vereniging Borstvoeding Natuurlijk, Postbus 119, Wijk bij Duurstede, 3960 BC, Netherlands. TEL 31-343-576626, info@borstvoedingnatuurlijk.nl, http://www.borstvoedingnatuurlijk.nl.

618 618.92 GBR ISSN 1746-4358
RJ216
➤ **INTERNATIONAL BREASTFEEDING JOURNAL.** Text in English. 2006. irreg. free (effective 2011). adv. back issues avail.; reprints avail. **Document type:** *Journal, Academic/Scholarly.* **Description:** Covers all aspects of breastfeeding.
Media: Online - full text.
Indexed: A01, A26, A34, A36, A37, A38, C06, C07, CA, CABA, D01, E12, GH, I05, LT, N02, N03, N04, P30, R12, RRTA, SCOPUS, T02, T05, VS, W11.
—**CCC.**
Published by: BioMed Central Ltd. (Subsidiary of: Springer Science+Business Media), 236 Gray's Inn Rd, London, WC1X 8HB, United Kingdom. TEL 44-20-31922000, FAX 44-20-31922010, info@biomedcentral.com, http://www.biomedcentral.com. Ed. Lisa Amir. Adv. contact Natasha Bailey TEL 44-20-31922231.

618.202 NLD
INTERNATIONAL CONFEDERATION OF MIDWIVES. ANNUAL REPORT. Text in English. 1993. a. **Description:** Includes summary of the Confederation's membership, activities,and finance over three years.
Formerly: International Confederation of Midwives. Triennial Report
Published by: International Confederation of Midwives/Confederation Internationale des Sages-femmes, Laan van Meerdervoort 70, The Hague, 2517 AN, Netherlands. TEL 31-70-3060520, FAX 31-70-3555561, info@internationalmidwives.org, http://www.internationalmidwives.org.

618 NLD
INTERNATIONAL CONFEDERATION OF MIDWIVES. POSITION STATEMENTS. Text in English. 1990. irreg. **Document type:** *Monographic series.* **Description:** Includes statements agreed by the Confederation on professional, clinical, ethical, and statutory issues relating to midwifery.
Related titles: Online - full text ed.
Published by: International Confederation of Midwives/Confederation Internationale des Sages-femmes, Laan van Meerdervoort 70, The Hague, 2517 AN, Netherlands. TEL 31-70-3060520, FAX 31-70-3555561, info@internationalmidwives.org, http://www.internationalmidwives.org.

618.2 USA ISSN 2156-5287
▼ ➤ **INTERNATIONAL JOURNAL OF CHILDBIRTH.** Text in English. 2011. 4/yr. USD 250 combined subscription to institutions (effective 2011). **Document type:** *Journal, Academic/Scholarly.* **Description:** Publishes research and theory papers on childbirth in the context of maternity care across the world.
Related titles: Online - full text ed.: ISSN 2156-5295. 2011.
—**CCC.**
Published by: Springer Publishing Company, 11 W 42nd St, 15th Fl, New York, NY 10036. TEL 212-431-4370, 877-687-7476, FAX 212-941-7842, contactus@springerpub.com, http://www.springerpub.com. Eds. Denis Walsh, Kerri Schuiling.

618 USA ISSN 0887-8625
RG973
➤ **INTERNATIONAL JOURNAL OF CHILDBIRTH EDUCATION.** Text in English. 1986. q. free to members (effective 2011). adv. bk.rev. bibl. back issues avail. **Document type:** *Journal, Academic/Scholarly.* **Description:** Covers maternity and infant care.
Formed by the merger of (19??-1986): I C E A News (0445-0485); (19??-1986): I C E A Forum/Sharing; (19??-1986): I C E A Review
Related titles: Online - full text ed.
Indexed: A04, A26, C06, C07, C08, C11, CA, CINAHL, CLFP, E08, F09, Faml, GW, H04, H11, H12, I05, P19, P24, P30, P48, PQC, T02.
—BLDSC (4542.165400), IE, Infotrieve, Ingenta.
Published by: International Childbirth Education Association, 1500 Sunday Dr, Ste 102, Raleigh, NC 27607. TEL 919-863-9487, 800-624-4934, FAX 919-787-4916, info@icea.org.

618 IRN ISSN 2008-076X
INTERNATIONAL JOURNAL OF FERTILITY AND STERILITY. Abbreviated title: I J F S. Text in English. q. **Document type:** *Journal, Academic/Scholarly.* **Description:** Aims is to disseminate information through publishing the most recent scientific research studies on Fertility and Sterility and other related topics.
Formerly (until 2007): Iranian Journal of Fertility and Sterility (1735-8094)
Related titles: Online - full text ed.: ISSN 2008-0778.
Indexed: A01, A29, B&BAb, B19, B20, B21, C06, C07, EMBASE, ESPM, P20, P48, P54, PQC, SCI, SCOPUS, T02, W07.
Published by: Ryan Institute of Iran, P O Box 19395-4644, Tehran, Iran. TEL 98-21-22510895, ijfs@royaninstitute.org. Ed. Mohammad H Nasr Esfahani.

618 613.04244 USA ISSN 1938-3622
QP251 CODEN: IFMEEV
➤ **INTERNATIONAL JOURNAL OF FERTILITY AND WOMEN'S MEDICINE (ONLINE).** Abbreviated title: I J F & W M. Text in English. 1955. bi-m. bibl.; charts; illus. index. back issues avail.; reprints avail. **Document type:** *Journal, Academic/Scholarly.* **Description:** Publishes scholarly articles on medical treatments, surgery, and pathology pertaining to human reproduction and general women's health.
Former titles (until 2008): International Journal of Fertility and Women's Medicine (Print) (1534-892X); (until 1997): International Journal of Fertility and Menopausal Studies (1069-3130); (until 1993): International Journal of Fertility (0020-725X)

Indexed: A20, A21, A22, ASCA, CIN, CLFP, ChemAb, ChemTitl, CurCont, DBA, DentInd, EMBASE, ExcerpMed, FR, FamI, IBR, IBZ, ISR, IndMed, Inpharma, MEDLINE, P30, P35, R10, RI-1, RI-2, Reac, SCI, SCOPUS, THA, W07, W09.
—BLDSC (4542.250040), CASDDS, GNLM, IE, Ingenta, INIST. **CCC.**
Published by: M S P International, Inc., 405 Main St, Ste 8, Port Washington, NY 11050. TEL 516-944-7340, FAX 516-944-8663, mspinter@aol.com. Circ: 7,000 (paid).

618 616.99 USA ISSN 1048-891X
RC280.G5 CODEN: IJGCEN
➤ **INTERNATIONAL JOURNAL OF GYNECOLOGICAL CANCER.** Text in English. 1991. 9/yr. USD 1,635 domestic to institutions; USD 1,853 foreign to institutions (effective 2011). adv. back issues avail.; reprints avail. **Document type:** *Journal, Academic/Scholarly.* **Description:** Covers topics relevant to detection, prevention, diagnosis, and treatment of gynecologic malignancies.
Related titles: Online - full text ed.: ISSN 1525-1438. GBP 725 to institutions; USD 962 in the Americas to institutions (effective 2008) (from IngentaConnect).
Indexed: A20, A22, A26, A36, ASCA, AgrForAb, B&BAb, B19, B21, BIOBASE, CA, CABA, CurCont, E01, E12, EMBASE, ExcerpMed, F08, F11, F12, GH, H12, H16, I05, IABS, ISR, Inpharma, MEDLINE, N02, N03, OGFA, P30, P32, P33, P35, R10, R12, RA&MP, RM&VM, Reac, RefZh, SCI, SCOPUS, T05, VS, W07.
—BLDSC (4542.273500), GNLM, IE, Infotrieve, Ingenta. **CCC.**
Published by: (International Gynecological Cancer Society), Lippincott Williams & Wilkins (Subsidiary of: Wolters Kluwer N.V.), 333 7th Ave, 19th Fl, New York, NY 10001. TEL 212-886-1200, FAX 212-886-1205, customerservice@lww.com, http://www.lww.com. Ed. Uziel Beller. Pub. David Myers. Circ: 1,780.

618.1 USA ISSN 0277-1691
RG77
➤ **INTERNATIONAL JOURNAL OF GYNECOLOGICAL PATHOLOGY.** Text in English. 1982. bi-m. USD 1,086 domestic to institutions; USD 1,262 foreign to institutions (effective 2011). adv. Index. back issues avail.; reprints avail. **Document type:** *Journal, Academic/Scholarly.* **Description:** Provides advances in the understanding and management of gynecological disease.
Related titles: Online - full text ed.: ISSN 1538-7151. USD 559 domestic academic site license; USD 626 foreign academic site license; USD 623.50 domestic corporate site license; USD 690.50 foreign corporate site license (effective 2002).
Indexed: A22, ASCA, B25, BIOBASE, BIOSIS Prev, CurCont, EMBASE, ExcerpMed, IABS, ISR, IndMed, Inpharma, MEDLINE, MycolAb, P30, P35, R10, Reac, SCI, SCOPUS, W07.
—BLDSC (4542.274000), GNLM, IE, Infotrieve, Ingenta, INIST. **CCC.**
Published by: (International Society of Gynecological Pathologists), Lippincott Williams & Wilkins (Subsidiary of: Wolters Kluwer N.V.), 530 Walnut St, Philadelphia, PA 19106. TEL 215-521-8300, FAX 215-521-8902, customerservice@lww.com, http://www.lww.com. Ed. Dr. Mark H Stoler TEL 434-924-9131. Pub. Kevin Anderer. Adv. contact Miriam Terron-Elder TEL 646-674-6538. Circ: 878.

618 IRL ISSN 0020-7292
RG1 CODEN: IJGOAL
➤ **INTERNATIONAL JOURNAL OF GYNECOLOGY & OBSTETRICS.** Text in English. 1963. 12/yr. EUR 2,302 in Europe to institutions; JPY 305,700 in Japan to institutions; USD 2,575 elsewhere to institutions (effective 2012). adv. bibl.; illus. index. back issues avail. **Document type:** *Journal, Academic/Scholarly.* **Description:** Publishes articles on all aspects of basic and clinical research in the fields of obstetrics and gynecology and related subjects, with emphasis on matters of worldwide interest.
Supersedes: International Federation of Gynaecology and Obstetrics. Journal (0020-6695)
Related titles: Microform ed.: (from PQC); Online - full text ed.: ISSN 1879-3479 (from IngentaConnect, ScienceDirect); Supplement(s): International Journal of Gynecology & Obstetrics. Supplement. ISSN 0924-8447. 1987.
Indexed: A01, A03, A08, A20, A22, A26, A34, A35, A36, AIDS Ab, ASCA, BIOBASE, BP, CA, CABA, CIN, CLFP, ChemAb, ChemTitl, CurCont, D01, DentInd, E12, EMBASE, ExcerpMed, F08, F09, FR, GH, H17, I05, IABS, INI, ISR, IndMed, Inpharma, LT, MEDLINE, N02, N03, NRN, P30, P33, P34, P35, P39, R08, R10, R12, RA&MP, RM&VM, RRTA, Reac, S12, SCI, SCOPUS, SoyAb, T02, T05, TAR, THA, W07, W09, W11.
—BLDSC (4542.273000), CASDDS, GNLM, IE, Infotrieve, Ingenta, INIST. **CCC.**
Published by: (International Federation of Gynaecology and Obstetrics GBR), Elsevier Ireland Ltd (Subsidiary of: Elsevier Science & Technology), Elsevier House, Brookvale Plaza, E. Park, Shannon, Co. Clare, Ireland. TEL 353-61-709600, FAX 353-61-709100. Ed. Dr. J J Sciarra. R&P Annette Moloney. Circ: 4,000. **Subscr. to:** Elsevier BV, Radarweg 29, PO Box 211, Amsterdam 1000 AE, Netherlands. TEL 31-20-4853757, FAX 31-20-4853432, JournalsCustomerServiceEMEA@elsevier.com, http://www.elsevier.nl.

618.2 610.736 NGA
▼ ➤ **INTERNATIONAL JOURNAL OF NURSING AND MIDWIFERY.** Text in English. 2010. m. free (effective 2010). adv. **Document type:** *Journal, Academic/Scholarly.*
Media: Online - full text.
Published by: Academic Journals, PO Box 73023, Victoria Island, Lagos, Nigeria. service@academicjournals.org. Eds. Dr. Alleene M Ferguson Pingenot, Dr. Andrew Crowther, Dr. Jacinta Kelly.

618 GBR ISSN 0959-289X
RG732 CODEN: IOANER
➤ **INTERNATIONAL JOURNAL OF OBSTETRIC ANESTHESIA.** Abbreviated title: I J O A. Text in English. 1991. q. EUR 617 in Europe to institutions; JPY 66,600 in Japan to institutions; USD 549 elsewhere to institutions (effective 2012). adv. back issues avail.; reprints avail. **Document type:** *Journal, Academic/Scholarly.* **Description:** Contains research papers on obstetric anaesthesia, analgesia and related topics.
Related titles: Online - full text ed.: ISSN 1532-3374 (from ScienceDirect).
Indexed: A22, A26, C06, C07, CA, CurCont, E01, EMBASE, ExcerpMed, I05, Inpharma, MEDLINE, P30, P35, R10, Reac, SCI, SCOPUS, T02, W07.
—BLDSC (4542.410500), GNLM, IE, Infotrieve, Ingenta. **CCC.**
Published by: (Obstetric Anaesthetists' Association), Churchill Livingstone (Subsidiary of: Elsevier Health Sciences), The Blvd, Langford Ln, Kidlington, OX5 1GB, United Kingdom. TEL 44-1865-843434, FAX 44-1865-843970, directenquiries@elsevier.com, http://www.elsevierhealth.com/imprint.jsp?iid=9. Eds. L C Tsen TEL 617-732-8216, Robin Russell TEL 44-1865-221590. Adv. contact David Dunnachie.

618 GBR ISSN 1179-1411
▼ ➤ **INTERNATIONAL JOURNAL OF WOMEN'S HEALTH.** Text in English. 2009. irreg. free (effective 2011). **Document type:** *Journal, Academic/Scholarly.* **Description:** Covers all aspects of women's healthcare including gynecology, obstetrics, and breast cancer.
Media: Online - full text.
Indexed: EMBASE, P30, SCOPUS.
—**CCC.**
Published by: Dove Medical Press Ltd., Beechfield House, Winterton Way, Macclesfield, SK11 0JL, United Kingdom. TEL 44-1625-509130, FAX 44-1625-617933. Ed. Elie D Al-Chaer.

618 NLD ISSN 1560-3296
RG950.A1
INTERNATIONAL MIDWIFERY. Text in English. 4/yr. EUR 47.50 (effective 2009). adv. 12 p./no. 2 cols./p.; back issues avail. **Document type:** *Journal, Trade.* **Description:** News and listings of events and publications both from member associations and relating to midwifery worldwide.
Former titles (until 1998): International Midwifery Matters (1025-1669); (until 1994): International Confederation of Midwives. Newsletter
Related titles: Online - full text ed.
Indexed: A26, B28, C06, C07, C08, CINAHL, CWI, E08, G08, H12, I05, S09.
Published by: International Confederation of Midwives/Confederation Internationale des Sages-femmes, Laan van Meerdervoort 70, The Hague, 2517 AN, Netherlands. TEL 31-70-3060520, FAX 31-70-3555561, info@internationalmidwives.org, http://www.internationalmidwives.org.

301.426 USA ISSN 1944-0391
HQ763
➤ **INTERNATIONAL PERSPECTIVES ON SEXUAL AND REPRODUCTIVE HEALTH.** Abbreviated title: Int Perspect Sex Reprod Health. Text in English. 1975. q. USD 40 domestic to individuals; USD 60 foreign to individuals (effective 2009); USD 50 to institutions (effective 2008). adv. charts; illus.; stat. back issues avail.; reprints avail. **Document type:** *Journal, Academic/Scholarly.* **Description:** Highlights population research and program achievements of prime interest to those concerned with the growing family planning challenges faced by developing countries.
Former titles (until 2009): International Family Planning Perspectives (0190-3187); (until 1979): International Family Planning Perspectives and Digest (0162-2749); (until 1978): International Family Planning Digest (0362-4056)
Related titles: Microfilm ed.: (from PQC); Online - full text ed.: ISSN 1944-0405. free (effective 2011); ♦ French ed.: Perspectives Internationales sur le Planning Familial; ♦ Spanish ed.: Perspectivas Internacionales en Planificacion Familiar. ISSN 0190-3195.
Indexed: A01, A03, A08, A20, A22, A26, A36, A39, ARDT, ASCA, ASSIA, BAS, BiolDig, C06, C07, C08, C27, C29, CA, CABA, CCME, CINAHL, CLFP, CWI, CurCont, D03, D04, E08, E13, EIP, EMBASE, ESPM, ExcerpMed, F09, FR, FamI, G08, GEOBASE, GH, H05, H11, H12, I05, IBSS, M01, M02, MEDLINE, P10, P19, P20, P22, P24, P30, P34, P48, P50, P53, P54, PAIS, PQC, PopulInd, R10, R12, R14, Reac, S02, S03, S09, S14, S15, S18, S21, SCOPUS, SFSA, SOPODA, SRI, SSA, SSCI, SSciA, SociolAb, T02, T05, W07, W09, W11.
—BLDSC (4540.150000), GNLM, IE, Infotrieve, Ingenta, INIST. **CCC.**
Published by: Alan Guttmacher Institute, 125 Maiden Ln, 7th Fl, New York, NY 10038. TEL 212-248-1111, 800-355-0244, FAX 212-248-1951, info@guttmacher.org. Ed. Patricia Donovan.

618 616.6 GBR ISSN 0937-3462
CODEN: IUJOEF
➤ **INTERNATIONAL UROGYNECOLOGY JOURNAL;** and pelvic floor dysfunction. Text in English. 1990. bi-m. EUR 1,740, USD 1,754 combined subscription to institutions (print & online eds.) (effective 2012). back issues avail.; reprint service avail. from PSC. **Document type:** *Journal, Academic/Scholarly.* **Description:** Emphasizes a clinical approach to urogynecological topics of interest to urologists, gynecologists, nurses and basic scientists.
Related titles: Microform ed.: (from PQC); Online - full text ed.: ISSN 1433-3023. 1999 (from IngentaConnect).
Indexed: A01, A03, A08, A22, A26, CA, CurCont, E01, EMBASE, ExcerpMed, IndMed, Inpharma, MEDLINE, P20, P22, P30, P35, P48, P54, PQC, R10, Reac, SCI, SCOPUS, T02, W07.
—BLDSC (4551.567800), GNLM, IE, Infotrieve, Ingenta. **CCC.**
Published by: Springer U K (Subsidiary of: Springer Science+Business Media), Ashbourne House, The Guildway, Old Portsmouth Rd, Guildford, Surrey GU3 1LP, United Kingdom. TEL 44-1483-734433, FAX 44-1483-734411, postmaster@svl.co.uk. Ed. Dr. Mickey M Karram. Adv. contact Clare Colwell. **Subscr. in the Americas to:** Springer New York LLC, Journal Fulfillment, PO Box 2485, Secaucus, NJ 07096. TEL 800-777-4643, 201-348-4033, FAX 201-348-4505, journals-ny@springer.com, http://www.springer.com; **Subscr. to:** Springer Distribution Center, Kundenservice Zeitschriften, Haberstr 7, Heidelberg 69126, Germany. TEL 49-6221-3454303, FAX 49-6221-3454229, subscriptions@springer.com.

618 USA ISSN 1528-8439
RG1
➤ **THE INTERNET JOURNAL OF GYNECOLOGY AND OBSTETRICS.** Text in English. 2000. s-a. free (effective 2011). adv. bk.rev. back issues avail. **Document type:** *Journal, Academic/Scholarly.* **Description:** Provides information from the field of gynecology and obstetrics; contains original articles, reviews, case reports, streaming slide shows, streaming videos, letters to the editor, press releases and meeting information.
Media: Online - full text.
Indexed: A01, A02, A03, A08, A26, C06, C07, CA, EMBASE, G08, H11, H12, I05, SCOPUS, T02.
Published by: Internet Scientific Publications, Llc., 23 Rippling Creek Dr, Sugar Land, TX 77479. TEL 832-443-1193, FAX 281-240-1533, wenker@ispub.com. Ed. Dr. Kelvin H. Tan.

618 IRN ISSN 1680-6433
RG133.5
IRANIAN JOURNAL OF REPRODUCTIVE MEDICINE. Text in English. 2003. irreg. **Document type:** *Journal, Academic/Scholarly.*
Related titles: Online - full text ed.: ISSN 2008-2177. free (effective 2011).
Indexed: A01, A34, A35, A36, A38, AgBio, AgrForAb, B&BAb, B21, CABA, E12, EMBASE, ExcerpMed, F08, GH, GenetAb, LT, N02, N03, P10, P20, P33, P39, P48, P53, P54, PQC, R10, R12, RA&MP, RRTA, Reac, SCI, SCOPUS, T02, T05, VS, VirolAbstr, W07.
Published by: Yazd Shahid Sadoughi University of Medical Sciences, Research and Clinical Center for Infertility, Bouali Av, Safaeyeh, Yazd, Iran. TEL 98-351-8247085, FAX 98-351-8247087, TELEX http://www.yazdivf.org, award@yazdivf.org. Ed. Abbas Aflatoonian.

613 IRL ISSN 2009-0846
IRISH CERVICAL SCREENING PROGRAMME. ANNUAL REPORT. Text in English. 2002. a.
Published by: Irish Cervical Screening Programme, South West Wing, Mulgrave St, Freepost LK 407, Limerick, Ireland. TEL 353-61-461390, icsp@hse.ie, http://www.icsp.ie.

618 ITA ISSN 1121-8339
ITALIAN JOURNAL OF GYNAECOLOGY & OBSTETRICS. Text in Italian. 1989. q. EUR 50 domestic; EUR 70 foreign (effective 2008). **Document type:** *Journal, Academic/Scholarly.*
Indexed: EMBASE, ExcerpMed, R10, Reac, RefZh, SCOPUS.
—BLDSC (4588.340430), GNLM, IE, Ingenta. **CCC.**
Published by: (Societa Italiana di Ginecologia e Ostetricia), C I C Edizioni Internazionali, Corso Trieste 42, Rome, 00198, Italy. TEL 39-06-8412673, FAX 39-06-8412688, info@gruppocic.it, http://www.gruppocic.it. Ed. A Ambrosini.

618.12 613.04244 NLD ISSN 1871-5745
JAARRAPPORTAGE VAN DE WET AFBREKING ZWANGERSCHAP. Text in Dutch. 2002. a.
Published by: Inspectie voor de Gezondheidszorg, Postbus 16119, The Hague, 2500 BC, Netherlands. TEL 31-70-3407911, FAX 31-70-3407834, bestel@igz.nl.

JATROS MEDIZIN FUER DIE FRAU. *see* WOMEN'S HEALTH

618 TUR ISSN 1016-5126
CODEN: JODEE
JINEKOLOJI VE OBSTETRIK DERGISI/JOURNAL OF GYNECOLOGY AND OBSTETRICS. Text in Turkish; Summaries in English. 1987. q. adv. **Document type:** *Journal, Academic/Scholarly.*
Indexed: EMBASE, ExcerpMed, R10, Reac, SCOPUS.
—BLDSC (4669.029380).
Published by: Logos Yayincilik Ticaret A.S., Yildiz Posta Cad., Sinan Apt. No.36 D 66-67, Gayrettepe, Istanbul, 34349, Turkey. TEL 90-212-2880541, FAX 90-212-2116185, info@logos.com.tr, http://www.logos.com.tr. Ed. Dr. Turgay Atasu. Adv. contact Sukran Oznalga.

618.2 SWE ISSN 0021-7468
JORDEMODERN/MIDWIFE. Text in Swedish. 1888. m. SEK 300 (effective 2003). adv. bk.rev. illus. 48 p./no.; **Document type:** *Journal, Trade.*
Indexed: INI, P30, SCOPUS.
—BLDSC (4673.940000), GNLM, IE, Infotrieve, Ingenta.
Published by: Svenska Barnmorskefoerbundet/Swedish Association of Midwives, Ostermalmsgatan 19, Stockholm, 11426, Sweden. TEL 46-8-10-70-88, FAX 46-8-24-49-46. Eds. Ingrid Cordesius, Ingela Radestad. Pub. Ingela Radestad. Adv. contact Kajse Westlund TEL 46-8-107088. color page SEK 11,500; trim 105 x 172. Circ: 7,700.

618.202 NOR ISSN 1503-8580
JORDMORA. Text in Norwegian. 2003. q. NOK 100 (effective 2006). **Document type:** *Magazine, Trade.*
Published by: Jordmorforbundet NSF, c/o Norsk Sykepleierforbund, Tollbugata 22, Oslo, 0104, Norway. TEL 47-22-043304, FAX 47-22-043240, post@sykepleierforbundet.no.

618.202 610.73 JPN ISSN 1347-8168
JOSAN ZASSHI/JAPANESE JOURNAL FOR MIDWIVES. Text in Japanese. 1952. m. JPY 15,600; JPY 20,600 combined subscription (print & online eds.) (effective 2010). adv. illus.
Formerly (until 2003): Josanpu Zasshi (0047-1836)
Related titles: Online - full text ed.: ISSN 1882-1421.
Indexed: F09, INI, P30, S02, S03.
—BLDSC (4656.510000), GNLM.
Published by: Igaku Shoin Ltd., 1-28-36 Hongo, Bunkyo-ku, Tokyo, 113-8719, Japan. TEL 81-3-3817-5600, FAX 81-3-3815-7791, info@igaku-shoin.co.jp. Circ: 12,000.

618.202 JPN ISSN 1347-684X
JOSANSHI/JAPANESE MIDWIVES' ASSOCIATION. JOURNAL. Text in Japanese. 1947. 4/yr. JPY 7,000 (effective 2007). **Document type:** *Journal, Academic/Scholarly.*
Formerly (until 2002): Josampu (0389-9063)
Published by: Nihon Josanpukai Shuppanbu/Japan Midwives Association, 1-8-21 Fujimi, Chiyoda-ku, Tokyo, 102-0071, Japan. TEL 81-3-32629910, FAX 81-3-32628933, sanba2@midwife.or.jp, http://www.midwife.or.jp/. Ed. Shigeko Horiuchi.

618 150 JPN ISSN 1345-2894
JOSEI SHINSHIN IGAKU/JAPANESE SOCIETY OF PSYCHOSOMATIC OBSTETRICS AND GYNECOLOGY. JOURNAL. Text in Japanese. 1996. 3/yr. JPY 8,820 (effective 2009). **Document type:** *Journal, Academic/Scholarly.*
Related titles: Online - full text ed.
—BLDSC (4674.901850). **CCC.**
Published by: Nihon Josei Shinshin Igakkai/Japanese Society of Psychosomatic Obstetrics and Gynecology, c/o Congress Corp., Kosaikaikan Bldg., 5-1 Kojimachi, Chiyoda-ku, Tokyo, 102-8481, Japan. TEL 81-3-32631369, FAX 81-3-32634033, jimukyoku@jspog.com.

618 FRA ISSN 0368-2315
CODEN: JGOBAC
JOURNAL DE GYNECOLOGIE OBSTETRIQUE ET BIOLOGIE DE LA REPRODUCTION. Text in French; Summaries in English, French. 1971. 8/yr. EUR 366 in Europe to institutions; EUR 326.15 in France to institutions; JPY 56,800 in Japan to institutions; USD 476 elsewhere to institutions (effective 2012). adv. bk.rev. abstr.; illus. index. reprints avail. **Document type:** *Journal, Academic/Scholarly.* **Description:** Focuses on the entire field of medical and surgical gynecology as well as obstetrics and perinatal medicine.

Formed by the merger of (1920-1971): Gynecologie et Obstetrique (0017-601X); (1951-1971): Federation des Societes de Gynecologie et d'Obstetrique de Langue Francaise. Bulletin (0046-3515)
Related titles: Microform ed.: (from PQC); Online - full text ed.: (from ScienceDirect).
Indexed: A22, ChemAb, EMBASE, ExcerpMed, F09, FR, INI, IndMed, MEDLINE, P30, R10, Reac, SCI, SCOPUS, W07, W09.
—BLDSC (4996.600000), CASDDS, GNLM, IE, Infotrieve, Ingenta, INIST. **CCC.**
Published by: (Federation des Gynecologues et Obstetriciens de Langue Francaise. College National des Gynecologues et Obstetriciens), Elsevier Masson (Subsidiary of: Elsevier Health Sciences), 62 Rue Camille Desmoulins, Issy les Moulineaux, Cedex 92442, France. TEL 33-1-71165500, infos@elsevier-masson.fr. Ed. Herve Fernandez. Circ: 5,000. **Subscr. to:** Societe de Periodiques Specialises, BP 22, Vineuil Cedex 41354, France. TEL 33-2-54504612, FAX 33-2-54504611.

612.6 AUT ISSN 1997-6690
➤ **JOURNAL FUER GYNAEKOLOGISCHE ENDOKRINOLOGIE (PRINT)**; Assistierte Reproduktion - Kontrazeption - Menopause. Text in German. 2008. q. **Document type:** *Journal, Academic/Scholarly.*
Formed by the merger of (1991-2008): Journal fuer Fertilitaet und Reproduktion (1019-066X); (1994-2008): Journal fuer Menopause (1023-0904)
Related titles: Online - full text ed.: Journal fuer Gynaekologische Endokrinologie (Online). ISSN 1996-1553. 2008. free (effective 2011).
Indexed: EMBASE, ExcerpMed, SCOPUS.
—BLDSC (4996.591000). **CCC.**
Published by: Krause & Pachernegg GmbH, Mozartgasse 10, Gablitz, 3003, Austria. TEL 43-2231-612580, FAX 43-2231-6125810, k_u_p@eunet.at, http://www.kup.at/verlag.htm. Ed. Dr. Franz Fischl.

618 AUT ISSN 1810-2107
RG133.5
JOURNAL FUER REPRODUKTIONSMEDIZIN UND ENDOKRINOLOGIE. Text in German. 2004. 4/yr. EUR 80 (effective 2006). **Document type:** *Journal, Academic/Scholarly.*
Related titles: Online - full text ed.: ISSN 1810-9292. 2004. free (effective 2011).
Indexed: EMBASE, ExcerpMed, R10, Reac, SCOPUS.
—BLDSC (5049.707500), IE, Ingenta. **CCC.**
Published by: Krause & Pachernegg GmbH, Mozartgasse 10, Gablitz, 3003, Austria. TEL 43-2231-612580, FAX 43-2231-6125810, k_u_p@eunet.at, http://www.kup.at/verlag.htm. Ed. Dr. Hermann Behre.

JOURNAL FUER UROLOGIE UND UROGYNAEKOLOGIE; Zeitschrift fuer Urologie und Urogynaekologie in Klinik und Praxis. *see* MEDICAL SCIENCES—Urology And Nephrology

618 USA ISSN 1058-0468
RG135 CODEN: JARGE4
➤ **JOURNAL OF ASSISTED REPRODUCTION AND GENETICS.** Text in English. 1984. m. EUR 1,690, USD 1,742 combined subscription to institutions (print & online eds.) (effective 2012). adv. back issues avail.; reprint service avail. from PSC. **Document type:** *Journal, Academic/Scholarly.* **Description:** Provides a journal format for the publication of novel cellular, molecular, genetic, and epigenetic findings that advances understanding of the biology of human gametes and preimplantation embryos.
Formerly (until 1992): Journal of in Vitro Fertilization and Embryo Transfer (0740-7769)
Related titles: Microfilm ed.: (from PQC); Online - full text ed.: ISSN 1573-7330 (from IngentaConnect).
Indexed: A01, A02, A03, A08, A20, A21, A22, A26, A34, A35, A36, A38, ASCA, AgBio, B&BAb, B19, B21, B25, BIOSIS Prev, BibLing, CA, CABA, CurCont, E01, E12, EMBASE, ExcerpMed, FR, GH, GenetAb, IndMed, Inpharma, MEDLINE, MycolAb, N02, N03, N04, P20, P22, P30, P35, P48, P50, P54, PN&I, PQC, R07, R10, R12, RI-1, RI-2, Reac, SCI, SCOPUS, SoyAb, T02, T05, VS, W07.
—BLDSC (4947.286000), GNLM, IE, Infotrieve, Ingenta, INIST. **CCC.**
Published by: (American Society for Reproductive Medicine), Springer New York LLC (Subsidiary of: Springer Science+Business Media), 233 Spring St, New York, NY 10013. TEL 212-460-1500, FAX 212-460-1575, service-ny@springer.com. Ed. David F Albertini.

➤ **JOURNAL OF DIAGNOSTIC MEDICAL SONOGRAPHY.** *see* MEDICAL SCIENCES—Radiology And Nuclear Medicine

618 ITA ISSN 2035-9969
▼ **JOURNAL OF ENDOMETRIOSIS.** Text in English. 2009. q. EUR 398 combined subscription in Europe to institutions (print & online eds.); EUR 426 combined subscription elsewhere to institutions (print & online eds.) (effective 2009). **Document type:** *Journal, Academic/Scholarly.*
Related titles: Online - full text ed.: ISSN 2036-282X.
Indexed: SCOPUS.
—**CCC.**
Published by: Wichtig Editore Srl, Via Friuli 72, Milan, MI 20135, Italy. TEL 39-02-55195443, FAX 39-02-55195971, info@wichtig-publisher.com, http://www.wichtig-publisher.com. Ed. Felice Patraglia.

618 IRL ISSN 1743-1050
RG1
➤ **JOURNAL OF EXPERIMENTAL & CLINICAL ASSISTED REPRODUCTION.** Abbreviated title: J E C A R. Text in English. 2004. irreg. free (effective 2011). back issues avail. **Document type:** *Journal, Academic/Scholarly.* **Description:** Covers reproductive endocrinology, infertility, bioethics and the advanced reproductive technologies.
Media: Online - full text.
Indexed: A01, A26, B&BAb, B19, CA, EMBASE, ExcerpMed, I05, P30, R10, Reac, SCOPUS, T02.
—**CCC.**
Published by: The Sims Institute Press Ltd, c/o Eric Scott Sills, Rosemount Hall, Dundrum Rd, Dundrum, Dublin, 14, Ireland. TEL 353-1299-3920, FAX 353-1296-8512, DrScottSills@sims.ie. Eds. Eric Scott Sills, Gianpiero D Palermo.

➤ **THE JOURNAL OF FAMILY HEALTH CARE.** *see* MEDICAL SCIENCES—Nurses And Nursing

618 613.9 IND ISSN 0022-1074
HQ750.A2
THE JOURNAL OF FAMILY WELFARE. Text in English. 1954. s-a. INR 100 domestic; USD 35 foreign (effective 2011). bk.rev. abstr.; charts. back issues avail.; reprints avail. **Document type:** *Journal, Academic/Scholarly.* **Description:** Devoted to discussing views and providing information on all aspects of sexual and reproductive health including family planning, HIV/AIDS and related issues.
Related titles: CD-ROM ed.; Online - full text ed.: 2004.
Indexed: ASCA, BAS, CA, CLFP, ExtraMED, F09, FamI, P30, PopulInd, S02, S03, S21, T02, W09.
—BLDSC (4983.750000), IE, Infotrieve, Ingenta.
Published by: Family Planning Association of India, Bajaj Bhavan, Nariman Pt, Mumbai, Maharashtra 400 021, India. TEL 91-22-40863101, FAX 91-22-40863201, fpai@fpaindia.org, http://www.fpaindia.org.

JOURNAL OF GYNECOLOGIC ONCOLOGY NURSING. *see* MEDICAL SCIENCES—Oncology

618.1059 USA ISSN 1042-4067
CODEN: JGYSEF
➤ **JOURNAL OF GYNECOLOGIC SURGERY.** Text in English. 1984. bi-m. USD 1,322 domestic to institutions; USD 1,608 foreign to institutions; USD 1,588 combined subscription domestic to institutions (print & online eds.); USD 1,873 combined subscription foreign to institutions (print & online eds.) (effective 2012). adv. bk.rev. abstr. reprint service avail. from PSC. **Document type:** *Journal, Academic/Scholarly.* **Description:** Provides a forum for clinical articles dealing with all aspects of operative and office gynecology, including colposcopy, hysteroscopy, laparoscopy, laser surgery, conventional surgery, female urology, microsurgery, in vitro fertilization, and infectious diseases.
Formerly (until 1989): Colposcopy and Gynecologic Laser Surgery (0741-6113)
Related titles: Online - full text ed.: ISSN 1557-7724. USD 1,371 to institutions (effective 2012).
Indexed: A01, A03, A08, A22, ASCA, C06, C07, CA, E01, EMBASE, ExcerpMed, FR, Inpharma, P30, R10, Reac, SCOPUS, T02.
—BLDSC (4996.595000), GNLM, IE, Infotrieve, Ingenta, INIST. **CCC.**
Published by: Mary Ann Liebert, Inc. Publishers, 140 Huguenot St, 3rd Fl, New Rochelle, NY 10801. TEL 914-740-2100, FAX 914-740-2101, 800-654-3237, info@liebertpub.com. Ed. Michael S Baggish. Adv. contact Harriet I Matysko TEL 914-740-2182. **Co-sponsors:** International Society for Gynecologic Endoscopy; British Society for Cervical Pathology; Gynecologic Surgery Society.

618 617 IND ISSN 0974-1216
▼ ➤ **JOURNAL OF GYNECOLOGICAL ENDOSCOPY AND SURGERY.** Text in English. 2009. s-a. INR 1,000 domestic; USD 150 foreign; INR 1,200 combined subscription domestic (print & online eds.); USD 180 combined subscription foreign (print & online eds.) (effective 2011). adv. **Document type:** *Journal, Academic/Scholarly.* **Description:** Covers technical, clinical and bio-engineering aspects of obstetric and gynecological endoscopy including endoscopic female sterilizations, as a part of maternal, child health and family welfare services and ethical and social issues. It publishes peer-reviewed original research papers, case reports, systematic reviews, meta-analysis, and debates.
Related titles: Online - full text ed.: ISSN 0974-7818. INR 800 domestic; USD 120 foreign (effective 2011).
Indexed: A01, A26, CA, EMBASE, ExcerpMed, H12, I05, P10, P48, P53, P54, PQC, SCOPUS, T02.
Published by: (Indian Association of Gynaecological Endoscopists), Medknow Publications and Media Pvt. Ltd., B-9, Kanara Business Ctr, Off Link Rd, Ghatkopar (E), Mumbai, Maharastra 400 075, India. TEL 91-22-66491816, FAX 91-22-66491817, http://www.medknow.com. Ed. Rakesh Sinha.

618.71 USA ISSN 0890-3344
RJ216 CODEN: JHLAE5
➤ **JOURNAL OF HUMAN LACTATION.** Text in English. 1984. q. USD 688, GBP 405 combined subscription to institutions (print & online eds.); USD 674, GBP 397 to institutions (effective 2011). adv. bk.rev.; film rev.; video rev. bibl.; illus. index. 96 p./no.; back issues avail.; reprint service avail. from PSC. **Document type:** *Journal, Academic/Scholarly.* **Description:** Publishes scientific articles and commentaries on human lactation and breastfeeding, and discussions of clinical case reports relevant to practicing lactation consultants.
Related titles: Online - full text ed.: ISSN 1552-5732. USD 619, GBP 365 to institutions (effective 2011).
Indexed: A22, A26, A36, B07, C06, C07, C08, CA, CABA, CINAHL, CurCont, D01, E01, E08, E12, EMBASE, ExcerpMed, F09, FS&TA, FamI, G08, GH, H04, H11, H12, I05, INI, MEDLINE, N02, N03, P30, R10, R12, Reac, S09, SCI, SCOPUS, SFSA, T02, T05, V02, VS, W07, W09, W11.
—BLDSC (5003.417000), GNLM, IE, Infotrieve, Ingenta. **CCC.**
Published by: (International Lactation Consultant Association), Sage Publications, Inc., 2455 Teller Rd, Thousand Oaks, CA 91320. TEL 805-499-9774, FAX 805-499-0871, info@sagepub.com. Ed. M Jane Heinig. adv.: B&W page USD 735, color page USD 1,125; trim 8.5 x 11. Circ: 4,694 (paid). **Subscr. overseas to:** Sage Publications Ltd., 1 Oliver's Yard, 55 City Rd, London EC1Y 1SP, United Kingdom. TEL 44-207-3248701, FAX 44-207-3248733, subscription@sagepub.co.uk.

618 616.6 USA ISSN 1089-2591
➤ **JOURNAL OF LOWER GENITAL TRACT DISEASE.** Text in English. 1968. q. USD 341 domestic to institutions; USD 407 foreign to institutions (effective 2011). adv. back issues avail.; reprints avail. **Document type:** *Journal, Academic/Scholarly.* **Description:** Uses for the exchange of information among interested health care providers from many different disciplines including pathology, cytology, cytogenetics, gynecologic oncology, endocrinology, preventive medicine, basic science, and clinical medicine.
Formerly (until 1997): The Colposcopist
Related titles: Online - full text ed.: ISSN 1526-0976. USD 191 to individuals (effective 2011).
Indexed: A22, A26, C06, C07, CA, CurCont, E01, EMBASE, ExcerpMed, MEDLINE, P30, R10, Reac, SCI, SCOPUS, T02, W07.
—BLDSC (5010.590000), IE, Infotrieve, Ingenta. **CCC.**
Published by: (American Society for Colposcopy and Cervical Pathology), Lippincott Williams & Wilkins (Subsidiary of: Wolters Kluwer N.V.), 333 7th Ave, 19th Fl, New York, NY 10001. TEL 646-674-6300, FAX 646-674-6500, customerservice@lww.com, http://www.lww.com. Ed. Dr. Edward J Wilkinson. Pub. Matthew Jozwiak. Circ: 3,807. **Co-sponsor:** International Federation of Cervical Pathology and Coloscopy.

618 GBR ISSN 1476-7058
➤ **THE JOURNAL OF MATERNAL - FETAL & NEONATAL MEDICINE.** Text in English. 2002. m. GBP 745, EUR 1,010, USD 1,260 combined subscription to institutions (print & online eds.); GBP 1,480, EUR 2,015, USD 2,520 combined subscription to corporations (print & online eds.) (effective 2010). adv. back issues avail.; reprint service avail. from PSC. **Document type:** *Journal, Academic/Scholarly.* **Description:** Features a wide range of research on the obstetric, medical, genetic, mental health and surgical complications of pregnancy and their effects on the mother, fetus and neonate. Research on audit, evaluation and clinical care in maternal-fetal and perinatal medicine is also featured.
Formed by the merger of (1992-2002): Journal of Maternal - Fetal Medicine (1057-0802); (1996-2002): Prenatal and Neonatal Medicine (1359-8635)
Related titles: Online - full text ed.: ISSN 1476-4954. 2001 (from IngentaConnect).
Indexed: A01, A03, A08, A22, BIOBASE, C06, C07, C08, CA, CINAHL, CurCont, E01, EMBASE, ExcerpMed, FamI, IABS, MEDLINE, P20, P22, P24, P30, P48, P54, PQC, R10, Reac, SCI, SCOPUS, T02, W07.
—IE, Ingenta. **CCC.**
Published by: (European Association of Perinatal Medicine POL), Informa Healthcare (Subsidiary of: T & F Informa plc), Telephone House, 69-77 Paul St, London, EC2A 4LQ, United Kingdom. TEL 44-20-70175000, FAX 44-20-70176792, healthcare.enquiries@informa.com. Eds. Dev Maulik, Gian C Di Renzo. Adv. contact Per Sonnerfeldt. **Subscr. in N. America to:** Taylor & Francis Inc., Customer Services Dept, 325 Chestnut St, 8th Fl, Philadelphia, PA 19106. TEL 215-625-8900, 800-354-1420, FAX 215-625-8914, customerservice@taylorandfrancis.com; **Subscr. outside N. America to:** Taylor & Francis Ltd., Journals Customer Service, Sheepen Pl, Colchester, Essex CO3 3LP, United Kingdom. TEL 44-20-70175544, FAX 44-20-70175198, tf.enquiries@tfinforma.com.

610.73 618 USA ISSN 1526-9523
CODEN: JNUMEQ
➤ **JOURNAL OF MIDWIFERY & WOMEN'S HEALTH.** Text in English. 1955. 6/yr. GBP 322 in United Kingdom to institutions; EUR 370 in Europe to institutions; USD 455 elsewhere to institutions; GBP 370 combined subscription in United Kingdom to institutions (print & online eds.); EUR 427 combined subscription in Europe to institutions (print & online eds.); USD 524 combined subscription elsewhere to institutions (print & online eds.) (effective 2012). adv. bk.rev. bibl.; charts; illus. cum.index. back issues avail.; reprint service avail. from PSC. **Document type:** *Journal, Academic/Scholarly.* **Description:** Includes the presentation of current knowledge in the fields of nurse-midwifery, parent-child health, obstetrics, well-woman gynecology, family planning and neonatology.
Former titles (2000): Journal of Nurse - Midwifery (0091-2182); (until 1973): American College of Nurse - Midwives. Bulletin (0002-8002); (until 1969): American College of Nurse - Midwifery. Bulletin (0098-3721)
Related titles: Microform ed.: (from PQC); Online - full text ed.: ISSN 1542-2011. GBP 322 in United Kingdom to institutions; EUR 370 in Europe to institutions; USD 455 elsewhere to institutions (effective 2012) (from IngentaConnect).
Indexed: A20, A22, A26, ASCA, ASSIA, B28, C06, C07, C08, CA, CINAHL, CurCont, EMBASE, ExcerpMed, F09, FamI, G10, H12, I05, INI, IndMed, JW-WH, MEDLINE, NurAb, P03, P24, P30, P48, PQC, PsycInfo, R10, Reac, SCI, SCOPUS, SSCI, T02, W07, W09.
—BLDSC (5019.935000), GNLM, IE, Infotrieve, Ingenta. **CCC.**
Published by: (American College of Nurse-Midwives), Wiley-Blackwell Publishing, Inc. (Subsidiary of: Wiley-Blackwell Publishing Ltd.), 111 River St, Hoboken, NJ 07030. TEL 201-748-6000, FAX 201-748-6088, info@wiley.com, http://www.wiley.com/WileyCDA/. adv.: B&W page USD 2,035, color page USD 3,580; trim 8 x 10.75. Circ: 9,000 (controlled).

618 USA ISSN 1553-4650
CODEN: JAALF3
➤ **JOURNAL OF MINIMALLY INVASIVE GYNECOLOGY.** Abbreviated title: J M I G. Text in English. 1993. bi-m. USD 336 in United States to institutions; USD 336 elsewhere to institutions (effective 2012). adv. bk.rev. Index. back issues avail.; reprints avail. **Document type:** *Journal, Academic/Scholarly.* **Description:** Provides a clinical forum for the exchange and dissemination of ideas, findings and techniques relevant to gynecologic endoscopy and other minimally invasive procedures.
Formerly (until 2005): American Association of Gynecologic Laparoscopists. Journal (1074-3804)
Related titles: Online - full text ed.: ISSN 1553-4669. USD 85 (effective 2005) (from ScienceDirect).
Indexed: A22, A26, ASCA, C06, C07, CA, CurCont, EMBASE, ExcerpMed, I05, IndMed, Inpharma, MEDLINE, P30, P35, R10, Reac, SCI, SCOPUS, T02, W07.
—BLDSC (5020.160000), GNLM, IE, Infotrieve, Ingenta, INIST. **CCC.**
Published by: (American Association of Gynecologic Laparoscopists), Elsevier Inc. (Subsidiary of: Elsevier Science & Technology), 1600 John F Kennedy Blvd, Philadelphia, PA 19103. TEL 215-239-3900, FAX 215-238-7883, JournalCustomerService-usa@elsevier.com, http://www.elsevier.com. Ed. Stephen L Corson. Circ: 4,075 (paid).

610.73 NLD ISSN 1934-5798
JOURNAL OF NEONATAL AND PERINATAL MEDICINE. Text in English. 2008 (Jul.). q. USD 471 combined subscription in North America (print & online eds.); EUR 335 combined subscription elsewhere (print & online eds.) (effective 2012). **Document type:** *Journal, Academic/Scholarly.* **Description:** Aims to strengthen research and education of the neonatal community on the optimal physical, mental and social health and well-being of infants through high quality publications on neonatal-perinatal medicine and to provide examples of best practices in order to improve the quality, safety and effectiveness of infants' healthcare worldwide.
Related titles: Online - full text ed.: ISSN 1878-4429.
Indexed: A01, A22, E01, EMBASE, P30, SCOPUS, T02.

—IE.
Published by: I O S Press, Nieuwe Hemweg 6B, Amsterdam, 1013 BG, Netherlands. TEL 31-20-6883355, FAX 31-20-6870019, info@iospress.nl, http://www.iospress.nl. Ed. Hany Z Aly TEL 202-715-5236.

JOURNAL OF NEONATAL NURSING. *see* MEDICAL SCIENCES—Nurses And Nursing

JOURNAL OF OBSTETRIC, GYNECOLOGIC, AND NEONATAL NURSING. *see* MEDICAL SCIENCES—Nurses And Nursing

618 GBR ISSN 0144-3615
RG1 CODEN: JOGYDW
➤ **JOURNAL OF OBSTETRICS AND GYNAECOLOGY.** Text in English. 1980. 8/yr. GBP 570, EUR 825, USD 1,030 combined subscription to institutions (print & online eds.); GBP 1,140, EUR 1,645, USD 2,060 combined subscription to corporations (print & online eds.) (effective 2010). adv. bk.rev. index. back issues avail.; reprint service avail. from PSC. **Document type:** *Journal, Academic/Scholarly.* **Description:** Describes an established forum for the entire field of obstetrics and gynaecology. It includes occasional supplements on clinical symposia.
Related titles: Online - full text ed.: ISSN 1364-6893 (from IngentaConnect).
Indexed: A01, A02, A03, A08, A22, A34, A36, AgrForAb, C11, CA, CABA, ChemAb, CurCont, D01, E01, E12, EMBASE, ExcerpMed, F08, F11, F12, FamI, GH, H04, H13, H17, IndVet, LT, MEDLINE, N02, N03, P02, P10, P20, P30, P33, P39, P48, P53, P54, PQC, R07, R08, R10, R12, RA&MP, RM&VM, Reac, S02, S03, SCI, SCOPUS, T02, T05, TAR, VS, W07.
—CASDDS, GNLM, IE, Infotrieve, Ingenta, INIST. **CCC.**
Published by: (Institute of Obstetrics and Gynaecology Trust), Informa Healthcare (Subsidiary of: T & F Informa plc), Telephone House, 69-77 Paul St, London, EC2A 4LQ, United Kingdom. TEL 44-20-70175000, FAX 44-20-70176792, healthcare.enquiries@informa.com. Ed. A B MacLean. Adv. contact Per Sonnerfeldt. **Subscr. in N. America to:** Taylor & Francis Inc., Customer Services Dept, 325 Chestnut St, 8th Fl, Philadelphia, PA 19106. TEL 215-625-8900, 800-354-1420, FAX 215-625-8914, customerservice@taylorandfrancis.com; **Subscr. outside N. America to:** Taylor & Francis Ltd., Journals Customer Service, Sheepen Pl, Colchester, Essex CO3 3LP, United Kingdom. TEL 44-20-70175544, FAX 44-20-70175198, tf.enquiries@tfinforma.com.

618 CAN ISSN 1701-2163
➤ **JOURNAL OF OBSTETRICS AND GYNAECOLOGY CANADA/ JOURNAL D'OBSTETRIQUE ET GYNECOLOGIE DU CANADA.** Short title: J O G C. Text in English, French. 1980. m. CAD 200 domestic; USD 200 foreign; CAD 125 domestic to students; USD 20 per issue (effective 2004). adv. bk.rev. **Document type:** *Journal, Academic/Scholarly.*
Former titles (until 2001): Journal S O G C (0849-5831); (until 1989): S O G C Bulletin (0837-0265); (until 1985): Society of Obstetricians and Gynaecologists of Canada. Bulletin (0837-0257)
Indexed: EMBASE, ExcerpMed, MEDLINE, P30, R10, Reac, SCOPUS, W09.
—BLDSC (4670.327000), IE, Infotrieve, Ingenta. **CCC.**
Published by: (Society of Obstetricians and Gynaecologists of Canada), Canadian Medical Association/Association Medicale Canadienne, 1867 Alta Vista Dr, Ottawa, ON K1G 3Y6, Canada. TEL 613-731-8610, 800 663-7336 ext.2295. Ed. Dr. Jeffrey Nisker. Circ: 200 (paid); 15,000 (controlled).

618 AUS ISSN 1447-0756
➤ **JOURNAL OF OBSTETRICS AND GYNAECOLOGY RESEARCH (ONLINE).** Text in English. 1970. bi-m. GBP 424 in United Kingdom to institutions; EUR 539 in Europe to institutions; USD 686 in the Americas to institutions; USD 830 elsewhere to institutions (effective 2012). **Document type:** *Journal, Academic/Scholarly.* **Description:** Provides a medium for the publication of articles in the fields of obstetrics and gynecology from within and beyond the Asia Pacific region.
Media: Online - full text (from IngentaConnect). **Related titles:** ◆ Print ed.: Journal of Obstetrics and Gynaecology Research (Print). ISSN 1341-8076.
—CCC.
Published by: (The Japan Society of Obstetrics and Gynecology JPN, The Asia and Oceania Federation of Obstetrics and Gynaecology PHL), Wiley-Blackwell Publishing Asia (Subsidiary of: Wiley-Blackwell Publishing Ltd.), 155 Cremorne St, Richmond, VIC 3121, Australia. TEL 61-3-92743100, FAX 61-3-92743101, melbourne@wiley.com, http://www.wiley.com/WileyCDA/. Ed. Takashi Okai.

618 AUS ISSN 1341-8076
RG1 CODEN: JOGRFD
➤ **JOURNAL OF OBSTETRICS AND GYNAECOLOGY RESEARCH (PRINT).** Text in English. 1970. bi-m. abstr. back issues avail.; reprints avail. **Document type:** *Journal, Academic/Scholarly.* **Description:** Provides a medium for the publication of articles in the fields of obstetrics and gynecology from within and beyond the Asia Pacific region.
Former titles (until 1995): Journal of Obstetrics and Gynaecology (1340-9654); (until 1994): Asia - Oceania Journal of Obstetrics and Gynaecology (0389-2328); (until 1978): Asian Federation of Obstetrics and Gynaecology. Journal (0377-0532)
Related titles: ◆ Online - full text ed.: Journal of Obstetrics and Gynaecology Research (Online). ISSN 1447-0756.
Indexed: A01, A03, A08, A22, A26, C06, C07, C08, CA, CINAHL, ChemAb, CurCont, E01, EMBASE, ExcerpMed, ExtraMED, H12, INI, IndMed, Inpharma, MEDLINE, P30, P35, R10, Reac, S02, S03, SCI, SCOPUS, T02, W07.
—BLDSC (5026.055000), CASDDS, GNLM, IE, Infotrieve, Ingenta, INIST. **CCC.**
Published by: (The Japan Society of Obstetrics and Gynecology JPN, The Asia and Oceania Federation of Obstetrics and Gynaecology PHL), Wiley-Blackwell Publishing Asia (Subsidiary of: Wiley-Blackwell Publishing Ltd.), 155 Cremorne St, Richmond, VIC 3121, Australia. TEL 61-3-92743100, FAX 61-3-92743101, subs@blackwellpublishingasia.com, http://www.wiley.com/WileyCDA/. Eds. Shingo Fujii, Takashi Okai, Dr. Yuji Murata. Circ: 3,000 (paid and controlled).

618 USA ISSN 1090-1213
JOURNAL OF OBSTETRICS AND GYNECOLOGY; a journal of advances in obstetrics and gynecology. Text in English. 1996. m. USD 9.99 (effective 2010). back issues avail. **Document type:** *Journal, Academic/Scholarly.*
Media: Online - full text.
Published by: Current Clinical Strategies Publishing Inc., 27071 Cabot Rd, Ste 126, Laguna Hills, CA 92653. TEL 949-348-8404, 800-331-8227, FAX 909-744-8071, 800-965-9420, info@ccspublishing.com, http://www.ccspublishing.com/ccs/.

618 IND ISSN 0022-3190
RG1 CODEN: JOBYA4
➤ **JOURNAL OF OBSTETRICS AND GYNECOLOGY OF INDIA.** Text in English. 1950. bi-m. EUR 259 combined subscription (print & online eds.) (effective 2011). adv. bk.rev. charts; illus.; stat. reprint service avail. from IRC. **Document type:** *Journal, Academic/Scholarly.*
Related titles: CD-ROM ed.; Online - full text ed.: ISSN 0971-9202.
Indexed: A22, CIN, ChemAb, ChemTitl, ExtraMED, P30, W09.
—CASDDS, GNLM.
Published by: (Federation of Obstetric & Gynaecological Societies of India), Springer (India) Private Ltd. (Subsidiary of: Springer Science+Business Media), 212, Deen Dayal Upadhyaya Marg, 3rd Fl, Gandharva Mahavidyalaya, New Delhi, 110 002, India. TEL 91-11-45755888, FAX 91-11-45755889. Ed. Mahendra N Parikh.

618 GBR ISSN 1757-2215
QP261
➤ **JOURNAL OF OVARIAN RESEARCH.** Text in English. 2008. irreg. free (effective 2011). adv. back issues avail. **Document type:** *Journal, Academic/Scholarly.* **Description:** Provides a forum for high-quality basic and clinical research on ovarian functions, abnormalities, as well as prevention and treatment of diseases afflicting the organ.
Media: Online - full text.
Indexed: A01, A26, E08, EMBASE, H12, I05, P30, S09, SCOPUS.
Published by: BioMed Central Ltd. (Subsidiary of: Springer Science+Business Media), 236 Gray's Inn Rd, London, WC1X 8HB, United Kingdom. TEL 44-20-31922000, FAX 44-20-31922010, info@biomedcentral.com, http://www.biomedcentral.com. Eds. David Curiel, Fumikazu Kotsuji, Sham S Kakar.

618 618.92 HKG ISSN 1012-8875
➤ **JOURNAL OF PAEDIATRICS, OBSTETRICS AND GYNAECOLOGY (HONG KONG EDITION).** Text and summaries in English. 1975. bi-m. HKD 346, SGD 80 to non-members; HKD 173, SGD 40 to members (effective 2002). adv. illus. **Document type:** *Magazine, Academic/Scholarly.* **Description:** Reviews papers in the field of pediatrics and in obstetrics and gynecology.
Formerly: Mother and Child
Related titles: ◆ Regional ed(s).: Journal of Paediatrics, Obstetrics and Gynaecology (Thailand Edition). ISSN 1015-4345; ◆ Journal of Paediatrics, Obstetrics and Gynaecology (Taiwan Edition). ISSN 1015-4337.
—GNLM, IE.
Published by: MediMedia Pacific Ltd. (Subsidiary of: United Business Media Limited), 35th Fl, Two ChinaChem Exchange Sq, 338 King's Rd, North Point, Hong Kong. TEL 852-2559-5888, FAX 852-2559-6910, enquiry@medimedia.com.hk, http://www.medimedia.com.hk/. Ed. Sarah Aguoniby. Pub. Edgar Richards. Circ: 17,100 (controlled).

618 618.92 TWN ISSN 1015-4337
JOURNAL OF PAEDIATRICS, OBSTETRICS AND GYNAECOLOGY (TAIWAN EDITION). Text and summaries in English. 1974. bi-m. **Document type:** *Academic/Scholarly.*
Related titles: ◆ Regional ed(s).: Journal of Paediatrics, Obstetrics and Gynaecology (Thailand Edition). ISSN 1015-4345; ◆ Journal of Paediatrics, Obstetrics and Gynaecology (Hong Kong Edition). ISSN 1012-8875.
Published by: MediMedia Pacific Ltd. (Subsidiary of: United Business Media Limited), 1st Fl, No. 3, Ln 130, Sec 4, Hsin Hai Rd, Taipei, Taiwan. TEL 886-2-8663-3101, FAX 886-2-8663-3103, enquiry@medimedia.com.tw, http://www.medimedia-asia.com/.

618 618.92 THA ISSN 1015-4345
JOURNAL OF PAEDIATRICS, OBSTETRICS AND GYNAECOLOGY (THAILAND EDITION). Text and summaries in English. 1974. bi-m. **Document type:** *Journal, Academic/Scholarly.*
Related titles: ◆ Regional ed(s).: Journal of Paediatrics, Obstetrics and Gynaecology (Taiwan Edition). ISSN 1015-4337; ◆ Journal of Paediatrics, Obstetrics and Gynaecology (Hong Kong Edition). ISSN 1012-8875.
Published by: C M P Medica Asia Pte. Ltd. (Subsidiary of: United Business Media Limited), 58-60 Sukhumvit 62a Bangjak, Prakanong, Bangkok, 10260, Thailand. TEL 66-2-7415354, FAX 66-2-7415360, http://asia.cmpmedica.com/.

JOURNAL OF PEDIATRIC AND ADOLESCENT GYNECOLOGY. *see* MEDICAL SCIENCES—Pediatrics

JOURNAL OF PEDIATRIC SURGERY. *see* MEDICAL SCIENCES—Surgery

JOURNAL OF PERINATAL AND NEONATAL NURSING. *see* MEDICAL SCIENCES—Nurses And Nursing

618 USA ISSN 1058-1243
RG973
➤ **THE JOURNAL OF PERINATAL EDUCATION.** Abbreviated title: J P E. Text in English. 1992. q. USD 60 to individuals; USD 180 to institutions; free to members (effective 2011). adv. **Document type:** *Journal, Academic/Scholarly.* **Description:** Covers breastfeeding, labor, birth, maternal child health, clinical issues and more.
Related titles: Online - full text ed.: ISSN 1548-8519. free (effective 2011) (from IngentaConnect).
Indexed: A04, C06, C07, C08, C11, CA, CINAHL, GW, P30, P48, PQC, T02.
—BLDSC (5030.549000), IE, Ingenta. **CCC.**
Published by: Journal of Perinatal Education, Lamaze International, 2025 M St, NW, Ste 800, Washington, DC 20036. TEL 202-367-1128, FAX 202-367-2128. Ed. Wendy C Budin. Adv. contact James Costello TEL 212-431-4370 ext 208. Circ: 2,600.

618 DEU ISSN 0300-5577
RG626 CODEN: JPEMAO
➤ **JOURNAL OF PERINATAL MEDICINE;** official journal of the World Association of Perinatal Medicine. Text in English. 1973. bi-m. EUR 701, USD 1,052 to institutions; EUR 807, USD 1,211 combined subscription to institutions (print & online eds.) (effective 2012). adv. abstr.; charts; illus. back issues avail.; reprint service avail. from PSC. **Document type:** *Journal, Academic/Scholarly.* **Description:** Covers the whole field of perinatal medicine and neonatalogy.
Related titles: Online - full text ed.: ISSN 1619-3997. EUR 701, USD 1,052 to institutions (effective 2012); Supplement(s): Journal of Perinatal Medicine. Supplement. ISSN 0936-174X.
Indexed: A01, A03, A08, A20, A22, A26, A36, ASCA, B25, BDM&CN, BIOSIS Prev, C06, C07, C08, CA, CABA, CINAHL, ChemAb, ChemTitl, CurCont, D01, E01, E12, EMBASE, ExcerpMed, FamI, GH, H12, I05, IBR, IBZ, ISR, IndMed, Inpharma, MEDLINE, MycolAb, N02, N03, P30, P33, P35, P39, R08, R10, R12, RM&VM, Reac, SCI, SCOPUS, T02, T05, THA, VS, W07.
—BLDSC (5030.550000), CASDDS, GNLM, IE, Infotrieve, Ingenta, INIST. **CCC.**
Published by: Walter de Gruyter GmbH & Co. KG, Genthiner Str 13, Berlin, 10785, Germany. TEL 49-30-260050, FAX 49-30-26005251, info@degruyter.com. Ed. Joachim Dudenhausen. Adv. contact Dietlind Makswitat TEL 49-30-260050. page EUR 645; trim 140 x 190. Circ: 2,500 (paid and controlled).

618.3 GBR ISSN 0743-8346
CODEN: JOPEEI
➤ **JOURNAL OF PERINATOLOGY.** Text in English. 1981. m. EUR 440 in Europe to institutions; USD 553 in the Americas to institutions; JPY 75,100 in Japan to institutions; GBP 284 to institutions in the UK & elsewhere (effective 2011). adv. bk.rev. charts; illus.; stat. index. back issues avail.; reprints avail. **Document type:** *Journal, Academic/Scholarly.* **Description:** Provides all members of the perinatal/neonatal health care team with information pertinent to improving maternal, fetal and neonatal care.
Formerly (until 1984): California Perinatal Association. Journal (0733-334X)
Related titles: Microform ed.: (from PQC); Online - full text ed.: ISSN 1476-5543.
Indexed: A01, A02, A03, A08, A22, A26, A29, B20, B21, C06, C07, C08, CA, CCIP, CINAHL, CurCont, E01, EMBASE, ESPM, ExcerpMed, FamI, H04, H12, I05, I10, IndMed, MEDLINE, P20, P22, P24, P30, P48, P50, P54, PQC, R10, Reac, SCI, SCOPUS, T02, ViroIAbstr, W07.
—BLDSC (5030.570000), GNLM, IE, Infotrieve, Ingenta, INIST. **CCC.**
Published by: Nature Publishing Group (Subsidiary of: Macmillan Publishers Ltd.), The MacMillan Bldg, 4 Crinan St, London, N1 9XW, United Kingdom. TEL 44-20-78334000, FAX 44-20-78334640. Ed. Edward E Lawson TEL 410-955-4574. Adv. contact Ben Harkinson TEL 617-475-9222. **Subscr. to:** Brunel Rd, Houndmills, Basingstoke, Hamps RG21 6XS, United Kingdom. TEL 44-1256-329242, FAX 44-1256-812358, subscriptions@nature.com. **Co-sponsor:** California Perinatal Association.

618.12 USA ISSN 2090-2727
▼ ➤ **JOURNAL OF PREGNANCY.** Text in English. 2010. q. USD 195 (effective 2011). **Document type:** *Journal, Academic/Scholarly.* **Description:** Publishes original research articles, review articles, and clinical studies related to all aspects of pregnancy.
Related titles: Online - full text ed.: ISSN 2090-2735. free (effective 2011).
Indexed: A01, P30, T02.
Published by: Hindawi Publishing Corporation, 410 Park Ave, 15th Fl, PMB 287, New York, NY 10022. FAX 866-446-3294, hindawi@hindawi.com.

618.2 613.9 USA ISSN 1097-8003
RG103.5 CODEN: PPPJE4
➤ **JOURNAL OF PRENATAL & PERINATAL PSYCHOLOGY & HEALTH.** Text in English. 1986. q. free to members (effective 2010). back issues avail.; reprints avail. **Document type:** *Journal, Academic/Scholarly.* **Description:** Explores the psychological dimensions of human reproduction and pregnancy and the mental and emotional development of the unborn and newborn child.
Formerly (until 1997): Pre- and Perinatal Psychology Journal (0883-3095)
Indexed: A22, E-psyche, P03, P24, P25, P48, P50, PQC, PsycInfo, PsycholAb, SFSA.
—BLDSC (5042.162000), GNLM, IE, Ingenta. **CCC.**
Published by: Association for Pre- & Perinatal Psychology and Health, PO Box 1398, Forestville, CA 95436. TEL 707-887-2838, FAX 707-887-2838, apppah@aol.com. Ed. Bobbi Jo Lyman TEL 360-479-3273.

618 IND ISSN 0976-1756
▼ **JOURNAL OF PRENATAL DIAGNOSIS AND THERAPY.** Text in English. 2010. s-a. INR 1,000 domestic; USD 10 foreign (effective 2010). bk.rev. abstr. reprints avail. **Document type:** *Journal, Academic/Scholarly.*
Related titles: Online - full text ed.: free (effective 2011).
Indexed: A01, P10, P48, P53, P54, PQC.
—CCC.
Published by: Medknow Publications and Media Pvt. Ltd., B-9, Kanara Business Ctr, Off Link Rd, Ghatkopar (E), Mumbai, Maharastra 400 075, India. TEL 91-22-66491816, 91-22-66491818, publishing@medknow.com, http://www.medknow.com. Ed. Adi E Dastur. Pub. Dr. D K Sahu. Adv. contact Kaushik Shah. Circ: 500.

618 ITA ISSN 1971-3282
JOURNAL OF PRENATAL MEDICINE. Text in English. 2007. q. **Document type:** *Journal, Academic/Scholarly.*
Related titles: Online - full text ed.: ISSN 1971-3290.
Published by: C I C Edizioni Internazionali, Corso Trieste 42, Rome, 00198, Italy. TEL 39-06-8412673, FAX 39-06-8412688, info@gruppocic.it, http://www.gruppocic.it.

618 GBR ISSN 0167-482X
CODEN: JPOGD

➤ **JOURNAL OF PSYCHOSOMATIC OBSTETRICS AND GYNECOLOGY.** Abbreviated title: J P O G. Text in English. 1982. q. GBP 450, EUR 625, USD 780 combined subscription to institutions (print & online eds.); GBP 895, EUR 1,240, USD 1,555 combined subscription to corporations (print & online eds.) (effective 2010). adv. bk.rev. charts; illus. back issues avail.; reprint service avail. from PSC.
Document type: *Journal, Academic/Scholarly.* **Description:** Provides a scientific forum for gynaecologists, psychiatrists and psychologists as well as for all those who are interested in the psychosocial and psychosomatic aspects of women's health.
Related titles: Online - full text ed.: ISSN 1743-8942 (from IngentaConnect).
Indexed: A01, A03, A08, A20, A22, A36, ASCA, CA, CABA, CurCont, D01, DokArb, E-psyche, E01, EMBASE, ExcerpMed, F08, F09, FR, Faml, GH, IndMed, Inpharma, LT, MEDLINE, N02, N03, P03, P20, P22, P25, P30, P33, P35, P43, P48, P54, PQC, PsycInfo, PsycholAb, R10, RA&MP, RM&VM, RRTA, Reac, SCI, SCOPUS, SSCI, T02, T05, W07, W09.
—BLDSC (5043.479000), GNLM, IE, Infotrieve, Ingenta, INIST. **CCC.**
Published by: (International Society of Psychosomatic Obstetrics and Gynecology ESP), Informa Healthcare (Subsidiary of: T & F Informa plc), Telephone House, 69-77 Paul St, London, EC2A 4LQ, United Kingdom. TEL 44-20-70175000, healthcare.enquiries@informa.com. Eds. Dr. Harry B M van de Wiel, Dr. Willibrord C M Weijmar Schultz. Circ: 500 (paid). **Subscr. to:** Taylor & Francis Inc., Customer Services Dept, 325 Chestnut St, 8th Fl, Philadelphia, PA 19106. TEL 215-625-8900, 800-354-1420, FAX 215-625-8914, customerservice@taylorandfrancis.com; Taylor & Francis Ltd., Journals Customer Service, Sheepen Pl, Colchester, Essex CO3 3LP, United Kingdom. TEL 44-20-70175544, FAX 44-20-70175198.

➤ **JOURNAL OF REPRODUCTIVE IMMUNOLOGY.** *see* MEDICAL SCIENCES—Allergology And Immunology

618.05 USA ISSN 0024-7758
RG1 CODEN: JRPMAP

➤ **JOURNAL OF REPRODUCTIVE MEDICINE**; for the obstetrician and gynecologist. Text in English. 1968. bi-m. USD 340 combined subscription domestic to individuals (print & online eds.); USD 463 combined subscription foreign to individuals (print & online eds.); USD 713, USD 828 combined subscription domestic to institutions (print & online eds.); USD 290, USD 413 foreign to individuals; USD 413 domestic to institutions; USD 528 foreign to institutions (effective 2011). adv. bk.rev. illus. index. 2 cols./p.; back issues avail.; reprints avail. **Document type:** *Journal, Academic/Scholarly.* **Description:** Provides medicinal information for obstetrics and gynecologists.
Formerly (until 1969): Lying-in (0096-7033)
Related titles: Microform ed.: (from PMC, PQC); Online - full text ed.: ISSN 1943-3565.
Indexed: A20, A22, A36, ASCA, B25, BIOSIS Prev, C06, C07, C08, CABA, CCIOG, CIN, CINAHL, CLFP, ChemAb, ChemTitl, CurCont, D01, E12, EMBASE, ExcerpMed, F08, F09, F11, F12, FR, Faml, G10, GH, IDIS, INI, ISR, IndMed, Inpharma, LT, MEDLINE, MS&D, MaizeAb, MycolAb, N02, N03, NRN, P30, P32, P33, P35, P37, P39, PGegResA, PHN&I, R08, R10, R12, R13, RA&MP, RM&VM, RRTA, Reac, RefZh, SCI, SCOPUS, T05, THA, VS, W07, W09.
—BLDSC (5049.700000), CASDDS, GNLM, IE, Infotrieve, Ingenta, INIST. **CCC.**
Published by: Journal of Reproductive Medicine, Inc., 8342 Olive Blvd., St. Louis, MO 63132. TEL 314-991-4440, FAX 314-991-4654. Eds. Daniel R Mishell Jr., Lawrence D Devoe.

618 649.10242 GBR ISSN 1478-4785
JUNIOR PREGNANCY & BABY. Text in English. 2002. bi-m. back issues avail. **Document type:** *Magazine, Consumer.* **Description:** Lifestyle magazine for mothers-to-be and new mothers covering conception, pregnancy and birth to caring for the new baby up to six months.
—**CCC.**
Published by: Magicalia Ltd., 15-18 White Lion St, Islington, London, N1 9PG, United Kingdom. TEL 44-20-78438800, FAX 44-20-78438999, customer.services@magicalia.com, http://www.magicalia.com/.

649.102 AUS
JUNIOR PREGNANCY AND BABY. Variant title: Junior Magazine Pregnancy & Baby. Text in English. bi-m. AUD 14.95 newsstand/cover (effective 2007). **Document type:** *Magazine, Consumer.*
Published by: Derwent Howard Media Pty Ltd., PO Box 1037, Bondi Junction, NSW 1355, Australia. TEL 61-2-83056900, FAX 61-2-83056999, enquiries@derwenthoward.com.au, http://www.derwenthoward.com.au. Ed. Victoria Lea. Adv. contact Rose Fulete. Circ: 40,000 (paid and controlled).

618 TUR ISSN 1301-1154
KADIN DOGUM DERGISI/JOURNAL OF WOMEN OF BIRTH/TURKISH JOURNAL OF OBSTETRICS AND GYNAECOLOGY. Text in Turkish; Summaries in English. 1985 (May). q. **Document type:** *Journal, Academic/Scholarly.*
Published by: Gunes Kitap Kirtasiye, DAU Rektorluk Karsisi No.278, Semt, Gazimagusa, Turkey. TEL 90-232-3650370, bemregul@mynet.com, http://www.bemregul.com.

618 JPN ISSN 0916-2747
KAGAKU RYOHO KENKYUJO KIYO/INSTITUTE OF CHEMOTHERAPY. BULLETIN. Text in English, Japanese. 1989. a.
—**CCC.**
Published by: Kagaku Ryoho Kenkyujo, 1-14 Kono-Dai 6-chome, Ichikawa-shi, Chiba-ken 272-0827, Japan.

618.2 FIN ISSN 0022-9415
KATILOLEHTI/TIDSKRIFT FOER BARNMORSKOR. Text in Finnish, Swedish; Summaries in English. 1896. 7/yr. EUR 55 (effective 2005). adv. bk.rev. charts; illus.; stat. **Document type:** *Magazine, Trade.*
Indexed: INI, P30, SCOPUS.
Published by: Suomen Katiloliitto/Federation of Finnish Midwives, Asemamiehenkatu 4, Helsinki, 00520, Finland. TEL 358-9-1552790, FAX 358-9-1462917, toimisto@suomenkatiloliitto.fi. Ed. Mervi Parviainen. adv.: B&W page EUR 610, color page EUR 1,090; 152 x 220. Circ: 4,200.

618 POL ISSN 1230-6576
KLINICZNA PERINATOLOGIA I GINEKOLOGIA. Text in Polish. 1991. q. EUR 50 foreign (effective 2006). **Document type:** *Journal, Academic/Scholarly.*
Published by: Polskie Towarzystwo Medycyny Perinatalnej, Akademia Medyczna im. Karola Marcinkowskiego, Klinika Perinatologii i Ginekologii, Polna 33, Poznan, 60535, Poland. TEL 48-61-8419283, FAX 48-61-8419204, gbrebor@gpsk.am.poznan.pl. Ed. Grzegorz H Breborowicz. **Dist. by:** Ars Polona, Obroncow 25, Warsaw 03933, Poland. TEL 48-22-5098609, FAX 48-22-5098610, arspolona@arspolona.com.pl, http://www.arspolona.com.pl.

618 DEU ISSN 0932-0601
KORASION. Text in German. 1986. q. **Document type:** *Magazine, Academic/Scholarly.*
Related titles: ◆ Supplement to: Gyne. ISSN 0179-9185.
—GNLM.
Published by: H U F Verlag, Lindenhof 47, Muehlheim, 45481, Germany. TEL 49-208-480027, FAX 49-208-485899, huf-verlag@ob.kamp.net.

618.202 JPN ISSN 1348-334X
KYOUTO DAIGAKU JOSAMPU DOUSOUKAIHOU/MIDWIVES ASSOCIATION OF KYOTO UNIVERSITY. ANNALS. Text in Japanese. a. **Document type:** *Journal, Academic/Scholarly.*
Formerly: Kyoto Daigaku Josanpu Dosokaishi (0917-3641)
Published by: Kyoto Daigaku Josanpu Dosokai, Kyoto Daigaku Igakubu, Fanfujinkagaku Kyoshitsu, Shogoin Kawaramachi, Sakyo-ku, Kyoto-shi, Kyoto 606, Japan.

618 USA
LAMAZE; pregnancy, birth & beyond. Text in English, Spanish. 1983. a. free to qualified personnel (effective 2009). adv. **Document type:** *Magazine, Consumer.* **Description:** Contains feature articles on pregnancy, child birth and parenting.
Formerly: Lamaze Parents' Magazine
Related titles: Online - full text ed.: free (effective 2009).
Published by: Lamaze International, Inc., 2025 M St NW, Ste 800, Washington, DC 20036. TEL 202-367-1128, 800-368-4404, FAX 202-367-2128, http://www.lamaze.org/. Ed. Nelson Pena.

618.45 USA
LAMAZE PARA PADRES. Text in Spanish. 1994. q. free to qualified personnel (effective 2005). adv. **Document type:** *Magazine, Consumer.* **Description:** Offers information to Spanish-speaking expectant couples on prenatal and postpartum care through Lamaze classes.
Published by: (American Society for Psychoprophylaxis in Obstetrics, Inc.), Lamaze Publishing Co., 2025 M St, Ste 800, Washington, DC 20036. TEL 202-367-1128, 800-368-4404, FAX 202-367-2128. Ed. Susan Strecker Richard. adv.: page USD 48,075. Circ: 575,028 (controlled).

618.45 USA
LAMAZEBABY. Text in English. 1993. s-a. **Document type:** *Magazine, Consumer.* **Description:** Addressed to new parents on baby's first year.
Published by: (Lamaze International, Inc.), Lamaze Publishing Co., 2025 M St, Ste 800, Washington, DC 20036. TEL 202-367-1128, 800-368-4404, FAX 202-367-2128.

618.1 AUT ISSN 1991-9220
LEADING OPINIONS. GYNAEKOLOGIE. Text in German. 2006. q. **Document type:** *Journal, Academic/Scholarly.*
Media: Online - full content.
Published by: Universimed Verlags- und Service GmbH, Markgraf-Ruediger-Str 8, Vienna, 1150, Austria. TEL 43-1-87679560, FAX 43-1-876795620, office@universimed.com, http://www.universimed.com.

618.1 FRA ISSN 0759-1594
➤ **LA LETTRE DU GYNECOLOGUE.** Text in French. 1984. m. EUR 114 in Europe to individuals; EUR 114 DOM-TOM to individuals; EUR 114 in Africa to individuals; EUR 126 elsewhere to individuals; EUR 138 in Europe to institutions; EUR 138 DOM-TOM to institutions; EUR 138 in Africa to institutions; EUR 150 elsewhere to institutions (effective 2009). Supplement avail. **Document type:** *Newsletter, Academic/Scholarly.*
—INIST.
Published by: Edimark S.A.S., 2 Rue Sainte-Marie, Courbevoie, Cedex 92418, France. TEL 33-1-41458000, FAX 33-1-41458025, contact@edimark.fr. Ed. P Madelenat. Pub. Claudie Damour-Terrasson.

618.12 NZL ISSN 1177-0910
LITTLIES PREGNANCY GUIDE. Variant title: Pregnancy Guide. Text in English. 2005. a. NZD 9.95 domestic; NZD 14.95 foreign (effective 2006).
Published by: Littlies Ltd., PO Box 55197, Mission Bay, Auckland, New Zealand. TEL 64-9-5783402, FAX 64-9-5783412.

618.12 ISL ISSN 1670-2670
LJOSMAEDRABLADID. Text in Icelandic. 1922. 3/yr. **Document type:** *Magazine, Trade.*
Published by: Ljosmaedrafelagid/Icelandic Midwives Association, Hamraborg 1, Kopavogi, 200, Iceland. TEL 354-564-6099, FAX 354-564-6098, formadur@ljosmaedrafelag, http://www.ljosmaedrafelag.is.

THE LOCAL BABY DIRECTORY: BRISTOL & BATH. *see* CHILDREN AND YOUTH—About

THE LOCAL BABY DIRECTORY: HERTS & MIDDLESEX; an a-z of everything for pregnant women, babies and children. *see* CHILDREN AND YOUTH—About

THE LOCAL BABY DIRECTORY: OXFORDSHIRE, BERKS & BUCKS; an a-z of everything for pregnant women, babies and children. *see* CHILDREN AND YOUTH—About

THE LOCAL BABY DIRECTORY: SOUTH WALES; an a-z of everything for pregnant women, babies and children. *see* CHILDREN AND YOUTH—About

THE LOCAL BABY DIRECTORY: SURREY; an a-z everything for pregnant women, babies and children. *see* CHILDREN AND YOUTH—About

THE LOCAL BABY DIRECTORY: SUSSEX & HAMPSHIRE; an a-z of everything for pregnant women, babies and children. *see* CHILDREN AND YOUTH—About

THE LONDON BABY DIRECTORY; an a-z of everything for pregnant women, babies and children. *see* CHILDREN AND YOUTH—About

618 ITA ISSN 1590-6353
LUCINA. Text in Italian. 1934. bi-m. free to members. adv. **Document type:** *Bulletin, Trade.* **Description:** It is the main means of contact among the members of the Federazione Nazionale dei Collegi delle Ostetriche. It covers the principal themes of interest in the field of obstetrics.
Published by: (Federazione Nazionale dei Collegi delle Ostetriche), Mattioli 1885 SpA, Via Coduro 1, Fidenza, PR 43036, Italy. TEL 39-0524-84547, FAX 39-0524-84751, http://www.mattioli1885.com. Circ: 17,000.

618.202 GBR ISSN 0961-5555
M I D I R S MIDWIFERY DIGEST. Text in English. 1986. q. GBP 54 domestic; GBP 65 in Europe; GBP 66 in Australia & New Zealand; GBP 72 elsewhere; GBP 13.50 per issue domestic; GBP 16.25 per issue in Europe; GBP 16.50 per issue in Australia & New Zealand; GBP 18 per issue elsewhere (effective 2009). adv. back issues avail.
Document type: *Journal, Academic/Scholarly.* **Description:** Contains news, reviews, original articles and reprints of the best maternity and infant care information from journals around the world.
Formerly (until 1991): M I D I R S Information Pack (0955-8683)
Related titles: Online - full text ed.: GBP 70 domestic to individuals; GBP 81 in Europe to individuals; GBP 82 in Australia & New Zealand to individuals; GBP 88 elsewhere to individuals; GBP 17.50 per issue domestic to individuals; GBP 20.25 per issue in Europe to individuals; GBP 20.50 per issue in Australia & New Zealand to individuals; GBP 22 per issue elsewhere to individuals (effective 2009).
Indexed: B28, C06, C07, C08, CINAHL.
—BLDSC (5761.413886), IE, Ingenta. **CCC.**
Published by: Midwives Information and Resource Service, 9 Elmdale Rd, Clifton, Bristol, Glos BS8 1SL, United Kingdom. TEL 44-117-9251791, FAX 44-117-9251792, sales@midirs.org, http://www.midirs.org. Ed. Sally Marchant. Adv. contact Sue Penn TEL 44-117-9077594. B&W page GBP 840, color page GBP 1,625; 165 x 255. Circ: 8,500.

618 USA
M I D S NEWSLETTER. (Miscarriage, Infant Death, and Stillbirth) Text in English. 1983. 4/yr. USD 30 (effective 2000). **Document type:** *Newsletter.* **Description:** Newsletter of announcements for families suffering miscarriages, infant deaths, and stillbirths.
Indexed: E-psyche.
Published by: M I D S Inc., 16 Crescent Dr, Parsippany, NJ 07054.

618 TUR ISSN 1304-7264
M N KLINIK BILIMLER AND DOKTOR. Text in English. 1995. m. **Document type:** *Journal, Academic/Scholarly.*
Supersedes in part (in 1997): Klinik Bilimler (1300-4743)
Published by: Medical Network, Public Sokak No.4/2, Ankara, 06420, Turkey. info@medicalnetwork.com.tr, http://www.medicalnetwork.com.tr.

M P R (HEMATOLOGY/ONCOLOGY EDITION). (Monthly Prescribing Reference) *see* PHARMACY AND PHARMACOLOGY

M P R (OBSTETRICIAN & GYNECOLOGIST EDITION). (Monthly Prescribing Reference) *see* PHARMACY AND PHARMACOLOGY

MAGAZYN PIELEGNIARKI I POLOZNEJ. *see* MEDICAL SCIENCES—Nurses And Nursing

610 HUN ISSN 0025-021X
CODEN: MNLAA8
MAGYAR NOORVOSOK LAPJA. Text in Hungarian; Summaries in English. 1937. bi-m. HUF 3,000 domestic; HUF 5,000 foreign (effective 2000). bibl.; charts; illus.
Indexed: A22, ChemAb, ChemTitl, IndMed, P30, R10, Reac, SCOPUS.
—BLDSC (5345.010000), CASDDS, IE, Ingenta.
Published by: Magyar Noorvos Tarsasag, Szabolcs utca 35, PO Box 112, Budapest, 1135, Hungary. TEL 36-1-3506502, FAX 36-1-3506502. Ed. Dr. Jozsef Doszpod. **Subscr. to:** Kultura, PO Box 149, Budapest 1389, Hungary.

616 ROM ISSN 1224-6492
MAMI. Text in Romanian. 1995. m. adv. **Document type:** *Magazine, Consumer.*
Published by: Sanoma - Hearst Romania srl, Str Argentina nr 41, sect 1, Bucharest, Romania. TEL 40-21-3138620, FAX 40-21-3138622.

MAMM; women, cancer and community. *see* WOMEN'S HEALTH

618.1 GBR ISSN 1460-1397
RG186
THE MANAGEMENT OF THE MENOPAUSE: ANNUAL REVIEW. Text in English. 1998. a., latest 2003, 3rd Ed. USD 129 per issue (effective 2003).
—**CCC.**
Published by: Parthenon Publishing Group (Subsidiary of: C R C Press, LLC), 23-25 Blades Court, Deodar Road, London, SW15 2NU, United Kingdom. TEL 44-20-8875-0909, FAX 44-20-8871-9996, mail@parthpub.com, http://www.parthpub.com/journal.html. Ed. John Studd.

618 USA ISSN 1091-5680
RG186
MANAGING MENOPAUSE. Text in English. 1997. s-a. free (effective 2010). adv. **Document type:** *Newsletter, Trade.*
Related titles: Online - full text ed.
Published by: American College of Obstetricians and Gynecologists, PO Box 96920, Washington, DC 20090. TEL 202-638-5577, publication@acog.org, http://www.acog.org.

618 USA ISSN 1092-7875
RJ102 CODEN: MCHJFB
➤ **MATERNAL AND CHILD HEALTH JOURNAL.** Text in English. 1997. bi-m. EUR 865, USD 928 combined subscription to institutions (print & online eds.) (effective 2012). adv. back issues avail.; reprint service avail. from PSC. **Document type:** *Journal, Academic/Scholarly.*
Description: Provides a forum for advancing scientific and professional knowledge of the maternal and child health (MCH) field.
Related titles: Online - full text ed.: ISSN 1573-6628 (from IngentaConnect).
Indexed: A01, A03, A08, A22, A26, B20, B21, BibLing, C06, C07, C08, C11, CA, CINAHL, CurCont, E01, E08, EMBASE, ESPM, ExcerpMed, F09, Faml, G08, H04, H05, H11, H12, I05, IndMed, MEDLINE, P03, P20, P22, P24, P30, P34, P48, P50, P54, PQC, PsycInfo, PsycholAb, R10, Reac, S02, S03, S09, SCOPUS, SSCI, T02, W07.
—BLDSC (5399.272500), IE, Infotrieve, Ingenta. **CCC.**

Published by: (Association of Maternal and Child Health Programs), Springer New York LLC (Subsidiary of: Springer Science+Business Media), 233 Spring St, New York, NY 10013. TEL 212-460-1500, FAX 212-460-1575, service-ny@springer.com, http://www.springer.com/. Eds. Donna J Petersen, Greg R Alexander. **Co-sponsors:** Association of Teachers of Maternal and Child Health; American Public Health Association, Maternal and Child Health Section; CityMatCH.

➤ **MATERNAL DEATH SERIES.** *see* POPULATION STUDIES

618.202 IRL ISSN 1649-847X
MATERNITY. Text in English. 1998. a. **Document type:** *Magazine, Trade.*
Published by: Ashville Media Group, Apollo House, Tara St., Dublin, 2, Ireland. TEL 353-1-4322200, FAX 353-1-6727100, info@ashville.com, http://www.ashville.com. Ed. Anthea Savage. Adv. contact Brian O'Neill.

618.202 ESP ISSN 1578-0740
MATRONAS PROFESION. Text in Spanish. 2000. q. free to qualified personnel; EUR 36 domestic (effective 2008). 52 p./no.; **Document type:** *Journal, Trade.*
Indexed: C06, C07, EMBASE, ExcerpMed, SCOPUS.
Published by: Ediciones Mayo S.A., Calle Aribau 185-187, 2a Planta, Barcelona, 08021, Spain. TEL 34-93-2090255, FAX 34-93-2020643, edmayo@ediciones.mayo.es, http://www.edicionesmayo.es. Circ: 5,000.

612.665 IRL ISSN 0378-5122
RG186 CODEN: MATUDK
➤ **MATURITAS.** Text in English. 1978. 12/yr. EUR 1,613 in Europe to institutions; JPY 214,200 in Japan to institutions; USD 1,804 elsewhere to institutions (effective 2012). bk.rev. reprints avail. **Document type:** *Journal, Academic/Scholarly.* **Description:** For gynecologists, endocrinologists, geriatricians, andrologists, sociologists, and psychologists. Publishes original research on the physiological, psychological and sociological changes in function related to the climacteric in both men and women.
Incorporates (1994-1998): European Menopause Journal (1381-2858)
Related titles: Microform ed.: (from PQC); Online - full text ed.: ISSN 1873-4111 (from IngentaConnect, ScienceDirect).
Indexed: A01, A03, A08, A20, A22, A26, A34, A35, A36, A38, ASCA, ASG, AgBio, B25, BIOBASE, BIOSIS Prev, C06, C07, CA, CABA, CIN, ChemAb, ChemTitl, CurCont, D01, E-psyche, E12, EMBASE, ExcerpMed, F08, F11, F12, FamI, GH, H16, I05, IABS, IBR, IBZ, IDIS, ISR, IndMed, IndVet, Inpharma, LT, MEDLINE, MycolAb, N02, N03, N04, P03, P30, P32, P33, P35, P40, PGegResA, PsycInfo, PsycholAb, R10, R12, R13, RA&MP, RRTA, Reac, SCI, SCOPUS, SoyAb, T02, T05, TriticAb, VS, W07, W09.
—BLDSC (5413.265000), CASDDS, GNLM, IE, Infotrieve, Ingenta, INIST. **CCC.**
Published by: (European Menopause and Andropause Society DNK), Elsevier Ireland Ltd (Subsidiary of: Elsevier Science & Technology), Elsevier House, Brookvale Plaza, E. Park, Shannon, Co. Clare, Ireland. TEL 353-61-709600, FAX 353-61-709100. Ed. Margaret Rees. R&P Annette Moloney. Circ: 453. **Subscr. to:** Elsevier BV, Radarweg 29, PO Box 211, Amsterdam 1000 AE, Netherlands. TEL 31-20-4853757, FAX 31-20-4853432, JournalsCustomerServiceEMEA@elsevier.com, http://www.elsevier.nl.

➤ **MEALEY'S EMERGING DRUGS & DEVICES.** *see* LAW—Corporate Law

➤ **MEALEY'S LITIGATION REPORT: HORMONE REPLACEMENT THERAPY.** *see* LAW

618 613 BGR ISSN 0204-0956
CODEN: AKGIBP
➤ **MEDITSINSKI PREGLED. AKUSHERSTVO I GINEKOLOGIIA.** Text in Bulgarian; Summaries in Bulgarian, English. 1970. q. BGL 14 domestic; USD 40 foreign (effective 2005). adv. bk.rev. abstr.; bibl. index. back issues avail. **Document type:** *Journal, Academic/Scholarly.* **Description:** Publishes original articles and abstracts of foreign publications on gynecologic diseases and obstetrics - pregnancy complications, risk factors, neonatal diseases and abnormalities.
Indexed: ABSML, IndMed.
—CASDDS.
Published by: Meditsinski Universitet - Sofia, Tsentralna Meditsinska Biblioteka, Tsentur za Informatsiia po Meditsina/Medical University - Sofia, Central Medical Library, Medical Information Center, 1 Sv Georgi Sofiiski ul, Sofia, 1431, Bulgaria. TEL 359-2-9522342, FAX 359-2-9522393, lydia@medun.acad.bg, http://www.medun.acad.bg/cmb_htm/cmb1_home_bg.htm. Ed. Dr. B Marinov. R&P, Adv. contact Lydia Tacheva. B&W page USD 50, color page USD 150; trim 160 x 110. Circ: 350.

618 POL
MEDYCYNA PRAKTYCZNA. GINEKOLOGIA I POLOZNICTWO. Text in Polish. bi-m. PLZ 120 (effective 2000).
Published by: Medycyna Praktyczna, ul Krakowska 41, Krakow, 31066, Poland. TEL 48-12-4305520, FAX 48-12-4305536, listy@mp.pl, http://www.mp.pl. Ed. Andrzej Bacz.

618.175 ITA ISSN 1123-699X
MENOPAUSA NEWS. Text in Italian. 1995. q. free to qualified personnel. adv. **Document type:** *Newsletter, Trade.*
Published by: (Societa Italiana della Menopausa), C I C Edizioni Internazionali, Corso Trieste 42, Rome, 00198, Italy. TEL 39-06-8412673, FAX 39-06-8412688, info@gruppocic.it, http://www.gruppocic.it.

618 USA ISSN 1072-3714
RG186 CODEN: MENOF2
➤ **MENOPAUSE.** Text in English. 1994. bi-m. USD 731 domestic to institutions; USD 806 foreign to institutions (effective 2011). adv. charts; illus. back issues avail. **Document type:** *Journal, Academic/Scholarly.* **Description:** Forum for new research and scholarly material relating to all aspects of the human female menopause, from physiological, pathological, sociocultural and medical perspectives.
Related titles: Microform ed.: (from PQC); Online - full text ed.: ISSN 1530-0374. USD 373.10 domestic academic site license; USD 402.10 foreign academic site license; USD 416.15 domestic corporate site license; USD 445.15 foreign corporate site license (effective 2002).
Indexed: A20, A22, A34, A36, A38, ASCA, C06, C07, C08, CABA, CINAHL, CurCont, D01, E-psyche, E12, EMBASE, ExcerpMed, F08, F11, F12, GH, H16, ISR, IndMed, Inpharma, JW-WH, LT, MEDLINE, N02, N03, N04, P30, P32, P35, P40, PGegResA, PHN&I, PN&I, R10, R12, RA&MP, RRTA, Reac, SCI, SCOPUS, SoyAb, T05, VS, W07, W09.
—BLDSC (5678.457030), IE, Infotrieve, Ingenta, INIST. **CCC.**
Published by: (North American Menopause Society), Lippincott Williams & Wilkins (Subsidiary of: Wolters Kluwer N.V.), 530 Walnut St, Philadelphia, PA 19106. TEL 215-521-8300, FAX 215-521-8902, customerservice@lww.com, http://www.lww.com. Eds. Wulf H Utian, Isaac Schiff. Pubs. Cordelia Slaughter TEL 410-528-4462, Marcia Serepy. R&P Margaret Becker. Adv. contact Ray Thibodeau. B&W page USD 1,030, color page USD 2,250. Circ: 2,344 (paid). **Subscr. to:** PO Box 1620, Hagerstown, MD 21741. TEL 301-223-2300, 800-638-3030, FAX 301-223-2365.

618.175 GBR ISSN 1754-0453
CODEN: JBMSFN
MENOPAUSE INTERNATIONAL. Text in English. 1995. q. USD 752 combined subscription in North America to institutions (print & online eds); EUR 512 combined subscription in Europe to institutions (print & online eds); GBP 368 combined subscription to institutions in the UK & elsewhere (print & online eds.) (effective 2012). adv. back issues avail. **Document type:** *Journal, Academic/Scholarly.* **Description:** Provides resource of news, research and opinion aimed at all those involved in the study and treatment of menopausal conditions.
Formerly (until 2007): British Menopause Society. Journal (1362-1807)
Related titles: Online - full text ed.: ISSN 1754-0461. USD 677 in North America to institutions; EUR 461 in Europe to institutions; GBP 331 to institutions in the UK & elsewhere (effective 2012).
Indexed: A22, C06, C07, CA, E01, EMBASE, ExcerpMed, G10, MEDLINE, P30, R10, Reac, SCOPUS, T02.
—BLDSC (5678.457033), IE, Ingenta. **CCC.**
Published by: (British Menopause Society), Royal Society of Medicine Press Ltd., 1 Wimpole St, London, W1G 0AE, United Kingdom. TEL 44-20-72902921, FAX 44-20-72902929, publishing@rsm.ac.uk, http://www.rsmpress.co.uk. Eds. Edward Morris, Heather Currie. **Subscr. to:** Portland Customer Services, Commerce Way, Colchester CO2 8HP, United Kingdom. TEL 44-1206-796351, FAX 44-1206-799331, sales@portland-services.com, http://www.portlandpress.com.

618.1 POL ISSN 1730-0029
MENOPAUZA. Text in Polish. 2002. q. **Document type:** *Journal, Academic/Scholarly.*
Related titles: Online - full text ed.: ISSN 1730-0010.
Published by: Blackhorse Scientific Publishers, Ltd., Zeganska 16, Warsaw, 04713, Poland. TEL 48-22-4999099, FAX 48-22-4995081, blackhorse@blackhorse.pl, http://blackhorse.pl/blackhorse.

618.2 EGY ISSN 1110-5690
RG133.5 CODEN: MEFJFF
➤ **MIDDLE EAST FERTILITY SOCIETY JOURNAL.** Text in English. 1996. 3/yr. adv. bk.rev. abstr.; charts; illus. back issues avail. **Document type:** *Journal, Academic/Scholarly.* **Description:** Provides information and advocacy for all areas of reproductive medicine.
Related titles: Online - full text ed.: 2005 (from ScienceDirect).
Indexed: A01, CA, EMBASE, ExcerpMed, R10, Reac, SCOPUS, T02.
—BLDSC (5761.374250), IE, Ingenta. **CCC.**
Published by: Middle East Fertility Society, 10 Geziret El Arab St., Mohandessin, Cairo, 12411, Egypt. TEL 202-3383049, info@mefs.org, http://www.mefs.org. Ed. Dr. Mohamed A Aboulghar. adv.: color page USD 1,480; 25.5 x 17.8. Circ: 1,500 (paid); 500 (controlled).

618 GBR ISSN 0266-6138
RG950
➤ **MIDWIFERY.** Text in English. 1984. bi-m. EUR 600 in Europe to institutions; JPY 65,100 in Japan to institutions; USD 537 elsewhere to institutions (effective 2012). adv. bk.rev. abstr. back issues avail.; reprints avail. **Document type:** *Journal, Academic/Scholarly.* **Description:** Provides an international and interdisciplinary forum for the discussion of advances, controversies and current research in midwifery.
Related titles: Online - full text ed.: ISSN 1532-3099 (from ScienceDirect).
Indexed: A20, A22, A26, ASCA, ASSIA, B28, C06, C07, C08, CA, CINAHL, CurCont, E01, EMBASE, ExcerpMed, F09, FamI, G10, H12, I05, IBR, IBZ, INI, MEDLINE, P30, R10, Reac, SCI, SCOPUS, SSCI, T02, W07, W09.
—BLDSC (5761.449220), GNLM, IE, Infotrieve, Ingenta. **CCC.**
Published by: Churchill Livingstone (Subsidiary of: Elsevier Health Sciences), The Blvd, Langford Ln, Kidlington, OX5 1GB, United Kingdom. TEL 44-1865-843434, FAX 44-1865-843970, directenquiries@elsevier.com, http://www.elsevierhealth.com/imprint.jsp?iid=9. Ed. Debra Bick. Adv. contact Deborah Watkins TEL 44-20-74244280.

➤ **MIDWIFERY MATTERS.** *see* MEDICAL SCIENCES—Nurses And Nursing

618.202 USA ISSN 1551-8892
MIDWIFERY TODAY; the heart and science of birth. Text in English. 1996. q. USD 55 domestic (effective 2008); USD 65 in Canada & Mexico; USD 75 elsewhere (effective 2006). adv. bk.rev.; video rev. bibl.; illus.; tr.lit. Index. back issues avail.; reprints avail. **Document type:** *Magazine, Consumer.* **Description:** Directs professionals and non-professionals alike; balances technical articles with personal accounts and photography to present a wide range of options and perspectives on current birth care issues.
Formerly (until 1997): Midwifery Today and Childbirth Education with International Midwife (1522-2888); Which was formed by the merger of (1987-1996): Midwifery Today (0891-7701); (1995-1996): International Midwife (1080-9023)
Related titles: Online - full text ed.
Indexed: A04, A26, C06, C07, C08, C11, CINAHL, CWI, EMBASE, ExcerpMed, FamI, FemPer, G06, G07, G08, GW, H12, I05, INI, M06, MEDLINE, P30, P48, PQC, R10, Reac, SCOPUS, T02, T03.
—BLDSC (5761.449240), GNLM, IE, Ingenta.
Published by: Midwifery Today with International Midwife, PO Box 2672, Eugene, OR 97402. TEL 541-344-7438, 800-743-0974, FAX 541-344-1422. Eds. Alice Evans, Jan Tritten. R&P Jan Tritten. adv.: B&W page USD 150; trim 10 x 7.5. Circ: 2,500.

618.202 GBR
➤ **MIDWIVES.** Text in English. 1888. m. GBP 97.50 domestic; GBP 132.20 in Europe; GBP 138 elsewhere; free to members (effective 2009). bk.rev. index. reprints avail. **Document type:** *Journal, Academic/Scholarly.* **Description:** Presents articles, features and news relevant to midwives, obstetricians and others interested in the health and care of mothers and infants.
Former titles (until 2008): R C M Midwives (1479-2915); (until 2002): R C M Midwives Journal (1462-138X); (until 1998): Midwives (1355-8404); (until 1995): Midwives Chronicle (0026-3524)
Related titles: Microform ed.: (from PQC); Online - full text ed.: free (effective 2009); ◆ Supplement(s): Evidence - Based Midwifery. ISSN 1479-4489.
Indexed: A22, A26, ASSIA, B28, C06, C07, C08, CINAHL, F09, FamI, H12, I05, IBR, IBZ, INI, P30, R10, Reac, SCOPUS, W09.
—BLDSC (7300.180800), GNLM, IE, Ingenta. **CCC.**
Published by: (Royal College of Midwives), Ten Alps Publishing (Subsidiary of: Ten Alps Group), Trelawney House, Chestergate, Macclesfield, Cheshire SK11 6DW, United Kingdom. TEL 44-1625-613000, FAX 44-1625-511446, info@tenalpspublishing.com, http://www.tenalpspublishing.com.

618 JPN
MIE-KEN SANFUJINKA IHO/MEI OBSTETRICS AND GYNECOLOGY. ANNUAL BULLETIN. Text in Japanese. 1982. a. **Document type:** *Academic/Scholarly.*
Published by: Mie-ken Sanfujinka Ikai/Mei Obstetrics and Gynecologiy, 2-191-4, Sakurabashi, Tsu-shi, Mie-ken 514-0003, Japan. TEL 81-59-2247321, FAX 81-59-2248661, http://www.mie-aog.jp/.

618 ITA ISSN 0026-4784
➤ **MINERVA GINECOLOGICA;** a journal on obstetrics and gynecology. Text in Italian; Summaries in English, Italian. 1949. bi-m. EUR 255 combined subscription in the European Union to institutions (print & online eds.); EUR 280 combined subscription elsewhere to institutions (print & online eds.) (effective 2011). adv. bk.rev. bibl.; charts; illus. index. **Document type:** *Journal, Academic/Scholarly.* **Description:** Covers obstetric and gynecological pathophysiology, clinical medicine and therapy.
Incorporates: Folia Gynaecologica; Ginecologia; Aggiornamenti di Ostetricia e Ginecologia (0002-0931)
Related titles: Microform ed.: (from PQC); Online - full text ed.: ISSN 1827-1650.
Indexed: A20, A22, CA, ChemAb, EMBASE, ExcerpMed, IndMed, MEDLINE, P30, R10, Reac, RefZh, SCOPUS, T02, W09.
—BLDSC (5794.185000), GNLM, IE, Infotrieve, Ingenta, INIST. **CCC.**
Published by: Edizioni Minerva Medica, Corso Bramante 83-85, Turin, 10126, Italy. TEL 39-011-678282, FAX 39-011-674502, journals.dept@minervamedica.it, http://www.minervamedica.it. Ed., Pub. Alberto Oliaro. adv.: B&W page USD 1,400, color page USD 2,300; trim 270 x 190. Circ: 4,000 (paid).

618 CZE ISSN 1214-5572
MODERNI BABICTVI. Text in Czech. 2003. 3/yr. CZK 75 domestic (effective 2010). **Document type:** *Journal, Trade.* **Description:** Designed for for midwives and nurses working in the fields of obstetrics and gynecology.
Related titles: Online - full text ed.
Published by: Levret s.r.o., Terronska 61, Prague 6, 16000, Czech Republic. TEL 420-224-318262 Fax, zaznamnik 233 344 719 E-mail sosnova@levret.cz Web WWW.LEVRET.CZ, FAX 420-233-344719, levret@levret.cz.

618 CZE ISSN 1211-1058
MODERNI GYNEKOLOGIE A PORODNICTVI. Text in Czech. 1991. q. CZK 520 domestic; EUR 27 foreign (effective 2010). **Document type:** *Journal, Academic/Scholarly.*
Related titles: Online - full text ed.
Published by: Levret s.r.o., Terronska 61, Prague 6, 16000, Czech Republic. TEL 420-224-318262 Fax, zaznamnik 233 344 719 E-mail sosnova@levret.cz Web WWW.LEVRET.CZ, FAX 420-233-344719, levret@levret.cz. Ed. Pavel Calda.

612.6 571.8 GBR ISSN 1360-9947
CODEN: MHREFD
➤ **MOLECULAR HUMAN REPRODUCTION:** basic science of reproductive medicine. Abbreviated title: M H R. Text in English. 1995. m. GBP 723 in United Kingdom to institutions; EUR 1,085 in Europe to institutions; USD 1,446 in US & Canada to institutions; GBP 723 elsewhere to institutions; GBP 788 combined subscription in United Kingdom to institutions (print & online eds.); EUR 1,183 combined subscription in Europe to institutions (print & online eds.); USD 1,577 combined subscription in US & Canada to institutions (print & online eds.); GBP 788 combined subscription elsewhere to institutions (print & online eds.) (effective 2012). adv. back issues avail.; reprint service avail. from PSC. **Document type:** *Journal, Academic/Scholarly.* **Description:** Covers the molecular control of development and senescence, paracrines in embryonic growth and reproductive organs, genetic factors in reproduction and development, cell proliferations and apoptosis, and transport systems within cells and across membranes.
Related titles: Online - full text ed.: ISSN 1460-2407. GBP 527 in United Kingdom to institutions; EUR 790 in Europe to institutions; USD 1,053 in US & Canada to institutions; GBP 527 elsewhere to institutions (effective 2012) (from IngentaConnect).
Indexed: A22, B21, B25, BIOSIS Prev, CA, CIN, CTA, ChemAb, ChemTitl, CurCont, E01, EMBASE, ExcerpMed, GenetAb, ISR, IndMed, Inpharma, MEDLINE, MycolAb, NucAcAb, P15, P20, P22, P30, P48, P52, P54, P56, PQC, R10, Reac, SCI, SCOPUS, W07.
—BLDSC (5900.817650), CASDDS, GNLM, IE, Infotrieve, Ingenta, INIST. **CCC.**
Published by: (European Society of Human Reproduction and Embryology BEL), Oxford University Press, Great Clarendon St, Oxford, OX2 6DP, United Kingdom. TEL 44-1865-556767, FAX 44-1865-556646, enquiry@oup.co.uk, http://www.oxfordjournals.org. Ed. Stephen G Hillier. Pub. Janet Boulin.

➤ **N A B C O BREAST CANCER RESOURCE LIST.** *see* MEDICAL SCIENCES—Oncology

➤ **N A B C O NEWS.** *see* MEDICAL SCIENCES—Oncology

➤ **N A N N CENTRAL.** *see* MEDICAL SCIENCES—Nurses And Nursing

➤ **N H S CERVICAL SCREENING PROGRAMME (YEAR).** (National Health Service) *see* WOMEN'S HEALTH

➤ **N M C NEWS.** *see* MEDICAL SCIENCES—Nurses And Nursing

618.1 JPN
NAGANOKEN SANKA FUJINKA IKAIHO/GYNECOLOGICAL SOCIETY OF NAGANO. BULLETIN. Text in Japanese. 1962. s-a. free.
Document type: *Bulletin.*
Published by: Naganoken Sanka Fujinka Ikai, Shinshu Daigaku Igakubu Sanfujinka Kyoshitsu, 1-1 Asahi 3-chome, Matsumoto-shi, Nagano-ken 390-0802, Japan. Ed. Hiroo Linumd.

NASHRIYYAH-I PARASTARI-I IRAN/IRAN JOURNAL OF NURSING. *see* MEDICAL SCIENCES—Nurses And Nursing

NATIONAL ASSOCIATION OF NEONATAL NURSES. POSITION STATEMENT. *see* MEDICAL SCIENCES—Nurses And Nursing

618.2 USA
NATIONAL PERINATAL ASSOCIATION. BULLETIN. Text in English. 1980. q. USD 75 membership (effective 2007). adv. bk.rev.
Document type: *Bulletin.* **Description:** Information for association members.
Published by: National Perinatal Association, 2090 Linglestown Rd, Ste 107, Harrisburg, PA 17110. TEL 888-971-3295, FAX 717-920-1390, npa@nationalperinatal.org, http://www.nationalperinatal.org. Ed. Julie A Leachman. Circ: 1,500.

618 NLD ISSN 0921-4011
NEDERLANDS TIJDSCHRIFT VOOR OBSTETRIE & GYNAECOLOGIE. Text in Dutch. 1980. 10/yr. EUR 180 domestic; EUR 275 foreign; EUR 80.50 to students (effective 2009). bk.rev. abstr.; charts; illus. reprints avail. **Document type:** *Journal, Academic/Scholarly.* **Description:** Informs association members about developments in the field of obstetrics and gynecology.
Incorporates (in 1987): Ob-Gyn Digest (English Edition) (0198-9197); Which was formed by the merger of (1976-1980): Medilex Digest Ob-Gyn (0921-402X); (1977-1980): Journal of Continuing Education in Obstetrics and Gynecology (0148-5164); Which superseded (1959-1977): Ob-Gyn Digest (0029-7429); And incorporated: Ob-Gyn Abstracts
Related titles: Microform ed.: (from PQC).
Indexed: R10, Reac, SCOPUS.
—CCC.
Published by: (Nederlandse Vereniging voor Obstetrie en Gynaecologie), DCHG Medische Communicatie, Zijlweg 70, Haarlem, 2013 DK, Netherlands. TEL 31-23-5514888, FAX 31-23-5515522, info@dchg.nl, http://www.dchg.nl. Ed. A A W Peters. Circ: 1,600.

618.12 613.04244 NLD
NEGEN MAANDEN MAGAZINE. Variant title: 9 Maanden Magazine. Text in Dutch. a. EUR 4.50 newsstand/cover (effective 2009). adv.
Document type: *Magazine, Consumer.*
Published by: Jonge Gezinnen b.v. (Subsidiary of: Sanoma Uitgevers B.V.), Postbus 790, Alphen aan den Rijn, 2400 AT, Netherlands. TEL 31-172-447857, FAX 31-172-448409, info@jongegezinnen.nl, http://www.jongegezinnen.nl. adv.: color page EUR 11,995; trim 215 x 282. Circ: 170,000.

618 618.92 USA ISSN 1062-2454
➤ **NEONATAL INTENSIVE CARE**; the journal of perinatology - neonatology. Text in English. 1988. bi-m. USD 80 in North America; USD 110 elsewhere (effective 2010). adv. back issues avail.
Document type: *Journal, Academic/Scholarly.* **Description:** Covers diagnostic techniques, case studies and research findings in perinatology and neonatology.
Related titles: Online - full text ed.: free (effective 2010).
Indexed: A22, C06, C07, C08, CINAHL, P30.
—BLDSC (6075.623500), IE, Infotrieve, Ingenta.
Published by: Goldstein and Associates, Inc., 10940 Wilshire Blvd, Ste 600, Los Angeles, CA 90024. TEL 310-443-4109, FAX 310-443-4110. Ed. Les Plesko. Pub. Steve Goldstein.

➤ **NEONATAL NETWORK**; the journal of neonatal nursing. *see* MEDICAL SCIENCES—Nurses And Nursing

571.86 612.64 CHE ISSN 1661-7800
RJ251 CODEN: BNEOBV
➤ **NEONATOLOGY**; fetal and neonatal research. Text in English. 1952. 8/yr. CHF 2,952, EUR 2,360, USD 2,894 to institutions; CHF 3,240, EUR 2,590, USD 3,174 combined subscription to institutions (print & online eds.) (effective 2012). adv. bibl.; charts; illus. back issues avail. **Document type:** *Journal, Academic/Scholarly.* **Description:** Original papers present laboratory findings from both human and animal studies covering the physiological and biochemical events taking place during the period leading up to and immediately following birth, whether fullterm or premature.
Former titles (until 2007): Biology of the Neonate (0006-3126); Which incorporated (1980-1995): Developmental Pharmacology and Therapeutics (0379-8305); (until 1980): Biologia Neonatorum (0523-6525); (until 1959): Etudes Neo-natales (0423-5789)
Related titles: Microform ed.: (from PQC); Online - full text ed.: ISSN 1661-7819. CHF 2,884, EUR 2,308, USD 2,800 to institutions (effective 2012).
Indexed: A01, A03, A08, A22, A34, A36, A38, ASCA, B21, B25, BDM&CN, BIOBASE, BIOSIS Prev, CA, CABA, CIN, ChemAb, ChemTitl, CurCont, D01, DBA, E01, E12, EMBASE, ExcerpMed, Faml, GH, H13, IABS, IBR, IBZ, ISR, IndMed, IndVet, Inpharma, MEDLINE, MycolAb, N02, N03, NSA, P10, P15, P20, P22, P26, P30, P33, P35, P39, P48, P52, P53, P54, P56, PN&I, PQC, R10, RA&MP, RM&VM, Reac, S12, SCI, SCOPUS, T02, T05, VS, VirolAbstr, W07.
—BLDSC (6075.625550), CASDDS, GNLM, IE, Infotrieve, Ingenta, INIST. **CCC.**
Published by: S. Karger AG, Allschwilerstr 10, Basel, 4055, Switzerland. TEL 41-61-3061111, FAX 41-61-3061234, karger@karger.ch, http://www.karger.ch. Eds. C Speer, H L Halliday. adv.: page CHF 1,730; trim 210 x 280. Circ: 900.

618 NPL ISSN 1999-9623
➤ **NEPAL JOURNAL OF OBSTETRICS AND GYNAECOLOGY.** Text in English. 2007. s-a. **Document type:** *Journal, Academic/Scholarly.* **Description:** Aims to provide forum for scientific and clinical professional communication in Obstetrics and Gynaecology throughout the world.
Related titles: Online - full text ed.: ISSN 1999-8546. free (effective 2011).
Published by: Nepal Society of Obstetricians and Gynecologists, OPD Bldg, 2nd Fl, Maternity Hospital, Thapathali, P O Box 10644, Kathmandu, Nepal. TEL 977-1-4252315, FAX 977-1-4252315, njog63@gmail.com, http://www.nesog.org.np. Ed. Dr. Ashma Rana.

618.1 305.4 FRA ISSN 1299-1929
NEUF MOIS MAGAZINE. Text in French. 2000. m. EUR 18 (effective 2009). **Document type:** *Magazine, Consumer.*
Published by: Bleucom Editions, 12-14 Rue de l'Eglise, Paris, 75015, France. direction@bleucom.net, http://www.bleucom.net/.

618 GBR ISSN 1476-4806
NEW DIGEST. Text in English. 1993. q. GBP 24.35 (effective 2009). adv. **Document type:** *Journal, Consumer.* **Description:** Covers latest developments affecting maternity and new parents' services; critical appraisal of recent research with a round-up of new research and policy; and day-to-day practice of identifying and responding to parents' needs during pregnancy, birth and the early days.
Formerly (until 1999): New Generation Digest (1350-2735)
Published by: National Childbirth Trust, Alexandra House, Oldham Terr, Acton, London, W3 6NH, United Kingdom. TEL 44-844-2436100, infocentre@nct.org.uk. Adv. contact George Pearce TEL 44-20-87522331.

618 GBR ISSN 0263-5429
NEW GENERATION. Text in English. 1982. q. free to members (effective 2009). adv. bk.rev. **Document type:** *Magazine, Consumer.*
—BLDSC (6084.210900), IE, Ingenta.
Published by: National Childbirth Trust, Alexandra House, Oldham Terr, Acton, London, W3 6NH, United Kingdom. TEL 44-844-2436100, infocentre@nct.org.uk, http://www.nct.org.uk. Adv. contact George Pearce TEL 44-20-87522331.

NEW MOTHER. *see* CHILDREN AND YOUTH—About

618.202 NZL ISSN 0114-7870
NEW ZEALAND COLLEGE OF MIDWIVES. JOURNAL. Text in English. 1989. s-a. NZD 12 newsstand/cover to non-members; NZD 7 newsstand/cover to members (effective 2009). adv. back issues avail.
Document type: *Journal, Academic/Scholarly.* **Description:** Contributes to the development of midwifery knowledge.
Related titles: Online - full text ed.: ISSN 1178-3893.
Indexed: A11, A26, C06, C07, C08, CA, CINAHL, H12, I05, T02.
—BLDSC (4832.958000), IE, Ingenta.
Published by: New Zealand College of Midwives, 376 Manchester St, PO Box 21 106, Christchurch, New Zealand. TEL 64-3-3772732, FAX 64-3-3775662, nzcom@nzcom.org.nz. Ed. Rhondda Davis. Adv. contact Janice Bateman. Circ: 2,750.

363.46 310 NZL ISSN 1179-1098
NEW ZEALAND. STATISTICS NEW ZEALAND. ABORTION STATISTICS (YEAR). Text in English. 1997. a. **Document type:** *Government.* **Description:** Contains statistics on the number of abortions performed in New Zealand.
Related titles: Online - full text ed.: ISSN 1178-0193.
Published by: Statistics New Zealand/Te Tari Tatau, Statistics House, The Blvd, Harbour Quays, PO Box 2922, Wellington, 6140, New Zealand. TEL 64-4-9314600, FAX 64-4-9314610, info@stats.govt.nz.

618.1 JPN ISSN 1347-8559
NIHON FUJINKA SHUYOU GAKKAI ZASSHI/JAPAN SOCIETY OF GYNECOLOGIC ONCOLOGY. JOURNAL. Text in Japanese; Summaries in English, Japanese. 1982. q.
Formerly (until Jun. 1998): Nihon Fujinka Byori Koruposukopi Gakkai Zasshi/Japan Society of Gynecologic Pathology and Colposcopy. Journal
Published by: Nihon Fujinka Shuyou Gakkai/Japan Society of Gynecologic Oncology, 5F, Dai 2 Izumi-shoji Bldg., 4-2-6 Kojimachi, Chiyoda-ku, Tokyo, 102-0083, Japan. TEL 81-3-32881033, FAX 81-3-52751192, gyne-oncol@jsgo.gr.jp, http://www.jsgo.gr.jp/.

618.202 JPN ISSN 0917-6357
RG965.J3
NIHON JOSAN GAKKAISHI/JAPAN ACADEMY OF MIDWIFERY. JOURNAL. Text in Japanese; Summaries in English, Japanese. 1987. s-a. **Document type:** *Journal, Academic/Scholarly.*
Indexed: C06, C07, C08, CINAHL.
—BLDSC (4804.142000). **CCC.**
Published by: Nihon Josan Gakkai/Japan Academy of Midwifery, Josanpu Kaikan, 1-8-21, Fujimi, Chiyoda-ku, 3F, Midwives Hall, Tokyo, 102-0071, Japan. jam1987@ninus.ocn.ne.jp, http://square.umin.ac.jp/jam/.

618 JPN ISSN 0914-6776
NIHON JUSEI CHAKUSHO GAKKAI ZASSHI/JOURNAL OF FERTILIZATION AND IMPLANTATION. Text in English, Japanese. 1984. a. JPY 8,000 membership (effective 2004). **Document type:** *Journal, Academic/Scholarly.*
—CCC.
Published by: Nihon Jusei Chakusho Gakkai/Japan Society of Fertilization and Implantation, c/o Convex Inc., Ichijoji Bldg, 2-3-22 Azabudai, Minato-ku, Tokyo, 106-0041, Japan. TEL 81-3-35893460, FAX 81-3-35052126. Ed. Masahiko Hiroi. Circ: 1,400.

618 616.9 JPN ISSN 0918-4031
NIHON SANFUJINKA KANSENSHO KENKYUKAI GAKUJUTSU KOENKAI KIROKUSHU/CONFERENCE ON OBSTETRICAL AND GYNECOLOGICAL INFECTION. PROCEEDINGS. Text in Japanese; Summaries in English, Japanese. 1983. a. **Document type:** *Proceedings, Academic/Scholarly.*
Published by: Nihon Sanfujinka Kansensho Kenkyukai/Japan Association of Obstetrical and Gynecological Infection, Koto Byoin Sanfujinka, 8-5 Ojima 6-chome, Koto-ku, Tokyo, 136-0072, Japan.

618 JPN ISSN 0916-8796
➤ **NIHON SANFUJINKA SHINSEIJI KETSUEKI GAKKAISHI/JAPANESE JOURNAL OF OBSTETRICAL, GYNECOLOGICAL AND NEONATAL HEMATOLOGY.** Text in English, Japanese. 1977. q. adv. bk.rev. **Document type:** *Journal, Academic/Scholarly.* **Description:** Contains papers with laboratory or clinical orientation, case reports and revew articles.
Former titles (until 1990): Sanfujinka, Shinseiji Ketsueki (0285-3027); (until 1980): Sanfujinka Ketsueki/Journal of Obstetrical & Gynecological Hematology (0389-1917)
Published by: Nihon Sanfujinka, Shinseiji Ketsueki Gakkai/Japanese Society of Obstetrical Gynecological and Neonatal Hematology, c/o University of Occupational and Environmental Health, Division of Child Health, 1-1 Iseigaoka, Yahatanishiku, Kitakyushu, 807-8555, Japan. Circ: 1,500.

618 360 JPN ISSN 1348-5938
NIHON SANFUJINKAI KAIHOU/J A O G NEWS. Text in Japanese. 1949. m. JPY 36,000 membership (effective 2007). adv. bk.rev. **Document type:** *Newsletter, Trade.*
Former titles (until May 1995): Nihon Bosei Hogo Sanfujinka Ikai; (until Mar. 1994): Nichibo Iho (0288-8270)
Published by: Nihon Sanfujinkaik/Japan Association of Obstetricians & Gynecologists, 1-2 Sadohara-cho, Ichigaya, Shinjuku-ku, Tokyo, 162-0842, Japan. TEL 81-3-32694739, FAX 81-3-32694730, jimu@jaog.or.jp, http://www.jaog.or.jp/. Circ: 14,800.

618 JPN ISSN 1341-8165
NIHON SANKA FUJINKA GAKKAI AKITA CHIHOBU KAISHI/AKITA SOCIETY OF OBSTETRICS AND GYNECOLOGY. JOURNAL. Text in Japanese. 1995. bi-m. free to members. **Document type:** *Journal, Academic/Scholarly.*
Published by: Nihon Sanka Fujinka Gakkai, Akita Chihoubu/Japan Society of Obstetrics and Gynecology, Akita Branch, Akita University School of Medicine, Department of Obstetrics & Gynecology, 1-1-1 Hondo, Akita, 010-8543, Japan. http://www.med.akita-u.ac.jp/~obgyn/tihobukai/index.html. Circ: 100.

618 JPN ISSN 0546-1790
NIHON SANKA FUJINKA GAKKAI CHUGOKU SHINKOKU GODO CHIHO BUKAI ZASSHI/JAPAN SOCIETY OF OBSTETRICS AND GYNECOLOGY. CHUGOKU AND SHIKOKU DISTRICTS JOURNAL. Text in Japanese. 1951. 3/yr. (1 (vol.52, no.2) issue in 2004, s-a. until 2003). **Document type:** *Journal, Academic/Scholarly.*
Indexed: INIS AtomInd.
Published by: Nihon Sanka Fujinka Gakkai, Chuoku Shikoku Godo Chiho Bukai/Japan Society of Obstetrics and Gynecology, Chugoku and Shikoku Districts, c/o Okayama University Medical School, Department of Obstetrics & Gynecology, 2-5-1 Shikata-cho, Okayama, 700-8558, Japan. TEL 81-86-2357320, FAX 81-86-2259570.

618 JPN ISSN 0910-2485
NIHON SANKA FUJINKA GAKKAI KANAGAWA CHIHO BUKAI KAISHI/JAPAN SOCIETY OF OBSTETRICS AND GYNECOLOGY. KANAGAWA DISTRICT JOURNAL. Text in Japanese. 1964. s-a.
Document type: *Journal, Academic/Scholarly.*
Published by: Nihon Sanka Fujinka Gakkai, Kanagawa Chiho Bukai/Japanese Obstetrical and Gynecological Society, Kanagawa District, Kanagawa Medical Association of Obstetrics & Gynecology, 3-1 Fujimicho Naka-ku, Sogo Iryo Kaikan 4F, d, Kanagawa-ken 231-0037, Japan. TEL 81-45-2424867, FAX 81-45-2423830, http://www.kaog.jp/.

618 JPN ISSN 0285-8096
CODEN: NKRKES
NIHON SANKA FUJINKA GAKKAI KANTO RENGO CHIHO BUKAI KAIHO/KANTO JOURNAL OF OBSTETRICS AND GYNECOLOGY. Text in Japanese. 1964. s-a. **Document type:** *Journal, Academic/Scholarly.*
Related titles: Online - full content ed.: ISSN 1348-1606.
Indexed: ChemAb.
—CASDDS.
Published by: Nihon Sanka Fujinka Gakkai, Kanto Rengo Chiho Bukai/Japan Society of Obstetrics and Gynecology, Kanto Branch, 1-1, Ichigaya-Sadohara-cho, Shinjuku-ku, Tokyo, 162-0842, Japan.

618 JPN ISSN 1341-5050
NIHON SANKA FUJINKA GAKKAI KUMAMOTO CHIHO BUKAI ZASSHI/JAPAN SOCIETY OF OBSTETRICS AND GYNECOLOGY. KUMAMOTO DISTRICT JOURNAL. Text in Japanese. 1949. a. adv.
Document type: *Academic/Scholarly.*
Formerly: Nihon Sanka Fujinka Gakkai Kumamoto Chiho Bukai Kaiho
Published by: Nihon Sanka Fujinka Gakkai, Kumamoto Chiho Bukai/Japan Society of Obstetrics and Gynecology, Kumamoto Branch, c/o Kumamoto University School of Medicine, Faculty of Medical & Pharmaceutical Science, OBGyn, 1-1-1 Honjo, Kumamoto, 860-8556, Japan.

618 JPN ISSN 0913-2368
NIHON SANKA FUJINKA GAKKAI KYUSHU RENGO CHIHO BUKAI ZASSHI/JAPAN SOCIETY OF OBSTETRICS AND GYNECOLOGY. KYUSHU DISTRICT JOURNAL. Text in Japanese. a. **Document type:** *Journal, Academic/Scholarly.*
Published by: Nihon Sanka Fujinka Gakkai, Kyushu Rengo Chiho Bukai/Japan Society of Obstetrics and Gynecology, Kumamoto University School of Medicine, Obstetrics and Gynecology, 1-1-1 Honjo, Kumamoto, 860-8556, Japan.

618 JPN ISSN 0285-3485
NIHON SANKA FUJINKA GAKKAI NIIGATA CHIHO BUKAI KAISSHI/JAPAN SOCIETY OF OBSTETRICS AND GYNECOLOGY. NIIGATA DISTRICTS JOURNAL. Text in Japanese. 1972. q. membership.
Document type: *Journal, Academic/Scholarly.*
Published by: Nihon Sanka Fujinka Gakkai, Niigata Chiho Bukai, c/o Niigata Daigaku Igakubu Sanfujinka Kyoshitsu, 1-757, Asahi-machi Dori, Niigata-shi, Niigata-ken 951, Japan.

618 JPN ISSN 0911-6281
NIHON SANKA FUJINKA GAKKAI SAITAMA CHIHO BUKAI KAISHI/JAPAN SOCIETY OF OBSTETRICS AND GYNECOLOGY. SAITAMA DISTRICT JOURNAL. Text in Japanese. 1971. s-a.
Document type: *Journal, Academic/Scholarly.*
Published by: Nihon Sanka Fujinka Gakkai, Saitama Chiho Bukai/Japan Society of Obstetrics and Gynecology, Saitama District, c/o Saitama Medical Association, 3-5-1 Naka-cho, Urawa-shi, Saitama-ken 336-0007, Japan. TEL 81-48-8242611.

618 JPN
NIHON SANKA FUJINKA GAKKAI TOHOKU RENGO CHIHO BUKAI KAISHI/TOHOKU JOURNAL OF OBSTETRICS AND GYNECOLOGY. Text in Japanese. 1956. a. **Document type:** *Journal, Academic/Scholarly.*
Former titles (until 2002): Nihon Sanka Fujinka Gakkai Tohoku Rengo Chiho Bukai Kaiho
Published by: Nihon Sanka Fujinka Gakkai, Tohoku Rengo Chihou Bukai/Japan Society of Obstetrics and Gynecology, Tohoku Branch, Tohoku University School of Medicine, 1-1 Seiryo-cho, Aoba-ku, Sendai-shi, Miyagi-ken 980-0872, Japan. TEL 81-22-2741111.

618 JPN ISSN 0288-5751
NIHON SANKA FUJINKA GAKKAI TOKYO CHIHO BUKAI KAISHI/TOKYO JOURNAL OF OBSTETRICS AND GYNECOLOGY. Text in Japanese. 1952. q. **Document type:** *Journal, Academic/Scholarly.*

Published by: Nihon Sanka Fujinka Gakkai, Tokyo Chiho Bunkai/Japan Society of Obstetrics and Gynecology, Tokyo Branch, c/o MA Conventional Consulting Inc., Dai 2 Izumi-Shoji Bldg. 5F, 4-2-6 Koji machi, Chiyoda-ku, Tokyo, 102-0083, Japan. TEL 81-3-32880366, aag19250@pop02.odn.ne.jp, http://www.jsog.or.jp/about_us/region/branch_open/t13/t13_top.html.

618 JPN ISSN 0300-9165
CODEN: NISFAY

NIHON SANKA FUJINKA GAKKAI ZASSHI/ACTA OBSTETRICA ET GYNAECOLOGICA JAPONICA. Text in English, Japanese. 1949. m. adv. bibl.; charts. Index. **Document type:** *Journal, Academic/Scholarly.*
Incorporates (in 1969): Acta Obstetrica et Gynaecologica Japonica (0001-6330); Which was formerly (1954-1968): Japanese Obstetrical and Gynecological Society. Journal (0388-0486); Formed by the merger of (1906-1949): Nihon Fujinka Gakkai Zasshi; (1936-1948): Sanka Fujinka Kiyo; Which was formerly (until 1936): Kinki Fujin Kagakukai Zasshi/Kinki Gynecological Society. Journal; (until 1922): Taisho Fujin Kagakukai Kurikaeshihou; (until 1919): Kinki Fujin Kagakukai Kurikaeshihou; (1915-1916): Kinki Fujin Kakai Kurikaeshihou
Indexed: A22, ChemAb, INIS AtomInd, IndMed, P30, SCOPUS.
—BLDSC (0641.571000), CASDDS, GNLM, IE, Infotrieve, Ingenta, INIST. **CCC.**
Published by: Nihon Sanka Fujinka Gakkai/Japan Society of Obstetrics and Gynecology, Twin View Ochanomizu Bldg. 3F, 2-3-9, Hongo,. Bunkgo-ku, Tokyo, 113-0033, Japan. TEL 81-3-58425452, FAX 81-3-58425470, nissanfu@jsog.or.jp. Circ: 2,500.

618 JPN

NIHON SANKA FUJINKA NAISHIKYO GAKKAI ZASSHI/JAPANESE JOURNAL OF GYNECOLOGIC AND OBSTETRIC ENDOSCOPY. Text in Japanese. 1985. irreg. **Document type:** *Journal, Academic/Scholarly.*
Published by: Nihon Sanka Fujinka Naishinkyo Gakkai/Japan Society of Gynecologic and Obstetric Endoscopy, c/o Medical Supply Japan Ltd., Natsume Bldg 4th Fl, 2-18-6 Yushima, Bunkyo-ku, Tokyo, 113-0034, Japan. TEL 81-3-38182177, FAX 81-3-38152644, http://jsgoe.umin.jp/.

618 617 JPN

NIHON SEISHOKU GEKA GAKKAI ZASSHI/JAPAN SOCIETY OF REPRODUCTIVE SURGERY. JOURNAL. Text in Japanese. a.
Formerly: Sanfujinka Maikuro Sajari Gakkai Zasshi/Japanese Journal of Gynecological Microsurgery
Published by: Nihon Seishoku Geka Gakkai/Japan Society of Reproductive Surgery, Kinki University School of Medicine, Nara Hospital, Obstetrics and Gynecology Department, 1248-1 Otuda-chou, Ikoma, Nara 630-0293, Japan. TEL 81-743-770880, FAX 81-743-770890.

NURSING UPDATE. *see* MEDICAL SCIENCES—Nurses And Nursing

618 658 USA ISSN 1044-307X
RG1

O B G MANAGEMENT. (Obstetrics and Gynecology) Text in English. 1989. m. USD 138 domestic; USD 178 foreign (effective 2010). adv. **Document type:** *Magazine, Trade.* **Description:** Contains evidence based articles that provide cutting-edge, clinical information. Also focuses on practice management issues.
Related titles: Online - full text ed.
Indexed: A26, B02, B15, B17, B18, CompD, E08, G04, G08, I05, S09.
—BLDSC (6196.954000), IE, Ingenta. **CCC.**
Published by: Quadrant HealthCom, 7 Century Dr, Ste 302, Parsippany, NJ 07054. TEL 973-206-3434, FAX 973-206-9378, http://www.quadranthealth.com. adv.: B&W page USD 5,345, color page USD 8,630; trim 8.1 x 11. Circ: 39,428 (paid and controlled).

618 USA ISSN 1543-6691

OB-GYN & REPRODUCTION WEEK. Text in English. 2003. w. USD 2,295 in US & Canada; USD 2,495 elsewhere; USD 2,525 combined subscription in US & Canada (print & online eds.); USD 2,755 combined subscription elsewhere (print & online eds.) (effective 2008). back issues avail. **Document type:** *Newsletter, Trade.*
Related titles: E-mail ed.; Online - full text ed.: ISSN 1543-6683. USD 2,295 combined subscription (online & email eds.); single user (effective 2008).
Indexed: A26, E08, G08, H11, H12, I05, S09.
—CIS.
Published by: NewsRx, 2727 Paces Ferry Rd SE, Ste 2-440, Atlanta, GA 30339. TEL 770-435-8286, 800-726-4550, FAX 770-435-6800, pressrelease@newsrx.com. Ed. Carol Kohn. Pub. Susan Hasty TEL 770-507-7777.

618 USA ISSN 0743-8354
RG1

OB/GYN CLINICAL ALERT. Text in English. 1982. m. USD 319 combined subscription (print & online eds.); USD 53 per issue (effective 2010). index. reprints avail. **Document type:** *Newsletter, Trade.* **Description:** Features abstracts of developments in obstetrics and gynecology, with expert commentary added by the physician editors.
Formerly (until 1984): Advances in Reproductive Medicine (0741-420X)
Related titles: Audio cassette/tape ed.; Online - full text ed.; Polish Translation: Nowosci Ginekologiczne. ISSN 1642-8080.
Indexed: A01, A26, E08, G08, H11, H12, I05, P20, P48, P54, PQC, S09.
—CCC.
Published by: A H C Media LLC (Subsidiary of: Thomson Corporation, Healthcare Information Group), 3525 Piedmont Rd, NE, Bldg 6, Ste 400, Atlanta, GA 30305. TEL 404-262-7436, 800-688-2421, FAX 404-262-7837, 800-284-3291, customerservice@ahcmedia.com, http://www.ahcmedia.com/. Ed. Dr. Leon Speroff. Pub. Brenda L Mooney TEL 404-262-5403. **Subscr. to:** PO Box 105109, Atlanta, GA 30348. TEL 404-262-5476, FAX 404-262-5560.

OB-GYN CODING ALERT; the practical monthly adviser for ethically optimizing coding reimbursement and efficiency in ob-gyn offices and clinics. *see* INSURANCE

618 USA ISSN 0029-7437
RG1

OB-GYN NEWS. Text in English. 1966. s-m. USD 146 in United States to institutions; USD 293 elsewhere to institutions (effective 2012). adv. bk.rev. back issues avail.; reprints avail. **Document type:** *Newspaper, Trade.* **Description:** Provides the practicing obstetrician/gynecologist with timely and relevant news and commentary about clinical developments in the field and about the impact of health care policy on the specialty and the physician's practice.
Related titles: Microform ed.: (from PQC); Online - full text ed.; Spanish ed.: ISSN 1135-8505.
Indexed: A22, A26, CLFP, G08, H11, H12, I05, P30, W09.
—CCC.
Published by: International Medical News Group (Subsidiary of: Elsevier Health Sciences), 5635 Fishers Ln, Ste 6000, Rockville, MD 20852. TEL 877-524-9337, FAX 240-221-4400, m.altier@elsevier.com, http://www.imng.com. Ed. Mary Jo M. Dales. Pub. Alan J Imhoff TEL 973-290-8216. Circ: 39,631. **Subscr. to:** Elsevier, Subscription Customer Service, 60 Columbia Rd, Bldg B, Morristown, NJ 07960. TEL 973-290-8200, FAX 973-290-8250, http://www.elsevier.com/.

▼ **THE OB-GYN NURSE.** *see* MEDICAL SCIENCES—Nurses And Nursing

618 IND ISSN 0971-8133

OBS. & GYNAE. TODAY. Variant title: Obstetrics and Gynaecology Today. Text in English. 1996. m. **Document type:** *Journal, Academic/Scholarly.*
Published by: C M P Medica (Subsidiary of: C M P Medica Ltd.), Sagar Tech Plz A 615-617, 6th Fl, Andheri Kurla Rd, Saki Naka Jct, Andheri E, Mumbai, 400 072, India. TEL 91-22-66122600, FAX 91-22-66122626, info.india@ubm.com, http://www.ubmindia.in/cmp-medica.asp.

OBSTETRIC ANESTHESIA DIGEST. *see* MEDICAL SCIENCES—Anaesthesiology

618.12 GBR ISSN 1753-495X

➤ **OBSTETRIC MEDICINE.** Text in English. 2008 (Sep.). q. USD 828 combined subscription in North America to institutions (print & online eds.); EUR 588 combined subscription in Europe to institutions (print & online eds.); GBP 382 combined subscription to institutions in the UK & elsewhere (print & online eds.) (effective 2012). adv. back issues avail. **Document type:** *Journal, Academic/Scholarly.* **Description:** Covers all aspects of medicine affecting the pregnant woman, including conditions that pre-exist and arise de novo in pregnancy, and the long-term implications of pregnancies, including those complicated by disease, for maternal health.
Related titles: Online - full text ed.: ISSN 1753-4968. USD 745 in North America to institutions; EUR 529 in Europe to institutions; GBP 344 to institutions in the UK & elsewhere (effective 2012).
Indexed: A01, T02.
—CCC.
Published by: (Society of Obstetric Medicine of Australia and New Zealand AUS, International Society of Obstetric Medicine CAN, MacDonald Obstetric Medicine Society, North American Society of Obstetric Medicine CAN), Royal Society of Medicine Press Ltd., 1 Wimpole St, London, W1G 0AE, United Kingdom. TEL 44-20-72902921, FAX 44-20-72902929, publishing@rsm.ac.uk, http://www.rsmpress.co.uk. Eds. Catherine Nelson-Piercy, Karen Rosene-Montella, Sandra Lowe. **Subscr. to:** Portland Customer Services, Commerce Way, Colchester CO2 8HP, United Kingdom. TEL 44-1206-796351, FAX 44-1206-799331, sales@portland-services.com, http://www.portlandpress.com.

618 ROM ISSN 1220-5532

OBSTETRICA SI GINECOLOGIE. Text in Romanian; Summaries in English, French, German, Russian. 1920. 4/yr. adv. bk.rev. bibl.; charts; illus. **Document type:** *Journal, Academic/Scholarly.*
Former titles (until 1990): Revista de Pediatrie, Obstetrica si Ginecologie. Obstetrica di Ginecologie (1220-0913); (until 1975): Obstetrica si Ginecologie (0029-781X); (until 1953): Revista de Obstetrica - Ginecologie (1220-5524); (until 1946): Revista de Obstetrica - Ginecologie, Puericultura (1220-5540)
Indexed: ChemAb, DentInd, EMBASE, ExcerpMed, P30, SCOPUS.
—GNLM, INIST.
Published by: (Asociatia Medicala Romana/Romanian Medical Association), Editura Didactica si Pedagogica, Strada Spiru Haret 12, Sector 1, Bucharest, 70738, Romania. TEL 40-21-3133470, comenzi@edituradp.ro, http://www.edituradp.ro.

618 USA ISSN 0029-7828
RG1 CODEN: OGSUA8

OBSTETRICAL & GYNECOLOGICAL SURVEY. Text in English. 1946. m. USD 732 domestic to institutions; USD 827 foreign to institutions (effective 2011). adv. bk.rev. abstr.; bibl.; charts; illus. back issues avail.; reprints avail. **Document type:** *Journal, Academic/Scholarly.* **Description:** Presents 20 or more summaries of the clinically relevant research being published worldwide.
Related titles: CD-ROM ed.; Online - full text ed.: ISSN 1533-9866. USD 430.30 domestic academic site license; USD 430.30 foreign academic site license; USD 479.95 domestic corporate site license; USD 479.95 foreign corporate site license (effective 2002).
Indexed: A22, C06, C07, CCIOG, CLFP, ChemAb, CurCont, EMBASE, ExcerpMed, INI, IndMed, MEDLINE, MS&D, NRN, P30, R10, Reac, SCI, SCOPUS, W07, W09.
—BLDSC (6208.172000), CASDDS, GNLM, IE, Infotrieve, Ingenta, INIST. **CCC.**
Published by: Lippincott Williams & Wilkins (Subsidiary of: Wolters Kluwer N.V.), Two Commerce Sq, 2001 Market St, Philadelphia, PA 19103. TEL 215-521-8300, FAX 215-521-8902, customerservice@lww.com, http://www.lww.com. Pub. Matthew Jozwiak. Adv. contact Michelle Smith TEL 646-674-6537. Circ: 2,019.

618.2 GBR ISSN 1467-2561

➤ **THE OBSTETRICIAN & GYNAECOLOGIST.** Abbreviated title: T O G. Text in English. 1999. q. GBP 138 in United Kingdom to institutions; EUR 161 in Europe to institutions; USD 197 elsewhere to institutions; GBP 159 combined subscription in United Kingdom to institutions (print & online eds.); EUR 185 combined subscription in Europe to institutions (print & online eds.); USD 226 combined subscription elsewhere to institutions (print & online eds.) (effective 2012). back issues avail. **Document type:** *Journal, Academic/Scholarly.* **Description:** Provides all health professionals working within the field of obstetrics and gynaecology with an up-to-date information resource delivered through a range of educational articles.
Related titles: Online - full text ed.: ISSN 1744-4667. GBP 138 in United Kingdom to institutions; EUR 161 in Europe to institutions; USD 197 elsewhere to institutions (effective 2012).
Indexed: A01.
—BLDSC (6208.178000), IE. **CCC.**
Published by: (Royal College of Obstetricians and Gynaecologists), Wiley-Blackwell Publishing Ltd. (Subsidiary of: John Wiley & Sons, Inc.), 9600 Garsington Rd, Oxford, OX4 2DQ, United Kingdom. TEL 44-1865-776868, FAX 44-1865-714591, customerservices@blackwellpublishing.com, http://www.wiley.com/.

618 ZAF ISSN 1029-1962

OBSTETRICS & GYNAECOLOGY FORUM. Text in English. 1990. q. free domestic; USD 60 foreign (effective 2001). adv. back issues avail. **Document type:** *Journal, Trade.* **Description:** Targets gynecologists and general practitioners with an interest in gynecology.
Related titles: Online - full text ed.
Indexed: A01, EMBASE, ExcerpMed, ISAP, SCOPUS, T02.
—BLDSC (6208.206800).
Published by: In House Publications, PO Box 412748, Craighall, Johannesburg 2024, South Africa. TEL 27-11-7889139, FAX 27-11-7889136, inhouse@iafrica.com, http://www.inhousepub.co.za. Ed. B G Lindeque. Pub., R&P A. Thomas. Adv. contact A Thomas. B&W page USD 887, color page USD 1,200; 210 x 297.

618 USA ISSN 0029-7844
RG1 CODEN: OBGNAS

➤ **OBSTETRICS AND GYNECOLOGY.** Variant title: The Green Journal. Text in English. 1952. m. USD 654 domestic to institutions; USD 925 foreign to institutions (effective 2011). adv. bk.rev. bibl.; charts; illus. s-a. index. back issues avail.; reprints avail. **Document type:** *Journal, Academic/Scholarly.* **Description:** Provides information on current developments in obstetrics, gynecology, and women's total health care.
Related titles: Microform ed.: (from PQC); Online - full text ed.: ISSN 1873-233X. USD 389 to individuals (effective 2011) (from IngentaConnect).
Indexed: A01, A03, A08, A20, A22, A26, A34, A36, A38, AIDS Ab, AIM, ASCA, B25, BDM&CN, BIOBASE, BIOSIS Prev, C06, C07, C08, CA, CABA, CCIOG, CIN, CINAHL, CLFP, ChemAb, ChemTitl, CurCont, D01, DBA, DentInd, DiabCont, E12, EMBASE, ExcerpMed, F09, FR, FamI, G08, GH, H11, H12, H16, H17, IABS, IDIS, INI, ISR, IndMed, IndVet, Inpharma, JW, JW-WH, Kidney, LT, MEDLINE, MS&D, MycolAb, N02, N03, N04, NRN, P30, P33, P34, P35, P37, P38, P39, R07, R08, R10, R12, RA&MP, RM&VM, RRTA, Reac, SCI, SCOPUS, T02, T05, TriticAb, VS, W07, W09, W11.
—BLDSC (6208.200000), CASDDS, GNLM, IE, Infotrieve, Ingenta, INIST. **CCC.**
Published by: (American College of Obstetricians and Gynecologists), Lippincott Williams & Wilkins (Subsidiary of: Wolters Kluwer N.V.), 530 Walnut St, Philadelphia, PA 19106. TEL 215-521-8300, FAX 215-521-8902, customerservice@lww.com, http://www.lww.com. Ed. Dr. James R Scott. Adv. contact Kathleen Harrison TEL 212-904-0372. B&W page USD 4,585, color page USD 7,370; trim 8 x 10.75. Circ: 45,629.

618 USA ISSN 0889-8545
RG1 CODEN: OGCAE8

➤ **OBSTETRICS AND GYNECOLOGY CLINICS OF NORTH AMERICA.** Text in English. 1974. q. USD 474 in United States to institutions; USD 598 elsewhere to institutions (effective 2012). adv. back issues avail.; reprints avail. **Document type:** *Journal, Academic/Scholarly.* **Description:** Updates you on the latest trends in patient management; keeps you up to date on the newest advances; and provides a sound basis for choosing treatment options.
Supersedes in part (in 1987): Clinics in Obstetrics and Gynaecology (0306-3356)
Related titles: Online - full text ed.: ISSN 1558-0474 (from ScienceDirect); ◆ Spanish Translation: Clinicas Obstetricas y Ginecologicas de Norteamerica. ISSN 0009-9333; Supplement(s): C M E Supplement to Obstetrics and Gynecology Clinics. ISSN 1557-816X. USD 175 per issue (effective 2006).
Indexed: A22, ASCA, BDM&CN, C06, C07, C08, CINAHL, CLFP, CurCont, DokArb, EMBASE, ExcerpMed, FR, INI, ISR, IndMed, Inpharma, MEDLINE, P30, R10, Reac, SCI, SCOPUS, W07.
—BLDSC (6208.206300), GNLM, IE, Infotrieve, Ingenta, INIST. **CCC.**
Published by: W.B. Saunders Co. (Subsidiary of: Elsevier Health Sciences), Elsevier, Health Sciences Division, Order Fulfillment, 3251 Riverport Ln, Maryland Heights, MO 63043. TEL 314-872-8370, 800-325-4177, FAX 314-432-1380, JournalCustomerService-usa@elsevier.com, http://www.us.elsevierhealth.com. Adv. contact John Marmero TEL 212-633-3657.

618 USA ISSN 1687-9589

▼ ➤ **OBSTETRICS AND GYNECOLOGY INTERNATIONAL.** Text in English. 2009. fortn. USD 395 (effective 2011). **Document type:** *Journal, Academic/Scholarly.* **Description:** Publishes original research articles as well as review articles in all areas of obstetrics and gynecology.
Related titles: Online - full text ed.: ISSN 1687-9597. free (effective 2011).
Indexed: A01, C06, C07, CA, P30, T02.
Published by: Hindawi Publishing Corporation, 410 Park Ave, 15th Fl, PMB 287, New York, NY 10022. FAX 215-893-4392, 866-446-3294, info@hindawi.com.

618 GBR ISSN 1751-7214
RG1 CODEN: COGYFP

OBSTETRICS, GYNECOLOGY AND REPRODUCTIVE MEDICINE. Text in English. 1991. m. EUR 823 in Europe to institutions; JPY 89,000 in Japan to institutions; USD 732 elsewhere to institutions (effective 2012). adv. back issues avail. **Document type:** *Journal, Academic/Scholarly.* **Description:** Provides relevant, up to date, review and reference material for candidates for MRCOG part II and specialists in obstetrics & gynaecology.
Formerly (until 2007): Current Obstetrics & Gynaecology (0957-5847)
Related titles: Online - full text ed.: ISSN 1879-3622 (from ScienceDirect).
Indexed: A22, A26, CA, E01, EMBASE, ExcerpMed, I05, P30, R10, Reac, SCOPUS, T02.
—BLDSC (6208.241000), GNLM, IE, Infotrieve, Ingenta. **CCC.**
Published by: The Medicine Publishing Company (Subsidiary of: Elsevier Ltd), The Boulevard, Langford Ln, Kidlington, Oxford, OX5 1GB, United Kingdom. TEL 44-1865-843154, FAX 44-1865-843965, JournalsCustomerServiceEMEA@elsevier.com, http://www.medicinepublishing.co.uk. Ed. Philip N Baker. Pub. Melanie Burton. Adv. contact Ellie Ostime TEL 44-20-74244971.

618 JPN ISSN 1341-4100

ONCHIKAI KAIHO/NEWS OF ONCHIKAI. Text in Japanese. a. **Document type:** *Academic/Scholarly.*
Published by: Onchikai, 4-48-6 Nishigahara, Kita-ku, Tokyo, 114-0024, Japan. http://www.onchikai.com/.

618 GBR ISSN 1179-1527
▼ ➤ **OPEN ACCESS JOURNAL OF CONTRACEPTION.** Text in English. 2010. irreg. free (effective 2011). **Document type:** *Journal, Academic/Scholarly.*
Media: Online - full text.
—CCC.
Published by: Dove Medical Press Ltd., Beechfield House, Winterton Way, Macclesfield, SK11 0JL, United Kingdom. TEL 44-1625-509130, FAX 44-1625-617933. Ed. Igal Wolman.

618 USA ISSN 2160-8792
▼ ➤ **OPEN JOURNAL OF OBSTETRICS AND GYNECOLOGY.** Abbreviated title: O J O G. Text in English. 2011. q. USD 156 (effective 2011). **Document type:** *Journal, Academic/Scholarly.*
Related titles: Online - full text ed.: ISSN 2160-8806. free (effective 2011).
Published by: Scientific Research Publishing, Inc., PO Box 54821, Irvine, CA 92619. service@scirp.org. Ed. Christos E Constantinou.

613.04244 618 NLD ISSN 1874-2912
RA564.85
➤ **THE OPEN WOMEN'S HEALTH JOURNAL.** Text in English. 2007. irreg. free (effective 2011). **Document type:** *Journal, Academic/Scholarly.* **Description:** Covers all areas of experimental and clinical research in gynaecology and obstetrics.
Media: Online - full text.
Indexed: A01, CTA.
Published by: Bentham Open (Subsidiary of: Bentham Science Publishers Ltd.), PO Box 294, Bussum, AG 1400, Netherlands. TEL 31-35-6923800, FAX 31-35-6980150, subscriptions@bentham.org. Ed. Robert R Freedman.

618.1 NLD ISSN 1873-894X
OVARIAN DISEASES. Text in English. 2008 (Jul.). q. USD 706 combined subscription in North America (print & online eds.); EUR 505 combined subscription elsewhere (print & online eds.) (effective 2012). **Document type:** *Journal, Academic/Scholarly.* **Description:** Aims to educate researchers and clinicians about our rapidly evolving understanding of the biology of the ovary.
Related titles: Online - full text ed.: ISSN 1875-9106.
Published by: I O S Press, Nieuwe Hemweg 6B, Amsterdam, 1013 BG, Netherlands. TEL 31-20-6883355, FAX 31-20-6870019, info@iospress.nl. Ed. Michael J Birrer.

PAEDIATRIA CROATICA; the journal for the paediatricians. *see* MEDICAL SCIENCES—Pediatrics

649 USA ISSN 1091-0387
RG525
PARENTING'S HEALTHY PREGNANCY. Key Title: Healthy Pregnancy. Text in English. 1990. s-a. USD 2.95 newsstand/cover domestic; USD 3.50 newsstand/cover in Canada (effective 2001). adv. illus. **Document type:** *Magazine, Consumer.* **Description:** Guide to a healthy pregnancy, labor and delivery, and taking care of a newborn.
Formerly (until 1996): Baby on the Way: Basics (1173-0269)
Published by: (American College of Obstetricians and Gynecologists), Time Publishing Ventures (Subsidiary of: Time Warner Inc.), 1325 Ave of the Americas, 27th Fl, New York, NY 10019. TEL 212-522-8989, FAX 212-522-8159. Ed. Susan Kane. Pub. Risa Crandell. adv.: B&W page USD 59,130, color page USD 73,910. Circ: 2,400,000.

618 USA ISSN 1558-5859
PARENTS EXPECTING. Text in English. 1967. s-a. bk.rev. illus. reprints avail. **Document type:** *Magazine, Consumer.* **Description:** Presents various health and beauty topics to expectant moms and dads.
Related titles: Microform ed.: (from PQC).
Published by: Meredith Corporation, 1716 Locust St, Des Moines, IA 50309. TEL 515-284-3000, patrick.taylor@meredith.com, http://www.meredith.com.

618 USA ISSN 1529-9961
RG525
PARENTS PREGNANCY. Text in English. 1999. s-a. **Document type:** *Magazine, Consumer.*
Published by: Meredith Corporation, 1716 Locust St, Des Moines, IA 50309. TEL 515-284-3000, patrick.taylor@meredith.com, http://www.meredith.com.

PEDIATRIYA, AKUSHERSTVO TA GINEKOLOGIYA. *see* MEDICAL SCIENCES—Pediatrics

618 616 ITA
PELVIPERINEOLOGY. Text in English. 1982. q. bk.rev. **Document type:** *Journal, Academic/Scholarly.*
Former titles (until 2006): Pelvi - Perineologia (1973-4921); (until 2004): Rivista Italiana di Colon - Proctologia (1973-493X); (until 2003): Italian Journal of Coloproctology (1973-4948); (until 1996): Rivista Italiana di Colon-Proctologia (0394-9109)
Related titles: Online - full text ed.: ISSN 1973-4913.
—GNLM.
Address: c/o Clinica Chirurgica 2, University of Padova, Padua, 35128, Italy.

618.12 NLD ISSN 1871-4846
PERINATALE ZORG IN NEDERLAND/PERINATAL CARE IN THE NETHERLANDS. Text in Dutch. 2005. a.
Published by: Stichting Perinatale Registratie Nederland, Postbus 8588, Utrecht, 3503 RN, Netherlands. TEL 31-30-2823165, FAX 31-30-2823170, info@perinatreg.nl, http://www.perinatreg.nl.

618.24 TUR ISSN 1300-5251
PERINATOLOJI DERGISI/JOURNAL OF PERINATOLOGY/PERINATAL JOURNAL. Text in Turkish; Summaries in English. 1993. q. **Document type:** *Journal, Academic/Scholarly.* **Description:** Publishes articles related to experimental and clinical research, case reports, comments, congress of perinatal and postgraduate training course presentations.
Related titles: Online - full text ed.
Indexed: A01.
Published by: Turk Perinatoloji Dernegi/Turkish Perinatology Society, Rumeli Cad 47/606, Nisantasi, Istanbul, Turkey. TEL 90-212-2246849, FAX 90-212-2960150, info@perinatology.org.tr, http://www.perinataljournal.com.

618 JPN ISSN 0910-8718
PERINEITARU KEA/PERINATAL CARE. Text in Japanese. 1982. m. JPY 20,412; JPY 1,890 newsstand/cover (effective 2007). Supplement avail. **Document type:** *Journal, Academic/Scholarly.*
Published by: Medicus Shuppan/Medicus Publishing Inc., 18-24 Hiroshiba-cho, Suita-shi, Osaka-fu 564-8580, Japan. TEL 81-6-63856911, FAX 81-6-63856873, http://www.medica.co.jp/. Ed. Takahiki Matsui.

613.9 USA ISSN 0190-3195
➤ **PERSPECTIVAS INTERNACIONALES EN PLANIFICACION FAMILIAR.** Text in Spanish. 1978. a. adv. abstr.; charts; illus.; stat. back issues avail.; reprints avail. **Document type:** *Journal, Academic/Scholarly.* **Description:** Focuses on the population concerns of Latin America.
Related titles: ◆ English ed.: International Perspectives on Sexual and Reproductive Health. ISSN 1944-0391; ◆ French ed.: Perspectives Internationales sur le Planning Familial.
Indexed: H21, P08, P30.
—CCC.
Published by: Alan Guttmacher Institute, 125 Maiden Ln, 7th Fl, New York, NY 10038. TEL 212-248-1111, 800-355-0244, FAX 212-248-1951, applytoguttmacher@guttmacher.org.

301.426 USA
➤ **PERSPECTIVES INTERNATIONALES SUR LE PLANNING FAMILIAL.** Text in French. 19??. a. adv. abstr.; charts; illus.; stat. reprints avail. **Document type:** *Journal, Academic/Scholarly.* **Description:** Focuses on the population concerns of francophone Africa.
Related titles: ◆ English ed.: International Perspectives on Sexual and Reproductive Health. ISSN 1944-0391; ◆ Spanish ed.: Perspectivas Internacionales en Planificacion Familiar. ISSN 0190-3195.
Published by: Alan Guttmacher Institute, 125 Maiden Ln, 7th Fl, New York, NY 10038. TEL 212-248-1111, 800-355-0244, FAX 212-248-1951, applytoguttmacher@guttmacher.org.

301.426 USA ISSN 1538-6341
HQ763 CODEN: FPGPA
➤ **PERSPECTIVES ON SEXUAL AND REPRODUCTIVE HEALTH.** Text in English. 1969. q. GBP 169 combined subscription in United Kingdom to institutions (print & online eds.); EUR 215 combined subscription in Europe to institutions (print & online eds.); USD 285 combined subscription in the Americas to institutions (print & online eds.); USD 330 combined subscription elsewhere to institutions (print & online eds.) (effective 2012). bk.rev. charts; illus. Index. back issues avail.; reprints avail. **Document type:** *Journal, Academic/Scholarly.* **Description:** Focuses on the country's most pressing reproductive health issues, providing key findings from the institute's research and work of other distinguished social scientists.
Formerly (until 2002): Family Planning Perspectives (0014-7354)
Related titles: Microfilm ed.: (from CIS, PQC); Online - full text ed.: ISSN 1931-2393. GBP 153 in United Kingdom to institutions; EUR 193 in Europe to institutions; USD 256 in the Americas to institutions; USD 297 elsewhere to institutions (effective 2012) (from IngentaConnect).
Indexed: A01, A02, A03, A08, A20, A22, A25, A26, A36, AMHA, ASCA, ASSIA, AbAn, Agr, BibAg, BiolDig, C06, C07, C08, C11, C12, CA, CABA, CINAHL, CLFP, CWI, Chicano, CurCont, D01, E01, E08, EMBASE, ESPM, EnvAb, EnvInd, ExcerpMed, F09, FR, FamI, G08, GH, H03, H04, H05, H11, H12, I05, I07, INI, IndMed, JW-WH, L03, LT, M01, M02, MEA&I, MEDLINE, N02, N03, P02, P03, P06, P10, P12, P13, P19, P20, P22, P24, P30, P33, P34, P39, P48, P50, P53, P54, PAIS, PQC, PRA, PopulInd, PsycInfo, PsycholAb, R10, RASB, Reac, RefZh, RiskAb, S02, S03, S08, S09, S11, S23, SCOPUS, SFSA, SOPODA, SRI, SRRA, SSCI, SWR&A, SociolAb, T02, T05, W07, W09.
—BLDSC (6428.163760), CIS, GNLM, IE, Infotrieve, Ingenta. **CCC.**
Published by: (Alan Guttmacher Institute), Wiley-Blackwell Publishing, Inc. (Subsidiary of: Wiley-Blackwell Publishing Ltd.), 111 River St, Hoboken, NJ 07030. TEL 201-748-6000, FAX 201-748-6088, info@wiley.com, http://www.wiley.com/WileyCDA/. Ed. Patricia Donovan. Adv. contact Kristin McCarthy TEL 201-748-7683.

➤ **PHARMA FOKUS GYNAEKOLOGIE.** *see* PHARMACY AND PHARMACOLOGY

618 USA ISSN 1938-3630
PLUM; something especially prized. Text in English. 2004. s-a. adv. back issues avail. **Document type:** *Magazine, Consumer.* **Description:** Serves as a comprehensive guide for the 35 and over mom-to-be to turn to again and again throughout pregnancy and into the first months of her baby's life.
Related titles: Online - full text ed.
Published by: (American College of Obstetricians and Gynecologists), Groundbreak Publishing, Inc., 276 Fifth Ave, Ste 712, New York, NY 10001. TEL 212-725-9201, FAX 212-725-9203.

618 USA ISSN 0194-3898
POSTGRADUATE OBSTETRICS & GYNECOLOGY. Text in English. 1979. bi-w. USD 794 domestic to institutions; USD 951 foreign to institutions (effective 2011). adv. back issues avail.; reprints avail. **Document type:** *Newsletter, Academic/Scholarly.*
Related titles: Online - full text ed.
—BLDSC (6563.905400), IE. **CCC.**
Published by: Lippincott Williams & Wilkins (Subsidiary of: Wolters Kluwer N.V.), 530 Walnut St, Philadelphia, PA 19106. TEL 215-521-8300, customerservice@lww.com. Ed. Dr. William Schlaff.

618 GBR ISSN 1461-3123
➤ **THE PRACTISING MIDWIFE.** Text in English. 1991. 11/yr. EUR 284 in Europe to institutions; JPY 54,500 in Japan to institutions; USD 386 elsewhere to institutions (effective 2012). bk.rev. back issues avail.; reprints avail. **Document type:** *Journal, Academic/Scholarly.* **Description:** Provides midwives with all the latest developments and guidelines that concern the profession, both in the UK and internationally.
Formerly (until 1998): Modern Midwife (0963-276X)
Related titles: Online - full text ed.
Indexed: B28, C06, C07, C08, CINAHL, EMBASE, ExcerpMed, F09, FamI, MEDLINE, P30, R10, Reac, SCOPUS, W09.
—BLDSC (6597.820000), GNLM, IE, Infotrieve, Ingenta. **CCC.**
Published by: Elsevier Ltd (Subsidiary of: Elsevier Science & Technology), 54 Siward Rd, Bromley, BR2 9JZ, United Kingdom. TEL 44-20-84640304, journalscustomerserviceemea@elsevier.com, http://www.elsevier.com. Ed. Jennifer Hall. Adv. contact Margaret Floate TEL 44-1483-824094.

618 SVK ISSN 1335-4221
➤ **PRAKTICKA GYNEKOLOGIA.** Text in Slovak. 1994. q. EUR 63.40 in Europe; EUR 74 elsewhere (effective 2011). **Document type:** *Journal, Academic/Scholarly.* **Description:** Publishes technical articles of domestic and foreign authors on curative and preventive gynecological care. Covers practical gynecology, as well as the history of gynecological science.
Published by: (Nemecko-Slovenska Spolocnost Edukacia v Gynekologii a Porodnictve/German-Slovak Association for Education in Obstetrics and Gynecology), Slovak Academic Press Ltd., Nam Slobody 6, PO Box 57, Bratislava, 81005, Slovakia. TEL 421-2-55421729, FAX 421-2-55565862, sap@sappress.sk, http://www.sappress.sk. Ed. Michal Valent. Circ: 1,800. **Dist. by:** Slovart G.T.G. s.r.o., Krupinska 4, PO Box 152, Bratislava 85299, Slovakia. TEL 421-2-63839472, FAX 421-2-63839485, info@slovart-gtg.sk, http://www.slovart-gtg.sk.

618 CZE ISSN 1211-6645
➤ **PRAKTICKA GYNEKOLOGIE.** Text in Czech. 1997. q. CZK 825 domestic; EUR 35 foreign (effective 2010). **Document type:** *Journal, Academic/Scholarly.* **Description:** Intended for professional and practical gynecologists. Publishes review articles, case studies and results of various surveys.
Related titles: Online - full text ed.: ISSN 1801-8750.
Published by: Medica Healthworld a.s., Bidlaky 20, Brno, 63900, Czech Republic. TEL 420-533-337311, FAX 420-533-337312, info@mhw.cz, http://www.mhw.cz. Ed. Robert Hudecek. Circ: 1,800.

618 USA ISSN 1540-8485
PREGNANCY. Text in English. 2000. m. USD 10 domestic; USD 15 in Canada (effective 2009). adv. Supplement avail.; back issues avail. **Document type:** *Magazine, Consumer.* **Description:** Covers preconception, breastfeeding, birthing, postpartum, nutrition, health & fitness, multiples, beauty & wellness, maternity fashion, Internet resources, your say, expert Q & A, working and pregnancy, fatherhood, time for mom, nurseries and product news.
—CCC.
Published by: Future U S, Inc. (Subsidiary of: Future Publishing Ltd.), 4000 Shoreline Ct, Ste 400, South San Francisco, CA 94080. TEL 650-872-1642, FAX 650-872-1643, http://www.futureus.com. Eds. Kendra Smith, Abigail Tuller. adv.: page USD 14,970; trim 8 x 10.5. Circ: 205,000 (paid).

618.2 AUS ISSN 1445-1255
PREGNANCY & BIRTH. Text in English. 1995. bi-m. AUD 33 domestic; AUD 40 in New Zealand; AUD 53 elsewhere; AUD 7.50 newsstand/cover (effective 2008). adv. **Document type:** *Magazine, Consumer.* **Description:** Guides the expectant mother through the nine months of pregnancy, informing and reassuring about the changes. It offers facts on changing bodies and lifestyles and gives insight into what they can expect from birth to their baby.
Published by: A C P Magazines Ltd. (Subsidiary of: P B L Media Pty Ltd.), 54-58 Park St, Sydney, NSW 2000, Australia. TEL 61-2-92828000, FAX 61-2-91263769, research@acpaction.com.au. Ed. Fiona Baker. Adv. contacts Rachael Ferrari TEL 61-3-98607906, Julie Hancock TEL 61-2-95819443. page AUD 3,554; bleed 215 x 285. Circ: 21,500 (paid).

618.12 618.92 USA
PREGNANCY AND NEWBORN. Text in English. 2006. m. USD 24 domestic; USD 37.50 in Canada; USD 44 elsewhere (effective 2010). adv. back issues avail. **Document type:** *Magazine, Consumer.* **Description:** Designed for expecting mothers for everything she needs to know for a healthy, happy pregnancy and her first year with her new arrival.
Related titles: Online - full text ed.
Published by: Halcyon Media, LLC, 280 Interstate N Cir, Ste 650, Atlanta, GA 30339. TEL 770-226-8472. Adv. contact Adam Woodman TEL 770-226-8413.

618.2 AUS ISSN 1328-5661
THE PREGNANCY BOOK. Text in English. 1986. a. free (effective 2009). adv. illus. **Document type:** *Magazine, Consumer.* **Description:** Provides a complete guide to pregnancy, approved and distributed by hospitals.
Published by: Bounty Services Pty. Ltd. (Subsidiary of: Emap International), Level 6, 187 Thomas St., Haymarket, NSW 2000, Australia. TEL 61-2-95819400, FAX 61-2-95819570. adv.: color page AUD 14,960; trim 148 x 210. Circ: 207,438.

618 GBR ISSN 0197-3851
RG628 CODEN: PRDIDM
➤ **PRENATAL DIAGNOSIS.** Text in English. 1981. 13/yr. GBP 1,772 in United Kingdom to institutions; EUR 2,239 in Europe to institutions; USD 3,470 elsewhere to institutions; GBP 2,038 combined subscription in United Kingdom to institutions (print & online eds.); EUR 2,575 combined subscription in Europe to institutions (print & online eds.); USD 3,990 combined subscription elsewhere to institutions (print & online eds.) (effective 2012). adv. back issues avail.; reprint service avail. from PSC. **Document type:** *Journal, Academic/Scholarly.* **Description:** Communicates the results of original research in a variety of clinical and scientific specialties concerned with human in utero diagnosis of fetal abnormality resulting from genetic and environmental factors.
Related titles: Microform ed.: (from PQC); Online - full text ed.: ISSN 1097-0223. 1996. GBP 1,772 in United Kingdom to institutions; EUR 2,239 in Europe to institutions; USD 3,470 elsewhere to institutions (effective 2012).
Indexed: A20, A22, A29, A36, ASCA, ASFA, B20, B21, B26, BDM&CN, BIOBASE, C06, C07, CABA, CIN, CTA, ChemAb, ChemTitl, CurCont, DentInd, E12, EMBASE, ESPM, ExcerpMed, F09, FamI, GH, GenetAb, HGA, I10, IABS, INI, ISR, IndMed, Inpharma, JW-WH, MEDLINE, MS&D, N02, N03, NSA, P30, P33, P35, P39, R10, R12, Reac, SCI, SCOPUS, T05, ViroIAbstr, W07, W11.
—BLDSC (6607.646000), CASDDS, GNLM, IE, Infotrieve, Ingenta, INIST. **CCC.**
Published by: (International Society for Prenatal Diagnosis USA), John Wiley & Sons Ltd. (Subsidiary of: John Wiley & Sons, Inc.), 1-7 Oldlands Way, PO Box 808, Bognor Regis, West Sussex PO21 9FF, United Kingdom. TEL 44-1865-778315, FAX 44-1243-843232, cs-journals@wiley.com, http://eu.wiley.com/WileyCDA/. Ed. D W Bianchi. **Subscr. in the Americas to:** John Wiley & Sons, Inc., 111 River St, Hoboken, NJ 07030. TEL 201-748-6645, subinfo@wiley.com; **Subscr. to:** 1-7 Oldlands Way, PO Box 809, Bognor Regis, West Sussex PO21 9FG, United Kingdom. TEL 44-1865-778054, cs-agency@wiley.com.

618 GBR ISSN 2042-7557
PRENATAL SCREENING PERSPECTIVES. Variant title: Prenatal Screening Review. Text in English. 1994. a. back issues avail. **Document type:** *Journal, Trade.*
Formerly (until 2009): Down's Screening News (1469-6150)
Published by: International Prenatal Screening Group, Leeds Screening Centre, Gemini Park, Sheepscar Way, Leeds, LS7 3JB, United Kingdom. TEL 44-113-2849230, FAX 44-113-2621658, http://www.leeds.ac.uk/idssg/index.htm. Ed. Phillipa Bloom.

618 DEU ISSN 1865-0058
PRIMA MAMA!; Magazin fuer moderne Muetter. Text in German. 2005. 4/yr. adv. **Document type:** *Magazine, Consumer.*
Published by: Fromm & Fromm GmbH, Achtern Felln 26, Hasloh, 25474, Germany. TEL 49-4106-63070, FAX 49-4106-630715, info@2xfromm.de, http://www.pmi-medien.de. Adv. contact Romy Demeter. Circ: 30,000 (controlled).

618.1 DEU
▼ **DER PRIVATARZT GYNAEKOLOGIE.** Text in German. 2010. bi-m. adv. **Document type:** *Journal, Trade.*
Published by: MiM Verlagsgesellschaft, Hans-Fleissner Str 80, Egelsbach, 63329, Germany. TEL 49-6103-300240, FAX 49-6103-3002429, info@mim-verlag.de. Ed. Angelika Ramm-Fischer. Adv. contact Sabrina Jantschik.

618 USA ISSN 2154-4751
▼ **PROCEEDINGS IN OBSTETRICS AND GYNECOLOGY.** Text in English. 2010. q. free (effective 2010). **Document type:** *Journal, Trade.* **Description:** Encompasses all areas of women's reproductive health, including clinical care, education of students, residents and fellows, and research.
Media: Online - full text.
Published by: University of Iowa, 130 N Madison, Iowa City, IA 52240. TEL 319-353-1538, http://www.uiowa.edu/.

618.202 FRA ISSN 1251-9839
PROFESSION SAGE-FEMME. Text in French. 1994. m. EUR 55 domestic to individuals; EUR 65 foreign to individuals; EUR 71 domestic to institutions; EUR 78 foreign to institutions; EUR 39 to students (effective 2009). bk.rev. bibl.; stat. back issues avail. **Document type:** *Academic/Scholarly.* **Description:** Features articles about obstetrics and midwifery. Informs readers about the profession as well as new technologies.
Published by: Paganelle, 94-96 bd. Magenta, Paris, 75010, France. TEL 33-140346473, FAX 33-140345938. Ed. Sandra Mignot. Pub. Jean Pascal Fix.

618 PRT ISSN 1646-4605
PROGRESO DE OBSTRECTICIA Y GINECOLOGIA. Text in Portuguese. 2006. irreg. **Document type:** *Journal, Trade.*
Published by: (Sociedad Espanola de Ginecologia y Obstetricia ESP), Medicografica Edicoes Medicas, Rua Camilo Castelo Branco 23-5, Lisbon, 1150-083, Portugal. geral@medicografica.pt, http://www.medicografica.pt.

618 ESP ISSN 0304-5013
➤ **PROGRESOS DE OBSTETRICIA Y GINECOLOGIA.** Text in Spanish; Summaries in English. 1958. m. EUR 229.02 combined subscription to individuals print & online eds.; EUR 579.79 to institutions print & online eds. (effective 2009). bk.rev. index. back issues avail.; reprints avail. **Document type:** *Journal, Academic/Scholarly.*
Related titles: Online - full text ed.: ISSN 1578-1453. 1996. EUR 171.04 (effective 2009) (from ScienceDirect); Supplement(s): Progresos de Obstetricia y Ginecologia. Suplemento. ISSN 1137-781X. 1995.
Indexed: A22, EMBASE, ExcerpMed, IME, R10, Reac, SCOPUS.
—BLDSC (6864.939800), GNLM, IE, Ingenta. **CCC.**
Published by: (Sociedad Espanola de Ginecologia y Obstetricia), Elsevier Doyma (Subsidiary of: Elsevier Health Sciences), Traversa de Gracia 17-21, Barcelona, 08021, Spain. TEL 34-932-418800, FAX 34-932-419020, editorial@elsevier.com. Ed. A. Fortuny Estivill. Circ: 5,500.

618 ESP ISSN 1695-811X
➤ **PROGRESOS EN DIAGNOSTICO Y TRATAMIENTO PRENATAL.** Text in Spanish; Summaries in English. 1989. 10/yr. EUR 106.99 to individuals; EUR 208.62 to institutions (effective 2009). bk.rev. index. back issues avail.; reprints avail. **Document type:** *Journal, Academic/Scholarly.*
Formerly (until 2003): Progresos en Diagnostico Prenatal (1130-0523)
Related titles: Online - full text ed.: ISSN 1695-999X. 1996. EUR 74.90 to individuals; EUR 112.34 to institutions (effective 2009).
Indexed: CA, L05, T02.
—**CCC.**
Published by: (Asociacion Espanola de Diagnostico Prenatal), Grupo Ars XXI de Comunicacion, SA, Muntaner 262 Atico 2a., Barcelona, 08021, Spain. TEL 34-90-2195484, FAX 34-93-2722902, info@arsxxi.com, http://www.arsxxi.com. Circ: 2,000.

341.1 CHE ISSN 1564-0655
PROGRESS IN HUMAN REPRODUCTION RESEARCH. Text in English. 1987. q. **Document type:** *Journal, Academic/Scholarly.*
Indexed: P30, SCOPUS.
Published by: World Health Organization, Department of Reproductive Health and Research, Genva 27, 1211, Switzerland. TEL 41-22-7913372, FAX 41-22-7914189, rhrpublications@who.int.

618 GBR ISSN 0261-0140
RG1
PROGRESS IN OBSTETRICS AND GYNAECOLOGY. Text in English. 1981. irreg., latest vol.18, 2008. price varies. adv. illus. back issues avail. **Document type:** *Monographic series, Academic/Scholarly.* **Description:** Discusses research and developments in the practice of obstetric and gynecological care.
—BLDSC (6871.250000), GNLM. **CCC.**
Published by: Churchill Livingstone (Subsidiary of: Elsevier Health Sciences), The Blvd, Langford Ln, Kidlington, OX5 1GB, United Kingdom. TEL 44-1865-843434, FAX 44-1865-843970, directenquiries@elsevier.com, http://www.elsevierhealth.com/imprint.jsp?iid=9. Ed. John Studd.

618 DEU ISSN 1614-9823
PROPRAXIS GYNAEKOLOGIE; Magazin fuer Medizin und Management. Text in German. 1985. 9/yr. adv. back issues avail. **Document type:** *Journal, Academic/Scholarly.* **Description:** Seminar papers including summaries of original articles, interviews and congress reports.
Former titles (until 2004): Jatros Gyn (1432-5128); (until 1996): Giatros Gynaekologie, Frauenheilkunde und Geburtshilfe (0944-6079); (until 1992): Giatros Gynaekologie, Geburtshilfe (0942-0959); (until 1992): Jatros Gynaekologie (0177-9109)
—GNLM. **CCC.**
Published by: Fromm & Fromm GmbH, Achtern Felln 26, Hasloh, 25474, Germany. TEL 49-4106-63070, FAX 49-4106-630715, info@2xfromm.de, http://www.pmi-medien.de. Adv. contact Romy Demeter. color page EUR 3,560; trim 184 x 250. Circ: 8,800 (paid and controlled).

618 POL ISSN 1731-8602
PRZEGLAD GINEKOLOGICZNO-POLOZNICZY. Text in Polish. 2001. s-a. **Document type:** *Journal, Academic/Scholarly.*
Formerly (until 2003): Kolposkopia (1641-6554)
Related titles: Online - full text ed.: ISSN 1733-7593.
Indexed: C06, C07.
Published by: (Polskie Towarzystwo Ginekologiczne/Polish Society of Gynaecology), Blackhorse Scientific Publishers, Ltd., Zeganska 16, Warsaw, 04713, Poland. TEL 48-22-4999099, FAX 48-22-4995081, blackhorse@blackhorse.pl, http://blackhorse.pl/blackhorse. Ed. Stefan Sajdak.

618.1 POL ISSN 1643-8876
PRZEGLAD MENOPAUZALNY/MENOPAUSE REVIEW. Text in Polish. 2002. m. PLZ 54 domestic (effective 2010). **Document type:** *Journal, Academic/Scholarly.*
Indexed: EMBASE, ExcerpMed, R10, Reac, SCI, SCOPUS, W07.
—BLDSC (6943.300000).
Published by: Termedia sp. z o.o./Termedia Publishing House, ul Wenedow 9/1, Poznan, 61614, Poland. TEL 48-61-8227781, FAX 48-61-8227781, termedia@termedia.pl. Ed. Tomasz Pertynski.

618.202 DEU
RATGEBER FUER SCHWANGERSCHAFT. Text in German. 1991. q. free (effective 2009). adv. **Document type:** *Magazine, Consumer.*
Formerly (until 2008): Ratgeber fuer Werdende Muetter
Published by: Bonus Marketing GmbH, Kleiner Hirschgraben 10-12, Frankfurt Am Main, 60311, Germany. TEL 49-69-20973730, FAX 49-69-209737350, info@bonus-marketing.de, http://www.bonus-marketing.de. adv.: page EUR 29,750. Circ: 130,257 (controlled).

618 FRA ISSN 1264-8809
REALITES EN GYNECOLOGIE-OBSTETRIQUE. Text in French. 1995. m. EUR 52 domestic to qualified personnel; EUR 42 domestic to students; EUR 65 foreign to students (effective 2008). **Document type:** *Journal, Trade.*
Published by: Performances Medicales, 91 Av. de la Republique, Paris, 75011, France. TEL 33-1-47006714, FAX 33-1-47006999.

618 CAN ISSN 1910-2062
REPERTOIRE DES MEDECINS DE FAMILLE ACCOUCHEURS DU QUEBEC. Text in French. 2006. irreg. **Document type:** *Directory, Consumer.*
Media: Online - full text.
Published by: (Federation des Medecins Omnipraticiens du Quebec/Federation of General Practitioners of Quebec), Association des Omnipraticiens en Perinatalite du Quebec, 505 blvd Adoncour, Bureau 200, Longueuil, PQ J4G 2M6, Canada. info@aopq.org, http://www.aopq.org.

618 NLD ISSN 2210-4348
REPRODUCTIEVE GENEESKUNDE, GYNAECOLOGIE EN OBSTETRIE. Text in Dutch. 2007. biennial.
Published by: DCHG Medische Communicatie, Hendrik Figeeweg 3G-20, Haarlem, 2031 BJ, Netherlands. TEL 31-23-5514888, FAX 31-23-5515522, info@dchg.nl, http://www.dchg.nl.

618 616.4 FRA ISSN 0994-3919
CODEN: RHHOED
REPRODUCTION HUMAINE ET HORMONES. Text in French. 1988. 4/yr. EUR 10 (effective 2009). **Document type:** *Journal, Academic/Scholarly.* **Description:** Publishes both cutting edge articles on the discoveries in the field and practical syntheses and analyses on contemporary issues in gynecologie.
Indexed: A22, EMBASE, ExcerpMed, P20, P54, PQC, R10, Reac, SCOPUS.
—BLDSC (7713.605000), GNLM, IE, Ingenta, INIST. **CCC.**
Published by: (Association Francaise pour l'Etude de la Menopause (A F E M)), Editions ESKA, 12 Rue du Quatre-Septembre, Paris, 75002, France. TEL 33-1-40942222, FAX 33-1-40942232, eska@eska.fr. Ed. Dr. Henri Rozenbaum.

618 GBR ISSN 1472-6483
RG1 CODEN: RBOEA6
➤ **REPRODUCTIVE BIOMEDICINE ONLINE;** an international journal devoted to biomedical research on human conception and the welfare of the human embryo. Abbreviated title: R B M Online. Text in English. 1991. bi-m. EUR 432 in Europe to institutions; JPY 57,400 in Japan to institutions; USD 617 elsewhere to institutions (effective 2012). adv. back issues avail. **Document type:** *Journal, Academic/Scholarly.* **Description:** Devoted to biomedical research and ethical issues surrounding human conception and the welfare of the human embryo.
Former titles (until Jan.2002): Reproductive Technologies (1528-4840); (until 2000): Assisted Reproduction (1522-3949); (until 1999): Assisted Reproduction Reviews (1051-2446)
Related titles: CD-ROM ed.; Online - full text ed.: ISSN 1472-6491. GBP 188, USD 338 to individuals; GBP 241, USD 434 to institutions (effective 2009) (from ScienceDirect).
Indexed: A01, A03, A08, A20, A21, C03, CA, CBCARef, CurCont, EMBASE, ExcerpMed, Inpharma, MEDLINE, P30, P35, P48, PQC, R10, RI-1, RI-2, Reac, SCI, SCOPUS, T02, W07.
—BLDSC (7713.705600), GNLM, IE, Ingenta, INIST. **CCC.**
Published by: (Alpha (Scientists in Reproductive Medicine) CHE, American College of Embryology (ACE) USA, Global Chinese Association for Reproductive Medicine (GCARM) USA, International Society for In Vitro Fertilization (ISIVF) CAN, Mediterranean Society for Reproductive Medicine (MSRM) ITA, Preimplantation Genetic Diagnosis International Society (PGDIS) USA), Elsevier Ltd (Subsidiary of: Elsevier Science & Technology), The Blvd, Langford Ln, Kidlington, Oxford, OX5 1GB, United Kingdom. TEL 44-1865-843434, FAX 44-1865-843970, customerserviceau@elsevier.com. Circ: 1,500.

➤ **REPRODUCTIVE HEALTH.** *see* MEDICAL SCIENCES

618 USA ISSN 1933-7191
RG1 CODEN: JSGIED
➤ **REPRODUCTIVE SCIENCES.** Text in English. 1994. m. USD 1,166, GBP 686 combined subscription to institutions (print & online eds.); USD 1,143, GBP 672 to institutions (effective 2011). back issues avail.; reprint service avail. from PSC. **Document type:** *Journal, Academic/Scholarly.* **Description:** Publishes timely and important scientific papers on all aspects of reproductive biology, including the disciplines of perinatology, obstetrics, gynecology, infertility and other related fields.
Formerly (until 2007): Society for Gynecologic Investigation. Journal (Print) (1071-5576)
Related titles: Microform ed.: (from PQC); Online - full text ed.: ISSN 1933-7205. USD 1,049, GBP 617 to institutions (effective 2011) (from IngentaConnect).
Indexed: A01, A03, A08, A22, A26, ASCA, BIOBASE, CA, CIN, ChemAb, ChemTitl, CurCont, E01, EMBASE, ExcerpMed, I05, IABS, ISR, IndMed, Inpharma, MEDLINE, P30, P35, R10, Reac, S21, SCI, SCOPUS, T02, W07.
—BLDSC (7713.706370), CASDDS, GNLM, IE, Infotrieve, Ingenta, INIST. **CCC.**
Published by: (Society for Gynecologic Investigation), Sage Publications, Inc., 2455 Teller Rd, Thousand Oaks, CA 91320. TEL 805-499-9774, FAX 805-499-0871, info@sagepub.com, http://www.sagepub.com/. Ed. Dr. Hugh S Taylor.

618.1 618.92 UKR
➤ **REPRODUKTIVNOE ZDOROV'YE ZHENSHCHINY;** vseukrainskii nauchno-prakticheskii zhurnal. Text in Russian. 2002. 5/yr. UAK 75 domestic; USD 79 foreign (effective 2007). **Document type:** *Journal, Academic/Scholarly.* **Description:** Covers midwifery, gynecology and pediatrics.
Published by: (Akademiya Medychnykh Nauk Ukrainy, Instytut Pedyatrii, Akusherstva i Hinekolohii/Academy of Medical Sciences of Ukraine, Institute of Paediatrics, Obstetrics and Gynaecology), Vydavnychyi Dim Professional, vul Yuriya Kotsyubyns'kogo 9A, Korpus 2, 8-i etazh, Kyiv, 04053, Ukraine. office@zdr.kiev.ua, http://www.zdr.kiev.ua. Ed. Yu P Vdovichenko. Circ: 6,000. **Dist. by:** East View Information Services, 10601 Wayzata Blvd, Minneapolis, MN 55305. TEL 952-252-1201, 800-477-1005, FAX 952-252-1202, info@eastview.com, http://www.eastview.com.

618.2 GBR ISSN 1179-9935
▼ ➤ **RESEARCH AND REPORTS IN NEONATOLOGY.** Text in English. 2011. irreg. free (effective 2011). **Document type:** *Journal, Academic/Scholarly.* **Description:** Contains research, reports, editorials, reviews and commentaries on neonatal health.
Media: Online - full text.
—**CCC.**
Published by: Dove Medical Press Ltd., Beechfield House, Winterton Way, Macclesfield, SK11 0JL, United Kingdom. TEL 44-1625-509130, FAX 44-1625-617933. Ed. Dr. Robert Schelonka.

618 PAK ISSN 1994-7925
➤ **RESEARCH JOURNAL OF OBSTETRICS AND GYNECOLOGY.** Text in English. 2008. 4/yr. **Document type:** *Journal, Academic/Scholarly.* **Description:** Provides a new forum to share the latest scientific development in the field of obstetrics and gynecology to the busy clinician. It covers all major topics in the filed such as fetal medicine, fertility, endocopic surgery, gynecologic oncology and pathology, and general obstetrics.
Related titles: Online - full text ed.: free (effective 2011).
Indexed: A01, A29, B20, B21, CABA, EMBASE, ESPM, ExcerpMed, GH, N02, N03, SCOPUS, T02, T05, ToxAb, VirolAbstr.
Published by: A N S I Network, 308 Lasani Town, Sargodha Rd, Faisalabad, 38090, Pakistan. TEL 92-41-8787087, FAX 92-41-8815544, sarwarm@ansimail.org, http://ansinet.com.

618 USA ISSN 1042-0290
RESOLVE NATIONAL NEWSLETTER. Text in English. q. free with membership. **Document type:** *Newsletter, Consumer.* **Description:** Covers all aspects of infertility with topics such as: medical information, adoption advise, advocacy, expert answers to reader questions.
Published by: RESOLVE: The National Infertility Association, 1310 Broadway, Somerville, MA 02144 . TEL 617-623-0744, FAX 617-623-0252, resolveinc@aol.com.

618 USA ISSN 1941-2797
REVIEWS IN OBSTETRICS AND GYNECOLOGY. Text in English. 2008 (Winter). q. includes with subscr. to Reviews in Cardiovascular Medicine, Reviews in Urology & Reviews in Neurological Diseases. **Document type:** *Journal, Academic/Scholarly.* **Description:** Includes information on advances in gynecology, including new treatments for menopause, new treatments for uterine cancer, prevention of cervical and uterine cancer, fertility control, contraception, obesity and STDs.
Related titles: Online - full text ed.: ISSN 2153-8166.
Indexed: P30.
Published by: MedReviews, Llc, 494 Eighth Ave, Ste 1000, New York, NY 10001. TEL 212-201-6860, FAX 212-201-6850, sblack@medreviews.com.

618 BRA ISSN 0100-7203
CODEN: RBGODX
REVISTA BRASILEIRA DE GINECOLOGIA E OBSTETRICIA. Abbreviated title: R B G O. Text in Portuguese. 1979. q. adv. **Document type:** *Journal, Academic/Scholarly.*
Related titles: Online - full text ed.: ISSN 1806-9339. 2000. free (effective 2011).
Indexed: A34, A35, A36, A38, AgBio, C01, CABA, D01, E12, EMBASE, ExcerpMed, F08, GH, H17, INIS AtomInd, LT, MEDLINE, N02, N03, P30, P33, P39, R10, R12, RM&VM, Reac, S12, S17, SCOPUS, SoyAb, T05, TAR, VS.
—CASDDS.
Published by: Federacao Brasileira das Sociedades de Ginecologia e Obstetricia (F E B R A S G O), Av das Americas 8445, Sala 711, Barra da Tijuca, Rio de Janeiro, 22793-081, Brazil. TEL 55-21-24876336, FAX 55-21-24295133, publicacoes@febrasgo.org.br, http://www.febrasgo.org.br/. Ed. Jurandyr Moreira de Andrade. Circ: 8,500.

618 CHL ISSN 0048-766X
REVISTA CHILENA DE OBSTETRICIA Y GINECOLOGIA. Text in Spanish. 1935. bi-m. CLP 40,000 domestic; USD 60 foreign. illus. **Document type:** *Journal, Academic/Scholarly.*
Supersedes (in 1961): Sociedad Chilena de Obstetricia y Ginecologia. Boletin (0366-3140)

Related titles: E-mail ed.; Fax ed.; Online - full text ed.: ISSN 0717-7526. 2002. free (effective 2011) (from SciELO).
Indexed: A22, CA, ChemAb, IndMed, P30, SCOPUS, T02.
—BLDSC (7848.930000), GNLM, IE, Infotrieve, Ingenta.
Published by: Sociedad Chilena de Obstetricia y Ginecologia, Roman Diaz 205, Of 205, Providencia, Santiago, Chile. TEL 56-2-2350133, FAX 56-2-2351294, sochog@entel-chile.net, http://www.sochog.cl. Ed. Mario Herrera.

618 CHL ISSN 0717-0815
REVISTA CHILENA DE OBSTETRICIA Y GINECOLOGIA INFANTIL Y DE LA ADOLESCENCIA. Text in Spanish. 1994. 3/yr. **Document type:** *Journal, Academic/Scholarly.*
Published by: Sociedad Chilena de Obstetricia y Ginecologia Infantil y de la Adolescencia, Avenida Profesor Zanartu 1030, Independencia, Santiago, Chile. http://www.cemera.uchile.cl. Ed. Ramiro Molina Cortes.

618 COL ISSN 0034-7434
➤ **REVISTA COLOMBIANA DE OBSTETRICIA Y GINECOLOGIA.** Text in Spanish, Portuguese. 1950. q. COP 177,000 domestic; USD 90 foreign (effective 2011). adv. bk.rev. bibl.; charts; illus. index. **Document type:** *Journal, Academic/Scholarly.*
Related titles: Online - full text ed.: 1998. free (effective 2011) (from SciELO).
Indexed: A22, A26, C01, CA, I04, I05, IndMed, P30, SCOPUS, T02.
—BLDSC (7851.405000), GNLM, IE, Infotrieve, Ingenta.
Published by: Sociedad Colombiana de Obstetricia y Ginecologia, Carrera 23, 39-82, Bogota, Colombia. TEL 57-1-2681485. Eds. Enrique Archila, Jose Gabriel Acuna. Circ: 2,000. **Co-sponsor:** Federacion Colombiana de Sociedades de Obstetricia y Ginecologia.

618 CUB ISSN 0138-600X
CODEN: RCOGBK
REVISTA CUBANA DE OBSTETRICIA Y GINECOLOGIA. Text in Spanish; Summaries in English, Spanish. 1974. q. USD 30 in North America; USD 32 in South America; USD 34 elsewhere (effective 2005). bibl.; charts; illus. index. back issues avail. **Document type:** *Journal, Academic/Scholarly.*
Related titles: Online - full text ed.: ISSN 1561-3062. 1995. free (effective 2011).
Indexed: A01, C01, CA, INIS AtomInd, SCOPUS, T02.
Published by: (Centro Nacional de Informacion de Ciencias Medicas (C N I C M), Cuba. Ministerio de Salud Publica), Editorial Ciencias Medicas, Linea Esq 1, 10o, Vedado, Havana, 10400, Cuba. TEL 53-7-8323863, ecimed@infomed.sld.cu. Eds. Dania Silva Hernandez, Fredesvinda Blanco. Circ: 2,000. **Co-sponsor:** Sociedad Cubana de Obstetricia y Ginecologia.

618 VEN ISSN 0048-7732
REVISTA DE OBSTETRICIA Y GINECOLOGIA DE VENEZUELA. Text in Spanish. 1941. q. adv. bk.rev. back issues avail. **Document type:** *Journal, Academic/Scholarly.*
Related titles: Online - full text ed.: free (effective 2011).
Indexed: C01, ChemAb, IBR, IBZ, IndMed, P30, SCOPUS.
—GNLM.
Published by: Sociedad de Obstetricia y Ginecologia de Venezuela, Biblioteca, Ave. San Martin, Apdo 20081, Caracas, DF 1020-A, Venezuela. TEL 58-2-4515955, FAX 58-2-4510895. Ed. Jacqueline Saulni de Jorges. Circ: 2,000.

618 ESP ISSN 1697-6436
REVISTA ESPANOLA DE OBSTETRICIA Y GINECOLOGIA. Text in Spanish. 1944. bi-m. **Document type:** *Journal, Academic/Scholarly.*
Former titles (until 2001): Obstetricia y Ginecologia Espanola (1130-7919); (until 1989): Revista Espanola de Obstetricia y Ginecologia (0034-9445)
Indexed: IBR, IBZ, P30.
—GNLM, INIST. **CCC.**
Published by: Sociedad de Obstetricia y Ginecologia de la Comunidad Valenciana (S O G C V), C/ Maestro Lope 59, Burjassot, Valencia 46100, Spain. http://www.sogcv.com.

618 ESP ISSN 1132-0249
REVISTA IBEROAMERICANA DE FERTILIDAD Y REPRODUCCION HUMANA. Text in Multiple languages. 1984. bi-m. EUR 53 domestic; EUR 82 foreign (effective 2009). **Document type:** *Journal, Academic/Scholarly.*
Formerly (until 1987): Revista Iberoamericana de Fertilidad (1132-0230)
Related titles: Online - full text ed.: ISSN 1695-3703. 2001.
Indexed: EMBASE, ExcerpMed, R10, Reac, SCOPUS.
—BLDSC (7858.821000), IE, Ingenta.
Published by: (Sociedad Espanola de Fertilidad, Sociedad Espanola de Contracepcion), Editorial Medica, C/ Gamonal 5, 5a Planta, No 9, Edificio Valencia, Madrid, 28031, Spain. contacto@editorialmedica.com, http://www.editorialmedica.com.

618 610.73 PER ISSN 1816-7713
REVISTA PERUANA DE OBSTETRICIA Y ENFERMERIA. Text in Spanish. 2005. s-a. **Document type:** *Journal, Academic/Scholarly.*
Published by: Universidad de San Martin de Porres, Facultad de Obstetricia y Enfermeria, Ciudad Universitaria, Av las Calandrias s/n, Santa Anita, Lima, Peru. TEL 51-1-3620064, http://www.usmp.edu.pe.

618.3 FRA ISSN 1965-0833
▼ ➤ **REVUE DE MEDECINE PERINATALE.** Text in French. 2009. q. EUR 209, USD 313 combined subscription to institutions (print & online eds.) (effective 2012). reprint service avail. from PSC. **Document type:** *Journal, Academic/Scholarly.*
Related titles: Online - full text ed.: ISSN 1965-0841. 2009 (from IngentaConnect).
Indexed: SCOPUS.
—IE. **CCC.**
Published by: Springer France (Subsidiary of: Springer Science+Business Media), 22 Rue de Palestro, Paris, 75002, France. TEL 33-1-53009860, FAX 33-1-53009861, sylvie.kamara@springer.com. Ed. Pierre Lequien.

618.202 FRA ISSN 1637-4088
LA REVUE SAGE - FEMME. Text in French. 2002. bi-m. EUR 173 in Europe to institutions; EUR 153.77 in France to institutions; JPY 27,700 in Japan to institutions; USD 225 elsewhere to institutions (effective 2012). **Document type:** *Journal, Trade.*
Related titles: Online - full text ed.: (from ScienceDirect).
Indexed: SCOPUS.
—**CCC.**
Published by: Elsevier Masson (Subsidiary of: Elsevier Health Sciences), 62 Rue Camille Desmoulins, Issy les Moulineaux, Cedex 92442, France. TEL 33-1-71165500, infos@elsevier-masson.fr.

618 JPN ISSN 0386-9865
CODEN: RFUSA4
RINSHO FUJINKA SANKA/CLINICAL GYNECOLOGY AND OBSTETRICS. Text in Japanese. 1946. m. JPY 37,800 per issue; JPY 49,200 combined subscription (print & online eds.) (effective 2010). **Document type:** *Journal, Academic/Scholarly.*
Related titles: Online - full text ed.: ISSN 1882-1294.
Indexed: ChemAb, ChemTitl, P30.
—BLDSC (3286.289000), CASDDS.
Published by: Igaku Shoin Ltd., 1-28-36 Hongo, Bunkyo-ku, Tokyo, 113-8719, Japan. TEL 81-3-3817-5600, FAX 81-3-3815-7791, info@igaku-shoin.co.jp. Circ: 3,000.

618 ITA ISSN 1724-6776
LA RIVISTA ITALIANA DI GINECOLOGIA E OSTETRICIA. Cover title: La Rivista Italiana di Ostetricia e Ginecologia. Text in Italian. 2004. q. free to qualified personnel (effective 2008). **Document type:** *Journal, Academic/Scholarly.*
Related titles: Online - full text ed.: ISSN 1824-0283.
Published by: M N L Publimed, Largo Respighi 8, Bologna, 40126, Italy. TEL 39-051-5877605, info@mnlpublimed.com, http://www.mnlpublimed.com.

618 RUS ISSN 1726-6122
➤ **ROSSIISKII VESTNIK AKUSHERA-GINEKOLOGA.** Text in Russian. 2001. bi-m. USD 164 in North America (effective 2010). **Document type:** *Journal, Academic/Scholarly.*
Related titles: Online - full text ed.
Indexed: RefZh.
Published by: Media Sfera, Dmitrovskoe shosse 46, korp 2, etazh 4, P.O. Box 54, Moscow, 127238, Russian Federation. TEL 7-095-4824329, FAX 7-095-4824312, podpiska@mediasphera.ru, http://mediasphera.ru. Ed. Lidiya Logutova. Circ: 2,000.

618 RUS ISSN 1027-4065
CODEN: VOMDAQ
➤ **ROSSIISKII VESTNIK PERINATOLOGII I PEDIATRII.** Text in Russian. 1956. bi-m. USD 255 in North America (effective 2010). adv. bk.rev. bibl.; illus.; charts. index. reprints avail. **Document type:** *Journal, Academic/Scholarly.* **Description:** For pediatricians, obstetricians and gynecologists, working in different fields of maternal and child health at maternity and pediatric health centers, hospitals, nurseries and kindergarten, schools, rural medical centers.
Former titles: Materinstvo i Detstvo (0869-2114); (until 1992): Voprosy Okhrany Materinstva i Detstva (0042-8825)
Related titles: E-mail ed.; Online - full content ed.
Indexed: B25, BDM&CN, BIOSIS Prev, ChemAb, IndMed, MycolAb, P30, RASB, RefZh, S02, S03, WBSS.
—CASDDS, GNLM. **CCC.**
Published by: Moskovskii Institut Pediatrii i Detskoi Khirurgii, ul Taldomskaya, dom 2, Moscow, 125412, Russian Federation. TEL 7-495-4837250, http://www.pedklin.ru. Ed. Aleksandr Tsaregorodtsev. Circ: 2,000 (paid). **Dist. by:** East View Information Services, 10601 Wayzata Blvd, Minneapolis, MN 55305. TEL 952-252-1201, 800-477-1005, FAX 952-252-1202, info@eastview.com, http://www.eastview.com.

618 362.11 IRL ISSN 1649-9174
ROTUNDA DELIVERY. Text in English. 2006. q. **Document type:** *Newsletter.*
Published by: (Rotunda Hospital), Harmonia Ltd., Rosemount House, Dundrum Rd, Dublin, 14, Ireland. TEL 353-1-2405300, FAX 353-1-6619757, http://www.harmonia.ie. Ed. Kieran Slevin.

618 GBR
ROYAL FREE AND UNIVERSITY COLLEGE MEDICAL SCHOOL. DEPARTMENT OF OBSTETRICS & GYNAECOLOGY. NEWSLETTER. Text in English. m. **Document type:** *Newsletter, Academic/Scholarly.*
Published by: Royal Free and University College Medical School. Department of Obstetrics & Gynaecology (Subsidiary of: University College London), 86-96 Chenies Mews, London, WC1E 6HX, United Kingdom. TEL 44-20-76796056, FAX 44-20-73837429.

618 ITA
S I E O G NEWS. (Societa Italiana di Ecografia Ostetrico-Ginecologica) Text in Italian. 1995. q. **Document type:** *Journal, Trade.*
Formerly (until 200?): Econews (1123-8399)
Published by: Societa Italiana di Ecografia Ostetrico-Ginecologica e Metodologie Biofisiche Correlate, Via dei Soldati 25, Rome, Italy. TEL 39-06-6875119, FAX 39-06-6868142, http://www.sieog.it.

618 ITA ISSN 1721-7016
S I G O NOTIZIE. (Societa Italiana di Ginecologia e Ostetrica) Text in Italian. 1987. q. free to qualified personnel. adv. **Document type:** *Newsletter, Trade.* **Description:** Provides information on the activities of the Societa Italiana di Ginecologia e Ostetrica.
Published by: (Societa Italiana di Ginecologia e Ostetrica), C I C Edizioni Internazionali, Corso Trieste 42, Rome, 00198, Italy. TEL 39-06-8412673, FAX 39-06-8412688, info@gruppocic.it, http://www.gruppocic.it.

613.99 CHE ISSN 1014-952X
SAFE MOTHERHOOD. Text in English. 1989. 3/yr. **Document type:** *Journal, Academic/Scholarly.*
Related titles: Online - full text ed.: ISSN 1564-1104; French ed.: ISSN 1014-9511.
Indexed: SCOPUS.
—**CCC.**
Published by: World Health Organization, Maternal and Newborn Health - Safe Motherhood Unit, Family and Reproductive Health, Avenue Appia 20, Geneva 27, 1211, Switzerland. TEL 41-22-7912111, FAX 41-22-7913111, http://www.safemotherhood.org.

618.2 FRA ISSN 1777-3741
SAGES - FEMMES. Text in French. 1946. q. adv. **Document type:** *Bulletin, Trade.*
Former titles (until 2004): Le Bulletin des Sages - Femmes (1273-2540); (until 1994): Association des Sages - Femmes de l'Ecole d'Accouchement de la Maternite de Nancy. Bulletin (1273-2559); (until 1971): Association des Eleves et Anciennes Eleves Sages - Femmes de l'Universite de Nancy (1278-7531); (until 1971): Association des Sages - Femmes de l'Ecole d'Accouchement de la Maternite de Nancy (1278-7523); (until 1963): Association Amicale des Eleves et Anciennes Eleves Sages - Femmes de l'Ecole d'Accouchement de la Maternite de Nancy (1278-7515); (until 1961): Amicale des Eleves et Anciennes Eleves Sages - Femmes de l'Ecole d'Accouchement de la Maternite de Nancy (1278-7507)
Published by: Association Amicale des Eleves et des Anciennes Eleves de l'Ecole d'Accouchement de la Maternite de Nancy, Rue du Docteur Heydendreich, Nancy, 54000, France.

618 JPN ISSN 0912-2966
SAITAMA-KEN SANFUJINKA IKAIHO/SAITAMA SOCIETY OF OBSTETRICIANS AND GYNECOLOGISTS. Text in Japanese. 1970. a. **Document type:** *Journal, Academic/Scholarly.*
Published by: Saitamaken Sanfujinka Ikai, c/o Saitama Medical Association, 3-5-1 Naka-cho 3-chome, Urawa, Saitama 330-0062, Japan. TEL 81-48-8242611, FAX 81-48-8228515, gaku@office.saitama.med.or.jp, http://ssi.umin.jp/.

618 JPN ISSN 0558-471X
CODEN: RKAKDK
SANFUJINKA CHIRYO/OBSTETRICAL AND GYNECOLOGICAL THERAPY. Text in Japanese. 1960. m. USD 354 (effective 2000). **Document type:** *Academic/Scholarly.*
Indexed: INIS AtomInd, P30.
—BLDSC (6208.173000), CASDDS.
Published by: Nagai Shoten Co. Ltd., 21-15 Fukushima 8-chome, Fukushima-ku, Osaka-shi, 553-0003, Japan. Ed. T Nagai.

618 JPN ISSN 0913-865X
SANFUJINKA KANPO KENKYU NO AYUMI/RECENT PROGRESS OF KANPO MEDICINE IN OBSTETRICS AND GYNECOLOGY. Text in Japanese. 1984. a., latest no.23, 2005. JPY 21,000 newsstand/cover (effective 2007). **Document type:** *Academic/Scholarly.*
Published by: Shindan to Chiryosha, Sanno Grand Bldg. 4F, 2-14-2 Nagata-cho, Chiyoda-ku, Tokyo, 100-0014, Japan. TEL 81-3-35802770, FAX 81-3-35802776, eigyobu@shindan.co.jp, http://www.shindan.co.jp/.

618 JPN ISSN 0558-4728
SANFUJINKA NO JISSAI/OBSTETRICAL AND GYNECOLOGICAL PRACTICE. Text in Japanese. 1952. m. JPY 42,000 (effective 2007). **Document type:** *Journal, Academic/Scholarly.*
Indexed: INIS AtomInd, P30.
—GNLM.
Published by: Kanehara Shuppan/Kanehara & Co. Ltd., 2-31-14 Yushima, Bunkyo-ku, Tokyo, 113-8687, Japan. TEL 81-3-38117184, FAX 81-3-38130288, http://www.kanehara-shuppan.co.jp/.

618 JPN ISSN 0386-9873
CODEN: SASEAU
SANFUJINKA NO SEKAI/WORLD OF OBSTETRICS AND GYNECOLOGY. Text in Japanese. 1949. m. JPY 23,940 (effective 2007). **Document type:** *Journal, Academic/Scholarly.*
Indexed: CIN, ChemAb, ChemTitl, INIS AtomInd.
—BLDSC (9356.900000), CASDDS.
Published by: Igaku no Sekaisha, Inc., 1-12-4 Kudan-Kita, Chiyoda-ku, Tokyo, 102-0073, Japan. TEL 81-3-32393258, FAX 81-3-32393259, iawase@igakunosekaisha.com.

618 617 JPN ISSN 0915-8375
SANFUJINKA SHUJUTSU/GYNECOLOGIC AND OBSTETRIC SURGERY. Text in Japanese. 1990. a. JPY 7,350 per issue (effective 2007). **Document type:** *Journal, Academic/Scholarly.* **Description:** Contains annual proceedings of the Society.
Published by: (Nihon Sanfujinka Shujutsu Kenkyukai/Japan Society of Gynecological and Obstetrical Surgery), Medical View Co. Ltd./Mejikaru Byusha, 2-30 Ichigaya-Honmura-cho, Shinjuku-ku, Tokyo, 162-0845, Japan. TEL 81-3-52282050, FAX 81-3-52282059, eigyo@medicalview.co.jp, http://www.medicalview.co.jp. Circ: 4,000 (controlled).

SCANDINAVIAN JOURNAL OF SURGERY. *see* MEDICAL SCIENCES—Surgery

618.2 DEU
SCHWANGERSCHAFT UND GEBURT. Variant title: Leben und Erziehen - Schwangerschaft und Geburt. Text in German. 1998. 4/yr. EUR 2.95 newsstand/cover (effective 2010). adv. **Document type:** *Magazine, Consumer.*
Published by: Bayard Media GmbH & Co. KG, Boeheimstr 8, Augsburg, 86153, Germany. TEL 49-821-45548181, FAX 49-821-45548110, redaktion@bayard-media.de, http://www.bayard-media.de. adv.: page EUR 8,250; trim 210 x 280. Circ: 95,000 (paid and controlled).

618.92 GBR ISSN 1744-165X
CODEN: SNEOFI
➤ **SEMINARS IN FETAL & NEONATAL MEDICINE.** Text in English. 1996. bi-m. EUR 523 in Europe to institutions; JPY 56,900 in Japan to institutions; USD 466 elsewhere to institutions (effective 2012). adv. 2 cols./p.; back issues avail.; reprints avail. **Document type:** *Journal, Academic/Scholarly.* **Description:** Each issue offers current, clinical information on a single topic in the care and treatment of the neonate.
Formerly (until 2004): Seminars in Neonatology (1084-2756)
Related titles: Online - full text ed.: ISSN 1878-0946 (from ScienceDirect).
Indexed: A22, A26, C06, C07, CA, CurCont, E01, EMBASE, ExcerpMed, I05, IndMed, MEDLINE, P30, R10, Reac, SCI, SCOPUS, T02, W07.
—BLDSC (8239.455100), GNLM, IE, Infotrieve, Ingenta, INIST. **CCC.**
Published by: W.B. Saunders Co. Ltd. (Subsidiary of: Elsevier Health Sciences), 32 Jamestown Rd, Camden, London, NW1 7BY, United Kingdom. TEL 44-20-74244200, FAX 44-20-74832293, elsols@elsevier.com. Ed. M I Levene TEL 44-113-92432799.

➤ **SEMINARS IN PERINATOLOGY.** *see* MEDICAL SCIENCES—Pediatrics

612.6 FRA ISSN 1158-1360
HQ23
➤ **SEXOLOGIES**; revue europeenne de sante sexuelle - european journal of sexual health. Text in English, French. 1991. q. EUR 159 in Europe to institutions; EUR 155.73 in France to institutions; JPY 19,000 in Japan to institutions; USD 178 elsewhere to institutions (effective 2012). **Document type:** *Journal, Academic/Scholarly.* **Description:** Contains articles on human sexuality, its dysfunctions and its management.
Related titles: Online - full text ed.: (from ScienceDirect).
Indexed: A26, CA, EMBASE, ExcerpMed, FR, I05, PsycInfo, R10, Reac, SCOPUS, T02.
—IE, Ingenta, INIST. **CCC.**
Published by: (European Federation of Sexology GBR), Elsevier Masson (Subsidiary of: Elsevier Health Sciences), 62 Rue Camille Desmoulins, Issy les Moulineaux, Cedex 92442, France. TEL 33-1-71165500, FAX 33-1-71165600, infos@elsevier-masson.fr, http://www.elsevier-masson.fr. Eds. Mireille Bonierbale, Robert Porto.

618 USA ISSN 1546-2501
QP251
➤ **SEXUALITY, REPRODUCTION & MENOPAUSE.** Abbreviated title: S R M. Text in English. 2003. q. free to members (effective 2010). adv. back issues avail. **Document type:** *Journal, Academic/Scholarly.* **Description:** Contains topical information, clinical reviews, and updates on the reproductive life span, from adolescence to old age.
Related titles: Online - full text ed.: ISSN 1878-7576. free (effective 2010); ◆ Supplement to: Fertility and Sterility. ISSN 0015-0282.
Indexed: A26, CA, EMBASE, ExcerpMed, I05, Inpharma, SCOPUS, T02.
—BLDSC (8254.485240), IE, Ingenta, INIST. **CCC.**
Published by: (American Society for Reproductive Medicine), Dowden Health Media, Inc (Subsidiary of: Lebhar-Friedman, Inc.), 110 Summit Ave, Montvale, NJ 07645. TEL 212-756-5000, FAX 201-391-2168, customerservice@dowdenhealth.com, http://www.dowdenhealth.com. Ed. Sandra A Carson.

➤ **SHARING (ST. CHARLES)**; the official newsletter of S H A R E. *see* PSYCHOLOGY

616.6 CHN ISSN 1004-3845
SHENGZHI YIXUE ZAZHI/JOURNAL OF REPRODUCTIVE MEDICINE. Text in Chinese. 1992. bi-m. USD 39 (effective 2009). **Document type:** *Journal, Academic/Scholarly.*
Related titles: Online - full text ed.
—BLDSC (8256.416000), East View.
Published by: Guojia Jihua Shengyu Weiyuanhui Kexue Jishu Yanjiusuo/ China National Research Institute for Family Planning, 12, Dahuisi Rd, Beijing, 100081, China. Ed. Qing-Sheng Ge. **Dist. by:** China International Book Trading Corp, 35 Chegongzhuang Xilu, Haidian District, PO Box 399, Beijing 100044, China. TEL 86-10-68412045, FAX 86-10-68412023, cibtc@mail.cibtc.com.cn, http://www.cibtc.com.cn.

618 CHN
SHIJIE HEXIN YIXUE QIKAN WENZHAI (FUCHANG KEXUE FENCE)/ DIGEST OF THE WORLD CORE MEDICAL JOURNALS (OBSTETRICS/GYNECOLOGY). Text in Chinese. 2004. bi-m. **Document type:** *Journal, Academic/Scholarly.*
Supersedes in part (in 2005): Shijie Zuixin Yixue Xinxi Wenzhai/Digest of the World Latest Medical Information (1671-3141)
Related titles: Online - full text ed.
—East View.
Published by: Shijie Tushu Chuban Xi'an Gongsi, 17, Nandajie, Xi'an, 710001, China. TEL 86-29-87265319, FAX 86-29-87265318, wzg1995@163.com, http://wuzhigang.bookonline.com.cn/. **Dist. by:** China International Book Trading Corp, 35 Chegongzhuang Xilu, Haidian District, PO Box 399, Beijing 100044, China. TEL 86-10-68412045, FAX 86-10-68412023, cibtc@mail.cibtc.com.cn, http://www.cibtc.com.cn.

618 CHN ISSN 1003-6946
RG1
SHIYONG FUCHANKE ZAZHI/JOURNAL OF PRACTICAL OBSTETRICS AND GYNECOLOGY. Text in Chinese. 1985. m. USD 49.20 (effective 2009). **Document type:** *Journal, Academic/Scholarly.*
Related titles: Online - full text ed.
—BLDSC (8267.297885), East View.
Published by: Sichuan Sheng Yixuehui/Schuan Medical Association, 80 Wenmiao Xijie, Chengdu, 610041, China. TEL 86-28-86136595, http://www.sma.org.cn/. **Dist. by:** China International Book Trading Corp, 35 Chegongzhuang Xilu, Haidian District, PO Box 399, Beijing 100044, China. TEL 86-10-68412045, FAX 86-10-68412023, cibtc@mail.cibtc.com.cn, http://www.cibtc.com.cn.

618 JPN ISSN 0386-9881
CODEN: SHUIAX
SHUSANKI IGAKU/PERINATAL MEDICINE. Text in Japanese. 1971. m. JPY 39,100 per issue (effective 2005). **Document type:** *Journal, Academic/Scholarly.*
—CASDDS.
Published by: Tokyo Igakusha Ltd., 35-4 Hongo 3-chome, Bunkyo-ku, Tokyo, 113-0033, Japan. TEL 81-3-38114119, FAX 81-3-38116135, shoge@tokyo-igakusha.co.jp.

618 JPN ISSN 1342-0526
SHUSANKIGAKU SHIMPOJIUMU/JAPAN SOCIETY OF PERINATOLOGY. YEAR BOOK. Text in Japanese. 1984. a. JPY 3,150 per issue (effective 2007). **Document type:** *Yearbook, Academic/Scholarly.* **Description:** Contains the annual proceedings of the Society.
Formerly (until 1992): Shusankigaku Symposium/Perinatology Symposium (0910-3570)
Published by: (Nihon Shusanki Gakkai/Japan Society of Perinatology), Medical View Co. Ltd./Mejikaru Byusha, 2-30 Ichigaya-Honmura-cho, Shinjuku-ku, Tokyo, 162-0845, Japan. TEL 81-3-52282050, FAX 81-3-52282059, eigyo@medicalview.co.jp, http://www.medicalview.co.jp. Circ: 5,000 (controlled).

618 SGP ISSN 0129-3273
CODEN: SJOGDE
SINGAPORE JOURNAL OF OBSTETRICS & GYNAECOLOGY. Text in English. 1967 (vol.6). 3/yr. USD 25 to individuals; USD 6 to students (effective 2000). adv. bk.rev. charts; illus. reprints avail. **Document type:** *Journal, Academic/Scholarly.* **Description:** Original and review articles on all aspects of obstetrics and gynaecology.
Formerly: Kandang Kerbau Hospital Bulletin (0022-8346)
Related titles: CD-ROM ed.
Indexed: ASCA, ChemAb, ExtraMED, P30.
—BLDSC (8285.463800), CASDDS, GNLM.
Published by: Obstetrical and Gynaecological Society of Singapore, c/o National University Hospital, Dept. of O & G, Lower Kent Ridge Rd, Singapore, 0511, Singapore. ogss@pacific.net.sg. Ed. Dr. Loganath K Annamalai. Circ: 1,000.

618 SVK ISSN 1335-0862
➤ **SLOVENSKA GYNEKOLOGIA A PORODNICTVO.** Text in Slovak, Czech. 1994. q. EUR 63.40 in Europe; EUR 72 elsewhere (effective 2011). **Document type:** *Journal, Academic/Scholarly.*
Published by: (Slovenska Gynekologicko Porodnicka Spolocnost), Slovak Academic Press Ltd., Nam Slobody 6, PO Box 57, Bratislava, 81005, Slovakia. TEL 421-2-55421729, FAX 421-2-55565862, sap@sappress.sk, http://www.sappress.sk. Ed. Helena Bernadicova. **Dist. by:** Slovart G.T.G. s.r.o., Krupinska 4, PO Box 152, Bratislava 85299, Slovakia. TEL 421-2-63839472, FAX 421-2-63839485, info@slovart-gtg.sk, http://www.slovart-gtg.sk.

618 ARG ISSN 0328-7947
SOCIEDAD ARGENTINA DE GINECOLOGIA INFANTO JUVENIL. REVISTA. Text in Spanish. 1994. 3/yr. **Document type:** *Journal, Academic/Scholarly.*
Published by: Sociedad Argentina de Ginecologia Infanto Juvenil, Sarmiento 1617, Local 39, Complejo La Plaza, Buenos Aires, Argentina. TEL 54-11-43713113, consultas@sagij.org.ar, http://www.sagij.org.ar.

618 ARG ISSN 0037-8542
SOCIEDAD DE OBSTETRICIA Y GINECOLOGIA DE BUENOS AIRES. REVISTA. Text in Spanish. 1922. m. bibl.; illus. **Document type:** *Journal, Academic/Scholarly.*
Formerly (until 1961): Sociedad de Obstetricia y Ginecologia de Buenos Aires. Boletin (0327-5191)
Indexed: C01.
Published by: Sociedad de Obstetricia y Ginecologia de Buenos Aires (S O GI B A), Peru 345, Piso 12, Buenos Aires, C1067AAG, Argentina. TEL 54-11-43455051, http://www.sogiba.org.ar.

618 ESP ISSN 1888-5640
SOCIEDAD ESPANOLA DE CONTRACEPCION. REVISTA. Text in Spanish. 2008. biennial. **Document type:** *Monographic series, Academic/Scholarly.*
Published by: Sociedad Espanola de Contracepcion, C Diego de Leon, 47, Madrid, 28006, Spain. TEL 34-902-195545, sec@sec.es, http://www.sec.es.

SONOACE-INTERNATIONAL. *see* MEDICAL SCIENCES—Radiology And Nuclear Medicine

618 ZAF ISSN 0038-2329
RG1 CODEN: SSAJGJ
➤ **SOUTH AFRICAN JOURNAL OF OBSTETRICS AND GYNAECOLOGY.** Abbreviated title: S A J O G. Text in English. 3/yr. USD 15 foreign (effective 2004). adv. illus. back issues avail. **Document type:** *Journal, Academic/Scholarly.* **Description:** Discusses clinical and experimental topics in obstetrics and gynecology.
Related titles: ◆ Supplement to: S A M J South African Medical Journal. ISSN 0256-9574.
Indexed: A01, A26, A29, A36, B20, B21, CABA, EMBASE, ESPM, ExcerpMed, GH, H12, I05, I10, ISAP, P30, P33, P39, R10, R12, RM&VM, Reac, SCI, SCOPUS, T05, ViroIAbstr, W07.
—BLDSC (8339.300000), INIST. **CCC.**
Published by: South African Medical Association, Block F Castle Walk Corporate Park, Nossob St, Erasmuskloof X3, Pretoria 7430, South Africa. TEL 27-12-4812000, FAX 27-12-4812100, publishing@samedical.org, http://www.samedical.org. R&P Peter Roberts. **Subscr. to:** PO Box 74789, Lynnwood Ridge, Pretoria 0040, South Africa.

618 IND ISSN 0974-8938
▼ ➤ **SOUTH ASIAN FEDERATION OF OBSTETRICS AND GYNECOLOGY. JOURNAL.** Variant title: S A F O G. Journal. Text in English. 2009. 3/yr. INR 1,500 domestic to individuals; USD 90 foreign to individuals; INR 2,500 domestic to institutions; USD 150 foreign to institutions (effective 2011). adv. bk.rev. illus. back issues avail. **Document type:** *Journal, Academic/Scholarly.* **Description:** The aim of this journal to provide platform for members to have access to scientific and peer reviewed clinically oriented guidelines for practice and professional updating of subject of obstetrics and gynecology.The scope of SAFOG journal is to cover the broad subject of obstetrics and gynecology and give out articles, information, and practice guidelines. The journal has fixed format of review articles, presentations as original studies by members and readers, operative skill reviews, case reports, and midwifery peer reviewed practice guidelines. In addition call upon experts and clinical authorities among member countries of SAFOG region to give out editorials on policy formulating topics such as maternal mortality, abortions, contraceptives, reproductive health preservation of women etc.
Related titles: Online - full text ed.: ISSN 0975-1920.
Indexed: A01, CA, P20, P48, P54, PQC, T02.
Published by: (South Asia Federation of Obstetrics and Gynaecology), Jaypee Brothers Medical Publishers Pvt. Ltd., 4838/24, Ansari Rd, Daryaganj, New Delhi, 110 002, India. TEL 91-11-43574357, FAX 91-11-43574314, jaypee@jaypeebrothers.com, http://www.jaypeebrothers.com. Ed. Narendra Malhotra. Adv. contact Abhinav Kumar.

➤ **SOUTH EAST THAMES PERINATAL MONITORING GROUP. PROVISIONAL STATISTICS.** *see* STATISTICS

▼ ➤ **SOUTHERN AFRICAN JOURNAL OF GYNAECOLOGICAL ONCOLOGY.** *see* MEDICAL SCIENCES—Oncology

618.202 USA ISSN 1083-5008
SPECIAL DELIVERY. Text in English. 1977. q. USD 20 domestic; USD 23 in Canada & Mexico; USD 25 elsewhere (effective 2007). adv. bk.rev. illus. back issues avail.; reprints avail. **Document type:** *Newsletter.* **Description:** Discusses midwifery, alternatives in birth, parenting, early childhood education, women's health.
Related titles: Online - full text ed.
Indexed: A26, G08, GW, H11, H12, HlthInd, I05, P19, P48, PQC.
Published by: Association of Labor Assistants & Childbirth Educators, PO Box 390436, Cambridge, MA 02139. TEL 617-441-2500, FAX 617-441-3167, info@alace.org. Ed. Annmarie Kalmar. Pub., R&P, Adv. contact Jessica Porter. Circ: 2,000 (paid).

612.6 AUT ISSN 1011-8772
RG1
SPECULUM; Geburtshilfe - Frauen-Heilkunde - Strahlen-Heilkunde Forschung - Konsequenzen. Text in German. 1983. q. EUR 36 (effective 2005). adv. abstr.; bibl. back issues avail. **Document type:** *Journal, Academic/Scholarly.*
Related titles: Online - full text ed.: ISSN 1810-4797. 2001. free (effective 2011).
—CCC.
Published by: Krause & Pachernegg GmbH, Mozartgasse 10, Gablitz, 3003, Austria. TEL 43-2231-612580, FAX 43-2231-6125810, k_u_p@eunet.at, http://www.kup.at/verlag.htm. Ed. Dr. Kinga Chalubinski.

618.202 RUS
SPRAVOCHNIK FEL'DSHERA I AKUSHERKI. Text in Russian. 2001. m. USD 1,518 domestic (effective 2007). **Document type:** *Journal, Trade.*
Published by: Mezhdunarodnyi Tsentr Finansovo-Ekonomicheskogo Razvitiya, ul Yaroslavskaya, dom 8, k 5, Moscow, 126106, Russian Federation. TEL 7-495-9379080, FAX 7-495-9379087, ap@mcfr.ru, http://www.zdrav.ru.

618 ESP ISSN 1885-0642
SUELO PELVICO. Text in Spanish. 2005. q. 32 p./no.; back issues avail. **Document type:** *Journal, Trade.*
Published by: Ediciones Mayo S.A., Calle Aribau 185-187, 2a Planta, Barcelona, 08021, Spain. TEL 34-93-2090255, FAX 34-93-2020643, edmayo@ediciones.mayo.es, http://www.edicionesmayo.es. Circ: 2,500.

SURGICAL INNOVATION. *see* MEDICAL SCIENCES—Surgery

SURGICAL LAPAROSCOPY, ENDOSCOPY AND PERCUTANEOUS TECHNIQUES. *see* MEDICAL SCIENCES—Surgery

618 HKG ISSN 1028-4559
➤ **TAIWANESE JOURNAL OF OBSTETRICS AND GYNECOLOGY.** Text and summaries in Chinese, English. 1962. q. EUR 210 in Europe to institutions; JPY 32,700 in Japan to institutions; USD 277 elsewhere to institutions (effective 2012). adv. reprints avail. **Document type:** *Journal, Academic/Scholarly.*
Formerly (until vol.36, no.1, 1997): Journal of Obstetrics and Gynecology of the Republic of China
Related titles: Microform ed.: (from PQC); Online - full text ed.: ISSN 1875-6263 (from ScienceDirect).
Indexed: A34, A36, A38, B21, CABA, D01, EMBASE, ExcerpMed, GH, H16, MEDLINE, N02, N03, P30, P33, R08, R10, R12, RA&MP, RM&VM, Reac, SCI, SCOPUS, T05, VS, ViroIAbstr, W07.
—BLDSC (8600.920000), IE. **CCC.**
Published by: (Taiwan Association of Obstetrics and Gynecology TWN), Elsevier (Singapore) Pte Ltd, Hong Kong Branch (Subsidiary of: Elsevier Health Sciences), 1601, 16/F, Leighton Centre, 77 Leighton Rd., Causeway Bay, Hong Kong. TEL 852-2965-1300, FAX 852-2976-0778, asiajournals@elsevier.com. Ed. Chih-Ping Chen. Circ: 2,400.

618.202 DNK ISSN 0106-1836
TIDSSKRIFT FOR JORDEMOEDRE. Text in Danish. 1891. m. DKK 515 (effective 2009). adv. back issues avail. **Document type:** *Magazine, Academic/Scholarly.* **Description:** Seeks to spread knowledge about professional and trade-political matters for the awareness of the profession of midwifery and its developments.
Related titles: Online - full text ed.
Published by: Jordemoderforeningen/Danish Association of Midwives, Sankt Annae Plads 30, PO Box 1217, Copenhagen K, 1250, Denmark. TEL 45-46-953400, sek@jordemoderforeningen.dk. Ed. Anne Marie Kjeldset TEL 45-46-953404. Circ: 2,150.

618.202 NOR ISSN 1503-3244
TIDSSKRIFT FOR JORDMOEDRE. Text in Norwegian. 1895. 9/yr. adv. bk.rev. illus. index. **Document type:** *Magazine, Trade.*
Former titles (until 2002): Jordmoedre (1502-1300); (until 2000): Tidsskrift for Jordmoedre (0040-7089); Which incorporated (1950-1966): Jordmorbladet (0332-9909)
Related titles: Online - full text ed.
Published by: Den Norske Jordmorforening/The Norwegian Association of Midwives, Tollbugata 35, Oslo, 0157, Norway. TEL 47-21-023372, FAX 47-21-023377, dnj@jordmorforeningen.no. Ed. Eddy Groenset. Adv. contact Dagfrid Hammersvik. Circ: 2,700 (paid and controlled).

618 NLD ISSN 0378-1925
TIJDSCHRIFT VOOR VERLOSKUNDIGEN. Text in Dutch. 1975. m. (11/yr.). EUR 122 domestic; EUR 136 foreign; EUR 96 to students (effective 2009). adv.
Formed by the merger of (1899-1975): Tijdschrift voor Praktische Verloskunde (0378-3332); (1955-1975): Verloskundige Gids (0926-1834)
Indexed: A22.
—IE.
Published by: Koninklijke Nederlandse Organisatie van Verloskundigen, Postbus 2001, Utrecht, 3500 GA, Netherlands. TEL 31-30-2823100, FAX 31-30-2823101, info@knov.nl, http://www.knov.nl. adv.: B&W page EUR 1,057; trim 210 x 297. Circ: 3,650.

305.42 CAN ISSN 1702-8590
TODAY'S PARENT, PREGNANCY & BIRTH. Text in English. 1972. 3/yr. CAD 12, USD 18 (effective 2000). adv. bk.rev. back issues avail. **Document type:** *Magazine, Consumer.* **Description:** Focus on pregnancy, birth, postpartum care, breastfeeding and parenting the newborn.
Formerly (until 2000): Great Expectations (0823-9266)
Related titles: Online - full text ed.; ◆ Supplement to: Canadian Today's Parent. ISSN 1912-0303.
Indexed: C03, CBCARef, H13, P10, P19, P20, P53, P54, PQC.
Published by: (Today's Parent Group), Professional Publishing Associates, 269 Richmond St W, Toronto, ON M5V 1X1, Canada. TEL 416-596-8680, FAX 416-596-1991. Ed. Holly Bennett. adv.: B&W page CAD 13,120, color page CAD 16,400. Circ: 200,000 (controlled).

618 JPN ISSN 0915-7204
TOKAI SANKA FUJINKA GAKKAI ZASSHI/TOKAI JOURNAL OF OBSTETRICS AND GYNECOLOGY. Text in English, Japanese. 1981. a. **Document type:** *Journal, Academic/Scholarly.*
Formerly: Tokai Sanka Fujinka Gakkaishi

Published by: Toukai Sanka Fujinka Gakkai/Tokai Society of Obstetrics and Gynecology, Nagoya University School of Medicine, 1-1-20, Daikominami, Higashi-ku, Nagoya, 461-0047, Japan. TEL 81-52-7231111 ext 564.

618 USA ISSN 0891-9925
CODEN: TRREEN

➤ **TROPHOBLAST RESEARCH.** Text in English. 1984. irreg. price varies. back issues avail. **Document type:** *Monographic series, Academic/Scholarly.*
Indexed: A22, CIN, ChemAb, ChemTitl.
—CASDDS, IE, Ingenta. **CCC.**
Published by: University of Rochester Press, 668 Mt Hope Ave, Rochester, NY 14620. TEL 585-275-0419, FAX 585-271-8778, boydell@boydellusa.net.

618 NGA ISSN 0189-5117
TROPICAL JOURNAL OF OBSTETRICS AND GYNAECOLOGY. Text in English. 1981. q. USD 60. **Document type:** *Journal, Academic/Scholarly.*
Related titles: Online - full text ed.
Published by: (International Federation of Gynaecology and Obstetrics GBR), Fourth Dimension Publishing Co. Ltd., House 16, Fifth Ave., PMB 01164, New Haven, Enugu State, Nigeria. TEL 234-42-459969, FAX 234-42-453739. Circ: 1,000. **Co-sponsor:** Society of Gynaecology and Obstetrics of Nigeria.

618 TUR ISSN 1307-699X
TURK JINEKOLOJI VE OBSTETRIK DERNEGI DERGISI. Text in Turkish. 2007. **Document type:** *Journal, Academic/Scholarly.*
Related titles: Online - full text ed.: ISSN 1307-7007. free (effective 2011).
Published by: Turkiye Klinikleri Jinekoloji Obsterik Dergisi, Cetin Emec Bulvari Harbiye Mahallesi, Hurriyet Caddesi 1/3 Ovecler, Ankara, 06230, Turkey. TEL 90-0312-4810606, FAX 90-0312-4812828, editor@tjod.org.

618.1 TUR ISSN 1309-0399
TURKISH-GERMAN GYNECOLOGICAL ASSOCIATION. JOURNAL. Text in English. 2000. q. free to qualified personnel (effective 2011). **Document type:** *Journal, Academic/Scholarly.* **Description:** Includes gynaecologists and primary care physicians interested in gynecology practice. It publishes original work on all aspects of gynecology.
Formerly (until 2003): Artemis (1303-9695)
Related titles: Online - full text ed.: ISSN 1309-0380. free (effective 2011).
Indexed: A01, A26, C06, C07, CA, E08, EMBASE, ExcerpMed, H12, I05, P20, P22, P48, P54, PQC, R10, Reac, SCOPUS, T02.
Published by: (Turkish-German Gynecological Association, Turkish Society of Reproductive Medicine (T S R M)), Turgut Yayincilik ve Ticaret A.S., Firin Sokak No: 61/2 Bomonti, Sisli, Istanbul, 34381, Turkey. TEL 90-212-2330223, FAX 90-212-2336545, tyryay@turyay.com.tr, http://www.turyay.com.tr. Eds. Cihat Unlu, Klaus Vetter.

618 616.07 GBR ISSN 0960-7692
RG527.5.U48 CODEN: UOGYFJ

➤ **ULTRASOUND IN OBSTETRICS AND GYNECOLOGY.** Text in English. 1991. 13/yr. GBP 691 in United Kingdom to institutions; EUR 873 in Europe to institutions; USD 1,353 elsewhere to institutions; GBP 794 combined subscription in United Kingdom to institutions (print & online eds.); EUR 1,004 combined subscription in Europe to institutions (print & online eds.); USD 1,557 combined subscription elsewhere to institutions (print & online eds.) (effective 2012). adv. bk.rev. back issues avail.; reprint service avail. from PSC. **Document type:** *Journal, Academic/Scholarly.* **Description:** Publishes clinical research in the field.
Related titles: Online - full text ed.: ISSN 1469-0705. GBP 691 in United Kingdom to institutions; EUR 873 in Europe to institutions; USD 1,353 elsewhere to institutions (effective 2012) (from IngentaConnect); Supplement(s): Ultrasound in Obstetrics & Gynecology. Supplement. ISSN 1472-1201.
Indexed: A01, A03, A08, A22, A26, ASCA, B&BAb, B19, B21, BioEngAb, C06, C07, CA, CurCont, E01, EMBASE, ExcerpMed, ISR, IndMed, Inpharma, MEDLINE, P30, R10, Reac, RefZh, SCI, SCOPUS, T02, W07.
—GNLM, IE, Infotrieve, Ingenta, INIST. **CCC.**
Published by: (International Society of Ultrasound in Obstetrics and Gynecology), John Wiley & Sons Ltd. (Subsidiary of: John Wiley & Sons, Inc.), 1-7 Oldlands Way, PO Box 808, Bognor Regis, West Sussex PO21 9FF, United Kingdom. TEL 44-1865-778315, FAX 44-1243-843232, cs-journals@wiley.com, http://eu.wiley.com/WileyCDA/. Ed. Yves Ville. **Subscr. to:** 1-7 Oldlands Way, PO Box 809, Bognor Regis, West Sussex PO21 9FG, United Kingdom. TEL 44-1865-778054, cs-agency@wiley.com.

618.1 ZAF ISSN 0254-184X
UNIVERSITY OF CAPE TOWN. DEPARTMENT OF OBSTETRICS AND GYNAECOLOGY. ANNUAL REPORT. Text in English. 1952. a. free. **Document type:** *Yearbook, Academic/Scholarly.* **Description:** Lists personnel, research in progress, publications and programs available in the department.
Formerly: University of Cape Town. Department of Gynaecology. Annual Report (0069-0228)
Published by: University of Cape Town, Department of Obstetrics and Gynaecology, Observatory, Cape Town 7925, South Africa. TEL 27-21-4044485, FAX 27-21-4486921, http://web.uct.ac.za/depts/doogie/. Circ: 100. **Co-sponsor:** Cape Provincial Administration.

618 SWE ISSN 1650-1756
VI FOERAELDRAR GRAVID. Text in Swedish. 2000. bi-m. SEK 45 newsstand/cover (effective 2010). adv. **Document type:** *Magazine, Consumer.*
Published by: Bonnier Tidskrifter AB, Sveavaegen 53, Stockholm, 10544, Sweden. TEL 46-8-7365200, FAX 46-8-7363842, info@bt.bonnier.se, http://www.bonniertidskrifter.se. Ed. Helena Roennberg.

618.202 371.42 FRA ISSN 1634-0760
VOCATION SAGE - FEMME. Text in French. 2002. 10/yr. EUR 109 in Europe to institutions; EUR 82.27 in France to institutions; JPY 10,600 in Japan to institutions; USD 132 elsewhere to institutions (effective 2012). **Document type:** *Journal, Academic/Scholarly.* **Description:** Deals with day-to-day midwife practice, providing the profession with the information it needs to enhance professional skills.
Related titles: Online - full text ed.
—**CCC.**
Published by: Elsevier Masson (Subsidiary of: Elsevier Health Sciences), 62 Rue Camille Desmoulins, Issy les Moulineaux, Cedex 92442, France. TEL 33-1-71165500, FAX 33-1-71165600, infos@elsevier-masson.fr.

WESTLAW JOURNAL. HEALTH LAW. *see* LAW—Civil Law

618.1 DEU ISSN 1866-2927
WIRTSCHAFTSTIP FUER GYNAEKOLOGEN. Text in German. 1996. m. EUR 21.40 (effective 2008). adv. **Document type:** *Magazine, Trade.*
Published by: Aerzte Zeitung Verlagsgesellschaft mbH (Subsidiary of: Springer Science+Business Media), Am Forsthaus Gravenbruch 5, Neu-Isenburg, 63263, Germany. TEL 49-6102-506157, FAX 49-6102-506123, info@aerztezeitung.de, http://www.aerztezeitung.de. adv.: B&W page EUR 3,190, color page EUR 4,420. Circ: 10,250 (controlled).

618.202 NLD ISSN 1871-5192
RG950.A1

➤ **WOMEN AND BIRTH.** Text in English. 1988. q. EUR 260 in Europe to institutions; JPY 36,800 in Japan to institutions; USD 331 elsewhere to institutions (effective 2012). adv. bk.rev.; video rev. stat.; tr.lit. back issues avail. **Document type:** *Journal, Academic/Scholarly.* **Description:** Provides a forum for the exchange of midwifery ideas, practice, and research.
Former titles (until 2006): Australian Midwifery (1448-8272); (until 2003): Australian Journal of Midwifery (1445-4386); (until 2001): A C M I Journal (1031-170X)
Related titles: Online - full text ed.: ISSN 1878-1799 (from ScienceDirect).
Indexed: A26, ASSIA, C06, C07, C08, CA, CINAHL, EMBASE, ExcerpMed, FamI, H12, I05, MEDLINE, P30, R10, Reac, SCOPUS, T02.
—BLDSC (9343.237300), GNLM, IE, Ingenta. **CCC.**
Published by: (Australian College of Midwives Inc. AUS), Elsevier BV (Subsidiary of: Elsevier Science & Technology), Radarweg 29, PO Box 211, Amsterdam, 1000 AE, Netherlands. TEL 31-20-4853911, FAX 31-20-4852457, JournalsCustomerServiceEMEA@elsevier.com, http://www.elsevier.nl. Ed. Kathleen Fahy. adv.: B&W page AUD 550. Circ: 3,000.

➤ **WOMEN'S HEALTH ADVISOR;** helping women over 40 make informed health decisions. *see* WOMEN'S HEALTH

➤ **WOMEN'S HEALTH ISSUES.** *see* WOMEN'S HEALTH

618.2 USA ISSN 1044-4890
RG631
YEAR BOOK OF NEONATAL AND PERINATAL MEDICINE. Text in English. 1987. a. USD 239 in United States to institutions; USD 259 elsewhere to institutions (effective 2012). adv. illus. reprints avail. **Document type:** *Yearbook, Academic/Scholarly.* **Description:** Presents abstracts of pertinent literature with commentary by leading experts in the field.
Formerly (until 1989): The Year Book of Perinatal / Neonatal Medicine (8756-5005)
Related titles: CD-ROM ed.; Online - full text ed.
—BLDSC (9414.624000), GNLM. **CCC.**
Published by: Mosby, Inc. (Subsidiary of: Elsevier Health Sciences), 1600 John F. Kennedy Blvd, Ste 1800, Philadelphia, PA 19103. TEL 215-239-3900, 800-523-1649, FAX 215-239-3990, elspcs@elsevier.com, http://www.us.elsevierhealth.com. Eds. Avroy A. Fanaroff, David K Stevenson, M Jeffrey Maisels.

618.1 618.082 USA ISSN 1090-798X
RG26
YEAR BOOK OF OBSTETRICS, GYNECOLOGY, AND WOMEN'S HEALTH. Text in English. 1901. a. USD 239 in United States to institutions; USD 259 elsewhere to institutions (effective 2012). adv. illus. **Document type:** *Yearbook, Academic/Scholarly.* **Description:** Presents abstracts of pertinent literature with commentary by leading experts in the field.
Former titles (until 1966): The Year Book of Obstetrics and Gynecology (0084-3911); (until 1933): Obstetrics. Gynecology
Related titles: CD-ROM ed.; Online - full text ed.
—BLDSC (9414.652500), GNLM. **CCC.**
Published by: Mosby, Inc. (Subsidiary of: Elsevier Health Sciences), 1600 John F. Kennedy Blvd, Ste 1800, Philadelphia, PA 19103. TEL 215-239-3900, 800-523-1649, FAX 215-239-3990, elspcs@elsevier.com, http://www.us.elsevierhealth.com. Ed. Lee P Shulman.

618.1 GBR ISSN 1476-220X
RG1
THE YEAR IN GYNAECOLOGY (YEAR). Text in English. 2001. a., latest 2003. USD 99.95 per issue in US & Canada; GBP 59.99 per issue elsewhere (effective 2009). 384 p./no.; back issues avail. **Document type:** *Journal, Academic/Scholarly.* **Description:** Aims to provide the external evidence from systematic research with individual clinical expertise to make effective decisions about patient treatment and care.
Related titles: Online - full text ed.
Indexed: P20, P22, P48, P54, PQC.
—**CCC.**
Published by: Clinical Publishing (Subsidiary of: Atlas Medical Publishing Ltd), Oxford Centre for Innovation, Mill St, Oxford, OX2 0JX, United Kingdom. TEL 44-1865-811116, FAX 44-1865-251550, info@clinicalpublishing.co.uk. Eds. J Barter, N Hampton. **Dist. by:** Marston Book Services Ltd., Unit 160, Milton Park, Abingdon, Oxfordshire OX14 4SD, United Kingdom. TEL 44-1235-465500, FAX 44-1235-465555, trade.orders@marston.co.uk, http://www.marston.co.uk/.

618.175 GBR ISSN 1742-3104
RG186
THE YEAR IN POST-MENOPAUSAL HEALTH (YEAR). Text in English. 2004 (Feb.). a. USD 99.95 per issue in US & Canada; GBP 59.99 per issue elsewhere (effective 2009). **Document type:** *Journal, Academic/Scholarly.* **Description:** Provides an overview of the advances in the treatment of conditions that can emerge post-menopause, including breast cancer, stroke, heart disease and arthritis.
Indexed: P20, P22, P48, P54, PQC.
—**CCC.**
Published by: Clinical Publishing (Subsidiary of: Atlas Medical Publishing Ltd), Oxford Centre for Innovation, Mill St, Oxford, OX2 0JX, United Kingdom. TEL 44-1865-811116, FAX 44-1865-251550, info@clinicalpublishing.co.uk. Eds. L G Keith, M Rees. **Dist. by:** Marston Book Services Ltd., Unit 160, Milton Park, Abingdon, Oxfordshire OX14 4SD, United Kingdom. TEL 44-1235-465500, FAX 44-1235-465555, trade.orders@marston.co.uk, http://www.marston.co.uk/.

618 GBR ISSN 1465-9255
RG1
YEARBOOK OF OBSTETRICS AND GYNAECOLOGY. Text in English. 1993. irreg., latest vol.12, 2007. GBP 48 per issue (effective 2009). back issues avail. **Document type:** *Yearbook, Academic/Scholarly.* **Description:** Features contributions from a large cross-section of clinical and scientific fields.
Formerly (until 1998): Royal College of Obstetricians and Gynaecologists. Yearbook (1351-4148)
—BLDSC (9414.648000), GNLM. **CCC.**
Published by: Royal College of Obstetricians and Gynaecologists, 27 Sussex Pl, Regent's Park, London, NW1 4RG, United Kingdom. TEL 44-20-77726200, FAX 44-20-77230575, publications@rcog.org.uk, http://www.rcog.org.uk/. Ed. Tim Hillard.

YOU AND YOUR FAMILY. *see* CHILDREN AND YOUTH—About

618 DEU ISSN 0948-2393
RG1 CODEN: ZGNEFR

➤ **ZEITSCHRIFT FUER GEBURTSHILFE UND NEONATOLOGIE.** Text in German; Summaries in English, German. 1877. bi-m. EUR 308 to institutions; EUR 424 combined subscription to institutions (print & online eds.); EUR 70 newsstand/cover (effective 2011). adv. bk.rev. charts; illus. index per vol. reprint service avail. from IRC. **Document type:** *Journal, Academic/Scholarly.*
Former titles (until 1995): Zeitschrift fuer Geburtshilfe und Perinatologie (0300-967X); (until 1972): Zeitschrift fuer Geburtshilfe und Gynaekologie (0044-278X); Which was formed by the merger of (1875-1877): Zeitschrift fuer Geburtshilfe und Frauenkrankheiten (0931-9697); (18??-1877): Beitraege zur Geburtshilfe und Gynaekologie
Related titles: Microfiche ed.: 1876 (from BHP); Online - full text ed.: ISSN 1439-1651. EUR 409 to institutions (effective 2011).
Indexed: A22, A36, ASCA, BDM&CN, CABA, ChemAb, D01, DentInd, E12, EMBASE, ExcerpMed, GH, IBR, IBZ, IndMed, Inpharma, MEDLINE, N02, N03, P30, P33, R10, R12, RM&VM, Reac, SCOPUS, T05.
—BLDSC (9462.452000), CASDDS, GNLM, IE, Infotrieve, Ingenta, INIST. **CCC.**
Published by: Georg Thieme Verlag, Ruedigerstr 14, Stuttgart, 70469, Germany. TEL 49-711-89310, 49-711-8931421, FAX 49-711-8931298, 49-711-8931410, leser.service@thieme.de. Ed. Stephan Schmidt. Adv. contact Ulrike Bradler. Circ: 1,900 (paid).

618.1 DEU ISSN 0044-4197
CODEN: ZEGYAX

➤ **ZENTRALBLATT FUER GYNAEKOLOGIE.** Text in German; Summaries in English. 1877. bi-m. EUR 235.80 domestic to institutions; EUR 245.80 in Europe to institutions; EUR 254.80 elsewhere to institutions; EUR 98 to students; EUR 40 newsstand/cover (effective 2007). adv. bk.rev. charts; illus. index. 75 p./no.; **Document type:** *Journal, Academic/Scholarly.* **Description:** Covers all areas of gynecology and obstetrics.
Related titles: Microfiche ed.: (from BHP); Online - full text ed.; ISSN 1438-9762.
Indexed: A20, A22, CIN, ChemAb, ChemTitl, DentInd, F09, G10, IndMed, P30, R10, Reac, S02, S03, SCOPUS, W09.
—CASDDS, GNLM, IE, Infotrieve, Ingenta, INIST. **CCC.**
Published by: Johann Ambrosius Barth Verlag in Medizinverlage Heidelberg GmbH & Co. KG, Ruedigerstr 14, Stuttgart, 70469, Germany. TEL 49-711-8931-0, FAX 49-711-8931422, kunden.service@thieme.de. Ed. M Kaufmann. Adv. contact Ulrike Bradler TEL 49-711-8931466. B&W page EUR 1,290, color page EUR 2,370; trim 180 x 256. Circ: 1,500 (paid).

➤ **ZHDU MALYSHA/EXPECTING A BABY.** *see* CHILDREN AND YOUTH—About

618 CHN ISSN 1673-3916
ZHONGGUO FUCHANKE LINCHUANG ZAZHI/CHINESE JOURNAL OF CLINICAL OBSTETRICS AND GYNECOLOGY. Text in Chinese. 2000. m.
Formerly (until 2003): Zhongguo Fuchanke Linchuang
Related titles: Online - full text ed.
Published by: Beijing Daxue Renmin Yiyuan/Peking University People's Hospital, 11, Xizhimen Nan Dajie, Beijing, 100044, China. TEL 86-10-88324270, FAX 86-10-88324179, http://www.phbjmu.edu.cn/.

618 CHN ISSN 1001-4411
ZHONGGUO FUYOU BAOJIAN/MATERNAL AND CHILD HEALTH CARE OF CHINA. Text in Chinese. 1982. s-a. USD 147.60 (effective 2009). **Document type:** *Journal, Academic/Scholarly.*
Related titles: Online - full text ed.
Indexed: A35, A36, B&BAb, B21, CABA, D01, E12, GH, H16, ImmunAb, N02, N03, OGFA, P32, P33, P39, R07, R08, R12, RA&MP, RM&VM, SoyAb, T05, VS, W10, W11.
—East View.
Published by: Zhongguo Fuyou Baojian Zazhishe, 971, Jianzheng Lu, Changchun, 130061, China. TEL 86-431-8929639, FAX 86-431-8967763.

ZHONGGUO SHENGYU JIANKANG ZAZHI/CHINESE JOURNAL FOR HEALTH OF WOMEN IN CHILDBIRTH. *see* BIRTH CONTROL

618 CHN ISSN 1005-2216

➤ **ZHONGGUO SHIYONG FUKE YU CHANKE ZAZHI/CHINESE JOURNAL OF PRACTICAL GYNECOLOGY AND OBSTETRICS.** Text in Chinese; Abstracts in English. 1985. m. USD 49.20 (effective 2009). adv. **Document type:** *Journal, Academic/Scholarly.* **Description:** Features new developments and methods of practical diagnosis, treatment, and prevention of gynecological and obstetrical diseases.
Formerly: Shiyong Fuke yu Chanke Zazhi - Journal of Practical Gynecology and Obstetrics (1001-0858)
Related titles: Online - full text ed.
Indexed: A35, A36, AgBio, CABA, D01, E12, GH, N02, N03, P33, P39, PN&I, R12, RA&MP, RM&VM, T05, VS, W11.
—BLDSC (3180.559800), East View.

Published by: Zhongguo Shiyong Yixue Zazhishe, 9, Nanjing Nan Jie, 5th Fl., Heping-qu, Shenyang, Liaoning 110001, China. TEL 86-24-23866489, FAX 86-24-23866481. Ed. Shu-Lan Zhang. adv.: page USD 1,500. Circ: 55,000.

➤ **ZHONGGUO YIXUE WENZHAI (JIHUA SHENGYU, FUCHAN KEXUE)/CHINA MEDICAL ABSTRACTS (BIRTH CONTROL AND GYNECOLOGY).** *see* MEDICAL SCIENCES—Abstracting, Bibliographies, Statistics

618 CHN ISSN 0529-567X
RG1 CODEN: CHFCA2
ZHONGHUA FUCHANKE ZAZHI/CHINESE JOURNAL OF OBSTETRICS AND GYNECOLOGY. Text in Chinese. 1953. m. USD 80.40 (effective 2009). back issues avail. **Document type:** *Journal, Academic/Scholarly.*
Related titles: CD-ROM ed.; Online - full text ed.
Indexed: A22, ChemAb, EMBASE, ExcerpMed, ExtraMED, IndMed, MEDLINE, P30, R10, Reac, SCOPUS.
—BLDSC (3180.440000), East View, IE, Infotrieve, Ingenta.
Published by: Zhonghua Yixuehui Zazhishe/Chinese Medical Association Publishing House, 42 Dongsi Xidajie, Beijing, 100710, China. http://www.medline.org.cn/. **Dist. by:** China International Book Trading Corp, 35 Chegongzhuang Xilu, Haidian District, PO Box 399, Beijing 100044, China. TEL 86-10-68412045, FAX 86-10-68412023, cibtc@mail.cibtc.com.cn, http://www.cibtc.com.cn.

ZHONGHUA NEIFENMI DAIXIE ZAZHI/CHINESE JOURNAL OF ENDOCRINOLOGY AND METABOLISM. *see* MEDICAL SCIENCES—Endocrinology

618 616.992 CHN ISSN 1674-0807
CODEN: ZRBZBZ
ZHONGHUA RUXIANBING ZAZHI (DIANZIBAN)/CHINESE JOURNAL OF BREAST DISEASE (ELECTRONIC VERSION). Text in Chinese. 1997. bi-m. CNY 228, USD 300; CNY 35 per issue (effective 2009). **Document type:** *Journal, Academic/Scholarly.* **Description:** Covers new technologies, surgical techniques, and disease related articles on domestic and foreign clinical practice and experience.
Media: CD-ROM.
Published by: Xinan Yiyuan/Southwest Hospital, 29, Gaotanyanzheng Jie, Shapingba-qu, Chongqing, 400038, China. TEL 86-23-68765277, FAX 86-23-65310689, http://www.swhospital.com/XNYYFore/default.aspx. Eds. Jun Jiang, Yan Sun. Circ: 3,200.

618.12 CHN ISSN 1007-9408
ZHONGHUA WEICHAN YIXUE ZAZHI/CHINESE JOURNAL OF PERINATAL MEDICINE. Text in Chinese. 1998. bi-m. **Document type:** *Journal, Academic/Scholarly.*
—BLDSC (9512.840050), East View.
Published by: Zhonghua Yixuehui/Chinese Medical Association, 1, Anmen Dajie, Beijing Yike Daxue, Fu-Er Yiyuan, Beijing, 100034, China. TEL 86-10-66171122 ext 3248, FAX 86-10-66513519.

618 618.92 RUS ISSN 1608-9650
9 MESYATSEV/9 MONTHS. Text in Russian. 2000. m. RUR 65 per issue (effective 2003). **Document type:** *Magazine, Consumer.*
Published by: Pressa Magazin, 1-ya Bukhvostova, dom 12/11, korp17, a/ya 14, Moscow, 107392, Russian Federation. TEL 7-095-9958080, FAX 7-095-9621177, info@9months.ru. Ed. Irina Zingerman. **Dist. by:** M K - Periodica, ul Gilyarovskogo 39, Moscow 129110, Russian Federation. TEL 7-095-2845008, FAX 7-095-2813798, info@periodicals.ru, http://www.mkniga.ru.

MEDICAL SCIENCES—Oncology

see also MEDICAL SCIENCES—Radiology And Nuclear Medicine

616.9 ESP ISSN 1133-3871
A E C C. Text in Spanish. 1993. q. free to members (effective 2008). **Document type:** *Bulletin, Consumer.* **Description:** Cover cancer issues and notices about association activities.
Published by: Asociacion Espanola Contra el Cancer, Amador de los Rios, 5, Madrid, 28010, Spain. TEL 34-91-3194138, FAX 34-91-3190966, http://www.aecc.es/. Ed. Lolina Perez Caballero. Circ: 20,000.

616.99 USA ISSN 0160-6344
A F I P ATLAS OF TUMOR PATHOLOGY. Text in English. 1949; N.S. 1990. irreg., latest 2007. price varies. back issues avail. **Document type:** *Monographic series, Academic/Scholarly.* **Description:** Reports on research in the treatment and management of various tumors.
Published by: (Armed Forces Institute of Pathology), American Registry of Pathology, 14th St & Alaska Ave, N W, Bldg 54, Washington, DC 20306. TEL 301-319-0093, FAX 301-319-0630, publications@arppress.org.

616.992 USA
A S C O ANNUAL MEETING PROCEEDINGS. Text in English. 1953. a. USD 80 per issue to non-members; free to members (effective 2009). **Document type:** *Proceedings, Trade.* **Description:** Contains all abstracts presented at the Annual Meeting and the titles and bylines of the abstracts.
Former titles (until 2004): American Society of Clinical Oncology. Meeting Proceedings; (until 2003): American Society of Clinical Oncology. Program / Proceedings (1081-0641); (until 1990): American Society of Clinical Oncology. Meeting Proceedings (0736-7589); Which superseded in part (in 1982): American Association for Cancer Research. Annual Meeting Proceedings (0197-016X); Which was formerly (until 1974): American Association for Cancer Research. Annual Meeting. Proceedings (0197-0151); (until 1971): American Association for Cancer Research. Proceedings (0569-2261)
Indexed: A22.
—BLDSC (6841.278200), IE, Ingenta, INIST. **CCC.**
Published by: American Society of Clinical Oncology, 2318 Mill Rd, Ste 800, Alexandria, VA 22314. TEL 571-483-1300, 888-282-2552, asco@asco.org.

616.992 USA ISSN 2155-2584
A S C O CONNECTION. Text in English. 19??. q. free to members (effective 2009). adv. back issues avail. **Document type:** *Magazine, Trade.* **Description:** Provides summaries of research from oncology-related meetings and the literature, including commentary on controversial issues by recognized experts in the field.
Former titles (until July 2010): A S C O News and Forum (1931-7646); (until 2006): A S C O News
Related titles: Online - full text ed.: ISSN 2155-2592.
Indexed: C06, C07, C08, CINAHL.
Published by: American Society of Clinical Oncology, 2318 Mill Rd, Ste 800, Alexandria, VA 22314. TEL 571-483-1300, 888-282-2552, FAX 571-366-9550, asco@asco.org, http://www.asco.org. Ed. Jonathan S Berek. Pub. Lisa Guttman Greaves.

616.992 USA ISSN 2154-3283
▼ **A S C O POST.** Variant title: ASCO Post. Text in English. 2010 (Aug.). m. **Document type:** *Newsletter, Trade.* **Description:** Reports on the latest news in clinical cancer research, patient care and policy, and includes timely commentary on the most important issues facing the field.
Related titles: Online - full text ed.: ISSN 2154-3291. 2010 (Aug.).
Published by: (American Society of Clinical Oncology), Harborside Press, 37 Main St, Cold Spring Harbor, NY 11724. TEL 631-692-0800, FAX 631-692-0805, info@harborsidepress.com, http://www.harborsidepress.com.

ACOUSTIC NEUROMA ASSOCIATION NOTES. *see* MEDICAL SCIENCES—Otorhinolaryngology

616.994 PER ISSN 1013-5545
ACTA CANCEROLOGICA. Text in Spanish; Summaries in English. 1960. s-a. adv. bibl.; charts; illus. **Document type:** *Journal, Academic/Scholarly.* **Description:** Covers the study and research of cancer.
Related titles: Online - full text ed.: ISSN 1810-8296.
Indexed: INIS AtomInd, P30.
Published by: Instituto de Enfermedades Neoplasicas, Ave. Angamos 2520, Lima, 34, Peru. TEL 51-1-7106900, spc@inen.sid.pe, http://www.inen.sid.pe. Ed. Dr. Juvenal Sanchez.

616.99 GBR ISSN 0284-186X
CODEN: ACTOEL
➤ **ACTA ONCOLOGICA.** Text in English. 1921. 8/yr. GBP 435, EUR 575, USD 720 combined subscription to institutions (print & online eds.); GBP 870, EUR 1,155, USD 1,440 combined subscription to corporations (print & online eds.) (effective 2010). adv. bk.rev. bibl.; illus. index, cum.index. reprint service avail. from PSC. **Document type:** *Journal, Academic/Scholarly.* **Description:** Focuses on all fields of clinical cancer research including cancer nursing and psychological and social aspects of cancer.
Former titles (until 1986): Acta Radiologica. Oncology (0349-652X); (until 1979): Acta Radiologica. Oncology, Radiation, Physics, Biology (0348-5196); (until 1977): Acta Radiologica. Therapy, Physics, Biology (0567-8064); Which superseded in part (in 1962): Acta Radiologica (0001-6926)
Related titles: Online - full text ed.: ISSN 1651-226X (from IngentaConnect); ◆ Supplement(s): Acta Oncologica. Supplement. ISSN 1100-1704.
Indexed: A01, A03, A08, A20, A22, ASCA, B&BAb, B19, B21, B25, BIOBASE, BIOSIS Prev, C06, C07, C08, CA, CINAHL, CTA, ChemAb, CurCont, DBA, DentInd, E01, EMBASE, ExcerpMed, GenetAb, IABS, IIL, INIS AtomInd, ISR, ImmunAb, IndMed, Inpharma, Inspec, MEDLINE, MS&D, MycolAb, NSA, OGFA, P30, P35, R10, Reac, SCI, SCOPUS, T02, W07.
—AskIEEE, CASDDS, GNLM, IE, Infotrieve, Ingenta, INIST. **CCC.**
Published by: (Acta Radiologica NOR), Informa Healthcare (Subsidiary of: T & F Informa plc), Telephone House, 69-77 Paul St, London, EC2A 4LQ, United Kingdom. TEL 44-20-70175000, healthcare.enquiries@informa.com, http://informahealthcare.com/, http://www.tandf.co.uk/journals/. Ed. Bengt Glimelius. Circ: 1,400. **Subscr. in N. America to:** Taylor & Francis Inc., Customer Services Dept, 325 Chestnut St, 8th Fl, Philadelphia, PA 19106. TEL 215-625-8900, 800-354-1420, FAX 215-625-2940, customerservice@taylorandfrancis.com; **Subscr. outside N. America to:** Taylor & Francis Ltd., Journals Customer Service, Sheepen Pl, Colchester, Essex CO3 3LP, United Kingdom. TEL 44-20-70175544, FAX 44-20-70175198, tf.enquiries@tfinforma.com.

616.99 BRA ISSN 0100-3127
ACTA ONCOLOGICA BRASILEIRA. Text in Portuguese. 1959. bi-m.
Formerly (until 1965): Boletim de Oncologia (0520-4038)
Indexed: INIS AtomInd.
Published by: Hospital do Cancer A C Camargo, Departamento de Oncologia Clinica, Rua Professor Antonio Prudente, 211 Bairro da Liberdade, Sao Paulo, Brazil.

616.99 SWE ISSN 1100-1704
CODEN: AOSPEZ
ACTA ONCOLOGICA. SUPPLEMENT. Text in Norwegian. 1988. irreg., latest vol.11, 1998. reprint service avail. from PSC. **Document type:** *Academic/Scholarly.*
Related titles: Online - full text ed.: ISSN 1651-2499; ◆ Supplement to: Acta Oncologica. ISSN 0284-186X.
Indexed: A01, A03, A08, INIS AtomInd, SCOPUS, T02.
—INIST. **CCC.**
Published by: Taylor & Francis A B (Subsidiary of: Taylor & Francis Group), PO Box 3255, Stockholm, 10365, Sweden. TEL 46-8-4408040, FAX 46-8-4408050.

ACUTE MYELOID LEUKEMIA RESEARCH TODAY. *see* MEDICAL SCIENCES—Hematology

616.992 USA ISSN 1946-0945
ADVANCED STUDIES IN ONCOLOGY. Variant title: J H A S I O. Johns Hopkins Advanced Studies in Oncology. Text in English. 2008. irreg.
Related titles: Online - full text ed.: ISSN 1946-0953.
Published by: Galen Publishing, LLC, 166 W Main St, PO Box 340, Somerville, NJ 08876. TEL 908-253-9001, FAX 908-253-9002, http://www.galenpublishing.com.

616.994 USA ISSN 0065-230X
RC267 CODEN: ACRSAJ
➤ **ADVANCES IN CANCER RESEARCH.** Text in English. 1953. irreg., latest vol.105, 2009. USD 156 per vol. (effective 2010). adv. back issues avail.; reprints avail. **Document type:** *Journal, Academic/Scholarly.*
Related titles: Online - full text ed.
Indexed: A22, AIDS&CR, ASCA, B21, BIOSIS Prev, CIN, ChemAb, ChemTitl, DBA, DentInd, EMBASE, ExcerpMed, IBR, IBZ, ISR, IndMed, MEDLINE, MycolAb, OGFA, P30, R10, Reac, SCI, SCOPUS, T02, Telegen, W07.
—BLDSC (0701.000000), CASDDS, GNLM, IE, Infotrieve, Ingenta, INIST, Linda Hall. **CCC.**
Published by: Academic Press (Subsidiary of: Elsevier Science & Technology), 3251 Riverport Ln, Maryland Heights, MO 63043. TEL 314-447-8010, FAX 314-447-8030, JournalCustomerService-usa@elsevier.com, http://www.elsevierdirect.com/imprint.jsp?iid=5. Eds. George F Vande Woude, George Klein. Adv. contact Tino DeCarlo TEL 212-633-3815.

➤ **ADVANCES IN GASTROINTESTINAL CANCERS.** *see* MEDICAL SCIENCES—Gastroenterology

616.992 USA ISSN 1529-4196
ADVANCES IN LUNG CANCER. Abbreviated title: A L C. Text in English. 1999. irreg. **Document type:** *Monographic series, Academic/Scholarly.*
—BLDSC (0709.322000).
Published by: Physicians' Education Resource, 3500 Maple Ave, Ste 700, Dallas, TX 75219. TEL 888-949-0045, FAX 214-367-3402, CustomerSupport@CancerLearning.com.

616.992 USA ISSN 2152-5129
▼ ➤ **ADVANCES IN LYMPHOMA, MYELOMA, AND LEUKEMIA.** Text in English. forthcoming 2011. bi-m. **Document type:** *Journal, Academic/Scholarly.*
Related titles: Online - full text ed.: ISSN 2152-5153. forthcoming 2011.
Published by: C I G Media Group, L.P., 3500 Maple Ave, Ste 750, Dallas, TX 75219. TEL 214-367-3348, FAX 214-367-3301, http://www.cigjournals.com/.

616.994 USA ISSN 1939-8468
ADVANCES IN PANCREATIC CANCER. Text in English. 2007. irreg. **Document type:** *Monographic series, Academic/Scholarly.*
Published by: Physicians' Education Resource, 3500 Maple Ave, Ste 700, Dallas, TX 75219. TEL 888-949-0045, FAX 214-367-3402, CustomerSupport@CancerLearning.com, http://www.cancerlearning.com.

AERZTE ZEITUNG FUER ONKOLOGEN - HAEMATOLOGEN. *see* MEDICAL SCIENCES—Hematology

616.992 DEU ISSN 1869-246X
AERZTLICHE PRAXIS. ONKOLOGIE. Text in German. 2008. 6/yr. adv. **Document type:** *Journal, Trade.*
Published by: Biermann Verlag GmbH, Otto-Hahn-Str 7, Cologne, 50997, Germany. TEL 49-2236-3760, FAX 49-2236-376999, info@biermann.net, http://www.biermann-verlag.de. Ed. Anke Anyadiegwu. Adv. contact Isabelle Becker. Circ: 7,800 (controlled).

616.992 DEU ISSN 1862-331X
AERZTLICHES JOURNAL REISE UND MEDIZIN ONKOLOGIE. Text in German. 2006. bi-m. EUR 21 (effective 2007). adv. **Document type:** *Journal, Trade.*
Published by: Otto Hoffmanns Verlag GmbH, Arnulfstr 10, Munich, 80335, Germany. TEL 49-89-5458450, FAX 49-89-54584530, info@ohv-online.de. adv.: B&W page EUR 2,250, color page EUR 3,300. Circ: 6,851 (paid and controlled).

AIBIAN, JIBIAN, TUBIAN/CARCINOGENESIS, TERATOGENESIS AND MUTAGENESIS. *see* ENVIRONMENTAL STUDIES

616.99 JPN ISSN 0916-068X
AICHI CANCER CENTER RESEARCH INSTITUTE. SCIENTIFIC REPORT. Text in English. 1968. biennial. free. **Document type:** *Government.* **Description:** Covers the scientific research activities conducted by the institute.
Formerly: Aichi Cancer Center Research Institute. Annual Report (0374-5295)
Related titles: Online - full content ed.
—GNLM.
Published by: Aichi Cancer Center Research Institute, 1-1 Kanokoden, Chikusa.ku, Nagoya, 464-8681, Japan. TEL 81-52-7626111, http://www.pref.aichi.jp/cancer-center/. Ed. Akio Matsukaga. Circ: 1,000.

616.99 CHN ISSN 1000-467X
RC261.A1 CODEN: AIZHENG
AIZHENG/CHINESE JOURNAL OF CANCER. Text in Chinese; Abstracts in English. 1982. m. USD 74.40 (effective 2009). **Document type:** *Journal, Academic/Scholarly.*
Related titles: Online - full text ed.; ◆ English ed.: Chinese Journal of Cancer. ISSN 1944-446X.
Indexed: EMBASE, ExcerpMed, P30, R10, Reac, SCOPUS.
—BLDSC (3180.297500), East View.
Published by: Zhongshan Yike Daxue, Zhongliuzhi Zhongxin, 651, Dongfeng Dong Lu, Guangzhou, 510060, China. TEL 86-20-87343065, FAX 86-20-87343336. Ed. Yixin Ceng. **Dist. by:** China International Book Trading Corp, 35 Chegongzhuang Xilu, Haidian District, PO Box 399, Beijing 100044, China. TEL 86-10-68412045, FAX 86-10-68412023, cibtc@mail.cibtc.com.cn, http://www.cibtc.com.cn. **Co-sponsor:** Shijie Weisheng Zuzhi Yanzheng Yanjiu Hezuo Zhongxin.

616.992 CHN ISSN 1672-1535
AIZHENG JINZHAN/ONCOLOGY PROGRESS. Text in Chinese. 2003. bi-m. **Document type:** *Journal, Academic/Scholarly.*
Related titles: Online - full text ed.
Published by: Zhongguo Xiehe Yike Daxue Chubanshe/Peking Union Medical College Press, 9, Dongdan 3-tiao, Beijing, 100730, China. TEL 86-10-65260426, FAX 86-10-65260426, pumcp@sohu.com.

AIZHENG KANGFU/CANCER REHABILITATION. *see* MEDICAL SCIENCES—Physical Medicine And Rehabilitation

616.99 DEU ISSN 0174-2744
CODEN: AKONFG
➤ **AKTUELLE ONKOLOGIE.** Text in German. 1981. irreg., latest vol.122, 2004. price varies. **Document type:** *Monographic series, Academic/Scholarly.*
Related titles: Online - full text ed.
—BLDSC (0785.778000), CASDDS. **CCC.**
Published by: W. Zuckschwerdt Verlag GmbH, Industriestr 1, Germering, 82110, Germany. TEL 49-89-8943490, FAX 49-89-89434950, post@zuckschwerdtverlag.de, http://www.zuckschwerdtverlag.de. Eds. G Jakse, H Borchers.

616.994 CAN ISSN 0839-8135
ALBERTA CANCER BOARD. ANNUAL REPORT. Text in English. 1983. a. **Document type:** *Corporate.*
Published by: Alberta Cancer Board, Provincial Office, Ste 1220, Standard Life Centre, 10405 Jasper Ave, Edmonton, AB T5J 3N4, Canada. TEL 780-412-6300, FAX 780-412-6326, info@cancerboard.ab.ca, http://www.cancerboard.ab.ca.

ALBERTA CANCER BOARD. BUSINESS PLAN. *see* BUSINESS AND ECONOMICS

616.99 USA ISSN 0197-016X
RC267

➤ **AMERICAN ASSOCIATION FOR CANCER RESEARCH. PROCEEDINGS OF THE ANNUAL MEETING.** Text in English. 1953. a. adv. **Document type:** *Proceedings, Academic/Scholarly.* **Description:** Publishes papers on original research presented at the annual meeting.
Former titles (until 1974): Annual Meeting of the American Association for Cancer Research. Proceedings (0197-0151); (until 1971): American Association for Cancer Research. Proceedings (0569-2261)
Indexed: A22, BIOSIS Prev, DBA, MycolAb.
—GNLM, IE, Infotrieve, Ingenta, INIST. **CCC.**
Published by: American Association for Cancer Research, 615 Chestnut St, 17th Fl, Philadelphia, PA 19106. TEL 215-440-9300, 866-423-3965, FAX 215-440-9313, aacr@aacr.org, http://www.aacr.org.

616.994 USA ISSN 0190-5147
RC261

AMERICAN CANCER SOCIETY. ANNUAL REPORT (ONLINE). Text in English. 19??. a. free (effective 2009). **Document type:** *Report, Trade.*
Formerly: American Cancer Society. Annual Report (Print)
Media: Online - full text.
Published by: American Cancer Society, Inc., 1599 Clifton Rd, N E, Atlanta, GA 30329. TEL 404-320-3333, 800-227-2345.

616.99 USA ISSN 1044-4580

AMERICAN INSTITUTE FOR CANCER RESEARCH. NEWSLETTER; on diet, nutrition and cancer prevention. Variant title: A I C R Newsletter. Text in English. 1983. q. looseleaf. free (effective 2009). charts; illus. 12 p./no.; back issues avail. **Document type:** *Newsletter, Consumer.* **Description:** Explains current cancer research as well as features recipes and menu ideas for healthy eating and practical advice to lower cancer risk.
Related titles: Online - full text ed.
Indexed: A26, C06, C07, C08, CHNI, CINAHL, H11, H12, I05.
Published by: American Institute for Cancer Research (A I C R), 1759 R St, NW, Washington, DC 20009. TEL 202-328-7744, 800-843-8114, FAX 202-328-7226, aicrweb@aicr.org. Ed. Catherine Wolz.

616.992 USA ISSN 2156-6976

▼ ➤ **AMERICAN JOURNAL OF CANCER RESEARCH.** Text in English. 2011. irreg. free (effective 2011). **Document type:** *Journal, Academic/Scholarly.*
Media: Online - full text.
Published by: E-Century Publishing Corporation, 40 White Oaks Ln, Madison, WI 53711. TEL 608-230-6435, FAX 608-230-6435, info@e-century.org, http://www.e-century.org/. Ed. Joseph H Antin.

616.99 USA ISSN 0277-3732
RC270.8 CODEN: AJCODI

➤ **AMERICAN JOURNAL OF CLINICAL ONCOLOGY.** Abbreviated title: A J C O. Text in English. 1978. bi-m. USD 949 domestic to institutions; USD 1,161 foreign to institutions (effective 2011). adv. bk.rev. charts; illus. index. back issues avail.; reprints avail. **Document type:** *Journal, Academic/Scholarly.* **Description:** Designed for cancer surgeons, radiation oncologists, medical oncologists, GYN oncologists, and pediatric oncologists.
Formerly (until 1982): Cancer Clinical Trials (0190-1206)
Related titles: Microform ed.; Online - full text ed.: ISSN 1537-453X. USD 577.20 domestic academic site license; USD 651.20 foreign academic site license; USD 643.80 domestic corporate site license; USD 717.80 foreign corporate site license (effective 2002).
Indexed: A22, ASCA, B25, BIOBASE, BIOSIS Prev, CIS, ChemAb, CurCont, DBA, DentInd, EMBASE, ExcerpMed, IABS, IDIS, ISR, IndMed, Inpharma, MEDLINE, MS&D, MycolAb, NRN, P30, P35, R10, Reac, SCI, SCOPUS, THA, Telegen, W07.
—BLDSC (0823.500000), CASDDS, GNLM, IE, Infotrieve, Ingenta, INIST. **CCC.**
Published by: Lippincott Williams & Wilkins (Subsidiary of: Wolters Kluwer N.V.), Two Commerce Sq, 2001 Market St, Philadelphia, PA 19103. TEL 215-521-8300, FAX 215-521-8902, customerservice@lww.com, http://www.lww.com. Ed. David E Wazer. Pub. David Myers. Adv. contact Joe Schuldner TEL 212-904-0377. Circ: 983.

616.99 USA ISSN 1939-6163
RC261.A1

➤ **THE AMERICAN JOURNAL OF HEMATOLOGY/ONCOLOGY.** Abbreviated title: A J H O. Text in English. 2002. m. back issues avail. **Document type:** *Journal, Trade.* **Description:** Designed for oncologists, hematology-oncologists and sub-specialists. Offers practical, clinical guidance and wide variety of continuing education opportunities.
Formerly (until 2006): The American Journal of Oncology Review (1542-9520)
Related titles: Online - full text ed.
Indexed: A26, C06, C07, C08, CA, CINAHL, EMBASE, ExcerpMed, H11, H12, I05, P20, P48, P50, P54, PQC, R10, Reac, SCOPUS, T02.
—BLDSC (0824.810000), IE, Ingenta. **CCC.**
Published by: Haymarket Media Inc. (Subsidiary of: Haymarket Group Ltd.), 114 W 26th St, 4th Fl, New York, NY 10001. TEL 646-638-6000, custserv@haymarketmedia.com, http://www.haymarket.com. Ed. Sara Elan TEL 212-755-4296 ext 404. Pub. Charles Benaiah TEL 212-755-4296 ext 212.

616.992 USA ISSN 1934-2233
R712.A1

AMERICA'S TOP DOCTORS FOR CANCER. Text in English. 2005. irreg. (3rd ed). USD 29.95 per issue softcover; USD 79.95 per issue hardcover (effective 2008). **Document type:** *Directory, Consumer.*
Published by: Castle Connolly Medical Ltd., 42 W 24th St., 2nd Flr, New York, NY 10010. TEL 212-367-8400, FAX 212-367-0964.

616.99 NLD ISSN 0969-6970
QP106.6 CODEN: AGIOFT

➤ **ANGIOGENESIS.** Text in English. 1997. q. EUR 537, USD 544 combined subscription to institutions (print & online eds.) (effective 2012). adv. reprint service avail. from PSC. **Document type:** *Journal, Academic/Scholarly.* **Description:** Encourages active research toward the development of practical therapies aimed at angiogenic diseases.
Incorporates (1998-1999): Angiogenesis Research (1386-2049)
Related titles: Online - full text ed.: ISSN 1573-7209 (from IngentaConnect).
Indexed: A22, A26, B&BAb, B19, B21, B25, BIOBASE, BIOSIS Prev, BibLing, CA, CurCont, E01, E08, EMBASE, ExcerpMed, I05, IABS, IndMed, M&PBA, MEDLINE, MycolAb, P20, P22, P30, P48, P54, PQC, R10, Reac, S09, SCI, SCOPUS, T02, W07.
—BLDSC (0902.630000), CASDDS, IE, Infotrieve, Ingenta, INIST. **CCC.**
Published by: Springer Netherlands (Subsidiary of: Springer Science+Business Media), Van Godewijckstraat 30, Dordrecht, 3311 GX, Netherlands. TEL 31-78-6576050, FAX 31-78-6576474, http://www.springer.com. Eds. Arjan Griffioen, Joyce Bischoff.

616.992 JPN ISSN 1344-6835
RC261.A1 CODEN: ACRTCO

ANNALS OF CANCER RESEARCH AND THERAPY. Text in English. 1992. s-a. back issues avail. **Document type:** *Journal, Academic/Scholarly.*
Related titles: Online - full text ed.: ISSN 1880-5469. 2005.
Indexed: B21, EMBASE, ExcerpMed, OGFA, R10, Reac, SCOPUS.
—IE, Ingenta. **CCC.**
Published by: Japanese Society of Strategies for Cancer Research and Therapy, Gastroenterological Surgery, Tokai University School of Medicine, Ogose Kiyouzi Shimoiti, Isehara, Kanagawa, 259-1193, Japan. TEL 81-463-966163, FAX 81-463-964120, info@q-life.org, http://q-life.org/jsct/. Ed. Kenji Ogawa TEL 81-3-38101111.

616.99 GBR ISSN 0923-7534
RC254.A1 CODEN: ANONE2

➤ **ANNALS OF ONCOLOGY.** Text in English. 1990. m. GBP 1,152 in United Kingdom to institutions; EUR 1,728 in Europe to institutions; USD 2,303 in US & Canada to institutions; GBP 1,152 elsewhere to institutions; GBP 1,256 combined subscription in United Kingdom to institutions (print & online eds.); EUR 1,885 combined subscription in Europe to institutions (print & online eds.); USD 2,513 combined subscription in US & Canada to institutions (print & online eds.); GBP 1,256 combined subscription elsewhere to institutions (print & online eds.) (effective 2012). adv. bk.rev. back issues avail.; reprint service avail. from PSC. **Document type:** *Journal, Academic/Scholarly.* **Description:** Publishes research in medical oncology, surgery, radiotherapy, pediatric oncology, basic research, and the comprehensive management of patients with malignant diseases.
Related titles: Microform ed.: (from PQC); Online - full text ed.: ISSN 1569-8041. GBP 1,006 in United Kingdom to institutions; EUR 1,510 in Europe to institutions; USD 2,013 in US & Canada to institutions; GBP 1,006 elsewhere to institutions (effective 2012) (from IngentaConnect); ◆ Spanish ed.: Annals of Oncology (Spanish Edition). ISSN 1132-0109; Supplement(s): Annals of Oncology. Supplement. ISSN 1572-610X.
Indexed: A01, A03, A08, A22, A36, AIDS Ab, ASCA, B21, BA, BIOBASE, CA, CABA, CurCont, E01, E12, EMBASE, ExcerpMed, F08, FR, GH, H16, H17, IABS, IDIS, INI, ISR, IndMed, Inpharma, MEDLINE, N02, N03, NRN, OGFA, P20, P22, P30, P33, P35, P38, P39, P48, P54, PQC, R08, R10, R12, RA&MP, RM&VM, Reac, S12, SCI, SCOPUS, T02, T05, W07, W11.
—BLDSC (1043.320000), GNLM, IE, Infotrieve, Ingenta, INIST. **CCC.**
Published by: (European Society for Medical Oncology CHE), Oxford University Press, Great Clarendon St, Oxford, OX2 6DP, United Kingdom. TEL 44-1865-556767, FAX 44-1865-556646, enquiry@oup.co.uk, http://www.oxfordjournals.org. Eds. David J Kerr, J B Vermorken TEL 44-3238-213375. adv.: B&W page GBP 1,400, B&W page USD 2,225, color page GBP 1,720, color page USD 2,720; trim 216 x 280. Circ: 4,345. **Co-sponsor:** Japanese Society of Medical Oncology.

616.99 ESP ISSN 1132-0109

ANNALS OF ONCOLOGY (SPANISH EDITION). Text in Spanish. 1992. bi-m. EUR 75 (effective 2005). back issues avail. **Document type:** *Journal, Academic/Scholarly.*
Related titles: ◆ English ed.: Annals of Oncology. ISSN 0923-7534.
Published by: Grupo Saned, Capitan Haya 60, 1o, Madrid, 28028, Spain. TEL 34-91-7499500, FAX 34-91-7499501, saned@medynet.com, http://www.gruposaned.com. Ed. Jordi Estape. Circ: 2,000.

ANNALS OF SURGICAL ONCOLOGY. *see* MEDICAL SCIENCES—Surgery

616.99 GBR ISSN 0348-8799
RG1

ANNUAL REPORT ON THE RESULTS OF TREATMENT IN GYNECOLOGICAL CANCER. Variant title: Annual Report Gynecological Cancer F I G O. Text in English. 1937. triennial. charts. back issues avail. **Document type:** *Monographic series, Academic/Scholarly.* **Description:** Contains report on the results of treatment in Gynecologic Cancer.
Former titles (until 1979): Annual Report on the Results of Treatment in Carcinoma of the Uterus, Vagina and Ovary (0346-7503); (until 1973): Annual Report on the Results of Treatment in Carcinoma of the Uterus and Vagina (0349-3164); (until 1964): Annual Report on the Results of Treatment in Carcinoma of the Uterus (0349-3156); (until 1953): Annual Report on the Results of Radiotherapy in Carcinoma of the Uterine Cervit
—GNLM.
Published by: International Federation of Gynaecology and Obstetrics, FIGO Secretariat, FIGO House, Ste 3, Waterloo Ct, 10 Theed St, London, SE1 8ST, United Kingdom. TEL 44-20-79281166, FAX 44-20-79287099, figo@figo.org.

616.994 NLD ISSN 1871-5206
RS431.A64 CODEN: AAMCE4

➤ **ANTI-CANCER AGENTS IN MEDICINAL CHEMISTRY.** Variant title: Anti-Cancer Agents. Text in English. 2001 (May). 10/yr. USD 1,990 combined subscription to institutions (print or online ed.) (effective 2012). adv. back issues avail.; reprints avail. **Document type:** *Journal, Academic/Scholarly.* **Description:** Aims to cover all the latest and outstanding developments in medicinal chemistry and rational drug design for the discovery of new anti-cancer agents.
Formerly (until 2006): Current Medicinal Chemistry. Anti-Cancer Agents (1568-0118)
Related titles: Online - full text ed.: ISSN 1875-5992 (from IngentaConnect).
Indexed: A01, A03, A08, AIDS&CR, B&BAb, B19, B21, BIOSIS Prev, BioEngAb, C33, CA, ChemAb, EMBASE, ESPM, ExcerpMed, M&PBA, MEDLINE, MycolAb, NucAcAb, OGFA, P30, R10, Reac, SCI, SCOPUS, T02, ToxAb, W07.
—BLDSC (1547.286000), IE, Infotrieve, Ingenta. **CCC.**
Published by: Bentham Science Publishers Ltd., PO Box 294, Bussum, 1400 AG, Netherlands. TEL 31-35-6923800, FAX 31-35-6980150, sales@bentham.org. Eds. Peter M Fischer, Sean Michael Kerwin, Michelle Prudhomme TEL 33-4-73407124. **Subscr. addr. in the US:** Bentham Science Publishers Ltd., c/o Richard E Morrissy, PO Box 446, Oak Park, IL 60301. TEL 312-413-5867, FAX 312-996-7107, subscriptions@bentham.org.

616.99 USA ISSN 0959-4973
RS431.A64 CODEN: ANTDEV

➤ **ANTI-CANCER DRUGS.** Text in English. 1990. 10/yr. USD 2,692 domestic to institutions; USD 2,841 foreign to institutions (effective 2011). adv. bk.rev. back issues avail.; reprints avail. **Document type:** *Journal, Academic/Scholarly.* **Description:** Aims to stimulate and report research on both toxic and non-toxic anti-cancer agents.
Related titles: CD-ROM ed.; Online - full text ed.: ISSN 1473-5741. USD 1,825 domestic academic site license; USD 1,825 foreign academic site license; USD 2,035.80 domestic corporate site license; USD 2,035.80 foreign corporate site license (effective 2002).
Indexed: A22, A35, A36, ASCA, AgBio, B&BAb, B19, B21, B25, BIOBASE, BIOSIS Prev, BP, BioEngAb, C30, C33, CABA, CIN, ChemAb, ChemTitl, CurCont, E01, E12, EMBASE, ESPM, ExcerpMed, F08, F11, F12, GH, H16, IABS, INI, ISR, IndMed, Inpharma, M&PBA, MEDLINE, MycolAb, N02, N03, NucAcAb, P30, P33, P35, P39, PGrRegA, PN&I, R10, R13, RA&MP, RM&VM, Reac, SCI, SCOPUS, SoyAb, T05, ToxAb, VS, ViroIAbstr, W07.
—BLDSC (1547.287300), CASDDS, GNLM, IE, Infotrieve, Ingenta, INIST. **CCC.**
Published by: (Netherlands Cancer Institute NLD), Lippincott Williams & Wilkins (Subsidiary of: Wolters Kluwer N.V.), 530 Walnut St, Philadelphia, PA 19106. TEL 215-521-8300, FAX 215-521-8902, customerservice@lww.com, http://www.lww.com. Ed. Dr. Mels Sluyser TEL 31-35-5259943. Pub. Phil Daly. Circ: 141.

616.99 GRC ISSN 0250-7005
RC261.A1 CODEN: ANTRD4

➤ **ANTICANCER RESEARCH**; international journal of cancer research and treatment. Text and summaries in English. 1981. bi-m. EUR 740 in Europe to individuals; EUR 800 elsewhere to individuals; EUR 1,530 in Europe to institutions; EUR 1,630 elsewhere to institutions (effective 2005). adv. bk.rev. index. back issues avail.; reprints avail. **Document type:** *Journal, Academic/Scholarly.* **Description:** Contains high-quality works on all aspects of experimental and clinical cancer research.
Related titles: Online - full text ed.: ISSN 1791-7530.
Indexed: A22, A34, A35, A36, A38, AIDS Ab, AIDS&CR, ASCA, AgBio, AgrForAb, B&BAb, B19, B21, B25, BIOBASE, BIOSIS Prev, BP, BioEngAb, BioIDig, C30, CABA, CIN, CTD, ChemAb, ChemTitl, CurCont, D01, E12, EMBASE, ESPM, ExcerpMed, F08, F11, F12, G10, GH, GenetAb, H16, H17, IABS, IBR, IBZ, ISR, IndMed, IndVet, Inpharma, M&PBA, MEDLINE, MycolAb, N02, N03, NRN, OGFA, P30, P32, P33, P35, P39, P40, PGegResA, R07, R08, R11, R13, RA&MP, RM&VM, RefZh, S17, SCI, SCOPUS, SoyAb, T05, THA, Telegen, ToxAb, VITIS, VS, W07, W10.
—BLDSC (1547.290000), CASDDS, GNLM, IE, Infotrieve, Ingenta, INIST. **CCC.**
Published by: International Institute of Anticancer Research, 1st km Kapandritiou-Kalamou Rd, PO Box 22, Kapandriti Attica, Attiki 190 14, Greece. TEL 30-22950-52945, FAX 30-22950-53389, http://www.iiar-anticancer.org. Ed., Pub., R&P, Adv. contact Dr. John G Delinassios. B&W page EUR 700; 173 x 230. Circ: 1,400.

➤ **ANTIMICROBIAL AGENTS AND CHEMOTHERAPY.** *see* BIOLOGY—Microbiology

616.99 SRB ISSN 0354-7310

➤ **ARCHIVE OF ONCOLOGY.** Text in English. 1993. q. adv. bk.rev. 72 p./no. 2 cols./p.; **Document type:** *Journal, Academic/Scholarly.* **Description:** Original articles, actual problems, review articles, case reports, brief communications (short reports), letters to the editor, news, books received, book reviews, congress reports, calendar of medical and scientific meetings, ONCONET, editorials.
Formerly: Onkoloski Arhiv (0354-2351)
Related titles: Online - full text ed.: ISSN 1450-9520. 2000. free (effective 2011); ◆ Supplement(s): Archive of Oncology. Supplement. ISSN 0354-8139.
Indexed: A01, CA, EMBASE, ExcerpMed, R10, Reac, SCOPUS, T02.
—BLDSC (1638.438000), IE, Ingenta.
Published by: Institut za Onkologiju/Institute of Oncology, Institutski put 4, Sremska Kamenica, 21204. TEL 381-21-611061, FAX 381-21-613714, onkons@eunet.yu, http://www.onk.ns.ac.yu. Ed. Vladimir V Baltic.

616.99 SRB ISSN 0354-8139

➤ **ARCHIVE OF ONCOLOGY. SUPPLEMENT.** Text in English. 1995. a. free with subscr. to Archive of Oncology. adv. back issues avail. **Document type:** *Report, Academic/Scholarly.* **Description:** Presents abstracts, sometimes combined with original articles, as well as actual cases, problems, review articles, and short reports.
Related titles: ◆ Supplement to: Archive of Oncology. ISSN 0354-7310.
Published by: Institut za Onkologiju/Institute of Oncology, Institutski put 4, Sremska Kamenica, 21204. TEL 381-21-611061, FAX 381-21-613714, baltic@uns.ns.ac.yu. Ed. Vladimir V Baltic. R&P, Adv. contact Ljiljana Zegarac TEL 381-21-615711 ext 316. Circ: 200.

616.99 BRA ISSN 0365-6268

ARQUIVOS DE ONCOLOGIA. Text in Portuguese, English. 1956. irreg. **Document type:** *Monographic series, Academic/Scholarly.*
Indexed: P30.
Published by: Liga Bahiaana Contra o Cancer, Hospital Aristides Maltez, Ave D. Joao Vi, 332, Brotas, Salvador de Bahia, Brazil.

616.992 GBR ISSN 1743-7555
RC254.A1
➤ **ASIA PACIFIC JOURNAL OF CLINICAL ONCOLOGY.** Variant title: Asia-Pacific Journal of Clinical Oncology. Text in English. 2004. q. GBP 374 in United Kingdom to institutions; EUR 475 in Europe to institutions; USD 606 in the Americas to institutions; USD 733 elsewhere to institutions; GBP 430 combined subscription in United Kingdom to institutions (print & online eds.); EUR 547 combined subscription in Europe to institutions (print & online eds.); USD 697 combined subscription in the Americas to institutions (print & online eds.); USD 843 combined subscription elsewhere to institutions (print & online eds.) (effective 2012). adv. back issues avail.; reprint service avail. from PSC. **Document type:** *Journal, Academic/Scholarly.* **Description:** Covers pre-clinical studies, translational research, clinical trials and epidemiological studies, describing new findings of clinical significance.
Related titles: Online - full text ed.: ISSN 1743-7563. GBP 374 in United Kingdom to institutions; EUR 475 in Europe to institutions; USD 606 in the Americas to institutions; USD 733 elsewhere to institutions (effective 2012) (from IngentaConnect).
Indexed: A01, A22, A26, B21, CA, E01, EMBASE, ExcerpMed, I05, MEDLINE, OGFA, P30, R10, Reac, SCI, SCOPUS, T02, W07.
—BLDSC (1742.260681), IE, Ingenta. **CCC.**
Published by: Wiley-Blackwell Publishing Ltd. (Subsidiary of: John Wiley & Sons, Inc.), 9600 Garsington Rd, Oxford, OX4 2DQ, United Kingdom. TEL 44-1865-776868, FAX 44-1865-714591, customerservices@blackwellpublishing.com. Eds. Alex Chang, Atsushi Ohtsu, Stephen Ackland.

616.992 616.15 GBR ISSN 1759-6637
▼ ➤ **ASIA PACIFIC JOURNAL OF ONCOLOGY & HEMATOLOGY.** Text in English. 2009 (Mar.). q. free. back issues avail.; reprints avail. **Document type:** *Journal, Academic/Scholarly.*
Related titles: Online - full text ed.: ISSN 1759-6645.
Indexed: A01, P20, P48, P54, PQC, T02.
Published by: San Lucas Medical Ltd., 11-12 Freetrade House, Lowther Rd, Stanmore, Middlesex HA7 1EP, United Kingdom. TEL 44-201-7938581, http://www.slm-oncology.com/. Ed. Jim Jones. Pub. John Gault. Circ: 14,106.

616.992 616.15 GBR ISSN 2040-5936
▼ ➤ **ASIA-PACIFIC ONCOLOGY AND HAEMATOLOGY.** Text in English. 2009. a. EUR 180, USD 225 to institutions (effective 2011). adv. illus. back issues avail.; reprints avail. **Document type:** *Journal, Academic/Scholarly.* **Description:** Contains review articles, case reports, practice guides, theoretical discussions, and original research; and features balanced and comprehensive articles written by leading authorities, addressing the most important and salient developments in the field of oncology and haematology.
Related titles: Online - full text ed.
Published by: Touch Briefings (Subsidiary of: Touch Group plc), Saffron House, 6-10 Kirby St, London, EC1N 8TS, United Kingdom. TEL 44-20-74525600, FAX 44-20-74525606, info@touchbriefings.com, http://www.touchbriefings.com/. Ed. Jonathan McKenna. Pub., Adv. contact Fergus Brunning. Circ: 10,000 (controlled).

616.992 THA ISSN 1513-7368
RC268
ASIAN PACIFIC JOURNAL OF CANCER PREVENTION. Text in English. 2001. bi-m. **Document type:** *Journal, Academic/Scholarly.* **Description:** Aims to promote an increased awareness in all areas of cancer prevention and to stimulate research and practical intervention approaches.
Related titles: Online - full text ed.: free (effective 2011).
Indexed: EMBASE, ExcerpMed, MEDLINE, P30, R10, Reac, SCI, SCOPUS, W07.
—BLDSC (1742.705270), IE, Ingenta. **CCC.**
Published by: Asian Pacific Organization for Cancer Prevention, c/o Malcolm A Moore, 268/1 Rama 6 Rd., Rajchathewee, Bangkok, 10400, Thailand. TEL 66-1-8097664, FAX 66-2-9559986, http://www.apocp.org/. Ed. Malcolm A. Moore.

616.9 ESP
ASOCIACION ESPANOLA CONTRA EL CANCER. MEMORIA. Text in Spanish. 1958. a. free. charts; stat. **Document type:** *Monographic series, Academic/Scholarly.*
Former titles: Asociacion Espanola Contra el Cancer. Memoria Tecnico-Administrativa; Asociacion Espanola Contra el Cancer. Memoria de la Asamblea General (0066-8540)
Published by: Asociacion Espanola Contra el Cancer, Amador de los Rios, 5, Madrid, 28010, Spain. TEL 34-1-3194138, FAX 34-1-3190966.

616.992 ITA ISSN 1121-936X
ATTUALITA IN SENOLOGIA. Text in Multiple languages. 1992. 3/yr. EUR 50 (effective 2009). **Document type:** *Journal, Academic/Scholarly.*
Published by: (Scuola Italiana di Senologia), Scientific Press, Viale G Matteotti 7, Florence, 50121, Italy. TEL 39-055-50351, FAX 39-055-5001912, http://www.oic.it.

616.99 USA ISSN 1350-9667
AUDIO JOURNAL OF ONCOLOGY. Text in English. 1995. bi-w. USD 9.99 per issue (effective 2009). adv. reprints avail. **Document type:** *Magazine, Trade.* **Description:** Features interviews about recent advances in cancer therapy and leading cancer conferences.
Media: CD-ROM. **Related titles:** Audio cassette/tape ed.: USD 6.99 per issue (effective 2009).
—**CCC.**
Published by: American Society of Clinical Oncology, 2318 Mill Rd, Ste 800, Alexandria, VA 22314. TEL 571-483-1300, 888-282-2552, asco@asco.org, http://www.asco.org.

616.99021 AUS
AUSTRALIA. BUREAU OF STATISTICS. CANCER IN AUSTRALIA. Text in English. 1996. a., latest 2001. **Document type:** *Government.* **Description:** Present comprehensive national data on cancer incidence and mortality and summary data on cancer screening, the cancer workforce and cancer expenditure in Australia.
Published by: Australian Bureau of Statistics, Locked Bag 10, Belconnen, ACT 2616, Australia. TEL 61-2-92684909, 61-2-62527037, 300-135-070, FAX 61-2-62528103, client.services@abs.gov.au.

AUSTRALIA. BUREAU OF STATISTICS. NATIONAL HEALTH SURVEY: CANCER SCREENING, AUSTRALIA (ONLINE). see MEDICAL SCIENCES—Abstracting, Bibliographies, Statistics

616.994 NLD ISSN 0304-419X
CODEN: BBACEU
➤ **B B A - REVIEWS ON CANCER.** Text in Dutch. 1963. 4/yr. EUR 1,241 in Europe to institutions; JPY 164,300 in Japan to institutions; USD 1,388 elsewhere to institutions (effective 2012). reprints avail. **Document type:** *Journal, Academic/Scholarly.* **Description:** Presents critical reviews on new developments in cancer investigation at the biochemical level.
Supersedes in part (in 1974): Biochimica et Biophysica Acta: N. Nucleic Acids and Protein Synthesis (0005-2787); Which was formerly (until 1965): Biochimical et Biophysica Acta. Specialized Section on Nucleic Acids and Related Subjects (0926-6550)
Related titles: Microform ed.: (from PQC); Online - full text ed.: (from IngentaConnect, ScienceDirect); ◆ Series of: Biochimica et Biophysica Acta. ISSN 0006-3002.
Indexed: A01, A03, A08, A22, A26, ASCA, B25, B27, BIOBASE, BIOSIS Prev, C33, CA, CurCont, DBA, EMBASE, ExcerpMed, FS&TA, I05, IABS, ISR, Inpharma, MycolAb, SCI, SCOPUS, T02, W07.
—GNLM, IE, Ingenta, INIST. **CCC.**
Published by: Elsevier BV (Subsidiary of: Elsevier Science & Technology), Radarweg 29, PO Box 211, Amsterdam, 1000 AE, Netherlands. TEL 31-20-4853911, FAX 31-20-4852457, JournalsCustomerServiceEMEA@elsevier.com, http://www.elsevier.nl.

616.992 FRA ISSN 1969-8771
▼ **B.COM BACLESSE.** Text in French. 2010. q. **Document type:** *Newsletter, Consumer.*
Published by: Centre Francois Baclesse, 3 Av General Harris, BP 5026, Caen Cedex 5, 14076, France. TEL 33-2-31455050, cfbcaen@baclesse.fr, http://www.baclesse.fr.

616.994 GBR ISSN 0007-0920
RC261.A1 CODEN: BJCAAI
➤ **B J C.** (British Journal of Cancer) Text in English. 1947. 24/yr. EUR 2,200 in Europe to institutions; USD 2,357 in the Americas to institutions; JPY 375,900 in Japan to institutions; GBP 1,418 to institutions in the UK & elsewhere (effective 2011). adv. bk.rev. illus. index. back issues avail.; reprints avail. **Document type:** *Journal, Academic/Scholarly.* **Description:** Presents the etiology of cancer and to improving the treatment and survival of patients.
Related titles: Microform ed.: (from PMC, PQC); Online - full text ed.: ISSN 1532-1827; Supplement(s): British Journal of Cancer. Supplement. ISSN 0306-9443. 1973.
Indexed: A01, A02, A03, A08, A20, A22, A35, A36, AIDS&CR, ASCA, AgBio, B21, B25, BIOBASE, BIOSIS Prev, CA, CABA, CIN, CIS, CISA, ChemAb, ChemTitl, CurCont, D01, DBA, DentInd, DokArb, E01, E12, EMBASE, ESPM, ExcerpMed, F08, FR, G10, GH, GeoRef, H&SSA, H16, H17, IABS, IBR, IBZ, INI, ISR, IndMed, Inpharma, LT, MEDLINE, MS&D, MycolAb, N02, N03, NRN, OGFA, P20, P22, P24, P30, P33, P35, P48, P50, P54, PHN&I, PN&I, PQC, R08, R10, R11, R12, RA&MP, RM&VM, RRTA, Reac, RiskAb, SAA, SCI, SCOPUS, SoyAb, T02, T05, THA, ToxAb, TriticAb, VS, VirolAbstr, W07.
—BLDSC (2307.000000), CASDDS, GNLM, IE, Infotrieve, Ingenta, INIST. **CCC.**
Published by: (Cancer Research), Nature Publishing Group (Subsidiary of: Macmillan Publishers Ltd.), The MacMillan Bldg, 4 Crinan St, London, N1 9XW, United Kingdom. TEL 44-20-78334000, FAX 44-20-78334640. Ed. Dr. Nicole Muller-Berat Killman TEL 33-1-40036769. Adv. contact Ben Harkinson TEL 617-475-9222. **Subscr. to:** Brunel Rd, Houndmills, Basingstoke, Hamps RG21 6XS, United Kingdom. TEL 44-1256-329242, FAX 44-1256-812358, subscriptions@nature.com.

616.992 GBR ISSN 1471-2407
CODEN: BCMACL
➤ **B M C CANCER.** (BioMed Central) Text in English. 2000. irreg. free (effective 2011). adv. back issues avail.; reprints avail. **Document type:** *Journal, Academic/Scholarly.* **Description:** Covers original research articles in all aspects of research relating to cancer, including molecular biology, genetics, pathophysiology, epidemiology, clinical reports, and controlled trials.
Media: Online - full text.
Indexed: A01, A02, A03, A08, A20, A26, A34, A35, A36, A38, AgBio, AgrForAb, C06, C07, C30, CA, CABA, CurCont, D01, E12, EMBASE, ExcerpMed, F08, F11, F12, GH, H16, H17, I05, IndVet, Inpharma, MEDLINE, N02, N03, OGFA, P20, P22, P30, P32, P33, P35, P39, P54, PQC, R07, R10, R12, RA&MP, RM&VM, Reac, S06, SCI, SCOPUS, SoyAb, T02, T05, VS, W07, W10.
—Infotrieve. **CCC.**
Published by: BioMed Central Ltd. (Subsidiary of: Springer Science+Business Media), 236 Gray's Inn Rd, London, WC1X 8HB, United Kingdom. TEL 44-20-31922000, FAX 44-20-31922010, info@biomedcentral.com. Ed. Dr. Melissa Norton. Adv. contact Natasha Bailey TEL 44-20-31922231.

616.994061 GBR ISSN 2045-6379
▼ **B O P A BULLETIN.** Text in English. 2010. 3/yr. back issues avail. **Document type:** *Bulletin, Trade.* **Description:** Provides a forum in which readers can share practice, encouraging networking and a collaborative approach to working.
Related titles: Online - full text ed.: ISSN 2045-6387. free (effective 2010).
Published by: (British Oncology Pharmacy Association), The Pharmacy Publishing Company, 4 Clark's Courtyard, 145 Granville St, Birmingham, B1 1SB, United Kingdom. TEL 44-121-6334691, FAX 44-121-6330055, info@pharmacypublishing.co.uk.

616.992 GRC ISSN 1107-0625
CODEN: JBUOFH
BALKAN UNION OF ONCOLOGY. JOURNAL. Variant title: The Journal of B U On. Text in English. 1996. q. USD 60 to individuals; USD 100 to institutions; USD 20 newsstand/cover (effective 2001); Free for members.
Indexed: A35, A36, AgBio, BIOBASE, CABA, D01, E12, EMBASE, ExcerpMed, GH, H16, I11, IABS, MEDLINE, N02, N03, P30, R10, RA&MP, Reac, S13, S16, SCI, SCOPUS, T05, VS, W07.
—BLDSC (4707.645500), IE, Ingenta.
Published by: (Balkan Union of Oncology), Zerbinis Medical Publications, 42 Antifilou St., Athens, 15771, Greece. TEL 30-1-7719600, FAX 30-1-7701207.

616.99 ISR
BAMAH (GIVATAYIM); journal for health professionals in the field of cancer. Text in Hebrew. 1983. a. free (effective 2008). **Document type:** *Bulletin, Trade.* **Description:** For health professionals who work with cancer patients.
Published by: Israel Cancer Association, Revivim 7, P O Box 437, Giv'atayim, 51304, Israel. TEL 972-3-5721616, FAX 972-3-5719578, debby@cancer.org.il. Ed. Miri Ziv. Circ: 10,000.

BARN OCH CANCER. see MEDICAL SCIENCES—Pediatrics

616.992 IRN ISSN 2228-5466
▼ ➤ **BASIC AND CLINICAL CANCER RESEARCH.** Text in English. 2010. q. Index. back issues avail. **Document type:** *Journal, Academic/Scholarly.* **Description:** Publishes original studies, reviews, and perspectives within the major topic areas of cancer; oncogenesis, prevention and epidemiology, early detection and screening, treatment modalities, patient quality of life. The bulletin comprises preclinical, clinical and field trial as well as translational research, with special attention given to molecular discoveries and an emphasis on building a translational bridge between the basic and clinical sciences.
Formerly (until 2010): Cancer Bulletin (2008-2568)
Media: Online - full text.
Published by: Tehran University of Medical Sciences, Cancer Institute, Imam Khomeini Hospital Complex, Keshavarz Bulvar, Tehran, Iran. TEL 98-21-66940021, FAX 98-21-66581638. Ed. Shams Shariat Torbagham.

616.99 USA ISSN 1073-0028
CODEN: BCLOEQ
BASIC AND CLINICAL ONCOLOGY. Text in English. 1993. irreg., latest 1999. price varies. back issues avail. **Document type:** *Monographic series, Trade.*
Indexed: CIN, ChemAb, ChemTitl.
—BLDSC (1863.914100), CASDDS, IE, Ingenta. **CCC.**
Published by: C R C Press, LLC (Subsidiary of: Taylor & Francis Group), 6000 Broken Sound Pky, NW, Ste 300, Boca Raton, FL 33487. TEL 800-272-7737, FAX 800-374-3401, orders@crcpress.com.

616.99449 AUS ISSN 1834-5921
THE BEACON. Text in English. 1997. q. free to qualified personnel (effective 2008). back issues avail. **Document type:** *Magazine, Consumer.* **Description:** Provides information and articles for those affected by breast cancer through communication, shared information and experiences, and education.
Related titles: Online - full text ed.: ISSN 1834-593X; Supplement(s): The Inside Story. ISSN 1834-5948. 2006.
Published by: Breast Cancer Network Australia, 293 Camberwell Rd, Camberwell, VIC 3124, Australia. TEL 61-3-98052500, FAX 61-3-98052599. Ed. Lyn Swinburne. Circ: 5,500 (controlled).

616.992 DEU
BEFUND KREBS; Deutsches Magazin fuer Tumorerkrankte. Text in German. 2003. 5/yr. adv. **Document type:** *Magazine, Consumer.*
Published by: G F M K GmbH & Co. KG Verlagsgesellschaft, Gezelinallee 37-39, Leverkusen, 51375, Germany. TEL 49-214-310570, FAX 49-214-3105719, info@gfmk.de, http://www.gfmk.de. Adv. contact Kirsten Caspari TEL 49-214-3105714. Circ: 30,000 (controlled).

616.992 DEU ISSN 0946-4565
➤ **BEST PRACTICE ONKOLOGIE.** Text in German. 2006. 2/yr. EUR 193, USD 240 combined subscription to institutions (print & online eds.) (effective 2012). adv. reprint service avail. from PSC. **Document type:** *Journal, Academic/Scholarly.*
Related titles: Online - full text ed.: ISSN 1862-8559 (from IngentaConnect).
Indexed: A22, A26, E01, E08, EMBASE, ExcerpMed, H12, S09, SCOPUS.
—IE, Ingenta. **CCC.**
Published by: Springer (Subsidiary of: Springer Science+Business Media), Tiergartenstr 17, Heidelberg, 69121, Germany. TEL 49-6221-4870, FAX 49-6221-345229, subscriptions@springer.com. Circ: 10,000 (paid).

616.992 NZL ISSN 1179-299X
▼ **BIOMARKERS IN CANCER.** Text in English. 2009. irreg. free (effective 2011). **Document type:** *Journal, Academic/Scholarly.*
Media: Online - full text.
Indexed: P30.
—**CCC.**
Published by: Libertas Academica Ltd., PO Box 300-874, Mairangi Bay, Auckland, 0751, New Zealand. TEL 64-9-4763930, FAX 64-9-3531397, enquiries@la-press.com. Ed. Barbara Guinn.

616.99419 GBR ISSN 1179-9889
▼ ➤ **BLOOD AND LYMPHATIC CANCER: TARGETS AND THERAPY.** Text in English. 2011. irreg. free (effective 2011). **Document type:** *Journal, Academic/Scholarly.*
—**CCC.**
Published by: Dove Medical Press Ltd., Beechfield House, Winterton Way, Macclesfield, SK11 0JL, United Kingdom. TEL 44-1625-509130, FAX 44-1625-617933. Ed. David Dingli.

616.9 USA ISSN 1538-4721
RC271.R27 CODEN: BRACC4
➤ **BRACHYTHERAPY.** Variant title: Brachytherapy International. Journal of Brachytherapy. Text in English. 1985. q. USD 558 in United States to institutions; USD 638 elsewhere to institutions (effective 2012). bk.rev. illus.; stat. back issues avail.; reprints avail. **Document type:** *Journal, Academic/Scholarly.* **Description:** Publishes original articles, reviews of selected subjects, and information on the techniques and clinical applications of interstitial irradiation, endovascular brachytherapy, systemic brachytherapy, and hyperthermia in the management of cancer, cardiac and other patients, including laboratory and experimental research relevant to clinical practice.
Former titles (until 2002): Journal of Brachytherapy International (1094-4540); (until 1997): Endocurietherapy - Hyperthermia Oncology (8756-1689)
Related titles: Online - full text ed.: ISSN 1873-1449 (from IngentaConnect, ScienceDirect).
Indexed: A01, A03, A08, A26, BIOBASE, CA, CurCont, EMBASE, ExcerpMed, I05, IABS, MEDLINE, P30, R10, Reac, SCI, SCOPUS, T02, W07.
—BLDSC (2265.884500), GNLM, IE, Ingenta. **CCC.**

Published by: (American Brachytherapy Society), Elsevier Inc. (Subsidiary of: Elsevier Science & Technology), 1600 John F Kennedy Blvd, Philadelphia, PA 19103. TEL 215-239-3900, FAX 215-238-7883, JournalCustomerService-usa@elsevier.com, http://www.elsevier.com. Ed. Dr. Michael J Zelefsky TEL 212-639-8838. Adv. contact Pat Hampton TEL 212-633-3181.

616.994 JPN ISSN 1433-7398
RD663 CODEN: BTPAFM
➤ **BRAIN TUMOR PATHOLOGY.** Text in English. 1983. 2/yr. EUR 214, USD 263 combined subscription to institutions (print & online eds.) (effective 2012). reprint service avail. from PSC. **Document type:** *Journal, Academic/Scholarly.* **Description:** Documents the latest research and topical debate in all clinical and experimental fields related to brain tumors.
Related titles: Online - full text ed.: ISSN 1861-387X (from IngentaConnect).
Indexed: A22, A26, B21, BIOBASE, CurCont, E-psyche, E01, EMBASE, ExcerpMed, I05, IABS, IndMed, MEDLINE, NSA, NSCI, P30, R10, Reac, SCI, SCOPUS, W07.
—BLDSC (2268.221500), CASDDS, IE, Infotrieve, Ingenta. **CCC.**
Published by: Springer Japan KK (Subsidiary of: Springer Science+Business Media), No 2 Funato Bldg, 1-11-11 Kudan-kita, Chiyoda-ku, Tokyo, 102-0073, Japan. TEL 81-3-68317000, FAX 81-3-68317001, http://www.springer.jp. Ed. Keiji Kawamoto. **Subscr. in the Americas to:** Springer New York LLC, Journal Fulfillment, PO Box 2485, Secaucus, NJ 07096. TEL 201-348-4033, 800-777-4643, FAX 201-348-4505, journals-ny@springer.com, http://www.springer.com; **Subscr. to:** Springer Distribution Center, Kundenservice Zeitschriften, Haberstr 7, Heidelberg 69126, Germany. TEL 49-6221-3454303, FAX 49-6221-3454229, subscriptions@springer.com.

616.992 CAN ISSN 1494-6831
BRAINSTORM. Text in English. 1989. q. **Document type:** *Newsletter.*
Formerly (until 1990): Brain Research Fund Newsletter
Published by: Brain Tumor Foundation of Canada, 620 Colborne St, Ste 301, London, ON N6B 3R9, Canada. TEL 519-642-7755, 800-265-5106, FAX 519-642-7192, btfc@btfc.org, http://www.braintumour.ca.

616.992 NZL ISSN 1178-2234
RC280.B8
➤ **BREAST CANCER**; basic and clinical research. Text in English. 2007. irreg. free (effective 2011). **Document type:** *Journal, Academic/Scholarly.* **Description:** Covers all areas of breast cancer research and treatment.
Media: Online - full text.
Indexed: A01, C06, C07, EMBASE, ExcerpMed, P30, SCOPUS, T02.
—CCC.
Published by: Libertas Academica Ltd., PO Box 302-624, North Harbour, Auckland, 1330, New Zealand. TEL 64-21-662617, FAX 64-21-740006, editorial@la-press.com, http://www.la-press.com. Ed. Coberdham P Dimri.

616.99419 JPN ISSN 1340-6868
RC280.B8
➤ **BREAST CANCER.** Variant title: Japanese Breast Cancer Society. Journal. Text in English. 1994. q. EUR 240, USD 558 combined subscription to institutions (print & online eds.) (effective 2012). reprint service avail. from PSC. **Document type:** *Journal, Academic/Scholarly.* **Description:** Contains original articles on clinical, epidemiological studies and laboratory investigations concerning breast cancer and related diseases.
Related titles: Online - full text ed.: ISSN 1880-4233 (from IngentaConnect).
Indexed: A22, A26, CurCont, E01, E08, EMBASE, ExcerpMed, H12, MEDLINE, P30, R10, Reac, S09, SCI, SCOPUS, W07.
—BLDSC (2277.493450), IE, Ingenta. **CCC.**
Published by: (Japanese Breast Cancer Society), Springer Japan KK (Subsidiary of: Springer Science+Business Media), No 2 Funato Bldg, 1-11-11 Kudan-kita, Chiyoda-ku, Tokyo, 102-0073, Japan. TEL 81-3-68317000, FAX 81-3-68317001, orders@springer.jp, http://www.springer.jp. Ed. Shinzaburo Noguchi. **Subscr. to:** Maruzen Co., Ltd., Export Dept., PO Box 5050, Tokyo International 100-3191, Japan. FAX 81-3-3278-9256, journal@maruzen.co.jp, http://www.maruzen.co.jp.

616.994 NZL ISSN 1179-1314
▼ ➤ **BREAST CANCER (AUCKLAND)**; targets and therapy. Text in English. 2009. a. free (effective 2011). back issues avail. **Document type:** *Journal, Academic/Scholarly.* **Description:** Focuses on breast cancer research.
Media: Online - full text.
Indexed: P30, SCOPUS.
—CCC.
Published by: Dove Medical Press Ltd., 2G, 5 Ceres Ct, Mairangi Bay, Albany, PO Box 300-008, Auckland, 0752, New Zealand. TEL 64-9-4766466, FAX 64-9-4766469, info@dovepress.com. Ed. Hava Avraham.

616.994 GBR ISSN 1758-1923
▼ ➤ **BREAST CANCER MANAGEMENT.** Text in English. forthcoming 2011. 3/m. GBP 350 combined subscription domestic to institutions (print & online eds.); USD 610 combined subscription in North America to institutions (print & online eds.); JPY 64,500 combined subscription in Japan to institutions (print & online eds.); EUR 490 combined subscription elsewhere to institutions (print & online eds.) (effective 2011). adv. **Document type:** *Journal, Academic/Scholarly.*
Related titles: Online - full text ed.: ISSN 1758-1931. forthcoming. GBP 310 domestic to institutions; USD 540 in North America to institutions; JPY 58,000 in Japan to institutions; EUR 435 elsewhere to institutions (effective 2011).
Published by: Future Medicine Ltd. (Subsidiary of: Future Science Ltd.), Unitec House, 2 Albert Pl, London, N3 1QB, United Kingdom. TEL 44-20-83716080, FAX 44-20-83716099, info@futuremedicine.com, http://www.futuremedicine.com/. Ed. Elisa Manzotti TEL 44-20-83716090. Pub. David Hughes. Adv. contact Simon Boisseau TEL 44-208-3716083.

616.994 GBR ISSN 1470-9031
RC280.B8
➤ **BREAST CANCER ONLINE.** Text in English. 1998. w. free (effective 2012). back issues avail.; reprints avail. **Document type:** *Journal, Academic/Scholarly.* **Description:** An educational service made available to users working in the numerous fields of breast cancer research and treatment.
Media: Online - full content.
Indexed: A22, E01, EMBASE, ExcerpMed, P20, P48, P50, P54, PQC, R10, Reac, RiskAb, SCOPUS.
Published by: Cambridge University Press, The Edinburgh Bldg, Shaftesbury Rd, Cambridge, CB2 8RU, United Kingdom. TEL 44-1223-312393, FAX 44-1223-315052, journals@cambridge.org, http://www.cambridge.org/uk. Ed. John Robertson.

616.992 GBR ISSN 1465-542X
➤ **BREAST CANCER RESEARCH (ONLINE).** Text in English. 1999. bi-m. price varies based on the number of users. **Document type:** *Journal, Academic/Scholarly.* **Description:** Aims to ensure that researchers and clinician have easy access to the latest research and analysis, particularly in the areas of genetic, biochemistry and cell biology.
Formerly (until 2005): Breast Cancer Research (Print) (1465-5411)
Media: Online - full text.
Indexed: A26, C06, C07, CurCont, I05, Inpharma, SCI, W07.
—CCC.
Published by: BioMed Central Ltd. (Subsidiary of: Springer Science+Business Media), Fl 6, 236 Gray's Inn Rd, London, WC1X 8HB, United Kingdom. TEL 44-20-31922009, 800-389-8136, FAX 44-20-31922010, info@biomedcentral.com, http://www.biomedcentral.com. Ed. Lewis A Chodosh.

616.99249 USA ISSN 0167-6806
CODEN: BCTRD6
➤ **BREAST CANCER RESEARCH AND TREATMENT.** Text in English. 1981. 18/yr. EUR 3,529, USD 3,631 combined subscription to institutions (print & online eds.) (effective 2012). adv. bk.rev. back issues avail.; reprint service avail. from PSC. **Document type:** *Journal, Academic/Scholarly.* **Description:** Seeks to develop a new focus and new perspectives for all those concerned with breast cancer.
Related titles: Microform ed.: (from PQC); Online - full text ed.: ISSN 1573-7217 (from IngentaConnect).
Indexed: A20, A22, A26, A34, A35, A36, A38, ASCA, AgBio, Agr, B21, B25, BIOBASE, BIOSIS Prev, BibLing, CA, CABA, CIN, CMCI, ChemAb, ChemTitl, CurCont, D01, E01, E12, EMBASE, ExcerpMed, F08, F11, F12, FR, G10, GH, H13, H16, I05, IABS, IBR, IBZ, ISR, IndMed, IndVet, Inpharma, LT, MEDLINE, MycolAb, N02, N03, NRN, OGFA, P02, P10, P20, P22, P30, P32, P33, P35, P48, P50, P53, P54, PGrRegA, PQC, R08, R10, R12, RA&MP, RM&VM, RRTA, Reac, SCI, SCOPUS, SoyAb, T02, T05, VS, W07.
—BLDSC (2277.494000), CASDDS, GNLM, IE, Infotrieve, Ingenta, INIST. **CCC.**
Published by: Springer New York LLC (Subsidiary of: Springer Science+Business Media), 233 Spring St, New York, NY 10013. TEL 212-460-1500, FAX 212-460-1575, service-ny@springer.com. Ed. Marc E Lippman.

616.994 NZL
▼ **BREAST CANCER RESEARCH REVIEW.** Text in English. 2010. bi-m. **Document type:** *Journal, Academic/Scholarly.*
Media: Online - full text.
Published by: Research Review Ltd., N Shore Mail Centre, PO Box 100116, Auckland, New Zealand. TEL 64-9-4102277, info@researchreview.co.nz.

616.99249 USA ISSN 1535-2749
BREAST CANCER WEEKLY. Text in English. 2000. w.
Indexed: CWI.
Published by: NewsRx, 2727 Paces Ferry Rd SE, Ste 2-440, Atlanta, GA 30339. TEL 770-435-8286, 800-726-4550, FAX 770-435-6800, pressrelease@newsrx.com, http://www.newsrx.com.

BREAST DISEASE. *see* MEDICAL SCIENCES—Obstetrics And Gynecology

BREAST DISEASE SERIES. *see* MEDICAL SCIENCES—Obstetrics And Gynecology

616.99249 AUS ISSN 1324-7077
BREAST NEWS. Text in English. 1995. q. free (effective 2007). **Document type:** *Newsletter, Consumer.* **Description:** Covers current research and issues in breast cancer management and control.
Related titles: Online - full text ed.
Published by: N H M R C National Breast Cancer Centre, 92 Parramatta Rd, Camperdown, NSW 2050, Australia. TEL 61-2-90363030, FAX 61-2-90363077, directorate@nbcc.org.au, http://www.nbcc.org.au/pages/info/resource/nbccpubs/brnews/contents.htm. Circ: 6,500.

616.992 CAN ISSN 1185-1031
BRITISH COLUMBIA CANCER RESEARCH CENTRE. ANNUAL REPORT. Text in English. 1950. a. free. **Document type:** *Corporate.*
Former titles (until 1990): British Columbia. Cancer Control Agency. Annual Report (0849-4703); British Columbia. Cancer Foundation. Annual Report (0068-1423)
Published by: British Columbia Cancer Agency, 600 W Tenth Ave, Vancouver, BC V5Z 4E6, Canada. TEL 604-877-6000, FAX 604-877-6146. Circ: 6,000. **Co-sponsor:** British Columbia Cancer Foundation.

616.994 FRA ISSN 1769-6917
➤ **BULLETIN DU CANCER (ONLINE).** Text and summaries in French. 2003. m. EUR 179 (effective 2011). **Document type:** *Journal, Academic/Scholarly.*
Incorporates (1999-2004): Electronic Journal of Oncology (1292-8933)
Media: Online - full text. **Related titles:** Microform ed.: (from PQC); ◆ Print ed.: Bulletin du Cancer (Print). ISSN 0007-4551.
Published by: (Societe Francaise du Cancer), John Libbey Eurotext, 127 Av. de la Republique, Montrouge, 92120, France. TEL 33-1-46730660, FAX 33-1-40840999, contact@jle.com.

616.994 FRA ISSN 0007-4551
CODEN: BUCABS
➤ **BULLETIN DU CANCER (PRINT).** Text and summaries in French. 1908. m. EUR 504 combined subscription domestic to institutions (print & online eds.); EUR 504 combined subscription in the European Union to institutions (print & online eds.); EUR 564 combined subscription elsewhere to institutions (print & online eds.) (effective 2011). adv. bk.rev. illus. index. reprints avail. **Document type:** *Journal, Academic/Scholarly.* **Description:** Publishes original articles on clinical oncology, basic cancer research and related fields. Includes review articles, editorials, brief notes, letters to the editor.
Formerly (until 1966): Association Francaise pour l'Etude du Cancer. Bulletin (0004-5497)
Related titles: Microform ed.: (from PQC); ◆ Online - full text ed.: Bulletin du Cancer (Online). ISSN 1769-6917; ◆ Series: Cancer Radiotherapie. ISSN 1278-3218.
Indexed: A22, ASCA, B25, BIOSIS Prev, ChemAb, CurCont, DBA, DentInd, EMBASE, ExcerpMed, FR, ISR, IndMed, Inpharma, MEDLINE, MycolAb, P30, P35, R10, Reac, SCI, SCOPUS, W07.
—BLDSC (2837.970000), CASDDS, GNLM, IE, Infotrieve, Ingenta, INIST. **CCC.**
Published by: (Societe Francaise du Cancer), John Libbey Eurotext, 127 Av. de la Republique, Montrouge, 92120, France. TEL 33-1-46730660, FAX 33-1-40840999, contact@jle.com, http://www.john-libbey-eurotext.fr. Ed. Jacques-Olivier Bay. Circ: 3,500.

616.994 FRA ISSN 1628-2205
BULLETIN INFIRMIER DU CANCER. Text in French. 2001. q. EUR 98 combined subscription domestic to institutions (print & online eds.); EUR 114 combined subscription in the European Union to institutions (print & online eds.); EUR 122 combined subscription elsewhere to institutions (print & online eds.) (effective 2011). **Document type:** *Journal, Trade.*
Related titles: Online - full text ed.: ISSN 2102-5983.
Published by: John Libbey Eurotext, 127 Av. de la Republique, Montrouge, 92120, France. TEL 33-1-46730660, FAX 33-1-40840999, contact@jle.com. Ed. Pascale Dielenseger.

616.994 USA ISSN 0007-9235
CODEN: CAMCAM
➤ **C A**; a cancer journal for clinicians. Text in English. 1950. bi-m. GBP 43 in United Kingdom to institutions; EUR 50 in Europe to institutions; USD 61 elsewhere to institutions (effective 2012). adv. bibl.; charts; illus. cum.index: 1971-80. reprint service avail. from PSC. **Document type:** *Journal, Academic/Scholarly.* **Description:** Covers all aspects of cancer management for clinicians in primary care, oncology and related specialties.
Related titles: Microform ed.: (from PQC); Online - full text ed.: ISSN 1542-4863.
Indexed: A20, A22, A26, AIM, B21, C06, C07, C08, CA, CINAHL, CurCont, E-psyche, E08, EMBASE, ExcerpMed, G08, H04, H11, H12, H13, I05, ISR, IndMed, Inpharma, M01, M02, MEDLINE, MS&D, P02, P10, P20, P30, P48, P53, P54, PQC, R10, Reac, RefZh, S09, SCI, SCOPUS, T02, ViroIAbstr, W07.
—BLDSC (2943.180000), GNLM, IE, Infotrieve, Ingenta, INIST. **CCC.**
Published by: (American Cancer Society, Inc.), John Wiley & Sons, Inc., 111 River St, Hoboken, NJ 07030. TEL 201-748-6000, FAX 201-748-6088, uscs-wis@wiley.com, http://www.wiley.com/WileyCDA/. Eds. Dr. Ted Gansler, Dr. Otis Webb Brawley. adv.: B&W page USD 5,340, color page USD 6,690; trim 8.125 x 10.875. Circ: 94,500 (controlled).

➤ **C A SELECTS PLUS. ANTITUMOR AGENTS.** *see* MEDICAL SCIENCES—Abstracting, Bibliographies, Statistics

616.992 616.994 GBR ISSN 1475-8075
C M E CANCER MEDICINE. (Continuing Medical Education) Variant title: Cancer Medicine. Text in English. 2002. 3/yr. GBP 45 per vol. domestic to individuals; GBP 60 per vol. foreign to individuals; GBP 60 per vol. domestic to institutions; GBP 90 per vol. foreign to institutions (effective 2009). adv. bk.rev.; Website rev. abstr. back issues avail. **Document type:** *Journal, Academic/Scholarly.* **Description:** Contains significant review articles on cancer medicine.
Formed by the merger of (1997-2002): C M E Bulletin Oncology (1367-9031); (1998-2002): C M E Bulletin Palliative Medicine (1462-8791)
Related titles: Online - full content ed.: GBP 30 per issue (effective 2009).
Indexed: EMBASE, ExcerpMed, R10, Reac, SCOPUS.
—BLDSC (3287.223042). **CCC.**
Published by: Rila Publications Ltd., 73 Newman St, London, W1A 4PG, United Kingdom. TEL 44-20-76311299, FAX 44-20-75807166, admin@rila.co.uk. Ed. Peter Barrett-Lee.

616.992 USA ISSN 1559-6397
RC261.A1
C R (PHILADELPHIA); learn and live. (Collaborations - Results) Text in English. 2006 (Mar.). q. USD 23.95 domestic; USD 39.95 foreign (effective 2009). adv. back issues avail.; reprints avail. **Document type:** *Magazine, Consumer.* **Description:** Provides essential, evidence-based information and perspectives on cancer research, advocacy and survivorship.
Related titles: Online - full text ed.: ISSN 1940-6592.
Published by: American Association for Cancer Research, 615 Chestnut St, 17th Fl, Philadelphia, PA 19106. TEL 215-440-9300, FAX 215-440-9313, aacr@aacr.org, http://www.aacr.org. Ed. Gwen Darien. Adv. contact Tracy Middleton TEL 215-440-9300 ext 138. B&W page USD 13,000, color page USD 15,000; trim 8.375 x 10.875.

CANADIAN CANCER STATISTICS. *see* MEDICAL SCIENCES—Abstracting, Bibliographies, Statistics

CANADIAN ONCOLOGY NURSING JOURNAL/REVUE CANADIENNE DE NURSING ONCOLOGIQUE. *see* MEDICAL SCIENCES—Nurses And Nursing

616.994 USA ISSN 0008-543X
RC261 CODEN: CANCAR
➤ **CANCER.** Text in English. 1948. 24/yr. GBP 581 in United Kingdom to institutions; EUR 735 in Europe to institutions; USD 898 in United States to institutions; USD 1,048 in Canada & Mexico to institutions; USD 1,138 elsewhere to institutions; GBP 671 combined subscription in United Kingdom to institutions (print & online eds.); EUR 848 combined subscription in Europe to institutions (print & online eds.); USD 1,034 combined subscription in United States to institutions (print & online eds.); USD 1,184 combined subscription in Canada & Mexico to institutions (print & online eds.); USD 1,274 combined subscription elsewhere to institutions (print & online eds.) (effective 2012). illus. index. back issues avail.; reprint service avail. from PSC. **Document type:** *Journal, Academic/Scholarly.* **Description:** Provides an international, interdisciplinary forum for the exchange of information among all specialists concerned with cancer prevention, early detection, diagnosis, cure, and rehabilitation.
Related titles: CD-ROM ed.: Cancer on Disk. ISSN 1045-7410; Microform ed.: (from PQC); Online - full text ed.: ISSN 1097-0142. 1998. GBP 459 in United Kingdom to institutions; EUR 580 in Europe to institutions; USD 898 elsewhere to institutions (effective 2012); Supplement(s): Cancer Cytopathology (Online). ISSN 1934-6638; Cancer Cytopathology. ISSN 1934-662X.

Indexed: A01, A03, A08, A20, A22, A26, A36, AIDS Ab, AIDS&CR, AIM, ASG, B21, B25, BIOBASE, BIOSIS Prev, BiolDig, C06, C07, C13, C30, CA, CABA, CIS, ChemAb, CurCont, D01, DBA, DentInd, DokArb, E08, E12, EMBASE, ESPM, ExcerpMed, FR, FamI, G06, G07, G08, GH, H&SSA, H11, H12, HospLI, I05, IABS, IBR, IBZ, IDIS, INI, ISR, IndMed, Inpharma, JW, JW-WH, Kidney, MEDLINE, MS&D, MycolAb, N02, N03, NRN, OGFA, P03, P30, P32, P33, P34, P35, PsycInfo, R10, R12, RA&MP, RM&VM, Reac, RiskAb, S09, SAA, SCI, SCOPUS, SoyAb, T02, T05, TAR, Telegen, ToxAb, VS, W07, W09, W10.
—BLDSC (3046.450000), CASDDS, GNLM, IE, Infotrieve, Ingenta, INIST. **CCC.**
Published by: (American Cancer Society, Inc.), John Wiley & Sons, Inc., 111 River St, Hoboken, NJ 07030. TEL 201-748-6000, FAX 201-748-6088, info@wiley.com, http://www.wiley.com/WileyCDA/. Ed. Dr. Fadlo Khuri. Adv. contact Stephen Donohue TEL 781-388-8511. **Subscr. outside the Americas to:** John Wiley & Sons Ltd.

616.992 CAN
CANCER ADVOCACY COALITION OF CANADA. REPORT CARD ON CANCER IN CANADA. Text in English. 1998. a. free. charts; stat. **Document type:** *Report.* **Description:** An independent evaluation of cancer system performance. Provides general information related to current events and topics relevant to cancer in Canada.
Formerly (until 2004): Report Card on Cancer Care in Canada
Related titles: Online - full content ed.
Published by: Cancer Advocacy Coalition of Canada, 60 St Clair Avenue E, Ste 204, Toronto, ON M4T 1N5, Canada. TEL 416-538-4874, 877-472-3436, info@canceradvocacy.ca. Ed. Coleen Savage.

616.99 USA ISSN 0167-7659
RC269.5 CODEN: CMRED4
➤ **CANCER AND METASTASIS REVIEWS.** Text in English. 1982. q. EUR 889, USD 975 combined subscription to institutions (print & online eds.) (effective 2012). adv. bk.rev. back issues avail.; reprint service avail. from PSC. **Document type:** *Journal, Academic/Scholarly.* **Description:** Reviews some of the more important and interesting recent developments in the biology and treatment of malignant disease, as well as to highlight new and promising directions, be theytechnological or conceptual.
Formerly: Cancer Metastasis
Related titles: Microform ed.: (from PQC); Online - full text ed.: ISSN 1573-7233 (from IngentaConnect).
Indexed: A22, A26, A35, A36, ASCA, B&BAb, B19, B21, BIOBASE, BIOSIS Prev, BibLing, C03, CA, CABA, CBCARef, CIN, CPerI, ChemAb, ChemTitl, D01, E01, E12, EMBASE, ExcerpMed, GH, H16, I05, IABS, ISR, IndMed, Inpharma, MEDLINE, MycolAb, N02, N03, OGFA, P20, P22, P30, P32, P40, P48, P50, P54, PQC, R10, Reac, SCI, SCOPUS, SoyAb, T02, W07.
—BLDSC (3046.455700), CASDDS, GNLM, IE, Infotrieve, Ingenta, INIST. **CCC.**
Published by: (The Metastasis Research Society), Springer New York LLC (Subsidiary of: Springer Science+Business Media), 233 Spring St, New York, NY 10013. TEL 212-460-1500, FAX 212-460-1575, service-ny@springer.com. Eds. Avraham Raz, Barbara Ann Karmanos, Kenneth V Honn.

616.992 GBR ISSN 1464-7591
CANCER B A C U P NEWS. (British Association of Cancer United Patients) Text in English. 1986. 3/yr. **Document type:** *Newsletter.*
Formerly (until 1998): B A C U P News (0269-8765)
—BLDSC (3046.697000). **CCC.**
Published by: CancerBACUP, 3 Bath Place, London, EC2A 3JR, United Kingdom. TEL 44-20-77392280, FAX 44-20-76969002.

▼ **CANCER BIOLOGY.** *see* BIOLOGY—Physiology

616.99 USA ISSN 1538-4047
RC268.48 CODEN: CBTAAO
➤ **CANCER BIOLOGY & THERAPY.** Text in English. 2002. bi-w. USD 2,900 combined subscription in US & Canada to institutions (print & online eds.); USD 3,020 combined subscription elsewhere to institutions (print & online eds.) (effective 2009). **Document type:** *Journal, Academic/Scholarly.* **Description:** Covers original research on the molecular basis of cancer, including articles with translational relevance to diagnosis or therapy, including reviews, op-ed pieces, and meeting reports of interest.
Related titles: Online - full text ed.: ISSN 1555-8576. USD 2,500 to institutions (effective 2009).
Indexed: B21, EMBASE, ExcerpMed, ImmunAb, MEDLINE, OGFA, P30, R10, Reac, SCI, SCOPUS, W07.
—BLDSC (3046.456700), IE, Ingenta, INIST. **CCC.**
Published by: Landes Bioscience, 1002 W Ave, Austin, TX 78701. TEL 512-637-6050, FAX 512-637-6079, info@landesbioscience.com. Ed. Wafik S El-Deiry.

616.994 572 NLD ISSN 1574-0153
RC255
CANCER BIOMARKERS; section of Disease Markers. Text in English. 2005 (June). m. USD 1,653 combined subscription in North America (print & online eds.); EUR 1,180 combined subscription elsewhere (print & online eds.) (effective 2012). **Document type:** *Journal, Academic/Scholarly.* **Description:** Concentrates on molecular biomarkers in cancer research. Publishes original research findings (and reviews solicited by the Editor) on the subject of the identification of markers associated with the disease processes whether or not they are an integral part of the pathological lesion.
Related titles: Online - full content ed.: EUR 510, USD 615 (effective 2007); Online - full text ed.: ISSN 1875-8592.
Indexed: A01, A22, A36, B21, B25, BIOBASE, BIOSIS Prev, CA, CABA, E01, E12, EMBASE, ESPM, ExcerpMed, GH, IABS, MEDLINE, MycolAb, N02, N03, OGFA, P30, P33, R10, RM&VM, Reac, SCI, SCOPUS, T02, T05, W07.
—BLDSC (3046.457200), IE, INIST. **CCC.**
Published by: I O S Press, Nieuwe Hemweg 6B, Amsterdam, 1013 BG, Netherlands. TEL 31-20-6883355, FAX 31-20-6870019, info@iospress.nl. Ed. Dr. Sudhir Srivastava.

616.99 USA ISSN 1084-9785
RC271.C5 CODEN: CBRAFJ
➤ **CANCER BIOTHERAPY & RADIOPHARMACEUTICALS.** Abbreviated title: C B R. Text in English. 1996. 10/yr. USD 1,889 domestic to institutions; USD 2,278 foreign to institutions; USD 2,267 combined subscription domestic to institutions (print & online eds.); USD 2,657 combined subscription foreign to institutions (print & online eds.) (effective 2012). adv. reprint service avail. from PSC. **Document type:** *Journal, Academic/Scholarly.* **Description:** Covers biotherapy and innovative investigations of methods to improve cancer therapy. Contains topics such as clinical trials in cancer research, tumor cell vaccines etc.
Formed by the merger of (1988-1996): Antibody, Immunoconjugates, and Radiopharmaceuticals (0892-7049); (1993-1996): Cancer Biotherapy (1062-8401); Which was formerly (until 1993): Selective Cancer Therapeutics (1043-0733); (until 1989): Cancer Drug Delivery (0732-9482)
Related titles: Online - full text ed.: ISSN 1557-8852. USD 1,887 to institutions (effective 2012).
Indexed: A01, A03, A08, A22, A26, A34, A36, ASCA, B&BAb, B19, B21, B25, BIOSIS Prev, BioEngAb, C06, C07, CA, CABA, CIN, CTA, ChemAb, ChemTitl, CurCont, DBA, E01, E12, EMBASE, ESPM, ExcerpMed, GH, H12, H13, I05, ISR, ImmunAb, IndMed, IndVet, Inpharma, M&PBA, MEDLINE, MycolAb, N02, N03, NSA, P10, P20, P22, P30, P35, P48, P50, P52, P53, P54, P56, PQC, R10, RA&MP, Reac, SCI, SCOPUS, T02, T05, Telegen, ToxAb, TriticAb, VITIS, VS, W07.
—BLDSC (3046.457600), CASDDS, GNLM, IE, Infotrieve, Ingenta, INIST. **CCC.**
Published by: Mary Ann Liebert, Inc. Publishers, 140 Huguenot St, 3rd Fl, New Rochelle, NY 10801. TEL 914-740-2100, FAX 914-740-2101, 800-654-3237, info@liebertpub.com. Ed. Dr. Robert K Oldham TEL 573-803-0776. Adv. contact Harriet I Matysko TEL 914-740-2182.

616.994 USA ISSN 1542-8206
CANCER CARE HEALTH MONITOR. Text in English. 1998. q. free. adv. **Document type:** *Magazine, Consumer.* **Description:** Patient education publication distributed in the waiting rooms of oncologists/ hematologists.
Related titles: Online - full content ed.
Published by: Data Centrum Communications, Inc., 650 From Rd, 2nd Fl, Paramus, NJ 07652. TEL 201-391-1911, FAX 201-225-1440, info@healthmonitor.com, http://www.healthmonitor.com. adv.: B&W page USD 11,130; trim 8 x 10.75.

362.1 616.994 CAN ISSN 1912-659X
CANCER CARE ONTARIO. ABORIGINAL CANCER CARE UNIT. NEWSLETTER. Text in English. 2003. a. **Document type:** *Newsletter, Consumer.*
Formerly (until 2004): Aboriginal Cancer Care Unit (1912-6581)
Published by: Cancer Care Ontario, 620 University Ave, Toronto, ON M5G 2L7, Canada. TEL 416-971-9800, FAX 416-971-6888, publicaffairs@cancercare.on.ca, http://www.cancercare.on.ca/ index.htm.

616.99 NLD ISSN 0957-5243
RC261.A1 CODEN: CCCNEN
➤ **CANCER CAUSES & CONTROL**; an international journal of studies of cancer in human populations. Text in English. 1990. 12/yr. EUR 2,580, USD 2,718 combined subscription to institutions (print & online eds.) (effective 2012). adv. reprint service avail. from PSC. **Document type:** *Journal, Academic/Scholarly.* **Description:** Reports and stimulates new avenues of investigation into the causes, control and subsequent prevention of cancer.
Related titles: CD-ROM ed.; Online - full text ed.: ISSN 1573-7225 (from IngentaConnect).
Indexed: A22, A26, A36, AESIS, ASCA, Agr, AgrForAb, B21, B25, BIOBASE, BIOSIS Prev, BibLing, CA, CABA, CurCont, D01, E01, E08, E12, EMBASE, ESPM, ExcerpMed, F08, F09, GH, H&SSA, H16, H17, I05, IABS, ISR, IndMed, Inpharma, LT, MEDLINE, MycolAb, N02, N03, NRN, P03, P20, P22, P24, P30, P33, P35, P37, P39, P48, P50, P54, PHN&I, PN&I, PQC, PsycInfo, R07, R08, R10, R12, R13, RM&VM, RRTA, Reac, RiskAb, S09, S12, S13, S16, SCI, SCOPUS, SoyAb, T02, T05, THA, ToxAb, VS, W07, W09, W10, W11.
—BLDSC (3046.464150), GNLM, IE, Infotrieve, Ingenta, INIST. **CCC.**
Published by: Springer Netherlands (Subsidiary of: Springer Science+Business Media), Van Godewijckstraat 30, Dordrecht, 3311 GX, Netherlands. TEL 31-78-6576050, FAX 31-78-6576474, http://www.springer.com. Ed. Edward Giovannucci.

616.992 616.994 USA ISSN 1535-6108
RC269.7 CODEN: CCAECI
➤ **CANCER CELL.** Text in English. 2002. m. EUR 1,432 in Europe to institutions; JPY 151,200 in Japan to institutions; USD 1,146 in US & Canada to institutions; USD 1,288 elsewhere to institutions (effective 2012). adv. back issues avail.; reprints avail. **Document type:** *Journal, Academic/Scholarly.* **Description:** Publishes research results ranging from molecular and cellular biology to clinical oncology.
Related titles: Online - full text ed.: ISSN 1878-3686. 200?. USD 140 to individuals (effective 2008) (from IngentaConnect, ScienceDirect).
Indexed: A01, A03, A08, A22, A26, B21, B25, BIOBASE, BIOSIS Prev, C33, CA, CTA, CurCont, EMBASE, ESPM, ExcerpMed, GenetAb, I05, IABS, ISR, Inpharma, MEDLINE, MycolAb, NucAcAb, OGFA, P30, P35, R10, Reac, SCI, SCOPUS, T02, ToxAb, W07.
—BLDSC (3046.464170), IE, Ingenta. **CCC.**
Published by: Cell Press (Subsidiary of: Elsevier Science & Technology), 600 Technology Sq, Cambridge, MA 02139. TEL 617-661-7057, FAX 617-661-7061, celleditor@cell.com. Eds. Li-Kuo Su, Emilie Marcus. Adv. contact Jim Secretario TEL 212-462-1928. Circ: 1,126. **Subscr. to:** 11830 Westline Industrial Dr, St. Louis, MO 63146. TEL 314-579-2880, 866-314-2355, FAX 314-523-5170, subs@cell.com; Elsevier BV.

616.994 GBR ISSN 1475-2867
QH573
➤ **CANCER CELL INTERNATIONAL.** Text in English. 2001. irreg. free (effective 2011). adv. back issues avail. **Document type:** *Journal, Academic/Scholarly.* **Description:** Publishes papers dealing with cell lines, transformed cells and cultures derived from malignant tissues.
Media: Online - full text.
Indexed: A01, A26, B19, B25, BIOSIS Prev, CA, EMBASE, ExcerpMed, I05, MycolAb, OGFA, P20, P22, P30, P48, P54, PQC, R10, Reac, S06, SCI, SCOPUS, T02, W07.
—Infotrieve. **CCC.**
Published by: (International Federation for Cell Biology), BioMed Central Ltd. (Subsidiary of: Springer Science+Business Media), 236 Gray's Inn Rd, London, WC1X 8HB, United Kingdom. TEL 44-20-31922000, FAX 44-20-31922010, info@biomedcentral.com, http:// www.biomedcentral.com. Ed. Denys Wheatley TEL 44-1467-670280. Adv. contact Natasha Bailey TEL 44-20-31922231.

616.99 DEU ISSN 0344-5704
RC271.C5 CODEN: CCPHDZ
➤ **CANCER CHEMOTHERAPY AND PHARMACOLOGY.** Text in English. 1978. m. EUR 5,126, USD 6,090 combined subscription to institutions (print & online eds.) (effective 2012). adv. index. back issues avail.; reprint service avail. from PSC. **Document type:** *Journal, Academic/Scholarly.* **Description:** Addresses a wide range of pharmacologic and oncologic concerns on both the experimental and clinical levels.
Related titles: Microform ed.: (from PQC); Online - full text ed.: ISSN 1432-0843 (from IngentaConnect); ◆ Supplement(s): Cancer Chemotherapy and Pharmacology. Supplement. ISSN 0943-9404.
Indexed: A01, A03, A08, A22, A26, ASCA, Agr, B21, B25, BIOBASE, BIOSIS Prev, C06, C07, CA, CIN, ChemAb, ChemTitl, CurCont, DBA, DentInd, E01, E12, EMBASE, ESPM, ExcerpMed, H12, I05, IABS, ISR, IndMed, Inpharma, MEDLINE, MycolAb, P20, P22, P30, P35, P48, P50, P54, PQC, R10, Reac, RefZh, SCI, SCOPUS, T02, ToxAb, W07.
—BLDSC (3046.467000), CASDDS, GNLM, IE, Infotrieve, Ingenta, INIST. **CCC.**
Published by: Springer (Subsidiary of: Springer Science+Business Media), Tiergartenstr 17, Heidelberg, 69121, Germany. TEL 49-6221-4870, FAX 49-6221-345229. Eds. Dr. D R Newell, Dr. M J Egorin. **Subscr. in the Americas to:** Springer New York LLC, Journal Fulfillment, PO Box 2485, Secaucus, NJ 07096. TEL 800-777-4643, 201-348-4033, FAX 201-348-4505, journals-ny@springer.com, http://www.springer.com; **Subscr. to:** Springer Distribution Center, Kundenservice Zeitschriften, Haberstr 7, Heidelberg 69126, Germany. TEL 49-6221-3454303, FAX 49-6221-3454229, subscriptions@springer.com.

616.99 DEU ISSN 0943-9404
CODEN: CCHSE
CANCER CHEMOTHERAPY AND PHARMACOLOGY. SUPPLEMENT. Text in German. 19??. irreg. price varies. **Document type:** *Monographic series, Academic/Scholarly.*
Related titles: ◆ Supplement to: Cancer Chemotherapy and Pharmacology. ISSN 0344-5704.
Indexed: A01, A03, A08, SCOPUS, T02.
—Infotrieve. **CCC.**
Published by: Springer (Subsidiary of: Springer Science+Business Media), Tiergartenstr 17, Heidelberg, 69121, Germany. TEL 49-6221-4870, FAX 49-6221-345229, subscriptions@springer.com, http://www.springer.com.

616.99 USA ISSN 1073-2748
CODEN: CACOFD
➤ **CANCER CONTROL.** Text in English. 1994. bi-m. USD 60 domestic to individuals; USD 75 foreign to individuals; USD 120 domestic to institutions; USD 135 foreign to institutions; USD 10 per issue domestic; USD 15 per issue foreign; free (effective 2011). back issues avail. **Document type:** *Journal, Academic/Scholarly.* **Description:** Contains articles on the spectrum of actions and approaches needed to reduce the impact of human malignancy.
Related titles: Online - full text ed.: ISSN 1526-2359. free (effective 2011).
Indexed: B21, C06, C07, EMBASE, ExcerpMed, ImmunAb, IndMed, Inpharma, MEDLINE, P30, R10, Reac, SCOPUS.
—BLDSC (3046.472100), GNLM, IE, Ingenta, INIST. **CCC.**
Published by: Moffitt Cancer Center & Research Institute H Lee, 12902 Magnolia Dr, Tampa, FL 33612. TEL 813-745-1349, FAX 813-745-4950. Ed. John Horton.

616 USA ISSN 0191-3794
CANCER CONTROL JOURNAL. Text in English. 1973. irreg. membership. bk.rev. back issues avail.
—**CCC.**
Published by: Cancer Control Society, Cancer Book House, 2043 N Berendo, Los Angeles, CA 90027. TEL 323-663-7801. Circ: 10,000.

616.99 616.15 USA
➤ **CANCER DRUG DISCOVERY AND DEVELOPMENT.** Text in English. 1996. irreg., latest 2007. price varies. illus. back issues avail. **Document type:** *Monographic series, Academic/Scholarly.* **Description:** Provides pharmacologists and oncologists with reviews of the latest research in the development of new pharmacological agents, or approaches to the treatment and cure of cancer.
Related titles: Online - full text ed.
Indexed: GenetAb, M&PBA, OGFA.
Published by: Humana Press, Inc. (Subsidiary of: Springer Science+Business Media), 233 Spring St, New York, NY 10013. TEL 212-460-1500, FAX 212-460-1575, service-ny@springer.com. Ed. Beverly A Teicher.

616.99 GBR ISSN 1369-7129
CANCER DRUG NEWS (C D N). Text in English. 1997. w. GBP 590, USD 1,120, EUR 885; GBP 35, USD 65, EUR 55 per issue (effective 2009). back issues avail. **Document type:** *Newsletter, Trade.* **Description:** Provides news reported on drugs for all cancer types.
Related titles: CD-ROM ed.: ISSN 1461-7617; E-mail ed.; Online - full text ed.: ISSN 1473-1568.
—**CCC.**
Published by: Espicom Business Intelligence, Lincoln House, City Fields Business Park, City Fields Way, Chichester, W Sussex PO20 2FS, United Kingdom. TEL 44-1243-533322, FAX 44-1243-533418, Annette_Bulbeck@espicom.com. Ed. Alice Rossiter.

616.994 USA ISSN 1877-7821
RC268 CODEN: CDPRD4
➤ **CANCER EPIDEMIOLOGY**; the international journal of cancer epidemiology, detection and prevention. Text in English. 1976. 6/yr. EUR 1,072 in Europe to institutions; JPY 142,300 in Japan to institutions; USD 1,200 elsewhere to institutions (effective 2012). adv. reprints avail. **Document type:** *Journal, Academic/Scholarly.* **Description:** Dedicated to advancing cancer prevention and control.
Formerly (until 2009): Cancer Detection and Prevention (0361-090X)
Related titles: Microfilm ed.; Online - full text ed.: ISSN 1877-783X (from IngentaConnect, ScienceDirect); Supplement(s): Cancer Detection and Prevention. Supplement. ISSN 1043-6995. 1987.

Indexed: A01, A03, A08, A22, A26, A34, A35, A36, A38, ASCA, AgBio, B&BAb, B19, B21, B25, BIOBASE, BIOSIS Prev, BioEngAb, CA, CABA, CIN, ChemAb, ChemTitl, CurCont, D01, DentInd, DokArb, E01, E12, EMBASE, ESPM, ExcerpMed, F08, GH, H&SSA, H16, H17, IABS, IndMed, Inpharma, LT, MEDLINE, MycolAb, N02, N03, P30, P32, P33, P39, P40, PHN&I, R07, R12, RA&MP, RRTA, RiskAb, S13, S16, SCI, SCOPUS, SoyAb, T02, T05, THA, ToxAb, W07.
—BLDSC (3046.477910), CASDDS, GNLM, IE, Infotrieve, Ingenta, INIST. **CCC.**
Published by: (International Society of Preventive Oncology), Elsevier Inc. (Subsidiary of: Elsevier Science & Technology), 360 Park Ave S, New York, NY 10010. TEL 212-989-5800, 888-437-4636, FAX 212-633-3990, usinfo-f@elsevier.com. Ed. J Schuez.

616.99 USA ISSN 1055-9965
RC268.48 CODEN: CEBPE4
➤ **CANCER EPIDEMIOLOGY, BIOMARKERS & PREVENTION.** Abbreviated title: C E B P. Text in English. 1991. m. USD 325 domestic to individuals; USD 385 foreign to individuals (effective 2011). adv. back issues avail. **Document type:** *Journal, Academic/Scholarly.* **Description:** Features research on cancer causation, mechanisms of carcinogenesis, prevention, and survivorship.
Related titles: Online - full text ed.: ISSN 1538-7755.
Indexed: A22, ASCA, B21, B25, BIOBASE, BIOSIS Prev, BioEngAb, CA, CIN, ChemAb, ChemTitl, CurCont, EMBASE, ESPM, ExcerpMed, G10, H&SSA, IABS, ISR, IndMed, Inpharma, MEDLINE, MycolAb, NRN, NucAcAb, OGFA, P30, P35, R10, Reac, RiskAb, SCI, SCOPUS, SD, T02, THA, ToxAb, W07, W09.
—BLDSC (3046.477930), CASDDS, GNLM, IE, Infotrieve, Ingenta, INIST. **CCC.**
Published by: American Association for Cancer Research, 615 Chestnut St, 17th Fl, Philadelphia, PA 19106. TEL 215-440-9300, 866-423-3965, FAX 215-440-9313, aacr@aacr.org, http://www.aacr.org. Ed. Timothy R Rebbeck. Adv. contact Dean Mather TEL 856-768-9360. B&W page USD 805, color page USD 945; bleed 7.625 x 10.8125. Circ: 3,060. **Distr. addr. in the UK:** Turpin Distribution Services Ltd.; **Distr. addr. in the US:** Turpin Distribution Services Ltd.

616.994 USA ISSN 0069-0147
RC261
CANCER FACTS AND FIGURES. Text in English. 1951. a. back issues avail. **Document type:** *Journal, Trade.* **Description:** Provides the latest estimates of cancer incidence and morality.
Related titles: Online - full text ed.: free (effective 2009).
Indexed: A36, E12, GH, N02, P50, SRI.
—GNLM.
Published by: American Cancer Society, Inc., 1599 Clifton Rd, N E, Atlanta, GA 30329. TEL 404-320-3333, 800-227-2345, http://www.cancer.org. Circ: 300,000 (controlled).

616.994 305.86 USA ISSN 1556-3685
CANCER FACTS & FIGURES FOR HISPANICS/LATINOS. Text in English. 19??. irreg., latest 2008. back issues avail. **Document type:** *Monographic series, Trade.* **Description:** Summarizes recent information on cancer occurrence and cancer screening in the Hispanic/Latino population.
Related titles: Online - full text ed.: free (effective 2009).
Published by: American Cancer Society, Inc., 1599 Clifton Rd, N E, Atlanta, GA 30329. TEL 404-320-3333, 800-227-2345.

616.992 USA
CANCER FIGHTERS THRIVE. Text in English. 2008. q. USD 16 (effective 2010). adv. illus. **Document type:** *Magazine, Consumer.* **Description:** Offers tips and insights for those living with and fighting cancer.
Related titles: Online - full text ed.
Published by: (Cancer Treatment Centers of America), Cancer Fighters Thrive, 6511 Oakton St, Morton Grove, IL 60053. TEL 917-816-7896. Ed. Edgar Staren. Adv. contact Tim Oldenburg TEL 972-447-0910.

616.99 AUS ISSN 0311-306X
RC261.A1
➤ **CANCER FORUM.** Text in English. 1974. 3/yr. free to members (effective 2008). bk.rev. abstr. back issues avail. **Document type:** *Journal, Academic/Scholarly.* **Description:** Contains original articles concerning medical, scientific, political, social, educational or administrative aspects of cancer.
Related titles: Online - full text ed.: free (effective 2008).
Indexed: EMBASE, ExcerpMed, R10, Reac, SCOPUS.
—BLDSC (3046.478200), GNLM, IE, Ingenta, INIST. **CCC.**
Published by: (Clinical Oncological Society of Australia), Cancer Council Australia, GPO Box 4708, Sydney, NSW 2001, Australia. TEL 61-2-80634100, FAX 61-2-80634101, info@cancer.org.au.

616.992 JPN ISSN 1344-8919
CANCER FRONTIER. Text in Japanese. 1999. a. JPY 2,940 newsstand/cover (effective 2005). **Document type:** *Journal, Academic/Scholarly.*
Published by: Iyaku Journal-sha/Medicine & Drug Journal Co., Ltd., Highness Awajimachi Bldg. 21/F, 3-1-5 Awajimachih, Chuo-Ku, Osaka, 541-0047, Japan. TEL 81-6-62027280, FAX 81-6-62025295, ij-main@iyaku-j.com, http://www.iyaku-j.com/.

616.994 GBR ISSN 0929-1903
CODEN: CGTHEG
➤ **CANCER GENE THERAPY.** Abbreviated title: C G T. Text in English. 1994. m. EUR 2,048 in Europe to institutions; USD 2,576 in the Americas to institutions; JPY 350,400 in Japan to institutions; GBP 1,321 to institutions in the UK & elsewhere (effective 2011). adv. abstr.; bibl.; charts; illus.; stat. back issues avail.; reprints avail. **Document type:** *Journal, Academic/Scholarly.* **Description:** Provides the results of laboratory investigations, preclinical studies, and clinical trials in the field of gene transfer or gene therapy as applied to cancer research.
Related titles: Online - full text ed.: ISSN 1476-5500.
Indexed: A01, A02, A03, A08, A22, A26, AIDS&CR, ASCA, B&BAb, B19, B21, B25, B26, BIOBASE, BIOSIS Prev, BioEngAb, C33, CA, CIN, CTA, ChemAb, ChemTitl, CurCont, DBA, E01, EMBASE, ExcerpMed, GenetAb, H12, I05, IABS, ISR, IndMed, Inpharma, M&PBA, MEDLINE, MycolAb, NSA, NucAcAb, OGFA, P15, P20, P22, P30, P35, P48, P50, P52, P54, P56, PQC, R10, Reac, SCI, SCOPUS, T02, ViroIAbstr, W07.
—CASDDS, GNLM, IE, Infotrieve, Ingenta. **CCC.**
Published by: Nature Publishing Group (Subsidiary of: Macmillan Publishers Ltd.), The MacMillan Bldg, 4 Crinan St, London, N1 9XW, United Kingdom. TEL 44-20-78334000, FAX 44-20-78334640. Eds. Kevin J. Scanlon, Robert E. Sobol. Adv. contact Ben Harkinson TEL 617-475-9222. **Subscr. to:** Brunel Rd, Houndmills, Basingstoke, Hamps RG21 6XS, United Kingdom. TEL 44-1256-329242, FAX 44-1256-812358, subscriptions@nature.com.

616.992 USA ISSN 1543-6829
CANCER GENE THERAPY WEEK. Text in English. 2003. w. USD 2,295 in US & Canada; USD 2,495 elsewhere; USD 2,525 combined subscription in US & Canada (print & online eds.); USD 2,755 combined subscription elsewhere (print & online eds.) (effective 2008). back issues avail. **Document type:** *Newsletter, Trade.* **Description:** Contains articles that feature the latest research in human gene therapy for cancers, including genetically engineered vaccines, gene delivery, vector development, antisense technology and pharmaceuticals.
Related titles: E-mail ed.; Online - full text ed.: ISSN 1543-6837. USD 2,295 combined subscription (online & email eds.); single user (effective 2008).
Indexed: A26, E08, G08, H11, H12, I05, S09.
—CIS.
Published by: NewsRx, 2727 Paces Ferry Rd SE, Ste 2-440, Atlanta, GA 30339. TEL 770-435-8286, 800-726-4550, FAX 770-435-6800, pressrelease@newsrx.com, http://www.newsrx.com. Pub. Susan Hasty TEL 770-507-7777.

616.99 USA ISSN 2210-7762
RC268.4 CODEN: CGCYDF
➤ **CANCER GENETICS.** Abbreviated title: C G C. Text in English. 1979. m. USD 4,362 in United States to institutions; USD 4,960 elsewhere to institutions (effective 2012). adv. back issues avail.; reprints avail. **Document type:** *Journal, Academic/Scholarly.* **Description:** Covers the cellular and molecular aspects of cancer research. Features articles focusing on the knowledge and advances in the area of cytogenetics and cancer genetics.
Formerly (until 2011): Cancer Genetics and Cytogenetics (0165-4608)
Related titles: Microform ed.: (from PQC); Online - full text ed.: ISSN 1873-4456. 199? (from IngentaConnect, ScienceDirect).
Indexed: A01, A03, A08, A22, A26, A34, A36, A38, ASCA, B21, B25, B26, BIOBASE, BIOSIS Prev, CA, CABA, ChemAb, CurCont, D01, DentInd, DokArb, EMBASE, ExcerpMed, GH, GenetAb, H17, HGA, I05, IABS, IBR, IBZ, ISR, ImmunAb, IndMed, IndVet, Inpharma, MEDLINE, MycolAb, N02, N03, P30, P33, P35, R10, R12, Reac, S01, SCI, SCOPUS, SoyAb, T02, T05, THA, VS, W07.
—BLDSC (3046.478400), CASDDS, GNLM, IE, Infotrieve, Ingenta, INIST. **CCC.**
Published by: Elsevier Inc. (Subsidiary of: Elsevier Science & Technology), 1600 John F Kennedy Blvd, Philadelphia, PA 19103. TEL 215-239-3900, FAX 215-238-7883, JournalCustomerService-usa@elsevier.com, http://www.elsevier.com. Ed. Jaclyn A Biegel.

616.994071 GRC ISSN 1109-6535
CODEN: CGPAC7
➤ **CANCER GENOMICS & PROTEOMICS.** Text in English. 2004. bi-m. EUR 800 to institutions; EUR 400 membership (effective 2005). adv. bk.rev. **Document type:** *Journal, Academic/Scholarly.* **Description:** Contains articles and reviews on the application of genomic and proteomic technology to basic, experimental and clinical cancer research.
Related titles: Online - full text ed.: ISSN 1790-6245.
Indexed: B&BAb, B19, B21, B25, BIOBASE, BIOSIS Prev, BiolDig, C33, EMBASE, ExcerpMed, GenetAb, IABS, M&PBA, MEDLINE, MycolAb, NucAcAb, OGFA, P30, R10, Reac, RefZh, SCI, SCOPUS, W07.
—IE. **CCC.**
Published by: International Institute of Anticancer Research, 1st km Kapandritiou-Kalamou Rd, PO Box 22, Kapandriti Attica, Attiki 190 14, Greece. TEL 30-22950-52945, FAX 30-22950-53389. Ed. A Seth. Pub., R&P, Adv. contact Dr. John G Delinassios.

616.992 NZL ISSN 1179-0644
▼ **CANCER GROWTH AND METASTASIS.** Text in English. 2010. irreg. free (effective 2011). **Document type:** *Journal, Academic/Scholarly.*
Media: Online - full text.
Indexed: C06, P30.
—**CCC.**
Published by: Libertas Academica Ltd., PO Box 300-874, Mairangi Bay, Auckland, 0751, New Zealand. TEL 64-9-4763930, FAX 64-9-3531397, enquiries@la-press.com. Ed. Marc D Basson.

616.9 NLD ISSN 1871-3238
CANCER GROWTH AND PROGRESSION. Text in English. 200?. irreg., latest vol.17, 2004. price varies. **Document type:** *Monographic series, Academic/Scholarly.*
Published by: Springer Netherlands (Subsidiary of: Springer Science+Business Media), Van Godewijckstraat 30, Dordrecht, 3311 GX, Netherlands. TEL 31-78-6576050, FAX 31-78-6576474. Eds. Aejaz Nasir, Hans E Kaiser.

616.992 GBR ISSN 1470-7330
➤ **CANCER IMAGING.** Text in English. 2000. irreg. ((frequent updates)). free to members (effective 2009). adv. back issues avail. **Document type:** *Journal, Academic/Scholarly.* **Description:** Provides articles on the current state of the art and standards in cancer imaging as a reference source and an educational tool for a wide audience.
Media: Online - full text. **Related titles:** Print ed.: ISSN 1740-5025.
Indexed: CurCont, EMBASE, ExcerpMed, R10, Reac, SCI, W07.
—Ingenta. **CCC.**
Published by: (International Cancer Imaging Society), e-MED Limited, PO Box 61053, London, SE16 7YZ, United Kingdom. TEL 44-20-77198989, FAX 44-560-1264446, publications@e-med.org.uk, http://www.e-med.org.uk/. Ed. Rodney H Reznek. Adv. contact Marie Bardsley TEL 44-207-2317773.

616.99 USA ISSN 1424-9634
RC268.3
CANCER IMMUNITY. Text in English. 2001. irreg. free (effective 2011). back issues avail. **Document type:** *Journal, Academic/Scholarly.*
Media: Online - full text.
Indexed: EMBASE, ExcerpMed, MEDLINE, P30, R10, Reac, SCOPUS.
Published by: Academy of Cancer Immunology, c/o Cancer Research Institute, One Exchange Plaza, 55 Broadway, Ste. 1802, New York, NY 10006. info@academycancerimmunology.org, http://www.academycancerimmunology.org/. Ed. Lloyd J Old.

616.994 DEU ISSN 0340-7004
RC261 CODEN: CIIMDN
➤ **CANCER IMMUNOLOGY, IMMUNOTHERAPY;** other biological response modifications. Text in English. 1976. m. EUR 4,550, USD 5,594 combined subscription to institutions (print & online eds.) (effective 2012). adv. back issues avail.; reprint service avail. from PSC. **Document type:** *Journal, Academic/Scholarly.* **Description:** Presents the latest research results and clinical findings in oncology and immunology, including the latest developments in understanding tumor-host interactions.
Related titles: Microfiche ed.: (from PQC); Online - full text ed.: ISSN 1432-0851 (from IngentaConnect).
Indexed: A01, A03, A08, A22, A26, A34, A35, A36, AIDS&CR, ASCA, AgBio, Agr, B&BAb, B19, B21, B25, BIOBASE, BIOSIS Prev, BioEngAb, CA, CABA, CIN, ChemAb, ChemTitl, CurCont, DBA, E01, E12, EMBASE, ExcerpMed, GH, H12, I05, IABS, IBR, IBZ, ISR, ImmunAb, IndMed, IndVet, Inpharma, M&PBA, MEDLINE, MycolAb, N02, N03, P20, P22, P30, P32, P33, P35, P40, P48, P50, P54, PQC, R08, R10, RM&VM, Reac, RefZh, SCI, SCOPUS, T02, Telegen, VS, W07.
—BLDSC (3046.478600), CASDDS, GNLM, IE, Infotrieve, Ingenta, INIST. **CCC.**
Published by: Springer (Subsidiary of: Springer Science+Business Media), Tiergartenstr 17, Heidelberg, 69121, Germany. TEL 49-6221-4870, FAX 49-6221-345229. Eds. Enrico Mihich TEL 716-845-8224, Graham Pawelec TEL 49-7071-2982805. **Subscr. in the Americas to:** Springer New York LLC, Journal Fulfillment, PO Box 2485, Secaucus, NJ 07096. TEL 800-777-4643, 201-348-4033, FAX 201-348-4505, journals-ny@springer.com, http://www.springer.com; **Subscr. to:** Springer Distribution Center, Kundenservice Zeitschriften, Haberstr 7, Heidelberg 69126, Germany. TEL 49-6221-3454303, FAX 49-6221-3454229, subscriptions@springer.com.

616.994021 CAN ISSN 1195-406X
CANCER IN CANADA. Text in English. 1969. a.
Former titles (until 1989): Health Reports. Supplement. Cancer in Canada (1180-3053); (until 1983): Cancer in Canada (0227-1788); (until 1975): New Primary Sites of Malignant Neoplasms in Canada (0315-5161)
Published by: Statistics Canada, Canadian Centre for Health Information (Subsidiary of: Statistics Canada/Statistique Canada), 1500 Rm, Main Bldg, Holland Ave, Ottawa, ON K1A 0T6, Canada. TEL 613-951-8116.

616.9 PRI ISSN 0896-9035
RC279.P8
CANCER IN PUERTO RICO. Text in English, Spanish. 1950. a. free. adv. bk.rev.
Published by: (Puerto Rico. Department of Health USA, Puerto Rico. Cancer Control Program USA, Puerto Rico. NCI-BIO Branch USA), Cancer Registry of Puerto Rico, Department of Health of Puerto Rico, PO Box 70184, San Juan, 00927, Puerto Rico. TEL 787-274-7866. Ed. Dr. Isidro Martinez. Circ: 1,000.

616.992 GBR ISSN 1464-2077
CANCER IN YORKSHIRE. Text in English. 1993. every 5 yrs. **Document type:** *Monographic series, Academic/Scholarly.*
Published by: Yorkshire Cancer Organisation, Cookridge Hospital, Arthington House, Cookridge Lane, Leeds, LS16 6QB, United Kingdom. TEL 44-113-2924401.

CANCER INCIDENCE IN SWEDEN (ONLINE EDITION). *see* MEDICAL SCIENCES—Abstracting, Bibliographies, Statistics

616.992 NZL ISSN 1176-9351
RC261.A1
➤ **CANCER INFORMATICS.** Text in English. 2005. irreg. free (effective 2011). **Document type:** *Journal, Academic/Scholarly.* **Description:** Covers advances in bioinformatics, computational biology, statistics, pathology informatics and software design and engineering in support of cancer research and clinical practice.
Media: Online - full text.
Indexed: A01, B&BAb, B19, B21, CA, EMBASE, ExcerpMed, OGFA, P30, R10, Reac, SCOPUS, T02.
—**CCC.**
Published by: Libertas Academica Ltd., PO Box 302-624, North Harbour, Auckland, 1330, New Zealand. TEL 64-21-662617, FAX 64-21-740006. Ed. Dr. Igor Jurisica.

616.99 USA ISSN 0735-7907
RC261.A1 CODEN: CINVD7
➤ **CANCER INVESTIGATION.** Text in English. 1983. 8/yr. GBP 2,470, EUR 3,255, USD 4,065 combined subscription to institutions (print & online eds.); GBP 4,935, EUR 6,510, USD 8,125 combined subscription to corporations (print & online eds.) (effective 2010). adv. bk.rev. charts; illus. index. back issues avail.; reprint service avail. from PSC. **Document type:** *Journal, Academic/Scholarly.* **Description:** Informs about the current state of progress in the cancer field with a broad background of reliable information necessary for effective decision making.
Related titles: Microform ed.: (from RPI); Online - full text ed.: ISSN 1532-4192 (from IngentaConnect).
Indexed: A01, A03, A08, A20, A22, A36, AIDS&CR, ASCA, B21, B25, BIOSIS Prev, BiolDig, C06, C07, CA, CABA, CIN, ChemAb, ChemTitl, CurCont, D01, DokArb, E01, E12, EMBASE, EnvAb, ExcerpMed, F08, F11, F12, FR, GH, H16, INI, INIS AtomInd, ISR, IndMed, Inpharma, MEDLINE, MycolAb, N02, N03, NRN, OGFA, P30, P33, P35, P39, PGrRegA, R08, R10, R12, RA&MP, RM&VM, Reac, RefZh, SCI, SCOPUS, T02, T05, THA, Telegen, VS, ViroIAbstr, W07.
—CASDDS, GNLM, IE, Infotrieve, Ingenta, INIST. **CCC.**
Published by: (Inter-American Society for Chemotherapy, Cancer Section), Informa Healthcare (Subsidiary of: T & F Informa plc), 52 Vanderbilt Ave, New York, NY 10017. TEL 212-262-8230, FAX 212-262-8234, healthcare.enquiries@informa.com, http://www.informahealthcare.com. Ed. Gary H Lyman. Adv. contact Daniel Wallen. **Subscr. outside N. America to:** Taylor & Francis Ltd. **Co-sponsor:** Chemotherapy Foundation.

616.99 USA ISSN 1528-9117
RC261.A1 CODEN: CAJOCB
➤ **THE CANCER JOURNAL.** Text in English. 1995. bi-m. USD 534 domestic to institutions; USD 545 foreign to institutions (effective 2011). adv. charts; illus. back issues avail.; reprints avail. **Document type:** *Journal, Academic/Scholarly.* **Description:** Provides a view of modern oncology across all disciplines.

Formerly (until 2000): The Cancer Journal from Scientific American (1081-4442)
Related titles: Online - full text ed.: ISSN 1540-336X.
Indexed: A20, A22, AIDS&CR, ASCA, B21, B25, BIOSIS Prev, C06, C07, C08, CA, CINAHL, CurCont, EMBASE, ExcerpMed, ISR, IndMed, Inpharma, MEDLINE, MycolAb, OGFA, P20, P22, P24, P30, P35, P48, P54, PQC, R10, Reac, SCI, SCOPUS, T02, ViroIAbstr, W07.
—BLDSC (3046.479850), GNLM, IE, Ingenta, INIST. **CCC.**
Published by: (American Radium Society), Lippincott Williams & Wilkins (Subsidiary of: Wolters Kluwer N.V.), 530 Walnut St, Philadelphia, PA 19106. TEL 215-521-8300, FAX 215-521-8902, customerservice@lww.com, http://www.lww.com. Eds. Dr. Steven A Rosenberg, Theodore S Lawrence, Vincent T DeVita.

616.99 344.041 USA ISSN 1551-5273
CANCER LAW WEEKLY. Text in English. 2004. w. USD 2,295 in US & Canada; USD 2,495 elsewhere; USD 2,525 combined subscription in US & Canada (print & online eds.); USD 2,755 combined subscription elsewhere (print & online eds.) (effective 2008). back issues avail. **Document type:** *Newsletter, Trade.*
Related titles: E-mail ed.; Online - full text ed.: ISSN 1551-5281. USD 2,295 combined subscription (online & email eds.); single user (effective 2008).
Published by: NewsRx, 2727 Paces Ferry Rd SE, Ste 2-440, Atlanta, GA 30339. TEL 770-435-8286, 800-726-4550, FAX 770-435-6800, pressrelease@newsrx.com, http://www.newsrx.com. Pub. Susan Hasty TEL 770-507-7777.

616.992 USA
CANCER LETTER (ONLINE). Text in English. 19??. w. (46/yr.). USD 395 (effective 2010). adv. back issues avail.; reprints avail. **Document type:** *Newsletter, Academic/Scholarly.*
Media: Online - full text.
Published by: Cancer Letter Inc., PO Box 9905, Washington, DC 20016. TEL 202-362-1809, FAX 202-379-1787, http://www.cancerletter.com/. Eds. Kirsten Boyd Goldberg, Paul Goldberg. Pub. Kirsten Boyd Goldberg.

616.994 IRL ISSN 0304-3835
RC261.A1 CODEN: CALEDQ
➤ **CANCER LETTERS.** Text in English. 1975. 28/yr. EUR 6,337 in Europe to institutions; JPY 841,700 in Japan to institutions; USD 7,087 elsewhere to institutions (effective 2012). adv. charts; illus.; abstr. index. back issues avail.; reprints avail. **Document type:** *Journal, Academic/Scholarly.* **Description:** Covers all areas of cancer research, including molecular biology of cancer, oncogenes, carcinogenesis, hormones and cancer; viral oncology; chemotherapy; epidemiology; and biology of cancer and metastasis.
Related titles: Microform ed.: (from PQC); Online - full text ed.: ISSN 1872-7980 (from IngentaConnect, ScienceDirect).
Indexed: A01, A03, A08, A22, A26, A34, A35, A36, AIDS&CR, ASCA, AgBio, AgrForAb, B21, B25, BIOBASE, BIOSIS Prev, BP, C06, C07, C30, C33, CA, CABA, CIN, ChemAb, ChemTitl, CurCont, D01, DentInd, E12, EMBASE, ESPM, ExcerpMed, F08, F11, F12, GH, H16, H17, I05, IABS, ISR, IndMed, IndVet, Inpharma, LT, MEDLINE, MS&D, MycolAb, N02, N03, NRN, OGFA, P30, P32, P33, P35, P39, P40, PGrRegA, PN&I, R07, R08, R10, R11, R12, R13, RA&MP, RM&VM, Reac, S17, SAA, SCI, SCOPUS, SoyAb, T02, T05, THA, Telegen, ToxAb, TriticAb, VITIS, VS, ViroIAbstr, W07, W10.
—BLDSC (3046.485000), CASDDS, GNLM, IE, Infotrieve, Ingenta, INIST. **CCC.**
Published by: Elsevier Ireland Ltd (Subsidiary of: Elsevier Science & Technology), Elsevier House, Brookvale Plaza, E. Park, Shannon, Co. Clare, Ireland. TEL 353-61-709600, FAX 353-61-709100. Ed. Dr. M Schwab. Pub. Dr. Peter W Harrison. Adv. contact Samantha Cimurs TEL 44-1865-843258. B&W page USD 1,060, color page USD 2,295; trim 7.5 x 10.25. Circ: 248 (paid); 88 (free). **Subscr. to:** Elsevier BV, Radarweg 29, PO Box 211, Amsterdam 1000 AE, Netherlands. JournalsCustomerServiceEMEA@elsevier.com, http://www.elsevier.nl.

616.992 GBR ISSN 1179-1322
▼ ➤ **CANCER MANAGEMENT AND RESEARCH.** Text in English. 2009. irreg. free (effective 2011). **Document type:** *Journal, Academic/Scholarly.* **Description:** Focuses on cancer research and the optimal use of preventative and integrated treatment interventions to achieve improved outcomes, enhanced survival and quality of life for the cancer patient.
Media: Online - full text.
Indexed: EMBASE, P30, SCOPUS.
—**CCC.**
Published by: Dove Medical Press Ltd., Beechfield House, Winterton Way, Macclesfield, SK11 0JL, United Kingdom. TEL 44-1625-509130, FAX 44-1625-617933. Ed. Kenan Onel.

616.992 CAN
CANCER MATTERS. Text in English. m. free. **Document type:** *Newsletter.* **Description:** Offers all kinds of information for people who are concerned about cancer.
Media: E-mail.
Published by: Canadian Cancer Society, 10 Alcorn Ave, Ste 200, Toronto, ON M4V 3B1, Canada. TEL 416-961-7223, FAX 416-961-4189, ccs@cancer.ca, http://www.cancer.ca.

616.992 NLD ISSN 1875-2292
➤ **CANCER MICROENVIRONMENT.** Text in English. 2008. 3/yr. EUR 261 combined subscription to institutions (print & online eds.) (effective 2011). reprint service avail. from PSC. **Document type:** *Journal, Academic/Scholarly.*
Related titles: Online - full text ed.: ISSN 1875-2284. 2008 (from IngentaConnect).
Indexed: A22, B21, E01, EMBASE, ExcerpMed, OGFA, P30, SCOPUS.
—IE. **CCC.**
Published by: Springer Netherlands (Subsidiary of: Springer Science+Business Media), Van Godewijckstraat 30, Dordrecht, 3311 GX, Netherlands. TEL 31-78-6576050, FAX 31-78-6576474. Ed. Isaac Witz.

616.992 AUT ISSN 1868-6958
▼ **CANCER NANOTECHNOLOGY;** basic,translational and clinical research. Text in English. 2010. bi-m. USD 836 combined subscription to institutions (print & online eds.) (effective 2011). **Document type:** *Journal, Academic/Scholarly.* **Description:** Covers basic research on the design and development of nanoparticles for oncology.
Related titles: Online - full text ed.: ISSN 1868-6966. 2010.
Indexed: H12, P30.
—**CCC.**
Published by: Springer Wien (Subsidiary of: Springer Science+Business Media), Sachsenplatz 4-6, Vienna, W 1201, Austria. TEL 43-1-33024150, FAX 43-1-3302426, springer@springer.at, http://www.springer.at. Ed. Raghuraman Kannan.

CANCER NURSING; an international journal for cancer care. *see* MEDICAL SCIENCES—Nurses And Nursing

CANCER NURSING PRACTICE. *see* MEDICAL SCIENCES—Nurses And Nursing

616.992 USA ISSN 1940-6207
➤ **CANCER PREVENTION RESEARCH.** Text in English. 2008 (Jun.). m. USD 325 domestic to individuals; USD 350 foreign to individuals (effective 2011). adv. back issues avail.; reprints avail. **Document type:** *Journal, Academic/Scholarly.* **Description:** Features original studies, reviews, and perspectives within the major topic areas of oncogenesis, risk factors and risk assessment, early detection research, and chemopreventive and other interventions, including the basic science behind them.
Related titles: Online - full text ed.: ISSN 1940-6215. 2008 (Jul.).
Indexed: B25, BIOSIS Prev, CurCont, EMBASE, ExcerpMed, MEDLINE, MycolAb, P30, R10, Reac, SCI, SCOPUS, W07.
—BLDSC (3046.492980), IE, INIST. **CCC.**
Published by: American Association for Cancer Research, 615 Chestnut St, 17th Fl, Philadelphia, PA 19106. TEL 215-440-9300, 866-423-3965, FAX 215-440-9313, aacr@aacr.org, http://www.aacr.org. Ed. Scott M Lippman. Adv. contact Dean Mather TEL 856-768-9360. B&W page USD 805, color page USD 945; bleed 7.625 x 10.8125. Circ: 3,060.

616.99 615.84 FRA ISSN 1278-3218
RC271.R3 CODEN: CARAFC
➤ **CANCER RADIOTHERAPIE.** Text in French, English; Summaries in English, French. 1990. 6/yr. EUR 325 in Europe to institutions; EUR 303.62 in France to institutions; JPY 41,300 in Japan to institutions; USD 432 elsewhere to institutions (effective 2012). back issues avail. **Document type:** *Journal, Academic/Scholarly.* **Description:** Provides a forum within the field of oncology for the dissemination of knowledge in all areas relating to therapeutic radiation oncology: technology, radiophysics, radiobiology and clinical radiotherapy.
Formerly (until 1997): Bulletin du Cancer - Radiotherapie (0924-4212); Which superseded in part (in 1990): Bulletin du Cancer (0007-4551)
Related titles: Microform ed.: (from PQC); Online - full text ed.: ISSN 1769-6658. 1999 (from IngentaConnect, ScienceDirect); ◆ Series: Bulletin du Cancer (Print). ISSN 0007-4551.
Indexed: A01, A03, A08, A22, A26, CA, EMBASE, ExcerpMed, FR, I05, INIS AtomInd, IndMed, MEDLINE, P30, R10, Reac, SCI, SCOPUS, T02, W07.
—BLDSC (3046.494000), GNLM, IE, Infotrieve, Ingenta, INIST. **CCC.**
Published by: (Societe Francaise de Radiotherapie Oncologique), Elsevier Masson (Subsidiary of: Elsevier Health Sciences), 62 Rue Camille Desmoulins, Issy les Moulineaux, Cedex 92442, France. TEL 33-1-71165500, FAX 33-1-71165600, infos@elsevier-masson.fr. Ed. Jean-Jacques Mazeron. Circ: 3,500.

616.994 USA ISSN 0008-5472
RC261 CODEN: CNREA8
➤ **CANCER RESEARCH.** Text in English. 1916. s-m. USD 845 domestic to individuals; USD 1,005 foreign to individuals (effective 2011). adv. abstr.; bibl.; charts; illus. index. back issues avail.; reprints avail. **Document type:** *Journal, Academic/Scholarly.* **Description:** Covers original studies in all areas of basic, clinical, translational, epidemiological, and prevention research devoted to the study of cancer and cancer-related biomedical sciences.
Incorporates (1953-1956): Cancer Research. Supplement (0576-6656); Former titles (until 1941): American Journal of Cancer; (until 1931): Journal of Cancer Research (0099-7013)
Related titles: Microfilm ed.: (from PMC); Online - full text ed.: ISSN 1538-7445.
Indexed: A22, A34, A35, A36, A38, ABC, AIDS Ab, AIDS&CR, ASCA, AgBio, B&BAb, B19, B21, B25, B27, BIOBASE, BIOSIS Prev, BP, C13, C30, C33, CABA, CBTA, CIN, CIS, ChemAb, ChemTitl, CurCont, D01, DBA, DentInd, DokArb, E12, EMBASE, ESPM, ExcerpMed, F08, F11, F12, FS&TA, G10, GH, GenetAb, H16, HGA, I12, IABS, IDIS, INI, INIS AtomInd, ISR, ImmunAb, IndMed, IndVet, Inpharma, M&PBA, MEDLINE, MS&D, MycolAb, N02, N03, N04, NRN, NucAcAb, OGFA, P30, P32, P33, P35, P39, P40, PN&I, R07, R08, R10, R12, RA&MP, RM&VM, Reac, S12, S13, S17, SAA, SCI, SCOPUS, SoyAb, T05, THA, Telegen, ToxAb, VITIS, VS, ViroIAbstr, W07.
—BLDSC (3046.500000), CASDDS, GNLM, IE, Infotrieve, Ingenta, INIST, Linda Hall. **CCC.**
Published by: American Association for Cancer Research, 615 Chestnut St, 17th Fl, Philadelphia, PA 19106. TEL 215-440-9300, 866-423-3965, FAX 215-440-9313, aacr@aacr.org, http://www.aacr.org. Ed. Dr. Frank J Rauscher III. Adv. contact Dean Mather TEL 856-768-9360. B&W page USD 1,790, color page USD 2,735; bleed 7.625 x 10.8125. Circ: 10,200. **Dist. addr. in the UK:** Turpin Distribution Services Ltd.; **Dist. addr. in the US:** Turpin Distribution Services Ltd.

616.992 KOR ISSN 1598-2998
CANCER RESEARCH AND TREATMENT. Text in English. 1966. bi-m. **Document type:** *Journal, Academic/Scholarly.*
Formerly (until 2001): Korean Cancer Research Association. Journal/Daehan Am'hag Hoeji (0496-6872)
Indexed: P30.
—BLDSC (3046.500750).
Published by: Korean Cancer Association, Rm 1824, Gwanghwamun Officia, 163 Sinmunno 1-ga, Jongno-gu, Seoul, 110-999, Korea, S. TEL 82-2-7921486, FAX 82-2-7921410, cancer@kams.or.kr, http://www.cancer.or.kr/. Ed. Yung-June Bang. Pub. Hyo Pyo Lee.

616.992 JPN ISSN 0388-0192
RC279.J35
CANCER RESEARCH INSTITUTE REPORT. Text in English. 1943. irreg. **Document type:** *Journal, Academic/Scholarly.*
Former titles (until 1970): Kanazawa Daigaku Gan Kenkyusho Nempo/Kanazawa University. Cancer Research Institute. Annual Report (0368-5047); (until 1967): Kanazawa Daigaku Kekkaku Kenkyujo Nenpo/Kanazawa University. Research Institute of Tuberculosis. Annual Report (0376-2564)
Published by: Kanazawa University, Cancer Research Institute, 13-1, Takara-machi, Kanazawa, Ishikawa 920-0934, Japan. TEL 81-76-2652799, http://www.kanazawa-u.ac.jp/~ganken/gankenhomejp.html.

616.994 USA ISSN 1935-2506
RC261.A1
CANCER RESEARCH JOURNAL. Text in English. 2007. q. USD 295 to institutions; USD 442 combined subscription to institutions (print & online eds.) (effective 2012). **Document type:** *Journal, Academic/Scholarly.*
Related titles: Online - full text ed.: 2007. USD 295 to institutions (effective 2012).
Indexed: RefZh.
Published by: Nova Science Publishers, Inc., 400 Oser Ave, Ste 1600, Hauppauge, NY 11788. TEL 631-231-7269, FAX 631-231-8175, main@novapublishers.com. Ed. Frank Columbus.

616.994 USA ISSN 1935-620X
CANCER REVIEWS ONLINE. Text in English. 2007 (Apr.). m. free to qualified personnel (effective 2009). back issues avail. **Document type:** *Journal, Academic/Scholarly.* **Description:** Features review articles on the topics such as cancer research, clinical cancer research, cancer epidemiology, biomarkers and prevention, molecular cancer therapeutics, molecular cancer research and cancer prevention research.
Media: Online - full content.
Indexed: B19.
—**CCC.**
Published by: American Association for Cancer Research, 615 Chestnut St, 17th Fl, Philadelphia, PA 19106. TEL 215-440-9300, 866-423-3965, FAX 215-440-7228, aacr@aacr.org, http://www.aacr.org. Ed. George Prendergast. Adv. contact Dean Mather TEL 856-768-9360.

616.992 GBR ISSN 1349-7006
➤ **CANCER SCIENCE (ONLINE).** Text in English. 1998. m. GBP 798 in United Kingdom to institutions; EUR 1,014 in Europe to institutions; USD 1,340 in the Americas to institutions; USD 1,718.20 in Australia to institutions; USD 1,562 elsewhere to institutions (effective 2012). back issues avail. **Document type:** *Journal, Academic/Scholarly.* **Description:** Publishes original articles, editorials, and letters to the editor, describing original research in the fields of basic, translational and clinical cancer research.
Formerly (until 2003): Japanese Journal of Cancer Research (Online) (1876-4673)
Media: Online - full text (from IngentaConnect). **Related titles:** Microform ed.: (from PMC, PQC).
—**CCC.**
Published by: (Japanese Cancer Association JPN), Wiley-Blackwell Publishing Japan (Subsidiary of: Wiley-Blackwell Publishing Ltd.), GS Chiyoda Bldg, 5F 3-11-14 Iidabashi, Chiyoda-ku, Tokyo, 102-0072, Japan. TEL 81-3-52153051, FAX 81-3-52153052, tokyo@blackwellpublishingasia.com. Ed. Yusuke Nakamura.

616.992 USA ISSN 1083-0774
CANCER SMART. Text in English. 1995. q. **Document type:** *Magazine, Consumer.*
Indexed: BiolDig.
Published by: Memorial Sloan-Kettering Cancer Center, 1275 York Ave, New York, NY 10021. TEL 212-639-2000, http://www.mskcc.org.

616.99 USA
CANCER SOURCEBOOK. Text in English. 1990. irreg., latest 2007, 5th ed. USD 84 5th ed. (effective 2008). illus.; stat. master index. **Document type:** *Magazine, Consumer.* **Description:** Offers basic information about the most common forms of cancer and their stages. Includes facts on primary and secondary neoplasms of all kinds, along with treatment options and advice on coping.
Former titles (until 1999): New Cancer Sourcebook; (until 1996): Cancer Sourcebook
Published by: Omnigraphics, Inc., PO Box 31-1640, Detroit, MI 48231. TEL 313-961-1340, 800-234-1340, FAX 313-961-1383, 800-875-1340, info@omnigraphics.com. Eds. Edward J Prucha, Karen Bellenir. Pub. Frederick G Ruffner Jr.

616.99 USA
CANCER SOURCEBOOK FOR WOMEN. Text in English. 1996. irreg., latest 2006, 3rd ed. USD 84 3rd ed. (effective 2008). charts; illus. master index. **Document type:** *Magazine, Consumer.* **Description:** Offers laypersons information on forms of cancer specific to women: breast cancer, cervical cancer, ovarian cancer, cancer of the uterus and uterine sarcoma, and cancer of the vulva, along with advice on coping and seeking treatment.
Published by: Omnigraphics, Inc., PO Box 31-1640, Detroit, MI 48231. TEL 313-961-1340, 800-234-1340, FAX 313-961-1383, 800-875-1340, info@omnigraphics.com. Eds. Amy L Sutton, Edward J Prucha. Pub. Frederick G Ruffner Jr.

616.992 AUS ISSN 1832-4096
CANCER SOUTH AUSTRALIA. Text in English. 1978. a. **Document type:** *Journal, Academic/Scholarly.* **Description:** Reports on the incidence and mortality patterns of cancer.
Former titles (until 2002): Epidemiology of Cancer in South Australia (0818-7207); (until 1984): Cancer in South Australia, Incidence and Mortality (0725-4091)
Published by: South Australia, Department of Health. South Australian Cancer Registry. Epidemiology Branch, PO Box 6, Adelaide, SA 5000, Australia. TEL 61-8-82266360, Epidemiology@health.sa.gov.au, http://www.dh.sa.gov.au/pehs/branches/branch-epidemiology.htm.

616.992 USA ISSN 1943-2534
CANCER SUMMARIES & COMMENTARIES. Text in English. 2008. irreg. **Document type:** *Monographic series, Academic/Scholarly.*
Published by: Physicians' Education Resource, 3500 Maple Ave, Ste 700, Dallas, TX 75219. TEL 888-949-0045, FAX 214-367-3402, CustomerSupport@CancerLearning.com, http://www.cancerlearning.com.

616.99 GRC ISSN 1543-9135
RC270.8
CANCER THERAPY. Text in English. 2/yr. **Document type:** *Journal, Academic/Scholarly.*
Related titles: Online - full text ed.: ISSN 1543-9143.
Indexed: A01, CA, P30, SCOPUS, T02.
—BLDSC (3046.617000).
Address: c/o Teni Boulikas, Chief Editor, Gregoriou Afxentiou 7, Alimos, Athens, 17455, Greece. TEL 30-210-9858454, 30-210-9853849, FAX 30-210-9858453, maria@cancer-therapy.org, teni@regulon.org. Ed. Teni Boulikas.

M

616.99 NZL ISSN 1174-5916
RM260
CANCER TODAY. Text in English. 1999. m. USD 315 to individuals; USD 1,345 to institutions (effective 2008). back issues avail. **Document type:** *Newsletter, Academic/Scholarly.* **Description:** Rapid alerts service on all aspects of drug therapy and disease management of cancer.
Indexed: A01, Inpharma.
—**CCC.**
Published by: Adis International Ltd. (Subsidiary of: Wolters Kluwer N.V.), 41 Centorian Dr, Mairangi Bay, Private Bag 65901, Auckland, 1311, New Zealand. TEL 64-9-4770700, FAX 64-9-4770764, queries@adisonline.com, http://www.adisonline.info/. Ed. Rachel McLeay. **Americas subscr. to:** Adis International Inc., Subscriptions Dept, Ste F 10, 940 Town Center Dr, Langhorne, PA 19047. TEL 877-234-7329.

616.99 NLD ISSN 0927-3042
CODEN: CTRREP
➤ **CANCER TREATMENT AND RESEARCH.** Text in English. 1981. irreg., latest vol.151, 2009. price varies. back issues avail. **Document type:** *Monographic series, Academic/Scholarly.*
Indexed: CIN, ChemAb, ChemTitl, EMBASE, ExcerpMed, IndMed, MEDLINE, P30, R10, Reac, SCOPUS.
—BLDSC (3046.625000), CASDDS, GNLM, IE, Infotrieve, Ingenta, INIST. **CCC.**
Published by: Springer Netherlands (Subsidiary of: Springer Science+Business Media), Van Godewijckstraat 30, Dordrecht, 3311 GX, Netherlands. TEL 31-78-6576050, FAX 31-78-6576474, http://www.springer.com. Ed. Steven T Rosen.

616.994 GBR ISSN 0305-7372
RC270.8 CODEN: CTREDJ
➤ **CANCER TREATMENT REVIEWS.** Text in English. 1974. 8/yr. EUR 701 in Europe to institutions; JPY 75,500 in Japan to institutions; USD 640 elsewhere to institutions (effective 2012). adv. illus. index. back issues avail.; reprint service avail. from PSC. **Document type:** *Journal, Academic/Scholarly.* **Description:** Devoted to important advances in the field of cancer treatment for oncologists and physicians.
Incorporates (1997-2002): Evidence - Based Oncology (1363-4054)
Related titles: Online - full text ed.: ISSN 1532-1967. USD 544 to institutions (effective 2009) (from ScienceDirect).
Indexed: A22, A26, ASCA, B21, BIOSIS Prev, C06, C07, CA, CIN, ChemAb, ChemTitl, CurCont, DentInd, E01, EMBASE, ESPM, ExcerpMed, I05, INI, ISR, IndMed, Inpharma, MEDLINE, MycolAb, OGFA, P30, R10, Reac, SCI, SCOPUS, T02, ToxAb, W07.
—BLDSC (3046.630000), CASDDS, GNLM, IE, Infotrieve, Ingenta, INIST. **CCC.**
Published by: W.B. Saunders Co. Ltd. (Subsidiary of: Elsevier Health Sciences), 32 Jamestown Rd, Camden, London, NW1 7BY, United Kingdom. TEL 44-20-74244200, FAX 44-20-74832293, elsols@elsevier.com. Eds. N Pavlidis, R A Stahel.

616.992 USA ISSN 1543-6810
CANCER VACCINE WEEK. Text in English. 2003. w. USD 2,295 in US & Canada; USD 2,495 elsewhere; USD 2,525 combined subscription in US & Canada (print & online eds.); USD 2,755 combined subscription elsewhere (print & online eds.) (effective 2008). back issues avail. **Document type:** *Newsletter, Trade.* **Description:** Covers the latest research from clinical trials for cancer vaccines, together with news on cancer vaccine development, immunization, monoclonal antibodies, efficacy and safety, FDA regulatory issues and approvals.
Related titles: E-mail ed.; Online - full text ed.: ISSN 1543-6802. USD 2,295 combined subscription (online & email eds.); single user (effective 2008).
Indexed: A26, E08, G08, H11, H12, I05, S09.
—CIS.
Published by: NewsRx, 2727 Paces Ferry Rd SE, Ste 2-440, Atlanta, GA 30339. TEL 770-435-8286, 800-726-4550, FAX 770-435-6800, pressrelease@newsrx.com, http://www.newsrx.com. Pub. Susan Hasty TEL 770-507-7777.

616.99 USA ISSN 1059-3802
CANCER WATCH; the monthly news and educational magazine of cancer research. Abbreviated title: C W. Text in English. 1992. m. USD 50 to individuals; USD 290 to institutions non-profit; USD 436 to corporations (effective 2010). adv. back issues avail. **Document type:** *Newsletter, Trade.*
Media: Online - full text.
Indexed: Inpharma.
—**CCC.**
Published by: Adenine Press, 2066 Central Ave, Schenectady, NY 12304. TEL 518-456-0784, FAX 518-452-4955, info@adeninepress.com, http://www.adeninepress.com. Ed. Mukti H Sarma TEL 518-442-4441.

616.99 USA
CANCER WEEKLY. Text in English. 1988. w. (43/yr.). USD 2,295 in US & Canada; USD 2,495 elsewhere; USD 2,525 combined subscription in US & Canada (print & online eds.); USD 2,755 combined subscription elsewhere (print & online eds.) (effective 2008). back issues avail. **Document type:** *Newsletter, Trade.* **Description:** Contains reports on all the latest oncology developments including prevention, diagnostics, genetics, screening, alternative medicines, risk factors, the latest cancer therapies, vaccines, and biotechnologies.
Former titles (until 2000): Cancer Weekly Plus; Cancer Researcher Weekly (1071-7226); (until 1993): Cancerweekly (1071-7218); (until 1991): N C I Cancer Weekly (0896-7385)
Related titles: E-mail ed.; Online - full text ed.: ISSN 1532-4567. USD 2,295 combined subscription (online & email eds.); single user (effective 2008).
Indexed: A26, B03, CWI, G08, H11, H12, H13, P10, P19, P20, P48, P50, P53, P54, PQC.
—CIS. **CCC.**
Published by: NewsRx, 2727 Paces Ferry Rd SE, Ste 2-440, Atlanta, GA 30339. TEL 770-435-8286, 800-726-4550, FAX 770-435-6800, pressrelease@newsrx.com. Pub. Susan Hasty TEL 770-507-7777.

616.9 CAN
CANCERCARE MANITOBA REPORT. Text in English. 1957. a. free. **Document type:** *Corporate.*
Formerly: Manitoba Cancer Treatment and Research Foundation. Report (0076-3802)
Published by: Manitoba Cancer Treatment and Research Foundation, 100 Olivia St, Winnipeg, MB R3E 0V9, Canada. TEL 204-787-2241, FAX 204-787-1184. Ed. Julia De Fehr. R&P Brent Schacter. Circ: 1,000.

616.992 616.3 FRA ISSN 1953-5171
CANCERO DIGEST. Text in French. 2003. s-a. back issues avail. **Document type:** *Journal, Academic/Scholarly.*
Published by: (Club de Reflexion des Cabinets et Groupes d'Hepato-Gastroenterologie (C R E G G)), A L N Editions, 127 Rue Saint-Dizier, Nancy, 54000, France.

616.994 MEX ISSN 1870-4573
➤ **CANCEROLOGIA.** Text in Spanish, English; Summaries in English. 1954. 4/yr. MXN 100 domestic to institutions; USD 60 foreign to institutions (effective 2005). adv. charts; illus.; stat. back issues avail. **Document type:** *Journal, Academic/Scholarly.* **Description:** Provides original papers and clininal case work on cancer.
Formerly (until 2006): Instituto Nacional de Cancerologia. Revista (0534-3828)
Related titles: CD-ROM ed.; Online - full text ed.: free (effective 2011).
Indexed: IndMed, Inpharma.
—Infotrieve, INIST.
Published by: Instituto Nacional de Cancerologia, Ave. San Fernando 22, Col. Tlalpan, Mexico City, DF 14000, Mexico. TEL 52-55-56551437, FAX 52-55-55733627, mohar@cenids.ssa.gob.mx, http://www.incan.edu.mx/. Ed. Dr. Alejandro Mohar Betancourt. R&P Alejandro Mohar Betancourt. Adv. contact Alicia Garfias Flores. Circ: 1,500 (paid). **Co-sponsors:** Sociedad Mexicana de Estudios Oncologicos; Federacion Latinoamericana de Sociedades Contra el Cancer; Union Internacional Contral el Cancer en Latinoamerica.

616.992 CHE ISSN 2072-6694
➤ **CANCERS.** Text in English. 2008. q. free (effective 2011). **Document type:** *Journal, Academic/Scholarly.*
Media: Online - full text.
Indexed: A01, A36, CABA, E12, F08, GH, N02, N03, P30.
Published by: M D P I AG, Postfach, Basel, 4005, Switzerland. TEL 41-61-6837734, FAX 41-61-3028918, http://www.mdpi.org/. Ed. Robert H Weiss.

616 GBR ISSN 0143-3334
RC268.5 CODEN: CRNGDP
➤ **CARCINOGENESIS**; integrative cancer research. Text in English. 1980. m. GBP 1,296 in United Kingdom to institutions; EUR 1,944 in Europe to institutions; USD 2,592 in US & Canada to institutions; GBP 1,296 elsewhere to institutions; GBP 1,414 combined subscription in United Kingdom to institutions (print & online eds.); EUR 2,120 combined subscription in Europe to institutions (print & online eds.); USD 2,827 combined subscription in US & Canada to institutions (print & online eds.); GBP 1,414 combined subscription elsewhere to institutions (print & online eds.) (effective 2012). adv. illus. index. back issues avail.; reprint service avail. from PSC. **Document type:** *Journal, Academic/Scholarly.* **Description:** Multi-disciplinary research journal in the areas of viral, physical and chemical carcinogenesis and mutagenesis.
Related titles: Online - full text ed.: ISSN 1460-2180. 1997. GBP 1,067 in United Kingdom to institutions; EUR 1,600 in Europe to institutions; USD 2,135 in US & Canada to institutions; GBP 1,067 elsewhere to institutions (effective 2012) (from IngentaConnect).
Indexed: A01, A03, A08, A22, A35, A36, AIDS&CR, AgBio, AgrForAb, B21, B25, B27, BA, BIOBASE, BIOSIS Prev, BP, C30, C33, CA, CABA, ChemAb, CurCont, D01, DBA, E01, E12, EMBASE, ESPM, ExcerpMed, F08, F11, F12, FS&TA, GH, GenetAb, H16, HGA, IABS, ISR, IndMed, Inpharma, MEDLINE, MaizeAb, MycolAb, N02, N03, NRN, NucAcAb, OGFA, P15, P20, P22, P30, P32, P33, P35, P37, P38, P39, P40, P48, P50, P52, P54, P56, PHN&I, PQC, R07, R08, R10, R12, R13, RA&MP, RM&VM, Reac, S17, SCI, SCOPUS, SoyAb, T02, T05, THA, ToxAb, VS, W07, W10.
—BLDSC (3051.007000), CASDDS, GNLM, IE, Infotrieve, Ingenta, INIST. **CCC.**
Published by: Oxford University Press, Great Clarendon St, Oxford, OX2 6DP, United Kingdom. TEL 44-1865-556767, FAX 44-1865-556646, enquiry@oup.co.uk, http://www.oxfordjournals.org. Eds. Alan Clarke, Dr. Curtis C Harris. Pub. Mandy Sketch. adv.: B&W page GBP 270, B&W page USD 485, color page GBP 490, color page USD 880; trim 279 x 216. Circ: 1,050.

616.99 USA
CARING4CANCER. Variant title: Caring For Cancer. Text in English. 2006. q. free to qualified personnel (effective 2008). adv. **Document type:** *Magazine, Consumer.* **Description:** Provides patients with their complete source of knowledge and support for chronic health conditions.
Related titles: Online - full text ed.
Published by: P4 Healthcare LLC, 6031 University Rd, Ste 335, Ellicott City, MD 21043. TEL 888-364-5220, admin@caring4cancer.com. adv.: color page USD 90,000; trim 8.375 x 10.875. Circ: 600,000 (controlled).

616.992 USA ISSN 2090-6706
▼ ➤ **CASE REPORTS IN ONCOLOGICAL MEDICINE.** Text in English. 2011. **Document type:** *Journal, Academic/Scholarly.* **Description:** Publishes case reports in all areas of oncological medicine.
Related titles: Online - full text ed.: ISSN 2090-6714. 2011. free (effective 2011).
Published by: Hindawi Publishing Corporation, 410 Park Ave, 15th Fl, PMB 287, New York, NY 10022. FAX 215-893-4392, 866-446-3294, info@hindawi.com.

616.992 CHE ISSN 1662-6575
RC254.A1
➤ **CASE REPORTS IN ONCOLOGY.** Text in English. 2008. irreg. free (effective 2011). **Document type:** *Monographic series, Academic/Scholarly.* **Description:** Publishes original case reports covering the entire spectrum of oncology.
Media: Online - full text.
Indexed: A22, E01, P30, SCOPUS.
—BLDSC (3058.144560), IE. **CCC.**
Published by: S. Karger AG, Allschwilerstr 10, Basel, 4055, Switzerland. TEL 41-61-3061111, FAX 41-61-3061234, karger@karger.ch, http://www.karger.ch. Ed. M Markman.

616.99249 ESP ISSN 2171-5483
▼ **CASOS CLINICOS EN CANCER DE MAMA.** Text in Spanish. 2009. 3/yr.
Published by: Madrid Accion Medica, C Fernandez de la Hoz, 61, Madrid, 28003, Spain. TEL 34-91-5360814, FAX 34-91-5360607, comercial@accionmedica.com, http://www.accionmedica.com/.

616.994 ESP ISSN 2171-5475
▼ **CASOS CLINICOS EN ONCOHEMATOLOGIA.** Text in Spanish. 2010. 3/yr. **Document type:** *Magazine, Consumer.*
Published by: Madrid Accion Medica, C Fernandez de la Hoz, 61, Madrid, 28003, Spain. TEL 34-91-5360814, FAX 34-91-5360607, comercial@accionmedica.com, http://www.accionmedica.com/.

616.994 ESP ISSN 2013-214X
CASOS CLINICOS EN ONCOHEMATOLOGIA. Text in Spanish. 2008. m. **Document type:** *Journal, Academic/Scholarly.*
Published by: Sanofi Aventis, Edif. Torre Diagona Mar, C. Josep Pla, 2, Barcelona, 08019, Spain. TEL 34-93-4859400, http://www.sanofi-aventis.es/.

616.992 DEU ISSN 1867-416X
➤ **CELLULAR THERAPY AND TRANSPLANTATION.** Text in English, Russian. 2008. irreg. **Document type:** *Journal, Academic/Scholarly.*
Related titles: Online - full text ed.: ISSN 1866-8836. free (effective 2011).
Indexed: EMBASE, P30, SCOPUS.
Published by: Universitaetsklinikum Hamburg - Eppendorf/University Medical Center Hamburg - Eppendorf, Martinstr 52, Hamburg, 20246, Germany.

616.99 USA
CENTER NEWS. Text in English. 1975. bi-m. free donation. **Document type:** *Newsletter.* **Description:** Reports on the latest advances in cancer research and treatment and the newest developments at Memorial Sloan-Kettering.
Indexed: GW.
Published by: (Department of Public Affairs), Memorial Sloan-Kettering Cancer Center, 1275 York Ave, New York, NY 10021. TEL 212-639-2000, PublicAffairs@mskcc.org. Ed. Debbie Rosenberg Bush. Circ: 250,000 (controlled).

616.99 USA
➤ **THE CHALLENGE (BANNING).** Text in English. 1978. q. bk.rev. back issues avail. **Document type:** *Journal, Academic/Scholarly.* **Description:** Covers cancer immunology and biological modifiers.
Published by: Cancer Federation, Inc., PO Box 1298, Banning, CA 92220. TEL 951-849-4325, FAX 951-849-0156, info@cancerfed.org, http://www.cancerfed.com. Circ: 2,000.

616.99 DEU ISSN 0940-6735
CODEN: CHJOFT
➤ **CHEMOTHERAPIE JOURNAL**; Epidemiologie, Diagnose und Therapie von Infektionskrankheiten. Text in German. 1992. bi-m. EUR 186; EUR 35 newsstand/cover (effective 2012). adv. **Document type:** *Journal, Academic/Scholarly.*
Related titles: Supplement(s): Chemotherapie Journal. Supplement. ISSN 0944-6486. 1993.
Indexed: A22, CIN, ChemAb, ChemTitl, EMBASE, ExcerpMed, R10, Reac, SCOPUS.
—BLDSC (3172.303000), CASDDS, GNLM, IE, Ingenta. **CCC.**
Published by: (Paul-Ehrlich-Gesellschaft fuer Chemotherapie e.V.), Wissenschaftliche Verlagsgesellschaft mbH, Postfach 101061, Stuttgart, 70009, Germany. TEL 49-711-25820, FAX 49-711-2582290, service@wissenschaftliche-verlagsgesellschaft.de. Ed. Heike Oberpichler-Schwenk. Circ: 4,290 (paid).

616.994061 USA ISSN 2090-2107
▼ **CHEMOTHERAPY RESEARCH AND PRACTICE.** Text in English. 2009. q. USD 195 (effective 2011). **Document type:** *Journal, Academic/Scholarly.*
Related titles: Online - full text ed.: ISSN 2090-2115. free (effective 2011).
Indexed: A01.
Published by: Hindawi Publishing Corporation, 410 Park Ave, 15th Fl, PMB 287, New York, NY 10022. FAX 215-893-4392, 866-446-3294, hindawi@hindawi.com.

616.992 USA ISSN 1944-446X
CHINESE JOURNAL OF CANCER. Text in English. m. **Document type:** *Journal, Academic/Scholarly.* **Description:** Publishes original research, reviews, extra views, perspectives, supplements, and spotlights in all areas of cancer research.
Media: Online - full content. **Related titles:** ◆ Chinese ed.: Aizheng. ISSN 1000-467X.
Indexed: MEDLINE, P30.
—**CCC.**
Published by: Landes Bioscience, 1002 W Ave, Austin, TX 78701. TEL 512-637-6050, FAX 512-637-6079, info@landesbioscience.com. **Co-publisher:** Sun Yatsen University Cancer Center/Zhongshan Daxue.

616.99 CHN ISSN 1000-9604
CODEN: CJCRFH
➤ **CHINESE JOURNAL OF CANCER RESEARCH/ZHONGGUO AIZHENG YANJIU.** Text in English. 1989. q. EUR 495, USD 598 combined subscription to institutions (print & online eds.) (effective 2012). back issues avail.; reprint service avail. from PSC. **Document type:** *Journal, Academic/Scholarly.* **Description:** Contains research papers, clinical observations and traditional Chinese medicine in the field of cancer research.
Related titles: CD-ROM ed.; Online - full text ed.: ISSN 1993-0631.
Indexed: A22, A26, B&BAb, B19, B21, E01, EMBASE, ExcerpMed, I05, OGFA, R10, Reac, SCI, SCOPUS, W07.
—BLDSC (3180.297700), CASDDS, GNLM, IE, Ingenta. **CCC.**
Published by: (Beijing Institute for Cancer Research), China Anti-Cancer Association/Zhongguo Kangyan Xiehui, 52, Fucheng Lu, Beijing, 100036, China. TEL 86-10-88118836. Ed. Qibo Ling. Circ: 300 (controlled). **Dist. outside of China by:** Springer, Haber Str 7, Heidelberg 69126, Germany. TEL 49-6221-3454303, FAX 49-6221-3454229, subscriptions@springer.com. **Co-publisher:** Springer.

616.99 USA
CHOICE (CHULA VISTA). Text in English. 1975. 3/yr. USD 16 (effective 1999). adv. bk.rev. illus.; stat. back issues avail. **Document type:** *Newsletter, Consumer.* **Description:** Devoted to news about medicine, medical politics, and "alternative" therapies.
Published by: Committee for Freedom of Choice in Medicine, Inc., c/o American Biologics, 1180 Walnut St, Chula Vista, CA 91911. TEL 619-429-8200, FAX 619-429-8004, cfcm@americanbiologics.com, http://www.americanbiologics.com. Ed., R&P Carole Bradford. adv.: B&W page USD 400. Circ: 8,000.

616.992 USA
➤ **CLASSIC PAPERS AND CURRENT COMMENTS**; highlights of cancer research. Text in English. 1996. q. **Document type:** *Journal, Academic/Scholarly.* **Description:** Compiles some of the most important papers on the diagnosis and management of particular disease states previously published in the Journal of Clinical Oncology.
Published by: American Society of Clinical Oncology, 2318 Mill Rd, Ste 800, Alexandria, VA 22314. TEL 571-483-1300, 888-282-2552, asco@asco.org, http://www.asco.org.

616.992 USA ISSN 1941-3718
CLINICAL ADVANCES IN BREAST CANCER. Text in English. 2008. irreg. **Document type:** *Monographic series, Academic/Scholarly.*
Related titles: Online - full text ed.: ISSN 1941-3726.
Published by: Physicians' Education Resource, 3500 Maple Ave, Ste 700, Dallas, TX 75219. TEL 888-949-0045, FAX 214-367-3402, CustomerSupport@CancerLearning.com, http://www.cancerlearning.com.

CLINICAL ADVANCES IN HEMATOLOGY & ONCOLOGY. *see* MEDICAL SCIENCES—Hematology

616.99 NLD ISSN 0262-0898
RC269.5 CODEN: CEXMD2
➤ **CLINICAL AND EXPERIMENTAL METASTASIS.** Text in English. 1982. 8/yr. EUR 1,719, USD 1,798 combined subscription to institutions (print & online eds.) (effective 2012). adv. bk.rev. index. reprint service avail. from PSC. **Document type:** *Journal, Academic/Scholarly.* **Description:** Focuses on the crucial process of dissemination and metastasis formation.
Related titles: CD-ROM ed.; Online - full text ed.: ISSN 1573-7276 (from IngentaConnect).
Indexed: A22, A26, AIDS&CR, ASCA, Agr, B21, B25, BIOBASE, BIOSIS Prev, BibLing, CIN, ChemAb, ChemTitl, CurCont, E01, EMBASE, ESPM, ExcerpMed, IABS, ISR, IndMed, Inpharma, MEDLINE, MycolAb, OGFA, P20, P22, P26, P30, P35, P48, P52, P54, P56, PQC, R10, Reac, SCI, SCOPUS, ToxAb, W07.
—BLDSC (3286.251400), CASDDS, GNLM, IE, Infotrieve, Ingenta, INIST. **CCC.**
Published by: Springer Netherlands (Subsidiary of: Springer Science+Business Media), Van Godewijckstraat 30, Dordrecht, 3311 GX, Netherlands. TEL 31-78-6576050, FAX 31-78-6576474, http://www.springer.com. Eds. Danny R Welch, Suzanne A Eccles, Tatsuro Irimura.

616.992 ITA ISSN 1699-048X
RD651
CLINICAL AND TRANSLATIONAL ONCOLOGY. Text in Multiple languages. 1999. bi-m. EUR 908, USD 1,104 combined subscription to institutions (print & online eds.) (effective 2012). reprint service avail. from PSC. **Document type:** *Journal, Academic/Scholarly.* **Description:** Devoted to fostering interaction between experimental and clinical oncology.
Formerly (until 2005): Revista de Oncologia (1575-3018)
Related titles: CD-ROM ed.: ISSN 1699-5384. 2004; Online - full text ed.: ISSN 1699-3055 (from IngentaConnect); Supplement(s): Revista de Oncologia. Suplemento. ISSN 1579-1971.
Indexed: A22, A26, E01, E08, EMBASE, ExcerpMed, MEDLINE, P30, R10, Reac, S09, SCI, SCOPUS, W07.
—BLDSC (3286.255000), IE, Ingenta. **CCC.**
Published by: (Federacion de Sociedades Espanolas de Oncologia ESP), Springer Italia Srl (Subsidiary of: Springer Science+Business Media), Via Decembrio 28, Milan, 20137, Italy. TEL 39-02-54259722, FAX 39-02-55193360, springer@springer.it. Ed. Andres Cervantes.

616.992 PRT ISSN 1645-9725
CLINICAL & TRANSLATIONAL ONCOLOGY (PORTUGUESE EDITION). Text in English. 2004. bi-m. **Document type:** *Journal, Academic/Scholarly.*
Published by: Medicografica Edicoes Medicas, Rua Camilo Castelo Branco 23-5, Lisbon, 1150-083, Portugal. geral@medicografica.pt, http://www.medicografica.pt.

616.994 USA ISSN 1526-8209
RC280.B8 CODEN: CBCLB7
➤ **CLINICAL BREAST CANCER.** Text in English. bi-m. USD 840 in United States to institutions; USD 890 elsewhere to institutions (effective 2012). adv. back issues avail. **Document type:** *Journal, Academic/Scholarly.* **Description:** Publishes original articles describing various aspects of clinical and translational research of breast cancer.
Related titles: Online - full text ed.: ISSN 1938-0666. USD 475 (effective 2009).
Indexed: A22, C06, C07, C08, CINAHL, CurCont, E01, EMBASE, ExcerpMed, MEDLINE, P30, R10, Reac, SCI, SCOPUS, W07.
—BLDSC (3286.263700), IE, Ingenta, INIST. **CCC.**
Published by: C I G Media Group, L.P., 3102 Oak Lawn Ave., Ste. 610, Dallas, TX 75219. TEL 214-367-3333, FAX 214-367-3301, http://www.cigjournals.com/. Ed. George Sledge.

616.992 USA
CLINICAL CANCER LETTER (ONLINE). Text in English. 200?. m. USD 125 (effective 2010). adv. back issues avail.; reprints avail. **Document type:** *Newsletter, Academic/Scholarly.* **Description:** Covers cancer clinical trials, incluidng newly opened cancer center trials, industry-sponsored studies, and NCI cooperative group trials. Also contains reports on clinical trials results presented at scientific conferences and published in medical journals.
Media: Online - full text.
Published by: Cancer Letter Inc., PO Box 9905, Washington, DC 20016. TEL 202-362-1809, FAX 202-379-1787, http://www.cancerletter.com/. Pub. Kirsten Boyd Goldberg.

616.99 USA ISSN 1078-0432
RC267 CODEN: CCREF4
➤ **CLINICAL CANCER RESEARCH.** Text in English. 1995. s-m. USD 425 domestic to individuals; USD 525 foreign to individuals (effective 2011). adv. back issues avail.; reprints avail. **Document type:** *Journal, Academic/Scholarly.* **Description:** Contains original articles that describes clinical research on the cellular and molecular characterization, prevention, diagnosis, and therapy of human cancer.
Related titles: Online - full text ed.: ISSN 1557-3265.
Indexed: A22, A34, A36, ASCA, B&BAb, B19, B21, B25, BIOBASE, BIOSIS Prev, CABA, CIN, ChemAb, ChemTitl, CurCont, DBA, EMBASE, ExcerpMed, G10, GH, IABS, IDIS, ISR, ImmunAb, IndMed, Inpharma, MEDLINE, MycolAb, N02, N03, NRN, OGFA, P30, P33, P35, R10, Reac, SCI, SCOPUS, T05, VirolAbstr, W07.
—BLDSC (3286.264750), CASDDS, GNLM, IE, Infotrieve, Ingenta, INIST. **CCC.**
Published by: American Association for Cancer Research, 615 Chestnut St, 17th Fl, Philadelphia, PA 19106. TEL 215-440-9300, 866-423-3965, FAX 215-440-9354, aacr@aacr.org, http://www.aacr.org. Adv. contact Dean Mather TEL 856-768-9360. B&W page USD 1,075, color page USD 2,020; bleed 7.625 x 10.8125. Circ: 5,180. **Dist. addr. in N. America to:** Turpin Distribution Services Ltd.; **Dist. addr. outside N. America to:** Turpin Distribution Services Ltd.

616.994 USA ISSN 1533-0028
RC280.C6 CODEN: CCCLCF
➤ **CLINICAL COLORECTAL CANCER.** Text in English. q. USD 525 in United States to institutions; USD 575 elsewhere to institutions (effective 2012). adv. back issues avail. **Document type:** *Journal, Academic/Scholarly.* **Description:** Publishes original articles describing various aspects of clinical and translational research of colorectal cancer.
Related titles: Online - full text ed.: ISSN 1938-0674. USD 475 to institutions (effective 2009).
Indexed: A22, C06, C07, C08, CINAHL, CurCont, E01, EMBASE, ExcerpMed, MEDLINE, P30, R10, Reac, SCI, SCOPUS, W07.
—BLDSC (3286.268450), IE, Ingenta, INIST. **CCC.**
Published by: C I G Media Group, L.P., 3102 Oak Lawn Ave., Ste. 610, Dallas, TX 75219. TEL 214-367-3333, FAX 214-367-3301, http://www.cigjournals.com/. Ed. Edward Chu.

➤ **CLINICAL DERMATOLOGY (LONDON)**; retinoids & other treatments. *see* MEDICAL SCIENCES—Dermatology And Venereology

616.992 USA ISSN 1938-0682
➤ **CLINICAL GENITOURINARY CANCER (ONLINE).** Text in English. 2005. s-a. free. Supplement avail.; back issues avail. **Document type:** *Journal, Academic/Scholarly.* **Description:** Publishes original articles describing various aspects of clinical and translational research of prostate, urinary, and renal cancers. Covers detection, diagnosis, prevention, and treatment of prostate, urinary, and renal cancers.
Media: Online - full text.
—CCC.
Published by: C I G Media Group, L.P., 3102 Oak Lawn Ave., Ste. 610, Dallas, TX 75219. TEL 214-367-3333, FAX 214-367-3301, http://www.cigjournals.com/. Eds. Oliver Sartor, Ronald M. Bukowski.

➤ **CLINICAL JOURNAL OF ONCOLOGY NURSING.** *see* MEDICAL SCIENCES—Nurses And Nursing

616.99419 USA ISSN 1938-0704
➤ **CLINICAL LEUKEMIA (ONLINE).** Text in English. 2006. q. free. back issues avail. **Document type:** *Journal, Academic/Scholarly.* **Description:** Publishes original articles describing various aspects of clinical and translational research of leukemia, including etection, diagnosis, prevention, and treatment of leukemia.
Media: Online - full text.
—CCC.
Published by: C I G Media Group, L.P., 3102 Oak Lawn Ave., Ste. 610, Dallas, TX 75219. TEL 214-367-3333, FAX 214-367-3301, http://www.cigjournals.com/. Ed. Jorge Cortez.

616 USA ISSN 1525-7304
RC280.L8 CODEN: CLCLCA
➤ **CLINICAL LUNG CANCER.** Text in English. 1999. bi-m. USD 840 in United States to institutions; USD 890 elsewhere to institutions (effective 2012). adv. back issues avail. **Document type:** *Journal, Academic/Scholarly.* **Description:** Publishes original articles describing various aspects of clinical and translational research of lung cancer, including detection, diagnosis, prevention, and treatment of lung cancer. The main emphasis is on recent scientific developments in all areas related to lung cancer.
Related titles: Online - full text ed.: ISSN 1938-0690. USD 760 (effective 2009).
Indexed: A22, C06, C07, C08, CINAHL, CurCont, E01, EMBASE, ExcerpMed, MEDLINE, P30, R10, Reac, SCI, SCOPUS, W07.
—BLDSC (3286.298200), IE, Ingenta, INIST. **CCC.**
Published by: C I G Media Group, L.P., 3102 Oak Lawn Ave., Ste. 610, Dallas, TX 75219. TEL 214-367-3333, FAX 214-367-3301, http://www.cigjournals.com/. Ed. David R. Gandara.

616.992 616.15 USA ISSN 2152-2650
RC280.L9 CODEN: CLLYAO
➤ **CLINICAL LYMPHOMA, MYELOMA & LEUKEMIA.** Text in English. 2000. bi-m. USD 840 in United States to institutions; USD 890 elsewhere to institutions (effective 2012). adv. back issues avail. **Document type:** *Journal, Academic/Scholarly.* **Description:** Publishes original articles describing various aspects of clinical and translational research of lymphoma and myeloma, including detection, diagnosis, prevention, and treatment of lymphoma, myeloma, and related disorders including macroglobulinemia, amyloidosis, and plasma-cell dyscrasias.
Former titles (until 2010): Clinical Lymphoma & Myeloma (1557-9190); (until 2005): Clinical Lymphoma (1526-9655)
Related titles: Online - full text ed.: ISSN 2152-2669. USD 190 to individuals (effective 2010).
Indexed: A22, A29, B20, B21, C06, C07, C08, CINAHL, CTA, CurCont, E01, EMBASE, ESPM, ExcerpMed, ImmunAb, Inpharma, MEDLINE, NSA, P30, P35, R10, Reac, SCI, SCOPUS, W07.
—BLDSC (3286.298280), IE, Ingenta, INIST. **CCC.**
Published by: C I G Media Group, L.P., 3102 Oak Lawn Ave., Ste. 610, Dallas, TX 75219. TEL 214-367-3333, FAX 214-367-3301, http://www.cigjournals.com/. Eds. Bruce D. Cheson, Sundar Jagannath.

616.992 NZL ISSN 1179-5549
RC254.A1
➤ **CLINICAL MEDICINE INSIGHTS: ONCOLOGY.** Text in Italian. 2007. irreg. free (effective 2011). **Document type:** *Journal, Academic/Scholarly.* **Description:** Brings out articles on all aspects of cancer research and treatment.
Formerly (until 2010): Clinical Medicine: Oncology (1177-9314)
Media: Online - full text.
Indexed: A01, C06, C07, EMBASE, ExcerpMed, P30, SCOPUS, T02.
—CCC.
Published by: Libertas Academica Ltd., PO Box 300-874, Mairangi Bay, Auckland, 0751, New Zealand. TEL 64-9-4763930, FAX 64-9-3531397, enquiries@la-press.com. Ed. William Chi-Shing Cho.

616.992 NZL ISSN 1179-2531
▼ **CLINICAL MEDICINE REVIEWS IN ONCOLOGY.** Text in English. 2009. irreg. free (effective 2011). **Document type:** *Journal, Academic/Scholarly.* **Description:** Publishes articles on all aspects of cancer research and treatment.
Media: Online - full text.
—CCC.
Published by: Libertas Academica Ltd., PO Box 300-874, Mairangi Bay, Auckland, 0751, New Zealand. TEL 64-9-4763930, FAX 64-9-3531397, editorial@la-press.com. Ed. Garry Walsh.

616.994 GBR ISSN 0936-6555
RC254.A1 CODEN: CLIOEH
➤ **CLINICAL ONCOLOGY.** Text in English. 1989. 10/yr. EUR 919 in Europe to institutions; JPY 98,800 in Japan to institutions; USD 863 elsewhere to institutions (effective 2012). adv. bk.rev. back issues avail.; reprints avail. **Document type:** *Journal, Academic/Scholarly.* **Description:** Publishes international, multidisciplinary research covering all aspects of the clinical management of cancer patients.
Related titles: Online - full text ed.: ISSN 1433-2981. USD 742 to institutions (effective 2009) (from IngentaConnect, ScienceDirect).
Indexed: A01, A03, A08, A22, A26, C06, C07, CA, CurCont, EMBASE, ExcerpMed, I05, INI, IndMed, Inpharma, MEDLINE, P30, P35, R10, Reac, SCI, SCOPUS, T02, W07.
—BLDSC (3286.317000), GNLM, IE, Infotrieve, Ingenta, INIST. **CCC.**
Published by: (Royal College of Radiologists), W.B. Saunders Co. Ltd. (Subsidiary of: Elsevier Health Sciences), 32 Jamestown Rd, Camden, London, NW1 7BY, United Kingdom. TEL 44-20-74244200, FAX 44-20-74832293, elsols@elsevier.com. Ed. P J Hoskins.

616.99 USA ISSN 0886-7186
RC254.A1
CLINICAL ONCOLOGY ALERT. Text in English. 1986. m. USD 319 combined subscription (print & online eds.); USD 53 per issue (effective 2010). index. reprints avail. **Document type:** *Newsletter, Trade.* **Description:** Covers abstracts of developments in oncology, combined with expert physician commentary. Special features by practicing oncologists give you important insights into the specialty.
Related titles: Online - full text ed.
Indexed: A26, C06, C07, CA, E08, G08, H11, H12, I05, P20, P24, P48, P54, PQC, S09, T02.
—CCC.
Published by: A H C Media LLC (Subsidiary of: Thomson Corporation, Healthcare Information Group), 3525 Piedmont Rd, NE, Bldg 6, Ste 400, Atlanta, GA 30305. TEL 404-262-7436, 800-688-2421, FAX 404-262-7837, 800-284-3291, customerservice@ahcmedia.com, http://www.ahcmedia.com/. Ed. William B Ershler. Pub. Brenda L Mooney TEL 404-262-5403. **Subscr. to:** PO Box 105109, Atlanta, GA 30348. TEL 404-262-5476, FAX 404-262-5560.

616.992 CHN ISSN 1674-5361
➤ **CLINICAL ONCOLOGY AND CANCER RESEARCH.** Text in English. 2004. bi-m. EUR 576, USD 699 combined subscription to institutions (print & online eds.) (effective 2011). reprint service avail. from PSC. **Document type:** *Journal, Academic/Scholarly.*
Formerly (until 2010): Chinese Journal of Clinical Oncology (1672-7118)
Related titles: Online - full text ed.: ISSN 1868-324X; ◆ Chinese ed.: Zhongguo Zhongliu Linchuang. ISSN 1000-8179.
Indexed: A22, A26, B25, BIOSIS Prev, E01, EMBASE, ExcerpMed, H12, I05, MycolAb.
—BLDSC (3286.317700), East View, IE. **CCC.**
Published by: Tianjin Yike Daxue Fushu Zhongliu Yiyuan/Tianjin Medical University Cancer Institute and Hospital, Ti-Yuan-Bei, Huanhu Xi Lu, Hexi-qu, Tianjin, 300060, China. **Co-publisher:** Springer.

616.992 GBR ISSN 2230-2263
▼ ➤ **CLINICAL ONCOLOGY IN ADOLESCENTS AND YOUNG ADULTS.** Text in English. 2011. irreg. free (effective 2011). **Document type:** *Journal, Academic/Scholarly.* **Description:** Contains research on all aspects of the epidemiology, diagnosis and treatment of cancers in adolescents and young adults.
Media: Online - full text.
—CCC.
Published by: Dove Medical Press Ltd., Beechfield House, Winterton Way, Macclesfield, SK11 0JL, United Kingdom. TEL 44-1625-509130, FAX 44-1625-617933. Ed. Dr. Mark Kieran.

616.992 USA ISSN 1933-0677
CLINICAL ONCOLOGY NEWS. Text in English. 2006. bi-m. USD 70 domestic; USD 90 foreign; USD 7 per issue domestic; USD 10 per issue foreign; free to qualified personnel (effective 2009). adv. back issues avail. **Document type:** *Magazine, Trade.* **Description:** Aims to serve the professional needs of oncologists, hematologist/ oncologists and oncology nurses.
Related titles: Online - full text ed.: ISSN 1948-111X.
Published by: McMahon Group, 545 W 45th St, 8th Fl, New York, NY 10036. TEL 212-957-5300, FAX 212-957-7230, mcmahon@med.com, http://www.mcmahongroup.com. Ed. Kate O'Rourke TEL 212-957-5300 ext 265. Pub. Raymond E McMahon. Adv. contact Nancy Parker TEL 212-957-5300 ext 260. Circ: 17,733.

616.992 USA
CLINICAL ONCOLOGY NEWS SPECIAL EDITION. Text in English. 199?. a. free to qualified personnel (effective 2010). adv. **Document type:** *Journal, Trade.* **Description:** Brings out collection of relevant clinical reviews devoted exclusively to exploring the drug information in succinct educational summaries.
Formerly: Oncology Special Edition
Published by: McMahon Group, 545 W 45th St, 8th Fl, New York, NY 10036. TEL 212-957-5300, FAX 212-957-7230, mcmahon@med.com, http://www.mcmahongroup.com.

616.992 USA ISSN 1543-6799
CLINICAL ONCOLOGY WEEK. Text in English. 2003. w. USD 2,295 in US & Canada; USD 2,495 elsewhere; USD 2,525 combined subscription in US & Canada (print & online eds.); USD 2,755 combined subscription elsewhere (print & online eds.) (effective 2008). back issues avail. **Document type:** *Newsletter, Trade.* **Description:** Contains clinical trial results and reports on current research in oncology, including cancer vaccines, new drug development, diagnostics, genetics and risk factors.

Related titles: E-mail ed.; Online - full text ed.: ISSN 1543-6780. USD 2,295 combined subscription (online & email eds.); single user (effective 2008).
Indexed: A26, E08, G08, H11, H12, I05, S09.
—CIS.
Published by: NewsRx, 2727 Paces Ferry Rd SE, Ste 2-440, Atlanta, GA 30339. TEL 770-435-8286, 800-726-4550, FAX 770-435-6800, pressrelease@newsrx.com, http://www.newsrx.com. Pub. Susan Hasty TEL 770-507-7777.

CLINICAL OVARIAN CANCER AND OTHER GYNECOLOGIC MALIGNANCIES. *see* MEDICAL SCIENCES—Obstetrics And Gynecology

CLINICAL RADIOLOGY. *see* MEDICAL SCIENCES—Radiology And Nuclear Medicine

616.992 616.4 USA ISSN 1534-8644
RC931.M45 CODEN: CRBMBF
➤ **CLINICAL REVIEWS IN BONE AND MINERAL METABOLISM.** Text and summaries in English. 2002. q. EUR 299, USD 366 combined subscription to institutions (print & online eds.) (effective 2012). bk.rev. illus. back issues avail.; reprint service avail. from PSC. **Document type:** *Journal, Academic/Scholarly.* **Description:** Focuses on a single theme that integrates new information, both basic and clinical science, into the context of clinical practice.
Related titles: Online - full text ed.: ISSN 1559-0119 (from IngentaConnect).
Indexed: A01, A22, Agr, B21, BIOBASE, CA, CTA, E01, EMBASE, ESPM, ExcerpMed, IABS, P30, R10, Reac, SCOPUS, T02, ToxAb.
—BLDSC (3286.374560), IE, Ingenta. **CCC.**
Published by: Humana Press, Inc. (Subsidiary of: Springer Science+Business Media), 999 Riverview Dr, Ste 208, Totowa, NJ 07512. TEL 973-256-1699, FAX 973-256-8341, humana@humanapr.com, http://humanapress.com/journals.pasp. Ed. Angelo Licata. Pub. Thomas B. Lanigan Jr. R&P Wendy A. Warren. Adv. contacts John Chasse, Thomas B. Lanigan Jr.

616.992 USA
CLINICAL TRIALS NEWS. Text in English. w. bk.rev. back issues avail. **Document type:** *Newsletter.* **Description:** Features special reports and clinical briefs dealing with all aspects of cancer.
Media: Online - full text.
Published by: University of Pennsylvania, Cancer Center Clinical Trials Group, 1223 Penn Tower, 3400 Spruce St, Philadelphia, PA 19104. FAX 215-349-8299. Ed. Maggie Hampshire.

616.992 AUS ISSN 1328-9454
CLINICAL UPDATE. Text in English. 1998. s-a. free to qualified personnel (effective 2007). **Document type:** *Newsletter, Trade.* **Description:** Provides surgeons, medical and radiation oncologists with information about recent breast cancer research with immediate signifance to clinical practice.
Related titles: Online - full text ed.
Published by: N H M R C National Breast Cancer Centre, 92 Parramatta Rd, Camperdown, NSW 2050, Australia. TEL 61-2-90363030, FAX 61-2-90363077, directorate@nbcc.org.au, http://www.nbcc.org.au/pages/info/resource/nbccpubs/brnews/contents.htm. Ed. Dr. Karen Luxford. Circ: 1,200.

616.992 USA ISSN 1947-8178
▼ **COLORECTAL CANCER;** bench to bedside. Text in English. 2009. 3/yr. **Document type:** *Journal, Academic/Scholarly.* **Description:** Research on colorectal cancer.
Published by: Wolters Kluwer Health, 530 Walnut St, Philadelphia, PA 19106. TEL 215-521-8300, info@wolterskluwer.com, http://www.wkhealth.com.

616.994 GBR ISSN 1758-194X
▼ ➤ **COLORECTAL CANCER.** Text in English. forthcoming 2011. 3/yr. GBP 350 combined subscription domestic to institutions (print & online eds.); USD 610 combined subscription in North America to institutions (print & online eds.); JPY 64,500 combined subscription in Japan to institutions (print & online eds.); EUR 490 combined subscription elsewhere to institutions (print & online eds.) (effective 2011). adv. **Document type:** *Journal, Academic/Scholarly.*
Related titles: Online - full text ed.: ISSN 1758-1958. forthcoming. GBP 310 domestic to institutions; USD 540 in North America to institutions; JPY 58,000 in Japan to institutions; EUR 435 elsewhere to institutions (effective 2011).
Published by: Future Medicine Ltd. (Subsidiary of: Future Science Ltd.), Unitec House, 2 Albert Pl, London, N3 1QB, United Kingdom. TEL 44-20-83716080, FAX 44-20-83716099, info@futuremedicine.com, http://www.futuremedicine.com/. Ed. Elisa Manzotti TEL 44-20-83716090. Pub. David Hughes. Adv. contact Simon Boisseau TEL 44-208-3716083.

616.992 NZL ISSN 1178-6094
COLORECTAL ONCOLOGY RESEARCH REVIEW. Text in English. 2006. q. free to qualified personnel (effective 2009). **Document type:** *Journal, Academic/Scholarly.*
Media: Online - full text.
Published by: Research Review Ltd., N Shore Mail Centre, PO Box 100116, Auckland, New Zealand. TEL 64-9-4102277, info@researchreview.co.nz.

616.99 USA ISSN 0743-5061
RA960 CODEN: HSOJEY
COMMUNITY CANCER PROGRAMS IN THE UNITED STATES. Text in English. 1980. a. USD 150 (effective 2001). back issues avail. **Document type:** *Directory.* **Description:** Summaries of close to 600 cancer programs in the U.S. Includes medical contacts, a cancer program narrative description, and cancer program data.
Published by: Association of Community Cancer Centers, 11600 Nebel St, Ste 201, Rockville, MD 20852-2557. TEL 301-984-9496, FAX 301-770-1949. Ed. Lee E Mortenson. R&P Donald Jewler.

616.992 USA ISSN 1548-5315
RC261.A1
➤ **COMMUNITY ONCOLOGY.** Text in English. 2004 (May). m. USD 363 in United States to institutions; USD 401 elsewhere to institutions (effective 2012). adv. back issues avail. **Document type:** *Journal, Academic/Scholarly.* **Description:** Features articles relating to research, quality of care, and practice management issues in the community setting.
Related titles: Online - full text ed.: free (effective 2010).
Indexed: C06, C07, EMBASE, ExcerpMed, P30, R10, Reac, SCOPUS.
—BLDSC (3363.646750). **CCC.**
Published by: Elsevier Oncology (Subsidiary of: International Medical News Group), 60 Columbia Rd, Bldg B, Morristown, NJ 07960. TEL 973-290-8200, FAX 631-424-8905, L.Kalish@Elsevier.com, http://www.elsevieroncology.com/. Eds. David H Henry, Linda D Bosserman, Lee S Schwartzberg. Circ: 26,300.

616.99 USA
➤ **CONTEMPORARY CANCER RESEARCH.** Text in English. 1998. irreg., latest 2007. price varies. illus. 500 p./no.; back issues avail.; reprints avail. **Document type:** *Monographic series, Academic/Scholarly.* **Description:** Provides state-of-the-art scientific and medical reviews on the subject of cutting-edge cancer research. Intended for all those conducting both basic and clinical cancer research.
Related titles: Online - full text ed.
Indexed: GenetAb, HGA.
Published by: Humana Press, Inc. (Subsidiary of: Springer Science+Business Media), 233 Spring St, New York, NY 10013. TEL 212-460-1500, FAX 212-460-1575, service-ny@springer.com. Ed. Jac A Nickoloff.

616.99 CHE ISSN 0250-3220
CODEN: COONEV
➤ **CONTRIBUTIONS TO ONCOLOGY/BEITRAEGE ZUR ONKOLOGIE.** Text in English, German. 1979. irreg., latest vol.56, 2002. price varies. index. **Document type:** *Monographic series, Academic/Scholarly.* **Description:** Describes the latest developments in various areas of oncology as well as future research directions.
Related titles: Online - full text ed.: ISSN 1662-2928.
Indexed: A22, CIN, ChemAb, ChemTitl, EMBASE, ExcerpMed.
—BLDSC (1887.090000), CASDDS, GNLM, IE, Ingenta, INIST. **CCC.**
Published by: S. Karger AG, Allschwilerstr 10, Basel, 4055, Switzerland. TEL 41-61-3061111, FAX 41-61-3061234, karger@karger.ch, http://www.karger.ch. Eds. W Queisser, W Scheithauer.

616.992 616.8 NLD ISSN 2210-5565
▼ **CONTROVERSIES IN NEURO-ONCOLOGY.** Text in English. 2010. irreg. **Document type:** *Monographic series, Academic/Scholarly.*
Media: Online - full text.
Published by: Bentham Science Publishers Ltd., PO Box 294, Bussum, 1400 AG, Netherlands. TEL 31-35-6923800, FAX 31-35-6980150, sales@bentham.org, http://www.bentham.org.

616.994 USA ISSN 1544-5488
RC261.A1
COPING WITH CANCER. Text in English. 1986. bi-m. USD 19 domestic; USD 35 foreign (effective 2010). adv. bk.rev. illus. 60 p./no. 3 cols./p.; back issues avail.; reprints avail. **Document type:** *Magazine, Consumer.* **Description:** Aims to inspire patients and survivors to assume greater responsibility for, and participation in, the many aspects of cancer.
Formerly (until 199?): Coping (1043-8637)
Indexed: C06, C07, C08, CINAHL.
Published by: Media America, Inc., PO Box 682268, Franklin, TN 37068. TEL 615-790-2400, FAX 615-794-0179, info@copingmag.com, http://www.copingmag.com.

616.992 616.15 FRA ISSN 1954-4820
CORRESPONDANCES EN ONCO-HEMATOLOGIE. Text in French. 2006. quadrennial. back issues avail. **Document type:** *Journal, Academic/Scholarly.*
—INIST.
Published by: Edimark S.A.S., 2 Rue Sainte-Marie, Courbevoie, Cedex 92418, France. TEL 33-1-46676300, FAX 33-1-46676310, contact@edimark.fr.

616.994 CAN ISSN 1922-5547
COURAGE. Text in English. 1997. s-a. free to qualified personnel (effective 2010). back issues avail. **Document type:** *Magazine, Consumer.* **Description:** Provides articles about cancer prevention and awareness to help improving survivorship.
Formerly (until 2009): Challenge (1209-661X)
Published by: Ottawa Regional Cancer Foundation, 704-265, Carling Ave, Ottawa, ON K1S 2E1, Canada. TEL 613-247-3527, FAX 613-247-3526, info@ottawacancer.ca. Ed. Louise Rachlis.

COURTROOM MEDICINE: CANCER. *see* LAW

616.99 USA ISSN 0893-9675
RC268.5 CODEN: CRONEI
➤ **CRITICAL REVIEWS IN ONCOGENESIS.** Text in English. 1989. q. USD 716 to institutions (effective 2010). adv. back issues avail.; reprints avail. **Document type:** *Journal, Academic/Scholarly.* **Description:** Contains reviews and theme issues on topics of current interest in basic and patient-oriented cancer research. Covers various fields of molecular oncology.
Indexed: A22, AIDS&CR, ASCA, B21, BIOBASE, BIOSIS Prev, CIN, ChemAb, ChemTitl, EMBASE, ExcerpMed, IABS, ISR, IndMed, Inpharma, MEDLINE, MycolAb, NSA, OGFA, P30, R10, Reac, SCOPUS.
—BLDSC (3487.478900), CASDDS, GNLM, IE, Infotrieve, Ingenta. **CCC.**
Published by: Begell House Inc., 50 Cross Hwy, Redding, CT 06896. TEL 203-938-1300, FAX 203-938-1304, orders@begellhouse.com. Ed. Ragnhild A Lothe.

616.99 616.15 IRL ISSN 1040-8428
RC254.A1 CODEN: CCRHEC
➤ **CRITICAL REVIEWS IN ONCOLOGY / HEMATOLOGY.** Text in English. 1981. 12/yr. EUR 2,146 in Europe to institutions; JPY 285,100 in Japan to institutions; USD 2,402 elsewhere to institutions (effective 2012). back issues avail. **Document type:** *Journal, Academic/Scholarly.* **Description:** Publishes scholarly, critical reviews in the fields of oncology and hematology.
Formerly: C R C Critical Reviews in Oncology - Hematology (0737-9587)
Related titles: Online - full text ed.: ISSN 1879-0461 (from IngentaConnect, ScienceDirect).
Indexed: A01, A03, A08, A22, A26, AIDS&CR, ASCA, B21, BIOBASE, BIOSIS Prev, CA, CurCont, EMBASE, ExcerpMed, I05, IABS, ISR, IndMed, Inpharma, MEDLINE, MycolAb, OGFA, P30, R10, Reac, SCI, SCOPUS, T02, Telegen, W07.
—BLDSC (3487.479000), GNLM, IE, Infotrieve, Ingenta, INIST. **CCC.**
Published by: Elsevier Ireland Ltd (Subsidiary of: Elsevier Science & Technology), Elsevier House, Brookvale Plaza, E. Park, Shannon, Co. Clare, Ireland. TEL 353-61-709600, FAX 353-61-709100. Ed. Dr. M S Aapro. Pub. Dr. Peter W Harrison. Circ: 168 (paid); 76 (free). **Subscr. to:** Elsevier BV, Radarweg 29, PO Box 211, Amsterdam 1000 AE, Netherlands. JournalsCustomerServiceEMEA@elsevier.com, http://www.elsevier.nl.

616.89 ESP ISSN 1889-7088
▼ **CUADERNOS DEL RESIDENTE EN ONCOLOGIA.** Text in Spanish. 2009. q. **Document type:** *Journal, Academic/Scholarly.*
Published by: Jarpyo Editores S.A., Ave de la Concha Espina, No. 9 Dcha., Madrid, 28016, Spain. TEL 34-91-3144338, editorial@jarpyo.es, http://www.jarpyo.es. Ed. Gumersindo Perez Manga. Circ: 1,000.

616.994 USA ISSN 1534-7664
RC254.A1
CURE. Variant title: Cancer Updates, Research & Education. Text in English. 2002. q. USD 20 elsewhere to individuals; USD 30 in Canada to individuals; USD 100 elsewhere to individuals; USD 75 domestic to institutions; USD 120 in Canada to institutions; USD 150 elsewhere to institutions; USD 10 newsstand/cover; free to patients & their caregivers (effective 2005). **Document type:** *Magazine, Consumer.*
Related titles: Online - full text ed.
Indexed: C06, C07, C08, CINAHL.
—BLDSC (3493.507000), IE. **CCC.**
Published by: Cure Media Group, LP., 3500 Maple Ave, Ste 750, Dallas, TX 75219. TEL 214-367-3500, 800-210-2873, FAX 214-367-3306.

616.994 FRA ISSN 1768-4463
CURIE@CTU. Text in French. 2004. q. free (effective 2007). back issues avail. **Document type:** *Newsletter, Consumer.*
Related titles: Online - full text ed.
Published by: Institut Curie, 26 Rue d'Ulm, Paris, 75248 Cedex 05, France. TEL 33-1-42346600.

CURRENT ADVANCES IN CANCER RESEARCH. *see* MEDICAL SCIENCES—Abstracting, Bibliographies, Statistics

616.99 616.1 NLD ISSN 2211-5528
▼ **CURRENT ANGIOGENESIS.** Text in English. forthcoming 2012. 3/yr. USD 540 to institutions (print or online ed.) (effective 2012). **Document type:** *Journal, Academic/Scholarly.* **Description:** Presents recent developments in angiogenesis research, covering all aspects from preclinical to clinical research pertaining to both neoplastic and non-neoplastic disorders.
Related titles: Online - full text ed.: ISSN 2211-5536. forthcoming.
Published by: Bentham Science Publishers Ltd., PO Box 294, Bussum, 1400 AG, Netherlands. TEL 31-35-6923800, FAX 31-35-6980150, sales@bentham.org, http://www.bentham.org. Ed. Dr. Dipak Panigrahy. **Subscr. to:** Bentham Science Publishers Ltd., c/o Richard E Morrissy, PO Box 446, Oak Park, IL 60301. TEL 312-413-5867, FAX 312-996-7107, subscriptions@bentham.org.

616.992 USA ISSN 1943-4588
RC280.B8
▼ ➤ **CURRENT BREAST CANCER REPORTS.** Text in English. 2009 (Mar.). q. reprint service avail. from PSC. **Document type:** *Journal, Academic/Scholarly.* **Description:** Aims to help the reader, by providing in a systematic manner, the views of experts on the current advances in the breast cancer field in a clear and readable form and by providing reviews which highlight the most important papers recently published from the wealth of original publications.
Related titles: Online - full text ed.: ISSN 1943-4596. 2009 (Mar.). USD 1,158 to institutions (effective 2010).
Indexed: EMBASE, P30, SCOPUS.
—IE. **CCC.**
Published by: Current Medicine Group LLC (Subsidiary of: Springer Science+Business Media), 400 Market St, Ste 700, Philadelphia, PA 19106. TEL 215-574-2266, 800-427-1796, FAX 215-574-2225, info@phl.cursci.com, http://www.current-medicine.com. Ed. D F Hayes.

616.994 NLD ISSN 1568-0096
RC271.C5 CODEN: CCDTB9
➤ **CURRENT CANCER DRUG TARGETS.** Text in English. 2001 (May). 9/yr. USD 1,840 to institutions (print or online ed.) (effective 2012). adv. back issues avail.; reprints avail. **Document type:** *Journal, Academic/Scholarly.* **Description:** Aims to cover all the latest and outstanding developments on the medicinal chemistry, pharmacology, molecular biology, genomics and biochemistry of contemporary molecular drug targets involved in cancer e.g. disease specific proteins, receptors, enzymes, genes.
Related titles: Online - full text ed.: ISSN 1873-5576 (from IngentaConnect).
Indexed: A01, A02, A03, A08, AIDS&CR, B&BAb, B19, B21, B26, B27, BIOBASE, BIOSIS Prev, BioEngAb, C33, CA, ChemAb, EMBASE, ESPM, ExcerpMed, IABS, M&PBA, MEDLINE, MycolAb, P30, R10, Reac, SCI, SCOPUS, T02, ToxAb, W07.
—BLDSC (3494.792500), IE, Infotrieve, Ingenta. **CCC.**
Published by: Bentham Science Publishers Ltd., PO Box 294, Bussum, 1400 AG, Netherlands. TEL 31-35-6923800, FAX 31-35-6980150, sales@bentham.org. Ed. John K Buolamwini TEL 901- 448-7533. **Subscr. addr. in the US:** Bentham Science Publishers Ltd., c/o Richard E Morrissy, PO Box 446, Oak Park, IL 60301. TEL 312-413-5867, FAX 312-996-7107, subscriptions@bentham.org.

616.99 DEU ISSN 0940-0745
RC267
CURRENT CANCER RESEARCH. Text in German. 1986. irreg. **Document type:** *Monographic series, Academic/Scholarly.*
—CCC.
Published by: Deutsches Krebsforschungszentrum, Im Neuenheimer Feld 280, Heidelberg, 69120, Germany. TEL 49-6221-424800, FAX 49-6221-424809, webmaster@dkfz.de, http://www.dkfz.de.

616.99 USA ISSN 1074-2816
RC270.8
CURRENT CANCER THERAPEUTICS. Text in English. 1994. irreg., latest 2008, 5th ed. USD 149 per issue (effective 2010). back issues avail.; reprints avail. **Document type:** *Monographic series, Academic/Scholarly.* **Description:** Features summaries and charts of topics such as pharmacokinetics, drug indications, and toxicities.
—CCC.

Published by: Current Medicine Group LLC (Subsidiary of: Springer Science+Business Media), 400 Market St, Ste 700, Philadelphia, PA 19106. TEL 215-574-2266, FAX 215-574-2225, service-ny@springer.com, http://www.current-medicine.com/. Eds. David S Ettinger, Ross Donehower.

616.994 615.1 NLD ISSN 1573-3947
RC261.A1
➤ **CURRENT CANCER THERAPY REVIEWS.** Text in English. 2005 (Jan). q. USD 480 to institutions (print or online ed.) (effective 2012). adv. back issues avail.; reprints avail. **Document type:** *Journal, Academic/Scholarly.* **Description:** Publishes frontier reviews on all the latest advances in clinical oncology, cancer therapy and pharmacology.
Related titles: Online - full text ed.: ISSN 1875-6301 (from IngentaConnect).
Indexed: A01, B&BAb, B19, CA, EMBASE, ExcerpMed, P30, R10, Reac, SCOPUS, T02.
—IE, Ingenta. **CCC.**
Published by: Bentham Science Publishers Ltd., PO Box 294, Bussum, 1400 AG, Netherlands. TEL 31-35-6923800, FAX 31-35-6980150, sales@bentham.org, http://www.bentham.org. Ed. Kurt S Zaenker. **Subscr. to:** Bentham Science Publishers Ltd., c/o Richard E Morrissy, PO Box 446, Oak Park, IL 60301. TEL 312-413-5867, FAX 312-996-7107, subscriptions@bentham.org.

616.99 616.15 USA
➤ **CURRENT CLINICAL ONCOLOGY.** Text in English. 1999. irreg., latest 2007. price varies. illus. back issues avail. **Document type:** *Monographic series, Academic/Scholarly.* **Description:** Covers the latest therapies and treatment regimens for physicians treating patients with cancer.
Related titles: Online - full text ed.
Indexed: GenetAb.
Published by: Humana Press, Inc. (Subsidiary of: Springer Science+Business Media), 233 Spring St, New York, NY 10013. TEL 212-460-1500, FAX 212-460-1575, service-ny@springer.com. Ed. Maurie Markman.

616.99 616.3 USA ISSN 1556-3790
CURRENT COLORECTAL CANCER REPORTS. Text in English. 2005 (Aug.). q. reprint service avail. from PSC. **Document type:** *Journal, Academic/Scholarly.* **Description:** Provides insightful reviews of recent literature in colorectal cancer.
Related titles: CD-ROM ed.: ISSN 2153-5833. 2010 (Mar.). USD 33.75 per issue (effective 2010); Online - full text ed.: ISSN 1556-3804. 2005 (Aug.). USD 1,158 to institutions (effective 2010).
Indexed: A22, A26, E01, E08, EMBASE, H12, P30, S09, SCOPUS.
—IE. **CCC.**
Published by: Current Medicine Group LLC (Subsidiary of: Springer Science+Business Media), 400 Market St, Ste 700, Philadelphia, PA 19106. TEL 215-574-2266, 800-427-1796, FAX 215-574-2225, info@phl.cursci.com, http://www.current-medicine.com. Ed. Jaffer Ajani.

016.992 GBR ISSN 0956-6511
RC280.B8 CODEN: CMBCEL
➤ **CURRENT MEDICAL LITERATURE. BREAST CANCER.** Text in English. 1989. q. GBP 60 to individuals; GBP 130 to institutions; free to qualified personnel (effective 2009). back issues avail. **Document type:** *Journal, Academic/Scholarly.* **Description:** Aims to provide physicians and allied healthcare professionals with rapid access to expert commentary and analysis on key topics in breast cancer.
Related titles: Online - full text ed.: ISSN 1759-8060.
Indexed: A01, A03, A08, CA, T02.
—CCC.
Published by: Remedica Medical Education and Publishing Ltd., Commonwealth House, 1 New Oxford St, London, WC1A 1NU, United Kingdom. TEL 44-20-77592999, FAX 44-20-77592951, info@remedica.com, http://www.remedica.com. Ed. Clare Byrne.

016.992 GBR ISSN 1364-4831
CODEN: CMCCFR
➤ **CURRENT MEDICAL LITERATURE. COLORECTAL CANCER.** Text in English. 1997. q. GBP 60 to individuals; GBP 130 to institutions; free to qualified personnel (effective 2009). back issues avail. **Document type:** *Journal, Academic/Scholarly.* **Description:** Aims to provide physicians and allied healthcare professionals with rapid access to expert commentary and analysis on key topics in colorectal cancer.
Related titles: Online - full text ed.: ISSN 1759-8079.
Indexed: A01, A03, A08, CA.
—CCC.
Published by: Remedica Medical Education and Publishing Ltd., Commonwealth House, 1 New Oxford St, London, WC1A 1NU, United Kingdom. TEL 44-20-77592999, FAX 44-20-77592951, info@remedica.com, http://www.remedica.com. Ed. Emma Beagley.

016.992 GBR ISSN 0969-7063
CODEN: LYMYEJ
➤ **CURRENT MEDICAL LITERATURE. LEUKAEMIA AND LYMPHOMA.** Text in English. 1993. q. GBP 60 to individuals; GBP 130 to institutions; free to qualified personnel (effective 2009). back issues avail. **Document type:** *Journal, Academic/Scholarly.* **Description:** Contains articles written on Leukaemia and Lymphoma.
Related titles: Online - full text ed.: ISSN 1759-8125; Hungarian Translation: Current Medical Literature. Leukaemia Es lymphoma. ISSN 1788-957X. 2007.
Indexed: A01, A03, A08, CA, T02.
—CCC.
Published by: Remedica Medical Education and Publishing Ltd., Commonwealth House, 1 New Oxford St, London, WC1A 1NU, United Kingdom. TEL 44-20-77592999, FAX 44-20-77592951, info@remedica.com, http://www.remedica.com. Ed. Emma Beagley.

➤ **CURRENT MEDICAL LITERATURE. LUNG CANCER.** *see* MEDICAL SCIENCES—Abstracting, Bibliographies, Statistics

616.99 CAN ISSN 1198-0052
RC261.A1 CODEN: CUONF6
➤ **CURRENT ONCOLOGY (TORONTO).** Text in English. 1994. q. CAD 125 to qualified personnel; CAD 225 to institutions (effective 2007). adv. **Document type:** *Journal, Academic/Scholarly.*
Related titles: Online - full text ed.: free (effective 2011).
Indexed: A01, C06, C07, EMBASE, ExcerpMed, P30, R10, Reac, SCI, SCOPUS, W07.
—BLDSC (3500.725000), GNLM, IE, Ingenta. **CCC.**
Published by: Multimed, Inc., 66 Martin St, Milton, ON L9T R2R, Canada. TEL 905-875-2456, 888-834-1001, FAX 905-875-2864, subscription@multi-med.com, http://www.multi-med.com. Ed. Michael McLean. Adv. contact Harriet Cooper.

616.1992 USA ISSN 1534-6269
RC254.A1
➤ **CURRENT ONCOLOGY REPORTS (ONLINE).** Text in English. 1999. bi-m. EUR 954, USD 1,270 to institutions (effective 2012). back issues avail. **Document type:** *Journal, Academic/Scholarly.* **Description:** Provides the views of experts on the advances in the oncology field.
Media: Online - full text.
—CCC.
Published by: Current Medicine Group LLC (Subsidiary of: Springer Science+Business Media), 400 Market St, Ste 700, Philadelphia, PA 19106. TEL 215-574-2266, FAX 215-574-2225, service-ny@springer.com, http://www.current-medicine.com/. Ed. Maurie Markman.

616.99 USA ISSN 1040-8746
RC254.A1 CODEN: CUOOE8
CURRENT OPINION IN ONCOLOGY. Text in English. 1989. bi-m. USD 1,254 domestic to institutions; USD 1,346 foreign to institutions (effective 2011). adv. bibl.; illus. back issues avail.; reprints avail. **Document type:** *Journal, Academic/Scholarly.* **Description:** Covers key subjects such as leukemia, endocrine tumors, cancer biology, transplantation, lung and mediastinum, melanoma and other skin neoplasms and the brain and nervous system.
Related titles: Online - full text ed.: ISSN 1531-703X. USD 266 to individuals (effective 2011); ◆ Czech Translation: Current Opinion in Oncology (Czech Edition). ISSN 1801-2671.
Indexed: A22, A35, A36, AIDS Ab, AgBio, BIOBASE, BIOSIS Prev, C06, C07, C08, CABA, CIN, CINAHL, ChemAb, ChemTitl, CurCont, E01, E12, EMBASE, ExcerpMed, F08, GH, IABS, ISR, IndMed, Inpharma, MEDLINE, MycolAb, N02, N03, P30, P33, P35, R08, RM&VM, SCI, SCOPUS, T05, W07.
—BLDSC (3500.776400), CASDDS, GNLM, IE, Infotrieve, Ingenta, INIST. **CCC.**
Published by: Lippincott Williams & Wilkins (Subsidiary of: Wolters Kluwer N.V.), 530 Walnut St, Philadelphia, PA 19106. TEL 215-521-8300, FAX 215-521-8902, customerservice@lww.com, http://www.lww.com. Ed. Jean Klastersky. Pub. Ian Burgess. Circ: 765.

616.992 CZE ISSN 1801-2671
CURRENT OPINION IN ONCOLOGY (CZECH EDITION). Text in Czech. 2007. q. **Document type:** *Journal, Academic/Scholarly.*
Related titles: ◆ Translation of: Current Opinion in Oncology. ISSN 1040-8746.
Published by: Medical Tribune CZ, s.r.o., Na Morani 5, Prague 2, 12800, Czech Republic. TEL 420-224-916916, FAX 420-224-922436, info@medical-tribune.cz, http://www.tribune.cz.

616.99 USA ISSN 0147-0272
RC261.A1 CODEN: CPRCDJ
➤ **CURRENT PROBLEMS IN CANCER.** Short title: C P Ca. Text in English. 1977. bi-m. USD 306 in United States to institutions; USD 361 elsewhere to institutions (effective 2012). adv. index. back issues avail.; reprints avail. **Document type:** *Journal, Academic/Scholarly.* **Description:** Features information from recognized experts on practical clinical care.
Related titles: Microform ed.: (from PQC); Online - full text ed.: ISSN 1535-6345 (from ScienceDirect); ◆ English ed.: Current Problems in Cancer (Spanish Edition). ISSN 1137-196X.
Indexed: A22, A26, ASCA, BIOSIS Prev, CA, CurCont, DentInd, DokArb, EMBASE, ExcerpMed, I05, ISR, IndMed, Inpharma, MEDLINE, MycolAb, P30, R10, Reac, SCI, SCOPUS, T02, W07.
—BLDSC (3501.345000), GNLM, IE, Infotrieve, Ingenta, INIST. **CCC.**
Published by: Mosby, Inc. (Subsidiary of: Elsevier Health Sciences), 1600 John F. Kennedy Blvd, Ste 1800, Philadelphia, PA 19103. TEL 215-239-3900, 800-523-1649, FAX 215-239-3990, elspcs@elsevier.com, http://www.us.elsevierhealth.com. Ed. Dr. Peter A.S. Johnstone. Adv. contact Kevin Edmonds TEL 215-239-3804.

616.99 ESP ISSN 1137-196X
CURRENT PROBLEMS IN CANCER (SPANISH EDITION). Text in English. 1997. bi-m. **Document type:** *Journal, Academic/Scholarly.*
Related titles: ◆ English ed.: Current Problems in Cancer. ISSN 0147-0272.
Published by: Jarpyo Editores S.A., Antonio Lopez Aguado 4, Madrid, 28029, Spain. TEL 34-91-3144338, FAX 34-91-3144499, editorial@jarpyo.es, http://www.jarpyo.es.

616.992 USA ISSN 1527-2729
CODEN: CTOOBW
CURRENT TREATMENT OPTIONS IN ONCOLOGY. Text in English. 2000. bi-m. EUR 331, USD 392 combined subscription to institutions (print & online eds.) (effective 2010). back issues avail.; reprint service avail. from PSC. **Document type:** *Journal, Academic/Scholarly.* **Description:** Aims to help the reader by providing a systematic manner: the views of experts on current treatment options in oncologic medicine in a clear and readable format and selections annotated by experts of the most interesting papers from the great wealth of original publications.
Related titles: Online - full text ed.: ISSN 1534-6277 (from IngentaConnect).
Indexed: A22, A26, CurCont, E01, EMBASE, ExcerpMed, H12, I05, MEDLINE, P30, R10, Reac, SCI, SCOPUS, W07.
—BLDSC (3504.936470), IE, Ingenta. **CCC.**
Published by: Springer New York LLC (Subsidiary of: Springer Science+Business Media), 233 Spring St, New York, NY 10013. TEL 212—460-1500, FAX 212-460-1575, service-ny@springer.com. Ed. David S Ettinger.

362.1 USA ISSN 0095-6775
RC267
DAMON RUNYON - WALTER WINCHELL CANCER RESEARCH FUND. ANNUAL REPORT. Text in English. 1973. a. free.
Formerly (until 1973): Damon Runyon Memorial Fund for Cancer Research. Annual Report (0416-6639)
Published by: Damon Runyon Walter Winchell Cancer Research Fund, 675 Third Ave, 25th Fl, New York, NY 10017. TEL 212-697-9100, FAX 212-697-4050, crfinfo@cancerresearchfund.org. Circ: 1,000.

616.992 NLD ISSN 1875-6093
DANIEL DEN HOED CANCER NEWS. Text in English. 2007. q.
Published by: (Erasmus MC - University Medical Center Rotterdam, Daniel den Hoed Cancer Center), DCHG Medische Communicatie, Zijlweg 70, Haarlem, 2013 DK, Netherlands. TEL 31-23-5514888, FAX 31-23-5515522, info@dchg.nl, http://www.dchg.nl.

DERMATOLOGIC SURGERY. *see* MEDICAL SCIENCES—Surgery

616.99 DEU ISSN 0947-0255
DEUTSCHE KREBSGESELLSCHAFT. FORUM. Text in German. 1986. 8/yr. EUR 164, USD 218 combined subscription to institutions (print & online eds.) (effective 2012). adv. **Document type:** *Journal, Academic/Scholarly.*
Formerly (until 1994): Deutsche Krebsgesellschaft. Mitteilungen (0932-7479)
Related titles: Online - full text ed.
—CCC.
Published by: (Deutsche Krebsgesellschaft e.V.), Springer (Subsidiary of: Springer Science+Business Media), Tiergartenstr 17, Heidelberg, 69121, Germany. TEL 49-6221-4870, FAX 49-6221-345229, subscriptions@springer.com. Ed. Dr. Carsten Bokemeyer. Circ: 6,651 (paid and controlled).

616.99 DEU ISSN 1617-5891
RC254.A1 CODEN: DZONEH
➤ **DEUTSCHE ZEITSCHRIFT FUER ONKOLOGIE/GERMAN JOURNAL OF ONCOLOGY.** Text in German; Summaries in English. 1971. q. EUR 74.90 to institutions; EUR 102 combined subscription to institutions (print & online eds.); EUR 24.90 newsstand/cover (effective 2011). adv. back issues avail. **Document type:** *Journal, Academic/Scholarly.*
Former titles (until 2001): Zeitschrift fuer Onkologie (1432-2919); (until 1996): Deutsche Zeitschrift fuer Onkologie (0931-0037); (until 1987): Krebsgeschehen (0340-5672)
Related titles: Online - full text ed.: ISSN 1439-0930. EUR 102 to institutions (effective 2011).
Indexed: A22, EMBASE, ExcerpMed, R10, Reac, RefZh, SCOPUS.
—BLDSC (3575.830000), GNLM, IE, Infotrieve, Ingenta. **CCC.**
Published by: (Deutsche Gesellschaft fuer Onkologie e.V.), Karl F. Haug Verlag in MVS Medizinverlage Stuttgart GmbH & Co. KG (Subsidiary of: Georg Thieme Verlag), Oswald-Hesse-Str 50, Stuttgart, 70469, Germany. TEL 49-711-89310, FAX 49-711-8931706, kunden.service@thieme.de, http://www.haug-verlag.de. adv.: B&W page EUR 1,700, color page EUR 2,900. Circ: 4,800 (paid).

616.99 NLD ISSN 0167-4927
CODEN: DEOND5
➤ **DEVELOPMENTS IN ONCOLOGY.** Text in English. 1980. irreg., latest vol.82, 2004. price varies. **Document type:** *Monographic series, Academic/Scholarly.*
Indexed: A22, CIN, ChemAb, ChemTitl.
—BLDSC (3579.085470), CASDDS, IE, Ingenta, INIST. **CCC.**
Published by: Springer Netherlands (Subsidiary of: Springer Science+Business Media), Van Godewijckstraat 30, Dordrecht, 3311 GX, Netherlands. TEL 31-78-6576050, FAX 31-78-6576474.

616.992 USA
DEVITA, HELLMAN, AND ROSENBERG'S CANCER: PRINCIPLES & PRACTICE OF ONCOLOGY. Text in English. 1982. irreg., latest 8th ed. price varies. 3200 p./no.; **Document type:** *Monographic series, Academic/Scholarly.* **Description:** Provides information on the science of oncology and the multimodality treatment of every cancer type.
Formerly (until 2008): Cancer Principles & Practice of Oncology (0892-0567)
Related titles: Online - full text ed.
Published by: Lippincott Williams & Wilkins (Subsidiary of: Wolters Kluwer N.V.), 333 7th Ave, 19th Fl, New York, NY 10001. TEL 212-886-1200, FAX 212-886-1205, customerservice@lww.com. Eds. Dr. Steven A Rosenberg, Theodore S Lawrence, Vincent T DeVita.

616.99 NLD ISSN 0278-0240
RB1 CODEN: DMARD3
➤ **DISEASE MARKERS.** Text in English. 1982. m. USD 2,318 combined subscription in North America (print & online eds.); EUR 1,605 combined subscription elsewhere (print & online eds.) (effective 2012). adv. bk.rev. charts; illus. index. reprints avail. **Document type:** *Journal, Academic/Scholarly.* **Description:** Addresses original research findings and reviews on the subject of the identification of markers associated with the disease process, whether they are an integral part of the pathological lesion.
Related titles: Online - full text ed.: ISSN 1875-8630 (from IngentaConnect).
Indexed: A01, A03, A08, A20, A22, A34, A36, ASCA, B&BAb, B19, B20, B21, B25, B26, BIOBASE, BIOSIS Prev, CA, CABA, CIN, ChemAb, ChemTitl, D01, E01, E12, EMBASE, ExcerpMed, FR, GH, GenetAb, IABS, ISR, IndMed, IndVet, Inpharma, MEDLINE, MycolAb, N02, N03, NSA, P30, R10, Reac, SCI, SCOPUS, T02, T05, Telegen, VS, W07.
—BLDSC (3598.090000), CASDDS, GNLM, IE, Infotrieve, Ingenta, INIST. **CCC.**
Published by: I O S Press, Nieuwe Hemweg 6B, Amsterdam, 1013 BG, Netherlands. TEL 31-20-6883355, FAX 31-20-6870019, info@iospress.nl. Ed. Dr. Sudhir Srivastava. Circ: 1,000. **Subscr. to:** I O S Press, Inc, 4502 Rachael Manor Dr, Fairfax, VA 22032-3631. iosbooks@iospress.com; Kinokuniya Co Ltd., Shinjuku 3-chome, Shinjuku-ku, Tokyo 160-0022, Japan. FAX 81-3-3439-1094, journal@kinokuniya.co.jp, http://www.kinokuniya.co.jp; Globe Publication Pvt. Ltd., C-62 Inderpuri, New Delhi 100 012, India. TEL 91-11-579-3211, 91-11-579-3212, FAX 91-11-579-8876, custserve@globepub.com, http://www.globepub.com.

616.992 USA
DOCTOR'S DIGEST, ONCOLOGY. Text in English. 2007. bi-m. USD 54 domestic; USD 108 foreign; USD 12 per issue domestic; USD 18 per issue foreign (effective 2011). **Document type:** *Magazine, Trade.* **Description:** Designed for physicians and healthcare professionals. Includes information on topics such as evidence-based medicine, medical practice operations, financial planning, emergency planning, health policy issues and career development.
Related titles: Online - full text ed.: USD 27 (effective 2011).
Published by: Brandofino Communications, LLC, 12 Spruce Park, Syosset, NY 11791. TEL 516-364-2575, http://brandofinocommunications.com/. Ed. Paula S Katz. Pub. Jeanette Brandofino.

DOORGANG. *see* MEDICAL SCIENCES—Gastroenterology

DRUG RESISTANCE UPDATES; reviews and commentaries in antimicrobial and anticancer chemotherapy. *see* MEDICAL SCIENCES

616.99 CHE ISSN 2211-7288
E S M O CONGRESS. Text in English. 1980. irreg. **Document type:** *Monographic series, Academic/Scholarly.*
Former titles (until 2000): European Society for Medical Oncology. Congress (2211-7296); (until 1990): European Society for Medical Oncology. Abstracts of the Congress (0937-8723); (until 1989): European Society for Medical Oncology. Abstracts of the Annual Meeting (0936-8191); (until 1980): Medical Oncology (0172-6595)
—CCC.
Published by: European Society for Medical Oncology, Via L Taddei 4, Viganello-Lugano, 6962, Switzerland. TEL 41-91-9731900, FAX 41-91-9731902, esmo@esmo.org, http://www.esmo.org.

616.992 ITA ISSN 1754-6605
RC261.A1
ECANCERMEDICALSCIENCE. Text in Italian. 2007. irreg. free (effective 2011). **Document type:** *Journal, Academic/Scholarly.*
Media: Online - full text.
Indexed: A01, CA, EMBASE, ExcerpMed, T02.
Published by: The European Institute of Oncology, Via Ripamonti 435, Milan, 20141, Italy. TEL 39-02-574891, FAX 39-02-57489208, http://www.ieo.it.

616.992 USA ISSN 1548-8748
RC261.A2
EDUCATIONAL BOOK. Text in English. 19??. a. USD 80 per issue (effective 2009). back issues avail. **Document type:** *Journal, Academic/Scholarly.* **Description:** Highlight the current standards of care, discuss existing technologies, and look toward future therapeutic possibilities and novel treatment modalities.
Related titles: CD-ROM ed.: ISSN 1930-7020. USD 65 per issue (effective 2009); Online - full text ed.: ISSN 1548-8756. free to members (effective 2009).
—CCC.
Published by: American Society of Clinical Oncology, 2318 Mill Rd, Ste 800, Alexandria, VA 22314. TEL 571-483-1300, 888-282-2552, FAX 571-366-9550, asco@asco.org, http://www.asco.org. Ed. Ramaswamy Govindan. Pub. Joy Curzio.

616.994 EGY ISSN 1110-0362
EGYPTIAN NATIONAL CANCER INSTITUTE. JOURNAL/MAGALLAT MA'HAD AL-QAWMI AL-MISRI. Text in English. 1982. q. **Document type:** *Journal, Academic/Scholarly.*
Related titles: Online - full text ed.: ISSN 1687-9996.
Indexed: EMBASE, ExcerpMed, MEDLINE, P30, R10, Reac, SCOPUS.
Published by: Cairo University. National Cancer Institute, Qassr El-Aini Str, Fum El-Khalig Square, Cairo, Egypt. TEL 02-3683360. Ed. Dr. Salah S Abdel-Hadi.

616.99 DEU ISSN 0933-128X
EINBLICK (HEIDELBERG). Text in German. 1987. 4/yr. free (effective 2009). **Document type:** *Journal, Trade.*
—GNLM.
Published by: Deutsches Krebsforschungszentrum, Im Neuenheimer Feld 280, Heidelberg, 69120, Germany. TEL 49-6221-424800, FAX 49-6221-424809, webmaster@dkfz.de.

616.992 USA ISSN 2151-4194
▼ **EMERGING CANCER THERAPEUTICS.** Text in English. 2010 (Mar.). 3/yr. USD 85 per issue (effective 2011). **Document type:** *Monographic series, Academic/Scholarly.* **Description:** Provides a thorough analysis of key clinical research related to cancer therapeutics, including a discussion and assessment of current evidence, current clinical best practice, and likely near future developments. Each volume focuses on one type of cancer.
Related titles: Online - full text ed.: ISSN 2151-8300. 2010 (Mar.) (from IngentaConnect).
Published by: Demos Medical Publishing, 11 W 42nd St, 15th Fl, New York, NY 10036. TEL 212-683-0072 x238, info@demospub.com.

616.994 NLD ISSN 2211-1379
EMERGO!. Text in Dutch. 1983. q. EUR 16 membership (effective 2010).
Formerly (until 2010): Merg en Been (0920-8011)
Published by: Contactgroep Myeloom en Waldenstrom Patienten, c/o Hans Boot, Sec., Heerbaan 59, Asten, 5721 LR, Netherlands. TEL 31-79-3618158. Ed. Hans Scheurer.

ENFERMERIA ONCOLOGICA. *see* MEDICAL SCIENCES—Nurses And Nursing

ETESIA STATISTIKE. EREVNA TOU KARKINOU/ANNUAL STATISTICAL SURVEY OF CANCER. *see* MEDICAL SCIENCES—Abstracting, Bibliographies, Statistics

616.992 FRA ISSN 1760-7248
ETUDES ET EXPERTISES. Text in French. 2007. irreg. **Document type:** *Monographic series, Academic/Scholarly.*
Published by: Institut National du Cancer, 52 Av Andre Morizet, Boulogne-Billancourt, 92513 Cedex, France. TEL 33-1-41105000, contact@institutcancer.fr, http://www.e-cancer.fr.

616.99 FRA ISSN 1253-0727
EUROCANCER (YEAR). Text in English. 1958. a. EUR 65 (effective 2010). **Document type:** *Monographic series, Academic/Scholarly.*
Supersedes in part (in 1995): Pathologie et Biologie (0369-8114); Which was formerly (until 1959): Archives de Biologie Medicale, Anales de la Recherche Medicale (0150-7265); Which was formed by the 1958 merger of: Annales de la Recherche Medicale (0997-4415); Societe Francaise de Biologie Medicale. Archives (0997-4423)
—INIST.
Published by: John Libbey Eurotext, 127 Av. de la Republique, Montrouge, 92120, France. TEL 33-1-46730660, FAX 33-1-40840999, contact@jle.com. Eds. Michel Boiron, Michel Marty.

616.994 GBR ISSN 0959-8049
RC261.A1 CODEN: EJCAEL
➤ **EUROPEAN JOURNAL OF CANCER.** Abbreviated title: E J C. Text in English. 1965. 18/yr. EUR 3,352 in Europe to institutions; JPY 445,300 in Japan to institutions; USD 3,751 elsewhere to institutions (effective 2012). adv. bk.rev. charts; illus. index. back issues avail. **Document type:** *Journal, Academic/Scholarly.* **Description:** Provides an integrated forum for publication of clinical and laboratory research in all specializations of oncology.
Former titles (until 1990): European Journal of Cancer and Clinical Oncology (0277-5379); (until 1981): European Journal of Cancer (0014-2964)
Related titles: Microfilm ed.: (from PQC); Online - full text ed.: ISSN 1879-0852. EUR 46 in Europe; JPY 6,100 in Japan; USD 52 elsewhere (effective 2004) (from IngentaConnect, ScienceDirect); Supplement(s): European Journal of Cancer. Supplement. ISSN 1359-6349. 1978.
Indexed: A01, A03, A08, A20, A22, A26, A35, A36, AHCMS, AIDS Ab, AIDS&CR, ASCA, AgBio, B21, B25, BIOBASE, BIOSIS Prev, C06, C07, C08, CA, CABA, CIN, CINAHL, ChemAb, ChemTitl, CurCont, D01, DBA, DentInd, DokArb, E12, EMBASE, ESPM, ExcerpMed, FR, G10, GH, H12, H16, H17, I05, IABS, INIS AtomInd, ISR, IndMed, Inpharma, LT, MEDLINE, MS&D, MycolAb, N02, N03, NRN, OGFA, OR, P30, P33, P35, P39, R07, R08, R10, R12, RA&MP, RM&VM, RRTA, Reac, SCI, SCOPUS, SoyAb, T02, T05, THA, ToxAb, TriticAb, VS, W07, W10, W11.
—BLDSC (3829.725100), CASDDS, GNLM, IE, Ingenta, INIST. **CCC.**
Published by: (European CanCer Organisation BEL, Federation of European Cancer Societies), Pergamon (Subsidiary of: Elsevier Science & Technology), The Blvd, Langford Ln, East Park, Kidlington, Oxford OX5 1GB, United Kingdom. TEL 44-1865-843000, FAX 44-1865-843010, JournalsCustomerServiceEMEA@elsevier.com. Ed. John Smyth. adv.: B&W page EUR 1,436, color page EUR 4,787. Circ: 1,278. **Subscr. to:** Elsevier BV, Radarweg 29, PO Box 211, Amsterdam 1000 AE, Netherlands. TEL 31-20-4853757, FAX 31-20-4853432, http://www.elsevier.nl. **Co-sponsors:** European Organization for Research on Treatment of Cancer; European Association for Cancer Research; European School of Oncology.

616.99 GBR ISSN 0961-5423
CODEN: EUCAEU
➤ **EUROPEAN JOURNAL OF CANCER CARE.** Text in English. 1992. bi-m. GBP 592 in United Kingdom to institutions; EUR 752 in Europe to institutions; USD 1,091 in the Americas to institutions; USD 1,270 elsewhere to institutions; GBP 681 combined subscription in United Kingdom to institutions (print & online eds.); EUR 865 combined subscription in Europe to institutions (print & online eds.); USD 1,256 combined subscription in the Americas to institutions (print & online eds.); USD 1,461 combined subscription elsewhere to institutions (print & online eds.) (effective 2012). adv. bk.rev. bibl.; illus. index. back issues avail.; reprint service avail. from PSC. **Document type:** *Journal, Academic/Scholarly.* **Description:** Provides a medium for communicating multiprofessional cancer care across Europe and internationally.
Related titles: Microform ed.: (from PQC); ◆ Online - full text ed.: European Journal of Cancer Care Online. ISSN 1365-2354; Translation: European Journal of Cancer Care (Dutch Edition). ISSN 0961-6446; French Translation: European Journal of Cancer Care (French Edition). ISSN 0961-6438; Translation: European Journal of Cancer Care (Italian Edition). ISSN 0961-6454; Supplement(s): European Journal of Cancer Care. Supplement. ISSN 1360-5801. 1995.
Indexed: A01, A02, A03, A08, A20, A22, A26, AMED, B&BAb, B19, B28, C06, C07, C08, C11, CA, CINAHL, CurCont, E-psyche, E01, EMBASE, ExcerpMed, H04, H12, I05, INI, Inpharma, MEDLINE, P03, P20, P30, P35, P48, P54, PQC, PsycInfo, PsycholAb, R10, Reac, SCI, SCOPUS, T02, W07.
—BLDSC (3829.725350), IE, Infotrieve, Ingenta. **CCC.**
Published by: Wiley-Blackwell Publishing Ltd. (Subsidiary of: John Wiley & Sons, Inc.), 9600 Garsington Rd, Oxford, OX4 2DQ, United Kingdom. TEL 44-1865-776868, FAX 44-1865-714591, customerservices@blackwellpublishing.com. Eds. Stephen J O'Connor, Pat Webb. Adv. contact Joanna Baker TEL 44-1865-476271.

616.99 GBR ISSN 1365-2354
RC261.A1
➤ **EUROPEAN JOURNAL OF CANCER CARE ONLINE.** Text in English. 1999. bi-m. GBP 592 in United Kingdom to institutions; EUR 752 in Europe to institutions; USD 1,091 in the Americas to institutions; USD 1,270 elsewhere to institutions (effective 2012). adv. back issues avail.; reprints avail. **Document type:** *Journal, Academic/Scholarly.* **Description:** Provides a medium for communicating multiprofessional cancer care across Europe and internationally.
Media: Online - full text (from IngentaConnect). **Related titles:** Microform ed.: (from PQC); ◆ Print ed.: European Journal of Cancer Care. ISSN 0961-5423.
—CCC.
Published by: Wiley-Blackwell Publishing Ltd. (Subsidiary of: John Wiley & Sons, Inc.), 9600 Garsington Rd, Oxford, OX4 2DQ, United Kingdom. TEL 44-1865-776868, FAX 44-1865-714591, customerservices@blackwellpublishing.com, http://www.wiley.com/.

616.99 USA ISSN 0959-8278
CODEN: EJPEEK
➤ **EUROPEAN JOURNAL OF CANCER PREVENTION.** Text in English. 1991. bi-m. USD 1,621 domestic to institutions; USD 1,730 foreign to institutions (effective 2011). adv. back issues avail.; reprints avail. **Document type:** *Journal, Academic/Scholarly.* **Description:** Aims to promote an increased awareness of all aspects of cancer prevention and to stimulate new ideas and innovations.
Related titles: CD-ROM ed.; Online - full text ed.: ISSN 1473-5709.
Indexed: A20, A22, A34, A35, A36, A37, ASCA, AgBio, AgrForAb, BIOBASE, C30, CABA, CurCont, D01, E01, E12, EMBASE, ExcerpMed, F08, F11, F12, FR, FS&TA, GH, H16, IABS, IndMed, Inpharma, LT, MEDLINE, MaizeAb, N02, N03, P30, P35, P37, PN&I, R07, R10, R12, RA&MP, RRTA, Reac, SCI, SCOPUS, SoyAb, T05, THA, TriticAb, VITIS, VS, W07, W10, W11.
—BLDSC (3829.725400), GNLM, IE, Infotrieve, Ingenta, INIST. **CCC.**
Published by: (European Cancer Prevention Organisation), Lippincott Williams & Wilkins (Subsidiary of: Wolters Kluwer N.V.), 530 Walnut St, Philadelphia, PA 19106. TEL 215-521-8300, FAX 215-521-8902, customerservice@lww.com, http://www.lww.com. Ed. Jaak Ph Janssens TEL 32-11-275734. Pub. Phil Daly. Circ: 113.

616.99 618.1 CAN ISSN 0392-2936
CODEN: EJGODE
➤ **EUROPEAN JOURNAL OF GYNECOLOGICAL ONCOLOGY.** Text in English. 1980. bi-m. USD 200 to individuals; USD 390 to institutions; USD 95 per issue (effective 2005). adv. bk.rev. back issues avail. **Document type:** *Journal, Academic/Scholarly.*
Indexed: A22, B25, BIOSIS Prev, CurCont, EMBASE, ExcerpMed, IndMed, Inpharma, MEDLINE, MycolAb, NRN, P30, P35, R10, Reac, SCI, SCOPUS, W07.
—BLDSC (3829.729600), GNLM, IE, Infotrieve, Ingenta, INIST. **CCC.**
Published by: (European Society of Gynecological Oncology), I R O G Canada, Inc., 4900 Cote St Luc, # 212, Montreal, PQ H3W 2H3, Canada. TEL 514-489-3242, FAX 514-485-4513, canlux@qc.aira.com. Eds. Antonio Onnis, P Bosze. Adv. contact Moriuz Morsoui. Circ: 600.

616.992 ITA ISSN 1128-6598
EUROPEAN JOURNAL OF ONCOLOGY/GIORNALE EUROPEO DI ONCOLOGIA. Text in English, Italian. 1996. q. EUR 78 in Europe to institutions; EUR 88 elsewhere to institutions (effective 2008). **Document type:** *Journal, Academic/Scholarly.*
Indexed: BIOBASE, EMBASE, ExcerpMed, IABS, R10, Reac, SCI, SCOPUS, W07.
—BLDSC (3829.733050), IE, Ingenta.
Published by: (Societa Italiana Tumori), Mattioli 1885 SpA, Via Coduro 1, Fidenza, PR 43036, Italy. TEL 39-0524-84547, FAX 39-0524-84751, http://www.mattioli1885.com. Ed. Jill V Brazier. Circ: 3,000.

EUROPEAN JOURNAL OF ONCOLOGY NURSING. *see* MEDICAL SCIENCES—Nurses And Nursing

616.992 BEL ISSN 1783-3914
EUROPEAN JOURNAL OF ONCOLOGY PHARMACY. Abbreviated title: E J O P. Text in English. 2007. s-a. EUR 42 in Europe to individuals; EUR 50 elsewhere to individuals; EUR 90 in Europe hospitals/universities; EUR 98 elsewhere hospitals/universities; EUR 114 in Europe to corporations; EUR 122 elsewhere to corporations (effective 2008). **Document type:** *Journal, Academic/Scholarly.*
Indexed: EMBASE, ExcerpMed, R10, Reac, SCOPUS.
—BLDSC (3668.430500). **CCC.**
Published by: Pharma Publishing & Media Europe, Postbus 10001, Mol, B-2400, Belgium. TEL 32-474-989572, editorial@ejop.eu, http://www.ejhp.eu. Ed. Klaus Meier.

616.994 GBR ISSN 0748-7983
RC261.A1
➤ **EUROPEAN JOURNAL OF SURGICAL ONCOLOGY.** Abbreviated title: E J S O. Text in English. 1975. m. EUR 929 in Europe to institutions; JPY 100,500 in Japan to institutions; USD 822 elsewhere to institutions (effective 2012). adv. illus. index. back issues avail.; reprint service avail. from PSC. **Document type:** *Journal, Academic/Scholarly.* **Description:** Presents original articles and state-of-the-art reviews of immediate interest to surgical oncologists.
Formerly (until 1985): Clinical Oncology (0305-7399)
Related titles: Online - full text ed.: ISSN 1532-2157. USD 707 to institutions (effective 2009) (from ScienceDirect).
Indexed: A20, A22, A26, AMED, CA, CurCont, E01, EMBASE, ExcerpMed, FR, I05, INI, IndMed, Inpharma, MEDLINE, P30, R10, Reac, SCI, SCOPUS, T02, W07.
—BLDSC (3829.745500), GNLM, IE, Infotrieve, Ingenta, INIST. **CCC.**
Published by: (British Association of Surgical Oncology), W.B. Saunders Co. Ltd. (Subsidiary of: Elsevier Health Sciences), 32 Jamestown Rd, Camden, London, NW1 7BY, United Kingdom. TEL 44-20-74244200, FAX 44-20-74832293, elsols@elsevier.com. Ed. David A Rew. **Co-sponsor:** European Society of Surgical Oncology.

616.992 GBR ISSN 2045-5275
➤ **EUROPEAN ONCOLOGY & HAEMATOLOGY.** Text in English. 200? (Sep.). s-a. EUR 100 combined subscription to individuals (print & online eds.); EUR 225 combined subscription to institutions (print & online eds.); EUR 30 combined subscription to qualified personnel (print & online eds.) (effective 2011). back issues avail. **Document type:** *Journal, Trade.* **Description:** Brings together industry experts in each specialized sector within Oncology, in order to provide physicians, nurses, surgeons and professionals with information on the innovations and developments they require to diagnose, treat and care for their patients.
Former titles (until 2011): European Oncology (1758-3853); (until 2008): European Oncological Disease (1753-4100); (until 2006): European Oncological Review
Related titles: CD-ROM ed.: ISSN 2045-5291; Online - full text ed.: ISSN 2045-5283. EUR 85 to individuals; EUR 210 to institutions; free to qualified personnel (effective 2011).
Published by: Touch Briefings (Subsidiary of: Touch Group plc), Saffron House, 6-10 Kirby St, London, EC1N 8TS, United Kingdom. TEL 44-20-74525600, FAX 44-20-74525606, info@touchbriefings.com, http://www.touchbriefings.com/.

616.99 NLD ISSN 1387-6589
EUROPEAN SCHOOL OF ONCOLOGY. SCIENTIFIC UPDATES. Text in English. 1997. irreg., latest vol.6, 2005. price varies. **Document type:** *Monographic series, Academic/Scholarly.* **Description:** Provides state of the art overviews from a panel of leading experts on important and rapidly developing topics in cancer research.
—BLDSC (3829.968450), IE, Ingenta.
Published by: (European School of Oncology DEU), Elsevier BV (Subsidiary of: Elsevier Science & Technology), Radarweg 29, PO Box 211, Amsterdam, 1000 AE, Netherlands. TEL 31-20-4853911, FAX 31-20-4852457, JournalsCustomerServiceEMEA@elsevier.com, http://www.elsevier.nl.

EUROPEAN UROLOGY. *see* MEDICAL SCIENCES—Urology And Nephrology

▼ **EVIDENCE-BASED ANTICANCER COMPLEMENTARY AND ALTERNATIVE MEDICINE.** *see* ALTERNATIVE MEDICINE

EXCERPTA MEDICA. SECTION 16: CANCER. *see* MEDICAL SCIENCES—Abstracting, Bibliographies, Statistics

616.99 UKR ISSN 1812-9269
CODEN: EKSODD
➤ **EXPERIMENTAL ONCOLOGY**; nauchno-teknicheskii zhurnal. Text in Russian, English, Ukrainian; Summaries in English, Russian. 1979. q. USD 95; USD 190 combined subscription (print & online eds.) (effective 2009). bk.rev. **Document type:** *Journal, Academic/Scholarly.* **Description:** Presents full research papers and short communications that deal with fundamental aspects of cancer in the areas of molecular biology, cell biology, biochemistry, biophysics, genetics, virology, endocrinology and immunology.
Formerly (until 2004): Eksperimental'naya Onkologiya (0204-3564)
Related titles: Online - full text ed.
Indexed: A34, A35, A36, A38, ASCA, AgBio, B25, BIOSIS Prev, CABA, ChemAb, D01, Djerelo, E12, EMBASE, ExcerpMed, GH, INIS AtomInd, ISR, IndMed, Inpharma, MEDLINE, MycolAb, N02, N03, P30, P32, P40, R10, RA&MP, Reac, SCOPUS, T05, VS.
—CASDDS, East View, GNLM, INIST, Linda Hall. **CCC.**

Published by: (Natsional'na Akademiya Nauk Ukrainy, Instytut Eksperymental'noi Patolohii, Onkolohii i Radiobiolohii im. R.E. Kavets'koho), Morion LLC, pr-kt M Bazhana, 10A, Kyiv, 02140, Ukraine. public@morion.kiev.ua, http://www.morion.kiev.ua. Ed. V F Chekhun. Circ: 300.

➤ **EXPERT REVIEW OF ANTICANCER THERAPY.** *see* PHARMACY AND PHARMACOLOGY

615.28 DEU ISSN 0722-7566
CODEN: FAACEX
F A C - FORTSCHRITTE DER ANTIMIKROBIELLEN UND ANTINEOPLASTISCHEN CHEMOTHERAPIE. Text in German. 1982. irreg. price varies. **Document type:** *Monographic series, Academic/Scholarly.*
Indexed: A22.
—CCC.
Published by: Paul-Ehrlich-Gesellschaft fuer Chemotherapie e.V., Immenburgstr 20, Bonn, 53121, Germany. TEL 49-228-4447060, FAX 49-228-44470616, geschaeftsstelle@p-e-g.org, http://www.p-e-g.org.

616.2 599.935 NLD ISSN 1389-9600
➤ **FAMILIAL CANCER.** Text in English. 2000. q. EUR 350, USD 355 combined subscription to institutions (print & online eds.) (effective 2012). adv. reprint service avail. from PSC. **Document type:** *Journal, Academic/Scholarly.* **Description:** Publishes research into the hereditary aspects of cancer, with material of interest to the clinician, geneticist, and counselor.
Related titles: Online - full text ed.: ISSN 1573-7292 (from IngentaConnect).
Indexed: A22, A26, B21, BIOBASE, BibLing, CA, CurCont, E01, EMBASE, ExcerpMed, GenetAb, H13, I05, IABS, MEDLINE, OGFA, P10, P20, P22, P30, P48, P53, P54, PQC, R10, Reac, SCI, SCOPUS, T02, W07.
—BLDSC (3865.553881), IE, Ingenta. **CCC.**
Published by: Springer Netherlands (Subsidiary of: Springer Science+Business Media), Van Godewijckstraat 30, Dordrecht, 3311 GX, Netherlands. TEL 31-78-6576050, FAX 31-78-6576474, http://www.springer.com. Eds. Fred H Menko, Hans F A Vasen, Henry T Lynch.

➤ **FETAL AND PEDIATRIC PATHOLOGY.** *see* MEDICAL SCIENCES—Pediatrics

616.992 DNK ISSN 1603-5712
FOKUS PAA KRAEFT OG SYGEPLEJE. Text in Danish. 198?. q. DKK 350 membership (effective 2009). adv. **Document type:** *Trade.* **Description:** Cancer and the nursing and care of cancer patients.
Formerly (until 2002): F S 13 Nyt (0909-5934)
Related titles: Online - full text ed.
Published by: Fagligt Selskab for Kraeftsygeplejersker/Danish Cancer Nursing Society, c/o Birgitte Grube, Sandparken 15, Vindinge, Roskilde, 4000, Denmark. TEL 45-46-363217, birgitte.grube@gmail.com, http://www.dsr.dk/fsk. Ed. Karen Buur Andersson. Circ: 1,300.

616.992 ITA ISSN 2035-4479
FONDAMENTALE. Text in Italian. 1973. 5/yr. **Document type:** *Magazine, Consumer.*
Former titles (until 1993): Associazione Italiana per la Ricerca sul Cancro. Notiziario (2035-4460); (until 1976): Associazione Italiana per la Promozione delle Ricerche sul Cancro. Notiziario (2035-4452)
Published by: Associazione Italiana per la Ricerca sul Cancro (A I R C), Via Corridoni 7, Milan, 20122, Italy. http://www.airc.it.

616.992 DEU
FORUM (FRANKFURT AM MAIN). Text in German. 7/yr. adv. **Document type:** *Magazine, Consumer.*
Published by: (Deutsche Krebsgesellschaft e.V.), Konzept Verlagsgesellschaft mbH, Ludwigstr 33-37, Frankfurt Am Main, 60327, Germany. TEL 49-69-97460621, FAX 49-69-974608621, hann.wagner@konzept-verlagsgesellschaft.de, http://www.konzept-verlagsgesellschaft.de. adv.: B&W page EUR 1,750, color page EUR 3,050. Circ: 6,647 (controlled).

616.992 GRC ISSN 1792-345X
FORUM OF CLINICAL ONCOLOGY. Abbreviated title: F C O. Text in English. 1997. q. **Document type:** *Journal, Academic/Scholarly.*
Formerly (until 2009): Vima Klinikis Ogkologias (1107-5384)
Related titles: Online - full text ed.: ISSN 1792-362X. free (effective 2011).
Published by: Hellenic Society of Medical Oncology, 105 Alexandras Ave, Athens, 11475, Greece. Ed. Vassileios Barbounis.

616.99 USA ISSN 1040-0303
RC267
FOX CHASE CANCER CENTER. SCIENTIFIC REPORT. Text in English. 1948. a., latest 2006. back issues avail. **Document type:** *Report, Academic/Scholarly.*
Former titles (until 1984): Institute for Cancer Research. Scientific Report (0091-7087); (until 1957): Institute for Cancer Research and the Lankenau Hospital Research Institute. Scientific Report (0098-6046); (until 1950): Institute for Cancer Research and the Lankenau Hospital Research Institute. Annual Report
—BLDSC (8197.249990).
Published by: Fox Chase Cancer Center, 333 Cottman Ave, Philadelphia, PA 19111. TEL 215-728-6900, 888-369-2427, info@fccc.edu.

▼ **FRONTIERS IN ANTI-CANCER DRUG DISCOVERY.** *see* PHARMACY AND PHARMACOLOGY

FRONTIERS OF RADIATION THERAPY AND ONCOLOGY. *see* MEDICAL SCIENCES—Radiology And Nuclear Medicine

616 USA ISSN 1082-331X
FUTURE ONCOLOGY; technology, products, markets, and service opportunities. Text in English. 1995. m. USD 1,040 domestic; USD 1,100 foreign (effective 2011). back issues avail. **Document type:** *Newsletter, Academic/Scholarly.* **Description:** Provides comprehensive, up-to-date analysis of scientific, technological, clinical and commercial developments in oncology.
Related titles: Online - full text ed.: USD 840 (effective 2011).
Published by: New Medicine, Inc., PO Box 909, Lake Forest, CA 92609. TEL 949-830-0448, FAX 949-830-0887, info@newmedinc.com, http://www.newmedinc.com.

616.992 GBR ISSN 1479-6694
RC270.8
➤ **FUTURE ONCOLOGY.** Text in English. 2005. m. GBP 1,095 combined subscription domestic (print & online eds.); USD 1,915 combined subscription in North America (print & online eds.); JPY 203,500 combined subscription in Japan (print & online eds.); EUR 1,530 combined subscription elsewhere (print & online eds.) (effective 2011). adv. back issues avail.; reprints avail. **Document type:** *Journal, Academic/Scholarly.* **Description:** Takes a forward-looking stance toward the scientific and clinical issues, together with the economic and policy issues, that confront us in a new era of cancer care. The journal includes news and views, literature awareness regarding new biomarkers, concise commentary and analysis, reports from the conference circuit and full review articles.
Related titles: Online - full text ed.: ISSN 1744-8301. GBP 985 domestic to institutions; USD 1,730 in North America to institutions; JPY 185,000 in Japan to institutions; EUR 1,385 elsewhere to institutions (effective 2011) (from IngentaConnect).
Indexed: A26, C06, C07, CA, CurCont, E08, EMBASE, ExcerpMed, H11, H12, I05, MEDLINE, P20, P22, P30, P48, P54, PQC, R10, Reac, SCI, SCOPUS, W07.
—BLDSC (4060.610420), IE, Ingenta. **CCC.**
Published by: Future Medicine Ltd. (Subsidiary of: Future Science Ltd.), Unitec House, 2 Albert Pl, London, N3 1QB, United Kingdom. TEL 44-20-83716080, FAX 44-20-83716099, info@futuremedicine.com. Ed. Elisa Manzotti TEL 44-20-83716090. Pub. David Hughes. Adv. contact Simon Boisseau TEL 44-208-3716083. Circ: 400.

616.99 USA
G I ONCOLOGY REVIEW & OUTLOOK. (Gastrointestinal) Text in English. 2004. 4/yr. free to members (effective 2010). back issues avail. **Document type:** *Newsletter, Academic/Scholarly.*
Related titles: Online - full text ed.: free (effective 2010).
Published by: International Society of Gastrointestinal Oncology, 200 Broadhollow Rd, Ste 207, Melville, NY 11747. TEL 631-390-8390, FAX 631-393-5026, mchoti@jhmi.edu. Ed. George A Rossetti. Pub. Robert Ross.

616.994 MEX ISSN 1665-9201
GACETA MEXICANA DE ONCOLOGIA. Text in Spanish. 2002. bi-m. back issues avail. **Document type:** *Journal, Academic/Scholarly.*
Related titles: Online - full text ed.
Indexed: A26, B02, B15, B17, B18, C01, G04, I04, I05, SCOPUS.
Published by: Sociedad Mexicana de Oncologia, A.C., Tuxpan # 59 PH, Col. Roma Sur, Mexico, D.F., 06760, Mexico. smeo@infosel.net.mx.

616.992 JPN ISSN 1347-6955
CODEN: GBHCAE
GAN BUNSHI HYOUTEKI CHIRYOU. Text in Japanese. 2003. q. JPY 10,500 (effective 2005). **Document type:** *Journal, Academic/Scholarly.*
Published by: Medikaru Rebyusha/Medical Review Co., Ltd., 1-7-3 Hirano-Machi, Chuo-ku, Yoshida Bldg., Osaka-shi, 541-0046, Japan. TEL 81-6-62231468, FAX 81-6-62231245.

616.992 JPN ISSN 0915-4639
GAN CHIRYO TO SHUKUSHU/FRONTIERS IN CANCER TREATMENT. Text in Japanese. 1989. q. JPY 7,560 (effective 2005). **Document type:** *Journal, Academic/Scholarly.*
Published by: Medikaru Rebyusha/Medical Review Co., Ltd., 1-7-3 Hirano-Machi, Chuo-ku, Yoshida Bldg., Osaka-shi, 541-0046, Japan. TEL 81-6-62231468, FAX 81-6-62231245.

616.994 JPN ISSN 1342-0569
GAN KANGO/JAPANESE JOURNAL OF CANCER CARE. Text in Japanese. bi-m. JPY 13,440 domestic; JPY 18,000 foreign (effective 2007). **Document type:** *Journal, Academic/Scholarly.*
Published by: Nankodo Co. Ltd., 3-42-6 Hongo, Bunkyo-ku, Tokyo, 113-8410, Japan. TEL 81-3-38117140, FAX 81-3-38117265, http://www.nankodo.co.jp/.

616.99 JPN ISSN 0918-8509
GAN KANJA TO TAISHO RYOHO/SYMPTOM CONTROL IN CANCER PATIENTS. Text in Japanese. 1989. s-a. JPY 4,830 (effective 2005). **Document type:** *Monographic series, Academic/Scholarly.*
Published by: Medikaru Rebyusha/Medical Review Co., Ltd., 1-7-3 Hirano-Machi, Chuo-ku, Yoshida Bldg., Osaka-shi, 541-0046, Japan. TEL 81-6-62231468, FAX 81-6-62231245.

616.994 JPN ISSN 0021-4949
CODEN: GANRAE
GAN NO RINSHO/JAPANESE JOURNAL OF CANCER CLINICS. Text in Japanese; Summaries in English. 1954. m. JPY 31,800 (effective 2005). adv. bk.rev. abstr.; charts; illus. Index. **Document type:** *Journal, Academic/Scholarly.*
Indexed: ChemAb, DentInd, INIS AtomInd, IndMed, Inpharma, P30, Telegen.
—BLDSC (4651.250000), CASDDS, GNLM.
Published by: Shinohara-Shuppan Shinsha/Shinoharashinsha Inc., 2-4-9 Yushima Bunkyo-ku, Tokyo, 113-0034, Japan. TEL 81-3-38165311, FAX 81-3-38165314, info@shinoharashinsha.co.jp. Circ: 3,800.

616.9 JPN ISSN 0385-0684
CODEN: GTKRDX
➤ **GAN TO KAGAKU RYOHO/JAPANESE JOURNAL OF CANCER AND CHEMOTHERAPY.** Text in Japanese; Summaries in English. 1974. m. JPY 24,570 (effective 2005). adv. bk.rev. Supplement avail.; back issues avail. **Document type:** *Journal, Academic/Scholarly.*
Related titles: Online - full text ed.: (from IngentaConnect).
Indexed: A22, CIN, ChemAb, ChemTitl, EMBASE, ExcerpMed, F09, INI, INIS AtomInd, IndMed, Inpharma, MEDLINE, P30, R10, Reac, SCOPUS.
—BLDSC (4651.230000), CASDDS, GNLM, IE, Infotrieve, Ingenta, INIST.
Published by: Japanese Journal of Cancer and Chemotherapy Publishers Inc., Risshu Bldg. 2/F, 2-2-3 Nihonbashi, Chuo-ku, Tokyo, 103-0027, Japan. TEL 81-3-32780052, FAX 81-3-32810435. Ed., Pub. Tetsuo Taguchi. Adv. contact Hachiro Sato. Circ: 6,000 (paid).

616.9 CHE ISSN 0072-0151
CODEN: GMCRDC
➤ **GANN MONOGRAPH ON CANCER RESEARCH.** Text in English. 1966. irreg., latest vol.53, 2004. price varies. bk.rev. **Document type:** *Monographic series, Academic/Scholarly.* **Description:** Includes collected contributions on current topics in cancer problems and allied fields.
Indexed: CIN, ChemAb, ChemTitl, INIS AtomInd, SCOPUS.
—BLDSC (4069.310500), CASDDS, GNLM, IE, Ingenta, INIST. **CCC.**
Published by: (Japanese Cancer Association JPN), S. Karger AG, Allschwilerstr 10, Basel, 4055, Switzerland. TEL 41-61-3061111, FAX 41-61-3061234, karger@karger.ch, http://www.karger.ch. Circ: 2,000 (paid and controlled).

616.992 GRC ISSN 1109-7655
➤ **GASTRIC AND BREAST CANCER.** Text in English. 2002. irreg. **Document type:** *Journal, Academic/Scholarly.* **Description:** Provides secondary-research articles on current best practice and future clinical and research directions on carcinogenesis-based prevention and early detection, and multidisciplinary, evidence-based management and treatment of breast cancer and gastric cancer.
Related titles: Online - full text ed.: ISSN 1109-7647.
Indexed: A01, CA, EMBASE, ExcerpMed, SCOPUS, T02.
Published by: University of Ioannina, Gastric Breast Cancer Editorial Office, Ioannina, 45110, Greece. TEL 30-265-1097423, FAX 30-265-1097094. Ed. Dimitrios H Roukos.

616.99 663 JPN ISSN 1436-3291
➤ **GASTRIC CANCER.** Text in English. 1999. q. (in 1 vol., 4 nos./vol.). EUR 265, USD 313 combined subscription to institutions (print & online eds.) (effective 2012). reprint service avail. from PSC. **Document type:** *Journal, Academic/Scholarly.* **Description:** Devoted exclusively to studies of stomach neoplasms.
Related titles: Online - full text ed.: ISSN 1436-3305 (from IngentaConnect).
Indexed: A01, A03, A08, A22, A26, Agr, BIOBASE, CA, CurCont, E01, EMBASE, ExcerpMed, H12, I05, IABS, MEDLINE, P20, P22, P30, P48, P50, P54, PQC, R10, Reac, SCI, SCOPUS, T02, W07.
—BLDSC (4088.700000), IE, Infotrieve, Ingenta. **CCC.**
Published by: (Japanese Gastric Cancer Association), Springer Japan KK (Subsidiary of: Springer Science+Business Media), No 2 Funato Bldg, 1-11-11 Kudan-kita, Chiyoda-ku, Tokyo, 102-0073, Japan. TEL 81-3-3812-0757, FAX 81-3-3812-0719, http://www.springer.jp. Eds. Dr. J Ruediger Siewert, Dr. Oichira Kobori. Adv. contact Stephan Kroeck TEL 49-30-827875739. **Subscr. in the Americas to:** Springer New York LLC, Journal Fulfillment, PO Box 2485, Secaucus, NJ 07096. TEL 800-777-4643, 201-348-4033, FAX 201-348-4505, journals-ny@springer.com, http://www.springer.com; **Subscr. to:** Springer Distribution Center, Kundenservice Zeitschriften, Haberstr 7, Heidelberg 69126, Germany. TEL 49-6221-3454303, FAX 49-6221-3454229, subscriptions@springer.com.

616.99 USA ISSN 1934-7820
➤ **GASTROINTESTINAL CANCER RESEARCH.** Abbreviated title: G C R. Text in English. 2007. bi-m. free to members (effective 2010). **Document type:** *Journal, Academic/Scholarly.*
Related titles: Online - full text ed.: ISSN 1934-7987.
Indexed: EMBASE, ExcerpMed, P30, SCOPUS.
—CCC.
Published by: International Society of Gastrointestinal Oncology, 200 Broadhollow Rd, Ste 207, Melville, NY 11747. TEL 631-390-8390, FAX 631-393-5026, mchoti@jhmi.edu, http://www.isgio.org. Pub. Robert Ross.

616.99 GBR ISSN 1179-9919
▼ ➤ **GASTROINTESTINAL CANCER: TARGETS AND THERAPY.** Text in English. 2011. irreg. free (effective 2011). **Document type:** *Journal, Academic/Scholarly.*
Media: Online - full text.
—CCC.
Published by: Dove Medical Press Ltd., Beechfield House, Winterton Way, Macclesfield, SK11 0JL, United Kingdom. TEL 44-1625-509130, FAX 44-1625-617933. Ed. Dr. Eileen O'Reilly.

616.992 599.9 USA ISSN 1947-6019
RC268.4
▼ **GENES & CANCER.** Text in English. 2010 (Jan.). m. USD 928, GBP 546 combined subscription to institutions (print & online eds.); USD 909, GBP 535 to institutions (effective 2011). **Document type:** *Journal, Trade.* **Description:** Features research on cancer research, signal transduction, and developmental biology.
Related titles: Online - full text ed.: ISSN 1947-6027. USD 835, GBP 491 to institutions (effective 2011).
Indexed: A22, E01, P30.
—CCC.
Published by: Sage Publications, Inc., 2455 Teller Rd, Thousand Oaks, CA 91320. TEL 805-499-9774, 800-818-7243, FAX 805-499-0871, 800-583-2665, info@sagepub.com. Ed. E Premkumar Reddy.

GENES, CHROMOSOMES & CANCER. *see* BIOLOGY—Genetics

616.99 ITA ISSN 0392-128X
GIORNALE ITALIANO DI ONCOLOGIA. Text in Italian; Summaries in English. 1981. q. EUR 50 domestic; USD 70 foreign (effective 2008). **Document type:** *Journal, Academic/Scholarly.*
Related titles: Online - full text ed.: ISSN 1971-1409.
Indexed: A22, P30, SCOPUS.
—BLDSC (4178.236000), GNLM, IE, Infotrieve, Ingenta. **CCC.**
Published by: C I C Edizioni Internazionali, Corso Trieste 42, Rome, 00198, Italy. TEL 39-06-8412673, FAX 39-06-8412688, info@gruppocic.it, http://www.gruppocic.it.

616.99 150 ITA ISSN 1128-5516
➤ **GIORNALE ITALIANO DI PSICO-ONCOLOGIA.** Text in Italian; Summaries in English. 1999. s-a. EUR 50 domestic to institutions; EUR 85 foreign to institutions (effective 2009). adv. bk.rev. abstr.; illus. 64 p./no.; back issues avail.; reprints avail. **Document type:** *Journal, Academic/Scholarly.* **Description:** Publishes original articles, case reports, editorials in the field of psycho-oncology. For oncologists and psychologists.
Related titles: Online - full text ed.: ISSN 1974-5184.
Published by: (Societa Italiana di Psico-Oncologica), C I C Edizioni Internazionali, Corso Trieste 42, Rome, 00198, Italy. TEL 39-06-8412673, FAX 39-06-8412688, http://www.gruppocic.it. Eds. Gabriella Morasso, Luigi Grassi. adv.: B&W page EUR 955, color page EUR 1,291; 21 x 28. Circ: 1,200.

➤ **GLOSSARIUM ONCOLOGIA.** *see* PHARMACY AND PHARMACOLOGY

616.994 NLD
GNRH ANALOGUES IN CANCER AND HUMAN REPRODUCTION. Text in English. irreg., latest vol.4, 1990. price varies. **Document type:** *Monographic series, Academic/Scholarly.*
Published by: Springer Netherlands (Subsidiary of: Springer Science+Business Media), Van Godewijckstraat 30, Dordrecht, 3311 GX, Netherlands. TEL 31-78-6576050, FAX 31-78-6576474, http://www.springer.com.

GREAT BRITAIN. GOVERNMENT STATISTICAL SERVICE. CANCER STATISTICS REGISTRATIONS. ENGLAND AND WALES. *see* MEDICAL SCIENCES—Abstracting, Bibliographies, Statistics

616.992 KWT ISSN 2078-2101
THE GULF JOURNAL OF ONCOLOGY. Text in English. 2007. s-a. **Document type:** *Journal, Academic/Scholarly.*
Indexed: MEDLINE, P30, SCOPUS.
Published by: The Gulf Federation for Cancer Control, PO Box 26733, Safat, 13128, Kuwait. TEL 965-2253-0186, gffccku@yahoo.com, http://www.gffcc.org/journal/index.htm. Ed. Dr. Khaled Al-Saleh.

616.992 CHN ISSN 1673-422X
➤ **GUOJI ZHONGLIUXUE ZAZHI/JOURNAL OF INTERNATIONAL ONCOLOGY.** Text in Chinese; Abstracts in Chinese, English. 1974. m. CNY 144, USD 21; CNY 12 newsstand/cover (effective 2009). **Document type:** *Journal, Academic/Scholarly.* **Description:** Covers the latest developments of theoretical and applied researches in the fields of cancer.
Former titles (until 2006): Guowai Yixue (Zhongliuxue Fence)/Foreign Medical Sciences (Cancer) (1000-8225); (until 1979): Guowai Yixue Cankao Ziliao, Zhongliuxue Fence/Foreign Medical Sciences Reference Materials, Oncology Section
Related titles: Online - full text ed.
Indexed: A34, A36, B&BAb, B20, B21, CABA, E12, ESPM, GH, ImmunAb, IndVet, N02, N03, NucAcAb, OGFA, P33, RA&MP, T05, VS.
—East View.
Published by: Shandong Sheng Yixueyuan, 89, Jingshi Lu, Jinan, 250062, China. TEL 86-531-82949227, FAX 86-531-82949227. Circ: 3,000. **Dist. by:** China International Book Trading Corp, 35 Chegongzhuang Xilu, Haidian District, PO Box 399, Beijing 100044, China. TEL 86-10-68412045, FAX 86-10-68412023, cibtc@mail.cibtc.com.cn, http://www.cibtc.com.cn.

➤ **HET H N P C C-LYNCH JOURNAAL.** (Hereditary Nonpolyposis Colorectal Cancer) *see* MEDICAL SCIENCES—Gastroenterology

➤ **HAEMATO-ONKOLOGISCHE NACHRICHTEN.** *see* MEDICAL SCIENCES—Hematology

616.994 JPN ISSN 0386-9628
HAIGAN. Text in Japanese. 1969. bi-m. (7/yr.). **Document type:** *Journal, Academic/Scholarly.*
Formerly: Haigan Kenkyukai Kiji
Related titles: Online - full text ed.: ISSN 1348-9992.
Indexed: EMBASE, ExcerpMed, INIS AtomInd, R10, Reac, RefZh, SCOPUS.
—BLDSC (4656.035000). **CCC.**
Published by: Nihon Haigan Gakkai/Japan Lung Cancer Society, 4-9-8-401 Chuo Chuo-ku Chibasi, Chiba, 260-0013, Japan. TEL 81-43-2223110, FAX 81-43-2220655, office@haigan.gr.jp, http://www.haigan.gr.jp/. Ed. Koichi Kobayashi.

616.992 572 USA
HANDBOOK OF IMMUNOHISTOCHEMISTRY AND IN SITU HYBRIDIZATION OF HUMAN CARCINOMAS. Text in English. 2002. irreg. price varies. **Document type:** *Monographic series, Academic/Scholarly.*
Related titles: Online - full text ed.: ISSN 1874-5784.
Published by: Academic Press (Subsidiary of: Elsevier Science & Technology), 3251 Riverport Ln, Maryland Heights, MO 63043. TEL 314-447-8010, FAX 314-447-8030, http://www.elsevierdirect.com/imprint.jsp?iid=5.

616.992 AUS ISSN 1446-7941
HANSON INSTITUTE. ANNUAL REPORT. Text in English. 1992. a. back issues avail. **Document type:** *Report, Trade.* **Description:** Aims to make fundamental biological and biomedical discoveries and to create a scientifically advanced working environment to attract the finest researchers.
Former titles (until 2001): Hanson Centre for Cancer Research. Annual Report (1329-2943); (until 1994): Hanson Centre for Cancer Research. Annual Review (1039-7981)
Published by: Hanson Institute, Frome Rd, Rundle Mall, PO Box 14, Adelaide, SA 5000, Australia. TEL 61-8-82223033, FAX 61-8-82223035, hanson@imvs.sa.gov.au, http://www.hansoninstitute.sa.gov.au/index.htm. Ed. Peter Coyle.

616.992 GBR ISSN 1758-3284
▼ ➤ **HEAD & NECK ONCOLOGY.** Text in English. 2009. irreg. free (effective 2011). **Document type:** *Journal, Academic/Scholarly.* **Description:** Covers all aspects of clinical practice, basic and translational research on the aetiology, pathophysiology, diagnosis, assessment, management, follow-up and prognosis of patients with head and neck tumors.
Media: Online - full text.
Indexed: A01, A26, C06, C07, E08, EMBASE, H12, I05, MEDLINE, OGFA, P30, S09, SCOPUS.
Published by: BioMed Central Ltd. (Subsidiary of: Springer Science+Business Media), 236 Gray's Inn Rd, London, WC1X 8HB, United Kingdom. TEL 44-20-31922000, FAX 44-20-31922010, info@biomedcentral.com, http://www.biomedcentral.com. Eds. Adel El-Naggar, Colin Hopper, Tahwinder Upile, Waseem Jerjes.

616.99 USA ISSN 1949-0593
HEADLINES ON THE PATH TO PROGRESS. Text in English. 1974. 3/yr. looseleaf. free (effective 2009). 24 p./no. 4 cols./p.; back issues avail. **Document type:** *Newsletter, Consumer.* **Description:** Updates on research advances in the treatment of brain tumors.
Formerly (until 2009): Message Line (1060-233X)
Related titles: Online - full text ed.: ISSN 1949-0607.
Published by: American Brain Tumor Association, 2720 River Rd, Ste 146, Des Plaines, IL 60018-4110. TEL 847-827-9910, 800-886-2282, FAX 847-827-9918, info@abta.org, http://hope.abta.org, http://www.abta.org. Circ: 40,000.

616.994 USA ISSN 1548-5072
RC261.A1
HEAL; living well with cancer. Text in English. 2007. 2/yr. USD 19.95 domestic; USD 34.95 in Canada; USD 44.95 elsewhere (effective 2007). adv. **Document type:** *Magazine, Consumer.* **Description:** Provides a guide for those who want to stay informed on the medical and practical issues emerging daily for patients who have had treatment for cancer in the past.
Published by: Cure Media Group, LP., 3500 Maple Ave, Ste 750, Dallas, TX 75219. TEL 214-367-3500, 800-210-2873, FAX 214-367-3306, subs@healtoday.com. Ed. Debu Tripathy. Pub. Susan McClure. Adv. contact Kristene Richardson. page USD 22,500; trim 9 x 10.875. Circ: 246,000.

HELICOBACTER (OXFORD). *see* BIOLOGY—Microbiology

▼ **HEM-ONC.** *see* MEDICAL SCIENCES—Hematology

HEM/ONC TODAY; clinical news in hematology and oncology. *see* MEDICAL SCIENCES—Hematology

HEMATOLOGY - ONCOLOGY AND STEM CELL THERAPY. *see* MEDICAL SCIENCES—Hematology

616.99 USA ISSN 0889-8588
RB145 CODEN: HCNAEQ
➤ **HEMATOLOGY / ONCOLOGY CLINICS OF NORTH AMERICA.** Text in English. 1987. bi-m. USD 541 in United States to institutions; USD 662 elsewhere to institutions (effective 2012). adv. back issues avail.; reprints avail. **Document type:** *Journal, Academic/Scholarly.* **Description:** Addresses the management of patients with cancer and systemic disease.
Formed by the merger of (1982-1987): Clinics in Oncology (0261-9873); (1972-1987): Clinics in Haematology (0308-2261)
Related titles: Microform ed.: (from PQC); Online - full text ed.: ISSN 1558-1977 (from ScienceDirect).
Indexed: A22, BIOSIS Prev, C06, C07, C08, CINAHL, ChemAb, CurCont, EMBASE, ExcerpMed, ISR, IndMed, Inpharma, MEDLINE, MycolAb, P30, P35, R10, Reac, SCI, SCOPUS, W07.
—BLDSC (4291.610000), CASDDS, GNLM, IE, Infotrieve, Ingenta, INIST. **CCC.**
Published by: (American Society for Clinical Oncology, American Society of Hematology), W.B. Saunders Co. (Subsidiary of: Elsevier Health Sciences), Elsevier, Health Sciences Division, Order Fulfillment, 3251 Riverport Ln, Maryland Heights, MO 63043. TEL 314-872-8370, 800-325-4177, FAX 314-432-1380, JournalCustomerService-usa@elsevier.com, http://www.us.elsevierhealth.com. Adv. contact John Marmero TEL 212-633-3657.

616.992 PRT ISSN 1647-2691
HEMATONCOLOGIA. Text in Portuguese. 2008. q. **Document type:** *Magazine, Trade.*
Published by: JAS Farma, Edificio Lisboa Oriente, Avenida Infante D Henrique 333, Lisbon, 1800-282, Portugal. TEL 351-21-8504000, FAX 351-21-8504009, http://www.jasfarma.pt.

HEPATO - GASTRO & ONCOLOGIE DIGESTIVE. *see* MEDICAL SCIENCES—Gastroenterology

616.992 GBR ISSN 1731-2302
➤ **HEREDITARY CANCER IN CLINICAL PRACTICE.** Text in English. 2003. q. free (effective 2010). back issues avail. **Document type:** *Journal, Academic/Scholarly.*
Related titles: Online - full text ed.: ISSN 1897-4287. free (effective 2011).
Indexed: A01, BIOBASE, EMBASE, ESPM, ExcerpMed, IABS, P30, R10, Reac, RiskAb, SCI, SCOPUS, W07.
Published by: (International Hereditary Cancer Centre POL), BioMed Central Ltd. (Subsidiary of: Springer Science+Business Media), 236 Gray's Inn Rd, London, WC1X 8HB, United Kingdom. TEL 44-20-31922000, FAX 44-20-31922010, info@biomedcentral.com, http://www.biomedcentral.com. Eds. Jan Lubinski, Rodney J Scott, Rolf Sijmons.

616.994 GBR ISSN 0309-0167
RB25 CODEN: HISTDD
➤ **HISTOPATHOLOGY.** Text in English. 1977. m. GBP 1,404 in United Kingdom to institutions; EUR 1,784 in Europe to institutions; USD 2,599 in the Americas to institutions; USD 3,034 elsewhere to institutions; GBP 1,615 combined subscription in United Kingdom to institutions (print & online eds.); EUR 2,053 combined subscription in Europe to institutions (print & online eds.); USD 2,989 combined subscription in the Americas to institutions (print & online eds.); USD 3,490 combined subscription elsewhere to institutions (print & online eds.) (effective 2012). adv. bk.rev. illus. index. back issues avail.; reprint service avail. from PSC. **Document type:** *Journal, Academic/Scholarly.* **Description:** Aims to publish advances in pathology, in particular those applicable to clinical practice and contributing to the better understanding of human disease.
Related titles: Online - full text ed.: ISSN 1365-2559. GBP 1,404 in United Kingdom to institutions; EUR 1,784 in Europe to institutions; USD 2,599 in the Americas to institutions; USD 3,034 elsewhere to institutions (effective 2012) (from IngentaConnect); Supplement(s): Histopathology. Supplement. ISSN 1478-2383.
Indexed: A01, A03, A08, A22, A26, A36, ASCA, B21, B25, B27, BIOBASE, BIOSIS Prev, CA, CABA, CTA, ChemoAb, CurCont, DentInd, DokArb, E01, EMBASE, ExcerpMed, GH, GenetAb, H12, H17, I05, IABS, ISR, IndMed, Inpharma, LT, MEDLINE, MycolAb, N02, N03, NSA, NucAcAb, P30, P33, P35, P39, R08, R10, R12, RM&VM, RRTA, Reac, SCI, SCOPUS, T02, T05, VS, W07.
—BLDSC (4316.027000), GNLM, IE, Infotrieve, Ingenta, INIST. **CCC.**
Published by: (International Academy of Pathology. British Division), Wiley-Blackwell Publishing Ltd. (Subsidiary of: John Wiley & Sons, Inc.), 9600 Garsington Rd, Oxford, OX4 2DQ, United Kingdom. TEL 44-1865-776868, FAX 44-1865-714591, customerservices@blackwellpublishing.com. Ed. Michael Wells TEL 44-114-2713332.

➤ **HORIZONS (LIVINGSTON).** *see* PHYSICAL FITNESS AND HYGIENE

▼ ➤ **HORMONES AND CANCER.** *see* MEDICAL SCIENCES—Endocrinology

616.992 ITA ISSN 1973-9656
HOT TOPICS IN ONCOLOGY. Text in Multiple languages. 2007. 3/yr. **Document type:** *Monographic series, Academic/Scholarly.*
Related titles: Online - full text ed.: ISSN 2036-0894.
Indexed: A01, EMBASE, SCOPUS.
Published by: F B Communication, Via Mascherella 19, Modena, 41121, Italy. TEL 39-059-4270122, FAX 39-059-4279368, info@fbcommunication.org. Eds. Chritopher P Cannon, Sergio Dalla Volta.

HUMAN ANTIBODIES. *see* MEDICAL SCIENCES—Allergology And Immunology

616.99 NLD ISSN 1389-2142
HUMAN CELL CULTURE. Text in English. 1999. irreg., latest vol.7, 2009. price varies. bk.rev. back issues avail. **Document type:** *Monographic series, Academic/Scholarly.*
—BLDSC (4336.034000).
Published by: Springer Netherlands (Subsidiary of: Springer Science+Business Media), Van Godewijckstraat 30, Dordrecht, 3311 GX, Netherlands. TEL 31-78-6576050, FAX 31-78-6576474.

616.9 JPN ISSN 0913-8927
HYOGO KENRITSU SEIJINBYO SENTA KIYO/HYOGO MEDICAL CENTER FOR ADULTS. BULLETIN. Text in Japanese; Summaries in English, Japanese. 1962. a. **Document type:** *Bulletin, Academic/Scholarly.*
Former titles (until 1984): Hyogo Kenritsu Byoin Gan Senta Kiyo - Hyogo Cancer Hospital. Bulletin (0387-0944); (until 1973): Hyogoken Gan Senta Nenpo (0441-537X)
Published by: Hyogo Kenritsu Seijinbyo Senta/Hyogo Medical Center for Adults, 13-70, Kitaohji-cho, Akashi, Hyogo 673-8558, Japan. TEL 81-78-9291151, FAX 81-78-9292380, http://www.hyogo-seijinbyo.jp/.

616.994 GBR
I A JOURNAL. Text in English. 1956. q. free to members (effective 2009). adv. pat.; stat. **Document type:** *Journal, Academic/Scholarly.* **Description:** Contains information about new products and appliance equipment, about ostomy management, and many other matters involving life with an ileostomy or internal pouch.
Published by: Ileostomy and Internal Pouch Support Group, Peverill House, 1 - 5 Mill Rd, Ballyclare, Co. Antrim BT39 9DR, United Kingdom. TEL 44-28-93344043, FAX 44-28-93324606, info@the-ia.org.uk. Circ: 12,000.

616.99 FRA ISSN 1014-5435
I A R C BIENNIAL REPORT. Text in English. 1987. biennial. **Document type:** *Journal, Trade.*
Formerly (until 199?): I A R C Annual Report (0250-8613)
Related titles: Microfiche ed.: (from CIS); Online - full text ed.: free; French ed.: ISSN 1017-3412.
Indexed: IIS.
—GNLM.
Published by: (International Agency for Research on Cancer), International Agency for Research on Cancer (IARC), 150 Cours Albert Thomas, Lyon, Cedex 8 69372, France. TEL 33-4-72738485, FAX 33-4-72738575, press@iarc.fr.

616.99 FRA ISSN 1027-5622
RC268
I A R C HANDBOOKS OF CANCER PREVENTION. (International Agency for Research on Cancer) Text in English. 1997. irreg., latest vol.12, 2008. USD 60 per issue (effective 2010).
—BLDSC (4359.536297).
Published by: World Health Organization, International Agency for Research on Cancer, 150 Cours Albert Thomas, Lyon, F-69372, France. TEL 33-4-72738485, FAX 33-4-72738575, http://www.iarc.fr.

616.994 FRA ISSN 1017-1606
RC268.6 CODEN: IARMB8
I A R C MONOGRAPHS ON THE EVALUATION OF CARCINOGENIC RISKS TO HUMANS. Text in English. 1972. irreg., latest vol.99, 2010. price varies. bibl. **Document type:** *Monographic series, Academic/Scholarly.* **Description:** Monographs comprise sections on physical and chemical data, technical products, use, occurrence and analysis, carcinogenicity in animals, other biological data, human epidemiological results and evaluations.
Former titles (until 1988): I A R C Monographs on the Evaluation of the Carcinogenic Risk of Chemicals to Humans (0250-9555); (until 1978): I A R C Monographs on the Evaluation of Carcinogenic Risk of Chemicals to Man (0301-3944)
Related titles: Supplement(s): I A R C Monographs on the Evaluation of Carcinogenic Risks to Humans. Supplement. ISSN 1014-711X. 1979.
Indexed: A22, A36, BIOBASE, CABA, E12, EMBASE, ExcerpMed, FS&TA, GH, IABS, IndMed, MEDLINE, NRN, P30, R10, Reac, SCOPUS, VS.
—BLDSC (4359.536700), CASDDS, GNLM, IE, Ingenta, INIST. **CCC.**
Published by: (International Agency for Research on Cancer), International Agency for Research on Cancer (IARC), 150 Cours Albert Thomas, Lyon, Cedex 8 69372, France. TEL 33-4-72738485, FAX 33-4-72738575, press@iarc.fr, http://www.iarc.fr. **Subscr. to:** I A R C Press or World Health Organization, Distribution and Sales Services, Geneva 27 1211, Switzerland.

616.994 FRA ISSN 0300-5038
CODEN: IARCCD
➤ **I A R C SCIENTIFIC PUBLICATIONS.** Text in French. 1971. irreg., latest vol.162, 2011. price varies. bk.rev. **Document type:** *Monographic series, Academic/Scholarly.* **Description:** Reviews issues concerning the epidemiology of cancer and the study of potential carcinogens in the human environment.
Indexed: A22, ChemAb, DentInd, DokArb, EMBASE, ExcerpMed, FS&TA, GeoRef, IndMed, MEDLINE, P30, R10, Reac, SCOPUS.
—BLDSC (4359.537000), CASDDS, GNLM, IE, Infotrieve, Ingenta, INIST. **CCC.**
Published by: (International Agency for Research on Cancer), International Agency for Research on Cancer (IARC), 150 Cours Albert Thomas, Lyon, Cedex 8 69372, France. TEL 33-4-72738485, FAX 33-4-72738575, press@iarc.fr. **U.S. subscr. to:** I A R C Press Oxford University Press, 200 Madison Ave, New York, NY 10016.

616.99 FRA ISSN 1012-7348
I A R C TECHNICAL REPORTS. Text mainly in French; Text occasionally in English, Spanish. 1988. irreg., latest vol.41, 2003. price varies. **Document type:** *Monographic series, Academic/Scholarly.*
Published by: (International Agency for Research on Cancer), International Agency for Research on Cancer (IARC), 150 Cours Albert Thomas, Lyon, Cedex 8 69372, France. TEL 33-4-72738485, FAX 33-4-72738575, press@iarc.fr.

616.994 NLD ISSN 1383-2298
I K R BULLETIN. Text in Dutch. 1976. q. **Document type:** *Bulletin, Trade.*
Published by: Integraal Kankercentrum Rotterdam, Postbus 289, Rotterdam, 3000 AG, Netherlands. TEL 31-10-4405803, FAX 31-10-4364784, http://www.ikcnet.nl/ikr. Eds. K van Dullemen, Dr. J C J Wereldsma.

616.99 362.1 DEU ISSN 0724-8016
ILCO-PRAXIS. Text in German. 1974. q. EUR 30 membership (effective 2009). adv. bk.rev. **Document type:** *Newsletter, Trade.*
Formerly (until 1982): Deutsche Ilco-Praxis (0724-8024)

Published by: Deutsche I L C O, Thomas-Mann-Str 40, Bonn, 53111, Germany. TEL 49-228-33889450, FAX 49-228-33889475, info@ilco.de. Ed. Helga Englert. Circ: 12,000 (controlled).

616.99 DEU ISSN 1435-7402
IM FOCUS ONKOLOGIE. Text in German. 1998. 10/yr. EUR 105, USD 127 to institutions (effective 2012). adv. **Document type:** *Journal, Academic/Scholarly.*
Indexed: A26.
—BLDSC (4368.590950). **CCC.**
Published by: Urban und Vogel Medien und Medizin Verlagsgesellschaft mbH (Subsidiary of: Springer Science+Business Media), Neumarkter Str 43, Munich, 81673, Germany. TEL 49-89-4372-1411, FAX 49-89-4372-1410, verlag@urban-vogel.de, http://www.urban-vogel.de. Ed. Dr. Doris Berger. Adv. contact Renate Senfft. B&W page EUR 2,650, color page EUR 4,250; trim 174 x 237. Circ: 11,333 (paid). **Subscr. to:** Springer Distribution Center, Kundenservice Zeitschriften, Haberstr 7, Heidelberg 69126, Germany. TEL 49-6221-3454303, FAX 49-6221-3454229, subscriptions@springer.com.

616.994 GBR ISSN 0306-4905
IMPERIAL CANCER RESEARCH FUND. SCIENTIFIC REPORT. Text in English. 1973. a. free to qualified personnel. **Document type:** *Report, Academic/Scholarly.*
Related titles: Online - full text ed.
Published by: Imperial Cancer Research Fund, Lincoln's Inn Fields, Imperial Cancer Research Fund, London, WC2A 3PX, United Kingdom. TEL 44-20-7269-3206, FAX 44-20-7269-3084. Ed., R&P Angela Aldam TEL 44-20-7269-3371. Circ: 1,700 (controlled).

616.99449 CAN ISSN 1700-0971
IN STRIDE; breast cancer & the road to recovery. Text in English. 2001. 3/yr. **Document type:** *Newsletter, Consumer.*
Related titles: French ed.: Parcours. ISSN 1700-0963.
Published by: Parkhurst Publishing, 400 McGill St, 3rd Fl, Montreal, PQ H2Y 2G1, Canada. TEL 514-397-8833, FAX 514-397-0228, contact@parkpub.com, http://www.parkpub.com. Ed. Dr. Maureen Trudeau.

616.9 SVN ISSN 0079-9580
INCIDENCA RAKA V SLOVENIJI/CANCER INCIDENCE IN SLOVENIA. Text in English, Slovenian. 1957. a., latest 2003. free (effective 2003). index. **Document type:** *Yearbook, Academic/Scholarly.*
Formerly: Rak v Sloveniji. Tabele
Published by: Onkoloski Institut Ljubljana/Institute of Oncology Ljubljana, Zaloska 2, Ljubljana, 1000, Slovenia. TEL 386-1-4314225, FAX 386-1-4314180, mzakelj@onko-i.si, http://www.onko-i.si. Ed., R&P Gregor Sersa. Circ: 750.

616.994 IND ISSN 0019-509X
CODEN: IJCAAR
➤ **INDIAN JOURNAL OF CANCER.** Text in English. 1963. q. INR 1,500 domestic to individuals; USD 150 foreign to individuals; INR 2,000 domestic to institutions; USD 250 foreign to institutions; INR 1,800 combined subscription domestic to individuals (print & online eds.); USD 120 combined subscription foreign to individuals (print & online eds.); INR 2,400 combined subscription domestic to institutions (print & online eds.); USD 300 combined subscription foreign to institutions (print & online eds.) (effective 2011). bk.rev. charts; illus.; stat. 60 p./no. 2 cols./p.; back issues avail.; reprint service avail. from IRC. **Document type:** *Journal, Academic/Scholarly.* **Description:** Contains researches in the field of cancer.
Related titles: CD-ROM ed.; Microfilm ed.: (from PQC); Online - full text ed.: ISSN 1998-4774. INR 1,200 domestic to individuals; USD 80 foreign to individuals; INR 1,600 domestic to institutions; INR 200 foreign to institutions (effective 2011).
Indexed: A01, A03, A08, A22, A26, A36, B25, BIOSIS Prev, C06, C07, CA, CABA, ChemAb, DentInd, E08, E12, EMBASE, ExcerpMed, ExtraMED, G08, GH, H11, H12, I05, INIS AtomInd, IndMed, MEDLINE, MycolAb, N02, N03, P10, P20, P22, P30, P33, P48, P53, P54, PHN&I, PQC, R10, R12, Reac, S09, SCI, SCOPUS, T02, T05, W07, W11.
—BLDSC (4410.550000), CASDDS, GNLM, IE, Infotrieve, Ingenta, INIST, Linda Hall. **CCC.**
Published by: (Indian Cancer Society), Medknow Publications and Media Pvt. Ltd., B-9, Kanara Business Ctr, Off Link Rd, Ghatkopar (E), Mumbai, Maharastra 400 075, India. TEL 91-22-66491816, FAX 91-22-66491817, http://www.medknow.com. Eds. D K Sahu, Purvish M Parikh. **Subscr. to:** I N S I O Scientific Books & Periodicals. **Co-sponsor:** Indian Association of Oncology.

616.15 IND ISSN 0971-4502
➤ **INDIAN JOURNAL OF HEMATOLOGY AND BLOOD TRANSFUSION.** Text in English. 1982. q. EUR 328, USD 263 combined subscription to institutions (print & online eds.) (effective 2012). **Document type:** *Journal, Academic/Scholarly.* **Description:** Publishes Original Articles, Case Reports, Correspondence, and Review Articles in the related fields of Hematology, Hemato Oncology, Molecular Hematology, Pediatric Hematology, Transfusion Medicine, Genetics, and Laboratory Hematology.
Related titles: Online - full text ed.: ISSN 0974-0449 (from IngentaConnect).
Indexed: A22, A26, A36, CABA, E01, E08, E12, EMBASE, ExcerpMed, GH, H12, N02, N03, P33, R08, R10, Reac, S09, SCI, SCOPUS, T05, W07.
—BLDSC (4414.100000), IE. **CCC.**
Published by: (Indian Society of Hematology and Blood Transfusion), Springer (India) Private Ltd. (Subsidiary of: Springer Science+Business Media), 212, Deen Dayal Upadhyaya Marg, 3rd Fl, Gandharva Mahavidyalaya, New Delhi, 110 002, India. TEL 91-11-45755888, FAX 91-11-45755889. Ed. A K Tripathi.

618.92994 IND ISSN 0971-5851
➤ **INDIAN JOURNAL OF MEDICAL & PAEDIATRIC ONCOLOGY.** Text in English. q. back issues avail. **Document type:** *Journal, Academic/Scholarly.* **Description:** Contains original articles, short communications, reviews, selected summary, treatment, case reports, and letters on pediatric oncology.
Related titles: Online - full text ed.: ISSN 0975-2129. free (effective 2011).
Indexed: A01, A26, E08, EMBASE, H12, I05, P10, P30, P48, P53, P54, PQC, SCOPUS, T02.
—**CCC.**
Published by: (Indian Society of Medical & Paediatric Oncology), Medknow Publications and Media Pvt. Ltd., B-9, Kanara Business Ctr, Off Link Rd, Ghatkopar (E), Mumbai, Maharastra 400 075, India. TEL 91-22-66491816, 91-22-66491818, publishing@medknow.com, journals@medknow.com, http://www.medknow.com. Ed. Dr. Lalit Kumar.

616.992 IND ISSN 0975-7651
▼ ➤ **INDIAN JOURNAL OF SURGICAL ONCOLOGY.** Text in English. 2010. q. EUR 210, USD 284 combined subscription to institutions (print & online eds.) (effective 2012). **Document type:** *Journal, Academic/Scholarly.* **Description:** Covers the specialized areas of oncology that engage surgeons in the treatment and management of cancer.
Related titles: Online - full text ed.: ISSN 0976-6952. 2010 (from IngentaConnect).
Indexed: A22, E01.
—IE. **CCC.**
Published by: (Indian Association of Surgical Oncology), Springer (India) Private Ltd. (Subsidiary of: Springer Science+Business Media), 212, Deen Dayal Upadhyaya Marg, 3rd Fl, Gandharva Mahavidyalaya, New Delhi, 110 002, India. TEL 91-11-45755888, FAX 91-11-45755889. Ed. K S Gopinath.

➤ **INDIAN JOURNAL OF UROLOGY.** *see* MEDICAL SCIENCES—Urology And Nephrology

616.994061 KOR ISSN 2093-2340
➤ **INFECTION & CHEMOTHERAPY.** Text in English, Korean. 2003. bi-m. membership. Supplement avail. **Document type:** *Journal, Academic/Scholarly.* **Description:** Contains original articles, reviews, notes, case reports and letter to editors. Covers pathogenesis, clinical investigation, epidemiology, medical microbiology, diagnosis, immune mechanisms, and the treatment of diseases caused by infectious agents.
Formerly (until 2010): Gam'yeom Gwa Hwahag Yo'beob/Infection and Chemotherapy (1598-8112); Which was formed by the merger of (1969-2003): Gam'yeom/Korean Journal of Infectious Diseases (0368-6221); (1982-2003): Daehan Hwahag Yo'beob Haghoeji/Korean Society for Chemotherapy. Journal (1225-7850)
Related titles: Online - full text ed.: ISSN 2092-6448.
Indexed: A29, A34, A36, B20, B21, ESPM, H&SSA, ImmunAb, P33, R08, T05.
—BLDSC (4478.713000).
Published by: (Korean Society of Infectious Diseases/Daehan Gamyeom Hakoe), Korean Society for Chemotherapy/Daehan Hwahag Yobeop Hakoe, #1203, Majellan 21 Aseuterium 158-10, Samseong-dong, Gangnam-gu, Seoul, 135-880, Korea, S. TEL 82-2-2055141, FAX 82-2-2055142, ksc@ksac.or.kr, http://www.ksac.or.kr/. Ed. Hee Jin Cheong.

616.992 GBR ISSN 1750-9378
RC268.57
➤ **INFECTIOUS AGENTS AND CANCER.** Text in English. 2006. irreg. free (effective 2011). adv. **Document type:** *Journal, Academic/Scholarly.* **Description:** Covers all aspects of the pathogenic mechanisms of chronic infections and progression to oncogenesis.
Media: Online - full text.
Indexed: A01, A26, A35, A36, AgBio, C06, C07, CA, CABA, E12, EMBASE, ExcerpMed, GH, I05, OGFA, P30, P33, P39, R12, SCOPUS, T02, T05, VS, VirolAbstr.
—**CCC.**
Published by: BioMed Central Ltd. (Subsidiary of: Springer Science+Business Media), 236 Gray's Inn Rd, London, WC1X 8HB, United Kingdom. TEL 44-20-31922000, FAX 44-20-31922010, info@biomedcentral.com, http://www.biomedcentral.com. Eds. Franco M Buonaguro, George K Lewis, Pier Giuseppe Pelicci.

616.994 DEU ISSN 1613-3633
INFO ONKOLOGIE. Text in German. 1998. bi-m. EUR 138, USD 184 to institutions (effective 2012). adv. **Document type:** *Journal, Academic/Scholarly.*
Former titles (until 2004): Interdisziplinaere Fortbildung Onkologie (1611-2326); (until 2002): InFo Onkologie (1435-2486)
Related titles: CD-ROM ed.; Online - full text ed.
Indexed: A26.
—**CCC.**
Published by: (Deutscher Krebsgesellschaft e.V., Arbeitsgemeinschaft Internistische Onkologie), Urban und Vogel Medien und Medizin Verlagsgesellschaft mbH (Subsidiary of: Springer Science+Business Media), Neumarkter Str 43, Munich, 81673, Germany. TEL 49-89-4372-1411, FAX 49-89-4372-1410, verlag@urban-vogel.de. Ed. Dr. U R Kleeberg. Adv. contact Renate Senfft. B&W page EUR 2,100, color page EUR 3,400; trim 174 x 245. Circ: 4,000 (paid and controlled). **Subscr. to:** Springer Distribution Center, Kundenservice Zeitschriften, Haberstr 7, Heidelberg 69126, Germany. TEL 49-6221-3454303, FAX 49-6221-3454229, subscriptions@springer.com.

616.992 CHE ISSN 1664-8390
▼ **INFO@ONKOLOGIE.** Text in German. 2011. bi-m. CHF 80 (effective 2011). **Document type:** *Journal, Trade.*
Published by: Aerzteverlag Medinfo AG, Seestr 141, Erlenbach, 8703, Switzerland. TEL 41-44-9157080, FAX 41-44-9157089, info@medinfo-verlag.ch. Circ: 4,000 (paid).

615.6 USA ISSN 1080-3858
INFUSION (ALEXANDRIA). Text in English. 1991. bi-m. USD 75 to individuals; free to qualified personnel (effective 2004). adv. back issues avail. **Document type:** *Journal, Academic/Scholarly.* **Description:** Provides information designed to assist infusion therapy professionals in providing high quality, cost-effective infusion care.
Indexed: C06, C07, C08, CINAHL, I12, IDIS.
—BLDSC (4499.539000), IE, Ingenta.
Published by: National Home Infusion Association, 100 Daingerfield Rd., Alexandria, VA 22314-2899. Circ: 15,000.

616.994 CAN ISSN 1713-6997
➤ **INNOVATIONS IN BREAST CANCER CARE.** Text in English. 2003. 3/yr. **Document type:** *Journal, Academic/Scholarly.* **Description:** Intended for dialogue on evidence-based current and emerging trends in diagnosis and treatment, along with practical management tools.
Published by: Parkhurst Publishing, 400 McGill St, 3rd Fl, Montreal, PQ H2Y 2G1, Canada. TEL 514-397-8833, FAX 514-397-0228, contact@parkpub.com, http://www.parkpub.com. Ed. Dr. Shalendra Verma.

616.994 FRA ISSN 1760-1266
INSTITUT CURIE. LE JOURNAL. Key Title: Le Journal de l'Institut Curie. Text in French. 2003. q. EUR 6 (effective 2009). back issues avail. **Document type:** *Magazine, Consumer.*
Formed by the merger of (1986-2003): Comprendre et Agir (0982-2313); (1989-2003): Institut Curie. La Lettre (1145-9131)
Published by: Institut Curie, 26 Rue d'Ulm, Paris, 75248 Cedex 05, France. TEL 33-1-42346600.

616.992 FRA ISSN 1950-9308
INSTITUT NATIONAL DU CANCER. LETTRE. Variant title: La Lettre de l'Institut National du Cancer. Text in French. 2006. irreg. back issues avail. **Document type:** *Bulletin, Consumer.*
Related titles: Online - full text ed.: free.
Published by: Institut National du Cancer, 52 Av Andre Morizet, Boulogne-Billancourt, 92513 Cedex, France. TEL 33-1-41105000, contact@institutcancer.fr, http://www.e-cancer.fr.

616.994 PER ISSN 1017-0642
INSTITUTO NACIONAL DE ENFERMEDADES NEOPLASTICAS. BOLETIN. Key Title: Boletin del INEN. Text in Spanish. 1979. s-a. back issues avail. **Document type:** *Bulletin, Academic/Scholarly.*
Related titles: Online - full text ed.
Published by: Instituto Nacional de Enfermedades Neoplasicas, Ave Angamos Este 2520, Surquillo, Lima, 34, Peru. TEL 51-1-7106900, FAX 51-1-6204991, postmaster@inen.sld.pe, http://www.inen.sld.pe/. Ed. Orlando Morales Quedena.

614 USA ISSN 1534-7354
RC271.A62 CODEN: ICTNAY
INTEGRATIVE CANCER THERAPIES. Text in English. 2002. q. USD 600, GBP 353 combined subscription to institutions (print & online eds.); USD 588, GBP 346 to institutions (effective 2011). adv. back issues avail.; reprint service avail. from PSC. **Document type:** *Journal, Trade.* **Description:** Focuses on a new and growing movement in cancer treatment that emphasizes scientific understanding of alternative medicine and traditional medicine therapies, and their responsible integration with conventional health care.
Related titles: Online - full text ed.: ISSN 1552-695X. USD 540, GBP 318 to institutions (effective 2011).
Indexed: A20, A22, A26, A34, A35, A36, AgBio, B07, BIOBASE, BP, C06, C07, C30, CA, CABA, E01, E08, E12, EMBASE, ExcerpMed, F08, F11, F12, G08, GH, H11, H12, H16, I05, I12, IABS, IndVet, MEDLINE, N02, N03, P30, P32, PHN&I, R10, R11, R12, RA&MP, Reac, S09, SCI, SCOPUS, SoyAb, T02, T05, VS, W07.
—BLDSC (4531.816572), IE, Ingenta. **CCC.**
Published by: Sage Publications, Inc., 2455 Teller Rd, Thousand Oaks, CA 91320. TEL 805-499-9774, FAX 805-499-0871, info@sagepub.com. Ed. Dr. Keith I Block. adv.: B&W page USD 495, color page USD 865; trim 8.5 x 11. Circ: 1,950. **Subscr. outside the Americas to:** Sage Publications Ltd., 1 Oliver's Yard, 55 City Rd, London EC1Y 1SP, United Kingdom. TEL 44-20-73248701, FAX 44-20-73248733, subscription@sagepub.co.uk.

616.992 USA ISSN 2090-3189
▼ ➤ **INTERNATIONAL JOURNAL OF BREAST CANCER.** Text in English. 2011. free (effective 2011). **Document type:** *Journal, Academic/Scholarly.*
Media: Online - full text.
Published by: Sage - Hindawi Access to Research, 410 Park Ave, 15th Fl, 287 PMB, New York, NY 10022. FAX 866-446-3294.

616.994 USA ISSN 0020-7136
RC261 CODEN: IJCNAW
➤ **INTERNATIONAL JOURNAL OF CANCER/JOURNAL INTERNATIONAL DU CANCER.** Variant title: Predictive Oncology. Text in English, French. 1936. 24/yr. GBP 2,409 in United Kingdom to institutions; EUR 3,045 in Europe to institutions; USD 4,720 elsewhere to institutions; GBP 2,770 combined subscription in United Kingdom to institutions (print & online eds.); EUR 3,502 combined subscription in Europe to institutions (print & online eds.); USD 5,428 combined subscription elsewhere to institutions (print & online eds.) (effective 2012). adv. bk.rev. charts; illus.; abstr. s-a. index. back issues avail.; reprint service avail. from PSC. **Document type:** *Journal, Academic/Scholarly.* **Description:** Examines all topics relevant to experimental and clinical cancer research, with an emphasis on fundamental studies that have relevance to the understanding of human cancer.
Incorporates (1993-199?): Radiation Oncology Investigation (1065-7541); Formerly (until 1966): Acta - Union Internationale Contra Cancrum (0365-3056)
Related titles: Microform ed.: (from PQC); Online - full text ed.: ISSN 1097-0215. GBP 2,409 in United Kingdom to institutions; EUR 3,045 in Europe to institutions; USD 4,720 elsewhere to institutions (effective 2012); ◆ Supplement(s): International Journal of Cancer. Supplement. ISSN 0898-6924.
Indexed: A20, A22, A34, A35, A36, A38, AIDS Ab, AIDS&CR, ASCA, AgBio, B&BAb, B19, B21, B25, BIOBASE, BIOSIS Prev, BP, C30, C33, CABA, CIN, CISA, ChemAb, ChemTitl, CurCont, D01, DBA, DentInd, DokArb, E12, EMBASE, ESPM, ExcerpMed, F08, F09, F11, F12, FR, G10, GH, H&SSA, H16, H17, IABS, IBR, IBZ, INI, ISR, ImmunAb, IndMed, IndVet, Inpharma, LT, M&PBA, MEDLINE, MS&D, MaizeAb, MycolAb, N02, N03, N04, NRN, OGFA, P30, P32, P33, P35, P37, P38, P39, P40, PN&I, R07, R08, R10, R12, R13, RA&MP, RM&VM, RRTA, Reac, RefZh, RiskAb, SAA, SCI, SCOPUS, SoyAb, T05, THA, Telegen, ToxAb, TriticAb, VITIS, VS, VirolAbstr, W07, W09, W10, W11.
—BLDSC (4542.156000), CASDDS, GNLM, IE, Infotrieve, Ingenta, INIST. **CCC.**
Published by: (International Union Against Cancer CHE, Deutsches Krebsforschungszentrum DEU), John Wiley & Sons, Inc., 111 River St, Hoboken, NJ 07030. TEL 201-748-6000, FAX 201-748-6088, info@wiley.com, http://www.wiley.com/WileyCDA/. Ed. Peter Lichter. Adv. contact Stephen Donohue TEL 781-388-8511. **Subscr. outside the Americas to:** John Wiley & Sons Ltd.

616.992 USA ISSN 1811-9727
RC261.A1
➤ **INTERNATIONAL JOURNAL OF CANCER RESEARCH.** Text in English. 2004. q. **Document type:** *Journal, Academic/Scholarly.* **Description:** Publishes original studies in all areas of basic, clinical, translational, epidemiological and prevention research devoted to the study of cancer and cancer-related biomedical sciences.
Related titles: Online - full text ed.: ISSN 1811-9735.

Indexed: A01, A34, A36, AgrForAb, B21, BP, C30, CA, CABA, D01, E12, EMBASE, ExcerpMed, F08, F11, F12, GH, GenetAb, H16, H17, MaizeAb, N02, N03, OGFA, P32, P33, P40, R08, R10, R11, R12, RA&MP, Reac, S12, SCOPUS, SoyAb, T02, T05, TriticAb, VS.
—BLDSC (4542.156800), IE.
Published by: Academic Journals Inc., 224, 5th Ave, No 2218, New York, NY 10001. FAX 888-777-8532, support@scialert.com.

616.992 USA ISSN 1554-1134
RC268.15
➤ **INTERNATIONAL JOURNAL OF CANCER RESEARCH AND PREVENTION.** Text in English. 2004. q. USD 505 to institutions; USD 757 combined subscription to institutions (print & online eds.) (effective 2012). **Document type:** *Journal, Academic/Scholarly.* **Description:** Focuses on advances in genetics, molecular medicine, biotechnologies, and behavioral sciences that have impact on primary, secondary and tertiary cancer prevention.
Related titles: Online - full text ed.: USD 505 to institutions (effective 2012).
Indexed: EMBASE, ExcerpMed, P30, SCOPUS.
Published by: (International Society of Cancer Chemoprevention), Nova Science Publishers, Inc., 400 Oser Ave, Ste 1600, Hauppauge, NY 11788. TEL 631-231-7269, FAX 631-231-8175, main@novapublishers.com. Ed. Alaa F Badawi.

616.994 JPN ISSN 1341-9625
RC254.A1 CODEN: IJCOF6
➤ **INTERNATIONAL JOURNAL OF CLINICAL ONCOLOGY.** Text in English, Japanese. 1996. bi-m. (in 1 vol., 6 nos./vol.). EUR 336, USD 384 combined subscription to institutions (print & online eds.) (effective 2012). adv. bk.rev. abstr.; bibl.; charts; illus. reprint service avail. from PSC. **Document type:** *Journal, Academic/Scholarly.* **Description:** Publishes original research papers on all aspects of clinical human oncology that report the results of novel and timely investigations. Experimental studies with relevance to clinical oncology will also be accepted.
Formerly (until 1996): Japan Society for Cancer Therapy. Journal (0021-4671)
Related titles: ◆ Online - full text ed.: International Journal of Clinical Oncology (Online). ISSN 1437-7772.
Indexed: A01, A03, A08, A22, A26, B21, CA, ChemAb, ChemTitl, DentInd, E01, EMBASE, ExcerpMed, H12, H13, I05, INIS AtomInd, IndMed, Inpharma, MEDLINE, OGFA, P10, P20, P22, P30, P48, P50, P53, P54, PQC, R10, Reac, RefZh, SCI, SCOPUS, T02, W07.
—BLDSC (4542.170500), CASDDS, GNLM, IE, Infotrieve, Ingenta, INIST. **CCC.**
Published by: (Japan Society of Clinical Oncology/Nihon Gan Chiryo Gakkai), Springer Japan KK (Subsidiary of: Springer Science+Business Media), No 2 Funato Bldg, 1-11-11 Kudan-kita, Chiyoda-ku, Tokyo, 102-0073, Japan. TEL 81-3-68317000, FAX 81-3-68317001, http://www.springer.jp. Ed. Masahiro Hiraoka. Adv. contact Stephan Kroeck TEL 49-30-827875739. **Subscr. in the Americas to:** Springer New York LLC, Journal Fulfillment, PO Box 2485, Secaucus, NJ 07096. TEL 800-777-4643, 201-348-4033, FAX 201-348-4505, journals-ny@springer.com, http://www.springer.com; **Subscr. to:** Springer Distribution Center, Kundenservice Zeitschriften, Haberstr 7, Heidelberg 69126, Germany. TEL 49-6221-3454303, FAX 49-6221-3454229, subscriptions@springer.com.

616.994 JPN ISSN 1437-7772
➤ **INTERNATIONAL JOURNAL OF CLINICAL ONCOLOGY (ONLINE).** Text in English. bi-m. **Document type:** *Journal, Academic/Scholarly.*
Media: Online - full text (from IngentaConnect). **Related titles:** ◆ Print ed.: International Journal of Clinical Oncology. ISSN 1341-9625.
—**CCC.**
Published by: Springer Japan KK (Subsidiary of: Springer Science+Business Media), No 2 Funato Bldg, 1-11-11 Kudan-kita, Chiyoda-ku, Tokyo, 102-0073, Japan. TEL 81-3-3812-0617, 81-3-68317000, 81-3-3812-0757, FAX 81-3-68317001, orders@springer.jp. **Subscr. in N. America to:** Springer New York LLC, Journal Fulfillment, PO Box 2485, Secaucus, NJ 07096. TEL 800-777-4643, FAX 201-348-4505; **Subscr. to:** Eastern Book Service, Inc., 3-13 Hongo 3-chome, Bunkyo-ku, Tokyo 113-8480, Japan.

➤ **INTERNATIONAL JOURNAL OF GYNECOLOGICAL CANCER.** *see* MEDICAL SCIENCES—Obstetrics And Gynecology

616.99 GBR ISSN 0265-6736
RC271.T5 CODEN: IJHYEQ
➤ **INTERNATIONAL JOURNAL OF HYPERTHERMIA.** Text in English. 1985. 8/yr. GBP 1,755, EUR 2,455, USD 3,065 combined subscription to institutions (print & online eds.); GBP 3,415, EUR 4,770, USD 5,955 combined subscription to corporations (print & online eds.) (effective 2010). adv. back issues avail.; reprint service avail. from PSC. **Document type:** *Journal, Academic/Scholarly.* **Description:** Provides a forum for the publication of research and clinical papers on hyperthermia, which fall largely into the three main categories: clinical studies, biological studies and techniques of heat delivery and temperature measurement.
Related titles: Online - full text ed.: ISSN 1464-5157 (from IngentaConnect).
Indexed: A01, A02, A03, A08, A22, A34, A35, A36, A37, ASCA, AgBio, B07, B25, BIOBASE, BIOSIS Prev, C11, CA, CABA, CIN, ChemAb, ChemTitl, CurCont, E01, E12, EMBASE, ExcerpMed, GH, H04, IABS, ISR, IndMed, Inpharma, Inspec, MEDLINE, MycolAb, N02, N03, P30, P35, PN&I, R10, RA&MP, Reac, SCI, SCOPUS, T02, T05, VS, W07.
—AskIEEE, CASDDS, GNLM, IE, Infotrieve, Ingenta, INIST. **CCC.**
Published by: (Society for Thermal Medicine USA, North American Hyperthermia Group), Informa Healthcare (Subsidiary of: T & F Informa plc), Telephone House, 69-77 Paul St, London, EC2A 4LQ, United Kingdom. TEL 44-20-70175000, FAX 44-20-70176792, healthcare.enquiries@informa.com. Ed. Mark W Dewhirst TEL 919-483-4180. Adv. contact Per Sonnerfeldt. **Subscr. in N. America to:** Taylor & Francis Inc., Customer Services Dept, 325 Chestnut St, 8th Fl, Philadelphia, PA 19106. TEL 215-625-8900, 800-354-1420, FAX 215-625-8914, customerservice@taylorandfrancis.com; **Subscr. outside N. America to:** Taylor & Francis Ltd., Journals Customer Service, Sheepen Pl, Colchester, Essex CO3 3LP, United Kingdom. TEL 44-20-70175544, FAX 44-20-70175198, tf.enquiries@tfinforma.com.

616.99 GRC ISSN 1019-6439
RC254.A1 CODEN: IJONES
➤ **INTERNATIONAL JOURNAL OF ONCOLOGY.** Text in English. 1992. m. USD 350 in Europe to individuals; USD 390 elsewhere to individuals; USD 720 in Europe to institutions; USD 770 elsewhere to institutions (effective 2003). adv. bk.rev. charts; illus. **Document type:** *Journal, Academic/Scholarly.* **Description:** Publishes original high-quality articles and reports in experimental and clinical cancer research.
Related titles: Online - full text ed.: ISSN 1791-2423.
Indexed: A22, A34, A35, A36, A38, AIDS&CR, ASCA, AgBio, AgrForAb, B&BAb, B19, B21, B25, BIOSIS Prev, C30, CABA, CIN, CTA, ChemAb, ChemTitl, CurCont, D01, E12, EMBASE, ExcerpMed, F08, F11, F12, GH, GenetAb, H16, ISR, IndMed, IndVet, Inpharma, MEDLINE, MycolAb, N02, N03, NSA, NucAcAb, OGFA, P30, P32, P33, P35, P39, P40, PGegResA, R07, R08, R10, R13, RA&MP, RM&VM, Reac, S12, SCI, SCOPUS, SoyAb, T05, TriticAb, VS, W07.
—BLDSC (4542.424600), CASDDS, GNLM, IE, Infotrieve, Ingenta, INIST. **CCC.**
Published by: Spandidos Publications, PO Box 18179, Athens, 116 10, Greece. TEL 30-210-7227809, FAX 30-210-7252922, contact@spandidos-publications.com, http://www.spandidos-publications.com. Circ: 700.

616.992 IND
➤ **INTERNATIONAL JOURNAL OF ONCOLOGY RESEARCH.** Text in English. s-a. USD 425 (effective 2011). **Document type:** *Journal, Academic/Scholarly.* **Description:** Publishes articles related to oncology research.
Related titles: Online - full text ed.: free (effective 2011).
Published by: Bioinfo Publications, 49/F-72, Vighnahar Complex, Front of Overseas Bank, Sector 12, Kharghar, Navi Mumbai, 410 210, India. TEL 91-22-27743967, FAX 91-22-66736413, editor@bioinfo.in, subscription@bioinfo.in.

616.99 571.4 GBR ISSN 0955-3002
QH652 CODEN: IJRBE7
➤ **INTERNATIONAL JOURNAL OF RADIATION BIOLOGY.** Abbreviated title: I J R B. Text and summaries in English, French, German. 1959. m. GBP 2,230, EUR 3,105, USD 3,880 combined subscription to institutions (print & online eds.); GBP 4,450, EUR 6,215, USD 7,760 combined subscription to corporations (print & online eds.) (effective 2010). adv. charts; illus. index. back issues avail.; reprint service avail. from PSC. **Document type:** *Journal, Academic/Scholarly.* **Description:** Contains original research and review papers on the effects of ionization, ultraviolet and visible radiation, accelerated particles, microwaves, ultrasound and heat and related modalities.
Formerly (until 1988): International Journal of Radiation Biology and Related Studies in Physics, Chemistry and Medicine (0020-7616)
Related titles: Microform ed.; Online - full text ed.: ISSN 1362-3095. 1996 (from IngentaConnect).
Indexed: A01, A02, A03, A08, A22, A34, A35, A36, A38, ASCA, AgBio, B&BAb, B07, B19, B21, B25, B27, BIOBASE, BIOSIS Prev, BP, C11, C25, C30, C33, CA, CABA, CIN, CIS, ChemAb, ChemTitl, CurCont, D01, E01, E12, EMBASE, ESPM, ExcerpMed, F08, FCA, FR, FS&TA, GH, H04, H16, IABS, IBR, IBZ, ISR, IndMed, IndVet, Inpharma, Inspec, MEDLINE, MaizeAb, MycolAb, N02, N03, N04, P30, P32, P33, P40, PGrRegA, PHN&I, R07, R08, R10, RA&MP, Reac, RefZh, S13, S17, SCI, SCOPUS, SoyAb, T02, T05, THA, ToxAb, VS, W07, W10.
—AskIEEE, CASDDS, GNLM, IE, Infotrieve, Ingenta, INIST, Linda Hall. **CCC.**
Published by: Informa Healthcare (Subsidiary of: T & F Informa plc), Telephone House, 69-77 Paul St, London, EC2A 4LQ, United Kingdom. TEL 44-20-70175000, healthcare.enquiries@informa.com, http://www.tandf.co.uk/journals/. Eds. A Michael Rauth, Richard Hill. **Subscr. in N. America to:** Taylor & Francis Inc., Customer Services Dept, 325 Chestnut St, 8th Fl, Philadelphia, PA 19106. TEL 215-625-8900, 800-354-1420, FAX 215-625-2940, customerservice@taylorandfrancis.com; **Subscr. outside N. America to:** Taylor & Francis Ltd., Journals Customer Service, Sheepen Pl, Colchester, Essex CO3 3LP, United Kingdom. TEL 44-20-70175544, FAX 44-20-70175198, tf.enquiries@tfinforma.com.

▼ ➤ **INTERNATIONAL JOURNAL OF SURGICAL ONCOLOGY.** *see* MEDICAL SCIENCES—Surgery

➤ **INTERNATIONAL JOURNAL OF SURGICAL PATHOLOGY.** *see* MEDICAL SCIENCES—Surgery

616.992 GBR ISSN 1477-7800
RD651
➤ **INTERNATIONAL SEMINARS IN SURGICAL ONCOLOGY.** Abbreviated title: I S S O. Text in English. 2004. irreg. adv. back issues avail. **Document type:** *Journal, Academic/Scholarly.* **Description:** Covers on all aspects of medical and surgical oncology, including the diagnosis and treatment of a patient with cancer, pathology, and techniques of cancer surgery.
Media: Online - full text.
Indexed: A01, A26, C06, C07, CA, EMBASE, ExcerpMed, I05, P30, R10, Reac, SCOPUS, T02.
—**CCC.**
Published by: BioMed Central Ltd. (Subsidiary of: Springer Science+Business Media), 236 Gray's Inn Rd, London, WC1X 8HB, United Kingdom. TEL 44-20-31922000, FAX 44-20-31922010, info@biomedcentral.com, http://www.biomedcentral.com. Eds. Gurpreet Singh-Ranger, Mohamad Hussein. Adv. contact Natasha Bailey TEL 44-20-31922231.

616.992 ITA ISSN 1125-632X
INTERNATIONAL TRENDS IN ONCOLOGY. Text in Multiple languages. 1997. q. EUR 10 domestic; EUR 20 foreign (effective 2008). adv. **Document type:** *Journal, Academic/Scholarly.*
Related titles: Online - full text ed.: ISSN 1971-3754. 2007.
Indexed: RefZh.
Published by: C I C Edizioni Internazionali, Corso Trieste 42, Rome, 00198, Italy. TEL 39-06-8412673, FAX 39-06-8412688, info@gruppocic.it, http://www.gruppocic.it. adv.: color page EUR 2,633.93, B&W page EUR 2,065.83; 275 x 375.

616.994 CHE ISSN 0074-9206
INTERNATIONAL UNION AGAINST CANCER. PROCEEDINGS OF CONGRESS. Text in Multiple languages. irreg. **Document type:** *Proceedings, Academic/Scholarly.*
Published by: International Union Against Cancer, 62 route de Frontenex, Geneva, 1207, Switzerland. TEL 41-22-8091811, FAX 41-22-8091810, info@uicc.ch, http://www.uicc.ch.

616.992 USA ISSN 1528-8331
RC1
➤ **THE INTERNET JOURNAL OF ONCOLOGY.** Text in English. 2000. s-a. free (effective 2011). adv. bk.rev. back issues avail. **Document type:** *Journal, Academic/Scholarly.* **Description:** Provides information from the field of oncology, cancer prevention and cancer treatment; contains original articles, reviews, case reports, streaming slide shows, streaming videos, letters to the editor, press releases, and meeting information.
Media: Online - full text.
Indexed: A01, A02, A03, A08, A26, C06, C07, CA, EMBASE, G08, H11, H12, I05, S06, SCOPUS, T02.
Published by: Internet Scientific Publications, Llc., 23 Rippling Creek Dr, Sugar Land, TX 77479. TEL 832-443-1193, FAX 281-240-1533, wenker@ispub.com. Ed. Claire Verschraegen.

➤ **THE INTERNET JOURNAL OF PAIN, SYMPTOM CONTROL AND PALLIATIVE CARE.** *see* MEDICAL SCIENCES—Anaesthesiology

➤ **INTERSCIENCE CONFERENCE ON ANTIMICROBIAL AGENTS AND CHEMOTHERAPY. ABSTRACTS.** *see* BIOLOGY—Microbiology

616.992 IRN ISSN 2008-2398
IRANIAN JOURNAL OF CANCER PREVENTION. Text in English. 2007. q. **Document type:** *Journal, Academic/Scholarly.*
Related titles: Online - full text ed.: ISSN 2008-2401. free (effective 2011).
Indexed: A34, A35, A36, AgBio, AgrForAb, C06, CABA, D01, F08, F12, GH, H16, N02, N03, P33, R08, R12, SCOPUS, T05.
Published by: Shahid Beheshti University of Medical Sciences, PO Box 19395, Tehran, 4618, Iran. TEL 98-21-22718505.

IRISH CERVICAL SCREENING PROGRAMME. ANNUAL REPORT. *see* MEDICAL SCIENCES—Obstetrics And Gynecology

616.992 USA ISSN 2090-5661
▼ ➤ **ISRN ONCOLOGY.** (International Scholarly Research Network) Text in English. 2011. **Document type:** *Journal, Academic/Scholarly.* **Description:** Publishes original research articles, review articles, and clinical studies in all areas of oncology.
Related titles: Online - full text ed.: ISSN 2090-567X. 2011. free (effective 2011).
Published by: Hindawi Publishing Corporation, 410 Park Ave, 15th Fl, PMB 287, New York, NY 10022. FAX 215-893-4392, 866-446-3294, info@hindawi.com.

➤ **J A S T R O NEWSLETTER.** *see* MEDICAL SCIENCES—Radiology And Nuclear Medicine

616.992 FRA ISSN 2106-8534
▼ **J O G, LE JOURNAL D'ONCOGERIATRIE.** Text in French. 2010. bi-m. **Document type:** *Journal, Academic/Scholarly.*
Related titles: Online - full text ed.: ISSN 2107-6669.
Published by: Kephren Publishing, 22 Rue Chanez, Paris, 75016, France. TEL 33-1-75772091, http://www.le-jog.com/index.php. Eds. O Guerin, V Girre.

616.99 158 AUT ISSN 0949-0213
➤ **JAHRBUCH DER PSYCHOONKOLOGIE.** Text in German. 1993. irreg., latest 1997. price varies. **Document type:** *Monographic series, Academic/Scholarly.*
Published by: (Oesterreichische Gesellschaft fuer Psychoonkologie), Springer Wien (Subsidiary of: Springer Science+Business Media), Sachsenplatz 4-6, Vienna, W 1201, Austria. TEL 43-1-3302415-0, FAX 43-1-330242665, books@springer.at, http://www.springer.at. R&P Angela Foessl TEL 43-1-3302415517. **Subscr. to:** Springer New York LLC, 233 Spring St, New York, NY 10013. TEL 800-777-4643, FAX 201-348-4505.

616.992 JPN
JAPAN JOURNAL OF MOLECULAR TUMOR MARKER RESEARCH. Text in Japanese. a. **Document type:** *Journal, Academic/Scholarly.*
Media: Online - full content.
Published by: Japan Science and Technology Corp., Kawaguchi Center Bldg, 1-8, Honcho 4-chome, Kawaguchi City, Saitama 332-0012, Japan. TEL 81-48-226-5601, 81-48-226-5630, FAX 81-48-226-5751, http://www.jst.go.jp/.

616.994 GBR ISSN 0368-2811
RC254 CODEN: JJCOAC
➤ **JAPANESE JOURNAL OF CLINICAL ONCOLOGY.** Abbreviated title: J J C O. Text in English. 1971. m. GBP 190 in United Kingdom to institutions; EUR 286 in Europe to institutions; USD 380 in US & Canada to institutions; GBP 190 elsewhere to institutions; GBP 208 combined subscription in United Kingdom to institutions (print & online eds.); EUR 312 combined subscription in Europe to institutions (print & online eds.); USD 416 combined subscription in US & Canada to institutions (print & online eds.); GBP 208 combined subscription elsewhere to institutions (print & online eds.) (effective 2012). adv. bibl.; charts; illus. back issues avail.; reprint service avail. from PSC. **Document type:** *Journal, Academic/Scholarly.* **Description:** Publishes original high-quality articles and reviews on all aspects of clinical oncology; also epidemiology notes, clinical trial notes, interesting case reports with merits for clinical oncologists, as well as data of basic research with relevance to clinical oncology are welcomed.
Related titles: CD-ROM ed.; Online - full text ed.: ISSN 1465-3621. 1997. GBP 164 in United Kingdom to institutions; EUR 247 in Europe to institutions; USD 328 in US & Canada to institutions; GBP 164 elsewhere to institutions (effective 2012) (from IngentaConnect).
Indexed: A22, A29, A36, ASCA, B20, B21, B25, BIOSIS Prev, CA, CABA, ChemAb, CurCont, DentInd, E01, EMBASE, ESPM, ExcerpMed, GH, I10, INIS AtomInd, IndMed, Inpharma, MEDLINE, MycolAb, N02, N03, NRN, OGFA, P20, P22, P30, P33, P35, P48, P54, PQC, R10, R12, RA&MP, Reac, SCI, SCOPUS, T05, THA, VirolAbstr, W07.
—BLDSC (4651.378000), GNLM, IE, Infotrieve, Ingenta, INIST. **CCC.**
Published by: Oxford University Press, Great Clarendon St, Oxford, OX2 6DP, United Kingdom. TEL 44-1865-556767, FAX 44-1865-556646, enquiry@oup.co.uk, http://www.oxfordjournals.org. Ed. Tadao Kakizoe.

➤ **JAPANESE JOURNAL OF RADIOLOGY.** *see* MEDICAL SCIENCES—Radiology And Nuclear Medicine

➤ **JAPANESE SOCIETY FOR THERAPEUTIC RADIATION AND ONCOLOGY. JOURNAL.** *see* MEDICAL SCIENCES—Radiology And Nuclear Medicine

➤ **JATROS HAEMATOLOGIE UND ONKOLOGIE.** *see* MEDICAL SCIENCES—Hematology

616.994 FRA ISSN 1965-0817
▼ ➤ **JOURNAL AFRICAIN DU CANCER/AFRICAN JOURNAL OF CANCER.** Text in French, English. 2009. q. EUR 142, USD 213 combined subscription to institutions (print & online eds.) (effective 2011). reprint service avail. from PSC. **Document type:** *Journal, Academic/Scholarly.*
Related titles: Online - full text ed.: ISSN 1965-0825. 2009 (from IngentaConnect).
Indexed: SCOPUS.
—IE. **CCC.**
Published by: Springer France (Subsidiary of: Springer Science+Business Media), 22 Rue de Palestro, Paris, 75002, France. TEL 33-1-53009860, FAX 33-1-53009861, sylvie.kamara@springer.com. Ed. Adama Ly.

616.992 USA ISSN 2156-5333
▼ ➤ **JOURNAL OF ADOLESCENT AND YOUNG ADULT ONCOLOGY.** Abbreviated title: J A Y A O. Text in English. 2011. q. USD 758 combined subscription domestic to individuals (print & online eds.); USD 871 combined subscription foreign to individuals (print & online eds.) (effective 2012). adv. reprints avail. **Document type:** *Journal, Academic/Scholarly.* **Description:** Focuses on the unique biological, clinical, psychosocial, and survivorship issues with 15-39 age group. Dedicated to improving adolescent and young adult cancer care management and outcomes through the promotion of interdisciplinary research, education, communication, and collaboration between health care professionals.
Related titles: Online - full text ed.: ISSN 2156-535X. USD 739 (effective 2012).
—CCC.
Published by: Mary Ann Liebert, Inc. Publishers, 140 Huguenot St, 3rd Fl, New Rochelle, NY 10801. TEL 914-740-2100, FAX 914-740-2101, 800-654-3237, info@liebertpub.com. Ed. Leonard S Sender. Adv. contact Harriet I Matysko TEL 914-740-2182.

616.99449 KOR ISSN 1738-6756
➤ **JOURNAL OF BREAST CANCER.** Text in English. 1998. q. **Document type:** *Journal, Academic/Scholarly.*
Formerly (until 2003): Han'gug Yubang am Haghoeji/Korean Breast Cancer Society. Journal (1598-3641)
Related titles: Online - full text ed.: ISSN 2092-9900.
Indexed: EMBASE, SCI, SCOPUS, W07.
Published by: Korean Breast Cancer Society/han-gug Yubang-am Hakoe, Gwanghwamun Officia 2024, Sinmunno 1-ga, Jongno-gu, Seoul, 110-999, Korea, S. TEL 82-2-34616060, FAX 82-2-34616061, kbcs1996@paran.com, http://www.kbcs.or.kr/. Ed. Se Jeong Oh.

616.992 AUS ISSN 1837-9664
▼ **JOURNAL OF CANCER.** Text in English. 2010. irreg. **Document type:** *Journal, Academic/Scholarly.*
Related titles: Online - full text ed.: free (effective 2011).
Indexed: P30.
Published by: Ivyspring International Publisher, PO Box 4546, Lake Haven, NSW 2263, Australia. TEL 61-2-43905688, FAX 61-2-43905660, info@ivyspring.com, http://www.ivyspring.com. Eds. Naoto T Veno, Yan-Gao Man.

616.99 USA ISSN 0885-8195
RC266.5
➤ **JOURNAL OF CANCER EDUCATION.** Text in English. 1986. q. EUR 315, USD 426 combined subscription to institutions (print & online eds.) (effective 2012). index. back issues avail.; reprint service avail. from PSC. **Document type:** *Journal, Academic/Scholarly.* **Description:** Addresses varied aspects of cancer education for physicians, dentists, nurses, students, social workers and other allied health professionals. Articles include reports of original results of educational research and discussions of current problems and techniques in cancer education.
Related titles: Microform ed.: (from PQC); Online - full text ed.: ISSN 1543-0154.
Indexed: A20, A22, C06, C07, C08, CA, CINAHL, CPE, CurCont, E01, EMBASE, ExcerpMed, FamI, INI, IndMed, MEDLINE, NRN, P03, P10, P20, P22, P24, P30, P48, P53, P54, PQC, PsycInfo, PsycholAb, R10, Reac, SCI, SCOPUS, T02, THA, W07.
—BLDSC (4954.843000), GNLM, IE, Infotrieve, Ingenta, INIST. **CCC.**
Published by: (American Association for Cancer Education), Springer New York LLC (Subsidiary of: Springer Science+Business Media), 233 Spring St, New York, NY 10013. TEL 212-460-1500, FAX 212-460-1575, journals-ny@springer.com. Ed. Joseph F O'Donnell. Circ: 1,000. **Co-sponsor:** European Association for Cancer Education.

616.992 USA ISSN 1687-8558
➤ **JOURNAL OF CANCER EPIDEMIOLOGY.** Text in English. 2007. q. USD 195 (effective 2011). **Document type:** *Journal, Academic/Scholarly.*
Formerly (until 2008): Molecular and Translational Cancer Epidemiology (1687-6458)
Related titles: Online - full text ed.: ISSN 1687-8566. free (effective 2011).
Indexed: A01, A36, B21, CA, CABA, ESPM, GH, GenetAb, ImmunAb, P30, RiskAb, SCOPUS, T02, ToxAb.
Published by: Hindawi Publishing Corporation, 410 Park Ave, 15th Fl, PMB 287, New York, NY 10022. FAX 215-893-4392, 866-446-3294, info@hindawi.com.

616.992 TWN ISSN 1816-0735
RC261.A1 CODEN: JCMOCF
➤ **JOURNAL OF CANCER MOLECULES.** Text in English. 2005. bi-m. TWD 2,800 domestic to institutions; USD 120 in China to institutions; USD 135 in Asia & the Pacific to institutions; USD 150 elsewhere to institutions (effective 2008). **Document type:** *Journal, Academic/Scholarly.* **Description:** Covers basic research and clinical practice in the molecular aspects of cancer.
Related titles: Online - full text ed.: ISSN 1817-4256.
Indexed: A01, C33, EMBASE, ExcerpMed, SCOPUS, T02.
—BLDSC (4954.846700), IE.
Published by: MedUnion Press, 4F, No 185, Kui-Sui St, Taipei, 103, Taiwan. FAX 886-2-25506718. Ed. Tze-Sing Huang.

616.992 IND
➤ **JOURNAL OF CANCER RESEARCH.** Text in English. s-a. USD 425 (effective 2011). **Document type:** *Journal, Academic/Scholarly.* **Description:** Publishes all the latest research articles, reviews and letters in all areas of cancer research.
Related titles: Online - full text ed.: free (effective 2011).
Published by: Bioinfo Publications, 49/F-72, Vighnahar Complex, Front of Overseas Bank, Sector 12, Kharghar, Navi Mumbai, 410 210, India. TEL 91-22-27743967, FAX 91-22-66736413, editor@bioinfo.in, subscription@bioinfo.in. Ed. Dr. Virendra S Gomase.

616.994 DEU ISSN 0171-5216
RC267 CODEN: JCROD7
➤ **JOURNAL OF CANCER RESEARCH AND CLINICAL ONCOLOGY.** Text in English. 1903. m. EUR 4,184, USD 5,167 combined subscription to institutions (print & online eds.) (effective 2012). adv. back issues avail.; reprint service avail. from PSC. **Document type:** *Journal, Academic/Scholarly.* **Description:** Contains up-to-date articles within the fields of experimental and clinical oncology.
Former titles (until 1979): Zeitschrift fuer Krebsforschung und Klinische Onkologie (0084-5353); (until 1971): Zeitschrift fuer Krebsforschung (0301-1585)
Related titles: Microform ed.: (from PQC); Online - full text ed.: ISSN 1432-1335 (from IngentaConnect); ◆ Supplement(s): Journal of Cancer Research and Clinical Oncology. Supplement. ISSN 0943-9382.
Indexed: A01, A03, A08, A22, A26, A35, A36, ASCA, AgBio, Agr, B21, B25, BIOBASE, BIOSIS Prev, BP, C30, CA, CABA, CIN, CISA, ChemAb, ChemTitl, CurCont, D01, DBA, E01, EMBASE, ExcerpMed, GH, H12, H13, I05, IABS, ISR, IndMed, Inpharma, MEDLINE, MS&D, MycolAb, N02, N03, NRN, OGFA, P02, P10, P20, P22, P30, P32, P35, P40, P48, P50, P53, P54, PQC, R10, RA&MP, Reac, SCI, SCOPUS, T02, T05, VS, W07.
—BLDSC (4954.851000), CASDDS, GNLM, IE, Infotrieve, Ingenta, INIST. **CCC.**
Published by: (Deutsche Krebsgesellschaft e.V.), Springer (Subsidiary of: Springer Science+Business Media), Tiergartenstr 17, Heidelberg, 69121, Germany. TEL 49-6221-4870, FAX 49-6221-345229. Ed. Dr. Klaus Hoeffken. adv.: B&W page EUR 790, color page EUR 1,830. Circ: 500 (paid and controlled). **Subscr. in the Americas to:** Springer New York LLC, Journal Fulfillment, PO Box 2485, Secaucus, NJ 07096. TEL 800-777-4643, 201-348-4033, FAX 201-348-4505, journals-ny@springer.com, http://www.springer.com; **Subscr. to:** Springer Distribution Center, Kundenservice Zeitschriften, Haberstr 7, Heidelberg 69126, Germany. TEL 49-6221-3454303, FAX 49-6221-3454229, subscriptions@springer.com.

616.994 DEU ISSN 0943-9382
CODEN: JCCSE
JOURNAL OF CANCER RESEARCH AND CLINICAL ONCOLOGY. SUPPLEMENT. Text in English. 1982. irreg., latest 2006. price varies. **Document type:** *Monographic series, Academic/Scholarly.*
Related titles: ◆ Supplement to: Journal of Cancer Research and Clinical Oncology. ISSN 0171-5216.
Indexed: SCOPUS.
—CCC.
Published by: (Deutsche Krebsgesellschaft e.V.), Springer (Subsidiary of: Springer Science+Business Media), Tiergartenstr 17, Heidelberg, 69121, Germany. TEL 49-6221-4870, FAX 49-6221-345229, subscriptions@springer.com, http://www.springer.com. **Subscr. in N. America to:** Springer New York LLC, Journal Fulfillment, PO Box 2485, Secaucus, NJ 07096. TEL 201-348-4033, FAX 201-348-4505.

616.992 NGA
➤ **JOURNAL OF CANCER RESEARCH AND EXPERIMENTAL ONCOLOGY.** Text in English. m. free (effective 2010). adv. **Document type:** *Journal, Academic/Scholarly.*
Media: Online - full text.
Published by: Academic Journals, PO Box 73023, Victoria Island, Lagos, Nigeria. service@academicjournals.org. Eds. Lalit Kumar, Mohamed Mabruk.

616.994 IND ISSN 0973-1482
RC261.A1
➤ **JOURNAL OF CANCER RESEARCH AND THERAPEUTICS.** Abbreviated title: J C R T. Text in English. 2005. q. INR 2,000 domestic to individuals; USD 250 foreign to individuals; INR 1,600 combined subscription domestic to institutions (print & online eds.); USD 200 combined subscription foreign to institutions (print & online eds.) (effective 2011). adv. **Document type:** *Journal, Academic/Scholarly.* **Description:** Dedicated to basic and clinical sciences in oncology including radiation oncology.
Related titles: Online - full text ed.: ISSN 1998-4138. free (effective 2011).
Indexed: A01, A26, A36, C06, C07, CA, CABA, E08, E12, EMBASE, ExcerpMed, F08, G08, GH, H11, H12, H16, I05, MEDLINE, N02, N03, P10, P20, P22, P30, P48, P53, P54, PQC, R10, R12, RA&MP, Reac, S09, SCI, SCOPUS, T02, T05, VS, W07.
—CCC.
Published by: (Association of Radiation Oncology of India), Medknow Publications and Media Pvt. Ltd., B-9, Kanara Business Ctr, Off Link Rd, Ghatkopar (E), Mumbai, Maharastra 400 075, India. TEL 91-22-66491818, 91-22-66491816, publishing@medknow.com, journals@medknow.com, http://www.medknow.com. Ed. Nagraj G Huilgol.

616.992 USA ISSN 1948-5956
RC261.A1
▼ ➤ **JOURNAL OF CANCER SCIENCE & THERAPY.** Text in English. 2009. bi-m. free (effective 2011). **Document type:** *Journal, Academic/Scholarly.* **Description:** Features new research and reviews on oncology, cancer research, and experimental therapies for cancer patients.
Media: Online - full text.
Indexed: A01, P30, SCOPUS, T02.
Published by: Omics Publishing Group, 5716 Corse Ave, Ste 110, Westlake, Los Angeles, CA 91362. TEL 650-268-9744, info@omicsonline.com, http://www.omicsonline.com.

616.994 USA ISSN 1932-2259
RC261.A1
➤ **JOURNAL OF CANCER SURVIVORSHIP.** Text in English. 2007 (Mar.). q. EUR 504, USD 614 combined subscription to institutions (print & online eds.) (effective 2012). back issues avail.; reprint service avail. from PSC. **Document type:** *Journal, Academic/Scholarly.* **Description:** Aims to advance knowledge and practice in areas related to improving the quality of care and quality of life of cancer survivors.
Related titles: Online - full text ed.: ISSN 1932-2267. 2007 (Mar.) (from IngentaConnect).
Indexed: A22, A26, C06, C07, E01, E08, EMBASE, ExcerpMed, H12, H13, MEDLINE, P02, P03, P10, P20, P22, P24, P30, P48, P53, P54, PQC, PsycInfo, R10, Reac, S09, SCOPUS.
—IE. **CCC.**
Published by: Springer New York LLC (Subsidiary of: Springer Science+Business Media), 233 Spring St, New York, NY 10013. TEL 212-460-1500, FAX 212-460-1575, service-ny@springer.com. Ed. Michael Feuerstein.

616.994 USA ISSN 2151-1934
▼ ➤ **JOURNAL OF CANCER THERAPY.** Abbreviated title: J C T. Text in English. 2009. q. adv. back issues avail.; reprints avail. **Document type:** *Journal, Academic/Scholarly.* **Description:** Provides a platform for doctors and academicians all over the world to promote, share, and discuss various new issues and developments in cancer related problems.
Related titles: Online - full text ed.: ISSN 2151-1942. free (effective 2011).
Indexed: A26, H11, H12, I05, P20, P48, P52, P54, PQC, SCOPUS.
Published by: Scientific Research Publishing, Inc., 5005 Paseo Segovia, Irvine, CA 92603. service@scirp.org. Ed. Yongde Liao.

616.994071 IND ISSN 0974-6773
➤ **JOURNAL OF CARCINOGENESIS.** Abbreviated title: J C. Text in English. 2001. q. USD 300, GBP 150, EUR 120 (effective 2011). **Document type:** *Journal, Academic/Scholarly.* **Description:** Publishes multi-disciplinary papers on carcinogenesis that include physical and chemical carcinogens and mutagenesis; processes such as DNA repair that influence or modulate carcinogenesis, genetics and nutrition; metabolism of carcinogens; the mechanism of action of carcinogens and modulating agents; epidemiological studies; and the formation, detection, identification and quantification of environmental carcinogens.
Related titles: Online - full text ed.: ISSN 1477-3163. free (effective 2009).
Indexed: A01, A26, B21, CA, E08, EMBASE, H12, I05, NucAcAb, OGFA, S09, SCOPUS, T02.
—CCC.
Published by: (Carcinogenesis Press), Medknow Publications and Media Pvt. Ltd., B-9, Kanara Business Ctr, Off Link Rd, Ghatkopar (E), Mumbai, Maharastra 400 075, India. TEL 91-22-66491816, FAX 91-22-66491817, http://www.medknow.com.

616.992 USA ISSN 2157-2518
▼ ➤ **JOURNAL OF CARCINOGENESIS & MUTAGENESIS.** Text in English. 2010. bi-m. free (effective 2011). **Document type:** *Journal, Academic/Scholarly.*
Media: Online - full text.
Published by: Omics Publishing Group, 5716 Corse Ave, Ste 110, Westlake, Los Angeles, CA 91362. TEL 650-268-9744, 800-216-6499, info@omicsonline.com.

616.99 615.8 616.2 ITA ISSN 1120-009X
CODEN: JCHEEU
➤ **JOURNAL OF CHEMOTHERAPY.** Text in English. 1982. bi-m. EUR 480 combined subscription domestic to institutions print & online eds.; EUR 520 combined subscription foreign to institutions print & online eds. (effective 2009). adv. abstr. index. back issues avail. **Document type:** *Journal, Academic/Scholarly.* **Description:** Publishes original articles on experimental and clinical studies in antimicrobial and oncologic chemotherapy.
Formerly (until 1989): Chemioterapia (0392-906X); Which was formed by the merger of (1978-1982): Chemoterapia Antimicrobica (0391-9862); (1977-1982): Chemoterapia Oncologica (0392-0968)
Related titles: CD-ROM ed.; Online - full text ed.: ISSN 1973-9478.
Indexed: A22, A34, A36, ASCA, B25, BIOSIS Prev, BP, CABA, CIN, ChemAb, ChemTitl, CurCont, D01, E12, EMBASE, ExcerpMed, FR, GH, H16, H17, IBR, IBZ, IndMed, IndVet, Inpharma, MEDLINE, MycolAb, N02, N03, P30, P33, P35, P39, PN&I, R08, R10, R12, R13, RA&MP, RM&VM, Reac, RefZh, S13, S16, SCI, SCOPUS, T05, VS, W07, W11.
—BLDSC (4957.390000), CASDDS, GNLM, IE, Infotrieve, Ingenta, INIST. **CCC.**
Published by: (Societa Italiana di Chemioterapia/Italian Society of Chemotherapy), E S I F T srl, Via Carlo del Greco 36, Florence, FI 50141, Italy. TEL 39-055-4271516, FAX 39-055-4271280. Eds. Andrea Novelli, Enrico Mini, Teresita Mazzei. R&P, Adv. contact Mary Forrest. Circ: 700.

616.992 USA ISSN 0732-183X
RC254.A1 CODEN: JCONDN
➤ **JOURNAL OF CLINICAL ONCOLOGY.** Abbreviated title: J C O. Text in English. 1983. 3/m. USD 578 combined subscription domestic to individuals (print & online eds.); USD 802 combined subscription foreign to individuals (print & online eds.); USD 817 combined subscription domestic to institutions (print & online eds.); USD 1,129 combined subscription foreign to institutions (print & online eds.); free to members (effective 2010). adv. abstr.; bibl.; charts; illus. index. back issues avail. **Document type:** *Journal, Academic/Scholarly.* **Description:** Contains articles from around the world discussing the diagnosis, management, treatment, and prevention of cancer.
Related titles: Online - full text ed.: ISSN 1527-7755. 1983. USD 735 to institutions Tier 1 (effective 2010); Chinese Translation: ISSN 2074-1057; French Translation: ISSN 1969-2420; Polish Translation: ISSN 1730-8801; Hungarian Translation: ISSN 1786-8084.
Indexed: A20, A22, A34, A36, A37, A38, AHCMS, AIDS Ab, ASCA, B21, BIOBASE, C06, C07, C08, C13, CABA, CIN, CINAHL, ChPerI, ChemAb, ChemTitl, CurCont, D01, DBA, DentInd, E12, EMBASE, ExcerpMed, FR, G10, GH, I12, IABS, IBR, IBZ, IDIS, ISR, IndMed, Inpharma, JW, JW-D, Kidney, LT, MEDLINE, MS&D, N02, N03, N04, NRN, OGFA, P30, P33, P35, R10, R12, RA&MP, RM&VM, RRTA, Reac, SCI, SCOPUS, SoyAb, T05, THA, VS, W07.
—BLDSC (4958.615000), CASDDS, GNLM, IE, Infotrieve, Ingenta, INIST. **CCC.**
Published by: American Society of Clinical Oncology, 2318 Mill Rd, Ste 800, Alexandria, VA 22314. TEL 571-483-1300, 703-797-1900, 888-282-2552, FAX 571-366-9550, 703-684-8720, asco@asco.org, http://www.asco.org. Ed. Daniel G. Haller. Pub. Theresa Van-Schaik. adv.: page USD 3,145; 6.8 x 9.175. Circ: 26,000.

➤ **JOURNAL OF ENVIRONMENTAL SCIENCE AND HEALTH. PART C: ENVIRONMENTAL CARCINOGENESIS & ECOTOXICOLOGY REVIEWS.** *see* ENVIRONMENTAL STUDIES—Toxicology And Environmental Safety

M

616.99 GBR ISSN 1756-9966
RC267 CODEN: JECRDN
➤ **JOURNAL OF EXPERIMENTAL AND CLINICAL CANCER RESEARCH (ONLINE).** Abbreviated title: J E C C R. Text in English. 1982. irreg. free (effective 2011). adv. back issues avail. **Document type:** *Journal, Academic/Scholarly.* **Description:** Features contributions dealing with basic and applied research in the field of experimental and clinical oncology.
Formerly (until 2008): Journal of Experimental and Clinical Cancer Research (Print) (0392-9078)
Media: Online - full text.
Indexed: A01, A22, A26, ASCA, CA, CIN, ChemAb, ChemTitl, CurCont, E08, EMBASE, ExcerpMed, H12, I05, IndMed, Inpharma, MEDLINE, NRN, P30, P35, R10, Reac, S09, SCI, SCOPUS, T02, W07.
—BLDSC (4979.740000), CASDDS, GNLM, IE, Infotrieve, Ingenta, INIST. **CCC.**
Published by: (Regina Elena Institute for Cancer Research ITA), BioMed Central Ltd. (Subsidiary of: Springer Science+Business Media), 236 Gray's Inn Rd, London, WC1X 8HB, United Kingdom. TEL 44-20-31922000, FAX 44-20-31922010, info@biomedcentral.com, http://www.biomedcentral.com. Ed. Mauro Castelli. Adv. contact Natasha Bailey TEL 44-20-31922231.

616.99 USA ISSN 1533-869X
➤ **JOURNAL OF EXPERIMENTAL THERAPEUTICS AND ONCOLOGY (ONLINE).** Text in English. 1996. q. adv. back issues avail. **Document type:** *Journal, Academic/Scholarly.* **Description:** Provides review articles, communications on all areas of cancer research, clinical experimental therapeutics, anticancer drug development etc.
Media: Online - full text. **Related titles:** ◆ Print ed.: Journal of Experimental Therapeutics and Oncology (Print). ISSN 1359-4117.
—CCC.
Published by: Old City Publishing, Inc., 628 N 2nd St, Philadelphia, PA 19123. TEL 215-925-4390, FAX 215-925-4371, info@oldcitypublishing.com. Ed. Dominic Fan.

616.99 USA ISSN 1359-4117
RC270.8 CODEN: JETOFX
➤ **JOURNAL OF EXPERIMENTAL THERAPEUTICS AND ONCOLOGY (PRINT).** Text in English. 1996. q. USD 108 in North America to individuals; USD 156 elsewhere to individuals; USD 527 combined subscription in North America to institutions (print & online eds.); USD 577 combined subscription elsewhere to institutions (print & online eds.) (effective 2011). adv. 80 p./no.; back issues avail. **Document type:** *Journal, Academic/Scholarly.* **Description:** Provides review articles, communications on all areas of cancer research, clinical experimental therapeutics, anticancer drug development etc.
Related titles: ◆ Online - full text ed.: Journal of Experimental Therapeutics and Oncology (Online). ISSN 1533-869X.
Indexed: A01, A03, A08, A22, A26, CA, CIN, ChemAb, ChemTitl, E01, EMBASE, ExcerpMed, MEDLINE, P30, R10, Reac, SCOPUS, T02.
—BLDSC (4982.800000), CASDDS, GNLM, IE, Infotrieve, Ingenta. **CCC.**
Published by: (Anticancer Therapeutics and Oncology Society GBR), Old City Publishing, Inc., 628 N 2nd St, Philadelphia, PA 19123. TEL 215-925-4390, FAX 215-925-4371, info@oldcitypublishing.com. Ed. Dominic Fan.

➤ **JOURNAL OF GASTROINTESTINAL CANCER.** *see* MEDICAL SCIENCES—Endocrinology

▼ ➤ **JOURNAL OF GASTROINTESTINAL ONCOLOGY.** *see* MEDICAL SCIENCES—Gastroenterology

616.992 USA ISSN 1879-4068
RC281.A34
▼ ➤ **JOURNAL OF GERIATRIC ONCOLOGY.** Text in English. 2010. 2/yr. EUR 496 in Europe to institutions; JPY 68,000 in Japan to institutions; USD 764 elsewhere to institutions (effective 2012). **Document type:** *Journal, Academic/Scholarly.* **Description:** Focuses on advancing research in the pathogenesis, biology, treatment, and survivorship issues of older adults with cancer.
Related titles: Online - full text ed.: ISSN 1879-4076 (from ScienceDirect).
Indexed: CurCont, P30, SCI, SCOPUS, T02, W07.
—CCC.
Published by: Elsevier Inc. (Subsidiary of: Elsevier Science & Technology), 360 Park Ave S, New York, NY 10010. TEL 212-989-5800, 888-437-4636, FAX 212-633-3990, usinfo-f@elsevier.com, http://www.elsevier.com. Ed. Dr. Arti Hurria.

616.992 618.1 USA ISSN 1536-9935
JOURNAL OF GYNECOLOGIC ONCOLOGY NURSING. Abbreviated title: J O G O N. Text in English. 19??. 3/yr. free to members (effective 2010). **Document type:** *Journal, Academic/Scholarly.*
Formerly (until 1998): Gynecologic Oncology Nursing
Indexed: A26, C06, C07, C08, CINAHL, H12, I05, SCOPUS.
Published by: Society of Gynecologic Nurse Oncologists, 6024 Welch Ave, Forth Worth, TX 76133. cwinslow@sgno.org.

JOURNAL OF HEMATOLOGY & ONCOLOGY. *see* MEDICAL SCIENCES—Hematology

616.992 CAN ISSN 1916-0518
➤ **JOURNAL OF INTERVENTIONAL ONCOLOGY.** Text in English. 2008. q. CAD 424 domestic to institutions; USD 424 in United States to institutions; USD 477 elsewhere to institutions; CAD 508.80 combined subscription domestic to institutions (print & online eds.); USD 508.80 combined subscription in United States to institutions (print & online eds.); USD 572.40 combined subscription elsewhere to institutions (print & online eds.) (effective 2010). adv. back issues avail. **Document type:** *Journal, Academic/Scholarly.* **Description:** Publishes articles that address technical and research developments in interventional oncology, as well as related organizational, regulatory, and financial aspects.
Related titles: Online - full text ed.: ISSN 1916-0526. CAD 466.40 domestic to institutions; USD 466.40 foreign to institutions (effective 2010).
Indexed: A01, CA, EMBASE, SCOPUS, T02.
—IE.
Published by: B.C. Decker Inc., 50 King St E, 2nd Fl, Hamilton, ON L8N 2A1, Canada. TEL 905-522-7017, 800-568-7281, FAX 905-522-7839, info@bcdecker.com. Eds. Peter Mueller, Yuman Fong. Adv. contact Jennifer Coates TEL 905-522-7017 ext 291. B&W page USD 920, color page USD 2,020; trim 8.125 x 10.875. Circ: 1,000 (paid).

616.99 USA ISSN 0167-594X
RC280.N43 CODEN: JNODD2
➤ **JOURNAL OF NEURO-ONCOLOGY.** Text in English. 1983. 15/yr. EUR 2,922, USD 2,998 combined subscription to institutions (print & online eds.) (effective 2012). adv. bk.rev. back issues avail.; reprint service avail. from PSC. **Document type:** *Journal, Academic/Scholarly.* **Description:** Contains clinical investigations in all research areas as they relate to cancer and the central nervous system.
Related titles: Microform ed.: (from PQC); Online - full text ed.: ISSN 1573-7373 (from IngentaConnect).
Indexed: A22, A26, ASCA, B21, BIOBASE, BibLing, CA, ChemAb, CurCont, E01, EMBASE, ExcerpMed, FR, I05, IABS, ISR, IndMed, Inpharma, MEDLINE, NSA, NSCI, P20, P22, P30, P35, P48, P50, P54, PQC, R10, Reac, SCI, SCOPUS, T02, W07.
—BLDSC (5021.650000), CASDDS, GNLM, IE, Infotrieve, Ingenta, INIST. **CCC.**
Published by: Springer New York LLC (Subsidiary of: Springer Science+Business Media), 233 Spring St, New York, NY 10013. TEL 212-460-1500, FAX 212-460-1575, service-ny@springer.com, http://www.springer.com/. Eds. Linda M Liau, Webster K Cavenee. **Subscr. to:** Journal Fulfillment, PO Box 2485, Secaucus, NJ 07096. TEL 201-348-4033, FAX 201-348-4505, journals-ny@springer.com.

616.992 USA ISSN 1687-8450
➤ **JOURNAL OF ONCOLOGY.** Text in English. 2008. irreg. USD 495 (effective 2011). **Document type:** *Journal, Academic/Scholarly.* **Description:** Publishes original research articles as well as review articles in all areas of oncology.
Related titles: Online - full text ed.: ISSN 1687-8469. 2008. free (effective 2011).
Indexed: A01, B21, C06, C07, CA, EMBASE, ExcerpMed, OGFA, P30, SCOPUS, T02.
Published by: Hindawi Publishing Corporation, 410 Park Ave, 15th Fl, PMB 287, New York, NY 10022. FAX 215-893-4392, 866-446-3294, orders@hindawi.com.

➤ **JOURNAL OF ONCOLOGY PHARMACY PRACTICE.** *see* PHARMACY AND PHARMACOLOGY

616.992 USA ISSN 1554-7477
JOURNAL OF ONCOLOGY PRACTICE. Abbreviated title: J O P. Text in English. 2005 (May). 6/yr. USD 200 domestic to institutions institutions; USD 250 foreign to institutions institutions; USD 30 per issue domestic institutions; USD 40 per issue foreign institutions (effective 2011). adv. back issues avail. **Document type:** *Journal, Academic/Scholarly.* **Description:** Provides information to oncology professionals about clinical and adminstrative issues in oncology health care.
Related titles: Online - full text ed.: ISSN 1935-469X.
Indexed: A01, C06, C07, EMBASE, ExcerpMed, Inpharma, P30, P35, R10, Reac, SCOPUS, T02.
—BLDSC (5026.314580), IE. **CCC.**
Published by: American Society of Clinical Oncology, 2318 Mill Rd, Ste 800, Alexandria, VA 22314. TEL 571-483-1300, 888-282-2552, asco@asco.org, http://www.asco.org. Ed. John V Cox. Pub. Theresa Van Schaik.

618.92 616.99 USA ISSN 1077-4114
RJ411 CODEN: JPHOFG
➤ **JOURNAL OF PEDIATRIC HEMATOLOGY / ONCOLOGY.** Abbreviated title: J P H O. Text in English. 1979. m. USD 1,198 domestic to institutions; USD 1,413 foreign to institutions (effective 2011). adv. bk.rev. abstr.; bibl.; charts; illus.; stat.; tr.lit. index. back issues avail.; reprints avail. **Document type:** *Journal, Academic/Scholarly.* **Description:** Brings out reports on advances in the diagnosis and treatment of cancer and blood diseases in children.
Formerly (until 1995): American Journal of Pediatric Hematology / Oncology (0192-8562)
Related titles: Microform ed.; Online - full text ed.: ISSN 1536-3678.
Indexed: A20, A22, A34, A36, ASCA, BIOBASE, CABA, CurCont, D01, DentInd, E12, EMBASE, ExcerpMed, F08, GH, IABS, INI, ISR, IndMed, IndVet, Inpharma, MEDLINE, N02, N03, P30, P33, P35, P39, R08, R10, R12, R13, RA&MP, RM&VM, Reac, SCI, SCOPUS, T05, VS, W07, W10.
—BLDSC (5030.183000), CASDDS, GNLM, IE, Infotrieve, Ingenta, INIST. **CCC.**
Published by: (American Society of Pediatric Hematology, Oncology), Lippincott Williams & Wilkins (Subsidiary of: Wolters Kluwer N.V.), Two Commerce Sq, 2001 Market St, Philadelphia, PA 19103. TEL 215-521-8300, FAX 215-521-8902, customerservice@lww.com, http://www.lww.com. Ed. Dr. Barton A Kamen. Pub. David Myers. Adv. contact Melissa Mooday. Circ: 343.

616.99 610.73 USA ISSN 1043-4542
CODEN: JONUEM
➤ **JOURNAL OF PEDIATRIC ONCOLOGY NURSING.** Text in English. 1984. bi-m. USD 376, GBP 222 combined subscription to institutions (print & online eds.); USD 368, GBP 218 to institutions (effective 2011). adv. bk.rev. bibl. reprint service avail. from PSC. **Document type:** *Journal, Academic/Scholarly.* **Description:** Stimulates and disseminates research in the treatment of young cancer patients with emphasis on holistic, family-centered care.
Formerly (until 1989): Association of Pediatric Oncology Nurses. Journal (0748-1802)
Related titles: Online - full text ed.: ISSN 1532-8457. USD 338, GBP 200 to institutions (effective 2011).
Indexed: A20, A22, A26, AMED, C06, C07, C08, CA, CINAHL, CurCont, E01, E08, EMBASE, ExcerpMed, F09, FamI, G08, H11, H12, I05, INI, IndMed, MEDLINE, P03, P30, PsycInfo, R10, Reac, S09, SCI, SCOPUS, SSCI, T02, W07.
—BLDSC (5030.195000), GNLM, IE, Infotrieve, Ingenta. **CCC.**
Published by: (Association of Pediatric Oncology Nurses), Sage Publications, Inc., 2455 Teller Rd, Thousand Oaks, CA 91320. TEL 805-499-9774, FAX 805-499-0871, info@sagepub.com. Ed. Dr. Nancy E Kline. adv.: color page USD 1,610, B&W page USD 1,070; trim 8.375 x 10.875. Circ: 2,550 (paid). **Subscr. overseas to:** Sage Publications Ltd., 1 Oliver's Yard, 55 City Rd, London EC1Y 1SP, United Kingdom. TEL 44-207-3248701, FAX 44-207-3248733, subscription@sagepub.co.uk.

616.9 USA ISSN 0734-7332
RC261.A1
➤ **JOURNAL OF PSYCHOSOCIAL ONCOLOGY.** Abbreviated title: J P O. Text in English. 1983. q. GBP 927 combined subscription in United Kingdom to institutions (print & online eds.); EUR 1,204, USD 1,213 combined subscription to institutions (print & online eds.) (effective 2012). adv. bk.rev. 120 p./no. 1 cols./p.; back issues avail.; reprint service avail. from PSC. **Document type:** *Journal, Academic/Scholarly.* **Description:** Publishes for health professionals responsible for psychosocial needs of cancer patients and their families.
Related titles: Microfiche ed.: (from PQC); Microform ed.; Online - full text ed.: ISSN 1540-7586. GBP 834 in United Kingdom to institutions; EUR 1,084, USD 1,091 to institutions (effective 2012).
Indexed: A01, A03, A20, A22, AMED, ASCA, AgeL, C06, C07, C08, CA, CINAHL, CurCont, E-psyche, E01, EMBASE, ExcerpMed, FR, FamI, H13, MEDLINE, P02, P03, P10, P20, P30, P48, P53, P54, PC&CA, PQC, PsycInfo, PsycholAb, RefZh, RehabLit, S02, S03, SCOPUS, SOPODA, SSA, SSCI, SWR&A, SociolAb, T02, W07.
—BLDSC (5043.476000), GNLM, IE, Infotrieve, Ingenta, INIST. **CCC.**
Published by: (Association of Oncology Social Work), Routledge (Subsidiary of: Taylor & Francis Group), 325 Chestnut St, Ste 800, Philadelphia, PA 19106. TEL 215-625-8900, 800-354-1420, FAX 215-625-8914, journals@routledge.com, http://www.routledge.com. Ed. James Zabora. adv.: B&W page USD 315, color page USD 550; trim 4.375 x 7.125. Circ: 1,295 (paid).

616.992 DEU ISSN 1948-7894
▼ **JOURNAL OF RADIATION ONCOLOGY.** Text in English. forthcoming 2010 (June). q. USD 200 (effective 2010). **Document type:** *Journal, Academic/Scholarly.*
Related titles: Online - full text ed.: ISSN 1948-7908. forthcoming 2010 (June).
Published by: Springer (Subsidiary of: Springer Science+Business Media), Tiergartenstr 17, Heidelberg, 69121, Germany. TEL 49-6221-4870, FAX 49-6221-345229, subscriptions@springer.com, http://www.springer.com.

616.992 USA ISSN 2090-2905
▼ ➤ **JOURNAL OF SKIN CANCER.** Text in English. 2010. q. USD 195 (effective 2011). **Document type:** *Journal, Academic/Scholarly.* **Description:** Publishes original research articles, review articles, and clinical studies related to all aspects of skin cancer.
Related titles: Online - full text ed.: ISSN 2090-2913. free (effective 2011).
Indexed: A01, P30, T02.
Published by: Hindawi Publishing Corporation, 410 Park Ave, 15th Fl, PMB 287, New York, NY 10022. FAX 866-446-3294, hindawi@hindawi.com.

616.992 USA ISSN 1544-6794
CODEN: JSOOBY
➤ **THE JOURNAL OF SUPPORTIVE ONCOLOGY;** quality of life-symptoms/side effects-palliative care. Abbreviated title: J S O. Text in English. 2003 (May/Jun.). bi-m. USD 334 in United States to institutions; USD 371 elsewhere to institutions (effective 2012). adv. back issues avail. **Document type:** *Journal, Academic/Scholarly.* **Description:** Brings out review articles and research relating to practical management issues in the supportive care of patients with neoplastic diseases.
Related titles: Online - full text ed.: ISSN 1879-596X. free (effective 2010) (from ScienceDirect).
Indexed: C06, C07, EMBASE, ExcerpMed, MEDLINE, P30, R10, Reac, SCOPUS.
—BLDSC (5067.270000), IE, Ingenta. **CCC.**
Published by: Elsevier Oncology (Subsidiary of: International Medical News Group), 60 Columbia Rd, Bldg B, Morristown, NJ 07960. TEL 973-290-8200, FAX 631-424-8905, L.Kalish@Elsevier.com, http://www.elsevieroncology.com/. Ed. Jamie H Von Roenn. Pub. Dan H Kim TEL 973-630-2039. Circ: 24,000.

➤ **JOURNAL OF SURGICAL ONCOLOGY.** *see* MEDICAL SCIENCES—Surgery

▼ ➤ **THE JOURNAL OF THE ADVANCED PRACTITIONER IN ONCOLOGY.** *see* MEDICAL SCIENCES—Nurses And Nursing

616.992 USA ISSN 1556-0864
JOURNAL OF THORACIC ONCOLOGY. Abbreviated title: J T O. Text in English. 2006 (Jan.). m. USD 1,456 domestic to institutions; USD 1,600 foreign to institutions (effective 2011). adv. back issues avail.; reprints avail. **Document type:** *Journal, Academic/Scholarly.* **Description:** Covers topics relevant to detection, prevention, diagnosis, and treatment of thoracic malignancies.
Related titles: Online - full text ed.: ISSN 1556-1380. 2006 (Jan.).
Indexed: C06, CurCont, EMBASE, ExcerpMed, Inpharma, MEDLINE, P30, P35, R10, Reac, SCI, SCOPUS, W07.
—BLDSC (5069.124000), IE. **CCC.**
Published by: (International Association for the Study of Lung Cancer), Lippincott Williams & Wilkins (Subsidiary of: Wolters Kluwer N.V.), Two Commerce Sq, 2001 Market St, Philadelphia, PA 19103. TEL 215-521-8300, FAX 215-521-8902, customerservice@lww.com, http://www.lww.com. Ed. James R Jett. Pub. David Myers. Adv. contact Joe Schuldner TEL 212-904-0377. Circ: 2,494.

JOURNAL OF TOXICOLOGY AND ENVIRONMENTAL HEALTH. PART A: CURRENT ISSUES. *see* ENVIRONMENTAL STUDIES—Toxicology And Environmental Safety

JOURNAL OF TOXICOLOGY AND ENVIRONMENTAL HEALTH. PART B: CRITICAL REVIEWS. *see* ENVIRONMENTAL STUDIES—Toxicology And Environmental Safety

616.99 AUT ISSN 0886-3849
CODEN: JTMOEY
➤ **JOURNAL OF TUMOR MARKER ONCOLOGY.** Text in English. 1986. bi-m. back issues avail.; reprints avail. **Document type:** *Journal, Academic/Scholarly.* **Description:** Covers tumor markers and their applications in the diagnosis and treatment of malignant neoplasms. Includes new markers for clinical application, and basic research on their physiological behavior and role in malignant neoplasms.
Indexed: A22, ASCA, Inpharma, SCOPUS.
—BLDSC (5071.250000), CASDDS, GNLM, IE, Infotrieve, Ingenta, INIST. **CCC.**
Published by: International Academy of Tumor Marker Oncology, Schwarzspanierstr. 15, Vienna, 1090, Austria.

616.992 DEU ISSN 1618-7687
JOURNAL ONKOLOGIE. Text in German. 2001. 8/yr. EUR 28 (effective 2007). adv. **Document type:** *Magazine, Trade.*
Published by: R S Media GmbH, Watmarkt 1, Regensburg, 93047, Germany. TEL 49-941-584030, FAX 49-941-5840379, adi.rixner@journalmed.de. adv.: B&W page EUR 2,510, color page EUR 3,840. Circ: 11,983 (paid).

616.99 616.15 USA ISSN 1527-1560
JOURNAL WATCH ONCOLOGY AND HEMATOLOGY. Text in English. 200?. m. USD 109 combined subscription domestic to individuals (print & online eds.); CAD 163.81 combined subscription in Canada to individuals (print & online eds.); USD 156 combined subscription elsewhere to individuals (print & online eds.); USD 179 combined subscription domestic to institutions (print & online eds.); CAD 252.38 combined subscription in Canada to institutions (print & online eds.); USD 216 combined subscription elsewhere to institutions (print & online eds.); USD 69 combined subscription domestic to students (print & online eds.); CAD 96.19 combined subscription in Canada to students (print & online eds.); USD 78 combined subscription elsewhere to students (print & online eds.) (effective 2009). **Document type:** *Newsletter, Academic/Scholarly.* **Description:** Explains wide variety of oncology and hematology topics, including leukemia. anemia, lymphoma, thrombosis, and hemochromatosis.
Related titles: Online - full text ed.: ISSN 1938-7768.
—CCC.
Published by: Massachusetts Medical Society, 860 Winter St, Waltham, MA 02451. TEL 781-893-4610, FAX 781-893-8009, info@massmed.org, http://www.massmed.org. Eds. Lowell A Goldsmith, Dr. William John Gradishar.

616.992 DEU ISSN 1610-2657
K. KREBS-JOURNAL. Variant title: Krebs-Journal. Text in German. 2001. q. adv. **Document type:** *Journal, Academic/Scholarly.*
Published by: Humanis Verlag fuer Gesundheit GmbH, Silcherstr 15, Moelsheim, 67591, Germany. TEL 49-6243-900704, FAX 49-6327-974332, info@humanis-verlag.de, http://www.humanis-verlag.de. adv.: B&W page EUR 1,300, color page EUR 2,550. Circ: 14,000 (controlled).

616.992 CHN ISSN 1008-3065
KANG'AI/ANTICANCER. Text in Chinese. 1988. q. USD 12 (effective 2009). **Document type:** *Journal, Academic/Scholarly.*
Related titles: Online - full text ed.
—East View.
Published by: Shanghai Shi Kang'ai Xiehui, 270, Dongan Lu, Shanghai, 200032, China. TEL 86-21-64175590 ext 3235. **Dist. by:** China International Book Trading Corp, 35 Chegongzhuang Xilu, Haidian District, PO Box 399, Beijing 100044, China. TEL 86-10-68412045, FAX 86-10-68412023, cibtc@mail.cibtc.com.cn, http://www.cibtc.com.cn.

616.994 NLD ISSN 1879-5617
▼ **KANKER BREED.** Text in Dutch. 2009. 6/yr. EUR 35 membership (effective 2010).
Published by: (Nederlandse Vereniging voor Oncologie), DCHG Medische Communicatie, Hendrik Figeeweg 3G-20, Haarlem, 2031 BJ, Netherlands. TEL 31-23-5514888, FAX 31-23-5515522, info@dchg.nl, http://www.dchg.nl.

KAREI IGAKU KENKYUSHO ZASSHI. *see* MEDICAL SCIENCES—Communicable Diseases

616.992 JPN ISSN 1346-1052
KAZOKUSEI SHUYO. Text in Japanese. 2001. s-a. **Document type:** *Journal, Academic/Scholarly.*
Related titles: Online - full content ed.
Published by: Kazokusei Shuyo Kenkyukai/Japanese Society for Familial Tumor, c/o Center for Academic Societies Japan, 14th Fl, Senri LC Bldg, 1-4-2 Shinsenrihigashi-machi, Toyonaka, Osaka 560-0082, Japan. TEL 81-6-68732301, FAX 81-6-68732300, http://jsft.bcasj.or.jp/.

KETSUEKI SHUYOKA/HEMATOLOGY & ONCOLOGY. *see* MEDICAL SCIENCES—Hematology

616.994 USA ISSN 1933-0863
KIDNEY CANCER JOURNAL. Text in English. 2003. q. free to qualified personnel (effective 2010). adv. back issues avail.; reprints avail. **Document type:** *Journal, Academic/Scholarly.* **Description:** Provides information on latest developments and research in kidney cancer treatment for oncologists, urologists and hematologists.
Related titles: Online - full text ed.: ISSN 1933-0871.
Published by: (Kidney Cancer Association), Genitourinary Publishing, 332 E 93rd St, Ste 1D, New York, NY 10128. TEL 516-356-5006, FAX 347-726-7813. Ed. Robert A Figlin.

616.99 CZE ISSN 0862-495X
CODEN: KLONEU
➤ **KLINICKA ONKOLOGIE.** Text in Czech. 1988. bi-m. CZK 540 domestic; EUR 22 foreign (effective 2010). **Document type:** *Journal, Academic/Scholarly.* **Description:** Publishes original works and reviews of the basic results of clinical research. Aims to contribute to increasing the effectiveness of prevention, diagnosis and treatment of cancer.
Related titles: Online - full content ed.: ISSN 1802-5307.
Indexed: A22, EMBASE, ExcerpMed, MEDLINE, P30, R10, Reac, SCOPUS.
—BLDSC (5099.284797), IE, Ingenta.
Published by: (Ceska Lekarska Spolecnost J.E. Purkyne, Ceska Onkologicka Spolecnost/Czech Medical Association of J.E. Purkyne, Czech Oncological Society, Slovenska Onkologicka Spolecnost SVN), Medica Healthworld a.s., Bidlaky 20, Brno, 63900, Czech Republic. TEL 420-533-337311, FAX 420-533-337312, info@mhw.cz, http://www.mhw.cz.

616.994 NLD ISSN 1876-0686
KRACHT. Text in Dutch. 2008. q. free (effective 2011). **Document type:** *Magazine, Consumer.*
Formed by the merger of (1992-2008): OverLeven (1380-0825); (1997-2008): K W F Journaal (1387-4454); (1978-2008): K W F Nieuws (1574-9878); Which was formerly (until 2003): Nederlandse Kankerbestrijding. Nieuws Brief (1382-2144); (1978-1989): K W F Nieuws Brief (1382-2136)
Related titles: Online - full text ed.: ISSN 1876-0694.
Published by: KWF Kankerbestrijding, Postbus 75508, Amsterdam, 1070 AM, Netherlands. TEL 31-20-5700500, FAX 31-20-6750302, info@kwfkanderbestrijding.nl, http://www.kwfkanderbestrijding.nl. Ed. Stan Termeer.

616.992 DEU ISSN 2190-2356
KREBS IN SCHLESWIG-HOLSTEIN. Text in German. 2001. a. EUR 10 (effective 2011). **Document type:** *Journal, Academic/Scholarly.*
Published by: (Institut fuer Krebsepidemiologie e.V.), Max Schmidt-Roemhild KG, Mengstr 16, Luebeck, 23552, Germany. TEL 49-451-703101, FAX 49-451-7031253, info@schmidt-roemhild.de, http://www.beleke.de/unternehmen/verlage/schmidtroemhild/index.html.

616.99 DEU ISSN 0177-0853
RC267
KREBSFORSCHUNG HEUTE. Text in German. 1978. irreg. **Document type:** *Monographic series, Academic/Scholarly.*
Formerly (until 1981): Deutsches Krebsforschungszentrum. Jahresbericht (0170-9356)
—GNLM. **CCC.**
Published by: Deutsches Krebsforschungszentrum, Im Neuenheimer Feld 280, Heidelberg, 69120, Germany. TEL 49-6221-424800, FAX 49-6221-424809, webmaster@dkfz.de, http://www.dkfz.de.

616.992 AUT
KREBS:HILFE!. Text in German. 6/yr. adv. **Document type:** *Magazine, Trade.*
Published by: Medizin Medien Austria GmbH, Wiedner Hauptstr 120-124, Vienna, 1050, Austria. TEL 43-1-54600, FAX 43-1-54600710, office@medizin-medien.at, http://www.medical-tribune.at. Adv. contact Martina Osterbauer. color page EUR 2,900; trim 210 x 297. Circ: 14,000 (controlled).

616.992 DEU ISSN 0173-9395
KREBSMEDIZIN. Text in German. 1980. q. EUR 40; EUR 34 to students; EUR 10 newsstand/cover (effective 2007). adv. **Document type:** *Journal, Trade.*
Published by: Juergen Hartmann Verlag GmbH, Seefeld 18, Hessdorf-Klebheim, 91093, Germany. TEL 49-9135-71230, FAX 49-9135-712340, kontakt@hartmann-medverlag.de, http://www.hartmann-medverlag.de. Adv. contact Markus Hartmann. B&W page EUR 1,675, color page EUR 2,442. Circ: 4,900 (paid).

616.994 NOR ISSN 1504-2553
KREFTFORENINGEN. RAPPORT. Text in Norwegian. 2001. a. back issues avail. **Document type:** *Monographic series.*
Formerly (until 2004): Den Norske Kreftforening. D N K-Rapport (1502-5527)
Related titles: Online - full text ed.
Published by: Kreftforeningen/The Norwegian Cancer Society, PO Box 4, Sentrum, Oslo, 0101, Norway. TEL 47-22-866600, FAX 47-22-866610, ervicetorget@kreftforeningen.no.

616.992 ITA ISSN 1722-7917
L I L T. (Lega Italiana per la Lotta Contro i Tumori) Text in Italian. 2003. q. free to qualified personnel. **Document type:** *Journal, Trade.*
Published by: (Lega Italiana per la Lotta contro i Tumori), C I C Edizioni Internazionali, Corso Trieste 42, Rome, 00198, Italy. TEL 39-06-8412673, FAX 39-06-8412688, info@gruppocic.it, http://www.gruppocic.it.

616.992 GBR ISSN 1470-2045
RC254.A1 CODEN: LOANBN
➤ **THE LANCET ONCOLOGY.** Text in English. 2000. m. EUR 1,497 in Europe to institutions; JPY 191,700 in Japan to institutions; USD 1,608 elsewhere to institutions (effective 2012). back issues avail. **Document type:** *Journal, Academic/Scholarly.* **Description:** Publishes interesting and informative reviews on any topic connected with oncology.
Related titles: Online - full text ed.: ISSN 1474-5488. 2000. EUR 874 in Europe to institutions; JPY 111,900 in Japan to institutions; USD 934 elsewhere to institutions (effective 2006) (from IngentaConnect, ScienceDirect); ◆ Supplement(s): The Lancet. ISSN 0140-6736.
Indexed: A01, A03, A08, A20, A22, A26, A36, B21, BIOBASE, C06, C07, C08, CA, CABA, CINAHL, CurCont, D01, E12, EMBASE, ExcerpMed, GH, H12, H17, I05, IABS, Inpharma, MEDLINE, N02, N03, OGFA, P20, P22, P24, P30, P33, P35, P48, P50, P54, PQC, R10, R12, RM&VM, Reac, SCI, SCOPUS, T02, T05, W07.
—BLDSC (5146.090000), IE, Infotrieve, Ingenta. **CCC.**
Published by: The Lancet Publishing Group (Subsidiary of: Elsevier Health Sciences), 32 Jamestown Rd, London, NW1 7BY, United Kingdom. TEL 44-1865-843077, FAX 44-1865-843970, custserv@lancet.com, http://www.thelancet.com. Ed. David Collingridge.

616.92 CZE ISSN 1213-9432
THE LANCET ONCOLOGY (CZECH EDITION). Text in Czech. 2002. q. **Document type:** *Journal, Academic/Scholarly.*
Published by: MedProGO, s.r.o., Anglicka 17, Prague 2, 12000, Czech Republic. TEL 420-2-22512649, FAX 420-2-24247568, contact@medprogo.cz. Ed. Vladimir Kocandrle.

616.992 PRT ISSN 1646-8910
THE LANCET ONCOLOGY (PORTUGUESE EDITION). Text in Portuguese. 2008. bi-m. **Document type:** *Journal, Academic/Scholarly.*
Published by: Publisaude Edicoes Medicas, Alameda Antonio Sergio, Edificio Amadeu S Cardoso, Miraflores, Alges, 1495-132, Portugal. TEL 351-214-135032, FAX 351-214-135007, http://publisaude.pai.pt.

LEADING OPINIONS. HAEMATOLOGIE UND ONKOLOGIE. *see* MEDICAL SCIENCES—Hematology

616.992 DEU
LEBEN? LEBEN!; Das Magazin fuer Frauen nach der Diagnose Krebs. Text in German. 2002. 4/yr. adv. **Document type:** *Magazine, Consumer.*
Published by: G F M K GmbH & Co. KG Verlagsgesellschaft, Gezelinallee 37-39, Leverkusen, 51375, Germany. TEL 49-214-310570, FAX 49-214-3105719, info@gfmk.de, http://www.gfmk.de. Ed. Holger Caspari. Adv. contact Kirsten Caspari TEL 49-214-3105714. Circ: 30,000 (controlled).

616.99 FRA ISSN 1165-113X
➤ **LA LETTRE DU CANCEROLOGUE.** Text in French. 1992. bi-m. EUR 114 in Europe; EUR 114 DOM-TOM; EUR 114 in Africa; EUR 126 elsewhere (effective 2009). Supplement avail. **Document type:** *Newsletter, Academic/Scholarly.*
—INIST.
Published by: Edimark S.A.S., 2 Rue Sainte-Marie, Courbevoie, Cedex 92418, France. TEL 33-1-41458000, FAX 33-1-41458025, contact@edimark.fr. Ed. J F Morere. Pub. Claudie Damour-Terrasson.

➤ **LEUKEMIA.** *see* MEDICAL SCIENCES—Hematology

➤ **LEUKEMIA AND LYMPHOMA.** *see* MEDICAL SCIENCES—Hematology

616.15 USA
LEUKEMIA INSIGHTS. Text in English. 1996. q. back issues avail. **Document type:** *Newsletter, Trade.* **Description:** Provides latest leukemia news, research and results from ongoing clinical trials, as well as available leukemia programs at MD Anderson.
Related titles: Online - full text ed.: free (effective 2010).
Published by: University of Texas, MD Anderson Cancer Center, 1515 Holcombe Blvd, Houston, TX 77030. TEL 713-792-2121, ckoller@mdanderson.org. Ed. Hagop Kantarjian.

LEUKEMIA RESEARCH; clinical and laboratory studies. *see* MEDICAL SCIENCES—Hematology

616.99 USA
LEUKEMIA SOCIETY OF AMERICA. NEWSLINE. Text in English. 1983. q. free. bk.rev. illus. back issues avail.; reprints avail. **Document type:** *Newsletter.* **Description:** Informs patients, volunteers, grantees, and the public about the society's programs and advances in research.
Formerly: Leukemia Society of America. Society News
Published by: Leukemia Society of America, Inc., 1311 Mamaroneck Ave, White Plains, NY 10605. TEL 914-949-5213, 800-955-4572, FAX 914-949-6691. Ed., R&P Julie Farin TEL 212-450-8861. Circ: 86,000 (controlled).

616.99419 NLD ISSN 1572-7947
LEUKONIEUWS. Text in Dutch. 200?. q. EUR 15 (effective 2010).
Published by: Stichting Contactgroep Leukemie, Het Rijpaard 32, Dronten, 8252 EV, Netherlands. TEL 31-30-2916090, info@leukemie.nfkpv.nl.

616 HRV ISSN 0300-8142
CODEN: LBOCB3
➤ **LIBRI ONCOLOGICI/CROATIAN JOURNAL OF ONCOLOGY.** Text in English; Summaries in Croatian. 1972. 3/yr. adv. back issues avail. **Document type:** *Journal, Academic/Scholarly.* **Description:** Examines primary and secondary prevention of malignant diseases, early diagnosis, screening, advances in treatments, terminal care, and basic research work in Molecular Biology, Genetics, Biochemistry & Immunology.
Indexed: A22, ChemAb, EMBASE, ExcerpMed, R10, Reac, SCOPUS.
—BLDSC (5207.350000), CASDDS, GNLM, IE, Ingenta.
Published by: Klinika za Tumore - Zagreb/University Hospital for Tumors in Zagreb, Ilica 197, Zagreb, 10000, Croatia. TEL 385-1-3783555, FAX 385-1-3775536, kzt@kzt.hr, http://www.kzt.hr. Ed. Marco Turic. Adv. contact Morana Simat. Circ: 300.

616.992 CHN ISSN 1009-0460
LINCHUANG ZHONGLIUXUE ZAZHI/CHINESE CLINICAL ONCOLOGY. Text in Chinese. 1995. m. CNY 10 newsstand/cover (effective 2006). **Document type:** *Journal, Academic/Scholarly.*
Related titles: Online - full text ed.
Indexed: A34, A35, A36, A37, AgBio, CABA, D01, E12, F08, GH, H16, N02, N03, P32, P33, R12, RA&MP, RM&VM, SoyAb, T05, VS.
Published by: Jiefangjun Di-81 Yiyuan, Yanggongjing 34 Biao, no.34, Nanjing, 210002, China. TEL 86-25-84400143.

616.99 USA
LIVE WELL WITH CANCER. Text in English. 1982. s-a. **Document type:** *Newsletter.* **Description:** Covers current activities related to cancer in the Western Pennsylvania region.
Formerly (until 1988): Cancer Challenge
Published by: Cancer Caring Center, 4117 Liberty Ave, Pittsburgh, PA 15224-1424. TEL 412-622-1212, FAX 412-622-1216. Ed. Rebecca Whitlinger. Circ: 10,000.

616.992 USA
▼ **LIVESTRONG QUARTERLY**; unity is strength, knowledge is power, attitude is everything. Text in English. 2009. q. adv. illus. **Document type:** *Magazine, Consumer.* **Description:** Provides the following: compelling profiles of advocates, survivors, and supporters in the fight against cancer; articles about health, fitness, and wellness; resources and information about preventing, treating, and raising awareness about cancer; building an engaged community to take meaningful action on cancer issues worldwide.
Related titles: Online - full text ed.: free (effective 2010).
Published by: Livingstrong Quarterly, National Mail Processing Center, P O Box 6003, Albert Lea, MN 56007-6603. TEL 407-253-4770, 1-877-932-7935, media@livestrong.org. Ed. Curt Pesmen.

616.99 IRL ISSN 0169-5002
RC280.L8 CODEN: TRESEY
➤ **LUNG CANCER.** Text in English. 1986. 12/yr. EUR 2,740 in Europe to institutions; JPY 320,800 in Japan to institutions; USD 3,064 elsewhere to institutions (effective 2012). adv. back issues avail.; reprints avail. **Document type:** *Journal, Academic/Scholarly.* **Description:** Reports new findings and advances in therapy, etiology and related aspects.
Related titles: Online - full text ed.: ISSN 1872-8332 (from IngentaConnect, ScienceDirect).
Indexed: A01, A03, A08, A22, A26, ASCA, BIOBASE, CA, CurCont, EMBASE, ExcerpMed, I05, IABS, ISR, IndMed, Inpharma, MEDLINE, P30, P35, R10, Reac, SCI, SCOPUS, T02, W07.
—BLDSC (5307.245000), GNLM, IE, Infotrieve, Ingenta, INIST. **CCC.**
Published by: (International Association for the Study of Lung Cancer USA), Elsevier Ireland Ltd (Subsidiary of: Elsevier Science & Technology), Elsevier House, Brookvale Plaza, E. Park, Shannon, Co. Clare, Ireland. TEL 353-61-709600, FAX 353-61-709100. Ed. Rolf A Stahel. adv.: B&W page USD 1,060, color page USD 2,295; trim 8.25 x 11. Circ: 1,395 (paid); 64 (free). **Subscr. to:** Elsevier BV, Radarweg 29, PO Box 211, Amsterdam 1000 AE, Netherlands. TEL 31-20-4853757, FAX 31-20-4853432, JournalsCustomerServiceEMEA@elsevier.com, http://www.elsevier.nl.

616.992 GBR ISSN 1179-2728
▼ ➤ **LUNG CANCER**; target and therapy. Text in English. 2010. irreg. free (effective 2011). **Document type:** *Journal, Academic/Scholarly.*
Media: Online - full text.
Indexed: SCOPUS.
—CCC.
Published by: Dove Medical Press Ltd., Beechfield House, Winterton Way, Macclesfield, SK11 0JL, United Kingdom. TEL 44-1625-509130, FAX 44-1625-617933. Ed. Rajagopal Ramesh.

616.994 GBR ISSN 1743-8047
LUNG CANCER IN PRACTICE. Text in English. 2004. q. back issues avail. **Document type:** *Journal, Academic/Scholarly.* **Description:** Provides a broad range of articles of interest to all those working in the therapeutic area.
Related titles: Online - full text ed.: GBP 55 to individuals; GBP 225 to institutions (effective 2009).
—CCC.
Published by: Hayward Medical Communications Ltd. (Subsidiary of: Hayward Group plc), 8-10 Dryden St, Covent Garden, London, WC2E 9NA, United Kingdom. TEL 44-20-72404493, FAX 44-20-72404479, edit@hayward.co.uk, http://www.hayward.co.uk. Ed. Michael D Peake.

616.994 GBR ISSN 1758-1966
▼ ➤ **LUNG CANCER MANAGEMENT.** Text in English. forthcoming 2011. 3/yr. GBP 350 combined subscription domestic to institutions (print & online eds.); USD 610 combined subscription in North America to institutions (print & online eds.); JPY 64,500 combined subscription in Japan to institutions (print & online eds.); EUR 490 combined subscription elsewhere to institutions (print & online eds.) (effective 2011). adv. **Document type:** *Journal, Academic/Scholarly.*
Related titles: Online - full text ed.: ISSN 1758-1974. forthcoming. GBP 310 domestic to institutions; USD 540 in North America to institutions; JPY 58,000 in Japan to institutions; EUR 435 elsewhere to institutions (effective 2011).
Published by: Future Medicine Ltd. (Subsidiary of: Future Science Ltd.), Unitec House, 2 Albert Pl, London, N3 1QB, United Kingdom. TEL 44-20-83716080, FAX 44-20-83716099, info@futuremedicine.com, http://www.futuremedicine.com/. Ed. Elisa Manzotti TEL 44-20-83716090. Pub. David Hughes. Adv. contact Simon Boisseau TEL 44-208-3716083.

➤ **LYMFO.** *see* MEDICAL SCIENCES—Endocrinology

362.19642 USA ISSN 1539-6851
RC646 CODEN: LRBYAD
➤ **LYMPHATIC RESEARCH AND BIOLOGY.** Abbreviated title: L R B. Text in English. 2003. q. USD 596 domestic to institutions; USD 693 foreign to institutions; USD 717 combined subscription domestic to institutions (print & online eds.); USD 819 combined subscription foreign to institutions (print & online eds.) (effective 2012). adv. reprint service avail. from PSC. **Document type:** *Journal, Academic/Scholarly.* **Description:** Provides a forum for the biomedical investigators to discuss current and anticipated developments in lymphatic biology and pathology.
Related titles: Online - full text ed.: ISSN 1557-8585. USD 596 to institutions (effective 2012).
Indexed: A22, B21, B25, BIOSIS Prev, CA, E01, EMBASE, ExcerpMed, ImmunAb, MEDLINE, MycolAb, P30, R10, Reac, SCI, SCOPUS, T02, VirolAbstr, W07.
—BLDSC (5310.995000), IE, Ingenta. **CCC.**
Published by: (Lymphatic Research Foundation, Inc.), Mary Ann Liebert, Inc. Publishers, 140 Huguenot St, 3rd Fl, New Rochelle, NY 10801. TEL 914-740-2100, FAX 914-740-2101, 800-654-3237, info@liebertpub.com. Ed. Stanley G Rockson TEL 650-725-7571. Adv. contact Harriet I Matysko TEL 914-740-2182.

616.99419 NZL ISSN 1179-2361
▼ ➤ **LYMPHOMA AND CHRONIC LYMPHOCYTIC LEUKEMIAS.** Text in English. 2009. irreg. free (effective 2011). **Document type:** *Journal, Academic/Scholarly.* **Description:** Covers all aspects of basic and clinical research into lymphoma and chronic lymphoid leukemia.
Media: Online - full text.
—CCC.
Published by: Libertas Academica Ltd., PO Box 300-874, Mairangi Bay, Auckland, 0751, New Zealand. TEL 64-9-4763930, FAX 64-9-3531397, editorial@la-press.com. Ed. Dr. Mitchell Smith.

➤ **LYMPHOMA / LEUKAEMIA REVIEW.** *see* MEDICAL SCIENCES—Hematology

616.992 613.04244 USA ISSN 1940-1329
M D ANDERSON BREAST MEDICAL ONCOLOGY. Text in English. 2002. q. free (effective 2010). **Document type:** *Newsletter, Academic/Scholarly.* **Description:** Describes developments of new drugs and advances in studies of breast cancer research and treatment.
Published by: (University of Texas, MD Anderson Cancer Center), J W C Covenant, Inc, PO Box 132919, The Woodlands, TX 77393. TEL 281-364-7387, FAX 281-292-4378, info@jwccinc.com, http://www.jwccinc.com.

616.992 616.15 USA ISSN 1940-7319
M.D. ANDERSON CLINICAL PERSPECTIVES. LYMPHOMA & MYELOMA. Text in English. 2007. q. back issues avail. **Document type:** *Newsletter, Academic/Scholarly.* **Description:** Contains information on lymphoma and myeloma protocols.
Published by: (University of Texas, MD Anderson Cancer Center), J W C Covenant, Inc, 35 S Crossed Birch Pl, The Woodlands, TX 77381. info@jwccinc.com, http://www.jwccinc.com.

616.992 GBR ISSN 2045-7324
M I M S ONCOLOGY & PALLIATIVE CARE. (Monthly Index of Medical Specialties) Text in English. 2007. q. GBP 50 domestic; EUR 240 in Europe; USD 212 elsewhere (effective 2010). adv. **Document type:** *Journal, Academic/Scholarly.* **Description:** Designed for primary and secondary care practitioners with an interest in the treatment and care of cancer patients.
Published by: Haymarket Business Media (Subsidiary of: Haymarket Media Group), 174 Hammersmith Rd, London, W6 7JP, United Kingdom. TEL 44-20-82675000, info@haymarket.com. Ed. Paula Hensler TEL 44-20-82674848. Adv. contact Robert Nuzzaci TEL 44-20-82674884. Circ: 8,000.

MACMILLAN NURSE. *see* MEDICAL SCIENCES—Nurses And Nursing

616.992 AUT ISSN 1865-5041
➤ **MAGAZINE OF EUROPEAN MEDICAL ONCOLOGY.** Variant title: Memo. Text in English. 2008. q. EUR 84, USD 110 combined subscription to institutions (print & online eds.) (effective 2012). adv. **Document type:** *Journal, Academic/Scholarly.* **Description:** Covers research and developments in the fields of hematology and oncology relevant for daily practice.
Related titles: Online - full text ed.: ISSN 1865-5076. 2008 (from IngentaConnect).
Indexed: A22, A26, E01, E08, EMBASE, ExcerpMed, H12, S09, SCOPUS.
—IE. **CCC.**
Published by: Springer Wien (Subsidiary of: Springer Science+Business Media), Sachsenplatz 4-6, Vienna, W 1201, Austria. TEL 43-1-33024150, FAX 43-1-3302426, journals@springer.at, http://www.springer.at. Ed. Wolfgang Hilbe. adv.: color page EUR 3,350; trim 210 x 297. Circ: 3,000 (paid).

610 HUN ISSN 0025-0244
RC254.A1 CODEN: MGONAD
➤ **MAGYAR ONKOLOGIA/HUNGARIAN ONCOLOGY.** Text in Hungarian; Summaries in English, Russian. 1957. q. EUR 113, USD 151 (effective 2011). bk.rev. bibl.; charts; illus. **Document type:** *Journal, Academic/Scholarly.*
Related titles: Online - full content ed.: free (effective 2011).
Indexed: ChemAb, EMBASE, ExcerpMed, IndMed, MEDLINE, P30, R10, Reac, SCOPUS.
—CASDDS.
Published by: (Magyar Onkologia Szerkesztosege), Akademiai Kiado Rt. (Subsidiary of: Wolters Kluwer N.V.), Prielle Kornelia u 19/D, Budapest, 1117, Hungary. TEL 36-1-4648222, FAX 36-1-4648221, journals@akkrt.hu, http://www.akademiai.com. Ed. Jozsef Timar. Circ: 500.

616.992 GBR ISSN 2044-799X
▼ ➤ **MALIGNANCY.** Text in English. 2009. 3/yr. (q. until 2011). free. adv. back issues avail.; reprints avail. **Document type:** *Journal, Academic/Scholarly.* **Description:** Publishes original research manuscripts and other works dealing with cancer and hematological malignancy management, diagnosis, staging, nursing and research.
Formerly (until 2011): European Journal of Clinical & Medical Oncology (1759-8958)
Related titles: E-mail ed.; Online - full text ed.: ISSN 2044-8007. free (effective 2011).
Indexed: A01, A36, CABA, GH, N02, N03, P30, P33, RM&VM, T02.
Published by: San Lucas Medical Ltd., 80-83 Long Lane Barbican, London, EC1A 9ET, United Kingdom. Ed. Jim Jones. Pub. Stephen Davidson. Adv. contact Ryan Joshi TEL 44-20-71930673. B&W page GBP 7,000, color page GBP 1,000.

616.99 AUT ISSN 1609-7041
➤ **MALIGNANT HYPERTHERMIA.** Text in English. 2000. q. adv. back issues avail. **Document type:** *Journal, Academic/Scholarly.* **Description:** Publishes articles, case reports, reviews, and letters on improving communications in understanding malignant hyperthermia reactions.
Related titles: Online - full text ed.
Indexed: SCOPUS.
Published by: V I C E R Publishing, PO Box 14, Vienna, A-1097, Austria. TEL 43-676-9568085, FAX 43-676-9568086, vicer@vicer.org, http://www.vicer.org. Ed., R&P Roland Hofbauer. adv.: B&W page USD 1,700, color page USD 2,200. Circ: 1,000 (paid and controlled).

➤ **MAMM**; women, cancer and community. *see* WOMEN'S HEALTH

616.992 JPN ISSN 1349-2179
MEBIO ONCOLOGY; principle, practice and research review. Text in Japanese. 2004. q. JPY 2,940 newsstand/cover (effective 2007). **Document type:** *Journal, Academic/Scholarly.*
Published by: Medical View Co. Ltd./Mejikaru Byusha, 2-30 Ichigaya-Honmura-cho, Shinjuku-ku, Tokyo, 162-0845, Japan. TEL 81-3-52282050, FAX 81-3-52282059, eigyo@medicalview.co.jp, http://www.medicalview.co.jp.

MECHANISMS OF B CELL NEOPLASIA. *see* BIOLOGY—Physiology

616.99 SWE ISSN 1400-7347
MEDDELANDE FRAAN S O F. (Svensk Onkologisk Foerening) Text in Swedish. 1995. 8/yr. **Document type:** *Journal, Academic/Scholarly.*
—CCC.
Published by: (Svensk Onkologisk Foerening), Taylor & Francis A B (Subsidiary of: Taylor & Francis Group), PO Box 3255, Stockholm, 10365, Sweden. TEL 46-8-4408040, FAX 46-8-4408050, journals@se.tandf.no. Ed. Jan-Erik Froedin.

616.99 USA ISSN 1357-0560
CODEN: MOTPE2
➤ **MEDICAL ONCOLOGY**; a leading journal in clinical oncology. Text and summaries in English. 1984. q. EUR 595, USD 725 combined subscription to institutions (print & online eds.) (effective 2012). adv. bk.rev. illus. back issues avail.; reprint service avail. from PSC. **Document type:** *Journal, Academic/Scholarly.* **Description:** Studies the chemistry, biochemistry, biology, epidemiology, pathology, virology, and genetics of malignant tumors, along with clinical aspects of cancer.
Formerly (until 1994): Medical Oncology and Tumor Pharmacotherapy (0736-0118)
Related titles: Microform ed.: (from PQC); Online - full text ed.: ISSN 1559-131X (from IngentaConnect).
Indexed: A22, A26, ASCA, ASFA, B21, B25, BIOBASE, BIOSIS Prev, C06, C07, CTA, CurCont, DBA, E01, E08, EMBASE, ESPM, ExcerpMed, H12, IABS, IndMed, Inpharma, MEDLINE, MycolAb, NSA, P20, P22, P30, P35, P48, P54, PQC, R10, Reac, S09, SCI, SCOPUS, T02, W07.
—BLDSC (5531.040500), CASDDS, GNLM, IE, Infotrieve, Ingenta, INIST. **CCC.**
Published by: Humana Press, Inc. (Subsidiary of: Springer Science+Business Media), 999 Riverview Dr, Ste 208, Totowa, NJ 07512. TEL 973-256-1699, FAX 973-256-8341, humana@humanapr.com, http://humanapress.com/journals.pasp. Eds. Anders Oesterborg, Peter H Wiernik. Pub. Thomas B. Lanigan Jr. R&P Wendy A. Warren. Adv. contacts John Chasse, Thomas B. Lanigan Jr.

616.992 DEU
MEDICAL TRIBUNE ONKOLOGIE - HAEMATOLOGIE. Text in German. 2007. 8/yr. adv. **Document type:** *Journal, Trade.*
Published by: Medical Tribune Verlagsgesellschaft mbH, Unter den Eichen 5, Wiesbaden, 65195, Germany. TEL 49-611-97460, FAX 49-611-9746303, online@medical-tribune.de, http://www.medical-tribune.de. adv.: B&W page EUR 3,550, color page EUR 4,330; trim 286 x 390. Circ: 12,000 (controlled).

616.992 NLD
MEDISCHE ONCOLOGIE. Text in Dutch. 6/yr. adv. **Document type:** *Magazine, Trade.*
Published by: Benecke, Arena Boulevard 61-75, Amsterdam, 1101 DL, Netherlands. TEL 31-20-7150600, FAX 31-20-6918446. Ed. Henri Neuvel. Adv. contact Linda van Iwaarden. color page EUR 2,740; 210 x 297. Circ: 3,000.

016.61699 BGR ISSN 1312-1111
➤ **MEDITSINSKI PREGLED. ONKOLOGIIA I RADIOLOGIIA/MEDICAL REVIEW. CLINICAL ONCOLOGY.** Text in Bulgarian. q. BGL 14 domestic; USD 40 foreign (effective 2005). adv. abstr.; bibl.; illus. 1 cols./p.; back issues avail. **Document type:** *Journal, Academic/Scholarly.* **Description:** Publishes original articles and abstracts of foreign publications on diagnosis and treatment of oncologic diseases.
Former titles (until 2003): Meditsinski Pregled. Klinichna Onkologiia (1311-4573); (until 1999): Onkologichen Pregled (1310-1714); Which superseded in part (in 1994): Onkologia, Rentgenologia, Radiologia (0204-7101); Which was formerly (until 1974): Zlokacestveni Novoobrazuvania (0323-908X); (until 1970): Zlokacestveni Tumori
Indexed: INIS AtomInd.
—GNLM.
Published by: Meditsinski Universitet - Sofia, Tsentralna Meditsinska Biblioteka, Tsentur za Informatsiia po Meditsina/Medical University - Sofia, Central Medical Library, Medical Information Center, 1 Sv Georgi Sofiiski ul, Sofia, 1431, Bulgaria. TEL 359-2-9522342, FAX 359-2-9522393, lydia@medun.acad.bg, http://www.medun.acad.bg/cmb_htm/cmb1_home_bg.htm. Ed. Dr. D Todorov. R&P, Adv. contact Lydia Tacheva. B&W page USD 50, color page USD 150; 12 x 18. Circ: 200.

➤ **MEDSCAPE HEMATOLOGY-ONCOLOGY.** *see* MEDICAL SCIENCES—Hematology

➤ **MELANOMA LETTER.** *see* MEDICAL SCIENCES—Dermatology And Venereology

616.99 USA ISSN 0960-8931
RC280.M37 CODEN: MREEEH
➤ **MELANOMA RESEARCH**; a journal for basic, translational and clinical research in melanoma. Text in English. 1990. bi-m. USD 1,683 domestic to institutions; USD 1,803 foreign to institutions (effective 2011). adv. back issues avail.; reprints avail. **Document type:** *Journal, Academic/Scholarly.* **Description:** Aims to encourage an informed and balanced view of experimental and clinical research and extend and stimulate communication and exchange of knowledge between investigators with differing areas of expertise.
Related titles: CD-ROM ed.: USD 1,168.70 domestic academic site license; USD 1,168.70 foreign academic site license; USD 1,303.55 domestic corporate site license; USD 1,303.55 foreign corporate site license (effective 2002); Online - full text ed.: ISSN 1473-5636.
Indexed: A22, A34, A35, A36, A38, ASCA, AgBio, B&BAb, B21, B25, BIOBASE, BIOSIS Prev, C30, CABA, ChemAb, ChemTitl, CurCont, E01, E12, EMBASE, ExcerpMed, GH, IABS, ISR, ImmunAb, IndMed, IndVet, Inpharma, MEDLINE, MS&D, MycolAb, N02, N03, OGFA, P30, P33, P35, P39, R10, RA&MP, Reac, SCI, SCOPUS, T05, VS, W07.
—BLDSC (5536.813450), CASDDS, GNLM, IE, Infotrieve, Ingenta. **CCC.**
Published by: Lippincott Williams & Wilkins (Subsidiary of: Wolters Kluwer N.V.), 530 Walnut St, Philadelphia, PA 19106. TEL 215-521-8300, FAX 215-521-8902, customerservice@lww.com, http://www.lww.com. Eds. Ferdy J Lejeune TEL 41-76-3261806, W J Storkus TEL 412-648-9981. Pub. Phil Daly. Circ: 170.

➤ **MELANOOM NIEUWS.** *see* MEDICAL SCIENCES—Dermatology And Venereology

616.99 USA
MEMORIAL SLOAN-KETTERING CANCER CENTER. ANNUAL REPORT. Text in English. a. free. charts; illus. **Document type:** *Corporate.* **Description:** Reviews research in the detection, prevention, and treatment of cancer conducted at Memorial Sloan-Kettering Cancer Center.
Published by: (Department of Public Affairs), Memorial Sloan-Kettering Cancer Center, 1275 York Ave, New York, NY 10021. TEL 212-639-2000, PublicAffairs@mskcc.org, http://www.mskcc.org.

616.992 ITA ISSN 2035-4819
▼ **MESOTHELIOMA TODAY.** Text in English. 2009. irreg. **Document type:** *Journal, Academic/Scholarly.*
Related titles: Online - full text ed.: ISSN 2035-4622.
Published by: Pagepress, Via Giuseppe Belli 4, Pavia, 27100, Italy. TEL 39-0382-1751762, FAX 39-0382-1750481, http://www.pagepress.org.

616.992 IRN ISSN 2008-6709
▼ **MIDDLE EAST JOURNAL OF CANCER.** Text in English. 2010. q. **Document type:** *Journal, Academic/Scholarly.*
Related titles: Online - full text ed.: ISSN 2008-6687. free (effective 2011).
Indexed: A01.
Published by: Shiraz University of Medical Sciences, Nemazee Hospital, Shiraz, 71934, Iran. TEL 98-71-660134, FAX 98-71-661001, vessalk@pearl.sums.ac.ir.

616.99 USA ISSN 1935-3855
MILESTONES IN ONCOLOGY. Text in English. 2006. irreg., latest 2006. free (effective 2010). **Document type:** *Journal, Academic/Scholarly.*
Media: Optical Disk - DVD.
Published by: AlphaMed Press, Inc., 318 Blackwell St, Ste 260, Durham, NC 27701. TEL 919-680-0011, FAX 919-680-4411, alphamedpress@alphamedpress.com, http://www.alphamedpress.org/.

616.992 GBR
MITOMYCIN-C KYOWA UPDATE. Text in English. 3/yr. **Document type:** *Journal, Academic/Scholarly.* **Description:** Provides information on recent clinical applications of mitomycin-C in relation to cancer.
Published by: Leeds Medical Information, University of Leeds, Leeds, W Yorks LS2 9JT, United Kingdom. TEL 44-113-233-5550, FAX 44-113-233-5568, lmi@leeds.ac.uk, http://www.leeds.ac.uk/lmi/intro.html. **Co-sponsor:** Kyowa Hakko U.K. Ltd.

616.992 GBR ISSN 1476-4598
RC261.A1
➤ **MOLECULAR CANCER.** Text in English. 2002. irreg. free (effective 2011). adv. back issues avail. **Document type:** *Journal, Academic/Scholarly.* **Description:** Contains reviews, original research, case reports, short communications and hypotheses on all aspects of cancer science.
Media: Online - full text.
Indexed: A01, A02, A03, A08, A26, B19, B25, B27, BIOSIS Prev, CA, CurCont, EMBASE, ExcerpMed, I05, MEDLINE, MycolAb, OGFA, P30, R10, Reac, SCI, SCOPUS, T02, W07.
—CCC.

Published by: BioMed Central Ltd. (Subsidiary of: Springer Science+Business Media), 236 Gray's Inn Rd, London, WC1X 8HB, United Kingdom. TEL 44-20-31922000, FAX 44-20-31922010, info@biomedcentral.com, http://www.biomedcentral.com. Ed. Dr. Alan Storey. Adv. contact Natasha Bailey TEL 44-20-31922231.

616.99 USA ISSN 1541-7786
RC261.A1 CODEN: MCROC5

➤ **MOLECULAR CANCER RESEARCH.** Text in English. 1990. m. USD 325 domestic to individuals; USD 355 foreign to individuals (effective 2011). adv. back issues avail.; reprints avail. **Document type:** *Journal, Academic/Scholarly.* **Description:** Features original research in all areas of the molecular biology of cancer.
Formerly (until 2002): Cell Growth & Differentiation (1044-9523)
Related titles: Online - full text ed.: ISSN 1557-3125. USD 615 (effective 2011).
Indexed: A22, ASCA, B21, B25, B27, BIOBASE, BIOSIS Prev, BioEngAb, C33, CIN, ChemAb, ChemTitl, CurCont, EMBASE, ESPM, ExcerpMed, IABS, ISR, IndMed, Inpharma, MEDLINE, MycolAb, OGFA, P30, R10, Reac, SCI, SCOPUS, THA, ToxAb, W07.
—BLDSC (5900.799750), CASDDS, GNLM, IE, Ingenta, INIST. **CCC.**
Published by: American Association for Cancer Research, 615 Chestnut St, 17th Fl, Philadelphia, PA 19106. TEL 215-440-9300, 866-423-3965, FAX 215-440-9411, aacr@aacr.org, http://www.aacr.org. Ed. Dr. Michael B. Kastan. Adv. contact Dean Mather TEL 856-768-9360. B&W page USD 1,010, color page USD 1,955; bleed 7.625 x 10.8125. Circ: 3,020. **Distr. addr. in N. America:** Turpin Distribution Services Ltd., The Bleachery, 143 W St, New Milford, CT 06776. TEL 860-350-0041, FAX 860-350-0036, turpinna@turpin-distribution.com, http://www.turpin-distribution.com; **Distr. addr.outside N. America:** Turpin Distribution Services Ltd., Pegasus Dr, Stratton Business Park, Biggleswade, Bedfordshire SG18 8QB, United Kingdom. TEL 44-1767-604954, FAX 44-1767-601640, custserv@turpin-distribution.com, http://www.turpin-distribution.com/.

616.992 USA ISSN 1535-7163
RC270.8 CODEN: MCTOCF

➤ **MOLECULAR CANCER THERAPEUTICS.** Text in English. 2001. m. USD 325 domestic to individuals; USD 430 foreign to individuals (effective 2011). adv. back issues avail.; reprints avail. **Document type:** *Journal, Academic/Scholarly.* **Description:** Focuses on basic research that has implications for cancer therapeutics in the following areas: experimental cancer therapeutics, identification of molecular targets, targets for chemoprevention, new models, cancer chemistry and drug discovery, molecular and cellular pharmacology, molecular classification of tumors, and bioinformatics and computational molecular biology.
Related titles: Online - full text ed.: ISSN 1538-8514. USD 615 (effective 2011).
Indexed: A22, B&BAb, B19, B21, B25, B26, B27, BIOSIS Prev, C33, CurCont, EMBASE, ESPM, ExcerpMed, GenetAb, Inpharma, M&PBA, MEDLINE, MycolAb, P30, P35, R10, Reac, SCI, SCOPUS, ToxAb, VirolAbstr, W07.
—IE, INIST. **CCC.**
Published by: American Association for Cancer Research, 615 Chestnut St, 17th Fl, Philadelphia, PA 19106. TEL 215-440-9300, 866-423-3965, FAX 215-440-9354, aacr@aacr.org, http://www.aacr.org. Ed. Dr. Daniel D Von Hoff. Adv. contact Dean Mather TEL 856-768-9360. B&W page USD 805, color page USD 1,750; bleed 7.625 x 10.8125. Circ: 2,930. **Subscr. in N. America to:** Turpin Distribution Services Ltd.; **Subscr. outside N. America to:** Turpin Distribution Services Ltd.

616.994071 USA ISSN 0899-1987
RC268.5 CODEN: MOCAE8

➤ **MOLECULAR CARCINOGENESIS.** Text in English. 1988. m. (in 3 vols., 4 nos./vol.). GBP 1,846 in United Kingdom to institutions; EUR 2,333 in Europe to institutions; USD 3,364 in United States to institutions; USD 3,532 in Canada & Mexico to institutions; USD 3,616 elsewhere to institutions; GBP 2,124 combined subscription in United Kingdom to institutions (print & online eds.); EUR 2,685 combined subscription in Europe to institutions (print & online eds.); USD 3,868 combined subscription in United States to institutions (print & online eds.); USD 4,036 combined subscription in Canada & Mexico to institutions (print & online eds.); USD 4,120 combined subscription elsewhere to institutions (print & online eds.) (effective 2012). adv. bk.rev. back issues avail.; reprint service avail. from PSC. **Document type:** *Journal, Academic/Scholarly.* **Description:** Devoted to the study of the molecular aspects of mechanisms involved in chemical, physical and viral (biological) carcinogenesis.
Related titles: Microform ed.: (from PQC); Online - full text ed.: ISSN 1098-2744. 1996. GBP 1,717 in United Kingdom to institutions; EUR 2,170 in Europe to institutions; USD 3,364 elsewhere to institutions (effective 2012).
Indexed: A22, A35, A36, AIDS&CR, ASCA, B21, B25, B26, B27, BIOBASE, BIOSIS Prev, BP, C33, CABA, CIN, ChemAb, ChemTitl, CurCont, EMBASE, ESPM, ExcerpMed, F08, F11, F12, FoMM, GH, GenetAb, H16, H17, HGA, IABS, INIS AtomInd, ISR, IndMed, Inpharma, MEDLINE, MycolAb, N02, N03, NucAcAb, OGFA, P30, P32, P33, R10, R13, RA&MP, RM&VM, Reac, RefZh, SCI, SCOPUS, SoyAb, T05, THA, ToxAb, VITIS, VS, W07.
—BLDSC (5900.802000), CASDDS, GNLM, IE, Infotrieve, Ingenta, INIST. **CCC.**
Published by: (University of Texas), John Wiley & Sons, Inc., 111 River St, Hoboken, NJ 07030. TEL 201-748-6000, FAX 201-748-6088, info@wiley.com, http://www.wiley.com/WileyCDA/. Ed. John DiGiovanni. **Subscr. outside the Americas to:** John Wiley & Sons Ltd.

616.992 NLD ISSN 1574-7891
RC261.A1

MOLECULAR ONCOLOGY. Text in English. 2007. q. EUR 892 in Europe to institutions; JPY 130,100 in Japan to institutions; USD 1,134 elsewhere to institutions (effective 2012). **Document type:** *Journal, Academic/Scholarly.* **Description:** Covers new discoveries, approaches, as well as technical developments, in basic, clinical and discovery-driven translational research.
Related titles: Online - full text ed.: ISSN 1878-0261 (from ScienceDirect).
Indexed: A26, B&BAb, B19, B21, B25, BIOBASE, BIOSIS Prev, CA, EMBASE, ExcerpMed, GenetAb, I05, IABS, ImmunAb, MEDLINE, MycolAb, OGFA, P30, SCI, SCOPUS, T02, W07.
—IE. **CCC.**

Published by: (Federation of European Biochemical Societies DNK), Elsevier BV (Subsidiary of: Elsevier Science & Technology), Radarweg 29, PO Box 211, Amsterdam, 1000 AE, Netherlands. TEL 31-20-4853911, FAX 31-20-4852457, JournalsCustomerServiceEMEA@elsevier.com, http://www.elsevier.nl. Ed. J Celis.

572.8 GBR ISSN 1525-0016
RB155.8 CODEN: MTOHCK

➤ **MOLECULAR THERAPY.** Text in English. 2000. m. EUR 1,561 in Europe to institutions; JPY 266,900 in Japan to institutions; USD 1,814 in the Americas to institutions; GBP 1,007 to institutions in the UK & elsewhere (effective 2011). adv. back issues avail.; reprints avail. **Document type:** *Journal, Academic/Scholarly.* **Description:** Publishes scientific meritorious papers in the areas of gene transfer, gene regulation, gene discovery, cell therapy, experimental models, correction of genetic and acquired diseases, clinical trials and significant methodological advances. Also publishes timely reviews, scientific correspondence and commentaries.
Related titles: Online - full text ed.: ISSN 1525-0024. 2000 (from IngentaConnect).
Indexed: A01, A03, A08, A22, A26, AIDS Ab, B&BAb, B19, B21, B25, B26, BIOBASE, BIOSIS Prev, BioEngAb, C33, CA, ChemAb, CurCont, E01, EMBASE, ExcerpMed, I05, IABS, ImmunAb, IndMed, Inpharma, M&PBA, MEDLINE, MycolAb, P30, P35, R10, Reac, S01, SCI, SCOPUS, T02, W07.
—BLDSC (5900.856500), IE, Infotrieve, Ingenta, INIST. **CCC.**
Published by: Nature Publishing Group (Subsidiary of: Macmillan Publishers Ltd.), The MacMillan Bldg, 4 Crinan St, London, N1 9XW, United Kingdom. TEL 44-20-78334000, FAX 44-20-78334640. Eds. Robert M Frederickson TEL 206-724-7760, Dr. Malcolm K Brenner TEL 832-824-4671. Adv. contact Ben Harkinson TEL 617-475-9222. **Subscr. to:** Brunel Rd, Houndmills, Basingstoke, Hamps RG21 6XS, United Kingdom. TEL 44-1256-329242, FAX 44-1256-812358, subscriptions@nature.com.

616.992 USA ISSN 1559-8438

MONOGRAPHS IN RENAL CELL CARCINOMA. Text in English. 2005. irreg. **Document type:** *Monographic series, Trade.*
Published by: Physicians' Education Resource, 3500 Maple Ave., Ste 700, Dallas, TX 75219. TEL 888-949-0045, FAX 214-367-3305, http://www.cancerpublications.com.

616.99424 JPN

MOOK: HAIGAN NO RINSHO/CLINICS OF LUNG CANCER: EPIDEMIOLOGY, DETECTION, DIAGNOSES, TREATMENTS. Text in Japanese. 1998. a. JPY 7,350 newsstand/cover (effective 2005).
Formerly (until 2003): Haigan no Rinsho/Japanese Journal of Lung Cancer Clinics (1343-9294)
Published by: Shinohara-Shuppan Shinsha/Shinoharashinsha. Inc., 2-4-9 Yushima Bunkyo-ku, Tokyo, 113-0034, Japan. TEL 81-3-38165311, FAX 81-3-38165314, info@shinoharashinsha.co.jp.

616.992 SWE ISSN 2000-7477

MUN & HALS. Text in Swedish. 1973. q. **Document type:** *Magazine, Consumer.*
Formerly (until 2010): Lary (0283-9725)
Related titles: Online - full text ed.
Published by: Mun- och Halscancerfoerbundet, Barks Vaeg 14, Solna, 17073, Sweden. TEL 46-8-6558310, FAX 46-8-6554610, kansli@mhcforbundet.se, info@mhcforbundet.se. Ed. Gunnar Schneider.

616.994 USA ISSN 1541-9762

MYELOMA TODAY. Text in English. 1992. bi-m. free domestic; USD 15 foreign (effective 2006). back issues avail. **Document type:** *Newsletter, Trade.* **Description:** Contains articles about the Foundation events and medical and psychological issues of interest to patients and caregivers, as well as scientific articles about oncology.
Related titles: Online - full text ed.: free worldwide (effective 2006).
Published by: International Myeloma Foundation, 12650 Riverside Dr., Ste. 206, Valley Village, CA 91607-3466. TEL 818-487-7455, FAX 818-487-7454, theimf@myeloma.org. Ed. Marya Kazakova.

616.994 USA ISSN 1526-5803

N A B C O BREAST CANCER RESOURCE LIST. Text in English. a. **Document type:** *Directory.* **Description:** Compiles books, brochures, hotlines, and video resources useful to breast cancer patients and professionals.
Published by: National Alliance of Breast Cancer Organizations, 9 E 37th St, 10th Fl, New York, NY 10016-2822. TEL 212-889-0606, FAX 212-689-1213.

616.99 USA

N A B C O NEWS. Text in English. 1987. q. bk.rev. index. back issues avail. **Document type:** *Newsletter.* **Description:** Contains updates on breast cancer research, treatment, policy programs, and detection.
Related titles: Online - full text ed.
Published by: National Alliance of Breast Cancer Organizations, 9 E 37th St, 10th Fl, New York, NY 10016-2822. TEL 212-889-0606, FAX 212-689-1213. Ed. Ruth Spear. Circ: 7,000.

616.994 USA

N C I CANCER BULLETIN. (National Cancer Institute) Text in English. 2004 (Jan.). w. free (effective 2006).
Related titles: Online - full content ed.: ISSN 1559-4394.
Published by: U.S. National Cancer Institute, Building. 31, Rm. 10A31, 31 Center Dr, MSC 2580, Bethesda, MD 20892-2580. TEL 800-422-6237, cancergovstaff@mail.nih.gov.

616.99 USA ISSN 0270-7950
RC267

N C I FACT BOOK. Text in English. a. **Document type:** *Government.*
Formerly: National Cancer Institute Fact Book
Published by: National Cancer Institute, Financial Management Branch, 9000 Rockville Pike, Bethesda, MD 20892.

616.994 GBR ISSN 1460-2105

NATIONAL CANCER INSTITUTE. JOURNAL (ONLINE). Text in English. 199?. m. GBP 482 in United Kingdom to institutions; EUR 709 in Europe to institutions; USD 722 in US & Canada to institutions; GBP 482 elsewhere to institutions (effective 2012). **Document type:** *Journal, Academic/Scholarly.*
Formerly (until 2007): J N C I Cancer Spectrum (Online) (1475-4029)
Media: Online - full text (from IngentaConnect). **Related titles:** Microfiche ed.: (from CIS); Microform ed.: (from PMC, PQC); ◆ Print ed.: National Cancer Institute. Journal (Print). ISSN 0027-8874.
—**CCC.**

Published by: (U.S. National Cancer Institute USA), Oxford University Press, Great Clarendon St, Oxford, OX2 6DP, United Kingdom. TEL 44-1865-556767, FAX 44-1865-556646, enquiry@oup.co.uk, http://www.oxfordjournals.org.

616.994 GBR ISSN 0027-8874
CODEN: JNCIEQ

➤ **NATIONAL CANCER INSTITUTE. JOURNAL (PRINT).** Text in English. 1940. s-m. GBP 597 in United Kingdom to institutions; EUR 897 in Europe to institutions; USD 897 in US & Canada to institutions; GBP 597 elsewhere to institutions; GBP 652 combined subscription in United Kingdom to institutions (print & online eds.); EUR 978 combined subscription in Europe to institutions (print & online eds.); USD 978 combined subscription in US & Canada to institutions (print & online eds.); GBP 652 combined subscription elsewhere to institutions (print & online eds.) (effective 2012). adv. bk.rev. bibl.; charts; illus. index. back issues avail.; reprint service avail. from PSC. **Document type:** *Journal, Academic/Scholarly.* **Description:** Contains original reports, articles, reviews, editorials, and commentaries on new findings in clinical and laboratory cancer research.
Incorporates (1976-1987): Cancer Treatment Reports (0361-5960); Which was formed by the merger of (1968-1975): Cancer Chemotherapy Reports. Part 1 (0069-0112); (1968-1975): Cancer Chemotherapy Reports. Part 2 (0069-0120); (1968-1975): Cancer Chemotherapy Reports. Part 3 (0069-0139); All of which superseded in part (in 1968): Cancer Chemotherapy Reports (0576-6559); Which incorporated (1958-1967): Cancer Chemotherapy Screening Data (0576-6583)
Related titles: Microfiche ed.: (from CIS); Microform ed.: (from PMC, PQC); ◆ Online - full text ed.: National Cancer Institute. Journal (Online). ISSN 1460-2105; ◆ Supplement(s): National Cancer Institute. Journal. Monographs. ISSN 1052-6773.
Indexed: A01, A02, A03, A08, A20, A22, A26, A35, A36, AIDS&CR, ASCA, AmStl, B21, B25, BIOBASE, BIOSIS Prev, C06, C07, C08, C13, CA, CABA, CIN, CINAHL, CIS, CISA, ChPerl, ChemAb, ChemTitl, CurCont, D01, DBA, DentInd, DokArb, E01, E08, E12, EMBASE, ESPM, ExcerpMed, FR, FS&TA, G08, G10, GH, H&SSA, H04, H11, H12, H13, I05, I12, IABS, IBR, IBZ, IDIS, INI, INIS AtomInd, ISR, IUSGP, IndMed, Inpharma, JW-D, JW-WH, LT, MEDLINE, MS&D, MycolAb, N02, N03, NRN, OGFA, P02, P06, P10, P15, P19, P20, P22, P24, P26, P30, P33, P34, P35, P39, P48, P50, P52, P53, P54, P56, PN&I, PQC, R07, R10, R12, RA&MP, RM&VM, RRTA, Reac, RiskAb, S09, SCI, SCOPUS, SRI, SoyAb, T02, T05, THA, Telegen, ToxAb, VS, VirolAbstr, W07, W09.
—BLDSC (4830.000000), CASDDS, CIS, GNLM, IE, Infotrieve, Ingenta, INIST, Linda Hall. **CCC.**
Published by: (U.S. National Cancer Institute USA), Oxford University Press, Great Clarendon St, Oxford, OX2 6DP, United Kingdom. TEL 44-1865-556767, FAX 44-1865-556646, enquiry@oup.co.uk, http://www.oxfordjournals.org. Ed. Barnett S Kramer.

616.994 USA ISSN 1052-6773
RC261.A2 CODEN: JNCME4

➤ **NATIONAL CANCER INSTITUTE. JOURNAL. MONOGRAPHS.** Text in English. 1986. irreg., latest vol.39, 2008. price varies. reprint service avail. from PSC. **Document type:** *Monographic series, Academic/Scholarly.* **Description:** Features manuscripts from key conferences dealing with cancer and closely related research fields, or a related group of papers on specific subjects of importance to cancer research.
Formerly (until 1990): N C I Monographs (0893-2751); Which was formed by the merger of (1983-1985): Cancer Treament Sympoia (0742-1761); (1959-1986): National Cancer Institute. Monographs (0083-1921)
Related titles: Online - full text ed.: ISSN 1745-6614 (from IngentaConnect); ◆ Supplement to: National Cancer Institute. Journal (Print). ISSN 0027-8874.
Indexed: A22, B21, B25, BIOBASE, BIOSIS Prev, ChPerl, EMBASE, ExcerpMed, IABS, ImmunAb, IndMed, Inpharma, MEDLINE, MycolAb, NucAcAb, OGFA, P30, P35, R10, Reac, SCOPUS.
—BLDSC (5914.670000), CASDDS, CIS, GNLM, IE, Infotrieve, Ingenta, INIST. **CCC.**
Published by: (U.S. National Cancer Institute), Oxford University Press (Subsidiary of: Oxford University Press), 2001 Evans Rd, Cary, NC 27513. TEL 919-677-0977, FAX 919-677-1303, orders.us@oup.com, http://www.us.oup.com. Ed. Barnett S Kramer.

616.9 CAN ISSN 0834-8855

NATIONAL CANCER INSTITUTE OF CANADA. ANNUAL REPORT. Text in English. 1947. a. free (effective 2006).
Formerly: National Cancer Institute of Canada. Report (0077-3689)
Published by: National Cancer Institute of Canada, 10 Alcorn Ave, Ste 200, Toronto, ON M4V 3B1, Canada. TEL 416-961-7223, FAX 416-961-4189, ncic@cancer.ca. Circ: 1,000.

616.994 USA ISSN 1540-1405
RC261.A1 CODEN: JNCCA4

➤ **NATIONAL COMPREHENSIVE CANCER NETWORK. JOURNAL.** Abbreviated title: J N C C N. Text in English. 2003. m. USD 460 domestic to individuals (print or online ed.); USD 570 foreign to individuals (print or online ed.); USD 720 domestic to institutions (print or online ed.); USD 830 foreign to institutions (print or online ed.); USD 510 combined subscription domestic to individuals (print & online eds.); USD 640 combined subscription foreign to individuals (print & online eds.); USD 790 combined subscription domestic to institutions (print & online eds.); USD 910 combined subscription foreign to institutions (print & online eds.); free to qualified personnel (effective 2011). adv. back issues avail. **Document type:** *Journal, Academic/Scholarly.* **Description:** Focuses on the publication of the NCCN Practice Guidelines in Oncology, outcomes data and the practical applications of standards of care in daily practice, and also publishes original research and discusses important issues in cancer care.
Related titles: Online - full text ed.: ISSN 1540-1413.
Indexed: C06, C07, CurCont, EMBASE, ExcerpMed, MEDLINE, P30, R10, Reac, SCI, SCOPUS, W07.
—BLDSC (4830.097000), IE, Ingenta, INIST. **CCC.**
Published by: (National Comprehensive Cancer Network), Harborside Press, 37 Main St, Cold Spring Harbor, NY 11724. TEL 631-692-0800, FAX 631-692-0805, info@harborsidepress.com, http://www.harborsidepress.com. Ed. Harold J Burstein. Pub. Jack A Gentile TEL 631-935-7655. Adv. contact Wendy McGullam TEL 631-692-0800 ext 303.

616.992 GBR ISSN 1474-175X
RC267 CODEN: NRCAC4

➤ **NATURE REVIEWS. CANCER.** Text in English. 2001 (Oct.). m. EUR 3,214 in Europe to institutions; USD 4,048 in the Americas to institutions; GBP 2,077 to institutions in the UK & elsewhere (effective 2011). adv. back issues avail.; reprints avail. **Document type:** *Journal, Academic/Scholarly.* **Description:** Provides information to researchers on the diagnosis, treatment and prevention of cancer.
Related titles: Online - full text ed.: ISSN 1474-1768.
Indexed: A01, A02, A03, A08, A22, A26, A36, AIDS&CR, B&BAb, B19, B21, BIOBASE, BIOSIS Prev, C33, CA, CABA, ChemAb, CurCont, D01, E12, EMBASE, ESPM, ExcerpMed, GH, GenetAb, H12, I05, IABS, ISR, M&PBA, MEDLINE, MycolAb, N02, N03, N05, NSA, NucAcAb, OGFA, P20, P22, P30, P48, P50, P54, PQC, R10, Reac, S13, S16, SCI, SCOPUS, T02, T05, ToxAb, W07.
—BLDSC (6047.223000), IE, Infotrieve, Ingenta. **CCC.**
Published by: Nature Publishing Group (Subsidiary of: Macmillan Publishers Ltd.), The MacMillan Bldg, 4 Crinan St, London, N1 9XW, United Kingdom. TEL 44-20-78334000, FAX 44-20-78334640, NatureReviews@nature.com. Eds. Nicola McCarthy, Dr. Philip Campbell. Adv. contact Andy Douglas TEL 44-22-78434975. **Subscr. in N. & S. America to:** Nature Publishing Group; **Subscr. to:** Brunel Rd, Houndmills, Basingstoke, Hamps RG21 6XS, United Kingdom. TEL 44-1256-329242, FAX 44-1256-812358, subscriptions@nature.com.

606.992 GBR ISSN 1759-4774

➤ **NATURE REVIEWS CLINICAL ONCOLOGY.** Text in English. 2004 (Nov.). m. EUR 1,224 in Europe to institutions; USD 1,257 in the Americas to institutions; GBP 741 to institutions in the UK & elsewhere (effective 2011). adv. back issues avail.; reprints avail. **Document type:** *Journal, Academic/Scholarly.* **Description:** Features unique content designed to be of real, practical value in making diagnosis and treatment decisions. Sections include editorial and opinion pieces, highlights from the current literature, commentaries on the application of recent research to practical patient care, comprehensive reviews, and in-depth case studies.
Formerly (until 2009): Nature Clinical Practice Oncology (1743-4254)
Related titles: Online - full text ed.: ISSN 1759-4782.
Indexed: A26, B21, C06, C07, C08, CA, CINAHL, CurCont, EMBASE, ExcerpMed, GenetAb, H12, I05, Inpharma, MEDLINE, OGFA, P30, P35, R10, Reac, SCI, SCOPUS, T02, W07.
—BLDSC (6046.280200), IE, Ingenta. **CCC.**
Published by: Nature Publishing Group (Subsidiary of: Macmillan Publishers Ltd.), The MacMillan Bldg, 4 Crinan St, London, N1 9XW, United Kingdom. TEL 44-20-78334000, FAX 44-20-78334640, NatureReviews@nature.com. Eds. Lisa Hutchinson, Dr. Philip Campbell. Adv. contact Andy Douglas TEL 44-22-78434975. **Subscr. to:** Brunel Rd, Houndmills, Basingstoke, Hamps RG21 6XS, United Kingdom. TEL 44-1256-329242, FAX 44-1256-812358, subscriptions@nature.com.

616.992 BRA ISSN 0104-6497
NAUPLIUS. Text in English. 1993. a.
Indexed: C01, Z01.
Published by: Sociedade Brasileira de Carcinologia/Brazilian Society of Carcinology, Departamento de Zoologia, Instituto de Biocencias, Universidade de Sao Paulo, Rua do Matao, Travessa 14 No.101, Sao Paulo, 05508-900, Brazil. sbueno@ib.usp.br, http://www.ib.usp.br/sbc.

616.992 NLD ISSN 1572-1604

➤ **NEDERLANDS TIJDSCHRIFT VOOR ONCOLOGIE/DUTCH JOURNAL OF ONCOLOGY.** Text in Dutch. 2004. 8/yr. **Document type:** *Journal, Trade.*
Published by: Ariez Medical Publishing, Kruislaan 419, Amsterdam, 1098 VA, Netherlands. TEL 31-20-5612070, FAX 31-20-5612051, info@ariezmp.nl, http://www.ariezmp.nl.

616.99 USA ISSN 1522-8002
RC261.A1 CODEN: NEOPFL

➤ **NEOPLASIA**; an international journal of oncology research. Text in English. 1999. m. USD 575 domestic; USD 750 foreign (effective 2010). abstr.; bibl.; charts; illus.; stat. back issues avail. **Document type:** *Journal, Academic/Scholarly.* **Description:** Publishes laboratory and clinical studies describing new molecular and genetic findings relating to the neoplastic phenotype.
Related titles: Online - full text ed.: ISSN 1476-5586. free (effective 2011).
Indexed: A01, A02, A03, A08, A22, AIDS&CR, B21, B25, BIOBASE, BIOSIS Prev, CA, CTA, CurCont, E01, EMBASE, ExcerpMed, GenetAb, IABS, IndMed, Inpharma, MEDLINE, MycolAb, NSA, OGFA, P30, P35, R10, Reac, SCI, SCOPUS, T02, W07.
—BLDSC (6075.628100), IE, Infotrieve, Ingenta, INIST. **CCC.**
Published by: Neoplasia Press, c/o Divya Khanna, University of Michigan Medical Ctr, 109 Zina Pitcher Pl, BSRB-A628, Ann Arbor, MI 48109. TEL 734-647-6679, FAX 734-615-5669. Ed. Alnawaz Rehemtulla. **Subscr. to:** Odyssey Press Inc., PO Box 7307, Gonic, NH 03839. TEL 603-749-4433, FAX 603-749-1425, https://www.odysseypress.com.

616.994 SVK ISSN 0028-2685
CODEN: NEOLA4

➤ **NEOPLASMA.** Text in English. 1954. bi-m. EUR 200 foreign; EUR 240 combined subscription foreign print & online eds. (effective 2006). bk.rev. charts; illus. index. reprints avail. **Document type:** *Journal, Academic/Scholarly.* **Description:** Publishes original works of Czechoslovak and foreign authors in the fields of experimental and clinical oncology. Covers the biochemistry of tumors, the biology and genetics of oncology, and significant causistry. Includes statistics of oncology.
Related titles: Online - full text ed.: EUR 40 foreign (effective 2006).
Indexed: A22, A29, ASCA, B20, B21, B25, BIOSIS Prev, CIN, CISA, CTA, ChemAb, ChemTitl, CurCont, DentInd, EMBASE, ESPM, ExcerpMed, FR, GenetAb, I10, INIS AtomInd, ISR, IndMed, Inpharma, MEDLINE, MycolAb, NRN, NSA, OGFA, P30, P35, R10, Reac, SCI, SCOPUS, ToxAb, VirolAbstr, W07.
—BLDSC (6075.630000), CASDDS, GNLM, IE, Infotrieve, Ingenta, INIST. **CCC.**
Published by: (Slovenska Akademia Vied, Ustav Experimentalnej Onkologie/Slovak Academy of Sciences, Cancer Research Institute), Vydavatel'stvo Slovenskej Akademie Vied Veda/Veda, Publishing House of the Slovak Academy of Sciences, Dubravska cesta 9, PO Box 106, Bratislava 45, 84005, Slovakia. TEL 421-2-54774253, FAX 421-2-54772682, veda@savba.sk, http://www.veda-sav.sk. Ed. Viliam Ujhazy.

616.99449 CAN ISSN 1481-0999
NETWORK NEWS (OTTAWA). Text in English. 1997. s-a. free.
Document type: *Newsletter.* **Description:** Offers a forum for women with breast cancer to share their experiences and wisdom with others.
Published by: Canadian Breast Cancer Network, 300-331 Cooper St, Ottawa, ON K2P 0G5, Canada. TEL 613-230-3044, 800-685-8820, FAX 613-230-4424, cbcn@cbcn.ca, http://www.cbcn.ca.

616.99383 USA
NEURO-FIBROMA-TOSIS NEWS. Text in English. q. USD 40 membership (effective 2005). **Document type:** *Newsletter.*
Formerly: Neuro-Fibroma-Tosis
Published by: National Neurofibromatosis Foundation, Inc., 95 Pine St, Fl 16, New York, NY 10005-1611. TEL 212-344-6633, FAX 212-747-0004. R&P Francine Morris. Circ: 35,000.

616.994 USA ISSN 1522-8517
RC280.B7 CODEN: NEURJR

➤ **NEURO-ONCOLOGY.** Text in English. 1999. m. GBP 369 in United Kingdom to institutions; EUR 553 in Europe to institutions; USD 702 in US & Canada to institutions; GBP 369 elsewhere to institutions; GBP 403 combined subscription in United Kingdom to institutions (print & online eds.); EUR 604 combined subscription in Europe to institutions (print & online eds.); USD 765 combined subscription in US & Canada to institutions (print & online eds.); GBP 403 combined subscription elsewhere to institutions (print & online eds.) (effective 2012). back issues avail.; reprint service avail. from PSC. **Document type:** *Journal, Academic/Scholarly.* **Description:** Dedicated to provide superior and rapid publication of information in all areas of neuro-oncology.
Related titles: Online - full text ed.: ISSN 1523-5866. GBP 323 in United Kingdom to institutions; EUR 484 in Europe to institutions; USD 613 in US & Canada to institutions; GBP 323 elsewhere to institutions (effective 2012).
Indexed: B19, CA, CurCont, EMBASE, ExcerpMed, IndMed, Inpharma, MEDLINE, NSCI, P30, P35, R10, Reac, SCI, SCOPUS, T02, W07.
—BLDSC (6081.288000), IE, Ingenta. **CCC.**
Published by: (World Federation of Neurology/Federation Mondiale de Neurologie GBR, Duke University Medical Center, Society for Neuro-Oncology, Japan Society for Neuro-Oncology JPN, European Association for Neuro-Oncology DEU), Oxford University Press (Subsidiary of: Oxford University Press), 2001 Evans Rd, Cary, NC 27513. TEL 919-677-0977, 800-445-9714, FAX 919-677-1303, custserv.us@oup.com, http://www.oup.com/us. Ed. W K Alfred Yung.

616.992 USA
NEW MEDICAL THERAPIES BRIEFS. BREAST CANCER. Text in English. 19??. irreg. free (effective 2009). **Document type:** *Newsletter, Academic/Scholarly.*
Media: Online - full content.
Published by: CenterWatch (Subsidiary of: Jobson Medical Information LLC.), 100 N Washington St, Ste 301, Boston, MA 02114. TEL 617-948-5100, 866-219-3440, customerservice@centerwatch.com.

616.992 USA
NEW MEDICAL THERAPIES BRIEFS. HEAD AND NECK CANCER. Text in English. 200?. irreg. free (effective 2009). **Document type:** *Newsletter, Trade.*
Media: Online - full content.
Published by: CenterWatch (Subsidiary of: Jobson Medical Information LLC.), 100 N Washington St, Ste 301, Boston, MA 02114. TEL 617-948-5100, 866-219-3440, customerservice@centerwatch.com.

616.992 USA
NEW MEDICAL THERAPIES BRIEFS. KIDNEY CANCER. Text in English. 200?. irreg. free (effective 2009). **Document type:** *Newsletter, Trade.*
Media: Online - full content.
Published by: CenterWatch (Subsidiary of: Jobson Medical Information LLC.), 100 N Washington St, Ste 301, Boston, MA 02114. TEL 617-948-5100, 866-219-3440, customerservice@centerwatch.com.

616.9942406 USA
NEW MEDICAL THERAPIES BRIEFS. LUNG CANCER. Text in English. 200?. irreg. free (effective 2009). **Document type:** *Newsletter, Academic/Scholarly.*
Media: Online - full content.
Published by: CenterWatch (Subsidiary of: Jobson Medical Information LLC.), 100 N Washington St, Ste 301, Boston, MA 02114. TEL 617-948-5100, 866-219-3440, customerservice@centerwatch.com.

616.992 JPN ISSN 0915-5988
NIHON KOKU SHUYO GAKKAISHI/JAPAN SOCIETY FOR ORAL TUMORS. JOURNAL. Text in English, Japanese. 1983. s-a. **Document type:** *Journal, Academic/Scholarly.* **Description:** Covers all aspects of oral oncology.
Former titles (until 1989): Koku SHuyo Kenkyukaishi (0914-7799); (until 1987): Koku Shuyo Kenyukai Kiroku (0911-6516); (until 1986): Koku Shuyo Konwakai Kiroku (0911-6508)
Indexed: INIS AtomInd.
—**CCC.**
Published by: Nihon Koku Shuyo Gakkai/Japan Society for Oral Tumors, c/o Hitotsubashi-Insatsu Gakkai-Jimu Center, 2-4-11 Fukagawa, Koto-ku, Tokyo, 135-0033, Japan. TEL 81-3-56201953, FAX 81-3-56201960, http://www.jsot.org/.

616 USA ISSN 2152-1492

➤ **NORTHWESTERN UNIVERSITY. ROBERT H. LURIE COMPREHENSIVE CANCER CENTER. JOURNAL.** Text in English. 1977. s-a. free to members (effective 2010). bk.rev. charts; illus. index. back issues avail. **Document type:** *Journal, Academic/Scholarly.* **Description:** Covers topics of interest to members of the center; faculty and staff of Northwestern University; oncologists, nurses, clinicians and officials of cancer centers as well as programs throughout the U.S.
Former titles (until vol.2, no.2., 1991): Northwestern University Cancer Center. Journal (1049-6025); (until 1990): Cancer Focus (0147-1155)
Related titles: Online - full text ed.: free (effective 2010).
Published by: Northwestern University, Robert H. Lurie Comprehensive Cancer Center, 676 N St Clair, 21st Fl, Ste 1200, Chicago, IL 60611. TEL 312-908-5250, 866-587-4322, cancer@northwestern.edu. Ed. Dr. Steven T Rosen.

616.992 CZE ISSN 1801-870X
NOVARTIS ONCOLOGY NEWS. Text in Czech. 2006. q. **Document type:** *Journal, Trade.*
Published by: MedProGO, s.r.o., Anglicka 17, Prague 2, 12000, Czech Republic. TEL 420-2-22512649, FAX 420-2-24247568, contact@medprogo.cz.

616.994 POL ISSN 0029-540X
CODEN: NOWOAL

➤ **NOWOTWORY.** Text in Polish; Summaries in English. 1923. bi-m. EUR 15 foreign (effective 2005). adv. bk.rev. index. reprints avail. **Document type:** *Journal, Academic/Scholarly.* **Description:** Highlights oncology, radio-chemotherapy and surgery, cancer biology, epidemiology and control.
Indexed: A22, CIN, ChemAb, ChemTitl, DentInd, EMBASE, ExcerpMed, INIS AtomInd, IndMed, P30, R10, Reac, SCOPUS.
—BLDSC (6180.479000), CASDDS, GNLM, IE, Infotrieve, Ingenta.
Published by: Instytut Onkologii im. Marii Sklodowskiej-Curie, Centrum Onkologii/Maria Sklodowska-Curie Memorial Cancer Center and Institute of Oncology, ul Roentgena 5, Warsaw, 02781, Poland. TEL 48-22-4229900, FAX 48-22-4226680, http://www.onkologia.krakow.pl. Ed. Edward Towpik. Adv. contact Danuta Sadowska Osmycka. Circ: 1,200. **Co-sponsor:** Polskie Towarzystwo Onkologiczne/Polish Oncological Society.

➤ **NUTRITION AND CANCER**; an international journal. *see* NUTRITION AND DIETETICS

616.99 618.082 JPN ISSN 0911-2251
NYUGAN NO RINSHO/JAPANESE JOURNAL OF BREAST CANCER. Text in Japanese. 1986. bi-m. JPY 13,800 per issue (effective 2005). **Document type:** *Journal, Academic/Scholarly.*
Indexed: INIS AtomInd.
—BLDSC (4651.120000).
Published by: Shinohara-Shuppan Shinsha/Shinoharashinsha. Inc., 2-4-9 Yushima Bunkyo-ku, Tokyo, 113-0034, Japan. TEL 81-3-38165311, FAX 81-3-38165314, info@shinoharashinsha.co.jp.

616.9 610.73 USA ISSN 1935-1623
O N S CONNECT. Text in English. 1986. m. USD 29.99, USD 39.99 to individuals; free to members (effective 2010). adv. 16 p./no. 3 cols./p.; back issues avail. **Document type:** *Magazine, Trade.* **Description:** Contains news and information of interest to Oncology Nursing Society members and other oncology nursing professionals.
Formerly (until 2007): O N S News (0890-5215)
Related titles: Online - full text ed.
Indexed: A01, A02, A03, A08, A26, C06, C07, C08, C11, CA, CINAHL, EMBASE, ExcerpMed, H04, H12, I05, INI, MEDLINE, P20, P22, P24, P30, P34, P48, P54, PQC, R10, Reac, SCOPUS, T02.
—BLDSC (6261.494500), IE. **CCC.**
Published by: Oncology Nursing Society, 125 Enterprise Dr, Pittsburgh, PA 15275. TEL 412-859-6100, 866-257-4667, FAX 412-859-6163, 877-369-5497, customer.service@ons.org, http://www.ons.org. Ed. Debra M Wujcik. Pub. Leonard Mafrica. Adv. contact Anthony J Jannetti TEL 856-256-2300.

O N S FOUNDATION NEWS. (Oncology Nursing Society) *see* MEDICAL SCIENCES—Nurses And Nursing

616.992 615.842 FRA ISSN 2106-5055
OBSERVATOIRE NATIONAL DE LA RADIOTHERAPIE. Text in French. 2008. a. **Document type:** *Academic/Scholarly.*
Published by: Institut National du Cancer, 52 Av Andre Morizet, Boulogne-Billancourt, 92513 Cedex, France. TEL 33-1-41105000, contact@institutcancer.fr, http://www.e-cancer.fr.

616.994 JPN ISSN 0918-4538
CODEN: SKBZAA
OKAYAMA GEKA BYORI ZASSHI/OKAYAMA SURGICAL PATHOLOGY ASSOCIATION. JOURNAL. Text in Japanese; Summaries in English. 1953. irreg. USD 5,000 membership (effective 2007). adv. reprints avail. **Document type:** *Journal, Academic/Scholarly.*
Former titles (until 1991): Okayama Geka Byori Kenkyukai Zasshi (0916-2186); (until 1988): Saibokaku Byorigaku Zasshi/Journal of Karyopathology (0022-2119)
Indexed: IndMed.
—CASDDS.
Published by: Okayama Geka Byori Kenkyukai/Okayama Surgical Pathology Association, c/o Kawasaki Medical School, Department of Pathology, Matsushima 577, Kurashiki, 701-0192, Japan. http://homepage2.nifty.com/NOS/osp.html.

616.994 GBR ISSN 0950-9232
CODEN: ONCNES

➤ **ONCOGENE**; including Oncogene Reviews. Text in English. 1987. w. EUR 7,002 in Europe to institutions; USD 8,809 in the Americas to institutions; JPY 1,197,300 in Japan to institutions; GBP 4,518 to institutions in the UK & elsewhere (effective 2011). adv. bk.rev. charts; illus.; stat. index. back issues avail.; reprints avail. **Document type:** *Journal, Academic/Scholarly.* **Description:** Covers all aspects of the structure and function of oncogenes, especially cellular oncogenes and their mechanism of activation.
Related titles: Microfilm ed.: (from PQC); Online - full text ed.: ISSN 1476-5594.
Indexed: A01, A02, A03, A08, A22, A26, AIDS Ab, AIDS&CR, ASCA, B21, B25, B26, BIOBASE, BIOSIS Prev, C33, CA, ChemAb, ChemTitl, CurCont, E01, EMBASE, ExcerpMed, FoMM, GenetAb, H12, H13, HGA, I05, IABS, ISR, IndMed, Inpharma, MEDLINE, MycolAb, NucAcAb, OGFA, P10, P15, P20, P22, P30, P35, P48, P50, P52, P53, P54, P56, PQC, R10, Reac, S01, SAA, SCI, SCOPUS, T02, THA, Telegen, VirolAbstr, W07.
—BLDSC (6256.782000), CASDDS, GNLM, IE, Infotrieve, Ingenta, INIST. **CCC.**
Published by: Nature Publishing Group (Subsidiary of: Macmillan Publishers Ltd.), The MacMillan Bldg, 4 Crinan St, London, N1 9XW, United Kingdom. TEL 44-20-78334000, FAX 44-20-78334640. Ed. Douglas R Green. Adv. contact Ben Harkinson TEL 617-475-9222. **Subscr. to:** Brunel Rd, Houndmills, Basingstoke, Hamps RG21 6XS, United Kingdom. TEL 44-1256-329242, FAX 44-1256-812358, subscriptions@nature.com.

616.992 616.15 ROM ISSN 2066-8716

▼ **ONCOLOG-HEMATOLOG.RO.** Text in Romanian. 2009. q. ROL 90 (effective 2011). adv. **Document type:** *Magazine, Trade.*
Related titles: Online - full text ed.: ISSN 2066-8260. 2009.
Published by: Versa Puls Media, s.r.l., Calea Rahovei 266-268, corp 1, etaj 2, Bucharest, 050912, Romania. TEL 40-31-4254040, FAX 40-31-4254041, office@pulsmedia.ro. Ed. Dr. Roxana Pioaru. Adv. contact George Pavel. Circ: 1,000 (paid).

616.99 ECU ISSN 1390-0110
➤ **ONCOLOGIA.** Text in Spanish. 1993. q. USD 50 domestic to doctors; USD 150 foreign to doctors; USD 100 domestic to institutions; USD 200 foreign to institutions (effective 2005). adv. back issues avail. **Document type:** *Journal, Academic/Scholarly.* **Description:** Publishes original research and study cases on oncology.
Related titles: Online - full text ed.
Indexed: AMED, C01, INIS AtomInd, SCOPUS.
Published by: Sociedad de Lucha contra el Cancer, Ave Pedro Menendez Gilbert, Apartado 09-01, Guayaquil, Guayas 5255, Ecuador. TEL 593-4-281744, FAX 593-4-287151, revista@solca.med.ed, http://www.solca.med.ec/. Ed. Jaime Sanchez Sabando. R&P Juan Tanca Campozano TEL 593-4-288-088 ext. 128-208. Adv. contact Amado Freire Torres.

616.992 NLD ISSN 0929-8703
ONCOLOGICA. Text in Dutch. 1993. q. adv. **Document type:** *Journal, Academic/Scholarly.*
Indexed: A22, P30, SCOPUS.
Published by: Verpleegkundigen en Verzorgenden Nederland, Postbus 8212, Utrecht, 3503 RE, Netherlands. TEL 31-30-2919050, FAX 31-30-2919059, info@venvn.nl, http://www.venvn.nl. adv.: B&W page EUR 1,191, color page EUR 1,812; trim 215 x 285. Circ: 2,600.

616.99 FRA ISSN 1292-3818 CODEN: CIOCEO
➤ **ONCOLOGIE.** Text in French. 1992. 8/yr. EUR 405, USD 578 combined subscription to institutions (print & online eds.) (effective 2012). reprint service avail. from PSC. **Document type:** *Journal, Academic/Scholarly.* **Description:** Gives information on recent advances in cancer therapy to clinicians and all related personnel.
Formerly (until 1999): Cahiers d'Oncologie (0941-3804)
Related titles: Microform ed.; Online - full text ed.: ISSN 1765-2839 (from IngentaConnect).
Indexed: A01, A22, A26, CA, E01, EMBASE, ExcerpMed, I05, R10, Reac, SCI, SCOPUS, T02, W07.
—BLDSC (6256.887500), GNLM, IE, Ingenta, INIST. **CCC.**
Published by: Springer France (Subsidiary of: Springer Science+Business Media), 22 Rue de Palestro, Paris, 75002, France. TEL 33-1-53009860, FAX 33-1-53009861, sylvie.kamara@springer.com. Ed. Dr. Daniel Serin. Adv. contact Stephan Kroeck TEL 49-30-827875739. **Subscr. in Americas to:** Springer New York LLC, Journal Fulfillment, PO Box 2485, Secaucus, NJ 07096. TEL 800-777-4643, 201-348-4033, FAX 201-348-4505, journals-ny@springer.com, http://www.springer.com; **Subscr. to:** Springer Distribution Center, Kundenservice Zeitschriften, Haberstr 7, Heidelberg 69126, Germany. TEL 49-6221-3454303, FAX 49-6221-3454229, subscriptions@springer.com.

616.992 NLD ISSN 2211-1794
▼ **HET ONCOLOGIE FORMULARIUM.** Text in Dutch. 2010. a. EUR 35 (effective 2010).
Published by: Bohn Stafleu van Loghum B.V. (Subsidiary of: Springer Science+Business Media), Postbus 246, Houten, 3990 GA, Netherlands. TEL 31-30-6383872, FAX 31-30-6383991, boekhandels@bsl.nl, http://www.bsl.nl.

616.992 NLD ISSN 1874-1827
ONCOLOGIE MAGAZINE. Text in Dutch. 2005. q. adv.
Formerly (until 2006): Script Oncologie (1871-0484)
Published by: Van Zuiden Communications B.V., Postbus 2122, Alphen aan den Rijn, 2400 CC, Netherlands. TEL 31-172-476191, FAX 31-172-471882, zuiden@zuidencomm.nl, http://www.zuidencomm.nl.

616.992 NLD ISSN 1874-7140
ONCOLOGISCH. Text in Dutch. 1988. q.
Former titles (until 2002): Regionaal Oncologisch Informatiebulletin voor Verpleegkundigen en Dietisten (1874-7116); (until 1999): Oncologisch Informatiebulletin voor Verpleegkundigen en Dietisten (1383-8806); (until 1995): I K Z Integraal (0922-0798)
Published by: Integraal Kankercentrum Zuid, Postbus 231, Eindhoven, 5600 AE, Netherlands. TEL 31-40-2971616, FAX 31-40-2971610.

616.99 616.15 USA ISSN 1083-7159 CODEN: OCOLF6
➤ **THE ONCOLOGIST.** Text in English. 1996. m. USD 450 to institutions; USD 245 combined subscription to individuals (print & online eds.) (effective 2010). adv. bk.rev. abstr. back issues avail.; reprints avail. **Document type:** *Journal, Academic/Scholarly.* **Description:** Designed for the practicing oncologist and hematologist. Reports on the multimodality diagnosis and treatment of the cancer patient.
Related titles: Online - full text ed.: ISSN 1549-490X. USD 145 to individuals (effective 2010).
Indexed: B21, BiolDig, C06, C07, C08, CA, CINAHL, CurCont, EMBASE, ExcerpMed, INI, IndMed, Inpharma, MEDLINE, OGFA, P30, P35, R10, Reac, S02, S03, SCI, SCOPUS, SWR&A, T02, W07.
—BLDSC (6256.890000), CASDDS, GNLM, IE, Infotrieve, Ingenta, INIST. **CCC.**
Published by: AlphaMed Press, Inc., 318 Blackwell St, Ste 260, Durham, NC 27701. TEL 919-680-0011, FAX 919-680-4411, alphamedpress@alphamedpress.com, http://www.alphamedpress.org/. Ed. Bruce A Chabner. Circ: 15,263. **Subscr. to:** Cambey & West Inc, PO Box 412, Congers, NY 10920. TEL 845-267-3079, FAX 845-267-3478, http://ful.cambeywest.com.

616.992 USA ISSN 2159-8401
▼ **THE ONCOLOGIST (EUROPEAN EDITION).** Text in English. 2011. m. **Document type:** *Journal, Trade.*
Published by: AlphaMed Press, Inc., 318 Blackwell St, Ste 260, Durham, NC 27701. TEL 919-680-0011, FAX 919-680-4411, alphamedpress@alphamedpress.com, http://www.alphamedpress.org/.

616.99 USA ISSN 0890-9091
RC254.A1 CODEN: OCLGE9
➤ **ONCOLOGY.** Text in English. 1987. m. free to qualified personnel (effective 2010). adv. bk.rev. cum.index. back issues avail. **Document type:** *Journal, Academic/Scholarly.* **Description:** Publishes articles reviewing recent trends in the clinical practice of oncology, original research or results of trials having clinical relevance.
Related titles: Online - full text ed.; Supplement(s): A Supplement to Oncology.
Indexed: A22, A26, AMED, C06, C07, C08, CA, CINAHL, CurCont, E08, EMBASE, ExcerpMed, G08, H11, H12, I05, INI, ISR, IndMed, Inpharma, MEDLINE, P20, P22, P24, P30, P48, P50, P54, PQC, R10, Reac, S09, SCI, SCOPUS, T02, W07.
—BLDSC (6256.930000), GNLM, IE, Infotrieve, Ingenta, INIST. **CCC.**
Published by: C M P Medica LLC, The Oncology Group (Subsidiary of: C M P Medica LLC), 535 Connecticut Ave, Ste 300, Norwalk, CT 06854. TEL 203-523-7000.

616.994 CHE ISSN 0030-2414
RC261 CODEN: ONCOBS
➤ **ONCOLOGY;** international journal of cancer research and treatment. Text in English. 1948. 12/yr. CHF 3,192, EUR 2,550, USD 3,141 to institutions; CHF 3,502, EUR 2,798, USD 3,441 combined subscription to institutions (print & online eds.) (effective 2012). adv. bk.rev. abstr.; bibl.; charts; illus. index. back issues avail. **Document type:** *Journal, Academic/Scholarly.* **Description:** Works to accelerate the adaptation of experimental results to the clinic.
Formerly (until 1966): Oncologia (0369-7606)
Related titles: Microform ed.; Online - full text ed.: ISSN 1423-0232. CHF 3,090, EUR 2,472, USD 3,000 to institutions (effective 2012).
Indexed: A01, A03, A08, A22, B21, B25, BIOSIS Prev, CA, CIN, ChemAb, ChemTitl, CurCont, DentInd, E01, EMBASE, ESPM, ExcerpMed, FR, H13, ISR, ImmunAb, IndMed, Inpharma, MEDLINE, MS&D, MycolAb, NRN, NSA, P02, P10, P19, P20, P22, P24, P30, P35, P48, P50, P53, P54, PQC, R10, Reac, SCI, SCOPUS, T02, Telegen, W07.
—BLDSC (6256.900000), CASDDS, GNLM, IE, Infotrieve, Ingenta, INIST. **CCC.**
Published by: S. Karger AG, Allschwilerstr 10, Basel, 4055, Switzerland. TEL 41-61-3061111, FAX 41-61-3061234, karger@karger.ch, http://www.karger.ch. Ed. M Markman. adv.: page CHF 1,730; trim 210 x 280. Circ: 1,300.

616.992 USA ISSN 2154-4581
▼ **ONCOLOGY (GLENDALE).** Text in English. 2010 (June). s-m. USD 399.89 domestic; USD 431.72 in Canada; USD 479.72 elsewhere (effective 2011). **Document type:** *Trade.*
Media: Audio CD. **Related titles:** Online - full text ed.: USD 359.72 (effective 2011).
Published by: Audio-Digest Foundation, 1577 E Chevy Chase Dr, Glendale, CA 91206. TEL 818-240-7500, FAX 818-240-7379, marmstrong@audiodigest.org, http://www.audio-digest.org.

616.99 USA
ONCOLOGY & BIOTECHNOLOGY NEWS. Text in English. 1987. m. USD 95 (effective 2009). **Document type:** *Magazine, Trade.* **Description:** Global coverage of cancer and related biotechnical topics.
Related titles: Online - full text ed.
Indexed: Telegen.
Published by: Intellisphere, LLC (Subsidiary of: MultiMedia Healthcare Inc.), Office Center at Princeton Meadows, 666 Plainsboro Rd, Bldg 300, Plainsboro, NJ 08536. TEL 609-716-7777, FAX 609-716-4747. Circ: 40,000.

ONCOLOGY & HEMATOLOGY CODING ALERT; the practical monthly adviser for ethically optimizing coding, reimbursement and efficiency in oncology and hematology practices. *see* INSURANCE

616.992 330 USA ISSN 1552-5635
ONCOLOGY BUSINESS WEEK. Text in English. 2004. w. USD 2,295 in US & Canada; USD 2,495 elsewhere; USD 2,525 combined subscription in US & Canada (print & online eds.); USD 2,755 combined subscription elsewhere (print & online eds.) (effective 2008). back issues avail. **Document type:** *Newsletter, Trade.* **Description:** Provides the biotech or pharma company executive with the latest news on new cancer drug development, as well as genetic and genomic discoveries, together with the business news of the companies active in the cancer treatment field: mergers, acquisitions, joint ventures, fiscal reports, new patents, regulatory announcements and new research targets.
Related titles: E-mail ed.; Online - full text ed.: ISSN 1552-5643. USD 2,295 combined subscription (online & email eds.); single user (effective 2008).
Indexed: A15, ABIn, B16, H13, P10, P20, P21, P48, P51, P53, P54, PQC.
Published by: NewsRx, 2727 Paces Ferry Rd SE, Ste 2-440, Atlanta, GA 30339. TEL 770-435-8286, 800-726-4550, FAX 770-435-6800, pressrelease@newsrx.com. Pub. Susan Hasty TEL 770-507-7777.

616.992 CAN ISSN 1705-2394
➤ **ONCOLOGY EXCHANGE;** essential reading in multidisciplinary cancer care. Text in English. 2002. q. CAD 32 domestic; CAD 90 in United States; CAD 112 elsewhere (effective 2011). adv. back issues avail. **Document type:** *Journal, Academic/Scholarly.*
Related titles: Online - full text ed.: ISSN 1925-7155. free (effective 2011).
Indexed: A01.
Published by: Parkhurst Publishing, 400 McGill St, 3rd Fl, Montreal, PQ H2Y 2G1, Canada. TEL 514-397-8833, FAX 514-397-0228, contact@parkpub.com, http://www.parkpub.com. Ed. Devon Phillips TEL 514-397-8833 ext 210. Pub. David Elkins. Adv. contact Debra Makuch TEL 514-397-8833 ext 117. Circ: 4,958.

616.99 USA ISSN 1046-3356
ONCOLOGY ISSUES. Text in English. 1986. bi-m. USD 20 to individuals; USD 40 to corporations (effective 2001). adv. back issues avail. **Document type:** *Journal, Trade.* **Description:** Provides economic, health policy and planning information to United States cancer programs.
Related titles: Online - full text ed.
—BLDSC (6256.972000), IE, Ingenta. **CCC.**
Published by: Association of Community Cancer Centers, 11600 Nebel St, Ste 201, Rockville, MD 20852-2557. TEL 301-984-9496, FAX 301-770-1949, http://www.accc-cancer.org/main2001.shtml. Adv. contact Mal Milburn TEL 301-984-9496. Circ: 17,000.

616.992 GRC ISSN 1792-1074
▼ **ONCOLOGY LETTERS.** Text in English. 2010. bi-m. **Document type:** *Journal, Trade.*
Related titles: Online - full text ed.: ISSN 1792-1082.
—**CCC.**
Published by: Spandidos Publications, PO Box 18179, Athens, 116 10, Greece. TEL 30-210-7227809, FAX 30-210-7252922, contact@spandidos-publications.com, http://www.spandidos-publications.com.

616.99 USA
ONCOLOGY NET GUIDE; internet guide to cancer sites. Text in English. 2000. m. USD 95; free to qualified personnel (effective 2009). back issues avail. **Document type:** *Handbook/Manual/Guide, Trade.* **Description:** Reviews, describes and compiles online resources for oncologists.
Related titles: ◆ E-mail ed.: Oncology Net Guide eNewsletter; Online - full content ed.: 2000. free (effective 2009).
Published by: Intellisphere, LLC (Subsidiary of: MultiMedia Healthcare Inc.), Office Center at Princeton Meadows, 666 Plainsboro Rd, Bldg 300, Plainsboro, NJ 08536. TEL 609-716-7777, FAX 609-716-4747, info@mdnetguide.com, http://www.hcplive.com. Ed. Mary Jardem.

616.99 USA
ONCOLOGY NET GUIDE ENEWSLETTER. Text in English. 2000. bi-m. **Document type:** *Newsletter, Trade.* **Description:** Provides information on headlines, upcoming events, and special promotions related to oncology.
Media: E-mail. **Related titles:** Online - full content ed.: 2000. free (effective 2009); ◆ Print ed.: Oncology Net Guide.
Published by: Intellisphere, LLC (Subsidiary of: MultiMedia Healthcare Inc.), Office Center at Princeton Meadows, 666 Plainsboro Rd, Bldg 300, Plainsboro, NJ 08536. TEL 609-716-7777, FAX 609-716-4747, info@mdnetguide.com, http://www.hcplive.com. Ed. Mary Jardem.

616.992 ITA ISSN 2039-0963
▼ **ONCOLOGY NEWS.** Text in Italian. 2010. s-a. **Document type:** *Journal, Trade.*
Published by: Wolters Kluwer Health Italy (Subsidiary of: Wolters Kluwer N.V.), Via B Lanino 5, Milan, 20144, Italy. http://www.wkhealth.it.

616.99 USA ISSN 1065-2957
ONCOLOGY NEWS INTERNATIONAL. Text in English. 1992. m. free to qualified personnel (effective 2010). adv. back issues avail. **Document type:** *Newspaper, Trade.* **Description:** Publishes timely reports on news and developments from around the world in all areas of interest to the cancer specialist.
Related titles: Online - full text ed.; Supplement(s): A Supplement to Oncology News International.
Indexed: A26, C06, C07, C08, CA, CINAHL, G08, H11, H12, I05.
—**CCC.**
Published by: C M P Medica LLC, The Oncology Group (Subsidiary of: C M P Medica LLC), 535 Connecticut Ave, Ste 300, Norwalk, CT 06854. TEL 203-523-7000.

616.992 NLD ISSN 1875-3795
ONCOLOGY NEWS INTERNATIONAL. Text in Dutch. 2007. bi-m. EUR 58 (effective 2008). adv.
Published by: C M P Medica Netherlands BV, Hogehilweg 8f, Amsterdam, 1101 CC, Netherlands. TEL 31-20-3123120, FAX 31-20-3123121. Eds. Dr. V Oppedijk, Dr. L M Bonapart. Pub. P A de l'Orme. Circ: 4,000.

THE ONCOLOGY NURSE. *see* MEDICAL SCIENCES—Nurses And Nursing

▼ **ONCOLOGY NURSE ADVISOR.** *see* MEDICAL SCIENCES—Nurses And Nursing

ONCOLOGY NURSING FORUM. *see* MEDICAL SCIENCES—Nurses And Nursing

ONCOLOGY NURSING NEWS. *see* MEDICAL SCIENCES—Nurses And Nursing

616.992 613.2 USA ISSN 1545-9896
ONCOLOGY NUTRITION CONNECTION. Text in English. 199?. q. USD 35 to individuals; USD 50 to institutions (effective 2009). **Document type:** *Newsletter.*
Formerly (until 2003): On-Line (1087-4364)
Indexed: C06, C07, C08, CINAHL.
—BLDSC (6256.982000), IE. **CCC.**
Published by: American Diatetic Association, Oncology Nutrition Dietetic Practice Group, c/o Marianne Grandon, 2075 Thornhill Dr, Akron, OH 44313. TEL 330-867-1264. Ed. Marianne Grandon.

THE ONCOLOGY PHARMACIST. *see* PHARMACY AND PHARMACOLOGY

616.992 USA ISSN 1548-5323
THE ONCOLOGY REPORT. Abbreviated title: T O R. Text in English. 2004 (Fall). bi-m. USD 150 domestic; USD 200 foreign; free to qualified personnel (effective 2010). adv. back issues avail. **Document type:** *Journal, Academic/Scholarly.* **Description:** Provides reports and commentary on the advances in cancer treatment from the oncology meetings.
Related titles: Online - full text ed.: free (effective 2010).
Indexed: EMBASE, ExcerpMed, R10, Reac, SCOPUS.
—BLDSC (6256.983200). **CCC.**
Published by: Elsevier Oncology (Subsidiary of: International Medical News Group), 60 Columbia Rd, Bldg B, Morristown, NJ 07960. TEL 973-290-8200, FAX 631-424-8905, L.Kalish@Elsevier.com, http://www.elsevieroncology.com/. Ed. Howard A Burris III. Pub. Dan H Kim TEL 973-630-2039. Circ: 14,350.

616.99 GRC ISSN 1021-335X
RC254.A1 CODEN: OCRPEW
➤ **ONCOLOGY REPORTS;** an international journal devoted to fundamental and applied research in oncology. Text in English. 1994. bi-m. adv. bk.rev. index. **Document type:** *Journal, Academic/Scholarly.* **Description:** Covers the spectrum of cancer research; aimed at a multidisciplinary readership.
Related titles: Online - full text ed.: ISSN 1791-2431.
Indexed: ASCA, B21, B25, BIOSIS Prev, CTA, ChemAb, ChemTitl, CurCont, EMBASE, ExcerpMed, GenetAb, ISR, ImmunAb, IndMed, Inpharma, MEDLINE, MycolAb, NSA, NucAcAb, OGFA, P30, P35, R10, Reac, SCI, SCOPUS, W07.
—BLDSC (6256.983350), CASDDS, GNLM, IE, Ingenta, INIST. **CCC.**
Published by: Spandidos Publications, PO Box 18179, Athens, 116 10, Greece. TEL 30-210-7227809, FAX 30-210-7252922, contact@spandidos-publications.com, http://www.spandidos-publications.com.

616.99 USA ISSN 0965-0407
RC261.A1 CODEN: ONREE8
➤ **ONCOLOGY RESEARCH;** featuring preclinical and clincal cancer therapeutics. Text in English. 1989. m. USD 1,225 combined subscription to institutions (print & online eds.) (effective 2011). back issues avail. **Document type:** *Journal, Academic/Scholarly.* **Description:** Rapid dissemination journal for full research papers and short communications contributing to the understanding of cancer in areas of molecular biology, cell biology, biochemistry, biophysics, genetics, virology, endocrinology and immunology.
Incorporates: Anti-Cancer Drug Design (0266-9536); Formerly (until 1992): Cancer Communications (0955-3541)
Related titles: Microfilm ed.: (from PQC); Online - full text ed.: ISSN 1555-3906. USD 1,100 (effective 2011) (from IngentaConnect).

Indexed: A22, ASCA, B&BAb, B21, B25, BIOBASE, BIOSIS Prev, CIN, ChemAb, ChemTitl, CurCont, EMBASE, ExcerpMed, GenetAb, IABS, ISR, IndMed, Inpharma, MEDLINE, MycolAb, NSA, P30, P35, R10, Reac, SCI, SCOPUS, W07.
—BLDSC (6256.983400), CASDDS, GNLM, IE, Infotrieve, Ingenta, INIST. **CCC.**
Published by: Cognizant Communication Corp., 18 Peeksill Hollow Rd, P O Box 37, Putnam Valley, NY 10579. TEL 845-603-6440, FAX 845-603-6442, cogcomm@aol.com. Eds. Alan C Sartorelli, Edward Chu. Pub. Robert N Miranda.

616.992 ITA ISSN 1970-5557
ONCOLOGY REVIEWS. Text in English. 2007. 4/yr. EUR 295, USD 359 combined subscription to institutions (print & online eds.) (effective 2011). reprint service avail. from PSC. **Document type:** *Journal, Academic/Scholarly.*
Related titles: Online - full text ed.: ISSN 1970-5565. 2007 (from IngentaConnect).
Indexed: A22, A26, E01, E08, EMBASE, ExcerpMed, H12, S09, SCOPUS.
—IE. **CCC.**
Published by: Springer Italia Srl (Subsidiary of: Springer Science+Business Media), Via Decembrio 28, Milan, 20137, Italy. TEL 39-02-54259722, FAX 39-02-55193360, springer@springer.it. Ed. C Porta.

616.99 USA ISSN 0276-2234
ONCOLOGY TIMES; the news center for the cancer care team. Text in English. 1979. s-m. USD 440 domestic to institutions; USD 558 foreign to institutions (effective 2011). adv. bk.rev. index. 64 p./no. 4 cols./p.; back issues avail.; reprints avail. **Document type:** *Journal, Academic/Scholarly.* **Description:** Covers all aspects of the diagnosis, treatment, and care of the cancer patient.
Related titles: Online - full text ed.: ISSN 1548-4688.
Indexed: A22, Agr, BiolDig, C06, C07, C08, CINAHL.
—IE. **CCC.**
Published by: Lippincott Williams & Wilkins (Subsidiary of: Wolters Kluwer N.V.), 333 7th Ave, 19th Fl, New York, NY 10001. TEL 646-674-6529, FAX 646-674-6500, customerservice@lww.com, http://www.lww.com. Ed. Robert C Young. Pub. David Myers. Adv. contact Frank Cox TEL 212-685-5010. Circ: 39,000.

616.99 GBR ISSN 1742-8009
ONCOLOGY TIMES (U.K. EDITION). Text in English. 2004. m. USD 177 domestic to institutions; USD 177 foreign to institutions (effective 2011). adv. back issues avail. **Document type:** *Journal, Academic/Scholarly.* **Description:** Provides news, information and commentary for cancer physicians.
—CCC.
Published by: Lippincott Williams & Wilkins, Ltd., 250 Waterloo Rd, London, SE1 8RD, United Kingdom. TEL 44-20-79810600, FAX 44-20-79810601, customerservice@lww.com. Eds. Gordon McVie, Mary Fogarty.

616.992 FRA ISSN 1950-2184
➤ **ONCOMAGAZINE.** Text in French. 2007. q. EUR 121, USD 145 combined subscription to institutions (print & online eds.) (effective 2011). reprint service avail. from PSC. **Document type:** *Journal, Academic/Scholarly.*
Related titles: Online - full text ed.: ISSN 1954-345X (from IngentaConnect).
—IE. **CCC.**
Published by: Springer France (Subsidiary of: Springer Science+Business Media), 22 Rue de Palestro, Paris, 75002, France. TEL 33-1-53009860, FAX 33-1-53009861, sylvie.kamara@springer.com. Ed. Dr. Daniel Serin.

616.992 USA ISSN 1949-2553
▼ ➤ **ONCOTARGET.** Text in English. 2010 (May). m. **Document type:** *Journal, Academic/Scholarly.* **Description:** Focuses on medical research related to atherosclerosis, hyperotrophic organ diseases, cancer, benign tumors, metabolic and other diseases.
Media: Online - full content.
Indexed: P30.
Published by: Impact Journals LLC, 6211 Tipton House, Ste 6, Albany, NY 12203. TEL 518-456-5316, publisher@impactjournals.com, http://impactjournals.com/.

616.992 GBR ISSN 1178-6930
➤ **ONCOTARGETS AND THERAPY.** Text in English. 2008. irreg. free (effective 2011). **Document type:** *Journal, Academic/Scholarly.* **Description:** Focuses on the pathological basis of all cancers, potential targets for therapy and treatment protocols employed to improve the management of cancer patients.
Media: Online - full text.
Indexed: B25, B26, BIOSIS Prev, EMBASE, ExcerpMed, P30, SCI, SCOPUS, W07.
—CCC.
Published by: Dove Medical Press Ltd., Beechfield House, Winterton Way, Macclesfield, SK11 0JL, United Kingdom. TEL 44-1625-509130, FAX 44-1625-617933. Ed. Hans-Joachim Schmoll.

616.992 SVK ISSN 1337-6950
ONKO MAGAZIN. Text in Slovak. 2007. q. **Document type:** *Magazine, Trade.*
Published by: MedMedia, s.r.o. herda@medmedia.sk. Ed. Tibor Mrocek.

616.994 FRA ISSN 2101-9495
▼ **ONKO +.** Text in French. 2009. m. (10/yr). **Document type:** *Journal, Trade.*
Published by: Expressions Groupe, 2 Rue de la Roquette, Cour de Mai, Paris, 75011, France. TEL 33-1-49292929, FAX 33-1-49292919, contact@expressions-sante.fr.

616.99 DEU ISSN 0947-8965
RD651
➤ **DER ONKOLOGE.** Text in German. 1995. m. EUR 346, USD 347 combined subscription to institutions (print & online eds.) (effective 2012). adv. back issues avail.; reprint service avail. from PSC. **Document type:** *Journal, Academic/Scholarly.*
Related titles: Online - full text ed.: ISSN 1433-0415 (from IngentaConnect).
Indexed: A22, A26, E01, EMBASE, ExcerpMed, I05, R10, Reac, SCI, SCOPUS, W07.
—BLDSC (6260.580000), GNLM, IE, Infotrieve, Ingenta. **CCC.**
Published by: (Deutsche Krebsgesellschaft e.V.), Springer (Subsidiary of: Springer Science+Business Media), Tiergartenstr 17, Heidelberg, 69121, Germany. TEL 49-6221-4870, FAX 49-6221-345229. Eds. Dr. Klaus Hoeffken, Dr. M Bamberg, Dr. P M Schlag. Adv. contact Stephan Kroeck TEL 49-30-827875739. B&W page EUR 1,840, color page EUR 3,030. Circ: 3,300 (paid and controlled). **Subscr. in the Americas to:** Springer New York LLC, Journal Fulfillment, PO Box 2485, Secaucus, NJ 07096. TEL 800-777-4643, 201-348-4033, FAX 201-348-4505, journals-ny@springer.com, http://www.springer.com; **Subscr. to:** Springer Distribution Center, Kundenservice Zeitschriften, Haberstr 7, Heidelberg 69126, Germany. TEL 49-6221-3454303, FAX 49-6221-3454229, subscriptions@springer.com.

616.992 SVK ISSN 1336-8176
➤ **ONKOLOGIA.** Text in Slovak. 2006. bi-m. EUR 18 (effective 2010). **Document type:** *Journal, Academic/Scholarly.*
Published by: Solen, s.r.o., Uprkova 23, Bratislava, 811 04, Slovakia. TEL 421-2-54650649, FAX 421-2-54651384, solen@solen.sk. Ed. Kamila Hudakova TEL 421-2-54131381.

616.992 POL ISSN 1505-6732
ONKOLOGIA POLSKA. Text in Polish. 1998. q. EUR 55 foreign (effective 2005). **Document type:** *Journal, Academic/Scholarly.*
Indexed: A22, BIOBASE, EMBASE, ExcerpMed, IABS, R10, Reac, SCOPUS.
—BLDSC (6260.600000), IE, Ingenta.
Published by: (Akademia Medyczna, Katedra Onkologii, Klinika Chemioterapii), Wydawnictwo Almamedia, ul Budowlanych 50, lok 24, Opole, 45124, Poland. TEL 48-77-4428905, FAX 48-77-4428906, biuro@almamedia.com.pl. Ed. Anna Pluzanska. **Dist. by:** Ars Polona, Obroncow 25, Warsaw 03933, Poland. TEL 48-22-5098609, FAX 48-22-5098610, arspolona@arspolona.com.pl, http://www.arspolona.com.pl.

616.992 POL ISSN 1734-3542
➤ **ONKOLOGIA W PRAKTYCE KLINICZNEJ.** Text in Polish, English. 2005. q. EUR 71 to individuals; EUR 104 to institutions (effective 2011). **Document type:** *Journal, Academic/Scholarly.* **Description:** Focuses mainly on education and is adressed to specialists in any branch of oncology and primary care physicians.
Related titles: Online - full text ed.: ISSN 1734-6460.
—BLDSC (6260.610000).
Published by: (Polskie Towarzystwo Onkologii Klinicznej), Wydawnictwo Via Medica, ul Swietokrzyska 73, Gdansk, 80180, Poland. TEL 48-58-3209494, FAX 48-58-3209460, redakcja@viamedica.pl, http://www.viamedica.pl. Ed. Marek Pawlicki.

616 CHE ISSN 0378-584X
RC254.A1 CODEN: ONKOD2
➤ **ONKOLOGIE**; international journal for cancer research and treatment. Text in English, German. 10/yr. CHF 452, EUR 283, USD 497.50 to institutions; CHF 524, EUR 333, USD 572.50 combined subscription to institutions (print & online eds.) (effective 2012). adv. illus. index. back issues avail. **Document type:** *Journal, Academic/Scholarly.*
Formerly (until 1978): Oesterreichische Zeitschrift fuer Onkologie (0377-2004)
Related titles: Microform ed.: (from PQC); Online - full text ed.: ISSN 1423-0240. CHF 367, EUR 253, USD 380 to institutions (effective 2012).
Indexed: A20, A22, ASCA, B21, B25, BIOSIS Prev, CurCont, DentInd, E01, EMBASE, ExcerpMed, IBR, IBZ, ISR, IndMed, Inpharma, MEDLINE, MycolAb, NSA, P30, P35, R10, Reac, RefZh, SCI, SCOPUS, W07.
—BLDSC (6260.650000), CASDDS, GNLM, IE, Infotrieve, Ingenta, INIST. **CCC.**
Published by: (Deutsche und Oesterreichische Gesellschaft fuer Haematologie und Onkologie), S. Karger AG, Allschwilerstr 10, Basel, 4055, Switzerland. TEL 41-61-3061111, FAX 41-61-3061234, karger@karger.ch, http://www.karger.ch. Ed. H.-J. Schmoll. adv.: B&W page EUR 3,100; trim 210 x 297. Circ: 5,000 (paid).
Co-sponsor: Oesterreichische Krebsgesellschaft-Krebsliga.

616.992 CZE ISSN 1802-4475
➤ **ONKOLOGIE.** Text in Czech. 2007. bi-m. CZK 480; CZK 80 per issue (effective 2010). **Document type:** *Journal, Academic/Scholarly.*
Related titles: Online - full text ed.: ISSN 1803-5345.
Published by: Solen s.r.o., Lazecka 297/51, Olomouc 51, 779 00, Czech Republic. TEL 420-582-396038, FAX 420-582-396099, solen@solen.cz, http://www.solen.cz. Ed. Eva Dokoupilova. Circ: 1,300.

616.99 AUT ISSN 1436-1280
➤ **ONKOLOGIE HEUTE.** Text in German. 1999. irreg., latest 2001. price varies. **Document type:** *Monographic series, Academic/Scholarly.*
Published by: Springer Wien (Subsidiary of: Springer Science+Business Media), Sachsenplatz 4-6, Vienna, W 1201, Austria. TEL 43-1-3302415-0, FAX 43-1-330242665, books@springer.at, http://www.springer.at. Eds. C Zielinski, R Jakesz. R&P Angela Foessl TEL 43-1-3302415517. **Subscr. to:** Springer New York LLC, 233 Spring St, New York, NY 10013. TEL 800-777-4643, FAX 201-348-4505.

616.99 AUT
ONKOLOGIE IN DER PRAXIS. Text in German. 4/yr. **Document type:** *Journal, Trade.* **Description:** Covers all aspects of cancer detection, treatment and research.
Published by: Aerzte Woche Zeitungsverlagsgesellschaft mbH (Subsidiary of: Springer Science+Business Media), Sachsenplatz 4-6, Postfach 33, Vienna, 1201, Austria. TEL 43-1-5131047, FAX 43-1-5134783. Ed. Dr. Monika Steinmassl-Wirrer.

616.992 SVN ISSN 1408-1741
ONKOLOGIJA. Text in Slovenian. 1997. s-a. free to qualified personnel (effective 2006). **Document type:** *Journal, Academic/Scholarly.* **Description:** Covers various theoretical and practical aspects of oncology, with a particular emphasis on the primary and secondary cancer prevention, early detection, treatment, rehabilitation and palliative care in oncological patients.
Related titles: Online - full content ed.: ISSN 1581-3215. 2000.
Published by: Onkoloski Institut Ljubljana/Institute of Oncology Ljubljana, Zaloska 2, Ljubljana, 1000, Slovenia. TEL 386-1-4314225, FAX 386-1-4314180, mzakelj@onko-i.si.

616.9 UKR ISSN 1562-1774
ONKOLOGIYA. Text in Russian, Ukrainian; Abstracts in English; Summaries in English. q. **Document type:** *Journal, Academic/Scholarly.*
Related titles: Online - full text ed.
—East View.
Published by: (Natsional'na Akademiya Nauk Ukrainy, Instytut Eksperymental'noi Patolohii, Onkolohii i Radiobiolohii im. R.E. Kavets'koho), Morion LLC, pr-kt M Bazhana, 10A, Kyiv, 02140, Ukraine. public@morion.kiev.ua, http://www.morion.kiev.ua. Ed. V F Chekhun.

616.992 DEU ISSN 1866-5861
➤ **ONKOPIPELINE.** Text in German. 2008. q. EUR 139.25, USD 209 combined subscription to institutions (print & online eds.) (effective 2010). adv. reprint service avail. from PSC. **Document type:** *Journal, Academic/Scholarly.*
Related titles: Online - full text ed.: ISSN 1866-587X. 2008.
Indexed: A22, E01.
—IE. **CCC.**
Published by: Urban und Vogel Medien und Medizin Verlagsgesellschaft mbH (Subsidiary of: Springer Science+Business Media), Neumarkter Str 43, Munich, 81673, Germany. TEL 49-89-4372-1411, FAX 49-89-4372-1410, verlag@urban-vogel.de. Ed. Heidrun Guthoehrlein. Adv. contact Renate Senfft. B&W page EUR 2,125, color page EUR 3,325; trim 174 x 247. Circ: 3,500 (paid).

616.992 NLD ISSN 1876-8172
▼ **THE OPEN BREAST CANCER JOURNAL.** Text in English. 2009. irreg. free (effective 2011). **Document type:** *Journal, Academic/Scholarly.*
Media: Online - full text.
Indexed: OGFA.
Published by: Bentham Open (Subsidiary of: Bentham Science Publishers Ltd.), PO Box 294, Bussum, AG 1400, Netherlands. TEL 31-35-6923800, FAX 31-35-6980150, subscriptions@bentham.org.

616.994 NLD ISSN 1876-4010
RC268.3
➤ **THE OPEN CANCER IMMUNOLOGY JOURNAL.** Text in English. 2008. irreg. free (effective 2011). **Document type:** *Journal, Academic/Scholarly.*
Media: Online - full text.
Indexed: SCOPUS.
Published by: Bentham Open (Subsidiary of: Bentham Science Publishers Ltd.), PO Box 294, Bussum, AG 1400, Netherlands. TEL 31-35-6923800, FAX 31-35-6980150, subscriptions@bentham.org.

616.992 NLD ISSN 1874-0790
RC261.A1
➤ **THE OPEN CANCER JOURNAL.** Text in English. 2007. irreg. free (effective 2011). **Document type:** *Journal, Academic/Scholarly.*
Media: Online - full text.
Indexed: A01, EMBASE, ExcerpMed, NSA, P30, SCOPUS.
Published by: Bentham Open (Subsidiary of: Bentham Science Publishers Ltd.), PO Box 294, Bussum, AG 1400, Netherlands. TEL 31-35-6923800, FAX 31-35-6980150, subscriptions@bentham.org. Ed. William E Carson.

616.992 NLD ISSN 1874-1894
RC267
➤ **THE OPEN CLINICAL CANCER JOURNAL.** Text in English. 2007. irreg. free (effective 2011). **Document type:** *Journal, Academic/Scholarly.*
Media: Online - full text.
Indexed: A01, CTA, EMBASE, ExcerpMed, NSA, P30, SCOPUS.
Published by: Bentham Open (Subsidiary of: Bentham Science Publishers Ltd.), PO Box 294, Bussum, AG 1400, Netherlands. TEL 31-35-6923800, FAX 31-35-6980150, subscriptions@bentham.org.

616.992 NLD ISSN 1876-8202
RC280.C6
▼ **THE OPEN COLORECTAL CANCER JOURNAL.** Text in English. 2009. irreg. free (effective 2011). **Document type:** *Journal, Academic/Scholarly.* **Description:** Covers all aspects of basic and clinical colorectal cancer research including therapy and surgery.
Media: Online - full text.
Indexed: A01, OGFA.
Published by: Bentham Open (Subsidiary of: Bentham Science Publishers Ltd.), PO Box 294, Bussum, AG 1400, Netherlands. TEL 31-35-6923800, FAX 31-35-6980150, subscriptions@bentham.org. Ed. Andrew P Zbar.

616.992 NLD ISSN 1876-8164
▼ **THE OPEN LEUKEMIA JOURNAL.** Text in English. 2010. irreg. free (effective 2011). **Document type:** *Journal, Academic/Scholarly.*
Media: Online - full text.
Published by: Bentham Open (Subsidiary of: Bentham Science Publishers Ltd.), PO Box 294, Bussum, AG 1400, Netherlands. TEL 31-35-6923800, FAX 31-35-6980150, subscriptions@bentham.org. Ed. Donna Hogge.

616.994 616.2 NLD ISSN 1876-8199
➤ **THE OPEN LUNG CANCER JOURNAL.** Text in English. 2008. irreg. free (effective 2011). **Document type:** *Journal, Academic/Scholarly.* **Description:** Covers all aspects of basic and clinical lung cancer research including therapy and surgery.
Media: Online - full text.
Indexed: A01, OGFA.
Published by: Bentham Open (Subsidiary of: Bentham Science Publishers Ltd.), PO Box 294, Bussum, AG 1400, Netherlands. TEL 31-35-6923800, FAX 31-35-6980150, subscriptions@bentham.org, http://www.bentham.org. Ed. G J Peters.

616.992 NLD ISSN 1876-8229
RC280.P7
▼ ➤ **OPEN PROSTATE CANCER JOURNAL.** Text in English. 2009. irreg. free (effective 2011). **Document type:** *Journal, Academic/Scholarly.*
Media: Online - full text.
Indexed: A01, OGFA.
Published by: Bentham Open (Subsidiary of: Bentham Science Publishers Ltd.), PO Box 294, Bussum, AG 1400, Netherlands. TEL 31-35-6923800, FAX 31-35-6980150, subscriptions@bentham.org.

➤ **THE OPEN SURGICAL ONCOLOGY JOURNAL.** *see* MEDICAL SCIENCES—Surgery

616.99 GBR ISSN 1368-8375
RC280.M6 CODEN: EJCCER
➤ **ORAL ONCOLOGY.** Text in English. 1992. 12/yr. EUR 1,438 in Europe to institutions; JPY 190,600 in Japan to institutions; USD 1,606 elsewhere to institutions (effective 2012). back issues avail. **Document type:** *Journal, Academic/Scholarly.* **Description:** Discusses issues relating to aetiopathogenesis, epidemiology, prevention and management of oral cancer.
Formerly (until 1997): European Journal of Cancer. Part B: Oral Oncology (0964-1955); Which superseded in part (in 1992): European Journal of Cancer (0959-8049); Which was formerly (until 1990): European Journal of Cancer and Clinical Oncology (0277-5379); (until 1981): European Journal of Cancer (0014-2964)
Related titles: Microfilm ed.: (from PQC); Online - full text ed.: Oral Oncology Extra. ISSN 1741-9409 (from IngentaConnect, ScienceDirect); ◆ Supplement(s): Oral Oncology. Supplement. ISSN 1744-7895.
Indexed: A01, A03, A08, A22, A26, A29, A36, AIDS&CR, ASCA, B20, B21, B23, B25, BIOBASE, BIOSIS Prev, BP, C06, C07, C30, CA, CABA, CIN, CTA, ChemAb, ChemTitl, CurCont, D02, DBA, E12, EMBASE, ESPM, ExcerpMed, F08, F11, F12, FR, GH, I05, I10, IABS, ISR, IndMed, Inpharma, MEDLINE, MycolAb, N02, N03, OGFA, P30, P33, P35, R10, R12, RA&MP, RM&VM, Reac, S12, SCI, SCOPUS, T02, T05, THA, VITIS, VS, VirolAbstr, W07.
—BLDSC (6277.592000), CASDDS, IE, Ingenta, INIST. **CCC.**
Published by: (International Academy of Oral Oncology, International Association of Oral Pathologists AUS), Pergamon (Subsidiary of: Elsevier Science & Technology), The Blvd, Langford Ln, East Park, Kidlington, Oxford OX5 1GB, United Kingdom. TEL 44-1865-843000, FAX 44-1865-843010, JournalsCustomerServiceEMEA@elsevier.com. Ed. Crispian Scully. **Subscr. to:** Elsevier BV, Radarweg 29, PO Box 211, Amsterdam 1000 AE, Netherlands. TEL 31-20-4853757, FAX 31-20-4853432, http://www.elsevier.nl.

616.992 GBR ISSN 1744-7895
RC280.M6
ORAL ONCOLOGY. SUPPLEMENT. Text in English. 2005 (Apr.). a. includes subscr with Oral Oncology. **Document type:** *Journal, Academic/Scholarly.*
Related titles: Online - full text ed.: (from ScienceDirect); ◆ Supplement to: Oral Oncology. ISSN 1368-8375.
Indexed: A29, B20, B21, CTA, ESPM, I10, OGFA, VirolAbstr.
—BLDSC (6277.594000), IE, INIST. **CCC.**
Published by: Pergamon (Subsidiary of: Elsevier Science & Technology), The Blvd, Langford Ln, East Park, Kidlington, Oxford OX5 1GB, United Kingdom. TEL 44-1865-843000, FAX 44-1865-843010, JournalsCustomerServiceEMEA@elsevier.com, http://www.elsevier.com.

616.99449 CAN
OUTREACH. Text in English. 8/yr. free. **Document type:** *Newsletter.*
Media: E-mail.
Published by: Canadian Breast Cancer Network, 300-331 Cooper St, Ottawa, ON K2P 0G5, Canada. TEL 613-230-3044, 800-685-8820, FAX 613-230-4424, cbcn@cbcn.ca, http://www.cbcn.ca.

616.992 USA ISSN 1938-6621
P P O FOCUS. (Principles and Practice of Oncology) Text in English. 2007. q. free (effective 2008). **Document type:** *Newsletter, Academic/Scholarly.* **Description:** Features summaries of new developments cancer treatment and therapies.
Published by: Lippincott Williams & Wilkins (Subsidiary of: Wolters Kluwer N.V.), 333 7th Ave, 19th Fl, New York, NY 10001. TEL 212-886-1200, FAX 212-886-1205, http://www.lww.com.

616.992 USA
▼ **P R E P SUBSPECIALTIES.** (Pediatrics Review and Education Program) Text in English. 2010. m. USD 199 to non-members; USD 179 to members (effective 2011). **Document type:** *Trade.*
Media: Online - full text.
Published by: American Academy of Pediatrics, 141 NW Pt Blvd, Elk Grove Village, IL 60007. TEL 847-434-4000, FAX 847-434-8000, journals@aap.org, http://www.aap.org. **Subscr. to:** 72139 Eagle Way, Chicago, IL 60678. TEL 866-843-2271, FAX 847-228-1281.

616.992 618.92 DEU
PAEDIATRISCHE ONKOLOGIE. Text in German. 2008. irreg., latest vol.6, 2010. price varies. **Document type:** *Monographic series, Academic/Scholarly.*
Published by: Shaker Verlag GmbH, Kaiserstr 100, Herzogenrath, 52134, Germany. TEL 49-2407-95960, FAX 49-2407-95969, info@shaker.de, http://www.shaker.de.

THE PAIN CLINIC. *see* MEDICAL SCIENCES—Anaesthesiology

616.992 JOR ISSN 2070-254X
➤ **PAN ARAB JOURNAL OF ONCOLOGY.** Text in English. 2008. q. **Document type:** *Journal, Academic/Scholarly.*
Published by: (The Arab Medical Association Against Cancer (A M A A C)), Pan Arab Publishing Company, P O Box: 2509, Amman, 11953, Jordan. TEL 9626-566-7853, FAX 9626-562-3853, info@e-pamj.com, http://www.e-pamj.com. Ed. Dr. Marwan Ghosn.

616.994 NLD ISSN 1219-4956
CODEN: POREFR
PATHOLOGY AND ONCOLOGY RESEARCH. Text in English. 1995. q. EUR 635, USD 859 combined subscription to institutions (print & online eds.) (effective 2012). adv. reprint service avail. from PSC. **Document type:** *Journal, Academic/Scholarly.* **Description:** Provides an international forum for the communication of reviews, original research and critical and topical reports in pathology and oncology covering basic research and clinicopathological developments.
Related titles: Online - full text ed.: ISSN 1532-2807 (from IngentaConnect).
Indexed: A22, A29, A36, B20, B21, B25, BIOSIS Prev, CABA, CurCont, E01, EMBASE, ESPM, ExcerpMed, GH, H17, I10, INI, IndMed, MEDLINE, MycolAb, N02, N03, P30, P33, PN&I, R10, RM&VM, Reac, RiskAb, SCI, SCOPUS, T05, VirolAbstr, W07.
—BLDSC (6412.824000), CASDDS, GNLM, IE, Infotrieve, Ingenta, INIST. **CCC.**
Published by: (Aranyi Lajos Foundation HUN), Springer Netherlands (Subsidiary of: Springer Science+Business Media), Van Godewijckstraat 30, Dordrecht, 3311 GX, Netherlands. TEL 31-78-6576050, FAX 31-78-6576474, http://www.springer.com. Eds. Jozsef Timar, Laszlo Kopper.

616.992 GBR ISSN 1752-5519
QP517.S85
PATHWAY INTERACTION DATABASE. Text in English. 2006. base vol. plus m. updates. **Document type:** *Database.* **Description:** Contains collection of information about known biomolecular interactions and key cellular processes assembled into signaling pathways.
Media: Online - full text.
Published by: Nature Publishing Group (Subsidiary of: Macmillan Publishers Ltd.), The MacMillan Bldg, 4 Crinan St, London, N1 9XW, United Kingdom. TEL 44-20-78334000, FAX 44-20-78433601, http://www.nature.com. Ed. Kira Anthony. Pub. Matthew Day. **Co-publisher:** National Cancer Institute.

616.992 CAN ISSN 1703-9290
PATIENT MANAGEMENT PROBLEMS IN CLINICAL ONCOLOGY. Text in English. 2003. q. CAD 309.50 domestic to individuals; USD 229 foreign to individuals (effective 2008). **Document type:** *Journal, Academic/Scholarly.*
Media: CD-ROM.
—CCC.
Published by: (American Cancer Society, Inc. USA), B.C. Decker Inc., 50 King St E, 2nd Fl, Hamilton, ON L8N 2A1, Canada. TEL 905-522-7017, 800-568-7281, FAX 905-522-7839, 888-311-4987, info@bcdecker.com.

616.992 USA
PATIENT RESOURCE CANCER GUIDE; a treatment & facilities guide for patients & their families. Text in English. 2007. a. USD 9.95 per issue (effective 2009). adv. **Document type:** *Guide, Consumer.* **Description:** Includes a comprehensive list of cancer treatment facilities in the U.S. and detailed sections about treatment options, cancer types, clinical trials and patient resources; plus removable treatment option charts for breast and colon cancer patients.
Published by: Patient Resource Publishing, 440 W 62nd St, Kansas City, MO 64113. TEL 816-333-3595, FAX 712-643-2207, prp@patientresource.net. Pub. Linette Atwood. adv.: page USD 18,640; trim 8 x 10.875. Circ: 734 (paid); 339,410.

616.994 618.92 USA ISSN 1545-5009
RC261.A1 CODEN: PBCEAQ
➤ **PEDIATRIC BLOOD & CANCER.** Text in English. 1975. 14/yr. GBP 2,582 in United Kingdom to institutions; EUR 3,266 in Europe to institutions; USD 4,767 in United States to institutions; USD 4,963 in Canada & Mexico to institutions; USD 5,061 elsewhere to institutions; GBP 2,971 combined subscription in United Kingdom to institutions (print & online eds.); EUR 3,757 combined subscription in Europe to institutions (print & online eds.); USD 5,483 combined subscription in United States to institutions (print & online eds.); USD 5,679 combined subscription in Canada & Mexico to institutions (print & online eds.); USD 5,777 combined subscription elsewhere to institutions (print & online eds.) (effective 2012). adv. charts; illus. index. back issues avail.; reprint service avail. from PSC. **Document type:** *Journal, Academic/Scholarly.* **Description:** Provides broad coverage of advances in clinical oncology in children and adults; presents original articles on the diagnosis and treatment of malignant cancerous diseases.
Formerly (until 2004): Medical and Pediatric Oncology (0098-1532)
Related titles: Microform ed.: (from PQC); Online - full text ed.: ISSN 1545-5017. 1996. GBP 2,432 in United Kingdom to institutions; EUR 3,076 in Europe to institutions; USD 4,767 elsewhere to institutions (effective 2012); ◆ Supplement(s): Medical and Pediatric Oncology. Supplement. ISSN 0740-8226.
Indexed: A20, A22, A34, A36, ASCA, B&BAb, B19, B21, B25, BIOBASE, BIOSIS Prev, C06, C07, CABA, CIS, CurCont, DentInd, E12, EMBASE, ExcerpMed, GH, GenetAb, H17, IABS, INI, ISR, ImmunAb, IndMed, Inpharma, LT, MEDLINE, MycolAb, N02, N03, NSA, OGFA, P30, P33, P35, P39, R07, R08, R10, R12, R13, RA&MP, RM&VM, RRTA, Reac, RefZh, SCI, SCOPUS, T05, THA, W07.
—BLDSC (6417.533500), CASDDS, GNLM, IE, Infotrieve, Ingenta, INIST. **CCC.**
Published by: (American Society of Pediatric Hematology, Oncology, International Society of Pediatric Oncology), John Wiley & Sons, Inc., 111 River St, Hoboken, NJ 07030. TEL 201-748-6000, FAX 201-748-6088, info@wiley.com, http://www.wiley.com/WileyCDA/. Ed. Robert J Arceci TEL 410-502-7756. **Subscr. outside the Americas to:** John Wiley & Sons Ltd., The Atrium, Southern Gate, Chichester, West Sussex PO19 8SQ, United Kingdom.

➤ **PEDIATRIC HEMATOLOGY & ONCOLOGY.** *see* MEDICAL SCIENCES—Pediatrics

618.92 616 USA ISSN 1054-2086
➤ **PEDIATRIC HEMATOLOGY - ONCOLOGY SERIES.** Text in English. 1988. irreg., latest 2001. price varies. reprints avail. **Document type:** *Monographic series, Academic/Scholarly.*
—CCC.
Published by: Lippincott Williams & Wilkins (Subsidiary of: Wolters Kluwer N.V.), 530 Walnut St, Philadelphia, PA 19106. TEL 215-521-8300, FAX 215-521-8902, customerservice@lww.com, http://www.lww.com. **Subscr. to:** PO Box 1620, Hagerstown, MD 21741.

616.992 DEU
PERSPEKTIVEN (LEVERKUSEN). Text in German. 2001. a. adv. **Document type:** *Magazine, Consumer.*
Published by: (Krebsgesellschaft Nordrhein-Westfalen e.V.), G F M K GmbH & Co. KG Verlagsgesellschaft, Gezelinallee 37-39, Leverkusen, 51375, Germany. TEL 49-214-310570, FAX 49-214-3105719, info@gfmk.de, http://www.gfmk.de. Circ: 10,000 (controlled).

616.992 NLD ISSN 1572-1000
RM835
➤ **PHOTODIAGNOSIS AND PHOTODYNAMIC THERAPY.** Text in English. 2004. 4/yr. EUR 332 in Europe to institutions; JPY 46,500 in Japan to institutions; USD 332 elsewhere to institutions (effective 2012). **Document type:** *Journal, Academic/Scholarly.* **Description:** Provides for the dissemination of scientific knowledge and clinical developments of photodiagnosis and photodynamic therapy in all medical specialties.
Related titles: Online - full text ed.: ISSN 1873-1597 (from ScienceDirect).
Indexed: A26, CA, CurCont, EMBASE, ExcerpMed, I05, MEDLINE, P30, R10, Reac, SCI, SCOPUS, T02, W07.
—BLDSC (6465.991700), IE, Ingenta. **CCC.**
Published by: Elsevier BV (Subsidiary of: Elsevier Science & Technology), Radarweg 29, PO Box 211, Amsterdam, 1000 AE, Netherlands. TEL 31-20-4853911, FAX 31-20-4852457, JournalsCustomerServiceEMEA@elsevier.com, http://www.elsevier.nl. Ed. K Moghissi.

616.994 613.04244 NLD ISSN 1574-2431
PINK RIBBON. Text in Dutch. 2004. a. EUR 4.99 (effective 2009). adv. **Document type:** *Magazine, Consumer.*
Published by: (Stichting Pink Ribbon), Sanoma Uitgevers B.V., Postbus 1900, Hoofddorp, 2130 JH, Netherlands. TEL 31-23-5566770, FAX 31-23-5565376, http://www.sanomamedia.nl. adv.: color page EUR 7,950; trim 220 x 290. Circ: 180,000.

616.992 USA ISSN 1879-8500
▼ ➤ **PRACTICAL RADIATION ONCOLOGY.** Text in English. 2011. 4/yr. USD 300 in United States to institutions; USD 320 elsewhere to institutions (effective 2012). adv. **Document type:** *Journal, Academic/Scholarly.* **Description:** Provides a forum for new techniques, evaluation of current practices, and publication of case reports involving radiation oncology.
Related titles: Online - full text ed.: 2011 (from ScienceDirect).
—CCC.
Published by: (American Society for Radiation Oncology), Elsevier Inc. (Subsidiary of: Elsevier Science & Technology), 360 Park Ave S, New York, NY 10010. TEL 212-633-3100, FAX 212-633-3140, usinfo-f@elsevier.com, http://www.elsevier.com. Ed. W. Robert Lee.

616.992 USA
PRESIDENT'S CANCER PANEL. ANNUAL REPORT. Text in English. 1973. a. free (effective 2011). back issues avail. **Document type:** *Report, Government.*
Former titles (until 2001): President's Cancer Panel. Report of the Chairman (0739-9987); (until 1982): President's Cancer Panel Submitted to the President of the United States. Report (0094-5684)
Related titles: Online - full text ed.
Published by: (National Cancer Institute), National Institutes of Health (Subsidiary of: U.S. Department of Health and Human Services), 9000 Rockville Pike, Bethesda, MD 20892. TEL 301-496-2125, 301-496-4000, nihinfo@od.nih.gov, http://www.nih.gov.

616.992 USA ISSN 1940-7629
PREVENTION PORTAL. Text in English. 2008. m. includes with subscr. to Cancer Prevention Package. back issues avail. **Document type:** *Journal, Academic/Scholarly.*
Formerly announced as: Cancer Prevention Central
Media: Online - full content.
—CCC.
Published by: American Association for Cancer Research, 615 Chestnut St, 17th Fl, Philadelphia, PA 19106. TEL 215-440-9300, 866-423-3965, FAX 215-440-7228, aacr@aacr.org, http://www.aacr.org.

616.9 USA ISSN 1533-5437
PRINCIPLES AND PRACTICE OF RADIATION ONCOLOGY UPDATES. Text in English. 1987. irreg., latest 2003. looseleaf. price varies. **Document type:** *Monographic series, Academic/Scholarly.* **Description:** Provides updated information for the textbook Principles and Practices of Oncology.
Related titles: CD-ROM ed.
Published by: Lippincott Williams & Wilkins (Subsidiary of: Wolters Kluwer N.V.), 530 Walnut St, Philadelphia, PA 19106. TEL 215-521-8300, FAX 215-521-8902, customerservice@lww.com, http://www.lww.com. Circ: 25,000 (controlled).

616.994 CAN ISSN 1912-3760
PROGRAMME QUEBECOIS DE DEPISTAGE DU CANCER DU SEIN. RAPPORT D'ACTIVITE. Text in French. 1999. a., latest 2005. **Document type:** *Report, Trade.*
Formerly (until 200?): Programme Quebecois de Depistage du Cancer du Sein. Rapport d'Activites des Annees (1498-9174)
Published by: Quebec, Ministere de la Sante et des Services Sociaux, 400, boul. Jean-Lesage, bureau 105, Quebec, PQ G1K 8W1, Canada. TEL 418-643-1344, 800-363-1363, http://www.msss.gouv.qc.ca/index.php.

616.994 CHE ISSN 0079-6263
RC254 CODEN: PEXTAR
➤ **PROGRESS IN EXPERIMENTAL TUMOR RESEARCH.** Text in English. 1960. irreg., latest vol.40, 2008. price varies. back issues avail.; reprints avail. **Document type:** *Monographic series, Academic/Scholarly.* **Description:** Overviews of experimental work in key areas of tumor research.
Related titles: Online - full text ed.: ISSN 1662-3916.
Indexed: A22, ASCA, BIOSIS Prev, ChemAb, ChemTitl, EMBASE, ExcerpMed, ISR, IndMed, MEDLINE, MycolAb, P30, R10, Reac, SCI, SCOPUS, W07.
—BLDSC (6868.380000), CASDDS, GNLM, IE, Infotrieve, Ingenta, INIST. **CCC.**
Published by: S. Karger AG, Allschwilerstr 10, Basel, 4055, Switzerland. TEL 41-61-3061111, FAX 41-61-3061234, karger@karger.ch, http://www.karger.ch. Ed. J R Bertino.

616.992 USA ISSN 1535-9980
RC261.A1 CODEN: PORNAF
PROGRESS IN ONCOLOGY (YEAR). Text in English. 2001. a., latest 2004. **Document type:** *Monographic series, Academic/Scholarly.* **Description:** Covers critical issues in clinical cancer care and research in a scholarly though readable style.
—BLDSC (6871.370000), IE. **CCC.**
Published by: Jones & Bartlett Learning, 40 Tall Pine Dr, Sudbury, MA 01776. TEL 978-443-5000, 800-832-0034, FAX 978-443-8000, info@jblearning.com.

616.99 GBR ISSN 0969-9260
R726.8 CODEN: PPCRCT
➤ **PROGRESS IN PALLIATIVE CARE;** science and the art of caring. Abbreviated title: P P C. Text in English. 1993. bi-m. GBP 389 combined subscription to institutions (print & online eds.); USD 637 combined subscription in United States to institutions (print & online eds.) (effective 2012). adv. back issues avail.; reprint service avail. from PSC. **Document type:** *Journal, Academic/Scholarly.* **Description:** Locates and reports the scholarly literature on all aspects of the management of the problems of end-stage disease, and issues pertinent to living with chronic or progressive disease.
Related titles: Online - full text ed.: ISSN 1743-291X. GBP 350 to institutions; USD 573 in United States to institutions (effective 2012) (from IngentaConnect).

Indexed: AMED, C06, C07, C08, CA, CINAHL, EMBASE, ExcerpMed, R10, Reac, SCOPUS, T02.
—BLDSC (6872.285000), IE, Infotrieve, Ingenta. **CCC.**
Published by: (International Observatory on End of Life Care), Maney Publishing, Ste 1C, Joseph's Well, Hanover Walk, Leeds, W Yorks LS3 1AB, United Kingdom. TEL 44-113-2432800, FAX 44-113-3868178, maney@maney.co.uk. Ed. Mellar Davis. adv.: B&W page GBP 320, color page GBP 650. **Subscr. in N. America to:** Maney Publishing, 875 Massachusetts Ave, 7th Fl, Cambridge, MA 02139. TEL 866-297-5154, FAX 617-354-6875, maney@maneyusa.com.

616.92 DEU ISSN 1860-5478
PROPRAXIS ONKOLOGIE - HAEMATOLOGIE. Text in German. 2000. 9/yr. adv. **Document type:** *Journal, Academic/Scholarly.*
Formerly (until 2005): Medical Expert Onkologie (1617-0105)
Published by: Fromm & Fromm GmbH, Achtern Felln 26, Hasloh, 25474, Germany. TEL 49-4106-63070, FAX 49-4106-630715, info@2xfromm.de, http://www.pmi-medien.de. adv.: color page EUR 3,650. Circ: 13,750 (controlled).

616.99 NLD ISSN 0924-1914
➤ **PROSTAGLANDINS, LEUKOTRIENES AND CANCER.** Text in English. 1985. irreg., latest vol.6, 1989. price varies. **Document type:** *Monographic series, Academic/Scholarly.*
—**CCC.**
Published by: Springer Netherlands (Subsidiary of: Springer Science+Business Media), Van Godewijckstraat 30, Dordrecht, 3311 GX, Netherlands. TEL 31-78-6576050, FAX 31-78-6576474.

➤ **THE PROSTATE.** *see* MEDICAL SCIENCES—Urology And Nephrology

616.65 USA ISSN 2090-3111
▼ ➤ **PROSTATE CANCER.** Text in English. 2011. USD 195 (effective 2011). **Document type:** *Journal, Academic/Scholarly.* **Description:** Publishes original research articles, review articles, and clinical studies related to all aspects of prostate cancer.
Related titles: Online - full text ed.: ISSN 2090-312X. 2011. free (effective 2011).
Indexed: A01.
Published by: Hindawi Publishing Corporation, 410 Park Ave, 15th Fl, PMB 287, New York, NY 10022. FAX 215-893-4392, 866-446-3294, info@hindawi.com.

616.65 GBR ISSN 1365-7852
RC280.P7 CODEN: PCPDFW
➤ **PROSTATE CANCER AND PROSTATIC DISEASES.** Text in English. 1997. q. EUR 998 in Europe to institutions; USD 1,257 in the Americas to institutions; JPY 170,900 in Japan to institutions; GBP 645 to institutions in the UK & elsewhere (effective 2011). adv. bk.rev. charts; illus.; stat. index. back issues avail.; reprints avail. **Document type:** *Journal, Academic/Scholarly.* **Description:** Covers all aspects of prostatic diseases, and also reports on exciting new developments being made in diagnosis, surgery, radiotherapy, drug discovery and medical management.
Related titles: Online - full text ed.: ISSN 1476-5608.
Indexed: A01, A02, A03, A08, A22, A26, B&BAb, B19, CA, CurCont, E01, EMBASE, ExcerpMed, G10, H12, I05, Inpharma, MEDLINE, P20, P22, P30, P35, P48, P50, P54, PQC, R10, Reac, SCI, SCOPUS, T02, W07.
—BLDSC (6935.194500), CASDDS, IE, Infotrieve, Ingenta. **CCC.**
Published by: Nature Publishing Group (Subsidiary of: Macmillan Publishers Ltd.), The MacMillan Bldg, 4 Crinan St, London, N1 9XW, United Kingdom. TEL 44-20-78334000, FAX 44-20-78334640. Ed. Stephen J Freedland. Adv. contact Ben Harkinson TEL 617-475-9222. **Subscr. to:** Brunel Rd, Houndmills, Basingstoke, Hamps RG21 6XS, United Kingdom. TEL 44-1256-329242, FAX 44-1256-812358, subscriptions@nature.com.

616.994 ESP ISSN 1696-7240
PSICOONCOLOGIA. Text in Spanish. 2003. 3/yr. EUR 35 to individuals; EUR 55 to institutions (effective 2009). back issues avail. **Document type:** *Journal, Academic/Scholarly.*
Indexed: A26, CA, EMBASE, ExcerpMed, H21, I04, I05, P03, P08, P20, P24, P25, P26, P48, P54, PQC, PsycInfo, SCOPUS, T02.
Published by: Asociacion de Psicooncologia de Madrid, Fac. de Psicologia Buzon 24, UCM, Madrid, 28223, Spain. TEL 34-91-3943126, FAX 34-91-3943189, psicooncologia@psi.ucm.es. Ed. Juan A Cruzado.

616.994 FRA ISSN 1778-3798
➤ **PSYCHO-ONCOLOGIE.** Text in French. 2002. q. EUR 201, USD 243 combined subscription to institutions (print & online eds.) (effective 2012). reprint service avail. from PSC. **Document type:** *Journal, Academic/Scholarly.*
Formerly (until 2007): Revue Francophone de Psycho-Oncologie (1760-4133)
Related titles: Online - full text ed.: ISSN 1778-381X (from IngentaConnect).
Indexed: A22, A26, E01, E08, EMBASE, ExcerpMed, FR, H12, I05, P03, PsycInfo, PsycholAb, R10, Reac, S09, SCI, SCOPUS, W07.
—IE, Ingenta, INIST. **CCC.**
Published by: Springer France (Subsidiary of: Springer Science+Business Media), 22 Rue de Palestro, Paris, 75002, France. TEL 33-1-53009860, FAX 33-1-53009861, sylvie.kamara@springer.com. Ed. Marie-Frederique Bacque. Adv. contact Stephan Kroeck TEL 49-30-827875739.

616.99 GBR ISSN 1057-9249
RC261.A1 CODEN: POJCEE
➤ **PSYCHO-ONCOLOGY;** journal of the psychological, social and behavioral dimensions of cancer. Text in English. 1992. m. GBP 924 in United Kingdom to institutions; EUR 1,168 in Europe to institutions; USD 1,810 elsewhere to institutions; GBP 1,063 combined subscription in United Kingdom to institutions (print & online eds.); EUR 1,344 combined subscription in Europe to institutions (print & online eds.); USD 2,082 combined subscription elsewhere to institutions (print & online eds.) (effective 2012). adv. back issues avail.; reprint service avail. from PSC. **Document type:** *Journal, Academic/Scholarly.* **Description:** Covers the the psychological, social, behavioral, and ethical aspects of cancer.
Related titles: Microform ed.: (from PQC); Online - full text ed.: ISSN 1099-1611. 1996. GBP 924 in United Kingdom to institutions; EUR 1,168 in Europe to institutions; USD 1,810 elsewhere to institutions (effective 2012).
Indexed: A01, A03, A08, A20, A22, ASSIA, B28, C06, C07, C08, CA, CINAHL, CurCont, E-psyche, EMBASE, ExcerpMed, F09, FamI, H13, INI, IndMed, Inpharma, MEDLINE, P02, P03, P10, P20, P30, P35, P43, P48, P53, P54, PQC, PsycInfo, PsycholAb, R10, Reac, RefZh, S02, S03, SCI, SCOPUS, SSCI, SociolAb, T02, W07.
—GNLM, IE, Infotrieve, Ingenta. **CCC.**
Published by: (International Psycho-Oncology Society USA, American Psychosocial Oncology Society USA, British Psycho-Oncology Society), John Wiley & Sons Ltd. (Subsidiary of: John Wiley & Sons, Inc.), 1-7 Oldlands Way, PO Box 808, Bognor Regis, West Sussex PO21 9FF, United Kingdom. TEL 44-1865-778315, FAX 44-1243-843232, cs-journals@wiley.com, http://eu.wiley.com/WileyCDA/. Eds. Jimmie C Holland TEL 646-888-0026, Maggie Watson TEL 44-2086-613009. **Subscr. in the Americas to:** John Wiley & Sons, Inc., 111 River St, Hoboken, NJ 07030. TEL 201-748-6645, subinfo@wiley.com; **Subscr. to:** 1-7 Oldlands Way, PO Box 809, Bognor Regis, West Sussex PO21 9FG, United Kingdom. TEL 44-1865-778054, cs-agency@wiley.com.

616.992 616.89 NLD ISSN 1570-7652
PSYCHOSOCIALE ONCOLOGIE. Text in Dutch. 1993. 3/yr. EUR 23.20 to individuals; EUR 59.60 to institutions (effective 2010). adv.
Former titles (until 2002): Nederlandse Vereniging voor Psychosociale Oncologie. Bulletin (1567-3839); (until 2000): Nederlandse Vereniging voor Psychosociale Oncologie. Nieuwsbulletin (0929-7278)
Published by: (Nederlandse Vereniging voor Psychosociale Oncologie), Koninklijke Van Gorcum BV/Royal Van Gorcum BV, PO Box 43, Assen, 9400 AA, Netherlands. TEL 31-592-379555, FAX 31-592-372064, info@vangorcum.nl, http://www.vangorcum.nl. Ed. Dr. E R Spelten. adv.: B&W page EUR 465, color page EUR 1,365; 180 x 255.

PUBLIC HEALTH REVIEWS (PRINT); an international quarterly. *see* PUBLIC HEALTH AND SAFETY

616.992 PRT ISSN 1647-3361
▼ **PUBLICACAO ONCOLOGICA PORTUGUESA.** Text in Portuguese. 2009. q. **Document type:** *Magazine, Trade.*
Published by: JRS Pharmarketing, Rua Alexandre Herculano, Edf 1, Linda-a Velha, 2795-240, Portugal. TEL 351-21-4389060, FAX 351-21-4389065, http://www.jrs.pt.

616.992 DEU
➤ **QUALITAETSSICHERUNG IN DER ONKOLOGIE.** Text in German. 1995. irreg., latest vol.11, 2002. price varies. **Document type:** *Monographic series, Academic/Scholarly.*
Published by: W. Zuckschwerdt Verlag GmbH, Industriestr 1, Germering, 82110, Germany. TEL 49-89-8943490, FAX 49-89-89434950, post@zuckschwerdtverlag.de, http://www.zuckschwerdtverlag.de.

616.992 USA ISSN 2151-4208
▼ **RADIATION MEDICINE ROUNDS.** Text in English. 2010 (Mar.). 3/yr. USD 85 per issue (effective 2011). **Document type:** *Monographic series, Academic/Scholarly.* **Description:** A review series for new scientific, technological, and clinical advances in all areas of radiation medicine.
Related titles: Online - full text ed.: ISSN 2151-4216. 2010 (Mar.) (from IngentaConnect).
Published by: Demos Medical Publishing, 11 W 42nd St, 15th Fl, New York, NY 10036. TEL 212-683-0072 x238, info@demospub.com.

616.994061 GBR ISSN 1748-717X
RC271.R3
➤ **RADIATION ONCOLOGY.** Text in English. 2006. irreg. free (effective 2011). adv. back issues avail. **Document type:** *Journal, Academic/Scholarly.* **Description:** Covers topics related to the treatment of cancer using radiation.
Media: Online - full text.
Indexed: A01, A26, B19, C06, C07, CA, CurCont, EMBASE, ExcerpMed, I05, MEDLINE, P30, R10, Reac, SCI, SCOPUS, T02, W07.
—**CCC.**
Published by: BioMed Central Ltd. (Subsidiary of: Springer Science+Business Media), 236 Gray's Inn Rd, London, WC1X 8HB, United Kingdom. TEL 44-20-31922000, FAX 44-20-31922010, info@biomedcentral.com, http://www.biomedcentral.com. Ed. Claus Belka.

➤ **RADIATION THERAPIST;** the journal of the radiation oncology sciences. *see* MEDICAL SCIENCES—Radiology And Nuclear Medicine

➤ **RADIOLOGY AND ONCOLOGY.** *see* MEDICAL SCIENCES—Radiology And Nuclear Medicine

➤ **RADIOTHERAPY & ONCOLOGY.** *see* MEDICAL SCIENCES—Radiology And Nuclear Medicine

616.992 ITA ISSN 2036-3605
▼ **RARE TUMORS.** Text in English. 2009. irreg. **Document type:** *Journal, Academic/Scholarly.*
Related titles: Online - full text ed.: ISSN 2036-3613. free (effective 2011).
Indexed: A01, EMBASE, P30, SCOPUS, T02.
Published by: Pagepress, Via Giuseppe Belli 4, Pavia, 27100, Italy. TEL 39-0382-1751762, FAX 39-0382-1750481. Ed. Robert C Miller.

616.994 NLD ISSN 1574-8928
RS431.A64 CODEN: RPADDY
➤ **RECENT PATENTS ON ANTI-CANCER DRUG DISCOVERY.** Text in English. 2006. 3/yr. USD 1,000 to institutions (print or online ed.) (effective 2012). adv. back issues avail.; reprints avail. **Document type:** *Journal, Academic/Scholarly.* **Description:** Publishes review articles on recent patents in the field of anti-cancer drug discovery e.g. on novel bioactive compounds, analogs & targets.
Related titles: Online - full text ed.: (from IngentaConnect).
Indexed: A01, A28, APA, B&BAb, B19, B21, BrCerAb, C&ISA, C33, CA, CA/WCA, CIA, CTA, CerAb, CivEngAb, CorrAb, E&CAJ, E11, EEA, EMA, EMBASE, ESPM, EnvEAb, ExcerpMed, H15, M&PBA, M&TEA, M09, MBF, MEDLINE, METADEX, NSA, P30, SCI, SCOPUS, SolStAb, T02, T04, W07, WAA.
—IE, Ingenta, Linda Hall. **CCC.**
Published by: Bentham Science Publishers Ltd., PO Box 294, Bussum, 1400 AG, Netherlands. TEL 31-35-6923800, FAX 31-35-6980150, sales@bentham.org. Ed. Khurshid Zaman. **Subscr. to:** Bentham Science Publishers Ltd., c/o Richard E Morrissy, PO Box 446, Oak Park, IL 60301. TEL 312-413-5867, FAX 312-996-7107, subscriptions@bentham.org.

616.994 IND
RECENT RESEARCH DEVELOPMENTS IN CANCER. Text in English. 1999. a. **Document type:** *Monographic series, Academic/Scholarly.*
Published by: Transworld Research Network, T C 37-661 (2), Fort Post Office, Trivandrum, Kerala 695 023, India. TEL 91-471-2452918, FAX 91-471-2573051, ggcom@vsnl.com, http://www.trnres.com.

616.994 USA ISSN 0080-0015
RC261 CODEN: RRCRBU
RECENT RESULTS IN CANCER RESEARCH/FORTSCHRITTE DER KREBSFORSCHUNG. Text in English; Text occasionally in French, German. 1965. irreg., latest vol.188, 2010. price varies. back issues avail.; reprints avail. **Document type:** *Monographic series, Academic/Scholarly.*
Indexed: A22, ChemAb, DentInd, EMBASE, ExcerpMed, IndMed, MEDLINE, P30, R10, Reac, SCOPUS, THA.
—BLDSC (7305.090000), CASDDS, GNLM, IE, Infotrieve, Ingenta, INIST, Linda Hall. **CCC.**
Published by: Springer New York LLC (Subsidiary of: Springer Science+Business Media), 233 Spring St, New York, NY 10013. TEL 212-460-1500, FAX 212-460-1575, service-ny@springer.com. Eds. Hans-Jorg Senn, Peter M Schlag.

REFERATIVNYI ZHURNAL. ONKOLOGIYA; razdel-tom. *see* MEDICAL SCIENCES—Abstracting, Bibliographies, Statistics

REFERATIVNYI ZHURNAL. ONKOLOGIYA EKSPERIMENTAL'NAYA; vypusk razdela-toma. *see* MEDICAL SCIENCES—Abstracting, Bibliographies, Statistics

REFERATIVNYI ZHURNAL. ONKOLOGIYA: TERAPIYA OPUKHOLEI; vypusk razdela-toma. *see* MEDICAL SCIENCES—Abstracting, Bibliographies, Statistics

616.992 POL ISSN 1507-1367
RC271.R3 CODEN: RPORA7
REPORTS ON PRACTICAL ONCOLOGY AND RADIOTHERAPY. Text in English. 1998. bi-m. EUR 200 in Europe to institutions; JPY 31,100 in Japan to institutions; USD 278 elsewhere to institutions (effective 2012). **Document type:** *Journal, Academic/Scholarly.*
Related titles: Online - full text ed.: (from ScienceDirect).
Indexed: BIOBASE, EMBASE, ExcerpMed, IABS, R10, Reac, RefZh, SCOPUS, T02.
—BLDSC (7661.954500), IE, Ingenta. **CCC.**
Published by: (Polish Society of Radiation Oncology, Czech Society of Radiation Oncology CZE, Hungarian Society of Radiation Oncology HUN, Slovenian Society for Radiotherapy and Oncology SVN, Polish Study Group of Head and Neck Cancer), Great Poland Cancer Center, Garbary 15th St, Poznan, 61866, Poland. TEL 48-61-8850500, FAX 48-61-8521948. Ed. Julian Malicki TEL 48-61-8540700.

616.99 ESP ISSN 0213-8573
➤ **REVISIONES EN CANCER.** Text in Spanish; Abstracts in Spanish, English. 1987. bi-m. EUR 69 to qualified personnel; EUR 110 to institutions; EUR 46 to students (effective 2007). adv. abstr.; bibl.; illus.; stat. back issues avail. **Document type:** *Journal, Academic/Scholarly.*
Indexed: A22, EMBASE, ExcerpMed, R10, Reac, SCOPUS.
—BLDSC (7800.572000), GNLM, IE, Ingenta. **CCC.**
Published by: Aran Ediciones, Castello 128, 1o, Madrid, 28006, Spain. TEL 34-91-7820030, FAX 34-91-5615787, edita@grupoaran.com, http://www.grupoaran.com. Ed. Dr. E. Diaz-Rubio. Pub. Jose Jimenez Marquez. R&P Maria Dolores Linares TEL 34-91-7820035. Circ: 3,000.

616.994 BRA ISSN 0034-7116
RC261.A1 CODEN: RVBCA7
REVISTA BRASILEIRA DE CANCEROLOGIA. Text in Portuguese; Summaries in English, Portuguese. 1947. bi-m. adv. bibl.; charts; illus. **Document type:** *Journal, Academic/Scholarly.*
Indexed: ChemAb, INIS AtomInd, IndMed.
—CASDDS, GNLM, INIST.
Published by: Instituto Nacional do Cancer (I N C A), Praca Cruz Vermelha 23, Rio de Janeiro, RJ 20230-130, Brazil.

REVISTA BRASILEIRA DE COLOPROCTOLOGIA. *see* MEDICAL SCIENCES—Surgery

616.992 BRA ISSN 1806-6054
REVISTA BRASILEIRA DE ONCOLOGIA CLINICA. Text in Portuguese. 2004. 3/yr. **Document type:** *Journal, Academic/Scholarly.*
Published by: Sociedade Brasileira de Oncologia Clinica (S B O C), Av dos Andradas 2287 sl 709, Centro, Belo Horizonte, MG 30120-010, Brazil. TEL 55-31-32412920, http://www.sboc.org.br.

616.992 616.99419 CHL ISSN 0717-3210
REVISTA CHILENA DE CANCEROLOGIA Y HEMATOLOGIA. Text in Spanish. 1991. 3/yr. **Document type:** *Journal, Academic/Scholarly.*
Formerly (until 1997): Revista Chilena de Cancerologia (0716-9027)
Published by: Sociedad Chilena de Cancerologia, Perez Valenzuela 1520, Of.502, Santiago, Chile. TEL 56-2-2358357.

616.994 COL ISSN 0123-9015
RC254.A1
REVISTA COLOMBIANA DE CANCEROLOGIA; publicacion cientifica del Instituto Nacional de Cancerologia. Text in Spanish. 1997. quadrennial. back issues avail. **Document type:** *Journal, Academic/Scholarly.*
Related titles: Online - full text ed.: free (effective 2011).
Published by: Instituto Nacional de Cancerologia, Calle 1 No 9-85, Apdo Aereo 17158, Bogota, Colombia. TEL 57-1-3341111, FAX 57-1-3341122, direccion@incancerologia.gov.co, http://www.incancerologia.gov.co.

615.28 ESP ISSN 1888-8844
REVISTA ESPANOLA DE QUIMIOTERAPIA. MONOGRAFIA. Text in Spanish. 2008. irreg. **Document type:** *Monographic series, Academic/Scholarly.*
Published by: Sociedad Espanola de Quimioterapia, Apartado de Correos 60139, Madrid, 28080, Spain. TEL 34-91-3941508, FAX 34-91-3941511, http:/www.seq.es.

616.99 VEN ISSN 0798-0582
RC261.A1
➤ **REVISTA VENEZOLANA DE ONCOLOGIA.** Text in Spanish, English. 1989. q. back issues avail. **Document type:** *Journal, Academic/Scholarly.*
Related titles: Online - full text ed.: free (effective 2011).
Indexed: EMBASE, ExcerpMed, SCOPUS.

Published by: Sociedad Venezolana de Oncologia, Edif. Torre del Colegio de Mexico, 2o Piso, Of. C-2 Ave Jose M. Vargas, Urb. Santa Fe, Caracas, 1080, Venezuela. TEL 58-212-9798635, FAX 58-212-9764941, svoncologia@cantv.net, http://www.oncology.org.ve. Ed. Carlos Pacheco Soler.

616.99 ITA
RIVISTA ITALIANA DI CURE PALLIATIVE. Text in Italian. 1993. 4/yr. **Document type:** *Journal, Academic/Scholarly.*
Formerly (until 2000): Quaderni di Cure Palliative (1122-0260)
Published by: Societa Italiana di Cure Palliative, Viale Piave 17, Milan, 20129, Italy. TEL 39-02-76013317, FAX 39-02-783325, ricp@healthsite.net, http://www.sicp.it.

616.992 USA
ROSEWELLNESS. Text in English. 3/yr. **Document type:** *Magazine, Consumer.*
Published by: Roswell Park Cancer Institute, Elm and Carlton St, Buffalo, NY 14263. TEL 716-845-2300.

616.99 RUS ISSN 1726-9865
➤ **ROSSIISKAYA AKADEMIYA MEDITSINSKIKH NAUK. ROSSIISKII ONKOLOGICHESKII NAUCHNYI TSENTR IMENI N. N. BLOKHINA. VESTNIK/RUSSIAN ACADEMY OF MEDICAL SCIENCES. N. N. BLOKHIN CANCER RESEARCH CENTER. HERALD.** Key Title: Vestnik Rossiiskogo Onkologicheskogo Nauchnogo Tsentra imeni N.N. Blohina R A M N. Text in Russian, English. 1990. q. USD 202 foreign (effective 2007). **Document type:** *Journal, Academic/Scholarly.*
Formerly (until 1998): Vsesoyuznyi Onkologicheskii Nauchnyi Tsentr A M N S S S R. Vestnik (0869-8910)
Related titles: Online - full content ed.
—East View.
Published by: Rossiiskaya Akademiya Meditsinskikh Nauk, Rossiiskii Onkologicheskii Nauchnyi Tsentr imeni N.N. Blokhina/Russian Academy of Medical Sciences, N.N.Blokhin Cancer Research Center, Kashirskoe shosse 24, Moscow, 115478, Russian Federation. TEL 7-495-3245537. Ed. M I Davydov. **Dist. by:** East View Information Services, 10601 Wayzata Blvd, Minneapolis, MN 55305. TEL 952-252-1201, 800-477-1005, FAX 952-252-1202, info@eastview.com, http://www.eastview.com.

616.99 RUS ISSN 1028-9984
ROSSIISKII ONKOLOGICHESKII ZHURNAL/RUSSIAN ONCOLOGICAL JOURNAL. Text in Russian; Summaries in English. 1996. bi-m. USD 221 foreign (effective 2005). adv. bk.rev. **Document type:** *Journal, Academic/Scholarly.* **Description:** Publishes papers on all aspects of cancer research, ranging from basic investigations to the results of experimental and clinical studies, new trends in the treatment of cancer and cancer control.
Indexed: RefZh.
—BLDSC (0154.059256), IE, Ingenta.
Published by: Izdatel'stvo Meditsina/Meditsina Publishers, ul B Pirogovskaya, d 2, str 5, Moscow, 119435, Russian Federation. TEL 7-095-2483324, meditsina@mtu-net.ru, http://www.medlit.ru. Ed. Valerii I Chissov. Pub. A M Stochik. R&P I Sokolova. Adv. contact O A Fadeeva TEL 7-095-923-51-40. **Dist. by:** East View Information Services, 10601 Wayzata Blvd, Minneapolis, MN 55305. TEL 952-252-1201, 800-477-1005, FAX 952-252-1202, info@eastview.com, http://www.eastview.com.

SARCOIDOSIS VASCULITIS AND DIFFUSE LUNG DISEASES. *see* MEDICAL SCIENCES—Respiratory Diseases

616.99 USA ISSN 1357-714X
CODEN: SARCFO
➤ **SARCOMA.** Text in English. 1997. irreg. USD 395 (effective 2011). **Document type:** *Journal, Academic/Scholarly.* **Description:** Publishes papers covering all aspects of connective tissue oncology research. Covers molecular biology and pathology and the clinical sciences of epidemiology, surgery, radiotherapy and chemotherapy.
Related titles: Online - full text ed.: ISSN 1369-1643. free (effective 2011) (from IngentaConnect).
Indexed: A01, A02, A03, A08, A22, A26, APA, B21, B25, BIOSIS Prev, C&ISA, C06, C07, C08, C11, CA, CINAHL, CorrAb, E&CAJ, E01, EEA, EMBASE, ESPM, EnvEAb, ExcerpMed, H04, H12, I05, MycolAb, OGFA, P30, R10, Reac, SCOPUS, SolStAb, T02, WAA.
—BLDSC (8076.026000), CASDDS, IE, Infotrieve, Ingenta. **CCC.**
Published by: Hindawi Publishing Corporation, 410 Park Ave, 15th Fl, PMB 287, New York, NY 10022. FAX 215-893-4392, 866-446-3294, hindawi@hindawi.com. Ed. Robert Grimer.

616.99 BGR ISSN 0582-3250
CODEN: SSCMBX
➤ **SCRIPTA SCIENTIFICA MEDICA.** Text in English. 1962. a. Supplement avail.; back issues avail. **Document type:** *Journal, Academic/Scholarly.*
Indexed: ABSML, BSLBiol, ChemAb, ChemTitl.
—CASDDS, GNLM.
Published by: Meditsinski Universitet "Profesor Doktor Paraskev Stoyanov" - Varna/Medical University in Varna Prof. Dr. Paraskev Stoyanov, ul Marin Drinov, 55, Varna, 9002, Bulgaria. TEL 359-52-650057, FAX 359-52-650019. Ed. Aneliya Klisarova.

➤ **SEMINARS IN CANCER BIOLOGY.** *see* BIOLOGY—Physiology

616.994 USA ISSN 0093-7754
RC261 CODEN: SOLGAV
➤ **SEMINARS IN ONCOLOGY.** Text in English. 1974 (Mar.). bi-m. USD 510 in United States to institutions; USD 633 elsewhere to institutions (effective 2012). adv. bibl.; charts; illus. index. back issues avail.; reprints avail. **Document type:** *Journal, Academic/Scholarly.* **Description:** Provides current, authoritative, and practical reviews of developments in the diagnosis and management of patients with cancer.
Related titles: Online - full text ed.: ISSN 1532-8708 (from ScienceDirect).
Indexed: A20, A22, AIDS&CR, ASCA, B21, BIOSIS Prev, C06, C07, C08, CIN, CINAHL, CISA, CTA, ChemAb, ChemTitl, CurCont, DentInd, EMBASE, ESPM, ExcerpMed, FR, ISR, ImmunAb, IndMed, Inpharma, MEDLINE, MycolAb, NRN, NSA, OGFA, P30, P35, R10, Reac, SCI, SCOPUS, ToxAb, W07.
—BLDSC (8239.456500), CASDDS, GNLM, IE, Infotrieve, Ingenta, INIST. **CCC.**
Published by: W.B. Saunders Co. (Subsidiary of: Elsevier Health Sciences), Elsevier, Health Sciences Division, Order Fulfillment, 3251 Riverport Ln, Maryland Heights, MO 63043. TEL 314-872-8370, 800-325-4177, FAX 314-432-1380, JournalCustomerService-usa@elsevier.com, http://www.us.elsevierhealth.com. Ed. Dr. Michael J Mastrangelo. Pub. Livia Berardi. Adv. contact John Marmero TEL 212-633-3657. Circ: 2,750.

616.994 ESP ISSN 1578-8792
SEMINARS IN ONCOLOGY (SPANISH EDITION). Text in Spanish. 2002. bi-m. **Document type:** *Journal, Academic/Scholarly.*
Published by: Spanish Publishers Associates, Edif. Vertice C Antonio Lopez, 249 1o-4o, Madrid, 28041, Spain. TEL 34-91-5002077, FAX 34-91-5002075, prodrug@drugfarma.com, http://www.drugfarma.com/espanol/03spa/index.htm.

SEMINARS IN ONCOLOGY NURSING. *see* MEDICAL SCIENCES—Nurses And Nursing

616.99 616.07 USA ISSN 1053-4296
RC254.A1 CODEN: SRONEO
➤ **SEMINARS IN RADIATION ONCOLOGY.** Text in English. 1991 (Oct.). q. USD 365 in United States to institutions; USD 480 elsewhere to institutions (effective 2012). back issues avail.; reprints avail. **Document type:** *Journal, Academic/Scholarly.* **Description:** Presenting definitive information on areas of rapid change and development on topics are tumor biology, diagnosis, medical and surgical management of the patient, and new technologies.
Related titles: Online - full text ed.: ISSN 1532-9461 (from ScienceDirect).
Indexed: A22, A26, C06, C07, C08, CINAHL, CurCont, EMBASE, ExcerpMed, H12, I05, INI, ISR, IndMed, Inpharma, MEDLINE, P30, R10, Reac, SCI, SCOPUS, T02, W07.
—BLDSC (8239.457300), GNLM, IE, Infotrieve, Ingenta. **CCC.**
Published by: W.B. Saunders Co. (Subsidiary of: Elsevier Health Sciences), Elsevier, Health Sciences Division, Order Fulfillment, 3251 Riverport Ln, Maryland Heights, MO 63043. TEL 314-872-8370, 800-325-4177, FAX 314-432-1380, JournalCustomerService-usa@elsevier.com, http://www.us.elsevierhealth.com. Ed. Dr. Joel E Tepper. Pub. Mary Heffner TEL 212-633-3953. Adv. contact Gene Conselyea TEL 732-970-0220. Circ: 1,275.

616.992 CHN ISSN 1001-5930
SHIYONG AIZHENG ZAZHI. Text in Chinese. 1985. bi-m. USD 31.20 (effective 2009). **Document type:** *Journal, Academic/Scholarly.*
Related titles: Online - full text ed.
—BLDSC (8267.297875), East View.
Published by: Jiangxi Sheng Zhongliu Yiyuan, 519, Beijing Donglu, Nanchang, 330029, China. **Dist. by:** China International Book Trading Corp, 35 Chegongzhuang Xilu, Haidian District, PO Box 399, Beijing 100044, China. TEL 86-10-68412045, FAX 86-10-68412023, cibtc@mail.cibtc.com.cn, http://www.cibtc.com.cn.

616.99 CHN ISSN 1001-1692
CODEN: SZZHAB
➤ **SHIYONG ZHONGLIU ZAZHI/JOURNAL OF PRACTICAL ONCOLOGY.** Text in Chinese. 1986. bi-m. USD 24.60 (effective 2009). **Document type:** *Journal, Academic/Scholarly.*
Related titles: Online - full text ed.
Indexed: A36, B21, CABA, D01, E12, EMBASE, ExcerpMed, F08, GH, GenetAb, ImmunAb, N02, N03, OGFA, P32, P40, PGegResA, RA&MP, SCOPUS, T05, VS.
—BLDSC (8267.297955), East View.
Published by: Zhejiang Daxue Yixueyuan, Fushu Di-2 Yiyuan, 88, Jiefang Lu, Hangzhou, 310009, China. TEL 86-571-87783654, FAX 86-571-87783659. **Dist. by:** China International Book Trading Corp, 35 Chegongzhuang Xilu, Haidian District, PO Box 399, Beijing 100044, China. TEL 86-10-68412045, FAX 86-10-68412023, cibtc@mail.cibtc.com.cn, http://www.cibtc.com.cn.

616.99 CHN ISSN 1002-3070
SHIYONG ZHONGLIUXUE ZAZHI/JOURNAL OF PRACTICAL ONCOLOGY. Variant title: Practical Oncology Journal. Text in Chinese. 1987. bi-m. USD 31.20 (effective 2009). **Document type:** *Journal, Academic/Scholarly.*
Related titles: Online - full text ed.
Published by: Heilongjiang Zhongliu Fangzhi Bangongshi/Heilongjiang Cancer Prevention and Treatment Office, 150, Heping LU, Ha'erbin, Heilongjiang 150040, China. TEL 86-451-86625603, FAX 86-451-86665003. Circ: 4,000. **Dist. by:** China International Book Trading Corp, 35 Chegongzhuang Xilu, Haidian District, PO Box 399, Beijing 100044, China. TEL 86-10-68412045, FAX 86-10-68412023, cibtc@mail.cibtc.com.cn, http://www.cibtc.com.cn.

616 RUS ISSN 1814-4861
➤ **SIBIRSKIJ ONKOLOGICESKIJ ZURNAL/SIBERIAN JOURNAL OF ONCOLOGY.** Text in Russian; Summaries in English. 2002. bi-m. RUR 400 (effective 2008). back issues avail. **Document type:** *Journal, Academic/Scholarly.* **Description:** Publishes articles involving research and clinical activity in the fields of cancer diagnosis, treatment and prevention.
Indexed: RefZh.
Published by: N I I Onkologii Tomskogo Naucnogo Centra S O - R A M N, 5, Kooperativny St, Tomsk, 634009, Russian Federation. TEL 7-3822-511039, FAX 7-3822-514097. Ed., Pub., R&P E Choinzonov.

616.99 DEU ISSN 0721-6831
SIGNAL; Leben mit Krebs. Text in German. 1982. 4/yr. EUR 25 to institutions (effective 2009). adv. **Document type:** *Journal, Academic/Scholarly.*
Related titles: Online - full text ed.
Indexed: AES.
—GNLM. **CCC.**
Published by: Karl F. Haug Verlag in MVS Medizinverlage Stuttgart GmbH & Co. KG (Subsidiary of: Georg Thieme Verlag), Oswald-Hesse-Str 50, Stuttgart, 70469, Germany. TEL 49-711-89310, FAX 49-711-8931706, kunden.service@thieme.de, http://www.haug-verlag.de. Ed. Dr. Sabine Tettenborn. Adv. contact Guenter Fecke. B&W page EUR 1,524, color page EUR 2,444; trim 190 x 255. Circ: 15,000 (paid and controlled).

616.994 FRA ISSN 1959-6324
LA SITUATION DU CANCER EN FRANCE EN (YEAR). Text in French. 2007. irreg. **Document type:** *Journal.*
Related titles: Online - full text ed.: free.
Published by: Institut National du Cancer, 52 Av Andre Morizet, Boulogne-Billancourt, 92513 Cedex, France. TEL 33-1-41105000, contact@institutcancer.fr.

616 PRT ISSN 0871-2549
SKIN CANCER. Text in Portuguese, English. 1986. q. USD 80 in the European Union; USD 160 elsewhere (effective 2005).
Related titles: Online - full text ed.
Indexed: EMBASE, ExcerpMed, R10, Reac, SCOPUS.
—BLDSC (8295.915000), IE, Ingenta.
Published by: (Associacao Portuguesa de Cancro Cutaneo), Revismedica, Av. Coronel Eduardo Galhardo, Lote A 2.2, Arm.2, Piso 3, Lisbon, 1170-105, Portugal. TEL 351-21-816-0690, FAX 351-21-814-9627.

616.994 JPN ISSN 0915-3535
CODEN: SNCAEX
SKIN CANCER. Text in Japanese. 1986. 3/yr. **Document type:** *Journal, Academic/Scholarly.*
Indexed: INIS AtomInd.
Published by: Nihon Hifu Akusei Shuyo Gakkai/Japanese Society for Skin Cancer, Shinshu University, School of Medicine, Department of Dermatology, 3-1-1 Asahi, Matsumoto, 390-8621, Japan. TEL 81-263-372647, FAX 81-263-372646, http://www.skincancer.jp/index.html.

616 USA ISSN 0898-6665
SKIN CANCER FOUNDATION JOURNAL. Text in English. 198?. a. USD 5 per issue to non-members; free to members (effective 2010). back issues avail. **Document type:** *Journal, Academic/Scholarly.* **Description:** Compiles short articles to strengthen public awareness of the importance of prevention and early detection of skin cancer.
Related titles: Online - full text ed.; Special ed(s).: Fourth World Congress of Cancers of the Skin.
Published by: Skin Cancer Foundation, 149 Madison Ave, Ste 901, New York, NY 10016. TEL 212-725-5176, FAX 212-725-5751, info@skincancer.org, http://www.skincancer.org. Pub. Perry Robins.

616.992 BRA ISSN 1415-6725
➤ **SOCIEDADE BRASILEIRA DE CANCEROLOGIA. REVISTA.** Text in Portuguese; Abstracts in Portuguese, English. 1998. q. free to qualified personnel. **Document type:** *Journal, Academic/Scholarly.*
Indexed: GH, T05.
Published by: Sociedade Brasileira de Cancerologia, Rua Alfredo Magalhaes 4-Barra, Salvador, BA 40140-140, Brazil. rsbc@atarde.com.br, http://www.sbcancer.org.br. Ed. Lair Barbosa de Castro Ribeiro. Circ: 5,500 (free).

616.992 CAN ISSN 1715-894X
RC271.A62
➤ **SOCIETY FOR INTEGRATIVE ONCOLOGY. JOURNAL.** Abbreviated title: J S I O. Text in English. 2003. q. CAD 348.75 domestic to institutions; USD 325.40 in United States to institutions; USD 421.90 elsewhere to institutions; CAD 303.15 combined subscription domestic to institutions (print & online eds.); USD 393.30 combined subscription in United States to institutions (print & online eds.); USD 510.90 combined subscription elsewhere to institutions (print & online eds.) (effective 2010). adv. back issues avail. **Document type:** *Journal, Academic/Scholarly.* **Description:** Provides oncology professionals with information about the data-based utility of complementary therapies.
Formerly (until 2005): Journal of Cancer Integrative Medicine (1544-6301)
Related titles: Online - full text ed.: ISSN 1715-8958. CAD 355 domestic to institutions; USD 339.20 foreign to institutions (effective 2010).
Indexed: A01, C06, C07, CA, EMBASE, ExcerpMed, MEDLINE, P30, R10, Reac, SCOPUS, T02.
—BLDSC (4889.380000), IE. **CCC.**
Published by: (Society for Integrative Oncology USA), B.C. Decker Inc., 50 King St E, 2nd Fl, Hamilton, ON L8N 2A1, Canada. TEL 905-522-7017, 800-568-7281, FAX 905-522-7839, info@bcdecker.com. Ed. Lorenzo Cohen TEL 713-745-4260. Adv. contact Jennifer Coates TEL 905-522-7017 ext 291. B&W page USD 920, color page USD 220; trim 8.125 x 10.875. Circ: 532.

616.992 JPN ISSN 1343-2443
SOKI DAICHOGAN/EARLY COLORECTAL CANCER. Text in Japanese. 1997. bi-m. JPY 15,750 (effective 2007). **Document type:** *Journal, Academic/Scholarly.*
Published by: Nihon Medikaru Senta/Nihon Medical Center, Inc., Kyowa Bldg., 1-64, Kanda-jinbo-cho, Chiyoda-ku, Tokyo, 101-0051, Japan. TEL 81-3-32913901, FAX 81-3-32913377, http://www.nmckk.co.jp/.

616.992 618.1 ZAF ISSN 2074-2835
▼ ➤ **SOUTHERN AFRICAN JOURNAL OF GYNAECOLOGICAL ONCOLOGY.** Abbreviated title: S A J G O. Text in English. 2009. 2/yr. **Document type:** *Journal, Academic/Scholarly.* **Description:** Focuses on all aspects of gynecological cancer prevention, detection, diagnosis and treatment.
Related titles: Online - full text ed.: ISSN 2220-105X. 2009.
Indexed: A01.
Published by: Medpharm Publications (Pty) Ltd, PO Box 14804, Lyttelton, 0140, South Africa. TEL 27-12-6647460, FAX 27-12-6646276, reception@medpharm.co.za, http://www.medpharm.co.za. Ed. Greta Dreyer.

616.992 NLD ISSN 2210-3368
SPREEKUUR ONCOLOGIE. Text in Dutch. 2004. q. free to qualified personnel (effective 2010). adv. **Document type:** *Journal, Trade.*
Formerly (until 2010): Oncologie Vademecum (1574-2377)
Published by: Bohn Stafleu van Loghum B.V. (Subsidiary of: Springer Science+Business Media), Postbus 246, Houten, 3990 GA, Netherlands. TEL 31-30-6383767, FAX 31-30-6383839, boekhandels@bsl.nl, http://www.bsl.nl. adv.: color page EUR 3,940; trim 210 x 297. Circ: 847.

616.994 NLD ISSN 2211-3002
STICHTING ZAADBALKANKER. Text in Dutch. 2006. s-a. EUR 15 membership (effective 2011). **Document type:** *Newsletter, Consumer.*
Formerly (until 2010): Stichting Kernzaak. Nieuwsbrief (2210-4208)
Address: Postbus 8152, Utrecht, 3503 RD, Netherlands. TEL 31-30-2916090, FAX 31-30-6046101, info@stichtingkernzaak.nl, http://www.stichtingkernzaak.nl.

616.99 DEU ISSN 0941-4355
RC271.P33 CODEN: SCCAEO
➤ **SUPPORTIVE CARE IN CANCER.** Text in English. 1992. m. EUR 1,177, USD 1,394 combined subscription to institutions (print & online eds.) (effective 2012). adv. back issues avail.; reprint service avail. from PSC. **Document type:** *Journal, Academic/Scholarly.*
Description: Provides the most recent scientific and social information on all aspects of supportive care for cancer patients.
Related titles: Microform ed.: (from PQC); Online - full text ed.: ISSN 1433-7339 (from IngentaConnect).
Indexed: A01, A03, A08, A20, A22, A26, A34, A35, A36, AMED, ASCA, AgBio, C06, C07, CA, CABA, CurCont, D01, E01, E12, EMBASE, ExcerpMed, F09, FR, GH, H16, I05, INI, ISR, IndMed, Inpharma, LT, MEDLINE, N02, N03, N04, OR, P20, P22, P24, P27, P30, P33, P35, P46, P48, P54, PQC, R10, R12, RA&MP, RM&VM, RRTA, Reac, S12, SCI, SCOPUS, T02, T05, W07, W10.
—BLDSC (8547.638620), GNLM, IE, Infotrieve, Ingenta, INIST. **CCC.**
Published by: (Multinational Association of Supportive Care in Cancer), Springer (Subsidiary of: Springer Science+Business Media), Tiergartenstr 17, Heidelberg, 69121, Germany. TEL 49-6221-4870, FAX 49-6221-345229. Eds. Fred Ashbury, H J Senn. **Subscr. in the Americas to:** Springer New York LLC, Journal Fulfillment, PO Box 2485, Secaucus, NJ 07096. TEL 800-777-4643, 201-348-4033, FAX 201-348-4505, journals-ny@springer.com, http://www.springer.com; **Subscr. to:** Springer Distribution Center, Kundenservice Zeitschriften, Haberstr 7, Heidelberg 69126, Germany. TEL 49-6221-3454303, FAX 49-6221-3454229, subscriptions@springer.com.

616.99 617 GBR ISSN 0960-7404
CODEN: SUOCEC
➤ **SURGICAL ONCOLOGY;** a review journal of cancer research & management. Text in English. 1992. 4/yr. EUR 747 in Europe to institutions; JPY 99,500 in Japan to institutions; USD 835 elsewhere to institutions (effective 2012). adv. bk.rev. illus. index. back issues avail.; reprints avail. **Document type:** *Journal, Academic/Scholarly.*
Description: Contains review articles that contribute to the advancement of knowledge in surgical oncology and related fields.
Related titles: Microform ed.: (from PQC); Online - full text ed.: ISSN 1879-3320 (from IngentaConnect, ScienceDirect); Supplement(s): Surgical Oncology. Supplement. ISSN 1350-7281.
Indexed: A01, A03, A08, A26, ASCA, BIOBASE, CA, CurCont, EMBASE, ExcerpMed, I05, IABS, IndMed, Inpharma, MEDLINE, P30, P35, R10, Reac, SCI, SCOPUS, T02, W07.
—BLDSC (8548.242000), GNLM, IE, Infotrieve, Ingenta. **CCC.**
Published by: Elsevier Ltd (Subsidiary of: Elsevier Science & Technology), The Blvd, Langford Ln, Kidlington, Oxford, OX5 1GB, United Kingdom. TEL 44-1865-843000, FAX 44-1865-843010, journalscustomerserviceemea@elsevier.com. Ed. Riccardo A Audisio. Circ: 180.

616.992 BEL
SURGICAL ONCOLOGY/ONCOLOGISCHE HEELKUNDE. Text in Dutch, English. 1995. irreg. price varies. **Document type:** *Monographic series, Academic/Scholarly.*
Published by: Leuven University Press, Blijde Inkomststraat 5, Leuven, 3000, Belgium. TEL 32-16-325345, FAX 32-16-325352, university.press@upers.kuleuven.ac.be, http://www.kuleuven.ac.be/upers.

616.99 617 USA ISSN 1055-3207
CODEN: SOCAF7
SURGICAL ONCOLOGY CLINICS OF NORTH AMERICA. Text in English. 1992. q. USD 357 in United States to institutions; USD 444 elsewhere to institutions (effective 2012). adv. index. back issues avail.; reprints avail. **Document type:** *Journal, Academic/Scholarly.*
Description: Discusses diagnostic techniques, surgical procedures, and radiation therapy for the treatment of cancer patients.
Related titles: Microform ed.: (from PQC); Online - full text ed.: ISSN 1558-5042 (from ScienceDirect).
Indexed: A22, C06, C07, C08, CINAHL, CurCont, EMBASE, ExcerpMed, INI, IndMed, MEDLINE, P30, R10, Reac, SCI, SCOPUS, W07.
—BLDSC (8548.242100), GNLM, IE, Infotrieve, Ingenta. **CCC.**
Published by: W.B. Saunders Co. (Subsidiary of: Elsevier Health Sciences), Elsevier, Health Sciences Division, Order Fulfillment, 3251 Riverport Ln, Maryland Heights, MO 63043. TEL 314-872-8370, 800-325-4177, FAX 314-432-1380, JournalCustomerService-usa@elsevier.com, http://www.us.elsevierhealth.com.

616.994 USA ISSN 0491-6263
SURVEY OF COMPOUNDS WHICH HAVE BEEN TESTED FOR CARCINOGENIC ACTIVITY. Text in English. a. USD 695 (effective 2004).
Media: CD-ROM.
Published by: G M A Industries, Inc, 60 West St., Ste. 203, Annapolis, MD 21401-2480. info@gmai.com, http://www.gmai.com/.

616.994 FIN ISSN 0356-3081
SYOPA/CANCER. Text in Finnish, Swedish. 1962. 6/yr. adv. bk.rev. 32 p./no. 3 cols./p.; **Document type:** *Magazine, Consumer.*
Description: Contains articles and information about the latest discoveries in cancer treatment, information on rehabilitation, personal stories and other material of interest to cancer patients and their families.
Former titles (until 1977): Syovantorjunta (0049-2787); (until 1969): Terveystyo
Related titles: Online - full text ed.
Published by: Suomen Syopayhdistys/Cancer Society of Finland, Liisankatu 21 B, Helsinki, 00170, Finland. TEL 358-9-135331. Ed. Seppo Pyrhoenen. Circ: 134,000.

616.992 FRA ISSN 1776-2596
RC254.A1
➤ **TARGETED ONCOLOGY;** biotherapies for the clinicians in oncology. Text in English. 2006. 4/yr. EUR 435, USD 538 combined subscription to institutions (print & online eds.) (effective 2012). reprint service avail. from PSC. **Document type:** *Journal, Academic/Scholarly.*
Description: Contains research on new cancer treatments emerging that target molecular pathways and inhibit tumor growth and progression.
Related titles: Online - full text ed.: ISSN 1776-260X (from IngentaConnect).
Indexed: A22, A26, B26, E01, EMBASE, ExcerpMed, I05, MEDLINE, P30, SCI, SCOPUS, W07.
—IE, Ingenta, INIST. **CCC.**
Published by: Springer France (Subsidiary of: Springer Science+Business Media), 22 Rue de Palestro, Paris, 75002, France. TEL 33-1-53009860, FAX 33-1-53009861, sylvie.kamara@springer.com. Ed. Jean-Francoise Morere.

616.994 USA ISSN 1533-0346
RC261.A1 CODEN: TCRTBS
➤ **TECHNOLOGY IN CANCER RESEARCH AND TREATMENT.** Abbreviated title: T C R T. Text in English. 2002. bi-m. USD 300 to individuals (print or online ed.); USD 1,242 to institutions (print or online ed.) non-profit; USD 1,531 to corporations (print or online ed.); USD 450 combined subscription to individuals (print & online eds.); USD 1,932 combined subscription to institutions (print & online eds.) non-profit; USD 2,163 combined subscription to corporations (print & online eds.) (effective 2010). back issues avail. **Document type:** *Journal, Academic/Scholarly.*
Related titles: Online - full text ed.: ISSN 1533-0338.
Indexed: B25, BIOSIS Prev, CurCont, EMBASE, ExcerpMed, MEDLINE, MycolAb, P30, R10, Reac, RefZh, SCI, SCOPUS, W07.
—BLDSC (8758.745210), IE, Ingenta, INIST. **CCC.**
Published by: Adenine Press, 2066 Central Ave, Schenectady, NY 12304. TEL 518-456-0784, FAX 518-452-4955, info@adeninepress.com, http://www.adeninepress.com. Ed. Mukti H Sarma TEL 518-442-4441.

616.992 GBR ISSN 1758-8340
RC270.8
▼ **THERAPEUTIC ADVANCES IN MEDICAL ONCOLOGY.** Text in English. 2009 (Jul.). bi-m. USD 1,071, GBP 579 combined subscription to institutions (print & online eds.); USD 1,050, GBP 567 to institutions (effective 2011). **Document type:** *Journal, Academic/Scholarly.* **Description:** Contains the latest research and reviews on systemic cancer treatments including chemotherapy, endocrine therapy, biological therapy and immunotherapy.
Related titles: Online - full text ed.: ISSN 1758-8359. USD 964, GBP 521 to institutions (effective 2011).
Indexed: A22, E01, EMBASE, P30, SCOPUS.
—**CCC.**
Published by: Sage Publications Ltd. (Subsidiary of: Sage Publications, Inc.), 1 Oliver's Yard, 55 City Rd, London, EC1Y 1SP, United Kingdom. TEL 44-20-73248500, FAX 44-20-73248600, info@sagepub.co.uk, http://www.uk.sagepub.com/home.nav. Ed. Charles Coombes.

616.992 JPN ISSN 1882-2576
CODEN: NHGAEO
THERMAL MEDICINE/JAPANESE JOURNAL OF HYPERTHERMIC ONCOLOGY. Text in Japanese. 1985. q. **Document type:** *Journal, Academic/Scholarly.*
Formerly (until 2007): Nihon Haipasamia Gakkaishi (0911-2529)
Related titles: Online - full text ed.: ISSN 1882-3750. free (effective 2011).
Indexed: INIS AtomInd.
Published by: Nihon Haipasamia Gakkai/Japanese Society of Hyperthermic Oncology, Nara Medical University School of Medicine, Department of Biology, Shijo-cho 840, Kashihara, Nara 634-8521, Japan. TEL 81-744-223051 ext 2264, FAX 81-744-253345, thermmed@naramed-u.ac.jp, http://www.jsho.jp/.

616.994 AUS ISSN 1759-7706
▼ **THORACIC CANCER.** Text in English. 2010. q. GBP 428 in United Kingdom to institutions; EUR 501 in Europe to institutions; USD 677 elsewhere to institutions (effective 2012). adv. back issues avail.; reprints avail. **Document type:** *Journal, Academic/Scholarly.*
Description: Aims to facilitate collaboration and exchange of information on basic, translational, and applied clinical research in lung cancer, esophageal cancer, mediastinal cancer, and other thoracic malignancies.
Related titles: Online - full text ed.: ISSN 1759-7714. GBP 428 in United Kingdom to institutions; EUR 501 in Europe to institutions; USD 677 elsewhere to institutions (effective 2012).
Indexed: A22, C06, E01.
Published by: Wiley-Blackwell Publishing Asia (Subsidiary of: Wiley-Blackwell Publishing Ltd.), 155 Cremorne St, Richmond, VIC 3121, Australia. TEL 61-3-92743100, FAX 61-3-92743101, melbourne@wiley.com, http://eu.wiley.com/WileyCDA/Section/index.html. Eds. Qinghua Zhou, Yan Sun. **Dist. by:** 33 Windorah St, Stafford, QLD 4053, Australia. TEL 61-7-33548455, FAX 61-7-33527109, brisbane@wiley.com.

616.994 NLD ISSN 0923-8018
TIJDSCHRIFT KANKER. Text in Dutch. 1977. 6/yr. EUR 35 (effective 2008). adv. bk.rev. **Document type:** *Journal, Academic/Scholarly.*
Formerly: K.W.F. Nieuws (0022-7447)
—IE, Infotrieve.
Published by: (Nederlandse Vereniging tot Steun aan het Koningin Wilhelmina Fonds voor de Kankerbestrijding), K B U Uitgevers B.V., Postbus 24, Oisterwyk, 5060 AA, Netherlands. TEL 31-13-5216665, FAX 31-13-5285255, kbu@vandenboogaardgroep.nl, http://www.vandenboogaardgroep.nl. Circ: 3,000.

616.992 JPN ISSN 1349-5747
CODEN: TOSHEG
TOKEIBU SHUYO/HEAD AND NECK CANCER. Text in Japanese. 1974. a. **Document type:** *Journal, Academic/Scholarly.*
Formerly (until 2004): Tokeibu Shuyo (Tokyo, 1974) (0911-4335)
Indexed: INIS AtomInd.
—**CCC.**
Published by: Nihon Tokeibu Shuyo Gakkai/Japan Society for Head and Neck Cancer, 2-4-11 Fukagawa Kotoku, Tokyo, 135-0033, Japan. TEL 81-3-56201953, FAX 81-3-56201960, jshnc-service@onebridge.co.jp, http://www.jshnc.umin.ne.jp/.

616.992 JPN ISSN 0915-8383
TOUKAI KOTSU NANBU SHUYOU/JOURNAL OF TOKAI BONE AND SOFT TISSUE TUMORS. Text in Japanese. 1989. a. **Document type:** *Journal, Academic/Scholarly.*
—**CCC.**
Published by: Toukai Kotsu Nanbu Shuyou Kenkyuukai/Tokai Bone and Soft Tissue Tumors, c/o Fujita Health University School of Medicine, Second Teaching Hospital, 3-6-10, Otoubashi, Nagoya, 454, Japan. TEL 81-52-3218171, FAX 81-52-3224734.

616.992 NZL ISSN 1177-2727
RC268.42
➤ **TRANSLATIONAL ONCOGENOMICS.** Text in English. 2006. irreg. free (effective 2011). **Document type:** *Journal, Academic/Scholarly.*
Description: Aims to assist in the dissemination of novel genetic, epigenetic and molecular pathway information related to clinical cancer.
Media: Online - full text.
Indexed: A01, CA, EMBASE, ExcerpMed, P30, SCOPUS, T02.
—**CCC.**
Published by: Libertas Academica Ltd., PO Box 302-624, North Harbour, Auckland, 1330, New Zealand. TEL 64-21-662617, FAX 64-21-740006. Ed. Robert Gallagher.

616.992 USA ISSN 1944-7124
RC254.A1
➤ **TRANSLATIONAL ONCOLOGY.** Text in English. 2008 (Sep.). m. USD 575 domestic; USD 750 foreign (effective 2010). back issues avail. **Document type:** *Journal, Academic/Scholarly.* **Description:** Bring out articles about laboratory studies of novel therapeutic interventions as well as clinical trials which evaluate new treatment paradigms for cancer.
Related titles: Online - full text ed.: ISSN 1936-5233. free (effective 2010).
Indexed: BIOSIS Prev, EMBASE, ExcerpMed, MycolAb, P30, SCI.
Published by: Neoplasia Press, c/o Divya Khanna, University of Michigan Medical Ctr, 109 Zina Pitcher Pl, BSRB-A628, Ann Arbor, MI 48109. TEL 734-647-6679, FAX 734-615-5669, info@neoplasia.com, http://www.neoplasia.com. Ed. Theodore S Lawrence.

616.992 GBR ISSN 2046-5807
▼ **TREATMENT STRATEGIES. ONCOLOGY.** Text in English. 2010. a. free to qualified personnel (effective 2011). adv. reprints avail. **Document type:** *Academic/Scholarly.* **Description:** Provides clinicians with information on the latest developments from the field of oncology with emphasis on both therapeutic and technological aspects.
Related titles: Online - full text ed.: ISSN 2046-5815. free (effective 2011).
Published by: Cambridge Research Centre, Coppergate House, 16 Brune St, London, E1 7NJ, United Kingdom. TEL 44-20-79538490, FAX 44-20-80430691, info@treatmentstrategies.co.uk. Ed., Adv. contact Rachel Holcroft.

616.992 IND ISSN 0973-1040
TRENDS IN CANCER RESEARCH. Text in English. 2005. a. EUR 134 in Europe; JPY 17,582 in Japan; USD 149 elsewhere (effective 2010). **Document type:** *Journal, Academic/Scholarly.* **Description:** Publishes review articles, original research papers and short communications on all aspects of cancer research at the clinical and experimental levels.
Related titles: CD-ROM ed.
Indexed: B&BAb, B19, B21, ESPM, I10, OGFA.
Published by: Research Trends (P) Ltd., T.C. 17 / 250 (3), Chadiyara Rd, Poojapura, Trivandrum, Kerala 695 012, India. TEL 91-471-2344424, FAX 91-471-2344423, info@researchtrends.net.

616.99 USA
TRIPLE I ONCOLOGY. Text in English. 19??. a. **Document type:** *Magazine, Trade.*
Published by: MediMedia USA, Inc. (Subsidiary of: United Business Media Limited), 350 Starke Rd., Carlstadt, NJ 07072-2108. TEL 201-727-9300, 800-969-7237, FAX 201-727-0099, http://www.medimedia.com.

616.992 NLD ISSN 1010-4283
CODEN: OBIMD4
➤ **TUMOR BIOLOGY.** Text in English. 1980. bi-m. EUR 1,531, USD 2,072 combined subscription to institutions (print & online eds.) (effective 2012). adv. back issues avail.; reprint service avail. from PSC. **Document type:** *Journal, Academic/Scholarly.* **Description:** Focuses on the basic biology of tumor markers, the crucial indicators of the onset of cancer. Reflects new approaches analyzing the structural and functional properties, differentiation status and lineage derivation of individual cells in normal and neoplastic populations.
Former titles (until 1987): Tumour Biology (0289-5447); (until 1984): Oncodevelopmental Biology and Medicine (0167-1618)
Related titles: Online - full text ed.: ISSN 1423-0380 (from IngentaConnect).
Indexed: A20, A22, AIDS&CR, ASCA, B&BAb, B19, B21, B25, BIOSIS Prev, CA, CurCont, E01, EMBASE, ExcerpMed, H13, IBR, IBZ, ISR, ImmunAb, IndMed, Inpharma, MEDLINE, MycolAb, OGFA, P10, P20, P22, P30, P35, P48, P50, P52, P53, P54, P56, PQC, R10, Reac, SCI, SCOPUS, T02, W07.
—BLDSC (9070.645500), CASDDS, GNLM, IE, Infotrieve, Ingenta, INIST. **CCC.**
Published by: (International Society for Oncodevelopmental Biology and Medicine CHE), Springer Netherlands (Subsidiary of: Springer Science+Business Media), Van Godewijckstraat 30, Dordrecht, 3311 GX, Netherlands. TEL 31-78-6576050, FAX 31-78-6576474. Ed. Torgny Stigbrand. adv.: page CHF 1,815; trim 210 x 280. Circ: 800 (controlled).

616.994 JPN ISSN 0041-4093
CODEN: TUREA6
➤ **TUMOR RESEARCH: EXPERIMENTAL AND CLINICAL/GAN KENKYU, JIKKEN TO RINSHO.** Text in English. 1966. a. per issue exchange basis. abstr.; bibl.; charts; illus.; stat. **Document type:** *Journal, Academic/Scholarly.*
Related titles: Microfilm ed.: (from PQC).
Indexed: B25, BIOBASE, BIOSIS Prev, ChemAb, EMBASE, ExcerpMed, IABS, INIS AtomInd, MycolAb, P30, R10, Reac, RefZh, SCOPUS.
—BLDSC (9070.650000), CASDDS, GNLM, INIST.
Published by: Sapporo Ika Daigaku, Gan Kenkyusho/Sapporo Medical University, Cancer Research Institute, 17 Minami-1Jo Nishi, Chuo-ku, Sapporo, Hokkaido 060-8556, Japan. TEL 81-11-6112111, FAX 81-11-6112299. Circ: 550.

616.99 DEU ISSN 0722-219X
RC254.A1
➤ **TUMORDIAGNOSTIK & THERAPIE.** Text in German; Summaries in English, German. 1980. bi-m. EUR 256 to institutions; EUR 337 combined subscription to institutions (print & online eds.); EUR 52 newsstand/cover (effective 2011). adv. **Document type:** *Journal, Academic/Scholarly.*
Formerly (until 1982): Tumordiagnostik (0173-086X)

Related titles: Online - full text ed.: ISSN 1439-1279. EUR 325 to institutions (effective 2011).
Indexed: A22, ASCA, EMBASE, ExcerpMed, IBR, IBZ, ISR, Inpharma, R10, Reac, SCOPUS.
—BLDSC (9070.675000), GNLM, IE, Infotrieve, Ingenta, INIST. **CCC.**
Published by: Georg Thieme Verlag, Ruedigerstr 14, Stuttgart, 70469, Germany. TEL 49-711-8931421, FAX 49-711-8931410, leser.service@thieme.de, http://www.thieme-connect.de. Eds. J Schuette, S Seeber. Adv. contact Ulrike Bradler. Circ: 5,700 (paid).

616.994 ITA ISSN 0300-8916
RC261.A1 CODEN: TUMOAB
➤ **TUMORI**; a journal of experimental and clinical oncology. Text in English; Abstracts in English. 1911. bi-m. EUR 170 domestic to institutions; EUR 250 foreign to institutions (effective 2009). adv. bk.rev. bibl.; illus. index, cum.index. 96 p./no.; back issues avail.; reprints avail. **Document type:** *Journal, Academic/Scholarly.*
Related titles: Online - full text ed.: ISSN 2038-2529.
Indexed: A22, ASCA, B25, BIOBASE, BIOSIS Prev, CIN, ChemAb, ChemTitl, CurCont, DentInd, EMBASE, ExcerpMed, IABS, ISR, IndMed, Inpharma, MEDLINE, MycolAb, P30, P35, R10, Reac, SCI, SCOPUS, W07.
—BLDSC (9070.700000), CASDDS, GNLM, IE, Infotrieve, Ingenta, INIST.
Published by: (Istituto Nazionale per lo Studio e la Cura dei Tumori), Il Pensiero Scientifico Editore, Via Bradano 3-C, Rome, 00199, Italy. TEL 39-06-862821, FAX 39-06-86282250. Circ: 3,700.

616.992 ITA ISSN 1828-6615
TUMORI FEMMINILI. Text in Multiple languages. 2006. bi-m. **Document type:** *Journal, Academic/Scholarly.*
Published by: Elsevier Masson (Subsidiary of: Elsevier Health Sciences), Via Paleocapa 7, Milan, 20121, Italy. TEL 39-02-881841, FAX 39-02-88184302, info@masson.it, http://www.masson.it.

616.992 DEU
➤ **TUMORZENTRUM MUENCHEN. MANUAL.** Text in German. 2000. a. EUR 19.90 per issue (effective 2010).
Related titles: Online - full text ed.
Published by: (Tumorzentrum Muenchen), W. Zuckschwerdt Verlag GmbH, Industriestr 1, Germering, 82110, Germany. TEL 49-89-8943490, FAX 49-89-89434950, post@zuckschwerdtverlag.de, http://www.zuckschwerdtverlag.de.

616.992 TUR ISSN 1300-7467
TURK ONKOLOJI DERGISI/TURKISH JOURNAL OF ONCOLOGY. Text in Turkish, English. 1986. q. **Document type:** *Journal, Academic/ Scholarly.*
Related titles: Print ed.: free (effective 2011).
Indexed: EMBASE, R10, Reac, SCOPUS.
Published by: KARE Publishing Ed. Erkan Topuz.

616.99 TUR ISSN 1019-3103
RC261.A1 CODEN: TJCAFH
➤ **TURKISH JOURNAL OF CANCER.** Text in English. 1967. 4/yr. TRY 60 domestic; USD 60 foreign (effective 2009). adv. bk.rev. back issues avail. **Document type:** *Journal, Academic/Scholarly.* **Description:** Contains scientific research articles, reviews, editorials, and letters to the editor in the fields of basic and clinical oncology.
Formerly (until 1992): Kanser (0377-9750)
Related titles: Online - full text ed.: free (effective 2009).
Indexed: A01, A03, A08, CA, EMBASE, ExcerpMed, P10, P20, P48, P50, P53, P54, PQC, R10, Reac, SCOPUS, T02.
—BLDSC (9072.468000), INIST.
Published by: Turkish Association of Cancer Research and the Council of War/Turk Kanser Arastirma ve Savas Kurumu, Atac 1st Sokak No.21/1, Yenisehir, Ankara, 06410, Turkey. TEL 90-312-4312950, FAX 90-312-4313958, info@turkkanser.org.tr, http://www.turkcancer.org.tr. Ed. Dr. Dincer Firat. Circ: 1,000 (paid).

616.994 616.15 TUR ISSN 1306-133X
RC633.A1
U H O D/INTERNATIONAL JOURNAL OF HEMATOLOGY AND ONCOLOGY; uluslararasi hematoloji-onkoloji dergisi. Text in Turkish, English. a. **Document type:** *Journal, Academic/Scholarly.* **Description:** Publishes papers describing original research, case reports as well as review articles. It covers areas of interest relating to radiation oncology, medical ongology, surgical oncology, and hematology.
Formerly (until 2005): Turk Hematoloji-Onkoloji Dergisi/Turkish Journal of Hematology and Oncology (1301-8825)
Related titles: Online - full text ed.: free (effective 2011).
Indexed: A01, BIOBASE, CA, EMBASE, ExcerpMed, IABS, R10, Reac, SCI, SCOPUS, T02, W07.
—BLDSC (9082.818402), IE, Ingenta.
Published by: Akademi Doktorlar Yayinevi, 4 Cadde 56, Sokak, No. 49-E, Hilal Cankaya, Ankara, 06550, Turkey. TEL 90-312-4402028, FAX 90-312-4404749, http://www.uhod.org. Ed. Dr. Ibrahim H Gullu.

U I C C INTERNATIONAL CALENDAR OF MEETINGS ON CANCER. (Union Internationale Contre le Cancer) *see* MEETINGS AND CONGRESSES

616.99 CHE
U I C C INTERNATIONAL DIRECTORY OF CANCER INSTITUTES AND ORGANIZATIONS. (Union Internationale Contre le Cancer) Text in English. 1976. quadrennial. **Document type:** *Directory, Trade.*
Formerly: International Directory of Specialized Cancer Research and Treatment Establishments
Published by: International Union Against Cancer, 62 route de Frontenex, Geneva, 1207, Switzerland. TEL 41-22-8091811, FAX 41-22-8091810, info@uicc.ch, http://www.uicc.ch.

616.992 USA ISSN 1551-8272
RC268.6
U.S. NATIONAL TOXICOLOGY PROGRAM. REPORT ON CARCINOGENS. Text in English. 1980. biennial. **Document type:** *Government.* **Description:** Identifies and discusses agents, substances, mixtures, or exposure circumstances that may pose a hazard to human health by virtue of their carcinogenicity.
Formerly: U.S. National Toxicology Program. Annual Report on Carcinogens (0272-2836); Which was formed by the merger of: Report on Carcinogens. Summary; Report on Carcinogens. Full Report
Related titles: Online - full text ed.: ISSN 1551-8280.
Indexed: EMBASE, ExcerpMed, MEDLINE, P30, R10, Reac, SCOPUS.
—BLDSC (7639.462000).
Published by: U.S. National Toxicology Program, PO Box 12233, Research Triangle Park, NC 27709. TEL 919-541-3419, ehis@niehs.nih.gov, http://ehis.niehs.nih.gov. Ed. C W Jameson.

616.992 GBR ISSN 2045-6344
➤ **U S ONCOLOGY & HEMATOLOGY.** Text in English. 2008. s-a. back issues avail. **Document type:** *Journal, Academic/Scholarly.* **Description:** Brings together industry experts in each specialized sector within oncology, providing readers with information on the latest innovations and developments.
Formed by the merger of (2008-2011): U S Hematology (1756-6126); (2008-2011): U S Oncology (1758-4027); Which was formerly (until 2008): U S Oncological Disease (1753-4011); (until 2006): U S Oncological Review
Related titles: Online - full text ed.: ISSN 2045-6352.
Published by: Touch Briefings (Subsidiary of: Touch Group plc), Saffron House, 6-10 Kirby St, London, EC1N 8TS, United Kingdom. TEL 44-20-74525600, FAX 44-20-74525606, info@touchbriefings.com, http://www.touchbriefings.com/.

616.992 GBR ISSN 0191-3123
RB25 CODEN: ULPAD3
➤ **ULTRASTRUCTURAL PATHOLOGY.** Text in English. 1980. bi-m. GBP 1,260, EUR 1,700, USD 2,070 combined subscription to institutions (print & online eds.); GBP 2,515, EUR 3,320, USD 4,145 combined subscription to corporations (print & online eds.) (effective 2010). adv. bk.rev. abstr.; bibl.; illus.; stat. index. back issues avail.; reprint service avail. from PSC. **Document type:** *Journal, Academic/Scholarly.* **Description:** Covers electron microscopy, immunohistochemistry, the study and diagnosis of human diseases, EM and oncology, theory, and possible applications.
Related titles: Microform ed.: (from PQC); Online - full text ed.: ISSN 1521-0758 (from IngentaConnect).
Indexed: A01, A02, A03, A08, A20, A22, ASCA, B25, BIOBASE, BIOSIS Prev, C11, CA, ChemAb, CurCont, DentInd, E01, EMBASE, ExcerpMed, H04, IABS, ISR, IndMed, Inpharma, MEDLINE, MS&D, MycolAb, P30, R10, Reac, SCI, SCOPUS, T02, W07.
—BLDSC (9082.816000), CASDDS, GNLM, IE, Infotrieve, Ingenta, INIST. **CCC.**
Published by: Informa Healthcare (Subsidiary of: T & F Informa plc), Telephone House, 69-77 Paul St, London, EC2A 4LQ, United Kingdom. TEL 44-20-70175000, FAX 44-20-70176792, healthcare.enquiries@informa.com. Ed. Jahn M Nesland TEL 47-22-935620. Circ: 750. **Subscr. in N. America to:** Taylor & Francis Inc., Customer Services Dept, 325 Chestnut St, 8th Fl, Philadelphia, PA 19106. TEL 215-625-8900, 800-354-1420, FAX 215-625-8914, customerservice@taylorandfrancis.com; **Subscr. outsdie N. America to:** Taylor & Francis Ltd., Journals Customer Service, Sheepen Pl, Colchester, Essex CO3 3LP, United Kingdom. TEL 44-20-70175544, FAX 44-20-70175198, tf.enquiries@tfinforma.com.

616.9 USA
UNIVERSITY OF TEXAS. M.D. ANDERSON CANCER CENTER. RESEARCH REPORT. Text in English. 1955. a. free (effective 2010). charts; illus.; pat. **Document type:** *Report, Academic/Scholarly.* **Description:** Compendium of research accomplishments at the center.
Former titles (until 1985): M.D. Anderson Hospital and Tumor Institute. Annual Research Report (0896-128X); (until 1977): M.D. Anderson Hospital and Tumor Institute. Research Report (0066-1635)
Related titles: Online - full text ed.
Published by: University of Texas, MD Anderson Cancer Center, 1515 Holcombe Blvd, Houston, TX 77030. TEL 713-792-2121, ckoller@mdanderson.org, http://www.mdanderson.org.

616.992 NLD ISSN 1872-115X
➤ **UPDATE ON CANCER THERAPEUTICS.** Text in English. 2006. 4/yr. EUR 391 in Europe to institutions; JPY 54,000 in Japan to institutions; USD 463 elsewhere to institutions (effective 2009). **Document type:** *Journal, Academic/Scholarly.* **Description:** Contains reviews on progress and achievements in clinical oncology and cancer therapeutics.
Media: Online - full content. **Related titles:** Online - full text ed.
Indexed: A26, CA, EMBASE, ExcerpMed, I05, P30, R10, Reac, SCOPUS, T02.
—IE, Ingenta. **CCC.**
Published by: Elsevier BV (Subsidiary of: Elsevier Science & Technology), Radarweg 29, PO Box 211, Amsterdam, 1000 AE, Netherlands. TEL 31-20-4853911, FAX 31-20-4852457, JournalsCustomerServiceEMEA@elsevier.com, http://www.elsevier.nl. Eds. Dr. G Giaccone, Dr. P Sondel, Dr. R Schilsky.

616.9 USA ISSN 1078-1439
RD670 CODEN: URONEC
➤ **UROLOGIC ONCOLOGY**; seminars and original investigations. Text in English. 1983. bi-m. USD 377 in United States to institutions; USD 483 elsewhere to institutions (effective 2012). adv. back issues avail.; reprints avail. **Document type:** *Journal, Academic/Scholarly.* **Description:** Features research from Urologic Oncology with the comprehensive overviews from Seminars in Urologic Oncology. Provides clinical research and reviews of critical scientific relevance.
Incorporates (1995-2002): Seminars in Urologic Oncology (1081-0943); Which was formerly (until 1995): Seminars in Urology (0730-9147)
Related titles: Online - full text ed.: ISSN 1873-2496 (from IngentaConnect, ScienceDirect).
Indexed: A01, A03, A08, A22, A26, BIOBASE, C06, C07, CA, CurCont, EMBASE, ExcerpMed, I05, IABS, Inpharma, MEDLINE, P30, R10, Reac, S01, SCI, SCOPUS, T02, W07.
—BLDSC (9124.627000), CASDDS, GNLM, IE, Infotrieve, Ingenta, INIST. **CCC.**
Published by: (Society of Urologic Oncology), Elsevier Inc. (Subsidiary of: Elsevier Science & Technology), 1600 John F Kennedy Blvd, Philadelphia, PA 19103. TEL 215-239-3900, FAX 215-238-7883, JournalCustomerService-usa@elsevier.com, http://www.elsevier.com. Ed. Michael J Droller. Adv. contact Kevin Dunn TEL 201-767-4170. Circ: 575.

616.992 USA ISSN 2153-4888
RC270.8
▼ **VALUE BASED CANCER CARE.** Text in English. 2010 (May). bi-m. USD 150 (effective 2011). **Document type:** *Journal, Academic/ Scholarly.*
Related titles: Online - full text ed.: ISSN 2153-4896. 2010 (May).
Published by: Engage Healthcare Communications, LLC, 241 Forsgate Dr, Ste 205A, Monroe Township, NJ 08831. TEL 732-992-1882, blanche@engagehc.com.

616.3 NLD ISSN 2210-2361
VAN GISTEREN NAAR MORGEN. Text in Dutch. 200?. q. **Document type:** *Newsletter.*
Published by: Contactgroep G I S T Nederland-Belgie, Postbus 8152, Utrecht, 3503 RD, Netherlands. info@contactgroepgist.nl.

616.99 GBR ISSN 2045-824X
▼ ➤ **VASCULAR CELL.** Text in English. 2009. irreg. free (effective 2011). adv. back issues avail. **Document type:** *Journal, Academic/ Scholarly.* **Description:** Publishes articles on recent advances in the understanding of the processes responsible for neovascularization and pathological angiogenesis.
Formerly (until 2011): Journal of Angiogenesis Research (2040-2384)
Media: Online - full text.
Indexed: A26, E08, EMBASE, H12, I05, P30, S09, SCOPUS.
Published by: BioMed Central Ltd. (Subsidiary of: Springer Science+Business Media), 236 Gray's Inn Rd, London, WC1X 8HB, United Kingdom. TEL 44-20-31922000, FAX 44-20-31922010, info@biomedcentral.com, http://www.biomedcentral.com. Eds. Jan Kitajewski, Mark Slevin, Yihai Cao.

➤ **VETERINARY AND COMPARATIVE ONCOLOGY.** *see* VETERINARY SCIENCE

616.992 ITA ISSN 2038-4483
▼ **VINCERE IL CANCRO SI PUO.** Text in Italian. 2010. m. **Document type:** *Magazine, Consumer.*
Published by: Sprea Editori Srl, Via Torino 51, Cernusco sul Naviglio, MI 20063, Italy. TEL 39-02-92432222, FAX 39-02-92432236, editori@sprea.it, http://www.sprea.it.

616.994 FRA ISSN 0249-0358
VIVRE. Text in French. 1923. q. EUR 3.81 (effective 2008). bk.rev. bibl.; charts; illus.; stat. **Document type:** *Magazine, Consumer.* **Description:** Information on cancer research, prevention, and treatments.
Formerly: Lutte Contre le Cancer (0024-7642)
Indexed: IndMed, P30.
—BLDSC (9244.470000), INIST.
Published by: Ligue Nationale Francaise Contre le Cancer, 14 rue Corvisart, Paris, 75013, France. TEL 33-1-53552427, FAX 33-1-53552553. Circ: 120,000.

616.994 RUS ISSN 0507-3758
CODEN: VOONAW
➤ **VOPROSY ONKOLOGII**; nauchno-prakticheskii zhurnal. Text in Russian; Summaries in Russian, English. 1955. bi-m. USD 294 foreign (effective 2005). adv. bk.rev. abstr.; bibl.; charts; illus.; stat. Index. back issues avail. **Document type:** *Journal, Academic/ Scholarly.* **Description:** Discusses problems of experimental and clinical oncology (origin, development, course, diagnosis and methods of treating neoplasms), the problems of the organization of oncological aid to the population, prevention and treatment of malignant tumors and precancerous conditions.
Related titles: Diskette ed.; E-mail ed.; Fax ed.; Online - full text ed.
Indexed: B25, BIOSIS Prev, CIN, ChemAb, ChemTitl, DBA, DentInd, DokArb, EMBASE, ExcerpMed, INIS AtomInd, IndMed, MEDLINE, MycolAb, P30, R10, Reac, RefZh, SCOPUS.
—CASDDS, East View, GNLM, INIST. **CCC.**
Published by: Redaktsiya Zhurnala Voprosy Onkologii, ul B Zelenina 43-a, St Petersburg, 197110, Russian Federation. TEL 7-812-2353009, FAX 7-812-2350986, aesculap@mail.wplus.net. Ed. Sergei V Kanayev. Pub. Catherine Tkalenko. R&P, Adv. contact Alexei Belkin TEL 7-812-235-1719. B&W page USD 600, color page USD 2,000; trim 205 x 210. Circ: 1,000. **Dist. by:** East View Information Services, 10601 Wayzata Blvd, Minneapolis, MN 55305. TEL 952-252-1201, 800-477-1005, FAX 952-252-1202, info@eastview.com, http://www.eastview.com.

616.994 USA ISSN 1557-5780
WOMEN & CANCER. Text in English. 2005. q. USD 24.95 (effective 2007). adv. illus. **Document type:** *Magazine, Consumer.*
Related titles: Online - full text ed.; Japanese Translation: Pink. 2007 (Oct.).
Published by: Omni Health Media, Llc., P O Box 2581, Ketchum, ID 83340. editor@womenandcancermag.com. Eds. Charles H Weaver, Juliana Hansen.

616.992 CHN ISSN 2218-4333
▼ ➤ **WORLD JOURNAL OF CLINICAL ONCOLOGY.** Text in English. 2010. m. free (effective 2011). **Document type:** *Journal, Academic/ Scholarly.*
Media: Online - full text.
Published by: Beijing Baishideng BioMed Scientific Co., Ltd (Subsidiary of: Baishideng Publishing Group Co., Limited), Rm 903, Bldg D, Ocean International Center, 62 Dongsihuan Zhonglu, Chaoyang District, Beijing, 100025, China. TEL 86-10-85381892, FAX 86-10-85381893, baishideng@wjgnet.com.

616.992 CHN ISSN 1948-5204
▼ ➤ **WORLD JOURNAL OF GASTROINTESTINAL ONCOLOGY.** Abbreviated title: W J G O. Text in English. 2010. m. free (effective 2011). **Document type:** *Journal, Academic/Scholarly.* **Description:** Features research on gastrointestinal oncology.
Media: Online - full text.
Indexed: P30.
Published by: Beijing Baishideng BioMed Scientific Co., Ltd (Subsidiary of: Baishideng Publishing Group Co., Limited), Rm 903, Bldg D, Ocean International Center, 62 Dongsihuan Zhonglu, Chaoyang District, Beijing, 100025, China. TEL 86-10-85381892, FAX 86-10-85381893, baishideng@wjgnet.com. Ed. Lian-Sheng Ma.

616.992 CAN ISSN 1920-4531
▼ ➤ **WORLD JOURNAL OF ONCOLOGY.** Text in English. 2010. bi-m. **Document type:** *Journal, Academic/Scholarly.*
Related titles: Online - full text ed.: ISSN 1920-454X. free (effective 2011).
Published by: Elmer Press, 8485 Rue Outaouais, Brossard, Montreal, PQ J4Y 3E2, Canada. TEL 514-467-3868, FAX 450-812-3126.

616.992 617 GBR ISSN 1477-7819
➤ **WORLD JOURNAL OF SURGICAL ONCOLOGY.** Text in English. 2003. irreg. free (effective 2010). adv. back issues avail. **Document type:** *Journal, Academic/Scholarly.* **Description:** Provides research articles on the super speciality of surgical oncology and broadly related subjects such as epidemiology, cancer research, biomarkers, prevention, pathology, radiology, cancer treatment, clinical trials, multimodality treatment and molecular biology.
Media: Online - full text.

Indexed: A01, A26, CA, CurCont, EMBASE, ExcerpMed, I05, MEDLINE, P20, P22, P30, P48, P54, PQC, R10, Reac, SCI, SCOPUS, T02, W07.
—CCC.
Published by: BioMed Central Ltd. (Subsidiary of: Springer Science+Business Media), 236 Gray's Inn Rd, London, WC1X 8HB, United Kingdom. TEL 44-20-31922000, FAX 44-20-31922010, info@biomedcentral.com, http://www.biomedcentral.com. Ed. Dr. Manoj Pandey TEL 91-542-2309511. Adv. contact Natasha Bailey TEL 44-20-31922231.

616.992 POL ISSN 1428-2526
WSPOLCZESNA ONKOLOGIA/CONTEMPORARY ONCOLOGY. Text in Polish. 1997. 10/yr. PLZ 50 domestic (effective 2010). **Document type:** *Journal, Academic/Scholarly.*
Related titles: Online - full text ed.: Contemporary Oncology / Wspolczesna Onkologia. free (effective 2011).
Indexed: EMBASE, ExcerpMed, R10, Reac, SCI, SCOPUS, W07.
—BLDSC (9364.934370).
Published by: (Fundacja Onkologii Doswiadczalnej i Klinicznej, Stowarzyszenie na Rzecz Walki z Rakiem Geny Zycia), Termedia sp. z o.o./Termedia Publishing House, ul Wenedow 9/1, Poznan, 61614, Poland. TEL 48-61-8227781, FAX 48-61-8227781, termedia@termedia.pl, http://www.termedia.pl. Ed. Andrzej Mackiewicz.

616.992 CHN ISSN 1672-4992
XIANDAI ZHONGLIU YIXUE/JOURNAL OF MODERN ONCOLOGY. Text in Chinese. 1999. q. USD 62.40 (effective 2009). **Document type:** *Journal, Academic/Scholarly.*
Formerly: Shaanxi Zhongliu Yixue/Shaanxi Oncology Medicine (1008-7001)
—BLDSC (9367.037380).
Address: 309 Yanta West Rd., Xian, Shaaxi 710061, China. TEL 86-29-85276012, FAX 86-29-85277356. Ed. Shu-ye Li. **Dist. by:** China International Book Trading Corp, 35 Chegongzhuang Xilu, Haidian District, PO Box 399, Beijing 100044, China. TEL 86-10-68412045, FAX 86-10-68412023, cibtc@mail.cibtc.com.cn, http://www.cibtc.com.cn.

616.994071 616.043 616.042 CHN
YANBIAN - JIBIAN - TUBIAN/CARCINOGENESIS, TERATOGENESIS AND MUTAGENESIS. Text in Chinese. 1989. q. CNY 24 (effective 2004). **Document type:** *Academic/Scholarly.*
Related titles: Online - full text ed.
Address: 22, Xinlin Lu, Shantou Daxue Yixueyuan, Shantou, Guangdong 515031, China. TEL 86-754-8900267, FAX 86-754-8557562. **Dist. by:** China International Book Trading Corp, 35 Chegongzhuang Xilu, Haidian District, PO Box 399, Beijing 100044, China. TEL 86-10-68412045, FAX 86-10-68412023, cibtc@mail.cibtc.com.cn, http://www.cibtc.com.cn.

YANKE XIN JINZHAN/RECENT ADVANCES IN OPHTHALMOLOGY. *see* MEDICAL SCIENCES—Ophthalmology And Optometry

616.994 USA ISSN 1040-1741
RC261 CODEN: YEONEX
YEAR BOOK OF ONCOLOGY. Text in English. 1957. a. USD 217 in United States to institutions; USD 235 elsewhere to institutions (effective 2012). adv. illus. **Document type:** *Yearbook, Academic/Scholarly.* **Description:** Presents abstracts of pertinent literature with commentary by leading experts in the field.
Formerly (until 1989): The Year Book of Cancer (0084-3679)
Related titles: CD-ROM ed.; Online - full text ed.
—GNLM, INIST. **CCC.**
Published by: Mosby, Inc. (Subsidiary of: Elsevier Health Sciences), 1600 John F. Kennedy Blvd, Ste 1800, Philadelphia, PA 19103. TEL 215-239-3900, 800-523-1649, FAX 215-239-3990, elspcs@elsevier.com, http://www.us.elsevierhealth.com. Ed. Dr. Patrick Loehrer Sr.

616.992 CHN ISSN 1674-5671
▼ **ZHONGGUO AIZHENG FANGZHI ZAZHI/CHINESE JOURNAL OF ONCOLOGY PREVENTION AND TREATMENT.** Text in Chinese. 2009. q. **Document type:** *Journal, Academic/Scholarly.*
Former titles (until 2009): Zhongguo Yixue Wenzhai (Zhongliuxue)/ Chinese medical Abstracts, Oncology (1003-7209); (until 1984): Yixue Wenzhai (Linchuang Zhongliu Fence)
Related titles: Online - full text ed.
Published by: Guangxi Zhongliu Fangzhi Yanjiusuo/Guangxi Cancer Institute, 71, Hedi Lu, Nanning, 530021, China. TEL 86-771-5332455. **Co-sponsor:** Zhongguo Yishi Xiehui.

ZHONGGUO GANRAN KONGZHI ZAZHI/CHINESE JOURNAL OF INFECTION AND CHEMOTHERAPY. *see* MEDICAL SCIENCES—Communicable Diseases

616.992 CHN ISSN 1004-0242
ZHONGGUO ZHONGLIU/BULLETIN OF CHINESE CANCER. Text in Chinese. 1992. m. USD 49.20 (effective 2009). **Document type:** *Journal, Academic/Scholarly.*
Related titles: Online - full text ed.
—BLDSC (3180.125300), East View.
Published by: Zhejiang Sheng Zhongliu Yiyuan, 38, Guangji Rd., Hangzhou, 310022, China. TEL 86-571-88122280, FAX 86-571-88147297.

616.99 CHN ISSN 1000-8179
CODEN: ZZLIEP
ZHONGGUO ZHONGLIU LINCHUANG. Text in Chinese; Abstracts in English. 1963. s-m. USD 86.40 (effective 2009). adv. **Document type:** *Academic/Scholarly.* **Description:** Publishes original articles pertaining to the clinical disciplines of oncology and the related laboratory studies.
Related titles: CD-ROM ed.; Online - full text ed.; ◆ English ed.: Clinical Oncology and Cancer Research. ISSN 1674-5361.
Indexed: ExtraMED, R10, Reac, SCOPUS.
—CASDDS, East View, GNLM.
Published by: Tianjin Yike Daxue Fushu Zhongliu Yiyuan/Tianjin Medical University Cancer Institute and Hospital, Ti-Yuan-Bei, Huanhu Xi Lu, Hexi-qu, Tianjin, 300060, China. Ed. Tian-Ze Zhang. Pub. Lian Zhong Zhao. Adv. contact Hong Xin Yang. color page CNY 6,000. Circ: 10,000. **Dist. overseas by:** China International Book Trading Corp, 35 Chegongzhuang Xilu, Haidian District, PO Box 399, Beijing 100044, China. TEL 86-10-68412045, FAX 86-10-68412023, cibtc@mail.cibtc.com.cn, http://www.cibtc.com.cn.

616.992 CHN ISSN 1007-385X
ZHONGGUO ZHONGLIU SHENGWU ZHILIAO ZAZHI/CHINESE JOURNAL OF CANCER BIOTHERAPY. Text in Chinese. 1994. bi-m. USD 24.60 (effective 2009). **Document type:** *Journal, Academic/Scholarly.*
Related titles: Online - full text ed.
Indexed: A34, A35, A36, AgBio, B&BAb, B19, CABA, E12, EMBASE, ExcerpMed, F08, F11, F12, GH, H17, N02, N03, P33, PN&I, R08, RA&MP, RM&VM, RefZh, SCOPUS, SoyAb, T05, VS.
—BLDSC (9512.835433), East View, IE.
Published by: Publishing House of Chinese Journal of Cancer Biotherapy, c/o Institution of Immunology, 800, Xiangyin Lu, Shanghai, 200433, China. Ed. Xue-Tao Cao.

616.992 616.07 CHN ISSN 1004-4221
ZHONGHUA FANGSHE ZHONGLIUXUE ZAZHI/CHINESE JOURNAL OF RADIATION ONCOLOGY. Text in Chinese. 1992. q. CNY 50 (effective 2004). **Document type:** *Journal, Academic/Scholarly.*
Related titles: Online - full text ed.
Indexed: INIS AtomInd.
—BLDSC (3180.630000).
Address: PO Box 2258, Beijing, 100021, China. TEL 86-10-67700737, FAX 86-10-67737011. **Dist. by:** China International Book Trading Corp, 35 Chegongzhuang Xilu, Haidian District, PO Box 399, Beijing 100044, China. TEL 86-10-68412045, FAX 86-10-68412023, cibtc@mail.cibtc.com.cn, http://www.cibtc.com.cn.

ZHONGHUA RUXIANBING ZAZHI (DIANZIBAN)/CHINESE JOURNAL OF BREAST DISEASE (ELECTRONIC VERSION). *see* MEDICAL SCIENCES—Obstetrics And Gynecology

ZHONGHUA SHENJING WAIKE ZAZHI/CHINESE JOURNAL OF NEUROSURGERY. *see* MEDICAL SCIENCES—Surgery

616.992 CHN ISSN 1673-5269
CODEN: ZZFZA8
ZHONGHUA ZHONGLIU FANGZHI ZAZHI/CHINESE JOURNAL OF CANCER PREVENTION AND TREATMENT. Text in Chinese; Abstracts in Chinese, English. 1994. s-a. USD 98.40 (effective 2009). **Document type:** *Journal, Academic/Scholarly.*
Former titles (until 2006): Zhongliu Fangzhi Zazhi/China Journal of Cancer Prevention and Treatment (1009-4571); (until 2000): Qilu Zhongliu Zazhi/Journal of Qilu Oncology (1006-9569)
Related titles: Online - full content ed.
Indexed: B&BAb, B19, B21, EMBASE, ExcerpMed, GenetAb, ImmunAb, OGFA, SCOPUS.
—BLDSC (9512.844057), East View.
Address: No.44, Jiyan Rd, Jinan, 250117, China. TEL 86-531-87984783, FAX 86-531-87984783. Ed. Jin-ming Yu. Circ: 5,000.

616.99 CHN ISSN 0253-3766
CODEN: CCLCDY
ZHONGHUA ZHONGLIU ZAZHI/CHINESE JOURNAL OF ONCOLOGY. Text in Chinese. bi-m. USD 117.60 (effective 2009). **Document type:** *Journal, Academic/Scholarly.*
Related titles: CD-ROM ed.; Online - full text ed.
Indexed: A22, B25, BIOSIS Prev, ChemAb, EMBASE, ExcerpMed, ExtraMED, IndMed, MEDLINE, MycolAb, P30, R10, Reac, SCOPUS.
—BLDSC (3180.460000), CASDDS, East View, GNLM, IE, Infotrieve, Ingenta.
Published by: Zhongguo Kexue Yixue Kexueyuan/Chinese Academy of Medical Sciences, Zhaoyang-qu, no.17 Panjiayuan, Beijing, 100021, China. **Dist. by:** China International Book Trading Corp, 35 Chegongzhuang Xilu, Haidian District, PO Box 399, Beijing 100044, China. TEL 86-10-68412045, FAX 86-10-68412023, cibtc@mail.cibtc.com.cn, http://www.cibtc.com.cn. **Co-publisher:** Zhonggo Xiehe Yike Daxue, Zhongliu Yiyuan.

616.992 CHN ISSN 1000-7431
CODEN: ZHONEV
ZHONGLIU/TUMOR. Text in Chinese. 1981. m. **Document type:** *Journal, Academic/Scholarly.*
Related titles: Online - full text ed.
Indexed: A35, A36, AgBio, B&BAb, B19, B21, BIOBASE, CABA, D01, E12, EMBASE, ExcerpMed, F08, F11, F12, GH, GenetAb, H16, IABS, ImmunAb, N02, N03, OGFA, P32, P33, P37, P39, P40, R08, R10, R12, RA&MP, RM&VM, Reac, SCOPUS, SoyAb, T05, VS.
—BLDSC (9070.645000), East View.
Published by: Shanghai Zhongliu Yanjiusuo, Xietu Lu 2200-Nong, no.25, Shanghai, 200032, China. TEL 86-21-64436792, FAX 86-21-64032388. Ed. Yu-tang Gao.

616.992 CHN ISSN 1000-8578
ZHONGLIU FANGZHI YANJIU/CANCER RESEARCH ON PREVENTION AND TREATMENT. Text in Chinese. 1973. m. USD 49.20 (effective 2009). **Document type:** *Journal, Academic/Scholarly.*
Related titles: Online - full text ed.
Indexed: A34, A35, A36, AgBio, AgrForAb, B&BAb, B19, B21, CABA, E12, ESPM, F08, F11, F12, GH, H16, ImmunAb, N02, N03, OGFA, P32, P33, P39, R12, RA&MP, RM&VM, T05, ToxAb, VS.
Published by: Zhongguo Kangai Xiehui/Chinese Anticancer Association, 116, Wuchangzhoudaoyuan Nanlu, Wuhan, 430079, China. TEL 86-27-87670126, FAX 86-27-87670122, http://www.lungca.org. **Dist. by:** China International Book Trading Corp, 35 Chegongzhuang Xilu, Haidian District, PO Box 399, Beijing 100044, China. TEL 86-10-68412045, FAX 86-10-68412023, cibtc@mail.cibtc.com.cn, http://www.cibtc.com.cn.

616.992 CHN ISSN 1673-5412
ZHONGLIU JICHU YU LINCHUANG/JOURNAL OF BASIC AND CLINICAL ONCOLOGY. Text in Chinese. 1990. bi-m. USD 24.60 (effective 2009). **Document type:** *Journal, Academic/Scholarly.*
Formerly (until 2006): Henan Zhongliuxue Zazhi/Henan Journal of Oncology (1003-1464)
Related titles: Online - full text ed.
—BLDSC (9512.844420), East View.
Published by: Henan Zhongliuxue Zazhi, 40, Daxue Road, Zhengzhou, Henan 450052, China. TEL 86-371-6658178. Ed. Liuxing Wang. **Dist. by:** China International Book Trading Corp, 35 Chegongzhuang Xilu, Haidian District, PO Box 399, Beijing 100044, China. TEL 86-10-68412045, FAX 86-10-68412023, cibtc@mail.cibtc.com.cn, http://www.cibtc.com.cn.

616.992 CHN ISSN 1006-9801
➤ **ZHONGLIU YANJIU YU LINCHUANG/CANCER RESEARCH AND CLINIC.** Text in English. 1986. m. CNY 72, USD 72; CNY 6 newsstand/cover (effective 2009). **Document type:** *Journal, Academic/Scholarly.* **Description:** Covers the latest developments of theoretical and applied researches in the fields of cancer.
Related titles: Online - full text ed.
Indexed: A35, A36, AgBio, AgrForAb, B&BAb, B19, B21, CABA, D01, E12, ESPM, F08, F11, F12, GH, GenetAb, ImmunAb, N02, N03, OGFA, OR, P33, R12, RA&MP, RM&VM, T05, ToxAb, VS, VirolAbstr.
—East View.
Published by: Shanxi Sheng Zhongliu Yiyuan, Shanxi Sheng Zhongliu Yanjiusuo/Shanxi Cancer Hospital, Shanxi Cancer Institute, 3, Zigong Xinjie, Taiyuan, Shanxi 030013, China. TEL 86-351-4650389, FAX 86-351-4651415. Ed. Xiao-bo Liang.

616.992 CHN ISSN 1674-0904
ZHONGLIU YUFANG YU ZHILIAO/JOURNAL OF CANCER CONTROL AND TREATMENT. Text in Chinese. 1973. q. CNY 40; CNY 10 per issue (effective 2009). **Document type:** *Journal, Academic/Scholarly.*
Formerly (until 2008): Sichuan Zhongliu Fangzhi/Sichuan Tumour Prevention and Treatment (1007-0281)
Related titles: Online - full text ed.
—East View.
Published by: Sichuan Sheng Zhongliu Yiyuan, Section 4, no.55, Remin Nanlu, Chengdu, 610041, China. TEL 86-28-85420233, FAX 86-28-85420115, http://www.sichuancancer.org/. **Dist. by:** China International Book Trading Corp, 35 Chegongzhuang Xilu, Haidian District, PO Box 399, Beijing 100044, China. TEL 86-10-68412045, FAX 86-10-68412023, cibtc@mail.cibtc.com.cn, http://www.cibtc.com.cn.

616.992 CHN ISSN 1671-170X
CODEN: ZZHAAB
ZHONGLIUXUE ZAZHI. Text in Chinese; Abstracts in Chinese, English. 1971. m. CNY 96, USD 96; CNY 9 per issue (effective 2010). **Document type:** *Journal, Academic/Scholarly.* **Description:** Provides a forum for communication and information for clinicians, researchers and educators. Publishes papers that focus on clinical treatment, research and control of common cancers in China such as ovarian and colorectal cancers. Also includes special reports and advertisements.
Former titles (until 2001): Zhejiang Zhongliu/Zhejiang Cancer Journal (1006-5504); (until 1992): Zhejiang Zhongliu Tongxun/Zhejiang Cancer; (until 1972): Zhongliu Gongzuo Qingkuang Huibao/Situation Report of Tumor Control
Related titles: Online - full text ed.
Published by: Zhejiang Sheng Zongliu Yiyuan/Zhejiang Provincial Cancer Hospital, No.38,Guangji Road, Banxianqiao, Hangzhou, 310022, China. TEL 86-571-88122280, FAX 86-571-88122282, http://www.zchospital.com/cms/default.aspx. Circ: 4,000.

MEDICAL SCIENCES—Ophthalmology And Optometry

617.7 USA
A R V O ANNUAL MEETING ABSTRACT SEARCH AND PROGRAM PLANNER. Text in English. 19??. a.
Published by: Association for Research in Vision and Ophthalmology, 12300 Twinbrook Pkwy, Ste 250, Rockville, MD 20852. TEL 240-221-2900, FAX 240-221-0370, arvo@arvo.org.

617.7 ESP ISSN 0210-4695
ACTA ESTRABOLOGICA. Text in Spanish. 1973. s-a. back issues avail. **Document type:** *Journal, Academic/Scholarly.*
Published by: Sociedad Espanola de Estrabologia, C Donoso Cortes, 73 1o., Madrid, 28015, Spain.

617.7 USA ISSN 1755-375X
RE1 CODEN: AOSCFV
➤ **ACTA OPHTHALMOLOGICA (PRINT).** Text in English. 1923. 8/yr. GBP 336 in United Kingdom to institutions; EUR 426 in Europe to institutions; USD 562 in the Americas to institutions; USD 657 elsewhere to institutions; GBP 386 combined subscription in United Kingdom to institutions (print & online eds.); EUR 491 combined subscription in Europe to institutions (print & online eds.); USD 647 combined subscription in the Americas to institutions (print & online eds.); USD 756 combined subscription elsewhere to institutions (print & online eds.) (effective 2012). bibl.; charts; illus. index, cum.index: vols.1-25. back issues avail.; reprint service avail. from PSC. **Document type:** *Journal, Academic/Scholarly.* **Description:** Publishes original scientific articles, major reviews, clinical reviews, cases and clinical series, letters, and transactions of the five Nordic ophthalmological societies.
Former titles (until 2008): Acta Ophthalmologica Scandinavica (1395-3907); Which incorporated (1981-1998): Oftalmolog (0108-5344); (until 1995): Acta Ophthalmologica (0001-639X)
Related titles: ◆ Online - full text ed.: Acta Ophthamologica (Online). ISSN 1755-3768; ◆ Supplement(s): Acta Ophthalmologica. Supplementum. ISSN 1755-3776.
Indexed: A01, A03, A08, A22, A26, ASCA, B21, B25, BIOSIS Prev, CA, CIN, ChemAb, ChemTitl, CurCont, DokArb, E01, EMBASE, ESPM, ExcerpMed, H&SSA, H12, I10, IBR, IBZ, INI, ISR, IndMed, Inpharma, MEDLINE, MycolAb, NSA, P30, P35, PsycholAb, R10, Reac, SCI, SCOPUS, T02, W07.
—BLDSC (0641.750500), CASDDS, GNLM, IE, Infotrieve, Ingenta, INIST. **CCC.**
Published by: (European Association for Vision and Eye Research BEL), Wiley-Blackwell Publishing, Inc. (Subsidiary of: Wiley-Blackwell Publishing Ltd.), Commerce Pl, 350 Main St, Malden, MA 02148. TEL 781-388-8200, FAX 781-388-8210, info@wiley.com, http://www.wiley.com/WileyCDA/. Ed. Einar Stefansson.

617.7 USA ISSN 1755-3776
CODEN: AOSSFB
➤ **ACTA OPHTHALMOLOGICA. SUPPLEMENTUM.** Text in English. 1932. irreg. free to subscribers to Acta Ophthalmologica. adv. back issues avail. **Document type:** *Monographic series, Academic/Scholarly.*
Former titles (until 2008): Acta Ophthalmologica Scandinavica. Supplementum (1395-3931); (until 1995): Acta Ophthalmologica. Supplementum (0065-1451)
Related titles: Online - full text ed.: ISSN 1600-5465; ◆ Supplement to: Acta Ophthalmologica (Print). ISSN 1755-375X.

Indexed: A22, DentInd, DokArb, IndMed, MEDLINE, P30, P35, R10, SCOPUS.
—BLDSC (0641.754000), CASDDS, IE, Ingenta, INIST. **CCC.**
Published by: Wiley-Blackwell Publishing, Inc. (Subsidiary of: Wiley-Blackwell Publishing Ltd.), Commerce Pl, 350 Main St, Malden, MA 02148. TEL 781-388-8200, FAX 781-388-8210, info@wiley.com, http://www.wiley.com/WileyCDA/.

617.7 USA ISSN 1755-3768
➤ **ACTA OPHTHAMOLOGICA (ONLINE).** Text in English. bi-m. GBP 336 in United Kingdom to institutions; EUR 426 in Europe to institutions; USD 562 in the Americas to institutions; USD 657 elsewhere to institutions (effective 2012). **Document type:** *Journal, Academic/Scholarly.*
Formerly (until 2008): Acta Ophthamologica Scandinavica (Online) (1600-0420)
Media: Online - full text (from IngentaConnect). **Related titles:** ◆ Print ed.: Acta Ophthalmologica (Print). ISSN 1755-375X.
—CCC.
Published by: (European Association for Vision and Eye Research BEL), Wiley-Blackwell Publishing, Inc. (Subsidiary of: Wiley-Blackwell Publishing Ltd.), Commerce Pl, 350 Main St, Malden, MA 02148. TEL 781-388-8200, FAX 781-388-8210, info@wiley.com, http://www.wiley.com/WileyCDA/.

617.7 658 USA ISSN 1087-2809
ADMINISTRATIVE EYECARE. Text in English. 1992. q. USD 100 domestic to non-members; USD 150 foreign to non-members; free to members (effective 2011). adv. back issues avail. **Document type:** *Magazine, Trade.* **Description:** Provides focused, up-to-date information on such topics as efficiency, marketing strategies, skill development, legal concerns, personnel issues, and legislative changes.
Formerly (until 1996): Administrative Ophthalmology (1060-5991)
Related titles: Online - full text ed.
Published by: American Society of Ophthalmic Administrators, 4000 Legato Rd, Ste 700, Fairfax, VA 22033. TEL 703-788-5777, 800-451-1339, FAX 703-591-5020, asoa@asoa.org, http://www.ascrs.org. Circ: 2,208.

617.7 USA ISSN 1558-0199
ADVANCED STUDIES IN OPHTHALMOLOGY. Text in English. 2004 (Oct.). irreg. USD 150 per issue domestic; USD 200 per issue foreign (effective 2010). **Document type:** *Journal, Academic/Scholarly.*
Related titles: Online - full text ed.: ISSN 1558-0202.
Indexed: C06, C07.
Published by: (Wilmer Ophthalmological Institute), Galen Publishing, LLC, 166 W Main St, PO Box 340, Somerville, NJ 08876. TEL 908-253-9001, FAX 908-253-9002, info@asimcme.com, http://www.galenpublishing.com. Ed. Neil M Bressler. Pub. Jack M Ciattarelli.

617.7 ITA ISSN 0390-5764
➤ **AGGIORNAMENTI DI TERAPIA OFTALMOLOGICA.** Text in Italian, English. 1949. 3/yr. adv. abstr. 64 p./no.; back issues avail. **Document type:** *Journal, Academic/Scholarly.*
Published by: (Farmigea SpA), Pacini Editore SpA, Via A Gherardesca 1, Ospedaletto, PI 56121, Italy. TEL 39-050-313011, FAX 39-050-3130300, pacini.editore@pacinieditore.it, http://www.pacinieditore.it.

617.7 PAN ISSN 1990-598X
ALCON EN IBEROAMERICA (SPANISH EDITION). Text in Spanish. 2006. 3/yr. **Document type:** *Journal, Academic/Scholarly.*
Related titles: Portuguese ed.: Alcon na Iberoamerica (Portuguese Edition). ISSN 1990-5998.
Published by: Highlights of Ophthalmology International, PO Box 0819-06890, El Dorado, Panama. TEL 507-3170161, FAX 507-3170155, http://www.thehighlights.com.

618.920977 USA ISSN 1091-8531
RE48.2.C5 CODEN: JAOAB2
➤ **AMERICAN ASSOCIATION FOR PEDIATRIC OPHTHALMOLOGY AND STRABISMUS. JOURNAL.** Key Title: Journal of A A P O S. Text in English. 1997. bi-m. USD 348 in United States to institutions; USD 427 elsewhere to institutions (effective 2012). adv. back issues avail.; reprints avail. **Document type:** *Journal, Academic/Scholarly.* **Description:** Presents expert information on children's eye diseases and on strabismus as it impacts all age groups.
Related titles: Online - full text ed.: ISSN 1528-3933 (from ScienceDirect).
Indexed: A20, A22, A26, CA, CurCont, E01, EMBASE, ExcerpMed, I05, IndMed, Inpharma, MEDLINE, P30, P35, R10, Reac, SCI, SCOPUS, T02, W07.
—BLDSC (4674.942000), IE, Infotrieve, Ingenta. **CCC.**
Published by: (American Association for Pediatric Ophthalmology and Strabismus), Mosby, Inc. (Subsidiary of: Elsevier Health Sciences), 1600 John F. Kennedy Blvd, Ste 1800, Philadelphia, PA 19103. TEL 215-239-3900, 800-523-1649, FAX 215-239-3990, elspcs@elsevier.com, http://www.us.elsevierhealth.com. Ed. David G Hunter.

617.7 USA ISSN 0002-9394
RE1 CODEN: AJOPAA
➤ **AMERICAN JOURNAL OF OPHTHALMOLOGY.** Abbreviated title: A J O. Text in English. 1884. m. USD 654 in US & Canada to institutions; USD 870 elsewhere to institutions (effective 2012). adv. bk.rev. abstr.; bibl.; illus. Index. back issues avail.; reprints avail. **Document type:** *Journal, Academic/Scholarly.* **Description:** Describes clinical investigations, clinical observations and clinically relevant laboratory investigations related to ophthalmology.
Incorporates (1922-1926): Ophthalmic Year Book; (1911-1917): Annals of Ophthalmology; (1891-1917): Ophthalmic Record; (1904-1917): Ophthalmology; (1911-1917): Ophthalmic Literature; (1898-1915): Anales de Oftalmologia
Related titles: CD-ROM ed.; Microform ed.: (from PQC); Online - full text ed.: ISSN 1879-1891. 200? (from IngentaConnect, ScienceDirect).
Indexed: A01, A03, A08, A22, A26, A36, AIM, ASCA, B25, BIOSIS Prev, BioDAb, C06, C07, CA, CABA, CIN, ChemAb, ChemTitl, CurCont, DBA, DentInd, DokArb, E08, E12, EMBASE, ExcerpMed, G08, GH, H11, H12, H17, I05, IDIS, ISR, IndMed, Inpharma, Kidney, MEDLINE, MS&D, MycolAb, N02, N03, P30, P33, P35, P39, PsycholAb, R08, R10, R12, R13, RM&VM, Reac, S09, SCI, SCOPUS, T02, T05, W07.
—BLDSC (0828.900000), CASDDS, GNLM, IE, Infotrieve, Ingenta, INIST. **CCC.**
Published by: (Mayo Clinic), Elsevier Inc. (Subsidiary of: Elsevier Science & Technology), 1600 John F Kennedy Blvd, Philadelphia, PA 19103. TEL 215-239-3900, FAX 215-238-7883, JournalCustomerService-usa@elsevier.com, http://www.elsevier.com. Ed. Dr. Thomas J Liesegang TEL 904-953-2555. Pub. Nancy Axelrod. Circ: 3,680.

617.7 USA ISSN 1545-6110
AMERICAN OPHTHALMOLOGICAL SOCIETY. TRANSACTIONS (ONLINE). Text in English. 2004. a. free to members (effective 2011). back issues avail. **Document type:** *Proceedings, Academic/Scholarly.*
Media: Online - full text.
Indexed: EMBASE, ExcerpMed.
—CCC.
Published by: American Ophthalmological Society, PO Box 193940, San Francisco, CA 94119. TEL 415-561-8578, FAX 415-561-8531, admin@aosonline.org.

617.752 USA
AMERICAN OPTICIAN. Text in English. 1950. q. free to members (effective 2010). bk.rev. back issues avail.; reprints avail. **Document type:** *Newsletter, Academic/Scholarly.*
Former titles (until Feb.1992): O A A News; (until 1987): Dispensing Optician (0194-2174); (until (1976): R X O - Journal of Opticianry; (19??): Guild Guide (0017-5382)
Related titles: E-mail ed.: free; Microform ed.: (from PQC); Online - full text ed.: free (effective 2010).
Published by: Opticians Association of America, 4064 E Fir Hill Dr, Lakeland, TN 38002. TEL 901-388-2423, FAX 901-388-2348, oaa@oaa.org.

617.7 USA ISSN 0094-9620
AMERICAN OPTOMETRIC ASSOCIATION NEWS. Text in English. 1961. 18/yr. USD 126 to individuals; USD 97 in United States to individuals (effective 2006). adv. 24 p./no. 4 cols./p.; **Document type:** *Magazine, Trade.* **Description:** Contains news and information for members of the American Optometric Association.
—CCC.
Published by: American Optometric Association, 243 N Lindbergh Blvd, St. Louis, MO 63141. TEL 314-991-4100, FAX 314-991-4101, http://www.aoa.org/. Ed. Robert Foster. Pub., R&P, Adv. contact Andrew L Miller. B&W page USD 4,240, color page USD 6,060; trim 9.625 x 13.375. Circ: 32,000 (paid and controlled).

617.7 USA ISSN 0065-955X
CODEN: AOJTAW
➤ **AMERICAN ORTHOPTIC JOURNAL.** Abbreviated title: A O J. Text in English. 1950. a. USD 130 combined subscription per issue to institutions (print & online eds.) (effective 2012). adv. cum.index: 1950-1960, 1971-1980. back issues avail.; reprints avail. **Document type:** *Journal, Academic/Scholarly.* **Description:** Provides a forum for the presentation of new material in the fields of pediatric ophthalmology, neuro-ophthalmology, amblyopia and strabismus.
Related titles: Microform ed.: (from PQC); Online - full text ed.: ISSN 1553-4448. USD 115 per issue to institutions (effective 2012).
Indexed: A01, A03, A08, A22, CA, MEDLINE, P30, SCOPUS, T02.
—BLDSC (0847.750000), GNLM, IE, Infotrieve, Ingenta. **CCC.**
Published by: (American Association of Certified Orthoptists, American Academy of Ophthalmology and Otolaryngology), University of Wisconsin Press, Journal Division, 1930 Monroe St, 3rd Fl, Madison, WI 53711. TEL 608-263-0668, 800 258-3632, FAX 608-263-1173, journals@uwpress.wisc.edu, http://www.uwpress.org. Ed. Dr. James D Reynolds. Adv. contact Adrienne Omen TEL 608-263-0534. Circ: 1,700. **Co-sponsor:** American Orthoptic Council.

➤ **ANDERS BEKEKEN.** *see* HANDICAPPED—Visually Impaired

617.7 ESP ISSN 1133-7737
ANNALS D'OFTALMOLOGIA; organ de les societats d'oftalmologia de Catalunya, Balears i Valencia. Text in Spanish. 1991. q. EUR 70 to institutions (effective 2009). **Document type:** *Journal, Academic/Scholarly.*
Published by: Nexus Medica Editores, C/ Passeig d'Amunt 38, Barcelona, 08024, Spain. TEL 34-93-5510260, FAX 34-93-2136672, redaccion@nexusmedica.com, http://www.nexusediciones.com.

617.754 670.29 FRA ISSN 1766-9766
LES ANNONCES DE L'OPTIQUE. Text in French. 2004. m. (10/yr). EUR 29.90 (effective 2009). **Document type:** *Magazine, Trade.*
Published by: Press Optic SARL, 31 Rue d'Alleray, Paris, 75015, France. TEL 33-1-45300804, FAX 33-1-45300834.

ANNUARIO OTTICO ITALIANO. *see* BUSINESS AND ECONOMICS—Trade And Industrial Directories

617.7 USA ISSN 0003-9950
RE1 CODEN: AROPAW
➤ **ARCHIVES OF OPHTHALMOLOGY.** Text in English. 1869. m. USD 690 domestic to institutions; USD 863 in the Americas to institutions; EUR 698 in Europe to institutions; GBP 592 elsewhere to institutions (effective 2012). bk.rev. charts; illus. index. back issues avail.; reprints avail. **Document type:** *Journal, Academic/Scholarly.* **Description:** Features original contributions and observations on the science of vision of interest to clinicians and researchers.
Former titles (until 1960): A M A Archives of Ophthalmology (0096-6339); (until 1950): Archives of Ophthalmology (0093-0326); Which superseded in part (in 1879): Archives of Ophthalmology and Otology (0092-5624)
Related titles: Microform ed.: (from PMC, PQC); Online - full text ed.: ISSN 1538-3601. free to members (effective 2012); ◆ Spanish Translation: Archives of Ophthalmology (Spanish Edition). ISSN 1130-5134.
Indexed: A20, A22, A26, A36, AIDS Ab, AIIM, AIM, ASCA, B21, B25, BIOSIS Prev, CABA, CIN, CISA, ChemAb, ChemTitl, CurCont, D01, DBA, DentInd, DiabCont, DokArb, E08, E12, EMBASE, ExcerpMed, F08, F11, F12, FR, G08, GH, H11, H12, H13, HRIS, I05, IBR, IBZ, IDIS, ISR, IndMed, Inpharma, JW, LT, MEDLINE, MS&D, MycolAb, N02, N03, NSA, P02, P10, P20, P22, P24, P30, P32, P33, P35, P39, P48, P53, P54, PQC, PsycholAb, R08, R10, R12, RA&MP, RM&VM, RRTA, Reac, S09, SAA, SCI, SCOPUS, T05, VITIS, W07.
—BLDSC (1638.450000), CASDDS, GNLM, IE, Infotrieve, Ingenta, INIST. **CCC.**
Published by: American Medical Association, 515 N State St, Chicago, IL 60654. TEL 312-464-4200, 800-621-8335, FAX 312-464-4142, journalsales@ama-assn.org, http://www.ama-assn.org. Eds. Dr. Daniel M. Albert TEL 608-262-7769, Dr. Catherine D DeAngelis. **Subscr. in the Americas to:** PO Box 10946, Chicago, IL 60654. TEL 312-670-7827, 800-262-2350, ama-subs@ama-assn.org; **Subscr. outside the Americas to:** American Medical Association, J A M A and Archive Journals.

617.7 ARG ISSN 0066-6777
ARCHIVOS DE OFTALMOLOGIA DE BUENOS AIRES. Text in Spanish. 1925. q. adv. **Document type:** *Journal, Academic/Scholarly.*
Indexed: P30.
—GNLM, Infotrieve.
Published by: Sociedad Argentina de Oftalmologia, Viamonte 1465, 7o, Buenos Aires, C1055ABA, Argentina. TEL 54-11-43738826, FAX 54-11-43738828. Ed. Edgardo Manzitti.

617.7 BRA ISSN 0004-2749
RE1 CODEN: AQBOAP
ARQUIVOS BRASILEIROS DE OFTALMOLOGIA. Text in Portuguese. 1938. bi-m. adv. bk.rev. abstr.; illus. back issues avail. **Document type:** *Journal, Academic/Scholarly.*
Related titles: Online - full text ed.: ISSN 1678-2925. free (effective 2011).
Indexed: A34, A35, A36, C01, CA, CABA, E12, EMBASE, ExcerpMed, GH, H16, H17, IndMed, LT, MEDLINE, N02, N03, P30, P33, P39, PN&I, R08, R10, R12, R13, RA&MP, RM&VM, RRTA, Reac, S12, SCI, SCOPUS, T02, T05, VS, W07.
—BLDSC (1695.240000), GNLM, INIST.
Published by: Belfort Editora, Caixa 4086, Rua Barao de Itapetininga, 297, Centro, Sao Paulo, SP 01042-001, Brazil. Ed. Rubens Belfort Mattos. Circ: 1,500.

617.7 SGP ISSN 0129-1653
➤ **ASIA - PACIFIC JOURNAL OF OPHTHALMOLOGY.** Text in English. 1987. q. USD 65 in Asia & the Pacific to individuals; USD 80 elsewhere to individuals; USD 130 in Asia & the Pacific to institutions; USD 160 elsewhere to institutions (effective 2003). adv. bk.rev. **Document type:** *Journal, Academic/Scholarly.* **Description:** Disseminates the latest research and development in surgical techniques, complications, management. Includes geographical and historical notes, and information on new implants and instruments.
Incorporates (in 1990): Implants in Ophthalmology (0218-0367)
Published by: Singapore National Eye Centre, 11 Third Hospital Ave, Singapore, 168751, Singapore. TEL 65-62277255, FAX 65-62277291, http://www.snec.com.sg. Ed. Arthur S M Lim. Adv. contact Julie Goh TEL 65-64666666. page USD 1,350; trim 210 x 297. Circ: 500.

617.7 HKG
ASIAN JOURNAL OF OPHTHALMOLOGY (ONLINE). Text in English. 1998. q. free. back issues avail. **Document type:** *Journal, Academic/Scholarly.*
Formerly: Asian Journal of Ophthalmology (Print) (1560-2133)
Media: Online - full text.
Indexed: SCOPUS.
—BLDSC (1742.525000).
Published by: South East Asia Glaucoma Interest Group (SEAGIG) info@seagig.org, http://www.seagig.org/. Ed. Paul Chew.

617.7 JPN ISSN 0910-1810
ATARASHII GANKA/JOURNAL OF THE EYE. Text in Japanese; Summaries in English, Japanese. 1984. m. JPY 35,280 (effective 2007). **Document type:** *Journal, Academic/Scholarly.*
Indexed: A22, ChemAb.
—BLDSC (4983.450000), IE, Ingenta.
Published by: Medikaru Aoi Shuppan/Medical-Aoi Publications, Inc., 2-39-5 Hongo, Bunkyo-ku, Kataoka Bldg. 5F, Tokyo, 113-0033, Japan. TEL 81-3-38110544.

617.7 016 USA ISSN 0271-1281
RE1
➤ **AUDIO-DIGEST OPHTHALMOLOGY.** Text in English. 1963. s-m. USD 449.81 domestic; USD 479.72 in Canada; USD 527.72 elsewhere (effective 2010). back issues avail. **Document type:** *Journal, Academic/Scholarly.*
Media: Audio cassette/tape. **Related titles:** Audio CD ed.: USD 399.89 domestic; USD 431.72 in Canada; USD 479.72 elsewhere (effective 2010); Online - full text ed.: USD 359.72 (effective 2010).
—Infotrieve.
Published by: Audio-Digest Foundation (Subsidiary of: California Medical Association), 1577 E Chevy Chase Dr, Glendale, CA 91206. TEL 818-240-7500, 800-423-2308, FAX 818-240-7379.

617.7 DEU ISSN 0004-7902
DER AUGENARZT. Text in German. 1967. 6/yr. adv. bk.rev. abstr.; illus. **Document type:** *Magazine, Trade.*
—GNLM.
Published by: (Berufsverband der Augenaerzte Deutschlands e.V.), Dr. R. Kaden Verlag GmbH & Co. KG, Ringstr 19 B, Heidelberg, 69115, Germany. TEL 49-6221-1377600, FAX 49-6221-29910, kaden@kaden-verlag.de, http://www.kaden-verlag.de. adv.: B&W page EUR 2,555, color page EUR 3,890; trim 178 x 230. Circ: 8,500 (paid and controlled).

617.752 DEU ISSN 1612-9865
AUGENLICHT; VisionCare. Text in German. 1994. q. EUR 17 domestic; EUR 22 foreign; EUR 5 newsstand/cover (effective 2010). adv. **Document type:** *Magazine, Consumer.* **Description:** Provides information on products and services offered by ophthalmologists and opticians.
Published by: Autentic.Info GmbH, Felder Str 15/3, Wangen, 88239, Germany. TEL 49-7522-931073, FAX 49-7522-771114, info@autentic.info, http://www.autentic.info.

617.7 DEU ISSN 0004-7929
DER AUGENOPTIKER. Text in German. 1946. 13/yr. EUR 84 domestic; EUR 91.80 foreign (effective 2011). adv. bk.rev. bibl.; charts; illus.; stat. **Document type:** *Magazine, Trade.*
—GNLM.
Published by: Konradin Verlag Robert Kohlhammer GmbH, Ernst Mey Str 8, Leinfelden-Echterdingen, 70771, Germany. TEL 49-711-75940, FAX 49-711-7594390, info@konradin.de, http://www.konradin.de. Ed. Theo Mahr. Adv. contact Ines Scholz. Circ: 9,822 (paid).

617.7 DEU ISSN 0004-7937
DER AUGENSPIEGEL; Zeitschrift fuer Klinik und Praxis. Text in German. 1955. 11/yr. EUR 83; EUR 47 to students; EUR 9.90 newsstand/cover (effective 2008). adv. bk.rev. charts; illus.; mkt.; stat.; tr.lit. **Document type:** *Magazine, Trade.*
—GNLM.
Published by: Augenspiegel Verlags GmbH, Papiermuehlenweg 74, Ratingen, 40882, Germany. TEL 49-2102-1678000, FAX 49-2102-1678030, info@mediawelt-services.de. Ed. Ulrike Luedtke. Adv. contact Karin Lilge. B&W page EUR 2,387, color page EUR 3,950. Circ: 6,082 (paid and controlled).

AUSTRALIA. BUREAU OF STATISTICS. OPTOMETRY AND OPTICAL DISPENSING SERVICES, AUSTRALIA (ONLINE). *see* MEDICAL SCIENCES—Abstracting, Bibliographies, Statistics

617.75 AUS ISSN 0726-5018
AUSTRALIAN OPTOMETRY. Text in English. 1980. m. free to qualified personnel (effective 2009). adv. tr.lit. **Document type:** *Newspaper, Trade.* **Description:** Provides news and features pertaining to optometry in Australia.
Related titles: Supplement(s): Practice (Carlton South); Optometry Pharma; Guide4Grads; Ophthalmic Lenses; Contact Lenses; Ophthalmic Equipment.
Published by: Optometrists Association Australia, 240 Drummond St, PO Box 185, Carlton South, VIC 3053, Australia. TEL 61-3-96688500, FAX 61-3-96637478, oaanat@optometrists.asn.au. Ed., Adv. contact Sandra Shaw TEL 61-3-96636833. B&W page AUD 2,722.50, color page AUD 4,917; 290 x 420. Circ: 4,000.

616.7 AUS ISSN 0814-0936
RE1
➤ **AUSTRALIAN ORTHOPTIC JOURNAL.** Text in English. 1967. s-a. AUD 70 to individuals; AUD 130 to institutions (effective 2007). **Document type:** *Journal, Academic/Scholarly.* **Description:** Covers areas of orthoptic clinical practice - strabismus, amblyopia, ocular motility and binocular vision anomalies; low vision and rehabilitation; paediatric ophthalmology; neuro-ophthalmology including nystagmus; ophthalmic technology and biometry; and public health agenda.
Indexed: A01.
—Ingenta.
Published by: Orthoptic Association of Australia Inc., PO Box 1175, Hampton North, VIC 3188, Australia. TEL 61-3-95219844, FAX 61-3-95989499, office@orthoptics.org.au.

617.7 GBR ISSN 1471-2415
RE1 CODEN: BOMPAC
➤ **B M C OPHTHALMOLOGY.** (BioMed Central) Text in English. 2001 (Apr.). irreg. free (effective 2011). adv. **Document type:** *Journal, Academic/Scholarly.* **Description:** Publishes original research articles in all aspects of the prevention, diagnosis and management of eye disorders, as well as related molecular genetics, pathophysiology, and epidemiology.
Media: Online - full text.
Indexed: A26, C06, C07, CA, CurCont, EMBASE, ExcerpMed, I05, MEDLINE, NSA, P30, R10, Reac, SCI, SCOPUS, T02, W07.
—Infotrieve. **CCC.**
Published by: BioMed Central Ltd. (Subsidiary of: Springer Science+Business Media), 236 Gray's Inn Rd, London, WC1X 8HB, United Kingdom. TEL 44-20-31922000, FAX 44-20-31922010, info@biomedcentral.com. Ed. Dr. Melissa Norton. Adv. contact Natasha Bailey TEL 44-20-31922231.

617.7 USA ISSN 1048-2725
BASIC AND CLINICAL SCIENCE COURSE. Text in English. 1989. irreg. **Document type:** *Monographic series, Academic/Scholarly.*
—BLDSC (1863.914400).
Published by: American Academy of Ophthalmology, PO Box 7424, San Francisco, CA 94120. TEL 415-561-8500, FAX 415-561-8533, customer_service@aao.org, http://www.aao.org.

617.7 IRN ISSN 1026-6399
RE46
BINA JOURNAL OF OPHTALOMOLOGY. Abbreviated title: Bina. Text in Persian, Modern, English. 1995. q. **Document type:** *Journal, Academic/Scholarly.*
Related titles: Online - full text ed.: free (effective 2011).
Published by: Central Eye Bank of Iran, Africa Ave, Yazdan Panah 27, Tehran, Iran. Ed. Mohammad Ali Javadi.

617.7 USA ISSN 1088-6281
CODEN: BVSQFV
➤ **BINOCULAR VISION & STRABISMUS QUARTERLY.** Text in English; Abstracts in Spanish, French, German. 1985. q. USD 84 (effective 2011). adv. bk.rev.; video rev. abstr.; illus. cum.index: 1985-2002 in vol.18, no.1. 80 p./no. 2 cols./p.; back issues avail.; reprints avail. **Document type:** *Journal, Academic/Scholarly.* **Description:** For the professional devoting his or her practice to strabismus, amblyopia, eye movements, and other disorders of binocular vision.
Former titles (until 1996): Binocular Vision and Eye Muscle Surgery Quarterly (1073-001X); (until 1991): Binocular Vision (0749-386X)
Related titles: Online - full text ed.
Indexed: EMBASE, ExcerpMed, IndMed, MEDLINE, P30, R10, Reac, SCOPUS.
—IE, Infotrieve, Ingenta, INIST.
Published by: Binoculus Publishing, Summit Haus, 740 Piney Acres Cir, PO Box 3727, Dillon, CO 80435. TEL 970-262-0753, FAX 970-262-0753, judyatbv@vail.net, http://binocularvision.net. Ed. Dr. Paul E Romano.

617.7 USA ISSN 2154-9176
R857.L37
▼ **BIOOPTICS WORLD.** Text in English. 2009. bi-m. **Document type:** *Magazine, Trade.* **Description:** Advances in optometry, lasers, optics, and imaging.
Published by: PennWell Corporation, 98 Spit Brook Rd, Nashua, NH 03062. TEL 603-891-9447, http://www.pennwell.com, http://de.pennnet.com/.

617.3 USA ISSN 0067-9283
BLUE BOOK OF OPTOMETRISTS. Text in English. 1912. biennial. USD 115 per issue; USD 165 print & CD-ROM eds. (effective 2007). index. **Document type:** *Directory.*
Related titles: CD-ROM ed.
Published by: Jobson Publishing LLC, One Meadowlands Pl, Ste 1020, E Rutherford, NJ 07073. TEL 201-623-0999, FAX 201-623-0991, http://www.jobson.com.

617.7 GBR ISSN 1743-9868
➤ **BRITISH AND IRISH ORTHOPTIC JOURNAL.** Abbreviated title: B I O J. Text in English. 1939. a. free to members (effective 2009). adv. bk.rev. cum.index every 5 yrs. back issues avail. **Document type:** *Journal, Academic/Scholarly.* **Description:** Covers subjects including orthoptics, binocular vision, ocular motility, pediatric ophthalmology, and neuro-ophthalmology.
Formerly (until 2004): British Orthoptic Journal (0068-2314)
Related titles: Online - full text ed.: free to members (effective 2009).
Indexed: A22, FR, P30.
—BLDSC (2287.920000), GNLM, IE, Infotrieve, Ingenta, INIST.
Published by: British and Irish Orthoptic Society, Tavistock House N, Tavistock Sq, London, WC1H 9 HX, United Kingdom. TEL 44-20-73877992, FAX 44-20-73832584, bios@orthoptics.org.uk. Ed. Catherine Stewart.

617.7 GBR ISSN 0007-1161
RE1 CODEN: BJOPAL
➤ **BRITISH JOURNAL OF OPHTHALMOLOGY**; a peer review journal for health professionals and researchers in ophthalmology. Abbreviated title: B J O. Text in English. 1917. m. GBP 478 to institutions; GBP 606 combined subscription to institutions small FTE (print & online eds.) (effective 2011). adv. bk.rev. abstr.; bibl.; charts; illus. index. back issues avail.; reprints avail. **Document type:** *Journal, Academic/Scholarly.* **Description:** Presents international papers from both clinicians and laboratory workers in ophthalmology.
Formed by the merger of (1881-1917): Ophthalmic Review (0266-3066); (1903-1917): Ophthalmoscope (0266-3430); (1880-1917): Royal London Ophthalmic Hospital Reports (0266-2906); Which was formerly (1857-1880): Royal London Ophthalmic Hospital. Reports and Journal
Related titles: Microform ed.: (from PQC); Online - full text ed.: B J O Online. ISSN 1468-2079. GBP 489 to institutions small FTE (effective 2011).
Indexed: A01, A03, A08, A20, A22, A26, A36, ASCA, B21, B25, BIOBASE, BIOSIS Prev, CA, CABA, ChemAb, CurCont, DiabCont, DokArb, E01, E08, E12, EMBASE, ESPM, ExcerpMed, G08, GH, H&SSA, H11, H12, H17, I05, IABS, IBR, IBZ, INI, ISR, IndMed, Inpharma, MEDLINE, MycolAb, N02, N03, NSA, P20, P22, P30, P33, P35, P39, P48, P54, PQC, R08, R10, R12, RM&VM, Reac, RefZh, S09, SCI, SCOPUS, T02, T05, W07, W11.
—BLDSC (2313.000000), GNLM, IE, Infotrieve, Ingenta, INIST. **CCC.**
Published by: B M J Group, BMA House, Tavistock Sq, London, WC1H 9JR, United Kingdom. TEL 44-20-73836373, FAX 44-20-73836668, http://group.bmj.com. Ed. Harminder Dua. Pub. Allison Lang TEL 44-20-73836212. Adv. contact Nick Gray TEL 44-20-73836386. Circ: 1,820. **Subscr. to:** PO Box 299, London WC1H 9TD, United Kingdom. TEL 44-20-73836270, FAX 44-20-73836402, support@bmjgroup.com.

➤ **BUSINESS RATIO REPORT. THE OPTICAL INDUSTRY.** *see* PHYSICS—Optics

617.7505 GBR ISSN 1367-899X
➤ **C E OPTOMETRY.** (Continuing Education) Text in English. 1997. 3/yr. GBP 45 per vol. domestic to individuals; GBP 60 per vol. foreign to individuals; GBP 60 per vol. domestic to institutions; GBP 90 per vol. foreign to institutions (effective 2009). back issues avail. **Document type:** *Journal, Academic/Scholarly.* **Description:** Contains significant review articles on optometry.
Related titles: Online - full text ed.: GBP 30 per vol. (effective 2009).
—**CCC.**
Published by: Rila Publications Ltd., 73 Newman St, London, W1A 4PG, United Kingdom. TEL 44-20-76311299, FAX 44-20-75807166, admin@rila.co.uk. Eds. David Hensen, Robert Harper.

617.7 CAN ISSN 0834-2245
C J O. CANADIAN JOURNAL OF OPTOMETRY/REVUE CANADIENNE D'OPTOMETRIE. Text in English, French. 1939. q. CAD 55 domestic; CAD 65 foreign (effective 2005). adv. bk.rev. **Document type:** *Journal, Trade.*
Former titles (until 1986): Optovision (0834-2237); (until 1986): Canadian Journal of Optometry (0045-5075)
—IE, Infotrieve. **CCC.**
Published by: Canadian Association of Optometrists, 234 Argyle Ave, Ottawa, ON K2P 1B9, Canada. TEL 888-263-4676, FAX 613-235-2025, info@opto.ca, http://www.opto.ca. Ed. Dr. Mitchell Samek. Adv. contact Ed Marriner. Circ: 4,000.

617.7 GBR ISSN 1367-0131
CODEN: CMEOF5
C M E JOURNAL. OPHTHALMOLOGY. (Continuing Medical Education) Text in English. 1997. irreg., latest 2007. GBP 45 per vol. domestic to individuals; GBP 60 per vol. foreign to individuals; GBP 60 per vol. domestic to institutions; GBP 90 per vol. foreign to institutions (effective 2010). back issues avail. **Document type:** *Journal, Academic/Scholarly.*
Related titles: Online - full text ed.: GBP 30 per vol. (effective 2010).
Indexed: R10, Reac, SCOPUS.
—**CCC.**
Published by: Rila Publications Ltd., 73 Newman St, London, W1A 4PG, United Kingdom. TEL 44-20-76311299, FAX 44-20-75807166, admin@rila.co.uk. Ed. Harminder S Dua.

617.75 USA ISSN 0273-804X
CALIFORNIA OPTOMETRY. Text in English. 1933. s-m. USD 35 to non-members (effective 2005). adv. bk.rev. illus. 32 p./no. 3 cols./p.; **Document type:** *Magazine, Trade.* **Description:** Informs members on the latest economic, educational and business trends that affect the profession.
Former titles (until 1980): California Optometrist (0361-7025); (until 1975): California Optometrist Association. Journal (0008-1337)
Published by: California Optometric Association, 2415 K St, Sacramento, CA 95816. TEL 916-441-3990, FAX 916-448-1423. Eds. Jessica Slivyak, Palmer Lee. adv.: page USD 550; trim 7.5 x 10. Circ: 3,500.

617.7 CAN ISSN 0008-4182
CODEN: CAJOBA
➤ **CANADIAN JOURNAL OF OPHTHALMOLOGY/JOURNAL CANADIEN D'OPHTALMOLOGIE.** Text in English, French. 1948. 6/yr. USD 150 in United States to institutions; USD 165 elsewhere to institutions (effective 2012). adv. bk.rev. illus. back issues avail.; reprints avail. **Document type:** *Journal, Academic/Scholarly.* **Description:** Contains scientific papers presented at annual meetings, and contributions from within and outside Canada.
Formerly (until 1966): Canadian Ophthalmological Society Annual Meeting. Transactions (0068-9408)
Related titles: Microform ed.: (from PQC).
Indexed: A20, A22, ASCA, ChemAb, CurCont, EMBASE, ExcerpMed, FR, ISR, IndMed, Inpharma, MEDLINE, OphLit, P30, P35, R10, Reac, SCI, SCOPUS, W07.
—BLDSC (3033.700000), CASDDS, GNLM, IE, Infotrieve, Ingenta, INIST. **CCC.**
Published by: Canadian Ophthalmological Society, 610-1525 Carling Ave, Ottawa, ON K1Z 8R9, Canada. TEL 613-729-6779, FAX 613-729-7209, cos@eyesite.ca. Ed. Dr. Miguel N Burnier Jr. Adv. contact Anne Keefer. B&W page CAD 855, color page CAD 959; trim 10.88 x 8.13. Circ: 330 (paid); 870 (controlled). **Subscr. in N. America to:** Allen Press Inc., PO Box 1897, Lawrence, KS 66044.

617.7 CHE ISSN 1663-2699
RE1
▼ ➤ **CASE REPORTS IN OPHTHALMOLOGY.** Text in English. 2010 (May). irreg. free (effective 2011). **Document type:** *Journal, Academic/Scholarly.* **Description:** Publishes original case reports covering the entire spectrum of ophthalmology.
Media: Online - full text.
Indexed: A22, P30.
—IE.
Published by: S. Karger AG, Allschwilerstr 10, Basel, 4055, Switzerland. TEL 41-61-3061111, FAX 41-61-3061234, karger@karger.ch, http://www.karger.ch. Ed. Anat Loewenstein.

617.7 EGY ISSN 1110-7499
CATARACT AND CORNEA. Text in English. 1995. a. **Document type:** *Journal, Academic/Scholarly.*
Published by: The Egyptian Society of Cataract and Corneal Diseases, Abrag Osman, Bldg No 2, Apt 11,, El-Maadi, Cairo, Egypt. FAX 20-2-5263398, info@escacod.org, http://escacod.org/society.htm. Ed. Dr. Amr Salah Al-Din Abdel-Hakim.

617.7 USA ISSN 1541-5619
RE451
CATARACT & REFRACTIVE SURGERY TODAY. Text in English. 2001 (Sept.). m. free (effective 2010). adv. back issues avail. **Document type:** *Magazine, Trade.* **Description:** Promotes continuing education by covering such topics as surgical pearls, complications management, technological advances, and practice management.
Related titles: Online - full text ed.
Published by: Bryn Mawr Communications, LLC (Subsidiary of: Bryn Mawr Communications Group LLC), 1008 Upper Gulph Rd, Ste 200, Wayne, PA 19087. TEL 484-581-1800, FAX 484-581-1818, http://www.bmctoday.com/. Ed. Gillian McDermott TEL 484-581-1812. Pub. David Cox TEL 484-581-1814.

617.7 CZE ISSN 1211-9059
➤ **CESKA A SLOVENSKA OFTALMOLOGIE/CZECH AND SLOVAK OPHTHALMOLOGY.** Text in Czech, Slovak; Summaries in Czech, English. 1943. 6/yr. CZK 426, EUR 33 (effective 2010). adv. bk.rev. abstr.; bibl.; illus. index. **Document type:** *Journal, Academic/Scholarly.* **Description:** Publishes original papers, results of research, reviews, case reports, postgraduate chapters, articles for practitioners, reports from congresses and symposia. Provides information on new diagnostic methods in the field of eye diseases and their conservative and surgical treatment.
Formerly: Ceskoslovenska Oftalmologie (0009-059X)
Related titles: Online - full text ed.
Indexed: ChemAb, DentInd, DokArb, EMBASE, ExcerpMed, IndMed, MEDLINE, P30, R10, Reac, SCOPUS.
—BLDSC (3120.258470), GNLM, INIST. **CCC.**
Published by: (Ceska Lekarska Spolecnost J.E. Purkyne/Czech Medical Association), Nakladatelske Stredisko C L S J.E. Purkyne, Sokolska 31, Prague, 12026, Czech Republic. nts@cls.cz. Ed. Eva Vlkova. adv.: B&W page CZK 19,900, color page CZK 31,000; 136 x 194. Circ: 2,000.

617.7 CHL ISSN 0716-1999
CIENCIA OFTALMOLOGICA. Text in Spanish. 1981. q. **Document type:** *Bulletin, Trade.*
Formerly (until 1984): Clinica Oftalmologica del Hospital del Salvador. Boletin Informativo (0716-1050)
Published by: Clinica Oftalmologica del Hospital del Salvador, Ave 11 de Septiembre 2155, Ofic 305 Torre C, Providencia, Santiago, Chile. TEL 56-2-3404265, FAX 56-2-2099714, cienciaoftalmol@vtr.net. Ed. Jorge Roberto Schliapiapinik.

617.7 AUS ISSN 1442-6404
RE1 CODEN: CEOPBW
➤ **CLINICAL AND EXPERIMENTAL OPHTHALMOLOGY.** Text in English. 1973. 9/yr. GBP 485 in United Kingdom to institutions; EUR 615 in Europe to institutions; USD 782 in the Americas to institutions; USD 949 elsewhere to institutions; GBP 558 combined subscription in United Kingdom to institutions (print & online eds.); EUR 708 combined subscription in Europe to institutions (print & online eds.); USD 899 combined subscription in the Americas to institutions (print & online eds.); USD 1,092 combined subscription elsewhere to institutions (print & online eds.) (effective 2012). adv. back issues avail.; reprint service avail. from PSC. **Document type:** *Journal, Academic/Scholarly.* **Description:** Provides reports of research from around the world in all areas of ophthalmology.
Formerly (until 1999): Australian and New Zealand Journal of Ophthalmology (0814-9763); Which was formed by the merger of (1947-1984): Transactions of the Ophthalmological Society of New Zealand (0300-8983); (1973-1984): Australian Journal of Ophthalmology (0310-1177); Which superseded (1960-1972): Australian College of Ophthalmologists. Transactions (0067-1789)
Related titles: Online - full text ed.: ISSN 1442-9071. GBP 485 in United Kingdom to institutions; EUR 615 in Europe to institutions; USD 782 in the Americas to institutions; USD 949 elsewhere to institutions (effective 2012) (from IngentaConnect).
Indexed: A01, A03, A08, A20, A22, A26, A36, ASCA, B&BAb, B19, B21, CA, CABA, CurCont, DentInd, E01, E12, EMBASE, ExcerpMed, GH, H12, H17, ISR, IndMed, Inpharma, MEDLINE, N02, N03, NSA, P30, P33, P35, P39, R08, R10, R12, R13, RA&MP, RM&VM, Reac, SCI, SCOPUS, SD, T02, T05, VS, W07.
—BLDSC (3286.251920), GNLM, IE, Infotrieve, Ingenta. **CCC.**
Published by: (Royal Australian and New Zealand College of Ophthalmologists), Wiley-Blackwell Publishing Asia (Subsidiary of: Wiley-Blackwell Publishing Ltd.), 155 Cremorne St, Richmond, VIC 3121, Australia. TEL 61-3-92743100, FAX 61-3-92743101, subs@blackwellpublishingasia.com, http://www.wiley.com/WileyCDA/. Ed. Charles N J McGhee. adv.: B&W page AUD 890, color page AUD 1,800; trim 210 x 275. Circ: 1,400.

617.75 GBR ISSN 0816-4622
RE1 CODEN: ASAYEY
➤ **CLINICAL AND EXPERIMENTAL OPTOMETRY.** Text in English. 1913. bi-m. GBP 249 combined subscription in United Kingdom to institutions (print & online eds.); EUR 315 combined subscription in Europe to institutions (print & online eds.); USD 420 combined subscription in the Americas to institutions (print & online eds.); USD 488 combined subscription elsewhere to institutions (print & online eds.) (effective 2012). adv. bk.rev. charts; illus.; stat.; abstr.; bibl. index. back issues avail.; reprints avail. **Document type:** *Journal, Academic/Scholarly.* **Description:** Aims to publish original research papers and reviews in clinical optometry and vision science.
Former titles (until 1986): Australian Journal of Optometry (0045-0642); (until 1959): Australasian Journal of Optometry (0817-881X); (until 1929): The Commonwealth Optometrist; (until 1914): New South Wales Institute of Optometrists. Journal
Related titles: Online - full text ed.: ISSN 1444-0938. GBP 217 in United Kingdom to institutions; EUR 275 in Europe to institutions; USD 366 in the Americas to institutions; USD 424 elsewhere to institutions (effective 2012) (from IngentaConnect).
Indexed: A01, A22, A26, B21, C06, C07, CA, CurCont, E01, EMBASE, ExcerpMed, H12, MEDLINE, NSA, P30, R10, Reac, SCI, SCOPUS, SD, T02, W07.
—BLDSC (3286.251940), CASDDS, GNLM, IE, Infotrieve, Ingenta. **CCC.**
Published by: (New Zealand Association of Optometrists NZL, Optometrists Association Australia AUS), Wiley-Blackwell Publishing Ltd. (Subsidiary of: John Wiley & Sons, Inc.), 9600 Garsington Rd, Oxford, OX4 2DQ, United Kingdom. TEL 44-1865-776868, FAX 44-1865-714591, customerservices@blackwellpublishing.com. Ed. Dr. H Barry Collin. R&P, Adv. contact Sandra Shaw TEL 61-3-96636833. Circ: 3,500.

617.75 CAN ISSN 1705-4850
CODEN: CROLA8
➤ **CLINICAL & REFRACTIVE OPTOMETRY.** Text in English. 1990. 10/yr. CAD 54 domestic; USD 58 in United States; USD 67 elsewhere (effective 2003). adv. bk.rev. illus. index. back issues avail. **Document type:** *Journal, Academic/Scholarly.* **Description:** Discusses diagnostic technologies, marketing techniques, co-management strategies, product news.
Formerly (until Mar. 2003): Practical Optometry (1181-6058)
Indexed: SCOPUS.
—BLDSC (3286.253800), IE, Ingenta. **CCC.**
Published by: Mediaconcept, Inc., 79 Alouette St, Montreal, PQ H9A 3G8, Canada. TEL 514-331-4561, FAX 514-336-1129. Ed. Barbara Caffery. Pub. Lawrence Goldstein. Adv. contact Brenda Demberg. Circ: 2,300 (controlled).

617.7 CAN ISSN 1705-4842
CODEN: OPPRFI
➤ **CLINICAL & SURGICAL OPHTHALMOLOGY.** Text in English. 1983. m. adv. bk.rev. index. **Document type:** *Journal, Academic/Scholarly.* **Description:** Studies ophthalmic surgery, ocular infection, intraocular lens implants, pediatric problems, technological advances.
Former titles (until 2003): Ophthalmic Practice (0832-9869); (until 1986): Current Canadian Ophthalmic Practice (0823-4744)
Indexed: SCOPUS.
—BLDSC (3286.253900), GNLM. **CCC.**
Published by: Mediaconcept, Inc., 79 Alouette St, Montreal, PQ H9A 3G8, Canada. TEL 514-331-4561, FAX 514-336-1129. Ed. Leon Solomon. Pub. Lawrence Goldstein. R&P Linda Armitage. Adv. contact Helen Kaplin. Circ: 1,200.

617.7 GBR ISSN 1177-5483
➤ **CLINICAL OPHTHALMOLOGY (ONLINE).** Text in English. 2007. irreg. free (effective 2011). back issues avail. **Document type:** *Journal, Academic/Scholarly.* **Description:** Covers all ophthalmology subspecialties, optometry, visual science, pharmacology and drug therapy in eye diseases, basic sciences such as cell biology and genetics, primary and secondary eye care, patient safety, and quality of care improvements.
Media: Online - full text.
—CCC.
Published by: Dove Medical Press Ltd., Beechfield House, Winterton Way, Macclesfield, SK11 0JL, United Kingdom. TEL 44-1625-509130, FAX 44-1625-617933. Ed. Scott Fraser.

617.7 GBR ISSN 1179-2752
▼ ➤ **CLINICAL OPTOMETRY.** Text in English. 2009. a. free (effective 2011). **Document type:** *Journal, Academic/Scholarly.*
Media: Online - full text.
—CCC.
Published by: Dove Medical Press Ltd., Beechfield House, Winterton Way, Macclesfield, SK11 0JL, United Kingdom. TEL 44-1625-509130, FAX 44-1625-617933. Ed. Simon Berry.

617.7 362.41 GBR ISSN 0953-6833
CODEN: CEHEF2
➤ **COMMUNITY EYE HEALTH;** an international journal to promote eye health worldwide. Variant title: Community Eye Health Journal. Text in English. 1988. q. GBP 50; free in developing nations (effective 2011). adv. bk.rev. abstr.; illus. back issues avail. **Document type:** *Journal, Academic/Scholarly.* **Description:** Contains articles on planning and management, appropriate technology, communication and advocacy, and new developments in community eye care.
Related titles: CD-ROM ed.: ISSN 1994-9413; Online - full text ed.: ISSN 1993-7288. free (effective 2011); ◆ French ed.: Revue de Sante Oculaire Communautaire. ISSN 1993-7210; ◆ Spanish ed.: Salud Ocular Comunitaria Revista. ISSN 1993-7229; ◆ Portuguese ed.: Jornal de Saude Ocular Comunitaria. ISSN 2041-188X; ◆ Chinese ed.: Shequ Yan Jiankang; Supplement(s): Community Eye Health Journal. Indian Supplement.
Indexed: A01, A36, C06, C07, CABA, FR, GH, H17, LT, N02, P30, P33, P39, R08, R10, R12, RM&VM, Reac, SCOPUS, T02, T05, W11.
—INIST. **CCC.**
Published by: International Centre for Eye Health, London School of Hygiene and Tropical Medicine, Keppel St, London, WC1E 7HT, United Kingdom. TEL 44-20-76127972, FAX 44-20-79588317, iceh@iceh.org.uk, http://www.iceh.org.uk/. Ed. Elmien Wolvaardt Ellison.

617.7 DEU
CONCEPT OPHTHALMOLOGIE. Text in German. 2007. bi-m. adv. **Document type:** *Magazine, Trade.*
Published by: Autentic.Info GmbH, Felder Str 15/3, Wangen, 88239, Germany. TEL 49-7522-931073, FAX 49-7522-771114, info@autentic.info, http://www.autentic.info. Adv. contact Karin Burghardt. Circ: 6,000 (controlled).

617.7 NLD ISSN 1367-0484
RE977.C6 CODEN: CLAEAB
➤ **CONTACT LENS & ANTERIOR EYE.** Text in English. 1977. 5/yr. EUR 378 in Europe to institutions; JPY 50,300 in Japan to institutions; USD 423 elsewhere to institutions (effective 2012). charts; illus. Index. back issues avail.; reprints avail. **Document type:** *Journal, Academic/Scholarly.* **Description:** Publishes original and research articles on all aspects of contact lens theory and practice.
Incorporates (1985-2000): International Contact Lens Clinic (0892-8967); Which was formerly (until 1987): International Eyecare (0884-4577); Which was formed by the merger of (1974-1985): International Contact Lens Clinic (0094-1840); (1919-1985): Optometric Monthly (0160-9254); Which was formerly (until 1978): Optometric Weekly (0030-4093); (until 1928): Optometric Weekly and the Optometrist & Optician (0092-6965); Formerly (until 1997): British Contact Lens Association. Journal (0141-7037); Which incorporated: British Contact Lens Association. Transactions
Related titles: Online - full text ed.: ISSN 1476-5411 (from IngentaConnect, ScienceDirect).
Indexed: A01, A03, A08, A22, A26, C06, C07, CA, E01, EMBASE, ExcerpMed, I05, MEDLINE, P30, R10, Reac, SCOPUS, T02.
—BLDSC (3424.971000), IE, Infotrieve, Ingenta, INIST. **CCC.**
Published by: (British Contact Lens Association GBR), Elsevier BV (Subsidiary of: Elsevier Science & Technology), Radarweg 29, PO Box 211, Amsterdam, 1000 AE, Netherlands. TEL 31-20-4853911, FAX 31-20-4852457, JournalsCustomerServiceEMEA@elsevier.com, http://www.elsevier.nl. Ed. Shehzad A Naroo.

617.752 USA ISSN 0885-9175
RE977.C6
CONTACT LENS SPECTRUM. Text in English. 1976. m. USD 55 domestic; USD 70 in Canada; USD 104 elsewhere; free to qualified personnel (effective 2010). back issues avail. **Document type:** *Magazine, Trade.* **Description:** Provides contact lens professionals with clinical and technical information concerning contact lenses and solutions, guidelines for effective patient care, coverage of industry developments and new products, and analyses of market trends.
Incorporates (1976-1990): Contact Lens Forum (0363-1621)
Indexed: A22, CA, T02.
—BLDSC (3424.984000), GNLM, IE, Ingenta. **CCC.**
Published by: Lippincott Williams & Wilkins, VisionCare Group (Subsidiary of: Lippincott Williams & Wilkins), 323 Norristown Rd, Ste 200, Ambler, PA 19002. TEL 215-646-8700, http://www.visioncareprofessional.com/. Pub. Roger Zimmer TEL 203-846-2827.

617.7 USA ISSN 1537-5846
CONTEMPORARY OPHTHALMOLOGY. Text in English. 2002 (Jan.). bi-w. USD 420 domestic to institutions; USD 511 foreign to institutions (effective 2011). back issues avail. **Document type:** *Newsletter, Academic/Scholarly.*
Related titles: Online - full text ed.
—CCC.
Published by: Lippincott Williams & Wilkins (Subsidiary of: Wolters Kluwer N.V.), 530 Walnut St, Philadelphia, PA 19106. TEL 215-521-8300, FAX 215-521-8902, customerservice@lww.com. Ed. C S Foster.

617.175 USA ISSN 1541-5783
CONTEMPORARY OPTOMETRY (HAGERSTOWN); a publication for continuing education in optometry. Text in English. 2003 (Jan.). 11/yr. USD 395 domestic to institutions; USD 548 foreign to institutions (effective 2011). back issues avail. **Document type:** *Newsletter, Academic/Scholarly.* **Description:** Contains case study, epidemiology with historical associations and risk factors, concise pathology review, discussion of diagnosis, and overview of therapeutic management options, and a useful update on current clinical research.
Related titles: Online - full text ed.
—CCC.
Published by: Lippincott Williams & Wilkins (Subsidiary of: Wolters Kluwer N.V.), 16522 Hunters Green Pky, Hagerstown, MD 21740. TEL 301-223-2300, FAX 301-223-2398, customerservice@lww.com. Ed. Deepak Gupta.

617.7 USA ISSN 0277-3740
R336 CODEN: CORNDB
➤ **CORNEA;** the journal of cornea and external disease. Text in English. 1982. 10/yr. USD 1,163 domestic to institutions; USD 1,280 foreign to institutions (effective 2011). adv. bk.rev. abstr.; charts; illus. Index. back issues avail.; reprints avail. **Document type:** *Journal, Academic/Scholarly.* **Description:** Provides the clinical and basic research on the cornea and the anterior segment of the eye.
Related titles: Microform ed.: (from PQC); Online - full text ed.: ISSN 1536-4798.
Indexed: A22, A34, A36, ASCA, CABA, ChemAb, CurCont, E12, EMBASE, ExcerpMed, F08, F12, GH, H17, ISR, IndMed, IndVet, Inpharma, MEDLINE, N02, N03, P30, P33, P35, P39, R07, R08, R10, R12, R13, RA&MP, RM&VM, Reac, S12, SCI, SCOPUS, T05, TAR, VS, W07, W10, W11.
—BLDSC (3470.927500), CASDDS, GNLM, IE, Infotrieve, Ingenta, INIST. **CCC.**
Published by: (The Cornea Society), Lippincott Williams & Wilkins (Subsidiary of: Wolters Kluwer N.V.), Two Commerce Sq, 2001 Market St, Philadelphia, PA 19103. TEL 215-521-8300, FAX 215-521-8902, customerservice@lww.com, http://www.lww.com. Ed. R Doyle Stulting TEL 770-255-3330. Pub. Nina J Chang. Adv. contact Michelle Smith TEL 646-674-6537. Circ: 1,146.

617.7 CAN
COUP D'OEIL. Text in English. 1982. 5/yr.
Published by: Les Productions CT Enr., 1048 rue d'Avaugour, Chicoutimi, PQ G7H 2T1, Canada. TEL 418-696-4805, FAX 514-359-0836. adv.: B&W page CAD 1,390, color page CAD 1,955; trim 10.88 x 8.75. Circ: 2,492.

COURTROOM MEDICINE: THE EYE. *see* LAW

617.7 GBR ISSN 0271-3683
QP476 CODEN: CEYRDM
➤ **CURRENT EYE RESEARCH.** Text in English. 1981. m. GBP 1,050, EUR 1,455, USD 1,820 combined subscription to institutions (print & online eds.); GBP 2,095, EUR 2,910, USD 3,645 combined subscription to corporations (print & online eds.) (effective 2010). adv. illus. Index. back issues avail.; reprint service avail. from PSC. **Document type:** *Journal, Academic/Scholarly.* **Description:** Brings out articles in all the areas of eye research. Includes clinical research, anatomy, physiology, biophysics, biochemistry, pharmacology, developmental biology, microbiology and immunology.
Related titles: Online - full text ed.: ISSN 1460-2202 (from IngentaConnect).
Indexed: A01, A03, A08, A22, ASCA, B21, CA, CurCont, E01, EMBASE, ExcerpMed, ISR, IndMed, Inpharma, MEDLINE, NSA, OphLit, P30, P35, P48, PQC, R10, Reac, SCI, SCOPUS, T02, W07.
—CASDDS, GNLM, IE, Infotrieve, Ingenta, INIST. **CCC.**
Published by: Informa Healthcare (Subsidiary of: T & F Informa plc), Telephone House, 69-77 Paul St, London, EC2A 4LQ, United Kingdom. TEL 44-20-70175000, FAX 44-20-70176792, healthcare.enquiries@informa.com, http://www.tandf.co.uk/journals/. Adv. contact Per Sonnerfeldt. **Subscr. in N America to:** Taylor & Francis Inc., Customer Services Dept, 325 Chestnut St, 8th Fl, Philadelphia, PA 19106. TEL 215-625-8900, 800-354-1420, FAX 215-625-8914, customerservice@taylorandfrancis.com; **Subscr. outside N. America to:** Taylor & Francis Ltd., Journals Customer Service, Sheepen Pl, Colchester, Essex CO3 3LP, United Kingdom. TEL 44-20-70175544, FAX 44-20-70175198, tf.enquiries@tfinforma.com.

➤ **CURRENT MEDICAL LITERATURE. OPHTHALMOLOGY.** *see* MEDICAL SCIENCES—Abstracting, Bibliographies, Statistics

617.7 USA ISSN 1040-8738
CODEN: COOTEF
CURRENT OPINION IN OPHTHALMOLOGY. Text in English. 1989. bi-m. USD 1,348 domestic to institutions; USD 1,449 foreign to institutions (effective 2011). adv. bibl.; illus. back issues avail.; reprints avail. **Document type:** *Journal, Academic/Scholarly.* **Description:** Covers key subjects such as cataract surgery and lens implantation, glaucoma, retinal, vitreous and macular disorders, corneal and external disorders, refractive surgery, oculoplastic and orbital surgery, neuro-ophthalmology.
Related titles: Online - full text ed.: ISSN 1531-7021. USD 346 to individuals (effective 2011); Optical Disk - DVD ed.: Current Opinion in Ophthalmology, with Evaluated MEDLINE. ISSN 1080-8132. 1995.
Indexed: A22, BIOBASE, C06, C07, C08, CINAHL, CurCont, E01, EMBASE, ExcerpMed, IABS, MEDLINE, P30, R10, Reac, SCI, SCOPUS, W07.
—BLDSC (3500.776500), GNLM, IE, Infotrieve, Ingenta. **CCC.**
Published by: Lippincott Williams & Wilkins (Subsidiary of: Wolters Kluwer N.V.), 530 Walnut St, Philadelphia, PA 19106. TEL 215-521-8300, FAX 215-521-8902, customerservice@lww.com, http://www.lww.com. Ed. Allen C Ho. Pub. Ian Burgess. Circ: 628.

CUTANEOUS AND OCULAR TOXICOLOGY. *see* PHARMACY AND PHARMACOLOGY

617.7 KOR ISSN 0378-6471
CODEN: TAHCDH
DAEHAN AN'GWA HAG'HOEJI/KOREAN OPHTHALMOLOGICAL SOCIETY. JOURNAL. Text in Korean. 1989. m. membership. **Document type:** *Journal, Academic/Scholarly.*
Related titles: Online - full text ed.
—BLDSC (4812.341240).
Published by: Korean Ophthalmological Society/Daehan An'gwa Haghoe, Seocho World Officetel #1007, 1355-3 Seocho-2-dong Seocho-ku, Seoul, 137-072, Korea, S. TEL 82-2-5836520, FAX 82-2-5836521, kos@ophthalmology.org. Ed. Sang In Khwarg.

617.752 DEU ISSN 0344-7103
RE1 CODEN: DDOPD4
DEUTSCHE OPTIKERZEITUNG. Text in German. 1945. m. EUR 69.70; EUR 22 to students (effective 2009). adv. bk.rev. back issues avail. **Document type:** *Magazine, Trade.*
Formerly (until 1978): Sueddeutsche Optikerzeitung (0344-7170)
Indexed: P30, TM.
—CASDDS. **CCC.**
Published by: D O Z Verlag - Optische Fachveroeffentlichung GmbH, Luisenstr 14, Heidelberg, 69115, Germany. TEL 49-6221-905170, FAX 49-6221-905171, doz@doz-verlag.de. Ed. Dieter Baust. Adv. contact Ralf Ritter. B&W page EUR 4,160; trim 185 x 258. Circ: 8,775 (paid and controlled).

617.7 CHE ISSN 0250-3751
RE14 CODEN: DEOPDB
➤ **DEVELOPMENTS IN OPHTHALMOLOGY.** Text in English. 1980. irreg., latest vol.48, 2011. price varies. back issues avail.; reprints avail. **Document type:** *Monographic series, Academic/Scholarly.* **Description:** Provides ophthalmologists, ophthalmic surgeons and practicing optometrists with expert summaries of international developments vital to progress in this field.
Incorporates (in 1979): Modern Problems in Ophthalmology (0077-0078); (in 1981): Advances in Ophthalmology (0065-3004); Which was formerly (until 1969): Fortschritte der Augenheilkunde (1421-5756); (in 1977): Bibliotheca Ophthalmologica (0067-8090); Which was formerly (until 1939): Abhandlungen aus der Augenheilkunde und ihren Grenzgebieten (1016-2739)
Related titles: Online - full text ed.: ISSN 1662-2790; ◆ Supplement to: Ophthalmologica. ISSN 0030-3755.
Indexed: A22, ChemAb, EMBASE, ExcerpMed, IndMed, MEDLINE, P30, R10, Reac, SCOPUS.
—BLDSC (3579.085480), CASDDS, GNLM, IE, Infotrieve, Ingenta, INIST. **CCC.**
Published by: S. Karger AG, Allschwilerstr 10, Basel, 4055, Switzerland. TEL 41-61-3061111, FAX 41-61-3061234, karger@karger.ch, http://www.karger.ch. Ed. F Bandello.

617.7 USA ISSN 1542-8958
➤ **DIGITAL JOURNAL OF OPHTHALMOLOGY.** Abbreviated title: D J O. Text in English. 1995. q. free (effective 2011). back issues avail. **Document type:** *Journal, Academic/Scholarly.* **Description:** Aims to serve as a resource for ophthalmologists and vision scientists throughout the world.
Media: Online - full text. **Related titles:** CD-ROM ed.

Published by: Massachusetts Eye and Ear Infirmary, 243 Charles St, Boston, MA 02114. Mark_Hatton@meei.harvard.edu. Ed. Carolyn Kloek.

617.7 MEX
DIMENSION OPTICA. Text in Spanish. bi-m. USD 350 (effective 2001). adv. back issues avail. **Document type:** *Academic/Scholarly.*
Related titles: Online - full text ed.: ISSN 1605-4970. 1999.
Published by: Corporacion Optica y Publicitaria, Paseo de Mexico No. 21, Col. Jardines de Atizapan, Atizapan de Zaragoza, Estado de Mexico 52978, Mexico. TEL 52-5-8258258, dimop@mail.com, dimensionoptica@usa.net. Ed. Rafael Balcazar Narro. Adv. contact Alejandra Moscoso Garcia.

616.7 GBR
DIRECTORY OF TRAINING POSTS IN OPHTHALMOLOGY. Text in English. 19??. a. GBP 16 per issue (effective 2010). **Document type:** *Directory, Academic/Scholarly.* **Description:** Contains information on training for ophthalmology in the UK.
Published by: (Royal College of Ophthalmologists), Hawker Publications Ltd., Culvert House, Culvert Rd, London, SW11 5DH, United Kingdom. TEL 44-20-77202108, FAX 44-20-74983023, suec@hawkerpublications.com, http://www.careinfo.org/.

617.7 DEU ISSN 0012-4486
RE14 CODEN: DOOPAA
➤ **DOCUMENTA OPHTHALMOLOGICA.** Text in English. 1938. bi-m. EUR 1,421, USD 1,511 combined subscription to institutions (print & online eds.) (effective 2012). adv. bk.rev. Supplement avail.; reprint service avail. from PSC. **Document type:** *Journal, Academic/Scholarly.* **Description:** Publishes studies on clinical and non-clinical ophthalmology.
Related titles: Microform ed.: (from PQC); Online - full text ed.: ISSN 1573-2622 (from IngentaConnect); ◆ Supplement(s): Documenta Ophthalmologica Proceedings Series. ISSN 0303-6405.
Indexed: A20, A22, A26, A34, A36, AEBA, ASCA, B21, B25, BIOSIS Prev, BibLing, CA, CABA, ChemAb, CurCont, E01, E12, EMBASE, ExcerpMed, FR, GH, GenetAb, IBR, IBZ, ISR, IndMed, IndVet, Inpharma, Inspec, M&PBA, MEDLINE, MycolAb, N02, N03, NSA, P20, P22, P30, P33, P35, P39, P48, P54, PQC, R07, R08, R10, Reac, SCI, SCOPUS, T02, T05, VS, W07.
—BLDSC (3609.560000), AskIEEE, CASDDS, GNLM, IE, Infotrieve, Ingenta, INIST. **CCC.**
Published by: (International Society for Clinical Electrophysiology of Vision NLD), Springer (Subsidiary of: Springer Science+Business Media), Tiergartenstr 17, Heidelberg, 69121, Germany. TEL 49-6221-4870, FAX 49-6221-345229, subscriptions@springer.com. Ed. Laura Frishman.

617.7 NLD ISSN 0303-6405
CODEN: DOPSBP
DOCUMENTA OPHTHALMOLOGICA PROCEEDINGS SERIES. Text in English. 1973. irreg., latest vol.62, 1998. price varies. **Document type:** *Proceedings, Academic/Scholarly.*
Related titles: ◆ Supplement to: Documenta Ophthalmologica. ISSN 0012-4486.
Indexed: P30, PsycholAb.
—BLDSC (3609.600000), CASDDS, GNLM. **CCC.**
Published by: Springer Netherlands (Subsidiary of: Springer Science+Business Media), Van Godewijckstraat 30, Dordrecht, 3311 GX, Netherlands. TEL 31-78-6576050, FAX 31-78-6576474.

617.7 KEN ISSN 1992-5832
➤ **EAST AFRICAN JOURNAL OF OPHTHALMOLOGY.** Text in English. 1976. a. USD 120, GBP 85 (effective 2007). **Document type:** *Journal, Academic/Scholarly.* **Description:** Covers all aspects of ophthalmology and community eye health.
Related titles: Online - full text ed.: ISSN 1994-6880. 2007.
Published by: Ophthalmological Society of Eastern Africa, Ralph Bunche Road, Upper Hill Medical Centre, 4th Floor, Suite 4E, PO Box 332-00200, Nairobi, Kenya. TEL 254-20-2727682, info@oseafrica.org. Ed. Dr. Jefitha Karimurio TEL 254-73-7381995.

362.1 617.7 NLD ISSN 1876-2425
EEN OGENBLIK. Text in Dutch. 1985. 3/yr. illus. 6 p./no. 2 cols./p.; back issues avail. **Document type:** *Newsletter.* **Description:** Reports on the foundation's activities to prevent and cure blindness in the Himalayan Central Asian region.
Formerly (until 2008): Op Ooghoogte (1384-0339)
Published by: Eye Care Foundation, Postbus 59021, Amsterdam, 1040 KA, Netherlands. TEL 31-20-6473879, FAX 31-20-4751467, info@eyecarefoundation.nl, http://www.eyecarefoundation.nl. Circ: 12,000.

617.7 EGY ISSN 1687-6997
THE EGYPTIAN JOURNAL OF CATARACT AND REFRACTIVE SURGERY. Abbreviated title: Egypt. J. Cataract Refract. Surg. Text in English. 199?. s-a. **Document type:** *Journal, Academic/Scholarly.*
Published by: The Egyptian Society of Ocular Implants and Refractive Surgery, University of Alexandria, Faculty of Medicine, Ophthalmology Dept, PO Box 1116, Alexandria, Egypt. TEL 203-486-2920. Ed. Dr. Alaa Atef Ghaith.

617.7 EGY ISSN 2090-0686
EGYPTIAN OPHTHALMOLOGICAL SOCIETY. JOURNAL. Short title: J E O S. Text in English. 2008. a. **Document type:** *Journal, Academic/Scholarly.*
Published by: Ophthalmological Society of Egypt, 42 Qassr Al-Aini St, Cairo, Egypt. eos@eyegypt.eg.net.

617.7 FRA ISSN 0246-0343
➤ **ENCYCLOPEDIE MEDICO-CHIRURGICALE. OPHTALMOLOGIE.** Cover title: Traite d'Ophtalmologie. Variant title: Encyclopedie Medico-Chirurgicale, Instantanes Medicaux. Ophtalmologie. Text in French. 1955. 6 base vols. plus q. updates. EUR 1,353 (effective 2006). bibl.; charts; illus. **Document type:** *Academic/Scholarly.* **Description:** Provides ophthalmologists with a comprehensive, up-to-date reference to diagnose and treat diseases and conditions of the eye.
Related titles: Online - full text ed.
—INIST. **CCC.**
Published by: Elsevier Masson (Subsidiary of: Elsevier Health Sciences), 62 Rue Camille Desmoulins, Issy les Moulineaux, Cedex 92442, France. TEL 33-1-71165500, FAX 33-1-71165600, infos@elsevier-masson.fr.

617.7 ITA ISSN 1120-6721
RE1 CODEN: EJOOEL
➤ **EUROPEAN JOURNAL OF OPHTHALMOLOGY.** Text in English. 1991. bi-m. EUR 280 combined subscription in Europe to institutions (print & online eds.); EUR 324 combined subscription elsewhere to institutions (print & online eds.) (effective 2009). adv. **Document type:** *Journal, Academic/Scholarly.* **Description:** Covers clinical and basic research in ophthalmology.
Related titles: Online - full text ed.: ISSN 1724-6016. EUR 80 to individuals; EUR 210 to institutions (effective 2008).
Indexed: A22, A36, CABA, CurCont, E12, EMBASE, ExcerpMed, F08, F11, F12, GH, H17, IndMed, Inpharma, MEDLINE, N02, N03, P30, P33, P39, R08, R10, R12, RA&MP, RM&VM, Reac, RefZh, SCI, SCOPUS, T05, W07.
—BLDSC (3829.733230), GNLM, IE, Infotrieve, Ingenta, INIST. **CCC.**
Published by: Wichtig Editore Srl, Via Friuli 72, Milan, MI 20135, Italy. TEL 39-02-55195443, FAX 39-02-55195971, info@wichtig-publisher.com, http://www.wichtig-publisher.com. Ed. Dr. Rosario Brancato. Circ: 3,000 (paid); 4,500 (controlled).

617.7 658 USA
EUROPEAN LENSES & TECHNOLOGY. Text in English. bi-m. free with subscr. to 20/20 Europe. **Document type:** *Magazine, Trade.* **Description:** Provides up-to-date ophthalmic lens information, including products, technology, marketing, business & educational features, plus interviews.
Related titles: ◆ Supplement to: 20/20 Europe. ISSN 1353-3290.
Published by: Jobson International (Subsidiary of: Jobson Publishing LLC), 100 Avenue of the Americas, 9th Fl, New York, NY 10013. TEL 212-274-7000, FAX 212-431-5579, subscriptions@2020europe.com, http://www.2020europe.com.

617.7 SWE ISSN 0301-326X
EUROPEAN OPHTHALMOLOGICAL SOCIETY. CONGRESS. Text in Multiple languages. 1960. biennial. **Document type:** *Proceedings, Academic/Scholarly.*
Published by: European Society of Ophthalmology/Societas Ophthalmologica Europaea (S O E), PO Box 5619, Stockholm, 114 86, Sweden. TEL 46-8-4596650, FAX 46-8-6619125, http://www.soevision.org. Ed. P D Trevor Roper.

617.7 USA ISSN 1555-9203
EVIDENCE - BASED OPHTHALMOLOGY; critical appraisals and healthcare economic analysis. Text in English. 1999. q. USD 274 domestic to institutions; USD 360 foreign to institutions (effective 2011). adv. back issues avail.; reprints avail. **Document type:** *Journal, Academic/Scholarly.* **Description:** Presents analyses in the categories of clinical studies or trials, medical socioeconomics, and politics as it relates to healthcare.
Formerly (until Jan.2005): Evidence - Based Eye Care (1525-8599)
Related titles: Online - full text ed.: ISSN 1555-9211.
Indexed: A01, A03, A08, CA, EMBASE, ExcerpMed, R10, Reac, SCOPUS, T02.
—BLDSC (3831.037505), IE, Infotrieve, Ingenta. **CCC.**
Published by: Lippincott Williams & Wilkins (Subsidiary of: Wolters Kluwer N.V.), Two Commerce Sq, 2001 Market St, Philadelphia, PA 19103. TEL 215-521-8300, FAX 215-521-8902, customerservice@lww.com, http://www.lww.com. Eds. Dr. Gary C Brown, Dr. Melissa M Brown, Peter J Kertes.

EXCERPTA MEDICA. SECTION 12: OPHTHALMOLOGY. *see* MEDICAL SCIENCES—Abstracting, Bibliographies, Statistics

617.7 GBR ISSN 0014-4835
QP474 CODEN: EXERA6
➤ **EXPERIMENTAL EYE RESEARCH.** Text in English. 1961. m. EUR 3,558 in Europe to institutions; JPY 384,200 in Japan to institutions; USD 3,162 elsewhere to institutions (effective 2012). adv. charts; illus.; stat. index. back issues avail.; reprint service avail. from PSC. **Document type:** *Journal, Academic/Scholarly.* **Description:** Publishes original research papers on all aspects of the anatomy, physiology, biochemistry, biophysics, molecular biology, pharmacology, developmental biology, microbiology, and immunology of the eye.
Related titles: Online - full text ed.: ISSN 1096-0007. USD 2,916 to institutions (effective 2009) (from IngentaConnect, ScienceDirect).
Indexed: A01, A03, A08, A22, A26, ASCA, B21, B25, BIOSIS Prev, C33, CA, CIN, ChemAb, ChemTitl, CurCont, DentInd, E01, EMBASE, ExcerpMed, I05, IBR, IBZ, ISR, IndMed, Inpharma, MEDLINE, MycolAb, NSA, P30, P35, R10, Reac, SCI, SCOPUS, T02, W07.
—BLDSC (3839.150000), CASDDS, GNLM, IE, Infotrieve, Ingenta, INIST. **CCC.**
Published by: (International Society for Eye Research USA), Academic Press (Subsidiary of: Elsevier Science & Technology), 32 Jamestown Rd, Camden, London, NW1 7BY, United Kingdom. TEL 44-20-74244200, FAX 44-20-74832293, corporatesales@elsevier.com. Ed. Dr. Joe G Hollyfield. R&P Catherine John. Adv. contact Nik Screen.

617.7 GBR ISSN 1746-9899
RE1
➤ **EXPERT REVIEW OF OPHTHALMOLOGY.** Text in English. 2006 (Oct.). bi-m. GBP 695 combined subscription domestic to institutions (print & online eds.); USD 1,220 combined subscription in North America to institutions (print & online eds.); JPY 129,000 combined subscription in Japan to institutions (print & online eds.); EUR 975 combined subscription elsewhere to institutions (print & online eds.) (effective 2011). adv. back issues avail.; reprints avail. **Document type:** *Journal, Academic/Scholarly.* **Description:** Provides an important platform for commentary and debate on current and emerging approaches in ocular medicine.
Related titles: Online - full text ed.: ISSN 1746-9902. GBP 615 domestic to institutions; USD 1,080 in North America to institutions; JPY 115,500 in Japan to institutions; EUR 865 elsewhere to institutions (effective 2011) (from IngentaConnect).
Indexed: A26, CA, E08, EMBASE, ExcerpMed, H11, H12, I05, P20, P30, P48, P54, PQC, R10, Reac, SCOPUS, T02.
—BLDSC (9830.009000), IE. **CCC.**
Published by: Expert Reviews Ltd. (Subsidiary of: Future Science Ltd.), Unitec House, 2 Albert Pl, London, N3 1QB, United Kingdom. TEL 44-20-83716080, FAX 44-20-83716099, info@expert-reviews.com. Ed. Elisa Manzotti TEL 44-20-83716090. Pub. David Hughes. Adv. contact Simon Boisseau. Circ: 350.

617.7 GBR ISSN 0950-222X
RE1 CODEN: EYEEEC
➤ **EYE.** Text in English. 1880. m. EUR 889 in Europe to institutions; USD 993 in the Americas to institutions; JPY 151,900 in Japan to institutions; GBP 573 to institutions in the UK & elsewhere (effective 2011). adv. bk.rev. index. back issues avail.; reprints avail. **Document type:** *Journal, Academic/Scholarly.* **Description:** Provides the practicing opthamologist with information on the latest clinical and laboratory-based research, including external eye disease; oculo-plastic surgery; oculo surface and corneal disorders; neuro-opthamology and opthalmic pathology.
Formerly (until 1987): Ophthalmological Society of the United Kingdom. Transactions (0078-5334)
Related titles: Microfiche ed.: (from BHP); Online - full text ed.: ISSN 1476-5454.
Indexed: A01, A02, A03, A08, A22, A36, AIDS Ab, B21, B25, BIOSIS Prev, C06, C07, CA, CABA, CurCont, D01, DentInd, E01, E12, EMBASE, ESPM, ExcerpMed, F08, F11, F12, FR, GH, H&SSA, H17, INI, ISR, IndMed, Inpharma, LT, MEDLINE, MycolAb, N02, N03, NSA, P20, P22, P30, P33, P35, P39, P48, P54, PQC, R08, R10, R12, RA&MP, RM&VM, RRTA, Reac, SCI, SCOPUS, T02, T05, VS, W07, W10, W11.
—CASDDS, GNLM, IE, Infotrieve, Ingenta, INIST. **CCC.**
Published by: (Royal College of Opthamologists), Nature Publishing Group (Subsidiary of: Macmillan Publishers Ltd.), The MacMillan Bldg, 4 Crinan St, London, N1 9XW, United Kingdom. TEL 44-20-78334000, FAX 44-20-78334640. Ed. Andrew Lotery. Adv. contact Ben Harkinson TEL 617-475-9222. **Subscr. addr.:** Brunel Rd, Houndmills, Basingstoke, Hamps RG21 6XS, United Kingdom. TEL 44-1256-329242, FAX 44-1256-812358, subscriptions@nature.com.

617.7 616.8 GBR ISSN 1179-2744
▼ ➤ **EYE AND BRAIN.** Text in English. 2009. irreg. free (effective 2011). **Document type:** *Journal, Academic/Scholarly.*
Media: Online - full text.
—**CCC.**
Published by: Dove Medical Press Ltd., Beechfield House, Winterton Way, Macclesfield, SK11 0JL, United Kingdom. TEL 44-1625-509130, FAX 44-1625-617933. Ed. Margaret Wong-Riley.

617.7 USA ISSN 1542-2321
RE977.C6 CODEN: CLAJEU
➤ **EYE AND CONTACT LENS**; science and clinical practice. Text in English. 1968. bi-m. USD 262 domestic to institutions; USD 367 foreign to institutions (effective 2011). adv. bk.rev. back issues avail.; reprints avail. **Document type:** *Journal, Academic/Scholarly.* **Description:** Addresses all aspects of refractive science - contact lenses, optical dispensing, refractive surgery and related anterior segment disease.
Former titles (until 2003): The C L A O Journal (0733-8902); (until 1983): Contact and Intraocular Lens Medical Journal (0360-1358); Which superseded (in 1975): Contact Lens Medical Bulletin (0010-728X)
Related titles: Microform ed.: (from PQC); Online - full text ed.: ISSN 1542-233X.
Indexed: A22, ChemAb, CurCont, EMBASE, ExcerpMed, IndMed, MEDLINE, P30, R10, Reac, SCI, SCOPUS, W07.
—BLDSC (3854.587000), CASDDS, GNLM, IE, Ingenta, INIST. **CCC.**
Published by: (Contact Lens Association of Ophthalmologists, University of Texas, Department of Opthalmology), Lippincott Williams & Wilkins (Subsidiary of: Wolters Kluwer N.V.), Two Commerce Sq, 2001 Market St, Philadelphia, PA 19103. TEL 215-521-8300, FAX 215-521-8902, customerservice@lww.com, http://www.lww.com. Ed. Desmond Fonn. Pub. Nina J Chang. **Co-publisher:** Contact Lens Association of Ophthalmologists.

617.7 ITA ISSN 2035-6900
▼ **EYE DOCTOR.** Text in Italian. 2009. bi-m. EUR 45 (effective 2010). **Document type:** *Journal, Academic/Scholarly.*
Published by: Casa Editrice Ariesdue, Via Airoldi 11, Carimate, CO 22060, Italy. TEL 39-031792135, FAX 39-031790743, info@ariesdue.it, http://www.ariesdue.it.

617.7 NZL
▼ **EYE HEALTH RESEARCH REVIEW.** Text in English. 2009. bi-m. free to qualified personnel (effective 2009). **Document type:** *Journal, Academic/Scholarly.*
Media: Online - full text.
Published by: Research Review Ltd., N Shore Mail Centre, PO Box 100116, Auckland, New Zealand. TEL 64-9-4102277, info@researchreview.co.nz.

617.7 USA
EYE LIGHTS. Text in English. q. free to members. **Document type:** *Newsletter, Trade.* **Description:** Covers organization news, events, continuing education, and calendar.
Supersedes in part: Viewpoints
Published by: Joint Commission on Allied Health Personnel in Ophthalmology, 2025 Woodlane Dr, St. Paul, MN MN 55125-2998. TEL 651-731-2944, 800-284-3937, FAX 651-731-0410, jcahpo@jcahpo.org, http://www.jcahpo.org/newsite/index.htm.

617.7 GBR ISSN 1368-8952
EYE NEWS. Text in English. 1995. bi-m. GBP 19 domestic; GBP 28 in Europe; GBP 42 elsewhere (effective 2009). adv. bk.rev. back issues avail.; reprints avail. **Document type:** *Magazine, Trade.* **Description:** Contains editorial topics, reviews of journals and reports on new products.
—BLDSC (3854.631000). **CCC.**
Published by: Pinpoint Scotland Ltd., 9 Gayfield St, Edinburgh, Scotland EH1 3NT, United Kingdom. TEL 44-131-5574184, FAX 44-131-5574701, info@pinpoint-scotland.com. Ed. Katie Labak TEL 44-131-5574184. Adv. contact Justin Chater TEL 44-131-5574184. Circ: 1,656 (paid); 2,954 (controlled).

617.75 USA
EYE ON OREGON. Text in English. 1934. q. free to members. bk.rev. **Document type:** *Newsletter.* **Description:** Filled with articles on upcoming industry, state and federal legislation, and information on upcoming events around the state.
Former titles (until vol.29, no.4, 1992): Oregon Optometry (0274-6549); Oregon Optometrist (0030-476X)
Related titles: Online - full text ed.
Published by: Oregon Optometric Physicians Association, 4404 SE King Rd Milwaukie, Milwaukie, OR 97222. TEL 503-654-5036, FAX 503-659-4189, info@oregonoptometry.org, http://www.oregonoptometry.org. Ed. J Gregg Mindt.

617.7 ITA ISSN 2039-4756
▼ ➤ **EYE REPORTS.** Text in English. 2011. irreg. **Document type:** *Journal, Academic/Scholarly.*
Media: Online - full text.
Published by: Pagepress, Via Giuseppe Belli 4, Pavia, 27100, Italy. TEL 39-0382-1751762, FAX 39-0382-1750481, http://www.pagepress.org. Ed. David Pow.

617.7 USA
EYE TO EYE. Text in English. 1971. a. free. **Document type:** *Newsletter.*
Former titles: International Eye Foundation - Society of Eye Surgeons. Newsletter; Eyelights
Published by: International Eye Foundation, 7801 Norfolk Ave, Bethesda, MD 20814. TEL 301-986-1830, FAX 301-986-1876, info@iefusa.org, http://www.iefusa.org. Ed. Calvin Baervelat. Circ: 1,500.

617.752 DEU ISSN 1613-186X
EYEBIZZ; optics - management - design - communication. Text in German. 2003. bi-m. EUR 24 domestic; EUR 30 foreign; EUR 7 newsstand/cover (effective 2011). adv. **Document type:** *Magazine, Trade.*
Published by: Ebner Verlag GmbH, Karlstr 41, Ulm, 89073, Germany. TEL 49-731-152002, FAX 49-731-1520188, info@ebnerverlag.de, http://www.ebnerverlag.de. Ed. Martin Graf. Adv. contact Dagmar Schwall. Circ: 12,167 (paid and controlled).

617.7 USA ISSN 1097-2986
EYENET. Text in English. 1978. m. USD 128 domestic to non-members; USD 180 foreign to non-members; free to members (effective 2010). adv. illus. back issues avail. **Document type:** *Magazine, Trade.* **Description:** Covers research and clinical developments in the field.
Former titles (until 1997): Argus (0194-8172); (until 1979): Academy Argus
Published by: American Academy of Ophthalmology, PO Box 7424, San Francisco, CA 94120. TEL 415-561-8500, FAX 415-561-8533, customer_service@aao.org. Ed. David W Parke. Pub. Jane Aguirre. Circ: 16,346.

617.7 USA ISSN 0891-8260
RE1
➤ **FOCAL POINTS (SAN FRANCISCO)**; clinical modules for opthalmologists. Variant title: Clinical Modules for Opthalmologists. Text in English. 1983. q. USD 252 combined subscription domestic to non-members (print & online eds.); USD 282 combined subscription foreign to non-members (print & online eds.); USD 187 combined subscription domestic to members (print & online eds.); USD 217 combined subscription foreign to members (print & online eds.) (effective 2011). back issues avail. **Document type:** *Journal, Academic/Scholarly.* **Description:** Provides the opthalmologist with concise clinical information on the diagnosis and treatment of ocular disease and injury.
Related titles: Online - full text ed.: USD 209 domestic to institutions; USD 155 foreign to institutions (effective 2011).
—IE.
Published by: American Academy of Opthalmology, PO Box 7424, San Francisco, CA 94120. TEL 415-561-8500, FAX 415-561-8533, aaoe@aao.org, http://www.aao.org.

617.7 DEU ISSN 0721-1600
FOCUS (RATINGEN). Text in German. 1981. 11/yr. EUR 6 newsstand/cover (effective 2007). adv. bk.rev. charts; illus. **Document type:** *Magazine, Trade.* **Description:** For optometrists and dispensing opticians: practice management, education and trade relations in political matters.
Published by: Spangemacher Verlags GmbH und Co. KG, Papiermuehlenweg 74, Ratingen, 40882, Germany. TEL 49-2102-16780, FAX 49-2102-167829. Ed. Joerg Spangemacher. Adv. contact Heike Bergfeld. B&W page EUR 2,604, color page EUR 4,164. Circ: 10,007 (paid and controlled).

617.752 658 USA
FRAMES DATA QUARTERLY. Text in English. 1968. q. USD 459 (effective 2007). adv. **Document type:** *Magazine, Trade.* **Description:** Serves as a reference for frame style information in the industry. Includes complete specifications on 50,000 currently available styles from 200 industry manufacturers and importers.
Formerly (until 1999): Frames
Indexed: AIAP.
Published by: Frames Data (Subsidiary of: Jobson Publishing LLC), 100 Avenue of the Americas, 9th Fl, New York, NY 10013. TEL 212-274-7000, 800-821-6069, FAX 212-274-0392, info@framesdata.com, http://www.framesdata.com. Pub. Thomas Lamond. Circ: 18,000.

617.7 JPN ISSN 1881-4263
FRONTIERS IN DRY EYE/RUIEKI KARA MITA OKYURA SAFESU. Text in Japanese. 2006. s-a. JPY 3,780 (effective 2007). **Document type:** *Journal, Academic/Scholarly.*
Published by: Medikaru Rebyusha/Medical Review Co., Ltd., 1-7-3 Hirano-Machi, Chuo-ku, Yoshida Bldg., Osaka-shi, 541-0046, Japan. TEL 81-6-62231468, FAX 81-6-62231245, http://www.m-review.co.jp/.

617.7 JPN ISSN 1345-854X
FRONTIERS IN GLAUCOMA. Text in Japanese. 2000. bi-m. JPY 8,380 (effective 2005). **Document type:** *Journal, Academic/Scholarly.*
Published by: Medikaru Rebyusha/Medical Review Co., Ltd., 1-7-3 Hirano-Machi, Chuo-ku, Yoshida Bldg., Osaka-shi, 541-0046, Japan. TEL 81-6-62231468, FAX 81-6-62231245.

617.175 ESP ISSN 0210-5284
GACETA OPTICA. Text in Spanish. 1971. m. back issues avail. **Document type:** *Bulletin, Consumer.*
Related titles: ◆ Supplement(s): Optometria Information (Castilla-La Mancha, Extremadura y Madrid Edition). ISSN 1885-4060; ◆ Optometria Informacion (Castilla y Leon Edition). ISSN 1885-4052.
Published by: Colegio Nacional de Opticos Optometristas de Espana/Spanish Council of Optometry, C Princesa, 25 4o, Edificio Hexagono, Madrid, 28008, Spain. TEL 34-91-5414403, FAX 34-91-5422397. Circ: 14,000.

617.7 615.7 JPN ISSN 0914-1405
GAN YAKURI/JAPANESE JOURNAL OF OCULAR PHARMACOLOGY. Text in English, Japanese. 1987. a. membership. **Document type:** *Journal, Academic/Scholarly.*
Published by: Nihon Gan Yakuri Gakkai/Japanese Society for Ocular Pharmacology, Showa University, School of Pharmaceutical Sciences, 1-5-8 Hatanodai, Shinagawa, Tokyo, 142-8555, Japan. TEL 81-3-37848128, FAX 81-3-37848129, ganyakuri@med.showa-u.ac.jp, http://jsop.umin.ne.jp/.

617.7 JPN ISSN 0016-4488
GANKA/OPHTHALMOLOGY. Text in Japanese. 1959. m. JPY 42,945 (effective 2007). bk.rev. cum.index. **Document type:** *Journal, Academic/Scholarly.*
Indexed: INIS AtomInd, ISR, JPI, P30.
—GNLM.
Published by: Kanehara Shuppan/Kanehara & Co. Ltd., 2-31-14 Yushima, Bunkyo-ku, Tokyo, 113-8687, Japan. TEL 81-3-38117184, FAX 81-3-38130288, http://www.kanehara-shuppan.co.jp/. Circ: 5,100.

617.7 JPN ISSN 1344-8293
GANKA KEA/JAPANESE JOURNAL OF OPHTHALMIC CARING. Text in Japanese. 1999. m. JPY 20,412; JPY 1,890 newsstand/cover (effective 2007). reprints avail. **Document type:** *Journal, Academic/Scholarly.*
Published by: Medicus Shuppan/Medicus Publishing Inc., 18-24 Hiroshiba-cho, Suita-shi, Osaka-fu 564-8580, Japan. TEL 81-6-63856911, FAX 81-6-63856873, http://www.medica.co.jp/.

617.7 JPN ISSN 0386-9601
GANKA RINSHO IHO/JAPANESE REVIEW OF CLINICAL OPHTHALMOLOGY. Text in Japanese; Summaries in English. 1906. m. JPY 15,000 (effective 2007). **Document type:** *Journal, Academic/Scholarly.*
Indexed: INIS AtomInd.
—BLDSC (4661.750000).
Published by: Ganka Rinsho Ihokai/Japanese Society of Clinical Ophthalmology, c/o Teikyo University, Department of Ophthalmology, 2-11-1 Kaga, Itabashi, Tokyo, 173-8605, Japan. TEL 03-3964-1211, FAX 03-3963-0303.

GELBE LISTE PHARMINDEX. OPHTHALMOLOGEN. *see* PHARMACY AND PHARMACOLOGY

617.7 DNK ISSN 1901-774X
GLAUCOM. Text in Danish. 199?. biennial. DKK 150 membership (effective 2008). **Document type:** *Magazine, Consumer.*
Formerly (until 2005): Dansk Glaucom Forening Informerer (1600-3489)
Published by: Dansk Glaukom Forening/Danish Glaucoma Association, PO Box 142, Kgs. Lyngby, 2800, Denmark. TEL 45-70-200393, post@glaukom.dk, http://www.glaukom.dk.

617.7 GBR ISSN 1465-5071
➤ **GLAUCOMA FORUM**; the IGA journal for interdisciplinary discussion. Text in English. 1999. q. free to members (effective 2009). adv. back issues avail.; reprints avail. **Document type:** *Journal, Academic/Scholarly.* **Description:** Discusses professional and clinical issues relating to glaucoma.
—BLDSC (4194.280000), IE, Ingenta.
Published by: International Glaucoma Association, Woodcote House, 15 Highpoint Business Village, Henwood, Ashford, Kent, TN24 8DH, United Kingdom. TEL 44-1233-648164, FAX 44-1233-648179, info@iga.org.uk, http://www.iga.org.uk/.

617.7 USA
GLAUCOMA TODAY. Text in English. 2003 (Feb.). bi-m. adv. back issues avail. **Document type:** *Journal, Trade.* **Description:** Acts as source of information and education for glaucoma subspecialists and general ophthalmologists who treat glaucoma patients. Delivers important information on recent research, surgical techniques, clinical strategies, and technology.
Related titles: Online - full content ed.
Published by: Bryn Mawr Communications, LLC (Subsidiary of: Bryn Mawr Communications Group LLC), 1008 Upper Gulph Rd, Ste 200, Wayne, PA 19087. TEL 484-581-1800, FAX 484-581-1818, http://www.bmctoday.com/. Ed. Gillian McDermott TEL 484-581-1812. Pub. David Cox TEL 484-581-1814.

617.7 NLD ISSN 1872-6658
GLAUCOOMMAGAZINE. Text in Dutch. q. EUR 22 (effective 2009).
Formerly (until 2006): Oogappel (1568-8046)
Published by: Nederlandse Vereniging van Glaucoompatienten, Jaarbeursplein 15, Utrecht, 3521 AM, Netherlands. TEL 31-30-2945444, FAX 31-30-2932544, informatie@glaucoomvereniging.nl, http://www.glaucoomvereniging.nl.

617.7 USA ISSN 1072-7906
GLEAMS. Text in English. 1982. 3/yr. free. bk.rev. charts; illus. back issues avail. **Document type:** *Newsletter, Consumer.* **Description:** Aims to educate the public and professionals about current glaucoma diagnosis, treatment, and research.
Related titles: Online - full text ed.
Published by: Glaucoma Research Foundation, 490 Post Street, Ste 1427, San Francisco, CA 94102. TEL 415-986-3162, 800-826-6693, FAX 415-986-3763, info@glaucoma.org. Ed. Joy Guihama. R&P Lisa Wagreich. Circ: 33,000.

617.7 NLD ISSN 1386-0194
GLOBAL CONTACT. Text in English. 1992. 3/yr. EUR 45 (effective 2009); free to qualified personnel. adv. illus. **Document type:** *Journal, Trade.* **Description:** Covers news affecting the contact lens industry worldwide, including new technologies, manufacturing, marketing and technical issues.
Formerly (until 1996): Contact (Hank) (1381-3676)
Related titles: E-mail ed.; Online - full content ed.
Indexed: R18.
Published by: E P S, Waterwilg 1, Zevenbergen, 4761 WN, Netherlands. TEL 31-168-329278, FAX 31-168-327069, info@gclabsite.com, http://www.gclabsite.com. Circ: 2,750 (controlled).

617.7 TUR ISSN 1305-9173
GLOKOM-KATARAKT/JOURNAL OF GLOKOM-CATARACT. Text in Turkish, English. 4/yr. TRY 150 to institutions; TRY 75 doctors (effective 2009). **Document type:** *Journal, Academic/Scholarly.* **Description:** Contains original research, innovation reviews, short articles and case reports on cataract.
Related titles: Online - full text ed.
Indexed: A01, CA, T02.
Published by: Gazi Eye Foundation, Tuna Cad. No. 26/15, Larissa, Ankara, Turkey. TEL 90-312-4318480, FAX 90-312-4310946, yaziisleri@glokomkatarakt.com.

617.7 DEU ISSN 0721-832X
RE1 CODEN: GACODL
➤ **GRAEFE'S ARCHIVE FOR CLINICAL AND EXPERIMENTAL OPHTHALMOLOGY.** Text in English. 1854. m. EUR 2,594, USD 3,169 combined subscription to institutions (print & online eds.) (effective 2012). adv. bibl.; charts; illus. index, cum.index: vols.1-138. back issues avail.; reprint service avail. from PSC. **Document type:** *Journal, Academic/Scholarly.* **Description:** Articles by leading ophthalmologists and vision research scientists provide rapid dissemination of clinical and clinically-related experimental information.
Former titles (until 1982): Albrecht von Graefes Archiv fuer Klinische und Experimentelle Ophthalmologie (0065-6100); (until 1965): Albrecht von Graefes Archiv fuer Ophthalmologie (0376-0200); (until 1871): Archiv fuer Ophtalmologie (0721-8494)
Related titles: Microform ed.: (from PQC); Online - full text ed.: ISSN 1435-702X (from IngentaConnect).
Indexed: A01, A03, A08, A22, A26, A34, A35, A36, ASCA, AgBio, B21, B25, BIOSIS Prev, CA, CABA, CIN, ChemAb, ChemTitl, CurCont, E01, EMBASE, ExcerpMed, F08, GH, H17, ISR, IndMed, IndVet, Inpharma, MEDLINE, MycolAb, N02, N03, NSA, P20, P22, P30, P33, P35, P39, P48, P54, PN&I, PQC, R08, R10, R12, RA&MP, RM&VM, Reac, S12, SCI, SCOPUS, T02, T05, VS, W07, W10.
—BLDSC (4207.850000), CASDDS, GNLM, IE, Infotrieve, Ingenta, INIST. **CCC.**
Published by: Springer (Subsidiary of: Springer Science+Business Media), Tiergartenstr 17, Heidelberg, 69121, Germany. TEL 49-6221-4870, FAX 49-6221-345229. Ed. Bernd Kirchhof. adv.: B&W page EUR 880, color page EUR 1,920. Circ: 1,100 (paid and controlled). **Subscr. in the Americas to:** Springer New York LLC, Journal Fulfillment, PO Box 2485, Secaucus, NJ 07096. TEL 800-777-4643, 201-348-4033, FAX 201-348-4505, journals-ny@springer.com, http://www.springer.com; **Subscr. to:** Springer Distribution Center, Kundenservice Zeitschriften, Haberstr 7, Heidelberg 69126, Germany. TEL 49-6221-3454303, FAX 49-6221-3454229, subscriptions@springer.com.

617.7 CHN ISSN 1672-5123
GUOJI YANKE ZAZHI/INTERNATIONAL JOURNAL OF OPHTHALMOLOGY. Text in English. 2000. bi-m. USD 106.80 (effective 2009). **Document type:** *Journal, Academic/Scholarly.*
Related titles: Online - full text ed.
Indexed: EMBASE, ExcerpMed, R10, Reac, SCI, SCOPUS, W07.
—BLDSC (4232.074720).
Published by: Zhonghua Yixuehui, Xian Fenhui, 269, Youyi Donglu, Xian, 710054, China. TEL 86-29-83085628, FAX 86-29-82245172. **Dist. by:** China International Book Trading Corp, 35 Chegongzhuang Xilu, Haidian District, PO Box 399, Beijing 100044, China. TEL 86-10-68412045, FAX 86-10-68412023, cibtc@mail.cibtc.com.cn, http://www.cibtc.com.cn.

617.7 CHN ISSN 1001-1196
GUOWAI YIXUE (YANKEXUE FENCE)/FOREIGN MEDICAL SCIENCES (OPHTHALMOLOGY). Text in Chinese. 1964. bi-m. CNY 60 domestic; CNY 25.20 foreign (effective 2005). **Document type:** *Journal, Academic/Scholarly.*
Related titles: Online - full text ed.
—East View.
Published by: Beijing Shi Yanke Yanjiusuo, 17, Chongnei Dajie Hougouhutong, Beijing, 100005, China. TEL 86-10-58265902. **Dist. by:** China International Book Trading Corp, 35 Chegongzhuang Xilu, Haidian District, PO Box 399, Beijing 100044, China. TEL 86-10-68412045, FAX 86-10-68412023, cibtc@mail.cibtc.com.cn, http://www.cibtc.com.cn.

HERPES. *see* MEDICAL SCIENCES—Communicable Diseases

617.7 JPN ISSN 0286-7486
HIKAKU GANKA KENKYU/ANIMAL'S EYE RESEARCH. Text in Japanese. 1982. s-a. membership.
Published by: Hikaku Ganka Gakkai/Japanese Society of Comparative Ophthalmology, Kokuritsu Yobo Eisei Kenkyujo, Tsukuba Igaku Jikken'yo Reichorui Senta, 1 Yahatadai, Tsukuba-shi, Ibaraki-ken 305-0000, Japan.

617.75 USA ISSN 1948-4984
HINDSIGHT; journal of optometry history. Text in English. 1970. q. free to members (effective 2009). **Document type:** *Journal, Academic/Scholarly.* **Description:** Features significant articles that cover the history of optometry.
Formerly (until 1992): Optometric Historical Society. Newsletter
Published by: Optometric Historical Society, 243 N Lindbergh Blvd, St. Louis, MO 63141.

617.7 HKG ISSN 1021-8947
HONG KONG OPTICAL. Text in English. 1992. a. adv. back issues avail. **Document type:** *Magazine, Trade.* **Description:** Covers optometric instruments, glasses, lenses, spectacles, mountings and accessories.
Related titles: Online - full content ed.
Published by: Hong Kong Trade Development Council, 38th Fl Office Tower, Convention Plaza, 1 Harbour Rd, Wanchai, Hong Kong. TEL 852-1830668, FAX 852-28240249, publications@tdc.org.hk, http://www.tdc.org.hk. adv.: color page HKD 1,300; 213 x 280. Circ: 15,000.

617.7 MEX ISSN 0018-5760
HOSPITAL OFTALMOLOGICO DE NUESTRA SENORA DE LA LUZ. BOLETIN. Text in Spanish. 1940. q. free. adv. charts; illus. index. **Document type:** *Bulletin, Trade.*
Indexed: C01, IndMed, P30.
Published by: Hospital Oftalmologico de Nuestra Senora de la Luz, Ezequiel Montes 135, Col Revolucion, Mexico City, DF 06030, Mexico. http://www.hospitaldelaluz.org. Ed. Dr. Arturo Lelo de Larrca.

617.75 USA
I O A NEWS. Text in English. m. free to members. adv. **Document type:** *Newsletter, Trade.*
Former titles (until 1993): Observer; Iowa Journal of Optometry
Published by: Iowa Optometric Association, 1454 30th St Ste 204, West Des Moines, IA 50266-1312. TEL 515-222-5679, FAX 515-222-9073, IAOptAssn@aol.com, http://www.iowaoptometry.org/. Circ: 600.

617.7 JPN ISSN 1341-3678
I O L & R S. (Intra-Ocular Lens & Refractive Surgery) Variant title: Japanese Journal of Cataract and Refractive Surgery. Nihon Gannai Renzu Kussetsu Shujutsu Gakkaishi. Text in Japanese; Summaries in English, Japanese. 1987. q. JPY 15,000 membership (effective 2006). **Document type:** *Journal, Academic/Scholarly.*

Formerly (until 1994): Nihon Gannai Renzu Gakkaishi/I O L: Intraocular Lens (0913-7270)
Published by: Nihon Gannai Renzu Gakkai/Japanese Intraocular Lens Implant Society, #501, Asai Bldg., 7-2-4, Hongo, Bunkyo-ku, Tokyo, 113-0033, Japan. TEL 81-3-38110309, FAX 81-3-38110676, info@jscrs.jp.

▼ **I-PERCEPTION.** *see* PSYCHOLOGY

617.7 USA ISSN 2090-5688
▼ ➤ **I S R N OPHTHALMOLOGY.** (International Scholarly Research Network) Text in English. 2011. **Document type:** *Journal, Academic/Scholarly.* **Description:** Publishes original research articles, review articles, and clinical studies in all areas of ophthalmology.
Related titles: Online - full text ed.: ISSN 2090-5696. 2011. free (effective 2011).
Published by: Hindawi Publishing Corporation, 410 Park Ave, 15th Fl, PMB 287, New York, NY 10022. FAX 215-893-4392, 866-446-3294, info@hindawi.com.

617.7 USA ISSN 0279-6422
RE1
ILLINOIS OPTOMETRIC ASSOCIATION. JOURNAL. Text in English. 1942. q. adv. charts. **Document type:** *Journal, Trade.*
Published by: Illinois Optometric Association, 304 W Washington, Springfield, IL 62701. TEL 217-525-8012, FAX 217-525-8018, ioa@ioaweb.org. Ed. Gary Gray. adv.: page USD 400; trim 7.5 x 10. Circ: 1,000.

617.7 FRA ISSN 1961-3172
IMAGES EN OPHTALMOLOGIE. Text in French. 2007. q. EUR 72 in Europe to individuals; EUR 72 DOM-TOM to individuals; EUR 72 in Africa to individuals; EUR 82 elsewhere to individuals; EUR 90 in Europe to institutions; EUR 90 DOM-TOM to institutions; EUR 90 in Africa to institutions; EUR 100 elsewhere to institutions; EUR 45 in Europe to students; EUR 45 DOM-TOM to students; EUR 45 in Africa to students; EUR 55 elsewhere to students (effective 2008). **Document type:** *Journal, Trade.*
—INIST.
Published by: Edimark S.A.S., 2 Rue Sainte-Marie, Courbevoie, Cedex 92418, France. TEL 33-1-46676300, FAX 33-1-46676310, contact@edimark.fr.

617.7 IND ISSN 0301-4738
RE1 CODEN: IJOMBM
➤ **INDIAN JOURNAL OF OPHTHALMOLOGY.** Abbreviated title: I J O. Text in English. 1953. bi-m. INR 2,000 domestic to individuals; USD 180 foreign to individuals; INR 3,000 domestic to institutions; USD 300 foreign to institutions; INR 2,400 combined subscription domestic to individuals (print & online eds.); USD 215 combined subscription foreign to individuals (print & online eds.); INR 3,600 combined subscription domestic to institutions (print & online eds.); USD 360 combined subscription foreign to institutions (print & online eds.) (effective 2011). adv. bk.rev. illus. cum.index: vols. 1-5 (1953-58); vols. 11-15 (1963-67). 130 p./no.; reprints avail. **Document type:** *Journal, Academic/Scholarly.* **Description:** Covers information on ophthalmology and vision science.
Formerly (until 1971): All India Ophthalmological Society. Journal (0044-7307)
Related titles: CD-ROM ed.; Online - full text ed.: ISSN 1998-3689. INR 1,600 domestic to individuals; USD 145 foreign to individuals; INR 2,400 domestic to institutions; USD 240 foreign to institutions (effective 2011).
Indexed: A01, A02, A03, A08, A22, A26, A36, B25, BIOSIS Prev, C06, C07, CA, CABA, DentInd, E08, E12, EMBASE, ExcerpMed, ExtraMED, G08, G11, GH, H11, H12, H17, I05, IndMed, MEDLINE, MycolAb, N02, N03, P10, P20, P22, P30, P33, P39, P48, P53, P54, PN&I, PQC, R08, R10, R12, R13, RA&MP, RM&VM, Reac, S09, SCI, SCOPUS, T02, T05, VS, W07, W10.
—BLDSC (4417.600000), GNLM, IE, Infotrieve, Ingenta, INIST. **CCC.**
Published by: (All India Ophthalmological Society), Medknow Publications and Media Pvt. Ltd., B-9, Kanara Business Ctr, Off Link Rd, Ghatkopar (E), Mumbai, Maharastra 400 075, India. TEL 91-22-66491816, FAX 91-22-66491817, http://www.medknow.com.

617.7 362 USA
INFOCUS (OWINGS MILLS). Text in English. 1973. 3/yr. free (effective 2009). bk.rev. **Document type:** *Newsletter, Consumer.* **Description:** Contains articles on retinitis pigmentosa, macular degeneration, Usher syndrome and other retinal degenerations. Includes personal profiles on people affected by these diseases.
Formerly (until 2004): Fighting Blindness News (0899-7756)
Related titles: Online - full text ed.; Large type ed. 14 pt.: free (effective 2009).
Published by: Foundation Fighting Blindness, 11435 Cronhill Dr, Owings Mills, MD 21117. TEL 410-568-0150, 888-394-3937, FAX 410-363-2393, info@blindness.org, http://www.blindness.org. Ed. Allie Laban-Baker. Circ: 70,000.

617.7 610.73 USA ISSN 1060-135X
RE88
➤ **INSIGHT (SAINT LOUIS).** Text in English. 1991. q. USD 53 domestic to individuals; USD 65 foreign to individuals; USD 93 domestic to institutions; USD 105 foreign to institutions (effective 2011). bk.rev. reprints avail. **Document type:** *Journal, Academic/Scholarly.* **Description:** Provides information about current professional nursing issues, legislative concerns, administrative announcements, as well as offering a forum for commentaries and viewpoint articles.
Related titles: Online - full text ed.
Indexed: A22, A26, C06, C07, C08, CINAHL, E01, EMBASE, ExcerpMed, H12, I05, INI, MEDLINE, P30, R10, Reac, SCOPUS.
—BLDSC (4518.174100), GNLM, IE, Infotrieve, Ingenta. **CCC.**
Published by: American Society of Ophthalmic Registered Nurses, Inc., PO Box 193030, San Francisco, CA 94119. TEL 415-561-8513, asorn@aao.org, http://webeye.ophth.uiowa.edu/ASORN/. Ed. Sarah Smith TEL 319-356-7218.

617.7 USA
INSIGHT (WASHINGTON, 1990). Text in English. 1961. bi-m. (plus annual newsletter). free. stat. back issues avail. **Document type:** *Newsletter.* **Description:** Covers latest issues in eye banking and corneal transplantation.
Formerly (until 1989): Foresight (Washington, 1961)
Published by: Eye Bank Association of America, 1015 18th St N W, Ste 1010, Washington, DC 20036. TEL 202-775-4999, FAX 202-429-6036, info@restoresight.org. Ed. Rick Rose. Circ: 1,000.

617.7 ESP ISSN 0020-3645
➤ **INSTITUTO BARRAQUER. ANALES.** Text in Multiple languages. 1959. q. adv. charts; illus. back issues avail. **Document type:** *Academic/Scholarly.*
Indexed: OphLit, P30.
—GNLM. **CCC.**
Published by: Instituto Barraquer, Laforja, 88, Barcelona, 08021, Spain. TEL 34-93-4146798, FAX 34-93-2099977. Eds. Rafael I Barraquer, Joaquin Barraquer. R&P Eva Luther. Circ: 2,000.

➤ **THE INTERNATIONAL DIRECTORY OF OPTICAL GOODS AND INSTRUMENTS IMPORTERS.** *see* BUSINESS AND ECONOMICS—Trade And Industrial Directories

617.7 NLD ISSN 0165-5701
RE1 CODEN: INOPDR
➤ **INTERNATIONAL OPHTHALMOLOGY.** Text in English. 1978. bi-m. EUR 1,073, USD 1,084 combined subscription to institutions (print & online eds.) (effective 2012). adv. bk.rev. illus. reprint service avail. from PSC. **Document type:** *Journal, Academic/Scholarly.* **Description:** Provides the clinician with articles on all the relevant subspecialties of ophthalmology, with a broad international scope. In addition to original research papers, the journal presents review articles, editorial comments, an international calendar of events and book reviews.
Related titles: Microform ed.: (from PQC); Online - full text ed.: ISSN 1573-2630 (from IngentaConnect).
Indexed: A22, A26, A29, ASCA, B20, B21, B25, BIOSIS Prev, BibLing, ChemAb, E01, EMBASE, ESPM, ExcerpMed, H&SSA, I10, IBR, IBZ, ISR, IndMed, Inpharma, MEDLINE, MycolAb, NSA, P20, P22, P30, P48, P54, PQC, R10, Reac, SCOPUS, ViroIAbstr.
—BLDSC (4544.804000), CASDDS, GNLM, IE, Infotrieve, Ingenta, INIST. **CCC.**
Published by: Springer Netherlands (Subsidiary of: Springer Science+Business Media), Van Godewijckstraat 30, Dordrecht, 3311 GX, Netherlands. TEL 31-78-6576050, FAX 31-78-6576474, http://www.springer.com. Eds. Carl P Herbort, Philippe Kestelyn.

617.7 USA ISSN 0020-8167
CODEN: IOPCAV
➤ **INTERNATIONAL OPHTHALMOLOGY CLINICS.** Text in English. 1961. q. USD 615 domestic to institutions; USD 836 foreign to institutions (effective 2011). adv. charts; illus.; stat. Index. back issues avail.; reprints avail. **Document type:** *Journal, Academic/Scholarly.* **Description:** Presents a review of a single topic in a new or changing area of ophthalmology. Provides ophthalmologists the opportunity to benefit from the knowledge of leading experts in this rapidly changing field.
Related titles: Microform ed.: (from PQC); Online - full text ed.: ISSN 1536-9617.
Indexed: A01, A03, A08, A22, ASCA, CA, DentInd, EMBASE, ExcerpMed, IndMed, Inpharma, MEDLINE, MycolAb, P30, R10, Reac, SCOPUS, T02.
—BLDSC (4544.805000), GNLM, IE, Infotrieve, Ingenta, INIST. **CCC.**
Published by: Lippincott Williams & Wilkins (Subsidiary of: Wolters Kluwer N.V.), 530 Walnut St, Philadelphia, PA 19106. TEL 215-521-8300, FAX 215-521-8902, customerservice@lww.com, http://www.lww.com. Ed. Mitchell H Friedlaender. Pub. Nina J Chang.

617.7 USA ISSN 1528-8269
RE1
➤ **THE INTERNET JOURNAL OF OPHTHALMOLOGY AND VISUAL SCIENCE.** Text in English. 2000. s-a. free (effective 2011). adv. bk.rev. back issues avail. **Document type:** *Journal, Academic/Scholarly.* **Description:** Contains information from the field of ophthalmology, including original articles, reviews, case reports, streaming slide shows, streaming videos, letters to the editor, press releases, and meeting information.
Media: Online - full text.
Indexed: A01, A02, A03, A08, A26, C06, C07, CA, G08, H11, H12, I05, T02.
Published by: Internet Scientific Publications, Llc., 23 Rippling Creek Dr, Sugar Land, TX 77479. TEL 832-443-1193, FAX 281-240-1533, wenker@ispub.com. Ed. Richard F. Bensinger.

617.7 USA ISSN 0146-0404
RE1 CODEN: IOVSDA
➤ **INVESTIGATIVE OPHTHALMOLOGY & VISUAL SCIENCE.** Variant title: I O V S. Text in English. 1962. m. USD 550 combined subscription domestic to individuals (print & online eds.); USD 775 combined subscription foreign to individuals (print & online eds.); USD 805 combined subscription domestic to institutions (print & online eds.); USD 985 combined subscription foreign to institutions (print & online eds.); USD 365 combined subscription domestic to students (print & online eds.); USD 585 combined subscription foreign to students (print & online eds.); free to members (effective 2009). adv. illus. index. **Document type:** *Journal, Academic/Scholarly.* **Description:** Contains original scientific articles concerning diagnosis, treatment and management of diseases of the ocular complex.
Formerly (until 1977): Investigative Ophthalmology (0020-9988)
Related titles: Microform ed.: (from PQC); Online - full text ed.: ISSN 1552-5783. USD 515 domestic to individuals; USD 725 foreign to individuals; USD 750 domestic to institutions; USD 895 foreign to institutions; USD 340 domestic to students; USD 535 foreign to students (effective 2009).
Indexed: A20, A22, A34, A35, A36, A37, A38, ASCA, AgBio, AgrForAb, B25, BA, BIOBASE, BIOSIS Prev, BP, CABA, ChemAb, CurCont, D01, DentInd, E12, EMBASE, ExcerpMed, F08, FR, GH, H16, H17, IABS, IBR, IBZ, IDIS, ISR, IndMed, IndVet, Inpharma, LT, MEDLINE, MaizeAb, MycolAb, N02, N03, P30, P32, P33, P35, P37, P39, PN&I, R08, R10, R12, R13, RA&MP, RM&VM, RRTA, Reac, S12, SAA, SCI, SCOPUS, SoyAb, T05, TriticAb, VS, W07.
—BLDSC (4560.220000), CASDDS, GNLM, IE, Infotrieve, Ingenta, INIST. **CCC.**
Published by: Association for Research in Vision and Ophthalmology, 12300 Twinbrook Pkwy, Ste 250, Rockville, MD 20852. TEL 240-221-2920, FAX 240-221-0355, arvo@arvo.org, http://www.arvo.org/. Ed. Paul L Kaufman. Adv. contact Mike Ryan TEL 781-455-9838. B&W page USD 1,265, color page USD 1,800; bleed 8.625 x 11.125. Circ: 6,800.

617.752 IRL ISSN 0791-3109
IRISH OPTICIAN. Text in English. 1990. bi-m. adv. **Document type:** *Magazine, Trade.* **Description:** Contains articles and information for optical professionals in Ireland.
Published by: Mac Communications, Taney Hall, Eglinton Terrace, Dundrum, Dublin, Dublin 14, Ireland. TEL 353-1-2960000, FAX 353-1-2960383, info@maccommunications.ie. Ed. Niall Hunter. adv.: B&W page EUR 686, color page EUR 1,270; trim 210 x 297. Circ: 1,200 (paid and controlled).

617.7 JPN ISSN 0021-5155
RE1 CODEN: JJOPA7
➤ **JAPANESE JOURNAL OF OPHTHALMOLOGY.** Text in English. 1957. bi-m. EUR 342, USD 420 combined subscription to institutions (print & online eds.) (effective 2012). adv. bk.rev. charts; illus. back issues avail.; reprint service avail. from PSC. **Document type:** *Journal, Academic/Scholarly.* **Description:** Carries papers on new developments in ophthalmology reported by authors of all nationalities.
Related titles: Microform ed.: (from PQC); Online - full text ed.: ISSN 1613-2246 (from IngentaConnect).
Indexed: A01, A03, A08, A22, A26, A29, A36, ASCA, B20, B21, CA, CABA, CIN, ChemAb, ChemTitl, CurCont, DentInd, E01, E12, EMBASE, ESPM, ExcerpMed, GH, H17, I10, INIS AtomInd, ISR, IndMed, Inpharma, MEDLINE, N02, N03, P20, P22, P30, P33, P35, P39, P48, P54, PQC, R08, R10, R12, RM&VM, Reac, RefZh, SCI, SCOPUS, T02, T05, VS, ViroIAbstr, W07.
—BLDSC (4656.770000), CASDDS, GNLM, IE, Infotrieve, Ingenta, INIST, Linda Hall. **CCC.**
Published by: (Japanese Ophthalmological Society), Springer Japan KK (Subsidiary of: Springer Science+Business Media), No 2 Funato Bldg, 1-11-11 Kudan-kita, Chiyoda-ku, Tokyo, 102-0073, Japan. TEL 81-3-68317000, FAX 81-3-68317001, orders@springer.jp, http://www.springer.jp. Ed. Yozo Miyake. Circ: 1,000.

617.7 JPN
CODEN: NGKYA3
➤ **JAPANESE SOCIETY FOR LOW-VISION RESEARCH AND REHABILITATION. JOURNAL.** Text in Japanese; Summaries in English. 1950. m. membership. adv. bk.rev. **Document type:** *Proceedings, Academic/Scholarly.*
Formerly (until 2001): Nippon Ganka Kiyo/Folia Ophthalmologica Japonica (0015-5667)
Related titles: Microform ed.; ◆ Supplement(s): Nihon Contact Lens Gakkaishi. ISSN 0374-9851.
Indexed: A22, INIS AtomInd, IndMed, P30, R10, Reac, SCOPUS.
—BLDSC (3971.824000), CASDDS, GNLM, IE, Infotrieve, Ingenta, INIST.
Published by: Japanese Society for Low-Vision Research and Rehabilitation, Kawasaki University of Medical Welfare, 288 Matsushima, Kurashiki, Okayama 701-0193, Japan. jsllr@mw.kawasaki-m.ac.jp, http://www.jsllr.org/. Ed. Yasuo Tano. Pub., Adv. contact Keiko Miyake. Circ: 2,700 (paid).

617.7 USA
JOINT COMMISSION ON ALLIED HEALTH PERSONNEL IN OPHTHALMOLOGY. PRESIDENT'S REPORT. Text in English. 1983. a. **Document type:** *Report, Trade.* **Description:** Activities of the Commission.
Formerly: Joint Commission on Allied Health Personnel in Ophthalmology. Annual Report
Published by: Joint Commission on Allied Health Personnel in Ophthalmology, 2025 Woodlane Dr, St. Paul, MN MN 55125-2998. TEL 651-731-2944, 800-284-3937, FAX 651-731-0410, jcahpo@jcahpo.org, http://www.jcahpo.org/newsite/index.htm.

617.7 367.41 GBR ISSN 2041-188X
▼ ➤ **JORNAL DE SAUDE OCULAR COMUNITARIA.** Text in Portuguese. 2009. s-a. GBP 50; free in developing nations (effective 2011). **Document type:** *Journal, Academic/Scholarly.*
Related titles: Online - full text ed.: ISSN 2041-1898; ◆ Chinese ed.: Shequ Yan Jiankang; ◆ Spanish ed.: Salud Ocular Comunitaria Revista. ISSN 1993-7229; ◆ English ed.: Community Eye Health. ISSN 0953-6833; ◆ French ed.: Revue de Sante Oculaire Communautaire. ISSN 1993-7210.
Published by: International Centre for Eye Health, London School of Hygiene and Tropical Medicine, Keppel St, London, WC1E 7HT, United Kingdom. TEL 44-20-76127964, 44-20-76127972, FAX 44-20-79588317, admin@cehjournal.org, http://www.iceh.org.uk/.

617.7 FRA ISSN 0181-5512
RE1
➤ **JOURNAL FRANCAIS D'OPHTALMOLOGIE.** Text in French. 1881. 10/yr. EUR 528 in Europe to institutions; EUR 380.02 in France to institutions; JPY 85,100 in Japan to institutions; USD 686 elsewhere to institutions (effective 2012). adv. bk.rev. abstr.; bibl.; illus. index. reprints avail. **Document type:** *Journal, Academic/Scholarly.* **Description:** Publishes original works, clinical or scientific facts, therapeutic notes, analyses of works, and reports on congresses.
Formed by the merger of (1838-1977): Annales d'Oculistique (0003-4371); (1976-1977): Archives d'Ophtalmologie (0399-4236); Which was formerly (until 1975): Archives d'Ophtalmologie. Revue Generale d'Ophtalmologie (0003-973X)
Related titles: Microform ed.: (from PQC); Online - full text ed.: ISSN 1773-0597 (from ScienceDirect).
Indexed: A20, A22, A34, A36, ASCA, CABA, ChemAb, CurCont, D01, DentInd, E12, EMBASE, ExcerpMed, GH, H17, IBR, IBZ, INI, IndMed, IndVet, Inpharma, MEDLINE, MaizeAb, N02, N03, N04, P30, P33, P35, P39, R08, R10, R13, RM&VM, Reac, SCI, SCOPUS, T05, VS, W07.
—BLDSC (4986.410000), GNLM, IE, Infotrieve, Ingenta, INIST. **CCC.**
Published by: Elsevier Masson (Subsidiary of: Elsevier Health Sciences), 62 Rue Camille Desmoulins, Issy les Moulineaux, Cedex 92442, France. TEL 33-1-71165500, infos@elsevier-masson.fr. Ed. Christophe Baudouin. Circ: 3,000.

617.7 FRA ISSN 0240-7914
JOURNAL FRANCAIS D'ORTHOPTIQUE. Text in French. 1969. a. **Document type:** *Journal, Trade.*
Related titles: Online - full text ed.
Indexed: FR.
—INIST.
Published by: Association Francaise d'Orthoptique, 20-22 Rue Edith Cavell, Le Creusot, 71200, France. FAX 31-3-88238390, http://www.association-orthoptique.fr.

617.7 USA ISSN 1045-8395
RE960
➤ **JOURNAL OF BEHAVIORAL OPTOMETRY.** Text in English. 1990. bi-m. index. back issues avail. **Document type:** *Journal, Academic/Scholarly.* **Description:** Publishes original scholarly and clinical articles in the field of behavioral optometry, with news of issues, meetings and products of interest to the profession.
Related titles: Online - full text ed.
Indexed: A01, CA, P03, P25, P48, PQC, PsycInfo, PsycholAb, T02.
—BLDSC (4951.265000), IE.
Published by: Optometric Extension Program Foundation, 1921 E Carnegie Ave, Ste 3-L, Santa Ana, CA 92705. TEL 949-250-8070, FAX 949-250-8157, GregoryKitchener@oep.org. Ed. W C Maples.

617.7 USA ISSN 0886-3350
RE451 CODEN: JCSUEV
➤ **JOURNAL OF CATARACT & REFRACTIVE SURGERY.** Abbreviated title: J C R S. Text in English. 1974. m. USD 481 in US & Canada to institutions; USD 695 elsewhere to institutions (effective 2012). adv. back issues avail.; reprints avail. **Document type:** *Journal, Academic/Scholarly.* **Description:** Brings out articles on all aspects of anterior segment surgery. Features a consultation section, practical techniques, important cases, and reviews as well as basic science articles.
Former titles (until 1986): American Intra-Ocular Implant Society Journal (0146-2776); (until 1976): American Intra-Ocular Implant Society. Newsletter (0361-235X); Incorporates (1986-1995): European Journal of Implant and Refractive Surgery (0983-5636); Which was formerly (until 1986): Implants et Micro-Chirurgie Oculaire (0765-6211)
Related titles: Online - full text ed.: ISSN 1873-4502 (from IngentaConnect, ScienceDirect).
Indexed: A01, A03, A08, A22, A26, ASCA, CA, CIN, ChemAb, ChemTitl, CurCont, EMBASE, ExcerpMed, I05, ISR, IndMed, Inpharma, MEDLINE, P30, P35, R10, Reac, SCI, SCOPUS, T02, W07.
—BLDSC (4954.900000), CASDDS, GNLM, IE, Infotrieve, Ingenta, INIST. **CCC.**
Published by: (American Society of Cataract and Refractive Surgery), Elsevier Inc. (Subsidiary of: Elsevier Science & Technology), 1600 John F Kennedy Blvd, Philadelphia, PA 19103. TEL 215-239-3900, FAX 215-238-7883, JournalCustomerService-usa@elsevier.com, http://www.elsevier.com. Eds. E S Rosen, Dr. N Mamalis. Adv. contact Pat Hampton TEL 212-633-3181. Circ: 13,635. **Co-sponsor:** European Society of Cataract and Refractive Surgeons.

617.7 USA ISSN 2155-9570
▼ ➤ **JOURNAL OF CLINICAL & EXPERIMENTAL OPHTHALMOLOGY.** Text in English. 2010. bi-m. free (effective 2011). **Document type:** *Journal, Academic/Scholarly.*
Media: Online - full text.
Published by: Omics Publishing Group, 5716 Corse Ave, Ste 110, Westlake, Los Angeles, CA 91362. TEL 650-268-9744, 800-216-6499, info@omicsonline.com, http://omicsonline.org.

617.7 IND ISSN 0974-0333
➤ **JOURNAL OF CURRENT GLAUCOMA PRACTICE.** Text in English. 2007. 3/yr. INR 3,000 domestic to individuals; USD 180 foreign to individuals; INR 4,500 domestic to institutions; USD 250 foreign to institutions (effective 2010). adv. bk.rev. illus. back issues avail.; reprints avail. **Document type:** *Journal, Academic/Scholarly.* **Description:** Contains articles on new technology for glaucoma diagnosis,effect of systematic diseases on glaucoma,management of primary angle closure glaucoma and the importance of follow up in glaucoma.
Related titles: Online - full text ed.
Indexed: A01, CA, P20, P48, P54, PQC, T02.
Published by: Jaypee Brothers Medical Publishers Pvt. Ltd., 4838/24, Ansari Rd, Daryaganj, New Delhi, 110 002, India. TEL 91-11-43574357, FAX 91-11-43574314, jaypee@jaypeebrothers.com, http://www.jaypeebrothers.com. Ed. Tanuj Dada. Pub. Jitendar Pal Vij. R&P Chetna Malhotra. Adv. contact Rakesh Sheoran TEL 91-997-1020680. page INR 20,000, page USD 400; trim 7 x 10.

617.7 ESP ISSN 2171-4703
JOURNAL OF EMMETROPIA. Text in Spanish. 1989. q. back issues avail. **Document type:** *Journal, Academic/Scholarly.*
Former titles (until 2008): Microcirugia Ocular (1134-654X); (until 1992): C E C O I R (1134-6558)
Related titles: Online - full text ed.
Published by: Sociedad Espanola de Cirugia Ocular Implanto-Refractiva, Donoso Cortes, 73 1o. Izq., Madrid, 28015, Spain. TEL 34-91-5448036, FAX 34-91-5441847, avpm@oftalmo.com. Ed. Carlos Palomino Bautista.

617.7 PRT ISSN 1647-7677
▼ **JOURNAL OF EYE TRACKING, VISUAL COGNITION AND EMOTION.** Abbreviated title: J E T V C E. Text in English. 2010. a. **Document type:** *Journal, Academic/Scholarly.*
Published by: Universidade Lusofona de Humanidades e Tecnologia, Edicoes Universitarias, Campo Grande 376, Lisbon, 1749-024, Portugal. TEL 351-217-515500, FAX 351-217-577006, http://ulusofona.pt.

617.741 USA ISSN 1057-0829
RE871 CODEN: JOGLES
➤ **JOURNAL OF GLAUCOMA.** Text in English. 1992. 9/yr. USD 739 domestic to institutions; USD 870 foreign to institutions (effective 2011). adv. bk.rev. illus. back issues avail.; reprints avail. **Document type:** *Journal, Academic/Scholarly.* **Description:** Provides a forum for discussion of clinical, scientific, and socioeconomic issues of greatest concern to clinicians who care for glaucoma patients.
Related titles: Online - full text ed.: ISSN 1536-481X.
Indexed: A22, CurCont, EMBASE, ExcerpMed, ISR, IndMed, Inpharma, MEDLINE, P30, P35, R10, RILM, Reac, SCI, SCOPUS, W07.
—BLDSC (4996.230000), GNLM, IE, Infotrieve, Ingenta. **CCC.**
Published by: Lippincott Williams & Wilkins (Subsidiary of: Wolters Kluwer N.V.), 530 Walnut St, Philadelphia, PA 19106. TEL 215-521-8300, FAX 215-521-8902, customerservice@lww.com, http://www.lww.com. Ed. G A Cioffi TEL 503-413-8373. Pub. Nina J Chang. Adv. contact Dan Marsh. Circ: 1,420.

617.7 SGP ISSN 1793-5458
R857.O6
JOURNAL OF INNOVATIVE OPTICAL HEALTH SCIENCES. Abbreviated title: J I O H S. Text in English. 2008. q. SGD 719, USD 461, EUR 364 combined subscription to institutions (print & online eds.) (effective 2012). adv. back issues avail. **Document type:** *Journal, Academic/Scholarly.* **Description:** Contains papers in all disciplines of photonics in biology and medicine including but not limited to: photonic therapeutics and diagnostics, optical clinical technologies and systems, tissue optics, laser-tissue interaction and tissue engineering, biomedical spectroscopy, advanced microscopy and imaging, nanobiophotonics and optical molecular imaging, multimodal and hybrid biomedical imaging, micro/nanofabrication and medical microsystem.
Related titles: Online - full text ed.: ISSN 1793-7205. SGD 654, USD 419, EUR 331 to institutions (effective 2012).
Indexed: A22, E01, P30.
—IE.
Published by: World Scientific Publishing Co. Pte. Ltd., 5 Toh Tuck Link, Singapore, 596224, Singapore. TEL 65-6466-5775, FAX 65-6467-7667, wspc@wspc.com.sg, http://www.worldscientific.com. **Dist. by:** World Scientific Publishing Ltd., 57 Shelton St, London WC2H 9HE, United Kingdom. TEL 44-207-8360888, FAX 44-207-8362020, sales@wspc.co.uk; World Scientific Publishing Co., Inc., 27 Warren St, Ste 401-402, Hackensack, NJ 07601. TEL 201-487-9655, 800-227-7562, FAX 201-487-9656, 888-977-2665, wspc@wspc.com.

617.7 USA ISSN 1070-8022
RE725 CODEN: JNEOEK
➤ **JOURNAL OF NEURO-OPHTHALMOLOGY.** Text in English. 1981. q. USD 817 domestic to institutions; USD 897 foreign to institutions (effective 2011). adv. bk.rev. charts; illus.; stat. Index. back issues avail.; reprints avail. **Document type:** *Journal, Academic/Scholarly.* **Description:** Brings out articles on both clinical and basic aspects of neuro-ophthalmology. Features include reviews, viewpoints, photoessays, editorials, letters, and special features including interviews, historical vignettes, and NANOS news.
Formerly (until 1994): Journal of Clinical Neuro-Ophthalmology (0272-846X)
Related titles: Online - full text ed.: ISSN 1536-5166.
Indexed: A22, ASCA, B21, CurCont, DentInd, E-psyche, EMBASE, ExcerpMed, IBR, IBZ, IndMed, Inpharma, JW-N, MEDLINE, NSA, NSCI, P30, P35, R10, Reac, SCI, SCOPUS, W07.
—BLDSC (5021.660000), GNLM, IE, Infotrieve, Ingenta, INIST. **CCC.**
Published by: (North American Neuro-Ophthalmology Society), Lippincott Williams & Wilkins (Subsidiary of: Wolters Kluwer N.V.), Two Commerce Sq, 2001 Market St, Philadelphia, PA 19103. TEL 215-521-8300, FAX 215-521-8902, customerservice@lww.com, http://www.lww.com. Ed. Lanning B Kline TEL 205-325-8660. Pub. Nina J Chang. Adv. contact Michelle Smith TEL 646-674-6537.

617.7 USA ISSN 1936-8437
➤ **JOURNAL OF OCULAR BIOLOGY, DISEASES, AND INFORMATICS.** Text in English. 2008 (Mar.). q. USD 309 to institutions (effective 2011). reprint service avail. from PSC. **Document type:** *Journal, Academic/Scholarly.* **Description:** Covers all aspects of research on ocular biology, including basic biology, clinical trials and new advances in etiology, genetics and progression of a range of eye diseases.
Related titles: Online - full text ed.: ISSN 1936-8445. 2008 (Mar.). EUR 218, USD 295 to institutions (effective 2010).
Indexed: P30, SCOPUS.
—IE. **CCC.**
Published by: Springer New York LLC (Subsidiary of: Springer Science+Business Media), 233 Spring St, New York, NY 10013. TEL 212-460-1500, FAX 212-460-1575, journals@springer-ny.com.

617.7 USA ISSN 1080-7683
RE994 CODEN: JOPTFU
➤ **JOURNAL OF OCULAR PHARMACOLOGY AND THERAPEUTICS.** Abbreviated title: J O P T. Text in English. 1985. bi-m. USD 1,279 domestic to institutions; USD 1,641 foreign to institutions; USD 1,495 combined subscription domestic to institutions (print & online eds.); USD 1,902 combined subscription foreign to institutions (print & online eds.) (effective 2012). adv. bk.rev. reprint service avail. from PSC. **Document type:** *Journal, Academic/Scholarly.* **Description:** Covers basic and clinical research about biopharmaceuticals that have the potential to prevent, treat, and/or diagnose, ocular diseases and disorders.
Formerly (until 1995): Journal of Ocular Pharmacology (8756-3320)
Related titles: Online - full text ed.: ISSN 1557-7732. USD 1,337 to institutions (effective 2012).
Indexed: A01, A03, A08, A22, A35, A36, ASCA, AgBio, B25, BIOBASE, BIOSIS Prev, BP, C06, C07, C33, CA, CABA, CIN, ChemAb, ChemTitl, CurCont, DBA, E01, E12, EMBASE, ExcerpMed, F08, F11, F12, GH, H16, IABS, IndMed, Inpharma, MEDLINE, MycolAb, N02, N03, OphLit, P30, P32, P33, P35, P39, P40, R08, R10, R13, RA&MP, RM&VM, Reac, SCI, SCOPUS, T02, T05, VS, W07.
—BLDSC (5026.155020), CASDDS, GNLM, IE, Infotrieve, Ingenta, INIST. **CCC.**
Published by: (Association for Ocular Pharmacology and Therapeutics), Mary Ann Liebert, Inc. Publishers, 140 Huguenot St, 3rd Fl, New Rochelle, NY 10801. TEL 914-740-2100, FAX 914-740-2101, 800-654-3237, info@liebertpub.com. Ed. Craig E Crosson. Adv. contact Harriet I Matysko TEL 914-740-2182.

617.7 IRN ISSN 2008-2010
➤ **JOURNAL OF OPHTHALMIC & VISION RESEARCH.** Text in English. 2005. q. free (effective 2009). **Document type:** *Journal, Academic/Scholarly.*
Formerly (until 2008): Iranian Journal of Ophthalmic Research (1735-4684)
Related titles: Online - full text ed.: ISSN 2008-322X. free (effective 2011).
Indexed: A36, B&BAb, B19, B21, C06, C07, CABA, GH, N02, N03, NSA, P20, P33, P54, R08, RA&MP, SCOPUS, T02, T05, VS.
Published by: Shaheed Beheshti Medical University, Ophthalmic Research Center, PO Box 14155-3651, Tehran, 16666, Iran. TEL 98-21-2258-5952, FAX 98-21-2259-0607, Editor@ijor.ir, http://www.IJOR.ir.

617.7 DEU ISSN 1869-5760
▼ ➤ **JOURNAL OF OPHTHALMIC INFLAMMATION AND INFECTION.** Text in English. 2011. **Document type:** *Journal, Academic/Scholarly.* **Description:** Presents current clinical and experimental research on ophthalmic inflammation and infection.
Media: Online - full text.
—**CCC.**
Published by: SpringerOpen (Subsidiary of: Springer Science+Business Media), Tiergartenstr 17, Heidelberg, 69121, Germany. info@springeropen.com, http://www.springeropen.com.

617.7 USA ISSN 1933-6535
➤ **JOURNAL OF OPHTHALMIC MEDICAL TECHNOLOGY.** Text in English. 2005. s-a. back issues avail. **Document type:** *Journal, Academic/Scholarly.* **Description:** Publish articles and presentations dealing with all aspects of ophthalmology with a special emphasis on providing information to ophthalmic medical personnel and to highlight student research from accredited training programs.
Media: Online - full text.
Published by: University of Arkansas for Medical Sciences, 4301 W Markham St, Little Rock, AR 72205. TEL 501-686-7000, http://www.uams.edu/. Ed. Michael N Wiggins.

617.7 USA ISSN 0198-6155
RE79.P54
➤ **THE JOURNAL OF OPHTHALMIC PHOTOGRAPHY.** Text in English. 1978. s-a. USD 20; free membership (effective 2005). **Document type:** *Journal, Trade.* **Description:** Provides a forum for ophthalmic photographers to share their work and ideas.
Indexed: P30.
Published by: Ophthalmic Photographers' Society, Inc., 1869 W Ranch Rd, Nixa, MO 65714-8262. TEL 417-725-0181, FAX 417-724-8450, ops@opsweb.org. Ed. Chris Barry.

617.7 USA ISSN 1091-2983
JOURNAL OF OPHTHALMIC PROSTHETICS. Text in English. 1972. a. USD 35 per issue in North America; USD 45 per issue elsewhere (effective 2011). 64 p./no.; **Document type:** *Journal, Academic/Scholarly.* **Description:** Provides a forum for the publication of original articles containing clinical and research information for professionals who serve patients that have suffered eye loss.
Former titles (until 1996): American Society of Ocularists. Journal (1055-5161); (until 1975): Todays Ocularist
—BLDSC (5026.349000), IE, Ingenta.
Published by: American Society of Ocularists, PO Box 608, Earlysville, VA 22936. TEL 866-973-4066, toniz@ocularist.org. Ed. Michael Hughes.

617.7 USA ISSN 2090-004X
▼ ➤ **JOURNAL OF OPHTHALMOLOGY.** Text in English. 2009. irreg. USD 195 (effective 2011). **Document type:** *Journal, Academic/Scholarly.* **Description:** Publishes original research articles, review articles, case reports, and clinical studies in all areas of ophthalmology.
Related titles: Online - full text ed.: ISSN 2090-0058. free (effective 2011).
Indexed: A01, B21, C06, CA, NSA, P30, T02.
Published by: Hindawi Publishing Corporation, 410 Park Ave, 15th Fl, PMB 287, New York, NY 10022. FAX 215-893-4392, 866-446-3294, info@hindawi.com.

617.7 ESP ISSN 1888-4296
JOURNAL OF OPTOMETRY. Text in English. 2008. irreg. **Document type:** *Journal, Academic/Scholarly.*
Related titles: Online - full text ed.: free (effective 2011) (from ScienceDirect).
Indexed: P30, SCOPUS.
—**CCC.**
Published by: Colegio Nacional de Opticos Optometristas de Espana/Spanish Council of Optometry, C Princesa, 25 4o, Edificio Hexagono, Madrid, 28008, Spain. TEL 34-91-5414403, FAX 34-91-5422397, http://www.cnoo.es/index.php.

617.7 618.92 USA ISSN 0191-3913
RE48.2.C5 CODEN: JPOSDR
➤ **JOURNAL OF PEDIATRIC OPHTHALMOLOGY & STRABISMUS.** Text in English. 1964. bi-m. USD 174 combined subscription domestic to individuals (print & online eds.); USD 287 combined subscription domestic to institutions (print & online eds.); USD 59 per issue (effective 2010). adv. bk.rev.; film rev. abstr.; bibl.; charts; illus.; stat. index. back issues avail.; reprints avail. **Document type:** *Journal, Academic/Scholarly.* **Description:** Provides information useful to the pediatric ophthalmologist for the diagnosis, treatment, correction, and prevention of eye disorders in infants, children, and adolescents.
Formerly (until 1978): Journal of Pediatric Ophthalmology (0022-345X)
Related titles: Microform ed.: (from PQC); Online - full text ed.: ISSN 1938-2405.
Indexed: A22, A29, ASCA, B20, B21, CA, CurCont, DentInd, EMBASE, ESPM, ExcerpMed, FR, I10, IndMed, Inpharma, MEDLINE, P20, P22, P26, P30, P35, P48, P54, PQC, R10, Reac, SCI, SCOPUS, T02, VirolAbstr, W07.
—BLDSC (5030.210000), GNLM, IE, Infotrieve, Ingenta, INIST. **CCC.**
Published by: Slack, Inc., 6900 Grove Rd, Thorofare, NJ 08086. TEL 856-848-1000, FAX 856-848-6091, customerservice@slackinc.com, http://www.slackinc.com. Eds. Dr. Leonard Nelson, Dr. Rudolph Wagner.

➤ **JOURNAL OF REFRACTIVE SURGERY.** *see* MEDICAL SCIENCES—Surgery

617.7 USA ISSN 1534-7362
RE1
➤ **JOURNAL OF VISION.** Text in English. 2001. irreg., latest vol.9, no.6. free (effective 2011). back issues avail. **Document type:** *Journal, Academic/Scholarly.* **Description:** Covers all aspects of visual function in humans and other organisms.
Media: Online - full text.
Indexed: A20, B21, CurCont, EMBASE, ExcerpMed, MEDLINE, NSA, P03, P30, PsycInfo, PsycholAb, R10, Reac, SCI, SCOPUS, W07.
—**CCC.**
Published by: Association for Research in Vision and Ophthalmology, 12300 Twinbrook Pkwy, Ste 250, Rockville, MD 20852. TEL 240-221-2900, FAX 240-221-0370, arvo@arvo.org, http://www.arvo.org/. Ed. Andrew B Watson.

617.7 DEU ISSN 1615-9241
JULIUS-HIRSCHBERG-GESELLSCHAFT ZUR GESCHICHTE DER AUGENHEILKUNDE. MITTEILUNGEN. Text in German. 2000. irreg. **Document type:** *Monographic series, Academic/Scholarly.*
Published by: Julius-Hirschberg-Gesellschaft zur Geschichte der Augenheilkunde, Kirchgasse 6, Thuengersheim, 97291, Germany. TEL 49-9364-811543, FAX 49-9364-811559, Frank.Krogmann@t-online.de, http://www.dog.org/jhg/index.html.

617.75 USA ISSN 1063-1623
RE1
KANSAS OPTOMETRIC JOURNAL. Text in English. 1929. q. adv. bk.rev. **Document type:** *Journal, Trade.*
Published by: Kansas Optometric Association, 1266 S W Topeka Blvd, Topeka, KS 66612. TEL 785-232-0225, FAX 785-232-6151, info@kansasoptometric.org, http://www.kansasoptometric.org. Ed. Dr. David R Reynolds. Circ: 550.

KEY NOTE MARKET ASSESSMENT. OPTICIANS AND OPTICAL GOODS. *see* BUSINESS AND ECONOMICS—Production Of Goods And Services

KEY NOTE MARKET REPORT: OPHTHALMIC GOODS & SERVICES. *see* BUSINESS AND ECONOMICS—Production Of Goods And Services

617.75 USA ISSN 0886-7666
KEYSTONER. Text in English. 1947. 10/yr. free to members. bk.rev. **Document type:** *Newsletter.* **Description:** Contains society news.
Published by: Pennsylvania Optometric Association, 218 North St, Harrisburg, PA 17105. TEL 717-233-6455, FAX 717-233-6833, mail@poaeyes.org, http://www.poaeyes.org. Ed. Deborah A Sohn. R&P Robert A Hall. Circ: 175.

617 JPN ISSN 0914-6806
KIKAN GANKA SHUJUTSU/JAPANESE SOCIETY OF OPHTHALMIC SURGEONS. JOURNAL. Text in Japanese; Summaries in English, Japanese. 1988. q. JPY 10,080 (effective 2007). **Document type:** *Journal, Academic/Scholarly.*
—BLDSC (4809.474200).
Published by: Medikaru Aoi Shuppan/Medical-Aoi Publications, Inc., 2-39-5 Hongo, Bunkyo-ku, Kataoka Bldg. 5F, Tokyo, 113-0033, Japan. TEL 81-3-38110544.

617.7 POL ISSN 0023-2157
CODEN: KOAOAE
KLINIKA OCZNA. Text in Polish; Summaries in English. 1923. m. EUR 116 foreign (effective 2006). adv. bk.rev. abstr.; illus. index. **Document type:** *Journal, Academic/Scholarly.*
Indexed: A22, CIN, ChemAb, ChemTitl, DentInd, DokArb, EMBASE, ExcerpMed, IndMed, MEDLINE, P30, R10, Reac, SCOPUS.
—BLDSC (5099.300000), CASDDS, GNLM, IE, Infotrieve, Ingenta, INIST.
Published by: (Polskie Towarzystwo Okulistyczne/Polish Ophthalmological Society), Oftal Sp. z o.o., ul Sierakowskiego 13 (Szpital), Warsaw, 03709, Poland. ored@okulistyka.com.pl. **Dist. by:** Ars Polona, Obroncow 25, Warsaw 03933, Poland. TEL 48-22-5098609, FAX 48-22-5098610, arspolona@arspolona.com.pl, http://www.arspolona.com.pl. **Co-sponsor:** Ministerstwo Zdrowia in Opieki Spolecznej.

617.7 DEU ISSN 0023-2165
RE67 CODEN: KMAUAI
➤ **KLINISCHE MONATSBLAETTER FUER AUGENHEILKUNDE.** Text and summaries in German; Summaries in English. 1863. m. EUR 352 to institutions; EUR 490 combined subscription to institutions (print & online eds.); EUR 46 newsstand/cover (effective 2011). adv. bk.rev. abstr.; charts; illus. index. Supplement avail.; reprint service avail. from IRC. **Document type:** *Journal, Academic/Scholarly.*
Incorporates (1976-1995): Aktuelle Augenheilkunde (0942-5276); Which was formerly (until 1992): Folia Ophthalmologica (0323-4932); Former titles (until 1963): Klinische Monatsblaetter fuer Augenheilkunde und Augenaerztliche Fortbildung (0344-6360); (until 192?): Klinische Monatsblaetter fuer Augenheilkunde (0344-6387)
Related titles: Online - full text ed.: ISSN 1439-3999. EUR 472 to institutions (effective 2011).
Indexed: A20, A22, ASCA, ChemAb, CurCont, DentInd, EMBASE, ExcerpMed, FR, IBR, IBZ, ISR, IndMed, Inpharma, MEDLINE, P30, R10, RILM, Reac, SCI, SCOPUS, W07.
—BLDSC (5099.450000), GNLM, IE, Infotrieve, Ingenta, INIST. **CCC.**
Published by: Georg Thieme Verlag, Ruedigerstr 14, Stuttgart, 70469, Germany. TEL 49-711-8931421, FAX 49-711-8931410, kunden.service@thieme.de. Eds. Dr. Gabriele Lang, Dr. Gerhard Lang. Adv. contact Christine Volpp TEL 49-711-8931603. Circ: 1,600 (paid).

617.75 DEU ISSN 0721-5096
DIE KONTAKTLINSE. Text in German. 1966. 10/yr. EUR 109 domestic; EUR 115 foreign (effective 2011). adv. bk.rev. **Document type:** *Journal, Trade.* **Description:** Publication for specialists devoted to contact lens technology featuring clinical articles, the latest in research and new products.
Formerly (until 1980): Die Contactlinse (0010-7336)
Indexed: TM.
—GNLM.
Published by: (Vereinigung Deutscher Contactlinsen-Spezialisten e.V.), Konradin Verlag Robert Kohlhammer GmbH, Ernst Mey Str 8, Leinfelden-Echterdingen, 70771, Germany. TEL 49-711-75940, FAX 49-711-7594390, info@konradin.de, http://www.konradin.de. Ed. Wolfgang Cagnolati. Adv. contact Ines Scholz. Circ: 2,908 (paid and controlled).

617.7 POL ISSN 1509-4251
KONTAKTOLOGIA I OPTYKA OKULISTYCZNA. Text in Polish. 2000. s-a. EUR 33 foreign (effective 2006). **Document type:** *Journal, Academic/Scholarly.*
Published by: Oftal Sp. z o.o., ul Sierakowskiego 13 (Szpital), Warsaw, 03709, Poland. ored@okulistyka.com.pl. Ed. Jozef Kaluzny. **Dist. by:** Ars Polona, Obroncow 25, Warsaw 03933, Poland. TEL 48-22-5098609, FAX 48-22-5098610, arspolona@arspolona.com.pl, http://www.arspolona.com.pl.

617.7 KOR ISSN 1011-8942
➤ **KOREAN JOURNAL OF OPHTHALMOLOGY.** Text in English. 1987. q. (s-a. until 2004). membership. **Document type:** *Journal, Academic/Scholarly.* **Description:** Contains original articles, case reports, clinical experiments, review articles and letters to the editor.
Related titles: Online - full text ed.
Indexed: EMBASE, ExcerpMed, MEDLINE, P30, R10, Reac, SCOPUS.
—BLDSC (5113.569800), IE, Ingenta.
Published by: Korean Ophthalmological Society/Daehan An'gwa Haghoe, Seocho World Officetel #1007, 1355-3 Seocho-2-dong Seocho-ku, Seoul, 137-072, Korea, S. TEL 82-2-5836520, FAX 82-2-5836521, kos@ophthalmology.org. Ed. Young Jae Hong.

617.7 658 USA
LABTALK. Text in English. 1992. 6/yr. free to qualified personnel; USD 15 per issue (effective 2009). back issues avail. **Document type:** *Magazine, Trade.* **Description:** Provides information, features and new product knowledge to optical laboratory managers, and owners, providing real solutions to the challenges facing optical laboratories.
Related titles: Online - full text ed.
Published by: Jobson Optical Group (Subsidiary of: Jobson Publishing LLC), 100 Ave of the Americas, New York, NY 10013. TEL 212-274-7000, FAX 212-431-0500, info@jmihealth.com, http://www.jmihealth.com/. Ed. Christie Walker TEL 909-866-5590. Circ: 4,555.

617.7 658 USA
LENSES. Text in English. s-a. USD 99 domestic; USD 119 in Canada; USD 129 elsewhere (effective 2007). **Document type:** *Magazine, Trade.* **Description:** Industry resource for information concerning ophthalmic lenses.
Published by: Frames Data (Subsidiary of: Jobson Publishing LLC), 100 Avenue of the Americas, 9th Fl, New York, NY 10013. TEL 212-274-7000, 800-821-6069, FAX 212-274-0392, info@framesdata.com, http://www.framesdata.com.

617.7 LTU ISSN 1648-5289
LIETUVOS OFTALMOLOGIJA. Text in Lithuanian. 2002. q. **Document type:** *Journal, Academic/Scholarly.*
Published by: Lietuvos Akiu Gydytoju Draugija, Eiveniu g 2, Kaunas, 3007, Lithuania. TEL 370-37-326828.

LIGHT (WHEATON). *see* HANDICAPPED—Visually Impaired

617.7 TUR
M N OFTALMOLOJI DERGISI/JOURNAL OF OPHTHALMOLOGY. Text in English. q. TRY 15 to individuals; TRY 60 to institutions; TRY 50 doctors; TRY 40 to students (effective 2010). **Document type:** *Journal, Academic/Scholarly.*
Related titles: Online - full text ed.: free (effective 2010).
Published by: Medical Network, Public Sokak No.4/2, Ankara, 06420, Turkey. info@medicalnetwork.com.tr.

617.7 POL
MAGAZYN OKULISTYCZNY. Text in Polish. q. PLZ 60 (effective 2005). **Document type:** *Journal.*
Published by: Agencja Wydawniczo-Reklamowa, ul Wadowicka 8a, Krakow, 30415, Poland. medicus@medicus.com.pl, http://www.medicus.com.pl.

617.7 IRN ISSN 1735-4153
MAJALLAH-I CHASHM PIZISHKI-I IRAN/IRANIAN JOURNAL OF OPHTHALMOLOGY. Text in Persian, Modern. 1985. q. **Document type:** *Journal, Academic/Scholarly.*
Published by: Iranian Society of Ophtalmology, 3 Ferdosi Alley, North Kargar St, Tehran, Iran. TEL 98-2-66919061, FAX 98-2-66942404, info@irso.org, http://www.irso.org.

687 DEU ISSN 1614-1598
MANUFACTURERS FORUM. Text in German. 2004. bi-m. **Document type:** *Magazine, Trade.*
Published by: MediaWelt Produktions und Agentur GmbH, Papiermuehlenweg 74, Ratingen, 40882, Germany. TEL 49-2102-1678000, FAX 49-2102-1678020, joerg.spangemacher@mediawelt-services.de, http://www.mediawelt-services.de.

617.7 IRN ISSN 2079-0090
▼ **MEDICAL HYPOTHESIS, DISCOVERY AND INNOVATION IN OPHTHALMOLOGY.** Text in English. 2010. s-a. **Document type:** *Journal, Academic/Scholarly.* **Description:** Publishes online mini-reviews, letters and research articles on new ideas, discoveries, hypothesis, minimally invasive surgical techniques, medications, software and new instruments.
Media: Online - full text.
Published by: Middle East Cancer Institute, Ophthalmology Department, PO Box 14155-1856, Tehran, Iran. TEL 60-143-686153, FAX 60-143-686153. Eds. Fatemeh Heidary, Reza Gharebaghi. Pub. Ali Ahmadiani.

617.75 USA ISSN 1071-1627
RE1
THE MICHIGAN OPTOMETRIST. Text in English. 1921. bi-m. USD 15 (effective 2007). adv. bk.rev. charts; stat.; illus. 32 p./no.; **Document type:** *Magazine, Trade.* **Description:** Contains news for and about optometrists, their field, and related ones.
Published by: Michigan Optometric Association, 530 W Ionia St, Ste A, Lansing, MI 48933. TEL 517-482-0616, FAX 517-482-1611. Ed., Pub., Adv. contact William D Dansby. page USD 299. Circ: 950 (controlled).

617.7 IND ISSN 0974-9233
➤ **MIDDLE EAST AFRICAN JOURNAL OF OPHTHALMOLOGY.** Abbreviated title: M E A J O. Text in English. 1993. q. INR 1,000 domestic to individuals; USD 100 foreign to individuals; INR 2,000 domestic to institutions; USD 250 foreign to institutions; INR 1,200 combined subscription domestic to individuals (print & online eds.); USD 120 combined subscription foreign to individuals (print & online eds.); INR 2,400 combined subscription domestic to institutions (print & online eds.); USD 300 combined subscription foreign to institutions (print & online eds.) (effective 2011). adv. **Document type:** *Journal, Academic/Scholarly.* **Description:** Covers all ophthalmology topics, which includes publication of original research of interest to ophthalmologists in the Middle East & Africa that describe clinical investigations, observations, and relevant laboratory investigations.
Related titles: Online - full text ed.: ISSN 0975-1599. INR 800 domestic to individuals; USD 80 foreign to individuals; INR 1,600 domestic to institutions; USD 200 foreign to institutions (effective 2011).
Indexed: A01, A26, E08, H11, H12, I05, P30, S09, T02.
—**CCC.**
Published by: (Middle East African Council of Ophthalmology), Medknow Publications and Media Pvt. Ltd., B-9, Kanara Business Ctr, Off Link Rd, Ghatkopar (E), Mumbai, Maharastra 400 075, India. TEL 91-22-66491816, 91-22-66491818, publishing@medknow.com, journals@medknow.com, http://www.medknow.com. Ed. Deepak P Edward.

617.7 ITA ISSN 0026-4903
MINERVA OFTALMOLOGICA; a journal on ophthalmology. Text in Italian; Summaries in English, Italian. 1958. q. EUR 240 combined subscription in the European Union to institutions print & online eds.; EUR 265 combined subscription elsewhere to institutions print & online eds. (effective 2011). adv. bk.rev. bibl.; charts; illus. index. **Document type:** *Journal, Academic/Scholarly.* **Description:** Covers ophthalmological pathophysiology, clinical medicine and therapy.
Related titles: Microform ed.: (from PQC); Online - full text ed.: ISSN 1827-1685. 2005.
Indexed: A22, IndMed, P30.
—GNLM, INIST.
Published by: Edizioni Minerva Medica, Corso Bramante 83-85, Turin, 10126, Italy. TEL 39-011-678282, FAX 39-011-674502, journals.dept@minervamedica.it, http://www.minervamedica.it. Pub. Alberto Oliaro. Circ: 3,000 (paid).

617.7 NLD ISSN 0167-8612
CODEN: MPTHDI
➤ **MONOGRAPHS IN OPHTHALMOLOGY.** Text in English. 1981. irreg., latest vol.15, 1994. price varies. **Document type:** *Monographic series, Academic/Scholarly.*
—**CCC.**
Published by: Springer Netherlands (Subsidiary of: Springer Science+Business Media), Van Godewijckstraat 30, Dordrecht, 3311 GX, Netherlands. TEL 31-78-6576050, FAX 31-78-6576474.

617.7 BRA ISSN 1678-1139
MUNDO DA OPTICA. Text in Portuguese. 2003. bi-m. 76 p./no.; **Document type:** *Magazine, Trade.*
Related titles: Online - full text ed.
Published by: Editorial Bolina Brasil (Subsidiary of: Grupo Editorial Bolina), Alameda Pucurui 51-59 B, Tamporere - Barueri, Sao Paulo, 06460-100, Brazil. Ed. Graziela Canella. Circ: 12,000.

617.7 659.52 BRA ISSN 1981-3368
MUNDO DA OPTICA NEWS. Text in Portuguese. 2006. bi-m. 32 p./no.; **Document type:** *Journal, Trade.*
Published by: Editorial Bolina Brasil (Subsidiary of: Grupo Editorial Bolina), Alameda Pucurui 51-59 B, Tamporere - Barueri, Sao Paulo, 06460-100, Brazil. Ed. Graziela Canella. Circ: 12,000.

617.75 ESP
MUNDO DE LA OPTICA. Text in Spanish. bi-m. EUR 42 (effective 2009). adv. **Document type:** *Magazine, Trade.*
Published by: Grupo Editorial Bolina, Calle Rufino Gonzales 13, 4o, Madrid, 28037, Spain. TEL 34-91-3273242, FAX 34-91-7542668, http://www.editorialbolina.com. Ed. Antonio Castillo. adv.: page EUR 2,140; trim 240 x 310.

617.7 NPL ISSN 2072-6805
▼ ➤ **NEPALESE JOURNAL OF OPHTHALMOLOGY.** Text in English. 2009. s-a. **Document type:** *Journal, Academic/Scholarly.*
Related titles: Online - full text ed.: free (effective 2011).
Indexed: MEDLINE, P30.
Published by: Nepal Ophthalmic Society, Tripureshwor, PO Box 23041, Kathmandu, Nepal. TEL 977-1-4225977, FAX 977-1-4720142, nepophsoc@yahoo.com. Ed. Badri P Badhu.

➤ **NEURO-OPHTHALMOLOGY.** *see* MEDICAL SCIENCES—Psychiatry And Neurology

➤ **NEW LITERATURE ON SIGHT PROBLEMS.** *see* HANDICAPPED—Abstracting, Bibliographies, Statistics

617.7 NLD ISSN 0077-8605
CODEN: TNOOA6
➤ **NEW ORLEANS ACADEMY OF OPHTHALMOLOGY. TRANSACTIONS.** Variant title: Symposia. Text in English. a. price varies. back issues avail. **Document type:** *Proceedings, Academic/Scholarly.*
Indexed: DentInd, IndMed, P30.
—**CCC.**
Published by: (New Orleans Adademy of Ophthalmology USA), Kugler Publications (Subsidiary of: Contributions to Zoology), PO Box 20538, Amsterdam, 1001 NN, Netherlands. TEL 31-20-6845700, FAX 31-20-6847788, info@kuglerpublications.com, http://www.kuglerpublications.com.

617.7 NGA ISSN 0189-9171
NIGERIAN JOURNAL OF OPHTHALMOLOGY. Text in English. 1992. a. NGN 1,000 domestic; GBP 50 in United Kingdom; USD 75 elsewhere (effective 2004). back issues avail. **Document type:** *Journal, Academic/Scholarly.*
Related titles: Online - full text ed.
Published by: Ophthalmological Society of Nigeria, Ojulowo Eye Hospital, PO Box 851, Ibadan, Nigeria. osnigeria@hotmail.com. Ed. O. Osuntokun.

617.7 JPN ISSN 0374-9851
CODEN: NSIZBD
➤ **NIHON CONTACT LENS GAKKAISHI.** Key Title: Nihon Kontakuto Renzu Gakkai Kaishi. Text in Japanese; Summaries in English. 1959. q. JPY 8,000 domestic; JPY 9,000 foreign. bk.rev. **Document type:** *Proceedings, Academic/Scholarly.*
Related titles: Microform ed.; ◆ Supplement to: Japanese Society for Low-Vision Research and Rehabilitation. Journal.
Indexed: P30.
—BLDSC (4804.740000), CASDDS, GNLM, INIST.
Published by: Japanese Society for Low-Vision Research and Rehabilitation, Kawasaki University of Medical Welfare, 288 Matsushima, Kurashiki, Okayama 701-0193, Japan. TEL 81-726-23-7878, FAX 81-726-23-6060, http://www.jslrr.org/. Ed. Yuichi Ohashi. Pub., R&P, Adv. contact Keiko Miyake. Circ: 2,250.

➤ **NIHON GAN YAKURI GAKKAI PUROGURAMU KOEN YOSHISHU/ JAPANESE SOCIETY FOR OCULAR PHARMACOLOGY. PROGRAM AND ABSTRACTS OF THE MEETING.** *see* MEDICAL SCIENCES—Abstracting, Bibliographies, Statistics

617.7 JPN
NIHON GANKOGAKU GAKKAI YOKOSHU/OPHTHALMOLOGICAL OPTICS SOCIETY OF JAPAN. PRELIMINARY PROGRAM. Text in Japanese. 1964. a. JPY 500. **Document type:** *Proceedings, Academic/Scholarly.*
Published by: Nihon Gankogaku Gakkai/Ophthalmological Optics Society of Japan, 7-5-10, Minamikasugaoka, 2nd Yamamoto Bldg. 203, Ibaraki, Osaka 100-0005, Japan. TEL 81-72-6313737, FAX 81-72-6313738, jmcfuji@ops.dti.ne.jp, http://www.gankougaku.gr.jp/.

617.3 JPN ISSN 0915-4302
NIHON HAKUNAISHO GAKKAISHI/JAPANESE SOCIETY FOR CATARACT RESEARCH. JOURNAL. Text in Japanese; Summaries in English, Japanese. 1989. a. **Document type:** *Journal, Academic/ Scholarly.*
Published by: Nihon Hakunaisho Gakkai, c/o Dokkyo Medical University, Department of Ophthalmology, 880 Kitakobayashi, Mibu-machi, Shimotsuga-gun, Tochigi, a 321-0293, Japan. TEL 81-282-861111 ext 2679, FAX 81-282-8-0630.

617.3 JPN ISSN 0289-3843
NIHON JAKUSHI SHASHI GAKKAI ZASSHI/JAPANESE ASSOCIATION OF STRABISMUS AND AMBLYOPIA. JOURNAL. Text in Japanese; Summaries in English, Japanese. 1973. a. **Document type:** *Journal, Academic/Scholarly.*
Published by: Nihon Jakushi Shashi Gakkai/Japanese Association of Strabismus and Amblyopia, 7-5-10, Minamikasugaoka, Daini-Yamamoto Bldg. 203, Ibaraki, 567-0046, Japan. TEL 81-72-6313737, FAX 81-72-6313738, jmcfuji@ops.dti.ne.jp, http://www.jasa-web.jp/. **Co-sponsor:** Ganka Rinsho Ihokai - Japanese Society of Clinical Ophthalmology.

617.3 JPN ISSN 0386-4200
NIHON JAKUSHI SHASHI GAKKAIHO/JAPANESE ASSOCIATION OF STRABISMUS AND AMBLYOPIA. BULLETIN. Text in Japanese. 1964. 3/yr. **Document type:** *Journal, Academic/Scholarly.*
Published by: Nihon Jakushi Shashi Gakkai/Japanese Association of Strabismus and Amblyopia, 7-5-10, Minamikasugaoka, Daini-Yamamoto Bldg. 203, Ibaraki, 567-0046, Japan. TEL 81-72-6313737, FAX 81-72-6313738, jmcfuji@ops.dti.ne.jp, http://www.jasa-web.jp/.

617.3 JPN ISSN 0285-1326
NIHON NO GANKA/JAPAN OPHTHALMOLOGISTS ASSOCIATION. JOURNAL. Text in Japanese. 1967. m. **Document type:** *Journal, Academic/Scholarly.*
Published by: Nihon Ganka Ikai, Ichiboshi-Shiba Bldg., 2-2-14 Shiba, Minato-ku, Tokyo, 101-0064, Japan. TEL 81-3-57657755, FAX 81-3-57657676, http://www.gankaikai.or.jp/.

617.7 JPN ISSN 0387-5172
NIHON SHINO KUNRENSHI KYOKAISHI/JAPANESE ORTHOPTIC JOURNAL. Text in Japanese; Summaries in English, Japanese. 1972. a. **Document type:** *Journal, Academic/Scholarly.*
Formerly (until 1977): Nihon Shino Kunrenshi Kyokai Kaiho/Japanese Association of Certified Orthoptist. Journal (0385-5341)
Published by: Nihon Shino Kenrenshi Kyokai/Japanese Association of Certified Orthoptists, 1-8-5 Kajicho, Chiyoda-ku, Shin-Kanda Bldg. 2F, Tokyo, 101-0044, Japan. TEL 81-3-52095251, FAX 81-3-68049233, http://www.jaco.or.jp/index.htm.

617.7 JPN ISSN 0029-0203
CODEN: NGZAA6
➤ **NIPPON GANKA GAKKAI ZASSHI/JAPANESE OPHTHALMOLOGICAL SOCIETY. JOURNAL.** Text in Japanese; Abstracts in English, Japanese. 1897. m. JPY 15,000 membership (effective 2004). adv. **Document type:** *Journal, Academic/Scholarly.*
Indexed: A22, B25, BIOSIS Prev, CIN, ChemAb, ChemTitl, DentInd, EMBASE, ExcerpMed, INIS AtomInd, IndMed, MEDLINE, MycolAb, P30, R10, Reac, SCOPUS.
—BLDSC (4809.365000), CASDDS, GNLM, IE, Infotrieve, Ingenta, INIST. **CCC.**
Published by: Nippon Ganka Gakkai/Japanese Ophthalmological Society, 2-4-11-402 Sarugakucho, Chiyoda-ku, Tokyo, 101-8346, Japan. TEL 81-3-32952360, FAX 81-3-32939384, ytano@ophthal.med.osaka-u.ac.jp. Circ: 12,000.

617.7 USA
NOVA JOURNAL OF EYE RESEARCH. Text in English. 2008 (Jan.). q. USD 245 to institutions; USD 367 combined subscription to institutions (print & online eds.) (effective 2012). **Document type:** *Journal, Academic/Scholarly.*
Formerly (until 2010): Journal of Macular Degeneration (1939-5892)
Related titles: Online - full text ed.: USD 245 to institutions (effective 2012).
Published by: Nova Science Publishers, Inc., 400 Oser Ave, Ste 1600, Hauppauge, NY 11788. TEL 631-231-7269, FAX 631-231-8175, main@novapublishers.com.

617.7 RUS
➤ **NOVOE V OFTAL'MOLOGII.** Text in Russian. 1995. q. USD 183 foreign (effective 2007). **Document type:** *Journal, Academic/ Scholarly.*
Published by: M N T K Mikrokhirurgiya Glaza, Beskudnikovskii bulv 59-a, Moscow, 127486, Russian Federation. TEL 7-095-4888427, FAX 7-095-4888409, info@mntk.ru. Ed. H P Takhchidi. Circ: 3,000. **Dist. by:** East View Information Services, 10601 Wayzata Blvd, Minneapolis, MN 55305. TEL 952-252-1201, 800-477-1005, FAX 952-252-1202, info@eastview.com, http://www.eastview.com.

617.7 GBR ISSN 0927-3948
RE68 CODEN: OIINEN
➤ **OCULAR IMMUNOLOGY AND INFLAMMATION.** Text in English. 1993. bi-m. GBP 590, EUR 775, USD 970 combined subscription to institutions (print & online eds.); GBP 1,180, EUR 1,545, USD 1,935 combined subscription to corporations (print & online eds.) (effective 2010). adv. back issues avail.; reprint service avail. from PSC. **Document type:** *Journal, Academic/Scholarly.* **Description:** Publishes original research papers, reviews and short communications on all aspects of basic and clinical research pertaining to the ocular inflammatory response and its control by the immune system.
Related titles: Microform ed.: (from PQC); Online - full text ed.: ISSN 1744-5078 (from IngentaConnect).
Indexed: A01, A03, A08, A22, A36, B21, C06, C07, CA, CABA, CurCont, E01, E12, EMBASE, ExcerpMed, F08, F12, GH, H17, ISR, ImmunAb, IndMed, Inpharma, MEDLINE, N02, NSA, P30, P33, P35, P39, R08, R10, RM&VM, Reac, SCI, SCOPUS, T02, T05, W07.
—BLDSC (6235.154200), CASDDS, GNLM, IE, Infotrieve, Ingenta. **CCC.**
Published by: (International Ocular Inflammation Society ESP), Informa Healthcare (Subsidiary of: T & F Informa plc), Telephone House, 69-77 Paul St, London, EC2A 4LQ, United Kingdom. TEL 44-20-70175000, FAX 44-20-70176792, healthcare.enquiries@informa.com. Ed. Manfred Zierhut TEL 49-7071-2984007. Adv. contact Per Sonnerfeldt. **Subscr. in N America to:** Taylor & Francis Inc., Customer Services Dept, 325 Chestnut St, 8th Fl, Philadelphia, PA 19106. TEL 215-625-8900, 800-354-1420, FAX 215-625-8914, customerservice@taylorandfrancis.com; **Subscr. outside N. America to:** Taylor & Francis Ltd., Journals Customer Service, Sheepen Pl, Colchester, Essex CO3 3LP, United Kingdom. TEL 44-20-70175544, FAX 44-20-70175198, tf.enquiries@tfinforma.com.

617.7 USA ISSN 1542-0124
➤ **THE OCULAR SURFACE**; a journal of review linking laboratory science, clinical science,and clinical practice. Text in English. 2003 (Jan.). q. USD 154 in US & Canada to individuals; USD 199 elsewhere to individuals; USD 249 in US & Canada to institutions; USD 299 elsewhere to institutions (effective 2010). adv. back issues avail.; reprints avail. **Document type:** *Journal, Academic/Scholarly.* **Description:** Addresses reviews of work in laboratory science, clinical science, and clinical practice, along with coverage of ongoing studies, patents pending, conference highlights, and more.
Related titles: Online - full text ed.: ISSN 1937-5913 (from IngentaConnect).
Indexed: CurCont, EMBASE, ExcerpMed, MEDLINE, P30, R10, Reac, SCI, SCOPUS, W07.
—BLDSC (6235.154400), IE, Ingenta. **CCC.**
Published by: Ethis Communications, Inc., 75 Maiden Ln, Ste 408, New York, NY 10038. TEL 212-791-1440, FAX 212-791-4980, http://ethiscommunications.com/. Eds. Gary N Foulks TEL 502-852-6150, David Kellner. Circ: 1,500.

617.7 USA ISSN 1938-5374
OCULAR SURGERY NEWS (CHINA EDITION). Text in Chinese. 1989. m.
Related titles: ◆ Regional ed(s).: Ocular Surgery News (Europe Edition). ISSN 2157-8567.
Published by: Slack, Inc., 6900 Grove Rd, Thorofare, NJ 08086. TEL 856-848-1000, FAX 856-848-6091, customerservice@slackinc.com, http://www.slackinc.com.

OCULAR SURGERY NEWS (EUROPE EDITION). *see* MEDICAL SCIENCES—Surgery

617.7 USA ISSN 1938-5366
OCULAR SURGERY NEWS (INDIA EDITION). Text in English. 2007. m. reprints avail. **Document type:** *Journal, Academic/Scholarly.* **Description:** Provides information about Ocular Surgery.
Related titles: ◆ Regional ed(s).: Ocular Surgery News (Europe Edition). ISSN 2157-8567; ◆ Ocular Surgery News (Japan Edition). ISSN 1533-0125; ◆ Ocular Surgery News (Latin America Edition). ISSN 1520-944X.
Published by: Slack, Inc., 6900 Grove Rd, Thorofare, NJ 08086. TEL 856-848-1000, 800-257-8290, FAX 856-848-6091, customerservice@slackinc.com, http://www.slackinc.com.

617.7 USA ISSN 1533-0125
OCULAR SURGERY NEWS (JAPAN EDITION). Text in English. 200?. m. reprints avail. **Description:** Covers information about Ocular Surgery.
Related titles: ◆ Regional ed(s).: Ocular Surgery News (Europe Edition). ISSN 2157-8567; ◆ Ocular Surgery News (India Edition). ISSN 1938-5366; ◆ Ocular Surgery News (Latin America Edition). ISSN 1520-944X.
Published by: Slack, Inc., 6900 Grove Rd, Thorofare, NJ 08086. TEL 856-848-1000, FAX 856-848-6091, customerservice@slackinc.com, http://www.slackinc.com.

617.7 USA ISSN 1520-944X
RE80
➤ **OCULAR SURGERY NEWS (LATIN AMERICA EDITION).** Text in Spanish, Portuguese. 1998. bi-m. USD 99 to individuals; USD 249 to institutions; USD 45 per issue (effective 2010). reprints avail. **Document type:** *Journal, Academic/Scholarly.* **Description:** Delivers news reports to ophthalmologists throughout Latin America. Presents the latest techniques and therapies in refractive surgery, cataract, glaucoma and all subspecialties of opthalmology.
Formerly: Ocular Surgery News (Edicion Internacional)
Related titles: ◆ Regional ed(s).: Ocular Surgery News (Europe Edition). ISSN 2157-8567; ◆ Ocular Surgery News (India Edition). ISSN 1938-5366; ◆ Ocular Surgery News (Japan Edition). ISSN 1533-0125.
Indexed: A01.
Published by: Slack, Inc., 6900 Grove Rd, Thorofare, NJ 08086. TEL 856-848-1000, FAX 856-848-6091, customerservice@slackinc.com, http://www.slackinc.com. Ed. Richard L Lindstrom.

➤ **OCULAR SURGERY NEWS (US EDITION).** *see* MEDICAL SCIENCES—Surgery

617.75 NLD ISSN 0029-8328
OCULUS. Text in Dutch. 1938. m. (10/yr.). adv. bk.rev. illus. **Document type:** *Trade.*
Formerly (until 1945): Mededeelingenblad van de Vakgroep Opticiens
Published by: Nederlandse Unie van Optiekbedrijven (NUVO), Postbus 643, Woerden, 3440 AP, Netherlands. TEL 31-348-436590, FAX 31-348-434755, info@nuvo.nl, http://www.nuvo.nl. adv.: color page EUR 1,695; trim 210 x 297. Circ: 2,100.

617.7 RUS ISSN 0235-4160
➤ **OFTAL'MOKHIRURGIYA.** Text in English, Russian. 1989. q. RUR 312 domestic; USD 60 foreign. adv. bk.rev. abstr.; bibl.; charts; illus.; pat.; stat. **Document type:** *Journal, Academic/Scholarly.* **Description:** Includes articles on corneal surgery, refractive surgery, surgical and laser management of glaucoma, cataract surgery and vitreoretinal surgery.
Indexed: RefZh.
—BLDSC (0128.632000), East View, GNLM.
Published by: M H T K Mikrokhirurgiya Glaza/I R T C Eye Microsurgery, Beskudnikovskii bulv 59-a, Moscow, 127486, Russian Federation. TEL 7-095-4888427, FAX 7-095-4888409. Ed. S N Fyodorov. Adv. contact L S Tumar. B&W page USD 600, color page USD 800; trim 297 x 210. Circ: 1,000 (paid and controlled). **Dist. by:** East View Information Services, 10601 Wayzata Blvd, Minneapolis, MN 55305. TEL 952-252-1201, 800-477-1005, FAX 952-252-1202, info@eastview.com, http://www.eastview.com.

617.7 UKR ISSN 0030-0675
CODEN: OFZHAV
OFTAL'MOLOGICHESKII ZHURNAL/OPHTHALMOLOGICAL JOURNAL. Text in Russian; Summaries in English. 1946. 6/yr. USD 173 foreign (effective 2005). bk.rev. bibl. index. **Document type:** *Journal, Academic/Scholarly.* **Description:** Publishes major clinical and laboratory reseach work from Russia, Ukraine, and other Eastern European countries related to clinical opthalmology and scientific opthalmology.
Indexed: ChemAb, IndMed, P30, RefZh.
—CASDDS, East View, GNLM. **CCC.**
Published by: Naukove Tovarystvo Oftal'mologiv Ukrainy/Ukrainian Ophthalmological Society, Filatov Institute of Eye Diseases & Tissue Therapy, Frantsuzskii bul 49/51, Odessa, 65061, Ukraine. TEL 380-482-222035. Ed. Ivan Logay. Pub. Valery Ponomarchuk. Adv. contact Svetlana Slobodyanik. Circ: 1,500. **Dist. by:** East View Information Services, 10601 Wayzata Blvd, Minneapolis, MN 55305. TEL 952-252-1201, 800-477-1005, FAX 952-252-1202, info@eastview.com, http://www.eastview.com.

617.7 POL ISSN 1505-2753
OKULISTYKA; kwartalnik medyczny. Text in Polish. 1998. q. EUR 42 foreign (effective 2005).
Published by: Oftal Sp. z o.o., ul Sierakowskiego 13 (Szpital), Warsaw, 03709, Poland. **Dist. by:** Ars Polona, Obroncow 25, Warsaw 03933, Poland. TEL 48-22-5098609, FAX 48-22-5098610, arspolona@arspolona.com.pl, http://www.arspolona.com.pl.

617.7 IND ISSN 0974-620X
OMAN JOURNAL OF OPHTALMOLOGY. Abbreviated title: O J O. Text in English. 2008. 3/yr. INR 2,000 domestic; USD 200 foreign (effective 2011). adv. **Document type:** *Journal, Academic/Scholarly.* **Description:** Provides a platform for scientific expression of the Oman Ophthalmic Society and the international Ophthalmic community and to provide opportunities for free exchange of ideas and information. It serves as a valuable resource for ophthalmologists, eye-care providers including optometrists, orthoptists, other health care professionals and research workers in all aspects of the field of visual science.
Related titles: Online - full text ed.: ISSN 0974-7842. INR 1,600 domestic; USD 160 foreign (effective 2011).
Indexed: A01, A26, E08, H12, I05, P10, P30, P48, P53, P54, PQC, S09, T02.
—IE. **CCC.**
Published by: (Oman Ophthalmic Society), Medknow Publications and Media Pvt. Ltd., B-9, Kanara Business Ctr, Off Link Rd, Ghatkopar (E), Mumbai, Maharastra 400 075, India. TEL 91-22-66491816, FAX 91-22-66491817, http://www.medknow.com. Ed. Abdulatif Al Raisi.

OOGLID. *see* HANDICAPPED—Visually Impaired

617.7 NLD ISSN 1874-3641
RE1
➤ **THE OPEN OPHTHALMOLOGY JOURNAL.** Text in English. 2007. irreg. free (effective 2011). **Document type:** *Journal, Academic/ Scholarly.* **Description:** Publishes research articles, reviews, and letters in all areas of experimental and clinical research in ophthalmology and vision science.
Media: Online - full text.
Indexed: A01, CA, NSA, P30, T02.
Published by: Bentham Open (Subsidiary of: Bentham Science Publishers Ltd.), PO Box 294, Bussum, AG 1400, Netherlands. TEL 31-35-6923800, FAX 31-35-6980150, subscriptions@bentham.org. Ed. Sue Lightman.

617.7 NZL ISSN 1179-1721
▼ **OPHTALMOLOGY AND EYE DISEASES.** Text in English. 2009. irreg. free (effective 2011). **Document type:** *Journal, Academic/Scholarly.*
Media: Online - full text.
Indexed: C06, C07, P30, T02.
—**CCC.**
Published by: Libertas Academica Ltd., PO Box 302-624, North Harbour, Auckland, 1330, New Zealand. TEL 64-21-662617, FAX 64-21-740006, editorial@la-press.com. Ed. Joshua Cameron.

617.75 GBR ISSN 0275-5408
RE939.2 CODEN: OPOPD5
➤ **OPHTHALMIC AND PHYSIOLOGICAL OPTICS.** Abbreviated title: O P O. Text in English. bi-m. GBP 826 in United Kingdom to institutions; EUR 1,048 in Europe to institutions; USD 1,526 in the Americas to institutions; USD 1,781 elsewhere to institutions; GBP 950 combined subscription in United Kingdom to institutions (print & online eds.); EUR 1,206 combined subscription in Europe to institutions (print & online eds.); USD 1,755 combined subscription in the Americas to institutions (print & online eds.); USD 2,048 combined subscription elsewhere to institutions (print & online eds.) (effective 2012). adv. bk.rev. charts; illus. index. back issues avail.; reprint service avail. from PSC. **Document type:** *Journal, Academic/Scholarly.* **Description:** Publishes international and interdisciplinary original research in aspects of pure and applied vision science.
Former titles (until 1981): British Journal of Physiological Optics (0007-1218); (until 1950): Dioptic Review and British Journal of Physiological Optics
Related titles: Microform ed.: (from PQC); Online - full text ed.: ISSN 1475-1313. GBP 826 in United Kingdom to institutions; EUR 1,048 in Europe to institutions; USD 1,526 in the Americas to institutions; USD 1,781 elsewhere to institutions (effective 2012) (from IngentaConnect).
Indexed: A01, A03, A08, A20, A22, A26, ASCA, B21, CA, CurCont, DentInd, E-psyche, E01, EMBASE, ErgAb, ExcerpMed, FR, H12, ISR, IndMed, Inpharma, Inspec, MEDLINE, NSA, P03, P30, P35, P43, PsycholAb, R10, Reac, SCI, SCOPUS, T02, W07.
—BLDSC (6270.870000), AskIEEE, GNLM, IE, Infotrieve, Ingenta, INIST. **CCC.**
Published by: (College of Optometrists), Wiley-Blackwell Publishing Ltd. (Subsidiary of: John Wiley & Sons, Inc.), 9600 Garsington Rd, Oxford, OX4 2DQ, United Kingdom. TEL 44-1865-776868, FAX 44-1865-714591, customerservices@blackwellpublishing.com. Ed. Dr. Christine Dickinson TEL 44-161-3063874. Adv. contact Craig Pickett TEL 44-1865-476267.

617.7 615 USA ISSN 1043-1780
RE994
OPHTHALMIC DRUG FACTS. Text in English. 1990. a. USD 77 per issue (effective 2009). **Document type:** *Report, Trade.* **Description:** Provides accurate, objective drug information for the eye care professionals, who need to make sound therapeutic decisions.

Published by: Facts and Comparisons (Subsidiary of: Wolters Kluwer N.V.), 77 West Port Plz, Ste 450, St. Louis, MO 63146. TEL 314-216-2100, 800-223-0554, FAX 317-735-5390.

617.7 GBR ISSN 0928-6586
RE91 CODEN: OPEPFP

➤ **OPHTHALMIC EPIDEMIOLOGY.** Text in Dutch. 1994. bi-m. GBP 655, EUR 935, USD 1,170 combined subscription to institutions (print & online eds.); GBP 1,310, EUR 1,870, USD 2,335 combined subscription to corporations (print & online eds.) (effective 2010). adv. back issues avail.; reprint service avail. from PSC. **Document type:** *Journal, Academic/Scholarly.* **Description:** Publishes research papers in ophthalmic research in the fields of epidemiology, public health, and the prevention of blindness.

Related titles: Online - full text ed.: ISSN 1744-5086 (from IngentaConnect).

Indexed: A01, A03, A08, A22, A34, A36, BA, CA, CABA, CurCont, E01, E12, EMBASE, ExcerpMed, GH, IndMed, LT, MEDLINE, N02, N03, P30, P33, P39, R08, R10, R12, RM&VM, RRTA, Reac, SCI, SCOPUS, T02, T05, VS, W07, W11.

—BLDSC (6270.880000), GNLM, IE, Infotrieve, Ingenta. **CCC.**

Published by: (International Society of Geographic and Epidemiological Ophthalmology (ISGEO) NLD), Informa Healthcare (Subsidiary of: T & F Informa plc), Telephone House, 69-77 Paul St, London, EC2A 4LQ, United Kingdom. TEL 44-20-70175000, healthcare.enquiries@informa.com, http://informahealthcare.com/. Ed. Dr. Sheila West. adv.: B&W page EUR 500; 17.5 x 22.8. **Subscr. in N America to:** Taylor & Francis Inc., Customer Services Dept, 325 Chestnut St, 8th Fl, Philadelphia, PA 19106. TEL 215-625-8900, 800-354-1420, FAX 215-625-2940, customerservice@taylorandfrancis.com; **Subscr. outside N. America to:** Taylor & Francis Ltd., Journals Customer Service, Sheepen Pl, Colchester, Essex CO3 3LP, United Kingdom. TEL 44-20-70175544, FAX 44-20-70175198, tf.enquiries@tfinforma.com.

617.7 618.92 GBR ISSN 1381-6810

➤ **OPHTHALMIC GENETICS.** Text in English. 1981. q. GBP 465, EUR 650, USD 805 combined subscription to institutions (print & online eds.); GBP 930, EUR 1,300, USD 1,610 combined subscription to corporations (print & online eds.) (effective 2010). adv. bk.rev. back issues avail.; reprint service avail. from PSC. **Document type:** *Journal, Academic/Scholarly.* **Description:** Contains review articles, research papers, and short communications on genetic ophthalmological problems of the newborn and of children, as well as adults.

Formerly (until 1994): Ophthalmic Paediatrics and Genetics (0167-6784)

Related titles: Microform ed.; Online - full text ed.: ISSN 1744-5094 (from IngentaConnect).

Indexed: A01, A03, A08, A22, ASCA, B21, CA, CurCont, E01, EMBASE, ExcerpMed, GenetAb, IBR, IBZ, IndMed, Inpharma, MEDLINE, P30, R10, Reac, SCI, SCOPUS, T02, W07.

—BLDSC (6270.893000), GNLM, IE, Infotrieve, Ingenta. **CCC.**

Published by: (International Society for Genetic Eye Disease and Retinoblastoma CAN), Informa Healthcare (Subsidiary of: T & F Informa plc), Telephone House, 69-77 Paul St, London, EC2A 4LQ, United Kingdom. TEL 44-20-70175000, FAX 44-20-70176792, healthcare.enquiries@informa.com. Ed. Elias I Traboulsi. Adv. contact Per Sonnerfeldt. **Subscr. to:** Taylor & Francis Ltd., Journals Customer Service, Sheepen Pl, Colchester, Essex CO3 3LP, United Kingdom. TEL 44-20-70175544, FAX 44-20-70175198; Taylor & Francis Inc., Customer Services Dept, 325 Chestnut St, 8th Fl, Philadelphia, PA 19106. TEL 215-625-8900, 800-354-1420, FAX 215-625-8914, customerservice@taylorandfrancis.com.
Co-sponsor: Ophthalmic Genetics Study Club, International Society of Paediatric Ophthalmology.

➤ **OPHTHALMIC NURSING**; international journal of ophthalmic nursing. *see* MEDICAL SCIENCES—Nurses And Nursing

617.7 617 USA ISSN 0740-9303
CODEN: CRIRDX

➤ **OPHTHALMIC PLASTIC AND RECONSTRUCTIVE SURGERY.** Text in English. 1985. bi-m. USD 826 domestic to institutions; USD 1,002 foreign to institutions (effective 2011). adv. bk.rev. illus. Index. back issues avail.; reprints avail. **Document type:** *Journal, Academic/Scholarly.* **Description:** Features articles and reviews on topics such as ptosis, eyelid reconstruction, orbital diagnosis and surgery, lacrimal problems, and eyelid malposition.

Related titles: Online - full text ed.: ISSN 1537-2677. USD 100 to individuals (effective 2008).

Indexed: A22, ASCA, CurCont, EMBASE, ExcerpMed, IndMed, Inpharma, MEDLINE, MS&D, P30, P35, R10, Reac, SCI, SCOPUS, W07.

—BLDSC (6271.430000), GNLM, IE, Infotrieve, Ingenta, INIST. **CCC.**

Published by: (American Society of Ophthalmic Plastic and Reconstructive Surgery), Lippincott Williams & Wilkins (Subsidiary of: Wolters Kluwer N.V.), Two Commerce Sq, 2001 Market St, Philadelphia, PA 19103. TEL 215-521-8300, FAX 215-521-8902, customerservice@lww.com, http://www.lww.com. Ed. Jonathan Dutton. Pub. Nina J Chang. Adv. contact Bethann H Sands TEL 215-521-8399. Circ: 1,034.

617.7 CHE ISSN 0030-3747
RE58 CODEN: OPRSAQ

➤ **OPHTHALMIC RESEARCH**; journal for research in experimental and clinical ophthalmology. Text in English. 1970. 8/yr. CHF 1,916, EUR 1,530, USD 1,888 to institutions; CHF 2,100, EUR 1,678, USD 2,066 combined subscription to institutions (print & online eds.) (effective 2012). adv. charts; illus.; stat. index. back issues avail. **Document type:** *Journal, Academic/Scholarly.* **Description:** Features original papers, reviews and short communications reporting basic and clinical experimental studies on ophthalmology.

Related titles: Microform ed.; Online - full text ed.: ISSN 1423-0259. 199?. CHF 1,848, EUR 1,478, USD 1,794 to institutions (effective 2012).

Indexed: A01, A03, A08, A22, A29, ASCA, B20, B21, B25, BIOSIS Prev, CA, ChemAb, ChemTitl, CurCont, DentInd, E01, EMBASE, ESPM, ExcerpMed, I10, IBR, IBZ, ISR, IndMed, Inpharma, MEDLINE, MycolAb, P20, P22, P30, P35, P48, P54, PQC, R10, Reac, SCI, SCOPUS, T02, VirolAbstr, W07.

—BLDSC (6271.450000), CASDDS, GNLM, IE, Infotrieve, Ingenta, INIST, Linda Hall. **CCC.**

Published by: S. Karger AG, Allschwilerstr 10, Basel, 4055, Switzerland. TEL 41-61-3061111, FAX 41-61-3061234, karger@karger.ch, http://www.karger.ch. Ed. U Pleyer. adv.: page CHF 1,730; trim 210 x 280. Circ: 800.

➤ **OPHTHALMIC SURGERY, LASERS AND IMAGING.** *see* MEDICAL SCIENCES—Surgery

617.7 DEU ISSN 0936-2517

OPHTHALMO CHIRURGIE. Text in German. 1989. 6/yr. EUR 81; EUR 41 to students; EUR 20 newsstand/cover (effective 2009). adv. bk.rev. back issues avail. **Document type:** *Journal, Academic/Scholarly.*

—GNLM.

Published by: Dr. R. Kaden Verlag GmbH & Co. KG, Ringstr 19 B, Heidelberg, 69115, Germany. TEL 49-6221-1377600, FAX 49-6221-29910, kaden@kaden-verlag.de, http://www.kaden-verlag.de. Adv. contact Petra Huebler. B&W page EUR 1,455, color page EUR 2,580; trim 178 x 230. Circ: 1,200 (paid and controlled).

617.7 DEU ISSN 0941-293X
RE1 CODEN: OHTHEJ

➤ **DER OPHTHALMOLOGE.** Text in German. 192?. m. EUR 551, USD 646 combined subscription to institutions (print & online eds.) (effective 2012). adv. back issues avail.; reprint service avail. from PSC. **Document type:** *Journal, Academic/Scholarly.* **Description:** Covers all fields of research, science, and practice in medical conditions and treatments of the eyes.

Former titles (until 1992): Fortschritte der Ophthalmologie (0723-8045); (until 1982): Deutsche Ophthalmologische Gesellschaft. Bericht ueber die Zusammenkunft (0070-427X)

Related titles: Microform ed.: (from PQC); Online - full text ed.: ISSN 1433-0423 (from IngentaConnect).

Indexed: A20, A22, A26, CIN, ChemAb, ChemTitl, CurCont, DentInd, DokArb, E01, EMBASE, ExcerpMed, FR, ISR, IndMed, Inpharma, MEDLINE, P30, P35, R10, Reac, SCI, SCOPUS, W07.

—BLDSC (6271.585000), CASDDS, GNLM, IE, Infotrieve, Ingenta, INIST. **CCC.**

Published by: Springer (Subsidiary of: Springer Science+Business Media), Tiergartenstr 17, Heidelberg, 69121, Germany. TEL 49-6221-4870, FAX 49-6221-345229. Ed. H E Voelcker. Adv. contact Stephan Kroeck TEL 49-30-827875739. B&W page EUR 1,710, color page EUR 2,900. Circ: 5,700 (paid and controlled). **Subscr. in the Americas to:** Springer New York LLC, Journal Fulfillment, PO Box 2485, Secaucus, NJ 07096. TEL 800-777-4643, 201-348-4033, FAX 201-348-4505, journals-ny@springer.com, http://www.springer.com; **Subscr. to:** Springer Distribution Center, Kundenservice Zeitschriften, Haberstr 7, Heidelberg 69126, Germany. TEL 49-6221-3454303, FAX 49-6221-3454229, subscriptions@springer.com.

617.7 CHE ISSN 0030-3755
RE1 CODEN: OPHTAD

➤ **OPHTHALMOLOGICA**; international journal of ophthalmology. Text in English. 1899. bi-m. CHF 2,006, EUR 1,602, USD 1,976 to institutions; CHF 2,200, EUR 1,758, USD 2,164 combined subscription to institutions (print & online eds.) (effective 2012). adv. bk.rev. bibl.; illus. index, cum.index vols.96-138. back issues avail. **Document type:** *Journal, Academic/Scholarly.* **Description:** Contains a selection of patient-oriented reports covering the etiology of eye diseases, diagnostic techniques, and advances in medical and surgical treatment.

Related titles: Microform ed.; Online - full text ed.: ISSN 1423-0267. 199?. CHF 1,938, EUR 1,550, USD 1,882 to institutions (effective 2012); ◆ Supplement(s): Developments in Ophthalmology. ISSN 0250-3751.

Indexed: A01, A03, A08, A22, ASCA, B21, B25, BIOSIS Prev, CA, ChemAb, ChemTitl, CurCont, E01, EMBASE, ESPM, ExcerpMed, H&SSA, H13, ISR, IndMed, Inpharma, MEDLINE, MycolAb, P10, P20, P22, P30, P35, P48, P53, P54, PQC, PsycholAb, R10, Reac, SCI, SCOPUS, T02, W07.

—BLDSC (6271.600000), CASDDS, GNLM, IE, Infotrieve, Ingenta, INIST. **CCC.**

Published by: (Netherlands Ophthalmological Society NLD), S. Karger AG, Allschwilerstr 10, Basel, 4055, Switzerland. TEL 41-61-3061111, FAX 41-61-3061234, karger@karger.ch, http://www.karger.ch. Ed. C Ohrloff. adv.: page CHF 1,730; trim 210 x 280. Circ: 1,000.

617.7 DEU ISSN 0943-898X

OPHTHALMOLOGISCHE NACHRICHTEN. Text in German. 1998. 16/yr. adv. **Document type:** *Journal, Trade.*

—**CCC.**

Published by: Biermann Verlag GmbH, Otto-Hahn-Str 7, Cologne, 50997, Germany. TEL 49-2236-3760, FAX 49-2236-376999, info@biermann.net, http://www.biermann-verlag.de. Ed. Dieter Kaulard. Adv. contact Michael Kesten.

617.7 USA ISSN 0161-6420
RE1

➤ **OPHTHALMOLOGY.** Text in English. 1907. m. USD 636 in US & Canada to institutions; USD 840 elsewhere to institutions (effective 2012). adv. illus. index. back issues avail.; reprints avail. **Document type:** *Journal, Academic/Scholarly.* **Description:** Covers topics such as new diagnostic and surgical techniques, treatment methods, instrument updates, the latest drug findings, results of clinical trials, and research findings.

Formerly (until vol.85, 1978): American Academy of Ophthalmology and Otolaryngology. Section on Ophthalmology. Transactions (0161-6978); Which superseded in part (in 1975): American Academy of Ophthalmology and Otolaryngology. Transactions (0002-7154); Which incorporated (in 1940): American Academy of Ophthalmology and Otolaryngology. Bulletin; American Academy of Ophthalmology and Otolaryngology. Transactions was formerly (until 1940): American Academy of Ophthalmology and Otolaryngology. Annual Meeting. Transactions (0163-593X); (until 1906): Ophthalmological Division of the American Academy of Ophthalmology and Otolaryngology at its Annual Meeting. Transactions (0190-7018); Which was formed by the merger of: Transactions of the Ophthalmological Division; Transactions of the Otological, Laryngological, and Rhinological Division

Related titles: CD-ROM ed.; Microform ed.: (from PQC); Online - full text ed.: ISSN 1549-4713 (from IngentaConnect, ScienceDirect); ◆ Spanish ed.: Ophthalmology (Spanish Edition). ISSN 1696-7631.

Indexed: A01, A03, A08, A20, A22, A26, A36, AIDS Ab, ASCA, B21, B25, BIOSIS Prev, CA, CABA, CISA, ChemAb, CurCont, DentInd, DokArb, E12, EMBASE, ESPM, ExcerpMed, FR, GH, H&SSA, H17, HospLI, I05, IBR, IBZ, IDIS, INI, ISR, IndMed, Inpharma, LT, MEDLINE, MS&D, MycolAb, N02, N03, NSA, P30, P33, P35, P39, R08, R10, R12, R13, RILM, RM&VM, RRTA, Reac, SCI, SCOPUS, T02, T05, W07.

—BLDSC (6271.805000), GNLM, IE, Infotrieve, Ingenta, INIST. **CCC.**

Published by: (American Academy of Ophthalmology), Elsevier Inc. (Subsidiary of: Elsevier Science & Technology), 1600 John F Kennedy Blvd, Philadelphia, PA 19103. TEL 215-239-3900, FAX 215-238-7883, JournalCustomerService-usa@elsevier.com, http://www.elsevier.com. Ed. Andrew P Schachat. Pub. Nancy Axelrod. Adv. contact Pat Hampton TEL 212-633-3181. Circ: 25,700.

617.7 ESP ISSN 1696-7631

OPHTHALMOLOGY (SPANISH EDITION). Text in Spanish. 2003. bi-m. EUR 75. **Document type:** *Journal, Academic/Scholarly.*

Related titles: ◆ English ed.: Ophthalmology. ISSN 0161-6420.

Published by: Grupo Saned, Capitan Haya 60, 1o, Madrid, 28028, Spain. TEL 34-91-7499500, FAX 34-91-7499501, saned@medynet.com, http://www.gruposaned.com. Ed. Teresa Dapena.

OPHTHALMOLOGY CODING ALERT; the practical adviser for ethically optimizing coding reimbursement and efficiency in ophthalmology practices. *see* INSURANCE

658 USA ISSN 1532-0316

OPHTHALMOLOGY MANAGEMENT. Text in English. 199?. m. USD 92 domestic; USD 101 in Canada; USD 144 elsewhere; free to qualified personnel (effective 2010). back issues avail. **Document type:** *Magazine, Trade.* **Description:** Delivers the essential strategies needed to navigate and grow today's ophthalmology practice.

—**CCC.**

Published by: Lippincott Williams & Wilkins, VisionCare Group (Subsidiary of: Lippincott Williams & Wilkins), 323 Norristown Rd, Ste 200, Ambler, PA 19002. TEL 215-646-8700, http://www.visioncareprofessional.com/. Ed. Jim Thomas TEL 215-367-2172. Pub. Doug Parry TEL 215-628-7747.

617.7 USA ISSN 1078-6392

OPHTHALMOLOGY ON C D. Text in English. 1995. a. **Document type:** *Journal, Academic/Scholarly.*

Media: CD-ROM.

Published by: (American Academy of Ophthalmology), Lippincott Williams & Wilkins (Subsidiary of: Wolters Kluwer N.V.), 530 Walnut St, Philadelphia, PA 19106. TEL 215-521-8300, FAX 215-521-8902, customerservice@lww.com, http://www.lww.com. **Subscr. to:** PO Box 1620, Hagerstown, MD 21741. TEL 800-638-3030.

617.7 USA

OPHTHALMOLOGY RESEARCH. Text in English. 2006. irreg., latest 2008. price varies. **Document type:** *Monographic series, Academic/Scholarly.* **Description:** Offers ophthalmic researchers a range of state-of-the-art titles to guide the advancement of knowledge in the field.

Related titles: Online - full text ed.

Published by: Humana Press, Inc. (Subsidiary of: Springer Science+Business Media), 233 Spring St, New York, NY 10013. TEL 212-460-1500, FAX 212-460-1575, service-ny@springer.com. Eds. Colin J Barnstable, Joyce Tombran-Tink.

617.7 USA ISSN 0193-032X

OPHTHALMOLOGY TIMES; all the clinical news in sight. Text in English. 1976. s-m. USD 200 domestic; USD 263 foreign; USD 17 newsstand/cover domestic; USD 19 newsstand/cover in Canada & Mexico; USD 23 newsstand/cover elsewhere (effective 2011). adv. back issues avail. **Document type:** *Magazine, Trade.* **Description:** Contains reports on current clinical and non-clinical news of interest to ophthalmologists in patient care practice in the United States.

Related titles: Microform ed.: (from PQC); Online - full text ed.: ISSN 2150-7333. free (effective 2011); ◆ Regional ed(s).: Ophthalmology Times Latin America; ◆ Ophthalmology Times China.

Indexed: A01, A03, A08, A15, A26, ABIn, B07, C11, C12, CA, E08, G06, G07, G08, H03, H04, H11, H12, I05, M01, M02, P16, P19, P26, P34, P48, P51, P53, P54, PQC, S09, T02, V02.

—BLDSC (6271.833000), GNLM, IE, Infotrieve. **CCC.**

Published by: Advanstar Communications, Inc., 6200 Canoga Ave, 2nd Fl, Woodland Hills, CA 91367. TEL 818-593-5000, FAX 818-593-5020, info@advanstar.com, http://www.advanstar.com. Ed. Mark Dlugoss TEL 440-891-2703. Pub. Lauri Jorgensen TEL 732-346-3013. Adv. contact Estelle Hofer TEL 440-891-2697. Circ: 21,234.

617.7 CHN

OPHTHALMOLOGY TIMES CHINA. Text in Chinese, English. 2002 (Spring). s-a. **Document type:** *Magazine, Academic/Scholarly.*

Related titles: ◆ Regional ed(s).: Ophthalmology Times Latin America; ◆ Ophthalmology Times. ISSN 0193-032X.

Published by: eSinoMed, Ltd., China Marine Tower, Suite 1305, 1 Pudong Avenue, Pudong, Shanghai, 200120, China. TEL 86-21-6886-1928, FAX 86-21-6886-0257, info@eSinoMed.com, http://www.esinomed.com/.

617.7 GBR ISSN 1753-3066

OPHTHALMOLOGY TIMES EUROPE. Abbreviated title: O T E. Text in English. 2005. 10/yr. GBP 140 domestic; GBP 100 foreign; GBP 20 newsstand/cover (effective 2011). adv. back issues avail. **Document type:** *Journal, Academic/Scholarly.* **Description:** Delivers a well-rounded package of surgical and clinical news, industry trends, dispensing and practice information, and insights and discoveries in all specialties.

Related titles: Online - full text ed.

—**CCC.**

Published by: Advanstar Communications (UK) Ltd. (Subsidiary of: Advanstar Communications, Inc.), Advanstar House, Park West, Sealand Rd, Chester, CH1 4RN, United Kingdom. TEL 44-1244-378888, FAX 44-1244-370011, info@advanstar.com, http://www.advanstar.com. Ed. Pamela Brook TEL 44-1244-393107. Pub. Andrew Davies TEL 44-1244-393408.

617.7 USA

OPHTHALMOLOGY TIMES LATIN AMERICA; all the clinical news in sight. Abbreviated title: O T L A. Text in Portuguese, English, Spanish. 1997. bi-m. free to qualified personnel (effective 2009). adv. back issues avail. **Description:** Covers clinical news about ophthalmology in the United States and Latin America.

Related titles: Ed.: Ophthalmology Times Latin America (Spanish Edition); Ed.: Ophthalmology Times Latin America (Portuguese Edition); ◆ Regional ed(s).: Ophthalmology Times. ISSN 0193-032X; ◆ Ophthalmology Times China.
Published by: Advanstar Communications, Inc., 6200 Canoga Ave, 2nd Fl, Woodland Hills, CA 91367. TEL 818-593-5000, FAX 818-593-5020, info@advanstar.com, http://www.advanstar.com. Ed. Mark L Dlugoss TEL 440-891-2703. Pub. Lauri Jorgensen TEL 732-346-3013. adv.: B&W page USD 3,774, color page USD 5,629; trim 8 x 10.75. Circ: 15,146 (controlled).

617.7 IND
OPHTHALMOLOGY TODAY. Text in English. 19??. bi-m. **Document type:** *Journal, Academic/Scholarly.*
Published by: C M P Medica (Subsidiary of: C M P Medica Ltd.), Sagar Tech Plz A 615-617, 6th Fl, Andheri Kurla Rd, Saki Naka Jct, Andheri E, Mumbai, 400 072, India. TEL 91-22-66122600, FAX 91-22-66122626, info.india@ubm.com, mediworld@bol.net.in, http://www.ubmindia.in/cmp-medica.asp.

617.7 DEU ISSN 1436-2155
OPTIC UND VISION; Magazin fuer wertige Augenoptik. Text in German. 1998. bi-m. adv. **Document type:** *Magazine, Trade.*
Published by: Autentic.Info GmbH, Felder Str 15/3, Wangen, 88239, Germany. TEL 49-7522-931073, FAX 49-7522-771114, info@autentic.info, http://www.autentic.info. Ed. Susanne Wolters. Adv. contact Karin Burghardt. Circ: 12,000 (paid and controlled).

617.7 GBR ISSN 0969-0018
OPTICAL PRACTITIONER; the business magazine for optical management. Text in English. 1992. bi-m. adv. bk.rev. **Document type:** *Magazine, Trade.* **Description:** Geared to the development of the optical practice as an effectively managed and successful business.
—**CCC.**
Published by: Optical World Ltd., 200 London Rd, Southend-on-Sea, Essex SS1 1PJ, United Kingdom. TEL 44-1702-345443, FAX 44-1702-431806. Ed., R&P Gerald Ward. Adv. contact Russell Ward. B&W page USD 1,100; trim 11 x 8.25. Circ: 5,000.

617.7 CAN ISSN 0824-3441
OPTICAL PRISM; Canada's optical business magazine. Text in English. 1983. 10/yr. adv. bk.rev. back issues avail. **Document type:** *Magazine, Trade.* **Description:** Provides information on practice management as well as coverage of Canada's optical industry to Canadian optometrists, opticians, ophthalmologists, suppliers and their sales personnel.
Related titles: Online - full text ed.
Published by: Nusand Publishing Inc., 250 The East Mall Ste 1113, Toronto, ON M9B 6L3, Canada. TEL 416-233-2487, FAX 416-233-1746. Ed., R&P Robert May. Adv. contact Monika Raepple. B&W page USD 1,353, color page USD 2,050; trim 10.88 x 8.13. Circ: 11,500 (controlled).

617.7 GBR ISSN 0969-1952
RE1
OPTICAL WORLD. Text in English. 1947. 9/yr. GBP 85 domestic; EUR 180 in Europe; GBP 135 elsewhere (effective 2009). bk.rev. charts; illus. back issues avail. **Document type:** *Magazine, Trade.* **Description:** Provides in-depth technical articles, product information, previews and reports of the world's major ophthalmic exhibitions as well as company and personality profiles.
Supersedes in part (in 1972): Manufacturing Optics International (0025-2581); Which was formerly (until 1969): Manufacturing Optician International; (until 1966): Manufacturing Optician
Related titles: Online - full text ed.: free (effective 2009).
—**CCC.**
Published by: Optical World Ltd., 258a Fairfax Dr, Westcliff-on-Sea, Essex SS0 9EJ, United Kingdom. TEL 44-1702-345443, FAX 44-1702-431806. Ed., Pub. Gerald Ward.

617.7 GBR ISSN 0030-3968
OPTICIAN; the weekly journal for optometrists and dispensing opticians. Text in English. 1891. w. GBP 199 domestic; EUR 300 in Europe; USD 350 elsewhere (effective 2010); subscr. includes Optician Directory. adv. bk.rev. back issues avail.; reprints avail. **Document type:** *Magazine, Trade.* **Description:** Contains exclusive news reports, clinical and technical features, practice management, new products, frames, and continuing education and training projects.
Former titles (until 1932): Optician and Scientific Instrument Maker; (until 1916): Optician and Photographic Trade Journal
Related titles: Online - full text ed.
Indexed: A01, A03, A15, A22, ABIn, B02, B07, B15, B17, B18, BRD, G03, G04, G06, G07, G08, GSA, GSI, HECAB, I05, Inspec, P30, P34, P48, P51, PQC, S04, S06, T02, W03, W05.
—BLDSC (6273.400000), IE, Ingenta. **CCC.**
Published by: Reed Business Information Ltd. (Subsidiary of: Reed Business), Quadrant House, The Quadrant, Sutton, Surrey SM2 5AS, United Kingdom. TEL 44-20-86523500, FAX 44-20-86528932, rbi.subscriptions@qss-uk.com, http://www.reedbusiness.co.uk/. Ed. Chris Bennett TEL 44-20-86528250. Adv. contact Lara Phelps TEL 44-20-86528755. page GBP 2,648; trim 210 x 297. **Subscr. to:** Quadrant Subscription Services, PO Box 302, Haywards Heath, W Sussex RH16 3YY, United Kingdom. qss.customer.services@quadrantsubs.com, http://www.quadrantsubs.com.

617.7 GBR ISSN 1474-6247
RE981
OPTICIAN DIRECTORY. Text in English. 1903. a. included with subscr. to Optician. adv. bibl.; stat. **Document type:** *Directory, Trade.*
Former titles (until 2001): Optical Yearbook (1357-9576); (until 1994): International Optical Year Book and Diary (1357-9568); (until 1976): British & International Optical Year Book (1357-972X); (until 1975): Optical Year Book
Related titles: Online - full text ed.
—**CCC.**
Published by: Reed Business Information Ltd. (Subsidiary of: Reed Business), Quadrant House, The Quadrant, Sutton, Surrey SM2 5AS, United Kingdom. TEL 44-20-86523500, FAX 44-20-86528932, rbi.subscriptions@qss-uk.com, http://www.reedbusiness.co.uk/. Ed. Chris Bennett TEL 44-20-86528250.

617.7 NLD ISSN 1570-8276
DE OPTICIEN; vakinformatie voor de totale optiek- en contactlensbranche. Text in Dutch. 2002. bi-m. EUR 42 domestic; EUR 51 in Europe (effective 2009). adv. **Document type:** *Magazine, Trade.*
Published by: GPmedia BV, Spoorstraat 152, Gennep, 6591 GW, Netherlands. TEL 31-485-540300, FAX 31-485-540411, info@gpmedia.nl, http://www.gpmedia.nl. Ed. Else Witten. Pub. Peter Peeters. Adv. contact Gerdo van de Peppel. B&W page EUR 1,340, color page EUR 2,335; 240 x 340. Circ: 2,800.

617.7 SWE
OPTIK. Text in Swedish. 1979. m. bk.rev. 3 cols./p.; back issues avail. **Document type:** *Magazine, Trade.*
Formerly (until 2005): Aktuell Optik och Optometri (0348-5730); Incorporates (1976-1986): Kontaktlinsaktuellt (0348-0097); (1956-1978): Aktuell Optik
Related titles: Online - full text ed.
Published by: (Optikerfoerbundet/Swedish Optometric Association SOR), Optikbranschen, Karlbergsvaegen 22, Stockholm, 11327, Sweden. TEL 46-8-6128960, FAX 46-8-6125690, kansli@optikbranschen.se. Ed. Micke Jaresand TEL 46-8-41066471. Adv. contact Lennart Uhlman TEL 46-8-50893800.

617.75 DNK ISSN 0900-2944
OPTIKEREN. Text in Danish. 1962. 6/yr. DKK 350 (effective 2008). adv. bk.rev. **Document type:** *Magazine, Trade.*
Formerly (until 1970): Specialoptikeren
Related titles: Online - full text ed.: 2007.
Published by: Danmarks Optikerforening, Vester Voldgade 96, Copenhagen V, 1552, Denmark. TEL 45-45-861533, FAX 45-45-766576. Ed. Bjarne Hansen TEL 45-45-162699.

617.752 ESP
OPTIMODA. Text in Spanish. 1994. m. (11/yr.). adv. back issues avail. **Document type:** *Magazine, Trade.* **Description:** Covers the optical industry: frames, lenses, machinery and accessories.
Published by: Astoria Ediciones S.L., Calle Girona 148 4o-2o, Barcelona, 08037, Spain. TEL 34-93-4581900, FAX 34-93-4592513, info@astoriaediciones.com, http://www.astoriaediciones.com/. Ed. Jose Martin. Adv. contact David Martin. Circ: 5,200 (paid).

617.75 DEU
OPTOINDEX. Text in German. 1991. a. adv. **Document type:** *Directory, Trade.*
Published by: MediaWelt Produktions und Agentur GmbH, Papiermuehlenweg 74, Ratingen, 40882, Germany. TEL 49-2102-1678000, FAX 49-2102-1678020, joerg.spangemacher@mediawelt-services.de, http://www.mediawelt-services.de. adv.: B&W page EUR 2,604, color page EUR 4,164. Circ: 13,600 (paid and controlled).

617.75 535 BEL
OPTOMAGAZINE. Text in French. 1970. 6/yr. EUR 45 domestic; EUR 60 foreign (effective 2005). adv. Supplement avail. **Document type:** *Newsletter.* **Description:** Covers optometry, contact lenses and business related matters.
Formerly: Association Professionnelle des Opticiens de Belgique. Bulletin d'Information Mensuel
Related titles: Dutch ed.
Published by: Algemene Professionele Opticiens en Optometristenbond van Belgie/Association Professionnelle des Opticiens et Optometristes de Belgique, Rue Capitaine Crespel 26, Brussels, 1050, Belgium. TEL 32-2-512-5526, FAX 32-2-502-3402. Ed. Ph Carlier. R&P B. Denis. Adv. contact B Denis. Circ: 2,500.

617.7 FIN ISSN 1456-7407
OPTOMETRIA. Text in Finnish. 1996. 5/yr. adv. bk.rev. **Document type:** *Journal, Trade.*
Formerly (until 1999): Uusi Optikko (1455-1586); Which was formed by the merger of (1960-1996): Optikko (0048-2021); (1984-1996): Pupilli (0781-3325)
Published by: Optiikka Media Oy, Paciuksenkatu 19, Helsinki, 00270, Finland. TEL 358-9-47335473, FAX 358-9-47335479, omo@optometria.fi. Ed., R&P Ilkka Liukkonen. Adv. contact Tarja Paussoi. Circ: 2,500.

617.175 ESP ISSN 1885-4052
OPTOMETRIA INFORMACION (CASTILLA Y LEON EDITION). Text in Spanish. 2004. q. **Document type:** *Bulletin, Consumer.*
Related titles: ◆ Supplement to: Gaceta Optica. ISSN 0210-5284.
Published by: Colegio Profesional de Opticos Optometristas de Castilla y Leon, Pasaje de la Marquesina, 9, Valladolid, 47004, Spain. TEL 34-983-298435, 34-983-391644, coocyle@coocyl.es, http://www.cnoo.es/.

617.175 ESP ISSN 1885-4060
OPTOMETRIA INFORMATION (CASTILLA-LA MANCHA, EXTREMADURA Y MADRID EDITION). Text in Spanish. 2004. q. back issues avail. **Document type:** *Bulletin, Consumer.*
Related titles: ◆ Supplement to: Gaceta Optica. ISSN 0210-5284.
Published by: Colegio Profesional de Opticos Optometristas de Espana, Primera Delegacion Regional, Jose Ortega y Gasset, 74 1o. A, Madrid, 28006, Spain. TEL 34-91-4015029, FAX 34-91-3091736, dr1@cnoo.es, http://www.cnoo.es/index.php.

617.7 USA ISSN 1933-8880
OPTOMETRIC EDUCATION (ONLINE). Text in English. 1991. 3/yr. free (effective 2011). **Document type:** *Journal, Academic/Scholarly.* **Description:** Publishes scholarly reports, papers, and other timely, informative materials relative to optometric education and professional health education.
Media: Online - full text.
Published by: Association of Schools and Colleges of Optometry, 6110 Executive Blvd, Ste 420, Rockville, MD 20852. TEL 301-231-5944, FAX 301-770-1828, pororurke@opted.org.

617.75 USA ISSN 0030-4085
OPTOMETRIC MANAGEMENT; the business and marketing magazine for optometry. Text in English. 1965. m. USD 42 domestic; USD 51 in Canada; USD 90 elsewhere; free to qualified personnel (effective 2010). charts; illus.; tr.lit. index. back issues avail.; reprints avail. **Document type:** *Magazine, Trade.* **Description:** Dedicated to helping optometrists improve their practice through relevant, actionable and practical columns that enhance patient outcomes and bolster the bottom line.
Related titles: Microform ed.: (from PQC); Online - full text ed.
Indexed: CA, P16, P48, P53, P54, PQC, T02.
—**CCC.**

Published by: Lippincott Williams & Wilkins, VisionCare Group (Subsidiary of: Lippincott Williams & Wilkins), 323 Norristown Rd, Ste 200, Ambler, PA 19002. TEL 215-646-8700, http://www.visioncareprofessional.com/. Ed. Jim Thomas TEL 215-367-2172. Pub. Roger Zimmer TEL 203-846-2827.

617.75 DEU ISSN 0030-4123
OPTOMETRIE. Text in German. 1952. q. EUR 49 (effective 2010). adv. bk.rev. charts; illus.; stat. index. **Document type:** *Magazine, Trade.*
Indexed: RASB.
—GNLM.
Published by: Wissenschaftliche Vereinigung fuer Augenoptik und Optometrie e.V., Mainzer Str 176, Mainz, 55124, Germany. TEL 49-6131-613061, FAX 49-6131-614872, info@wvao.org. Ed. Hartmut Glaser. adv.: B&W page EUR 1,750, color page EUR 2,400; trim 184 x 251. Circ: 2,500 (controlled).

617.7 CAN ISSN 0708-3173
L'OPTOMETRISTE. Text in English. 1978. 6/yr. free to qualified personnel. adv. **Document type:** *Journal, Trade.* **Description:** News for French speaking optometrists in Quebec.
Published by: Association des Optometristes du Quebec, 1265 Berri St, local 740, Montreal, PQ H2L 4X4, Canada. TEL 514-288-6272, FAX 514-288-7071. Ed. Dr. Jean Pierre Lagace. R&P, Adv. contact Lucie English. B&W page CAD 975, color page CAD 1,125; trim 10.88 x 8.13. Circ: 3,400.

617.75 USA
OPTOMETRIST'S PATIENT NEWSLETTER. Text in English. 1988. q. price varies. index. **Document type:** *Newsletter, Trade.* **Description:** Offers relationship marketing through newsletters.
Published by: Newsletters Ink, Corp., 450 N Prince St, P O Box 4008, Lancaster, PA 17604. TEL 717-393-1000, 800-379-5585, FAX 717-393-4702, info@newslettersink.com, http://www.newslettersink.com. Pub. Lynn McDowell.

617.75 USA ISSN 1557-4113
RE1
➤ **OPTOMETRY AND VISION DEVELOPMENT.** Abbreviated title: O V D. Text in English. 1970. q. free to members (effective 2010). adv. bk.rev. abstr.; charts; illus.; bibl. index. back issues avail.; reprints avail. **Document type:** *Journal, Academic/Scholarly.*
Former titles (until 2005): Journal of Optometric Vision Development (0149-886X); (until 1976): Journal of Optometric Vision Therapy (0149-8940); (until 1975): Journal of Optometric Vision Development (0099-1171); (until 1974): Journal of Optometric Vision Therapy (0091-4177)
Related titles: Online - full text ed.: free (effective 2011).
Indexed: A01, A22, BibInd, CA, CDA, E-psyche, ECER, P03, PsycInfo, PsycholAb, T02.
—BLDSC (6276.440500), GNLM, IE. **CCC.**
Published by: College of Optometrists in Vision Development, 215 W Garfield Rd, Ste 200, Aurora, OH 44202. TEL 330-995-0718, 888-268-3770, FAX 330-995-0719, info@covd.org. Ed. Dominick M Maino TEL 312-949-7282. Adv. contact Jackie Cencer.

617.75 USA ISSN 1040-5488
RE939.2 CODEN: OVSCET
➤ **OPTOMETRY AND VISION SCIENCE.** Text in English. 1924. m. USD 606 domestic to institutions; USD 814 foreign to institutions (effective 2011). adv. bk.rev. abstr.; bibl.; charts; illus.; stat. index. back issues avail.; reprints avail. **Document type:** *Journal, Academic/Scholarly.* **Description:** Presents research and clinical findings in optometry, as well as case reports and instrument and technique reviews.
Former titles (until 1989): American Journal of Optometry and Physiological Optics (0093-7002); (until 1974): American Journal of Optometry and Archives of American Academy of Optometry (0002-9408); (until 1941): The American Journal of Optometry (0271-4469); (until 1925): Northwest Journal of Optometry
Related titles: Online - full text ed.: ISSN 1538-9235.
Indexed: A20, A22, ASCA, C06, C07, CISA, CPEI, CurCont, EMBASE, EngInd, ExcerpMed, FR, IBR, IBZ, ISR, IndMed, Inpharma, Inspec, MEDLINE, P30, P35, PsycholAb, R10, Reac, SCI, SCOPUS, SPPI, TM, W07.
—BLDSC (6276.450000), AskIEEE, GNLM, IE, Infotrieve, Ingenta, INIST. **CCC.**
Published by: (American Academy of Optometry), Lippincott Williams & Wilkins (Subsidiary of: Wolters Kluwer N.V.), 530 Walnut St, Philadelphia, PA 19106. TEL 215-521-8300, FAX 215-521-8902, customerservice@lww.com, http://www.lww.com. Ed. Anthony J Adams. Pub. Nina J Chang.

➤ **OPTOMETRY CODING & BILLING ALERT.** *see* INSURANCE

617.175 GBR ISSN 1467-9051
➤ **OPTOMETRY IN PRACTICE.** Text in English. 2000. q. free to members (effective 2009). **Document type:** *Journal, Academic/Scholarly.* **Description:** Provides articles of interest to practising optometrists.
Incorporates (in 200?): In Focus
—BLDSC (6276.470000), IE, Ingenta.
Published by: (College of Optometrists), Distance Learning (UK) Ltd., PO Box 6, Skelmersdale, Lancs WN8 9FW, United Kingdom. TEL 44-1695-554209, FAX 44-1695-554210, http://www.distance-learning-uk.net/. Ed. Stephen Parrish. Circ: 86,000.

617.75 USA ISSN 1529-1839
RE1 CODEN: JAOPBD
➤ **OPTOMETRY - JOURNAL OF THE AMERICAN OPTOMETRIC ASSOCIATION.** Text in English. 1929. m. USD 258 in United States to institutions; USD 317 elsewhere to institutions (effective 2012). adv. bk.rev. abstr.; charts; illus.; stat.; tr.lit. index. back issues avail.; reprints avail. **Document type:** *Journal, Academic/Scholarly.* **Description:** Covers a range of topics with an emphasis in primary care optometry, contact lenses, sports vision, low vision, pharmaceuticals, and practice enhancement.
Formerly (until 2000): American Optometric Association. Journal (0003-0244)
Related titles: Online - full text ed.: ISSN 1558-1527 (from ScienceDirect).
Indexed: A22, A26, A29, B20, B21, C06, C07, CA, CTA, ChemoAb, DokArb, E-psyche, EMBASE, ESPM, ExcerpMed, FR, I05, I10, INI, IndMed, Inspec, MEDLINE, NSA, P03, P30, PsycholAb, R10, Reac, SCOPUS, T02, VirolAbstr.
—BLDSC (6276.440000), GNLM, IE, Infotrieve, Ingenta, INIST. **CCC.**

Published by: (American Optometric Association), Elsevier Inc. (Subsidiary of: Elsevier Science & Technology), 1600 John F Kennedy Blvd, Philadelphia, PA 19103. TEL 215-239-3900, FAX 215-238-7883, JournalCustomerService-usa@elsevier.com, http://www.elsevier.com. Ed. Paul B Freeman TEL 412-749-2568. Adv. contact Aileen Rivera TEL 212-633-3721. Circ: 28,230.

617.7 GBR ISSN 1757-6148
THE OPTOMETRY RED BOOK. Text in English. 2008. s-a. **Document type:** *Journal, Academic/Scholarly.* **Description:** Provides references about optometry in Scotland and Northern Ireland.
Published by: (Association of Optometrists), Ten Alps Publishing (Subsidiary of: Ten Alps Group), One New Oxford St, London, WC1A 1NU, United Kingdom. TEL 44-20-78782300, FAX 44-20-73797118, info@tenalpspublishing.com, http://www.tenalpspublishing.com. Ed. David Challinor TEL 44-20-72028164. Adv. contact Vanya Palczewski TEL 44-20-78782347.

617.7 ITA ISSN 2039-473X
▼ ➤ **OPTOMETRY REPORTS.** Text in English. 2010. irreg. **Document type:** *Journal, Academic/Scholarly.*
Media: Online - full text.
Published by: Pagepress, Via Giuseppe Belli 4, Pavia, 27100, Italy. TEL 39-0382-1751762, FAX 39-0382-1750481, http://www.pagepress.org. Ed. Raul Martin Herranz.

617.75 USA
▼ **OPTOMETRY TIMES.** Text in English. 2009. 9/yr. USD 49 domestic; USD 59 in Canada & Mexico; USD 89 elsewhere; USD 9 newsstand/cover domestic; USD 11 newsstand/cover in Canada & Mexico; USD 14 newsstand/cover elsewhere (effective 2011). adv. **Document type:** *Magazine, Trade.* **Description:** Disseminates news and information of a clinical, scientific, socioeconomic, and political nature in a timely and accurate manner for members of the optometry community.
Related titles: Online - full text ed.
Indexed: CA.
Published by: Advanstar Communications, Inc., 6200 Canoga Ave, 2nd Fl, Woodland Hills, CA 91367. TEL 818-593-5000, FAX 818-593-5020, info@advanstar.com, http://www.advanstar.com. Ed. Mark Dlugoss TEL 440-891-2703. Pub. Lauri Jorgensen TEL 732-346-3013. adv.: B&W page USD 4,460, color page USD 6,815; trim 9 x 12. Circ: 35,187.

617.7 IND ISSN 0048-203X
OPTOMETRY TODAY; eye and hearing-care quarterly journal. Text in English. 196?. q. INR 680 (effective 2011). bk.rev. abstr.; bibl.; tr.lit. reprints avail. **Document type:** *Journal, Academic/Scholarly.* **Description:** Covers information about ophthalmic medicine.
Incorporates (1977-2003): Hearing Aid Journal (0971-0949); Former titles (until 1970): Indian Optometric Association. Journal (0378-8164); (until 1969): Indian Journal of Optometry
Related titles: Microform ed.: (from PQC).
—BLDSC (6276.500000).
Published by: Dr. Narendra Kumar Ed. & Pub., C4F/216, Janakpuri, New Delhi, 110 058, India. TEL 91-11-25599839, FAX 91-11-25612301, kumars@vsnl.com.

617.7 GBR ISSN 0268-5485
RE1
➤ **OPTOMETRY TODAY**; optometry today/optics today. Abbreviated title: O T. Text in English. 1961. fortn. GBP 130 domestic to non-members; GBP 175 foreign to non-members; free to members (effective 2009). adv. bk.rev. 60 p./no. 3 cols./p.; back issues avail. **Document type:** *Journal, Trade.* **Description:** Provides all optometrists, dispensing opticians, key personnel in the industry, political bodies and students in the UK as well as overseas practitioners with all the latest news and information in the market place.
Formerly (until 1985): Ophthalmic Optician (0030-3739); Which was formed by the merger of (195?-1961): Association of Optometrists News; Which was formerly (19??-195?): A O P Newsletter; (1930-1961): Dioptric News
Related titles: Online - full text ed.
Indexed: A01, A26, CISA, H12, HECAB, I05.
—BLDSC (6276.480000), GNLM, IE, Ingenta. **CCC.**
Published by: (Association of Optometrists, Words and Images), Ten Alps Publishing (Subsidiary of: Ten Alps Group), Trelawney House, Chestergate, Macclesfield, Cheshire SK11 6DW, United Kingdom. TEL 44-1625-613000, FAX 44-1625-511446, info@tenalpspublishing.com, http://www.tenalpspublishing.com. Ed. David Challinor TEL 44-20-72028164. Adv. contact Vanya Palczewski TEL 44-20-78782347. page GBP 2,730; trim 210 x 297. Circ: 19,442.

617.7 616.21 GBR ISSN 0167-6830
CODEN: CONRD3
➤ **ORBIT.** Text in English. 1981. bi-m. GBP 590, EUR 780, USD 975 combined subscription to institutions (print & online eds.); GBP 1,180, EUR 1,555, USD 1,945 combined subscription to corporations (print & online eds.) (effective 2010). adv. bk.rev. index, cum.index. back issues avail.; reprint service avail. from PSC. **Document type:** *Journal, Academic/Scholarly.* **Description:** Contains review articles, research papers, and short communications on orbital disorders, ophthalmology, otolaryngology, reconstructive and maxillofacial surgery, endocrinology, radiology, radiotherapy, oncology, neurology, neuro-ophthalmology, neurosurgery, pathology, immunology, and hematology.
Related titles: Microform ed.; Online - full text ed.: ISSN 1744-5108 (from IngentaConnect).
Indexed: A01, A03, A08, A22, CA, E01, EMBASE, ExcerpMed, MEDLINE, P30, R10, Reac, S&VD, SCOPUS, T02.
—BLDSC (6277.869600), GNLM, IE, Infotrieve, Ingenta. **CCC.**
Published by: (International Society on Orbital Disorders NLD), Informa Healthcare (Subsidiary of: T & F Informa plc), Telephone House, 69-77 Paul St, London, EC2A 4LQ, United Kingdom. TEL 44-20-70175000, FAX 44-20-70176792, healthcare.enquiries@informa.com. Ed. David H Verity. **Subscr. to:** Taylor & Francis Inc., Customer Services Dept, 325 Chestnut St, 8th Fl, Philadelphia, PA 19106. TEL 215-625-8900, 800-354-1420, FAX 215-625-8914, customerservice@taylorandfrancis.com; Taylor & Francis Ltd., Journals Customer Service, Sheepen Pl, Colchester, Essex CO3 3LP, United Kingdom. TEL 44-20-70175544, FAX 44-20-70175198. **Co-sponsor:** European Society for Orbital Plastic and Reconstructive Surgery.

617.7 ITA
OTTICO. Text in Italian. 1975 (no.114). bi-m. adv. bk.rev. charts; illus. **Document type:** *Magazine, Trade.*
Published by: Associazione Italiana Ottici, Via Giusti 2, Sesto Fiorentino, FI 50019, Italy. http://www.associazioneitalianaottici.it.

617.7 ARG ISSN 1515-7202
PAGINAS DE ACTUALIZACION EN OFTALMOLOGIA. Text in Spanish. 2000. bi-m. back issues avail.
Media: Online - full text.
Published by: Consejo Argentino de Oftalmologia, Tte. Gral. Juan D. Peron 725, 6o. Piso, Buenos Aires, 1038, Argentina. TEL 54-114-3255553, FAX 54-114-3250128, secretaria@oftalmologos.org.ar, http://www.oftalmologos.org.ar/.

PERCEPTION. *see* PSYCHOLOGY

617.7 PHL ISSN 0031-7659
RE1
PHILIPPINE JOURNAL OF OPHTHALMOLOGY. Text in English. 1969. q. PHP 500, USD 20 (effective 2003). adv. bk.rev. abstr. index. 50 p./no. 2 cols./p.; reprints avail. **Document type:** *Journal, Academic/Scholarly.*
Related titles: CD-ROM ed.; Microform ed.: (from PQC).
Indexed: ChemAb, ExtraMED, OphLit, P30.
—GNLM.
Published by: Philippine Academy of Ophthalmology, Unit 15 Medical Plaza Makati, Amorsold Cor. Dela Rosa Streets, Legaspi Village, Makati City, 1209, Philippines. TEL 63-2-8135324, FAX 63-2-8135331, pao@pao.org.ph, http://www.pao.org.ph. Ed. Dr. Rossina Lydia A Ramirez. adv.: page USD 120. Circ: 1,000.

617.7 USA ISSN 1535-461X
RE994
PHYSICIANS' DESK REFERENCE FOR OPHTHALMIC MEDICINES. Variant title: P D R Ophthalmic Medicines. Text in English. 1972. a. USD 69.95 per issue (effective 2010). **Document type:** *Monographic series, Trade.* **Description:** Contains product information relating to optometry and ophthalmology.
Formerly (until 2001): Physicians' Desk Reference for Ophthalmology (0091-6803)
Related titles: Online - full text ed.
—**CCC.**
Published by: Thomson P D R, Five Paragon Dr, Montvale, NJ 07645. TEL 888-227-6469, FAX 201-722-2680, TH.customerservice@thomson.com, http://www.pdr.net.

PITTSBURGH VISION SERVICES. NEWSLETTER. *see* HANDICAPPED—Visually Impaired

617.7 FRA ISSN 2106-9735
PRATIQUES EN OPHTALMOLOGIE; revue didactique medico-chirurgicale. Text in French. 2007. m. **Document type:** *Journal, Trade.*
Formerly (until 2010): Ophtalmologies (1956-2594)
Published by: Expressions Groupe, 2 Rue de la Roquette, Cour de Mai, Paris, 75011, France. TEL 33-1-49292929, FAX 33-1-49292919, contact@expressions-sante.fr.

617.7 USA ISSN 2153-1951
▼ **PREMIER SURGEON**; enhancing your pratice of opthalmology. Text in English. 2010. bi-m. free (effective 2010). **Document type:** *Journal, Trade.* **Description:** The information source for cataract and refractive surgeons who strive to be market leaders in the arena of premium Intraocular Lens (IOL) and who wishe to provide unparalleled patient care and outcomes.
Published by: Slack, Inc., 6900 Grove Rd, Thorofare, NJ 08086. TEL 609-848-1000, FAX 856-848-6091, customerservice@slackinc.com, http://www.slackinc.com.

PREVENT BLINDNESS NEWS. *see* PUBLIC HEALTH AND SAFETY

617.75 USA ISSN 1081-6437
RE1
PRIMARY CARE OPTOMETRY NEWS. Text in English. 1996. m. USD 299 to individuals; USD 479 to institutions; USD 39 per issue (effective 2010). adv. 44 p./no.; back issues avail.; reprints avail. **Document type:** *Newspaper, Academic/Scholarly.* **Description:** Provides information related to clinical and socioeconomic developments in the field of optometry.
Indexed: A01, P20, P48, P54, PQC.
—**CCC.**
Published by: Slack, Inc., 6900 Grove Rd, Thorofare, NJ 08086. TEL 856-848-1000, FAX 856-848-6091, customerservice@slackinc.com, http://www.slackinc.com. Eds. Michael D DePaolis, Nancy Hemphill.

617.7 GBR ISSN 1350-9462
QP479 CODEN: PRTRES
➤ **PROGRESS IN RETINAL AND EYE RESEARCH.** Text in English. 1982. 6/yr. EUR 1,217 in Europe to institutions; JPY 161,400 in Japan to institutions; USD 1,361 elsewhere to institutions (effective 2012). back issues avail. **Document type:** *Journal, Academic/Scholarly.* **Description:** Covers Information on relevant developments and current advances in retinal science for clinicians and scientists.
Formerly (until 1994): Progress in Retinal Research (0278-4327)
Related titles: Microfilm ed.: (from PQC); Online - full text ed.: ISSN 1873-1635 (from IngentaConnect, ScienceDirect).
Indexed: A01, A03, A08, A22, A26, ASCA, B21, BIOBASE, C06, C07, CA, ChemAb, ChemTitl, CurCont, EMBASE, ExcerpMed, I05, IABS, ISR, IndMed, Inpharma, MEDLINE, NSA, NSCI, P30, R10, Reac, SCI, SCOPUS, T02, W07.
—BLDSC (6924.525590), CASDDS, GNLM, IE, Infotrieve, Ingenta, INIST. **CCC.**
Published by: Pergamon (Subsidiary of: Elsevier Science & Technology), The Blvd, Langford Ln, East Park, Kidlington, Oxford OX5 1GB, United Kingdom. TEL 44-1865-843000, FAX 44-1865-843010, JournalsCustomerServiceEMEA@elsevier.com. Eds. Gerald J Chader, Dr. Neville N Osborne. **Subscr. to:** Elsevier BV, Radarweg 29, PO Box 211, Amsterdam 1000 AE, Netherlands. TEL 31-20-4853757, FAX 31-20-4853432, http://www.elsevier.nl.

617.7 FRA ISSN 1242-0018
REALITES OPHTALMOLOGIQUES. Text in French. 1992. m. EUR 52 domestic to qualified personnel; EUR 42 domestic to students; EUR 65 foreign (effective 2008). **Document type:** *Journal, Trade.*
Published by: Performances Medicales, 91 Av. de la Republique, Paris, 75011, France. TEL 33-1-47006714, FAX 33-1-47006999.

617.7 USA
RE22
RED BOOK OF OPHTHALMOLOGISTS. Text in English. 1915. biennial. USD 125. adv. **Document type:** *Directory.*
Former titles (until 1996): Red Book of Ophthalmology (0146-4582); (until 1977): Red Book of Eye, Ear, Nose and Throat Specialists (0146-4590)
Published by: Jobson Publishing LLC, One Meadowlands Pl, Ste 1020, E Rutherford, NJ 07073. TEL 201-623-0999, FAX 201-623-0991, http://www.jobson.com.

617.7 USA ISSN 1931-7905
REFRACTIVE EYECARE. Text in English. 1997 (Sum.). m. USD 139 domestic; USD 169 in Canada & Mexico; USD 205 elsewhere (effective 2010). adv. back issues avail.; reprints avail. **Document type:** *Journal, Trade.* **Description:** Contains articles which focuses on clinical and management topics, with an emphasis on improving both clinical outcomes and bottom line results.
Formerly (until Aug.2005): Refractive Eyecare for Ophthalmologists (1094-6616)
Related titles: Online - full text ed.
Published by: Ethis Communications, Inc., 75 Maiden Ln, Ste 408, New York, NY 10038. TEL 212-791-1440, FAX 212-791-4980, http://ethiscommunications.com/. Eds. Robert C Campbell, David Kellner. Pub. LaVon Kellner TEL 212-791-1440.

617.7 USA ISSN 0275-004X
RE501 CODEN: RETIDX
➤ **RETINA**; the journal of retinal and vitreous diseases. Text in English. 1981. 10/yr. USD 911 domestic to institutions; USD 1,007 foreign to institutions (effective 2011). adv. illus. Index. back issues avail.; reprints avail. **Document type:** *Journal, Academic/Scholarly.* **Description:** Provides information on diagnostic and therapeutic techniques.
Related titles: Microform ed.: (from PQC); Online - full text ed.: ISSN 1539-2864.
Indexed: A22, A36, ASCA, B25, BIOSIS Prev, CABA, CurCont, DentInd, E12, EMBASE, ExcerpMed, GH, H17, IBR, IBZ, ISR, IndMed, Inpharma, MEDLINE, MycolAb, N02, N03, NSCI, P30, P33, P35, P39, R08, R10, R13, RM&VM, Reac, SCI, SCOPUS, T05, W07.
—BLDSC (7785.510300), GNLM, IE, Ingenta. **CCC.**
Published by: Lippincott Williams & Wilkins (Subsidiary of: Wolters Kluwer N.V.), 530 Walnut St, Philadelphia, PA 19106. TEL 215-521-8300, FAX 215-521-8902, customerservice@lww.com, http://www.lww.com. Ed. Dr. Alexander J Brucker. Pub. Nina J Chang. Circ: 2,237.

617.7 USA ISSN 1942-1257
RETINA TODAY. Text in English. 2006. 8/yr. free to qualified personnel. adv. **Document type:** *Journal, Academic/Scholarly.* **Description:** Delivers the latest research and clinical developments from areas such as medical retina, retinal surgery, vitreous, diabetes, retinal imaging, posterior segment oncology and ocular trauma.
Related titles: Online - full text ed.; Supplement(s):.
Published by: Bryn Mawr Communications, LLC (Subsidiary of: Bryn Mawr Communications Group LLC), 1008 Upper Gulph Rd, Ste 200, Wayne, PA 19087. TEL 484-581-1800, FAX 484-581-1818, http://www.bmctoday.com/. Ed. Rachel Renshaw TEL 484-581-1858. Pubs. Alan Guralnick TEL 484-581-1832, David Cox TEL 484-581-1814. adv.: color page USD 5,150; trim 8 x 10.75. Circ: 5,350.

617.7 ITA ISSN 1825-0572
RETINA TODAY. Text in Multiple languages. 2004. s-a. **Document type:** *Journal, Academic/Scholarly.*
Media: Online - full text.
Published by: Universita Vita-Salute San Raffaele, Via Olgettina 58, Milan, Italy. http://www.unisr.it.

617.7 TUR ISSN 1300-1256
➤ **RETINA - VITREUS/JOURNAL OF RETINA - VITREOUS.** Text in Turkish. 1993. q. TRY 150 to institutions; TRY 75 doctors (effective 2010). **Document type:** *Journal, Academic/Scholarly.* **Description:** Publishes articles related to retina and vitreous. It includes reviews, short editorials articles, original case reports and figures covering fundamental innovations dealing with education.
Related titles: Online - full text ed.: free (effective 2010); English ed.
Indexed: A01, CA, EMBASE, SCOPUS, T02.
Published by: Gazi Eye Foundation, Tuna Cad. No. 26/15, Larissa, Ankara, Turkey. TEL 90-312-4318480, FAX 90-312-4310946, abone@retinavitreus.com, yazisleri@glokomkatarakt.com, http://www.glokomkatarakt.com/. Ed. Berati Hasanreisoglu.

617.7 USA ISSN 1935-1089
➤ **RETINAL CASES & BRIEF REPORTS.** Text in English. 2007. q. USD 283 domestic to institutions; USD 306 foreign to institutions (effective 2011). adv. back issues avail.; reprints avail. **Document type:** *Journal, Academic/Scholarly.* **Description:** Designed for ophthalmologist to improve their diagnostic and therapeutic skills.
Related titles: Online - full text ed.: ISSN 1937-1578.
Indexed: CA, P30, T02.
—IE. **CCC.**
Published by: Lippincott Williams & Wilkins (Subsidiary of: Wolters Kluwer N.V.), 530 Walnut St, Philadelphia, PA 19106. TEL 215-238-4200, FAX 215-238-4227, customerservice@lww.com, http://www.lww.com. Ed. Dr. Alexander J Brucker. Pub. Nina J Chang. Circ: 469.

617.7 USA ISSN 1552-812X
RETINAL PHYSICIAN. Text in English. 2004. 9/yr. USD 98 domestic; USD 107 in Canada; USD 149 elsewhere; free to qualified personnel (effective 2010). back issues avail. **Document type:** *Journal, Academic/Scholarly.* **Description:** Focuses on current and future treatment strategies in medical and surgical retina care.
Indexed: CA, T02.
—**CCC.**
Published by: Lippincott Williams & Wilkins, VisionCare Group (Subsidiary of: Lippincott Williams & Wilkins), 323 Norristown Rd, Ste 200, Ambler, PA 19002. TEL 215-646-8700, http://www.visioncareprofessional.com/. Ed. Jim Thomas TEL 215-367-2172. Pub. Doug Parry TEL 215-628-7747.

617.7 FRA ISSN 1278-9534
LE RETINO. Text in French. 1992. q. EUR 46 membership; EUR 4 newsstand/cover (effective 2009). **Document type:** *Journal, Academic/Scholarly.*
Formerly (until 199?): Le Retinopathe (1166-2891)
—**CCC.**
Published by: Association Francaise Retinitis Pigmentosa, 2, Chemin du Cabirol, BP 62, Colomiers Cedex, 31771, France. TEL 33-810-302050, FAX 33-5-61789100, communication@retina.fr.

617.754 USA
REVIEW OF CORNEA AND CONTACT LENSES. Text in English. 9/yr. **Document type:** *Magazine, Trade.*
Indexed: H01, H02.
Published by: Jobson Optical Group (Subsidiary of: Jobson Publishing LLC), 100 Ave of the Americas, New York, NY 10013. TEL 212-274-7000, FAX 212-431-0500, info@jmihealth.com, http://www.jmihealth.com/.

617.7 USA ISSN 1081-0226
RE1
REVIEW OF OPHTHALMOLOGY. Text in English. 1994. m. USD 55 domestic; USD 85 in Canada; USD 135 elsewhere (effective 2007). adv. cum.index. back issues avail. **Document type:** *Magazine, Trade.* **Description:** Magazine for office and hospital ophthalmologists, residents and staff with information and research on clinical, patient care and practice management topics.
Incorporates (2000-2005): Review of Refractive Surgery (1559-4696)
Related titles: Online - full text ed.: ISSN 1945-6204.
Indexed: A01, A02, A03, A08, A26, C11, CA, H04, T02.
—BLDSC (7793.816000), IE, Ingenta. **CCC.**
Published by: Jobson Optical Group (Subsidiary of: Jobson Publishing LLC), 100 Ave of the Americas, New York, NY 10013. TEL 212-274-7000, FAX 212-274-0392, http://www.jobson.com. Ed. Christopher Glen. adv.: page USD 3,550, color page USD 5,770. Circ: 21,284 (controlled).

617.75 USA ISSN 1930-160X
RE1
REVIEW OF OPTOMETRY. Abbreviated title: R O. Text in English. 1910. m. USD 46 domestic; USD 70 in Canada; USD 136 elsewhere (effective 2009). adv. bk.rev. illus. Index. back issues avail.; reprints avail. **Document type:** *Magazine, Trade.* **Description:** Targets the professionals who provide eye care services as well as ophthalmic products such as frames, ophthalmic lenses and contact lenses.
Former titles (until 1998): Chilton's Review of Optometry (0147-7633); (until 1977): Optical Journal and Review of Optometry (0030-3925); Which was formed by the merger of (1907-1910): Optical Review; (1885-1910): Optical Journal (0092-6973); Which incorporated: Focus; Optical Instrument Monthly
Related titles: Microfiche ed.: (from PQC); Microfilm ed.: (from PQC); Online - full text ed.
Indexed: A01, A02, A03, A08, A15, A26, ABIn, C11, CA, E08, G08, H04, H11, H12, I05, P19, P30, P48, P51, PQC, S09, T02.
—BLDSC (7793.818000), IE, Ingenta. **CCC.**
Published by: Jobson Optical Group (Subsidiary of: Jobson Publishing LLC), 100 Ave of the Americas, New York, NY 10013. info@jmihealth.com, http://www.jmihealth.com/. Ed. Amy Hellem TEL 610-492-1006. Circ: 35,100 (controlled).

617.7 NLD ISSN 0168-8375
CODEN: ROCREC
➤ **REVIEWS OF OCULOMOTOR RESEARCH.** Text in English. 1985. irreg., latest vol.5, 1993. price varies. back issues avail. **Document type:** *Monographic series, Academic/Scholarly.* **Description:** Surveys new research in the oculomotor system.
Indexed: E-psyche, EMBASE, ExcerpMed, IndMed, MEDLINE, P30, R10, Reac.
—GNLM. **CCC.**
Published by: Elsevier BV (Subsidiary of: Elsevier Science & Technology), Radarweg 29, PO Box 211, Amsterdam, 1000 AE, Netherlands. TEL 31-20-4853911, FAX 31-20-4852457, JournalsCustomerServiceEMEA@elsevier.com, http://www.elsevier.nl. Eds. D A Robinson, H Collewijn.

617.7 BRA ISSN 0034-7280
RE1 CODEN: RBOFA9
REVISTA BRASILEIRA DE OFTALMOLOGIA. Text in Portuguese; Summaries in English. 1942. q. adv. bk.rev. abstr.; bibl. index. **Document type:** *Journal, Academic/Scholarly.*
Related titles: Online - full text ed.: free (effective 2011).
Indexed: ChemAb, IBR, IBZ, IndMed, P30, SCI, SCOPUS, W07.
—GNLM.
Published by: Sociedade Brasileira de Oftalmologia, Rua Sao Salvador 107, Laranjeiras, Rio de Janeiro, RJ 22231-170, Brazil. TEL 55-21-22057728, FAX 55-21-22052240, http://www.sboportal.org.br. Ed. Riuitiro Yamane.

617.7 COL ISSN 1692-8415
REVISTA CIENCIA Y TECNOLOGIA PARA LA SALUD VISUAL Y OCULAR. Text in Spanish. 2003. s-a. back issues avail. **Document type:** *Journal, Academic/Scholarly.*
Published by: Universidad de la Salle, Facultad de Optometria, Sede Chapinero, Cra. 5 No. 59A-44, Edif. Administrativo Piso 3ro., Bogota, Colombia. TEL 57-1-3488000 ext. 1224, FAX 57-1-2170885, publicaciones@lasalle.edu.co, http://www.lasalle.edu.co/. Ed. Jairo Garcia Touchie.

618 CUB ISSN 0864-2176
REVISTA CUBANA DE OFTALMOLOGIA. Text in Spanish; Summaries in English, Spanish, Portuguese. 1995. s-a. USD 34 in North America; USD 42 in Europe; USD 50 elsewhere (effective 2006). back issues avail. **Document type:** *Journal, Academic/Scholarly.* **Description:** Covers ophthalmology and, in particular, the treatment of pigmentary retinosis.
Related titles: Online - full text ed.: ISSN 1561-3070. 1995. free (effective 2011).
Indexed: A01, C01, CA, T02.
Published by: (Centro Nacional de Informacion de Ciencias Medicas (C N I C M), Cuba. Ministerio de Salud Publica), Editorial Ciencias Medicas, Linea Esq 1, 10o, Vedado, Havana, 10400, Cuba. TEL 53-7-8323863, ecimed@infomed.sld.cu. Ed. Grisell Concepcion. Circ: 1,000. **Co-sponsor:** Sociedad Cubana de Oftalmologia.

617.7 MEX ISSN 0187-4519
CODEN: RMOFEM
➤ **REVISTA MEXICANA DE OFTALMOLOGIA.** Text in Spanish; Abstracts in English, Spanish. 1987. bi-m. MXN 500 domestic; USD 80 foreign (effective 2006). adv. index. back issues avail. **Document type:** *Journal, Academic/Scholarly.* **Description:** Contains original research articles and clinical studies.
Formed by the merger of (1890-1987): Sociedad Mexicana de Oftalmologia. Anales (0185-4224); (1942-1987): Asociacion para Evitar la Ceguera de Mexico. Archivos (0004-489X)
Related titles: Online - full text ed.
Indexed: C01, SCOPUS.
—GNLM.
Published by: Sociedad Mexicana de Oftalmologia, Boston No. 99, Mexico, Col. Noche Buena, Mexico, D.F., 03720, Mexico. revistamexoftal@smo.org.mx. Ed. Rogelio Herreman. Circ: 1,500. **Subscr. to:** Composicion Editorial Laser, S.A. de C.V., LAGO ABERTO 442-7, Col. Anahuac, Mexico City, DF 11320, Mexico. TEL 525-2600250, FAX 525-2600048.

617.7 VEN ISSN 0484-8039
REVISTA OFTALMOLOGICA VENEZOLANA. Text in Spanish. 1955. 3/yr. **Document type:** *Journal, Academic/Scholarly.*
Indexed: C01.
Published by: Sociedad Venezolana de Oftalmologia, Av Principal de los Ruices, Centro Empresarial de los Ruices, Piso 5o, Of 507, Caracas, Venezuela. TEL 58-212-2398127, svo@svo.org.ve, http://www.svo.org.ve.

617.7 PER ISSN 1810-8482
REVISTA PERUANA DE OFTALMOLOGIA. Text in Spanish. 199?. irreg. **Document type:** *Journal, Academic/Scholarly.*
Published by: Sociedad Peruana de Oftalmologia, Parque Luis F Villaran 957, San Isidro, Lima, Peru. TEL 51-1-4406740, FAX 51-1-4402698, http://www.spo.org.pe.

617.7 362.41 GBR ISSN 1993-7210
➤ **REVUE DE SANTE OCULAIRE COMMUNAUTAIRE.** Text in French. 2004. s-a. GBP 50; free in developing nations (effective 2011). **Document type:** *Journal, Academic/Scholarly.*
Related titles: Online - full text ed.: ISSN 1993-7237; ♦ Chinese ed.: Shequ Yan Jiankang; ♦ Portuguese ed.: Jornal de Saude Ocular Comunitaria. ISSN 2041-188X; ♦ English ed.: Community Eye Health. ISSN 0953-6833; ♦ Spanish ed.: Salud Ocular Comunitaria Revista. ISSN 1993-7229.
Published by: International Centre for Eye Health, London School of Hygiene and Tropical Medicine, Keppel St, London, WC1E 7HT, United Kingdom. TEL 44-20-76127964, 44-20-76127972, FAX 44-20-79588317, admin@cehjournal.org, http://www.iceh.org.uk/.

617.7 FRA ISSN 0246-0831
REVUE INTERNATIONALE DU TRACHOME ET DE PATHOLOGIE OCULAIRE TROPICALE ET SUBTROPICALE ET DE SANTE PUBLIQUE. Text in French. 1923. q. free. adv. bk.rev. bibl.; illus.
Former titles (until 1980): Revue Internationale du Trachome et de Pathologie Tropicale et Subtropicale et de Sante Publique (0249-7026); (until 1974): Revue Internationale du Trachome (0301-5017); (until 1926): Revue du Trachome (0301-5009); Revue Internationale du Trachome et des Maladies Oculaires des Pays Tropicaux et Sub Tropicaux (0035-3531)
Indexed: ChemAb, EMBASE, ExcerpMed, FR, IndMed, MEDLINE, P30, R10, Reac, SCOPUS.
—GNLM, INIST. **CCC.**
Published by: Ligue contre le Trachome, La Bergere, Route de Grenoble, Aspres Sur Buech, 05140, France. TEL 33-4-92586560, FAX 331-45-17-52-27, TELEX 345023. Ed. Georges Cornand. **Subscr. to:** CIBA Vision Ophthalmics, B.P. 1129, Toulouse Cedex 31036, France.

617.7 JPN ISSN 0370-5579
CODEN: RIGAA3
RINSHO GANKA/JAPANESE JOURNAL OF CLINICAL OPHTHALMOLOGY. Text in Japanese; Summaries in English. 1946. m. JPY 41,660; JPY 54,300 combined subscription (print & online eds.) (effective 2010). **Document type:** *Journal, Academic/Scholarly.*
Related titles: Online - full text ed.: ISSN 1882-1308.
Indexed: A22, INIS AtomInd, MycolAb, P30, R10, Reac, SCOPUS.
—BLDSC (4651.380000), GNLM, IE, Ingenta.
Published by: Igaku Shoin Ltd., 1-28-36 Hongo, Bunkyo-ku, Tokyo, 113-8719, Japan. TEL 81-3-3817-5600, FAX 81-3-3815-7791, info@igaku-shoin.co.jp. Circ: 5,000.

617.7 RUS ISSN 2072-0076
➤ **ROSSIISKII OFTAL'MOLOGICHESKII ZHURNAL.** Text in Russian. 2008. q. RUR 1,600 (effective 2011). bk.rev. **Document type:** *Journal, Academic/Scholarly.*
Related titles: Online - full text ed.
Indexed: RefZh.
Published by: Moskovskii Nauchno-Issledovatel'skii Institut Glaznykh Boleznei im. Gelmgoltsa/The Helmholtz Moscow Research Institute of Eye Disaseases, Sadovaya-Chernogryazskaya 14/19, Moscow, Russian Federation. TEL 7-495-6253256. Ed. V V Neroev. Pub. Tatiana Logvinenko.

617.7 JPN ISSN 0917-4338
RYOKUNAISHO/JAPAN GLAUCOMA SOCIETY. JOURNAL. Text in English, Japanese. 1990. a. **Document type:** *Journal, Academic/Scholarly.*
Published by: (Nihon Ryokunaisho/Japan Glaucoma Society), Medikaru Aoi Shuppan/Medical-Aoi Publications, Inc., 2-39-5 Hongo, Bunkyo-ku, Kataoka Bldg. 5F, Tokyo, 113-0033, Japan. TEL 81-3-38110544, http://www.medical-aoi.co.jp/.

617.7 362.41 GBR ISSN 1993-7229
➤ **SALUD OCULAR COMUNITARIA REVISTA.** Text in Spanish. 2006. s-a. GBP 50; free in developing nations (effective 2011). **Document type:** *Journal, Academic/Scholarly.*
Related titles: Online - full text ed.: ISSN 1993-7245; ♦ Chinese ed.: Shequ Yan Jiankang; ♦ Portuguese ed.: Jornal de Saude Ocular Comunitaria. ISSN 2041-188X; ♦ English ed.: Community Eye Health. ISSN 0953-6833; ♦ French ed.: Revue de Sante Oculaire Communautaire. ISSN 1993-7210.
Published by: International Centre for Eye Health, London School of Hygiene and Tropical Medicine, Keppel St, London, WC1E 7HT, United Kingdom. TEL 44-20-76127964, 44-20-76127972, FAX 44-20-79588317, admin@cehjournal.org, http://www.iceh.org.uk/.

617.7 NLD ISSN 1319-4534
➤ **SAUDI JOURNAL OF OPHTHALMOLOGY.** Abbreviated title: S J O. Text in English. 1987. q. **Document type:** *Journal, Academic/Scholarly.* **Description:** Publishes original papers, clinical studies, reviews and case reports related to Ophthalmology.
Related titles: Online - full text ed.: free (effective 2011) (from ScienceDirect).
Indexed: EMBASE, SCOPUS, T02.
—BLDSC (8076.974350), IE. **CCC.**
Published by: (Saudi Ophthalmological Society SAU), Elsevier BV (Subsidiary of: Elsevier Science & Technology), Radarweg 29, PO Box 211, Amsterdam, 1000 AE, Netherlands. http://www.elsevier.nl. Ed. A A Al-Rajhi.

617.7 CHE
SCHWEIZER OPTIKER. Text in German. 1925. m. adv. bk.rev. **Document type:** *Journal, Trade.*
Published by: Maihof Verlag AG, Postfach, Luzern, 6002, Switzerland. TEL 41-41-4295252, FAX 41-41-4295367. Ed. Kurt Butikofer. Circ: 2,300.

617.7 NLD ISSN 1874-9623
SCOPE. Text in Dutch. 3/yr. **Document type:** *Magazine, Trade.*
Published by: Medical Workshop b.v., PO Box 461, Groningen, 9700 AL, Netherlands. TEL 31-50-5276999, FAX 31-50-5276958, service@medicalworkshop.nl.

617.7 GBR ISSN 0882-0538
RE56 CODEN: SEOPE7
➤ **SEMINARS IN OPHTHALMOLOGY.** Text in English. 1986. bi-m. GBP 515, EUR 675, USD 850 combined subscription to institutions (print & online eds.); GBP 1,030, EUR 1,350, USD 1,700 combined subscription to corporations (print & online eds.) (effective 2010). adv. bibl.; charts; illus. index. back issues avail.; reprint service avail. from PSC. **Document type:** *Journal, Academic/Scholarly.* **Description:** Each issue focuses on a particular therapeutic or surgical technique through high-level clinical reviews geared toward trainee and practicing eye specialists.
Related titles: Online - full text ed.: ISSN 1744-5205 (from IngentaConnect).
Indexed: A01, A03, A08, A22, C06, C07, C08, CA, CINAHL, E01, EMBASE, ExcerpMed, FR, IndMed, MEDLINE, P30, R10, Reac, SCOPUS, T02.
—GNLM, IE, Infotrieve, Ingenta, INIST. **CCC.**
Published by: Informa Healthcare (Subsidiary of: T & F Informa plc), Telephone House, 69-77 Paul St, London, EC2A 4LQ, United Kingdom. TEL 44-20-70175000, FAX 44-20-70176792, healthcare.enquiries@informa.com. Ed. Thomas R Friberg. Adv. contact Per Sonnerfeldt. **Subscr. to:** Taylor & Francis Inc., Customer Services Dept, 325 Chestnut St, 8th Fl, Philadelphia, PA 19106. TEL 215-625-8900, 800-354-1420, FAX 215-625-8914, customerservice@taylorandfrancis.com; Taylor & Francis Ltd., Journals Customer Service, Sheepen Pl, Colchester, Essex CO3 3LP, United Kingdom. TEL 44-20-70175544, FAX 44-20-70175198, tf.enquiries@tfinforma.com.

➤ **SHANDONG DAXUE ERBIHOUYAN XUEBAO/JOURNAL OF OTOLARYNGOLOGY AND OPHTHALMOLOGY OF SHANDONG UNIVERSITY.** *see* MEDICAL SCIENCES—Otorhinolaryngology

617.7 362.41 GBR
➤ **SHEQU YAN JIANKANG.** Text in Chinese. s-a. GBP 50; free in developing nations (effective 2011). **Document type:** *Journal, Academic/Scholarly.*
Related titles: Online - full text ed.; ♦ Portuguese ed.: Jornal de Saude Ocular Comunitaria. ISSN 2041-188X; ♦ Spanish ed.: Salud Ocular Comunitaria Revista. ISSN 1993-7229; ♦ English ed.: Community Eye Health. ISSN 0953-6833; ♦ French ed.: Revue de Sante Oculaire Communautaire. ISSN 1993-7210.
Published by: International Centre for Eye Health, London School of Hygiene and Tropical Medicine, Keppel St, London, WC1E 7HT, United Kingdom. TEL 44-20-76127964, 44-20-76127972, FAX 44-20-79588317, admin@cehjournal.org, http://www.iceh.org.uk/.

617.7 CHN
SHIJIE HEXIN YIXUE QIKAN WENZHAI (YANKEXUE FENCE)/DIGEST OF THE WORLD CORE MEDICAL JOURNALS (OPHTHALMOLOGY). Text in Chinese. 2004. bi-m. **Document type:** *Journal, Academic/Scholarly.*
Supersedes in part (in 2005): Shijie Zuixin Yixue Xinxi Wenzhai/Digest of the World Latest Medical Information (1671-3141)
Related titles: Online - full text ed.
—East View.
Published by: Shijie Tushu Chuban Xi'an Gongsi, 17, Nandajie, Xi'an, 710001, China. TEL 86-29-87265319, FAX 86-29-87265318, wzg1995@163.com, http://wuzhigang.bookonline.com.cn/. **Dist. by:** China International Book Trading Corp, 35 Chegongzhuang Xilu, Haidian District, PO Box 399, Beijing 100044, China. TEL 86-10-68412045, FAX 86-10-68412023, cibtc@mail.cibtc.com.cn, http://www.cibtc.com.cn.

617.7 JPN ISSN 0916-8273
SHIKAKU NO KAGAKU/JAPANESE JOURNAL OF VISUAL SCIENCE. Text in Japanese; Summaries in English. 1980. a. free to members. **Document type:** *Journal, Academic/Scholarly.*
Formerly (until 1991): Nihon Gankogaku Gakkaishi/Ophtalmological Optics Society of Japan. Journal (0917-611X)
—**CCC.**
Published by: Nihon Gankogaku Gakkai/Ophthalmological Optics Society of Japan, 7-5-10, Minamikasugaoka, 2nd Yamamoto Bldg. 203, Ibaraki, Osaka 100-0005, Japan. TEL 81-72-6313737, FAX 81-72-6313738, jmcfuji@ops.dti.ne.jp, http://www.gankougaku.gr.jp/.

SHIKAKU SHOGAI RIHABIRITEISHON. *see* HANDICAPPED—Visually Impaired

617.7 JPN ISSN 0289-7024
CODEN: UIJOFU
➤ **SHINKEI GANKA/NEURO-OPHTHALMOLOGY JAPAN.** Text in English, Japanese. 1984. q. JPY 13,000 per issue membership (effective 2004); subscr. incld. with membership. adv. bk.rev. reprints avail. **Document type:** *Journal, Academic/Scholarly.*
Indexed: E-psyche, EMBASE, ExcerpMed, INIS AtomInd, R10, Reac, SCOPUS.
—BLDSC (6081.511000), GNLM. **CCC.**
Published by: Nihon Shinkei Ganka Gakkai/Japanese Neuro-Ophthalmology Society, Kitasato University School of Allied Health Sciences, 15-1 Kitaza-To 1-chome, Sagamihara, Kanagawa 228-8555, Japan. TEL 81-42-7789416, FAX 81-42-7789417. Ed. Kazuo Mukuno. Adv. contact M Wakakura. Circ: 1,500.

➤ **SIGHT AND SOUND NEWS.** *see* HEALTH FACILITIES AND ADMINISTRATION

➤ **SKULL BASE;** an interdisciplinary approach. *see* MEDICAL SCIENCES—Surgery

117.7 COL ISSN 0037-8364
S599.4.G72S6 CODEN: SEESEY
SOCIEDAD AMERICANA DE OFTALMOLOGIA Y OPTOMETRIA. ARCHIVOS/AMERICAN SOCIETY FOR OPHTHALMOLOGY AND OPTOMETRY. ARCHIVES. Text in Multiple languages. 1958. q. adv. bk.rev. illus.; stat. index, cum.index every 10 yrs. **Document type:** *Journal, Academic/Scholarly.*
Indexed: C01.
Published by: Sociedad Americana de Oftalmologia y Optometria, Apartado Aereo 091019, Bogota, DE 8, Colombia.

617.7 ESP ISSN 0211-2698
SOCIEDAD CANARIA DE OFTALMOLOGIA. ARCHIVOS. Text in Spanish. 1976. a. back issues avail. **Document type:** *Journal, Academic/Scholarly.*
Related titles: Online - full text ed.: ISSN 1989-7294. 1986.
Published by: Sociedad Canaria de Oftalmologia, El Humo 1, 1o A, Santa Cruz de Tenerife, 38003, Spain. http://www.oftalmo.com/sco/index.htm. Ed. Alfredo Amigo Rodriguez.

617.7 COL ISSN 0120-0453
SOCIEDAD COLOMBIANA DE OFTALMOLOGIA. REVISTA. Text in Multiple languages. 1969. 3/yr. **Document type:** *Journal, Academic/Scholarly.*
Published by: Sociedad Colombiana de Oftalmologia, Transversal 21 No 100-20, Of 305, Bogota, Colombia. TEL 57-1-6369868, FAX 57-1-6218547, http://www.socoftal.com.

617.7 ESP ISSN 0365-6691
SOCIEDAD ESPANOLA DE OFTALMOLOGIA. ARCHIVOS. Text in Spanish; Summaries in English, French, German, Spanish. 1901. m. EUR 339 in Europe to institutions; GBP 294 in United Kingdom to institutions; JPY 44,500 in Japan to institutions; USD 473 elsewhere to institutions (effective 2012). adv. bk.rev. abstr.; bibl.; illus. index. back issues avail. **Document type:** *Journal, Academic/Scholarly.*
Former titles (until 1971): Sociedad Oftalmologica Hispano-Americana. Archivos (0365-7051); (until 1936): Archivos de Oftalmologia Hispano-Americanos (0365-5210)
Related titles: Online - full text ed.: ISSN 1989-7286. free (effective 2011) (from ScienceDirect).
Indexed: A22, EMBASE, ExcerpMed, IndMed, MEDLINE, P30, R10, Reac, SCOPUS.
—BLDSC (1653.990000), GNLM, IE, Infotrieve, Ingenta, INIST. **CCC.**
Published by: Sociedad Espanola de Oftalmologia, C Donoso Cortes, 73 1o Izq, Madrid, 28015, Spain. TEL 34-91-5445879, FAX 34-91-5441847, archivosdelaseo@infonegocio.com.

617.7 ESP ISSN 1132-3701
SOCIEDAD OFTALMOLOGICA DE MADRID. BOLETIN. Text in Spanish. 1960. a. **Document type:** *Journal, Academic/Scholarly.*
Published by: Sociedad Oftalmologica de Madrid, Donoso Cortes 73, 1a izq, Madrid, 28015, Spain. TEL 34-91-5445879, avpm@oftalmo.com.

617.7 BEL ISSN 0081-0746
RE1
SOCIETE BELGE D'OPHTALMOLOGIE. BULLETIN. Text in French. 1896. q. EUR 102 domestic; EUR 115 in the European Union; EUR 127 elsewhere (effective 2007). adv. **Document type:** *Bulletin, Trade.*
Indexed: A22, DentInd, EMBASE, ExcerpMed, FR, IndMed, MEDLINE, P30, R10, Reac, SCOPUS.
—BLDSC (2727.220000), GNLM, IE, Infotrieve, Ingenta, INIST. **CCC.**
Published by: Societe Belge d'Ophtalmologie, Marlene Verlaeckt, Kapucijnenvoer 33, Leuven, 3000, Belgium. TEL 32-16-332398, FAX 32-16-332678. Ed. M Hanssens.

617.7 FRA ISSN 0081-1270
CODEN: BSOFAK
SOCIETES D'OPHTALMOLOGIE DE FRANCE. BULLETIN. Text in French. 1888. q. abstr.
Formerly (until 1948): Societe d'Ophtalmologie de Paris. Bulletin (0366-3485)
Indexed: A22, ChemAb, FR, IndMed, P30.
—BLDSC (2758.240000), GNLM, IE, Infotrieve, Ingenta, INIST. **CCC.**
Published by: Diffusion Generale de Librairie, 11 rue Moliere, Marseille, 13001, France. TEL 33-4-91335718, FAX 33-4-91335727. **Subscr. to:** B.P. 60, Marseille Cedex 20 13486, France.

617.75 ZAF ISSN 0378-9411
➤ **SOUTH AFRICAN OPTOMETRIST/SUID-AFRIKAANSE OOGKUNDIGE.** Text in English. 1941. q. membership. adv. bk.rev. charts; illus. **Document type:** *Journal, Academic/Scholarly.*
Indexed: ISAP.
Published by: South African Optometric Association, PO Box 2925, Halfway House, 1685, South Africa. TEL 27-11-8054517, FAX 27-11-8053882, pro@saoa.co.za. Ed. Alan Rubin. Circ: 2,000.

617.7 AUT ISSN 0930-4282
RE46
➤ **SPEKTRUM DER AUGENHEILKUNDE**; Zeitschrift der Oesterreichischen Ophthalmologischen Gesellschaft. Text in German; Summaries in English. 1987. bi-m. EUR 284, USD 307 combined subscription to institutions (print & online eds.) (effective 2012). adv. bk.rev. abstr.; illus. back issues avail.; reprint service avail. from PSC. **Document type:** *Journal, Academic/Scholarly.*
Description: Informs ophthalmologists about developments in research and clinical practice that are relevant to their practices.
Related titles: Microform ed.: (from PQC); Online - full text ed.: ISSN 1613-7523 (from IngentaConnect).
Indexed: A22, A26, E01, INIS AtomInd, SCI, SCOPUS, W07.
—BLDSC (8411.400150), GNLM, IE, Ingenta. **CCC.**
Published by: (Oesterreichische Ophthalmologische Gesellschaft), Springer Wien (Subsidiary of: Springer Science+Business Media), Sachsenplatz 4-6, Vienna, W 1201, Austria. TEL 43-1-33024150, FAX 43-1-3302426, journals@springer.at, http://www.springer.at. Ed. S Binder. Adv. contact Margit Hauser. color page EUR 1,750; 210 x 297. Circ: 1,000 (paid). **Subscr. in the Americas to:** Springer New York LLC, Journal Fulfillment, PO Box 2485, Secaucus, NJ 07096. TEL 800-777-4643, 201-348-4033, FAX 201-348-4505, journals-ny@springer.com, http://www.springer.com; **Subscr. to:** Springer Distribution Center, Kundenservice Zeitschriften, Haberstr 7, Heidelberg 69126, Germany. TEL 49-6221-3454303, FAX 49-6221-3454229, subscriptions@springer.com.

617.7 GBR ISSN 0927-3972
RE771 CODEN: SRABFL
➤ **STRABISMUS (LONDON).** Text in English. 1993. q. GBP 360, EUR 475, USD 590 combined subscription to institutions (print & online eds.); GBP 720, EUR 950, USD 1,185 combined subscription to corporations (print & online eds.) (effective 2010). adv. abstr. back issues avail.; reprint service avail. from PSC. **Document type:** *Journal, Academic/Scholarly.* **Description:** Features papers and review articles on strabismus and related fields, including neurophysiology.
Related titles: Microform ed.: (from PQC); Online - full text ed.: ISSN 1744-5132 (from IngentaConnect).
Indexed: A01, A03, A08, A22, CA, E-psyche, E01, EMBASE, ExcerpMed, IndMed, MEDLINE, P30, R10, Reac, SCOPUS, T02.
—IE, Infotrieve, Ingenta. **CCC.**
Published by: Informa Healthcare (Subsidiary of: T & F Informa plc), Telephone House, 69-77 Paul St, London, EC2A 4LQ, United Kingdom. TEL 44-20-70175000, FAX 44-20-70176792, healthcare.enquiries@informa.com. Ed. H J Simonsz TEL 31-10-7040704. Adv. contact Per Sonnerfeldt. **Subscr. to:** Taylor & Francis Inc., Customer Services Dept, 325 Chestnut St, 8th Fl, Philadelphia, PA 19106. TEL 215-625-8900, 800-354-1420, FAX 215-625-8914, customerservice@taylorandfrancis.com; Taylor & Francis Ltd., Journals Customer Service, Sheepen Pl, Colchester, Essex CO3 3LP, United Kingdom. TEL 44-20-70175544, FAX 44-20-70175198, tf.enquiries@tfinforma.com.

➤ **STUDIES IN VISUAL INFORMATION PROCESSING.** *see* MEDICAL SCIENCES—Psychiatry And Neurology

617.7 ESP ISSN 0210-8720
STUDIUM OPHTHALMOLOGICUM. Text in Spanish. 1979. q. back issues avail. **Document type:** *Journal, Academic/Scholarly.*
Published by: Audiovisual y Marketing, S.L., C Donoso Cortes, 73 1o., Madrid, 28015, Spain. TEL 34-91-5440252, FAX 34-91-5441847, avpm@oftalmo.com, http://www.oftalmo.com/estrabologia/. Ed. Miguel Zato Gomez de Liano.

617.7 SDN ISSN 1858-540X
➤ **SUDANESE JOURNAL OF OPHTHALMOLOGY.** Text in English. s-a. **Document type:** *Journal, Academic/Scholarly.* **Description:** Publishes original, peer-reviewed reports of research in ophthalmology, including basic scientific papers, clinical studies and interesting case reports.
Related titles: Online - full text ed.: ISSN 1858-5418.
Published by: Sudan Eye Center, Street No 43, Amarat, Khartoum, 11111, Sudan. TEL 249-919-519413, FAX 249-183-469691, kamal@sudaneyecenter.com. Ed. Dr. Nadir Ali.

617.7 TUR ISSN 1308-9552
➤ **SULEYMAN DEMIREL UNIVERSITESI. VIZYONER DERGISI/S D U VISIONARY JOURNAL.** Text in Turkish. s-a. free (effective 2011). **Document type:** *Journal, Academic/Scholarly.*
Media: Online - full text.
Published by: Suleyman Demirel University, Senirkent Vocational School/Suleyman Demirel Universitesi, Senirkent Meslek Yuksekokulu, Senirkent, Isparta, 32600, Turkey. TEL 90-246-2113057, kayalar@iibf.sdu.edu.tr. Ed. Murat Kayalar.

➤ **SUNGLASS ASSOCIATION OF AMERICA. NEWSLETTER.** *see* CLOTHING TRADE

617.7 USA ISSN 1087-299X
HD9707.5.S85
SUNWEAR. Text in English. 1996. q. **Document type:** *Magazine, Trade.*
Published by: Jobson Optical Group (Subsidiary of: Jobson Publishing LLC), 100 Ave of the Americas, New York, NY 10013. TEL 212-274-7000, FAX 212-431-0500, info@jmihealth.com, http://www.jmihealth.com/. Circ: 30,000.

SURVEY OF OPHTHALMOLOGY. *see* MEDICAL SCIENCES—Abstracting, Bibliographies, Statistics

617.7 HUN ISSN 0039-8101
SZEMESZET/OPHTHALMOLOGICA HUNGARICA. Summaries in English, German, Russian. 1864. q. illus. **Document type:** *Journal, Academic/Scholarly.*
Indexed: ChemAb, IndMed, P30.
—GNLM.
Published by: Magyar Szemorvostarsasag/Hungarian Society of Ophthalmology, Tomo ut 25 - 29, Budapest, Hungary. TEL 36-1-3039435.

617.752 ITA
TECH INTERNATIONAL. Text in French, Spanish, Italian, English. 1992. 8/yr. EUR 52 (effective 2009). adv. back issues avail. **Document type:** *Magazine, Trade.* **Description:** Covers raw materials, machinery, equipment and components for the eyewear industry.
Published by: Edizioni Ariminum, Via Negroli 51, Milan, MI 20133, Italy. TEL 39-02-730091, FAX 39-02-717346, welcome@vedere.it, http://www.vedere.it. Pub., Adv. contact Isabella Morpurgo. Circ: 4,000.

617.7 USA ISSN 1542-1929
TECHNIQUES IN OPHTHALMOLOGY. Text in English. 2003 (Mar.). q. USD 420 domestic to institutions; USD 503 foreign to institutions (effective 2011). adv. back issues avail.; reprints avail. **Document type:** *Journal, Academic/Scholarly.* **Description:** Provides reviews of current surgical techniques and instrumentation in each of the ophthalmologic subspecialties - Cataract surgery, Refractive surgery, Corneal surgery, Glaucoma surgery, Oculoplastic surgery, Retinal surgery, and Pediatric Surgery.
Related titles: Online - full text ed.: ISSN 1542-1937.
Indexed: C06, C07, EMBASE, ExcerpMed, R10, Reac, SCOPUS.
—**CCC.**
Published by: Lippincott Williams & Wilkins (Subsidiary of: Wolters Kluwer N.V.), Two Commerce Sq, 2001 Market St, Philadelphia, PA 19103. TEL 215-521-8300, FAX 215-521-8902, customerservice@lww.com, http://www.lww.com. Ed. Thomas John. Pub. Nina J Chang. Adv. contact Michelle Smith TEL 646-674-6537. Circ: 176.

617.7 USA ISSN 0738-7644
TEXAS OPTOMETRY. Text in English. 1945. 3/yr. USD 12 (effective 2005). adv. bk.rev. charts; stat.; illus. **Document type:** *Magazine, Trade.*
Formerly: Texas Optometric Association. Journal
Published by: Texas Optometric Association, 1503 S.I. Hwy. 35, Austin, TX 78741. TEL 512-707-2020, FAX 512-326-8504. Ed. Clarke Newman. adv.: B&W page USD 365, color page USD 965; trim 10.88 x 8.13. Circ: 1,600.

THYROBULLETIN. *see* MEDICAL SCIENCES—Endocrinology

TID OG SYN. *see* JEWELRY, CLOCKS AND WATCHES

TIFLOLOGIA PER L'INTEGRAZIONE. *see* HANDICAPPED—Visually Impaired

617.7 TUR ISSN 1300-0659
CODEN: TOFGA
➤ **TURK OFTALMOLOJI GAZETESI/TURKISH JOURNAL OF OPHTHALMOLOGY.** Text in Turkish. 1929. bi-m. **Document type:** *Journal, Academic/Scholarly.*
Related titles: Online - full text ed.: free (effective 2009).
Indexed: A01, A26, E08, H12, I05.
—GNLM.
Published by: Turkish Ophthalmological Society/Turk Oftalmoloji Dernegi, Millet Caddesi Gulsen Ap.21/9 Kat 4, Aksaray, Istanbul, 34000, Turkey. TEL 90-212-5307133, FAX 90-212-5307166, nusretozdemir@aol.com, http://www.tod-net.org/. Ed. Dr. Ercan Ongor.

617.7 NLD ISSN 1574-6534
UITZICHT (UTRECHT). Text in Dutch. q. EUR 13 to non-members; EUR 20.50 membership (effective 2009).
Published by: Retina Nederland, Postbus 2061, Utrecht, 3500 GB, Netherlands. TEL 31-30-2980697, FAX 31-30-2980927, secretariaat@retinanederland.org, http://www.retinanederland.org.

617.7 658 BRA
UNIVERSO VISUAL. Text in Portuguese. bi-m. **Document type:** *Magazine, Trade.* **Description:** Contains technical primary care information of interest to the Brazilian visual care professionals.
Published by: Jobson Brasil Ltda. (Subsidiary of: Jobson Publishing LLC), Rua Conego Eugeno leite 920, Pinheiros, Sao Paulo, 050414-011, Brazil. TEL 55-11-30619025, FAX 55-11-8833288, http://www.2020brasil.com.br. Circ: 11,200.

V H L FAMILY FORUM. (Von Hippel-Lindau Disease) *see* MEDICAL SCIENCES—Psychiatry And Neurology

617.7 USA ISSN 1550-0004
VAUGHAN & ASBURY'S GENERAL OPHTHALMOLOGY. Text in English. 1958-1999; resumed 2004. irreg., latest 2007, 17th ed. USD 75.95 per issue (print or online ed.) (effective 2010). 480 p./no.; **Document type:** *Journal, Academic/Scholarly.* **Description:** Covers the diagnosis and treatment of all major ophthalmic diseases, as well as neurological and systemic diseases causing visual disturbance.
Formerly (until 2004): General Ophthalmology (0891-2084)
Related titles: Online - full text ed.
Published by: McGraw-Hill Professional (Subsidiary of: McGraw-Hill Companies, Inc.), Two Penn Plz, 23rd Fl, New York, NY 10121. TEL 212-904-2000, FAX 212-904-6030, customer.service@mcgraw-hill.com, http://www.mhprofessional.com/index.php.

617.7 ITA ISSN 0302-6256
VEDERE INTERNATIONAL; international journal on optics, frame industry and optical instruments. Text in English, French, Spanish, Italian. 1953. 8/yr. EUR 52 (effective 2009). adv. tr.lit. back issues avail. **Document type:** *Magazine, Trade.* **Description:** Covers the optical industry.
Formerly (until 1971): Vedere (0503-7565)
Published by: Edizioni Ariminum, Via Negroli 51, Milan, MI 20133, Italy. TEL 39-02-730091, FAX 39-02-717346, welcome@vedere.it, http://www.vedere.it. Pub., Adv. contact Isabella Morpurgo. Circ: 8,500.

617.7 617.89 ESP ISSN 0212-4394
VER Y OIR. Text in Spanish. 1983. q. **Document type:** *Magazine, Trade.*
Related titles: Online - full text ed.
Published by: Publicaciones Nacionales Tecnicas y Extranjeras (PUNTEX), Padilla 323, Barcelona, 08025, Spain. TEL 34-934-462820, FAX 34-934-462064, puntex@puntex.es. Circ: 3,000.

617.7 RUS ISSN 0042-465X
RE1 CODEN: VEOFA6
VESTNIK OFTAL'MOLOGII/ANNALS OF OPHTHALMOLOGY. Text in Russian; Summaries in English. 1884. q. USD 110 foreign (effective 2005). adv. bk.rev. illus.; abstr. index. **Document type:** *Journal, Academic/Scholarly.* **Description:** Publishes materials on the diagnosis and treatment of eye diseases, hygiene of vision, prevention of ophthalmic infections, ophthalmological techniques.
Indexed: ChemAb, DentInd, DokArb, EMBASE, ExcerpMed, IndMed, Inpharma, MEDLINE, P30, PlantSci, R10, Reac, RefZh, SCOPUS.
—CASDDS, East View, GNLM, Infotrieve, INIST. **CCC.**
Published by: Izdatel'stvo Meditsina/Meditsina Publishers, ul B Pirogovskaya, d 2, str 5, Moscow, 119435, Russian Federation. TEL 7-095-2483324, meditsina@mtu-net.ru, http://www.medlit.ru. Ed. Mikhail M Krasnov. Pub. A M Stochik. R&P V Sinitsina. Adv. contact V I Sinitsina. Circ: 2,000. **Dist. by:** M K - Periodica, ul Gilyarovskogo 39, Moscow 129110, Russian Federation. TEL 7-095-2845008, FAX 7-095-2813798, info@periodicals.ru, http://www.mkniga.ru.

VETERINARY OPHTHALMOLOGY. *see* VETERINARY SCIENCE

617.7 658 BRA
VIEW MAGAZINE/REVISTA VIEW. Text in Portuguese. 8/yr. **Document type:** *Magazine, Trade.* **Description:** Optical business magazine serving the Brazilian optical market.
Published by: Jobson Brasil Ltda. (Subsidiary of: Jobson Publishing LLC), Rua Conego Eugeno leite 920, Pinheiros, Sao Paulo, 050414-011, Brazil. TEL 55-11-30619025, FAX 55-11-8833288, http://www.2020brasil.com.br. Circ: 15,000.

617.7 USA
VIEWPOINTS. Text in English. 2006. q. membership. **Document type:** *Magazine, Trade.*
Published by: Association of Technical Personnel in Ophthalmology, 2025 Woodlane Dr., St Paul, MN 55125-2998. TEL 800-482-4858, FAX 651-731-0410, ATPOmembership@jcahpo.org.

617.7 USA ISSN 1549-6716
VISION CARE PRODUCT NEWS. Abbreviated title: V C P N. Text in English. 2000. m. free to qualified personnel (effective 2010). back issues avail. **Document type:** *Magazine, Consumer.* **Description:** Provides information on opthalmic products.
Related titles: Online - full text ed.

Published by: First Vision Media Group Inc., 25 E Spring Valley Ave, Ste 290, Maywood, NJ 07607. TEL 201-587-9460, FAX 201-587-9464, fg@visioncareproducts.com, http://www.firstvisionmedia.com/.

617.7 658.8 USA ISSN 1054-7665
VISION MONDAY; the home page for optical industry news. Text in English. 1987. m. USD 125.95 (effective 2009); subscr. includes VMail Extra. adv. back issues avail.; reprints avail. **Document type:** *Magazine, Trade.* **Description:** Covers news and information about the world-wide optical industry.
Formerly (until 19??): 20/20's VisionMonday (0891-1770)
Related titles: Online - full text ed.
Indexed: A26, B01, B07, H01, H02, T02.
—CCC.
Published by: Jobson Optical Group (Subsidiary of: Jobson Publishing LLC), 100 Ave of the Americas, New York, NY 10013. TEL 212-274-7000, FAX 212-431-0500, info@jmihealth.com, http://www.jmihealth.com/. Ed. Deirdre Carroll TEL 212-274-7076. Pub. Bill Scott TEL 212-274-7131. adv.: color page USD 6,180; trim 10 x 12.

617.7 GBR ISSN 0042-6989
QP474 CODEN: VISRAM
➤ **VISION RESEARCH.** Text in English, French, German, Russian. 1961. 24/yr. EUR 4,104 in Europe to institutions; JPY 544,900 in Japan to institutions; USD 4,589 elsewhere to institutions (effective 2012). adv. bk.rev. charts; illus. index. back issues avail. **Document type:** *Journal, Academic/Scholarly.* **Description:** Features original research in functional aspects of the neurobiology, psychophysics and behavioral physiology of human, vertebrate and invertebrate vision, as well as computational vision research.
Incorporates (1986-1993): Clinical Vision Science (0887-6169)
Related titles: Microfilm ed.: (from PQC); Online - full text ed.: ISSN 1878-5646 (from IngentaConnect, ScienceDirect).
Indexed: A01, A03, A08, A20, A22, A26, ASCA, ApMecR, ApicAb, B21, B25, BIOBASE, BIOSIS Prev, C06, C07, CA, CIN, CMCI, CRFR, CTA, ChemAb, CurCont, E-psyche, EMBASE, ErgAb, ExcerpMed, FR, I05, IABS, IBR, IBZ, IBuildSA, ISR, IndMed, Inpharma, Inspec, MEDLINE, MycolAb, NSA, NSCI, P03, P30, PhysBer, PsycInfo, PsycholAb, R10, Reac, RefZh, SCI, SCOPUS, T02, W07, WildRev.
—BLDSC (9240.925000), AskIEEE, CASDDS, GNLM, IE, Infotrieve, Ingenta, INIST. **CCC.**
Published by: Pergamon (Subsidiary of: Elsevier Science & Technology), The Blvd, Langford Ln, East Park, Kidlington, Oxford OX5 1GB, United Kingdom. TEL 44-1865-843000, FAX 44-1865-843010, JournalsCustomerServiceEMEA@elsevier.com. Ed. D M Levi. **Subscr. to:** Elsevier BV, Radarweg 29, PO Box 211, Amsterdam 1000 AE, Netherlands. TEL 31-20-4853757, FAX 31-20-4853432, http://www.elsevier.nl.

617.7 USA ISSN 1554-3048
VISION UPDATE. Text in English. 1998. bi-m. free. adv. **Document type:** *Newsletter, Trade.* **Description:** Presents timely issues relating to eye health and vision care from a variety of scientific studies and viewpoints.
Media: Online - full content.
Published by: C L E Contact Lenses Inc., 16 E 52nd St, Ste 503, New York, NY 10022. TEL 212-752-1212, FAX 212-752-8507, president@clecontactlenses.com. Ed. Ted Roxan. Pub. Jay Stockman. Circ: 8,100 (controlled).

610 617.7 613.7 USA
VISIONARY. Text in English. 1962. 2/yr. looseleaf. free. bk.rev. charts; illus.; stat. back issues avail. **Document type:** *Newsletter.*
Published by: Illinois Society for the Prevention of Blindness, 211 W Wacker Dr, Ste 17, Chicago, IL 60606. TEL 312 922-8710, 800-433-4772, FAX 312-922-8713, ispb@ehil.org. Circ: 12,000.

VISUAL NEUROSCIENCE. *see* MEDICAL SCIENCES—Psychiatry And Neurology

617.75 NLD ISSN 1382-1210
VISUS. Text in Dutch. 1985. q. EUR 32 (effective 2010). adv. bk.rev. **Document type:** *Journal, Trade.*
Published by: Optometristen Vereniging Nederland, Postbus 10417, Weert, 6000 GK, Netherlands. TEL 31-495-585748, info@optometrie.nl. adv.: color page EUR 950; trim 210 x 297. Circ: 1,000.

WEITERSEHEN. *see* HANDICAPPED—Visually Impaired

617.7 CHN ISSN 1004-4469
YANKE. Text in Chinese. 1992. bi-m. USD 31.20 (effective 2009). **Document type:** *Journal, Academic/Scholarly.*
Related titles: Online - full text ed.
Indexed: SCOPUS.
—BLDSC (9371.572353), East View.
Published by: Beijing Shi Yanke Yanjiusuo, 17, Chongnei Dajie Hougouhutong, Beijing, 100005, China. TEL 86-10-58265902. **Dist. by:** China International Book Trading Corp, 35 Chegongzhuang Xilu, Haidian District, PO Box 399, Beijing 100044, China. TEL 86-10-68412045, FAX 86-10-68412023, cibtc@mail.cibtc.com.cn, http://www.cibtc.com.cn.

617.7 CHN ISSN 1003-5141
YANKE XIN JINZHAN/RECENT ADVANCES IN OPHTHALMOLOGY. Text in Chinese; Abstracts and contents page in English. 1980. bi-m. USD 49.20 (effective 2009). adv. back issues avail. **Document type:** *Journal, Academic/Scholarly.* **Description:** Covers recent advances in Opthalmology, basic and clinical research of with columns of original articles, clinical reports, short reports, case reports and review.
Related titles: E-mail ed.; Online - full text ed.
—East View.
Published by: Xinxiang Yixueyuan/Xinxiang Medical College, Xinyan Road, Xinxiang, 453003, China. TEL 86-373-3029404, FAX 86-373-3831371. adv.: B&W page USD 1,000, color page USD 2,000; trim 284 x 207. Circ: 4,500. **Dist. by:** China International Book Trading Corp, 35 Chegongzhuang Xilu, Haidian District, PO Box 399, Beijing 100044, China. TEL 86-10-68412045, FAX 86-10-68412023, cibtc@mail.cibtc.com.cn, http://www.cibtc.com.cn.

617.7 CHN ISSN 1000-4432
RE1 CODEN: YAXUE
➤ **YANKE XUEBAO/EYE SCIENCE.** Text in Chinese. 1985. q. USD 14.40 (effective 2009). **Document type:** *Journal, Academic/Scholarly.*
Related titles: Online - full text ed.
Indexed: A22, EMBASE, ExcerpMed, IndMed, MEDLINE, P30, R10, Reac, SCOPUS.
—BLDSC (3854.635000), CASDDS, East View, GNLM, IE, Infotrieve, Ingenta.
Published by: Zhongshan Yike Daxue, Zhongshan Yanke Zhongxin/Sun Yat-sen University of Medical Sciences, Zhongshan Ophthalmic Center, 54 Xianlie Nanlu, Guangzhou, Guangdong 510060, China. **Dist. by:** China International Book Trading Corp, 35 Chegongzhuang Xilu, Haidian District, PO Box 399, Beijing 100044, China. TEL 86-10-68412045, FAX 86-10-68412023, cibtc@mail.cibtc.com.cn, http://www.cibtc.com.cn.

617.7 CHN ISSN 1003-0808
YANKE YANJIU/CHINESE OPHTHALMIC RESEARCH. Text in Chinese. 1983. bi-m. **Document type:** *Journal, Academic/Scholarly.*
Related titles: Online - full text ed.
Indexed: EMBASE, ExcerpMed, R10, Reac, SCOPUS.
—BLDSC (3181.031000), East View, IE, Ingenta.
Published by: Henan Sheng Yike Yanjiusuo, 7, Weiwu Lu, Zhengzhou, 450003, China. TEL 86-371-65580157, FAX 86-371-65580157, webhnyks@126.com. **Dist. by:** China International Book Trading Corp, 35 Chegongzhuang Xilu, Haidian District, PO Box 399, Beijing 100044, China. TEL 86-10-68412045, FAX 86-10-68412023, cibtc@mail.cibtc.com.cn, http://www.cibtc.com.cn.

617.7 CHN ISSN 1004-6461
YANWAISHANG ZHIYE YANBING ZAZHI/JOURNAL OF OPHTHALMIC TRAUMA AND OCCUPATIONAL OCULAN DISEASES. Text in Chinese. 1979. m. USD 43.20 (effective 2009). **Document type:** *Journal, Academic/Scholarly.*
Related titles: Online - full text ed.
Address: 1, Jianshe Lu, Henan Yike Daxue, Di-1 Fushu Yiyuan, Zhengzhou, 450052, China. TEL 86-371-6993497, FAX 86-371-6982899. **Dist. by:** China International Book Trading Corp, 35 Chegongzhuang Xilu, Haidian District, PO Box 399, Beijing 100044, China. TEL 86-10-68412045, FAX 86-10-68412023, cibtc@mail.cibtc.com.cn, http://www.cibtc.com.cn.

617.705 USA ISSN 0084-392X
RE6
YEAR BOOK OF OPHTHALMOLOGY. Text in English. 1958. a. USD 239 in United States to institutions; USD 259 elsewhere to institutions (effective 2012). adv. illus. reprints avail. **Document type:** *Yearbook, Academic/Scholarly.* **Description:** Presents abstracts of pertinent literature with commentary by leading experts in the field.
Supersedes in part (in 1958): Yearbook of the Eye, Ear, Nose, and Throat
Related titles: Online - full text ed.
—GNLM. **CCC.**
Published by: Mosby, Inc. (Subsidiary of: Elsevier Health Sciences), 1600 John F. Kennedy Blvd, Ste 1800, Philadelphia, PA 19103. TEL 215-239-3900, 800-523-1649, FAX 215-239-3990, elspcs@elsevier.com, http://www.us.elsevierhealth.com. Ed. Christopher J Rapuano.

617.7 DEU ISSN 1436-0322
CODEN: ZPAUD3
Z P A - ZEITSCHRIFT FUER PRAKTISCHE AUGENHEILKUNDE UND AUGENAERZTLICHE FORTBILDUNG. Text in German. 1996. 11/yr. EUR 108 domestic; EUR 110 foreign; EUR 10 newsstand/cover (effective 2009). adv. bk.rev. back issues avail. **Document type:** *Magazine, Trade.*
Formed by the merger of (1979-1996): Zeitschrift fuer Praktische Augenheilkunde (0173-2595); (1972-1996): Augenaerztliche Fortbildung (0341-1486)
—CASDDS, GNLM. **CCC.**
Published by: Dr. R. Kaden Verlag GmbH & Co. KG, Ringstr 19 B, Heidelberg, 69115, Germany. TEL 49-6221-1377600, FAX 49-6221-29910, kaden@kaden-verlag.de, http://www.kaden-verlag.de. Adv. contact Petra Huebler. B&W page EUR 2,205, color page EUR 3,540; trim 210 x 275. Circ: 5,000 (paid and controlled).

617.7 CHN ISSN 1006-4443
ZHONGGUO SHIYONG YANKE ZAZHI/CHINESE JOURNAL OF PRACTICAL OPHTHALMOLOGY. Text in Chinese. 1983. m. USD 62.40 (effective 2009). **Document type:** *Journal, Academic/Scholarly.*
Formerly (until 1993): Shiyong Yanke Zazhi (1003-5079)
Related titles: Online - full text ed.
—BLDSC (9512.798900).
Published by: Zhongguo Yike Daxue, Fushu Di-1 Yiyuan, 155, Nanjing Bei Jie, Beijing, 110001, China. TEL 86-24-23256666 ext 6183, FAX 86-24-23250064. **Dist. by:** China International Book Trading Corp, 35 Chegongzhuang Xilu, Haidian District, PO Box 399, Beijing 100044, China. TEL 86-10-68412045, FAX 86-10-68412023, cibtc@mail.cibtc.com.cn, http://www.cibtc.com.cn.

617.7 CHN ISSN 1002-4379
ZHONGGUO ZHONGYI YANKE ZAZHI/JOURNAL OF TRADITIONAL CHINESE OPHTHALMOLOGY. Text in Chinese. 1991. q. USD 37.20 (effective 2009). **Document type:** *Journal, Academic/Scholarly.*
Related titles: Online - full text ed.
—East View.
Address: 9, Lugu Lu, Beijing, 100040, China. TEL 86-10-68668940.

617.7 TWN ISSN 1021-3120
ZHONGHUA MINGGUO YANKE YIXUEHUI ZAZHI/ OPHTHALMOLOGICAL SOCIETY OF TAIWAN. JOURNAL. Text in Chinese. 1962. a. membership. adv. cum.index. **Document type:** *Journal, Academic/Scholarly.*
Formerly (until 1992): Zhonghua Mingguo Yanke Yixuehui Xuekan/ Ophthalmological Society of the Republic of China. Transactions
Indexed: OphLit.
—BLDSC (0584.022300).
Published by: Zhonghua Mingguo Yanke Yixuehui/Ophthalmological Society of Taiwan, 32 Gongyuan Lu, 11/F, Taipei, Taiwan. TEL 882-2-23146694, FAX 882-2-23146835, oph4@oph.org.tw, http://www.oph.org.tw/. adv.: B&W page TWD 10,000, color page TWD 20,000. Circ: 400.

617.7 CHN ISSN 1005-1015
CODEN: ZYAZEE
➤ **ZHONGHUA YANDIBING ZAZHI/CHINESE JOURNAL OF OCULAR FUNDUS DISEASES.** Text in Chinese, English. 1985. bi-m. (q. until 2003). USD 31.20 (effective 2009). adv. abstr.; bibl.; charts; illus.; stat. index. 64 p./no.; back issues avail. **Document type:** *Report, Academic/Scholarly.* **Description:** Clinical reports and research works on ocular fundus diseases relating to the infections of the interior eye and systemic involvements.
Formerly (until 1992): Yandi Bing/Ocular Fundus (1001-4071)
Related titles: Online - full text ed.
—BLDSC (9512.841900), East View.
Published by: (West China Hospital, Sichuan University), Zhonghua Yixuehui Zazhishe/Chinese Medical Association Publishing House, 42 Dongsi Xidajie, Beijing, 100710, China. Ed. Mi Yan. Pub., R&P Chunyi Wei. Adv. contact Jian Tang. Circ: 5,000. **Dist. outside China by:** China International Book Trading Corp, 35 Chegongzhuang Xilu, Haidian District, PO Box 399, Beijing 100044, China. TEL 86-10-68412045, FAX 86-10-68412023, cibtc@mail.cibtc.com.cn, http://www.cibtc.com.cn.

617.7 CHN ISSN 0412-4081
ZHONGHUA YANKE ZAZHI/CHINESE JOURNAL OF OPHTHALMOLOGY. Key Title: Chung-Hua Yen K'o Tsa Chih. Text in Chinese. 1951. bi-m. USD 96 (effective 2009). **Document type:** *Academic/Scholarly.*
Related titles: Online - full text ed.
Indexed: A22, EMBASE, ExcerpMed, IndMed, MEDLINE, P30, R10, Reac, SCOPUS.
—BLDSC (3180.462000), East View, IE, Infotrieve, Ingenta.
Published by: Zhonghua Yixuehui Zazhishe/Chinese Medical Association Publishing House, 42 Dongsi Xidajie, Beijing, 100710, China. Ed. Mei-Yu Li. **Dist. by:** China International Book Trading Corp, 35 Chegongzhuang Xilu, Haidian District, PO Box 399, Beijing 100044, China. TEL 86-10-68412045, FAX 86-10-68412023, cibtc@mail.cibtc.com.cn, http://www.cibtc.com.cn.

617.7 CHN ISSN 1674-845X
RE1
ZHONGHUA YANSHIGUANGXUE YU SHIJUE KEXUE ZAZHI/CHINESE JOURNAL OF OPTOMETRY OPHTHALMOLOGY AND VISUAL SCIENCE. Text in Chinese. 1980. bi-m. **Document type:** *Journal, Academic/Scholarly.* **Description:** Covers the combined application of Western and traditional Chinese medicine in ophthalmology.
Former titles (until 2010): Yanshi Guangxue Zazhi/Chinese Journal of Optometry & Ophthalmology (1008-1801); (until 1992): Zhong-Xiyi Jiehe Yanke Zazhi/Journal of Ophthalmology, Combination of Chinese Traditional Medicine and Western Medicine (1007-1946); (until 1988): Yanke Tongxun
Related titles: Online - full text ed.
Indexed: Inspec.
—BLDSC (9371.575250), East View, IE.
Published by: (Zhonghua Yixuehui/Chinese Medical Association), Zhonghua Yanshiguangxue yu Shijue Kexue Zazhi Bianji Weiyuanhui, Chashan Gaojiaoyuan-qu, Wenzhou Yixueyuan, Tongren-lou B-509, Wenzhou, 325035, China. TEL 86-577-86699366, FAX 86-577-86699366.

617.7 658 USA ISSN 0192-1304
20/20. Text in English. 1974. m. free to qualified personnel (effective 2009). adv. illus. Supplement avail.; back issues avail.; reprints avail. **Document type:** *Magazine, Trade.*
Related titles: Online - full text ed.
Indexed: A26, B01, B07, H01, H02, T02.
—CCC.
Published by: Jobson Optical Group (Subsidiary of: Jobson Publishing LLC), 100 Ave of the Americas, New York, NY 10013. TEL 212-274-7000, FAX 212-431-0500, info@jmihealth.com, http://www.jmihealth.com/. Ed. James J Spina. Pub. Jim Vitkus. Circ: 49,536.

617.7 658 GBR ISSN 1367-5982
20/20 ASIA. Text in English, Japanese, Korean, Chinese. 1996. a. EUR 28 per issue in Asia; EUR 31 per issue elsewhere (effective 2009). adv. **Document type:** *Magazine, Trade.* **Description:** Provides coverage of the latest business and marketing ideas as well as optical industry data analysis.
Published by: Jobson International (Subsidiary of: Jobson Publishing LLC), c/o Andrew Martin, Jobson House, Holbrooke Pl, Hill Rise, Richmond, Surrey TW10 6UD, United Kingdom. TEL 44-20-83344541, FAX 44-20-83326918. Circ: 16,000.

617.7 BRA
20/20 BRASIL. Text in Portuguese. m. **Document type:** *Magazine, Trade.* **Description:** Covers all aspects of eyewear and eye care dispensing activities for ophthalmologists, optometrists and opticians.
Published by: Jobson Brasil Ltda. (Subsidiary of: Jobson Publishing LLC), Rua Conego Eugeno leite 920, Pinheiros, Sao Paulo, 050414-011, Brazil. TEL 55-11-30619025, FAX 55-11-8833288, jobsonbrasil@uol.com.br. Ed. Lilian Liang. Pub. Flavio Bitelman.

617.7 USA ISSN 1353-3290
20/20 EUROPE. Text in English. 1974. bi-m. EUR 120 in Europe; EUR 300 elsewhere (effective 2007). **Document type:** *Magazine, Trade.*
Related titles: French ed.; German ed.; Italian ed.; Spanish ed.; ◆ Supplement(s): European Lenses & Technology.
—CCC.
Published by: Jobson International (Subsidiary of: Jobson Publishing LLC), 100 Avenue of the Americas, 9th Fl, New York, NY 10013. TEL 212-274-7000, FAX 212-431-5579, subscriptions@2020europe.com.

MEDICAL SCIENCES—Orthopedics And Traumatology

617.3 USA ISSN 1935-6765
A A O S NOW. Text in English. 1952. m. free to members (effective 2010). 68 cols./p.; back issues avail. **Document type:** *Bulletin, Trade.* **Description:** Covers clinical news, practice management, regulatory, reimbursement, research updates.
Formerly (until 2007): American Academy of Orthopaedic Surgeons. Bulletin (1049-9741)
Related titles: Online - full text ed.: ISSN 1935-6773.
Indexed: A01, A26, E08, H12, I05.
Published by: American Academy of Orthopaedic Surgeons, 6300 N River Rd, Rosemont, IL 60018. TEL 847-823-7186, FAX 847-823-8125, custserv@aaos.org. Ed. S Terry Canale.

616.025 USA ISSN 1551-9171
A C E P NEWS. Text in English. 1981. m. USD 175 to non-members; free to members (effective 2010). adv. back issues avail. **Document type:** *Newspaper, Trade.* **Description:** Provides clinical articles, helpful emergency medicine practice ideas and articles on issues facing emergency medicine.
Related titles: Online - full text ed.: free (effective 2010).

Published by: (American College of Emergency Physicians), Elsevier Society News Group (Subsidiary of: Elsevier Inc.), 5635 Fishers Ln, Ste 6000, Rockville, MD 20852. TEL 240-221-4500, FAX 240-221-4400, m.branca@elsevier.com, http://www.esng-meded.com. Adv. contact Jim Brady TEL 516-742-7960.

617 CHE
A O DIALOGUE. (Arbeitsgemeinschaft fuer Osteosynthesefragen) Text in English. s-a. **Document type:** *Journal, Academic/Scholarly.*
Description: Provides general information about the AO Group as well as issues of interest in orthopedics and trauma care.
Published by: A O Foundation, Clavadelerstr 8, Davos Platz, 7270, Switzerland. TEL 41-81-4142801, FAX 41-81-4142280, foundation@aofoundation.org, http://www.aofoundation.org.

617.585 USA ISSN 8750-2585
A P M A NEWS. Text in English. 1980. 10/yr. free to members (effective 2010). charts; illus.; stat.; tr.lit. **Document type:** *Newsletter, Trade.*
Description: Contains information on the podiatric medical profession, including columns on practice enhancement and insurance advice.
Formerly (until 1984): A P A Report (0272-7722)
Indexed: SD.
Published by: American Podiatric Medical Association, 9312 Old Georgetown Rd, Bethesda, MD 20814. TEL 301-571-9200, FAX 301-530-2752, publications@apma.org, http://www.apma.org. Adv. contact Rachel Richards.

616.025 USA ISSN 1069-6563
RC86 CODEN: AEMEF5
➤ **ACADEMIC EMERGENCY MEDICINE.** Abbreviated title: A E M. Text in English. 1994. m. GBP 174 combined subscription in United Kingdom to institutions (print & online eds.); EUR 221 combined subscription in Europe to institutions (print & online eds.); USD 331 combined subscription in the Americas to institutions (print & online eds.); USD 342 combined subscription elsewhere to institutions (print & online eds.) (effective 2012). adv. bk.rev.; software rev.; video rev. abstr.; charts; illus.; stat. Index. back issues avail.; reprint service avail. from PSC. **Document type:** *Journal, Academic/Scholarly.* **Description:** Publishes material relevant to the practice, education, and investigation of emergency medicine, and reaches a wide audience of emergency care practitioners and educators.
Related titles: Online - full text ed.: ISSN 1553-2712. GBP 153 in United Kingdom to institutions; EUR 193 in Europe to institutions; USD 289 in the Americas to institutions; USD 297 elsewhere to institutions (effective 2012) (from IngentaConnect).
Indexed: A20, A22, ASCA, AddicA, C06, C07, C08, CA, CINAHL, CurCont, E01, EMBASE, ExcerpMed, INI, ISR, IndMed, Inpharma, JW-EM, MEDLINE, P16, P20, P22, P24, P30, P35, P48, P53, P54, PQC, R10, Reac, SCI, SCOPUS, T02, W07.
—BLDSC (0570.511250), GNLM, IE, Infotrieve, Ingenta, INIST. **CCC.**
Published by: (Society for Academic Emergency Medicine), Wiley-Blackwell Publishing, Inc. (Subsidiary of: Wiley-Blackwell Publishing Ltd.), 111 River St, Hoboken, NJ 07030. TEL 201-748-6000, FAX 201-748-6088, info@wiley.com. Ed. David C Cone. Adv. contact Stephen Donohue TEL 781-388-8511.

617 CZE ISSN 0001-5415
CODEN: ACOTA7
➤ **ACTA CHIRURGIAE ORTHOPAEDICAE ET TRAUMATOLOGIAE CECHOSLOVACA.** Text in Czech, Slovak; Summaries in English, Russian. 1934. 6/yr. CZK 600 (effective 2010). bk.rev. 74 p./no.; **Document type:** *Journal, Academic/Scholarly.*
Related titles: Online - full text ed.
Indexed: A22, CISA, DentInd, EMBASE, ExcerpMed, IndMed, MEDLINE, P30, R10, Reac, SCI, SCOPUS, W07.
—BLDSC (0611.050000), CASDDS, GNLM, IE, Infotrieve, Ingenta, INIST. **CCC.**
Published by: (Slovenska Ortopedicka a Traumatologicka Spolocnost SVK, Ceska Spolecnost pro Ortopedii a Traumatologii), Galen, spol. s r.o., Na Belidle 34, Prague 5, 15000, Czech Republic. TEL 420-2-57326178, FAX 420-2-57326170, objednavky@galen.cz, http://www.galen.cz. Ed. Martin Krbec.

617.3 BRA ISSN 0104-7795
➤ **ACTA FISIATRICA.** Text in Portuguese. 1993. s-a. adv. bk.rev. back issues avail. **Document type:** *Journal, Academic/Scholarly.*
Related titles: Online - full text ed.
Published by: (Universidade de Sao Paulo, Faculdade de Medicina, Hospital das Clinicas), Lemos Editorial & Graficos Ltda., Rua Rui Barbosa, 70, B Vista, Sao Paulo, SP 01326-010, Brazil. TEL 55-11-251-4300, FAX 55-11-251-4300, lemospl@netpoint.com.br, http://www.lemos.com.br.

617.3 GBR ISSN 1745-3682
ACTA ORTHOPAEDICA (ONLINE). Text in English. bi-m. free (effective 2011). **Document type:** *Journal, Academic/Scholarly.*
Formerly (until 2005): Acta Orthopaedica Scandinavica (Online) (1651-1964)
Media: Online - full text (from IngentaConnect). **Related titles:** ◆ Print ed.: Acta Orthopaedica (Print). ISSN 1745-3674.
—BLDSC (0642.055000). **CCC.**
Published by: Taylor & Francis Ltd. (Subsidiary of: Taylor & Francis Group), 4 Park Sq, Milton Park, Abingdon, Oxfordshire OX14 4RN, United Kingdom. TEL 44-1235-828600, FAX 44-1235-829000, info@tandf.co.uk, http://www.tandf.co.uk/journals.

617.3 GBR ISSN 1745-3674
CODEN: AOSAAK
➤ **ACTA ORTHOPAEDICA (PRINT).** Text in English. 1930. bi-m. GBP 365, EUR 475, USD 595 combined subscription to institutions (print & online eds.); GBP 720, EUR 950, USD 1,190 combined subscription to corporations (print & online eds.) (effective 2010). adv. bk.rev. bibl.; charts; illus. index. back issues avail.; reprint service avail. from PSC. **Document type:** *Journal, Academic/Scholarly.* **Description:** Presents original articles of basic research interest, as well as clinical studies in the field of orthopedics and related subdisciplines.
Formerly (until 2005): Acta Orthopaedica Scandinavica (Print) (0001-6470)
Related titles: ◆ Online - full text ed.: Acta Orthopaedica (Online). ISSN 1745-3682; ◆ Supplement(s): Acta Orthopaedica. Supplementum (Print Edition). ISSN 1745-3690.
Indexed: A01, A03, A08, A22, A36, AMED, ASCA, B21, B25, BDM&CN, BIOSIS Prev, C06, C07, C08, C11, CA, CABA, CINAHL, CTA, ChemAb, CurCont, DentInd, E01, E12, EMBASE, ExcerpMed, FR, FoSS&M, GH, H04, IBR, IBZ, ISR, IndMed, Inpharma, MEDLINE, MycolAb, N02, N03, P30, R09, R10, Reac, SCI, SCOPUS, SD, T02, W07.
—CASDDS, GNLM, IE, Infotrieve, Ingenta, INIST. **CCC.**
Published by: (Nordic Orthopaedic Federation DNK, Scandinavian Orthopaedic Association NOR), Taylor & Francis Ltd. (Subsidiary of: Taylor & Francis Group), 4 Park Sq, Milton Park, Abingdon, Oxfordshire OX14 4RN, United Kingdom. TEL 44-20-70176000, FAX 44-20-70176336, subscriptions@tandf.co.uk, http://www.taylorandfrancis.com. Ed. Anders Rydholm Lund. Adv. contact Linda Hann. **Subscr. to:** Journals Customer Service, Sheepen Pl, Colchester, Essex CO3 3LP, United Kingdom. TEL 44-20-70175544, FAX 44-20-70175198, tf.enquiries@tfinforma.com.

617.3 BEL ISSN 1784-407X
RD701
ACTA ORTHOPAEDICA BELGICA. Text in English. 1945. 6/yr. EUR 130 domestic to institutions; EUR 150 foreign to institutions (effective 2011). bk.rev. abstr.; bibl. index. **Document type:** *Journal, Academic/Scholarly.*
Formerly (until 2003): Acta Orthopaedica Belgica (Bilingual Edition) (0001-6462)
Related titles: ◆ Supplement(s): Acta Orthopaedica Belgica. Supplementum. ISSN 0772-7623.
Indexed: A22, B21, BDM&CN, C06, C07, CTA, EMBASE, ExcerpMed, IndMed, MEDLINE, P30, R10, Reac, SCI, SCOPUS, W07.
—BLDSC (0642.060000), GNLM, IE, Infotrieve, Ingenta, INIST. **CCC.**
Published by: (Association Royale des Societes Scientifiques Medicales Belges/Koninklijke Vereniging van de Belgische Medische Wetenschappelijke Genootschappen), Acta Medica Belgica, Avenue Winston Churchill 11/30, Brussels, 1180, Belgium. TEL 32-2-3745158, FAX 32-2-3749628, amb@skynet.be, http://www.ulb.ac.be/medecine/loce/amb.htm.

617.3 BEL ISSN 0772-7623
ACTA ORTHOPAEDICA BELGICA. SUPPLEMENTUM. Text in English. 1946. irreg.
Related titles: ◆ Supplement to: Acta Orthopaedica Belgica. ISSN 1784-407X.
Published by: Acta Medica Belgica, Avenue Winston Churchill 11/30, Brussels, 1180, Belgium. Ed. J Dequeker.

616.7 TUR ISSN 1017-995X
RD701
➤ **ACTA ORTHOPAEDICA ET TRAUMATOLOGICA TURCICA.** Abbreviated title: A O T T. Text in English, Turkish. 1962. 5/yr. **Document type:** *Journal, Academic/Scholarly.* **Description:** Publishes diagnostic, treatment and prevention methods related to orthopedics and traumatology.
Related titles: Online - full text ed.: free (effective 2011).
Indexed: EMBASE, ExcerpMed, MEDLINE, P30, R10, Reac, SCI, SCOPUS, W07.
Published by: Istanbul Medical Faculty, Istanbul School of Medicine, Department of Orthopaedics and Traumatology, Topkapi, Istambul, 34390, Turkey. TEL 90-212-5241053, FAX 90-212-6352835, info@aott.org.tr. Ed. Mehmet Demirhan.

617.3 SRB ISSN 0350-2309
➤ **ACTA ORTHOPAEDICA IUGOSLAVICA.** Text mainly in Serbian; Text occasionally in English; Summaries in English. 1969. s-a. EUR 10 to individuals; EUR 25 to institutions (effective 2003). adv. bk.rev. back issues avail. **Document type:** *Academic/Scholarly.* **Description:** Includes general reviews, original scientific papers, professional papers, case reports and other contributions from the fields of orthopaedic surgery, traumatology and related medical branches.
Indexed: SCOPUS.
Published by: Udruzenje Ortopeda i Traumatologa, c/o Institut za Ortopedsko-Hirurske Bolesti "Banjica", Mihajla Avramovica 28, Belgrade, 11041. TEL 381-11-666447, FAX 381-11-667321. Ed., R&P, Adv. contact Zoran Vukasinovic. Circ: 200 (paid); 300 (controlled). **Co-sponsor:** Ministarstvo za Nauku i Tehnologiju Republike Srbije.

616.7005 SWE ISSN 1745-3704
ACTA ORTHOPAEDICA. SUPPLEMENTUM (ONLINE EDITION). Text in Norwegian. irreg. **Document type:** *Monographic series, Academic/Scholarly.*
Formerly (until 2005): Acta Orthopaedica Scandinavica. Supplementum (Online Edition) (1651-2650)
Media: Online - full text. **Related titles:** ◆ Print ed.: Acta Orthopaedica. Supplementum (Print Edition). ISSN 1745-3690.
—CCC.
Published by: Taylor & Francis A B (Subsidiary of: Taylor & Francis Group), PO Box 3255, Stockholm, 10365, Sweden. TEL 46-8-4408040, FAX 46-8-4408050, journals@se.tandf.no, http://www.tandf.co.uk.

617.3 SWE ISSN 1745-3690
CODEN: AOSUAC
ACTA ORTHOPAEDICA. SUPPLEMENTUM (PRINT EDITION). Text in Norwegian. 1934. irreg., latest 2002. free to subscribers of Acta Orthopaedica Scandinavica. adv. reprints avail. **Document type:** *Monographic series, Academic/Scholarly.*
Formerly (until 2005): Acta Orthopaedica Scandinavica. Supplementum (Print Edition) (0300-8827)
Related titles: ◆ Online - full text ed.: Acta Orthopaedica. Supplementum (Online Edition). ISSN 1745-3704; ◆ Supplement to: Acta Orthopaedica (Print). ISSN 1745-3674.
Indexed: A01, A03, A08, A22, C06, C07, C08, C11, CA, CINAHL, EMBASE, ExcerpMed, H04, IndMed, MEDLINE, P30, R09, SCOPUS, SD, T02.
—IE, Ingenta, INIST. **CCC.**
Published by: (Scandinavian Orthopaedic Association NOR), Taylor & Francis A B (Subsidiary of: Taylor & Francis Group), PO Box 3255, Stockholm, 10365, Sweden. TEL 46-8-4408040, FAX 46-8-4408050.

617.3 BRA ISSN 1413-7852
ACTA ORTOPEDICA BRASILEIRA. Text in Portuguese. 1993. q. **Document type:** *Journal, Academic/Scholarly.* **Description:** Devoted to publishing information related to orthopedics.
Related titles: Online - full text ed.: free (effective 2011).
Indexed: C01, SCI, SCOPUS, W07.
Published by: Instituto de Ortopedia e Traumatologia, R Dr Ovidio Pires de Campos 333, Pinheiros, Sao Paulo, 05403-010, Brazil. http://www.hcnet.usp.br/iot/.

616.7 MEX
ACTA ORTOPEDICA MEXICANA. Text in Spanish. 1987. bi-m. USD 50 domestic to non-members; USD 80 foreign to non-members; free to members (effective 2005). back issues avail. **Document type:** *Journal, Academic/Scholarly.*
Formerly: Revista Mexicana de Ortopedia y Traumatologia (0187-7593)
Related titles: Online - full content ed.; Online - full text ed.
Indexed: A01, C01.
Published by: Sociedad Mexicana de Ortopedia, Edificio World Trade Center, Montecito 38, Piso 25, Oficina 23-27, Col Napoles, Mexico D.F., Mexico. http://www.smo.edu.mx/. Ed. Dr. Octavio Sierra Martinez.

617.3 ESP ISSN 1699-3543
ACTUALIZACIONES EN CIRUGIA ORTOPEDICA Y TRAUMATOLOGIA. Text in Spanish. 1999. a. price varies. **Document type:** *Monographic series, Academic/Scholarly.*
Formerly (until 2004): Sociedad Espanola de Cirugia Ortopedica y Traumatologia. Actualizaciones (1699-3535)
Published by: Sociedad Espanola de Cirugia Ortopedica y Traumatologia, C Fernandez de los Rios 108 - 2o, Madrid, 28015, Spain. TEL 34-91-5441062, FAX 34-91-4550475, secot@secot.es, http://www.secot.es/.

616.71 ARG ISSN 1669-8975
ACTUALIZACIONES EN OSTEOLOGIA. Text in Spanish. 2005. 3/yr. back issues avail. **Document type:** *Journal, Academic/Scholarly.*
Related titles: Online - full text ed.: ISSN 1669-8983. 2005.
Indexed: CA, EMBASE, SCOPUS, T02.
Published by: Asociacion Argentina de Osteologia y Metabolismo Mineral, Cosquin 1673, Barrio Jardin, Cordoba, 5014, Argentina. TEL 34-11-48611807, info@aaomm.org.ar, http://www.aaomm.org.ar/. Ed. Ariel Sanchez.

616.025 USA ISSN 1931-4485
➤ **ADVANCED EMERGENCY NURSING JOURNAL.** Text in English. 1979. q. USD 347.51 domestic to institutions; USD 459 foreign to institutions (effective 2011). adv. back issues avail.; reprints avail. **Document type:** *Journal, Academic/Scholarly.* **Description:** Designed to meet the information needs of practice clinicians, clinical nurse specialists, nurse practitioners, health care professionals, and clinical and academic educators in emergency nursing.
Formerly (until 2006): Topics in Emergency Medicine (0164-2340)
Related titles: Online - full text ed.: ISSN 1931-4493.
Indexed: A01, A03, A08, A22, A26, C06, C07, C08, CA, CINAHL, E08, EMBASE, ExcerpMed, G08, H11, H12, I05, MEDLINE, P16, P20, P22, P24, P26, P30, P48, P53, P54, PQC, S09, SCOPUS, T02.
—BLDSC (0696.849000), GNLM, IE, Infotrieve, Ingenta. **CCC.**
Published by: Lippincott Williams & Wilkins (Subsidiary of: Wolters Kluwer N.V.), Two Commerce Sq, 2001 Market St, Philadelphia, PA 19103. TEL 215-521-8300, FAX 215-521-8902, customerservice@lww.com, http://www.lww.com. Eds. Jean A Proehl, K Sue Hoyt. Pub. Kathleen M Phelan. Circ: 1,914.

616.02 USA ISSN 1524-0134
ADVANCED RESCUE TECHNOLOGY. Text in English. 1995. bi-m. free (effective 2008). adv. software rev.; video rev.; bk.rev. illus.; tr.lit. Supplement avail.; back issues avail.; reprints avail. **Document type:** *Magazine, Trade.* **Description:** Addresses the education needs of today's rescue personnel.
Formerly: E M S Rescue Technology
Related titles: Online - full text ed.: free (effective 2008).
Indexed: CA, P24, P48, PQC.
—CCC.
Published by: Cygnus Business Media, Inc., 1233 Janesville Ave, PO Box 803, Fort Atkinson, WI 53538. TEL 920-563-6388, 800-547-7377, FAX 920-563-1702, http://www.cygnusb2b.com. Ed. Harvey Eisner TEL 631-963-6252. Circ: 20,000.

616.7 USA ISSN 2090-3472
RD701
▼ ➤ **ADVANCES IN ORTHOPEDICS.** Text in English. 2011. free (effective 2011). **Document type:** *Journal, Academic/Scholarly.*
Description: Covers all areas of orthopedics.
Media: Online - full text.
Published by: Sage - Hindawi Access to Research, 410 Park Ave, 15th Fl, 287 PMB, New York, NY 10022. FAX 866-446-3294.

616 GBR ISSN 1753-3805
➤ **ADVANCES IN PAIN MANAGEMENT.** Text in English. 2007. q. EUR 150 in Europe; USD 200 elsewhere (effective 2009). back issues avail. **Document type:** *Journal, Academic/Scholarly.* **Description:** Aims to promote a better understanding of pain medicine by providing an active forum for the discussion of clinical and healthcare issues.
Related titles: Online - full text ed.
—BLDSC (0709.575250), IE.
Published by: Remedica Medical Education and Publishing Ltd., Commonwealth House, 1 New Oxford St, London, WC1A 1NU, United Kingdom. TEL 44-20-77592999, FAX 44-20-77592951, info@remedica.com, http://www.remedica.com. Eds. Lara Dhingra, Ricardo A Cruciani. Pub. Ian Ackland-Snow.

616.7 USA ISSN 2162-1918
▼ **ADVANCES IN WOUND CARE.** Text in English. 2012. bi-m. USD 1,394 combined subscription domestic (print & online eds.); USD 1,590 combined subscription foreign (print & online eds.) (effective 2012). back issues avail. **Document type:** *Journal, Academic/Scholarly.*
Related titles: Online - full text ed.: ISSN 2162-1934. USD 1,245 (effective 2012).
Published by: Mary Ann Liebert, Inc. Publishers, 140 Huguenot St, 3rd Fl, New Rochelle, NY 10801. TEL 914-740-2100, FAX 914-740-2101, 800-654-3237, info@liebertpub.com. Ed. Chandan K Sen.

616.7 DEU
AERZTLICHES JOURNAL REISE UND MEDIZIN ORTHOPAEDIE. Text in German. 2000. bi-m. EUR 21; EUR 4.60 newsstand/cover (effective 2007). adv. **Document type:** *Magazine, Trade.*
Published by: Otto Hoffmanns Verlag GmbH, Arnulfstr 10, Munich, 80335, Germany. TEL 49-89-5458450, FAX 49-89-54584530, info@ohv-online.de. Adv. contact Edeltraud Koller. B&W page EUR 1,640, color page EUR 2,690. Circ: 4,020 (paid and controlled).

616 ITA ISSN 1970-6839
➤ **AGGIORNAMENTI C I O.** (Club Italiano Osteosintesi) Text in Italian. 1991. s-a. EUR 55, USD 92 combined subscription to institutions (print & online eds.) (effective 2012). **Document type:** *Journal, Academic/Scholarly.*
Formerly (until 2003): C I O D Aggiornamenti (1121-693X)
Related titles: Online - full text ed.: ISSN 1970-6847. 1995.
—CCC.
Published by: Springer Italia Srl (Subsidiary of: Springer Science+Business Media), Via Decembrio 28, Milan, 20137, Italy. TEL 39-02-54259722, FAX 39-02-55193360, springer@springer.it. Ed. P Maniscalco. **Subscr. to:** Springer New York LLC, Journal Fulfillment, PO Box 2485, Secaucus, NJ 07096. TEL 201-348-4033, 800-777-4643, FAX 201-348-4505, journals-ny@springer.com, http://www.springer.com.

616.025 TUR ISSN 1309-534X
▼➤ **AKADEMIK ACIL TIP OLGU SUNUMLARI DERGISI/JOURNAL OF ACADEMIC EMERGENCY MEDICINE CASE REPORTS.** Text in English, Turkish. 2010. q. free. back issues avail. **Document type:** *Journal, Academic/Scholarly.* **Description:** Publishes original case reports and brief reports.
Related titles: Online - full text ed.
—CCC.
Published by: Acil Tip Uzmanlari Dernegi Yukari Ayranci Guleryuz Sk./Emergency Medicine Physicians' Association of Turkey, No:26/19 Cankaya, Ankara, 06550, Turkey. TEL 90-312-4261214, FAX 90-312-4261244. Ed. Yusuf Yurumez.

616.7 CAN
ALIGNMENT. Text in English. a. adv. **Description:** Includes clinical methods, technical procedures, member listing, accredited facility listing, and CAPO news.
Published by: (Canadian Association of Prosthetists and Orthotists), Pappin Communications, The Victoria Centre, 84 Isabella St, Pembroke, ON K8A 5S5, Canada. TEL 613-735-0952, FAX 613-735-7983, info@pappin.com, http://www.pappin.com. Ed. Kirsten Simonsen. Pub. Bruce Pappin. Adv. contact Heather Coughlin. B&W page CAD 510, color page CAD 1,120.

AMBULANCE IRELAND. *see* HEALTH FACILITIES AND ADMINISTRATION

362.18 GBR
AMBULANCE TODAY. Text in English. 2004 (vol.4). bi-m. adv. **Document type:** *Magazine, Trade.*
—BLDSC (0809.210500).
Address: 41 Canning St, Liverpool, Merseyside L8 7NN, United Kingdom. Ed. Declan Heneghan.

AMBULANCE U K. *see* HEALTH FACILITIES AND ADMINISTRATION

617.3 USA ISSN 0065-6895
RD711
AMERICAN ACADEMY OF ORTHOPAEDIC SURGEONS. COMMITTEE ON INSTRUCTIONAL COURSES. INSTRUCTIONAL COURSE LECTURES. Text in English. 1948. a. free to members (effective 2010). reprints avail. **Document type:** *Proceedings, Academic/Scholarly.*
Indexed: A22, EMBASE, ExcerpMed, IndMed, MEDLINE, P30, R10, Reac, SCOPUS.
—BLDSC (4524.930000), GNLM, IE, Infotrieve, Ingenta.
Published by: American Academy of Orthopaedic Surgeons, 6300 N River Rd, Rosemont, IL 60018. TEL 847-823-7186, FAX 847-823-8125, custserv@aaos.org, http://www.aaos.org. Circ: 542,005.

617.3 USA
AMERICAN ACADEMY OF ORTHOPAEDIC SURGEONS. FIND AN ORTHOPAEDIST. Text in English. 1933. biennial. **Document type:** *Directory, Trade.*
Supersedes in part (in 2004): American Academy of Orthopaedic Surgeons. Directory and Bylaws (Print); Which was formerly (until 1998): American Academy of Orthopaedic Surgeons. Directory (0516-8856)
Media: Online - full text.
Published by: American Academy of Orthopaedic Surgeons, 6300 N River Rd, Rosemont, IL 60018. TEL 847-384-4015, FAX 847-823-8125, jaaos@ebsco.com, http://www.aaos.org.

617.3 USA ISSN 1067-151X
RD736
➤ **AMERICAN ACADEMY OF ORTHOPAEDIC SURGEONS. JOURNAL.** Text in English; Abstracts in Multiple languages. 1993. m. USD 206 domestic to individuals; USD 248 foreign to individuals; USD 385 domestic to institutions; USD 433 foreign to institutions (effective 2010). adv. abstr.; bibl.; illus. 112 p./no.; back issues avail.; reprints avail. **Document type:** *Journal, Academic/Scholarly.* **Description:** Covers the latest developments in the clinical practice of orthopedics, focusing on diagnosis and management of orthopedic conditions.
Related titles: CD-ROM ed.: ISSN 1095-8762. 1997; Online - full text ed.: ISSN 1940-5480; ♦ Spanish ed.: American Academy of Orthopaedic Surgeons. Journal (Spanish Edition). ISSN 1579-2080.
Indexed: A22, A26, C06, C07, CurCont, E08, EMBASE, ExcerpMed, H12, I05, INI, IndMed, MEDLINE, P30, R10, Reac, SCI, SCOPUS, W07.
—BLDSC (4683.732000), GNLM, IE, Infotrieve, Ingenta.
Published by: American Academy of Orthopaedic Surgeons, 6300 N River Rd, Rosemont, IL 60018. TEL 847-823-7186, FAX 847-823-8125, jaaos@ebsco.com, custserv@aaos.org, http://www.aaos.org. Ed. Jeffrey S Fischgrund. Circ: 31,527 (controlled). **Subscr. to:** PO Box 361, Birmingham, AL 35201. TEL 205-995-1567, 800-633-4931, FAX 205-995-1588.

617.3 ESP ISSN 1579-2080
AMERICAN ACADEMY OF ORTHOPAEDIC SURGEONS. JOURNAL (SPANISH EDITION). Text in Spanish. 2002. bi-m. EUR 173.63 to individuals; EUR 320.11 to institutions (effective 2009). back issues avail. **Document type:** *Journal, Academic/Scholarly.*
Related titles: Online - full text ed.: ISSN 1695-0275. 2002. EUR 114.91 to individuals; EUR 172.37 to institutions (effective 2009); ♦ English ed.: American Academy of Orthopaedic Surgeons. Journal. ISSN 1067-151X.
Indexed: A01, CA, F03, F04, T02.
Published by: Grupo Ars XXI de Comunicacion, SA, Muntaner 262 Atico 2a., Barcelona, 08021, Spain. TEL 34-90-2195484, FAX 34-93-2722902, info@arsxxi.com. Ed. William P Cooney.

617.11 USA ISSN 0361-7726
AMERICAN BURN ASSOCIATION. ANNUAL MEETING. PROCEEDING. Text in English. 1967. a. USD 25. **Document type:** *Proceedings.*
Published by: American Burn Association, 625 N Michigan Ave, Ste 2550, Chicago, IL 60611. TEL 312-642-9260, 800-548-2876, FAX 312-642-9130, info@ameriburn.org, http://www.ameriburn.org. Circ: 4,000.

616.7 USA ISSN 1876-4983
▼➤ **THE AMERICAN COLLEGE OF CERTIFIED WOUND SPECIALISTS. JOURNAL.** Text in English. 2009. 4/yr. USD 248 in North America to institutions; USD 303 elsewhere to institutions (effective 2012). **Document type:** *Journal, Academic/Scholarly.*
Related titles: Online - full text ed.: ISSN 1876-4991 (from ScienceDirect).
Indexed: CA, EMBASE, ExcerpMed, P30, R10, Reac, SCOPUS, T02.
—CCC.
Published by: (The American College of Certified Wound Specialists), Elsevier Inc. (Subsidiary of: Elsevier Science & Technology), 360 Park Ave S, New York, NY 10010. TEL 212-989-5800, 888-437-4636, FAX 212-633-3990, usinfo-f@elsevier.com. Ed. Steve Abraham.

617.3 USA
AMERICAN COLLEGE OF FOOT AND ANKLE ORTHOPEDICS AND MEDICINE NEWSLETTER. Variant title: A C F A O M Newsletter. Text in English. 1964. q. looseleaf. membership. bk.rev. abstr.; charts; illus. **Document type:** *Newsletter, Trade.*
Formerly (until Oct. 1993): American College of Foot Orthopedists Newsletter (0002-7987)
Published by: American College of Foot and Ankle Orthopedics and Medicine, 5272 River Rd., Ste. 630, Bethesda, MD 20816. TEL 301-718-6505, 800-265-8263, FAX 301-656-0989, info@acfaom.org, http://www.acfaom.org/. Ed. Judith A Baerg. Circ: 1,100.

AMERICAN JOURNAL OF CRITICAL CARE. *see* MEDICAL SCIENCES—Nurses And Nursing

616.025 USA ISSN 0735-6757
RC86 CODEN: AJEMEN
➤ **AMERICAN JOURNAL OF EMERGENCY MEDICINE.** Abbreviated title: A J E M. Text in English. 1983. 7/yr. USD 529 in United States to institutions; USD 711 elsewhere to institutions (effective 2012). adv. bk.rev. abstr.; bibl.; charts; illus. index. back issues avail.; reprints avail. **Document type:** *Journal, Academic/Scholarly.* **Description:** Covers all aspects of emergency medicine with clinical articles, case studies, reviews, worldwide news items, and editorials.
Related titles: Microform ed.: (from PQC); Online - full text ed.: ISSN 1532-8171 (from ScienceDirect).
Indexed: A22, A26, A34, A36, ASCA, C06, C07, C08, CA, CABA, CINAHL, CurCont, E01, E12, EMBASE, ExcerpMed, FR, Faml, GH, H12, H16, H17, I05, IDIS, IndMed, Inpharma, Inspec, JW-EM, MEDLINE, MS&D, N02, N03, P30, P32, P33, P35, P39, R07, R08, R10, R12, RA&MP, RILM, RM&VM, Reac, SCI, SCOPUS, T02, T05, VS, W07, W10.
—BLDSC (0824.480000), GNLM, IE, Ingenta, INIST. **CCC.**
Published by: W.B. Saunders Co. (Subsidiary of: Elsevier Health Sciences), Elsevier, Health Sciences Division, Order Fulfillment, 3251 Riverport Ln, Maryland Heights, MO 63043. TEL 314-872-8370, 800-325-4177, FAX 314-432-1380, JournalCustomerService-usa@elsevier.com, http://www.us.elsevierhealth.com. Ed. Dr. J Douglas White. Pub. Theresa Monturano. Adv. contact John Marmero TEL 212-633-3657. Circ: 500.

617.3 USA ISSN 1078-4519
CODEN: AJORFL
➤ **THE AMERICAN JOURNAL OF ORTHOPEDICS.** Text in English. 1972. m. USD 128 domestic to individuals; USD 165 in Canada & Mexico to individuals; USD 185 elsewhere to individuals; USD 184 domestic to institutions; USD 232 in Canada & Mexico to institutions; USD 297 elsewhere to institutions (effective 2007). adv. bk.rev. charts; illus.; stat. index. back issues avail.; reprints avail. **Document type:** *Journal, Academic/Scholarly.*
Formerly (until 1995): Orthopaedic Review (0094-6591)
Related titles: Microform ed.: (from PQC); Online - full text ed.: ISSN 1934-3418.
Indexed: A22, C06, C07, EMBASE, ExcerpMed, INI, IndMed, MEDLINE, P30, R10, Reac, SCOPUS.
—BLDSC (0829.190000), GNLM, IE, Infotrieve, Ingenta, INIST. **CCC.**
Published by: Quadrant HealthCom, 7 Century Dr, Ste 302, Parsippany, NJ 07054. TEL 973-206-3434, FAX 973-206-9251, http://www.qhc.com. Eds. Barbara Ready TEL 973-206-8971, Peter McCann. Adv. contact Tim LaPella TEL 866-312-8805 ext 138. B&W page USD 2,555, color page USD 4,095; trim 7.875 x 10.75. Circ: 29,000 (paid).

617.585 USA ISSN 8750-7315
RD563.A2 CODEN: JAPAEA
➤ **AMERICAN PODIATRIC MEDICAL ASSOCIATION. JOURNAL.** Abbreviated title: J A P M A. Text in English. 1907. bi-m. USD 75 to members; USD 195 combined subscription domestic to non-members (print & online eds.); USD 230 combined subscription foreign to non-members (print & online eds.); USD 40 per issue to non-members (effective 2010). adv. bk.rev. bibl.; illus. cum.index: 1973-1984. 128 p./no. 2 cols./p.; back issues avail. **Document type:** *Journal, Academic/Scholarly.* **Description:** Publishes research studies, case reports, literature reviews, special communications, clinical correspondence, letters to the editor, book reviews, and various other types of submissions.
Incorporates: Podiatric Medicine and Surgery; Former titles (until 1985): American Podiatry Association. Journal (0003-0538); (until 1958): National Association of Chiropodists. Journal (0360-1684); (until 1949): National Association of Chiropodists Podiatrists. Journal; (until 1940): National Association of Chiropodists. Journal; (until 1921): The Pedic Items
Related titles: Microfilm ed.; Online - full text ed.: ISSN 1930-8264. USD 145 domestic to individuals; USD 170 foreign to individuals; USD 175 domestic to institutions; USD 210 foreign to institutions (effective 2010); ♦ Spanish ed.: Pedologia Clinica. ISSN 1578-0716.
Indexed: A20, A22, A36, AMED, ASCA, C06, C07, C08, CABA, CINAHL, CurCont, DentInd, E12, EMBASE, ExcerpMed, GH, HospLI, INI, IndMed, Inpharma, LT, MEDLINE, MS&D, N02, N03, P30, P33, P35, R08, R10, R12, RM&VM, RRTA, Reac, SCI, SCOPUS, T05, VS, W07.
—BLDSC (4692.040000), GNLM, IE, Infotrieve, Ingenta, INIST.
Published by: American Podiatric Medical Association, 9312 Old Georgetown Rd, Bethesda, MD 20814. TEL 301-571-9200, FAX 301-530-2752, publications@apma.org, http://www.apma.org. Ed. Warren S Joseph.

616.025 FRA ISSN 2108-6524
▼ **ANNALES FRANCAISES DE MEDECINE D'URGENCE.** Text in French. 2011. bi-m. EUR 315, USD 387 combined subscription to institutions (print & online eds.) (effective 2012). **Document type:** *Journal, Academic/Scholarly.*
Related titles: Online - full text ed.: ISSN 2108-6591. 2011.
—IE. **CCC.**
Published by: Springer France (Subsidiary of: Springer Science+Business Media), 22 Rue de Palestro, Paris, 75002, France. TEL 33-1-53009860, FAX 33-1-53009861, sylvie.kamara@springer.com. Ed. Bruno Riou.

616.025 USA ISSN 0196-0644
RC86 CODEN: AEMED3
➤ **ANNALS OF EMERGENCY MEDICINE.** Text in English. 1972. m. USD 456 in United States to institutions; USD 556 elsewhere to institutions (effective 2012). bk.rev. back issues avail.; reprints avail. **Document type:** *Journal, Academic/Scholarly.* **Description:** Presents pertinent information encompassing clinical studies, case reports, basic research, and discussion.
Formerly (until 1980): J A C E P (0361-1124)
Related titles: Microfilm ed.; Online - full text ed.: ISSN 1097-6760 (from ScienceDirect).
Indexed: A20, A22, A26, A36, AHCMS, AIM, ASCA, B21, C06, C07, C08, CA, CABA, CINAHL, CurCont, D01, DentInd, E01, E08, E12, EMBASE, ESPM, ExcerpMed, FAMLI, FR, G08, GH, H&SSA, H11, H12, I05, IDIS, INI, ISR, IndMed, Inpharma, JW, JW-EM, Kidney, MEDLINE, N02, N03, P30, P33, P35, P39, PN&I, R07, R08, R10, R12, RM&VM, Reac, RiskAb, S02, S03, S09, S12, S13, S16, SCI, SCOPUS, T02, T05, W07, W11.
—BLDSC (1040.425000), GNLM, IE, Infotrieve, Ingenta, INIST. **CCC.**
Published by: (American College of Emergency Physicians), Mosby, Inc. (Subsidiary of: Elsevier Health Sciences), 1600 John F. Kennedy Blvd, Ste 1800, Philadelphia, PA 19103. TEL 215-239-3900, 800-523-1649, FAX 215-239-3990, elspcs@elsevier.com, http://www.us.elsevierhealth.com. Ed. Dr. Michael L. Callaham.

617.3 DEU ISSN 0936-8051
CODEN: AOTSEF
➤ **ARCHIVES OF ORTHOPAEDIC AND TRAUMA SURGERY.** Text in English. 1903. 10/yr. EUR 3,411, USD 4,098 combined subscription to institutions (print & online eds.) (effective 2012). adv. bk.rev. bibl.; charts; illus. index. back issues avail.; reprint service avail. from PSC. **Document type:** *Journal, Academic/Scholarly.* **Description:** Reports on the latest advances in all areas of orthopedics, including accident related injuries, experimental bone and joint surgery, and problems related to rehabilitation.
Former titles: Archives of Orthopaedic and Traumatic Surgery (0344-8444); (until 1978): Archiv fuer Orthopaedische und Unfallchirurgie (0003-9330)
Related titles: Microform ed.: (from PQC); Online - full text ed.: ISSN 1434-3916 (from IngentaConnect).
Indexed: A01, A03, A08, A20, A22, A26, ASCA, B21, B25, BIOSIS Prev, C06, C07, CA, CTA, ChemAb, CurCont, DentInd, E01, EMBASE, ExcerpMed, FoSS&M, H12, IBR, IBZ, ISR, IndMed, Inpharma, MEDLINE, MycolAb, P30, P35, R09, R10, Reac, SCI, SCOPUS, SD, T02, W07.
—BLDSC (1638.494900), GNLM, IE, Infotrieve, Ingenta, INIST. **CCC.**
Published by: (Deutsche Gesellschaft fuer Unfallheilkunde, Versicherungs-, Versorgungs- und Verkehrsmedizin), Springer (Subsidiary of: Springer Science+Business Media), Tiergartenstr 17, Heidelberg, 69121, Germany. TEL 49-6221-4870, FAX 49-6221-345229. Eds. Dr. J Goldhahn, Dr. Michael J Strobel, Dr. Michael Blauth. adv.: B&W page EUR 790, color page EUR 1,830. Circ: 650 (paid and controlled). **Subscr. in the Americas to:** Springer New York LLC, Journal Fulfillment, PO Box 2485, Secaucus, NJ 07096. TEL 800-777-4643, 201-348-4033, FAX 201-348-4505, journals-ny@springer.com, http://www.springer.com; **Subscr. to:** Springer Distribution Center, Kundenservice Zeitschriften, Haberstr 7, Heidelberg 69126, Germany. TEL 49-6221-3454303, FAX 49-6221-3454229, subscriptions@springer.com.

617.3 616.742 ITA ISSN 0390-7368
RD701
➤ **ARCHIVIO DI ORTOPEDIA E REUMATOLOGIA.** Text in Italian; Summaries in English. 1884. q. EUR 87, USD 106 combined subscription to institutions (print & online eds.) (effective 2011). adv. bk.rev. abstr.; bibl.; illus. index. **Document type:** *Journal, Academic/Scholarly.*
Formerly (until 1974): Archivio di Ortopedia (0004-0118)
Related titles: Online - full text ed.: ISSN 1592-7113 (from IngentaConnect).
Indexed: A22, A26, ChemAb, E01, IndMed, P30.
—GNLM, IE. **CCC.**
Published by: (Istituto Ortopedico "Gaetano Pini"), Springer Italia Srl (Subsidiary of: Springer Science+Business Media), Via Decembrio 28, Milan, 20137, Italy. TEL 39-02-54259722, FAX 39-02-55193360, springer@springer.it. Eds. G Peretti, V Corrao, Marco d'Imporzano. Adv. contact Stephan Kroeck TEL 49-30-827875739. Circ: 500. **Subscr. in the Americas to:** Springer New York LLC, Journal Fulfillment, PO Box 2485, Secaucus, NJ 07096. TEL 800-777-4643, 201-348-4033, FAX 201-348-4505, journals-ny@springer.com, http://www.springer.com; **Subscr. to:** Springer Distribution Center, Kundenservice Zeitschriften, Haberstr 7, Heidelberg 69126, Germany. TEL 49-6221-3454303, FAX 49-6221-3454229, subscriptions@springer.com, http://link.springer.de.

616.7 FRA ISSN 1957-7729
ARGOSPINE NEWS & JOURNAL. Text in English. 2000. 2/yr. EUR 168, USD 223 combined subscription to institutions (print & online eds.) (effective 2012). reprint service avail. from PSC. **Document type:** *Journal, Academic/Scholarly.*
Formerly (until 2007): Argos Spine News (1774-6701)
Related titles: Online - full text ed.: ISSN 1957-7737 (from IngentaConnect).
Indexed: SCOPUS.
—IE. **CCC.**

M

Published by: Springer France (Subsidiary of: Springer Science+Business Media), 22 Rue de Palestro, Paris, 75002, France. TEL 33-1-53009860, FAX 33-1-53009861, sylvie.kamara@springer.com, http://www.springer.com. Eds. Christian Mazel, Dr. Pierre Kehr.

617 USA ISSN 0749-8063
RD686 CODEN: ARTHE3
➤ **ARTHROSCOPY: THE JOURNAL OF ARTHROSCOPY AND RELATED SURGERY.** Text in English. 1985. m. USD 913 in United States to institutions; USD 1,114 elsewhere to institutions (effective 2012). adv. bk.rev. charts; illus. index. back issues avail.; reprints avail. **Document type:** *Journal, Academic/Scholarly.* **Description:** Explores trends and innovations in both diagnostic and operative arthroscopy.
Related titles: Online - full text ed.: ISSN 1526-3231 (from ScienceDirect).
Indexed: A22, A26, B25, BIOSIS Prev, C06, C07, CA, CurCont, E01, EMBASE, ExcerpMed, FR, FoSS&M, I05, ISR, IndMed, Inpharma, MEDLINE, MycolAb, P30, P35, R10, Reac, SCI, SCOPUS, T02, W07.
—BLDSC (1733.940000), GNLM, IE, Infotrieve, Ingenta, INIST. **CCC.**
Published by: (Arthroscopy Association of North America), W.B. Saunders Co. (Subsidiary of: Elsevier Health Sciences), Elsevier, Health Sciences Division, Order Fulfillment, 3251 Riverport Ln, Maryland Heights, MO 63043. TEL 314-872-8370, 800-325-4177, FAX 314-432-1380, JournalCustomerService-usa@elsevier.com, http://www.us.elsevierhealth.com. Ed. Dr. Gary G Poehling. Adv. contact Nicole Johnson TEL 215-239-3168. Circ: 5,400. **Co-sponsor:** International Arthroscopy Association.

616.73 KOR ISSN 1976-1902
ASIAN SPINE JOURNAL. Text in English. 2007. s-a. **Document type:** *Journal, Academic/Scholarly.*
Related titles: Online - full text ed.: ISSN 1976-7846.
Indexed: P30.
—BLDSC (1742.746458).
Published by: Korean Society of Spine Surgery, Department of Orthopaedic Surgery, Yonsei University, College of Medicine, #134 Shinchon-dong, Soedaemun-ku, Seoul, 120-752, Korea, S. TEL 82-2-22282180, FAX 82-2-3631139, Koreaspine@yumc.yonsei.ac.kr, http://www.spine.or.kr/. Ed. Jae-Yoon Chung.

616.7 617.6 ARG ISSN 0326-5404
ASOCIACION ARGENTINA DE ORTOPEDIA FUNCIONAL DE LOS MAXILARES. REVISTA. Text in Spanish. 1964. q. **Document type:** *Journal, Academic/Scholarly.*
Published by: Asociacion Argentina de Ortopedia Funcional de los Maxilares (A A O F M), Av Directorio 1824, Buenos Aires, C1406GZU, Argentina. TEL 54-11-46326926, FAX 54-11-46328138, aaofm@sion.com.ar.

616.7 ARG ISSN 1515-1786
ASOCIACION ARGENTINA DE ORTOPEDIA Y TRAUMATOLOGIA. REVISTA. Text in English. 1936. q. **Document type:** *Journal, Academic/Scholarly.*
Former titles (until 1983): Sociedad Argentina de Ortopedia y Traumatologia. Boletines y Trabajos (0325-1578); (until 1949): Sociedad Argentina de Cirugia Ortopedica. Boletines y Trabajos (1515-4769)
Related titles: Online - full text ed.: ISSN 1852-7434. 1936 (from SciELO).
Published by: Asociacion Argentina de Ortopedia y Traumatologia (A A O T), Vicente Lopez 1878, Buenos Aires, 1128, Argentina. TEL 54-11-4801 2320, FAX 54-11-4801 7703, publicaciones@aaot.org.ar, http://www.aaot.com.ar. Circ: 2,500.

616.7 IRL ISSN 1649-6264
ATLANTIC ORTHOPAEDIC CLUB. PROCEEDINGS. Text in English. 2004. a.
Related titles: ◆ Supplement to: National Institute of Health Sciences. Research Bulletin. ISSN 1649-0681.
Published by: (Atlantic Orthopaedic Club), National Institute of Health Sciences, St Camillus Hospital, Limerick, Ireland. TEL 353-61-483981, FAX 353-61-483974, http://www.nihs.ie.

617.5 POL ISSN 1895-281X
➤ **ATROSKOPIA I CHIRURGIA STAWOW/ARTHROSCOPY AND JOINT SURGERY.** Text and summaries in English, Polish. 2005. q. PLZ 120 domestic to institutions; EUR 99 in Europe to institutions; USD 145 elsewhere to institutions (effective 2011). adv. abstr.; illus. back issues avail. **Document type:** *Journal, Academic/Scholarly.* **Description:** Covers a wide spectrum of issues connected with orthopedics, traumatology, and arthroscopic treatment of rehabilitation for patients with orthopedic and traumatological disorders.
Related titles: Online - full text ed.
Indexed: A01.
Published by: (Polskie Towarzystwo Chirurgii Artroskopowej/Polish Society of Arthroscopic Surgery), Index Copernicus International S.A., Al. Jerozolimskie 146 C, Warsaw, 02-305, Poland. TEL 48-22-3475077, FAX 48-22-3475086, j.lewczuk@indexcopernicus.com, http://indexcopernicus.com/pages/view/id/32. Ed. Jaroslaw Deszczynski. Pub., R&P Joanna Lewczuk. Circ: 500 (paid).

617.3 USA ISSN 0748-8947
➤ **AUDIO-DIGEST EMERGENCY MEDICINE.** Text in English. 1984. s-m. USD 449.81 domestic; USD 527.72 elsewhere (effective 2010). back issues avail. **Document type:** *Journal, Academic/Scholarly.*
Media: Audio cassette/tape. **Related titles:** Audio CD ed.: USD 399.89 domestic; USD 431.72 in Canada; USD 479.72 elsewhere (effective 2010); Online - full text ed.: USD 359.72 (effective 2010).
Published by: Audio-Digest Foundation (Subsidiary of: California Medical Association), 1577 E Chevy Chase Dr, Glendale, CA 91206. TEL 818-240-7500, 800-423-2308, FAX 818-240-7379.

617.3 USA ISSN 0271-132X
➤ **AUDIO-DIGEST ORTHOPAEDICS.** Text in English. 1978. s-m. USD 449.81 domestic; USD 479.72 in Canada; USD 527.72 elsewhere (effective 2010). back issues avail. **Document type:** *Journal, Academic/Scholarly.*
Media: Audio cassette/tape. **Related titles:** Audio CD ed.: USD 399.89 domestic; USD 431.72 in Canada; USD 479.72 elsewhere (effective 2010); Online - full text ed.: USD 359.72 (effective 2010).
Published by: Audio-Digest Foundation (Subsidiary of: California Medical Association), 1577 E Chevy Chase Dr, Glendale, CA 91206. TEL 818-240-7500, 800-423-2308, FAX 818-240-7379.

➤ **AUSTRALASIAN EMERGENCY NURSING JOURNAL.** *see* MEDICAL SCIENCES—Nurses And Nursing

616.02 NZL ISSN 1174-4707
HV1
➤ **AUSTRALASIAN JOURNAL OF DISASTER AND TRAUMA STUDIES.** Text in English. 1997. 2/yr. free (effective 2011). bk.rev. back issues avail. **Document type:** *Journal, Academic/Scholarly.* **Description:** Provides a forum for the publication of original research, reviews and commentaries. Includes disaster and trauma mitigation and prevention, response, support, recovery, treatment, policy formulation and planning and their implications at the individual, group, organizational and community level.
Media: Online - full text.
Indexed: B21, ESPM, H&SSA, P03, PsycInfo, PsycholAb, RiskAb, SCOPUS.
—**CCC.**
Published by: Massey University, School of Psychology, Private Bag 11-222, Palmerston North, New Zealand. TEL 64-6-3569099, FAX 64-6-3505673. Ed. Douglas Paton. Pub., R&P Harvey Jones.

➤ **AVANCES EN TRAUMATOLOGIA, CIRUGIA, REHABILITACION, MEDICINA PREVENTIVA Y DEPORTIVA.** *see* MEDICAL SCIENCES—Surgery

616.7 GBR ISSN 1471-227X
RC1 CODEN: BEMMC3
➤ **B M C EMERGENCY MEDICINE.** (BioMed Central) Text in English. 2001 (Jun.). irreg. free (effective 2011). adv. back issues avail.; reprints avail. **Document type:** *Journal, Academic/Scholarly.* **Description:** Features original research articles on all aspects of emergency medicine, trauma, and pre-hospital care.
Media: Online - full text.
Indexed: A01, A26, C06, C07, CA, EMBASE, ESPM, ExcerpMed, I05, MEDLINE, P20, P22, P30, PQC, R10, Reac, SCOPUS, T02.
—**CCC.**
Published by: BioMed Central Ltd. (Subsidiary of: Springer Science+Business Media), 236 Gray's Inn Rd, London, WC1X 8HB, United Kingdom. TEL 44-20-31922000, FAX 44-20-31922010, info@biomedcentral.com. Ed. Dr. Melissa Norton. Adv. contact Natasha Bailey TEL 44-20-31922231.

617.3 GBR ISSN 1471-2474
QM1 CODEN: BMDMCE
➤ **B M C MUSCULOSKELETAL DISORDERS.** (BioMed Central) Text in English. 2000 (Oct.). irreg. free (effective 2011). adv. back issues avail. **Document type:** *Journal, Academic/Scholarly.* **Description:** Features original research articles in all aspects of the prevention, diagnosis and management of musculoskeletal and associated disorders, as well as related molecular genetics, pathophysiology, and epidemiology.
Media: Online - full text.
Indexed: A01, A02, A03, A08, A26, A36, C06, C07, C25, CA, CABA, CTA, CurCont, EMBASE, ExcerpMed, F08, F11, F12, GH, I05, LT, MEDLINE, N02, N03, NSA, P20, P22, P30, P33, R08, R10, R12, RA&MP, RRTA, Reac, SCI, SCOPUS, SoyAb, T02, T05, W07.
—Infotrieve. **CCC.**
Published by: BioMed Central Ltd. (Subsidiary of: Springer Science+Business Media), 236 Gray's Inn Rd, London, WC1X 8HB, United Kingdom. TEL 44-20-31922000, FAX 44-20-31922010, info@biomedcentral.com. Ed. Dr. Melissa Norton. Adv. contact Natasha Bailey TEL 44-20-31922231.

616 USA ISSN 0894-7376
THE BACK LETTER. Key Title: The Backletter. Text in English. 198?. m. USD 398 domestic to institutions; USD 484 foreign to institutions (effective 2011). adv. back issues avail. **Document type:** *Newsletter, Trade.* **Description:** Covers all aspects of spine function, disease and injury.
Related titles: Online - full text ed.: ISSN 2161-5179.
Indexed: A26, C06, C07, C08, CINAHL, E08, G05, G06, G07, G08, H11, H12, I05, S09.
—IE. **CCC.**
Published by: Lippincott Williams & Wilkins (Subsidiary of: Wolters Kluwer N.V.), 530 Walnut St, Philadelphia, PA 19106. TEL 215-521-8300, FAX 215-521-8902, customerservice@lww.com. Ed. Sam W Wiesel.

617.13 USA ISSN 1549-6252
RD771.B217
BACK PAIN AND OSTEOPOROSIS. Text in English. 1998. a. USD 19.95 per issue (effective 2010). back issues avail. **Document type:** *Monographic series, Academic/Scholarly.*
Formerly (until 2003): Low Back Pain and Osteoporosis (1542-1872)
Published by: (Johns Hopkins Medical Institutions), Medletter Associates, 6 Trowbridge Dr, Bethel, CT 06801.

616.7 GBR
THE BACKCARE JOURNAL. Text in English. 1974. q. GBP 3.95 per issue (effective 2011). **Document type:** *Magazine, Trade.* **Description:** Publishes interdisciplinary work, research, case studies, outcomes and ideas on back pain.
Former titles (until 1999): Talkback (1750-1016); (until 1988): Talk Back (0144-3798)
Related titles: Online - full text ed.
Published by: Backcare, 16 Elmtree Rd., Teddington, TW11 8ST, United Kingdom.

617.3 JPN ISSN 0287-1645
CODEN: SEGEAW
BESSATSU SEIKEI GEKA/ORTHOPEDIC SURGERY. SPECIAL ISSUE. Text in Japanese. 1982. s-a. JPY 48,615 combined subscription includes Seikei Geka. **Document type:** *Journal, Academic/Scholarly.*
Published by: Nankodo Co. Ltd., 3-42-6 Hongo, Bunkyo-ku, Tokyo, 113-8410, Japan. TEL 81-3-38117140, FAX 81-3-38117265, http://www.nankodo.co.jp/.

616.7 FRA ISSN 1951-3550
BIBLIOTHEQUE DE L'AUTRE. COLLECTION TRAUMA. Text in French. 2006. irreg.
Published by: Editions La Pensee Sauvage, 12 Place Notre Dame, Grenoble, 38002, France. penseesauvage@wanadoo.fr, http://www.ardm.asso.fr/liens/petitx/penssauv.htm.

617.3 CAN ISSN 1205-562X
BODY CAST. Text in English. 1986. q. CAD 37.45, USD 42.80 in North America; USD 53.50 elsewhere (effective 2002 - 2003). adv.
Indexed: C06, C07, C08, CINAHL.
Published by: Canadian Society of Orthopaedic Technologists, 18 Wynford Dr, Ste 516, North York, ON M3C 3S2, Canada. TEL 416-445-4516.

617.3 JPN ISSN 0914-7047
CODEN: BONEFN
THE BONE. Text in Japanese. 1987. bi-m. JPY 12,570 (effective 2005). 100 p./no.; **Document type:** *Journal, Academic/Scholarly.*
—BLDSC (2247.332000), CASDDS.
Published by: Medikaru Rebyusha/Medical Review Co., Ltd., 1-7-3 Hirano-Machi, Chuo-ku, Yoshida Bldg., Osaka-shi, 541-0046, Japan. TEL 81-6-62231468, FAX 81-6-62231245.

617.6 616.4 USA ISSN 8756-3282
QP88.2 CODEN: BONEDL
➤ **BONE.** Text in English. 1979. m. EUR 3,206 in Europe to institutions; JPY 425,300 in Japan to institutions; USD 3,582 elsewhere to institutions (effective 2012). abstr.; illus. back issues avail.; reprints avail. **Document type:** *Journal, Academic/Scholarly.* **Description:** Provides a forum for publication of experimental or clinical studies and review articles dealing with both normal and pathological processes which occur in bone or in other tissues affecting bone metabolism.
Incorporates (1986-1994): Bone and Mineral (0169-6009); Formerly (until 1985): Metabolic Bone Disease and Related Research (0221-8747)
Related titles: Microfilm ed.: ISSN 1873-2763 (from PQC); Online - full text ed.: (from IngentaConnect, ScienceDirect).
Indexed: A01, A03, A08, A22, A26, A34, A36, ASCA, B21, B25, BIOBASE, BIOSIS Prev, BioEngAb, CA, CABA, CIN, CTA, ChemAb, ChemTitl, CurCont, D01, DentInd, E12, EMBASE, ESPM, ExcerpMed, F08, F11, F12, FR, GH, GeoRef, I05, IABS, INI, ISR, IndMed, IndVet, Inpharma, LT, MEDLINE, MycolAb, N02, N03, N04, NRN, P30, P35, P37, R10, R12, RA&MP, RRTA, Reac, S12, SAA, SCI, SCOPUS, SoyAb, T02, T05, ToxAb, VS, W07, W10.
—BLDSC (2247.330000), CASDDS, GNLM, IE, Infotrieve, Ingenta, INIST. **CCC.**
Published by: (International Bone and Mineral Society), Elsevier Inc. (Subsidiary of: Elsevier Science & Technology), 1600 John F Kennedy Blvd, Philadelphia, PA 19103. TEL 215-239-3900, FAX 215-238-7883, JournalCustomerService-usa@elsevier.com. Eds. Masaki Noda, Rene Rizzoli, Dr. Roland Baron.

616.7 USA
BONEZONE; strategic sourcing for the orthopaedic industry. Text in English. 2002 (Aug.). q. USD 150; USD 25 per issue; free to qualified personnel (effective 2008). adv. **Document type:** *Magazine, Trade.* **Description:** Focuses upon strategic sourcing issues relevant to the industry.
Published by: Knowledge Enterprises, Inc., 8401 Chagrin Rd, Ste 18, Chagrin Falls, OH 44023. TEL 440-543-2101, FAX 440-543-2122. Ed. Julie Vetalice. adv.: color page USD 2,995; trim 8.125 x 10.75. Circ: 2,541 (paid); 2,300 (controlled).

628 USA ISSN 1093-4758
BRAIN INJURY ASSOCIATION. T B I CHALLENGE!. (Traumatic Brain Injury) Text in English. 1982. 6/yr. back issues avail. **Document type:** *Magazine, Consumer.* **Description:** Covers topics related to rehabilitation, prevention and legislation as they pertain to the needs and rights of persons with brain injuries and their families.
Formerl titles (until 199?): The National Head Injury Foundation. T B I Challenge! (1071-6262); (until 1993): N H I F Newsletter
Published by: Brain Injury Association of America, 8201 Greensboro Dr, Ste 611, Mc Lean, VA 22102-3816. TEL 703-761-0750, 800-444-6443, FAX 703-761-0755, publications@biausa.org. Ed. Monique J Marino. R&P Rosy McGillan. Circ: 12,000.

BREATHE; continuing medical education for respiratory professionals. *see* MEDICAL SCIENCES—Respiratory Diseases

617.11 USA ISSN 1069-675X
RA975.5.B87
BURN CARE RESOURCES IN NORTH AMERICA. Text in English. 1984. biennial. USD 50 (effective 2008). **Document type:** *Directory.* **Description:** Lists burn care facilities, skin banks, foundations and available fellowships in U.S. and Canada.
Published by: American Burn Association, 625 N Michigan Ave, Ste 2550, Chicago, IL 60611. TEL 312-642-9260, 800-548-2876, FAX 312-642-9130, info@ameriburn.org. Circ: 4,500.

617.11 360 USA ISSN 1544-1857
BURN SUPPORT NEWS. Text in English. 1980. q. free (effective 2006). adv. bk.rev. back issues avail. **Document type:** *Newsletter, Consumer.* **Description:** For burn survivors, their families and professionals in fields related to burn injuries. Features news regarding prevention, treatment and rehabilitation, personal stories, listing of resource materials available.
Former titles (until 2001): Phoenix Society Newsletter; Icarus File (1081-4396)
Published by: Phoenix Society, Inc., 2153 Wealthy S E, Ste 215, East, Grand Rapids, MI 49506. TEL 616-458-2773, FAX 616-458-2831, info@phoenix-society.org, http://www.phoenix-society.org. Ed. Kathy Edwards. Pub., R&P Amy Acton. Adv. contact Wendy Hunt. Circ: 9,000.

617.95 GBR ISSN 0305-4179
RC87.7 CODEN: BURND8
➤ **BURNS.** Text in English. 1974. 8/yr. EUR 1,104 in Europe to institutions; JPY 146,400 in Japan to institutions; USD 1,234 elsewhere to institutions (effective 2012). adv. bk.rev. index. back issues avail. **Document type:** *Journal, Academic/Scholarly.* **Description:** Focuses on the scientific, clinical and social aspects of burns. Includes clinical and scientific papers, and case reports.
Related titles: Microform ed.: (from PQC); Online - full text ed.: ISSN 1879-1409 (from IngentaConnect, ScienceDirect).
Indexed: A01, A03, A08, A20, A22, A26, A34, A36, ASCA, AgrForAb, B21, C06, C07, C08, CA, CABA, CINAHL, CurCont, DentInd, E12, EMBASE, ESPM, ExcerpMed, F08, F09, FR, GH, H&SSA, H12, H16, I05, IndMed, IndVet, Inpharma, LT, MEDLINE, MycolAb, N02, N03, P30, P33, P35, PN&I, R07, R08, R10, R12, R13, RA&MP, RM&VM, RRTA, Reac, RiskAb, SCI, SCOPUS, SoyAb, T02, T05, VS, W07, W10.
—BLDSC (2931.728000), GNLM, IE, Infotrieve, Ingenta, INIST. **CCC.**

Published by: (International Society for Burn Injuries USA), Pergamon (Subsidiary of: Elsevier Science & Technology), The Blvd, Langford Ln, East Park, Kidlington, Oxford OX5 1GB, United Kingdom. TEL 44-1865-843000, FAX 44-1865-843010, JournalsCustomerServiceEMEA@elsevier.com. Ed. S Wolf. Circ: 940. **Subscr. to:** Elsevier BV, Radarweg 29, PO Box 211, Amsterdam 1000 AE, Netherlands. TEL 31-20-4853757, FAX 31-20-4853432, http://www.elsevier.nl.

616.025 CAN ISSN 1481-8035
➤ **C J E M**; Canadian journal of emergency medicine. Text in French, English. 1999 (Jan.). bi-m. CAD 95 domestic to individuals; USD 175 in United States to individuals; CAD 130 domestic to institutions; USD 210 in United States to institutions (effective 2005). **Document type:** *Journal, Academic/Scholarly.* **Description:** Contains original research, review articles, clinical updates, literature reviews and news for emergency physicians.
Related titles: Online - full text ed.: ISSN 1481-8043.
Indexed: A01, A03, A08, C03, C05, C06, C07, C08, CA, CBCARef, CINAHL, EMBASE, ExcerpMed, H13, I12, MEDLINE, P10, P20, P22, P24, P30, P48, P53, P54, PQC, R10, Reac, SCI, SCOPUS, SD, T02, W07.
—BLDSC (3274.273200), IE, Ingenta. **CCC.**
Published by: (Canadian Association of Emergency Physicians), Canadian Medical Association/Association Medicale Canadienne, 1867 Alta Vista Dr, Ottawa, ON K1G 3Y6, Canada. TEL 613-731-8610, 888-855-2555, FAX 613-236-8864, http://www.cma.ca. Ed. Jennifer Raiche. Adv. contact Beverley Kirkpatrick.

617.3 GBR ISSN 1367-8957
C M E ORTHOPAEDICS. (Continuing Medical Education) Text in English. 1999. irreg., latest 2007. GBP 45 per vol. domestic to individuals; GBP 60 per vol. foreign to individuals; GBP 60 per vol. domestic to institutions; GBP 90 per vol. foreign to institutions (effective 2010). back issues avail. **Document type:** *Bulletin, Academic/Scholarly.*
Related titles: Online - full text ed.: GBP 30 per vol. (effective 2010).
Indexed: R10, Reac, SCOPUS.
—BLDSC (3287.223070). **CCC.**
Published by: Rila Publications Ltd., 73 Newman St, London, W1A 4PG, United Kingdom. TEL 44-20-76311299, FAX 44-20-75807166, admin@rila.co.uk. Ed. Nicola Maffulli.

CALCIFIED TISSUE INTERNATIONAL. *see* MEDICAL SCIENCES—Endocrinology

616.02 CAN ISSN 0847-947X
CANADIAN EMERGENCY NEWS. Text in English. 1978. 6/yr. CAD 30 domestic; USD 40 in United States (effective 2005). adv. bk.rev.; software rev. illus.; tr.lit. 3 cols./p.; back issues avail. **Document type:** *Magazine, Trade.* **Description:** For emergency medical prehospital care professionals and allied professions.
Formerly: Canadian Emergency Services News (0706-9278)
—CCC.
Published by: Pendragon Publishing Ltd., 1121 Newcastle Rd, Drumheler, AB TOJ OY2, Canada. TEL 403-823-2290. Ed., Pub., R&P, Adv. contact Lyle Blumhagen. B&W page CAD 1,100, color page CAD 1,740; trim 10.88 x 8.25. Circ: 4,000.

616.7 CAN ISSN 1488-1543
➤ **CANADIAN JOURNAL OF EMERGENCY MEDICINE/JOURNAL CANADIEN DE LA MEDICINE D'URGENCE.** Abbreviated title: C J E M. Text in English, French. 1999 (Apr.). bi-m. CAD 399 domestic to institutions; USD 449 foreign to institutions (effective 2009). **Document type:** *Journal, Academic/Scholarly.* **Description:** Covers the clinical practice of emergency medicine and political & societal changes which affect the delivery of emergency health care.
Related titles: Online - full text ed.
Indexed: A26, CPerI, E08, G08, H11, H12, I05, JW-EM, S09, SD.
—CCC.
Published by: Canadian Association of Emergency Physicians, Ste 104, 1785 Alta Vista Dr, Ottawa, ON K1G 3Y6, Canada. TEL 613-523-3343, FAX 613-532-0190, admin@caep.ca, http://www.caep.ca. Ed. James Ducharme.

616.7 CHN ISSN 1008-1275
RD92
➤ **CHINESE JOURNAL OF TRAUMATOLOGY.** Text in English. 1998. bi-m. EUR 201 in Europe to institutions; JPY 32,000 in Japan to institutions; USD 297 elsewhere to institutions (effective 2011). **Document type:** *Journal, Academic/Scholarly.*
Related titles: Online - full text ed.: (from ScienceDirect); ◆ Chinese ed.: Zhonghua Chuangshang Zazhi. ISSN 1001-8050.
Indexed: C06, C07, CA, EMBASE, ExcerpMed, MEDLINE, P30, R10, Reac, SCOPUS, T02.
—BLDSC (3180.680950), East View, IE, Ingenta. **CCC.**
Published by: Zhonghua Changshang Zazhi Bianjibu, Editorial Board of Chinese Journal of Trauma, Daping Changjiangzhi Lu, 10, Yuzhong-qu, Chongching, 400042, China. **Subscr. to:** Elsevier BV, Radarweg 29, PO Box 211, Amsterdam 1000 AE, Netherlands.

617.3 POL ISSN 0009-479X
CODEN: CNROA4
CHIRURGIA NARZADOW RUCHU I ORTOPEDIA POLSKA. Text in Polish. 1928. bi-m. EUR 145 foreign (effective 2006). bk.rev. **Document type:** *Journal, Academic/Scholarly.* **Description:** Contains review papers on the physiology and pathology of the locomotive system.
Indexed: DentInd, EMBASE, ExcerpMed, IndMed, MEDLINE, P30, R10, Reac, SCOPUS.
—BLDSC (3181.200000), GNLM, INIST.
Published by: Polskie Towarzystwo Ortopedyczne i Traumatologiczne/ Polish Society or Orthopedic Surgery and Traumatology, Katedra i Oddz Kliniczny Ortopedii SI AM, Szpital Wojewodzki Nr 5 im Sw Barbary, pl Medykow 1, Sosnowiec, 41200, Poland. TEL 48-32-2918663, http://www.ptoitr.pl. **Dist. by:** Ars Polona, Obroncow 25, Warsaw 03933, Poland. TEL 48-22-5098609, FAX 48-22-5098610, arspolona@arspolona.com.pl, http://www.arspolona.com.pl.

CHUANGSHANG WAIKE ZAZHI/JOURNAL OF TRAUMATIC SURGERY. *see* MEDICAL SCIENCES—Surgery

CHUBU NIPPON SEIKEI GEKA SAIGAI GEKA GAKKAI SHOROKU/ CENTRAL JAPAN ASSOCIATION OF ORTHOPAEDIC AND TRAUMATIC SURGERY. ABSTRACTS. *see* MEDICAL SCIENCES—Abstracting, Bibliographies, Statistics

617.3 JPN ISSN 0008-9443
CHUBU NIPPON SEIKEI GEKA SAIGAI GEKA GAKKAI ZASSHI/ CENTRAL JAPAN JOURNAL OF ORTHOPAEDIC SURGERY & TRAUMATOLOGY. Text in Japanese. 1958. bi-m. membership. adv. **Document type:** *Journal, Academic/Scholarly.*
Related titles: Online - full text ed.: ISSN 1349-0885.
Indexed: INIS AtomInd.
—BLDSC (3106.144100), GNLM. **CCC.**
Published by: Chubu Nippon Seikei Geka Saigai Geka Gakkai/Central Japan Association of Orthopaedic Surgery and Traumatology, 4F, Imadegawa-kudaru, Teramachi-dori, Kamigyo-ku, Kyoto, 602-0848, Japan. TEL 81-75-2317599, FAX 81-75-2317499, chubuseisai@nacos.com, http://www.nacos.com/cjot/. Circ: 3,600.

617.3 JPN ISSN 0915-2695
CHUGOKU SHIKOKU SEIKEI GEKA GAKKAI ZASSHI/CHUGOKU-SHIKOKU ORTHOPAEDIC ASSOCIATION. JOURNAL. Text in Japanese; Summaries in English. 1989. s-a. JPY 10,000 membership (effective 2007). **Document type:** *Journal, Academic/Scholarly.*
Related titles: Online - full text ed.: ISSN 1347-5606.
—CCC.
Published by: Chugoku Shikoku Seikei Geka Gakkai, 7-13 Oka-Machi, Okayama-shi, 700-0867, Japan. TEL 81-86-2274628, chushi@md.okayama-u.ac.jp, http://www.chushi.gr.jp/.

CLINICAL BIOMECHANICS. *see* MEDICAL SCIENCES—Chiropractic, Homeopathy, Osteopathy

CLINICAL JOURNAL OF SPORT MEDICINE. *see* MEDICAL SCIENCES—Sports Medicine

616.7 NZL ISSN 1179-5603
➤ **CLINICAL MEDICINE INSIGHTS: TRAUMA AND INTENSIVE MEDICINE.** Text in English. 2008. irreg. free (effective 2010). **Document type:** *Journal, Academic/Scholarly.* **Description:** Covers all aspects of trauma and intensive medicine.
Formerly (until 2010): Clinical Medicine: Trauma and Intensive Medicine (1178-2161)
Media: Online - full text.
Indexed: C06, C07, T02.
—CCC.
Published by: Libertas Academica Ltd., PO Box 300-874, Mairangi Bay, Auckland, 0751, New Zealand. TEL 64-9-4763930, FAX 64-9-3531397, enquiries@la-press.com. Ed. Philip Stahel.

617.3 USA ISSN 0009-921X
RD701 CODEN: CORTBR
➤ **CLINICAL ORTHOPAEDICS AND RELATED RESEARCH.** Text in English. 1953. m. EUR 784, USD 1,051 combined subscription to institutions (print & online eds.) (effective 2012). adv. illus. Index. back issues avail.; reprint service avail. from PSC. **Document type:** *Journal, Academic/Scholarly.* **Description:** Publishes original articles on general orthopaedics and specialty topics covering the latest advances in current research and practice.
Formerly (until 1963): Clinical Orthopaedics (0095-8654)
Related titles: Microform ed.: (from PQC); Online - full text ed.: ISSN 1528-1132 (from IngentaConnect).
Indexed: A01, A03, A08, A20, A22, AIM, AMED, ASCA, AbAn, B21, BDM&CN, C06, C07, C08, CA, CINAHL, CTA, ChemAb, CurCont, DentInd, DokArb, E01, EMBASE, ExcerpMed, FR, FoSS&M, HospLI, INI, ISR, ImmunAb, IndMed, Inpharma, MEDLINE, P20, P22, P24, P30, P35, P48, P54, PQC, R10, Reac, SCI, SCOPUS, T02, TM, W07.
—BLDSC (3286.323000), CASDDS, GNLM, IE, Infotrieve, Ingenta, INIST. **CCC.**
Published by: (The Association of Bone and Joint Surgeons, Musculoskeletal Tumor Society), Springer New York LLC (Subsidiary of: Springer Science+Business Media), 233 Spring St, New York, NY 10013. TEL 212-460-1500, FAX 212-460-1575, service-ny@springer.com. Ed. Richard Brand. adv.: B&W page USD 1,905, color page USD 2,980; trim 9.94 x 6.63. Circ: 5,916 (paid).

➤ **CLINICAL PEDIATRIC EMERGENCY MEDICINE.** *see* MEDICAL SCIENCES—Pediatrics

617.585 USA ISSN 1559-6486
RD563
CLINICS IN PODIATRIC MEDICINE AND SURGERY OF NORTH AMERICA. Text in English. 1984. q. USD 385 in United States to institutions; USD 477 elsewhere to institutions (effective 2012). adv. back issues avail.; reprints avail. **Document type:** *Journal, Academic/Scholarly.* **Description:** Focuses on a single topic relevant to practice, from arthrodesis techniques to reconstruction of failed hindfoot, ankle and lower leg surgery.
Former titles (until 2004): Clinics in Podiatric Medicine and Surgery (0891-8422); (until 1986): Clinics in Podiatry (0742-0668)
Related titles: Microfilm ed.; Online - full text ed.: ISSN 1558-2302 (from ScienceDirect).
Indexed: A22, C06, C07, C08, CINAHL, EMBASE, ExcerpMed, FR, IndMed, MEDLINE, P30, R10, Reac, SCOPUS.
—BLDSC (3286.590650), GNLM, IE, Infotrieve, Ingenta, INIST. **CCC.**
Published by: W.B. Saunders Co. (Subsidiary of: Elsevier Health Sciences), Elsevier, Health Sciences Division, Order Fulfillment, 3251 Riverport Ln, Maryland Heights, MO 63043. TEL 314-872-8370, 800-325-4177, FAX 314-432-1380, JournalCustomerService-usa@elsevier.com, http://www.us.elsevierhealth.com. Adv. contact John Marmero TEL 212-633-3657.

616.71 ARG ISSN 1667-9164
COLECCION TRABAJOS DISTINGUIDOS. SERIE OSTEOPOROSIS Y OSTEOPATIAS MEDICAS. Text in Spanish. 1994. 6/yr. back issues avail. **Document type:** *Journal, Academic/Scholarly.*
Media: Online - full text.
Published by: Sociedad Iberoamericana de Informacion Cientifica (S I I C), Ave Belgrano 430, Buenos Aires, C1092AAR, Argentina. TEL 54-11-43424901, FAX 54-11-43313305, atencionallector@siicsalud.com, http://www.siicsalud.com. Ed. Rafael Bernal Castro.

COMMON DIAGNOSTIC PROCEDURES: ORTHOPEDICS AND NEUROLOGY. *see* LAW

616.7 USA ISSN 1559-5315
COMPLETE GLOBAL SERVICE DATA FOR ORTHOPAEDIC SURGERY. Text in English. 1996. a. (in 2 vols.). **Document type:** *Guide, Trade.* **Description:** An inclusive global billing guide for orthopaedic practices.

Published by: American Academy of Orthopaedic Surgeons, 6300 N River Rd, Rosemont, IL 60018. TEL 847-823-7186, 800-346-2267, FAX 847-823-8125, custserv@aaos.org.

617.3 USA ISSN 0887-1736
COMPLICATIONS IN ORTHOPEDICS. Text in English. 1986. irreg. (2-3/yr). USD 55 per issue (effective 2011). **Description:** Seeks to help orthopedic surgeons maximize their clinical judgement and skill. Provides practical reports from the scientific and clinical arenas.
—CCC.
Published by: American Academy of Orthopaedic Surgeons, 6300 N River Rd, Rosemont, IL 60018. TEL 847-384-4015, 800-346-2267, FAX 847-823-8033, custserv@aaos.org, http://www.aaos.org.

616.025 USA ISSN 1543-9003
CONTEMPORARY CRITICAL CARE; a monthly publication for continuing medical education in critical care. Text in English. 2003 (Jun.). m. USD 404 domestic to institutions; USD 496 foreign to institutions (effective 2011). back issues avail. **Document type:** *Newsletter, Academic/Scholarly.* **Description:** Designed for continuing medical education in critical care.
Related titles: Online - full text ed.
—CCC.
Published by: Lippincott Williams & Wilkins (Subsidiary of: Wolters Kluwer N.V.), 16522 Hunters Green Pky, Hagerstown, MD 21740. TEL 301-223-2300, FAX 301-223-2398, customerservice@lww.com. Ed. Todd Dorman.

CONTEMPORARY SPINE SURGERY. *see* MEDICAL SCIENCES—Surgery

616.7 USA ISSN 1879-9043
CORE KNOWLEDGE IN ORTHOPAEDICS. Text in English. 2005. irreg., latest 2008. price varies. **Document type:** *Monographic series, Academic/Scholarly.*
Published by: Mosby, Inc. (Subsidiary of: Elsevier Health Sciences), 11830 Westline Industrial Dr, St Louis, MO 63146-3318. TEL 314-453-7041, 800-654-2452, FAX 314-453-5170, http://www.us.elsevierhealth.com.

617.3 USA
CRANIAL LETTER. Text in English. 1946. q. USD 155 membership; USD 25 to students (effective 2006). adv. bk.rev. **Document type:** *Newsletter, Trade.*
Formerly: Cranial Academy Newsletter (0011-0825)
Published by: Cranial Academy, 8202 Clearvista Pkwy, Ste 9D, Indianapolis, IN 46256-1457. TEL 317-594-0411, FAX 317-594-9299, info@cranialacademy.org, http://www.cranialacademy.org/. Ed. Patricia S Crampton. Circ: 1,200 (paid).

616.025 USA ISSN 1067-9502
RT120.I5
CRITICAL CARE ALERT. Text in English. 1993. m. USD 319 combined subscription (print & online eds.); USD 53 per issue (effective 2010). **Document type:** *Newsletter, Trade.* **Description:** Features key findings that can improve the way you deliver patient care.
Incorporates (1993-1995): Critical Care Management (1070-4523)
Related titles: Online - full text ed.: ISSN 1945-1555.
Indexed: A25, A26, C06, C07, CA, E08, G08, H11, H12, I05, S08, S09, T02.
—CCC.
Published by: A H C Media LLC (Subsidiary of: Thomson Corporation, Healthcare Information Group), 3525 Piedmont Rd, NE, Bldg 6, Ste 400, Atlanta, GA 30305. TEL 404-262-7436, 800-688-2421, FAX 404-262-7837, 800-284-3291, customerservice@ahcmedia.com, http://www.ahcmedia.com/. Ed. Dr. David J Pierson. Pub. Brenda L Mooney TEL 404-262-5403. **Subscr. to:** PO Box 105109, Atlanta, GA 30348. TEL 404-262-5476, FAX 404-262-5560.

616.02 AUS ISSN 1441-2772
➤ **CRITICAL CARE AND RESUSCITATION.** Text in English. 1999. q. AUD 110 domestic to individuals; AUD 120 foreign to individuals; AUD 165 domestic to institutions; AUD 200 foreign to institutions (effective 2008). adv. back issues avail.; reprints avail. **Document type:** *Journal, Academic/Scholarly.* **Description:** Covers original articles of scientific and clinical interest in specialties such as critical care, intensive care, anesthesia, emergency medicine and related disciplines.
Related titles: CD-ROM ed.; Online - full text ed.
Indexed: EMBASE, ExcerpMed, MEDLINE, P30, R10, Reac, SCOPUS.
—BLDSC (3487.450670), IE, Ingenta. **CCC.**
Published by: Australasian Academy of Critical Care Medicine, 630 St Kilda Rd, Melbourne, VIC 3004, Australia. TEL 61-3-95302861, FAX 61-3-95302862, jficm@anzca.edu.au. Eds. Peter V van Heerden, Rinaldo Bellomo. Adv. contact Laura Fernandez.

610.7361099405 USA ISSN 1445-6753
CRITICAL TIMES. Abbreviated title: C T. Text in English. 1998. q. free to members (effective 2010). adv. back issues avail. **Document type:** *Newspaper, Academic/Scholarly.* **Description:** Aims to provide news and views about Australian critical care nursing.
Related titles: Online - full text ed.: free (effective 2010).
Published by: (Australian College of Critical Care Nurses Ltd. AUS), Elsevier Inc. (Subsidiary of: Elsevier Science & Technology), 1600 John F Kennedy Blvd, Philadelphia, PA 19103. TEL 215-239-3900, FAX 215-238-7883, JournalCustomerService-usa@elsevier.com, http://www.elsevier.com. Adv. contact Tricia Croxen TEL 61-2-94228594.

617.3 USA
CURRENT DIAGNOSIS & TREATMENT EMERGENCY MEDICINE. Text in English. 1983. irreg., latest 2007, 6th ed. USD 79.95 per issue (effective 2010). **Document type:** *Monographic series, Trade.*
Formerly (until 2008): Current Emergency Diagnosis and Treatment (0894-2293)
Published by: McGraw-Hill Education (Subsidiary of: McGraw-Hill Companies, Inc.), 148 Princeton-Hightstown Rd, Hightstown, NJ 08520. TEL 609-426-5793, FAX 609-426-7917, customer.service@mcgraw-hill.com, http://www.mheducation.com/.

617 USA ISSN 1070-5295
RC86 CODEN: COCCF7
CURRENT OPINION IN CRITICAL CARE. Text in English. 1994. bi-m. USD 1,112 domestic to institutions; USD 1,198 foreign to institutions (effective 2011). adv. bibl. back issues avail.; reprints avail. **Document type:** *Journal, Academic/Scholarly.* **Description:** Covers key subjects such as the respiratory system, neuroscience, cardiopulmonary resuscitation, the surgical patient, trauma, and infectious diseases.

Related titles: Online - full text ed.: ISSN 1531-7072. USD 270 to individuals (effective 2011); Optical Disk - DVD ed.: Current Opinion in Critical Care, with Evaluated MEDLINE. ISSN 1080-8183. 1995.
Indexed: A22, C06, C07, CurCont, E01, EMBASE, ExcerpMed, Inpharma, MEDLINE, P30, R10, Reac, SCI, SCOPUS, W07.
—BLDSC (3500.773800), GNLM, IE, Infotrieve, Ingenta. **CCC.**
Published by: Lippincott Williams & Wilkins (Subsidiary of: Wolters Kluwer N.V.), 530 Walnut St, Philadelphia, PA 19106. TEL 215-521-8300, FAX 215-521-8902, customerservice@lww.com, http://www.lww.com. Ed. Dr. Jean-Louis Vincent. Pub. Ian Burgess. Circ: 920.

617.3 USA ISSN 1940-7041 CODEN: COORE9
➤ **CURRENT ORTHOPAEDIC PRACTICE**; a review and research journal. Text in English. 1989. bi-m. USD 1,265 domestic to institutions; USD 1,265 foreign to institutions (effective 2011). adv. bibl.; illus. back issues avail.; reprints avail. **Document type:** *Journal, Academic/Scholarly.* **Description:** Designed to translates clinical research into practices for diagnosing, treating, and managing musculoskeletal disorders.
Formerly (until 2008): Current Opinion in Orthopaedics (1041-9918)
Related titles: Online - full text ed.: ISSN 1941-7551. USD 405 domestic to individuals; USD 413 foreign to individuals (effective 2008).
Indexed: A22, B21, C06, C07, C08, CINAHL, CTA, ChemoAb, E01, EMBASE, ExcerpMed, NSA, P30, R10, Reac, SCOPUS.
—BLDSC (3500.835000), GNLM, IE, Infotrieve, Ingenta. **CCC.**
Published by: Lippincott Williams & Wilkins (Subsidiary of: Wolters Kluwer N.V.), Two Commerce Sq, 2001 Market St, Philadelphia, PA 19103. TEL 215-521-8300, FAX 215-521-8902, customerservice@lww.com, http://www.lww.com. Ed. Andrew H Crenshaw TEL 901-759-3270. Pub. Marcia Serepy. Circ: 434.

616.7 USA ISSN 1544-2241
➤ **CURRENT OSTEOPOROSIS REPORTS (ONLINE).** Text in English. 2003. q. EUR 954, USD 1,270 to institutions (effective 2012). back issues avail. **Document type:** *Journal, Academic/Scholarly.* **Description:** Provides the views of experts on the advances in the osteoporosis field.
Media: Online - full text.
—CCC.
Published by: Current Medicine Group LLC (Subsidiary of: Springer Science+Business Media), 400 Market St, Ste 700, Philadelphia, PA 19106. TEL 215-574-2266, FAX 215-574-2225, service-ny@springer.com, http://www.current-medicine.com/. Ed. Thomas J Schnitzer.

616.7 USA ISSN 1935-973X
CURRENT REVIEWS IN MUSCULOSKELETAL MEDICINE. Text in English. 2008 (Mar.). q. reprint service avail. from PSC. **Document type:** *Journal, Academic/Scholarly.*
Related titles: Online - full text ed.: ISSN 1935-9748. 2008 (Mar.).
Indexed: A22, Agr, B21, E01, EMBASE, ESPM, ExcerpMed, H&SSA, P30.
—CCC.
Published by: Springer Publishing Company, 11 W 42nd St, 15th Fl, New York, NY 10036. TEL 212-431-4370, FAX 212-941-7842, http://www.springerpub.com. Ed. W F Curtis.

617.472 USA ISSN 1068-4107
CURRENT TECHNIQUES IN ARTHROSCOPY. Text in English. 1994. irreg., latest 1998. reprints avail. **Document type:** *Monographic series, Academic/Scholarly.*
—CCC.
Published by: Current Medicine Group LLC (Subsidiary of: Springer Science+Business Media), 400 Market St, Ste 700, Philadelphia, PA 19106. TEL 215-574-2266, 800-427-1796, FAX 215-574-2225, info@phl.cursci.com. Ed. J Serge Parisien. **Co-publisher:** Thieme Medical Publishers, Incorporated.

D.C. TRACTS. (Doctor of Chiropractic) *see* MEDICAL SCIENCES—Chiropractic, Homeopathy, Osteopathy

616.025 KOR ISSN 1226-4334
DAEHAN EUNG'GEUB YIHAGHOEJI/KOREAN SOCIETY OF EMERGENCY MEDICINE. JOURNAL. Text in Korean. 1990. q. **Document type:** *Journal, Academic/Scholarly.*
—BLDSC (3510.220000).
Published by: Daehan Eung'geub Yihaghoe/Korean Society of Emergency Medicine, University of Ulsan, Asan Medical Center, Emergency Medical Center, 388-1 Pungnap-2dong, Songpa-gu, Seoul, 138-736, Korea, S. TEL 82-2-30108533, FAX 82-2-30108533, ksem2amc.seoul.kr, http://www.emergency.or.kr/.

THE DIABETIC FOOT. *see* MEDICAL SCIENCES—Endocrinology

▼ **DIABETIC FOOT & ANKLE.** *see* MEDICAL SCIENCES—Endocrinology

DISASTER MANAGEMENT & RESPONSE. *see* MEDICAL SCIENCES—Nurses And Nursing

616.7 ROM ISSN 1220-8752
DUREREA. Text in Romanian. 1991. q. ROL 90 to non-members (effective 2011).
Published by: Versa Puls Media, s.r.l., Calea Rahovei 266-268, corp 1, etaj 2, Bucharest, 050912, Romania. TEL 40-31-4254040, FAX 40-31-4254041, office@pulsmedia.ro. Circ: 1,000 (controlled).

362.18 362 USA ISSN 1081-4507
E M S INSIDER. (Emergency Medical Services) Text in English. 1973. m. USD 215 in United States to institutions; USD 255 elsewhere to institutions (effective 2012). adv. back issues avail.; reprints avail. **Document type:** *Newsletter, Trade.* **Description:** Provides the latest legislative issues, grants, new drugs and products, current trends and controversies in the field.
Formerly (until 1990): E M S Communicator (0275-0716)
Related titles: Online - full text ed.: ISSN 1532-1541. USD 158 (effective 2011).
Indexed: C06, C07, C08, CINAHL, SCOPUS.
—CCC.
Published by: Elsevier Public Safety (Subsidiary of: Elsevier Inc.), 525 B St, Ste 1800, San Diego, CA 92101. TEL 619-687-3272, 888-456-5367, FAX 619-699-6396, http://www.elsevier.com/wps/find/nfp.cws_home/PublicSafety/DEFAULT. Ed. Jennifer Doyle.

616.02 USA ISSN 2158-7833
RA645.5
E M S WORLD. (Emergency Medical Services) Text in English. 1972. m. USD 40 domestic; USD 55 in Canada & Mexico; USD 80 elsewhere; USD 7 newsstand/cover; free to qualified personnel (effective 2011). adv. bk.rev.; software rev.; video rev. 112 p./no. 3 cols./p.; back issues avail.; reprints avail. **Document type:** *Magazine, Trade.* **Description:** Provides EMS news and training for paramedics and EMTs, as well as for other prehospital practitioners and public safety responders.
Former titles (until 2010): E M S Magazine (1946-4967); (until 2007): Emergency Medical Services (0094-6575)
Related titles: Online - full text ed.: ISSN 2159-3078. free (effective 2011).
Indexed: A10, A22, A26, C06, C07, C08, CA, CINAHL, E08, EMBASE, G06, G07, G08, H12, I02, I05, IndMed, MEDLINE, P20, P22, P24, P30, P48, P54, PQC, R10, Reac, S09, SCOPUS, T02, V03.
—BLDSC (3737.896500), GNLM, IE, Infotrieve, Ingenta.
Published by: Cygnus Business Media, Inc., 1233 Janesville Ave, PO Box 803, Fort Atkinson, WI 53538. TEL 920-563-6388, 800-547-7377, FAX 920-563-1702, http://www.cygnusb2b.com. Ed. Nancy Perry TEL 800-547-7377 ext 1110. Pub. Scott Cravens.

617.3 EGY ISSN 1110-1148
EGYPTIAN ORTHOPAEDIC JOURNAL/AL-MAJALLAH AL-MISRIYYAH LI-JIRAHAT AL-'ITHAM. Text in Arabic, English, French. 1966. q. USD 80. adv. bk.rev. abstr.; bibl.; charts; illus. **Document type:** *Proceedings, Academic/Scholarly.* **Description:** Publishes original research articles, news, and proceedings.
Formerly: Egyptian Orthopaedic Journal (0013-242X)
Related titles: CD-ROM ed.
Indexed: ExtraMED.
Published by: Egyptian Orthopaedic Association, P O Box 4, Alexandria, 21111, Egypt. TEL 20-3-4225626. Ed. Amin M Rida. Circ: 4,000.

616.02 DEU
EINSATZ (STUTTGART). Text in German. q. adv. **Document type:** *Magazine, Trade.*
Published by: (Deutsche Rettungsflugwacht e.V.), Redaktionsbuero Syntax Stuttgart GmbH, Birkenhofstr 10, Stuttgart, 70599, Germany. TEL 49-711-45103310, FAX 49-711-45103311, info@syntax-verlag.de, http://www.syntaxverlag.de. adv.: B&W page EUR 3,375, color page EUR 4,360. Circ: 198,421 (controlled).

617.3 TUR ISSN 1305-8282
EKLEM HASTALIKLAN VE CERRAHISI/JOINT DISEASES & RELATED SURGERY. Text in English. 1990. s-a. **Document type:** *Journal, Academic/Scholarly.*
Formerly: Artroplasti Artroskopik Cerrahi/Journal of Arthroplasty Arthroscopic Surgery (1300-0594)
Related titles: Online - full text ed.: ISSN 1309-0313. free (effective 2009).
Indexed: EMBASE, ExcerpMed, MEDLINE, P30, SCI, SCOPUS, SD, W07.
Published by: Turkiye Eklem Hastaliklari Tedavi Vakfi/Turkish Joint Diseases Foundation, c/o O. Sahap Atik, MD, Bugday Sokak, 6/27, Kavaklidere, Ankara, 06700, Turkey. TEL 90-312-4679686, FAX 90-312-4676269, satikmd@gmail.com. Ed. Dr. O. Sahap Atik.

616.7 BRA ISSN 1981-335X
EMERGENCIA CLINICA. Text in Portuguese. 2005. q. 32 p./no.; **Document type:** *Magazine, Trade.*
Formerly (until 2006): Emergencia (1809-2497)
Indexed: C06, C07.
Published by: Editorial Bolina Brasil (Subsidiary of: Grupo Editorial Bolina), Alameda Pucurui 51-59 B, Tamporere - Barueri, Sao Paulo, 06460-100, Brazil. Ed. Fabricio Guimaraes. Circ: 10,000.

616.02 ESP ISSN 1137-6821
RC86
EMERGENCIAS. Text in Spanish. 1988. bi-m. EUR 95 (effective 2009). **Document type:** *Journal, Trade.* **Description:** Covers various aspects of emergency medicine.
Indexed: SCI, SCOPUS, W07.
—CCC.
Published by: (Sociedad Espanola de Medicina de Urgencias y Emergencias), Grupo Saned, Capitan Haya 60, 1o, Madrid, 28028, Spain. TEL 34-91-7499500, FAX 34-91-7499501, saned@medynet.com, http://www.gruposaned.com. Ed. Oscar Miro i Andreu. Circ: 8,000.

616.025 610.736 GBR ISSN 2042-6437
EMERGENCY & URGENT CARE TODAY. Text in English. 1995. q. GBP 24 domestic to individuals; GBP 48 foreign to individuals; GBP 40 domestic to institutions; GBP 72 foreign to institutions; free to qualified personnel (effective 2010). adv. **Document type:** *Journal, Trade.* **Description:** Provides information about emergency & urgent care in medical field.
Formerly (until 2009): Today's Emergency (1360-1938)
—CCC.
Published by: Media Publishing Company, Media House, 48 High St, Swanley, Kent BR8 8BQ, United Kingdom. TEL 44-1322-660434, FAX 44-1322-666539, mediajournals@aol.com. adv.: B&W page GBP 800, color page GBP 1,200; trim 210 x 297. Circ: 2,612.

616.025 JPN ISSN 1349-6557
EMERGENCY CARE/EMAJENSHI KEA; Nihon Kyuukyuu Kango Gakkai junkikanshi. Text in Japanese. 1988. m. JPY 20,412; JPY 1,890 newsstand/cover (effective 2007). Supplement avail. **Document type:** *Journal, Academic/Scholarly.*
Formerly (until 2004): Emergency Nursing/Emajenshi Nashingu (0915-4213)
Published by: (Nihon Kyuukyuu Kango Gakkai/Japanese Association for Emergency Nursing), Medicus Shuppan/Medicus Publishing Inc., 18-24 Hiroshiba-cho, Suita-shi, Osaka-fu 564-8580, Japan. TEL 81-6-63856911, FAX 81-6-63856873, http://www.medica.co.jp/.

616.025 658 USA ISSN 1044-9167
RC86
EMERGENCY DEPARTMENT MANAGEMENT. Key Title: E D Management. Text in English. 1989. m. USD 499 combined subscription (print & online eds.); USD 82 per issue (effective 2010). **Document type:** *Newsletter, Trade.* **Description:** Keeps emergency department directors, administrators, physicians, and nurse supervisors on top of developments in the business and management of emergency medical care in a concise.
Incorporates (1990-1991): Reports in Emergency Nursing (1050-8759)
Related titles: Online - full text ed.; ◆ Supplement(s): Trauma Reports. ISSN 1531-1082.
Indexed: A26, C06, C07, C08, CINAHL, EMBASE, ExcerpMed, G08, H11, H12, I05, MEDLINE, P20, P22, P24, P30, P48, P54, PQC, R10, Reac, SCOPUS.
—BLDSC (3659.744700). **CCC.**
Published by: A H C Media LLC (Subsidiary of: Thomson Corporation, Healthcare Information Group), 3525 Piedmont Rd, NE, Bldg 6, Ste 400, Atlanta, GA 30305. TEL 404-262-7436, 800-688-2421, FAX 404-262-7837, 800-284-3291, customerservice@ahcmedia.com, http://www.ahcmedia.com/. Pub. Brenda L Mooney TEL 404-262-5403. **Subscr. to:** PO Box 105109, Atlanta, GA 30348. TEL 404-262-5476, FAX 404-262-5560.

616.025 USA ISSN 0013-6654
RC86
EMERGENCY MEDICINE; acute medicine for the primary-care physician. Text in English. 1969. m. USD 109 domestic to individuals; USD 142 in Canada & Mexico to individuals; USD 157 elsewhere to individuals; USD 129 domestic to institutions; USD 168 in Canada & Mexico to institutions; USD 186 elsewhere to institutions (effective 2007). adv. bk.rev. charts; illus. index. back issues avail.; reprints avail. **Document type:** *Journal, Academic/Scholarly.* **Description:** Emphasizes acute-care medicine for primary-care physicians.
Related titles: Microform ed.: (from PQC); Online - full text ed.
Indexed: A20, A22, C06, C07, C08, CINAHL, HospLI, Inpharma, P16, P24, P26, P30, P48, P53, P54, PQC, SCOPUS.
—BLDSC (3733.190000), GNLM, IE, Infotrieve, Ingenta, INIST. **CCC.**
Published by: Quadrant HealthCom, 7 Century Dr, Ste 302, Parsippany, NJ 07054. TEL 973-206-3434, FAX 973-206-9251, http://www.qhc.com. Eds. Melissa Steiger TEL 973-206-8096, Vincent A DeLeo. Adv. contact Carolann Mitchell. B&W page USD 3,465, color page USD 5,290; trim 7.875 x 10.75. Circ: 41,000 (paid).

616.02 617.1 AUS ISSN 1742-6723
RC86
EMERGENCY MEDICINE AUSTRALASIA (ONLINE). Text in English. 5/yr. GBP 480 in United Kingdom to institutions; EUR 609 in Europe to institutions; USD 779 in the Americas to institutions; USD 939 elsewhere to institutions (effective 2012). **Document type:** *Journal, Academic/Scholarly.*
Formerly: Emergency Medicine (Online Edition) (1442-2026)
Media: Online - full text (from IngentaConnect). **Related titles:** ◆ Print ed.: Emergency Medicine Australasia (Print). ISSN 1742-6731.
—Ingenta. **CCC.**
Published by: Wiley-Blackwell Publishing Asia (Subsidiary of: Wiley-Blackwell Publishing Ltd.), 155 Cremorne St, Richmond, VIC 3121, Australia. TEL 61-3-92743100, FAX 61-3-92743101, subs@blackwellpublishingasia.com, http://www.wiley.com/WileyCDA/.

616.02 617.1 AUS ISSN 1742-6731
RC86 CODEN: EMEMFL
➤ **EMERGENCY MEDICINE AUSTRALASIA (PRINT).** Abbreviated title: E M A. Text in English. 1989. bi-m. GBP 480 in United Kingdom to institutions; EUR 609 in Europe to institutions; USD 779 in the Americas to institutions; USD 939 elsewhere to institutions; GBP 552 combined subscription in United Kingdom to institutions (print & online eds.); EUR 701 combined subscription in Europe to institutions (print & online eds.); USD 896 combined subscription in the Americas to institutions (print & online eds.); USD 1,080 combined subscription elsewhere to institutions (print & online eds.) (effective 2012). adv. charts; illus. back issues avail.; reprint service avail. from PSC. **Document type:** *Journal, Academic/Scholarly.* **Description:** Presents information on emergency medicine for the medical community in Australia.
Former titles (until 2003): Emergency Medicine (1035-6851); (until 1990): Emergency Doctor (1035-1167)
Related titles: ◆ Online - full text ed.: Emergency Medicine Australasia (Online). ISSN 1742-6723.
Indexed: A01, A02, A03, A08, A22, A26, A34, A36, B21, C06, C07, C08, C11, CA, CABA, CINAHL, E01, E12, EMBASE, ESPM, ExcerpMed, GH, GeoRef, H&SSA, H04, H12, H16, H17, IndVet, LT, MEDLINE, N02, N03, P30, P33, P37, P39, R08, R10, R12, RA&MP, RM&VM, RRTA, Reac, RiskAb, S13, S16, SCI, SCOPUS, SD, T02, T05, TAR, ToxAb, VS, W07, W10, W11.
—BLDSC (3733.190300), IE, Infotrieve, Ingenta. **CCC.**
Published by: (Australasian College for Emergency Medicine, Australasian Society for Emergency Medicine), Wiley-Blackwell Publishing Asia (Subsidiary of: Wiley-Blackwell Publishing Ltd.), 155 Cremorne St, Richmond, VIC 3121, Australia. TEL 61-3-92743100, FAX 61-3-92743101, melbourne@wiley.com, http://www.wiley.com/WileyCDA/. Ed. Anthony F T Brown. adv.: B&W page AUD 920, color page AUD 1,870; trim 210 x 275.

616.025 USA ISSN 0733-8627 CODEN: EMCAD7
EMERGENCY MEDICINE CLINICS OF NORTH AMERICA. Text in English. 1983. q. USD 455 in United States to institutions; USD 549 elsewhere to institutions (effective 2012). adv. back issues avail.; reprints avail. **Document type:** *Journal, Academic/Scholarly.* **Description:** Focuses on a single topic relevant to your practice, from wilderness medicine to bioterrorism.
Related titles: Microform ed.: (from PQC); Online - full text ed.: ISSN 1558-0539 (from ScienceDirect); ◆ Spanish Translation: Clinicas de Medicina de Urgencias de Norteamerica; Supplement(s): Continuing Medical Education Supplement to Emergency Medicine Clinics of North America. ISSN 1557-8151.
Indexed: A20, A22, C06, C07, C08, CINAHL, CurCont, DokArb, EMBASE, ExcerpMed, FR, INI, IndMed, MEDLINE, P30, R10, Reac, SCI, SCOPUS, W07.
—BLDSC (3733.190400), GNLM, IE, Infotrieve, Ingenta, INIST. **CCC.**
Published by: W.B. Saunders Co. (Subsidiary of: Elsevier Health Sciences), Elsevier, Health Sciences Division, Order Fulfillment, 3251 Riverport Ln, Maryland Heights, MO 63043. TEL 314-872-8370, 800-325-4177, FAX 314-432-1380, JournalCustomerService-usa@elsevier.com, http://www.us.elsevierhealth.com. Adv. contact John Marmero TEL 212-633-3657.

616.025 USA ISSN 2090-2840
▼ ➤ **EMERGENCY MEDICINE INTERNATIONAL.** Text in English. 2010. irreg. USD 195 (effective 2011). **Document type:** *Journal, Academic/Scholarly.* **Description:** Publishes original research articles, review articles, case reports, and clinical studies in all areas of emergency medicine.

Related titles: Online - full text ed.: ISSN 2090-2859. 2010. free (effective 2011).
Indexed: A01, T02.
Published by: Hindawi Publishing Corporation, 410 Park Ave, 15th Fl, PMB 287, New York, NY 10022. FAX 866-446-3294, orders@hindawi.com.

616.025 GBR ISSN 1472-0205
RC86 CODEN: EMJMB8
➤ **EMERGENCY MEDICINE JOURNAL**; an international peer-reviewed journal for health professionals and researchers in emergency medicine. Abbreviated title: E M J. Text in English. 1983. m. GBP 478 to institutions; GBP 595 combined subscription to institutions small FTE (print & online eds.) (effective 2011). adv. bk.rev. abstr.; bibl.; illus. index. back issues avail.; reprints avail. **Document type:** *Journal, Academic/Scholarly.* **Description:** Provides a forum for education, research, and debate on all aspects of emergency medicine.
Former titles (until 2001): Journal of Accident and Emergency Medicine (1351-0622); (until 1994): Archives of Emergency Medicine (0264-4924); Incorporates (in 2001): Pre-Hospital Immediate Care (1364-4882); Which was formerly (until 1997): British Association for Immediate Care. Journal (0267-3258); (until 1980): British Association of Immediate Care Schemes. Journal
Related titles: Microform ed.: (from PQC); Online - full text ed.: E M J Online. ISSN 1472-0213. 1999. GBP 488 to institutions small FTE (effective 2011).
Indexed: A22, A26, ASCA, AddicA, B28, C06, C07, C08, CINAHL, CurCont, E01, E08, EMBASE, ExcerpMed, FR, G08, GeoRef, H11, H12, I05, INI, ISR, IndMed, Inpharma, JW-EM, MEDLINE, P16, P20, P22, P24, P30, P35, P48, P50, P53, P54, PQC, R10, Reac, S09, SCI, SCOPUS, W07.
—BLDSC (3733.190420), GNLM, IE, Infotrieve, Ingenta, INIST. **CCC.**
Published by: (College of Emergency Medicine, British Association for Accident and Emergency Medicine), B M J Group, BMA House, Tavistock Sq, London, WC1H 9JR, United Kingdom. TEL 44-20-73836373, FAX 44-20-73836668, membership@bma.org.uk, http://group.bmj.com. Ed. Geoff Hughes. Pub. Janet O'Flaherty TEL 44-20-73836154. Adv. contact Nick Gray TEL 44-20-73836386. Circ: 3,645. **Subscr. to:** PO Box 299, London WC1H 9TD, United Kingdom. TEL 44-20-73836270, FAX 44-20-73836402, support@bmjgroup.com.

616.025 USA ISSN 1054-0725
EMERGENCY MEDICINE NEWS. Abbreviated title: E M N. Text in English. 1979. m. USD 444 domestic to institutions; USD 553 foreign to institutions (effective 2011). adv. back issues avail.; reprints avail. **Document type:** *Magazine, Academic/Scholarly.* **Description:** Disseminates information in all areas of emergency medicine, as well as emergency departments and ambulatory care centers.
Former titles (until 1989): Emergency Medicine and Ambulatory Care News (1042-7023); (until Aug.1986): Emergency Department News (0195-3281)
Related titles: Online - full text ed.: ISSN 1552-3624. 19??.
Indexed: CA, P30, T02.
—CCC.
Published by: Lippincott Williams & Wilkins (Subsidiary of: Wolters Kluwer N.V.), 530 Walnut St, Philadelphia, PA 19106. TEL 215-521-8300, FAX 215-521-8902, customerservice@lww.com, http://www.lww.com. Ed. Lisa Hoffman TEL 646-674-6544. Pub. John Ewers. Adv. contact James Nagle. Circ: 29,851.

616.025 USA ISSN 0746-2506
EMERGENCY MEDICINE REPORTS; the practical journal for primary-care physicians. (Annual Emergency Medicine Reports Rapid Reference Cards also avail.) Text in English. 1980. q. USD 399 combined subscription (print & online eds.); USD 67 per issue (effective 2010). **Document type:** *Newsletter, Trade.* **Description:** Features review articles on important clinical issues in emergency medicine, with practical treatment recommendations. Topics covered include cardiology, trauma, infectious diseases, hormonal and metabolic disorders, orthopedics, etc.
Formerly (until 1983): E R Reports (0732-9628)
Related titles: CD-ROM ed.: USD 399; USD 114 per issue (effective 2010); Online - full text ed.; ◆ Supplement(s): Trauma Reports. ISSN 1531-1082.
Indexed: A01, A26, G08, H11, H12, I05, P30.
—BLDSC (3733.190700). **CCC.**
Published by: A H C Media LLC (Subsidiary of: Thomson Corporation, Healthcare Information Group), 3525 Piedmont Rd, NE, Bldg 6, Ste 400, Atlanta, GA 30305. TEL 404-262-7436, 800-688-2421, FAX 404-262-7837, 800-284-3291, customerservice@ahcmedia.com, http://www.ahcmedia.com/. Pub. Brenda L Mooney TEL 404-262-5403. **Subscr. to:** PO Box 105109, Atlanta, GA 30348. TEL 404-262-5476, FAX 404-262-5560.

EMERGENCY PRODUCT BUYER. *see* MEDICAL SCIENCES—Surgery

ENCYCLOPEDIE MEDICO-CHIRURGICALE. APARATO LOCOMOTOR. *see* MEDICAL SCIENCES—Rheumatology

ENCYCLOPEDIE MEDICO-CHIRURGICALE. APPAREIL LOCOMOTEUR; vers le retour a la motricite. *see* MEDICAL SCIENCES—Rheumatology

617.585 FRA ISSN 0292-062X
➤ **ENCYCLOPEDIE MEDICO-CHIRURGICALE. PODOLOGIE.** Cover title: Traite de Podologie. Text in French. 2 base vols. plus updates 4/yr. EUR 374.81 (effective 2003). bibl.; charts; illus. **Document type:** *Academic/Scholarly.* **Description:** Offers podiatrists a comprehensive reference for diagnosing and treating conditions affecting the feet.
Related titles: Online - full text ed.
Published by: Elsevier Masson (Subsidiary of: Elsevier Health Sciences), 62 Rue Camille Desmoulins, Issy les Moulineaux, Cedex 92442, France. TEL 33-1-71165500, FAX 33-1-71165600, infos@elsevier-masson.fr.

➤ **ENCYCLOPEDIE MEDICO-CHIRURGICALE. RADIOLOGIE ET IMAGERIE MEDICALE. MUSCULOSQUELETTIQUE - NEUROLOGIQUE - MAXILLOFACIALE.** *see* MEDICAL SCIENCES—Radiology And Nuclear Medicine

➤ **ENCYCLOPEDIE MEDICO-CHIRURGICALE. TECHNIQUES CHIRURGICALES. ORTHOPEDIE - TRAUMATOLOGIE.** *see* MEDICAL SCIENCES—Surgery

616.02 FRA ISSN 1241-8234
➤ **ENCYCLOPEDIE MEDICO-CHIRURGICALE. URGENCES.** Cover title: Traite d'Urgences. Variant title: Encyclopedie Medico-Chirurgicale, Instantanes Medicaux. Urgences. Text in French. 1939. 2 base vols. plus q. updates. EUR 374.81 (effective 2003). bibl.; charts; illus. **Document type:** *Academic/Scholarly.* **Description:** Provides emergency-medicine practitioners with a comprehensive and up-to-date reference source to diagnose and treat medical conditions.
Former titles (until 1991): Encyclopedie Medico-Chirurgicale. Urgences Medicales et Chirurgicales (0246-0580); (until 1942): Encyclopedie Medico-Chirurgicale. Urgences (0246-0750)
Related titles: ◆ Italian ed.: Encyclopedie Medico-Chirurgicale. Urgenze. ISSN 1286-9341.
—INIST.
Published by: Elsevier Masson (Subsidiary of: Elsevier Health Sciences), 62 Rue Camille Desmoulins, Issy les Moulineaux, Cedex 92442, France. TEL 33-1-71165500, FAX 33-1-71165600, infos@elsevier-masson.fr, http://www.elsevier-masson.fr.

616.02 ITA ISSN 1286-9341
➤ **ENCYCLOPEDIE MEDICO-CHIRURGICALE. URGENZE.** Short title: Urgenze. Text in Italian. 2 base vols. plus q. updates. EUR 396.81 (effective 2003). bibl.; charts; illus. **Document type:** *Academic/ Scholarly.* **Description:** Provides emergency-medicine practitioners with a comprehensive and up-to-date reference to diagnose and treat a variety of medical conditions.
Related titles: ◆ French ed.: Encyclopedie Medico-Chirurgicale. Urgences. ISSN 1241-8234.
Published by: Elsevier Masson (Subsidiary of: Elsevier Health Sciences), Via Paleocapa 7, Milan, 20121, Italy. TEL 39-02-881841, FAX 39-02-88184302, info@masson.it, http://www.masson.it.

617.585 FRA ISSN 2102-7153
ENTRETIENS DE BICHAT. ENTRETIENS DE REEDUCATION. PODOLOGIE. Text in French. 2005. a. **Document type:** *Trade.*
Formerly (until 2008): Podologie, Medecine Orthopedique et de Reeducation, Medecine du Sport (1760-9828); Which was formed by the merger of (1985-2005): Podologie (0767-953X); (1986-2005): Medecine du Sport (0767-9521); (2000-2005): Journee de Medecine Orthopedique et de Reeducation (1624-074X); Which was formerly (until 2000): Reeducation (0034-2211); (until 1983): Journee de Medecine Physique et de Reeducation (0755-3951); (1958-1978): Journee de Reeducation (0075-4420)
Published by: Expansion Scientifique Francaise, 15 Rue Saint-Benoit, Paris, 75278 Cedex 06, France. TEL 33-1-45484260, FAX 33-1-45448155, expansionscientifiquefrancaise@wanadoo.fr, http://www.expansionscientifique.com.

616.7 DEU ISSN 0721-3506
EUROPAEISCHE HOCHSCHULSCHRIFTEN. REIHE 7: MEDIZIN. ABTEILUNG C: ORTHOPAEDIE. Text in German. 1977. irreg., latest vol.3, 1981. price varies. **Document type:** *Monographic series, Academic/Scholarly.*
Published by: Peter Lang GmbH (Subsidiary of: Peter Lang Publishing Group), Eschborner Landstr 42-50, Frankfurt Am Main, 60489, Germany. TEL 49-69-7807050, FAX 49-69-78070550, zentrale.frankfurt@peterlang.com, http://www.peterlang.com.

616.025 GBR ISSN 2042-7840
▼ **EUROPEAN CRITICAL CARE & EMERGENCY MEDICINE.** Text in English. 2009. a. **Document type:** *Journal, Trade.*
Related titles: Online - full text ed.: ISSN 2042-7859. free (effective 2010).
Published by: Touch Briefings (Subsidiary of: Touch Group plc), Saffron House, 6-10 Kirby St, London, EC1N 8TS, United Kingdom. TEL 44-20-74525600, FAX 44-20-74525606, info@touchbriefings.com. Ed. Amy Brewerton TEL 44-20-74525008.

616.7 GBR ISSN 1359-2335
EUROPEAN INSTRUCTIONAL COURSE LECTURES. Text in English. 1993. biennial. price varies. adv. back issues avail.; reprints avail. **Document type:** *Journal, Academic/Scholarly.* **Description:** Designed to provide a concise summary of the major advances in orthopaedics and traumatology.
—BLDSC (3829.720903), IE, Ingenta. **CCC.**
Published by: (European Federation of National Associations of Orthopaedics and Trauma (EFORT) CHE), British Editorial Society of Bone and Joint Surgery, 22 Buckingham St, London, WC2N 6ET, United Kingdom. TEL 44-20-77820010, FAX 44-20-77820995, info@jbjs.org.uk. Adv. contacts Pam Pam Noble TEL 44-1620-823383, Amber Howard TEL 781-449-9780.

617 GBR ISSN 0969-9546
RC86
➤ **EUROPEAN JOURNAL OF EMERGENCY MEDICINE.** Abbreviated title: E J E M. Text in English. 1994. bi-m. USD 1,069 domestic to institutions; USD 1,131 foreign to institutions (effective 2011). adv. back issues avail.; reprints avail. **Document type:** *Journal, Academic/ Scholarly.* **Description:** Features articles devoted to serve the European emergency medicine community and to promote European standards of training, diagnosis and care.
Related titles: Online - full text ed.: ISSN 1473-5695. USD 717.60 domestic academic site license; USD 717.60 foreign academic site license; USD 800.40 domestic corporate site license; USD 800.40 foreign corporate site license (effective 2002).
Indexed: A22, CurCont, E01, EMBASE, ExcerpMed, INI, IndMed, MEDLINE, P30, R10, Reac, SCI, SCOPUS, W07.
—BLDSC (3829.728600), GNLM, IE, Infotrieve, Ingenta. **CCC.**
Published by: (European Society of Emergency Medicine BEL), Lippincott Williams & Wilkins, Ltd., 250 Waterloo Rd, London, SE1 8RD, United Kingdom. TEL 44-20-79810600, FAX 44-20-79810601, customerservice@lww.com, http://www.lww.com. Ed. Colin A Graham. Pub. Phil Daly. Adv. contact Melissa Moody. B&W page USD 965, color page USD 1,275; trim 8.125 x 10.875.

617.3 FRA ISSN 1633-8065
➤ **EUROPEAN JOURNAL OF ORTHOPAEDIC SURGERY & TRAUMATOLOGY.** Text in English; Abstracts in French. 1990. q. EUR 583, USD 693 combined subscription to institutions (print & online eds.) (effective 2012). reprint service avail. from PSC. **Document type:** *Journal, Academic/Scholarly.* **Description:** Original basic and clinical research articles on all aspects of orthopaedic surgery and traumatology.
Formerly (until 1995): Orthopedie - Traumatologie (0948-4817)
Related titles: Microform ed.: (from PQC); Online - full text ed.: ISSN 1432-1068 (from IngentaConnect).
Indexed: A01, A03, A08, A22, A26, C06, C07, CA, E01, EMBASE, ExcerpMed, R10, Reac, RefZh, SCI, SCOPUS, T02, W07.
—BLDSC (3829.733320), GNLM, IE, Infotrieve, Ingenta, INIST. **CCC.**
Published by: Springer France (Subsidiary of: Springer Science+Business Media), 22 Rue de Palestro, Paris, 75002, France. TEL 33-1-53009860, FAX 33-1-53009861, sylvie.kamara@springer.com. Ed. Dr. Pierre Kehr. Adv. contact Stephan Kroeck TEL 49-30-827875739. **Subscr. in Americas to:** Springer New York LLC, Journal Fulfillment, PO Box 2485, Secaucus, NJ 07096. TEL 201-348-4033, 800-777-4643, FAX 201-348-4505, journals-ny@springer.com; **Subscr. to:** Springer Distribution Center, Kundenservice Zeitschriften, Haberstr 7, Heidelberg 69126, Germany. TEL 49-6221-3454303, FAX 49-6221-3454229, subscriptions@springer.com, http://link.springer.de. **Co-sponsors:** Societe d'Orthopedie et de Traumatologie de l'Est; Association of European Research Groups for Spinal Osteosynthesis; Group d'Etude pour la Chirurgie Osseuse European.

617.1 DEU ISSN 1863-9933
RD92 CODEN: EJTRFM
➤ **EUROPEAN JOURNAL OF TRAUMA AND EMERGENCY SURGERY.** Text in English, German; Summaries in English. 1975. bi-m. EUR 265, USD 349 combined subscription to institutions (print & online eds.) (effective 2012). adv. reprint service avail. from PSC. **Document type:** *Journal, Academic/Scholarly.*
Former titles (until 2007): European Journal of Trauma (1439-0590); (until 2000): Unfallchirurgie (0340-2649)
Related titles: Online - full text ed.: ISSN 1863-9941 (from IngentaConnect).
Indexed: A22, A26, C06, C07, C08, CA, CINAHL, E01, H12, H13, IBR, IBZ, IndMed, P02, P10, P20, P24, P30, P48, P53, P54, PQC, SCI, SCOPUS, T02, W07.
—GNLM, IE, Infotrieve, Ingenta. **CCC.**
Published by: (European Society for Trauma and Emergency Surgery (E S T E S) AUT), Urban und Vogel Medien und Medizin Verlagsgesellschaft mbH (Subsidiary of: Springer Science+Business Media), Neumarkter Str 43, Munich, 81673, Germany. TEL 49-89-4372-1411, FAX 49-89-4372-1410, verlag@urban-vogel.de, http://www.urban-vogel.de. Ed. Daniela Oesterle. Adv. contact Peter Urban. B&W page EUR 1,700, color page EUR 2,990; trim 174 x 240. Circ: 3,500 (paid). **Subscr. to:** Springer Distribution Center, Kundenservice Zeitschriften, Haberstr 7, Heidelberg 69126, Germany. TEL 49-6221-345-0, FAX 49-6221-345-4229, subscriptions@springer.com.

616.7 GBR ISSN 1754-5072
EUROPEAN MUSCULOSKELETAL REVIEW. Text in English. 2006. s-a. back issues avail. **Document type:** *Journal, Trade.* **Description:** Focuses on latest developments within the European musculoskeletal disease market from a scientific, clinical and objective perspective.
Related titles: Online - full text ed.: ISSN 1754-5080.
Published by: Touch Briefings (Subsidiary of: Touch Group plc), Saffron House, 6-10 Kirby St, London, EC1N 8TS, United Kingdom. TEL 44-20-74525600, FAX 44-20-74525606, info@touchbriefings.com.

616.7 DEU ISSN 1867-4569
▼ ➤ **EUROPEAN ORTHOPAEDICS AND TRAUMATOLOGY.** Text in English. 2010 (May). bi-m. EUR 513, USD 770 combined subscription to institutions (print & online eds.) (effective 2012). **Document type:** *Journal, Academic/Scholarly.*
Related titles: Online - full text ed.: ISSN 1867-4577. 2010.
Indexed: A22, A26, H12, SCOPUS.
—IE. **CCC.**
Published by: Springer (Subsidiary of: Springer Science+Business Media), Tiergartenstr 17, Heidelberg, 69121, Germany. TEL 49-6221-4870, FAX 49-6221-345229, subscriptions@springer.com.

➤ **EXCERPTA MEDICA. SECTION 19: REHABILITATION AND PHYSICAL MEDICINE.** *see* MEDICAL SCIENCES—Abstracting, Bibliographies, Statistics

➤ **EXCERPTA MEDICA. SECTION 33: ORTHOPEDIC SURGERY.** *see* MEDICAL SCIENCES—Abstracting, Bibliographies, Statistics

➤ **EXTRACTA ORTHOPAEDICA.** *see* MEDICAL SCIENCES—Abstracting, Bibliographies, Statistics

616.7 USA ISSN 1554-3196
FIRST AID FOR THE ORTHOPAEDIC BOARDS. Text in English. 2006. irreg., latest 2nd ed. USD 69.95 2nd ed. (effective 2008). 304 p./no.; back issues avail. **Document type:** *Monographic series, Trade.*
Published by: McGraw-Hill Companies, Inc., 1221 Ave of the Americas, 43rd fl, New York, NY 10020. TEL 212-512-2000, customer.service@mcgraw-hill.com, http://www.mcgraw-hill.com.

618.92 ESP ISSN 1579-7864
FISIOTERAPIA. Text in Spanish. 2002. s-m. **Document type:** *Journal, Academic/Scholarly.*
Related titles: Online - full text ed.: ISSN 1989-6360.
Published by: Universidad Catolica San Antonio, Facultad de Ciencias de la Salud, de la Actividad Fisica y del Deporte, Campus de los Jeronimos s/n, Guadalupe, Murcia 30107, Spain. TEL 34-968-278806, FAX 34-968-278820, info@ucam.edu, http://www.ucam.edu.

617.3 DNK ISSN 0901-0408
FODTERAPEUTEN. Text in Danish. 1948. 10/yr. adv. bk.rev. **Document type:** *Magazine, Trade.*
Formerly (until 1972): Tidsskrift for Fodplejere (0901-0394)
Published by: Landsforeningen af Statsautoriserede Fodterapeuter, Holsbjergvej 29, Albertslund, 2620, Denmark. TEL 45-43-205120, FAX 45-43-632440, lasf@lasf.dk, http://www.lasf.dk. Ed. Jann Pristed. Adv. contact Karin Birk. page DKK 7,725.

617.1 GBR ISSN 0958-2592
CODEN: FOOTEE
➤ **THE FOOT.** Text in English. 1991. q. EUR 448 in Europe to institutions; JPY 48,600 in Japan to institutions; USD 400 elsewhere to institutions (effective 2012). adv. back issues avail.; reprints avail. **Document type:** *Journal, Academic/Scholarly.* **Description:** Contains primary articles and commissioned reviews on disorders of the foot and their medical or surgical treatment.
Related titles: Online - full text ed.: ISSN 1532-2963 (from ScienceDirect).
Indexed: A22, A26, AMED, C06, C07, C08, CA, CINAHL, E01, EMBASE, ExcerpMed, H12, I05, MEDLINE, P30, R10, Reac, SCOPUS, T02.
—BLDSC (3984.840000), GNLM, IE, Infotrieve, Ingenta. **CCC.**

Published by: Churchill Livingstone (Subsidiary of: Elsevier Health Sciences), The Blvd, Langford Ln, Kidlington, OX5 1GB, United Kingdom. TEL 44-1865-843434, FAX 44-1865-843970, directenquiries@elsevier.com, http://www.elsevierhealth.com/imprint.jsp?iid=9. Pub. Susan Young. Adv. contact Emma Steel TEL 44-207-4244221. Circ: 936.

617.3 USA ISSN 1083-7515
➤ **FOOT AND ANKLE CLINICS.** Text in English. 1996. q. USD 357 in United States to institutions; USD 422 elsewhere to institutions (effective 2012). adv. back issues avail.; reprints avail. **Document type:** *Journal, Academic/Scholarly.* **Description:** Focuses on a single topic relevant to foot and ankle, orthopedic surgery, and podiatric practice, from innovative approaches to peripheral nerve problems to external fixation techniques.
Related titles: Online - full text ed.: ISSN 1558-1934 (from ScienceDirect).
Indexed: C06, C07, CurCont, EMBASE, ExcerpMed, IndMed, MEDLINE, P30, R10, Reac, SCI, SCOPUS, W07.
—BLDSC (3984.854000), IE, Infotrieve, Ingenta. **CCC.**
Published by: W.B. Saunders Co. (Subsidiary of: Elsevier Health Sciences), Elsevier, Health Sciences Division, Order Fulfillment, 3251 Riverport Ln, Maryland Heights, MO 63043. TEL 314-872-8370, 800-325-4177, FAX 314-432-1380, JournalCustomerService-usa@elsevier.com, http://www.us.elsevierhealth.com. Adv. contact John Marmero TEL 212-633-3657.

617.3 USA ISSN 1071-1007
CODEN: FAINE4
➤ **FOOT & ANKLE INTERNATIONAL.** Abbreviated title: F A I. Text in English. 1980. m. USD 325 domestic to institutions; USD 385 foreign to institutions; USD 500 combined subscription domestic to institutions (print & online eds.); USD 550 combined subscription in Canada to institutions (print & online eds.); USD 560 combined subscription elsewhere to institutions (print & online eds.) (effective 2010). adv. bk.rev. back issues avail. **Document type:** *Journal, Academic/Scholarly.* **Description:** Emphasizes surgical and medical management as well as basic clinical research related to foot and ankle problems.
Formerly (until 1994): Foot and Ankle (0198-0211)
Related titles: Online - full text ed.: ISSN 1944-7876. USD 219 to individuals; USD 465 to institutions (effective 2010); Optical Disk - DVD ed.: USD 289 to non-members; USD 214 to members (effective 2010).
Indexed: A20, A22, AMED, ASCA, C06, C07, C08, CA, CINAHL, CurCont, EMBASE, ExcerpMed, FoSS&M, IBR, IBZ, IndMed, Inpharma, MEDLINE, P30, R10, Reac, SCI, SCOPUS, SD, SportS, T02, W07.
—BLDSC (3984.860000), GNLM, IE, Infotrieve, Ingenta, INIST. **CCC.**
Published by: (American Orthopaedic Foot and Ankle Society), Data Trace Publishing Company, PO Box 1239, Brooklandville, MD 21022. TEL 410-494-4994, 800-342-0454, FAX 410-494-0515, info@datatrace.com, http://www.datatrace.com. Ed. David B Thordarson. Adv. contact Frank M Tufariello TEL 410-494-4994.

617.3 USA ISSN 1941-6806
➤ **FOOT & ANKLE JOURNAL.** Abbreviated title: F A O J. Text in English. 2007. m. free (effective 2011). back issues avail. **Document type:** *Journal, Academic/Scholarly.* **Description:** Contains articles of foot and ankle medicine and surgery.
Formerly (until 2008): Podiatry Internet Journal
Media: Online - full text.
Published by: Al. Kline, Ed. & Pub., Barry University School of Podiatric Medicine, Doctors Regional Medical Ctr, Corpus Christi, TX 78411. picomstaff@hotmail.com. Eds. Al Kline, Sarah A Curran.

617.3 USA ISSN 1068-3100
FOOT AND ANKLE QUARTERLY; the seminar journal. Abbreviated title: F A Q. Text in English. 1988. q. USD 99 to individuals; USD 295 to institutions (effective 2010). back issues avail. **Document type:** *Journal, Academic/Scholarly.* **Description:** Contains four journal issues, two lectures per issue on CD, four sets of questions and answer forms etc.
Formerly (until 1993): Podiatry Tracts (0894-6116)
Related titles: Online - full text ed.: USD 60 per issue (effective 2010).
Indexed: C06, C07, C08, CINAHL.
—BLDSC (3984.870000). **CCC.**
Published by: Data Trace Publishing Company, PO Box 1239, Brooklandville, MD 21022. TEL 410-494-4994, 800-342-0454, FAX 410-494-0515, info@datatrace.com. Ed. Stephanie C Wu.

617.585 USA ISSN 1938-6400
➤ **FOOT AND ANKLE SPECIALIST**; a multidisciplinary journal dedicated to the advancement of foot and anle care. Text in English. 2008 (Feb.). bi-m. USD 178, GBP 105 combined subscription to institutions (print & online eds.); USD 174, GBP 103 to institutions (effective 2011). adv. reprint service avail. from PSC. **Document type:** *Journal, Academic/Scholarly.* **Description:** Offers the latest techniques and advancements in foot and ankle treatment through research reports and reviews, technical perspectives, case studies, and other evidence-based articles.
Related titles: Online - full text ed.: ISSN 1938-7636. 2008 (Feb.). USD 160, GBP 95 to institutions (effective 2011).
Indexed: A22, B21, CTA, E01, EMBASE, ExcerpMed, MEDLINE, P30, SCOPUS.
—IE. **CCC.**
Published by: Sage Publications, Inc., 2455 Teller Rd, Thousand Oaks, CA 91320. TEL 805-499-9774, FAX 805-499-0871, info@sagepub.com. Eds. Babak Baravarian, Dr. Gregory C Berlet. adv.: B&W page USD 1,395; trim 8.125 x 10.875. Circ: 10,500 (controlled).

617.585 SWE ISSN 1654-8388
FORKIRURGISK TIDSKRIFT. Text in Swedish. 2007. s-a. SEK 200; SEK 300 membership (effective 2008). adv. **Document type:** *Magazine, Trade.*
Published by: Svenska Fotkirurg Saellskapet/Swedish Foot and Ankle Society, c/o Department of Orthopaedics, University Hospital, Lund, 22185, Sweden. FAX 46-46-177167, http://www.musconline.org/Default.aspx?ContID=1848. Ed. Bjoern Kullenberg. Adv. contact Boerje Ohlsson.

616.7 TWN ISSN 2210-7940
RC925.A1
▼ ➤ **FORMOSAN JOURNAL OF MUSCULOSKELETAL DISORDERS.** Text in English. 2011. 4/yr. EUR 210 in Europe to institutions; JPY 32,950 in Japan to institutions; USD 280 elsewhere to institutions (effective 2012). **Document type:** *Journal, Academic/Scholarly.* **Description:** Offers readers the most updated clinical and basic researches that contribute to today's orthopaedic practice and improve treatment results or orthopedic diseases.
Related titles: Online - full text ed.: (from ScienceDirect).
—**CCC.**
Published by: (Taiwan Orthopaedic Association), Elsevier Taiwan LLC. (Subsidiary of: Elsevier BV), 96 Chung Shan North Rd, Section 2, Ste N-412, 4th Fl, Chia Hsin Cement Building, Taipei, Taiwan. TEL 886-2522-5900, FAX 886-2522-1885. Ed. Jinn Lin.

616.7 DEU
➤ **FORTBILDUNG ORTHOPAEDIE, TRAUMATOLOGIE.** Text in German. 1999. irreg., latest vol.12, 2007. price varies. **Document type:** *Monographic series, Academic/Scholarly.*
Formerly (until 2003): Fortbildung Orthopaedie
Published by: Dr. Dietrich Steinkopff Verlag (Subsidiary of: Springer Science+Business Media), Tiergartenstr 17, Heidelberg, 69121, Germany. TEL 49-6221-4878821, FAX 49-6221-4878830, info.steinkopff@springer.com, http://www.steinkopff.com.

617.585 DEU
DER FUSS. Text in German. 1996. bi-m. EUR 40.40 domestic; EUR 46.80 foreign; EUR 7 newsstand/cover (effective 2009). adv. **Document type:** *Journal, Academic/Scholarly.*
Published by: C. Maurer Druck und Verlag, Schubartstr 21, Geislingen, 73312, Germany. TEL 49-7331-9300, FAX 49-7331-930190, info@maurer-online.de, http://www.maurer-online.de. Adv. contact Sybille Lutz. B&W page EUR 1,715, color page EUR 2,885; trim 185 x 282. Circ: 8,340 (paid and controlled).

617.585 DEU ISSN 1619-9987
RD781
➤ **FUSS & SPRUNGGELENK**; German journal of foot and ankle surgery. Text in English, German. 2003. q. EUR 457 in Europe to institutions; EUR 457 to institutions in Germany, Austria and Switzerland; JPY 62,900 in Japan to institutions; USD 504 elsewhere to institutions (effective 2012). adv. bk.rev. abstr. back issues avail.; reprint service avail. from PSC. **Document type:** *Journal, Academic/Scholarly.*
Related titles: Online - full text ed.: ISSN 1619-9995 (from IngentaConnect, ScienceDirect).
Indexed: A22, A26, CA, E01, SCOPUS, T02.
—BLDSC (4059.742000), IE, Ingenta. **CCC.**
Published by: Urban und Fischer Verlag (Subsidiary of: Elsevier GmbH), Loebdergraben 14a, Jena, 07743, Germany. TEL 49-3641-626444, FAX 49-3641-626443, info@urbanfischer.de, http://www.urbanfischer.de. Ed. Renee A Fuhrmann. Adv. contact Eva Kraemer TEL 49-89-5383704. B&W page EUR 1,600, color page EUR 2,920; trim 175 x 240. Circ: 1,500.

617.95 FRA ISSN 1951-5839
G E C O. COLLECTION. (Groupe d'Etude pour la Chirurgie Osseuse) Text in French. 2006. irreg., latest 2010. price varies. back issues avail. **Document type:** *Monographic series, Academic/Scholarly.*
Published by: Springer France (Subsidiary of: Springer Science+Business Media), 22 Rue de Palestro, Paris, 75002, France. TEL 33-1-53009860, FAX 33-1-53009861, sylvie.kamara@springer.com.

GAIT & POSTURE. *see* MEDICAL SCIENCES

GELBE LISTE PHARMINDEX. ORTHOPAEDEN. *see* PHARMACY AND PHARMACOLOGY

617.3 RUS ISSN 1028-4427
GENII ORTOPEDII. Text in Russian. 1995. q.
Indexed: RefZh.
—East View.
Published by: Redaktsiya Genii Ortopedii, Ul M Ul'yanovoi 6, Kurgan, 640005, Russian Federation. TEL 35222-3-33-10, FAX 35222-3-60-46. Ed. V I Shevtsov. **Dist. by:** East View Information Services, 10601 Wayzata Blvd, Minneapolis, MN 55305. TEL 952-252-1201, 800-477-1005, FAX 952-252-1202, info@eastview.com, http://www.eastview.com.

▼ **GERIATRIC ORTHOPAEDIC SURGERY & REHABILITATION.** *see* MEDICAL SCIENCES—Surgery

617.3 ITA ISSN 0390-0134
GIORNALE ITALIANO DI ORTOPEDIA E TRAUMATOLOGIA. Text in Italian. 1975. 4/yr. EUR 97 domestic; EUR 122 foreign (effective 2009). adv. bk.rev. Supplement avail. **Document type:** *Journal, Academic/Scholarly.* **Description:** Covers current thought, practice and research in the science of orthopedics and traumatology.
Related titles: ◆ English ed.: Journal of Orthopaedics and Traumatology. ISSN 1590-9921.
Indexed: DentInd, IndMed.
—GNLM.
Published by: Pacini Editore SpA, Via A Gherardesca 1, Ospedaletto, PI 56121, Italy. TEL 39-050-313011, FAX 39-050-3130300, pacini.editore@pacinieditore.it, http://www.pacinimedicina.it.

616.02 USA ISSN 0017-1565
GOLD CROSS. Text in English. 1930. q. free to qualified personnel. adv. **Document type:** *Magazine, Trade.*
Published by: (New Jersey State First Aid Council, Inc. GBR), Leonard Publications, Inc., 10 W Hanover Ave, Mt. Freedom, NJ 07970-0553. TEL 973-895-6000, FAX 973-895-3297. Ed. Julie Aberger. Circ: 6,700.

617.3 ESP ISSN 1576-1622
GUIA PUNTEX. ANUARIO ESPANOL DE ORTOPEDIA Y GERONTOLOGIA. Text in Spanish. 1997. a. EUR 69 domestic; EUR 98 in Europe; EUR 125 elsewhere (effective 2008). adv. back issues avail. **Document type:** *Yearbook, Consumer.*
Formerly (until 1998): Guia Puntex. Anuario Espanol de Ortopedia (1576-1630)
Published by: Publicaciones Nacionales Tecnicas y Extranjeras (PUNTEX), Padilla 323, Barcelona, 08025, Spain. TEL 34-934-462820, FAX 34-934-462064, puntex@puntex.es, http://www.puntex.es. Ed. Martin Yolanda. adv.: B&W page EUR 925; 170 x 240. Circ: 8,000.

617.585 ESP ISSN 1576-1649
GUIA PUNTEX. ANUARIO ESPANOL DE PODOLOGIA. Text in Spanish. 1997. a. EUR 52 domestic; EUR 81 in Europe; EUR 107 elsewhere (effective 2007). adv. back issues avail. **Document type:** *Yearbook, Consumer.*
Formerly (until 1998): Guia Puntex. Anuario de Podologia (1576-2769)
Published by: Publicaciones Nacionales Tecnicas y Extranjeras (PUNTEX), Padilla 323, Barcelona, 08025, Spain. TEL 34-934-462820, FAX 34-934-462064, puntex@puntex.es, http://www.puntex.es. Ed. Martin Yolanda. adv.: color page EUR 920; trim 170 x 240. Circ: 3,000.

616.7 CHN
GUKE DONGTAI/JOURNAL OF BONE & JOINT SURGERY. Text in Chinese. q. **Document type:** *Journal, Academic/Scholarly.*
Published by: Tianjin Yiyuan, 406, Jiefang Nanlu, Tianjin, 300211, China. TEL 86-22-28334734, FAX 86-22-28241184.

616.7 CHN ISSN 1009-9255
GUOWAI YIXUE (GUKEXUE FENCE)/FOREIGN MEDICAL SCIENCES (ORTHOPAEDICS). Text in Chinese. 1964. bi-m. CNY 30 domestic; USD 19.20 foreign (effective 2005). **Document type:** *Journal, Academic/Scholarly.*
Formerly (until 2000): Guowai Yixue (Chuangshang yu Waike Jiben Wenti Fence) (1001-1161)
Related titles: Online - full text ed.
—East View.
Published by: Shanghai Shi Yixue Kexue Jishu Qingbao Yanjiusuo, 602, Jianguo Xilu, Shanghai, 200031, China. TEL 86-21-64728661 ext 20, FAX 86-21-64667456. **Dist. by:** China International Book Trading Corp, 35 Chegongzhuang Xilu, Haidian District, PO Box 399, Beijing 100044, China. TEL 86-10-68412045, FAX 86-10-68412023, cibtc@mail.cibtc.com.cn, http://www.cibtc.com.cn.

616.7 TUR ISSN 1018-0877
HACETTEPE ORTOPEDI DERGISI/HACETTEPE JOURNAL OF ORTHOPAEDIC SURGERY. Text in Turkish. 1991. q. **Document type:** *Journal, Academic/Scholarly.*
Related titles: English ed.
Published by: Hacettepe Universitesi, Hacettepe Universitesi Tanitim Ofisi, Beytepe - Ankara, 06532, Turkey. e-dergi@hacettepe.edu.tr, info@hacettepe.edu.tr, http://hacettepe.edu.tr.

617 JPN ISSN 0917-365X
HAMAMATSU SEIKEI GEKA KIYO/HAMAMATSU UNIVERSITY. ANNUAL OF ORTHOPAEDIC SURGERY. Text in Japanese. 1990. a. **Document type:** *Bulletin, Academic/Scholarly.*
Published by: Hamamatsu Ika Daigaku, Seikei Gekagaku Kyoshitsu/Hamamatsu University, School of Medicine, Department of Orthopaedics, 1-20-1 Handayama, Hamamatsu-shi, Shizuoka-ken 431-3192, Japan. TEL 81-53-435-2299, FAX 81-53-435-2296.

617 USA ISSN 0749-0712
RC951
➤ **HAND CLINICS.** Text in English. 1985. q. USD 540 in United States to institutions; USD 617 elsewhere to institutions (effective 2012). adv. back issues avail.; reprints avail. **Document type:** *Journal, Academic/Scholarly.* **Description:** Focuses on a single topic relevant to hand and orthopedic surgery practice, from tumors of the upper extremity to thoracic outlet syndrome.
Related titles: Microfilm ed.; Online - full text ed.: ISSN 1558-1969 (from ScienceDirect).
Indexed: A20, A22, ASCA, C06, C07, C08, CINAHL, CurCont, EMBASE, ExcerpMed, FR, IndMed, Inpharma, MEDLINE, P30, R10, RILM, Reac, SCI, SCOPUS, W07.
—BLDSC (4241.558000), GNLM, IE, Infotrieve, Ingenta, INIST. **CCC.**
Published by: W.B. Saunders Co. (Subsidiary of: Elsevier Health Sciences), Elsevier, Health Sciences Division, Order Fulfillment, 3251 Riverport Ln, Maryland Heights, MO 63043. TEL 314-872-8370, 800-325-4177, FAX 314-432-1380, JournalCustomerService-usa@elsevier.com, http://www.us.elsevierhealth.com. Adv. contact John Marmero TEL 212-633-3657.

➤ **HAND THERAPY.** *see* MEDICAL SCIENCES—Physical Medicine And Rehabilitation

616.7 DEU ISSN 1432-3648
HANDBUCH REHA- UND VORSORGE-EINRICHTUNGEN. Text in German. 1996. a. EUR 25 (effective 2007). adv. **Document type:** *Directory, Trade.*
Published by: Medizinische Medien Informations GmbH, Am Forsthaus Gravenbruch 7, Neu-Isenburg, 63263, Germany. TEL 49-6102-5020, FAX 49-6102-502243, info@mmi.de. adv.: page EUR 5,200. Circ: 30,000 (paid and controlled).

617.3 JPN ISSN 1342-7784
HIGASHI NIHON SEIKEI SAIGAI GEKA GAKKAI ZASSHI/EASTERN JAPAN ASSOCIATION OF ORTHOPAEDICS AND TRAUMATOLOGY. JOURNAL. Text in Japanese. 1989. q. JPY 10,000 membership (effective 2007).
Formerly (until 1996): Higashinihon Rinsho Seikei Geka Gakkai Zasshi/Eastern Japan Journal of Clinical Orthopaedics (0915-8855)
—**CCC.**
Published by: Higashi Nihon Seikei Saigai Geka Gakkai/Eastern Japan Association of Orthopaedics and Traumatology, 30-1 Oyaguchi-Kamimachi, Itabashi-ku, Tokyo, 173-8610, Japan. TEL 81-3-59959118, FAX 81-3-59959119, hnseisai@muse.ocn.ne.jp, http://www.ejaot.jp/.

617.3 JPN ISSN 0389-3634
HIP JOINT. Text in Japanese. 1975. a. JPY 9,000 per issue.
Published by: Nihon Kokansetsu Gakkai/Japanese Hip Society, University of yamanashi, Faculty of Medicine, Department of Orthopaedic Surgery, 1110 Shimo-Gato, Nakakoma-gun, Tamaho-cho, Yamanashi-ken 409-3898, Japan. TEL 81-55-2736768, FAX 81-55-2739241.

616.7 CZE ISSN 1802-6400
➤ **HOJENI RAN.** Text in Czech; Summaries in English. 2007. q. CZK 200 domestic (effective 2010). **Document type:** *Journal, Academic/Scholarly.* **Description:** Covers wound healing problems viewed from different perspectives. Includes review articles, studies, case reports.
Published by: (Ceska Spolecnost pro Lecbu Rany/Czech Society for Treatment of Wounds), Nakladatelstvi GEUM, s.r.o., Nadrazni 66, Semily, 51301, Czech Republic. FAX 420-481-312858, geum@geum.org. Ed. Karel Vizner.

617.3 JPN ISSN 0914-6083
HOKKAIDO SEIKEI GEKA GAISHO KENKYUKAI KAISHI/HOKKAIDO ORTHOPAEDIC TRAUMATOLOGY ASSOCIATION. JOURNAL. Text in Japanese. 1985. a. **Document type:** *Journal, Academic/Scholarly.*
Published by: Hokkaido Seikei Geka Gaisho Kenkyukai/Hokkaido Orthopaedic Traumatology Association, Ito Orthopedic Hospital, S2, W10, 5-chome, Chuo-ku, Sapporo, Hokkaido 060-0062, Japan. TEL 81-11-2415461.

617.3 JPN ISSN 1343-3873
HOKKAIDO SEIKEI SAIGAI GEKA GAKKAI ZASSHI/HOKKAIDO JOURNAL OF ORTHOPAEDICS AND TRAUMATOLOGY. Text in English, Japanese. 1954. a. **Document type:** *Journal, Academic/Scholarly.*
Formerly (until 1996): Hokkaido Seikei Saigai Geka Zasshi/Hokkaido Journal of Orthopedic & Traumatic Surgery (0018-3377)
Indexed: SCOPUS.
—CCC.
Published by: Hokkaido Seikei Saigai Geka Gakkai/Hokkaido Orthopedic and Traumatic Surgery Society, c/o Hokkaido University, School of Medicine, North 15, West 7, Kita-ku, Sapporo, Hokkaido 060-8638, Japan. TEL 81-11-7162111 ext 5936, FAX 81-11-7066054. Circ: 750.

616.02 HKG ISSN 1024-9079
HONG KONG JOURNAL OF EMERGENCY MEDICINE. Text in English. 1994. q. adv. **Document type:** *Journal, Academic/Scholarly.*
Related titles: Online - full text ed.: free (effective 2011).
Indexed: EMBASE, ExcerpMed, R10, Reac, SCI, SCOPUS, W07.
—BLDSC (4326.385655).
Published by: (Hong Kong College of Emergency Medicine, Hong Kong Society for Emergency Medicine and Surgery), Medcom Limited, Rm 808, Two Chinachem Exchange Sq, 338 King's Rd, North Point, Hong Kong. TEL 852-25783833, FAX 852-25783929, mcl@medcom.com.hk, http://www.medcom.com.hk. Ed. Chin Hung Chung.

617.3 USA ISSN 1070-7778
HUGHSTON HEALTH ALERT. Text in English. 1989. q. free. 2 p./no.; **Document type:** *Newsletter, Consumer.* **Description:** Presents information on musculoskeletal health and fitness for all ages.
Indexed: SD, T02.
—BLDSC (4335.844055).
Published by: Hughston Sports Medicine Foundation, 6262 Veterans Pkwy, PO Box 9517, Columbus, GA 31908. TEL 706-494-3345. Ed. Dr. David C Rehak.

616.025 USA ISSN 2090-5629
▼ ➤ **I S R N EMERGENCY MEDICINE.** (International Scholarly Research Network) Text in English. 2011. **Document type:** *Journal, Academic/Scholarly.* **Description:** Publishes original research articles, review articles, and clinical studies in all areas of emergency medicine.
Related titles: Online - full text ed.: ISSN 2090-5637. 2011. free (effective 2011).
Published by: Hindawi Publishing Corporation, 410 Park Ave, 15th Fl, PMB 287, New York, NY 10022. FAX 215-893-4392, 866-446-3294, info@hindawi.com.

616.7 USA ISSN 2090-6161
▼ ➤ **I S R N ORTHOPEDICS.** Text in English. 2011. **Document type:** *Journal, Academic/Scholarly.* **Description:** Publishes original research articles, review articles, and clinical studies in all areas of orthopedics.
Related titles: Online - full text ed.: ISSN 2090-617X. 2011. free (effective 2011).
Published by: Hindawi Publishing Corporation, 410 Park Ave, 15th Fl, PMB 287, New York, NY 10022. FAX 215-893-4392, 866-446-3294, info@hindawi.com.

616.7 NZL ISSN 1177-4347
I T R U REPORT. (Interdisciplinary Trauma Research Unit) Text in English. 2006. irreg., latest vol.4, 2006. **Document type:** *Monographic series, Academic/Scholarly.*
Related titles: Online - full text ed.: ISSN 1177-5424.
Published by: Auckland University of Technology, Interdisciplinary Trauma Research Unit, Private Bag 92006, Auckland, 1142, New Zealand. TEL 64-9-9219796, http://www.aut.ac.nz/about/faculties/health_and_environmental_sciences/research_centres_and_institutes/interdisciplinary_trauma_research_unit/.

616.025 JPN ISSN 0912-2125
IBARAKI-KEN KYUKYU IGAKKAI ZASSHI. Text in Japanese. 1977. a. **Document type:** *Academic/Scholarly.*
Formerly (until 1978): Ibarakiken Kyukyu Igakkai Zasshi/Ibaraki Journal of Acute Medicine (0912-117X)
Published by: (Kyukyu Iryo Kyokai), Ibarakiken Ishikai/Ibaraki Medical Association, 489 Kasahara-cho, Mito-shi, Ibaraki-ken 310-0852, Japan. TEL 81-29-2418446, http://www.ibaraki.med.or.jp/.

617.3 IND ISSN 0019-5413
RD701 CODEN: INJOAU
➤ **INDIAN JOURNAL OF ORTHOPAEDICS.** Abbreviated title: I J O. Text in English. 1967 (June). q. INR 1,500 domestic to individuals; USD 150 foreign to individuals; INR 2,500 domestic to institutions; USD 250 foreign to institutions; INR 1,800 combined subscription domestic to individuals (print & online eds.); USD 180 combined subscription foreign to individuals (print & online eds.); INR 3,000 combined subscription domestic to institutions (print & online eds.); USD 300 combined subscription foreign to institutions (print & online eds.) (effective 2011). adv. bk.rev. bibl.; charts; illus. index. back issues avail. **Document type:** *Journal, Academic/Scholarly.*
Related titles: Online - full text ed.: ISSN 1998-3727. INR 1,200 domestic to individuals; USD 120 foreign to individuals; INR 2,000 domestic to institutions; USD 200 foreign to institutions (effective 2011).
Indexed: A01, A26, A36, C06, C07, CA, CABA, E12, GH, H17, I05, ISA, N02, N03, P10, P30, P33, P48, P53, P54, PQC, R12, R13, SCI, SCOPUS, T02, T05, VS, W07.
—GNLM, IE. **CCC.**
Published by: (Indian Orthopaedic Association), Medknow Publications and Media Pvt. Ltd., B-9, Kanara Business Ctr, Off Link Rd, Ghatkopar (E), Mumbai, Maharastra 400 075, India. TEL 91-22-66491816, FAX 91-22-66491817, http://www.medknow.com. Ed. Anil K Jain.

616.8 NLD ISSN 1871-2789
INFOCUS. Text in Dutch. 1984. q. EUR 25 (effective 2010).
Formerly (until 2005): En Toch (1383-1364)
Published by: Vereniging van Mensen met Brandwonden, Postbus 264, Beverwijk, 1940 EA, Netherlands. TEL 31-6-28924494, info@brandwondenvereniging.nl.

617 GBR ISSN 0020-1383
RD92 CODEN: INJUBF
➤ **INJURY;** international journal of the care of the injured. Text in English. 1969. 12/yr. EUR 1,267 in Europe to institutions; JPY 168,100 in Japan to institutions; USD 1,416 elsewhere to institutions (effective 2012). adv. bk.rev. abstr.; bibl.; illus. index. back issues avail. **Document type:** *Journal, Academic/Scholarly.* **Description:** Deals with all aspects of trauma, including fractures and soft-tissue injuries, and covers problems in the accident unit.
Related titles: Microform ed.: (from PQC); Online - full text ed.: ISSN 1879-0267 (from IngentaConnect, ScienceDirect); Supplement(s): Injury Extra. ISSN 1572-3461. 2003 (from IngentaConnect, ScienceDirect).
Indexed: A01, A03, A08, A20, A22, A26, A28, AMED, APA, ASCA, ASG, B21, BrCerAb, C&ISA, C06, C07, CA, CA/WCA, CIA, CerAb, CivEngAb, CorrAb, CurCont, DentInd, DokArb, E&CAJ, E11, EEA, EMA, EMBASE, ESPM, EnvEAb, ExcerpMed, FR, FamI, GeoRef, H&SSA, H15, HRIS, I05, INI, IndMed, Inpharma, M&TEA, M09, MBF, MEDLINE, METADEX, P30, P35, PEI, R10, Reac, RiskAb, S02, S03, SCI, SCOPUS, SD, SolStAb, T02, T04, W07, WAA.
—BLDSC (4514.400000), GNLM, IE, Infotrieve, Ingenta, INIST. **CCC.**
Published by: (British Trauma Society, Australasian Trauma Society (A T S) AUS, Saudi Orthopedic Association in Trauma SAU, Institute of Accident Surgery), Elsevier Ltd (Subsidiary of: Elsevier Science & Technology), The Blvd, Langford Ln, Kidlington, Oxford, OX5 1GB, United Kingdom. TEL 44-1865-843000, FAX 44-1865-843010. Ed. S. J. Krikler. **Subscr. to:** Elsevier BV, Radarweg 29, PO Box 211, Amsterdam 1000 AE, Netherlands. TEL 31-20-4853757, FAX 31-20-4853432, JournalsCustomerServiceEMEA@elsevier.com, http://www.elsevier.nl.

616.7 DEU ISSN 1662-3282
INSPINE. Text in English. 2005. q. EUR 67 to individuals; EUR 187 to institutions (effective 2011). **Document type:** *Journal, Academic/Scholarly.* **Description:** Aimed at the whole spine community, which differs radically from traditional medical publications. Covers controversial spine-related questions, profiles of significant surgeons or institutions, and case study reports.
Published by: Georg Thieme Verlag, Ruedigerstr 14, Stuttgart, 70469, Germany. TEL 49-711-8931421, FAX 49-711-8931410, kunden.service@thieme.de. Ed. Michael E Janssen.

616.25 GBR ISSN 1751-1437
INTENSIVE CARE SOCIETY. JOURNAL. Text in English. 1999. q. GBP 100 domestic to individuals; GBP 110 foreign to individuals; GBP 160 domestic to institutions; GBP 170 foreign to institutions; free to members (effective 2009). adv. back issues avail. **Document type:** *Journal, Academic/Scholarly.* **Description:** Covers papers, review articles, critically appraised topics, case reports and audits of interest to all those involved in caring for critically ill patients.
Related titles: Online - full text ed.: free (effective 2009).
Indexed: SCOPUS.
—BLDSC (4802.062200), IE, Ingenta. **CCC.**
Published by: Intensive Care Society, Churchill House, 35 Red Lion Sq, London, WC1R 4SG, United Kingdom. TEL 44-20-72804350, FAX 44-20-72804369, http://www.ics.ac.uk/. Ed. Jane Harper. Adv. contact Christine Bishop TEL 44-1279-714510. B&W page GBP 945, color page GBP 1,470; trim 210 x 297.

616.025 DEU ISSN 1865-1380
➤ **INTERNATIONAL JOURNAL OF EMERGENCY MEDICINE (ONLINE).** Text in English. 2008. irreg. free (effective 2011). **Document type:** *Journal, Academic/Scholarly.*
Media: Online - full text (from IngentaConnect).
Indexed: P20, P30, P48, P54, PQC.
—CCC.
Published by: (American Academy for Emergency Medicine in India USA, Malaysian Association of Emergency Medicine MYS, Nederlandse Vereniging van Spoedeisende Hulp Artsen NLD), SpringerOpen (Subsidiary of: Springer Science+Business Media), Tiergartenstr 17, Heidelberg, 69121, Germany. info@springeropen.com, http://www.springeropen.com. Eds. Latha Ganti, Wyatt Decker.

➤ **INTERNATIONAL JOURNAL OF GERONTOLOGY.** *see* GERONTOLOGY AND GERIATRICS

616.7 USA ISSN 2042-0099
RB131
▼ **INTERNATIONAL JOURNAL OF INFLAMMATION.** Text in English. 2010. irreg. free (effective 2011). back issues avail. **Document type:** *Journal, Academic/Scholarly.* **Description:** Brings out research articles, review articles, case reports, and clinical studies in all areas of inflammation.
Media: Online - full text.
Indexed: A01, P30, T02.
Published by: Sage - Hindawi Access to Research, 410 Park Ave, 15th Fl, 287 PMB, New York, NY 10022. FAX 866-446-3294.

616.7 NZL ISSN 1902-8016
INTERNATIONAL JOURNAL OF MECHANICAL DIAGNOSIS AND THERAPY. Text in English. 3/yr. membership. **Document type:** *Journal, Academic/Scholarly.*
Formerly (until 2006): McKenzie Institut Danmark. Nyhedsbrev (1601-4790)
—BLDSC (4542.340000).
Published by: McKenzie Institute International, 1 Alexander Rd, PO Box 2026, Raumati Beach, 5255, New Zealand. TEL 64-4-2996645, FAX mckinst@xtra.co.nz, 64-4-2997010. Ed. Helen Clare.

INTERNATIONAL JOURNAL OF ORTHOPAEDIC AND TRAUMA NURSING. *see* MEDICAL SCIENCES—Nurses And Nursing

616.716 GBR ISSN 1746-0689
RZ341
➤ **INTERNATIONAL JOURNAL OF OSTEOPATHIC MEDICINE.** Abbreviated title: I J O M. Text in English. 1997. 4/yr. EUR 284 in Europe to institutions; JPY 37,700 in Japan to institutions; USD 318 elsewhere to institutions (effective 2012). back issues avail. **Document type:** *Journal, Academic/Scholarly.* **Description:** Contains research articles and review papers on osteopathic medicine with emphasis on basic science research, clinical epidemiology and health social science in relation to osteopathy and neuromusculoskeletal medicine.
Former titles (until 2005): Journal of Osteopathic Medicine (1443-8461); (until 2000): Australasian Osteopathic Medicine Review (1329-1491)
Related titles: Online - full text ed.: ISSN 1878-0164 (from ScienceDirect).
Indexed: A26, C06, C07, C08, CA, CINAHL, EMBASE, ExcerpMed, H12, I05, P30, PEI, R10, Reac, SCI, SCOPUS, T02, W07.
—BLDSC (4542.440650), IE, Ingenta. **CCC.**
Published by: Elsevier Ltd (Subsidiary of: Elsevier Science & Technology), The Blvd, Langford Ln, Kidlington, Oxford, OX5 1GB, United Kingdom. TEL 44-1865-843000, FAX 44-1865-843010, journalscustomerserviceemea@elsevier.com. Eds. Nicholas Lucas, Robert Moran, Steven Vogel.

616.7 PAK ISSN 1994-5442
➤ **INTERNATIONAL JOURNAL OF OSTEOPOROSIS AND METABOLIC DISORDERS.** Text in English. 2008. 4/yr. **Document type:** *Journal, Academic/Scholarly.* **Description:** Provides a forum for the communication and exchange of current ideas concerning osteoporosis and metabolic disorders. The mission of this journal is to keep those interested individuals informed of all the latest exciting advancements that are essential to their research or clinical practice.
Related titles: Online - full text ed.: free (effective 2011).
Indexed: A36, CABA, EMBASE, ExcerpMed, GH, N02, N03, T05, VS.
Published by: A N S I Network, 308 Lasani Town, Sargodha Rd, Faisalabad, 38090, Pakistan. TEL 92-41-8787087, FAX 92-41-8815544, sarwarm@ansimail.org, http://ansinet.com.

➤ **INTERNATIONAL JOURNAL OF SHOULDER SURGERY.** *see* MEDICAL SCIENCES—Surgery

616.7 GBR ISSN 1753-6146
RC925.A1
➤ **INTERNATIONAL MUSCULOSKELETAL MEDICINE.** Abbreviated title: I M M. Text in English. 1979. q. GBP 194 combined subscription to institutions (print & online eds.); USD 355 combined subscription in United States to institutions (print & online eds.) (effective 2012). adv. bk.rev. back issues avail.; reprint service avail. from PSC. **Document type:** *Journal, Academic/Scholarly.* **Description:** Publishes research and review papers about pain and dysfunction in the musculoskeletal system.
Formerly (until 2008): Journal of Orthopaedic Medicine (1355-297X)
Related titles: Online - full text ed.: ISSN 1753-6154. GBP 177 to institutions; USD 325 in United States to institutions (effective 2012) (from IngentaConnect).
Indexed: A01, C06, C07, CA, P30, T02.
—BLDSC (4544.379000), IE, Ingenta. **CCC.**
Published by: (British Institute of Musculoskeletal Medicine, Society of Orthopaedic Medicine, F I M M Academy/International Federation of Manual/Musculoskeletal Medicine), Maney Publishing, Ste 1C, Joseph's Well, Hanover Walk, Leeds, W Yorks LS3 1AB, United Kingdom. TEL 44-113-2432800, FAX 44-113-3868178, maney@maney.co.uk, http://www.maney.co.uk. Ed. Richard Ellis. **Subscr. in N. America to:** Maney Publishing, 875 Massachusetts Ave, 7th Fl, Cambridge, MA 02139. TEL 866-297-5154, FAX 617-354-6875, maney@maneyusa.com.

617.3 DEU ISSN 0341-2695
RD701
➤ **INTERNATIONAL ORTHOPAEDICS.** Text in English, French. 1977. bi-m. EUR 2,053, USD 2,452 combined subscription to institutions (print & online eds.) (effective 2012). adv. illus. index. reprint service avail. from PSC. **Document type:** *Journal, Academic/Scholarly.* **Description:** Presents articles dealing with clinical orthopedic surgery or basic research directly connected with orthopedic surgery.
Supersedes (1929-1972): International Society of Orthopaedic Surgery and Traumatology. Proceedings of Congresses (0074-8552)
Related titles: Microform ed.: (from PQC); Online - full text ed.: ISSN 1432-5195 (from IngentaConnect).
Indexed: A01, A03, A08, A22, A26, A36, ASCA, ASG, B21, C06, C07, CA, CABA, CTA, CurCont, E01, EMBASE, ExcerpMed, GH, INI, ISR, IndMed, Inpharma, MEDLINE, N02, N03, P30, P35, R10, R12, Reac, SCI, SCOPUS, T02, T05, W07.
—BLDSC (4544.856000), GNLM, IE, Infotrieve, Ingenta, INIST. **CCC.**
Published by: (Societe Internationale de Chirurgie Orthopedique et de Traumatologie BEL), Springer (Subsidiary of: Springer Science+Business Media), Tiergartenstr 17, Heidelberg, 69121, Germany. TEL 49-6221-4870, FAX 49-6221-345229. Ed. Dr. Marko Pecina. adv.: B&W page EUR 1,650, color page EUR 2,690. Circ: 2,800 (paid and controlled). **Subscr. in the Americas to:** Springer New York LLC, Journal Fulfillment, PO Box 2485, Secaucus, NJ 07096. TEL 201-348-4033, 800-777-4643, FAX 201-348-4505, journals-ny@springer.com, http://www.springer.com; **Subscr. to:** Springer Distribution Center, Kundenservice Zeitschriften, Haberstr 7, Heidelberg 69126, Germany. TEL 49-6221-3454303, FAX 49-6221-3454229, subscriptions@springer.com.

617.1 GBR ISSN 1742-4801
RD92
➤ **INTERNATIONAL WOUND JOURNAL.** Abbreviated title: I W J. Text in English; Abstracts in French, German, Italian, Spanish. 2004 (Apr.). bi-m. GBP 369 in United Kingdom to institutions; EUR 468 in Europe to institutions; USD 683 in the Americas to institutions; USD 798 elsewhere to institutions; GBP 426 combined subscription in United Kingdom to institutions (print & online eds.); EUR 539 combined subscription in Europe to institutions (print & online eds.); USD 786 combined subscription in the Americas to institutions (print & online eds.); USD 917 combined subscription elsewhere to institutions (print & online eds.) (effective 2012). adv. back issues avail.; reprint service avail. from PSC. **Document type:** *Journal, Academic/Scholarly.* **Description:** Focuses on providing the best quality information, research data and education on all aspects of wounds and wound healing.

Related titles: Online - full text ed.: ISSN 1742-481X. GBP 369 in United Kingdom to institutions; EUR 468 in Europe to institutions; USD 683 in the Americas to institutions; USD 798 elsewhere to institutions (effective 2012) (from IngentaConnect).
Indexed: A22, A26, C06, C07, C08, CINAHL, CurCont, E01, EMBASE, ExcerpMed, H12, MEDLINE, P30, R10, Reac, SCI, SCOPUS, W07.
—BLDSC (4552.230800), IE, Ingenta. **CCC.**
Published by: (Medicalhelplines.com Inc. CAN), Wiley-Blackwell Publishing Ltd. (Subsidiary of: John Wiley & Sons, Inc.), 9600 Garsington Rd, Oxford, OX4 2DQ, United Kingdom. TEL 44-1865-776868, FAX 44-1865-714591, customerservices@blackwellpublishing.com, http://www.wiley.com/WileyCDA/. Eds. Dr. Douglas Queen, Dr. Keith Harding. Adv. contact Mia Scott Ruddock TEL 44-1865-476354.

616.02 USA ISSN 1092-4051
RC86
➤ **THE INTERNET JOURNAL OF EMERGENCY AND INTENSIVE CARE MEDICINE.** Text in English. 1996. s-a. free (effective 2011). adv. bk.rev. back issues avail. **Document type:** *Journal, Academic/Scholarly.* **Description:** Contains information from the field of critical care and intensive care medicine, including original articles, reviews, case reports, streaming slide shows, streaming videos, letters to the editor, press releases, and meeting information.
Media: Online - full text.
Indexed: A01, A02, A03, A08, A26, C06, C07, C08, CA, CINAHL, G08, H11, H12, I05, T02.
Published by: Internet Scientific Publications, Llc., 23 Rippling Creek Dr, Sugar Land, TX 77479. TEL 832-443-1193, FAX 281-240-1533, wenker@ispub.com. Ed. Joseph Nates.

616.025 USA ISSN 1935-9551
➤ **THE INTERNET JOURNAL OF EMERGENCY MEDICINE.** Text in English. 2004. s-a. free (effective 2011). **Document type:** *Journal, Academic/Scholarly.*
Media: Online - full text.
Indexed: A01, A26, A39, C06, C07, C27, C29, CA, D03, D04, E13, G08, H11, H12, I05, R14, S14, S15, S18, T02.
Published by: Internet Scientific Publications, Llc., 23 Rippling Creek Dr, Sugar Land, TX 77479. TEL 832-443-1193, FAX 281-240-1533, wenker@ispub.com. Ed. Tom Vo.

617.47 USA ISSN 1531-2968
RD701
➤ **THE INTERNET JOURNAL OF ORTHOPEDIC SURGERY.** Text in English. 2001. s-a. free (effective 2011). adv. bk.rev. back issues avail. **Document type:** *Journal, Academic/Scholarly.* **Description:** Provides information from the field of orthopedic surgery; contains original articles, reviews, case reports, streaming slide shows, streaming videos, letters to the editor, press releases, and meeting information.
Media: Online - full text.
Indexed: A01, A02, A03, A08, A26, C06, C07, CA, G08, H11, H12, I05, T02.
Published by: Internet Scientific Publications, Llc., 23 Rippling Creek Dr, Sugar Land, TX 77479. TEL 832-443-1193, FAX 281-240-1533, wenker@ispub.com. Ed. Dr. Nahshon Rand.

617.585 USA ISSN 2155-7403
▼➤ **THE INTERNET JOURNAL OF PODIATRY.** Text in English. forthcoming 2011. s-a. free (effective 2011). **Document type:** *Journal, Trade.*
Media: Online - full text.
Indexed: A01.
Published by: Internet Scientific Publications, Llc., 23 Rippling Creek Dr, Sugar Land, TX 77479. TEL 832-443-1193, FAX 281-240-1533, wenker@ispub.com.

616.02 USA ISSN 1531-2992
RA645.5
➤ **THE INTERNET JOURNAL OF RESCUE AND DISASTER MEDICINE.** Text in English. 1998. s-a. free (effective 2011). adv. back issues avail. **Document type:** *Journal, Academic/Scholarly.* **Description:** Contains information from the fields of rescue medicine, traumatology, air rescue, aeromedical transportation, and disaster medicine, including original articles, reviews, case reports, streaming slide shows, streaming videos, letters to the editor, press releases, and meeting information.
Formed by the merger of (1997-1998): Internet Journal of Aeromedical Transportation; (1997-1998): Internet Journal of Disaster Medicine
Media: Online - full text.
Indexed: A01, A02, A03, A08, A26, C06, C07, C08, CA, CINAHL, G08, H11, H12, I02, I05, T02.
Published by: Internet Scientific Publications, Llc., 23 Rippling Creek Dr, Sugar Land, TX 77479. TEL 832-443-1193, FAX 281-240-1533, wenker@ispub.com. Ed. Amado Alejandro Baez.

617.3 USA ISSN 1541-5457
➤ **THE IOWA ORTHOPAEDIC JOURNAL.** Text in English. 1981. a. adv. illus. **Document type:** *Journal, Academic/Scholarly.* **Description:** Publishes articles relevant to orthopedic science, surgery and teaching.
Related titles: Online - full text ed.: ISSN 1555-1377. free (effective 2011).
Indexed: EMBASE, ExcerpMed, IndMed, MEDLINE, P30, R10, Reac, SCOPUS.
Published by: University of Iowa, Department of Orthopaedics, 200 Hawkins Dr, Iowa City, IA 52242. **Co-sponsor:** Iowa Orthopaedic Society.

➤ **ISOKINETICS AND EXERCISE SCIENCE.** *see* MEDICAL SCIENCES—Sports Medicine

➤ **J O H N S: JOURNAL OF OTOLARYNGOLOGY, HEAD AND NECK SURGERY/JIBI INKOKA, TOKEIBU GEKA.** *see* MEDICAL SCIENCES—Otorhinolaryngology

616.025 USA ISSN 1938-0011
➤ **J U C M.** (Journal of Urgent Care Medicine) Text in English. 2006 (Oct.). 11/yr. free to qualified personnel; USD 50 to individuals; USD 105 to institutions (effective 2008). adv. **Document type:** *Journal, Academic/Scholarly.* **Description:** Carries a mix of clinical and practice management articles that address the unique clinical and practice needs of urgent care medicine clinicians.
Related titles: Online - full text ed.: ISSN 1938-002X.
Published by: (Urgent Care Association of America), Braveheart Publishing, 2 Split Rock Rd, Mahwah, NJ 07430. TEL 201-529-4004, FAX 201-529-4007. Eds. Harris Fleming, Dr. Lee Resnick. Pubs. Peter Murphy, Stuart Williams. adv.: B&W page USD 3,080; trim 8 x 10.75. Circ: 10,989 (controlled); 1,724 (paid).

617.3 JPN
➤ **JAPAN KNEE SOCIETY. JOURNAL.** Text in Japanese; Summaries in English, Japanese. s-a. adv. **Document type:** *Proceedings, Academic/Scholarly.*
Formerly (until 1999): Tokyo Hiza Kansetsu Gakkai Kaishi
Published by: Japan Knee Society, Dept of Orthopaedic Surgery School of Medicine, University, 1-8-1 Inohana, Chuo-ku, Chiba-shi, 260-0856, Japan. TEL 81-43-226-2338, FAX 81-43-226-2369, moriyati@doc.ho.chiba-u.ac.jp. Ed., R&P, Adv. contact Hideshige Moriya.

617.3 AUT
JATROS ORTHOPAEDIE. Text in German. 1999. bi-m. EUR 28 (effective 2007). adv. **Document type:** *Journal, Academic/Scholarly.*
Related titles: Online - full text ed.: ISSN 1991-9174.
Published by: Universimed Verlags- und Service GmbH, Markgraf-Ruediger-Str 8, Vienna, 1150, Austria. TEL 43-1-87679560, FAX 43-1-876795620, office@universimed.com, http://www.universimed.com. Ed. Christine Dominkus. Adv. contact Christian Gallei. Circ: 3,500 (paid).

616.025 CHN ISSN 1006-463X
JIZHEN YIXUE/JOURNAL OF EMERGENCY MEDICINE. Text in Chinese. 1990. bi-m. **Document type:** *Journal, Academic/Scholarly.*
Related titles: Online - full content ed.; Online - full text ed.
Published by: Zhonghua Yixuehui, Jizhen Yixue Fenhui, 68, Jiefang Lu, Hangzhou, 310009, China. TEL 86-571-7077272 ext 5323, FAX 86-571-7228649, jzyx@mail.hz.zj.cn. Ed. Deyun Ding. **Dist. by:** China International Book Trading Corp, 35 Chegongzhuang Xilu, Haidian District, PO Box 399, Beijing 100044, China. TEL 86-10-68412045, FAX 86-10-68412023, cibtc@mail.cibtc.com.cn, http://www.cibtc.com.cn.

616.7 FRA ISSN 1297-319X
RC932 CODEN: JBSPFA
JOINT BONE SPINE. Text in English. 6/yr. EUR 424 in Europe to institutions; EUR 366.82 in France to institutions; JPY 52,900 in Japan to institutions; USD 564 elsewhere to institutions (effective 2012). **Document type:** *Journal, Academic/Scholarly.*
Related titles: Online - full text ed.: ISSN 1778-7254 (from IngentaConnect, ScienceDirect).
Indexed: A01, A03, A08, A26, B21, C06, C07, CA, CTA, CurCont, EMBASE, ExcerpMed, I05, ISR, IndMed, Inpharma, MEDLINE, P30, P35, R10, Reac, SCI, SCOPUS, T02, W07.
—BLDSC (4672.250420), IE, Infotrieve, Ingenta, INIST. **CCC.**
Published by: Elsevier Masson (Subsidiary of: Elsevier Health Sciences), 62 Rue Camille Desmoulins, Issy les Moulineaux, Cedex 92442, France. TEL 33-1-71165500, FAX 33-1-71165600, infos@elsevier-masson.fr.

616.7 AUS ISSN 1838-255X
JOINT NEWS. Text in English. 200?. q. free to members (effective 2011). **Document type:** *Newsletter, Trade.*
Published by: Arthritis Queensland, 1 Cartwright St, PO Box 2121, Windsor, QLD 4030, Australia. TEL 61-7-38574300, 800-242-141, info@arthritis.org.au, http://www.arthritis.org.au. Adv. contact Lee Ryan TEL 61-7-38574200.

616.7 FRA ISSN 1621-7853
LE JOURNAL DE L'ORTHOPEDIE. Text in French. 1998. q. EUR 44.21 domestic to individuals & European Union; EUR 63.27 elsewhere to individuals; EUR 132.63 domestic to institutions & European Union; EUR 151.69 elsewhere to institutions; EUR 36.59 domestic to students & European Union; EUR 55.64 elsewhere to students (effective 2009). **Document type:** *Journal, Trade.*
—INIST.
Published by: I S P O FRANCE, 5 Rue de la Claire, Lyon, 69009, France. TEL 33-4-3764-2166, FAX 33-4-3764-2168. Ed. Jean-Pierre Lissac.

616 FRA ISSN 0993-9857
CODEN: JEURE
JOURNAL EUROPEEN DES URGENCES/EUROPEAN JOURNAL OF EMERGENCIES. Variant title: J E U R. Text in English, French. 1988. 4/yr. EUR 260 in Europe to institutions; EUR 228.21 in France to institutions; JPY 40,200 in Japan to institutions; USD 338 elsewhere to institutions (effective 2012). adv. back issues avail. **Document type:** *Journal, Academic/Scholarly.* **Description:** Includes original articles, brief reviews, clinical cases and letters. Practical guide to emergency medicine for hospital practitioners.
Related titles: Online - full text ed.
Indexed: EMBASE, ExcerpMed, R10, Reac, SCOPUS.
—BLDSC (4979.640500), GNLM, IE, Ingenta, INIST. **CCC.**
Published by: Elsevier Masson (Subsidiary of: Elsevier Health Sciences), 62 Rue Camille Desmoulins, Issy les Moulineaux, Cedex 92442, France. TEL 33-1-71165500, infos@elsevier-masson.fr. Ed. Pierre Carli. Circ: 1,500. **Subscr. to:** Societe de Periodiques Specialises, BP 22, Vineuil Cedex 41354, France. TEL 33-2-54504612, FAX 33-2-54504611.

JOURNAL OF APPLIED BIOMECHANICS. *see* BIOLOGY—Physiology

617.3 USA ISSN 0883-5403
CODEN: JOAREG
➤ **JOURNAL OF ARTHROPLASTY.** Text in English. 1986. 8/yr. USD 802 in United States to institutions; USD 1,012 elsewhere to institutions (effective 2012). adv. charts; illus.; tr.lit. index. back issues avail.; reprints avail. **Document type:** *Journal, Academic/Scholarly.* **Description:** Presents basic scientific and clinical information on joint replacement surgery. Covers surgical techniques, prosthetic design, biomechanics, biomaterials, metallurgy, and the biologic response to arthroplasty materials in vivo and in vitro.
Related titles: Microfilm ed.: 1986; Online - full text ed.: ISSN 1532-8406 (from ScienceDirect).
Indexed: A22, A26, A28, APA, ASCA, B21, BrCerAb, C&ISA, C06, C07, CA, CA/WCA, CIA, CTA, CerAb, CivEngAb, CorrAb, CurCont, E&CAJ, E01, E11, EEA, EMA, EMBASE, ESPM, EnvEAb, ExcerpMed, H15, I05, INI, IndMed, Inpharma, M&TEA, M09, MBF, MEDLINE, METADEX, P30, P35, R10, Reac, SCI, SCOPUS, SolStAb, T02, T04, W07, WAA.
—BLDSC (4947.211500), GNLM, IE, Infotrieve, Ingenta, INIST. **CCC.**
Published by: (American Association of Hip and Knee Surgeons), Churchill Livingstone (Subsidiary of: Elsevier Health Sciences), 1600 John F Kennedy Blvd, Ste 1800, Philadelphia, PA 19103. TEL 215-239-3900, 800-523-1649, FAX 215-239-3990, JournalsOnlineSupport-usa@elsevier.com, http://www.us.elsevierhealth.com. Ed. Dr. Richard H Rothman. Adv. contact Nicole Johnson TEL 215-239-3168. **Subscr. to:** Elsevier, Subscription Customer Service.

617.3 NLD ISSN 1053-8127
RD771.B217 CODEN: JBMRFK
➤ **JOURNAL OF BACK AND MUSCULOSKELETAL REHABILITATION.** Text in English. 1991. q. USD 686 combined subscription in North America (print & online eds.); EUR 490 combined subscription elsewhere (print & online eds.) (effective 2012). back issues avail. **Document type:** *Journal, Academic/Scholarly.* **Description:** Provides clinicians with a current guide to the assessment, diagnosis, and management of back and musculoskeletal disorders.
Related titles: Microform ed.: (from PQC); Online - full text ed.: ISSN 1878-6324 (from IngentaConnect).
Indexed: A01, A03, A08, A22, AMED, ASCA, B21, C06, C07, C08, CA, CINAHL, CTA, E01, EMBASE, ESPM, ExcerpMed, FoSS&M, H&SSA, H04, MEDLINE, P30, PEI, R09, R10, Reac, RiskAb, SCI, SCOPUS, SD, T02, W07.
—BLDSC (4950.900000), GNLM, IE, Infotrieve, Ingenta, Linda Hall. **CCC.**
Published by: I O S Press, Nieuwe Hemweg 6B, Amsterdam, 1013 BG, Netherlands. TEL 31-20-6883355, FAX 31-20-6870019, info@iospress.nl. Ed. Dr. Hermie J Hermens TEL 31-53-4875702. **Subscr. to:** I O S Press, Inc, 4502 Rachael Manor Dr, Fairfax, VA 22032-3631. sales@iospress.com.

617.3 USA ISSN 1094-5903
JOURNAL OF BONE AND JOINT SURGERY: AMERICAN AND BRITISH VOLUMES ON CD-ROM. Text in English. 1990. q. USD 311 (effective 2010). back issues avail. **Document type:** *Journal, Academic/Scholarly.* **Description:** Contains the full text of American and British volumes, 1996 to present.
Formerly (until 1997): Journal of Bone and Joint Surgery: American Volume on CD-ROM (1058-2436)
Media: CD-ROM. **Related titles:** International ed. of: Journal of Bone and Joint Surgery: British Volume on CD-ROM. ISSN 0968-7300. 1984.
—**CCC.**
Published by: Journal of Bone and Joint Surgery, 20 Pickering St, Needham, MA 02492. TEL 781-449-9780, FAX 781-449-9742, editorial@jbjs.org, http://www.jbjs.org. Ed. Dr. James D Heckman. Adv. contact Amber Howard TEL 781-449-9780 ext 1233.
Co-publisher: British Editorial Society of Bone and Joint Surgery.

617.3 USA ISSN 0021-9355
RD684 CODEN: JBJSA3
➤ **JOURNAL OF BONE AND JOINT SURGERY: AMERICAN VOLUME.** Text in English. 1889. m. USD 169 combined subscription domestic to individuals (print & online eds.); USD 191 combined subscription foreign to individuals (print & online eds.); USD 311 combined subscription worldwide to individuals includes British Volume (print & online eds.) (effective 2010). adv. bk.rev. bibl.; charts; illus.; abstr. index. back issues avail.; reprints avail. **Document type:** *Journal, Academic/Scholarly.* **Description:** Provides the general orthopaedic surgeon and the subspecialist with an ability to assess his or her continuing competence in orthopaedics through the acquisition of contemporary scientific information.
Supersedes in part (in 1948): Journal of Bone and Joint Surgery (0375-9229); Which was formerly (until 1922): The Journal of Orthopaedic Surgery (1545-1496); (until 1919): The American Journal of Orthopedic Surgery (1049-1961); (until 1903): American Orthopedic Association. Transactions (1938-0623)
Related titles: Online - full text ed.: ISSN 1535-1386.
Indexed: A01, A02, A03, A08, A22, A26, A29, AHCMS, AIM, AMED, ASCA, AbAn, B&BAb, B19, B20, B21, BDM&CN, C06, C07, C08, C11, CA, CINAHL, CTA, ChemAb, CurCont, DentInd, EMBASE, ESPM, ExcerpMed, FR, FoSS&M, G08, H04, H11, H12, ISR, IndMed, Inpharma, JW, MEDLINE, P20, P22, P24, P26, P30, P34, P35, P48, P54, PQC, R09, R10, Reac, SCI, SCOPUS, SD, T02, VirolAbstr, W07.
—BLDSC (4954.250000), CASDDS, GNLM, IE, Infotrieve, Ingenta, INIST. **CCC.**
Published by: Journal of Bone and Joint Surgery, 20 Pickering St, Needham, MA 02492. TEL 781-449-9780, FAX 781-449-9742, editorial@jbjs.org. Ed. Dr. Vernon Tolo. Adv. contact Amber Howard TEL 781-449-9780 ext 1233. B&W page USD 3,060; trim 8.3125 x 10.875. Circ: 31,792 (paid).

617.3 GBR ISSN 0301-620X
RD684 CODEN: JBSUAK
➤ **JOURNAL OF BONE AND JOINT SURGERY: BRITISH VOLUME.** Abbreviated title: J B J S. Text in English. 1889. m. GBP 86 combined subscription (print, CD-ROM & online eds.) (effective 2011); subscr. includes supplements. adv. bk.rev. bibl.; charts; illus. index. back issues avail.; reprints avail. **Document type:** *Journal, Academic/Scholarly.* **Description:** Covers all aspects of orthopaedic and trauma surgery.
Supersedes in part (in 1948): Journal of Bone and Joint Surgery (0375-9229); Which was formerly (until 1922): The Journal of Orthopaedic Surgery (1545-1496); (until 1919): The American Journal of Orthopedic Surgery (1049-1961); (until 1903): American Orthopedic Association. Transactions (1938-0623)
Related titles: CD-ROM ed.: Journal of Bone and Joint Surgery: British Volume on CD-ROM. ISSN 0968-7300. 1984; Microform ed.: (from PQC); Online - full text ed.: ISSN 2044-5377. 1997; ◆ Supplement(s): Journal of Bone and Joint Surgery. British Volume. Orthopaedic Proceedings. ISSN 1358-992X.
Indexed: A22, A36, AIDS Ab, AIM, AMED, ASCA, B21, BDM&CN, C06, C07, C08, CABA, CINAHL, CTA, ChemAb, CurCont, DentInd, E12, EMBASE, ExcerpMed, FR, FoSS&M, GH, ISR, IndMed, Inpharma, LT, MEDLINE, N02, N03, P20, P22, P24, P30, P33, P35, P48, P54, PQC, R08, R10, R12, RRTA, Reac, SCI, SCOPUS, T05, W07.
—BLDSC (4954.255000), CASDDS, IE, Infotrieve, Ingenta, INIST. **CCC.**
Published by: British Editorial Society of Bone and Joint Surgery, 22 Buckingham St, London, WC2N 6ET, United Kingdom. TEL 44-20-77820010, FAX 44-20-77820995, info@jbjs.org.uk, http://www.jbjs.org.uk. Adv. contact Amber Howard TEL 781-449-9780.
Subscr. in the U.S. to: Journal of Bone and Joint Surgery.

617.3 GBR ISSN 1358-992X
JOURNAL OF BONE AND JOINT SURGERY. BRITISH VOLUME. ORTHOPAEDIC PROCEEDINGS. Text in English. 199?. irreg. includes with subscr. to Journal of Bone and Joint Surgery. British Volume. adv. back issues avail.; reprints avail. **Document type:** *Proceedings, Trade.* **Description:** Contains abstracts of papers presented at recent scientific meetings organised by orthopaedic associations and specialist societies.
Related titles: ◆ Supplement to: Journal of Bone and Joint Surgery: British Volume. ISSN 0301-620X.
—INIST. **CCC.**
Published by: British Editorial Society of Bone and Joint Surgery, 22 Buckingham St, London, WC2N 6ET, United Kingdom. TEL 44-20-77820010, FAX 44-20-77820995, info@jbjs.org.uk, http://www.jbjs.org.uk. Adv. contacts Pam Pam Noble TEL 44-1620-823383, Amber Howard TEL 781-449-9780.

616.7 USA ISSN 0884-0431
QP88.2 CODEN: JBMREJ
➤ **JOURNAL OF BONE AND MINERAL RESEARCH.** Text in English. 1986. m. GBP 552 in United Kingdom to institutions; EUR 648 in Europe to institutions; USD 840 in United States to institutions; USD 902 in Canada & Mexico to institutions; USD 902 elsewhere to institutions; GBP 635 combined subscription in United Kingdom to institutions (print & online eds.); EUR 745 combined subscription in Europe to institutions (print & online eds.); USD 966 combined subscription in United States to institutions (print & online eds.); USD 1,028 combined subscription in Canada & Mexico to institutions (print & online eds.); USD 1,028 combined subscription elsewhere to institutions (print & online eds.) (effective 2012). adv. back issues avail.; reprint service avail. from PSC. **Document type:** *Journal, Academic/Scholarly.* **Description:** Publishes papers on all areas of calcium regulation, skeletal physiology, and metabolic bone diseases.
Related titles: Online - full text ed.: ISSN 1523-4681. GBP 514 in United Kingdom to institutions; EUR 603 in Europe to institutions; USD 840 elsewhere to institutions (effective 2012).
Indexed: A20, A22, A34, A36, A38, ASCA, B21, B25, B27, BIOSIS Prev, C30, CA, CABA, CIN, CTA, ChemAb, ChemTitl, CurCont, D01, E12, EMBASE, ExcerpMed, GH, INI, ISR, IndMed, IndVet, Inpharma, Kidney, LT, MEDLINE, MycolAb, N02, N03, N04, P30, P35, P37, PEI, R10, R12, RA&MP, RRTA, Reac, SCI, SCOPUS, SD, SoyAb, T02, T05, VS, W07.
—BLDSC (4954.255530), CASDDS, GNLM, IE, Infotrieve, Ingenta, INIST. **CCC.**
Published by: (American Society for Bone and Mineral Research), Wiley-Blackwell Publishing, Inc. (Subsidiary of: Wiley-Blackwell Publishing Ltd.), Commerce Pl, 350 Main St, Malden, MA 02148. TEL 781-388-8200, FAX 781-388-8210, info@wiley.com, http://www.wiley.com/WileyCDA/. Ed. Thomas L Clemens. **Co-sponsor:** National Osteoporosis Foundation.

➤ **JOURNAL OF BURN CARE & RESEARCH.** *see* MEDICAL SCIENCES

618.92 DEU ISSN 1863-2521
RD732.3.C48
➤ **JOURNAL OF CHILDREN'S ORTHOPAEDICS.** Text in English. 2007. 6/yr. EUR 709, USD 864 combined subscription to institutions (print & online eds.) (effective 2012). reprint service avail. from PSC. **Document type:** *Journal, Academic/Scholarly.* **Description:** Provides a forum for the advancement of the knowledge and education in pediatric orthopaedics and traumatology across geographical borders. Advocates an increased worldwide involvement in preventing and treating musculoskeletal diseases in children and adolescents.
Related titles: Online - full text ed.: ISSN 1863-2548 (from IngentaConnect).
Indexed: A22, A26, E01, E08, H12, P30, S09, SCOPUS.
—IE. **CCC.**
Published by: (European Paediatric Orthopaedic Society CHE), Springer (Subsidiary of: Springer Science+Business Media), Tiergartenstr 17, Heidelberg, 69121, Germany. TEL 49-6221-4870, FAX 49-6221-345229, subscriptions@springer.com. Ed. Shlomo Wientroub.

917.3 IND ISSN 0976-5662
▼ ➤ **JOURNAL OF CLINICAL ORTHOPAEDICS AND TRAUMA.** Text in English. 2010. s-a. **Document type:** *Journal, Academic/Scholarly.*
Related titles: Online - full text ed.
—**CCC.**
Published by: (Delhi Orthopaedic Association), Elsevier Health Sciences (Subsidiary of: Reed Elsevier India Pvt. Ltd.), 14th Fl, Building No. 10B, DLF Cyber City, Phase II, Gurgaon, 122002, India. TEL 91-124-4774444, FAX 91-124-4774201, Indiacontact@elsevier.com, http://www.elsevier.co.in/web/default.aspx. Eds. Bedi Bedi, Lalit Maini, Vivek Trikha.

616.73 617.95 IND ISSN 0974-8237
JOURNAL OF CRANIOVERTEBRAL JUNCTION AND SPINE. Text in English. s-a. **Document type:** *Journal, Academic/Scholarly.*
Related titles: Online - full text ed.: free (effective 2011).
Indexed: A01, A26, E08, H12, I05, P10, P30, P48, P53, P54, PQC, T02.
Published by: Medknow Publications and Media Pvt. Ltd., B-9, Kanara Business Ctr, Off Link Rd, Ghatkopar (E), Mumbai, Maharastra 400 075, India. TEL 91-22-66491816, 91-22-66491818, publishing@medknow.com, journals@medknow.com, http://www.medknow.com.

610 USA ISSN 0883-9441
RC86 CODEN: JCCAER
➤ **JOURNAL OF CRITICAL CARE**; improving patient care by integrating critical care systems knowledge into practice behavior. Text in English. 1986 (Mar.). q. USD 516 in United States to institutions; USD 638 elsewhere to institutions (effective 2012). adv. abstr.; bibl.; charts; illus. index. back issues avail.; reprints avail. **Document type:** *Journal, Academic/Scholarly.* **Description:** Provides a articles with the goal of improving patient care by integrating critical care systems knowledge into practice behavior and includes biomedical research, epidemiology, biostatistics, health policy research, social sciences, technology development, and relevant legal and ethical concerns.
Incorporates (1998-2007): Seminars in Anesthesia, Perioperative Medicine, and Pain (1547-9951)
Related titles: Online - full text ed.: ISSN 1557-8615 (from ScienceDirect).
Indexed: A22, A26, ASCA, C06, C07, C08, CA, CIN, CINAHL, ChemAb, ChemTitl, CurCont, E-psyche, EMBASE, ExcerpMed, FR, H12, I05, INI, ISR, IndMed, Inpharma, MEDLINE, P30, P35, R10, Reac, SCI, SCOPUS, T02, W07.
—BLDSC (4965.630000), CASDDS, GNLM, IE, Infotrieve, Ingenta, INIST. **CCC.**
Published by: (World Federation of Societies of Intensive and Critical Care Medicine), W.B. Saunders Co. (Subsidiary of: Elsevier Health Sciences), Elsevier, Health Sciences Division, Order Fulfillment, 3251 Riverport Ln, Maryland Heights, MO 63043. TEL 314-872-8370, 800-325-4177, FAX 314-432-1380, JournalCustomerService-usa@elsevier.com, http://www.us.elsevierhealth.com. Ed. Philip D Lumb. Pub. Kate Williamson. Adv. contact John Marmero TEL 212-633-3657.

616.7 IND ISSN 0974-2700
➤ **JOURNAL OF EMERGENCIES, TRAUMA, AND SHOCK**; synergizing basic science, clinical medicine, & global health. Text in English. 2008. q. INR 1,500 domestic to individuals; USD 100 foreign to individuals; INR 2,000 domestic to institutions; USD 250 foreign to institutions; INR 1,800 combined subscription domestic to individuals (print & online eds.); USD 120 combined subscription foreign to individuals (print & online eds.); INR 2,400 combined subscription domestic to institutions (print & online eds.); USD 300 combined subscription foreign to institutions (print & online eds.) (effective 2011). adv. bk.rev. abstr. reprints avail. **Document type:** *Journal, Academic/Scholarly.* **Description:** Covers emergency medicine, emergency surgery, pre-hospital care, trauma, and shock.
Related titles: Online - full text ed.: ISSN 0974-519X. INR 1,200 domestic to individuals; USD 80 foreign to individuals; INR 1,600 domestic to institutions; WST 200 foreign to institutions (effective 2011).
Indexed: A01, A26, A34, A36, C06, CA, CABA, E08, E12, F08, F11, F12, GH, H12, H17, I05, LT, N02, N03, P10, P30, P33, P39, P48, P53, P54, PQC, R07, R08, R12, RA&MP, RM&VM, S09, S12, S13, S16, T02, T05, TAR, W11.
—**CCC.**
Published by: (INDO-US Emergency and Trauma Collaborative), Medknow Publications and Media Pvt. Ltd., B-9, Kanara Business Ctr, Off Link Rd, Ghatkopar (E), Mumbai, Maharastra 400 075, India. TEL 91-22-66491816, FAX 91-22-66491817, http://www.medknow.com. Eds. Kelly P O'Keefe, Praveen Aggarwal, Tracy Sanson.

616.025 USA ISSN 1090-1280
JOURNAL OF EMERGENCY MEDICINE (LAGUNA HILLS). Variant title: Journal of Emergency Medicine and Acute Primary Care. Text in English. 1996. irreg. USD 9.99 (effective 2010). **Document type:** *Journal, Academic/Scholarly.*
Media: Online - full text.
Published by: Current Clinical Strategies Publishing Inc., 27071 Cabot Rd, Ste 126, Laguna Hills, CA 92653. TEL 949-348-8404, 800-331-8227, FAX 909-744-8071, 800-965-9420, info@ccspublishing.com, http://www.ccspublishing.com/ccs/.

616.025 USA ISSN 0736-4679
RC86
➤ **THE JOURNAL OF EMERGENCY MEDICINE (PHILADELPHIA).** Abbreviated title: J E M. Text in English. 1983. 8/yr. USD 1,294 in United States to institutions; USD 1,362 elsewhere to institutions (effective 2012). adv. abstr. back issues avail.; reprints avail. **Document type:** *Journal, Academic/Scholarly.* **Description:** Publishes clinical and research articles, along with reviews, on all facets of emergency medicine practice and management.
Related titles: Microfilm ed.: (from PQC); Online - full text ed.: (from IngentaConnect, ScienceDirect).
Indexed: A01, A03, A08, A20, A22, A26, A34, A36, B21, C06, C07, CA, CABA, CurCont, E12, EMBASE, ESPM, ExcerpMed, FR, GH, H&SSA, H12, H17, I05, IBR, IBZ, IndMed, IndVet, Inpharma, JW-EM, LT, MEDLINE, MS&D, N02, N03, P30, P33, P35, P39, R07, R08, R10, R12, R13, RA&MP, RM&VM, RRTA, Reac, RiskAb, SCI, SCOPUS, T02, T05, ToxAb, VS, ViroIAbstr, W07, W10.
—BLDSC (4977.250000), GNLM, IE, Infotrieve, Ingenta, INIST. **CCC.**
Published by: (American Academy of Emergency Medicine), Elsevier Inc. (Subsidiary of: Elsevier Science & Technology), 1600 John F Kennedy Blvd, Philadelphia, PA 19103. TEL 215-239-3900, FAX 215-238-7883, JournalCustomerService-usa@elsevier.com, http://www.elsevier.com. Ed. Stephen R Hayden. Pub. Theresa Monturano. Adv. contact John Marmero Jr. TEL 212-633-3657. Circ: 5,675.

617.6 USA ISSN 1082-1821
CODEN: JFSPF4
THE JOURNAL OF FACIAL AND SOMATO PROSTHETICS. Text in English. 1995. s-a. USD 70 domestic; USD 85 foreign (effective 2005).
Indexed: EMBASE, ExcerpMed, R10, Reac, SCOPUS.
—BLDSC (4983.623000), IE, Ingenta.
Published by: (American Anaplastology Association), A B I Professional Publications, PO Box 17446, Clearwater, FL 33762. TEL 727-556-0950, FAX 727-556-2560, webmaster@vandamere.com.

617.585 GBR ISSN 1757-1146
RD792
➤ **JOURNAL OF FOOT AND ANKLE RESEARCH.** Text in English. 2008. irreg. free (effective 2011). adv. back issues avail. **Document type:** *Journal, Academic/Scholarly.* **Description:** Encompasses all aspects of policy, organization, delivery and clinical practice related to the assessment, diagnosis, prevention and management of foot and ankle disorders.
Media: Online - full text.
Indexed: A01, A26, CA, E08, H12, I05, P30, S09, SCOPUS, T02.
—**CCC.**
Published by: (Society of Chiropodists and Podiatrists, Australasian Podiatry Council AUS), BioMed Central Ltd. (Subsidiary of: Springer Science+Business Media), 236 Gray's Inn Rd, London, WC1X 8HB, United Kingdom. TEL 44-20-31922000, FAX 44-20-31922010, info@biomedcentral.com, http://www.biomedcentral.com. Eds. Hylton Menz, Michael Potter. Adv. contact Natasha Bailey TEL 44-20-31922231.

617 USA ISSN 0885-9701
CODEN: JABOEG
➤ **JOURNAL OF HEAD TRAUMA REHABILITATION.** Text in English. 1986. bi-m. USD 370.51 domestic to institutions; USD 549 foreign to institutions (effective 2011). adv. back issues avail.; reprints avail. **Document type:** *Journal, Academic/Scholarly.* **Description:** Provides information on clinical management and rehabilitation of persons with head injuries for the practicing professional.
Related titles: Online - full text ed.: ISSN 1550-509X.
Indexed: A20, A22, A26, AMED, ASCA, B21, C06, C07, C08, CA, CINAHL, CTA, CurCont, E-psyche, E08, ECER, EMBASE, ExcerpMed, FamI, G08, H11, H12, I05, INI, IndMed, MEDLINE, NSA, NSCI, P03, P20, P22, P24, P25, P30, P48, P54, PQC, PsycInfo, PsycholAb, R09, R10, Reac, S09, SCI, SCOPUS, SD, SSCI, T02, W07.
—BLDSC (4996.672000), GNLM, IE, Infotrieve, Ingenta, INIST. **CCC.**
Published by: (Brain Injury Association of America), Lippincott Williams & Wilkins (Subsidiary of: Wolters Kluwer N.V.), Two Commerce Sq, 2001 Market St, Philadelphia, PA 19103. TEL 215-521-8300, FAX 215-521-8902, customerservice@lww.com, http://www.lww.com. Ed. John Corrigan. Pub. Sandra Kasko. Adv. contact Irene Anthony. Circ: 2,250.

➤ **JOURNAL OF KNEE SURGERY.** *see* MEDICAL SCIENCES—Surgery

➤ **JOURNAL OF MANIPULATIVE AND PHYSIOLOGICAL THERAPEUTICS.** *see* MEDICAL SCIENCES—Chiropractic, Homeopathy, Osteopathy

612.7 NLD ISSN 0142-4319
QP321 CODEN: JMRMD3
➤ **JOURNAL OF MUSCLE RESEARCH AND CELL MOTILITY.** Text in English. 1980. 6/yr. EUR 2,550, USD 2,709 combined subscription to institutions (print & online eds.) (effective 2012). adv. bk.rev. bibl.; illus. index. reprint service avail. from PSC. **Document type:** *Journal, Academic/Scholarly.* **Description:** Publishes original research on the excitation and contraction of muscle, the analysis of the processes involved, and the processes underlying cell contractility and motility.
Related titles: Online - full text ed.: ISSN 1573-2657 (from IngentaConnect).
Indexed: A22, A26, A34, A35, A38, ASCA, AgBio, Agr, B21, B25, B27, BIOBASE, BIOSIS Prev, BibLing, C30, CA, CABA, CTA, ChemAb, ChemTitl, CurCont, DentInd, E01, EMBASE, ExcerpMed, GH, GenetAb, IABS, ISR, IndMed, IndVet, Inpharma, MEDLINE, MycolAb, N05, P20, P22, P24, P30, P48, P52, P54, P56, PN&I, PQC, R10, Reac, SCI, SCOPUS, T02, VS, W07, Z01.
—BLDSC (5021.120000), CASDDS, GNLM, IE, Infotrieve, Ingenta, INIST. **CCC.**
Published by: Springer Netherlands (Subsidiary of: Springer Science+Business Media), Van Godewijckstraat 30, Dordrecht, 3311 GX, Netherlands. TEL 31-78-6576050, FAX 31-78-6576474, http://www.springer.com. Eds. C C Ashley, D J Manstein, M Gautel.

616.7 GRC
➤ **THE JOURNAL OF MUSCULOSKELETAL AND NEURONAL INTERACTIONS.** Text in English. 1990. q. free (effective 2004). **Document type:** *Journal, Academic/Scholarly.* **Description:** Publishes original papers of research and clinical experience in all areas of the musculoskeletal system and its interactions with the nervous system, especially metabolic bone diseases, with particular emphasis on osteoporosis.
Former titles: Journal of Musculoskeletal Interactions (1108-7161); (until 2000): Ostoun (1106-109X)
Related titles: Online - full text ed.: free (effective 2011).
Indexed: B21, B25, BIOSIS Prev, BiolDig, CTA, EMBASE, ExcerpMed, Inpharma, MEDLINE, MycolAb, NSA, P30, PEI, R10, Reac, SCI, SCOPUS, W07.
—BLDSC (5021.122000), IE, Ingenta.
Published by: The International Society of Musculoskeletal and Neuronal Interactions, 7 Spiliadou Sq, Nafplion, 21 100, Greece. TEL 30-752-99342, FAX 30-752-99343, jmni@ismni.org. Eds. George Lyritis, Webster S. Jee. Adv. contact Susan Clarkson.

617.3 USA ISSN 0899-2517
RC925.A1
➤ **THE JOURNAL OF MUSCULOSKELETAL MEDICINE.** Text in English. 1983. m. free to qualified personnel (effective 2009). adv. charts; illus. Index. back issues avail.; reprints avail. **Document type:** *Journal, Academic/Scholarly.* **Description:** Provides practical information on diagnosis and management of a wide variety of common musculoskeletal disorders.
Related titles: Online - full text ed.
Indexed: A22, A26, C06, C07, C08, CA, CINAHL, E08, G06, G07, G08, H11, H12, I05, P24, P48, PQC, S09, T02.
—BLDSC (5021.125000), GNLM, IE, Ingenta. **CCC.**
Published by: C M P Medica LLC (Subsidiary of: United Business Media Limited), 535 Connecticut Ave, Ste 300, Norwalk, CT 06854. TEL 203-523-7000, FAX 203-662-6420, http://www.cmpmedica.com. Ed. Leo Robert. adv.: color page USD 9,570, B&W page USD 7,000; trim 7.75 x 10.75. Circ: 64,396.

617 USA ISSN 1058-2452
RC927.3 CODEN: JMPAEQ
➤ **JOURNAL OF MUSCULOSKELETAL PAIN**; innovations in research, theory & clinical practice. Abbreviated title: J M P. Text in English. 1993. q. GBP 300, EUR 395, USD 535 combined subscription to institutions (print & online eds.); GBP 635, EUR 835, USD 1,140 combined subscription to corporations (print & online eds.) (effective 2010). adv. bk.rev. charts; illus.; stat. 120 p./no. 1 cols./p.; back issues avail.; reprint service avail. from PSC. **Document type:** *Journal, Academic/Scholarly.* **Description:** Addresses all aspects related to chronic soft-tissue pain, including the psychological dimensions of pain; trigger point therapy; muscle pain and aging; central sensitization; pain coping strategies; clinical physiotherapy; clinical neurology; muscle pain, sleep variables, and depression; and the development of widespread pain after injuries.
Related titles: Microfiche ed.: (from PQC); Microform ed.; Online - full text ed.: ISSN 1540-7012 (from IngentaConnect); Supplement(s): Journal of Musculoskeletal Pain. Supplement. ISSN 1082-6025. 1995.
Indexed: A01, A03, A20, A22, AbAn, B21, BiolDig, C06, C07, C08, CA, CINAHL, CurCont, E-psyche, E01, EMBASE, ESPM, ErgAb, ExcerpMed, H&SSA, H13, Inpharma, P02, P03, P10, P20, P48, P53, P54, PEI, PQC, Perlslam, PsycInfo, PsycholAb, R09, R10, Reac, RefZh, SCI, SCOPUS, SD, T02, W07.
—BLDSC (5021.126000), GNLM, IE, Infotrieve, Ingenta. **CCC.**

Published by: Informa Healthcare (Subsidiary of: T & F Informa plc), 52 Vanderbilt Ave, New York, NY 10017. TEL 212-262-8230, FAX 212-262-8234, healthcare.enquiries@informa.com, http://www.informahealthcare.com. Ed. I Jon Russell. adv.: B&W page USD 315, color page USD 550; trim 4.375 x 7.125. Circ: 712 (paid).

617.3 SGP ISSN 0218-9577
QM100 CODEN: JMURFZ

➤ **JOURNAL OF MUSCULOSKELETAL RESEARCH.** Abbreviated title: J M R. Text in English. 1997. q. SGD 463, USD 271, EUR 254 combined subscription to institutions (print & online eds.) (effective 2012). adv. back issues avail. **Document type:** *Journal, Academic/Scholarly.* **Description:** Explores all facets of musculoskeletal disorders with emphasis on both the clinical and basic aspects of study. Also covers basic and clinical research in the fields of orthopaedics, rheumatology and rehabilitation, biomechanics, biomaterials and related areas.
Related titles: Online - full text ed.: ISSN 1793-6497. SGD 421, USD 246, EUR 231 to institutions (effective 2012).
Indexed: A01, A03, A08, A22, B21, B25, BIOSIS Prev, CA, CTA, E01, EMBASE, ESPM, ExcerpMed, H&SSA, Inspec, MycolAb, P30, PEI, R09, R10, Reac, S01, SCOPUS, SD, T02.
—BLDSC (5021.126500), IE, Ingenta. **CCC.**
Published by: World Scientific Publishing Co. Pte. Ltd., 5 Toh Tuck Link, Singapore, 596224, Singapore. TEL 65-6466-5775, FAX 65-6467-7667, wspc@wspc.com.sg, http://www.worldscientific.com. Eds. Kai-Nan An TEL 507-538-1717, Po-Quang Chen TEL 886-2239-70800 ext 5271. **Dist. by:** World Scientific Publishing Co., Inc., 27 Warren St, Ste 401-402, Hackensack, NJ 07601. TEL 201-487-9655, 800-227-7562, FAX 201-487-9656, 888-977-2665, wspc@wspc.com; World Scientific Publishing Ltd., 57 Shelton St, London WC2H 9HE, United Kingdom. TEL 44-207-8360888, FAX 44-207-8362020, sales@wspc.co.uk.

617.1 USA ISSN 0897-7151
RD593 CODEN: JNEUE4

➤ **JOURNAL OF NEUROTRAUMA.** Text in English. 1984. 18/yr. USD 2,874 domestic to institutions; USD 3,554 foreign to institutions; USD 3,342 combined subscription domestic to institutions (print & online eds.); USD 4,112 combined subscription foreign to institutions (print & online eds.) (effective 2012). adv. bk.rev. reprint service avail. from PSC. **Document type:** *Journal, Academic/Scholarly.* **Description:** Brings out articles on the advances in both the clinical and laboratory investigation of traumatic brain and spinal cord injury.
Formerly (until 1988): Central Nervous System Trauma (0737-5999)
Related titles: Online - full text ed.: ISSN 1557-9042. USD 2,874 to institutions (effective 2012).
Indexed: A01, A03, A08, A22, A26, ASCA, B25, BIOSIS Prev, CA, CurCont, E-psyche, E01, E07, EMBASE, ExcerpMed, H12, I05, ISR, IndMed, Inpharma, MEDLINE, MycolAb, NSCI, P02, P03, P10, P20, P22, P30, P35, P48, P53, P54, PQC, PsycInfo, R10, Reac, SCI, SCOPUS, T02, W07.
—BLDSC (5022.270000), GNLM, IE, Infotrieve, Ingenta, INIST. **CCC.**
Published by: (National Neurotrauma Society), Mary Ann Liebert, Inc. Publishers, 140 Huguenot St, 3rd Fl, New Rochelle, NY 10801. TEL 914-740-2100, FAX 914-740-2101, 800-654-3237, info@liebertpub.com. Ed. John T Povlishock TEL 804-828-9623. Adv. contact Harriet I Matysko TEL 914-740-2182.

617.3 DEU ISSN 1434-5293

➤ **JOURNAL OF OROFACIAL ORTHOPEDICS.** Text in English, German. 1931. bi-m. EUR 302, USD 307 combined subscription to institutions (print & online eds.) (effective 2012). adv. bk.rev. bibl.; charts; illus. index. back issues avail.; reprint service avail. from PSC. **Document type:** *Journal, Academic/Scholarly.*
Formerly (until 1995): Fortschritte der Kieferorthopaedie (0015-816X)
Related titles: Online - full text ed.: ISSN 1615-6714 (from IngentaConnect).
Indexed: A22, A26, CA, CTD, D02, DentInd, E01, EMBASE, ExcerpMed, IBR, IBZ, IndMed, MEDLINE, P30, R10, Reac, SCI, SCOPUS, T02, W07.
—BLDSC (5027.520000), GNLM, IE, Infotrieve, Ingenta. **CCC.**
Published by: (Deutsche Gesellschaft fuer Kieferorthopaedie), Urban und Vogel Medien und Medizin Verlagsgesellschaft mbH (Subsidiary of: Springer Science+Business Media), Neumarkter Str 43, Munich, 81673, Germany. TEL 49-89-4372-1411, FAX 49-89-4372-1410, verlag@urban-vogel.de. Eds. Dr. Elisabeth Renatus, Dr. I Jonas, Dr. P Diedrich. R&P Oliver Renn. Adv. contact Paul Berger TEL 49-89-4372-1342. B&W page EUR 1,550, color page EUR 2,600; trim 174 x 240. Circ: 3,400 (paid and controlled). **Subscr. to:** Springer New York LLC. TEL 800-777-4643, journals-ny@springer.com; Springer Distribution Center, Kundenservice Zeitschriften, Haberstr 7, Heidelberg 69126, Germany. TEL 49-6221-3454303, FAX 49-6221-3454229, subscriptions@springer.com.

➤ **JOURNAL OF ORTHOPAEDIC AND SPORTS PHYSICAL THERAPY.** *see* MEDICAL SCIENCES—Sports Medicine

616.7 USA ISSN 1942-5082
RD725

➤ **JOURNAL OF ORTHOPAEDIC HISTORY.** Text in English. 2008 (Oct.). q. **Document type:** *Journal, Academic/Scholarly.* **Description:** Aimed at filling a void in orthopedic literature, namely the detailing and recounting of the events and individuals who helped mold the field into the rich and diverse profession that it has become today.
Related titles: Online - full text ed.: ISSN 1942-5090.
Published by: Aragon Publishers, 241 Nokomis Ave S, Venice, FL 34285. TEL 941-408-4135. Ed. Dr. Julio Gonzalez.

617.3 USA ISSN 0736-0266
RD701 CODEN: JOREDR

➤ **JOURNAL OF ORTHOPAEDIC RESEARCH;** a journal for musculoskeletal investigation. Text in English. 1983. m. GBP 509 in United Kingdom to institutions; EUR 643 in Europe to institutions; USD 744 in United States to institutions; USD 912 in Canada & Mexico to institutions; USD 996 elsewhere to institutions; GBP 587 combined subscription in United Kingdom to institutions (print & online eds.); EUR 741 combined subscription in Europe to institutions (print & online eds.); USD 856 combined subscription in United States to institutions (print & online eds.); USD 1,024 combined subscription in Canada & Mexico to institutions (print & online eds.); USD 1,108 combined subscription elsewhere to institutions (print & online eds.) (effective 2012). adv. illus. index. back issues avail.; reprint service avail. from PSC. **Document type:** *Journal, Academic/Scholarly.* **Description:** Covers experimental, theoretical and clinical aspects of orthopaedics.
Related titles: Online - full text ed.: ISSN 1554-527X. GBP 380 in United Kingdom to institutions; EUR 480 in Europe to institutions; USD 744 elsewhere to institutions (effective 2012) (from IngentaConnect).
Indexed: A01, A03, A08, A22, A26, A34, A35, A36, A38, AMED, ASCA, AgBio, B&BAb, B21, B25, BIOSIS Prev, BioEngAb, C&ISA, CA, CABA, CIN, CTA, ChemAb, ChemTitl, CurCont, DokArb, E&CAJ, EMBASE, ExcerpMed, GH, I05, ISMEC, ISR, ImmunAb, IndMed, IndVet, Inpharma, MEDLINE, MycolAb, N02, N03, P20, P22, P26, P30, P35, P48, P54, PEI, PN&I, PQC, R10, RA&MP, Reac, SCI, SCOPUS, SolStAb, T02, VS, W07.
—BLDSC (5027.665000), CASDDS, GNLM, IE, Infotrieve, Ingenta, INIST. **CCC.**
Published by: (Orthopaedic Research Society), John Wiley & Sons, Inc., 111 River St, Hoboken, NJ 07030. TEL 201-748-6000, FAX 201-748-6088, info@wiley.com, http://www.wiley.com/WileyCDA/. Eds. Dr. Joseph A Buckwalter TEL 319-356-2595, Dr. Timothy M Wright TEL 212-606-1093. Adv. contact Stephen J Max TEL 215-481-9450. Circ: 2,543.

617.3 JPN ISSN 0949-2658
RD701 CODEN: JOSCFS

➤ **JOURNAL OF ORTHOPAEDIC SCIENCE.** Text in English. 1996. bi-m. (in 1 vol., 6 nos./vol.). EUR 360, USD 427 combined subscription to institutions (print & online eds.) (effective 2012). reprint service avail. from PSC. **Document type:** *Journal, Academic/Scholarly.* **Description:** Documents the latest research and topical debates in all fields of clinical and experimental orthopedics.
Related titles: Online - full text ed.: ISSN 1436-2023 (from IngentaConnect).
Indexed: A01, A03, A08, A22, A26, C06, C07, CA, CurCont, E01, EMBASE, ExcerpMed, INIS AtomInd, IndMed, Inpharma, MEDLINE, P20, P22, P24, P30, P35, P48, P54, PQC, R10, Reac, SCI, SCOPUS, T02, W07.
—BLDSC (5027.668000), GNLM, IE, Infotrieve, Ingenta, INIST. **CCC.**
Published by: (Japanese Orthopaedic Association/Nippon Seikei Geka Gakkai), Springer Japan KK (Subsidiary of: Springer Science+Business Media), No 2 Funato Bldg, 1-11-11 Kudan-kita, Chiyoda-ku, Tokyo, 102-0073, Japan. TEL 81-3-68317000, FAX 81-3-68317001, http://www.springer.jp. Ed. Dr. Tetsuya Tamaki. Adv. contact Stephan Kroeck TEL 49-30-827875739. Circ: 2,800. **Subscr. in the Americas to:** Springer New York LLC, Journal Fulfillment, PO Box 2485, Secaucus, NJ 07096. TEL 201-348-4033, 800-777-4643, FAX 201-348-4505, journals-ny@springer.com, http://www.springer.com; **Subscr. to:** Springer Distribution Center, Kundenservice Zeitschriften, Haberstr 7, Heidelberg 69126, Germany. TEL 49-6221-3454303, FAX 49-6221-3454229, subscriptions@springer.com.

617.3 HKG ISSN 1022-5536
RD701 CODEN: JOTSEC

➤ **JOURNAL OF ORTHOPAEDIC SURGERY.** Text in English. 1962. 3/yr. HKD 624, USD 80; free to qualified personnel (effective 2010). adv. bk.rev. charts; illus. reprints avail. **Document type:** *Journal, Academic/Scholarly.* **Description:** Serves as an international forum for scientific research to allow orthopedic surgeons and scientists of the Asia Pacific Region to update themselves with the latest discoveries and advances of orthopedic surgery.
Formerly (until 1992): Western Pacific Orthopaedic Association. Journal (0043-4019)
Related titles: Online - full text ed.: free (effective 2011).
Indexed: C06, C07, EMBASE, ExcerpMed, HongKongiana, MEDLINE, P20, P22, P24, P26, P30, P48, P54, PQC, R10, Reac, SCOPUS.
—BLDSC (5027.669000), IE, Infotrieve, Ingenta.
Published by: (Asia Pacific Orthopaedic Association), Hong Kong Academy of Medicine Press, Rm.901, 9/F, HKAM Bldg., 99 Wong Hunk Hang Rd., Aberdeen, Hong Kong. TEL 852-28718807, FAX 852-25159061, hkampress@hkam.org.hk, http://www.hkampress.org. Ed. David Fang. Circ: 2,000 (controlled).

616.7 GBR ISSN 1749-799X
RD701

➤ **JOURNAL OF ORTHOPAEDIC SURGERY AND RESEARCH.** Abbreviated title: J O S R. Text in English. 2006. irreg. free (effective 2011). adv. back issues avail. **Document type:** *Journal, Academic/Scholarly.* **Description:** Covers on all aspects of research related to musculoskeletal issues.
Media: Online - full text.
Indexed: A01, A26, C06, C07, CA, I05, P30, SCOPUS, T02.
—CCC.
Published by: (International Chinese Hard Tissue Society USA, Chinese Speaking Orthopaedics Society/Huayi Guke Xuehui HKG), BioMed Central Ltd. (Subsidiary of: Springer Science+Business Media), 236 Gray's Inn Rd, London, WC1X 8HB, United Kingdom. TEL 44-20-31922000, FAX 44-20-31922010, info@biomedcentral.com, http://www.biomedcentral.com. Eds. Cheng-Kung Chen TEL 886-2-28267355, Kai-Ming Chan.

617.3 USA ISSN 0890-5339
CODEN: JORTE5

➤ **JOURNAL OF ORTHOPAEDIC TRAUMA.** Abbreviated title: J O T. Text in English. 1987. m. USD 982 domestic to institutions; USD 1,134 foreign to institutions (effective 2011). adv. bk.rev. charts; illus. index. back issues avail.; reprints avail. **Document type:** *Journal, Academic/Scholarly.* **Description:** Provides the information on diagnostic techniques, new and improved surgical instruments and procedures, surgical implants and prosthetic devices, bioplastics and biometals, and physical therapy and rehabilitation.
Related titles: Online - full text ed.: ISSN 1531-2291.
Indexed: A22, A34, A36, ASCA, C06, C07, C08, CABA, CINAHL, CurCont, EMBASE, ExcerpMed, FoSS&M, GH, ISR, IndMed, IndVet, Inpharma, JW-EM, MEDLINE, N02, N03, P30, R10, Reac, SCI, SCOPUS, VS, W07.
—BLDSC (5027.675000), GNLM, IE, Infotrieve, Ingenta, INIST. **CCC.**
Published by: (Orthopaedic Trauma Association), Lippincott Williams & Wilkins (Subsidiary of: Wolters Kluwer N.V.), Two Commerce Sq, 2001 Market St, Philadelphia, PA 19103. TEL 215-521-8300, FAX 215-521-8902, customerservice@lww.com, http://www.lww.com. Ed. Dr. Roy W Sanders TEL 813-253-2068. Pub. Marcia Serepy. Circ: 2,859. **Co-sponsor:** International Society for Fracture Repair.

616.7 IND ISSN 0972-978X

➤ **JOURNAL OF ORTHOPAEDICS.** Text in English. 2004. q. free (effective 2011). back issues avail. **Document type:** *Journal, Academic/Scholarly.* **Description:** Covers tropical Orthopaedics information. Aims to publish material of the highest quality reflecting world wide or provocative issues and perspectives.
Media: Online - full text.
Indexed: C06, C07.
Published by: (Calicut Ortho Alumni Association), Calicut Medical College, Medical College P O, Calicut, Kerala 673 008, India. TEL 91-495-2356531, FAX 91-495-2355331, pvramachandran@calicutmedicalcollege.ac.in, http://calicutmedicalcollege.ac.in. Eds. C M Kumaran, Dr. P Gopinathan TEL 91-94470-59014. **Co-sponsor:** Surendran Memorial Educational Foundation.

617.3 ITA ISSN 1590-9921
CODEN: IJOTD

➤ **JOURNAL OF ORTHOPAEDICS AND TRAUMATOLOGY.** Text in English. 1975. 3/yr. reprint service avail. from PSC. **Document type:** *Journal, Academic/Scholarly.* **Description:** Covers current thought, practice and research in the field of orthopaedics and traumatology.
Former titles (until 2000): Orthopaedics and Traumatology (1129-3853); (until 1999): Italian Journal of Orthopaedics and Traumatology (0390-5489)
Related titles: Microform ed.: (from PQC); Online - full text ed.: ISSN 1590-9999. free (effective 2011) (from IngentaConnect); ◆ Italian ed.: Giornale Italiano di Ortopedia e Traumatologia. ISSN 0390-0134.
Indexed: A01, A03, A08, A22, A26, B&BAb, B19, B21, C06, C07, CA, CTA, E01, EMBASE, ExcerpMed, MEDLINE, P30, R10, Reac, SCOPUS, T02.
—BLDSC (5027.675200), GNLM, IE, Ingenta, INIST. **CCC.**
Published by: Springer Italia Srl (Subsidiary of: Springer Science+Business Media), Via Decembrio 28, Milan, 20137, Italy. Ed. Marco d'Imporzano. **Subscr. in the Americas to:** Springer New York LLC, Journal Fulfillment, PO Box 2485, Secaucus, NJ 07096. TEL 201-348-4033, 800-777-4643, FAX 201-348-4505, journals-ny@springer.com, http://www.springer.com; **Subscr. to:** Springer Distribution Center, Kundenservice Zeitschriften, Haberstr 7, Heidelberg 69126, Germany. TEL 49-6221-3454303, FAX 49-6221-3454229, subscriptions@springer.com.

617.3 NLD ISSN 2210-4917

JOURNAL OF ORTHOPAEDICS, TRAUMA AND REHABILITATION. Text in English. 1997. s-a. EUR 142 in Europe to institutions; JPY 22,500 in Japan to institutions; USD 180 elsewhere to institutions (effective 2012). **Document type:** *Journal, Academic/Scholarly.*
Formerly (until 2010): Hong Kong Journal of Orthopaedic Surgery (1028-2637)
Related titles: Online - full text ed.: ISSN 2210-4925 (from ScienceDirect).
—BLDSC (4326.385770). **CCC.**
Published by: (Hong Kong Orthopaedic Association HKG), Elsevier BV (Subsidiary of: Elsevier Science & Technology), Radarweg 29, PO Box 211, Amsterdam, 1000 AE, Netherlands. TEL 31-20-4853911, FAX 31-20-4852457, JournalsCustomerServiceEMEA@elsevier.com, http://www.elsevier.com.

616.7 ITA

▼ ➤ **JOURNAL OF ORTHOPEDICS.** Text in English. 2010. 3/yr. **Document type:** *Journal, Academic/Scholarly.*
Published by: Biolife, Via S Stefano 39 bis, Silvi Marina, TE 66100, Italy. TEL 39-0871-3554805, FAX 39-0871-3554804, biolife_sas@yahoo.it, http://www.biolifesas.org. Ed. Giuliano Cerulli.

616.7 570.285 ITA ISSN 2036-6795

▼ **JOURNAL OF OSTEOLOGY AND BIOMATERIALS.** Text in English. 2010. 3/yr. **Document type:** *Journal, Academic/Scholarly.*
Related titles: Online - full text ed.: ISSN 2036-6809.
Published by: Biomaterials Clinical and Histological Research Association (Bio C R A)/Associazione di Ricerca Clinica ed Istologica sui Biomateriali, c/o ST Massei, Via Bardonecchia 29, Turin, 10139, Italy. http://www.biocra.com. Ed. Paolo Trisi.

616.7 USA ISSN 2042-0064
RC931.O73

▼ **JOURNAL OF OSTEOPOROSIS.** Text in English. 2010. irreg. free (effective 2011). **Document type:** *Journal, Academic/Scholarly.*
Media: Online - full text.
Indexed: A01, A26, B19, CTA, E08, H12, I05, P30, T02.
Published by: Sage - Hindawi Access to Research, 410 Park Ave, 15th Fl, 287 PMB, New York, NY 10022. FAX 866-446-3294.

616.025 GBR ISSN 1759-1376

➤ **JOURNAL OF PARAMEDIC PRACTICE;** the clinical monthly for emergency care professionals. Text in English. 2008 (Oct.). m. GBP 104 domestic to individuals; GBP 133 in Europe to individuals; GBP 174 elsewhere to individuals; GBP 286 in Europe to institutions; GBP 374 elsewhere to institutions (effective 2009). adv. **Document type:** *Journal, Academic/Scholarly.* **Description:** Essential reading for all those who are serious about developing their own career, as well as providing the best possible support for the people in their care.
Related titles: Online - full text ed.
Indexed: C06, C07, T02.
—BLDSC (5028.640000), IE. **CCC.**
Published by: M A Healthcare Ltd. (Subsidiary of: Mark Allen Publishing Ltd.), St. Jude's Church, Dulwich Rd, London, SE24 0PB, United Kingdom. TEL 44-20-77385454, FAX 44-20-77332325, healthcare/index.html. Ed. Andrea Porter TEL 44-1722-716997.

▼ ➤ **JOURNAL OF PEDIATRIC INTENSIVE CARE.** *see* MEDICAL SCIENCES—Pediatrics

617.3 USA ISSN 0271-6798
RD732.3.C48 CODEN: JPORDO

➤ **JOURNAL OF PEDIATRIC ORTHOPAEDICS.** Text in English. 1981. 8/yr. USD 1,206 domestic to institutions; USD 1,243 foreign to institutions (effective 2011). adv. bk.rev. illus. index. back issues avail.; reprints avail. **Document type:** *Journal, Academic/Scholarly.* **Description:** Focuses specifically on traumatic injuries to give hands-on coverage of a fast-growing field.
Related titles: Online - full text ed.: ISSN 1539-2570.
Indexed: A20, A22, ASCA, BDM&CN, C06, C07, CurCont, EMBASE, ExcerpMed, FR, IndMed, Inpharma, MEDLINE, P30, PsycholAb, R10, Reac, SCI, SCOPUS, W07.
—BLDSC (5030.225000), GNLM, IE, Infotrieve, Ingenta, INIST. **CCC.**

Published by: (The Pediatric Orthopaedic Society of North America), Lippincott Williams & Wilkins (Subsidiary of: Wolters Kluwer N.V.), Two Commerce Sq, 2001 Market St, Philadelphia, PA 19103. TEL 215-521-8300, FAX 215-521-8902, customerservice@lww.com, http://www.lww.com. Eds. Dr. George H Thompson, Dr. Robert N Hensinger. Pub. Marcia Serapy TEL 207-828-0162. Circ: 1,577.

617.3 USA ISSN 1060-152X
RD732.3.C48 CODEN: JPOBFC

➤ **JOURNAL OF PEDIATRIC ORTHOPAEDICS. PART B.** Text in English. 1992. bi-m. USD 903 domestic to institutions; USD 967 foreign to institutions (effective 2011). adv. charts; illus. back issues avail.; reprints avail. **Document type:** *Journal, Academic/Scholarly.* **Description:** Publishes recent developments in the treatment of musculoskeletal disorders in children, with an emphasis on advances from the European Community.
Related titles: Microform ed.: (from PQC); Online - full text ed.: ISSN 1473-5865.
Indexed: A22, ASCA, C06, C07, CurCont, EMBASE, ExcerpMed, IndMed, Inpharma, MEDLINE, P30, R10, Reac, SCI, SCOPUS, W07.
—BLDSC (5030.230000), IE, Infotrieve, Ingenta. **CCC.**
Published by: (The Pediatric Orthopaedic Society of North America, European Paediatric Orthopaedic Society CHE), Lippincott Williams & Wilkins (Subsidiary of: Wolters Kluwer N.V.), 530 Walnut St, Philadelphia, PA 19106. TEL 215-521-8300, FAX 215-521-8902, customerservice@lww.com, http://www.lww.com. Ed. Ashok N Johari. Pub. Phil Daly.

➤ **THE JOURNAL OF PHYSIOLOGY.** *see* BIOLOGY—Physiology

617.3 USA ISSN 1040-8800
RD130

➤ **JOURNAL OF PROSTHETICS AND ORTHOTICS.** Variant title: J P O. Text in English. 1988. q. USD 350 domestic to institutions; USD 432 foreign to institutions (effective 2011). adv. bk.rev. back issues avail. **Document type:** *Journal, Academic/Scholarly.* **Description:** Presents research articles and reports from professionals on current topics in orthotics and prosthetics.
Formed by the merger of (1967-1988): Orthotics and Prosthetics (0030-5928); Which was formerly (until 1967): Orthopedic and Prosthetic Appliance Journal; (until 1952): O A L M A. Journal; (1982-1988): Clinical Prosthetics and Orthotics (0735-0090); Which was formerly (until 1982): Newsletter, Prosthetics and Orthotics Clinic (0279-6910); Which superseded (in 19??): Newsletter, Amputee Clinics
Related titles: Microfilm ed.: (from PQC); Online - full text ed.: ISSN 1534-6331.
Indexed: A01, A22, AMED, ASCA, BioEngAb, C06, C07, C08, CA, CINAHL, P30, R09, SCOPUS, SD, T02.
—BLDSC (5042.910000), GNLM, IE, Infotrieve, Ingenta. **CCC.**
Published by: (The American Academy of Orthotists & Prosthetists, American Orthotic & Prosthetic Assocciation), Lippincott Williams & Wilkins (Subsidiary of: Wolters Kluwer N.V.), 530 Walnut St, Philadelphia, PA 19106. TEL 215-521-8300, FAX 215-521-8902, customerservice@lww.com, http://www.lww.com. Ed. David Boone.

617.3 USA ISSN 0748-7711
RD130 CODEN: JRRDEC

➤ **JOURNAL OF REHABILITATION RESEARCH AND DEVELOPMENT.** Text in English. 1964. q. free. bk.rev. abstr.; bibl.; charts; illus.; pat.; stat. Index. reprints avail. **Document type:** *Journal, Academic/Scholarly.* **Description:** Disseminates ideas in rehabilitation research and development that further efforts to meet the needs of people with disabilities.
Former titles (until 198?): Journal of Rehabilitation R and D (0742-3241); (until 1982): Prosthetics Research. Bulletin (0007-506X)
Related titles: Microform ed.: (from PQC); Online - full text ed.: ISSN 1938-1352. free (effective 2011).
Indexed: A01, A02, A03, A08, A20, A22, A26, AMED, ASCA, ApMecR, B&BAb, B19, B21, BioEngAb, C&ISA, C06, C07, C08, C11, CA, CBRI, CINAHL, CMCI, CPEI, CurCont, E&CAJ, ECER, EMBASE, ESPM, EngInd, ExcerpMed, H&SSA, H04, H11, H12, H13, HRIS, I05, INI, ISMEC, IndMed, Inpharma, MEDLINE, NSA, P02, P10, P20, P22, P24, P26, P30, P48, P53, P54, PEI, PQC, R09, R10, Reac, RefZh, RehabLit, SCI, SCOPUS, SD, SSCI, SolStAb, T02, W07.
—BLDSC (5048.970000), GNLM, IE, Infotrieve, Ingenta, INIST, Linda Hall.
Published by: (Office of Research and Development), Department of Veterans Affairs, Veterans Health Administration, 103 S Gay St, Baltimore, MD 21202-3517. TEL 410-962-1800, FAX 410-962-9670, mail@rehab-balt.med.va.gov, http://www.va.gov. Circ: 27,000.

617.3 USA ISSN 1536-0652
RC400 CODEN: JSDIEW

➤ **JOURNAL OF SPINAL DISORDERS & TECHNIQUES.** Text in English. 1988. bi-m. USD 817 domestic to institutions; USD 947 foreign to institutions (effective 2011). adv. charts; illus. back issues avail.; reprints avail. **Document type:** *Journal, Academic/Scholarly.* **Description:** Features research and clinical articles on diagnosis, management, and treatment of lumbar spine disorders.
Formerly (until 2002): Journal of Spinal Disorders (0895-0385)
Related titles: Online - full text ed.: ISSN 1539-2465.
Indexed: A01, A03, A08, A22, AMED, ASCA, CA, CurCont, EMBASE, ExcerpMed, FR, IndMed, Inpharma, MEDLINE, P30, R10, Reac, SCI, SCOPUS, W07.
—BLDSC (5066.182500), GNLM, IE, Infotrieve, Ingenta, INIST. **CCC.**
Published by: Lippincott Williams & Wilkins (Subsidiary of: Wolters Kluwer N.V.), Two Commerce Sq, 2001 Market St, Philadelphia, PA 19103. TEL 215-521-8300, FAX 215-521-8902, customerservice@lww.com, http://www.lww.com. Ed. Thomas Zdeblick. Pub. Marcia Serepy.

➤ **JOURNAL OF SPORT TRAUMATOLOGY & ALLIED SPORTS SCIENCES.** *see* MEDICAL SCIENCES—Sports Medicine

➤ **JOURNAL OF SPORTS TRAUMATOLOGY.** *see* MEDICAL SCIENCES—Sports Medicine

617.3 USA ISSN 1548-825X

➤ **JOURNAL OF SURGICAL ORTHOPAEDIC ADVANCES.** Abbreviated title: J S O A. Text in English. 1992. q. USD 99 to individuals; USD 179 to institutions (effective 2010). adv. back issues avail.; reprints avail. **Document type:** *Journal, Academic/Scholarly.* **Description:** Provides a forum for the exchange of information and presents new techniques and procedures, and also contains updates about the ongoing educational activities of interest to all practicing orthopedists.
Formerly (until 2003): Southern Orthopaedic Association. Journal (1059-1052)
Related titles: Online - full text ed.: ISSN 2158-3811. USD 99 to individuals; USD 329 to institutions (effective 2010).
Indexed: EMBASE, ExcerpMed, IndMed, MEDLINE, P30, R10, Reac, SCOPUS.
—BLDSC (5067.382000), GNLM, IE, Infotrieve, Ingenta. **CCC.**
Published by: (Southern Orthopaedic Association), Data Trace Publishing Company, PO Box 1239, Brooklandville, MD 21022. TEL 410-494-4994, 800-342-0454, FAX 410-494-0515, info@datatrace.com. Ed. Dr. L Andrew Koman. Adv. contact Frank M Tufariello TEL 410-494-4994.

617 USA ISSN 0022-5282
RD92 CODEN: JOTRA5

➤ **JOURNAL OF TRAUMA;** injury, infection, and critical care. Text in English. 1961. m. USD 842 domestic to institutions; USD 1,028 foreign to institutions (effective 2011). adv. abstr.; charts; illus.; stat.; tr.lit. Index. back issues avail.; reprints avail. **Document type:** *Journal, Academic/Scholarly.* **Description:** Focuses on traumatic injuries. Articles cover everything from the nature of the injury to the effects of new drug therapies.
Related titles: CD-ROM ed.; Online - full text ed.: ISSN 1529-8809.
Indexed: A22, A36, AIM, ASCA, B21, B25, BIOSIS Prev, C06, C07, C08, CABA, CIN, CINAHL, CISA, CLI, ChemAb, ChemTitl, CurCont, DentInd, E-psyche, E12, EMBASE, ESPM, ExcerpMed, F08, F09, F11, F12, FR, GH, H&SSA, HRIS, INI, ISR, IndMed, Inpharma, JW-EM, LT, MEDLINE, MycolAb, N02, N03, P30, P33, P35, PEI, PN&I, R10, RA&MP, RM&VM, RRTA, Reac, S02, S03, S12, SCI, SCOPUS, T05, W07, W11.
—CASDDS, GNLM, Ingenta, INIST. **CCC.**
Published by: (American Association for the Surgery of Trauma), Lippincott Williams & Wilkins (Subsidiary of: Wolters Kluwer N.V.), 351 W Camden St, Baltimore, MD 21201. TEL 410-528-4000, FAX 410-528-4312, customerservice@lww.com, http://www.lww.com. Ed. Basil A Pruitt Jr. Pub. John Ewers. Adv. contact Bethann H Sands TEL 215-521-8399.

616.7 GBR ISSN 1752-2897
RD92

➤ **JOURNAL OF TRAUMA MANAGEMENT & OUTCOMES.** Abbreviated title: J T M O. Text in English. 2007. irreg. free (effective 2011). adv. back issues avail. **Document type:** *Journal, Academic/Scholarly.* **Description:** Covers all aspects of trauma, focusing on interventions demonstrating efficacy and effectiveness in improving clinically relevant outcomes for severely injured patients.
Media: Online - full text.
Indexed: A01, A26, A39, C27, C29, CA, D03, D04, E13, H12, I05, P30, R14, S14, S15, S18, T02.
—**CCC.**
Published by: BioMed Central Ltd. (Subsidiary of: Springer Science+Business Media), 236 Gray's Inn Rd, London, WC1X 8HB, United Kingdom. TEL 44-20-31922000, FAX 44-20-31922010, info@biomedcentral.com, http://www.biomedcentral.com. Ed. Axel Ekkernkamp.

➤ **JOURNAL OF TRAUMA NURSING.** *see* MEDICAL SCIENCES—Nurses And Nursing

➤ **JOURNAL OF VETERINARY EMERGENCY AND CRITICAL CARE.** *see* VETERINARY SCIENCE

617.1 GBR ISSN 0969-0700
RD94

➤ **JOURNAL OF WOUND CARE.** Abbreviated title: J W C. Text in English. 1992. m. GBP 119 combined subscription domestic to individuals (print & online eds.); EUR 186 combined subscription in Europe to individuals (print & online eds.); USD 295 combined subscription elsewhere to individuals (print & online eds.); GBP 99 domestic to individuals; EUR 156 in Europe to individuals; USD 229 elsewhere to individuals (effective 2010). adv. bk.rev. charts; illus.; pat. cum.index. back issues avail.; reprints avail. **Document type:** *Journal, Academic/Scholarly.* **Description:** Designed for all wound-care specialists - nurses, doctors and researchers - who are keen to keep up-to-date with all developments in wound management and tissue viability.
Related titles: Online - full text ed.: GBP 90, EUR 99, USD 175 to individuals (effective 2010).
Indexed: B28, C06, C07, C08, CA, CINAHL, EMBASE, ExcerpMed, INI, MEDLINE, P30, R10, Reac, SCOPUS, T02.
—BLDSC (5072.695000), GNLM, IE, Infotrieve, Ingenta, INIST. **CCC.**
Published by: Mark Allen Publishing Ltd., St Jude's Church, Dulwich Rd, London, SE24 0PB, United Kingdom. TEL 44-20-77385454, FAX 44-20-79788316, subscriptions@markallengroup.com, http://www.markallengroup.com. Ed. Tracy Cowan. Pub., Adv. contact Anthony Kerr.

016.6167 USA ISSN 1521-6535
JOURNAL WATCH EMERGENCY MEDICINE. (Contains about 23 abstracts per issue) Text in English. 1997 (Sep.). m. USD 179 domestic for physicians; CAD 172 in Canada for physicians; USD 149 elsewhere for physicians; USD 179 domestic to institutions; CAD 265 in Canada to institutions; USD 216 elsewhere to institutions; USD 69 domestic for residents/students/nurses; USD 101 in Canada for residents/students/nurses; USD 75 elsewhere for residents/students/nurses (effective 2009). 8 p./no.; **Document type:** *Newsletter.* **Description:** Presents concise summaries of important research appearing in the emergency medicine literature.
Related titles: Online - full text ed.: ISSN 1533-7952.
—BLDSC (5072.523150), IE. **CCC.**
Published by: Massachusetts Medical Society, 860 Winter St, Waltham, MA 02451. TEL 781-893-3800 ext 5515, 800-843-6356, FAX 781-893-0413, http://www.massmed.org. Ed. Dr. Ron M Walls.

617.3 JPN ISSN 1348-043X
KANAGAWA SEIKEI SAIGAI GEKA KENKYUUKAI ZASSHI/KANAGAWA JOURNAL OF ORTHOPEDICS AND TRAUMATOLOGY. Text in Japanese. 1988. a. **Document type:** *Journal, Academic/Scholarly.*
Formerly: Kanagawa Seikei Saigai Geka Ikai Zasshi (0915-1451)
—**CCC.**
Published by: Kanagawa Seikei Saigai Geka Ikai/Kanagawa Society of Orthopedics and Traumatology, c/o Showa University Fujigaoka Hospital, Department of Orthopedics, 1-30 Fujigaoka, Aoba-Ku, Yokohama, Kanagawa 227-8501, Japan. TEL 81-45-9746365, FAX 81-45-9744610, kots-office@umin.ac.jp, http://kots.umin.jp/.

617.3 JPN ISSN 0286-5394

➤ **KANSETSU GEKA/JOURNAL OF JOINT SURGERY.** Text in Japanese. 1981. m. JPY 35,910 (effective 2007). **Document type:** *Journal, Academic/Scholarly.*
—BLDSC (5085.654050).
Published by: Medical View Co. Ltd./Mejikaru Byusha, 2-30 Ichigaya-Honmura-cho, Shinjuku-ku, Tokyo, 162-0845, Japan. TEL 81-3-52282050, FAX 81-3-52282059, http://www.medicalview.co.jp. Circ: 8,000.

617.3 JPN ISSN 0285-6255
KANSETSU NO GEKA/SURGERY OF JOINTS. Text in Japanese. 1974. q. **Document type:** *Journal, Academic/Scholarly.*
Published by: Shizen Kagakusha Co. Ltd., 2-1-4 Iida-Bashi, Chiyoda-ku, Tokyo, 102-0072, Japan. TEL 81-3-32344121, FAX 81-3-32344127, http://www.shizenkagaku.com/.

617.1 616.7 JPN ISSN 0910-223X
KANSETSUKYO/ARTHROSCOPY. Text in Japanese; Summaries in English. 1976. s-a. membership. adv. back issues avail. **Document type:** *Journal, Academic/Scholarly.* **Description:** Publishes proceedings of the annual meeting and original papers.
Published by: Nippon Kansetsukyo Gakkai/Japan Arthroscopy Association, c/o Chiba University, School of Medicine, Department of Surgery, 1-8-1 Inohana, Chuo-ku, Chiba-shi, 260-8670, Japan. TEL 81-43-2227171, FAX 81-43-2262116, http://www.jaaa.gr.jp/. Circ: 1,500.

617.3 JPN ISSN 0389-7087
CODEN: KSSZDW
KANTO SEIKEI SAIGAI GEKA GAKKAI ZASSHI/KANTO JOURNAL OF ORTHOPEDICS AND TRAUMATOLOGY. Text in Japanese. 1970. bi-m. membership.
Indexed: INIS AtomInd.
Published by: Kanto Seikei Saigai Geka Gakkai/Kanto Society of Orthopedics and Traumatology, Jikeikai Ika Daigaku Seikei Gekagaku Kyoshitsu, 25-8 Nishi-Shinbashi 3-chome, Minato-ku, Tokyo, 105-0003, Japan.

616.7 JPN ISSN 0910-4461
KATAKANSETSU/SHOULDER JOINT. Text in Japanese. 1977. a. **Document type:** *Journal, Academic/Scholarly.*
Related titles: Online - full text ed.
—BLDSC (5086.793600).
Published by: Katakansetsu Kenkyukai/Japan Shoulder Society, Fukuoka University, Department of Orthopaedic Surgery, 7-45-1 Nanakuma, Jonan-ku, Fukuoka City, 814-0180, Japan. TEL 81-92-8011011 ext 3465, 3466, FAX 81-92-8649055, office@j-shoulder-s.com, http://www.j-shoulder-s.com/.

THE KNEE. *see* BIOLOGY—Physiology

617.3 JPN ISSN 0287-2285
KOSSETSU/FRACTURE. Text in Japanese. 1978. a. adv. bk.rev. back issues avail. **Document type:** *Abstract/Index.*
Related titles: Fax ed.
Published by: Nihon Kossetsu Chiryo Gakkai/Japan Fracture Society, Kitasato Daigaku Igakubu Seikei Geka, 15-1 Kitaza-To 1-chome, Sagamihara-shi, Kanagawa-ken 228-0829, Japan. TEL 81-42-778-9343, 81-42-778-8111, FAX 81-42-778-8050. Ed., Adv. contact Moritoshi Itoman. R&P Kumiko Akikaze. Circ: 2,000 (paid).

610 JPN ISSN 0022-5274
CODEN: KOIGAU
KOTSU IGAKU/JOURNAL OF TRANSPORTATION MEDICINE. Text in Japanese. 1947. bi-m. membership. adv. **Document type:** *Journal, Academic/Scholarly.*
Indexed: CISA, INIS AtomInd, IndMed, SCOPUS.
—CASDDS. **CCC.**
Published by: Nihon Kotsu Igakkai/Japanese Association of Transportation Medicine, 3-3-11, Nishi-shinjuku, Shinjuku-ku, Tokyo, 160-0023, Japan. TEL 81-3-53397286, FAX 81-3-53397285, jatm@iva.jp, http://jatm.umin.jp/. Circ: 600 (controlled).

KOTSU KANSETSU JINTAI/JOURNAL OF MUSCULOSKELETAL SYSTEM. *see* MEDICAL SCIENCES—Rheumatology

617.3 JPN
KOTSU KEITO SHIKKAN KENKYUKAI SHOROKU/JAPANESE SOCIETY FOR SKELETAL DYSPLASIAS. PROCEEDINGS OF THE MEETING. Text in English, Japanese. 1989. a. **Document type:** *Proceedings.*
Published by: (Kotsu Keito Shikkan Kenkyukai), Kagawa Ikadaigaku Seikeigeka, 1750-1 Oaza-Ikedo, Kita-gun, Miki-cho, Kagawa-ken 761-0700, Japan. TEL 81-878-98-5111, FAX 81-878-91-0116.

616.7 POL ISSN 1230-1043
KWARTALNIK ORTOPEDYCZNY/ORTHOPEDIC QUARTERLY. Text in Polish. 1991. q. EUR 41 foreign (effective 2006). **Document type:** *Journal, Academic/Scholarly.*
Published by: (Polskie Towarzystwo Ortopedyczne i Traumatologiczne/ Polish Society or Orthopedic Surgery and Traumatology), Wydawnictwo Skamed, ul Zeromskiego 113, Lodz, 90549, Poland. TEL 48-42-6393511, info@kwartalnikortopedyczny.pl. Ed. Krystian Zolynski. **Dist. by:** Ars Polona, Obroncow 25, Warsaw 03933, Poland. TEL 48-22-5098609, FAX 48-22-5098610, arspolona@arspolona.com.pl, http://www.arspolona.com.pl.

616 360 GBR
L A S NEWS. (London Ambulance Service) Text in English. 1966. m. free to qualified personnel. back issues avail. **Document type:** *Newsletter.*
Formerly: Londam
Published by: London Ambulance Service, 220 Waterloo Rd, London, SE1 8SD, United Kingdom. TEL 44-20-79215113, FAX 44-20-74632590, Communications@lond-amb.nhs.uk, http://www.londonambulance.nhs.uk/. Ed. Andrew Faith. Circ: 3,000.

616.7 617.06 362.4 NLD ISSN 1574-9525
LANDELIJKE VERENIGING VAN GEAMPUTEERDEN NIEUWSBRIEF. Key Title: L V v G Nieuwsbrief. Text in Dutch. 1986. q. EUR 18.50 (effective 2009).
Formerly (until 2004): Nieuwsbrief Beenprothesegebruikers (1387-0335)
Published by: Landelijke Vereniging van Geamputeerden, c/o Willem Broos, Koningin Julianalaan 23, Leusden-Zuid, 3832 BA, Netherlands. http://www.lvvg.nl.

617.3 AUT ISSN 1991-279X
LEADING OPINIONS. ORTHOPAEDIE. Text in German. 2006. 4/yr. adv. **Document type:** *Journal, Academic/Scholarly.*

Published by: Universimed Verlags- und Service GmbH, Markgraf-Ruediger-Str 8, Vienna, 1150, Austria. TEL 43-1-87679560, FAX 43-1-876795620, office@universimed.com, http://www.universimed.com. Ed. Christine Dominkus. Adv. contact Christian Gallei. Circ: 1,500 (controlled).

617.1 POL ISSN 1733-4101
LECZENIE RAN/WOUND MANAGEMENT. Text in Polish. 2004. s-a. **Document type:** *Journal, Academic/Scholarly.*
Related titles: Online - full text ed.: ISSN 1733-7607.
Published by: (Polskie Towarzystwo Leczenia Ran, Polskie Towarzystwo Chirurgii Plastycznej, Rekonstrukcyjnej i Estetycznej), Blackhorse Scientific Publishers, Ltd., Zeganska 16, Warsaw, 04713, Poland. TEL 48-22-4999099, FAX 48-22-4995081, blackhorse@blackhorse.pl, http://blackhorse.pl/blackhorse. Ed. Andrzej Cencora.

616.7 CHN ISSN 1008-0287
LINCHUANG GUKE ZAZHI. Text in Chinese. 1998. q. USD 31.20 (effective 2009). **Document type:** *Journal, Academic/Scholarly.*
Related titles: Online - full text ed.
—BLDSC (5220.198500).
Published by: Anhui Yike Daxue/Anhui Medical University, Meishan Lu, Anhui, 230032, China. TEL 86-551-2923133, FAX 86-511-3664966.

616.025 CHN ISSN 1009-5918
LINCHUANG JIZHEN ZAZHI/JOURNAL OF CLINICAL EMERGENCE CALL. Text in Chinese. 2000. bi-m. **Document type:** *Journal, Academic/Scholarly.*
Related titles: Online - full text ed.: (from WanFang Data Corp.).
—BLDSC (5220.203300), East View.
Published by: Huazhong Keji Daxue Tongji Yixueyuan Fushu Xiehe Yiyuan/Tongji Medical University, Union Hospital, 1277, Jiefang Dadao, Wuhan, 430022, China. TEL 86-27-85726342 ext 8817, FAX 86-27-85727988, http://www.whuh.com/. **Dist. by:** China International Book Trading Corp, 35 Chegongzhuang Xilu, Haidian District, PO Box 399, Beijing 100044, China. TEL 86-10-68412045, FAX 86-10-68412023, cibtc@mail.cibtc.com.cn, http://www.cibtc.com.cn.

616 USA
LIPPINCOTT'S BONE AND JOINT NEWSLETTER; the newsletter on musculoskeletal medicine. Text in English. 1995. m. (11/yr.). USD 201.98 domestic to individuals; USD 297.98 foreign to individuals; USD 380.98 domestic to institutions; USD 499.98 foreign to institutions (effective 2011). 12 p./no.; **Document type:** *Newsletter, Trade.* **Description:** Covers joint function, disease and injury.
Former titles (until 2007): Bone & Joint (1543-9879); (until 2003): The Joint Letter (1078-6260)
Related titles: Online - full text ed.
Indexed: C06, C07, C08, CINAHL.
—CCC.
Published by: Lippincott Williams & Wilkins (Subsidiary of: Wolters Kluwer N.V.), Two Commerce Sq, 2001 Market St, Philadelphia, PA 19103. TEL 215-521-8300, 800-638-3030, FAX 215-521-8902, customerservice@lww.com. Ed. Dr. Stanley A Herring.

617.3 617.95 HUN ISSN 1217-3231
MAGYAR TRAUMATOLOGIA, ORTHOPEDIA, KEZSEBESZET ES PLASZTIKAI SEBESZET. Text in Hungarian; Summaries in English, German, Russian. 1958. q. adv. bk.rev. charts; illus.; pat. index. **Document type:** *Academic/Scholarly.*
Formerly (until no.4, 1992): Magyar Traumatologia, Orthopedia es Helyreallito-Sebeszet (0025-0317)
Indexed: IndMed, P30, SCOPUS.
—BLDSC (5345.850000), GNLM, IE, Ingenta.
Published by: Hungarian Traumatology Society, Karolina u 27, Budapest, 1113, Hungary. Ed., Pub., R&P, Adv. contact Dr. Tibor Vizkelety TEL 36-1-4666059. Circ: 1,000. **Co-sponsor:** Hungarian Orthopaedic Society.

MEDICINE AND SPORT SCIENCE. *see* MEDICAL SCIENCES—Sports Medicine

617.585 NLD ISSN 1877-9433
DE MEDISCHE VOET. Text in Dutch. 2008. bi-m. EUR 27.50 (effective 2010). adv. **Document type:** *Magazine, Trade.*
Published by: Uitgeverij Supplement BV, Paulus Potterstraat 30-2, Amsterdam, 1071 DA, Netherlands. TEL 31-20-6705000, FAX 31-20-4711007, info@sup.nl. Circ: 5,000.

617.11 ITA ISSN 1592-9558
➤ **MEDITERRANEAN COUNCIL FOR BURNS AND FIRE DISASTERS. ANNALS.** Variant title: Burns and Fire Disasters. Annals. Text in English, French; Summaries in English, French. 1987. q. EUR 15 to non-members; free to members (effective 2009). adv. bk.rev. bibl.; illus.; stat. back issues avail. **Document type:** *Journal, Academic/Scholarly.* **Description:** Specializes in burns as individual pathology and in fire disaster as societal pathology (mass burns).
Formerly (until 1995): Mediterranean Burns Club. Annals (1121-1539)
Related titles: Online - full text ed.: ISSN 1592-9566.
—BLDSC (1040.140000), IE, Ingenta.
Published by: Mediterranean Council for Burns and Fire Disasters, Via C. Lazzaro, Palermo, PA 90127, Italy. TEL 39-091-6663631, FAX 39-091-596404, mbcpa@medbc.com.

616.025 UKR
➤ **MEDITSINA NEOTLOZHNYKH SOSTOYANII**; spetsializirovannyi nauchno-prakticheskii zhurnal. Text in Russian. 2005. 6/yr. USD 104 foreign (effective 2006). **Document type:** *Journal, Academic/Scholarly.* **Description:** Publishes articles about the first aid in the practice of a wide range of doctors.
Published by: Zaslavskii Izdatel'skii Dom, ul Oktyabrya, 14, Donetsk, 83030, Ukraine. Ed. A Yu Zaslavskii. **Dist. by:** East View Information Services, 10601 Wayzata Blvd, Minneapolis, MN 55305. TEL 952-252-1201, 800-477-1005, FAX 952-252-1202, info@eastview.com, http://www.eastview.com. **Co-sponsors:** Khar'kovskaya Meditsinskaya Akademiya Poslediplomnogo Obrazovaniya; Khar'kovskii Nauchno-Issledovatel'skii Institut Obshchei i Neotlozhnoi Khirurgii; Khar'kovskaya Gorodskaya Klinicheskaya Bol'nitsa Skoroi i Neotlozhnoi Pomoshchi.

617.3 DEU ISSN 0340-5508
MEDIZINISCH-ORTHOPAEDISCHE TECHNIK. Text in German. 1880. bi-m. EUR 13.80 newsstand/cover (effective 2008). adv. bk.rev. charts; illus.; pat. index. **Document type:** *Journal, Academic/Scholarly.*
Indexed: A22.
—BLDSC (5535.073800), GNLM, IE, Ingenta. **CCC.**

Published by: Verlagsgesellschaft Tischler GmbH, Kaunstr 34, Berlin, 14163, Germany. TEL 49-30-8011018, FAX 49-30-8016661, media-service@firmengruppe-tischler.de. adv.: B&W page EUR 1,300, color page EUR 2,300. Circ: 6,550 (paid and controlled).

617.3 USA ISSN 1532-0421
➤ **MEDSCAPE ORTHOPEDICS & SPORTS MEDICINE.** Text in English. 1997. w. **Document type:** *Journal, Academic/Scholarly.* **Description:** Features clinical news, full-text articles, and other features covering prevention, diagnosis, and treatment of patients with orthopedic complaints.
Media: Online - full text.
Indexed: SD.
Published by: WebMD Medscape Health Network, 224 W 30th St, New York, NY 10001. TEL 888-506-6098, medscapecustomersupport@webmd.net.

616.025 POL ISSN 1506-4077
MEDYCYNA INTENSYWNA I RATUNKOWA/INTENSIVE CARE & EMERGENCY MEDICINE. Text in Polish; Abstracts in English. 1998. q. EUR 37 foreign (effective 2005). bk.rev. **Document type:** *Journal, Academic/Scholarly.*
Indexed: SCOPUS.
Published by: (Polskie Towarzystwo Anestezjologii i Intensywnej Terapii/Polish Society of Anaesthesiology and Intensive Therapy), Wydawnictwo Medyczne Urban i Partner, ul Marii Sklodowskiej-Curie 55-61, Wroclaw, 50950, Poland. TEL 48-71-3285487, FAX 48-71-3284391. Ed. Andrzej Kubler. Circ: 700. **Dist. by:** Ars Polona, Obroncow 25, Warsaw 03933, Poland. TEL 48-22-5098609, FAX 48-22-5098610, arspolona@arspolona.com.pl, http://www.arspolona.com.pl.

617.3 ITA ISSN 0394-3410
CODEN: MIORA5
MINERVA ORTOPEDICA E TRAUMATOLOGICA; a journal on orthopedics and traumatology. Text in Italian; Summaries in English, Italian. 1950. bi-m. EUR 255 combined subscription in the European Union to institutions (print & online eds.); EUR 280 combined subscription elsewhere to institutions (print & online eds.) (effective 2011). adv. bk.rev. bibl.; charts; illus. index. **Document type:** *Journal, Academic/Scholarly.* **Description:** Covers orthopedical and traumatological pathophysiology, clinical medicine and therapy.
Formerly: Minerva Ortopedica (0026-4911)
Related titles: Online - full text ed.: ISSN 1827-1707.
Indexed: A22, ChemAb, IndMed, P30, SCI, SCOPUS, W07.
—BLDSC (5794.315000), GNLM, IE, Ingenta, INIST.
Published by: (Societa Piemontese - Ligure - Lombarda di Ortopedia e Traumatologia), Edizioni Minerva Medica, Corso Bramante 83-85, Turin, 10126, Italy. TEL 39-011-678282, FAX 39-011-674502, journals.dept@minervamedica.it, http://www.minervamedica.it. Ed., Pub. Alberto Oliaro. Circ: 4,000 (paid).

617.3 JPN ISSN 0914-8124
MONTHLY BOOK ORTHOPAEDICS. Text in Japanese. 1988. m. price varies. **Document type:** *Monographic series, Academic/Scholarly.*
Published by: Zennihon Byoin Shuppankai, 3-16-4 Hongo, Bunkyo-Ku, 7F, Tokyo, 113-0033, Japan. TEL 81-3-56895989, FAX 81-3-56898030, http://www.zenniti.com/.

616.7 DEU ISSN 0178-0352
MUSKELREPORT. Text in German. 1972. q. EUR 20 (effective 2009). adv. **Document type:** *Journal, Academic/Scholarly.*
Published by: Deutsche Gesellschaft fuer Muskelkranke e.V., Im Moos 4, Freiburg, 79112, Germany. TEL 49-7665-94470, FAX 49-7665-944720, info@dgm.org. adv.: B&W page EUR 660, color page EUR 985. Circ: 8,500 (controlled).

617.3 USA ISSN 1936-9719
CODEN: BHJDEI
➤ **N Y U HOSPITAL FOR JOINT DISEASES. BULLETIN.** (New York University) Text in English. 1940. q. adv. bk.rev. charts; illus. cum.index: 1965-81; 1982-85; 1986-89. reprints avail. **Document type:** *Journal, Academic/Scholarly.* **Description:** Publishes clinical and basic science articles in orthopaedic surgery.
Former titles (until 2006): Hospital for Joint Diseases. Bulletin (0018-5647); (until 1992): Hospital for Joint Diseases Orthopaedic Institute. Bulletin (0883-9344)
Related titles: Online - full text ed.: ISSN 1936-9727.
Indexed: A22, A26, CA, EMBASE, ExcerpMed, H12, I05, IndMed, MEDLINE, P30, R09, R10, Reac, SCOPUS, SD, T02.
—BLDSC (2661.569500), GNLM, IE, Ingenta, INIST. **CCC.**
Published by: (N Y U Hospital for Joint Diseases), J Michael Ryan Publishing, Inc., 24 Crescent Dr N, Andover, NJ 07821. TEL 973-786-7777, FAX 973-786-7776, info@jmichaelryan.com, http://www.jmichaelryan.com/. Ed. William L Jaffe. Circ: 2,500.

617.1 USA
NATIONAL DIRECTORY OF BRAIN INJURY REHABILITATION SERVICES. Text in English. 1984. a., latest 2006. USD 25 (effective 2007). **Document type:** *Directory, Trade.* **Description:** State by state listing of providers of services for people with traumatic brain injury, including rehabilitation programs and individual professionals.
Former titles: B I A National Directory of Brain Injury Rehabilitation Services (1089-2982); (until 1995): National Directory of Brain Injury Rehabilitation Services (1089-2974); (until 1991): National Directory of Head Injury Rehabilitation Services (0892-6972)
Published by: Brain Injury Association of America, 8201 Greensboro Dr, Ste 611, Mc Lean, VA 22102-3816. TEL 703-761-0750, 800-444-6443, FAX 703-761-0755, publications@biausa.org, http://www.biausa.org.

NATIONAL DIRECTORY OF FIRE CHIEFS & E M S ADMINISTRATORS. *see* FIRE PREVENTION

616 NLD ISSN 0929-8622
NEDERLANDS TIJDSCHRIFT VOOR TRAUMATOLOGIE. Text in Dutch. 1993. bi-m. EUR 72, USD 108 to institutions (effective 2009). adv. **Document type:** *Journal, Academic/Scholarly.*
Related titles: Online - full text ed.: ISSN 1876-5505.
Published by: Bohn Stafleu van Loghum B.V. (Subsidiary of: Springer Science+Business Media), Postbus 246, Houten, 3990 GA, Netherlands. TEL 31-30-6383872, FAX 31-30-6383991, boekhandels@bsl.nl, http://www.bsl.nl. adv.: page EUR 1,544; trim 210 x 297. Circ: 1,168.

616.7 USA ISSN 1934-9866
NEUROAXIS; das Journal zur Rueckengesundheit. Text in German. 2006. m. **Document type:** *Journal, Consumer.*
Media: Online - full text.

Published by: Daniel Hertle

NIHON FUKUBU KYUKYU IGAKKAI ZASSHI/JOURNAL OF ABDOMINAL EMERGENCY MEDICINE. *see* MEDICAL SCIENCES—Surgery

617 JPN ISSN 1340-6264
➤ **NIHON GAISHO GAKKAI ZASSHI/JAPANESE ASSOCIATION FOR THE SURGERY OF TRAUMA. JOURNAL.** Text in Japanese; Abstracts in English. 1987. 4/yr. JPY 2,000 (effective 2003). adv. **Document type:** *Academic/Scholarly.*
Formerly (until 1994): Nihon Gaisho Kenkyukaishi (0914-4927)
—BLDSC (4809.095000). **CCC.**
Published by: Nihon Gaisho Gakkai/Japanese Association for the Surgery of Trauma, Rakuyo Bldg 4F, 519 Wasedatsurumakicho, Shinjuku-ku, Tokyo, 162-0041, Japan. TEL 81-3-52916259, FAX 81-3-52912176, jast@shunkosha.com, http://jast-hp.org/. Ed. Kazuhiko Maekawa. Pub. Kunio Kobayashi. Adv. contact Toshio Nakatani. page JPY 30,000. Circ: 1,350 (controlled).

➤ **NIHON GAISHOU SHIGAKKAI ZASSHI/JAPAN ASSOCIATION OF DENTAL TRAUMATOLOGY. JOURNAL.** *see* MEDICAL SCIENCES—Dentistry

617.3 JPN ISSN 1340-8852
NIHON GAKU TOGAI KINO GAKKAISHI/JAPAN ASSOCIATION OF CRANIO-MANDIBULAR ORTHOPEDICS. JOURNAL. Text in Multiple languages. 1988. a. back issues avail. **Document type:** *Journal, Academic/Scholarly.*
Formerly (until 1994): Nihon Gaku Togai Kino Kenkyukaishi (0915-8766)
—CCC.
Published by: Nihon Gaku Togai Kino Kenkyukai, c/o Center for Academic Societies Japan, Osaka, 14th Fl, Senri Life Science Center Bldg., 1-4-2 Shinsenrihigashi-machi, Togonaka, 560-0082, Japan.

617.3 JPN ISSN 1881-9893
➤ **NIHON KOTSU, KANSETSU KANSENSHOU GAKKAI ZASSHI/JAPANESE SOCIETY FOR STUDY OF BONE AND JOINT INFECTIONS. JOURNAL.** Text in Japanese. 1978. a. membership. **Document type:** *Journal, Academic/Scholarly.*
Former titles (until 2005): Nihon Kotsu, Kansetsu Kansenshou Kenkyuukai Zasshi (1345-8922); (until 1997): Kotsu, Kansetsu Kansenshou/Japanese Society for Study of Bone and Joint Infections. Proceedings of the Annual Meeting; Nihon Kotsu Kansetsu Kansensho Kenkyukai
Published by: Nihon Kotsu Kansetsu Kansensho Kenkyukai/Japanese Society of Rheumatism and Joint Surgery, c/o Kyorin University School of Medicine, Department of Orthopaedics, 6-20-2 Shinkawa, Mitaka, Tokyo, 181-8611, Japan. TEL 81-422-475511 ext 3622, FAX 81-422-484206.

617.3 JPN ISSN 0917-4648
NIHON KOTSU KEITAI KEISOKU GAKKAI ZASSHI/JAPANESE SOCIETY OF BONE MORPHOMETRY. JOURNAL. Text in Japanese; Summaries in English, Japanese. 1991. 2/yr.
Indexed: INIS AtomInd.
—CCC.
Published by: Nihon Kotsu Keitai Keisoku Gakkai/Japanese Society for Bone Morphometry, c/o Kawasaki Medical School, Department of Radiology, 577 Matsushima, Kurashiki, Okayama 701-0192, Japan. TEL 81-86-4621111, FAX 81-86-4641192, e-jsbm@med.kawasaki-m.ac.jp, http://www.e-jsbm.com/. Circ: 1,000 (controlled).

616.025 JPN ISSN 1348-0928
NIHON KYUUKYUU KANGO GAKKAI ZASSHI. Text in Japanese. 1999. s-a. **Document type:** *Journal, Academic/Scholarly.*
Published by: Nihon Kyuukyuu Kango Gakkai/Japanese Association for Emergency Nursing, c/o Medicus Shuppan, 18-24, Hiroshiba-cho,, Suita, Osaka 564-0052, Japan. jaen-adm@umin.ac.jp.

617.3 JPN ISSN 1340-9018
NIHON RINSHO BAIOMEKANIKUSU GAKKAISHI/JAPANESE SOCIETY FOR CLINICAL BIOMECHANICS AND RELATED RESEARCH. PROCEEDINGS OF ANNUAL MEETING. Text in English, Japanese; Summaries in English. 1980. a. JPY 8,000 membership (effective 2006). **Document type:** *Proceedings, Academic/Scholarly.*
Formerly (until 1992): Seikei Geka Baiomekanikusu/Japanese Society for Orthopaedic Biomechanics. Proceedings of Annual Meeting (0289-1565)
—CCC.
Published by: Nihon Rinsho Baiomekanikusu Gakkai/Japanese Society for Clinical Biomechanics, Osaka University, Graduate School of Medicine, Department of Orthopedics, 2-2 Yamadaoka, Suita, 565-0871, Japan. TEL 81-6-68793552, FAX 81-6-68793559, biomecha@ort.med.osaka-u.ac.jp, http://www.clin-biomechanics.org/.

617.3 JPN ISSN 0912-0580
NIHON RINSHO SEIKEI GEKAIKAI KAISHI/JAPANESE CLINICAL ORTHOPAEDIC ASSOCIATION. JOURNAL. Text in Japanese. 1976. 3/yr. **Document type:** *Journal, Academic/Scholarly.*
Published by: Nihon Rinsho Seikei Geka Ikai/Japanese Clinical Orthopaedic Association, 4-26-8 Taito Taitoku, Tokyo, 110-0016, Japan. TEL 81-3-38395363, FAX 81-3-38395366, zimu@jcoa.gr.jp, http://www.jcoa.gr.jp/.

617.3 616.075 JPN ISSN 0915-7107
➤ **NIHON SEIKEI GEKA CHOONPA KENKYUKAI KAISHI/JAPANESE SOCIETY OF ORTHOPEDIC ULTRASONICS. JOURNAL.** Text in Japanese. 1989. a. **Document type:** *Journal, Academic/Scholarly.*
Published by: Nihon Seikei Geka Choonpa Kenkyukai/Japanese Society of Orthopedic Ultrasoics, Surugadai Nihon University Hospital, Department of Orthopaedic Surgery, 1-8-13 Kandasurugadai, Chiyoda-ku, Tokyo, 101-8309, Japan. TEL 81-3-32931711 ext 425, FAX 81-3-32920307, orthecho@med.nihon-u.ac.jp, http://ortho.med.nagoya-u.ac.jp/jasou/. Ed. Hiromi Matsuzaki.

617 JPN ISSN 0916-1643
NIHON SEIKEI GEKA SUPOTSU IGAKKAISHI/JAPANESE JOURNAL OF ORTHOPEDIC SPORTS MEDICINE. Text in Japanese. 1982. a. membership.
Published by: Nihon Seikei Geka Supotsu Igakkai/Japanese Orthopedic Society for Sports Medicine, Yokohama Shiritsu Kowan Byoin Seikei Geka, 2-3, Shin'yamashita 3-chome, Naka-ku, Yokohama-shi, Kanagawa-ken 231, Japan.

617.3 JPN ISSN 1346-4876
NIHON SEKITSUI SEKIZUIBYOU GAKKAI ZASSHI/JAPAN SPINE RESEARCH SOCIETY. JOURNAL. Text in English, Japanese. 1990. a. **Document type:** *Journal, Academic/Scholarly.*

ormerly (until 2000): Nihon Sekitsui Geka Gakkai Zasshi/Japan Spine Research Society. Journal (0915-6496)
—BLDSC (6113.049800), IE, Ingenta.
ublished by: Nihon Sekitsui Geka Gakkai/Japan Spine Research Society, TH Bldg. 2F, 2-40-8 Hongo, Bunkyo-ku, Tokyo, 160-0016, Japan. TEL 81-3-38152270, FAX 81-3-38152495, http://www.jsrs.jp.

617.3 616.89 JPN ISSN 1348-3242
IHON SEKIZUI SHOUGAI IGAKKAI ZASSHI/JAPAN MEDICAL SOCIETY OF PARAPLEGIA. JOURNAL. Text in English, Japanese; Summaries in English. 1988. a. **Document type:** *Journal, Academic/ Scholarly.*
ormerly (until 2002): Nihon Parapurejia Igakkai Zasshi (0914-6822)
ndexed: E-psyche.
ublished by: Nihon Parapurejia Igakkai/Japan Medical Society of Paraplegia, 3-13-20 Katase-Kaigan, Tokyo, Kanagawa 251-0035, Japan. TEL 81-466-279724, FAX 81-466-279723.

IHON SHONI SEIKEI GEKA GAKKAI ZASSHI/JAPANESE PAEDIATRIC ORTHOPEDIC ASSOCIATION. JOURNAL. *see* MEDICAL SCIENCES—Pediatrics

617.3 JPN ISSN 1342-3495
IHON SOGAI KOTEI, KOTSU ENCHO GAKKAI ZASSHI/JAPANESE ASSOCIATION OF EXTERNAL FIXATION AND LIMB LENGTHENING. JOURNAL. Text in Japanese; Summaries in English. 1990. a. **Document type:** *Journal, Academic/Scholarly.*
ormerly (until 1996): Nihon Sogai Kotei Kenkyukaishi/Japanese Society of External Fixation. Journal (0915-4906)
ublished by: Nihon Sogai Kotei, Kotsu Encho Gakkai/Japanese Association of External Fixation and Limb Lengthening, Yamauchi Hospital, 3-7-22 Ichihashi, Gifu, 500-8381, Japan. TEL 81-58-2680567, FAX 81-58-2680568, http://ortho.aa2.netvolante.jp/jaefll/.

617.3 JPN ISSN 0910-5700
IHON TE NO GEKA GAKKAI ZASSHI/JAPANESE SOCIETY FOR SURGERY OF THE HAND. JOURNAL. Text in Japanese; Summaries in English. 1984. 6/yr. **Document type:** *Journal, Academic/Scholarly.*
dexed: A22, INIS AtomInd.
-BLDSC (4809.518000), IE, Ingenta.
ublished by: Nihon Te no Geka Gakkai/Japanese Society for Surgery of the Hand, c/o His Brains, Inc., 1013 Otokikiyama, Tempaku-ku, Nagoya, 468-0063, Japan. TEL 81-52-8363511, FAX 81-52-8363510, info@jssh.gr.jp.

615.82 JPN ISSN 1345-9074
IHON YOTSU GAKKAI ZASSHI/JAPANESE SOCIETY FOR LUMBAR SPINE DISORDERS. JOURNAL. Text in Japanese. 1995. a. **Document type:** *Journal, Academic/Scholarly.*
ormerly (until 2000): Nihon Yotsu Kenkyukai Zasshi (1341-7355)
elated titles: Online - full text ed.: ISSN 1882-1863.
ublished by: Nihon Yotsu Gakkai/Japanese Society for Lumbar Spine Disorders, Nippon Medical School Hospital, 1-1-5 Sendagi, Bunkyo-ku, Tokyo, 113-0022, Japan. TEL 81-3-38222131, FAX 81-3-56851796.

617.3 JPN ISSN 0914-6636
IGATA SEIKEI GEKA KENKYUKAI KAISHI/NIIGATA SOCIETY FOR ORTHOPAEDIC SURGERY. ARCHIVES. Text in Japanese. 1983. a. **Document type:** *Journal, Academic/Scholarly.*
ublished by: Niigata Seikei Geka Kenkyukai/Niigata Society for Orthopaedic Surgery, Niigata University, Faculty of Medicine, Department of Orthopaedic Surgery, 1, Asahimachi Dori, Niigata-shi, Niigata-ken 951, Japan.

617.3 JPN ISSN 0021-5325
CODEN: NSGZA2
PPON SEIKEI GEKA GAKKAI ZASSHI/JAPANESE ORTHOPAEDIC ASSOCIATION. JOURNAL. Text in Japanese. 1926. m. JPY 20,000 domestic; EUR 200 to elsewhere other than Japan and the Americas (effective 2003). **Document type:** *Journal, Academic/Scholarly.* **Description:** Documents the latest research and topical debates in all fields of clinical and experimental orthopedics. Topics include original articles, rapid short communications, instructional lectures, review articles, and letters to the editor.
elated titles: Online - full content ed.
dexed: A22, INIS AtomInd, P30, SCOPUS.
BLDSC (4809.370000), Infotrieve, INIST.
ublished by: (Nippon Seikei Geka Gakkai/Japanese Orthopaedic Association), Springer Japan KK (Subsidiary of: Springer Science+Business Media), No 2 Funato Bldg, 1-11-11 Kudan-kita, Chiyoda-ku, Tokyo, 102-0073, Japan. TEL 81-3-3812-0617, FAX 81-3-3812-4699, http://www.springer.jp. Ed. Tetsuya Tamaki. **Subscr. in US & the Americas to:** Springer New York LLC, 233 Spring St, New York, NY 10013. TEL 201-348-4033, 800-777-4643, FAX 201-348-4505, http://www.springer.com/.

617.3 JPN ISSN 0287-1092
SHINIHON SEKITSUI KENKYUKAISHI/WESTERN JAPANESE RESEARCH SOCIETY FOR SPINE. JOURNAL. Text in Japanese. a. JPY 6,000.
blished by: Nishinihon Sekitsui Kenkyukai/Western Japanese Research Society for Spine, Yamaguchi University School of Medicine, Department of Orthopaedic Surgery, 1-1-1 Minami-Kogushi, Ube, Yamaguchi 755-8505, Japan.

616.7 DEU ISSN 1614-3078
T DURCH HIRNVERLETZUNG, SCHLAGANFALL ODER SONSTIGE ERWORBENE HIRNSCHAEDEN. Variant title: Not. Text in German. 1992. bi-m. EUR 30 domestic; EUR 40 foreign; EUR 6.50 newsstand/cover (effective 2008). adv. **Document type:** *Magazine, Trade.*
rmer titles (until 2003): Not der Schaedel-Hirnverletzten und Schlaganfall-Patienten (1616-2234); (until 1998): Not (0947-4315)
blished by: H W - Studio Weber, Gewerbegebiet 39, Leimersheim, 76774, Germany. TEL 49-7272-92750, FAX 49-7272-927544, info@hw-studio.de, http://www.hw-studio.de. adv.: B&W page EUR 1,296, color page EUR 1,796; trim 184 x 258. Circ: 9,486 (paid and controlled).

610 DEU ISSN 1865-0791
NOTFALL UND HAUSARZTMEDIZIN. Text in German. 2006. m. EUR 116 to institutions; EUR 157 to institutions (print & online eds.); EUR 18 newsstand/cover (effective 2010). **Document type:** *Journal, Academic/Scholarly.*
Formed by the merger of (1975-2006): Notfall und Hausarztmedizin. Fokus auf Hausarztmedizin (1612-8583); (1975-2006): Notfall und Hausarztmedizin. Fokus auf Notfallmedizin (1612-8591); Both of which superseded in part (in 2004): Notfall-Medizin in der Taeglichen Praxis (1617-0482); Which was formerly (until 2000): Notfall-Medizin (0341-2903)
Related titles: Online - full text ed.: ISSN 1865-0805. 2006. EUR 151 to institutions (effective 2010).
—CCC.
Published by: Georg Thieme Verlag, Ruedigerstr 14, Stuttgart, 70469, Germany. TEL 49-711-8931421, FAX 49-711-8931410, leser.service@thieme.de, http://www.thieme.de.

616.025 DEU ISSN 1434-6222
RC86
➤ **NOTFALL UND RETTUNGSMEDIZIN**; German interdisciplinary journal of emergency medicine. Variant title: Notfall. Text in German. 1998. 8/yr. EUR 254, USD 288 combined subscription to institutions (print & online eds.) (effective 2012). adv. back issues avail.; reprint service avail. from PSC. **Document type:** *Journal, Academic/ Scholarly.* **Description:** Contains new developments and information on the practices and procedures of emergency medicine.
Related titles: Online - full text ed.: ISSN 1436-0578 (from IngentaConnect).
Indexed: A22, A26, E01, EMBASE, ExcerpMed, SCI, SCOPUS, W07.
—BLDSC (6170.075000), IE, Infotrieve, Ingenta. **CCC.**
Published by: Springer (Subsidiary of: Springer Science+Business Media), Tiergartenstr 17, Heidelberg, 69121, Germany. TEL 49-6221-4870, FAX 49-6221-345229. Circ: 3,300 (paid and controlled). **Subscr. in the Americas to:** Springer New York LLC, Journal Fulfillment, PO Box 2485, Secaucus, NJ 07096. TEL 800-777-4643, 201-348-4033, FAX 201-348-4505, journals-ny@springer.com, http://www.springer.com; **Subscr. to:** Springer Distribution Center, Kundenservice Zeitschriften, Haberstr 7, Heidelberg 69126, Germany. TEL 49-6221-3454303, FAX 49-6221-3454229, subscriptions@springer.com.

610 DEU ISSN 1611-6550
RC86
NOTFALLMEDIZIN UP2DATE. Text in German. 2006. 4/yr. EUR 140 to institutions; EUR 192 combined subscription to institutions (print & online eds.); EUR 44 newsstand/cover (effective 2011). adv. **Document type:** *Journal, Academic/Scholarly.*
Related titles: Online - full text ed.: ISSN 1862-6955. 2006. EUR 185 to institutions (effective 2011).
—IE. **CCC.**
Published by: Georg Thieme Verlag, Ruedigerstr 14, Stuttgart, 70469, Germany. TEL 49-711-8931421, FAX 49-711-8931410, leser.service@thieme.de. Circ: 3,000 (paid).

617.3 USA ISSN 1061-4621
O & P ALMANAC; the magazine for the orthotics & prosthetics industry. (Orthotics and Prosthetics) Text in English. 1951. m. adv. 84 p./no.; back issues avail. **Document type:** *Magazine, Trade.* **Description:** Covers professional, business, association and government activities affecting the field.
Formerly (until 1991): American Orthotic and Prosthetic Association. Almanac (0279-6953)
Indexed: H01.
Published by: American Orthotic & Prosthetic Asssociation, 330 John Carlyle St., Ste 200, Alexandria, VA 22314. TEL 571-431-0816, FAX 571-431-0899. Ed., R&P Lisa L Gough. Pub. Tyler J Wilson. Adv. contact Amy Clontz TEL 888-557-7277. B&W page USD 1,310, color page USD 2,800; bleed 8.5 x 11.125. Circ: 8,500 (paid).

617.23 330 USA ISSN 1060-3220
O & P BUSINESS NEWS. (Orthotics & Prosthetics) Text in English. 1992. s-m. USD 149 to individuals; USD 239 to institutions; USD 39 per issue (effective 2010). adv. reprints avail. **Document type:** *Magazine, Trade.* **Description:** Delivers timely coverage of the most important advances in the field of orthotics and prosthetics.
Related titles: Online - full content ed.
Indexed: CA, P20, P24, P48, P54, PQC, SD, T02.
—CCC.
Published by: Slack, Inc., 6900 Grove Rd, Thorofare, NJ 08086. TEL 856-848-1000, FAX 856-848-6091, customerservice@slackinc.com, http://www.slackinc.com.

616.7 DEU ISSN 1862-6599
RD557
➤ **OBERE EXTREMITAET**; Schulter - Ellenbogen - Hand. Text in German. 2006. 4/yr. EUR 361, USD 434 combined subscription to institutions (print & online eds.) (effective 2012). adv. reprint service avail. from PSC. **Document type:** *Journal, Academic/Scholarly.*
Related titles: Online - full text ed.: ISSN 1862-6602.
Indexed: A22, A26, E01, SCOPUS.
—BLDSC (6196.728000), IE, Ingenta. **CCC.**
Published by: Dr. Dietrich Steinkopff Verlag (Subsidiary of: Springer Science+Business Media), Tiergartenstr 17, Heidelberg, 69121, Germany. TEL 49-6221-4878821, FAX 49-6221-4878830, info.steinkopff@springer.com, http://www.steinkopff.com. Ed. Dr. Markus Loew. adv.: B&W page EUR 1,440, color page EUR 2,480; trim 210 x 279. Circ: 980 (paid).

616.025 NLD ISSN 1876-5424
RC86
➤ **THE OPEN EMERGENCY MEDICINE JOURNAL.** Text in English. 2008. irreg. free (effective 2011). **Document type:** *Journal, Academic/Scholarly.*
Media: Online - full text.
Published by: Bentham Open (Subsidiary of: Bentham Science Publishers Ltd.), PO Box 294, Bussum, AG 1400, Netherlands. TEL 31-35-6923800, FAX 31-35-6980150, subscriptions@bentham.org.

616.7 NLD ISSN 1874-3250
RD701
➤ **THE OPEN ORTHOPAEDICS JOURNAL.** Text in English. 2007. irreg. free (effective 2011). **Document type:** *Journal, Academic/Scholarly.* **Description:** Publishes research articles, reviews and letters in all areas of experimental and clinical research and surgery in orthopaedics.
Media: Online - full text.
Indexed: A01, CA, CTA, P30, T02.
Published by: Bentham Open (Subsidiary of: Bentham Science Publishers Ltd.), PO Box 294, Bussum, AG 1400, Netherlands. TEL 31-35-6923800, FAX 31-35-6980150, subscriptions@bentham.org. Ed. Philippe Hernigou.

616.7 NLD ISSN 1876-5327
RD768
➤ **THE OPEN SPINE JOURNAL.** Text in English. 2008. irreg. free (effective 2011). **Document type:** *Journal, Academic/Scholarly.*
Media: Online - full text.
Indexed: CTA, NSA.
Published by: Bentham Open (Subsidiary of: Bentham Science Publishers Ltd.), PO Box 294, Bussum, AG 1400, Netherlands. TEL 31-35-6923800, FAX 31-35-6980150, subscriptions@bentham.org. Ed. Toru Hasegawa.

617.3 DEU ISSN 0934-6694
RD701 CODEN: OOTPAK
➤ **OPERATIVE ORTHOPAEDIE UND TRAUMATOLOGIE**; Standardeingriffe und neue Verfahren. Text in German. 1989. 5/yr. EUR 347, USD 291 combined subscription to institutions (print & online eds.) (effective 2012). adv. bk.rev. back issues avail.; reprint service avail. from PSC. **Document type:** *Journal, Academic/ Scholarly.*
Related titles: Online - full text ed.: ISSN 1439-0981 (from IngentaConnect); ◆ Spanish Translation: Tecnicas Quirurgicas en Ortopedia y Traumatologia. ISSN 1132-1954.
Indexed: A22, A26, E01, EMBASE, ExcerpMed, MEDLINE, P30, R10, Reac, SCI, SCOPUS, W07.
—BLDSC (6269.380500), GNLM, IE, Infotrieve, Ingenta. **CCC.**
Published by: Urban und Vogel Medien und Medizin Verlagsgesellschaft mbH (Subsidiary of: Springer Science+Business Media), Neumarkter Str 43, Munich, 81673, Germany. TEL 49-89-4372-1411, FAX 49-89-4372-1410, verlag@urban-vogel.de. Ed. Anna-Maria Worsch. Adv. contact Peter Urban. B&W page EUR 1,900, color page EUR 3,100; trim 174 x 240. Circ: 3,500 (paid and controlled). **Subscr. to:** Springer Distribution Center, Kundenservice Zeitschriften, Haberstr 7, Heidelberg 69126, Germany. TEL 49-6221-3454303, FAX 49-6221-3454229, subscriptions@springer.com.

617 USA ISSN 1048-6666
RD701 CODEN: OTOPAU
➤ **OPERATIVE TECHNIQUES IN ORTHOPAEDICS.** Text in English. 1991. q. USD 547 in United States to institutions; USD 639 elsewhere to institutions (effective 2012). adv. illus. back issues avail.; reprints avail. **Document type:** *Journal, Academic/Scholarly.* **Description:** Resources that keeps practitioners informed of significant advances in all areas of surgical management and offering alternate approaches to the same procedure.
Related titles: Online - full text ed.: ISSN 1558-3848 (from ScienceDirect); Translation: Tecniche di Chirurgia Ortopedica. ISSN 1593-6910.
Indexed: A22, A26, C06, C07, C08, CA, CINAHL, EMBASE, ExcerpMed, H12, I05, P30, R10, Reac, SCOPUS, T02.
—BLDSC (6269.381500), GNLM, IE, Ingenta. **CCC.**
Published by: W.B. Saunders Co. (Subsidiary of: Elsevier Health Sciences), Elsevier, Health Sciences Division, Order Fulfillment, 3251 Riverport Ln, Maryland Heights, MO 63043. TEL 314-872-8370, 800-325-4177, FAX 314-432-1380, JournalCustomerService-usa@elsevier.com, http://www.us.elsevierhealth.com. Ed. Dr. Freddie Fu. Pub. Jason Miller. Adv. contact John Marmero TEL 212-633-3657.

616.7 USA
ORTHOCAROLINA. Text in English. 2008. 2/yr. adv. **Document type:** *Magazine, Trade.* **Description:** Provides up-to-date information on the latest medical advances, research, patient care, practice and physician achievements.
Published by: (OrthoCarolina), G L C Custom Publishing, 900 Skokie Blvd, Ste 200, Northbrook, IL 60062. TEL 847-205-3000, 800-641-3912, FAX 847-564-8197, jcimba@glcomm.com, http://www.glcomm.com. Circ: 25,000 (controlled).

616.7 DEU ISSN 1865-5181
ORTHODOC. Text in German. 2000. bi-m. EUR 3 per issue (effective 2009). adv. **Document type:** *Magazine, Consumer.*
Former titles (until 2007): Orthoprof (1613-4486); (until 2004): Orthodoc (1616-3745)
Published by: (Deutsche Gesellschaft fuer Orthopaedie und Orthopaedische Chirurgie, Berufsverband der Fachaerzte fuer Orthopaedie e.V.), Edition Nymphenburg GmbH & Co. KG, Jakob-Endl-Str. 10, Passau, 94032, Germany. TEL 49-851-7201857, FAX 49-851-7201859, edition.nymhenburg@t-online.de. Ed. Heinz Weichselgartner. adv.: page EUR 3,525. Circ: 5,907 (paid and controlled).

617.13 USA
ORTHOKINETIC REVIEW. Text in English. 1984. m. free to qualified personnel (effective 2004). adv. bk.rev. charts; illus. **Document type:** *Magazine, Trade.* **Description:** Provides a source for the most up-to-date news on products, services and technology for podiatrists.
Former titles (until 2000): Podiatric Products (0890-3972); (until 1986): Podiatry Products Report
—CCC.
Published by: Novicom, Inc. (Subsidiary of: Allied Healthcare Group), 6100 Center Dr., # 1000, Los Angeles, CA 90045-9200. Ed. Greg Thompson. Pub. Tony Ramos. adv.: B&W page USD 1,453, color page USD 2,153; trim 8.125 x 10.825. Circ: 14,000 (controlled).

617.3 DEU ISSN 0085-4530
CODEN: ORHPBG
➤ **DER ORTHOPAEDE.** Text in German. 1972. m. EUR 550, USD 607 combined subscription to institutions (print & online eds.) (effective 2012). adv. back issues avail.; reprint service avail. from PSC. **Document type:** *Journal, Academic/Scholarly.* **Description:** Offers information and continuing education for the orthopedic physician. Each issue treats one leding topic from orthopedics or a neighboring discipline and gives an overview of the current state of the science and practice.
Related titles: Microform ed.: (from PQC); Online - full text ed.: ISSN 1433-0431 (from IngentaConnect).
Indexed: A20, A22, A26, ASCA, CA, CurCont, E01, EMBASE, ExcerpMed, INI, IndMed, Inpharma, MEDLINE, P30, P35, R10, Reac, SCI, SCOPUS, T02, W07.
—BLDSC (6296.114000), IE, Infotrieve, Ingenta, INIST. **CCC.**
Published by: Springer (Subsidiary of: Springer Science+Business Media), Tiergartenstr 17, Heidelberg, 69121, Germany. TEL 49-6221-4870, FAX 49-6221-345229. Eds. Dr. C J Wirth, Dr. V Ewerbeck. Adv. contact Stephan Kroeck TEL 49-30-827875739. B&W page EUR 1,660, color page EUR 2,850. Circ: 4,100 (paid and controlled). **Subscr. in the Americas to:** Springer New York LLC,

Journal Fulfillment, PO Box 2485, Secaucus, NJ 07096. TEL 800-777-4643, 201-348-4033, FAX 201-348-4505, journals-ny@springer.com, http://www.springer.com; **Subscr. to:** Springer Distribution Center, Kundenservice Zeitschriften, Haberstr 7, Heidelberg 69126, Germany. TEL 49-6221-3454303, FAX 49-6221-3454229, subscriptions@springer.com.

617.3 JPN ISSN 0289-2855
ORTHOPAEDIC CERAMIC IMPLANTS. Text in English, Japanese; Summaries in English. 1981. a. **Document type:** *Proceedings, Academic/Scholarly.*
Published by: Seikei Geka Seramikku Inpuranto Kenkyukai/Japanese Society of Orthopaedic Ceramic Implants, Kyoto University Hospital, Department of Orthopaedic Surgery, 54 Shogoin-Kawarachou, Sakyou-ku, Kyoto, 606-8507, Japan.

616.7 USA ISSN 1940-4093
ORTHOPAEDIC KNOWLEDGE ONLINE. Abbreviated title: O K O. Text in English. 2002. m. USD 168 to non-members; free to members (effective 2010). **Document type:** *Newsletter, Trade.*
Media: Online - full text.
Published by: American Academy of Orthopaedic Surgeons, 6300 N River Rd, Rosemont, IL 60018. TEL 847-823-7186, 800-346-2267, FAX 847-823-8125, custserv@aaos.org, http://www.aaos.org.

ORTHOPAEDIC NURSING JOURNAL. *see* MEDICAL SCIENCES—Nurses And Nursing

617.3 615.82 USA ISSN 1532-0871
ORTHOPAEDIC PHYSICAL THERAPY PRACTICE. Text in English. 1989. q. adv. bk.rev. **Document type:** *Newsletter.*
Indexed: AMED, C06, C07, C08, CINAHL.
—BLDSC (6296.125550), IE, Ingenta.
Published by: Orthopaedic Section A P T A, 2920 East Ave S, La Crosse, WI 54601-7202. TEL 608-788-3982, FAX 608-788-3965, orthostaff@centuryinter.net. Ed. Jonathan M Cooperman. R&P Sharon L Klinski. Circ: 12,500 (paid).

617.3 GBR ISSN 0954-4755
ORTHOPAEDIC PRODUCT NEWS. Text in English. 1987. 5/yr. GBP 37.99 domestic; GBP 47.99 in Europe; GBP 61.99 elsewhere (effective 2008). adv. illus.; tr.lit. back issues avail. **Document type:** *Magazine, Trade.* **Description:** Provides details of new products and reviews of products for orthopedic surgeons in Europe.
Related titles: Online - full text ed.
Published by: Pelican Magazines Ltd., 2 Cheltenham Mount, Harrogate, HG1 1DL, United Kingdom. TEL 44-1423-569676, FAX 44-1423-569677. Adv. contact Debbie Hall. B&W page GBP 1,100, color page GBP 1,520, B&W page USD 2,400, color page USD 3,750; trim 210 x 297. Circ: 8,500. **Dist. in US by:** Knowledge Enterprises, Inc., 8401 Chagrin Rd, Ste 18, Chagrin Falls, OH 44023. TEL 440-543-2101, FAX 440-543-2122.

616.7 USA ISSN 0149-6433
RD715
ORTHOPAEDIC RESEARCH SOCIETY. TRANSACTIONS OF THE ANNUAL MEETING. Text in English. a. USD 75 per issue (effective 2005). **Document type:** *Proceedings.*
Related titles: CD-ROM ed.: USD 50 (effective 2005).
Indexed: A22.
—BLDSC (9020.228000), IE, Ingenta. **CCC.**
Published by: Orthopaedic Research Society, 6300 N River Rd, Ste 727, Rosemont, IL 60018. TEL 847-698-1625, FAX 847-823-4921, Ors@ors.org, http://www.ors.org.

617.2 GBR ISSN 1877-1327
RD701 CODEN: CUOREH
➤ **ORTHOPAEDICS AND TRAUMA.** Text in English. 1986. 6/yr. EUR 949 in Europe to institutions; JPY 102,500 in Japan to institutions; USD 844 elsewhere to institutions (effective 2012). adv. illus. back issues avail.; reprints avail. **Document type:** *Journal, Academic/Scholarly.* **Description:** Reviews topics in orthopedics for qualified and trainee orthopedic surgeons.
Formerly (until 2009): Current Orthopaedics (0268-0890)
Related titles: Microfilm ed.; Online - full text ed.: ISSN 1877-1335 (from ScienceDirect).
Indexed: A22, A26, AMED, ASCA, C06, C07, C08, CA, CINAHL, E01, EMBASE, ExcerpMed, H12, I05, P30, R10, Reac, SCOPUS, T02.
—BLDSC (6296.127650), GNLM, IE, Infotrieve, Ingenta. **CCC.**
Published by: The Medicine Publishing Company (Subsidiary of: Elsevier Ltd), The Boulevard, Langford Ln, Kidlington, Oxford, OX5 1GB, United Kingdom. TEL 44-1865-843154, FAX 44-1865-843965, JournalsCustomerServiceEMEA@elsevier.com, http://www.medicinepublishing.co.uk. Ed. Roger Wayman. Circ: 1,395.

616.7 FRA ISSN 1877-0568
RD701
▼ **ORTHOPAEDICS & TRAUMATOLOGY: SURGERY & RESEARCH.** Text in English. 2009. irreg. EUR 580 in Europe to institutions; JPY 69,600 in Japan to institutions; USD 754 elsewhere to institutions (effective 2011). **Document type:** *Journal, Academic/Scholarly.*
Media: Online - full text (from ScienceDirect).
Indexed: CurCont, EMBASE, ExcerpMed, MEDLINE, P30, SCI, SCOPUS, W07.
—BLDSC (6296.127800), IE. **CCC.**
Published by: Elsevier Masson (Subsidiary of: Elsevier Health Sciences), 62 Rue Camille Desmoulins, Issy les Moulineaux, Cedex 92442, France. TEL 33-1-71165500, FAX 33-1-71165600, infos@elsevier-masson.fr, http://www.elsevier-masson.fr. Ed. Jean-Michel Thomine.

616.7 IND
ORTHOPAEDICS TODAY. Text in English. 19??. q. **Document type:** *Journal, Academic/Scholarly.*
Published by: C M P Medica (Subsidiary of: C M P Medica Ltd.), Sagar Tech Plz A 615-617, 6th Fl, Andheri Kurla Rd, Saki Naka Jct, Andheri E, Mumbai, 400 072, India. TEL 91-22-66122600, FAX 91-22-66122626, info.india@ubm.com, http://www.ubmindia.in/cmp-medica.asp.

617.3 USA ISSN 1942-6275
➤ **ORTHOPAEDICS TODAY EUROPE.** Text in English. 1997. bi-m. USD 199 to individuals; USD 329 to institutions; USD 39 per issue (effective 2009). adv. **Document type:** *Newspaper, Academic/Scholarly.* **Description:** The official newspaper of EFORT focuses on news coverage of the latest studies and newest techniques in orthopaedic surgery as presented at scientific meetings throughout the world.
Formerly (until 2008): Orthopaedics Today International (1095-4341)
Related titles: Online - full content ed.
Indexed: A01, P20, P48, P54, PQC.
—**CCC.**
Published by: (European Federation of National Associations of Orthopaedics and Trauma (EFORT) CHE), Slack, Inc., 6900 Grove Rd, Thorofare, NJ 08086. TEL 856-848-1000, 800-257-8290, FAX 856-848-6091, customerservice@slackinc.com, http://www.slackinc.com. Ed. David Hamblen. Pub. John C. Carter. adv.: B&W page USD 4,860; trim 10.5 x 14. Circ: 16,877 (paid).

617.3 DEU ISSN 1439-2542
➤ **ORTHOPAEDIE MITTEILUNGEN (STUTTGART).** Text in German. 1996. bi-m. EUR 188 to institutions; EUR 38 newsstand/cover (effective 2011). adv. **Document type:** *Journal, Academic/Scholarly.*
Formerly (until 1998): Orthopaedie (Stuttgart) (1430-3388); Which was formed by the merger of (19??-1996): Orthopaedie-Mitteilungen (0941-214X); Which was formerly (until 1991): Deutsche Gesellschaft fuer Orthopaedie und Traumatologie. Mitteilungsblatt (0723-8002); (19??-1996): Berufsverband der Aerzte fuer Orthopaedie. Informationen (0931-6779); Which was formerly (until 1985): Berufsverband der Fachaerzte fuer Orthopaedie. Informationen (0723-7073)
—BLDSC (6296.114575).
Published by: Georg Thieme Verlag, Ruedigerstr 14, Stuttgart, 70469, Germany. TEL 49-711-8931421, FAX 49-711-8931410, leser.service@thieme.de. Adv. contact Christine Volpp TEL 49-711-8931603. Circ: 8,700 (paid and controlled).

615.477 DEU ISSN 0340-5591
ORTHOPAEDIE-TECHNIK. Text in German. 1949. m. EUR 109 domestic; EUR 143 foreign; EUR 9.50 newsstand/cover (effective 2009). adv. **Document type:** *Journal, Academic/Scholarly.*
Indexed: A22, TM.
—BLDSC (6296.115000), IE, Ingenta.
Published by: Bundesinnungsverband fuer Orthopaedie-Technik, Reinoldistr 7-9, Dortmund, 44135, Germany. TEL 49-231-55705050, FAX 49-231-55705070. Ed. Dirk Boecker. Adv. contact Gudrun Bramsiepe. B&W page EUR 1,560, color page EUR 2,760; trim 185 x 265. Circ: 5,004 (paid and controlled).

617.3 DEU
➤ **ORTHOPAEDIE TECHNIK QUARTERLY.** Text in English. 2000. q. back issues avail. **Document type:** *Journal, Academic/Scholarly.* **Description:** Covers all aspects of prosthetics, orthotics, and rehabilitation technology.
Media: Online - full text.
Published by: Bundesinnungsverband fuer Orthopaedie-Technik, Reinoldistr 7-9, Dortmund, 44135, Germany. TEL 49-231-55705050, FAX 49-231-55705070, info@ot-forum.de. Ed. Dirk Boecker.

617.3 DEU ISSN 1435-0017
➤ **ORTHOPAEDIE UND RHEUMA.** Text in German. 1998. bi-m. EUR 122, USD 133 to institutions (effective 2012). adv. **Document type:** *Journal, Academic/Scholarly.*
Former titles: Orthopaedie und Rheuma Praxisinformation; Orthopaedie und Rheuma Nachrichten
Indexed: A26.
—IE. **CCC.**
Published by: Urban und Vogel Medien und Medizin Verlagsgesellschaft mbH (Subsidiary of: Springer Science+Business Media), Neumarkter Str 43, Munich, 81673, Germany. TEL 49-89-4372-1411, FAX 49-89-4372-1410, verlag@urban-vogel.de, http://www.urban-vogel.de. Ed. Claudia Maeck. Adv. contact Paul Berger TEL 49-89-4372-1342. B&W page EUR 2,100, color page EUR 3,350; trim 174 x 237. Circ: 6,500 (paid). **Subscr. to:** Springer Distribution Center, Kundenservice Zeitschriften. subscriptions@springer.com.

616.7 DEU ISSN 1611-7859
ORTHOPAEDIE UND UNFALLCHIRURGIE UP2DATE. Text in German. 2006. bi-m. EUR 172 to institutions; EUR 233 combined subscription to institutions (print & online eds.); EUR 35 newsstand/cover (effective 2011). adv. **Document type:** *Journal, Academic/Scholarly.*
Related titles: Online - full text ed.: ISSN 1861-1982. EUR 223 to institutions (effective 2011).
—**CCC.**
Published by: Georg Thieme Verlag, Ruedigerstr 14, Stuttgart, 70469, Germany. TEL 49-711-8931421, FAX 49-711-8931410, kunden.service@thieme.de. Adv. contact Christine Volpp TEL 49-711-8931603. Circ: 4,950 (paid and controlled).

616.7 DEU ISSN 1437-2193
ORTHOPAEDISCHE NACHRICHTEN. Text in German. 1996. m. adv. **Document type:** *Journal, Trade.*
Published by: Biermann Verlag GmbH, Otto-Hahn-Str 7, Cologne, 50997, Germany. TEL 49-2236-3760, FAX 49-2236-376999, info@biermann.net, http://www.biermann-verlag.de. Ed. Felix Hoefele. Adv. contact Larissa Apisa. Circ: 8,421 (controlled).

617.3 DEU ISSN 0030-588X
CODEN: OPBAAS
ORTHOPAEDISCHE PRAXIS; mit Traumatologie, Rheumatologie, physikalischer, physiotherapeutischer und balneologischer Therapie des Bewegungsapparates. Text in German. 1965. m. EUR 116.10; EUR 87.10 to students; EUR 11.80 newsstand/cover (effective 2008). adv. bk.rev. charts; illus. index, cum.index. back issues avail. **Document type:** *Journal, Academic/Scholarly.*
Indexed: A22, IBR, IBZ.
—GNLM, IE, Ingenta. **CCC.**
Published by: (Vereinigung Sueddeutscher Orthopaeden e.V.), Medizinisch Literarische Verlagsgesellschaft mbH, Postfach 1151-1152, Uelzen, 29501, Germany. TEL 49-581-808151, FAX 49-581-808158, mlverlag@mlverlag.de. Eds. Dr. D Clemens, Dr. G Rompe. adv.: B&W page EUR 1,550, color page EUR 2,700. Circ: 5,500 (paid and controlled).

617.3 USA ISSN 0030-5898
CODEN: OCLNAQ
➤ **ORTHOPEDIC CLINICS OF NORTH AMERICA.** Text in English. 1970. q. USD 513 in United States to institutions; USD 615 elsewhere to institutions (effective 2012). adv. charts; illus. index. back issues avail.; reprints avail. **Document type:** *Journal, Academic/Scholarly.* **Description:** Discusses the practical information on the diagnosis and treatment of conditions affecting the musculoskeletal system.
Related titles: Microform ed. (from PQC); Online - full text ed.: ISSN 1558-1373 (from ScienceDirect).
Indexed: A22, AIM, AMED, ASCA, B21, BDM&CN, C06, C07, C08, CINAHL, CTA, CurCont, EMBASE, ExcerpMed, FR, ISR, IndMed, Inpharma, MEDLINE, P30, R10, Reac, SCI, SCOPUS, W07.
—BLDSC (6296.135000), GNLM, IE, Infotrieve, Ingenta, INIST. **CCC.**
Published by: W.B. Saunders Co. (Subsidiary of: Elsevier Health Sciences), Elsevier, Health Sciences Division, Order Fulfillment, 3251 Riverport Ln, Maryland Heights, MO 63043. TEL 314-872-8370, 800-325-4177, FAX 314-432-1380, JournalCustomerService-usa@elsevier.com, http://www.us.elsevierhealth.com. Adv. contact John Marmero TEL 212-633-3657.

616.7 368.382 USA ISSN 1941-7837
ORTHOPEDIC CODER'S PINK SHEET. Text in English. 19??. m. USD 450 combined subscription (print & online eds.) (effective 2011). adv. **Document type:** *Newsletter, Trade.* **Description:** Devoted exclusively to coding and billing orthopedic services.
Formerly (until 2003): Orthopaedic Practice Coder
Related titles: Online - full text ed.: ISSN 1941-7853.
Published by: DecisionHealth (Subsidiary of: United Communications Group), Two Washingtonian Ctr, 9737 Washingtonian Blvd, Ste 100, Gaithersburg, MD 20878. TEL 855-225-5341, FAX 301-287-2535, customer@decisionhealth.com, http://www.decisionhealth.com. Ed. Laura Evans.

ORTHOPEDIC CODING ALERT; Your practical adviser for ethically optimizing coding, reimbursement, and efficiency for orthopedic practices. *see* INSURANCE

616.7 338 USA ISSN 2157-1449
ORTHOPEDIC DESIGN & TECHNOLOGY. Abbreviated title: O D T. Text in English. 2005. bi-m. free to qualified personnel (effective 2010). back issues avail. **Document type:** *Magazine, Trade.* **Description:** Covers the design and manufacturing of orthopedic products. Contains comprehensive articles, industry news, trends and technological advances and developments.
Related titles: Online - full text ed.
Indexed: V03.
Published by: Rodman Publishing, Corp., 70 Hilltop Rd, 3rd Fl, Ramsey, NJ 07446. TEL 201-825-2552, FAX 201-825-0553, info@rodpub.com, http://www.rodmanpublishing.com. Ed. Tom Branna TEL 201-880-2223. Adv. contact Howard A Revitch TEL 201-880-2243. Circ: 7,500.

317.305 USA ISSN 1059-311X
ORTHOPEDIC NETWORK NEWS. Text in English. 1990. q. **Document type:** *Newsletter, Trade.* **Description:** Collects and reports information on procedures, pricing, manufacturer market share, payments to hospitals and physicians.
Published by: Mendenhall Associates, 1500 Cedar Bend Dr, Ann Arbor, MI 48105. TEL 734-741-4710, FAX 734-741-7277. Ed., Pub. Stan Mendenhall. **Subscr. enquiries to:** PO Box 830430, Birmingham, AL 35823-0430. TEL 800-633-4931, FAX 205-995-1588.

616.0754 USA
ORTHOPEDIC, NEUROLOGICAL AND CHIROPRACTIC PHYSICAL EXAMINATIONS: TECHNIQUE AND SIGNIFICANCE. Text in English. 1988. irreg., latest 1988. USD 55 per issue (effective 2008). 80 p./no.; **Document type:** *Monographic series, Trade.* **Description:** Includes an alphabetical listing of the various types of examinations, a summary of different conditions and which examinations might be performed to detect them, and a diagram setting out the planes of the body.
Related titles: Online - full text ed.
Indexed: E-psyche.
Published by: Michie Company (Subsidiary of: LexisNexis North America), 701 E Water St, Charlottesville, VA 22902. TEL 434-972-7600, 800-446-3410, FAX 434-972-7677, customer.support@lexisnexis.com, http://www.michie.com. Ed. Barry Creighton.

616.7 GBR ISSN 1179-1462
▼ **ORTHOPEDIC RESEARCH AND REVIEWS.** Text in English. 2009. irreg. free (effective 2011). **Document type:** *Journal, Academic/Scholarly.*
Media: Online - full text.
Indexed: P30.
—**CCC.**
Published by: Dove Medical Press Ltd., Beechfield House, Winterton Way, Macclesfield, SK11 0JL, United Kingdom. TEL 44-1625-509130, FAX 44-1625-617933. Ed. Clark T Hung.

616.7 ITA ISSN 2035-8237
▼ **ORTHOPEDIC REVIEWS.** Text in English. 2009. irreg. **Document type:** *Journal, Academic/Scholarly.*
Related titles: Online - full text ed.: ISSN 2035-8164. free (effective 2011).
Indexed: A01, T02.
Published by: Pagepress, Via Giuseppe Belli 4, Pavia, 27100, Italy. TEL 39-0382-1751762, FAX 39-0382-1750481. Ed. Marcus Jaeger.

616.7 CHE ISSN 1612-8060
ORTHOPEDIC TRAUMA DIRECTIONS. Text in English. 2003. bi-m. EUR 446 to institutions; EUR 565 combined subscription to institutions (print & online eds.); EUR 76 newsstand/cover (effective 2011). **Document type:** *Journal, Academic/Scholarly.* **Description:** Contains articles on advances in orthopedic surgery.
Related titles: Online - full text ed.: ISSN 1612-8087. EUR 545 to institutions (effective 2011).
—IE. **CCC.**
Published by: A O Foundation, Clavadelerstr 8, Davos Platz, 7270, Switzerland. TEL 41-81-4142801, FAX 41-81-4142280, foundation@aofoundation.org, http://www.aofoundation.org. Ed. Rick Buckley. **Subscr. to:** Thieme Medical Publishers, 333 Seventh Ave, New York, NY 10001. TEL 800-782-3488, custserv@thieme.com, http://www.thieme.com/journals.

617.3 USA ISSN 0147-7447
RD701
➤ **ORTHOPEDICS.** Text in English. 1978. m. USD 299 to individuals; USD 479 to institutions; USD 39 per issue (effective 2010). 85 p./no. 3 cols./p.; back issues avail.; reprints avail. **Document type:** *Journal, Academic/Scholarly.* **Description:** Covers the entire spectrum of orthopedic surgery and treatment.
Related titles: Online - full text ed.: ISSN 1938-2367. free (effective 2011).

Indexed: A20, A22, ASCA, B&BAb, B19, B21, BDM&CN, BioEngAb, C06, C07, C08, CA, CINAHL, CTA, CurCont, EMBASE, ExcerpMed, FR, INI, IndMed, Inpharma, MEDLINE, P20, P22, P24, P26, P30, P35, P48, P54, PEI, PQC, R10, Reac, SCI, SCOPUS, T02, W07. —BLDSC (6296.146000), GNLM, IE, Infotrieve, Ingenta, INIST. **CCC.**
Published by: Slack, Inc., 6900 Grove Rd, Thorofare, NJ 08086. TEL 856-848-1000, FAX 856-848-6091, customerservice@slackinc.com, http://www.slackinc.com.

617.3 USA ISSN 0279-5647 CODEN: DUCRE2
ORTHOPEDICS TODAY. Text in English. 1981. m. USD 299 to individuals; USD 479 to institutions; USD 39 per issue (effective 2010). adv. illus. reprints avail. **Document type:** *Newspaper, Academic/Scholarly.* **Description:** Features reports from scientific meetings covering the broad spectrum of orthopedic interests.
Related titles: Online - full text ed.
Indexed: C06, C07, C08, CINAHL, P20, P24, P48, P54, PQC. —BLDSC (6296.163000), IE, Ingenta. **CCC.**
Published by: Slack, Inc., 6900 Grove Rd, Thorofare, NJ 08086. TEL 856-848-1000, FAX 856-848-6091, customerservice@slackinc.com, http://www.slackinc.com. Ed. Lee Beadling.

685.31 617.3 NLD ISSN 2210-7894
ORTHOPEDISCHE TECHNIEK. Text in Dutch. 1981. 3/yr. EUR 35 (effective 2010). adv. bk.rev. **Document type:** *Magazine, Trade.* **Description:** Discusses orthopedic shoes and boots, foot diseases, and orthopedic surgery.
Formerly (until 2010): Orthopedische Schoentechniek (1382-8533)
Published by: N V O S-Orthobanda, Postbus 120, Soest, 3760 AC, Netherlands. TEL 31-35-5880495, FAX 31-35-6025170, info@nvos-orthobanda.nl, http://www.nvos.nl. Ed. Rob Verwaard. adv.: color page EUR 800; 190 x 270. Circ: 1,500.

616.7 DEU
ORTHOPRESS. Text in German. 1994. q. EUR 17.50; free newsstand/cover (effective 2007). adv. **Document type:** *Magazine, Trade.*
Related titles: Online - full text ed.
Published by: Fiwa Verlag GmbH, Lothringer Str 85, Cologne, 50677, Germany. TEL 49-221-940820, FAX 49-221-9408211. Ed. Curt Findeisen. adv.: B&W page EUR 13,500, color page EUR 19,957; trim 210 x 285. Circ: 896,198 (controlled).

617 610.73 CAN ISSN 1207-2842
ORTHOSCOPE. Text in English. 1978. q. CAD 35. adv. bk.rev. index. back issues avail. **Document type:** *Newsletter.*
Former titles (until 1995): C O N A Newsletter (1207-2834); (until 1994): C O N A Journal (0708-6474)
Indexed: A22, C06, C07, C08, CINAHL.
Published by: (Canadian Orthopaedic Nurses Association), Pappin Communications, The Victoria Centre, 84 Isabella St, Pembroke, ON K8A 5S5, Canada. TEL 613-735-0952, FAX 613-735-7983. Ed., R&P Bill Grudecki. Circ: 600.

616.7 USA ISSN 2153-9782
RD701
▼ **ORTHOTEC**; orthopedic trends, technology & manufacturing. Text in English. 2010 (May). s-a. **Document type:** *Trade.*
Related titles: Online - full text ed.: ISSN 2153-9790. 2010 (May). free (effective 2011).
Indexed: B02, G04, G08, I05.
Published by: Canon Communications LLC (Subsidiary of: Apprise Media LLC), 11444 W Olympic Blvd, Ste 900, Los Angeles, CA 90064. TEL 310-445-4200, FAX 310-445-4299, info@cancom.com, http://www.cancom.com.

617.3 ITA ISSN 1123-6531
ORTOPEDIA NEWS. Text in Italian. 1995. 3/yr. free to qualified personnel. adv. **Document type:** *Newsletter, Trade.*
Published by: C I C Edizioni Internazionali, Corso Trieste 42, Rome, 00198, Italy. TEL 39-06-8412673, FAX 39-06-8412688, info@gruppocic.it, http://www.gruppocic.it.

617.3 POL ISSN 1509-3492
ORTOPEDIA, TRAUMATOLOGIA, REHABILITACJA. Text in Polish. 1999. q.
Indexed: EMBASE, ExcerpMed, MEDLINE, P30, R10, Reac, SCOPUS. —BLDSC (6296.305000).
Published by: MedSportPress, ul Marymoncka 34 skr. 23, Warsaw, 01813, Poland. TEL 48-22-8346772, FAX 48-22-8340431, nauka@medsport.pl, http://www.medsport.pl.

617.3 ITA ISSN 0030-5979
ORTOPEDICI E SANITARI. Text in Italian. 1964. m. (9/yr.). EUR 35 domestic; EUR 70 in Europe; EUR 90 elsewhere (effective 2011). adv. illus.; pat. **Document type:** *Magazine, Trade.* **Description:** Deals with new products in orthopedic field.
Related titles: Online - full text ed.
Published by: Tecniche Nuove SpA, Via Eritrea 21, Milan, MI 201, Italy. TEL 39-02-390901, FAX 39-02-7570364, info@tecnichenuove.com. Ed. Cristina Suzzani. Circ: 10,000.

616.7 CZE ISSN 1802-1727
ORTOPEDIE. Text in Czech. 2007. bi-m. CZK 480 (effective 2009). **Document type:** *Magazine, Trade.*
Published by: Medakta s.r.o., Evropska 57, Prague 6, 160 00, Czech Republic. TEL 420-311612650, medakta@medakta.cz.

617.3 SWE ISSN 0349-733X
ORTOPEDISKT MAGASIN; nordisk tidskrift foer ortopedi och rehabilitering. Text in Swedish. 1977. q. SEK 170 (effective 2007). adv. back issues avail. **Document type:** *Magazine, Academic/Scholarly.*
Formerly (until 1982): O M. Ortopediskt Meddelande
Related titles: Online - full text ed.
Address: PO Box 89, Tomelilla, 27322, Sweden. TEL 46-708-626176, FAX 46-417-31261. Ed. Boerje Ohlsson TEL 46-417-31026. Adv. contact Eva Evedius. color page SEK 13,300. Circ: 2,000.

OSTEOARTHRITIS AND CARTILAGE. *see* MEDICAL SCIENCES—Rheumatology

617.3 CZE ISSN 1211-3778
➤ **OSTEOLOGICKY BULLETIN.** Text in Czech. 1996. q. EUR 41.70 (effective 2009). **Document type:** *Journal, Academic/Scholarly.*
Indexed: EMBASE, ExcerpMed, R10, Reac, SCOPUS. —BLDSC (6303.858915).
Published by: (Spolecnost pro Metabolicka Onemocneni Skeletu), Trios s.r.o., Zakourilova 142, Prague 4, 14900, Czech Republic. TEL 420-2-67912030, FAX 420-2-67915563, redakce@trios.cz, http://www.trios.cz. Ed. Alena Mechurova. **Dist. by:** Kubon & Sagner Buchexport - Import GmbH, Hessstr 39-41, Munich 80798, Germany. TEL 49-89-542180, FAX 49-89-54218218, postmaster@kubon-sagner.de, http://www.kubon-sagner.de.

617.3 DEU ISSN 1019-1291 CODEN: OSTEFK
➤ **OSTEOLOGIE**; interdisziplinaere Zeitschrift fuer Knochen und Gelenke. Text in German, English. 1992. q. EUR 142 to individuals; EUR 255 to institutions; EUR 74 to students (effective 2011). adv. abstr.; bibl.; charts; illus. 72 p./no.; **Document type:** *Journal, Academic/Scholarly.*
Related titles: Online - full text ed.
Indexed: EMBASE, ExcerpMed, IBR, IBZ, R10, Reac, SCI, SCOPUS, W07. —GNLM.
Published by: (Deutsche Gesellschaft fuer Osteologie CHE), Schattauer GmbH, Hoelderlinstr 3, Stuttgart, 70174, Germany. TEL 49-711-229870, FAX 49-711-2298750, info@schattauer.de, http://www.schattauer.com. Ed. Dr. Peter Burkhardt. Adv. contact Jasmin Thurner. Circ: 2,050 (controlled).

616.71 JPN ISSN 0919-6307
OSTEOPOROSIS JAPAN. Text in Japanese. 1993. q. JPY 6,800; JPY 1,700 newsstand/cover (effective 2004). Supplement avail. **Document type:** *Journal, Academic/Scholarly.* —BLDSC (6303.873550).
Published by: Raifu Saiensu Shuppan K.K./Life Science Publishing Co. Ltd., Daisen Bldg, 11-7 Nihonbashikobuna-cho, Chuo-ku, Tokyo, 103-0024, Japan. TEL 81-3-36647917, info@lifescience.co.jp.

617 USA ISSN 0889-5899
RD94
➤ **OSTOMY - WOUND MANAGEMENT.** Abbreviated title: O W M. Text in English. 1980. m. USD 85 domestic; USD 140 foreign; free domestic to qualified personnel (effective 2010). adv. charts; illus.; stat. back issues avail.; reprints avail. **Document type:** *Journal, Academic/Scholarly.* **Description:** Contains clinical, practical and professional information relating to skin, wound, ostomy and incontinence care.
Formerly (until 198?): Ostomy Management (0274-7944)
Related titles: Online - full text ed.: ISSN 1943-2720. free (effective 2010).
Indexed: A22, C06, C07, C08, CINAHL, CurCont, EMBASE, ExcerpMed, INI, MEDLINE, P24, P30, P48, PQC, R10, Reac, SCI, SCOPUS, W07. —BLDSC (6312.377000), GNLM, IE, Infotrieve, Ingenta, INIST. **CCC.**
Published by: H M P Communications, LLC (Subsidiary of: Alta Communications), 83 General Warren Blvd, Ste 100, Malvern, PA 19355. TEL 610-560-0500, 800-237-7285, FAX 610-560-0502, http://www.hmpcommunications.com. Ed. Barbara Zeiger TEL 800-237-7285 ext 244. Pub. Jeremy Bowden TEL 800-237-7285 ext 219.

616.025 GBR ISSN 1363-0938
OXFORD HANDBOOKS IN EMERGENCY MEDICINE. Text in English. 1991. irreg., latest 2001. price varies. back issues avail. **Document type:** *Monographic series, Academic/Scholarly.* —**CCC.**
Published by: Oxford University Press, Great Clarendon St, Oxford, OX2 6DP, United Kingdom. TEL 44-1865-556767, FAX 44-1865-556646, enquiry@oup.co.uk, http://www.oup-usa.org/catalogs/general/series/.

616.7 CAN ISSN 1705-0022
PATIENT MANAGEMENT PROBLEMS IN TRAUMA AND CRITICAL CARE. Text in English. 2001. q. CAD 309 domestic to individuals; USD 229 foreign to individuals (effective 2008).
Formerly (until 2003): Trauma Patient Management Problems (1713-0263)
Media: CD-ROM. —**CCC.**
Published by: (American College of Surgeons USA); B.C. Decker Inc., 50 King St E, 2nd Fl, Hamilton, ON L8N 2A1, Canada. TEL 905-522-7017, 800-568-7281, FAX 905-522-7839, 888-311-4987, info@bcdecker.com. Ed. Rao R Ivatury.

PATOLOGIA DEL APARATO LOCOMOTOR. *see* MEDICAL SCIENCES—Rheumatology

PEDIATRIC EMERGENCY CARE. *see* MEDICAL SCIENCES—Pediatrics

616.025 618.92 USA ISSN 1082-3344
RJ370
PEDIATRIC EMERGENCY MEDICINE REPORTS. Text in English. 1996. m. USD 439 combined subscription (print & online eds.); USD 65 per issue (effective 2010). **Document type:** *Newsletter, Trade.* **Description:** Contains reviews of current issues faced by physicians dealing with pediatric emergencies. Topics include airway emergencies, trauma, metabolic disorders, fevers, toxicology, and more.
Related titles: Online - full text ed.: ISSN 1945-0370; ◆ Supplement(s): Trauma Reports. ISSN 1531-1082.
Indexed: A01, A26, G08, H11, H12, I05, P20, P48, P54, PQC. —**CCC.**
Published by: A H C Media LLC (Subsidiary of: Thomson Corporation, Healthcare Information Group), 3525 Piedmont Rd, NE, Bldg 6, Ste 400, Atlanta, GA 30305. TEL 404-262-7436, 800-688-2421, FAX 404-262-7837, 800-284-3291, customerservice@ahcmedia.com. Ed. Ann Dietrich. Pub. Brenda L Mooney TEL 404-262-5403. **Subscr. to:** PO Box 105109, Atlanta, GA 30348. TEL 404-262-5476, FAX 404-262-5560.

617.585 ESP ISSN 1578-0716
PEDOLOGIA CLINICA. Text in Spanish. 2000. bi-m. EUR 67 domestic; EUR 85 in Europe; EUR 107 elsewhere (effective 2009). back issues avail. **Document type:** *Journal, Academic/Scholarly.*
Related titles: ◆ English ed.: American Podiatric Medical Association. Journal. ISSN 8750-7315.
Published by: Ediciones Especializadas Europeas, Mila i Fontanals 14-26 3o. 1a, Barcelona, 08012, Spain. TEL 34-93-4587207, FAX 34-93-2082001, http://www.edicionesee.com/. Ed. Joan Estape i Llop.

617.585 CAN ISSN 1922-9429
PEDORTHICS QUARTERLY. Text in English. 199?. q. free to members (effective 2011). **Document type:** *Journal, Academic/Scholarly.*
Formerly (until 2009): Pedorthics Canada (1499-7673)
Published by: Pedorthic Association of Canada, Ste 503, 386 Broadway, Winnipeg, MB R3C 3R6, Canada. TEL 204-975-8200, 888-268-4404, FAX 866-994-9925, info@pedorthic.ca, http://www.pedorthic.ca.

617.585 USA
PODIATRIST'S PATIENT NEWSLETTER. Text in English. 1983. q. 4 p./no. 3 cols./p.; **Document type:** *Newsletter, Trade.*
Published by: Newsletters Ink, Corp., 450 N Prince St, P O Box 4008, Lancaster, PA 17604. TEL 717-393-1000, 800-379-5585, FAX 717-393-4702, info@newslettersink.com, http://www.newslettersink.com. Ed. Ann Mead Ash. Pub. Gregory A Gilson.

617.585 USA ISSN 0744-3528 CODEN: DJSHD8
PODIATRY MANAGEMENT. Text in English. 1982. 9/yr. free (effective 2007). adv. bk.rev. pat.; stat. back issues avail. **Document type:** *Magazine, Trade.* **Description:** Publishes articles and features of interest to the podiatric community.
Related titles: Online - full text ed.
Indexed: A26, C06, C07, C08, CA, CINAHL, G08, H11, H12, I05, T02. —BLDSC (6541.498070), IE, Ingenta.
Published by: Kane Communications, Inc., 10 E Athens Ave, Ste 208, Ardmore, PA 19003. TEL 610-645-6940, FAX 610-645-6943, touristmag@aol.com, http://www.kanec.com. Ed. Dr. Barry H Block. Pub., R&P Scott C Borowsky. Adv. contact David Kagan TEL 610-734-2427. color page USD 2,600, B&W page USD 1,800. Circ: 15,066.

615.585 GBR ISSN 1460-731X
➤ **PODIATRY NOW.** Text in English. 1998. m. free to members (effective 2009). adv. bk.rev. abstr.; charts; illus.; mkt.; stat.; tr.lit. back issues avail. **Document type:** *Journal, Academic/Scholarly.* **Description:** Contains important issues affecting the profession are highlighted, including current issues in legislation and continuing professional development.
Supersedes in part (in 1998): Journal of British Podiatric Medicine (0961-6055); Which was formerly (until 1991): Chiropodist (0009-4706); British Journal of Podiatric Medicine and Surgery (0955-8160); Which was formerly (until 1989): Podiatric Society. Journal
Indexed: A26, C06, C07, C08, CA, CINAHL, H12, I05, T02. —**CCC.**
Published by: Society of Chiropodists and Podiatrists, 1 Fellmongers Path, Tower Bridge Rd, London, SE1 3LY, United Kingdom. TEL 44-845-4503741, FAX 44-20-72348621, eg@scpod.org, http://www.feetforlife.org. Adv. contact Tina Davies TEL 44-20-72348639. page GBP 50.

617.3 USA ISSN 1045-7860
PODIATRY TODAY. Text in English. 1988. m. USD 100 domestic; USD 140 foreign; free domestic to qualified personnel (effective 2010). adv. back issues avail.; reprints avail. **Document type:** *Journal, Trade.* **Description:** Contains informative and how-to clinical articles as well as practice management features.
Formerly (until 1989): Podiatric Staff (1040-6859)
Related titles: Online - full text ed.: free (effective 2010).
Indexed: C06. —BLDSC (6541.498100), IE. **CCC.**
Published by: H M P Communications, LLC (Subsidiary of: Alta Communications), 83 General Warren Blvd, Ste 100, Malvern, PA 19355. TEL 610-560-0500, 800-237-7285, FAX 610-560-0501, http://www.hmpcommunications.com. Pub. Jeremy Bowden TEL 800-237-7285 ext 219.

617.585 AUS
PODIATRY UPDATE BULLETIN. Text in English. 1998. bi-m. adv. back issues avail. **Document type:** *Bulletin, Trade.*
Formerly (until 1999): Australian Podiatry Council. Bulletin
Related titles: Online - full text ed.
Published by: Australasian Podiatry Council, 89 Nicholson St, Brunswick E, Moreland, VIC 3057, Australia. TEL 61-3-94163111, FAX 61-3-94163188, apodc@apodc.com.au. Ed., Adv. contact Karen Fitzgerald. color page AUD 1,529; bleed 220 x 307.

617.585 ESP ISSN 1135-9552
EL PODOLOGO. Text in Multiple languages. 1995. q. back issues avail. **Document type:** *Journal, Academic/Scholarly.*
Published by: Colegio Oficial de Podologos de la Comunidad Valenciana, c/ Doctor Zamenhof 41, Bajo Izqda, Valencia, 46008, Spain. TEL 34-96-3854890, FAX 34-96-3850551.

616.7 RUS ISSN 1819-1495
➤ **POLITRAVMA/POLYTRAUMA**; scientific practical review journal. Text in Russian; Summaries in Russian, English. 2006 (Jun.). 4/yr. RUR 300 per issue (effective 2008). Index. back issues avail. **Document type:** *Journal, Academic/Scholarly.* **Description:** Published for clinicians, scientists and health authorities leaders. Presents fundamental and applied theoretic, clinical and experimental studies, practical notes, discussions, literature reviews, information about problems associated with polytrauma.
Indexed: RefZh.
Published by: Federal'noe Gosudarstvennoe Lechebno-Profilakticheskoe Uchrezhdenie, Nauchno-Klinicheskii Tsentr Okhrany Zdorov'ya Shakhterov/Federal State Medical Institute "Clinical Center of Miners' Health Protection", Mikrorayon 7, # 9, Leninsk-Kuznetsky, Kemerovo Region 652509, Russian Federation. TEL 7-384-5634000, FAX 7-384-5630750, info@gnkc.lnk.kuzbass.net, http://www.mine-med.ru. Ed. Vagram V Agadzhanyan. Circ: 1,000 (paid).

616.025 USA ISSN 1930-1103 CODEN: TMEIE3
PRACTICAL SUMMARIES IN ACUTE CARE. Text in English. 1994. m. USD 299 combined subscription (print & online eds.); USD 50 per issue (effective 2010). 8 p./no.; **Document type:** *Newsletter, Trade.* **Description:** Offers a concise review of articles and reports on advanced emergency medicine.
Formerly (until 2006): Emergency Medicine Alert (1075-6914); Which incorporated (in 1997): Emergency Medicine Desk Reference; Which superseded (in 1994): Advanced Cardiac Life Support Alert (1041-7974)
Related titles: Online - full text ed.
Indexed: A26, E08, G08, H04, H11, H12, I05, S09.

Published by: A H C Media LLC (Subsidiary of: Thomson Corporation, Healthcare Information Group), 3525 Piedmont Rd, NE, Bldg 6, Ste 400, Atlanta, GA 30305. TEL 404-262-7436, 800-688-2421, FAX 404-262-7837, 800-284-3291, customerservice@ahcmedia.com, http://www.ahcmedia.com/. Pub. Brenda L Mooney TEL 404-262-5403. **Subscr. to:** PO Box 105109, Atlanta, GA 30348. TEL 404-262-5476, FAX 404-262-5560.

614.8 USA ISSN 1049-023X
➤ **PREHOSPITAL AND DISASTER MEDICINE**; an international journal. Text in English. 1981. bi-m. GBP 313, USD 516 combined subscription to institutions (print & online eds.) (effective 2012). adv. bk.rev. abstr.; bibl.; stat. **Document type:** *Journal, Academic/Scholarly.* **Description:** Establishes, maintains, and promulgates the sciences associated with the delivery of emergency services to one or multiple victims of sudden illness or injury through the stimulation and dissemination of quality research in the areas of prehospital emergency medical care and disaster medicine.
Former titles (until 1989): Journal of Prehospital Medicine; (until 1987): World Association for Emergency and Disaster Medicine. Journal (0882-7397)
Related titles: Online - full text ed.: ISSN 1945-1938. GBP 227, USD 375 to institutions (effective 2012).
Indexed: A34, A35, A36, AgBio, C06, C07, C08, CABA, CINAHL, D01, E12, EMBASE, ExcerpMed, F08, GH, IndVet, JW-EM, LT, MEDLINE, N02, N03, P30, P33, P37, P39, R08, R10, R12, RM&VM, RRTA, Reac, S13, S16, SCOPUS, T05, TAR, VS, W11.
—BLDSC (6605.910000), GNLM, IE, Infotrieve, Ingenta. **CCC.**
Published by: (World Association for Disaster and Emergency Medicine), Cambridge University Press, 32 Ave of the Americas, New York, NY 10013. TEL 212-337-5000, FAX 212-691-3239, information@cambridge.org, http://us.cambridge.org.

616.025 GBR ISSN 1090-3127
CODEN: PEMCFS
➤ **PREHOSPITAL EMERGENCY CARE.** Text in English. 1997. q. GBP 125, EUR 160, USD 200 combined subscription to institutions (print & online eds.); GBP 245, EUR 320, USD 400 combined subscription to corporations (print & online eds.) (effective 2010). adv. back issues avail.; reprint service avail. from PSC. **Document type:** *Journal, Academic/Scholarly.* **Description:** Delivers up-to-date clinical and research information on advances in medical care in the out-of-hospital setting.
Related titles: Online - full text ed.: ISSN 1545-0066 (from IngentaConnect); ♦ Spanish ed.: Prehospital Emergency Care (Spanish Edition). ISSN 1888-4024.
Indexed: A22, C06, C07, C08, CA, CINAHL, CurCont, E01, EMBASE, ExcerpMed, IndMed, JW-EM, MEDLINE, P16, P20, P22, P24, P26, P30, P48, P53, P54, PQC, R10, Reac, SCI, SCOPUS, T02, W07.
—BLDSC (6605.917000), GNLM, IE, Infotrieve, Ingenta. **CCC.**
Published by: (National Association of E M S Physicians USA, National Association of State E M S Officials USA, National Association of E M S Educators USA, National Association of E M Ts USA), Informa Healthcare (Subsidiary of: T & F Informa plc), Telephone House, 69-77 Paul St, London, EC2A 4LQ, United Kingdom. TEL 44-20-70175000, FAX 44-20-70176792, healthcare.enquiries@informa.com. Ed. James J Menegazzi TEL 412-647-7992. Adv. contact Per Sonnerfeldt. **SUbscr. outside N. America to:** Taylor & Francis Ltd., Journals Customer Service, Sheepen Pl, Colchester, Essex CO3 3LP, United Kingdom. TEL 44-20-70175544, FAX 44-20-70175198, tf.enquiries@tfinforma.com; **Subscr. in N. America to:** Taylor & Francis Inc., Customer Services Dept, 325 Chestnut St, 8th Fl, Philadelphia, PA 19106. TEL 215-625-8900, 800-354-1420, FAX 215-625-8914, customerservice@taylorandfrancis.com.

616.025 ESP ISSN 1888-4024
PREHOSPITAL EMERGENCY CARE (SPANISH EDITION). Text in Spanish. 2008. q. EUR 88.91 combined subscription to individuals; EUR 225.10 combined subscription to institutions (effective 2009).
Related titles: Online - full text ed.: ISSN 1989-9084. EUR 74.07 (effective 2009); ♦ English ed.: Prehospital Emergency Care. ISSN 1090-3127.
Published by: Elsevier Doyma (Subsidiary of: Elsevier Health Sciences), Traversa de Gracia 17-21, Barcelona, 08021, Spain. TEL 34-932-418800, FAX 34-932-419020, editorial@elsevier.com. Ed. J. Gonzalez Uriarte. Circ: 2,500.

617.3 617.58 GBR ISSN 0309-3646
RD755 CODEN: POIND7
➤ **PROSTHETICS AND ORTHOTICS INTERNATIONAL.** Text in English. 1964. q. GBP 275, EUR 385, USD 485 combined subscription to institutions (print & online eds.); GBP 550, EUR 770, USD 968 combined subscription to corporations (print & online eds.) (effective 2010). adv. bk.rev. illus. index. back issues avail.; reprint service avail. from PSC. **Document type:** *Journal, Academic/Scholarly.* **Description:** Features scientific articles on prosthetics, orthotics and related topics.
Former titles (until 1977): I S P O Bulletin (0302-4229); (until 1971): Prosthetics International (0555-4837)
Related titles: Online - full text ed.: ISSN 1746-1553.
Indexed: A22, AMED, ASCA, B&BAb, B19, B21, BDM&CN, BioEngAb, C06, C07, CA, CTA, CurCont, E01, EMBASE, ExcerpMed, IndMed, Inpharma, Inspec, MEDLINE, P30, PEI, R10, Reac, SCI, SCOPUS, T02, W07.
—BLDSC (6935.500000), AskIEEE, GNLM, IE, Infotrieve, Ingenta, INIST. **CCC.**
Published by: (International Society for Prosthetics and Orthotics BEL), Sage Publications Ltd. (Subsidiary of: Sage Publications, Inc.), 1 Oliver's Yard, 55 City Rd, London, EC1Y 1SP, United Kingdom. TEL 44-20-73248500, FAX 44-20-73248600, info@sagepub.co.uk, http://www.uk.sagepub.com/home.nav. Ed. Margrit R. Meier.

616.02 ESP ISSN 1576-0316
➤ **PUESTA AL DIA EN URGENCIAS, EMERGENCIAS Y CATASTROFES.** Text in Spanish; Abstracts in Spanish, English. 1999. q. EUR 60 to institutions; EUR 105 domestic to institutions; EUR 256 in Europe to institutions; EUR 347 elsewhere to institutions (effective 2007). adv. abstr.; bibl.; illus.; stat. back issues avail. **Document type:** *Journal, Academic/Scholarly.*
Indexed: B21, ESPM, H&SSA, R10, Reac, RiskAb, SCOPUS.
Published by: Aran Ediciones, Castello 128, 1o, Madrid, 28006, Spain. TEL 34-91-7820030, FAX 34-91-5615787, edita@grupoaran.com, http://www.grupoaran.com. Ed. C. Alvarez Leiva. Pub. Jose Jimenez Marquez. R&P Maria Dolores Linares TEL 34-91-7820035. Circ: 10,000.

616.7 ESP
PUNTEX ORTOPEDIA; la revista del sector. Text in Spanish. 3/yr. adv. back issues avail. **Document type:** *Magazine, Consumer.*
Published by: Publicaciones Nacionales Tecnicas y Extranjeras (PUNTEX), Padilla 323, Barcelona, 08025, Spain. TEL 34-934-462820, FAX 34-934-462064, puntex@puntex.es, http://www.puntex.es. Ed. Raul Sanahuja. adv.: B&W page EUR 615; trim 240 x 330. Circ: 4,000.

RACHIS; revue de pathologie vertebrale. *see* MEDICAL SCIENCES—Rheumatology

REANIMATION. *see* MEDICAL SCIENCES—Anaesthesiology

RESPONSE. *see* HEALTH FACILITIES AND ADMINISTRATION

616.7 DEU ISSN 1430-1873
RETTUNGS-MAGAZIN. Text in German. 1995. bi-m. EUR 25 domestic; EUR 30 foreign; EUR 4.50 newsstand/cover (effective 2011). adv. **Document type:** *Magazine, Trade.*
Published by: Ebner Verlag GmbH, Karlstr 41, Ulm, 89073, Germany. TEL 49-731-152002, FAX 49-731-1520188, info@ebnerverlag.de, http://www.ebnerverlag.de. Ed. Lars Schmitz-Eggen. Adv. contact Ulrike Gross. Circ: 13,553 (paid and controlled).

616.7 ARG ISSN 1666-5139
REVISTA ARGENTINA DE OSTEOLOGIA. Text in Spanish. 2002. 3/yr.
Published by: Sociedad Argentina de Osteoporosis, Calle Thames 2484, Buenos Aires, Argentina. TEL 54-11-47729987.

616.8 ARG ISSN 0326-4823
REVISTA ARGENTINA DE QUEMADURAS. Text in Spanish. 1983. 3/yr. **Document type:** *Journal, Academic/Scholarly.*
Related titles: Online - full text ed.
Published by: Fundacion Benaim, Alberti 1093, Buenos Aires, C1223AAK, Argentina. info@fundacionbenaim.org.ar, http://www.fundacionbenaim.org.ar.

617.3 BRA ISSN 0102-3616
REVISTA BRASILEIRA DE ORTOPEDIA/BRAZILIAN JOURNAL OF ORTHOPAEDICS. Text in Portuguese. 1939-1943; resumed 1966. m. adv. bibl. **Document type:** *Journal, Academic/Scholarly.* **Description:** Describes research in orthopedic medicine and traumatology.
Supersedes (1939-1943): Revista Brasileira de Orthopedia e Traumatologia (0102-2326)
Related titles: Online - full text ed.: free (effective 2011).
Indexed: C01, SCOPUS.
Published by: (Sociedade Brasileira de Ortopedia e Traumatologia), Redprint Editora Ltda., Rua Domingos de Morais 2777 - 13o, Sao Paulo, SP, 04035-001, Brazil. TEL 55-11-5724813, FAX 55-11-5711719, redprint@uol.com.br. Ed. Carlos Giesta.

616.7 618.92 BRA ISSN 1518-8698
REVISTA BRASILEIRA DE ORTOPEDIA PEDIATRICA. Text in Portuguese. 2000. s-a. **Document type:** *Journal, Academic/Scholarly.*
Published by: Sociedade Brasileira de Ortopedia Pediatrica, Al Lorena 427, 14o Andar, Sao Paulo, 01424-000, Brazil. http://www.sbop.org.br.

616.025 CHL ISSN 0717-5833
REVISTA CHILENA DE MEDICINA INTENSIVA. Text in Spanish. 1985. q. **Document type:** *Journal, Academic/Scholarly.*
Published by: Sociedad Chilena de Medicina Intensiva, Bernardo Morin 488, 2o Piso, Providencia, Santiago, Chile. TEL 56-2-2253082, FAX 56-2-3440358, http://www.medicina-intensiva.cl.

616.7 CHL ISSN 0716-4548
REVISTA CHILENA DE ORTOPEDIA Y TRAUMATOLOGIA. Text in Spanish. 1949. q. **Document type:** *Journal, Academic/Scholarly.*
Published by: Sociedad Chilena de Ortopedia y Traumatologia, Evaristo Lillo 78, Of 81, Las Condes, Santiago, Chile. TEL 56-2-2072151, FAX 56-2-2069820, schot@schot.cl.

616.7 COL ISSN 0120-8845
REVISTA COLOMBIANA DE ORTOPEDIA Y TRAUMATOLOGIA. Text and summaries in Spanish. 1987. q. **Document type:** *Journal, Academic/Scholarly.*
Published by: Sociedad Colombiana de Cirugia Ortopedica y Traumatologia, Calle 134 #13-83, Of 201, Bogota, Colombia. TEL 57-1-6257445, http://www.sccot.org.co.

616.7 CUB ISSN 1810-2352
REVISTA CUBANA DE MEDICINA INTENSIVA Y EMERGENCIAS. Text in English. 2002. q. **Document type:** *Journal, Academic/Scholarly.*
Media: Online - full text.
Published by: Editorial Ciencias Medicas, Linea Esq 1, 10o, Vedado, Havana, 10400, Cuba. TEL 53-7-8323863, ecimed@infomed.sld.cu.

617.3 CUB ISSN 0864-215X
REVISTA CUBANA DE ORTOPEDIA Y TRAUMATOLOGIA. Text in Spanish; Abstracts in English, French, Spanish. 1987. s-a. USD 30 in North America; USD 32 in South America; USD 34 elsewhere (effective 2005). back issues avail. **Document type:** *Journal, Academic/Scholarly.*
Related titles: Online - full text ed.: ISSN 1561-3100. 1995. free (effective 2011).
Indexed: C01, SCOPUS, T02.
Published by: (Centro Nacional de Informacion de Ciencias Medicas (C N I C M), Cuba. Ministerio de Salud Publica), Editorial Ciencias Medicas, Linea Esq 1, 10o, Vedado, Havana, 10400, Cuba. TEL 53-7-8323863, ecimed@infomed.sld.cu. Ed. Yolanda Sarzo Gonzalez. Circ: 1,300. **Co-sponsors:** Sociedad Cubana de Ortopedia y Traumatologia; Hospital de Ortopedia y Traumatologia "Frank Pais".

617.3 ESP ISSN 1888-4415
➤ **REVISTA ESPANOLA DE CIRUGIA ORTOPEDICA Y TRAUMATOLOGIA.** Text in Spanish. 1944. bi-m. EUR 195.74 combined subscription to individuals print & online eds.; EUR 495.55 combined subscription to institutions print & online eds. (effective 2009). back issues avail.; reprints avail. **Document type:** *Journal, Academic/Scholarly.*
Former titles (until 2007): Revista de Ortopedia y Traumatologia (Print) (0482-5985); (until 1957): Acta Ortopedica Traumatologica Iberica (0400-4094); (until 1952): Cirugia del Aparato Locomotor (0210-6280)
Related titles: Online - full text ed.: ISSN 1988-8856. 1996. EUR 146.18 (effective 2009) (from ScienceDirect); Supplement(s): Revista de Ortopedia y Traumatologia. Suplemento. ISSN 1130-5614. 1990.
Indexed: SCOPUS.
—BLDSC (7853.930950), GNLM, IE, INIST. **CCC.**
Published by: (Sociedad Espanola de Cirugia Ortopedica y Traumatologia), Elsevier Doyma (Subsidiary of: Elsevier Health Sciences), Traversa de Gracia 17-21, Barcelona, 08021, Spain. TEL 34-932-418800, FAX 34-932-419020, editorial@elsevier.com. Ed. E.C. Rodriguez Merchan. Circ: 4,500.

617.585 ESP ISSN 0210-1238
REVISTA ESPANOLA DE PODOLOGIA. Text in Spanish. 1961. bi-m. **Document type:** *Journal, Academic/Scholarly.*
Formerly (until 1967): Revista Nacional de Podologia (0484-7970)
Published by: Federacion Espanola de Podologos, San Bernardo 74, Madrid, 28015, Spain. TEL 34-91-5315044.

617.3 FRA ISSN 1877-0517
➤ **REVUE DE CHIRURGIE ORTHOPEDIQUE ET TRAUMATOLOGIQUE.** Text in French; Summaries in English. 1890. 8/yr. EUR 351 in Europe to institutions; EUR 305.58 in France to institutions; JPY 54,700 in Japan to institutions; USD 456 elsewhere to institutions (effective 2012). bk.rev. illus. index. reprints avail. **Document type:** *Journal, Academic/Scholarly.* **Description:** Publishes original articles of clinical facts, technical notes, publication analyses, reports of meetings and congresses.
Former titles (until 2008): Revue de Chirurgie Orthopedique et Reparatrice de l'Appareil Moteur (0035-1040); (until 1950): Revue d'Orthopedie et de Chirurgie de l'Appareil Moteur (1243-2504); (until 1927): Revue d'Orthopedie (1243-2512)
Related titles: Microform ed.: (from PQC); Online - full text ed.: ISSN 1877-0525 (from ScienceDirect); Supplement(s): Revue de Chirurgie Orthopedique et Reparatrice de l'Appareil Moteur. Supplement. ISSN 0150-9780.
Indexed: A20, A22, ASCA, BDM&CN, DentInd, EMBASE, IndMed, Inpharma, MEDLINE, P30, SCOPUS.
—BLDSC (7897.155000), GNLM, IE, Infotrieve, Ingenta, INIST. **CCC.**
Published by: (Societe Francaise de Chirurgie Orthopedique et Traumatologique (S O F C O T)), Elsevier Masson (Subsidiary of: Elsevier Health Sciences), 62 Rue Camille Desmoulins, Issy les Moulineaux, Cedex 92442, France. TEL 33-1-71165500, FAX 33-1-71165600, infos@elsevier-masson.fr, http://www.elsevier-masson.fr. Ed. Jean-Michel Thomine. Circ: 6,100. **Subscr. to:** Societe de Periodiques Specialises, BP 22, Vineuil Cedex 41354, France. TEL 33-2-54504612, FAX 33-2-54504611.

617.585 FRA ISSN 1766-7313
➤ **REVUE DU PODOLOGUE.** Text in French. 2005. 6/yr. EUR 86 in Europe to institutions; EUR 81.29 in France to institutions; JPY 12,400 in Japan to institutions; USD 112 elsewhere to institutions (effective 2012). **Document type:** *Journal, Academic/Scholarly.*
Related titles: Online - full text ed.
Indexed: SCOPUS.
—CCC.
Published by: Elsevier Masson (Subsidiary of: Elsevier Health Sciences), 62 Rue Camille Desmoulins, Issy les Moulineaux, Cedex 92442, France. TEL 33-1-71165500, FAX 33-1-71165600, infos@elsevier-masson.fr.

617.3 JPN ISSN 0557-0433
RINSHO SEIKEI GEKA/CLINICAL ORTHOPAEDIC SURGERY. Text in Japanese. 1966. m. JPY 29,400 per issue; JPY 38,300 combined subscription (print & online eds.) (effective 2010). **Document type:** *Journal, Academic/Scholarly.*
Related titles: Online - full text ed.: ISSN 1882-1286.
Indexed: INIS AtomInd.
—BLDSC (3286.319000).
Published by: Igaku Shoin Ltd., 1-28-36 Hongo, Bunkyo-ku, Tokyo, 113-8719, Japan. TEL 81-3-3817-5600, FAX 81-3-3815-7791, info@igaku-shoin.co.jp. Circ: 9,000.

616.7 NOR ISSN 1500-757X
RYGGSTOETTEN. Text in Norwegian. 1998. q. NOK 225 membership (effective 2006). **Document type:** *Magazine, Consumer.*
Published by: Ryggforeningen i Norge, PO Box 6725, Etterstad, 0609, Norway. TEL 47-23-034561, 47-23-034560, ryggforeningenon@ryggforeningen. Ed. Inger Ljoestad.

616.7 ZAF ISSN 1681-150X
S A ORTHOPAEDIC JOURNAL. (South Africa) Text in English. 2002. q. **Document type:** *Journal, Academic/Scholarly.*
Related titles: Online - full text ed.: free (effective 2011).
Published by: South African Orthopaedic Association, University of Pretoria, Pretoria Academic Hospital, Private Bag X 169, Pretoria, South Africa.

S A S JOURNAL. *see* MEDICAL SCIENCES—Surgery

617.3 ITA ISSN 1122-715X
S O T I M I. ATTI E MEMORIE. (Societa di Ortopedia e Traumatologia dell'Italia Meridionale ed Insulare) Text in Italian; Summaries in English, French. 1937. s-a. **Document type:** *Journal, Academic/Scholarly.*
Formerly (until 1985): Societa di Ortopedia e Traumatologia dell'Italia Meridionale ed Insulare. Atti e Memorie (0394-0713)
Published by: (Societa di Ortopedia e Traumatologia dell'Italia Meridionale ed Insulare (S O T I M I)), Casa Editrice Idelson Gnocchi, Via Michele Pietravalle 85, Naples, NA 80131, Italy. TEL 39-081-5524733, FAX 39-081-5518295, informazioni@idelson-gnocchi.com, http://www.idelson-gnocchi.com.

617.585 FRA ISSN 1961-571X
SANTE DU PIED. Text in French. 2006. bi-m. EUR 10 (effective 2008). **Document type:** *Magazine, Consumer.*
Published by: Union Francaise pour la Sante du Pied, 17 Rue de l'Echiquier, Paris, 75010, France. info@sante-du-pied.org, http://www2.sante-du-pied.org.

617.3 ITA ISSN 0390-5276
➤ **LO SCALPELLO.** Text in Italian. 1971. 3/yr. EUR 124, USD 137 combined subscription to institutions (print & online eds.) (effective 2012). reprint service avail. from PSC. **Document type:** *Journal, Academic/Scholarly.*
Related titles: Online - full text ed.: ISSN 1970-6812 (from IngentaConnect).

Indexed: A22, A26, E01, E08, S09.
—IE. **CCC.**
Published by: Springer Italia Srl (Subsidiary of: Springer Science+Business Media), Via Decembrio 28, Milan, 20137, Italy. TEL 39-02-54259722, FAX 39-02-55193360, springer@springer.it. Ed. N Pace.

616.025 GBR ISSN 1757-7241
RA645.5
➤ **SCANDINAVIAN JOURNAL OF TRAUMA, RESUSCITATION AND EMERGENCY MEDICINE.** Abbreviated title: S J T R E M. Text in English. 1994. irreg. free (effective 2011). adv. back issues avail. **Document type:** *Journal, Academic/Scholarly.* **Description:** Covers all aspects of the epidemiology, etiology, pathophysiology, diagnosis, treatment, rehabilitation and prevention of acute illnesses and trauma.
Former titles (until 2008): Akuttjournalen (Online) (1500-7480); (until 2007): Akuttjournalen (Print) (0805-6129)
Media: Online - full text.
Indexed: A26, E08, EMBASE, H12, I05, MEDLINE, P30, S09, SCI, SCOPUS, W07.
—CCC.
Published by: BioMed Central Ltd. (Subsidiary of: Springer Science+Business Media), 236 Gray's Inn Rd, London, WC1X 8HB, United Kingdom. TEL 44-20-31922000, FAX 44-20-31922010, info@biomedcentral.com, http://www.biomedcentral.com. Eds. Hans Morten Lossius, Kjetil Soreide.

616.7 GBR ISSN 1748-7161
RD771.S3
➤ **SCOLIOSIS.** Text in English. 2005. irreg. free (effective 2011). adv. back issues avail. **Document type:** *Journal, Academic/Scholarly.* **Description:** Covers all aspects of the prevention, control, and conservative treatment of scoliosis and other spinal deformities.
Media: Online - full text.
Indexed: A01, A26, C06, C07, CA, CTA, I05, P30, PEI, SCOPUS, T02.
—CCC.
Published by: BioMed Central Ltd. (Subsidiary of: Springer Science+Business Media), 236 Gray's Inn Rd, London, WC1X 8HB, United Kingdom. TEL 44-20-31922000, FAX 44-20-31922010, info@biomedcentral.com, http://www.biomedcentral.com. Ed. Theodoros B Grivas. Adv. contact Natasha Bailey TEL 44-20-31922231.

617.3 JPN ISSN 0030-5901
SEIKEI GEKA/ORTHOPEDIC SURGERY. Text in Japanese. 1950. m. JPY 36,015 domestic; JPY 66,000 foreign; JPY 5,775 newsstand/cover (effective 2007). adv. charts; illus. Index. Supplement avail. **Document type:** *Journal, Academic/Scholarly.*
Indexed: INIS AtomInd, IndMed, P30.
—GNLM.
Published by: Nankodo Co. Ltd., 3-42-6 Hongo, Bunkyo-ku, Tokyo, 113-8410, Japan. TEL 81-3-38117140, FAX 81-3-38117265, http://www.nankodo.co.jp/. Circ: 8,500.

SEIKEI-GEKA KANGO/JAPANESE JOURNAL OF ORTHOPEDIC NURSING. *see* MEDICAL SCIENCES—Nurses And Nursing

617.3 JPN ISSN 0037-1033
SEIKEI GEKA TO SAIGAI GEKA/ORTHOPEDICS AND TRAUMATOLOGY. Text in English, Japanese. 1952. s-a. membership. adv. **Document type:** *Journal, Academic/Scholarly.*
Related titles: Online - full text ed.: ISSN 1349-4333.
Indexed: INIS AtomInd.
Published by: Nishi Nihon Seikei Saigai Geka Gakkai/West Japan Society of Orthopedics and Traumatology, c/o Dept of Orthopedic Surgery, Kyushu University, 3-1-1, Maidashi, Higashi-Ku, Fukuoka-shi, 812-0054, Japan. TEL 81-92-6425489, FAX 81-92-6425507. Ed. Yoichi Sugioka. Circ: 1,000.

610 JPN ISSN 0387-4095
SEKEI SAIGAI GEKA/ORTHOPAEDIC SURGERY AND TRAUMATOLOGY. Text in English, Japanese. 1958. m. JPY 38,115 (effective 2007). bk.rev. Index. **Document type:** *Journal, Academic/Scholarly.*
Formerly (until 1979): Journal of Accidental Medicine (0036-2689)
Indexed: CISA, INIS AtomInd, JPI.
Published by: Kanehara Shuppan/Kanehara & Co. Ltd., 2-31-14 Yushima, Bunkyo-ku, Tokyo, 113-8687, Japan. TEL 81-3-38117184, FAX 81-3-38130288, http://www.kanehara-shuppan.co.jp/. Circ: 7,100.

617.3 JPN ISSN 0911-6826
SEKICHU HENKEI/SPINAL DEFORMITY. Text in English, Japanese. 1986. a.
—CCC.
Published by: Nihon Sokuwansho Kenkyukai/Japanese Scoliosis Society, 10F Fujimi Highness Bldg., 2-7-5 Fujimi, Chuo-ku, Chiba, 260-0015, Japan. jss@soteria.cc, http://www.sokuwan.jp/index.html.

617.3 JPN ISSN 0914-4412
SEKITSUI SEKIZUI JANARU/SPINE AND SPINAL CORD. Text in Japanese. 1988. m. JPY 30,660; JPY 2,310 newsstand/cover (effective 2007). **Document type:** *Journal, Academic/Scholarly.*
Published by: Miwa-Shoten Ltd., 6-17-9 Hongo, Bunkyo-ku, Hongou Tsuna Bldg. 4F, Tokyo, 113-0033, Japan. TEL 81-3-38167796, FAX 81-3-38167756, info@miwapubl.com, http://www.miwapubl.com/.

617.3 JPN ISSN 0914-6024
RD533
SEKIZUI GEKA/SPINAL SURGERY. Text in English, Japanese; Summaries in English. 1987. a. **Document type:** *Journal, Academic/Scholarly.*
—BLDSC (8413.899000).
Published by: Nihon Sekizui Geka Kenkyukai Oosaka/Japanese Society of Spinal Surgery, Hokkaido University School of Medicine, Department of Neurosurgery, North 15, West 7, Kita-ku, Sapporo, 060-8638, Japan. TEL 81-3-63826891, 81-11-7065987, FAX 81-11-7087737, 81-3-63826892, js-hoku@med.hokudai.ac.jp, http://www.m-tsuda.com/jssshc/index.html.

SEMINARS IN ARTHRITIS AND RHEUMATISM. *see* MEDICAL SCIENCES—Rheumatology

617.3 USA ISSN 1045-4527
RD686 CODEN: SAERCZ
SEMINARS IN ARTHROPLASTY. Text in English. 1990. q. USD 416 in United States to institutions; USD 568 elsewhere to institutions (effective 2012). back issues avail.; reprints avail. **Document type:** *Journal, Academic/Scholarly.* **Description:** Provides a comprehensive, current overview of a single topic in arthroplasty and addresses orthopedic surgeons, providing authoritative reviews with emphasis on new developments relevant to their practice.
Related titles: Online - full text ed.: ISSN 1558-4437 (from ScienceDirect).
Indexed: EMBASE, ExcerpMed, P30, R10, Reac, SCOPUS.
—BLDSC (8239.448100), GNLM, IE, Infotrieve, Ingenta. **CCC.**
Published by: W.B. Saunders Co. (Subsidiary of: Elsevier Health Sciences), Elsevier, Health Sciences Division, Order Fulfillment, 3251 Riverport Ln, Maryland Heights, MO 63043. TEL 314-872-8370, 800-325-4177, FAX 314-432-1380, JournalCustomerService-usa@elsevier.com, http://www.us.elsevierhealth.com. Eds. A Seth Greenwald, Peter F Sharkey. Adv. contact Nicole Johnson TEL 215-239-3168.

SEMINARS IN ROENTGENOLOGY. *see* MEDICAL SCIENCES—Radiology And Nuclear Medicine

617 USA ISSN 1040-7383
RD768 CODEN: SSPSEH
SEMINARS IN SPINE SURGERY. Text in English. 1989. q. USD 383 in United States to institutions; USD 531 elsewhere to institutions (effective 2012). back issues avail.; reprints avail. **Document type:** *Journal, Academic/Scholarly.* **Description:** Topics includes basic anatomy, pathophysiology, clinical presentation, management options and follow-up of the condition under consideration and providing summaries of articles from other journals that are of relevance to the understanding of ongoing research related to the treatment of spinal disorders.
Related titles: Online - full text ed.: ISSN 1558-4496 (from ScienceDirect).
Indexed: EMBASE, ExcerpMed, P30, R10, Reac, SCOPUS.
—BLDSC (8239.468000), GNLM, IE, Ingenta. **CCC.**
Published by: W.B. Saunders Co. (Subsidiary of: Elsevier Health Sciences), Elsevier, Health Sciences Division, Order Fulfillment, 3251 Riverport Ln, Maryland Heights, MO 63043. TEL 314-872-8370, 800-325-4177, FAX 314-432-1380, JournalCustomerService-usa@elsevier.com, http://www.us.elsevierhealth.com. Eds. Dr. Sam W Wiesel, Scott D Boden. Pub. Jason Miller.

SEMINARS IN ULTRASOUND, C T AND M R I. (Computerized Tomography and Magnetic Resonance) *see* MEDICAL SCIENCES—Radiology And Nuclear Medicine

616.7 CHN ISSN 1672-5972
SHENGWU GUKE CAILIAO YU LINCHUANG YANJIU/ORTHOPAEDIC BIOMECHANICS MATERIALS AND CLINICAL STUDY. Text in Chinese. 2003. bi-m. CNY 9.80 newsstand/cover (effective 2006). **Document type:** *Journal, Academic/Scholarly.*
Related titles: Online - full text ed.
Address: 28, Shucheng Lu, Wuhan, 430070, China. TEL 86-27-87678738, FAX 86-27-87393955.

SHINKEI GAISHO/NEUROTRAUMATOLOGY. *see* MEDICAL SCIENCES—Psychiatry And Neurology

616.7 CHN ISSN 1008-5572
SHIYONG GUKE ZAZHI/JOURNAL OF PRACTICAL ORTHOPEDICS. Text in Chinese. 1994. bi-m. USD 49.20 (effective 2009). **Document type:** *Journal, Academic/Scholarly.*
Related titles: Online - full text ed.
—East View.
Published by: Zhonghua Yixuehui, Shanxi Fenhui/Chinese Medical Association, Shanxi Branch, 382, Wuyi Lu, Taiyuan, China. TEL 86-351-3365705, FAX 86-351-3072133. **Dist. by:** China International Book Trading Corp, 35 Chegongzhuang Xilu, Haidian District, PO Box 399, Beijing 100044, China. TEL 86-10-68412045, FAX 86-10-68412023, cibtc@mail.cibtc.com.cn, http://www.cibtc.com.cn.

SHOCK (PHILADELPHIA); injury, inflammation, and sepsis: laboratory and clinical approaches. *see* MEDICAL SCIENCES

616.7 GBR ISSN 1758-5732
▼ ➤ **SHOULDER AND ELBOW.** Text in English. 2009. s-a. GBP 203 in United Kingdom to institutions; EUR 238 in Europe to institutions; USD 316 elsewhere to institutions (effective 2012). **Document type:** *Journal, Academic/Scholarly.* **Description:** Devoted to the advancement of the science of diagnosis and management of shoulder and elbow disorders.
Related titles: Online - full text ed.: ISSN 1758-5740. 2009. GBP 203 in United Kingdom to institutions; EUR 238 in Europe to institutions; USD 316 elsewhere to institutions (effective 2012).
Indexed: A01, A22, CA, E01, T02.
—CCC.
Published by: (British Elbow and Shoulder Society), Wiley-Blackwell Publishing Ltd. (Subsidiary of: John Wiley & Sons, Inc.), 9600 Garsington Rd, Oxford, OX4 2DQ, United Kingdom. TEL 44-1865-776868, FAX 44-1865-714591, customerservices@blackwellpublishing.com, http://www.wiley.com/WileyCDA/. Ed. Ian Trail.

615.822 CHN ISSN 1004-6569
SHUANGZU YU BAOJIAN/CHINA REFLEXOLOGY JOURNAL. Text in Chinese. 1992. bi-m. USD 18 (effective 2009). **Document type:** *Journal, Academic/Scholarly.*
—East View.
Published by: Zhongguo Zubu Fanshequ Jiankangfa Yanjiuhui/China Reflexology Association, PO Box 2002, Beijing, 100026, China. TEL 86-10-65068310, FAX 86-10-65068309, crazhang@public.bta.net.cn. **Dist. by:** China International Book Trading Corp, 35 Chegongzhuang Xilu, Haidian District, PO Box 399, Beijing 100044, China. TEL 86-10-68412045, FAX 86-10-68412023, cibtc@mail.cibtc.com.cn, http://www.cibtc.com.cn.

616.7 GBR ISSN 2044-5040
▼ ➤ **SKELETAL MUSCLE.** Text in English. 2011. irreg. free (effective 2011). adv. back issues avail. **Document type:** *Journal, Academic/Scholarly.* **Description:** Publishes articles investigating molecular mechanisms underlying the biology of skeletal muscle.
Media: Online - full text.
Indexed: A01, A26, H12, I05.
Published by: BioMed Central Ltd. (Subsidiary of: Springer Science+Business Media), 236 Gray's Inn Rd, London, WC1X 8HB, United Kingdom. TEL 44-20-31922000, FAX 44-20-31922010, info@biomedcentral.com, http://www.biomedcentral.com. Eds. David J Glass, Kevin P Campbell, Michael A Rudnicki.

▼ ➤ **SKULL BASE REPORTS.** *see* MEDICAL SCIENCES—Surgery

617.2 ESP ISSN 0212-0771
➤ **SOCIEDAD ANDALUZA DE TRAUMATOLOGIA Y ORTOPEDIA. REVISTA.** Text in Spanish. 1981. s-a. back issues avail.; reprints avail. **Document type:** *Journal, Academic/Scholarly.*
Related titles: Online - full text ed.: 1996.
—INIST.
Published by: (Sociedad Andaluza de Traumatologia y Ortopedia), Elsevier Doyma (Subsidiary of: Elsevier Health Sciences), Traversa de Gracia 17-21, Barcelona, 08021, Spain. TEL 34-932-418800, FAX 34-932-419020, editorial@elsevier.com, http://www.elsevier.es/. Ed. Manuel Zabala Gamara. Circ: 1,000.

617.3 FRA ISSN 0081-1033
SOCIETE FRANCAISE DE CHIRURGIE ORTHOPEDIQUE ET TRAUMATOLOGIQUE. CONFERENCES D'ENSEIGNEMENT. Text in French. 1967. a. price varies.
Published by: (Societe Francaise de Chirurgie Orthopedique et Traumatologique (S O F C O T)), Elsevier Masson (Subsidiary of: Elsevier Health Sciences), 62 Rue Camille Desmoulins, Issy les Moulineaux, Cedex 92442, France. TEL 33-1-71165500, FAX 33-1-71165600, infos@elsevier-masson.fr, http://www.elsevier-masson.fr.

616.02 ZAF
➤ **SOUTH AFRICAN JOURNAL OF CRITICAL CARE.** Text in English. s-a. USD 10 foreign (effective 2003). illus. **Document type:** *Journal, Academic/Scholarly.* **Description:** Publishes clinical and experimental research in all areas of critical care medicine.
Indexed: ISAP.
Published by: South African Medical Association, Block F Castle Walk Corporate Park, Nossob St, Erasmuskloof X3, Pretoria 7430, South Africa. TEL 27-12-4812000, FAX 27-12-4812100, publishing@samedical.org, http://www.samedical.org. **Subscr. to:** PO Box 74789, Lynnwood Ridge, Pretoria 0040, South Africa.

610 USA
SPINAL COLUMN (ATLANTA). Text in English. q.
Published by: Shepherd Center, 2020 Peachtree Rd NW, Atlanta, GA 30309-1402.

610.73 618.92 USA
SPINAL CONNECTION. Text in English. 1984. s-a. free. adv. bk.rev. back issues avail. **Document type:** *Newsletter.* **Description:** Provides medical information on scoliosis, including an overview of the foundation's activities and services.
Published by: National Scoliosis Foundation, 5 Cabot Pl, Stoughton, MA 02072. TEL 781-341-6333, FAX 781-341-8333. Circ: 25,000.

SPINAL CORD. *see* MEDICAL SCIENCES—Psychiatry And Neurology

617.375 USA ISSN 0362-2436
RD768 CODEN: SPINDD
➤ **SPINE (PHILADELPHIA, 1976).** Text in English. 1976. s-m. USD 2,239 domestic to institutions; USD 2,934 foreign to institutions (effective 2011). adv. illus. index. back issues avail.; reprints avail. **Document type:** *Journal, Academic/Scholarly.* **Description:** Designed for the treatment of spinal disorders.
Related titles: CD-ROM ed.; Microform ed.: (from PQC); Online - full text ed.: ISSN 1528-1159.
Indexed: A01, A03, A08, A20, A22, AMED, B21, B25, BDM&CN, BIOSIS Prev, C06, C07, C08, CA, CINAHL, ChemAb, CurCont, DentInd, DokArb, EMBASE, ErgAb, ExcerpMed, FR, FoSS&M, HospLI, IBR, IBZ, INI, IndMed, Inpharma, MEDLINE, MycolAb, P30, P35, R10, Reac, SCI, SCOPUS, T02, W07.
—BLDSC (8413.903000), CASDDS, GNLM, IE, Infotrieve, Ingenta, INIST. **CCC.**
Published by: Lippincott Williams & Wilkins (Subsidiary of: Wolters Kluwer N.V.), 530 Walnut St, Philadelphia, PA 19106. TEL 215-521-8300, FAX 215-521-8902, customerservice@lww.com, http://www.lww.com. Ed. James N Weinstein. Pub. Marcia E Serepy TEL 207-828-0162. Circ: 4,310.

616.7 617.06 NLD ISSN 1529-9430
RD768 CODEN: SJPOA6
THE SPINE JOURNAL. Text in English. 2001. 12/yr. USD 401 in United States to institutions; USD 463 elsewhere to institutions (effective 2012). adv. **Document type:** *Journal, Academic/Scholarly.* **Description:** Publishes original articles on research and treatment related to spine and spine care, including basic science and clinical investigations.
Related titles: Online - full text ed.: ISSN 1878-1632 (from IngentaConnect, ScienceDirect).
Indexed: A01, A03, A08, A26, C06, C07, CA, CurCont, EMBASE, ExcerpMed, I05, MEDLINE, P30, R10, Reac, SCI, SCOPUS, T02, W07.
—BLDSC (8413.903500), IE, Ingenta. **CCC.**
Published by: (North American Spine Society USA), Elsevier BV (Subsidiary of: Elsevier Science & Technology), Radarweg 29, PO Box 211, Amsterdam, 1000 AE, Netherlands. TEL 31-20-4853911, FAX 31-20-4852457, JournalsCustomerServiceEMEA@elsevier.com, http://www.elsevier.nl. Ed. Eugene J Carragee.

617 USA ISSN 1062-8592
CODEN: SMARCV
➤ **SPORTS MEDICINE AND ARTHROSCOPY REVIEW.** Text in English. 1993. q. USD 561 domestic to institutions; USD 651 foreign to institutions (effective 2011). adv. illus. index. back issues avail.; reprints avail. **Document type:** *Journal, Academic/Scholarly.* **Description:** Designed for physicians to digest the clinical literature in sports medicine and arthroscopy, identify the new developments, and apply new information effectively in clinical practice.
Related titles: Microform ed.; Online - full text ed.: ISSN 1538-1951.
Indexed: A01, A03, A08, ASCA, B21, C06, C07, CA, EMBASE, ESPM, ExcerpMed, FoSS&M, H&SSA, MEDLINE, P30, PEI, R09, R10, Reac, SCI, SCOPUS, SD, T02, W07.
—BLDSC (8419.837370), GNLM, IE, Infotrieve, Ingenta. **CCC.**
Published by: Lippincott Williams & Wilkins (Subsidiary of: Wolters Kluwer N.V.), 530 Walnut St, Philadelphia, PA 19106. TEL 215-521-8300, FAX 215-521-8902, customerservice@lww.com, http://www.lww.com. Eds. Kenneth E DeHaven TEL 716-275-2970, Dr. W Dilworth Cannon TEL 415-353-7566. Pub. Kevin Anderer. Circ: 401.

616.7 ITA ISSN 1828-8936
➤ **STRATEGIES IN TRAUMA AND LIMB RECONSTRUCTION.** Text in English. 2006. 3/yr. free (effective 2011). reprint service avail. from PSC. **Document type:** *Journal, Academic/Scholarly.*
Related titles: Online - full text ed.: ISSN 1828-8928 (from IngentaConnect).
Indexed: A22, A26, B21, CTA, E01, I05, P30, SCOPUS.
—IE, Ingenta. **CCC.**
Published by: Springer Italia Srl (Subsidiary of: Springer Science+Business Media), Via Decembrio 28, Milan, 20137, Italy. TEL 39-02-54259722, FAX 39-02-55193360, springer@springer.it. Eds. Konrad Mader, Selvadurai Nayagam.

616.7 SWE ISSN 1654-2363
STUDIES IN OSTEOLOGY. Text in English. 2005. irreg., latest vol.1, 2005. **Document type:** *Monographic series, Academic/Scholarly.*
Published by: (Lunds Universitet, Institutionen foer Arkeologi och Antikens Historia/Lund University. Department of Archaeology and Ancient History), Almqvist & Wiksell International, P O Box 7634, Stockholm, 10394, Sweden. TEL 46-8-6136133, 46-8-6136100, info@akademibokhandeln.se, http://www.akademibokhandeln.se.

SWISS KNIFE. *see* MEDICAL SCIENCES—Surgery

616.7 JPN ISSN 0915-3004
T M J NIHON GAKU KANSETSU GAKKAI ZASSHI. Text in Japanese. 1980. s-a. **Document type:** *Journal, Academic/Scholarly.*
Formerly (until 1988): Gakukansetsu Kenkyukaishi (0914-4870)
Related titles: Online - full text ed.
Indexed: P30.
Published by: Nihon Gaku Kansetsu Gakkai/Japanese Society for Temporomandibular Joint, Komagome TS Bldg., 1-43-9 Komagome, Toshima-ku, Tokyo, 170-0003, Japan. TEL 81-3-39478891, FAX 81-3-39478341.

616.7 ITA ISSN 1970-741X
TABLOID DI ORTOPEDIA. Text in Italian. 2006. 9/yr. **Document type:** *Magazine, Trade.*
Published by: Griffin Srl, Via Airoldi 11, Carimate, Como 22060, Italy. TEL 39-031-789085, FAX 39-031-790743, redazione@griffineditore.it, http://www.griffineditore.it.

616.7 KOR
TAEHAN CHONGHYONG OEKWA HAKHOECHI/KOREAN ORTHOPEDIC ASSOCIATION. JOURNAL. Text in Korean. 1966. bi-m. **Document type:** *Journal, Academic/Scholarly.*
Formerly (until 198?): Taehan Chonghyong Oekwa Hakhoe Chapchi
Related titles: Online - full text ed.
Published by: Taehan Chonghyong Oekwa Hakhoe/Korean Orthopedic Association, Yoeido-Dong Youngdeungpo-Gu, Seoul, 150-732, Korea, S. TEL 82-2-7802765, FAX 82-2-7802767, ortho@koa.or.kr, http://www.koa.or.kr/main/.

616.7 CAN ISSN 1922-3447
TALKBACK. Text in English. 1985. q. free to members (effective 2010). **Document type:** *Newsletter, Trade.* **Description:** Provides information about happenings in the world of Arthritis.
Formerly (until 2009): Ontario Spondylitis Association. Newsletter (0831-7631)
Related titles: Online - full text ed.
Published by: Canadian Spondylitis Association, 18 Long Cres, Toronto, ON M4E 1N6, Canada. info@spondylitis.ca, http://www.spondylitis.ca. Ed. Christy MacPhail.

TECHNIQUES IN FOOT & ANKLE SURGERY. *see* MEDICAL SCIENCES—Surgery

TECHNIQUES IN KNEE SURGERY. *see* MEDICAL SCIENCES—Surgery

617.3 USA ISSN 0885-9698
RD701
➤ **TECHNIQUES IN ORTHOPAEDICS.** Text in English. 1986. q. USD 561 domestic to institutions; USD 671 foreign to institutions (effective 2011). adv. illus. index. back issues avail.; reprints avail. **Document type:** *Journal, Academic/Scholarly.* **Description:** Brings out technique oriented articles covering operations, manipulations and instruments being developed and applied in such areas as arthroscopy, arthroplasty and trauma.
Related titles: Microform ed.; Online - full text ed.
Indexed: A22, C06, C07, EMBASE, ExcerpMed, R10, Reac, SCOPUS.
—BLDSC (8745.278000), GNLM, IE, Infotrieve, Ingenta. **CCC.**
Published by: Lippincott Williams & Wilkins (Subsidiary of: Wolters Kluwer N.V.), Two Commerce Sq, 2001 Market St, Philadelphia, PA 19103. TEL 215-521-8300, FAX 215-521-8902, customerservice@lww.com, http://www.lww.com. Ed. Bruce D Browner. Pub. Kevin Anderer. Adv. contact Renee Artuso TEL 516-741-1772. Circ: 404.

617.3 ESP ISSN 1132-1954
TECNICAS QUIRURGICAS EN ORTOPEDIA Y TRAUMATOLOGIA. Text in Spanish. 1992. q. EUR 155.75 combined subscription to individuals print & online eds.; EUR 394.31 combined subscription to institutions print & online eds. (effective 2009). **Document type:** *Journal, Academic/Scholarly.*
Related titles: Online - full text ed.: EUR 129.75 (effective 2009); ◆ Translation of: Operative Orthopaedie und Traumatologie. ISSN 0934-6694.
Published by: Elsevier Doyma (Subsidiary of: Elsevier Health Sciences), Traversa de Gracia 17-21, Barcelona, 08021, Spain. TEL 34-932-418800, FAX 34-932-419020, editorial@elsevier.com. Ed. A. Navarro Quillis. Circ: 1,300.

616.7 ITA ISSN 1971-1905
TECNICHE CHIRURGICHE IN ORTOPEDIA E TRAUMATOLOGIA. Text in Multiple languages. 2003. 3/yr. **Document type:** *Journal, Trade.*
Media: Online - full text.
Published by: C I C Edizioni Internazionali, Corso Trieste 42, Rome, 00198, Italy. TEL 39-06-8412673, FAX 39-06-8412688, info@gruppocic.it, http://www.gruppocic.it.

616.7 GBR ISSN 1759-720X
RC925.A1
▼ **THERAPEUTIC ADVANCES IN MUSCULOSKELETAL DISEASE.** Text in English. 2009 (Oct.). bi-m. USD 1,071, GBP 579 combined subscription to institutions (print & online eds.); USD 1,050, GBP 567 to institutions (effective 2011). **Document type:** *Journal, Academic/Scholarly.* **Description:** For professionals concerned with research into, and the practice of, musculoskeletal disease and is a forum for all views on related subjects.
Related titles: Online - full text ed.: ISSN 1759-7218. USD 964, GBP 521 to institutions (effective 2011).
Indexed: A22, E01, P30.
—CCC.
Published by: Sage Publications Ltd. (Subsidiary of: Sage Publications, Inc.), 1 Oliver's Yard, 55 City Rd, London, EC1Y 1SP, United Kingdom. TEL 44-20-73248500, FAX 44-20-73248600, info@sagepub.co.uk, http://www.uk.sagepub.com/home.nav. Ed. Phillip Sambrook.

616.7 USA ISSN 1938-6311
TODAY'S WOUND CLINIC; contemporary approaches to wound clinic management. Text in English. 2007. irreg., latest 2010. USD 99 per issue domestic; USD 200 per issue foreign (effective 2010). adv. back issues avail.; reprints avail. **Document type:** *Magazine, Trade.* **Description:** Features business and medical advice on improving outpatient wound treatment centers.
Related titles: Online - full text ed.: free (effective 2010).
—CCC.
Published by: H M P Communications, LLC (Subsidiary of: Alta Communications), 83 General Warren Blvd, Ste 100, Malvern, PA 19355. TEL 610-560-0500, 800-237-7285, FAX 610-560-0502, http://www.hmpcommunications.com. Eds. Caroline E Fife, Dot Weir.

617.3 JPN ISSN 0915-2253
➤ **TOHKAI SEIKEI GEKA GAISHO KENKYU KAISHI/TOHKAI ORTHOPAEDIC SOCIETY OF TRAUMATOLOGY. JOURNAL.** Text in Japanese. 1988. a. JPY 5,000 to non-members; JPY 1,000 per issue. adv. back issues avail. **Document type:** *Academic/Scholarly.* **Description:** Publishes proceedings of medical meetings and original articles on traumatology, including fractures, dislocations and other injuries in the orthopaedic field.
Related titles: CD-ROM ed.; Fax ed.
Published by: Tohkai Seikei Geka Gaisho Kenkyukai/Tohkai Orthopaedic Society of Traumatology, Gifu Kenritsu Tajimi Byoin Seikei Geka, 5-161 Maebata-cho, Tajimi-shi, Gifu-ken 507-0042, Japan. TEL 81-572-22-5311, FAX 81-572-25-1246. Ed. Toshiyuki Muro. Circ: 1,000 (controlled).

617.3 JPN ISSN 0913-476X
➤ **TOHKAI SEKITSUI GEKA/JOURNAL OF TOHKAI SPINAL SURGERY.** Text in Japanese; Summaries in English, Japanese. 1987. a. JPY 5,000 to non-members. adv. **Document type:** *Academic/Scholarly.* **Description:** Contains proceedings of medical meetings, original articles, and historical reviews on spinal surgery.
Related titles: CD-ROM ed.; Online - full text ed.
Published by: Tohkai Sekitsui Geka Kenkyukai/Society of Tohkai Spinal Surgery, Gifu Kenritsu Tajimi Byoin, 5-161 Maebata-cho, Tajimi-shi, Gifu-ken 507-0042, Japan. TEL 81-3-3334-7625, FAX 81-3-3334-0497. Ed. Dr. Toshiyuki Muro. Circ: 600 (controlled).

617.3 JPN ISSN 1348-8694
TOUHOKU SEIKEI SAIGAI GEKA GAKKAI ZASSHI/TOHOKU SEIKEI SAIGAI GEKA KIYO. Text in Japanese. 1957. s-a. membership. bk.rev. abstr.; bibl.; charts; illus. index, cum.index.
Former titles (until 2003): Tohoku Seikei Saigai Geka Kiyo/Tohoku Archives of Orthopaedic Surgery and Traumatology (0040-8751); (until vol.20, 1977): Tohoku Archivo por Orthopedia Kej Akcidenta Hirurgio
Published by: Tohoku Society of Orthopaedic Surgery and Traumatology/Tohoku Seikei Saigai Geka Gakkai, c/o Dept of Orthopaedic Surgery, Tohoku University School of Medicine, 1-1 Seiryo-cho, Aoba-ku, Sendai-shi, Miyagi-ken 980-8574, Japan. TEL 81-22-7177245, FAX 81-22-7177248. Circ: 650 (controlled).

616.02 MEX ISSN 1405-1001
TRAUMA. Text in Spanish; Summaries in English, Spanish. 1992. q. USD 40. **Document type:** *Academic/Scholarly.* **Description:** Contains original articles, research reports, review articles, clinical cases and notices related to emergency medicine.
Indexed: C01.
Published by: Asociacion Mexicana de Medicina y Cirugia del Trauma, Hospital Espanol Sala 8 Cons. 5, Ave Ejercito Nacional 613, Col. Granada, Mexico, D.F., 11520, Mexico. TEL 52-55-52505094, http://www.asemde.com/ammct/Asociacion.htm. Ed. Alberto Basilio Olivares. Circ: 2,000.

617.1 616.02 GBR ISSN 1460-4086
➤ **TRAUMA.** Text in English. 1999. q. USD 598, GBP 323 combined subscription to institutions (print & online eds.); USD 586, GBP 317 to institutions (effective 2011). adv. back issues avail.; reprint service avail. from PSC. **Document type:** *Journal, Academic/Scholarly.* **Description:** Covers all aspects of trauma care from prevention through rehabilitation.
Related titles: Online - full text ed.: ISSN 1477-0350. USD 538, GBP 291 to institutions (effective 2011).
Indexed: A01, A02, A03, A08, A22, C06, C07, C11, CA, E-psyche, E01, EMBASE, ExcerpMed, H04, P16, P20, P24, P48, P53, P54, PEI, PQC, R10, Reac, SCOPUS, T02.
—BLDSC (9026.856800), IE, Infotrieve, Ingenta. **CCC.**
Published by: Sage Publications Ltd. (Subsidiary of: Sage Publications, Inc.), 1 Oliver's Yard, 55 City Rd, London, EC1Y 1SP, United Kingdom. TEL 44-20-73248500, FAX 44-20-73248600, info@sagepub.co.uk, http://www.uk.sagepub.com/home.nav. Eds. Ian Greaves, James M Ryan, Keith M Porter. adv.: B&W page GBP 450; 160 x 215.

617.1 USA ISSN 1531-1082
TRAUMA REPORTS. Text in English. 2000. bi-m. USD 249 combined subscription (print & online eds.); USD 42 per issue (effective 2010). **Document type:** *Newsletter, Trade.* **Description:** Focuses on emergency care of adult and pediatric patients with moderate and severe traumatic injuries.
Related titles: Online - full text ed.: ISSN 1945-7391; ◆ Supplement to: Emergency Department Management. ISSN 1044-9167; ◆ Supplement to: Pediatric Emergency Medicine Reports. ISSN 1082-3344; ◆ Supplement to: Emergency Medicine Reports. ISSN 0746-2506.
Indexed: A01, A26, CA, E08, G08, H11, H12, I05, P20, P48, P54, PQC, S09, T02.
—BLDSC (9026.857310). **CCC.**
Published by: A H C Media LLC (Subsidiary of: Thomson Corporation, Healthcare Information Group), 3525 Piedmont Rd, NE, Bldg 6, Ste 400, Atlanta, GA 30305. TEL 404-262-7436, 800-688-2421, FAX 404-262-7837, 800-284-3291, customerservice@ahcmedia.com, http://www.ahcmedia.com/. Ed. Ann Dietrich. Pub. Brenda L Mooney TEL 404-262-5403. **Subscr. to:** PO Box 105109, Atlanta, GA 30348. TEL 404-262-5476, FAX 404-262-5560.

617 ZAF
TRAUMA REVIEW. Text in English. q. free. **Document type:** *Newsletter.*
Indexed: ISAP.
Published by: (National Trauma Research Programme), Medical Research Council, PO Box 19070, Tygerberg, 7505, South Africa. TEL 27-21-9380911, FAX 27-21-9380381, http://www.mrc.ac.za/. Ed., R&P Johan van der Spuy.

617.1 DEU ISSN 1436-6274
➤ **TRAUMA UND BERUFSKRANKHEIT.** Text in German. 1998. q. EUR 221, USD 229 combined subscription to institutions (print & online eds.) (effective 2012). adv. back issues avail.; reprint service avail. from PSC. **Document type:** *Journal, Academic/Scholarly.* **Description:** Covers all aspects of trauma and emergency medicine.
Related titles: Online - full text ed.: ISSN 1436-6282 (from IngentaConnect).
Indexed: A01, A03, A08, A22, A26, CA, E01, SCOPUS, T02, TM.
—BLDSC (9026.857320), IE, Infotrieve, Ingenta. **CCC.**
Published by: Springer (Subsidiary of: Springer Science+Business Media), Tiergartenstr 17, Heidelberg, 69121, Germany. TEL 49-6221-4870, FAX 49-6221-345229. Adv. contact Stephan Kroeck TEL 49-30-827875739. Circ: 650 (paid and controlled). **Subscr. in the Americas to:** Springer New York LLC, Journal Fulfillment, PO Box 2485, Secaucus, NJ 07096. TEL 201-348-4033, 800-777-4643, FAX 201-348-4505, journals-ny@springer.com, http://www.springer.com; **Subscr. to:** Springer Distribution Center, Kundenservice Zeitschriften, Haberstr 7, Heidelberg 69126, Germany. TEL 49-6221-3454303, FAX 49-6221-3454229, subscriptions@springer.com.

➤ **TRAUMA UND GEWALT**; Forschung und Praxisfelder. *see* PSYCHOLOGY

353.6 610 USA ISSN 1524-8380
HV6626.5
TRAUMA, VIOLENCE & ABUSE; a review journal. Text in English. q. adv. reprint service avail. from PSC. **Document type:** *Journal, Academic/Scholarly.* **Description:** Devoted to organizing, synthesizing and expanding knowledge on all forms of trauma, violence and abuse. Dedicated to professionals and advanced students in clinical training who work in all forms of trauma, violence and abuse and is intended to compile knowledge that impacts practice, policy and research.
Related titles: Online - full text ed.: ISSN 1552-8324. USD 462, GBP 272 to institutions (effective 2011).
Indexed: A01, A02, A03, A08, A22, B07, C06, C07, C08, CA, CINAHL, CJA, CJPI, CurCont, E-psyche, E01, EMBASE, ESPM, ExcerpMed, FamI, H04, MEDLINE, P03, P30, PQC, PsycInfo, PsycholAb, RiskAb, S02, S03, SCOPUS, SFSA, SSA, SSCI, SWR&A, SociolAb, T02, V&AA, V02, W07, W09.
—BLDSC (9026.857330), IE, Infotrieve, Ingenta. **CCC.**
Published by: Sage Publications, Inc., 2455 Teller Rd, Thousand Oaks, CA 91320. TEL 805-499-9774, 800-818-7243, FAX 805-499-0871, 800-583-2665, info@sagepub.com. Ed. Jon R Conte. **Subscr. to:** Sage Publications Ltd., 1 Oliver's Yard, 55 City Rd, London EC1Y 1SP, United Kingdom. TEL 44-207-3248701, FAX 44-207-3248733, subscription@sagepub.co.uk.

617.3 USA
TRAUMA WATCH. Text in English. 19??. bi-w. free to members (effective 2010). **Document type:** *Newsletter, Consumer.* **Description:** Covers information on trauma care across the nation.
Related titles: Online - full text ed.: free (effective 2010).
Published by: American Trauma Society, 7611 S Osborne Rd, Ste 202, Upper Marlboro, MD 20772. TEL 301-574-4300, 800-556-7890, FAX 301-574-4301, info@amtrauma.org, http://www.amtrauma.org. Ed. Heidi Atlas.

617.3 USA
TRAUMAGRAM. Text in English. 19??. q. free to members (effective 2010). **Document type:** *Newsletter, Consumer.*
Published by: American Trauma Society, 7611 S Osborne Rd, Ste 202, Upper Marlboro, MD 20772. TEL 301-574-4300, 800-556-7890, FAX 301-574-4301, info@amtrauma.org, http://www.amtrauma.org.

617.1 USA ISSN 1085-9373
➤ **TRAUMATOLOGY (ONLINE).** Text in English. q. USD 440, GBP 259 to institutions (effective 2011). **Document type:** *Journal, Academic/Scholarly.* **Description:** Reference for professionals all over the world who study and treat people exposed to highly stressful and traumatic events, such as terrorist bombings, war disasters, fires, accidents, criminal and familial abuse, hostage-taking, hospitalization, major illness, abandonment, and sudden unemployment.
Media: Online - full text.
—CCC.
Published by: Sage Publications, Inc., 2455 Teller Rd, Thousand Oaks, CA 91320. TEL 805-499-9774, FAX 805-499-0871, info@sagepub.com, http://www.sagepub.com/.

616.7 UKR ISSN 1608-1706
➤ **TRAVMA/TRAUMA**; naukovo-praktychnyi zhurnal. Text in Ukrainian. 2000. s-a. USD 92 in United States (effective 2007). **Document type:** *Journal, Academic/Scholarly.*
—BLDSC (0181.577500), East View.
Published by: Ministerstvo Okhorony Zdorov'ya Ukrainy, Donets'kyi Derzhavnyi Medychnyi Universytet im. M. Hor'kogo, Naukovo-Doslidnyi Instytut Travmatolohii ta Ortopedii/Ministry of Health Service of Ukraine, Donetsk State Medical University named after M. Gorky, Research and Development Institute of Traumatology and Orthopedics, vul Artema 106, Donets'k, 83048, Ukraine. TEL 380-62-3351461, FAX 380-62-2551141. Ed. V G Klymovyts'kyi. Circ: 150. **Dist. by:** East View Information Services, 10601 Wayzata Blvd, Minneapolis, MN 55305. TEL 952-252-1201, 800-477-1005, FAX 952-252-1202, info@eastview.com, http://www.eastview.com.

➤ **TURK ANESTEZIYOLOJI VE REANIMASYON DERNEGI DERGISI/TURKISH ANESTHESIOLOGY AND REANIMATION SOCIETY. JOURNAL.** *see* MEDICAL SCIENCES—Anaesthesiology

616.7 GBR ISSN 1753-4143
U S MUSCULOSKELETAL REVIEW. (United States) Text in English. 2006 (Jun.). s-a. adv. back issues avail. **Document type:** *Journal, Trade.* **Description:** Focuses on latest developments within the US musculoskeletal disease market from a scientific and clinical perspectives.
Related titles: Online - full text ed.: ISSN 1753-4151.
Published by: Touch Briefings (Subsidiary of: Touch Group plc), Saffron House, 6-10 Kirby St, London, EC1N 8TS, United Kingdom. TEL 44-20-74525600, FAX 44-20-74525606, info@touchbriefings.com. Circ: 15,000.

616.025 384.64 TUR ISSN 1306-696X
ULUSAL TRAVMA VE ACIL CERRAHI DERGISI/TURKISH JOURNAL OF TRAUMA & EMERGENCY SURGERY. Text in Turkish. 1995. s-a. **Document type:** *Journal, Academic/Scholarly.*
Formerly (until 200?): Ulusal Travma Dergisi (1300-6738)
Indexed: A22, P30, SCOPUS.
—BLDSC (9082.818300), IE, Ingenta.
Published by: Istanbul Universitesi, Ulusal Travma ve Acil Cerrahi Dernegi, Deniz Abdal Mah. Koprulu Mehmet Pasa Sok, Dadasoglu Apt. No. 25/1, Sehremini, Istanbul, 34104, Turkey. TEL 90-212-5886246, FAX 90-212-5331882, info@travma.org.tr. Ed. Erhan Aysan.

616.028 617.1 DEU ISSN 0177-5537
R51 CODEN: UNFAE2
➤ **DER UNFALLCHIRURG.** Text in German. 1894. m. EUR 657, USD 712 combined subscription to institutions (print & online eds.) (effective 2012). adv. back issues avail.; reprint service avail. from PSC. **Document type:** *Journal, Academic/Scholarly.* **Description:** Covers all aspects of trauma and emergency surgery.
Former titles (until 1985): Unfallheilkunde (0341-5694); (until 1976): Monatsschrift fuer Unfallheilkunde (0340-1669); (until 1974): Monatsschrift fuer Unfallheilkunde, Versicherungs-, Versorgungs- und Verkehrsmedizin (0026-9336); (until 1963): Monatsschrift fuer Unfallheilkunde und Versicherungsmedizin (0373-5222)
Related titles: Microform ed.: (from PQC); Online - full text ed.: ISSN 1433-044X (from IngentaConnect).
Indexed: A22, A26, ASCA, CurCont, E01, EMBASE, ExcerpMed, FR, IndMed, Inpharma, MEDLINE, P30, R10, Reac, SCI, SCOPUS, W07.
—BLDSC (9090.235280), GNLM, IE, Infotrieve, Ingenta, INIST. **CCC.**
Published by: (Deutsche Gesellschaft fuer Unfallheilkunde), Springer (Subsidiary of: Springer Science+Business Media), Tiergartenstr 17, Heidelberg, 69121, Germany. TEL 49-6221-4870, FAX 49-6221-345229. Eds. Dr. C Krettek, Dr. W Mutschler. Adv. contact Stephan Kroeck TEL 49-30-827875739. Circ: 4,100 (paid and controlled). **Subscr. in the Americas to:** Springer New York LLC, Journal Fulfillment, PO Box 2485, Secaucus, NJ 07096. TEL 800-777-4643, 201-348-4033, FAX 201-348-4505, journals-ny@springer.com, http://www.springer.com; **Subscr. to:** Springer Distribution Center, Kundenservice Zeitschriften, Haberstr 7, Heidelberg 69126, Germany. TEL 49-6221-3454303, FAX 49-6221-3454229, subscriptions@springer.com.

616.7 USA
➤ **UNIVERSITY OF PENNSYLVANIA ORTHOPAEDIC JOURNAL (ONLINE).** Short title: U P O J. Text in English. 1985. a. free (effective 2011). **Document type:** *Journal, Academic/Scholarly.* **Description:** Emphasizes research with strong scientific content and experimentation, as well as literature directed towards advancement of the discipline by focusing on new clinical observations and developments from laboratory investigations.
Formerly (until 1996): University of Pennsylvania Orthopaedic Journal (Print) (0885-4904)
Media: Online - full text.
—CCC.
Published by: University of Pennsylvania, Department of Orthopaedic Surgery, 36th & Spruce Sts., Philadelphia, PA 19104. Eds. Chancellor F Gray, Mara L Schenker.

616.025 FRA ISSN 1244-1791
URGENCE PRATIQUE. Text in French. 1992. bi-m. EUR 70 (effective 2010). **Document type:** *Journal, Academic/Scholarly.*
—CCC.
Published by: Urgence Pratique Publications, BP 26, Ganges, 34190, France. TEL 33-04-67735361, FAX 33-04-67738636. Ed., Adv. contact Jean-Claude Deslandes.

616.025 CAN ISSN 1914-5802
L'URGENTISTE. Text in French. 1996. m. **Document type:** *Journal, Trade.*
Former titles (until 2007): Archives de la Medecine d'Urgence Quebecoise (1711-134X); (until 2003): Medecine d'Urgence (1701-2155)
Published by: Association des Medecins d'Urgence du Quebec, 750 Bd Charest Est, Bureau 515, Quebec, PQ G1K 3J7, Canada. TEL 418-658-7679, FAX 418-658-6545, amuq@amuq.qc.ca, http://www.amuq.qc.ca.

617 NLD ISSN 2212-1714
VAKBLAD V & V N AMBULANCEZORG. Text in Dutch. 1978; N.S. 1999. q. EUR 40 (effective 2009). adv. back issues avail. **Description:** Covers topics relating to emergency medicine and ambulances.
Former titles (until 2008): Vakblad Beroeps Vereniging Ambulancezorg (1573-5885); (until 2004): Ambulance (1389-2614); Which was formed by the 1999 merger of (1996-1998): De Ambulancekrant (1384-9883); (1980-1998): N T S R (1380-3522); Which was formerly (until 1994): Ambulance (0167-9589); Ambulance incorporated (1999-2000): N A I Bulletin (1568-3982)
—IE.
Published by: V & V N Ambulancezorg, Churchillaan 11, Utrecht, 3527 GV, Netherlands. TEL 31-30-2919050, info@beroepsverenigingambulancezorg.nl, http://www.beroepsverenigingambulancezorg.nl. Eds. Piet Hoving, Chris de Vogel.

617.3 RUS ISSN 0869-8678
VESTNIK TRAVMATOLOGII I ORTOPEDII IM. N.N. PRIOROVA. Text in Russian; Summaries in English. 1927. q. USD 162 foreign (effective 2005). bk.rev. bibl. **Document type:** *Journal, Academic/Scholarly.* **Description:** Discusses basic theoretical and practical problems of orthopedics, traumatology and prosthetics.
Formerly (until 1994): Ortopediya, Travmatologiya i Protezirovanie (0030-5987)
Indexed: DentInd, IndMed, P30, RefZh.
—BLDSC (0036.550000), East View, GNLM, INIST. **CCC.**
Published by: Izdatel'stvo Meditsina/Meditsina Publishers, ul B Pirogovskaya, d 2, str 5, Moscow, 119435, Russian Federation. TEL 7-095-2483324, meditsina@mtu-net.ru, http://www.medlit.ru. Ed. Sergey P Mironov. R&P L Tikhomirova. Circ: 2,500. **Dist. by:** East View Information Services, 10601 Wayzata Blvd, Minneapolis, MN 55305. TEL 952-252-1201, 800-477-1005, FAX 952-252-1202, info@eastview.com, http://www.eastview.com.

VETERINARY AND COMPARATIVE ORTHOPAEDICS AND TRAUMATOLOGY. *see* VETERINARY SCIENCE

617.33 USA ISSN 1524-9778
VIDEO JOURNAL OF ORTHOPAEDICS. Text in English. 1986. q. USD 495 to individuals; USD 695 to institutions (effective 2002). back issues avail.
Media: Optical Disk - DVD. **Related titles:** CD-ROM ed.; Online - full text ed.; Optical Disk - DVD ed.: USD 595 to individuals; USD 795 to institutions (effective 2002).
Address: P O Box 4367, Santa Barbara, CA 93140. TEL 805-962-3410, FAX 805-962-1260, customersupport@vjortho.com.

362.18 USA
VITALCARE. Text in English. 2008. q. adv. **Document type:** *Magazine, Consumer.* **Description:** Offers readers health, safety, and emergency medical information.
Published by: (American College of Emergency Physicians Foundation), The Pohly Co., 99 Bedford St, Fl 5, Boston, MA 02111. TEL 617-451-1700, 800-383-0888, FAX 617-338-7767, info@pohlyco.com, http://www.pohlyco.com. adv.: B&W page USD 15,080, color page USD 16,400; trim 8.125 x 10.875. Circ: 250,000 (free).

616.025 USA ISSN 1936-900X
WESTERN JOURNAL OF EMERGENCY MEDICINE. Text in English. 2000. q. adv. back issues avail. **Document type:** *Journal, Academic/Scholarly.* **Description:** Provides research and review articles in patient care through clinical decision-making, efficiency of evaluation and treatment, medical education and promotion of patient safety.
Formerly (until 2007): The California Journal of Emergency Medicine (1948-3384)
Related titles: Online - full text ed.: ISSN 1936-9018. free (effective 2011).
Indexed: B21, C06, ESPM, H&SSA, P30, RiskAb.
Published by: (American Academy of Emergency Medicine, California Chapter), eScholarship (Subsidiary of: California Digital Library), 300 Lakeside Dr, 7th Fl, Oakland, CA 94612. TEL 510-587-6439, FAX 510-987-0243, info@escholarship.org, http://www.escholarship.org. Eds. Mark I Langdorf TEL 714-456-2326, Suleman Ahmed TEL 714-456-6389. Adv. contact June Casey TEL 714-456-5922. **Co-sponsor:** University of California, Irvine, Department of Emergency Medicine.

616.71 NLD ISSN 1878-898X
WHIPLASH MAGAZINE. Text in Dutch. 3/yr. EUR 6.50 to non-members; EUR 4.75 to members (effective 2010).
Formerly (until 2009): Whiplash Rapport (1871-6180)
Published by: Whiplash Stichting Nederland, Postbus 105, Bunnik, 3980 CC, Netherlands. TEL 31-30-6565000, FAX 31-30-6565252, http://www.whiplashstichting.nl, info@whiplashstichting.nl.

616.7 DEU ISSN 1616-3877
WIRTSCHAFTSMAGAZIN FUER DEN ORTHOPAEDEN. Text in German. 1996. bi-m. EUR 22.50 (effective 2011). adv. **Document type:** *Magazine, Trade.*
Formerly (until 2000): Wirtschaftsbrief fuer den Orthopaeden (1439-2984)
Published by: W P V- Wirtschafts- und Praxisverlag GmbH, Otto-Hahn-Str 7, Koeln, 50997, Germany. TEL 49-2236-376711, FAX 49-2236-37692530, info@wpv.de. Adv. contact Isabelle Becker TEL 49-2236-376711. Circ: 2,794 (controlled).

616.7 DEU ISSN 1866-2846
WIRTSCHAFTSTIP FUER ORTHOPAEDEN - RHEUMATOLOGEN. Text in German. 2004. m. EUR 21.40 (effective 2008). adv. **Document type:** *Journal, Trade.*
Published by: Aerzte Zeitung Verlagsgesellschaft mbH (Subsidiary of: Springer Science+Business Media), Am Forsthaus Gravenbruch 5, Neu-Isenburg, 63263, Germany. TEL 49-6102-506157, FAX 49-6102-506123, info@aerztezeitung.de, http://www.aerztezeitung.de. adv.: color page EUR 3,440, B&W page EUR 2,210. Circ: 4,818 (controlled).

616.7 GBR ISSN 1369-2607
➤ **WORLD WIDE WOUNDS.** Text in English. 1997. s-m. free (effective 2011). **Document type:** *Journal, Academic/Scholarly.* **Description:** Seeks to monitor and raise the standard of reference material available to professionals with an interest in wound management.
Media: Online - full content.
Indexed: C06, C07, C08, CINAHL, EMBASE, ExcerpMed, R10, Reac, SCOPUS.
Published by: Surgical Materials Testing Laboratory, Princess of Wales Hospital, Coity Rd, Bridgend, S Wales CF31 1RQ, United Kingdom. TEL 44-1656-752820, FAX 44-1656-752830, pete@smtl.co.uk, http://www.smtl.co.uk. **Co-sponsor:** Medical Education Partnership.

616.7 USA ISSN 2157-9148
▼ **WOUND CARE & HYPERBARIC MEDICINE.** Text in English. 2010. q. USD 65 (effective 2010). adv. **Document type:** *Magazine, Trade.* **Description:** Provides reports and comments on the current state of knowledge and advances in science and technology encompassing hyperbaric oxygen therapy, wound care, and diving medicine.
Published by: American Baromedical Corporation, 2700 PGA Blvd, Ste 104, Palm Beach Gardens, FL 33410. TEL 561-776-4004, FAX 561-776-4008, info@AmericanBaromedical.com, http://www.americanbaromedical.com/. Ed., Pub. Kenneth R Locklear.

617.1 GBR ISSN 1757-7519
WOUND CARE HANDBOOK (YEARS). Text in English. 2008. a. free domestic to qualified personnel; GBP 19.99 per issue; free to subscribers of Journal of Wound Care, British Journal of Nursing and British Journal of Community Nursing (effective 2008). **Document type:** *Handbook/Manual/Guide, Trade.* **Description:** Essential resource, providing an easy-to-use and comprehensive reference to over 475 products available to the UK wound care practitioner.
—BLDSC (9364.529154). **CCC.**
Published by: M A Healthcare Ltd. (Subsidiary of: Mark Allen Publishing Ltd.), St. Jude's Church, Dulwich Rd, London, SE24 0PB, United Kingdom. TEL 44-20-77385454, FAX 44-20-77332325. Ed. Tom Pollard.

617.1 ZAF ISSN 1998-8885
➤ **WOUND HEALING.** Text in English. 2008. 2/yr. **Document type:** *Journal, Academic/Scholarly.* **Description:** Publishes articles related to wound healing and wound care.
Related titles: Online - full text ed.: ISSN 2076-8893. 2008.
Indexed: A01, A36, CABA, E12, GH, N02, N03, T05.
Published by: Medpharm Publications (Pty) Ltd, PO Box 14804, Lyttelton, 0140, South Africa. TEL 27-12-6647460, FAX 27-12-6646276, reception@medpharm.co.za, http://www.medpharm.co.za. Ed. Alan Widgerow. Adv. contact Sandy Laranja.

617.14 AUS ISSN 1837-6304
➤ **WOUND PRACTICE & RESEARCH.** Text in English. 1993. q. AUD 143 to individuals; AUD 286 to institutions; AUD 35.75 per issue; free to members (effective 2010). adv. back issues avail. **Document type:** *Journal, Academic/Scholarly.* **Description:** Focuses on discussing and portraying issues on wound management within Australia and surrounding countries.
Formerly (until 2008): Primary Intention (1323-2495)
Related titles: Online - full text ed.
Indexed: C06, C07, C08, CA, CINAHL, T02.
—BLDSC (9364.529315), IE, Ingenta.
Published by: (Australian Wound Management Association), Cambridge Publishing (Subsidiary of: Cambridge Media), 10 Walters Dr, Osborne Park, W.A. 6017, Australia. TEL 61-8-63145222, FAX 61-8-63145299, mail@cambridgemedia.com.au, http://www.cambridgemedia.com.au. Eds. Allison Cowin TEL 61-8-81617077, Michael Woodward. Adv. contact Simon Henriques TEL 61-8-93823911.

617.1 USA ISSN 1067-1927
RD94 CODEN: WREREU
➤ **WOUND REPAIR AND REGENERATION.** Text in English. 1993. bi-m. GBP 443 in United Kingdom to institutions; EUR 561 in Europe to institutions; USD 604 in Canada & Mexico to institutions; USD 561 in the Americas to institutions; USD 865 elsewhere to institutions; GBP 509 combined subscription in United Kingdom to institutions (print & online eds.); EUR 646 combined subscription in Europe to institutions (print & online eds.); USD 695 combined subscription in Canada & Mexico to institutions (print & online eds.); USD 646 combined subscription in the Americas to institutions (print & online eds.); USD 996 combined subscription elsewhere to institutions (print & online eds.) (effective 2012). adv. abstr.; illus. back issues avail.; reprint service avail. from PSC. **Document type:** *Journal, Academic/Scholarly.* **Description:** Provides extensive international coverage of cellular and molecular biology, connective tissue, and biological mediator studies in the field of tissue repair and regeneration.
Related titles: Online - full text ed.: ISSN 1524-475X. 1999. GBP 443 in United Kingdom to institutions; EUR 561 in Europe to institutions; USD 604 in Canada & Mexico to institutions; USD 561 in the Americas to institutions; USD 865 elsewhere to institutions (effective 2012) (from IngentaConnect).
Indexed: A01, A02, A03, A08, A22, A26, A34, A35, A36, AgBio, B25, BIOSIS Prev, C06, C07, C08, C11, C25, C30, CA, CABA, CINAHL, CurCont, D01, E01, E12, EMBASE, ExcerpMed, F08, GH, H04, H12, INI, ISR, IndMed, IndVet, Inpharma, MEDLINE, MycolAb, N02, N03, P30, P32, P33, P35, P40, PN&I, R08, R10, R11, RA&MP, Reac, RefZh, SCI, SCOPUS, T02, T05, VS, W07.
—BLDSC (9364.529320), GNLM, IE, Infotrieve, Ingenta, INIST. **CCC.**
Published by: (Wound Healing Society), Wiley-Blackwell Publishing, Inc. (Subsidiary of: Wiley-Blackwell Publishing Ltd.), 111 River St, Hoboken, NJ 07030. TEL 201-748-6000, FAX 201-748-6088, info@wiley.com. Ed. Patricia A Hebda. Adv. contact Karl Franz TEL 781-388-8470. **Co-sponsors:** European Tissue Repair Society; Australian Wound Management Association; Japanese Society for Wound Healing.

617.1 USA
WOUND SOURCE; the Kestrel wound product sourcebook. Text in English. 200?. a. USD 34.95 per issue (effective 2009). adv. **Document type:** *Directory, Trade.*
Related titles: Online - full text ed.: ISSN 2151-2116.
Published by: Kestrel Health Information, Inc., 206 Commerce St, PO Box 189, Hinesburg, VT 05461. TEL 802-482-4000, FAX 802-329-2077, info@kestrelhealthinfo.com, http://www.kestrelhealthinfo.com/. Ed. Diane Krasner. Pub., Adv. contact Jeanne Cunningham TEL 802-482-4000 ext 224. B&W page USD 3,981, color page USD 5,481; trim 8.125 x 10.875. Circ: 24,678.

616.02 USA ISSN 1044-7946
➤ **WOUNDS;** a compendium of clinical research and practice. Text in English. 1989. m. USD 85 domestic; USD 140 foreign; free domestic to qualified personnel (effective 2010). adv. back issues avail. **Document type:** *Journal, Academic/Scholarly.* **Description:** Provides information on current research, treatment methodology, and protocol in the field of wound care.
Related titles: Online - full text ed.: ISSN 1943-2704. free (effective 2010).
Indexed: A22, ASCA, C06, C07, C08, CINAHL, CurCont, Inpharma, SCI, SCOPUS, W07.
—BLDSC (9364.529340), GNLM, IE, Ingenta. **CCC.**
Published by: H M P Communications, LLC (Subsidiary of: Alta Communications), 83 General Warren Blvd, Ste 100, Malvern, PA 19355. TEL 610-560-0500, 800-237-7285, FAX 610-560-0502, http://www.hmpcommunications.com. Pub., Adv. contact Jeremy Bowden TEL 800-237-7285 ext 219.

616.7 GBR ISSN 2044-0057
▼ **WOUNDS INTERNATIONAL;** the essential wound management resource for clinicians worldwide. Text in English. 2009. q. free (effective 2010). back issues avail. **Document type:** *Journal, Trade.* **Description:** Aims to provide a service that quickly updates the clinician on the developments in wound management.
Media: Online - full text.
Indexed: C06.
Address: c/o Schofield Healthcare Media Ltd, 3.05 Enterprise House, 1-2 Hatfields, London, SE1 9PG, United Kingdom. TEL 44-20-76271510, FAX 44-20-76271570. Ed. Suzie Calne. Pub. Kathy Day.

616.7 GBR ISSN 1746-6814
➤ **WOUNDS U K.** Text in English. 2005 (May). q. free to members (effective 2011). back issues avail. **Document type:** *Journal, Academic/Scholarly.* **Description:** Aims to provide cutting-edge articles and information on wound healing/management to all professionals working in wound care.
Related titles: Online - full text ed.

Indexed: B28, C06, EMBASE, ExcerpMed, R10, Reac, SCOPUS.
—BLDSC (9364.539330), IE, Ingenta.
Published by: Healthcomm U K, 36 Upperkirkgate, Ste 3.1, Aberdeen, AB10 1BA, United Kingdom. TEL 44-1224-637371, furtherinfo@wounds-uk.com.

616.7 DEU
➤ **WUNDMANAGEMENT.** Text in German; Summaries in English. 1995. bi-m. EUR 31.20; EUR 8.85 newsstand/cover (effective 2007). adv. back issues avail. **Document type:** *Journal, Academic/Scholarly.* **Description:** Provides information on all areas of wound care and the nursing of patients with chronic wounds.
Former titles (until 2007): Zeitschrift fuer Wundheilung (1439-670X); (until 2000): Zeitschrift fuer Wundbehandlung (1436-2171)
Indexed: A01, SCOPUS, T02.
—BLDSC (9495.222000), IE, Ingenta. **CCC.**
Published by: M H P Verlag GmbH, Marktplatz 13, Wiesbaden, 65183, Germany. TEL 49-611-505930, FAX 49-611-5059311, info@mhp-verlag.de. Eds. Dr. Barbara Springer, E S Debus, R U Peter. adv.: B&W page EUR 1,330, color page EUR 2,325; trim 179 x 234. Circ: 4,693 (controlled).

616.025 USA ISSN 0271-7964
RC86
YEAR BOOK OF EMERGENCY MEDICINE. Text in English. 1981. a. USD 239 in United States to institutions; USD 259 elsewhere to institutions (effective 2012). adv. **Document type:** *Yearbook, Academic/Scholarly.* **Description:** Presents abstracts of pertinent literature with commentary by leading experts in the field.
Related titles: CD-ROM ed.; Online - full text ed.
—GNLM. **CCC.**
Published by: Mosby, Inc. (Subsidiary of: Elsevier Health Sciences), 1600 John F. Kennedy Blvd, Ste 1800, Philadelphia, PA 19103. TEL 215-239-3900, 800-523-1649, FAX 215-239-3990, elspcs@elsevier.com, http://www.us.elsevierhealth.com. Ed. Richard J Hamilton.

YEAR BOOK OF HAND AND UPPER LIMB SURGERY. *see* MEDICAL SCIENCES—Surgery

YEAR BOOK OF ORTHOPEDICS. *see* MEDICAL SCIENCES—Abstracting, Bibliographies, Statistics

616.7 DEU ISSN 1864-6697
➤ **ZEITSCHRIFT FUER ORTHOPAEDIE UND UNFALLCHIRURGIE.** Text in German. 2007. bi-m. EUR 348 to institutions; EUR 485 to institutions (print & online eds.); EUR 72 newsstand/cover (effective 2011). adv. **Document type:** *Journal, Academic/Scholarly.*
Formed by the merger of (1971-2007): Aktuelle Traumatologie (0044-6173); (1936-2007): Zeitschrift fuer Orthopaedie und Ihre Grenzgebiete (0044-3220); Which incorporated (1969-1991): Deutsche Gesellschaft fuer Orthopaedie und Ihre Grenzgebiete. Verhandlungen (0070-4091); Which was formerly (1913-1969): Verhandlungen der Deutschen Orthopaedischen Gesellschaft (0070-4288)
Related titles: Online - full text ed.: ISSN 1864-6743. EUR 470 to institutions (effective 2011).
Indexed: CurCont, EMBASE, MEDLINE, P30, SCI, SCOPUS, W07.
—INIST. **CCC.**
Published by: Georg Thieme Verlag, Ruedigerstr 14, Stuttgart, 70469, Germany. TEL 49-711-8931421, FAX 49-711-8931410, leser.service@thieme.de. Adv. contact Christine Volpp TEL 49-711-8931603.

616.7 617 CHN ISSN 1009-7147
ZHEJIANG CHUANGSHANG WAIKE/ZHEJIANG JOURNAL OF TRAUMATIC SURGERY. Text in Chinese. 1994. bi-m. USD 24.60 (effective 2009). **Document type:** *Journal, Academic/Scholarly.*
Related titles: Online - full text ed.
Published by: Wenzhou Yixueyuan/Wenzhou Institute of Medical Sciences, 82, Xueyuan Xilu, Wenzhou, 325027, China. **Dist. by:** China International Book Trading Corp, 35 Chegongzhuang Xilu, Haidian District, PO Box 399, Beijing 100044, China. TEL 86-10-68412045, FAX 86-10-68412023, cibtc@mail.cibtc.com.cn, http://www.cibtc.com.cn.

616.7 CHN ISSN 1672-9935
ZHONGGUO GU YU GUANJIE SUNSHANG ZAZHI/CHINESE JOURNAL OF BONE AND JOINT INJURY. Text in Chinese. 1986. m. USD 62.40 (effective 2009). **Document type:** *Journal, Academic/Scholarly.*
Formerly: Gu yu Guanjie Sunshang Zazhi/Journal of Bone and Joint Injury (1003-9562)
Related titles: Online - full text ed.; Print ed.
Indexed: B&BAb, B19, B20, B21, CTA, ESPM, ViroIAbstr.
—East View.
Published by: Gu yu Guanjie Sunshang Zazhi, 175 Yiyuan, Zhangzhou, 363000, China. TEL 86-596-2989185, FAX 86-596-2975585. **Dist. by:** China International Book Trading Corp, 35 Chegongzhuang Xilu, Haidian District, PO Box 399, Beijing 100044, China. TEL 86-10-68412045, FAX 86-10-68412023, cibtc@mail.cibtc.com.cn, http://www.cibtc.com.cn.

617 CHN ISSN 1674-1439
ZHONGGUO GU YU GUANJIE WAIKE/CHINESE BONE AND JOINT SURGERY. Text in Chinese. 2008. bi-m. **Document type:** *Journal, Academic/Scholarly.*
Related titles: Online - full text ed.
Published by: (Beijing Xiehe Yixueyuan Guke/Peking Union Medical College, Department of Orthopaedics), Zhongguo Xiehe Yike Daxue Chubanshe/Peking Union Medical College Press, 9, Dong Dan San Tiao, Dongcheng District, Beijing, 100730, China. TEL 86-10-65281306, FAX 86-10-65286276, pumcp@sohu.com, http://www.pumcp.com/index.html.

616.7 CHN ISSN 1003-0034
ZHONGGUO GUSHANG/CHINA JOURNAL OF ORTHOPAEDICS AND TRAUMATOLOGY. Text in Chinese. 1987. m. CNY 15 per issue (effective 2011). back issues avail. **Document type:** *Journal, Academic/Scholarly.*
Related titles: Online - full text ed.
Indexed: EMBASE, ExcerpMed, MEDLINE, P30, R10, Reac, SCOPUS.
—BLDSC (3180.184000), East View.
Published by: (Zhongguo Zhongxiyi Jiehe Xuehui/Chinese Association of Integrative Medicine), Zhongguo Zhongyi Yanjiuyuan/Chinese Academy of Traditional Chinese Medicine, 16, Nan Xiaojiejia, Zhongzhimen Nei, Beijing, 100700, China. TEL 86-10-84020925, FAX 86-10-84036581, http://www.cintcm.ac.cn/. **Dist. by:** China International Book Trading Corp, 35 Chegongzhuang Xilu, Haidian District, PO Box 399, Beijing 100044, China. TEL 86-10-68412045, FAX 86-10-68412023, cibtc@mail.cibtc.com.cn, http://www.cibtc.com.cn.

ZHONGGUO GUZHI SHUSONG ZAZHI/CHINESE JOURNAL OF OSTEOPOROSIS. *see* GERONTOLOGY AND GERIATRICS

616.7 CHN ISSN 1005-8478
ZHONGGUO JIAOXING WAIKE ZAZHI/ORTHOPEDIC JOURNAL OF CHINA. Text in Chinese; Abstracts in Chinese, English. 1994. s-m. USD 160.80 (effective 2009). **Document type:** *Journal, Academic/Scholarly.*
Formerly (until 1993): Xiaoer Mabi Yanjiu/Research of Infantile Paralysis (1002-1191)
Related titles: Online - full text ed.
Indexed: A28, A34, A35, A36, A38, APA, AgBio, B&BAb, B19, B21, BrCerAb, C&ISA, CA/WCA, CABA, CIA, CTA, CerAb, CivEngAb, CorrAb, E&CAJ, E11, E12, EEA, EMA, ESPM, EnvEAb, F08, GH, H15, H17, IndVet, LT, M&TEA, M09, MBF, METADEX, N02, P33, P37, P39, PN&I, R12, RA&MP, RRTA, RefZh, S12, SolStAb, SoyAb, T04, T05, TAR, VS, WAA.
—BLDSC (9512.737518), East View, Linda Hall.
Published by: Zhongguo Renmin Jiefangjun Guke Zhongxin (88 Yiyuan), Taian, 271000, China. TEL 86-538-6213228, FAX 86-538-6213427. Ed. Zhi-jie Ning.

617.375 CHN ISSN 1004-406X
ZHONGGUO JIZHU JISUI ZAZHI/CHINESE JOURNAL OF SPINE AND SPINAL CORD. Text in Chinese; Abstracts in Chinese, English. 1991. m. USD 80.40 (effective 2009). adv. bibl.; illus. **Document type:** *Journal, Academic/Scholarly.* **Description:** Covers clinical diagnosis, treatment techniques, rehabilitation techniques and experimental studies, osteonosus, deformation and tumors of spine and spinal cord.
Related titles: Online - full text ed.
—East View.
Published by: Zhongri Youhao Yiyuan, Heping Jie Bei-kou Yinghua Dong Jie no.2, Beijing, 100029, China. adv.: page USD 3,000. **Dist. by:** China International Book Trading Corp, 35 Chegongzhuang Xilu, Haidian District, PO Box 399, Beijing 100044, China. TEL 86-10-68412045, FAX 86-10-68412023, cibtc@mail.cibtc.com.cn, http://www.cibtc.com.cn. **Co-sponsor:** Chinese Association of Rehabilitation Medicine, Special Board of Spine and Spinal Cord Injury.

616.7 615.82 CHN ISSN 1673-6567
ZHONGGUO SHANGCAN YIXUE/CHINESE JOURNAL OF TRAUMA AND DISABILITY MEDICINE. Text in Chinese. 1993. q. USD 31.20 (effective 2009). **Document type:** *Journal, Academic/Scholarly.*
Formerly: Shangcan Yixue Zazhi/Medical Journal of Trauma and Disability (1007-0354)
Related titles: Online - full text ed.
—BLDSC (9512.796302).
Published by: Heilongjiang Sheng Jietan Yanjiusuo/Paralegia Research Institute of Heilongjiang Province, 23 Youzheng Rd., Ha'erbin, 150001, China. Ed. Changrong Liu. **Co-sponsor:** Zhongguo Kangfu Yixuehui/Chinese Rehabilitation Medical Association.

616.02 CHN ISSN 1001-0726
➤ **ZHONGGUO SHAOSHANG CHUANGSHANG ZAZHI/CHINESE JOURNAL OF BURNS, WOUNDS & SURFACE ULCERS.** Text in Chinese; Summaries in Chinese, English. 1989. q. USD 16.40 (effective 2009). adv. bk.rev. charts; abstr.; illus.; stat. back issues avail. **Document type:** *Academic/Scholarly.* **Description:** Provides a forum to exchange information among all engaged in the treatment and care of burn injuries. Regular features include: Medical philosophy, basic medical science, case reports, burn care in practice, state of the art reviews.
Related titles: E-mail ed.; Online - full text ed.
—East View.
Published by: Zhongguo Shaoshang Chuangshang Keji Zhongxin/Chinese Science and Technology Center for Burns, Wounds & Surface Ulcers Society, No 54 Xibianmennei St, Xuanwu-qu, Beijing, 100053, China. FAX 86-10-6304-2420. Ed. Rongxiang Xu. R&P, Adv. contact Mengjie Zhu TEL 86-10-6304-2423.

➤ **ZHONGGUO XIAOER JIJIU YIXUE/CHINESE PEDIATRIC EMERGENCY MEDICINE.** *see* MEDICAL SCIENCES—Pediatrics

➤ **ZHONGGUO XIUFU CHONGJIAN WAIKE ZAZHI/CHINESE JOURNAL OF REPARATIVE AND RECONSTRUCTIVE SURGERY.** *see* MEDICAL SCIENCES—Surgery

➤ **ZHONGGUO ZHONGYI GUSHANGKE ZAZHI/CHINESE JOURNAL OF TRADITIONAL MEDICAL TRAUMATOLOGY & ORTHOPEDICS.** *see* ALTERNATIVE MEDICINE

616.7 CHN ISSN 1004-745X
ZHONGGUO ZHONGYI JIZHENG/JOURNAL OF EMERGENCY IN TRADITIONAL CHINESE MEDICINE. Text in Chinese. 1992. m. USD 62.40 (effective 2009). **Document type:** *Journal, Academic/Scholarly.*
Related titles: Online - full text ed.
—BLDSC (9512.835445), East View.
Address: Yuzhong-qu, 1, Beiqu Lu, Chongqing, 400013, China. **Dist. by:** China International Book Trading Corp, 35 Chegongzhuang Xilu, Haidian District, PO Box 399, Beijing 100044, China. TEL 86-10-68412045, FAX 86-10-68412023, cibtc@mail.cibtc.com.cn, http://www.cibtc.com.cn.

616.7 CHN ISSN 1671-7600
ZHONGHUA CHUANGSHANG GUKE ZAZHI/CHINESE JOURNAL OF ORTHOPAEDIC TRAUMA. Text in Chinese. 1999. m. USD 85.20 (effective 2009). **Document type:** *Journal, Academic/Scholarly.*
Related titles: Online - full text ed.
—East View.
Published by: Di-1 Junyi Daxue, Nanfang Yiyuan, 1838, Guangzhou Dadao Bei, Guangzhou, 510515, China. TEL 020-61641748, FAX 020-61360066.

617.1 CHN ISSN 1001-8050
CODEN: ZCZAFD
➤ **ZHONGHUA CHUANGSHANG ZAZHI/CHINESE JOURNAL OF TRAUMA.** Text in Chinese, English. 1985 (Sep.). m. USD 85.20 (effective 2009). adv. bk.rev. bibl.; illus.; abstr.; charts; mkt.; pat.; stat. 80 p./no.; back issues avail. **Document type:** *Journal, Academic/Scholarly.*
Formerly (until 1989): Chuangshang Zazhi (1001-229X)
Related titles: ◆ CD-ROM ed.: Chinese Academic Journals Full-Text Database. Medicine & Hygiene; Online - full content ed.; Online - full text ed.; ◆ English ed.: Chinese Journal of Traumatology. ISSN 1008-1275.
Indexed: CIN, ChemAb, ChemTitl.
—BLDSC (3180.680800), CASDDS, East View.
Published by: (Zhonghua Yixuehui/Chinese Medical Association, Di-3 Junyi Daxue Yezhan, Waike Yanjiusuo/Third Military Medical University, Research Institute of Surgery), Zhonghua Changshang Zazhi Bianjibu, Editorial Board of Chinese Journal of Trauma, Daping Changjiangzhi Lu, 10, Yuzhong-qu, Chongching, 400042, China. TEL 68-23-68757458. Ed., R&P Zhengguo Wang TEL 86-23-6875-7424. Adv. contact Yong Xiang. B&W page USD 420, color page USD 1,200; 210 x 290. Circ: 6,000. **Subscr. to:** Jialingqiao Xicuen No 83, Chongqing, Sichuan, China. **Dist. overseas by:** China International Book Trading Corp, 35 Chegongzhuang Xilu, Haidian District, PO Box 399, Beijing 100044, China. TEL 86-10-68412045, FAX 86-10-68412023, cibtc@mail.cibtc.com.cn, http://www.cibtc.com.cn.

617.3 CHN ISSN 0253-2352
ZHONGHUA GUKE ZAZHI/CHINESE JOURNAL OF ORTHOPEDICS. Text in Chinese. 1981. m. USD 80.40 (effective 2009). **Document type:** *Journal, Academic/Scholarly.*
Related titles: CD-ROM ed.; Online - full text ed.
Indexed: A22, A35, A36, A37, AgBio, B&BAb, B19, B21, CABA, CTA, D01, E12, ExtraMED, GH, H17, ImmunAb, LT, N02, NucAcAb, P33, PN&I, RRTA, RefZh, T05, VS.
—BLDSC (3180.463500), East View, IE, Ingenta.
Published by: (Zhonghua Yixuehui/Chinese Medical Association), Tianjin Yiyuan, 406, Jiefang Nanlu, Tianjin, 300211, China. TEL 86-22-28334734, FAX 86-22-28241184. Ed. Geng-Ting Dang. **Dist. by:** China International Book Trading Corp, 35 Chegongzhuang Xilu, Haidian District, PO Box 399, Beijing 100044, China. TEL 86-10-68412045, FAX 86-10-68412023, cibtc@mail.cibtc.com.cn, http://www.cibtc.com.cn.

616.7 CHN ISSN 1674-2591
ZHONGHUA GUZHI SHUSONG HE GUKUANGYAN JIBING ZAZHI/CHINESE JOURNAL OF OSTEOPOROSIS AND BONE MINERAL RESEARCH. Text in English. 2008. q. **Document type:** *Journal, Academic/Scholarly.*
Related titles: Online - full text ed.
Published by: Zhongguo Yixue Kexueyuan Beijing Xiehe Yiyuan/Chinese Academy of Medical Sciences (CAMS), Peking Union Medical College (PUMC) Hospital, 1 Shuaifuyuan Wang, Beijing, 100730, China. TEL 86-10-65295071, FAX 86-10-65296872, http://www.pumch.ac.cn/.

616.025 CHN ISSN 1671-0282
➤ **ZHONGHUA JIZHEN YIXUE ZAZHI/CHINESE JOURNAL OF EMERGENCY MEDICINE.** Text in Chinese; Summaries in Chinese, English. 1990. m. CNY 120, USD 120; free to qualified personnel (effective 2008). **Document type:** *Journal, Academic/Scholarly.* **Description:** Covers all aspects of prehospital rescue, trauma, resuscitation, poisoning, and emergency care.
Related titles: Online - full text ed.
Indexed: A29, A36, B&BAb, B19, B20, B21, CABA, CTA, E12, ESPM, GH, ImmunAb, N02, N03, NSA, NucAcAb, P33, R07, R12, RA&MP, S13, S16, SCOPUS, T05, W10.
—BLDSC (9512.839412), East View.
Published by: Zhonghua Yixuehui/Chinese Medical Association, 88, Jiefang Road, Hangzhou, Zhejiang 310009, China. TEL 86-571-87783951, FAX 86-571-87783647. Ed. Dr. Yu-Guan Jiang. Circ: 4,800 (paid). **Dist. by:** China International Book Trading Corp, 35 Chegongzhuang Xilu, Haidian District, PO Box 399, Beijing 100044, China. TEL 86-10-68412045, FAX 86-10-68412023, cibtc@mail.cibtc.com.cn, http://www.cibtc.com.cn.

➤ **ZHONGHUA SHAOSHANG ZAZHI/CHINESE JOURNAL OF BURNS.** *see* MEDICAL SCIENCES—Dermatology And Venereology

617.3 615.5 CHN ISSN 1001-6015
➤ **ZHONGYI ZHENGGU/JOURNAL OF TRADITIONAL CHINESE ORTHOPEDICS AND TRAUMATOLOGY.** Text in Chinese. 1989. m. CNY 120 (effective 2011 & 2012). bk.rev. illus. 8064 p./no.; back issues avail. **Document type:** *Journal, Academic/Scholarly.* **Description:** Covers the application of traditional Chinese medicine in orthopedics and traumatology, including diagnosis and treatment.
Related titles: Online - full text ed.
—East View.
Published by: Henansheng Zheng-gu Yanjiuyuan, 82, Qiming Nan Lu, Luoyang, Henan 471002, China. TEL 86-379-3953520, FAX 86-379-3953520. Ed. Weihai Guo. Circ: 6,000. **Dist. overseas by:** China International Book Trading Corp, 35 Chegongzhuang Xilu, Haidian District, PO Box 399, Beijing 100044, China. **Co-sponsor:** Zhongguo Zhongyiyao Xuehui.

MEDICAL SCIENCES—Otorhinolaryngology

➤ **A A O A NEWS.** *see* MEDICAL SCIENCES—Allergology And Immunology

616.28 ESP ISSN 1137-8174
A E L F A. BOLETIN. (Asociacion Espanola de Logopedia, Foniatria y Audiologia. Boletin) Text in Spanish. 1996. 3/yr. back issues avail. **Document type:** *Bulletin, Academic/Scholarly.*
Related titles: Online - full text ed.: ISSN 1695-0224 (from ScienceDirect).
Indexed: A01, F03, F04, T02.
—**CCC.**
Published by: Grupo Ars XXI de Comunicacion, SA, Muntaner 262 Atico 2a., Barcelona, 08021, Spain. TEL 34-90-2195484, FAX 34-93-2722902, info@arsxxi.com. Ed. Enrique Salesa.

616.21 USA ISSN 0742-3152
ABSTRACTS OF THE MIDWINTER RESEARCH MEETING. Text in English. 1983. a.

Formerly (until 1984): Program and Abstracts of the Midwinter Research Meeting (0742-3144)
Published by: Association for Research in Otolaryngology, 19 Mantua Rd, Mt. Royal, NJ 08601. TEL 856-423-0041, headquarters@aro.org, http://www.aro.org.

616.21 USA
RF297
➤ **ACADEMY OF REHABILITATIVE AUDIOLOGY. JOURNAL (CD-ROM).** Short title: J A R A. Text in English. 1969. a. free to members (effective 2010). bk.rev. **Document type:** *Journal, Academic/Scholarly.* **Description:** Forum for the exchange of ideas on, knowledge of, and experience with habilitative and rehabilitative aspects of audiology.
Former titles (until 2003): Academy of Rehabilitative Audiology. Journal (Print) (0149-8886); (until 1970): Academy of Rehabilitative Audiology. Newsletter (0149-8878)
Media: CD-ROM.
Indexed: A22, AMED, C06, C07, C08, CINAHL, E-psyche, ECER, P30, PsycholAb, SCOPUS, SOPODA.
—BLDSC (4674.984000), GNLM, IE, Ingenta. **CCC.**
Published by: Academy of Rehabilitative Audiology, PO Box 2323, Albany, NY 12220. ara@audrehab.org. Ed. Kathleen M Cienkowski TEL 860-486-3289. Circ: 500 (paid).

616.31 617 USA
ACOUSTIC NEUROMA ASSOCIATION NOTES. Text in English. 1981. q. USD 35 membership (effective 2006). **Document type:** *Newsletter.* **Description:** Provides support and information for patients who have been diagnosed with or treated for acoustic neuromas or other benign cranial nerve tumors.
Published by: Acoustic Neuroma Association, PO Box 12402, Atlanta, GA 30355. TEL 404-237-8023, FAX 404-237-2704. Ed. Lois V White. Circ: 5,000.

616.21 GBR ISSN 0001-6489
RF1 CODEN: AOLAAJ
➤ **ACTA OTO-LARYNGOLOGICA.** Text in English. 1918. m. GBP 605, EUR 795, USD 995 combined subscription to institutions (print & online eds.); GBP 1,210, EUR 1,595, USD 1,990 combined subscription to corporations (print & online eds.) (effective 2010). adv. charts; illus. index. back issues avail.; reprint service avail. from PSC. **Document type:** *Journal, Academic/Scholarly.* **Description:** Presents original articles of basic research interest, as well as clinical studies in the field of otorhinolaryngology and related subdisciplines.
Related titles: Online - full text ed.: ISSN 1651-2553 (from IngentaConnect); ◆ Supplement(s): Acta Oto-Laryngologica. Supplement. ISSN 0365-5237.
Indexed: A01, A03, A08, A20, A22, A26, A34, A36, A37, A38, ASCA, B&BAb, B19, B21, BIOBASE, C06, C07, C08, C11, CA, CABA, CINAHL, CISA, ChemAb, CurCont, DBA, DentInd, DokArb, E01, E12, EMBASE, EnerRA, ExcerpMed, F08, F11, F12, G08, GH, H04, H11, H12, IABS, IBR, IBSS, IBZ, ISR, IndMed, Inpharma, L&LBA, MEDLINE, N02, N03, NBA, NPPA, NSA, P03, P30, P33, P35, P43, PN&I, PsycholAb, R08, R10, R12, RA&MP, RM&VM, Reac, RefZh, SCI, SCOPUS, SOPODA, T02, T05, THA, VS, W07, W10.
—CASDDS, GNLM, IE, Infotrieve, Ingenta, INIST. **CCC.**
Published by: (Scandinavian Oto-Laryngological Society NOR), Informa Healthcare (Subsidiary of: T & F Informa plc), Telephone House, 69-77 Paul St, London, EC2A 4LQ, United Kingdom. TEL 44-20-70175000, healthcare.enquiries@informa.com, http://www.tandf.co.uk/journals/. Ed. Matti Anniko. **Subscr. outside N. America to:** Taylor & Francis Ltd., Journals Customer Service, Sheepen Pl, Colchester, Essex CO3 3LP, United Kingdom. TEL 44-20-70175544, FAX 44-20-70175198, tf.enquiries@tfinforma.com; **Subscr. in N. America to:** Taylor & Francis Inc., Customer Services Dept, 325 Chestnut St, 8th Fl, Philadelphia, PA 19106. TEL 215-625-8900, 800-354-1420, FAX 215-625-2940, customerservice@taylorandfrancis.com.

616.21 GBR ISSN 0365-5237
RF20 CODEN: AOLSA5
ACTA OTO-LARYNGOLOGICA. SUPPLEMENT. Text in Norwegian. 1918. irreg., latest 1995. price varies. adv. reprint service avail. from PSC. **Document type:** *Monographic series, Academic/Scholarly.*
Related titles: Online - full text ed.: ISSN 1651-2464; ◆ Supplement to: Acta Oto-Laryngologica. ISSN 0001-6489.
Indexed: A01, A03, A08, A22, A36, C06, C07, C08, C11, CA, CABA, CINAHL, E12, EMBASE, ExcerpMed, GH, H04, IndMed, MEDLINE, N02, N03, P30, P33, P35, P43, R10, RM&VM, Reac, SCOPUS, T02.
—IE, Infotrieve, Ingenta, INIST. **CCC.**
Published by: (Scandinavian Oto-Laryngological Society NOR), Taylor & Francis Ltd. (Subsidiary of: Taylor & Francis Group), 4 Park Sq, Milton Park, Abingdon, Oxfordshire OX14 4RN, United Kingdom. TEL 44-1235-828600, FAX 44-1235-829000, info@tandf.co.uk, http://www.tandf.co.uk/journals. Circ: 1,900.

616.21 ITA ISSN 0392-100X
RF1 CODEN: AOITDU
ACTA OTORHINOLARYNGOLOGICA ITALICA. Text in Italian. 1900. bi-m. EUR 83 domestic; EUR 93 foreign (effective 2009). **Document type:** *Journal, Academic/Scholarly.*
Formerly (until 1981): Annali di Laringologia, Otologia, Rinologia, Faringologia (0066-2267)
Related titles: Online - full text ed.: ISSN 1827-675X. free (effective 2011); ◆ Supplement(s): Acta Otorhinolaryngologica Italica. Supplement. ISSN 0393-7976.
Indexed: A22, EMBASE, ExcerpMed, IndMed, MEDLINE, NBA, P30, R10, Reac, SCI, SCOPUS, W07.
—BLDSC (0642.280000), GNLM, IE, Infotrieve, Ingenta, INIST.
Published by: Pacini Editore SpA, Via A Gherardesca 1, Ospedaletto, PI 56121, Italy. TEL 39-050-313011, FAX 39-050-3130300, pacini.editore@pacinieditore.it, http://www.pacinimedicina.it. Ed. F Chiesa.

616.21 ITA ISSN 0393-7976
CODEN: AOTOE
ACTA OTORHINOLARYNGOLOGICA ITALICA. SUPPLEMENT. Text in Italian. 1982. irreg. **Document type:** *Journal, Academic/Scholarly.*
Related titles: ◆ Supplement to: Acta Otorhinolaryngologica Italica. ISSN 0392-100X.
Indexed: IndMed.
—BLDSC (0642.280100), IE, Ingenta, INIST.
Published by: Pacini Editore SpA, Via A Gherardesca 1, Ospedaletto, PI 56121, Italy. TEL 39-050-313011, FAX 39-050-3130300, pacini.editore@pacinieditore.it, http://www.pacinimedicina.it.

616.21 ESP ISSN 0001-6519
➤ **ACTA OTORRINOLARINGOLOGICA ESPANOLA.** Text in Spanish. 1949. m. EUR 132.06 combined subscription to individuals print & online eds.; EUR 334 combined subscription to institutions print & online eds. (effective 2009). bk.rev. bibl.; charts; illus. back issues avail.; reprints avail. **Document type:** *Academic/Scholarly.*
Related titles: Online - full text ed.: ISSN 1988-3013. EUR 110 (effective 2009) (from ScienceDirect).
Indexed: A22, A29, B20, B21, EMBASE, ESPM, ExcerpMed, IME, IndMed, MEDLINE, NSA, P30, R10, Reac, SCOPUS, ViroIAbstr.
—BLDSC (0642.300000), GNLM, IE, Infotrieve, Ingenta. **CCC.**
Published by: (Sociedad Espanola de Otorrinolaringologia), Elsevier Doyma (Subsidiary of: Elsevier Health Sciences), Traversa de Gracia 17-21, Barcelona, 08021, Spain. TEL 34-932-418800, FAX 34-932-419020, editorial@elsevier.com. Circ: 3,000.

616.85 USA ISSN 1062-5747
ADVANCE FOR SPEECH - LANGUAGE PATHOLOGISTS AND AUDIOLOGISTS. Text in English. 1991. w. free to qualified personnel (effective 2008). adv. back issues avail.; reprints avail. **Document type:** *Magazine, Trade.* **Description:** Contains articles on products, jobs and events in the field of speech, language and audiology.
Related titles: Online - full text ed.: free to qualified personnel (effective 2008).
Indexed: C06.
Published by: Merion Publications, Inc., 2900 Horizon Dr, PO Box 61556, King of Prussia, PA 19406. TEL 610-278-1400, 800-355-5627, FAX 610-278-1421, advance@merion.com, http://www.advanceweb.com. Ed. Sherry Fox. Adv. contact Cynthia Caramanico. B&W page USD 1,990, color page USD 2,790; trim 8.125 x 10.5. Circ: 61,106.

616.21 CHE ISSN 0065-3071
RF16 CODEN: ADORB9
➤ **ADVANCES IN OTO-RHINO-LARYNGOLOGY.** Text in English. 1953. irreg., latest vol.72, 2011. price varies. reprints avail. **Document type:** *Monographic series, Academic/Scholarly.* **Description:** Contains results from basic research and clinical studies pertaining to the pathophysiology, diagnosis, clinical symptoms, course, prognosis and therapy of a variety of ear, nose and throat disorders.
Formerly (until 1970): Bibliotheca Oto-Rhino-Laryngologica (0301-3286)
Related titles: Online - full text ed.: ISSN 1662-2847.
Indexed: A22, A29, ASCA, B20, B21, C06, C07, CTA, ChemAb, DentInd, EMBASE, ESPM, ExcerpMed, IndMed, MEDLINE, NSA, P30, R10, Reac, SCOPUS, ViroIAbstr.
—BLDSC (0709.570000), CASDDS, GNLM, IE, Infotrieve, Ingenta, INIST. **CCC.**
Published by: S. Karger AG, Allschwilerstr 10, Basel, 4055, Switzerland. TEL 41-61-3061111, FAX 41-61-3061234, karger@karger.ch, http://www.karger.ch. Ed. G Randolph.

617.89 USA ISSN 1050-0545
RF286 CODEN: JAAAE3
➤ **AMERICAN ACADEMY OF AUDIOLOGY. JOURNAL.** Abbreviated title: J A A A. Text in English; Abstracts in English, Spanish. 1989. 10/yr. USD 337 domestic to individuals; USD 466 domestic to institutions; USD 391 combined subscription to individuals (print & online eds.); USD 516 combined subscription to institutions (print & online eds.) (effective 2010). adv. abstr.; charts; illus. 78 p./no.; back issues avail.; reprints avail. **Document type:** *Journal, Academic/Scholarly.* **Description:** Features original contributions, abstracts, research reports, case studies and a clinical forum.
Related titles: Microfiche ed.; Online - full text ed.: ISSN 2157-3107. USD 306 to individuals; USD 424 to institutions (effective 2010) (from IngentaConnect).
Indexed: A01, A03, A08, A20, A22, A26, C06, C07, C08, CA, CINAHL, CurCont, EMBASE, ExcerpMed, H04, H11, H12, I05, IndMed, MEDLINE, P03, P20, P22, P24, P30, P48, P54, PQC, PsycInfo, PsycholAb, R10, Reac, SCI, SCOPUS, SOPODA, SociolAb, T02, W07.
—BLDSC (4683.670000), GNLM, IE, Infotrieve, Ingenta. **CCC.**
Published by: American Academy of Audiology, 11730 Plz America Dr, Ste 300, Reston, VA 20190. TEL 703-790-8466, 800-222-2336, FAX 703-790-8631, jwilson@audiology.org. Ed. James Jerger. Adv. contact Christy Hanson TEL 703-226-1062.

616.21 USA ISSN 0731-8359
AMERICAN ACADEMY OF OTOLARYNGOLOGY - HEAD AND NECK SURGERY. BULLETIN. Text in English. 1982. m. USD 25 domestic to members; USD 55 domestic to non-members; USD 52 foreign to members; USD 65 foreign to non-members (effective 2005). adv. tr.lit. index. **Document type:** *Bulletin, Trade.* **Description:** Features governmental and socioeconomic affairs plus practice management tips and information of interest to otolaryngologists. Provides information about meetings, publications, policies and activities and news. Contains employment listings and a calendar of courses, meetings and workshops.
Published by: American Academy of Otolaryngology - Head and Neck Surgery, Inc., One Prince St, Alexandria, VA 22314. TEL 703-519-1562, FAX 703-519-1587, http://www.entnet.org. Ed., Pub. G Richard Holt. R&P Michele Finley TEL 703-519-1597. Adv. contact Lisette Bassett. B&W page USD 930, color page USD 1,900; trim 11 x 8.5. Circ: 10,100 (paid).

616.21 USA ISSN 0196-0709
RF1 CODEN: AJOTDP
➤ **AMERICAN JOURNAL OF OTOLARYNGOLOGY**; head and neck medicine and surgery. Text in English. 1979. bi-m. USD 435 in United States to institutions; USD 649 elsewhere to institutions (effective 2012). adv. back issues avail.; reprints avail. **Document type:** *Journal, Academic/Scholarly.* **Description:** Provides original reports on the developments in the fields of otology, neurotology, audiology, allergology, laryngology, speech science, bronchoesophagology, facial plastic surgery, and head and neck surgery.
Related titles: Online - full text ed.: ISSN 1532-818X (from ScienceDirect).
Indexed: A22, A26, A36, ASCA, C06, C07, C08, CA, CABA, CIN, CINAHL, ChemAb, ChemTitl, CurCont, DentInd, E01, E12, EMBASE, ExcerpMed, F08, GH, H12, H17, I05, IBR, IBZ, IndMed, Inpharma, MEDLINE, N02, N03, NBA, P30, P33, P35, P39, R07, R08, R10, RM&VM, Reac, SCI, SCOPUS, T02, T05, THA, VS, W07.
—BLDSC (0829.300000), CASDDS, GNLM, IE, Infotrieve, Ingenta, INIST. **CCC.**
Published by: W.B. Saunders Co. (Subsidiary of: Elsevier Health Sciences), Elsevier, Health Sciences Division, Order Fulfillment, 3251 Riverport Ln, Maryland Heights, MO 63043. TEL 314-872-8370, 800-325-4177, FAX 314-432-1380, JournalCustomerService-usa@elsevier.com, http://www.us.elsevierhealth.com. Ed. Peter C. Weber. Pub. Alexandra Gavenda. Adv. contact Janine Castle TEL 44-1865-843844.

616.21 USA ISSN 1945-8924
CODEN: AJRHE5
➤ **AMERICAN JOURNAL OF RHINOLOGY & ALLERGY.** Text in English. 1987. bi-m. USD 548 combined subscription domestic to institutions (print & online eds.); USD 608 combined subscription foreign to institutions (print & online eds.) (effective 2011); includes archives. adv. **Document type:** *Journal, Academic/Scholarly.* **Description:** Clinical discussions regarding medical and surgical aspects of the nose.
Formerly (until Jan.2009): American Journal of Rhinology (1050-6586)
Related titles: Online - full text ed.: ISSN 1945-8932. USD 515 to institutions (effective 2011); includes archives (from IngentaConnect).
Indexed: A22, A34, A36, ASCA, AgrForAb, CA, CABA, CurCont, E12, EMBASE, ExcerpMed, F08, F11, F12, GH, ISR, IndMed, Inpharma, MEDLINE, N02, N03, P20, P22, P30, P33, P35, P48, P54, PQC, R08, R10, R12, RA&MP, RM&VM, Reac, RefZh, S12, SCI, SCOPUS, T02, T05, VS, W07, W10.
—BLDSC (0836.700000), CASDDS, GNLM, IE, Infotrieve, Ingenta, INIST. **CCC.**
Published by: OceanSide Publications, Inc., 95 Pitman St, Providence, RI 02906. TEL 401-331-2510, FAX 401-331-0223, subscriptions@oceansidepubl.com. Eds. Alexander Chiu, Rakesh Chandra. Circ: 3,016.

636.08 616.21 USA ISSN 0891-1940
AMERICAN LARYNGOLOGICAL ASSOCIATION. TRANSACTIONS OF THE ANNUAL MEETING. Text in English. 1879. a., latest 2008. back issues avail. **Document type:** *Proceedings, Academic/Scholarly.* **Description:** Contains minutes of business meetings and summary of historical data relating to membership, officers, etc. No manuscripts have been published since 1995.
Indexed: P30.
Published by: American Laryngological Association, Animal Scientific Program, PO Box 128186, Nashville, TN 37212. TEL 615-509-5525, FAX 615-322-9102, alahns@comcast.net. Ed. Mark S Courey TEL 415-885-7700.

617.8 USA ISSN 0096-6851
RF1 CODEN: TAOTAW
➤ **AMERICAN OTOLOGICAL SOCIETY. TRANSACTIONS.** Text in English. 1868. a., latest 2006. free (effective 2011). back issues avail. **Document type:** *Proceedings, Academic/Scholarly.* **Description:** Abstracts of papers and discussions presented at the meeting of the society.
Indexed: P30.
—GNLM, Linda Hall.
Published by: American Otological Society, c/o Clough Shelton, University of Utah School of Medicine, Salt Lake City, UT 84132.

616.21 MEX ISSN 0188-8323
ANALES DE OTORRINOLARINGOLOGIA MEXICANA. Text in Spanish. 1949. q. back issues avail. **Document type:** *Journal, Academic/Scholarly.*
Formerly (until 1956): Sociedad Mexicana de Otorrinolaringologia. Anales (0583-7596)
Related titles: Online - full content ed.; Online - full text ed.
Indexed: C01.
Published by: Sociedad Mexicana de Otorrinolaringologia y Cirugia de Cabeza y Cuello, Montes Urales 723-402, Mexico D.F, CP 11000, Mexico. Ed. Rafael Navarro Meneses.

616.21 FRA ISSN 1879-7261
▼ **ANNALES FRANCAISES D'OTO-RHINO-LARYNGOLOGIE ET DE PATHOLOGIE CERVICO-FACIALE.** Text in French. 2010. bi-m. EUR 407 in Europe to institutions; EUR 324.19 in France to institutions; JPY 63,300 in Japan to institutions; USD 529 elsewhere to institutions (effective 2012). **Document type:** *Journal, Academic/Scholarly.*
Formed by the merger of (1963-2009): Annales d'Oto-Laryngologie et de Chirurgie Cervico-Faciale (0003-438X); (2005-2009): Oto-Rhino-Laryngologie Francaise (1778-1108)
Related titles: Online - full text ed.: ISSN 1879-727X (from ScienceDirect).
—BLDSC (0974.405000), IE. **CCC.**
Published by: Elsevier Masson (Subsidiary of: Elsevier Health Sciences), 62 Rue Camille Desmoulins, Issy les Moulineaux, Cedex 92442, France. TEL 33-1-71165500, FAX 33-1-71165600, infos@elsevier-masson.fr, http://www.elsevier-masson.fr.

616.21 USA ISSN 0003-4894
CODEN: AORHA2
➤ **ANNALS OF OTOLOGY, RHINOLOGY AND LARYNGOLOGY.** Text in English. 1892. m. USD 240 domestic to individuals; USD 255 in Canada & Mexico to individuals; USD 265 elsewhere to individuals; USD 400 domestic to institutions; USD 420 in Canada & Mexico to institutions; USD 430 elsewhere to institutions (effective 2010); subscr. includes online access. adv. bk.rev.; software rev. charts. index. 112 p./no. 2 cols./p.; back issues avail.; reprints avail. **Document type:** *Journal, Academic/Scholarly.* **Description:** Publishes original manuscripts of clinical and research importance in otolaryngology - head and neck medicine and surgery, broncho-esophagology, maxillofacial surgery, audiology, speech pathology, and related specialties.
Supersedes in part: Annals of Ophthalmology and Otology
Related titles: CD-ROM ed.: 1998. USD 202 domestic to individuals; USD 215 in Canada & Mexico to individuals; USD 227 elsewhere to individuals; USD 305 domestic to institutions; USD 318 in Canada & Mexico to institutions; USD 330 elsewhere to institutions; USD 122 domestic residents/students; USD 131 in Canada & Mexico residents/students; USD 140 elsewhere residents/students (effective 2006); Online - full text ed.: ISSN 1943-572X; Supplement(s): Annals of Otology, Rhinology & Laryngology. Supplement. ISSN 0096-8056. 1971.

M

Indexed: A01, A02, A03, A08, A20, A22, A26, A36, AIM, ASCA, AbAn, B25, BIOSIS Prev, C06, C07, C08, C11, CA, CABA, CINAHL, ChemAb, CurCont, D01, DentInd, DokArb, EMBASE, ExcerpMed, F08, G08, GH, H04, H11, H12, IDIS, ISR, IndMed, Inpharma, L&LBA, MEDLINE, MLA-IB, MycolAb, N02, N03, NBA, NPPA, P20, P22, P24, P26, P30, P33, P35, P43, P48, P54, PQC, PsycholAb, R08, R10, RA&MP, RILM, RM&VM, Reac, SCI, SCOPUS, SOPODA, T02, T05, THA, VS, W07, W10.
—BLDSC (1043.400000), GNLM, IE, Infotrieve, Ingenta, INIST.
Published by: (American Laryngological Association), Annals Publishing Co., 4507 Laclede Ave, St. Louis, MO 63108. TEL 314-367-4987, FAX 314-367-4988, manager@annals.com. Ed. Dr. Richard J H Smith. R&P Michol L Sheridan. Adv. contact Jim Cunningham. B&W page USD 765; trim 8.375 x 11. Circ: 5,623.

616.21 016 USA ISSN 0886-4470
RF1 CODEN: AONSEJ
➤ **ARCHIVES OF OTOLARYNGOLOGY - HEAD & NECK SURGERY.** Text in English. 1925. m. USD 670 domestic to institutions; USD 838 in the Americas to institutions; EUR 678 in Europe to institutions; GBP 575 elsewhere to institutions (effective 2012). bk.rev. bibl.; charts; illus. index. back issues avail.; reprints avail. **Document type:** *Journal, Academic/Scholarly.* **Description:** Provides timely information for physicians and scientists concerned with diseases of the head and neck through original articles and clinical observations relevant to the practice of otolaryngology.
Former titles (until 1986): Archives of Otolaryngology (0003-9977); (until 1960): A M A Archives of Otolaryngology (0096-6894); (until 1950): Archives of Otolaryngology (0276-0673)
Related titles: Microform ed.: (from PQC); Online - full text ed.: ISSN 1538-361X. free to members (effective 2012).
Indexed: A22, A26, A34, A36, AIM, ASCA, AbAn, B&BAb, B21, C06, C07, C08, CA, CABA, CINAHL, CISA, CTA, ChemAb, CurCont, DentInd, E08, E12, ECER, EMBASE, ExcerpMed, F08, F11, F12, FR, G05, G06, G07, G08, GH, H11, H12, H13, I05, IBR, IBZ, INI, ISR, IndMed, Inpharma, Kidney, MEDLINE, MLA-IB, MS&D, N02, N03, N04, NBA, NPPA, NSA, P02, P10, P20, P22, P24, P30, P33, P35, P48, P53, P54, PQC, R08, R10, RA&MP, RILM, RM&VM, Reac, S09, SCI, SCOPUS, T05, VS, W07.
—BLDSC (1638.510000), CASDDS, GNLM, IE, Infotrieve, Ingenta, INIST. **CCC.**
Published by: American Medical Association, 515 N State St, Chicago, IL 60654. TEL 312-464-4200, 800-621-8335, FAX 312-464-4142, journalsales@ama-assn.org, http://www.ama-assn.org. Eds. Dr. Paul A Levine, Dr. Catherine D DeAngelis. **Subscr. in the Americas to:** PO Box 10946, Chicago, IL 60654. TEL 312-670-7827, 800-262-2350, ama-subs@ama-assn.org; **Subscr. outside the Americas to:** American Medical Association, J A M A and Archive Journals.

617.5 BRA ISSN 0103-555X
ASSOCIACAO WILLIAN HOUSE DE OTOLOGIA. ACTA. Key Title: Acta AWHO. Text in Portuguese. 1982. q. back issues avail. **Document type:** *Journal, Academic/Scholarly.*
Related titles: Online - full text ed.
Published by: Associacao Willian House de Otologia, Av Brig Faria Lima 2639 Conj 31, Sao Paulo, 01452-902, Brazil. TEL 55-11-30329258, FAX 55-11-38141122, http://www.awho.org.br/. Ed. Pedro Luis Mangabeira Albernaz.

616.2 ITA ISSN 0066-9865
ASSOCIAZIONE ITALIANA LARINGECTOMIZZATI. ATTI (DEL) CONVEGNO NAZIONALE. Text in Italian. 1957. irreg. **Document type:** *Proceedings, Trade.* **Description:** Addresses all laryngectomees and their families with news about Association life and medical advice.
Published by: Associazione Italiana Laringectomizzati, Via Friuli 28, Milan, 20135, Italy. TEL 39-02-5510819, FAX 39-02-54122104, http://www.laringect.it.

616.21 USA
➤ **AUDIO-DIGEST OTOLARYNGOLOGY - HEAD AND NECK SURGERY.** Text in English. 19??. s-m. USD 449.81 domestic; USD 479.72 in Canada; USD 527.72 elsewhere (effective 2010). back issues avail. **Document type:** *Journal, Academic/Scholarly.*
Former titles (until 1981): Audio-Digest Otorhinolaryngology - Head and Neck Surgery (0271-1354); (until 1968): Audio-Digest Otorhinolaryngology (0030-6673)
Media: Audio cassette/tape. **Related titles:** Audio CD ed.: USD 399.89 domestic; USD 431.72 in Canada; USD 479.72 elsewhere (effective 2010); Online - full text ed.: USD 359.72 (effective 2010).
Published by: Audio-Digest Foundation (Subsidiary of: California Medical Association), 1577 E Chevy Chase Dr, Glendale, CA 91206. TEL 818-240-7500, 800-423-2308, FAX 818-240-7379.

617.89 ESP ISSN 1887-8679
AUDIOLOGIA PRACTICA. Text in Spanish. 2007. 3/yr. free to qualified personnel (effective 2009). 16 p./no.; **Document type:** *Journal, Trade.*
Published by: Ediciones Mayo S.A., Calle Aribau 185-187, 2a Planta, Barcelona, 08021, Spain. TEL 34-93-2090255, FAX 34-93-2020643, edmayo@ediciones.mayo.es, http://www.edicionesmayo.es. Circ: 30,000.

617.89 GBR ISSN 1651-386X
RF286
➤ **AUDIOLOGICAL MEDICINE.** Text in English. 2003. q. GBP 300, EUR 400, USD 500 combined subscription to institutions (print & online eds.); GBP 605, EUR 795, USD 1,000 combined subscription to corporations (print & online eds.) (effective 2010). adv. back issues avail.; reprint service avail. from PSC. **Document type:** *Journal, Academic/Scholarly.* **Description:** Aims to provide a forum for clinical audiologists in continuing medical education as well as professionals within other fields involving communication disorders.
Related titles: Online - full text ed.: ISSN 1651-3835 (from IngentaConnect).
Indexed: A22, C06, C07, C08, CINAHL, E01, EMBASE, ExcerpMed, L&LBA, P03, P30, PsycInfo, SCOPUS.
—BLDSC (1789.067000), IE, Ingenta. **CCC.**
Published by: (Societa Italiana di Audiologia ITA), Informa Healthcare (Subsidiary of: T & F Informa plc), Telephone House, 69-77 Paul St, London, EC2A 4LQ, United Kingdom. TEL 44-20-70175000, FAX 44-20-70176792, healthcare.enquiries@informa.com. Ed. Alessandro Martini. Adv. contact Per Sonnerfeldt. **Subscr. in N. America to:** Taylor & Francis Inc., Customer Services Dept, 325 Chestnut St, 8th Fl, Philadelphia, PA 19106. TEL 215-625-8900, 800-354-1420, FAX 215-625-8914, customerservice@taylorandfrancis.com; **Subscr. outside N. America to:** Taylor & Francis Ltd., Journals Customer Service, Sheepen Pl, Colchester, Essex CO3 3LP, United Kingdom. TEL 44-20-70175544, FAX 44-20-70175198, tf.enquiries@tfinforma.com.

617.8 CHE
RF290 CODEN: ANEOFO
➤ **AUDIOLOGY AND NEUROTOLOGY**; basic research and clinical applications. Text in English. 1996. bi-m. CHF 1,596, EUR 1,275, USD 1,570.50 to institutions; CHF 1,751, EUR 1,399, USD 1,720.50 combined subscription to institutions (print & online eds.) (effective 2012). adv. abstr.; bibl.; illus. index, cum.index. back issues avail. **Document type:** *Journal, Academic/Scholarly.* **Description:** Provides a forum for the presentation of outstanding papers on the auditory and vestibular systems.
Formerly (until 2005): Audiology and Neuro-Otology (1420-3030)
Related titles: Microfilm ed.; Online - full text ed.: ISSN 1421-9700. CHF 1,545, EUR 1,236, USD 1,500 to institutions (effective 2012).
Indexed: A01, A03, A08, A20, A22, ASCA, AcoustA, B21, BDM&CN, C06, C07, CA, CurCont, DokArb, E-psyche, E01, EMBASE, ExcerpMed, ISR, IndMed, Inpharma, MEDLINE, NBA, NPPA, NSA, NSCI, P03, P20, P22, P24, P25, P30, P35, P48, P54, PQC, PsycInfo, PsycholAb, R10, Reac, SCI, SCOPUS, SOPODA, T02, W07.
—BLDSC (1789.081500), CASDDS, GNLM, IE, Infotrieve, Ingenta, INIST. **CCC.**
Published by: (International Society of Audiology CAN), S. Karger AG, Allschwilerstr 10, Basel, 4055, Switzerland. TEL 41-61-3061111, FAX 41-61-3061234, karger@karger.ch, http://www.karger.ch. Ed. J P Harris. adv.: page CHF 1,730; trim 210 x 280. Circ: 900.

617.89 ITA ISSN 2039-4330
▼ ➤ **AUDIOLOGY RESEARCH.** Text in English. 2010. irreg. **Document type:** *Journal, Academic/Scholarly.*
Related titles: Online - full text ed.: ISSN 2039-4349. free (effective 2011).
Published by: Pagepress, Via Giuseppe Belli 4, Pavia, 27100, Italy. TEL 39-0382-1751762, FAX 39-0382-1750481, http://www.pagepress.org. Ed. Gabriella Tognola.

617.89 USA ISSN 1535-2609
RF286
AUDIOLOGY TODAY; the magazine of, by, and for audiologists. Text in English. 1988. bi-m. USD 54 domestic to individuals (print or online ed.); USD 102 foreign to individuals (print or online ed.); USD 112 domestic to institutions; USD 134 foreign to institutions; USD 59.50 combined subscription domestic to individuals (print & online eds.); USD 112 combined subscription foreign to individuals (print & online eds.) (effective 2010). adv. back issues avail.; reprints avail. **Document type:** *Magazine, Academic/Scholarly.* **Description:** Covers all aspects of audiology and related topics on hearing and balance including clinical activities, hearing research, current events, news items, professional issues and events.
Related titles: Online - full text ed.
Indexed: A26, C06, C07, C08, CA, CINAHL, H11, H12, I05, P24, P48, PQC, T02.
—BLDSC (1789.084300), IE. **CCC.**
Published by: American Academy of Audiology, 11730 Plz America Dr, Ste 300, Reston, VA 20190. TEL 703-790-8466, 800-222-2336, FAX 703-790-8631, jwilson@audiology.org. Adv. contact Christy Hanson TEL 703-226-1062. **Subscr. to:** 11654 Plz America Dr 507, Reston, VA 20190.

616.21 NLD ISSN 0385-8146
RF1 CODEN: ANLADF
AURIS NASUS LARYNX. Text in English, French, German; Summaries in English. 1973. 6/yr. EUR 446 in Europe to institutions; JPY 59,400 in Japan to institutions; USD 500 elsewhere to institutions (effective 2012). adv. charts; illus. back issues avail. **Document type:** *Journal, Academic/Scholarly.* **Description:** Provides rapid and reviewed publications concerning the basic and clinical aspects of otorhinolaryngology and related fields such as: otology, neurotology, equilibrium sciences, bronchoesophagology, laryngology, neurolaryngology, rhinology, allergology, head and neck medicine and oncologic surgery, maxillofacial and plastic surgery, audiology, speech science and communication disorders.
Related titles: Online - full text ed.: ISSN 1879-1476 (from IngentaConnect, ScienceDirect).
Indexed: A01, A03, A08, A22, A26, C06, C07, CA, CurCont, DentInd, EMBASE, ExcerpMed, I05, IndMed, Inpharma, MEDLINE, P30, P35, R10, Reac, SCI, SCOPUS, T02, W07.
—BLDSC (1792.760000), CASDDS, GNLM, IE, Infotrieve, Ingenta. **CCC.**
Published by: (The Oto-Rhino-Laryngological Society of Japan, Inc./Nihon Jibi Inkoka Gakkai JPN), Elsevier BV (Subsidiary of: Elsevier Science & Technology), Radarweg 29, PO Box 211, Amsterdam, 1000 AE, Netherlands. TEL 31-20-4853911, FAX 31-20-4852457, JournalsCustomerServiceEMEA@elsevier.com, http://www.elsevier.nl. Ed. T Yamasoba.

AUSTRALIAN AND NEW ZEALAND JOURNAL OF AUDIOLOGY. *see* HANDICAPPED—Hearing Impaired

617.89 AUS ISSN 1832-9691
AUSTRALIAN HEARING. ANNUAL REPORT. Text in English. 1987. a. back issues avail. **Document type:** *Government.*
Former titles (until 1998): Australian Hearing Services. Annual Report (1444-3317); (until 1993): Australia. Department of Health, Housing, Local Government and Community Services. Annual Report (1321-4950); (until 1992): Australia. Department of Health, Housing and Community Services. Annual Report (1037-4825); (until 1990): Australia. Department of Community Services and Health. Annual Report (1032-1659); Which was formed by the merger of (1986-1987): Australia. Department of Community Services. Annual Report (1032-7916); Which was formerly (in 1985): Australia. Department of Community Services. Report for the Period (0815-8894); (1985-1987): Australia. Commonwealth Deaprtment of Health. Annual Report (0816-7621); Which was formerly (1963-1984): Australia. Department of Health. Annual Report of the Director General of Health (0312-4827); (1954-1962): Australia. Report of the Director-General of Health (0519-5977)
Related titles: Online - full content ed.
Published by: Australia. Department of Human Services, 126 Greville St, Chatswood, NSW 2067, Australia. TEL 61-2-94126800, FAX 61-2-94133855, mediaenquiries@hearing.com.au.

616.21 BEL ISSN 1781-782X
RF1 CODEN: AORLAE
B - E N T. (Belgian Ear Nose Throat) Text in Multiple languages. 1896. bi-m. EUR 100 domestic; EUR 125 foreign (effective 2006). Supplement avail. **Document type:** *Journal, Academic/Scholarly.*
Former titles (until 2005): Acta Oto-Rhino-Laryngologica Belgica (0001-6497); (until 1933): Societe Belge d'Otologie, de Laryngologie et de Rhinologie. Bulletin (0770-1357); (until 1897): Societe Belge d'Otologie et de Laryngologie. Bulletin (0770-1306)
Indexed: A20, A22, ChemAb, CurCont, DentInd, EMBASE, ExcerpMed, IndMed, MEDLINE, NBA, P30, R10, Reac, SCI, SCOPUS, SOPODA, W07.
—BLDSC (1854.162000), GNLM, IE, Infotrieve, Ingenta, INIST. **CCC.**
Published by: Societe Royale Belge d'Oto - Rhino - Laryngologie et de Chirurgie Cervico - Faciale, PO Box 1248, Louvain, Belgium. TEL 32-473-352780, secretary@orl-nko.be, http://www.orl-nko.be. Eds. Bernard Bertrand, Mark Jorissen.

616.21 GBR ISSN 1472-6815
RF1 CODEN: BENTCT
➤ **B M C EAR, NOSE AND THROAT DISORDERS.** (BioMed Central) Text in English. 2001 (Nov.). irreg. free (effective 2011). adv. back issues avail.; reprints avail. **Document type:** *Journal, Academic/Scholarly.* **Description:** Covers original research articles in all aspects of the prevention, diagnosis and management of ear, nose and throat disorders, as well as related molecular genetics, pathophysiology, and epidemiology.
Media: Online - full text.
Indexed: A01, A26, C06, C07, CA, EMBASE, ExcerpMed, I05, P20, P22, P30, PQC, R10, Reac, SCOPUS, T02.
—Infotrieve. **CCC.**
Published by: BioMed Central Ltd. (Subsidiary of: Springer Science+Business Media), 236 Gray's Inn Rd, London, WC1X 8HB, United Kingdom. TEL 44-20-31922000, FAX 44-20-31922010, info@biomedcentral.com. Ed. Dr. Melissa Norton. Adv. contact Natasha Bailey TEL 44-20-31922231.

617.89 USA
BETTER HEARING NEWS. Text in English. 1973. q. **Document type:** *Newsletter.* **Description:** Highlights of current institute activities.
Formerly: Communicator
Published by: Better Hearing Institute, 515 Kings St, Ste 420, Alexandria, VA 22314. TEL 703-684-3391, 800-327-9355, FAX 703-684-3394, mail@betterhearing.org. Ed., Pub., R&P Michele D Hartlove. Circ: 2,500.

616.21 BRA ISSN 1808-8694
CODEN: RBORAB
➤ **BRAZILIAN JOURNAL OF OTORHINOLARYNGOLOGY.** Abbreviated title: B J O R L. Text in English. 1933. bi-m. adv. abstr.; bibl.; illus. index. 150 p./no.; back issues avail.; reprints avail. **Document type:** *Journal, Academic/Scholarly.* **Description:** Contains original papers and case reports from otolaryngology, head and neck surgery and related areas.
Former titles (until 2006): Revista Brasileira de Otorrinolaringologia (0034-7299); (until 1938): Revista Oto-Laringologica de Sao Paulo (0101-0689)
Related titles: Online - full text ed.: ISSN 1808-8686. 2001. free (effective 2011).
Indexed: A22, C01, ChemAb, EMBASE, IndMed, MEDLINE, P30, R10, RILM, Reac, SCOPUS.
—BLDSC (7845.425000), IE, Ingenta.
Published by: Associacao Brasileira de Otorrinolaringologia e Cirurgia Cervicofacial, Av Indianapolis 740, Sao Paulo, SP 04062-001, Brazil. TEL 55-11-50529515, FAX 55-11-50521025. Ed. Joao Ferreira Melo.

616.21 CAN ISSN 1199-0538
C A D CHAT (ONLINE EDITION). Text in English, French. 1989. 10/yr. CAD 25 (effective 2005). back issues avail. **Document type:** *Newsletter, Consumer.*
Formerly (until 2005): C A D Chat (Print Edition)
Media: Online - full content.
Published by: Canadian Association of the Deaf, 251 Bank St, Ste 203, Ottawa, ON K1V 7P2, Canada. TEL 613-565-2882, FAX 613-565-1207, cad@cad.ca. Ed. Jim Roots. Circ: 1,000.

616.2 401 BRA ISSN 1516-1846
C E F A C REVISTA. (Centro de Especializacao em Fonoaudiologia Clinica) Text in Portuguese. 1998. s-a. **Document type:** *Journal, Academic/Scholarly.*
Related titles: Online - full text ed.: free (effective 2011).
Indexed: A26, I04, I05, T02.
Published by: Centro de Especializacao em Fonoaudiologia Clinica (C E F A C), Rua Cayowaa 664, Sao Paulo, 05018-000, Brazil. TEL 55-11-38680818.

617.8 PRT ISSN 1646-7205
CLINICA E INVESTIGACAO EM OTORRINOLARINGOLOGIA. Text in Portuguese. 2007. q. **Document type:** *Journal, Academic/Scholarly.*
Published by: Medicografica Edicoes Medicas, Rua Camilo Castelo Branco 23-5, Lisbon, 1150-083, Portugal. geral@medicografica.pt, http://www.medicografica.pt.

617.8 KOR ISSN 1976-8710
➤ **CLINICAL AND EXPERIMENTAL OTORHINOLARYNGOLOGY.** Text in Korean. 2008. q. **Document type:** *Journal, Academic/Scholarly.* **Description:** Publishes original articles relating to both clinical and basic researches, reviews, clinical trials, and case reports, encompassing the whole topics of otorhinolaryngology-head and neck surgery.
Related titles: Online - full text ed.: ISSN 2005-0720. free (effective 2011).
Indexed: P30, SCI, SCOPUS, W07.
Published by: Korean Society of Otorhinolaryngology-Head and Neck Surgery/Daehan Ibi-inhugwa Haghoe, Samsung Medical Center, Department of Otolaryngology-Head & Neck Surgery, 50 Ilwon-dong, Gangnam-gu, Seoul, 135-710, Korea, S. TEL 82-2-34103577, FAX 82-2-34106987. Ed. Dr. Chung-Hwan Baek.

617.8 NZL ISSN 1179-5506
➤ **CLINICAL MEDICINE INSIGHTS: EAR, NOSE AND THROAT.** Text in English. 2008. irreg. free (effective 2011). **Document type:** *Journal, Academic/Scholarly.* **Description:** Covers all aspects of the diagnosis, management and prevention of disorders of the ear, nose and throat, in addition to related genetic, pathophysiological and epidemiological topics.

Formerly (until 2010): Clinical Medicine: Ear, Nose and Throat (1178-1211)
Media: Online - full text.
Indexed: C06, C07, EMBASE, T02.
—CCC.
Published by: Libertas Academica Ltd., PO Box 300-874, Mairangi Bay, Auckland, 0751, New Zealand. TEL 64-9-4763930, FAX 64-9-3531397, enquiries@la-press.com. Ed. Liu Xue Zhong.

616.21 GBR ISSN 1749-4478
CODEN: COTSD2

➤ **CLINICAL OTOLARYNGOLOGY.** Text in English. 1976. bi-m. GBP 1,041 in United Kingdom to institutions; EUR 1,322 in Europe to institutions; USD 1,924 in the Americas to institutions; USD 2,248 elsewhere to institutions; GBP 1,198 combined subscription in United Kingdom to institutions (print & online eds.); EUR 1,522 combined subscription in Europe to institutions (print & online eds.); USD 2,214 combined subscription in the Americas to institutions (print & online eds.); USD 2,585 combined subscription elsewhere to institutions (print & online eds.) (effective 2012). adv. bk.rev. charts; illus. index. back issues avail.; reprint service avail. from PSC. **Document type:** *Journal, Academic/Scholarly.* **Description:** Contains clinical and clinically oriented research papers dealing with current otorhinolaryngological practice, audiology, speech pathology, and related specialties.
Formerly (until 2005): Clinical Otolaryngology and Allied Sciences (0307-7772)
Related titles: Microform ed.: (from PQC); Online - full text ed.: ISSN 1749-4486. GBP 1,041 in United Kingdom to institutions; EUR 1,322 in Europe to institutions; USD 1,924 in the Americas to institutions; USD 2,248 elsewhere to institutions (effective 2012) (from IngentaConnect).
Indexed: A01, A02, A03, A08, A22, A26, ASCA, C11, CA, CurCont, E01, EMBASE, ExcerpMed, H04, H12, IBR, IBZ, ISR, IndMed, Inpharma, MEDLINE, NBA, P30, P35, R10, Reac, SCI, SCOPUS, T02, W07.
—BLDSC (3286.324050), GNLM, IE, Infotrieve, Ingenta, INIST. **CCC.**
Published by: (British Association of Otorhinolaryngologists, Oto-Rhino-Laryngology Research Society, Nederlandse Vereniging voor Keel-Neus- Oorheelkunde en Heelkunde van het Hoofd- Halsgebied NLD), Wiley-Blackwell Publishing Ltd. (Subsidiary of: John Wiley & Sons, Inc.), 9600 Garsington Rd, Oxford, OX4 2DQ, United Kingdom. TEL 44-1865-776868, FAX 44-1865-714591, customerservices@blackwellpublishing.com. Ed. G G Browning. Pub. Elizabeth Whelan. Adv. contact Jenny Applin. Circ: 1,735.

617.89 USA
RC423.A1

➤ **CONTEMPORARY ISSUES IN COMMUNICATION SCIENCE & DISORDERS (ONLINE).** Abbreviated title: C I C S D. Text in English. 1973. s-a. free (effective 2010). adv. back issues avail. **Document type:** *Journal, Academic/Scholarly.* **Description:** Focuses on recent advances in the discipline and serves as a supplemental training tool for communication science students.
Former titles (until 2009): Contemporary Issues in Communication Science & Disorders (Print) (1092-5171); (until 1997): N S S L H A Journal (1097-7449); (until 1983): National Student Speech Language Hearing Association. Journal (0736-0312)
Media: Online - full text.
Indexed: C06, C07, C08, CA, CINAHL, L&LBA, P20, P24, P30, P48, P54, PQC, T02.
—BLDSC (3425.184117). **CCC.**
Published by: (National Student Speech Language Hearing Association), American Speech - Language - Hearing Association, 2200 Research Blvd, Rockville, MD 20850-3289. TEL 301-296-5700, 800-638-8255, FAX 301-296-8580, actioncenter@asha.org, http://www.asha.org. Ed. Dale Evan Metz. Adv. contact Pamela J Leppin.

➤ **CORRIERE DEI LARINGECTOMIZZATI.** *see* SOCIAL SERVICES AND WELFARE

616.21 617 USA ISSN 1068-9508
CODEN: COOSFD

CURRENT OPINION IN OTOLARYNGOLOGY & HEAD AND NECK SURGERY. Text in English. 1993. bi-m. USD 943 domestic to institutions; USD 1,013 foreign to institutions (effective 2011). adv. back issues avail.; reprints avail. **Document type:** *Journal, Academic/Scholarly.* **Description:** Covers key subjects such as the nose and paranasal sinuses, head and neck oncology, speech therapy and rehabilitation, hearing science, allergy, head and neck reconstruction, laryngology and bronchoesophagology and facial plastic surgery.
Related titles: Online - full text ed.: ISSN 1531-6998. USD 224 to individuals (effective 2011); Optical Disk - DVD ed.: Current Opinion in Otolaryngology & Head and Neck Surgery, with Evaluated MEDLINE. ISSN 1080-8086. 1995.
Indexed: A20, A22, C06, C07, C08, CINAHL, CurCont, E01, EMBASE, ExcerpMed, MEDLINE, P30, R10, Reac, SCI, SCOPUS, W07.
—BLDSC (3500.776700), GNLM, IE, Infotrieve, Ingenta. **CCC.**
Published by: Lippincott Williams & Wilkins (Subsidiary of: Wolters Kluwer N.V.), 530 Walnut St, Philadelphia, PA 19106. TEL 215-521-8300, FAX 215-521-8902, customerservice@lww.com, http://www.lww.com. Eds. Patrick J Bradley, Dr. Paul J Donald. Pub. Ian Burgess. Circ: 480.

616.21 AUS ISSN 1120-8694
CODEN: DIESE

➤ **DISEASES OF THE ESOPHAGUS.** Text in English. 1988-1992; resumed 1994. 8/yr. GBP 679 in United Kingdom to institutions; EUR 861 in Europe to institutions; USD 1,103 in the Americas to institutions; USD 1,329 elsewhere to institutions; GBP 781 combined subscription in United Kingdom to institutions (print & online eds.); EUR 991 combined subscription in Europe to institutions (print & online eds.); USD 1,269 combined subscription in the Americas to institutions (print & online eds.); USD 1,529 combined subscription elsewhere to institutions (print & online eds.) (effective 2011). adv. bk.rev. abstr.; bibl. back issues avail.; reprint service avail. from PSC. **Document type:** *Journal, Academic/Scholarly.* **Description:** Explores original and review material covering all aspects of esophageal disorders, their etiology, investigation and diagnosis, and both medical and surgical treatment.
Incorporates (in July 1993): Gullet (0952-0643)
Related titles: Microform ed.: (from PQC); Online - full text ed.: ISSN 1442-2050. GBP 679 in United Kingdom to institutions; EUR 861 in Europe to institutions; USD 1,103 in the Americas to institutions; USD 1,329 elsewhere to institutions (effective 2011) (from IngentaConnect).
Indexed: A01, A03, A08, A22, A26, CA, CurCont, E01, EMBASE, ExcerpMed, H12, IndMed, Inpharma, MEDLINE, P30, P35, R10, Reac, SCI, SCOPUS, T02, W07.
—BLDSC (3598.210000), GNLM, IE, Infotrieve, Ingenta. **CCC.**
Published by: (International Society for Diseases of the Esophagus USA), Wiley-Blackwell Publishing Asia (Subsidiary of: Wiley-Blackwell Publishing Ltd.), 155 Cremorne St, Richmond, VIC 3121, Australia. TEL 61-3-92743100, FAX 61-3-92743101, subs@blackwellpublishingasia.com, http://www.wiley.com/WileyCDA/. Eds. Brenda Levos-Beale, Claude Deschamps, Kenneth Wang. Circ: 990. **Subscr. to:** Wiley-Blackwell Publishing Ltd., Journal Customer Services, 9600 Garsington Rd, PO Box 1354, Oxford OX4 2XG, United Kingdom.

➤ **DISTURBIOS DE COMUNICACAO.** *see* COMMUNICATIONS

616.21 USA ISSN 0179-051X
RC815.2 CODEN: DYSPE2

➤ **DYSPHAGIA;** an international multidisciplinary journal devoted to swallowing and its disorders. Text in English. 1986. q. EUR 775, USD 800 combined subscription to institutions (print & online eds.) (effective 2012). adv. Supplement avail.; back issues avail.; reprint service avail. from PSC. **Document type:** *Journal, Academic/Scholarly.* **Description:** Surveys all aspects of normal and dysphagic ingestion involving the mouth, pharynx, and esophagus. Draws on expertise from a variety of disciplines including gastroenterology, neurology, otolaryngology, radiology, dentistry, rehabilitation medicine, speech pathology, nursing, dietetics, medical administration and the basic biomedical sciences.
Related titles: Microform ed.: (from PQC); Online - full text ed.: ISSN 1432-0460 (from IngentaConnect).
Indexed: A22, A26, AMED, ASCA, B21, B25, BIOSIS Prev, C06, C07, C08, CA, CINAHL, CurCont, E01, E08, EMBASE, ExcerpMed, H12, I05, ISR, IndMed, Inpharma, MEDLINE, MycolAb, NSA, P20, P22, P24, P30, P48, P54, PQC, R10, Reac, S09, SCI, SCOPUS, T02, W07.
—BLDSC (3637.270000), GNLM, IE, Infotrieve, Ingenta, INIST. **CCC.**
Published by: (Dysphagia Research Society, The Japanese Society of Dysphagia Rehabilitation), Springer New York LLC (Subsidiary of: Springer Science+Business Media), 233 Spring St, New York, NY 10013. TEL 212-460-1500, FAX 212-460-1575, service-ny@springer.com. Ed. Dr. Bronwyn Jones.

617.51005 GBR ISSN 2042-2156

E N T & AUDIOLOGY NEWS. (Ear Nose and Throat) Text in English. 1992. bi-m. GBP 19 domestic; GBP 28 in Europe; GBP 42 elsewhere (effective 2009). adv. bk.rev.; Website rev.; software rev.; video rev. abstr.; tr.lit. reprints avail. **Document type:** *Magazine, Consumer.* **Description:** Provides reviews of otolaryngology, audiology and related journals in a high quality glossy magazine. Combining first class articles and clearly referenced reviews, it provides an invaluable forum for the communication of news and information.
Formerly (until Sep.2009): E N T News (1368-8944)
Related titles: E-mail ed.; Online - full text ed.; Spanish ed.: E N T News Espanol.
—BLDSC (3776.420750). **CCC.**
Published by: Pinpoint Scotland Ltd., 9 Gayfield St, Edinburgh, Scotland EH1 3NT, United Kingdom. TEL 44-131-5574184, FAX 44-131-5574701. Ed. Joseph Crossland TEL 44-131-4788401. Adv. contact Heather McLaughlin TEL 44-131-4788401. Circ: 19,500 (controlled).

617.51 616.21 USA ISSN 1559-4939

E N T TODAY. (Ear Nose and Throat) Variant title: E N Today. Text in English. 2006 (Apr.). m. GBP 84 in United Kingdom to institutions; EUR 98 in Europe to institutions; USD 136 elsewhere to institutions (effective 2012). adv. back issues avail. **Document type:** *Newspaper, Trade.* **Description:** Covers news about otolaryngology-head and neck surgery, ready to be used by those involved with the full spectrum of disorders of the head and neck and related structures.
Related titles: Online - full text ed.: ISSN 1932-5312.
Indexed: CA, T02.
—CCC.
Published by: Lippincott Williams & Wilkins (Subsidiary of: Wolters Kluwer N.V.), 530 Walnut St, Philadelphia, PA 19106. TEL 215-521-8300, FAX 215-521-8902, customerservice@lww.com, http://www.lww.com. Ed. Stephanie Cajigal. Pub. Vickie Thaw.

617.89 USA ISSN 0196-0202
RF286 CODEN: EAHEDS

➤ **EAR AND HEARING.** Text in English. 1975. bi-m. USD 399 domestic to institutions; USD 515 foreign to institutions (effective 2011). adv. illus. index. back issues avail.; reprints avail. **Document type:** *Journal, Academic/Scholarly.* **Description:** Focuses on assessment, diagnosis and management of auditory disorders.
Former titles (until 1980): American Auditory Society. Journal (0164-5080); (until 1978): American Audiology Society. Journal (0360-9294)
Related titles: Online - full text ed.: ISSN 1538-4667. 19??.
Indexed: A20, A22, ASCA, AcoustA, B25, BIOSIS Prev, C06, C07, C08, CINAHL, ChPerI, CurCont, EMBASE, ExcerpMed, FR, ISR, IndMed, Inpharma, MEDLINE, MLA-IB, MycolAb, NBA, NPPA, NSCI, P30, R10, Reac, SCI, SCOPUS, SOPODA, W07.
—BLDSC (3642.866000), GNLM, IE, Infotrieve, Ingenta, INIST. **CCC.**
Published by: (American Auditory Society), Lippincott Williams & Wilkins (Subsidiary of: Wolters Kluwer N.V.), 530 Walnut St, Philadelphia, PA 19106. TEL 215-521-8300, FAX 215-521-8902, customerservice@lww.com, http://www.lww.com. Ed. Brenda M Ryals. Pub. Marcia Serepy. Circ: 2,695.

616.21 USA ISSN 0145-5613
RF1

➤ **EAR, NOSE & THROAT JOURNAL.** Variant title: E N T Journal. Text in English. 1921. m. free domestic to qualified personnel; USD 255 foreign (effective 2010). adv. bk.rev. charts; illus. index. back issues avail.; reprints avail. **Document type:** *Journal, Academic/Scholarly.* **Description:** Publishes recent, scientific, clinical articles and case reports in otolaryngology and head and neck surgery; provides practical hands-on information for today's busy physician.
Formerly (until 1976): Eye, Ear, Nose and Throat Monthly (0014-5491); Which incorporated (1941-1942): Diseases of the Eye, Ear, Nose & Throat
Related titles: Microfilm ed.: (from PQC); Online - full text ed.: ISSN 1942-7522.
Indexed: A01, A02, A03, A08, A22, A26, C06, C07, C11, CA, ChemAb, CurCont, DentInd, E08, EMBASE, ExcerpMed, G06, G07, G08, H03, H04, H11, H12, I05, IndMed, M01, M02, MEDLINE, P20, P22, P24, P30, P48, P54, PQC, R10, Reac, S09, SCI, SCOPUS, T02, THA, W07.
—BLDSC (3642.867000), GNLM, IE, Infotrieve, Ingenta, INIST. **CCC.**
Published by: Vendome Group, LLC, 3800 Lakeside Ave, E Ste 201, Cleveland, OH 44114. TEL 216-373-1200, FAX 216-391-9200, info@vendomegrp.com, http://www.vendomegrp.com/. Ed. Robert T Sataloff TEL 215-732-6100. Pub. Michael W O'Donnell TEL 216-373-1209. Circ: 13,000 (controlled).

➤ **ECHO (ONLINE).** *see* HANDICAPPED—Hearing Impaired

616.21 EGY ISSN 2090-0740

EGYPTIAN JOURNAL OF EAR NOSE THROAT AND ALLIED SCIENCES/AL-MAJALLAT AL-'ILMIYYAT LIL-JAM'IYYAT AL-MISRIYYAT LIL-UZUN WA-AL-ANF WA-AL-HANJARAT WA-AL-'ULUM AL-MUSHTARAKAT. Text in English. 2000. 3/yr. **Document type:** *Journal, Academic/Scholarly.*
Formerly (until 2009): Egyptian Journal of E N T and Allied Sciences (1110-6670)
Published by: Egyptian Society of Otolaryngology and Allied Sciences, Ain Shams Specialized Hospital, Otolaryngology Department, El-Khalifa El-Maamoun St., Abbassiya, P O Box 11588, Cairo, Egypt. TEL 20-2-4039012, FAX 20-2-2605805. Ed. Dr. Mohammed Abdel-Ismail Lottfi.

616.21 EGY ISSN 1012-5574

THE EGYPTIAN JOURNAL OF OTOLARYNGOLOGY. Text in English. 1984. q. **Document type:** *Journal, Academic/Scholarly.*
Published by: The Egyptian Society of Otorhinolaryngology, Dar El-Hekma, 42 Qasr El-Aini Str, Cairo, Egypt.

616.21 FRA ISSN 0246-0351

➤ **ENCYCLOPEDIE MEDICO-CHIRURGICALE. OTO-RHINO-LARYNGOLOGIE.** Cover title: Traite d'Oto-Rhino-Laryngologie. Variant title: Encyclopedie Medico-Chirurgicale, Instantanes Medicaux. Oto-Rhino-Laryngologie. Text in French. 1951. 6 base vols. plus q. updates. EUR 1,353 (effective 2006). bibl.; charts; illus. **Document type:** *Academic/Scholarly.* **Description:** Provides otorhinolaryngologists with a comprehensive and up-to-date reference source for diagnosing and treating disorders of the ears, nose, and throat.
Related titles: Online - full text ed.
—INIST.
Published by: Elsevier Masson (Subsidiary of: Elsevier Health Sciences), 62 Rue Camille Desmoulins, Issy les Moulineaux, Cedex 92442, France. TEL 33-1-71165500, FAX 33-1-71165600, infos@elsevier-masson.fr.

➤ **ENCYCLOPEDIE MEDICO-CHIRURGICALE. TECHNIQUES CHIRURGICALES. TETE ET COU.** *see* MEDICAL SCIENCES—Surgery

➤ **ENCYCLOPEDIE MEDICO-CHIRURGICALE. TECHNIQUES CHIRURGICALES. THORAX.** *see* MEDICAL SCIENCES—Surgery

➤ **ENCYCLOPEDIE MEDICO-CHIRURGICALE. TECNICHE CHIRURGICHE. CHIRURGIA O R L E CERVICO-FACCIALE.** (Oto-Rhino-Laryngologia) *see* MEDICAL SCIENCES—Surgery

➤ **ENCYCLOPEDIE MEDICO-CHIRURGICALE. TECNICHE CHIRURGICHE. TORACE.** *see* MEDICAL SCIENCES—Surgery

616.21 JPN ISSN 1346-2067

ENTONI. Variant title: Monthly Book Entoni. Text in Japanese. 2001. m. price varies. **Document type:** *Monographic series, Academic/Scholarly.*
Published by: Zennihon Byoin Shuppankai, 3-16-4 Hongo, Bunkyo-Ku, 7F, Tokyo, 113-0033, Japan. TEL 81-3-56895989, FAX 81-3-56898030, http://www.zenniti.com/.

617.8 FRA ISSN 1879-7296

▼ **EUROPEAN ANNALS OF OTORHINOLARYNGOLOGY, HEAD AND NECK DISEASES.** Text in English, French. 2011. q. EUR 480 in Europe to institutions; EUR 480 in France to institutions; JPY 57,600 in Japan to institutions; USD 624 elsewhere to institutions (effective 2012). **Document type:** *Journal, Academic/Scholarly.* **Description:** Publishes scientific articles in all areas of your specialty: otology, laryngology rhinology, and head and neck surgery allowing you to deepen and broaden your knowledge.
Related titles: Online - full text ed.: ISSN 1879-730X.
Indexed: MEDLINE, P30, SCOPUS, T02.
—CCC.
Published by: Elsevier Masson (Subsidiary of: Elsevier Health Sciences), 62 Rue Camille Desmoulins, Issy les Moulineaux, Cedex 92442, France. TEL 33-1-71165500, FAX 33-1-71165600, infos@elsevier-masson.fr, http://www.elsevier-masson.fr. Ed. C Martin.

616.21 DEU ISSN 0937-4477
RF1 CODEN: EAOTE7

➤ **EUROPEAN ARCHIVES OF OTO-RHINO-LARYNGOLOGY.** Text in English, German. 1864. 12/yr. EUR 4,662, USD 5,785 combined subscription to institutions (print & online eds.) (effective 2012). adv. bibl.; charts; illus. index. back issues avail.; reprint service avail. from PSC. **Document type:** *Journal, Academic/Scholarly.* **Description:** Focuses on original clinical reports and clinically relevant experimental studies in the fields of oto-rhino-laryngology, and head and neck surgery.
Former titles (until 1989): Archives of Oto-Rhino-Laryngology (0302-9530); (until 1973): Archiv fuer Klinische und Experimentelle Ohren-, Nasen- und Kehlkopfheilkunde (0003-9195); (until 1965): Archiv fuer Ohren-, Nasen- und Kehlkopfheilkunde (0365-5245); Which incorporated (1922-1944): Zeitschrift fuer Hals-Nasen-Ohren-und-Ohrenheilkunde (0372-8978); (until 1915): Archiv fuer Ohrenheilkunde
Related titles: Microform ed.: (from PQC); Online - full text ed.: ISSN 1434-4726 (from IngentaConnect); Supplement(s): European Archives of Oto-Rhino-Laryngology. Supplement. ISSN 0942-8992. 1983.
Indexed: A01, A03, A08, A20, A22, A26, A34, A36, ASCA, B25, BIOSIS Prev, CA, CABA, CurCont, DentInd, E01, E12, EMBASE, ExcerpMed, F08, F11, GH, H12, H17, IBR, IBZ, ISR, IndMed, IndVet, Inpharma, MEDLINE, MycolAb, N02, N03, P30, P33, P35, P39, R08, R10, R12, RA&MP, RM&VM, Reac, SCI, SCOPUS, T02, T05, VS, W07, W10.
—BLDSC (3829.488540), CASDDS, GNLM, IE, Ingenta, INIST. **CCC.**

Published by: (European Federation of Oto-Rhino-Laryngological Societies), Springer (Subsidiary of: Springer Science+Business Media), Tiergartenstr 17, Heidelberg, 69121, Germany. TEL 49-6221-4870, FAX 49-6221-345229. Eds. Jan Olofsson, Jochen A Werner. adv.: B&W page EUR 790, color page EUR 1,830. Circ: 500 (paid and controlled). **Subscr. in the Americas to:** Springer New York LLC, Journal Fulfillment, PO Box 2485, Secaucus, NJ 07096. TEL 800-777-4643, 201-348-4033, FAX 201-348-4505, journals-ny@springer.com, http://www.springer.com; **Subscr. to:** Springer Distribution Center, Kundenservice Zeitschriften, Haberstr 7, Heidelberg 69126, Germany. TEL 49-6221-3454303, FAX 49-6221-3454229, subscriptions@springer.com. **Co-sponsor:** European Laryngological Society.

➤ **EVIDENCE-BASED COMMUNICATION ASSESSMENT AND INTERVENTION.** *see* MEDICAL SCIENCES

➤ **EXCERPTA MEDICA. SECTION 11: OTORHINOLARYNGOLOGY.** *see* MEDICAL SCIENCES—Abstracting, Bibliographies, Statistics

616.21 ARG ISSN 1666-9398
FEDERACION ARGENTINA DE SOCIEDADES DE OTORRINOLARINGOLOGIA. REVISTA. Text in Spanish. 1994. q. **Document type:** *Magazine, Trade.*
Published by: Federacion Argentina de Sociedades de Otorrinolaringologia, Angel Carranza 2382, Buenos Aires, 1425, Argentina. TEL 54-11-47736447, FAX 54-11-47726410, Faso1@ciudad.com.ar, http://www.faso.org.ar.

617.8 CHE ISSN 1021-7762
RC423 CODEN: FPLOEP
➤ **FOLIA PHONIATRICA ET LOGOPAEDICA**; international journal of phoniatrics, speech therapy and communication pathology. Text in English, French, German; Summaries in English. 1947. bi-m. CHF 1,378, EUR 1,101, USD 1,358.50 to institutions; CHF 1,511, EUR 1,207, USD 1,487.50 combined subscription to institutions (print & online eds.) (effective 2012). adv. bk.rev. bibl.; charts; illus. index. back issues avail. **Document type:** *Journal, Academic/Scholarly.* **Description:** Provides a survey of international research in physiology and pathology of speech and the voice organs.
Formerly: Folia Phoniatrica (0015-5705)
Related titles: Microform ed.; Online - full text ed.: ISSN 1421-9972. CHF 1,327, EUR 1,062, USD 1,288 to institutions (effective 2012).
Indexed: A01, A03, A08, A20, A22, AMED, ASCA, BDM&CN, C06, C07, C08, CA, CINAHL, ChemAb, CurCont, DentInd, E-psyche, E01, EMBASE, ExcerpMed, IBR, IBZ, INI, IndMed, L&LBA, L11, MEA&I, MEDLINE, MLA, MLA-IB, NBA, P03, P15, P20, P22, P24, P25, P26, P30, P48, P54, PQC, PsycInfo, PsycholAb, R10, RASB, Reac, SCI, SCOPUS, SSCI, T02, W07.
—BLDSC (3973.560000), GNLM, IE, Infotrieve, Ingenta, INIST. **CCC.**
Published by: (International Association of Logopedics and Phoniatrics), S. Karger AG, Allschwilerstr 10, Basel, 4055, Switzerland. TEL 41-61-3061111, FAX 41-61-3061234, karger@karger.ch, http://www.karger.ch. Ed. H. K. Schutte. adv.: page CHF 1,730; trim 210 x 280. Circ: 900.

616.21 DEU ISSN 1439-717X
FORUM HALS-, NASEN-, OHRENHEILKUNDE. Text in German. 1999. bi-m. EUR 50; EUR 15 newsstand/cover (effective 2010). adv. **Document type:** *Magazine, Trade.*
Published by: OmniMed Verlagsgesellschaft mbH, Borsteler Chaussee 85-99a, Haus 16, Hamburg, 22453, Germany. TEL 49-40-232334, FAX 49-40-230292, info@omnimedonline.de, http://www.omnimedonline.de. Ed. Dr. T Grundmann. Adv. contact Vanessa Baack. Circ: 5,469 (paid and controlled).

617.8 ITA ISSN 2038-4793
▼ **FRONTIERA O R L.** (Otorinolaringoiatria) Text in Italian. 2010. q. **Document type:** *Journal, Trade.*
Related titles: Online - full text ed.: ISSN 2038-4785.
Address: Via Fuga 64, Caserta, Italy.

616.21 HUN ISSN 0016-237X
CODEN: FOGGAX
FUL-, ORR-, GEGEGYOGYASZAT/OTORHINOLARYNGOLOGIA HUNGARICA. Text in Hungarian; Summaries in English, German, Russian. 1955. q. HUF 1,000 (effective 2006). illus. **Document type:** *Journal, Academic/Scholarly.*
Indexed: IndMed, P30.
—BLDSC (4055.290000), GNLM.
Published by: Magyar Ful-, Orr-, Gegeorvosok Egyesulete/Hungarian Oto-, Rhino-, Laryngological Society, Szigony u 36, Budapest, 1083, Hungary. TEL 36-1-3342384, FAX 36-1-3333316, http://www.orl.hu. Ed. Miklos Becske.

616.21 617 DEU ISSN 1865-1038
G M S CURRENT POSTERS IN OTORHINOLARYNGOLOGY, HEAD AND NECK SURGERY. (German Medical Science) Text in English. 2005. a. **Document type:** *Journal, Academic/Scholarly.*
Media: Online - full content.
Indexed: A01, T02.
Published by: (Deutsche Gesellschaft fuer Hals-Nasen-Ohren-Heilkunde, Kopf- und Hals-Chirurgie), German Medical Science (G M S), Ubierstr 20, Duesseldorf, 40223, Germany. TEL 49-211-312828, FAX 49-211-316819, info@egms.de.

616.21 DEU ISSN 1865-1011
RF1
G M S CURRENT TOPICS IN OTORHINOLARINGOLOGY - HEAD AND NECK SURGERY. (German Medical Science) Text in English. 2004. a. free (effective 2011). **Document type:** *Journal, Academic/Scholarly.*
Media: Online - full text.
Indexed: A01, C06.
Published by: German Medical Science (G M S), Ubierstr 20, Duesseldorf, 40223, Germany. TEL 49-211-312828, FAX 49-211-316819, info@egms.de.

617.89 NLD ISSN 1874-6993
GEHOOR IN ONDERZOEK. Text in Dutch. 2006. a.
Published by: (Initiatiefgroep HoorPlatform), HoorPlatform, Rijnsburgerweg 10, Leiden, 2333 AA, Netherlands. TEL 31-71-5234245, FAX 31-71-5234243, info@hoorplatform.nl, http://www.hoorplatform.nl.

GELBE LISTE PHARMINDEX. H N O-AERZTE. (Hals-Nasen-Ohren) *see* PHARMACY AND PHARMACOLOGY

616.21 CHN ISSN 1001-1102
GUOWAI YIXUE (ER BI YANHOU KEXUE FENCE)/FOREIGN MEDICAL SCIENCES (OTOLARYNGOLOGY). Text in Chinese. 1964. bi-m. USD 31.20 (effective 2009). **Document type:** *Journal, Academic/Scholarly.*
Related titles: Online - full text ed.
—East View.
Published by: Beijing Shi Er Bi Yanhouke Yanjiusuo, 17, Chongneihougouhutong, Beijing, 100005, China. TEL 86-10-65596373, FAX 86-10-65596001. **Dist. by:** China International Book Trading Corp, 35 Chegongzhuang Xilu, Haidian District, PO Box 399, Beijing 100044, China. TEL 86-10-68412045, FAX 86-10-68412023, cibtc@mail.cibtc.com.cn, http://www.cibtc.com.cn.

616.21 DEU ISSN 0017-6192
RF1 CODEN: HBZHAS
➤ **H N O (BERLIN)**; Hals-, Nasen-, Ohren-Heilkunde, Kopf- und Halschirurgie. (Hals-, Nasen-, Ohren-Heilkunde) Text in German; Summaries in English, German. 1947. m. EUR 474, USD 529 combined subscription to institutions (print & online eds.) (effective 2012). adv. bk.rev. bibl.; charts; illus. index. reprint service avail. from PSC. **Document type:** *Journal, Academic/Scholarly.* **Description:** Contains research articles and papers on all aspects of surgery and medical treatments in the field of otorhinolaryngology.
Formerly: H N O: Wegweiser fuer Die Fachaerztliche Praxis
Related titles: Microform ed.: (from PQC); Online - full text ed.: ISSN 1433-0458 (from IngentaConnect).
Indexed: A20, A22, A26, CurCont, E01, EMBASE, ExcerpMed, FR, INI, IndMed, Inpharma, MEDLINE, P30, P35, R10, Reac, SCI, SCOPUS, W07.
—BLDSC (4319.500000), GNLM, IE, Infotrieve, Ingenta, INIST. **CCC.**
Published by: (Deutsche Gesellschaft fuer Hals-Nasen-Ohren-Heilkunde, Kopf- und Hals-Chirurgie), Springer (Subsidiary of: Springer Science+Business Media), Tiergartenstr 17, Heidelberg, 69121, Germany. TEL 49-6221-4870, FAX 49-6221-345229. Circ: 2,100 (paid and controlled). **Subscr. in the Americas to:** Springer New York LLC, Journal Fulfillment, PO Box 2485, Secaucus, NJ 07096. TEL 800-777-4643, 201-348-4033, FAX 201-348-4505, journals-ny@springer.com, http://www.springer.com; **Subscr. to:** Springer Distribution Center, Kundenservice Zeitschriften, Haberstr 7, Heidelberg 69126, Germany. TEL 49-6221-3454303, FAX 49-6221-3454229, subscriptions@springer.com.

616.21 DEU ISSN 0344-9319
➤ **H N O INFORMATIONEN.** (Hals - Nase - Ohren) Text in German. 1976. q. EUR 87 to institutions; EUR 21.75 newsstand/cover (effective 2009). adv. **Document type:** *Journal, Academic/Scholarly.*
—GNLM. **CCC.**
Published by: (Deutsche Gesellschaft fuer Hals-Nasen-Ohren-Heilkunde, Kopf- und Hals-Chirurgie), Deutscher Aerzte-Verlag GmbH, Dieselstr 2, Cologne, 50859, Germany. TEL 49-2234-70110, FAX 49-2234-7011460, verlag@aerzteblatt.de. Ed. Heinrich Rudert. Adv. contact Nicole Ohmann. B&W page EUR 1,650, color page EUR 2,650; trim 185 x 260. Circ: 4,183 (paid and controlled).

616.21 DEU
H N O KOMPAKT. (Hals - Nase - Ohren) Text in German. 1993. 6/yr. EUR 70; EUR 35 to students; EUR 18 newsstand/cover (effective 2009). adv. index. back issues avail. **Document type:** *Journal, Academic/Scholarly.*
Formerly (until 2007): H N O Aktuell (0943-0121)
—GNLM.
Published by: Dr. R. Kaden Verlag GmbH & Co. KG, Ringstr 19 B, Heidelberg, 69115, Germany. TEL 49-6221-1377600, FAX 49-6221-29910, kaden@kaden-verlag.de, http://www.kaden-verlag.de. Adv. contact A Siegmann. color page EUR 2,330, B&W page EUR 1,415; trim 210 x 275. Circ: 3,500 (controlled).

616.21 DEU ISSN 0939-6381
H N O - MITTEILUNGEN. (Hals Nase Ohren) Text in German. 1950. bi-m. EUR 28.80; EUR 4.80 newsstand/cover (effective 2009). adv. **Document type:** *Newsletter, Trade.*
Formerly (until 1990): H N O (Cologne) (0341-9746)
Indexed: DentInd.
—GNLM. **CCC.**
Published by: (Deutsche Berufsverband der Hals-, Nasen-, Ohrenaerzte e.V.), Deutscher Aerzte-Verlag GmbH, Dieselstr 2, Cologne, 50859, Germany. TEL 49-2234-70110, FAX 49-2234-7011460, froitzheim@aerzteverlag.de. Ed. Dr. Detlef Walter. Adv. contact Nicole Ohmann. B&W page EUR 1,700, color page EUR 2,700; trim 185 x 260. Circ: 4,875 (paid and controlled).

616.21 DEU ISSN 0177-1000
H N O - NACHRICHTEN; Praxisinformation fuer den HNO-Arzt. (Hals Nase Ohren) Text in German. 1971. bi-m. EUR 51, USD 57 to institutions (effective 2012). adv. **Document type:** *Newsletter, Academic/Scholarly.*
Indexed: A26.
—BLDSC (4319.507000), GNLM. **CCC.**
Published by: Urban und Vogel Medien und Medizin Verlagsgesellschaft mbH (Subsidiary of: Springer Science+Business Media), Neumarkter Str 43, Munich, 81673, Germany. TEL 49-89-4372-1411, FAX 49-89-4372-1410, verlag@urban-vogel.de, http://www.urban-vogel.de. Ed. Claudia Maeck. Adv. contact Renate Senfft. B&W page EUR 1,800, color page EUR 3,050; trim 174 x 237. Circ: 5,200 (paid and controlled). **Subscr. in N. America to:** Springer Distribution Center, Kundenservice Zeitschriften, Haberstr 7, Heidelberg 69126, Germany. TEL 49-6221-3454303, FAX 49-6221-3454229, subscriptions@springer.com.

616.21 NLD ISSN 0378-5955
QP460 CODEN: HERED3
➤ **HEARING RESEARCH.** Text in English. 1978. 24/yr. EUR 6,001 in Europe to institutions; JPY 796,300 in Japan to institutions; USD 6,716 elsewhere to institutions (effective 2012). adv. bk.rev. back issues avail.; reprints avail. **Document type:** *Journal, Academic/Scholarly.* **Description:** Publishes papers concerned with basic auditory mechanisms.
Related titles: Microform ed.: (from PQC); Online - full text ed.: ISSN 1878-5891 (from IngentaConnect, ScienceDirect).
Indexed: A01, A03, A08, A20, A22, A26, A34, A35, A36, ASCA, AcoustA, AgBio, B21, B25, BIOSIS Prev, CA, CABA, CIN, ChemAb, ChemTitl, CurCont, DentInd, E12, EMBASE, ExcerpMed, FR, GH, I05, IBR, IBZ, ISR, IndMed, IndVet, Inpharma, Inspec, MEDLINE, MycolAb, N02, N03, N04, NBA, NPPA, NSA, NSCI, P03, P30, P35, P37, PsycInfo, R10, Reac, S13, S16, SCI, SCOPUS, SoyAb, T02, T05, VS, W07, W10, WildRev, Z01.
—BLDSC (4275.286700), AskIEEE, CASDDS, GNLM, IE, Infotrieve, Ingenta, INIST, Linda Hall. **CCC.**
Published by: Elsevier BV (Subsidiary of: Elsevier Science & Technology), Radarweg 29, PO Box 211, Amsterdam, 1000 AE, Netherlands. TEL 31-20-4853911, FAX 31-20-4852457, JournalsCustomerServiceEMEA@elsevier.com, http://www.elsevier.nl. Ed. Joe Eggermont.

617.8 NZL ISSN 1178-6698
HEARING REVIEW. Variant title: N Z Hearing Review. Text in English. 2007. bi-m. free to qualified personnel (effective 2009).
Media: Online - full text.
Published by: Research Review Ltd., N Shore Mail Centre, PO Box 100116, Auckland, New Zealand. TEL 64-9-4102277, info@researchreview.co.nz.

617.89 USA ISSN 1074-5734
QP460
THE HEARING REVIEW. Text in English. 1994. 13/yr. free to qualified personnel (effective 2011). adv. **Document type:** *Magazine, Trade.* **Description:** Covers news and trends on products and services for hearing health care professionals.
Related titles: Online - full content ed.
Indexed: A10, A26, C06, C07, H12, I05, V03.
—BLDSC (4275.286900), IE, Ingenta. **CCC.**
Published by: Allied Healthcare Group (Subsidiary of: Ascend Media), 6100 Ctr Dr, Ste 1020, Los Angeles, CA 90045. TEL 310-642-4400, FAX 310-641-4444, cagulnek@ascendmedia.com, http://www.alliedhealthjournals.com. Ed. Karl Strom TEL 218-525-5558. Pub. David Galuppo TEL 303-494-5493. Adv. contact Tom Madorna TEL 610-544-3568.

371.91 USA ISSN 0300-6883
I A L NEWS. Text in English. 1955. 3/yr. free. bk.rev. illus. **Document type:** *Newsletter.*
Indexed: RehabLit.
Published by: International Association of Laryngectomees, c/o Gary L. Miner Sr., 1203 Wolf Swamp Rd, Jacksonville, NC 28546. TEL 910-340-4519, ialhq@larynxlink.com. Ed. Karen Smith. Circ: 20,000.

I F H O H JOURNAL. *see* HANDICAPPED—Hearing Impaired

617.8 USA ISSN 2090-5742
▼➤ **I S R N OTOLARYNGOLOGY.** (International Scholarly Research Network) Text in English. 2011. **Document type:** *Journal, Academic/Scholarly.* **Description:** Publishes original research articles, review articles, and clinical studies in all areas of otolaryngology.
Related titles: Online - full text ed.: ISSN 2090-5750. 2011. free (effective 2011).
Published by: Hindawi Publishing Corporation, 410 Park Ave, 15th Fl, PMB 287, New York, NY 10022. FAX 215-893-4392, 866-446-3294, info@hindawi.com.

616.21 IND
CODEN: IJOLBJ
➤ **INDIAN JOURNAL OF OTOLARYNGOLOGY AND HEAD AND NECK SURGERY.** Text in English. 1948. q. EUR 214, USD 260 combined subscription to institutions (print & online eds.) (effective 2011). adv. bk.rev. abstr. index. 105 p./no. 2 cols./p.; reprint service avail. from PSC. **Document type:** *Journal, Academic/Scholarly.* **Description:** Provides the details of the clinical and research work done by the Otolaryngologists community in India and around the world. It features clinical reports, clinical studies, research articles in basic and applied Otolaryngology, short communications, clinical records reporting unusual presentations or lesions and new surgical techniques.
Former titles (until 1993): Indian Journal of Otolaryngology and Head and Neck; Indian Journal of Otolaryngology (0019-5421)
Related titles: Online - full text ed.: ISSN 0973-7707 (from IngentaConnect).
Indexed: A01, A22, A26, A36, CA, CABA, E01, E08, E12, GH, H11, H12, H17, N02, N03, P30, P33, R08, R10, R12, RM&VM, Reac, S09, SCI, SCOPUS, T02, T05, W07.
—CASDDS, IE. **CCC.**
Published by: (Association of Otolaryngologists of India), Springer (India) Private Ltd. (Subsidiary of: Springer Science+Business Media), 212, Deen Dayal Upadhyaya Marg, 3rd Fl, Gandharva Mahavidyalaya, New Delhi, 110 002, India. TEL 91-11-45755888, FAX 91-11-45755889. Ed. D Dwarakanatha Reddy. adv.: B&W page INR 8,000, color page INR 12,000. Circ: 3,500.

617.89 IND ISSN 0971-7749
INDIAN JOURNAL OF OTOLOGY. Text in English. 1995. q. INR 2,000 domestic to individuals; USD 200 foreign to individuals; INR 3,000 domestic to institutions; USD 300 foreign to institutions (effective 2011). adv. back issues avail. **Document type:** *Journal, Academic/Scholarly.* **Description:** Covers cover technical and clinical studies related to health, ethical and social issues in field of Otology, Neuro-otology, audiology, anatomy.
Related titles: Online - full text ed.: INR 1,600 domestic to individuals; USD 160 foreign to individuals; INR 2,400 domestic to institutions; USD 240 foreign to institutions (effective 2011).
Indexed: SCOPUS.
—BLDSC (4417.810000).
Published by: (Indian Institute of Ear Diseases), Medknow Publications and Media Pvt. Ltd., B-9, Kanara Business Ctr, Off Link Rd, Ghatkopar (E), Mumbai, Maharastra 400 075, India. TEL 91-22-66491818, FAX 91-22-66491817, journals@medknow.com, http://www.medknow.com. Ed. M K Taneja TEL 91-11-26275102.

616.21 BRA ISSN 1809-9777
INTERNATIONAL ARCHIVES OF OTORHINOLARYNGOLOGY. Text in Portuguese. 2002. q. back issues avail. **Document type:** *Journal, Academic/Scholarly.*
Former titles (until 2006): Arquivos Internacionais de Otorrinolaringologia (Print) (1809-4872); (until 2005): Arquivos de Otorrinolaringologia (1677-7530)
Related titles: Online - full text ed.: ISSN 1809-4864. 1997. free (effective 2011).

Published by: Fundacao Otorrinolaringologia, Rua Teodoro Sampaio 417 Cj 52, Sao Paulo, 05405, Brazil. TEL 55-11-30689855, FAX 55-11-30796769, revista@arquivosdeorl.org.br, http://www.forl.org.br/ . Ed. Marcelo M Hueb.

617.8 GBR ISSN 1499-2027
RF286 CODEN: IJANGS

➤ **INTERNATIONAL JOURNAL OF AUDIOLOGY.** Text in English. 2002. m. GBP 580, EUR 835, USD 1,035 combined subscription to institutions (print & online eds.); GBP 1,155, EUR 1,660, USD 2,070 combined subscription to corporations (print & online eds.) (effective 2010). adv. bk.rev. index. back issues avail.; reprint service avail. from PSC. **Document type:** *Journal, Academic/Scholarly.*
Formed by the merger of (1973-2002): British Journal of Audiology (0300-5364); (1971-2002): Audiology (0020-6091); Which was formerly (until 1971): International Audiology (0538-4915); (1972-2002): Scandinavian Audiology (0105-0397); Which was formerly (until 1972): Nordisk Audiologi (0105-0400); (until 1961): Nordisk Tidsskrift for Praktisk Audiologi (0105-1865)
Related titles: Online - full text ed.: ISSN 1708-8186 (from IngentaConnect).
Indexed: A01, A02, A03, A08, A20, A22, A29, ASFA, ASSIA, AcoustA, B07, B20, B21, B25, BIOBASE, BIOSIS Prev, C03, C06, C07, C08, C11, CA, CBCARef, CINAHL, CMM, CTA, ChemoAb, CurCont, DSHAb, DokArb, E-psyche, E01, E03, EMBASE, ERI, ESPM, ExcerpMed, FR, H04, I10, IABS, IBR, IBZ, IndMed, Inpharma, Inspec, MEDLINE, MLA-IB, MycolAb, NPPA, NSA, P03, P10, P20, P22, P25, P30, P43, P48, P53, P54, PQC, PsycInfo, PsycholAb, R10, Reac, SCI, SCOPUS, SOPODA, T02, VirolAbstr, W07.
—BLDSC (4542.115000), AskIEEE, GNLM, IE, Ingenta, INIST. **CCC.**
Published by: (International Society of Audiology CAN, British Society of Audiology, Nordisk Audiologisk Selskab/Nordic Audiological Society NOR), Informa Healthcare (Subsidiary of: T & F Informa plc), Telephone House, 69-77 Paul St, London, EC2A 4LQ, United Kingdom. TEL 44-20-70175000, FAX 44-20-70176792, healthcare.enquiries@informa.com. Ed. Ross J Roeser. Adv. contact Per Sonnerfeldt. **Subscr. in N America to:** Taylor & Francis Inc., Customer Services Dept, 325 Chestnut St, 8th Fl, Philadelphia, PA 19106. TEL 215-625-8900, 800-354-1420, FAX 215-625-8914, customerservice@taylorandfrancis.com; **Subscr. outside N America to:** Taylor & Francis Ltd., Journals Customer Service, Sheepen Pl, Colchester, Essex CO3 3LP, United Kingdom. TEL 44-20-70175544, FAX 44-20-70175198, tf.enquiries@tfinforma.com.

616.855 GBR ISSN 1368-2822
RC423.A1 CODEN: IJLDFI

➤ **INTERNATIONAL JOURNAL OF LANGUAGE AND COMMUNICATION DISORDERS.** Text in English. 1966. bi-m. GBP 686 in United Kingdom to institutions; EUR 989 in Europe to institutions; USD 1,236 elsewhere to institutions; GBP 789 combined subscription in United Kingdom to institutions (print & online eds.); EUR 1,137 combined subscription in Europe to institutions (print & online eds.); USD 1,422 combined subscription elsewhere to institutions (print & online eds.) (effective 2012). adv. bk.rev. abstr.; bibl.; charts; illus.; stat. index. back issues avail.; reprints avail. **Document type:** *Journal, Academic/Scholarly.* **Description:** Covers all aspects of speech, language, communication disorders and speech and language therapy.
Former titles (until 1998): European Journal of Disorders of Communication (0963-7273); (until 1992): British Journal of Disorders of Communication (0007-098X); Which incorporated (1958-1965): Speech Pathology and Therapy (0584-8687)
Related titles: Online - full text ed.: ISSN 1460-6984. 1999. GBP 686 in United Kingdom to institutions; EUR 989 in Europe to institutions; USD 1,236 elsewhere to institutions (effective 2012) (from IngentaConnect).
Indexed: A01, A02, A03, A08, A20, A22, A36, AMED, ASCA, AmHI, B01, B06, B07, B09, B29, BDM&CN, C06, C07, C08, CA, CINAHL, CMM, CPE, CurCont, DentInd, E-psyche, E01, E03, ECER, EMBASE, ERI, ERIC, ExcerpMed, FR, FamI, GH, H07, IBR, IBZ, INI, IndMed, L&LBA, L11, LT&LA, MEDLINE, MLA-IB, P03, P30, PsycInfo, PsycholAb, R10, Reac, RehabLit, SCOPUS, SOPODA, SSCI, T02, W07.
—GNLM, IE, Infotrieve, Ingenta, INIST. **CCC.**
Published by: (Royal College of Speech and Language Therapists), John Wiley & Sons Ltd. (Subsidiary of: John Wiley & Sons, Inc.), 9600 Garsington Rd, Oxford, OX4 2DQ, United Kingdom. TEL 44-1865-776868, FAX 44-1865-714591, cs-journals@wiley.com, http://onlinelibrary.wiley.com/.

616.21 USA ISSN 1687-9201

➤ **INTERNATIONAL JOURNAL OF OTOLARYNGOLOGY.** Text in English. 2008. irreg. USD 195 (effective 2011). **Document type:** *Journal, Academic/Scholarly.* **Description:** Publishes original research articles as well as review articles in all areas of otolaryngology.
Related titles: Online - full text ed.: ISSN 1687-921X. 2008. free (effective 2011).
Indexed: A01, C06, C07, CA, P30, T02.
Published by: Hindawi Publishing Corporation, 410 Park Ave, 15th Fl, PMB 287, New York, NY 10022. FAX 215-893-4392, 866-446-3294, orders@hindawi.com.

616.21 618.92 GBR ISSN 0165-5876
RF47.C4 CODEN: IPOTDJ

➤ **INTERNATIONAL JOURNAL OF PEDIATRIC OTORHINOLARYNGOLOGY.** Text in English. 1979. 12/yr. EUR 3,252 in Europe to institutions; JPY 431,700 in Japan to institutions; USD 3,638 elsewhere to institutions (effective 2012). bk.rev. back issues avail. **Document type:** *Journal, Academic/Scholarly.* **Description:** Provides a medium for clinical and basic contributions in all of the areas of pediatric otorhinolaryngology.
Related titles: Microform ed.: (from PQC); Online - full text ed.: ISSN 1872-8464 (from IngentaConnect, ScienceDirect); Supplement(s): International Journal of Pediatric Otorhinolaryngology Extra. ISSN 1871-4048 (from ScienceDirect).
Indexed: A01, A03, A08, A20, A22, A26, A29, A34, A36, ASCA, AgrForAb, B20, B21, BIOBASE, CA, CABA, CIS, CurCont, D01, DentInd, E12, EMBASE, ESPM, ExcerpMed, F08, F12, FR, GH, H16, H17, I05, I10, IABS, ISR, IndMed, IndVet, Inpharma, LT, MEDLINE, N02, N03, NBA, OR, P30, P32, P33, P35, P39, R08, R10, R12, RA&MP, RM&VM, Reac, S12, S13, S16, SCI, SCOPUS, T02, T05, VS, VirolAbstr, W07, W10.
—BLDSC (4542.451000), GNLM, IE, Infotrieve, Ingenta, INIST. **CCC.**
Published by: Elsevier Ltd (Subsidiary of: Elsevier Science & Technology), The Blvd, Langford Ln, Kidlington, Oxford, OX5 1GB, United Kingdom. TEL 44-1865-843000, FAX 44-1865-843010, journalscustomerserviceemea@elsevier.com. Ed. Dr. R J Ruben. Pub. Fiona Barratt. Adv. contact Fiona Macnab TEL 44-207-4244259. **Subscr. to:** Elsevier BV, Radarweg 29, PO Box 211, Amsterdam 1000 AE, Netherlands. TEL 31-20-4853757, FAX 31-20-4853432, http://www.elsevier.nl.

616.21 USA ISSN 0946-5448
RF293.8 CODEN: ITJOF9

➤ **INTERNATIONAL TINNITUS JOURNAL.** Text in English. 1995. s-a. bk.rev. index. back issues avail. **Document type:** *Journal, Academic/Scholarly.* **Description:** Articles provide experimental and operational reports, clinical studies, reviews, and theoretical papers relating to tinnitus. Aims to facilitate the exchange of information and ideas among interested professionals in the areas of audiology, otology, otolaryngology and neuropsychology.
Related titles: Online - full text ed.
Indexed: C06, C07, CA, EMBASE, ExcerpMed, IndMed, MEDLINE, P30, R10, Reac, SCOPUS, T02.
—BLDSC (4551.030000), CASDDS, IE, Infotrieve, Ingenta.
Published by: (Martha Entenmann Tinnitus Research Center, Inc.), SUNY Downstate Medical Center, Office of Institutional Advancement, 450 Clarkson Ave, Brooklyn, NY 11203. TEL 718-270-1176, FAX 718-270-3160, http://www.downstate.edu/ia/index.html.

616.21 USA ISSN 1528-8420
RF1

➤ **THE INTERNET JOURNAL OF OTORHINOLARYNGOLOGY.** Text in English. 2000. s-a. free (effective 2011). adv. bk.rev. back issues avail. **Document type:** *Journal, Academic/Scholarly.* **Description:** Provides information from the field of ear, nose and throat medicine/surgery, otorhinolaryngology; contains original articles, reviews, case reports, streaming slide shows, streaming videos, letters to the editor, press releases and meeting information.
Media: Online - full text.
Indexed: A01, A02, A03, A08, A26, C06, C07, CA, G08, H11, H12, I05, T02.
Published by: Internet Scientific Publications, Llc., 23 Rippling Creek Dr, Sugar Land, TX 77479. TEL 832-443-1193, FAX 281-240-1533, wenker@ispub.com. Ed. Joginder Singh Gulia.

616.21 USA ISSN 1525-3961
RF1 CODEN: JJARBC

➤ **J A R O.** (Journal of the Association for Research in Otolaryngology) Text in English. 2000. q. EUR 354, USD 370 combined subscription to institutions (print & online eds.) (effective 2012). adv. back issues avail.; reprint service avail. from PSC. **Document type:** *Journal, Academic/Scholarly.* **Description:** Brings out research findings from disciplines related to otolaryngology and communications sciences.
Related titles: Online - full text ed.: ISSN 1438-7573 (from IngentaConnect).
Indexed: A22, A26, B21, B25, BIOSIS Prev, CA, CurCont, E01, EMBASE, ExcerpMed, H12, Inpharma, MEDLINE, MycolAb, NSA, NSCI, P20, P22, P24, P30, P48, P54, PQC, R10, Reac, SCI, SCOPUS, T02, W07.
—BLDSC (4663.110000), IE, Infotrieve, Ingenta. **CCC.**
Published by: (Association for Research in Otolaryngology), Springer New York LLC (Subsidiary of: Springer Science+Business Media), 233 Spring St, New York, NY 10013. TEL 212-460-1500, service-ny@springer.com. Ed. Ruth Anne Eatock.

617 JPN ISSN 0910-6820

J O H N S: JOURNAL OF OTOLARYNGOLOGY, HEAD AND NECK SURGERY/JIBI INKOKA, TOKEIBU GEKA. Text in Japanese. 1985. m. JPY 33,900 (effective 2005).
Indexed: INIS AtomInd.
Published by: Tokyo Igakusha Ltd., 35-4 Hongo 3-chome, Bunkyo-ku, Tokyo, 113-0033, Japan. TEL 81-3-38114119, FAX 81-3-38116135, shoge@tokyo-igakusha.co.jp.

616.21 JPN ISSN 0032-6313
CODEN: JIBIAG

JIBI INKOKA RINSHO/PRACTICAOTO-RHINO-LARYNGOLOGICA. Text in Japanese; Summaries in English. 1908. m. membership. adv. abstr.; bibl.; charts; illus. Index. **Document type:** *Journal, Academic/Scholarly.*
Formerly: Jibi Inkouka Kyouto Rinshou
Related titles: ◆ Supplement(s): Practica Otologica Kyoto. Supplement. ISSN 0912-1870.
Indexed: A22, INIS AtomInd, SCOPUS.
—BLDSC (6593.830000), GNLM, IE, Ingenta, INIST. **CCC.**
Published by: Society of Practical Otolaryngology, 39 Kawabata-higashi, Marutamachi-dori, Sakyo-ku, Kyoto 606-8395, Japan. TEL 81-75-7712301, FAX 81-75-7612373, postmaster@jibirin.gr.jp. Circ: 1,500.

616.21 JPN ISSN 0386-9687
CODEN: JITEBR

JIBI INKOKA TEMBO/OTORHINOLARYNGOLOGY TOKYO. Text in Japanese. 1958. bi-m. Supplement avail. **Document type:** *Journal, Academic/Scholarly.*
Related titles: Online - full content ed.
Indexed: A22, EMBASE, ExcerpMed, INIS AtomInd, R10, Reac, SCOPUS.
—BLDSC (6313.620000), IE, Ingenta.
Published by: Jibi Inkoka Tembokai/Society of Otorhinolaryngology Tokyo, 3-25-8 Nishi-Shinbashi, Minato-Ku, Jikei University School of Medicine, Department of Otorhinolaryngology, Tokyo, 105-8461, Japan. TEL 81-3-34331111 ext 3608, http://www.jibitenbou.gr.jp/thome.html.

616.21 JPN ISSN 0914-3491

JIBI INKOKA, TOKEIBU GEKA/OTOLARYNGOLOGY - HEAD AND NECK SURGERY. Text in Japanese; Summaries in English. 1928. m. (13/yr.). JPY 39,950; JPY 52,000 combined subscription per academic year (print & online eds.) (effective 2010). **Document type:** *Journal, Academic/Scholarly.*
Formerly (until 1987): Jibi Inkoka/Otolaryngology (0386-9679)
Related titles: Online - full text ed.: ISSN 1882-1316.
Indexed: A22, INIS AtomInd, P30, SCOPUS.
—BLDSC (6313.524000), GNLM, IE, Ingenta.
Published by: Igaku Shoin Ltd., 1-28-36 Hongo, Bunkyo-ku, Tokyo, 113-8719, Japan. TEL 81-3-3817-5600, FAX 81-3-3815-7791, info@igaku-shoin.co.jp. Circ: 4,000.

617.8 BRA ISSN 1517-5308

JORNAL BRASILEIRO DE FONOAUDIOLOGIA. Text in Portuguese. 1999. q. **Document type:** *Journal, Academic/Scholarly.*
Published by: Editora Maio Ltda., Rua Itupava, Curitiba, 80240-000, Brazil. editoramaio@editoramaio.com.br.

617.89 BRA ISSN 0101-9252

JORNAL BRASILEIRO DE REABILITACAO. Text in Portuguese. 1979. q. **Document type:** *Journal, Academic/Scholarly.*
Formerly (until 1981): Jornal Brasileiro de Reabilitacao Vocal (0101-9139)
Published by: Sociedade Brasileira de Fonoaudiologia, Rua Barao do Bananal 819, Sao Paulo, 05024-000, Brazil. TEL 55-11-38734211, socfono@terra.com.br, http://www.sbfa.org.br.

JOURNAL OF BRONCHOLOGY & INTERVENTIONAL PULMONOLOGY. see MEDICAL SCIENCES—Respiratory Diseases

617.8 TUR ISSN 1308-7649

THE JOURNAL OF INTERNATIONAL ADVANCED OTOLOGY. Abbreviated title: I A O. Text in English. 3/yr. EUR 50 (effective 2010). **Document type:** *Journal, Academic/Scholarly.*
Formerly (until 2008): The Mediterranean Journal of Otology (1305-5267)
Related titles: Online - full text ed.: free (effective 2010).
Indexed: SCOPUS.
Published by: The Journal of International Advanced Otology, Bahcelievler, P O Box 108, Ankara, Turkey. FAX 90-312-2354100, iao@advancedotology.org. Ed. O Nuri Ozgirgin.

616.21 GBR ISSN 0022-2151
RF1 CODEN: JLOTAX

➤ **JOURNAL OF LARYNGOLOGY AND OTOLOGY.** Text in English. 1887. m. GBP 414, USD 827 combined subscription to institutions (print & online eds.) (effective 2012). adv. bibl.; illus. index, cum.index every 10 yrs. back issues avail.; reprint service avail. from PSC. **Document type:** *Journal, Academic/Scholarly.* **Description:** Contains original scientific articles and clinical records in all fields of otology, rhinology and laryngology.
Former titles (until 1921): The Journal of Laryngology, Rhinology, and Otology (1755-1463); (until 1892): The Journal of Laryngology and Rhinology (1755-1455)
Related titles: Microform ed.: (from PQC); Online - full text ed.: ISSN 1748-5460. GBP 356, USD 712 to institutions (effective 2012); Supplement(s): Journal of Laryngology and Otology. Supplement. ISSN 0144-2945. price varies.
Indexed: A01, A03, A08, A20, A22, A26, A36, AIM, ASCA, B21, B25, BIOSIS Prev, C06, C07, C08, CA, CABA, CINAHL, ChemAb, CurCont, DentInd, E01, E12, EMBASE, ExcerpMed, F08, FR, G08, GH, H11, H12, H17, INI, ISR, IndMed, Inpharma, MEDLINE, MLA-IB, MycolAb, N02, N03, NBA, NSA, P20, P22, P24, P26, P30, P33, P35, P39, P48, P54, PN&I, PQC, R08, R10, R12, RA&MP, RM&VM, Reac, SCI, SCOPUS, T02, T05, THA, W07, W10, W11.
—BLDSC (5010.100000), GNLM, IE, Infotrieve, Ingenta, INIST. **CCC.**
Published by: (The Journal of Laryngology & Otology (1984) Ltd.), Cambridge University Press, The Edinburgh Bldg, Shaftesbury Rd, Cambridge, CB2 8RU, United Kingdom. TEL 44-1223-312393, FAX 44-1223-315052, journals@cambridge.org, http://www.cambridge.org/uk. Eds. Guy Kenyon, Robin Youngs. adv.: B&W page GBP 555, B&W page USD 1,045, color page GBP 1,170, color page USD 2,225.

➤ **JOURNAL OF MAXILLOFACIAL AND ORAL SURGERY.** see MEDICAL SCIENCES—Surgery

616.855 USA ISSN 1065-1438
RC423.A1 CODEN: JSLPEP

➤ **JOURNAL OF MEDICAL SPEECH - LANGUAGE PATHOLOGY.** Text in English. 1993. q. USD 165; USD 49.95 per issue (effective 2010). **Document type:** *Journal, Academic/Scholarly.* **Description:** Contains clinical and theoretical articles, clinical notes and dialogue covering all aspects of human communication disorders encountered in medical settings — from pediatric issues to the increasing challenges of the elderly.
Related titles: Online - full text ed.
Indexed: A22, A26, C06, C07, C08, CINAHL, E-psyche, E08, EMBASE, ExcerpMed, G08, H11, H12, I05, L&LBA, NSCI, P03, P30, PsycInfo, PsycholAb, S09, SCI, SCOPUS, SOPODA, W07.
—BLDSC (5017.087500), GNLM, IE, Ingenta.
Published by: (Academy of Neurologic Communication Disorders and Sciences), Delmar Cengage Learning (Subsidiary of: Cengage Learning), PO Box 6904, Florence, KY 41022. TEL 800-354-9706, FAX 800-487-8488, schoolcustomerservice@cengage.com, http://www.delmarhealthcare.com.

616.21 CAN ISSN 1916-0208
CODEN: JOTODX

➤ **JOURNAL OF OTOLARYNGOLOGY - HEAD & NECK SURGERY.** Text in English, French. 1947. bi-m. CAD 286.20 domestic to institutions; USD 275 in United States to institutions; USD 337.10 elsewhere to institutions; CAD 331.80 combined subscription domestic to institutions (print & online eds.); USD 314.80 combined subscription in United States to institutions (print & online eds.); USD 393.25 combined subscription elsewhere to institutions (print & online eds.) (effective 2010). adv. bk.rev. index. back issues avail. **Document type:** *Journal, Academic/Scholarly.* **Description:** Devoted to all aspects of the field, as well as a broad range of related activities.
Former titles (until 2008): The Journal of Otolaryngology (0381-6605); (until 1976): Canadian Journal of Otolaryngology (0045-5083); (until 1972): Canadian Otolaryngological Society. Annual Meeting. Proceedings (0068-9416); (until 1958): Canadian Otolaryngological Society. Annual Meeting. Papers and Discussions (0380-5565)
Related titles: Online - full text ed.: ISSN 1916-0216. CAD 275.60 domestic to institutions; USD 265 foreign to institutions (effective 2010); ◆ Supplement(s): Journal of Otolaryngology. Supplement. ISSN 0707-7270.
Indexed: A01, A03, A08, A20, A22, A29, ASCA, B20, B21, C03, CA, CBCARef, ChemoAb, DokArb, ESPM, FR, I10, IndMed, Inpharma, NBA, P20, P22, P30, P48, P54, PQC, SCOPUS, SOPODA, T02, THA, VirolAbstr.
—BLDSC (5027.715500), GNLM, IE, Infotrieve, Ingenta, INIST. **CCC.**
Published by: (Canadian Society of Otolaryngology - Head and Neck Surgery), B.C. Decker Inc., 50 King St E, 2nd Fl, Hamilton, ON L8N 2A1, Canada. TEL 905-522-7017, 800-568-7281, FAX 905-522-7839, info@bcdecker.com. Ed. Hadi Seikaly TEL 780-407-3691. Adv. contact Jennifer Coates TEL 905-522-7017 ext 291. B&W page USD 1,160, color page USD 2,260; trim 8.125 x 10.875. Circ: 873.

616.21 JPN ISSN 0030-6622
RF1
➤ **JOURNAL OF OTOLARYNGOLOGY OF JAPAN/NIHON JIBI INKOKA GAKKAI KAIHO.** Text in Japanese; Summaries in English. 1890. m. JPY 15,600, USD 200 (effective 2003). adv. **Document type:** *Academic/Scholarly.*
Related titles: Online - full text ed.: ISSN 1883-0854.
Indexed: EMBASE, ExcerpMed, INIS AtomInd, IndMed, MEDLINE, P30, R10, Reac, SCOPUS.
—BLDSC (5027.720000), GNLM, IE, Infotrieve, Ingenta, INIST. **CCC.**
Published by: The Oto-Rhino-Laryngological Society of Japan, Inc./Nihon Jibi Inkoka Gakkai, 3-23-14-807 Takanawa, Minato-ku, Tokyo, 108-0074, Japan. TEL 81-3-3443-3085, FAX 81-3-3443-3037. Ed. Takuya Uemura. Circ: 10,800.

616.21 CAN ISSN 0707-7270
JOURNAL OF OTOLARYNGOLOGY. SUPPLEMENT. Text in English. 1974. irreg., latest 2003.
Formerly (until 1977): Canadian Journal of Otolaryngology. Supplement (0707-7289)
Related titles: ◆ Supplement to: Journal of Otolaryngology - Head & Neck Surgery. ISSN 1916-0208.
Indexed: P30.
—BLDSC (5027.710500), Ingenta, INIST.
Published by: B.C. Decker Inc., 50 King St E, 2nd Fl, Hamilton, ON L8N 2A1, Canada. TEL 905-522-7017, 800-568-7281, FAX 905-522-7839, 888-311-4987, info@bcdecker.com, http://www.bcdecker.com.

616.21 USA ISSN 0892-1997
QP306 CODEN: JOVOEA
➤ **THE JOURNAL OF VOICE.** Text in English. 1987. bi-m. USD 436 in United States to institutions; USD 482 elsewhere to institutions (effective 2012). adv. charts; illus. back issues avail.; reprints avail. **Document type:** *Journal, Academic/Scholarly.* **Description:** Publishes articles on the development and care of the professional voice.
Supersedes (1978-1985): Annual Symposium on Care of the Professional Voice. Transcripts
Related titles: Online - full text ed.: ISSN 1873-4588 (from IngentaConnect, ScienceDirect).
Indexed: A20, A22, A26, AMED, ASCA, AcoustA, C06, C07, C08, CA, CINAHL, CMM, CommAb, CurCont, E-psyche, E07, E08, EMBASE, ExcerpMed, G08, H11, H12, I05, IBT&D, IIMP, IndMed, Inpharma, L&LBA, M11, MEDLINE, MusicInd, P03, P30, P35, PCI, PsycInfo, PsycholAb, R10, RILM, Reac, S09, SCI, SCOPUS, T02, W07.
—BLDSC (5072.512700), GNLM, IE, Infotrieve, Ingenta, INIST. **CCC.**
Published by: (International Association of Phonosurgeons, Voice Foundation), Mosby, Inc. (Subsidiary of: Elsevier Health Sciences), 1600 John F. Kennedy Blvd, Ste 1800, Philadelphia, PA 19103. TEL 215-239-3900, 800-523-1649, FAX 215-239-3990, elspcs@elsevier.com, http://www.us.elsevierhealth.com. Ed. Dr. Robert Thayer Sataloff.

616.21 TUN ISSN 1737-7803
JOURNAL TUNISIEN D'O R L, DE CHIRURGIE CERVICO - FACIALE ET D'AUDIOPHONOLOGIE/JAM'IYAT 'AT-TUNISIYAT LI-TIB 'AL-'UDIN WA'AL-'ANIF WA'AL-HUNJURAT/MAJALLAT 'AL-JAM'IYAT 'AT-TUNISIYAT LI-TIB 'AL-'UDIN WA'AL-'ANIF WA'AL-HUNJURAT. (Oto - Rhino - Laryngologie) Text in French. 1998. m. **Document type:** *Journal, Academic/Scholarly.*
Related titles: Online - full text ed.: free (effective 2011).
Published by: Societe Tunisienne d'O R L et de Chirurgie Cervico - Faciale, Rue de Touraine 16, Tunis, 1082, Tunisia. info@journal-storl.org.

616.855 616.8 401 JPN ISSN 1347-8451
➤ **KOMINIKEISYON SYOIGAIGAKU/JAPANESE JOURNAL OF COMMUNICATION DISORDERS.** Text in Japanese; Summaries in English, Japanese. 1983. 3/yr. JPY 2,000. bk.rev. 70 p./no.; **Document type:** *Journal, Academic/Scholarly.*
Formerly (until 2003): Chono Gengogaku Kenkyu (0912-8204)
Published by: Nihon Chono Gengo Gakkai/Japanese Association of Communication Disorders, 2-15-6-202 Minami-cho, Kokubunji-shi, Tokyo-to 185-0021, Japan. TEL 81-42-324-7397, FAX 81-42-328-7071, jslha@cd.inbox.ne.jp. Ed. Bensaku Nishimura.

617.89 DEU ISSN 1436-1175
KOMMUNIKATIONSSTOERUNGEN - BERICHTE AUS PHONIATRIE UND PAEDAUDIOLOGIE. Text in German. 1998. irreg., latest vol.18, 2008. price varies. **Document type:** *Monographic series, Academic/Scholarly.*
Published by: Shaker Verlag GmbH, Kaiserstr 100, Herzogenrath, 52134, Germany. TEL 49-2407-95960, FAX 49-2407-95969, info@shaker.de.

616.855 USA ISSN 1558-9129
➤ **LANGUAGE, SPEECH AND HEARING SERVICES IN SCHOOLS (ONLINE).** Text in English. 1971. q. USD 69 to individuals non-members; USD 170 to institutional members (effective 2011). adv. **Document type:** *Journal, Academic/Scholarly.* **Description:** Archival journal for research and practice in educational settings.
Media: Online - full text.
Indexed: P18, P20, P22, P24, P25, P54, P55.
—**CCC.**
Published by: American Speech - Language - Hearing Association, 2200 Research Blvd, Rockville, MD 20850-3289. TEL 301-296-5700, 800-638-8255, FAX 301-296-8580, http://www.asha.org. Ed. Marilyn A Nippold TEL 541-346-2587.

616.21 DEU ISSN 0935-8943
CODEN: LROTEX
➤ **LARYNGO- RHINO- OTOLOGIE**; Zeitschrift fuer Hals-Nasen-Ohrenheilkunde, Kopf- und Halschirurgie. Text in German; Summaries in English, German. 1975. m. EUR 286 to institutions; EUR 400 combined subscription to institutions; EUR 31 newsstand/cover (effective 2011). adv. bk.rev. abstr.; bibl.; charts; illus.; stat. index. back issues avail.; reprints avail. **Document type:** *Journal, Academic/Scholarly.*
Formerly (until 1989): Laryngologie, Rhinologie, Otologie und Ihre Grenzgebiete Vereinigt mit Monatsschrift fuer Ohrenheilkunde (0340-1588); Which was formed by the merger of (1948-1975): Laryngologie, Rhinologie, Otologie und Ihre Grenzgebiete (0302-9379); Which was formerly (until 1974): Zeitschrift fuer Laryngologie, Rhinologie, Otologie und Ihre Grenzgebiete (0044-3018); (1867-1975): Monatsschrift fuer Ohrenheilkunde und Laryngo-Rhinologie (0026-9328)
Related titles: Online - full text ed.: ISSN 1438-8685. EUR 386 to institutions (effective 2011); Supplement(s): Laryngo- Rhino- Otologie. Supplement. ISSN 1615-0007. 2000.
Indexed: A20, A22, ASCA, CISA, CurCont, DentInd, EMBASE, ExcerpMed, FR, IBR, IBZ, INIS AtomInd, IndMed, Inpharma, MEDLINE, MLA-IB, NBA, P30, P35, R10, Reac, S02, S03, SCI, SCOPUS, W07.
—BLDSC (5156.150000), GNLM, IE, Infotrieve, Ingenta, INIST. **CCC.**
Published by: (Deutsche Gesellschaft fuer Hals-Nasen-Ohren-Heilkunde, Kopf- und Hals-Chirurgie), Georg Thieme Verlag, Ruedigerstr 14, Stuttgart, 70469, Germany. TEL 49-711-8931421, FAX 49-711-8931410, leser.service@thieme.de, http://www.thieme-connect.de. Eds. Dr. G Rettinger, Dr. H Stammberger. R&P Peter Eich. Adv. contact Irmgard Mayer TEL 49-711-8931469. Circ: 2,150 (paid and controlled). **Co-sponsor:** Oesterreichische Gesellschaft fuer Hals-Nasen-Ohrenheilkunde, Kopf- und Halschirurgie.

616.21 USA ISSN 0023-852X
RF1 CODEN: LARYA8
➤ **THE LARYNGOSCOPE.** Text in English. 1896. m. GBP 410 in United Kingdom to institutions; EUR 518 in Europe to institutions; USD 741 in the Americas to institutions; USD 803 elsewhere to institutions; GBP 471 combined subscription in United Kingdom to institutions (print & online eds.); EUR 596 combined subscription in Europe to institutions (print & online eds.); USD 853 combined subscription in the Americas to institutions (print & online eds.); USD 924 combined subscription elsewhere to institutions (print & online eds.) (effective 2012). adv. bk.rev. bibl.; illus. index. back issues avail.; reprint service avail. from PSC. **Document type:** *Journal, Academic/Scholarly.* **Description:** Features in broncho-esophagology, communicative disorders, head and neck surgery, plastic and reconstructive facial surgery, oncology, speech and hearing defects.
Related titles: CD-ROM ed.: ISSN 1091-756X. 1997; Microfilm ed.: (from PQC); Online - full text ed.: ISSN 1531-4995. GBP 410 in United Kingdom to institutions; EUR 518 in Europe to institutions; USD 741 in the Americas to institutions; USD 803 elsewhere to institutions (effective 2012); Supplement(s): The Laryngoscope. Supplement. ISSN 1066-8349.
Indexed: A20, A22, A26, A34, A35, A36, A38, ASCA, AgBio, C06, C07, C08, CABA, CIN, CINAHL, ChemAb, ChemTitl, CurCont, D01, DentInd, DokArb, E12, EMBASE, ExcerpMed, FR, G08, GH, H11, H12, INI, ISR, IndMed, IndVet, Inpharma, MEDLINE, MLA-IB, MS&D, N02, N03, NBA, NPPA, P30, P32, P33, P35, PN&I, R08, R10, R12, R13, RILM, RM&VM, Reac, S12, SCI, SCOPUS, T02, T05, VS, W07, W10, W11.
—BLDSC (5156.200000), CASDDS, GNLM, IE, Infotrieve, Ingenta, INIST. **CCC.**
Published by: (American Laryngological, Rhinological and Otological Society), John Wiley & Sons, Inc., 111 River St, Hoboken, NJ 07030. TEL 201-748-6000, FAX 201-748-5915, info@wiley.com, http://www.wiley.com/WileyCDA/. Ed. Jonas T Johnson. Pub. Kim Thompkins TEL 212-850-6921. Adv. contact Rich Devanna TEL 201-767-4170.

616.21 FRA ISSN 0754-7188
LA LETTRE D'OTO-RHINO-LARYNGOLOGIE; et de chirurgie cervico-faciale. Text in French. 1985. m. EUR 75 in Europe; EUR 75 DOM-TOM; EUR 75 in Africa; EUR 87 elsewhere (effective 2009). Supplement avail. **Document type:** *Newsletter, Academic/Scholarly.*
—INIST.
Published by: Edimark S.A.S., 2 Rue Sainte-Marie, Courbevoie, Cedex 92418, France. TEL 39-1-41458000, FAX 33-1-41458025, contact@edimark.fr. Ed. Y Manac'h. Pub. Claudie Damour-Terrasson.

617.51 CHN
LINCHUANG ERBI YANHOU WAIKE ZAZHI/JOURNAL OF CLINICAL OTORHINOLARYNGOLOGY HEAD AND NECK SURGERY. Text in Chinese. 1987. s-m. (q. until 1993; bi-m. until 1997; m. until 2006). **Document type:** *Journal, Academic/Scholarly.*
Formerly (until 2009): Lingchuang Erbiyuanhouke Zazhi (1001-1781)
Related titles: Online - full text ed.
Indexed: A22, MEDLINE, P30, SCOPUS.
—BLDSC (4958.632500), East View, IE, Ingenta.
Published by: Huazhong Keji Daxue Tongji Yixueyuan Fushu Xiehe Yiyuan/Tongji Medical University, Union Hospital, 1277, Jiefang Dadao, Wuhan, 430022, China. TEL 86-27-85726342 ext 8818, FAX 86-27-85727988, http://www.whuh.com/.

617.8 GBR ISSN 1401-5439
RC423.A1 CODEN: LPVOF6
➤ **LOGOPEDICS PHONIATRICS VOCOLOGY.** Text in English; Summaries in Danish, Finnish, Norwegian, Swedish. 1936. q. GBP 170, EUR 230, USD 285 combined subscription to institutions (print & online eds.); GBP 350, EUR 460, USD 570 combined subscription to corporations (print & online eds.) (effective 2010). adv. back issues avail.; reprint service avail. from PSC. **Document type:** *Journal, Academic/Scholarly.* **Description:** Serves as an international forum for research reports and information within the area of communication disorders.
Former titles (until 1996): Scandinavian Journal of Logopedics and Phoniatrics (0803-5032); (until 1991): Nordisk Tidsskrift for Logopedi og Foniatri (0105-1539); (until 1976): Nordisk Tidsskrift for Tale og Stemme (0029-1552)
Related titles: Online - full text ed.: ISSN 1651-2022 (from IngentaConnect).
Indexed: A01, A03, A08, A22, C06, C07, C08, CA, CINAHL, CMM, E01, EMBASE, ExcerpMed, IndMed, L&LBA, L11, MEDLINE, P30, R10, Reac, SCI, SCOPUS, SOPODA, T02, W07.
—BLDSC (5292.364000), IE, Infotrieve, Ingenta. **CCC.**
Published by: Informa Healthcare (Subsidiary of: T & F Informa plc), Telephone House, 69-77 Paul St, London, EC2A 4LQ, United Kingdom. TEL 44-20-70175000, FAX 44-20-70176792, healthcare.enquiries@informa.com. Ed. David Howard. Adv. contact Per Sonnerfeldt. **Subscr. in N. America to:** Taylor & Francis Inc., Customer Services Dept, 325 Chestnut St, 8th Fl, Philadelphia, PA 19106. TEL 215-625-8900, 800-354-1420, FAX 215-625-8914, customerservice@taylorandfrancis.com; **Subscr. outside N. America to:** Taylor & Francis Ltd., Journals Customer Service, Sheepen Pl, Colchester, Essex CO3 3LP, United Kingdom. TEL 44-20-70175544, FAX 44-20-70175198, tf.enquiries@tfinforma.com. **Co-sponsor:** British Voice Association.

616.21 ARG ISSN 1669-8924
METAVOCES. Text in Spanish. 2005. s-a. **Document type:** *Journal, Academic/Scholarly.*
Published by: Universidad Nacional de San Luis, Facultad de Ciencias Humanas, Avenida Ejercito de los Andes 950, IV Bloque, San Luis, 5700, Argentina. TEL 54-652-435512, 54-652-30224, histopsi@unsl.edu.ar, http://humanas.unsl.edu.ar/. Eds. Hugo Klappenbach, Maria Beatriz Forcade.

616.855 USA
MINNESOTA SPEECH - LANGUAGE - HEARING ASSOCIATION. NEWSLETTER. Text in English. 1955. bi-m. free to members (effective 2007). adv. **Document type:** *Newsletter, Trade.*
Former titles: Minnesota Speech and Hearing Association. Newsletter; (until 1976): Minnesota Speech and Hearing Association Journal
Related titles: Online - full content ed.: free (effective 2007).
Published by: Minnesota Speech - Language - Hearing Association, 1821 University Ave W, Ste S256, St. Paul, MN 55104. TEL 651-999-5350, FAX 651-917-1835, office@msha.net, http://www.msha.net. Ed. Maxine Slobof. Adv. contact Frances Laven. Circ: 650.

610 NZL ISSN 1175-107X
RC423
➤ **NEW ZEALAND JOURNAL OF SPEECH-LANGUAGE THERAPY.** Text in English. 1946-1997; resumed 1998. a. free to members. adv. bk.rev. reprints avail. **Document type:** *Journal, Academic/Scholarly.* **Description:** Includes research papers, conference proceedings and reviews.
Former titles (until 1997): New Zealand Speech-Language Therapists Journal (0110-571X); (until May 1983): New Zealand Speech Therapists Journal (0028-8713)
Related titles: Microfilm ed.: (from PQC).
Indexed: A22, BEL&L, DSHAb, INZP, L&LBA, RehabLit.
—**CCC.**
Published by: New Zealand Speech-Language Therapists Association, Suite 369, 63 Remuera Rd, Newmarket, Auckland, New Zealand. TEL 64-3-3831518, nzsta@speechtherapy.org.nz. Ed. Dr. Marleen Westerveld. Circ: 320.

616.21 JPN ISSN 0913-3976
NIHON JIBI INKOKA KANSENSHO KENKYUKAI KAISHI/JAPAN SOCIETY FOR INFECTIOUS DISEASES IN OTOLARYNGOLOGY. JOURNAL. Text in Japanese. 1983. a. back issues avail. **Document type:** *Journal, Academic/Scholarly.*
—BLDSC (4807.510000).
Published by: Nihon Jibi Inkoka Kansensho Kenkyukai/Japan Society for Infectious Diseases in Otolaryngology, Fujita Health University, 2ndTeaching Hospital, 3-6-10 Otoubashi, Nakagawa-ku, Nagoya, Aichi 454-8509, Japan.

617.89 613.62 IND ISSN 1463-1741
RA772.N7 CODEN: NHOEA4
➤ **NOISE & HEALTH**; a bimonthly inter-disciplinary international journal. Text in English. 1998. bi-m. INR 2,500 domestic to individuals; USD 350 foreign to individuals; INR 3,500 domestic to institutions; USD 450 foreign to institutions; INR 3,000 combined subscription domestic to individuals (print & online eds.); USD 420 combined subscription foreign to individuals (print & online eds.); INR 4,200 combined subscription domestic to institutions (print & online eds.); USD 540 combined subscription foreign to institutions (print & online eds.) (effective 2011). bk.rev. abstr.; illus. back issues avail.; reprints avail. **Document type:** *Journal, Academic/Scholarly.* **Description:** Examines and disseminates research on all aspects of noise and its effects on human health from the perspectives of multiple disciplines. Covers a broad range of topics related to noise pollution and its medical effects, ranging from basic experimental research to clinical evaluation and treatment, along with technical aspects of noise-reduction systems and public health policy solutions to related environmental and social issues.
Related titles: Online - full text ed.: ISSN 1998-4030. free (effective 2011) (from IngentaConnect).
Indexed: A01, A26, A36, A37, B21, C06, C07, CA, CABA, CurCont, E12, EMBASE, ESPM, ExcerpMed, GH, H&SSA, H11, H12, I05, LT, MEDLINE, P10, P20, P22, P24, P30, P48, P50, P53, P54, PQC, PollutAb, RRTA, S13, S16, SCI, SCOPUS, T02, T05, VS, W07, W11.
—BLDSC (6115.797000), IE, Infotrieve, Ingenta. **CCC.**
Published by: (European Commission, Directorate General - Health and Consumer Protection BEL), Medknow Publications and Media Pvt. Ltd., B-9, Kanara Business Ctr, Off Link Rd, Ghatkopar (E), Mumbai, Maharastra 400 075, India. TEL 91-22-66491816, FAX 91-22-66491817, http://www.medknow.com. Ed. Dr. Deepak Prasher.

616.2 FRA ISSN 0983-8201
O P A PRATIQUE. (O R L, Pneumo, Allergo) Text in French. m. (10/yr.). **Document type:** *Newspaper, Trade.*
Published by: L E N Medical - Axis Sante, 15 Rue des Sablons, Paris, 75116, France. TEL 33-1-47553131, FAX 33-1-47553132, info@len-medical.fr, http://www.len-medical.fr.

616.2 CHE ISSN 0301-1569
RF1 CODEN: ORLJAH
➤ **O R L**; journal for oto-rhino-laryngology and its related specialties. (Oto Rhino Laryngology) Text in English. 1938. bi-m. CHF 1,565, EUR 1,250, USD 1,540.50 to institutions; CHF 1,716, EUR 1,371, USD 1,687.50 combined subscription to institutions (print & online eds.) (effective 2012). adv. bk.rev. back issues avail.; reprints avail. **Document type:** *Journal, Academic/Scholarly.* **Description:** Contains original scientific papers of interest for both clinicians and researchers in otorhinolaryngology and head and neck surgery.
Formerly: Practica Oto-Rhino-Laryngologica (0032-6305)
Related titles: Microform ed.; Online - full text ed.: ISSN 1423-0275. CHF 1,514, EUR 1,211, USD 1,470 to institutions (effective 2012).
Indexed: A01, A03, A08, A22, B25, BIOSIS Prev, C06, CA, ChemAb, CurCont, DentInd, E01, EMBASE, ExcerpMed, H13, IndMed, Inpharma, MEDLINE, MycolAb, NBA, NPPA, P10, P20, P22, P24, P30, P35, P48, P53, P54, PQC, R10, Reac, SCI, SCOPUS, T02, W07.
—BLDSC (6291.378000), CASDDS, GNLM, IE, Infotrieve, Ingenta, INIST. **CCC.**
Published by: S. Karger AG, Allschwilerstr 10, Basel, 4055, Switzerland. TEL 41-61-3061111, FAX 41-61-3061234, karger@karger.ch, http://www.karger.ch. Ed. B.W. O'Malley. adv.: page CHF 1,730; trim 210 x 280. Circ: 800 (controlled).

617.89 CHE
O R L - AKTUELL. (Otorhinolaryngologie) Text in German. irreg., latest vol.30, 2007. price varies. **Document type:** *Monographic series, Academic/Scholarly.*

Published by: E M H Schweizerischer Aerzteverlag AG, Farnsburgerstr 8, Muttenz, 4132, Switzerland. TEL 41-61-4678555, FAX 41-61-4678556, verlag@emh.ch, http://www.emh.ch.

616.21 ESP ISSN 1576-9127
O.R.L. ARAGON. (Otorrinolaringologia Aragon) Text in Spanish. 1998. s-a. back issues avail. **Document type:** *Bulletin, Consumer.*
Published by: Sociedad Aragonesa de Otorrinolaringologia, P. Ruisenores, 2, Zaragoza, 50006, Spain. TEL 34-976-388011, info@saorl.org, http://www.saorl.org/.

616.2 CHE
O R L - PRAXIS. (Oto Rhino Laryngologie) Text in German. 1994. bi-m. CHF 80; CHF 40 to students; CHF 25 newsstand/cover (effective 2007). adv. **Document type:** *Journal, Academic/Scholarly.*
Formerly: O R L Highlights (1022-7709)
Published by: Springer Medizin Verlag Schweiz AG (Subsidiary of: Springer Science+Business Media), Nordstr 31, Zurich, 8006, Switzerland. TEL 41-44-2502800, FAX 41-44-2502803, verlag@springer-medizin.ch, http://www.springer-medizin.ch.

617.8 JPN ISSN 0030-2813
ONSEI GENGO IGAKU/JAPAN JOURNAL OF LOGOPEDICS AND PHONIATRICS. Text in Japanese; Summaries in English. 1960. 4/yr. membership. adv. bk.rev. **Document type:** *Journal, Academic/Scholarly.*
Indexed: SCOPUS.
Published by: Nihon Onsei Gengo Igakkai/Japan Society of Logopedics and Phoniatrics, Hakuo Bldg, 5F, 2-3-10 Koraku, Bunkyo-ku, Tokyo, 112-0004, Japan. TEL 81-3-56845958, FAX 81-3-56845954, onsei@jslp.org, http://wwwsoc.nii.ac.jp/jslp/. Ed. Hiroyuki Fukuda. Circ: 1,850 (controlled).

THE OPEN ACOUSTICS JOURNAL. *see* PHYSICS—Sound

616.21 NLD ISSN 1874-4281
RF1
➤ **THE OPEN OTORHINOLARYNGOLOGY JOURNAL.** Text in English. 2007. irreg. free (effective 2011). **Document type:** *Journal, Academic/Scholarly.* **Description:** Covers all areas of experimental, clinical and surgical otorhinolaryngology; including the prevention, diagnosis, treatment and cure of otorhinolaryngological disorders.
Media: Online - full text.
Indexed: A01, CA, T02.
Published by: Bentham Open (Subsidiary of: Bentham Science Publishers Ltd.), PO Box 294, Bussum, AG 1400, Netherlands. TEL 31-35-6923800, FAX 31-35-6980150, subscriptions@bentham.org.

616.21 USA ISSN 1043-1810
CODEN: OTONAO
➤ **OPERATIVE TECHNIQUES IN OTOLARYNGOLOGY - HEAD AND NECK SURGERY.** Text in English. 1990. q. USD 469 in United States to institutions; USD 602 elsewhere to institutions (effective 2012). adv. illus. back issues avail.; reprints avail. **Document type:** *Journal, Academic/Scholarly.* **Description:** Presents detailed illustrations of new surgical procedures and techniques in otology, rhinology, laryngology, reconstructive head and neck surgery, and facial plastic surgery.
Related titles: Online - full text ed.: ISSN 1557-9395 (from ScienceDirect).
Indexed: A22, A26, C06, C07, C08, CINAHL, EMBASE, ExcerpMed, H12, I05, R10, Reac, SCOPUS, T02.
—BLDSC (6269.382000), GNLM, IE, Infotrieve, Ingenta. **CCC.**
Published by: W.B. Saunders Co. (Subsidiary of: Elsevier Health Sciences), Elsevier, Health Sciences Division, Order Fulfillment, 3251 Riverport Ln, Maryland Heights, MO 63043. TEL 314-872-8370, 800-325-4177, FAX 314-432-1380, JournalCustomerService-usa@elsevier.com, http://www.us.elsevierhealth.com. Ed. Dr. Michael Friedman. Pub. Alexandra Gavenda. Adv. contact Aileen Rivera TEL 212-633-3721. Circ: 510.

➤ **OPHTHALMOLOGY ON C D.** *see* MEDICAL SCIENCES—Ophthalmology And Optometry

616.21 617 DEU ISSN 1865-1550
CODEN: MKGEFD
➤ **ORAL AND MAXILLOFACIAL SURGERY.** Text in English. 1997. bi-m. EUR 321, USD 379 combined subscription to institutions (print & online eds.) (effective 2012). adv. bk.rev. abstr.; charts; illus. back issues avail.; reprint service avail. from PSC. **Document type:** *Journal, Academic/Scholarly.* **Description:** Provides information concerning current developments in the subject fields of surgery in support of professional continuing education.
Formerly (until 2008): Mund-, Kiefer- und Gesichtschirurgie (1432-9417); Which was formed by the merger of (1977-1997): Deutsche Zeitschrift fuer Mund-, Kiefer- und Gesichtschirurgie (0343-3137); (1955-1997): Fortschritte der Kiefer- und Gesichtschirurgie (0071-7916)
Related titles: Online - full text ed.: ISSN 1865-1569 (from IngentaConnect).
Indexed: A22, A26, CTD, E01, E08, EMBASE, ExcerpMed, H12, IBR, IBZ, IndMed, MEDLINE, P20, P22, P30, P48, P54, PQC, R10, Reac, S09, SCOPUS.
—BLDSC (6277.441490), GNLM, IE, Infotrieve, Ingenta, INIST. **CCC.**
Published by: (Deutsche Gesellschaft fuer Mund-, Kiefer- und Gesichtschirurgie), Springer (Subsidiary of: Springer Science+Business Media), Tiergartenstr 17, Heidelberg, 69121, Germany. TEL 49-6221-4870, FAX 49-6221-345229. Ed. Dr. Friedrich W Neukam. Adv. contact Sabine Weidner. B&W page EUR 1,080, color page EUR 2,120. Circ: 1,650 (controlled). **Subscr. in the Americas to:** Springer New York LLC, Journal Fulfillment, PO Box 2485, Secaucus, NJ 07096. TEL 800-777-4643, 201-348-4033, FAX 201-348-4505, journals-ny@springer.com, http://www.springer.com; **Subscr. to:** Springer Distribution Center, Kundenservice Zeitschriften, Haberstr 7, Heidelberg 69126, Germany. TEL 49-6221-3454303, FAX 49-6221-3454229, subscriptions@springer.com. **Co-sponsor:** Berufsverband Deutscher Aerzte fuer Mund-Kiefer-Gesichtschirurgie e.V.

➤ **ORBIT.** *see* MEDICAL SCIENCES—Ophthalmology And Optometry

617.8 ROM ISSN 2067-6530
ORL.RO. Text in Romanian. 2008. q. ROL 90 (effective 2011). adv. **Document type:** *Magazine, Trade.*
Published by: Versa Puls Media, s.r.l., Calea Rahovei 266-268, corp 1, etaj 2, Bucharest, 050912, Romania. TEL 40-31-4254040, FAX 40-31-4254041, office@pulsmedia.ro. Ed. Dr. Madalina Georgescu. Adv. contact George Pavel. Circ: 1,000 (paid).

616.21 POL ISSN 0030-6657
CODEN: OTPOAW
OTOLARYNGOLOGIA POLSKA/POLISH JOURNAL OF OTOLARYNGOLOGY. Text in Polish; Summaries in English. 1947. bi-m. EUR 289 in Europe to institutions; JPY 45,000 in Japan to institutions; USD 402 elsewhere to institutions (effective 2012). adv. bk.rev. index. **Document type:** *Journal, Academic/Scholarly.* **Description:** Publishes original papers, case reports, history and summaries of doctor theses.
Related titles: Online - full text ed.: (from ScienceDirect).
Indexed: ChemAb, DentInd, EMBASE, ExcerpMed, IndMed, MEDLINE, P30, R10, Reac, SCOPUS.
—CASDDS, GNLM. **CCC.**
Published by: (Polskie Towarzystwo Otolaryngologow - Chirurgow Glowy i Szyi), Wydawnictwo Medyczne Urban i Partner, ul Marii Sklodowskiej-Curie 55-61, Wroclaw, 50950, Poland. TEL 48-71-3285487, FAX 48-71-3284391, http://www.urbanpartner.pl. Ed. Zygmunt Szmeja. Circ: 1,450. **Dist. by:** Ars Polona, Obroncow 25, Warsaw 03933, Poland. TEL 48-22-5098609, FAX 48-22-5098610, arspolona@arspolona.com.pl, http://www.arspolona.com.pl.

616.21 USA ISSN 0030-6665
RF1 CODEN: OCNAB
➤ **OTOLARYNGOLOGIC CLINICS OF NORTH AMERICA.** Text in English. 1968. bi-m. USD 590 in United States to institutions; USD 741 elsewhere to institutions (effective 2012). adv. back issues avail.; reprints avail. **Document type:** *Journal, Academic/Scholarly.* **Description:** Updates you on the latest trends in patient management and provides a sound basis for choosing treatment options.
Related titles: Microform ed.: (from MIM, PQC); Online - full text ed.: ISSN 1557-8259 (from ScienceDirect).
Indexed: A22, A36, ASCA, C06, C07, C08, CABA, CINAHL, CurCont, D01, DentInd, EMBASE, ExcerpMed, GH, INI, ISR, IndMed, Inpharma, MEDLINE, N02, N03, P30, P33, R10, RILM, RM&VM, Reac, SCI, SCOPUS, T05, W07.
—BLDSC (6313.510000), GNLM, IE, Infotrieve, Ingenta, INIST. **CCC.**
Published by: W.B. Saunders Co. (Subsidiary of: Elsevier Health Sciences), Elsevier, Health Sciences Division, Order Fulfillment, 3251 Riverport Ln, Maryland Heights, MO 63043. TEL 314-872-8370, 800-325-4177, FAX 314-432-1380, JournalCustomerService-usa@elsevier.com, http://www.us.elsevierhealth.com. Adv. contact John Marmero TEL 212-633-3657.

➤ **OTOLARYNGOLOGY CODING ALERT**; your practical adviser for ethically optimizing coding, payment, and efficiency in otolaryngology practices. *see* INSURANCE

617.51 USA ISSN 0194-5998
RD521 CODEN: OHNSDL
➤ **OTOLARYNGOLOGY - HEAD AND NECK SURGERY.** Text in English. 1903. q. USD 640 domestic to institutions; USD 708 foreign to institutions (effective 2010). adv. bk.rev. s-a. index. Supplement avail.; reprint service avail. from PSC. **Document type:** *Journal, Academic/Scholarly.* **Description:** Publishes scientific articles to meet the clinical and continuing educational needs of all specialists in head and neck surgery.
Former titles (until 1981): Otolaryngology (0161-6439); (until 1978): American Academy of Ophthalmology and Otolaryngology. Transactions-Otolaryngology (0161-696X); Which superseded in part (in 1975): American Academy of Ophthalmology and Otolaryngology. Transactions (0002-7154); Which was formerly (until 1940): American Academy of Ophthalmology and Otolaryngology. Transactions of the Annual Meeting (0163-593X); (until 1906): American Academy of Ophthalmology and Otolaryngology. Transactions of the Ophthalmologic Division at the Annual Meeting (0190-7018)
Related titles: CD-ROM ed.: ISSN 1085-8679. 199?; Microfilm ed.: (from PQC); Online - full text ed.: ISSN 1097-6817 (from IngentaConnect).
Indexed: A20, A22, A26, A34, A36, ASCA, C06, C07, C08, CA, CABA, CINAHL, ChemAb, CurCont, D01, E01, E12, EMBASE, ExcerpMed, F08, F11, F12, GH, H12, H17, I05, INI, ISR, IndMed, Inpharma, MEDLINE, N02, N03, N04, NBA, OR, P30, P33, P35, PN&I, R08, R10, R12, RA&MP, RILM, RM&VM, Reac, S13, S16, SCI, SCOPUS, T02, T05, VS, W07, W11.
—BLDSC (6313.523000), CASDDS, GNLM, IE, Infotrieve, Ingenta, INIST. **CCC.**
Published by: (American Academy of Otolaryngology - Head and Neck Surgery Foundation, Inc.), Mosby, Inc. (Subsidiary of: Elsevier Health Sciences), 1600 John F. Kennedy Blvd, Ste 1800, Philadelphia, PA 19103. TEL 215-239-3900, 800-523-1649, FAX 215-239-3990, elspcs@elsevier.com, http://www.us.elsevierhealth.com. Ed. Richard M Rosenfeld. Adv. contact Aileen Rivera. **Co-sponsor:** American Academy of Otolaryngic Allergy.

616.21 JPN
➤ **OTOLOGIA FUKUOKA - JIBI TO RINSHO.** Text in Japanese; Summaries in English. 1955. bi-m. JPY 6,000 (effective 2003). adv. bk.rev. back issues avail. **Document type:** *Journal, Academic/Scholarly.*
Formerly: Jibi to Rinsho (0447-7227)
Indexed: INIS AtomInd, Inpharma.
—BLDSC (6313.525000), GNLM.
Published by: Jibi to Rinsho Co., Department of Otorhinolaryngology, Kyushu University, Fukuoka-shi, 812-8582, Japan. TEL 81-92-642-5668, FAX 81-92-642-5685. Ed. Takashi Nakagawa. Pub. Sohtaro Komiyama. R&P, Adv. contact Otologia Fukuoka. Circ: 1,500.

616.21 USA ISSN 1531-7129
RF1 CODEN: ONTEAE
➤ **OTOLOGY & NEUROTOLOGY.** Text in English. 1979. 8/yr. USD 706 domestic to institutions; USD 815 foreign to institutions (effective 2011). adv. bk.rev. bibl.; illus. back issues avail.; reprints avail. **Document type:** *Journal, Academic/Scholarly.* **Description:** Brings out articles relating to both clinical and basic science aspects of otology, neurotology, and cranial base surgery.
Formerly (until 2001): American Journal of Otology (0192-9763)
Related titles: Microform ed.: (from PQC); Online - full text ed.: ISSN 1537-4505.
Indexed: A20, A22, ASCA, B25, BIOSIS Prev, C06, C07, CurCont, DentInd, EMBASE, ExcerpMed, ISR, IndMed, Inpharma, MEDLINE, MycolAb, NPPA, NSCI, P30, P35, R10, Reac, SCI, SCOPUS, SOPODA, W07.
—BLDSC (6313.528000), GNLM, IE, Infotrieve, Ingenta, INIST. **CCC.**
Published by: (American Otological Society), Lippincott Williams & Wilkins (Subsidiary of: Wolters Kluwer N.V.), Two Commerce Sq, 2001 Market St, Philadelphia, PA 19103. TEL 215-521-8300, FAX 215-521-8902, customerservice@lww.com, http://www.lww.com. Ed. John K Niparko. Pub. Marcia Serepy. Adv. contact Martha McGarity TEL 646-674-6535. Circ: 2,358. **Co-sponsors:** European Academy of Otology and Neurotology; American Neurotology Society.

617.8 JPN ISSN 0917-2025
CODEN: OTJAEW
OTOLOGY JAPAN. Text in English, Japanese. 1991.
Formed by the merger of (1974-1990): Rinsho Jika/Clinical Otology, Japan (0387-8848); (1981-1990): Ear Research Japan (0288-9781); Which was formerly (1970-1980): Naiji Seikagaku (0288-9773)
Indexed: INIS AtomInd.
—**CCC.**
Published by: Nihon Jika Gakkai/Otological Society of Japan, 2-14-14-707 Takanawa, Minato-ku, Tokyo, 108-0074, Japan. TEL 81-3-34433537, FAX 81-3-34457880, otology@blue.ocn.ne.jp, http://www.otology.gr.jp/.

M

617.51 GBR ISSN 1752-9360
➤ **THE OTORHINOLARYNGOLOGIST.** Text in English. 1996. irreg., latest 2008. GBP 45 per vol. domestic to individuals; GBP 60 per vol. foreign to individuals; GBP 60 per vol. domestic to institutions; GBP 90 per vol. foreign to institutions (effective 2010). back issues avail. **Document type:** *Journal, Academic/Scholarly.*
Former titles (until 2006): C M E Journal. Otorhinolaryngology, Head & Neck Surgery (1752-8828); (until 2006): C M E Bulletin. Otorhinolaryngology Head & Neck Surgery (1364-8829)
Related titles: Online - full text ed.: ISSN 1752-9379. GBP 30 per vol. (effective 2010).
Indexed: EMBASE, ExcerpMed, R10, Reac, SCOPUS.
—BLDSC (6313.609000), IE. **CCC.**
Published by: (Young Consultant Otolaryngologists Head & Neck Surgeons, Association of Otolaryngologists in Training), Rila Publications Ltd., 73 Newman St, London, W1A 4PG, United Kingdom. TEL 44-20-76311299, FAX 44-20-75807166, admin@rila.co.uk. Ed. Sanjai Sood.

617.8 IND ISSN 0975-444X
▼ ➤ **OTORHINOLARYNGOLOGY CLINICS: AN INTERNATIONAL JOURNAL.** Text in English. 2009. 3/yr. INR 3,000 domestic to individuals; USD 180 foreign to individuals; INR 4,500 domestic to institutions; USD 250 foreign to institutions (effective 2010). adv. bk.rev. abstr.; illus. Index. reprints avail. **Document type:** *Journal, Academic/Scholarly.* **Description:** Dedicated to the purpose of furthering medical education in the field of otorhinolaryngology and head & neck surgery, designed to encourage analysis of data from various centers using Standardized Protocols to develop an international consensual perspective on the management of disorders related to the field.
Related titles: Online - full text ed.: ISSN 0975-6957.
Indexed: A01, P20, P54, T02.
Published by: Jaypee Brothers Medical Publishers Pvt. Ltd., 4838/24, Ansari Rd, Daryaganj, New Delhi, 110 002, India. TEL 91-11-43574357, FAX 91-11-43574314, jaypee@jaypeebrothers.com, http://www.jaypeebrothers.com. Ed. Bachi T Hathiram. Pub. Rohit Gorawara. R&P Chetna Malhotra. Adv. contact Rakesh Sheoran TEL 91-997-1020680. Circ: 3,100.

616.21 ITA ISSN 0392-6621
➤ **OTORINOLARINGOLOGIA**; a journal on otorhinolaryngology, head and neck surgery, plastic reconstructive surgery, otoneurosurgery. Text in Italian; Summaries in English, Italian. 1981. q. EUR 240 combined subscription in the European Union to institutions (print & online eds.); EUR 265 combined subscription elsewhere to institutions (print & online eds.) (effective 2011). adv. bk.rev. bibl.; charts; illus. index. **Document type:** *Journal, Academic/Scholarly.*
Formed by the merger of (1951-1980): Minerva Otorinolaringologica (0026-4938); (1930-1980): Oto-rino-laringologia Italiana (0030-6630); (1950-1980): Bollettino delle Malattie dell'Orecchio, della Gola, del Naso (0392-7024); Which was formerly (1930-1949): Bollettino delle Malattie dell'Orecchio, della Gola, del Naso di Tracheo-Bronco-Esofagoscopia e di Fonetica (0392-7016); (1883-1929): Bollettino delle Malattie dell'Orecchio, della Gola, del Naso (1883) (0006-6567); (1973-1980): Nuovo Archivio Italiano di Otologia, Rinologia e Laringologia (0301-3693); Which was formerly (1967-1971): Archivio Italiano di Otologia, Rinologia Laringologia e Patologia Cervico-Facciale (0301-3685); (1893-1967): Archivio Italiano di Otologia, Rinologia e Laringologia (0004-0258)
Related titles: Online - full text ed.: ISSN 1827-188X. 2005.
Indexed: ChemAb, IndMed, L&LBA, NBA, P30, SCOPUS, SOPODA.
—BLDSC (6313.635000), GNLM, IE, Ingenta, INIST. **CCC.**
Published by: Edizioni Minerva Medica, Corso Bramante 83-85, Turin, 10126, Italy. TEL 39-011-678282, FAX 39-011-674502, journals.dept@minervamedica.it, http://www.minervamedica.it. Ed., Pub. Alberto Oliaro. Circ: 3,000 (paid).

616.21 617 SVK ISSN 1337-2181
➤ **OTORINOLARYNGOLOGIA A CHIRURGIA HLAVY A KRKU.** Text in Slovak. 2003. 3/yr. EUR 9 (effective 2009). **Document type:** *Journal, Academic/Scholarly.*
Published by: (Slovenska Spolocnost pre ORL a Chirurgiu Hlavy a Krku), Samedi s.r.o., Racianska 20, Bratislava, 839 27, Slovakia. TEL 421-2-55645901, FAX 421-2-55645902, samedi@samedi.sk. Ed. Eva Ochabova.

616.21 CZE ISSN 1210-7867
CODEN: CEOTA9
➤ **OTORINOLARYNGOLOGIE A FONIATRIE/OTORHINOLARYNGOLOGY AND PHONIATRICS.** Text in Czech, Slovak; Summaries in Czech, English. 1952. q. CZK 440, EUR 27.20 (effective 2010). adv. bk.rev. abstr. index. **Document type:** *Journal, Academic/Scholarly.* **Description:** Publishes original papers, results of research and reviews. contains information on surgical treatment of tumors of ENT organs, pananasal sinuses, larynx and soft parts of the neck.
Former titles (until 1994): Cesko-Slovenska Otorinolaryngologie a Foniatrie (1210-5988); (until 1991): Ceskoslovenska Otolaryngologie (0009-0603)
Related titles: Online - full text ed.
Indexed: A01, CISA, DentInd, IndMed, MLA-IB, P30, SCOPUS.
—CASDDS, GNLM, INIST. **CCC.**

Published by: (Ceska Lekarska Spolecnost J.E. Purkyne/Czech Medical Association), Nakladatelske Stredisko C L S J.E. Purkyne, Sokolska 31, Prague, 12026, Czech Republic. nts@cls.cz. Ed. J Astl. adv.: B&W page CZK 29,500, color page CZK 41,500; 244 x 166. Circ: 1,200. **Co-sponsor:** Ceskoslovanska Otolaryngologicka Spolesnost.

617.8 TUR ISSN 1302-2792
OTOSKOP DERGISI. Text in Turkish. 1999. q. **Document type:** *Journal, Academic/Scholarly.* **Description:** Publishes articles related to audiology.
Related titles: Online - full text ed.
Published by: Otoscope, Sedat Simavi Sok. 86/A Blok No.13, Cankaya, Ankara, Turkey. TEL 90-312-4426792, otoskop@cty.com.tr. Ed. Dr. Bulent Gursel.

616.21 PAK ISSN 0257-4985
PAKISTAN JOURNAL OF OTOLARYNGOLOGY. Text in English. 1985. q. PKR 250, USD 40, GBP 30. adv. bk.rev. **Document type:** *Journal, Academic/Scholarly.* **Description:** Publishes scientific research and articles.
Related titles: CD-ROM ed.
Indexed: ExtraMED, Perlslam.
—GNLM. **CCC.**
Published by: Pakistan Society of Otolaryngology, c/o Dr. M.H.A. Beg F.R.C.S., Modern Ear Nose and Throat Hospital, B-10 Block 13-A, Opposite PIA Planetarium, University Rd., Karachi, 74400, Pakistan. TEL 92-21-4971762, FAX 92-21-4971763. Circ: 2,000.

616.21 CAN ISSN 1188-0236
PATIENT OF THE MONTH PROGRAM. Short title: P M P. Variant title: Otolaryngology - Patient of the Month Program. (Also avail. in latent-image print version) Text in English. 1971. 8/yr. USD 410 combined subscription to individuals (print & online eds.); USD 666 combined subscription to institutions (print & online eds.) (effective 2010). abstr.; charts. **Document type:** *Journal, Trade.* **Description:** Aims to perfect clinical decision-making skills by simulating clinical situations with a personal computer.
Related titles: CD-ROM ed.: ISSN 1708-1572. USD 555 to individuals; USD 834 to institutions; USD 666 combined subscription to individuals (CD-ROM & online eds.); USD 779 combined subscription to institutions (CD-ROM & online eds.) (effective 2010); Online - full text ed.: USD 399 to individuals; USD 649 to institutions (effective 2010).
Indexed: C06, C07, C08, CA, CINAHL, T02.
—CCC.
Published by: (American Academy of Otolaryngology - Head and Neck Surgery, Inc. USA), B.C. Decker Inc., 50 King St E, 2nd Fl, Hamilton, ON L8N 2A1, Canada. TEL 905-522-7017, 800-568-7281, FAX 905-522-7839, info@bcdecker.com. Ed. Daniel J Kirse.

PERSPECTIVES ON AURAL REHABILITATION AND ITS INSTRUMENTATION (ONLINE). *see* HANDICAPPED—Hearing Impaired

616.21 USA ISSN 1940-7661
PERSPECTIVES ON HEARING AND HEARING DISORDERS. RESEARCH AND DIAGNOSTICS (ONLINE). Text in English. 2002. s-a. USD 40 to individuals; USD 75 to institutions; free to members (effective 2010). adv. back issues avail. **Document type:** *Newsletter, Academic/Scholarly.* **Description:** Provides the forum in which the clinician can suggest areas in need of further research and perhaps develop productive collaborations with the researchers.
Media: Online - full text.
Published by: American Speech - Language - Hearing Association, 2200 Research Blvd, Rockville, MD 20850-3289. TEL 301-296-5700, 800-638-8255, FAX 301-296-8580, actioncenter@asha.org, http://www.asha.org. Ed. Richard Wilson. Adv. contact Pamela J Leppin. **Subscr. to:** PO Box 1160, Rockville, MD 20849. subscribe@asha.org.

PERSPECTIVES ON HEARING CONSERVATION AND OCCUPATIONAL AUDIOLOGY (ONLINE). *see* HANDICAPPED—Hearing Impaired

612.14 USA ISSN 1940-7572
PERSPECTIVES ON SPEECH SCIENCE AND OROFACIAL DISORDERS. Text in English. 1992. s-a. USD 40 to individuals; USD 75 to institutions; free to members (effective 2010). adv. back issues avail. **Document type:** *Newsletter, Academic/Scholarly.* **Description:** Provides an opportunity for interaction among colleagues concerning specific areas of mutual interest.
Formerly (until 2002): American Speech - Language - Hearing Association. Special Interest Divisions. Division 5: Speech Science and Orofacial Disorders Newsletter
Related titles: Online - full text ed.: ISSN 1940-7580.
Indexed: C06, C07, P30.
Published by: American Speech - Language - Hearing Association, 2200 Research Blvd, Rockville, MD 20850-3289. TEL 301-296-5700, 800-638-8255, FAX 301-296-8580, actioncenter@asha.org, http://www.asha.org. Ed. Richard D Andreatta. Adv. contact Pamela J Leppin. **Subscr. to:** PO Box 1160, Rockville, MD 20849. subscribe@asha.org.

612 USA ISSN 1940-7556
PERSPECTIVES ON SWALLOWING AND SWALLOWING DISORDERS. Text in English. 1992. q. USD 55 to individuals; USD 85 to institutions; free to members (effective 2010). adv. back issues avail. **Document type:** *Newsletter, Academic/Scholarly.* **Description:** Aims to provide leadership and advocacy for issues in swallowing and swallowing disorders and to serve affiliates who evaluate and manage individuals with swallowing and feeding disorders.
Formerly (until 2002): American Speech - Language - Hearing Association. Special Interest Divisions. Division 13: Swallowing and Swallowing Disorders
Related titles: Online - full text ed.: ISSN 1940-7564.
Indexed: C06, C07.
Published by: American Speech - Language - Hearing Association, 2200 Research Blvd, Rockville, MD 20850-3289. TEL 301-296-5700, 800-638-8255, FAX 301-296-8580, actioncenter@asha.org, http://www.asha.org. Ed. Lori A Davis. Adv. contact Pamela J Leppin. **Subscr. to:** PO Box 1160, Rockville, MD 20849. subscribe@asha.org.

616.21 JPN ISSN 0912-1870
CODEN: JIRHET
PRACTICA OTOLOGICA KYOTO. SUPPLEMENT/JIBI INKOKA RINSHO. HOSATSU. Text in Japanese; Summaries in English. 1986. irreg. **Document type:** *Monographic series, Academic/Scholarly.*
Related titles: ◆ Supplement to: Jibi Inkoka Rinsho. ISSN 0032-6313.
Indexed: SCOPUS.
—BLDSC (6593.812000), INIST. **CCC.**
Published by: Kyoto University, Faculty Of Medicine, Department of Otolaryngology/Kyoto Daigaku Igakubu Jibi Inkoka Kyoshitsu, 39 Kawabata-Higashi, Marutamachi-St. Sakyo-ku, Kyoto, 606-8395, Japan. TEL 81-75-7712301, FAX 81-75-7612373, http://web.kyoto-inet.or.jp/org/jibirin/. Ed. Iwao Houjo.

616.21 BRA ISSN 0104-5687
➤ **PRO-FONO;** revista de atualizacao cientifica. Text in Portuguese. 1989. 3/yr. BRL 110 (effective 2005). **Document type:** *Journal, Academic/Scholarly.* **Description:** Contributes to the advance of knowledge in the field of speech, language, and hearing.
Related titles: CD-ROM ed.: ISSN 1679-3919; Online - full text ed.: ISSN 1809-399X. free (effective 2011).
Indexed: EMBASE, ExcerpMed, L&LBA, MEDLINE, P30, R10, Reac, SCOPUS.
Published by: Pro-Fono Produtos Especializados para Fonoaudiologia, Rue Gemeos 22, Alphaville Conde 1, Barueri, SP 06473-020, Brazil. TEL 55-11-46882220, FAX 55-11-46880147, profono@profono.com.br, http://www.profono.com.br/. Ed. Claudia Regina Furquim de Andrade. Circ: 1,000.

617.8 FRA ISSN 0034-222X
➤ **REEDUCATION ORTHOPHONIQUE.** Text in French. 1963. q. EUR 96 domestic to non-members; EUR 106 foreign to non-members; EUR 73 domestic to members; EUR 46 domestic to students; EUR 56 foreign to students (effective 2009). adv. bk.rev. bibl.; charts; illus.; stat.; tr.lit. **Document type:** *Journal, Academic/Scholarly.* **Description:** Covers hearing, speech, language and voice disorders.
Indexed: FR.
—INIST. **CCC.**
Published by: Federation Nationale des Orthophonistes (F N O), 145 Bd Magenta, Paris, 75010, France. TEL 33-1-40374144, FAX 33-1-40374142. Ed., Pub. Jacques Roustit. Circ: 3,000.

617.89 CHL ISSN 0717-4659
REVISTA CHILENA DE FONOAUDIOLOGIA. Text in Spanish. 1999. s-a. **Document type:** *Journal, Academic/Scholarly.*
Published by: Universidad de Chile, Facultad de Medicina, Escuela de Fonoaudiologia, Independencia 1027, Santiago, Chile. http://www.med.uchile.cl. Ed. Mariangela Maggiolo.

▼ **REVISTA DE INVESTIGACION EN LOGOPEDIA.** *see* LINGUISTICS

617.8 ESP ISSN 0214-4603
➤ **REVISTA DE LOGOPEDIA, FONIATRIA Y AUDIOLOGIA.** Text in Spanish. 1982. q. EUR 86.03 to individuals; EUR 153.32 to institutions (effective 2009). adv. bk.rev. bibl. back issues avail.; reprints avail. **Document type:** *Journal, Academic/Scholarly.*
Formerly (until 1986): Revista de Logopedia y Fonoaudiologia (0211-6146)
Related titles: Online - full text ed.: ISSN 1578-1712. 1996. EUR 55.04 to individuals; EUR 82.56 to institutions (effective 2009) (from ScienceDirect).
Indexed: A01, CA, F03, F04, L11, P03, PsycInfo, PsycholAb, SCOPUS, T02.
—CCC.
Published by: (Asociacion Espanola de Logopedia, Foniatria y Audiologia), Grupo Ars XXI de Comunicacion, SA, Muntaner 262 Atico 2a., Barcelona, 08021, Spain. TEL 34-90-2195484, FAX 34-93-2722902, info@arsxxi.com. Ed. Enrique Salesa. Circ: 3,000.

616.21 CHL ISSN 0716-4084
REVISTA DE OTORRINOLARINGOLOGIA Y CIRUGIA DE CABEZA Y CUELLO. Text in Spanish; Summaries in English. 1941. 3/yr. adv. bk.rev. bibl.; charts; illus.; stat. index. **Document type:** *Journal, Academic/Scholarly.*
Formerly: Revista de Otorrinolaringologia (0034-8643)
Related titles: Online - full text ed.: ISSN 0718-4816. 2007. free (effective 2011) (from SciELO).
Indexed: ChemAb, P30.
—GNLM.
Published by: Sociedad Chilena de Otorrinolaringologia Medicina y Cirugia de Cabeza y Cuello, Avda Nueva Los Leones 07 of. 801, Casilla 260, Providencia, Correo 35, Santiago, Chile. TEL 56-2-3359236, FAX 56-2-3359237, revistainformativa@sochiorl.cl, http://www.sochiorl.cl/. Ed. Jorge Caro.

616.21 401 COL ISSN 0121-652X
REVISTA MENSAJE. Text in Spanish. 1980. a. **Document type:** *Magazine, Trade.*
Published by: Asociacion Colombiana de Fonoaudiologia y Terapia del Lenguaje, Calle 79 No 18-18, Of 206, Bogota, Colombia. TEL 57-1-2185109, http://www.asofono.org.

616.21 ROM ISSN 1583-9443
REVISTA ROMANA DE O R L. (Oto-Rino-Laringologia) Text in Romanian. 1974. q. **Document type:** *Journal, Academic/Scholarly.*
Former titles (until 2002): Oto-Rino-Laringologia (1223-2505); (until 1990): Revista de Chirurgie, Oncologie, Radiologie, ORL, Oftalmologie, Stomatologie. Oto-rino-laringologia (1220-0867); Which superseded in part (in 1974): Oto-Rino-Laringologie si Oftalmologie (0303-5123); Which was formed by the merger of (1956-1974): Oto-Rino-Laringologie (0030-6649); (1956-1974): Oftalmologia (0030-0667)
Indexed: P30.
—GNLM, INIST.
Published by: (Societatea de Otorinolaringologie), Asociatia Medicala Romana/Romanian Medical Association, Str Ionel Perlea 10, Sector 1, Bucharest, 70754, Romania. amr@medica.ro, http://www.medica.ro.

616.21 FRA ISSN 0035-1334
REVUE DE LARYNGOLOGIE - OTOLOGIE - RHINOLOGIE. Text and summaries in English, French. 1881. 5/yr. (plus 1 about phoniatrics). EUR 150 to individuals; EUR 180 to institutions; EUR 170 combined subscription to individuals print & online eds.; EUR 200 combined subscription to institutions print & online eds.; EUR 80 combined subscription to qualified personnel print & online eds. (effective 2009). adv. bk.rev. abstr.; bibl.; charts; illus.; stat. index. **Document type:** *Journal, Academic/Scholarly.*
Former titles (until 1919): Revue Hebdomadaire de Laryngologie, d'Otologie et de Rhinologie (0302-1394); (until 1896): Revue de Laryngologie, d'Otologie et de Rhinologie (0376-2157); (until 1889): Revue Mensuelle de Laryngologie, d'Otologie et de Rhinologie (0301-8466)
Related titles: Online - full text ed.: USD 80; USD 40 to qualified personnel (effective 2009).
Indexed: A22, DentInd, EMBASE, ExcerpMed, IndMed, MEDLINE, MLA-IB, NBA, P30, R10, Reac, SCOPUS, SOPODA.
—BLDSC (7926.450000), GNLM, IE, Infotrieve, Ingenta, INIST. **CCC.**
Published by: Revue de Laryngologie, 114 av. d'Ares, Bordeaux, Cedex 33074, France. TEL 33-5-56243015, FAX 33-5-57815848, orl.bordeaux@wanadoo.fr. Ed. Jacques Verhulst. Circ: 2,200.

616.21 NLD ISSN 0300-0729
CODEN: RNGYA8
➤ **RHINOLOGY.** Text in English. 1963. q. EUR 88 to members (effective 2009). adv. bk.rev. index. back issues avail. **Document type:** *Journal, Academic/Scholarly.* **Description:** Contains papers dealing with physiology, diagnostics, pathology, medical therapy and surgery of the nose and paranasal sinuses, including allergology.
Formerly (until 1971): International Rhinology (0300-0737)
Related titles: Online - full text ed.; Supplement(s): Rhinology. Supplement. ISSN 1013-0047. 1981.
Indexed: A22, B25, BIOSIS Prev, CIS, CurCont, DentInd, EMBASE, ExcerpMed, IndMed, Inpharma, MEDLINE, MycolAb, P30, P35, R10, Reac, SCI, SCOPUS, W07.
—BLDSC (7960.743000), GNLM, IE, Infotrieve, Ingenta, INIST. **CCC.**
Published by: International Rhinologic Society, PO Box 2233, Amersfoort, 3800 CE, Netherlands. FAX 31-84-7304986. Ed. Valerie J Lund.

616.21 617.89 ITA ISSN 0392-1360
RIVISTA ITALIANA DI OTORINOLARINGOLOGIA, AUDIOLOGIA E FONIATRIA. Text in Italian; Summaries in English. 1980. q. adv. **Document type:** *Journal, Academic/Scholarly.*
Indexed: A22, NBA, SCOPUS.
—GNLM, IE, Ingenta, INIST. **CCC.**
Published by: C I C Edizioni Internazionali, Corso Trieste 42, Rome, 00198, Italy. TEL 39-06-8412673, FAX 39-06-8412688, info@gruppocic.it, http://www.gruppocic.it. Eds. D. Passali, T. Marullo. adv.: B&W page EUR 1,239.50, color page EUR 1,704.31; 210 x 280.

616.21 RUS ISSN 0869-5474
➤ **ROSSIISKAYA RINOLOGIYA;** nauchno-prakticheskii zhurnal. Text in Russian. 1993. q. USD 139 foreign (effective 2006). **Document type:** *Journal, Academic/Scholarly.*
Indexed: RefZh.
—BLDSC (0154.059073), East View.
Published by: Rossiiskoe Obshchestvo Rinologov, Ivan'kovskoe shosse, d 7, Moscow, 125367, Russian Federation. TEL 7-095-4900449, jap@cch.pmc.ru, http://www.rhinology.ru. Ed. G Z Piskunov. **Dist. by:** East View Information Services, 10601 Wayzata Blvd, Minneapolis, MN 55305. TEL 952-252-1201, 800-477-1005, FAX 952-252-1202, info@eastview.com, http://www.eastview.com.

616 USA ISSN 0734-0451
RF286 CODEN: SEMHE7
➤ **SEMINARS IN HEARING.** Text in English. 1980. q. USD 486 domestic to institutions; USD 498 foreign to institutions; USD 592 combined subscription domestic to institutions (print & online eds.); USD 618 combined subscription foreign to institutions (print & online eds.) (effective 2011). adv. reprints avail. **Document type:** *Journal, Academic/Scholarly.* **Description:** Publishes topic-specific issues in the field of audiology including areas such as hearing loss, auditory disorders and psychoacoustics.
Supersedes in part (in 1983): Seminars in Speech, Language and Hearing (0196-108X)
Related titles: Microfilm ed.; Online - full text ed.: ISSN 1098-8955. USD 572 domestic to institutions; USD 586 foreign to institutions (effective 2011).
Indexed: A01, A03, A08, A22, BIOSIS Prev, C06, C07, C08, CA, CINAHL, E01, EMBASE, ExcerpMed, L&LBA, MycolAb, P30, R10, Reac, SCOPUS, T02.
—BLDSC (8239.449800), GNLM, IE, Infotrieve, Ingenta. **CCC.**
Published by: Thieme Medical Publishers (Subsidiary of: Georg Thieme Verlag), 333 Seventh Ave, New York, NY 10001. TEL 212-760-0888, 800-782-3488, FAX 212-947-1112, info@thieme.com. Ed. Dr. Catherine V Palmer TEL 412-647-6089. Adv. contact James C Cunningham TEL 201-767-4170. Circ: 2,025.

617.89 USA ISSN 0734-0478
RC423.A1 CODEN: SSLAEB
➤ **SEMINARS IN SPEECH AND LANGUAGE.** Text in English. 1980. q. USD 482 domestic to institutions; USD 494 foreign to institutions; USD 587 combined subscription domestic to institutions (print & online eds.); USD 613 combined subscription foreign to institutions (print & online eds.) (effective 2011). adv. abstr.; bibl.; illus. reprints avail. **Document type:** *Journal, Academic/Scholarly.* **Description:** Reports on clinical advances in speech and language pathology, offering diagnostic procedures, screening and assessment techniques, treatment protocols, and short- and long-term management practices.
Supersedes in part (in 1983): Seminars in Speech, Language and Hearing (0196-108X)
Related titles: Microfilm ed.; Online - full text ed.: ISSN 1098-9056. USD 567 domestic to institutions; USD 581 foreign to institutions (effective 2011).
Indexed: A01, A03, A08, A22, AMED, BIOSIS Prev, C06, C07, C08, CA, CINAHL, CMM, E01, EMBASE, ExcerpMed, IndMed, L&LBA, MEDLINE, MycolAb, P03, P30, PsycInfo, PsycholAb, SCOPUS, T02.
—BLDSC (8239.462000), GNLM, IE, Infotrieve, Ingenta. **CCC.**
Published by: Thieme Medical Publishers (Subsidiary of: Georg Thieme Verlag), 333 Seventh Ave, New York, NY 10001. TEL 212-760-0888, 800-782-3488, FAX 212-947-1112, info@thieme.com. Eds. Dr. Audrey L Holland TEL 520-621-3208, Dr. Nan Bernstein Ratner TEL 301-405-4217. Adv. contact James C Cunningham TEL 201-767-4170. Circ: 1,047.

616.21 617.7 CHN ISSN 1673-3770
SHANDONG DAXUE ERBIHOUYAN XUEBAO/JOURNAL OF OTOLARYNGOLOGY AND OPHTHALMOLOGY OF SHANDONG UNIVERSITY. Text in Chinese. 1987. bi-m. CNY 42 (effective 2009). **Document type:** *Journal, Academic/Scholarly.*
Formerly (until 2005): Shandong Daxue Jichu Yixueyuan Xuebao/Preclinical Medicine College of Shandong University. Journal (1673-6001); (until 2002): Shandong Yi-Da Jichu Xueyuan Xuebao (1008-8202); (until 1999): Erbihouyan Xuebao
Related titles: Online - full text ed.

Indexed: A34, A35, A36, AgBio, B&BAb, B19, B21, CABA, E12, GH, N02, N03, NSA, NucAcAb, P33, R08, R12, RA&MP, RM&VM, T05, VS, W10.
—BLDSC (8254.588428).
Published by: Shandong Daxue, 73, Jingshi Lu, Jinan, 250061, China. TEL 86-531-88395259, FAX 86-531-88392495.

617.8 IRN ISSN 1735-1936
SHINAVAYI/SHINASI/AUDIOLOGY. Text in Persian, Modern. 1992. s-a. **Document type:** *Journal, Academic/Scholarly.* **Description:** Publishes articles relating to both clinical and basic science aspects of auditory and balance system in form of full-length paper, short communications, letter to editor, and reviews. This journal is of primary interest to audiologists, otologists, speech therapists, neurologists, pediatricians, linguistists, and educators.
Related titles: Online - full text ed.: ISSN 2008-2657.
Indexed: A01, C06, C07, CA, T02.
Published by: Danishgah-i Ulum-i Pizishki-i Tihran/Tehran University of Medical Sciences, Department of Audiology, Faculty of Rehabilitation, Enghelab Ave., PO Box 15615-341, Tehran, 1148965141, Iran. TEL 98-21-77621188, FAX 98-21-77621188. Ed. Mohammad Akbari.

SIGHT AND SOUND NEWS. *see* HEALTH FACILITIES AND ADMINISTRATION

617.8 ESP ISSN 2171-9381
▼ **SOCIEDAD OTORRINOLARINGOLOGICA DE CASTILLA Y LEON, CANTABRIA Y LA RIOJA. REVISTA.** Text in Spanish. 2010. a. free (effective 2011). **Document type:** *Journal, Academic/Scholarly.*
Media: Online - full text.
Published by: Sociedad Otorrinolaringologica de Castilla y Leon, Cantabria y La Rioja, Facultad de Medicina, Calle Ramon y Cajal 7, Valladolid, 47005, Spain.

617.89 BRA ISSN 1516-8034
SOCIEDADE BRASILEIRA DE FONOAUDIOLOGIA. Text in Portuguese. 1997. s-a. **Document type:** *Journal, Academic/Scholarly.*
Related titles: Online - full text ed.: free (effective 2011).
Address: Rua Barao do Bananal 819, Sao Paulo, 05024-000, Brazil. TEL 55-11-38734211, socfono@terra.com.br, http://www.sbfa.org.br. Eds. Ana Luiza Gomes Pinto Navas, Fernanda Dreux Miranda Fernandes.

616.21 USA
SOCIETY OF OTORHINOLARYNGOLOGY AND HEAD-NECK NURSES. UPDATE. Key Title: Update. Text in English. 1980. q. adv. **Document type:** *Newsletter, Trade.* **Description:** Focuses on updating members of the Society on news, events, and activities taking place within their organization. Contents include, President's message, annual conference news, member news, achievements & appreciation, awards/grants and scholarship committee updates and information.
Published by: Magellan Publishing (Subsidiary of: Woodward Communications Inc.), PO Box 388, Dubuque, IL 52004-0388. TEL 563-588-3850, 800-977-0474, FAX 563-588-3848. Ed. Sandra Bailey TEL 386-428-1695. Adv. contact Karen Ruden TEL 563-588-3855. B&W page USD 695; trim 8.5 x 11. Circ: 1,200 (paid).

SPRACHE - STIMME - GEHOER; Zeitschrift fuer Kommunikationsstoerungen. *see* EDUCATION—Special Education And Rehabilitation

616.21 USA ISSN 0947-2657
SPRINGER HANDBOOK OF AUDITORY RESEARCH. Text in English. 1992. irreg., latest vol.36, 2010. price varies. back issues avail. **Document type:** *Monographic series, Academic/Scholarly.*
—BLDSC (8424.721500), IE, Ingenta.
Published by: Springer New York LLC (Subsidiary of: Springer Science+Business Media), 233 Spring St, New York, NY 10013. TEL 212-460-1500, FAX 212-460-1575, service-ny@springer.com. Eds. Arthur Popper, Richard Fay.

SWIAT CISZY; czasopismo polskich inwalidow sluchu. *see* HANDICAPPED—Hearing Impaired

616.21 HRV ISSN 1330-0296
SYMPOSIA OTORHINOLARYNGOLOGICA. Text in Croatian; Summaries in English. 1966. 3/yr. adv. bk.rev.
Formerly (until 1991): Symposia Otorhinolaryngologica Iugoslavica (0586-9145)
Indexed: IndMed.
—GNLM.
Published by: (Klinicka Bolnica "Sestre Milosrdnice", Klinika za Otorinolaringologiju i Cervikofacijalnu Kirurgiju), Zavod za Proucavanje i Zastitu Uha i Disnih Organa, Vinogradska 29, Zagreb, 10000, Croatia. Ed. Boris Pegan. Circ: 300 (paid). **Co-sponsor:** Ministarstva Znanosti i Tehnologije Republike Hrvatske.

616.21 CHN ISSN 1006-7299
TINGLIXUE JI YANYU JIBING ZAZHI/JOURNAL OF AUDIOLOGY AND SPEECH PATHOLOGY. Text in Chinese. 1993. bi-m. USD 31.20 (effective 2009). **Document type:** *Journal, Academic/Scholarly.*
Related titles: Online - full text ed.
—BLDSC (4949.320000), East View.
Published by: Wuhan Daxue Remin Yiyuan, 5, Wuchangziyang Road, Wuhan, 430060, China. http://www.hbsti.ac.cn/. **Dist. by:** China International Book Trading Corp, 35 Chegongzhuang Xilu, Haidian District, PO Box 399, Beijing 100044, China. TEL 86-10-68412045, FAX 86-10-68412023, cibtc@mail.cibtc.com.cn, http://www.cibtc.com.cn.

TINNITUS-FORUM. *see* HANDICAPPED—Hearing Impaired

616.21 USA ISSN 0897-6368
TINNITUS TODAY. Text in English. 1975. q. USD 35 domestic membership; USD 50 foreign membership (effective 2006). adv. bk.rev. 2 cols./p.; back issues avail. **Document type:** *Journal, Consumer.* **Description:** Serves professionals and laypeople with scientific and anecdotal articles.
Formerly (until 1988): A T A Newsletter
Related titles: Online - full content ed.: ISSN 1530-6569.
Indexed: C06, C07.
Published by: American Tinnitus Association, PO Box 5, Portland, OR 97207. TEL 503-248-9985, 800-634-8978, FAX 503-248-0024. Ed., R&P, Adv. contact Barbara Tabachnick Sanders TEL 503-248-9985 ext 216. Circ: 170,000.

TOUKEIBU GEKA/JAPAN SOCIETY FOR HEAD AND NECK SURGERY. JOURNAL. *see* MEDICAL SCIENCES—Surgery

616.21 USA ISSN 1084-7138
RF300 CODEN: TAMPFF
➤ **TRENDS IN AMPLIFICATION.** Text in English. 1996. q. USD 638, GBP 375 combined subscription to institutions (print & online eds.); USD 625, GBP 368 to institutions (effective 2011). adv. index. back issues avail.; reprint service avail. from PSC. **Document type:** *Journal, Academic/Scholarly.* **Description:** For audiologists, otolaryngologists, and hearing aid dispensers. Covers current topics in amplification and hearing aids.
Related titles: Online - full text ed.: ISSN 1940-5588. USD 574, GBP 338 to institutions (effective 2011).
Indexed: A22, A26, C06, C07, C08, CA, CINAHL, E01, E08, EMBASE, ExcerpMed, G08, H11, H12, I05, MEDLINE, P30, R10, Reac, S09, SCOPUS, T02.
—BLDSC (9049.528900), IE, Ingenta. **CCC.**
Published by: Sage Publications, Inc., 2455 Teller Rd, Thousand Oaks, CA 91320. TEL 805-499-9774, FAX 805-499-0871, info@sagepub.com, http://www.sagepub.com/. Ed. Charles J Limb. adv.: page USD 875; trim 8 x 10.75. Circ: 1,000 (paid).

616.21 USA
TRIOLOGISTICS (ONLINE). Text in English. 1976. 3/yr. free to members. **Document type:** *Newsletter.* **Description:** Society information relating to the field of otolaryngology.
Formerly: Triologistics (Print)
Media: Online - full content.
Published by: Triological Society, 555 N 30th St, Omaha, NE 68131-2136. TEL 402-346-5500, FAX 402-346-5300, info@triological.org.

616.21 TUR ISSN 0304-4793
➤ **TURK OTOLARENGOLOJI ARSIVI/TURKISH ARCHIVES OF OTOLARYNGOLOGY.** Text in English, Turkish. 1962. q. EUR 60 to individuals; EUR 120 to institutions (effective 2009). **Document type:** *Journal, Academic/Scholarly.* **Description:** Official journal of the Turkish Otorhinolaryngology & Head and Neck Surgery Foundation.
Related titles: Online - full text ed.: ISSN 1303-6289.
Indexed: A01.
Published by: (Turkish Otorhinolaryngology & Head and Neck Surgery Foundation), Deomed Medical Publishing, Acibadem Cad. Ismail Hakki Bey Sok. Ismail Hakki Bey Sok. 7/1, Kadikoy, Istanbul, 34718, Turkey. TEL 90-216-4148343, FAX 90-216-4148342, medya@deomed.com, ilknurd@deomed.com, http://www.deomed.com. Ed. Irfan Devranoglu.

616.21 ITA ISSN 0042-2371
IL VALSALVA. Text in Italian; Summaries in English. 1923. q. adv. bk.rev. **Document type:** *Journal, Academic/Scholarly.* **Description:** Covers all aspects of otorhinolaryngology.
Indexed: ChemAb, DentInd, IndMed, NBA, P30.
—GNLM, INIST.
Published by: Edizioni Luigi Pozzi s.r.l., Via Panama 68, Rome, 00198, Italy. TEL 39-06-8553548, FAX 39-06-8554105, edizioni_pozzi@tin.it. Circ: 1,000.

VER Y OIR. *see* MEDICAL SCIENCES—Ophthalmology And Optometry

616.21 RUS ISSN 0042-4668
CODEN: VORLA7
VESTNIK OTORINOLARINGOLOGII/ANNALS OF OTORHINOLARYNGOLOGY. Text in Russian; Summaries in English. 1936. bi-m. USD 234 in North America (effective 2010). adv. bk.rev. bibl. index. reprints avail. **Document type:** *Journal, Academic/Scholarly.* **Description:** Publishes original papers of clinical, laboratory, experimental and theoretical nature dedicated to problems of etiology, pathogenesis, diagnosis of different otorhinolaryngological diseases, their relation to other infections.
Related titles: Online - full content ed.
Indexed: B25, BIOSIS Prev, ChemAb, DentInd, DokArb, EMBASE, ExcerpMed, IndMed, MEDLINE, MycolAb, P30, R10, Reac, RefZh, SCOPUS.
—East View, GNLM, INIST. **CCC.**
Published by: (Vsesoyuznoe Nauchnoe Obshchestvo Otorinolaringologov), Media Sfera, Dmitrovskoe shosse 46, korp 2, etazh 4, P.O. Box 54, Moscow, 127238, Russian Federation. TEL 7-095-4824329, FAX 7-095-4824312, podpiska@mediasphera.ru, http://mediasphera.ru. Ed. Vladimir Pal'chun. Circ: 3,000 (paid). **Dist. by:** East View Information Services, 10601 Wayzata Blvd, Minneapolis, MN 55305. TEL 952-252-1201, 800-477-1005, FAX 952-252-1202, info@eastview.com, http://www.eastview.com. **Co-sponsor:** Ministerstvo Zdravookhraneniya Rossiiskoi Federatsii/Ministry of Public Health of Russian Federation.

616.21 USA
VOICES (HILLSBOROUGH). Text in English. 1969. irreg. (approx. 4/yr.). free to members. **Document type:** *Newsletter.* **Description:** Covers current and future activities within NJSHA and the industry.
Formerly (until 199?): New Jersey Speech and Hearing Association. Newsletter (0077-8516)
Published by: New Jersey Speech and Hearing Association, 203 Towne Center Dr, Hillsborough, NJ 08844. TEL 908-359-5308, FAX 908-450-1119, info@njsha.org, http://www.njsha.org. Ed. Wendy Webber. Circ: 1,400.

616.21 USA ISSN 1948-9579
WORLD ARTICLES IN EAR NOSE AND THROAT; bringing the world together for the betterment of healthcare. Text in English. 2008 (Dec.). irreg. free (effective 2011). back issues avail. **Document type:** *Journal, Academic/Scholarly.* **Description:** Offers easy access and dissemination of interesting cases and substantive research from around the world.
Media: Online - full text.
Published by: Cumberland Otolaryngology Consultants, 402 Bogle St, Somerset, KY 42503. TEL 606-679-7426. Ed. Sudhakar Vaidya TEL 91-734-2525435. Pub. Kevin T Kavanagh.

616.21 USA ISSN 1041-892X
RF11
YEAR BOOK OF OTOLARYNGOLOGY - HEAD AND NECK SURGERY. Text in English. 1900. a. USD 217 in United States to institutions; USD 235 elsewhere to institutions (effective 2012). adv. illus. **Document type:** *Yearbook, Academic/Scholarly.* **Description:** Presents abstracts of pertinent literature in the field with commentary by leading experts.
Former titles (until 1985): The Year Book of Otolaryngology (0146-7247); (until 1976): The Year Book of the Ear, Nose and Throat (0084-4055); (until 1959): Year Book of the Ear, Nose & Throat and Maxillofacial Surgery
Related titles: CD-ROM ed.; Online - full text ed.
—GNLM. **CCC.**
Published by: Mosby, Inc. (Subsidiary of: Elsevier Health Sciences), 1600 John F. Kennedy Blvd, Ste 1800, Philadelphia, PA 19103. TEL 215-239-3900, 800-523-1649, FAX 215-239-3990, elspcs@elsevier.com, http://www.us.elsevierhealth.com. Eds. Markus Gapany, Dr. Michael Paparella.

616.21 CHN ISSN 1007-1520
ZHONGGUO ER-BI-YANHOU-LUDI WAIKE ZAZHI/CHINESE JOURNAL OF OTORHINOLARYNGOLOGY-SKULL BASE SURGERY. Text in Chinese. 1995. bi-m. USD 37.20 (effective 2009). **Document type:** *Journal, Academic/Scholarly.*
Related titles: Online - full text ed.
Indexed: A28, APA, B&BAb, B19, B21, BrCerAb, C&ISA, CA/WCA, CIA, CTA, CerAb, CivEngAb, CorrAb, E&CAJ, E11, EEA, EMA, ESPM, EnvEAb, H15, M&TEA, M09, MBF, METADEX, SolStAb, T04, WAA.
—East View, Linda Hall.
Published by: (Zhonghua Renmin Gongheguo Weishengbu/Ministry of Health People's Republic of China), Zhongnan Daxue/Central South University, 87, Xiangya Lu, Changsha, 410008, China. http://www.csu.edu.cn/chinese/. **Dist. by:** China International Book Trading Corp, 35 Chegongzhuang Xilu, Haidian District, PO Box 399, Beijing 100044, China. TEL 86-10-68412045, FAX 86-10-68412023, cibtc@mail.cibtc.com.cn, http://www.cibtc.com.cn.

616.21 617 CHN ISSN 1672-7002
ZHONGGUO ER-BI-YANHOU-TOU-JING WAIKE/CHINESE ARCHIVES OF OTOLARYNGOLOGY HEAD AND NECK SURGERY. Text in Chinese. 1994. m. USD 80.40 (effective 2009). **Document type:** *Journal, Academic/Scholarly.*
Formerly (until 2003): Er-Bi-Yanhou-Tou-Jing Waike (1005-3565)
Related titles: Online - full text ed.
Published by: Beijing Shi Er-Bi-Yanhouke Yanjiusuo, 17, Chongneihou Guohutong, Beijing, 100005, China. TEL 86-10-65596373, FAX 86-10-65596001.

ZHONGGUO YIXUE WENZHAI (ER-BI-YANHOU KEXUE)/CHINA MEDICAL ABSTRACTS. OTORHINOLARYNGOLOGY. *see* MEDICAL SCIENCES—Abstracting, Bibliographies, Statistics

616.21 CHN ISSN 1007-4856
ZHONGGUO ZHONGXIYI JIEHE ERBIYANHOUKE ZAZHI/CHINESE OTORHINOLARYNGOLOGYICAL JOURNAL OF INTEGRATIVE MEDICINE. Text in Chinese. 1993. bi-m. USD 31.20 (effective 2009). **Document type:** *Journal, Academic/Scholarly.*
Related titles: Online - full text ed.
—East View.
Published by: Zhongguo Zhong-Xiyi Jiehe Xuehui/China Association of Integrative Medicine, 42, Xiaosu Lu, Anqing, 246004, China. TEL 86-556-5519852, FAX 86-556-5545966. **Dist. by:** China International Book Trading Corp, 35 Chegongzhuang Xilu, Haidian District, PO Box 399, Beijing 100044, China. TEL 86-10-68412045, FAX 86-10-68412023, cibtc@mail.cibtc.com.cn, http://www.cibtc.com.cn.

616.21 CHN ISSN 1673-0860
ZHONGHUA ER-BI-YAN-HOU-TOU-JING WAIKE ZAZHI/CHINESE JOURNAL OF OTORHINOLARYNGOLOGY HEAD AND NECK SURGERY. Text in Chinese. 1953. m. USD 85.20 (effective 2009). **Document type:** *Journal, Academic/Scholarly.*
Formerly (until 2005): Zhonghua Er-Bi-Yanhouke Zazhi/Chinese Journal of Otorhinolaryngology (0412-3948)
Related titles: Online - full text ed.
Indexed: EMBASE, ExcerpMed, IndMed, MEDLINE, P30, R10, Reac, SCOPUS.
—BLDSC (9512.838500), East View.
Published by: Zhonghua Yixuehui/Chinese Medical Association, 42 Dong Si Xi Dajie, Beijing, 100710, China.

616.21 CHN ISSN 1672-2922
ZHONGHUA ERKEXUE ZAZHI/CHINESE JOURNAL OF OTOLOGY. Text in Chinese. 2003. q. CNY 16 newsstand/cover (effective 2006). **Document type:** *Journal, Academic/Scholarly.*
Published by: Jiefangjun Er-bi-yanhouke Yanjiusuo/Chinese P L A, Institute of Otolaryngology, 28, Fuxin Lu, Beijing, 100853, China. TEL 86-10-66939502, FAX 86-10-68286148.

616.21 TWN ISSN 1019-6102
ZHONGHUA MINGUO ERBIHOUKE YIXUEHUI ZAZHI/OTOLARYNGOLOGICAL SOCIETY OF THE REPUBLIC OF CHINA. JOURNAL. Text in Chinese. 1966. q. **Document type:** *Journal, Academic/Scholarly.*
Indexed: SCOPUS.
Published by: Zhonghua Minguo Erbihouke Yixuehui/Taiwan Otolaryngological Society, Zhongzheng District, 6, Hengyang Road, Room 507, 5th Floor, Taipei, 100, Taiwan. TEL 886-2-23141618, FAX 886-2-23141621, http://www.tos.org.tw/.

616.21 UKR ISSN 0044-4650
CODEN: ZUNBA9
➤ **ZHURNAL USHNYKH, NOSOVYKH I GORLOVYKH BOLEZNEI/JOURNAL OF EAR, NOSE AND NECK DISEASES.** Text in Ukrainian. 1924. bi-m. USD 134 in United States (effective 2007). abstr.; bibl.; charts; illus.; stat. index. **Document type:** *Journal, Academic/Scholarly.* **Description:** Concerns matters of otorhinolaryngology, and adjacent specialties; current questions of etiology, pathogenesis, diagnosis, prophylaxis and management of related diseases, ENT-head and neck surgeons, pathologists, neurologists, immunologists, radiologists, dentists, biochemists and students.
Related titles: Fax ed.; Online - full text ed.; Abridged ed.
Indexed: ChemAb, IndMed, P30, SCOPUS.
—CASDDS, East View, GNLM. **CCC.**
Published by: Ministerstvo Okhorony Zdorov'ya Ukrainy/Ministry of Health of Ukraine, vul Hrushevs'kogo, 7, Kyiv, 01021, Ukraine. TEL 380-44-2535602, FAX 380-44-2536975, moz@moz.gov.ua, http://www.moz.gov.ua. **Dist. by:** East View Information Services, 10601 Wayzata Blvd, Minneapolis, MN 55305. TEL 952-252-1201, 800-477-1005, FAX 952-252-1202, info@eastview.com, http://www.eastview.com. **Co-sponsor:** Ukrainskoe Nauchnoe Obshchestvo Otolaringologov.

MEDICAL SCIENCES—Pediatrics

➤ **A A I M H I NEWSLETTER.** (Australian Association for Infant Mental Health Inc) *see* MEDICAL SCIENCES—Psychiatry And Neurology

618.92 USA ISSN 1073-0397
A A P NEWS. Text in English. 19??. m. USD 89 combined subscription to non-members (print & online eds.); USD 10 per issue to non-members; free to members (effective 2010). adv. charts; illus.; stat.; abstr. 40 p./no.; back issues avail.; reprints avail. **Document type:** *Magazine, Trade.* **Description:** Contains news reports, clinical policy statements, legislation news, and practice management tips.
Former titles (until 1985): News and Comment - American Academy of Pediatrics (0094-8209); (until 1973): American Academy of Pediatrics. Newsletter (0094-8217)
Related titles: Online - full text ed.: ISSN 1556-3332. 2000 (Aug). USD 69 to non-members (effective 2010).
Indexed: P30.
—**CCC.**
Published by: American Academy of Pediatrics, 141 NW Pt Blvd, Elk Grove Village, IL 60007. TEL 847-434-4000, FAX 847-434-8000, journals@aap.org, http://www.aap.org. Ed. Anne Hegland.

618.92 USA ISSN 1934-5135
➤ **A A P PEDIATRIC CODING NEWSLETTER.** Text in English. 2005. irreg. USD 219.95 to non-members (print or online ed.); USD 199.95 to members (effective 2008). **Document type:** *Newsletter, Academic/Scholarly.*
Formerly (until 2006): Pediatric Coding Companion (1556-3049)
Related titles: Online - full text ed.: ISSN 1934-5143.
Published by: American Academy of Pediatrics, 141 NW Pt Blvd, Elk Grove Village, IL 60007. TEL 847-434-4000, FAX 847-434-8000, journals@aap.org, http://www.aap.org. Pub. Robert Perelman.

➤ **A MOTHER'S GIFT.** *see* NUTRITION AND DIETETICS

▼ ➤ **A P S P JOURNAL OF CASE REPORTS.** (Association of Paediatric Surgeons of Pakistan) *see* MEDICAL SCIENCES—Surgery

618.92 USA ISSN 1876-2859
RJ1 CODEN: APMECB
➤ **ACADEMIC PEDIATRICS.** Text in English. 1964. bi-m. USD 318 in United States to institutions; USD 400 elsewhere to institutions (effective 2012). adv. back issues avail.; reprints avail. **Document type:** *Journal, Academic/Scholarly.* **Description:** Focuses on the education of pediatricians, child health research, emergency medicine, research methodology, complementary and alternative medicine, child health policy and adolescent medicine.
Former titles (until 2009): Ambulatory Pediatrics (1530-1567); (until 2001): Ambulatory Pediatric Association. Journal; (until 1998): Ambulatory Pediatric Association. Newsletter (0002-7006)
Related titles: Online - full text ed.: ISSN 1876-2867. 2001 (from ScienceDirect).
Indexed: A20, A22, A26, A36, B21, C06, C07, C08, C22, CA, CABA, CINAHL, CurCont, D01, E01, EMBASE, ESPM, ExcerpMed, F09, FamI, GH, H12, H13, I05, LT, MEDLINE, N02, N03, P02, P10, P16, P20, P22, P24, P30, P48, P50, P53, P54, PEI, PQC, R12, RRTA, S12, SCI, SCOPUS, T02, T05, ToxAb, W07.
—BLDSC (0570.513973), IE, Ingenta. **CCC.**
Published by: (Ambulatory Pediatric Association), Elsevier Inc. (Subsidiary of: Elsevier Science & Technology), 360 Park Ave S, New York, NY 10010. TEL 212-989-5800, FAX 212-633-3990, usinfo-f@elsevier.com, http://www.elsevier.com. Ed. Dr. Peter Szilagyi.

➤ **ACTA DE ODONTOLOGIA PEDIATRICA**; una revista internacional para la odontologia pediatrica. *see* MEDICAL SCIENCES—Dentistry

618.92 GBR ISSN 0803-5253
RJ1 CODEN: APAEEL
➤ **ACTA PAEDIATRICA**; promoting child health. Text in English. 1921. m. GBP 575 in United Kingdom to institutions; EUR 731 in Europe to institutions; USD 984 in the Americas to institutions; USD 1,127 elsewhere to institutions; GBP 662 combined subscription in United Kingdom to institutions (print & online eds.); EUR 841 combined subscription in Europe to institutions (print & online eds.); USD 1,133 combined subscription in the Americas to institutions (print & online eds.); USD 1,297 combined subscription elsewhere to institutions (print & online eds.) (effective 2012). adv. bk.rev. charts; illus. cum.index: vols.1-30 (1921-1943). Supplement avail.; back issues avail.; reprint service avail. from PSC. **Document type:** *Journal, Academic/Scholarly.* **Description:** Covers both clinical and experimental research in all areas of pediatrics including neonatal medicine, developmental medicine, adolescent medicine, child health and environment, psychosomatic pediatrics, and child health in developing countries.
Former titles (until 1991): Acta Paediatrica Scandinavica (0001-656X); (until 1965): Acta Paediatrica (0365-1436)
Related titles: Online - full text ed.: ISSN 1651-2227. GBP 575 in United Kingdom to institutions; EUR 731 in Europe to institutions; USD 984 in the Americas to institutions; USD 1,127 elsewhere to institutions (effective 2012) (from IngentaConnect); Supplement(s): Acta Paediatrica. Supplement. ISSN 0803-5326. 1921.
Indexed: A01, A02, A03, A08, A20, A22, A29, A34, A36, A38, AIDS Ab, ASCA, B20, B21, B23, B25, BDM&CN, BIOBASE, BIOSIS Prev, C06, C07, C11, CA, CABA, CISA, ChemAb, CurCont, D01, DentInd, DiabCont, DokArb, E01, E12, EMBASE, ESPM, ExcerpMed, F08, F09, F12, FR, FamI, GH, GeoRef, H04, H16, H17, I10, IABS, INI, ISR, IndMed, IndVet, Inpharma, Kidney, LT, MEDLINE, MS&D, MaizeAb, MycolAb, N02, N03, NRN, NSA, P03, P30, P33, P34, P35, P39, PsycInfo, R07, R08, R10, R12, RA&MP, RM&VM, RRTA, Reac, S12, SCI, SCOPUS, SoyAb, SpeleolAb, T02, T05, TAR, VS, VirolAbstr, W07, W10, W11.
—BLDSC (0642.400000), CASDDS, GNLM, IE, Infotrieve, Ingenta, INIST. **CCC.**
Published by: (Foundation Acta Paediatrica, Japan Pediatric Society JPN), Wiley-Blackwell Publishing Ltd. (Subsidiary of: John Wiley & Sons, Inc.), 9600 Garsington Rd, Oxford, OX4 2DQ, United Kingdom. TEL 44-1865-776868, FAX 44-1865-714591, customerservices@blackwellpublishing.com. Ed. Hugo Lagercrantz. Circ: 2,000. **Subscr. to:** 1-7 Oldlands Way, PO Box 809, Bognor Regis PO21 9FG, United Kingdom. TEL 44-1865-778054.

618.9 CRI ISSN 1409-0090
ACTA PEDIATRICA COSTARRICENSE. Text in Spanish. 1987. a. back issues avail. **Document type:** *Journal, Academic/Scholarly.*
Related titles: Online - full text ed.
Published by: Asociacion Costarricense de Pediatria, Apdo. de Correos 1654, San Jose, 1000, Costa Rica. TEL 506-255-2239, FAX 506-221-6821, rrivera@hnn.sa.cr. Ed. Ramon Rivera.

618.92 MEX ISSN 0186-2391
RJ1
ACTA PEDIATRICA DE MEXICO. Text in Spanish. 1980. bi-m. MXN 350 domestic; USD 45 foreign (effective 2005). back issues avail. **Document type:** *Journal, Academic/Scholarly.*
Related titles: Online - full text ed.
Indexed: A01, C01, CA, T02.
Published by: Instituto Nacional de Pediatria, Ave Insurgentes Sur No 3700-C, Col Insurgentes Cuicuilco, Mexico D.F., 04530, Mexico. TEL 52-55-10840900, http://www.pediatria.gob.mx/. Ed. Jorge Espino Vela.

618.92 ESP ISSN 0001-6640
➤ **ACTA PEDIATRICA ESPANOLA.** Text in Spanish. 1943. m. EUR 80 domestic; EUR 115 foreign (effective 2009). adv. **Document type:** *Journal, Academic/Scholarly.* **Description:** Contains original articles on pediatric medicine and translated abstracts from prominent literature.
Formerly (until 1945): Acta Pediatrica (0301-5203)
Related titles: Online - full text ed.
Indexed: A22, ChemAb, EMBASE, ExcerpMed, IME, P02, P20, P30, P48, P54, PQC, R10, Reac, SCOPUS.
—BLDSC (0644.300000), GNLM, IE, Infotrieve, Ingenta. **CCC.**
Published by: Ediciones Mayo S.A., Calle Aribau 185-187, 2a Planta, Barcelona, 08021, Spain. TEL 34-93-2090255, FAX 34-93-2020643, edmayo@ediciones.mayo.es, http://www.edicionesmayo.es. Circ: 8,000 (controlled).

618.92 ITA ISSN 0393-6392
ACTA PEDIATRICA MEDITERRANEA. Text in English, Italian. 1960. 3/yr. adv. abstr.; bibl.; illus.; stat. index. **Document type:** *Journal, Academic/Scholarly.* **Description:** Comntains clinical cases of pediatrics and newborns are reviewed and discussed.
Formerly: Archivio Siciliano di Medicina e Chirurgia (Sezione Pediatrica)
Published by: Carbone Editore, Via Quintino Sella 68, Palermo, PA 90139, Italy. TEL 39-91-321273, FAX 39-91-321782, info@carboneeditore.com, http://carboneeditore.com. Circ: 3,000.

618.92 PRT ISSN 0873-9781
ACTA PEDIATRICA PORTUGUESA; revista da Sociedade Portuguesa de Pediatria. Abbreviated title: A P P. Text in Multiple languages. 1970. bi-m. **Document type:** *Journal, Academic/Scholarly.*
Formerly (until 1994): Revista Portuguesa de Pediatria (0301-147X)
Related titles: Online - full text ed.: free (effective 2011).
Indexed: P30.
Published by: Sociedade Portuguesa de Pediatria, Rua Amilcar Cabral 15, Lisbon, 1750-018, Portugal. TEL 351-21-7574680, FAX 351-21-7577617.

618.92 GBR ISSN 1179-318X
▼ ➤ **ADOLESCENT HEALTH, MEDICINE AND THERAPEUTICS.** Text in English. 2010. irreg. free (effective 2011). **Document type:** *Journal, Academic/Scholarly.*
—**CCC.**
Published by: Dove Medical Press Ltd., Beechfield House, Winterton Way, Macclesfield, SK11 0JL, United Kingdom. TEL 44-1625-509130, FAX 44-1625-617933. Ed. Steven L Youngentob.

618.92 USA ISSN 1934-4287
RJ550 CODEN: AMSRER
➤ **ADOLESCENT MEDICINE (ELK GROVE)**; state of the art reviews. Text in English. 1990. 3/yr. USD 174.95 to institutions; USD 124.95 to non-members; USD 114.95 to members (effective 2010). abstr.; charts; illus.; stat. 200 p./no. 1 cols./p.; back issues avail. **Document type:** *Monographic series, Academic/Scholarly.* **Description:** Contains a series of clinical reviews that detail advances in the diagnosis and management of a wide range of health problems affecting adolescents.
Former titles (until 2007): Adolescent Medicine Clinics (1547-3368); (until 2004): Adolescent Medicine (1041-3499)
Related titles: Online - full text ed.: ISSN 1545-0058.
Indexed: C06, C07, C08, CCIP, CINAHL, EMBASE, ExcerpMed, IndMed, MEDLINE, P20, P22, P24, P26, P30, P48, P54, PQC, R10, Reac, SCOPUS.
—BLDSC (0696.585900), GNLM, IE, Infotrieve, Ingenta. **CCC.**
Published by: (American Academy of Pediatrics), W.B. Saunders Co. (Subsidiary of: Elsevier Health Sciences), Elsevier, Health Sciences Division, Order Fulfillment, 3251 Riverport Ln, Maryland Heights, MO 63043. TEL 314-872-8370, 800-325-4177, FAX 314-432-1380, JournalCustomerService-usa@elsevier.com, http://www.us.elsevierhealth.com.

➤ **ADONG GANHO HAGHOEJI/KOREAN ACADEMY OF CHILD HEALTH NURSING. JOURNAL.** *see* MEDICAL SCIENCES—Nurses And Nursing

➤ **ADVANCES IN CHILD DEVELOPMENT AND BEHAVIOR.** *see* PSYCHOLOGY

610 USA ISSN 1536-0903
ADVANCES IN NEONATAL CARE. Abbreviated title: A N C. Text in English. 2001. bi-m. USD 230.51 domestic to institutions; USD 305 foreign to institutions (effective 2011). adv. back issues avail.; reprints avail. **Document type:** *Journal, Academic/Scholarly.* **Description:** Promotes care and outcomes for the tiniest patients and their families. Includes visual and teaching aids, such as family teaching toolbox, research to practice, cultivating clinical expertise, and online features.
Related titles: Online - full text ed.: ISSN 1536-0911.
Indexed: A26, C06, C07, C08, CA, CINAHL, EMBASE, ExcerpMed, I05, MEDLINE, P30, R10, Reac, SCOPUS, T02.
—BLDSC (0709.463000), IE, Ingenta. **CCC.**
Published by: (National Association of Neonatal Nurses), Lippincott Williams & Wilkins (Subsidiary of: Wolters Kluwer N.V.), Two Commerce Sq, 2001 Market St, Philadelphia, PA 19103. TEL 215-521-8300, FAX 215-521-8902, customerservice@lww.com, http://www.lww.com. Ed. Catherine L Witt. Pub. Beth L Guthy. Adv. contact Mark Harling. Circ: 8,400.

618.92 USA ISSN 0065-3101
RJ23
ADVANCES IN PEDIATRICS. Text in English. 1942. a. USD 202 in United States to institutions; USD 219 elsewhere to institutions (effective 2012). adv. illus. reprints avail. **Document type:** *Journal, Academic/Scholarly.* **Description:** Presents a collection of original, fully referenced clinical review articles in pediatrics.
Related titles: Microfilm ed.: (from PQC); Online - full text ed.: ISSN 1878-1926 (from ScienceDirect).
Indexed: A22, A26, CA, DentInd, EMBASE, ExcerpMed, FR, I05, IndMed, MEDLINE, P30, R10, Reac, SCOPUS, T02.
—BLDSC (0709.590000), GNLM, IE, Infotrieve, Ingenta, INIST. **CCC.**
Published by: Mosby, Inc. (Subsidiary of: Elsevier Health Sciences), 1600 John F. Kennedy Blvd, Ste 1800, Philadelphia, PA 19103. TEL 215-239-3900, 800-523-1649, FAX 215-239-3990, elspcs@elsevier.com, http://www.us.elsevierhealth.com. Ed. Dr. Michael S Kappy.

618.92 DEU ISSN 1436-2651
AERZTLICHE PRAXIS. PAEDIATRIE. Short title: Ae P Paediatrie. Text in German. 1988. bi-m. adv. **Document type:** *Journal, Trade.*
Former titles (until 1998): T und E Paediatrie (1435-1099); (until 1997): T W Paediatrie (0935-3216)
Indexed: A22, SCOPUS.
—BLDSC (1567.785500), GNLM, IE, Ingenta. **CCC.**
Published by: Biermann Verlag GmbH, Otto-Hahn-Str 7, Cologne, 50997, Germany. TEL 49-2236-3760, FAX 49-2236-376999, info@biermann.net, http://www.biermann-verlag.de.

AERZTLICHER RATGEBER FUER WERDENDE UND JUNGE ELTERN; die Schwangerschaft, Geburt und Babyzeit. *see* MEDICAL SCIENCES—Obstetrics And Gynecology

618.92 617 IND ISSN 0189-6725
RD137.A1
➤ **AFRICAN JOURNAL OF PAEDIATRIC SURGERY.** Text in English. 2004. s-a. INR 1,500 domestic to individuals; USD 150 foreign to individuals; INR 3,000 domestic to institutions; USD 250 foreign to institutions; INR 1,800 domestic to individuals (print & online eds.); USD 180 foreign to individuals (print & online eds.); INR 3,600 domestic to institutions (print & online eds.); USD 300 foreign to institutions (print & online eds.) (effective 2011). **Document type:** *Journal, Academic/Scholarly.* **Description:** Aims to promote research, post-graduate training and further education among paediatric surgeons, paediatric surgical trainees and paramedical personnel in the surgery of newborn infants and children particularly in Africa and other tropical regions of the world.
Related titles: Online - full text ed.: ISSN 0974-5998. INR 1,200 domestic to individuals; USD 120 foreign to individuals; INR 2,400 domestic to institutions; USD 200 foreign to institutions (effective 2011).
Indexed: A01, A26, A36, C06, CA, CABA, E08, EMBASE, ExcerpMed, GH, H12, H17, I05, MEDLINE, P10, P20, P22, P30, P33, P48, P53, P54, PQC, R12, S09, SCOPUS, T02, T05.
—**CCC.**
Published by: (Pan-African Paediatric Surgical Association KEN, Association of Paediatric Surgeons of Nigeria NGA), Medknow Publications and Media Pvt. Ltd., B-9, Kanara Business Ctr, Off Link Rd, Ghatkopar (E), Mumbai, Maharastra 400 075, India. TEL 91-22-66491816, FAX 91-22-66491817, http://www.medknow.com.

➤ **ALERGIA, ASMA E INMUNOLOGIA PEDIATRICAS.** *see* MEDICAL SCIENCES—Allergology And Immunology

618.92 USA ISSN 1080-0131
RJ401
AMERICAN ACADEMY OF PEDIATRICS. COMMITTEE ON INFECTIOUS DISEASES. RED BOOK (YEAR). Text in English. 1938. irreg., latest 2006, 27th ed. USD 109.95 to non-members 27th ed.; USD 94.95 to members 27th ed. (effective 2008). **Document type:** *Monographic series, Academic/Scholarly.* **Description:** Includes the latest in clinical manifestations, etiology, epidemiology, diagnostic tests, and treatments for over 200 infectious diseases.
Formerly (until 1991): Report of the Committee on Infectious Diseases (0065-6909)
Related titles: CD-ROM ed.; Online - full text ed.: ISSN 1544-9300; Special ed(s).: Red Book Mobile. ISSN 1947-2927. 2009. USD 114.95 per issue to non-members; USD 99.85 per issue to members (effective 2009).
—BLDSC (7405.555000), IE, Ingenta. **CCC.**
Published by: American Academy of Pediatrics, 141 NW Pt Blvd, Elk Grove Village, IL 60007. TEL 847-434-4000, FAX 847-434-8000, journals@aap.org, http://www.aap.org. Ed. Larry K Pickering. Pub. Robert Perelman.

AMERICAN ASSOCIATION FOR PEDIATRIC OPHTHALMOLOGY AND STRABISMUS. JOURNAL. *see* MEDICAL SCIENCES—Ophthalmology And Optometry

618.92 ESP ISSN 1695-4033
CODEN: APNECG
ANALES DE PEDIATRIA. Text in Spanish. 1968. m. EUR 128.70 combined subscription to individuals print & online eds.; EUR 328.82 combined subscription to institutions print & online eds. (effective 2009). **Document type:** *Journal, Academic/Scholarly.*
Formerly (until 2002): Anales Espanoles de Pediatria (0302-4342)
Related titles: Online - full text ed.: ISSN 1695-9531. 2000 (from ScienceDirect); Supplement(s): Anales Espanoles de Pediatria. Suplemento. ISSN 0213-9146. 1974.
Indexed: A22, A34, A35, A36, CABA, ChemAb, D01, DentInd, E12, EMBASE, ExcerpMed, GH, IME, IndMed, LT, MEDLINE, N02, N03, P30, P33, P39, R08, R10, Reac, SCI, SCOPUS, T05, W07.
—BLDSC (0890.157000), CASDDS, GNLM, IE, Infotrieve, Ingenta, INIST. **CCC.**
Published by: (Asociacion Espanola de Pediatria), Elsevier Doyma (Subsidiary of: Elsevier Health Sciences), Traversa de Gracia 17-21, Barcelona, 08021, Spain. TEL 34-932-418800, FAX 34-932-419020, doyma@doyma.es, http://www.doyma.es. Circ: 8,800.

618.92 ESP ISSN 1696-2818
ANALES DE PEDIATRIA CONTINUADA. Text in Spanish. 2003. bi-m. EUR 216.60 domestic to individuals; EUR 573.27 foreign to individuals; EUR 734.24 to institutions (effective 2009). back issues avail. **Document type:** *Journal, Academic/Scholarly.*
Related titles: Online - full text ed.: ISSN 1696-4608. 2003 (from ScienceDirect); ◆ Supplement(s): Anales de Pediatria Continuada. Monografias. ISSN 1886-306X.
Indexed: EMBASE, ExcerpMed, SCOPUS.
—**CCC.**
Published by: Elsevier Doyma (Subsidiary of: Elsevier Health Sciences), Traversa de Gracia 17-21, Barcelona, 08021, Spain. TEL 34-932-418800, FAX 34-932-419020, editorial@elsevier.com, http://www.elsevier.es/.

618.92 ESP ISSN 1886-306X
ANALES DE PEDIATRIA CONTINUADA. MONOGRAFIAS. Text in Spanish. 2006. 3/yr.

Related titles: ♦ Supplement to: Anales de Pediatria Continuada. ISSN 1696-2818.
Published by: Elsevier Doyma (Subsidiary of: Elsevier Health Sciences), Traversa de Gracia 17-21, Barcelona, 08021, Spain. TEL 34-932-418800, FAX 34-932-419020, editorial@elsevier.com, http://www.elsevier.es/.

ANESTESIA PEDIATRICA E NEONATALE. *see* MEDICAL SCIENCES—Anaesthesiology

ANNALS OF PEDIATRIC CARDIOLOGY. *see* MEDICAL SCIENCES—Cardiovascular Diseases

618.92 155.4 USA ISSN 1075-5217
HQ767.8
ANNUAL EDITIONS: CHILD GROWTH & DEVELOPMENT. Text in English. 1994. a. USD 22.25 per issue (effective 2010). back issues avail. **Document type:** *Journal, Academic/Scholarly.*
Related titles: Online - full text ed.
Indexed: E-psyche.
Published by: McGraw-Hill, Contemporary Learning Series (Subsidiary of: McGraw-Hill Companies, Inc.), 1221 Ave of the Americas, New York, NY 10020. TEL 212-904-2000, FAX 212-512-2000, customer.service@mcgraw-hill.com, http://www.mhhe.com/cls/.

618.92 FRA ISSN 0929-693X
RJ1 CODEN: APEDE4
➤ **ARCHIVES DE PEDIATRIE.** Text in French; Summaries in English, French. 1993. 12/yr. EUR 452 in Europe to institutions; EUR 400.59 in France to institutions; JPY 55,200 in Japan to institutions; USD 588 elsewhere to institutions (effective 2012). adv. bk.rev. charts; illus. index. reprints avail. **Document type:** *Journal, Academic/Scholarly.* **Description:** Publishes clinical and research articles in all areas of pediatric medicine.
Incorporates (in 1999): Annales de Pediatrie (0066-2097); Formed by the merger of (1912-1993): Pediatrie (0031-4021); (1942-1993): Archives Francaises de Pediatrie (0003-9764); Which incorporated (1898-1940): Archives de Medecine des Enfants (0365-4311)
Related titles: Microfilm ed.: (from PQC); Online - full text ed.: ISSN 1769-664X. 1999 (from IngentaConnect, ScienceDirect).
Indexed: A01, A03, A08, A20, A22, A26, A29, A34, A36, ASCA, B20, B21, B25, BDM&CN, BIOSIS Prev, CA, CABA, ChemAb, CurCont, D01, DentInd, E12, EMBASE, ESPM, ExcerpMed, F09, FR, G11, GH, H17, I05, IBR, IBZ, INI, ISR, IndMed, IndVet, Inpharma, LT, MEDLINE, MycolAb, N02, N03, NSA, P30, P33, P37, P39, PN&I, R08, R10, R11, R12, RM&VM, RRTA, Reac, S12, SCI, SCOPUS, SoyAb, T02, T05, TriticAb, VS, W07, W10, W11.
—BLDSC (1638.965000), CASDDS, GNLM, IE, Infotrieve, Ingenta, INIST. **CCC.**
Published by: (Societe Francaise de Pediatrie), Elsevier Masson (Subsidiary of: Elsevier Health Sciences), 62 Rue Camille Desmoulins, Issy les Moulineaux, Cedex 92442, France. TEL 33-1-71165500, FAX 33-1-71165600, infos@elsevier-masson.fr. Circ: 3,200.

618.92 GBR ISSN 0003-9888
CODEN: ADCHAK
➤ **ARCHIVES OF DISEASE IN CHILDHOOD**; an international peer-reviewed journal for health professionals and researchers covering conception to adolescence. Abbreviated title: A D C. Text in English. 1904. m. GBP 628 to institutions; GBP 774 combined subscription to institutions small FTE (print & online eds.) (effective 2011); subscr. includes Fetal and Neonatal Edition & Education and Practice Edition. adv. bk.rev. charts; illus. index. back issues avail.; reprints avail. **Document type:** *Journal, Academic/Scholarly.* **Description:** Features a wide range of papers on all aspects of childhood health and disease for UK pediatricians and others worldwide.
Incorporates (1997-200?): Paediatric and Perinatal Drug Therapy (1463-0095); (1904-1944): British Journal of Children's Diseases (0366-2837)
Related titles: CD-ROM ed.; Microfilm ed.; Online - full text ed.: e A D C. ISSN 1468-2044. 1997. GBP 644 to institutions small FTE (effective 2011); ♦ Supplement(s): Archives of Disease in Childhood. Education and Practice Edition. ISSN 1743-0585; ♦ Archives of Disease in Childhood. Fetal and Neonatal Edition. ISSN 1359-2998.
Indexed: A01, A03, A08, A20, A22, A26, A34, A36, AHCMS, AIM, AMED, AbAn, B20, B21, B25, B28, BIOBASE, BIOSIS Prev, C06, C07, C08, C28, CA, CABA, CINAHL, CLFP, ChemAb, CurCont, D01, DentInd, DiabCont, DokArb, E01, E07, E08, E12, EMBASE, ESPM, ExcerpMed, F08, F09, FR, Faml, G08, GH, H&SSA, H11, H12, I05, I07, IABS, IDIS, INI, ISR, IndMed, IndVet, Inpharma, Kidney, LT, MEDLINE, MS&D, MycolAb, N02, N03, NRN, OR, P07, P18, P20, P22, P24, P26, P30, P33, P34, P35, P37, P39, P48, P50, P53, P54, P55, PQC, PsycholAb, R07, R08, R10, R11, R12, RA&MP, RM&VM, RRTA, Reac, RiskAb, S02, S03, S09, S23, SCI, SCOPUS, SoyAb, T02, T05, THA, VS, VirolAbstr, W07, W11.
—BLDSC (1634.200000), CASDDS, GNLM, IE, Infotrieve, Ingenta, INIST. **CCC.**
Published by: (Royal College of Paediatrics and Child Health), B M J Group, BMA House, Tavistock Sq, London, WC1H 9JR, United Kingdom. TEL 44-20-73836373, FAX 44-20-73836668, membership@bma.org.uk, http://group.bmj.com. Ed. Howard Bauchner. Pub. Janet O'Flaherty TEL 44-20-73836154. Adv. contact Nick Gray TEL 44-20-73836386. Circ: 10,800. **Subscr. to:** PO Box 299, London WC1H 9TD, United Kingdom. TEL 44-20-73836270, FAX 44-20-73836402, support@bmjgroup.com.

618.92 GBR ISSN 1743-0585
RJ33.5
➤ **ARCHIVES OF DISEASE IN CHILDHOOD. EDUCATION AND PRACTICE EDITION**; an international peer-reviewed journal that keeps health professionals and others up to date in all areas of paediatrics. Abbreviated title: E P. Text in English. 2004. bi-m. Included with subscr. to Archives of Disease in Childhood. adv. back issues avail.; reprints avail. **Document type:** *Journal, Academic/Scholarly.* **Description:** Dedicated to the continuing professional development of pediatricians.
Related titles: Online - full text ed.: ISSN 1743-0593; ♦ Supplement to: Archives of Disease in Childhood. ISSN 0003-9888.
Indexed: A01, A03, A08, A22, C06, C07, CA, CurCont, EMBASE, ExcerpMed, MEDLINE, P30, R10, Reac, SCI, SCOPUS, T02, W07.
—BLDSC (1634.200400), IE, Ingenta, INIST. **CCC.**
Published by: (Royal College of Paediatrics and Child Health), B M J Group, BMA House, Tavistock Sq, London, WC1H 9JR, United Kingdom. TEL 44-20-73836373, FAX 44-20-73836668, membership@bma.org.uk, http://group.bmj.com. Ed. Howard Bauchner. Pub. Janet O'Flaherty TEL 44-20-73836154. Adv. contact Nick Gray TEL 44-20-73836386. **Subscr. to:** PO Box 299, London WC1H 9TD, United Kingdom. TEL 44-20-73836270, FAX 44-20-73836402.

➤ **ARCHIVES OF DISEASE IN CHILDHOOD. FETAL AND NEONATAL EDITION**; an international peer-reviewed journal for health professionals and researchers covering neonatal and perinatal medicine. *see* MEDICAL SCIENCES—Obstetrics And Gynecology

618.92 USA ISSN 1072-4710
RJ1 CODEN: APAMEB
➤ **ARCHIVES OF PEDIATRICS & ADOLESCENT MEDICINE.** Text in English. 1911. m. USD 630 domestic to institutions; USD 788 in the Americas to institutions; EUR 637 in Europe to institutions; GBP 540 elsewhere to institutions (effective 2012). bk.rev. abstr.; bibl.; charts; illus. Index. back issues avail.; reprints avail. **Document type:** *Journal, Academic/Scholarly.* **Description:** Provides a forum for dialogue on clinical, scientific, advocacy and humanistic issues relevant to the care of pediatric patients from infancy to young adulthood.
Former titles (until Jan.1994): A J D C - American Journal of Diseases of Children (0002-922X); (until 1960): A M A Journal of Diseases of Children (0096-6916); (until 1956): A M A American Journal of Diseases of Children (0096-8994)
Related titles: Microform ed.: (from PQC); Online - full text ed.: ISSN 1538-3628. free to members (effective 2012).
Indexed: A20, A22, A26, A34, A36, AIDS Ab, AIIM, AIM, AMHA, ASCA, AbAn, AddicA, AgrForAb, B21, B25, BDM&CN, BIOSIS Prev, BiolDig, C06, C07, C08, CABA, CCIP, CDA, CINAHL, CTA, ChemAb, ChemoAb, Chicano, CurCont, D01, DBA, DokArb, E08, E12, ECER, EMBASE, ESPM, ExcerpMed, F08, F09, FAMLI, FR, Faml, G06, G07, G08, GH, H&SSA, H11, H12, H13, H16, H17, HRIS, I05, IDIS, INI, ISR, IndMed, Inpharma, JW, JW-D, JW-EM, JW-ID, JW-P, JW-WH, Kidney, LT, MEDLINE, MS&D, MaizeAb, MycolAb, N02, N03, NRN, NSA, P02, P10, P20, P21, P22, P24, P30, P32, P33, P35, P38, P39, P40, P48, P50, P53, P54, PN&I, PQC, PsycholAb, R08, R10, R12, RM&VM, RRTA, Reac, RiskAb, S02, S03, S09, S12, SCI, SCOPUS, SoyAb, T05, THA, VS, W07, W11.
—BLDSC (1638.960000), CASDDS, GNLM, IE, Infotrieve, Ingenta, INIST. **CCC.**
Published by: American Medical Association, 515 N State St, Chicago, IL 60654. TEL 312-464-4200, 800-621-8335, FAX 312-464-4142, journalsales@ama-assn.org, http://www.ama-assn.org. Eds. Dr. Frederick P Rivara TEL 206-685-3573, Dr. Catherine D DeAngelis. **Subscr. in the Americas to:** PO Box 10946, Chicago, IL 60654. TEL 312-670-7827, 800-262-2350, ama-subs@ama-assn.org; **Subscr. outside the Americas to:** American Medical Association, J A M A and Archive Journals.

618.92 ARG ISSN 0325-0075
➤ **ARCHIVOS ARGENTINOS DE PEDIATRIA.** Text in Spanish. 1930. bi-m. ARS 30 domestic to individuals; ARS 50 foreign to individuals; ARS 50 domestic to institutions; ARS 60 foreign to institutions (effective 2010). **Document type:** *Journal, Academic/Scholarly.*
Formerly (until 1930): Archivos Latino Americanos de Pediatria (0004-0487)
Related titles: Online - full text ed.: ISSN 1668-3501. 1998. free (effective 2011) (from SciELO).
Indexed: EMBASE, ExcerpMed, MEDLINE, P30, R10, Reac, SCI, SCOPUS, W07.
Published by: Sociedad Argentina de Pediatria, Av Coronel Diaz 1971/75, Buenos Aires, C1425DQF, Argentina. Ed. Carlos G Wahren.

618.92 URY ISSN 0004-0584
CODEN: APURAK
ARCHIVOS DE PEDIATRIA DEL URUGUAY. Text in Spanish; Summaries in English. 1929. q. adv. bk.rev. abstr.; bibl.; charts; illus. index. back issues avail. **Document type:** *Journal, Academic/Scholarly.*
Related titles: Online - full text ed.: ISSN 1688-1249. free (effective 2011).
Indexed: C01, INIS AtomInd, IndMed, P30.
—CASDDS, GNLM.
Published by: Sociedad Uruguaya de Pediatria, Blvd Artigas 1550 1er Piso, Montevideo, Uruguay. TEL 598-2-7091801, FAX 598-2-7085213, paediatrica@telefonica.net.pe, http://www.sup.org.uy/. Ed. Raul Bustos. Circ: 1,250.

618.92 DOM ISSN 0004-0606
ARCHIVOS DOMINICANOS DE PEDIATRIA. Text in Spanish; Summaries in English. 1965. q. adv. bk.rev. charts; illus.; bibl. index, cum.index every 10 yrs. reprints avail. **Document type:** *Journal, Academic/Scholarly.*
Indexed: C01, IndMed, P30, SCOPUS.
Published by: Sociedad Dominicana de Pediatricas, Calle Santiago 702, Zona Universitaria, Santo Domingo, Dominican Republic. TEL 809-688-9414, FAX 809-685-9200, http://www.sdp.org.do. Ed. Emilio Mena Castro.

618.92 VEN ISSN 0004-0649
RJ502.V4
ARCHIVOS VENEZOLANOS DE PUERICULTURA Y PEDIATRIA. Text in Spanish; Summaries in English. 1939. q. adv. bk.rev. bibl.; charts; illus. index. back issues avail. **Document type:** *Journal, Academic/Scholarly.*
Related titles: Online - full text ed.
Indexed: CA, ChemAb, P30, T02.
Published by: Sociedad Venezolana de Puericultura y Pediatria, Apdo de Correos 3122, Caracas, 1010A, Venezuela. TEL 58-212-2637778, FAX 58-212-2676078, svpp@reacciun.ve. Ed. Ingrid Soto de Sanabria. Circ: 2,000.

618.92 ITA ISSN 1591-0075
AREA PEDIATRICA. Text in Italian. 2000. m. **Document type:** *Magazine, Trade.* **Description:** This is the training and information venue of the Societa Italiana di Pediatria.
Related titles: Online - full text ed.
Indexed: SCOPUS.
Published by: Elsevier Masson (Subsidiary of: Elsevier Health Sciences), Via Paleocapa 7, Milan, 20121, Italy. TEL 39-02-881841, FAX 39-02-88184302, info@masson.it, http://www.masson.it. Ed. Paolo Becherucci.

618.92 ITA ISSN 2039-1374
ASSOCIAZIONE CULTURALE PEDIATRI. QUADERNI. Text in Multiple languages. 1994. bi-m. **Document type:** *Journal, Trade.*
Formed by the merger of (1990-1994): Associazione Culturale Pediatri. Bollettino (2039-1366); (1993-1994): Ausili Didattici per il Pediatra
Related titles: Online - full text ed.: ISSN 2039-1382.
Published by: Associazione Culturale Pediatri http://www.acp.it.

618.92 USA ISSN 0271-1346
➤ **AUDIO-DIGEST PEDIATRICS.** Text in English. 1955. s-m. USD 449.81 domestic; USD 479.72 in Canada; USD 527.72 elsewhere (effective 2010). back issues avail. **Document type:** *Journal, Academic/Scholarly.*
Media: Audio cassette/tape. **Related titles:** Audio CD ed.: USD 399.89 domestic; USD 431.72 in Canada; USD 479.72 elsewhere (effective 2010); Online - full text ed.: USD 359.72 (effective 2010).
—**CCC.**
Published by: Audio-Digest Foundation (Subsidiary of: California Medical Association), 1577 E Chevy Chase Dr, Glendale, CA 91206. TEL 818-240-7500, 800-423-2308, FAX 818-240-7379.

➤ **AUSTRALIA. BUREAU OF STATISTICS. CHILDREN'S HEALTH SCREENING (ONLINE).** *see* MEDICAL SCIENCES—Abstracting, Bibliographies, Statistics

➤ **AUSTRALIA. BUREAU OF STATISTICS. CHILDREN'S IMMUNISATION, AUSTRALIA (ONLINE).** *see* MEDICAL SCIENCES—Abstracting, Bibliographies, Statistics

618.92 USA ISSN 2161-0746
RC553.A88
AUTISM ASPERGER'S DIGEST. Text in English. 1999. bi-m. USD 49.95 in US & Canada; USD 59.95 elsewhere (effective 2011). adv. back issues avail. **Document type:** *Magazine, Consumer.*
Published by: Future Horizons, Inc., PO Box 1519, Waynesville, NC 28786. TEL 828-454-0229, http://www.fhautism.com. Ed. Veronica Zysk.

618.92 EGY ISSN 1110-7774
AL AZHAR JOURNAL OF PEDIATRICS/MAGALLAT TIB ATFAL AL-AZHAR. Text in English. 1997. bi-m. **Document type:** *Journal, Academic/Scholarly.*
Published by: Al-Azhar University, Faculty of Medicine, Pediatric Department, Al-Azhar Pediatric Society, Al-Hussein University Hospital, El-Darassah, Cairo, Egypt. TEL 20-2-5104345, FAX 20-2-2756298. Ed. Dr. Khalil Mustafa El-Diwani.

618.92 GBR ISSN 1471-2431
RJ1 CODEN: BPMEBL
➤ **B M C PEDIATRICS.** (BioMed Central) Text in English. 2001 (Feb.). irreg. free (effective 2011). adv. back issues avail.; reprints avail. **Document type:** *Journal, Academic/Scholarly.* **Description:** Publishes original research articles in all aspects of health care in neonates, children and adolescents, as well as related molecular genetics, pathophysiology, and epidemiology.
Media: Online - full text.
Indexed: A26, A36, C06, C07, CA, CABA, CurCont, D01, E12, EMBASE, ESPM, ExcerpMed, GH, I05, LT, MEDLINE, N02, N03, P20, P22, P30, P33, P39, R08, R10, R12, RA&MP, Reac, S12, SCI, SCOPUS, SoyAb, T02, T05, W07, W11.
—Infotrieve. **CCC.**
Published by: BioMed Central Ltd. (Subsidiary of: Springer Science+Business Media), 236 Gray's Inn Rd, London, WC1X 8HB, United Kingdom. TEL 44-20-31922000, FAX 44-20-31922010, info@biomedcentral.com. Ed. Dr. Melissa Norton. Adv. contact Natasha Bailey TEL 44-20-31922231.

618.9 649 USA
BABY MAGAZINE INFANT CARE GUIDE. Text in English. 1989. m. free to new parents (effective 2007). adv. back issues avail. **Document type:** *Magazine, Consumer.* **Description:** Offers new parents tips on caring for their baby.
Formerly (until Aug. 1996): Bounty Infant Care Guide
Published by: Baby Magazine, 375 Lexington Ave, New York, NY 10017. TEL 212-499-2000. Ed. Jeanne Muchnick. Pub. Suzanne Robotti. R&P Dina Kaliko. Adv. contact John Knecht. B&W page USD 78,500, color page USD 103,500; trim 7.5 x 5.25. Circ: 3,700,000 (controlled).

BABY POST. *see* CHILDREN AND YOUTH—About

618.92 AUS ISSN 1326-1665
BABYCARE BOOK. Text in English. 1984. a. adv. **Document type:** *Handbook/Manual/Guide, Consumer.* **Description:** Focuses on 1st years of a baby's life.
Published by: Bounty Services Pty. Ltd. (Subsidiary of: Emap International), Level 6, 187 Thomas St., Haymarket, NSW 2000, Australia. TEL 61-2-95819555. adv.: page AUD 14,760; trim 210 x 148. Circ: 230,000.

BABYS ERSTES JAHR. *see* CHILDREN AND YOUTH—About

BABYS RICHTIG FOERDERN. *see* CHILDREN AND YOUTH—About

618.92 616.99 SWE ISSN 0284-7507
BARN OCH CANCER. Text in Swedish. 1987. bi-m. SEK 200 (effective 2007). **Document type:** *Magazine, Trade.*
Published by: Barncancerfonden, PO Box 5408, Stockholm, 11484, Sweden. TEL 46-8-58420900, FAX 46-8-58410900, info@barncancerfonden.se. Ed. Victoria Wahlberg TEL 46-8-6102000.

618.92 610.73 SWE ISSN 0349-1994
BARNBLADET; tidskrift foer Sveriges barnsjukskoeterskor. Text in Swedish. 1976. q. SEK 150; SEK 40 newsstand/cover. **Document type:** *Trade.*
Published by: (Riksfoereningen foer Barnsjukskoeterskor/Swedish Association of Pediatric Nurses), Via Media, PO Box 640, Landskrona, 26125, Sweden. TEL 46-418-10780, FAX 46-418-12394. Ed. Kerstin Hedberg Nyqvist. Circ: 2,600.

BEFORE BIRTH AND BEYOND; community newsletter. *see* CHILDREN AND YOUTH—About

618.92 POL ISSN 0303-7827
BIBLIOTEKA PEDIATRY. Text in Polish. 1974. irreg. price varies. **Document type:** *Monographic series, Academic/Scholarly.*
Published by: (Polskie Towarzystwo Pediatryczne), Wydawnictwo Lekarskie PZWL, Domaniewska 41, Warsaw, 02672, Poland. krystyna.regulska@pzwl.pl, http://www.pzwl.pl. Ed. Krystyna Bozkowa.

BIRTH ANOMALIES SERIES. *see* POPULATION STUDIES

618.92 PER
BOLETIN DE NINO. Text in Spanish. 1939. q.
Formerly: Hospital del Nino. Revista (0301-3790)
Indexed: P30.
Published by: Instituto Nacional de Salud del Nino, Ave Brasil, 600, Brena, Lima, Peru. TEL 51-1-3300066, http://www.isn.gob.pe/homepage.htm.

618.92 ESP ISSN 0214-2597
RJ1
➤ **BOLETIN DE PEDIATRIA.** Variant title: Boletin de Pediatria de Asturias, Cantabria, Castilla y Leon. Text in Spanish; Summaries in English, Spanish. 1960. q. free to qualified personnel (effective 2009). adv. bk.rev. abstr.; charts; illus. index. **Document type:** *Journal, Academic/Scholarly.*
Formerly (until 1987): Sociedad Castellano-Astur-Leonosa de Pediatria. Boletin (0037-8429)
Related titles: Online - full text ed.: 1997. free (effective 2011).
—CCC.
Published by: (Sociedad de Pediatria de Asturias, Cantabria, Castilla y Leon), Ediciones Ergon S.A., C/ Arboleda 1, Majadahonda, Madrid, Madrid 28220, Spain. TEL 34-91-6362930, FAX 34-91-6362931, ergon@ergon.es, http://www.ergon.es. Circ: 1,000.

➤ **BRAIN & DEVELOPMENT.** *see* MEDICAL SCIENCES—Psychiatry And Neurology

➤ **BRITISH NATIONAL FORMULARY FOR CHILDREN.** *see* PHARMACY AND PHARMACOLOGY

362.7 USA ISSN 1527-8395
RJ504.7
BROWN UNIVERSITY CHILD & ADOLESCENT PSYCHOPHARMACOLOGY UPDATE. Text in English. 1997. m. GBP 801 in United Kingdom to institutions; EUR 1,012 in Europe to institutions; USD 1,500 in United States to institutions; USD 1,548 in Canada & Mexico to institutions; USD 1,566 elsewhere to institutions; GBP 922 combined subscription in United Kingdom to institutions (print & online eds.); EUR 1,165 combined subscription in Europe to institutions (print & online eds.); USD 1,727 combined subscription in United States to institutions (print & online eds.); USD 1,775 combined subscription in Canada & Mexico to institutions (print & online eds.); USD 1,793 combined subscription elsewhere to institutions (print & online eds.) (effective 2012). adv. 8 p./no.; back issues avail.; reprint service avail. from PSC. **Document type:** *Newsletter, Trade.* **Description:** Contains updates on new drugs, their uses, typical doses, side effects and interactions, examines generic vs. name brand drugs, reports on new research and new indications for existing medications.
Formerly: Children's Services Report (1098-5182)
Related titles: Online - full text ed.: ISSN 1556-7567. GBP 767 in United Kingdom to institutions; EUR 969 in Europe to institutions; USD 1,500 elsewhere to institutions (effective 2012).
Indexed: A01, A03, A08, A26, C06, C07, C08, CA, CINAHL, E-psyche, E07, E08, G08, H01, H11, H12, I05, S09, T02.
—IE. CCC.
Published by: John Wiley & Sons, Inc., 111 River St, Hoboken, NJ 07030. TEL 201-748-6000, FAX 201-748-6088, info@wiley.com, http://www.wiley.com/WileyCDA/. Ed. Christopher Kratochvil. Pub. Sue Lewis.

618.92 USA
C H I - P A C C UPDATE. (Children's Hospice International) Text in English. q. free to members (effective 2007). back issues avail. **Document type:** *Newsletter.* **Description:** Pediatric hospice care issues.
Formerly: Children's Hospice International Newsletter
Published by: Children's Hospice International, 1101 King St, Ste 360, Alexandria, VA 22314. TEL 703-684-0330, 800-242-4453, info@chionline.org, http://www.chionline.org. Circ: 5,000.

618.92 CAN ISSN 1205-5298
C P S NEWS. Text in English. 1954. bi-m. membership only. adv. bk.rev. **Document type:** *Newsletter.* **Description:** Promotes and highlights the accomplishments and activities of the society and its members. Provides members with information on services and coming events.
Formerly: Canadian Paediatric Society. News Bulletin (0831-7682)
Related titles: French ed.: Gazette S C P. ISSN 0831-7674.
Published by: Canadian Paediatric Society, 2204 Walkley Rd, Ste 100, Ottawa, ON K1G 4G8, Canada. TEL 613-526-9397, FAX 613-526-3332. Ed. Elizabeth Moreau. Adv. contact Paige Raymond. Circ: 2,500.

CADERNOS DE POS-GRADUACAO EM DISTURBIOS DO DESENVOLVIMENTO. *see* MEDICAL SCIENCES—Psychiatry And Neurology

CANADIAN ACADEMY OF CHILD AND ADOLESCENT PSYCHIATRY. JOURNAL. *see* MEDICAL SCIENCES—Psychiatry And Neurology

618.92 CAN ISSN 1199-7044
CANADIAN PAEDIATRIC SOCIETY. ANNUAL REPORT. Text in English. a. **Document type:** *Corporate.*
Related titles: French ed.: Societe Canadienne de Pediatrie. Rapport Annuel. ISSN 1191-1980.
Published by: Canadian Paediatric Society, 2204 Walkley Rd, Ste 100, Ottawa, ON K1G 4G8, Canada. TEL 613-526-9397, FAX 613-526-3332.

618.92 ESP ISSN 1131-6128
CANARIAS PEDIATRICA. Text in Spanish. 1966. s-a. free to qualified personnel. adv. bk.rev. charts; illus. **Document type:** *Journal, Academic/Scholarly.*
Formerly (until 1991): Sociedad Canaria de Pediatria. Boletin (0037-8410)
Related titles: Online - full text ed.
—CCC.
Published by: Sociedad Canaria de Pediatria, Avda Universidad 27, La Laguna, Santa Cruz 38205, Spain. TEL 34-922-678000, FAX 34-922-319307. Ed. Victor Manuel Garcia Nieto. Circ: 1,000.

618.92 USA ISSN 2090-6803
▼ ➤ **CASE REPORTS IN PEDIATRICS.** Text in German. 2011. **Document type:** *Journal, Academic/Scholarly.* **Description:** Publishes case reports in all areas of pediatrics.
Related titles: Online - full text ed.: ISSN 2090-6811. 2011. free (effective 2011).
Published by: Hindawi Publishing Corporation, 410 Park Ave, 15th Fl, PMB 287, New York, NY 10022. FAX 215-893-4392, 866-446-3294, info@hindawi.com.

618.92 CZE ISSN 0069-2328
CODEN: CEPEA3
➤ **CESKO-SLOVENSKA PEDIATRIE/CZECHO-SLOVAK PEDIATRICS.** Key Title: Ceskoslovenska Pediatrie. Text in Czech, Slovak; Summaries in Czech, English. 1945. m. CZK 1,032, EUR 51.60 (effective 2010). adv. bk.rev. abstr. **Document type:** *Journal, Academic/Scholarly.* **Description:** Presents original papers, research results, case reports, review articles, reports on the new books and congresses from the field of general pediatrics and specialized pediatric disciplines.
Formerly: Pediatrice Listy
Related titles: Online - full text ed.
Indexed: A01, A22, CDA, ChemAb, DentInd, F09, IndMed, P30, R10, Reac, SCOPUS.
—BLDSC (3122.480000), CASDDS, GNLM, IE, Infotrieve, Ingenta, INIST. CCC.
Published by: (Ceska Lekarska Spolecnost J.E. Purkyne/Czech Medical Association), Nakladatelske Stredisko C L S J.E. Purkyne, Sokolska 31, Prague, 12026, Czech Republic. nts@cls.cz. Ed. Oldrich Pozler. adv.: B&W page CZK 38,700, color page CZK 50,300; 250 x 165. Circ: 4,200.

618.92 JPN
CHIBA DAIGAKU SHONI GEKA NENPO/CHIBA UNIVERSITY. SCHOOL OF MEDICINE. PEDIATRIC SURGICAL DEPARTMENT. ANNUAL REPORT. Text in Japanese. 1978. a.
Published by: Chiba Daigaku, Igakubu, 8-1 Inohana 1-chome, Chuo-ku, Chiba-shi, 260-0856, Japan.

618.92 362.7 AUS ISSN 1442-4886
CHILD & ADOLESCENT HEALTH CARE. Text in English. 1998. q. AUD 25 membership (effective 2006). bk.rev. back issues avail. **Document type:** *Newsletter, Consumer.* **Description:** Provides updates and information on pediatric health care, non-medical and psychosocial needs of children and adolescents in the health care system of Australia.
Published by: Association for the Welfare of Child Health, Gladesville Hospital, Bldg 7, Cnr Victoria & Punt Rd, Gladesville, NSW 2111, Australia. TEL 61-2-98172439, FAX 61-2-98794346, awch@awch.com.au. Ed. Anne Cutler. Circ: 400.

618.92 155.5 GBR ISSN 1740-1135
CHILD & ADOLESCENT MENTAL HEALTH IN PRIMARY CARE; for professionals working with children & adolescents. Text in English. 2003. q. **Document type:** *Journal, Academic/Scholarly.* **Description:** Publishes articles offering up-to-date information on clinical topics, including theory and clinical management.
—IE, Ingenta.
Published by: Primary Care Mental Health Education, The Old Stables, 2a Laurel Ave, Twickenham, Middx TW1 4JA, United Kingdom. TEL 44-20-88916593, FAX 44-20-88916729, info@primhe.org, http://www.primhe.org/. Eds. Dr. Margaret Thompson, Dr. Phil Hill.

618.92 616.89 USA ISSN 1056-4993
RJ499.A1 CODEN: CAPAF2
➤ **CHILD AND ADOLESCENT PSYCHIATRIC CLINICS OF NORTH AMERICA.** Text in English. 1992. q. USD 425 in United States to institutions; USD 513 elsewhere to institutions (effective 2012). adv. index. back issues avail.; reprints avail. **Document type:** *Journal, Academic/Scholarly.* **Description:** Delivers practical advice from experts in each specialty covered with a fresh perspective on problems and controversies.
Related titles: Microform ed.: (from PQC); Online - full text ed.: ISSN 1558-0490 (from ScienceDirect).
Indexed: A20, A22, CurCont, E-psyche, EMBASE, ExcerpMed, F09, FamI, INI, IndMed, MEDLINE, P03, P30, PsycInfo, PsycholAb, R10, Reac, SCOPUS, SSCI, W07.
—BLDSC (3172.913600), GNLM, IE, Infotrieve, Ingenta. CCC.
Published by: W.B. Saunders Co. (Subsidiary of: Elsevier Health Sciences), Elsevier, Health Sciences Division, Order Fulfillment, 3251 Riverport Ln, Maryland Heights, MO 63043. TEL 314-872-8370, 800-325-4177, FAX 314-432-1380, JournalCustomerService-usa@elsevier.com, http://www.us.elsevierhealth.com. Adv. contact Don Scholz TEL 215-239-3537.

➤ **CHILD & ADOLESCENT PSYCHIATRY ALERTS.** *see* MEDICAL SCIENCES—Psychiatry And Neurology

➤ **CHILD AND ADOLESCENT PSYCHOPHARMACOLOGY NEWS.** *see* MEDICAL SCIENCES—Psychiatry And Neurology

618.92 GBR ISSN 0305-1862
RJ101 CODEN: CCHDDH
➤ **CHILD: CARE, HEALTH AND DEVELOPMENT.** Text in English. 1975. bi-m. GBP 772 in United Kingdom to institutions; EUR 981 in Europe to institutions; USD 1,423 in the Americas to institutions; USD 1,662 elsewhere to institutions; GBP 889 combined subscription in United Kingdom to institutions (print & online eds.); EUR 1,128 combined subscription in Europe to institutions (print & online eds.); USD 1,637 combined subscription in the Americas to institutions (print & online eds.); USD 1,912 combined subscription elsewhere to institutions (print & online eds.) (effective 2012). adv. bk.rev. bibl.; charts; illus. index. back issues avail.; reprint service avail. from PSC. **Document type:** *Journal, Academic/Scholarly.* **Description:** Covers all aspects of the health and development of children and young people.
Incorporates (1995-2002): Ambulatory Child Health (1355-5626)
Related titles: Microform ed.: (from PQC); Online - full text ed.: ISSN 1365-2214. GBP 772 in United Kingdom to institutions; EUR 981 in Europe to institutions; USD 1,423 in the Americas to institutions; USD 1,662 elsewhere to institutions (effective 2012) (from IngentaConnect); Supplement(s): Child: Care, Health and Development (Supplement). ISSN 1478-1972.
Indexed: A01, A02, A03, A08, A20, A22, A26, A36, AMED, ASCA, ASSIA, Agr, AgrForAb, B21, B28, BDM&CN, BibAg, C06, C07, C08, C11, C28, CA, CABA, CDA, CINAHL, CMM, CurCont, D01, E-psyche, E01, E03, E07, E12, ECER, EMBASE, ERI, ESPM, ExcerpMed, F08, F09, FamI, GH, H&SSA, H04, H05, H12, I14, INI, IndMed, Inpharma, LT, MEDLINE, N02, N03, P02, P03, P04, P18, P30, P33, P34, P35, P43, P48, P50, P53, P54, P55, PAIS, PQC, PsycInfo, PsycholAb, R07, R10, R12, RA&MP, RM&VM, RRTA, Reac, RiskAb, S02, S03, SCI, SCOPUS, SOPODA, SSCI, SociolAb, T02, T05, TAR, VirolAbstr, W07, W11, YAE&RB.
—BLDSC (3172.925000), GNLM, IE, Infotrieve, Ingenta, INIST. CCC.
Published by: (B A A C H, European Society for Social Pediatrics, Swiss Paediatric Society CHE), Wiley-Blackwell Publishing Ltd. (Subsidiary of: John Wiley & Sons, Inc.), 9600 Garsington Rd, Oxford, OX4 2DQ, United Kingdom. TEL 44-1865-776868, FAX 44-1865-714591, customerservices@blackwellpublishing.com. Ed. Stuart Logan. Pub. Elaine Stott. R&P Sophie Savage. Adv. contact Craig Pickett TEL 44-1865-476267. Circ: 720.

➤ **CHILD CARE IN PRACTICE.** *see* CHILDREN AND YOUTH—About

➤ **CHILD DEVELOPMENT.** *see* CHILDREN AND YOUTH—About

618.92 ITA ISSN 2036-5888
▼ **CHILD DEVELOPMENT & DISABILITIES.** Text in Multiple languages. 2009. 3/yr.
Media: Online - full text.
Published by: Franco Angeli Edizioni, Viale Monza 106, Milan, 20127, Italy. TEL 39-02-2837141, FAX 39-02-26144793, redazioni@francoangeli.it, http://www.francoangeli.it.

▼ **CHILD HEALTH AND EDUCATION**; an interdisciplinary journal/revue interdisciplinaire. *see* CHILDREN AND YOUTH—About

CHILD PSYCHIATRY & HUMAN DEVELOPMENT. *see* MEDICAL SCIENCES—Psychiatry And Neurology

CHILDREN & SOCIETY; the international journal of childhood and children's services. *see* CHILDREN AND YOUTH—About

CHILDREN'S NURSERIES U K MARKET REPORT (YEAR). *see* BUSINESS AND ECONOMICS—Production Of Goods And Services

618.92 USA
THE CHILD'S DOCTOR (ONLINE). Text in English. 1983. s-a. **Document type:** *Journal, Academic/Scholarly.*
Formerly: The Child's Doctor (Print) (0882-2301)
Media: Online - full text.
Published by: Children's Memorial Hospital, 2300 Children's Plz, Chicago, IL 60614. TEL 773-880-4000, 800-543-7362, KIDSDOC@childrensmemorial.org, http://www.childrensmemorial.org/default.asp. Eds. Vita Lerman, Dr. Edward S Ogata.

CHILD'S NERVOUS SYSTEM. *see* MEDICAL SCIENCES—Psychiatry And Neurology

CHILD'S PLAY. *see* CHILDREN AND YOUTH—About

CHIROPRACTIC PEDIATRICS (GAINESVILLE). *see* MEDICAL SCIENCES—Chiropractic, Homeopathy, Osteopathy

CIRUGIA PEDIATRICA. *see* MEDICAL SCIENCES—Surgery

618.92 NZL ISSN 1179-5565
➤ **CLINICAL MEDICINE INSIGHTS: PEDIATRICS.** Text in English. 2008. irreg. free (effective 2011). **Document type:** *Journal, Academic/Scholarly.* **Description:** Contains manuscripts on all aspects of the diagnosis, management and prevention of disorders specific to children and adolescents, in addition to related genetic, pathophysiological and epidemiological topics.
Formerly (until 2010): Clinical Medicine: Pediatrics (1178-220X)
Media: Online - full text.
Indexed: A01, C06, C07, P30, T02.
—CCC.
Published by: Libertas Academica Ltd., PO Box 300-874, Mairangi Bay, Auckland, 0751, New Zealand. TEL 64-9-4763930, FAX 64-9-3531397, enquiries@la-press.com. Ed. Pietro Galassetti.

618.92 616.02 USA ISSN 1522-8401
RJ370 CODEN: CPEMBG
CLINICAL PEDIATRIC EMERGENCY MEDICINE. Abbreviated title: C P E M. Text in English. 1999. q. USD 289 in United States to institutions; USD 382 elsewhere to institutions (effective 2012). adv. back issues avail.; reprints avail. **Document type:** *Journal, Academic/Scholarly.* **Description:** Devoted to helping pediatricians and emergency physicians provide the best possible care for their young patients.
Related titles: Online - full text ed.: ISSN 1558-2310 (from ScienceDirect).
Indexed: A26, C06, C07, CA, EMBASE, ExcerpMed, I05, P30, R10, Reac, SCOPUS, T02.
—BLDSC (3286.324370), IE, Ingenta. CCC.
Published by: W.B. Saunders Co. (Subsidiary of: Elsevier Health Sciences), Elsevier, Health Sciences Division, Order Fulfillment, 3251 Riverport Ln, Maryland Heights, MO 63043. TEL 314-872-8370, 800-325-4177, FAX 314-432-1380, JournalCustomerService-usa@elsevier.com, http://www.us.elsevierhealth.com. Ed. Steven E Krug. Pub. Theresa Monturano. Adv. contact Hank Blaney TEL 212-633-3648.

618.92 616.4 JPN ISSN 0918-5739
RJ418 CODEN: CPENFN
CLINICAL PEDIATRIC ENDOCRINOLOGY. Text in English, Japanese. 1989. s-a. adv. **Document type:** *Journal, Academic/Scholarly.* **Description:** Serves as the official journal for the society. Includes case reports and clinical investigations.
Related titles: Online - full content ed.: ISSN 1347-7358. 1998. free (effective 2011); Online - full text ed.
Indexed: A01, EMBASE, ExcerpMed, R10, Reac, SCOPUS.
—BLDSC (3286.324400), IE, Ingenta. CCC.
Published by: Nihon Shoninaibunpi Gakkai/Japanese Society for Pediatric Endocrinology, c/o IPEC, Inc., 1-24-11 Sugamo, Toshima-ku, Tokyo, 170-0002, Japan. TEL 81-3-53959610, FAX 81-3-59784068, 003@ipec-pub.co.jp. Ed. Susumu Yokoya.

618.92 USA ISSN 0009-9228
RJ1 CODEN: CPEDAM
➤ **CLINICAL PEDIATRICS.** Text in English. 1962. m. USD 898, GBP 528 combined subscription to institutions (print & online eds.); USD 880, GBP 517 to institutions (effective 2011). adv. illus. Index. 3 cols./p.; back issues avail.; reprint service avail. from PSC. **Document type:** *Journal, Academic/Scholarly.* **Description:** For practitioners in all areas of child care. Contains articles on pediatric practice, clinical research, behavioral and educational problems, community health and subspecialty or affiliated specialty applications.
Formed by the merger of (1884-1962): Archives of Pediatrics (0096-6630); (1946-1962): Quarterly Review of Pediatrics (0097-0107); (1950-1962): American Practitioner (0517-4465); Which was formerly (until 1961): American Practitioner and Digest of Treatment (0097-658X)
Related titles: Microform ed.: (from PQC); Online - full text ed.: ISSN 1938-2707. USD 808, GBP 475 to institutions (effective 2011).

dexed: A01, A02, A03, A08, A20, A22, A26, A29, A34, A36, A37, AIM, ASCA, Agr, AgrForAb, B20, B21, BDM&CN, BIOBASE, C06, C07, C08, CA, CABA, CCIP, CDA, CINAHL, CTA, ChemAb, ChemoAb, CurCont, D01, DentInd, E-psyche, E01, E03, E07, E08, E12, EMBASE, ERI, ESPM, ExcerpMed, F08, F09, F12, FR, FamI, G08, GH, H04, H11, H12, H13, H17, HospLI, I05, I10, IABS, IDIS, INI, ISR, IndMed, Inpharma, LT, M01, M02, MEDLINE, MS&D, N02, N03, NRN, NSA, P03, P10, P20, P22, P24, P25, P26, P30, P33, P34, P35, P37, P39, P48, P50, P53, P54, PQC, PsycholAb, R08, R11, R12, RA&MP, RM&VM, RRTA, S02, S03, S09, SCI, SCOPUS, SoyAb, T02, T05, VS, VirolAbstr, W07, W10, W11.
-BLDSC (3286.325000), GNLM, IE, Infotrieve, Ingenta, INIST, Linda Hall. **CCC.**
ublished by: Sage Publications, Inc., 2455 Teller Rd, Thousand Oaks, CA 91320. TEL 805-499-9774, 800-818-7243, FAX 805-499-0871, 800-583-2665, info@sagepub.com, http://www.sagepub.com. Ed. Dr. Russell W Steele. Circ: 9,000.

618.92 ESP ISSN 0186-159X
LINICAS PEDIATRICAS DE NORTEAMERICA. Text in Spanish. 1964. bi-m. charts; illus. index. **Document type:** *Directory, Academic/ Scholarly.*
elated titles: ◆ English ed.: Pediatric Clinics of North America. ISSN 0031-3955.
ublished by: Elsevier Doyma (Subsidiary of: Elsevier Health Sciences), Traversa de Gracia 17-21, Barcelona, 08021, Spain. TEL 34-932-418800, FAX 34-932-419020, doyma@doyma.es, http://www.doyma.es.

612 GBR ISSN 0069-4835
RJ1 CODEN: CDVMAG
LINICS IN DEVELOPMENTAL MEDICINE. Text in English. 1959. irreg. back issues avail. **Document type:** *Monographic series, Academic/ Scholarly.* **Description:** Provides a comprehensive study of the theoretical and clinical aspects of a specific childhood condition or disorder.
ndexed: A22, E-psyche, FR.
-BLDSC (3286.550000), GNLM, IE, Infotrieve, Ingenta, INIST. **CCC.**
ublished by: Mac Keith Press, 6 Market Rd, London, N7 9PW, United Kingdom. TEL 44-20-76197199, FAX 44-20-76197207, allat@mackeith.co.uk.

LINICS IN MOTHER AND CHILD HEALTH. *see* MEDICAL SCIENCES—Obstetrics And Gynecology

617 TUR ISSN 1305-5194
CODEN: PCEDE
OCUK CERRAHISI DERGISI/PEDIATRIC SURGERY. Text in Turkish; Summaries in English. 1987. 3/yr. USD 45 (effective 2009). adv. **Document type:** *Journal, Academic/Scholarly.*
ormerly (until 2005): Pediatrik Cerrahi Dergisi/Pediatric Surgery (1016-5142)
elated titles: Online - full text ed.
ndexed: P30, R10, Reac, SCOPUS.
ublished by: (Turkiye Cocuk Cerrahisi Dernegi), Logos Yayincilik Ticaret A.S., Yildiz Posta Cad., Sinan Apt. No.36 D 66-67, Gayrettepe, Istanbul, 34349, Turkey. TEL 90-212-2885022, 90-212-2880541, FAX 90-212-2116185, logos@logos.com.tr, info@logos.com.tr. Ed. Dr. Cenk Buyukunal. Adv. contact Sukran Oznalga.

618.92 TUR ISSN 1302-9940
OCUK DERGISI/JOURNAL OF THE CHILD. Text in Turkish. 2001. m. **Document type:** *Journal, Academic/Scholarly.*
elated titles: Online - full text ed.: free (effective 2009).
ndexed: A01, T02.
ublished by: Logos Yayincilik Ticaret A.S., Yildiz Posta Cad., Sinan Apt. No.36 D 66-67, Gayrettepe, Istanbul, 34349, Turkey. TEL 90-212-2885022, 90-212-2880541, FAX 90-212-2116185, logos@logos.com.tr, info@logos.com.tr.

618.92 616 TUR ISSN 1307-1068
➤ **COCUK ENFEKSIYON DERGISI/JOURNAL OF PEDIATRIC INFECTIONS.** Text in Turkish. 2007. q. **Document type:** *Journal, Academic/Scholarly.*
elated titles: Online - full text ed.: ISSN 1308-5271. free (effective 2011); Supplement(s):.
ndexed: A26, C06, C07, CA, EMBASE, ExcerpMed, H12, I05, R10, Reac, SCOPUS, T02.
ublished by: (Uludag Universitesi, Tip Fakultesi/Uludag University, Faculty of Medicine), Aves Yayincilik, Kizilelma Cad 5/3, Findikazade, Istanbul, 34096, Turkey. TEL 90-212-5890053, FAX 90-212-5890094, info@avesyayincilik.com, http://www.avesyayincilik.com. Eds. Mehmet Ceyhan, Mustafa Hacimustaoglu.

618.92 TUR ISSN 0010-0161
RJ1 CODEN: CSHDAO
➤ **COCUK SAGLIGI VE HASTALIKLARI DERGISI.** Text in Turkish; Summaries in English. 1958. q. free (effective 2008). adv. bk.rev. abstr.; bibl.; charts; illus. index. **Document type:** *Journal, Academic/ Scholarly.*
elated titles: Online - full text ed.: free (effective 2011).
ndexed: A01, A22, A34, A36, B25, BIOSIS Prev, CA, CABA, D01, E12, EMBASE, ExcerpMed, GH, H17, IndVet, LT, MycolAb, N02, N03, P33, P37, P39, R08, R10, R12, RM&VM, Reac, S12, SCOPUS, SoyAb, T02, T05, VS.
—BLDSC (3292.760800), GNLM, IE, Ingenta.
Published by: International Children's Center (I C C)/Uluslararasi Cocuk Sagligi Merkezi, Bilkent University, Main Campus, Library Bldg, Bilkent, Ankara, 06800, Turkey. TEL 90-312-2902366, FAX 90-312-2664678, icc@icc.org.tr, http://www.icc.org.tr. Ed. Dr. Murat Yurdakok. Circ: 1,500. **Co-sponsors:** Hacettepe Universitesi, Institute of Child Health; Turkish National Pediatric Society.

618 ARG ISSN 1667-9148
COLECCION TRABAJOS DISTINGUIDOS. SERIE PEDIATRIA. Text in Spanish. 1998. 6/yr. back issues avail. **Document type:** *Journal, Academic/Scholarly.*
Media: Online - full text.
Published by: Sociedad Iberoamericana de Informacion Cientifica (S I I C), Ave Belgrano 430, Buenos Aires, C1092AAR, Argentina. TEL 54-11-43424901, FAX 54-11-43313305, atencionallector@siicsalud.com, http://www.siicsalud.com. Ed. Rafael Bernal Castro.

618.92 CAN ISSN 1715-9326
COMMENT S I P P E' RENDRE?. (Services Integres en Perinatalite et pour la Petite Enfance) Text in French. 2004. 3/yr. **Document type:** *Bulletin, Trade.*
Formerly (until 2005): Services Integres. Bulletin (1910-0132)
Published by: Agence de Developpement de Reseaux Locaux de Sante et de Services Sociaux de Montreal, Direction de Sante Publique, Centre de documentation, a/s Sossee Zerdelian, 1301, rue Sherbrooke Est, Montreal, PQ H2L 1M3, Canada. TEL 514-528-2400, SZerdeli@santepub-mtl.qc.ca.

618 ARG ISSN 1851-5037
CONEXION PEDIATRICA. Text in Spanish. 2008. q.
Media: Online - full text.
Published by: Hospital Italiano de Buenos Aires, Departamento de Pediatria, Gascon 450, Buenos Aires, C1181ACH, Argentina. TEL 54-11-49590200, conexion.pediatrica@hospitalitaliano.org.ar, http://www.hospitalitaliano.org.ar/. Ed. Carmen De Cunto.

CONGENITAL CARDIOLOGY TODAY. *see* MEDICAL SCIENCES—Cardiovascular Diseases

CONGENITAL HEART DISEASE; clinical studies from fetus to adulthood. *see* MEDICAL SCIENCES—Cardiovascular Diseases

618.92 USA ISSN 1545-8539
➤ **CONSULTANT FOR PEDIATRICIANS.** Text in English. 2002 (Mar.). m. USD 80 domestic; USD 90 foreign; free to qualified personnel (effective 2009). adv. back issues avail.; reprints avail. **Document type:** *Journal, Academic/Scholarly.* **Description:** Features review articles that describe the state-of-the-art on diagnosis and management.
Related titles: Online - full text ed.
Indexed: A26, G08, H11, H12, I05, T02.
—CCC.
Published by: C M P Medica LLC (Subsidiary of: United Business Media Limited), 535 Connecticut Ave, Ste 300, Norwalk, CT 06854. TEL 203-523-7000, FAX 203-662-6420, subscriptions@cmpmedica.com, http://www.cmpmedica.com. adv.: B&W page USD 3,925, color page USD 4,585. Circ: 63,081.

618.92 USA ISSN 8750-0507
RJ1 CODEN: PRADER
➤ **CONTEMPORARY PEDIATRICS**; practical information for today's pediatrician. Text in English. 1984. m. USD 89 domestic; USD 105 foreign; USD 17 newsstand/cover domestic; USD 21 newsstand/ cover in Canada & Mexico; USD 23 newsstand/cover elsewhere (effective 2011). adv. charts; illus.; stat. index. back issues avail.; reprints avail. **Document type:** *Journal, Trade.* **Description:** Contains clinical articles on prevention, diagnosis and treatment of illness from infancy through young adulthood; also reports on important trends in pediatric practices, including innovations in practice management.
Related titles: Microform ed.: (from PQC, RPI); Online - full text ed.: ISSN 2150-6345.
Indexed: A22, A26, C06, C07, C08, CA, CCIP, CINAHL, E08, FamI, G06, G07, G08, H11, H12, I05, NRN, P30, S09, S23, SCOPUS, T02.
—BLDSC (3425.197900), GNLM, IE, Infotrieve, Ingenta. **CCC.**
Published by: Advanstar Communications, Inc., 6200 Canoga Ave, 2nd Fl, Woodland Hills, CA 91367. TEL 818-593-5000, FAX 818-593-5020, info@advanstar.com, http://www.advanstar.com. Ed. Toby Jane Hindin TEL 212-951-6628. Adv. contact Steve Farrell TEL 201-690-5462. B&W page USD 4,085, color page USD 6,990.

➤ **CRITICAL ISSUES IN DEVELOPMENTAL & BEHAVIORAL PEDIATRICS.** *see* PSYCHOLOGY

616 ESP ISSN 1989-9793
CUADERNOS DE PEDIATRIA SOCIAL. Text in Spanish. 2003. 3/yr. **Document type:** *Journal, Academic/Scholarly.*
Media: Online - full text.
Published by: Asociacion Espanola de Pediatria, Seccion de Pediatria Social, C Alcalde Sainz de Baranda, 34, Madrid, 28009, Spain. TEL 34-91-5044256. Ed. Jesus Garcia Perez.

618.92 USA ISSN 1944-6004
RJ1
CURRENT DIAGNOSIS & TREATMENT PEDIATRICS. Text in English. 1970. irreg., latest 2010, 20th ed. USD 74.95 per vol. (effective 2011). back issues avail. **Document type:** *Monographic series, Trade.* **Description:** Offers practical, up-to-date, well-referenced coverage of the care of children from birth through infancy and adolescence in an easy-to-use, find-it-now presentation.
Formerly (until 2009): Current Pediatric Diagnosis and Treatment (0093-8556)
Related titles: CD-ROM ed.
Published by: McGraw-Hill Education (Subsidiary of: McGraw-Hill Companies, Inc.), 148 Princeton-Hightstown Rd, Hightstown, NJ 08520. TEL 609-426-5793, FAX 609-426-7917, customer.service@mcgraw-hill.com, http://www.mheducation.com/.

618.92 USA ISSN 1940-0691
CURRENT ESSENTIALS OF PEDIATRICS. Text in English. 2007 (Dec.). irreg., latest 2007, 1st ed. USD 39.95 1st ed. (effective 2008). **Document type:** *Monographic series, Trade.* **Description:** Provides synoptic information for 600 common or important diseases and syndromes seen in children, from birth through infancy and adolescence.
Related titles: Online - full text ed.: USD 34.95 per issue (effective 2008).
Published by: McGraw-Hill Companies, Inc., 1221 Ave of the Americas, 43rd fl, New York, NY 10020. TEL 212-512-2000, customer.service@mcgraw-hill.com, http://www.mcgraw-hill.com.

618.92 USA ISSN 1040-8703
RJ1 CODEN: COPEE9
CURRENT OPINION IN PEDIATRICS. Text in English. 1989. bi-m. USD 917 domestic to institutions; USD 918 foreign to institutions (effective 2011). adv. bibl.; illus. back issues avail.; reprints avail. **Document type:** *Journal, Academic/Scholarly.* **Description:** Covers key subjects such as hematology and oncology, orthopedics, infectious disease and immunization, office pediatrics, neonatology and perinatology etc.
Related titles: Online - full text ed.: ISSN 1531-698X. USD 224 to individuals (effective 2011); Optical Disk - DVD ed.: Current Opinion in Pediatrics, with Evaluated MEDLINE. ISSN 1080-8116. 1995; Supplement(s): Current Opinion in Pediatrics. Current World Literature. ISSN 1074-5572. 1994.
Indexed: A22, BIOSIS Prev, C06, C07, C08, CINAHL, CurCont, E01, EMBASE, ExcerpMed, F09, INI, IndMed, Inpharma, MEDLINE, MycolAb, P30, R10, Reac, SCI, SCOPUS, W07.
—BLDSC (3500.776800), GNLM, IE, Infotrieve, Ingenta, INIST. **CCC.**
Published by: Lippincott Williams & Wilkins (Subsidiary of: Wolters Kluwer N.V.), 530 Walnut St, Philadelphia, PA 19106. TEL 215-521-8300, FAX 215-521-8902, customerservice@lww.com, http://www.lww.com. Ed. Richard B Johnston Jr. Pub. Ian Burgess. Circ: 543.

618.92 IND ISSN 0971-9032
➤ **CURRENT PEDIATRIC RESEARCH**; international journal of pediatrics. Text in English. 1997. s-a. INR 3,000 domestic to institutions; USD 150 foreign to institutions (effective 2011). adv. bk.rev. 100 p./no.; back issues avail. **Document type:** *Journal, Academic/Scholarly.* **Description:** Publishes original research work in all major disciplines of pediatrics.
Related titles: Online - full text ed.
Indexed: A36, C06, C07, CA, CABA, D01, EMBASE, ExcerpMed, GH, N02, N03, P33, R10, R12, Reac, SCOPUS, T02, T05.
—BLDSC (3500.870000). **CCC.**
Published by: Scientific Publishers, 5-A, New Pali Rd, PO Box 91, Jodhpur, Rajasthan 342 001, India. TEL 91-291-2433323, FAX 91-291-2624154, info@scientificpub.com, http://www.scientificpub.com. Eds. Abdulrahman Al-Frayh, Vishnu Bhat.

618.92 NLD ISSN 1573-3963
RJ1
➤ **CURRENT PEDIATRIC REVIEWS.** Text in English. 2005 (Jan). q. USD 480 to institutions (print or online ed.) (effective 2012). adv. back issues avail.; reprints avail. **Document type:** *Journal, Academic/ Scholarly.* **Description:** Publishes frontier reviews on all the latest advances in pediatric medicine.
Related titles: Online - full text ed.: ISSN 1875-6336 (from IngentaConnect).
Indexed: A01, B20, B21, C06, C07, CA, EMBASE, ESPM, ExcerpMed, ImmunAb, NSA, R10, Reac, SCOPUS, T02, VirolAbstr.
—IE, Ingenta. **CCC.**
Published by: Bentham Science Publishers Ltd., PO Box 294, Bussum, 1400 AG, Netherlands. TEL 31-35-6923800, FAX 31-35-6980150, sales@bentham.org, http://www.bentham.org. Ed. Anne Greenough.
Subscr. to: Bentham Science Publishers Ltd., c/o Richard E Morrissy, PO Box 446, Oak Park, IL 60301. TEL 312-413-5867, FAX 312-996-7107, subscriptions@bentham.org.

618.92 USA ISSN 1934-5119
RJ52
CURRENT PEDIATRIC THERAPY. Text in English. 1964. biennial, latest 2006, 18th ed. USD 125 per issue (effective 2010). adv. back issues avail.; reprints avail. **Document type:** *Monographic series, Trade.* **Description:** Provides with the recent advances in therapeutic care which includes medical and surgical therapies, preventive medicine, adolescent gynecology, and behavioral issues.
Former titles (until 2006): Gellis & Kagan's Current Pediatric Therapy (1069-2460); (until 1993): Current Pediatric Therapy (0070-2021)
Related titles: Online - full text ed.
—CCC.
Published by: W.B. Saunders Co. (Subsidiary of: Elsevier Health Sciences), Elsevier, Health Sciences Division, Order Fulfillment, 3251 Riverport Ln, Maryland Heights, MO 63043. TEL 314-872-8370, 800-325-4177, FAX 314-432-1380, JournalCustomerService-usa@elsevier.com, http://www.us.elsevierhealth.com.

618.92 USA ISSN 1538-5442
➤ **CURRENT PROBLEMS IN PEDIATRIC AND ADOLESCENT HEALTH CARE.** Text in English. 1970. 10/yr. USD 290 in United States to institutions; USD 332 elsewhere to institutions (effective 2012). adv. illus. cum.index. back issues avail.; reprints avail. **Document type:** *Journal, Academic/Scholarly.* **Description:** Provides monthly monographic clinical reviews from authorities in the field, intended for practitioners.
Formerly (until 2001): Current Problems in Pediatrics (0045-9380)
Related titles: Microform ed.: (from PQC); Online - full text ed.: ISSN 1538-3199 (from ScienceDirect).
Indexed: A22, A26, AMHA, C06, C07, CA, EMBASE, ExcerpMed, I05, IndMed, MEDLINE, P30, R10, Reac, SCOPUS, T02.
—BLDSC (3501.390100), GNLM, IE, Ingenta, INIST. **CCC.**
Published by: Mosby, Inc. (Subsidiary of: Elsevier Health Sciences), 1600 John F. Kennedy Blvd, Ste 1800, Philadelphia, PA 19103. TEL 215-239-3900, 800-523-1649, FAX 215-239-3990, elspcs@elsevier.com, http://www.us.elsevierhealth.com. Ed. Arthur H Fierman. Pub. Pamela Poppalardo TEL 212-633-3911.

618.92 SVK ISSN 1335-0838
➤ **DETSKY LEKAR.** Text in Slovak. 1994. q. EUR 8 (effective 2009). **Document type:** *Journal, Academic/Scholarly.*
Published by: (Slovenska Pediatricka Spolocnost), Samedi s.r.o., Racianska 20, Bratislava, 839 27, Slovakia. TEL 421-2-55645901, FAX 421-2-55645902, samedi@samedi.sk. Ed. Eva Ochabova.

618.92 616.8 GBR ISSN 0012-1622
RJ1 CODEN: DMCNAW
➤ **DEVELOPMENTAL MEDICINE AND CHILD NEUROLOGY.** Abbreviated title: D M C N. Text in English. 1958. m. GBP 332 in United Kingdom to institutions; EUR 422 in Europe to institutions; USD 583 in the Americas to institutions; USD 713 elsewhere to institutions; GBP 383 combined subscription in United Kingdom to institutions (print & online eds.); EUR 485 combined subscription in Europe to institutions (print & online eds.); USD 670 combined subscription in the Americas to institutions (print & online eds.); USD 820 combined subscription elsewhere to institutions (print & online eds.) (effective 2012). bk.rev.; software rev. abstr. 72 p./no. 2 cols./p.; back issues avail.; reprint service avail. from PSC. **Document type:** *Journal, Academic/Scholarly.* **Description:** Covers a wide range of clinical topics involving diseases and neurological disabilities of children.
Formerly (until 1962): Cerebral Palsy Bulletin
Related titles: Microfilm ed.: (from PQC); Online - full text ed.: ISSN 1469-8749. GBP 332 in United Kingdom to institutions; EUR 422 in Europe to institutions; USD 583 in the Americas to institutions; USD 713 elsewhere to institutions (effective 2012) (from IngentaConnect); Supplement(s): ISSN 0419-0238.

Indexed: A01, A03, A08, A20, A22, A26, A36, AMED, ASCA, B21, B25, B28, BDM&CN, BIOBASE, BIOSIS Prev, BibInd, C06, C07, C08, CA, CABA, CDA, CINAHL, Cadscan, CurCont, D01, DSHAb, DentInd, DokArb, E-psyche, E01, ECER, EMBASE, ExcerpMed, F09, FR, FamI, G08, GH, H11, H12, IABS, ISR, IndMed, Inpharma, LT, LeadAb, MEDLINE, MLA-IB, MRefA, MS&D, MycolAb, N02, N03, NRN, NSA, NSCI, P03, P20, P22, P24, P25, P26, P30, P33, P35, P39, P48, P54, PQC, PsycInfo, PsycholAb, R08, R10, R12, RRTA, Reac, RehabLit, SCI, SCOPUS, SoyAb, T02, T05, W07, W11, Zincscan.
—BLDSC (3579.055000), GNLM, IE, Infotrieve, Ingenta, INIST. **CCC.**
Published by: (American Academy for Cerebral Palsy and Developmental Medicine USA), Mac Keith Press, 6 Market Rd, London, N7 9PW, United Kingdom. TEL 44-20-76197199, FAX 44-20-76197207, allat@mackeith.co.uk. Eds. Hilary M Hart, Peter Baxter. **Subscr. to:** Wiley-Blackwell Publishing Ltd. **Co-sponsor:** British Paediatric Neurology Association.

➤ **DEVELOPMENTAL NEUROREHABILITATION.** *see* MEDICAL SCIENCES—Physical Medicine And Rehabilitation

618.92 DEU
DOCUMENTA PAEDIATRIE. Text in German. 1976. irreg., latest vol.21, 1994. EUR 12 newsstand/cover (effective 2005). **Document type:** *Monographic series, Academic/Scholarly.*
Published by: Hansisches Verlagskontor, Mengstr 16, Luebeck, 23552, Germany. TEL 49-451-703101, FAX 49-451-7031253, http://www.beleke.de/verlagsgruppe/ind_hvk.html.

618.92 575 AUS ISSN 1833-0606
DOWN SYNDROME RESEARCH TODAY. Text in English. 2004. m. free (effective 2008). adv. back issues avail. **Document type:** *Journal, Consumer.* **Description:** Contains the latest research about down syndrome, including details about education, symptoms, treatment, information.
Media: Online - full text.
Published by: Research Today Publications ad@researchtoday.net, http://www.researchtoday.net.

DUCTUS. *see* MEDICAL SCIENCES—Cardiovascular Diseases

618.92 GBR ISSN 2045-5003
E S P E NEWSLETTER (ONLINE). (European Society for Paediatric Endocrinology) Text in English. 2005. s-a. free (effective 2010). back issues avail. **Document type:** *Newsletter, Trade.* **Description:** Aims to promote the highest levels of knowledge, research, education and clinical practice of paediatric endocrinology and metabolism throughout the world.
Formerly (until 2010): E S P E newsletter (Print) (2045-4996)
Media: Online - full text.
Published by: BioScientifica Ltd., Euro House, 22 Apex Ct, Woodlands, Bradley Stoke, Bristol, BS32 4JT, United Kingdom. TEL 44-1454-642246, FAX 44-1454-642222, info@bioscientifica.com, http://www.bioscientifica.com. Ed. Jesus Argente.

EARLY CHILD DEVELOPMENT AND CARE. *see* CHILDREN AND YOUTH—About

EARLY HUMAN DEVELOPMENT. *see* MEDICAL SCIENCES—Obstetrics And Gynecology

618.92 EGY ISSN 1110-6638
EGYPTIAN PAEDIATRIC ASSOCIATION. GAZETTE. Text in English. 1945. q. **Document type:** *Journal, Academic/Scholarly.*
Indexed: P30.
Published by: Egyptian Pediatric Association, Children Hospital, Mounira, Cario, Egypt. TEL 20-2-3646718, http://www.gazped.eg.net. Ed. Dr. Salah Ahmad Shuhayeb.

ELTERN-INFO. *see* CHILDREN AND YOUTH—About

618.92 FRA ISSN 1245-1789
➤ **ENCYCLOPEDIE MEDICO-CHIRURGICALE. PEDIATRIA/ ENCYCLOPEDIE MEDICO-QUIRURGICA. PEDIATRIA.** Cover title: Tratado de Pediatria. Text in Spanish. 1998. 7 base vols. plus q. updates. EUR 1,311.83 (effective 2003). bibl.; charts; illus. **Document type:** *Academic/Scholarly.* **Description:** Offers Spanish-speaking pediatricians a comprehensive and up-to-date reference for diagnosing and treating childhood ailments.
Related titles: ◆ French ed.: Encyclopedie Medico-Chirurgicale. Pediatrie. ISSN 0246-0513.
Published by: Elsevier Masson (Subsidiary of: Elsevier Health Sciences), 62 Rue Camille Desmoulins, Issy les Moulineaux, Cedex 92442, France. TEL 33-1-71165500, FAX 33-1-71165600, infos@elsevier-masson.fr, http://www.elsevier-masson.fr.

618.92 FRA ISSN 0246-0513
➤ **ENCYCLOPEDIE MEDICO-CHIRURGICALE. PEDIATRIE.** Cover title: Traite de Pediatrie. Variant title: Encyclopedie Medico-Chirurgicale, Instantanes Medicaux. Pediatrie. Receuil Periodique de l'Encyclopedie Medico-Chirurgicale. Pediatrie. Text in French. 1960. 7 base vols. plus q. updates. EUR 1,577 (effective 2006). bibl.; charts; illus. **Document type:** *Academic/Scholarly.* **Description:** Offers pediatricians a comprehensive and up-to-date reference for diagnosing and treating diseases and conditions in their young patients.
Formed by the merger of (1950-1960): Encyclopedie Medico-Chirurgicale. Pediatrie, La Seconde Enfance (0246-0505); (1934-1960): Encyclopedie Medico-Chirurgicale. Pediatrie, La Premiere Enfance (0246-0491); Which was formerly (until 1949): Encyclopedie Medico-Chirurgicale. Pediatrie (0246-0483)
Related titles: Online - full text ed.; ◆ Spanish ed.: Encyclopedie Medico-Chirurgicale. Pediatria. ISSN 1245-1789.
—INIST.
Published by: Elsevier Masson (Subsidiary of: Elsevier Health Sciences), 62 Rue Camille Desmoulins, Issy les Moulineaux, Cedex 92442, France. TEL 33-1-71165500, FAX 33-1-71165600, infos@elsevier-masson.fr.

➤ **ENDOCRINE DEVELOPMENT.** *see* MEDICAL SCIENCES—Endocrinology

➤ **ENFANCE;** psychologie, pedagogie, neuro-psychiatrie, sociologie. *see* CHILDREN AND YOUTH—About

618.92 615 CHN ISSN 1672-108X
ERKE YAOXUE ZAZHI/JOURNAL OF PEDIATRIC PHARMACY. Text in Chinese. 1999. bi-m. USD 21.60 (effective 2009).
Formerly (until 2002): Erke Yaoxue/Journal of Pediatric Pharmacy (1009-6884)
Related titles: Online - full text ed.
—BLDSC (3810.168000), East View, IE.
Published by: Chongqing Yike Daxue, Ertong Yiyuan/Children's Hospital of Chongqing University of Medical Sciences, Yuzhong-qu, 136, Zhongshan Erlu, Chongqing, 400014, China. TEL 86-23-63626877, FAX 86-23-63626877. Ed. Ting-yu Li. **Dist. by:** China International Book Trading Corp, 35 Chegongzhuang Xilu, Haidian District, PO Box 399, Beijing 100044, China. TEL 86-10-68412045, FAX 86-10-68412023, cibtc@mail.cibtc.com.cn, http://www.cibtc.com.cn.

EUROPAEISCHER ARBEITSKREIS FUER PRAE- UND POSTNATALE ENTWICKLUNGSFORSCHUNG. SCHRIFTENREIHE. *see* MEDICAL SCIENCES—Obstetrics And Gynecology

EUROPEAN ARCHIVES OF PAEDIATRIC DENTISTRY. *see* MEDICAL SCIENCES—Dentistry

EUROPEAN JOURNAL OF PAEDIATRIC DENTISTRY. *see* MEDICAL SCIENCES—Dentistry

618.92 GBR ISSN 1090-3798
RJ486 CODEN: EJPNFO
EUROPEAN JOURNAL OF PAEDIATRIC NEUROLOGY. Text in English. 1997. bi-m. EUR 590 in Europe to institutions; JPY 63,500 in Japan to institutions; USD 525 elsewhere to institutions (effective 2012). back issues avail.; reprints avail. **Document type:** *Journal, Academic/Scholarly.* **Description:** Offers articles on clinical and experimental research.
Related titles: Online - full text ed.: ISSN 1532-2130. USD 449 to institutions (effective 2009) (from ScienceDirect).
Indexed: A22, A26, B21, CA, CurCont, E-psyche, E01, EMBASE, ExcerpMed, I05, IndMed, Inpharma, JW-N, MEDLINE, NSA, NSCI, P30, P35, R10, Reac, SCI, SCOPUS, T02, W07.
—BLDSC (3829.733370), GNLM, IE, Infotrieve, Ingenta. **CCC.**
Published by: (European Paediatric Neurology Society), Elsevier Ltd (Subsidiary of: Elsevier Science & Technology), The Blvd, Langford Ln, Kidlington, Oxford, OX5 1GB, United Kingdom. TEL 44-1865-843000, FAX 44-1865-843010, customerserviceau@elsevier.com. Ed. L Lagae.

EUROPEAN JOURNAL OF PEDIATRIC DERMATOLOGY (ENGLISH EDITION). *see* MEDICAL SCIENCES—Dermatology And Venereology

EUROPEAN JOURNAL OF PEDIATRIC DERMATOLOGY (ITALIAN EDITION). *see* MEDICAL SCIENCES—Dermatology And Venereology

EUROPEAN JOURNAL OF PEDIATRIC SURGERY. *see* MEDICAL SCIENCES—Surgery

EUROPEAN JOURNAL OF PEDIATRIC SURGERY. SUPPLEMENT. *see* MEDICAL SCIENCES—Surgery

618.92 DEU ISSN 0340-6199
RJ1 CODEN: EJPEDT
➤ **EUROPEAN JOURNAL OF PEDIATRICS.** Text in English. 1910. m. EUR 4,096, USD 4,945 combined subscription to institutions (print & online eds.) (effective 2012). adv. charts; illus. back issues avail.; reprint service avail. from PSC. **Document type:** *Journal, Academic/Scholarly.* **Description:** Covers the whole broad field of pediatrics in all its aspects.
Former titles (until 1975): Zeitschrift fuer Kinderheilkunde (0044-2917); (until 1921): Zeitschrift fuer Kinderheilkunde. Originalien (0178-4919); (until 1912): Zeitschrift fur Kinderheilkunde (0178-4935); Incorporated (19??-1981): Acta Paediatrica Belgica (0001-6535); (1945-1988): Helvetica Paediatrica Acta (0018-022X)
Related titles: Microform ed.: (from PQC); Online - full text ed.: ISSN 1432-1076 (from IngentaConnect); ◆ Supplement(s): European Journal of Pediatrics. Supplement. ISSN 0943-9676.
Indexed: A01, A02, A03, A08, A20, A22, A26, A34, A36, ASCA, B21, B23, B25, BDM&CN, BIOSIS Prev, C11, CA, CABA, CIN, ChemAb, ChemTitl, CurCont, D01, DBA, DentInd, E01, E12, EMBASE, ESPM, ExcerpMed, F08, F09, FR, FamI, GH, H&SSA, H04, H12, H17, IBR, IBZ, ISR, IndMed, Inpharma, Kidney, LT, MEDLINE, MS&D, MycolAb, N02, N03, NRN, NSA, OR, P20, P22, P30, P32, P33, P35, P39, P40, P48, P50, P54, PQC, R08, R10, R12, RA&MP, RM&VM, RRTA, Reac, S12, S13, S16, SCI, SCOPUS, T02, T05, THA, VS, W07, W10.
—BLDSC (3829.733500), CASDDS, GNLM, IE, Infotrieve, Ingenta, INIST. **CCC.**
Published by: (Belgian Pediatric Association), Springer (Subsidiary of: Springer Science+Business Media), Tiergartenstr 17, Heidelberg, 69121, Germany. TEL 49-6221-4870, FAX 49-6221-345229. Eds. Dr. Beat Steinmann TEL 41-1-2667167, Dr. Willem Proesmans TEL 32-16-343971. adv.: B&W page EUR 990, color page EUR 2,030. Circ: 1,250 (paid and controlled). **Subscr. in the Americas to:** Springer New York LLC, Journal Fulfillment, PO Box 2485, Secaucus, NJ 07096. TEL 800-777-4643, 201-348-4033, FAX 201-348-4505, journals-ny@springer.com, http://www.springer.com; **Subscr. to:** Springer Distribution Center, Kundenservice Zeitschriften, Haberstr 7, Heidelberg 69126, Germany. TEL 49-6221-3454303, FAX 49-6221-3454229, subscriptions@springer.com.

618.92 DEU ISSN 0943-9676
CODEN: EJPSF
EUROPEAN JOURNAL OF PEDIATRICS. SUPPLEMENT. Text in German. 19??. irreg. price varies. **Document type:** *Monographic series, Academic/Scholarly.*
Related titles: ◆ Supplement to: European Journal of Pediatrics. ISSN 0340-6199.
Indexed: A01, A02, A03, A08, C11, H04, SCOPUS, T02.
—Infotrieve, INIST. **CCC.**
Published by: Springer (Subsidiary of: Springer Science+Business Media), Tiergartenstr 17, Heidelberg, 69121, Germany. TEL 49-6221-4870, FAX 49-6221-345229, orders-hd-individuals@springer.com, http://www.springer.com. **Subscr. in N. America to:** Springer New York LLC, Journal Fulfillment, PO Box 2485, Secaucus, NJ 07096. TEL 212-460-1500, FAX 212-473-6272.

618.92 GBR ISSN 1557-6272
EVIDENCE-BASED CHILD HEALTH; a cochrane review journal. Text in English. 2006 (Sum.). q. GBP 211 in United Kingdom to institutions; EUR 327 in Europe to institutions; USD 414 elsewhere to institutions (effective 2012). adv. back issues avail.; reprint service avail. from PSC. **Document type:** *Journal, Academic/Scholarly.* **Description:** Targets medical and healthcare practitioners, parents, patients and other child health advocates. Supplies the latest clinical decision-making and policy development research evidence.
Media: Online - full content.
Indexed: P30.
—BLDSC (3831.036610), IE.
Published by: (The Cochrane Collaboration, European Paediatric Association), John Wiley & Sons Ltd. (Subsidiary of: John Wiley & Sons, Inc.), 1-7 Oldlands Way, PO Box 808, Bognor Regis, West Sussex PO21 9FF, United Kingdom. TEL 44-1865-778315, FAX 44-1243-843232, cs-journals@wiley.com, http://eu.wiley.com/WileyCDA/. Eds. Martin Offringa, Terry Klassen. **Subscr. to:** 1-7 Oldlands Way, PO Box 809, Bognor Regis, West Sussex PO21 9FG, United Kingdom. TEL 44-1865-778054, cs-agency@wiley.com.

EXCERPTA MEDICA. SECTION 7: PEDIATRICS AND PEDIATRIC SURGERY. *see* MEDICAL SCIENCES—Abstracting, Bibliographies, Statistics

618.92 688.72 DEU ISSN 1431-9543
FAMILIE & CO. Text in German. 1996. m. EUR 2.50 newsstand/cover (effective 2010). adv. **Document type:** *Magazine, Consumer.*
Related titles: Online - full text ed.; Supplement(s): Urlaub. 2005.
Published by: Family Media GmbH & Co. KG, Schnewlinstr 6, Freiburg, 79098, Germany. TEL 49-761-705780, FAX 49-761-70578651, http://www.kinderzeit.com. Adv. contact Sabine Mecklenburg. page EUR 15,900; trim 210 x 265. Circ: 241,937 (paid).

FETAL AND MATERNAL MEDICINE REVIEW. *see* MEDICAL SCIENCES—Obstetrics And Gynecology

618.92 GBR ISSN 1551-3815
CODEN: PPMMFX
➤ **FETAL AND PEDIATRIC PATHOLOGY.** Text in English. 1983. bi-m. GBP 790, EUR 1,035, USD 1,290 combined subscription to institutions (print & online eds.); GBP 1,570, EUR 2,060, USD 2,575 combined subscription to corporations (print & online eds.) (effective 2010). adv. bk.rev. bibl.; charts; illus. index. back issues avail.; reprint service avail. from PSC. **Document type:** *Journal, Academic/Scholarly.* **Description:** Covers the study of disease in the developing human.
Former titles (until 2004): Pediatric Pathology & Molecular Medicine (1522-7952); (until 1999): Pediatric Pathology & Laboratory Medicine (1077-1042); (until 1995): Pediatric Pathology (0277-0938)
Related titles: Microform ed.: (from PQC); Online - full text ed.: ISSN 1551-3823 (from IngentaConnect).
Indexed: A01, A02, A03, A08, A22, ASCA, B25, BIOSIS Prev, C11, CA, CurCont, E01, EMBASE, ExcerpMed, H04, ISR, IndMed, Inpharma, MEDLINE, MycolAb, P30, R10, Reac, SCI, SCOPUS, T02, W07.
—BLDSC (3910.846050), GNLM, IE, Infotrieve, Ingenta, INIST. **CCC.**
Published by: Informa Healthcare (Subsidiary of: T & F Informa plc), Telephone House, 69-77 Paul St, London, EC2A 4LQ, United Kingdom. TEL 44-20-70175000, FAX 44-20-70176792, healthcare.enquiries@informa.com. Ed. Dr. Enid Gilbert-Barness. Adv. contact Per Sonnerfeldt. **Subscr. in N. America to:** Taylor & Francis Inc., Customer Services Dept, 325 Chestnut St, 8th Fl, Philadelphia, PA 19106. TEL 215-625-8900, 800-354-1420, FAX 215-625-8914, customerservice@taylorandfrancis.com; **Subscr. outside N. America to:** Taylor & Francis Ltd., Journals Customer Service, Sheepen Pl, Colchester, Essex CO3 3LP, United Kingdom. TEL 44-20-70175544, FAX 44-20-70175198. **Co-sponsor:** International Pediatric Pathology Association.

618 ESP ISSN 1888-8062
FORMACION ACTIVA EN PEDIATRIA DE ATENCION PRIMARIA. Text in Spanish. 2008. q. EUR 92.08 to individuals; EUR 188.46 to institutions (effective 2009). back issues avail. **Document type:** *Journal, Academic/Scholarly.*
Related titles: Online - full text ed.: ISSN 2171-6811. 2008.
Published by: Grupo Ars XXI de Comunicacion, SA, Muntaner 262 Atico 2a., Barcelona, 08021, Spain. Ed. Begona Dominguez-Aurrecoechea.

618.92 ESP ISSN 1885-2483
FORO PEDIATRICO. Text in Spanish. 1999. q. free (effective 2010). back issues avail. **Document type:** *Journal, Academic/Scholarly.*
Related titles: Online - full text ed.: ISSN 1885-2491. 1999. free (effective 2011).
—**CCC.**
Published by: Sociedad de Pediatria de Atencion Primaria de Extremadura, Avenida de Cristobal Colon 21, Badajoz, 06005, Spain. jjmorell@spapex.org.

618.92 ITA ISSN 0390-5845
CODEN: GSLNAG
GASLINI; a journal on pediatrics and pediatric specialties. Text in Italian. 1969-1996; N.S. 1998. 3/yr. EUR 147 combined subscription domestic to individuals print & online eds.; EUR 160 combined subscription foreign to individuals print & online eds.; EUR 227 combined subscription domestic to institutions print & online eds.; EUR 249 combined subscription foreign to institutions print & online eds. (effective 2009). adv. **Document type:** *Journal, Academic/Scholarly.* **Description:** Covers medical and surgical issues in the field of pediatrics.
Related titles: Online - full text ed.: ISSN 1970-8920.
Indexed: SCOPUS.
—CASDDS, GNLM.
Published by: (Istituto Pediatrico Giannina Gaslini di Genova), Edizioni Minerva Medica, Corso Bramante 83-85, Turin, 10126, Italy. TEL 39-011-678282, FAX 39-011-674502, journals.dept@minervamedica.it, http://www.minervamedica.it.

GEBURTSVORBEREITUNG. *see* CHILDREN AND YOUTH—About

GELBE LISTE PHARMINDEX. PAEDIATER. *see* PHARMACY AND PHARMACOLOGY

GESUNDHEIT, MEIN KIND!. *see* CHILDREN AND YOUTH—About

618.92 ITA ISSN 2036-8275
GIORNALE ITALIANO DI INFETTIVOLOGIA PEDIATRICA. Text in Italian. 1999. q. **Document type:** *Journal, Trade.*
Published by: Edizioni Medico Scientifiche, Via Riviera 39, Pavia, 27100, Italy. TEL 39-0382-526253, FAX 39-0382-423120, edint@edimes@tin.it.

618.92 CAN ISSN 1192-9073
GLOBAL CHILD HEALTH NEWS & REVIEW. Text in English. 1993. q.
Indexed: C06, C07, C08, CINAHL, P30.
Published by: Global Child Health Society, 113-990 Beach Ave, Vancouver, BC V6E 4M2, Canada.

362.1 618.92 USA
GUIDELINES FOR HEALTH SUPERVISION. Variant title: Guidelines for Health Supervision Three. Text in English. 1985. irreg., latest 2002, 3rd ed. USD 59.95 per issue (effective 2009). adv. **Document type:** *Monographic series, Consumer.* **Description:** Guidelines of doctor visits for children, newborn through age 21.
Published by: American Academy of Pediatrics, 141 NW Pt Blvd, Elk Grove Village, IL 60007. TEL 847-434-4000, FAX 847-434-8000, journals@aap.org.

618.92 TUR ISSN 1304-9054
➤ **GUNCEL PEDIATRI/JOURNAL OF CURRENT PEDIATRICS.** Text in Turkish, English. 2003. 3/yr. free to qualified personnel (effective 2010). **Document type:** *Journal, Academic/Scholarly.* **Description:** Publishes original research articles in the field of both clinical and scientific pediatrics. The content of the journal is intended to encompass reviews of new developments in education, brief editorial manuscripts, case reports, original photographs, letters concerning experiences in the field of child health and diseases (pediatrics), and special feature articles in the field of social pediatrics.
Related titles: Online - full text ed.: free (effective 2011).
Indexed: A01, A26, C06, C07, CA, EMBASE, ExcerpMed, I05, R10, Reac, SCOPUS, T02.
Published by: (Uludag Universitesi, Tip Fakultesi/Uludag University, Faculty of Medicine), Galenos Yayincilik, Molla Gurani Cad.22/2, Findikzade-Istanbul, 34093, Turkey. TEL 90-212-6219925, FAX 90-212-6219927, info@galenos.com.tr, http://www.galenos.com.tr.

618.92 CHN ISSN 1001-3512
GUOWAI YIXUE (ERKEXUE FENCE)/FOREIGN MEDICAL SCIENCES (PEDIATRICS). Text in Chinese. 1974. bi-m. USD 24.60 (effective 2009). **Document type:** *Journal, Academic/Scholarly.*
Related titles: Online - full text ed.
—East View.
Published by: Zhongguo Yike Daxue, Erke Yanjiusuo/China Medical University, Pediatrics Research Institute, 36 Sanhao Jie, Shenyan, 110004, China. TEL 86-24-83956563, FAX 86-24-23845727. **Dist. by:** China International Book Trading Corp, 35 Chegongzhuang Xilu, Haidian District, PO Box 399, Beijing 100044, China. TEL 86-10-68412045, FAX 86-10-68412023, cibtc@mail.cibtc.com.cn, http://www.cibtc.com.cn.

618.92 HUN ISSN 0017-5900
GYERMEKGYOGYASZAT. Text in Hungarian; Summaries in German, Russian. 1950. q. adv. index.
Indexed: ChemAb, IndMed, P30.
—GNLM.
Published by: Magyar Gyermekorvosok Tarsasaga, Petofi u 4, Mosdos, 7257, Hungary. gyermekorvostarsasag@doki.net, http://www.gyermekorvostarsasag.hu. Circ: 1,750.

618.92 HUN ISSN 1589-0309
GYERMEKORVOS TOVABBKEPZES. Text in Hungarian. 1967. q. adv. bk.rev. **Document type:** *Magazine, Consumer.*
Former titles (until 2002): Pediater (1216-3821); (until 1992): Magyar Pediater (0303-5042)
Published by: Promenade Publishing House, Istenhegyi ut 29, Pf 804, Budapest, 1535, Hungary. TEL 36-1-2245450, FAX 36-1-2245457, recepcio@promenade.hu, http://www.promenade.hu. Ed. Veress Palma. Circ: 1,000.

HALLO BABY. *see* CHILDREN AND YOUTH—About

618.92 USA
HANDBOOK OF COMMON POISONINGS IN CHILDREN. Variant title: Common Poisonings in Children. Text in English. 1976. irreg. USD 44.95 (effective 2008). adv. **Document type:** *Handbook/Manual/Guide, Consumer.* **Description:** Includes essential information on poison prevention, general management of acute poisoning, drugs used in poisoned patients, toxicity calculations, and specific poisons.
Published by: American Academy of Pediatrics, 141 NW Pt Blvd, Elk Grove Village, IL 60007. TEL 847-434-4000, FAX 847-434-8000, journals@aap.org, http://www.aap.org.

618.92 DEU
HAUNER-JOURNAL. Text in German. 2/yr. EUR 4 per issue (effective 2011). adv. **Document type:** *Magazine, Trade.*
Related titles: Online - full text ed.
Published by: Verlag Volker Witthoff, Beethovenstr 15, Neusaess, 86356, Germany. TEL 49-821-541075, FAX 49-821-541093. Ed., Pub. Volker Witthoff. adv.: color page EUR 2,000. Circ: 6,000 (controlled).

HIV IN CHILDREN. *see* MEDICAL SCIENCES—Allergology And Immunology

HOME CARE FAMILY NEWSLETTER. *see* SOCIAL SERVICES AND WELFARE

618.92 HKG ISSN 1013-9923
HONG KONG JOURNAL OF PAEDIATRICS. Text in English. 1996. q. adv. **Document type:** *Journal, Academic/Scholarly.*
Related titles: Online - full text ed.: free (effective 2011).
Indexed: BAS, EMBASE, ExcerpMed, R10, Reac, SCI, SCOPUS, W07.
—BLDSC (4326.385800).
Published by: Medcom Limited, Rm 808, Two Chinachem Exchange Sq, 338 King's Rd, North Point, Hong Kong. TEL 852-25783833, FAX 852-25783929, mcl@medcom.com.hk, http://www.medcom.com.hk. Ed. Yeung Chap Yung.

618.92 ARG ISSN 0521-517X
➤ **HOSPITAL DE NINOS. REVISTA.** Text in Spanish. 1959. 5/yr. adv. bk.rev. **Document type:** *Journal, Academic/Scholarly.*
Published by: Asociacion Medica del Hospital de Ninos, Gallo 1330, Buenos Aires, 1425, Argentina. TEL 54-114-9614609, FAX 54-114-9614609.

618.92 CAN ISSN 1494-1015
THE HOSPITAL FOR SICK CHILDREN JOURNAL. Text in English. 1984. q.
Supersedes in part (in 1999): Kaleidoscope (Toronto) (0828-2730); Which was formerly (until 1984): What's New - Hospital for Sick Children (0049-7533); (until 1970): What's New at H S C? (0827-1232)
Published by: Hospital for Sick Children, 555 University Ave, Toronto, ON M5G 1X8, Canada. FAX 416-813-5328. Ed. John Pires TEL 416-813-5328. Circ: 30,000.

HOSPITAL FOR SICK CHILDREN, TORONTO. RESEARCH INSTITUTE. ANNUAL REPORT. *see* HEALTH FACILITIES AND ADMINISTRATION

HOSPITAL INFANTIL DE MEXICO. BOLETIN MEDICO. *see* HEALTH FACILITIES AND ADMINISTRATION

HOSPITAL INFANTIL DEL ESTADO DE SONORA. BOLETIN CLINICO. *see* MEDICAL SCIENCES

HOSPITAL MATERNO INFANTIL RAMON SARDA. REVISTA. *see* MEDICAL SCIENCES—Obstetrics And Gynecology

618.92 CRI ISSN 1017-8546
HOSPITAL NACIONAL DE NINOS DR. CARLOS SAEZ HERRERA. REVISTA MEDICA. Text in Spanish. 1966. s-a. **Document type:** *Journal, Academic/Scholarly.*
Related titles: Online - full text ed.
Indexed: C01.
Published by: Hospital Nacional de Ninos Dr. Carlos Saez Herrera, Apdo de Correos 1654, San Jose, 1000, Costa Rica. Ed. Cecilia Lizano.

618.92 USA ISSN 2154-1663
HOSPITAL PEDIATRICS. Text in English. 200?. s-a. free (effective 2010). **Document type:** *Newsletter, Trade.* **Description:** News and information from the American Academy of Pediatrics Section on Hospital Medicine.
Formerly (until 2007): Section on Hospital Medicine News
Related titles: Online - full text ed.: ISSN 2154-1671.
Published by: American Academy of Pediatrics, 141 NW Pt Blvd, Elk Grove Village, IL 60007. TEL 847-434-4000, FAX 847-434-8000, journals@aap.org, http://www.aap.org.

▼ **I C A N**; infant, child & adolescent nutrition. (Infant, Child & Adolescent Nutrition) *see* NUTRITION AND DIETETICS

618.92 USA ISSN 2090-469X
▼ ➤ **I S R N PEDIATRICS.** (International Scholarly Research Network) Text in English. 2011. q. **Document type:** *Journal, Academic/Scholarly.*
Related titles: Online - full text ed.: ISSN 2090-4703. free (effective 2011).
Published by: Hindawi Publishing Corporation, 410 Park Ave, 15th Fl, PMB 287, New York, NY 10022. FAX 215-893-4392, 866-446-3294, hindawi@hindawi.com.

618.9212 MLT ISSN 1729-441X
RJ421
IMAGES IN PAEDIARIC CARDIOLOGY. Text in English. 1999. q.
Media: Online - full content.
Published by: Government of Malta, Department of Health Information, St. Luke's Hospital, Guadamangia, MSD09, Malta. TEL 356-212-40176, FAX 356-212-41251. Ed. Victor Grech.

618.92 617 IND ISSN 0971-9261
INDIAN ASSOCIATION OF PEDIATRIC SURGEONS. JOURNAL. Text in English. 1995. q. INR 3,000 domestic to individuals; USD 300 foreign to individuals; INR 3,600 combined subscription domestic to institutions (print & online eds.); USD 360 combined subscription foreign to institutions (print & online eds.) (effective 2011). adv. **Document type:** *Journal, Academic/Scholarly.* **Description:** Publishes original articles, case reports, review articles and technical innovations. Special issues on different subjects are published every year. There have been several contributions from overseas experts.
Related titles: Online - full text ed.: ISSN 1998-3891. free (effective 2011).
Indexed: A01, A26, A34, A36, C06, C07, CA, CABA, E08, G08, GH, H11, H12, H17, I05, IndVet, N02, N03, P10, P30, P33, P48, P53, P54, PQC, R12, S09, S12, SCOPUS, T02, T05, VS.
—IE. **CCC.**
Published by: (Indian Association of Pediatric Surgeons), Medknow Publications and Media Pvt. Ltd., B-9, Kanara Business Ctr, Off Link Rd, Ghatkopar (E), Mumbai, Maharastra 400 075, India. TEL 91-22-66491816, FAX 91-22-66491817, http://www.medknow.com. Ed. K L N Rao.

INDIAN JOURNAL OF MEDICAL & PAEDIATRIC ONCOLOGY. *see* MEDICAL SCIENCES—Oncology

618.92 IND ISSN 0019-5456
RJ1 CODEN: IJPEA2
THE INDIAN JOURNAL OF PEDIATRICS. Text in English. 1933. m. EUR 590, USD 721 combined subscription to institutions (print & online eds.) (effective 2012). adv. bk.rev. abstr.; charts. index. reprint service avail. from PSC. **Document type:** *Journal, Academic/Scholarly.* **Description:** Features discussions on pediatric emergencies, current issues, clinical, advances in pediatrics and technological techniques and neonatology. Includes pharmacology and nutrition.
Related titles: Microfilm ed.: (from PQC); Online - full text ed.: ISSN 0973-7693 (from IngentaConnect).
Indexed: A22, A26, A36, B25, BA, BIOSIS Prev, C06, C07, CABA, CDA, ChemAb, CurCont, D01, DSHAb, DentInd, E01, E08, E12, EMBASE, ExcerpMed, F09, FR, GH, H12, H17, IndMed, MEDLINE, MycolAb, N02, N03, P30, P33, P39, PN&I, R08, R10, R12, REE&TA, RM&VM, Reac, S09, SCI, SCOPUS, T05, W07, W11.
—BLDSC (4418.000000), GNLM, IE, Infotrieve, Ingenta, INIST. **CCC.**
Published by: (All India Institute of Medical Sciences, Department of Pediatrics), Indian Journal of Pediatrics, 125, 2nd Fl, Gautam Nagar, P O Box 3875, New Delhi, 110 049, India. TEL 91-11-26568098, FAX 91-11-26857587, ijpsubs@airtelbroadband.in, ijp.journal.vsnl@vsnl.net. Ed. Dr. I C Verma. Circ: 10,000. **Subscr. to:** I N S I O Scientific Books & Periodicals, PO Box 7234, Indraprastha HPO, New Delhi 110 002, India. iihm@ap.nic.in, http://iihm.ap.nic.in/. **Co-publisher:** Springer (India) Private Ltd.

618.92 IND ISSN 0972-9607
➤ **INDIAN JOURNAL OF PRACTICAL PEDIATRICS.** Text in English. 1993. q. free to members (effective 2011). **Document type:** *Journal, Academic/Scholarly.*
Indexed: A36, BP, CABA, D01, E12, GH, H17, N02, N03, P33, P39, PN&I, R08, R10, R12, RM&VM, Reac, SCOPUS, T05.
—BLDSC (4420.230000).
Published by: Indian Academy of Pediatrics, Kailas Darshan, Kennedy Bridge, Mumbai, Maharastra 400 007, India. TEL 91-22-23889565, FAX 91-22-23851713, centraloffice@iapindia.org, http://www.iapindia.org.

618.92 IND ISSN 0019-6061
RJ1 CODEN: INPDAR
INDIAN PEDIATRICS. Text in English. 1964. m. EUR 533, USD 720 combined subscription to institutions (print & online eds.) (effective 2012). adv. bk.rev. charts; illus. reprint service avail. from IRC. **Description:** Promotes the science and practice of Pediatrics.
Formed by the merger of (1952-1963): Indian Journal of Child Health (0445-7684); (1962-1963): Indian Pediatric Society. Journal (0537-2380)
Related titles: Online - full text ed.: ISSN 0974-7559. free (effective 2011) (from IngentaConnect).
Indexed: A22, A34, A36, AgrForAb, BP, CA, CABA, ChemAb, CurCont, D01, DentInd, E01, E12, EMBASE, ExcerpMed, F08, F09, FR, GH, H17, ISA, IndMed, IndVet, MEDLINE, N02, N03, N04, P30, P33, P37, P39, PN&I, R08, R10, R12, RM&VM, Reac, S12, SCI, SCOPUS, SoyAb, T02, T05, TAR, VS, W07, W10, W11.
—BLDSC (4425.280000), CASDDS, GNLM, IE, Infotrieve, Ingenta, INIST. **CCC.**
Published by: Indian Academy of Pediatrics, Kailas Darshan, Kennedy Bridge, Mumbai, Maharastra 400 007, India. TEL 91-22-23889565, FAX 91-22-23851713, iapcoff@bom5.vsnl.net.in, http://www.iapindia.org. Ed. Piyush Gupta. adv.: B&W page INR 8,000, color page INR 14,000. Circ: 4,800. **Co-publisher:** Springer (India) Private Ltd.

INFANCY. *see* CHILDREN AND YOUTH—About

618.92 GBR ISSN 1745-1205
INFANT; for neonatal and paediatric healthcare professionals. Text in English. 2005. bi-m. GBP 46 domestic to individuals; GBP 60 foreign to individuals; GBP 130 domestic to institutions; GBP 145 foreign to institutions; GBP 56 combined subscription domestic to individuals (print & online eds.); GBP 70 combined subscription foreign to individuals (print & online eds.); GBP 195 combined subscription domestic to institutions (print & online eds.); GBP 205 combined subscription foreign to institutions (print & online eds.) (effective 2010). adv. back issues avail. **Document type:** *Journal, Academic/Scholarly.* **Description:** Designed for the multidisciplinary team that cares for vulnerable sick or premature babies in their first year of life.
Related titles: Online - full text ed.: ISSN 1745-1213. GBP 40 to individuals; GBP 150 to institutions (effective 2010); Supplement(s): Infant Grapevine.
Indexed: B28, C06, C07, C08, CINAHL, T02.
—BLDSC (4478.256500), IE. **CCC.**
Published by: Stansted News Ltd., 134 South St, Bishop's Stortford, Herts CM23 3BQ, United Kingdom. TEL 44-1279-714511, FAX 44-1279-714519, http://www.stanstednews.com/. Pub. Christine Bishop TEL 44-1279-714510. Adv. contact Mark Ranger TEL 44-1279-714509. B&W page GBP 1,110, color page GBP 1,683; trim 210 x 297.

INFANT BEHAVIOR AND DEVELOPMENT. *see* PSYCHOLOGY

155.422 USA ISSN 0163-9641
RJ502.5 CODEN: IMHJDZ
➤ **INFANT MENTAL HEALTH JOURNAL.** Abbreviated title: I M H J. Text in English. 1980. bi-m. GBP 337 in United Kingdom to institutions; EUR 428 in Europe to institutions; USD 618 in United States to institutions; USD 666 in Canada & Mexico to institutions; USD 666 elsewhere to institutions; GBP 388 combined subscription in United Kingdom to institutions (print & online eds.); EUR 492 combined subscription in Europe to institutions (print & online eds.); USD 711 combined subscription in United States to institutions (print & online eds.); USD 759 combined subscription in Canada & Mexico to institutions (print & online eds.); USD 759 combined subscription elsewhere to institutions (print & online eds.) (effective 2012). adv. back issues avail.; reprint service avail. from PSC. **Document type:** *Journal, Academic/Scholarly.* **Description:** Focuses on infant social-emotional development, caregiver-infant interactions, contextual and cultural influences on infant and family development, and all conditions that place infants and their families at risk for less than optimal development.
Related titles: Online - full text ed.: ISSN 1097-0355. GBP 313 in United Kingdom to institutions; EUR 397 in Europe to institutions; USD 618 elsewhere to institutions (effective 2012).
Indexed: A01, A03, A08, A22, ASCA, C06, C07, C08, C28, CA, CDA, CINAHL, CurCont, E-psyche, EMBASE, ExcerpMed, F09, FR, Faml, IPsyAb, P03, P30, P43, PsycInfo, PsycholAb, R10, Reac, SCOPUS, SFSA, SSCI, T02, W07.
—BLDSC (4478.274000), GNLM, IE, Infotrieve, Ingenta, INIST. **CCC.**
Published by: (World Association for Infant Mental Health FIN, Michigan Association for Infant Mental Health), John Wiley & Sons, Inc., 111 River St, Hoboken, NJ 07030. TEL 201-748-6000, FAX 201-748-6088, info@wiley.com, http://www.wiley.com/WileyCDA/. Ed. Hiram E Fitzgerald. Pub., Adv. contact Kim Thompkins TEL 212-850-6921. **Subscr. outside the Americas to:** John Wiley & Sons Ltd.

618.92 GBR ISSN 1369-8036
INFANT OBSERVATION; the international journal of infant observation and its applications. Variant title: International Journal of Infant Observation. Text in English. 1997. 3/yr. GBP 190 combined subscription in United Kingdom to institutions (print & online eds.); EUR 279, USD 347 combined subscription to institutions (print & online eds.) (effective 2012). adv. back issues avail.; reprint service avail. from PSC. **Document type:** *Journal, Academic/Scholarly.* **Description:** Reflects the way in which the disciplines of psychology, psychiatry and the social sciences may be aided and enhanced by the depth of psychoanalytical infant observation.
Related titles: Online - full text ed.: ISSN 1745-8943. 2005. GBP 172 in United Kingdom to institutions; EUR 251, USD 313 to institutions (effective 2012) (from IngentaConnect).
Indexed: A01, A22, CA, CPE, E01, P03, P50, PsycInfo, T02.
—IE, Ingenta. **CCC.**
Published by: (Tavistock Clinic Foundation), Routledge (Subsidiary of: Taylor & Francis Group), 4 Park Sq, Milton Park, Abingdon, Oxon OX14 4RN, United Kingdom. TEL 44-20-70176000, FAX 44-20-70176336, subscriptions@tandf.co.uk, http://www.routledge.com. Ed. Lisa Miller. Adv. contact Linda Hann TEL 44-1344-779945. **Subscr. to:** Taylor & Francis Ltd., Journals Customer Service, Sheepen Pl, Colchester, Essex CO3 3LP, United Kingdom. TEL 44-20-70175544, FAX 44-20-70175198. **Co-sponsor:** University of East London Press.

618.92 BRA ISSN 1413-0270
INFANTO. Text in Portuguese. 1993. 3/yr.
Indexed: EMBASE, ExcerpMed, R10, Reac, SCOPUS.
Published by: Lemos Editorial & Graficos Ltda., Rua Rui Barbosa, 70, B Vista, Sao Paulo, SP 01326-010, Brazil. TEL 55-11-251-4300, http://www.lemos.com.br.

618.92 649 USA ISSN 0896-3746
RJ102 CODEN: IYCHEL
➤ **INFANTS AND YOUNG CHILDREN**; an interdisciplinary journal of special care. Abbreviated title: I Y C. Text in English. 1988. q. USD 347 domestic to institutions; USD 508 foreign to institutions (effective 2011). adv. back issues avail.; reprints avail. **Document type:** *Journal, Academic/Scholarly.* **Description:** Focuses on vulnerable children from birth to five years of age and their families. Articles addresses issues involving policy, professional training, new conceptual models, and related matters.
Related titles: Online - full text ed.: ISSN 1550-5081.
Indexed: A22, A26, ASCA, C06, C07, C08, C22, C28, CA, CINAHL, CMM, CurCont, E-psyche, E03, E07, E08, E09, ECER, ERI, F09, FamI, G08, G09, H11, H12, I05, I06, I07, NurAb, P02, P03, P10, P18, P24, P30, P48, P50, P53, P54, P55, PQC, PsycInfo, S02, S03, S09, S23, SCOPUS, SOPODA, SSCI, SociolAb, T02, W07.
—BLDSC (4478.283000), IE, Infotrieve, Ingenta. **CCC.**
Published by: Lippincott Williams & Wilkins (Subsidiary of: Wolters Kluwer N.V.), Two Commerce Sq, 2001 Market St, Philadelphia, PA 19103. TEL 215-521-8300, FAX 215-521-8902, customerservice@lww.com, http://www.lww.com. Ed. Mary Beth Bruder. Pub. Paul Gee. Circ: 1,485.

618.92 616.9 USA ISSN 1044-9779
RJ401
➤ **INFECTIOUS DISEASES IN CHILDREN.** Text in English. 1988. m. USD 299 to individuals; USD 479 to institutions; USD 39 per issue (effective 2010). adv. reprints avail. **Document type:** *Journal, Academic/Scholarly.* **Description:** Covers new drugs and procedures for diagnosing and treating pediatric infectious diseases.
Related titles: Online - full text ed.: free to members (effective 2010).
Indexed: A01, P20, P48, P54, PQC.
—CCC.
Published by: Slack, Inc., 6900 Grove Rd, Thorofare, NJ 08086. TEL 856-848-1000, FAX 856-848-6091, customerservice@slackinc.com, http://www.slackinc.com. Eds. Dr. Philip A Brunell, Marie Rosenthal.

▼ ➤ **GLI INFERMIERI DEI BAMBINI. GIORNALE ITALIANO DI SCIENZE INFERMIERISTICHE PEDIATRICHE.** *see* MEDICAL SCIENCES—Nurses And Nursing

614.19 USA
INFORMATION EXCHANGE. Text in English. 1983. s-a. free. **Document type:** *Newsletter, Consumer.* **Description:** Provides a national forum for exchange of information and resources on SIDS, death investigation, apnea, grief of parents and the role of professionals dealing with families suffering a SIDS loss.
Related titles: Online - full content ed.
Published by: National Sudden Infant Death Syndrome Resource Center, 8280 Greensboro Dr, Ste 300, McLean, VA 22102. TEL 703-821-8955, 866-866-7437, FAX 703-821-2098, sids@circlesolutions.com. Circ: 2,600.

618.92 GBR ISSN 1353-8047
HV675.72
➤ **INJURY PREVENTION**; an international peer-reviewed journal for health professionals and others in injury prevention. Abbreviated title: I P. Text in English. 1995. bi-m. GBP 377 to institutions; GBP 483 combined subscription to institutions small FTE (print & online eds.) (effective 2011). adv. bk.rev. charts; illus. index. back issues avail.; reprints avail. **Document type:** *Journal, Academic/Scholarly.* **Description:** Features papers that focus on the prevention of unintentional or intentional injury at young age.
Related titles: Microfilm ed.: (from PQC); Online - full text ed.: ISSN 1475-5785. GBP 321 to institutions small FTE (effective 2011).
Indexed: A01, A03, A08, A22, A26, A34, A36, A37, ASG, B21, C06, C07, C08, C28, CA, CABA, CINAHL, CurCont, E01, E08, E12, EMBASE, ESPM, ExcerpMed, F08, F11, F12, G08, GH, H&SSA, H11, H12, HRIS, I05, INI, IndMed, LT, MEDLINE, N02, N03, P20, P22, P24, P30, P34, P48, P50, P54, PEI, PQC, PsycInfo, R10, R12, R13, RA&MP, RRTA, Reac, RiskAb, S02, S03, S09, S13, S16, SCI, SCOPUS, SD, SSCI, T02, T05, TAR, VS, W07, W11.
—BLDSC (4514.435000), GNLM, IE, Infotrieve, Ingenta. **CCC.**
Published by: (International Society for Childhood and Adolescent Injury Prevention), B M J Group, BMA House, Tavistock Sq, London, WC1H 9JR, United Kingdom. TEL 44-20-73836373, FAX 44-20-73836668, http://group.bmj.com. Ed. Brian Johnston. Pub. Christiane Notarmarco TEL 44-20-78747096. Adv. contact Nick Gray TEL 44-20-73836386. Circ: 740. **Subscr. to:** PO Box 299, London WC1H 9TD, United Kingdom. TEL 44-20-73836270, FAX 44-20-73836402, support@bmjgroup.com.

➤ **INTERNATIONAL BREASTFEEDING JOURNAL.** *see* MEDICAL SCIENCES—Obstetrics And Gynecology

618.92 DEU ISSN 0334-0139
CODEN: IJAHE8
➤ **INTERNATIONAL JOURNAL OF ADOLESCENT MEDICINE AND HEALTH.** Text in English. 1985. q. EUR 344, USD 516 to institutions; EUR 396, USD 594 combined subscription to institutions (print & online eds.) (effective 2012). adv. bk.rev. back issues avail. **Document type:** *Journal, Academic/Scholarly.* **Description:** Provides an international and interdisciplinary forum for the dissemination of new information in the field of adolescence.
Related titles: Online - full text ed.: ISSN 2191-0278. EUR 344, USD 516 to institutions (effective 2012).
Indexed: A36, C06, C07, CABA, D01, E-psyche, E12, EMBASE, ExcerpMed, F09, GH, H17, IBR, IBZ, LT, MEDLINE, N02, N03, P03, P30, P33, P39, PsycInfo, PsycholAb, R08, R10, R12, RA&MP, RM&VM, RRTA, Reac, SCOPUS, T05, VirolAbstr, W11.
—BLDSC (4541.565000), GNLM, IE, Infotrieve, Ingenta, INIST.
Published by: Walter de Gruyter GmbH & Co. KG, Genthiner Str 13, Berlin, 10785, Germany. TEL 49-30-26005220, FAX 49-30-26005251, info@degruyter.com, http://www.degruyter.de. Ed. Joav Merrick. Circ: 1,000.

618.92 USA ISSN 1939-5930
RJ101
➤ **INTERNATIONAL JOURNAL OF CHILD AND ADOLESCENT HEALTH.** Text in English. 2008 (Jan.). q. USD 295 to institutions; USD 442 combined subscription to institutions (print & online eds.) (effective 2012). **Document type:** *Journal, Academic/Scholarly.* **Description:** Aimed at the scientific community interested in the broad area of child health, adolescent health and human development. Provides an international multidisciplinary forum with a holistic approach to public health issues, health and medicine, health and social policy, service aspects.
Related titles: Online - full text ed.: USD 295 to institutions (effective 2012).
Indexed: C06, C07, P03, P30, PsycInfo.
Published by: Nova Science Publishers, Inc., 400 Oser Ave, Ste 1600, Hauppauge, NY 11788. TEL 631-231-7269, FAX 631-231-8175, main@novapublishers.com. Ed. Joav Merrick.

618.92 USA ISSN 1939-5965
HQ767.9
INTERNATIONAL JOURNAL OF CHILD HEALTH AND HUMAN DEVELOPMENT. Text in English. 2008 (Jan.). q. USD 295 to institutions; USD 442 combined subscription to institutions (print & online eds.) (effective 2012). **Document type:** *Journal, Academic/Scholarly.* **Description:** Provides an international multidisciplinary forum with a holistic approach to public health issues; health and medicine; health and social policy; service aspects, developmental aspects, epidemiology, rehabilitation; family and social issues; quality of life, genetics and all other aspects of human development over the whole age spectrum.
Related titles: Online - full text ed.: USD 295 to institutions (effective 2012).
Indexed: C06, C07, P03, P30, PsycInfo.
Published by: Nova Science Publishers, Inc., 400 Oser Ave, Ste 1600, Hauppauge, NY 11788. TEL 631-231-7269, FAX 631-231-8175, main@novapublishers.com. Ed. Joav Merrick.

INTERNATIONAL JOURNAL OF CHILDBIRTH EDUCATION. *see* MEDICAL SCIENCES—Obstetrics And Gynecology

INTERNATIONAL JOURNAL OF CLINICAL PEDIATRIC DENTISTRY. *see* MEDICAL SCIENCES—Dentistry

▼ **INTERNATIONAL JOURNAL OF PEDIATRIC ENDOCRINOLOGY.** *see* MEDICAL SCIENCES—Endocrinology

INTERNATIONAL JOURNAL OF PEDIATRIC OTORHINOLARYNGOLOGY. *see* MEDICAL SCIENCES—Otorhinolaryngology

618.92 USA ISSN 1687-9740
▼ ➤ **INTERNATIONAL JOURNAL OF PEDIATRICS.** Text in English. 2009. irreg. USD 395 (effective 2011). **Document type:** *Journal, Academic/Scholarly.* **Description:** Publishes original research articles, review articles, case reports, and clinical studies in all areas of pediatric research.
Related titles: Online - full text ed.: ISSN 1687-9759. free (effective 2011).
Indexed: A01, A36, B21, C06, C07, CA, CABA, D01, E12, GH, ImmunAb, LT, N02, N03, NSA, P30, P33, R08, R12, T02, T05.
Published by: Hindawi Publishing Corporation, 410 Park Ave, 15th Fl, PMB 287, New York, NY 10022. FAX 215-893-4392, 866-446-3294, hindawi@hindawi.com.

618.92 CHE ISSN 0074-7300
INTERNATIONAL PEDIATRIC ASSOCIATION. PROCEEDINGS OF CONGRESS. Text in English. triennial. **Document type:** *Proceedings, Academic/Scholarly.*
Published by: International Pediatric Association/Association Internationale de Pediatrie, 1-3, rue de Chantepoulet, PO Box 1726, Geneva 1, 1211, Switzerland. TEL 41-22-9069152, FAX 41-22-7322852, adminoffice@ipa-world.org, http://www.ipa-world.org.

INTERNATIONAL PEDIATRICS. *see* MEDICAL SCIENCES—Surgery

INTERNATIONAL PERSPECTIVES ON CHILD AND ADOLESCENT MENTAL HEALTH. *see* MEDICAL SCIENCES—Psychiatry And Neurology

INTERNATIONAL REVIEWS OF CHILD NEUROLOGY SERIES. *see* MEDICAL SCIENCES—Psychiatry And Neurology

INTERNATIONAL SEMINARS IN PAEDIATRIC GASTROENTEROLOGY AND NUTRITION. *see* MEDICAL SCIENCES—Gastroenterology

618.92 649.1 USA ISSN 1537-9140
THE INTERNET GUIDE TO BABY HEALTH. Text in English. 2002. a.
Related titles: Online - full text ed.: ISSN 1537-9132.
Published by: eMedguides.com, 15 Roszel Rd., Princeton, NJ 08540. TEL 609-520-2001. Pub. Daniel R. Goldenson.

618.92 USA ISSN 1528-8374
RJ1
➤ **THE INTERNET JOURNAL OF PEDIATRICS AND NEONATOLOGY.** Text in English. 2001. s-a. free (effective 2011). adv. Website rev.; bk.rev. back issues avail. **Document type:** *Journal, Academic/Scholarly.* **Description:** Provides information from the field of pediatrics and neonatology; contains original articles, reviews, case reports, streaming slide shows, streaming videos, letters to the editor, press releases and meeting information.
Formerly: The Internet Journal of Neonatology
Media: Online - full text.
Indexed: A01, A02, A03, A08, A26, C06, C07, CA, EMBASE, G08, H11, H12, I05, SCOPUS, T02.
Published by: Internet Scientific Publications, Llc., 23 Rippling Creek Dr, Sugar Land, TX 77479. TEL 832-443-1193, FAX 281-240-1533, wenker@ispub.com. Ed. Akshaya Vachharajani.

618.92 IRN ISSN 2008-2142
➤ **IRANIAN JOURNAL OF PEDIATRICS.** Text in English. 2007. q. **Document type:** *Journal, Academic/Scholarly.* **Description:** Publishes basic, biomedical and clinical investigations on prevalent diseases relevant to pediatrics. Following categories are the main areas of the interest: clinical management on subspecialties of pediatric fields, nutrition, epidemiology, child health and genetics.
Related titles: Online - full content ed.: ISSN 2008-2150. free (effective 2011).
Indexed: A36, CABA, D01, E12, GH, H16, H17, LT, MaizeAb, N02, N03, P33, P39, R08, R11, R12, SCI, T05, TAR, W07.
Published by: Tehran University of Medical Sciences Publications, P O Box 14155-6386, Tehran, Iran. TEL 98-21-66595522, FAX 98-21-66595525, http://diglib.tums.ac.ir/pub/journals.asp. Ed. Gholam-Reza Walizadeh.

➤ **ISSUES IN COMPREHENSIVE PEDIATRIC NURSING.** *see* MEDICAL SCIENCES—Nurses And Nursing

618.92 GBR ISSN 1824-7288
RJ1
THE ITALIAN JOURNAL OF PEDIATRICS (ONLINE). Text in Italian. 2002. irreg. free (effective 2011).
Media: Online - full text.
Indexed: MEDLINE, P30.
Published by: (Societa Italiana di Pediatria ITA), BioMed Central Ltd. (Subsidiary of: Springer Science+Business Media), 236 Gray's Inn Rd, London, WC1X 8HB, United Kingdom. TEL 44-20-31922000, FAX 44-20-31922010, info@biomedcentral.com, http://www.biomedcentral.com.

618.92 NLD ISSN 1567-8644
J G Z. (Jeugd Gezondheids Zorg) Variant title: Tijdschrift voor Jeugdgezondheidszorg. Text in Dutch. 1968. 6/yr. EUR 104, USD 156 to institutions (effective 2009). adv. **Document type:** *Journal, Academic/Scholarly.*
Former titles (until 1999): Tijdschrift voor Jeugdgezondheidszorg (0165-1870); (until 1978): J G Z (1567-7966)
—IE.
Published by: Bohn Stafleu van Loghum B.V. (Subsidiary of: Springer Science+Business Media), Postbus 246, Houten, 3990 GA, Netherlands. TEL 31-30-6383872, FAX 31-30-6383991, boekhandels@bsl.nl, http://www.bsl.nl. Ed. R A Hira Sing. adv.: page EUR 881; trim 210 x 297. Circ: 1,509 (paid).

618.92 649 DEU ISSN 1619-3911
JA ZUM BABY; medizinischer Ratgeber fuer werdende und junge Eltern. Text in German. 1982. 2/yr. EUR 1.50 newsstand/cover (effective 2011). adv. **Document type:** *Magazine, Consumer.*
Formerly (until 1996): Ja Zum Kind (0936-9945)
Published by: Marken Verlag GmbH, Hansaring 97, Cologne, 50670, Germany. TEL 49-221-9574270, FAX 49-221-9574777, marken-info@markenverlag.de, http://www.markenverlag.de. Adv. contact Frank Krauthaeuser. Circ: 400,000 (paid and controlled).

618.92 BRA ISSN 0021-7557
JORNAL DE PEDIATRIA; the official journal of the Brazilian Pediatric Society. Text in Portuguese; Summaries in English, Portuguese. 1934. bi-m. free (effective 2005). adv. bk.rev. abstr.; bibl.; charts; illus.; stat. index. back issues avail.; reprints avail. **Document type:** *Journal, Academic/Scholarly.*
Related titles: CD-ROM ed.; Microform ed.: (from PQC); Online - full text ed.: ISSN 1678-4782. free (effective 2011).
Indexed: A34, A36, A37, A38, C01, CABA, D01, E12, EMBASE, ExcerpMed, F09, GH, H16, H17, IndMed, IndVet, LT, MEDLINE, N02, N03, N04, P30, P33, P39, R08, R10, R12, RM&VM, RRTA, Reac, S12, SCI, SCOPUS, T05, TAR, VS, W07, W11.
—GNLM, INIST.
Published by: Sociedade Brasileira de Pediatria, Rua Santa Clara, 292, Copacabana, Rio De Janeiro, RJ 22041-010, Brazil. TEL 55-21-25481999, FAX 55-21-25473567, http://www.jpes.com.br. Ed. Dr. Jefferson Pedro Piva. Adv. contact Yantemi Pinnerio TEL 55-11-3667-2336. page USD 1,500. Circ: 15,000.

618.92 FRA ISSN 1297-5354
LE JOURNAL DES PROFESSIONNELS DE L'ENFANCE. Text in French. 1999. bi-m. EUR 31 domestic to individuals; EUR 41 in Europe to individuals; EUR 41 DOM-TOM to individuals; EUR 51 elsewhere to individuals; EUR 45 domestic to institutions (effective 2009). **Document type:** *Journal, Trade.*
Indexed: SCOPUS.
Published by: T P M A, 40 Av. Saint Jacques, Savigny-sur-Orge, 91600, France. TEL 33-1-69445370.

JOURNAL FOR SPECIALISTS IN PEDIATRIC NURSING. *see* MEDICAL SCIENCES—Nurses And Nursing

618.92 EGY ISSN 1110-0672
JOURNAL OF ARAB CHILD/MAGALLAT AL-TEFL AL-'ARABI. Text in English. 1990. q. EGP 25 domestic; USD 45 foreign (effective 2004). **Document type:** *Journal, Academic/Scholarly.*
Published by: Association of Arab Pediatric Societies, New Children's Hospital, Cairo University, Cairo, Egypt. TEL 202-364-0513. Ed. Dr. Hussein Kamel Bahaa- El-Din.

JOURNAL OF CHILD AND ADOLESCENT PSYCHOPHARMACOLOGY. *see* MEDICAL SCIENCES—Psychiatry And Neurology

618.92 GBR ISSN 1367-4935
RJ245
➤ **JOURNAL OF CHILD HEALTH CARE.** Text in English. 1997. q. USD 828, GBP 447 combined subscription to institutions (print & online eds.); USD 811, GBP 438 to institutions (effective 2011). adv. back issues avail.; reprint service avail. from PSC. **Document type:** *Journal, Academic/Scholarly.* **Description:** A professionally focused, research-based journal which addresses child health issues from a multi-disciplinary perspective. It aims to foster critical understanding of the neonate, child and adolescent in health and illness.
Related titles: Online - full text ed.: ISSN 1741-2889. USD 745, GBP 402 to institutions (effective 2011).
Indexed: A22, B28, C06, C07, C08, CA, CINAHL, CurCont, E-psyche, E01, EMBASE, ExcerpMed, FamI, INI, L&LBA, MEDLINE, P03, P30, PAIS, PsycInfo, PsycholAb, R10, Reac, SCI, SCOPUS, SFSA, SSCI, SociolAb, T02, W07.
—BLDSC (4957.520000), IE, Infotrieve, Ingenta. **CCC.**
Published by: (Association of British Paediatric Nurses), Sage Publications Ltd. (Subsidiary of: Sage Publications, Inc.), 1 Oliver's Yard, 55 City Rd, London, EC1Y 1SP, United Kingdom. TEL 44-20-73248500, FAX 44-20-73248600, info@sagepub.co.uk, http://www.uk.sagepub.com/home.nav. Ed. Bernie Carter. adv.: B&W page GBP 350; 140 x 210. **Subscr. in the Americas to:** Sage Publications, Inc., 2455 Teller Rd, Thousand Oaks, CA 91320. TEL 805-499-9774, FAX 805-499-0871, journals@sagepub.com.

➤ **JOURNAL OF CHILD NEUROLOGY.** *see* MEDICAL SCIENCES—Psychiatry And Neurology

➤ **JOURNAL OF CHILDREN'S ORTHOPAEDICS.** *see* MEDICAL SCIENCES—Orthopedics And Traumatology

➤ **JOURNAL OF CLINICAL CHIROPRACTIC PEDIATRICS.** *see* MEDICAL SCIENCES—Chiropractic, Homeopathy, Osteopathy

➤ **JOURNAL OF CLINICAL PEDIATRIC DENTISTRY.** *see* MEDICAL SCIENCES—Dentistry

618.92 JPN ISSN 0035-550X
CODEN: RSHIAY
JOURNAL OF CLINICAL PEDIATRICS/RINSHO SHONI IGAKU. Text in Japanese. 1953. bi-m. JPY 5,000, USD 6.60. adv. bk.rev. abstr.; bibl.; charts; illus.; stat. index. **Document type:** *Trade.*
Indexed: ChemAb, INIS AtomInd.
Published by: Association for the Care of the Child/Shoni Aiiku Kyokai, c/o Dept of Pediatrics, School of Medicine, Sapporo Medical University, Minami-1, Nishi-16-chome, Chuo-ku, Sapporo, 060, Japan. Ed. Shunzo Chiba. Circ: 575.

JOURNAL OF DENTISTRY FOR CHILDREN (ONLINE). *see* MEDICAL SCIENCES—Dentistry

618.92 155.4 USA ISSN 0196-206X
RJ1 CODEN: JDBPD5
➤ **JOURNAL OF DEVELOPMENTAL AND BEHAVIORAL PEDIATRICS.** Abbreviated title: J D B P. Text in English. 1980. bi-m. USD 648 domestic to institutions; USD 743 foreign to institutions (effective 2011). adv. bk.rev. back issues avail.; reprints avail. **Document type:** *Journal, Academic/Scholarly.* **Description:** Covers some of the disorders affecting child development and behavior, including ADHD, eating disorders etc, for clinicians, teachers, and researchers involved in pediatric healthcare.
Related titles: Online - full text ed.: ISSN 1536-7312.
Indexed: A20, A22, A26, A36, ASCA, B25, BDM&CN, BIOSIS Prev, BibInd, C06, C07, C22, CABA, CDA, ChPerI, CurCont, D01, E-psyche, E03, E07, E08, EMBASE, ERI, ExcerpMed, F09, FR, FamI, G08, GH, H11, H12, H13, HRIS, I05, INI, IndMed, Inpharma, LT, MEDLINE, MycolAb, N02, N03, P02, P03, P10, P20, P30, P33, P35, P39, P48, P50, P53, P54, PQC, PsycInfo, PsycholAb, R10, R12, RRTA, Reac, S02, S03, S09, SCI, SCOPUS, SSCI, T05, W07, W11, YAE&RB.
—BLDSC (4969.280000), GNLM, IE, Infotrieve, Ingenta, INIST. **CCC.**
Published by: (Society for Developmental and Behavioral Pediatrics, Society for Behavioral Pediatrics), Lippincott Williams & Wilkins (Subsidiary of: Wolters Kluwer N.V.), 530 Walnut St, Philadelphia, PA 19106. TEL 215-521-8300, FAX 215-521-8902, customerservice@lww.com, http://www.lww.com. Ed. Suzanne D Dixon. Pub. Sandy Kasko. Circ: 1,182.

618.92 370.72 GBR ISSN 1476-718X
HQ767.8
➤ **JOURNAL OF EARLY CHILDHOOD RESEARCH.** Text in English. 2003 (May). 3/yr. USD 625, GBP 338 combined subscription to institutions (print & online eds.); USD 613, GBP 331 to institutions (effective 2011). adv. back issues avail.; reprint service avail. from PSC. **Document type:** *Journal, Academic/Scholarly.* **Description:** Provides an international forum for the dissemination of early childhood research, bridging cross-disciplinary areas and applying theory and research within the professional community.
Related titles: Online - full text ed.: ISSN 1741-2927. USD 563, GBP 304 to institutions (effective 2011).
Indexed: A22, AEI, B29, CA, CPE, E01, E03, EAA, ERIC, FamI, SCOPUS, T02.
—BLDSC (4970.701700), IE, Ingenta. **CCC.**
Published by: Sage Publications Ltd. (Subsidiary of: Sage Publications, Inc.), 1 Oliver's Yard, 55 City Rd, London, EC1Y 1SP, United Kingdom. TEL 44-20-73248500, FAX 44-20-73248600, info@sagepub.co.uk, http://www.uk.sagepub.com/home.nav. adv.: B&W page GBP 350; 140 x 210. **Subscr. in the Americas to:** Sage Publications, Inc., 2455 Teller Rd, Thousand Oaks, CA 91320. TEL 805-499-9774, FAX 805-499-0871, journals@sagepub.com.

618.92 NLD ISSN 0141-8955
RC627.8 CODEN: JIMDDP
➤ **JOURNAL OF INHERITED METABOLIC DISEASE.** Text in English. 1978. 6/yr. EUR 1,580, USD 1,664 combined subscription to institutions (print & online eds.) (effective 2012). adv. bk.rev. charts; illus. index. reprint service avail. from PSC. **Document type:** *Journal, Academic/Scholarly.* **Description:** Publishes original work, in the form of papers, short reports and case reports, covering all aspects of inherited metabolic disorderss in man and higher animals: clinical, biochemical, genetic, experimental, epidemiological and ethical.
Incorporates: Society for the Study of Inborn Errors of Metabolism. Symposia
Related titles: Microform ed.: (from PQC); Online - full text ed.: ISSN 1573-2665 (from IngentaConnect).
Indexed: A22, A26, A34, A35, A36, A38, ASCA, Agr, B21, B25, BDM&CN, BIOBASE, BIOSIS Prev, BibLing, CABA, CIN, CTA, ChemAb, ChemTitl, CurCont, D01, E01, EMBASE, ExcerpMed, F08, GH, H17, IABS, IBR, IBZ, ISR, IndMed, IndVet, Inpharma, MEDLINE, MaizeAb, MycolAb, N02, N03, N04, NSA, P20, P22, P30, P33, P35, P39, P48, P54, PQC, R08, R10, R12, RA&MP, Reac, RefZh, S12, SCI, SCOPUS, SoyAb, T05, VS, W07.
—BLDSC (5006.950000), CASDDS, GNLM, IE, Infotrieve, Ingenta, INIST. **CCC.**
Published by: (Society for the Study of Inborn Errors of Metabolism), Springer Netherlands (Subsidiary of: Springer Science+Business Media), Van Godewijckstraat 30, Dordrecht, 3311 GX, Netherlands. TEL 31-78-6576050, FAX 31-78-6576474, http://www.springer.com. Eds. Georg F Hoffmann, Johannes Zschocke.

➤ **JOURNAL OF NEONATAL AND PERINATAL MEDICINE.** *see* MEDICAL SCIENCES—Obstetrics And Gynecology

618.9201 IND ISSN 0973-2179
JOURNAL OF NEONATOLOGY. Text in English. 2000. q. back issues avail. **Document type:** *Journal, Academic/Scholarly.* **Description:** Encourages the advance knowledge study and practice of the science of neonatology.
Related titles: Online - full text ed.: ISSN 0973-2187.
Indexed: EMBASE, ExcerpMed, SCOPUS.
Published by: National Neonatology Forum, 803, 8th Fl, GD-ITL, Northex Tower A-9, Netaji Subhash Place, Ring Rd, Pitampura, New Delhi, 110 034, India. TEL 91-11-27353535, secnnf@vsnl.com, http://www.nnfi.org. **Subscr. to:** Indianjournals.com.

618.92 GBR ISSN 1034-4810
RJ101 CODEN: JPCHE3
➤ **JOURNAL OF PAEDIATRICS AND CHILD HEALTH.** Text in English. 1965. m. ((2 combined)). GBP 804 in United Kingdom to institutions; EUR 1,021 in Europe to institutions; USD 1,300 in the Americas to institutions; USD 1,577 elsewhere to institutions; GBP 925 combined subscription in United Kingdom to institutions (print & online eds.); EUR 1,175 combined subscription in Europe to institutions (print & online eds.); USD 1,495 combined subscription in the Americas to institutions (print & online eds.); USD 1,814 combined subscription elsewhere to institutions (print & online eds.) (effective 2012). adv. bk.rev. charts; illus. index. back issues avail.; reprint service avail. from PSC. **Document type:** *Journal, Academic/Scholarly.* **Description:** Covers original contributions concerned with both the formal aspects of pediatric medicine and the broader fields of children's health.
Formerly (until 1990): Australian Paediatric Journal (0004-993X)
Related titles: Microfiche ed.: (from PQC); Online - full text ed.: ISSN 1440-1754. GBP 804 in United Kingdom to institutions; EUR 1,021 in Europe to institutions; USD 1,300 in the Americas to institutions; USD 1,577 elsewhere to institutions (effective 2012) (from IngentaConnect).
Indexed: A01, A03, A08, A20, A22, A26, A34, A36, AMHA, ASCA, B21, BDM&CN, C06, C07, C08, CA, CABA, CINAHL, ChemAb, CurCont, D01, E01, E12, EMBASE, ESPM, ExcerpMed, F09, FR, FamI, GH, H&SSA, H12, H13, H17, INI, ISR, IndMed, IndVet, Inpharma, LT, MEDLINE, N02, N03, NRN, P02, P03, P10, P20, P30, P32, P33, P35, P39, P40, P48, P50, P53, P54, PGegResA, PQC, PsycInfo, PsycholAb, R08, R10, R12, RA&MP, RM&VM, RRTA, Reac, RiskAb, S02, S03, SCI, SCOPUS, SoyAb, T02, T05, VS, W07, W11.
—BLDSC (5027.778000), CASDDS, GNLM, IE, Infotrieve, Ingenta, INIST. **CCC.**
Published by: (Royal College of Physicians, Paediatrics & Child Health Division AUS, Perinatal Society of Australia and New Zealand, Paediatric Research Society of Australia, Australasian Association of Paediatric Surgeons AUS), Wiley-Blackwell Publishing Ltd. (Subsidiary of: John Wiley & Sons, Inc.), 9600 Garsington Rd, Oxford, OX4 2DQ, United Kingdom. TEL 44-1865-776868, FAX 44-1865-714591, customerservices@blackwellpublishing.com. Ed. David Isaacs.

➤ **JOURNAL OF PAEDIATRICS, OBSTETRICS AND GYNAECOLOGY (HONG KONG EDITION).** *see* MEDICAL SCIENCES—Obstetrics And Gynecology

➤ **JOURNAL OF PAEDIATRICS, OBSTETRICS AND GYNAECOLOGY (TAIWAN EDITION).** *see* MEDICAL SCIENCES—Obstetrics And Gynecology

➤ **JOURNAL OF PAEDIATRICS, OBSTETRICS AND GYNAECOLOGY (THAILAND EDITION).** *see* MEDICAL SCIENCES—Obstetrics And Gynecology

618.92 USA ISSN 1083-3188
RJ478 CODEN: JPAGFP
➤ **JOURNAL OF PEDIATRIC AND ADOLESCENT GYNECOLOGY.** Text in Dutch. 1988. bi-m. USD 710 in United States to institutions; USD 747 elsewhere to institutions (effective 2012). adv. back issues avail.; reprints avail. **Document type:** *Journal, Academic/Scholarly.* **Description:** Covers all aspects of clinical and basic science research in pediatric and adolescent gynecology, as well as molecular biology research as applied to the field.
Formerly (until 1996): Adolescent and Pediatric Gynecology (0932-8610)
Related titles: Microform ed.: (from PQC); Online - full text ed.: ISSN 1873-4332 (from IngentaConnect, ScienceDirect).
Indexed: A01, A03, A08, A22, A26, ASCA, CA, CCIOG, CCIP, ChPerI, CurCont, E01, EMBASE, ExcerpMed, F09, FR, I05, INI, IndMed, JW-WH, MEDLINE, P30, R10, Reac, SCI, SCOPUS, T02, W07.
—BLDSC (5030.154000), GNLM, IE, Infotrieve, Ingenta, INIST. **CCC.**
Published by: (North American Society for Pediatric and Adolescent Gynecology), Elsevier Inc. (Subsidiary of: Elsevier Science & Technology), 1600 John F Kennedy Blvd, Philadelphia, PA 19103. TEL 215-239-3900, FAX 215-238-7883, JournalCustomerService-usa@elsevier.com, http://www.elsevier.com. Ed. Dr. Joseph S Sanfilippo TEL 412-641-1204. Adv. contact Carol Clark TEL 212-633-3719. Circ: 575. **Co-sponsor:** International Federation of Infantile and Juvenile Gynecology.

618.92 612.015 NLD ISSN 1879-5390
▼ ➤ **JOURNAL OF PEDIATRIC BIOCHEMISTRY.** Text in English. 2010. q. USD 446 combined subscription in North America to institutions (print & online eds.); EUR 320 combined subscription elsewhere to institutions (print & online eds.) (effective 2012). **Document type:** *Journal, Academic/Scholarly.* **Description:** Covers child biochemistry, pediatric laboratory medicine and biochemical aspects in the study of childhood diseases.
Related titles: Online - full text ed.: ISSN 1879-5404.
Indexed: A22, E01.
Published by: I O S Press, Nieuwe Hemweg 6B, Amsterdam, 1013 BG, Netherlands. TEL 31-20-6883355, FAX 31-20-6870019, info@iospress.nl, http://www.iospress.nl. Eds. Husein Caksen, Mustafa Cemek.

➤ **JOURNAL OF PEDIATRIC ENDOCRINOLOGY & METABOLISM.** *see* MEDICAL SCIENCES—Endocrinology

▼ ➤ **JOURNAL OF PEDIATRIC EPILEPSY.** *see* MEDICAL SCIENCES—Psychiatry And Neurology

➤ **JOURNAL OF PEDIATRIC GASTROENTEROLOGY AND NUTRITION.** *see* NUTRITION AND DIETETICS

618.92 599.9 NLD ISSN 2146-4596
▼ ➤ **JOURNAL OF PEDIATRIC GENETICS.** Text in English. 2011. q. USD 376 combined subscription in North America (print & online eds.); EUR 270 combined subscription elsewhere (print & online eds.) (effective 2012). bk.rev. **Document type:** *Journal, Academic/Scholarly.* **Description:** Covers all aspects of genetics in childhood and the genetics of experimental models.
Related titles: Online - full text ed.: ISSN 2146-460X.
Published by: (World Society of Child Science TUR), I O S Press, Nieuwe Hemweg 6B, Amsterdam, 1013 BG, Netherlands. TEL 31-20-6883355, FAX 31-20-6870019, info@iospress.nl, http://www.iospress.nl. Eds. Husein Caksen, Stephanie M Ware.

618.92 USA ISSN 0891-5245
RJ1 CODEN: JPHCED
➤ **JOURNAL OF PEDIATRIC HEALTH CARE.** Text in English. 1987. bi-m. USD 288 in United States to institutions; USD 330 elsewhere to institutions (effective 2012). adv. abstr.; charts; illus. index. back issues avail.; reprints avail. **Document type:** *Journal, Academic/Scholarly.* **Description:** Provides information on examination and developmental assessments, treatment, and coordination of care for various childhood illnesses.
Related titles: Microform ed.: (from PQC); Online - full text ed.: ISSN 1532-656X (from ScienceDirect).
Indexed: A22, A26, C06, C07, C08, CA, CINAHL, CurCont, E01, EMBASE, ExcerpMed, F09, FamI, H12, I05, INI, MEDLINE, NurAb, P03, P30, PsycInfo, PsycholAb, R10, Reac, SCI, SCOPUS, SSCI, T02, W07.
—BLDSC (5030.180000), GNLM, IE, Infotrieve, Ingenta. **CCC.**
Published by: (National Association of Pediatric Nurse Associates & Practitioners), Mosby, Inc. (Subsidiary of: Elsevier Health Sciences), 1600 John F. Kennedy Blvd, Ste 1800, Philadelphia, PA 19103. TEL 215-239-3900, 800-523-1649, FAX 215-239-3990, elspcs@elsevier.com, http://www.us.elsevierhealth.com. Ed. Martha K Swartz. Adv. contact Kerri Petrakis TEL 856-768-9360.

➤ **JOURNAL OF PEDIATRIC HEMATOLOGY / ONCOLOGY.** *see* MEDICAL SCIENCES—Oncology

618.92 USA ISSN 2150-6272
▼ ➤ **JOURNAL OF PEDIATRIC HOSPITAL MEDICINE.** Text in English. forthcoming 2010 (Mar.). bi-m. USD 250 (effective 2010). **Document type:** *Journal, Academic/Scholarly.*
Related titles: Online - full text ed.: ISSN 2150-6280. forthcoming 2010 (Mar.).
Published by: John Wiley & Sons, Inc., 111 River St, Hoboken, NJ 07030. TEL 201-748-6000, FAX 201-748-5915, info@wiley.com, http://www.wiley.com/WileyCDA/.

➤ **JOURNAL OF PEDIATRIC INFECTIOUS DISEASES.** *see* MEDICAL SCIENCES—Communicable Diseases

618.92 617.1 NLD ISSN 2146-4618
▼ ➤ **JOURNAL OF PEDIATRIC INTENSIVE CARE.** Text in English. 2011. q. USD 376 combined subscription in North America (print & online eds.); EUR 270 combined subscription elsewhere (print & online eds.) (effective 2012). bk.rev. **Document type:** *Journal, Academic/Scholarly.* **Description:** Covers the latest techniques in intensive care in childhood.
Related titles: Online - full text ed.: ISSN 2146-4626.
Published by: (World Society of Child Science TUR), I O S Press, Nieuwe Hemweg 6B, Amsterdam, 1013 BG, Netherlands. TEL 31-20-6883355, FAX 31-20-6870019, info@iospress.nl, http://www.iospress.nl. Eds. Husein Caksen, Mark J Heulitt.

618.92 USA ISSN 2153-2559
▼ **JOURNAL OF PEDIATRIC, MATERNAL & FAMILY HEALTH.** Abbreviated title: J P M F H. Text in English. 2009. q. USD 150 to individuals; USD 75 to members; USD 50 per issue (effective 2010). back issues avail. **Document type:** *Journal, Academic/Scholarly.*
Media: Online - full text.
Published by: McCoy Press, 4390 Bells Ferry Rd, Kennesaw, GA 30144. TEL 404-247-2550, FAX 678-445-1459, matthewmccoy@comcast.net, http://mccoypress.net/. Ed. Matthew McCoy.

618.92 NLD ISSN 1304-2580
RJ486 CODEN: JPNOA7
➤ **JOURNAL OF PEDIATRIC NEUROLOGY.** Text and summaries in English. 2003. q. USD 406 combined subscription in North America (print & online eds.); EUR 290 combined subscription elsewhere (print & online eds.) (effective 2012). adv. bk.rev. abstr. Index. back issues avail. **Document type:** *Journal, Academic/Scholarly.* **Description:** Publishes articles in the fields of child neurology, pediatric neurosurgery, pediatric neuroradiology, child psychiatry and pediatric neuroscience.
Related titles: Online - full text ed.: ISSN 1875-9041.
Indexed: A22, A29, A35, A36, AgBio, B20, B21, C06, C07, CABA, D01, E01, E12, EMBASE, ESPM, ExcerpMed, GH, H13, H17, LT, N02, N03, NSA, P02, P03, P10, P20, P30, P33, P39, P48, P53, P54, PN&I, PQC, PsycInfo, PsycholAb, R08, R10, R12, RRTA, Reac, S13, S16, SCOPUS, T05, VirolAbstr.
—BLDSC (5030.185000), IE, Ingenta. **CCC.**
Published by: (The Society of Pediatric Science TUR), I O S Press, Nieuwe Hemweg 6B, Amsterdam, 1013 BG, Netherlands. TEL 31-20-6883355, FAX 31-20-6870019, info@iospress.nl, http://www.iospress.nl. Ed. Husein Caksen. adv.: B&W page USD 1,000, color page USD 3,000. Circ: 500 (paid and controlled). **Subscr. to:** The Society of Pediatric Science, P O Box 2, Van 65100, Turkey. jpn@yyu.edu.tr.

618.92 616.07 NLD ISSN 1309-6680
▼ ➤ **JOURNAL OF PEDIATRIC NEURORADIOLOGY.** Text in English. 2011. q. USD 376 combined subscription in North America (print & online eds.); EUR 270 combined subscription elsewhere (print & online eds.) (effective 2012). bk.rev. **Document type:** *Journal, Academic/Scholarly.* **Description:** Covers all topics related to child neuroradiology including diagnostic, functional and therapeutic imaging of the brain, head, neck and spine, congenital central nervous system malformations, and pediatric ophthalmological and otorhinolaryngologic imaging.
Related titles: Online - full text ed.: ISSN 1309-6745.
Published by: (World Society of Child Science TUR), I O S Press, Nieuwe Hemweg 6B, Amsterdam, 1013 BG, Netherlands. TEL 31-20-6883355, FAX 31-20-6870019, info@iospress.nl, http://www.iospress.nl. Eds. Husein Caksen, Monica S Pearl.

➤ **JOURNAL OF PEDIATRIC NEUROSCIENCES.** *see* MEDICAL SCIENCES—Psychiatry And Neurology

➤ **JOURNAL OF PEDIATRIC NURSING;** nursing care of children and families. *see* MEDICAL SCIENCES—Nurses And Nursing

➤ **JOURNAL OF PEDIATRIC OPHTHALMOLOGY & STRABISMUS.** *see* MEDICAL SCIENCES—Ophthalmology And Optometry

➤ **JOURNAL OF PEDIATRIC ORTHOPAEDICS.** *see* MEDICAL SCIENCES—Orthopedics And Traumatology

➤ **JOURNAL OF PEDIATRIC ORTHOPAEDICS. PART B.** *see* MEDICAL SCIENCES—Orthopedics And Traumatology

618.92 615.1 USA ISSN 1551-6776
RJ560
➤ **JOURNAL OF PEDIATRIC PHARMACOLOGY AND THERAPEUTICS.** Abbreviated title: J P P T. Text in English. 1996. q. USD 250 to individuals; USD 300 to institutions; free to members (effective 2010). adv. back issues avail. **Document type:** *Journal, Academic/Scholarly.*
Formerly (until 2001): Journal of Pediatric Pharmacy Practice (1087-0539)
Indexed: I12.
—BLDSC (5030.235000), IE, Ingenta.
Published by: Pediatric Pharmacy Advocacy Group, Inc., 7953 Stage Hills Blvd, Ste 101, Memphis, TN 38133. TEL 901-380-3617, FAX 901-266-4751, http://www.ppag.org/. Ed. Stephanie J Phelps. Adv. contact Matthew Helms.

➤ **JOURNAL OF PEDIATRIC PSYCHOLOGY.** *see* PSYCHOLOGY

618.92 NLD ISSN 1874-5393
➤ **JOURNAL OF PEDIATRIC REHABILITATION MEDICINE.** Text in English. 2007. q. USD 546 combined subscription in North America (print & online eds.); EUR 390 combined subscription elsewhere (print & online eds.) (effective 2012). **Document type:** *Journal, Academic/Scholarly.*
Related titles: Online - full text ed.: ISSN 1875-8894. USD 120, EUR 100 in North America to individuals (effective 2011).
Indexed: A01, A22, E01, EMBASE, P30, SCOPUS, T02.
—BLDSC (5030.270000), IE. **CCC.**
Published by: I O S Press, Nieuwe Hemweg 6B, Amsterdam, 1013 BG, Netherlands. TEL 31-20-6883355, FAX 31-20-6870019, info@iospress.nl. Ed. Jacob A Neufeld TEL 510-428-3655.

618.92 TUR ISSN 1309-1247
▼ ➤ **JOURNAL OF PEDIATRIC SCIENCES.** Text in English. 2009. irreg. free (effective 2011). **Document type:** *Journal, Academic/Scholarly.*
Description: Publishes research articles, reviews, and case reports regarding all disorders and diseases in neonates, children and adolescents, as well as related molecular genetics, pathophysiology, and epidemiology.
Media: Online - full text.
Address: H. Dedelek cd., Kent Park Konaklari Acelya Apt no.9, Eskisehir, Turkey. TEL 90-507-2334108, bilalyn@yahoo.com, enercagri@gmail.com. Eds. Dr. Bilal Yildiz, Dr. Ener Cagri Dinleyici.

➤ **JOURNAL OF PEDIATRIC SURGERY.** *see* MEDICAL SCIENCES—Surgery

618.92 617 ROM
➤ **JOURNAL OF PEDIATRIC SURGICAL SPECIALTIES.** Text in English. 3/yr. EUR 120 in Europe; EUR 128 elsewhere (effective 2010). back issues avail. **Document type:** *Journal, Academic/Scholarly.* **Description:** Covers surgery, orthopedics, urology, otorhinolaryngology, neurosurgery, anesthesia, intensive care, oncology, cardiovascular surgery, imagery, perinatology, embryology, anatomo-pathology. We intend to issue it quarterly and it will cover: editorials, original articles, case presentations, reviews, retrospective studies, clinical research and announcements for future medical meetings.
Related titles: Online - full text ed.
Published by: PRO-ARTE Foundation, 22A Mozart St., Ap. 9, Sector 2, Bucharest, Romania. Ed. Dr. Sebastian Ionescu.

➤ **JOURNAL OF PEDIATRIC UROLOGY.** *see* MEDICAL SCIENCES—Urology And Nephrology

618.92 USA ISSN 0022-3476
RJ1 CODEN: JOPDAB
➤ **THE JOURNAL OF PEDIATRICS.** Text in English. 1932. m. USD 767 in United States to institutions; USD 870 elsewhere to institutions (effective 2012). adv. bk.rev. abstr.; bibl.; charts; illus. s-a. index. back issues avail.; reprints avail. **Document type:** *Journal, Academic/Scholarly.* **Description:** Offers practical guidance for physicians who diagnose and treat disorders in infants and children.
Supersedes (in 1932): American Academy of Pediatrics. Transactions
Related titles: CD-ROM ed.: ISSN 1085-8695; Microfilm ed.: (from PMC, PQC); Online - full text ed.: ISSN 1097-6833 (from ScienceDirect).
Indexed: A20, A22, A26, A29, A34, A36, AIDS Ab, AIM, ASCA, Agr, B20, B21, B25, BDM&CN, BIOBASE, BIOSIS Prev, BibAg, BiolDig, C06, C07, C08, CA, CABA, CCIP, CDA, CIN, CINAHL, ChemAb, ChemTitl, CurCont, D01, DBA, DiabCont, DokArb, E01, E12, ECER, EMBASE, ESPM, ExcerpMed, F09, FR, FS&TA, Faml, G08, GH, GenetAb, H11, H12, H17, HospLI, I10, IABS, IBR, IBZ, IDIS, INI, ISR, IndMed, Inpharma, JW-D, JW-EM, JW-ID, Kidney, LT, MEDLINE, MS&D, MaizeAb, MycolAb, N02, N03, N04, NRN, P03, P16, P18, P30, P32, P33, P35, P39, P40, P50, P53, P54, P55, PQC, PsycInfo, R08, R10, R12, RA&MP, RM&VM, RRTA, Reac, S02, S03, S12, SCI, SCOPUS, SoyAb, T02, T05, THA, VS, VirolAbstr, W07, W10, W11.
—BLDSC (5030.300000), CASDDS, GNLM, IE, Ingenta, INIST. **CCC.**
Published by: Mosby, Inc. (Subsidiary of: Elsevier Health Sciences), 1600 John F. Kennedy Blvd, Ste 1800, Philadelphia, PA 19103. TEL 215-239-3900, 800-523-1649, FAX 215-239-3990, elspcs@elsevier.com, http://www.us.elsevierhealth.com. Ed. Dr. William F Balistreri. Adv. contact Pat Hampton TEL 212-633-3181.

618.92 USA
JOURNAL OF PEDIATRICS AND ADOLESCENT MEDICINE; a journal of current diagnosis and treatment in pediatrics. Text in English. 1996. m. USD 9.99 (effective 2010). back issues avail. **Document type:** *Journal, Academic/Scholarly.*
Formerly: Journal of Pediatrics On-Line (1090-123X)
Media: Online - full text.
Published by: Current Clinical Strategies Publishing Inc., 27071 Cabot Rd, Ste 126, Laguna Hills, CA 92653. TEL 949-348-8404, 800-331-8227, FAX 909-744-8071, 800-965-9420, info@ccspublishing.com, http://www.ccspublishing.com/ccs/.

JOURNAL OF PERINATOLOGY. *see* MEDICAL SCIENCES—Obstetrics And Gynecology

618.92 GBR ISSN 0142-6338
RJ1 CODEN: JTRPAO
➤ **JOURNAL OF TROPICAL PEDIATRICS.** Text in English. 1955. bi-m. GBP 362 in United Kingdom to institutions; EUR 543 in Europe to institutions; USD 723 in US & Canada to institutions; GBP 362 elsewhere to institutions; GBP 395 combined subscription in United Kingdom to institutions (print & online eds.); EUR 593 combined subscription in Europe to institutions (print & online eds.); USD 788 combined subscription in US & Canada to institutions (print & online eds.); GBP 395 combined subscription elsewhere to institutions (print & online eds.) (effective 2012). adv. bk.rev. charts; illus. index. Supplement avail.; back issues avail.; reprint service avail. from PSC. **Document type:** *Journal, Academic/Scholarly.* **Description:** Covers all aspects of child health nutrition, including locality and quality of environment.
Former titles (until 1980): Journal of Tropical Pediatrics and Environmental Child Health (0300-9920); (until 1971): Journal of Tropical Pediatrics (0267-0593); (until 1967): Journal of Tropical Pediatrics and African Child Health (0368-4512); (until 1959): Journal of Tropical Pediatrics (0449-3281)
Related titles: Online - full text ed.: ISSN 1465-3664. GBP 329 in United Kingdom to institutions; EUR 494 in Europe to institutions; USD 657 in US & Canada to institutions; GBP 329 elsewhere to institutions (effective 2012) (from IngentaConnect).
Indexed: A01, A03, A08, A20, A22, A29, A34, A36, AIDS Ab, ARDT, ASCA, ASD, AbAn, AgrForAb, B20, B21, BIOBASE, C25, CA, CABA, CurCont, D01, DentInd, E01, E12, EMBASE, ESPM, ExcerpMed, F08, F09, FR, GH, H&SSA, H13, H16, H17, IABS, INI, ISR, IndMed, IndVet, Inpharma, MEDLINE, N02, N03, P10, P20, P22, P30, P33, P35, P37, P39, P48, P50, P53, P54, PN&I, PQC, R08, R10, R12, RA&MP, RM&VM, Reac, S02, S03, SCI, SCOPUS, SPPI, SoyAb, T02, T05, TAR, VS, VirolAbstr, W07, W11.
—BLDSC (5071.090000), IE, Infotrieve, Ingenta, INIST. **CCC.**
Published by: Oxford University Press, Great Clarendon St, Oxford, OX2 6DP, United Kingdom. TEL 44-1865-556767, FAX 44-1865-556646, enquiry@oup.co.uk, http://www.oxfordjournals.org. Eds. A J R Waterston, D Simkiss, Dr. G J Ebrahim.

618.92 USA ISSN 1538-3571
JOURNAL WATCH PEDIATRICS & ADOLESCENT MEDICINE. Text in English. 2002. m. USD 99 combined subscription domestic to individuals (print & online eds.); CAD 127.62 combined subscription in Canada to individuals (print & online eds.); USD 123 combined subscription elsewhere to individuals (print & online eds.); USD 179 combined subscription domestic to institutions (print & online eds.); CAD 224.76 combined subscription in Canada to institutions (print & online eds.); USD 179 combined subscription elsewhere to institutions (print & online eds.); USD 69 combined subscription domestic to students (print & online eds.); CAD 89.52 combined subscription in Canada to students (print & online eds.); USD 69 combined subscription elsewhere to students (print & online eds.) (effective 2009). **Document type:** *Newsletter, Academic/Scholarly.*
Description: Provides latest information on all aspects of the medical care of children and adolescents including ADHD, autism, depression, eating disorders, genetic disease, obesity, otitis media, sexually transmitted diseases, SIDS, and vaccination.
Related titles: Online - full text ed.: ISSN 1538-358X.
—**CCC.**
Published by: Massachusetts Medical Society, 860 Winter St, Waltham, MA 02451. TEL 781-893-4610, FAX 781-893-8009, info@massmed.org, http://www.massmed.org. Ed. F Bruder Stapleton. Pub. Alberta L Fitzpatrick.

618.92 FRA ISSN 0399-029X
CODEN: JPPEDO
JOURNEES PARISIENNES DE PEDIATRIE. Text in French. 1966. a. price varies. **Document type:** *Journal, Academic/Scholarly.*
—CASDDS, GNLM.
Published by: (Hopital des Enfants Malades, Centre d'Etudes sur les Maladies du Metabolisme chez l'Enfant), Editions Flammarion, 87 Quai Panhard et Levassor, Paris, 75647 Cedex 13, France. TEL 33-1-40513100, http://www.flammarion.com. Ed. P Royer. **U.S. subscr. addr.:** S.F.P.A., c/o Mr Benech, 14 E 60th St, New York, NY 10022.

918.6 DEU ISSN 1612-6084
JUNG UND GESUND; Zeitschrift fuer Kinder und Jugendgesundheit. Text in German. 2003. 4/yr. **Document type:** *Magazine, Consumer.*
Published by: (Berufsverband der Kinder- und Jugendaerzte e.V.), Hansisches Verlagskontor, Mengstr 16, Luebeck, 23552, Germany. TEL 49-451-703101, FAX 49-451-7031253, eickershoff@beleke.de, http://www.beleke.de/verlagsgruppe/ind_hvk.html. Circ: 115,000 (controlled).

618.92 688.72 DEU ISSN 0179-3489
JUNGE FAMILIE; das Baby-Journal. Text in German. 1969. bi-m. EUR 9; EUR 1.20 newsstand/cover (effective 2007). adv. back issues avail. **Document type:** *Magazine, Consumer.*
Published by: Junior-Verlag GmbH und Co. KG, Raboisen 30, Hamburg, 20095, Germany. TEL 49-40-344434, FAX 49-40-352540, info@junior-verlag.de, http://www.junior-verlag.de. Ed. Dagmar von Schweinitz. Pub. Manfred Zedler. Adv. contact Birgit Koenig. B&W page EUR 10,500, color page EUR 18,900; trim 185 x 250. Circ: 269,252 (paid and controlled).

618.92 ROM ISSN 2065-4855
RD137.A1
JURNALUL PEDIATRULUI. Text in English. 1993. s-a. free (effective 2011). **Document type:** *Journal, Academic/Scholarly.*
Formerly (until 1998): Stirea Express (Print) (1221-7212)
Media: Online - full text.
Indexed: A01.
Published by: Fundatia "Profilaxis", Gospodarilor St 42, Timisoara, 300778, Romania. TEL 40-256-439441.

JUST KIDS. *see* CHILDREN AND YOUTH—About

618.92 028.5 USA
KID'S HEALTH. Text in English. 3/yr. free. back issues avail. **Document type:** *Newsletter, Consumer.*
Related titles: Online - full text ed.
Published by: Children's Hospital of Orange County, 455 S. Main St., Orange, CA 92613-3874. TEL 714-997-3000, FAX 714-289-4087. Ed. Susan Thomas. Circ: 135,000 (controlled and free).

618.92 CAN ISSN 1493-7832
KIDS' HEALTH. Text in English. 1984. 3/yr.
Supersedes in part (in 1999): Kaleidoscope (Toronto) (0828-2730); Which was formerly (until 1984): What's New - Hospital for Sick Children (0049-7533); (until 1970): What's New at H S C? (0827-1232)
Published by: Hospital for Sick Children, 555 University Ave, Toronto, ON M5G 1X8, Canada. TEL 416-813-1500, FAX 416-813-5328, http://www.sickkids.on.ca.

KIDS' HEALTH MATTERS. *see* CHILDREN AND YOUTH—About

KIDS WITH FOOD ALLERGIES E-NEWS. *see* MEDICAL SCIENCES—Allergology And Immunology

618.92 NLD ISSN 0167-2436
CODEN: IGKEES
KIND EN ADOLESCENT. Text in Dutch. 1980. q. EUR 134, USD 201 combined subscription to institutions (print & online eds.) (effective 2009). adv. **Document type:** *Journal, Academic/Scholarly.*
Related titles: Online - full text ed.: ISSN 1876-5998.
Indexed: A22, E-psyche, E01, P03, PsycInfo, PsycholAb, S02, S03, SCOPUS.
—IE, Infotrieve.
Published by: Bohn Stafleu van Loghum B.V. (Subsidiary of: Springer Science+Business Media), Postbus 246, Houten, 3990 GA, Netherlands. TEL 31-30-6383872, FAX 31-30-6383991, boekhandels@bsl.nl, http://www.bsl.nl. Ed. Dr. F Boer. adv.: page EUR 825; trim 163 x 245. Circ: 1,550.

618.92 ISSN 1571-4136
KIND EN ADOLESCENT PRAKTIJK. Text in Dutch. 2002. q. EUR 134, USD 201 combined subscription to institutions (print & online eds.) (effective 2009). **Document type:** *Journal, Academic/Scholarly.*
Related titles: Online - full text ed.: ISSN 1875-7065.
Indexed: A22.
Published by: Bohn Stafleu van Loghum B.V. (Subsidiary of: Springer Science+Business Media), Postbus 246, Houten, 3990 GA, Netherlands. TEL 31-30-6383872, FAX 31-30-6383991, boekhandels@bsl.nl. Ed. Dr. Else de Haan.

618.92 NLD ISSN 1571-4969
KIND EN ADOLESCENT REVIEW. Text in Dutch. 2002. q. EUR 232, USD 348 to institutions (effective 2009). **Document type:** *Journal, Academic/Scholarly.*
Published by: Bohn Stafleu van Loghum B.V. (Subsidiary of: Springer Science+Business Media), Postbus 246, Houten, 3990 GA, Netherlands. TEL 31-30-6383872, FAX 31-30-6383991, boekhandels@bsl.nl, http://www.bsl.nl. Ed. J Hermanns.

618.92 NLD ISSN 0169-7072
KIND EN ZIEKENHUIS. Text in Dutch. 1977. q. EUR 35 (effective 2009). adv. bk.rev. 32 p./no.; back issues avail.; reprints avail. **Document type:** *Magazine, Trade.*
Formerly (until 1980): Vereniging Kind en Ziekenhuis. Nieuwsbrief (0165-9642)
—IE, Infotrieve.
Published by: (Vereniging Kind en Ziekenhuis), Landelijke Vereniging Kind en Ziekenhuis, Korte Kalkhaven 9, Dordrecht, 3311 JM, Netherlands. info@kindenziekenhuis.nl. adv.: B&W page EUR 320, color page EUR 1,510; trim 183 x 265. Circ: 1,600.

KIND & GESUNDHEIT. *see* CHILDREN AND YOUTH—About

KINDER; fuer Eltern, Erzieher und Kinder. *see* CHILDREN AND YOUTH—About

618.92 DEU ISSN 1617-0288
➤ **KINDER- UND JUGENDMEDIZIN.** Text in German. 1997. 6/yr. EUR 140 to individuals; EUR 240 to institutions; EUR 70 to students; EUR 32 newsstand/cover (effective 2011). adv. **Document type:** *Journal, Academic/Scholarly.*
Formerly (until 2001): Sozialpaediatrie Kinder- und Jugendheilkunde (1432-9247); Which superseded in part (1994-1997): Sozialpaediatrie und Kinderaerztliche Praxis (0945-7712); Which was formed by the merger of (1930-1994): Kinderaerztliche Praxis (0023-1495); (1979-1994): Sozialpaediatrie in der Paediatrie (0944-2375); Which was formerly (until 1993): Sozialpaediatrie in Praxis und Klinik (0171-9327)
—IE. **CCC.**
Published by: Schattauer GmbH, Hoelderlinstr 3, Stuttgart, 70174, Germany. TEL 49-711-229870, FAX 49-711-2298750, info@schattauer.de, http://www.schattauer.com. Ed. Wieland Kiess. Adv. contact Jasmin Thurner. Circ: 20,898 (paid and controlled).

618.92 DEU ISSN 1432-3605
CODEN: SKIPEJ
KINDERAERZTLICHE PRAXIS; Soziale Paediatrie und Jugendmedizin. Text in German. 1979. 6/yr. EUR 46.50; EUR 9 newsstand/cover (effective 2010). adv. **Document type:** *Journal, Academic/Scholarly.*
Former titles (until 1997): Sozialpaediatrie und Kinderaerztliche Praxis (0945-7712); (until 1993): Sozialpaediatrie in der Paediatrie fuer Praxis und Klinik (0944-2375); (until 1992): Sozial Paediatrie in Praxis und Klinik (0171-9327)
—GNLM.
Published by: (Deutsche Gesellschaft fuer Sozialpaediatrie und Jugendmedizin e.V.), Verlag Kirchheim und Co. GmbH, Kaiserstr 41, Mainz, 55116, Germany. TEL 49-6131-960700, FAX 49-6131-9607070, info@kirchheim-verlag.de, http://www.kirchheim-verlag.de. Ed. Dr. Ruediger von Kries. Circ: 9,800 (paid and controlled).

KINDERKRANKENSCHWESTER. *see* MEDICAL SCIENCES—Nurses And Nursing

KINDEROPVANG. *see* CHILDREN AND YOUTH—About

618.92 DEU ISSN 0942-5403
KINDHEIT UND ENTWICKLUNG; Zeitschrift fuer klinische Kinderpsychologie. Text in German. 1992. q. EUR 81.95 to individuals; EUR 145.95 to institutions; EUR 36.95 newsstand/cover (effective 2011). adv. **Document type:** *Journal, Academic/Scholarly.*
Related titles: Online - full text ed.: ISSN 2190-6246.
Indexed: CurCont, DIP, E-psyche, ERA, IBR, IBZ, M12, P03, PsycInfo, PsycholAb, S20, S21, SCOPUS, SSCI, W07.
—BLDSC (5095.753000), GNLM, IE. **CCC.**
Published by: Hogrefe Verlag GmbH & Co. KG, Rohnsweg 25, Goettingen, 37085, Germany. TEL 49-551-496090, FAX 49-551-4960988, verlag@hogrefe.de. Ed. Ulrike Petermann. Adv. contact Carmen Bergmann. Circ: 2,200 (paid).

618.92 TUR
➤ **KLINIK PEDIATRI DERGISI.** Text in Turkish. 2002. 3/yr. **Document type:** *Journal, Academic/Scholarly.*
Formerly (in 200?): Klinik Pediatri (1303-5312)
Related titles: Online - full text ed.
Published by: Klinik Psikiyatri Dergisi, Sedat Simavi sok. 86/A Blok No.13, Ankara, Turkey. klinikpsikiyatri@cty.com.tr, http://www.klinikpsikiyatri.org/. Ed. Mehmet Vehbi Sahin.

618.92 POL ISSN 1230-7637
KLINIKA PEDIATRYCZNA. Text in Polish. 1993. q. EUR 186 foreign (effective 2006). **Document type:** *Journal, Academic/Scholarly.*
Published by: Wydawnictwo Medyczne Agama, ul Poligonowa 2/37, Warsaw, 04051, Poland. klinika@klinika.com.pl. Ed. M Grabek. **Dist. by:** Ars Polona, Obroncow 25, Warsaw 03933, Poland. TEL 48-22-5098609, FAX 48-22-5098610, arspolona@arspolona.com.pl, http://www.arspolona.com.pl.

618.92 DEU ISSN 0300-8630
RJ1 CODEN: KLPDB2
➤ **KLINISCHE PAEDIATRIE**; clinical research and practice in pediatrics. Text in German; Summaries in English, German. 1880. 7/yr. EUR 379 to institutions; EUR 512 combined subscription to institutions (print & online eds.); EUR 68 newsstand/cover (effective 2011). adv. bk.rev. abstr.; charts; illus. reprint service avail. from IRC. **Document type:** *Journal, Academic/Scholarly.*
Formerly (until 1972): Archiv fuer Kinderheilkunde (0003-9179)
Related titles: Microfiche ed.: (from BHP); Online - full text ed.: ISSN 1439-3824. EUR 495 to institutions (effective 2011).
Indexed: A22, A34, A36, ASCA, B21, BDM&CN, CABA, CTA, ChemAb, CurCont, D01, DBA, EMBASE, ExcerpMed, F09, FR, GH, IBR, IBZ, INI, ISR, IndMed, IndVet, Inpharma, MEDLINE, N02, N03, NSA, OR, P30, P33, P35, R07, R08, R10, R12, RM&VM, Reac, SCI, SCOPUS, T05, VS, VirolAbstr, W07, W10.
—BLDSC (5099.460000), CASDDS, GNLM, IE, Infotrieve, Ingenta, INIST. **CCC.**
Published by: Georg Thieme Verlag, Ruedigerstr 14, Stuttgart, 70469, Germany. TEL 49-711-8931421, FAX 49-711-8931410, kunden.service@thieme.de. Eds. Dr. Ludwig Gortner, Dr. U Goebel. Adv. contact Irmgard Mayer TEL 49-711-8931469. Circ: 900 (paid and controlled).

618.92 KOR ISSN 1738-1061
KOREAN JOURNAL OF PEDIATRICS/SOA'GWA. Text in Korean; Abstracts in English. 1958. m. **Document type:** *Journal, Academic/Scholarly.*
Formerly (until 2004): Soakwa/Korean Pediatric Society. Journal (0560-3560)
Indexed: P30.
—BLDSC (4812.341600).
Published by: Taehan Soakwa Hakhoe/Korean Pediatric Society, Rm 1606, Seocho World Officetel, 1355-3 Seocho-2dong, Seocho-gu, Seoul, 137-862, Korea, S. TEL 82-2-34737305, FAX 82-2-34737307. Ed. Duk Hi Kim. Pub. Hyung Ro Moon.

L D ESSENTIALS. (Learning Disabilities) *see* EDUCATION—Special Education And Rehabilitation

618.92 CHN ISSN 1000-3606
LINCHUANG ERKE ZAZHI/JOURNAL OF CLINICAL PEDIATRICS. Text in Chinese. 1983. m. USD 56.40 (effective 2009). **Document type:** *Journal, Academic/Scholarly.*
Related titles: Online - full text ed.
Published by: Shanghai Shi Erke Yixue Yanjiusuo/Shanghai Institute for Pediatric Research, 1665, Kongjiang Lu, Shanghai, 200092, China. TEL 86-21-65790000 ext 3406, FAX 86-21-55964560. **Dist. by:** China International Book Trading Corp, 35 Chegongzhuang Xilu, Haidian District, PO Box 399, Beijing 100044, China. TEL 86-10-68412045, FAX 86-10-68412023, cibtc@mail.cibtc.com.cn, http://www.cibtc.com.cn.

LISA FAMILY. *see* CHILDREN AND YOUTH—About

LJOSMAEDRABLADID. *see* MEDICAL SCIENCES—Obstetrics And Gynecology

M P R (PEDIATRICIANS' EDITION). (Monthly Prescribing Reference) *see* PHARMACY AND PHARMACOLOGY

MAGASINET VOKSNE FOR BARN. *see* PSYCHOLOGY

618.92 RUS
MAMA, PAPA, YA; nauchno-populyarnaya meditsinskaya gazeta. Text in Russian. m. free (effective 2004). **Document type:** *Newspaper, Consumer.* **Description:** Contains advices, recommendations and consultations of the best medical specialists in pediatrics.
Related titles: Online - full content ed.
Published by: Redaktsiya Gazety Mama, Papa, Ya, ul Taldomskaya 2, Moscow, 125412, Russian Federation. TEL 7-095-2298668, mamapapa@macuser.ru. Ed. Anatolii Khavkin. **Co-sponsor:** Komitet po Delam Semii i Molodezhi Pravitel'stva Moskvy.

MATERNAL AND CHILD HEALTH JOURNAL. *see* MEDICAL SCIENCES—Obstetrics And Gynecology

618.92 FRA ISSN 0291-0233
➤ **MEDECINE ET ENFANCE.** Text in French. 1981. 10/yr. EUR 50 (effective 2009). adv. bk.rev. **Document type:** *Journal, Academic/Scholarly.* **Description:** A post-graduate medical journal directed at pediatricians, GP's and institutions.
Related titles: CD-ROM ed.
Indexed: FR.
—INIST.
Published by: Edition et Communication Medicales, 23 rue Saint Ferdinand, Paris, 75017, France. TEL 33-1-45744465. Ed. C Geselson.

618.92 FRA ISSN 1286-5494
MEDECINE THERAPEUTIQUE PEDIATRIE. Key Title: M T P. Medecine Therapeutique Pediatrie. Text in French. 1998. bi-m. EUR 406 combined subscription domestic to institutions (print & online eds.); EUR 430 combined subscription in the European Union to institutions (print & online eds.); EUR 442 combined subscription elsewhere to institutions (print & online eds.) (effective 2011). **Document type:** *Journal, Academic/Scholarly.* **Description:** Publishes only reviews and synoptic articles aimed at both practicing doctors and students.
Related titles: Online - full text ed.: ISSN 1952-4188.
Indexed: SCOPUS.
—BLDSC (5487.965000), IE, Ingenta, INIST. **CCC.**
Published by: John Libbey Eurotext, 127 Av. de la Republique, Montrouge, 92120, France. TEL 33-1-46730660, FAX 33-1-40840999, contact@jle.com, http://www.john-libbey-eurotext.fr. Ed. Philippe Reinert.

MEDICAL STAFF. ALLERGOLOGIE PEDIATRIE. *see* MEDICAL SCIENCES—Allergology And Immunology

618.92 ITA ISSN 1591-3090
MEDICO E BAMBINO; rivista di formazione e aggiornamento professionale per il pediatra. Text in Italian. 1981. m. (10/yr.). EUR 45 (effective 2008). adv. **Document type:** *Magazine, Consumer.*
Indexed: EMBASE, ExcerpMed, R10, Reac, SCOPUS.
—BLDSC (5534.179000).
Published by: (Associazione Culturale Pediatri), Edifarm SpA, Via P. Palagi 4, Milan, 20129, Italy. TEL 39-02-29520315, FAX 39-02-29520449, http://www.edifarm.com. Circ: 8,500 (paid).

618.92 BGR ISSN 0324-1122
➤ **MEDITSINSKI PREGLED. DETSKI BOLESTI/MEDICAL REVIEW. CHILDREN'S DISEASES.** Text in Bulgarian; Summaries in Bulgarian, English. 1972. q. BGL 14 domestic; USD 40 foreign (effective 2005). adv. bk.rev. abstr.; bibl. index. 48 p./no.; **Document type:** *Journal, Academic/Scholarly.* **Description:** Presents original articles and abstracts of foreign publications in the field of pediatrics - diagnosis, treatment and prevention of children's diseases, new drugs, child health.
Indexed: ABSML.
Published by: Meditsinski Universitet - Sofia, Tsentralna Meditsinska Biblioteka, Tsentur za Informatsiia po Meditsina/Medical University - Sofia, Central Medical Library, Medical Information Center, 1 Sv Georgi Sofiiski ul, Sofia, 1431, Bulgaria. TEL 359-2-9522342, FAX 359-2-9522393, lydia@medun.acad.bg, http://www.medun.acad.bg/cmb_htm/cmb1_home_bg.htm. Ed. Dr. A Anadoliiska. R&P, Adv. contact Lydia Tacheva. B&W page USD 50, color page USD 200; 12 x 18. Circ: 450.

618.92 POL
MEDYCYNA PRAKTYCZNA. PEDIATRIA. Text in Polish. 1995. bi-m.
Published by: Medycyna Praktyczna, ul Krakowska 41, Krakow, 31066, Poland. TEL 48-12-4305520, FAX 48-12-4305536, listy@mp.pl, http://www.mp.pl. Ed. Jacek Mrukowicz.

618.92 POL ISSN 1428-345X
MEDYCYNA WIEKU ROZWOJOWEGO. Text in Polish. 1997. q. EUR 51 foreign (effective 2005). **Document type:** *Journal, Academic/Scholarly.*
Former titles (until 1997): Problemy Medycyny Wieku Rozwojowego (0303-2264); (until 1972): Instytut Matki i Dziecka. Prace i Materialy Naukowe (0511-1382)
Indexed: EMBASE, ExcerpMed, F09, MEDLINE, P30, R10, Reac, SCOPUS.
—BLDSC (5536.082000), Linda Hall.
Published by: Instytut Matki i Dziecka, ul Kasprzaka 17a, Warsaw, 01211, Poland. TEL 48-22-3277197, medroz@imid.med.pl, http://www.imid.med.pl. **Dist. by:** Ars Polona, Obroncow 25, Warsaw 03933, Poland. TEL 48-22-5098609, FAX 48-22-5098610, arspolona@arspolona.com.pl, http://www.arspolona.com.pl.

METIERS DE LA PETITE ENFANCE; eveil et developpement de l'enfant. *see* CHILDREN AND YOUTH—About

MIDWIFERY. *see* MEDICAL SCIENCES—Obstetrics And Gynecology

618.92 ITA ISSN 0026-4946
CODEN: MIPEA5
➤ **MINERVA PEDIATRICA**; a journal on pediatrics, neonatology, adolescent medicine, child and aolescent psychiatry. Text in Italian; Summaries in English, Italian. 1949. bi-m. EUR 255 combined subscription in the European Union to institutions (print & online eds.); EUR 280 combined subscription elsewhere to institutions (print & online eds.) (effective 2011). adv. bk.rev. abstr.; bibl.; illus. index. **Document type:** *Journal, Academic/Scholarly.* **Description:** Covers pediatric neonatology, adolescent medicine, child and adolescent psychiatry.
Incorporates: Policlinico Infantile (0391-0474); Pediatria del Medico Pratico (0391-0393); Medicina Italiana (0369-0415); Il Lattante (0023-8864); Rivista di Clinica Pediatrica (0035-6077)
Related titles: Microform ed.: (from PQC); Online - full text ed.: ISSN 1827-1715; ◆ Supplement(s): Notiziario Pediatrico. ISSN 0392-0615.
Indexed: A22, A34, A36, C25, CABA, ChemAb, D01, DentInd, E12, EMBASE, ExcerpMed, F09, GH, H16, IndMed, LT, MEDLINE, N02, N03, P30, P33, P39, R08, R10, R11, R12, RA&MP, RM&VM, RRTA, Reac, RefZh, SCOPUS, SoyAb, T05, VS.
—BLDSC (5794.400000), CASDDS, GNLM, IE, Infotrieve, Ingenta, INIST. **CCC.**
Published by: Edizioni Minerva Medica, Corso Bramante 83-85, Turin, 10126, Italy. TEL 39-011-678282, FAX 39-011-674502, journals.dept@minervamedica.it, http://www.minervamedica.it. Circ: 5,000 (paid).

618.92 DEU ISSN 0026-9298
CODEN: MOKIAY
➤ **MONATSSCHRIFT KINDERHEILKUNDE**; Zeitschrift fuer Kinder- und Jugendmedizin. Text in German. 1903. m. EUR 587, USD 659 combined subscription to institutions (print & online eds.) (effective 2012). adv. bk.rev. bibl.; charts. back issues avail.; reprint service avail. from PSC. **Document type:** *Journal, Academic/Scholarly.* **Description:** Serves the continuing education of pediatricians in hospitals and practice.
Related titles: Microform ed.: (from PQC); Online - full text ed.: ISSN 1433-0474 (from IngentaConnect).
Indexed: A20, A22, A26, A34, A36, BDM&CN, BP, CABA, ChemAb, CurCont, D01, E01, E12, EMBASE, ExcerpMed, FR, GH, H17, ISR, IndMed, IndVet, Inpharma, LT, N02, N03, N04, P30, P33, P35, P39, PN&I, R08, R10, R13, RM&VM, RRTA, Reac, S02, S03, S12, SCI, SCOPUS, T05, VS, W07, W11.
—BLDSC (5906.400000), CASDDS, GNLM, IE, Infotrieve, Ingenta, INIST. **CCC.**
Published by: (Deutschen Gesellschaft fuer Kinderheilkunde und Jugendmedizin), Springer (Subsidiary of: Springer Science+Business Media), Tiergartenstr 17, Heidelberg, 69121, Germany. TEL 49-6221-4870, FAX 49-6221-345229. Ed. D Reinhardt. Adv. contact Stephan Kroeck TEL 49-30-827875739. Circ: 13,500 (paid and controlled). **Subscr. in the Americas to:** Springer New York LLC, Journal Fulfillment, PO Box 2485, Secaucus, NJ 07096. TEL 800-777-4643, 201-348-4033, FAX 201-348-4505, journals-ny@springer.com, http://www.springer.com; **Subscr. to:** Springer Distribution Center, Kundenservice Zeitschriften, Haberstr 7, Heidelberg 69126, Germany. TEL 49-6221-3454303, FAX 49-6221-3454229, subscriptions@springer.com.

618.92 ESP ISSN 0212-1603
MONOGRAFIAS DE PEDIATRIA. Text in Spanish. 1982. 6/yr. EUR 72 (effective 2009). **Document type:** *Journal, Academic/Scholarly.*
Related titles: Cumulative ed(s).: EUR 30 (effective 2009).
Published by: Grupo Aula Medica S.A., C Isabel Colbrand, 10 Nave 78, Planta 2a, Madrid, 28050, Spain. TEL 34-91-3586478, FAX 34-91-3589979, informacion@grupoaulamedica.com. Ed. Dr. Angel Nogales Espert.

MR. NO-NO SAYS, "DON'T TOUCH, STAY AWAY". *see* CHILDREN AND YOUTH—About

N A N N CENTRAL. *see* MEDICAL SCIENCES—Nurses And Nursing

617.463 USA
N O C I R C ANNUAL NEWSLETTER. Text in English. 1986. a. back issues avail.; reprints avail. **Document type:** *Newsletter.* **Description:** Provides parents, health-care professionals, and other concerned individuals with current medical and legal information on routine neonatal circumcision and female genital mutilation, and focuses on efforts to reduce the frequency of the practice, protecting the rights of infants and children.
Formerly: N O C I R C Newsletter (1070-3721)
Related titles: Online - full text ed.
Published by: National Organization of Circumcision Information Resource Centers, PO Box 2512, San Anselmo, CA 94979-2512. TEL 415-488-9883, FAX 415-488-9660, nocirc@concentric.net, http://www.nocirc.org. Ed., R&P Marilyn Fayre Milos. Circ: 15,000.

618 PRT ISSN 0872-0754
NASCER E CRESCER. Text in Portuguese. 1992. q. back issues avail. **Document type:** *Journal, Academic/Scholarly.*
Related titles: Online - full text ed.
Indexed: A22, EMBASE, ExcerpMed, R10, Reac, SCOPUS.
—BLDSC (6015.553500), IE.
Published by: Hospital Central Especializado de Criancas Maria Pia, Rua de Boavista, No. 827, Porto, 4050-111, Portugal. TEL 351-22-6089900, FAX 351-22-6000841, hmaria@hmariapia.min-saude.pt. Ed. Silvia Alvarez.

NASH MALYSH. *see* CHILDREN AND YOUTH—About

NATIONAL ASSOCIATION OF NEONATAL NURSES. POSITION STATEMENT. *see* MEDICAL SCIENCES—Nurses And Nursing

618.92 JPN ISSN 1341-4577
NEONATAL CARE/NEONEITARU KEA. Text in Japanese. 1987. m. JPY 20,412; JPY 1,800 newsstand/cover (effective 2007). Supplement avail. **Document type:** *Journal, Academic/Scholarly.*
Formerly (until vol.7, no.4, 1994): N I C U: Japanese Journal of Neonatal Care (0914-2533)
Published by: Medicus Shuppan/Medicus Publishing Inc., 18-24 Hiroshiba-cho, Suita-shi, Osaka-fu 564-8580, Japan. TEL 81-6-63856911, FAX 81-6-63856873, http://www.medica.co.jp/.

NEONATAL INTENSIVE CARE; the journal of perinatology - neonatology. *see* MEDICAL SCIENCES—Obstetrics And Gynecology

NEONATAL NETWORK; the journal of neonatal nursing. *see* MEDICAL SCIENCES—Nurses And Nursing

NEONATAL, PAEDIATRIC AND CHILD HEALTH NURSING. *see* MEDICAL SCIENCES—Nurses And Nursing

618.92 GBR ISSN 2045-0818
NEONATAL SURVEY REPORT. Text in English. 19??. a. back issues avail. **Document type:** *Report, Academic/Scholarly.*
Formerly (until 2005): Trent Neonatal Survey Report
Related titles: Online - full text ed.: free (effective 2010).
Published by: University of Leicester, Department of Health Sciences, The Neonatal Survey, 22-28 Princess Rd W, Leicester, LE1 6TP, United Kingdom. TEL 44-116-2525468, FAX 44-116-2523272, timms@leicester.ac.uk, http://www2.le.ac.uk/departments/health-sciences/research/ships/timms/images/tns-small.gif/view.

618.92 USA ISSN 1932-7129
NEONATOLOGY TODAY. Text in English. 2006. m. free to qualified personnel (effective 2011). back issues avail. **Document type:** *Newsletter, Academic/Scholarly.* **Description:** Provides news and information to Board Certified Neonatologists and Perinatologists regarding the care of newborns and the diagnosis and treatment of premature and/or sick infants.
Related titles: Online - full text ed.: ISSN 1932-7137.
Address: 824 Elmcroft Blvd, Rockville, MD 20850. Info@Neonate.biz. Ed., Pub. Richard Koulbanis.

618.92 USA ISSN 1526-9906
➤ **NEOREVIEWS.ORG.** Text in English. 2000 (Jan.). m. USD 122 to non-members; USD 109 to members (effective 2011). charts; illus.; stat. back issues avail.; reprints avail. **Document type:** *Journal, Academic/Scholarly.* **Description:** Focuses on neonatal and perinatal topics. Delivers 3-4 reviews, case discussions, basic science insights, and on the horizon pieces each month.
Media: Online - full text.
Indexed: P30, SCOPUS.
—CCC.
Published by: American Academy of Pediatrics, 141 NW Pt Blvd, Elk Grove Village, IL 60007. TEL 847-434-4000, FAX 847-434-8000, journals@aap.org, http://www.aap.org. Ed. Alistair G S Philip.

618.92 USA
NEOREVIEWSPLUS. Variant title: NeoReviews Plus. Text in English. 2004. m. USD 215 to non-members; USD 193 to members (effective 2010). back issues avail. **Document type:** *Journal, Academic/Scholarly.*
Media: Online - full text.
Published by: American Academy of Pediatrics, 141 NW Pt Blvd, Elk Grove Village, IL 60007. TEL 847-434-4000, FAX 847-434-8000, journals@aap.org, http://www.aap.org. **Subscr. to:** 72139 Eagle Way, Chicago, IL 60678. TEL 866-843-2271, FAX 847-228-1281.

618.92 NPL ISSN 1990-7974
RJ1
➤ **NEPAL PAEDIATRIC SOCIETY. JOURNAL.** Variant title: NEPAS Journal. Text in English. 1981. s-a. **Document type:** *Journal, Academic/Scholarly.* **Description:** Aims to publish work by members of the society and also by non-members or organizations who have worked in the field of Paediatrics.
Related titles: Online - full text ed.: ISSN 1990-7982. 2002. free (effective 2011).
Indexed: A01, CA, CABA, D01, EMBASE, ExcerpMed, GH, N02, N03, P33, R08, SCOPUS, T02, T05, W10, W11.
Published by: Nepal Paediatric Society, Kanti Children's Hospital, Maharajguj, G P O Box No 2668, Kathmandu, Nepal. TEL 977-1-4412648, 977-1-4271965, FAX 977-1-4427449, arunneopane@hotmail.com, nepas@healthnet.org.np, http://www.nepas.org.np/. Ed. Arun Neopane.

616.8 DEU ISSN 1619-3873
➤ **NEUROPAEDIATRIE IN KLINIK UND PRAXIS.** Text in German. 2002. q. EUR 46; EUR 12 newsstand/cover (effective 2011). adv. **Document type:** *Journal, Academic/Scholarly.*

M

Published by: Max Schmidt-Roemhild KG, Mengstr 16, Luebeck, 23552, Germany. TEL 49-451-703101, FAX 49-451-7031253, info@schmidt-roemhild.de, http://www.beleke.de/unternehmen/verlage/schmidtroemhild/index.html.

616.8 DEU ISSN 0174-304X
RD1 CODEN: NRPDDB

➤ **NEUROPEDIATRICS**; journal of pediatric neurobiology, neurology and neurosurgery. Text in English. 1970. bi-m. EUR 449 to institutions; EUR 602 combined subscription to institutions (print & online eds.); EUR 83 per issue (effective 2011). adv. **Document type:** *Journal, Academic/Scholarly.* **Description:** Designed for pediatricians, neurologists, neurosurgeons, neurogeneticians, and neurobiologists. Covers current developments and trends in pediatric neurology.
Formerly: Neuropaediatrie (0028-3797)
Related titles: Online - full text ed.: ISSN 1439-1899. EUR 580 to institutions (effective 2011).
Indexed: A01, A03, A08, A22, ASCA, B21, B25, BDM&CN, BIOSIS Prev, CA, CDA, ChemAb, CurCont, E-psyche, EMBASE, ExcerpMed, GenetAb, ISR, ImmunAb, IndMed, Inpharma, MEDLINE, MycolAb, NSA, NSCI, P30, P35, R10, Reac, SCI, SCOPUS, T02, W07.
—BLDSC (6081.515500), CASDDS, GNLM, IE, Infotrieve, Ingenta, INIST. **CCC.**
Published by: (Gesellschaft fuer Neuropaediatrie/Society for Neuropediatrics), Georg Thieme Verlag, Ruedigerstr 14, Stuttgart, 70469, Germany. TEL 49-711-8931421, FAX 49-711-8931410, kunden.service@thieme.de. Eds. Dr. E Boltshauser, G F Hoffmann. adv.: B&W page EUR 990, color page EUR 2,085. Circ: 1,580 (paid). **Subscr. to:** Thieme Medical Publishers, 333 Seventh Ave, New York, NY 10001. TEL 212-760-0888, 800-782-3488, 800-782-3488, FAX 212-947-1112, custserv@thieme.com, http://www.thieme.com/journals.

616.8 FRA ISSN 0222-9617
RJ486.A1 CODEN: PMECD8

NEUROPSYCHIATRIE DE L'ENFANCE ET DE L'ADOLESCENCE. Text in French. 1953. 8/yr. EUR 393 in Europe to institutions; EUR 352.60 in France to institutions; JPY 46,800 in Japan to institutions; USD 497 elsewhere to institutions (effective 2012). adv. bk.rev. bibl.; charts; illus. **Document type:** *Journal, Academic/Scholarly.*
Formerly: Revue de Neuropsychiatrie Infantile et d'Hygiene Mentale de l'Enfance (0035-1628)
Related titles: Microform ed.; Online - full text ed.: (from IngentaConnect, ScienceDirect).
Indexed: A01, A03, A08, A20, A22, CA, E-psyche, EMBASE, ExcerpMed, FR, IndMed, P03, P30, PsycInfo, PsycholAb, R10, Reac, S02, S03, SCOPUS, SOPODA, SociolAb, T02.
—BLDSC (6081.536000), GNLM, IE, Infotrieve, Ingenta, INIST. **CCC.**
Published by: (Societe Francaise de Psychiatrie de l'Enfant et de l'Adolescent), Elsevier Masson (Subsidiary of: Elsevier Health Sciences), 62 Rue Camille Desmoulins, Issy les Moulineaux, Cedex 92442, France. TEL 33-1-71165500, FAX 33-1-71165600, infos@elsevier-masson.fr. Ed. Michel Basquin. Circ: 5,000.

616.8588 NZL ISSN 1177-6323

NEW ZEALAND DOWN SYNDROME JOURNAL. Variant title: N Z D S A Journal. Text in English. 1990. q. **Document type:** *Journal, Consumer.*
Former titles (until 2006): New Zealand Down Syndrome News; (until 1998): New Zealand Down Syndrome Association. Series; (until 1995): Down's Association. Newsletter
Published by: New Zealand Down Syndrome Association, PO Box 4142, Auckland, New Zealand. TEL 800-693-724, FAX 64-3-3602867, national.coordinator@nzdsa.org.nz, http://www.nzdsa.org.nz.

NEWBORN AND INFANT NURSING REVIEWS. *see* MEDICAL SCIENCES—Nurses And Nursing

618.92 JPN ISSN 1346-1680

NIHON S I D S GAKKAI ZASSHI/JAPAN S I D S RESEARCH SOCIETY. JOURNAL. (Sudden Infant Death Syndrome) Text in Japanese. 2001. a. **Document type:** *Journal, Academic/Scholarly.*
—BLDSC (6113.100000).
Published by: Nihon S I D S Gakkai/Japan S I D S Research Society, 8-1 Kawadacho, Shinjuku-ku, Tokyo Women's Medical College, Tokyo, 162-8666, Japan. TELEX 81-3-52697346.

618.92 JPN ISSN 0288-609X

NIHON SHONI GEKA GAKKAI ZASSHI/JAPANESE SOCIETY OF PEDIATRIC SURGEONS. JOURNAL. Text in Japanese; Summaries in English. 1965. 7/yr. JPY 2,000 per issue. **Document type:** *Journal, Academic/Scholarly.*
Indexed: INIS AtomInd.
—BLDSC (4809.476000). **CCC.**
Published by: Nihon Shoni Geka Gakkai/Japanese Society of Pediatric Surgeons, 26-1-B03 Kaitai-cho, Shinjuku-ku, Tokyo, 162-0802, Japan. TEL 81-3-52066009, FAX 81-3-52066008, http://www.jsps.gr.jp/.

NIHON SHONI HOSHASEN GAKKAI ZASSHI/JAPANESE SOCIETY OF PEDIATRIC RADIOLOGY. JOURNAL. *see* MEDICAL SCIENCES—Radiology And Nuclear Medicine

NIHON SHONI KETSUEKI GAKKAI ZASSHI/JAPANESE JOURNAL OF PEDIATRIC HEMATOLOGY. *see* MEDICAL SCIENCES—Hematology

618.92 617.3 JPN ISSN 0917-6950

NIHON SHONI SEIKEI GEKA GAKKAI ZASSHI/JAPANESE PAEDIATRIC ORTHOPAEDIC ASSOCIATION. JOURNAL. Text in English, Japanese. 1991. s-a. JPY 10,000 membership (effective 2006). **Document type:** *Journal, Academic/Scholarly.*
—BLDSC (6113.091850). **CCC.**
Published by: Nihon Shoni Seikei Geka Gakkai/Japanese Paediatric Orthopaedic Association, TH Bldg, 2nd Fl., 2-40-8 Hongo, Bunkyo-ku, Tokyo, 113-0033, Japan. TEL 81-3-58037071, FAX 81-3-58037072, jpoa@jpoa.org, http://www.jpoa.org/.

618.92 610 JPN ISSN 1348-964X

➤ **NIHON SHUUSANKI SHINSEIJI IGAKKAI ZASSHI/JAPAN SOCIETY OF PERINATAL AND NEONATAL MEDICINE. JOURNAL.** Text in Japanese; Summaries in English, Japanese. 1965. q. JPY 8,000 membership (effective 2005). adv. bk.rev. bibl. cum.index. back issues avail. **Document type:** *Journal, Academic/Scholarly.*
Formerly (until 2003): Nihon Shinseiji Gakkai Zasshi/Acta Neonatologica Japonica (0029-0386)
Indexed: INIS AtomInd, SCOPUS.
—BLDSC (6113.098500), GNLM.
Published by: Nihon Shinseiji Gakkai/Japan Society of Neonatology, c/o Toho University School of Medicine, Department of Neonatology, 6-11-1 Omori-Nishi, Ota-ku, Tokyo, 143-0015, Japan. TEL 81-3-37620841, FAX 81-3-37620842. Ed. Dr. Hiroshi Tada. Adv. contact Nihon Igaku Koukokusha. Circ: 4,000 (controlled).

618.92 SVK ISSN 1337-0634

NOVINKY. Variant title: Novinky Detskej Fakultnej Nemocnice s Poliklinikou Banska Bystrica. Text in Slovak. 2006. q. **Document type:** *Magazine, Trade.*
Published by: Detska Fakultna Nemocnica s Poliklinikou Banska Bystrica, Nam L Svobodu c 4, Banska Bystrica, 974 09, Slovakia. TEL 421-48-4726501, dfn@dfnbb.sk. Ed. Ladislav Laho.

618.92 POL ISSN 1428-1848

➤ **NOWA PEDIATRIA.** Text in Polish. 1997. q. PLZ 50 domestic (effective 2008). **Document type:** *Journal, Academic/Scholarly.*
Related titles: Online - full content ed.: ISSN 1731-2493.
Indexed: A36, CABA, E12, GH, H16, N02, N03, P33, P39.
Published by: Wydawnictwo Medyczne Borgis, ul Walbrzyska 3/5, Warsaw, 02739, Poland. wydawnictwo@borgis.pl, http://www.borgis.pl. Ed. Artur A Gadomski. Circ: 8,000.

610.7362 GBR ISSN 1476-136X

NURSERY MANAGEMENT TODAY. Text in English. 2002. bi-m. GBP 65 domestic; GBP 80 in Europe; GBP 90 elsewhere (effective 2009). adv. bk.rev. 48 p./no.; back issues avail. **Document type:** *Magazine, Trade.* **Description:** Contains management information for senior staff of children's nurseries.
Published by: Hawker Publications Ltd., Culvert House, Culvert Rd, London, SW11 5DH, United Kingdom. TEL 44-20-77202108, FAX 44-20-74983023, suec@hawkerpublications.com, http://www.careinfo.org/. Ed. Alison Gordon TEL 44-1225-466950. Adv. contact Chris Banner TEL 44-1323-740701. **Subscr. to:** ESCO Business Services Ltd., Trinity House, Sculpins Ln, Wethersfield, Braintree, Essex CM7 4AY, United Kingdom. TEL 44-1371-810433, FAX 44-1371-851808, enquiries@esco.co.uk, http://www.esco.co.uk.

NYUUYOUJI IGAKU, SHINRIGAKU KENKYUU/JAPANESE JOURNAL OF MEDICAL AND PSYCHOLOGICAL STUDY OF INFANTS. *see* PSYCHOLOGY

ODONTOLOGIA PEDIATRICA. *see* MEDICAL SCIENCES—Dentistry

618.92 USA ISSN 2160-8741

▼ ➤ **OPEN JOURNAL OF PEDIATRICS.** Text in English. 2011. q. USD 156 (effective 2011). **Document type:** *Journal, Academic/Scholarly.* **Description:** Provides a platform for scientists and academicians all over the world to promote, share, and discuss various new issues and developments in different areas of pediatrics.
Related titles: Online - full text ed.: ISSN 2160-8776. free (effective 2011).
Published by: Scientific Research Publishing, Inc., PO Box 54821, Irvine, CA 92619. service@scirp.org. Ed. Constantinos J Stefanidis.

618.92 NLD ISSN 1874-3099
RJ1

➤ **THE OPEN PEDIATRIC MEDICINE JOURNAL.** Text in English. 2007. irreg. free (effective 2011). **Document type:** *Journal, Academic/Scholarly.* **Description:** Covers all areas of experimental and clinical research in pediatric medicine.
Media: Online - full text.
Indexed: A01, P30, SCOPUS.
Published by: Bentham Open (Subsidiary of: Bentham Science Publishers Ltd.), PO Box 294, Bussum, AG 1400, Netherlands. TEL 31-35-6923800, FAX 31-35-6980150, subscriptions@bentham.org.

➤ **OPHTHALMIC GENETICS.** *see* MEDICAL SCIENCES—Ophthalmology And Optometry

➤ **ORTHOSCOPE.** *see* MEDICAL SCIENCES—Orthopedics And Traumatology

➤ **OSLO UNIVERSITETSSYKEHUS. ULLEVAAL, KLINIKK FOR PSYKISK HELSE - BARN OG UNGDOM. MONOGRAFISERIEN.** *see* MEDICAL SCIENCES—Psychiatry And Neurology

618.92 USA ISSN 1943-0949

P R E P (YEAR) SELF ASSESSMENT. (Pediatrics Review and Education Program) Text in English. 2000. a. USD 373 per issue to non-members; USD 260 per issue to members (effective 2011). back issues avail. **Document type:** *Journal, Trade.* **Description:** Contains compilation of clinically relevant questions and critiques that assist participants in acquiring and updating the knowledge and skills needed to provide health supervision, and manage acute and chronic illnesses in infants, children, adolescents, and young adults.
Media: Online - full text. **Related titles:** CD-ROM ed.: ISSN 1943-0957; ◆ Print ed.: P R E P, the Curriculum. ISSN 1943-0965.
Published by: American Academy of Pediatrics, 141 NW Pt Blvd, Elk Grove Village, IL 60007. TEL 847-434-4000, FAX 847-434-8000, journals@aap.org, http://www.aap.org. **Subscr. to:** 72139 Eagle Way, Chicago, IL 60678. TEL 866-843-2271, FAX 847-228-1281.

618.92 USA ISSN 1559-0356

P R E P AUDIO. (Pediatrics Review and Education Program) Text in English. 2006. m. USD 317 combined subscription to institutions (CD-ROM & MP3 eds.); USD 295 combined subscription to non-members (CD-ROM & MP3 eds.); USD 247 combined subscription to members (CD-ROM & MP3 eds.) (effective 2011). back issues avail. **Document type:** *Journal, Trade.*
Media: CD-ROM. **Related titles:** Online - full text ed.: ISSN 1559-0364. 2006. USD 275 to non-members; USD 225 to members (effective 2011).
Published by: American Academy of Pediatrics, 141 NW Pt Blvd, Elk Grove Village, IL 60007. TEL 847-434-4000, FAX 847-434-8000, journals@aap.org, http://www.aap.org. Ed. Kurt Metzl. **Subscr. to:** 72139 Eagle Way, Chicago, IL 60678. TEL 866-843-2271, FAX 847-228-1281.

618.92 USA ISSN 2150-783X

▼ ➤ **P R E P DBPEDS.** (Pediatrics Review and Education Program) Text in English. 2009. m. USD 199 to non-members; USD 179 to members (effective 2011). **Document type:** *Journal, Academic/Scholarly.* **Description:** Provides developmental and behavioral pediatric specialists the tools, knowledge and vital education resources for success in their practice.
Media: Online - full text.
Published by: American Academy of Pediatrics, 141 NW Pt Blvd, Elk Grove Village, IL 60007. TEL 847-434-4000, FAX 847-434-8000, journals@aap.org, http://www.aap.org. Eds. Franklin Trimm, Sydney Rice. **Subscr. to:** 72139 Eagle Way, Chicago, IL 60678. TEL 866-843-2271, FAX 847-228-1281.

618.92 USA

▼ ➤ **P R E P E-MED**; the premier emergency medicine self-assessment. (Pediatrics Review and Education Program) Text in English. 2009. m. USD 199 to non-members; USD 179 to members (effective 2011). **Document type:** *Journal, Academic/Scholarly.*
Media: Online - full text.
Published by: American Academy of Pediatrics, 141 NW Pt Blvd, Elk Grove Village, IL 60007. TEL 847-434-4000, FAX 847-434-8000, journals@aap.org, http://www.aap.org. Eds. Douglas Baker, James Wilde, Jeffrey Avner. **Subscr. to:** 72139 Eagle Way, Chicago, IL 60678. TEL 866-843-2271, FAX 847-228-1281.

▼ ➤ **P R E P ENDOCRINOLOGY**; the premier endocrinology self-assessment. (Pediatrics Review and Education Program) *see* MEDICAL SCIENCES—Endocrinology

618.92 USA

➤ **P R E P ICU**; the premier critical care self-assessment. (Pediatrics Review and Education Program) Text in English. 2008. m. USD 199 to non-members; USD 179 to members (effective 2011). back issues avail. **Document type:** *Journal, Academic/Scholarly.*
Media: Online - full text.
Published by: American Academy of Pediatrics, 141 NW Pt Blvd, Elk Grove Village, IL 60007. TEL 847-434-4000, FAX 847-434-8000, journals@aap.org, http://www.aap.org. Eds. Jeremy Garrett, Otwell Timmons, Richard Fiser. **Subscr. to:** 72139 Eagle Way, Chicago, IL 60678. TEL 866-843-2271, FAX 847-228-1281.

▼ ➤ **P R E P INFECTIOUS DISEASES**; the premier infectious diseases self-assessment. (Pediatrics Review and Education Program) *see* MEDICAL SCIENCES—Communicable Diseases

618.92 USA ISSN 1556-3227

P R E P REFERENCE ON CD-ROM. (Pediatric Review and Education Program) Text in English. 2005. a. USD 339 to non-members; USD 326 to members (effective 2010). back issues avail. **Document type:** *Handbook/Manual/Guide, Trade.*
Media: CD-ROM.
Published by: American Academy of Pediatrics, 141 NW Pt Blvd, Elk Grove Village, IL 60007. TEL 847-434-4000, FAX 847-434-8000, journals@aap.org, http://www.aap.org.

618.92 USA ISSN 1943-0965

P R E P, THE CURRICULUM; growing your knowledge of pediatrics never ends. (Pediatrics Review and Education Program) Text in English. 1997. a. USD 215 combined subscription to institutions (print & CD-ROM eds.) (effective 2011). **Document type:** *Journal, Academic/Scholarly.*
Related titles: CD-ROM ed.: ISSN 1943-0957; ◆ Online - full text ed.: P R E P (Year) Self Assessment. ISSN 1943-0949.
Published by: American Academy of Pediatrics, 141 NW Pt Blvd, Elk Grove Village, IL 60007. TEL 847-434-4000, FAX 847-434-8000, journals@aap.org, http://www.aap.org.

618.92 DEU ISSN 0949-7641

PAED; praktische Paediatrie. Text in German. 1995. bi-m. EUR 50; EUR 15 newsstand/cover (effective 2010). adv. **Document type:** *Magazine, Trade.*
Published by: OmniMed Verlagsgesellschaft mbH, Borsteler Chaussee 85-99a, Haus 16, Hamburg, 22453, Germany. TEL 49-40-232334, FAX 49-40-230292, info@omnimedonline.de, http://www.omnimedonline.de. Ed. M Zinke. Adv. contact Vanessa Baack. Circ: 10,895 (paid and controlled).

618.92 HRV ISSN 1330-1403
CODEN: PCROE6

➤ **PAEDIATRIA CROATICA**; the journal for the paediatricians. Text and summaries in Croatian, English. 1957. q. EUR 60 foreign (effective 2012). adv. bk.rev. 70 p./no. 3 cols./p.; back issues avail. **Document type:** *Journal, Academic/Scholarly.* **Description:** Publishes original scientific articles on the child development, pathology and health care, from the pre-natal period to full biological, emotional and social maturity.
Formerly: Arhiv za Zastitu Majke i Djeteta - Archives for Mother and Child Health (0004-1289)
Related titles: Online - full text ed.
Indexed: EMBASE, ExcerpMed, P30, R10, Reac, RefZh, SCI, SCOPUS, W07.
—BLDSC (6333.399170), GNLM, IE, Ingenta.
Published by: (Hrvatsko Pedijatrijsko Drustvo), Klinika za Djecje Bolesti Zagreb/Children's Hospital in Zagreb, Klaiceva 16, Zagreb, 10000, Croatia. TEL 385-1-4600162, FAX 385-091-4600268, ibarisic@kob.hr, http://www.kdb.hr. Ed. Ingeborg Barisic. Circ: 900.

➤ **PAEDIATRIC ANAESTHESIA.** *see* MEDICAL SCIENCES—Anaesthesiology

➤ **PAEDIATRIC ANAESTHESIA ONLINE.** *see* MEDICAL SCIENCES—Anaesthesiology

618.92 GBR ISSN 1365-3016

➤ **PAEDIATRIC AND PERINATAL EPIDEMIOLOGY (ONLINE).** Text in English. 1999. bi-m. GBP 723 in United Kingdom to institutions; EUR 917 in Europe to institutions; USD 1,332 in the Americas to institutions; USD 1,552 elsewhere to institutions (effective 2012). adv. back issues avail. **Document type:** *Journal, Academic/Scholarly.* **Description:** Focuses to ensure that the most important paediatric, reproductive, obstetric and perinatal studies reach those researchers and clinicians for whom the results are especially relevant.
Media: Online - full text (from IngentaConnect). **Related titles:** Microform ed.: (from PQC); ◆ Print ed.: Paediatric and Perinatal Epidemiology (Print). ISSN 0269-5022.
—**CCC.**
Published by: (Society for Paediatric and Perinatal Epidemiologic Research USA), Wiley-Blackwell Publishing Ltd. (Subsidiary of: John Wiley & Sons, Inc.), 9600 Garsington Rd, Oxford, OX4 2DQ, United Kingdom. TEL 44-1865-776868, FAX 44-1865-714591, customerservices@blackwellpublishing.com, http://www.wiley.com/. Eds. Jean Golding, Tim J Peters. Adv. contact Craig Pickett TEL 44-1865-476267.

618.92 GBR ISSN 0269-5022
RJ106
➤ **PAEDIATRIC AND PERINATAL EPIDEMIOLOGY (PRINT).** Text in English. 1988. bi-m. GBP 723 in United Kingdom to institutions; EUR 917 in Europe to institutions; USD 1,332 in the Americas to institutions; USD 1,552 elsewhere to institutions; GBP 833 combined subscription in United Kingdom to institutions (print & online eds.); EUR 1,055 combined subscription in Europe to institutions (print & online eds.); USD 1,532 combined subscription in the Americas to institutions (print & online eds.); USD 1,786 combined subscription elsewhere to institutions (print & online eds.) (effective 2012). adv. bk.rev. illus. index. back issues avail.; reprint service avail. from PSC. **Document type:** *Journal, Academic/Scholarly.* **Description:** Crosses the boundaries between the epidemiologist and the paediatrician, obstetrician or specialist in child health.
Related titles: Microform ed.: (from PQC); ◆ Online - full text ed.: Paediatric and Perinatal Epidemiology (Online). ISSN 1365-3016; Supplement(s): Paediatric and Perinatal Epidemiology. Supplement. ISSN 1353-663X.
Indexed: A01, A02, A03, A08, A22, A26, A36, ASCA, B21, C11, CA, CABA, CurCont, D01, E01, E12, EMBASE, ESPM, ExcerpMed, F09, FR, GH, H&SSA, H04, H12, INI, ISR, IndMed, Inpharma, LT, MEDLINE, MS&D, N02, N03, P30, P33, P35, P39, R07, R08, R10, R12, RM&VM, Reac, RiskAb, SCI, SCOPUS, SoyAb, T02, T05, TAR, VS, W07, W11.
—BLDSC (6333.399710), GNLM, IE, Infotrieve, Ingenta. **CCC.**
Published by: (Society for Paediatric and Perinatal Epidemiologic Research USA), Wiley-Blackwell Publishing Ltd. (Subsidiary of: John Wiley & Sons, Inc.), 9600 Garsington Rd, Oxford, OX4 2DQ, United Kingdom. TEL 44-1865-776868, FAX 44-1865-714591, customerservices@blackwellpublishing.com. Eds. Jean Golding, Tim J Peters.

➤ **PAEDIATRIC DRUGS.** *see* PHARMACY AND PHARMACOLOGY

618.92 NZL ISSN 1179-7304
▼ **PAEDIATRIC VACCINES RESEARCH REVIEW.** Text in English. 2010. q. free (effective 2010). back issues avail. **Document type:** *Journal, Academic/Scholarly.*
Media: Online - full text.
Published by: Research Review Ltd., N Shore Mail Centre, PO Box 100116, Auckland, New Zealand. TEL 64-9-4102277, FAX 64-9-5248653, info@researchreview.co.nz.

618.92 PER ISSN 1728-239X
➤ **PAEDIATRICA.** Text in Spanish. 1998. s-a. back issues avail. **Document type:** *Journal, Academic/Scholarly.* **Description:** It aims at becoming a forum for the publication and discussion of works on pediatrics.
Related titles: Online - full text ed.: ISSN 1728-2403.
Indexed: CA, T02.
Published by: Asociacion de Medicos Residentes del Instituto Especializado de Salud del Nino, Av Brasil 600 Brena, Lima, 5, Peru. paediatrica@telefonica.net.pe, http://www.paediatrica.org/. Ed. Juan Pablo Chalco Orrego.

618.92 IDN ISSN 0030-9311
RJ1 CODEN: PIDOA8
PAEDIATRICA INDONESIANA; journal of the Indonesian Society of Pediatricians. Text and summaries in English. 1961. bi-m. adv. bk.rev. abstr.; bibl.; charts; illus.; stat. reprints avail. **Document type:** *Journal, Academic/Scholarly.*
Related titles: CD-ROM ed.; Microfiche ed.; Microfilm ed.: (from PQC).
Indexed: IndMed, P30.
—GNLM, INIST.
Published by: Indonesian Society of Pediatrician, c/o University of Indonesia, Medical School, Department of Child health, Salemba 6, Jakarta, 10430, Indonesia. pi@idai.or.id, http://www.idai.or.id. Circ: 2,000.

618.92 CAN ISSN 1205-7088
➤ **PAEDIATRICS AND CHILD HEALTH**; the journal of the Canadian Paediatric Society. Text in English. 1996. 10/yr. CAD 200 domestic to individuals; USD 200 in United States to individuals; USD 240 elsewhere to individuals; CAD 250 domestic to institutions; USD 250 in United States to institutions; USD 290 elsewhere to institutions (effective 2005). adv. bk.rev. back issues avail. **Document type:** *Journal, Academic/Scholarly.* **Description:** Advocates for the health of all children and youth in Canada, and provides educational material and information to all concerned with the health care of Canadian children.
Former titles (until 1996): Canadian Journal of Pediatrics (0843-4263); (until 1988): Contemporary Pediatrics Canada (0832-7831)
Related titles: Online - full text ed.
Indexed: C03, CBCARef, EMBASE, ExcerpMed, P30, P48, PQC, R10, Reac, SCI, SCOPUS, W07.
—BLDSC (6333.450500), IE, Ingenta. **CCC.**
Published by: (Canadian Paediatric Society), Pulsus Group Inc., 2902 S Sheridan Way, Oakville, ON L6J 7L6, Canada. TEL 905-829-4770, FAX 905-829-4799, pulsus@pulsus.com. Eds. Dr. Norman Jones, Dr. Noni MacDonald TEL 613-526-9397. Adv. contact Lisa Robb. B&W page USD 2,325, color page USD 4,100. Circ: 15,500 (paid).

618.92 GBR ISSN 1751-7222
RJ1 CODEN: CUPAF6
PAEDIATRICS AND CHILD HEALTH; the continuously updated review of paediatrics and child health. Text in English. 1991. m. EUR 992 in Europe to institutions; JPY 107,600 in Japan to institutions; USD 884 elsewhere to institutions (effective 2012). adv. back issues avail. **Document type:** *Journal, Academic/Scholarly.* **Description:** Provides all pediatricians and child health care specialists with up-to-date reviews on all aspects of hospital/community pediatrics and neonatology, including investigations and technical procedures.
Formerly (until 2007): Current Paediatrics (0957-5839)
Related titles: Online - full text ed.: ISSN 1878-206X (from ScienceDirect).
Indexed: A22, A26, CA, E01, E08, EMBASE, ExcerpMed, H11, H12, I02, R10, Reac, S09, SCOPUS, T02.
—BLDSC (6333.450600), GNLM, IE, Infotrieve, Ingenta. **CCC.**
Published by: The Medicine Publishing Company (Subsidiary of: Elsevier Ltd), The Boulevard, Langford Ln, Kidlington, Oxford, OX5 1GB, United Kingdom. TEL 44-1865-843154, FAX 44-1865-843965, JournalsCustomerServiceEMEA@elsevier.com, http://www.medicinepublishing.co.uk. Ed. Patrick Cartlidge. Pub. Melanie Burton. Adv. contact Ellie Ostime TEL 44-20-74244971.

618.92 GBR ISSN 2046-9047
CODEN: ATPAD9
➤ **PAEDIATRICS AND INTERNATIONAL CHILD HEALTH.** Text in English. 1981. q. USD 921 combined subscription in United States to institutions (print & online eds.) (effective 2011); GBP 499 combined subscription elsewhere to institutions (print & online eds.) (effective 2012). adv. bk.rev. back issues avail.; reprint service avail. from PSC. **Document type:** *Journal, Academic/Scholarly.* **Description:** Provides an international forum for problems and achievements in child health and pediatrics in the tropics and subtropics.
Formerly (until 2012): Annals of Tropical Paediatrics (0272-4936)
Related titles: Online - full text ed.: Paediatrics and International Child Health (Online). ISSN 2046-9055. USD 845 in United States to institutions; GBP 457 elsewhere to institutions (effective 2012) (from IngentaConnect).
Indexed: A01, A03, A08, A22, A34, A36, ASCA, AbAn, B20, B21, B25, BIOSIS Prev, CA, CABA, CurCont, D01, DentInd, E01, E12, EMBASE, ESPM, ExcerpMed, FR, GH, H&SSA, H17, INI, ImmunAb, IndMed, IndVet, Inpharma, LT, MEDLINE, MycolAb, N02, NRN, P20, P22, P26, P30, P33, P35, P39, P48, P54, PQC, R08, R10, R12, RM&VM, RRTA, Reac, RiskAb, S21, SCI, SCOPUS, SoyAb, T02, T05, VS, VirolAbstr, W07, W11.
—BLDSC (1045.100000), GNLM, IE, Infotrieve, Ingenta, INIST. **CCC.**
Published by: Maney Publishing, Ste 1C, Joseph's Well, Hanover Walk, Leeds, W Yorks LS3 1AB, United Kingdom. TEL 44-113-2432800, FAX 44-113-3868178, maney@maney.co.uk, http://www.maney.co.uk. Ed. Brian Coulter. adv.: B&W page GBP 320, color page GBP 650.

618.92 GBR ISSN 1755-3172
PAEDIATRICS.ME; today's children - tomorrow's adults. Text in English. 1996. q. GBP 40 (effective 2010). adv. **Document type:** *Journal, Trade.* **Description:** Features articles related to child care in the Middle East.
Formerly (until 2007): Middle East Paediatrics (1368-5937)
Indexed: EMBASE, ExcerpMed, SCOPUS.
—BLDSC (6333.521000), IE, Ingenta. **CCC.**
Published by: Pharmedia International, 6 Tobin Close, Epsom, Surrey KT19 8AE, United Kingdom. TEL 44-1372-742347, FAX 44-1372-745187, info@pharmedia.co.uk. adv.: page GBP 2,500; trim 210 x 297.

618.92 IND ISSN 0972-0537
PAEDIATRICS TODAY. Text in English. 1998. bi-m. **Document type:** *Journal, Academic/Scholarly.*
Published by: C M P Medica (Subsidiary of: C M P Medica Ltd.), Sagar Tech Plz A 615-617, 6th Fl, Andheri Kurla Rd, Saki Naka Jct, Andheri E, Mumbai, 400 072, India. TEL 91-22-66122600, FAX 91-22-66122626, info.india@ubm.com, http://www.ubmindia.in/cmp-medica.asp.

618.92 616.5 DEU ISSN 1437-1782
PAEDIATRIE HAUTNAH. Text in German. 1989. 6/yr. EUR 87, USD 123 to institutions (effective 2012). adv. **Document type:** *Journal, Academic/Scholarly.*
Formerly (until 1998): Hautnah Paediatrie (0935-3453)
Indexed: A26.
—GNLM, IE. **CCC.**
Published by: Urban und Vogel Medien und Medizin Verlagsgesellschaft mbH (Subsidiary of: Springer Science+Business Media), Neumarkter Str 43, Munich, 81673, Germany. TEL 49-89-4372-1411, FAX 49-89-4372-1410, verlag@urban-vogel.de. Ed. Markus Seidl. Adv. contact Kornelia Echsel. B&W page EUR 2,070, color page EUR 3,670; trim 174 x 237. Circ: 7,968 (paid). **Subscr. to:** Springer Distribution Center, Kundenservice Zeitschriften, Haberstr 7, Heidelberg 69126, Germany. TEL 49-6221-3454303, FAX 49-6221-3454229, subscriptions@springer.com.

618.92 AUT ISSN 0030-9338
RJ499.A1 CODEN: PAPAB5
➤ **PAEDIATRIE UND PAEDOLOGIE**; oesterreichische Zeitschrift fuer Kinder- und Jugendheilkunde. Text in German. 1965. bi-m. EUR 86, USD 98 combined subscription to institutions (print & online eds.) (effective 2012). adv. bk.rev. charts; illus. index. reprint service avail. from PSC. **Document type:** *Journal, Academic/Scholarly.* **Description:** Covers research in children's health and development.
Related titles: Microform ed.: (from PQC); Online - full text ed.: ISSN 1613-7558 (from IngentaConnect).
Indexed: A22, A26, BDM&CN, ChemAb, E01, IBR, IBZ, INIS AtomInd, IndMed, MycolAb, P30, SCOPUS.
—BLDSC (6333.230000), CASDDS, GNLM, IE, Infotrieve, Ingenta, INIST. **CCC.**
Published by: Springer Wien (Subsidiary of: Springer Science+Business Media), Sachsenplatz 4-6, Vienna, W 1201, Austria. TEL 43-1-33024150, FAX 43-1-3302426, journals@springer.at, http://www.springer.at. Ed. R Kerbl. Adv. contact Gabriele Popernitsch. color page EUR 3,130; 210 x 297. Circ: 7,250 (paid). **Subscr. in the Americas to:** Springer New York LLC, Journal Fulfillment, PO Box 2485, Secaucus, NJ 07096. TEL 800-777-4643, 201-348-4033, FAX 201-348-4505, journals-ny@springer.com, http://www.springer.com; **Subscr. to:** Springer Distribution Center, Kundenservice Zeitschriften, Haberstr 7, Heidelberg 69126, Germany. TEL 49-6221-3454303, FAX 49-6221-3454229, subscriptions@springer.com.

618.92 DEU ISSN 1611-6445
RJ1
PAEDIATRIE UP2DATE. Text in German. 2007. 4/yr. EUR 140 to institutions; EUR 192 combined subscription to institutions (print & online eds.); EUR 44 newsstand/cover (effective 2011). adv. **Document type:** *Journal, Academic/Scholarly.*
Related titles: Online - full text ed.: ISSN 1862-9393. 2006. EUR 185 to institutions (effective 2011).
—IE. **CCC.**
Published by: Georg Thieme Verlag, Ruedigerstr 14, Stuttgart, 70469, Germany. TEL 49-711-8931421, FAX 49-711-8931410, leser.service@thieme.de. Ed. Dr. Fred Zepp. Adv. contact Irmgard Mayer TEL 49-711-8931469. Circ: 3,150 (controlled).

PAEDIATRISCHE ALLERGOLOGIE IN KLINIK UND PRAXIS. *see* MEDICAL SCIENCES—Allergology And Immunology

PAEDIATRISCHE ONKOLOGIE. *see* MEDICAL SCIENCES—Oncology

618.92 DEU ISSN 0030-9346
PAEDIATRISCHE PRAXIS; Zeitschrift fuer Kinder- und Jugendmedizin in Klinik und Praxis. Text in German. 1962. 4/yr. EUR 175 (effective 2010). bk.rev. abstr.; bibl.; charts; illus. index, cum.index every 5 yrs. reprints avail. **Document type:** *Journal, Academic/Scholarly.* **Description:** Practical information of interest to specialists in pediatrics. Features current research, questions and answers, and photographs.
Related titles: Microfilm ed.: (from PQC).
Indexed: A22, EMBASE, ExcerpMed, R10, Reac, SCOPUS.
—BLDSC (6333.300000), GNLM, IE, Infotrieve, Ingenta. **CCC.**
Published by: Hans Marseille Verlag GmbH, Buerkleinstr 12, Munich, 80538, Germany. TEL 49-89-227988, FAX 49-89-2904643, marseille-verlag@t-online.de. Ed. S Wirth. Circ: 4,500 (controlled).

M

618.92 DEU
PAEDIATRISCHE ZEITUNG. Text in German. bi-m. adv. **Document type:** *Magazine, Trade.*
Published by: Neupunkt Verlag, Virnicherstr 100, Mechernich, 53984, Germany. adv.: B&W page EUR 2,700, color page EUR 3,810. Circ: 7,400 (controlled).

618.92 GRC ISSN 1105-2325
PAIDIATRIKE BOREIOU ELLADOS. Text in Greek. 1989. q. **Document type:** *Journal, Academic/Scholarly.*
Published by: Paidiatrike Etaireia Boreiou Ellados/Paediatric Society of Northern Greece, Al.Papanastasiou & 1 Lidias Str, Thessaloniki, 544 53, Greece. info@peve.gr, http://www.peve.gr/.

618.92 NOR ISSN 1503-5360
PAIDOS; tidsskrift for Norsk barnelegeforening. Text in Norwegian. 1985. q. back issues avail. **Document type:** *Magazine, Trade.*
Former titles (until 2002): N B F - Nytt (0804-1687); (until 1992): N P S - Nytt (0801-7182)
Related titles: Online - full text ed.: ISSN 1503-867X.
Published by: Norsk Barnelegeforening/Norwegian Association of Pediatrics, c/o Leif Brunvand, Barneintensiv Avd., Ullevaal Universitetssykehus, Oslo, 0407, Norway. TEL 47-22-118080, leder@barnelegeforeningen.no. Ed. Tomas Nordheim Alme. Circ: 750.

618.92 PAK ISSN 0048-2722
PAKISTAN PEDIATRIC JOURNAL. Text in English. 1971. q. adv. bk.rev. bibl.; charts; illus. **Document type:** *Journal, Academic/Scholarly.*
Related titles: Online - full text ed.
Published by: Pakistan Pediatricians Association, c/o Prof. Said ul Haque, 72/A, Block-G, Gulberg-III, P O Box 308, G.P.O., Lahore, Pakistan. ppj@ma-tech.com. Ed. Dr. Abdul Jamil Khan.

PARENTS HEALTHY KIDS. *see* CHILDREN AND YOUTH—About

618.92 ITA ISSN 1970-4240
IL PEDIATRA. Text in Italian. 1997. bi-m. EUR 30 domestic; EUR 60 in Europe; EUR 80 elsewhere (effective 2011). **Document type:** *Journal, Trade.*
Formerly (until 2006): Occhio Clinico. Pediatria (1592-1093)
Related titles: Online - full text ed.
Indexed: SCOPUS.
Published by: Tecniche Nuove SpA, Via Eritrea 21, Milan, MI 201, Italy. TEL 39-02-390901, FAX 39-02-7570364, info@tecnichenuove.com. Ed. Marina Pagani.

618.92 SVK ISSN 1336-863X
➤ **PEDIATRIA.** Text in Slovak. 2006. bi-m. EUR 14.97 (effective 2009). **Document type:** *Journal, Academic/Scholarly.*
Published by: Samedi s.r.o., Racianska 20, Bratislava, 839 27, Slovakia. TEL 421-2-55645901, FAX 421-2-55645902, samedi@samedi.sk. Ed. Dr. Peter Banovcin.

618.92 PRY ISSN 1683-979X
PEDIATRIA. Text in Spanish. 2000. s-a. back issues avail. **Document type:** *Journal, Academic/Scholarly.*
Related titles: Online - full text ed.: ISSN 1683-9803. free (effective 2011) (from SciELO).
Published by: Sociedad Paraguaya de Pediatria, Mcal. Estigarribia 1764, C. Rca Francesa, Asuncion, Paraguay. TEL 595-21-447493, FAX 595-21-226795.

618.92 BGR ISSN 0479-7876
CODEN: PDTAAB
PEDIATRIA. Text in Bulgarian; Summaries in English, Russian. 1962. bi-m. **Document type:** *Journal, Academic/Scholarly.*
Indexed: ABSML, DentInd, IndMed, SCOPUS.
—CASDDS, GNLM, INIST.
Published by: (Bulgaria. Ministerstvo na Narodnoto Zdrave), Izdatelstvo Meditsina i Fizkultura, 11 Slaveikov Sq, Sofia, 1080, Bulgaria. TEL 359-2-9884068, FAX 359-2-9871308, medpubl@abv.bg. Ed. Sh Ninjo. Circ: 1,950. **Co-sponsor:** Nauchno Druzhestvo po Pediatria.

618.92 COL ISSN 0031-3882
CODEN: PEDSA
PEDIATRIA. Text in Spanish. 1942. q. **Document type:** *Journal, Academic/Scholarly.*
Former titles (until 1965): Sociedad Colombiana de Pediatria y Puericultura. Revista (0120-8756); (until 1958): Revista Colombiana de Pediatria y Puericultura (0120-0402)
Indexed: C01, P30.
—INIST.
Published by: Sociedad Colombiana de Pediatria, Cra 20 No 84-14, Of 304, Bogota, Colombia. scp@scp.com.co, http://www.scp.com.co.

618.92 POL ISSN 1734-1531
➤ **PEDIATRIA & MEDYCYNA RODZINNA.** Text in Polish; Contents page in English, Polish. 2005. q. PLZ 60 domestic; USD 25 foreign (effective 2007). **Document type:** *Journal, Academic/Scholarly.* **Description:** Publishes original articles that constitute significant contributions to the advancements of paediatrics and family medicine.
Indexed: EMBASE, ExcerpMed, R10, Reac, SCOPUS.
—BLDSC (6417.476700).
Published by: Medical Communications, ul Ojcowska 11, Warsaw, 02918, Poland. TEL 48-22-6159783, FAX 48-22-8425363. Ed. Anna Jung.

618.92 BRA ISSN 0103-2712
PEDIATRIA ATUAL. Text in Portuguese. 1988. 11/yr. abstr.; bibl. Index.
Published by: Editora de Publicacoes Cientificas Ltda., Rua Major Suckow 30, Rocha, Rio de Janeiro, RJ 20911-160, Brazil. TEL 55-21-2013722, 55-21-5010057, FAX 55-21-2613749. Eds. Almir L de Fonseca, J M Melo. R&P, Adv. contact Ana Paula. Circ: 12,000.

618.92 ESP ISSN 1135-8831
CODEN: BSCPDR

PEDIATRIA CATALANA. Text in Spanish. 1928. bi-m. adv. **Document type:** *Journal, Trade.*
Former titles (until 1996): Societat Catalana de Pediatria. Butlleti (0210-721X); (until 1977): Sociedad Catalana de Pediatria. Boletin (1132-4899); (until 1959): Suplemento de Pediatria (1132-4902); (until 1952): Sociedad Catalana de Pediatria. Boletin (0304-498X); (until 1948): Asociacion de Pediatras de Cataluna. Boletin (0210-718X); (until 1937): Societat Catalana de Pediatria. Butlleti (0210-7201)
Related titles: Online - full text ed.
Indexed: EMBASE, ExcerpMed, IME, P30, R10, Reac, SCOPUS.
—BLDSC (6417.475000), CASDDS, GNLM. **CCC.**
Published by: Societat Catalana de Pediatria, Major de Can Caralleu 1-7, Barcelona, 08017, Spain. TEL 34-93-2030312, FAX 34-93-2123569, scpediatria@academia.cat. Ed. Antoni Martinez Roig.

616 ESP ISSN 1135-4542

PEDIATRIA INTEGRAL. Text in Spanish. 1995. m. **Document type:** *Journal, Academic/Scholarly.*
Indexed: EMBASE, ExcerpMed, R10, Reac, SCOPUS.
—BLDSC (6417.477000).
Published by: (Asociacion Espanola de Pediatria, Seccion de Pediatria Extrahospitalaria), Ediciones Ergon S.A., C/ Arboleda 1, Majadahonda, Madrid, Madrid 28220, Spain. TEL 34-91-6362930, FAX 34-91-6362931, ergon@ergon.es, http://www.ergon.es. Circ: 6,000.

618.92 BRA ISSN 0031-3920
CODEN: RBMEAU

➤ **PEDIATRIA MODERNA.** Text in Portuguese; Summaries in English, Portuguese. 1966. m. BRL 250, USD 300 (effective 2009); free to qualified personnel. adv. bk.rev.; Website rev. abstr.; bibl.; charts; illus.; stat. cum.index. back issues avail. **Document type:** *Journal, Academic/Scholarly.*
Indexed: A22, A36, CABA, D01, E12, GH, H17, LT, N02, N03, P33, P39, PN&I, R07, R08, R12, RA&MP, RM&VM, RRTA, T05, TAR.
Published by: Grupo Editorial Moreira Jr., Rua Henrique Martins, 493, Jd Paulista, Sao Paulo, SP 04504-000, Brazil. TEL 55-11-38849911, FAX 55-11-38849993, editora@moreirajr.com.br, http://www.moreirajr.com.br/. Ed. Friederich T Simon. Pub., R&P Americo Moreira Junior. Adv. contact Maria Rachel Bellusci. Circ: 20,000 (controlled).

618.92 617.3 ITA ISSN 0391-898X

PEDIATRIA OGGI MEDICA E CHIRURGICA. Text in Italian; Summaries in English. 1980. q. free to qualified personnel. adv. **Document type:** *Journal, Academic/Scholarly.*
Indexed: A22, SCOPUS.
—BLDSC (6417.488000), GNLM, IE, Ingenta, INIST. **CCC.**
Published by: C I C Edizioni Internazionali, Corso Trieste 42, Rome, 00198, Italy. TEL 39-06-8412673, FAX 39-06-8412688, info@gruppocic.it, http://www.gruppocic.it.

618.92 POL ISSN 0031-3939
CODEN: PEPOA6

➤ **PEDIATRIA POLSKA.** Text in Polish; Summaries in English. 1921. m. EUR 289 in Europe to institutions; JPY 45,000 in Japan to institutions; USD 402 elsewhere to institutions (effective 2012). bk.rev. index. **Document type:** *Journal, Academic/Scholarly.* **Description:** Publishes original papers on advances in pediatrics as well as clinical reports.
Related titles: Online - full text ed.: (from ScienceDirect).
Indexed: ChemAb, DentInd, EMBASE, ExcerpMed, IndMed, P30, R10, Reac, SCOPUS.
—BLDSC (6417.500000), CASDDS, GNLM, INIST. **CCC.**
Published by: (Polskie Towarzystwo Pediatryczne), Wydawnictwo Medyczne Urban i Partner, ul Marii Sklodowskiej-Curie 55-61, Wroclaw, 50950, Poland. TEL 48-71-3285487, FAX 48-71-3284391, http://www.urbanpartner.pl. Ed. Teresa Wyszynska. Circ: 3,500. **Dist. by:** Ars Polona, Obroncow 25, Warsaw 03933, Poland. TEL 48-22-5098609, FAX 48-22-5098610, arspolona@arspolona.com.pl, http://www.arspolona.com.pl. **Co-sponsor:** Instytut Matki i Dziecka.

618.92 SVK ISSN 1336-8168

➤ **PEDIATRIA PRE PRAX.** Text in Slovak. 2006. bi-m. EUR 18 (effective 2010). **Document type:** *Journal, Academic/Scholarly.*
Published by: Solen, s.r.o., Uprkova 23, Bratislava, 811 04, Slovakia. TEL 421-2-54650649, FAX 421-2-54651384, solen@solen.sk. Ed. Jana Repiska.

618.92 ESP ISSN 1135-4410

PEDIATRIA RURAL Y EXTRAHOSPITALARIA. Text in Spanish. 1971. m. EUR 30 domestic; USD 100 foreign (effective 2009). back issues avail. **Document type:** *Journal, Academic/Scholarly.*
Formerly (until 1994): Pediatria Rural (1131-4354)
Related titles: Online - full text ed.
Published by: Asociacion para la Docencia e Investigacion en Pediatria Extrahospitalaria, Mallorca, 272-276, Madrid, 08037, Spain. TEL 34-93-2159034, FAX 34-93-4874064, med010302@saludalia.com. Ed. Antonio Portugal Ramirez. Circ: 7,050.

618.92 POL ISSN 1507-5532

PEDIATRIA WSPOLCZESNA. Text in Polish. 1999. q. EUR 52 foreign (effective 2005). **Document type:** *Journal, Academic/Scholarly.*
Indexed: A22, EMBASE, ExcerpMed, R10, Reac, SCOPUS.
—BLDSC (6417.521000), IE, Ingenta.
Published by: (Polskie Towarzystwo Gastroenterologii, Hepatologii i Zywienia Dzieci, Akademia Medyczna w Warszawie, Klinika Gastroenterologii i Zywienia Dziecka), Leximed s.c., ul Moniuszki 7, Nysa, 48300, Poland. biuro@leximed.ac.pl, http://www.leximed.ac.pl. Ed. Tadeusz Zalewski. **Dist. by:** Ars Polona, Obroncow 25, Warsaw 03933, Poland. TEL 48-22-5098609, FAX 48-22-5098610, arspolona@arspolona.com.pl, http://www.arspolona.com.pl.

618.92 USA ISSN 0160-0184
RJ1

PEDIATRIC ALERT. Text in English. 1976. s-m. looseleaf. 6 p./no.; back issues avail. **Document type:** *Newsletter.*
Related titles: Online - full text ed.
Indexed: A01, A03, A08, A22, M01, M02, P30, T02.
—IE, Infotrieve.
Published by: Medical Alert, Inc., PO Box 610228, Newton, MA 02461-0228. TEL 781-239-1762, FAX 781-239-1762, alertsus@mediaone.net. Ed. Dr. Allen A Mitchell. R&P Katherrine Bicknell.

618.92 616.97 GBR ISSN 0905-6157
RJ385 CODEN: PALUEE

➤ **PEDIATRIC ALLERGY AND IMMUNOLOGY.** Text in English. 1990. 8/yr. GBP 784 in United Kingdom to institutions; EUR 997 in Europe to institutions; USD 1,317 in the Americas to institutions; USD 1,535 elsewhere to institutions; GBP 901 combined subscription in United Kingdom to institutions (print & online eds.); EUR 1,146 combined subscription in Europe to institutions (print & online eds.); USD 1,515 combined subscription in the Americas to institutions (print & online eds.); USD 1,766 combined subscription elsewhere to institutions (print & online eds.) (effective 2012). adv. charts; illus. back issues avail.; reprint service avail. from PSC. **Document type:** *Journal, Academic/Scholarly.* **Description:** Promotes communication between scientists engaged in basic research and clinicians working with children, we publish both clinical and experimental work.
Related titles: Online - full text ed.: ISSN 1399-3038. GBP 784 in United Kingdom to institutions; EUR 997 in Europe to institutions; USD 1,317 in the Americas to institutions; USD 1,535 elsewhere to institutions (effective 2012) (from IngentaConnect); ◆ Supplement(s): Pediatric Allergy and Immunology. Supplementum. ISSN 0906-5784.
Indexed: A01, A03, A08, A22, A26, A34, A36, ASCA, AgrForAb, B21, BIOBASE, CA, CABA, CurCont, D01, E01, E12, EMBASE, ExcerpMed, F08, F12, GH, H12, H16, H17, IABS, ISR, ImmunAb, IndMed, IndVet, Inpharma, MEDLINE, MaizeAb, N02, N03, OR, P30, P32, P33, P35, P39, PN&I, R08, R10, R11, R12, RA&MP, RM&VM, Reac, S13, S16, SCI, SCOPUS, SoyAb, T02, T05, TriticAb, VS, W07, W10, W11.
—BLDSC (6417.527000), GNLM, IE, Infotrieve, Ingenta, INIST. **CCC.**
Published by: (European Society of Pediatric Allergy and Clinical Immunology FRA), Wiley-Blackwell Publishing Ltd. (Subsidiary of: John Wiley & Sons, Inc.), 9600 Garsington Rd, Oxford, OX4 2DQ, United Kingdom. TEL 44-1865-776868, FAX 44-1865-714591, customerservices@blackwellpublishing.com. Ed. John Warner.

618.92 616.97 GBR ISSN 0906-5784
CODEN: PAIUE

➤ **PEDIATRIC ALLERGY AND IMMUNOLOGY. SUPPLEMENTUM.** Text in English. 1991. irreg. includes with subscr. to Pediatric Allergy and Immunology. back issues avail. **Document type:** *Monographic series, Academic/Scholarly.*
Related titles: Online - full text ed.: ISSN 1600-5562; ◆ Supplement to: Pediatric Allergy and Immunology. ISSN 0905-6157.
Indexed: SCOPUS.
—BLDSC (6417.527001), IE, Ingenta, INIST. **CCC.**
Published by: (European Society of Pediatric Allergy and Clinical Immunology FRA), Wiley-Blackwell Publishing Ltd. (Subsidiary of: John Wiley & Sons, Inc.), 9600 Garsington Rd, Oxford, OX4 2DQ, United Kingdom. TEL 44-1865-776868, FAX 44-1865-714591, customerservices@blackwellpublishing.com, http://www.wiley.com/. Ed. John Warner.

➤ **PEDIATRIC ALLERGY FOR CLINICIANS.** *see* MEDICAL SCIENCES—Allergology And Immunology

618.92 USA ISSN 2151-321X
CODEN: PAAIEP

➤ **PEDIATRIC ALLERGY, IMMUNOLOGY, AND PULMONOLOGY.** Text in English. 1987. q. USD 1,153 domestic to institutions; USD 1,478 foreign to institutions; USD 1,345 combined subscription domestic to institutions (print & online eds.); USD 1,713 combined subscription foreign to institutions (print & online eds.) (effective 2012). adv. reprint service avail. from PSC. **Document type:** *Journal, Academic/Scholarly.* **Description:** Emphasizes the developmental implications of the morphologic, physiologic, and sociologic components of these problems in infants, children, and adolescents, as well as the impact of the disease processes on their families.
Formerly (until 2010): Pediatric Asthma, Allergy & Immunology (0883-1874)
Related titles: Online - full text ed.: ISSN 2151-3228. USD 1,254 to institutions (effective 2012).
Indexed: A01, A03, A08, A22, A26, A36, ASCA, B21, B25, BIOSIS Prev, C06, C07, C08, CA, CABA, CINAHL, ChPerI, CurCont, D01, E01, E07, E12, EMBASE, ExcerpMed, F08, FR, GH, H12, I05, I12, ImmunAb, Inpharma, MycolAb, N02, N03, P30, P33, R08, R10, RM&VM, Reac, SCI, SCOPUS, T02, T05, W07, W11.
—BLDSC (6417.532000), GNLM, IE, Infotrieve, Ingenta, INIST. **CCC.**
Published by: Mary Ann Liebert, Inc. Publishers, 140 Huguenot St, 3rd Fl, New Rochelle, NY 10801. TEL 914-740-2100, FAX 914-740-2101, 800-654-3237, info@liebertpub.com. Ed. Harold J Farber. Adv. contact Harriet I Matysko TEL 914-740-2182.

618.92 CHE ISSN 1017-5989
RJ23 CODEN: PEAMEV

➤ **PEDIATRIC AND ADOLESCENT MEDICINE.** Text in English. 1954. irreg., latest vol.15, 2011. price varies. reprints avail. **Document type:** *Monographic series, Academic/Scholarly.* **Description:** Seeks to clarify and evaluate difficult and evolving issues in pediatric and adolescent medicine.
Incorporates (1975-1989): Modern Problems in Paediatrics (0303-884X); (1971-1989): Monographs in Paediatrics (0077-0914); Which was formerly (1945-1968): Bibliotheca Paediatrica (0301-357X); (1924-1937): Abhandlungen aus der Kinderheilkunde und ihren Grenzgebieten (0365-3749)
Related titles: Online - full text ed.: ISSN 1662-3886.
Indexed: ChemAb, IndMed, P30, SCOPUS.
—BLDSC (6417.528400), CASDDS, IE, Ingenta, INIST. **CCC.**
Published by: S. Karger AG, Allschwilerstr 10, Basel, 4055, Switzerland. TEL 41-61-3061111, FAX 41-61-3061234, karger@karger.ch, http://www.karger.ch. Eds. D Branski, W Kiess.

618.92 616.07 USA ISSN 1093-5266
CODEN: PDPAFU

➤ **PEDIATRIC AND DEVELOPMENTAL PATHOLOGY.** Text in English. 1973. bi-m. (in 1 vol., 6 nos./vol.). USD 985 combined subscription domestic to institutions (print & online eds.); USD 1,022 combined subscription foreign to institutions (print & online eds.) (effective 2010). adv. back issues avail.; reprints avail. **Document type:** *Journal, Academic/Scholarly.* **Description:** Features with the pathology of disease from conception through adolescence.
Formerly (until 1998): Perspectives in Pediatric Pathology (0091-2921)
Related titles: Online - full text ed.: ISSN 1615-5742. USD 897 to institutions (effective 2010) (from IngentaConnect).
Indexed: A01, A03, A08, A20, A22, A26, CA, CurCont, E01, E08, EMBASE, ExcerpMed, G08, H11, H12, I05, ISR, IndMed, Inpharma, MEDLINE, P20, P22, P30, P35, P48, P54, PQC, R10, Reac, S09, SCI, SCOPUS, T02, W07.
—BLDSC (6417.528500), CASDDS, IE, Infotrieve, Ingenta. **CCC.**
Published by: Alliance Communications Group (Subsidiary of: Allen Press Inc.), 810 E 10th St, PO Box 368, Lawrence, KS 66044. TEL 785-843-1234, 800-627-0932, FAX 785-843-1226, info@allenpress.com. Ed. Miguel Reyes-Mugica TEL 412-692-3268. Adv. contact Valerie Pierce TEL 800-627-0932 ext 226. **Subscr. to:** PO Box 7075, Lawrence, KS 66044. TEL 785-843-1235, FAX 785-843-1274. **Co-sponsors:** Paediatric Pathology Society; Society for Pediatric Pathology.

618.92 USA ISSN 0090-4481
RJ1

➤ **PEDIATRIC ANNALS;** a journal of continuing pediatric education. Text in English. 1972. m. USD 229 to individuals; USD 379 to institutions; USD 39 per issue (effective 2010). adv. bk.rev. bibl.; illus.; stat. index. reprints avail. **Document type:** *Journal, Academic/Scholarly.* **Description:** Provides a thorough, practical review of a single topic in pediatrics.
Related titles: Microfilm ed.: (from PQC); Online - full text ed.: ISSN 1938-2359.
Indexed: A20, A22, A34, A36, ASCA, BDM&CN, C06, C07, CA, CABA, CCIP, CurCont, D01, E03, E12, EMBASE, ExcerpMed, F09, FamI, GH, H13, H17, INI, IndMed, IndVet, Inpharma, LT, MEDLINE, N02, N03, NRN, P02, P10, P18, P20, P22, P24, P26, P30, P32, P33, P35, P39, P40, P48, P50, P53, P54, P55, PN&I, PQC, R08, R10, R12, RM&VM, RRTA, Reac, SCI, SCOPUS, T02, T05, VS, W07.
—BLDSC (6417.530000), GNLM, IE, Infotrieve, Ingenta, INIST. **CCC.**
Published by: Slack, Inc., 6900 Grove Rd, Thorofare, NJ 08086. TEL 856-848-1000, FAX 856-848-6091, customerservice@slackinc.com, http://www.slackinc.com. Ed. Stanford Shulman. Adv. contact Matt Dechen TEL 877-307-5255 ext 346.

➤ **PEDIATRIC BLOOD & CANCER.** *see* MEDICAL SCIENCES—Oncology

➤ **PEDIATRIC CARDIAC SURGERY ANNUAL OF THE SEMINARS IN THORACIC AND CARDIOVASCULAR SURGERY.** *see* MEDICAL SCIENCES—Cardiovascular Diseases

➤ **PEDIATRIC CARDIOLOGY.** *see* MEDICAL SCIENCES—Cardiovascular Diseases

618.92 USA ISSN 1942-2024
RJ33.6

PEDIATRIC CLINICAL PRACTICE GUIDELINES & POLICIES. Text in English. 2001. irreg., latest 2007, 8th ed. USD 99.95 combined subscription per issue to non-members (print & CD-ROM ed.); USD 84.95 combined subscription per issue to members (print & CD-ROM ed.) (effective 2008); includes CD-ROM. **Document type:** *Bulletin, Trade.* **Description:** Includes the full text of all AAP policy statements, practice parameters, model bills, and clinical practice guidelines for 17 pediatric conditions.
Formed by the merger of (1984-2001): American Academy of Pediatrics. Policy Reference Guide (1522-4716); (19??-2001): American Academy of Pediatrics. Clinical Practice Guidelines
Related titles: CD-ROM ed.
Published by: American Academy of Pediatrics, 141 NW Pt Blvd, Elk Grove Village, IL 60007. TEL 847-434-4000, FAX 847-434-8000, journals@aap.org, http://www.aap.org. Pub. Robert Perelman.

618.92 NLD ISSN 0928-7868

PEDIATRIC CLINICS AMSTERDAM. Text in English. 1990. q. **Document type:** *Journal, Academic/Scholarly.*
Published by: DCHG Medische Communicatie, Zijlweg 70, Haarlem, 2013 DK, Netherlands. TEL 31-23-5514888, FAX 31-23-5515522, info@dchg.nl, http://www.dchg.nl.

618.92 USA ISSN 0031-3955
RJ23 CODEN: PCNAA8

➤ **PEDIATRIC CLINICS OF NORTH AMERICA.** Text in English. 1954. bi-m. USD 423 in United States to institutions; USD 563 elsewhere to institutions (effective 2012). adv. back issues avail.; reprints avail. **Document type:** *Journal, Academic/Scholarly.* **Description:** Provides the latest clinical information on health issues for children and adolescents. Each issue focuses on a single topic and is written by pediatricians with proven experience. Features expert reviews of current diagnosis and treatment that can be applied directly to practice.
Related titles: Microform ed.: (from PQC); Online - full text ed.: ISSN 1557-8240 (from IngentaConnect, ScienceDirect); ◆ Spanish ed.: Clinicas Pediatricas de Norteamerica. ISSN 0186-159X; Supplement(s): Continuing Medical Education Supplement to Pediatric Clinics of North America. ISSN 1557-8135.
Indexed: A20, A22, A29, AIDS Ab, AIM, AMHA, ASCA, B20, B21, BDM&CN, BIOSIS Prev, C06, C07, C08, CCIP, CINAHL, ChemAb, CurCont, ECER, EMBASE, ESPM, ExcerpMed, F09, FR, FamI, I10, INI, ISR, IndMed, Inpharma, MEDLINE, MycolAb, P30, R10, Reac, SCI, SCOPUS, VirolAbstr, W07.
—BLDSC (6417.550000), GNLM, IE, Infotrieve, Ingenta, INIST. **CCC.**
Published by: W.B. Saunders Co. (Subsidiary of: Elsevier Health Sciences), Elsevier, Health Sciences Division, Order Fulfillment, 3251 Riverport Ln, Maryland Heights, MO 63043. TEL 314-872-8370, 800-325-4177, FAX 314-432-1380, JournalCustomerService-usa@elsevier.com, http://www.us.elsevierhealth.com. Adv. contact John Marmero TEL 212-633-3657.

➤ **PEDIATRIC CODING ALERT;** the practical adviser for ethically optimizing coding reimbursement and efficiency for pediatric practices. *see* INSURANCE

618.92 USA ISSN 1529-7535
RJ370

➤ **PEDIATRIC CRITICAL CARE MEDICINE.** Abbreviated title: P C C M. Text in English. 2000. bi-m. USD 394 domestic to institutions; USD 431 foreign to institutions (effective 2011). adv. back issues avail.; reprints avail. **Document type:** *Journal, Academic/Scholarly.* **Description:** Focuses exclusively on pediatric critical care medicine and critical care neonatology.
Related titles: Online - full text ed.: ISSN 1947-3893.
Indexed: C06, C07, CurCont, EMBASE, ExcerpMed, MEDLINE, P30, R10, Reac, SCI, SCOPUS, W07.
—IE, Infotrieve. **CCC.**

Published by: (Society of Critical Care Medicine, World Federation of Pediatric Intensive and Critical Care Societies CAN), Lippincott Williams & Wilkins (Subsidiary of: Wolters Kluwer N.V.), 351 W Camden St, Baltimore, MD 21201. TEL 410-528-4000, customerservice@lww.com, http://www.lww.com. Ed. Dr. Patrick M Kochanek. Pub. John Ewers. adv.: B&W page USD 965, color page USD 1,455; trim 8.125 x 10.875. Circ: 2,385.

➤ **PEDIATRIC DENTAL JOURNAL.** *see* MEDICAL SCIENCES—Dentistry

➤ **PEDIATRIC DENTISTRY TODAY.** *see* MEDICAL SCIENCES—Dentistry

➤ **PEDIATRIC DERMATOLOGY.** *see* MEDICAL SCIENCES—Dermatology And Venereology

➤ **PEDIATRIC DERMATOLOGY (SPANISH EDITION).** *see* MEDICAL SCIENCES—Dermatology And Venereology

618.92 616.46 USA ISSN 1399-5448
➤ **PEDIATRIC DIABETES (ONLINE).** Text in English. 2000. bi-m. GBP 507 in United Kingdom to institutions; EUR 645 in Europe to institutions; USD 853 in the Americas to institutions; USD 993 elsewhere to institutions (effective 2012). adv. **Document type:** *Journal, Academic/Scholarly.*
Media: Online - full text (from IngentaConnect). **Related titles:** ◆ Print ed.: Pediatric Diabetes (Print). ISSN 1399-543X.
—CCC.
Published by: Wiley-Blackwell Publishing, Inc. (Subsidiary of: Wiley-Blackwell Publishing Ltd.), Commerce Pl, 350 Main St, Malden, MA 02148. TEL 781-388-8200, FAX 781-388-8210, info@wiley.com, http://www.wiley.com/WileyCDA/. Ed. Mark A Sperling. Adv. contact Claire Rogers.

618.92 616.46 USA ISSN 1399-543X
RJ420.D5 CODEN: PDEIBT
➤ **PEDIATRIC DIABETES (PRINT).** Text in English. 2000. bi-m. GBP 507 in United Kingdom to institutions; EUR 645 in Europe to institutions; USD 853 in the Americas to institutions; USD 993 elsewhere to institutions; GBP 584 combined subscription in United Kingdom to institutions (print & online eds.); EUR 742 combined subscription in Europe to institutions (print & online eds.); USD 981 combined subscription in the Americas to institutions (print & online eds.); USD 1,143 combined subscription elsewhere to institutions (print & online eds.) (effective 2012). adv. back issues avail.; reprint service avail. from PSC. **Document type:** *Journal, Academic/Scholarly.* **Description:** Devoted to disseminating new knowledge related to the epidemiology, etiology, pathogenesis, management, complications and prevention of diabetes in childhood and adolescence.
Related titles: ◆ Online - full text ed.: Pediatric Diabetes (Online). ISSN 1399-5448.
Indexed: A01, A03, A08, A22, A26, B21, C06, C07, CA, CurCont, E01, EMBASE, ExcerpMed, H12, ImmunAb, MEDLINE, P30, R10, Reac, SCI, SCOPUS, T02, W07.
—BLDSC (6417.584000), IE, Infotrieve, Ingenta. **CCC.**
Published by: (International Society for Pediatric and Adolescent Diabetes), Wiley-Blackwell Publishing, Inc. (Subsidiary of: Wiley-Blackwell Publishing Ltd.), Commerce Pl, 350 Main St, Malden, MA 02148. TEL 781-388-8200, FAX 781-388-8210, info@wiley.com, http://www.wiley.com/WileyCDA/. Ed. Mark A Sperling. Adv. contact Claire Rogers.

618.92 616.46 USA ISSN 1745-1426
➤ **PEDIATRIC DIABETES. SUPPLEMENT (PRINT).** Text in English. 2004. irreg., latest vol.13, 2009. back issues avail. **Document type:** *Monographic series, Academic/Scholarly.*
Related titles: Online - full text ed.
Published by: Wiley-Blackwell Publishing, Inc. (Subsidiary of: Wiley-Blackwell Publishing Ltd.), Commerce Pl, 350 Main St, Malden, MA 02148. TEL 781-388-8200, FAX 781-388-8210, info@wiley.com, http://www.wiley.com/WileyCDA/.

➤ **PEDIATRIC DOSAGE HANDBOOK.** *see* PHARMACY AND PHARMACOLOGY

618.92 616.02 USA ISSN 0749-5161
RJ370 CODEN: PECAE5
➤ **PEDIATRIC EMERGENCY CARE.** Text in English. 1985. m. USD 663 domestic to institutions; USD 779 foreign to institutions (effective 2011). adv. back issues avail.; reprints avail. **Document type:** *Journal, Academic/Scholarly.* **Description:** Features clinically relevant articles with an EM perspective on the care of acutely ill or injured children and adolescents.
Related titles: Online - full text ed.: ISSN 1535-1815.
Indexed: A20, A22, A36, ASCA, C06, C07, C08, CABA, CINAHL, CurCont, D01, E12, EMBASE, ExcerpMed, FR, GH, H17, INI, IndMed, Inpharma, JW-EM, LT, MEDLINE, N02, N03, P30, P33, P35, P39, PN&I, R08, R10, RA&MP, RM&VM, RRTA, Reac, SCI, SCOPUS, T05, VS, W07, W10.
—BLDSC (6417.586000), GNLM, IE, Infotrieve, Ingenta, INIST. **CCC.**
Published by: Lippincott Williams & Wilkins (Subsidiary of: Wolters Kluwer N.V.), 530 Walnut St, Philadelphia, PA 19106. TEL 215-521-8300, FAX 215-521-8902, customerservice@lww.com, http://www.lww.com. Eds. Gary R Fleisher, Dr. Stephen Ludwig. Pub. Sandra Kasko. Circ: 928.

618.92 USA ISSN 1549-9650
PEDIATRIC EMERGENCY MEDICINE PRACTICE; an evidence-based approach to pediatric emergency medicine. Text in English. 2004. m. USD 299 (effective 2010). back issues avail. **Document type:** *Journal, Academic/Scholarly.*
Related titles: Online - full text ed.: ISSN 1549-9669.
Published by: E B Medicine, 5550 Triangle Pky, Ste 150, Norcross, GA 30092. TEL 678-366-7933, 800-249-5770, FAX 770-500-1316, ebm@ebmedicine.net. Ed. Martin I Herman.

PEDIATRIC EMERGENCY MEDICINE REPORTS. *see* MEDICAL SCIENCES—Orthopedics And Traumatology

PEDIATRIC ENDOCRINOLOGY REVIEWS; diabetes, nutrition, metabolism. *see* MEDICAL SCIENCES—Endocrinology

618.92 USA ISSN 0899-8493
RJ133 CODEN: PEXSFT
➤ **PEDIATRIC EXERCISE SCIENCE.** Short title: P E S. Text in English. 1989. q. USD 368 domestic to institutions; USD 378 foreign to institutions; USD 426 combined subscription domestic to institutions (print & online eds.); USD 436 combined subscription foreign to institutions (print & online eds.) (effective 2012). adv. bk.rev. charts; illus. back issues avail.; reprint service avail. from PSC. **Document type:** *Journal, Academic/Scholarly.* **Description:** Addresses the importance of exercise during childhood and adolescence to scientists, health-care providers, and physical educators.
Related titles: Online - full text ed.: ISSN 1543-2920. USD 368 to institutions (effective 2012).
Indexed: A20, A22, AMED, ASCA, C06, C07, C08, CA, CDA, CINAHL, DIP, EMBASE, ESPM, ExcerpMed, FoSS&M, IBR, IBZ, MEDLINE, P30, PEI, R09, R10, Reac, RiskAb, SCI, SCOPUS, SD, SportS, T02, W07.
—BLDSC (6417.590000), GNLM, IE, Infotrieve, Ingenta. **CCC.**
Published by: (North American Society of Pediatric Exercise Medicine), Human Kinetics, 1607 N Market St, Champaign, IL 61820. TEL 800-747-4457, FAX 217-351-2674, info@hkusa.com, http://www.humankinetics.com. Ed. Dr. Thomas W Rowland TEL 413-794-7350. Pub. Rainer Martens. R&P Martha Gullo TEL 217-403-7534. Adv. contact Amy Bleich TEL 217-403-7803.

618.92 GBR ISSN 1745-5111
➤ **PEDIATRIC HEALTH.** Text in English. 2007. bi-m. GBP 605 combined subscription domestic (print & online eds.); USD 1,160 combined subscription in North America (print & online eds.); JPY 126,000 combined subscription in Japan (print & online eds.); EUR 755 combined subscription elsewhere (print & online eds.) (effective 2010). adv. back issues avail.; reprints avail. **Document type:** *Journal, Academic/Scholarly.* **Description:** Features articles on all aspects of pediatric healthcare, from neonate to young adult, including pediatric oncology, neurology, cardiology, nephrology and infectious diseases.
Related titles: Online - full text ed.: ISSN 1745-512X. GBP 535 domestic; USD 1,030 in North America; JPY 112,500 in Japan; EUR 670 elsewhere (effective 2010) (from IngentaConnect).
Indexed: A26, B21, E08, EMBASE, ESPM, ExcerpMed, G08, H&SSA, H12, I05, P20, P24, P30, P48, P50, P54, PQC, RiskAb, SCOPUS.
—BLDSC (6417.598750), IE. **CCC.**
Published by: Future Medicine Ltd. (Subsidiary of: Future Science Ltd.), Unitec House, 2 Albert Pl, London, N3 1QB, United Kingdom. TEL 44-20-83716080, FAX 44-20-83716099, info@futuremedicine.com. Eds. Tarryn Greenberg, Elisa Manzotti TEL 44-20-83716090. Pub. David Hughes.

618.92 GBR ISSN 1179-9927
▼ ➤ **PEDIATRIC HEALTH, MEDICINE AND THERAPEUTICS.** Text in English. 2010. irreg. free (effective 2011). **Document type:** *Journal, Academic/Scholarly.*
Media: Online - full text.
—CCC.
Published by: Dove Medical Press Ltd., Beechfield House, Winterton Way, Macclesfield, SK11 0JL, United Kingdom. TEL 44-1625-509130, FAX 44-1625-617933. Ed. Dr. Claire Wainwright.

618.92 USA ISSN 1067-9413
PEDIATRIC HEALTH MONITOR. Text in English. 1995. q. free. **Document type:** *Magazine, Consumer.*
Published by: Data Centrum Communications, Inc., 650 From Rd, 2nd Fl, Paramus, NJ 07652. TEL 201-391-1911, FAX 201-225-1440, info@healthmonitor.com, http://www.healthmonitor.com.

618.92 GBR ISSN 0888-0018
RJ411 CODEN: PHONEN
➤ **PEDIATRIC HEMATOLOGY & ONCOLOGY.** Text in English. 1984. 8/yr. GBP 905, EUR 1,195, USD 1,495 combined subscription to institutions (print & online eds.); GBP 1,810, EUR 2,390, USD 2,990 combined subscription to corporations (print & online eds.) (effective 2010). adv. bk.rev. back issues avail.; reprint service avail. from PSC. **Document type:** *Journal, Academic/Scholarly.* **Description:** Features experimental, biochemical and clinical articles covering immunology, pathology and pharmacology.
Incorporates (1994-2002): International Journal of Pediatric Hematology - Oncology (1070-2903); Formerly (until 1986): European Paediatric Haematology and Oncology (0800-2789)
Related titles: Microform ed.: (from PQC); Online - full text ed.: ISSN 1521-0669 (from IngentaConnect).
Indexed: A01, A03, A08, A22, A34, A36, ASCA, B21, B25, BIOBASE, BIOSIS Prev, CA, CABA, ChemAb, ChemTitl, CurCont, D01, E01, E12, EMBASE, ESPM, ExcerpMed, FR, GH, H&SSA, H17, IABS, ISR, IndMed, Inpharma, MEDLINE, MS&D, MycolAb, N02, N03, P30, P33, P35, P39, R08, R10, R12, RM&VM, Reac, SCI, SCOPUS, T02, T05, W07.
—BLDSC (6417.599500), CASDDS, GNLM, IE, Infotrieve, Ingenta, INIST. **CCC.**
Published by: Informa Healthcare (Subsidiary of: T & F Informa plc), Telephone House, 69-77 Paul St, London, EC2A 4LQ, United Kingdom. TEL 44-20-70175000, FAX 44-20-70176792, healthcare.enquiries@informa.com. Ed. Dr. Elliott Vichinsky. Adv. contact Per Sonnerfeldt. **Subscr. in N. America to:** Taylor & Francis Inc., Customer Services Dept, 325 Chestnut St, 8th Fl, Philadelphia, PA 19106. TEL 215-625-8900, 800-354-1420, FAX 215-625-8914, customerservice@taylorandfrancis.com; **Subscr. outside N. America to:** Taylor & Francis Ltd., Journals Customer Service, Sheepen Pl, Colchester, Essex CO3 3LP, United Kingdom. TEL 44-20-70175544, FAX 44-20-70175198, tf.enquiries@tfinforma.com.

➤ **PEDIATRIC HEMATOLOGY - ONCOLOGY SERIES.** *see* MEDICAL SCIENCES—Oncology

618.92 USA ISSN 1947-2412
▼ **PEDIATRIC I C D-9-C M CODING POCKET GUIDE.** (International Classification of Diseases, Ninth Revision, Clinical Modification) Text in English. 2009. a. USD 39.95 per issue to members; USD 44.95 per issue to non-members (effective 2009). **Document type:** *Handbook/ Manual/Guide, Trade.* **Description:** A quick reference for pediatric coding diagnosis.
Formerly (until 2009): Pedatric I C D-9-C M Coding Flip Chart (1557-0827)
Published by: American Academy of Pediatrics, 141 NW Pt Blvd, Elk Grove Village, IL 60007. TEL 847-434-4000, FAX 847-434-8000, journals@aap.org, http://www.aap.org.

618.92 616.9 USA ISSN 0891-3668
RJ1 CODEN: PIDJEV
➤ **THE PEDIATRIC INFECTIOUS DISEASE JOURNAL.** Abbreviated title: P I D J. Text in English. 1982. m. USD 755 domestic to institutions; USD 881 foreign to institutions (effective 2011). adv. bk.rev. Index. back issues avail.; reprints avail. **Document type:** *Journal, Academic/Scholarly.* **Description:** Brings out insights on combating disease in children - from state-of-the-art diagnostic techniques to the effective drug therapies and other treatment protocols.
Formerly (until 1987): Pediatric Infectious Disease (0277-9730)
Related titles: Online - full text ed.: ISSN 1532-0987; Supplement(s): Pediatric Infectious Disease Journal International Newsletter. ISSN 1073-3175. 1994.
Indexed: A22, A29, A34, A35, A36, ASCA, AbAn, AgBio, AgrForAb, B20, B21, B25, BA, BDM&CN, BIOSIS Prev, CABA, CCIP, CurCont, D01, DentInd, DokArb, E12, EMBASE, ESPM, ExcerpMed, F08, F09, FR, FamI, GH, H17, IBR, IBZ, IDIS, ISR, ImmunAb, IndMed, IndVet, Inpharma, JW-EM, JW-ID, LT, MEDLINE, MS&D, MycolAb, N02, N03, N04, NRN, P30, P32, P33, P35, P37, P39, P40, PN&I, R08, R10, R12, R13, RM&VM, RRTA, Reac, S12, S13, S16, SAA, SCI, SCOPUS, T05, TAR, VS, VirolAbstr, W07, W11.
—BLDSC (6417.601600), GNLM, IE, Infotrieve, Ingenta, INIST. **CCC.**
Published by: (Pediatric Infectious Diseases Society, European Society for Paediatric Infectious Diseases NLD), Lippincott Williams & Wilkins (Subsidiary of: Wolters Kluwer N.V.), Two Commerce Sq, 2001 Market St, Philadelphia, PA 19103. TEL 215-521-8300, FAX 215-521-8902, customerservice@lww.com, http://www.lww.com. Ed. Dr. John D Nelson TEL 214-648-2520. Pub. Kim Jansen. Adv. contact Bethann H Sands TEL 215-521-8399. Circ: 3,116.

618.92 GBR
▼ **PEDIATRIC INFECTIOUS DISEASES SOCIETY. JOURNAL.** Text in English. forthcoming 2012. q. EUR 1,690 combined subscription in Europe to institutions (print & online eds.); USD 2,089 combined subscription in the Americas to institutions (print & online eds.); GBP 1,420 combined subscription to institutions in the UK & elsewhere; (print & online eds.) (effective 2012). **Document type:** *Journal, Academic/Scholarly.* **Description:** Dedicated to perinatal, childhood, and adolescent infectious diseases.
Related titles: Online - full text ed.: forthcoming.
Published by: (Pediatric Infectious Diseases Society USA), Oxford University Press, Great Clarendon St, Oxford, OX2 6DP, United Kingdom. TEL 44-1865-556767, FAX 44-1865-556646, enquiry@oup.co.uk, http://www.oup.co.uk/. Ed. Dr. Theoklis Zaoutis.

PEDIATRIC LENGTH OF STAY BY DIAGNOSIS & OPERATION, UNITED STATES. *see* HEALTH FACILITIES AND ADMINISTRATION—Abstracting, Bibliographies, Statistics

▼ **PEDIATRIC N P / P A.** *see* MEDICAL SCIENCES—Nurses And Nursing

PEDIATRIC NEPHROLOGY. *see* MEDICAL SCIENCES—Urology And Nephrology

618.92 USA ISSN 0887-8994
RJ486
➤ **PEDIATRIC NEUROLOGY.** Text in English. 1985. m. USD 974 in United States to institutions; USD 1,083 elsewhere to institutions (effective 2012). adv. back issues avail.; reprints avail. **Document type:** *Journal, Academic/Scholarly.* **Description:** Brings out clinical and research articles covering all aspects of the developing nervous system.
Related titles: Microform ed.: (from PQC); Online - full text ed.: ISSN 1873-5150 (from IngentaConnect, ScienceDirect).
Indexed: A01, A03, A08, A22, A26, A36, ASCA, B21, BIOBASE, C06, CA, CABA, CurCont, E-psyche, E12, EMBASE, ExcerpMed, FR, GH, H17, I05, IABS, ISR, IndMed, Inpharma, JW-N, LT, MEDLINE, N02, N03, NSA, NSCI, P30, P33, P35, R07, R08, R10, R12, RM&VM, RRTA, Reac, SCI, SCOPUS, SoyAb, T02, T05, W07, W10.
—BLDSC (6417.604300), GNLM, IE, Infotrieve, Ingenta, INIST. **CCC.**
Published by: Elsevier Inc. (Subsidiary of: Elsevier Science & Technology), 1600 John F Kennedy Blvd, Philadelphia, PA 19103. TEL 215-239-3900, FAX 215-238-7883, JournalCustomerService-usa@elsevier.com, http://www.elsevier.com. Ed. Dr. Kenneth F Swaiman. Pub. Virginia Prada Lopez. Adv. contact Pat Hampton TEL 212-633-3181.

618.92 USA ISSN 0031-398X
RJ1
PEDIATRIC NEWS. Text in English. 1967. m. USD 114 in United States to institutions; USD 182 elsewhere to institutions (effective 2012). adv. bk.rev. charts; illus. back issues avail.; reprints avail. **Document type:** *Newspaper, Trade.* **Description:** Provides the practicing pediatrician with news and commentary about clinical developments in the field and about the impact of health care policy on the specialty and the physician's practice.
Related titles: Microform ed.: (from PQC); Online - full text ed.
Indexed: A26, G08, H11, H12, I05, P30.
—BLDSC (6417.605000), Infotrieve. **CCC.**
Published by: International Medical News Group (Subsidiary of: Elsevier Health Sciences), 5635 Fishers Ln, Ste 6000, Rockville, MD 20852. TEL 877-524-2341, FAX 240-221-4400, m.altier@elsevier.com, http://www.imng.com. Ed. Mary Jo M. Dales. Pub. Alan J Imhoff TEL 973-290-8216. Circ: 53,485. **Subscr. to:** Elsevier, Subscription Customer Service, 60 Columbia Rd, Bldg B, Morristown, NJ 07960. TEL 973-290-8200, FAX 973-290-8250, http://www.elsevier.com/.

618.92 USA
PEDIATRIC NUTRITION HANDBOOK. Text in English. 1979. irreg., latest 2009, 6th ed. USD 84.95 to non-members 6th ed.; USD 74.95 to members 6th ed. (effective 2009). **Document type:** *Handbook/ Manual/Guide, Trade.*
Published by: American Academy of Pediatrics, 141 NW Pt Blvd, Elk Grove Village, IL 60007. TEL 847-434-4000, FAX 847-434-8000, journals@aap.org, http://www.aap.org. Ed. Ronald e Kleinman. Pub. Robert Perelman.

618.92 IND ISSN 0973-0966
➤ **PEDIATRIC ON CALL;** a complete child health care. Text in English. 2000. m. free (effective 2011). Index. back issues avail. **Document type:** *Journal, Academic/Scholarly.* **Description:** Contains scientific articles, case reports, spot diagnosis, letters to editors, and more. The audience is international and predominantly from India, USA, Canada, Turkey and Iran.
Related titles: Online - full text ed.: ISSN 0973-0958.

Indexed: A36, CABA, D01, E12, GH, N02, N03, P33, R08, R12, T05.
Published by: Levioza, 1/B Saguna, 271/B St Francis Rd., Vile Parle (W), Mumbai, 400056, India. TEL 91-22-32905610, FAX 91-22-26171392. Ed., Pub. Ira Shah. R&P Santosh Singh. Adv. contact Alok Singh.

618.92 615.19 USA
PEDIATRIC PHARMACOTHERAPY; a monthly review for health care professionals. Text in English. 1995. m. **Document type:** *Newsletter, Trade.* **Description:** Provides a brief, referenced source of continuing medication information specifically related to children. Focuses on the initiation and monitoring of medications in the primary care setting.
Related titles: Online - full text ed.
Published by: University of Virginia Health Sciences Center, Children's Medical Center, Box 800674, Charlottesville, VA 22908. TEL 434-982-0921, FAX 434-982-1682, mlb3u@virginia.edu, http://www.hsc.virginia.edu.

618.92 615.82 USA ISSN 0898-5669
RJ53.P5 CODEN: PPTHEI
➤ **PEDIATRIC PHYSICAL THERAPY.** Abbreviated title: P P T. Text in English. 1989. q. USD 345 domestic to institutions; USD 446 foreign to institutions (effective 2011). adv. Index. back issues avail.; reprints avail. **Document type:** *Journal, Academic/Scholarly.* **Description:** Presents articles that address developmental, orthopedic and respiratory concerns, thoughtful discussions of professional issues, and reports on promising research.
Related titles: Online - full text ed.: ISSN 1538-005X.
Indexed: A22, AMED, C06, C07, C08, CINAHL, ECER, EMBASE, ExcerpMed, MEDLINE, P30, R10, Reac, SCOPUS.
—BLDSC (6417.605700), GNLM, IE, Infotrieve, Ingenta. **CCC.**
Published by: (American Physical Therapy Association, Section on Pediatrics), Lippincott Williams & Wilkins (Subsidiary of: Wolters Kluwer N.V.), Two Commerce Sq, 2001 Market St, Philadelphia, PA 19103. TEL 215-521-8300, FAX 215-521-8902, customerservice@lww.com, http://www.lww.com. Ed. Ann F VanSant TEL 215-204-3378. Pub. Paul Gee. Adv. contact Pat Wendelken. Circ: 5,330.

618.92 616.2 USA ISSN 8755-6863
RJ431 CODEN: PEPUES
➤ **PEDIATRIC PULMONOLOGY.** Text in English. 1985. m. GBP 1,462 in United Kingdom to institutions; EUR 1,847 in Europe to institutions; USD 2,611 in United States to institutions; USD 2,779 in Canada & Mexico to institutions; USD 2,863 elsewhere to institutions; GBP 1,682 combined subscription in United Kingdom to institutions (print & online eds.); EUR 2,126 combined subscription in Europe to institutions (print & online eds.); USD 3,003 combined subscription in United States to institutions (print & online eds.); USD 3,171 combined subscription in Canada & Mexico to institutions (print & online eds.); USD 3,255 combined subscription elsewhere to institutions (print & online eds.) (effective 2012). adv. bk.rev. back issues avail.; reprint service avail. from PSC. **Document type:** *Journal, Academic/Scholarly.* **Description:** Covers various aspects of respiratory system disorders in infants and children.
Related titles: Online - full text ed.: ISSN 1099-0496. 1996. GBP 1,333 in United Kingdom to institutions; EUR 1,684 in Europe to institutions; USD 2,611 elsewhere to institutions (effective 2012); Supplement(s): Pediatric Pulmonology. Supplement. ISSN 1054-187X. 1987.
Indexed: A22, A34, A36, ASCA, CABA, CurCont, D01, E12, EMBASE, ExcerpMed, F09, FR, GH, H17, INI, ISR, IndMed, Inpharma, MEDLINE, N02, N03, N04, P30, P33, P35, P39, R10, R12, R13, RA&MP, RM&VM, Reac, RefZh, SCI, SCOPUS, SoyAb, T05, VS, W07.
—BLDSC (6417.605800), GNLM, IE, Infotrieve, Ingenta, INIST. **CCC.**
Published by: John Wiley & Sons, Inc., 111 River St, Hoboken, NJ 07030. TEL 201-748-6000, FAX 201-748-6088, info@wiley.com, http://www.wiley.com/WileyCDA/. Ed. Victor Chernick. Pub. Colette Bean. **Subscr. outside the Americas to:** John Wiley & Sons Ltd., The Atrium, Southern Gate, Chichester, West Sussex PO19 8SQ, United Kingdom. TEL 44-1243-779777, 800-243407, FAX 44-1243-775878, cs-journals@wiley.com.

➤ **PEDIATRIC RADIOLOGY**; roentgenology, nuclear medicine, ultrasonics, CT, MRI. *see* MEDICAL SCIENCES—Radiology And Nuclear Medicine

618.92 ITA ISSN 2036-749X
▼ **PEDIATRIC REPORTS.** Text in English. 2009. irreg. **Document type:** *Journal, Academic/Scholarly.*
Related titles: Online - full text ed.: ISSN 2036-7503. free (effective 2011).
Indexed: A01, T02.
Published by: Pagepress, Via Giuseppe Belli 4, Pavia, 27100, Italy. TEL 39-0382-1751762, FAX 39-0382-1750481.

618.92 USA ISSN 0031-3998
RJ1 CODEN: PEREBL
➤ **PEDIATRIC RESEARCH**; international journal of human developmental biology. Text in English. 1857. m. USD 1,059 domestic to institutions; USD 1,276 foreign to institutions (effective 2011). adv. bk.rev. charts; illus. Index. back issues avail.; reprints avail. **Document type:** *Journal, Academic/Scholarly.* **Description:** Covers advances in the understanding and management of pediatric pulmonary, endocrinological, gastroenterological, and nutritional disorders.
Former titles (until 1967): Annales Paediatrici (0365-4966); (until 1938): Jahrbuch fur Kinderheilkunde (0368-1203); (until 1932): Jahrbuch fur Kinderheilkunde und Physische Erziehung (1421-1025)
Related titles: Online - full text ed.: ISSN 1530-0447.
Indexed: A20, A22, A34, A35, A36, A38, ASCA, AgBio, B25, BDM&CN, BIOBASE, BIOSIS Prev, CABA, CCIP, CDA, ChPerl, ChemAb, ChemTitl, CurCont, D01, DentInd, E12, EMBASE, ExcerpMed, F09, FR, Faml, GH, IABS, IBR, IBZ, ISR, IndMed, IndVet, Inpharma, Kidney, MEDLINE, MycolAb, N02, N03, N04, N05, NRN, P30, P33, P35, P39, PN&I, R07, R08, R10, R13, RA&MP, RM&VM, Reac, S12, S13, S16, SCI, SCOPUS, SoyAb, T05, THA, TriticAb, VS, W07.
—BLDSC (6417.620000), CASDDS, GNLM, IE, Infotrieve, Ingenta, INIST. **CCC.**
Published by: (International Pediatric Research Foundation Inc.), Lippincott Williams & Wilkins (Subsidiary of: Wolters Kluwer N.V.), Two Commerce Sq, 2001 Market St, Philadelphia, PA 19103. TEL 215-521-8300, FAX 215-521-8902, customerservice@lww.com, http://www.lww.com. Ed. Sherin U Devaskar. Pub. Sandra Kasko. **Co-sponsors:** American Pediatric Society; Society for Pediatric Research; European Society for Pediatric Research.

618.92 ITA ISSN 2035-827X
▼ **PEDIATRIC REVIEWS.** Text in English. 2009. irreg. **Document type:** *Monographic series, Academic/Scholarly.*
Related titles: Online - full text ed.: ISSN 2035-8121.
Published by: Pagepress, Via Giuseppe Belli 4, Pavia, 27100, Italy. TEL 39-0382-1751762, FAX 39-0382-1750481, http://www.pagepress.org.

PEDIATRIC RHEUMATOLOGY ONLINE JOURNAL. *see* MEDICAL SCIENCES—Rheumatology

PEDIATRIC SURGERY INTERNATIONAL. *see* MEDICAL SCIENCES—Surgery

PEDIATRIC SURGERY UPDATE. *see* MEDICAL SCIENCES—Surgery

617.98 USA ISSN 1397-3142
RD120.77.C45 CODEN: PETRF6
➤ **PEDIATRIC TRANSPLANTATION.** Text in English. 1997. 8/yr. GBP 671 in United Kingdom to institutions; EUR 853 in Europe to institutions; USD 1,129 in the Americas to institutions; USD 1,316 elsewhere to institutions; GBP 772 combined subscription in United Kingdom to institutions (print & online eds.); EUR 981 combined subscription in Europe to institutions (print & online eds.); USD 1,299 combined subscription in the Americas to institutions (print & online eds.); USD 1,514 combined subscription elsewhere to institutions (print & online eds.) (effective 2012). adv. illus. back issues avail.; reprint service avail. from PSC. **Document type:** *Journal, Academic/Scholarly.* **Description:** Deals with clinical experience and basic research in transplantation of tissues and solid organs in infants, children and adolescents.
Related titles: Online - full text ed.: ISSN 1399-3046. 1999. GBP 671 in United Kingdom to institutions; EUR 853 in Europe to institutions; USD 1,129 in the Americas to institutions; USD 1,316 elsewhere to institutions (effective 2012) (from IngentaConnect); Supplement(s): Pediatric Transplantation. Supplement. ISSN 1398-2265. 1999.
Indexed: A01, A03, A08, A20, A22, A26, B21, CA, CurCont, E01, EMBASE, ExcerpMed, H12, INI, ImmunAb, IndMed, Inpharma, MEDLINE, P30, P35, R10, Reac, SCI, SCOPUS, T02, W07.
—BLDSC (6417.628330), GNLM, IE, Infotrieve, Ingenta, INIST. **CCC.**
Published by: (International Pediatric Transplantation Association DNK), Wiley-Blackwell Publishing, Inc. (Subsidiary of: Wiley-Blackwell Publishing Ltd.), Commerce Pl, 350 Main St, Malden, MA 02148. TEL 781-388-8200, FAX 781-388-8210, info@wiley.com, http://www.wiley.com/WileyCDA/. Ed. Richard N Fine.

618.92 USA
PEDIATRICLINX. Text in English. d. adv. **Document type:** *Newsletter.* **Description:** Includes pediatric news and medical information for physicians and healthcare professionals.
Media: Online - full text. **Related titles:** E-mail ed.
Published by: MDLinx.com Inc, 1232 22nd St NW, Washington, DC 20037-1202. info@mdlinx.com. Ed. Dave Rothenberg.

618.92 USA ISSN 0031-4005
RJ1 CODEN: PEDIAU
➤ **PEDIATRICS (ENGLISH EDITION).** Text in English. 1948. m. USD 611 combined subscription domestic to institutions (print & online eds.); USD 668 combined subscription foreign to institutions (print & online eds.) (effective 2010). adv. bk.rev. illus.; abstr. s-a. index. 250 p./no.; back issues avail.; reprints avail. **Document type:** *Journal, Academic/Scholarly.* **Description:** Contains original research and special features in the field of pediatrics. Articles cover various topics including nutrition, surgery, dentistry, public health, genetics, psychosocial development, education and nursing.
Related titles: CD-ROM ed.; Microfiche ed.; Online - full text ed.: ISSN 1098-4275. 1996. USD 549 to institutions Tier 1 (effective 2010); ◆ Spanish ed.: Pediatrics (Spanish Edition). ISSN 0210-5721; Arabic ed.; Hungarian ed.; Russian ed.; Portuguese ed.; Ed.: Pediatrics (Chinese Edition). ISSN 1938-9191; Regional ed(s).: Pediatrics (Indian Edition).
Indexed: A01, A02, A03, A08, A20, A22, A25, A26, A29, A34, A36, A37, AHCMS, AIDS Ab, AIM, Agr, AgrForAb, B20, B21, B25, BA, BDM&CN, BIOBASE, BIOSIS Prev, BP, C06, C07, C08, C11, CA, CABA, CCIP, CINAHL, ChemAb, Chicano, CurCont, D01, DBA, DentInd, DiabCont, DokArb, E03, E07, E08, E12, ECER, EMBASE, ERI, ESPM, ExcerpMed, F08, F09, FAMLI, FR, FS&TA, Faml, G05, G06, G07, G08, G10, GH, H&SSA, H03, H04, H11, H12, H13, H16, H17, HospLI, I05, I07, I12, IABS, IDIS, INI, ISR, IndMed, IndVet, Inpharma, JW, JW-D, JW-EM, JW-ID, JW-WH, Kidney, LT, M01, M02, M06, MEDLINE, MS&D, MaizeAb, MycolAb, N02, N03, N04, NRN, O01, P02, P03, P10, P16, P19, P20, P21, P22, P24, P26, P30, P32, P33, P34, P35, P39, P40, P43, P48, P50, P53, P54, PEI, PHN&I, PN&I, PQC, PsycInfo, R07, R08, R10, R11, R12, R13, RA&MP, RM&VM, RRTA, Reac, RiskAb, S02, S03, S08, S09, S12, S13, S16, S23, SCI, SCOPUS, SoyAb, T02, T05, TriticAb, V02, VS, VirolAbstr, W07, W10, W11.
—BLDSC (6417.650000), CASDDS, CIS, GNLM, IE, Infotrieve, Ingenta, INIST. **CCC.**
Published by: American Academy of Pediatrics, 141 NW Pt Blvd, Elk Grove Village, IL 60007. TEL 847-434-4000, FAX 847-434-8000, journals@aap.org, http://www.aap.org. Eds. Dr. Jerold F Lucey, Lewis R First. adv.: B&W page USD 3,750; trim 8.125 x 10.875. Circ: 60,000 (paid).

618.92 ITA ISSN 1120-7507
PEDIATRICS (ITALIAN EDITION). Variant title: Pediatrics Edizione Italiana. Text in Italian. 1989. m. EUR 60 (effective 2008). **Document type:** *Journal, Academic/Scholarly.* **Description:** Italian edition of the American Academy of Pediatrics' journal.
Related titles: Online - full text ed.
Indexed: BibAg, ISR, JW-D.
Published by: Centro Studi Humana (C S H), Viale Liguria 20-22, Milan, 20143, Italy. http://www.humana.it.

618.9 ESP ISSN 0210-5721
➤ **PEDIATRICS (SPANISH EDITION).** Text in Spanish. 1976. m. EUR 142.15 combined subscription to individuals print & online eds.; EUR 359.87 combined subscription to institutions print & online eds. (effective 2009). back issues avail.; reprints avail. **Document type:** *Journal, Academic/Scholarly.* **Description:** Covers infectious illnesses, immunity, nutrition, community medicine, premature and newborn babies, neurology, psychiatry, cardiology, endocrinology and toxicology.
Related titles: Online - full text ed.; ◆ English ed.: Pediatrics (English Edition). ISSN 0031-4005; Russian ed.; Portuguese ed.; Ed.: Pediatrics (Chinese Edition). ISSN 1938-9191; Arabic ed.; Hungarian ed.
Indexed: DokArb, ISR.
—IE, Infotrieve. **CCC.**
Published by: (American Academy of Pediatrics USA), Elsevier Doyma (Subsidiary of: Elsevier Health Sciences), Traversa de Gracia 17-21, Barcelona, 08021, Spain. TEL 34-932-418800, FAX 34-932-419020, editorial@elsevier.com. Ed. A. Gallart Catala. Circ: 6,700.

618.92 TWN ISSN 1875-9572
▼ ➤ **PEDIATRICS AND NEONATOLOGY.** Text in Chinese. 2009. bi-m. EUR 387 in Europe to institutions; JPY 58,800 in Japan to institutions; USD 499 elsewhere to institutions (effective 2012). adv. **Document type:** *Journal, Academic/Scholarly.*
Formed by the merger of (1994-2009): Clinical Neonatology (1381-3390); (1999-2009): Acta Paediatrica Taiwanica (1608-8115); Which was formerly (1960-1999): Xiao'erke Yixuehui Zazhi/Acta Paediatrica Sinica (0001-6578)
Related titles: Online - full text ed.: ISSN 2212-1692 (from ScienceDirect).
Indexed: A36, B&BAb, B19, B20, B21, B25, BIOSIS Prev, CA, CABA, CTA, D01, E12, EMBASE, ESPM, ExcerpMed, GH, ImmunAb, MEDLINE, MycolAb, N02, N03, NSA, P30, P33, R08, R10, RA&MP, RM&VM, Reac, SCI, SCOPUS, T02, T05, ToxAb, W07.
—BLDSC (6417.652650), IE. **CCC.**
Published by: Taiwan Xiao'erke Yixuehui/Taiwan Pediatric Association, 10F-1, No. 69, Sec. 1, Hang Chow S. Rd., Taipei, 10055, Taiwan. TEL 886-2-23516446, FAX 886-2-23516448, pediatr@www.pediatr.org.tw, http://www.pediatr.org.tw/. Ed. Dr. Yen-Hsuan Ni.

618.92 USA ISSN 0730-6725
RJ1
PEDIATRICS FOR PARENTS; the newsletter for people who care for children. Abbreviated title: P F P. Text in English. 1980. m. looseleaf. USD 25 (effective 2010). adv. 12 p./no.; back issues avail. **Document type:** *Newsletter, Consumer.* **Description:** Features articles written by pediatricians and other healthcare professionals for parents of children of all ages.
Incorporates (1983-2010): Child Health Alert (1064-4849)
Related titles: Microform ed.: (from PQC); Online - full text ed.: USD 5 (effective 2010).
Indexed: A26, C11, C12, E07, G05, G06, G07, G08, H03, H11, H12, H13, HlthInd, I05, I07, M01, M02, M06, P07, P10, P18, P19, P20, P48, P53, P54, P55, PQC, S06, S23, T02.
—BLDSC (6417.656700), IE. **CCC.**
Published by: Pediatrics for Parents, Inc., 120 Western Ave, Gloucester, MA 01930. TEL 215-253-4543, FAX 973-302-8187, issues@pedsforparents.com, http://www.moms-refuge.com/. Ed. Dr. Richard J Sagall. adv.: page USD 1,700. Circ: 60,000. **Subscr. to:** PO Box 63716, Philadelphia, PA 19147.

618.92 USA ISSN 0191-9601
RJ47 CODEN: PDREFI
➤ **PEDIATRICS IN REVIEW.** Text in English. 1979. m. USD 222 combined subscription to non-members (print & online eds.); USD 177 combined subscription to members (print & online eds.) (effective 2010). abstr.; charts; illus. cum.index. Supplement avail.; back issues avail.; reprints avail. **Document type:** *Journal, Academic/Scholarly.* **Description:** Provides information on new developments in pediatric medicine.
Related titles: Online - full text ed.: ISSN 1526-3347. USD 172 to non-members; USD 135 to members (effective 2011).
Indexed: A20, A22, C06, C07, CCIP, CurCont, EMBASE, ExcerpMed, IndMed, MEDLINE, NRN, P30, R10, Reac, SCI, SCOPUS, W07.
—BLDSC (6417.657000), GNLM, IE, Infotrieve, Ingenta. **CCC.**
Published by: American Academy of Pediatrics, 141 NW Pt Blvd, Elk Grove Village, IL 60007. TEL 847-434-4000, FAX 847-434-8000, journals@aap.org, http://www.aap.org. Ed. Lawrence F Nazarian. Circ: 31,000.

618.92 AUS ISSN 1328-8067
CODEN: JAMMFW
➤ **PEDIATRICS INTERNATIONAL.** Text in English. 1958. bi-m. GBP 555 in United Kingdom to institutions; EUR 705 in Europe to institutions; USD 899 in the Americas to institutions; USD 1,088 elsewhere to institutions; GBP 639 combined subscription in United Kingdom to institutions (print & online eds.); EUR 811 combined subscription in Europe to institutions (print & online eds.); USD 1,034 combined subscription in the Americas to institutions (print & online eds.); USD 1,252 combined subscription elsewhere to institutions (print & online eds.) (effective 2012). adv. bk.rev. abstr.; bibl.; charts; illus. index. back issues avail.; reprint service avail. from PSC. **Document type:** *Journal, Academic/Scholarly.* **Description:** Contains scientific articles, clinical and laboratory studies, and case reports in the field of pediatrics and child health.
Former titles (until 1999): Acta Paediatrica Japonica. Overseas Edition (0374-5600); (until 1961): Paediatrica Japonica
Related titles: Microform ed.: (from PQC); Online - full text ed.: ISSN 1442-200X. GBP 555 in United Kingdom to institutions; EUR 705 in Europe to institutions; USD 899 in the Americas to institutions; USD 1,088 elsewhere to institutions (effective 2012) (from IngentaConnect); Japanese ed.: Nippon Shonika Gakkai Zasshi. ISSN 0001-6543.
Indexed: A01, A03, A08, A22, A26, A34, A36, A38, B20, B21, B25, BIOSIS Prev, C06, C07, C08, CA, CABA, CIN, CINAHL, ChemAb, ChemTitl, CurCont, D01, E01, E12, EMBASE, ESPM, ExcerpMed, F09, GH, H&SSA, H12, H13, H17, IndMed, Inpharma, Kidney, LT, MEDLINE, MycolAb, N02, N03, NRN, P02, P10, P20, P30, P33, P35, P38, P39, P48, P53, P54, PHN&I, PN&I, PQC, R08, R10, R12, R13, RA&MP, RM&VM, RRTA, Reac, RiskAb, SCI, SCOPUS, T02, T05, VS, VirolAbstr, W07, W10, W11.
—BLDSC (6417.655800), CASDDS, GNLM, IE, Infotrieve, Ingenta, INIST. **CCC.**
Published by: (Japan Pediatric Society JPN), Wiley-Blackwell Publishing Asia (Subsidiary of: Wiley-Blackwell Publishing Ltd.), 155 Cremorne St, Richmond, VIC 3121, Australia. TEL 61-3-92743100, FAX 61-3-92743101, subs@blackwellpublishingasia.com, http://www.wiley.com/WileyCDA/. Ed. Norikazu Shimizu. adv.: B&W page AUD 950, color page AUD 1,950; trim 210 x 275. Circ: 1,000.

618.92 USA ISSN 1556-6927
RJ48
PEDIATRICS ON CALL. Text in English. 2005. triennial. USD 43.95 per issue (effective 2010). **Document type:** *Journal, Trade.*
Related titles: Online - full text ed.

Published by: McGraw-Hill Professional (Subsidiary of: McGraw-Hill Companies, Inc.), Two Penn Plz, 23rd Fl, New York, NY 10121. TEL 212-904-2000, FAX 212-904-6030, customer.service@mcgraw-hill.com, http://www.mhprofessional.com/index.php.

618.92 USA ISSN 1944-2637
PEDIATRICS WEEK. Text in English. 2008 (Jan.). w. USD 2,295 in US & Canada; USD 2,495 elsewhere; USD 2,525 combined subscription in US & Canada (print & online eds.); USD 2,755 combined subscription elsewhere (print & online eds.) (effective 2011). adv. back issues avail. **Document type:** *Newsletter, Trade.* **Description:** Provides coverage of significant drug, device and biotechnology developments for the treatment of children and childhood diseases.
Related titles: E-mail ed.; Online - full text ed.: ISSN 1944-2645. USD 2,295 combined subscription (online & e-mail eds.) (effective 2011).
Indexed: P20, P48, P54, PQC.
Published by: NewsRx, 2727 Paces Ferry Rd SE, Ste 2-440, Atlanta, GA 30339. TEL 770-435-8286, 800-726-4550, FAX 770-435-6800, pressrelease@newsrx.com, http://www.newsrx.com. Pub., Adv. contact Susan Hasty TEL 770-507-7777.

618.92 FRA ISSN 0993-9717
PEDIATRIE PRATIQUE. Text in French. 1988. m. (10/yr.). **Document type:** *Newspaper, Trade.*
Published by: L E N Medical - Axis Sante, 15 Rue des Sablons, Paris, 75116, France. TEL 33-1-47553131, FAX 33-1-47553132, info@len-medical.fr, http://www.len-medical.fr.

618.92 CZE ISSN 1213-0494
➤ **PEDIATRIE PRO PRAXI.** Text in Czech. 2000. bi-m. CZK 480; CZK 80 per issue (effective 2010). **Document type:** *Journal, Academic/Scholarly.*
Related titles: Online - full text ed.: ISSN 1803-5264.
Published by: Solen s.r.o., Lazecka 297/51, Olomouc 51, 779 00, Czech Republic. TEL 420-582-396038, FAX 420-582-396099, solen@solen.cz, http://www.solen.cz. Ed. Iva Dankova. Circ: 3,500.

618.92 RUS ISSN 0031-403X CODEN: PEDTAT
➤ **PEDIATRIYA/PEDIATRICS**; journal named after G.N. Speranskii. Text in Russian; Summaries in English. 1922. bi-m. USD 221 foreign (effective 2005). bk.rev. bibl. index. **Document type:** *Journal, Academic/Scholarly.* **Description:** Covers major problems of modern pediatrics in the Soviet Union and other countries. Includes articles and reviews devoted to the etiology, pathogenesis, clinical picture, prophylaxis and treatment of childhood diseases, surgery, neuropathology, psychiatry and other branches of pediatrics.
Related titles: Online - full text ed.
Indexed: B25, BDM&CN, BIOSIS Prev, ChemAb, F09, ISR, IndMed, MycolAb, P30, RefZh, S02, S03.
—CASDDS, East View, GNLM, INIST. **CCC.**
Published by: Mezhdunarodnyi Fond Okhrany Zdorov'ya Materi i Rebenka, Novyi Arbat 5, Moscow, 121019, Russian Federation. Ed. N S Kislyak. **Dist. by:** East View Information Services, 10601 Wayzata Blvd, Minneapolis, MN 55305. TEL 952-252-1201, 800-477-1005, FAX 952-252-1202, info@eastview.com, http://www.eastview.com. **Co-sponsor:** Soyuz Pediatrov Rossii.

618 UKR ISSN 0031-4048 CODEN: PDAGA2
PEDIATRIYA, AKUSHERSTVO TA GINEKOLOGIYA. Text in Ukrainian; Summaries in Russian. 1936. bi-m. UAK 92.94 domestic; USD 25 foreign (effective 2007). adv. bk.rev. index. **Document type:** *Journal, Academic/Scholarly.* **Description:** Provides scientific and practical information on pediatrics, obstetrics and gynecology.
Indexed: ChemAb, IndMed, P30, S02, S03.
—CASDDS, GNLM, INIST.
Published by: (Ukraine. Ministerstvo Okhorony Zdorov'ya Ukrainy/ Ministry of Health of Ukraine), Pediatriya, Akusherstvo ta Ginekologiya, vul L Tolstogo, 10, Kyiv 4, 01034, Ukraine. Ed. Vitaly G Maidannik. adv.: page USD 500. Circ: 2,000.

618.92 ROM ISSN 1841-5164
PEDIATRU.RO. Text in Romanian. q. ROL 90 (effective 2011). adv. **Document type:** *Magazine, Trade.*
Related titles: Online - full text ed.: ISSN 2066-8252. 2009.
Published by: Versa Puls Media, s.r.l., Calea Rahovei 266-268, corp 1, etaj 2, Bucharest, 050912, Romania. TEL 40-31-4254040, FAX 40-31-4254041, office@pulsmedia.ro. Ed. Dr. Mircea Nanulescu. Adv. contact George Pavel. Circ: 2,000 (paid).

618.92 616.97 USA ISSN 1934-4031
PERINATAL HIV PREVENTION. Text in English. 2006. irreg. free (effective 2007). **Document type:** *Bulletin, Trade.* **Description:** Contains recommendations and guidelines for healthcare and HIV prevention from mothers to their infants.
Related titles: CD-ROM ed.: ISSN 1934-404X; Online - full text ed.: ISSN 1934-4058.
Published by: California Perinatal Quality Care Collaboration, 750 Welch Rd, Ste 224, Palo Alto, CA 94304. TEL 650-723-5763, FAX 650-723-2829, info@cpqcc.org, http://www.cpqcc.org/.

PESQUISA BRASILEIRA EM ODONTOPEDIATRIA E CLINICA INTEGRADA/BRAZILIAN RESEARCH IN PEDIATRIC DENTISTRY AND INTEGRATED CLINIC. *see* MEDICAL SCIENCES—Dentistry

618.92 PHL ISSN 0031-7667
PHILIPPINE JOURNAL OF PEDIATRICS. Text in English. 1950. bi-m. PHP 70, USD 20. adv. bk.rev. abstr. index.
Indexed: P30.
—GNLM.
Published by: Philippine Pediatric Society, P.O. Box 3527, Manila, Philippines. Ed. Dr. Felix A Estrada. Circ: 2,000.

618.92 615.82 USA ISSN 0194-2638
RJ53.P5 CODEN: POTPDY
➤ **PHYSICAL & OCCUPATIONAL THERAPY IN PEDIATRICS**; a quarterly journal of developmental therapy. Abbreviated title: P O T P. Text in English. 1980. q. GBP 485, EUR 640, USD 865 combined subscription to institutions (print & online eds.); GBP 970, EUR 1,280, USD 1,725 combined subscription to corporations (print & online eds.) (effective 2010). adv. bk.rev. 120 p./no. 1 cols./p.; back issues avail.; reprint service avail. from PSC. **Document type:** *Journal, Academic/Scholarly.* **Description:** Brings information to all therapists involved in the developmental and physical rehabilitation of infants and children. Covers current clinical research and practical applications.
Related titles: Microfiche ed.: (from PQC); Microform ed.; Online - full text ed.: ISSN 1541-3144.
Indexed: A01, A03, A22, AMED, ASSIA, BibInd, C06, C07, C08, CA, CDA, CINAHL, E01, E03, ECER, EMBASE, ERI, ExcerpMed, Faml, M02, MEDLINE, P30, PEI, PsycholAb, R09, R10, Reac, RehabLit, S02, S03, SCOPUS, SD, SWR&A, T02, YAE&RB.
—BLDSC (6475.280000), GNLM, IE, Infotrieve, Ingenta. **CCC.**
Published by: Informa Healthcare (Subsidiary of: T & F Informa plc), 52 Vanderbilt Ave, New York, NY 10017. TEL 212-262-8230, FAX 212-262-8234, healthcare.enquiries@informa.com, http://www.informahealthcare.com. Eds. Annette Majnemer, Robert J Palisano. adv.: B&W page USD 315, color page USD 550; trim 4.375 x 7.125. Circ: 743 (paid).

➤ **PNEUMOLOGIA PEDIATRICA.** *see* MEDICAL SCIENCES—Respiratory Diseases

618.92 MEX ISSN 1405-1168
PRACTICA PEDIATRICA. Text in Spanish; Summaries in English. 1929. bi-m. MXN 450 domestic; USD 85 in Latin America; USD 95 in US & Canada; USD 105 elsewhere (effective 2007). adv. bk.rev. abstr.; illus. index. **Document type:** *Magazine, Trade.*
Formerly (until 1993): Revista Mexicana de Pediatria (0035-0052)
Related titles: Online - full text ed.
Indexed: A01, C01, CA, ChemAb, EMBASE, ExcerpMed, R10, Reac, RefZh, SCOPUS, T02.
—GNLM.
Published by: Sociedad Mexicana de Pediatria, Tehuantepec 86 - 503, Col. Roma, Mexico, D.F., 06720, Mexico. TEL 52-55-55647739, FAX 52-55-55648371, emyc@medigraphic.com, http://www.socmexped.com/. Ed. Leopoldo Vega Franco. Circ: 5,000.

PRACTICE MANAGEMENT AND MARKETING NEWS IN PEDIATRIC DENTISTRY. *see* MEDICAL SCIENCES—Dentistry

618.92 NLD ISSN 1876-3782
PRAKTISCHE PEDIATRIE. Text in Dutch. 2007. q. EUR 265 (effective 2011). adv. **Document type:** *Magazine, Trade.*
Related titles: Online - full text ed.: ISSN 1876-3774.
Published by: Prelum Uitgevers, Postbus 545, Houten, 3990 GH, Netherlands. TEL 31-30-6355060, FAX 31-30-6355069, info@prelum.nl, http://www.prelum.nl. Ed. S Thurmer. Pubs. Dr. A D van Kempen, Dr. C A L Dumas. Adv. contact Harry Velthuis. B&W page EUR 695, color page EUR 1,950; trim 210 x 297. Circ: 1,063.

618.92 DEU ISSN 1866-6981
PRAXISFIEBER; Magazin fuer die Medizinischen Fachangestellten in der Kinder- und Jugendarztpraxis. Text in German. 2006. 2/yr. **Document type:** *Magazine, Trade.*
Published by: Hansisches Verlagskontor, Mengstr 16, Luebeck, 23552, Germany. TEL 49-451-703101, FAX 49-451-7031253, eickershoff@beleke.de, http://www.beleke.de/verlagsgruppe/ind_hvk.html. Circ: 20,000 (controlled).

PREGNANCY & BIRTH. *see* MEDICAL SCIENCES—Obstetrics And Gynecology

PREGNANCY AND NEWBORN. *see* MEDICAL SCIENCES—Obstetrics And Gynecology

THE PREGNANCY BOOK. *see* MEDICAL SCIENCES—Obstetrics And Gynecology

362.76 USA ISSN 1942-7743
PREVENTING SEXUAL VIOLENCE; an educational toolkit for health care professionals. Text in English. 2008 (Aug.). irreg., latest 2008. USD 65 per issue to non-members; USD 55 per issue to members (effective 2010). **Document type:** *Monographic series, Trade.* **Description:** Practical new video shows doctors how to talk to patients and parents about sexual violence prevention.
Media: CD-ROM.
Published by: American Academy of Pediatrics, 141 NW Pt Blvd, Elk Grove Village, IL 60007. TEL 847-434-4000, FAX 847-434-8000, journals@aap.org, http://www.aap.org. Ed. Dr. Nancy Kellogg.

618.92 USA ISSN 1040-2497
➤ **PRIMARY CARE REPORTS.** Text in English. 1985. m. USD 369 combined subscription (print & online eds.); USD 62 per issue (effective 2010). **Document type:** *Newsletter, Academic/Scholarly.* **Description:** Features latest treatment protocols and diagnostic methods.
Formerly (until 1988): Advanced Clinical Updates (0893-9837); Which was formed by the merger of (1983-1985): Family Medicine Reports (0746-2514); (1984-1985): Internal Medicine Reports (0891-835X)
Related titles: Online - full text ed.
Indexed: A01, A26, C06, C07, G08, H11, H12, I05, P20, P24, P48, P54, PQC.
—**CCC.**
Published by: A H C Media LLC (Subsidiary of: Thomson Corporation, Healthcare Information Group), 3525 Piedmont Rd, NE, Bldg 6, Ste 400, Atlanta, GA 30305. TEL 404-262-7436, 800-688-2421, FAX 404-262-7837, 800-284-3291, customerservice@ahcmedia.com, http://www.ahcmedia.com/. Ed. Gregory Wise. Pub. Brenda L Mooney TEL 404-262-5403. **Subscr. to:** PO Box 105109, Atlanta, GA 30348. TEL 404-262-5476, FAX 404-262-5560.

➤ **PROFESSION SAGE-FEMME.** *see* MEDICAL SCIENCES—Obstetrics And Gynecology

618.92 USA ISSN 1527-5884
BF719
PROGRESS IN INFANCY RESEARCH. Text in English. 2000. a., latest vol.2, 2002. price varies. back issues avail. **Document type:** *Journal, Academic/Scholarly.*
Related titles: Online - full text ed.
—BLDSC (6868.520500).
Published by: Psychology Press (Subsidiary of: Taylor & Francis Inc.), 325 Chestnut St, Ste 800, Philadelphia, PA 19106. TEL 800-354-1420, FAX 215-625-2940, orders@taylorandfrancis.com, http://www.psypress.com.

PROGRESS IN PEDIATRIC CARDIOLOGY. *see* MEDICAL SCIENCES—Cardiovascular Diseases

618.92 POL ISSN 0137-723X
RJ1 CODEN: PPEDFY
PRZEGLAD PEDIATRYCZNY. Text in Polish. q. **Document type:** *Journal, Academic/Scholarly.*
Formerly (until 1971): Polskie Towarzystwo Pediatryczne. Lodzki Oddzial. Biuletyn
Related titles: Online - full text ed.: free (effective 2011).
Indexed: A01, CA, EMBASE, ExcerpMed, R10, Reac, SCOPUS, T02.
Published by: (Polskie Towarzystwo Pediatryczne), Wydawnictwo Cornetis, ul Dlugosza 2-6, Wroclaw, 51162, Poland. TEL 48-71-3252808, FAX 48-71-3252803, sekretariat@cornetis.com.pl. Ed. Jerzy Bodalski. **Dist. by:** Ars Polona, Obroncow 25, Warsaw 03933, Poland. TEL 48-22-5098609, FAX 48-22-5098610, arspolona@arspolona.com.pl, http://www.arspolona.com.pl.

618.92 155.4 FRA ISSN 0079-726X
RJ499.A1 CODEN: PSYEAH
➤ **LA PSYCHIATRIE DE L'ENFANT.** Text in French; Abstracts in French, English. 1958. s-a. EUR 90 foreign to institutions (effective 2012). cum.index. reprint service avail. from SCH. **Document type:** *Journal, Academic/Scholarly.* **Description:** Original works in the clinical, technical and social psychological areas.
Related titles: Online - full text ed.: ISSN 2102-5320.
Indexed: A22, ASCA, E-psyche, FR, IBR, IBZ, IndMed, P03, P30, PCI, PsycInfo, PsycholAb, S02, S03, SCI, SCOPUS, SSCI, W07.
—BLDSC (6946.243000), GNLM, IE, Infotrieve, Ingenta, INIST. **CCC.**
Published by: Presses Universitaires de France, 6 Avenue Reille, Paris, 75685, France. TEL 33-1-58103161, FAX 33-1-45897530, revues@puf.com, http://www.puf.com. Ed. Pierre Sullivan.

618.92 649 TWN ISSN 1818-2828
QINGSHAONIAN YIXUE JI BAOJIAN TONGXUN/NEWSLETTER OF ADOLESCENT MEDICINE & HEALTH. Text in Chinese. 2006. q. **Document type:** *Newsletter, Academic/Scholarly.*
Published by: Taiwan Qingshaonian Yixue ji Baojian Xuehui/Taiwan Society for Adolescent Medicine and Health, Section 1, no. 110, Chien-Kuo North Road, Taichung, 402, Taiwan. TEL 886-4-24721859, FAX 886-4-23248137, http://www.tsam.org.tw/.

RATGEBER FUER BABYS ERSTE MONATE. *see* CHILDREN AND YOUTH—About

618.92 FRA ISSN 1266-3697
REALITES PEDIATRIQUES. Text in French. 1995. m. EUR 52 domestic to qualified personnel; EUR 42 domestic to students; EUR 65 foreign (effective 2008). **Document type:** *Journal, Trade.*
Published by: Performances Medicales, 91 Av. de la Republique, Paris, 75011, France. TEL 33-1-47006714, FAX 33-1-47006999.

618.92 GBR ISSN 0309-0140
RJ1
RECENT ADVANCES IN PAEDIATRICS. Text in English. 1954. a. price varies. back issues avail. **Document type:** *Monographic series, Academic/Scholarly.* **Description:** Provides a comprehensive update of key topics in pediatrics and child health.
—BLDSC (7303.882000), GNLM, IE, Ingenta. **CCC.**
Published by: Royal Society of Medicine Press Ltd., 1 Wimpole St, London, W1G 0AE, United Kingdom. TEL 44-20-72902921, FAX 44-20-72902929, publishing@rsm.ac.uk. Ed. Timothy J David.

618.92 USA ISSN 0737-7282
RJ21
REPORT OF THE ROSS ROUNDTABLE ON CRITICAL APPROACHES TO COMMON PEDIATRIC PROBLEMS IN COLLABORATION WITH THE AMBULATORY PEDIATRIC ASSOCIATION. Text in English. 1969. irreg.
Published by: Ross Laboratories, 625 Cleveland Ave, Columbus, OH 43215-1724. TEL 614-624-7485, 800-986-8510, FAX 614-624-7899, http://www.ross.com.

REPRODUKTIVNOE ZDOROV'YE ZHENSHCHINY; vseukrainskii nauchno-prakticheskii zhurnal. *see* MEDICAL SCIENCES—Obstetrics And Gynecology

RETT SYNDROME ASSOCIATION OF AUSTRALIA. NEWSLETTER. *see* MEDICAL SCIENCES—Psychiatry And Neurology

REVISTA ARGENTINA DE PSIQUIATRIA Y PSICOLOGIA DE LA INFANCIA Y DE LA ADOLESCENCIA. *see* MEDICAL SCIENCES—Psychiatry And Neurology

618.92 BRA ISSN 0104-1282
➤ **REVISTA BRASILEIRA DE CRESCIMENTO E DESENVOLVIMENTO HUMANO.** Text in Portuguese, Spanish; Summaries in English, Portuguese. 1991. s-a. adv. bk.rev. abstr.; bibl.; illus.; stat. 100 p./no.; reprints avail. **Document type:** *Journal, Academic/Scholarly.* **Description:** Publishes interdisciplinary works in health, education, psychology, sociology and anthropology. Observes the relationship between human growth and developmental processes, highlighting children and adolescents.
Related titles: Online - full text ed.: ISSN 2175-3598. free (effective 2011).
Indexed: C01, CA, S02, S03, SCOPUS, SociolAb, T02.
Published by: Universidade de Sao Paulo, Faculdade de Saude Publica, Av Dr Arnaldo 715, Sao Paulo, 01246-904, Brazil. Ed. Arnaldo Augusto Franco de Siqueira.

➤ **REVISTA BRASILEIRA DE ORTOPEDIA PEDIATRICA.** *see* MEDICAL SCIENCES—Orthopedics And Traumatology

618.92 CHL ISSN 0370-4106
REVISTA CHILENA DE PEDIATRIA. Text in Spanish; Summaries in English, Spanish. 1930-1977 (no.4); resumed. bi-m. CLP 64,780 domestic; USD 170 in the Americas; USD 210 elsewhere. adv. bk.rev. abstr.; charts; illus. index. **Document type:** *Journal, Academic/Scholarly.* **Description:** Contains statistical, educational, and original information for professionals studying in the fields of public health and pediatrics.
Related titles: Microform ed.: (from PQC); Online - full text ed.: ISSN 0717-6228. 1998. free (effective 2011) (from SciELO).
Indexed: A22, C01, CA, ChemAb, DentInd, EMBASE, ExcerpMed, IndMed, P30, R10, Reac, SCOPUS, T02.
—BLDSC (7848.950000), IE, Infotrieve, Ingenta.
Published by: Sociedad Chilena de Pediatria, Alcalde Eduardo Castillo Velasco 1838, Casilla 593-11, Santiago, Nunoa, Chile. TEL 56-2-2379757, FAX 56-2-2380046. Eds. Dr. Francisca Ugarte, Dr. Francisco Cano. Circ: 12,000.

618.92 CUB ISSN 0034-7531
REVISTA CUBANA DE PEDIATRIA. Text in Spanish; Summaries in English, Spanish. 1929. q. CUP 12 domestic; USD 34 in North America; USD 36 in South America; USD 38 elsewhere (effective 2005). bibl.; charts; illus. back issues avail. **Document type:** *Journal, Academic/Scholarly.* **Description:** Covers child development including infant-newborn diseases, child nutrition, respiratory tract diseases, infant mortality, airway obstruction, low birth weight, heart and congenital defects.
Formerly (until 1945): Sociedad Cubana de Pediatria. Boletin (1017-9801)

M

Related titles: Online - full text ed.: ISSN 1561-3119. 1995. free (effective 2011).
Indexed: A01, C01, CA, ChemAb, FR, IBR, IBZ, IndMed, P30, SCOPUS, T02.
—GNLM, INIST.
Published by: (Centro Nacional de Informacion de Ciencias Medicas (C N I C M), Cuba. Ministerio de Salud Publica), Editorial Ciencias Medicas, Linea Esq 1, 10o, Vedado, Havana, 10400, Cuba. TEL 53-7-8323863, ecimed@infomed.sld.cu. Ed. Fidel Araujo. Circ: 3,000. **Co-sponsor:** Sociedad Cubana de Pediatria.

REVISTA DE CIRUGIA INFANTIL. *see* MEDICAL SCIENCES—Surgery

618.92 MEX ISSN 1405-0749
REVISTA DE ENFERMEDADES INFECCIOSAS EN PEDIATRIA. Text in Spanish. 1986. q. free to members (effective 2006). **Document type:** *Journal, Academic/Scholarly.*
Related titles: Online - full text ed.
Indexed: A01, C01, CA, T02.
Published by: Grupo Galo, Alfonso Esparza Oteo, 153, Col. Guadalupe Inn, Mexico, D.F., 01020, Mexico. TEL 52-55-30004600, FAX 52-55-30004612, editor@grupogalo.com, http://www.grupogalo.com/. Ed. Napoleon Gonzalo Saldana.

REVISTA DE PSIQUIATRIA INFANTO-JUVENIL. *see* MEDICAL SCIENCES—Psychiatry And Neurology

618.92 ESP ISSN 0034-947X
CODEN: REPEAW
➤ **REVISTA ESPANOLA DE PEDIATRIA.** Text in Spanish. 1936. bi-m. bk.rev. abstr.; bibl.; illus. back issues avail.; reprints avail. **Document type:** *Journal, Academic/Scholarly.*
Related titles: Online - full text ed.: ISSN 1578-1542. 1996.
Indexed: A22, ChemAb, EMBASE, ExcerpMed, IME, P30, R10, Reac, SCOPUS.
—BLDSC (7854.200000), CASDDS, GNLM, IE, Infotrieve, Ingenta, INIST. **CCC.**
Published by: Ediciones Ergon S.A., C/ Arboleda 1, Majadahonda, Madrid, Madrid 28220, Spain. TEL 34-91-6362930, FAX 34-91-6362931, ergon@ergon.es, http://www.ergon.es. Circ: 4,000.

618.92 BRA ISSN 0103-0582
RJ1
REVISTA PAULISTA DE PEDIATRIA. Text in Portuguese. 1982. q. **Document type:** *Journal, Academic/Scholarly.*
Related titles: Online - full text ed.: free (effective 2011).
Indexed: SCOPUS.
—BLDSC (7869.570600), IE, Ingenta.
Published by: Sociedade de Pediatria de Sao Paulo, Al Santos 211, Cerq cesar, Sao Paulo, Brazil. TEL 55-11-32849809, http://www.spsp.org.br. Ed. Ruth Guinsburg. Circ: 5,500.

618.92 ESP ISSN 1139-7632
➤ **REVISTA PEDIATRIA DE ATENCION PRIMARIA/JOURNAL OF PRIMARY CARE PEDIATRICS.** Variant title: Pediatria Atencion Primaria. Text in Spanish; Summaries in English, Spanish. 1999. q. EUR 39 to individuals; EUR 83 to institutions (effective 2010). adv. Index. back issues avail. **Document type:** *Journal, Academic/Scholarly.* **Description:** Contains original research, clinical notes, reviews, criticism and comments to articles published in other journals, and professional news.
Related titles: Online - full text ed.: free (effective 2011).
Indexed: SCOPUS.
Published by: (Asociacion Espanola de Pediatria de Atencion Primaria/ Spanish Association of Primary Care Pediatric), Exlibris Ediciones, S.L., C. Infanta Mercedes, 92-bajo, Madrid, 28020, Spain. TEL 34-91-5717051, FAX 34-91-5716913, exlibris@exlibrisediciones.com, http://www.exlibrisediciones.com/inicio.htm. Pub. Daniel Sanchez Martinezq. R&P, Adv. contact Francisca Hernandez Plaza. B&W page EUR 850, color page EUR 1,150. Circ: 2,500 (paid); 4,000.

618.92 CHL ISSN 0718-0918
CODEN: PEDSAQ
REVISTA PEDIATRIA ELECTRONICA. Text in Spanish; Summaries in English. 1958. q. adv. bk.rev. abstr.; bibl.; illus.; stat. index. back issues avail.; reprints avail. **Document type:** *Journal, Academic/Scholarly.*
Formerly (until 2004): Pediatria (Print) (0375-9563)
Media: Online - full text.
Indexed: C01, DentInd, IndMed, P30.
—GNLM.
Published by: Universidad de Chile, Departamento de Pediatria, Zanatu, 1085, Santiago, Chile. TEL 56-2-4791144, FAX 56-2-4791047, http://www.med.uchile.cl/departamentos/norte/pediatria/. Ed. Jorge Torres Pereira. Circ: 1,000.

618 PER ISSN 1993-6826
REVISTA PERUANA DE PEDIATRIA. Text in Spanish. 2005. q. **Document type:** *Journal, Academic/Scholarly.*
Related titles: Online - full text ed.: ISSN 1993-6834. 2005. free (effective 2011).
Published by: Sociedad Peruana de Pediatria, Calle Los Geranios, 151, Urbanizacion Jardin, Lima, Peru. TEL 51-1-4226397, FAX 51-1-4411570, pediatria@rednextel.com.per, http://www.pediatriaperuana.org/. Ed. Angela Castillo Vilela.

618.92 ROM ISSN 1454-0398
CODEN: RPOPD
REVISTA ROMANA DE PEDIATRIE. Text in Romanian; Summaries in English, French, German, Russian. 1952. q. adv. bk.rev. abstr.; charts; illus. **Document type:** *Journal, Academic/Scholarly.*
Former titles (until 1996): Pediatria (1220-580X); (until 1990): Revista de Pediatrie, Obstetrica si Ginecologie. Seria Pediatrie (0303-8416); (until 1974): Pediatria (0031-3904)
Indexed: A01, CA, ChemAb, IndMed, P30, SCOPUS, T02.
—CASDDS, GNLM, INIST.
Published by: Asociatia Medicala Romana/Romanian Medical Association, Str Ionel Perlea 10, Sector 1, Bucharest, 70754, Romania. amr@medica.ro, http://www.medica.ro. **Subscr. to:** ILEXIM, Str. 13 Decembrie 3, PO Box 136-137, Bucharest 70116, Romania.

616.858 618.928 ESP ISSN 1132-1911
REVISTA SINDROME DE DOWN. Text in Spanish. 1984. q. back issues avail. **Document type:** *Magazine, Consumer.*
Formerly (until 1991): Sindrome de Down. Noticias (0214-3607)
Published by: Fundacion Sindrome de Down de Cantabria, Avenida General Davila 24 A, 1o C, Santander, 39005, Spain. TEL 34-942-278028, FAX 34-942-276564, downcan@infonegocio.com. Ed. Jesus Flores.

LA REVUE DES AUXILIAIRES DE PUERICULTURE. *see* CHILDREN AND YOUTH—About

618.92 TUN ISSN 0330-7611
REVUE MAGHREBINE DE PEDIATRIE/AL-MAGALLAAT AL-MAGARIBIYAT LI-TIB AL-'ATFAL. Text in French. 1991. bi-m.
Indexed: A36, CABA, FR, GH, N02, P33, RM&VM, T05.
—INIST.
Published by: Hopital d'Enfants, Tunis Jebbari, 1007, Tunisia. TEL 216-71-563 626, http://www.stim.org/stp/accueil.htm.

618.92 ITA ISSN 2035-0678
RIVISTA ITALIANA DI MEDICINA DELL'ADOLESCENZA. Text in Multiple languages. 2003. 3/yr. **Document type:** *Journal, Academic/Scholarly.*
Indexed: EMBASE.
Published by: Edizioni Scripta Manent, Via Bassini 41, Milan, 20133, Italy.

ROSS CONFERENCE ON PEDIATRIC RESEARCH. REPORT. *see* NUTRITION AND DIETETICS

618.92 RUS ISSN 1560-9561
ROSSIISKII PEDIATRICHESKII ZHURNAL/RUSSIAN JOURNAL OF PEDIATRICS. Text in Russian; Summaries in English. 1998. bi-m. USD 333 foreign (effective 2005). adv. bk.rev. abstr.; bibl.; illus. back issues avail. **Document type:** *Journal, Academic/Scholarly.* **Description:** Covers issues of experimental and clinical pediatrics; diagnosis and prevention of childhood diseases; and management of pediatric services.
Related titles: Fax ed.
Indexed: RefZh.
Published by: Izdatel'stvo Meditsina/Meditsina Publishers, ul B Pirogovskaya, d 2, str 5, Moscow, 119435, Russian Federation. TEL 7-095-2483324, meditsina@mtu-net.ru, http://www.medlit.ru. Ed. Aleksandr A Baranov. Pub. A M Stochik. R&P Yu Isakov. Adv. contact O A Fadeeva TEL 7-095-923-51-40. Circ: 620. **Dist. by:** East View Information Services, 10601 Wayzata Blvd, Minneapolis, MN 55305. TEL 952-252-1201, 800-477-1005, FAX 952-252-1202, info@eastview.com, http://www.eastview.com.

ROSSIISKII VESTNIK PERINATOLOGII I PEDIATRII. *see* MEDICAL SCIENCES—Obstetrics And Gynecology

RUND UMS BABY. *see* CHILDREN AND YOUTH—About

S R C D DEVELOPMENTS NEWSLETTER. *see* CHILDREN AND YOUTH—About

618.92 USA
SCHOOL HEALTH: POLICY AND PRACTICE. Text in English. 1972. irreg., latest 2004, 6th ed. USD 44.95 to non-members 6th ed.; USD 39.95 to members 6th ed. (effective 2008). **Document type:** *Monographic series, Trade.*
Formerly: School Health: A Guide for Health Professionals
Published by: American Academy of Pediatrics, 141 NW Pt Blvd, Elk Grove Village, IL 60007. TEL 847-434-4000, FAX 847-434-8000, journals@aap.org. Pub. Robert Perelman.

610.7362 618.92 USA ISSN 1072-3722
SCHOOL HEALTH PROFESSIONAL. Text in English. 1994. s-m. USD 147 (effective 2006). 8 p./no.; **Document type:** *Newsletter, Trade.* **Description:** Covers pediatric medicine, school health, physical and nutritional education, school nursing, student rights and records, violence prevention, sexuality counseling and education, drug abuse prevention and testing, health insurance and Medicaid.
—**CCC.**
Published by: PaperClip Communications, 125 Paterson Ave, Little Falls, NJ 07424. TEL 973-256-1333, FAX 973-256-8088, info@paper-clip.com.

SEMINARS IN FETAL & NEONATAL MEDICINE. *see* MEDICAL SCIENCES—Obstetrics And Gynecology

SEMINARS IN PEDIATRIC NEUROLOGY. *see* MEDICAL SCIENCES—Psychiatry And Neurology

SEMINARS IN PEDIATRIC SURGERY. *see* MEDICAL SCIENCES—Surgery

618.92 USA ISSN 0146-0005
CODEN: SEMPDU
➤ **SEMINARS IN PERINATOLOGY.** Text in English. 1977. bi-m. USD 598 in United States to institutions; USD 785 elsewhere to institutions (effective 2012). adv. bibl.; charts; illus. index. back issues avail.; reprints avail. **Document type:** *Journal, Academic/Scholarly.* **Description:** Provides authoritative and comprehensive reviews of a single topic of interest to professionals who care for the mother, the fetus, and the newborn.
Related titles: Online - full text ed.: ISSN 1558-075X (from ScienceDirect).
Indexed: A22, A26, A36, ASCA, BDM&CN, BIOSIS Prev, C06, C07, C08, CABA, CINAHL, CurCont, D01, E12, EMBASE, ExcerpMed, GH, H12, I05, ISR, IndMed, Inpharma, MEDLINE, MycolAb, N02, N03, P30, P33, R10, R12, RM&VM, Reac, SCI, SCOPUS, T02, T05, W07.
—BLDSC (8239.456800), GNLM, IE, Infotrieve, Ingenta, INIST. **CCC.**
Published by: W.B. Saunders Co. (Subsidiary of: Elsevier Health Sciences), Elsevier, Health Sciences Division, Order Fulfillment, 3251 Riverport Ln, Maryland Heights, MO 63043. TEL 314-872-8370, 800-325-4177, FAX 314-432-1380, JournalCustomerService-usa@elsevier.com, http://www.us.elsevierhealth.com. Eds. Ian Gross, Dr. Mary D'Alton. Pub. Alexandra Gavenda.

➤ **SHAKEN BABY ALLIANCE**; dedicated to prevention, support and justice. *see* CHILDREN AND YOUTH—About

618.92 CHN ISSN 1003-515X
SHIYONG ERKE LINCHUANG ZAZHI/JOURNAL OF APPLIED CLINICAL PEDIATRICS. Text in Chinese. 1986. m. USD 91.20 (effective 2009). **Document type:** *Journal, Academic/Scholarly.*
Related titles: Online - full text ed.
Indexed: A22.
—BLDSC (4942.366000), East View, IE, Ingenta.
Published by: Xinxiang Yixueyuan/Xinxiang Medical College, Xinyan Road, Xinxiang, 453003, China. **Dist. by:** China International Book Trading Corp, 35 Chegongzhuang Xilu, Haidian District, PO Box 399, Beijing 100044, China. TEL 86-10-68412045, FAX 86-10-68412023, cibtc@mail.cibtc.com.cn, http://www.cibtc.com.cn.

SHONI GEKA/JAPANESE JOURNAL OF PEDIATRIC SURGERY. *see* MEDICAL SCIENCES—Surgery

SHONI HOKEN KENKYU/JOURNAL OF CHILD HEALTH. *see* PHYSICAL FITNESS AND HYGIENE

SHONI KANGO/JAPANESE JOURNAL OF CHILD NURSING, MONTHLY. *see* MEDICAL SCIENCES—Nurses And Nursing

618.92 JPN ISSN 0385-6305
SHONI NAIKA/JAPANESE JOURNAL OF PEDIATRIC MEDICINE. Text in Japanese. 1969. m. JPY 40,000 (effective 2005). **Document type:** *Academic/Scholarly.*
Supersedes in part (in 1976): Shoni Geka, Naika/Japanese Journal of Pediatric Surgery and Medicine (0387-2386)
Published by: Tokyo Igakusha Ltd., 35-4 Hongo 3-chome, Bunkyo-ku, Tokyo, 113-0033, Japan. TEL 81-3-38114119, FAX 81-3-38116135, shoge@tokyo-igakusha.co.jp. Ed. Naoyoshi Minami. Circ: 6,000.

SHONI NO NOSHINKEI/NERVOUS SYSTEM IN CHILDREN. *see* MEDICAL SCIENCES—Psychiatry And Neurology

SHONI SHIKAGAKU ZASSHI/PEDIATRIC DENTAL JOURNAL. *see* MEDICAL SCIENCES—Dentistry

618.92 JPN ISSN 0037-4121
SHONIKA/PEDIATRICS OF JAPAN. Text in Japanese. 1960. m. JPY 39,690 (effective 2007). bk.rev. Index. **Document type:** *Journal, Academic/Scholarly.*
Indexed: P30.
Published by: Kanehara Shuppan/Kanehara & Co. Ltd., 2-31-14 Yushima, Bunkyo-ku, Tokyo, 113-8687, Japan. TEL 81-3-38117184, FAX 81-3-38130288, http://www.kanehara-shuppan.co.jp/. Circ: 6,200.

618.92 JPN ISSN 0021-518X
SHONIKA RINSHO/JAPANESE JOURNAL OF PEDIATRICS. Text in Japanese. 1948. m. JPY 39,585 (effective 2007). **Document type:** *Journal, Academic/Scholarly.*
Indexed: ChemAb, INIS AtomInd.
—BLDSC (4656.950000), IE, Ingenta, INIST.
Published by: Nihon Shoni Iji Shuppansha, 5-24-18, Nishishinjuku, Shinjuku-ku, Tokyo, 160-8306, Japan. TEL 81-3-53885195, FAX 81-3-53885193, shoni-ijied@wakodo.co.jp.

618.92 JPN ISSN 0386-9806
CODEN: SHSHAK
SHONIKA SHINRYO. Text in Japanese. 1935. m. **Document type:** *Journal, Academic/Scholarly.*
Formerly (until 1953): Jika Shinryo/Journal for Pediatric Praxis (0386-9970)
Indexed: INIS AtomInd.
—BLDSC (5030.250000).
Published by: Shindan to Chiryosha, Sanno Grand Bldg. 4F, 2-14-2 Nagata-cho, Chiyoda-ku, Tokyo, 100-0014, Japan. TEL 81-3-35802770, FAX 81-3-35802776, eigyobu@shindan.co.jp, http://www.shindan.co.jp/.

616 HRV ISSN 1334-5605
➤ **SIGNA VITAE.** Text in English. 2006. s-a. HRK 300; HRK 150 newsstand/cover; free to qualified personnel (effective 2007). adv. Index. back issues avail. **Document type:** *Journal, Academic/Scholarly.* **Description:** Publishes articles involving neonatal, pediatric, and adult intensive care, along with the emergency medicine.
Related titles: Online - full text ed.: ISSN 1845-206X. free (effective 2011).
Indexed: A01, A36, A37, CA, CABA, EMBASE, ExcerpMed, GH, N02, N03, PN&I, SCI, T02, T05, VS, W07.
—**CCC.**
Published by: Pharmamed Mado Ltd., Zatisje 8g, Zagreb, 10000, Croatia. TEL 385-1-3776116, FAX 385-1-3776066, http://pharmamed.com. Ed. Julije Mestrovic. Pub. Marko Goricki. Adv. contact Neda Stimac.

618.92 BOL ISSN 1024-0675
SOCIEDAD BOLIVIANA DE PEDIATRIA. REVISTA. Text in Spanish. 1961. q. **Document type:** *Journal, Academic/Scholarly.*
Related titles: Online - full text ed.: ISSN 1727-7361. 2000 (from SciELO).
Published by: Sociedad Boliviana de Pediatria, Calle Pastor Sainz s-n, Edif. Colegio Medico Departamental, Sucre, Bolivia. TEL 591-4-6439977, FAX 591-4-6441670. Ed. Manuel Pantoja Luduena.

SOCIEDAD CHILENA DE ODONTOPEDIATRIA. REVISTA. *see* MEDICAL SCIENCES—Dentistry

618.92 ESP ISSN 0489-3824
SOCIEDAD VALENCIANA DE PEDIATRIA. BOLETIN. Text in Spanish. 1959. a. **Document type:** *Journal, Academic/Scholarly.*
Indexed: P30.
Published by: Sociedad Valenciana de Pediatria, Ave de la Plata, 20, Valencia, 46013, Spain. TEL 34-96-3745568, http://www.socvaped.org.

618.92 ESP ISSN 0037-8658
SOCIEDAD VASCO-NAVARRA DE PEDIATRIA. BOLETIN. Text in Spanish. 1966. q. adv. charts; illus.; stat. **Document type:** *Bulletin, Trade.*
—**CCC.**
Published by: (Sociedad Vasco Navarra de Pediatria), Ediciones Ergon S.A., C/ Arboleda 1, Majadahonda, Madrid, Madrid 28220, Spain. TEL 34-91-6362930, FAX 34-91-6362931, ergon@ergon.es, http://www.ergon.es. Circ: 1,000.

618.92 ZAF ISSN 1994-3032
➤ **SOUTH AFRICAN JOURNAL OF CHILD HEALTH.** Variant title: S A J C H. Text in English. 2007. q. **Document type:** *Journal, Academic/Scholarly.*
Related titles: Online - full text ed.: ISSN 1999-7671. free (effective 2011).
Indexed: A01, A26, B21, EMBASE, ESPM, ExcerpMed, H&SSA, H12, I05, P30, R10, Reac, SCOPUS.
Published by: Health and Medical Publishing Group, 21 Dreyer St, Claremont, 7700, South Africa. TEL 27-21-6578200, FAX 27-21-6834509, publishing@hmpg.co.za, http://www.hmpg.co.za. Ed. Nonhlanhla P Khumalo.

618.92 UKR
SOVREMENNAYA PEDIATRIYA. Text in Russian. 2003. q. USD 80 foreign (effective 2006). **Document type:** *Journal, Academic/Scholarly.*

Published by: (Ministerstvo Okhorony Zdorov'ya Ukrainy, Ukrains'kyi Instytut Hromads'koho Zdorov'ya), Vydavnytstvo Ekspert, a/ya 32, Kyiv 210, 04210, Ukraine. **Dist. by:** East View Information Services, 10601 Wayzata Blvd, Minneapolis, MN 55305. TEL 952-252-1201, 800-477-1005, FAX 952-252-1202, info@eastview.com, http://www.eastview.com.

SPINAL CONNECTION. *see* MEDICAL SCIENCES—Orthopedics And Traumatology

618.92 ITA ISSN 1721-5471
THE SUFFERING CHILD. Text in English. 2002. 3/yr. **Document type:** *Journal, Academic/Scholarly.* **Description:** Its aims are to explore all aspects of nociception, to combat the prejudice that still conditions doctors when faced with a situation of pain (especially in newborn and pre-term babies) and to formulate guidelines for acute and chronic pain.
Media: Online - full text.
Published by: The Suffering Child Association, Riv San Benedetto 118, Padua, 35134, Italy. TEL 39-049-8726540, FAX 39-049-8726077, info@thesufferingchild.net, http://www.thesufferingchild.net. Ed. Fabrizia Zingales.

618.92 TZA ISSN 0856-311X
RJ27.5.T43
TANZANIA JOURNAL OF PAEDIATRICS. Text in English. 1989. 2/yr. adv. **Document type:** *Newsletter, Academic/Scholarly.* **Description:** Includes information on the current situation of health in children.
Indexed: PLESA.
Published by: Tanzania Publishing House, PO Box 65370, Dar Es Salaam, Tanzania. Ed., Adv. contact Dr. Karim P Manji. Circ: 200.

618.92 DEU
TELE-FORUM KINDERARZT. Text in German. q. EUR 24.50 to non-members; EUR 9.95 to members (effective 2005). **Document type:** *Journal, Academic/Scholarly.*
Published by: Hansisches Verlagskontor, Mengstr 16, Luebeck, 23552, Germany. TEL 49-451-7031101, FAX 49-451-7031253, http://www.beleke.de/verlagsgruppe/ind_hvk.html.

618.92 DEU
THEMEN DER KINDERHEILKUNDE. Text in German. 1986. irreg., latest vol.13, 1999. price varies. **Document type:** *Monographic series, Academic/Scholarly.*
Published by: Max Schmidt-Roemhild KG, Mengstr 16, Luebeck, 23552, Germany. TEL 49-451-7031101, FAX 49-451-7031253, info@schmidt-roemhild.de, http://www.beleke.de/unternehmen/verlage/schmidtroemhild/index.html.

618.92 NLD ISSN 0376-7442
CODEN: TIKID4
TIJDSCHRIFT VOOR KINDERGENEESKUNDE. Text in Dutch, English. 1920. bi-m. EUR 124, USD 186 combined subscription to institutions (print & online eds.) (effective 2009). adv. bk.rev. charts; illus.; stat. index. **Document type:** *Journal, Academic/Scholarly.*
Former titles (until 1976): Maandschrift voor Kindergeneeskunde (0024-869X); (until 1931): Nederlandsch Maandschrift voor Geneeskunde (0369-3724)
Related titles: Online - full text ed.: ISSN 1875-6840.
Indexed: A22, ChemAb, DentInd, E01, EMBASE, ExcerpMed, IBR, IBZ, IndMed, P30, R10, Reac, SCOPUS.
—BLDSC (8842.300000), GNLM, IE, Infotrieve, Ingenta, INIST.
Published by: Bohn Stafleu van Loghum B.V. (Subsidiary of: Springer Science+Business Media), Postbus 246, Houten, 3990 GA, Netherlands. TEL 31-30-6383830, FAX 31-30-6383999, boekhandels@bsl.nl, http://www.bsl.nl. Circ: 2,236.

TIJDSCHRIFT VOOR ORTHOPEDAGOGIEK, KINDERPSYCHIATRIE EN KLINISCHE KINDERPSYCHOLOGIE. *see* MEDICAL SCIENCES—Psychiatry And Neurology

TODAY'S PARENT, BABY & TODDLER. *see* CHILDREN AND YOUTH—About

618.92 USA ISSN 0892-0435
TOPICS IN PEDIATRICS. Text in English. 1982. 3/yr. free. **Description:** For physicians, nurses, and psychosocial professionals who care for children.
Published by: Minneapolis Children's Medical Center, 2525 Chicago Ave S, Minneapolis, MN 55404. TEL 612-863-6222, FAX 612-863-6674. Ed. Dr. John MacDonald. Circ: 10,000 (controlled).

618.92 TUR ISSN 1306-0015
➤ **TURK PEDIATRI ARSIVI/TURKISH ARCHIVES OF PEDIATRICS.** Text in Turkish. 2002. q. free to qualified personnel (effective 2007). **Document type:** *Journal, Academic/Scholarly.* **Description:** Covers children's health and diseases.
Related titles: Online - full text ed.: free (effective 2011).
Indexed: A01, A26, C06, C07, CA, H12, I05, SCI, SCOPUS, T02, W07.
Published by: Galenos Yayincilik, Barbaros Bulvari, Salim Aktas Is Hani, No. 85 D:3, Besiktas, Istanbul, 80690, Turkey. TEL 90-212-2369054, FAX 90-212-2369052, info@galenos.com.tr, http://www.galenos.com.tr. Ed. Nil Arisoy.

618.92 TUR ISSN 0041-4301
RJ1
➤ **TURKISH JOURNAL OF PEDIATRICS.** Text in English. 1958. q. adv. bk.rev. abstr.; bibl.; charts; illus. index. **Document type:** *Journal, Academic/Scholarly.* **Description:** Publishes original articles, case reports, reviews of the literature, case of the month, short communications, clinicopathological exercises and letter to the editor in the field of pediatrics.
Related titles: Online - full text ed.: free (effective 2011).
Indexed: A20, A22, A34, A36, ASCA, CA, CABA, D01, DentInd, E12, EMBASE, ExcerpMed, GH, H17, IndMed, IndVet, Inpharma, LT, MEDLINE, N02, N03, P10, P20, P22, P30, P33, P39, P48, P53, P54, PQC, R08, R10, R12, RM&VM, RRTA, Reac, S12, SCI, SCOPUS, T02, T05, VS, W07.
—BLDSC (9072.480000), GNLM, IE, Infotrieve, Ingenta.
Published by: International Children's Center (I C C)/Uluslararasi Cocuk Sagligi Merkezi, Bilkent University, Main Campus, Library Bldg, Bilkent, Ankara, 06800, Turkey. TEL 90-312-2902366, FAX 90-312-2664678, icc@icc.org.tr, http://www.icc.org.tr. Ed. Dr. Turgay Coskun. Circ: 1,500. **Co-sponsors:** Hacettepe Universitesi, Institute of Child Health; Turkish National Pediatric Society.

618.92 ITA ISSN 1971-7296
➤ **TUTOR.** Text in Italian. 2001. 3/yr. **Document type:** *Journal, Academic/Scholarly.*
Former titles (until 1993): Pedagogia Medica (1120-8627); (until 1987): La Formazione del Medico
Related titles: Online - full text ed.: ISSN 1971-8551.
Published by: (Societa Italiana di Pedagogia Medica), Centro Scientifico Editore, Via Borgone 57, Turin, 10139, Italy. TEL 39-011-3853656, FAX 39-011-3853244, cse@cse.it, http://www.cse.it. Ed. Cesare Scandellari.

➤ **TWIN RESEARCH AND HUMAN GENETICS.** *see* BIOLOGY—Genetics

614.47 MEX
VACUNACION HOY. Text in Spanish. 1993. bi-m. MXN 380 (effective 2007). back issues avail. **Document type:** *Magazine, Consumer.*
Formerly: Revista Mexicana de Puericultura y Pediatria (1405-0730)
Indexed: A01, C01, CA, T02.
Published by: Ediciones Franco (Subsidiary of: Grupo Galo), Alfonso Esparza Oteo, No. 153, Col. Guadalupe Inn, Mexico, D.F., 01020, Mexico. TEL 52-55-30004600, FAX 52-55-30004612, editorial@grupogalo.com, http://www.grupogalo.com/index.php?option=com_content&task=view&id=30&Itemid=48. Ed. Demostenes Gomez Barreto. Circ: 500.

618.92 362.76 USA ISSN 1532-4443
HV6626.52
VISUAL DIAGNOSIS OF CHILD ABUSE ON CD-ROM. Text in English. 2001. irreg., latest 3rd ed. USD 175 to non-members 3rd ed.; USD 150 to members 3rd ed. (effective 2008). **Document type:** *Monographic series, Trade.* **Description:** Provides a complete set of reference materials and powerful teaching, learning, and diagnostic tools. Includes informative articles, more than 375 photographic images with audio commentary, AAP policy statements, parent education materials, and much more, fully searchable and cross-referenced for fast access.
Media: CD-ROM.
Published by: American Academy of Pediatrics, 141 NW Pt Blvd, Elk Grove Village, IL 60007. TEL 847-434-4000, FAX 847-434-8000, journals@aap.org, http://www.aap.org. Pub. Robert Perelman.

WILLKOMMEN BABY. *see* CHILDREN AND YOUTH—About

330 618.92 DEU ISSN 1611-2644
WIRTSCHAFTSMAGAZIN FUER DEN KINDERARZT. Text in German. 1996. bi-m. EUR 22.50 (effective 2011). adv. **Document type:** *Magazine, Trade.*
Formerly (until 2000): Wirtschaftsbrief fuer den Kinderarzt (1439-2968)
Published by: W P V- Wirtschafts- und Praxisverlag GmbH, Otto-Hahn-Str 7, Koeln, 50997, Germany. TEL 49-2236-376711, FAX 49-2236-37692530, info@wpv.de. Adv. contact Isabelle Becker TEL 49-2236-376711. Circ: 5,832 (controlled).

618.92 DEU ISSN 1866-2919
WIRTSCHAFTSTIP FUER PAEDIATER. Text in German. 1996. m. EUR 21.40 (effective 2008). adv. **Document type:** *Journal, Trade.*
Published by: Aerzte Zeitung Verlagsgesellschaft mbH (Subsidiary of: Springer Science+Business Media), Am Forsthaus Gravenbruch 5, Neu-Isenburg, 63263, Germany. TEL 49-6102-506157, FAX 49-6102-506123, info@aerztezeitung.de, http://www.aerztezeitung.de. adv.: B&W page EUR 2,210, color page EUR 3,440. Circ: 6,058 (controlled).

649.1 DEU
WO BEKOMME ICH MEIN BABY?. Text in German. 1985. a. free newsstand/cover (effective 2009). adv. **Document type:** *Magazine, Consumer.*
Published by: Buettner Medien GmbH, Sigmund-Freud-Str 77a, Frankfurt Am Main, 60435, Germany. TEL 49-69-7561900, FAX 49-69-75619041, sbuettner@buemed.de, http://www.buemed.de. Pub., Adv. contact Sven Buettner. B&W page EUR 23,860, color page EUR 38,200; trim 180 x 264. Circ: 298,768 (paid and controlled).

▼ **WORLD JOURNAL FOR PEDIATRIC AND CONGENITAL HEART SURGERY.** *see* MEDICAL SCIENCES—Surgery

618.9 CHN ISSN 1708-8569
➤ **WORLD JOURNAL OF PEDIATRICS.** Text in English. 2005. q. EUR 382, USD 572 combined subscription to institutions (print & online eds.) (effective 2012). adv. **Document type:** *Journal, Academic/Scholarly.* **Description:** Covers clinical practice, basic sciences, experimental work, and research in pediatrics, including subject areas in medical, surgical, radiological, pathological, biochemical, physiological and historical aspect, as well as those relevant to preventive healthcare, pharmacology, and stomatology.
Related titles: Online - full text ed.: ISSN 1867-0687 (from IngentaConnect).
Indexed: A22, E01, EMBASE, ExcerpMed, MEDLINE, P30, R10, Reac, RefZh, SCI, SCOPUS, W07.
—BLDSC (8256.496770), IE. **CCC.**
Published by: Zhejiang University, School of Medicine Children's Hospital, 57 Zhugan Xiang, Hangzhou, 310003, China. TEL 86-571-87084307, FAX 86-571-87084307. Ed. Zheng-Yan Zhao. **Co-publisher:** Springer.

618.92 USA ISSN 0084-3954
RJ16
YEAR BOOK OF PEDIATRICS. Text in English. 1901. a. USD 239 in United States to institutions; USD 259 elsewhere to institutions (effective 2012). adv. illus. reprints avail. **Document type:** *Yearbook, Academic/Scholarly.* **Description:** Presents abstracts of pertinent literature with commentary by leading experts in the field.
Formerly (until 1933): Pediatrics
Related titles: CD-ROM ed.; Online - full text ed.
—BLDSC (9414.800000), GNLM. **CCC.**
Published by: Mosby, Inc. (Subsidiary of: Elsevier Health Sciences), 1600 John F. Kennedy Blvd, Ste 1800, Philadelphia, PA 19103. TEL 215-239-3900, 800-523-1649, FAX 215-239-3990, elspcs@elsevier.com, http://www.us.elsevierhealth.com. Ed. Dr. James A Stockman III.

YEARBOOK OF PEDIATRIC ENDOCRINOLOGY. *see* MEDICAL SCIENCES—Endocrinology

618.92 613.2 RUS
ZA OBE SHCHECHKI; zhurnal o pitanii i zdorovie malyshei. Text in Russian. bi-m. **Document type:** *Magazine, Consumer.*
Related titles: Online - full text ed.
Published by: Izdatel'skii Dom Stranitsa, ul Mishina, dom 35, 4-i etazh, ofis 401, Moscow, 127083, Russian Federation. TEL 7-095-2122191, dmitri@paradigma.ru.

618.92 CHN ISSN 1008-8830
ZHONGGUO DANGDAI ERKE ZAZHI/CHINESE JOURNAL OF CONTEMPORARY PEDIATRICS. Text in Chinese. bi-m. USD 74.40 (effective 2009). back issues avail. **Document type:** *Journal, Academic/Scholarly.*
Related titles: Online - full text ed.
Indexed: EMBASE, ExcerpMed, MEDLINE, P30, R10, Reac, SCOPUS.
—BLDSC (9512.727068), East View.
Published by: Zhongnan Daxue/Central South University, 87, Xiangya Lu, Changsha, 410008, China. TEL 86-731-4327402, FAX 86-731-4327922, http://www.csu.edu.cn/chinese/. **Dist. by:** China International Book Trading Corp, 35 Chegongzhuang Xilu, Haidian District, PO Box 399, Beijing 100044, China. TEL 86-10-68412045, FAX 86-10-68412023, cibtc@mail.cibtc.com.cn, http://www.cibtc.com.cn.

618.92 CHN ISSN 1008-6579
ZHONGGUO ERTONG BAOJIAN ZAZHI/CHINESE JOURNAL OF CHILD HEALTH CARE. Text in Chinese. 1993. bi-m. USD 31.20 (effective 2009). **Document type:** *Journal, Academic/Scholarly.*
Formerly: Zhonghua Ertong Baojian Zazhi
Related titles: Online - full text ed.
—East View.
Address: 157, Xi-Wu Lu Zhong Duan, Xi'an, 710004, China. TEL 86-29-87679391, FAX 86-29-87276092.

ZHONGGUO FUYOU WEISHENG ZAZHI/CHINESE JOURNAL OF WOMEN AND CHILDREN HEALTH. *see* WOMEN'S HEALTH

618.92 CHN ISSN 1005-2224
➤ **ZHONGGUO SHIYONG ERKE ZAZHI/CHINESE JOURNAL OF PRACTICAL PEDIATRICS.** Text in Chinese; Abstracts in English. 1986. m. USD 49.20 (effective 2009). adv. reprints avail. **Document type:** *Journal, Academic/Scholarly.* **Description:** Features new developments and methods of practical diagnosis, treatment, and prevention of pediatric diseases.
Formerly: Shiyong Erke Zashi - Journal of Practical Pediatrics (1001-0866)
Related titles: Online - full text ed.
Indexed: A29, A36, B&BAb, B19, B21, CABA, CTA, D01, E12, GH, ImmunAb, N02, N03, NSA, NucAcAb, P33, R08, R12, RM&VM, T05, ViroIAbstr.
—BLDSC (9512.798780).
Published by: Zhongguo Shiyong Yixue Zazhishe, 9, Nanjing Nan Jie, 5th Fl., Heping-qu, Shenyang, Liaoning 110001, China. Ed. Xin-Dong Xue. Circ: 35,000. **Dist. by:** China International Book Trading Corp, 35 Chegongzhuang Xilu, Haidian District, PO Box 399, Beijing 100044, China. TEL 86-10-68412045, FAX 86-10-68412023, cibtc@mail.cibtc.com.cn, http://www.cibtc.com.cn.

618.92 616.025 CHN
ZHONGGUO XIAOER JIJIU YIXUE/CHINESE PEDIATRIC EMERGENCY MEDICINE. Text in Chinese; Abstracts in English. 1994. bi-m. CNY 8 newsstand/cover (effective 2007). 96 p./no.; **Document type:** *Journal, Academic/Scholarly.*
Formerly: Xiaoer Jijiu Yixue/Pediatric Emergency Medicine (1007-9459)
Related titles: Online - full text ed.
—East View.
Published by: Zhongguo Yike Daxue, Erke Yanjiusuo/China Medical University, Pediatrics Research Institute, 36 Sanhao Jie, Shenyan, 110004, China. TEL 86-24-83956553, FAX 86-24-23926295. Ed. Qun Zhao. Circ: 7,000 (paid); 1,000 (controlled). **Dist. by:** China International Book Trading Corp, 35 Chegongzhuang Xilu, Haidian District, PO Box 399, Beijing 100044, China. TEL 86-10-68412045, FAX 86-10-68412023, cibtc@mail.cibtc.com.cn, http://www.cibtc.com.cn.

618.92 CHN ISSN 1673-6710
ZHONGGUO XINSHENG ERKE ZAZHI/CHINESE JOURNAL OF NEONATOLOGY. Text in Chinese. 1986. bi-m. CNY 48; CNY 8 per issue (effective 2010). **Document type:** *Journal, Academic/Scholarly.*
Formerly (until 2006): Xinsheng Erke Zazhi/Journal of Neonatology (1002-1213)
Related titles: Online - full text ed.
—East View.
Published by: Beijing Daxue Di-Yi Yiyuan/Peking University First Hospital, 1, Xianmen Dajie, Xichang-qu, Beijing, 100034, China. TEL 86-10-66181701, FAX 86-10-66181701. **Dist. by:** China International Book Trading Corp, 35 Chegongzhuang Xilu, Haidian District, PO Box 399, Beijing 100044, China. TEL 86-10-68412045, FAX 86-10-68412023, cibtc@mail.cibtc.com.cn, http://www.cibtc.com.cn.

618.2 CHN ISSN 0578-1310
ZHONGHUA ERKE ZAZHI/CHINESE JOURNAL OF PEDIATRICS. Text in Chinese. 1950. m. USD 80.40 (effective 2009). **Document type:** *Journal, Academic/Scholarly.*
Related titles: CD-ROM ed.; Online - full text ed.
Indexed: EMBASE, ExcerpMed, ExtraMED, MEDLINE, P30, R10, Reac, SCOPUS.
—BLDSC (3180.470000), East View.
Published by: Zhonghua Yixuehui/Chinese Medical Association, 42 Dong Si Xi Dajie, Beijing, 100710, China. TEL 86-10-85158220. **Dist. by:** China International Book Trading Corp, 35 Chegongzhuang Xilu, Haidian District, PO Box 399, Beijing 100044, China. TEL 86-10-68412045, FAX 86-10-68412023, cibtc@mail.cibtc.com.cn, http://www.cibtc.com.cn.

617.98 CHN ISSN 0253-3006
ZHONGHUA XIAOER WAIKE ZAZHI/CHINESE JOURNAL OF PEDIATRIC SURGERY. Text in Chinese. 1980. bi-m. USD 56.40 (effective 2009). **Document type:** *Journal, Academic/Scholarly.*
Related titles: Online - full text ed.
—East View.
Published by: Zhonghua Yixuehui/Chinese Medical Association, 177, Shenglijie, Wuhan, 430014, China. TEL 86-27-82846835, FAX 86-27-82837652, cmj@cma.org.cn, http://www.cmj.org. **Dist. by:** China International Book Trading Corp, 35 Chegongzhuang Xilu, Haidian District, PO Box 399, Beijing 100044, China. TEL 86-10-68412045, FAX 86-10-68412023, cibtc@mail.cibtc.com.cn, http://www.cibtc.com.cn.

9 MESYATSEV/9 MONTHS. *see* MEDICAL SCIENCES—Obstetrics And Gynecology

MEDICAL SCIENCES—Physical Medicine And Rehabilitation

615.8515 CAN
A A R O T - A C O T NEWS. Text in English. 1976. q. **Document type:** *Trade.*
Former titles (until 2006): A A R O T News (1910-720X); (until 2006): Transitions (1711-2850); (until 2003): Perspectives (1193-1248); (until 1992): A A R O T Newsletter (0831-6031); (until 1978): Alberta Association of Registered Occupational Therapists Newsletter (0831-6023); (until 1977): Alberta Society of Occupational Therapists Newsletter (0831-6015)
Published by: Alberta College of Occupational Therapists, Ste 302, 8657 - 51 Ave, Edmonton, AB T6E 6A8, Canada. TEL 780-436-8381, 800-561-5429, FAX 780-434-0658, info@acot.ca, http://www.acot.ca/pages/home.

A A T A NEWSLETTER. (American Art Therapy Association) *see* ART

615.82 USA
A D T A NEWSLETTER (ONLINE EDITION). Text in English. 1967. q. free (effective 2007). bk.rev. bibl. **Document type:** *Newsletter.*
Description: Contains communications from ADTA President and membership, regional news, committee news, theory and philosophy, listing of courses, workshops, and job opportunities available.
Formerly: A D T A Newsletter (Print Edition)
Media: Online - full text.
Published by: American Dance Therapy Association, 2000 Century Plaza, Ste 108, 10632 Little Patuxent Pkwy, Columbia, MD 21044. TEL 410-997-4040, FAX 410-997-4048, info@adta.org, http://www.adta.org. Ed. Kyle Buckley.

615.82 ITA ISSN 1827-5842
A E R. Key Title: Abilitazione e Riabilitazione. Text in Italian. 1992. s-a. **Document type:** *Magazine, Trade.*
Published by: Centro di Riabilitazione Extraospedaliera Paolo VI, Via G Lugano 40, Casalnoceto, AL 15052, Italy. TEL 39-0131-808111, FAX 39-0131-808102.

615.82 USA
A T R A NEWSLETTER. Text in English. 198?. bi-m. free to members (effective 2010). adv. back issues avail. **Document type:** *Newsletter, Trade.*
Related titles: Online - full text ed.
Published by: American Therapeutic Recreation Association, 629 N Main St, Hattiesburg, MS 39401. TEL 601-450-2872, FAX 601-582-3354, national@atra-online.com. Ed. Jean Folkerth. Circ: 1,900.

ACTA OF BIOENGINEERING AND BIOMECHANICS. *see* BIOLOGY—Bioengineering

615.8515 CAN ISSN 1481-5923
ACTUALITES ERGOTHERAPIQUES. Text in French. 1995. bi-m. CAD 44 domestic to institutions; CAD 63 in United States to customers; CAD 74 to customers (effective 2005). adv. **Document type:** *Journal, Academic/Scholarly.*
Formerly (until 1999): Association Canadienne des Ergotherapeutes. National (1206-0720)
Related titles: Online - full text ed.; ◆ English ed.: Occupational Therapy Now. ISSN 1481-5532.
Published by: Canadian Association of Occupational Therapists, CTTC Bldg, Ste 3400, 1125 Colonel By Dr, Ottawa, ON K1S 5R1, Canada. TEL 613-523-2268, FAX 613-523-2552, subsrciptions@caot.ca. Ed. Mary Clark Green. R&P, Adv. contact Lisa Sheehan TEL 613-523-2268, ext. 232.

615.82 613.62 USA ISSN 1099-9507
ADVANCE FOR OCCUPATIONAL THERAPY PRACTITIONERS. Text in English. 1985. bi-w. free to qualified personnel (effective 2008). adv. back issues avail.; reprints avail. **Document type:** *Magazine, Trade.*
Description: Designed to help therapists enhance their impact on healthcare industry.
Supersedes in part (in 1998): Advance (0890-6521)
Related titles: Online - full text ed.: free to qualified personnel (effective 2008).
Indexed: C06, P30.
Published by: Merion Publications, Inc., 2900 Horizon Dr, PO Box 61556, King of Prussia, PA 19406. TEL 610-278-1400, 800-355-5627, FAX 610-278-1421, advance@merion.com, http://www.advanceweb.com. Ed. E J Brown. Adv. contact Cynthia Caramanico. B&W page USD 2,328, color page USD 3,128; trim 8.125 x 10.5. Circ: 60,117.

615.8 USA ISSN 2161-4288
ADVANCE FOR PHYSICAL THERAPY & REHAB MEDICINE. Text in English. 1988. bi-w. free to qualified personnel (effective 2011). adv. back issues avail.; reprints avail. **Document type:** *Magazine, Trade.*
Description: Features information on physical therapy.
Former titles (until 2009): Advance for Physical Therapists and P T Assistants (1099-9493); (until 1998): Advance for Physical Therapists (1053-7597); Which superseded in part (in 199?): Advance (0890-6521)
Related titles: Online - full text ed.
Published by: Merion Publications, Inc., 2900 Horizon Dr, King of Prussia, PA 19406. TEL 800-355-5627. Ed. Lisa Lombardo.

ADVANCES IN OCCUPATIONAL ERGONOMICS AND SAFETY. *see* OCCUPATIONAL HEALTH AND SAFETY

615.82 GBR ISSN 1403-8196
RM695 CODEN: APDHA7
ADVANCES IN PHYSIOTHERAPY. Text in Norwegian. 1999. q. GBP 210, EUR 275, USD 345 combined subscription to institutions (print & online eds.); GBP 415, EUR 550, USD 690 combined subscription to corporations (print & online eds.) (effective 2010). reprint service avail. from PSC. **Document type:** *Journal, Academic/Scholarly.*
Description: New international journal covering all aspects of physiotherapy.
Related titles: Online - full text ed.: ISSN 1651-1948 (from IngentaConnect).
Indexed: A01, A03, A08, A22, AMED, C06, C07, C08, CA, CINAHL, E01, EMBASE, ErgAb, ExcerpMed, P30, PEI, R09, R10, Reac, SCOPUS, SD, T02.
—IE, Infotrieve, Ingenta. **CCC.**
Published by: (Taylor & Francis A B SWE), Informa Healthcare (Subsidiary of: T & F Informa plc), Telephone House, 69-77 Paul St, London, EC2A 4LQ, United Kingdom. TEL 44-20-70175000, healthcare.enquiries@informa.com, http://informahealthcare.com/. Ed. Gunnevi Sundelin. **Subscr. in N. America to:** Taylor & Francis Inc., Customer Services Dept, 325 Chestnut St, 8th Fl, Philadelphia, PA 19106. TEL 215-625-8900, 800-354-1420, FAX 215-625-2940, customerservice@taylorandfrancis.com; **Subscr. outside N. America to:** Taylor & Francis Ltd., Journals Customer Service, Sheepen Pl, Colchester, Essex CO3 3LP, United Kingdom. TEL 44-20-70175544, FAX 44-20-70175198.

615.82 616.992 CHN ISSN 1007-8193
AIZHENG KANGFU/CANCER REHABILITATION. Variant title: Rehabilitation of Cancer Victims. Text in Chinese. 1990. bi-m. USD 16.40 (effective 2009). **Document type:** *Journal, Academic/Scholarly.*
—East View.
Published by: Zhongguo Kangai Xiehui/Chinese Anticancer Association, 52, Fucheng Lu, Beijing, 100036, China. http://www.lungca.org. **Dist. by:** China International Book Trading Corp, 35 Chegongzhuang Xilu, Haidian District, PO Box 399, Beijing 100044, China. TEL 86-10-68412045, FAX 86-10-68412023, cibtc@mail.cibtc.com.cn, http://www.cibtc.com.cn.

613.82 USA ISSN 0065-8022
AMERICAN DANCE THERAPY ASSOCIATION. (NO.) ANNUAL CONFERENCE PROCEEDINGS. Text in English. 1967. a., latest vol.27, 1992. USD 30 to non-members; USD 25 to members (effective 2007). **Document type:** *Proceedings.*
Published by: American Dance Therapy Association, 2000 Century Plaza, Ste 108, 10632 Little Patuxent Pkwy, Columbia, MD 21044. TEL 410-997-4040, 800-777-4643, FAX 410-997-4048, info@adta.org, http://www.adta.org.

615.8 USA ISSN 0894-9115
RM735.A1 CODEN: AJPREP
➤ **AMERICAN JOURNAL OF PHYSICAL MEDICINE AND REHABILITATION.** Text in English. 1921. m. USD 563 domestic to institutions; USD 733 foreign to institutions (effective 2011). adv. bk.rev. charts; illus.; tr.lit. back issues avail.; reprints avail. **Document type:** *Journal, Academic/Scholarly.* **Description:** Focuses on the practice, research and educational aspects of physical medicine and rehabilitation.
Former titles (until 1988): American Journal of Physical Medicine (0002-9491); (until 1952): Occupational Therapy and Rehabilitation; (until 1925): Archives of Occupational Therapy
Related titles: Online - full text ed.: ISSN 1537-7385.
Indexed: A01, A03, A08, A22, AIM, AMED, ASCA, B&BAb, B21, BDM&CN, BioEngAb, C06, C07, C08, CA, CINAHL, CTA, ChemAb, CurCont, E-psyche, EMBASE, ErgAb, ExcerpMed, FR, FoSS&M, IBR, IBZ, ISR, ISRS, IndMed, Inpharma, Inspec, MEDLINE, P30, P35, PEI, PsycholAb, R09, R10, Reac, RehabLit, SCI, SCOPUS, SD, SportS, T02, W07.
—BLDSC (0832.160000), AskIEEE, CASDDS, GNLM, IE, Infotrieve, Ingenta, INIST, Linda Hall. **CCC.**
Published by: (Association of Academic Physiatrists), Lippincott Williams & Wilkins (Subsidiary of: Wolters Kluwer N.V.), 530 Walnut St, Philadelphia, PA 19106. TEL 215-521-8300, FAX 215-521-8902, customerservice@lww.com, http://www.lww.com. Ed. Walter R Frontera. Pub. Jason Pointe. Circ: 2,253.

615.82 USA ISSN 1539-4131
RM736.7
➤ **AMERICAN JOURNAL OF RECREATION THERAPY.** Text in English. 2002. q. USD 167 to individuals; USD 171 to institutions (effective 2010). adv. back issues avail.; reprints avail. **Document type:** *Journal, Academic/Scholarly.* **Description:** Provides Certified Therapeutic Recreation Specialists (CTRS) with the techniques and advances in the use of recreational intervention to improve their client's health and well-being.
Indexed: C06, C07, C08, CINAHL.
—BLDSC (0836.200000), IE. **CCC.**
Published by: Weston Medical Publishing, LLC, 470 Boston Post Rd, Weston, MA 02493. TEL 781-899-2702, 800-743-7206, FAX 781-899-4900, brenda_devito@pnpco.com, subscription@pnpco.com, http://www.wmpllc.org. Ed. Linda L Buettner. Pub. Richard A DeVito Sr. TEL 781-899-2702 ext 107.

615.8 362 FRA ISSN 1877-0657
RM695 CODEN: ARMPEQ
➤ **ANNALS OF PHYSICAL AND REHABILITATION MEDICINE.** Text in English. 1957. 9/yr. EUR 481 in Europe to institutions; EUR 444.66 in France to institutions; JPY 60,400 in Japan to institutions; USD 625 elsewhere to institutions (effective 2012). adv. bk.rev. Index. reprints avail. **Document type:** *Journal, Academic/Scholarly.* **Description:** Publishes clinical, paraclinical and basic research papers pertaining to all aspects of the medicine of readaptation and rehabilitation.
Former titles (until 2009): Annales de Readaptation et de Medecine Physique (0168-6054); (until 1983): Annales de Medecine Physique (0402-4621)
Related titles: Microform ed.: (from PQC); Online - full text ed.: ISSN 1877-0665. 2000 (from IngentaConnect, ScienceDirect).
Indexed: A01, A03, A08, A22, A26, B25, BIOSIS Prev, CA, EMBASE, ExcerpMed, FR, I05, MEDLINE, MycolAb, P30, SCOPUS, T02.
—BLDSC (1043.439000), GNLM, IE, Infotrieve, Ingenta, INIST. **CCC.**
Published by: (Societe Francaise de Reeducation Fonctionnelle de Readaptation et de Medecine Physique), Elsevier Masson (Subsidiary of: Elsevier Health Sciences), 62 Rue Camille Desmoulins, Issy les Moulineaux, Cedex 92442, France. TEL 33-1-71165500, FAX 33-1-71165600, infos@elsevier-masson.fr. Circ: 3,000.

615.82 JPN ISSN 0918-1431
AOMORIKEN SAGYO RYOHO KENKYU/BULLETIN OF AOMORI OCCUPATIONAL THERAPY. Text in Japanese. 1992. a. **Document type:** *Journal, Academic/Scholarly.*
Published by: Aomoriken Sagyo Ryohoshikai/Association of Aomori-ken Occupational Therapists, c/o Hirosaki University, School of Health Sciences, Department of Occupational Therapy, Hon-Cho 66-1, Hirosaki, 036-8564, Japan. http://aomoriot.org/.

APPLIED PHYSIOLOGY, NUTRITION AND METABOLISM/ PHYSIOLOGIE APPLIQUEE, NUTRITION ET METABOLISME. *see* MEDICAL SCIENCES—Sports Medicine

615.82 615.853 GBR
AQUALINES. Text in English. s-a. free to members (effective 2005). **Document type:** *Journal, Trade.*
Published by: The Hydrotherapy Association of Chartered Physiotherapists, c/o Anne Jackson, Ed., Worthing Hospital, Physiotherapy Hospital, Lyndhurst Rd, Worthing, W Sussex BN11 2DH, United Kingdom. TEL 44-1903-286778.

615.82 SWE ISSN 1101-8259
ARBETSTERAPEUTEN PUBLICERAR SIG. Text in Swedish. 1990. irreg. price varies. **Document type:** *Monographic series, Trade.*
Published by: Foerbundet Sveriges Arbetsterapeuter (FSA)/Swedish Association of Occupational Therapists, Planiavaegen 13, PO Box 760, Nacka, 13124, Sweden. TEL 46-8-4662440, FAX 46-8-4662424, fsa@akademikerhuset.se, http://www.fsa.akadmikerhuset.se.

615.8 USA ISSN 0003-9993
RM845 CODEN: APMHAI
➤ **ARCHIVES OF PHYSICAL MEDICINE AND REHABILITATION.** Text in English. 1918. m. USD 585 in United States to institutions; USD 726 elsewhere to institutions (effective 2012). adv. bk.rev. charts; illus. Index. back issues avail.; reprints avail. **Document type:** *Journal, Academic/Scholarly.* **Description:** Concerns the therapeutic use of physical and pharmaceutical agents in providing comprehensive care for persons with disabilities and chronic illnesses.
Former titles (until 1953): Archives of Physical Medicine (0096-6622); (until 1945): Archives of Physical Therapy (0096-6037); (until 1938): Archives of Physical Therapy, X-Ray, Radium; (until 1926): Journal of Radiology (0095-9596); (until 1920): The Journal of Roentgenology
Related titles: Online - full text ed.: ISSN 1532-821X (from ScienceDirect); Supplement(s): American Congress of Physical Medicine & Rehabilitation. Education Issue; American Academy of Physical Medicine & Rehabilitation. Study Guide.
Indexed: A20, A22, A26, AHCMS, AIM, AMED, ASCA, BDM&CN, C06, C07, C08, CA, CINAHL, CISA, ChemAb, CurCont, DentInd, E01, EMBASE, ErgAb, ExcerpMed, F09, FR, FoSS&M, H12, HospLI, I05, IBR, IBZ, INI, ISR, IndMed, Inpharma, MEDLINE, MLA-IB, P30, P35, PEI, R09, R10, RILM, Reac, RehabLit, SCI, SCOPUS, SD, SportS, T02, W07.
—BLDSC (1639.000000), GNLM, IE, Infotrieve, Ingenta, INIST. **CCC.**
Published by: (American Congress of Rehabilitation Medicine, American Academy of Physical Medicine and Rehabilitation), W.B. Saunders Co. (Subsidiary of: Elsevier Health Sciences), Elsevier, Health Sciences Division, Order Fulfillment, 3251 Riverport Ln, Maryland Heights, MO 63043. TEL 314-872-8370, 800-325-4177, FAX 314-432-1380, JournalCustomerService-usa@elsevier.com, http://www.us.elsevierhealth.com. Ed. Jeffrey R Basford. Pub. Shannon Magee TEL 215-239-3730. Adv. contact Michael Targowski TEL 212-633-3693. Circ: 3,030.

615.85156 USA ISSN 0742-1656
RC489.A7
➤ **ART THERAPY.** Text in English. 1983. q. GBP 171 combined subscription in United Kingdom to institutions (print & online eds.); EUR 225, USD 281 combined subscription to institutions (print & online eds.) (effective 2012). adv. bk.rev. back issues avail.; reprint service avail. from PSC. **Document type:** *Journal, Academic/Scholarly.* **Description:** Aims to advance the understanding of how visual art functions in the treatment, education, development, and enrichment of people.
Supersedes in part: American Journal of Art Therapy (0007-4764)
Related titles: Online - full text ed.: GBP 153 in United Kingdom to institutions; EUR 202, USD 253 to institutions (effective 2012).
Indexed: A22, A30, A31, ABCT, ABM, AMED, C06, C07, C08, CA, CINAHL, E-psyche, E03, E07, ECER, ERI, ERIC, P03, PsycInfo, PsycholAb, SCOPUS, T02.
—BLDSC (1733.473800), IE, Ingenta.
Published by: American Art Therapy Association, Inc., 225 N Fairfax St, Alexandria, VA 22314. TEL 703-548-5860, 888-290-0878, FAX 703-783-8468, info@arttherapy.org, http://www.americanarttherapyassociation.org/. Ed. Lynn Kaplan. adv.: page USD 625; trim 8.5 x 11.

615.82 JPN ISSN 1347-3476
ASIAN JOURNAL OF OCCUPATIONAL THERAPY. Text in Japanese. 2001. a. **Document type:** *Journal, Academic/Scholarly.*
Related titles: Online - full content ed.: ISSN 1347-3484. free (effective 2011); Online - full text ed.
Published by: Japanese Association of Occupational Therapists, c/o Tsuyoshi Sato, PhD, OTR, School of Health Sciences, Sapporo Medical University, Sapporo, 060-8556, Japan. FAX 81-11-611-2155, nyukai@jaot.or.jp, http://www.jaot.or.jp/index.html. Ed. Tsuyoshi Sato.

618.0462 617.06 GBR ISSN 1367-7845
ASSOCIATION OF CHARTERED PHYSIOTHERAPISTS IN WOMEN'S HEALTH. JOURNAL. Text in English. 1995. s-a. free to members. **Document type:** *Journal, Academic/Scholarly.* **Description:** Contains a number of papers sent in by individuals currently involved in research related to women's health. The journal also contains news and reports about ACPWH, details of forthcoming events, and is a forum for members to communicate with one another.
Indexed: C06, C07, C08, CINAHL.
—BLDSC (4702.889000), IE, Ingenta.
Published by: Association of Chartered Physiotherapists in Women's Health, ACPWH Secretariat, c/o Fitwise Management Ltd, Drumcross Hall, Bathgate, West Lothian, EH48 4JT, United Kingdom. TEL 44-1506-811077, FAX 44-1506-811477. Ed. Mrs. Ros Thomas.

615.8 GBR ISSN 1368-7360
➤ **ASSOCIATION OF PAEDIATRIC CHARTERED PHYSIOTHERAPISTS. JOURNAL.** Text in English. 1973. q. free to members (effective 2009). adv. bk.rev. back issues avail. **Document type:** *Journal, Academic/Scholarly.* **Description:** Aims to raise the profile of paediatric physiotherapy and to achieve excellence in the treatment and management of children and young people.
Formerly (until 1994): Association of Paediatric Chartered Physiotherapists. Newsletter
—**CCC.**
Published by: Association of Paediatric Chartered Physiotherapists, PO Box 610, Huntingdon, PE29 9FJ, United Kingdom. va@apcp.org.uk. Ed. Melanie Lindley. **Co-sponsor:** Chartered Society of Physiotherapists.

615.82 AUS ISSN 1440-3994
➤ **AUSTRALASIAN REHABILITATION NURSES ASSOCIATION. OFFICIAL JOURNAL.** Abbreviated title: J A R N A. Text in English. 1993. q. AUD 100 to individuals for membership; AUD 300 to corporations for membership (effective 2008). adv. abstr. 32 p./no.; back issues avail. **Document type:** *Journal, Academic/Scholarly.* **Description:** Provides information on contemporary practice, policy and professional issues related to rehabilitation nursing.
Formerly (until 1997): Australian Rehabilitation Nurses Association. Bulletin
Indexed: A11, C06, C07, C08, CA, CINAHL, R09, T02.
—BLDSC (4662.940000), IE, Ingenta.
Published by: Australasian Rehabilitation Nurses Association Inc., PO Box 193, Surrey Hills, VIC 3127, Australia. TEL 61-3-98954483, FAX 61-3-98980249, arna@pams.org.au. Ed. Sarah Mott. Adv. contacts Felicity Shiel-Jones TEL 61-3-98954483, Jenny Rossi.

➤ **AUSTRALIA. BUREAU OF STATISTICS. PHYSIOTHERAPY SERVICES, AUSTRALIA (ONLINE).** *see* MEDICAL SCIENCES—Abstracting, Bibliographies, Statistics

➤ **AUSTRALIAN AND NEW ZEALAND CONTINENCE JOURNAL.** *see* MEDICAL SCIENCES—Urology And Nephrology

616.822 AUS ISSN 1448-997X
➤ **AUSTRALIAN ASSOCIATION OF MASSAGE THERAPISTS. JOURNAL.** Text in English. 2003. q. AUD 66 to non-members; free to members (effective 2008). adv. back issues avail. **Document type:** *Journal, Trade.* **Description:** Provides news and articles that focus on therapeutic massage industry, issues related to massage industry and relevant research based articles.
Indexed: C06, C07.
Published by: Australian Association of Massage Therapists Ltd., Level 6, 85 Queen St, Melbourne, VIC 3000, Australia. TEL 61-3-96913700, FAX 61-3-96023088, info@aamt.com.au, http://www.aamt.com.au. Adv. contact Alison Patience TEL 61-3-98202676. page AUD 1,210; 210 x 275. Circ: 7,000.

➤ **THE AUSTRALIAN JOURNAL OF REHABILITATION COUNSELLING.** *see* EDUCATION—Special Education And Rehabilitation

615.82 AUS ISSN 0045-0766
➤ **AUSTRALIAN OCCUPATIONAL THERAPY JOURNAL.** Variant title: Australian Association of Occupational Therapists. Journal. A O T Journal. Text in English. q. GBP 259 in United Kingdom to institutions; EUR 330 in Europe to institutions; USD 419 in the Americas to institutions; USD 508 elsewhere to institutions; GBP 297 combined subscription in United Kingdom to institutions (print & online eds.); EUR 379 combined subscription in Europe to institutions (print & online eds.); USD 483 combined subscription in the Americas to institutions (print & online eds.); USD 585 combined subscription elsewhere to institutions (print & online eds.) (effective 2012). adv. bk.rev. index. back issues avail.; reprint service avail. from PSC. **Document type:** *Journal, Academic/Scholarly.* **Description:** Examines the practice, theory, and professional education in occupational therapy in Australia.
Former titles (until 1962): Australian Association of Occupational Therapists. Bulletin; Occupational Therapists' Club. Bulletin
Related titles: Microfilm ed.: (from PQC); Online - full text ed.: ISSN 1440-1630. GBP 259 in United Kingdom to institutions; EUR 330 in Europe to institutions; USD 419 in the Americas to institutions; USD 508 elsewhere to institutions (effective 2012) (from IngentaConnect).
Indexed: A01, A02, A03, A08, A11, A22, A26, AEI, AMED, ASSIA, B21, C06, C07, C08, C11, CA, CINAHL, E-psyche, E01, EMBASE, ESPM, ExcerpMed, H&SSA, H04, H12, MEDLINE, P03, P30, P43, PEI, PsycInfo, PsycholAb, R10, Reac, SCI, SCOPUS, T02, W07.
—BLDSC (1815.950000), GNLM, IE, Infotrieve, Ingenta. **CCC.**
Published by: (Australian Association of Occupational Therapists), Wiley-Blackwell Publishing Asia (Subsidiary of: Wiley-Blackwell Publishing Ltd.), 155 Cremorne St, Richmond, VIC 3121, Australia. TEL 61-3-92743100, FAX 61-3-92743101, subs@blackwellpublishingasia.com, http://www.wiley.com/WileyCDA/. Eds. Elspeth Froude, Janet Fricke. Adv. contact Daniel Nash TEL 61-3-83591071. B&W page AUD 1,012, color page AUD 2,057; trim 210 x 275. Circ: 4,100.

➤ **AVANCES EN TRAUMATOLOGIA, CIRUGIA, REHABILITACION, MEDICINA PREVENTIVA Y DEPORTIVA.** *see* MEDICAL SCIENCES—Surgery

616.822 CAN ISSN 1195-3292
B C MASSAGE PRACTITIONER. Text in English. 1981. q. CAD 20 domestic; USD 20 foreign (effective 2006). adv. **Document type:** *Journal, Trade.*
Published by: B C M P Journal Society, PO Box 8844, Victoria, BC V8W 3Z1, Canada. TEL 250-208-4981. adv.: page CAD 300; 7.25 x 9.75.

615.82 JPN ISSN 1347-5568
BAIOFIRIA RIHABIRITESHON KENKYUU/BIOPHILIA REHABILITATION JOURNAL. Text in Japanese. a. **Document type:** *Journal, Academic/Scholarly.*
Related titles: Online - full text ed.
Published by: Baiofiria Rihabiriteshon Gakkai/Biophilia Rehabilitation Academy, 7-5-4 Zengyo, Fujisawa, 251-0871, Japan. TEL 81-466-840204, FAX 81-466-818815, http://www.biophilia.info/.

615.82 POL ISSN 0005-4402
CODEN: BAPOBT
BALNEOLOGIA POLSKA/POLISH BALNEOLOGY. Text in Polish; Summaries in English, Polish. 1950. q. PLZ 50 domestic; USD 20 foreign (effective 2007). adv. bk.rev. illus. index. **Document type:** *Journal, Academic/Scholarly.* **Description:** Consists of research articles in the areas of physical medicine, balneology, climatology, balneochemistry, balneotechnic and rehabilitation.
Formerly: Wiadomosci Uzdrowiskowe
Indexed: FR.
—CASDDS.
Published by: Polskie Towarzystwo Balneologii i Medycyny Fizykalnej/Polish Association of Balneology and Physical Medicine, Lesna 3, Ciechocinek, 87720, Poland. TEL 48-54-2833945, FAX 48-54-2833915, balneo@logonet.com.pl. Ed. Irena Ponikowska. Circ: 700 (controlled).

615.82 NLD ISSN 1871-2290
BEWEEGREDEN. Text in Dutch. 2004. q. EUR 35 (effective 2009). adv.
Formed by the merger of (1970-2004): Cesar Magazine (1380-5894); Which was formerly (until 1995): Cesar Oefentherapie (1380-5886); (until 1990): Cesar (0925-4226); (19??-2004): Nederlands Tijdschrift voor Oefentherapie-Mensendieck (0923-5876); Which was formerly (until 1989): Oefentherapie-Mensendieck (0926-468X); (until 1977): Nederlandsche Mensendieck Bond. Contactblad (1383-5386)
Published by: Nederlandse Vereniging van Oefentherapeuten Cesar en Mensendieck, Kaap Hoorndreef 54, Utrecht, 3563 AV, Netherlands. TEL 31-30-2625627, FAX 31-30-2623145, info@vvocm.nl, http://www.vvocm.nl. Ed. Ingrid de Wilt.

615.82 JPN
BIOPHILIA REHABILITATION ACADEMY. INTERNATIONAL CONFERENCE. PROCEEDINGS. Text in Japanese. a. **Document type:** *Proceedings, Academic/Scholarly.*
Related titles: Online - full text ed.
Published by: Baiofiria Rihabiriteshon Gakkai/Biophilia Rehabilitation Academy, 7-5-4 Zengyo, Fujisawa, 251-0871, Japan. TEL 81-466-840204, FAX 81-466-818815, http://www.biophilia.info/.

BODY, MOVEMENT AND DANCE IN PSYCHOTHERAPY; an international journal for theory, research and practice. *see* DANCE

BRAILLE JOURNAL OF PHYSIOTHERAPY. *see* HANDICAPPED—Visually Impaired

615.85154 GBR ISSN 1359-4575
ML3919
BRITISH JOURNAL OF MUSIC THERAPY. Text in English. 1968. s-a. free to members (effective 2009). adv. bk.rev. index. back issues avail. **Document type:** *Journal, Academic/Scholarly.* **Description:** Contains articles reflecting the broad spectrum of ideas and approaches to music therapy in this country.
Formerly (until 1995): Journal of British Music Therapy (0951-5038); Which superseded in part (in 1987): British Journal of Music Therapy (0308-244X)
Indexed: A22, AMED, DIP, IBR, IBZ, RILM.
—BLDSC (2311.900000), GNLM, IE, Ingenta. **CCC.**
Published by: (Association of Professional Music Therapists), British Society for Music Therapy, 24-27 White Lion St, London, N1 9PD, United Kingdom. TEL 44-20-78376100, FAX 44-20-78376142, info@bsmt.org. Ed. Simon Procter. Circ: 800.

615.53 EGY ISSN 1110-6611
CAIRO UNIVERSITY. FACULTY OF PHYSICAL THERAPY. BULLETIN. Text in English. 1996. s-a. EGP 20 domestic; USD 20 foreign (effective 2009). **Document type:** *Bulletin, Academic/Scholarly.*
Published by: Cairo University, Faculty of Physical Therapy, Murour St, Cairo, Egypt. Ed. Ebtesam Khattab.

615.82 CAN
CANADIAN HEALTHCARE BUSINESS NEWS. Text in English. 1994. s-a. **Document type:** *Magazine, Trade.* **Description:** Focusing on the business side of home healthcare, durable goods in rehabilitation, pharmacies specializing in homecare products.
Published by: B C S Communications Ltd., 101 Thorncliffe Park Dr, Toronto, ON M4H 1M2, Canada. TEL 416-421-7944, 800-798-6282, FAX 416-421-0966. Ed. Helmut Dostal. Pub. Caroline Tapp McDougall. Circ: 5,000 (controlled).

615.82 CAN ISSN 0008-4174
RM735
➤ **CANADIAN JOURNAL OF OCCUPATIONAL THERAPY/REVUE CANADIENNE D'ERGOTHERAPIE.** Abbreviated title: C J O T. Text mainly in English; Text occasionally in French; Abstracts in English, French. 1933. 5/yr. CAD 82 domestic to institutions; CAD 88 in United States to institutions; CAD 108 elsewhere to institutions; CAD 15 per issue domestic; CAD 20 per issue foreign (effective 2005). adv. bk.rev. bibl.; illus. index. reprints avail. **Document type:** *Journal, Academic/Scholarly.* **Description:** Promotes the advancement and growth of theory and practice in occupational therapy and fosters excellence in research and education.
Former titles (until 1939): Canadian Journal of Occupational Therapy and Physiotherapy (0315-1034); (until 1937): Canadian Journal of Occupational Therapy (0315-1026)
Related titles: Online - full text ed.: ISSN 1911-9828 (from IngentaConnect).
Indexed: A22, A26, AMED, B21, C03, C06, C07, C08, CA, CBCARef, CINAHL, CPerI, CurCont, E-psyche, E08, ECER, EMBASE, ESPM, ExcerpMed, H&SSA, H11, H12, HRA, I05, IndMed, MEDLINE, P03, P18, P20, P22, P24, P25, P30, P48, P53, P54, PQC, PsycInfo, PsycholAb, R10, Reac, RehabLit, RiskAb, S09, SCI, SCOPUS, SD, SSCI, T02, W07.
—BLDSC (3033.600000), GNLM, IE, Infotrieve, Ingenta. **CCC.**
Published by: Canadian Association of Occupational Therapists, CTTC Bldg, Ste 3400, 1125 Colonel By Dr, Ottawa, ON K1S 5R1, Canada. TEL 613-523-2268, 800-434-2268, FAX 613-523-2552, subsrciptions@caot.ca. Ed. F Swedlove. R&P, Adv. contact Lisa Sheehan TEL 613-523-2268, ext. 232. B&W page CAD 815; trim 9.5 x 7. Circ: 434 (paid); 8,000 (controlled).

616.1 615.8 USA ISSN 1541-7891
RC702
CARDIOPULMONARY PHYSICAL THERAPY JOURNAL. Text in English. 1986. q. USD 70 domestic to institutions; USD 85 in US & Canada to institutions; USD 100 elsewhere to institutions; USD 10 per issue domestic; USD 20 per issue foreign (effective 2010). adv. back issues avail. **Document type:** *Journal, Academic/Scholarly.*
Formerly (until 1990): Cardiopulmonary Record
Related titles: Online - full text ed.: free (effective 2010).
Indexed: A26, C06, C07, C08, CINAHL, H12, I05, P24, P30, P48, PQC, R09.
—BLDSC (3051.437050), IE, Ingenta. **CCC.**
Published by: American Physical Therapy Association, Cardiovascular & Pulmonary Section, 3437 Caroline St, St. Louis, MO 63104. office@cardiopt.org, http://www.cardiopt.org. Ed. Anne K Swisher. Adv. contact Kristen Mullins TEL 304-293-3610. Circ: 1,100.

CHIRYOGAKU/BIOMEDICINE & THERAPEUTICS. *see* BIOLOGY—Bioengineering

615.7 GBR ISSN 2230-2026
▼ ➤ **CHRONOPHYSIOLOGY AND THERAPY.** Text in English. 2011. irreg. free (effective 2011). **Document type:** *Journal, Academic/Scholarly.*
Media: Online - full text.
—CCC.
Published by: Dove Medical Press Ltd., Beechfield House, Winterton Way, Macclesfield, SK11 0JL, United Kingdom. TEL 44-1625-509130, FAX 44-1625-617933. Ed. Dr. Marc Hebert.

615.8 ITA ISSN 0390-8712
CODEN: CLTM-A
LA CLINICA TERMALE. Text in Italian. 1941. q. EUR 38.70 (effective 2008). **Document type:** *Journal, Academic/Scholarly.*
Indexed: P30.
—GNLM.
Published by: (Associazione Italiana di Idroclimatologia, Talassologia e Terapia Fisica), Societa Editrice Universo, Via Giovanni Battista Morgagni 1, Rome, RM 00161, Italy. TEL 39-06-44231171, FAX 39-06-4402033, amministrazione@seu-roma.it, http://www.seuroma.com.

613.7 USA
RD795 CODEN: CLKIE9
➤ **CLINICAL KINESIOLOGY (ONLINE).** Text in English. 1947. q. USD 75 to institutions; USD 30 to non-members (effective 2010). adv. bk.rev. bibl.; charts; illus. index. back issues avail.; reprints avail. **Document type:** *Journal, Academic/Scholarly.* **Description:** Features papers relevant to anatomy, physiology, biomechanics, adaptive equipment, motor control, psychology, health/pathology, neurology, orthopedics, geriatrics, pediatrics, etc. as they relate to exercise/education and disability/rehabilitation.
Former titles (until 2003): Clinical Kinesiology (Print) (0896-9620); (until 1988): American Corrective Therapy Journal (0002-8088); (until 1967): Association for Physical and Mental Rehabilitation. Journal (0098-8448); (until 1949): Physical & Mental Rehabilitation Journal; (until 1948): Association for Physical and Mental Rehabilitation. Journal
Media: Online - full text. **Related titles:** Microform ed.: (from PQC).
Indexed: A22, A26, AMED, AMHA, C06, C07, C08, CA, CINAHL, EMBASE, ExcerpMed, H12, HRIS, HospLI, I05, IndMed, P20, P24, P30, P48, P54, PEI, PQC, PsycholAb, RehabLit, SCOPUS, SD, SportS, T02, YAE&RB.
—GNLM, IE, Ingenta.
Published by: American Kinesiotherapy Association, 118 College Dr, #5142, Hattiesburg, MD 39406. info@akta.org, http://www.akta.org.

616.822 NZL ISSN 1179-559X
▼ ➤ **CLINICAL MEDICINE INSIGHTS: THERAPEUTICS.** Text in English. 2009. irreg. free (effective 2011). **Document type:** *Journal, Academic/Scholarly.* **Description:** Focuses on the role of therapeutics in human clinical medicine.
Formerly (until 2010): Clinical Medicine: Therapeutics (1179-1713)
Media: Online - full text.
Indexed: C06, C07, P30, SCOPUS, T02.
—CCC.
Published by: Libertas Academica Ltd., PO Box 300-874, Mairangi Bay, Auckland, 0751, New Zealand. TEL 64-9-4763930, FAX 64-9-3531397, enquiries@la-press.com. Ed. Garry Walsh.

615.82 GBR ISSN 0269-2155
RM930.A1 CODEN: CEHAEN
➤ **CLINICAL REHABILITATION.** Text in English. 1987. m. USD 1,947, GBP 1,053 combined subscription to institutions (print & online eds.); USD 1,908, GBP 1,032 to institutions (effective 2011). adv. back issues avail.; reprint service avail. from PSC. **Document type:** *Journal, Academic/Scholarly.* **Description:** Provides a forum for ideas and information for persons concerned with rehabilitation.
Incorporates (in 1996): Journal of Rehabilitation Sciences (0929-6719); Which was formerly (1987-1990): Tijdschrift voor Revalidatiewetenschappen (0923-0211)
Related titles: Online - full text ed.: ISSN 1477-0873. USD 1,752, GBP 948 to institutions (effective 2011).
Indexed: A01, A02, A03, A08, A22, AMED, ASSIA, C06, C07, C08, C11, CA, CINAHL, CurCont, E-psyche, E01, EMBASE, ExcerpMed, FR, H04, INI, ISR, IndMed, Inpharma, MEDLINE, P03, P19, P20, P22, P24, P25, P27, P30, P35, P43, P48, P54, PEI, PQC, PsycInfo, PsycholAb, R09, R10, RILM, Reac, RefZh, SCI, SCOPUS, SD, SociolAb, T02, W07.
—BLDSC (3286.351500), GNLM, IE, Infotrieve, Ingenta, INIST. **CCC.**
Published by: Sage Publications Ltd. (Subsidiary of: Sage Publications, Inc.), 1 Oliver's Yard, 55 City Rd, London, EC1Y 1SP, United Kingdom. TEL 44-20-73248500, FAX 44-20-73248600, info@sagepub.co.uk, http://www.uk.sagepub.com/home.nav. Ed. Derick T Wade. adv.: B&W page GBP 550; 160 x 215.

615.8515 AUS ISSN 1832-7605
CONNECTIONS (FITZROY); occupational therapy. Text in English. 2005. bi-m. adv. **Document type:** *Magazine, Trade.* **Description:** Provides information on industrial and professional representation issues and activities, CPD events and news, and the latest products and technologies relating to all aspects of the OT profession and operating environment.
Published by: Australian Association of Occupational Therapists, 6/340 Gore St, Fitzroy, VIC 3065, Australia. TEL 61-3-94152900, FAX 61-3-94161421, info@ausot.com.au. adv.: page AUD 2,497; 192 x 263.

615.82 USA ISSN 1040-2217
RM930.A1 CODEN: CPRHEZ
CONTEMPORARY PERSPECTIVES IN REHABILITATION. Text in English. 1986. irreg., latest 4th ed. price varies. back issues avail. **Document type:** *Monographic series, Trade.*
Indexed: A22.
—CCC.
Published by: F.A. Davis Company, 1915 Arch St, Philadelphia, PA 19103. TEL 215-568-2270, 800-523-4049, FAX 215-568-5065, info@fadavis.com.

615.82 USA ISSN 1075-9298
CONTEMPORARY REHAB. Text in English. 19??. bi-m. free to members (effective 2010). adv. **Document type:** *Magazine, Academic/Scholarly.*
Former titles (until 199?): National Rehabilitation Association Newsletter (1075-9301); (until 198?): N R A Newsletter (0279-5507)
Related titles: Online - full text ed.: free (effective 2010).
Indexed: C06, C07, C08, CINAHL, R09, SCOPUS.
Published by: National Rehabilitation Association, 633 S Washington St, Alexandria, VA 22314. TEL 703-836-0850, FAX 703-836-0848, info@nationalrehab.org, http://www.nationalrehab.org.

615.82 USA ISSN 0896-2960
CODEN: CRPHE5
CRITICAL REVIEWS IN PHYSICAL & REHABILITATION MEDICINE. Text in English. 1989. q. USD 937 to institutions (effective 2010). adv. back issues avail.; reprints avail. **Document type:** *Journal, Academic/Scholarly.* **Description:** Provides reviews of diagnostic methods, clinical modalities and techniques and physical and rehabilitation medicine.
Related titles: Online - full text ed.
Indexed: A22, AMED, C06, C07, C08, CINAHL, EMBASE, ExcerpMed, R10, Reac, SCOPUS.
—BLDSC (3487.479800), GNLM, IE, Ingenta. **CCC.**
Published by: Begell House Inc., 50 Cross Hwy, Redding, CT 06896. TEL 203-938-1300, FAX 203-938-1304, orders@begellhouse.com. Eds. Ernest J Henley, Martin Grabois.

615.82 ESP ISSN 1135-8599
CUESTIONES DE FISIOTERAPIA; revista universitaria de informacion e investigacion en fisioterapia. Text in Spanish. 1995. a. **Document type:** *Journal, Academic/Scholarly.*
Incorporates (2000-2004): Fisiterapia Actual (1576-141X)
Published by: (Universidad de Sevilla, Area de Fisioterapia), Universidad de Sevilla, Secretariado de Publicaciones, Calle Porvenir 27, Sevilla, 41013, Spain. TEL 34-95-4487444, FAX 34-95-4487443, secpub10@us.es, http://www.us.es/publius/inicio.html.

615.82 MKD ISSN 1409-6099
DEFECTOLOSKA TEORIJA I PRAKTIKA. Text in Multiple languages. 1997. q. **Document type:** *Journal, Academic/Scholarly.*
Related titles: Online - full text ed.: Journal of Special Education and Rehabilitation. ISSN 1857-663X. free (effective 2011).
Indexed: CA, E03, T02.
Published by: Ss. Cyril and Methodius University in Skopje, Institute of Special Education and Rehabilitation, Faculty of Philosophy, Bull. Krste Misirkov, Skopje, 1000, Macedonia. TEL 389-2-3116520, FAX 389-2-3118143. Ed. Vladimir Trajkovski.

DEVELOPMENTAL MOVEMENT PLAY JOURNAL. *see* DANCE

615.82 GBR ISSN 1751-8423
RJ496.B7 CODEN: PEREFP
➤ **DEVELOPMENTAL NEUROREHABILITATION.** Text in English. 1997. bi-m. GBP 405, EUR 570, USD 645 combined subscription to institutions (print & online eds.); GBP 810, EUR 1,135, USD 1,275 combined subscription to corporations (print & online eds.) (effective 2010). adv. back issues avail.; reprint service avail. from PSC. **Document type:** *Journal, Academic/Scholarly.* **Description:** Aims to enhance recovery and rehabilitation in children with brain injury and neurological disorders.
Formerly (until 2007): Pediatric Rehabilitation (1363-8491)
Related titles: Online - full text ed.: ISSN 1751-8431 (from IngentaConnect).
Indexed: A01, A02, A03, A08, A22, AMED, C06, C07, C08, C11, CA, CINAHL, E01, EMBASE, ExcerpMed, FamI, H04, IndMed, MEDLINE, P03, P30, PsycInfo, PsycholAb, R09, R10, Reac, SCI, SCOPUS, SD, T02, W07.
—IE, Infotrieve, Ingenta, INIST. **CCC.**
Published by: Informa Healthcare (Subsidiary of: T & F Informa plc), Telephone House, 69-77 Paul St, London, EC2A 4LQ, United Kingdom. TEL 44-20-70175000, FAX 44-20-70176792, healthcare.enquiries@informa.com. Ed. Dr. Jeff Sigafoos TEL 64-4-4639772. Adv. contact Per Sonnerfeldt. **Subscr. in N. America to:** Taylor & Francis Inc., Customer Services Dept, 325 Chestnut St, 8th Fl, Philadelphia, PA 19106. TEL 215-625-8900, 800-354-1420, FAX 215-625-8914, customerservice@taylorandfrancis.com; **Subscr. outside N. America to:** Taylor & Francis Ltd., Journals Customer Service, Sheepen Pl, Colchester, Essex CO3 3LP, United Kingdom. TEL 44-20-70175544, FAX 44-20-70175198, tf.enquiries@tfinforma.com.

615.82 USA ISSN 1061-7558
DIRECTIONS IN REHABILITATION COUNSELING. Text in English. 199?. m. USD 200 per vol. (effective 2010). **Document type:** *Journal, Academic/Scholarly.* **Description:** Provides a home-study course for rehabilitation counselors, case managers, disability management specialists, and rehabilitation nurses.
Published by: Hatherleigh Co. Ltd., 62545 State Hwy 10, Hobart, NY 13788. support@hatherleigh.com.

DISABILITY AND REHABILITATION. *see* HANDICAPPED

617.087 USA ISSN 1748-3107
RM950
DISABILITY AND REHABILITATION: ASSISTIVE TECHNOLOGY. Text in English. 2006. q. GBP 480, EUR 680, USD 845 combined subscription to institutions (print & online eds.); GBP 935, EUR 1,335, USD 1,660 combined subscription to corporations (print & online eds.) (effective 2010). adv. back issues avail.; reprint service avail. from PSC. **Document type:** *Journal, Academic/Scholarly.* **Description:** Devoted to the broad range of technological developments and related issues which enhance the rehabilitation process.
Related titles: Online - full text ed.: ISSN 1748-3115.
Indexed: ASSIA, C06, C07, C08, CINAHL, CPE, EMBASE, ExcerpMed, MEDLINE, P03, P30, PsycInfo, R09, R10, Reac.
—IE, Ingenta. **CCC.**
Published by: Informa Healthcare (Subsidiary of: T & F Informa plc), 52 Vanderbilt Ave, New York, NY 10017. TEL 212-262-8230, FAX 212-262-8234, healthcare.enquiries@informa.com, http://www.informahealthcare.com. Ed. Marcia Scherer TEL 585-671-3461. Adv. contact Daniel Wallen. **Subscr. outside N. America to:** Taylor & Francis Ltd.

DISABILITY, C B R AND INCLUSIVE DEVELOPMENT. (Community Based Rehabilitation) *see* SOCIAL SERVICES AND WELFARE

615.8 NLD
DUTCH JOURNAL OF PHYSICAL THERAPY. Text in Dutch. 1966. bi-m. EUR 50 domestic; EUR 90 foreign (effective 2007). adv. **Document type:** *Journal, Academic/Scholarly.*
Formerly (until 2007): Nederlands Tijdschrift voor Fysiotherapie (0377-208X)
Indexed: A22, AMED, C06, C07, C08, CINAHL.
—BLDSC (6071.500000), IE, Infotrieve, Ingenta.
Published by: (Koninklijk Nederlands Genootschap voor Fysiotherapie), Bohn Stafleu van Loghum B.V. (Subsidiary of: Springer Science+Business Media), Postbus 246, Houten, 3990 GA, Netherlands. TEL 31-30-6383830, FAX 31-30-6383999, boekhandels@bsl.nl, http://www.bsl.nl. adv.: page EUR 2,312; trim 210 x 297.

615.82 JPN ISSN 0919-5602
HD7757
E I R E C KENKYU HOKOKUSHU/ROSAI REHABILITATION ENGINEERING CENTER. ANNUAL REPORT. (Employment Injuries Rehabilitation Engineering Center) Text in Japanese; Summaries in English. 1986. a., latest 2005. **Document type:** *Academic/Scholarly.*
Formerly (until 1991): Rosai Rihabiriteshon Kogaku Senta Kenkyu Hokokushu (0912-7488)
Published by: Rosai Rehabilitation Engineering Center, 1-10-5 Komei, Minato-ku, Nagoya-shi, Aichi-ken 455-0018, Japan. TEL 81-52-6525831, FAX 81-52-6526275, http://www.lwc-eirec.go.jp/.

E-MOTION. *see* DANCE

616.822 FRA ISSN 2100-0808
▼ **EDUCATION THERAPEUTIQUE DU PATIENT/THERAPEUTIC PATIENT EDUCATION.** Text in English, French. 2009. s-a. EUR 141 combined subscription in Europe (print & online eds.); EUR 206 combined subscription elsewhere (print & online eds.) (effective 2012). **Document type:** *Journal, Academic/Scholarly.*
Related titles: Online - full text ed.: ISSN 2100-0816. EUR 109 in the European Union; EUR 130 elsewhere (effective 2011).
Indexed: P30.
Published by: E D P Sciences, 17 Ave du Hoggar, Parc d'Activites de Courtaboeuf, BP 112, Cedex A, Les Ulis, F-91944, France. TEL 33-1-69187575, FAX 33-1-69860678, subscribers@edpsciences.org, http://www.edpsciences.org.

EDUCATIONAL THERAPY & THERAPEUTIC TEACHING. *see* EDUCATION—Special Education And Rehabilitation

615.82 FRA ISSN 1293-2965
➤ **ENCYCLOPEDIE MEDICO-CHIRURGICALE. KINESITERAPIA - MEDICINA FISICA**; como recuperar la autonomia del paciente. Cover title: Tratado de Kinesiterapia - Medicina Fisica. Variant title: Encyclopedia Medico-Quirurgica. Kinesiterapia - Medicina Fisica. Text in Spanish. 1999. 4 base vols. plus q. updates. EUR 749.62 (effective 2003). bibl.; charts; illus. **Document type:** *Academic/Scholarly.* **Description:** Provides an up-to-date reference for topics in all areas of physical medicine and rehabilitation, including rheumatology, physical therapy, occupational therapy, orthopedics, and neurology.
Related titles: ◆ Italian ed.: Encyclopedie Medico-Chirurgicale. Medicina Riabilitativa. ISSN 1283-078X; ◆ French ed.: Encyclopedie Medico-Chirurgicale. Kinesitherapie - Medecine Physique - Readaptation. ISSN 1283-0887.
Published by: Elsevier Masson (Subsidiary of: Elsevier Health Sciences), 62 Rue Camille Desmoulins, Issy les Moulineaux, Cedex 92442, France. TEL 33-1-71165500, FAX 33-1-71165600, infos@elsevier-masson.fr, http://www.elsevier-masson.fr.

615.82 FRA ISSN 1283-0887
ENCYCLOPEDIE MEDICO-CHIRURGICALE. KINESITHERAPIE - MEDECINE PHYSIQUE - READAPTATION; de l'evaluation du handicap a la readaptation. Cover title: Traite de Kinesitherapie - Medecine Physique - Readaptation. Text in French. 1968. 4 base vols. plus q. updates. EUR 749.62 (effective 2003). bibl.; charts; illus. **Document type:** *Academic/Scholarly.* **Description:** Provides an up-to-date reference for topics in all areas of physical medicine and rehabilitation, including rheumatology, physical therapy, occupational therapy, orthopedics, and neurology.
Formerly (until 1998): Encyclopedie Medico-Chirurgicale. Kinesitherapie, Reeducation Fonctionelle (0246-0408)
Related titles: Online - full text ed.; ◆ Spanish ed.: Encyclopedie Medico-Chirurgicale. Kinesiterapia - Medicina Fisica. ISSN 1293-2965; ◆ Italian ed.: Encyclopedie Medico-Chirurgicale. Medicina Riabilitativa. ISSN 1283-078X.
—INIST. **CCC.**
Published by: Elsevier Masson (Subsidiary of: Elsevier Health Sciences), 62 Rue Camille Desmoulins, Issy les Moulineaux, Cedex 92442, France. TEL 33-1-71165500, FAX 33-1-71165600, infos@elsevier-masson.fr.

615.82 FRA ISSN 1283-078X
➤ **ENCYCLOPEDIE MEDICO-CHIRURGICALE. MEDICINA RIABILITATIVA**; dalla valutazione dell'handicap alla rieducazione. Key Title: Encyclopedie Medico-Chirurgicale. Kinesiterapia - Medicina Riabilitativa. Cover title: Trattato di Medicina Riabilitativa. Text in Italian. 1998. 4 base vols. plus q. updates. EUR 749.62 (effective 2003). bibl.; charts; illus. **Document type:** *Academic/Scholarly.* **Description:** Provides an up-to-date reference for topics in all areas of physical medicine and rehabilitation, including rheumatology, physical therapy, occupational therapy, orthopedics, and neurology.
Related titles: ◆ Spanish ed.: Encyclopedie Medico-Chirurgicale. Kinesiterapia - Medicina Fisica. ISSN 1293-2965; ◆ French ed.: Encyclopedie Medico-Chirurgicale. Kinesitherapie - Medecine Physique - Readaptation. ISSN 1283-0887.
Published by: Elsevier Masson (Subsidiary of: Elsevier Health Sciences), 62 Rue Camille Desmoulins, Issy les Moulineaux, Cedex 92442, France. TEL 33-1-71165500, FAX 33-1-71165600, infos@elsevier-masson.fr, http://www.elsevier-masson.fr.

615.82 FRA ISSN 1247-0074
ENTRETIENS DE BICHAT. THERAPEUTIQUE. Text in French. 1954. a. price varies. **Document type:** *Monographic series, Trade.*
Former titles (until 1991): Entretiens de Bichat Pitie Salpetriere. Therapeutique (0750-6767); (until 1975): Entretiens de Bichat. Therapeutique (0423-247X)
Indexed: P30.
—INIST.
Published by: Expansion Scientifique Francaise, 15 Rue Saint-Benoit, Paris, 75278 Cedex 06, France. TEL 33-1-45484260, FAX 33-1-45448155, expansionscientifiquefrancaise@wanadoo.fr, http://www.expansionscientifique.com.

615.82 DEU ISSN 1439-2283
ERGOPRAXIS. Text in German. 2008. 12/yr. EUR 91 to institutions; EUR 125 combined subscription to institutions (print & online eds.); EUR 20 newsstand/cover (effective 2011). **Document type:** *Journal, Academic/Scholarly.*
Related titles: Online - full text ed.: EUR 121 to institutions (effective 2011); ◆ Supplement(s): Praxisprofi.
Published by: Georg Thieme Verlag, Ruedigerstr 14, Stuttgart, 70469, Germany. TEL 49-711-8931421, FAX 49-711-8931410, leser.service@thieme.de, http://www.thieme.de.

615.82 DEU ISSN 1861-6348
ERGOSCIENCE; Wissenschaft & Forschung in der Ergotherapie. Text in German. 2006. 4/yr. EUR 92 to institutions; EUR 123 combined subscription to institutions (print & online eds.); EUR 30 newsstand/cover (effective 2010). adv. **Document type:** *Journal, Academic/Scholarly.*
Related titles: Online - full text ed.: ISSN 1861-6356. EUR 119 to institutions (effective 2010).
—BLDSC (3808.802305), IE. **CCC.**
Published by: Georg Thieme Verlag, Ruedigerstr 14, Stuttgart, 70469, Germany. TEL 49-711-8931421, FAX 49-711-8931410, leser.service@thieme.de. Circ: 1,800 (paid and controlled).

615.82 DEU ISSN 1438-9347
ERGOTHERAPIE; Zeitschrift fuer angewandte Wissenschaft. Text in German. 2000. s-a. EUR 16; EUR 9 newsstand/cover (effective 2011). adv. **Document type:** *Journal, Academic/Scholarly.*
Indexed: DIP, IBR, IBZ.
Published by: Verlag Modernes Lernen Borgmann KG, Schleefstr 14, Dortmund, 44287, Germany. TEL 49-231-128008, FAX 49-231-125640, info@verlag-modernes-lernen.de. Ed. Dorothea Becker. Pub. Dieter Borgmann.

615.82 CHE ISSN 0258-672X
ERGOTHERAPIE. Text in French, German. 1964. m. CHF 103 (effective 2003). adv. 48 p./no. 3 cols./p.; back issues avail. **Document type:** *Journal, Academic/Scholarly.*
Published by: Ergotherapeutinnen Verband Schweiz, Postgasse 17, Bern 8, 3000, Switzerland. TEL 41-31-3138844, FAX 41-31-3138899, evs-ase@ergotherapie.ch, http://www.ergotherapie.ch. Ed. Claudia Galli. adv.: page CHF 1,030; trim 182 x 243. Circ: 5,000 (controlled).
Dist. by: Staempfli und Cie AG. TEL 41-31-3006699.

615.82 NLD ISSN 1877-5381
ERGOTHERAPIE; magazine voor ergotherapeuten. Text in Dutch. 1973. 6/yr. EUR 75 domestic; EUR 89 foreign (effective 2009). adv. bk.rev. **Document type:** *Journal, Academic/Scholarly.*
Formerly (until 2009): Nederlands Tijdschrift voor Ergotherapie (0166-4751)
—IE, Infotrieve.
Published by: (Ergotherapie Nederland), Bohn Stafleu van Loghum B.V. (Subsidiary of: Springer Science+Business Media), Postbus 246, Houten, 3990 GA, Netherlands. TEL 31-30-6383838, FAX 31-30-6383839, http://www.bsl.nl.

616.07 FRA ISSN 1636-7073
ERGOTHERAPIES. Text in French. 1965. q. EUR 113 in the European Union to institutions; EUR 128 foreign to institutions (effective 2009). **Document type:** *Journal, Academic/Scholarly.* **Description:** Publishes theoretical and practical articles dealing with physiotherapy techniques.
Formerly (until 2000): Journal d'Ergotherapie (0249-6550)
Related titles: Microform ed.: (from PQC); Online - full text ed.
Indexed: FR.
—GNLM, INIST. **CCC.**
Published by: (Association Nationale Francaise des Ergotherapeutes), Editions Solal, 111 Rue Sainte Cecile, Marseille, 13005, France. TEL 33-4-91257785, FAX 33-4-91802958, editions.solal@wanadoo.fr. Circ: 2,100.

615.82 ITA ISSN 1125-890X
ERRE COME RIABILITAZIONE. Text in Italian. 1990. q. **Document type:** *Journal, Trade.*
Published by: Societa Erre Srl, Via Ardeatina 306, Rome, RM 00179, Italy. TEL 39-06-5191675, FAX 39-06-5032097. Ed. Giuseppe Tagliapietra.

615.82 ITA ISSN 1973-9087
CODEN: EUMPA
➤ **EUROPEAN JOURNAL OF PHYSICAL AND REHABILITATION MEDICINE**; a journal of physical medicine and rehabilitation after pathological events. Variant title: European Journal of Physical and Rehabilitation Medicine - Europa Medicophysica. Text in English, Italian. 1965. q. EUR 260 combined subscription in the European Union to institutions (print & online eds.); EUR 285 combined subscription elsewhere to institutions (print & online eds.) (effective 2011). adv. bk.rev. bibl.; charts; illus. index. **Document type:** *Journal, Academic/Scholarly.* **Description:** Covers physical medicine and rehabilitation.
Formerly (until 2007): Europa Medicophysica (0014-2573)
Related titles: Microform ed.: (from PQC); Online - full text ed.: ISSN 1827-1804. 2005.
Indexed: AMED, C06, C07, C08, CINAHL, CurCont, EMBASE, MEDLINE, P20, P22, P26, P30, P48, P54, PQC, R10, SCI, SCOPUS, W07.
—BLDSC (3829.734600), GNLM, IE, Ingenta, INIST. **CCC.**
Published by: (European Federation of Physical Medicine and Rehabilitation), Edizioni Minerva Medica, Corso Bramante 83-85, Turin, 10126, Italy. TEL 39-011-678282, FAX 39-011-674502, journals.dept@minervamedica.it, http://www.minervamedica.it. Ed. S Negrini. Circ: 3,000 (paid). **Co-sponsor:** Italian Society of Physical Medicine and Rehabilitation.

➤ **EXCERPTA MEDICA. SECTION 19: REHABILITATION AND PHYSICAL MEDICINE.** *see* MEDICAL SCIENCES—Abstracting, Bibliographies, Statistics

610 616.9 GBR ISSN 1478-7210
RC109
➤ **EXPERT REVIEW OF ANTI-INFECTIVE THERAPY.** Text in English. 2003 (June). m. GBP 1,095 combined subscription domestic (print & online eds.); USD 1,915 combined subscription in North America (print & online eds.); JPY 203,500 combined subscription in Japan (print & online eds.); EUR 1,530 combined subscription elsewhere (print & online eds.) (effective 2011). adv. back issues avail.; reprints avail. **Document type:** *Journal, Academic/Scholarly.* **Description:** Aims to provide critical commentary and analysis of the latest approaches to the management of bacterial, viral, fungal and parasitic infectious diseases.

Related titles: Online - full text ed.: ISSN 1744-8336. GBP 985 domestic to institutions; USD 1,730 in North America to institutions; JPY 185,000 in Japan to institutions; EUR 1,385 elsewhere to institutions (effective 2011) (from IngentaConnect).
Indexed: A26, A34, A35, A36, C06, C07, CA, CABA, CurCont, D01, E08, E12, EMBASE, ExcerpMed, GH, H11, H12, I05, MEDLINE, N02, N03, P20, P22, P30, P33, P48, P54, PQC, R08, R10, Reac, SCI, SCOPUS, T05, W07.
—BLDSC (3842.002981), IE, Ingenta. **CCC.**
Published by: Expert Reviews Ltd. (Subsidiary of: Future Science Ltd.), Unitec House, 2 Albert Pl, London, N3 1QB, United Kingdom. TEL 44-20-83716080, FAX 44-20-83716099, info@expert-reviews.com. Ed. Elisa Manzotti TEL 44-20-83716090. Pub. David Hughes. Adv. contact Simon Boisseau. Circ: 875.

➤ **EXPERT REVIEW OF CARDIOVASCULAR THERAPY.** *see* MEDICAL SCIENCES—Cardiovascular Diseases

616.822 FRA ISSN 1778-915X
F M T MAG. Variant title: Fichier Magazine Technique Mag. Text in French. 2005. q. free (effective 2009). **Document type:** *Magazine, Trade.*
Formerly: F M T Medical (0766-5024)
Related titles: Online - full content ed.
Published by: S.A.S. Groupe 76, 15 rue de Teheran, Paris, 75008, France. TEL 33-1-56881676. Ed. Philippe Goethals. Adv. contact Oriane Martin TEL 33-1-56881671.

615.8 CHE ISSN 1660-5209
FISIO ACTIVE/FISIOTERAPIA. Text in French, German, Italian. 1933. m. CHF 95 domestic; CHF 121 foreign (effective 2006). bk.rev. charts; illus.; stat. **Document type:** *Trade.*
Former titles (until 2001): Physiotherapie (1423-4092); (until 1993): Der Physiotherapeut (0257-7690); (until 1961): Der Heilmasseur-Physiopraktiker (1423-4106)
Published by: Schweizerischer Physiotherapeuten-Verband, Geschaftsstel, Stadthof / Bahnhofstrasse 7b, Sursee, 6210, Switzerland. TEL 41-41-9260780, FAX 41-41-9260799, info@fisio.org, http://www.fisio.org/. Ed. Rene Huber. Pub. Hans Walker. Adv. contact Henri Haeckel. Circ: 7,700.

615.8 ESP ISSN 2013-6056
FISIOGLOBAL. Text in Spanish. 2008. s-a. **Document type:** *Journal, Academic/Scholarly.*
Formerly (until 2008): Revista Cientifica Iberoamericana Fisioterapia Mexieres (2172-1416)
Related titles: Online - full text ed.: ISSN 2013-6064.
Published by: Instituto de Fisioterapia Global Mezieres, Guillem Tell, 40 Entlo 2a., Barcelona, 08006, Spain. TEL 34-93-2016513, ifgm@kimenez.com.

FISIOTERAPIA; revista de salud, discapacidad y terapeutica fisica. *see* MEDICAL SCIENCES—Nurses And Nursing

FISIOTERAPIA. MONOGRAFICO. *see* MEDICAL SCIENCES—Nurses And Nursing

615.82 ESP ISSN 1575-4847
➤ **FISIOTERAPIA Y CALIDAD DE VIDA.** Text and summaries in Spanish. 1998. q. adv. abstr.; bibl.; illus.; stat. back issues avail. **Document type:** *Academic/Scholarly.*
Related titles: Print ed.: ISSN 1989-6433. 2000.
Published by: (Physiotherapeutics' College), Ilustre Colegio de Fisioterapeutas de la Region de Murcia, C Maria Guerrero, 13 Bajo, Murcia, 30002, Spain. TEL 34-968-223079, FAX 34-968-223079, secretaria@cfsiomurcia.com, http://www.cfsiomurcia.com/. Circ: 5,000.

615.82 TUR ISSN 1300-6614
CODEN: FTRDE
➤ **FIZIK TEDAVI REHABILITASYON DERGISI/JOURNAL OF PHYSICAL MEDICINE AND REHABILITATION.** Text in Turkish. 1958. q. adv. bk.rev. **Document type:** *Journal, Academic/Scholarly.* **Description:** Publishes original articles, case reports, reviews and abstract of articles published in other journals.
Indexed: SCOPUS.
Published by: Turkiye Fiziksel Tip ve Rehabilitasyon Dernegi, Barbaros Bulvari Salim Aktas Is Hani, No:85 D. 3 Besiktas, Istanbul, 34390, Turkey. TEL 90-212-2369052, FAX 90-212-2369054, ftrdernek@ftr.org.tr, http://www.ftr.org.tr. Ed. Dr. Fikret Tuxun. Circ: 1,000.

615.82 RUS ISSN 1681-3456
FIZIOTERAPIYA, BOL'NEOLOGIYA I REABILITATSIYA. Text in Russian. 2002. bi-m. USD 165 foreign (effective 2005). **Document type:** *Journal, Academic/Scholarly.* **Description:** Published articles of interest to experts of physical rehabilitation, manual therapy, sanatoria and health resort physiotherapy and rehabilitation services.
—East View.
Published by: Izdatel'stvo Meditsina/Meditsina Publishers, ul B Pirogovskaya, d 2, str 5, Moscow, 119435, Russian Federation. TEL 7-095-2483324, meditsina@mtu-net.ru, http://www.medlit.ru. Ed. Vasiliy M Bogolyubov. **Dist. by:** East View Information Services, 10601 Wayzata Blvd, Minneapolis, MN 55305. TEL 952-252-1201, 800-477-1005, FAX 952-252-1202, info@eastview.com, http://www.eastview.com.

615.82 RUS
FIZIOTERAPIYA ROSSII; ezhegodnyi spravochnik. Text in Russian. a. **Document type:** *Directory.*
Published by: Chelovek, Malyi Prospekt VO, dom 26, ofis 2, Sankt-Peterburg, 199004, Russian Federation. zakaz@mirmed.ru. Ed. Gennadii Ponomarenko.

615.82 POL ISSN 1230-8323
FIZJOTERAPIA. Text in Polish. 1993. q. **Document type:** *Journal, Academic/Scholarly.*
Indexed: CA, EMBASE, ExcerpMed, R09, R10, Reac, SCOPUS, SD, T02.
—BLDSC (3949.663000).
Published by: (Polskie Towarzystwo Fizjoterapii), Akademia Wychowania Fizycznego we Wroclawiu/University School of Physical Education in Wroclaw, ul Banacha 11, Wroclaw, 51617, Poland. TEL 48-71-3473121. Ed. Tadeusz Skolimowski.

615.8 POL ISSN 1642-0136
FIZJOTERAPIA POLSKA/POLISH JOURNAL OF PHYSIOTHERAPY; organ Polskiego Towarzystwa Fizjoterapii. Text in Polish. 2001. q. EUR 58 foreign (effective 2006). **Document type:** *Journal, Academic/Scholarly.*
Indexed: R10, Reac, SCOPUS.
—BLDSC (3949.666000).
Published by: (Polskie Towarzystwo Fizjoterapii), MedSportPress, ul Marymoncka 34 skr. 23, Warsaw, 01813, Poland. TEL 48-22-8346772, FAX 48-22-8340431, nauka@medsport.pl, http://www.medsport.pl. **Dist. by:** Ars Polona, Obroncow 25, Warsaw 03933, Poland. TEL 48-22-5098609, FAX 48-22-5098610, arspolona@arspolona.com.pl, http://www.arspolona.com.pl.

617.06 TUR ISSN 1300-8757
FIZYOTERAPI REHABILITASYON/TURKISH JOURNAL OF PHYSIOTHERAPY REHABILITATION. Text in English. 1974. a. **Document type:** *Journal, Academic/Scholarly.*
Indexed: AMED, C06, C07, C08, CINAHL, EMBASE, ExcerpMed, SCOPUS, SD.
—BLDSC (3949.678000), IE, Ingenta.
Published by: (Hacettepe Universitesi), Turkey Association of Physiotherapists, 6 Cadde 39. Sokak No:33, Bahcelievler, Ankara, 06100, Turkey. TEL 90-312-3054055, FAX 90-530-4091428, tfd@fizyoterapi.org, tfd@e-fizyoterapist.com, http://www.e-fizyoterapist.com.

FOCAL POINT (PORTLAND); research, policy, and practice in children's mental health. *see* HANDICAPPED

616.85154 SWE ISSN 1650-3953
FOERBUNDET FOER MUSIKTERAPI I SVERIGE. Text in Swedish. 1978. 3/yr. SEK 200 membership. **Document type:** *Bulletin, Trade.*
Formerly (until 2000): Musikterapi (0349-7240)
Published by: Svenska Foerbundet foer Musikterapi/National Federation for Music Therapy in Sweden, PO Box 812, Stockholm, 10136, Sweden. info@musikterapi.se.

615.83 DNK ISSN 1903-0320
➤ **FORSKNING I FYSIOTERAPI (ONLINE).** Text in Danish. 1992. irreg. back issues avail. **Document type:** *Academic/Scholarly.*
Formerly (until 2003): Nyt om Forskning (Print) (1395-5454)
Media: Online - full content.
Indexed: AMED.
Published by: Danske Fysioterapeuter, Noerre Voldgade 90, Copenhagen K, 1358, Denmark. TEL 45-33-414620, FAX 45-33-414616, fysio@fysio.dk, http://www.fysio.dk. Eds. Henning Langberg TEL 45-26-127913, Vibeke Pilmark TEL 45-33-414631.

615.8 GBR ISSN 2045-4910
RM695
FRONTLINE (LONDON). Text in English. 1995. s-m. free to members (effective 2011). adv. back issues avail. **Document type:** *Magazine, Trade.* **Description:** Features news, reports, course information, and employment opportunities of interest to physiotherapists.
Formerly (until 2010): Physiotherapy Frontline (1356-9791)
Related titles: Online - full text ed.
Indexed: AMED, C06, C07, C08, CINAHL, SD.
—IE, Infotrieve. **CCC.**
Published by: Chartered Society of Physiotherapists, 14 Bedford Row, London, WC1R 4ED, United Kingdom. TEL 44-20-73066666, FAX 44-20-73066611, membership@csp.org.uk.

▼ **FYSIOPENSIOENACTUEEL.** *see* LABOR UNIONS

615.83 NLD ISSN 0927-5983
FYSIOPRAXIS. Text in Dutch. 1980. m. EUR 106 (effective 2011). adv. **Document type:** *Magazine, Trade.*
Formerly (until 1992): Fysiovisie (0922-1573)
Related titles: Online - full text ed.: ISSN 1876-5718.
Published by: (Koninklijk Nederlands Genootschap voor Fysiotherapie), Bohn Stafleu van Loghum B.V. (Subsidiary of: Springer Science+Business Media), Postbus 246, Houten, 3990 GA, Netherlands. TEL 31-30-6383872, FAX 31-30-6383991, http://www.bsl.nl. Ed. Saskia Bon. Circ: 22,530.

615.8 NOR ISSN 0016-3384
FYSIOTERAPEUTEN. Text in Norwegian. 1934. m. NOK 1,000 domestic to individuals; NOK 1,020 foreign to individuals; NOK 875 to institutions (effective 2011). adv. bk.rev. illus. back issues avail. **Document type:** *Magazine, Trade.*
Formerly (until 1958): Sykegymnasten (0802-5967)
Related titles: Online - full text ed.: ISSN 0807-9277. 1996.
Indexed: AMED.
—**CCC.**
Published by: Norsk Fysioterapeutforbund, St. Hanshaugen, PO Box 2704, Oslo, 0103, Norway. TEL 47-22933050, FAX 47-22465825, nff@fysio.no, http://www.fysio.no. Ed. Dagrun Lindvaag TEL 47-22-933059.

615.82 DNK ISSN 1601-1465
➤ **FYSIOTERAPEUTEN.** Text in Danish. 1918. 20/yr. DKK 1,017 in Scandinavia; DKK 1,211 in Europe; DKK 1,435 elsewhere; DKK 55 newsstand/cover (effective 2009). adv. bk.rev. **Document type:** *Magazine, Academic/Scholarly.*
Former titles (until 2001): Danske Fysioterapeuter (0105-0648); (until 1974): Tidsskrift for Danske Fysioterapeuter (0040-7054); (until 1966): Tidsskrift for Danske Fysioterapeuter (0105-1849); (until 1953): Tidsskrift for den Almindelige Danske Massageforening (0105-1857)
Related titles: Online - full text ed.
—**CCC.**
Published by: Danske Fysioterapeuter, Noerre Voldgade 90, Copenhagen K, 1358, Denmark. TEL 45-33-414620, FAX 45-33-414616, fysio@fysio.dk. Ed. Vibeke Pilmark TEL 45-33-414631. adv.: color page DKK 7.90; 210 x 270. Circ: 9,118 (controlled).

615.8 FIN ISSN 0789-5232
➤ **FYSIOTERAPIA.** Text in Finnish; Summaries in English. 1954. 8/yr. EUR 61 domestic; EUR 66 foreign (effective 2003). adv. bk.rev. charts; illus. **Document type:** *Magazine, Academic/Scholarly.* **Description:** Covers physiotherapy, movement and health, rehabilitation.
Former titles: Laakintavoimistelija (0039-5579); Suomen Laakintavoimistelija
Published by: Suomen Fysioterapeuttiliitto/Finnish Association of Physiotherapists, Asemamiehenkatu 4, Helsinki, 00520, Finland. TEL 358-9-87704710, FAX 358-9-1483054. Ed. Tarja Mansikkamaki. adv.: B&W page EUR 959, color page EUR 1,649; 175 x 260. Circ: 8,800.

➤ **GOOD MEDICINE.** *see* MEDICAL SCIENCES

615.82 FRA ISSN 2108-4084
▼ **LE GUIDE (YEAR) DES FORMATIONS KINES.** Text in French. 2010. a. **Document type:** *Trade.*
Published by: Profession Kine - Groupe Kalistene, 5, Route de Nanfray, Cran-Gevrier, 74960, France. TEL 33-4-50690197, FAX 33-4-50691780, contact@professionkine.com, http://www.professionkine.com.

615.892 362.29 USA ISSN 1070-8200
GUIDEPOINTS; acupuncture in recovery. Text in English. 1993. m. USD 180; USD 185 in Canada & Mexico; USD 190 elsewhere. bk.rev.; software rev.; video rev. charts; stat. back issues avail. **Document type:** *Newsletter, Trade.* **Description:** Provides information for professionals concerned with acupuncture in the treatment and recovery of people with addictive and mental problems.
Related titles: Online - full text ed.
Indexed: A04, T02.
Published by: J & M Reports, 7402 NE 58th St, Vancouver, WA 98662-5207. TEL 360-254-0186, FAX 360-260-8620. Ed., Pub., R&P Jay Renaud.

615.82 SWE ISSN 1650-3732
HAELSAHOEGSKOLAN I JOENKOEPING. AVDELINGEN FOER REHABILITERING. FORSKNINGSRAPPORT. Text in Swedish. 2002. irreg. **Document type:** *Monographic series, Academic/Scholarly.*
Published by: Haelsahoegskolan i Joenkoeping, Avdelingen foer Rehabilitering/University of Joenkoeping. School of Health Sciences. Department of Rehabilitation, PO Box 1026, Joenkoeping, 55111, Sweden. TEL 46-36-101000, FAX 46-36-101180, http://www.hhj.hj.se/doc/3148.

615.822 GBR ISSN 1758-9983
➤ **HAND THERAPY.** Text in English. 1991. q. USD 480 combined subscription in North America to institutions (print & online eds.); EUR 358 combined subscription in Europe to institutions (print & online eds.); GBP 246 combined subscription to institutions in the UK & elsewhere (print & online eds.) (effective 2012). adv. bk.rev. bibl.; charts; illus. back issues avail. **Document type:** *Journal, Academic/Scholarly.* **Description:** Publishes original articles and short reports on the theory and practice of hand therapy and related fields.
Formerly (until 2009): The British Journal of Hand Therapy (1369-9571)
Related titles: Online - full text ed.: ISSN 1758-9991. USD 432 in North America to institutions; EUR 322 in Europe to institutions; GBP 221 to institutions in the UK & elsewhere (effective 2012).
Indexed: C06, C07, C08, CINAHL, T02.
—BLDSC (4241.595650), IE, Ingenta. **CCC.**
Published by: (European Federation of Societies for Hand Therapy (E F S H T), British Association of Hand Therapists Ltd.), Royal Society of Medicine Press Ltd., 1 Wimpole St, London, W1G 0AE, United Kingdom. TEL 44-20-72902921, FAX 44-20-72902929, publishing@rsm.ac.uk, http://www.rsmpress.co.uk. Ed. Christina Jerosch-Herold. **Subscr. to:** Portland Customer Services, Commerce Way, Colchester CO2 8HP, United Kingdom. TEL 44-1206-796351, FAX 44-1206-799331, sales@portland-services.com, http://www.portlandpress.com.

651.82 615.5 USA ISSN 1547-5115
HEALING LIFESTYLES & SPAS. Text in English. bi-m. USD 19.95 domestic; USD 29.95 in Canada; USD 44.95 in Europe; USD 4.95 newsstand/cover domestic; USD 6.95 newsstand/cover in Canada (effective 2007). adv. back issues avail. **Document type:** *Magazine, Consumer.* **Description:** Provides information on spas, resort hotels, and other similar destinations around the world, including information on healthy living, alternative therapy, and events coverage.
Formerly (until Jan./Feb. 2003): Healing Retreats & Spas (1547-5107)
Related titles: Online - full content ed.
Published by: J L D Publications Inc., 899 Water St, Indiana, PA 15701. TEL 724-465-0643, FAX 724-349-4550. Ed. Melissa B Williams. Adv. contact Shanon Hoffman.

615.8 JPN ISSN 0912-1455
HOKKAIDO RIGAKU RYOHO/HOKKAIDO JOURNAL OF PHYSICAL THERAPY. Text in Japanese. 1984. a. JPY 1,500. **Document type:** *Journal, Academic/Scholarly.*
Published by: Nihon Rigaku Ryohoshi Kyokai, Hokkaido Shikai/Japanese Physical Therapy Association, Hokkaido Chapter, 3-2, N24 E1, Higashi-ku, Higuchi Bldg. 4/F, Sapporo, 065-0024, Japan. office@pt-hokkaido.jp, http://www.pt-hokkaido.jp/web/index.php.

615.82 JPN ISSN 0304-2081
HOKKAIDO RIHABIRITESHON GAKKAI ZASSHI/HOKKAIDO REHABILITATION ASSOCIATION. JOURNAL. Text in Japanese. 1964. a., latest 2005. JPY 4,000. adv. **Document type:** *Journal, Academic/Scholarly.*
Formerly (until 1972): Hokkaido Rihabiriteshon/Hokkaido Rehabilitation (0304-2073)
Published by: Hokkaido Rihabiriteshon Gakkai/Hokkaido Rehabilitation Association, c/o Sapporo Medical University, School of Medicine, Nishi 17-chome, Minami 1-jo, Chuo-ku, Sapporo-shi, Hokkaido 060, Japan.

615.8 JPN ISSN 1349-4317
HOKKAIDOU SAGYOU RYOUHOU/HOKKAIDO JOURNAL OF OCCUPATIONAL THERAPY. Text in Japanese. 1984. a. **Document type:** *Journal, Academic/Scholarly.*
Formerly (until 1997): Hokkaido Sagyo Ryoho Gakkaishi/Hokkaido Association of Occupational Therapists. Journal (0915-6429)
Published by: Hokkaido Sagyo Ryoho Shikai/Hokkaido Association of Occupational Therapists, Sapporo Ika Daigaku Eisei Tanki Daigakubu, 6-17-3, Megumino-Nishi, Eniwa, Hokkaido 061-1373, Japan. TEL http://www.north-wind.ne.jp/~haot/.

615.8515 NLD ISSN 1569-1861
RM735.A1
HONG KONG JOURNAL OF OCCUPATIONAL THERAPY. Text in English. s-a. EUR 158 in Europe to institutions; JPY 24,900 in Japan to institutions; USD 200 elsewhere to institutions (effective 2012). **Document type:** *Journal, Academic/Scholarly.*
Related titles: Online - full text ed.: ISSN 1876-4398 (from ScienceDirect).
Indexed: CA, EMBASE, ExcerpMed, PEI, R09, R10, Reac, SCI, SCOPUS, SD, T02, W07.
—BLDSC (4326.385760), IE. **CCC.**

Published by: (Hong Kong Occupational Therapy Association HKG), Elsevier BV (Subsidiary of: Elsevier Science & Technology), PO Box 1527, Amsterdam, 1000, Netherlands. TEL 31-20-4853852, FAX 31-20-4853342, JournalsCustomerServiceEMEA@elsevier.com, http://www.elsevier.nl. Ed. Dr. Kenneth N K Fong. **Subscr. to:** Elsevier (Singapore) Pte Ltd, 3 Killiney Rd, #08-01 Winsland House, Singapore 239519, Singapore. TEL 65-6349-0222, FAX 65-337-2230.

615.8 HKG ISSN 1013-7025
RM695 CODEN: HKPJFI
➤ **HONG KONG PHYSIOTHERAPY JOURNAL.** Text in English. 1978. a. EUR 83 in Europe to institutions; JPY 13,000 in Japan to institutions; USD 117 elsewhere to institutions (effective 2012). **Document type:** *Journal, Academic/Scholarly.*
Related titles: Online - full text ed.: ISSN 1876-441X (from ScienceDirect).
Indexed: AMED, C06, C07, C08, CINAHL, EMBASE, ExcerpMed, R10, Reac, SCOPUS, SD.
—IE. **CCC.**
Published by: (Hong Kong Physiotherapy Association), Elsevier (Singapore) Pte Ltd, Hong Kong Branch (Subsidiary of: Elsevier Health Sciences), 1601, 16/F, Leighton Centre, 77 Leighton Rd., Causeway Bay, Hong Kong. TEL 852-2965-1300, FAX 852-2976-0778, asiajournals@elsevier.com, http://asia.elsevierhealth.com/. Ed. Dr. Gladys Cheing TEL 852-27666738.

617.03 BRA ISSN 0103-6475
HOSPITAL DE PRONTO SOCORRO. REVISTA. Text in Portuguese. 1939. a. **Document type:** *Magazine, Academic/Scholarly.*
Formerly: Medicina e Cirugia (0102-9533)
Published by: Secretaria Municipal de Saude, Hospital de Pronto Socorro, Av Joa Pesso, 325, Porto Alegre, Brazil. TEL 55-51-32892899, http://www2.portoalegre.rs.gov.br/sms/default.php?p_secao=175.

615.82 HRV ISSN 1331-3010
RM930.A1
➤ **HRVATSKA REVIJA ZA REHABILITACIJSKA ISTRAZIVANJA/ CROATIAN REVIEW OF REHABILITATION RESEARCH.** Text in Croatian. 1965. s-a. **Document type:** *Journal, Academic/Scholarly.*
Formerly (until 1996): Defektologija (0351-1839)
Indexed: A26, CPE, ERA, I05, L&LBA, P03, PsycInfo, PsycholAb, S21, SCOPUS, YAE&RB.
Published by: Sveuciliste u Zagrebu, Edukacijsko-Rehabilitacijski Fakultet, Kuslanova 59-a, Zagreb, Croatia. TEL 385-1-2338022, FAX 385-1-2329950, dekan@erf.hr, http://www.erf.hr. Ed. Milko Mejovsek.

➤ **HULI YU KANGFU/NURSING AND REHABILITATION JOURNAL.** *see* MEDICAL SCIENCES—Nurses And Nursing

➤ **I T - INVALIDITYOE.** *see* SOCIAL SERVICES AND WELFARE

615.82 IND ISSN 0973-2209
INDIAN JOURNAL OF PHYSICAL MEDICINE AND REHABILITATION. Text in English. 1993. s-a. adv. **Document type:** *Journal, Academic/Scholarly.* **Description:** For service providers, professionals, applied researchers and educators in the field of physical medicine and rehabilitation.
Related titles: Online - full text ed.: free (effective 2011).
Published by: Indian Association of Physical Medicine and Rehabilitation, c/o Department of Physical Medicine and Rehabilitation, All India Institute of Medical Sciences, New Delhi, 110 029, India. TEL 91-11-26594916, FAX 91-11-26588663. Ed. U Singh.

615.82 615.8515 IND ISSN 0973-5666
➤ **INDIAN JOURNAL OF PHYSIOTHERAPY AND OCCUPATIONAL THERAPY.** Text in English. 2006. q. INR 6,000 domestic; USD 400 foreign; INR 8,000 combined subscription domestic (print & online eds.); USD 500 combined subscription foreign (print & online eds.) (effective 2011). adv. **Document type:** *Journal, Academic/Scholarly.* **Description:** Brings latest research about the field of physiotherapy & occupational therapy. It welcomes scientific articles, news, group discussions and information about latest equipments.
Related titles: Online - full text ed.: ISSN 0973-5674. INR 4,500 domestic; USD 300 foreign (effective 2011).
Indexed: C06, C07.
Published by: World Information Syndicate, 41/48, DSIDC, Pocket-II, Mayur Vihar, Phase-I, PO Box 9108, New Delhi, 110 091, India. TEL 91-11-55270068, FAX 91-11-22790315, contact@wis-india.com, http://www.wis-india.com/.

➤ **INTERFACE (CHICAGO, 1978).** *see* LIBRARY AND INFORMATION SCIENCES

615 GBR ISSN 1745-4832
➤ **INTERNATIONAL JOURNAL OF ART THERAPY.** Text in English. 1977. s-a. GBP 103 combined subscription in United Kingdom to institutions (print & online eds.); EUR 149, USD 187 combined subscription to institutions (print & online eds.) (effective 2012). adv. back issues avail.; reprint service avail. from PSC. **Document type:** *Journal, Academic/Scholarly.* **Description:** A forum dedicated to the growing and diverse field of art therapy and publishes articles from around the world on research, theory, practice and professional development.
Formerly (until 2005): Inscape (0264-7141)
Related titles: Online - full text ed.: ISSN 1745-4840. GBP 93 in United Kingdom to institutions; EUR 134, USD 168 to institutions (effective 2012).
Indexed: A22, A30, A31, ABM, AMED, C06, C07, CA, E01, E03, ERI, S21, SCOPUS, T02.
—BLDSC (4542.104650), IE, Ingenta. **CCC.**
Published by: (British Association of Art Therapists), Routledge (Subsidiary of: Taylor & Francis Group), 4 Park Sq, Milton Park, Abingdon, Oxon OX14 4RN, United Kingdom. TEL 44-20-70176000, FAX 44-20-70176336, subscriptions@tandf.co.uk, http://www.routledge.com. Ed. Tim Wright. Adv. contact Linda Hann TEL 44-1344-779945. **Subscr. to:** Taylor & Francis Ltd., Journals Customer Service, Sheepen Pl, Colchester, Essex CO3 3LP, United Kingdom. TEL 44-20-70175544, FAX 44-20-70175198.

615.82 IND ISSN 0976-4852
▼ ➤ **INTERNATIONAL JOURNAL OF CONTEMPORARY RESEARCH AND REVIEW.** Abbreviated title: I J C R R. Text in English. 2010. m. **Document type:** *Journal, Academic/Scholarly.*
Media: Online - full text.
Published by: Vivek Daniel, Ed.& Pub, Behind DVM School, HX 83 Kityani, Mandsaur, Madhya Pradesh 458 001, India. TEL 91-07422-407517. Ed. Vivek Daniel.

615.82 GBR ISSN 2041-3807
▼ ➤ **INTERNATIONAL JOURNAL OF PHYSIOTHERAPY AND REHABILITATION.** Text in English. 2010. irreg. free (effective 2011). **Document type:** *Journal, Academic/Scholarly.*
Media: Online - full text. Eds. Markus Froehiling, Sionnadh McLean.

617.06 USA ISSN 0342-5282
RM695 CODEN: IJRRDK
➤ **INTERNATIONAL JOURNAL OF REHABILITATION RESEARCH.** Text in English, French, German; Summaries in English, French, German, Spanish. 1977. q. USD 638 domestic to institutions; USD 685 foreign to institutions (effective 2011). adv. bk.rev. charts; illus. Index. back issues avail.; reprints avail. **Document type:** *Journal, Academic/Scholarly.* **Description:** Provides an interdisciplinary forum for research into disability and handicaps people in both industrial and developing nations face.
Related titles: Online - full text ed.: ISSN 1473-5660.
Indexed: A20, A22, AMED, ASCA, B&BAb, C06, C07, C08, CA, CDA, CINAHL, CPEI, CurCont, E01, E03, ECER, EMBASE, ERI, ERIC, EngInd, ErgAb, ExcerpMed, F09, FR, FamI, H13, IBR, IBZ, INI, IndMed, MEDLINE, P10, P20, P30, P48, P53, P54, PQC, PsycholAb, R10, Reac, RehabLit, SCOPUS, SSCI, W07, YAE&RB.
—BLDSC (4542.526000), GNLM, IE, Infotrieve, Ingenta, INIST. **CCC.**
Published by: (European Federation for Research in Rehabilitation LVA, Rehabilitation International), Lippincott Williams & Wilkins (Subsidiary of: Wolters Kluwer N.V.), 530 Walnut St, Philadelphia, PA 19106. TEL 215-521-8300, FAX 215-521-8902, customerservice@lww.com, http://www.lww.com. Ed. Crt Marincek. Pub. Phil Daly. Circ: 349.

615.82 USA ISSN 1945-2020
▼ ➤ **INTERNATIONAL JOURNAL OF TELEREHABILITATION.** Text in English. 2009 (Sep.). s-a. free (effective 2011). **Document type:** *Journal, Academic/Scholarly.* **Description:** Dedicated to advancing telerehabilitation.
Media: Online - full text.
Indexed: R09, T02.
Published by: University of Pittsburgh, University Library System, Coordinator of Library Instruction, 207 Hillman Library, Pittsburgh, PA 15260. TEL 412-648-7732, FAX 412-648-7733. Ed. Ellen R Cohn.

615.82 GBR ISSN 1741-1645
➤ **INTERNATIONAL JOURNAL OF THERAPY AND REHABILITATION.** Abbreviated title: I J T R. Text in English. 1994. m. GBP 157 combined subscription domestic to individuals (print & online eds.); EUR 246 combined subscription in Europe to individuals (print & online eds.); USD 381 combined subscription elsewhere to individuals (print & online eds.); GBP 123 combined subscription domestic to students (print & online eds.); EUR 199 combined subscription in Europe to students (print & online eds.); USD 312 combined subscription elsewhere to students (print & online eds.); GBP 140 domestic to individuals; EUR 211 in Europe to individuals; USD 312 elsewhere to individuals (effective 2010). adv. back issues avail.; reprints avail. **Document type:** *Journal, Academic/Scholarly.* **Description:** Promotes interdisciplinary practice through the publication of high quality original research, clinical reviews and evidence-based articles from a range of disciplines.
Formerly (until Apr.2003): British Journal of Therapy & Rehabilitation (1354-8581)
Related titles: Online - full text ed.: ISSN 1759-779X. GBP 129 to individuals; GBP 99 to students (effective 2010).
Indexed: A01, A02, A03, A08, AMED, B28, C06, C07, C08, C11, CA, CINAHL, ErgAb, H04, P34, R09, T02.
—BLDSC (4542.695120), IE, Ingenta. **CCC.**
Published by: Mark Allen Publishing Ltd., St Jude's Church, Dulwich Rd, London, SE24 0PB, United Kingdom. TEL 44-20-77385454, FAX 44-20-79788316, subscriptions@markallengroup.com, http://www.markallengroup.com. Eds. Olivia Wood, Alison Rushton. Adv. contact Adrian Johnston.

▼ ➤ **INTERNATIONAL SOCIETY FOR OCCUPATIONAL ERGONOMICS AND SAFETY. NEWSLETTER.** *see* OCCUPATIONAL HEALTH AND SAFETY

➤ **THE INTERNET JOURNAL OF PAIN, SYMPTOM CONTROL AND PALLIATIVE CARE.** *see* MEDICAL SCIENCES—Anaesthesiology

615.82 USA ISSN 2155-6741
▼ ➤ **THE INTERNET JOURNAL OF REHABILITATION.** Text in English. 2010 (Sept.). s-a. free (effective 2011). **Document type:** *Journal, Trade.* **Description:** Presents new developments in the broad field of rehabilitation including technical orthopedics for physical therapists, occupational therapists, chiropractors, osteopaths, and physiatrists.
Media: Online - full text.
Indexed: A01.
Published by: Internet Scientific Publications, Llc., 23 Rippling Creek Dr, Sugar Land, TX 77479. TEL 832-443-1193, FAX 281-240-1533, wenker@ispub.com. Ed. Dr. Hans-Rudolf Weiss.

615.82 IRN ISSN 1735-3602
IRANIAN REHABILITATION JOURNAL. Text in English. 2004. s-a. **Document type:** *Journal, Academic/Scholarly.*
Related titles: Online - full text ed.: ISSN 1735-3610. free (effective 2011).
Published by: University of Social Welfare and Rehabilitation Sciences, Evin, Kudakyar Ave, Tehran, 1985713831, Iran. Ed. Asghar Dadkhah.

615.8515 ISR ISSN 0792-7002
THE ISRAELI JOURNAL OF OCCUPATIONAL THERAPY/KETAV 'ET YISRE'ELI LE-RIPPUY BE-'ISSUQ. Abbreviated title: I J O T. Text in English, Hebrew. 1991. q. ILS 275 domestic to individuals; ILS 290 domestic to institutions; ILS 175 domestic to students (effective 2008); USD 80 foreign (effective 2007); free to members (effective 2008). back issues avail. **Document type:** *Journal, Academic/ Scholarly.* **Description:** Provides a platform for professionals desiring to present their views and a description of their clinical work and research to their colleagues and to the general public. It deals with a variety of subjects and includes theoretical articles, research summaries, case and group studies, outlines of techniques used for diagnosis and treatment, and reviews of professional literature.
Indexed: C06, C07, C08, CINAHL.
—BLDSC (4583.812700).
Published by: (The Israeli Society of Occupational Therapy), A H V A Publisher, P O Box 9120, Haifa, 31090, Israel. TEL 972-4-8522970, FAX 972-4-8520432. Ed. Dr. Orit Shenker.

JAPAN SOCIETY OF PAIN CLINICS. JOURNAL/NIHON PEIN KURINIKKU GAKKAISHI. *see* HEALTH FACILITIES AND ADMINISTRATION

615.82 JPN ISSN 1881-3526
➤ **JAPANESE JOURNAL OF REHABILITATION MEDICINE.** Text in Japanese. 1964. m. JPY 22,000 (effective 2010). Index. 90 p./no.; back issues avail. **Document type:** *Journal, Academic/Scholarly.*
Formerly (until 2007): Rihabiriteshon Igaku (0034-351X)
Related titles: Online - full text ed.: ISSN 1881-8560.
—**CCC.**
Published by: (Japanese Association of Rehabilitation Medicine/Nippon Rihabiriteshon Igakkai), Igaku Shoin Ltd., 1-28-36 Hongo, Bunkyo-ku, Tokyo, 113-8719, Japan. TEL 81-3-3817-5600, FAX 81-3-3815-7791, info@igaku-shoin.co.jp. Ed. Masami Akai. Circ: 9,700 (paid).

615.82 JPN ISSN 1344-1272
RM695
JAPANESE PHYSICAL THERAPY ASSOCIATION. JOURNAL. Text in English. 1998. a. **Document type:** *Journal, Academic/Scholarly.* **Description:** Publishes papers that deal with clinical practice, education, research, administration, public issues or historical perspectives, and pertain to rehabilitation.
Related titles: Online - full content ed.: free (effective 2011); Online - full text ed.
Indexed: C06, C07, PEI, SCOPUS.
—BLDSC (4809.380000).
Published by: Nihon Rigaku Ryohoshi Kyokai/Japanese Physical Therapy Association, 1-2-2 Kasumigaseki, Chiyoda-ku, Tokyo, 100-8916, Japan. TEL 86-3-5253-1111 ext 2577, FAX 86-3-3595-2204, jpta-international@japan.email.ne.jp, http://www.ne.jp/asahi/jpta/international/.

615.82 FRA ISSN 0242-648X
JOURNAL DE READAPTATION MEDICALE; pratique et formation en medicine physique et de readaptation. Text in French. q. EUR 267 in Europe to institutions; EUR 222.33 in France to institutions; JPY 40,400 in Japan to institutions; USD 342 elsewhere to institutions (effective 2012). **Document type:** *Journal, Academic/Scholarly.* **Description:** Deals with different therapies, as well as the material problems in kinesitherapy, ergotherapy and orthophony.
Related titles: Online - full text ed.: (from ScienceDirect).
Indexed: SCOPUS.
—INIST. **CCC.**
Published by: Elsevier Masson (Subsidiary of: Elsevier Health Sciences), 62 Rue Camille Desmoulins, Issy les Moulineaux, Cedex 92442, France. TEL 33-1-71165500, infos@elsevier-masson.fr. Ed. Claude Hamonet. Circ: 1,000.

610 USA ISSN 2158-8686
➤ **JOURNAL OF ACUTE CARE PHYSICAL THERAPY.** Abbreviated title: J A C P T. Text in English. 1993. 3/yr. USD 75 to non-members; free to members (effective 2011). adv. back issues avail.; reprints avail. **Document type:** *Journal, Academic/Scholarly.* **Description:** Promotes evidence-based practice and the literature specific to acute care physical therapy practice grows.
Formerly (until 2010): Acute Care Perspectives (1551-9147)
Related titles: Online - full text ed.: ISSN 2159-0524.
Indexed: C06, C07, C08, CA, CINAHL, H12, I05, T02.
—BLDSC (0678.060000).
Published by: American Physical Therapy Association, Acute Care Section, 1100 US Hwy 130, Ste 3, Robbinsville, NJ 08691. TEL 609-208-0981, 888-762-2427, FAX 609-208-1090, acute@acutept.org. Ed. Dr. Glenn Irion TEL 251-434-3575.

615.82 USA
➤ **JOURNAL OF AQUATIC PHYSICAL THERAPY.** Text in English. 1993. s-a. USD 50 (effective 2011). **Document type:** *Magazine, Trade.* **Description:** Publishes research reports, clinic and practice reports, and literature reviews on the aquatic physical therapy. Also includes calendar updates, continuing education and organization information.
Related titles: Online - full text ed.
Published by: American Physical Therapy Association, Aquatic Physical Therapy Section, 1111 N. Fairfax St., Alexandria, VA 22314. TEL 800-999-2782 ext 8512, FAX 703-706-8575, aquaticsPT@apta.org, http://www.aquaticpt.org/.

➤ **JOURNAL OF BACK AND MUSCULOSKELETAL REHABILITATION.** *see* MEDICAL SCIENCES—Orthopedics And Traumatology

615.8 GBR ISSN 1360-8592
RM724 CODEN: JBOTF2
➤ **JOURNAL OF BODYWORK AND MOVEMENT THERAPIES.** Text in English. 1997. q. EUR 395 in Europe to institutions; JPY 42,500 in Japan to institutions; USD 348 elsewhere to institutions (effective 2012). adv. bk.rev. 72 p./no. 2 cols./p.; back issues avail.; reprints avail. **Document type:** *Journal, Academic/Scholarly.* **Description:** Covers practical approaches to musculoskeletal dysfunction applicable across all bodywork, movement and manual therapies.
Related titles: Online - full text ed.: ISSN 1532-9283 (from ScienceDirect).
Indexed: A22, A26, AMED, B21, C06, C07, C08, CA, CINAHL, CTA, E01, EMBASE, ExcerpMed, H12, MEDLINE, NSA, P30, PEI, R10, Reac, SCOPUS, SD, T02.
—BLDSC (4954.235000), IE, Ingenta. **CCC.**
Published by: (Australian Pilates Method Association AUS), Churchill Livingstone (Subsidiary of: Elsevier Health Sciences), The Blvd, Langford Ln, Kidlington, OX5 1GB, United Kingdom. TEL 44-1865-843434, FAX 44-1865-843970, directenquiries@elsevier.com, http://www.elsevierhealth.com/imprint.jsp?iid=9. Ed. Leon Chaitow. R&P Sharon Boyle TEL 44-131-5241747. Adv. contact Deborah Watkins TEL 44-20-74244280.

615.82 JPN ISSN 0918-5259
JOURNAL OF CLINICAL REHABILITATION. Text in Japanese. 1992. m. JPY 2,205 newsstand/cover (effective 2007). **Document type:** *Magazine, Trade.*
Published by: Ishiyoku Shuppan K.K./Ishiyaku Publishers Inc., 1-7-10 Honkomagome, Bunkyo-ku, Tokyo, 113-0021, Japan.

617.06 USA ISSN 1939-9782
➤ **JOURNAL OF COGNITIVE REHABILITATION (ONLINE);** a publication for the therapist, family and patient. Text in English. 1991. q. USD 50 to individuals; USD 100 to institutions (effective 2011). adv. back issues avail. **Document type:** *Journal, Academic/Scholarly.* **Description:** Designed for the therapist, family and patient covering all aspects of the diagnosis and treatment of brain injury from any source including traumatic injury, stroke, attention deficit, tumor, encephalitis, multiple sclerosis or other brain anomaly.

Media: Online - full text.
Published by: NeuroScience Publishers, 6555 Carrollton Ave, Indianapolis, IN 46220. TEL 317-257-9672, FAX 317-257-9674, nsc@neuroscience.cnter.com, http://www.neuroscience.cnter.com. Ed. Odie L Bracy III. Adv. contact Nancy Bracy.

615.85155 USA ISSN 1089-313X
RC1220.D35
➤ **JOURNAL OF DANCE MEDICINE & SCIENCE.** Text in English. 1997. q. USD 95 domestic to non-members (print or online ed.); USD 115 foreign to non-members (print or online ed.); USD 142 combined subscription domestic to non-members (print & online eds.); USD 172 combined subscription foreign to non-members (print & online eds.); free to members (effective 2010). adv. bk.rev. **Document type:** *Journal, Academic/Scholarly.* **Description:** Focuses on bringing you the current results of clinical and experimental research and provides you with one source for up-to-date information.
Related titles: Online - full text ed.: (from IngentaConnect).
Indexed: A26, C06, C07, C08, CA, CINAHL, EMBASE, ExcerpMed, H12, I05, IBT&D, MEDLINE, P30, R09, SCOPUS, SD, T02.
—BLDSC (4967.360000), IE, Ingenta. **CCC.**
Published by: (International Association for Dance Medicine & Science), J Michael Ryan Publishing, Inc., 24 Crescent Dr N, Andover, NJ 07821. TEL 973-786-7777, FAX 973-786-7776, info@jmichaelryan.com, http://www.jmichaelryan.com/. Eds. John Solomon, Ruth Solomon. Adv. contact James Costello. Circ: 1,200 (paid).

➤ **JOURNAL OF DISABILITY AND ORAL HEALTH.** *see* HANDICAPPED

➤ **JOURNAL OF GERIATRIC PHYSICAL THERAPY.** *see* GERONTOLOGY AND GERIATRICS

615.82 USA ISSN 0894-1130
RC951 CODEN: JHTHFX
➤ **JOURNAL OF HAND THERAPY.** Text in English. 1987. q. USD 193 in United States to institutions; USD 232 elsewhere to institutions (effective 2012). adv. illus. back issues avail. **Document type:** *Journal, Academic/Scholarly.* **Description:** Designed for hand therapists, occupational and physical therapists, and other hand specialists involved in the rehabilitation of disabling hand problems.
Related titles: Online - full text ed.: ISSN 1545-004X (from ScienceDirect).
Indexed: A22, C06, C07, C08, CINAHL, CurCont, EMBASE, ErgAb, ExcerpMed, IndMed, Inpharma, MEDLINE, P20, P22, P24, P30, P48, P54, PQC, R10, RILM, Reac, SCI, SCOPUS, W07.
—BLDSC (4996.623500), GNLM, IE, Infotrieve, Ingenta. **CCC.**
Published by: (American Society of Hand Therapists), Hanley & Belfus, Inc. (Subsidiary of: Elsevier Health Sciences), 210 S 13th St, Philadelphia, PA 19107. TEL 215-546-7293, 800-962-1892, FAX 215-790-9330, http://www.elsevierhealth.com. Ed. Paul LaStayo. Pub. Chris Baumle. Adv. contact Danny Wang TEL 212-633-3158.

➤ **JOURNAL OF IMAGERY RESEARCH IN SPORT AND PHYSICAL ACTIVITY.** *see* PSYCHOLOGY

➤ **JOURNAL OF KNEE SURGERY.** *see* MEDICAL SCIENCES—Surgery

615.82 USA
➤ **JOURNAL OF LIFE CARE PLANNING.** Text in English. 2008. q. USD 85 to non-members; free to members (effective 2010). adv. **Document type:** *Journal, Academic/Scholarly.* **Description:** Published manuscripts relevant to the practice and processes of life care planning, and provides a forum for the debate and discussion of practice issues related to certification, ethics, standards and methodologies.
Indexed: CA.
Published by: (Association of Life Care Planning), Elliott & Fitzpatrick, Inc., 1135 Cedar Shoals Dr, Athens, GA 30605. TEL 800-843-4977, FAX 706-227-2204, myorder@elliottfitzpatrick.com. Circ: 500.

616.822 GBR ISSN 1066-9817
CODEN: JMMTFZ
➤ **THE JOURNAL OF MANUAL & MANIPULATIVE THERAPY.** Text in English. 1993. q. GBP 203 combined subscription to institutions (print & online eds.); USD 341 combined subscription in United States to institutions (print & online eds.) (effective 2012). back issues avail.; reprint service avail. from PSC. **Document type:** *Journal, Academic/Scholarly.* **Description:** Aims to improve patient care through clinically relevant articles on manual therapy.
Related titles: Online - full text ed.: ISSN 2042-6186. GBP 183 to institutions; USD 307 in United States to institutions (effective 2012) (from IngentaConnect).
Indexed: A01, A02, A03, A08, C06, C07, C08, C11, CA, CINAHL, EMBASE, ExcerpMed, H04, P30, R09, R10, Reac, SCOPUS, SD, T02.
—BLDSC (5011.603000), IE, Ingenta. **CCC.**
Published by: (American Academy of Orthopaedic Manual Physical Therapists USA), Maney Publishing, Ste 1C, Joseph's Well, Hanover Walk, Leeds, W Yorks LS3 1AB, United Kingdom. TEL 44-113-2432800, FAX 44-113-3868178, maney@maney.co.uk, http://www.maney.co.uk.

616.85154 USA ISSN 0022-2917
CODEN: JMUTA2
➤ **JOURNAL OF MUSIC THERAPY.** Text in English. 1962. q. USD 20 per issue; free to members (effective 2009). adv. bk.rev. charts; illus. index. back issues avail.; reprints avail. **Document type:** *Journal, Academic/Scholarly.* **Description:** Contains reports on research in the areas of music therapy and the use of music in treatment and rehabilitation settings.
Supersedes (in 1964): National Association for Music Therapy. Bulletin
Related titles: Microform ed.: (from PQC); Online - full text ed.
Indexed: A20, A22, ASCA, B04, BRD, C06, C07, CA, CurCont, DIP, E-psyche, E02, E03, E06, ECER, EMBASE, ERI, EdA, EdI, ExcerpMed, FamI, HospLI, IBR, IBZ, IIMP, IndMed, M11, MAG, MEDLINE, MusicInd, P03, P10, P18, P20, P22, P24, P25, P30, P48, P53, P54, PQC, PsycInfo, PsycholAb, RILM, SCOPUS, SSCI, T02, W03, W05, W07.
—BLDSC (5021.160000), GNLM, IE, Infotrieve, Ingenta.
Published by: American Music Therapy Association, 8455 Colesville Rd, Ste 1000, Silver Spring, MD 20910. TEL 301-589-3300, FAX 301-589-5175, info@musictherapy.org. Ed. Jayne Standley. **Subscr. to:** Allen Press Inc., PO Box 1897, Lawrence, KS 66044. http://www.allenpress.com.

➤ **JOURNAL OF NEUROENGINEERING AND REHABILITATION.** *see* MEDICAL SCIENCES—Psychiatry And Neurology

➤ **JOURNAL OF OCCUPATIONAL REHABILITATION.** *see* OCCUPATIONAL HEALTH AND SAFETY

615.8515 AUS ISSN 1442-7591
➤ **JOURNAL OF OCCUPATIONAL SCIENCE.** Abbreviated title: J O S. Text in English. 1993. 3/yr. GBP 222 combined subscription in United Kingdom to institutions (print & online eds.); EUR 293, AUD 359, USD 366 combined subscription to institutions (print & online eds.) (effective 2012). adv. bk.rev. back issues avail.; reprint service avail. from PSC. **Document type:** *Journal, Academic/Scholarly.* **Description:** Brings out discussion papers and research articles and promotes the study of humans as occupational beings.
Formerly (until 1998): Journal of Occupational Science: Australia (1320-0038)
Related titles: Online - full text ed.: ISSN 2158-1576. GBP 199 in United Kingdom to institutions; EUR 263, AUD 323, USD 330 to institutions (effective 2012).
Indexed: AMED, AgeL, AmHI, C06, C07, C08, CA, CINAHL, H07, P03, PsycInfo, PsycholAb, S02, S03, SCOPUS, SD, SOPODA, SociolAb, T02.
—BLDSC (5026.130000), IE, Ingenta. **CCC.**
Published by: (Association of Occupational Science Inc.), Taylor & Francis Australasia (Subsidiary of: Taylor & Francis Group), Level 2, 11 Queens Rd, Melbourne, VIC 3004, Australia. TEL 61-3-98662811, FAX 61-3-98668822, enquiries@tandf.com.au, http://www.tandf.co.uk.

➤ **JOURNAL OF OCCUPATIONAL THERAPY, SCHOOLS AND EARLY INTERVENTION;** innovations in practice, theory, and research. *see* EDUCATION—Special Education And Rehabilitation

➤ **JOURNAL OF ORTHOPAEDIC AND SPORTS PHYSICAL THERAPY.** *see* MEDICAL SCIENCES—Sports Medicine

615.8 IND ISSN 2079-0015
▼ ➤ **JOURNAL OF PHYSICAL THERAPY.** Text and summaries in English. 2010 (Apr.). q. looseleaf. USD 200 (effective 2011). adv. bk.rev. abstr.; bibl.; charts; illus.; stat. Index. back issues avail.; reprints avail. **Document type:** *Journal, Academic/Scholarly.* **Description:** Dedicated to physical therapy profession.
Related titles: Online - full text ed.: ISSN 2079-9209. free (effective 2011).
Indexed: C06.
Address: B-6, KMC Staff Quarters, Light house Hill Rd, Mangalore, Karnataka 575 001, India. TEL 91-9448039501, senthil.kumar@manipal.edu. Ed. Senthil P Kumar. Pub. Arun Balasubbramaniam.

615.82 USA ISSN 0899-1855
➤ **JOURNAL OF PHYSICAL THERAPY EDUCATION.** Abbreviated title: J O P T E. Text in English. 1987. 3/yr. USD 75 domestic to individuals; USD 90 foreign to individuals; USD 100 domestic to institutions; USD 115 foreign to institutions; free to members (effective 2011). **Document type:** *Journal, Academic/Scholarly.*
Related titles: Online - full text ed.: ISSN 1938-3533.
Indexed: A22, AMED, C06, C07, C08, CINAHL, P24, P48, PQC, R09.
—BLDSC (5036.215800), IE, Ingenta. **CCC.**
Published by: American Physical Therapy Association, Section on Education, 1111 N Fairfax St, Alexandria, VA 22314. TEL 800-999-2782 ext 3230, FAX 703-706-8575, EducationSection@apta.org. Ed. Judith Stoecker.

615.8 JPN ISSN 0915-5287
JOURNAL OF PHYSICAL THERAPY SCIENCE. Text in English. 1989. s-a. membership. abstr.; charts; illus. index. **Document type:** *Journal, Academic/Scholarly.* **Description:** Publishes original papers that deal with significant areas of physical therapy and exercise physiology.
Related titles: Online - full content ed.: free (effective 2011); Online - full text ed.
Indexed: AMED, C06, C07, C08, CA, CINAHL, PEI, R09, SCI, SCOPUS, SD, T02, W07.
—BLDSC (5036.216000), IE, Ingenta.
Published by: (Society of Physical Therapy Science/Rigaku Ryoho Kagakugakkai), I P E C Inc., 1-24-11 Sugamo, Toshima-ku, Tokyo, 170-0002, Japan. TEL 81-3-5978-4067, FAX 81-3-5978-4068. Ed., R&P Hitoshi Maruyama. Circ: 1,800. **Dist. overseas by:** Japan Publications Trading Co., Ltd., Book Export II Dept, PO Box 5030, Tokyo International, Tokyo 101-3191, Japan. TEL 81-3-32923753, FAX 81-3-32920410, infoserials@jptco.co.jp, http://www.jptco.co.jp.

615.8 AUS ISSN 1836-9553
RM695
➤ **JOURNAL OF PHYSIOTHERAPY.** Abbreviated title: A J B. Text in English. 1954. q. AUD 176 domestic to individuals; AUD 210 foreign to individuals; AUD 346.50 domestic to institutions; AUD 370 foreign to institutions (effective 2010). adv. bk.rev.; video rev. index. 88 p./no.; back issues avail. **Document type:** *Journal, Academic/Scholarly.* **Description:** Contains original scientific articles, book reviews, details on upcoming events and letters.
Formerly (until 2010): Australian Journal of Physiotherapy (0004-9514)
Related titles: Online - full text ed.: ISSN 1836-9561 (from ScienceDirect).
Indexed: A11, A22, A26, AMED, C06, C07, C08, CA, CINAHL, CurCont, EMBASE, ExcerpMed, FoSS&M, H11, H12, I05, MEDLINE, P20, P22, P24, P30, P48, P54, PQC, R10, Reac, SCI, SCOPUS, SD, T02, W07.
—BLDSC (1811.100000), GNLM, IE, Infotrieve, Ingenta. **CCC.**
Published by: Australian Physiotherapy Association, Level 1, 1175 Toorak Rd, Camberwell, Melbourne, VIC 3124, Australia. TEL 61-3-90920888, FAX 61-3-90920899, national.office@physiotherapy.asn.au, http://apa.advsol.com.au. Eds. Judy Waters, Linda Denehy, Louise Ada, Dr. Rob Herbert. Adv. contact Dominic Bruton-Gibney TEL 61-3-90920834. color page AUD 1,565; trim 210 x 297. Circ: 11,000.

615.8 362 USA ISSN 0022-4154
HD7255.A2 CODEN: JOREA
➤ **JOURNAL OF REHABILITATION.** Text in English. 1935. q. USD 95 domestic to non-members; USD 105 in Canada to non-members; USD 125 elsewhere to non-members; free to members (effective 2010). bk.rev. illus.; pat. index. 64 p./no.; back issues avail. **Document type:** *Journal, Academic/Scholarly.* **Description:** Covers counseling, restorative services, retraining, and placement of persons disabled by physical, mental, emotional or social disabilities. Provides articles deal with supervisory role, legislative concerns, consumer, current trends in rehabilitation etc.
Formerly (until 1945): National Rehabilitation News (0093-1756)
Related titles: Audio cassette/tape ed.; Braille ed.; Microfilm ed.: (from PQC); Online - full text ed.
Indexed: A01, A02, A03, A08, A20, A22, A25, A26, AMED, AMHA, ASCA, B04, B14, B28, BRD, BRI, C06, C07, C08, C11, C12, CA, CINAHL, CISA, CurCont, E08, ECER, F09, FamI, G08, H04, H09, H11, H12, H13, HlthInd, HospLI, I05, IndMed, P02, P10, P13, P19, P20, P24, P26, P27, P30, P48, P50, P53, P54, PCI, PQC, PsycholAb, R09, RehabLit, S02, S03, S05, S08, S09, SCOPUS, SD, SSAI, SSAb, SSCI, SSI, T02, W03, W05, W07.
—BLDSC (5048.850000), GNLM, IE, Infotrieve, Ingenta.
Published by: National Rehabilitation Association, 633 S Washington St, Alexandria, VA 22314. TEL 703-836-0850, FAX 703-836-0848, info@nationalrehab.org, http://www.nationalrehab.org. Eds. Paul J Toriello, Paul P Alston TEL 252-744-6300.

615.82 USA ISSN 0148-3846
HD7255.A2
➤ **JOURNAL OF REHABILITATION ADMINISTRATION.** Abbreviated title: J R A. Text in English. 1977. s-a. USD 85 to non-members; free to members (effective 2010). index. back issues avail. **Document type:** *Journal, Academic/Scholarly.* **Description:** Publishes theoretical papers, applied research studies, and practice reports designed to improve the practice of administration, management and supervision in a wide variety of human service settings.
Formerly (until 1977): Rehabilitation Administration
Indexed: AMED, CA, E-psyche, PsycholAb, R09, SD, T02.
—BLDSC (5048.870000), IE, Ingenta.
Published by: Elliott & Fitzpatrick, Inc., 1135 Cedar Shoals Dr, Athens, GA 30605. TEL 800-843-4977, FAX 706-227-2204, myorder@elliottfitzpatrick.com. Circ: 500.

615.82 JPN ISSN 1348-6756
JOURNAL OF REHABILITATION AND HEALTH SCIENCES. Text in Japanese. 2003. a. **Document type:** *Journal, Academic/Scholarly.*
Related titles: Online - full text ed.
Published by: Oosaka Furitsu Kango Daigaku, Sougou Rihabiriteshon Gakubu/Osaka Prefecture University, School of Comprehensive Rehabilitation, 3-7-30, Habikino, Habikino City, 583-8555, Japan. TEL 82-72-9502111, FAX 82-72-9502131.

615.82 AUS ISSN 1834-2612
RA645.T62
➤ **JOURNAL OF SMOKING CESSATION.** Text in English. 2006. s-a. AUD 150 domestic; AUD 165 foreign (effective 2011). back issues avail. **Document type:** *Journal, Academic/Scholarly.* **Description:** Provides observational studies for assisting smokers to quit.
Media: Online - full text. **Related titles:** Print ed.
Indexed: A01, P30, SCOPUS.
Published by: (Australian Association of Smoking Cessation Professionals), Australian Academic Press Pty. Ltd., 32 Jeays St, Bowen Hills, QLD 4006, Australia. TEL 61-7-32571176, FAX 61-7-32525908, aap@australianacademicpress.com.au, http://www.australianacademicpress.com.au. Ed. Renee Bittoun.

615.82 USA ISSN 1079-0268
CODEN: JSCMC3
➤ **JOURNAL OF SPINAL CORD MEDICINE.** Abbreviated title: J S C M. Text in English. 1978. bi-m. GBP 298 combined subscription to institutions (print & online eds.); USD 428 combined subscription in United States to institutions (print & online eds.) (effective 2012). adv. bk.rev. abstr. back issues avail.; reprint service avail. from PSC. **Document type:** *Journal, Academic/Scholarly.* **Description:** For physicians, researchers and health professionals who work in the spinal cord injury field.
Formerly (until 1995): American Paraplegia Society. Journal (0195-2307)
Related titles: Online - full text ed.: ISSN 2045-7723. GBP 267 to institutions; USD 377 in United States to institutions (effective 2012) (from IngentaConnect).
Indexed: A22, C06, C07, C08, CINAHL, CurCont, E-psyche, EMBASE, ExcerpMed, INI, IndMed, MEDLINE, NSCI, P30, R10, Reac, SCI, SCOPUS, W07.
—BLDSC (5066.181500), GNLM, IE, Infotrieve, Ingenta. **CCC.**
Published by: (Academy of Spinal Cord Injury Professionals (A S C I P)), Maney Publishing, Ste 1C, Joseph's Well, Hanover Walk, Leeds, W Yorks LS3 1AB, United Kingdom. TEL 44-113-2432800, FAX 44-113-3868178, maney@maney.co.uk, http://www.maney.co.uk. Ed. Donald R Bodner.

➤ **JOURNAL OF SPORT REHABILITATION.** *see* MEDICAL SCIENCES—Sports Medicine

617.1 615.82 GBR ISSN 2044-0707
JOURNAL OF SPORTS THERAPY; tri-annual review of sports therapy theory and practice. Abbreviated title: J S T. Text in English. 2008. 3/yr. free (effective 2010). back issues avail. **Document type:** *Journal, Academic/Scholarly.* **Description:** Contains articles on sports medicine, biomechanics, performance analysis, strength and conditioning, nutrition, and sports psychology.
Media: Online - full text.
Published by: University College Birmingham, Summer Row, Birmingham, B3 1JB, United Kingdom. TEL 44-121-6041000, international@ucb.ac.uk, http://www.ucb.ac.uk.

JOURNAL OF THERAPEUTIC HORTICULTURE. *see* GARDENING AND HORTICULTURE

613.7 USA ISSN 1936-7007
➤ **JOURNAL OF UNDERGRADUATE KINESIOLOGY RESEARCH.** Text in English. 2005. s-a. free (effective 2011). back issues avail. **Document type:** *Journal, Academic/Scholarly.* **Description:** Dedicated to promoting original undergraduate research in kinesiology.
Media: Online - full text.
Indexed: PEI.
Published by: University of Wisconsin at Eau Claire, Department of Kinesiology, McPhee Physical Education Center, Eau Claire, WI 54702-4004. TEL 715-836-3840, kinesiology@uwec.edu, http://www.uwec.edu/kin.

615.82 JPN ISSN 0919-195X
KANAGAWAKEN RIGAKU RYOHOSHIKAI NYUSU/KANAGAWA PHYSICAL THERAPY ASSOCIATION. NEWS. Text in Japanese. bi-m. **Document type:** *Journal, Academic/Scholarly.*
Published by: Kanagawaken Rigaku Ryohoshikai/Kanagawa Physical Therapy Association, 4-12 Kusunoki-cho, Nishi-ku, Aariajin 20, no. 101, Yokohama, Kanagawa 220-0003, Japan. TEL 81-45-3263225, FAX 81-45-3263226, http://www.pt-kanagawa.or.jp/.

615.82 CHN ISSN 1005-832X
KANG FU/REHABILITATION. Text in Chinese. 1986. s-m. USD 36 (effective 2009).
Published by: Shanghai Jiaoyu Baokan Zongshe/Shanghai Educational Press Group, no.36, Alley 491, Changning Lu, Shanghai, 200050, China. TEL 86-21-62525555, FAX 86-21-62525560, http://www.snb.sh.cn/. **Dist. by:** China International Book Trading Corp, 35 Chegongzhuang Xilu, Haidian District, PO Box 399, Beijing 100044, China. TEL 86-10-68412045, FAX 86-10-68412023, cibtc@mail.cibtc.com.cn, http://www.cibtc.com.cn.

615.82 JPN ISSN 1346-9606
KANSAI RIGAKU RYOUHOU/JOURNAL OF KANSAI PHYSICAL THERAPY. Text in Japanese. a. **Document type:** *Journal, Academic/Scholarly.*
Related titles: Online - full text ed.: ISSN 1349-9572.
Published by: Kansai rigaku Ryouhou Kenkyuukai/Academy for Kansei Physical Therapy, Geriatric Health Services Facility, Kosumosu-rakujuen, Geriatric Rehabilitation Group, 858, Mori, Kaizuka-City, Osaka 597-0044, Japan. TEL 81-724-470007 ext 444, FAX 81-724-470015, inquiry@enro.info, http://www.enro.info/.

616.07 FRA ISSN 0766-2262
KINE ACTUALITE. Text in French. 1927. 43/yr. EUR 125 domestic; EUR 127 foreign (effective 2009). adv. **Document type:** *Magazine, Trade.* **Description:** Professional news about physiotherapy, the social system, health, reports on congresses, conferences, seminars. Information on Minitel, French telematic system.
Formerly (until 1984): Kinesitherapie Actualite (0754-2038); Which superseded in part (in 1970): Kinesitherapie (0246-0769); Which was formerly (until 1962): Revue des Kinesitherapeutes (0482-7945); (until 1957): Revue des Masseurs-Kinesitherapeutes (0761-1447); (until 1966): Revue des Masseurs-Kinesitherapeutes, Infirmiers et Pedicures (0761-1390); (until 1950): Revue des Professions Medicales Auxiliaires (0761-1382); (until 1948): Technicien Medical (0761-1374); (until 1947): Auxiliaire Medical (0761-1188)
Published by: Societe de Presse et d'Edition de la Kinesitherapie, 3 Rue Lespagnol, Paris, 75020, France. TEL 33-1-44-83-46-46, FAX 33-1-44-83-46-47, ka@kineactu.com. Ed. Franck Gougeon. R&P Gerard Colnat. Adv. contact Vincent Deperrest. Circ: 12,432.

616.822 FRA ISSN 1772-8827
KINE POINT PRESSE. Text in French. 1985. q. EUR 20 (effective 2010). **Document type:** *Magazine, Trade.*
Former titles (until 2005): Kine Presse (1292-7589); (until 1997): Le Magazine des Kinesitherapeutes (1262-2303); (until 1995): Kine Presse (0769-2560)
Published by: (Association de Presse et d'Edition en Kinesitherapie), Syndicat National des Masseurs Kinesitherapeutes Reeducateurs, 15 Rue de l'Epee de Bois, Paris, 75005, France. TEL 33-1-45358245, FAX 33-1-47077023, secretariat@snmkr.fr, http://www.snmkr.fr. Ed. Tristan Marechal.

615.825 FRA ISSN 1958-4385
KINER. Text in Multiple languages. 199?. a. price varies. **Document type:** *Journal, Academic/Scholarly.*
Former titles (until 2006): Kinerea (0999-9183); (until 1999): Kinerea Actualites (1164-2890)
—INIST.
Published by: Societe de Kinesitherapie de Reanimation, c/o Mr. Bourges, 141 Rue Lourmel, Paris, 75015, France. http://www.skrea.org. Ed. P. Burtin.

617.1 FRA ISSN 1779-0123
➤ **KINESITHERAPIE. LA REVUE.** Text in French. 2006. m. EUR 303 in Europe to institutions; EUR 257.59 in France to institutions; JPY 48,000 in Japan to institutions; USD 394 elsewhere to institutions (effective 2012). **Document type:** *Journal, Academic/Scholarly.*
Formed by the merger of (2001-2006): Kinesitherapie. Les Cahiers (1632-8337); Which was formerly (1962-2000): Cahiers de Kinesitherapie (0007-9782); (2001-2006): Kinesitherapie. Les Annales (1632-8345); Which was formerly (1974-2001): Annales de Kinesitherapie (0302-427X); Which was formed by the merger of (1952-1974): Journal de Kinesitherapie (0021-7751); (1936-1974): Revue de Kinesitherapie (0035-1172)
Related titles: Online - full text ed.: (from ScienceDirect).
Indexed: C06, C07, C08, CINAHL, SD.
—BLDSC (5096.047000), IE, Ingenta, INIST. **CCC.**
Published by: Elsevier Masson (Subsidiary of: Elsevier Health Sciences), 62 Rue Camille Desmoulins, Issy les Moulineaux, Cedex 92442, France. TEL 33-1-71165500, infos@elsevier-masson.fr. Ed. Pierre Trudelle.

615.8 FRA ISSN 0023-1576 CODEN: KNTSAC
KINESITHERAPIE SCIENTIFIQUE. Text in French. 1965. 11/yr. EUR 120 domestic; EUR 123 foreign (effective 2009). adv. charts; illus. **Document type:** *Magazine, Trade.* **Description:** Clinical practice articles, research in physiotherapy, analysis, scientific information.
Supersedes in part: Kinesitherapie (0246-0769)
Related titles: Online - full text ed.: ISSN 1958-5373.
Indexed: A22, FR, SD.
—BLDSC (5096.070000), IE, Infotrieve, Ingenta, INIST. **CCC.**
Published by: Societe de Presse et d'Edition de la Kinesitherapie, 3 Rue Lespagnol, Paris, 75020, France. TEL 33-1-44834646, FAX 33-1-44834647, ks@kinephysio.com, http://www.kinephysio.com. Ed. Patrick Michaud. Adv. contact Vincent Deperrest. Circ: 15,000.

615.82 JPN ISSN 1342-8551
KOCHI RIHABIRITESHON GAKUIN RIGAKU RYOHO GAKKA SOTSUGYO KENKYU RONBUNSHU/KOCHI REHABILITATION INSTITUTE. DEPARTMENT OF PHYSICAL THERAPY. GRADUATION THESES. Text in Japanese. a. **Document type:** *Journal, Academic/Scholarly.*
Formerly (until 1995): Kochi Rihabiriteshon Gakuin Sotsugyo Ronbunshu/Kochi Rehabilitation Institute. College of Physical Therapy. Bulletin of Graduate Study (0912-5825)
Published by: Kochi Rihabiriteshon Gakuin, Rigaku Ryoho Gakka/Kochi Rehabilitation Institute, Department of Physical Therapy, 1139-3, Takaoka-cho, Tosa-shi, Kochi-shi, 781-1102, Japan. TEL 81-88-8502311, FAX 81-88-8502323, kochi-reha@kochireha.ac.jp, http://www.kochireha.ac.jp/.

KOKURITSU SHINTAI SHOGAISHA RIHABIRITESHON SENTA KENKYU KIYO/NATIONAL REHABILITATION CENTER FOR PERSONS WITH DISABILITIES. RESEARCH BULLETIN. *see* HANDICAPPED

LANDELIJKE VERENIGING VAN GEAMPUTEERDEN NIEUWSBRIEF. *see* MEDICAL SCIENCES—Orthopedics And Traumatology

615.82 FRA ISSN 1778-4298
LA LETTRE DE MEDECINE PHYSIQUE ET DE READAPTATION. Text in French. 198?. q. EUR 244, USD 297 combined subscription to institutions (print & online eds.) (effective 2012). reprint service avail. from PSC. **Document type:** *Journal, Academic/Scholarly.*
Former titles (until 2006): 3 R - Reeducation Readaptation Reinsertion (1164-5970); (until 1992): R R R Sante (1156-2978)
Related titles: Online - full text ed.: ISSN 1778-4301 (from IngentaConnect).
Indexed: A22, A26, E01, SCOPUS.
—IE, Ingenta. **CCC.**
Published by: Springer France (Subsidiary of: Springer Science+Business Media), 22 Rue de Palestro, Paris, 75002, France. TEL 33-1-53009860, FAX 33-1-53009861, sylvie.kamara@springer.com.

615.82 ITA ISSN 1827-1995
M R; giornale italiano di medicina riabilitativa. (Medicina Riabilitativa) Text in Italian. 1987. q. EUR 240 combined subscription in the European Union to institutions (print & online eds.); EUR 265 combined subscription elsewhere to institutions (print & online eds.) (effective 2011). **Document type:** *Journal, Academic/Scholarly.*
Related titles: Online - full text ed.: ISSN 1827-1871.
Published by: Edizioni Minerva Medica, Corso Bramante 83-85, Turin, 10126, Italy. TEL 39-011-678282, FAX 39-011-674502, journals.dept@minervamedica.it, http://www.minervamedica.it.

615.82 GBR ISSN 1356-689X CODEN: MATHFH
➤ **MANUAL THERAPY.** Text in English. 1995. bi-m. EUR 706 in Europe to institutions; JPY 76,400 in Japan to institutions; USD 629 elsewhere to institutions (effective 2012). adv. bk.rev. abstr.; bibl. back issues avail.; reprints avail. **Document type:** *Journal, Academic/Scholarly.* **Description:** Designed to serve as a resource tool for all those engaged in the many diverse aspects of manual therapy.
Related titles: Online - full text ed.: ISSN 1532-2769 (from ScienceDirect).
Indexed: A22, A26, AMED, C06, C07, C08, CA, CINAHL, E01, EMBASE, ExcerpMed, FoSS&M, H12, I05, IndMed, MEDLINE, P30, PEI, R09, R10, Reac, SCI, SCOPUS, SD, T02, W07.
—BLDSC (5365.380000), IE, Infotrieve, Ingenta. **CCC.**
Published by: (Manipulation Association of Chartered Physiotherapists), Churchill Livingstone (Subsidiary of: Elsevier Health Sciences), The Blvd, Langford Ln, Kidlington, OX5 1GB, United Kingdom. TEL 44-1865-843434, FAX 44-1865-843970, directenquiries@elsevier.com, http://www.elsevierhealth.com/imprint.jsp?iid=9. Eds. Ann Moore, Gwendolen A Jull. Adv. contact Deborah Watkins TEL 44-20-74244280.

615.8 DEU ISSN 0025-2514
RZ301
➤ **MANUELLE MEDIZIN**; Chirotherapie, Manuelle Therapie. Text in German. 1963. bi-m. EUR 386, USD 463 combined subscription to institutions (print & online eds.) (effective 2012). adv. bk.rev. index. back issues avail.; reprint service avail. from PSC. **Document type:** *Journal, Academic/Scholarly.* **Description:** Covers all aspects of physiotherapy and related fields.
Formerly (until 2001): Manuelle Medizin und Osteopathische Medizin
Related titles: Microform ed.: (from PQC); Online - full text ed.: ISSN 1433-0466 (from IngentaConnect).
Indexed: A22, A26, AMED, E01, SCOPUS.
—BLDSC (5365.766000), GNLM, IE, Infotrieve, Ingenta, INIST. **CCC.**
Published by: (Deutsche Gesellschaft fuer Manuelle Medizin), Springer (Subsidiary of: Springer Science+Business Media), Tiergartenstr 17, Heidelberg, 69121, Germany. TEL 49-6221-4870, FAX 49-6221-345229. Circ: 10,900 (paid). **Subscr. in the Americas to:** Springer New York LLC, Journal Fulfillment, PO Box 2485, Secaucus, NJ 07096. TEL 800-777-4643, 201-348-4033, FAX 201-348-4505, journals-ny@springer.com, http://www.springer.com; **Subscr. to:** Springer Distribution Center, Kundenservice Zeitschriften, Haberstr 7, Heidelberg 69126, Germany. TEL 49-6221-3454303, FAX 49-6221-3454229, subscriptions@springer.com.

615.8 DEU ISSN 1433-2671
➤ **MANUELLE THERAPIE**; Physiotherapeutische Zeitschrift. Text in German. 1997. 5/yr. EUR 109 to institutions; EUR 145 combined subscription to institutions (print & online eds.); EUR 30 newsstand/cover (effective 2011). adv. **Document type:** *Journal, Academic/Scholarly.*
Related titles: Online - full text ed.: ISSN 1439-2348. EUR 139 to institutions (effective 2011).
Indexed: C06, C07, C08, CINAHL.
—GNLM, IE. **CCC.**
Published by: Georg Thieme Verlag, Ruedigerstr 14, Stuttgart, 70469, Germany. TEL 49-711-8931421, FAX 49-711-8931410, leser.service@thieme.de. Ed. Jochen Schomacher. Circ: 3,500 (paid).

615.82 USA ISSN 1057-378X
MASSAGE. Text in English. 1985. bi-m. USD 26 domestic; USD 51 foreign (effective 2005). adv. bk.rev.; film rev. bibl.; illus.; stat. back issues avail. **Document type:** *Magazine, Trade.* **Description:** Covers the art and science of massage therapy and related healing arts, supporting readers promoting the benfits of healing touch.
Former titles (until 1991): Massage Magazine (1045-4268); Massage and Healing Arts Magazine; Massage and Bodywork Magazine
Related titles: CD-ROM ed.; Online - full text ed.
Indexed: A04, A10, C06, C07, C11, R09, SD, T02, V03.
—Ingenta.
Published by: Massage Magazine, 5150 Palm Valley Rd, Ponte Vedra, FL 32082. TEL 904-285-6020, 800-533-4263. Ed., R&P Karen Menehan TEL 831-477-1176. Pub. Kate Spencer. Adv. contact Jeff Schmidt. Circ: 45,000 (paid).

615.82 615.53 AUS ISSN 1328-8431
MASSAGE AUSTRALIA. Text in English. 1992. q. free to members (effective 2009). adv. bk.rev. back issues avail. **Document type:** *Magazine, Trade.* **Description:** Covers professional massage therapy, news and information.
Formerly (until issue 21): Touch Australia (1037-6801)
Related titles: Online - full text ed.
Indexed: A04, A10, A11, C11, T02, V03.
—IE.
Published by: Massage Australia Pty. Ltd., PO Box 198, Bargo, NSW 2528, Australia.

616.822 NLD ISSN 1877-4423
MASSAGE MAGAZINE; vakblad voor wellness en therapie. Text in Dutch. 2008. bi-m. EUR 40.25 domestic; EUR 41.50 in Belgium (effective 2010). adv. **Document type:** *Magazine, Trade.*
Published by: Koggeschip Vakbladen B.V., Hettenheuvelweg 41-43, Postbus 1198, Amsterdam, 1000 BD, Netherlands. TEL 31-20-6916666, FAX 31-20-6960396, http://www.koggeschip-vakbladen.nl. Ed. Marco D M Jouret. Pub. Anthony van Trigt. adv.: page EUR 2,540; trim 210 x 297. Circ: 10,740.

616.822 CAN ISSN 1499-8084
MASSAGE THERAPY CANADA. Text in English. 2002. 3/yr. CAD 20.13 domestic; USD 25 in United States; USD 55 elsewhere (effective 2005). **Document type:** *Magazine, Trade.*
Published by: M T Publishing, 1088 Fennell Ave E, 2nd Fl, Hamilton, ON L8T 1R8, Canada. TEL 888-247-2176.

616.822 CAN ISSN 1911-8813
MASSAGE THERAPY TODAY. Text in English. 2007 (Jan.). bi-m. adv. **Document type:** *Magazine, Trade.*
Indexed: SD.
Published by: Ontario Massage Therapist Association, 2 Carlton St., Ste 1304, Toronto, ON M5B 1J3, Canada. TEL 416-979-2010, 800-668-2022, FAX 416-979-1144, info@omta.com, http://www.omta.com.

616.822 USA ISSN 1531-8079
MASSAGE TODAY. Text in English. 2001. m. USD 48 (effective 2009). **Document type:** *Magazine, Trade.*
Related titles: Online - full text ed.
Indexed: A26, C06, C07, C08, CINAHL, H12, I05.
Published by: M P A Media, PO Box 4139, Huntington Beach, CA 92605-4139. TEL 714-230-3150, 800-324-7758, FAX 714-899-4273, editorial@mpamedia.com, http://www.mpamedia.com. Ed. Ramon McLeod.

616.822 NLD ISSN 1877-5241
MASSAGE ZAKEN. Text in Dutch. 2006. bi-m. EUR 39 domestic; EUR 49 foreign (effective 2011). adv. **Document type:** *Magazine, Trade.*
Published by: Body Biz International B.V., Postbus 178, Gennep, 6590 AD, Netherlands. TEL 31-485-513316, FAX 31-485-518461, info@bodybiz.nl, http://www.body-meets-beauty.nl.

615.82 ESP ISSN 0214-8714
MEDICINA DE REHABILITACION. Text in Spanish. 1986. q. EUR 35 domestic; USD 60 foreign (effective 2003). **Document type:** *Magazine, Academic/Scholarly.*
—IE, Ingenta.
Published by: (Liga para el Desarrollo de la Rehabilitacion), Editores Medicos, S.A., Alsasua 16, Madrid, 28013, Spain. TEL 34-91-3768140, FAX 34-91-3769907, edimsa@edimsa.es, http://www.edimsa.es. Circ: 3,000.

615.82 ARG ISSN 0374-9045
MEDICINA FISICA Y REHABILITACION. Text in Spanish. 1950. irreg. **Document type:** *Monographic series, Academic/Scholarly.*
Indexed: P30.
Published by: Sociedad Argentina de Medicina y Rehabilitacion, Echeverria, 955, Buenos Aires, 1428, Argentina. TEL 54-11-4782608, samfyr@volsinectis.com.ar, http://www.samfyr.com.ar/index.htm.

615.82 RUS ISSN 1560-9537
MEDIKO-SOTSYAL'NAYA EKSPRETIZA I REABILITATSIYA/MEDICOSOCIAL EXPERTISE AND REHABILITATION. Text in Russian; Contents page in English. 1998. q. USD 273 foreign (effective 2005). adv. Website rev. abstr. reprints avail. **Document type:** *Journal, Academic/Scholarly.* **Description:** Covers disability prevention, medical and social examinations; medical, social and everyday rehabilitation of disabled persons, specialization of doctors in this field.
Indexed: RefZh.
—East View.
Published by: Izdatel'stvo Meditsina/Meditsina Publishers, ul B Pirogovskaya, d 2, str 5, Moscow, 119435, Russian Federation. TEL 7-095-2483324, meditsina@mtu-net.ru, http://www.medlit.ru. Ed. Sergey N Puzin. Pub. A M Stochik. R&P Valerii I Chissov. **Dist. by:** East View Information Services, 10601 Wayzata Blvd, Minneapolis, MN 55305. TEL 952-252-1201, 800-477-1005, FAX 952-252-1202, info@eastview.com, http://www.eastview.com.

615.82 UKR
MEDITSINSKAYA REABILITATSIYA, KURORTOLOGIYA, FIZIOTERAPIYA/MEDICAL REHABILITATION, BALNEOLOGY, PHYSIOTHERAPY. Text in Russian. 1994. q. USD 134 foreign (effective 2007). **Document type:** *Journal, Academic/Scholarly.*
Published by: Vseukrains'ka Asotsiatsiya Fizioterapevtiv i Kurortolohiv, Per Lermontovskii 6, Odessa, Ukraine. **Dist. by:** East View Information Services, 10601 Wayzata Blvd, Minneapolis, MN 55305. TEL 952-252-1201, 800-477-1005, FAX 952-252-1202, info@eastview.com, http://www.eastview.com.

615.82 USA ISSN 2153-5736
▼ ➤ **MINDFULNESS (BROCKTON)**; a journal of the here and now. Text in English. 2009. q. free (effective 2010). **Document type:** *Journal, Academic/Scholarly.* **Description:** Covers information about mindfulness and therapeutic Practice.
Media: Online - full text.
—Linda Hall.
Published by: Rem Wholisystems http://www.remwholisystems.com/about.html.

615.82 JPN ISSN 1346-0773
MONTHLY BOOK MEDICAL REHABILITATION. Text in Japanese. 2001. m. price varies. **Document type:** *Monographic series, Academic/Scholarly.*
Published by: Zennihon Byoin Shuppankai, 3-16-4 Hongo, Bunkyo-Ku, 7F, Tokyo, 113-0033, Japan. TEL 81-3-56895989, FAX 81-3-56898030, http://www.zenniti.com/.

613.7 USA ISSN 1087-1640
QP303
➤ **MOTOR CONTROL.** Text in English. 1997. q. USD 446 domestic to institutions; USD 456 foreign to institutions; USD 528 combined subscription domestic to institutions (print & online eds.); USD 538 combined subscription foreign to institutions (print & online eds.) (effective 2012). adv. bk.rev.; software rev.; video rev. charts; illus.; stat. back issues avail.; reprint service avail. from PSC. **Document type:** *Journal, Academic/Scholarly.* **Description:** Designed to provide an international and multidisciplinary forum for the exchange of scientific information on the control of movement across the lifespan, including issues related to motor disorders.
Related titles: Online - full text ed.: ISSN 1543-2696. USD 446 to institutions (effective 2012).
Indexed: A22, B21, C06, C07, C08, CA, CINAHL, DIP, E-psyche, EMBASE, ErgAb, ExcerpMed, FoSS&M, IBR, IBZ, IndMed, MEDLINE, NSA, P03, P30, PEI, PsycInfo, PsycholAb, R09, R10, Reac, SCI, SCOPUS, SD, T02, W07.
—BLDSC (5972.910000), IE, Infotrieve, Ingenta. **CCC.**
Published by: Human Kinetics, 1607 N Market St, Champaign, IL 61820. TEL 800-747-4457, FAX 217-351-2674, info@hkusa.com, http://www.humankinetics.com. Ed. T Richard Nichols TEL 404-894-3986. Pub. Rainer Martens. R&P Martha Gullo TEL 217-403-7534. Adv. contact Amy Bleich TEL 217-403-7803.

615.837 ESP ISSN 0214-7572
MUSICA, TERAPIA Y COMUNICACION. Text in Spanish. 1987. s-a. back issues avail. **Document type:** *Journal, Academic/Scholarly.*
Indexed: RILM.
Published by: Centro de Investigaciones Musicoterapeuticas, Ribera, 8 Interior 1o Izq, Bilbao, 45005, Spain.

615.82 DNK ISSN 1902-9977
MUSKULOSKELETAL FYSIOTERAPI. Text in Danish, English. 2001. q. DKK 300 (effective 2008). adv. bk.rev. **Document type:** *Magazine, Trade.*
Formerly (until 2008): Muskuloskeletalt Forum (1602-608X); Which was formed by the merger of (1981-2001): Manuel Medicin (0107-9190); (1978-2001): M T Nyt (1602-6071)
Related titles: Online - full text ed.: ISSN 1902-9985. 2002.
—CCC.
Published by: (Dansk Selskab for Muskuloskeletal Medicin), Danske Fysioterapeuters Faggruppe for Manuel Terapi, c/o Martin B. Josefsen, Overgade 3, Skjalbjerg, Vissenbjerg, 5492, Denmark. TEL 45-61-706629, mbj@rygfys.dk. Eds. Per Kjaer, Martin B Josefsen.

615.83 NLD ISSN 1871-7241
N V G N MAGAZINE GEESTELIJKE GENEZER. Text in Dutch. 1966. 4/yr. EUR 20 (effective 2009).
Formerly (until 2003): De Geestelijke Genezer (0928-320X)
Published by: Nederlandse Vereniging voor Geestelijke- en Natuurgeneeswijzen, Postbus 53282, Amsterdam, 1007 RG, Netherlands. TEL 31-182-383854, info@nvgn.nl, http://www.nvgn.nl.

615.82 NLD ISSN 1874-2726
NEDERLANDS TIJDSCHRIFT VOOR KINDERFYSIOTHERAPIE. Text in Dutch. q. EUR 60 (effective 2009). adv. **Document type:** *Magazine, Trade.*
Formerly (until 2006): Kinderfysiotherapie (1571-6716)
Published by: Nederlandse Vereniging voor Fysiotherapie in de Kinder- en Jeugdgezondheidszorg, Postbus 248, Amersfoort, 3800 AE, Netherlands. TEL 31-33-4672900, info@nvfk.nl, http://www.nvfk.nl. Circ: 1,200.

NEUROCONNECTIONS. *see* MEDICAL SCIENCES—Psychiatry And Neurology

NEW BULLETIN (LONDON). *see* HANDICAPPED

615.8 NZL ISSN 0303-7193
RM695
➤ **NEW ZEALAND JOURNAL OF PHYSIOTHERAPY.** Text in English. 1938. 3/yr. NZD 55 domestic to non-members; NZD 80 foreign to non-members; free to members (effective 2011). adv. bk.rev. abstr.; charts; illus.; stat. back issues avail. **Document type:** *Journal, Academic/Scholarly.* **Description:** Covers all aspect of the theory and practice of physiotherapy.
Related titles: Online - full text ed.: ISSN 2230-4886. free (effective 2011).
Indexed: A22, A26, AMED, C06, C07, C08, CINAHL, H12, I05, INZP, Inpharma, P24, P35, P48, PQC, R09, R10, Reac.
—BLDSC (6094.640000), IE, Ingenta. **CCC.**
Published by: New Zealand Society of Physiotherapists Inc., Marion Sq, PO Box 27386, Wellington, 6141, New Zealand. TEL 64-4-8016500, FAX 64-4-8015571, nzsp@physiotherapy.org.nz. Ed. Leigh Hale. Adv. contact Amy Macklin.

615.8 NGA ISSN 0331-3735
➤ **NIGERIA SOCIETY OF PHYSIOTHERAPY. JOURNAL.** Abbreviated title: J N S P. Text in English. 1972. s-a. NGN 250, USD 20. adv. **Document type:** *Journal, Academic/Scholarly.* **Description:** Contains articles dealing with the pathology and research aspects of physiotherapy.
Indexed: A26, C06, C07, C08, CINAHL, E08, H12, I05, S09.
Published by: Nigeria Society of Physiotherapy, Department of Physiotherapy, College of Medicine, University of, Idi-Araba, Lagos, Lagos, Nigeria. FAX 234-1-837630, TELEX 0027636 NG. Ed., Adv. contact Dr. Isaac O Owoeye. Circ: 1,000.

615.85154 GBR ISSN 0809-8131
➤ **NORDIC JOURNAL OF MUSIC THERAPY/NORDISK TIDSSKRIFT FOR MUSIKKETERAPI.** Text mainly in English; Text occasionally in Danish, Norwegian, Swedish. 1992. s-a. GBP 194 combined subscription in United Kingdom to institutions (print & online eds.); EUR 310, USD 390 combined subscription to institutions (print & online eds.) (effective 2012). adv. bk.rev.; music rev. abstr. back issues avail.; reprint service avail. from PSC. **Document type:** *Journal, Academic/Scholarly.* **Description:** Publishes new research, theoretical developments, meta-reflections and discussions in the broad field of music therapy.
Formerly (until 2001): Norsk Tidsskrift for Musikkterapi (0803-9828)
Related titles: Online - full text ed.: ISSN 1944-8260. GBP 175 in United Kingdom to institutions; EUR 280, USD 352 to institutions (effective 2012).
Indexed: A01, A26, C06, C07, C08, CA, CINAHL, E-psyche, H12, I05, M11, MusicInd, P03, P48, PQC, PsycInfo, PsycholAb, RILM, SCOPUS, SSCI, T02, W07.
—BLDSC (6117.927010), IE. **CCC.**
Published by: (Griegakademiets Senter for Musikkterapiforsking NOR), Routledge (Subsidiary of: Taylor & Francis Group), 4 Park Sq, Milton Park, Abingdon, Oxon OX14 4RN, United Kingdom. info@routledge.co.uk, http://www.tandf.co.uk. Ed. Christian Gold. Pub., R&P, Adv. contact Rune Rolvsjord. page USD 240; trim 140 x 205. Circ: 575 (paid and controlled).

615.82 USA ISSN 1558-6170
NORTH AMERICAN JOURNAL OF SPORTS PHYSICAL THERAPY (ONLINE). Text in English. 2006. q. USD 60 to individuals; USD 150 to institutions; free to members (effective 2010). adv.
Media: Online - full text.
Published by: American Physical Therapy Association, Sports Physical Therapy Section, 9002 N Meridian St, Ste 112A, Indianapolis, IN 46260. TEL 317-846-5757, 877-732-5009, FAX 317-846-5775, tjackson@spts.org. Ed. Michael L Voight.

615.8515 GBR ISSN 0969-5095
OCCUPATIONAL THERAPY NEWS. Abbreviated title: O T N. Text in English. 1993. m. free to members (effective 2009). adv. **Document type:** *Magazine, Trade.* **Description:** Aims to keep members up to date with industry news and professional developments, as well as providing a tool through which members can share their knowledge, views and advice.
—CCC.
Published by: College of Occupational Therapists Ltd., 106-114 Borough High St, SouthWark, London, SE1 1LB, United Kingdom. TEL 44-20-73576480, 800-389-4873, FAX 44-20-74502299, ProfessionalEnquiries@cot.co.uk. Ed. Tracey Samuels TEL 44-20-74502339. Adv. contact Steven Meertens TEL 44-20-74502341. page GBP 1,200; trim 210 x 297.

615.82 CAN ISSN 1481-5532
OCCUPATIONAL THERAPY NOW. Text in English. 1979. 6/yr. CAD 44 domestic to institutions; CAD 63 in United States to institutions; CAD 74 elsewhere to institutions; CAD 8.50 newsstand/cover to institutions (effective 2005). back issues avail. **Document type:** *Magazine, Academic/Scholarly.* **Description:** Provides articles on clinical applications of recent research and theory, evidence-based practice, product reviews, socio-cultural, political and economic influences on occupational therapy as well as other information relevant to the profession at large.
Formerly (until 1999): Canadian Association of Occupational Therapists. National (0820-3008)
Related titles: Online - full text ed.; ♦ French ed.: Actualites Ergotherapiques. ISSN 1481-5923.
Indexed: A26, AMED, C06, C07, C08, CINAHL, E-psyche, H12, I05, P24, P48, PQC, SCOPUS, SD.
—BLDSC (6231.260570), IE, Ingenta. **CCC.**
Published by: Canadian Association of Occupational Therapists, CTTC Bldg, Ste 3400, 1125 Colonel By Dr, Ottawa, ON K1S 5R1, Canada. TEL 613-523-2268, FAX 613-523-2552, subscriptions@caot.ca, lsheehan@caot.ca. Ed. Mary Clark Green. R&P, Adv. contact Lisa Sheehan TEL 613-523-2268, ext. 232.

615.82 NLD ISSN 1566-3647
OEDEMINUS. Text in Dutch. 1998. q. EUR 34 (effective 2010). adv. **Document type:** *Journal, Trade.*
Published by: Nederlandse Vereniging voor Fysiotherapie binnen de Lymfologie, Impalastraat 32, Utrecht, 3523 PN, Netherlands. info@nvfl.nl, http://www.nvfl.nl. Ed. Jolanda Dekker. adv.: B&W page EUR 699, color page EUR 799; trim 210 x 297. Circ: 1,200.

615.82 ITA ISSN 2035-0384
OIKIA; esperienze e prospettive in pratica riabilitativa. Text in Multiple languages. 2008. s-a. **Document type:** *Journal, Academic/Scholarly.*
Published by: Fondazione Istituto Antoniano, Via Madonnelle 15, Ercolano, NA 80056, Italy. info@istitutoantoniano.it, http://www.istitutoantoniano.it.

615.82 NLD ISSN 1874-9437
RM735.A1
➤ **THE OPEN REHABILITATION JOURNAL.** Text in English. 2008. irreg. free (effective 2011). **Document type:** *Journal, Academic/Scholarly.*
Media: Online - full text.
Indexed: A01, NSA.
Published by: Bentham Open (Subsidiary of: Bentham Science Publishers Ltd.), PO Box 294, Bussum, AG 1400, Netherlands. TEL 31-35-6923800, FAX 31-35-6980150, subscriptions@bentham.org. Ed. Susanne Iwarsson.

➤ **ORTHOPAEDIC PHYSICAL THERAPY PRACTICE.** *see* MEDICAL SCIENCES—Orthopedics And Traumatology

615.82 USA ISSN 1934-1482
▼ ➤ **P M & R (PHILADELPHIA, 2009)**; the journal of injury, function and rehabilitation. (Physical Medicine and Rehabilitation) Text in English. 2009 (Jan.). m. USD 495 in US & Canada to institutions; USD 495 elsewhere to institutions (effective 2012). adv. back issues avail.; reprints avail. **Document type:** *Journal, Academic/Scholarly.* **Description:** Covers topics such as acute and chronic musculoskeletal disorders and pain, neurologic conditions involving the central and peripheral nervous systems, rehabilitation of impairments associated with disabilities in adults and children, and neurophysiology and electrodiagnosis.
Related titles: Online - full text ed.: ISSN 1934-1563. 2009 (from ScienceDirect).
Indexed: C06, CA, EMBASE, ExcerpMed, MEDLINE, P30, R10, Reac, SCOPUS, T02.
—IE. **CCC.**
Published by: (American Academy of Physical Medicine and Rehabilitation), Elsevier Inc. (Subsidiary of: Elsevier Science & Technology), 1600 John F Kennedy Blvd, Philadelphia, PA 19103. TEL 215-239-3900, FAX 215-238-7883, JournalCustomerService-usa@elsevier.com, http://www.elsevier.com. Ed. Dr. Stuart M Weinstein. Pub. Jami Walker TEL 314-447-8987.

615.82 USA ISSN 1949-3711
RM690
P T IN MOTION. (Physical Therapy) Text in English. 1993. m. USD 89 domestic to individuals; USD 109 foreign to individuals; USD 119 domestic to institutions; USD 139 foreign to institutions; free to members (effective 2009). adv. back issues avail.; reprints avail. **Document type:** *Magazine, Trade.* **Description:** Provides legislative, health care, human interest, and association news and serves as a forum for discussion of professional issues, ideas, and innovations in clinical practice.
Formerly (until 2009): P T - Magazine of Physical Therapy (1065-5077)
Related titles: Online - full text ed.
Indexed: A01, A03, A08, A22, A26, AMED, ASG, B04, BRD, C06, C07, C08, C11, CA, CINAHL, E08, G03, G08, GSA, GSI, H04, H11, H12, I05, P02, P10, P19, P24, P26, P34, P48, P53, P54, PQC, R09, S09, S10, SD, T02, W03.
—BLDSC (6946.563020), IE, Ingenta. **CCC.**
Published by: American Physical Therapy Association, 1111 N Fairfax St, Alexandria, VA 22314. TEL 703-684-2782, 800-999-2782, FAX 703-684-7343, aps@apta.org. Ed. Donald N Tepper. Adv. contact Julie Hilgenberg TEL 703-706-3197. color page USD 4,430; trim 8.25 x 10.875. Circ: 70,340 (paid).

615.82 RUS
PALLIATIVNAYA MEDITSINA I REABILITATSIYA/PALLIATIVE MEDICINE AND REHABILITATION. Text in Russian. 1996. q. USD 274 foreign (effective 2007). **Document type:** *Journal, Academic/Scholarly.*
Published by: Obshcherossiiskoe Obshchestvennoe Dvizhenie Meditsina za Kachestvo Zhizni, a-ya 118, Moscow, 105082, Russian Federation. moql@mail.ru. Ed. G A Novikov. **Dist. by:** East View Information Services, 10601 Wayzata Blvd, Minneapolis, MN 55305. TEL 952-252-1201, 800-477-1005, FAX 952-252-1202, info@eastview.com, http://www.eastview.com.

PEDIATRIC PHYSICAL THERAPY. *see* MEDICAL SCIENCES—Pediatrics

617.06 DEU ISSN 0948-1842
PFLEGEPARTNER. Text in German. 1995. 6/yr. adv. **Document type:** *Magazine, Trade.*
Published by: Vincentz Verlag, Plathnerstr 4c, Hannover, 30175, Germany. TEL 49-511-9910000, FAX 49-511-9910099, info@vincentz.de, http://www.vincentz.de. Ed. Sonja Markgraf. adv.: B&W page EUR 3,680, color page EUR 4,000; trim 185 x 258. Circ: 85,000 (controlled).

615.82 USA
THE PHYSIATRIST. Text in English. 1984. 10/yr. free to qualified personnel membership (effective 2007). adv. **Document type:** *Newsletter, Trade.* **Description:** Covers education, research, practice and legislation issues of interest to residents and practitioners in PM&R.
Published by: American Academy of Physical Medicine and Rehabilitation, 330 N Wabash Ave, Ste 2500, Chicago, IL 60611-3514. TEL 312-464-9700, FAX 312-464-0227, info@aapmr.org, http://www.aapmr.org. Ed. Dr. Claire V Wolfe. R&P John Wilson. Adv. contact Kris Rowland. Circ: 5,700.

PHYSICAL & OCCUPATIONAL THERAPY IN PEDIATRICS; a quarterly journal of developmental therapy. *see* MEDICAL SCIENCES—Pediatrics

PHYSICAL MEDICINE & REHAB CODING ALERT; the practical monthly adviser for ethically optimizing coding reimbursement and efficiency for physical medicine and rehabilitation practices and clinics. *see* INSURANCE

615.82 USA ISSN 1047-9651
RM695 CODEN: PMRAFZ
PHYSICAL MEDICINE AND REHABILITATION CLINICS OF NORTH AMERICA. Text in English. 1990. q. USD 414 in United States to institutions; USD 540 elsewhere to institutions (effective 2012). adv. index. back issues avail.; reprints avail. **Document type:** *Journal, Academic/Scholarly.* **Description:** Updates you on the latest trends in patient management and provides a sound basis for choosing treatment options.
Incorporates (1987-2002): Physical Medicine & Rehabilitation (0888-7357)
Related titles: Microform ed.: (from PQC); Online - full text ed.: ISSN 1558-1381 (from ScienceDirect).
Indexed: A22, AMED, C06, C07, C08, CINAHL, CurCont, EMBASE, ExcerpMed, INI, IndMed, MEDLINE, P30, R10, Reac, SCI, SCOPUS, W07.
—BLDSC (6475.637000), GNLM, IE, Infotrieve, Ingenta, INIST. **CCC.**
Published by: W.B. Saunders Co. (Subsidiary of: Elsevier Health Sciences), Elsevier, Health Sciences Division, Order Fulfillment, 3251 Riverport Ln, Maryland Heights, MO 63043. TEL 314-872-8370, 800-325-4177, FAX 314-432-1380, JournalCustomerService-usa@elsevier.com, http://www.us.elsevierhealth.com. Adv. contact John Marmero TEL 212-633-3657.

615.8 USA ISSN 0031-9023
RM695 CODEN: PTHEA
➤ **PHYSICAL THERAPY.** Abbreviated title: P T J. Text in English. 1921. m. USD 99 domestic to individuals; USD 119 foreign to individuals; USD 129 domestic to institutions; USD 149 foreign to institutions; free to members (effective 2009). adv. bk.rev. abstr.; charts; illus. index. 124 p./no. 3 cols./p.; back issues avail.; reprints avail. **Document type:** *Journal, Academic/Scholarly.* **Description:** Contributes to and documents the evolution and expansion of the scientific and professional body of knowledge in physical therapy.
Former titles (until 1964): American Physical Therapy Association. Journal; Which superseded in part (in 1962): The Physical Therapy Review (0735-7435); Which was formerly (until 1948): Physiotherapy Review; (until 1927): P.T.Review
Related titles: Microform ed.: (from PQC); Online - full text ed.: ISSN 1538-6724.
Indexed: A01, A02, A03, A08, A09, A10, A20, A22, A25, A26, AHCMS, AIM, AMED, ASCA, ASG, B04, BDM&CN, BRD, C06, C07, C08, C11, CA, CINAHL, CurCont, E08, ECER, EMBASE, ExcerpMed, FoSS&M, G03, G06, G07, G08, GSA, GSI, H03, H04, H11, H12, H13, HlthInd, HospLI, I05, I07, IBR, IBZ, INI, ISR, IndMed, Inpharma, M01, M02, M06, MEDLINE, MS&D, P02, P10, P16, P19, P20, P22, P24, P26, P30, P48, P53, P54, PEI, PQC, R09, R10, Reac, S06, S08, S09, S23, SCI, SCOPUS, SD, SportS, T02, V02, V03, V04, W03, W07.
—BLDSC (6476.350000), GNLM, IE, Infotrieve, Ingenta, INIST. **CCC.**
Published by: American Physical Therapy Association, 1111 N Fairfax St, Alexandria, VA 22314. TEL 703-684-2782, 800-999-2782, FAX 703-684-7343, aps@apta.org, subscriptions@apta.org, http://www.apta.org. Ed. Rebecca L Craik. Adv. contact Julie Hilgenberg TEL 703-706-3197. color page USD 4,235; trim 8.25 x 10.875. Circ: 57,631.

615.8 USA ISSN 1059-096X
RM700
PHYSICAL THERAPY PRODUCTS. Text in English. 199?. m. free to qualified personnel (effective 2011). adv. back issues avail. **Document type:** *Magazine, Trade.* **Description:** Covers the introductions of new physical therapy products, with advisory columns discussing new procedures, and other topics of interest to professionals.
Indexed: A26, H12, I05, R09, SD.
—CCC.
Published by: Allied Healthcare Group (Subsidiary of: Ascend Media), 6100 Ctr Dr, Ste 1020, Los Angeles, CA 90045. TEL 310-642-4400, FAX 310-641-4444, http://www.alliedhealthjournals.com. Eds. Judy O'Rourke TEL 818-716-6873, Stephen Noonoo TEL 310-642-4400 ext 237. Pub. Jody Rich TEL 310-642-4400 ext 243. adv.: B&W page USD 3,020, color page USD 3,870; trim 8.125 x 10.825. Circ: 30,000 (controlled).

PHYSICAL THERAPY REIMBURSEMENT NEWS (ONLINE). *see* INSURANCE

615.8 GBR ISSN 1083-3196
RM695
➤ **PHYSICAL THERAPY REVIEWS.** Abbreviated title: P T R. Text in English. 1996. bi-m. GBP 476 combined subscription to institutions (print & online eds.); USD 901 combined subscription in United States to institutions (print & online eds.) (effective 2012). adv. bk.rev. back issues avail.; reprint service avail. from PSC. **Document type:** *Journal, Academic/Scholarly.* **Description:** Aims to publish contemporary informed reviews and editorials within physical therapy.
Related titles: Online - full text ed.: ISSN 1743-288X. GBP 433 to institutions; USD 818 in United States to institutions (effective 2012) (from IngentaConnect).
Indexed: A01, A02, A03, A08, AMED, C06, C07, C08, C11, CA, CINAHL, H04, R09, T02.
—BLDSC (6476.350600), IE, Ingenta, INIST. **CCC.**
Published by: Maney Publishing, Ste 1C, Joseph's Well, Hanover Walk, Leeds, W Yorks LS3 1AB, United Kingdom. TEL 44-113-2432800, FAX 44-113-3868178, maney@maney.co.uk. Ed. G David Baxter. adv.: B&W page GBP 420, color page GBP 700. **Subscr. in N. America to:** Maney Publishing, 875 Massachusetts Ave, 7th Fl, Cambridge, MA 02139. TEL 866-297-5154, FAX 617-354-6875, maney@maneyusa.com.

615.82 NZL ISSN 1179-7967
PHYSIO MATTERS. Text in English. 1982. 11/yr. free to members (effective 2010). adv. **Document type:** *Newsletter, Trade.*
Formerly (until 2009): New Zealand Society of Physiotherapists. Newsletter
Related titles: Online - full text ed.: ISSN 1179-7975.
Published by: New Zealand Society of Physiotherapists Inc., Marion Sq, PO Box 27386, Wellington, 6141, New Zealand. TEL 64-4-8016500, FAX 64-4-8015571, nzsp@physiotherapy.org.nz, http://www.physiotherapy.org.nz. Adv. contact Amy Macklin. page USD 560; bleed 216 x 303. Circ: 3,000.

615.8 ZAF
PHYSIOFORUM. Text in English. 7/yr. ZAR 400 domestic; ZAR 700 foreign (effective 2006). **Document type:** *Magazine, Trade.*
Published by: (South African Society of Physiotherapy/Suid-Afrikaanse Fisiotherapie Vereiniging), Physiotherapy Publications, PO Box 92125, Norwood, Johannesburg 2117, South Africa. TEL 27-11-4851467, FAX 27-11-4851613, http://www.physiosa.org.za/.

617.06 DEU ISSN 1439-023X
➤ **PHYSIOPRAXIS.** Text in German. 2003. m. EUR 105 to institutions; EUR 149 combined subscription to institutions (print & online eds.); EUR 20 newsstand/cover (effective 2011). adv. **Document type:** *Journal, Academic/Scholarly.*
Related titles: Online - full text ed.: EUR 143 to institutions (effective 2011); ◆ Supplement(s): Praxisprofi.
—BLDSC (6488.493000), IE, Ingenta.
Published by: Georg Thieme Verlag, Ruedigerstr 14, Stuttgart, 70469, Germany. TEL 49-711-8931421, FAX 49-711-8931410, kunden.service@thieme.de. Ed. Elke Baumann. Adv. contact Irmgard Mayer TEL 49-711-8931469. Circ: 15,600 (paid and controlled).

615.82 NLD ISSN 1878-9609
▼ **PHYSIOS.** Text in Dutch. 2009. q. EUR 175 domestic to individuals; EUR 210 foreign to individuals (effective 2010).
Related titles: Online - full text ed.: ISSN 1878-9617.
Published by: Prelum Uitgevers, Postbus 545, Houten, 3990 GH, Netherlands. TEL 31-30-6355060, FAX 31-30-6355069, info@prelum.nl, http://www.prelum.nl. Ed. Martin Moons.

617.06 DEU ISSN 1860-3092
PHYSIOSCIENCE. Text in German. 2005. q. EUR 95 to institutions; EUR 128 combined subscription to institutions (print & online eds.); EUR 30 newsstand/cover (effective 2011). adv. **Document type:** *Journal, Academic/Scholarly.*
Related titles: Online - full text ed.: ISSN 1860-3351. EUR 124 to institutions (effective 2011).
—IE. **CCC.**
Published by: Georg Thieme Verlag, Ruedigerstr 14, Stuttgart, 70469, Germany. TEL 49-711-8931421, FAX 49-711-8931410, kunden.service@thieme.de. Adv. contact Irmgard Mayer TEL 49-711-8931469. Circ: 7,800 (paid and controlled).

615.8 IND ISSN 0973-6549
➤ **PHYSIOTHERAPY.** Variant title: Indian Association of Physiotherapists. Journal. Text in English. 2005. s-a. free to members (effective 2011). Index. back issues avail.; reprints avail. **Document type:** *Journal, Academic/Scholarly.* **Description:** Serves as a channel of communication among physiotherapists and others interested in the clinical aspects of physiotherapy and rehabilitation.
Related titles: Online - full text ed.
Published by: Indian Association of Physiotherapists, c/o Sanjiv Kumar, 415 Gulab bagh Near Shiv Convent School, Near Bombay Hospital, Indore, 452 010, India. sanjivkjha@physiotherapyindia.org. Ed. Arun G Maiya.

615.8 GBR ISSN 0031-9406
RM695
➤ **PHYSIOTHERAPY.** Text in English. 1915. 4/yr. EUR 446 in Europe to institutions; JPY 49,600 in Japan to institutions; USD 417 elsewhere to institutions (effective 2012). adv. bk.rev.; video rev. abstr.; illus. index. back issues avail. **Document type:** *Journal, Academic/Scholarly.* **Description:** Contains peer-reviewed articles by national and international experts in the fields of physiotherapy, medicine, education, and other professions.
Former titles (until 1948): Chartered Society of Physiotherapy. Journal; (until 1944): Chartered Society of Massage and Medical Gymnastics. Journal; (until 1920): Incorporated Society of Trained Masseuses. Journal
Related titles: Audio cassette/tape ed.; Braille ed.; Online - full text ed.: ISSN 1873-1465 (from ScienceDirect).
Indexed: A22, A26, AMED, ASSIA, B28, BDM&CN, C06, C07, C08, CA, CINAHL, CurCont, DokArb, EMBASE, ExcerpMed, FR, H12, I05, IndMed, MEDLINE, P30, PEI, R10, Reac, SCI, SCOPUS, SD, T02, W07.
—BLDSC (6489.000000), GNLM, IE, Infotrieve, Ingenta, INIST. **CCC.**
Published by: (Chartered Society of Physiotherapists), Elsevier Ltd (Subsidiary of: Elsevier Science & Technology), The Blvd, Langford Ln, Kidlington, Oxford, OX5 1GB, United Kingdom. TEL 44-1865-843000, FAX 44-1865-843010, journalscustomerserviceemea@elsevier.com. Ed. Michele Harms. adv.: B&W page GBP 1,540, color page GBP 1,840; trim 300 x 210. Circ: 34,000; 3,000 (paid); 31,000 (controlled).

615.82 AUS
PHYSIOTHERAPY BOARD OF SOUTH AUSTRALIA. ANNUAL REPORT YEAR ENDED. Text in English. 200?. a. free (effective 2009). **Document type:** *Report, Trade.*
Formerly (until 2007): Physiotherapists Board of South Australia. Annual Report Year Ended .. (1832-8865)
Media: Online - full text.
Published by: The Physiotherapists Board of South Australia, GPO Box 1270, Adelaide, SA 5001, Australia. TEL 61-8-82741488, FAX 61-8-83726677, jbailey@gtsa.com.au.

615.8 CAN ISSN 0300-0508
RM695 CODEN: PTHCAZ
➤ **PHYSIOTHERAPY CANADA/PHYSIOTHERAPIE CANADA.** Abbreviated title: P T C. Text in English, French. 1923. q. USD 185 domestic to institutions; USD 205 foreign to institutions; USD 215 combined subscription domestic to institutions (print & online eds.); USD 235 combined subscription foreign to institutions (print & online eds.) (effective 2011). adv. bk.rev. index. back issues avail.; reprints avail. **Document type:** *Journal, Academic/Scholarly.*
Formerly (until 1972): Canadian Physiotherapy Association Journal - Association Canadienne de Physiotherapie Revue (0008-4751)
Related titles: Microform ed.: 1923 (from PQC); Online - full text ed.: ISSN 1708-8313. USD 160 to institutions (effective 2011).
Indexed: A22, AMED, C06, C07, C08, CINAHL, HospLI, P30, R09, RehabLit, SCI, SCOPUS, W07.
—BLDSC (6489.100000), GNLM, IE, Infotrieve, Ingenta. **CCC.**
Published by: (Canadian Physiotherapy Association), University of Toronto Press, Journals Division, 5201 Dufferin St, Toronto, ON M3H 5T8, Canada. TEL 416-667-7810, FAX 416-667-7881, journals@utpress.utoronto.ca. Ed. Dina Brooks. R&P Jessica Shulist TEL 416-667-7777 ext 7849. Circ: 504.

615.8 GBR
PHYSIOTHERAPY EFFECTIVENESS BULLETIN. Text in English. 1999. q. **Document type:** *Bulletin.*
Indexed: AMED.
—BLDSC (6489.102500).
Published by: Chartered Society of Physiotherapists, 14 Bedford Row, London, WC1R 4ED, United Kingdom. TEL 44-20-73066666, FAX 44-20-73066611, http://www.csp.org.uk.

PHYSIOTHERAPY IRELAND. *see* MEDICAL SCIENCES—Abstracting, Bibliographies, Statistics

615.82 HKG
PHYSIOTHERAPY NEWS BULLETIN. Text in English. irreg. **Document type:** *Bulletin, Academic/Scholarly.*
Published by: Hong Kong Physiotherapy Association, PO Box 10139, Hong Kong, Hong Kong. Ed. Dr. Gladys Cheing TEL 852-27666738.

615.8 GBR ISSN 1358-2267
RM695
➤ **PHYSIOTHERAPY RESEARCH INTERNATIONAL.** Text in English. 1996. q. GBP 273 in United Kingdom to institutions; EUR 345 in Europe to institutions; USD 534 elsewhere to institutions; GBP 314 combined subscription in United Kingdom to institutions (print & online eds.); EUR 397 combined subscription in Europe to institutions (print & online eds.); USD 614 combined subscription elsewhere to institutions (print & online eds.) (effective 2012). adv. bk.rev. abstr. back issues avail.; reprint service avail. from PSC. **Document type:** *Journal, Academic/Scholarly.* **Description:** Publishes original research papers on a wide range of topics in physiotherapy and other related material.
Related titles: Online - full text ed.: ISSN 1471-2865. GBP 273 in United Kingdom to institutions; EUR 345 in Europe to institutions; USD 534 elsewhere to institutions (effective 2012).
Indexed: A01, A02, A03, A08, A22, AMED, C06, C07, C08, C11, CA, CINAHL, EMBASE, ExcerpMed, H04, IndMed, MEDLINE, P24, P26, P30, P48, P54, PQC, R09, R10, Reac, SCOPUS, SD, T02.
—BLDSC (6489.119000), IE, Infotrieve, Ingenta. **CCC.**
Published by: John Wiley & Sons Ltd. (Subsidiary of: John Wiley & Sons, Inc.), 1-7 Oldlands Way, PO Box 808, Bognor Regis, West Sussex PO21 9FF, United Kingdom. TEL 44-1865-778315, FAX 44-1243-843232, cs-journals@wiley.com, http://eu.wiley.com/WileyCDA/. Ed. Fiona Jones. **Subscr. to:** 1-7 Oldlands Way, PO Box 809, Bognor Regis, West Sussex PO21 9FG, United Kingdom. TEL 44-1865-778054, cs-agency@wiley.com. **Dist. by:** Turpin Distribution Services Ltd.

615.82 SGP ISSN 0219-1091
PHYSIOTHERAPY SINGAPORE. Text in English. q. **Document type:** *Journal, Academic/Scholarly.*
Indexed: AMED, C06, C07, C08, CINAHL, EMBASE, ExcerpMed, R10, Reac, SCOPUS.
—BLDSC (6489.129000), IE, Ingenta.
Published by: Singapore Physiotherapy Association, PO Box 442, Singapore, 912415, Singapore.

615.8 USA ISSN 0959-3985
RM695 CODEN: PTHPEA
➤ **PHYSIOTHERAPY THEORY AND PRACTICE**; an international journal of physical therapy. Text in English. 1985. bi-m. GBP 610, EUR 795, USD 995 combined subscription to institutions (print & online eds.); GBP 1,220, EUR 1,590, USD 1,990 combined subscription to corporations (print & online eds.) (effective 2010). adv. bk.rev. back issues avail.; reprint service avail. from PSC. **Document type:** *Journal, Academic/Scholarly.* **Description:** Provides a forum for recent developments and current research in physiotherapy.
Formerly (until 1990): Physiotherapy Practice (0266-6154)
Related titles: Online - full text ed.: ISSN 1532-5040 (from IngentaConnect).
Indexed: A01, A02, A03, A08, A22, AMED, ASSIA, B25, BIOSIS Prev, C06, C07, C08, C11, CA, CINAHL, E01, EMBASE, ExcerpMed, H04, MEDLINE, MycolAb, P30, R09, R10, Reac, SCOPUS, SD, T02.
—GNLM, IE, Infotrieve, Ingenta. **CCC.**
Published by: Informa Healthcare (Subsidiary of: T & F Informa plc), 52 Vanderbilt Ave, New York, NY 10017. TEL 212-262-8230, FAX 212-262-8234, healthcare.enquiries@informa.com, http://www.informahealthcare.com. Ed. Dr. Scott Hasson. Adv. contact Daniel Wallen. **Subscr. in N. America to:** Taylor & Francis Inc.; **Subscr. outside N. America to:** Taylor & Francis Ltd.

615.82 FRA ISSN 1624-8597
➤ **PHYTOTHERAPIE**; de la recherche a la pratique. Text in French. 1999. bi-m. EUR 163, USD 212 combined subscription to institutions (print & online eds.) (effective 2012). reprint service avail. from PSC. **Document type:** *Journal, Academic/Scholarly.* **Description:** Focuses on the fast-growing field of herbal medicine.
Formerly (until 2002): Cahiers de Phytotherapie (1295-4535)
Related titles: Online - full text ed.: ISSN 1765-2847 (from IngentaConnect).
Indexed: A22, A26, B25, BIOBASE, BIOSIS Prev, E01, EMBASE, ExcerpMed, IABS, MycolAb, R10, Reac, SCOPUS.
—BLDSC (6497.052500), IE, Ingenta, INIST. **CCC.**
Published by: Springer France (Subsidiary of: Springer Science+Business Media), 22 Rue de Palestro, Paris, 75002, France. TEL 33-1-53009860, FAX 33-1-53009861, sylvie.kamara@springer.com. Ed. Paul Goetz. Adv. contact Stephan Kroeck TEL 49-30-827875739. **Subscr. in Americas to:** Springer New York LLC, Journal Fulfillment, PO Box 2485, Secaucus, NJ 07096. TEL 800-777-4643, 201-348-4033, FAX 201-348-4505, journals-ny@springer.com, http://www.springer.com; **Subscr. to:** Springer Distribution Center, Kundenservice Zeitschriften, Haberstr 7, Heidelberg 69126, Germany. TEL 49-6221-3454303, FAX 49-6221-3454229, subscriptions@springer.com.

615.82 USA ISSN 1567-7575
PLENUM SERIES IN REHABILITATION AND HEALTH. Text in English. 1996. irreg., latest 2004. price varies. back issues avail. **Document type:** *Monographic series.* **Description:** Focuses on research issues in the field of rehabilitation, including rehabilitation and psychology, physical therapy, biofeedback, ergonomics, vocational and psychiatric rehabilitation, occupational health and therapy.
Indexed: E-psyche.
Published by: Springer New York LLC (Subsidiary of: Springer Science+Business Media), 233 Spring St, New York, NY 10013. TEL 212-460-1500, FAX 212-460-1575, service-ny@springer.com.

POST ACUTE CARE STRATEGY REPORT; the newsletter for integrating post acute services. *see* MEDICAL SCIENCES—Nurses And Nursing

615.82 POL ISSN 0860-6161
➤ **POSTEPY REHABILITACJI.** Text in Polish; Summaries in English. 1987. q. EUR 65 foreign (effective 2008). 80 p./no.; **Document type:** *Journal, Academic/Scholarly.* **Description:** Publishes papers in therapeutic rehabilitation and related disciplines, information on advances in rehabilitation of various diseases and on new rehabilitation equipment.
Related titles: Online - full text ed.: Advances in Rehabilitation. ISSN 1734-4948. 2005.
Indexed: EMBASE, ExcerpMed, SCOPUS, SD.
—BLDSC (6563.808000), GNLM.
Published by: (Akademia Wychowania Fizycznego Jozefa Pilsudskiego w Warszawie), Polskie Towarzystwo Rehabilitacji, ul Wierzejewskiego 12, Konstancin, 05511, Poland. ptreh@home.pl. Ed. Aleksander Ronikier. **Dist. by:** Ars Polona, Obroncow 25, Warsaw 03933, Poland. TEL 48-22-5098609, FAX 48-22-5098610, arspolona@arspolona.com.pl, http://www.arspolona.com.pl.

615.82 DEU ISSN 2190-6726
PRAEVENTION, REHABILITATION, INTEGRATION FUER DIE PRAXIS DER KINDER-REHA. Text in German. 2006. a. EUR 10 newsstand/cover (effective 2011). adv. **Document type:** *Journal, Trade.*
Formerly (until 2010): Praxis der Kinder-Reha (1861-7239)
Published by: Verlag Modernes Lernen Borgmann KG, Schleefstr 14, Dortmund, 44287, Germany. TEL 49-231-128008, FAX 49-231-125640, info@verlag-modernes-lernen.de. Ed. Dorothea Becker. Pub. Dieter Borgmann.

PRAEVENTION UND REHABILITATION. *see* MEDICAL SCIENCES

615.82 DEU ISSN 0933-842X
PRAXIS DER KLINISCHEN VERHALTENSMEDIZIN UND REHABILITATION. Text in German. 1988. q. EUR 49; EUR 43 to students; EUR 14 newsstand/cover (effective 2011). adv. bk.rev. **Document type:** *Journal, Academic/Scholarly.*
Indexed: DIP, E-psyche, IBR, IBZ.
—GNLM.
Published by: Pabst Science Publishers, Am Eichengrund 28, Lengerich, 49525, Germany. TEL 49-5484-97234, FAX 49-5484-550, pabst@pabst-publishers.com, http://www.pabst-publishers.de. Ed. Manfred Zielke.

615.82 DEU ISSN 0932-9692
PRAXIS ERGOTHERAPIE; Fachzeitschrift fuer Beschaeftigungs- und Arbeitstherapie. Text in German. 1988. 6/yr. EUR 36; EUR 30 to students; EUR 6.50 newsstand/cover (effective 2011). adv. **Document type:** *Journal, Academic/Scholarly.* **Description:** Covers all subjects to occupational therapy professionals.
Indexed: DIP, IBR, IBZ.
—GNLM.
Published by: Verlag Modernes Lernen Borgmann KG, Schleefstr 14, Dortmund, 44287, Germany. TEL 49-231-128008, FAX 49-231-125640, info@verlag-modernes-lernen.de. Ed. Dorothea Becker. Pub. Dieter Borgmann.

615.82 DEU
PRAXIS PHYSIOTHERAPIE. Text in German. 2008. 4/yr. EUR 34 (effective 2010). adv. **Document type:** *Journal, Trade.*
Published by: Verlag Modernes Lernen Borgmann KG, Schleefstr 14, Dortmund, 44287, Germany. TEL 49-231-128008, FAX 49-231-125640, info@verlag-modernes-lernen.de, http://www.verlag-modernes-lernen.de. Ed. Dorothea Becker. Pub. Dieter Borgmann.

615.8 DEU ISSN 1611-3497
PRAXISFUEHRUNG PROFESSIONELL. Text in German. 2003. m. EUR 61.50 for 6 mos. (effective 2010). **Document type:** *Journal, Trade.*
Related titles: Online - full text ed.
Published by: (I W W - Institut fuer Wirtschaftspublizistik), Vogel Business Media GmbH & Co.KG, Max-Planck-Str 7-9, Wuerzburg, 97064, Germany. TEL 49-931-4180, FAX 49-931-4182750, info@vogel.de, http://www.vogel-media.de. Ed. Stephann Voss.

▼ **PRAXISPROFI**; Praxisfuehrung - Marketing - Finanzen. *see* HEALTH FACILITIES AND ADMINISTRATION

615.82 POL ISSN 0867-6348
➤ **PROBLEMY TERAPII MONITOROWANEJ.** Text in Polish. 1990. q. PLZ 30 to individuals; PLZ 40 to institutions (effective 2008). **Document type:** *Journal, Academic/Scholarly.*
Indexed: A01, CA, T02.
—BLDSC (6617.959450), IE.
Published by: Towarzystwo Terapii Monitorowanej, ul Kniaziewicza 1/5, Lodz, Poland. TEL 48-42-2516003, FAX 48-42-6511059, ttm@ttm.org.pl, http://www.ttm.org.pl. Ed. Julita Chojnowska-Jezierska.

615.85153 AUS
R D A NEWS. Text in English. 1991. s-a. back issues avail. **Document type:** *Newsletter.* **Description:** Promotes equestrian activities for people with disability.
Published by: Riding for the Disabled Association of Australia, 402 Queens Parade, Clifton Hill, VIC 3068, Australia. TEL 61-3-94865755, FAX 61-3-94865766, admin@rdav.asn.au, http://www.rda.org.au. Ed., Pub., R&P, Adv. contact Susan Cusack.

617.06 USA ISSN 1067-9111
R E S N A CONFERENCE. PROCEEDINGS. (Rehabilitation Engineering & Assistive Technology Society of North America) Text in English. 1982. a. back issues avail. **Document type:** *Proceedings, Trade.*
Former titles (until 1989): Annual Conference on Rehabilitation Technology. Proceedings (0883-4741); (until 1985): Annual Conference on Rehabilitation Engineering. Proceedings (0733-5482)
Related titles: Online - full text ed.: free (effective 2010).
—IE, Ingenta.
Published by: Rehabilitation Engineering and Assistive Technology Society of North America (RESNA), 1700 N Moore St, Ste 1540, Arlington, VA 22209. TEL 703-524-6686, FAX 703-524-6630, publications@resna.org, http://www.resna.org.

615.82 GBR ISSN 0268-0548
HD7256.G7
RE-HAB NETWORK. Text in English. 1986. q.
Published by: City University, Rehabilitation Resource Centre, Department of Systems Science, Northampton Square, London, EC1 0HB, United Kingdom. TEL 44-20-7040-8377, FAX 44-20-7040-8356, rrc@city.ac.uk.

REHA-EINKAUFSFUEHRER. *see* BUSINESS AND ECONOMICS—Trade And Industrial Directories

615.82 362.15 CAN ISSN 1192-2508
REHAB & COMMUNITY CARE MANAGEMENT. Text in English. 1992. q. CAD 25.58; USD 49.50 foreign. adv. bk.rev. **Document type:** *Magazine, Trade.* **Description:** Covers technological advances, therapeutic trends, management issues and government legislative changes for those dedicated to improving the quality of daily life for Canadians challenged by injury, illness or aging.
Published by: B C S Communications Ltd., 101 Thorncliffe Park Dr, Toronto, ON M4H 1M2, Canada. TEL 416-421-7944, 800-798-6282, FAX 416-421-0966. Ed. H Dostal. Pub., R&P Caroline Tapp McDougall. Adv. contact Anita Boyle Evans. B&W page CAD 2,345, color page CAD 3,545; trim 10.88 x 8.13. Circ: 20,000 (controlled).

617.06 USA ISSN 0899-6237
RM930.A1
REHAB MANAGEMENT; the interdisciplinary journal of rehabilitation. Text in English. 1988. 10/yr. free to qualified personnel (effective 2011). adv. back issues avail. **Document type:** *Journal, Trade.* **Description:** Directed toward physical therapists, directors and managers of rehabilitation hospitals, and occupational therapists. Features the business aspects of rehabilitation, plus case histories.
Related titles: Online - full text ed.
Indexed: A26, C06, C07, C08, CINAHL, EMBASE, ExcerpMed, H12, I05, MEDLINE, P30, PEI, R09, R10, Reac, SCOPUS, SD, T02.
—IE, Infotrieve, Ingenta. **CCC.**
Published by: Allied Healthcare Group (Subsidiary of: Ascend Media), 6100 Ctr Dr, Ste 1020, Los Angeles, CA 90045. TEL 310-642-4400, FAX 310-641-4444, cagulnek@ascendmedia.com, http://www.alliedhealthjournals.com. Eds. Judy O'Rourke TEL 818-716-6873, Rogena Schuyler-Silverman TEL 310-642-4400 ext 245. Pub. Jody Rich TEL 310-642-4400 ext 243. Circ: 20,000 (controlled).

617.03 616.977 SVK ISSN 0375-0922
REHABILITACIA/REHABILITATION. Text in Slovak, Czech; Summaries in English, German, Slovak. 1967. 4/yr. bk.rev.; film rev. bibl.; charts; illus. index. back issues avail. **Document type:** *Bulletin, Trade.* **Description:** Focuses on rehabilitation, physical and psychosocial therapies.
Indexed: SCOPUS.
—GNLM.
Published by: (Slovenske Postgradualna Akademie Mediciny/Academy of Further Education of Physicians and Pharmaceutists), Vydavatelsvo Liecreh Guth, Cervenova 34, Bratislava, 81103, Slovakia. TEL 421-7-59545243, FAX 421-7-54414700, http://www.rehabilit@cla.sk. Ed. Anton Guth. Circ: 2,800 (paid).

615.82 ESP ISSN 0048-7120
➤ **REHABILITACION.** Text in Spanish; Summaries in English, Spanish. 1967. bi-m. EUR 174.72 combined subscription to individuals print & online eds.; EUR 537.59 to institutions print & online eds. (effective 2009). bk.rev. abstr.; bibl.; illus.; stat. index. back issues avail.; reprints avail. **Document type:** *Journal, Academic/Scholarly.*
Related titles: Online - full text ed.: ISSN 1578-3278. 1996. EUR 128.92 (effective 2009) (from ScienceDirect).
Indexed: A22, AMED, C06, C07, C08, CINAHL, IME, SCOPUS.
—BLDSC (7350.070000), GNLM, IE, Ingenta, INIST. **CCC.**
Published by: (Sociedad Espanola de Rehabilitacion y Medicina Fisica), Elsevier Doyma (Subsidiary of: Elsevier Health Sciences), Traversa de Gracia 17-21, Barcelona, 08021, Spain. TEL 34-932-418800, FAX 34-932-419020, editorial@elsevier.com. Ed. A. Esclarin de Ruiz. Circ: 2,200.

615.82 POL ISSN 1427-9622
➤ **REHABILITACJA MEDYCZNA.** Text in Polish, English. 1997. q. **Document type:** *Journal, Academic/Scholarly.*
Indexed: SCOPUS, SD.
—BLDSC (7350.080000).
Published by: Elipsa - Jaim s.c., ul Gontyna 10/1, Krakow, 30203, Poland. http://www.rehmed.pl. Ed. Janusz Bromboszcz.
Co-sponsors: Uniwersytet Jagiellonski, Collegium Medicum; Akademia Wychowanie Fizycznego im. Bronislawa Czecha w Krakowie.

615.82 POL ISSN 1895-4146
REHABILITACJA W PRAKTYCE. Text in Polish. 2006. q. PLZ 108 domestic (effective 2011). **Document type:** *Magazine, Trade.* **Description:** Promote the art and the technology used in rehabilitation, physiotherapy, and massage treatments.
Related titles: Online - full text ed.
Published by: Wydawnictwo Elamed, Al Rozdzienskiego 188, Katowice, 40203, Poland. TEL 48-32-2580361, FAX 48-32-2039356, elamed@elamed.com.pl, http://www.elamed.com.pl. Ed. Damian Hegenbarth.

617.06 DEU ISSN 0034-3536
➤ **DIE REHABILITATION**; Zeitschrift fuer Praxis und Forschung in der Rehabilitation. Text in German; Summaries in English, German. 1961. bi-m. EUR 205 to institutions; EUR 282 combined subscription to institutions (print & online eds.); EUR 46 newsstand/cover (effective 2011). adv. bk.rev. bibl.; charts; illus.; stat. index. back issues avail.; reprints avail. **Document type:** *Journal, Academic/Scholarly.*
Related titles: Microform ed.: (from PQC); Online - full text ed.: ISSN 1439-1309. EUR 272 to institutions (effective 2011).
Indexed: A20, A22, AMED, C06, C07, C08, CINAHL, EMBASE, ExcerpMed, F09, IBR, IBZ, IndMed, MEDLINE, P30, R10, Reac, SCI, SCOPUS, W07.
—BLDSC (7350.210000), GNLM, IE, Infotrieve, Ingenta, INIST. **CCC.**
Published by: (Deutsche Vereinigung fuer die Rehabilitation Behinderter), Georg Thieme Verlag, Ruedigerstr 14, Stuttgart, 70469, Germany. TEL 49-711-8931421, FAX 49-711-8931410, kunden.service@thieme.de. Eds. F Schliehe, K A Jochheim. R&P Peter Eich. Adv. contact Andreas Schweiger TEL 49-711-8931245. color page EUR 2,260, B&W page EUR 1,150; 175 x 250. Circ: 1,500 (paid).

➤ **REHABILITATION & SPORTS MEDICINE SOURCE.** *see* MEDICAL SCIENCES—Abstracting, Bibliographies, Statistics

➤ **REHABILITATION NURSING.** *see* MEDICAL SCIENCES—Nurses And Nursing

617.06 NZL ISSN 1179-5727
➤ **REHABILITATION PROCESS AND OUTCOME.** Text in English. 2008. irreg. free (effective 2011). **Document type:** *Journal, Academic/Scholarly.* **Description:** Covers all aspects of the rehabilitation process.
Media: Online - full text.
—**CCC.**
Published by: Libertas Academica Ltd., PO Box 300-874, Mairangi Bay, Auckland, 0751, New Zealand. TEL 64-9-4763930, FAX 64-9-3531397, editorial@la-press.com. Ed. Dr. Thilo Kroll.

615.82 USA
REHABILITATION PROFESSIONAL. Text in English. 1990. q. adv. bk.rev. **Document type:** *Journal, Academic/Scholarly.* **Description:** Contains research and discussion articles on topics pertinent to private sector rehabilitation along with product reviews.
Former titles (until 1997): N A R P P S Journal; (until 1993): N A R P P S Journal & News; Which was formed by the merger of (19??-1990): Journal of Private Sector Rehabilitation; N A R P P S News (0896-8640)
Published by: (International Association of Rehabilitation Professionals), Elliott & Fitzpatrick, Inc., 1135 Cedar Shoals Dr, Athens, GA 30605. TEL 800-843-4977, FAX 706-227-2204, myorder@elliottfitzpatrick.com. Ed. Cloie Johnson TEL 425-486-4040. Circ: 2,500.

REHABILITATION R & D PROGRESS REPORTS. (Research & Development) *see* MILITARY

615.82 CAN ISSN 1910-6831
REHABILITATION RESEARCH. REPORT. Text in English. 2005. a. **Document type:** *Report, Trade.*
Formerly (until 2006): Toronto Rehabilitation Institute. Project (1715-0477)
Published by: Toronto Rehabilitation Institute, University Centre, 550 University Ave, Toronto, ON M5G 2A2, Canada. TEL 416-597-3422, http://www.torontorehab.on.ca.

617.0305 NZL ISSN 1170-3415
REHABILITATION RESEARCH REVIEW. Text in English. 2008. bi-m. free to qualified personnel (effective 2009). back issues avail. **Document type:** *Journal, Academic/Scholarly.*
Media: Online - full text.
Published by: Research Review Ltd., N Shore Mail Centre, PO Box 100116, Auckland, New Zealand. TEL 64-9-4102277, info@researchreview.co.nz.

617.06 USA ISSN 0172-6412
REHABILITATION UND PRAEVENTION. Text in English. 1977. irreg., latest 2003. price varies. back issues avail.; reprints avail. **Document type:** *Monographic series, Academic/Scholarly.*
—**CCC.**
Published by: Springer New York LLC (Subsidiary of: Springer Science+Business Media), 233 Spring St, New York, NY 10013. TEL 212-460-1500, FAX 212-460-1575, service-ny@springer.com.

615.82 FRA ISSN 1774-9743
RELIANCE. Text in French. 2000. q. EUR 42 domestic to individuals; EUR 54 domestic to institutions; EUR 60 foreign (effective 2009). **Document type:** *Journal, Trade.*
Related titles: Online - full text ed.: ISSN 1951-6282. 2006.
Published by: Editions Eres, 33 Av. Marcel Dassault, Toulouse, 31500, France. TEL 33-5-61751576, FAX 33-5-61735289, eres@edition-eres.com.

615.85 NLD ISSN 1383-3464
REVALIDATA. Text in Dutch. 1979. 6/yr. **Document type:** *Journal, Academic/Scholarly.*
Published by: (Nederlandse Vereniging van Artsen voor Revalidatie en Physische Geneeskunde), DCHG Medische Communicatie, Zijlweg 70, Haarlem, 2013 DK, Netherlands. TEL 31-23-5514888, FAX 31-23-5515522, info@dchg.nl, http://www.dchg.nl.

REVALIDATIE BRANCHERAPPORT. *see* SOCIAL SERVICES AND WELFARE

▼ **REVALIDATIE - REUMATOLOGIE MAGAZINE.** *see* MEDICAL SCIENCES—Rheumatology

615.82 BRA ISSN 1413-3555
➤ **REVISTA BRASILEIRA DE FISIOTERAPIA.** Text in Portuguese, English. 1996. s-a. BRL 95 domestic to individuals; USD 90 foreign to individuals; BRL 190 domestic to institutions; USD 90 foreign to institutions (effective 2006). **Document type:** *Journal, Academic/Scholarly.* **Description:** Publishes articles related to physical therapy and covers basic and applied studies on the prevention and treatment of movement disorders.
Related titles: Online - full text ed.: ISSN 1809-9246. free (effective 2011).
Indexed: A01, C06, C07, CA, F03, F04, FoSS&M, MEDLINE, P30, PEI, R09, SCI, SCOPUS, SD, T02, W07.
Published by: (Associacao Brasileira de Fisioterapia), Universidade Federal de Sao Carlos, Departamento de Fisioterapia, Rod Washington Luis, Km 235, Sao Carlos, SP 13565-905, Brazil. TEL 55-16-33518755, rbfisio@power.ufscar.br. Ed. Helenice Jane Cote Gil Coury.

615.8515 CHL ISSN 0717-6767
REVISTA CHILENA DE TERAPIA OCUPACIONAL. Text in Spanish. 2001. a. **Document type:** *Journal, Academic/Scholarly.*
Published by: Universidad de Chile, Facultad de Medicina, Escuela de Terapia Ocupacional, Independencia 1027, Santiago, Chile. http://www.med.uchile.cl.

615.82 BRA ISSN 1413-7879
REVISTA DE FISIOTERAPIA DA UNIVERSIDADE DE SAO PAULO. Text in Portuguese; Abstracts in English, Portuguese. 1994. s-a. **Document type:** *Journal, Academic/Scholarly.*
Indexed: C01, C06, C07, C08, CINAHL.
Published by: Universidade de Sao Paulo, Faculdade de Medicina, Av Dr Arnaldo 455, Cerqueira Cesar, Sao Paulo, SP 01246-903, Brazil.

615.82 ESP ISSN 1576-5385
REVISTA ELECTRONICA DE INFORMATICA EN TERAPIA OCUPACIONAL. Text in Spanish, English. 1998. m. free (effective 2009). **Document type:** *Journal, Academic/Scholarly.*
Media: Online - full text.
Published by: Universidad Rey Juan Carlos, Facultad de Ciencias de la Salud, Avda Atenas s-n, Madrid, 26922, Spain. TEL 34-91-4888800, Revista_REITO@hotmail.com, http://www.cs.urcj.es/. Ed. Ricardo Moreno Rodriguez.

615.82 ESP ISSN 1138-6045
➤ **REVISTA IBEROAMERICANA DE FISIOTERAPIA Y KINESIOLOGIA.** Text in Spanish. 1998. s-a. EUR 50.45 combined subscription to individuals print & online eds.; EUR 127.73 combined subscription to institutions print & online eds. (effective 2009). adv. back issues avail.; reprints avail. **Document type:** *Journal, Academic/Scholarly.*
Related titles: Online - full text ed.: ISSN 1578-1941 (from ScienceDirect).
Indexed: C06, C07, C08, CINAHL, SCOPUS.
—BLDSC (7858.821500). **CCC.**
Published by: (Asociacion Espanola de Fisioterapeutas), Elsevier Doyma (Subsidiary of: Elsevier Health Sciences), Traversa de Gracia 17-21, Barcelona, 08021, Spain. TEL 34-932-418800, FAX 34-932-419020, editorial@elsevier.com. Ed. R. Fernandez Cervantes. Circ: 7,000 (paid).

615.82 BRA ISSN 1808-3269
REVISTA INTENSIVA. Text in Multiple languages. 2005. q. 32 p./no.; **Document type:** *Magazine, Trade.*
Related titles: Online - full text ed.: ISSN 1807-152X. 2005.
Published by: Editorial Bolina Brasil (Subsidiary of: Grupo Editorial Bolina), Alameda Pucurui 51-59 B, Tamporere - Barueri, Sao Paulo, 06460-100, Brazil. Ed. Fabricio Guimaraes. Circ: 10,000.

613.7 MEX ISSN 1405-8790
REVISTA MEXICANA DE MEDICINA FISICA Y REHABILITACION. Text in Spanish. 1988. s-a. back issues avail. **Document type:** *Journal, Academic/Scholarly.*
Indexed: C01.
Published by: Sociedad Mexicana de Medicina Fisica y Rehabilitacion, A.C., Apdo Postal 75-403, Mexico, D.F., 07300, Mexico. TEL 52-55-5586-5575, FAX 52-55-5119-2995. Ed. Ignacio Devesa Gutierrez.

615 BRA ISSN 1677-5937
REVISTA TERAPIA MANUAL. Text in Portuguese. 2002. quadrennial. BRL 120 (effective 2006). back issues avail. **Document type:** *Journal, Academic/Scholarly.*
Related titles: Online - full text ed.
Indexed: C06, C07.
Published by: Escola de Terapia Manual e Postural, Ave Higienopolis, 2554 Sala 2, Parque Guanabara, Londrina, Parana, 86050-000, Brazil. TEL 55-43-33299500, revista@terapiamanual.net. Ed. Luis Vicente Franco de Oliveira. Circ: 3,000.

615 ITA ISSN 1120-379X
CODEN: RIPRE
RICERCA & PRATICA. Text in Italian. 1967. bi-m. EUR 130 domestic to institutions; EUR 200 foreign to institutions (effective 2009). bibl. index. 48 p./no.; back issues avail. **Document type:** *Journal, Academic/Scholarly.*
Formerly (until 2003): Negri News
Related titles: Online - full text ed.: ISSN 2038-2480.
Indexed: EMBASE, ExcerpMed, R10, Reac, SCOPUS.
—BLDSC (7963.915000), GNLM.
Published by: (Istituto di Ricerche Farmacologiche Mario Negri), Il Pensiero Scientifico Editore, Via Bradano 3-C, Rome, 00199, Italy. TEL 39-06-862821, FAX 39-06-86282250, pensiero@pensiero.it, http://www.pensiero.it. Circ: 2,000.

615.82 JPN ISSN 0910-0059
RIGAKU RYOHO/JOURNAL OF PHYSICAL THERAPY. Text in Japanese. 1984. m. JPY 21,000 (effective 2007). **Document type:** *Journal, Academic/Scholarly.*
Published by: Medikaru Puresu/Medical Press Ltd., 1-12-17 Hikawadai, Nerima-ku, Tokyo, 179-0084, Japan. TEL 81-3-35506400, FAX 81-3-35506260, hanbai@medicalpress.co.jp, http://www.medicalpress.co.jp/.

615.8 JPN ISSN 0915-0552
RIGAKU RYOHO JANARU/JAPANESE JOURNAL OF PHYSICAL THERAPY. Text in Japanese; Summaries in English. 1967. m. JPY 20,880; JPY 27,200 combined subscription (print & online eds.) (effective 2010). **Document type:** *Journal, Academic/Scholarly.*
Supersedes in part (in 1989): Rigaku Ryoho to Sagyo Ryoho/Japanese Journal of Physical Therapy and Occupational Therapy (0386-9849)
Related titles: Online - full text ed.: ISSN 1882-1359.
Published by: Igaku Shoin Ltd., 1-28-36 Hongo, Bunkyo-ku, Tokyo, 113-8719, Japan. TEL 81-3-3817-5600, FAX 81-3-3815-7791, info@igaku-shoin.co.jp. Circ: 7,500.

615.8 JPN ISSN 1346-1710
RIGAKU RYOUHOU KYOUTO/KYOTO JOURNAL OF PHYSICAL THERAPY. Text in English, Japanese. 1971. a. **Document type:** *Journal, Academic/Scholarly.*
Formerly (until 2000): Kyoto Rigaku Ryohoshikai Kaishi (0915-6739)
Published by: Nihon Rigaku Ryohoshi Kyokai, Kyoto Rigaku Ryohoshikai, Kyoto University School of Medicine Hospital, Department of Rehabilitation, 54 Kawaracho, Shogoin, Sakyo-ku, Kyoto, 603-0000, Japan. TEL 81-75-7513571, FAX 81-75-7513308, http://www.kpta.jp/.

615.82 JPN ISSN 1341-1667
RM695
RIGAKURYOHO KAGAKU. Text in Japanese. 1986. q. **Document type:** *Journal, Academic/Scholarly.*
Formerly (until 1994): Rigaku Ryoho no Tame no Undo Seiri (0912-7100)
Related titles: Online - full content ed.: free (effective 2011); Online - full text ed.
Indexed: CA, PEI, SCOPUS, SD, T02.
—BLDSC (7970.680510).
Published by: Society of Physical Therapy Science, Publication Center OPT Bldg. 3F, 1-24-11, Sugamo, Toshima-ku, Tokyo, 170-0002, Japan.

RIVISTA DI CHIRURGIA DELLA MANO. *see* MEDICAL SCIENCES—Surgery

615.82 ITA ISSN 1826-2708
RIVISTA ITALIANA DI FISIOTERAPIA E RIABILITAZIONE RESPIRATORIA. Text in Italian. 2002. 3/yr. **Document type:** *Journal, Academic/Scholarly.*
Published by: Midia Srl, Via Santa Maddalena 1, Monza, 20052, Italy. TEL 39-039-2304440, FAX 39-039-2304442, http://www.mediaonline.it.

ROMATOLOJI VE TIBBI REHABILITASYON DERGISI/JOURNAL OF RHEUMATOLOGY AND MEDICAL REHABILITATION. *see* MEDICAL SCIENCES—Rheumatology

617.06 ITA ISSN 1590-6647
SCIENZA DELLA RIABILITAZIONE. Text in Multiple languages. 2000. q. EUR 47.17 (effective 2008). **Document type:** *Journal, Academic/Scholarly.*
Published by: Societa Editrice Universo, Via Giovanni Battista Morgagni 1, Rome, RM 00161, Italy. TEL 39-06-44231171, FAX 39-06-4402033, amministrazione@seu-roma.it, http://www.seuroma.com.

615.82 ITA ISSN 1828-3942
SCIENZA RIABILITATIVA. Text in Multiple languages. 1997. q. **Document type:** *Journal, Academic/Scholarly.*
Indexed: A26, C06, C07, C08, CA, CINAHL, E08, H12, I05, R09, S09, T02.
—BLDSC (8205.197000), IE.
Published by: Associazione Italiana Fisioterapisti (A I F I), Via Claterna 18, Rome, 00183, Italy. TEL 39-06-77201020, FAX 39-06-77077364, info@aifi.net, http://www.aifi.net.

615.8515 USA ISSN 1093-7250
RM735.A1
SENSORY INTEGRATION SPECIAL INTEREST SECTION QUARTERLY. Text in English. 1989. q. free to members (effective 2010). adv. **Document type:** *Newsletter, Trade.* **Description:** Offers leadership, resources, and information to occupational therapists, occupational therapy assistants, and students on sensory integration, as well as occupational therapy theory and clinical tools based on research and clinical practice.
Former titles (until 1997): Sensory Integration Special Interest Section Newsletter (0279-4128); (until 1981): American Occupational Therapy Association. Sensory Integration Specialty Section. Newsletter (0194-6358)
Related titles: Online - full text ed.; ◆ Series: Developmental Disabilities Special Interest Section Quarterly. ISSN 1093-7196; ◆ Gerontology Special Interest Section Quarterly. ISSN 1093-717X; ◆ Technology Special Interest Section Quarterly. ISSN 1093-7137; ◆ Work & Industry Special Interest Section Quarterly; ◆ Education Special Interest Section Quarterly. ISSN 1093-7188; ◆ Physical Disabilities Special Interest Section Quarterly. ISSN 1093-7234; ◆ Administration & Management Special Interest Section Quarterly. ISSN 1093-720X; ◆ Mental Health Special Interest Section Quarterly. ISSN 1093-7226.
Indexed: C06, C07, C08, CINAHL, P24, P48, PQC.
—CCC.
Published by: American Occupational Therapy Association, Inc., 4720 Montgomery Ln, PO Box 31220, Bethesda, MD 20824. TEL 301-652-2682, 800-377-8555, FAX 301-652-7711, members@aota.org. Ed. Stacey Reynolds.

615.82 CHN
SHENJING SUNSHANG YU GONGNENG CHONGJIAN/NEURAL INJURY AND FUNCTIONAL RECONSTRUCTION. Text in Chinese. 1981. q. **Document type:** *Journal, Academic/Scholarly.*
Formerly (until 2006): Guowai Yixue (Wuli Yixue yu Kangfuxue Fence)/ Foreign Medical Sciences (Physical Medicine & Rehabilitation) (1001-117X)
Related titles: Online - full text ed.: (from WanFang Data Corp.).
—East View.
Published by: Huazhong Keji Daxue Tongji Yixueyuan/Huazhong University of Science and Technology, Tongji Medical College, 1095 Jiefang Dadao, Wuhan, 430030, China. TEL 86-27-83662639, FAX 86-27-83662639, http://www.tjmu.edu.cn/. **Dist. by:** China International Book Trading Corp, 35 Chegongzhuang Xilu, Haidian District, PO Box 399, Beijing 100044, China. TEL 86-10-68412045, FAX 86-10-68412023, cibtc@mail.cibtc.com.cn, http://www.cibtc.com.cn.

617.06 GBR ISSN 2045-3590
SHIATSU SOCIETY JOURNAL. Text in English. 198?. q. **Document type:** *Journal, Trade.*
Formerly (until 2010): Shiatsu Society News (1366-2813)
Indexed: A10, AMED, V03.
Published by: Shiatsu Society, PO Box 4580, Rugby, Warwickshire CV21 9EL, United Kingdom. TEL 44-845-1304560, FAX 44-1788-547111, admin@shiatsusociety.org, http://www.shiatsusociety.org/.

615.82 NLD ISSN 1871-0794
SIGNALERINGSRAPPORT HULPMIDDELEN. Text in Dutch. 2001. a. free (effective 2008).
Published by: College voor Zorgverzekeringen, Postbus 320, Diemen, 1110 AH, Netherlands. TEL 31-20-7978555, FAX 31-20-7978500, info@cvz.nl, http://www.cvz.nl.

615.8515 EGY ISSN 1687-868X
AL-SIHHAT AL-MIHANIYYAT WA-AL-SALAMAT FI AL-MUNSHA'AT AL-TA'LIMIYYAT/OCCUPATIONAL HEALTH AND SAFETY IN EDUCATIONAL ESTABLISHMENTS. NEWSLETTER. Text in Arabic. 2008. q. **Document type:** *Newsletter, Academic/Scholarly.*
Published by: Zagazig University, Faculty of Medicine. Occupational and Environmental Health Services Center, Zagazig, Egypt. TEL 20-55-2302809, FAX 20-55-2307830. Ed. Ahmed-Refat AG Ahmed-Refat.

615.82 JPN ISSN 0386-9822
SOGO RIHABIRITESHON/SOGO REHABILITATION. Text in Japanese. 1973. m. JPY 25,680; JPY 33,500 combined subscription (print & online eds.) (effective 2010). **Document type:** *Journal, Academic/ Scholarly.* **Description:** Studies rehabilitation medicine and related medical fields.
Related titles: Online - full text ed.: ISSN 1882-1340.
Published by: Igaku Shoin Ltd., 1-28-36 Hongo, Bunkyo-ku, Tokyo, 113-8719, Japan. TEL 81-3-3817-5600, FAX 81-3-3815-7791, info@igaku-shoin.co.jp. Circ: 6,000.

615.8 ZAF ISSN 0379-6175
RM695
SOUTH AFRICAN JOURNAL OF PHYSIOTHERAPY. Text in English. 1925. q. ZAR 350 domestic; ZAR 650 foreign (effective 2006). adv. bk.rev. back issues avail. **Document type:** *Journal, Academic/ Scholarly.*
Indexed: A22, AMED, C06, C07, C08, CINAHL, ISAP, SCOPUS.
—BLDSC (8339.700000), GNLM, IE, Ingenta.
Published by: (South African Society of Physiotherapy/Suid-Afrikaanse Fisiotherapie Vereiniging), Physiotherapy Publications, PO Box 92125, Norwood, Johannesburg 2117, South Africa. TEL 27-11-4851467, FAX 27-11-4851613, pr@saphysio.co.za, http://www.physiosa.org.za/. Ed. J Beenhakker. Circ: 2,700.

THE SPINE JOURNAL. *see* MEDICAL SCIENCES—Orthopedics And Traumatology

615.8 NLD ISSN 1877-2102
STANDAARD BEWEEGINTERVENTIE. Variant title: K N G F - Standaard Beweeginterventie. Text in Dutch. 2008. irreg. free (effective 2011).
Media: Online - full text.
Published by: Koninklijk Nederlands Genootschap voor Fysiotherapie, Stadsring 159b, Amersfoort, 3817 BA, Netherlands. TEL 31-33-4672900, FAX 31-33-4672999, hoofdkantoor@kngf.nl.

615.8 NLD ISSN 0929-0591
STIMULUS. Text in Dutch. 1982. q. EUR 161, USD 242 to institutions (effective 2009). **Document type:** *Journal, Trade.*
Related titles: Online - full text ed.: ISSN 1876-5599.
Indexed: SCOPUS.
Published by: Bohn Stafleu van Loghum B.V. (Subsidiary of: Springer Science+Business Media), Postbus 246, Houten, 3990 GA, Netherlands. TEL 31-30-6383872, FAX 31-30-6383991, boekhandels@bsl.nl.

615.82 GBR ISSN 1360-8371
STROKE NEWS. Text in English. 1984. q. free (effective 2009). adv. bk.rev. back issues avail. **Document type:** *Magazine, Consumer.* **Description:** Features interviews with people who have been affected by stroke, plus topical stroke stories and ways to get involved with fundraising events. Articles report on health related issues, new stroke research and Stroke Association campaigns.
Formerly (until 1991): C H S A News (Chest, Heart and Stroke Association) (1360-838X)
Related titles: Audio cassette/tape ed.; Online - full text ed.
Published by: Stroke Association, 240 City Rd, London, EC1V 2PR, United Kingdom. TEL 44-20-75660300, FAX 44-20-74902686, info@stroke.org.uk. Ed. Maggie Warburton.

615.85 NLD ISSN 0924-3631
SYSTEEMTHERAPIE. Text in Dutch. 1989. q. EUR 62.50 domestic to individuals; EUR 71 foreign to individuals; EUR 100 domestic to institutions; EUR 107 foreign to institutions; EUR 33 to students (effective 2009). adv. **Document type:** *Journal, Academic/Scholarly.*
—IE.
Published by: Boom Uitgevers Amsterdam, Prinsengracht 747-751, Amsterdam, 1017 JX, Netherlands. TEL 31-20-6226107, FAX 31-20-6253327, info@uitgeverijboom.nl, http://www.uitgeverijboom.nl. Adv. contact Michiel Klaasen TEL 31-20-5200122. page EUR 375; trim 119 x 186.5. Circ: 2,300.

615.82 ESP ISSN 1885-527X
RM735.A1
T O G; revista terapia ocupacional Galicia. (Terapia Ocupacional Galicia) Text in Spanish. 2004. irreg. free (effective 2011). back issues avail. **Document type:** *Journal, Academic/Scholarly.*
Media: Online - full text.
Published by: Asociacion Profesional Gallega de Terapeutas Ocupacionales (A P G T O), Faro Finisterre 2, La Coruna, 15002, Spain. TEL 34-981-205770, FAX 34-669-088487. Ed. Miguel Angel Talavera Valverde.

617.06 IRN ISSN 2008-2576
➤ **TAVANBAKHSHI-I NUVIN/MODERN REHABILITATION.** Text in Persian, Modern; Abstracts in English, Persian, Modern. 2007. q. IRR 10,000 (effective 2011). abstr. back issues avail.; reprints avail. **Document type:** *Journal, Academic/Scholarly.* **Description:** Publishes articles relating to both clinical and basic science aspects of rehabilitation medicine in form of full-length paper, short communications, letter to editor, and reviews. It aims to be a wide forum for different areas of research in rehabilitation medicine, including functional assessment and intervention studies, clinical studies in various patient groups, papers on methodology in physical and rehabilitation medicine, epidemiological studies on disabling conditions and reports on vocational and sociomedical aspects of rehabilitation.
Related titles: Online - full text ed.: ISSN 2008-2584.
Published by: Danishgah-i Ulum-i Pizishki-i Tihran, Danishkadah-i Tavanbakhshi/Tehran University of Medical Sciences, School of Rehabilitation, Enghelab Ave., Pich-e-Shemiran, Tehran, 16115-316, Iran. TEL 98-21-77533939, FAX 98-21-77534133. Ed. Gholam Reza Olyaei. Pub. Payam Kabiri.

➤ **TECHNOLOGY AND DISABILITY.** *see* HANDICAPPED

➤ **THERAPEUTISCHES REITEN.** *see* SPORTS AND GAMES—Horses And Horsemanship

617.06 DEU ISSN 1432-7872
THERAPIE UND PRAXIS. Text in German. 1988. bi-m. EUR 35 (effective 2006). adv. **Document type:** *Magazine, Trade.*
Published by: V D B - Physiotherapieverband, Prinz-Albert-Str 41, Bonn, 53113, Germany. TEL 49-228-210506, FAX 49-228-210552, vdb.bundesverband@gmx.de. adv.: B&W page EUR 1,240. Circ: 4,000 (paid and controlled).

THERMOLOGY INTERNATIONAL. *see* PHYSICS—Heat

TIMISOARA PHYSICAL EDUCATION AND REHABILITATION JOURNAL. *see* EDUCATION

615.82 USA ISSN 2150-9972
TODAY IN P T. (Physical Therapy) Text in English. 2007. m. free to qualified personnel (effective 2009). adv. **Document type:** *Magazine, Trade.* **Description:** Features news and information covering cardiopulmonary, geriatrics and home health, neurology, pediatrics, and sports and orthopedics.
—CCC.
Published by: Gannett Healthcare Group, 2353 Hassell Rd, Ste 110, Hoffman Estates, IL 60195. TEL 847-839-1700, http://www.gannetthg.com. Ed. Anne Ahlman. Adv. contact Rodrick Rogers.

TOPICS IN GERIATRIC REHABILITATION. *see* GERONTOLOGY AND GERIATRICS

617 USA ISSN 1082-0744
CODEN: TSIRFP
➤ **TOPICS IN SPINAL CORD INJURY REHABILITATION.** Text in English. 1995. q. USD 219 combined subscription to individuals (print & online eds.); USD 347 combined subscription to institutions (print & online eds.) (effective 2010). adv. back issues avail.; reprints avail. **Document type:** *Journal, Academic/Scholarly.* **Description:** Covers rehabilitation techniques and care.
Related titles: Online - full text ed.: ISSN 1945-5763. USD 179 to individuals; USD 307 to institutions (effective 2010).
Indexed: AMED, C06, C07, C08, CA, CINAHL, EMBASE, ExcerpMed, P30, R10, Reac, SCOPUS, T02.
—BLDSC (8867.489300), IE, Ingenta. **CCC.**
Published by: Thomas Land Publishers, Inc., 255 Jefferson Rd, St Louis, MO 63119. TEL 314-963-7445, FAX 314-963-9345, publisher@thomasland.com, http://www.thomasland.com/. Ed. Dr. David F Apple Jr. Adv. contact Steve West TEL 856-432-1555. **Subscr. to:** PO Box 361, Birmingham, AL 35201. TEL 205-995-1567, 800-633-4931, FAX 205-995-1588; EBSCO Information Services.

➤ **TOPICS IN STROKE REHABILITATION.** *see* MEDICAL SCIENCES—Cardiovascular Diseases

615.82 TUR ISSN 1302-0234
➤ **TURKIYE FIZIKSEL TIP VE REHABILITASYON DERGISI/TURKISH JOURNAL OF PHYSICAL MEDICINE AND REHABILITATION.** Text in English, Turkish. 1998. q. free to qualified personnel (effective 2008). **Document type:** *Journal, Academic/Scholarly.* **Description:** Publishes original research papers on physical medicine and rehabilitation. Additionally, educational material, reviews on basic developments, editorial short notes, case reports, original views and letters from specialists on physical medicine, rheumatology, and rehabilitation medicine covering their experience and comments as well as social subjects.
Related titles: Online - full text ed.: ISSN 1308-6316. free (effective 2011).
Indexed: A26, C06, C07, CA, EMBASE, ExcerpMed, H12, I05, R09, R10, Reac, SCI, SCOPUS, SD, T02, W07.
Published by: Turkiye Fiziksel Tip ve Rehabilitasyon Dernegi/Turkish Society of Physical Medicine and Rehabilitation, Barbaros Bulvari, Salim Aktas, Is Hani, No.85 D:3, 80690 Besiktas, Istanbul, Turkey. TEL 90-212-2369052, FAX 90-212-2369054, ftrdernek@ftr.org.tr, http://www.ftr.org.tr/. Ed. Dilsad Sindel.

615.851 BRA ISSN 1415-9104
UNIVERSIDADE DE SAO PAULO. REVISTA DE TERAPIA OCUPACIONAL. Text in Portuguese. 1990. 3/yr. per issue exchange basis. bk.rev. bibl. **Document type:** *Academic/Scholarly.*
Published by: Universidade de Sao Paulo, Faculdade de Medicina, Curso de Terapia Ocupacional, Rua Cipotanea 51, Cidade Universitaria Armando Salles de Oliveira, Sao Paulo, SP 05508-900, Brazil.

616.822 ROM ISSN 2068-1712
UNIVERSITATEA DIN ORADEA. ANALELE. KINETOTERAPIE (ONLINE)/ROMANIAN JOURNAL OF PHYSICAL THERAPY. Text in Multiple languages. 1995. s-a. free (effective 2011).
Formerly (until 2010): Universitatea din Oradea. Analele. Kinetoterapie (Print) (1224-6220)
Media: Online - full text.
Published by: Editura Universitatii din Oradea/University of Oradea Publishing House, Str Universitatii 1, Geotermal Bldg., 2nd Fl., Oradea, Jud.Bihor 410087, Romania. TEL 40-259-408171, FAX 40-259-408404, editura@uoradea.ro, http://webhost.uoradea.ro/editura/.

615.82 NZL ISSN 1176-2098
UPBEAT. Text in English. 2000. s-a. free to members (effective 2011). back issues avail. **Document type:** *Newsletter, Consumer.*
Description: Contains news, research and events for people with early-onset Parkinson's.
Related titles: Online - full text ed.: ISSN 2230-2727. free (effective 2011).
Published by: Parkinsons New Zealand, Level 3, James Smith Bldg, 55 Cuba St, Manners St, PO Box 11067, Wellington, 6142, New Zealand. TEL 64-4-4722796, FAX 64-4-4722162, info@parkinsons.org.nz.

615.82 USA ISSN 1046-5642
VOICE (FT. LAUDERDALE). Text in English. 1987. m. adv. **Document type:** *Newspaper.* **Description:** Contains rehabilitation information for case managers, managed care workers, nurses, physicians, adjusters, consumers with disabilities and caregivers.
Published by: Cary - Joy Communications, 1405 S.E. First St., Ft. Lauderdale, FL 33301. TEL 954-463-5556, FAX 954-463-2674. Ed., Pub. Ray Brasted. Adv. contact Melanie Kornblatt. page USD 1,195. Circ: 70,000 (controlled).

615.8 RUS ISSN 0042-8787
RM819 CODEN: VKFLAL
VOPROSY KURORTOLOGII, FIZIOTERAPII I LECHEBNOI FIZICHESKOI KUL'TURY/PROBLEMS OF HEALTH RESORTS, PHYSIOTHERAPY AND EXERCISE THERAPY. Text in Russian. 1923. bi-m. USD 105 foreign (effective 2005). adv. bk.rev.; Website rev. illus. index. **Document type:** *Journal, Academic/Scholarly.*
Description: Examines the mechanisms of physiological and therapeutic effects of physical and health resort factors, methods and results of their employment; also covers theoretical and practical problems involved in the use of exercise therapy in the complex treatment of different diseases.
Indexed: ChemAb, DentInd, EMBASE, ExcerpMed, INI, IndMed, MEDLINE, P30, R10, Reac, SCOPUS.
—CASDDS, East View, GNLM, INIST. **CCC.**
Published by: Izdatel'stvo Meditsina/Meditsina Publishers, ul B Pirogovskaya, d 2, str 5, Moscow, 119435, Russian Federation. TEL 7-095-2483324, meditsina@mtu-net.ru, http://www.medlit.ru. Ed. Vasiliy M Bogolyubov. Pub. A M Stochik. R&P O Rozhenetskaya. Circ: 3,300. **Dist. by:** M K - Periodica, ul Gilyarovskogo 39, Moscow 129110, Russian Federation. TEL 7-095-2845008, FAX 7-095-2813798, info@periodicals.ru, http://www.mkniga.ru.

615.8515 NLD ISSN 1876-3227
WETENSCHAPPELIJK TIJDSCHRIFT VOOR ERGOTHERAPIE. Text in Dutch. 2008. q. EUR 55 combined subscription (print & online eds.) (effective 2011). **Document type:** *Magazine, Trade.*
Related titles: Online - full text ed.: ISSN 1876-3235.
Published by: Boom Lemma Uitgeverij, Postbus 85576, The Hague, 2508 CG, Netherlands. TEL 31-70-3307033, FAX 31-70-3307030, http://www.boomlemma.nl.

615.85156 DEU ISSN 1861-9762
WISSENSCHAFTLICHE GRUNDLAGEN DER KUNSTTHERAPIE. Text in German. 2007. irreg., latest vol.3, 2010. price varies. **Document type:** *Monographic series, Academic/Scholarly.*
Published by: Peter Lang GmbH (Subsidiary of: Peter Lang Publishing Group), Eschborner Landstr 42-50, Frankfurt Am Main, 60489, Germany. TEL 49-69-7807050, FAX 49-69-78070550, zentrale.frankfurt@peterlang.com, http://www.peterlang.com. Ed. Peter Sinapius.

615.82 DEU ISSN 0939-3889
CODEN: ZMPHEJ
ZEITSCHRIFT FUER MEDIZINISCHE PHYSIK. Text in German, English, French. 1990. 4/yr. EUR 116 in Europe to institutions; EUR 116 to institutions in Germany, Austria and Switzerland; JPY 17,100 in Japan to institutions; USD 154 elsewhere to institutions (effective 2012). adv. **Document type:** *Journal, Academic/Scholarly.*
Related titles: Online - full text ed.: ISSN 1876-4436 (from ScienceDirect).
Indexed: CA, EMBASE, ExcerpMed, INIS AtomInd, Inspec, MEDLINE, P30, R10, Reac, SCI, SCOPUS, T02, TM, W07.
—BLDSC (9469.890000), CASDDS, GNLM, IE. **CCC.**
Published by: Urban und Fischer Verlag (Subsidiary of: Elsevier GmbH), Loebdergraben 14a, Jena, 07743, Germany. TEL 49-3641-626430, FAX 49-3641-626432, info@urbanfischer.de, http://www.urbanundfischer.de. Ed. Lothar Schad. Adv. contact Eva Kraemer TEL 49-89-5383704. B&W page EUR 1,170, color page EUR 2,490; trim 210 x 280. Circ: 2,800 (paid and controlled). **Subscr. to:** Nature Publishing Group, Brunel Rd, Houndmills, Basingstoke, Hamps RG21 6XS, United Kingdom. TEL 44-1256-302629, FAX 44-1256-476117 **Co-sponsor:** Deutsche Gesellschaft fuer Medizinische Physik.

615.8 DEU ISSN 1614-0397
➤ **ZEITSCHRIFT FUER PHYSIOTHERAPEUTEN.** Variant title: P T. Text in German. 1948. m. EUR 98.40 domestic; EUR 112.80 foreign; EUR 8.80 newsstand/cover (effective 2008). adv. bk.rev. abstr.; charts; illus. index. **Document type:** *Journal, Academic/Scholarly.*
Formerly (until 2004): Krankengymnastik (0023-4494)
Related titles: Online - full text ed.
Indexed: A22, AMED, C06, C07, C08, CINAHL, P30.
—BLDSC (9484.120000), GNLM, IE, Ingenta. **CCC.**
Published by: (Deutscher Verband fuer Physiotherapie - Zentralverband der Physiotherapeuten - Krankengymnasten (ZvK) e.V.), Richard Pflaum Verlag GmbH und Co. KG, Lazarettstr 4, Munich, 80636, Germany. TEL 49-89-126070, FAX 49-89-12607202, info@pflaum.de, http://www.pflaum.de. Ed. Michael Dietl. Adv. contact Beate Altmann. B&W page EUR 2,420, color page EUR 3,830; trim 185 x 256. Circ: 26,901 (paid and controlled).

615.82 CHN ISSN 1006-9771
ZHONGGUO KANGFU LILUN YU SHIJIAN/CHINESE JOURNAL OF REHABILITATION THEORY & PRACTICE. Text in Chinese. 1995. q. USD 49.20 (effective 2009). **Document type:** *Academic/Scholarly.*
Related titles: Online - full content ed.; Online - full text ed.
—BLDSC (9512.738850), East View.
Published by: Zhongguo Kangfu Yanjiu Zhongxin, Fengtai Qu, 10, Jiaomen Bei Lu, Beijing, 100077, China. TEL 86-10-67213322 ext 6310, crrc@public.bta.net.cn, http://www.crrc.com.cn. Ed. Hong Shi Mou. **Dist. by:** China International Book Trading Corp, 35 Chegongzhuang Xilu, Haidian District, PO Box 399, Beijing 100044, China. TEL 86-10-68412045, FAX 86-10-68412023, cibtc@mail.cibtc.com.cn, http://www.cibtc.com.cn.

ZHONGGUO SHANGCAN YIXUE/CHINESE JOURNAL OF TRAUMA AND DISABILITY MEDICINE. *see* MEDICAL SCIENCES—Orthopedics And Traumatology

615.82 CHN ISSN 1673-8225
ZHONGGUO ZUZHI GONGCHENG YU LINCHUANG KANGFU/JOURNAL OF CLINICAL REHABILITATIVE TISSUE ENGINEERING RESEARCH. Text in Chinese. 1997. w. USD 322.40 (effective 2009). **Document type:** *Journal, Academic/Scholarly.*
Description: Focuses on the latest theory, prospective hi-tech achievements and applied subjects about tissue engineering, aims to report the innovative and applied researches about biomaterials, tissue construction, stem cells, organ transplantation, artificial prosthesis,artificial organ, orthopedic implants, vascular implants and techniques of rehabilitation engineering for tissue repair, and functional recovery and reconstruction in clinical rehabilitation.
Former titles: Zhongguo Linchuang Kangfu (1671-5926); (until 2002): Xiandai Kangfu (1007-5496)
Related titles: Online - full text ed.
Indexed: A28, APA, B&BAb, B19, B21, BrCerAb, C&ISA, CA/WCA, CIA, CerAb, CivEngAb, CorrAb, E&CAJ, E11, EEA, EMA, EMBASE, ESPM, EnvEAb, ExcerpMed, H15, M&TEA, M09, MBF, METADEX, NSA, R10, Reac, SCOPUS, SolStAb, T04, WAA.
—BLDSC (9512.835497), East View, IE, Ingenta, Linda Hall.
Published by: Zhongguo Kangfu Yixuehui/Chinese Rehabilitation Medical Association, Post Box 1200, Shenyang, 110004, China. TEL 86-24-23384352, FAX 86-24-23388105. **Dist. by:** China International Book Trading Corp, 35 Chegongzhuang Xilu, Haidian District, PO Box 399, Beijing 100044, China. TEL 86-10-68412045, FAX 86-10-68412023, cibtc@mail.cibtc.com.cn, http://www.cibtc.com.cn.

610 530 CHN
➤ **ZHONGHUA WULI YIXUE YU KANGFU ZAZHI/CHINESE JOURNAL OF PHYSICAL MEDICINE AND REHABILITATION.** Text in Chinese. 1979. m. USD 62.40 (effective 2009). adv. **Document type:** *Journal, Academic/Scholarly.* **Description:** Covers the latest development in physical medicine and rehabilitation.
Incorporated (1978-2002): Zhonghua Liliao Zazhi/Chinese Journal of Physical Therapy (0254-1408); Formerly: Zhonghua Wuli Yixue Zazhi/Chinese Journal of Physical Medicine (0254-1424)
Related titles: CD-ROM ed.; Online - full text ed.
Indexed: ExtraMED.
—BLDSC (3180.475200), East View.
Published by: Zhonghua Yixuehui/Chinese Medical Association, c/o Tongji Yiyuan, 1095, Jiefang Dadao, Wuhan, 430030, China. TEL 86-27-83662874, FAX 86-27-83662264. adv.: B&W page CNY 5,000, color page CNY 8,000. Circ: 9,000. **Dist. overseas by:** China International Book Trading Corp, 35 Chegongzhuang Xilu, Haidian District, PO Box 399, Beijing 100044, China.

MEDICAL SCIENCES—Psychiatry And Neurology

616.8 USA ISSN 1948-7088
A A C N BOLD VOICES. Text in English. 1993. m. USD 15 per issue; USD 100 to institutions (effective 2009). adv. **Document type:** *Newspaper, Trade.*
Formerly (until 2009): A A C N News (1075-7732)
Related titles: Online - full text ed.: ISSN 1948-7096.
Indexed: A26, C06, C07, C08, CINAHL, H12, I05.
Published by: American Association of Critical-Care Nurses, 101 Columbia, Aliso Viejo, CA 92656-4109. TEL 949-362-2000, 800-899-2226, FAX 949-362-2020, http://www.aacn.org/. adv.: B&W page USD 6,030, color page USD 7,480. Circ: 83,000 (paid).

616.8 618.92 AUS ISSN 1449-9509
A A I M H I NEWSLETTER. (Australian Association for Infant Mental Health Inc) Text in English. 2004. q. back issues avail. **Document type:** *Newsletter, Academic/Scholarly.*
Media: Online - full text. **Related titles:** Print ed.: ISSN 1442-701X.
Published by: Australian Association for Infant Mental Health, PO Box 846, Ashfield, NSW 1800, Australia. TEL 61-2-95157845. Ed. Shelley Reid.

616.8 USA ISSN 1934-645X
RD1
➤ **A A N S NEUROSURGEON.** (American Association of Neurological Surgeons) Text in English. 1975. q. free (effective 2010). adv. back issues avail.; reprints avail. **Document type:** *Journal, Academic/Scholarly.* **Description:** Focuses on issues related to legislation, workforce and practice management as they affect the specialty of neurosurgery.
Former titles (until 2007): A A N S Bulletin (1072-0456); (until 1992): A A N S Newsletter
Related titles: Online - full text ed.: ISSN 1934-6468.
Published by: American Association of Neurological Surgeons, 5550 Meadowbrook Dr, Rolling Meadows, IL 60008. TEL 847-378-0500, FAX 847-378-0600, info@aans.org. Ed. William T Couldwell. Adv. contact Greg Pessagno TEL 443-512-8899 ext 109.

616.8 FRA ISSN 1767-5936
A B C NEUROLOGIES. (Actualites Bibliographiques Commentees) Text in French. 2004. irreg. **Document type:** *Journal, Trade.*
Published by: Expressions Groupe, 2 Rue de la Roquette, Cour de Mai, Paris, 75011, France. TEL 33-1-49292929, FAX 33-1-49292919, contact@expressions-sante.fr, http://www.expressions-groupe.fr.

A B P CONTACT. (Association Belge des Paralyses) *see* HANDICAPPED

616.8 USA
A C O NEWSLETTER. Text in English. 1968. s-a. bk.rev. **Document type:** *Newsletter, Consumer.*
Related titles: Microform ed.: (from PQC).
Indexed: E-psyche.
Published by: American College of Orgonomy, PO Box 490, Princeton, NJ 08542. TEL 732-821-1144, FAX 732-821-0174, aco@orgonomy.orgaco@orgonomy.org, http://www.orgonomy.org.

616.858 AUS
A D A NEWSLETTER. Text in English. 1992. q. AUD 25 (effective 2007). **Document type:** *Newsletter, Trade.*
Formerly: O C D - The Hidden Disorder
Indexed: E-psyche.
Published by: Anxiety Disorders Alliance, Level 5, 80 William St, East Sydney, NSW 2011, Australia. TEL 61-2-93396093, top@ada.mentalhealth.asn.au, http://ada.mentalhealth.asn.au. Circ: 500. **Co-sponsor:** New South Wales Association for Mental Health.

616.858 AUT ISSN 1866-6116
➤ **A D H D - ATTENTION DEFICIT AND HYPERACTIVITY DISORDERS.** Text in English. 2008. 4/yr. EUR 520, USD 782 combined subscription to institutions (print & online eds.) (effective 2012). adv. reprint service avail. from PSC. **Document type:** *Journal, Academic/Scholarly.*
Description: Publishes the results of basic and clinical research contributing to the understanding, diagnosis and treatment of attention-deficit hyperactivity disorder.
Related titles: Online - full text ed.: ISSN 1866-6647. 2008.
Indexed: A22, E01, P30, SCOPUS.
—IE. **CCC.**
Published by: Springer Wien (Subsidiary of: Springer Science+Business Media), Sachsenplatz 4-6, Vienna, W 1201, Austria. TEL 43-1-33024150, FAX 43-1-3302426, journals@springer.at, http://www.springer.at. Ed. M Gerlach. Adv. contact Irene Hofmann. B&W page EUR 1,290; trim 170 x 230. Circ: 300 (paid).

616.858 USA ISSN 1065-8025
➤ **A D H D REPORT.** (Attention Deficit Hyperactivity Disorder) Text in English. 1993. bi-m. USD 79 combined subscription domestic to individuals (print & online eds.); USD 89 combined subscription foreign to individuals (print & online eds.); USD 240 combined subscription domestic to institutions (print & online eds.); USD 250 combined subscription foreign to institutions (print & online eds.) (effective 2011). bk.rev. abstr.; bibl. index. **Document type:** *Journal, Academic/Scholarly.* **Description:** Offers relevant information from research, workshops, and clinical work on ADHD, as well as from recent scientific publications and conferences from around the world.
Related titles: Online - full text ed.: ISSN 1943-2747.
Indexed: A01, A03, A08, A22, E-psyche, E01, P19, P25, P48, PQC, T02.
—BLDSC (0680.614000), IE, Ingenta.
Published by: Guilford Publications, Inc., 72 Spring St, 4th Fl, New York, NY 10012. TEL 800-365-7006, FAX 212-966-6708, info@guilford.com. Ed. Russell A Barkley. R&P Kathy Kuehl. Adv. contact Marian Robinson. Circ: 2,500 (paid).

616.8 AUS ISSN 1833-0576
A D H D RESEARCH TODAY. (Attention-Deficit Hyperactivity Disorder) Text in English. 2004. m. free (effective 2008). adv. back issues avail. **Document type:** *Journal, Consumer.* **Description:** Details on attention-deficit hyperactivity disorder, drugs, treatment, symptoms.
Media: Online - full text.
Published by: Research Today Publications ad@researchtoday.net, http://www.researchtoday.net.

616.8 FRA ISSN 1775-8297
A H F HUNTINGTON FRANCE; aimer, c'est agir. (Association Huntington France) Text in French. 1991. irreg. EUR 2.29 per issue (effective 2006). **Document type:** *Journal, Consumer.*
Former titles (until 2003): A H F; Association Huntington
Published by: Association Huntington France, 44 rue du Chateau-des-Rentiers, Paris, 75013, France. TEL 33-1-53600879, FAX 33-1-53600899, huntingtonfrance@wanadoo.fr, http://huntington.fr.

362.2 USA ISSN 0001-1436
A H R C CHRONICLE. (Association for the Help of Retarded Children) Text in English. 1949. q. free. adv. bk.rev. illus. **Document type:** *Newsletter, Consumer.* **Description:** Provides information for AHRC families and friends about news in the field and services for children who are developmentally disabled and their parents.
Indexed: E-psyche.
Published by: Association for the Help of Retarded Children, New York City Chapter, 83 Maiden Lane, New York, NY 10038. TEL 212-780-2500, FAX 212-473-2225. Ed., R&P, Adv. contact Shirley Berenstein TEL 212-780-2619. Circ: 15,000.

616.858 ITA ISSN 1970-6618
A I R I M NEWS. (Associazione Italiana per il Ritardo Mentale) Text in Italian. 2006. bi-m. **Document type:** *Newsletter, Consumer.*
Published by: (Associazione Italiana per il Ritardo Mentale (A I Ri M)), Vannini Editrice, Via Leonardo da Vinci 6, Gussago, BS 25064, Italy. TEL 39-030-313374, FAX 39-030-314078, http://www.vanninieditrice.it.

616.8 170 USA ISSN 2150-7740
R725.5
▼ ➤ **A J O B NEUROSCIENCE.** (American Journal of Bioethics) Variant title: American Journal of Bioethics Neuroscience. Text in English. 2010. q. GBP 32, EUR 42, USD 52 to individuals; GBP 175, EUR 230, EUR 288 combined subscription to institutions (print & online eds.) (effective 2010). **Document type:** *Journal, Academic/Scholarly.*
Description: Provides research for scholars, practitioners, and others interested in ethics and the brain sciences.
Related titles: Online - full text ed.: ISSN 2150-7759. GBP 30, EUR 42, USD 52 to individuals; GBP 166, EUR 219, USD 274 to institutions (effective 2010); ◆ Supplement to: The American Journal of Bioethics. ISSN 1526-5161.
Indexed: A01, C06, P30, P48, PQC, T02.
—**CCC.**
Published by: Taylor & Francis Inc. (Subsidiary of: Taylor & Francis Group), 325 Chestnut St, Ste 800, Philadelphia, PA 19106. TEL 215-625-8900, FAX 215-625-8914, customerservice@taylorandfrancis.com, http://www.taylorandfrancis.com.

616.8 FRA ISSN 0999-792X
CODEN: AANAE3
➤ **A N A E;** actualites de neuropsychologie de l'enfant. (Approche Neuropsychologique des Apprentissages chez l'Enfant) Text in English, French. 5/yr. EUR 120 domestic; EUR 200 foreign (effective 2003). back issues avail. **Document type:** *Journal, Academic/Scholarly.* **Description:** For researchers and clinicians.
Indexed: E-psyche, EMBASE, ExcerpMed, FR, L&LBA, P03, PsycInfo, PsycholAb, R10, Reac, SCOPUS, SOPODA.
—BLDSC (1580.615000), IE, Ingenta, INIST. **CCC.**
Published by: P D G Communication, 30 rue d'Armaille, Paris, 75017, France. TEL 33-01-40550595, FAX 33-01-45746567, pdg.com@wanadoo.fr. Ed. Dr. Claude Jeanne Madelin. Pub. Patrick de Gavre.

616.89 USA
A N D I NEWS. Text in English. q. free (effective 2007). back issues avail.
Document type: *Newsletter, Consumer.* **Description:** Includes research updates, conference summaries, new product advisories, articles by parents and professionals, and recipes.
Indexed: E-psyche.
Published by: Autism Network for Dietary Intervention, PO Box 17711, Rochester, NY 14617-0711. autismndi@aol.com.

301.19 167 USA
A N R E D. (Anorexia Nervosa & Related Eating Disorders) Text in English. 1979. m. free (effective 2003). bk.rev. back issues avail.
Document type: *Newsletter, Consumer.* **Description:** Causes, consequences, symptoms and treatment of anorexia nervosa and bulimia nervosa.
Formerly (until 1997): A N R E D Alert (Print)
Media: Online - full text.
Indexed: E-psyche.
Published by: Anorexia Nervosa & Related Eating Disorders, Inc., PO Box 5102, Eugene, OR 97405. TEL 541-344-1144. Ed. Dr. J. Bradley Rubel. R&P Dr. J Bradley Rubel.

616.8 USA ISSN 0886-5620
A S E T NEWSLETTER. Variant title: A S E T News. Text in English. 1976. q. looseleaf. free to members (effective 2010). back issues avail.
Document type: *Newsletter, Trade.* **Description:** Contains news of the society, educational articles, and calendar of events.
Related titles: Online - full text ed.
Indexed: E-psyche.
Published by: American Society of Electroneurodiagnostic Technologists, Inc., 402 E Bannister Rd, Ste A, Kansas City, MO 64131. TEL 816-931-1120, FAX 816-931-1145, info@aset.org.

616.80711 USA ISSN 1042-9670
RC336 CODEN: ACPSFE
➤ **ACADEMIC PSYCHIATRY.** Abbreviated title: A P. Text in English. 1977. bi-m. USD 223 combined subscription domestic to individuals (print & online eds.); USD 335 combined subscription foreign to individuals (print & online eds.); USD 363 combined subscription domestic to institutions (print & online eds.); USD 388 combined subscription foreign to institutions (print & online eds.) (effective 2011). adv. bk.rev. bibl.; charts; illus. back issues avail.; reprints avail. **Document type:** *Journal, Academic/Scholarly.* **Description:** Brings out scholarly work focused on innovative psychiatric education, professional development in academic psychiatry, and leadership by psychiatrists in the field of medicine.
Formerly (until 1989): Journal of Psychiatric Education (0363-1907)
Related titles: Microform ed.: (from PQC); Online - full text ed.: ISSN 1545-7230. USD 205 to individuals (effective 2011).
Indexed: A20, A22, ASCA, C06, C07, CPE, CPLI, CurCont, E-psyche, EMBASE, ERIC, ExcerpMed, F09, Faml, IBR, IBZ, MEA&I, MEDLINE, P03, P20, P22, P25, P30, P48, P54, PQC, PsycInfo, PsycholAb, R10, Reac, SCOPUS, SSCI, W07.
—BLDSC (0570.514150), GNLM, IE, Infotrieve, Ingenta. **CCC.**
Published by: (American Association of Directors of Psychiatric Residency Training), American Psychiatric Publishing, Inc., 1000 Wilson Blvd, Ste 1825, Arlington, VA 22209. TEL 703-907-7856, 800-368-5777, FAX 703-907-1092, appi@psych.org, http://www.appi.org. Eds. Dr. Laura Weiss Roberts, Michael D Roy. Adv. contact Valentin Torres TEL 212-904-0375. **Subscr. to:** PO Box 97250, Washington, DC 20090. **Co-sponsor:** Association for Academic Psychiatry.

570 616.8 POL ISSN 0065-1400
QP351 CODEN: ANEXAC
➤ **ACTA NEUROBIOLOGIAE EXPERIMENTALIS.** Text in English. 1928. q. EUR 214 foreign (effective 2006). adv. abstr. index. reprints avail.
Document type: *Journal, Academic/Scholarly.* **Description:** Publishes the results of original brain research in English.
Formerly (until 1970): Acta Biologiae Experimentalis (0365-0820)
Related titles: Online - full text ed.: ISSN 1689-0035. free (effective 2011).
Indexed: A20, A22, ASCA, ASFA, AgrAg, AgrLib, AnBeAb, B21, B25, BIOSIS Prev, ChemAb, CurCont, DentInd, E-psyche, EMBASE, ESPM, ExcerpMed, ISR, IndMed, Inpharma, MEDLINE, MycolAb, NSA, NSCI, P03, P30, PsycInfo, PsycholAb, R10, Reac, RefZh, SCI, SCOPUS, ToxAb, W07.
—BLDSC (0639.800000), CASDDS, GNLM, IE, Infotrieve, Ingenta, INIST.
Published by: Polska Akademia Nauk, Instytut Biologii Doswiadczalnej im. M. Nenckiego/Polish Academy of Sciences, M. Nencki Institute of Experimental Biology, ul Ludwika Pasteura 3, Warsaw, 02093, Poland. TEL 48-22-5892207, FAX 48-22-8225342, dyrekcja@nencki.gov.pl. Ed., R&P Krzysztof Turlejski. Adv. contact Krystyna Szlenk. B&W page USD 150, color page USD 300. **Dist. by:** Ars Polona, Obroncow 25, Warsaw 03933, Poland. TEL 48-22-5098609, FAX 48-22-5098610, arspolona@arspolona.com.pl, http://www.arspolona.com.pl.

➤ **ACTA NEUROCHIRURGICA**; the European journal of neurosurgery. *see* MEDICAL SCIENCES—Surgery

616.8 AUT ISSN 0065-1419
CODEN: ANCSBM
➤ **ACTA NEUROCHIRURGICA. SUPPLEMENTUM.** Text in English. 1950. irreg., latest vol.85, 2003. price varies. adv. reprints avail.
Document type: *Monographic series, Academic/Scholarly.*
Related titles: Microform ed.: (from PQC); ◆ Supplement to: Acta Neurochirurgica. ISSN 0001-6268.
Indexed: A22, ASCA, B&BAb, B19, B21, E-psyche, EMBASE, ExcerpMed, INIS AtomInd, IndMed, Inpharma, MEDLINE, NSA, P30, P35, R10, Reac, SCOPUS.
—BLDSC (0639.851000), IE, Ingenta, INIST. **CCC.**
Published by: Springer Wien (Subsidiary of: Springer Science+Business Media), Sachsenplatz 4-6, Vienna, W 1201, Austria. TEL 43-1-3302415-0, FAX 43-1-330242665, journals@springer.at, http://www.springer.at. Ed. H-J Reulen. R&P Angela Foessl TEL 43-1-3302415517. Adv. contact Michael Katzenberger TEL 43-1-3302415220. B&W page EUR 1,000; 170 x 250. **Subscri. in N. America to:** Springer New York LLC, Journal Fulfillment, PO Box 2485, Secaucus, NJ 07096. TEL 800-777-4643, 201-348-4033, FAX 201-348-4505, journals-ny@springer.com.

616.8 BEL ISSN 0300-9009
RC321 CODEN: ANUBBR
➤ **ACTA NEUROLOGICA BELGICA.** Text in English, French. 1900. 4/yr. EUR 120 domestic; EUR 130 foreign (effective 2011). Supplement avail. **Document type:** *Journal, Academic/Scholarly.*
Supersedes in part: Acta Neurologica et Psychiatrica Belgica (0001-6284)
Indexed: A22, A29, ASCA, B20, B21, BDM&CN, ChemAb, CurCont, E-psyche, EMBASE, ESPM, ExcerpMed, GeoRef, IndMed, Inpharma, MEDLINE, NSA, NSCI, P03, P30, P35, PsycInfo, PsycholAb, R10, Reac, SCI, SCOPUS, SpeleolAb, VirolAbstr, W07.
—BLDSC (0639.902000), CASDDS, GNLM, IE, Infotrieve, Ingenta, INIST. **CCC.**
Published by: (Association Royale des Societes Scientifiques Medicales Belges/Koninklijke Vereniging van de Belgische Medische Wetenschappelijke Genootschappen), Acta Medica Belgica, Avenue Winston Churchill 11/30, Brussels, 1180, Belgium. TEL 32-2-3745158, FAX 32-2-3749628, amb@skynet.be, http://www.ulb.ac.be/medecine/loce/amb.htm.

616.8 COL ISSN 0120-8748
ACTA NEUROLOGICA COLOMBIANA. Text in Spanish. 1985. quadrennial. back issues avail. **Document type:** *Journal, Academic/Scholarly.*
Related titles: Online - full text ed.
Published by: Asociacion Colombiana de Neurologia, Carrera 11-B No. 99-54 of 401, Bogota, Colombia. TEL 57-1-6112051, FAX 57-1-2363751. Ed. German Enrique Perez.

616.8 USA ISSN 0001-6314
RC321 CODEN: ANRSAS
➤ **ACTA NEUROLOGICA SCANDINAVICA.** Text in English. 1926. m. GBP 803 in United Kingdom to institutions; EUR 1,020 in Europe to institutions; USD 1,347 in the Americas to institutions; USD 1,574 elsewhere to institutions; GBP 924 combined subscription in United Kingdom to institutions (print & online eds.); EUR 1,174 combined subscription in Europe to institutions (print & online eds.); USD 1,549 combined subscription in the Americas to institutions (print & online eds.); USD 1,810 combined subscription elsewhere to institutions (print & online eds.) (effective 2012). bk.rev. bibl.; charts; illus. index. reprint service avail. from PSC. **Document type:** *Journal, Academic/Scholarly.* **Description:** Presents original clinical, diagnostic or experimental work in neuroscience, especially those which bring new knowledge and observations from the application of therapies or techniques in the combating of a broad spectrum of neurological disease and neurodegenerative disorders.
Supersedes in part (in 1961): Acta Psychiatrica et Neurologica Scandinavica (0365-5598); Which was formerly (until 1950): Acta Psychiatrica et Neurologica (0365-558X)
Related titles: Online - full text ed.: ISSN 1600-0404. GBP 803 in United Kingdom to institutions; EUR 1,020 in Europe to institutions; USD 1,347 in the Americas to institutions; USD 1,574 elsewhere to institutions (effective 2012) (from IngentaConnect); ◆ Supplement(s): Acta Neurologica Scandinavica. Supplementum. ISSN 0065-1427.
Indexed: A01, A02, A03, A08, A20, A22, A26, A36, ASCA, B21, B25, BDM&CN, BIOBASE, BIOSIS Prev, CA, CABA, CIN, ChemAb, ChemTitl, CurCont, DBA, DentInd, DokArb, E-psyche, E01, E12, EMBASE, ExcerpMed, FR, Faml, GH, H12, H17, IABS, ISR, IndMed, Inpharma, JW-N, MEDLINE, MycolAb, N02, N03, NRN, NSA, NSCI, P03, P30, P33, P35, P39, P43, PN&I, PsycInfo, PsycholAb, R08, R10, R12, Reac, S13, S16, SCI, SCOPUS, SSCI, T02, T05, THA, VS, W07, W10.
—BLDSC (0639.910000), CASDDS, GNLM, IE, Infotrieve, Ingenta, INIST. **CCC.**
Published by: Wiley-Blackwell Publishing, Inc. (Subsidiary of: Wiley-Blackwell Publishing Ltd.), Commerce Pl, 350 Main St, Malden, MA 02148. TEL 781-388-8200, FAX 781-388-8210, info@wiley.com, http://www.wiley.com/WileyCDA/. Ed. Elinor Ben-Menachem TEL 47-31-3423100.

616.8 USA ISSN 0065-1427
CODEN: ANSLAC
➤ **ACTA NEUROLOGICA SCANDINAVICA. SUPPLEMENTUM.** Text in English. 1951. irreg., latest vol.189, 2009. free with subscription to Acta Neurologica Scandinavica. reprint service avail. from PSC.
Document type: *Monographic series, Academic/Scholarly.*
Supersedes in part (in 1962): Acta Psychiatrica et Neurologica Scandinavica. Supplementum (0365-5067)
Related titles: Online - full text ed.: ISSN 1600-5449. 2000 (from IngentaConnect); ◆ Supplement to: Acta Neurologica Scandinavica. ISSN 0001-6314.
Indexed: A22, B21, ChemAb, E-psyche, EMBASE, ExcerpMed, IndMed, Inpharma, MEDLINE, NSA, P30, P35, R10, Reac, SCOPUS.
—BLDSC (0639.912000), CASDDS, IE, Infotrieve, Ingenta, INIST. **CCC.**
Published by: Wiley-Blackwell Publishing, Inc. (Subsidiary of: Wiley-Blackwell Publishing Ltd.), Commerce Pl, 350 Main St, Malden, MA 02148. TEL 781-388-8200, FAX 781-388-8210, info@wiley.com, http://www.wiley.com/WileyCDA/. Ed. Elinor Ben-Menachem TEL 47-31-3423100.

616.8 TWN ISSN 1028-768X
ACTA NEUROLOGICA TAIWANICA. Text in English. 1997. q. **Document type:** *Journal, Academic/Scholarly.*
Formerly (until 1997): Acta Neurologica Sinica (1019-6099)
Indexed: EMBASE, ExcerpMed, MEDLINE, P30, R10, Reac, SCOPUS.
—BLDSC (0639.916000), IE, Ingenta.
Published by: Taiwan Neurological Society, Ting Jou Lu section 3 no 8, Taipei, 100, Taiwan. TEL 886-2-2364-9217, FAX 886-2-2364-9218, gant@mail.hato.com.tw, http://www.neuro.org.tw/.

616.8 DEU ISSN 0001-6322
RC347 CODEN: ANPTAL
➤ **ACTA NEUROPATHOLOGICA.** Text in English. 1961. m. EUR 6,201, USD 7,382 combined subscription to institutions (print & online eds.) (effective 2012). bibl.; charts; illus. index. reprint service avail. from PSC. **Document type:** *Journal, Academic/Scholarly.* **Description:** Provides information on subjects related to nerve tissue research based on modern investigative techniques, including histochemistry, electron microscopy, immunology, tissue culture, biophysics, neurochemistry, and experimental neuropathology.
Related titles: Microform ed.: (from PQC); Online - full text ed.: ISSN 1432-0533 (from IngentaConnect).
Indexed: A01, A03, A08, A22, A26, A34, A35, A36, A38, AIDS&CR, ASCA, AgBio, B21, B25, BIOBASE, BIOSIS Prev, CA, CABA, CIN, ChemAb, ChemTitl, CurCont, DentInd, E-psyche, E01, E12, EMBASE, ExcerpMed, F08, F11, F12, GH, H12, I05, IABS, IBR, IBZ, ISR, IndMed, IndVet, Inpharma, JW-N, Kidney, MEDLINE, MycolAb, N02, NSA, NSCI, P03, P20, P22, P30, P33, P37, P39, P48, P54, PQC, PsycInfo, R10, RA&MP, RM&VM, Reac, SAA, SCI, SCOPUS, T02, T05, VS, VirolAbstr, W07, W10, WildRev.
—BLDSC (0639.920000), CASDDS, GNLM, IE, Infotrieve, Ingenta, INIST. **CCC.**
Published by: (World Federation of Neurology/Federation Mondiale de Neurologie GBR), Springer (Subsidiary of: Springer Science+Business Media), Tiergartenstr 17, Heidelberg, 69121, Germany. TEL 49-6221-4870, FAX 49-6221-345229. Ed. Dr. Werner A Paulus. **Subscr. in the Americas to:** Springer New York LLC, Journal Fulfillment, PO Box 2485, Secaucus, NJ 07096. TEL 800-777-4643, 201-348-4033, FAX 201-348-4505, journals-ny@springer.com, http://www.springer.com; **Subscr. to:** Springer Distribution Center, Kundenservice Zeitschriften, Haberstr 7, Heidelberg 69126, Germany. TEL 49-6221-3454303, FAX 49-6221-3454229, subscriptions@springer.com.

616.89 USA ISSN 1601-5215
➤ **ACTA NEUROPSYCHIATRICA (ONLINE).** Text in English. 1989. bi-m. GBP 261 in United Kingdom to institutions; EUR 331 in Europe to institutions; USD 437 in the Americas to institutions; USD 511 elsewhere to institutions (effective 2012). **Document type:** *Journal, Academic/Scholarly.* **Description:** Informs members of scientific developments in research in neuropsychiatry.
Media: Online - full text (from IngentaConnect).
—**CCC.**
Published by: (Scandinavian College of Neuro-Psychopharmacology DNK), Wiley-Blackwell Publishing, Inc. (Subsidiary of: Wiley-Blackwell Publishing Ltd.), Commerce Pl, 350 Main St, Malden, MA 02148. TEL 781-388-8200, FAX 781-388-8210, info@wiley.com. Ed. Gregers Gregers.

616.8 POL ISSN 1730-7503
➤ **ACTA NEUROPSYCHOLOGICA.** Text in Polish. 2003. q. PLZ 20 per issue domestic; EUR 5 per issue foreign (effective 2008). **Document type:** *Journal, Academic/Scholarly.* **Description:** Features original articles concerned with all aspects of the brain-behavior relationship, including neurobehavioral disturbances.
Related titles: Online - full text ed.: free (effective 2006).
Indexed: EMBASE, ExcerpMed, PsycInfo, R10, Reac, SCOPUS.
—BLDSC (0639.980000).
Published by: (Polskie Towarzystwo Neuropsychologiczne/Polish Neuropsychological Society), MedSportPress, ul Marymoncka 34 skr. 23, Warsaw, 01813, Poland. TEL 48-22-8346772, FAX 48-22-8340431, nauka@medsport.pl. Ed. Maria Pachalska.

616.89 ARG ISSN 0001-6896
RC321 CODEN: APQPAS
➤ **ACTA PSIQUIATRICA Y PSICOLOGICA DE AMERICA LATINA.** Text in Spanish. 1954. q. ARS 50 domestic to individuals; USD 75 foreign to individuals; ARS 80 domestic to institutions; USD 90 foreign to institutions (effective 2010). adv. bk.rev. abstr.; charts; illus. index. Supplement avail.; reprint service avail. from IRC. **Document type:** *Academic/Scholarly.* **Description:** Devoted to psychiatry and psychology issues relevant to Latin America.
Former titles (until 1963): Acta Psiquiatrica y Psicologica Argentina (0365-5636); (until 1961): Acta Neuropsiquiatrica Argentina (0365-5091)
Indexed: A20, A22, ASCA, C01, ChemAb, E-psyche, IBR, IBZ, IndMed, P03, P30, PsycInfo, PsycholAb, S02, S03, SCOPUS.
—BLDSC (0661.399000), GNLM, IE, Infotrieve, Ingenta, INIST.
Published by: Fundacion Acta Fondo para la Salud Mental, Malabia, 2274 13 A, Buenos Aires, 1425, Argentina. TEL 54-114-48548209, FAX 54-114-48573151. Eds. Dr. Guillermo Vidal, Fernando Lolas Stepke. R&P Dr. Guillermo Vidal. Adv. contact Dr. Diana Vidal. Circ: 2,000.

616.89 USA ISSN 0001-690X
RC321 CODEN: APYSA9
➤ **ACTA PSYCHIATRICA SCANDINAVICA.** Text in English. 1926. m. GBP 814 in United Kingdom to institutions; EUR 1,035 in Europe to institutions; USD 1,367 in the Americas to institutions; USD 1,595 elsewhere to institutions; GBP 936 combined subscription in United Kingdom to institutions (print & online eds.); EUR 1,191 combined subscription in Europe to institutions (print & online eds.); USD 1,572 combined subscription in the Americas to institutions (print & online eds.); USD 1,834 combined subscription elsewhere to institutions (print & online eds.) (effective 2012). adv. bk.rev. charts; illus. index. back issues avail.; reprint service avail. from PSC. **Document type:** *Journal, Academic/Scholarly.* **Description:** Articles in English representing clinical and clinically relevant experimental work in psychiatry.
Supersedes in part (in 1961): Acta Psychiatrica et Neurologica Scandinavica (0365-5598); Which was formerly (until 1950): Acta Psychiatrica et Neurologica (0365-558X)
Related titles: Online - full text ed.: ISSN 1600-0447. GBP 814 in United Kingdom to institutions; EUR 1,035 in Europe to institutions; USD 1,367 in the Americas to institutions; USD 1,595 elsewhere to institutions (effective 2012) (from IngentaConnect); ◆ Supplement(s): Acta Psychiatrica Scandinavica. Supplementum. ISSN 0065-1591.
Indexed: A01, A02, A03, A08, A20, A22, A26, A36, AC&P, AHCMS, AMHA, ASCA, AddicA, AgeL, B21, B25, BDM&CN, BIOBASE, BIOSIS Prev, CA, CABA, CIN, ChemAb, ChemTitl, CurCont, DBA, DentInd, DokArb, E-psyche, E01, E12, EMBASE, ExcerpMed, F09, FR, Faml, GH, H12, H13, H17, IABS, IBR, IBZ, INI, IPsyAb, ISR, IndMed, Inpharma, JW-P, Kidney, LT, MEA&I, MEDLINE, MycolAb, N02, N03, NSA, P02, P03, P10, P20, P30, P33, P35, P39, P43, P48, P53, P54, PQC, PsycInfo, PsycholAb, R10, R12, RRTA, Reac, S02, S03, SCI, SCOPUS, SSCI, T02, T05, THA, W07.
—BLDSC (0661.470000), CASDDS, GNLM, IE, Infotrieve, Ingenta, INIST. **CCC.**
Published by: Wiley-Blackwell Publishing, Inc. (Subsidiary of: Wiley-Blackwell Publishing Ltd.), Commerce Pl, 350 Main St, Malden, MA 02148. TEL 781-388-8200, FAX 781-388-8210, info@wiley.com, http://www.wiley.com/WileyCDA/. Ed. Povl Munk-Joergensen.

616.8 USA ISSN 0065-1591
RC321 CODEN: ASSUA6
➤ **ACTA PSYCHIATRICA SCANDINAVICA. SUPPLEMENTUM.** Text in English. 1951. irreg., latest vol.439, 2009. free with subscription to Acta Psychiatrica Scandinavica. adv. back issues avail.; reprint service avail. from PSC. **Document type:** *Monographic series, Academic/Scholarly.*
Supersedes in part (in 1961): Acta Psychiatrica et Neurologica Scandinavica (0365-5067)
Related titles: Online - full text ed.: ISSN 1600-5473; ◆ Supplement to: Acta Psychiatrica Scandinavica. ISSN 0001-690X.

Indexed: A01, A02, A03, A08, A22, CIN, ChemAb, ChemTitl, E-psyche, EMBASE, ExcerpMed, F09, FR, INI, IndMed, Inpharma, MEA&I, MEDLINE, P30, P35, P43, R10, Reac, SCOPUS, SSCI, T02, V&AA.
—BLDSC (0661.472000), CASDDS, IE, Infotrieve, Ingenta, INIST. **CCC.**
Published by: Wiley-Blackwell Publishing, Inc. (Subsidiary of: Wiley-Blackwell Publishing Ltd.), Commerce Pl, 350 Main St, Malden, MA 02148. TEL 781-388-8200, FAX 781-388-8210, info@wiley.com, http://www.wiley.com/WileyCDA/. Ed. Povl Munk-Joergensen.

616.8 ESP ISSN 1139-9287
CODEN: ALNPAJ
➤ **ACTAS ESPANOLAS DE PSIQUIATRIA.** Text in Spanish. 1940. bi-m. EUR 112.84 domestic to individuals; EUR 195.98 foreign to individuals; EUR 133.65 domestic to institutions; EUR 231.93 foreign to institutions (effective 2009). back issues avail.; reprints avail. **Document type:** *Journal, Academic/Scholarly.*
Former titles (until 1999): Actas Luso Espanolas de Neurologia Psiquiatria y Ciencias Afines (0300-5062); (until 1971): Actas Luso Espanolas de Neurologia y Psiquiatria (0001-7329); (until 1946): Actas Espanolas de Neurologia y Psiquiatria (0300-5054)
Related titles: Online - full text ed.: ISSN 1578-2735. 1996. EUR 70.34 domestic; EUR 105.53 foreign (effective 2009); ◆ Series: Actas Espanolas de Psiquiatria. Monografias. ISSN 1575-071X.
Indexed: A01, A22, ASCA, CA, E-psyche, EMBASE, ExcerpMed, F03, F04, IME, IndMed, MEDLINE, NSCI, P03, P30, PsycInfo, PsycholAb, R10, Reac, S02, S03, SCI, SCOPUS, T02, W07.
—BLDSC (0615.507000), CASDDS, GNLM, IE, Infotrieve, Ingenta, INIST. **CCC.**
Published by: Grupo Ars XXI de Comunicacion, SA, Muntaner 262 Atico 2a., Barcelona, 08021, Spain. TEL 34-90-2195484, FAX 34-93-2722902, info@arsxxi.com, http://www.stmeditores.com. Circ: 2,000.

616.8 ESP ISSN 1575-071X
ACTAS ESPANOLAS DE PSIQUIATRIA. MONOGRAFIAS. Text in Spanish. 1999. quadrennial. **Document type:** *Monographic series, Academic/Scholarly.*
Related titles: ◆ Series of: Actas Espanolas de Psiquiatria. ISSN 1139-9287.
—CCC.
Published by: Grupo Ars XXI de Comunicacion, SA, Muntaner 262 Atico 2a., Barcelona, 08021, Spain. TEL 34-90-2195484, FAX 34-93-2722902, info@arsxxi.com, http://www.arsxxi.com.

616.8 CZE ISSN 1802-9698
CODEN: HOMOEB
➤ **ACTIVITAS NERVOSA SUPERIOR**; journal for neuroscience and cognitive research. Text in English. 1959. bi-m. EUR 60 (effective 2009). adv. bk.rev. illus. index. **Document type:** *Journal, Academic/Scholarly.* **Description:** devoted to studies of integrative brain functions in homeostasis, their adaptation to environmental and psychosocial conditions, and underlying mechanisms ranging from molecular to systemic processes and behavior.
Former titles (until 2008): Homeostasis (0960-7560); (until vol.33, 1991): Activitas Nervosa Superior (0001-7604)
Indexed: A01, A20, A29, ASCA, ASFA, B20, B21, CISA, ChemAb, E-psyche, EMBASE, ESPM, ExcerpMed, I10, ISR, IndMed, MLA-IB, NSA, P03, P25, P30, P48, PQC, PsycInfo, PsycholAb, PsychopharAb, R10, Reac, SCOPUS, ViroIAbstr.
—BLDSC (0676.105000), CASDDS, GNLM, IE, Infotrieve, Ingenta, INIST. **CCC.**
Published by: (Collegium Internationale Activitatis Nervosae Superioris), Neuroscientia o.s., Center for Neuropsychiatric Research of traumatic Stress, Dept of Psychiatry, 1st Faculty of Medicine, Charles University, Prague, 12900, Czech Republic. Ed. Peter Fedor-Freybergh.

616.92 USA ISSN 1531-7277
RC523
➤ **ACTIVITIES DIRECTORS' QUARTERLY FOR ALZHEIMER'S & OTHER DEMENTIA PATIENTS.** Text in English. 2000. q. USD 117 to individuals; USD 152 to institutions (effective 2010). adv. 40 p./no.; reprints avail. **Document type:** *Journal, Trade.* **Description:** Designed to serve the day-to-day needs of activities directors serving Alzheimer's and other dementia patients. We reach several thousand activities directors each issue.
Indexed: AgeL, C06, C07.
—BLDSC (0676.474810). **CCC.**
Published by: Weston Medical Publishing, LLC, 470 Boston Post Rd, Weston, MA 02493. TEL 781-899-2702, 800-743-7206, FAX 781-899-4900, brenda_devito@pnpco.com, subscription@pnpco.com, http://www.wmpllc.org. Ed. Linda L Buettner. Pub. Richard A DeVito Sr. TEL 781-899-2702 ext 107.

616.8 IRL ISSN 1393-7472
ACTIVITIES OF IRISH PSYCHIATRIC SERVICES (YEAR). Text in English. 1972. a. **Document type:** *Journal, Academic/Scholarly.* **Description:** Psychiatric in-patient admission, community psychiatric services, diagnosis.
Formerly (until 1997): Activities of Irish Psychiatric Hospitals and Units (Year) (0332-2602)
Indexed: E-psyche.
Published by: Mental Health Division, Health Research Board, 73 Lower Baggot St., Dublin, 2, Ireland. TEL 353-1-6761176, FAX 353-1-6611856, mental_health@hrb.ie, http://www.hrb.ie. Ed. Joan Moore. Circ: 1,000.

616.8 FRA ISSN 0567-882X
ACTUALITES NEUROPHYSIOLOGIQUES/TRENDS IN NEUROPHYSIOLOGY. Text in French. 1959. irreg. **Document type:** *Journal, Academic/Scholarly.*
Indexed: P30.
Published by: Elsevier Masson (Subsidiary of: Elsevier Health Sciences), 62 Rue Camille Desmoulins, Issy les Moulineaux, Cedex 92442, France. TEL 33-1-71165500, infos@elsevier-masson.fr, http://www.elsevier-masson.fr.

616.8 BEL ISSN 1386-8977
ACTUELE THEMATA UIT DE PSYCHOMOTORISCHE THERAPIE. Text in Dutch. 1994. a. price varies.
Published by: Uitgeverij Acco, Brusselsestraat 153, Leuven, 3000, Belgium. TEL 32-16-628000, FAX 32-16-628001, uitgeverij@acco.be, http://www.acco.be.

616.8 362.7 FRA ISSN 0751-7696
BF724
ADOLESCENCE. Text in French. 1983. q. EUR 80 in Europe; EUR 90 elsewhere; EUR 70 to students (effective 2009). back issues avail. **Document type:** *Journal, Academic/Scholarly.*
Related titles: Online - full text ed.
Indexed: A22, CDA, FR, PsycInfo, THA, WSI.
—IE, Infotrieve, INIST. **CCC.**
Published by: Groupe de Recherche et d'Enseignement Universitaires de Psychopathologie et Psychanalyse (G R E U P P), 3 Av. Vavin, Paris, 75006, France. TEL 33-1-45516003, greuppado@club-internet.fr.

616.8 USA ISSN 0065-2008
RJ499.A1
➤ **ADOLESCENT PSYCHIATRY.** Variant title: American Society for Adolescent Psychiatry. Annals. Text in English. 1971. a., latest vol.30, 2007. price varies. back issues avail.; reprints avail. **Document type:** *Monographic series, Academic/Scholarly.* **Description:** Reports on specific clinical and theoretical issues, as well as considerations of social, cultural, and political themes. Contains scholarly articles from contributors in a variety of disciplines.
Related titles: Microfilm ed.: (from PMC); Online - full text ed.
Indexed: A01, A03, A08, A09, A10, A20, A22, ASCA, CA, E-psyche, P10, P16, P26, P30, P43, P48, P53, P54, PQC, PsycholAb, S02, S03, SCOPUS, SSCI, T02, V02, V03, V04, W07.
—BLDSC (0696.589000), GNLM, IE, Infotrieve, Ingenta. **CCC.**
Published by: (American Society for Adolescent Psychiatry), Routledge (Subsidiary of: Taylor & Francis Group), 270 Madison Ave, New York, NY 10016. TEL 212-216-7800, 800-634-7064, FAX 212-244-1563, journals@routledge.com, http://www.routledge.com.

616.89 NLD ISSN 2210-6766
▼ ➤ **ADOLESCENT PSYCHIATRY.** Text in English. 2011. q. USD 450 to institutions (print or online ed.) (effective 2012). **Document type:** *Journal, Academic/Scholarly.*
Related titles: Online - full text ed.: ISSN 2210-6774.
—CCC.
Published by: Bentham Science Publishers Ltd., PO Box 294, Bussum, 1400 AG, Netherlands. TEL 31-35-6923800, FAX 31-35-6980150, sales@bentham.org, http://www.bentham.org. Ed. Lois T Flaherty. **Subscr. to:** Bentham Science Publishers Ltd., c/o Richard E Morrissy, PO Box 446, Oak Park, IL 60301. TEL 312-413-5867, FAX 312-996-7107, subscriptions@bentham.org.

➤ **ADVANCE (RICHMOND).** *see* SOCIAL SERVICES AND WELFARE

616.8 SGP ISSN 1793-0863
ADVANCED SERIES IN NEUROSCIENCE. Text in English. 1988. irreg., latest vol.5, 1997. price varies. back issues avail. **Document type:** *Monographic series, Academic/Scholarly.*
Indexed: CCMJ, E-psyche.
Published by: World Scientific Publishing Co. Pte. Ltd., 5 Toh Tuck Link, Singapore, 596224, Singapore. TEL 65-6466-5775, FAX 65-6467-7667, wspc@wspc.com.sg, http://www.worldscientific.com. **Dist. by:** World Scientific Publishing Co., Inc., 27 Warren St, Ste 401-402, Hackensack, NJ 07601. TEL 201-487-9655, 800-227-7562, FAX 201-487-9656, 888-977-2665, wspc@wspc.com; World Scientific Publishing Ltd., 57 Shelton St, London WC2H 9HE, United Kingdom. TEL 44-207-8360888, FAX 44-207-8362020, sales@wspc.co.uk.

616.8 AUT ISSN 0095-4829
RD593
➤ **ADVANCES AND TECHNICAL STANDARDS IN NEUROSURGERY.** Text in English. 1974. irreg., latest vol.29, 2004. price varies. reprints avail. **Document type:** *Monographic series, Academic/Scholarly.* **Description:** Presents fields of neurosurgery and related areas in which important recent progress has been made.
Indexed: A22, E-psyche, EMBASE, ExcerpMed, IndMed, MEDLINE, P30, R10, Reac, SCOPUS.
—BLDSC (0698.820000), GNLM, IE, Infotrieve, Ingenta, INIST. **CCC.**
Published by: Springer Wien (Subsidiary of: Springer Science+Business Media), Sachsenplatz 4-6, Vienna, W 1201, Austria. TEL 43-1-3302415O, FAX 43-1-3302426, books@springer.at, http://www.springer.at. Ed. J Pickard. R&P Angela Foessl TEL 43-1-3302415517. **Subscr. to:** Springer New York LLC, Journal Fulfillment, PO Box 2485, Secaucus, NJ 07096. TEL 201-348-4033, 800-777-4643, FAX 201-348-4505, http://www.springer.com.

616.8 GBR ISSN 0965-1802
ADVANCES IN A L S - M N D. (Amyotrophic Lateral Sclerosis - Motor Neuron Disease) Text in English. 1991. irreg. **Document type:** *Monographic series, Academic/Scholarly.*
Indexed: E-psyche.
—CCC.
Published by: Smith-Gordon and Co. Ltd., Media House, Burrel Rd, St Ives, Cambridgeshire PE27 3LE, United Kingdom. TEL 44-1480-465233, FAX 44-1480-466053, publishing@smith-gordon-publishing.com.

616.8 CHE ISSN 0378-7354
CODEN: ABPSD5
➤ **ADVANCES IN BIOLOGICAL PSYCHIATRY.** Text in English. 1978. irreg., latest vol.26, 2010. price varies. reprints avail. **Document type:** *Monographic series, Academic/Scholarly.* **Description:** Focuses on interdisciplinary collaboration in which methodological contributions from the biological and psychological sciences are juxtaposed with clinical and more practical updates.
Related titles: Online - full text ed.: ISSN 1662-2774.
Indexed: CIN, ChemAb, ChemTitl, E-psyche, PsycholAb.
—BLDSC (0700.070000), CASDDS, IE, Ingenta, INIST. **CCC.**
Published by: S. Karger AG, Allschwilerstr 10, Basel, 4055, Switzerland. TEL 41-61-3061111, FAX 41-61-3061234, karger@karger.ch, http://www.karger.ch. Eds. D. Ebert, K. P. Ebmeier, Wolfgang P. Kaschka.

616.8 GBR ISSN 1473-9348
ADVANCES IN CLINICAL NEUROSCIENCE AND REHABILITATION. Text in English. 2001. bi-m. free to qualified personnel; GBP 75 foreign (effective 2009). **Document type:** *Journal, Academic/Scholarly.*
Indexed: P30.
—BLDSC (0578.686210). **CCC.**
Published by: Whitehouse Publishing, 1 The Lynch, Mere, Wiltshire, BA12 6DQ, United Kingdom. TEL 44-1747-860168, FAX 44-1747-860168, rachael@acnr.co.uk. Ed. Roger Barker. Pub. Rachael Hansford.

616.8 USA ISSN 1944-4001
QP351
ADVANCES IN COMPUTATIONAL MOTOR CONTROL. Variant title: (Year) Advances in Computational Motor Control. Text in English. 2002. a. free (effective 2009).
Media: Online - full content.
Published by: Emo Todorov & Reza Shadmehr, Eds. & Pubs., Department of Cognitive Science, University of California San Diego, Mail Code 0515, 9500 Gilman Dr, La Jolla, CA 92093. Eds. Emo Todorov, Reza Shadmehr.

ADVANCES IN CONSCIOUSNESS RESEARCH. *see* PSYCHOLOGY

362.2905 GBR ISSN 1757-0972
ADVANCES IN DUAL DIAGNOSIS; policy, practice and research in mental health and substance use. Text in English. 2008 (Aug.). q. EUR 689 combined subscription in Europe (print & online eds.); USD 889 combined subscription in the Americas (print & online eds.); GBP 529 combined subscription in the UK & elsewhere (print & online eds.); AUD 999 combined subscription in Australasia (print & online eds.) (effective 2012). adv. back issues avail. **Document type:** *Journal, Academic/Scholarly.* **Description:** Provides practical information to help improve services for people with dual diagnosis.
Related titles: Online - full text ed.: ISSN 2042-8324.
—BLDSC (0704.325000), IE. **CCC.**
Published by: Pier Professional Ltd. (Subsidiary of: Emerald Group Publishing Ltd.), Ste N4, The Old Market, Upper Market St, Hove, BN3 1AS, United Kingdom. TEL 44-1273-783720, FAX 44-1273-783723, info@pierprofessional.com. Eds. Cheryl Kipping, Graham Durcan, Liz Hughes. adv.: B&W page GBP 350; 160 x 245.

ADVANCES IN HUMAN FACTORS - ERGONOMICS. *see* PSYCHOLOGY

362.2 AUS ISSN 1838-7357
➤ **ADVANCES IN MENTAL HEALTH.** Text in English. 2002. 3/yr. AUD 175 to individuals includes Australia, Newzealand and the Pacific; USD 175 elsewhere to individuals; AUD 399 to institutions includes Australia, Newzealand and the Pacific; USD 399 elsewhere to institutions; AUD 499 combined subscription to institutions (print & online eds.); includes Australia, Newzealand and the Pacific; USD 499 combined subscription to institutions (print & online eds.) (effective 2011). **Document type:** *Journal, Academic/Scholarly.* **Description:** Aims to nurture and encourage understanding of mental health promotion, prevention and early intervention within a multidisciplinary forum.
Related titles: Online - full text ed.: ISSN 1837-4905.
Indexed: A01, A39, ASSIA, C06, C07, C08, C27, C29, CINAHL, D03, D04, E13, IBSS, P03, PsycholAb, R14, S14, S15, S18, T02.
Published by: (Auseinet), eContent Management Pty Ltd, PO Box 1027, Maleny, QLD 4552, Australia. TEL 61-7-54352900, FAX 61-7-54352911, info@e-contentmanagement.com, http://www.e-contentmanagement.com. Ed. Graham Martin.

362.30941 371.92 GBR ISSN 2044-1282
➤ **ADVANCES IN MENTAL HEALTH AND INTELLECTUAL DISABILITIES.** Text in English. 2007 (Mar.). bi-m. (q. until 2011). EUR 689 combined subscription in Europe (print & online eds.); USD 889 combined subscription in the Americas (print & online eds.); GBP 529 combined subscription in the UK & elsewhere (print & online eds.); AUD 999 combined subscription in Australasia (print & online eds.) (effective 2012). adv. back issues avail. **Document type:** *Journal, Academic/Scholarly.* **Description:** Integrates current research with practice. Keeps professionals up to date with a variety of different perspectives on developments in the field.
Formerly (until 2010): Advances in Mental Health and Learning Disabilities (1753-0180)
Related titles: Online - full text ed.: ISSN 2044-1290.
Indexed: B28, B29, CA, E03, ERI, PsycInfo, T02.
—BLDSC (0709.378250), IE. **CCC.**
Published by: Pier Professional Ltd. (Subsidiary of: Emerald Group Publishing Ltd.), Ste N4, The Old Market, Upper Market St, Hove, BN3 1AS, United Kingdom. TEL 44-1273-783720, FAX 44-1273-783723, info@pierprofessional.com. Eds. Jane McCarthy, Steve Hardy. Adv. contact Paul Somerville TEL 44-1273-783724. B&W page GBP 350; 160 x 245.

➤ **ADVANCES IN NEUROCHEMISTRY.** *see* BIOLOGY—Biochemistry

616.8 ITA ISSN 2035-8946
▼ **ADVANCES IN NEUROPSYCHIATRY.** Text in Italian. 2009. q. **Document type:** *Journal, Academic/Scholarly.*
Published by: Wolters Kluwer Health Italy (Subsidiary of: Wolters Kluwer N.V.), Via B Lanino 5, Milan, 20144, Italy. http://www.wkhealth.it.

616.8 GBR ISSN 1355-5146
RC321 CODEN: APTDA7
ADVANCES IN PSYCHIATRIC TREATMENT. Abbreviated title: A P T. Text in English. 1994. bi-m. GBP 151 combined subscription in Europe to institutions (print & online eds.); USD 260 combined subscription in United States to institutions (print & online eds.); GBP 163 combined subscription elsewhere to institutions (print & online eds.) (effective 2012). adv. back issues avail.; reprints avail. **Document type:** *Journal, Academic/Scholarly.* **Description:** Promotes the continuing professional development of consultant psychiatrists.
Related titles: Online - full text ed.: Advances in Psychiatric Treatment (Online). ISSN 1472-1481. 2000. GBP 138 to institutions; USD 213 in United States to institutions (effective 2012).
Indexed: E-psyche, EMBASE, ExcerpMed, R10, Reac, SCOPUS.
—BLDSC (0711.018000), IE, Ingenta. **CCC.**
Published by: Royal College of Psychiatrists, 17 Belgrave Sq, London, SW1X 8PG, United Kingdom. TEL 44-20-72352351, FAX 44-20-72451231, rcpsych@rcpsych.ac.uk, http://www.rcpsych.ac.uk/. Ed. Joe Bouch. Circ: 2,500. **Subscr. in N. America to:** Maney Publishing; **Subscr. outside N. America to:** Maney Publishing, Ste 1C, Joseph's Well, Hanover Walk, Leeds, W Yorks LS3 1AB, United Kingdom. TEL 44-113-2432800, FAX 44-113-3868178, subscriptions@maney.co.uk, http://www.maney.co.uk.

616.8 CHE ISSN 0065-3268
➤ **ADVANCES IN PSYCHOSOMATIC MEDICINE.** Text in English. 1960. irreg., latest vol.31, 2011. price varies. back issues avail.; reprints avail. **Document type:** *Monographic series, Academic/Scholarly.* **Description:** Explores areas where knowledge from psychosomatic medicine may aid in the prevention of specific diseases or help meet the emotional demands of hospitalized patients.

Formerly (until 1967): Fortschritte der Psychosomatischen Medizin (1421-4466)
Related titles: Online - full text ed.: ISSN 1662-2855.
Indexed: A22, ASCA, C06, C07, ChemAb, E-psyche, EMBASE, ExcerpMed, IndMed, MEDLINE, P30, R10, Reac, SCI, SCOPUS, W07.
—BLDSC (0711.100000), GNLM, IE, Infotrieve, Ingenta, INIST. **CCC.**
Published by: S. Karger AG, Allschwilerstr 10, Basel, 4055, Switzerland. TEL 41-61-3061111, FAX 41-61-3061234, karger@karger.ch, http://www.karger.ch. Ed. T N Wise.

362.20425 USA ISSN 1554-4494
HV6545
ADVANCING SUICIDE PREVENTION. Text in English. 2005. 6/yr. USD 47; USD 29.95 to students (effective 2005). **Description:** Targets healthcare and related professionals whose work impacts suicidal individuals, including social and human service specialists, public policy and government relations executives, educators, researchers, legal and law enforcement professionals in such fields as violence prevention, benefits administration and emergency and crisis intervention.
Related titles: Online - full text ed.: ISSN 1554-4508.
Published by: P D V Communications, 629 North 8th Street, Sheboygan, WI 53081-4502. TEL 920-457-4033, FAX 920-457-4011. Ed. Denise Pazur. Circ: 20,000 (controlled).

616.8 DEU ISSN 1866-2986
AERZTE ZEITUNG FUER NEUROLOGEN - PSYCHIATER. Text in German. 2007. m. EUR 21.40 (effective 2008). adv. **Document type:** *Magazine, Trade.*
Published by: Aerzte Zeitung Verlagsgesellschaft mbH (Subsidiary of: Springer Science+Business Media), Am Forsthaus Gravenbruch 5, Neu-Isenburg, 63263, Germany. TEL 49-6102-506157, FAX 49-6102-506123, info@aerztezeitung.de, http://www.aerztezeitung.de. adv.: B&W page EUR 2,900, color page EUR 4,130. Circ: 6,800 (controlled).

616.8 DEU ISSN 1436-2643
CODEN: TWNPE3
AERZTLICHE PRAXIS. NEUROLOGIE PSYCHIATRIE. Short title: Ae P Neurologie Psychiatrie. Text in German. 1987. bi-m. adv. **Document type:** *Journal, Trade.*
Former titles (until 1998): T und E Neurologie Psychiatrie (1435-1072); (until 1997): T W Neurologie - Psychiatrie (0935-3224)
Indexed: E-psyche, SCOPUS.
—GNLM, IE. **CCC.**
Published by: Biermann Verlag GmbH, Otto-Hahn-Str 7, Cologne, 50997, Germany. TEL 49-2252-9410-0, 49-2236-3760, FAX 49-2236-376999, info@biermann.net. Ed. Nadine Eckert. Adv. contact Isabelle Becker. Circ: 6,527 (paid and controlled).

616.8 DEU
AERZTLICHES JOURNAL REISE UND MEDIZIN NEUROLOGIE - PSYCHIATRIE. Text in German. 2000. bi-m. EUR 21; EUR 4.60 newsstand/cover (effective 2007). adv. **Document type:** *Magazine, Trade.*
Published by: Otto Hoffmanns Verlag GmbH, Arnulfstr 10, Munich, 80335, Germany. TEL 49-89-5458450, FAX 49-89-54584530, info@ohv-online.de. adv.: B&W page EUR 1,900, color page EUR 2,950. Circ: 5,800 (paid and controlled).

616.8 FRA ISSN 1015-8618
AFRICAN JOURNAL OF NEUROLOGICAL SCIENCES. Text in English, French. 1995. s-a. **Document type:** *Journal, Academic/Scholarly.* **Description:** Publishes scientific papers of any aspects of neurological sciences.
Related titles: Online - full text ed.: ISSN 1992-2647. free (effective 2011).
Indexed: A36, BIOBASE, CABA, EMBASE, ExcerpMed, GH, H17, IABS, N02, N03, P33, P39, R08, R10, R12, RM&VM, Reac, SCOPUS, T05.
Published by: Pan American Association of Neurological Sciences, CMCO Cote d'Opale, Route de Desvres, St Martin - Boulogne, 62280, France. Ed. Gilbert Dechambenoit.

616.8 ZAF ISSN 1994-8220
➤ **AFRICAN JOURNAL OF PSYCHIATRY.** Text in English. 1998. q. reprints avail. **Document type:** *Journal, Academic/Scholarly.*
Former titles (until 2007): South African Psychiatry Review (1811-7805); (until 2001): Journal of Depression and Anxiety (1560-0181)
Related titles: Online - full content ed.
Indexed: EMBASE, ExcerpMed, ISAP, MEDLINE, P03, P30, PsycInfo, PsycholAb, R10, Reac, SCI, SCOPUS, SSCI, W07.
Published by: In House Publications, PO Box 412748, Craighall, Johannesburg 2024, South Africa. TEL 27-11-7889139, FAX 27-11-7889136, inhouse@iafrica.com, http://www.inhousepub.co.za. Circ: 2,000.

616.8 USA ISSN 1044-0534
AFTERLOSS; the monthly newsletter to comfort and care for those who mourn. Text in English. 1989. m. USD 48 (effective 2005). index. back issues avail. **Document type:** *Newsletter, Consumer.* **Description:** Deals with the management of and education about grief following the death of a loved one. Functions to help the survivors deal with the death of a spouse, child, other relations and friends.
Indexed: E-psyche.
Published by: Afterloss, Inc., 79-301 Country Club Dr, Ste 100, Bermuda Dunes, CA 92201. TEL 800-423-8811, FAX 888-443-5732. Ed., Pub. Barbara Lesstrang. Circ: 6,000.

AGGRESSION AND VIOLENT BEHAVIOR. *see* PSYCHOLOGY

AGING & MENTAL HEALTH. *see* GERONTOLOGY AND GERIATRICS

618.97 CAN ISSN 1706-581X
➤ **THE AGING BRAIN**; clinical approaches for Canadian specialists. Text in English. 2001. q. **Document type:** *Journal, Academic/Scholarly.*
Related titles: French ed.: Cerveau et Vieillissement. ISSN 1713-6334. 2001.
Published by: Parkhurst Publishing, 400 McGill St, 3rd Fl, Montreal, PQ H2Y 2G1, Canada. TEL 514-397-8833, FAX 514-397-0228, contact@parkpub.com, http://www.parkpub.com.

➤ **AGORA (RIO DE JANEIRO)**; estudos em teoria psicanalitica. *see* PSYCHOLOGY

612 TUR ISSN 1300-0012
➤ **AGRI/TURKISH SOCIETY OF ALGOLOGY. JOURNAL**; Turk algoloji dernegi'nin yayin organidir. Text in Turkish; Summaries in English. 1989. q. adv. bk.rev. abstr. **Document type:** *Journal, Academic/Scholarly.* **Description:** Reports on new medical and technical issues affecting regional anesthesiologists.
Related titles: Online - full text ed.: free (effective 2009).
Indexed: A22, E-psyche, EMBASE, ExcerpMed, MEDLINE, P30, R10, Reac, SCOPUS.
—BLDSC (0738.780000), GNLM, IE, Ingenta.
Published by: Turk Algoloji Dernegi/Turkish Society of Algology, Istanbul Universitesi Istanbul Tip Falultesi Algoloji ABD, Istanbul, 34390, Turkey. TEL 90-212-5313147, FAX 90-212-6310541, algotur@superonline.com, http://www.algoloji.org.tr. Ed., R&P Dr. Serdar Erdine. Adv. contact Dr. Suleyman Ozyalcin. page USD 500. Circ: 1,000 (paid); 500 (controlled).

➤ **AICHI IKA DAIGAKU KAREI IKAGAKU KENKYUJO KIYO/AICHI MEDICAL UNIVERSITY. INSTITUTE FOR MEDICAL SCIENCE OF AGING. BULLETIN.** *see* GERONTOLOGY AND GERIATRICS

➤ **AIDS CARE**; psychological and socio-medical aspects of AIDS-HIV. (Acquired Immune Deficiency Syndrome) *see* MEDICAL SCIENCES—Communicable Diseases

616.8 DEU ISSN 0949-622X
AKTIV (HANNOVER). Text in German. 1953. q. adv. **Document type:** *Magazine, Consumer.*
Former titles (until 1993): D M S G Aktiv (0177-8293); (until 1984): Deutsche Multiple Sklerose Gesellschaft. Mitteilungen (0175-7334)
Published by: Deutsche Multiple Sklerose Gesellschaft e.V., Kuesterstr 8, Hannover, 30519, Germany. TEL 49-511-968340, FAX 49-511-9683450, dmsg@dmsg.de. adv.: B&W page EUR 2,550, color page EUR 3,240. Circ: 50,000 (controlled).

616.8 DEU ISSN 0302-4350
RC346
➤ **AKTUELLE NEUROLOGIE.** Text in German; Summaries in English, German. 1974. 10/yr. EUR 306 to institutions; EUR 421 combined subscription to institutions (print & online eds.); EUR 45 newsstand/cover (effective 2011). adv. index. back issues avail.; reprints avail. **Document type:** *Journal, Academic/Scholarly.*
Related titles: Online - full text ed.: ISSN 1438-9428. EUR 407 to institutions (effective 2011).
Indexed: A22, ASCA, B21, B25, BIOSIS Prev, CurCont, E-psyche, EMBASE, ExcerpMed, IBR, IBZ, Inpharma, MycolAb, NSA, NSCI, P35, R10, Reac, SCI, SCOPUS, W07.
—BLDSC (0785.775000), GNLM, IE, Infotrieve, Ingenta, INIST. **CCC.**
Published by: Georg Thieme Verlag, Ruedigerstr 14, Stuttgart, 70469, Germany. TEL 49-711-8931421, FAX 49-711-8931410, kunden.service@thieme.de. Ed. G Kraemer. Adv. contact Andreas Schweiger TEL 49-711-8931245. Circ: 6,200 (paid and controlled).

616.8 150 SRB ISSN 0354-2726
➤ **AKTUELNOSTI IZ NEUROLOGIJE, PSIHIJATRIJE I GRANICNIH PRODUCJA/CURRENT TOPICS IN NEUROLOGY, PSYCHIATRY AND RELATED DISCIPLINES.** Text in English, Serbian. 1993. irreg. **Document type:** *Journal, Academic/Scholarly.*
Related titles: Online - full text ed.: free (effective 2011).
Published by: Institut za Neurologiju, Psihijatriju i Mentalno Zdravlje, Hajduk Veljika 1, Novi Sad, 21000. TEL 381-64-2954236, FAX 381-64-526520.

616.89 ARG ISSN 0327-3954
ALCMEON. Text in Spanish. 1990. q. back issues avail.
Related titles: Online - full text ed.: ISSN 1514-9862. 1990.
Published by: Fundacion Argentina de Clinica Neuropsiquiatrica, Mitre 339, Quilmes, Buenos Aires, 1878, Argentina. TEL 54-114-42542261, alcmeon@alcmeon.com.ar, http://www.alcmeon.com.ar/. Ed. Hugo Marietan.

616.8 200 USA ISSN 2150-2722
▼ **ALEPH OMEGA**; journal of spiritual neuroscience. Text in English. 2011. q. USD 900; USD 225 per issue (effective 2011). **Document type:** *Journal, Academic/Scholarly.* **Description:** Covers spirituality and neuroscience, including mysticism, worship, and the numinous experience.
Media: Online - full content.
Published by: Kaiser Peer Publishing, PO Box 734, Churchville, NY 14428. TEL 585-393-1464, davidkaiser@spiritualneuroscience.org, http://brainandcosmos.com/info.htm.

616.8 USA
ALLIANCE (WISCONSIN). Text in English. irreg.
Media: Online - full text.
Indexed: E-psyche.
Published by: Alliance for Medical and Psychosocial Support, 10410 52nd St South, Wisconsin Rapids, WI 54494. TEL 715-325-7537, info@growthhouse.org. Ed. Sarah Skiba.

612.67 USA ISSN 0893-0341
RC523 CODEN: ADADE2
➤ **ALZHEIMER DISEASE AND ASSOCIATED DISORDERS.** Text in English. 1987. q. USD 706 domestic to institutions; USD 856 foreign to institutions (effective 2011). adv. bk.rev. charts; illus. back issues avail.; reprints avail. **Document type:** *Journal, Academic/Scholarly.* **Description:** Covers reports of research findings and approaches to diagnosis and treatment.
Formerly: Alzheimer's Research
Related titles: Online - full text ed.: ISSN 1546-4156.
Indexed: A20, A22, A36, ASCA, AgeL, BIOBASE, C06, C07, CA, CABA, CIN, ChemAb, ChemTitl, CurCont, E-psyche, EMBASE, ExcerpMed, FR, FamI, GH, IABS, INI, IPsyAb, ISR, IndMed, Inpharma, MEDLINE, N02, N03, NSCI, P03, P30, P35, PsycInfo, PsycholAb, R10, Reac, SCI, SCOPUS, T02, T05, THA, W07.
—BLDSC (0806.255300), CASDDS, GNLM, IE, Infotrieve, Ingenta, INIST. **CCC.**
Published by: Lippincott Williams & Wilkins (Subsidiary of: Wolters Kluwer N.V.), 530 Walnut St, Philadelphia, PA 19106. TEL 215-521-8300, FAX 215-521-8902, customerservice@lww.com, http://www.lww.com. Ed. Charles DeCarli TEL 916-734-8413. Pub. Harry Dean. Circ: 321.

616.8 USA ISSN 1552-5260
RC523
➤ **ALZHEIMER'S & DEMENTIA.** Text in English. 2005 (July). bi-m. USD 332 in United States to institutions; USD 341 elsewhere to institutions (effective 2012). adv. back issues avail.; reprints avail. **Document type:** *Journal, Academic/Scholarly.* **Description:** Covers all aspects of dementia research and clinical care, from molecular biology, through drug and non-drug therapies, to the psycho-social aspects of care.
Related titles: Online - full text ed.: ISSN 1552-5279 (from ScienceDirect).
Indexed: A26, ASSIA, B21, CA, CurCont, EMBASE, ExcerpMed, I05, MEDLINE, NSA, NSCI, P03, P30, PsycInfo, R10, Reac, SCI, SCOPUS, T02, W07.
—BLDSC (0806.255333), IE, Ingenta. **CCC.**
Published by: (Alzheimer's Association, Inc.), Elsevier Inc. (Subsidiary of: Elsevier Science & Technology), 1600 John F Kennedy Blvd, Philadelphia, PA 19103. TEL 215-239-3900, FAX 215-238-7883, JournalCustomerService-usa@elsevier.com, http://www.elsevier.com. Ed. Zaven Khachaturian TEL 301-294-7201. Adv. contact Jim Breuning TEL 609-397-5522.

➤ **ALZHEIMER'S CARE GUIDE**; published especially for those who care for people with Alzheimer's disease and related disorders. *see* GERONTOLOGY AND GERIATRICS

616.8 362.6 USA ISSN 1936-3001
➤ **ALZHEIMER'S CARE TODAY**; best practices in dementia care. Text in English. 2000. q. USD 315.51 domestic to institutions; USD 420 foreign to institutions (effective 2011). adv. back issues avail.; reprints avail. **Document type:** *Journal, Academic/Scholarly.* **Description:** Provides information on dementia care practices that can be incorporated into the day-to-day activities of health care professionals.
Formerly (until 2007): Alzheimer's Care Quarterly (1525-3279)
Related titles: Online - full text ed.: ISSN 1936-6760. 2000.
Indexed: A01, A03, A08, A26, C06, C07, C08, C11, CA, CINAHL, E08, G08, H04, H11, H12, H13, I05, P10, P20, P26, P30, P53, P54, PQC, S09, SCOPUS, T02.
—BLDSC (0806.255337), IE, Ingenta. **CCC.**
Published by: Lippincott Williams & Wilkins (Subsidiary of: Wolters Kluwer N.V.), Two Commerce Sq, 2001 Market St, Philadelphia, PA 19103. TEL 215-521-8300, FAX 215-521-8902, customerservice@lww.com, http://www.lww.com. Ed. Peg Gray-Vickrey TEL 239-590-1094. Pub. Beth Guthy.

616.8 USA ISSN 1935-2514
RC523
ALZHEIMER'S DISEASE RESEARCH JOURNAL. Text in English. 2007. q. USD 300 to institutions; USD 450 combined subscription to institutions (print & online eds.) (effective 2012). **Document type:** *Journal, Academic/Scholarly.* **Description:** Aimed at understanding why AD occurs and who is at greatest risk of developing it, improving the accuracy of diagnosis and the ability to identify those at risk, discovering, developing, and testing new treatments,.
Related titles: Online - full text ed.: 2007. USD 300 to institutions (effective 2012).
Published by: Nova Science Publishers, Inc., 400 Oser Ave, Ste 1600, Hauppauge, NY 11788. TEL 631-231-7269, FAX 631-231-8175, main@novapublishers.com. Eds. Alireza Minagar, Miao-Kun Sun.

616.8 USA
ALZHEIMER'S DISEASE SOURCEBOOK. Text in English. 1993. irreg., latest 4th ed. USD 84 4th ed. (effective 2008). charts; illus.; stat. Index. **Document type:** *Magazine, Consumer.* **Description:** Offers basic information for the layperson on Alzheimer's disease and related neurological disorders, along with treatment and care options.
Formerly: Alzheimer's, Stroke and 29 Other Neurological Disorders
Related titles: ◆ Series of: Omnigraphics Health Reference Series.
Indexed: E-psyche.
Published by: Omnigraphics, Inc., PO Box 31-1640, Detroit, MI 48231. TEL 313-961-1340, 800-234-1340, FAX 313-961-1383, 800-875-1340, info@omnigraphics.com. Ed. Karen Bellenir. Pub. Frederick G Ruffner Jr. R&P Laurie Lanzen Harris.

616.831 NZL ISSN 1173-4361
ALZHEIMERS NEWS. Text in English. 1988. q. NZD 10 (effective 2008). adv. bk.rev. back issues avail. **Document type:** *Newsletter.*
Formerly (1988-1994): A D A R D S New Zealand News (Alzheimers Disease and Related Disorders Society) (1170-5426)
Related titles: Online - full text ed.: free (effective 2008).
Published by: Alzheimers New Zealand, Level 3, Adelphi Finance House, 15 Courtenay Pl, 71 Armagh St, PO Box 3643, Christchurch, New Zealand. TEL 64-4-3812362, FAX 64-4-3812365, nationaloffice@alzheimers.org.nz. Ed. Robyn Peel.

612.67 GBR ISSN 1758-9193
▼ ➤ **ALZHEIMER'S RESEARCH & THERAPY.** Text in English. 2009. irreg. price varies based on the number of users. adv. **Document type:** *Journal, Academic/Scholarly.* **Description:** Provides forum for translational research into Alzheimer's disease.
Media: Online - full text.
Indexed: A01, A26, E08, EMBASE, H11, H12, I05, P30, SCOPUS.
Published by: BioMed Central Ltd. (Subsidiary of: Springer Science+Business Media), Fl 6, 236 Gray's Inn Rd, London, WC1X 8HB, United Kingdom. TEL 44-20-31922009, 800-389-8136, FAX 44-20-31922010, info@biomedcentral.com, http://www.biomedcentral.com. Eds. Douglas R Galasko, Gordon K Wilcock, Todd E Golde.

616.8 362.6 USA
ALZHEIMER'S RESEARCH REVIEW. Text in English. q. charts; illus. **Document type:** *Newsletter, Consumer.* **Description:** Describes the research sponsored by the organization into this debilitating disease.
Indexed: E-psyche.
Published by: Alzheimer's Disease Research, American Health Assistance Foundation, 22512 Gateway Center Dr., Clarksburg, MD 20871-2005. TEL 800-437-AHAF. Ed., R&P Eve Herold TEL 301-948-3244.

616.8 618.97 362.1 SWE ISSN 1652-0297
ALZHEIMERTIDNINGEN. Text in Swedish. 1987. q. SEK 200 to members (effective 2007). **Document type:** *Magazine, Consumer.*
Formerly (until 2002): Alzheimerfoereningen (1100-0899)
Indexed: E-psyche.

Published by: Alzheimerfoereningen, Karl XII Gata 1, PO Box 197, Lund, 22100, Sweden. TEL 46-46-147318, FAX 46-46-188976, http://www.alzheimerforeningen.se.

616.89 NLD ISSN 0890-8567
RJ499.A1 CODEN: JAAPEE
➤ **AMERICAN ACADEMY OF CHILD AND ADOLESCENT PSYCHIATRY. JOURNAL.** Text in English. 1962. m. USD 523 in United States to institutions; USD 641 elsewhere to institutions (effective 2012). adv. bk.rev. abstr.; bibl.; charts; illus. Index. back issues avail.; reprints avail. **Document type:** *Journal, Academic/Scholarly.* **Description:** Presents original papers in psychiatric research and the treatment of children and adolescents.
Formerly (until 1986): American Academy of Child Psychiatry. Journal (0002-7138)
Related titles: CD-ROM ed.; Online - full text ed.: ISSN 1527-5418 (from ScienceDirect).
Indexed: A01, A02, A03, A08, A20, A22, A26, AMHA, ASCA, ASSIA, B04, B21, B25, BDM&CN, BIOSIS Prev, BRD, C06, C07, C28, CA, CCIP, CDA, CurCont, DentInd, DokArb, E-psyche, E02, E03, E06, E07, E08, EMBASE, ERI, ERIC, EdA, EdI, ExcerpMed, F09, FR, FamI, G08, H11, H12, H13, I05, IDIS, INI, IPsyAb, ISR, IndMed, Inpharma, JW-P, M06, MEA&I, MEDLINE, MLA-IB, MycolAb, NRN, NSA, P02, P03, P10, P12, P20, P27, P30, P34, P35, P48, P50, P53, P54, PQC, PsycInfo, PsycholAb, R10, RILM, Reac, S02, S03, S09, SCI, SCOPUS, SSAI, SSAb, SSCI, SSI, SWR&A, T02, W01, W02, W03, W05, W07.
—BLDSC (4683.690000), GNLM, IE, Infotrieve, Ingenta, INIST. **CCC.**
Published by: (American Academy of Child and Adolescent Psychiatry USA), Elsevier BV (Subsidiary of: Elsevier Science & Technology), Radarweg 29, PO Box 211, Amsterdam, 1000 AE, Netherlands. JournalsCustomerServiceEMEA@elsevier.com, http://www.elsevier.nl. Ed. Dr. Andres Andres Martin. adv.: B&W page USD 1,680; trim 8.125 x 10.875. Circ: 7,634 (paid).

616.89 340 USA ISSN 1093-6793
RA1151
AMERICAN ACADEMY OF PSYCHIATRY AND THE LAW. JOURNAL. Text in English. 1969. q. USD 130 to individuals; USD 185 to institutions (effective 2010). bk.rev. bibl. reprints avail. **Document type:** *Journal, Academic/Scholarly.*
Former titles (until 1997): American Academy of Psychiatry and the Law. Bulletin (0091-634X); (until 1972): American Academy of Psychiatry and the Law. Newsletter
Related titles: Microfiche ed.: (from WSH); Microfilm ed.: (from WSH); Microform ed.: (from PQC, WSH); Online - full text ed.: ISSN 1943-3662.
Indexed: A20, A22, A26, ABRCLP, AC&P, AMHA, ASCA, CA, CJA, CLI, CurCont, DokArb, E-psyche, EMBASE, ExcerpMed, FamI, G08, HlthInd, I05, IndMed, LRI, LegCont, MEDLINE, P03, P30, P34, PsycInfo, PsycholAb, R10, Reac, S02, S03, SCOPUS, SSCI, T02, W07.
—BLDSC (4683.732750), GNLM, IE, Infotrieve, Ingenta. **CCC.**
Published by: American Academy of Psychiatry and the Law, One Regency Dr, PO Box 30, Bloomfield, CT 06002. TEL 860-242-5450, 800-331-1389, FAX 860-286-0787, execoff@aapl.org. Circ: 1,750.

616.89 150 USA ISSN 0065-860X
BF173.A2 CODEN: AMIAAO
➤ **AMERICAN IMAGO;** psychoanalysis and the human sciences. Text in English. 1939. q. USD 165 to institutions; USD 231 combined subscription to institutions (print & online eds.); USD 50 per issue to institutions (effective 2012). adv. bk.rev. bibl.; charts; illus. index. 120 p./no.; back issues avail.; reprint service avail. from PSC. **Document type:** *Journal, Academic/Scholarly.* **Description:** Features articles and book reviews that explore the relevance of Freud's legacy across the disciplines.
Related titles: Microform ed.: (from PMC, PQC); Online - full text ed.: ISSN 1085-7931. USD 175 to institutions (effective 2012).
Indexed: A01, A02, A03, A08, A20, A21, A22, A26, AES, ASCA, AmHI, ArtHuCI, BEL&L, CA, ChLitAb, ChemAb, CurCont, DIP, E-psyche, E01, E08, FR, G05, G06, G07, G08, H07, H14, I05, IBR, IBT&D, IBZ, IndMed, M01, M02, MEA&I, MLA, MLA-IB, MagInd, P02, P03, P10, P25, P30, P48, P53, P54, PCI, PQC, PsycInfo, PsycholAb, R04, RI-1, RI-2, RILM, S02, S03, S09, SCOPUS, T02, W07.
—BLDSC (0819.300000), GNLM, IE, Infotrieve, Ingenta, INIST. **CCC.**
Published by: (Association for Applied Psychoanalysis), The Johns Hopkins University Press, 2715 N Charles St, Baltimore, MD 21218. TEL 410-516-6900, FAX 410-516-6968. Ed. Peter L Rudnytsky. Pub. William M Breichner. **Subscr. to:** PO Box 19966, Baltimore, MD 21211. TEL 410-516-6987, 800-548-1784, FAX 410-516-3866, jrnlcirc@press.jhu.edu.

➤ **AMERICAN INDIAN AND ALASKA NATIVE MENTAL HEALTH RESEARCH (ONLINE).** *see* NATIVE AMERICAN STUDIES

616.804 USA ISSN 1086-508X
RC349.E53 CODEN: AJETFB
➤ **AMERICAN JOURNAL OF ELECTRONEURODIAGNOSTIC TECHNOLOGY.** Abbreviated title: A J E T. Text in English. 1960. q. USD 110 domestic to individuals; USD 130 foreign to individuals; USD 150 domestic to institutions; USD 180 foreign to institutions; free to members (effective 2010). adv. bk.rev. charts; illus. index, cum.index. back issues avail. **Document type:** *Journal, Academic/Scholarly.* **Description:** Features clinical and technical aspects of electroneurodiagnostics which includes EEG, evoked potentials, polysomnography, and nerve conduction studies and specialized applications.
Formerly (until 1996): American Journal of E E G Technology (0002-9238)
Related titles: Online - full text ed.
Indexed: A01, A02, A03, A08, A22, C06, C07, C08, C11, CA, CINAHL, CPEI, E-psyche, EMBASE, EngInd, ExcerpMed, H04, Inspec, MEDLINE, P03, P20, P24, P25, P30, P43, P48, P54, PQC, PsycInfo, PsycholAb, R10, Reac, RefZh, SCOPUS, T02.
—BLDSC (0824.430000), AskIEEE, GNLM, IE, Infotrieve, Ingenta, INIST.
Published by: American Society of Electroneurodiagnostic Technologists, Inc., 402 E Bannister Rd, Ste A, Kansas City, MO 64131. TEL 816-931-1120, FAX 816-931-1145, info@aset.org. Adv. contact Lucy Sullivan TEL 417-253-5838.

➤ **AMERICAN JOURNAL OF GERIATRIC PSYCHIATRY.** *see* GERONTOLOGY AND GERIATRICS

616.89 USA ISSN 1947-2951
AMERICAN JOURNAL OF NEUROPROTECTION AND NEUROREGENERATION. Text in English. 3/yr. **Document type:** *Journal, Academic/Scholarly.*
Related titles: Online - full text ed.: ISSN 1947-296X.
Published by: American Scientific Publishers, 26650 The Old Rd, Ste 208, Valencia, CA 91381. TEL 661-799-7200, FAX 661-254-1207, order@aspbs.com, editor@aspbs.com. **Subscr. to:** 25650 N Lewis Way, Stevenson Ranch, CA 91381.

616.8 USA ISSN 1548-7768
RC439.5
➤ **AMERICAN JOURNAL OF PSYCHIATRIC REHABILITATION.** Text in English. 1996. q. GBP 237 combined subscription in United Kingdom to institutions (print & online eds.); EUR 320, USD 404 combined subscription to institutions (print & online eds.) (effective 2012). back issues avail.; reprint service avail. from PSC. **Document type:** *Journal, Academic/Scholarly.* **Description:** Features research papers on psychiatric rehabilitation.
Formerly (until 2004): Psychiatric Rehabilitation Skills (1097-3435)
Related titles: Online - full text ed.: ISSN 1548-7776. GBP 213 in United Kingdom to institutions; EUR 288, USD 363 to institutions (effective 2012) (from IngentaConnect).
Indexed: A01, A22, C06, C07, C08, CA, CINAHL, E01, EMBASE, ExcerpMed, P03, P30, P48, P50, PQC, PsycInfo, PsycholAb, R09, R10, Reac, SCOPUS, T02.
—BLDSC (0834.900000), IE, Ingenta. **CCC.**
Published by: (University of Chicago, Center for Psychiatric Rehabilitation), Routledge (Subsidiary of: Taylor & Francis Group), 325 Chestnut St, Ste 800, Philadelphia, PA 19106. TEL 800-354-1420, FAX 215-625-2940, journals@routledge.com, http://www.routledge.com. Ed. Patrick W Corrigan TEL 312-567-6751. Adv. contact Linda Hann TEL 44-1344-779945.

616.89 USA ISSN 0002-953X
RC321 CODEN: AJPSAO
➤ **THE AMERICAN JOURNAL OF PSYCHIATRY.** Abbreviated title: A J P. Text in English. 1844. m. USD 244 combined subscription domestic to individuals (print & online eds.); USD 368 combined subscription foreign to individuals (print & online eds.); USD 350 combined subscription domestic to institutions (print & online eds.); USD 466 combined subscription foreign to institutions (print & online eds.) (effective 2011). adv. bk.rev. bibl.; charts; illus. index. back issues avail.; reprints avail. **Document type:** *Journal, Academic/Scholarly.* **Description:** Presents clinical research and discussion on current psychiatric issues for psychiatrists and other mental health professionals.
Formerly (until 1921): The American Journal of Insanity (1044-4815)
Related titles: CD-ROM ed.; Microform ed.: (from PMC, PQC); Online - full text ed.: ISSN 1535-7228. USD 220 to individuals (effective 2011); ◆ Spanish ed.: The American Journal of Psychiatry (Spanish Edition). ISSN 1139-3475.
Indexed: A01, A02, A03, A08, A20, A21, A22, A26, A36, AC&P, AHCMS, AIM, ASCA, ASG, AbAn, AddicA, AgeL, B04, B21, B25, B28, BAS, BDM&CN, BIOSIS Prev, BRD, BiolDig, C06, C07, C08, CA, CABA, CBRI, CINAHL, CISA, ChPerI, ChemAb, Chicano, CurCont, D01, DBA, DIP, DentInd, E-psyche, E08, E12, EMBASE, ERA, ESPM, ExcerpMed, F08, F09, F11, F12, FAMLI, FR, FamI, G08, G10, GH, H&SSA, H09, H11, H12, H13, HRA, HRIS, HospLI, I05, I12, IBR, IBZ, IDIS, INI, IPARL, IPsyAb, ISR, IndMed, Inpharma, JW, JW-P, JW-WH, L09, M06, MCR, MEA&I, MEDLINE, MLA-IB, MycolAb, N02, N03, NRN, NSA, P02, P03, P10, P12, P13, P20, P21, P22, P24, P25, P26, P27, P30, P33, P34, P35, P39, P48, P53, P54, PC&CA, PCI, PQC, PsycInfo, PsycholAb, R10, R12, RA&MP, RI-1, RI-2, RILM, Reac, RiskAb, S02, S03, S05, S09, S20, S21, SCI, SCOPUS, SOPODA, SSAI, SSAb, SSCI, SSI, SWR&A, SociolAb, T02, T05, ToxAb, W03, W07, W09.
—BLDSC (0835.000000), CASDDS, CIS, GNLM, IE, Infotrieve, Ingenta, INIST. **CCC.**
Published by: (American Psychiatric Association), American Psychiatric Publishing, Inc., 1000 Wilson Blvd, Ste 1825, Arlington, VA 22209. TEL 703-907-7885, 800-368-5777, FAX 703-907-1096, appi@psych.org, http://www.appi.org. Eds. Robert Freedman, Michael D Roy. Adv. contact Valentin Torres TEL 212-904-0375. **Subscr. to:** PO Box 97250, Washington, DC 20090.

616.89 ESP ISSN 1139-3475
THE AMERICAN JOURNAL OF PSYCHIATRY (SPANISH EDITION). Text in Spanish. 1998. bi-m. **Document type:** *Journal, Academic/Scholarly.*
Related titles: Online - full text ed.: ISSN 1695-0259; ◆ English ed.: The American Journal of Psychiatry. ISSN 0002-953X.
Indexed: A01, CA, F03, F04, T02.
Published by: Grupo Ars XXI de Comunicacion, SA, Muntaner 262 Atico 2a., Barcelona, 08021, Spain. TEL 34-90-2195484, FAX 34-93-2722902, info@arsxxi.com.

THE AMERICAN JOURNAL OF PSYCHOANALYSIS. *see* PSYCHOLOGY

616.8 USA ISSN 0002-9564
RC321 CODEN: AJPTAR
➤ **AMERICAN JOURNAL OF PSYCHOTHERAPY.** Abbreviated title: A J P. Text in English. 1946. q. USD 133 domestic to institutions; USD 144 in Canada to institutions; USD 150 elsewhere to institutions; USD 43 per issue (effective 2011). bk.rev. abstr.; bibl. index, cum.index: 1941-1965. back issues avail.; reprints avail. **Document type:** *Journal, Academic/Scholarly.*
Incorporates (1992-2001): The Journal of Psychotherapy Practice and Research
Related titles: Microform ed.: (from RPI); Online - full text ed.: (from IngentaConnect).
Indexed: A01, A02, A03, A08, A20, A21, A22, A26, AC&P, AMHA, ASCA, ASSIA, B04, BAS, BRD, C12, CA, ChemAb, Chicano, E-psyche, E08, EMBASE, ExcerpMed, F09, FR, FamI, G08, H11, H12, H13, I05, IBR, IBZ, INI, IPsyAb, ISR, IndMed, JW-P, M01, M02, MEA&I, MEDLINE, MLA-IB, P02, P03, P10, P12, P20, P22, P25, P26, P27, P30, P43, P48, P53, P54, PCI, PQC, PsycInfo, PsycholAb, R05, R10, RI-1, RI-2, Reac, RefZh, S02, S03, S09, SCOPUS, SOPODA, SSA, SSAI, SSAb, SSCI, SSI, SWR&A, SociolAb, T02, W03, W05.
—BLDSC (0835.600000), GNLM, IE, Infotrieve, Ingenta, INIST.
Published by: Association for the Advancement of Psychotherapy, Belfer Education Center, 1300 Morris Park Ave, Rm 402, Bronx, NY 10461. TEL 718-430-3503, FAX 718-430-8907, info@ajp.org. Ed. T Byram Karasu.

➤ **AMERICAN JOURNAL ON ADDICTIONS.** *see* DRUG ABUSE AND ALCOHOLISM

616.858 USA ISSN 1944-7515
RC326 CODEN: MPLIEG
➤ **AMERICAN JOURNAL ON INTELLECTUAL AND DEVELOPMENTAL DISABILITIES.** Abbreviated title: A J I D D. Text in English. 1876. bi-m. USD 287 combined subscription domestic to institutions print & online eds. for schools & public libraries; USD 344 combined subscription foreign to institutions print & online eds. for schools & public libraries (effective 2009). adv. bk.rev. bibl.; charts; illus.; stat. index. back issues avail. **Document type:** *Journal, Academic/Scholarly.* **Description:** Current research on biological, behavioral and educational sciences in mental retardation and related developmental disabilities.
Former titles (until 2008): American Journal on Mental Retardation (Print) (0895-8017); (until 1987): American Journal of Mental Deficiency (0002-9351); (until 1939): American Association on Mental Deficiency. Proceedings and Addresses of the Annual Session (0191-1740)
Related titles: Microfiche ed.; Microfilm ed.: (from PQC); Online - full text ed.: ISSN 1944-7558. USD 106 to individuals; USD 218 to institutions (effective 2005); ◆ Regional ed(s).: American Journal on Intellectual and Developmental Disabilities (Italian Edition). ISSN 2036-220X.
Indexed: A20, A22, AMHA, ASCA, B04, B28, BDM&CN, BRD, BRI, C06, C07, C28, CA, CBRI, CDA, ChPerI, ChemAb, Chicano, CurCont, DentInd, E-psyche, E02, E03, E06, EAA, ECER, EMBASE, ERA, ERI, ERIC, EdA, EdI, ExcerpMed, F09, FR, FamI, INI, ISR, IndMed, MEA&I, MEDLINE, MLA-IB, NRN, P03, P30, PCI, PsycInfo, PsycholAb, R10, Reac, RehabLit, S02, S03, S21, SCOPUS, SOPODA, SSCI, SWR&A, SociolAb, T02, W03, W05, W07.
—BLDSC (0826.790000), CASDDS, GNLM, IE, Ingenta, INIST. **CCC.**
Published by: American Association on Intellectual and Developmental Disabilities, 501 3rd St, NW, Ste 200, Washington, DC 20001. TEL 202-387-1968, 800-424-3688, FAX 202-387-2193, orders@allenpress.com, http://www.allenpress.com. Ed. Leonard Abbeduto. adv.: B&W page USD 920; trim 8.25 x 10.875. Circ: 8,000. **Subscr.to:** Allen Press Inc., PO Box 1897, Lawrence, KS 66044. TEL 785-843-1235, FAX 785-843-1274, orders@allenpress.com, http://www.allenpress.com.

616.858 ITA ISSN 2036-220X
AMERICAN JOURNAL ON INTELLECTUAL AND DEVELOPMENTAL DISABILITIES (ITALIAN EDITION). Abbreviated title: A J I D D. Text in Multiple languages. 2002. 3/yr. **Document type:** *Journal, Academic/Scholarly.*
Formerly (until 2008): American Journal of Mental Retardation (1721-3959)
Related titles: Online - full text ed.; ◆ Regional ed(s).: American Journal on Intellectual and Developmental Disabilities. ISSN 1944-7515.
Published by: (American Association on Intellectual and Developmental Disabilities USA), Vannini Editrice, Via Leonardo da Vinci 6, Gussago, BS 25064, Italy. TEL 39-030-313374, FAX 39-030-314078, http://www.vanninieditrice.it.

616.8 USA ISSN 2153-3709
▼ **AMERICAN NEUROFEEDBACK ASSOCIATION. JOURNAL.** Text in English. forthcoming 2011 (Jan.). q. USD 900 (effective 2011). **Document type:** *Journal, Academic/Scholarly.*
Media: Online - full text.
Published by: (American Neurofeedback Association), Kaiser Peer Publishing, PO Box 734, Churchville, NY 14428. TEL 585-393-1464, davidkaiser@spiritualneuroscience.org, http://brainandcosmos.com/info.htm.

616.8 USA
AMERICAN NEUROMODULATION SOCIETY. NEWSLETTER. Text in English. 19??. s-a. free to members (effective 2011). back issues avail. **Document type:** *Newsletter, Academic/Scholarly.* **Description:** Discusses news and topics in neuromodulation.
Related titles: Online - full content ed.: free (effective 2011); free.
Published by: American Neuromodulation Society, 4700 W Lake Ave, Glenview, IL 60025. TEL 847-375-4714, FAX 847-375-6424, cwelber@connect2amc.com. Ed. Ashwini Sharan.

616.8 USA ISSN 2153-3717
▼ **AMERICAN NEUROTHERAPY ASSOCIATION. JOURNAL.** Text in English. forthcoming 2011 (Jan.). q. USD 900 (effective 2011). **Document type:** *Journal, Academic/Scholarly.*
Media: Online - full text.
Published by: (American Neurotherapy Association), Kaiser Peer Publishing, PO Box 734, Churchville, NY 14428. TEL 585-393-1464, davidkaiser@spiritualneuroscience.org, http://brainandcosmos.com/info.htm.

AMERICAN PARKINSON DISEASE ASSOCIATION. NEWSLETTER. *see* SOCIAL SERVICES AND WELFARE

616.89 USA
AMERICAN PSYCHIATRIC ASSOCIATION. ANNUAL MEETING. Text in English. 19??. a. free to members (effective 2010). back issues avail. **Document type:** *Proceedings, Academic/Scholarly.*
Related titles: Online - full text ed.
Published by: (American Psychiatric Association), American Psychiatric Publishing, Inc., 1000 Wilson Blvd, Ste 1825, Arlington, VA 22209. TEL 703-907-7300, 800-368-5777, FAX 703-907-1091, appi@psych.org, http://www.appi.org.

616.89 USA ISSN 1048-4159
AMERICAN PSYCHIATRIC ASSOCIATION. TASK FORCE REPORTS. Text in English. 1970. irreg., latest 2009. price varies. back issues avail. **Document type:** *Monographic series, Academic/Scholarly.* **Description:** Features analysis and evaluation of problems, programs, issues, and practices in a given area of concern.
Related titles: Online - full text ed.: free (effective 2010).
Indexed: E-psyche.
—**CCC.**
Published by: (American Psychiatric Association), American Psychiatric Publishing, Inc., 1000 Wilson Blvd, Ste 1825, Arlington, VA 22209. TEL 703-907-7300, 800-368-5777, FAX 703-907-1091, appi@psych.org, http://www.appi.org. **Subscr. to:** PO Box 97250, Washington, DC 20090.

AMERICAN PSYCHIATRIC NURSES ASSOCIATION. JOURNAL. *see* MEDICAL SCIENCES—Nurses And Nursing

AMERICAN PSYCHOANALYTIC ASSOCIATION. JOURNAL. *see* PSYCHOLOGY

616.89 USA ISSN 0091-7389
RC626
AMERICAN PSYCHOPATHOLOGICAL ASSOCIATION. ANNUAL MEETING PROCEEDINGS. Text in English. 1945. a. reprints avail. **Document type:** *Proceedings, Academic/Scholarly.*
Indexed: E-psyche, P30.
—CCC.
Published by: (American Psychopathological Association), American Psychiatric Publishing, Inc., 1000 Wilson Blvd, Ste 1825, Arlington, VA 22209. TEL 703-907-7322, 800-368-5777, FAX 703-907-1091, appi@psych.org, http://www.appi.org.

616.8 USA
➤ **AMERICAN PSYCHOPATHOLOGICAL ASSOCIATION SERIES.** Text in English. 1978. irreg., latest 2007. price varies. reprints avail. **Document type:** *Monographic series, Academic/Scholarly.*
Indexed: E-psyche.
Published by: (American Psychopathological Association), American Psychiatric Publishing, Inc., 1000 Wilson Blvd, Ste 1825, Arlington, VA 22209. TEL 703-907-7322, 800-368-5777, FAX 703-907-1091, appi@psych.org, http://www.appi.org.

616.891 USA ISSN 1535-4075
RC451.4
➤ **AMERICAN PSYCHOTHERAPY ASSOCIATION. ANNALS.** Text in English. 19??. bi-m. USD 29.95 domestic to non-members; USD 54.95 foreign to non-members; free to members (effective 2010). adv. bk.rev. back issues avail. **Document type:** *Journal, Academic/Scholarly.* **Description:** Contains articles and columns on treatment modalities, trends, research and cutting-edge techniques as well as practice management tips and legal issues.
Formerly (until 1998): American Psychotherapy Association. Newsletter
Related titles: Online - full text ed.
Indexed: A01, A26, CA, E-psyche, E08, G08, I05, P03, PsycInfo, PsycholAb, S02, S03, S09, T02.
—BLDSC (1018.860000).
Published by: American Psychotherapy Association, 2750 E Sunshine St, Springfield, MO 65804. TEL 417-823-0173, FAX 800-205-9165, info@americanpsychotherapy.com, http://www.americanpsychotherapy.com.

616.8 USA
AMERICAN SOCIETY FOR ADOLESCENT PSYCHIATRY. NEWSLETTER. Abbreviated title: A S A P Newsletter. Text in English. 1967. q. USD 10 in US & Canada; USD 15 elsewhere; free to members (effective 2007). adv. bk.rev. stat. **Document type:** *Newsletter.* **Description:** Covers issues related to adolescent psychiatry.
Indexed: E-psyche.
Published by: American Society for Adolescent Psychiatry, P O Box 570218, Dallas, TX 75357-0218. TEL 972-686-6166, FAX 972-613-5532, info@adolpsych.org. Ed., R&P Dr. Leonard Henschel TEL 718-849-6339. Adv. contact Frances Roton. Circ: 2,700.

AMYLOID; the journal of protein folding disorders. *see* MEDICAL SCIENCES—Rheumatology

616.3995 GBR ISSN 1748-2968
RC406.A24
AMYOTROPHIC LATERAL SCLEROSIS; the official publication of the World Federation of Neurology Research Group on motor neuron disease. Text in English. 1999. bi-m. GBP 675, EUR 895, USD 1,110 combined subscription to institutions (print & online eds.); GBP 1,345, EUR 1,775, USD 2,220 combined subscription to corporations (print & online eds.) (effective 2010). adv. bk.rev. Index. back issues avail.; reprint service avail. from PSC. **Document type:** *Journal, Academic/Scholarly.* **Description:** Covers new treatment research and management issues in ALS and related motor neuron diseases.
Formerly (until 2006): Amyotrophic Lateral Sclerosis and Other Motor Neuron Disorders (1466-0822)
Related titles: Online - full text ed.: ISSN 1471-180X (from IngentaConnect).
Indexed: A01, A03, A08, A22, B21, CA, CurCont, E-psyche, E01, EMBASE, ExcerpMed, Inpharma, MEDLINE, NSA, NSCI, P30, P35, R10, Reac, SCI, SCOPUS, T02, W07.
—IE, Infotrieve, Ingenta. **CCC.**
Published by: (World Federation of Neurology/Federation Mondiale de Neurologie), Informa Healthcare (Subsidiary of: T & F Informa plc), Telephone House, 69-77 Paul St, London, EC2A 4LQ, United Kingdom. TEL 44-20-70175000, FAX 44-20-70176792, healthcare.enquiries@informa.com. Ed. Orla Hardiman. Adv. contact Per Sonnerfeldt. **Subscr. in N. America to:** Taylor & Francis Inc., Customer Services Dept, 325 Chestnut St, 8th Fl, Philadelphia, PA 19106. TEL 215-625-8900, 800-354-1420, FAX 215-625-8914, customerservice@taylorandfrancis.com; **Subscr. outside N. America to:** Taylor & Francis Ltd., Journals Customer Service, Sheepen Pl, Colchester, Essex CO3 3LP, United Kingdom. TEL 44-20-70175544, FAX 44-20-70175198, tf.enquiries@tfinforma.com.

616.8 TUR ISSN 1302-6631
ANADOLU PSIKIYATRI DERGISI/ANATOLIAN JOURNAL OF PSYCHIATRY. Text in Turkish, English. 2000. 4/yr. **Document type:** *Journal, Academic/Scholarly.* **Description:** Covers original studies in the field of psychiatry.
Related titles: Online - full text ed.
Indexed: A01, EMBASE, ExcerpMed, P03, P20, PQC, PsycInfo, R10, Reac, SCI, SCOPUS, W07.
Published by: Cumhuriyet Universitesi, Medical Faculty, Department of Psychiatry, Sivas, Turkey. TEL 90-346-2191010, FAX 90-346-2191110, editor.cap@gmail.com. Ed. Orhan Dogan.

616.89 ESP ISSN 0213-0599
CODEN: APSIEL
➤ **ANALES DE PSIQUIATRIA.** Text in Spanish; Abstracts in Spanish, English. 1984. 10/yr. EUR 63 to qualified personnel; EUR 97 to institutions; EUR 42 to students (effective 2007). adv. abstr.; bibl.; illus.; stat. back issues avail. **Document type:** *Journal, Academic/Scholarly.*
Indexed: A36, C06, C07, CABA, E-psyche, EMBASE, ExcerpMed, FR, GH, N02, N03, P03, PsycInfo, PsycholAb, R10, R12, RA&MP, Reac, S02, S03, SCOPUS, T05.
—BLDSC (0890.170000), GNLM, INIST. **CCC.**
Published by: Aran Ediciones, Castello 128, 1o, Madrid, 28006, Spain. TEL 34-91-7820030, FAX 34-91-5615787, edita@grupoaran.com, http://www.grupoaran.com. Ed. Barcia D Salorio. Pub. Jose Jimenez Marquez. R&P Maria Dolores Linares TEL 34-91-7820035. Circ: 3,000.

616.8 FRA ISSN 1253-1472
ANALYSE FREUDIENNE PRESSE; revue de l'Association Analyse Freudienne. Text in French. 1992. s-a. EUR 38 domestic; EUR 48 foreign (effective 2011). back issues avail. **Document type:** *Journal, Academic/Scholarly.*
Related titles: Online - full text ed.
Published by: (Association Analyse Freudienne), Editions Eres, 33 Av. Marcel Dassault, Toulouse, 31500, France. TEL 33-5-61751576, FAX 33-5-61735289, eres@edition-eres.com. Circ: 700.

616.8 ITA ISSN 1827-4439
ANNALI DI NEUROLOGIA E PSICHIATRIA. PSICHIATRIA. Text in Italian. 1996. biennial. **Document type:** *Journal, Academic/Scholarly.*
Supersedes in part (in 1996): Annuali di Neurologia e Psichiatria (1827-4412); Which was formerly (until 1981): Annuali di Neurologia e Psichiatria e Annali Ospedale Psichiatrico di Perugia (1827-4404); (until 1955): Ospedale Psichiatrico di Perugia. Annali (1827-4390); (until 1930): Ospedale Psichiatrico Provinciale di Perugia. Annali (1827-4382); (1907-1922): Manicomio Provinciale di Perugia. Annali (1827-4374)
Published by: Azienda Ospedaliera di Perugia, Via Brunamonti 51, Perugia, 06122, Italy. TEL 39-075-5781, FAX 39-075-5783531, http://www.ospedale.perugia.it.

616.8 USA ISSN 1040-1237
RC321 CODEN: APSYEZ
➤ **ANNALS OF CLINICAL PSYCHIATRY.** Text in English. 1989. q. USD 250 domestic to institutions; USD 275 foreign to institutions; USD 150 combined subscription domestic to individuals (print & online eds.); USD 175 combined subscription foreign to individuals (print & online eds.); free to members (effective 2010). back issues avail.; reprints avail. **Document type:** *Journal, Academic/Scholarly.* **Description:** Provides clinical practitioners with the results of current research into the phenomenology and treatment of psychiatric disorders.
Related titles: Online - full text ed.: ISSN 1547-3325. GBP 280, USD 461 to institutions (effective 2007) (from IngentaConnect).
Indexed: A01, A03, A08, A22, B21, BibLing, CA, CurCont, E-psyche, E01, EMBASE, ExcerpMed, FR, FamI, INI, IndMed, Inpharma, MEDLINE, NSA, P03, P20, P22, P25, P30, P48, P54, PQC, PsycInfo, PsycholAb, R10, Reac, SCI, SCOPUS, SSCI, T02, W07.
—GNLM, IE, Infotrieve, Ingenta, INIST. **CCC.**
Published by: (American Academy of Clinical Psychiatrists), Dowden Health Media, Inc (Subsidiary of: Lebhar-Friedman, Inc.), 110 Summit Ave, Montvale, NJ 07645. TEL 201-740-6100, 800-707-7040, FAX 201-391-2778, http://www.dowdenhealth.com. Eds. Alice V Luddington, Dr. Donald W Black TEL 319-353-4431. Pub. Kenneth A Sylvia.

616.89 GBR ISSN 1744-859X
➤ **ANNALS OF GENERAL PSYCHIATRY.** Text in English. 2002. irreg. free (effective 2011). adv. **Document type:** *Journal, Academic/Scholarly.* **Description:** Publishes original research papers concerning all aspects of psychiatry with emphasis on general hospital psychiatry.
Formerly (until 2004): Annals of General Hospital Psychiatry (1475-2832)
Media: Online - full text.
Indexed: A01, A26, C06, C07, CA, EMBASE, ExcerpMed, I05, NSA, P03, P20, P22, P30, PsycInfo, R10, Reac, SCOPUS, T02.
—CCC.
Published by: BioMed Central Ltd. (Subsidiary of: Springer Science+Business Media), 236 Gray's Inn Rd, London, WC1X 8HB, United Kingdom. TEL 44-20-31922000, FAX 44-20-31922010, info@biomedcentral.com, http://www.biomedcentral.com. Ed. Konstantinos Fountoulakis.

616.8 USA ISSN 0364-5134
RC321 CODEN: ANNED3
➤ **ANNALS OF NEUROLOGY.** Text in English. 1977. m. GBP 591 in United Kingdom to institutions; EUR 746 in Europe to institutions; USD 904 in United States to institutions; USD 1,072 in Canada & Mexico to institutions; USD 1,156 elsewhere to institutions; GBP 681 combined subscription in United Kingdom to institutions (print & online eds.); EUR 860 combined subscription in Europe to institutions (print & online eds.); USD 1,039 combined subscription in United States to institutions (print & online eds.); USD 1,207 combined subscription in Canada & Mexico to institutions (print & online eds.); USD 1,291 combined subscription elsewhere to institutions (print & online eds.) (effective 2012). bk.rev. abstr.; charts; illus.; stat. index. back issues avail.; reprint service avail. from PSC. **Document type:** *Journal, Academic/Scholarly.* **Description:** Brings out articles in understanding the mechanisms and treatment of diseases of the human nervous system.
Related titles: Microform ed.: (from PQC); Online - full text ed.: ISSN 1531-8249. GBP 462 in United Kingdom to institutions; EUR 583 in Europe to institutions; USD 904 elsewhere to institutions (effective 2012); Ed.: ISSN 1885-0162; Translation: ISSN 1881-8056.
Indexed: A20, A22, A26, A34, A35, A36, AIDS Ab, AIIM, ASCA, ASFA, AgBio, B21, B25, BDM&CN, BIOBASE, BIOSIS Prev, BiolDig, C06, C07, C08, CABA, CIN, CINAHL, ChemAb, ChemTitl, CurCont, DentInd, DiabCont, DokArb, E-psyche, E12, EMBASE, ESPM, ExcerpMed, FR, G08, GH, H11, H12, H17, IABS, IBR, IBZ, IDIS, ISR, IndMed, Inpharma, JW, JW-N, JW-P, MEDLINE, MycolAb, N02, N03, NSA, NSCI, P03, P30, P33, P35, P39, PsycInfo, PsycholAb, R08, R10, RILM, Reac, SCI, SCOPUS, T05, THA, ToxAb, VS, W07.
—BLDSC (1043.140000), CASDDS, CIS, GNLM, IE, Infotrieve, Ingenta, INIST. **CCC.**
Published by: (American Neurological Association), John Wiley & Sons, Inc., 111 River St, Hoboken, NJ 07030. TEL 201-748-6000, FAX 201-748-6088, info@wiley.com, http://www.wiley.com/WileyCDA/. Ed. Stephen L Hauser. Adv. contact James G Pattis. **Subscr. addr. outside the Americas:** John Wiley & Sons Ltd. **Co-sponsor:** Child Neurology Society.

616.8 IND ISSN 0972-7531
➤ **ANNALS OF NEUROSCIENCES.** Text and summaries in English. 1993. q. INR 800 domestic; USD 80 foreign (effective 2011). adv. bk.rev. bibl.; illus. back issues avail. **Document type:** *Journal, Academic/Scholarly.* **Description:** Aims to cover new advances in neurosciences. It provides a platform for papers that range from computational and experimental work in the neurosciences to those that fit the interface between experiments and clinic.
Related titles: Online - full text ed.: ISSN 0976-3260. free (effective 2011).
Indexed: A01, T02.
Published by: Indian Academy of Neurosciences, Neuroscience Research Lab, Department of neurology, PGIMER, Chandigarh, 160 012, India. TEL 91-172-2756090, FAX 91-1722748399. Ed., Pub. Dr. Akshay Anand. Circ: 1,500 (paid).

➤ **ANNUAL OF PSYCHOANALYSIS.** *see* PSYCHOLOGY

618.928 USA ISSN 0066-4030
RJ499.A1
➤ **ANNUAL PROGRESS IN CHILD PSYCHIATRY AND CHILD DEVELOPMENT.** Text in English. 1968. a., latest 2002. USD 95.50 per issue (effective 2010). **Document type:** *Journal, Academic/Scholarly.* **Description:** Provides the most current research and scholarship available in the field of child psychiatry and child development.
Indexed: A22, E-psyche, PsycholAb.
—BLDSC (1091.400000), GNLM, IE, Ingenta, INIST. **CCC.**
Published by: Routledge (Subsidiary of: Taylor & Francis Group), 325 Chestnut St, Ste 800, Philadelphia, PA 19106. TEL 800-354-1420, FAX 215-625-2940, journals@routledge.com. Eds. Ellen Farber, Margaret E Hertzig. Adv. contact Linda Hann TEL 44-1344-779945.

362.13 USA ISSN 1554-8716
R119.9
ANNUAL REVIEW OF CYBERTHERAPY AND TELEMEDICINE. Text in English. 2003. a. **Document type:** *Journal, Academic/Scholarly.* **Description:** Covers a wide variety of topics of interest to the mental health, neuroscience, and rehabilitation communities.
Related titles: Print ed.: free (effective 2011).
Indexed: EMBASE, ExcerpMed, P03, PsycInfo, SCOPUS.
—BLDSC (1522.282500), IE. **CCC.**
Published by: (Universita Cattolica del Sacro Cuore ITA), Interactive Media Institute, 6160 Cornerstone Ct E, Ste 155, San Diego, CA 92121. TEL 858-642-0267, 866-822-8762, FAX 858-642-0285, frontoffice@vrphobia.com, http://www.vrphobia.com/imi/cybertherapy.htm. Eds. Brenda Wiederhold, Giuseppe Riva.

616.8 USA ISSN 0147-006X
QP351 CODEN: ARNSD5
➤ **ANNUAL REVIEW OF NEUROSCIENCE.** Text in English. 1978. a. USD 272 combined subscription per issue to institutions (print & online eds.); USD 227 per issue to institutions (print or online ed.) (effective 2012). bibl.; abstr. index, cum.index. back issues avail.; reprint service avail. from PSC. **Document type:** *Journal, Academic/Scholarly.* **Description:** Reviews filter and synthesize primary research to identify the principal contributions in neuroscience.
Related titles: Microfilm ed.: (from PQC); Online - full text ed.: ISSN 1545-4126.
Indexed: A01, A03, A08, A22, A26, A34, A35, ASCA, ASFA, AgBio, Agr, AnBeAb, B&AI, B10, B21, BIOBASE, BIOSIS Prev, BRD, C13, C33, CA, CABA, CIN, CTA, ChemAb, ChemTitl, ChemoAb, CompAb, CurCont, E-psyche, E08, EMBASE, ExcerpMed, G03, G08, GH, GSA, GSI, I05, IABS, IBR, IBZ, ISR, IndMed, IndVet, Inpharma, Inspec, MEDLINE, MycolAb, N03, N04, N05, NSA, NSCI, P03, P10, P15, P20, P22, P25, P26, P30, P33, P43, P48, P52, P53, P54, P56, PQC, PsycInfo, PsycholAb, R07, R08, R10, Reac, S04, S09, S13, S16, SCI, SCOPUS, T02, THA, VS, W03, W05, W07, Z01.
—BLDSC (1523.350000), CASDDS, GNLM, IE, Infotrieve, Ingenta, INIST. **CCC.**
Published by: Annual Reviews, PO Box 10139, Palo Alto, CA 94303. TEL 650-493-4400, FAX 650-424-0910, 800-523-8635, service@annualreviews.org. Eds. Steven E Hyman TEL 617-496-5100, Samuel Gubins.

616.8 JPN
ANNUAL REVIEW SHINKEI/ANNUAL REVIEW. NERVE. Text in Japanese. 1988. a. JPY 9,400 per issue (effective 2007). adv. **Document type:** *Academic/Scholarly.*
Indexed: E-psyche.
Published by: Chugai Igakusha, 62 Yarai-cho, Shinjuku-ku, Tokyo, 162-0805, Japan. TEL 81-3-32682701, FAX 81-3-32682722, http://www.chugaiigaku.jp/.

616.8 ITA ISSN 1827-4420
ANNUALI DI NEUROLOGIA E PSICHIATRIA. NEUROLOGIA. Text in Italian. 1996. biennial. **Document type:** *Journal, Academic/Scholarly.*
Supersedes in part (in 1996): Annuali di Neurologia e Psichiatria (1827-4412); Which was formerly (until 1981): Annali di Neurologia e Psichiatria e Annali Ospedale Psichiatrico di Perugia. (1827-4404); (until 1955): Ospedale Psichiatrico di Perugia. Annali (1827-4390); (until 1930): Ospedale Psichiatrico Provinciale di Perugia. Annali (1827-4382); (1907-1922): Manicomio Provinciale di Perugia. Annali (1827-4374)
Published by: Azienda Ospedaliera di Perugia, Via Brunamonti 51, Perugia, 06122, Italy. TEL 39-075-5781, FAX 39-075-5783531, http://www.ospedale.perugia.it.

616.89 ESP ISSN 1134-7937
ANSIEDAD Y ESTRES/ANXIETY AND STRESS. Text in Spanish. 1995. s-a. EUR 70 domestic to institutions; free to members (effective 2009). back issues avail. **Document type:** *Journal, Academic/Scholarly.*
Related titles: Online - full text ed.: ISSN 2174-0437. 1994.
Indexed: A01, A22, CA, F03, F04, P03, PsycInfo, PsycholAb, SCOPUS, T02.
—BLDSC (1542.024000), IE, Ingenta.
Published by: Sociedad Espanola para el Estudio de la Ansiedad y el Estres, Buzon 23, Campus de Somosaguas, Madrid, 28223, Spain. TEL 34-91-3943111, FAX 34-91-3943024, seas@psi.ucm.es, http://www.ucm.es/info/seas/index.htm. Ed. Antonio Cano-Vindel.

616.8 GBR ISSN 0268-7038
RC425
➤ **APHASIOLOGY.** Text in English. 1987. m. GBP 1,529 combined subscription in United Kingdom to institutions (print & online eds.); EUR 2,018, USD 2,534 combined subscription to institutions (print & online eds.) (effective 2012). bk.rev. bibl.; charts; illus. back issues avail.; reprint service avail. from PSC. **Document type:** *Journal, Academic/Scholarly.* **Description:** Provides information on all aspects of brain damage-related language problems for neurologists, speech therapists, psychologists in universities, and hospitals and clinics.
Related titles: Online - full text ed.: ISSN 1464-5041. GBP 1,376 in United Kingdom to institutions; EUR 1,816, USD 2,281 to institutions (effective 2012) (from IngentaConnect).

Indexed: A01, A03, A08, A20, A22, AMED, ASCA, B21, BibLing, C06, C07, C08, CA, CINAHL, CMM, CurCont, E-psyche, E01, EMBASE, ExcerpMed, Inpharma, L&LBA, L11, MLA-IB, NSA, NSCI, P03, P30, PsycInfo, PsycholAb, R10, RASB, Reac, SCI, SCOPUS, SOPODA, T02, W07.
—GNLM, IE, Infotrieve, Ingenta. **CCC.**
Published by: Psychology Press (Subsidiary of: Taylor & Francis Ltd.), 27 Church Rd, Hove, E Sussex BN3 2FA, United Kingdom. TEL 44-20-70176000, FAX 44-20-70176717, info@psypress.co.uk, http://www.psypress.com. Ed. Chris Code. Adv. contact Linda Hann TEL 44-1344-779945. **Subscr. to:** Taylor & Francis Ltd., Journals Customer Service, Sheepen Pl, Colchester, Essex CO3 3LP, United Kingdom. TEL 44-20-70175544, FAX 44-20-70175198, subscriptions@tandf.co.uk, http://www.tandf.co.uk/journals.

616.8 USA ISSN 1931-4159
APPLIED NEUROLOGY. Text in English. 2005 (Jan.). irreg., latest 2006. adv. **Document type:** *Journal, Academic/Scholarly.* **Description:** Provides a forum and source of information for primary care physicians who treat neurological disorders including Alzheimer's disease, MS, and pain.
Related titles: Online - full text ed.: ISSN 1931-4256.
Indexed: A26, G08, H11, H12, I05.
—CCC.
Published by: C M P Medica LLC (Subsidiary of: United Business Media Limited), 535 Connecticut Ave, Ste 300, Norwalk, CT 06854. TEL 203-523-7000, FAX 203-662-6420, http://www.ubmmedica.com/.

616 616.8 USA ISSN 0908-4282
QP360 CODEN: ANEUF8
➤ **APPLIED NEUROPSYCHOLOGY.** Text in English. 1994. q. GBP 412, EUR 550, USD 691 combined subscription to institutions (print & online eds.) (effective 2011). adv. back issues avail.; reprint service avail. from PSC. **Document type:** *Journal, Academic/Scholarly.* **Description:** Publishes clinical neuropsychological articles concerning assessment, brain functioning and neuroimaging, and neuropsychological treatment and rehabilitation.
Related titles: Online - full text ed.: ISSN 1532-4826. GBP 371, EUR 495, USD 622 to institutions (effective 2011).
Indexed: A01, A03, A08, A22, B21, C06, C07, CA, E-psyche, E01, EMBASE, ExcerpMed, IndMed, L&LBA, MEDLINE, NSA, NSCI, P03, P30, P43, PsycInfo, PsycholAb, R10, Reac, SCI, SCOPUS, T02, W07.
—BLDSC (1576.231000), GNLM, IE, Infotrieve, Ingenta. **CCC.**
Published by: (American College of Professional Neuropsychology), Psychology Press (Subsidiary of: Taylor & Francis Inc.), 325 Chestnut St, Ste 800, Philadelphia, PA 19106. TEL 800-354-1420, FAX 215-625-2940, orders@taylorandfrancis.com, http://www.psypress.com. Ed. Arthur MacNeill Horton. Adv. contact Linda Hann TEL 44-1344-779945.

➤ **APPLIED PSYCHOLINGUISTICS**; psychological and linguistic studies across languages and learners. *see* LINGUISTICS

616.8 362.2 AUS
ARAFMI NEWS; providing support for carers of people with mental disorders. Text in English. 1982. q. free to members (effective 2009). bk.rev. back issues avail. **Document type:** *Newsletter.* **Description:** Provides information on developments in the field of mental health, events and activities.
Indexed: E-psyche.
Published by: Arafmi Queensland Inc., PO Box 248, New Farm, QLD 4005, Australia. TEL 61-7-32541881, info@arafmiqld.org, http://www.arafmiqld.org/. Ed. Barbara Kimber.

THE ARC INSIGHT. *see* SOCIAL SERVICES AND WELFARE

612.8 ITA ISSN 0003-9829
QH301 CODEN: AIBLAS
➤ **ARCHIVES ITALIENNES DE BIOLOGIE**; a journal of neuroscience. Text in English. 1882. q. EUR 104 domestic (effective 2009). adv. bk.rev. abstr.; bibl.; charts; illus. index. back issues avail. **Document type:** *Journal, Academic/Scholarly.* **Description:** Publishes basic research work in neuroanatomy, neurophysiology, neurobiology, neurochemistry and behavioral science.
Related titles: Microfiche ed.: (from BHP); Online - full text ed.
Indexed: A22, ASCA, ASFA, AnBeAb, B21, B25, BIOBASE, BIOSIS Prev, ChemAb, CurCont, E-psyche, EMBASE, ExcerpMed, IABS, IBR, IBZ, ISR, IndMed, Inpharma, MEDLINE, MycolAb, NSA, NSCI, P30, PhysBer, PsycholAb, R10, Reac, RefZh, SCI, SCOPUS, W07.
—BLDSC (1637.200000), CASDDS, GNLM, IE, Infotrieve, Ingenta, INIST, Linda Hall. **CCC.**
Published by: (Universita degli Studi di Pisa, Dipartimento di Fisiologia e Biochimica), Edizioni Plus - Universita di Pisa (Pisa University Press), Lungarno Pacinotti 43, Pisa, Italy. TEL 39-050-2212056, FAX 39-050-2212945, http://www.edizioniplus.it. Ed., R&P Ottavio Pompeiano TEL 39-050-554070. Circ: 300 (paid and controlled).

616.8 150 GBR ISSN 0887-6177
➤ **ARCHIVES OF CLINICAL NEUROPSYCHOLOGY.** Text in English. 1986. 8/yr. GBP 576 in United Kingdom to institutions; EUR 559 in Europe to institutions; USD 865 in US & Canada to institutions; GBP 576 elsewhere to institutions; GBP 629 combined subscription in United Kingdom to institutions (print & online eds.); EUR 610 combined subscription in Europe to institutions (print & online eds.); USD 943 combined subscription in US & Canada to institutions (print & online eds.); GBP 629 combined subscription elsewhere to institutions (print & online eds.) (effective 2012). back issues avail.; reprint service avail. from PSC. **Document type:** *Journal, Academic/Scholarly.* **Description:** Publishes original contributions dealing with psychological aspects of the etiology, diagnosis and treatment of disorders arising out of dysfunction of the central nervous system.
Related titles: Microfilm ed.: (from PQC); Online - full text ed.: ISSN 1873-5843. GBP 524 in United Kingdom to institutions; EUR 508 in Europe to institutions; USD 786 in US & Canada to institutions; GBP 524 elsewhere to institutions (effective 2012) (from IngentaConnect, ScienceDirect).
Indexed: A01, A03, A08, A20, A22, A26, ASCA, B21, CA, CDA, CurCont, E-psyche, EMBASE, FR, FamI, I05, MEDLINE, NSA, NSCI, P03, P30, PsycInfo, PsycholAb, R10, Reac, SCI, SCOPUS, SSCI, T02, W07.
—BLDSC (1634.090000), GNLM, IE, Infotrieve, Ingenta, INIST. **CCC.**
Published by: (National Academy of Neuropsychology USA), Oxford University Press, Great Clarendon St, Oxford, OX2 6DP, United Kingdom. TEL 44-1865-556767, FAX 44-1865-556646, enquiry@oup.co.uk, http://www.oxfordjournals.org. Ed. Robert J McCaffrey.

616.89 USA ISSN 0003-990X
RC321 CODEN: ARGPAQ
➤ **ARCHIVES OF GENERAL PSYCHIATRY.** Text in English. 1919. m. USD 745 domestic to institutions; USD 931 in the Americas to institutions; EUR 753 in Europe to institutions; GBP 639 elsewhere to institutions (effective 2012). adv. bk.rev. bibl.; charts; illus. Index. back issues avail.; reprints avail. **Document type:** *Journal, Academic/Scholarly.* **Description:** Features original state-of-the-art studies and commentaries of general interest to clinicians, scholars, and research scientists, on psychiatry, mental health, behavioral science, and allied fields.
Formerly (until 1960): A M A Archives of General Psychiatry (0375-8532); Which superseded in part (in 1959): A M A Archives of Neurology and Psychiatry (0096-6886); Which was formerly (1919-1950): Archives of Neurology and Psychiatry (0096-6754)
Related titles: Microform ed.: (from PQC); Online - full text ed.: ISSN 1538-3636. free to members (effective 2012).
Indexed: A20, A22, A26, ABS&EES, AHCMS, AIM, AMED, AMHA, ASCA, AddicA, B21, B25, BDM&CN, BIOSIS Prev, C28, CA, CDA, CIN, ChPerI, ChemAb, ChemTitl, Chicano, CurCont, DBA, DentInd, E-psyche, E08, EMBASE, ExcerpMed, F09, FR, FamI, G08, G10, H11, H12, H13, I05, I12, IBR, IBZ, IDIS, IPARL, ISR, IndMed, Inpharma, JW, JW-P, JW-WH, MEA&I, MEDLINE, MS&D, MycolAb, NRN, NSA, P02, P03, P10, P20, P21, P22, P24, P30, P35, P48, P53, P54, PQC, PsycInfo, PsycholAb, R10, RILM, Reac, S02, S03, S09, SCI, SCOPUS, SSCI, T02, W07, W09.
—BLDSC (1634.350000), CASDDS, GNLM, IE, Infotrieve, Ingenta, INIST. **CCC.**
Published by: American Medical Association, 515 N State St, Chicago, IL 60610. journalsales@ama-assn.org, http://www.ama-assn.org. Eds. Dr. Joseph T. Coyle TEL 617-855-2170, Dr. Catherine D DeAngelis. **Subscr. in the Americas to:** PO Box 10946, Chicago, IL 60654. TEL 312-670-7827, 800-262-2350, ama-subs@ama-assn.org; **Subscr. outside the Americas to:** American Medical Association, J A M A and Archive Journals.

616.8 016 USA ISSN 0003-9942
RC321 CODEN: ARNEAS
➤ **ARCHIVES OF NEUROLOGY.** Text in English. 1919. m. USD 750 domestic to institutions; USD 938 in the Americas to institutions; EUR 758 in Europe to institutions; GBP 643 elsewhere to institutions (effective 2012). bk.rev. charts; illus. index. back issues avail.; reprints avail. **Document type:** *Journal, Academic/Scholarly.* **Description:** Features scholarly papers on Neurology as well as Neurological reviews, clinical trials, case reports.
Formerly (until 1960): A M A Archives of Neurology (0375-8540); Which superseded in part (in 1959): A M A Archives of Neurology and Psychiatry (0096-6886); Which was formerly (1919-1950): Archives of Neurology and Psychiatry (0096-6754)
Related titles: Microform ed.: (from PMC, PQC); Online - full text ed.: ISSN 1538-3687. free to members (effective 2012).
Indexed: A20, A22, A26, A34, A36, AIDS Ab, AIIM, AIM, ASCA, AgrForAb, B21, B25, BDM&CN, BIOBASE, BIOSIS Prev, C06, C07, C08, CABA, CINAHL, CIS, ChemAb, CurCont, D01, DBA, DentInd, DokArb, E-psyche, E12, EMBASE, ESPM, ExcerpMed, F08, FR, G08, GH, H11, H12, H13, H17, IABS, IBR, IBZ, ISR, IndMed, IndVet, Inpharma, JW, JW-N, JW-P, LT, MEDLINE, MS&D, MycolAb, N02, N03, NSA, NSCI, P02, P03, P10, P20, P22, P24, P30, P33, P35, P48, P53, P54, PN&I, PQC, PsycInfo, PsycholAb, R07, R08, R10, RM&VM, RRTA, Reac, SCI, SCOPUS, SPPI, T05, THA, ToxAb, VS, W07.
—BLDSC (1638.400000), CASDDS, GNLM, IE, Infotrieve, Ingenta, INIST. **CCC.**
Published by: American Medical Association, 515 N State St, Chicago, IL 60654. TEL 312-464-4200, 800-621-8335, FAX 312-464-4142, journalsales@ama-assn.org, http://www.ama-assn.org. Eds. Dr. Roger N Rosenberg TEL 214-648-9383, Dr. Catherine D DeAngelis. **Subscr. in the Americas to:** PO Box 10946, Chicago, IL 60654. TEL 312-670-7827, 800-262-2350, ama-subs@ama-assn.org; **Subscr. outside of the Americas to:** American Medical Association, J A M A and Archive Journals.

➤ **ARCHIVES OF PSYCHIATRIC NURSING.** *see* MEDICAL SCIENCES—Nurses And Nursing

616.8 150 POL ISSN 1509-2046
RC321
➤ **ARCHIVES OF PSYCHIATRY AND PSYCHOTHERAPY.** Text and summaries in English. 1999. q. USD 40 foreign to individuals; USD 100 foreign to institutions (effective 2008). adv. abstr.; bibl. 80 p./no. 1 cols./p.; back issues avail. **Document type:** *Journal, Academic/Scholarly.* **Description:** Publishes clinical, experimental, theoretical papers and case reports on psychiatry and psychotherapy.
Indexed: A01, CA, EMBASE, ExcerpMed, P03, PsycInfo, PsycholAb, R10, Reac, SCOPUS, T02.
—BLDSC (1640.425000), IE.
Published by: Polskie Towarzystwo Psychiatryczne, ul Jana Sobieskiego 9, Warsaw, 02957, Poland. psych@kom-red-wyd-ptp.com.pl. Ed., Pub., R&P Jerzy W Aleksandrowicz. Adv. contact Magdalena Sikora. **Dist. by:** Ars Polona, Obroncow 25, Warsaw 03933, Poland. TEL 48-22-5098609, FAX 48-22-5098610, arspolona@arspolona.com.pl, http://www.arspolona.com.pl.

➤ **ARCHIVES OF SUICIDE RESEARCH.** *see* PSYCHOLOGY

616.8 MEX ISSN 1028-5938
➤ **ARCHIVOS DE NEUROCIENCIAS/ARCHIVES OF NEUROSCIENCES.** Text in Spanish. 1966. q. MXN 250 domestic to institutions; USD 50 foreign (effective 2011). adv. bk.rev. back issues avail. **Document type:** *Journal, Academic/Scholarly.* **Description:** Includes articles and research work on neurosciences.
Former titles (until 1995): Instituto Nacional de Neurologia y Neurocirugia. Archivos (0187-4705); (until 1980): Instituto Nacional de Neurologia. Revista
Related titles: Online - full text ed.
Indexed: A01, A22, B21, C01, C06, C07, C08, CA, CINAHL, E-psyche, EMBASE, ExcerpMed, ImmunAb, IndMed, NSA, R10, Reac, RefZh, SCOPUS, T02.
—BLDSC (1655.451000), IE, Ingenta.
Published by: Instituto Nacional de Neurologia y Neurocirugia Manuel Velasco Suarez, Insurgentes Sur 3877, Col La Fama, Mexico, D.F., DF 14269, Mexico. TEL 52-55-56063822, FAX 52-55-54241396, arcneuro@hotmail.com.mx, http://www.innn.edu.mx/inicio.html. Ed. Ricardo Colin Piana.

616.8 ESP ISSN 1576-0367
CODEN: ADEPFP
ARCHIVOS DE PSIQUIATRIA. Text in Spanish; Summaries in English. 1920. bi-m. EUR 50 domestic to individuals; EUR 80 foreign to individuals; EUR 70 domestic to institutions; EUR 100 foreign to institutions. **Document type:** *Journal, Academic/Scholarly.*
Formerly (until 1999): Archivos de Neurobiologia (0004-0576)
Related titles: Supplement(s): Archivos de Psiquiatria. Suplementos. ISSN 1576-0359. 1929.
Indexed: A20, A22, DentInd, E-psyche, EMBASE, ExcerpMed, IME, IndMed, MLA-IB, P03, P30, PsycholAb, R10, Reac, SCOPUS, SOPODA, YAE&RB.
—GNLM, INIST. **CCC.**
Published by: Editorial Triacastela, C Guzman El Bueno 27, 1o. Dcha., Madrid, 28015, Spain. TEL 34-902-151242, FAX 34-902-151317, editorial@triacastela.com, http://www.triacastela.com. Ed. Victor La Fora.

616.8 URY ISSN 1510-2718
ARCHIVOS DEL INSTITUTO DE NEUROLOGIA. Text in Spanish. 1998. 3/yr. **Document type:** *Monographic series, Academic/Scholarly.*
Related titles: Online - full text ed.
Published by: Instituto de Neurologia, Hospital de Clinicas "Dr. M. Quintela", Ave Italia, s-n Piso 2, Montevideo, Uruguay. TEL 598-2-4871515 ext. 2244, bibneu@hc.edu.uy. Ed. Eduardo Wilson. Circ: 400.

616.8 ITA ISSN 1122-6994
AREAANALISI; rivista italiana di psicodramma analitico. Text in Italian. 1987. s-a. **Document type:** *Journal, Academic/Scholarly.*
Published by: Edizioni dell' Orso, Via Urbano Rattazzi 47, Alessandria, 15100, Italy. TEL 39-0131-252349, FAX 39-0131-257567, direzione.editoriale@ediorso.it, http://www.ediorso.it.

616.8 USA ISSN 2155-3203
AREADNE. PROCEEDINGS. Text in English. 2006. biennial. **Document type:** *Proceedings, Trade.* **Description:** Proceedings of the Areadne Foundation Conference for recent findings on functioning of neuronal ensembles.
Related titles: CD-ROM ed.: ISSN 2155-319X; Online - full text ed.: ISSN 2154-6819.
Published by: Areadne Foundation, 366 Broadway, Cambridge, MA 02139. info@areadne.org, http://www.areadne.org.

616.8 ITA ISSN 0391-7274
GLI ARGONAUTI. Text in Italian. 1979. q. EUR 54.90 (effective 2009). **Document type:** *Journal, Academic/Scholarly.*
Related titles: Supplement(s): Quaderni de gli Argonauti. ISSN 1722-3962. 2001.
Published by: C I S Editore S.r.l., Via San Siro 1, Milan, 20149, Italy. TEL 39-02-4694542, FAX 39-02-48193584, http://www.ciseditore.it. Ed. Carlo Zucca Alessandrelli.

616.8 BRA ISSN 1518-3327
ARQUIVOS BRASILEIROS DE PSIQUIATRIA, NEUROLOGIA E MEDICINA LEGAL. Text in Portuguese. 1999. q. back issues avail. **Document type:** *Journal, Academic/Scholarly.*
Related titles: Online - full text ed.
Published by: Associacao Psiquiatrica do Estado do Rio de Janeiro, Ave Nossa Sra de Copacabana, 613, Rio de Janeiro, 22050-001, Brazil. TEL 55-21-22352125, FAX 55-21-25489439, aperj@aperj.com.br.

616.89 BRA ISSN 0004-282X
CODEN: ANPIAM
➤ **ARQUIVOS DE NEURO-PSIQUIATRIA.** Text in Portuguese, English. 1943. q. BRL 120 domestic; USD 80 foreign (effective 2005). adv. bk.rev. abstr.; bibl.; charts. index, cum.index: 1943-1999. 180 p./no.; back issues avail. **Document type:** *Journal, Academic/Scholarly.* **Description:** Publishes original and refereed articles on science and technology covering medical fields of neurology, neurosciences, and psychiatry.
Related titles: CD-ROM ed.; E-mail ed.; Online - full text ed.: ISSN 1678-4227. free (effective 2011).
Indexed: A20, A22, A36, ASCA, B21, C01, CA, CABA, D01, DentInd, E-psyche, E12, EMBASE, ExcerpMed, GH, H17, IBR, IBZ, INI, INIS AtomInd, IndMed, MEDLINE, N02, N03, NSA, NSCI, P03, P30, P33, P39, PsycInfo, PsycholAb, R08, R10, R12, RM&VM, Reac, RefZh, SCI, SCOPUS, T02, T05, VS, W07.
—BLDSC (1695.630000), GNLM, IE, Infotrieve, Ingenta, INIST. **CCC.**
Published by: (Academia Brasileira de Neurologia/Brazilian Academy of Neurology), Associacao Arquivos de Neuro-Psiquiatria, Praca Amadeu Amaral, 47-33, B Vista, Sao Paulo, SP 01327-010, Brazil. TEL 55-11-287-6600, FAX 55-11-289-8879. Ed. Oswaldo Lange. R&P Adriana Machado. Adv. contact Marilia Spina-Franca. Circ: 1,800 (paid); 200 (controlled).

616.8 PRT ISSN 1646-3943
ARQUIVOS DE PSIQUIATRIA. Text in Portuguese. 2006. s-a. **Document type:** *Journal, Academic/Scholarly.*
Published by: Universidade do Porto, Faculdade de Medicina, Alameda Prof Hernani Monteiro 4200, Oporto, 4200-319, Portugal. http://sigarra.up.pt/fmup/.

616.8 150 BRA ISSN 0103-0809
➤ **ARQUIVOS DE SAUDE MENTAL DO ESTADO DE SAO PAULO.** Text in Portuguese; Summaries in English. 1924. biennial. bk.rev. charts; illus. **Document type:** *Journal, Academic/Scholarly.*
Formerly (until 1987): Sao Paulo. Coordenadoria de Saude Mental. Arquivos (0101-1693)
Related titles: ◆ Supplement(s): Arquivos de Saude Mental do Estado de Sao Paulo. Suplemento. ISSN 0103-0817.
Indexed: E-psyche.
Published by: Biblioteca do Hospital de Juqueri, Franco da Rocha E.F.S.J., Franco Da Rocha, SP 07780-000, Brazil. TEL 55-11-432-5111 ext. 135, FAX 55-11-432-5444, TELEX 11-79736.

616.5 BRA ISSN 0103-0817
ARQUIVOS DE SAUDE MENTAL DO ESTADO DE SAO PAULO. SUPLEMENTO. Text in Portuguese. 1987. a.
Related titles: ◆ Supplement to: Arquivos de Saude Mental do Estado de Sao Paulo. ISSN 0103-0809.
Published by: Biblioteca do Hospital de Juqueri, Franco da Rocha E.F.S.J., Franco Da Rocha, SP 07780-000, Brazil. TEL 55-11-432-5111 ext. 135, FAX 55-11-432-5444.

616.891 GBR ISSN 2044-7221
▼ **ART THERAPY ONLINE.** Abbreviated title: A T O L. Text in English. 2009. s-a. free (effective 2010). back issues avail. **Document type:** *Journal, Academic/Scholarly.*

Published by: University of London, Goldsmiths' College, Lewisham Way, New Cross, London, SE14 6NW, United Kingdom. TEL 44-20-79197171, international-office@gold.ac.uk, http://www.gold.ac.uk.

616.89 AUS ISSN 1758-5864
▼ ➤ **ASIA-PACIFIC PSYCHIATRY.** Text in English. 2009 (Jul.). q. GBP 112 in United Kingdom to institutions; EUR 130 in Europe to institutions; USD 158 elsewhere to institutions (effective 2012).
Document type: *Journal, Academic/Scholarly.*
Related titles: Online - full text ed.: ISSN 1758-5872. 2009. GBP 112 in United Kingdom to institutions; EUR 130 in Europe to institutions; USD 158 elsewhere to institutions (effective 2012).
Indexed: A01, A22, E01, EMBASE, SCI, SCOPUS, SSCI, W07.
—CCC.
Published by: (Pacific Rim College of Pyschiatry JPN), Wiley-Blackwell Publishing Asia (Subsidiary of: Wiley-Blackwell Publishing Ltd.), 155 Cremorne St, Richmond, VIC 3121, Australia. Eds. Allan Tasman, Edmond Chiu, Ee Hoek Kua.

616.89 NLD ISSN 1876-2018
RC321
➤ **ASIAN JOURNAL OF PSYCHIATRY.** Text in English. 2008. 4/yr. EUR 235 in Europe to institutions; JPY 37,700 in Japan to institutions; USD 348 elsewhere to institutions (effective 2012). **Document type:** *Journal, Academic/Scholarly.* **Description:** Provides information on psychiatric research of relevance to Asia whether or not it originates from within the continent.
Related titles: Online - full text ed.: ISSN 1876-2026 (from ScienceDirect).
Indexed: CA, EMBASE, ExcerpMed, P30, SCOPUS, T02.
—IE. **CCC.**
Published by: (Asian Federation of Psychiatric Associations AUS), Elsevier BV (Subsidiary of: Elsevier Science & Technology), Radarweg 29, PO Box 211, Amsterdam, 1000 AE, Netherlands. TEL 31-20-4853911, FAX 31-20-4852457, JournalsCustomerServiceEMEA@elsevier.com, http://www.elsevier.com. Ed. Matcheri Keshavan.

616.8 RUS ISSN 1999-6489
➤ **ASIMMETRIYA**; journal of asymmetry. Text in Russian, English. 2007. q. free. abstr. back issues avail. **Document type:** *Journal, Academic/Scholarly.* **Description:** Publishes research results in the field of brain assymetry and related fields.
Media: Online - full text.
Published by: Assimetriya, b. Nikolovorob'inskii pereulok, 7, Moscow, Russian Federation. TEL 7-495-9170765, FAX 7-495-9170765. Ed. Vitalii Fokin.

616.891 ARG ISSN 0326-0704
ASOCIACION ESCUELA ARGENTINA DE PSICOTERAPIA PARA GRADUADOS. REVISTA. Text in Spanish. 1976. a. **Document type:** *Journal, Academic/Scholarly.*
Published by: Asociacion Escuela Argentina de Psicoterapia para Graduados, Julian Alvarez 1933, Buenos Aires, CDHA1425, Argentina. TEL 54-11-48661602, http://www.aeapg.org.ar.

616.9 ESP ISSN 0210-8194
ASOCIACION ESPANOLA DE NEUROPSIQUIATRIA. BOLETIN. Text in Spanish. 1978. s-a. **Document type:** *Bulletin, Academic/Scholarly.*
Published by: Asociacion Espanola de Neuropsiquiatria, Calle Magallanes 1, Sotano 2, Local 4, Madrid, 28015, Spain. TEL 34-957-480575, FAX 34-91-8473182, revistaaen@terra.es, http://www.pulso.com/aen/.

616.89 ESP ISSN 0211-5735
RC321
ASOCIACION ESPANOLA DE NEUROPSIQUIATRIA. REVISTA. Text in Spanish. 1981. 3/yr. EUR 18 (effective 2008). back issues avail. **Document type:** *Journal, Academic/Scholarly.*
Related titles: Online - full text ed.: free (effective 2011).
Indexed: A01.
—INIST.
Published by: Asociacion Espanola de Neuropsiquiatria, Calle Magallanes 1, Sotano 2, Local 4, Madrid, 28015, Spain. TEL 34-957-480575, revistaaen@terra.es, http://www.pulso.com/aen/. Ed. Fernando Codina.

ASSESSMENT. *see* PSYCHOLOGY

THE ASSESSMENT AND TREATMENT OF CHILD PSYCHOPATHOLOGY AND DEVELOPMENTAL DISABILITIES. *see* CHILDREN AND YOUTH—About

ASSOCIATION FOR APPLIED PSYCHOPHYSIOLOGY AND BIOFEEDBACK. PROCEEDINGS OF THE ANNUAL MEETING. *see* PSYCHOLOGY

ASSOCIATION OF NEUROPHYSIOLOGICAL SCIENTISTS. JOURNAL. *see* BIOLOGY—Physiology

616.8 ITA ISSN 1828-5317
ASSOCIAZIONE ITALIANA NEURODISABILI. Text in Italian. 2006. bi-m.
Media: Online - full text.
Published by: Associazione Italiana Neurodisabili (A I N), Via Filocomo 78D, Catania, Italy.

616.8 CAN ISSN 1910-1341
ATOUT HASARD. Text in French. 1999. irreg. **Document type:** *Bulletin, Academic/Scholarly.*
Published by: Universite Laval, Ecole de Psychologie. Centre Quebecois d'Excellence pour la Prevention et le Traitement du Jeu, Pavillon Felix-Antoine-Savard, Quebec, PQ G1K 7P4, Canada. TEL 418-656-5383, FAX 418-656-3646.

616.858 USA ISSN 1551-0980
ATTENTION!; for families & adults with attention-deficit/hyperactivity disorder. Text in English. 1995. bi-m. USD 45 domestic to individual members; USD 100 foreign to individual members (effective 2008). adv. illus. **Document type:** *Magazine, Consumer.* **Description:** Provides relevant, timely, and science-based information to families and adults with Attention-Deficit/Hyperactivity Disorder.
Indexed: E-psyche.
Published by: Children and Adults with Attention Deficit - Hyperactivity Disorders, 8181 Professional Pl., Ste. 201, Landover, MD 20785-2226. TEL 301-306-7070, 800-233-4050, FAX 301-306-7090. adv.: B&W page USD 2,736, color page USD 3,796; trim 8.375 x 10.875. Circ: 52,573.

610 016 USA ISSN 0271-1311
➤ **AUDIO-DIGEST PSYCHIATRY.** Text in English. 1971. s-m. USD 449.81 domestic; USD 479.72 in Canada; USD 527.72 elsewhere (effective 2010). back issues avail. **Document type:** *Journal, Academic/Scholarly.*
Media: Audio cassette/tape. **Related titles:** Audio CD ed.: USD 399.89 domestic; USD 431.72 in Canada; USD 479.72 elsewhere (effective 2010); Online - full text ed.: USD 359.72 (effective 2010).
Indexed: AddicA, E-psyche.
Published by: Audio-Digest Foundation (Subsidiary of: California Medical Association), 1577 E Chevy Chase Dr, Glendale, CA 91206. TEL 818-240-7500, 800-423-2308, FAX 818-240-7379.

616.89 ESP ISSN 1577-2950
AULA MEDICA PSIQUIATRIA. Text in Spanish. 1999. bi-m. EUR 36 (effective 2009). **Document type:** *Journal, Academic/Scholarly.*
Related titles: Online - full text ed.: EUR 30 (effective 2009).
Published by: Grupo Aula Medica S.A., C Isabel Colbrand, 10 Nave 78, Planta 2a, Madrid, 28050, Spain. TEL 34-91-3586478, FAX 34-91-3589979, informacion@grupoaulamedica.com. Ed. Jose Manuel Crespo Blanco.

616.8 AUS ISSN 1032-335X
RC350.5
➤ **AUSTRALASIAN JOURNAL OF NEUROSCIENCE.** Text in English. 1988. s-a. AUD 100 membership (effective 2008). **Document type:** *Journal, Academic/Scholarly.* **Description:** Contains articles on advances in neurosurgical and neurological techniques and commentary on the role of the neuroscience nurse in the health care team.
Indexed: A11, C06, C07, C08, CA, CINAHL, P24, P48, PQC, T02.
—BLDSC (1794.972000), IE, Ingenta.
Published by: Australasian Neuroscience Nurses' Association, PO Box 61, Mt Colah, NSW 2079, Australia. TEL 61-2-88378926, FAX 61-2-88379275, annaexecutive@anna.asn.au. Ed. Jennifer Blundell.

➤ **AUSTRALASIAN JOURNAL OF PSYCHOTHERAPY.** *see* PSYCHOLOGY

616.8 GBR ISSN 1039-8562
RC451.A788 CODEN: AUPSF4
➤ **AUSTRALASIAN PSYCHIATRY.** Text in English. 1993. bi-m. GBP 165, EUR 230, USD 290 combined subscription to institutions (print & online eds.); GBP 335, EUR 465, USD 580 combined subscription to corporations (print & online eds.) (effective 2010). adv. bk.rev. back issues avail.; reprint service avail. from PSC. **Document type:** *Journal, Academic/Scholarly.* **Description:** Aims to promote the art of psychiatry and its maintenance in practice.
Related titles: Online - full text ed.: ISSN 1440-1665 (from IngentaConnect).
Indexed: A01, A02, A03, A08, A11, A22, A26, C06, C07, C08, C11, CA, CINAHL, E-psyche, E01, EMBASE, ExcerpMed, H04, MEDLINE, P03, P30, P34, P43, PsycInfo, PsycholAb, R10, Reac, SCI, SCOPUS, SOPODA, SSCI, T02, W07.
—IE, Infotrieve, Ingenta. **CCC.**
Published by: (Royal Australian and New Zealand College of Psychiatrists AUS), Informa Healthcare (Subsidiary of: T & F Informa plc), Telephone House, 69-77 Paul St, London, EC2A 4LQ, United Kingdom. TEL 44-20-70175000, FAX 44-20-70176792, healthcare.enquiries@informa.com. Ed. Gary Walter. Adv. contact Per Sonnerfeldt.

616.89 GBR ISSN 0004-8674
RC321 CODEN: ANZPBQ
➤ **AUSTRALIAN & NEW ZEALAND JOURNAL OF PSYCHIATRY.** Text in English. 1967. m. GBP 585, EUR 815, USD 1,020 combined subscription to institutions (print & online eds.); GBP 1,165, EUR 1,630, USD 2,035 combined subscription to corporations (print & online eds.) (effective 2010). adv. bk.rev. abstr.; charts; illus. Index. Supplement avail.; back issues avail.; reprint service avail. from PSC. **Document type:** *Journal, Academic/Scholarly.* **Description:** Provides clinical and research papers and case studies in all areas of psychiatry.
Related titles: Online - full text ed.: ISSN 1440-1614 (from IngentaConnect).
Indexed: A01, A02, A03, A08, A11, A20, A22, A26, A35, A36, AMHA, ASCA, AddicA, B25, BIOSIS Prev, C06, C07, C08, C11, CA, CABA, CINAHL, CurCont, DokArb, E-psyche, E01, E12, EMBASE, ExcerpMed, F09, FR, FamI, GH, H04, H12, INI, INZP, IPsyAb, ISR, IndMed, Inpharma, JW-P, LT, MEA&I, MEDLINE, MycolAb, N02, N03, P03, P30, P34, P35, P43, PhilInd, PsycInfo, PsycholAb, R10, R12, Reac, RefZh, S02, S03, SCI, SCOPUS, SPPI, SSCI, T02, T05, W07, W09, W11.
—BLDSC (1796.893000), GNLM, IE, Infotrieve, Ingenta, INIST. **CCC.**
Published by: (Royal Australian and New Zealand College of Psychiatrists AUS), Informa Healthcare (Subsidiary of: T & F Informa plc), Telephone House, 69-77 Paul St, London, EC2A 4LQ, United Kingdom. TEL 44-20-70175000, FAX 44-20-70176792, healthcare.enquiries@informa.com. Ed. Peter Joyce. Adv. contact Per Sonnerfeldt.

616.89 155 GBR ISSN 1362-3613
RC553.A88 CODEN: AUTIFS
➤ **AUTISM**; the international journal of research and practice. Text in English. 1997. bi-m. USD 1,049, GBP 567 combined subscription to institutions (print & online eds.); USD 1,028, GBP 556 to institutions (effective 2011). adv. bk.rev. back issues avail.; reprint service avail. from PSC. **Document type:** *Journal, Academic/Scholarly.* **Description:** Provides a major new international forum for research of direct and practical relevance to improving the quality of life for individuals with autism or autism-related disorders.
Related titles: Online - full text ed.: ISSN 1461-7005. USD 944, GBP 510 to institutions (effective 2011).
Indexed: A01, A03, A08, A20, A22, ASSIA, B07, B21, B29, C06, C07, C08, CA, CINAHL, CPE, CurCont, E-psyche, E01, E03, EMBASE, ERI, ERIC, ExcerpMed, FR, H04, L&LBA, MEDLINE, NSA, P03, P04, P30, PsycInfo, PsycholAb, R10, Reac, S02, S03, SCOPUS, SSCI, SWR&A, T02, V02, W07.
—BLDSC (1825.520000), IE, Infotrieve, Ingenta, INIST. **CCC.**
Published by: (The National Autistic Society), Sage Publications Ltd. (Subsidiary of: Sage Publications, Inc.), 1 Oliver's Yard, 55 City Rd, London, EC1Y 1SP, United Kingdom. TEL 44-20-73248500, FAX 44-20-73248600, info@sagepub.co.uk, http://www.uk.sagepub.com/home.nav. Eds. Dermot M Bowler, Dougal Julian Hare, Lonnie Zwaigenbaum. **Subscr. in the Americas to:** Sage Publications, Inc., 2455 Teller Rd, Thousand Oaks, CA 91320. TEL 805-499-9774, FAX 805-499-0871, journals@sagepub.com.

616.85882 USA ISSN 1947-1203
RJ506.A9
AUTISM ADVOCATE. Text in English. 199?. q. free membership (effective 2009). adv. back issues avail. **Document type:** *Magazine, Consumer.* **Description:** Offers a diverse collection of the latest issues in autism (e.g., education, environmental health, therapies/interventions, adult issues, caregiving, etc.), Autism Society news, personal perspectives of families and individuals living with autism, and tips from parents and professionals.
Formerly (until 1992): Advocate
Related titles: Online - full text ed.: ISSN 1947-1211.
Published by: Autism Society of America, 7910 Woodmont Ave, Ste 300, Bethesda, MD 20814. TEL 301-657-0881, 800-328-8476, FAX 301-657-0869, media@autism-society.org.

▼ **AUTISM EYE.** *see* EDUCATION—Special Education And Rehabilitation

616.89 GBR ISSN 1468-5175
THE AUTISM FILE. Text in English. q. GBP 26.50 domestic; GBP 39.95 foreign (effective 2010). **Document type:** *Journal, Academic/Scholarly.* **Description:** Covers articles on safety for autistic children and the shocking lack of basic human rights for individuals with autism in many countries.
Related titles: ◆ International ed.: The Autism File USA.
Published by: The Autism File, P O Box 144, Hampton, TW12 2FF, United Kingdom. TEL 44-20-89792525, info@autismfile.com. Ed. Polly Tommey.

616.89 USA
THE AUTISM FILE USA. Text in English. 2008. q. USD 32.99 in North America; USD 62.99 elsewhere (effective 2010). **Document type:** *Journal, Academic/Scholarly.* **Description:** Covers articles on safety for autistic children and the shocking lack of basic human rights for individuals with autism in many countries.
Related titles: ◆ International ed. of: The Autism File. ISSN 1468-5175.
Published by: The Autism File USA, 800 Connecticut Ave, Norwalk, CT 06854-1631. TEL 800-424-7887, info@autismfile.com. Eds. Teri Arranga, Polly Tommey.

616.8 NZL ISSN 1179-5964
▼ ➤ **AUTISM INSIGHTS.** Text in English. 2010. free (effective 2011). **Document type:** *Journal, Academic/Scholarly.*
Media: Online - full text.
Indexed: C06.
—CCC.
Published by: Libertas Academica Ltd., PO Box 300-874, Mairangi Bay, Auckland, 0751, New Zealand. TEL 64-9-4763930, FAX 64-9-3531397, enquiries@la-press.com. Ed. Anthony J Russo.

618.9289 USA
THE AUTISM PERSPECTIVE. Text in English. q. USD 24 (effective 2005). **Document type:** *Magazine, Consumer.* **Description:** Focuses on the subject of autism spectrum disorders, for parents, professionals and persons with autism.
Published by: The Autism Perspective, 10153 1/2 Riverside Dr, Ste 243, Toluca Lake, CA 91602. TEL 310-709-0941.

616.85 USA ISSN 1939-3792
RC553.A88
AUTISM RESEARCH. Text in English. 2008 (Feb.). bi-m. GBP 569 in United Kingdom to institutions; EUR 656 in Europe to institutions; USD 806 elsewhere to institutions (effective 2012). adv. back issues avail.; reprint service avail. from PSC. **Document type:** *Journal, Academic/Scholarly.* **Description:** Covers the developmental disorders known as Pervasive Developmental Disorders (or autism spectrum disorders (ASDs). Focuses on basic genetic, neurobiological and psychological mechanisms and how these influence developmental processes in ASDs.
Related titles: Online - full text ed.: ISSN 1939-3806. GBP 569 in United Kingdom to institutions; EUR 656 in Europe to institutions; USD 806 elsewhere to institutions (effective 2012).
Indexed: B25, BIOSIS Prev, CurCont, EMBASE, ExcerpMed, MEDLINE, MycolAb, P03, P30, PsycInfo, SCI, SSCI, W07.
—IE. **CCC.**
Published by: (International Society for Autism Research), John Wiley & Sons, Inc., 111 River St, Hoboken, NJ 07030. TEL 201-748-6000, FAX 201-748-6088, info@wiley.com, http://www.wiley.com/WileyCDA/. Ed. Anthony J Bailey.

616.85 USA ISSN 2090-1925
▼ ➤ **AUTISM RESEARCH AND TREATMENT.** Text in English. 2011. irreg. USD 195 (effective 2011). **Document type:** *Journal, Academic/Scholarly.* **Description:** Publishes original research articles, review articles, and clinical studies related to all aspects of autism.
Related titles: Online - full text ed.: ISSN 2090-1933. 2011. free (effective 2011).
Indexed: A01.
Published by: Hindawi Publishing Corporation, 410 Park Ave, 15th Fl, PMB 287, New York, NY 10022. FAX 215-893-4392, 866-446-3294, info@hindawi.com.

616.89 155 USA ISSN 0893-8474
RC553.A88
AUTISM RESEARCH REVIEW INTERNATIONAL. Text in English. 1987. q. USD 18 domestic; USD 20 foreign (effective 2005). bk.rev. back issues avail. **Document type:** *Newsletter.* **Description:** Contains summaries and reviews of world literature pertaining to autistic children, with emphasis on research pertaining to cause and treatment.
Indexed: E-psyche.
—BLDSC (1825.569000), GNLM.
Published by: Autism Research Institute, 4182 Adams Ave, San Diego, CA 92116. TEL 619-281-7165, FAX 619-563-6840. Eds. Alison Blake, Bernard Rimland. Pub., R&P Bernard Rimland. Circ: 10,000 (paid).

616.85882 USA ISSN 1551-448X
AUTISM SPECTRUM QUARTERLY. Abbreviated title: A S Q. Text in English. 2004 (Aug.). q. USD 29.95 in US & Canada; USD 32 in United Kingdom; KWD 15 in the Middle East; ZAR 200 in South Africa; AUD 55 in Australia; NZD 65 in New Zealand; SGD 95 in Malaysia; SGD 80 in Singapore; SGD 100 in Philippines (effective 2010). adv. 56 p./no.; **Document type:** *Magazine, Consumer.* **Description:** Covers important issues relating to Autism Spectrum Disorders.
Former titles (until 2004): Jenison Autism Journal; (until 2002): The Morning News
Published by: Starfish Specialty Press, PO Box 799, Higganum, CT 06441. TEL 877-782-7347 ext 3, FAX 860-345-4471. Ed. Diane Twachtman-Cullen. Adv. contact Kim R Newgass. col. inch USD 1,800; 6.92 x 9.42. **Subscr. in Australia to:** Giant Steps Tasmania, 37 West Church St, Deloraine, TAS 7304, Australia. TEL 61-3-63622522; **Subscr. in Canada to:** Autism Today Education Corporation, 2016 Sherwood Dr, Ste 3, Sherwood Park, AB T8A 3X3, Canada. TEL 877-482-1555, sales@autismtoday.com; **Subscr. in Malaysia, Philippines & Singapore to:** Bloomberg Inspirations Pte Ltd. asqbloomins@yahoo.com.sg; **Subscr. in New Zealand to:** Autism New Zealand - National Office, Tower Junction, Addington, PO Box 42052, Christchurch 8149, New Zealand. TEL 64-3-3321038; **Subscr. in South Africa to:** Autism South Africa, PO Box 84209, Greenside 2034, South Africa. TEL 27-11-4849909, FAX 27-11-4843171, info@autismsouthafrica.org; **Subscr. in the Middle East to:** Kuwait Centre for Autism, PO Box 33425, Al-Rawda 73455, Kuwait. TEL 965-2540351, FAX 965-2540247, http://www.q8autism.com; **Subscr. in the UK & Europe to:** Autism Independent UK, 199-203 Blandford Ave, Kettering, Northants NN16 9AT, United Kingdom. TEL 44-1536-523274, http://www.autismuk.com/; **Subscr. in the US to:** PO Box 4618, Apache Junction, AZ 85278. TEL 877-782-7347, FAX 480-671-5160; **Subscr. rest of the world to:** Starfish Specialty Press, PO Box 4618, Apache Junction, AL 85278. TEL 860-345-2155; **Subscr. to:** Hei Kidz International Pte Ltd., Joyce Ng, 9 Rivervale Crest #15-31, Singapore 545086, Singapore. TEL 65-9785-7718, FAX 65-6875-5074, asqbloomins@yahoo.com.sg.

616 ITA ISSN 1722-4071
AUTISMO E DISTURBI DELLO SVILUPPO; giornale italiano di ricerca clinica e psicoeducativa. Text in Italian. 2003. 3/yr. EUR 32.50 to individuals; EUR 43.50 domestic to institutions; EUR 55 foreign to institutions (effective 2008). **Document type:** *Journal, Academic/Scholarly.*
Published by: Edizioni Erickson, Via Praga 5, Settore E, Gardolo, TN 38100, Italy. TEL 39-0461-950690, FAX 39-0461-950698, info@erickson.it. Ed. Giuseppe Maurizio Arduino.

616.89 DEU
AUTISMUS; Studien, Materialien und Quellen. Text in German. 2001. irreg., latest vol.21, 2010. price varies. **Document type:** *Monographic series, Academic/Scholarly.*
Published by: Weidler Buchverlag Berlin, Luebecker Str 8, Berlin, 10559, Germany. TEL 49-30-3948668, FAX 49-30-3948698, weidler_verlag@yahoo.de. Ed. Brita Schirmer.

616.8 NLD ISSN 1566-0702
CODEN: ANUEB2
➤ **AUTONOMIC NEUROSCIENCE: BASIC AND CLINICAL.** Text in English. 1979. 14/yr. EUR 3,792 in Europe to institutions; JPY 503,900 in Japan to institutions; USD 4,242 elsewhere to institutions (effective 2012). adv. bk.rev. charts; illus. back issues avail.; reprints avail. **Document type:** *Journal, Academic/Scholarly.* **Description:** Presents papers that deal with any aspect of the autonomic nervous system, including structure, physiology, pharmacology, biochemistry, development, evolution, aging, behavioral aspects, integrative role, and its influence on emotional and physical states of the body.
Supersedes (in 2000): Journal of the Autonomic Nervous System (0165-1838)
Related titles: Microform ed.: (from PQC); Online - full text ed.: ISSN 1872-7484 (from IngentaConnect, ScienceDirect).
Indexed: A01, A03, A08, A22, A26, A34, A35, A36, A38, ASCA, ASFA, AgBio, B21, B25, BIOBASE, BIOSIS Prev, CA, CABA, CIN, ChemAb, ChemTitl, CurCont, DentInd, E12, EMBASE, ESPM, ExcerpMed, F08, F11, F12, FR, GH, H16, H17, I05, IABS, ISR, IndMed, IndVet, Inpharma, MEDLINE, MycolAb, N02, N03, NSA, NSCI, P30, P33, P39, PN&I, R10, RA&MP, Reac, S01, SCI, SCOPUS, T02, T05, VS, W07.
—CASDDS, GNLM, IE, Infotrieve, Ingenta, INIST. **CCC.**
Published by: Elsevier BV (Subsidiary of: Elsevier Science & Technology), Radarweg 29, PO Box 211, Amsterdam, 1000 AE, Netherlands. TEL 31-20-4853911, FAX 31-20-4852457, JournalsCustomerServiceEMEA@elsevier.com, http://www.elsevier.nl. Ed. Dr. G Burnstock.

362.2 FRA ISSN 1954-507X
UN AUTRE REGARD. Text in French. 196?. q. EUR 39 (effective 2007). back issues avail. **Document type:** *Journal.*
Formerly (until 199?): Bulletin de Liaison Trimestriel (U N A F A M) (0992-3713)
Published by: Union Nationale des Amis et Familles de Malades Psychiques (U N A F A M), 12 Villa Compoint, Paris, 75017, France. TEL 33-1-53063043, FAX 33-1-42634400.

616.8 ESP ISSN 2172-430X
▼ **AVANCES EN NEUROLOGIA.** Text in Spanish. 2010. a. free (effective 2010). **Document type:** *Journal, Academic/Scholarly.*
Media: Online - full text.
Published by: InterSalud, Apdo de Correos 227, Palmova, Mallorca, 07181, Spain. info@intersalud.es, http://www.intersalud.es/. Ed. Virgili Paez Cervi.

616.8 GBR ISSN 1471-2377
CODEN: BNMEC8
➤ **B M C NEUROLOGY.** (BioMed Central) Text in English. 2001 (Jan.). irreg. free (effective 2011). adv. back issues avail.; reprints avail. **Document type:** *Journal, Academic/Scholarly.* **Description:** Publishes original research articles in all aspects of the prevention, diagnosis and management of neurological disorders, as well as related molecular genetics, pathophysiology, and epidemiology.
Media: Online - full text.
Indexed: A01, A02, A03, A08, A26, A36, C06, C07, CA, CABA, CurCont, E12, EMBASE, ExcerpMed, GH, H17, I05, LT, MEDLINE, N02, N03, NSA, NSCI, P03, P20, P22, P30, P33, P39, PsycInfo, R08, R10, R12, RA&MP, Reac, SCI, SCOPUS, T02, T05, W07, W10.
—Infotrieve. **CCC.**
Published by: BioMed Central Ltd. (Subsidiary of: Springer Science+Business Media), 236 Gray's Inn Rd, London, WC1X 8HB, United Kingdom. TEL 44-20-31922000, FAX 44-20-31922010, info@biomedcentral.com. Ed. Dr. Melissa Norton. Adv. contact Natasha Bailey TEL 44-20-31922231.

➤ **B M C NEUROSCIENCE.** (BioMed Central) *see* BIOLOGY—Physiology

616.89 GBR ISSN 1471-244X
RC321 CODEN: BPMSCU
➤ **B M C PSYCHIATRY.** (BioMed Central) Text in English. 2001 (Jun.). irreg. free (effective 2011). adv. back issues avail.; reprints avail. **Document type:** *Journal, Academic/Scholarly.* **Description:** Publishes original research articles in all aspects of the prevention, diagnosis and management of psychiatric disorders, as well as related molecular genetics, pathophysiology, and epidemiology.
Media: Online - full text.
Indexed: A01, A02, A03, A08, A26, CA, CurCont, EMBASE, ExcerpMed, I05, MEDLINE, NSA, P03, P20, P22, P30, PsycInfo, R10, Reac, SCI, SCOPUS, T02, W07.
—Infotrieve. **CCC.**
Published by: BioMed Central Ltd. (Subsidiary of: Springer Science+Business Media), 236 Gray's Inn Rd, London, WC1X 8HB, United Kingdom. TEL 44-20-31922000, FAX 44-20-31922010, info@biomedcentral.com. Ed. Dr. Melissa Norton. Adv. contact Natasha Bailey TEL 44-20-31922231.

616.89 DEU ISSN 1439-5142
BALINT-JOURNAL. Text in German. 2000. q. EUR 106 to institutions; EUR 142 combined subscription to institutions (print & online eds.); EUR 34 newsstand/cover (effective 2011). adv. **Document type:** *Journal, Academic/Scholarly.*
Related titles: Online - full text ed.: ISSN 1439-9008. EUR 137 to institutions (effective 2011).
Indexed: A22.
—IE, Infotrieve. **CCC.**
Published by: (Deutsche Balint-Gesellschaft e.V.), Georg Thieme Verlag, Ruedigerstr 14, Stuttgart, 70469, Germany. TEL 49-711-8931421, FAX 49-711-8931410, kunden.service@thieme.de. Ed. Dr. G Bergmann. Adv. contact Andreas Schweiger TEL 49-711-8931245. Circ: 1,600 (paid and controlled).

BARDZIEJ KOCHANI; magazyn poswiecony problemom osob z zespolem Downa i ich rodzin. *see* EDUCATION—Special Education And Rehabilitation

616.8 USA ISSN 1539-1914
BARROW QUARTERLY. Text in English. 1985. q. free to individuals; USD 20 to institutions (effective 2005).
Formerly (until 2002): B N I Quarterly (0894-5799)
Indexed: P30.
—BLDSC (1863.826552).
Published by: Barrow Neurological Institute, 350 West Thomas Rd, Phoenix, AZ 85013-4496. TEL 602-406-3593, neuropub@chw.edu. Eds. Shelley A Kick, Robert F Spetzler.

616.83 NLD ISSN 2210-5336
▼ ➤ **BASAL GANGLIA.** Text in English. 2011 (Mar.). 4/yr. EUR 399 in Europe to institutions; EUR 399 to institutions in Germany, Austria and Switzerland; JPY 52,200 in Japan to institutions; USD 559 elsewhere to institutions (effective 2012). **Document type:** *Journal, Academic/Scholarly.* **Description:** Focuses on all scientific aspects related to diseases of basal ganglia, especially movement disorders.
Related titles: Online - full text ed.
Published by: (L I M P E (Lega Italiana per la Lotta Contro la Malattia di Parkinson, le Sindromi Extrapiramidali e le Demenze) ITA), Elsevier BV (Subsidiary of: Elsevier Science & Technology), Radarweg 29, PO Box 211, Amsterdam, 1000 AE, Netherlands. JournalsCustomerServiceEMEA@elsevier.com. Ed. Wolfgang H Jost.

616.8 IRN ISSN 2228-7442
▼ ➤ **BASIC AND CLINICAL NEUROSCIENCE.** Text in English. 2009. q. IRR 200,000 domestic; USD 60 foreign (effective 2011). bk.rev. abstr.; illus.; stat. Index. back issues avail.; reprints avail. **Document type:** *Journal, Academic/Scholarly.* **Description:** Publishes editorials, original full-length research articles, short communications, reviews, methodological papers, commentaries, perspectives and "news and reports" in the broad fields of developmental, molecular, cellular, systems, computational, behavioral, cognitive, and clinical neurosciences.
Formerly (until 2011): Iranian Journal of Neuroscience (2008-126X)
Related titles: Online - full text ed.
Published by: (Danishgah-i Ulum-i Pizishki va Khadamat-i Bihdashti-Darmani-i shahid Bihishti/Shaheed Beheshti University of Medical Sciences), Danishgah-i Ulum-i Pizishki-i Tihran/Tehran University of Medical Sciences, School of Medicine, Department of Anatomy, Neuroscience Section, Hemmat Campus, Shaheed Hemmat Hwy., Tehran, Iran. TEL 98-21-82944576, FAX 98-21-88622709, journals@tums.ac.ir, http://journals.tums.ac.ir. Eds. Ali Shahbazi, Hamed Ekhtiari, Sobhan Rezaee. Pub. Mohammad Taghi Joghataei. R&P Payam Kabiri.

616.834 DEU
BEFUND M S. (Multiple Sklerose) Text in German. 2005. 3/yr. adv. **Document type:** *Magazine, Consumer.*
Published by: G F M K GmbH & Co. KG Verlagsgesellschaft, Gezelinallee 37-39, Leverkusen, 51375, Germany. TEL 49-214-310570, FAX 49-214-3105719, info@gfmk.de. Circ: 15,000 (controlled).

616.8 GBR ISSN 1744-9081
QP351
➤ **BEHAVIORAL AND BRAIN FUNCTIONS.** Text in English. 2005. irreg. free (effective 2011). adv. back issues avail.; reprints avail. **Document type:** *Journal, Academic/Scholarly.* **Description:** Covers all aspects of neurobiology and behavior.
Media: Online - full text.
Indexed: A01, A26, AnBeAb, CA, EMBASE, ExcerpMed, I05, MEDLINE, NSA, NSCI, P03, P30, PsycInfo, R10, Reac, SCI, SCOPUS, T02, W07.
—**CCC.**
Published by: BioMed Central Ltd. (Subsidiary of: Springer Science+Business Media), 236 Gray's Inn Rd, London, WC1X 8HB, United Kingdom. TEL 44-20-31922000, FAX 44-20-31922010, info@biomedcentral.com, http://www.biomedcentral.com. Ed. Terje Sagvolden. Adv. contact Natasha Bailey TEL 44-20-31922231.

➤ **BEHAVIORAL AND BRAIN SCIENCES**; an international journal of current research and theory with open peer commentary. *see* PSYCHOLOGY

➤ **BEHAVIORAL HEALTH BUSINESS NEWS.** *see* INSURANCE

616.8 GBR ISSN 1072-0847
RJ505.B4 CODEN: BEHIE2
➤ **BEHAVIORAL INTERVENTIONS**; theory and practice in residential and community-based clinical programs. Text in English. 1986. q. GBP 526 in United Kingdom to institutions; EUR 664 in Europe to institutions; USD 1,028 elsewhere to institutions; GBP 606 combined subscription in United Kingdom to institutions (print & online eds.); EUR 764 combined subscription in Europe to institutions (print & online eds.); USD 1,182 combined subscription elsewhere to institutions (print & online eds.) (effective 2012). adv. back issues avail.; reprint service avail. from PSC. **Document type:** *Journal, Academic/Scholarly.* **Description:** Publishes reports of research involving the utilization of behavioral techniques in applied settings.
Formerly (until 1994): Behavioral Residential Treatment (0884-5581)
Related titles: Microform ed.: (from PQC); Online - full text ed.: ISSN 1099-078X. GBP 526 in United Kingdom to institutions; EUR 664 in Europe to institutions; USD 1,028 elsewhere to institutions (effective 2012).
Indexed: A01, A03, A08, A22, AMED, B21, C06, C07, CA, CurCont, E-psyche, Faml, H13, L&LBA, NSA, P02, P03, P10, P12, P20, P43, P48, P52, P53, P54, P56, PQC, PsycInfo, PsycholAb, SCOPUS, SSCI, T02, W07.
—GNLM, IE, Infotrieve, Ingenta. **CCC.**
Published by: John Wiley & Sons Ltd. (Subsidiary of: John Wiley & Sons, Inc.), 1-7 Oldlands Way, PO Box 808, Bognor Regis, West Sussex PO21 9FF, United Kingdom. TEL 44-1865-778315, FAX 44-1243-843232, cs-journals@wiley.com, http://eu.wiley.com/WileyCDA/. Ed. Richard M Foxx. **Subscr. in the Americas to:** John Wiley & Sons, Inc., 111 River St, Hoboken, NJ 07030. TEL 201-748-6645, subinfo@wiley.com; **Subscr. to:** 1-7 Oldlands Way, PO Box 809, Bognor Regis, West Sussex PO21 9FG, United Kingdom. TEL 44-1865-778054, cs-agency@wiley.com.

➤ **BEHAVIORAL MEDICINE**; relating behavior and health. *see* PSYCHOLOGY

➤ **BEHAVIORAL NEUROSCIENCE.** *see* PSYCHOLOGY

616.8 NLD ISSN 0166-4328
QP360 CODEN: BBREDI
➤ **BEHAVIOURAL BRAIN RESEARCH.** Text in English. 1980. 20/yr. EUR 6,199 in Europe to institutions; JPY 823,600 in Japan to institutions; USD 6,934 elsewhere to institutions (effective 2012). charts; illus. back issues avail.; reprints avail. **Document type:** *Journal, Academic/Scholarly.* **Description:** Publishes articles in the neurosciences, with special emphasis on neural mechanisms of behavior.
Related titles: Microform ed.: (from PQC); Online - full text ed.: ISSN 1872-7549 (from IngentaConnect, ScienceDirect).
Indexed: A01, A03, A08, A20, A22, A26, A34, A36, A38, ASFA, AnBeAb, B21, B25, BIOBASE, BIOSIS Prev, BibInd, CA, CABA, CIN, ChemAb, ChemTitl, CurCont, D01, DentInd, E-psyche, E12, EMBASE, ESPM, ExcerpMed, F08, F11, F12, FR, GH, H16, I05, IABS, IPsyAb, ISR, IndMed, IndVet, Inpharma, MEDLINE, MycolAb, N02, N03, N04, N05, NSA, NSCI, P03, P30, P33, P35, P37, P39, PGrRegA, PN&I, PsycInfo, PsycholAb, R07, R08, R10, RA&MP, Reac, S01, S12, S13, S16, SCI, SCOPUS, SoyAb, T02, ToxAb, VS, W07, W08, YAE&RB.
—BLDSC (1877.320000), CASDDS, GNLM, IE, Infotrieve, Ingenta, INIST. **CCC.**
Published by: Elsevier BV (Subsidiary of: Elsevier Science & Technology), Radarweg 29, PO Box 211, Amsterdam, 1000 AE, Netherlands. TEL 31-20-4853911, FAX 31-20-4852457, JournalsCustomerServiceEMEA@elsevier.com, http://www.elsevier.nl. Eds. Joe Huston, T E Robinson.

616.8 NLD ISSN 0953-4180
RC386 CODEN: BNEUEI
➤ **BEHAVIOURAL NEUROLOGY**; an international journal on the relationship between disordered human behavior and underlying biological mechanisms. Text in English. 1988. 4/yr. USD 951 combined subscription in North America (print & online eds.); EUR 680 combined subscription elsewhere (print & online eds.) (effective 2012). adv. bk.rev. index. **Document type:** *Journal, Academic/Scholarly.* **Description:** Publishes original and review papers of a predominantly clinical nature, with emphasis on the meaning of expression of disordered human behavior.
Related titles: Online - full text ed.: ISSN 1875-8584 (from IngentaConnect).
Indexed: A01, A03, A08, A20, A22, ASCA, B21, BIOBASE, CA, E-psyche, E01, EMBASE, ExcerpMed, IABS, Inpharma, MEDLINE, NSA, NSCI, P03, P30, PsycInfo, PsycholAb, R10, RILM, Reac, SCI, SCOPUS, T02, W07.
—BLDSC (1877.590000), GNLM, IE, Infotrieve, Ingenta, INIST. **CCC.**
Published by: I O S Press, Nieuwe Hemweg 6B, Amsterdam, 1013 BG, Netherlands. TEL 31-20-6883355, FAX 31-20-6870019, info@iospress.nl. Eds. Argye E Hillis, Stefano Cappa. Circ: 400. **Subscr. to:** I O S Press, Inc, 4502 Rachael Manor Dr, Fairfax, VA 22032-3631. iosbooks@iospress.com; Kinokuniya Co Ltd., Shinjuku 3-chome, Shinjuku-ku, Tokyo 160-0022, Japan. FAX 81-3-3439-1094, journal@kinokuniya.co.jp, http://www.kinokuniya.co.jp; Globe Publication Pvt. Ltd., C-62 Inderpuri, New Delhi 100 012, India. TEL 91-11-579-3211, 91-11-579-3212, FAX 91-11-579-8876, custserv@globepub.com, http://www.globepub.com.

616.8 NLD ISSN 0376-6357
QL750 CODEN: BPRODA
➤ **BEHAVIOURAL PROCESSES.** Text in English. 1977. 9/yr. EUR 2,296 in Europe to institutions; JPY 304,800 in Japan to institutions; USD 2,570 elsewhere to institutions (effective 2012). adv. bk.rev. bibl.; illus. Index. back issues avail.; reprints avail. **Document type:** *Journal, Academic/Scholarly.* **Description:** Covers comparative ethology, behavioral ecology, theoretical and quantitative ethology, neuroethology, experimental analysis and operant conditioning.
Incorporates (1981-1983): Behaviour Analysis Letters (0166-4794)

Related titles: Microform ed.: (from PQC); Online - full text ed.: ISSN 1872-8308 (from IngentaConnect, ScienceDirect).
Indexed: A01, A03, A08, A20, A22, A26, A34, A35, A36, A37, A38, ASCA, ASFA, AgBio, AnBeAb, B21, B23, B25, BIOBASE, BIOSIS Prev, BP, C25, C30, CA, CABA, CurCont, D01, E-psyche, E12, EMBASE, EntAb, ExcerpMed, F08, F11, F12, FR, G11, GEOBASE, GH, GeoRef, H17, I05, IABS, IPsyAb, ISR, IndVet, Inpharma, LT, MEDLINE, MycolAb, N02, N03, N04, NSA, OR, P03, P30, P33, P37, P39, PHN&I, PsycInfo, PsycholAb, R07, R08, R10, R12, RA&MP, RRTA, Reac, S01, S13, S16, S17, SCI, SCOPUS, SSCI, T02, T05, VS, W07, W08, Z01.
—BLDSC (1877.700000), CASDDS, GNLM, IE, Infotrieve, Ingenta, INIST. **CCC.**
Published by: Elsevier BV (Subsidiary of: Elsevier Science & Technology), Radarweg 29, PO Box 211, Amsterdam, 1000 AE, Netherlands. TEL 31-20-4853911, FAX 31-20-4852457, JournalsCustomerServiceEMEA@elsevier.com, http://www.elsevier.nl. Eds. C D L Wynne, F Cezilly. **Subscr. to:** Elsevier, Subscription Customer Service, 6277 Sea Harbor Dr, Orlando, FL 32887-4800. TEL 407-345-4020, 877-839-7126, FAX 407-363-1354.

362.25 DEU ISSN 0932-4674
BEITRAEGE ZUR ERFORSCHUNG SELBSTDESTRUKTIVEN VERHALTENS. Text in German. 1984. irreg., latest vol.22, 1993. price varies. **Document type:** *Monographic series, Academic/Scholarly.*
Published by: S. Roderer Verlag, In der Obern Au 12, Regensburg, 93055, Germany. TEL 49-941-7992270, FAX 49-941-795198, info@roderer-verlag.de, http://roderer-verlag.de.

616.8 USA ISSN 1553-555X
RA790.A1
➤ **BEST PRACTICES IN MENTAL HEALTH.** Text in English. 2005. s-a. USD 40 domestic to individuals; USD 55 foreign to individuals; USD 90 domestic to institutions; USD 105 foreign to institutions (effective 2009). **Document type:** *Journal, Academic/Scholarly.* **Description:** Provides mental health teachers and practitioners with articles that promote best practices in mental health.
Related titles: Online - full text ed.
Indexed: A01, A03, A08, BRD, CA, P03, PsycInfo, S02, S03, SSA, SSAI, SSAb, SSI, SWR&A, T02, W03, W05.
—BLDSC (1942.327870), IE. **CCC.**
Published by: Lyceum Books, Inc., 341 N Charlotte St, Lombard, IL 60148. TEL 630-620-7132, FAX 630-620-7522, lyceum@lyceumbooks.com, http://www.lyceumbooks.com.

616.8 ITA ISSN 1972-0238
BIBLIOTECA. INFANZIA, PSICOANALISI E ISTITUZIONI. Text in Italian. 1981. irreg. **Document type:** *Monographic series, Academic/Scholarly.*
Published by: Liguori Editore, Via Posillipo 394, Naples, 80123, Italy. TEL 39-081-7206111, FAX 39-081-7206244, liguori@liguori.it, http://www.liguori.it.

616.89 ITA ISSN 1972-0262
BIBLIOTECA. LO SPECCHIO DI PSICHE. Text in Italian. 1997. irreg., latest vol.4, 1999. price varies. adv. **Document type:** *Monographic series, Academic/Scholarly.*
Indexed: E-psyche.
Published by: Liguori Editore, Via Posillipo 394, Naples, 80123, Italy. TEL 39-081-7206111, FAX 39-081-7206244, liguori@liguori.it. Pub. Guido Liguori. Adv. contact Maria Liguori.

616.89 POL ISSN 1425-0640
BIBLIOTEKA PSYCHIATRII POLSKIEJ. Text in Polish. 1995. irreg. price varies. **Document type:** *Monographic series, Academic/Scholarly.*
Published by: Polskie Towarzystwo Psychiatryczne, ul Jana Sobieskiego 9, Warsaw, 02957, Poland. TEL 48-12-6331203, FAX 48-12-6334067, psych@kom-red-wyd-ptp.com.pl. Ed., Pub. Jerzy W Aleksandrowicz. Adv. contact Magdalena Sikora.

BIOFEEDBACK. *see* PSYCHOLOGY

616.89 USA ISSN 0006-3223
RC321 CODEN: BIPCBF
➤ **BIOLOGICAL PSYCHIATRY.** Text in English. 1958. 24/yr. USD 2,944 in United States to institutions; USD 3,098 elsewhere to institutions (effective 2012). adv. bk.rev. charts; illus. index. back issues avail.; reprints avail. **Document type:** *Journal, Academic/Scholarly.* **Description:** Covers the whole range of psychiatric research interest; presents major clinical, behavioral, epidemiological and normative studies in all subdisciplines relevant to psychiatry.
Formerly (until 1969): Recent Advances in Biological Psychiatry (0376-2122)
Related titles: CD-ROM ed.: ISSN 1086-7694; Microfilm ed.: (from PQC); Online - full text ed.: ISSN 1873-2402 (from IngentaConnect, ScienceDirect).
Indexed: A01, A03, A08, A20, A22, A26, A36, AMHA, ASCA, AddicA, B21, B25, BDM&CN, BIOBASE, BIOSIS Prev, BibInd, CA, CABA, CIN, ChemAb, ChemTitl, CurCont, DentInd, E-psyche, E12, EMBASE, ESPM, ExcerpMed, F09, FR, FamI, FoP, GH, I05, IABS, IPsyAb, ISR, IndMed, Inpharma, JW-P, MEDLINE, MycolAb, N02, N03, NSA, NSCI, P03, P30, P33, P35, P39, P40, PsycInfo, PsycholAb, R10, RA&MP, Reac, S01, SCI, SCOPUS, SSCI, T02, T05, ToxAb, VS, W07.
—BLDSC (2077.550000), CASDDS, GNLM, IE, Infotrieve, Ingenta, INIST. **CCC.**
Published by: (Society of Biological Psychiatry), Elsevier Inc. (Subsidiary of: Elsevier Science & Technology), 1600 John F Kennedy Blvd, Philadelphia, PA 19103. TEL 215-239-3900, FAX 215-238-7883, JournalCustomerService-usa@elsevier.com. Ed. Dr. John H Krystal TEL 214-648-0880.

616.89 USA ISSN 1044-422X
BIOLOGICAL THERAPIES IN PSYCHIATRY NEWSLETTER. Text in English. 1977. m. USD 78 to individuals; USD 115 to institutions (effective 2007). back issues avail. **Document type:** *Newsletter, Trade.* **Description:** Provides updates on the clinical use of psychotropic drugs to practicing psychiatrists, psychiatric house staff, residents, and students.
Former titles: Biological Therapies in Psychiatry (0895-8262); Massachusetts General Hospital Biological Therapies in Psychiatry Newsletter (0199-2716)
Related titles: Online - full text ed.: USD 60 (effective 2007).
—BLDSC (2081.270000), GNLM. **CCC.**

Published by: Gelenberg Consulting & Publishing, L.L.C., PO Box 42650, Tucson, AZ 85733-2650. TEL 520-572-2039, 800-700-9589, FAX 520-626-4070, subscriptions@btpnews.com. Ed. Alan J Gelenberg. Circ: 4,500 (paid).

616.895 USA ISSN 1399-5618
➤ **BIPOLAR DISORDERS (ENGLISH EDITION, ONLINE).** Text in English. 1999. 8/yr. GBP 489 in United Kingdom to institutions; EUR 622 in Europe to institutions; USD 822 in the Americas to institutions; USD 958 elsewhere to institutions (effective 2012). adv. **Document type:** *Journal, Academic/Scholarly.*
Media: Online - full text (from IngentaConnect). **Related titles:** ◆ Print ed.: Bipolar Disorders (English Edition, Print). ISSN 1398-5647; Ed.: Bipolar Disorders (Spanish Edition, Online). ISSN 1696-2559. 2003.
—**CCC.**
Published by: (International Society for Bipolar Disorders), Wiley-Blackwell Publishing, Inc. (Subsidiary of: Wiley-Blackwell Publishing Ltd.), Commerce Pl, 350 Main St, Malden, MA 02148. TEL 781-388-8200, FAX 781-388-8210, info@wiley.com, http://www.wiley.com/WileyCDA/. Eds. Roy K N Chengappa, Samuel Gershon.

616.895 USA ISSN 1398-5647
RC516 CODEN: BDIIAU
➤ **BIPOLAR DISORDERS (ENGLISH EDITION, PRINT)**; an international journal of psychiatry and neurosciences. Text in English. 1999. 8/yr. GBP 489 in United Kingdom to institutions; EUR 622 in Europe to institutions; USD 822 in the Americas to institutions; USD 958 elsewhere to institutions; GBP 563 combined subscription in United Kingdom to institutions (print & online eds.); EUR 715 combined subscription in Europe to institutions (print & online eds.); USD 946 combined subscription in the Americas to institutions (print & online eds.); USD 1,102 combined subscription elsewhere to institutions (print & online eds.) (effective 2012). adv. back issues avail.; reprint service avail. from PSC. **Document type:** *Journal, Academic/Scholarly.* **Description:** Publishes all research of relevance for the basic mechanisms, clinical aspects, or treatment of bipolar disorders. It intends to provide a single international outlet for new research in this area.
Related titles: ◆ Online - full text ed.: Bipolar Disorders (English Edition, Online). ISSN 1399-5618; ◆ Spanish ed.: Bipolar Disorders (Spanish Edition, Print). ISSN 1695-3568; Chinese ed.: Bipolar Disorders (Chinese Edition). ISSN 1990-8180. 2006; ◆ Supplement(s): Bipolar Disorders. Supplement. ISSN 1399-2406.
Indexed: A01, A03, A08, A22, A26, B21, CA, CurCont, E-psyche, E01, E07, EMBASE, ExcerpMed, H12, Inpharma, JW-P, MEDLINE, NSA, NSCI, P03, P30, P35, PsycInfo, PsycholAb, R10, Reac, SCI, SCOPUS, T02, W07.
—BLDSC (2090.475000), IE, Infotrieve, Ingenta, INIST. **CCC.**
Published by: (International Society for Bipolar Disorders), Wiley-Blackwell Publishing, Inc. (Subsidiary of: Wiley-Blackwell Publishing Ltd.), Commerce Pl, 350 Main St, Malden, MA 02148. TEL 781-388-8200, FAX 781-388-8210, info@wiley.com, http://www.wiley.com/WileyCDA/. Eds. Roy K N Chengappa, Samuel Gershon.

616.895 ESP ISSN 1695-3568
BIPOLAR DISORDERS (SPANISH EDITION, PRINT). Text in Spanish. 2003. 3/yr. EUR 83.44 to individuals; EUR 156.62 to institutions (effective 2009). back issues avail. **Document type:** *Journal, Academic/Scholarly.*
Related titles: Online - full text ed.: Bipolar Disorders (Spanish Edition, Online). ISSN 1696-2559. 2003; ◆ English ed.: Bipolar Disorders (English Edition, Print). ISSN 1398-5647; Chinese ed.: Bipolar Disorders (Chinese Edition). ISSN 1990-8180. 2006.
Published by: Grupo Ars XXI de Comunicacion, SA, Muntaner 262 Atico 2a., Barcelona, 08021, Spain. TEL 34-90-2195484, FAX 34-93-2722902, info@arsxxi.com.

616.895 USA ISSN 1399-2406
➤ **BIPOLAR DISORDERS. SUPPLEMENT.** Text in English. 2002. irreg. **Document type:** *Monographic series, Academic/Scholarly.*
Related titles: Online - full text ed.: ISSN 1600-5511; ◆ Supplement to: Bipolar Disorders (English Edition, Print). ISSN 1398-5647.
Indexed: SCOPUS.
—BLDSC (2090.475100). **CCC.**
Published by: Wiley-Blackwell Publishing, Inc. (Subsidiary of: Wiley-Blackwell Publishing Ltd.), Commerce Pl, 350 Main St, Malden, MA 02148. TEL 781-388-8200, FAX 781-388-8210, info@wiley.com, http://www.wiley.com/WileyCDA/.

616.8 GBR ISSN 1877-1831
BLUE BOOKS OF NEUROLOGY. Text in English. 2007. irreg., latest vol.35, 2009. price varies. **Document type:** *Monographic series, Academic/Scholarly.*
Related titles: Online - full text ed.: ISSN 1877-184X.
Published by: W.B. Saunders Co. Ltd. (Subsidiary of: Elsevier Health Sciences), 32 Jamestown Rd, Camden, London, NW1 7BY, United Kingdom. TEL 44-20-74244200, FAX 44-20-74832293, http://www.elsevier.com.

BODY, MOVEMENT AND DANCE IN PSYCHOTHERAPY; an international journal for theory, research and practice. *see* DANCE

616.8 ESP
BRAIN. Text in Spanish. 2007. q. EUR 88 domestic; EUR 143 foreign (effective 2009). **Document type:** *Journal, Academic/Scholarly.*
Published by: Ediciones Mayo S.A., Calle Aribau 185-187, 2a Planta, Barcelona, 08021, Spain. TEL 34-93-2090255, FAX 34-93-2020643, edmayo@ediciones.mayo.es, http://www.edicionesmayo.es. Circ: 3,500.

616.8 GBR ISSN 0006-8950
RC321 CODEN: BRAIAK
➤ **BRAIN**; a journal of neurology. Text in English. 1878. m. GBP 637 in United Kingdom to institutions; EUR 955 in Europe to institutions; USD 1,273 in US & Canada to institutions; GBP 637 elsewhere to institutions; GBP 695 combined subscription in United Kingdom to institutions (print & online eds.); EUR 1,042 combined subscription in Europe to institutions (print & online eds.); USD 1,388 combined subscription in US & Canada to institutions (print & online eds.); GBP 695 combined subscription elsewhere to institutions (print & online eds.) (effective 2012). adv. bk.rev. bibl.; illus. index. back issues avail.; reprint service avail. from PSC. **Document type:** *Journal, Academic/Scholarly.* **Description:** Provides original papers in clinical neurology and related disciplines.

Related titles: Microfiche ed.: (from IDC); Microform ed.: (from PMC, PQC); Online - full text ed.: ISSN 1460-2156. 199?. GBP 489 in United Kingdom to institutions; EUR 733 in Europe to institutions; USD 978 in US & Canada to institutions; GBP 489 elsewhere to institutions (effective 2012) (from IngentaConnect).
Indexed: A01, A03, A08, A20, A22, A26, AIM, AMED, ASCA, B21, B25, BDM&CN, BIOBASE, BIOSIS Prev, C06, C07, C08, CA, CINAHL, CTA, ChemAb, ChemoAb, CurCont, DBA, DiabCont, E-psyche, E01, EMBASE, ERIC, ErgAb, ExcerpMed, G08, H11, H12, IABS, ISR, IndMed, Inpharma, JW-N, L&LBA, MEDLINE, MLA-IB, MycolAb, NSA, NSCI, P03, P20, P22, P24, P25, P30, P35, P48, P54, PQC, PsycInfo, PsycholAb, R10, RILM, Reac, SCI, SCOPUS, SOPODA, SPPI, T02, W07.
—BLDSC (2268.000000), CASDDS, GNLM, IE, Infotrieve, Ingenta, INIST. **CCC.**
Published by: Oxford University Press, Great Clarendon St, Oxford, OX2 6DP, United Kingdom. TEL 44-1865-556767, FAX 44-1865-556646, enquiry@oup.co.uk, http://www.oxfordjournals.org. Ed. Alastair Compston. Pub. Mandy Sketch. adv.: B&W page GBP 440, B&W page USD 790; trim 216 x 279. Circ: 2,115.

616.8 530 USA ISSN 2150-2714
▼ ➤ **BRAIN AND COSMOS.** Text in English. 2010 (Jan.). q. USD 225 per issue (effective 2010). **Document type:** *Journal, Academic/Scholarly.* **Description:** Studies the principles shared by neuroscience and physics.
Media: Online - full content.
Published by: Kaiser Peer Publishing, PO Box 734, Churchville, NY 14428. TEL 585-393-1464, davidkaiser@spiritualneuroscience.org. Ed. Dr. Moninder S Modgil.

616.8 618.92 NLD ISSN 0387-7604
RJ486 CODEN: NTHAA7
➤ **BRAIN & DEVELOPMENT.** Text in English. 1969. 10/yr. EUR 678 in Europe to institutions; JPY 89,900 in Japan to institutions; USD 758 elsewhere to institutions (effective 2012). abstr. back issues avail. **Document type:** *Journal, Academic/Scholarly.* **Description:** Contains both clinical and basic studies in the field of child neurology.
Related titles: Microform ed.: (from PQC); Online - full text ed.: ISSN 1872-7131 (from IngentaConnect, ScienceDirect); ◆ Japanese ed.: No to Hattatsu. ISSN 0029-0831.
Indexed: A01, A03, A08, A20, A22, A26, ASCA, B21, B25, BDM&CN, BIOBASE, BIOSIS Prev, CA, CurCont, E-psyche, EMBASE, ExcerpMed, I05, IABS, ISR, IndMed, Inpharma, MEDLINE, MycolAb, NSA, NSCI, P03, P30, P35, PsycInfo, PsycholAb, R10, Reac, SCI, SCOPUS, T02, W07.
—BLDSC (2268.032900), GNLM, IE, Infotrieve, Ingenta, INIST. **CCC.**
Published by: (Nihon Shoni Shinkei Gakkai/Japanese Society of Child Neurology JPN), Elsevier BV (Subsidiary of: Elsevier Science & Technology), Radarweg 29, PO Box 211, Amsterdam, 1000 AE, Netherlands. TEL 31-20-4853911, FAX 31-20-4852457, JournalsCustomerServiceEMEA@elsevier.com, http://www.elsevier.nl. Ed. M Kaga.

616.8 JPN ISSN 1881-6096
BRAIN AND NERVE/SHINKEI KENKYUU NO SHIMPO. Text in English. 2007. m. JPY 35,460; JPY 46,100 combined subscription (print & online eds.) (effective 2010). **Document type:** *Journal, Academic/Scholarly.*
Formed by the merger of (1948-2006): No To Shinkei/Brain and Nerve (0006-8969); (1956-2006): Shinkei Kenkyu No Shimpo/Advances in Neurological Sciences (0001-8724)
Related titles: Online - full text ed.: ISSN 1344-8129.
Indexed: B25, BIOSIS Prev, EMBASE, ExcerpMed, MEDLINE, MycolAb, P30, R10, Reac, SCOPUS.
—BLDSC (8256.797000), IE.
Published by: Igaku Shoin Ltd., 1-28-36 Hongo, Bunkyo-ku, Tokyo, 113-8719, Japan. TEL 81-3-3817-5600, FAX 81-3-3815-7791, info@igaku-shoin.co.jp.

616.8 USA ISSN 1941-4099
BRAIN, BEHAVIOR AND EVOLUTION. Text in English. 2008 (Jul.). irreg., latest 2008. USD 44.95, GBP 31.95 per issue (effective 2010). **Document type:** *Monographic series, Academic/Scholarly.*
Published by: Praeger Publishers (Subsidiary of: Greenwood Publishing Group Inc.), 88 Post Rd W, Westport, CT 06881. TEL 800-368-6868, tech.support@greenwood.com. Ed. Patrick McNamara.

616.8 CHE ISSN 0006-8977
QL750 CODEN: BRBEBE
➤ **BRAIN, BEHAVIOR AND EVOLUTION.** Text in English. 1968. 8/yr. CHF 3,438, EUR 2,748, USD 3,366 to institutions; CHF 3,776, EUR 3,018, USD 3,694 combined subscription to institutions (print & online eds.) (effective 2012). adv. bk.rev. bibl.; illus. index. back issues avail.; reprints avail. **Document type:** *Journal, Academic/Scholarly.* **Description:** Aims to understand the evolution of nervous systems and how they subserve behavior.
Related titles: Microform ed.: (from RPI); Online - full text ed.: ISSN 1421-9743. CHF 3,370, EUR 2,696, USD 3,272 to institutions (effective 2012).
Indexed: A01, A03, A08, A22, ASCA, ASFA, AbAn, AnBeAb, B21, B25, BIOSIS Prev, CA, CurCont, DentInd, E-psyche, E01, EMBASE, ExcerpMed, FR, GenetAb, GeoRef, IBR, IBZ, ISR, IndMed, Inpharma, MEDLINE, MycolAb, NSA, NSCI, P03, P11, P20, P22, P25, P26, P30, P43, P48, P52, P54, P56, PQC, PsycInfo, PsycholAb, R10, Reac, SCI, SCOPUS, SpeleolAb, T02, W07, W08, WildRev, Z01.
—BLDSC (2268.100000), GNLM, IE, Infotrieve, Ingenta, INIST. **CCC.**
Published by: S. Karger AG, Allschwilerstr 10, Basel, 4055, Switzerland. TEL 41-61-3061111, FAX 41-61-3061234, karger@karger.ch, http://www.karger.ch. Ed. W Wilczynski. adv.: page CHF 1,815; trim 210 x 280. Circ: 800.

616.8
BRAIN BRIEFINGS. Text in English. 1994. m. free to members (effective 2010). **Document type:** *Newsletter, Trade.* **Description:** Explains how basic neuroscience discoveries lead to clinical applications.
Related titles: Online - full text ed.: free (effective 2010).
Published by: Society for Neuroscience, 1121 14th St, NW, Ste 1010, Washington, DC 20005. TEL 202-962-4000, FAX 202-962-4941, info@sfn.org. Pub. Carol Barnes.

616.8 USA ISSN 2158-0014
▼ **BRAIN CONNECTIVITY.** Text in English. 2011. bi-m. USD 1,780 combined subscription domestic (print & online eds.); USD 2,015 combined subscription foreign (print & online eds.) (effective 2012). adv. reprints avail. **Document type:** *Journal, Academic/Scholarly.* **Description:** Provides information on brain mapping, modeling, novel research techniques, and the translation of research discoveries from the laboratory to the clinic.
Related titles: Online - full text ed.: ISSN 2158-0022. USD 1,715 (effective 2012); Abridged ed.: ISSN 2158-0022. USD 1,715 (effective 2012).
Published by: Mary Ann Liebert, Inc. Publishers, 140 Huguenot St, 3rd Fl, New Rochelle, NY 10801. TEL 914-740-2100, FAX 914-740-2101, 800-654-3237, info@liebertpub.com. Eds. Bharat B Biswal, Christopher P Pawela.

616.8 USA ISSN 1931-7557
RC386.6.D52
➤ **BRAIN IMAGING AND BEHAVIOR.** Text in English. 2007. q. USD 950 combined subscription to institutions (print & online eds.) (effective 2011). adv. back issues avail.; reprint service avail. from PSC. **Document type:** *Journal, Academic/Scholarly.* **Description:** Publishes behavioral research based on a variety of neuroimaging methods.
Related titles: Online - full text ed.: ISSN 1931-7565 (from IngentaConnect).
Indexed: A22, A26, Agr, CurCont, E01, EMBASE, H12, I05, MEDLINE, NSCI, P03, P30, PsycInfo, SCI, SCOPUS, W07.
—BLDSC (2268.128000), IE. **CCC.**
Published by: Springer New York LLC (Subsidiary of: Springer Science+Business Media), 233 Spring St, New York, NY 10013. TEL 212—460-1500, FAX 212-460-1575, service-ny@springer.com. Ed. Andrew J Saykin.

616.8 AUS ISSN 1443-9646
RC347
➤ **BRAIN IMPAIRMENT.** Text in English. 2000. 3/yr. AUD 237 combined subscription domestic to institutions (print & online eds.); AUD 260 combined subscription foreign to institutions (print & online eds.) (effective 2011). adv. abstr.; stat. Index. back issues avail.; reprints avail. **Document type:** *Journal, Academic/Scholarly.* **Description:** Covers neurology, neuropsychology, psychiatry, clinical psychology, neuropathology, occupational therapy, physiotherapy, speech pathology and anatomy.
Related titles: Online - full text ed.
Indexed: A01, A11, CA, P03, P30, PsycInfo, SCI, SCOPUS, T02, W07.
—BLDSC (2268.129000), IE, Ingenta.
Published by: (Australian Society for the Study of Brain Impairment, Inc.), Australian Academic Press Pty. Ltd., 32 Jeays St, Bowen Hills, QLD 4006, Australia. TEL 61-7-32571176, FAX 61-7-32525908, aap@australianacademicpress.com.au, http://www.australianacademicpress.com.au. Eds. Dr. Jacinta Douglas, Robyn Tate. Adv. contact Margaret Eagers.

616.8 GBR ISSN 0269-9052
RC387.5 CODEN: BRAIEO
➤ **BRAIN INJURY.** Text in English. 1987. 14/yr. GBP 1,670, EUR 2,350, USD 2,940 combined subscription to institutions (print & online eds.); GBP 3,305, EUR 4,655, USD 5,830 combined subscription to corporations (print & online eds.) (effective 2010). adv. back issues avail.; reprint service avail. from PSC. **Document type:** *Journal, Academic/Scholarly.* **Description:** Covers all aspects of brain injury, ranging from basic scientific research to epidemiology, neuropathology, neurosurgical and other medical procedures, assessment methods, rehabilitation, and outcome.
Related titles: Online - full text ed.: ISSN 1362-301X (from IngentaConnect).
Indexed: A01, A02, A03, A08, A20, A22, AMED, ASCA, B21, B25, BIOSIS Prev, C06, C07, C08, C11, CA, CINAHL, CurCont, E-psyche, E01, EMBASE, ESPM, ExcerpMed, F09, FR, H&SSA, H04, INI, IndMed, Inpharma, L&LBA, MEDLINE, MycolAb, NSA, NSCI, P03, P30, P35, P43, PsycInfo, PsycholAb, R10, RILM, Reac, SCI, SCOPUS, SSCI, T02, W07.
—BLDSC (2268.132000), GNLM, IE, Infotrieve, Ingenta, INIST. **CCC.**
Published by: Informa Healthcare (Subsidiary of: T & F Informa plc), Telephone House, 69-77 Paul St, London, EC2A 4LQ, United Kingdom. TEL 44-20-70175000, FAX 44-20-70176792, healthcare.enquiries@informa.com, http://www.tandf.co.uk/journals/. Eds. Jeffrey s Kreutzer, Nathan D Zasler. **Subscr. in N. America to:** Taylor & Francis Inc., Customer Services Dept, 325 Chestnut St, 8th Fl, Philadelphia, PA 19106. TEL 215-625-8900, 800-354-1420, FAX 215-625-8914; **Subscr. outside N. America to:** Taylor & Francis Ltd., Journals Customer Service, Sheepen Pl, Colchester, Essex CO3 3LP, United Kingdom. TEL 44-20-70175544, FAX 44-20-70175198, tf.enquiries@tfinforma.com.

617.481 USA
➤ **BRAIN INJURY PROFESSIONAL.** Text in English. 2004. q. free to members (effective 2010). adv. back issues avail. **Document type:** *Magazine, Academic/Scholarly.* **Description:** Features information about the subject of brain injury.
Related titles: Online - full text ed.: free (effective 2010).
Published by: (North American Brain Injury Society), H D I Publishers, PO Box 131401, Houston, TX 77219. TEL 713-526-6900, FAX 713-526-7787, mail@hdipub.com, http://www.hdipub.com. Ed. Ronald Savage. Pub. Chas Haynes. Adv. contact Joyce Parker.

➤ **BRAIN NURSING/BUREIN NASHINGU.** *see* MEDICAL SCIENCES—Nurses And Nursing

616.8 USA ISSN 1015-6305
RC347 CODEN: BRPAE7
➤ **BRAIN PATHOLOGY.** Text in English. 1990. bi-m. GBP 173 in United Kingdom to institutions; EUR 219 in Europe to institutions; USD 309 in the Americas to institutions; USD 373 elsewhere to institutions; GBP 200 combined subscription in United Kingdom to institutions (print & online eds.); EUR 252 combined subscription in Europe to institutions (print & online eds.); USD 356 combined subscription in the Americas to institutions (print & online eds.); USD 429 combined subscription elsewhere to institutions (print & online eds.) (effective 2012). adv. bk.rev. back issues avail.; reprint service avail. from PSC. **Document type:** *Journal, Academic/Scholarly.* **Description:** Investigates diseases of the nervous system.
Related titles: Online - full text ed.: ISSN 1750-3639. GBP 173 in United Kingdom to institutions; EUR 219 in Europe to institutions; USD 309 in the Americas to institutions; USD 373 elsewhere to institutions (effective 2012) (from IngentaConnect).
Indexed: A22, A26, A34, A35, A36, ASCA, AgBio, B21, B25, BIOBASE, BIOSIS Prev, CA, CABA, CIN, ChemAb, ChemTitl, CurCont, E-psyche, E01, E12, EMBASE, ExcerpMed, GH, H12, IABS, ISR, IndMed, IndVet, Inpharma, MEDLINE, MycolAb, N02, N03, NSA, NSCI, P30, P33, PN&I, R08, R10, Reac, SCI, SCOPUS, T02, VS, W07.
—BLDSC (2268.175000), CASDDS, GNLM, IE, Infotrieve, Ingenta, INIST. **CCC.**
Published by: (International Society of Neuropathology), Wiley-Blackwell Publishing, Inc. (Subsidiary of: Wiley-Blackwell Publishing Ltd.), 111 River St, Hoboken, NJ 07030. TEL 201-748-6000, FAX 201-748-6088, info@wiley.com. Ed. Arie Perry.

616.8 NLD ISSN 0006-8993
QP376 CODEN: BRREAP
➤ **BRAIN RESEARCH.** Text in English. 1966. 60/yr. EUR 20,904 in Europe to institutions; JPY 2,782,400 in Japan to institutions; USD 23,446 elsewhere to institutions (effective 2012). adv. bk.rev. abstr.; bibl.; illus. index, cum.index: 1966-1977. back issues avail. **Document type:** *Journal, Academic/Scholarly.* **Description:** Covers neuroanatomy, neurochemistry, neurophysiology, neuroendocrinology, neuropharmacology, neurotoxicology, neurocommunications, behavioral sciences, neurology and biocybernetics.
Incorporates (1986-2006): Molecular Brain Research (0169-328X); (1997-2006): Brain Research Protocols (1385-299X); (1992-2006): Cognitive Brain Research (0926-6410); (1981-2006): Developmental Brain Research (0165-3806)
Related titles: Microform ed.: (from PQC); Online - full text ed.: ISSN 1872-6240 (from IngentaConnect, ScienceDirect); ◆ Series: Brain Research Reviews. ISSN 0165-0173; ◆ Developmental Brain Research. ISSN 0165-3806; ◆ Molecular Brain Research. ISSN 0169-328X; ◆ Gene Expression Patterns. ISSN 1567-133X; ◆ Supplement(s): Cognitive Brain Research. ISSN 0926-6410; ◆ Gene Expression Patterns. ISSN 1567-133X; ◆ I B R O News. ISSN 0361-0713.
Indexed: A01, A03, A08, A20, A22, A26, A34, A35, A36, A37, A38, AIDS Ab, ASCA, ASFA, AbAn, AgBio, AnBeAb, ApicAb, B21, B25, B27, BIOBASE, BIOSIS Prev, BP, C13, C30, C33, CA, CABA, CIN, ChemAb, ChemTitl, CurCont, D01, DBA, DentInd, E-psyche, E12, EMBASE, ESPM, ExcerpMed, F08, F11, F12, GH, H16, H17, I05, IABS, IBR, IBZ, IPsyAb, ISR, IndMed, IndVet, Inpharma, L&LBA, MEDLINE, MaizeAb, MycolAb, N02, N03, N04, N05, NSA, NSCI, P03, P30, P32, P33, P35, P37, P39, PN&I, PsycInfo, PsycholAb, R07, R08, R10, R12, RA&MP, RM&VM, Reac, RefZh, S12, S13, S16, SCI, SCOPUS, SoyAb, T02, T05, THA, ToxAb, VS, W07, W08, W10, WildRev.
—BLDSC (2268.200000), CASDDS, GNLM, IE, Infotrieve, Ingenta, INIST. **CCC.**
Published by: Elsevier BV (Subsidiary of: Elsevier Science & Technology), Radarweg 29, PO Box 211, Amsterdam, 1000 AE, Netherlands. TEL 31-20-4853911, FAX 31-20-4852457, JournalsCustomerServiceEMEA@elsevier.com, http://www.elsevier.nl. Ed. Floyd E Bloom.

616.89 USA ISSN 0361-9230
QP376 CODEN: BRBUDU
➤ **BRAIN RESEARCH BULLETIN.** Abbreviated title: B R B. Text in English. 1976. 18/yr. EUR 4,371 in Europe to institutions; JPY 550,500 in Japan to institutions; USD 4,890 elsewhere to institutions (effective 2012). adv. bk.rev. illus. index. back issues avail.; reprints avail. **Document type:** *Journal, Academic/Scholarly.* **Description:** Emphasizes research on the effects of genetic and epigenetic interactions on behavior, cognitive functions and disease.
Incorporates (1972-1987): Journal of Electrophysiological Techniques (0361-0209)
Related titles: Microfilm ed.: (from PQC); Online - full text ed.: ISSN 1873-2747. 1995 (from IngentaConnect, ScienceDirect).
Indexed: A01, A03, A08, A22, A26, A34, A35, A36, A38, ASCA, ASFA, AgBio, AgrForAb, AnBeAb, B21, B25, BIOBASE, BIOSIS Prev, CA, CABA, CIN, ChemAb, ChemTitl, ChemoAb, CurCont, D01, DentInd, E-psyche, E12, EMBASE, ExcerpMed, F08, F11, F12, GH, H16, I05, IABS, IBR, IBZ, ISR, IndMed, IndVet, Inpharma, Inspec, MEDLINE, MycolAb, N02, N03, NSA, NSCI, P03, P30, P33, P37, PsycInfo, PsycholAb, R07, R08, R10, RA&MP, Reac, S01, S12, SCI, SCOPUS, SoyAb, T02, T05, TAR, THA, VS, W07, W10, Z01.
—BLDSC (2268.201000), CASDDS, GNLM, IE, Infotrieve, Ingenta, INIST. **CCC.**
Published by: Elsevier Inc. (Subsidiary of: Elsevier Science & Technology), 1600 John F Kennedy Blvd, Philadelphia, PA 19103. TEL 215-239-3900, FAX 215-238-7883, JournalCustomerService-usa@elsevier.com. Ed. Andres Buonanno.

616.8 USA
BRAIN RESEARCH FOUNDATION ANNUAL REPORT. Text in English. 1983. a. free. **Document type:** *Corporate.* **Description:** Presents financial statement, year's activities, list of the foundation's grants to scientists at University of Chicago's Brain Research Institute, donors lists, and scientific articles highlighting a specific area of research at the institute.
Related titles: Supplement(s): Brainwaves Newsletter.
Indexed: E-psyche.
Published by: Brain Research Foundation, 5812 S Ellis Ave, MC 7112, Rm J-141, Chicago, IL 60637. TEL 773-834-6750, FAX 773-834-6751, info@brainresearchfdn.org, http://www.brainresearchfdn.org. Ed. Nancy W Hohfeler. Circ: 1,100.

573.86 USA ISSN 1935-2875
QP376
BRAIN RESEARCH JOURNAL. Text in English. 2007. q. USD 295 to institutions; USD 442 combined subscription to institutions (print & online eds.) (effective 2012). **Document type:** *Journal, Academic/Scholarly.*
Related titles: Online - full text ed.: USD 295 to institutions (effective 2012).
Published by: Nova Science Publishers, Inc., 400 Oser Ave, Ste 1600, Hauppauge, NY 11788. TEL 631-231-7269, FAX 631-231-8175, main@novapublishers.com. Ed. Frank Columbus.

616.8 NLD ISSN 0165-0173
QP376 CODEN: BRERD2
➤ **BRAIN RESEARCH REVIEWS.** Text and summaries in English. 1980. 6/yr. EUR 1,591 in Europe to institutions; JPY 211,300 in Japan to institutions; USD 1,777 elsewhere to institutions (effective 2012). adv. abstr. back issues avail.; reprints avail. **Document type:** *Journal, Academic/Scholarly.* **Description:** Publishes articles and research papers which give analytical surveys that define heuristic hypotheses and provide new insights into brain mechanisms.
Related titles: Microform ed.: (from PQC); Online - full text ed.: ISSN 1872-6321 (from IngentaConnect, ScienceDirect); ◆ Series of: Brain Research. ISSN 0006-8993.
Indexed: A01, A03, A08, A22, A26, A34, A36, A38, ASCA, ASFA, AnBeAb, B21, BIOBASE, BIOSIS Prev, CA, CABA, CIN, ChemAb, ChemTitl, CurCont, DBA, E-psyche, E12, EMBASE, ExcerpMed, GH, I05, IABS, IBR, IBZ, ISR, IndMed, IndVet, Inpharma, MEDLINE, MycolAb, N02, N03, N05, NSA, NSCI, P03, P30, P33, P37, PN&I, PsycInfo, PsycholAb, R08, R10, RA&MP, Reac, S13, S16, SCI, SCOPUS, SoyAb, T02, THA, VS, W07, W10, Z01.
—BLDSC (2268.205000), CASDDS, GNLM, IE, Infotrieve, Ingenta, INIST. **CCC.**
Published by: Elsevier BV (Subsidiary of: Elsevier Science & Technology), Radarweg 29, PO Box 211, Amsterdam, 1000 AE, Netherlands. TEL 31-20-4853911, FAX 31-20-4852457, JournalsCustomerServiceEMEA@elsevier.com, http://www.elsevier.nl. Ed. Floyd E Bloom.

616.8 CHE ISSN 2076-3425
▼ ➤ **BRAIN SCIENCES.** Text in English. 2010 (Jul.). q. free (effective 2011). **Description:** Publishes original articles, critical reviews, research notes and short communications in the areas of cognitive neuroscience, developmental neuroscience, molecular and cellular neuroscience, neural engineering, neuroimaging, neurolinguistics, neuropathy, systems neuroscience, and theoretical and computational neuroscience.
Media: Online - full text.
Published by: M D P I AG, Postfach, Basel, 4005, Switzerland. TEL 41-61-6837734, FAX 41-61-3028918, http://www.mdpi.org/. Ed. German Barrionuevo.

612.8 USA ISSN 1935-861X
➤ **BRAIN STIMULATION**; basic, translational and clinical research in neuromodulation. Text in English. 2007 (Nov.). q. USD 618 in United States to institutions; USD 750 elsewhere to institutions (effective 2012). adv. back issues avail.; reprints avail. **Document type:** *Journal, Academic/Scholarly.* **Description:** Covers the entire field of brain stimulation, including noninvasive and invasive techniques and technologies that alter brain function through the use of electrical, magnetic, radiowave, or focally targeted pharmacologic stimulation.
Related titles: Online - full text ed.: ISSN 1876-4754. 2007 (from ScienceDirect).
Indexed: B25, BIOSIS Prev, CA, CurCont, EMBASE, ExcerpMed, MEDLINE, MycolAb, NSCI, P03, P30, PsycInfo, SCI, SCOPUS, T02, W07.
—IE. **CCC.**
Published by: Elsevier Inc. (Subsidiary of: Elsevier Science & Technology), 1600 John F Kennedy Blvd, Philadelphia, PA 19103. TEL 215-239-3900, FAX 215-238-7883, JournalCustomerService-usa@elsevier.com, http://www.elsevier.com. Ed. Dr. Mark George. Adv. contact Pat Hampton TEL 212-633-3181.

616.8 USA ISSN 0896-0267
RC386.6.B7 CODEN: BRTOEZ
➤ **BRAIN TOPOGRAPHY**; a journal of cerebral function and dynamics. Text in English. 1988. q. EUR 1,319, USD 1,366 combined subscription to institutions (print & online eds.) (effective 2012). adv. back issues avail.; reprint service avail. from PSC. **Document type:** *Journal, Academic/Scholarly.* **Description:** Reviews new research in the areas of EEG, MEG, psychiatry, and neuropsychology, and explores new methodology and techniques of data analysis and manipulation.
Related titles: Microform ed.: (from PQC); Online - full text ed.: ISSN 1573-6792 (from IngentaConnect).
Indexed: A22, A26, Agr, B21, B25, BIOBASE, BIOSIS Prev, BibLing, CA, CurCont, E-psyche, E01, EMBASE, ExcerpMed, I05, IABS, ISR, IndMed, Inpharma, L&LBA, MEDLINE, MycolAb, NSA, NSCI, P03, P15, P20, P22, P25, P30, P48, P52, P54, P56, PQC, PsycInfo, PsycholAb, R10, Reac, SCI, SCOPUS, T02, W07.
—BLDSC (2268.221200), GNLM, IE, Infotrieve, Ingenta, INIST. **CCC.**
Published by: Springer New York LLC (Subsidiary of: Springer Science+Business Media), 233 Spring St, New York, NY 10013. TEL 212-460-1500, FAX 212-460-1575, service-ny@springer.com. Eds. Christoph M Michel, Micah M Murray.

➤ **BRAIN TUMOR PATHOLOGY.** *see* MEDICAL SCIENCES—Oncology

612 USA ISSN 2151-1780
▼ **BRAIN WORLD.** Text in English. 2009. q. free to members (effective 2009). adv. **Document type:** *Magazine, Trade.* **Description:** Includes features on cutting-edge neuroscience alongside articles on healthy aging, art and culture, education and global issues.
Published by: International Brain Education Association, 866 United Nations Plz, Ste 479, New York, NY 10017. TEL 212-319-0848, FAX 212-319-8671, info@ibrea.org, http://www.ibrea.org. Ed. Andy Hunter.

616.8 ITA ISSN 2035-7109
QP376
➤ **BRAINFACTOR.** Text in Italian. 2008. d. free (effective 2011). **Document type:** *Journal, Academic/Scholarly.*
Media: Online - full text. Ed. Marco Mozzoni.

616.8 DEU ISSN 1861-1680
QP360.5
➤ **BRAINS, MINDS AND MEDIA.** Text in English. 2004. irreg. free (effective 2011). **Document type:** *Journal, Academic/Scholarly.* **Description:** Aims to promote an intelligible and thorough understanding of neural and cognitive concepts.
Media: Online - full content.
Indexed: P30.
—CCC.
Published by: Di P P - N R W, Juelicher Str 6, Cologne, 50674, Germany. TEL 49-221-400750, FAX 49-221-40075180, dipp@hbz-nrw.de, http://www.dipp.nrw.de. Ed. Martin Egelhaaf.

616.8 ITA ISSN 1973-3291
BRIDGING EASTERN AND WESTERN PSYCHIATRY. Text in Multiple languages. 2003. s-a. **Document type:** *Journal, Trade.*
Published by: Centro Studi Psichiatria e Territorio, Via Montauti 2, Forte dei Marmi, LU 55042, Italy.

616.8 GBR ISSN 1354-4187
RC394.L37
➤ **BRITISH JOURNAL OF LEARNING DISABILITIES.** Abbreviated title: B J L D. Text in English. 1973. q. GBP 306 in United Kingdom to institutions; EUR 387 in Europe to institutions; USD 561 in the Americas to institutions; USD 655 elsewhere to institutions; GBP 352 combined subscription in United Kingdom to institutions (print & online eds.); EUR 446 combined subscription in Europe to institutions (print & online eds.); USD 646 combined subscription in the Americas to institutions (print & online eds.); USD 753 combined subscription elsewhere to institutions (print & online eds.) (effective 2012). adv. back issues avail.; reprint service avail. from PSC. **Document type:** *Journal, Academic/Scholarly.* **Description:** Aims to promote better lifestyles and high quality services for adults and children with intellectual disabilities wordwide.
Former titles (until 1993): Mental Handicap (0261-9997); (until Mar.1982): Apex (0141-2205)
Related titles: Online - full text ed.: ISSN 1468-3156. GBP 306 in United Kingdom to institutions; EUR 387 in Europe to institutions; USD 561 in the Americas to institutions; USD 655 elsewhere to institutions (effective 2012) (from IngentaConnect).
Indexed: A01, A02, A03, A08, A22, A26, AMED, ASG, B28, B29, C06, C07, C08, C11, CA, CINAHL, CPE, CurCont, E-psyche, E01, E03, E07, ERI, ERIC, FamI, H04, H12, P03, P04, P43, PAIS, PsycInfo, PsycholAb, RehabLit, SCOPUS, SSCI, T02, W07.
—BLDSC (2311.125000), IE, Infotrieve, Ingenta. **CCC.**
Published by: (B I L D), Wiley-Blackwell Publishing Ltd. (Subsidiary of: John Wiley & Sons, Inc.), 9600 Garsington Rd, Oxford, OX4 2DQ, United Kingdom. TEL 44-1865-776868, FAX 44-1865-714591, customerservices@blackwellpublishing.com. Ed. Duncan Mitchell TEL 44-7974-726235. Pub. Elaine Stott. R&P Sophie Savage. Adv. contact Joanna Baker TEL 44-1865-476271. Circ: 3,700.

616.8 610.736 GBR ISSN 1747-0307
➤ **BRITISH JOURNAL OF NEUROSCIENCE NURSING.** Text in English. 2005 (Apr.). bi-m. GBP 116.10 to individuals in UK & Ireland; EUR 193 in Europe to individuals; USD 297 elsewhere to individuals; GBP 82.80 to students in UK & Ireland; EUR 143.10 in Europe to students; USD 234 elsewhere to students (effective 2008). adv. **Document type:** *Journal, Academic/Scholarly.* **Description:** Aims to keep nurses up to date with clinical, professional and policy developments, as well as providing a forum for sharing research and innovation.
Related titles: Online - full text ed.
Indexed: B28, C06, C07, C08, CA, CINAHL, T02.
—BLDSC (2311.935000), IE, Ingenta. **CCC.**
Published by: M A Healthcare Ltd. (Subsidiary of: Mark Allen Publishing Ltd.), St. Jude's Church, Dulwich Rd, London, SE24 0PB, United Kingdom. TEL 44-20-77385454, FAX 44-20-77332325. Eds. Liam Benison, Sue Woodward. Pub. Matt Cianfarani. **Subscr. to:** Jesses Farm, Snow Hill, Dinton, Salisbury, Wilts SP3 5HN, United Kingdom. TEL 44-1722-716997, FAX 44-1722-716926.

616.89 GBR ISSN 0007-1250
RC321 CODEN: BJPYAJ
➤ **BRITISH JOURNAL OF PSYCHIATRY.** Abbreviated title: B J P. Text in English. 1853. m. GBP 326 combined subscription in Europe to institutions (print & online eds.); USD 607 combined subscription in United States to institutions (print & online eds.); GBP 380 combined subscription elsewhere to institutions (print & online eds.) (effective 2012). adv. bk.rev. bibl.; charts; illus. index. back issues avail.; reprints avail. **Document type:** *Journal, Academic/Scholarly.* **Description:** Covers all branches of psychiatry, with emphasis on the clinical aspects of various topics in field.
Former titles (until 1963): Journal of Mental Science (0368-315X); (until 1858): Asylum Journal of Psychiatry
Related titles: CD-ROM ed.; Online - full text ed.: ISSN 1472-1465. GBP 268 to institutions; USD 428 in United States to institutions (effective 2012); Supplement(s): British Journal of Psychiatry. Supplement. ISSN 0960-5371. 1988.
Indexed: A20, A22, A26, A34, A36, AHCMS, AMED, AMHA, ASCA, ASSIA, AddicA, AgeL, B21, B25, B28, BDM&CN, BIOBASE, BIOSIS Prev, C06, C07, C08, C28, CA, CABA, CINAHL, ChemAb, CurCont, DBA, DiabCont, DokArb, E-psyche, E12, EMBASE, ExcerpMed, F08, F09, F11, F12, FR, FamI, G08, G10, GH, H11, H12, H17, HospAb, IABS, IDIS, INI, IPsyAb, ISR, IndMed, Inpharma, JW-P, JW-WH, LT, MEA&I, MEDLINE, MycolAb, N02, N03, N04, NSA, P03, P10, P12, P20, P33, P34, P35, P48, P53, P54, PQC, PsycInfo, PsycholAb, R08, R10, R12, RA&MP, RRTA, Reac, S02, S03, S21, SCI, SCOPUS, SOPODA, SPPI, SSCI, SociolAb, T02, T05, TAR, THA, W07, W09, W11.
—BLDSC (2320.800000), CASDDS, GNLM, IE, Infotrieve, Ingenta, INIST. **CCC.**
Published by: Royal College of Psychiatrists, 17 Belgrave Sq, London, SW1X 8PG, United Kingdom. TEL 44-20-72352351, FAX 44-20-72451231, rcpsych@rcpsych.ac.uk, http://www.rcpsych.ac.uk/. Ed. Peter Tyrer. Adv. contact Peter Mell. Circ: 15,800. **Subscr. in N. America to:** Maney Publishing; **Subscr. outside N. America to:** Maney Publishing, Ste 1C, Joseph's Well, Hanover Walk, Leeds, W Yorks LS3 1AB, United Kingdom. TEL 44-113-2432800, FAX 44-113-3868178, subscriptions@maney.co.uk, http://www.maney.co.uk.

616.891 GBR ISSN 0265-9883
HD2745
➤ **BRITISH JOURNAL OF PSYCHOTHERAPY.** Abbreviated title: B J P. Text in English. 1984. q. GBP 148 combined subscription in United Kingdom to institutions (print & online eds.); EUR 187 combined subscription in Europe to institutions (print & online eds.); USD 271 combined subscription in the Americas to institutions (print & online eds.); USD 289 combined subscription elsewhere to institutions (print & online eds.) (effective 2012). adv. bk.rev. 160 p./no. 1 cols./p.; back issues avail.; reprint service avail. from PSC. **Document type:** *Journal, Academic/Scholarly.* **Description:** Contains a unique place in the field of psychotherapy journals with an Editorial Board drawn from a wide range of psychotherapy training organisations.
Related titles: Online - full text ed.: ISSN 1752-0118. GBP 135 in United Kingdom to institutions; EUR 171 in Europe to institutions; USD 246 in the Americas to institutions; USD 264 elsewhere to institutions (effective 2012) (from IngentaConnect).
Indexed: A01, A22, ASSIA, B21, CA, E-psyche, E01, EMBASE, ExcerpMed, FamI, NSA, P03, PsycInfo, PsycholAb, R10, Reac, S02, S03, SCOPUS, SWR&A, T02.
—BLDSC (2321.200000), GNLM, IE, Ingenta, INIST. **CCC.**
Published by: (British Association of Psychotherapists), Wiley-Blackwell Publishing Ltd. (Subsidiary of: John Wiley & Sons, Inc.), 9600 Garsington Rd, Oxford, OX4 2DQ, United Kingdom. TEL 44-1865-776868, FAX 44-1865-714591, customerservices@blackwellpublishing.com. Circ: 2,800.

616.8914 GBR
➤ **BRITISH JOURNAL OF PSYCHOTHERAPY INTEGRATION.** Text in English. 2004. s-a. free to members. back issues avail. **Document type:** *Journal, Academic/Scholarly.*
—BLDSC (2321.300000).
Published by: United Kingdom Association for Psychotherapy Integration, Ealing, PO Box 2512, London, W5 2QG, United Kingdom. enquiries@ukapi.com.

362.4 616.835 GBR ISSN 0007-1633
BRITISH POLIO FELLOWSHIP. BULLETIN. Text in English. 1946. bi-m. GBP 12 per issue to non-members; free to members (effective 2009). adv. bk.rev. illus. **Document type:** *Bulletin, Consumer.* **Description:** Covers a vast range of topics including clinical information on polio and post polio syndrome.
Formerly (until 1963): I P F Bulletin
Indexed: E-psyche.
Published by: British Polio Fellowship, Eagle Office Centre, The Runway, South Ruislip, Midds HA4 6SE, United Kingdom. TEL 800-018-0586, FAX 44-20-88420555, info@britishpolio.org.uk. Ed. Nicola Hill. Adv. contact Peter Hirst.

616.8 JPN ISSN 1345-9082
BUNSHI SEISHIN IGAKU/JAPANESE JOURNAL OF MOLECULAR PSYCHIATRY. Text in Japanese. 2001. q. JPY 9,660 (effective 2005). **Document type:** *Journal, Academic/Scholarly.*
—BLDSC (2930.658100).
Published by: Sentan Igaku-sha, 1-9-7 Higashi-Nihonbashi, Chuo-ku, Tokyo, 103-0004, Japan. TEL 81-3-58202100, FAX 81-3-58202501, book@sentan.com.

616.89 JPN ISSN 0910-4798
➤ **BYOIN, CHIIKI SEISHIN IGAKU/JAPANESE JOURNAL OF HOSPITAL AND COMMUNITY PSYCHIATRY.** Text in Japanese. 1958. q. JPY 12,000 membership (effective 2007). bk.rev. **Document type:** *Journal, Academic/Scholarly.*
Formerly (until 1984): Byoin Seishin Igaku (0910-478X)
Indexed: E-psyche.
Published by: Byoin Chiiki Seishin Igakkai/Japanese Hospital and Community Psychiatry Association, 4-6-1 Yotsuya, Shinjuku-ku, 609 Yotsuya Sun Heights, Tokyo, Tokyo-to 160-0004, Japan. info@byochi.org, http://www.byochi.org/.

616.8 AUS ISSN 1838-8817
C C D N NEWS. (Cassava Cyanide Diseases Network) Variant title: C C D N N News. Text in English. 2003. s-a. free to members (effective 2011). back issues avail. **Document type:** *Newsletter, Trade.*
Related titles: Online - full text ed.: ISSN 1838-8825. free (effective 2011).
Published by: Cassava Cyanide Diseases and Neurolathyrism Network, c/o J Howard Bradbury, Australian National University, Canberra, ACT 0020, Australia. TEL 61-2-61250775, FAX 61-2-61255573, Howard.Bradbury@anu.edu.au.

616.8 617 USA ISSN 1068-9230
C I N N REPORT. Text in English. 1989. 2/yr. free. **Document type:** *Report, Trade.* **Description:** Contains information on neurosurgery and related considerations.
Formerly (until 1994): C N C Report
Indexed: E-psyche.
Published by: Chicago Institute of Neurosurgery and Neuroresearch, 2515 n Clark St, Ste 800, Chicago, IL 60614. TEL 773-388-7700, 800-411-2466, FAX 773-935-2132, connobd@suba.com, http://www.cinn.org. Ed. Heather L French. Circ: 15,000.

616 617.087 USA ISSN 1067-0181
THE C M T A REPORT. Text in English. 1983. bi-m.
Published by: Charcot-Marie-Tooth Association, 2700 Chestnut St, Chester, PA 19013-4867. TEL 800-606-CMTA, FAX 610-499-9267, staff@charcot-marie-tooth.org, http://www.charcot-marie-tooth.org/. Ed. Patricia Dreibelbis.

616.8 NLD ISSN 1871-5273
RM315 CODEN: CNDDA3
➤ **C N S & NEUROLOGICAL DISORDERS - DRUG TARGETS.** (Central Nervous System) Text in English. 2002 (Feb). 8/yr. USD 1,580 to institutions (print or online ed.) (effective 2012). adv. back issues avail.; reprints avail. **Document type:** *Journal, Academic/Scholarly.* **Description:** Aims to cover all the latest and outstanding developments on the medicinal chemistry, pharmacology, molecular biology, genomics and biochemistry of contemporary molecular targets involved in neurological and central nervous system (CNS) disorders e.g. disease specific proteins, receptors, enzymes, genes.
Formerly (until 2006): Current Drug Targets. C N S & Neurological Disorders (1568-007X)
Related titles: Online - full text ed.: ISSN 1996-3181 (from IngentaConnect).
Indexed: A01, A03, A08, B&BAb, B19, B21, BIOSIS Prev, BioEngAb, C33, CA, CTA, ChemAb, ChemoAb, CurCont, EMBASE, ExcerpMed, GenetAb, M&PBA, MEDLINE, MycolAb, NSA, NSCI, P03, P30, PsycholAb, R10, Reac, SCI, SCOPUS, T02, W07.
—BLDSC (3287.314338), IE, Infotrieve, Ingenta. **CCC.**
Published by: Bentham Science Publishers Ltd., PO Box 294, Bussum, 1400 AG, Netherlands. TEL 31-35-6923800, FAX 31-35-6980150, sales@bentham.org. Eds. Claire F Evans, John H Kehne, Stephen D Skaper. **Subscr. addr. in the US:** Bentham Science Publishers Ltd., c/o Richard E Morrissy, PO Box 446, Oak Park, IL 60301. TEL 312-413-5867, FAX 312-996-7107, subscriptions@bentham.org.

616.8 NZL ISSN 1174-5908
RC360
C N S DISORDERS TODAY. (Central Nervous System) Text in English. 1999. m. USD 315 to individuals; USD 1,345 to institutions (effective 2008). back issues avail. **Document type:** *Newsletter, Academic/Scholarly.* **Description:** Rapid alerts service on all aspects of drug therapy and disease management of psychiatric and neurological disorders.
Indexed: A01, E-psyche, Inpharma.
—**CCC.**
Published by: Adis International Ltd. (Subsidiary of: Wolters Kluwer N.V.), 41 Centorian Dr, Mairangi Bay, Private Bag 65901, Auckland, 1311, New Zealand. TEL 64-9-4770700, FAX 64-9-4770764, queries@adisonline.com, http://www.adisonline.info/. Ed. Suzanne Sullivan. **Americas subscr. to:** Adis International Inc., Subscriptions Dept, Ste F 10, 940 Town Center Dr, Langhorne, PA 19047. TEL 877-872-2347.

C N S DRUGS. (Central Nervous System) *see* PHARMACY AND PHARMACOLOGY

C N S NEUROSCIENCE & THERAPEUTICS. *see* PHARMACY AND PHARMACOLOGY

616.8 USA ISSN 1092-8529
RC346 CODEN: CNSPFH
➤ **C N S SPECTRUMS**; first in applied neuroscience. Text in English. 1996. m. USD 120 (effective 2010). **Document type:** *Journal, Academic/Scholarly.* **Description:** Designed to bridge the needs of practicing psychiatrists and neurologists, it publishes original scientific literature and reviews on a wide variety of neuroscientific topics of interest to the clinician.
Indexed: A20, C06, C07, CA, EMBASE, ExcerpMed, MEDLINE, NSCI, P03, P30, PsycInfo, PsycholAb, R10, Reac, SCI, SCOPUS, T02, W07.
—BLDSC (3287.314356), IE, Infotrieve, Ingenta. **CCC.**
Published by: M B L Communications, 333 Hudson St, 7th fl, New York, NY 10013. TEL 212-328-0800, FAX 212-328-0600, primepsych@aol.com, http://www.mblcommunications.com. Ed. Andrew A Nierenberg TEL 212-328-0800 ext 220. Pub. Darren Brodeur TEL 212-328-0800 ext 227.

616.8 GBR ISSN 1464-2514
➤ **C P D BULLETIN. OLD AGE PSYCHIATRY.** (Continuing Professional Development) Text in English. 1998. irreg., latest 2003. GBP 45 per vol. domestic to individuals; GBP 60 per vol. foreign to individuals; GBP 60 per vol. domestic to institutions; GBP 90 per vol. foreign to institutions (effective 2010). back issues avail. **Document type:** *Journal, Academic/Scholarly.*
Related titles: Online - full text ed.: GBP 30 per vol. (effective 2010).
Indexed: R10, Reac, SCOPUS.
—**CCC.**
Published by: Rila Publications Ltd., 73 Newman St, London, W1A 4PG, United Kingdom. TEL 44-20-76311299, FAX 44-20-75807166, admin@rila.co.uk. Ed. Dr. Roger Bullock TEL 44-1793-481182.

616.8 618.92 BRA ISSN 1519-0307
➤ **CADERNOS DE POS-GRADUACAO EM DISTURBIOS DO DESENVOLVIMENTO.** Abstracts in English; Text in Portuguese. 2001. a. free (effective 2005). **Document type:** *Journal, Academic/Scholarly.*
Indexed: C01.
Published by: Universidade Presbiteriana Mackenzie (Subsidiary of: Instituto Presbiteriano Mackenzie), Rua da Consolacao 896, Pr.2, Sao Paulo-SP, SP 01302-907, Brazil. FAX 55-11-32142582, 55-11-32368302, biblio.per@mackenzie.br, http://www.mackenzie.com.br. Ed. Nelson Francisco Annunciato.

616.8 FRA ISSN 1952-241X
CAHIER MARCE. Text in French. 2006. irreg. back issues avail. **Document type:** *Monographic series, Academic/Scholarly.*
Published by: L' Harmattan, 5 Rue de l'Ecole Polytechnique, Paris, 75005, France. TEL 33-1-43257651, FAX 33-1-43258203.

616.8 FRA ISSN 2108-2219
▼ **LES CAHIERS DE MYOLOGIE.** Text in French. 2009. 3/yr. **Document type:** *Journal, Academic/Scholarly.*
Published by: (Association Francaise contre les Myopathies (A F M)), Institut de Myologie, 47-83 Bd de l'Hopital, Paris Cedex 13, 75651, France. TEL 33-1-42165858, http://www.institut-myologie.org.

CAHIERS DE PSYCHOLOGIE CLINIQUE; une revue interdisciplinaire en psychologie clinique et psychotherapie. *see* PSYCHOLOGY

CANADA. STATISTICS CANADA. MENTAL HEALTH STATISTICS. *see* SOCIAL SERVICES AND WELFARE

616.9289 CAN ISSN 1719-8429
➤ **CANADIAN ACADEMY OF CHILD AND ADOLESCENT PSYCHIATRY. JOURNAL.** Abbreviated title: L'Academie Canadienne de Psychiatrie de l'Enfant et de l'Adolescent. Journal. Text in English, French. 1992. q. **Document type:** *Journal, Academic/Scholarly.* **Description:** Covers topics relevant to child and adolescent mental health.
Former titles (until 2006): The Canadian Child and Adolescent Psychiatry Review (1716-9119); (until 2002): Canadian Child Psychiatric Review (1209-7268); (until 1997): Canadian Child Psychiatric Bulletin (1188-7605)
Related titles: Online - full text ed.: free (effective 2011).
Indexed: A01, C06, C07, CA, EMBASE, ExcerpMed, P03, P30, PsycInfo, PsycholAb, R10, Reac, SCOPUS, T02.
—**CCC.**
Published by: Canadian Academy of Child and Adolescent Psychiatry, 701-141 Laurier Ave W, Ottawa, ON K1P 5J3, Canada. TEL 613-288-0408, FAX 613-234-9857, cacap@cpa-apc.org, http://www.canacad.org. Ed. Mary Nixon.

616.8 CAN
THE CANADIAN ALZHEIMER DISEASE REVIEW. Text in English, French. 1998. 3/yr. free (effective 2005). back issues avail.
Related titles: Online - full text ed.
Published by: S T A Communications Inc., 955 Blvd St Jean, Ste 306, Pointe Claire, PQ H9R 5K3, Canada. TEL 514-695-7623, FAX 514-695-8554. Ed. Carlo Viola. Pub. Paul F Brand.

616.8 CAN ISSN 0317-1671
RC321 CODEN: CJNSA2
➤ **CANADIAN JOURNAL OF NEUROLOGICAL SCIENCES/JOURNAL CANADIEN DES SCIENCES NEUROLOGIQUES.** Text in English, French. 1974. q. CAD 120 combined subscription domestic to individuals (print & online eds.); USD 140 combined subscription foreign to individuals (print & online eds.); CAD 150 combined subscription domestic to institutions (print & online eds.); USD 170 combined subscription foreign to institutions (print & online eds.) (effective 2010). adv. bk.rev. abstr.; bibl. index. 140 p./no. 2 cols./p.; back issues avail.; reprints avail. **Document type:** *Journal, Academic/Scholarly.* **Description:** Presents original work in the clinical and basic neurosciences.
Related titles: Microform ed.: (from PQC); Online - full text ed.: 1999.

Indexed: A22, ASCA, B21, B25, BIOBASE, BIOSIS Prev, CA, ChemAb, CurCont, DentInd, E-psyche, EMBASE, ExcerpMed, FR, IABS, IBR, IBZ, ISR, IndMed, Inpharma, JW-N, MEDLINE, MycolAb, NRN, NSA, NSCI, P03, P30, P35, PsycInfo, PsycholAb, R10, Reac, RefZh, SCI, SCOPUS, T02, W07.
—BLDSC (3033.300000), CASDDS, GNLM, IE, Infotrieve, Ingenta, INIST. **CCC.**
Published by: Canadian Journal of Neurological Sciences, Inc., 7015 Macleod Trail SW, Ste 709, Calgary, AB T2H 2K6, Canada. TEL 403-229-9575, FAX 403-229-1661. Ed., R&P Dr. G B Young. adv.: page CAD 1,043; 7 x 10. Circ: 1,400 (paid); 200 (controlled).
Co-sponsors: Canadian Neurological Society; Canadian Neurosurgical Society; Canadian Association of Child Neurology; Canadian Society of Clinical Neurophysiologists.

616.89 CAN ISSN 0706-7437
RC321 CODEN: CPAJAK
➤ **THE CANADIAN JOURNAL OF PSYCHIATRY/REVUE CANADIENNE DE PSYCHIATRIE.** Text in English, French. 1956. m. CAD 150 domestic; CAD 161.21 domestic in NF, NB, NS; CAD 190 foreign (effective 2005). adv. bk.rev. bibl.; charts; illus. index. back issues avail.; reprints avail. **Document type:** *Journal, Academic/Scholarly.* **Description:** Provides a forum for a broad spectrum of scholarly presentations, case reports, position papers, editorial contributions and current perspectives.
Formerly: Canadian Psychiatric Association Journal (0008-4824)
Related titles: Microform ed.: (from PQC); Online - full text ed.: ISSN 1497-0015.
Indexed: A01, A02, A03, A08, A20, A22, A36, AMHA, ASCA, AddicA, BAS, BDM&CN, C03, C05, C06, C07, C08, C11, CA, CABA, CBCARef, CDA, CINAHL, ChemAb, CurCont, DokArb, E-psyche, E03, E12, EMBASE, ERI, ExcerpMed, F09, FR, FamI, GH, H04, H13, INI, ISR, IndMed, Inpharma, LT, MEA&I, MEDLINE, N02, N03, NRN, P02, P03, P10, P12, P20, P22, P25, P30, P34, P35, P43, P48, P53, P54, PQC, PsycInfo, PsycholAb, R10, R12, RILM, RRTA, Reac, S02, S03, SCI, SCOPUS, SFSA, SOPODA, SPPI, SSCI, SociolAb, T02, T05, W07, W11, YAE&RB.
—BLDSC (3034.800000), GNLM, IE, Infotrieve, Ingenta, INIST. **CCC.**
Published by: Canadian Psychiatric Association, Suite 701 - 141 Laurier Ave West, Ottawa, ON K1P-5J3, Canada. TEL 613-234-2815, FAX 613-234-9857, http://www.allenpress.com. Ed. Dr. Quentin Rae-Grant. Pub., Adv. contact Sharon Petrie. B&W page CAD 1,035, color page CAD 2,010; trim 10.88 x 8.13. Circ: 3,500. **Subscr. to:** 260 - 441 MacLaren St, Ottawa, ON K2P 2H3, Canada. subscriptions@cpa-apc.org.

616.89 CAN ISSN 1195-3330
➤ **CANADIAN JOURNAL OF PSYCHOANALYSIS/REVUE CANADIENNE DE PSYCHANALYSE.** Text in English. 1993. s-a. CAD 50 domestic to individuals; CAD 60 foreign to individuals; CAD 65 domestic to institutions; CAD 70 foreign to institutions (effective 2005). bk.rev. **Document type:** *Journal, Academic/Scholarly.*
Indexed: A01, C03, CA, CBCARef, E-psyche, P03, P10, P12, P20, P25, P48, P53, P54, PQC, PsycInfo, PsycholAb, T02.
—BLDSC (3034.850000), IE, Ingenta. **CCC.**
Published by: (Canadian Psychoanalytic Society/Societe Canadienne de Psychanalyse), Becker Associates, Station Q, PO Box 507, Toronto, ON M4T 2M5, Canada. TEL 416-483-7282, FAX 416-489-1713, journals@interlog.com, http://www.interlog.com/~jbecker. Ed., Adv. contact Donald Carveth. Circ: 500 (paid).

616.8 CAN ISSN 0839-671X
CANADIAN REGISTER OF HEALTH SERVICE PROVIDERS IN PSYCHOLOGY. DIRECTORY/REPERTOIRE CANADIEN DES PSYCHOLOGUES OFFRANT DES SERVICES DE SANTE. Text in English, French. 1986. a. CAD 26.75 per issue (effective 2007). **Document type:** *Directory, Trade.*
Formerly (until 1987): Canadian Register of Health Service Providers in Psychology. Directory (0839-6701)
Related titles: CD-ROM ed.: ISSN 1912-063X.
Published by: Canadian Register of Health Service Providers in Psychology, 368 Dalhousie St, Ste 300, Ottawa, ON K1N 7G3, Canada. TEL 613-562-0900, FAX 613-562-0902, info@crhspp.ca, http://www.crhspp.ca.

616.1 616.8 USA ISSN 2090-0163
▼ ➤ **CARDIOVASCULAR PSYCHIATRY AND NEUROLOGY.** Text in English. 2009. q. USD 195 (effective 2011). **Document type:** *Journal, Academic/Scholarly.* **Description:** Covers pre-clinical/basic and clinical research on biological mechanisms of and treatments for co-occurring cardiovascular disorders and disorders of the central nervous system, including alterations in behavior, emotion, and cognition.
Related titles: Online - full text ed.: ISSN 2090-0171. free (effective 2011).
Indexed: A01, B21, C06, C07, CA, NSA, P30, T02.
Published by: Hindawi Publishing Corporation, 410 Park Ave, 15th Fl, PMB 287, New York, NY 10022. FAX 866-446-3294, hindawi@hindawi.com. Ed. Hari Manev.

618.97 USA
CARE ADVANTAGE. Text in English. 2004. q. free. **Document type:** *Magazine, Trade.* **Description:** Provides information, advice and support to improve quality of life for individuals and their caregivers. Topics include: Managing stress, at-home cognitive therapies, handling difficult behaviors, coping with family issues, Alzheimer's disease prevention, advice columns, legal, financial, practical issues, and more.
Formerly: Vantage (New York) (1556-1429)
Published by: Alzheimer's Foundation of America, 322 8th Ave., 6th Fl., New York, NY 10001. TEL 866-232-8484, FAX 646-638-1546, media@alzfdn.org, http://www.alzfdn.org/. Ed. Carol Steinberg.

616.8 150 FRA ISSN 1260-5921
LE CARNET PSY. Text in French. 1994. m. **Document type:** *Journal, Trade.*
Related titles: Online - full text ed.: ISSN 2107-0954. 2010.
Published by: Editions Cazaubon, 8 Av Jean-Baptiste, Clement, Boulogne 92100, France. TEL 33-1-46047435, FAX 33-1-46047400, http://www.carnetpsy.com/Default.aspx. Ed. Manuelle Missonnier.

616.8 USA ISSN 2090-6668
▼ ➤ **CASE REPORTS IN NEUROLOGICAL MEDICINE.** Text in English. 2011. **Document type:** *Journal, Academic/Scholarly.* **Description:** Publishes case reports in all areas of neurological medicine.
Related titles: Online - full text ed.: ISSN 2090-6676. 2011. free (effective 2011).
Published by: Hindawi Publishing Corporation, 410 Park Ave, 15th Fl, PMB 287, New York, NY 10022. FAX 215-893-4392, 866-446-3294, info@hindawi.com.

616.8 CHE ISSN 1662-680X
RC346
▼ ➤ **CASE REPORTS IN NEUROLOGY.** Text in English. 2009. irreg. free (effective 2011). **Document type:** *Monographic series, Academic/Scholarly.* **Description:** Publishes original case reports covering the entire spectrum of neurology.
Media: Online - full text.
Indexed: A22, P30.
—BLDSC (3058.144550), IE.
Published by: S. Karger AG, Allschwilerstr 10, Basel, 4055, Switzerland. TEL 41-61-3061111, FAX 41-61-3061234, karger@karger.ch, http://www.karger.ch. Ed. T Tatlisumak.

616.89 USA ISSN 2090-682X
▼ ➤ **CASE REPORTS IN PSYCHIATRY.** Text in English. 2011. **Document type:** *Journal, Academic/Scholarly.* **Description:** Publishes case reports in all areas of psychiatry.
Related titles: Online - full text ed.: ISSN 2090-6838. 2011. free (effective 2011).
Published by: Hindawi Publishing Corporation, 410 Park Ave, 15th Fl, PMB 287, New York, NY 10022. FAX 215-893-4392, 866-446-3294, info@hindawi.com.

616.8 GBR ISSN 1357-8944
CATNAP. Text in English. 1986. q. GBP 10 in Europe; GBP 15 elsewhere (effective 2009). back issues avail.; reprints avail. **Document type:** *Newsletter, Trade.* **Description:** Aims to promote awareness of narcolepsy and provide authoritative information about it to narcoleptics, to the medical profession and the public.
Formerly (until 1992): Narcolepsy Association. Newsletter (1357-8936)
Indexed: E-psyche.
Published by: Narcolepsy Association, Craven House, 121 Kingsway, London, WC2B 6PA, United Kingdom. info@narcolepsy.org.uk.

616.8 USA ISSN 0272-4340
QP351 CODEN: CMNEDI
➤ **CELLULAR AND MOLECULAR NEUROBIOLOGY.** Text in English. 1981. 8/yr. EUR 1,637, USD 1,736 combined subscription to institutions (print & online eds.) (effective 2012). adv. back issues avail.; reprint service avail. from PSC. **Document type:** *Journal, Academic/Scholarly.* **Description:** Examines the anatomic, genetic, physiologic, pharmacologic, and biochemical approaches to the analysis of neuronal and brain function at the cellular and subcellular levels.
Related titles: Microfilm ed.: (from PQC); Online - full text ed.: ISSN 1573-6830 (from IngentaConnect).
Indexed: A01, A03, A08, A22, A26, A34, A35, A36, A38, ASCA, AgBio, Agr, AgrForAb, B21, B25, B27, BIOBASE, BIOSIS Prev, BibLing, C30, CA, CABA, CIN, CTA, ChemAb, ChemTitl, ChemoAb, CurCont, D01, E-psyche, E01, E12, EMBASE, ExcerpMed, F08, F11, F12, GH, GenetAb, H16, H17, I05, IABS, ISR, IndMed, IndVet, Inpharma, MEDLINE, MycolAb, N02, N03, N04, NSA, NSCI, P03, P30, P32, P33, P37, P40, PGrRegA, PsycInfo, R07, R08, R10, RA&MP, Reac, RefZh, SCI, SCOPUS, SoyAb, T02, T05, VS, W07.
—BLDSC (3097.925000), CASDDS, GNLM, IE, Infotrieve, Ingenta, INIST. **CCC.**
Published by: Springer New York LLC (Subsidiary of: Springer Science+Business Media), 233 Spring St, New York, NY 10013. TEL 212-460-1500, FAX 212-460-1575, service-ny@springer.com. Ed. Juan M Saavedra.

616.8 USA ISSN 1868-4904
➤ **CENTRAL EUROPEAN NEUROSURGERY.** Text and summaries in English, German. 1936. q. USD 403 to institutions; USD 511 combined subscription to institutions (print & online eds.) (effective 2011). adv. bk.rev. abstr.; illus. index per vol. 60 p./no.; reprints avail. **Document type:** *Journal, Academic/Scholarly.* **Description:** Provides comprehensive information on all clinical, research and practical aspects of neurosurgery.
Formerly (until 2009): Zentralblatt fuer Neurochirurgie (0044-4251)
Related titles: Online - full text ed.: ISSN 1868-4912. USD 492 to institutions (effective 2011).
Indexed: A22, ASCA, DentInd, E-psyche, EMBASE, ExcerpMed, IBR, IBZ, IndMed, MEDLINE, NSCI, P30, R10, Reac, SCI, SCOPUS, W07.
—BLDSC (9511.300000), GNLM, IE, Infotrieve, Ingenta, INIST. **CCC.**
Published by: Thieme Medical Publishers (Subsidiary of: Georg Thieme Verlag), 333 Seventh Ave, New York, NY 10001. TEL 212-760-0888, 800-782-3488, FAX 212-947-1112, info@thieme.com.

616.8 NLD ISSN 1871-5249
RM315 CODEN: CNSAC3
CENTRAL NERVOUS SYSTEM AGENTS IN MEDICINAL CHEMISTRY; the journal for current and in-depth reviews on central nervous systerm agents. Variant title: Central Nervous System Agents. Text in English. 2001 (May). q. USD 820 to institutions (print or online ed.) (effective 2012). adv. back issues avail.; reprints avail. **Document type:** *Journal, Academic/Scholarly.* **Description:** Aims to cover all the latest and outstanding developments in medicinal chemistry and rational drug design for the discovery of new central nervous system agents.
Formerly (until 2005): Current Medicinal Chemistry. Central Nervous System Agents (1568-0150)
Related titles: Online - full text ed.: ISSN 1875-6166 (from IngentaConnect).
Indexed: A01, A03, A08, B&BAb, B19, B21, BIOBASE, BIOSIS Prev, C33, CA, ChemAb, EMBASE, ExcerpMed, IABS, MEDLINE, MycolAb, NSA, P30, R10, Reac, SCOPUS, T02.
—BLDSC (3106.149500), IE, Infotrieve, Ingenta. **CCC.**
Published by: Bentham Science Publishers Ltd., PO Box 294, Bussum, 1400 AG, Netherlands. TEL 31-35-6923800, FAX 31-35-6980150, sales@bentham.org. Eds. Gregory S Hamilton, Maria Luz Lopez Rodriguez. **Subscr. to:** Bentham Science Publishers Ltd., c/o Richard E Morrissy, PO Box 446, Oak Park, IL 60301. TEL 312-413-5867, FAX 312-996-7107, subscriptions@bentham.org.

616.8 GBR ISSN 0333-1024
RC392 CODEN: CEPHDF
➤ **CEPHALALGIA;** an international journal of headache. Text in English. 1981. m. USD 1,813, GBP 980 combined subscription to institutions (print & online eds.); USD 1,777, GBP 960 to institutions (effective 2011). adv. index. back issues avail.; reprint service avail. from PSC. **Document type:** *Journal, Academic/Scholarly.* **Description:** Contains original papers on all aspects of headache.
Related titles: Microform ed.: (from PQC); Online - full text ed.: ISSN 1468-2982. USD 1,632, GBP 882 to institutions (effective 2011) (from IngentaConnect); ◆ Supplement(s): Cephalalgia. Supplement. ISSN 0800-1952.
Indexed: A01, A02, A03, A08, A20, A22, A26, A36, ASCA, B21, B25, BIOSIS Prev, C06, C07, C11, CA, CABA, ChemAb, CurCont, D01, DentInd, E-psyche, E01, E12, EMBASE, ExcerpMed, F08, GH, H04, H12, I05, ISR, IndMed, Inpharma, JW-N, MEDLINE, MycolAb, N02, N03, NRN, NSA, NSCI, P03, P30, P33, P35, PsycInfo, R10, R12, RM&VM, Reac, SCI, SCOPUS, T02, T05, VITIS, W07, W10.
—BLDSC (3113.691000), CASDDS, GNLM, IE, Infotrieve, Ingenta, INIST. **CCC.**
Published by: (International Headache Society), Sage Publications Ltd. (Subsidiary of: Sage Publications, Inc.), 1 Oliver's Yard, 55 City Rd, London, EC1Y 1SP, United Kingdom. TEL 44-20-73248500, FAX 44-20-73248600, info@sagepub.co.uk, http://www.uk.sagepub.com/home.nav. Ed. David W Dodick. Circ: 1,500.

616.8 GBR ISSN 0800-1952
CEPHALALGIA. SUPPLEMENT. Text in English. 1983. irreg. reprints avail. **Document type:** *Journal, Academic/Scholarly.*
Related titles: ◆ Supplement to: Cephalalgia. ISSN 0333-1024.
Indexed: A22, SCOPUS.
—BLDSC (3113.691100), IE, Ingenta, INIST. **CCC.**
Published by: (International Headache Society), Wiley-Blackwell Publishing Ltd. (Subsidiary of: John Wiley & Sons, Inc.), 9600 Garsington Rd, Oxford, OX4 2DQ, United Kingdom. TEL 44-1865-776868, FAX 44-1865-714591, customerservices@blackwellpublishing.com, http://www.wiley.com/.

616.8 USA ISSN 1473-4222
QP379 CODEN: CERECF
➤ **THE CEREBELLUM.** Text in English. 2001. q. EUR 604, USD 811 combined subscription to institutions (print & online eds.) (effective 2012). adv. back issues avail.; reprint service avail. from PSC. **Document type:** *Journal, Academic/Scholarly.* **Description:** Devoted to the science of the cerebellum and its role in ataxia and other medical disorders.
Related titles: Online - full text ed.: ISSN 1473-4230 (from IngentaConnect).
Indexed: A01, A03, A08, A22, B21, BIOBASE, CA, E01, EMBASE, ExcerpMed, IABS, MEDLINE, NSA, NSCI, P03, P30, PsycInfo, R10, Reac, RefZh, SCI, SCOPUS, T02, W07.
—IE, Ingenta. **CCC.**
Published by: (Society for Research on the Cerebellum), Springer New York LLC (Subsidiary of: Springer Science+Business Media), 233 Spring St, New York, NY 10013. TEL 212-460-1500, FAX 212-460-1575, service-ny@springer.com, http://www.springer.com. Ed. Mario-Ubaldo Manto.

616.8 GBR ISSN 2044-5970
CEREBRA NEWSBEAT. Text in English. 1995. q. free to members (effective 2010). back issues avail. **Document type:** *Newsletter, Consumer.* **Description:** Contains updates on research developments and useful resources as well as articles on a wide range of topics for children.
Former titles (until 2009): Cerebra Bulletin (1753-2043); (until 2005): Parnet Bulletin (1360-9319)
Related titles: Online - full text ed.: free (effective 2010).
Published by: Cerebra, 2nd Fl Offices, Lyric Bldg, King St, Carmarthen, SA31 1BD, United Kingdom. TEL 44-1267-244200, FAX 44-1267-244201, info@cerebra.org.uk.

616.8 GBR ISSN 1047-3211
QP383
➤ **CEREBRAL CORTEX.** Text in English. 1991. m. GBP 1,274 in United Kingdom to institutions; EUR 1,913 in Europe to institutions; USD 2,549 in US & Canada to institutions; GBP 1,274 elsewhere to institutions; GBP 1,390 combined subscription in United Kingdom to institutions (print & online eds.); EUR 2,087 combined subscription in Europe to institutions (print & online eds.); USD 2,780 combined subscription in US & Canada to institutions (print & online eds.); GBP 1,390 combined subscription elsewhere to institutions (print & online eds.) (effective 2012). adv. bk.rev. Supplement avail.; back issues avail.; reprint service avail. from PSC. **Document type:** *Journal, Academic/Scholarly.* **Description:** Interdisciplinary journal publishing papers on the development, organization, plasticity, and function of the cerebral cortex.
Related titles: Online - full text ed.: ISSN 1460-2199. GBP 973 in United Kingdom to institutions; EUR 1,461 in Europe to institutions; USD 1,946 in US & Canada to institutions; GBP 973 elsewhere to institutions (effective 2012) (from IngentaConnect).
Indexed: A20, A22, ASCA, B21, B25, BIOBASE, BIOSIS Prev, CA, CMCI, ChemoAb, CurCont, E-psyche, E01, EMBASE, ESPM, ExcerpMed, IABS, ISR, IndMed, Inpharma, MEDLINE, MycolAb, NSA, NSCI, P03, P20, P22, P25, P30, P48, P54, PQC, PsycInfo, PsycholAb, R10, Reac, SCI, SCOPUS, ToxAb, W07.
—BLDSC (3120.027550), GNLM, IE, Infotrieve, Ingenta, INIST. **CCC.**
Published by: Oxford University Press, Great Clarendon St, Oxford, OX2 6DP, United Kingdom. TEL 44-1865-556767, FAX 44-1865-556646, enquiry@oup.co.uk, http://www.oxfordjournals.org. Ed. Dr. Pasko Rakic. adv.: B&W page GBP 230, B&W page USD 415, color page GBP 430, color page USD 740; trim 215 x 280. Circ: 450.

616.836 USA ISSN 1544-9939
CEREBRAL PALSY MAGAZINE. Text in English. 2003 (Jun.). q. USD 19 domestic; USD 22 in Canada; USD 39 elsewhere (effective 2003). adv. **Document type:** *Magazine, Consumer.* **Description:** Focuses on issues related to Cerebral Palsy.
Published by: Therasuit, LLC, P. O. Box 7005, West Bloomfield, MI 48302. TEL 248-706-1026, FAX 248-706-1049, suittherapy@aol.com, http://www.suittherapy.com/. Ed. Izabela Koscielny.

616.836 NZL ISSN 1171-6142
CEREBRAL PALSY SOCIETY OF NEW ZEALAND. REVIEW. Text in English. 1990. q. free to qualified personnel (effective 2011). back issues avail. **Document type:** *Magazine, Consumer.* **Description:** Contains articles related to the disability sector including services available, new products, personal experiences/points of view and news within the Cerebral Palsy Society of New Zealand.
Former titles (until 1991): Cerebral Palsy Review (1171-0292); Cerebral Palsy Society. Newsletter (1170-909X)
Related titles: Online - full text ed.: ISSN 1179-9986. free (effective 2011).
Published by: Cerebral Palsy Society of New Zealand, 14 Erson Ave, Royal Oak, PO Box 24759, Auckland, 1345, New Zealand. TEL 800-503-603, FAX 64-9-6241802, cpsociety@cpsociety.org.nz. Ed. Ross Flood.

616.89 BRA ISSN 1414-3690
CEREBRO E MENTE. Text in Portuguese. 1997. m. **Document type:** *Journal, Academic/Scholarly.*
Related titles: Ed.: ISSN 1414-4018.
Published by: Universidade Estadual de Campinas, Nucleo de Informatica Biomedica, Caixa Postal 6005, Sao Paulo, Campinas 13081-970, Brazil. TEL 55-19-3788-5102, FAX 55-19-3788-5103, http://www.nib.unicamp.br/. Ed. Mario Maccari Filho.

616.8 616.15 CHE ISSN 1015-9770
RC388.5 CODEN: CDISE7
➤ **CEREBROVASCULAR DISEASES.** Text in English. 1991. 12/yr. CHF 5,440, EUR 4,348, USD 5,323 to institutions; CHF 5,974, EUR 4,776, USD 5,841 combined subscription to institutions (print & online eds.) (effective 2012). adv. back issues avail. **Document type:** *Journal, Academic/Scholarly.* **Description:** Involves a variety of specialties such as neurology, internal medicine, surgery, radiology, epidemiology, cardiology, hematology, psychology and rehabilitation. Deals with all aspects of stroke and cerebrovascular diseases. Contains original contributions, reviews of selected topics and clinical investigative studies, recent meetings reports and work-in-progress as well as discussions on controversial issues.
Related titles: Microform ed.: (from PQC); Online - full text ed.: ISSN 1421-9786. CHF 5,338, EUR 4,270, USD 5,182 to institutions (effective 2012).
Indexed: A01, A03, A08, A22, A36, AgrForAb, B21, CA, CABA, CurCont, D01, E-psyche, E01, E12, EMBASE, ExcerpMed, F08, GH, ISR, IndMed, Inpharma, JW-N, LT, MEDLINE, N02, N03, NSA, NSCI, P20, P22, P30, P33, P35, P48, P54, PQC, R08, R10, R12, RA&MP, RRTA, Reac, SCI, SCOPUS, T02, T05, W07.
—BLDSC (3120.037790), GNLM, IE, Infotrieve, Ingenta. **CCC.**
Published by: S. Karger AG, Allschwilerstr 10, Basel, 4055, Switzerland. TEL 41-61-3061111, FAX 41-61-3061234, karger@karger.ch, http://www.karger.ch. Ed. M Hennerici. adv.: page CHF 1,815; trim 210 x 280. Circ: 4,300 (paid and controlled).

616.8 USA ISSN 1524-6205
CEREBRUM. Text in English. 1998. bi-m. back issues avail. **Document type:** *Journal, Academic/Scholarly.* **Description:** Contains articles, debates, interviews, color visual features by top scientists and other thinkers in brain science.
Related titles: Online - full text ed.: ISSN 1943-3859. free (effective 2010).
Indexed: BiolDig, P30, SCOPUS.
—BLDSC (3120.038700), IE.
Published by: The Dana Press, 745 Fifth Ave, Ste 900, New York, NY 10151. TEL 212-223-4040, FAX 212-317-8721, danainfo@dana.org. Ed. Johanna Goldberg. **Subscr. to:** Cerebrum Subscriber Services. **Co-sponsor:** The Charles A. Dana Foundation.

616.8 617.48 CZE ISSN 1210-7859
CODEN: CKNNAS
➤ **CESKA A SLOVENSKA NEUROLOGIE A NEUROCHIRURGIE.** Text in Czech, Slovak; Summaries in Czech, English. 1937. 6/yr. CZK 600 domestic; EUR 24 foreign (effective 2010). adv. bk.rev. abstr.; bibl.; charts; illus. index. **Document type:** *Journal, Academic/Scholarly.* **Description:** Publishes original papers from the whole range of neurology and neurosurgery.
Former titles (until 1993): Ceskoslovenska Neurologie a Neurochirurgie (0301-0597); (until 1972): Ceskoslovenska Neurologie (0009-0581)
Related titles: Online - full text ed.: ISSN 1802-4041. 2007.
Indexed: A20, ASCA, B21, CISA, ChemAb, DentInd, E-psyche, EMBASE, ExcerpMed, IndMed, NSA, NSCI, P30, R10, Reac, SCI, SCOPUS, W07.
—BLDSC (3120.258450), CASDDS, GNLM, INIST. **CCC.**
Published by: (Ceska Neurologicka Spolecnost C L S J.E. Purkyne/ Czech Neurology Society, Ceska Neurochirurgicka Spolecnost C L S J.E. Purkyne/Czech Neurosurgery Society, Ceska Spolecnost Detske Neurologie C L S J.E. Purkyne/Czech Society of Children Neurosurgery), Medica Healthworld a.s., Bidlaky 20, Brno, 63900, Czech Republic. TEL 420-533-337311, FAX 420-533-337312, info@mhw.cz, http://www.mhw.cz. Ed. J Bednarik. adv.: B&W page CZK 25,700, color page CZK 36,400; 246 x 173. Circ: 1,600.

616.8 CZE ISSN 1212-0383
➤ **CESKA A SLOVENSKA PSYCHIATRIE/CZECH AND SLOVAK PSYCHIATRY.** Text in Czech, Slovak; Summaries in Czech, English. 1904. 8/yr. CZK 520 (effective 2010). adv. bk.rev. abstr. **Document type:** *Journal, Academic/Scholarly.* **Description:** Publishes original papers from the area of general and special psychiatry concerned with problems of theoretical and special psychiatry.
Formerly (until 1993): Cesko-Slovenska Psychiatrie (0069-2336)
Related titles: Online - full text ed.
Indexed: A22, CISA, E-psyche, EMBASE, ExcerpMed, IndMed, P03, P30, PsycInfo, PsycholAb, R10, Reac, S02, S03, SCOPUS.
—BLDSC (3120.258480), GNLM, IE, Ingenta, INIST. **CCC.**
Published by: (Ceska Lekarska Spolecnost J.E. Purkyne/Czech Medical Association), Nakladatelske Stredisko C L S J.E. Purkyne, Sokolska 31, Prague, 12026, Czech Republic. nts@cls.cz. Ed. M Anders. adv.: B&W page CZK 30,100, color page CZK 42,000; 198 x 135. Circ: 2,700.

616.89 FRA ISSN 1266-5371
CHAMP PSYCHOSOMATIQUE. Text in French; Summaries in English. 1959. q. EUR 80 domestic; EUR 90 foreign (effective 2009). **Document type:** *Monographic series, Academic/Scholarly.*
Former titles (until 1996): Revue de Medecine Psychosomatique (0298-3850); (until 1983): Revue de Medecine Psychosomatique et de Psychologie Medicale (0397-930X); (until 1965): Revue de Medecine Psychosomatique (0035-1547)
Related titles: Online - full text ed.: ISSN 1961-8638.
Indexed: E-psyche, FR, IBR, IBZ, IndMed, P30, PsycholAb, S02, S03, SCOPUS.
—GNLM, INIST.
Published by: (Champ Psychosomatique), Editions L' Esprit du Temps, 115 Rue Anatole France, B P 107, Le Bouscat, 33491 Cedex, France. TEL 33-5-56028419, FAX 33-5-56029131, info@lespritdutemps.com.

616.8 150 FRA ISSN 0994-2424
CHE VUOI?. Text in French. 1988. s-a. EUR 35.10 domestic; EUR 41.20 foreign (effective 2008). **Document type:** *Journal, Academic/ Scholarly.*
Published by: (Cercle Freudien), L' Harmattan, 5 Rue de l'Ecole Polytechnique, Paris, 75005, France. TEL 33-1-43257651, FAX 33-1-43258203.

CHILD AND ADOLESCENT PSYCHIATRIC CLINICS OF NORTH AMERICA. *see* MEDICAL SCIENCES—Pediatrics

616.8 618.9289 USA ISSN 1522-3817
CHILD & ADOLESCENT PSYCHIATRY ALERTS. Text in English. 1999 (Jan.). m. USD 89 domestic to individuals; USD 97.50 in Canada to individuals; USD 107.50 elsewhere to individuals; USD 141 to institutions (effective 2010). **Document type:** *Newsletter, Trade.* **Description:** Provides appropriate therapy, diagnose, assess, and manage psychiatric and behavioral disorders.
Published by: M.J. Powers & Co. Publishers, 65 Madison Ave, Morristown, NJ 07960. TEL 973-898-1200, FAX 973-898-1201.

616.8 GBR ISSN 1753-2000
RJ499.A1
CHILD AND ADOLESCENT PSYCHIATRY AND MENTAL HEALTH. Text in English. 2007. irreg. free (effective 2011). adv. back issues avail.; reprints avail. **Document type:** *Journal, Academic/Scholarly.* **Description:** International platform for rapid and comprehensive scientific communication on child and adolescent mental health across different cultural backgrounds.
Media: Online - full text.
Indexed: A01, A26, CA, EMBASE, ExcerpMed, H12, I05, NSA, P03, P30, PsycInfo, SCOPUS, T02.
—**CCC.**
Published by: BioMed Central Ltd. (Subsidiary of: Springer Science+Business Media), 236 Gray's Inn Rd, London, WC1X 8HB, United Kingdom. TEL 44-20-31922000, FAX 44-20-31922010, info@biomedcentral.com, http://www.biomedcentral.com. Ed. Joerg M Fegert.

616.8 615 618.92 USA ISSN 1085-0295
➤ **CHILD AND ADOLESCENT PSYCHOPHARMACOLOGY NEWS.** Text in English. 1996. bi-m. USD 150 combined subscription domestic to individuals (print & online eds.); USD 160 combined subscription foreign to individuals (print & online eds.); USD 290 combined subscription domestic to institutions (print & online eds.); USD 305 combined subscription foreign to institutions (print & online eds.) (effective 2011). bk.rev. abstr.; bibl. index. back issues avail.; reprints avail. **Document type:** *Journal, Academic/Scholarly.* **Description:** Addresses clinical and research information on issues related to psychopharmacology for children and adolescents, such as which drugs work, drug interactions and treatment plans.
Formerly: Child and Adolescent Psychopharmacology Newsletter
Related titles: Microform ed.: (from PQC); Online - full text ed.: ISSN 1943-2739.
Indexed: A01, A03, A08, A22, CA, E-psyche, E01, P19, P25, P48, PQC, T02.
—BLDSC (3172.913800), IE, Ingenta. **CCC.**
Published by: Guilford Publications, Inc., 72 Spring St, 4th Fl, New York, NY 10012. TEL 800-365-7006, FAX 212-966-6708, info@guilford.com. Ed. Robert L Findling. R&P Kathy Kuehl. Adv. contact Marian Robinson. Circ: 600 (paid).

616.89 USA ISSN 0009-398X
RJ499.A1 CODEN: CPHDA3
➤ **CHILD PSYCHIATRY & HUMAN DEVELOPMENT.** Text in English. 1970. q. EUR 1,108, USD 1,187 combined subscription to institutions (print & online eds.) (effective 2012). adv. bibl. index. back issues avail.; reprint service avail. from PSC. **Document type:** *Journal, Academic/Scholarly.* **Description:** Serves allied professional groups of specialists in child psychiatry, social science, pediatrics, psychology, and human development.
Related titles: Microform ed.: (from PQC); Online - full text ed.: ISSN 1573-3327 (from IngentaConnect).
Indexed: A01, A03, A08, A20, A22, A26, ABS&EES, AC&P, AMHA, ASCA, ASSIA, Agr, B04, B21, B25, BDM&CN, BIOSIS Prev, BRD, BibLing, C06, C07, C28, CA, CDA, Chicano, CurCont, E-psyche, E01, E02, E03, E06, E07, ECER, EMBASE, ERI, ERIC, EdA, EdI, ExcerpMed, F09, FR, FamI, H12, IBR, IBZ, IndMed, Inpharma, L&LBA, MEDLINE, MycolAb, NSA, P03, P20, P22, P27, P30, P43, P48, P50, P54, PQC, PsycInfo, PsycholAb, R10, Reac, S02, S03, SCOPUS, SFSA, SOPODA, SSAI, SSAb, SSCI, SSI, SWR&A, SociolAb, T02, V&AA, W03, W05, W07, WSA.
—BLDSC (3172.945000), GNLM, IE, Infotrieve, Ingenta, INIST. **CCC.**
Published by: (American Association of Psychiatric Services for Children), Springer New York LLC (Subsidiary of: Springer Science+Business Media), 233 Spring St, New York, NY 10013. TEL 212-460-1500, FAX 212-460-1575, service-ny@springer.com. Ed. Kenneth Tarnowski.

618.92 612 DEU ISSN 0256-7040
RJ486 CODEN: CNSYE9
➤ **CHILD'S NERVOUS SYSTEM.** Text in English. 1972. m. EUR 3,210, USD 3,915 combined subscription to institutions (print & online eds.) (effective 2012). adv. bibl.; charts; illus. back issues avail.; reprint service avail. from PSC. **Document type:** *Journal, Academic/ Scholarly.* **Description:** Encompasses all aspects of the pediatric neurosciences including development and growth, trauma, degenerative disorders, hereditary diseases, neurophysiology, neurology and neurosurgery.
Superseded in part (in 1985): Child's Brain (0302-2803)
Related titles: Microform ed.: (from RPI); Online - full text ed.: ISSN 1433-0350 (from IngentaConnect).
Indexed: A01, A03, A08, A20, A22, A26, ASCA, Agr, B21, B25, BDM&CN, BIOSIS Prev, CA, CurCont, DentInd, E-psyche, E01, E08, EMBASE, ExcerpMed, I05, IBR, IBZ, INI, ISR, IndMed, Inpharma, MEDLINE, MycolAb, NSA, NSCI, P30, P35, R10, Reac, S09, SCI, SCOPUS, T02, W07.
—BLDSC (3172.993080), GNLM, IE, Infotrieve, Ingenta, INIST. **CCC.**
Published by: (International Society for Pediatric Neurosurgery), Springer (Subsidiary of: Springer Science+Business Media), Tiergartenstr 17, Heidelberg, 69121, Germany. TEL 49-6221-4870, FAX 49-6221-345229. Ed. Concezio Di Rocco. Circ: 1,125. **Subscr. in the Americas to:** Springer New York LLC, Journal Fulfillment, PO Box 2485, Secaucus, NJ 07096. TEL 800-777-4643, 201-348-4033, FAX 201-348-4505, journals-ny@springer.com, http://www.springer.com; **Subscr. to:** Springer Distribution Center, Kundenservice Zeitschriften, Haberstr 7, Heidelberg 69126, Germany. TEL 49-6221-3454303, FAX 49-6221-3454229, subscriptions@springer.com. **Co-sponsors:** Japanese Society for Pediatric Neurosurgery; European Society for Paediatric Neurosurgery.

616.8 ITA ISSN 1721-0151
CICLO EVOLUTIVO E DISABILITA. Text in Italian. 1998. s-a. EUR 25.80 (effective 2009). **Document type:** *Journal, Academic/Scholarly.*
Related titles: Print ed.: Life Span and Disability. ISSN 2035-5963. 2009. free (effective 2011).
—BLDSC (3192.644500).
Published by: Oasi Editrice, Via Conte Ruggero 73, Troina, EN 94018, Italy. http://www.oasi.en.it.

▼ **CLINICAL AND EXPERIMENTAL NEUROIMMUNOLOGY.** *see* MEDICAL SCIENCES—Allergology And Immunology

616.891 USA ISSN 1534-6501
RC465
CLINICAL CASE STUDIES. Text in English. 2002 (Jan.). bi-m. adv. reprint service avail. from PSC. **Document type:** *Journal, Academic/ Scholarly.* **Description:** Publishes case reports of therapeutic interventions across the age spectrum for a variety of problems and in all appropriate milieus, and covers individual therapy, couples therapy, family therapy, assessment cases and case series that present direct and systematic replications.
Related titles: Online - full text ed.: ISSN 1552-3802. USD 540, GBP 317 to institutions (effective 2011).
Indexed: A01, A03, A08, A22, CA, E01, EMBASE, ExcerpMed, FamI, P03, P30, PsycInfo, PsycholAb, R10, Reac, SCOPUS, T02.
—BLDSC (3286.266300), IE, Ingenta. **CCC.**
Published by: Sage Publications, Inc., 2455 Teller Rd, Thousand Oaks, CA 91320. TEL 805-499-9774, 800-818-7243, FAX 805-499-0871, 800-583-2665, info@sagepub.com. Ed. Michael Hersen. **Subscr. outside the Americas to:** Sage Publications Ltd., 1 Oliver's Yard, 55 City Rd, London EC1Y 1SP, United Kingdom. TEL 44-20-73248701, FAX 44-20-73248733, subscription@sagepub.co.uk.

616.8047547 USA ISSN 1550-0594
CODEN: CEEGA
CLINICAL E E G AND NEUROSCIENCE. (Electroencephalography) Text in English. 1970. q. USD 125 domestic to non-members; USD 158 foreign to non-members; free to members (effective 2011). adv. back issues avail. **Document type:** *Journal, Academic/Scholarly.* **Description:** Aims to convey clinically relevant research and development in electroencephalography and neuroscience.
Formerly (until 2004): Clinical E E G Electroencephalography (0009-9155)
Related titles: Online - full text ed.
Indexed: A22, B&BAb, B19, B21, CurCont, EMBASE, ExcerpMed, MEDLINE, NSA, NSCI, P20, P22, P24, P30, P48, P54, PQC, R10, Reac, SCI, SCOPUS, W07.
—BLDSC (3286.273930), GNLM, IE, Ingenta, INIST.
Published by: Electroencephalography and Clinical Neuroscience Society, 805 W Liberty Dr, Wheaton, IL 60187. FAX 630-653-6233, ChattaNeuro@aol.com. Ed. Norman C Moore. Adv. contact Kevin Kjellberg TEL 630-653-2244.

616.8 USA ISSN 0749-8047
RB127
➤ **CLINICAL JOURNAL OF PAIN.** Text in English. 1985. 9/yr. USD 751 domestic to institutions; USD 835 foreign to institutions (effective 2011). adv. bk.rev. charts; illus. Index. back issues avail.; reprints avail. **Document type:** *Journal, Academic/Scholarly.* **Description:** Explores all aspects of pain and its treatment, and the insights of leading anesthesiologists, surgeons, internists, neurologists, orthopedists, psychiatrists and psychologists, clinical pharmacologists, and rehabilitation medicine specialists.
Related titles: Online - full text ed.: ISSN 1536-5409.
Indexed: A20, A22, AMED, ASCA, C06, C07, C08, CINAHL, CurCont, E-psyche, EMBASE, ExcerpMed, FR, I12, INI, IndMed, Inpharma, MEDLINE, NSCI, P03, P30, P35, PsycInfo, PsycholAb, R10, Reac, SCI, SCOPUS, W07.
—BLDSC (3286.294200), GNLM, IE, Infotrieve, Ingenta, INIST. **CCC.**
Published by: (American Academy of Pain Medicine), Lippincott Williams & Wilkins (Subsidiary of: Wolters Kluwer N.V.), 530 Walnut St, Philadelphia, PA 19106. TEL 215-521-8300, FAX 215-521-8902, customerservice@lww.com, http://www.lww.com. Ed. Dennis C Turk TEL 206-616-2626. Pub. Nancy Megley.

616.8 GBR ISSN 0269-9206
RC423.A1
➤ **CLINICAL LINGUISTICS & PHONETICS.** Text in English. 1987. m. GBP 1,015, EUR 1,430, USD 1,780 combined subscription to institutions (print & online eds.); GBP 2,025, EUR 2,855, USD 3,570 combined subscription to corporations (print & online eds.) (effective 2010). adv. bk.rev. back issues avail.; reprint service avail. from PSC. **Document type:** *Journal, Academic/Scholarly.* **Description:** Covers all aspects of linguistics and phonetics of disorders of speech and language. Clinical dialectology and sociolinguistics.
Incorporates (2003-2007): Journal of Multilingual Communication Disorders (1476-9670)
Related titles: Online - full text ed.: ISSN 1464-5076 (from IngentaConnect).
Indexed: A01, A02, A03, A08, A20, A22, AMED, ASCA, BibLing, C06, C07, C08, CA, CINAHL, CMM, CurCont, E-psyche, E01, E03, EMBASE, ERI, ERIC, ExcerpMed, FR, FamI, H04, L&LBA, L11, MEDLINE, P03, P30, PsycInfo, PsycholAb, R10, Reac, SCOPUS, SOPODA, SSCI, T02, W07.
—GNLM, IE, Infotrieve, Ingenta, INIST. **CCC.**

Published by: Informa Healthcare (Subsidiary of: T & F Informa plc), Telephone House, 69-77 Paul St, London, EC2A 4LQ, United Kingdom. TEL 44-20-70175000, FAX 44-20-70176792, healthcare.enquiries@informa.com. Eds. Martin J Ball, Nicole Muller, Thomas W Powell. **Subscr. in N. America to:** Taylor & Francis Inc., Customer Services Dept, 325 Chestnut St, 8th Fl, Philadelphia, PA 19106. TEL 215-625-8900, 800-354-1420, FAX 215-625-8914; **Subscr. outside N. America to:** Taylor & Francis Ltd., Journals Customer Service, Sheepen Pl, Colchester, Essex CO3 3LP, United Kingdom. TEL 44-20-70175544, FAX 44-20-70175198, tf.enquiries@tfinforma.com.

616.89 NZL ISSN 1179-5573
➤ **CLINICAL MEDICINE INSIGHTS: PSYCHIATRY.** Text in English. 2008. irreg. free (effective 2011). **Document type:** *Journal, Academic/Scholarly.*
Formerly (until 2011): Clinical Medicine: Psychiatry (1178-6590)
Media: Online - full text.
Indexed: C06.
—**CCC.**
Published by: Libertas Academica Ltd., PO Box 300-874, Mairangi Bay, Auckland, 0751, New Zealand. TEL 64-9-4763930, FAX 64-9-3531397, editorial@la-press.com.

616.8 USA
RC346
CLINICAL NEUROANATOMY. Text in English. 1952. triennial. USD 47.95 per issue (effective 2008). **Document type:** *Journal, Trade.*
Description: Discusses the latest advances in molecular and cellular biology in the context of neuroanatomy.
Formerly (until 2001): Correlative Neuroanatomy (1042-0398); Which superseded (in 1988): Correlative Neuroanatomy and Functional Neurology (0892-1237); Correlative Neuroanatomy
Indexed: E-psyche.
Published by: McGraw-Hill Companies, Inc., 1221 Ave of the Americas, 43rd fl, New York, NY 10020. TEL 212-512-2000, FAX 212-426-7087, customer.service@mcgraw-hill.com, http://www.mcgraw-hill.com. Ed. Stephen G Waxman.

616.8 617 NLD ISSN 0303-8467
RC346 CODEN: CNNSBV
➤ **CLINICAL NEUROLOGY AND NEUROSURGERY.** Text in English. 1975. 10/yr. EUR 853 in Europe to institutions; JPY 113,100 in Japan to institutions; USD 953 elsewhere to institutions (effective 2012). adv. bk.rev. back issues avail. **Document type:** *Journal, Academic/Scholarly.* **Description:** Covers developments in the field of clinical neurology and neurosurgery, including invited reviews, original research, and brief case histories of unusual clinical syndromes or diseases.
Related titles: Microform ed.: (from PQC); Online - full text ed.: ISSN 1872-6968 (from IngentaConnect, ScienceDirect).
Indexed: A01, A03, A08, A20, A22, A26, A34, A36, ASCA, B21, BDM&CN, CA, CABA, CurCont, E-psyche, E12, EMBASE, ESPM, ExcerpMed, GH, H17, I05, IBR, IBZ, IndMed, IndVet, Inpharma, MEDLINE, N02, N03, NSA, NSCI, P03, P30, P33, P35, P39, PN&I, PsycholAb, R07, R08, R10, RA&MP, RM&VM, Reac, SCI, SCOPUS, T02, T05, ToxAb, VS, W07.
—BLDSC (3286.310100), GNLM, IE, Infotrieve, Ingenta, INIST. **CCC.**
Published by: Elsevier BV (Subsidiary of: Elsevier Science & Technology), Radarweg 29, PO Box 211, Amsterdam, 1000 AE, Netherlands. TEL 31-20-4853911, FAX 31-20-4852457, JournalsCustomerServiceEMEA@elsevier.com, http://www.elsevier.nl. Ed. Peter Paul De Deyn.

616.8 USA ISSN 1553-3212
CLINICAL NEUROLOGY NEWS. Text in English. 2005 (Jan.). m. USD 103 domestic; USD 164 foreign (effective 2009). adv. back issues avail.; reprints avail. **Document type:** *Newspaper, Trade.*
Description: Provides latest studies in neurovascular disorders, epilepsy, dementias and demyelinating disorders.
Related titles: Online - full text ed.: free (effective 2009).
—**CCC.**
Published by: International Medical News Group (Subsidiary of: Elsevier Health Sciences), 5635 Fishers Ln, Ste 6000, Rockville, MD 20852. TEL 240-221-4500, 800-445-6975, FAX 240-221-4400, m.altier@elsevier.com, http://www.imng.com. Ed. Mary Jo M. Dales. Pub. Alan J Imhoff TEL 973-290-8216. Circ: 17,229. **Subscr. to:** Elsevier, Subscription Customer Service, 60 Columbia Rd, Bldg B, Morristown, NJ 07960. TEL 973-290-8200, FAX 973-290-8250, http://www.elsevier.com/.

616.8 DEU ISSN 0722-5091
CODEN: CLNPDA
➤ **CLINICAL NEUROPATHOLOGY.** Text in English. 1982. bi-m. USD 282 to institutions; USD 324 combined subscription to institutions (print & online eds.) (effective 2011). adv. back issues avail.; reprints avail. **Document type:** *Journal, Academic/Scholarly.* **Description:** Publishes reviews and editorials, original papers, short communications and reports on recent advances in the entire field of clinical neuropathology.
Related titles: Online - full text ed.: USD 324 to institutions (effective 2011).
Indexed: A22, ASCA, BIOBASE, CA, CurCont, DentInd, E-psyche, EMBASE, ExcerpMed, IABS, IBR, IBZ, ISR, IndMed, Inpharma, MEDLINE, NSCI, P30, R10, Reac, RefZh, SCI, SCOPUS, T02, W07.
—BLDSC (3286.310400), GNLM, IE, Infotrieve, Ingenta, INIST. **CCC.**
Published by: Dustri-Verlag Dr. Karl Feistle, Bajuwarenring 4, Oberhaching, 82041, Germany. TEL 49-89-6138610, FAX 49-89-6135412, info@dustri.de, http://www.dustri.de. Ed. J Hainfellner.

➤ **CLINICAL NEUROPHARMACOLOGY.** *see* PHARMACY AND PHARMACOLOGY

616.8 IRL ISSN 1388-2457
RC321 CODEN: CNEUFU
➤ **CLINICAL NEUROPHYSIOLOGY.** Text in English, French. 1999. 12/yr. EUR 1,250 in Europe to institutions; JPY 165,900 in Japan to institutions; USD 1,397 elsewhere to institutions (effective 2012). adv. bk.rev. abstr.; charts; illus. Index. back issues avail. **Document type:** *Journal, Academic/Scholarly.* **Description:** Fosters research and disseminates information on all aspects of clinical neurophysiology, both normal and abnormal. Publishes scholarly reports on human physiology and pathophysiology of both the central and the peripheral nervous system.
Formerly (until 1999): Electroencephalography and Clinical Neurophysiology Including Evoked Potentials and Electromyography and Motor Control; Which was formed by the merger of (1991-1999): Electroencephalography and Clinical Neurophysiology: Electromyography and Motor Control (0924-980X); (1984-1999): Electroencephalographyy and Clinical Neurophysiology: Evoked Potentials (0168-5597); (1949-1999): Electroencephalography and Clinical Neurophysiology (0013-4694); Which incorporated (1967-1971): Index to Current E E G Literature (0424-8147)
Related titles: Microform ed.: (from PQC); Online - full text ed.: ISSN 1872-8952 (from IngentaConnect, ScienceDirect); ◆ Supplement(s): Clinical Neurophysiology. Supplement. ISSN 1567-424X.
Indexed: A01, A03, A08, A20, A22, A26, A29, ASCA, B20, B21, B25, BDM&CN, BIOBASE, BIOSIS Prev, CA, CIN, CISA, CMCI, ChemAb, ChemTitl, CurCont, DentInd, E-psyche, EMBASE, ESPM, ErgAb, ExcerpMed, I05, I10, IABS, ISR, IndMed, Inpharma, Inspec, MEDLINE, MycolAb, NSA, NSCI, P03, P30, P35, PEI, PsycInfo, PsycholAb, R10, RILM, Reac, SCI, SCOPUS, T02, VirolAbstr, W07.
—BLDSC (3286.310645), AskIEEE, CASDDS, GNLM, IE, Infotrieve, Ingenta, INIST, Linda Hall. **CCC.**
Published by: (International Federation of Clinical Neurophysiology), Elsevier Ireland Ltd (Subsidiary of: Elsevier Science & Technology), Elsevier House, Brookvale Plaza, E. Park, Shannon, Co. Clare, Ireland. TEL 353-61-709600, FAX 353-61-709100. Ed. Dr. M. Hallett. **Subscr. to:** Elsevier BV, Radarweg 29, PO Box 211, Amsterdam 1000 AE, Netherlands. TEL 31-20-4853757, FAX 31-20-4853432, JournalsCustomerServiceEMEA@elsevier.com, http://www.elsevier.nl.

616.8 NLD ISSN 1567-424X
RC321 CODEN: EECSB3
➤ **CLINICAL NEUROPHYSIOLOGY. SUPPLEMENT.** Text in English. 1950. irreg., latest vol.57, 2004. price varies. back issues avail. **Document type:** *Monographic series, Academic/Scholarly.*
Description: Offers insight in the use of electroencephalography (EEC) in a clinical neurophysiology setting.
Formerly (until 2000): Electroencephalography and Clinical Neurophysiology. Supplements (0424-8155)
Related titles: ◆ Supplement to: Clinical Neurophysiology. ISSN 1388-2457.
Indexed: A22, E-psyche, EMBASE, ExcerpMed, IndMed, MEDLINE, P30, P35, R10, Reac, SCOPUS.
—BLDSC (3286.310647), CASDDS, IE, INIST. **CCC.**
Published by: (International Federation of Clinical Neurophysiology IRL), Elsevier BV (Subsidiary of: Elsevier Science & Technology), Radarweg 29, PO Box 211, Amsterdam, 1000 AE, Netherlands. TEL 31-20-4853911, FAX 31-20-4852457, JournalsCustomerServiceEMEA@elsevier.com, http://www.elsevier.nl.

616.8 ITA ISSN 1724-4935
CLINICAL NEUROPSYCHIATRY; journal of treatments evaluation. Text in English. 2004 (Jun.). bi-m. EUR 95 in Europe to institutions; EUR 100 in United States to institutions; EUR 107 elsewhere to institutions (effective 2008). **Document type:** *Journal, Academic/Scholarly.*
Description: Aims to critically (without ideological bias) evaluate the current achievements in every field of neuropsychiatry, particularly illness course and treatments effectiveness.
Indexed: EMBASE, ExcerpMed, P03, PsycInfo, PsycholAb, R10, Reac, SCOPUS.
—BLDSC (3286.310655).
Published by: Giovanni Fioriti Editore, Via Archimede 179, Rome, 00197, Italy. TEL 39-06-8072063, FAX 39-06-80664609, info@fioriti.it, http://www.fioriti.it.

CLINICAL NEURORADIOLOGY. *see* MEDICAL SCIENCES—Radiology And Nuclear Medicine

617.48 USA ISSN 0069-4827
RD593.A1 CODEN: CLNEA8
CLINICAL NEUROSURGERY. Variant title: Congress of Neurological Surgeons. Proceedings. Text in English. 1953. a., latest vol.56, 2009. price varies. back issues avail. **Document type:** *Proceedings, Academic/Scholarly.* **Description:** Expresses as a official compendium of the platform presentations at the annual meeting of the Congress of Neurological Surgeons.
Related titles: Online - full text ed.: free (effective 2010).
Indexed: A22, E-psyche, EMBASE, ExcerpMed, IndMed, MEDLINE, P30, R10, Reac, SCOPUS.
—BLDSC (3286.311000), CASDDS, GNLM, IE, Infotrieve, Ingenta, INIST. **CCC.**
Published by: (Congress of Neurological Surgeons), Lippincott Williams & Wilkins (Subsidiary of: Wolters Kluwer N.V.), 530 Walnut St, Philadelphia, PA 19106. TEL 215-521-8300, FAX 215-521-8902, customerservice@lww.com. Ed. Gerald A Grant.

CLINICAL PRACTICE AND EPIDEMIOLOGY IN MENTAL HEALTH. *see* PSYCHOLOGY

616.89 USA ISSN 0270-6644
RC321 CODEN: EJRADR
CLINICAL PSYCHIATRY NEWS. Text in English. 1973. m. USD 114 in United States to institutions; USD 182 elsewhere to institutions (effective 2012). adv. bk.rev. back issues avail.; reprints avail. **Document type:** *Newspaper, Trade.* **Description:** Provides the practicing psychiatrist with news and commentary about clinical developments in the field and about the impact of health care policy on the specialty and the physicians practice.
Related titles: Microform ed.: (from PQC); Online - full text ed.
Indexed: A22, A26, E-psyche, G08, H11, H12, I05.
—**CCC.**
Published by: International Medical News Group (Subsidiary of: Elsevier Health Sciences), 5635 Fishers Ln, Ste 6000, Rockville, MD 20852. TEL 877-524-9335, FAX 240-221-4400, m.altier@elsevier.com, http://www.imng.com. Ed. Mary Jo M. Dales. Pub. Alan J Imhoff TEL 973-290-8216. Circ: 42,167. **Subscr. to:** Elsevier, Subscription Customer Service, 60 Columbia Rd, Bldg B, Morristown, NJ 07960. TEL 973-290-8200, FAX 973-290-8250, http://www.elsevier.com/.

616.8 615 KOR ISSN 1738-1088
➤ **CLINICAL PSYCHOPHARMACOLOGY AND NEUROSCIENCE.** Text in English. 2003. 3/yr. USD 200 to institutions (effective 2011). adv. bk.rev. abstr. back issues avail. **Document type:** *Journal, Academic/Scholarly.* **Description:** Aims to publish evidence-based, scientifically written articles related to clinical and preclinical studies in the field of psychopharmacology and neuroscience.
Related titles: Online - full text ed.: free.
Indexed: EMBASE, PsycInfo, SCOPUS.
—BLDSC (3286.346650), IE.
Published by: Korean College of Neuropsychopharmacology/Daehan Jeongsin Yangmul Hakoe, 1003 Life Officetel, 61-3 Yeouido-dong, Yeondeungpo-gu, Seoul, 150-731, Korea, S. TEL 82-2-7842742, FAX 82-2-7845542, secretariat@kcnp.or.kr, http://kcnp.or.kr/. Ed., R&P Young-Chul Chung. Pub. Jin-Sang Yoon. Adv. contact Woo-Im Lee. Circ: 800.

➤ **CLINICS IN DEVELOPMENTAL MEDICINE.** *see* MEDICAL SCIENCES—Pediatrics

616.89 AUT
CLINICUM PSY. Text in German. 6/yr. adv. **Document type:** *Magazine, Trade.*
Published by: Medizin Medien Austria GmbH, Wiedner Hauptstr 120-124, Vienna, 1050, Austria. TEL 43-1-54600, FAX 43-1-54600710, office@medizin-medien.at, http://www.medical-tribune.at. Adv. contact Martina Osterbauer. color page EUR 2,900; trim 210 x 297. Circ: 10,000 (controlled).

616.8 FRA ISSN 1770-7749
CLINIQUE DU TRANSFERT. Text in French. 2004. irreg. price varies. back issues avail. **Document type:** *Monographic series, Consumer.*
Published by: Editions Eres, 33 Av. Marcel Dassault, Toulouse, 31500, France. TEL 33-5-61751576, FAX 33-5-61735289, eres@edition-eres.com.

616.8 FRA ISSN 1288-6629
BF173.A2
➤ **LA CLINIQUE LACANIENNE.** Text in French. 1996. s-a. EUR 50 domestic to individuals; EUR 52 domestic to institutions; EUR 55 foreign (effective 2011). back issues avail. **Document type:** *Journal, Academic/Scholarly.*
Related titles: Online - full text ed.: ISSN 1776-2782.
Published by: Editions Eres, 33 Av. Marcel Dassault, Toulouse, 31500, France. TEL 33-5-61751576, FAX 33-5-61735289, eres@edition-eres.com. Circ: 1,100.

616.8 FRA ISSN 2115-8177
▼ **CLINIQUES**; paroles de praticiens en institution. Text in French. 2011. s-a. EUR 20 domestic; EUR 30 foreign (effective 2011). back issues avail. **Document type:** *Journal, Academic/Scholarly.*
Published by: Editions Eres, 33 Av. Marcel Dassault, Toulouse, 31500, France. TEL 33-5-61751576, FAX 33-5-61735289, eres@edition-eres.com, http://www.edition-eres.com.

616.8 FRA ISSN 0762-7491
➤ **CLINIQUES MEDITERRANEENNES**; psychanalyse et psychopathologie freudiennes. Text in French. 1984. s-a. EUR 50 domestic to individuals; EUR 52 foreign to institutions (effective 2011); EUR 36 domestic to students (effective 2009); EUR 58 foreign (effective 2011). back issues avail. **Document type:** *Journal, Academic/Scholarly.*
Related titles: Online - full text ed.: ISSN 1776-2790.
Indexed: FR, P03, PsycInfo, SCOPUS.
Published by: (Centre Inter-Regional de Recherches en Psychopathologie Clinique), Editions Eres, 33 Av. Marcel Dassault, Toulouse, 31500, France. TEL 33-5-61751576, FAX 33-5-61735289, eres@edition-eres.com. Eds. Roland Gori, Yves Poinso. Circ: 700.

616.8 TUR ISSN 1301-3904
COCUK VE GENCLIK RUH SAGLIGI DERGISI/TURKISH JOURNAL OF CHILD AND ADOLESCENT MENTAL HEALTH. Text in Turkish. 1994. 3/yr. **Document type:** *Journal, Academic/Scholarly.*
Indexed: P03, PsycInfo.
Published by: Cocuk ve Genclik Ruh Sagligi Dernegi/Turkish Child and Adolescent Mental Health Association, Cinnah Cad, No.38/17, Cankaya - Ankara, 06700, Turkey. TEL 90-312-3885015, FAX 90-312-3091430, admin@cgrsder.org. Ed. Dr. Bahar Gokler. **Subscr. to:** P K 67, Samanpazari - Ankara 06242, Turkey. crsdergi@hacettepe.edu.tr.

616.8 GBR ISSN 1467-5919
COGNITION AND BRAIN SCIENCES UNIT. ANNUAL REPORT. Abbreviated title: C B U A R. Variant title: C B U Annual Report. Text in English. 19??. a. back issues avail. **Document type:** *Report, Trade.*
Former titles (until 1999): Human Performance Reports (0461-5905); (until 1960): Human Performance Progress Report
Related titles: Online - full text ed.: free (effective 2009).
Published by: Medical Research Council, Cognition and Brain Science Unit, 15 Chaucer Rd, Cambridge, CB2 7EF, United Kingdom. TEL 44-1223-355294, FAX 44-1223-359062, info@mrc-cbu.cam.ac.uk.

362.2 JPN ISSN 1346-8685
COGNITION AND DEMENTIA. Text in Japanese. 2002. q. JPY 8,764 (effective 2005). **Document type:** *Journal, Academic/Scholarly.*
Published by: Medikaru Rebyusha/Medical Review Co., Ltd., 1-7-3 Hirano-Machi, Chuo-ku, Yoshida Bldg., Osaka-shi, 541-0046, Japan. TEL 81-6-62231468, FAX 81-6-62231245.

616.8 USA ISSN 1543-3633
RC321 CODEN: CBNOA2
➤ **COGNITIVE AND BEHAVIORAL NEUROLOGY.** Text in English. 1988. q. USD 664 domestic to institutions; USD 840 foreign to institutions (effective 2011). adv. charts; illus. back issues avail.; reprints avail. **Document type:** *Journal, Academic/Scholarly.* **Description:** Presents research articles on basic brain processes, critical review articles, case reports, and brief reports on preliminary studies and pertinent clinical issues.
Formerly (until 2003): Neuropsychiatry, Neuropsychology and Behavioral Neurology (0894-878X)
Related titles: Online - full text ed.: ISSN 1543-3641.
Indexed: A20, A22, ASCA, B21, CurCont, E-psyche, EMBASE, ExcerpMed, FR, IndMed, Inpharma, MEDLINE, NSA, NSCI, P03, P30, P35, PsycInfo, PsycholAb, R10, RILM, Reac, SCI, SCOPUS, W07.
—BLDSC (3292.872870), GNLM, IE, Ingenta, INIST. **CCC.**
Published by: (Society for Behavioral and Cognitive Neurology, Behavioral Neurology Society), Lippincott Williams & Wilkins (Subsidiary of: Wolters Kluwer N.V.), Two Commerce Sq, 2001 Market St, Philadelphia, PA 19103. TEL 215-521-8300, FAX 215-521-8902, customerservice@lww.com, http://www.lww.com. Ed. Dr. Murray Grossman TEL 215-349-8463. Pub. Harry Dean. Adv. contact Michelle Smith TEL 646-674-6537. Circ: 163.

616.8 USA ISSN 1866-9956
BF309
▼ ➤ **COGNITIVE COMPUTATION.** Text in English. 2009. q. USD 441 combined subscription to institutions (print & online eds.) (effective 2011). back issues avail.; reprint service avail. from PSC. **Document type:** *Journal, Academic/Scholarly.*
Related titles: Online - full text ed.: ISSN 1866-9964 (from IngentaConnect).
Indexed: A22, CPEI, E01, P03, P30, PsycInfo, SCOPUS.
—IE. **CCC.**
Published by: Springer New York LLC (Subsidiary of: Springer Science+Business Media), 233 Spring St, New York, NY 10013. TEL 212-460-1500, FAX 212-460-1575, service-ny@springer.com. Eds. Amir Hussain, I Aleksander.

➤ **COGNITIVE NEURODYNAMICS.** see BIOLOGY—Physiology

616.8 GBR ISSN 0264-3294
QP360 CODEN: COGNEP
➤ **COGNITIVE NEUROPSYCHOLOGY.** Text in English. 1984. 8/yr. GBP 1,229 combined subscription in United Kingdom to institutions (print & online eds.); EUR 1,620, USD 2,036 combined subscription to institutions (print & online eds.) (effective 2012). adv. bk.rev. illus. Index. back issues avail.; reprint service avail. from PSC. **Document type:** *Journal, Academic/Scholarly.* **Description:** Covers cognitive processes from a neuropsychological perspective.
Related titles: Online - full text ed.: ISSN 1464-0627. 1996. GBP 1,106 in United Kingdom to institutions; EUR 1,458, USD 1,832 to institutions (effective 2012) (from IngentaConnect).
Indexed: A01, A03, A08, A20, A22, AMED, ASCA, ASSIA, B21, B25, BDM&CN, BIOSIS Prev, CA, CurCont, E-psyche, E01, EMBASE, ExcerpMed, FR, L&LBA, L11, MEDLINE, MLA-IB, MycolAb, NSA, NSCI, P03, P30, P43, PsycInfo, PsycholAb, R10, RILM, Reac, SCI, SCOPUS, SOPODA, SSCI, T02, W07.
—GNLM, IE, Infotrieve, Ingenta, INIST. **CCC.**
Published by: Psychology Press (Subsidiary of: Taylor & Francis Ltd.), 27 Church Rd, Hove, E Sussex BN3 2FA, United Kingdom. TEL 44-20-70176000, FAX 44-20-70176717, info@psypress.co.uk, http://www.psypress.com. Ed. Alfonso Caramazza. Adv. contact Linda Hann TEL 44-1344-779945.

616.8 GBR ISSN 1758-8928
QP360.5
▼ **COGNITIVE NEUROSCIENCE.** Text in English. 2010. q. GBP 223 combined subscription in United Kingdom to institutions (print & online eds.); EUR 294, USD 367 combined subscription to institutions (print & online eds.) (effective 2012). **Document type:** *Journal, Academic/Scholarly.* **Description:** Aims to publish empirical and theoretical papers on any topic in the field of cognitive neuroscience.
Related titles: Online - full text ed.: ISSN 1758-8936. GBP 201 in United Kingdom to institutions; EUR 265, USD 331 to institutions (effective 2012).
Indexed: A01, B21, NSA, P30, PsycInfo, SCI, W07.
—**CCC.**
Published by: Psychology Press (Subsidiary of: Taylor & Francis Ltd.), 27 Church Rd, Hove, E Sussex BN3 2FA, United Kingdom. TEL 44-20-70177747, FAX 44-20-70176717, info@psypress.co.uk. Ed. Jamie Ward.

616.8 ITA ISSN 1724-4927
COGNITIVISMO CLINICO. Text in Italian. 2004. s-a. EUR 18 to individuals; EUR 28 to institutions (effective 2008). **Document type:** *Journal, Academic/Scholarly.*
Indexed: A26, I05.
Published by: Giovanni Fioriti Editore, Via Archimede 179, Rome, 00197, Italy. TEL 39-06-8072063, FAX 39-06-80664609, info@fioriti.it, http://www.fioriti.it.

616.8 ARG ISSN 1667-9105
COLECCION TRABAJOS DISTINGUIDOS. SERIE SALUD MENTAL. Text in Spanish. 1998. 6/yr. back issues avail. **Document type:** *Journal, Academic/Scholarly.*
Media: Online - full text.
Published by: Sociedad Iberoamericana de Informacion Cientifica (S I I C), Ave Belgrano 430, Buenos Aires, C1092AAR, Argentina. TEL 54-11-43424901, FAX 54-11-43313305, atencionallector@siicsalud.com, http://www.siicsalud.com. Ed. Rafael Bernal Castro.

COLLANA DI PSICOLOGIA CLINICA E PSICOTERAPIA PSICOANALITICA. see PSYCHOLOGY

COMMON DIAGNOSTIC PROCEDURES: ORTHOPEDICS AND NEUROLOGY. see LAW

COMMUNICATION OUTLOOK; focusing on communication aids and techniques. see COMPUTERS—Artificial Intelligence

COMMUNITY MENTAL HEALTH JOURNAL. see SOCIAL SERVICES AND WELFARE

COMMUNITY MENTAL HEALTH REPORT. see SOCIAL SERVICES AND WELFARE

616.834 CAN ISSN 1495-1932
COMPASS; navigating life with multiple sclerosis. Text in English. 2000. q. **Document type:** *Magazine, Consumer.*
Related titles: French ed.: Compas. ISSN 1495-1940.
Published by: Parkhurst Publishing, 400 McGill St, 3rd Fl, Montreal, PQ H2Y 2G1, Canada. TEL 514-397-8833, FAX 514-397-0228, contact@parkpub.com, http://www.parkpub.com.

COMPASS (WOKINGHAM); the global MS nurse journal. see MEDICAL SCIENCES—Nurses And Nursing

COMPREHENSIVE ACCREDITATION MANUAL FOR BEHAVIORAL HEALTH CARE. see SOCIAL SERVICES AND WELFARE

616.89 USA ISSN 0010-440X
RC321 CODEN: COPYAV
➤ **COMPREHENSIVE PSYCHIATRY.** Text in English. 1960. bi-m. USD 658 in United States to institutions; USD 785 elsewhere to institutions (effective 2012). adv. bk.rev. abstr.; bibl.; charts; illus. index. back issues avail.; reprints avail. **Document type:** *Journal, Academic/Scholarly.* **Description:** Covers developments in clinical and basic investigations, as well as new diagnostic and therapeutic practices.
Related titles: Online - full text ed.: ISSN 1532-8384 (from ScienceDirect).
Indexed: A20, A22, A26, A34, A36, AMHA, ASCA, AbAn, AddicA, B25, BIOSIS Prev, C06, C07, C08, CA, CABA, CINAHL, ChemAb, CurCont, DentInd, E-psyche, E01, E12, EMBASE, ExcerpMed, F09, FR, FamI, GH, H12, I05, IBR, IBZ, ISR, IndMed, Inpharma, JW-P, MEA&I, MEDLINE, MycolAb, N02, N03, NRN, P03, P30, P35, PsycInfo, PsycholAb, R10, R12, Reac, S02, S03, SCI, SCOPUS, SSCI, T02, T05, VS, W07.
—BLDSC (3366.390000), GNLM, IE, Infotrieve, Ingenta, INIST. **CCC.**
Published by: (American Psychopathological Association), W.B. Saunders Co. (Subsidiary of: Elsevier Health Sciences), Elsevier, Health Sciences Division, Order Fulfillment, 3251 Riverport Ln, Maryland Heights, MO 63043. TEL 314-872-8370, 800-325-4177, FAX 314-432-1380, JournalCustomerService-usa@elsevier.com, http://www.us.elsevierhealth.com. Ed. Dr. David L Dunner. Pub. Peter Bakker. Adv. contact John Marmero TEL 212-633-3657.

616.8 GBR ISSN 1029-2136
CONCEPTUAL ADVANCES IN BRAIN RESEARCH. Text in English. 2000. irreg., latest 2009. price varies. back issues avail.; reprints avail. **Document type:** *Monographic series, Academic/Scholarly.*
Related titles: Online - full text ed.: ISSN 2155-2517.
—BLDSC (3399.414520).
Published by: Routledge (Subsidiary of: Taylor & Francis Group), 4 Park Sq, Milton Park, Abingdon, Oxon OX14 4RN, United Kingdom. TEL 44-20-70176000, FAX 44-20-70176336, subscriptions@tandf.co.uk, http://www.routledge.com. **Subscr. to:** Taylor & Francis Ltd., Journals Customer Service, Sheepen Pl, Colchester, Essex CO3 3LP, United Kingdom. TEL 44-20-70175544, FAX 44-20-70175198, tf.enquiries@tfinforma.com.

616.6 ITA ISSN 1122-0279
➤ **CONFINIA CEPHALALGICA.** Text in Italian. 1992. 4/yr. free to members. adv. **Document type:** *Journal, Academic/Scholarly.*
Indexed: A20, A22, ASCA, E-psyche, EMBASE, ExcerpMed, R10, Reac, SCOPUS.
—GNLM, IE, Ingenta. **CCC.**
Published by: Centro Italiano Ricerche Neurologiche Applicate, Via L Porta, Pavia, 27100, Italy. FAX 39-0382-303044, cirna@cefalea.it, http://www.cefalea.it.

➤ **CONGRESS QUARTERLY.** see MEDICAL SCIENCES—Surgery

616.8 USA
➤ **CONTEMPORARY CLINICAL NEUROSCIENCE.** Text in English. 2000. irreg., latest 2006. price varies. illus. back issues avail.; reprints avail. **Document type:** *Monographic series, Academic/Scholarly.* **Description:** Covers all aspects of clinical neuroscience and neurology.
Related titles: Online - full text ed.
Published by: Humana Press, Inc. (Subsidiary of: Springer Science+Business Media), 233 Spring St, New York, NY 10013. TEL 212-460-1500, FAX 212-460-1575, service-ny@springer.com. Eds. Helen Baghdoyan, Ralph Lydic.

616.8 GBR ISSN 0069-9446
CODEN: CNRSAG
➤ **CONTEMPORARY NEUROLOGY SERIES.** Text in English. 1966. irreg., latest 2008. price varies. back issues avail. **Document type:** *Monographic series, Academic/Scholarly.*
Indexed: A22, ChemAb, E-psyche, IndMed, P30.
—BLDSC (3425.193000), CASDDS, GNLM, IE, Infotrieve, Ingenta. **CCC.**
Published by: Oxford University Press, Great Clarendon St, Oxford, OX2 6DP, United Kingdom. TEL 44-1865-556767, FAX 44-1865-556646, enquiry@oup.co.uk, http://www.oup.co.uk/. Ed. Sid Gilman.

616.8 USA ISSN 1061-5954
➤ **CONTEMPORARY NEUROSCIENCE.** Text and summaries in English. 1983. irreg., latest 2006. price varies. back issues avail. **Document type:** *Monographic series, Academic/Scholarly.* **Description:** Offers the latest news and concepts in neuroscience.
Related titles: Online - full text ed.
Indexed: E-psyche.
—**CCC.**
Published by: Humana Press, Inc. (Subsidiary of: Springer Science+Business Media), 233 Spring St, New York, NY 10013. TEL 212-460-1500, FAX 212-460-1575, service-ny@springer.com.

➤ **CONTEMPORARY NEUROSURGERY.** see MEDICAL SCIENCES—Surgery

616.89 USA ISSN 1080-2371
CONTINUUM (BALTIMORE); lifelong learning in neurology. Text in English. 1994. bi-m. USD 1,059 domestic to institutions; USD 1,188 foreign to institutions (effective 2011). back issues avail. **Document type:** *Journal, Academic/Scholarly.* **Description:** Provides an interactive continuing medical education program in neurology.
Related titles: Online - full text ed.: ISSN 1538-6899.
Indexed: E-psyche, EMBASE, ExcerpMed, P03, PsycInfo, R10, Reac, SCOPUS.
—BLDSC (3425.720520), IE, Ingenta. **CCC.**
Published by: (American Academy of Neurology), Lippincott Williams & Wilkins (Subsidiary of: Wolters Kluwer N.V.), 351 W Camden St, Baltimore, MD 21201. TEL 410-528-4000, FAX 410-528-4312, customerservice@lww.com. Ed. Dr. Aaron E Miller.

616.891 ITA ISSN 1590-0223
CONTRAPPUNTI. Text in Italian. 1987. 2/yr. bk.rev. **Document type:** *Monographic series, Academic/Scholarly.* **Description:** The periodical hosts a number of original studies on the problematics of psychotherapeutic techniques or psychopsychology.
Published by: Edizioni Cadmo, Via Benedetto da Maiano 3, Fiesole, FI 50014, Italy. TEL 39-055-5018206, FAX 39-055-5018201, cadmo@casalini.it, http://www.cadmo.com. **Dist. by:** Casalini Libri, Via Benedetto da Maiano 3, Fiesole, FI 50014, Italy.

▼ **CONTROVERSIES IN NEURO-ONCOLOGY.** see MEDICAL SCIENCES—Oncology

616.8 100 301 FRA ISSN 0335-7899
➤ **LE COQ HERON.** Text in French. 1969. q. EUR 60 domestic to individuals; EUR 65 domestic to institutions; EUR 72 foreign (effective 2011). back issues avail. **Document type:** *Journal, Academic/Scholarly.*
Related titles: Online - full text ed.: ISSN 1951-6290. 2006.
Indexed: FR.
—INIST.
Published by: (Le Coq Heron), Editions Eres, 33 Av. Marcel Dassault, Toulouse, 31500, France. TEL 33-5-61751576, FAX 33-5-61735289, eres@edition-eres.com. Circ: 1,000.

➤ **CORRECTIONAL MENTAL HEALTH REPORT.** see CRIMINOLOGY AND LAW ENFORCEMENT

➤ **CORRESPONDANCES EN NEUROLOGIE VASCULAIRE.** see MEDICAL SCIENCES—Cardiovascular Diseases

616.8 ITA ISSN 0010-9452
QP351
➤ **CORTEX.** Text in English. 1964. 10/yr. EUR 1,249 in Europe to institutions; JPY 197,600 in Japan to institutions; USD 1,873 elsewhere to institutions (effective 2012). adv. bk.rev. charts. index. reprints avail. **Document type:** *Journal, Academic/Scholarly.* **Description:** Devoted to the study of the nervous system and behaviour.
Related titles: Microform ed.: (from PQC, SWZ); Online - full text ed.: ISSN 1973-8102. 1997 (from ScienceDirect).
Indexed: A20, A22, A29, AMED, ASCA, B20, B21, B25, BAS, BDM&CN, BIOBASE, BIOSIS Prev, BibInd, C06, C07, C08, CA, CINAHL, ChemoAb, CurCont, DentInd, E-psyche, EMBASE, ESPM, ErgAb, ExcerpMed, I10, IABS, ISR, IndMed, Inpharma, L&LBA, MEDLINE, MycolAb, NSA, NSCI, P03, P30, PsycInfo, PsycholAb, R10, Reac, SCI, SCOPUS, ViroIAbstr, W07, YAE&RB.
—BLDSC (3477.150000), GNLM, IE, Infotrieve, Ingenta, INIST. **CCC.**
Published by: Elsevier Masson (Subsidiary of: Elsevier Health Sciences), Via Paleocapa 7, Milan, 20121, Italy. TEL 39-02-881841, FAX 39-02-88184302, info@masson.it, http://www.masson.it. Ed. Sergio Della Sala.

616.891 ITA ISSN 1721-9612
➤ **COSTRUZIONI PSICOANALITICHE.** Text in Italian. 2001. s-a. EUR 39.50 combined subscription domestic to institutions (print & online eds.); EUR 51 combined subscription foreign to institutions (print & online eds.) (effective 2009). **Document type:** *Journal, Academic/Scholarly.*
Related titles: Online - full text ed.: ISSN 1972-5744.
Published by: (Istituto di Psicoterapia Psicoanalitica della Cooperativa Sociale Icaro 2000), Franco Angeli Edizioni, Viale Monza 106, Milan, 20127, Italy. TEL 39-02-2837141, FAX 39-02-26144793, redazioni@francoangeli.it, http://www.francoangeli.it.

616.891 GBR ISSN 2045-4260
COUNSELLING CHILDREN AND YOUNG PEOPLE. Text in English. 19??. q. free to members (effective 2010). **Document type:** *Journal, Trade.* **Description:** Promotes and access research into counselling with children and young people.
Formerly (until 2005): Counselling in Education Journal
Published by: British Association for Counselling & Psychotherapy, BACP House, 15 St John's Business Park, Lutterworth, Leicestershire LE17 4HB, United Kingdom. TEL 44-1455-883300, FAX 44-1455-550243, bacp@bacp.co.uk, http://www.bacp.co.uk.

COUNSELLING PSYCHOLOGY QUARTERLY. see PSYCHOLOGY

362.29 362.2 FRA ISSN 1294-2561
LE COURRIER DES ADDICTIONS. Text in Multiple languages. 1998. q. EUR 75 in Europe to individuals; EUR 75 DOM-TOM to individuals; EUR 75 in Africa to individuals; EUR 87 elsewhere to individuals; EUR 96 in Europe to institutions; EUR 96 DOM-TOM to institutions; EUR 96 in Africa to institutions; EUR 108 elsewhere to institutions (effective 2009). **Document type:** *Journal, Academic/Scholarly.*
—INIST.
Published by: Edimark S.A.S., 2 Rue Sainte-Marie, Courbevoie, Cedex 92418, France. TEL 33-1-46676300, FAX 33-1-46676310, contact@edimark.fr.

COURTROOM MEDICINE: PSYCHIC INJURIES. see LAW

616.8 364 GBR ISSN 0957-9664
HV6080 CODEN: CBMHEE
➤ **CRIMINAL BEHAVIOUR AND MENTAL HEALTH.** Abbreviated title: C M B H. Text in English. 1991. 5/yr. GBP 337 in United Kingdom to institutions; EUR 427 in Europe to institutions; USD 662 elsewhere to institutions; GBP 387 combined subscription in United Kingdom to institutions (print & online eds.); EUR 491 combined subscription in Europe to institutions (print & online eds.); USD 762 combined subscription elsewhere to institutions (print & online eds.) (effective 2012). adv. bk.rev. charts; illus.; stat. index. back issues avail.; reprint service avail. from PSC. **Document type:** *Journal, Academic/Scholarly.* **Description:** This journal is intended for psychiatrists and psychologists who work with mentally abnormal offenders, violent patients, or who are engaged in research or teaching on crime or the criminal justice system.
Related titles: Online - full text ed.: ISSN 1471-2857. GBP 337 in United Kingdom to institutions; EUR 427 in Europe to institutions; USD 662 elsewhere to institutions (effective 2012) (from IngentaConnect).
Indexed: A01, A02, A03, A08, A22, AC&P, ASSIA, AddicA, C06, C07, CA, CJA, CJPI, CurCont, E-psyche, EMBASE, ExcerpMed, IBR, IBZ, MEDLINE, P03, P25, P30, P43, P48, PAIS, PQC, PsycInfo, PsycholAb, R10, Reac, S02, S03, SCOPUS, SOPODA, SSA, SSCI, SociolAb, T02, W07.
—BLDSC (3487.346200), IE, Infotrieve, Ingenta. **CCC.**
Published by: John Wiley & Sons Ltd. (Subsidiary of: John Wiley & Sons, Inc.), 1-7 Oldlands Way, PO Box 808, Bognor Regis, West Sussex PO21 9FF, United Kingdom. TEL 44-1865-778315, FAX 44-1243-843232, cs-journals@wiley.com, http://eu.wiley.com/WileyCDA/. Eds. David Farrington, John Gunn, Mary McMurran. **Subscr. to:** 1-7 Oldlands Way, PO Box 809, Bognor Regis, West Sussex PO21 9FG, United Kingdom. TEL 44-1865-778054, cs-agency@wiley.com.

616.832 ESP ISSN 1695-7377
CUADERNOS DE ESCLEROSIS MULTIPLE. Text in Spanish. 1998. q. **Document type:** *Journal, Trade.*
—**CCC.**
Published by: Fundacion Espanola de Esclerosis Multiple, c/ Principe de Vergara 58, Madrid, 28006, Spain. TEL 34-91-4312604, FAX 34-91-4313933, fedem@mx2.redestb.es.

616 ESP ISSN 1695-4246
CUADERNOS DE MEDICINA PSICOSOMATICA Y PSIQUIATRIA. Text in Spanish. 1984. q. EUR 46 domestic; USD 64 foreign (effective 2009). **Document type:** *Magazine, Consumer.*
Former titles (until 1995): Cuadernos de Medicina Psicosomatica (1132-0273); (until 1987): Cuadernos de Medicina Psicosomatica y Sexologia (1132-0281); (until 1985): Cuadernos de Medicina Conductal y Sexologica (0213-1218)
Related titles: Online - full text ed.: ISSN 1695-4238. 2001.
Published by: Editorial Medica, C/ Gamonal 5, 5a Planta, No 9, Edificio Valencia, Madrid, 28031, Spain. contacto@editorialmedica.com.

616.8 CHL
CUADERNOS DE NEUROLOGIA. Text in Spanish. irreg. back issues avail.
Related titles: Online - full text ed.
Published by: Pontificia Universidad Catolica de Chile, Escuela de Medicina, Ave. Vicuna Mackenna 4360, Santiago, Chile.

616.89 ESP ISSN 1578-9594
CUADERNOS DE PSIQUIATRIA COMUNITARIA. Text in Spanish. 2001. s-a. EUR 18 (effective 2007). back issues avail. **Document type:** *Journal, Academic/Scholarly.*
Related titles: Online - full text ed.
Published by: Asociacion Asturiana de Neuropsiquiatria y Salud Mental, C Magellanes, 1 Sotano 2 Local 4, Madrid, Asturias 28015, Spain. TEL 34-91-6367255, FAX 34-91-8473182, aen@aen.es, http://www.aen.es/. Ed. Fernando Colina.

616.89 ESP ISSN 1575-5967
CUADERNOS DE PSIQUIATRIA Y PSICOTERAPIA DEL NINO Y DEL ADOLESCENTE. Text in Spanish. 1985. s-a. **Document type:** *Journal, Academic/Scholarly.*
Formerly (until 1998): Cuadernos de Psiquiatria y Psicoterapia Infantil (1133-0805)
Published by: Sociedad Espanola de Psiquiatria y Psicoterapia del Nino y del Adolescente, Villanueva, 11 2o., Madrid, 28001, Spain. sepypna@inicia.es.

CULTURE, MEDICINE AND PSYCHIATRY; an international journal of comparative cross-cultural research. *see* ANTHROPOLOGY

CURRENT ADVANCES IN NEUROSCIENCE. *see* MEDICAL SCIENCES—Abstracting, Bibliographies, Statistics

616.8 NLD ISSN 1567-2050
RC523 CODEN: CARUBY
➤ **CURRENT ALZHEIMER RESEARCH.** Text in English. 2004. 10/yr. USD 1,030 to institutions (print or online ed.) (effective 2012). adv. back issues avail.; reprints avail. **Document type:** *Journal, Academic/Scholarly.* **Description:** Publishes frontier review and research articles on all areas of Alzheimer's disease.
Related titles: Online - full text ed.: ISSN 1875-5828 (from IngentaConnect).
Indexed: A01, A03, A08, A20, ASG, B21, BIOBASE, BIOSIS Prev, C33, CA, EMBASE, ExcerpMed, IABS, MEDLINE, MycolAb, NSA, NSCI, P03, P30, PsycInfo, PsycholAb, R10, Reac, RefZh, SCI, SCOPUS, T02, W07.
—BLDSC (3494.127500), IE, Ingenta. **CCC.**
Published by: Bentham Science Publishers Ltd., PO Box 294, Bussum, 1400 AG, Netherlands. TEL 31-35-6923800, FAX 31-35-6980150, sales@bentham.org. Ed. Debomoy K Lahiri. **Subscr. to:** Bentham Science Publishers Ltd., c/o Richard E Morrissy, PO Box 446, Oak Park, IL 60301. TEL 312-413-5867, FAX 312-996-7107, subscriptions@bentham.org.

616.8 USA ISSN 1559-0585
➤ **CURRENT CLINICAL NEUROLOGY.** Text and summaries in English. 1997. irreg., latest 2010. price varies. bk.rev. illus. back issues avail. **Document type:** *Monographic series, Academic/Scholarly.* **Description:** Discusses treatment protocols for neurological diseases and conditions.
Related titles: Online - full text ed.
Published by: Humana Press, Inc. (Subsidiary of: Springer Science+Business Media), 233 Spring St, New York, NY 10013. TEL 212-460-1500, FAX 212-460-1575, service-ny@springer.com. Ed. Daniel Tarsy.

616.8 USA ISSN 1932-1074
RC348
CURRENT DIAGNOSIS AND TREATMENT IN NEUROLOGY. Text in English. 2006 (Sept.). irreg., latest 2006, 1st ed. USD 64.95 1st ed. (effective 2008). **Document type:** *Handbook/Manual/Guide, Trade.* **Description:** Provides a reference for primary care physicians managing patients with neurologic disorders.
Published by: McGraw-Hill Companies, Inc., 1221 Ave of the Americas, 43rd fl, New York, NY 10020. TEL 212-512-2000, customer.service@mcgraw-hill.com, http://www.mcgraw-hill.com.

616.0472 NLD ISSN 0923-2354
CODEN: CMPAEH
➤ **CURRENT MANAGEMENT OF PAIN.** Text in English. 1988. irreg., latest vol.9, 1991. price varies. **Document type:** *Monographic series, Academic/Scholarly.* **Description:** Aims to provide up-to-date information on advances in the clinical management of acute and chronic pain and related research.
Indexed: E-psyche.
—CCC.
Published by: Springer Netherlands (Subsidiary of: Springer Science+Business Media), Van Godewijckstraat 30, Dordrecht, 3311 GX, Netherlands. TEL 31-78-6576050, FAX 31-78-6576474. Ed. Raj P Prithvi.

016.8 GBR ISSN 1356-6237
CODEN: CMLNEZ
➤ **CURRENT MEDICAL LITERATURE. NEUROLOGY.** Text in English. 1984. q. GBP 60 to individuals; GBP 130 to institutions; free to qualified personnel (effective 2009). back issues avail. **Document type:** *Journal, Academic/Scholarly.* **Description:** Aims to provide physicians and allied healthcare professionals with rapid access to expert commentary and analysis on key topics in neurology.
Former titles (until 1994): Current Medical Literature. Neurology and Neurosurgery (1356-6245); (until 1991): Current Medical Literature. Neurology (0267-0445)
Related titles: Online - full text ed.: ISSN 1759-815X.
Indexed: A01, A03, A08, CA, E-psyche, T02.
—CCC.
Published by: Remedica Medical Education and Publishing Ltd., Commonwealth House, 1 New Oxford St, London, WC1A 1NU, United Kingdom. TEL 44-20-77592999, FAX 44-20-77592951, info@remedica.com, http://www.remedica.com. Ed. Andrew McCormick.

016.8 GBR ISSN 0957-770X
CODEN: CMLPF9
➤ **CURRENT MEDICAL LITERATURE. PSYCHIATRY.** Text in English. 1990. q. GBP 60 to individuals; GBP 130 to institutions; free to qualified personnel (effective 2009). back issues avail. **Document type:** *Journal, Academic/Scholarly.* **Description:** Aims to provide physicians and allied healthcare professionals with rapid access to expert commentary and analysis on key topics in psychiatry.
Related titles: Online - full text ed.: ISSN 1759-8184.
Indexed: A01, A03, A08, CA, E-psyche, T02.
—CCC.
Published by: Remedica Medical Education and Publishing Ltd., Commonwealth House, 1 New Oxford St, London, WC1A 1NU, United Kingdom. TEL 44-20-77592999, FAX 44-20-77592951, info@remedica.com, http://www.remedica.com. Ed. Lesley Ezekiel.

➤ **CURRENT NEUROLOGIC DRUGS.** *see* PHARMACY AND PHARMACOLOGY

610 USA ISSN 1528-4042
RC346
CURRENT NEUROLOGY AND NEUROSCIENCE REPORTS. Text in English. 6/yr. reprint service avail. from PSC. **Document type:** *Journal, Academic/Scholarly.*
Related titles: Online - full text ed.: ISSN 1534-6293. EUR 870, USD 1,158 to institutions (effective 2010).
Indexed: A22, A26, E01, EMBASE, ExcerpMed, H12, I05, MEDLINE, NSCI, P20, P22, P25, P30, P48, P54, PQC, SCI, SCOPUS, W07.
—BLDSC (3500.632000), IE, Ingenta. **CCC.**
Published by: Current Medicine Group LLC (Subsidiary of: Springer Science+Business Media), 400 Market St, Ste 700, Philadelphia, PA 19106. TEL 215-574-2266, 800-427-1796, FAX 215-574-2225, info@phl.cursci.com, http://www.current-medicine.com. Eds. John Brust, Stanley Fahn.

616.8 615.1 NLD ISSN 1570-159X
RM315 CODEN: CNUEAN
➤ **CURRENT NEUROPHARMACOLOGY.** Text in English. 2003 (Mar.). q. USD 820 to institutions (print or online ed.) (effective 2012). adv. back issues avail.; reprints avail. **Document type:** *Journal, Academic/Scholarly.* **Description:** Aims to provide current, timely and comprehensive reviews of all areas of neuropharmacology and related matters of neuroscience.
Related titles: Online - full text ed.: ISSN 1875-6190 (from IngentaConnect).
Indexed: A01, A03, A08, B21, BIOSIS Prev, C33, CA, EMBASE, ExcerpMed, MycolAb, NSA, NSCI, P03, P30, PsycInfo, PsycholAb, R10, Reac, SCI, SCOPUS, T02, W07.
—BLDSC (3500.636000), IE, Ingenta. **CCC.**
Published by: Bentham Science Publishers Ltd., PO Box 294, Bussum, 1400 AG, Netherlands. TEL 31-35-6923800, FAX 31-35-6980150, sales@bentham.org, http://www.bentham.org. Ed. Thomas E Salt. **Subscr. to:** Bentham Science Publishers Ltd., c/o Richard E Morrissy, PO Box 446, Oak Park, IL 60301. TEL 312-413-5867, FAX 312-996-7107, subscriptions@bentham.org.

616.8 NLD ISSN 1567-2026
RC388.5
CURRENT NEUROVASCULAR RESEARCH. Abbreviated title: C N R. Text in English. 2004. q. USD 610 to institutions (print or online ed.) (effective 2012). adv. back issues avail.; reprints avail. **Document type:** *Journal, Academic/Scholarly.* **Description:** Provides a cross platform for the publication of scientifically rigorous research that addresses disease mechanisms of both neuronal and vascular origins in neuroscience.
Related titles: Online - full text ed.: ISSN 1875-5739 (from IngentaConnect).
Indexed: A01, A03, A08, B21, B25, BIOBASE, BIOSIS Prev, CA, CurCont, EMBASE, ExcerpMed, IABS, Inpharma, MEDLINE, MycolAb, NSA, NSCI, P30, P35, R10, Reac, SCI, SCOPUS, T02, W07.
—IE, Ingenta. **CCC.**
Published by: Bentham Science Publishers Ltd., PO Box 294, Bussum, 1400 AG, Netherlands. TEL 31-35-6923800, FAX 31-35-6980150, sales@bentham.org, http://www.bentham.org. Ed. Kenneth Maiese. **Subscr. to:** Bentham Science Publishers Ltd., c/o Richard E Morrissy, PO Box 446, Oak Park, IL 60301. TEL 312-413-5867, FAX 312-996-7107, subscriptions@bentham.org.

616.8 573.8 GBR ISSN 0959-4388
QP351 CODEN: COPUEN
➤ **CURRENT OPINION IN NEUROBIOLOGY.** Text in English. 1991. bi-m. EUR 1,742 in Europe to institutions; JPY 241,600 in Japan to institutions; USD 1,947 elsewhere to institutions (effective 2012). adv. bibl.; illus. back issues avail. **Document type:** *Journal, Academic/Scholarly.* **Description:** Provides infromation to researchers, educators and students of neurobiology. Presents review articles, followed by annotated bibliographies of references consulted. Includes a "Paper Alert" section, giving brief summaries of relevant papers recently published in other journals.
Related titles: CD-ROM ed.; Online - full text ed.: ISSN 1873-6882 (from IngentaConnect, ScienceDirect).
Indexed: A01, A03, A08, A20, A22, A26, ASCA, AnBeAb, B21, BIOBASE, BIOSIS Prev, C33, CA, CIN, CMCI, ChemAb, ChemTitl, ChemoAb, CurCont, E-psyche, E01, EMBASE, ExcerpMed, GenetAb, I05, IABS, ISR, IndMed, Inpharma, MEDLINE, MycolAb, NSA, NSCI, NucAcAb, P03, P30, PsycInfo, PsycholAb, R10, Reac, S01, SCI, SCOPUS, T02, W07.
—BLDSC (3500.775850), CASDDS, GNLM, IE, Infotrieve, Ingenta, INIST. **CCC.**
Published by: Elsevier Ltd., Current Opinion Journals (Subsidiary of: Elsevier Science & Technology), 84 Theobald's Rd, London, WC1X 8RR, United Kingdom. TEL 44-20-76114000, FAX 44-20-76114485, JournalsCustomerServiceEMEA@elsevier.com. Eds. Marc Tessier-Lavigne, Tobias Bonhoeffer.

616.8 USA ISSN 1350-7540
RC346 CODEN: CONEEX
➤ **CURRENT OPINION IN NEUROLOGY.** Text in English. 1988. bi-m. USD 1,254 domestic to institutions; USD 1,346 foreign to institutions (effective 2011). adv. bibl.; illus. back issues avail.; reprints avail. **Document type:** *Journal, Academic/Scholarly.* **Description:** Covers key subjects such as neuro-ophthalmology and neuro-otology, cerebrovascular disease, developmental disorders, seizure disorders, demyelinating diseases, headache, and degenerative diseases.
Formerly (until 1993): Current Opinion in Neurology and Neurosurgery (0951-7383)
Related titles: Diskette ed.; Online - full text ed.: ISSN 1473-6551. USD 266 to individuals (effective 2011); Optical Disk - DVD ed.: Current Opinion in Neurology, with Evaluated MEDLINE. ISSN 1080-8248.
Indexed: A22, ASCA, B21, BIOBASE, BIOSIS Prev, C06, C07, C08, CINAHL, CurCont, E-psyche, E01, EMBASE, ExcerpMed, IABS, IBR, IBZ, ISR, IndMed, Inpharma, MEDLINE, MycolAb, NSA, NSCI, P30, R10, Reac, SCI, SCOPUS, W07.
—BLDSC (3500.775870), GNLM, IE, Infotrieve, Ingenta, INIST. **CCC.**
Published by: Lippincott Williams & Wilkins (Subsidiary of: Wolters Kluwer N.V.), 530 Walnut St, Philadelphia, PA 19106. TEL 215-521-8300, FAX 215-521-8902, customerservice@lww.com, http://www.lww.com. Ed. Richard S J Frackowiak. Pub. Ian Burgess. Circ: 909.

616.8 USA ISSN 0951-7367
RC321 CODEN: COPPE8
➤ **CURRENT OPINION IN PSYCHIATRY.** Text in English. 1987. bi-m. USD 1,248 domestic to institutions; USD 1,342 foreign to institutions (effective 2011). adv. bibl.; illus. back issues avail.; reprints avail. **Document type:** *Journal, Academic/Scholarly.* **Description:** Covers key subjects such as personality disorders and neuroses, mood disorders, center for health studies, schizophrenia, behavioural medicine, addictive disorders, neuropsychiatry, child and adolescent psychiatry etc.
Related titles: Diskette ed.; Online - full text ed.: ISSN 1473-6578. USD 273 to individuals (effective 2011); Optical Disk - DVD ed.: Current Opinion in Psychiatry, with Evaluated MEDLINE. ISSN 1080-8191. 1995. USD 317 (effective 2006).
Indexed: A20, A22, ASCA, AddicA, B21, C06, C07, C08, CINAHL, CurCont, E-psyche, E01, EMBASE, ExcerpMed, FoP, FamI, H13, Inpharma, MEDLINE, NSA, P02, P03, P10, P20, P30, P48, P53, P54, PQC, PsycInfo, PsycholAb, R10, Reac, SCI, SCOPUS, SSCI, W07.
—BLDSC (3500.777000), GNLM, IE, Infotrieve, Ingenta. **CCC.**
Published by: Lippincott Williams & Wilkins (Subsidiary of: Wolters Kluwer N.V.), 530 Walnut St, Philadelphia, PA 19106. TEL 215-521-8300, FAX 215-521-8902, customerservice@lww.com, http://www.lww.com. Eds. Dr. David J Kupfer, Dr. Norman Sartorius. Pub. Ian Burgess. Circ: 512.

616 USA ISSN 1531-3433
RC392
CURRENT PAIN AND HEADACHE REPORTS. Text in English. 1994. bi-m. bibl.; illus. reprint service avail. from PSC. **Document type:** *Journal, Academic/Scholarly.* **Description:** Covers pain management and headache; topics include: chronic visceral pain, cluster headache, neuropathic pain, migraine headache, cancer pain, uncommon headache, syndrome, fibromyalgia, cervicogenic headache, myofascial pain, tension-type headache, anesthetic techniques in, pain management, chronic daily headache.
Formerly (until 2001): Current Review of Pain (1069-5850)
Related titles: Online - full text ed.: ISSN 1534-3081. EUR 870, USD 1,158 to institutions (effective 2010).
Indexed: A20, A22, A26, C06, C07, CurCont, E-psyche, E01, EMBASE, ExcerpMed, H12, I05, IndMed, MEDLINE, NSCI, P30, R10, Reac, SCI, SCOPUS, W07.
—BLDSC (3500.950000), IE, Infotrieve, Ingenta. **CCC.**
Published by: Current Medicine Group LLC (Subsidiary of: Springer Science+Business Media), 400 Market St, Ste 700, Philadelphia, PA 19106. TEL 215-574-2266, 800-427-1796, FAX 215-574-2225, info@phl.cursci.com, http://www.current-medicine.com. Ed. Stephen Silberstein.

616.853 FRA ISSN 0950-4591
CODEN: CPEPES
CURRENT PROBLEMS IN EPILEPSY. Text in English. 1983. irreg. price varies. **Document type:** *Monographic series, Academic/Scholarly.*
Indexed: IBR, IBZ.
—BLDSC (3501.383400), IE, Ingenta.
Published by: John Libbey Eurotext, 127 Av. de la Republique, Montrouge, 92120, France. TEL 33-1-46730660, FAX 33-1-40840999, contact@jle.com.

616.8 USA ISSN 1934-8584
CURRENT PROTOCOLS IN NEUROSCIENCE. Abbreviated title: C P N S. Text in English. 1997. 3 base vols. plus q. updates. USD 725 to individuals base vols. & updates (effective 2010). adv. back issues avail.; reprints avail. **Document type:** *Journal, Academic/Scholarly.* **Description:** Helps to finding and adapting the best models and methods for all types of neuroscience experiments.
Related titles: CD-ROM ed.: USD 595 combined subscription to institutions for base vol. & updates; USD 350 renewals to institutions (effective 2006); Online - full text ed.: ISSN 1934-8576.
Indexed: EMBASE, MEDLINE, P30, R10, SCOPUS.
Published by: John Wiley & Sons, Inc., 111 River St, Hoboken, NJ 07030. TEL 201-748-6000, FAX 201-748-6088, info@wiley.com, http://www.wiley.com/WileyCDA/. **Subscr. outside the Americas to:** John Wiley & Sons Ltd.

616.89 USA ISSN 1537-8276
RC331
CURRENT PSYCHIATRY. Text in English. 2002 (Jan.). m. USD 110 domestic; USD 124 foreign (effective 2010). adv. **Document type:** *Journal, Academic/Scholarly.* **Description:** Provides clinicians with evidence-based, practical advise by leading authorities emphasizing solutions to common clinical problems.
Indexed: A26, G06, G07, H11, H12, I05, P30.
—BLDSC (3501.555000), IE, Ingenta. **CCC.**
Published by: Quadrant HealthCom, 7 Century Dr, Ste 302, Parsippany, NJ 07054. TEL 973-206-3434, FAX 973-206-9378, http://www.quadranthealth.com. adv.: B&W page USD 4,755, color page USD 6,800; trim 7.8 x 10.75. Circ: 39,203 (paid and controlled).

616.8 USA ISSN 1556-3162
RC321
CURRENT PSYCHIATRY IN PRIMARY CARE. Text in English. 2005. m. USD 110 domestic; USD 124 foreign; free to qualified personnel (effective 2010). adv. back issues avail.; reprints avail. **Document type:** *Journal, Academic/Scholarly.* **Description:** Features practical clinical reviews that present the evidence on diagnosing and treating psychiatric disorders in a concise style.
Related titles: Online - full text ed.: ISSN 1556-3170.
Published by: Dowden Health Media, Inc (Subsidiary of: Lebhar-Friedman, Inc.), 110 Summit Ave, Montvale, NJ 07645. TEL 212-756-5000, FAX 201-391-2168, customerservice@dowdenhealth.com, http://www.dowdenhealth.com. Ed. Jeff Bauer. Pub. Kenneth A Sylvia. Adv. contact Maria Walsh TEL 201-740-6190.

616.89 USA ISSN 1523-3812
RC321
CURRENT PSYCHIATRY REPORTS. Text in English. 8/yr. reprint service avail. from PSC. **Document type:** *Journal, Academic/Scholarly.*
Related titles: Online - full text ed.: ISSN 1535-1645. EUR 870, USD 1,158 to institutions (effective 2010).

Indexed: A22, A26, C06, C07, CurCont, E01, E08, EMBASE, ExcerpMed, H12, IndMed, MEDLINE, P30, R10, Reac, S09, SCI, SCOPUS, SSCI, W07.
—BLDSC (3501.560000), IE, Infotrieve, Ingenta. **CCC.**
Published by: Current Medicine Group LLC (Subsidiary of: Springer Science+Business Media), 400 Market St, Ste 700, Philadelphia, PA 19106. TEL 215-574-2266, 800-427-1796, FAX 215-574-2225, info@phl.cursci.com, http://www.current-medicine.com. Eds. Dwight Evans, Robert Friedel. **Subscr. outside N America to:** Current Medicine Group Ltd., Middlesex House, 34-42 Cleveland St, London W1T 4LB, United Kingdom. TEL 44-20-73230323, FAX 44-20-75801938.

616.89 NLD ISSN 1573-4005
RC321
➤ **CURRENT PSYCHIATRY REVIEWS.** Text in English. 2005 (Jan). q. USD 480 to institutions (print or online ed.) (effective 2012). adv. back issues avail.; reprints avail. **Document type:** *Journal, Academic/Scholarly.* **Description:** Publishes frontier reviews on all the latest advances on clinical psychiatry and its related areas such as pharmacology, epidemiology, clinical care, and therapy.
Related titles: Online - full text ed.: ISSN 1875-6441 (from IngentaConnect).
Indexed: A01, CA, EMBASE, ExcerpMed, P03, P30, PsycInfo, PsycholAb, R10, Reac, SCOPUS, T02.
—BLDSC (3501.564000), IE, Ingenta. **CCC.**
Published by: Bentham Science Publishers Ltd., PO Box 294, Bussum, 1400 AG, Netherlands. TEL 31-35-6923800, FAX 31-35-6980150, sales@bentham.org, http://www.bentham.org. Ed. Michael E Thase TEL 215-746-6680. **Subscr. to:** Bentham Science Publishers Ltd., c/o Richard E Morrissy, PO Box 446, Oak Park, IL 60301. TEL 312-413-5867, FAX 312-996-7107, subscriptions@bentham.org.

▼ ➤ **CURRENT PSYCHOPHARMACOLOGY.** see PHARMACY AND PHARMACOLOGY

616.8 USA ISSN 1068-4093
CURRENT TECHNIQUES IN NEUROSURGERY. Text in English. 1993. irreg., latest 1998, 3rd ed. USD 275 per issue (effective 2010). back issues avail.; reprints avail. **Document type:** *Handbook/Manual/Guide, Academic/Scholarly.*
Indexed: E-psyche.
—GNLM. **CCC.**
Published by: Current Medicine Group LLC (Subsidiary of: Springer Science+Business Media), 400 Market St, Ste 700, Philadelphia, PA 19106. TEL 215-574-2266, FAX 215-574-2225, service-ny@springer.com, http://www.current-medicine.com/. Ed. Michael Salcman. **Subscr. outside N. America to:** Current Medicine Group Ltd.

616.8 USA ISSN 0891-7922
RC321
CURRENT THERAPY IN NEUROLOGIC DISEASE. Text in English. 1986. irreg., latest 2005. price varies. back issues avail. **Document type:** *Monographic series, Academic/Scholarly.*
Related titles: CD-ROM ed.
Indexed: E-psyche.
—CCC.
Published by: Mosby, Inc. (Subsidiary of: Elsevier Health Sciences), 1600 John F. Kennedy Blvd, Ste 1800, Philadelphia, PA 19103. http://www.us.elsevierhealth.com.

616.8 DEU ISSN 1866-3370
▼ **CURRENT TOPICS IN BEHAVIORAL NEUROSCIENCES.** Text in English. 2009. irreg., latest vol.8, 2011. price varies. **Document type:** *Monographic series, Academic/Scholarly.* **Description:** Provides a forum for research in important areas of behavioral neuroscience research.
Related titles: Online - full text ed.: ISSN 1866-3389. 2009.
—CCC.
Published by: Springer (Subsidiary of: Springer Science+Business Media), Tiergartenstr 17, Heidelberg, 69121, Germany. TEL 49-6221-4870, FAX 49-6221-345229, subscriptions@springer.com. Eds. Bart Ellenbroek, Charles Marsden, Mark A Geyer.

CURRENT TOPICS IN NEUROCHEMISTRY. see BIOLOGY—Biochemistry

616.8 USA ISSN 1092-8480
CODEN: CTONBT
CURRENT TREATMENT OPTIONS IN NEUROLOGY. Text in English. 1999. 6/yr. reprint service avail. from PSC.
Related titles: Online - full text ed.: ISSN 1534-3138. EUR 870, USD 1,158 to institutions (effective 2010).
Indexed: A22, A26, CurCont, E01, EMBASE, ExcerpMed, H12, I05, NSCI, P30, R10, Reac, SCI, SCOPUS, W07.
—BLDSC (3504.936450), IE, Infotrieve, Ingenta. **CCC.**
Published by: Current Medicine Group LLC (Subsidiary of: Springer Science+Business Media), 400 Market St, Ste 700, Philadelphia, PA 19106. TEL 215-574-2266, 800-427-1796, FAX 215-574-2225, http://www.current-medicine.com. Ed. William J Weiner. **Subscri. outside N America to:** Current Medicine Group Ltd., Middlesex House, 34-42 Cleveland St, London W1T 4LB, United Kingdom. TEL 44-20-73230323, FAX 44-20-75801938.

616.8 IND ISSN 0972-8252
➤ **CURRENT TRENDS IN NEUROLOGY.** Text in English. 2005. a. INR 6,854 domestic; EUR 134.10 in Europe; JPY 17,582 in Japan; USD 149 elsewhere (effective 2010). adv. bk.rev. abstr.; bibl.; charts; illus.; maps; stat. back issues avail.; reprints avail. **Document type:** *Journal, Academic/Scholarly.* **Description:** Contains review articles, original research papers and short communications in all branches of neuroscience, from the molecular to the behavioral levels.
Related titles: CD-ROM ed.; Online - full text ed.
Indexed: B21, ESPM, ImmunAb, NSA.
Published by: Research Trends (P) Ltd., T.C. 17 / 250 (3), Chadiyara Rd, Poojapura, Trivandrum, Kerala 695 012, India. TEL 91-471-2344424, FAX 91-471-2344423, info@researchtrends.net. Circ: 1,000.

616.89 USA ISSN 1545-8644
CYBER THERAPY. Text in English. 2003 (Fall). a.
Published by: Interactive Media Institute, 6160 Cornerstone Ct E, Ste 155, San Diego, CA 92121. TEL 858-642-0267, 866-822-8762, FAX 858-642-0285, http://www.vrphobia.com/imi/cybertherapy.htm.

616.8 DEU ISSN 0176-1218
D G S P SCHRIFTENREIHE. (Deutsche Gesellschaft fuer Soziale Psychiatrie) Text in German. 1984. irreg., latest vol.9, 1991. price varies. **Document type:** *Monographic series, Academic/Scholarly.*
Published by: Deutsche Gesellschaft fuer Soziale Psychiatrie e.V., Zeltinger Str 9, Cologne, 50969, Germany. TEL 49-221-511002, FAX 49-221-529903, dgsp@psychiatrie.de, http://www.psychiatrie.de/website/index.php?/f,11955,12000/.

616.8 ARG ISSN 1853-0893
▼ **A D I N A ROSARIO. ANUARIO.** (Asociacion de Docencia e Investigaciones en Neuropsicologia y Afasiologia) Text in Spanish. 2010. a. back issues avail. **Document type:** *Yearbook, Academic/Scholarly.*
Media: Online - full text.
Published by: A D I N A, Vias de Comunicacion s-n, Rosario, Argentina. TEL 54-341-4210072, FAX 54-341-4217831, info@adinarosario.com.

D W D NEWSLETTER. see GERONTOLOGY AND GERIATRICS

616.834 DEU
DABEI. Text in German. 1984. q. free to members (effective 2010). **Document type:** *Magazine, Consumer.*
Formerly (until 1994): Wir in Hessen
Published by: Deutsche Multiple Sklerose Gesellschaft, Landesverband Hessen e.V., Wittelsbacherallee 86, Farnkfurt am Main, 60385, Germany. TEL 49-69-4058980, FAX 49-69-40589840, dmsg@dmsg-hessen.de.

LE DECHAINE. see POLITICAL SCIENCE—Civil Rights

616.8 GBR ISSN 1179-9900
▼ ➤ **DEGENERATIVE NEUROLOGICAL AND NEUROMUSCULAR DISEASE.** Text in English. 2011. irreg. free (effective 2011). **Document type:** *Journal, Academic/Scholarly.*
Media: Online - full text.
—CCC.
Published by: Dove Medical Press Ltd., Beechfield House, Winterton Way, Macclesfield, SK11 0JL, United Kingdom. TEL 44-1625-509130, FAX 44-1625-617933. Ed. Dr. Glenn Lopate.

616.8 GBR ISSN 1471-3012
HV689
➤ **DEMENTIA.** Text in English. 2002 (Feb.). q. USD 821, GBP 444 combined subscription to institutions (print & online eds.); USD 805, GBP 435 to institutions (effective 2011). adv. bk.rev. back issues avail.; reprint service avail. from PSC. **Document type:** *Journal, Academic/Scholarly.* **Description:** Focuses on the social experience of dementia. It provides a forum for social research of direct relevance to improving the quality of life and care of people with dementia and their families, and will publish papers from the fields of public health, social policy, social work and sociology.
Related titles: Online - full text ed.: ISSN 1741-2684. USD 739, GBP 400 to institutions (effective 2011).
Indexed: A22, A26, ASG, AgeL, B07, C06, C07, C08, CA, CINAHL, E-psyche, E01, E08, FamI, G08, H11, H12, I05, P03, P30, PsycInfo, PsycholAb, S02, S03, S09, SCOPUS, SSA, SociolAb, T02.
—BLDSC (3550.524500), IE, Ingenta. **CCC.**
Published by: Sage Publications Ltd. (Subsidiary of: Sage Publications, Inc.), 1 Oliver's Yard, 55 City Rd, London, EC1Y 1SP, United Kingdom. TEL 44-20-73248500, FAX 44-20-73248600, info@sagepub.co.uk, http://www.uk.sagepub.com/home.nav. Eds. John Keady, Phyllis Braudy Harris. **Subscr. in the Americas to:** Sage Publications, Inc., 2455 Teller Rd, Thousand Oaks, CA 91320. TEL 805-499-9774, FAX 805-499-0871, journals@sagepub.com.

616.8 CHE ISSN 1420-8008
RC521 CODEN: DGCDFX
➤ **DEMENTIA AND GERIATRIC COGNITIVE DISORDERS.** Text in English. 1990. 12/yr. CHF 5,140, EUR 4,108, USD 5,033 to institutions; CHF 5,644, EUR 4,512, USD 5,521 combined subscription to institutions (print & online eds.) (effective 2012). adv. bibl.; charts; stat. **Document type:** *Journal, Academic/Scholarly.* **Description:** Examines the neural bases of cognitive dysfunction. Concentrates on neuro-degenerative diseases such as Alzheimer's and Parkinson's diseases, as well as Huntington's chorea. Covers topics of interest to professional in neurobiology, pharmacology, genetics, gerontology, and psychiatry.
Formerly (until 1996): Dementia (1013-7424)
Related titles: Microform ed.: (from PQC); Online - full text ed.: ISSN 1421-9824. CHF 5,038, EUR 4,030, USD 4,892 to institutions (effective 2012).
Indexed: A01, A03, A08, A20, A22, A35, A36, ASCA, ASG, AgBio, B21, C06, C07, C08, CA, CABA, CINAHL, CorrAb, CurCont, D01, E-psyche, E01, E12, EMBASE, ExcerpMed, F08, F11, F12, GH, INI, ISR, IndMed, Inpharma, LT, MEDLINE, N02, N03, NSA, NSCI, P03, P20, P22, P24, P25, P26, P27, P30, P33, P35, P48, P54, PHN&I, PQC, PsycInfo, PsycholAb, R08, R10, R12, RA&MP, RRTA, Reac, SCI, SCOPUS, SoyAb, T02, T05, W07, WAA.
—BLDSC (3550.525300), CASDDS, GNLM, IE, Infotrieve, Ingenta, INIST. **CCC.**
Published by: S. Karger AG, Allschwilerstr 10, Basel, 4055, Switzerland. TEL 41-61-3061111, FAX 41-61-3061234, karger@karger.ch, http://www.karger.ch. Ed. V Chan-Palay. adv.: page CHF 1,815; trim 210 x 280. Circ: 1,000 (paid and controlled).

➤ **DEPRESSION AND ANXIETY (HOBOKEN).** see PSYCHOLOGY

616.13 USA ISSN 1542-1880
RC537
DEPRESSION AND ANXIETY (NEW YORK). Text in English. 19??. a. USD 19.95 per issue (effective 2010). **Document type:** *Monographic series, Academic/Scholarly.*
Published by: (Johns Hopkins Medical Institutions), Medletter Associates, 6 Trowbridge Dr, Bethel, CT 06801.

362.25 JPN ISSN 1347-8893
DEPRESSION FRONTIER. Text in Japanese. 2002. a. JPY 2,940 newsstand/cover (effective 2005). **Document type:** *Journal, Academic/Scholarly.*
Published by: Iyaku Journal-sha/Medicine & Drug Journal Co., Ltd., Highness Awajimachi Bldg. 21/F, 3-1-5 Awajimachih, Chuo-Ku, Osaka, 541-0047, Japan. TEL 81-6-62027280, FAX 81-6-62025295, ij-main@iyaku-j.com, http://www.iyaku-j.com/.

155.904 USA ISSN 2090-1321
▼ ➤ **DEPRESSION RESEARCH AND TREATMENT.** Text in English. 2009. irreg. USD 195 (effective 2011). **Document type:** *Journal, Academic/Scholarly.* **Description:** Publishes original research articles, review articles, case reports, and clinical studies related to all aspects of depression.
Related titles: Online - full text ed.: ISSN 2090-133X. free (effective 2011).
Indexed: A01, P30, T02.
Published by: Hindawi Publishing Corporation, 410 Park Ave, 15th Fl, PMB 287, New York, NY 10022. FAX 215-893-4392, 866-446-3294, info@hindawi.com.

➤ **DEUTSCHE BEHINDERTENZEITSCHRIFT.** see EDUCATION—Special Education And Rehabilitation

616.8 DEU ISSN 1430-8339
RC438
DEUTSCHE GESELLSCHAFT FUER GESCHICHTE DER NERVENHEILKUNDE. SCHRIFTENREIHE. Text in German. 1996. irreg., latest vol.16, 2010. price varies. **Document type:** *Monographic series, Academic/Scholarly.*
Published by: (Deutsche Gesellschaft fuer Geschichte der Nervenheilkunde e.V.), Verlag Koenigshausen und Neumann GmbH, Leistenstr 7, Wuerzburg, 97082, Germany. TEL 49-931-3298700, FAX 49-931-83620, info@koenigshausen-neumann.de, http://koenigshausen-neumann.gebhardt-riegel.de.

DEVELOPMENT AND PSYCHOPATHOLOGY. see PSYCHOLOGY

616.8 USA ISSN 0892-8150
CODEN: DCPPE3
DEVELOPMENTAL CLINICAL PSYCHOLOGY AND PSYCHIATRY. Text in English. 1985. irreg., latest 2003. price varies. **Document type:** *Monographic series, Academic/Scholarly.*
Indexed: A22.
—BLDSC (3579.054270), IE, Ingenta. **CCC.**
Published by: Sage Publications, Inc., 2455 Teller Rd, Thousand Oaks, CA 91320. TEL 805-499-9774, 800-818-7243, FAX 805-499-0871, 800-583-2665, info@sagepub.com.

616.8 GBR ISSN 1878-9293
▼ ➤ **DEVELOPMENTAL COGNITIVE NEUROSCIENCE;** a journal for cognitive, affective and social developmental neuroscience. Text in English. forthcoming 2011. q. EUR 548 in Europe to institutions; JPY 82,300 in Japan to institutions; USD 838 elsewhere to institutions (effective 2012). **Document type:** *Journal, Academic/Scholarly.* **Description:** Publishes theoretical and research papers on cognitive brain development, from infancy through childhood and adolescence to old age. It will cover neurocognitive development and neurocognitive processing in both typical and atypical development, including social and affective aspects.
Related titles: Online - full text ed.: ISSN 1878-9307. forthcoming (from ScienceDirect).
Indexed: P30.
—CCC.
Published by: Elsevier Ltd (Subsidiary of: Elsevier Science & Technology), The Blvd, Langford Ln, Kidlington, Oxford, OX5 1GB, United Kingdom. TEL 44-1865-843434, FAX 44-1865-843970, customerserviceau@elsevier.com.

371.928 CAN ISSN 1184-0412
➤ **DEVELOPMENTAL DISABILITIES BULLETIN.** Text in English. 1972. s-a. CAD 19.25 domestic to individuals; USD 18 foreign to individuals; CAD 32.10 domestic to institutions; USD 28 foreign to institutions (effective 2007). adv. bk.rev. **Document type:** *Bulletin, Trade.* **Description:** Articles with both research and direct application to the education of, and provision of services for persons with mental retardation, learning disability and multiple handicaps.
Former titles (until 1990): Mental Retardation and Learning Disability Bulletin (0822-4277); (until 1983): Mental Retardation Bulletin (0707-9761); (until 1976): C S M R Bulletin (0707-977X)
Related titles: Online - full text ed.
Indexed: A01, A22, C03, CEI, E-psyche, ECER, ERIC, P03, P18, P25, P48, P53, P54, PQC, PsycInfo, PsycholAb, YAE&RB.
—BLDSC (3579.054450), GNLM, IE, Ingenta. **CCC.**
Published by: University of Alberta, Developmental Disabilities Centre, 6 123D Education North, Edmonton, AB T6G 2H1, Canada. TEL 780-492-1151, FAX 780-492-1318, http://www.ualberta.ca/~jpdasddc/INDEX.html. Eds. Rauno K Parrila, Sheila Mansell. R&P Dick Sobsey. Adv. contact Henny Degroot. Circ: 250.

616.858 USA ISSN 1940-5510
RC569.7 CODEN: MRDRFI
➤ **DEVELOPMENTAL DISABILITIES RESEARCH REVIEWS.** Text in English. 1995. q. GBP 428 in United Kingdom to institutions; EUR 540 in Europe to institutions; USD 755 in United States to institutions; USD 811 in Canada & Mexico to institutions; USD 839 elsewhere to institutions; GBP 493 combined subscription in United Kingdom to institutions (print & online eds.); EUR 622 combined subscription in Europe to institutions (print & online eds.); USD 869 combined subscription in United States to institutions (print & online eds.); USD 925 combined subscription in Canada & Mexico to institutions (print & online eds.); USD 953 combined subscription elsewhere to institutions (print & online eds.) (effective 2012). adv. back issues avail.; reprint service avail. from PSC. **Document type:** *Journal, Academic/Scholarly.* **Description:** Provides a focus for communication among neuroscientists, geneticists, neurodevelopmental pediatricians, and behavioral scientists interested in clinical or basic science research in aspects of brain development and function.
Formerly (until 2008): Mental Retardation and Developmental Disabilities Research Reviews (1080-4013)
Related titles: Microform ed.: (from PQC); Online - full text ed.: ISSN 1940-5529. 1996. GBP 385 in United Kingdom to institutions; EUR 486 in Europe to institutions; USD 755 elsewhere to institutions (effective 2012).
Indexed: A01, A03, A08, A36, AMED, B21, C06, C07, CA, CABA, CDA, CTA, CurCont, EMBASE, ExcerpMed, FR, GH, ISR, IndMed, LT, MEDLINE, N02, N03, NSA, NSCI, P03, P30, P33, P43, PsycInfo, PsycholAb, R10, RM&VM, RRTA, Reac, SCI, SCOPUS, T02, W07.
—BLDSC (3579.054458), GNLM, IE, Infotrieve, Ingenta, INIST. **CCC.**
Published by: (Society for Developmental Pediatrics), John Wiley & Sons, Inc., 111 River St, Hoboken, NJ 07030. TEL 201-748-6000, FAX 201-748-6088, info@wiley.com, http://www.wiley.com/WileyCDA/. Eds. Marc Yudkoff, Marilee C Allen. Adv. contact Kim Thompkins TEL 212-850-6921. **Subscr. outside the Americas to:** John Wiley & Sons Ltd., The Atrium, Southern Gate, Chichester, West Sussex PO19 8SQ, United Kingdom. TEL 44-1243-779777, 800-243407, FAX 44-1243-775878, cs-journals@wiley.com.

➤ **DEVELOPMENTAL MEDICINE AND CHILD NEUROLOGY.** see MEDICAL SCIENCES—Pediatrics

➤ **DEVELOPMENTAL NEUROBIOLOGY.** see BIOLOGY—Physiology

616.8 CHE ISSN 0378-5866
RC321 CODEN: DENED7
➤ **DEVELOPMENTAL NEUROSCIENCE.** Text in French. 1979. bi-m. CHF 1,596, EUR 1,275, USD 1,570.50 to institutions; CHF 1,751, EUR 1,399, USD 1,720.50 combined subscription to institutions (print & online eds.) (effective 2012). adv. illus. index. back issues avail. **Document type:** *Journal, Academic/Scholarly.* **Description:** Publishes neuroscience papers covering all stages of invertebrate, vertebrate and human development.
Related titles: Microform ed.: (from PQC); Online - full text ed.: ISSN 1421-9859. CHF 1,545, EUR 1,236, USD 1,500 to institutions (effective 2012).
Indexed: A22, ASCA, B21, B25, BIOSIS Prev, C33, CA, CIN, ChemAb, ChemTitl, ChemoAb, CurCont, E-psyche, E01, EMBASE, ESPM, ExcerpMed, GenetAb, IBR, IBZ, ISR, IndMed, Inpharma, MEDLINE, MycolAb, NSA, NSCI, P03, P20, P22, P30, P48, P54, PQC, PsycInfo, PsycholAb, R10, Reac, SCI, SCOPUS, T02, ToxAb, W07.
—BLDSC (3579.057500), CASDDS, GNLM, IE, Infotrieve, Ingenta, INIST. **CCC.**
Published by: S. Karger AG, Allschwilerstr 10, Basel, 4055, Switzerland. TEL 41-61-3061111, FAX 41-61-3061234, karger@karger.ch, http://www.karger.ch. Ed. S W Levison. adv.: page CHF 1,730; trim 210 x 280. Circ: 800 (paid and controlled).

➤ **DEVELOPMENTS IN MENTAL HEALTH LAW.** *see* LAW

616.8 NLD ISSN 0166-5960
CODEN: DEVND6
DEVELOPMENTS IN NEUROLOGY. Text in Dutch. 1978. irreg., latest vol.13, 1997. price varies. illus. back issues avail. **Document type:** *Monographic series, Academic/Scholarly.* **Description:** Disseminates clinical and applied research in the medical specialty of neurology.
Indexed: ChemAb, E-psyche.
—BLDSC (3579.085380), CASDDS, INIST.
Published by: Elsevier BV (Subsidiary of: Elsevier Science & Technology), Radarweg 29, PO Box 211, Amsterdam, 1000 AE, Netherlands. TEL 31-20-4853911, FAX 31-20-4852457, JournalsCustomerServiceEMEA@elsevier.com, http://www.elsevier.nl.

▼ **DEVELOPPEMENTS**; revue interdisciplinaire du developpement cognitif normal et pahologique. *see* PSYCHOLOGY

616.89 362.2 NLD ISSN 1381-0782
DEVIANT; tijdschrift tussen psychiatrie en maatschappij. Text in Dutch. 1984. q. EUR 22 to individuals; EUR 39 to institutions (effective 2008). adv. **Document type:** *Magazine, Trade.*
Formerly (until 1994): Platform Geestelijke Gezondheidszorg. Nieuwsbrief (1381-0790)
Published by: Koninklijke Van Gorcum BV/Royal Van Gorcum BV, PO Box 43, Assen, 9400 AA, Netherlands. TEL 31-592-379555, FAX 31-592-372064, info@vangorcum.nl, http://www.vangorcum.nl. Eds. Barbara Boudenwijnse, Michi Almer. adv.: page EUR 450.

616.89 NLD ISSN 1574-3535
DIAGNOSE EN THERAPIE. Text in Dutch. 2004. a. EUR 122.30 (effective 2008).
Published by: Bohn Stafleu van Loghum B.V. (Subsidiary of: Springer Science+Business Media), Postbus 246, Houten, 3990 GA, Netherlands. TEL 31-30-6383838, FAX 31-30-6383839, boekhandels@bsl.nl.

616.89 ARG ISSN 1668-5474
DIAGNOSIS. Text in Spanish. 2004. a. **Document type:** *Monographic series, Academic/Scholarly.*
Published by: Fundacion Prosam, Rodriguez Pena, 1046, Buenos Aires, C1020ADV, Argentina. TEL 54-11-49644560, prosam@prosam.org.ar, http://www.prosam.org.ar/. Ed. Ruth Melnistzky.

DIALECT. *see* SOCIAL SERVICES AND WELFARE

616.8 FRA ISSN 1294-8322
RC321
DIALOGUES IN CLINICAL NEUROSCIENCE. Text in English. 1999. q. **Document type:** *Journal, Academic/Scholarly.*
Related titles: Online - full text ed.: ISSN 1958-5969.
Indexed: BIOBASE, EMBASE, ExcerpMed, IABS, MEDLINE, P30, R10, Reac, SCOPUS.
—BLDSC (3579.775712), IE, Ingenta, INIST. **CCC.**
Published by: Les Laboratoires Servier, 22 rue Garnier, Neuilly sur Seine, 92578, France. TEL 33-1-55726000, http://www.servier.com.

DIALOGUES IN PHILOSOPHY, MENTAL AND NEURO SCIENCES. *see* PHILOSOPHY

DIGEST OF NEUROLOGY & PSYCHIATRY (ONLINE). *see* MEDICAL SCIENCES—Abstracting, Bibliographies, Statistics

616.891 USA ISSN 0891-3870
➤ **DIRECTIONS IN PSYCHIATRY.** Text in English. 1981. a. USD 300 per vol. (effective 2010). bk.rev. index. back issues avail.; reprints avail. **Document type:** *Journal, Academic/Scholarly.* **Description:** Publishes scholarly, jargon-free articles on developments in psychiatry. Continuing medical education credits are available.
Indexed: E-psyche, P03, PsycInfo, PsycholAb.
—BLDSC (3590.362000).
Published by: Hatherleigh Co. Ltd., 62545 State Hwy 10, Hobart, NY 13788. support@hatherleigh.com.

➤ **DIRECTORY OF MENTAL HEALTH SERVICES (YEARS).** *see* HEALTH FACILITIES AND ADMINISTRATION

616.8 USA ISSN 0740-8250
RC459.5.U6
DIRECTORY OF PSYCHIATRY RESIDENCY TRAINING PROGRAMS. Text in English. 1982. irreg., latest 1997, 7th ed. USD 76.50 per issue to members (effective 2010). **Document type:** *Directory, Academic/Scholarly.* **Description:** Provides a description of residency programs in general and child and adolescent psychiatry that will help residents to select the programs that interest them.
Indexed: E-psyche.
—**CCC.**
Published by: (American Psychiatric Association), American Psychiatric Publishing, Inc., 1000 Wilson Blvd, Ste 1825, Arlington, VA 22209. TEL 703-907-7322, 800-368-5777, FAX 703-907-1091, appi@psych.org.

DIRECTORY OF SUICIDE PREVENTION AND CRISIS INTERVENTION CENTERS. *see* PSYCHOLOGY

616.748 ITA ISSN 0012-4087
DISTROFIA MUSCOLARE. Short title: D M. Text in Italian; Summaries in English, Italian. 1962. q. free (effective 2009). bk.rev. bibl.; charts; illus. **Document type:** *Newsletter, Consumer.* **Description:** Presents research papers from various doctors interested in the field of muscular dystrophy. Also features articles on how to deal with victims of this illness as well as how to make their lives easier and more autonomous.
Indexed: E-psyche.
Published by: Unione Italiana Lotta alla Distrofia Muscolare, Via P.P. Vergerio 19, Padua, PD 35126, Italy. TEL 39-49-8021002, FAX 39-49-8022509. Circ: 60,000.

612.88 MEX
DOLOR, CLINICA Y TERAPIA. Text in Spanish. 2002. m. back issues avail. **Document type:** *Journal, Academic/Scholarly.*
Related titles: Online - full text ed.
Published by: Centro Nacional de Capacitacion en Terapia del Dolor, Rancho de la Laguna No 138, Frac Sta Cecilia, Coyoacan, Mexico, D.F., 04930, Mexico. TEL 52-55-55943101, sociedadneurologica@arnet.com.ar. Ed. Cesar Erosa Gonzalez.

DOULEUR & SANTE MENTALE. *see* PHARMACY AND PHARMACOLOGY

DOWN & UP. *see* HANDICAPPED

616.85 296 305.8924 USA ISSN 1545-4991
RC571
DOWN SYNDROME AMONGST US. Text in English. 1996. irreg.
Published by: DSAU, Inc., 32 Rutledge St., Brooklyn, NY 11211. downsyndrome@earthlink.net. Ed. Sarah Sander.

616.858842 USA ISSN 0161-0716
DOWN SYNDROME NEWS. Text in English. 1976. 6/yr. USD 25 membership (effective 2007). bk.rev.; film rev.; video rev. bibl. index. **Document type:** *Newsletter.* **Description:** Contains parent-oriented information on Down syndrome, including medical research, education issues, resources, articles by and for parents.
Indexed: E-psyche.
—**CCC.**
Published by: National Down Syndrome Congress, 1370 Center Dr, Ste 102, Atlanta, GA 30338-4132. TEL 770-604-9500, 800-232-NDSC, FAX 770-604-9898, info@ndsccenter.org, http://www.ndscenter.org. Ed. Julie Anderson. Circ: 10,000.

616.8 USA ISSN 1087-1756
DOWN SYNDROME QUARTERLY. Text in English. 1996. q. USD 24 domestic to individuals; USD 30 in Canada & Mexico to individuals; USD 34 elsewhere to individuals; USD 48 domestic to institutions; USD 54 in Canada & Mexico to institutions; USD 58 elsewhere to institutions (effective 2005). bk.rev. back issues avail. **Document type:** *Journal, Academic/Scholarly.* **Description:** Covers the medical, behavioral, and social scientific aspects of Down syndrome research.
Address: c/o Samuel J Thios, Denison University, Granville, OH 43023. FAX 740-587-6601. Ed. Samuel J Thois.

616.858 150 GBR ISSN 0968-7912
➤ **DOWN SYNDROME RESEARCH AND PRACTICE.** Text in English. 1992. 3/yr. GBP 40 to individuals; GBP 100 to institutions; GBP 30 to individual members; GBP 85 to institutional members (effective 2009). back issues avail. **Document type:** *Journal, Academic/Scholarly.* **Description:** Aims to inform researchers, education and health professionals and the families of people with Down syndrome of research findings and the implications for practice.
Incorporates (1998-2007): Down Syndrome News and Update (1463-6212)
Related titles: Online - full text ed.: ISSN 1753-7606.
Indexed: CPE, E-psyche, EMBASE, ERIC, ExcerpMed, IndMed, MEDLINE, P03, P30, PsycInfo, PsycholAb, R10, Reac, SCOPUS.
—BLDSC (3620.077000), IE, Infotrieve, Ingenta. **CCC.**
Published by: Down Syndrome Educational Trust, Sarah Duffen Centre, Belmont St, Southsea, Hants PO5 1NA, United Kingdom. TEL 44-23-92855330, FAX 44-23-92855320, enquiries@downsed.org, http://www.downsed.org. Ed. Sue Buckley.

➤ **DREAMING.** *see* PSYCHOLOGY

➤ **DRIFT**; tidsskrift for psychoanalyse. *see* PSYCHOLOGY

➤ **DRUG INFORMATION HANDBOOK FOR PSYCHIATRY.** *see* PHARMACY AND PHARMACOLOGY

616.8 TUR ISSN 1018-8681
➤ **DUSUNEN ADAM/JOURNAL OF PSYCHIATRY AND NEUROLOGICAL SCIENCES**; psikiyatri ve norolojik bilimler dergisi. Text in Turkish. 1984. q. adv. back issues avail. **Document type:** *Journal, Academic/Scholarly.* **Description:** Contains research articles for scientists, specialists and students working in the fields of psychiatry, psychology, neurology, neurosurgery, pharmacology, molecular biology, genetics, neuroscience and other related areas.
Related titles: Online - full text ed.: ISSN 1309-5749. free (effective 2011).
Indexed: A01, P02, P10, P48, P53, P54, PQC.
Published by: (Bakirkoy Ruh Sagligi ve Sinir Hastalikalari Egitim ve Arastirma Hastanesi/Bakirkoy Research and Training Hospital for Psychiatry, Neurology and Neurosurgery), Yerkure Tanitim ve Yayincilik Hizmetleri A.S., Cumhuriyet Cad 48, 3B, Harbiye, Istanbul, 34367, Turkey. TEL 90-212-2416820, FAX 90-212-2416820, yerkure@yerkure.com.tr, http://www.kure.com.tr. Ed. Cuneyt Evren. Pub. Nuket Dilmen Korkmaz. R&P Erhan Kurt. Circ: 1,500.

616.89 DEU ISSN 0012-740X
CODEN: DYPSAQ
➤ **DYNAMISCHE PSYCHIATRIE/DYNAMIC PSYCHIATRY**; internationale Zeitschrift fuer Psychiatrie und Psychoanalyse. Text and summaries in English, German. 1968. 3/yr. EUR 60; EUR 20 per issue (effective 2009). adv. bk.rev. bibl. index. cum.index. **Document type:** *Journal, Academic/Scholarly.* **Description:** Publishes international research results in the area of psychiatry and psychoanalysis on the basis of a humanistic concept of psychiatry.
Indexed: A20, A22, AC&P, ASCA, DIP, E-psyche, IBR, IBZ, P30, PsycholAb, PsycholRG, RefZh, SCOPUS.
—BLDSC (3637.140000), GNLM, IE, Infotrieve, Ingenta. **CCC.**
Published by: (World Association for Dynamic Psychiatry CHE, Deutschen Gruppenpsychotherapeutischen Gesellschaft, Deutschen Gesellschaft fuer Psychosomatische Medizin, Deutsche Akademie fuer Psychoanalyse), Pinel-Verlag fuer Humanistische Psychiatrie und Philosophie, Kantstr 120-121, Berlin, 10625, Germany. TEL 49-30-3132893, FAX 49-30-3136959, pinelverlag@web.de, http://www.dynpsych.de/pinel/index.htm. Ed. Dr. Maria Ammon. Pub. Werner Feja. adv.: page EUR 96; trim 120 x 190. Circ: 380 (paid and controlled).

➤ **DYSLEXIA.** *see* EDUCATION—Special Education And Rehabilitation

➤ **DYSLEXIA HANDBOOK.** *see* EDUCATION—Special Education And Rehabilitation

➤ **DYSLEXIA REVIEW.** *see* EDUCATION—Special Education And Rehabilitation

616.832 GBR ISSN 1478-1506
➤ **DYSPRAXIA FOUNDATION PROFESSIONAL JOURNAL.** Text in English. 2002. a. free to members (effective 2009). back issues avail. **Document type:** *Journal, Academic/Scholarly.* **Description:** Provides information on current practices, research and facilitates continuing education for all professionals working with those affected by Dyspraxia.
Indexed: AMED.
—BLDSC (3637.275000).
Published by: Dyspraxia Foundation, 8 West Alley, Hitchin, Herts SG5 1EG, United Kingdom. TEL 44-1462-454986, FAX 44-1462-455052, dyspraxia@dyspraxiafoundation.org.uk. Ed. Michele G Lee TEL 44-1462-455016.

616.8 FRA ISSN 1778-6959
➤ **E M C - NEUROLOGIE (ONLINE).** (Encyclopedie Medico Chirurgicale) Text in French. 2004. 4/yr. EUR 268 domestic to institutions; EUR 273 in Europe to institutions; JPY 36,400 in Japan to institutions; USD 306 elsewhere to institutions (effective 2008). **Document type:** *Journal, Academic/Scholarly.*
Formerly (until 2005): E M C - Neurologie (Print) (1762-4231)
Media: Online - full content. **Related titles:** Online - full text ed.
Indexed: A26, I05, SCOPUS.
—IE. **CCC.**
Published by: Elsevier Masson (Subsidiary of: Elsevier Health Sciences), 62 Rue Camille Desmoulins, Issy les Moulineaux, Cedex 92442, France. TEL 33-1-71165500, FAX 33-1-71165600, infos@elsevier-masson.fr.

616.89 FRA
RC321
E M C - PSYCHIATRIE (ONLINE). (Encyclopedie Medico-Chirurgicale) Text in French. 2004. 4/yr. USD 284 in Europe to institutions; JPY 31,300 in Japan to institutions; USD 284 elsewhere to institutions (effective 2008). **Document type:** *Journal, Academic/Scholarly.*
Formerly (until 2005): E M C - Psychiatrie (Print) (1762-5718)
Media: Online - full content. **Related titles:** Online - full text ed.
Indexed: A26, CA, I05, SCOPUS.
—IE, Ingenta. **CCC.**
Published by: Elsevier Masson (Subsidiary of: Elsevier Health Sciences), 62 Rue Camille Desmoulins, Issy les Moulineaux, Cedex 92442, France. TEL 33-1-71165500, FAX 33-1-71165600, infos@elsevier-masson.fr.

▼ **E M M-A**; tidsskrift for miljoearbeid. *see* SOCIAL SERVICES AND WELFARE

616.833 GBR
E P D A PLUS. Text in English. 3/yr. free to qualified personnel. adv. **Document type:** *Magazine, Trade.*
Related titles: Online - full text ed.
Published by: European Parkinson's Disease Association, 4 Golding Rd, Sevenoaks, Kent TN13 3NJ, United Kingdom. TEL 44-1732-457683, info@epda.eu.com. Ed. Llzzie Graham TEL 44-1732-457683.

616.89 AUS ISSN 1326-2610
E P P I C INFORMATION SHEET. Text in English. irreg. free. **Document type:** *Monographic series, Consumer.* **Description:** Aimed at addressing the needs of older adolescent and young adults with emerging psychotic disorders in the Western Metropolitan region of Melbourne, Victoria.
Media: Online - full text.
Published by: Early Psychosis Prevention and Intervention Centre, Locked Bag 10, Parville, VIC 3056, Australia. TEL 61-3-9389-2403, FAX 61-3-9387-3003, info@eppic.org.au.

616.8 AUS ISSN 1751-7885
RC321
➤ **EARLY INTERVENTION IN PSYCHIATRY**; the development, onset and treatment of emerging mental disorders. Text in English. 2007. q. GBP 134 in United Kingdom to institutions; EUR 169 in Europe to institutions; USD 254 in the Americas to institutions; USD 261 elsewhere to institutions; GBP 154 combined subscription in United Kingdom to institutions (print & online eds.); EUR 194 combined subscription in Europe to institutions (print & online eds.); USD 292 combined subscription in the Americas to institutions (print & online eds.); USD 300 combined subscription elsewhere to institutions (print & online eds.) (effective 2012). adv. back issues avail.; reprint service avail. from PSC. **Document type:** *Journal, Academic/Scholarly.* **Description:** Focuses on the early diagnosis and treatment of all mental health problems and disorders, early intervention in psychiatry promotes the importance of early intervention in psychiatric practice.
Related titles: Online - full text ed.: ISSN 1751-7893. GBP 134 in United Kingdom to institutions; EUR 169 in Europe to institutions; USD 254 in the Americas to institutions; USD 261 elsewhere to institutions (effective 2012) (from IngentaConnect).
Indexed: A01, A22, CA, CurCont, E01, EMBASE, ExcerpMed, MEDLINE, P03, P30, PsycInfo, SCI, SCOPUS, SSCI, T02, W07.
—IE, Ingenta. **CCC.**
Published by: (International Early Psychosis Association), Wiley-Blackwell Publishing Asia (Subsidiary of: Wiley-Blackwell Publishing Ltd.), 155 Cremorne St, Richmond, VIC 3121, Australia. TEL 61-3-92743100, FAX 61-3-92743101, melbourne@wiley.com, http://www.wiley.com/WileyCDA/. Ed. Patrick McGorry. Adv. contact Yasemin Caglar TEL 61-3-92743165.

M

616.89 AUS ISSN 1326-0871
EARLY PSYCHOSIS NEWS. Text in English. 1994. s-a. free (effective 2009). back issues avail. **Document type:** *Newsletter, Consumer.* **Description:** Provides a link for those who work with young people across different areas of practice, including clinical practice, research, groupwork, consumer and carer participation, resource development, and service development.
Media: Online - full content.
Published by: Early Psychosis Prevention and Intervention Centre, 35 Poplar Rd, Parkville, VIC 3052, Australia. TEL 800-888-320, info@eppic.org.au.

616.8 HKG ISSN 2078-9947
➤ **EAST ASIAN ARCHIVES OF PSYCHIATRY.** Text in Chinese. 1991. q. HKD 1,000 domestic; USD 150 foreign (effective 2011). adv. bk.rev. back issues avail. **Document type:** *Journal, Academic/Scholarly.* **Description:** Publishes original articles, review papers, and case reports related to the clinical practice and research in psychiatry and related disciplines.
Former titles (until 2009): Hong Kong Journal of Psychiatry (1026-2121); (until 1993): Hong Kong College of Psychiatrists. Journal (1023-0130)
Indexed: A01, A26, C06, C07, C08, CA, CINAHL, E-psyche, EMBASE, ExcerpMed, H12, HongKongiana, I05, P03, P25, P48, PQC, PsycInfo, PsychoIAb, R10, Reac, RefZh, SCOPUS, T02.
—BLDSC (3645.922700), IE, Ingenta.
Published by: (Hong Kong College of Psychiatrists), Hong Kong Academy of Medicine Press, Rm.901, 9/F, HKAM Bldg., 99 Wong Hunk Hang Rd., Aberdeen, Hong Kong. TEL 852-28718822, FAX 852-25159061, hkampress@hkam.org.hk, http://www.hkampress.org. Ed. Linda CW Lam. Adv. contact Samuel T.K. Lai TEL 852-27873068. Circ: 5,000.

616.8526 ITA ISSN 1590-1262
EATING AND WEIGHT DISORDERS (ONLINE); studies on anorexia, bulimia and obesity. Text in Italian. 1996. q. EUR 120 (effective 2011). back issues avail. **Document type:** *Journal, Academic/Scholarly.* **Description:** Contains clinical and experimental studies, special sections, discussions and reviews of new treaties on the common, specific problems relating to the causes, epidemiology, treatment and prevention of eating disorders and obesity.
Media: Online - full text.
Indexed: PsycholAb.
Published by: Editrice Kurtis s.r.l., Via Luigi Zoja 30, Milan, 20153, Italy. TEL 39-02-48202740, FAX 39-02-48201219, info@kurtis.it. Ed. Massimo Cuzzolaro.

616.8526 USA ISSN 1048-6984
RC552.E18
EATING DISORDERS REVIEW; current clinical information for the professional treating eating disorders. Text in English. 1990. bi-m. USD 65 domestic to non-members; USD 75 in Canada to non-members; USD 83 elsewhere to non-members; USD 52 domestic to members; USD 62 in Canada to members; USD 70 elsewhere to members (effective 2010). adv. 8 p./no.; back issues avail. **Document type:** *Newsletter, Academic/Scholarly.* **Description:** Presents clinical information for the professional treating eating disorders and features summaries of relevant research from journals and unpublished studies.
Related titles: Online - full text ed.: USD 39.95 (effective 2010).
Indexed: A01, A03, A08, CA, E-psyche, T02.
—CCC.
Published by: Gurze Books, PO Box 2238, Carlsbad, CA 92018. TEL 760-434-7533, 800-756-7533, FAX 760-434-5476, Melissa@gurze.net. Ed. Dr. Joel Yager. Pub., Adv. contact Leigh Cohn.

700 370 ESP ISSN 1695-8403
EDUCACION ARTISTICA; revista de investigacion. Text in Multiple languages. 2003. a. **Document type:** *Journal, Academic/Scholarly.*
Published by: Universitat de Valencia, Institut de Creativitat i Innovacions Educatives/Universidad de Valencia, Instituto de Creatividad e Innovaciones Educativas, Blsco Ibanez 32, Valencia, Spain. TEL 34-96-3864132, iucie@uv.es, http://www.uv.es/icie/.

EDUCATION AND TRAINING IN AUTISM AND DEVELOPMENTAL DISABILITIES. *see* EDUCATION—Special Education And Rehabilitation

616.8 150 EGY ISSN 1110-1075
THE EGYPTIAN JOURNAL OF MENTAL HEALTH. Text in English. 1961. a. **Document type:** *Journal, Academic/Scholarly.*
Published by: The Egyptian Association for Mental Health, 31 Orabi Str, El-Azbakia, Cairo, Egypt. TEL 20-2-5796823. Ed. Dr. Fatma Mousa.

616.8 150 EGY ISSN 1110-1083
➤ **THE EGYPTIAN JOURNAL OF NEUROLOGY, PSYCHIATRY, AND NEUROSURGERY.** Text in English. 1960. s-a.
Related titles: Online - full text ed.: ISSN 1687-8329. 2007.
Indexed: EMBASE, ExcerpMed, SCOPUS.
Published by: The Egyptian Society of Neurology, Psychiatry, and Neurosurgery, Dr. Ahmed Abdelalim, Department of Neurology, Cairo University, Cairo, 11562, Egypt. TEL 201-0519-0834, info@esnpn.org, http://www.esnpn.org. Ed. Mohamed S El-Tamawy.

616.89 EGY ISSN 1110-1105
THE EGYPTIAN JOURNAL OF PSYCHIATRY. Text in English, Arabic. 1978. s-a. free. **Document type:** *Journal, Academic/Scholarly.*
Published by: Egyptian Psychiatric Association, PO Box 6, Cairo, 11657, Egypt. Ed. Dr. Momtaz Abdel-Wahab.

616.891 IRL ISSN 1393-3582
EISTEACH; a quarterly journal of counselling and psychotherapy. Text in English. 198?. q.
Former titles (until 1996): Irish Association for Counselling and Therapy. Journal (0791-8763); (until 1994): Irish Association for Counselling. Newsletter (1393-1776)
—BLDSC (3668.140000), IE, Ingenta.
Published by: Irish Association for Counselling and Psychotherapy, 8 Cumberland St, Dun Laoghaire, Dublin, Ireland. TEL 353-1-2300061, FAX 353-1-2300064, iact@irish-counselling.ie, http://www.irish-counselling.ie.

612.8 BEL ISSN 0301-150X
RC77.5 CODEN: EMCNA9
ELECTROMYOGRAPHY AND CLINICAL NEUROPHYSIOLOGY. Text in English. 1961. 8/yr. abstr.; bibl.; charts; illus. index. **Document type:** *Journal, Academic/Scholarly.*
Formerly (until 1971): Electromyography (0013-4732)
Indexed: A22, E-psyche, EMBASE, ExcerpMed, IndMed, Inspec, MEDLINE, P30, R10, Reac, RefZh, SCOPUS.
—BLDSC (3699.720000), AskIEEE, GNLM, IE, Infotrieve, Ingenta, INIST.
Published by: Editions Nauwelaerts SA, Rue de l' Eglise St Suplice 19, Beauvechain, 1320, Belgium. TEL 32-10-866737, FAX 32-10-861655. Eds. F Bruyninckx, N Rosselle.

616.8 ARG ISSN 0328-0446
➤ **ELECTRONEUROBIOLOGIA.** Text in Multiple languages. 1993. q. **Document type:** *Journal, Academic/Scholarly.*
Related titles: Online - full text ed.: ISSN 1850-1826. free (effective 2011).
—IE.
Published by: Hospital Neuropsiquiatrico "Dr. Jose Tiburcio Borda", Laboratorio de Investigaciones Electroneurobiologicas, Ramon Carrillo 375, Buenos Aires, 1275, Argentina. postmaster@neurobiol.cyt.edu.ar.

➤ **THE ELECTRONIC JOURNAL OF COMMUNICATIVE PSYCHOANALYSIS**; an independent multilingual international publication. *see* PSYCHOLOGY

616.8 USA ISSN 0734-9890
CODEN: EBMOEN
➤ **EMOTIONS AND BEHAVIOR. MONOGRAPH.** Text in English. 1983. irreg., latest vol.10. price varies. back issues avail. **Document type:** *Monographic series, Academic/Scholarly.* **Description:** Experiences with brief psychotherapy, especially the author's investigations of The Twenty-Minute Hour, the teaching of psychotherapy to non-psychiatric physicians, and the combining of drugs and psychotherapy.
Indexed: E-psyche, PsycholAb.
Published by: (Chicago Institute for Psychoanalysis), International Universities Press, Inc., 59 Boston Post Rd, Box 1524, PO Box 389, Madison, CT 06443. TEL 203-245-4000, FAX 203-245-0775, info@iup.com.

616.89 SWE ISSN 1102-3104
EMPATI; tidning foer information, debatt och forskning om schizofreni och andra psykiska handicapp. Text in Swedish. 1991. q. SEK 200 domestic; NOK 280 in Scandinavia (effective 2003). adv. bk.rev. **Document type:** *Journal, Academic/Scholarly.*
Indexed: E-psyche.
Published by: Stiftelsen Sympatikus, Hagalundsgatan 46, Solna, 16955, Sweden. TEL 46-8-7350211, FAX 46-8-822395. Ed. Kristina Hollox. Adv. contact Margarethe Weckman.

616.89 FRA ISSN 0013-7006
CODEN: ENCEAN
➤ **L'ENCEPHALE**; revue de psychiatrie clinique biologique et therapeutique. Text in French; Summaries in English, French. 1906; N.S. 1973. 6/yr. EUR 273 in Europe to institutions; EUR 233.10 in France to institutions; JPY 40,400 in Japan to institutions; USD 355 elsewhere to institutions (effective 2012). adv. bk.rev. charts; tr.lit. index. reprints avail. **Document type:** *Journal, Academic/Scholarly.*
Related titles: Microform ed.: (from PQC); Online - full text ed.: (from ScienceDirect).
Indexed: A20, A22, CIN, ChemAb, ChemTitl, CurCont, E-psyche, EMBASE, ExcerpMed, F09, FR, IBR, IBZ, INI, IndMed, Inpharma, MEDLINE, NSCI, P03, P30, P35, PsycInfo, PsycholAb, R10, Reac, S02, S03, SCI, SCOPUS, SOPODA, SociolAb, W07.
—BLDSC (3738.390000), CASDDS, GNLM, IE, Infotrieve, Ingenta, INIST. **CCC.**
Published by: Elsevier Masson (Subsidiary of: Elsevier Health Sciences), 62 Rue Camille Desmoulins, Issy les Moulineaux, Cedex 92442, France. TEL 33-1-71165500, infos@elsevier-masson.fr. Circ: 1,200.

➤ **ENCOR RESPONDENCE.** *see* EDUCATION—Special Education And Rehabilitation

616.89 ARG ISSN 1851-4812
ENCUENTRO ARGENTINO DE HISTORIA DE LA PSIQUIATRIA, LA PSICOLOGIA Y EL PSICOANALISIS. ACTAS. Text in Spanish. 2007. a. **Document type:** *Proceedings, Academic/Scholarly.*
Media: CD-ROM.
Published by: Universidad Nacional de Mar del Plata, Facultad de Psicologia, Complejo Universitario - Funes 3250, Cuerpo V - Nivel II, Mar de Plata, Argentina. psisecoo@mdp.edu.ar, http://www2.mdp.edu.ar/psicologia/.

ENCUENTRO DE AVANCES EN PSICOLOGIA, GERONTOLOGIA Y NEUROCIENCIAS. *see* PSYCHOLOGY

616.8 FRA ISSN 0246-0378
RC346
➤ **ENCYCLOPEDIE MEDICO-CHIRURGICALE. NEUROLOGIE.** Cover title: Traite de Neurologie. Variant title: Encyclopedie Medico-Chirurgicale, Instantanes Medicaux. Neurologie. Receuil Periodique de l'Encyclopedie Medico-Chirurgicale. Neurologie. Text in French. 1939. 7 base vols. plus q. updates. EUR 1,577 (effective 2006). bibl.; charts; illus. **Document type:** *Academic/Scholarly.* **Description:** Offers neurologists a comprehensive, up-to-date reference for diagnosing and treating various neurological disorders.
Related titles: Online - full text ed.
—INIST. **CCC.**
Published by: Elsevier Masson (Subsidiary of: Elsevier Health Sciences), 62 Rue Camille Desmoulins, Issy les Moulineaux, Cedex 92442, France. TEL 33-1-71165500, FAX 33-1-71165600, infos@elsevier-masson.fr.

616.89 FRA ISSN 0246-1072
➤ **ENCYCLOPEDIE MEDICO-CHIRURGICALE. PSYCHIATRIE.** Text in French. 1955. 6 base vols. plus q. updates. EUR 1,353 (effective 2006). bibl.; charts; illus. **Document type:** *Academic/Scholarly.* **Description:** Offers psychiatrists an up-to-date, comprehensive reference for diagnosing and treating psychiatric disorders.
Related titles: Online - full text ed.
—INIST.
Published by: Elsevier Masson (Subsidiary of: Elsevier Health Sciences), 62 Rue Camille Desmoulins, Issy les Moulineaux, Cedex 92442, France. TEL 33-1-71165500, FAX 33-1-71165600, infos@elsevier-masson.fr.

➤ **ENCYCLOPEDIE MEDICO-CHIRURGICALE. RADIOLOGIE ET IMAGERIE MEDICALE. MUSCULOSQUELETTIQUE - NEUROLOGIQUE - MAXILLOFACIALE.** *see* MEDICAL SCIENCES—Radiology And Nuclear Medicine

616.8 SRB ISSN 0351-2665
ENGRAMI. Text in Serbo-Croatian; Summaries in English, Russian. 1979. q. **Document type:** *Journal, Academic/Scholarly.*
Indexed: E-psyche.
Published by: (Udruzenje Psihijatara Srbije/Serbian Psychiatric Association), Klinicki Centar Srbije, Institut za Psihijatriju, Pasterova br 2, Belgrade, 11000. TEL 381-11-657955, psihin@net.yu, http://www.klinicki-centar.co.yu. Ed. Dimitrije Milovanovic. Circ: 500.

616.89 FRA ISSN 0750-6791
ENTRETIENS DE BICHAT. CHIRURGIE-SPECIALITES. Text in French. 1948. a. EUR 140 (effective 2008 & 2009). **Document type:** *Monographic series, Trade.*
Incorporates (1974-2006): Entretiens de Bichat Pitie Salpetriere. Odontologie et Stomatologie (0151-6531); Former titles (until 1977): Entretiens de Bichat Pitie Salpetriere. Chirurgie Specialites Psychiatrie (0750-6783); (until 1975): Les Entretiens de Bichat. Chirurgie Specialites Psychiatrie (0750-6775); (until 1972): Entretiens de Bichat. Chirurgie-Specialites (0423-2453)
—INIST.
Published by: Expansion Scientifique Francaise, 15 Rue Saint-Benoit, Paris, 75278 Cedex 06, France. TEL 33-1-45484260, FAX 33-1-45448155, expansionscientifiquefrancaise@wanadoo.fr, http://www.expansionscientifique.com.

EPIDEMIOLOGY AND PSYCHIATRIC SCIENCES. *see* PUBLIC HEALTH AND SAFETY

616.853 362.196 DNK ISSN 0107-2668
EPILEPSI. Text in Danish. 1967. q. DKK 250 to individual members; DKK 500 to institutional members (effective 2008). adv. bk.rev. illus. **Document type:** *Newsletter, Consumer.* **Description:** Publishes medical and general information about epilepsy, advocacy and activities in the organization.
Formerly (until 1980): Tidsskrift for Epilepsi (0105-0680)
Indexed: E-psyche.
Published by: Dansk Epilepsiforening/Danish Epilepsy Association, Kongensgade 68, Odense C, 5000, Denmark. TEL 45-66-119091, FAX 45-66-117177, epilepsi@epilepsiforeningen.dk.

616.853 TUR ISSN 1300-7157
EPILEPSI. Text in Turkish, English. 1995. 3/yr. **Document type:** *Journal, Academic/Scholarly.*
Related titles: Online - full text ed.: free (effective 2011).
Published by: (Turk Epilepsi ile Savas Dernegi/Turkish Chapter of International League against Epilepsy), KARE Publishing http://www.onkder.org.

616.853 USA ISSN 0013-9580
RC395 CODEN: EPILAK
➤ **EPILEPSIA.** Text in English. 1960. m. GBP 1,095 in United Kingdom to institutions; EUR 1,391 in Europe to institutions; USD 1,572 in the Americas to institutions; USD 2,146 elsewhere to institutions; GBP 1,260 combined subscription in United Kingdom to institutions (print & online eds.); EUR 1,600 combined subscription in Europe to institutions (print & online eds.); USD 1,809 combined subscription in the Americas to institutions (print & online eds.); USD 2,468 combined subscription elsewhere to institutions (print & online eds.) (effective 2012). adv. bk.rev. charts; illus. back issues avail.; reprint service avail. from PSC. **Document type:** *Journal, Academic/Scholarly.* **Description:** Provides current clinical and research results on all aspects of epilepsy.
Related titles: Online - full text ed.: ISSN 1528-1167. GBP 1,095 in United Kingdom to institutions; EUR 1,391 in Europe to institutions; USD 1,572 in the Americas to institutions; USD 2,146 elsewhere to institutions (effective 2012) (from IngentaConnect).
Indexed: A01, A03, A08, A20, A22, A26, A34, A36, ASCA, B21, B25, BDM&CN, BIOBASE, BIOSIS Prev, CA, CABA, CIN, ChemAb, ChemTitl, CurCont, D01, DBA, DentInd, E-psyche, E01, E12, EMBASE, ExcerpMed, F08, GH, H12, H17, I12, IABS, IDIS, INI, ISR, IndMed, IndVet, Inpharma, JW-N, LT, MEDLINE, MycolAb, N02, N03, NSA, NSCI, P03, P30, P33, P35, P39, P43, PN&I, PsycInfo, PsycholAb, R08, R10, R12, RA&MP, RM&VM, RRTA, Reac, S12, SCI, SCOPUS, T02, T05, VS, W07.
—BLDSC (3793.700000), CASDDS, GNLM, IE, Infotrieve, Ingenta, INIST. **CCC.**
Published by: (International League Against Epilepsy), Wiley-Blackwell Publishing, Inc. (Subsidiary of: Wiley-Blackwell Publishing Ltd.), 111 River St, Hoboken, NJ 07030. TEL 201-748-6000, FAX 201-748-6088, info@wiley.com, http://www.wiley.com/. Eds. Philip A Schwartzkroin, Simon D Shorvon. Adv. contact Joann Mitchell TEL 212-904-0364. **Subscr. to:** Wiley-Blackwell Publishing Ltd.

616.853 362.1 FIN ISSN 0780-0150
EPILEPSIA-LEHTI. Text in Finnish; Summaries in English, Swedish. 1968. q. EUR 49 (effective 2005). adv. bk.rev. **Document type:** *Journal, Consumer.*
Formerly (until 1983): Epilepsia (0356-598X)
Indexed: E-psyche.
Published by: Epilepsialiitto/Finnish Epilepsy Association, Malmin Kauppatie 26, Helsinki, 00700, Finland. TEL 358-9-3508230, FAX 358-9-35082322.

616.853 CHE
EPILEPSIE. Text and summaries in French, German, Italian. 1983. 2/yr. adv. bk.rev. **Document type:** *Journal, Academic/Scholarly.* **Description:** Covers medical and social aspects, featuring research in treatment, diagnosis, therapy, and heredity, as well as social and educational problems of different age groups. Includes list of events.
Indexed: E-psyche.
Published by: epi-suisse, Seefeldstr 84, Zurich, 8034, Switzerland. TEL 41-43-4886880, FAX 41-43-4886881, info@epi-suisse.ch, http://www.epi-suisse.ch. Ed. Margret Becker. R&P, Adv. contact Ernst Zweifel. Circ: 800.

616.853 FRA ISSN 1149-6576
EPILEPSIES. Text in French. q. EUR 268 combined subscription domestic to institutions (print & online eds.); EUR 284 combined subscription in the European Union to institutions (print & online eds.); EUR 292 combined subscription elsewhere to institutions (print & online eds.) (effective 2011). **Document type:** *Journal, Academic/Scholarly.* **Description:** Provides a forum for neurologists, specialised institutions, general practitioners, nurses, technicians and electroencephalographers.
Related titles: Online - full text ed.: ISSN 1950-6937.
Indexed: A22, E-psyche, EMBASE, ExcerpMed, NSCI, R10, Reac, SCI, SCOPUS, W07.

—BLDSC (3793.740000), GNLM, IE, Ingenta, INIST. **CCC.**
Published by: (Ligue Francaise Contre l'Epilepsie), John Libbey Eurotext, 127 Av. de la Republique, Montrouge, 92120, France. TEL 33-1-46730660, FAX 33-1-40840999, contact@jle.com, http://www.john-libbey-eurotext.fr. Ed. Michele Bureau.

616.853 JPN ISSN 1882-5567
RC372.A1
EPILEPSY & SEIZURE. Text in English. 2008. irreg. free (effective 2008). **Document type:** *Journal, Academic/Scholarly.*
Media: Online - full content.
Indexed: EMBASE, ExcerpMed, SCOPUS.
—CCC.
Published by: Nihon Tenkan Gakkai/Japan Epilepsy Society, 4-6-15 Ogawahigashi-cho Kodaira, Tokyo, 187-0031, Japan. jessec@szec.hosp.go.jp. Ed. Kousuke Kanemoto.

616.853 USA ISSN 1535-7597
RC372.A1
EPILEPSY CURRENTS (ENGLISH EDITION). Text in English. 2001. bi-m. GBP 154 in United Kingdom to institutions; EUR 196 in Europe to institutions; USD 191 in the Americas to institutions; USD 302 elsewhere to institutions; GBP 178 combined subscription in United Kingdom to institutions (print & online eds.); EUR 226 combined subscription in Europe to institutions (print & online eds.); USD 220 combined subscription in the Americas to institutions (print & online eds.); USD 348 combined subscription elsewhere to institutions (print & online eds.) (effective 2011). adv. back issues avail.; reprint service avail. from PSC. **Document type:** *Journal, Academic/Scholarly.* **Description:** Provides reviews, commentaries and abstracts from the worlds literature on the research and treatment of epilepsy.
Related titles: Online - full text ed.: ISSN 1535-7511. GBP 154 in United Kingdom to institutions; EUR 196 in Europe to institutions; USD 191 in the Americas to institutions; USD 302 elsewhere to institutions (effective 2011) (from IngentaConnect); ◆ Spanish ed.: Epilepsy Currents (Spanish Edition). ISSN 1886-9777.
Indexed: A01, A03, A08, A22, A26, B21, CA, CurCont, E01, NSA, P30, RefZh, SCI, T02, W07.
—BLDSC (3793.801000), IE, Ingenta. **CCC.**
Published by: (American Epilepsy Society), Wiley-Blackwell Publishing, Inc. (Subsidiary of: Wiley-Blackwell Publishing Ltd.), 111 River St, Hoboken, NJ 07030. TEL 201-748-6000, FAX 201-748-6088, info@wiley.com. Eds. Gregory K Bergey, Michael A Rogawski. Adv. contact Karl Franz TEL 781-388-8470.

616.853 ESP ISSN 1886-9777
EPILEPSY CURRENTS (SPANISH EDITION). Text in Spanish. 2006. 3/yr. back issues avail. **Document type:** *Journal, Academic/Scholarly.*
Related titles: Online - full text ed.: ISSN 1886-9890. 2006; ◆ English ed.: Epilepsy Currents (English Edition). ISSN 1535-7597.
Published by: Grupo Ars XXI de Comunicacion, SA, Muntaner 262 Atico 2a., Barcelona, 08021, Spain. TEL 34-90-2195484, FAX 34-93-2722902, info@arsxxi.com. Ed. Antonio Gil-Nagel.

616.853 NLD ISSN 0920-1211
RC372 CODEN: EPIRE8
➤ **EPILEPSY RESEARCH.** Text in English. 1987. 15/yr. EUR 3,289 in Europe to institutions; JPY 436,700 in Japan to institutions; USD 3,678 elsewhere to institutions (effective 2012). adv. bk.rev. index. back issues avail.; reprints avail. **Document type:** *Journal, Academic/Scholarly.* **Description:** Provides for rapid publication of high-quality articles in both experimental and clinical epileptology, where the principal emphasis of the research is concerned with brain mechanisms in epilepsy.
Incorporates (1988-1999): Journal of Epilepsy (0896-6974)
Related titles: Microform ed.: (from PQC); Online - full text ed.: ISSN 1872-6844 (from IngentaConnect, ScienceDirect).
Indexed: A01, A03, A08, A20, A22, A26, A34, A35, A36, A37, A38, ASCA, ASG, AgBio, B21, B25, BIOBASE, BIOSIS Prev, CA, CABA, CIN, ChemAb, ChemTitl, CurCont, D01, E-psyche, EMBASE, ExcerpMed, GH, H17, I05, IABS, ISR, IndMed, Inpharma, MEDLINE, MycolAb, N02, N03, N04, NSA, NSCI, P30, P33, P35, P39, PN&I, R08, R10, R12, RA&MP, Reac, SCI, SCOPUS, SoyAb, T02, T05, VS, W07.
—BLDSC (3793.805000), CASDDS, GNLM, IE, Infotrieve, Ingenta, INIST. **CCC.**
Published by: Elsevier BV (Subsidiary of: Elsevier Science & Technology), Radarweg 29, PO Box 211, Amsterdam, 1000 AE, Netherlands. TEL 31-20-4853911, FAX 31-20-4852457, JournalsCustomerServiceEMEA@elsevier.com, http://www.elsevier.nl. Eds. A Pitkanen, W H Theodore.

616.853 USA ISSN 2090-1348
▼ ➤ **EPILEPSY RESEARCH AND TREATMENT.** Text in English. 2009. irreg. USD 195 (effective 2011). **Document type:** *Journal, Academic/Scholarly.* **Description:** Publishes original research articles, review articles, case reports, and clinical studies related to all aspects of epilepsy.
Related titles: Online - full text ed.: ISSN 2090-1356. free (effective 2011).
Indexed: A01, T02.
Published by: Hindawi Publishing Corporation, 410 Park Ave, 15th Fl, PMB 287, New York, NY 10022. FAX 215-893-4392, 866-446-3294, info@hindawi.com.

616.853 GBR ISSN 0958-496X
EPILEPSY TODAY. Text in English. 1976. bi-m. GBP 17 to non-members; GBP 3.50 per issue to non-members; free to members (effective 2009). adv. bk.rev. **Document type:** *Magazine, Consumer.* **Description:** Features informative articles on epilepsy.
Former titles (until 1987): Epilepsy Now! (0262-5474); (until 1981): Epilepsy News (0308-9703)
Related titles: Online - full text ed.: free to members (effective 2009).
Indexed: E-psyche.
—CCC.
Published by: British Epilepsy Association, New Anstey House, Gate Way Dr, Yeadon, Leeds, LS19 7XY, United Kingdom. TEL 44-113-2108800, 808-800-5050, FAX 44-113-3910300, epilepsy@epilepsy.org.uk. Circ: 21,500.

616.853 USA ISSN 1060-9369
EPILEPSY U S A. Text in English. 1972 (vol.5). 6/yr. USD 15 (effective 2008). bk.rev. illus. reprints avail. **Document type:** *Magazine, Consumer.* **Description:** Covers medical, legal, and legislative news and features for people with epilepsy.
Formerly (until 1991): National Spokesman (0091-2387)
Indexed: E-psyche, RehabLit.
Published by: Epilepsy Foundation of America, 8301 Professional Pl, Landover, MD 20785-2238. TEL 301-459-3700. Ed. Lisa Boylan.

616.853 AUS ISSN 0729-7823
EPILEPSY VICTORIA. Text in English. 1980. q. bk.rev. back issues avail. **Document type:** *Newsletter, Consumer.* **Description:** Covers all aspects of epilepsy, including research, human interest, medicine, fundraising and welfare.
Indexed: E-psyche.
Published by: Epilepsy Foundation of Victoria, 818 Burke Rd, Camberwell, VIC 3124, Australia. TEL 61-3-98059111, FAX 61-3-98827159, epilepsy@epilepsy.asn.au, http://www.epinet.org.au. Ed. Gail Chrisfield. Circ: 2,500.

616.853 FRA ISSN 1294-9361
CODEN: EPDIFP
➤ **EPILEPTIC DISORDERS**; international epilepsy journal with videotape. Text in English. 1999. q. USD 698 combined subscription domestic to institutions (print & online eds.); USD 722 combined subscription in Europe to institutions (print & online eds.); USD 734 combined subscription elsewhere to institutions (print & online eds.) (effective 2011). adv. bk.rev. back issues avail. **Document type:** *Journal, Academic/Scholarly.* **Description:** Publishes clinical and review articles on all facets of epilepsy and related disorders.
Related titles: Online - full text ed.: ISSN 1950-6945 (from IngentaConnect).
Indexed: A22, B21, CurCont, E01, EMBASE, ExcerpMed, IndMed, Inpharma, MEDLINE, NSA, NSCI, P03, P30, P35, PsycInfo, PsycholAb, R10, Reac, SCI, SCOPUS, W07.
—BLDSC (3793.807200), IE, Infotrieve, Ingenta, INIST. **CCC.**
Published by: (Hopital Robert-Debre, Neurologie Pediatrique), John Libbey Eurotext, 127 Av. de la Republique, Montrouge, 92120, France. TEL 33-1-46730660, FAX 33-1-40840999, contact@jle.com, http://www.john-libbey-eurotext.fr. Ed. Alexis Arzimanoglou.

616.853 POL ISSN 1230-5294
➤ **EPILEPTOLOGIA.** Text in Polish. 1993. q. EUR 53 foreign (effective 2006). **Document type:** *Journal, Academic/Scholarly.*
Published by: Fundacja Epileptologii, ul Wiertnicza 122, Warsaw, 02952, Poland. TEL 48-22-8582907, FAX 48-22-6427434, fundacja@epilepsy.org.pl. Ed. Jerzy Majkowski. **Dist. by:** Ars Polona, Obroncow 25, Warsaw 03933, Poland. TEL 48-22-5098609, FAX 48-22-5098610, arspolona@arspolona.com.pl, http://www.arspolona.com.pl.

616.8 FRA ISSN 1287-258X
ESSAIM; revue de psychanalyse. Text in French. 1998. s-a. EUR 50 domestic; EUR 58 foreign (effective 2011). back issues avail. **Document type:** *Journal, Academic/Scholarly.*
Related titles: Online - full text ed.: ISSN 1776-2839.
Indexed: SCOPUS.
Published by: Editions Eres, 33 Av. Marcel Dassault, Toulouse, 31500, France. TEL 33-5-61751576, FAX 33-5-61735289, eres@edition-eres.com. Ed. Erik Porge. Circ: 700.

616.8 360 USA ISSN 1559-4343
BF76.4 CODEN: EHSSF6
➤ **ETHICAL HUMAN PSYCHOLOGY AND PSYCHIATRY**; an international journal of critical inquiry. Text in English; Abstracts in Spanish, French. 1999. 3/yr. USD 75 domestic to individuals; USD 110 foreign to individuals; USD 210 domestic to institutions; USD 240 foreign to institutions; USD 113 combined subscription domestic to individuals (print & online eds.); USD 165 combined subscription foreign to individuals (print & online eds.); USD 300 combined subscription domestic to institutions (print & online eds.); USD 360 combined subscription foreign to institutions (print & online eds.) (effective 2009). adv. bk.rev.; software rev.; video rev. abstr.; bibl.; charts; illus.; stat. 120 p./no.; back issues avail.; reprints avail. **Document type:** *Journal, Academic/Scholarly.* **Description:** Publishes interdisciplinary and international critiques of theory and practice across the fields of health and social sciences seeking to raise the level of ethical awareness.
Formerly (until Spr.2004): Ethical Human Sciences and Services (1523-150X)
Related titles: Online - full text ed.: ISSN 1938-9000. USD 70 domestic to individuals; USD 100 foreign to individuals; USD 200 domestic to institutions; USD 230 foreign to institutions (effective 2009) (from IngentaConnect).
Indexed: A01, A03, CA, EMBASE, ExcerpMed, P03, P20, P22, P25, P27, P30, P43, P48, P50, P54, PAIS, PQC, PhilInd, PsycInfo, PsycholAb, R10, Reac, S02, S03, SCOPUS, SSA, SWR&A, SociolAb, T02.
—BLDSC (3814.640650), IE, Ingenta. **CCC.**
Published by: Springer Publishing Company, 11 W 42nd St, 15th Fl, New York, NY 10036. TEL 212-431-4370, FAX 212-941-7842, contactus@springerpub.com, http://www.springerjournals.com. Eds. Brian Keane, James A. Tucker, Leighton Whitaker. adv.: B&W page USD 280; trim 6.75 x 10. Circ: 376 (paid). **Co-sponsor:** International Center for the Study of Psychiatry and Psychology.

616.8 FRA ISSN 1272-3509
ETUDES, RECHERCHES, ACTIONS EN SANTE MENTALE EN EUROPE. Variant title: E R A S M E. Text in French. 1996. irreg. back issues avail. **Document type:** *Monographic series, Consumer.*
Published by: Editions Eres, 33 Av. Marcel Dassault, Toulouse, 31500, France. TEL 33-5-61751576, FAX 33-5-61735289, eres@edition-eres.com.

616.8 DEU ISSN 0940-1334
CODEN: EAPNES
➤ **EUROPEAN ARCHIVES OF PSYCHIATRY AND CLINICAL NEUROSCIENCE**; official organ of the German society for biological psychiatry. Text in English. 1868. bi-m. EUR 1,807, USD 2,212 combined subscription to institutions (print & online eds.) (effective 2012). abstr.; bibl. 50 p./no. 2 cols./p.; back issues avail.; reprint service avail. from PSC. **Document type:** *Journal, Academic/Scholarly.* **Description:** Covers clinical psychiatry, psychopathology, and epidemiology, as well as neuropathological, neurophysiological, and neurochemical studies of psychiatric disorders.
Former titles (until 1990): European Archives of Psychiatry and Neurological Sciences (0175-758X); (until 1984): Archiv fuer Psychiatrie und Nervenkrankheiten (0003-9373); Which incorporated (19??-1944): Zeitschrift fuer die Gesamte Neurologie und Psychiatrie (0303-4194); Which was formerly (until 1910): Zentralblatt fuer Nervenheilkunde und Psychiatrie (0340-3378)
Related titles: Microfiche ed.: (from BHP); Microform ed.: (from PQC); Online - full text ed.: ISSN 1433-8491 (from IngentaConnect).
Indexed: A01, A03, A08, A20, A22, A26, ASCA, B21, CA, ChemAb, CurCont, E-psyche, E01, E08, EMBASE, ExcerpMed, GJP, H12, I05, INI, ISR, IndMed, Inpharma, MEDLINE, NSA, NSCI, P03, P20, P22, P25, P30, P35, P43, P48, P54, PQC, PsycInfo, PsycholAb, R10, Reac, S02, S03, S09, SCI, SCOPUS, T02, W07.
—BLDSC (3829.488545), CASDDS, GNLM, IE, Infotrieve, Ingenta, INIST. **CCC.**
Published by: (Gesamtverband Deutscher Nervenaerzte), Dr. Dietrich Steinkopff Verlag (Subsidiary of: Springer Science+Business Media), Tiergartenstr 17, Heidelberg, 69121, Germany. TEL 49-6221-4878821, FAX 49-6221-4878830, info.steinkopff@springer.com, http://www.steinkopff.com. Eds. Dr. J FW Deakin, Dr. H.-J. Moeller. Circ: 500 (controlled). **Subscr. in the Americas to:** Springer New York LLC, Journal Fulfillment, PO Box 2485, Secaucus, NJ 07096. TEL 201-348-4033, FAX 201-348-4505; **Subscr. to:** Springer Distribution Center, Kundenservice Zeitschriften, Haberstr 7, Heidelberg 69126, Germany. TEL 49-6221-3454303, FAX 49-6221-3454229, subscriptions@springer.com.

M

616.8 DEU ISSN 1018-8827
RJ499.A1 CODEN: EAPSE9
➤ **EUROPEAN CHILD & ADOLESCENT PSYCHIATRY**; official journal of the European Society for Child and Adolescent Psychiatry. Text in English. 1992. bi-m. EUR 804, USD 943 combined subscription to institutions (print & online eds.) (effective 2012). adv. bk.rev. abstr.; bibl. back issues avail.; reprint service avail. from PSC. **Document type:** *Journal, Academic/Scholarly.* **Description:** Aims to promote the growth of empirically based clinical child and adolescent psychiatry, not only in Europe but throughout the world.
Related titles: Online - full text ed.: ISSN 1435-165X (from IngentaConnect); Supplement(s): ISSN 1433-5719.
Indexed: A01, A02, A03, A08, A22, A26, ASCA, ASSIA, B21, C06, C07, C08, C11, C28, CA, CINAHL, CurCont, DIP, E-psyche, E01, E07, EMBASE, ExcerpMed, F09, FR, FamI, H04, H12, IBR, IBZ, INI, IndMed, MEDLINE, NSA, P03, P10, P12, P20, P22, P24, P25, P27, P30, P43, P48, P53, P54, PQC, PsycInfo, PsycholAb, R10, Reac, S02, S03, S21, SCI, SCOPUS, SOPODA, SSCI, SociolAb, T02, W07.
—BLDSC (3829.600600), GNLM, IE, Infotrieve, Ingenta, INIST. **CCC.**
Published by: (European Society for Child and Adolescent Psychiatry), Dr. Dietrich Steinkopff Verlag (Subsidiary of: Springer Science+Business Media), Tiergartenstr 17, Heidelberg, 69121, Germany. TEL 49-6221-4878821, FAX 49-6221-4878830, info.steinkopff@springer.com, http://www.steinkopff.com. Ed. Jan K Buitelaar. Pub. Dietrich Steinkopff. adv.: B&W page EUR 830, color page EUR 1,870; trim 210 x 279. Circ: 590 (controlled). **Subscr. in the Americas to:** Springer New York LLC, Journal Fulfillment, PO Box 2485, Secaucus, NJ 07096. TEL 201-348-4033, FAX 201-348-4505, journals-ny@springer.com; **Subscr. to:** Springer Distribution Center, Kundenservice Zeitschriften, Haberstr 7, Heidelberg 69126, Germany. TEL 49-6221-3454303, FAX 49-6221-3454229, subscriptions@springer.com.

616.8 150 ITA ISSN 1973-6266
EUROPEAN JOURNAL OF AUTOGENIC AND BIONOMIC STUDIES. Text in English. 2007. s-a. **Document type:** *Journal, Academic/Scholarly.*
Published by: Formist, Viale Regina Margherita 56, Cagliari, 09124, Italy. TEL 39-070-653060, formist@tiscali.it, http://www.formist.eu.

EUROPEAN JOURNAL OF CLINICAL PSYCHOLOGY AND PSYCHIATRY. *see* PSYCHOLOGY

616.8 HUN ISSN 1788-4934
➤ **EUROPEAN JOURNAL OF MENTAL HEALTH**; individual, family, community and society. Text in English, German. 2006. s-a. EUR 250, USD 348 combined subscription (print & online eds.) (effective 2011). **Document type:** *Journal, Academic/Scholarly.*
Related titles: Online - full content ed.: ISSN 1788-7119. free (effective 2011).
Indexed: EMBASE, ExcerpMed, P03, PsycInfo, SCOPUS.
—IE.
Published by: Akademiai Kiado Rt. (Subsidiary of: Wolters Kluwer N.V.), Prielle Kornelia u 19/D, Budapest, 1117, Hungary. TEL 36-1-4648222, FAX 36-1-4648221, journals@akkrt.hu. Eds. Norbert Mette, Teodora Tomcsanyi.

616.8 GBR ISSN 1351-5101
RC321 CODEN: EJNEFL
➤ **EUROPEAN JOURNAL OF NEUROLOGY.** Text in English. 1994. m. GBP 1,439 in United Kingdom to institutions; EUR 1,826 in Europe to institutions; USD 2,306 in the Americas to institutions; USD 2,819 elsewhere to institutions; GBP 1,655 combined subscription in United Kingdom to institutions (print & online eds.); EUR 2,100 combined subscription in Europe to institutions (print & online eds.); USD 2,653 combined subscription in the Americas to institutions (print & online eds.); USD 3,242 combined subscription elsewhere to institutions (print & online eds.) (effective 2012). adv. bk.rev. Index. back issues avail.; reprint service avail. from PSC. **Document type:** *Journal, Academic/Scholarly.* **Description:** Covers all areas of clinical and basic research in neurology, including pre-clinical research of immediate translational value for new potential treatments.
Related titles: Online - full text ed.: ISSN 1468-1331. 1994. GBP 1,439 in United Kingdom to institutions; EUR 1,826 in Europe to institutions; USD 2,306 in the Americas to institutions; USD 2,819 elsewhere to institutions (effective 2012) (from IngentaConnect); Spanish ed.: ISSN 1579-2528; Supplement(s): ISSN 1471-0552.
Indexed: A01, A02, A03, A08, A20, A22, A26, A34, A36, AIDS Ab, ASCA, B21, B25, BIOBASE, BIOSIS Prev, C11, CA, CABA, CurCont, E-psyche, E01, E12, EMBASE, ESPM, ExcerpMed, F08, F11, F12, GH, H04, H12, I05, IABS, IndMed, IndVet, Inpharma, JW-N, MEDLINE, MycolAb, N02, N03, NSA, NSCI, P03, P30, P33, P35, P39, P43, PN&I, PsycInfo, PsycholAb, R08, R10, R12, RA&MP, RILM, RM&VM, Reac, RefZh, SCI, SCOPUS, T02, T05, ToxAb, VS, W07, W10.
—BLDSC (3829.731680), GNLM, IE, Infotrieve, Ingenta, INIST. **CCC.**
Published by: (European Federation of Neurological Societies AUT), Wiley-Blackwell Publishing Ltd. (Subsidiary of: John Wiley & Sons, Inc.), 9600 Garsington Rd, Oxford, OX4 2DQ, United Kingdom. TEL 44-1865-776868, FAX 44-1865-714591, customerservices@blackwellpublishing.com. Eds. Anthony Schapira, Matti Hillbom.

616.8 GBR ISSN 0953-816X
QP351 CODEN: EJONEI
➤ **EUROPEAN JOURNAL OF NEUROSCIENCE.** Abbreviated title: E J N. Text in English. 1989. s-m. GBP 3,393 in United Kingdom to institutions; EUR 4,312 in Europe to institutions; USD 6,271 in the Americas to institutions; USD 7,317 elsewhere to institutions; GBP 3,902 combined subscription in United Kingdom to institutions (print & online eds.); EUR 4,958 combined subscription in Europe to institutions (print & online eds.); USD 7,212 combined subscription in the Americas to institutions (print & online eds.); USD 8,418 combined subscription elsewhere to institutions (print & online eds.) (effective 2012). adv. back issues avail.; reprint service avail. from PSC. **Document type:** *Journal, Academic/Scholarly.* **Description:** Aims to advance our understanding of organization and function of the nervous system in health and disease, thereby improving the diagnosis and treatment of neuropsychiatric and neurodegenerative disorders.
Related titles: Microfiche ed.: (from PQC); Online - full text ed.: ISSN 1460-9568. GBP 3,393 in United Kingdom to institutions; EUR 4,312 in Europe to institutions; USD 6,271 in the Americas to institutions; USD 7,317 elsewhere to institutions (effective 2012) (from IngentaConnect); ◆ Supplement(s): European Journal of Neuroscience. Supplement. ISSN 1470-8566.
Indexed: A01, A02, A03, A08, A20, A22, A26, A34, A35, A36, A38, ASCA, AgBio, B21, B25, BIOBASE, BIOSIS Prev, C11, CA, CABA, CTA, ChemoAb, CurCont, D01, E-psyche, E01, E12, EMBASE, ExcerpMed, GH, H04, H12, H16, I05, IABS, ISR, IndMed, IndVet, Inpharma, MEDLINE, MycolAb, N02, N03, N04, NSA, NSCI, P03, P25, P30, P33, P35, P37, P39, P43, P48, PHN&I, PQC, PsycInfo, PsycholAb, R07, R08, R10, RA&MP, Reac, RefZh, S12, SCI, SCOPUS, SoyAb, T02, VS, W07.
—BLDSC (3829.731700), GNLM, IE, Infotrieve, Ingenta, INIST. **CCC.**
Published by: (Federation of European Neuroscience Societies DEU), Wiley-Blackwell Publishing Ltd. (Subsidiary of: John Wiley & Sons, Inc.), 9600 Garsington Rd, Oxford, OX4 2DQ, United Kingdom. TEL 44-1865-776868, FAX 44-1865-714591, customerservices@blackwellpublishing.com. Eds. Jean-Marc Fritschy, Martin Sarter. Adv. contact Joanna Baker TEL 44-1865-476271. **Co-sponsor:** European Neuroscience Association.

616.8 GBR ISSN 1470-8566
EUROPEAN JOURNAL OF NEUROSCIENCE. SUPPLEMENT. Text in English. 1989. irreg. includes with subscr. to European Journal of Neuroscience. **Document type:** *Journal, Academic/Scholarly.*
Formerly (until 2000): Supplement to the European Journal of Neuroscience (1359-5962)
Related titles: ◆ Supplement to: European Journal of Neuroscience. ISSN 0953-816X.
Indexed: EMBASE, ExcerpMed, IndMed, MEDLINE, P30.
—INIST. **CCC.**
Published by: Wiley-Blackwell Publishing Ltd. (Subsidiary of: John Wiley & Sons, Inc.), 9600 Garsington Rd, Oxford, OX4 2DQ, United Kingdom. TEL 44-1865-776868, FAX 44-1865-714591, customerservices@blackwellpublishing.com, http://www.wiley.com/.

EUROPEAN JOURNAL OF PAEDIATRIC NEUROLOGY. *see* MEDICAL SCIENCES—Pediatrics

616.89 GBR ISSN 1754-3207
RB127
EUROPEAN JOURNAL OF PAIN SUPPLEMENTS. Text in English. 2007. a.
Related titles: Online - full text ed.: ISSN 1878-0075 (from ScienceDirect); ◆ Supplement to: European Journal of Pain. ISSN 1090-3801.
Indexed: CA, EMBASE, ExcerpMed, SCOPUS, T02.
—BLDSC (3829.733384), IE. **CCC.**
Published by: Elsevier Ltd (Subsidiary of: Elsevier Science & Technology), The Blvd, Langford Ln, Kidlington, Oxford, OX5 1GB, United Kingdom. TEL 44-1865-843000, FAX 44-1865-843010.

616.89 ESP ISSN 0213-6163
RC321 CODEN: EJOPEO
➤ **THE EUROPEAN JOURNAL OF PSYCHIATRY.** Text in English. 1986. q. EUR 140 (effective 2009). adv. bk.rev. **Document type:** *Journal, Academic/Scholarly.* **Description:** Reports the scientific activity of European psychiatrists. Presents an eclectic orientation in its scientific approach and is open to Psychiatry, Mental Health and all related fields.
Related titles: Online - full text ed.: 2005. free (effective 2011).
Indexed: A20, A22, ASCA, ASSIA, B25, BIOSIS Prev, CurCont, E-psyche, EMBASE, ExcerpMed, FR, Faml, MycolAb, P03, PsycInfo, PsycholAb, R10, Reac, SCOPUS, SOPODA, SSCI, SociolAb, W07.
—BLDSC (3829.737700), GNLM, IE, Infotrieve, Ingenta, INIST. **CCC.**
Published by: Universidad de Zaragoza, Facultad de Medicina, Domingo Miral s/n, Zaragoza, 50009, Spain. TEL 34-976-762068, FAX 34-976-761664, http://wzar.unizar.es/. Ed. A Lobo.

616.891 GBR
➤ **EUROPEAN JOURNAL OF PSYCHOTHERAPY AND COUNSELLING.** Text in English. 1998. q. GBP 406 combined subscription in United Kingdom to institutions (print & online eds.); EUR 535, USD 672 combined subscription to institutions (print & online eds.) (effective 2012). adv. back issues avail.; reprint service avail. from PSC. **Document type:** *Journal, Academic/Scholarly.* **Description:** Investigates links between the different traditions of health care, counselling, and psychotherapy; the relationship of physical to mental health; and interactions among the psychotherapists, counsellors, and health care providers.
Formerly (until 2006): European Journal of Psychotherapy, Counselling and Health (1364-2537)
Related titles: Online - full text ed.: GBP 365 in United Kingdom to institutions; EUR 482, USD 604 to institutions (effective 2012) (from IngentaConnect).
Indexed: A01, A02, A03, A08, A22, CA, E-psyche, E01, Faml, P03, P43, P54, PsycInfo, PsycholAb, S21, T02.
—IE, Infotrieve, Ingenta. **CCC.**
Published by: Routledge (Subsidiary of: Taylor & Francis Group), 4 Park Sq, Milton Park, Abingdon, Oxon OX14 4RN, United Kingdom. TEL 44-20-70176000, FAX 44-20-70176336, subscriptions@tandf.co.uk, http://www.routledge.com. Ed. Del Lowenthal. Adv. contact Linda Hann TEL 44-1344-779945. **Subscr. to:** Taylor & Francis Ltd., Journals Customer Service, Sheepen Pl, Colchester, Essex CO3 3LP, United Kingdom. TEL 44-20-70175544, FAX 44-20-70175198, tf.enquiries@tfinforma.com.

616.8 GBR ISSN 2041-8000
▼ ➤ **THE EUROPEAN NEUROLOGICAL JOURNAL.** Text in English. 2009 (Oct.). s-a. free. adv. back issues avail.; reprints avail. **Document type:** *Journal, Academic/Scholarly.* **Description:** Provides information for neurologists and other related health care professionals who practice in Europe. Covers clinical and experimental aspects of neurological diseases and disorders. The journal is designed to ensure patient level changes occur regarding management & diagnosis and addresses the impact of recent developments on best practices in Europe.
Related titles: E-mail ed.; Online - full text ed.: free (effective 2011).
Indexed: A01, A36, CABA, GH, N02, N03, T02.
Published by: San Lucas Medical Ltd., 11-12 Freetrade House, Lowther Rd, Stanmore, Middlesex HA7 1EP, United Kingdom. TEL 44-20-70840330, FAX 44-20-70840330, http://www.slm-oncology.com/. Ed. Jim Jones. Pub. Stephen Davidson. Adv. contact Ryan Joshi TEL 44-20-71930673. B&W page GBP 7,000, color page GBP 10,000. Circ: 9,000.

616.8 GBR ISSN 1758-3837
EUROPEAN NEUROLOGICAL REVIEW. Text in English. 2006. s-a. EUR 80 combined subscription in Europe to individuals (print & online eds.); USD 100 combined subscription in United States to individuals (print & online eds.); EUR 180 combined subscription in Europe to institutions (print & online eds.); USD 225 combined subscription in United States to institutions (print & online eds.) (effective 2009). adv. back issues avail. **Document type:** *Journal, Trade.* **Description:** Focuses on latest developments in clinical neuroscience and medical practice with special reference to drug therapy for diseases of the brain, central nervous system and associated mental health issues.
Formerly (until 2008): European Neurological Disease (1753-3953)
Related titles: Online - full text ed.: ISSN 1758-3845. EUR 70 in Europe to individuals; EUR 85 in United States to individuals; EUR 170 in Europe to institutions; EUR 210 in United States to institutions (effective 2009).
Published by: Touch Briefings (Subsidiary of: Touch Group plc), Saffron House, 6-10 Kirby St, London, EC1N 8TS, United Kingdom. TEL 44-20-74525600, FAX 44-20-74525606, info@touchbriefings.com, http://www.touchbriefings.com/.

616.8 CHE ISSN 0014-3022
RC321 CODEN: EUNEAP
➤ **EUROPEAN NEUROLOGY.** Text in English. 1897. 12/yr. CHF 3,646, EUR 2,914, USD 3,581 to institutions; CHF 4,000, EUR 3,196, USD 3,925 combined subscription to institutions (print & online eds.) (effective 2012). adv. bk.rev. index. back issues avail. **Document type:** *Journal, Academic/Scholarly.* **Description:** Covers clinical aspects of diseases of the nervous system and muscles, as well as their neuropathological, biochemical, and electrophysiological basis.
Supersedes in part (in 1968): Psychiatria et Neurologia (0370-1956); Which was formerly (until 1957): Monatsschrift fuer Psychiatrie und Neurologie (0369-1519)
Related titles: Microform ed.; Online - full text ed.: ISSN 1421-9913. CHF 3,544, EUR 2,836, USD 3,440 to institutions (effective 2012).
Indexed: A01, A02, A03, A08, A20, A22, ASCA, B21, B25, BDM&CN, BIOSIS Prev, CA, CIN, ChemAb, ChemTitl, CurCont, DentInd, E-psyche, E01, EMBASE, ExcerpMed, ISR, IndMed, Inpharma, MEDLINE, MycolAb, NSA, NSCI, P03, P20, P22, P25, P26, P30, P35, P43, P48, P54, PQC, PsycInfo, PsycholAb, R10, Reac, SCI, SCOPUS, SSCI, T02, W07.
—BLDSC (3829.765000), CASDDS, GNLM, IE, Infotrieve, Ingenta, INIST. **CCC.**
Published by: S. Karger AG, Allschwilerstr 10, Basel, 4055, Switzerland. TEL 41-61-3061111, FAX 41-61-3061234, karger@karger.ch, http://www.karger.ch. Ed. Julien Bogousslavsky. adv.: page CHF 1,815; trim 210 x 280. Circ: 1,100.

616.8 615.1 NLD ISSN 0924-977X
RM315 CODEN: EURNE8
➤ **EUROPEAN NEUROPSYCHOPHARMACOLOGY.** Text in English. 1990. 12/yr. EUR 1,317 in Europe to institutions; JPY 191,400 in Japan to institutions; USD 1,609 elsewhere to institutions (effective 2012). adv. bk.rev. abstr. back issues avail.; reprints avail. **Document type:** *Journal, Academic/Scholarly.* **Description:** Publishes clinical and basic research articles in the field of neuropsychopharmacology, with particular focus on the effects of centrally acting agents.
Related titles: Microform ed.: (from PQC); Online - full text ed.: ISSN 1873-7862 (from IngentaConnect, ScienceDirect).
Indexed: A01, A03, A08, A20, A22, A26, A35, A36, ASCA, AddicA, AgBio, B21, B25, BIOBASE, BIOSIS Prev, C33, CA, CABA, CIN, ChemAb, ChemTitl, CurCont, DBA, E-psyche, EMBASE, ExcerpMed, FoP, GH, H16, I05, IABS, INI, IPsyAb, ISR, IndMed, Inpharma, MEDLINE, MycolAb, N02, N03, NSA, NSCI, P03, P30, P35, PsycInfo, PsycholAb, R10, RA&MP, Reac, SCI, SCOPUS, T02, T05, VS, W07.
—BLDSC (3829.765350), CASDDS, GNLM, IE, Infotrieve, Ingenta, INIST. **CCC.**
Published by: (European College of Neuropsychopharmacology), Elsevier BV (Subsidiary of: Elsevier Science & Technology), Radarweg 29, PO Box 211, Amsterdam, 1000 AE, Netherlands. TEL 31-20-4853911, FAX 31-20-4852457, JournalsCustomerServiceEMEA@elsevier.com, http://www.elsevier.nl. Eds. Dr. J M van Ree, Dr. S A Montgomery.

616.8 FRA ISSN 0924-9338
CODEN: EUPSED
➤ **EUROPEAN PSYCHIATRY.** Text in English. 1986. 8/yr. EUR 742 in Europe to institutions; EUR 697.63 in France to institutions; JPY 101,600 in Japan to institutions; USD 968 elsewhere to institutions (effective 2012). adv. bk.rev. back issues avail. **Document type:** *Journal, Academic/Scholarly.* **Description:** Presents original research in psychopathology, nosography, chemotherapy, psychotherapy, clinical methodology, biological disorders and mental pathology, psychophysiology, neuropsychology, and animal behavior.
Formerly (until 1991): Psychiatry and Psychobiology (0767-399X)
Related titles: Microform ed.: (from PQC); Online - full text ed.: ISSN 1778-3585 (from IngentaConnect, ScienceDirect); ◆ Spanish Translation: European Psychiatry (Spanish Edition).
Indexed: A01, A03, A08, A20, A22, A26, ASCA, B25, BIOSIS Prev, CA, CurCont, E-psyche, EMBASE, ExcerpMed, FR, Faml, I05, IndMed, Inpharma, MEDLINE, MycolAb, P03, P30, P35, PsycInfo, PsycholAb, R10, Reac, SCI, SCOPUS, SSCI, T02, W07.
—BLDSC (3829.842700), GNLM, IE, Infotrieve, Ingenta, INIST. **CCC.**
Published by: (Association of European Psychiatrists), Elsevier Masson (Subsidiary of: Elsevier Health Sciences), 62 Rue Camille Desmoulins, Issy les Moulineaux, Cedex 92442, France. TEL 33-1-71165500, FAX 33-1-71165600, infos@elsevier-masson.fr. Eds. Philip Gorwood, Reinhard Heun, Sophia Frangou. Circ: 3,000.

616.8 ESP
EUROPEAN PSYCHIATRY (SPANISH EDITION). Text in Spanish. 1994. 8/yr. EUR 80 (effective 2005). back issues avail. **Document type:** *Academic/Scholarly.* **Description:** Covers various clinical and research topics in psychiatry and psychiatric medicine.
Related titles: ◆ Translation of: European Psychiatry. ISSN 0924-9338.
Indexed: E-psyche.
—**CCC.**
Published by: (Asociacion Europea de Psiquiatria FRA), Grupo Saned, Capitan Haya 60, 1o, Madrid, 28028, Spain. TEL 34-91-7499500, FAX 34-91-7499501, saned@medynet.com, http://www.gruposaned.com. Ed. Dr. Carlos Ballus. Circ: 3,000.

EUROPEAN SPINE JOURNAL. *see* MEDICAL SCIENCES—Surgery

616.8 150 GBR ISSN 1362-0347
RA790.A1
EVIDENCE - BASED MENTAL HEALTH; an international digest of the evidence for mental health clinicians. Text in English. 1998. q. GBP 259 to institutions; GBP 312 combined subscription to institutions small FTE (print & online eds.) (effective 2011). adv. back issues avail.; reprints avail. **Document type:** *Journal, Academic/Scholarly.* **Description:** Designed to keep clinicians up to date with most reliable and important clinically relevant papers from an expanded range of journals.
Related titles: Online - full text ed.: ISSN 1468-960X. GBP 254 to institutions small FTE (effective 2011); Spanish ed.: Evidence - Based Mental Health (Espanola Edition). ISSN 1885-1177.
Indexed: A01, A03, A08, A22, A26, C06, C07, C08, CA, CINAHL, E-psyche, E08, EMBASE, ESPM, ExcerpMed, G08, H11, H12, I05, MEDLINE, P30, R10, Reac, RiskAb, S09, SCOPUS, T02.
—BLDSC (3831.037200), IE, Infotrieve, Ingenta. **CCC.**
Published by: (The British Psychological Society), B M J Group, BMA House, Tavistock Sq, London, WC1H 9JR, United Kingdom. TEL 44-20-73836373, FAX 44-20-73836668, membership@bma.org.uk, http://group.bmj.com. Ed. Graham Towl. Pub. Allison Lang TEL 44-20-73836212. Adv. contact Nick Gray TEL 44-20-73836386. Circ: 1,370. **Subscr. to:** PO Box 299, London WC1H 9TD, United Kingdom. TEL 44-20-73836270, FAX 44-20-73836402, support@bmjgroup.com.

616.89 FRA ISSN 0014-3855
RC321 CODEN: EVPSAG
➤ **L'EVOLUTION PSYCHIATRIQUE.** Text in French. 1925. 4/yr. EUR 297 in Europe to institutions; EUR 265.43 in France to institutions; JPY 35,500 in Japan to institutions; USD 379 elsewhere to institutions (effective 2012). adv. bibl. **Document type:** *Academic/Scholarly.* **Description:** Exposes psychiatry to the various currents in scientific and philosophical thought, clinical research and critical reflection, as they develop both in this field and in related areas.
Related titles: Online - full text ed.: (from IngentaConnect, ScienceDirect).
Indexed: A01, A03, A08, A20, A22, A26, ASCA, CA, CurCont, DIP, E-psyche, EMBASE, ExcerpMed, FR, I05, IBR, IBZ, IndMed, P03, P30, PsycInfo, PsycholAb, R10, Reac, S02, S03, SCOPUS, SSCI, T02, W07.
—BLDSC (3834.320000), GNLM, IE, Infotrieve, Ingenta, INIST. **CCC.**
Published by: (Association Francaise d'Etudes et de Recherches Psychiatriques), Elsevier Masson (Subsidiary of: Elsevier Health Sciences), 62 Rue Camille Desmoulins, Issy les Moulineaux, Cedex 92442, France. TEL 33-1-71165500, FAX 33-1-71165600, infos@elsevier-masson.fr. Ed. Richard Rechtman.

➤ **EXCERPTA MEDICA. SECTION 32: PSYCHIATRY.** *see* MEDICAL SCIENCES—Abstracting, Bibliographies, Statistics

➤ **EXCERPTA MEDICA. SECTION 50: EPILEPSY ABSTRACTS.** *see* MEDICAL SCIENCES—Abstracting, Bibliographies, Statistics

➤ **EXCERPTA MEDICA. SECTION 8: NEUROLOGY AND NEUROSURGERY.** *see* MEDICAL SCIENCES—Abstracting, Bibliographies, Statistics

616.8 AUT ISSN 1024-7033
➤ **EXISTENZANALYSE.** Text in German. 1984. s-a. EUR 25 (effective 2003). bk.rev. 100 p./no.; back issues avail. **Document type:** *Academic/Scholarly.*
Formerly: Gesellschaft fuer Logotherapie und Existenzanalyse. Bulletin (0258-5383)
Indexed: E-psyche.
Published by: Internationale Gesellschaft fuer Logotherapie und Existenzanalyse, Ed.-Suess-Gasse 10, Vienna, W 1150, Austria. TEL 43-1-9859566, FAX 43-1-9824845, gle@existenzanalyse.org, http://www.existenzanalyse.org. Ed. Silvia Laengle. Circ: 1,850 (controlled).

616.8 DEU ISSN 0014-4819
QP376 CODEN: EXBRAP
➤ **EXPERIMENTAL BRAIN RESEARCH.** Text in English. 1966. 32/yr. EUR 10,257, USD 12,327 combined subscription to institutions (print & online eds.) (effective 2012). adv. bibl.; charts; illus. index. back issues avail.; reprint service avail. from PSC. **Document type:** *Journal, Academic/Scholarly.* **Description:** Takes an interdisciplinary approach to the study of the central and peripheral nervous systems. Covers the fields of morphology, physiology, behavior, neurochemistry, developmental neurobiology, and experimental pathology relevant to general problems of brain function.
Related titles: Microform ed.: (from PQC); Online - full text ed.: ISSN 1432-1106 (from IngentaConnect).
Indexed: A01, A03, A08, A20, A22, A26, A34, A35, A36, A38, ASCA, AbAn, AgBio, Agr, ApicAb, B21, B25, BDM&CN, BIOBASE, BIOSIS Prev, CA, CABA, CIN, CTA, ChemAb, ChemTitl, ChemoAb, CurCont, DentInd, E-psyche, E01, E12, EMBASE, ExcerpMed, F08, GH, GenetAb, H12, I05, IABS, IBR, IBZ, ISR, IndMed, IndVet, Inpharma, MEDLINE, MycolAb, N02, N03, NSA, NSCI, NucAcAb, P03, P20, P22, P24, P27, P30, P33, P35, P37, P48, P54, PQC, PsycInfo, PsycholAb, R07, R08, R10, RA&MP, RILM, Reac, SCI, SCOPUS, T02, THA, VS, W07, WildRev.
—BLDSC (3838.800000), CASDDS, GNLM, IE, Infotrieve, Ingenta, INIST, Linda Hall. **CCC.**

Published by: Springer (Subsidiary of: Springer Science+Business Media), Tiergartenstr 17, Heidelberg, 69121, Germany. TEL 49-6221-4870, FAX 49-6221-345229. Ed. John C Rothwell. **Subscr. in the Americas to:** Springer New York LLC, Journal Fulfillment, PO Box 2485, Secaucus, NJ 07096. TEL 800-777-4643, 201-348-4033, FAX 201-348-4505, journals-ny@springer.com, http://www.springer.com; **Subscr. to:** Springer Distribution Center, Kundenservice Zeitschriften, Haberstr 7, Heidelberg 69126, Germany. TEL 49-6221-3454303, FAX 49-6221-3454229, subscriptions@springer.com.

616.8 USA ISSN 0014-4886
RC321 CODEN: EXNEAC
➤ **EXPERIMENTAL NEUROLOGY.** Text in English. 1959. m. EUR 4,749 in Europe to institutions; JPY 496,000 in Japan to institutions; USD 3,686 elsewhere to institutions (effective 2012). adv. index. back issues avail.; reprints avail. **Document type:** *Journal, Academic/Scholarly.* **Description:** Features the results and conclusions of original research in neuroscience with emphasis on novel findings in neural development, regeneration, plasticity, and transplantation.
Incorporates (1992-1997): Neurodegeneration (1055-8330)
Related titles: Online - full text ed.: ISSN 1090-2430 (from IngentaConnect, ScienceDirect); Supplement(s): ISSN 0531-559X.
Indexed: A01, A03, A08, A22, A26, A34, A35, A36, A38, ASCA, AgBio, B21, B25, BDM&CN, BIOBASE, BIOSIS Prev, BP, CA, CABA, CIN, CRFR, ChemAb, ChemTitl, CurCont, D01, DentInd, E-psyche, E01, E12, EMBASE, ExcerpMed, F08, GH, H16, I05, IABS, IBR, IBZ, ISR, IndMed, IndVet, Inpharma, MEDLINE, MycolAb, N02, N03, NSA, NSCI, P30, P33, P35, P37, P39, PN&I, PsycholAb, R07, R08, R10, RA&MP, Reac, SCI, SCOPUS, SoyAb, T02, T05, THA, VS, W07, W10.
—BLDSC (3839.850000), CASDDS, GNLM, IE, Infotrieve, Ingenta, INIST. **CCC.**
Published by: Academic Press (Subsidiary of: Elsevier Science & Technology), 3251 Riverport Ln, Maryland Heights, MO 63043. TEL 314-447-8010, FAX 314-447-8030, JournalCustomerService-usa@elsevier.com, http://www.elsevierdirect.com/imprint.jsp?iid=5. Ed. S Gilman. Adv. contact Tino DeCarlo TEL 212-633-3815.

➤ **EXPERT REVIEW OF NEUROTHERAPEUTICS.** *see* PHARMACY AND PHARMACOLOGY

616.8 AUS ISSN 1837-798X
▼➤ **EXPLORATIONS: AN E-JOURNAL OF NARRATIVE PRACTICE.** Text in English. 2009. a. free (effective 2010). adv. **Document type:** *Journal, Academic/Scholarly.* **Description:** Contains forum for narrative therapy and narrative practice.
Media: Online - full text.
Published by: Dulwich Centre Foundation, Hutt St, PO Box 7192, Adelaide, SA 5000, Australia. TEL 61-8-82233966, FAX 61-8-82324441, dulwich@dulwichcentre.com.au.

616.89 CAN ISSN 0834-129X
EXPRESS (MONTREAL). Text in English, French. 1983. q. CAD 25. bk.rev. **Document type:** *Journal, Trade.*
Formerly (until 1986): Express de la Montagne (0821-669X)
Indexed: E-psyche.
Published by: Quebec Society for Autism/Societe Quebecoise de l'Autisme, 65 de Castelnau ouest, Montreal, PQ H2R 2W3, Canada. TEL 514-270-7386, FAX 514-270-9261.

▼ **EYE AND BRAIN.** *see* MEDICAL SCIENCES—Ophthalmology And Optometry

616.8 IRN ISSN 1028-6918
FA INAMAH-I 'ILMI-PIZHUHISHI U UL-I BINDASHT-I RAVANI/JOURNAL OF FUNDAMENTALS OF MENTAL HEALTH. Text in Persian, Modern. 1997. q. **Document type:** *Journal, Academic/Scholarly.*
Related titles: Online - full text ed.: ISSN 1684-4300. free (effective 2011).
Published by: Mashhad University of Medical Sciences, Ebne-sina Hospital, PO Box 91959, Mashhad, 83134, Iran. Ed. Mohammad Reza Fayyazi Bordbar.

616.8 ITA ISSN 1591-0083
FACTS, NEWS & VIEWS. Text in Italian. 2000. 3/yr. **Document type:** *Magazine, Trade.* **Description:** House organ of the Societa Italiana di Neuropsicofarmacologia.
Indexed: EMBASE, ExcerpMed, SCOPUS.
Published by: Elsevier Masson (Subsidiary of: Elsevier Health Sciences), Via Paleocapa 7, Milan, 20121, Italy. TEL 39-02-881841, FAX 39-02-88184302, info@masson.it, http://www.masson.it. Ed. Giorgio Racagni.

616.8 ESP ISSN 0213-7429
FACULTAD DE MEDICINA DE BARCELONA. REVISTA DE PSIQUIATRIA. Key Title: Revista de Psiquiatria de la Facultad de Medicina de Barcelona. Text in Spanish; Summaries in English, Spanish. 1973. bi-m. bk.rev. illus.; charts; stat. index. Supplement avail.; back issues avail. **Document type:** *Journal, Academic/Scholarly.* **Description:** Original research articles on various topics in psychiatry, medicine and psychology.
Formerly (until 1986): Facultad de Medicina de Barcelona. Departamento de Psiquiatria. Revista (0210-1793)
Indexed: E-psyche, Inpharma, P03, PsycholAb, SCOPUS.
—GNLM, IE, Ingenta. **CCC.**
Published by: (Universitat de Barcelona, Facultad de Medicina), Hospital Clinico y Provincial de Barcelona, Departamento de Psiquiatria y Psicologia Medica, C/ Villaroel 170, Barcelona, 08036, Spain. TEL 34-93-2275400, FAX 34-93-2275454, http://www.hospitalclinic.org.

FAMILY SUPPORT BULLETIN. *see* HANDICAPPED—Physically Impaired

616.8 USA ISSN 1070-0609
RC488.5
➤ **FAMILY SYSTEMS;** a journal of natural systems thinking in psychiatry and the sciences. Text in English. 1994. s-a. USD 32 domestic to individuals; USD 38 foreign to individuals; USD 45 to institutions (effective 2010). bk.rev. 96 p./no.; **Document type:** *Journal, Academic/Scholarly.* **Description:** Aims to advance the understanding of human emotional functioning and behavior based on Bowen theory.
Indexed: E-psyche, ESPM, FamI, HPNRM, SSciA.
Published by: Georgetown Family Center, 4400 MacArthur Blvd, N W, Ste 103, Washington, DC 20007. TEL 202-965-4400, 800-432-6882, FAX 202-965-1765, info@thebowencenter.org. Ed. Dr. Michael E Kerr.

616.8 615 POL ISSN 1234-8279
FARMAKOTERAPIA W PSYCHIATRII I NEUROLOGII. Text in Polish. 1992. q. **Document type:** *Journal, Academic/Scholarly.*
Formerly (until 1995): Leki Psychotropowe (1232-0293)
Published by: Instytut Psychiatrii i Neurologii w Warszawie, Zespol Profilaktyki i Leczenia Uzaleznien/Institute of Psychiatry and Neurology, Department of Studies on Alcoholism and Drug Dependence, Al Sobieskiego 9, Warszawa, 02957, Poland. habratb@ipin.edu.pl, http://www.ipin.edu.pl/ain. **Dist. by:** Ars Polona, Obronców 25, Warsaw 03933, Poland. TEL 48-22-5098609, FAX 48-22-5098610, arspolona@arspolona.com.pl, http://www.arspolona.com.pl.

616.8 FRA ISSN 1623-3883
FIGURES DE LA PSYCHANALYSE; Logos Ananke, nouvelle serie. Text in French. 1999. s-a. EUR 44 domestic; EUR 50 foreign; EUR 36 domestic to students (effective 2009). back issues avail. **Document type:** *Journal, Academic/Scholarly.*
Formerly (until 2001): Logos Ananke (1290-3493)
Related titles: Online - full text ed.: ISSN 1776-2847.
Indexed: SCOPUS.
Published by: Editions Eres, 33 Av. Marcel Dassault, Toulouse, 31500, France. TEL 33-5-61751576, FAX 33-5-61735289, eres@edition-eres.com. Circ: 1,000.

616.891 CAN ISSN 1192-1412
FILIGRANE; revue de psychanalyse. Variant title: Ecoutes Psychotherapiques. Text in French. 1992. s-a. CAD 29.91 to individuals; CAD 32.21 to institutions; CAD 23.01 to students (effective 2004).
Indexed: A01, E-psyche, FR, T02.
—INIST.
Published by: Ecoutes Therapeutiques, C.P. 548, succ. Place d'Armes, Montreal, PQ H2Y 3H3, Canada. TEL 514-523-0607, FAX 514-523-0797, rsmq@cam.org. Ed. Helene Richard.

616.89 USA
FIRST PERSON MAGAZINE (ONLINE). Text in English. irreg. GBP 20 for 6 mos. (effective 2009). **Document type:** *Magazine, Consumer.* **Description:** Aims to provide a forum for opinions and to let people share their experiences relating to mental, emotional and spiritual health.
Media: Online - full content.
Published by: First Person Magazine, 2315 Folsom St, San Francisco, CA 94110. Ed. Alex Vulliamy.

616.8 GBR ISSN 2045-8118
➤ **FLUIDS AND BARRIERS OF THE C N S.** (Central Nervous System) Text in English. 2004. irreg. free (effective 2011). adv. back issues avail.; reprints avail. **Document type:** *Journal, Academic/Scholarly.* **Description:** Publishes on all aspects of cerebrospinal fluid in health and disease.
Formerly (until 2011): Cerebrospinal Fluid Research (1743-8454)
Media: Online - full text.
Indexed: A01, A26, CA, EMBASE, ExcerpMed, H11, H12, I05, NSA, P30, R10, Reac, SCOPUS, T02.
—**CCC.**
Published by: BioMed Central Ltd. (Subsidiary of: Springer Science+Business Media), 236 Gray's Inn Rd, London, WC1X 8HB, United Kingdom. TEL 44-20-31922000, FAX 44-20-31922010, info@biomedcentral.com, http://www.biomedcentral.com. Eds. Hazel C Jones, Tetsuya Terasaki.

➤ **FOCAL POINT (PORTLAND);** research, policy, and practice in children's mental health. *see* HANDICAPPED

616.89 USA ISSN 1541-4094
RC516
➤ **FOCUS (ARLINGTON, 2003);** the journal of lifelong learning in psychiatry. Text in English. 2003 (Jan.). q. USD 505 combined subscription domestic to individuals (print & online eds.); USD 585 combined subscription foreign to individuals (print & online eds.); USD 375 combined subscription domestic to institutions Tier 1 (print & online eds.); USD 408 combined subscription foreign to institutions Tier 1 (print & online eds.) (effective 2011). adv. back issues avail.; reprints avail. **Document type:** *Journal, Academic/Scholarly.* **Description:** Provides a review of current clinical practice based on the content outlined by the ABPN recertification exam.
Related titles: Online - full text ed.: ISSN 1541-4108. USD 454 to individuals (effective 2011).
—BLDSC (3964.185330), IE, Ingenta. **CCC.**
Published by: American Psychiatric Publishing, Inc., 1000 Wilson Blvd, Ste 1825, Arlington, VA 22209. TEL 703-907-7895, 800-368-5777, FAX 703-907-1096, appi@psych.org, http://www.appi.org. Eds. Deborah J Hales, Mark Hyman Rapaport. **Subscr. to:** PO Box 97250, Washington, DC 20090.

618.97 AUT ISSN 1864-1954
FOCUS NEUROGERIATRIE. Text in German. 2007. 4/yr. EUR 40, USD 54 combined subscription to institutions (print & online eds.) (effective 2010). adv. **Document type:** *Journal, Academic/Scholarly.*
Related titles: Online - full text ed.: ISSN 1864-1962. 2007.
Indexed: A22, A26, E01, E08, S09.
—IE. **CCC.**
Published by: Springer Wien (Subsidiary of: Springer Science+Business Media), Sachsenplatz 4-6, Vienna, W 1201, Austria. TEL 43-1-33024150, FAX 43-1-3302426, journals@springer.at, http://www.springer.at. Ed. Dr. Andreas Winkler. adv.: color page EUR 3,130; trim 210 x 297. Circ: 10,000 (paid). **Subscr. to:** Springer Distribution Center, Kundenservice Zeitschriften, Haberstr 7, Heidelberg 69126, Germany. TEL 49-6221-3454303, FAX 49-6221-3454229, subscriptions@springer.com.

616.8982 USA ISSN 1088-3576
RJ506.A9 CODEN: FAODF5
➤ **FOCUS ON AUTISM AND OTHER DEVELOPMENTAL DISABILITIES.** Text in English. 1986. q. USD 180, GBP 106 combined subscription to institutions (print & online eds.); USD 176, GBP 104 to institutions (effective 2011). adv. bk.rev. bibl.; abstr.; illus. 64 p./no.; back issues avail.; reprint service avail. from PSC. **Document type:** *Journal, Academic/Scholarly.* **Description:** Publishes practitioner-oriented articles for professionals involved in the education and treatment of children and youth with autism and pervasive developmental disorders.
Formerly (until vol.11, 1996): Focus on Autistic Behavior (0887-1566)
Related titles: Microfilm ed.: (from PQC); Online - full text ed.: ISSN 1538-4829. USD 162, GBP 95 to institutions (effective 2011).
Indexed: A01, A02, A03, A08, A22, A25, A26, B04, B21, BRD, C06, C07, C11, CA, CPE, CurCont, DIP, E-psyche, E01, E02, E03, E07, E08, ECER, EMBASE, ERA, ERI, ERIC, EdA, EdI, ExcerpMed, G08, H03, H04, I05, IBR, IBZ, M01, M02, M12, MLA-IB, NSA, P03, P04, P18, P25, P26, P30, P34, P43, P48, P53, P54, PAIS, PQC, PsycInfo, PsycholAb, S08, S09, S20, S21, SCOPUS, SOPODA, SSCI, SociolAb, T02, W03, W05, W07.
—BLDSC (3964.203810), GNLM, IE, Ingenta. **CCC.**
Published by: Sage Publications, Inc., 2455 Teller Rd, Thousand Oaks, CA 91320. TEL 805-499-9774, 800-818-7243, FAX 805-499-0871, 800-583-2665, info@sagepub.com, http://www.sagepub.com. Eds. Juane Heflin, Paul Alberto. Circ: 5,700 (paid and free).

616.891 362.82 NOR ISSN 0332-5415
FOKUS PAA FAMILIEN; tidsskrift for familiebehandling. Text in Danish, Norwegian, Swedish, English. 1972. q. NOK 479 to individuals; NOK 860 to institutions; NOK 279 to students (effective 2010). bk.rev. **Document type:** *Journal, Academic/Scholarly.* **Description:** Covers theoretical and practical family therapy and related fields including family sociology, family education and family politics.
Related titles: Online - full content ed.: ISSN 0807-7487. 1995. NOK 960 (effective 2010).
Indexed: DIP, E-psyche, IBR, IBZ.
—**CCC.**
Published by: Universitetsforlaget AS/Scandinavian University Press (Subsidiary of: Aschehoug & Co.), Sehesteds Gate 3, P O Box 508, Sentrum, Oslo, 0105, Norway. TEL 47-24-147500, FAX 47-24-147501, post@universitetsforlaget.no. Circ: 2,700.

616.891 700 FRA ISSN 1772-1024
FOL'ART. Text in French. 2003. q. **Document type:** *Magazine.* **Description:** Aims to bring relief to mental disease through the use of art.
Published by: Association Fol'Art, 22 Rue Geo Lefevre, Caen, 14000, France.

616.8 POL ISSN 1641-4640
CODEN: NUPOBT
FOLIA NEUROPATHOLOGICA. Text in Multiple languages; Summaries in English, Polish. 1963. q. EUR 70 foreign to individuals; EUR 140 foreign to institutions (effective 2010). bk.rev. bibl.; illus. index, cum.index. back issues avail. **Document type:** *Journal, Academic/Scholarly.* **Description:** Publishes papers devoted to achievements in experimental and clinical neuropathology.
Formerly (until 1994): Neuropatologia Polska (0028-3894)
Related titles: Online - full text ed.: ISSN 1509-572X. free (effective 2011).
Indexed: A22, A29, ASCA, B20, B21, CA, CIN, ChemAb, ChemTitl, E-psyche, EMBASE, ESPM, ExcerpMed, I10, IBR, IBZ, IndMed, MEDLINE, NSA, NSCI, P30, R10, Reac, SCI, SCOPUS, T02, ViroIAbstr, W07.
—BLDSC (3971.636000), CASDDS, GNLM, IE, Ingenta, INIST.
Published by: (Stowarzyszenie Neuropatologow Polskich/Polish Association of Neuropathologists), Termedia sp. z o.o./Termedia Publishing House, ul Wenedow 9/1, Poznan, 61614, Poland. TEL 48-61-8227781, termedia@termedia.pl. Ed. Ewa Matyja.

FOLIA PHONIATRICA ET LOGOPAEDICA; international journal of phoniatrics, speech therapy and communication pathology. *see* MEDICAL SCIENCES—Otorhinolaryngology

616.8 CAN ISSN 1712-8021
FONDATION DES MALADIES MENTALES. BULLETIN. Text in French. 2000. s-a. **Document type:** *Bulletin, Trade.*
Formerly (until 2003): Fondation Quebecoise des Maladies Mentales. Bulletin (1910-3301)
Media: Online - full text. **Related titles:** Print ed.: ISSN 1712-8013; ◆ English ed.: The Pearl. ISSN 1924-5580.
Published by: Mental Illness Foundation/Fondation des Maladies Mentales, 401-2120 Sherbrooke St E, Montreal, PQ H2K 1C3, Canada. TEL 514-529-5354, FAX 514-529-9877, info@fmm-mif.ca.

616.8 CAN ISSN 1910-0973
FONDATION QUEBECOISE DES MALADIES MENTALES. RAPPORT D'ACTIVITES. Text in French. 2001. a. **Document type:** *Report, Trade.*
Media: Online - full text.
Published by: (Fondation Quebecoise des Maladies Mentales/Mental Illness Foundation), Mental Illness Foundation/Fondation des Maladies Mentales, 401-2120 Sherbrooke St E, Montreal, PQ H2K 1C3, Canada. TEL 514-529-5354, FAX 514-529-9877, info@fmm-mif.ca, http://www.fmm-mif.ca.

616.8 NLD ISSN 1875-2551
FONDS PSYCHISCHE GEZONDHEID. NIEUWSBRIEF. Text in Dutch. 1994. 3/yr.
Formerly (until 2006): Nationaal Fonds voor de Geestelijke Volksgezondheid. Nieuwsbrief (1385-674X)
Published by: Fonds Psychische Gezondheid, Postbus 5103, Utrecht, 3502 JC, Netherlands. TEL 31-30-2971197, FAX 31-30-2971198, info@fondspsychischegezondheid.nl, http://www.fondspsychischegezondheid.nl.

616.8 GBR
FORENSIC FOCUS. Text in English. 1995. irreg., latest 2009. price varies. back issues avail. **Document type:** *Monographic series, Academic/Scholarly.* **Description:** Provides a forum for the presentation of theoretical and clinical issues.
Indexed: E-psyche.
—BLDSC (3987.726600).
Published by: Jessica Kingsley Publishers, 116 Pentonville Rd, London, N1 9JB, United Kingdom. TEL 44-20-78332307, FAX 44-20-78372917, post@jkp.com. Ed. Gwen Adshead.

616.89 DEU ISSN 1862-7072
➤ **FORENSISCHE PSYCHIATRIE, PSYCHOLOGIE, KRIMINOLOGIE.** Text in German. 2007. 4/yr. EUR 361, USD 438 combined subscription to institutions (print & online eds.) (effective 2012). reprint service avail. from PSC. **Document type:** *Journal, Academic/Scholarly.*
Related titles: Online - full text ed.: ISSN 1862-7080.
Indexed: A22, A26, E01, P03, PsycInfo, S09, SCOPUS.
—BLDSC (3987.770500), IE, Ingenta. **CCC.**
Published by: Dr. Dietrich Steinkopff Verlag (Subsidiary of: Springer Science+Business Media), Tiergartenstr 17, Heidelberg, 69121, Germany. TEL 49-6221-4878821, FAX 49-6221-4878830, info.steinkopff@springer.com, http://www.steinkopff.com. Adv. contact Sabine Weidner.

616.89 158 DEU ISSN 0945-2540
➤ **FORENSISCHE PSYCHIATRIE UND PSYCHOTHERAPIE.** Text in English, German; Summaries in English, French, German. 1994. 3/yr. EUR 30 (effective 2011). adv. bk.rev. **Document type:** *Journal, Academic/Scholarly.*
Indexed: E-psyche.
—GNLM.
Published by: Pabst Science Publishers, Am Eichengrund 28, Lengerich, 49525, Germany. TEL 49-5484-97234, FAX 49-5484-550, pabst@pabst-publishers.com, http://www.pabst-publishers.de. Ed. Heinfried Duncker. Circ: 1,200.

616.08 616.8914 DEU ISSN 1612-930X
FORSCHUNGSARBEITEN UND ERGEBNISSE AUS DER PSYCHOSOMATISCHEN MEDIZIN UND PSYCHOTHERAPIE. Text in German. 2004. irreg., latest vol.3, 2006. price varies. **Document type:** *Monographic series, Academic/Scholarly.*
Published by: Verlag Dr. Kovac, Leverkusenstr 13, Hamburg, 22761, Germany. TEL 49-40-3988800, FAX 49-40-39888055, info@verlagdrkovac.de. Ed. Manfred Beutel.

616.8 DEU
➤ **FORTSCHRITTE DER NEUROLOGIE, PSYCHIATRIE.** Text in German; Summaries in English, German. 1931. m. EUR 255 to institutions; EUR 357 combined subscription to institutions (print & online eds.); EUR 32 newsstand/cover (effective 2011). adv. bk.rev. bibl.; charts; illus.; stat. index. Supplement avail.; back issues avail.; reprints avail. **Document type:** *Journal, Academic/Scholarly.*
Former titles (until 1981): Fortschritte der Neurologie, Psychiatrie und ihrer Grenzgebiete; Fortschritte der Neurologie - Psychiatrie (0720-4299); (until 1980): Fortschritte der Neurologie, Psychiatrie und Ihrer Grenzgebiete (0015-8194)
Related titles: Online - full text ed.: ISSN 1439-3522. EUR 344 to institutions (effective 2011).
Indexed: A20, A22, ASCA, B21, B25, BIOSIS Prev, ChemAb, CurCont, E-psyche, EMBASE, ExcerpMed, F09, FR, GJP, ISR, IndMed, Inpharma, MEDLINE, MycolAb, NSA, NSCI, P03, P30, P35, PsycInfo, PsycholAb, R10, RILM, Reac, S02, S03, SCI, SCOPUS, SSCI, W07.
—BLDSC (4022.380000), GNLM, IE, Ingenta, INIST. **CCC.**
Published by: (Victor von Weizsaecker Gesellschaft), Georg Thieme Verlag, Ruedigerstr 14, Stuttgart, 70469, Germany. TEL 49-711-8931421, FAX 49-711-8931410, kunden.service@thieme.de. Ed. G R Fink. Adv. contact Andreas Schweiger TEL 49-711-8931245. Circ: 3,700 (paid).

616.8 DEU ISSN 0944-680X
➤ **FORTSCHRITTE IN DER NEUROTRAUMATOLOGIE UND KLINISCHEN NEUROPSYCHOLOGIE.** Text in German. 1993. irreg., latest vol.3, 1999. price varies. **Document type:** *Monographic series, Academic/Scholarly.*
Published by: W. Zuckschwerdt Verlag GmbH, Industriestr 1, Germering, 82110, Germany. TEL 49-89-8943490, FAX 49-89-89434950, post@zuckschwerdtverlag.de, http://www.zuckschwerdtverlag.de.

616.893 ITA ISSN 1971-0399
FORUM. JOURNAL OF INTERNATIONAL ASSOCIATION OF GROUP THERAPY. Text in English. 2006. a. EUR 29.50 combined subscription domestic to institutions (print & online eds.); EUR 42 combined subscription foreign to institutions (print & online eds.) (effective 2009). **Document type:** *Journal, Academic/Scholarly.*
Related titles: Online - full text ed.: ISSN 1972-5051.
Published by: Franco Angeli Edizioni, Viale Monza 106, Milan, 20127, Italy. TEL 39-02-2837141, FAX 39-02-26144793, redazioni@francoangeli.it, http://www.francoangeli.it.

616.8 DEU ISSN 1436-5758
FORUM STRESS- UND SCHLAFFORSCHUNG. Text in German. 1993. irreg., latest vol.5, 1996. price varies. **Document type:** *Monographic series, Academic/Scholarly.*
Published by: Lit Verlag, Grevener Str/Fresnostr 2, Muenster, 48159, Germany. TEL 49-251-235091, FAX 49-251-231972, lit@lit-verlag.de, http://www.lit-verlag.de.

617.48 NLD ISSN 0922-4386
FOUNDATIONS OF NEUROLOGICAL SURGERY. Text in English. 1988. irreg., latest vol.3, 1990. price varies. **Document type:** *Monographic series, Academic/Scholarly.*
Indexed: E-psyche.
Published by: Springer Netherlands (Subsidiary of: Springer Science+Business Media), Van Godewijckstraat 30, Dordrecht, 3311 GX, Netherlands. TEL 31-78-6576050, FAX 31-78-6576474.

616.89 NLD ISSN 0924-8935
FOUNDATIONS OF NEUROLOGY. Text in English. 1990. irreg., latest vol.2, 1992. price varies. **Document type:** *Monographic series, Academic/Scholarly.*
Indexed: E-psyche.
—CCC.
Published by: Springer Netherlands (Subsidiary of: Springer Science+Business Media), Van Godewijckstraat 30, Dordrecht, 3311 GX, Netherlands. TEL 31-78-6576050, FAX 31-78-6576474.

616.89 NLD ISSN 0924-0179
FOUNDATIONS OF NEUROPSYCHOLOGY. Text in English. 1989. irreg., latest vol.4, 1991. price varies. **Document type:** *Monographic series, Academic/Scholarly.*
Indexed: E-psyche.
Published by: Springer Netherlands (Subsidiary of: Springer Science+Business Media), Van Godewijckstraat 30, Dordrecht, 3311 GX, Netherlands. TEL 31-78-6576050, FAX 31-78-6576474.

616.858 GBR ISSN 2044-5938
FRAGILE X SOCIETY. NEWS. Text in English. 1990. 3/yr. free to members (effective 2010). **Document type:** *Newsletter, Trade.*
Formerly (until 2009): Fragile X Society. Newsletter (1745-1469)
Published by: Fragile X Society, Rood End House, 6 Stortford Rd, Great Dunmow, Essex CM6 1DA, United Kingdom. TEL 44-1371-875100, FAX 44-1371-859915, info@fragilex.org.uk.

616.89 ESP ISSN 1577-7200
FRENIA; revista de historia de psicologia. Text in Spanish. 2001. s-a. EUR 25 (effective 2008). back issues avail. **Document type:** *Journal, Academic/Scholarly.*
Published by: (Consejo Superior de Investigaciones Cientificas (C S I C), Instituto de Historia), Paradox, S.L., C Santa Teresa, 2, Madrid, 28004, Spain. TEL 34-91-7004042, FAX 34-91-3195926, paradox@paradox.es. Ed. Olga Vilasanta.

616.890 ITA ISSN 2037-1853
FRENIS ZERO. Text in Multiple languages. 2003. s-a. **Document type:** *Journal, Academic/Scholarly.*
Media: Online - full text.
Published by: Centro Psicoterapia Dinamica "Mauro Mancia", Via Lombardia 18, Lecce, 73100, Italy. FAX 39-083-2933507. Ed. Giuseppe Leo.

618 DEU
FREUD HEUTE; Wendepunkte und Streitfragen. Text in German. 1996. irreg., latest vol.3, 2001. price varies. **Document type:** *Monographic series, Academic/Scholarly.*
Published by: Frommann-Holzboog Verlag e.K., Koenig-Karl-Str 27, Stuttgart, 70372, Germany. TEL 49-711-9559690, FAX 49-711-9559691, info@frommann-holzboog.de, http://www.frommann-holzboog.de.

618 ESP ISSN 1131-5776
FREUDIANA. Text in Spanish. 1991. 3/yr. back issues avail. **Document type:** *Journal, Academic/Scholarly.*
Published by: Escuela Europea de Psicoanalisis del Campo Freudiano, Ave. Diagonal 333, 3o. 1o., Barcelona, Cataluna 08037, Spain. TEL 34-93-2075619, FAX 34-93-4593254, cdcelp@ilimit.es, http://www.cdcelp.org/freudiana. Ed. Myruam Chang.

616.8 CHE ISSN 1663-4365
▼ ➤ **FRONTIERS IN AGING NEUROSCIENCE.** Text in English. 2009. irreg. free (effective 2011). **Document type:** *Journal, Academic/Scholarly.* **Description:** Aims to understand the mechanistic processes associated with CNS aging and age-related neuronal diseases.
Media: Online - full text.
Indexed: P30.
Published by: Frontiers Research Foundation, Science Park PSE-A, Lausanne, 1015, Switzerland. TEL 41-21-6939202, FAX 41-21-6939201, info@frontiersin.org, http://frontiersin.org. Eds. Gemma Casadesus, Mark A Smith.

612.67 CHE
▼ ➤ **FRONTIERS IN ALZHEIMER'S DISEASE.** Text in English. 2010. irreg. free (effective 2010). **Document type:** *Journal, Academic/Scholarly.*
Media: Online - full text.
Published by: Frontiers Research Foundation, Science Park PSE-A, Lausanne, 1015, Switzerland. TEL 41-21-6939202, FAX 41-21-6939201, info@frontiersin.org, http://frontiersin.org. Ed. Einar Sigurdsson.

616.8 CHE
▼ ➤ **FRONTIERS IN AUTONOMIC NEUROSCIENCE.** Text in English. 2010. irreg. free (effective 2010). **Document type:** *Journal, Academic/Scholarly.* **Description:** Devoted to advancing understanding of the development, function and dysfunction of the autonomic nervous system.
Media: Online - full text.
Published by: Frontiers Research Foundation, Science Park PSE-A, Lausanne, 1015, Switzerland. TEL 41-21-6939202, FAX 41-21-6939201, info@frontiersin.org, http://frontiersin.org. Ed. Janet Keast.

616.8 CHE ISSN 1662-5153
QP360.5
➤ **FRONTIERS IN BEHAVIORAL NEUROSCIENCE.** Text in English. 2007. m. **Document type:** *Journal, Academic/Scholarly.*
Related titles: Online - full text ed.: free (effective 2011).
Indexed: AnBeAb, CTA, ChemoAb, NSA, P03, P30, PsycInfo, SCI, SCOPUS, W07, Z01.
Published by: Frontiers Research Foundation, Science Park PSE-A, Lausanne, 1015, Switzerland. TEL 41-21-6939202, FAX 41-21-6939201, info@frontiersin.org, http://frontiersin.org. Ed. Carmen Sandi.

616.8 CHE ISSN 1662-5102
➤ **FRONTIERS IN CELLULAR NEUROSCIENCE.** Text in English. 2007. m. **Document type:** *Journal, Academic/Scholarly.* **Description:** Devoted to better understanding the cellular mechanisms underlying the functions of the cells composing the nervous system - neural and non-neuronal - across all species.
Related titles: Online - full text ed.: free (effective 2011).
Indexed: B21, B25, BIOSIS Prev, NSA, P30, SCI, SCOPUS, W07, Z01.
Published by: Frontiers Research Foundation, Science Park PSE-A, Lausanne, 1015, Switzerland. TEL 41-21-6939202, FAX 41-21-6939201, info@frontiersin.org, http://frontiersin.org. Ed. Alexander Borst.

616.8 004 CHE ISSN 1662-5188
QP357.5
➤ **FRONTIERS IN COMPUTATIONAL NEUROSCIENCE.** Text in English. 2007. q. **Document type:** *Journal, Academic/Scholarly.* **Description:** Devoted to promoting theoretical modeling of brain function and fostering interdisciplinary interactions between theoretical and experimental neuroscience.
Related titles: Online - full text ed.: free (effective 2011).
Indexed: B21, B25, BIOSIS Prev, CPEI, NSA, P30, SCI, SCOPUS, W07.
Published by: Frontiers Research Foundation, Science Park PSE-A, Lausanne, 1015, Switzerland. TEL 41-21-6939202, FAX 41-21-6939201, info@frontiersin.org, http://frontiersin.org. Ed. Misha Tsodyks.

616.8 CHE ISSN 1663-4608
▼ ➤ **FRONTIERS IN ENTERIC NEUROSCIENCE.** Text in English. 2009. irreg. free (effective 2010). **Document type:** *Journal, Academic/Scholarly.* **Description:** Aims to publish key findings about the neural and neurobiological control of gastrointestinal functions.
Media: Online - full text.
Published by: Frontiers Research Foundation, Science Park PSE-A, Lausanne, 1015, Switzerland. TEL 41-21-6939202, FAX 41-21-6939201, info@frontiersin.org, http://frontiersin.org. Ed. Joel Bornstein.

616.8 CHE ISSN 1663-070X
▼ ➤ **FRONTIERS IN EVOLUTIONARY NEUROSCIENCE.** Text in English. 2009. irreg. free (effective 2011). **Document type:** *Journal, Academic/Scholarly.*
Media: Online - full text.
Indexed: B21, NSA, P30.
Published by: Frontiers Research Foundation, Science Park PSE-A, Lausanne, 1015, Switzerland. TEL 41-21-6939202, FAX 41-21-6939201, info@frontiersin.org, http://frontiersin.org. Ed. Steven M Platek.

616.8 CHE ISSN 1662-5161
QP351
➤ **FRONTIERS IN HUMAN NEUROSCIENCE.** Text in English. 2008. q. **Document type:** *Journal, Academic/Scholarly.* **Description:** Devoted to understanding the brain mechanisms supporting cognitive and social behavior in humans.
Related titles: Online - full text ed.: free (effective 2011).
Indexed: A20, B21, B25, BIOSIS Prev, MycolAb, NSA, NSCI, P03, P30, PsycInfo, SCI, SCOPUS, W07.
Published by: Frontiers Research Foundation, Science Park PSE-A, Lausanne, 1015, Switzerland. TEL 41-21-6939202, FAX 41-21-6939201, info@frontiersin.org, http://frontiersin.org. Ed. Robert T Knight.

616.8 CHE ISSN 1662-5145
RC343
➤ **FRONTIERS IN INTEGRATIVE NEUROSCIENCE.** Text in English. 2007. q. **Document type:** *Journal, Academic/Scholarly.* **Description:** Focuses on synthesizing multiple facets of brain structure and function to understand how multiple diverse functions are integrated to produce complex behaviors.
Related titles: Online - full text ed.: free (effective 2011).
Indexed: NSA, P03, P30, PsycInfo, SCOPUS.
Published by: Frontiers Research Foundation, Science Park PSE-A, Lausanne, 1015, Switzerland. info@frontiersin.org, http://frontiersin.org. Ed. Sidney A Simon.

616.8 CHE ISSN 1662-5099
➤ **FRONTIERS IN MOLECULAR NEUROSCIENCE.** Text in English. 2008. q. **Document type:** *Journal, Academic/Scholarly.* **Description:** Devoted to identifying key molecules, as well as their functions and interactions, that underlie the structure, design and function of the brain across all levels.
Related titles: Online - full text ed.: free (effective 2011).
Indexed: NSA, P30, SCOPUS.
Published by: Frontiers Research Foundation, Science Park PSE-A, Lausanne, 1015, Switzerland. info@frontiersin.org, http://frontiersin.org. Ed. Peter H Seeburg.

616.8 CHE ISSN 1662-5110
QP363.3
➤ **FRONTIERS IN NEURAL CIRCUITS.** Text in English. 2007. q. **Document type:** *Journal, Academic/Scholarly.* **Description:** Devoted to understanding the emergent properties of neural circuits.
Related titles: Online - full text ed.: free (effective 2011).
Indexed: B21, NSA, P30, SCI, SCOPUS, W07.
Published by: Frontiers Research Foundation, Science Park PSE-A, Lausanne, 1015, Switzerland. TEL 41-21-6939202, FAX 41-21-6939201, info@frontiersin.org, http://frontiersin.org. Ed. Rafael Yuste.

616.8 CHE ISSN 1662-5129
QM451
➤ **FRONTIERS IN NEUROANATOMY.** Text in English. 2007. q. **Document type:** *Journal, Academic/Scholarly.* **Description:** Publishes articles addressing important aspects of the anatomical organization of all nervous systems across all species.
Related titles: Online - full text ed.: free (effective 2011).
Indexed: B21, NSA, P30, SCOPUS.
Published by: Frontiers Research Foundation, Science Park PSE-A, Lausanne, 1015, Switzerland. TEL 41-21-6939202, FAX 41-21-6939201, info@frontiersin.org, http://frontiersin.org. Ed. Xavier De Felipe.

612.8 GBR ISSN 1353-6508
CODEN: FNEUES
➤ **FRONTIERS IN NEUROBIOLOGY.** Text in English. 1994. irreg. price varies. **Document type:** *Monographic series, Academic/Scholarly.*
Indexed: CIN, ChemAb, ChemTitl, E-psyche.
—CASDDS. **CCC.**
Published by: Portland Press Ltd., 3rd Fl, Eagle House, 16 Procter St, London, WC1V 6NX, United Kingdom. TEL 44-20-72804100, FAX 44-20-72804169, sales@portlandpress.com. Ed. A J Turner. R&P Adam Marshall. **Subscr. to:** Portland Customer Services, Commerce Way, Colchester CO2 8HP, United Kingdom. TEL 44-1206-796351, FAX 44-1206-799331, sales@portland-services.com, http://www.portland-services.com.

616.8 CHE ISSN 1662-6427
▼ ➤ **FRONTIERS IN NEUROENERGETICS.** Text in English. 2009. irreg. free (effective 2011). **Document type:** *Journal, Academic/Scholarly.* **Description:** Provides a forum for publication and discussion of cutting-edge articles reporting observations that will contribute to the understanding of how information processing and energy fluxes are coupled in the brain.
Media: Online - full text.
Indexed: NSA, P30.
Published by: Frontiers Research Foundation, Science Park PSE-A, Lausanne, 1015, Switzerland. TEL 41-21-6939202, FAX 41-21-6939201, info@frontiersin.org, http://frontiersin.org. Ed. Pierre Magistretti.

616.8 CHE ISSN 1662-6443
R856.A1
➤ **FRONTIERS IN NEUROENGINEERING.** Text in English. 2008. irreg. free (effective 2011). **Document type:** *Journal, Academic/Scholarly.* **Description:** Promotes research integrating neuroengineering, nanotechnologies and neurosciences.
Indexed: B&BAb, B19, B21, NSA, P30, SCOPUS.
Published by: Frontiers Research Foundation, Science Park PSE-A, Lausanne, 1015, Switzerland. TEL 41-21-6939202, FAX 41-21-6939201, info@frontiersin.org, http://frontiersin.org. Ed. Laura Ballerini.

616.8 CHE ISSN 1663-800X
▼ ➤ **FRONTIERS IN NEUROGENESIS.** Text in English. 2009. irreg. free (effective 2010). **Document type:** *Journal, Academic/Scholarly.* **Description:** Publishinges new and important findings in the rapidly expanding field of neurogenesis.
Media: Online - full text.
Published by: Frontiers Research Foundation, Science Park PSE-A, Lausanne, 1015, Switzerland. TEL 41-21-6939202, FAX 41-21-6939201, info@frontiersin.org, http://frontiersin.org. Eds. Angelique Bordey, Maria Donoghue.

616.8 CHE ISSN 1663-7763
▼ ➤ **FRONTIERS IN NEUROGENOMICS.** Text in English. 2009. irreg. free (effective 2010). **Document type:** *Journal, Academic/Scholarly.*
Media: Online - full text.

Published by: Frontiers Research Foundation, Science Park PSE-A, Lausanne, 1015, Switzerland. TEL 41-21-6939202, FAX 41-21-6939201, info@frontiersin.org, http://frontiersin.org. Ed. Robert Williams.

616.8 CHE ISSN 1662-5196
QP357.5
➤ **FRONTIERS IN NEUROINFORMATICS.** Text in English. 2007. q. free (effective 2010). **Description:** Devoted to studies on the creation of neuroscience data and knowledge bases, together with the development and use of numerical models and analytical tools for the sharing, integration and analysis of experimental data and the advancement of theories of nervous system function.
Related titles: Online - full text ed.: free (effective 2011).
Indexed: B21, NSA, P30, SCOPUS.
Published by: Frontiers Research Foundation, Science Park PSE-A, Lausanne, 1015, Switzerland. TEL 41-21-6939202, FAX 41-21-6939201, info@frontiersin.org, http://frontiersin.org. Ed. Jan G Bjaalie.

616.8 CHE ISSN 1664-2295
▼ ➤ **FRONTIERS IN NEUROLOGY.** Text in English. 2010. irreg. free (effective 2011). **Document type:** *Journal, Academic/Scholarly.* **Description:** Aims to bring all relevant specialties in neurology together on a single platform.
Media: Online - full text.
Indexed: P30.
Published by: Frontiers Research Foundation, Science Park PSE-A, Lausanne, 1015, Switzerland. TEL 41-21-6939202, FAX 41-21-6939201, info@frontiersin.org, http://frontiersin.org. Ed. Jose Biller.

616.8 CHE ISSN 1663-375X
▼ ➤ **FRONTIERS IN NEUROMETHODS.** Text in English. 2009. irreg. free (effective 2010). **Document type:** *Journal, Academic/Scholarly.*
Media: Online - full text.
Published by: Frontiers Research Foundation, Science Park PSE-A, Lausanne, 1015, Switzerland. TEL 41-21-6939202, FAX 41-21-6939201, info@frontiersin.org, http://frontiersin.org.

616.8 CHE ISSN 1662-9957
▼ ➤ **FRONTIERS IN NEUROPROSTHETICS.** Text in English. 2009. irreg. free (effective 2010). **Document type:** *Journal, Academic/Scholarly.* **Description:** Devoted to studies of brain-machine interfaces (BMI) and neuroprostheses.
Media: Online - full text.
Published by: Frontiers Research Foundation, Science Park PSE-A, Lausanne, 1015, Switzerland. TEL 41-21-6939202, FAX 41-21-6939201, info@frontiersin.org, http://frontiersin.org. Eds. Eilon Vaadia, Niels Birbaumer.

616.8 004 CHE ISSN 1662-5218
TJ211.37
➤ **FRONTIERS IN NEUROROBOTICS.** Text in English. 2007. q. **Document type:** *Journal, Academic/Scholarly.* **Description:** Publishes cutting edge research in the science and technology of embodied autonomous neural systems.
Related titles: Online - full text ed.: free (effective 2011).
Indexed: B21, NSA, P30.
Published by: Frontiers Research Foundation, Science Park PSE-A, Lausanne, 1015, Switzerland. TEL 41-21-6939202, FAX 41-21-6939201, info@frontiersin.org, http://frontiersin.org. Ed. Frederic Kaplan.

616.8 CHE ISSN 1662-4548
➤ **FRONTIERS IN NEUROSCIENCE.** Text in English. 2007. q. **Document type:** *Journal, Academic/Scholarly.*
Related titles: Online - full text ed.: ISSN 1662-453X. free (effective 2011).
Indexed: B21, CTA, ChemoAb, NSA, P30.
Published by: Frontiers Research Foundation, Science Park PSE-A, Lausanne, 1015, Switzerland. TEL 41-21-6939202, FAX 41-21-6939201, info@frontiersin.org, http://frontiersin.org. Ed. Idan Segev.

616.8 CHE ISSN 1664-0640
▼ **FRONTIERS IN PSYCHIATRY.** Text in English. 2009. irreg. free (effective 2011). **Document type:** *Journal, Academic/Scholarly.*
Media: Online - full text.
Indexed: P30.
Published by: Frontiers Research Foundation, Science Park PSE-A, Lausanne, 1015, Switzerland. TEL 41-21-6939202, FAX 41-21-6939201, info@frontiersin.org, http://frontiersin.org. Ed. Bankole Johnson.

616.8 CHE ISSN 1663-3563
▼ ➤ **FRONTIERS IN SYNAPTIC NEUROSCIENCE.** Text in English. 2009. irreg. free (effective 2011). **Document type:** *Journal, Academic/Scholarly.*
Media: Online - full text.
Indexed: P30.
Published by: Frontiers Research Foundation, Science Park PSE-A, Lausanne, 1015, Switzerland. TEL 41-21-6939202, FAX 41-21-6939201, info@frontiersin.org, http://frontiersin.org. Ed. Mary Kennedy.

616.8 CHE ISSN 1662-5137
QP376
➤ **FRONTIERS IN SYSTEMS NEUROSCIENCE.** Text in English. 2007. q. **Document type:** *Journal, Academic/Scholarly.* **Description:** Devoted to understanding whole systems of the brain.
Related titles: Online - full text ed.: free (effective 2011).
Indexed: B21, NSA, P30, SCOPUS.
Published by: Frontiers Research Foundation, Science Park PSE-A, Lausanne, 1015, Switzerland. TEL 41-21-6939202, FAX 41-21-6939201, info@frontiersin.org, http://frontiersin.org. Ed. Ranulfo Romo.

616.8 CHE ISSN 1660-4431
CODEN: MNUSB6
➤ **FRONTIERS OF NEUROLOGY AND NEUROSCIENCE.** Text in English. 1972. irreg., latest vol.29, 2010. price varies. reprints avail. **Document type:** *Monographic series, Academic/Scholarly.* **Description:** Provides a broad, interdisciplinary approach to the neural sciences, advancing current information vital for the management of various neurological diseases.
Former titles (until 2005): Monographs in Clinical Neuroscience (1420-2441); (until 1997): Monographs in Neural Sciences (0300-5186); Monographs in Basic Neurology (0077-0779)
Related titles: Online - full text ed.: ISSN 1662-2804.
Indexed: CIN, ChemAb, ChemTitl, E-psyche, EMBASE, ExcerpMed, IndMed, MEDLINE, P30, R10, Reac, SCOPUS.
—BLDSC (4042.041000), CASDDS, GNLM, IE, Ingenta, INIST. **CCC.**
Published by: S. Karger AG, Allschwilerstr 10, Basel, 4055, Switzerland. TEL 41-61-3061111, FAX 41-61-3061234, karger@karger.ch, http://www.karger.ch. Ed. Julien Bogousslavsky.

616.8 ITA ISSN 0393-5264
➤ **FUNCTIONAL NEUROLOGY.** Text in English. 1985. q. EUR 70 domestic to individuals; EUR 90 foreign to individuals; EUR 100 to institutions (effective 2008). adv. bk.rev. back issues avail. **Document type:** *Journal, Academic/Scholarly.* **Description:** Publishes scientific contributions dealing with all aspects of functional neurology. Focuses on the interaction of the nervous system with the environment, including neurochemistry, physiology and more.
Related titles: Online - full text ed.: ISSN 1971-3274.
Indexed: A20, A22, AMED, ASCA, BIOBASE, E-psyche, EMBASE, ExcerpMed, IABS, IndMed, MEDLINE, NSCI, P03, P20, P22, P25, P30, P48, P54, PQC, PsycInfo, PsycholAb, R10, Reac, RefZh, SCI, SCOPUS, W07.
—BLDSC (4055.619500), GNLM, IE, Infotrieve, Ingenta, INIST. **CCC.**
Published by: C I C Edizioni Internazionali, Corso Trieste 42, Rome, 00198, Italy. TEL 39-06-8412673, FAX 39-06-8412688, info@gruppocic.it, http://www.gruppocic.it. Ed. S Bastianello.

616.8 USA ISSN 2156-941X
▼ **FUNCTIONAL NEUROLOGY, REHABILITATION, AND ERGONOMICS.** Text in English. 2011. q. USD 295; USD 442 combined subscription (print & online eds.) (effective 2012). **Document type:** *Journal, Academic/Scholarly.* **Description:** Aims to provide a forum for the research papers in the fields of Biomedical and Rehabilitation Engineering, Neuropsychology, Clinical Neurology, Human Factors and Ergonomics, and vocational assessment & training to present critical ideas, theories, proof-of-concept for technology solutions, and data-based evaluative research to facilitate return to work or more effective functional development in children and adults.
Related titles: Online - full text ed.
Published by: (International Association of Functional Neurology and Rehabilitation), Nova Science Publishers, Inc., 400 Oser Ave, Ste 1600, Hauppauge, NY 11788. TEL 631-231-7269, FAX 631-231-8175, journals@novapublishers.com. Eds. Gerry Leisman, Robert Melillo.

616.8 ARG ISSN 0329-1367
FUNDACION ARGENTINA DE PSICOTERAPIA SIMBOLICA. REVISTA. Text in Spanish. 1997. a. **Document type:** *Magazine, Trade.*
Published by: Fundacion Argentina de Psicoterapia Simbolica, Av Rivadavia 1611, Piso 4o, Buenos Aires, Argentina.

616.8 GBR ISSN 1479-6708
RC346
➤ **FUTURE NEUROLOGY.** Text in English. 2006. bi-m. GBP 695 combined subscription domestic (print & online eds.); USD 1,220 combined subscription in North America (print & online eds.); JPY 129,000 combined subscription in Japan (print & online eds.); EUR 975 combined subscription elsewhere (print & online eds.) (effective 2011). adv. back issues avail.; reprints avail. **Document type:** *Journal, Academic/Scholarly.* **Description:** Provides a forum to address most important challenges and advances, highlighting their relevance in the clinical setting.
Related titles: Online - full text ed.: ISSN 1748-6971. GBP 615 domestic to institutions; USD 1,080 in North America to institutions; JPY 115,000 in Japan to institutions; EUR 865 elsewhere to institutions (effective 2011) (from IngentaConnect).
Indexed: A26, B21, CA, E08, EMBASE, ExcerpMed, H11, H12, I05, NSA, P20, P22, P30, P48, P54, PQC, SCOPUS.
—BLDSC (4060.610250), IE, Ingenta. **CCC.**
Published by: Future Medicine Ltd. (Subsidiary of: Future Science Ltd.), Unitec House, 2 Albert Pl, London, N3 1QB, United Kingdom. TEL 44-20-83716080, FAX 44-20-83716099, info@futuremedicine.com. Eds. Victoria Lane, Elisa Manzotti TEL 44-20-83716090. Adv. contact Simon Boisseau TEL 44-208-3716083. Circ: 550.

616.89 NLD ISSN 1875-3868
G G Z IN TABELLEN. Text in Dutch. 2005. a. EUR 24.50 (effective 2009).
Published by: Trimbos Instituut, De Costakade 45, Postbus 725, Utrecht, 3500 AS, Netherlands. TEL 31-30-2971100, FAX 31-30-2971111, info@trimbos.nl, http://www.trimbos.nl.

616.8 DEU ISSN 1860-5214
➤ **G M S PSYCHO - SOCIAL - MEDICINE.** (German Medical Science) Text in English. 2004. irreg. free (effective 2011). **Document type:** *Journal, Academic/Scholarly.* **Description:** Publishes articles from the whole area of psychosocial research in medicine.
Formerly (until 2005): Psycho - Social - Medicine (1614-2934)
Media: Online - full text.
Indexed: A01, P03, P30, PsycInfo, T02.
Published by: Arbeitsgemeinschaft der Wissenschaftlichen Medizinischen Fachgesellschaften/Association of the Scientific Medical Societies in Germany, Ubierstr 20, Duesseldorf, 40223, Germany. TEL 49-211-312828, FAX 49-211-316819, awmf@awmf.org, http://www.awmf.org.

616.8 USA ISSN 1947-6116
▼ **G N I BULLETIN.** Text in English. 2009. s-a. free (effective 2010). back issues avail. **Document type:** *Bulletin, Academic/Scholarly.* **Description:** Provides information about clinical trials in PD underway involving sleep, neuroprotection, and general well being.
Media: Online - full text.
Published by: Georgia Neurosurgical Institute, 840 Pine St, Ste 880, Macon, GA 31201. TEL 478-743-7092, FAX 478-743-0523, info@ganeurosurg.org, http://www.ganeurosurg.org.

616.8 CAN ISSN 1918-381X
G P PSYCHOTHERAPIST. (General Practice) Text in English. 1990. q. free to members (effective 2010). **Document type:** *Newsletter, Trade.*
Published by: General Practice Psychotherapy Association, c/o Dr. Victoria Winterton, President, 1717 2nd Ave E, Owen Sound, ON N4K 6V4, Canada. TEL 519-372-2511, drvwinterton@bellnet.ca. Ed. Howard Schneider.

616.8 150 FRA ISSN 1636-2667
G R A P P A F. CAHIERS. (Groupe de Recherche et d'Application des Concepts Psychanalytiques a la Psychiatrie en Afrique Franc) Key Title: Psychanalise et Traditions. Text in French. 2001. irreg. **Document type:** *Journal, Academic/Scholarly.*
Published by: (Groupe de Recherche et d'Application des Concepts Psychanalytiques a la Psychiatrie en Afrique Francophone (G R A P P A F)), L' Harmattan, 5 Rue de l'Ecole Polytechnique, Paris, 75005, France. TEL 33-1-43257651, FAX 33-1-43258203.

616.89 CHL ISSN 0718-4476
GACETA DE PSIQUIATRIA UNIVERSITARIA. Text in Spanish. 2005. q. back issues avail. **Document type:** *Journal, Academic/Scholarly.*
Related titles: Online - full text ed.
Published by: Universidad de Chile, Facultad de Medicina, Independencia 1027, Santiago, 1027, Chile. TEL 56-2-9786223, FAX 56-2-9786332, http://www.med.uchile.cl.

363.420994505 AUS ISSN 1449-1923
GAMBLING MATTERS. Abbreviated title: G M. Text in English. 2000. m. back issues avail. **Document type:** *Magazine, Consumer.* **Description:** Provides counseling for gambling related issues through a variety of feature articles.
Published by: Gambler's Help Southern, Gardeners Rd, PO Box 30, Bentleigh East, VIC 3165, Australia. TEL 61-3-95755353, FAX 61-3-95755380.

616.8 ISL ISSN 1022-4920
➤ **GEDVERND**; arsrit Gedverndarfelags Islands. Text in Icelandic. 1966. a. adv. bk.rev. **Document type:** *Academic/Scholarly.*
Indexed: E-psyche.
Published by: Gedverndarfelag Islands, Hatuni 10, Reykjavik, 105, Iceland. TEL 354-552-5508, http://www.obi.is. Ed. Eirikur Oern Arnarson.

➤ **GELBE LISTE PHARMINDEX. NEUROLOGEN, PSYCHIATER.** *see* PHARMACY AND PHARMACOLOGY

➤ **GENDER & PSYCHOANALYSIS**; an interdisciplinary journal. *see* PSYCHOLOGY

616.8 USA ISSN 0163-8343
RC439 CODEN: GHPSDB
➤ **GENERAL HOSPITAL PSYCHIATRY**; psychiatry, medicine and primary care. Text in English. 1979. bi-m. USD 1,042 in United States to institutions; USD 1,184 elsewhere to institutions (effective 2012). adv. back issues avail.; reprints avail. **Document type:** *Journal, Academic/Scholarly.* **Description:** Emphasizes a biopsychosocial approach to illness and health. Provides a forum for professionals with clinical, academic, and research interests in psychiatry's role in the mainstream of medicine.
Related titles: Microform ed.: (from PQC); Online - full text ed.: ISSN 1873-7714. 199? (from IngentaConnect, ScienceDirect).
Indexed: A01, A03, A08, A20, A22, A26, AHCMS, ASCA, C06, C07, C08, CA, CINAHL, CurCont, E-psyche, EMBASE, ExcerpMed, F09, FR, FamI, H12, I05, INI, IPsyAb, ISR, IndMed, Inpharma, JW-P, JW-WH, MEDLINE, P03, P30, P35, PsycInfo, PsycholAb, R10, Reac, SCI, SCOPUS, SSCI, SWR&A, T02, W07.
—BLDSC (4104.344000), GNLM, IE, Infotrieve, Ingenta, INIST. **CCC.**
Published by: Elsevier Inc. (Subsidiary of: Elsevier Science & Technology), 1600 John F Kennedy Blvd, Philadelphia, PA 19103. TEL 215-239-3900, FAX 215-238-7883, JournalCustomerService-usa@elsevier.com. Ed. Wayne J Katon. Pub. Herb Niemirow TEL 212-633-3141. Adv. contact John Marmero TEL 212-633-3657.

616.8 USA
GENERATIONS (WAYZATA). Text in English. 1957. q. USD 25; USD 30 foreign. bk.rev. 48 p./no.; back issues avail. **Document type:** *Newsletter.* **Description:** Covers meetings, current research, events and activities and other Foundation news relating to hereditary ataxias.
Indexed: A25, E-psyche, HlthInd, R05.
Published by: National Ataxia Foundation, 2600 Fernbrook Ln., N., Ste. 119, Plymouth, MN 55447-4752. TEL 763-553-0020, FAX 763-553-0167. Ed. Donna Gruetzmacher. Circ: 10,000 (controlled).

GENES, BRAIN AND BEHAVIOR. *see* BIOLOGY—Genetics

616.89 DEU ISSN 1433-1055
➤ **GERMAN JOURNAL OF PSYCHIATRY.** Text in German. 1998. irreg. free (effective 2011). back issues avail. **Document type:** *Journal, Academic/Scholarly.* **Description:** Covers all fields of psychiatry.
Media: Online - full text.
Indexed: A01, EMBASE, ExcerpMed, P03, PsycInfo, PsycholAb, R10, Reac, SCOPUS.
—CCC.
Published by: Georg-August-Universitaet Goettingen, Department of Psychiatry, Von-Siebold-Str 5, Goettingen, 37075, Germany. TEL 49-551-396601, FAX 49-551-3922798. Ed. Borwin Bandelow.

➤ **GEROPSYCH**; the journal of gerontopsychology and geriatric psychiatry. *see* GERONTOLOGY AND GERIATRICS

➤ **GESTALT REVIEW.** *see* PSYCHOLOGY

615.85 NLD ISSN 1566-0206
GEZINSTHERAPIE WERELDWIJD. Text in Dutch. 1990. q. EUR 229, USD 344 to institutions (effective 2009). adv. **Document type:** *Journal, Academic/Scholarly.*
Formerly (until 1999): Gezinstherapie (0924-8080)
Published by: Bohn Stafleu van Loghum B.V. (Subsidiary of: Springer Science+Business Media), Postbus 246, Houten, 3990 GA, Netherlands. TEL 31-30-6383872, FAX 31-30-6383991, boekhandels@bsl.nl, http://www.bsl.nl. Eds. Dr. P van der Kaaij, Dr. A Lange. Circ: 2,000.

616.8 NLD ISSN 1872-1141
GEZOND NU. Text in Dutch. 1963. m. EUR 45.95; EUR 4.45 newsstand/cover (effective 2009). adv.
Former titles (until 2005): Gezondheid (Harderwijk) (1574-227X); (until 2004): Gezondheidsnieuws (0165-3245)
Published by: Mix Media, Postbus 16, Lelystad, 8200 AA, Netherlands. TEL 31-320-265080, FAX 31-320-259199, http://www.mixmedia.nl. Circ: 92,454.

616.8 ITA ISSN 0392-4483
GIORNALE DI NEUROPSICHIATRIA DELL'ETA EVOLUTIVA. Text in English, Italian. 1980. 3/yr. EUR 64 domestic; EUR 74 foreign (effective 2009). **Document type:** *Journal, Academic/Scholarly.*
Indexed: A22, ASCA, E-psyche, IBR, IBZ, PsycholAb.
—BLDSC (4178.470000), IE, Ingenta. **CCC.**
Published by: (Societa Italiana di Neuropsichiatria Infantile (S I N P I A)), Pacini Editore SpA, Via A Gherardesca 1, Ospedaletto, PI 56121, Italy. TEL 39-050-313011, FAX 39-050-3130300, pacini.editore@pacinieditore.it, http://www.pacinimedicina.it. Ed. Roberto Milterni.

616 ITA ISSN 0391-9048
➤ **GIORNALE DI NEUROPSICOFARMACOLOGIA.** Text in Italian; Summaries in Italian, English. 1979. q. EUR 15 domestic; USD 30 foreign (effective 2008). adv. bk.rev. back issues avail. **Document type:** *Journal, Academic/Scholarly.*
Related titles: Online - full text ed.: ISSN 1971-1387.
Indexed: A22, ASCA, E-psyche, EMBASE, ExcerpMed, FoP, P03, PsycholAb, RefZh, SCOPUS.
—BLDSC (4178.475000), GNLM, IE, Ingenta. **CCC.**
Published by: C I C Edizioni Internazionali, Corso Trieste 42, Rome, 00198, Italy. TEL 39-06-8412673, FAX 39-06-8412688, info@gruppocic.it, http://www.gruppocic.it. adv.: B&W page EUR 1,707.92, color page EUR 2,169.12; 210 x 290.

➤ **GIORNALE ITALIANO DI PSICOLOGIA E PSICHIATRIA.** *see* PSYCHOLOGY

616.8 ITA ISSN 1592-1107
RC454.4 CODEN: GIPIAJ
GIORNALE ITALIANO DI PSICOPATOLOGIA. Text in Italian. 1995. q. EUR 68 domestic; EUR 83 foreign (effective 2009). **Document type:** *Journal, Academic/Scholarly.*
Related titles: Online - full text ed.
Indexed: E-psyche, EMBASE, ExcerpMed, P03, PsycInfo, R10, Reac, SCOPUS.
—BLDSC (4588.341350).
Published by: (Societa Italiana di Psicopatologia), Pacini Editore SpA, Via A Gherardesca 1, Ospedaletto, PI 56121, Italy. TEL 39-050-313011, FAX 39-050-3130300, pacini.editore@pacinieditore.it, http://www.pacinimedicina.it.

616.8 USA ISSN 0894-1491
QP363.2 CODEN: GLIAEJ
➤ **GLIA.** Text in English. 1988. 16/yr. GBP 2,708 in United Kingdom to institutions; EUR 3,426 in Europe to institutions; USD 4,973 in United States to institutions; USD 5,197 in Canada & Mexico to institutions; USD 5,309 elsewhere to institutions; GBP 3,116 combined subscription in United Kingdom to institutions (print & online eds.); EUR 3,942 combined subscription in Europe to institutions (print & online eds.); USD 5,719 combined subscription in United States to institutions (print & online eds.); USD 5,943 combined subscription in Canada & Mexico to institutions (print & online eds.); USD 6,055 combined subscription elsewhere to institutions (print & online eds.) (effective 2012). adv. back issues avail.; reprint service avail. from PSC. **Document type:** *Journal, Academic/Scholarly.* **Description:** Devoted to the study of the form and function of neuroglial cells in health and disease.
Related titles: Microform ed.: (from PQC); Online - full text ed.: ISSN 1098-1136. GBP 2,537 in United Kingdom to institutions; EUR 3,209 in Europe to institutions; USD 4,973 elsewhere to institutions (effective 2012).
Indexed: A22, A29, ASCA, B20, B21, B25, BIOBASE, BIOSIS Prev, CurCont, E-psyche, EMBASE, ESPM, ExcerpMed, I10, IABS, ISR, IndMed, Inpharma, MEDLINE, MycolAb, NSA, NSCI, P03, P30, PsycInfo, R10, Reac, RefZh, SCI, SCOPUS, VirolAbstr, W07.
—BLDSC (4195.208000), GNLM, IE, Infotrieve, Ingenta, INIST. **CCC.**
Published by: John Wiley & Sons, Inc., 111 River St, Hoboken, NJ 07030. TEL 201-748-6000, FAX 201-748-6088, info@wiley.com, http://www.wiley.com/WileyCDA/. Eds. Bruce R Ransom TEL 206-543-2340, Helmut Kettermann TEL 49-30-94063325. Adv. contact Kim Thompkins TEL 212-850-6921. **Subscr. outside the Americas to:** John Wiley & Sons Ltd., The Atrium, Southern Gate, Chichester, West Sussex PO19 8SQ, United Kingdom. TEL 44-1243-779777, FAX 44-1243-775878, cs-journals@wiley.com.

➤ **GRANTS FOR MENTAL HEALTH, ADDICTIONS & CRISIS SERVICES (ONLINE).** *see* EDUCATION—School Organization And Administration

616.891 NLD ISSN 1871-1146
GROEPEN. Text in Dutch. 1967. q. EUR 90 (effective 2009). **Document type:** *Magazine, Trade.*
Former titles (until 2006): Groepspsychotherapie (0924-381X); (until 1992): N V G P (1571-4071); (until 1989): Nederlandse Vereniging voor Groeps-Psychotherapie en de Nederlandse Vereniging voor Relatie- en Gezinstherapie. Dokumentatieblad (0924-3836); (until 1983): Nederlandse Vereniging voor Groepspsychotherapie. Documentatiebladen (1569-5220)
Published by: Nederlandse Vereniging voor Groepsdynamica en Groepspsychotherapie, Maliebaan 50B, Utrecht, 3581 CS, Netherlands. TEL 31-30-6701425, FAX 31-30-6700890, nvgp.7@planet.nl, http://www.groepspsychotherapie.nl. Eds. C van Manen, A ter Haar.

616.8 FRA ISSN 1952-7519
GROUPEMENT D'ASSISTANCE ET DE COOPERATION DOCUMENTAIRES EN PSYCHIATRIE. NOUVELLES; bulletin d'information du reseau documentaire en sante mentale. Key Title: Des Nouvelles d'Ascodocpsy. Text in French. 2002. q. **Document type:** *Bulletin.*
Published by: Groupement d'Assistance et de Cooperation Documentaires en Psychiatrie (A S C O D O C P S Y), 290 Route de Vienne, Lyon, 69373 Cedex 8, France. TEL 33-4-37901307, FAX 33-4-37901337, http://www.ascodocpsy.org.

GRUPPENANALYSE; Zeitschrift fuer gruppenanalytische Psychotherapie, Beratung und Supervision. *see* PSYCHOLOGY

616.89 DEU ISSN 0017-4947
➤ **GRUPPENPSYCHOTHERAPIE UND GRUPPENDYNAMIK**; Beitraege zur Sozialpsychologie und therapeutischen Praxis. Text in German; Summaries in English, German. 1968. a. (in 1 vol., 4 nos./vol.). EUR 82 to individuals; EUR 164 to institutions; EUR 62 to students; EUR 24.90 per issue (effective 2011). adv. **Document type:** *Journal, Academic/Scholarly.*
Indexed: A20, ASCA, CurCont, DIP, E-psyche, GJP, IBR, IBZ, SCOPUS, SSCI, W07.
—GNLM, IE, Infotrieve. **CCC.**
Published by: Vandenhoeck und Ruprecht, Theaterstr 13, Goettingen, 37073, Germany. TEL 49-551-508440, FAX 49-551-5084422, info@v-r.de. Ed. Kay Niebank. Circ: 1,600 (paid and controlled).

616.8 CHN ISSN 1528-2996
GUOJI ZHONGHUA SHENJING JINGSHEN YIXUE ZAZHI/ INTERNATIONAL CHINESE NEUROPSYCHIATRY MEDICINE JOURNAL. Text in Chinese. 2000. q. abstr. **Document type:** *Journal, Academic/Scholarly.*
Related titles: Online - full content ed.
Published by: Guoji Huaren Yixuejia Shenlixuejia Lianhehui/International Association of Chinese Medical Specialists & Psychologists, PO Box 18, Tangshang, Hebei 063000, China. iacmsp@juno.com. Ed. Jianming Li. Circ: 1,000 (paid); 500 (controlled).

616.8 CHN ISSN 1001-120X
GUOWAI YIXUE (JINGSHENBINGXUE FENCE)/FOREIGN MEDICAL SCIENCES (PSYCHIATRY). Text in Chinese. 1974. q. CNY 24 domestic; USD 11.60 foreign (effective 2005). **Document type:** *Journal, Academic/Scholarly.*
Related titles: Online - full text ed.
—East View.
Published by: Zhongnan Daxue/Central South University, 139, Renmin Zhonglu, Xiangya 2 Yiyuan, Changsha, 410011, China. TEL 86-731-5531571. **Dist. by:** China International Book Trading Corp, 35 Chegongzhuang Xilu, Haidian District, PO Box 399, Beijing 100044, China. TEL 86-10-68412045, FAX 86-10-68412023, cibtc@mail.cibtc.com.cn, http://www.cibtc.com.cn.

616.8 CHN ISSN 1004-6690
GUOWAI YIXUE (NAOXIEGUAN JIBING)/FOREIGN MEDICAL SCIENCES (CEREBROVASCULAR DISEASES). Text in Chinese. 1993. m. CNY 129.60 domestic; USD 64.80 foreign (effective 2005). **Document type:** *Journal, Academic/Scholarly.*
Related titles: Online - full text ed.
—East View.
Published by: Haijun Yixue Gaodeng Zhuanke Xuexiao, Jiangning-qu, PO Box 9, Nanjing, 211135, China. TEL 86-25-84121542 ext 802, FAX 86-25-84199486 ext 801. **Dist. by:** China International Book Trading Corp, 35 Chegongzhuang Xilu, Haidian District, PO Box 399, Beijing 100044, China. TEL 86-10-68412045, FAX 86-10-68412023, cibtc@mail.cibtc.com.cn, http://www.cibtc.com.cn.

616.8 CHN ISSN 1001-1056
GUOWAI YIXUE (SHENJINGBINGXUE SHENJING WAIKEXUE FENCE)/FOREIGN MEDICINE (NEUROLOGY, NEUROSURGERY). Text in Chinese. 1974. bi-m. CNY 58.80 domestic; USD 24.60 foreign (effective 2005). **Document type:** *Journal, Academic/Scholarly.*
Related titles: Online - full text ed.
Published by: Zhongnan Daxue/Central South University, 87, Xiangya Lu, Changsha, 410008, China. http://www.csu.edu.cn/chinese/. **Dist. by:** China International Book Trading Corp, 35 Chegongzhuang Xilu, Haidian District, PO Box 399, Beijing 100044, China. TEL 86-10-68412045, FAX 86-10-68412023, cibtc@mail.cibtc.com.cn, http://www.cibtc.com.cn.

616.891 JPN ISSN 0916-3662
HAKONIWA RYOHOGAKU KENKYU/ARCHIVES OF SANDPLAY THERAPY. Text in English, Japanese; Summaries in English. 1988. a. **Document type:** *Journal, Academic/Scholarly.*
Indexed: E-psyche.
Published by: Nihon Hakoniwa Ryoho Gakkai/Japan Association of Sandplay Therapy, c/o Kyoto University, Graduate School of Education, Department of Clinical Psychology, Yoshida-Honmachi, Sakyo-ku, Kyoto, 606-8501, Japan. FAX 81-75-7533059.

616.8 NLD ISSN 1569-7339
RC343.4 CODEN: TBSCEC
➤ **HANDBOOK OF BEHAVIOURAL NEUROSCIENCE.** Text in English. 1987. irreg., latest vol.18, 2008. price varies. bibl. back issues avail. **Document type:** *Monographic series, Academic/Scholarly.* **Description:** Describes in detail experiments in the theoretical and applied behavioral and neural sciences, discussing the merits of various experimental techniques and methods.
Formerly (until 2007): Techniques in the Behavioral and Neural Sciences (0921-0709)
Related titles: Online - full text ed.: ISSN 2212-1080.
Indexed: A22, CIN, ChemAb, ChemTitl, E-psyche, SCOPUS.
—BLDSC (4250.340050), CASDDS, IE, Ingenta, INIST. **CCC.**
Published by: Elsevier BV (Subsidiary of: Elsevier Science & Technology), Radarweg 29, PO Box 211, Amsterdam, 1000 AE, Netherlands. TEL 31-20-4853911, FAX 31-20-4852457, JournalsCustomerServiceEMEA@elsevier.com, http://www.elsevier.nl. Eds. Alexander Easton, Ekrem Dere, Joe Huston.

616.8 540 NLD ISSN 0924-8196
➤ **HANDBOOK OF CHEMICAL NEUROANATOMY.** Text in English. 1983. irreg., latest vol.20, 2002. price varies. illus. back issues avail. **Document type:** *Monographic series, Academic/Scholarly.* **Description:** Offers medical researchers and practitioners invaluable information on the localization and function of putative transmitter substances in the nervous system.
Related titles: Online - full text ed.
Indexed: E-psyche, SCOPUS.
—BLDSC (4250.397000).
Published by: Elsevier BV (Subsidiary of: Elsevier Science & Technology), Radarweg 29, PO Box 211, Amsterdam, 1000 AE, Netherlands. TEL 31-20-4853911, FAX 31-20-4852457, JournalsCustomerServiceEMEA@elsevier.com, http://www.elsevier.nl. Eds. A Bjorklund, T Hoekfelt.

616.8 NLD ISSN 0072-9752
RC332 CODEN: HACNEU
➤ **HANDBOOK OF CLINICAL NEUROLOGY**; revised series. Text in English. 1969; N.S. 1985. irreg., latest vol.92, 2009. price varies. cum index: vols1-43 in vol 44, 1982. back issues avail. **Document type:** *Monographic series, Academic/Scholarly.* **Description:** Provides a comprehensive reverence for understanding and treating neurologic disorders, research, and trends.
Related titles: Online - full text ed.
Indexed: E-psyche, EMBASE, ExcerpMed, MEDLINE, P30, R10, Reac, SCOPUS.
—BLDSC (4250.405000), IE, Ingenta. **CCC.**
Published by: Elsevier BV (Subsidiary of: Elsevier Science & Technology), Radarweg 29, PO Box 211, Amsterdam, 1000 AE, Netherlands. TEL 31-20-4853911, FAX 31-20-4852457, JournalsCustomerServiceEMEA@elsevier.com, http://www.elsevier.nl. Eds. D F Swaab, F Boller, M J Aminoff.

616.8 NLD ISSN 1567-4231
HANDBOOK OF CLINICAL NEUROPHYSIOLOGY. Text in English. 2004. irreg., latest vol.8, 2008. price varies. **Document type:** *Monographic series, Academic/Scholarly.* **Description:** Presents new and emerging concepts in the area of clinical neurophysiology.
Indexed: SCOPUS.
Published by: Elsevier BV (Subsidiary of: Elsevier Science & Technology), Radarweg 29, PO Box 211, Amsterdam, 1000 AE, Netherlands. TEL 31-20-4853911, FAX 31-20-4852457, JournalsCustomerServiceEMEA@elsevier.com, http://www.elsevier.com. Eds. F Mauguiere, J R Daube.

616.8 NLD
➤ **HANDBOOK OF NEUROPSYCHOLOGY.** Text in English. 1988. irreg., latest vol.11, 1997. price varies. back issues avail. **Document type:** *Monographic series, Academic/Scholarly.* **Description:** Offers a comprehensive reference of both the experimental and clinical aspects of neuropsychology.
Indexed: E-psyche.
Published by: Elsevier BV (Subsidiary of: Elsevier Science & Technology), Radarweg 29, PO Box 211, Amsterdam, 1000 AE, Netherlands. TEL 31-20-4853911, FAX 31-20-4852457, JournalsCustomerServiceEMEA@elsevier.com, http://www.elsevier.nl. Eds. F Boller, J Grafman.

616.8 573.8 USA ISSN 0194-0880
CODEN: HBNEEV
➤ **HANDBOOKS OF BEHAVIORAL NEUROBIOLOGY.** Text in English. 1978. irreg., latest vol.14, 2004. price varies. back issues avail. **Document type:** *Monographic series, Academic/Scholarly.*
Indexed: A22, E-psyche.
—BLDSC (4250.340000). **CCC.**
Published by: Springer New York LLC (Subsidiary of: Springer Science+Business Media), 233 Spring St, New York, NY 10013. TEL 212-460-1500, FAX 212-460-1575, service-ny@springer.com. Ed. Norman T Adler.

616.8 USA
THE HARVARD BRAIN; an undergraduate journal of musings on mind at Harvard University. Variant title: Journal of Neuroscience. Text in English. 1991. a. free (effective 2010). back issues avail. **Document type:** *Journal, Academic/Scholarly.* **Description:** Includes interdisciplinary articles on neurosciences.
Related titles: Online - full text ed.
Indexed: E-psyche.
Published by: Harvard Society for Mind, Brain and Behavior, 275 William James Hall, 33 Kirkland St, Cambridge, MA 02138. http://www.hcs.harvard.edu/~hsmbb. Eds. Amy Chen, Sarah Zhang.

616.8 USA ISSN 1057-5022
THE HARVARD MENTAL HEALTH LETTER. Text in English. 1984. m. USD 59 combined subscription (print & online eds.) (effective 2009). illus. 8 p./no.; back issues avail.; reprints avail. **Document type:** *Newsletter, Academic/Scholarly.* **Description:** Features articles on significant mental health issues.
Formerly (until 1990): Harvard Medical School Mental Health Letter (0884-3783)
Related titles: Online - full text ed.: ISSN 1943-5118. USD 55 (effective 2009).
Indexed: A01, A02, A03, A08, A25, A26, BiolDig, C06, C07, C08, C11, C12, CA, CHNI, CINAHL, E-psyche, E08, EMBASE, ExcerpMed, G08, H03, H04, H11, H12, I05, I07, M01, M02, M06, MASUSE, MEDLINE, P30, P43, R10, Reac, S08, S09, S23, SCOPUS, T02.
—BLDSC (4268.280000). **CCC.**
Published by: Harvard Health Publications Group (Subsidiary of: Harvard Medical School), 10 Shattuck St, Ste 612, Boston, MA 02115. TEL 877-649-9457, hhp@hms.harvard.edu, http://www.health.harvard.edu. Eds. Ann MacDonald, Anthony L Komaroff, Michael Craig Miller.

616.89 USA ISSN 1067-3229
RC321 CODEN: HRPSEP
➤ **HARVARD REVIEW OF PSYCHIATRY.** Text in English. 1993. bi-m. GBP 295, EUR 390, USD 485 combined subscription to institutions (print & online eds.); GBP 590, EUR 775, USD 970 combined subscription to corporations (print & online eds.) (effective 2010). adv. bk.rev. back issues avail.; reprint service avail. from PSC. **Document type:** *Journal, Academic/Scholarly.* **Description:** Examines a wide variety of subjects, emphasizing the integration of research findings with clinical care. Articles cover the diagnosis and treatment of a full range of psychiatric disorders.
Incorporates (1976-1993): McLean Hospital Journal
Related titles: Online - full text ed.: ISSN 1465-7309 (from IngentaConnect).
Indexed: A01, A02, A03, A08, A20, A22, ASCA, CA, CurCont, E-psyche, E01, EMBASE, ESPM, ExcerpMed, FamI, INI, IndMed, Inpharma, MEDLINE, P03, P30, P43, PsycInfo, PsycholAb, R10, Reac, RiskAb, SCOPUS, SSCI, T02, W07.
—GNLM, IE, Infotrieve, Ingenta, INIST. **CCC.**
Published by: Informa Healthcare (Subsidiary of: T & F Informa plc), 52 Vanderbilt Ave, New York, NY 10017. TEL 212-262-8230, FAX 212-262-8234, healthcare.enquiries@informa.com, http://www.informahealthcare.com. Ed. Dr. Sally F Greenfield. Adv. contact Daniel Wallen. **Subscr. outside N. America to:** Taylor & Francis Ltd.

616.857 USA ISSN 0017-8748
RC392 CODEN: HEADAE
➤ **HEADACHE**; the journal of head and face pain. Text in English. 1961. 10/yr. GBP 377 in United Kingdom to institutions; EUR 478 in Europe to institutions; USD 455 in the Americas to institutions; USD 736 elsewhere to institutions; GBP 433 combined subscription in United Kingdom to institutions (print & online eds.); EUR 550 combined subscription in Europe to institutions (print & online eds.); USD 524 combined subscription in the Americas to institutions (print & online eds.); USD 847 combined subscription elsewhere to institutions (print & online eds.) (effective 2012). adv. bk.rev. abstr.; charts; illus.; stat. cum.index. back issues avail.; reprint service avail. from PSC. **Document type:** *Journal, Academic/Scholarly.* **Description:** Publishes original manuscripts (clinical studies, case reports, base research), and other scientific materials concerned with the diagnosis and treatment of headache, in its many aspects, and head and face pain.
Related titles: CD-ROM ed.; Diskette ed.; Magnetic Tape ed.; Microform ed.: (from PQC); Online - full text ed.: ISSN 1526-4610. 1961. GBP 377 in United Kingdom to institutions; EUR 478 in Europe to institutions; USD 455 in the Americas to institutions; USD 736 elsewhere to institutions (effective 2012) (from IngentaConnect).

Indexed: A01, A03, A08, A20, A22, A26, ASCA, B21, B25, BIOBASE, BIOSIS Prev, C06, C07, C08, CA, CINAHL, CTD, ChemAb, CurCont, DentInd, E-psyche, E01, EMBASE, ESPM, ExcerpMed, FR, H12, I05, IABS, IDIS, ISR, IndMed, Inpharma, JW-N, MEDLINE, MycolAb, NRN, NSA, NSCI, P03, P30, P34, P35, P43, P48, PQC, PsycInfo, PsycholAb, R09, R10, Reac, RefZh, SCI, SCOPUS, SD, T02, THA, ToxAb, W07.
—BLDSC (4274.640000), CASDDS, GNLM, IE, Infotrieve, Ingenta, INIST. **CCC.**
Published by: (American Headache Society), Wiley-Blackwell Publishing, Inc. (Subsidiary of: Wiley-Blackwell Publishing Ltd.), 111 River St, Hoboken, NJ 07030. TEL 201-748-6000, FAX 201-748-6088, info@wiley.com, http://www.wiley.com/. Ed. John F Rothrock. Adv. contact Jennifer Johnson TEL 781-388-8512. **Subscr. to:** Wiley-Blackwell Publishing Ltd.

616.857 USA ISSN 2090-1909
▼ ➤ **HEADACHE RESEARCH AND TREATMENT.** Text in English. 2009. irreg. USD 195 (effective 2011). **Document type:** *Journal, Academic/Scholarly.* **Description:** Publishes original research articles, review articles, case reports, and clinical studies related to all aspects of headache.
Related titles: Online - full text ed.: ISSN 2090-1917. free (effective 2011).
Indexed: A01, T02.
Published by: Hindawi Publishing Corporation, 410 Park Ave, 15th Fl, PMB 287, New York, NY 10022. FAX 215-893-4392, 866-446-3294, info@hindawi.com.

616.8 GBR ISSN 0954-2027
HEALTH PSYCHOLOGY UPDATE. Text in English. 1988. q. free to members (effective 2009). adv. **Document type:** *Journal, Academic/Scholarly.* **Description:** Serve as a forum for discussion of issues related to the scientific analysis of psychological processes of health, illness and health care and the development of professional skills in research, practice, consultancy and teaching/training.
Related titles: Online - full text ed.: GBP 4.02 per issue to non-members; GBP 3.45 per issue to members (effective 2009).
—BLDSC (4275.105250), IE, Ingenta.
Published by: The British Psychological Society, St Andrews House, 48 Princess Rd E, Leicester, LE1 7DR, United Kingdom. TEL 44-116-2549568, FAX 44-116-2271314, enquiries@bps.org.uk.

616.8 NLD ISSN 1574-8731
HEALTHDIRECT NEUROLOGIE. Text in Dutch. 2005. 6/yr. EUR 70.75 (effective 2009). adv. **Document type:** *Journal, Trade.*
Related titles: Supplement(s): HealthDirect Agenda Neurologie. ISSN 1574-874X. 2005.
Published by: Elsevier Gezondheidszorg bv (Subsidiary of: Reed Business bv), Postbus 1110, Maarssen, 3600 BC, Netherlands. TEL 31-314-358358, http://www.elseviergezondheidszorg.nl. Circ: 1,383.

316.8588 DEU ISSN 0017-9647
HEILPAEDAGOGISCHE FORSCHUNG; Zeitschrift fuer Paedagogik und Psychologie bei Behinderungen. Text in German. 1964. q. EUR 56; EUR 15 newsstand/cover (effective 2007). bk.rev. abstr. 60 p./no.; back issues avail. **Document type:** *Journal, Academic/Scholarly.*
Indexed: A20, DIP, E-psyche, IBR, IBZ.
—IE. **CCC.**
Published by: Universitaet Potsdam, Institut fuer Sonderpaedagogik, Postfach 601553, Potsdam, 14415, Germany. TEL 49-331-9772597, FAX 49-331-9772195, goetze@rz.uni_potsdam.de, http://www.uni_potsdam.de/u/sonderpaed/spd/index/htm. Ed., Pub., Adv. contact Dr. Herbert Goetze.

616.8 CHN ISSN 1008-2360
HENAN SHIYONG SHENJING JIBING ZAZHI/HENAN JOURNAL OF PRACTICAL NERVOUS DISEASES. Text in Chinese. 1998. bi-m. CNY 10 newsstand/cover domestic (effective 2006). **Document type:** *Journal, Academic/Scholarly.*
Related titles: Online - full text ed.
—East View.
Address: 2, Jingba Lu, Zhengzhou, 450014, China. TEL 86-371-63974256. **Dist. by:** China International Book Trading Corp, 35 Chegongzhuang Xilu, Haidian District, PO Box 399, Beijing 100044, China. TEL 86-10-68412045, FAX 86-10-68412023, cibtc@mail.cibtc.com.cn, http://www.cibtc.com.cn.

616.8 NLD
HISTORY OF NEUROSCIENCE IN AUTOBIOGRAPHY. Text in English. 1998. irreg., latest vol.5, 2006. price varies. **Document type:** *Monographic series, Academic/Scholarly.*
Related titles: Online - full text ed.: ISSN 1874-6055.
—CCC.
Published by: Elsevier BV (Subsidiary of: Elsevier Science & Technology), Radarweg 29, PO Box 211, Amsterdam, 1000 AE, Netherlands. TEL 31-20-4853911, FAX 31-20-4852457, JournalsCustomerServiceEMEA@elsevier.com, http://www.elsevier.com.

616.8 GBR ISSN 0957-154X
RC438
➤ **HISTORY OF PSYCHIATRY.** Text in English. 1990. q. USD 826, GBP 446 combined subscription to institutions (print & online eds.); USD 809, GBP 437 to institutions (effective 2011). adv. back issues avail.; reprint service avail. from PSC. **Document type:** *Journal, Academic/Scholarly.* **Description:** Publishes research articles, analysis, information, and reviews on the history of mental illness as well as the forms of medicine, cultural response, and social policy that have evolved to understand and treat it.
Related titles: Online - full text ed.: ISSN 1740-2360. USD 743, GBP 401 to institutions (effective 2011).
Indexed: A01, A03, A08, A20, A22, ASCA, AmH&L, AmHI, B21, BrHumI, CA, CurCont, E-psyche, E01, EMBASE, ExcerpMed, FamI, H07, HistAb, I14, MEDLINE, NSA, P03, P30, PCI, PsycInfo, PsycholAb, SCOPUS, SSCI, T02, W07.
—BLDSC (4318.408000), GNLM, IE, Infotrieve, Ingenta. **CCC.**
Published by: Sage Publications Ltd. (Subsidiary of: Sage Publications, Inc.), 1 Oliver's Yard, 55 City Rd, London, EC1Y 1SP, United Kingdom. TEL 44-20-73248500, FAX 44-20-73248600, info@sagepub.co.uk, http://www.uk.sagepub.com/home.nav. Ed. G E Berrios. adv.: B&W page GBP 350; 140 x 210. **Subscr. in the Americas to:** Sage Publications, Inc., 2455 Teller Rd, Thousand Oaks, CA 91320. TEL 805-499-9774, FAX 805-499-0871, journals@sagepub.com.

616.8 NLD ISSN 0018-4705
HOOFDLIJNEN. Text in Dutch. 1965. q. EUR 55 domestic; EUR 57.50 foreign (effective 2009). adv. bk.rev. charts; illus. **Document type:** *Journal, Trade.*
Indexed: E-psyche.
Published by: Nederlandse Vereniging van Laboranten Klinische Neurofysiologie/Dutch Association of Electro-Encephalographic Technicians, Postbus 10500, Zwolle, 8000 DM, Netherlands. bestuur@nvlknf.nl, http://www.nvlknf.nl. Ed. Pieter Ingenhoest. Adv. contact Maria de Jong.

616.857 NLD ISSN 0920-0037
HOOFDZAKEN; nieuwsblad over migraine, hoofd- en aangezichtspijnen. Text in Dutch. 1981. 5/yr. EUR 27 (effective 2009). adv. bk.rev. back issues avail. **Document type:** *Newspaper, Consumer.* **Description:** Discusses migraine and other headaches persons suffering from these disorders.
Indexed: E-psyche.
Published by: Nederlandse Vereniging van Hoofdpijnpatienten, Postbus 2185, Amersfoort, 3800 CD, Netherlands. TEL 31-900-2020590, FAX 31-33-4224037, info@hoofdpijnpatienten.nl, http://www.hoofdpijnpatienten.nl.

616.8 CAN ISSN 0827-7605
HORIZON (CAMBRIDGE). Text in English. 1973. s-a. back issues avail. **Document type:** *Newsletter, Consumer.* **Description:** Relays items of interest about Huntington disease and the Society to families, supporters and health care professionals.
Related titles: Online - full text ed.: free.
Indexed: E-psyche.
Published by: Huntington Society of Canada/Societe Huntington du Canada, 151 Frederick St, Ste 400, Kitchener, ON N2H 2M2, Canada. TEL 519-749-7063, FAX 519-749-8965. Ed. Katie Reid. Circ: 10,000.

616.8 USA ISSN 2159-113X
▼ **HORIZONS IN NEUROSCIENCE RESEARCH.** Text in English. 2010. irreg., latest 2011. price varies. back issues avail. **Document type:** *Monographic series, Trade.* **Description:** Presents study results on the leading edge of neuroscience research.
Published by: Nova Science Publishers, Inc., 400 Oser Ave, Ste 1600, Hauppauge, NY 11788. TEL 631-231-7269, FAX 631-231-8175, journals@novapublishers.com.

362.2 CAN ISSN 1910-0337
HOSPITAL MENTAL HEALTH SERVICES IN CANADA. Text in English. 2001. biennial. **Document type:** *Trade.*
Media: Online - full text. **Related titles:** Print ed.: ISSN 1912-7812; ◆ French ed.: Services de Sante Mentale en Milieu Hospitalier au Canada. ISSN 1910-0345.
Published by: Canadian Institute for Health Information/Institut Canadien d'Information sur la Sante, 377 Dalhousie St, Ste 200, Ottawa, ON K1N 9N8, Canada. TEL 613-241-7860, FAX 613-241-8120, http://www.cihi.ca.

616.89 CUB ISSN 0138-7103
RC440
➤ **HOSPITAL PSIQUIATRICO DE LA HABANA. REVISTA.** Text in Spanish; Summaries in English. 1959. 3/yr. adv. bk.rev. abstr. 100 p./no.; back issues avail. **Document type:** *Academic/Scholarly.* **Description:** Covers general, pediatric, and geriatric psychiatry, rehabilitation, forensics, neurology and other topics in the field of mental health.
Indexed: C01, E-psyche, PsycholAb, R10, Reac, SCOPUS.
Published by: Hospital Psiquiatrico de la Habana, Avenida de la Independencia No. 26520, Mazorra, Boyeros, Ciudad De La Habana CP 19220, Cuba. TEL 537-451688, FAX 537-558692. Ed. Dr. Luis Calzadilla Fierro. Adv. contact Eduardo Bernabe Ordaz Ducunge. Circ: 8,000.

616.8 ITA ISSN 1974-7640
▼ **HOT TOPICS IN NEUROLOGY AND PSYCHIATRY.** Text in Multiple languages. 2009. 3/yr. **Document type:** *Monographic series, Academic/Scholarly.*
Related titles: Online - full text ed.: ISSN 2036-0916.
Indexed: A01, EMBASE.
Published by: F B Communication, Via Mascherella 19, Modena, 41121, Italy. TEL 39-059-4270122, FAX 39-059-4279368, info@fbcommunication.org. Eds. Chritopher P Cannon, Sergio Dalla Volta.

612.8 USA ISSN 1065-9471
RC386.6.B7 CODEN: HBMAEE
➤ **HUMAN BRAIN MAPPING.** Text in English. 1993. m. GBP 1,225 in United Kingdom to institutions; EUR 1,547 in Europe to institutions; USD 2,144 in United States to institutions; USD 2,312 in Canada & Mexico to institutions; USD 2,396 elsewhere to institutions; GBP 1,410 combined subscription in United Kingdom to institutions (print & online eds.); EUR 1,781 combined subscription in Europe to institutions (print & online eds.); USD 2,466 combined subscription in United States to institutions (print & online eds.); USD 2,634 combined subscription in Canada & Mexico to institutions (print & online eds.); USD 2,718 combined subscription elsewhere to institutions (print & online eds.) (effective 2012). adv. back issues avail.; reprint service avail. from PSC. **Document type:** *Journal, Academic/Scholarly.* **Description:** Publishes basic, clinical, technical, and theoretical research in the interdisciplinary field of human brain mapping. Includes imaging modalities such as positron-emission tomography, single-photon emission, event-related potentials, magnetoencephalography, magnetic resonance imaging, and x-ray computed tomography.
Related titles: Microform ed.: (from PQC); Online - full text ed.: ISSN 1097-0193. GBP 1,096 in United Kingdom to institutions; EUR 1,384 in Europe to institutions; USD 2,144 elsewhere to institutions (effective 2012).
Indexed: A20, A22, ASCA, B21, B25, BIOBASE, BIOSIS Prev, ChemoAb, CurCont, E-psyche, EMBASE, ESPM, ExcerpMed, IABS, IndMed, Inspec, MEDLINE, MycolAb, NSA, NSCI, P03, P30, PsycInfo, PsycholAb, R10, Reac, RefZh, SCI, SCOPUS, T02, ToxAb, W07.
—BLDSC (4336.031000), GNLM, IE, Infotrieve, Ingenta, INIST. **CCC.**
Published by: John Wiley & Sons, Inc., 111 River St, Hoboken, NJ 07030. TEL 201-748-6000, FAX 201-748-6088, info@wiley.com, http://www.wiley.com/WileyCDA/. Eds. Jack L Lancaster, Peter T Fox. Adv. contact Kim Thompkins TEL 212-850-6921. **Subscr. outside the Americas to:** John Wiley & Sons Ltd, The Atrium, Southern Gate, Chichester, West Sussex PO19 8SQ, United Kingdom. TEL 44-1243-779777, 800-243407, FAX 44-1243-775878, cs-journals@wiley.com.

616.8 615 GBR ISSN 0885-6222
CODEN: HUPSEC
➤ **HUMAN PSYCHOPHARMACOLOGY: CLINICAL AND EXPERIMENTAL.** Text in English. 1986. 8/yr. GBP 1,035 in United Kingdom to institutions; EUR 1,306 in Europe to institutions; USD 2,025 elsewhere to institutions; GBP 1,191 combined subscription in United Kingdom to institutions (print & online eds.); EUR 1,503 combined subscription in Europe to institutions (print & online eds.); USD 2,329 combined subscription elsewhere to institutions (print & online eds.) (effective 2012). adv. back issues avail.; reprint service avail. from PSC. **Document type:** *Journal, Academic/Scholarly.* **Description:** Communicates the results of clinical and experimental studies relevant to the understanding of new and established psychotropic drugs.
Related titles: Microform ed.: (from PQC); Online - full text ed.: ISSN 1099-1077. GBP 1,035 in United Kingdom to institutions; EUR 1,306 in Europe to institutions; USD 2,025 elsewhere to institutions (effective 2012).
Indexed: A01, A03, A08, A22, A36, ASCA, AddicA, B21, B25, BIOBASE, BIOSIS Prev, CA, CABA, CIN, ChemAb, ChemTitl, CurCont, DBA, E-psyche, E12, EMBASE, ESPM, ExcerpMed, F08, F11, F12, FoP, GH, H16, IABS, ISR, Inpharma, MEDLINE, MycolAb, N02, N03, NSA, NSCI, P03, P30, P35, P43, PsycInfo, PsycholAb, R10, RA&MP, Reac, SCI, SCOPUS, SoyAb, T02, T05, ToxAb, W07.
—CASDDS, GNLM, IE, Infotrieve, Ingenta, INIST. **CCC.**
Published by: John Wiley & Sons Ltd. (Subsidiary of: John Wiley & Sons, Inc.), 1-7 Oldlands Way, PO Box 808, Bognor Regis, West Sussex PO21 9FF, United Kingdom. TEL 44-1865-778315, FAX 44-1243-843232, cs-journals@wiley.com, http://eu.wiley.com/WileyCDA/. Eds. C Lindsay DeVane, Stephen Curran. **Subscr. to:** John Wiley & Sons, Inc., 111 River St, Hoboken, NJ 07030. TEL 201-748-6645, subinfo@wiley.com; **Subscr. to:** 1-7 Oldlands Way, PO Box 809, Bognor Regis, West Sussex PO21 9FG, United Kingdom. TEL 44-1865-778054, cs-agency@wiley.com.

➤ **HYPER ACTIVITIES.** *see* EDUCATION—Special Education And Rehabilitation

616.8 FRA ISSN 0361-0713
I B R O NEWS. (International Brain Research Organization) Text in English. 1962. a. price varies. **Document type:** *Newsletter, Trade.*
Formerly (until 1973): I B R O Bulletin (0536-1192)
Related titles: ◆ Supplement to: Neuroscience. ISSN 0306-4522; ◆ Supplement to: Brain Research. ISSN 0006-8993.
—BLDSC (4360.162000).
Published by: International Brain Research Organization, c/o Stephanie de la Rochefoucauld, 255 rue Saint-Honore, Paris, 75001, France. TEL 33-1-46479292, FAX 33-1-46474250, admin@ibro.org, http://www.ibro.org/.

616.8 USA ISSN 1939-3911
I N S N E T; International Neuropsychological Society Liaison Committee newsletter. Text in English. 1996. s-a. free (effective 2007). **Document type:** *Newsletter, Trade.*
Related titles: Online - full text ed.: ISSN 1939-392X.
Published by: International Neuropsychological Society, 700 Ackerman Rd, Ste 625, Columbus, OH 43202. TEL 614-263-4200, FAX 614-263-4366, ins@osu.edu, http://www.the-ins.org. Ed. Helen Haanes.

616.8 USA ISSN 2090-5505
▼ ➤ **I S R N NEUROLOGY.** (International Scholarly Research Network) Text in English. 2011. **Document type:** *Journal, Academic/Scholarly.* **Description:** Publishes original research articles, review articles, and clinical studies in all areas of neurology.
Related titles: Online - full text ed.: ISSN 2090-5513. 2011. free (effective 2011).
Published by: Hindawi Publishing Corporation, 410 Park Ave, 15th Fl, PMB 287, New York, NY 10022. FAX 215-893-4392, 866-446-3294, info@hindawi.com.

616.8 USA
I T F NEWSLETTER. Text in English. 1988. q. free membership (effective 2006). adv. bk.rev.; Website rev. charts; illus.; stat. back issues avail. **Document type:** *Newsletter.* **Description:** Reports recent advances in research in layman's terms for patient and family education.
Related titles: E-mail ed.; Fax ed.
Indexed: E-psyche.
Published by: International Essential Tremor Foundation, PO Box 14005, Lenexa, KS 66285-4005. TEL 913-341-4880, FAX 913-341-1296, staff@essentialtremor.org, http://www.essentialtremor.org. Ed., Pub., R&P, Adv. contact Catherine S Rice. Circ: 6,000 (paid).

616.891 USA ISSN 0899-403X
➤ **I U P STRESS AND HEALTH SERIES.** (International Universities Press) Text in English. 198?. irreg., latest vol.9. price varies. back issues avail. **Document type:** *Monographic series, Academic/Scholarly.* **Description:** Act as a handbook of psychosomatic Medicine is an essential tool for clincians in every specialty, a comprehensive work on a highly complex subject.
Indexed: E-psyche.
Published by: International Universities Press, Inc., 59 Boston Post Rd, Box 1524, PO Box 389, Madison, CT 06443. TEL 203-245-4000, FAX 203-245-0775, info@iup.com.

616.891 ITA ISSN 1592-193X
IDEE IN PSICHIATRIA. Text in Italian. 2001. q. **Document type:** *Journal, Academic/Scholarly.*
Published by: Societa Editrice Universo, Via Giovanni Battista Morgagni 1, Rome, RM 00161, Italy. TEL 39-06-44231171, FAX 39-06-4402033, amministrazione@seu-roma.it, http://www.seuroma.com.

616.891 ITA ISSN 1974-059X
IDEE IN PSICOTERAPIA. Text in Multiple languages. 2008. q. EUR 45 (effective 2010). **Document type:** *Journal, Trade.*
Published by: Alpes Italia, Via Cipro 77, Rome, 00136, Italy. info@alpesitalia.it, http://www.alpesitalia.it.

INCLUSION (ENGLISH EDITION). *see* PSYCHOLOGY

616.891 GBR ISSN 2045-4244
THE INDEPENDENT PRACTITIONER. Text in English. 2006. q. free (effective 2010). back issues avail. **Document type:** *Journal, Trade.* **Description:** Provides information about latest counselling developments in psychotherapy, a forum for debate about counselling, and opportunities for professional development.
Related titles: Online - full text ed.
Published by: British Association for Counselling & Psychotherapy, BACP House, 15 St John's Business Park, Lutterworth, Leicestershire LE17 4HB, United Kingdom. TEL 44-1455-883300, FAX 44-1455-550243, bacp@bacp.co.uk, http://www.bacp.co.uk. Ed. Margaret Akmakjian-Pitz TEL 44-1994-232142.

616.8 IND ISSN 0972-2327
➤ **INDIAN ACADEMY OF NEUROLOGY. ANNALS.** Text in English. 1998. q. INR 2,000 domestic; USD 150 foreign to individuals; USD 200 foreign to institutions; INR 2,400 combined subscription domestic; USD 180 combined subscription foreign to individuals (print & online eds.); USD 240 combined subscription foreign to institutions (print & online eds.) (effective 2011). adv. **Document type:** *Journal, Academic/Scholarly.* **Description:** Disseminates scientific information and contributes to the advancement of knowledge in neurosciences.
Related titles: Online - full text ed.: ISSN 1998-3549. INR 1,600 domestic; USD 120 foreign to individuals; USD 160 foreign to institutions (effective 2011).
Indexed: A01, A26, A36, B21, C06, C07, CA, CABA, E08, EMBASE, ExcerpMed, G08, GH, H11, H12, H17, I05, N02, N03, NSA, P10, P30, P33, P39, P48, P53, P54, PN&I, PQC, R08, R10, R12, RA&MP, RM&VM, Reac, S09, SCI, SCOPUS, T02, T05, W07.
—BLDSC (1026.850000), IE. **CCC.**
Published by: (Indian Academy of Neurology), Medknow Publications and Media Pvt. Ltd., B-9, Kanara Business Ctr, Off Link Rd, Ghatkopar (E), Mumbai, Maharastra 400 075, India. TEL 91-22-66491816, FAX 91-22-66491817, http://www.medknow.com. Ed. Sanjeev V Thomas TEL 91-471-2524468.

616.8 IND ISSN 0973-0508
THE INDIAN JOURNAL OF NEUROTRAUMA. Text in English. 2004. s-a. INR 1,000 domestic to individuals; USD 100 foreign to individuals; INR 3,000 domestic to institutions; USD 300 foreign to institutions; free to members (effective 2011). bk.rev. back issues avail. **Document type:** *Journal, Academic/Scholarly.* **Description:** Provides a platform for the accumulation and dissemination of ideas and information related to the field of neurotrauma.
Related titles: Online - full text ed.: free (effective 2011).
—IE.
Published by: Neurotrauma Society of India, K-20, First Fl Lajpat Nagar-III, New Delhi, 110 024, India. ydewan@yahoo.com, http://www.ntsi.in. Ed. Harjinder S Bhatoe TEL 91-20-26306112.

616.89 IND ISSN 0019-5545
RC321 CODEN: IJRPAB
➤ **INDIAN JOURNAL OF PSYCHIATRY.** Text in English. 1949. q. INR 3,000 domestic to individuals; USD 120 foreign to individuals; INR 4,000 domestic to institutions; USD 250 foreign to institutions; INR 3,600 combined subscription domestic to individuals (print & online eds.); USD 145 combined subscription foreign to individuals (print & online eds.); INR 4,800 combined subscription domestic to institutions (print & online eds.); USD 300 combined subscription foreign to institutions (print & online eds.) (effective 2011). bk.rev. charts; illus.; stat. index. **Document type:** *Journal, Academic/Scholarly.* **Description:** Original articles, review articles, case reports, letter to editor in psychiatry and related disciplines.
Formerly (until 1959): Indian Journal of Neurology and Psychiatry
Related titles: CD-ROM ed.; Online - full text ed.: ISSN 1998-3794. INR 2,400 domestic to individuals; USD 95 foreign to individuals; INR 3,200 domestic to institutions; USD 200 foreign to institutions (effective 2011).
Indexed: A01, A22, A26, B21, C06, C07, CA, ChemAb, E-psyche, EMBASE, ESPM, ExcerpMed, ExtraMED, H12, I05, NSA, P10, P30, P48, P53, P54, PQC, PsycholAb, R10, Reac, RiskAb, SCOPUS, T02.
—BLDSC (4420.280000), CASDDS, GNLM, IE, Infotrieve, Ingenta. **CCC.**
Published by: (Indian Psychiatric Society), Medknow Publications and Media Pvt. Ltd., B-9, Kanara Business Ctr, Off Link Rd, Ghatkopar (E), Mumbai, Maharastra 400 075, India. TEL 91-22-66491816, FAX 91-22-66491817, http://www.medknow.com.

616.8 IND ISSN 0253-7176
CODEN: IJPMEU
INDIAN JOURNAL OF PSYCHOLOGICAL MEDICINE. Text in English. 1978. s-a. INR 1,200 domestic; USD 100 foreign; INR 1,500 combined subscription domestic (print & online eds.); USD 120 combined subscription foreign (print & online eds.) (effective 2011). adv. bk.rev. abstr.; bibl.; charts; illus.; stat. reprints avail. **Document type:** *Journal, Academic/Scholarly.* **Description:** Research and review articles, and conference papers in various areas of psychiatry and related subjects.
Formerly (until 1978): Indian Journal of Psychology (0019-5553)
Related titles: Online - full text ed.: ISSN 0975-1564. INR 1,000 domestic; USD 80 foreign (effective 2011).
Indexed: A01, A26, BAS, CA, CIS, E-psyche, E08, H11, H12, I05, IPsyAb, ISA, P10, P30, P48, P53, P54, PCI, PQC, PRA, PsycholAb, S02, S03, S09, T02.
—Ingenta. **CCC.**
Published by: (Indian Psychiatric Society, South Zone), Medknow Publications and Media Pvt. Ltd., B-9, Kanara Business Ctr, Off Link Rd, Ghatkopar (E), Mumbai, Maharastra 400 075, India. TEL 91-22-66491816, FAX 91-22-66491817, http://www.medknow.com.

616.8 IND ISSN 0972-6748
INDUSTRIAL PSYCHIATRY JOURNAL. Text in English. 1991. s-a. INR 1,000, USD 200 (effective 2010). adv. abstr. reprints avail. **Document type:** *Journal, Academic/Scholarly.* **Description:** Covers industrial psychiatry and psychology, work psychology, occupational psychology, personnel psychology, human resources development and other disciplines such as social psychology, personality psychology and quantitative psychology. Audience includes psychiatrists and psychologists.
Related titles: Online - full text ed.: ISSN 0976-2795. free (effective 2011).
Indexed: A26, B01, E08, H12, I05, P10, P30, P48, P53, P54, PQC, S09, T02.
—**CCC.**
Published by: (Association of Industrial Psychiatry of India), Medknow Publications and Media Pvt. Ltd., B-9, Kanara Business Ctr, Off Link Rd, Ghatkopar (E), Mumbai, Maharastra 400 075, India. TEL 91-22-66491818, 91-22-66491816, publishing@medknow.com, http://www.medknow.com. Ed. Dr. Kalpana Srivastava. Pub. Dr. D K Sahu. Circ: 600.

616.8 155.5 ITA ISSN 1594-5146
INFANZIA E ADOLESCENZA; psicodinamica e psicopatologia. Text in Multiple languages. 2002. 3/yr. **Document type:** *Journal, Academic/Scholarly.*
Related titles: Online - full text ed.: ISSN 2038-1808.
Indexed: P03, PsycInfo.
Published by: Il Pensiero Scientifico Editore, Via Bradano 3-C, Rome, 00199, Italy. TEL 39-06-862821, FAX 39-06-86282250, http://www.pensiero.it.

616.8 CHE ISSN 1661-2671
INFO NEUROLOGIE UND PSYCHIATRIE. Text in German. 2003. bi-m. CHF 80 (effective 2007). **Document type:** *Journal, Academic/Scholarly.*
Published by: Springer Medizin Verlag Schweiz AG (Subsidiary of: Springer Science+Business Media), Nordstr 31, Zurich, 8006, Switzerland. TEL 41-44-2502800, FAX 41-44-2502803, verlag@springer-medizin.ch.

616.8 DEU ISSN 1437-062X
INFO NEUROLOGIE UND PSYCHIATRIE. Text in German. 1999. bi-m. EUR 117, USD 154 to institutions (effective 2012). adv. back issues avail. **Document type:** *Journal, Academic/Scholarly.*
Indexed: A26, E-psyche.
—**CCC.**
Published by: Urban und Vogel Medien und Medizin Verlagsgesellschaft mbH (Subsidiary of: Springer Science+Business Media), Neumarkter Str 43, Munich, 81673, Germany. TEL 49-89-4372-1411, FAX 49-89-4372-1410, verlag@urban-vogel.de, http://www.urban-vogel.de. Ed. Brigitte Mueller-Moreano. Adv. contact Peter Urban. B&W page EUR 2,080, color page EUR 3,380; trim 174 x 247. Circ: 14,000 (paid and controlled). **Subscr. to:** Springer Distribution Center, Kundenservice Zeitschriften, Haberstr 7, Heidelberg 69126, Germany. TEL 49-6221-3454303, FAX 49-6221-3454229, subscriptions@springer.com.

616.8 CAN ISSN 1910-0469
INFO PARKINSON. Text in English, French. 1988. q. **Document type:** *Bulletin, Consumer.*
Former titles (until 2002): Dopamien (1485-8010); (until 1998): Dopamien Parkinson (1198-7812)
Published by: Parkinson Society Quebec, 550, Sherbrooke West, Ste 1470, Montreal, PQ H3A 1B9, Canada. TEL 514-861-4422, 800 720-1307, FAX 514-861-4510, info@infoparkinson.org, http://www.infoparkinson.org.

616.8 BRA ISSN 0101-4331
INFORMACAO PSIQUIATRICA. Text in Portuguese; Summaries in English, Portuguese. 1980-1983 (vol.4, no.4); resumed. triennial. adv. bk.rev. index, cum.index. back issues avail. **Document type:** *Academic/Scholarly.* **Description:** Presents studies in clinical psychiatry.
Indexed: C01, E-psyche, SCOPUS.
—INIST.
Published by: (Universidade do Estado do Rio de Janeiro, Universidade do Estado do Rio de Janeiro, Departamento de Psiquiatria e Psicopatologia), Editora Cientifica Nacional Ltda. (E C N), Rua da Gloria 366, 3o Andar, Gloria, Rio de Janeiro, RJ 20241-180, Brazil. Ed. Jorge Alberto Costa e Silva. R&P, Adv. contact Maria Luiza Carvalho. Circ: 5,000.

616.89 ESP ISSN 0210-7279
INFORMACIONES PSIQUIATRICAS. Text in Spanish. 1955. q. back issues avail. **Document type:** *Bulletin, Academic/Scholarly.*
—**CCC.**
Published by: Benito Menni. Complejo Asistencia en Salud Mental, Dr. Pujadas, 38, Sant Boi de Llobregat, Barcelona, 08830, Spain. TEL 34-93-6529999, FAX 34-93-6400268, hscbmeni@comb.es. Ed. Jose Miguel Cebamanos Martin.

INFORMATION PLUS REFERENCE SERIES. WEIGHT IN AMERICA; obesity, eating disorders, and other health risks. *see* PHYSICAL FITNESS AND HYGIENE

616.8 FRA ISSN 0020-0204
L'INFORMATION PSYCHIATRIQUE. Text in French. 1908. m. (10/yr.). EUR 310 combined subscription domestic to institutions (print & online eds.); EUR 350 combined subscription in the European Union to institutions (print & online eds.).; EUR 370 combined subscription elsewhere to institutions (print & online eds.) (effective 2011). back issues avail. **Document type:** *Journal, Academic/Scholarly.*
Former titles (until 1940): L' Alieniste Francais (1246-6522); (until 1927): Association Amicale des Medecins des Etablissements Publics d'Alienes de France. Bulletin (1246-6514)
Related titles: Online - full text ed.: ISSN 1952-4056.
Indexed: A22, E-psyche, FR, IBR, IBZ, P30, PsycholAb, R10, Reac, S02, S03, SCOPUS.
—BLDSC (4493.920000), GNLM, IE, Infotrieve, Ingenta, INIST. **CCC.**
Published by: John Libbey Eurotext, 127 Av. de la Republique, Montrouge, 92120, France. TEL 33-1-46730660, FAX 33-1-40840999, contact@jle.com, http://www.john-libbey-eurotext.fr. Ed. Thierry Tremine.

616.8 USA ISSN 0737-125X
INNOVATIONS IN CLINICAL PRACTICE. Text in English. 1982. a. price varies.
Published by: Professional Resource Press, PO Box 15560, Sarasota, FL 34277-1560. TEL 800-443-3364, FAX 941-343-9201.

616.8 NOR ISSN 1890-4556
INNSIKT; tidsskrift om ad/hd, tourettes syndrom og narkolepsi. Text in Norwegian. 1996. q. free. back issues avail. **Document type:** *Magazine, Consumer.*
Formerly (until 2007): N K-Info (0809-0521)
Related titles: Online - full text ed.: ISSN 1890-4564. 1999.
Published by: Nasjonalt Kompetansesenter for AD/HD, Tourettes Syndrom og Narkolepsi/National Research Center for AD/HD, Tourette Syndrome and Narcolepsy, c/o Ullevaal Universitetssykehus HF, Bygg 29, Oslo, 0407, Norway. TEL 47-23-016030, FAX 47-23-016031, post@nasjkomp.no. Ed. Staale Tvete Vollan. Circ: 3,500.

616.858 USA
INSIDE CHADD. Text in English. 1993. q. USD 45 to members. **Document type:** *Newsletter.*
Formerly: Chadder Box
Indexed: E-psyche.
Published by: Children and Adults with Attention Deficit - Hyperactivity Disorders, 8181 Professional Pl., Ste. 201, Landover, MD 20785-2226. TEL 301-306-7070, 800-233-4050, FAX 301-306-7090. Ed. Jennifer Garner.

616.8914 BRA ISSN 0103-9083
RC475
➤ **INSIGHT-PSICOTERAPIA.** Text in Portuguese. 1990. m. adv. bk.rev. back issues avail. **Document type:** *Journal, Academic/Scholarly.*
Related titles: Online - full text ed.
Indexed: E-psyche.
Published by: Lemos Editorial & Graficos Ltda., Rua Rui Barbosa, 70, B Vista, Sao Paulo, SP 01326-010, Brazil. TEL 55-11-251-4300, FAX 55-11-251-4300, lemospl@netpoint.com.br, http://www.lemos.com.br.

612.8 USA ISSN 8755-3252
RZ460
INSTITUTE FOR ORGONOMIC SCIENCE. ANNALS. Text in English. 1984. a. USD 15. bk.rev.
Indexed: E-psyche.
Published by: Institute for Orgonomic Science, 205 Knapp Rd, Lansdale, PA 19446. TEL 215-368-2678. Circ: 600.

612.8 USA ISSN 1932-4502
BF1 CODEN: IPBSEK
➤ **INTEGRATIVE PSYCHOLOGICAL & BEHAVIORAL SCIENCE.** Abbreviated title: I P B S. Text in English. 1966. q. EUR 527, USD 719 combined subscription to institutions (print & online eds.) (effective 2012). index. back issues avail.; reprint service avail. from PSC. **Document type:** *Journal, Academic/Scholarly.* **Description:** Explores the cultural nature of human conduct and its evolutionary history, anthropology, ethology, communication processes between people, and within, as well as between, societies.
Former titles (until 2007): Integrative Physiological and Behavioral Science (1053-881X); (until 1991): Pavlovian Journal of Biological Science (0093-2213); (until 1974): Conditional Reflex (0010-5392)
Related titles: Microform ed.: (from PQC); Online - full text ed.: ISSN 1936-3567 (from IngentaConnect).
Indexed: A01, A02, A03, A08, A20, A22, A26, ASCA, BAS, BibInd, C11, CA, CIS, CRFR, ChemAb, DIP, DentInd, E-psyche, E01, E08, EMBASE, ExcerpMed, G08, H04, H12, HospLI, I05, IBR, IBZ, IndMed, MEDLINE, MycolAb, NSCI, P03, P25, P30, P43, P48, PQC, PsycInfo, PsycholAb, R10, Reac, S09, SCOPUS, SSCI, T02, W07.
—CASDDS, GNLM, IE, Infotrieve, Ingenta, INIST. **CCC.**
Published by: Springer New York LLC (Subsidiary of: Springer Science+Business Media), 233 Spring St, New York, NY 10013. TEL 212-460-1500, FAX 212-460-1575, service-ny@springer.com. Ed. Jaan Valsiner.

➤ **INTELLECTUAL AND DEVELOPMENTAL DISABILITIES**; journal of policy, practice, and perspectives. *see* EDUCATION—Special Education And Rehabilitation

➤ **INTERNATIONAL ABSTRACTS. ALZHEIMER'S DISEASE & OTHER DEMENTIAS.** *see* MEDICAL SCIENCES—Abstracting, Bibliographies, Statistics

616.855 CHE ISSN 0074-1655
INTERNATIONAL ASSOCIATION OF LOGOPEDICS AND PHONIATRICS. REPORTS OF CONGRESS. Text in English. 1947. triennial. USD 30 (effective 2003). adv. bk.rev. **Document type:** *Journal, Academic/Scholarly.*
Indexed: E-psyche.
Published by: International Association of Logopedics and Phoniatrics, c/o Dr. A. Muller, 43 R Louis de Savoie, Morges, 1110, Switzerland. TEL 41-21-8030800, FAX 41-21-3209300.

616.8 IRL ISSN 0074-3631
INTERNATIONAL CONGRESS OF ELECTROENCEPHALOGRAPHY AND CLINICAL NEUROPHYSIOLOGY (PROCEEDINGS). Text in English. irreg., latest 2000, Dec. price varies. Supplement avail.; back issues avail. **Document type:** *Proceedings, Academic/Scholarly.*
Indexed: E-psyche, IndMed, Inspec.
Published by: (International Federation of Clinical Neurophysiology), Elsevier Ireland Ltd (Subsidiary of: Elsevier Science & Technology), Elsevier House, Brookvale Plaza, E. Park, Shannon, Co. Clare, Ireland. TEL 353-61-709600, FAX 353-61-709100. R&P Annette Moloney. **Subscr. to:** Elsevier BV, Radarweg 29, PO Box 211, Amsterdam 1000 AE, Netherlands. TEL 31-20-4853757, FAX 31-20-4853432, JournalsCustomerServiceEMEA@elsevier.com, http://www.elsevier.nl.

616.8 CHE
INTERNATIONAL FEDERATION FOR PSYCHOTHERAPY. CONGRESS REPORTS. Text in English. 1972. irreg. **Document type:** *Proceedings, Trade.*
Formerly: International Federation for Medical Psychotherapy. Congress Reports (0074-5847)
Indexed: E-psyche.
Published by: International Federation for Psychotherapy, Culmannstr 8, Zurich, 8091, Switzerland. TEL 41-44-2555251, FAX 41-44-2554408, secretariat@ifp.name, http://www.ifp.name.

INTERNATIONAL GESTALT JOURNAL. *see* PSYCHOLOGY

612.67 USA ISSN 2090-0252
RC523
▼ ➤ **INTERNATIONAL JOURNAL OF ALZHEIMER'S DISEASE.** Text in English. 2009. irreg. free (effective 2011). **Document type:** *Journal, Academic/Scholarly.* **Description:** Publishes original research articles, review articles, case reports, and clinical studies in all areas of Alzheimer's disease.
Media: Online - full text.
Indexed: A01, A26, B19, C06, C07, CTA, E08, H11, H12, I05, NSA, P30, S09, T02.
Published by: Sage - Hindawi Access to Research, 410 Park Ave, 15th Fl, 287 PMB, New York, NY 10022. FAX 866-446-3294.

616.8 570.285 IND
➤ **INTERNATIONAL JOURNAL OF BIOENGINEERING, NEUROSCIENCES AND TECHNOLOGY.** Abbreviated title: I J B N S T. Text in English. free (effective 2011). **Document type:** *Journal, Academic/Scholarly.* **Description:** Contains research articles in the field of bioengineering, neurosciences and technology.

Media: Online - full text.
Published by: A.Prabhu Britto, Ed. & Pub., 18A, Nataraja Thevar Colony, Ramanathapuram, Coimbatore, Tamil Nadu 641 045, India. prabhu.britto@gmail.com, britto@prabhubritto.org, http://www.ijblst.org.

▼ ➤ **INTERNATIONAL JOURNAL OF BIOSCIENCES, PSYCHIATRY AND TECHNOLOGY.** *see* BIOLOGY

➤ **INTERNATIONAL JOURNAL OF DEVELOPMENTAL DISABILITIES.** *see* EDUCATION—Special Education And Rehabilitation

616.8 GBR ISSN 0736-5748
QP363.5 CODEN: IJDND6
➤ **INTERNATIONAL JOURNAL OF DEVELOPMENTAL NEUROSCIENCE.** Abbreviated title: I J D N. Text in English. 1983. 8/yr. EUR 1,943 in Europe to institutions; JPY 258,400 in Japan to institutions; USD 2,174 elsewhere to institutions (effective 2012). back issues avail. **Document type:** *Journal, Academic/Scholarly.* **Description:** Features research on basic and clinical aspects of the developing nervous system.
Related titles: Microfilm ed.: (from PQC); Online - full text ed.: ISSN 1873-474X (from IngentaConnect, ScienceDirect).
Indexed: A01, A03, A08, A22, A26, A34, A35, A36, A37, A38, ASCA, AgBio, B21, B25, BIOBASE, BIOSIS Prev, CA, CABA, CIN, ChemAb, ChemTitl, ChemoAb, CurCont, D01, E-psyche, E12, EMBASE, ESPM, ExcerpMed, F08, F11, F12, GH, I05, IABS, IBR, IBZ, IPsyAb, ISR, IndMed, IndVet, Inpharma, MEDLINE, MycolAb, N02, N03, N04, NSA, NSCI, P03, P30, PsycInfo, PsycholAb, R10, RA&MP, Reac, S01, SCI, SCOPUS, SoyAb, T02, T05, ToxAb, VS, W07.
—BLDSC (4542.185100), CASDDS, GNLM, IE, Infotrieve, Ingenta, INIST. **CCC.**
Published by: (International Society for Developmental Neuroscience CAN), Pergamon (Subsidiary of: Elsevier Science & Technology), The Blvd, Langford Ln, East Park, Kidlington, Oxford OX5 1GB, United Kingdom. TEL 44-1865-843000, FAX 44-1865-843010, JournalsCustomerServiceEMEA@elsevier.com. Ed. Dr. J Regino Perez-Polo. **Subscr. to:** Elsevier BV, Radarweg 29, PO Box 211, Amsterdam 1000 AE, Netherlands. TEL 31-20-4853757, FAX 31-20-4853432, http://www.elsevier.nl.

616.8 150 DEU ISSN 1866-7953
INTERNATIONAL JOURNAL OF DREAM RESEARCH; psychological aspects of sleep and dreaming. Abbreviated title: I J O D R. Text in English. 2008. s-a. free (effective 2011). **Document type:** *Journal, Academic/Scholarly.*
Media: Online - full text.
Published by: Universitaet Heidelberg, Central Institute of Mental Health, J 5, Mannheim, 68159, Germany. http://www.zi-mannheim.de. Ed. Michael Schredl.

616.8 USA ISSN 1522-4821
RC480.6
➤ **INTERNATIONAL JOURNAL OF EMERGENCY MENTAL HEALTH.** Text in English. 1999. q. USD 82 domestic to individuals; USD 128 foreign to individuals; USD 390 domestic to institutions; USD 485 foreign to institutions (effective 2011). back issues avail. **Document type:** *Journal, Academic/Scholarly.* **Description:** Publishes manuscripts on relevant topics including psychological trauma, disaster psychology, traumatic stress, etc.
Indexed: C06, C07, EMBASE, ExcerpMed, F09, IndMed, MEDLINE, P03, P30, PsycInfo, PsycholAb, R10, Reac, SCOPUS.
—BLDSC (4542.232700), IE, Infotrieve, Ingenta. **CCC.**
Published by: Chevron Publishing Corporation, PO Box 6274, Ellicott City, MD 21042. TEL 410-418-8002, FAX 410-418-8006, office@chevronpublishing.com.

➤ **INTERNATIONAL JOURNAL OF GERIATRIC PSYCHIATRY.** *see* GERONTOLOGY AND GERIATRICS

➤ **INTERNATIONAL JOURNAL OF GROUP PSYCHOTHERAPY.** *see* PSYCHOLOGY

616.8 USA ISSN 2156-9703
▼ **INTERNATIONAL JOURNAL OF INTEGRATIVE PSYCHOTHERAPY.** Text in English. 2010. bi-m. free (effective 2011). **Document type:** *Journal, Academic/Scholarly.*
Media: Online - full text.
Published by: International Integrative Psychotherapy Association http://www.integrativeassociation.com. Ed. Gregor Zvelc.

INTERNATIONAL JOURNAL OF LAW AND PSYCHIATRY. *see* LAW

616.834 USA ISSN 1537-2073
RC377
➤ **INTERNATIONAL JOURNAL OF M S CARE**; adjunctive treatment for cognitive problems. (Multiple Sclerosis) Text in English. 1999. q. USD 60 to non-members; free to members (effective 2011). adv. **Document type:** *Journal, Academic/Scholarly.* **Description:** Contains clinical and original research articles on topics of interest to MS care providers, including physician care, nursing care, rehabilitation, and psychosocial care.
Related titles: Online - full text ed.: free (effective 2008).
Indexed: C06, C07.
—BLDSC (4542.365900), IE.
Published by: (Consortium of Multiple Sclerosis Centers), Delaware Media Group, 66 S. Maple Ave, Ridgewood, NJ 07450. TEL 201-612-7676, FAX 201-612-8282, info@delmedgroup.com, http://www.delmedgroup.com. Ed. Nancy Monson. Pubs. Frank M Marino, Joseph J D'Onofrio. Circ: 4,735.

616.8 610.73 AUS ISSN 1445-8330
RC440
➤ **INTERNATIONAL JOURNAL OF MENTAL HEALTH NURSING.** Text in English. 1980. bi-m. GBP 335 in United Kingdom to institutions; EUR 427 in Europe to institutions; USD 549 in the Americas to institutions; USD 658 elsewhere to institutions; GBP 385 combined subscription in United Kingdom to institutions (print & online eds.); EUR 490 combined subscription in Europe to institutions (print & online eds.); USD 630 combined subscription in the Americas to institutions (print & online eds.); USD 756 combined subscription elsewhere to institutions (print & online eds.) (effective 2012). adv. back issues avail.; reprint service avail. from PSC. **Document type:** *Journal, Academic/Scholarly.* **Description:** Examines developments and trends in mental health nursing.
Former titles (until 2001): Australian and New Zealand Journal of Mental Health Nursing (1324-3780); (until 1994): Australian Journal of Mental Health Nursing (1035-8374); (until 1990): Australian Congress of Mental Health Nurses. Journal (0727-4173)
Related titles: Online - full text ed.: ISSN 1447-0349. 1999. GBP 335 in United Kingdom to institutions; EUR 427 in Europe to institutions; USD 549 in the Americas to institutions; USD 658 elsewhere to institutions (effective 2012) (from IngentaConnect).
Indexed: A01, A02, A03, A08, A22, A26, ASSIA, B28, C06, C07, C08, C11, CA, CINAHL, CurCont, E-psyche, E01, EMBASE, ExcerpMed, H04, H12, INI, MEDLINE, P03, P30, P43, PsycInfo, PsycholAb, R10, Reac, SCI, SCOPUS, SSCI, T02, V&AA, W07.
—BLDSC (4542.352030), IE, Ingenta. **CCC.**
Published by: (Australian and New Zealand College of Mental Health Nurses Inc.), Wiley-Blackwell Publishing Asia (Subsidiary of: Wiley-Blackwell Publishing Ltd.), 155 Cremorne St, Richmond, VIC 3121, Australia. TEL 61-3-92743100, FAX 61-3-92743101, subs@blackwellpublishingasia.com, http://www.wiley.com/WileyCDA/. Ed. Brenda Happell. adv.: B&W page AUD 935, color page AUD 2,057; trim 210 x 275.

616.8 GBR ISSN 1752-4458
RA790.A1
➤ **INTERNATIONAL JOURNAL OF MENTAL HEALTH SYSTEMS.** Text in English. 2007. irreg. free (effective 2011). adv. **Document type:** *Journal, Academic/Scholarly.* **Description:** Covers mental health legislation and policy, mental health system financing and governance, mental health service design implementation and evaluation, human resource development, effective mental health systems research transfer, and the human rights of people with mental illness.
Media: Online - full text.
Indexed: A01, A26, CA, H05, H12, I05, P03, P30, PsycInfo, R10, Reac, SCOPUS, T02.
—**CCC.**
Published by: BioMed Central Ltd. (Subsidiary of: Springer Science+Business Media), 236 Gray's Inn Rd, London, WC1X 8HB, United Kingdom. TEL 44-20-31922000, FAX 44-20-31922010, info@biomedcentral.com, http://www.biomedcentral.com. Ed. I H Minas. Adv. contact Natasha Bailey TEL 44-20-31922231.

616.8 GBR ISSN 1049-8931
RC337 CODEN: IPSREY
➤ **INTERNATIONAL JOURNAL OF METHODS IN PSYCHIATRIC RESEARCH.** Text in English. 1991-1996; N.S. 1998. q. GBP 386 in United Kingdom to institutions; EUR 489 in Europe to institutions; USD 756 elsewhere to institutions; GBP 444 combined subscription in United Kingdom to institutions (print & online eds.); EUR 563 combined subscription in Europe to institutions (print & online eds.); USD 870 combined subscription elsewhere to institutions (print & online eds.) (effective 2011). adv. bk.rev. abstr. back issues avail.; reprint service avail. from PSC. **Document type:** *Journal, Academic/Scholarly.* **Description:** Contains articles pertaining to important issues in the methods of psychiatric research, the measurement of psychiatric phenomena and related biological variables.
Related titles: Microform ed.: N.S. (from PQC); Online - full text ed.: ISSN 1557-0657. GBP 386 in United Kingdom to institutions; EUR 489 in Europe to institutions; USD 756 elsewhere to institutions (effective 2011) (from IngentaConnect).
Indexed: A01, A03, A08, ASCA, B21, CA, CurCont, E-psyche, EMBASE, ExcerpMed, FamI, MEDLINE, NSA, P03, P30, P43, PsycInfo, PsycholAb, R10, Reac, SCI, SCOPUS, SSCI, T02, W07.
—BLDSC (4542.352300), GNLM, IE, Infotrieve, Ingenta. **CCC.**
Published by: John Wiley & Sons Ltd. (Subsidiary of: John Wiley & Sons, Inc.), 1-7 Oldlands Way, PO Box 808, Bognor Regis, West Sussex PO21 9FF, United Kingdom. TEL 44-1865-778315, FAX 44-1243-843232, cs-journals@wiley.com, http://eu.wiley.com/WileyCDA/. Ed. Dr. Hans Ulrich Wittchen TEL 49-351-46336983. **Subscr. to:** 1-7 Oldlands Way, PO Box 809, Bognor Regis, West Sussex PO21 9FG, United Kingdom. TEL 44-1865-778054, cs-agency@wiley.com. **Distr. addr.:** Turpin Distribution Services Ltd.

616.8 GBR ISSN 0020-7454
QP351 CODEN: IJNUB7
➤ **INTERNATIONAL JOURNAL OF NEUROSCIENCE.** Text in French. 1970. m. (in 6 vols., 4 nos./vol.). GBP 6,535, EUR 7,300, USD 9,125 combined subscription to institutions (print & online eds.); GBP 13,070, EUR 14,600, USD 18,250 combined subscription to corporations (print & online eds.) (effective 2010). adv. bk.rev. index. back issues avail.; reprint service avail. from PSC. **Document type:** *Journal, Academic/Scholarly.* **Description:** Publishes papers concerned with problems of nervous tissue, the nervous system, and behavior.
Related titles: CD-ROM ed.: ISSN 1026-7085. 1995; Microform ed.; Online - full text ed.: ISSN 1563-5279 (from IngentaConnect).
Indexed: A01, A02, A03, A08, A20, A22, ASCA, B21, BIOBASE, CA, ChemAb, ChemoAb, DentInd, E-psyche, E01, EMBASE, ESPM, ExcerpMed, FR, IABS, IPsyAb, ISR, IndMed, MEDLINE, NSA, NSCI, P03, P30, P43, PsycInfo, PsycholAb, R10, RILM, Reac, SCI, SCOPUS, T02, ToxAb, W07.
—BLDSC (4542.386000), CASDDS, GNLM, IE, Infotrieve, Ingenta, INIST. **CCC.**
Published by: Informa Healthcare (Subsidiary of: T & F Informa plc), Telephone House, 69-77 Paul St, London, EC2A 4LQ, United Kingdom. TEL 44-20-70175000, healthcare.enquiries@informa.com, http://www.tandf.co.uk/journals/. Eds. Kelly E Lyons, Rajesh Pahwa. **Subscr. in N. America to:** Taylor & Francis Inc., Customer Services Dept, 325 Chestnut St, 8th Fl, Philadelphia, PA 19106. TEL 215-625-8900, 800-354-1420, FAX 215-625-2940, customerservice@taylorandfrancis.com; **Subscr. to:** Taylor & Francis Ltd., Journals Customer Service, Sheepen Pl, Colchester, Essex CO3 3LP, United Kingdom. TEL 44-20-70175544, FAX 44-20-70175198, tf.enquiries@tfinforma.com.

616.8 USA ISSN 2150-2749
▼ **INTERNATIONAL JOURNAL OF NEUROTHERAPY.** Text in English. forthcoming 2011 (Jan.). q. **Document type:** *Journal, Academic/Scholarly.* **Description:** Features studies on neurotherapy and neuromodulatory.
Media: Online - full content.
Published by: Kaiser Peer Publishing, PO Box 734, Churchville, NY 14428. TEL 585-393-1464, davidkaiser@spiritualneuroscience.org, http://brainandcosmos.com/info.htm.

INTERNATIONAL JOURNAL OF OFFENDER THERAPY AND COMPARATIVE CRIMINOLOGY. *see* CRIMINOLOGY AND LAW ENFORCEMENT

616.89 GBR ISSN 1365-1501
RA790.A1 CODEN: IJPCFZ
➤ **INTERNATIONAL JOURNAL OF PSYCHIATRY IN CLINICAL PRACTICE.** Text in English. 1997. q. GBP 415, EUR 550, USD 685 combined subscription to institutions (print & online eds.); GBP 835, EUR 1,100, USD 1,370 combined subscription to corporations (print & online eds.) (effective 2010). adv. bk.rev. index. back issues avail.; reprint service avail. from PSC. **Document type:** *Journal, Academic/Scholarly.* **Description:** Covers new developments in International Cardiology.
Related titles: Online - full text ed.: ISSN 1471-1788 (from IngentaConnect); ◆ Spanish ed.: International Journal of Psychiatry in Clinical Practice (Spanish Edition). ISSN 1579-3737.
Indexed: A01, A03, A08, A22, AddicA, C06, C07, CA, CurCont, E-psyche, E01, EMBASE, ExcerpMed, Inpharma, P03, P30, P35, P43, PsycInfo, PsycholAb, R10, Reac, SCI, SCOPUS, T02, W07.
—CASDDS, GNLM, IE, Infotrieve, Ingenta. **CCC.**
Published by: Informa Healthcare (Subsidiary of: T & F Informa plc), Telephone House, 69-77 Paul St, London, EC2A 4LQ, United Kingdom. TEL 44-20-70175000, FAX 44-20-70176792, healthcare.enquiries@informa.com. Eds. David Baldwin, Siegfried Kasper. Adv. contact Per Sonnerfeldt. **Subscr. in N. America to:** Taylor & Francis Inc., Customer Services Dept, 325 Chestnut St, 8th Fl, Philadelphia, PA 19106. TEL 215-625-8900, 800-354-1420, FAX 215-625-8914; **Subscr. outside N. America to:** Taylor & Francis Ltd., Journals Customer Service, Sheepen Pl, Colchester, Essex CO3 3LP, United Kingdom. TEL 44-20-70175544, FAX 44-20-70175198, tf.enquiries@tfinforma.com.

616.89 ESP ISSN 1579-3737
INTERNATIONAL JOURNAL OF PSYCHIATRY IN CLINICAL PRACTICE (SPANISH EDITION). Text in Spanish. 2002. bi-m. **Document type:** *Journal, Academic/Scholarly.*
Related titles: ◆ English ed.: International Journal of Psychiatry in Clinical Practice. ISSN 1365-1501.
Published by: Spanish Publishers Associates, Edif. Vertice C Antonio Lopez, 249 1o-4o, Madrid, 28041, Spain. TEL 34-91-5002077, FAX 34-91-5002075, prodrug@drugfarma.com, http://www.drugfarma.com/espanol/03spa/index.htm.

616.89 USA ISSN 0091-2174
RC321 CODEN: IJMEDO
➤ **THE INTERNATIONAL JOURNAL OF PSYCHIATRY IN MEDICINE.** Abbreviated title: I J P M. Text in English. 1970. q. USD 158 combined subscription to individuals (print & online eds.); USD 560 combined subscription to institutions (print & online eds.) (effective 2011). bk.rev. bibl.; charts; illus.; stat. Index. back issues avail.; reprints avail. **Document type:** *Journal, Academic/Scholarly.* **Description:** Contains articles which apply the methods of psychiatry and psychology to the further understanding of disorders which are primarily psychiatric in nature.
Formerly (until 1973): Psychiatry in Medicine (0033-278X)
Related titles: Online - full text ed.: ISSN 1541-3527. USD 151 to individuals; USD 532 to institutions (effective 2011).
Indexed: A20, A22, A34, A36, AHCMS, ASCA, AbAn, C06, C07, C08, CA, CABA, CINAHL, CurCont, DIP, E-psyche, E12, EMBASE, ExcerpMed, F09, FR, FamI, GH, H13, IBR, IBZ, IndMed, Inpharma, MEA&I, MEDLINE, N02, N03, N04, P03, P10, P20, P22, P24, P25, P30, P33, P35, P48, P53, P54, PQC, PsycInfo, PsycholAb, R10, R12, RA&MP, RM&VM, Reac, S02, S03, SCI, SCOPUS, SSCI, SWR&A, T02, T05, VS, W07.
—BLDSC (4542.495000), GNLM, IE, Infotrieve, Ingenta, INIST. **CCC.**
Published by: Baywood Publishing Co., Inc., 26 Austin Ave, PO Box 337, Amityville, NY 11701. TEL 631-691-1270, 800-638-7819, FAX 631-691-1770, Baywood@baywood.com. Ed. Dana King.

➤ **INTERNATIONAL JOURNAL OF PSYCHOPATHOLOGY, PSYCHOPHARMACOLOGY, AND PSYCHOTHERAPY.** *see* PSYCHOLOGY

616.89 GBR ISSN 0020-7640
RC321
➤ **INTERNATIONAL JOURNAL OF SOCIAL PSYCHIATRY.** Abbreviated title: I J S P. Text in English. 1954. bi-m. GBP 554, USD 1,025 to institutions; GBP 565, USD 1,046 combined subscription to institutions (print & online eds.) (effective 2012). adv. bk.rev. illus.; stat. index. back issues avail.; reprint service avail. from PSC. **Document type:** *Journal, Academic/Scholarly.* **Description:** Publishes articles on psychiatric problems, strategies for survival, drug abuse, psychiatry, social psychiatry, and psychotherapy.
Related titles: Online - full text ed.: ISSN 1741-2854. GBP 509, USD 941 to institutions (effective 2012).
Indexed: A01, A02, A03, A08, A20, A22, A26, AHCMS, AMHA, ASCA, ASSIA, B04, BAS, BRD, C06, C07, C08, CA, CINAHL, CurCont, E-psyche, E01, E08, EMBASE, ExcerpMed, F09, FR, FamI, G08, H04, H09, H12, H13, I05, I14, IBSS, INI, IPsyAb, IndMed, MEA&I, MEDLINE, MLA-IB, P02, P03, P10, P12, P20, P25, P27, P30, P34, P48, P53, P54, PCI, PQC, PsycInfo, PsycholAb, R10, Reac, S02, S03, S05, S09, SCOPUS, SOPODA, SSA, SSAI, SSAb, SSCI, SSI, SociolAb, T02, W01, W02, W03, W05, W07.
—BLDSC (4542.560000), GNLM, IE, Infotrieve, Ingenta, INIST. **CCC.**
Published by: Sage Publications Ltd. (Subsidiary of: Sage Publications, Inc.), 1 Oliver's Yard, 55 City Rd, London, EC1Y 1SP, United Kingdom. TEL 44-20-73248500, FAX 44-20-73248600, info@sagepub.co.uk, http://www.uk.sagepub.com/home.nav. Ed. Dinesh Bhugra. **Subscr. in the Americas to:** Sage Publications, Inc., 2455 Teller Rd, Thousand Oaks, CA 91320. TEL 805-499-9774, FAX 805-499-0871, journals@sagepub.com.

616.834 GBR ISSN 1352-8963
RC377
➤ **THE INTERNATIONAL M S JOURNAL.** (Multiple Sclerosis) Text in English. 1994. 3/yr. GBP 95 in Europe; GBP 110 elsewhere (effective 2009). bk.rev. back issues avail. **Document type:** *Journal, Academic/Scholarly.* **Description:** Contains review articles dealing with the biochemical, pathophysiological and clinical aspects of multiple sclerosis and related conditions.
Related titles: Online - full text ed.: ISSN 1469-3410. 1999.
Indexed: A26, B02, B15, B17, B18, E08, EMBASE, ExcerpMed, G04, I05, MEDLINE, P30, R10, Reac, SCOPUS.
—BLDSC (4544.364500), IE, Ingenta. **CCC.**
Published by: (Schering AG DEU), Cambridge Medical Publications, Wicker House, High St, Worthing, W Sussex BN11 1DJ, United Kingdom. TEL 44-1903-288000, FAX 44-1903-288292, cmp@hbase.com. Ed. Douglas Goodin.

616.8 GBR ISSN 1355-6177
QP360 CODEN: JINSF9

➤ **INTERNATIONAL NEUROPSYCHOLOGICAL SOCIETY. JOURNAL.** Abbreviated title: J I N S. Text in English. 1995. bi-m. GBP 399, USD 718 to institutions; GBP 441, USD 799 combined subscription to institutions (print & online eds.) (effective 2012). adv. bk.rev. Supplement avail.; back issues avail.; reprint service avail. from PSC. **Document type:** *Journal, Academic/Scholarly.* **Description:** Publishes primary research articles reflecting all areas of neuropsychology, including development of cognitive processes, brain-behaviour relationships, adult and child neuropsychology, developmental neuropsychology and disorders of speech and language.
Related titles: Online - full text ed.: ISSN 1469-7661. 1998. GBP 342, USD 615 to institutions (effective 2012).
Indexed: A01, A03, A08, A22, B21, CA, CurCont, E-psyche, E01, EMBASE, ExcerpMed, ISR, IndMed, Inpharma, JW-P, L&LBA, MEDLINE, NSA, NSCI, P03, P20, P22, P25, P30, P35, P48, P54, PQC, PsycInfo, PsycholAb, R10, Reac, SCI, SCOPUS, SOPODA, T02, W07.
—BLDSC (4802.325000), GNLM, IE, Infotrieve, Ingenta. **CCC.**
Published by: (International Neuropsychological Society USA), Cambridge University Press, The Edinburgh Bldg, Shaftesbury Rd, Cambridge, CB2 8RU, United Kingdom. TEL 44-1223-312393, FAX 44-1223-315052, journals@cambridge.org, http://www.cambridge.org/uk. Ed. Kathleen Y Haaland. R&P Linda Nicol TEL 44-1223-325702. Adv. contact Rebecca Roberts TEL 44-1223-325083. **Subscr. to:** Cambridge University Press, 32 Ave of the Americas, New York, NY 10013. TEL 212-337-5000, FAX 212-691-3239, journals_subscriptions@cup.org.

618.9289 USA ISSN 1874-5911

INTERNATIONAL PERSPECTIVES ON CHILD AND ADOLESCENT MENTAL HEALTH. Text in English. 2000. irreg., latest vol.2, 2002. price varies. back issues avail. **Document type:** *Monographic series, Academic/Scholarly.* **Description:** Designed to provide a forum for mental health and educational experts from various disciplines and countries.
Indexed: SCOPUS.
—**CCC.**
Published by: Elsevier Inc. (Subsidiary of: Elsevier Science & Technology), 1600 John F Kennedy Blvd, Philadelphia, PA 19103. TEL 215-239-3900, FAX 215-238-7883, JournalCustomerService-usa@elsevier.com. Ed. N Singh.

616.8 GBR ISSN 1749-3676

➤ **INTERNATIONAL PSYCHIATRY.** Abbreviated title: I P. Running title: Board of International Affairs of the Royal College of Psychiatrists. Bulletin. Text in English. 2004. q. GBP 30 to institutions; USD 54 in United States to institutions (effective 2012). back issues avail. **Document type:** *Journal, Academic/Scholarly.* **Description:** Provides an overview of current policy and practice in psychiatry in different countries.
Related titles: Online - full text ed.: ISSN 1749-3684. 2003.
Indexed: ASSIA, P30.
—BLDSC (4545.280000). **CCC.**
Published by: (Board of International Affairs), Royal College of Psychiatrists, 17 Belgrave Sq, London, SW1X 8PG, United Kingdom. TEL 44-20-72352351, FAX 44-20-72451231, rcpsych@rcpsych.ac.uk. Ed. Hamid Ghodse. Circ: 13,200. **Subscr. in N. America to:** Maney Publishing, 875 Massachusetts Ave, 7th Fl, Cambridge, MA 02139. TEL 866-297-5154, FAX 617-354-6875, maney@maneyusa.com; **Subscr. to:** Maney Publishing, Ste 1C, Joseph's Well, Hanover Walk, Leeds, W Yorks LS3 1AB, United Kingdom. TEL 44-113-2432800, FAX 44-113-3868178, maney@maney.co.uk, http://www.maney.co.uk.

618.97 GBR ISSN 1041-6102
CODEN: INPSE8

➤ **INTERNATIONAL PSYCHOGERIATRICS.** Text in English. 1989. 8/yr. GBP 542, USD 1,002 to institutions; GBP 585, USD 1,082 combined subscription to institutions (print & online eds.) (effective 2012). adv. bk.rev.; software rev.; video rev. abstr. 120 p./no.; Supplement avail.; back issues avail.; reprint service avail. from PSC. **Document type:** *Journal, Academic/Scholarly.* **Description:** Serves as a multidisciplinary and interdisciplinary forum for advances in psychogeriatric practice, research, service development and education worldwide.
Related titles: Online - full text ed.: ISSN 1741-203X. GBP 458, USD 847 to institutions (effective 2012).
Indexed: A20, A22, ASG, AgeL, B21, C06, C07, C08, CA, CINAHL, CurCont, E-psyche, E01, EMBASE, ExcerpMed, FR, FamI, H13, INI, IPsyAb, IndMed, Inpharma, MEDLINE, NSA, P03, P10, P12, P20, P22, P24, P25, P27, P30, P35, P48, P53, P54, PQC, PsycInfo, PsycholAb, R10, Reac, S02, S03, SCI, SCOPUS, SOPODA, SSCI, SWR&A, SociolAb, T02, W07.
—BLDSC (4545.345000), GNLM, IE, Infotrieve, Ingenta, INIST. **CCC.**
Published by: (International Psychogeriatric Association USA), Cambridge University Press, The Edinburgh Bldg, Shaftesbury Rd, Cambridge, CB2 8RU, United Kingdom. TEL 44-1223-312393, FAX 44-1223-315052, journals@cambridge.org, http://www.cambridge.org/uk. Ed. David Ames. R&P Linda Nicol TEL 44-1223-325702. Adv. contact Rebecca Roberts TEL 44-1223-325083. **Subscr. to:** Cambridge University Press, 32 Ave of the Americas, New York, NY 10013. TEL 212-337-5000, FAX 212-691-3239, journals_subscriptions@cup.org.

616.8 USA ISSN 0074-7742
RC341 CODEN: IRNEAE

➤ **INTERNATIONAL REVIEW OF NEUROBIOLOGY.** Text in English. 1959. irreg., latest vol.89, 2009. USD 192 per vol. (effective 2010). adv. index. back issues avail.; reprints avail. **Document type:** *Monographic series, Academic/Scholarly.* **Description:** Summarizes new advances schizophrenia research that focus on the field of neural and synaptic plasticity.
Related titles: Online - full text ed.; Supplement(s): International Review of Neurobiology. Supplement. ISSN 0091-5432. 1972.
Indexed: A22, ASCA, B21, BIOSIS Prev, CIN, CTA, ChemAb, ChemTitl, ChemoAb, DentInd, E-psyche, EMBASE, ExcerpMed, IBR, IBZ, ISR, IndMed, MEDLINE, MycolAb, NSA, P30, R10, Reac, SCI, SCOPUS, W07.
—BLDSC (4547.400000), CASDDS, GNLM, IE, Infotrieve, Ingenta, INIST, Linda Hall. **CCC.**
Published by: Academic Press (Subsidiary of: Elsevier Science & Technology), 3251 Riverport Ln, Maryland Heights, MO 63043. TEL 314-447-8010, FAX 314-447-8030, JournalCustomerService-usa@elsevier.com, http://www.elsevierdirect.com/imprint.jsp?iid=5. Adv. contact Tino DeCarlo TEL 212-633-3815.

616.8 GBR ISSN 0954-0261
CODEN: IRPSE2

➤ **INTERNATIONAL REVIEW OF PSYCHIATRY.** Text in English. 1989. bi-m. GBP 1,185, EUR 1,755, USD 2,195 combined subscription to institutions (print & online eds.); GBP 2,365, EUR 3,515, USD 4,395 combined subscription to corporations (print & online eds.) (effective 2010). adv. bk.rev. back issues avail.; reprint service avail. from PSC. **Document type:** *Journal, Academic/Scholarly.* **Description:** Covers undergraduate-level reviews of topics in psychiatry.
Related titles: Microfiche ed.; Online - full text ed.: ISSN 1369-1627 (from IngentaConnect).
Indexed: A01, A02, A03, A08, A20, A22, ASCA, B21, BIOSIS Prev, C11, CA, CPE, CurCont, E-psyche, E01, EMBASE, ExcerpMed, FamI, H04, H13, IPsyAb, MEDLINE, MycolAb, NSA, P02, P03, P10, P12, P20, P25, P30, P43, P48, P53, P54, PQC, PsycInfo, PsycholAb, R10, Reac, S02, S03, SCOPUS, SOPODA, SSCI, SociolAb, T02, W07.
—GNLM, IE, Infotrieve, Ingenta. **CCC.**
Published by: Informa Healthcare (Subsidiary of: T & F Informa plc), Telephone House, 69-77 Paul St, London, EC2A 4LQ, United Kingdom. TEL 44-20-70175000, FAX 44-20-70176792, healthcare.enquiries@informa.com. Eds. Constantine G Lyketsos, Dinesh Bhugra. Adv. contact Per Sonnerfeldt. **Subscr. in N America to:** Taylor & Francis Inc., Customer Services Dept, 325 Chestnut St, 8th Fl, Philadelphia, PA 19106. TEL 215-625-8900, 800-354-1420, FAX 215-625-8914, customerservice@taylorandfrancis.com; **Subscr. outside N. America to:** Taylor & Francis Ltd., Journals Customer Service, Sheepen Pl, Colchester, Essex CO3 3LP, United Kingdom. TEL 44-20-70175544, FAX 44-20-70175198, tf.enquiries@tfinforma.com.

371.928 USA ISSN 0074-7750
RC570

➤ **INTERNATIONAL REVIEW OF RESEARCH IN MENTAL RETARDATION.** Text in English. 1966. irreg., latest vol.38, 2009. USD 192 per vol. (effective 2010). adv. back issues avail.; reprints avail. **Document type:** *Monographic series, Academic/Scholarly.*
Related titles: Online - full text ed.
Indexed: A22, ASCA, BIOSIS Prev, CA, E-psyche, E03, ERI, MycolAb, P30, SCOPUS, SSCI, T02, W07.
—BLDSC (4547.600000), Ingenta, INIST. **CCC.**
Published by: Academic Press (Subsidiary of: Elsevier Science & Technology), 3251 Riverport Ln, Maryland Heights, MO 63043. TEL 314-447-8010, FAX 314-447-8030, JournalCustomerService-usa@elsevier.com, http://www.elsevierdirect.com/imprint.jsp?iid=5.

616.8 618.92 GBR ISSN 0899-3653

➤ **INTERNATIONAL REVIEWS OF CHILD NEUROLOGY SERIES.** Text in English. 1982. irreg., latest 2009. price varies. back issues avail.; reprints avail. **Document type:** *Monographic series, Academic/Scholarly.* **Description:** Aims to improve the quality of care provided for children with neurological disorders by child neurologists and professionals in allied disciplines.
Indexed: E-psyche.
Published by: (International Child Neurology Association USA), Mac Keith Press, 6 Market Rd, London, N7 9PW, United Kingdom. TEL 44-20-76197199, FAX 44-20-76197207, allat@mackeith.co.uk. **Dist. by:** Cambridge University Press.

616.8 USA ISSN 1531-295X
RC346

➤ **THE INTERNET JOURNAL OF NEUROLOGY.** Text in English. 2001. s-a. free (effective 2011). adv. bk.rev. back issues avail. **Document type:** *Journal, Academic/Scholarly.* **Description:** Provides information from the field of neurology; contains original articles, reviews, case reports, streaming slide shows, streaming videos, letters to the editor, press releases and meeting information.
Media: Online - full text.
Indexed: A01, A02, A03, A08, A26, C06, C07, CA, EMBASE, G08, H11, H12, I05, SCOPUS, T02.
Published by: Internet Scientific Publications, Llc., 23 Rippling Creek Dr, Sugar Land, TX 77479. TEL 832-443-1193, FAX 281-240-1533, wenker@ispub.com. Ed. Dr. H. Foyaca-Sibat.

616.8 USA ISSN 1531-300X
RD52.N48

➤ **THE INTERNET JOURNAL OF NEUROMONITORING.** Text in English. 2000. s-a. free (effective 2011). adv. **Document type:** *Journal, Academic/Scholarly.*
Media: Online - full text.
Indexed: A01, A02, A03, A08, A26, C06, C07, CA, G08, H11, H12, I05, T02.
Published by: Internet Scientific Publications, Llc., 23 Rippling Creek Dr, Sugar Land, TX 77479. TEL 832-443-1193, FAX 281-240-1533, wenker@ispub.com. Ed. Gerhard Litscher.

➤ **THE INTERNET JOURNAL OF NEUROSURGERY.** *see* MEDICAL SCIENCES—Surgery

616.8 USA ISSN 2155-7349

▼ ➤ **THE INTERNET JOURNAL OF PSYCHIATRY.** Text in English. 2010 (Sept.). s-a. free (effective 2011). **Document type:** *Journal, Trade.*
Media: Online - full text.
Indexed: A01.
Published by: Internet Scientific Publications, Llc., 23 Rippling Creek Dr, Sugar Land, TX 77479. TEL 832-443-1193, FAX 281-240-1533, wenker@ispub.com. Ed. Dr. Ahmed Rady.

615.851 ESP ISSN 1575-6483

INTERSUBJETIVO; revista de psicoterapia psicoanalitica y salud. Text in Spanish. 1999. s-a. back issues avail. **Document type:** *Journal, Academic/Scholarly.*
Indexed: P03, PsycInfo, PsycholAb.
Published by: Quipu. Instituto de Formacion en Psicoterapia Piscoanalitica y Salud Mental, C. Principe de Vergara, 35 Bajo Derecha, Madrid, 28001, Spain. TEL 34-91-5776039, FAX 34-91-5779734.

616.8 CHE ISSN 1664-9737

▼ **INTERVENTIONAL NEUROLOGY.** Text in English. forthcoming 2012. 4/yr. CHF 1,424, EUR 1,138, USD 1,397 to institutions (effective 2012). **Document type:** *Journal, Academic/Scholarly.*
Related titles: Online - full text ed.: ISSN 1664-5545. forthcoming 2012.
Published by: S. Karger AG, Allschwilerstr 10, Basel, 4055, Switzerland. TEL 41-61-3061111, FAX 41-61-3061234, karger@karger.ch, http://www.karger.ch. Ed. X Liu.

615.851 ESP ISSN 0214-7424

INTUS; revista de las Catedras de Psicologia Medica y Psiquiatria e Historia de la Medicina. Text in Spanish. 1989. s-a. **Document type:** *Journal, Academic/Scholarly.*
Published by: (Universidad de Cordoba, Facultad de Medicina), Universidad de Cordoba, Servicio de Publicaciones, Campus Universitario de Rabanales, Ctra Nacional IV, Km 396, Cordoba, 14071, Spain. TEL 34-957-218126, FAX 34-957-218196, publicaciones@uco.es.

616.8 IRN ISSN 1735-4668

IRANIAN JOURNAL OF CHILD NEUROLOGY. Text in English. 2006. q. **Document type:** *Journal, Academic/Scholarly.*
Related titles: Online - full text ed.: ISSN 2008-0700. free (effective 2011).
Indexed: A36, B21, C06, C07, CA, CABA, D01, E12, EMBASE, GH, N02, N03, NSA, R12, SCOPUS, T02, T05.
Published by: (Shahid Beheshti University of Medical Sciences), Iranian Child Neurology Society, 3d Fl, Child Neurology Office, Mofid Children Hospital, Tehran, 15468-15514, Iran. TEL 98-21-22909559, FAX 98-21-22909559.

616.8 IRN ISSN 1735-4587

➤ **IRANIAN JOURNAL OF PSYCHIATRY.** Text in English. 2006. q. free. charts. Index. back issues avail. **Document type:** *Journal, Academic/Scholarly.* **Description:** Publishes articles realted to psychopathology, biological psychiatry, cross-cultural psychiatry, psychopharmacology, social & community psychiatry, epidemiology, child & adolescent psychiatry, psychotherapy, neuropsychiatry, psychology, spiritual therapy, as well as animal studies in psychiatry and psychology.
Related titles: Online - full text ed.: ISSN 2008-2215.
Indexed: P20, P54.
Published by: (Iranian Psychiatric Association), Tehran University of Medical Sciences, Psychiatry and Psychology Research Center, Roozbeh Hospital, South Kargar Ave., Tehran, 13337, Iran. TEL 98-21-55413540, FAX 98-21-55413540.

616.8 IRN ISSN 1735-8639

IRANIAN JOURNAL OF PSYCHIATRY AND BEHAVIORAL SCIENCES. Text in English. 2006. s-a. **Document type:** *Journal, Academic/Scholarly.*
Related titles: Online - full text ed.: ISSN 1735-9287.
Indexed: SCOPUS.
Published by: Mazandaran University of Medical Sciences, Moalem Sq, Sari, Iran. TEL 98-151-3257230, FAX 98-151-3261244, http://www.mazums.ac.ir. Ed. Dr. Gholam Reza Mir-Sepassi.

616.89 IRL ISSN 0790-9667
CODEN: IPMEEX

➤ **IRISH JOURNAL OF PSYCHOLOGICAL MEDICINE.** Text in English. 1982. q. EUR 117 (effective 2006). bk.rev. charts. reprints avail. **Document type:** *Journal, Academic/Scholarly.* **Description:** Publishes original scientific contributions in psychiatry, psychological medicine, and related basic sciences (neurosciences, biological, psychological and social sciences).
Former titles: Irish Journal of Psychotherapy and Psychosomatic Medicine (0790-0848); Irish Journal of Psychotherapy
Related titles: Microform ed.: (from PQC); Online - full text ed.
Indexed: A20, A22, A36, ASCA, AddicA, B25, BIOSIS Prev, C06, C07, C08, CABA, CINAHL, E-psyche, EMBASE, ExcerpMed, FamI, GH, MycolAb, N02, N03, P03, P30, PsycInfo, PsycholAb, R10, RILM, Reac, SCOPUS, SOPODA, SWR&A, SociolAb.
—BLDSC (4572.180000), GNLM, IE, Infotrieve, Ingenta, INIST. **CCC.**
Published by: (Irish Institute of Psychological Medicine), MedMedia Ltd., 25 Adelaide St, Dun Laoghaire, Co. Dublin, Ireland. TEL 353-1-2803967, FAX 353-1-2807076. Ed. Brian Lawlor. Adv. contact Leon Ellison. Circ: 3,000. **Dist. by:** Turpin Distribution Services Ltd., Pegasus Dr, Stratton Business Park, Biggleswade, Bedfordshire SG18 8QB, United Kingdom. TEL 44-1767-604800, FAX 44-1767-601640, custserv@turpin-distribution.com, http://www.turpin-distribution.com/.

616.89 IRL ISSN 1649-4261

IRISH PSYCHIATRIST. Text in English. 2000. bi-m. EUR 66 (effective 2005). adv. **Document type:** *Magazine, Trade.* **Description:** Presents articles by leading Irish authorities highlighting specialities in many specific clinical areas of psychiatry.
Published by: Eireann Healthcare Publications, 25-26 Windsor Pl., Dublin, 2, Ireland. TEL 353-1-4753300, FAX 353-1-4753311, mhenderson@eireannpublications.ie, http://www.eireannpublications.ie. Ed. Maura Henderson. Adv. contact Cliodna O'Hanlon. B&W page EUR 1,685; trim 204 x 288. Circ: 3,322 (paid and controlled).

616.8 ISR ISSN 0333-7308
RC321 CODEN: IPRDAH

➤ **ISRAEL JOURNAL OF PSYCHIATRY AND RELATED SCIENCES.** Text in English. 1963. q. USD 55 in US & Canada to individuals; USD 75 elsewhere to individuals; USD 75 to institutions; USD 20 per issue (effective 2008). adv. bk.rev. charts; illus. index. back issues avail.; reprints avail. **Document type:** *Journal, Academic/Scholarly.* **Description:** Articles dealing with the bio-psycho-social aspects of mobility, relocation, acculturation, ethnicity, stress situations in war and peace, victimology and mental health in developing countries.
Supersedes (in 1979): Israel Annals of Psychiatry and Related Disciplines (0021-1958)
Related titles: Online - full text ed.
Indexed: A20, A22, AMED, ASCA, C06, C07, CDA, ChemAb, CurCont, E-psyche, EMBASE, ExcerpMed, F09, FamI, IndMed, MEDLINE, MLA-IB, P03, P20, P22, P25, P30, P48, P54, PQC, PhilInd, PsycholAb, R10, Reac, SCI, SCOPUS, SSCI, W07.
—BLDSC (4583.813000), GNLM, IE, Infotrieve, Ingenta, INIST.
Published by: (Israel Psychiatric Association USA), Gefen Publishing House Ltd., P O Box 36004, Jerusalem, 91360, Israel. TEL 972-2-5380247, FAX 972-2-5388423, info@gefenpublishing.com, gefenbooks@compuserve.com. Ed. Dr. David Greenberg. Pub. Ilan Greenfield. Circ: 950.

616.8 USA ISSN 2150-7864
ISSUES IN CLINICAL NEUROSCIENCES. Text in English. 2007. 3/yr. free to qualified personnel (effective 2009). back issues avail. **Document type:** *Journal, Trade.* **Description:** Provides information concerning all aspects of neuroscience and neurosurgical science.
Related titles: Online - full text ed.: ISSN 2150-7872.
Published by: Roosevelt Hospital, Department of Neurosurgery, 110 E 59th St, 10th Fl, New York, NY 10019. TEL 212-523-6720. Ed. Charles J Ippolito TEL 212-523-6097.

ISSUES IN MENTAL HEALTH NURSING. *see* MEDICAL SCIENCES—Nurses And Nursing

ISSUES IN PSYCHOANALYTIC PSYCHOLOGY. *see* PSYCHOLOGY

616.891 ITA ISSN 1128-3963
ISTITUTO DI PSICOTERAPIA DEL BAMBINO E DELL'ADOLESCENTE. QUADERNO. Text in Italian. 1991. s-a. **Document type:** *Journal, Academic/Scholarly.*
Published by: Istituto di Psicoterapia del Bambino e dell'Adolescente, Via Fratelli Bronzetti 28, Milan, 28129, Italy. TEL 39-02-7382045, FAX 39-02-70100112, http://www.psiba.it.

J C A H O ADVISOR FOR BEHAVIORAL HEALTH CARE PROVIDERS. (Joint Commission on Accreditation of Healthcare Organizations) *see* HEALTH FACILITIES AND ADMINISTRATION

616.8 USA ISSN 1548-7040
J C P C N S CAPSULES. (Journal Clinical Psychiatry Central Nervous System) Text in English. 1999 (Jul.). irreg., latest vol.5, no.1, 2004. back issues avail. **Document type:** *Monographic series, Academic/Scholarly.*
Related titles: Online - full text ed.: free (effective 2010).
Published by: Physicians Postgraduate Press, Inc., PO Box 752870, Memphis, TN 38175. TEL 901-751-3800, FAX 901-751-3444, circulation@psychiatrist.com.

617.4 USA ISSN 1558-8726
J H N JOURNAL. (Jefferson Hospital for Neuroscience) Text in English. 2005. 3/yr. **Document type:** *Journal, Academic/Scholarly.*
Published by: Thomas Jefferson University, Department of Neurological Surgery, 1020 Walnut St, Philadelphia, PA 19107. TEL 215-955-6000, jcgs-info@jefferson.edu, http://www.jefferson.edu/neurosurgery/.

JAMES ARTHUR LECTURE ON THE EVOLUTION OF THE HUMAN BRAIN. *see* BIOLOGY—Genetics

616.89 JPN ISSN 0289-0968
JAPANESE JOURNAL OF CHILD & ADOLESCENT PSYCHIATRY/JIDO SEINEN SEISHIN IGAKU TO SONO KINSETSU RYOIKI. Text in Japanese; Summaries in English. 1960. 5/yr. adv. bk.rev. abstr.; charts. index. back issues avail. **Document type:** *Academic/Scholarly.* **Description:** Addresses problems, issues, treatments, trends, and syndromes unique to child and adolescent psychology.
Formerly: Japanese Journal of Child Psychiatry (0021-4957)
Indexed: A22, CDA, E-psyche, P03, PsycholAb.
—BLDSC (4651.358000), GNLM, IE, Ingenta.
Published by: Japanese Society for Child and Adolescent Psychiatry, c/o Department of Neuropsychiatry, School of Medicine, Kyoto University, Sakyo-ku, Kyoto-shi, 606, Japan. Ed. Dr. Sadanobu Ushizima. R&P Dr. Yoshiki Ishikawa TEL 81-75-751-3388. Adv. contact Dr. Yoshiki Ishisaka. Circ: 2,000. **Subscr. to:** Maruzen Co., Ltd., Import & Export Dept, PO Box 5050, Tokyo International, Tokyo 100-3191, Japan.

616.8 AUT
JATROS NEUROLOGIE - PSYCHIATRIE. Text in German. 1999. 8/yr. EUR 37 (effective 2007). adv. **Document type:** *Journal, Academic/Scholarly.*
Related titles: Online - full text ed.: ISSN 1991-9158.
Published by: Universimed Verlags- und Service GmbH, Markgraf-Ruediger-Str 8, Vienna, 1150, Austria. TEL 43-1-87679560, FAX 43-1-876795620, office@universimed.com, http://www.universimed.com. Ed. Friederike Hoerandl. Adv. contact Antje Fresdorf. Circ: 3,100 (paid).

616.8 USA ISSN 1935-0783
RC321
JEFFERSON JOURNAL OF PSYCHIATRY (ONLINE). Text in English. 1983. a. **Document type:** *Journal, Academic/Scholarly.* **Description:** Contains clinical research and clinical writing by residents in psychiatry everywhere.
Formerly (until 2006): Jefferson Journal of Psychiatry (Print)
Media: Online - full text.
Published by: Thomas Jefferson University Hospital, Department of Psychiatry and Human Behavior, c/o Daniel Lieberman, 833 Chestnut St, Ste 210, Philadelphia, PA 19107. TEL 215-955-6912, http://www.tju.edu/psych/. Ed. Muhammad A Abbas TEL 215-955-6104.

JOINT COMMISSION ADVISOR FOR BEHAVIORAL HEALTH. *see* LAW—Civil Law

616.89 BRA ISSN 0047-2085
RC321 CODEN: JBPSAX
JORNAL BRASILEIRO DE PSIQUIATRIA/BRAZILIAN JOURNAL OF PSYCHIATRY. Text in Portuguese; Summaries in English, Portuguese. 1942. q. adv. bk.rev. bibl.; charts; illus.; stat. index, cum.index. back issues avail. **Document type:** *Journal, Academic/Scholarly.* **Description:** Studies in clinical psychiatry.
Formerly (until 1947): Universidade do Brasil. Instituto de Psiquiatria. Anais (0100-5340)
Related titles: Microform ed.: (from PQC); Online - full text ed.: free (effective 2011).
Indexed: A22, C01, ChemAb, E-psyche, EMBASE, ExcerpMed, IBR, IBZ, IndMed, MLA-IB, P03, P30, PsycInfo, PsycholAb, R10, Reac, S02, S03, SCOPUS.
—GNLM, IE, Infotrieve, Ingenta, INIST.
Published by: (Universidade Federal do Rio de Janeiro, Instituto de Psiquiatria), Editora Cientifica Nacional Ltda. (E C N), Rua da Gloria 366, 3o Andar, Gloria, Rio de Janeiro, RJ 20241-180, Brazil. ecn@rj.sol.com.br. Circ: 5,000.

616.89 FRA ISSN 1155-1704
JOURNAL DE THERAPIE COMPORTAMENTALE ET COGNITIVE. Text in English, French. 1991. q. EUR 223 in Europe to institutions; EUR 161.61 in France to institutions; JPY 36,700 in Japan to institutions; USD 296 elsewhere to institutions (effective 2012). adv. bk.rev. **Document type:** *Journal, Academic/Scholarly.* **Description:** Contains a clinical section with a didactical aspect, as well as international reports on advances in behavioural science and cognition.
Related titles: Online - full text ed.: (from ScienceDirect).
Indexed: E-psyche, FR, P03, PsycInfo, PsycholAb, SCOPUS.
—INIST. **CCC.**
Published by: (Association Francaise de Therapie Comportementale et Cognitive), Elsevier Masson (Subsidiary of: Elsevier Health Sciences), 62 Rue Camille Desmoulins, Issy les Moulineaux, Cedex 92442, France. TEL 33-1-71165500, infos@elsevier-masson.fr. Ed. Patrick Legeron. Circ: 1,500.

616.8 USA ISSN 2151-3244
▼ ➤ **JOURNAL FOR THE ADVANCEMENT OF BRAIN ANALYSIS.** Text in English. forthcoming 2011. q. **Document type:** *Journal, Academic/Scholarly.* **Description:** Features research on psychological electroencephalography (EEG) and clinical neuroscience.
Media: Online - full text.
Published by: (Society for the Advancement of Brain Analysis), Kaiser Peer Publishing, PO Box 734, Churchville, NY 14428. TEL 585-393-1464, davidkaiser@spiritualneuroscience.org, http://brainandcosmos.com/info.htm.

616.8 FRA ISSN 1260-5999
JOURNAL FRANCAIS DE PSYCHIATRIE; clinique, scientifique & psychanalitique. Text in French. 1995. q. EUR 6 domestic to individuals; EUR 70 domestic to institutions; EUR 75 foreign (effective 2011). back issues avail. **Document type:** *Journal, Academic/Scholarly.* **Description:** Contains articles on psychiatry.
Related titles: Online - full text ed.: ISSN 1776-2855. 2005; Supplement(s): Les Dossiers du J F P. ISSN 1763-2234. 2003.
Published by: Editions Eres, 33 Av. Marcel Dassault, Toulouse, 31500, France. TEL 33-5-61751576, FAX 33-5-61735289, eres@edition-eres.com, http://www.edition-eres.com. Eds. Charles Melman, Marcel Czermak. Circ: 1,800.

616.8 AUT ISSN 1608-1587
RC346
➤ **JOURNAL FUER NEUROLOGIE, NEUROCHIRURGIE UND PSYCHIATRIE;** Zeitschrift fuer Erkrankungen des Nervensystems. Text in German. 2000. q. EUR 36; EUR 10 newsstand/cover (effective 2005). adv. bk.rev. abstr.; bibl. 32 p./no. 3 cols./p.; back issues avail. **Document type:** *Journal, Academic/Scholarly.* **Description:** Contains research on all aspects of neurology, neurosurgery and psychiatry.
Related titles: Online - full text ed.: ISSN 1680-9440. 2001. free (effective 2011).
Indexed: BIOBASE, EMBASE, ExcerpMed, IABS, R10, Reac, SCOPUS.
—BLDSC (5021.577500), IE, Ingenta. **CCC.**
Published by: Krause & Pachernegg GmbH, Mozartgasse 10, Gablitz, 3003, Austria. TEL 43-2231-612580, FAX 43-2231-6125810, k_u_p@eunet.at, http://www.kup.at/verlag.htm. Ed. B Mamoli. Circ: 1,800 (paid).

➤ **JOURNAL FUER PHILOSOPHIE UND PSYCHIATRIE.** *see* PHILOSOPHY

616.89 USA ISSN 1877-5365
▼ **JOURNAL OF A D H D & RELATED DISORDERS.** (Attention Deficit Hyperactivity Disorder) Text in English. 2009. q. USD 78 domestic; USD 114 foreign (effective 2011). **Document type:** *Journal, Academic/Scholarly.* **Description:** Provides a forum for the exchange of information on best practices, effective treatment strategies to help patients achieve optimal outcomes, patient education, and treatment considerations for different patient populations.
Related titles: Online - full text ed.: ISSN 1877-5373.
Published by: (American Professional Society of A D H D and Related Disorders), Elsevier Inc. (Subsidiary of: Elsevier Science & Technology), 360 Park Ave S, New York, NY 10010. TEL 888-437-4636, JournalCustomerService-usa@elsevier.com, http://www.elsevier.com. Eds. Joseph Biederman, Stephen V Faraone.

JOURNAL OF ABNORMAL CHILD PSYCHOLOGY. *see* PSYCHOLOGY

616.8 NLD ISSN 0165-0327
RC537 CODEN: JADID7
➤ **JOURNAL OF AFFECTIVE DISORDERS.** Text in Dutch. 1979. 24/yr. EUR 3,893 in Europe to institutions; JPY 517,200 in Japan to institutions; USD 4,353 elsewhere to institutions (effective 2012). illus. back issues avail.; reprints avail. **Document type:** *Journal, Academic/Scholarly.* **Description:** Publishes papers concerned with affective disorders in the widest sense: depression, mania, anxiety and panic.
Related titles: Microform ed.: (from PQC); Online - full text ed.: ISSN 1573-2517 (from IngentaConnect, ScienceDirect).
Indexed: A01, A03, A08, A20, A22, A26, A34, A36, AMHA, ASCA, ASSIA, AddicA, AgeL, B25, BIOBASE, BIOSIS Prev, C06, C07, C25, CA, CABA, ChemAb, Chicano, CurCont, D01, E-psyche, E12, EMBASE, ExcerpMed, F08, F09, F11, F12, FR, Faml, GH, I05, IABS, IBR, IBZ, IPsyAb, ISR, IndMed, Inpharma, JW-P, LT, MEDLINE, MycolAb, N02, N03, N04, P03, P30, P35, PsycInfo, PsycholAb, R10, R12, R13, RA&MP, RRTA, Reac, S02, S03, SCI, SCOPUS, SSCI, T02, T05, W07.
—BLDSC (4919.986000), CASDDS, GNLM, IE, Infotrieve, Ingenta, INIST. **CCC.**
Published by: Elsevier BV (Subsidiary of: Elsevier Science & Technology), Radarweg 29, PO Box 211, Amsterdam, 1000 AE, Netherlands. TEL 31-20-4853911, FAX 31-20-4852457, JournalsCustomerServiceEMEA@elsevier.com, http://www.elsevier.nl. Eds. Dr. C Katona, Dr. H S Akiskal.

616.8 NLD ISSN 1387-2877
RC523 CODEN: JADIF9
➤ **JOURNAL OF ALZHEIMER'S DISEASE.** Abbreviated title: J A D. Text in English. 1999. 20/yr. USD 3,598 combined subscription in North America (print & online eds.); EUR 2,560 combined subscription elsewhere (print & online eds.) (effective 2012); incl. subscr. to Journal of Parkinson's Disease. **Document type:** *Journal, Academic/Scholarly.* **Description:** Focuses on providing timely information for the growing number of individuals and institutions active in research on and the treatment of Alzheimer's disease.
Related titles: Online - full text ed.: ISSN 1875-8908 (from IngentaConnect).
Indexed: A01, A03, A08, A22, A35, A36, AgBio, AgrForAb, B21, B25, BIOSIS Prev, C06, C07, C30, CA, CABA, CurCont, D01, E-psyche, E01, E12, EMBASE, ESPM, ExcerpMed, F08, F11, F12, GH, LT, MEDLINE, MycolAb, N02, N03, N05, NSA, NSCI, P03, P30, P33, PsycInfo, R10, RA&MP, RM&VM, Reac, S13, S16, SCI, SCOPUS, T02, T05, ToxAb, VS, W07.
—BLDSC (4927.204000), IE, Infotrieve, Ingenta. **CCC.**
Published by: I O S Press, Nieuwe Hemweg 6B, Amsterdam, 1013 BG, Netherlands. TEL 31-20-6883355, FAX 31-20-6870019, info@iospress.nl, http://www.iospress.nl. Ed. Dr. George Perry. Circ: 500. **Subscr. to:** I O S Press, Inc, 4502 Rachael Manor Dr, Fairfax, VA 22032-3631. iosbooks@iospress.com; Globe Publication Pvt. Ltd., C-62 Inderpuri, New Delhi 100 012, India. TEL 91-11-579-3211, 91-11-579-3212, FAX 91-11-579-8876, custserve@globepub.com, http://www.globepub.com; Kinokuniya Co Ltd., Shinjuku 3-chome, Shinjuku-ku, Tokyo 160-0022, Japan.

➤ **JOURNAL OF ANXIETY DISORDERS.** *see* PSYCHOLOGY

616.8 ITA ISSN 1825-2001
JOURNAL OF APPLIED RADICAL BEHAVIOR ANALYSIS. Abbreviated title: J A R B A. Text in Multiple languages. 2005. 3/yr. **Document type:** *Journal, Academic/Scholarly.*
Media: Online - full text.
Published by: Association for Advancement of Radical Behavior Analysis (A A R B A), Corso Sempione 52, Milan, 20154, Italy. TEL 39-02-33600455, info@aarba.it.

616.858 GBR ISSN 1360-2322
➤ **JOURNAL OF APPLIED RESEARCH IN INTELLECTUAL DISABILITIES.** Abbreviated title: J A R I D. Text in English. 1987. bi-m. GBP 420 in United Kingdom to institutions; EUR 533 in Europe to institutions; USD 775 in the Americas to institutions; USD 906 elsewhere to institutions; GBP 484 combined subscription in United Kingdom to institutions (print & online eds.); EUR 613 combined subscription in Europe to institutions (print & online eds.); USD 892 combined subscription in the Americas to institutions (print & online eds.); USD 1,042 combined subscription elsewhere to institutions (print & online eds.) (effective 2012). adv. back issues avail.; reprint service avail. from PSC. **Document type:** *Journal, Academic/Scholarly.* **Description:** Contains a forum for the dissemination of ideas to promote valued lifestyles for people with intellectual disabilities.
Formerly (until 1996): Mental Handicap Research (0952-9608)
Related titles: Online - full text ed.: ISSN 1468-3148. GBP 420 in United Kingdom to institutions; EUR 533 in Europe to institutions; USD 775 in the Americas to institutions; USD 906 elsewhere to institutions (effective 2012) (from IngentaConnect).
Indexed: A01, A02, A03, A08, A20, A22, A26, AMED, ASCA, B28, B29, C06, C07, CA, CPE, CurCont, E-psyche, E01, E03, E07, ERI, ERIC, Faml, P03, P04, P30, P34, P43, PCI, PsycInfo, PsycholAb, S02, S03, S21, SCOPUS, SSCI, SWR&A, SociolAb, T02, W07.
—BLDSC (4947.046000), GNLM, IE, Infotrieve, Ingenta. **CCC.**
Published by: (B I L D), Wiley-Blackwell Publishing Ltd. (Subsidiary of: John Wiley & Sons, Inc.), 9600 Garsington Rd, Oxford, OX4 2DQ, United Kingdom. TEL 44-1865-776868, FAX 44-1865-714591, customerservices@blackwellpublishing.com. Eds. David Felce TEL 44-2920-691795, Glynis Murphy TEL 44-1524-592127. Adv. contact Joanna Baker TEL 44-1865-476271.

616.85889 371.93 USA ISSN 1087-0547
RJ506.H9
➤ **JOURNAL OF ATTENTION DISORDERS;** a journal of theoretical and applied science. Text in English. 1996. bi-m. USD 543, GBP 319 combined subscription to institutions (print & online eds.); USD 532, GBP 313 to institutions (effective 2011). adv. bk.rev. back issues avail.; reprint service avail. from PSC. **Document type:** *Journal, Academic/Scholarly.*
Related titles: Online - full text ed.: ISSN 1557-1246. USD 489, GBP 287 to institutions (effective 2011).
Indexed: A22, B21, C06, C07, CurCont, E-psyche, E01, EMBASE, ERIC, ExcerpMed, F09, MEDLINE, NSA, P03, P30, PsycInfo, PsycholAb, SCI, SCOPUS, SSCI, W07.
—BLDSC (4949.240000), IE, Ingenta. **CCC.**
Published by: Sage Publications, Inc., 2455 Teller Rd, Thousand Oaks, CA 91320. TEL 805-499-9774, 800-818-7243, FAX 805-499-0871, 800-583-2665, info@sagepub.com. Eds. Jack Naglieri, Sam Goldstein. adv.: B&W page USD 550; trim 8.375 x 10.875. Circ: 283 (paid). **Subscr. outside the Americas to:** Sage Publications Ltd., 1 Oliver's Yard, 55 City Rd, London EC1Y 1SP, United Kingdom. TEL 44-20-73248701, FAX 44-20-73248733, subscription@sagepub.co.uk.

➤ **JOURNAL OF AUTISM AND DEVELOPMENTAL DISORDERS.** *see* EDUCATION—Special Education And Rehabilitation

616.89 GBR ISSN 0005-7916
RC489.B4 CODEN: JBTEAB
➤ **JOURNAL OF BEHAVIOR THERAPY AND EXPERIMENTAL PSYCHIATRY;** a journal of experimental psychopathology. Text in English. 1970. 4/yr. EUR 903 in Europe to institutions; JPY 120,000 in Japan to institutions; USD 1,012 elsewhere to institutions (effective 2012). bk.rev. index. back issues avail.; reprints avail. **Document type:** *Journal, Academic/Scholarly.* **Description:** Covers all aspects of behavior therapy and its applications in clinical psychiatry. Includes research articles, reviews, and case studies.
Related titles: Microfilm ed.: (from PQC); Online - full text ed.: ISSN 1873-7943 (from IngentaConnect, ScienceDirect).
Indexed: A01, A03, A08, A20, A22, A26, AC&P, AMHA, ASCA, ASSIA, AddicA, B25, BIOSIS Prev, C06, C07, CA, CDA, CurCont, E-psyche, EMBASE, ExcerpMed, F09, FR, HEA, IBR, IBZ, IndMed, L&LBA, MEA&I, MEDLINE, MycolAb, P03, P30, PsycInfo, PsycholAb, R10, Reac, S02, S03, SCOPUS, SSCI, SociolAb, T02, THA, W07.
—BLDSC (4951.250000), GNLM, IE, Infotrieve, Ingenta, INIST. **CCC.**
Published by: Pergamon (Subsidiary of: Elsevier Science & Technology), The Blvd, Langford Ln, East Park, Kidlington, Oxford OX5 1GB, United Kingdom. TEL 44-1865-843000, FAX 44-1865-843010, JournalsCustomerServiceEMEA@elsevier.com. Eds. A Arntz, M van den Hout. **Subscr. to:** Elsevier BV, Radarweg 29, PO Box 211, Amsterdam 1000 AE, Netherlands. TEL 31-20-4853757, FAX 31-20-4853432, JournalsCustomerServiceEMEA@elsevier.com.

616.8 USA ISSN 2160-5866
▼ ➤ **JOURNAL OF BEHAVIORAL AND BRAIN SCIENCE.** Abbreviated title: J B B S. Text in English. 2011. q. USD 156 (effective 2011). **Document type:** *Journal, Academic/Scholarly.* **Description:** Publishes original research articles and reviews in the general field of behavioural and brain function.
Related titles: Online - full text ed.: ISSN 2160-5874. free (effective 2011).
Published by: Scientific Research Publishing, Inc., PO Box 54821, Irvine, CA 92619. service@scirp.org. Ed. Juan J Canales.

M

616.8 USA ISSN 0160-7715
R726.5 CODEN: JBMEDD
➤ **JOURNAL OF BEHAVIORAL MEDICINE.** Text in English. 1978. bi-m. EUR 1,251, USD 1,306 combined subscription to institutions (print & online eds.) (effective 2012). adv. back issues avail.; reprint service avail. from PSC. **Document type:** *Journal, Academic/Scholarly.* **Description:** Furthers the understanding of physical health and illness through the techniques and knowledge of the behavioral sciences. Includes papers from a wide range of disciplines.
Related titles: Microfilm ed.: (from PQC); Online - full text ed.: ISSN 1573-3521 (from IngentaConnect).
Indexed: A01, A03, A08, A20, A22, A26, AMHA, ASCA, ASSIA, AddicA, B21, B25, BIOSIS Prev, BibLing, C06, C07, C08, C11, CA, CINAHL, CurCont, DentInd, E-psyche, E01, E08, EMBASE, ERA, ExcerpMed, F09, FR, Faml, G08, H04, H11, H12, H13, I05, IBR, IBZ, IndMed, M12, MEDLINE, MycolAb, NRN, NSA, P03, P10, P12, P20, P22, P24, P25, P30, P43, P48, P50, P53, P54, PQC, PsycInfo, PsycholAb, R10, RILM, Reac, RefZh, S02, S03, S09, S20, S21, SCOPUS, SOPODA, SSCI, SWR&A, SociolAb, T02, THA, W07.
—BLDSC (4951.262000), GNLM, IE, Infotrieve, Ingenta, INIST. **CCC.**
Published by: Springer New York LLC (Subsidiary of: Springer Science+Business Media), 233 Spring St, New York, NY 10013. TEL 212-460-1500, FAX 212-460-1575, service-ny@springer.com. Ed. Kevin S Masters.

616.8 USA ISSN 0748-7304
QH527 CODEN: JBRHEE
➤ **JOURNAL OF BIOLOGICAL RHYTHMS.** Abbreviated title: J B R. Text in English. 1985. bi-m. USD 1,124, GBP 661 combined subscription to institutions (print & online eds.); USD 1,102, GBP 648 to institutions (effective 2011). adv. bibl.; charts; illus. index. 88 p./no.; back issues avail.; reprint service avail. from PSC. **Document type:** *Journal, Academic/Scholarly.* **Description:** Reports on nature and functions of biological rhythms, using genetic, biochemical, physiological behavioral, and modeling approaches.
Related titles: Online - full text ed.: ISSN 1552-4531. USD 1,012, GBP 595 to institutions (effective 2011).
Indexed: A01, A02, A03, A08, A22, A26, A29, A34, A35, A36, A38, ASCA, AgBio, Agr, AnBeAb, B07, B20, B21, B23, B25, BIOBASE, BIOSIS Prev, CA, CABA, CurCont, D01, E-psyche, E01, E08, E12, EMBASE, ESPM, ErgAb, ExcerpMed, F08, F12, G08, GH, GenetAb, H04, H11, H12, H13, I05, I10, IABS, ISR, IndMed, IndVet, Inpharma, Inspec, MEDLINE, MycolAb, N02, N03, N04, NSA, P02, P03, P10, P11, P12, P15, P20, P25, P26, P30, P32, P33, P39, P40, P48, P52, P53, P54, P56, PQC, PsycInfo, PsycholAb, R07, R08, R10, Reac, S09, SCI, SCOPUS, T02, T05, V02, VS, ViroIAbstr, W07, W08, W10, Z01.
—BLDSC (4953.260000), AskIEEE, CASDDS, GNLM, IE, Infotrieve, Ingenta, INIST, Linda Hall. **CCC.**
Published by: (Society for Research on Biological Rhythms), Sage Publications, Inc., 2455 Teller Rd, Thousand Oaks, CA 91320. TEL 805-499-9774, FAX 805-499-0871, info@sagepub.com. Ed. Martin Zatz. adv.: color page USD 775, B&W page USD 385; 7 x 10. Circ: 700 (paid and free). **Subscr. outside the Americas to:** Sage Publications Ltd., 1 Oliver's Yard, 55 City Rd, London EC1Y 1SP, United Kingdom. TEL 44-207-3248701, FAX 44-207-3248733, subscription@sagepub.co.uk.

616.8 GBR ISSN 1749-7221
RD595
JOURNAL OF BRACHIAL PLEXUS AND PERIPHERAL NERVE INJURY. Abbreviated title: J B P P N I. Text in English. 2006. irreg. free (effective 2011). adv. back issues avail.; reprints avail. **Document type:** *Journal, Academic/Scholarly.* **Description:** Covers on all aspects of basic and clinical research findings, in the area of brachial plexus and peripheral nerve injury.
Media: Online - full text.
Indexed: A01, A26, C06, C07, CA, I05, NSA, P30, SCOPUS, T02.
—CCC.
Published by: BioMed Central Ltd. (Subsidiary of: Springer Science+Business Media), 236 Gray's Inn Rd, London, WC1X 8HB, United Kingdom. TEL 44-20-31922000, FAX 44-20-31922010, info@biomedcentral.com, http://www.biomedcentral.com. Eds. Rahul K Nath, Rolfe Birch. Adv. contact Natasha Bailey TEL 44-20-31922231.

616.8 NZL ISSN 1179-5735
▼ **JOURNAL OF CENTRAL NERVOUS SYSTEM DISEASE.** Text in English. 2009. irreg. free (effective 2011). **Document type:** *Journal, Academic/Scholarly.*
Media: Online - full text.
Indexed: C06.
—CCC.
Published by: Libertas Academica Ltd., PO Box 300-874, Mairangi Bay, Auckland, 0751, New Zealand. TEL 64-9-4763930, FAX 64-9-3531397, enquiries@la-press.com. Ed. Maria I Aguilar.

616.8 USA ISSN 0271-678X
QP108.5.C4 CODEN: JCBMDN
➤ **JOURNAL OF CEREBRAL BLOOD FLOW AND METABOLISM.** Abbreviated title: J C B F M. Text in English. 1981. m. EUR 1,188 in Europe to institutions; USD 1,247 in the Americas to institutions; JPY 202,400 in Japan to institutions; GBP 765 to institutions in the UK & elsewhere (effective 2011). adv. bk.rev. charts; illus. index. back issues avail.; reprints avail. **Document type:** *Journal, Academic/Scholarly.* **Description:** Stands at the interface between basic and clinical neurovascular research, and features timely and relevant research highlighting experimental, theoretical, and clinical aspects of brain circulation, metabolism and imaging.
Related titles: Online - full text ed.: ISSN 1559-7016.
Indexed: A01, A03, A08, A22, ASCA, B21, B25, B27, BIOBASE, BIOSIS Prev, CA, CIN, ChemAb, ChemTitl, CurCont, E-psyche, E01, EMBASE, ExcerpMed, IABS, ISR, IndMed, Inpharma, MEDLINE, MycolAb, NSA, NSCI, P15, P20, P22, P30, P35, P48, P52, P54, P56, PQC, R10, Reac, SCI, SCOPUS, T02, THA, W07.
—CASDDS, GNLM, IE, Infotrieve, Ingenta, INIST. **CCC.**
Published by: (International Society of Cerebral Blood Flow and Metabolism CHE), Nature Publishing Group (Subsidiary of: Macmillan Publishers Ltd.), 75 Varick St, 9th Fl, New York, NY 10013. TEL 212-726-9200, FAX 212-726-9006, subscriptions@nature.com. Eds. Martin Lauritzen TEL 45-43-232500, Ulrich Dirnagl TEL 49-30-450560134. Adv. contact Ben Harkinson TEL 212-726-9360. **Subscr. in the Americas to:** PO Box 5161, Brentwood, TN 37024-5161. TEL 615-850-5315, 800-524-0384, FAX 615-377-0525.

616.8 NLD ISSN 0891-0618
QM451 CODEN: JCNAEE
➤ **JOURNAL OF CHEMICAL NEUROANATOMY.** Text in Dutch. 1988. 8/yr. EUR 1,458 in Europe to institutions; JPY 193,300 in Japan to institutions; USD 1,628 elsewhere to institutions (effective 2012). reprints avail. **Document type:** *Journal, Academic/Scholarly.* **Description:** Publishes scientific reports relating to the functional and biochemical aspects of the nervous system, with emphasis on microanatomical organization.
Related titles: Microform ed.: (from PQC); Online - full text ed.: ISSN 1873-6300 (from IngentaConnect, ScienceDirect).
Indexed: A01, A03, A08, A22, A26, A29, A34, A35, A36, A37, A38, ASCA, AgBio, B20, B21, B25, B27, BIOBASE, BIOSIS Prev, C30, CA, CABA, CIN, CTA, ChemAb, ChemTitl, ChemoAb, CurCont, D01, E-psyche, EMBASE, ESPM, ExcerpMed, GH, H16, I05, I10, IABS, ISR, IndMed, IndVet, Inpharma, MEDLINE, MycolAb, N02, N03, N04, NSA, NSCI, P30, P37, R10, RA&MP, Reac, S01, SCI, SCOPUS, T02, VS, ViroIAbstr, W07, Z01.
—BLDSC (4956.850000), CASDDS, GNLM, IE, Infotrieve, Ingenta. **CCC.**
Published by: Elsevier BV (Subsidiary of: Elsevier Science & Technology), Radarweg 29, PO Box 211, Amsterdam, 1000 AE, Netherlands. TEL 31-20-4853911, FAX 31-20-4852457, JournalsCustomerServiceEMEA@elsevier.com, http://www.elsevier.nl. Ed. Harry W M Steinbusch.

616.8900835 ZAF ISSN 1728-0583
JOURNAL OF CHILD AND ADOLESCENT MENTAL HEALTH. Text in English. 1989. s-a. GBP 243 combined subscription in United Kingdom to institutions (print & online eds.); EUR 353, USD 440 combined subscription to institutions (print & online eds.) (effective 2012). reprint service avail. from PSC. **Document type:** *Journal, Academic/Scholarly.* **Description:** Publishes papers contributing to the improvement of mental health of children and adolescents, with an emphasis on epidemiology, mental health prevention and promotion, psychotherapy, pharmacotherapy, and policy and risk behavior.
Formerly (until 2003): Southern African Journal of Child and Adolescent Mental Health (1682-6108)
Related titles: Online - full text ed.: ISSN 1728-0591. GBP 219 in United Kingdom to institutions; EUR 317, USD 396 to institutions (effective 2012) (from IngentaConnect).
Indexed: A01, A36, C06, C07, CA, CABA, EMBASE, ExcerpMed, F09, Faml, GH, ISAP, LT, N02, N03, P03, PsycInfo, PsycholAb, R10, R12, RRTA, Reac, S02, S03, SCOPUS, SSA, SociolAb, T02, T05, TAR.
—BLDSC (4957.422000), IE, Ingenta. **CCC.**
Published by: (South African Association for Child and Adolescent Psychiatry), National Inquiry Services Centre, 19 Worcester St., PO Box 377, Grahamstown, 6140, South Africa. TEL 27-46-6229698, FAX 27-46-6229550, publishing@nisc.co.za. Ed. Alan J Flisher. **Co-publisher:** Routledge.

JOURNAL OF CHILD AND ADOLESCENT PSYCHIATRIC NURSING. *see* MEDICAL SCIENCES—Nurses And Nursing

616.8 USA ISSN 1044-5463
CODEN: JADPET
➤ **JOURNAL OF CHILD AND ADOLESCENT PSYCHOPHARMACOLOGY.** Text in English. 1990. bi-m. USD 818 domestic to institutions; USD 998 foreign to institutions; USD 981 combined subscription domestic to institutions (print & online eds.); USD 1,138 combined subscription foreign to institutions (print & online eds.) (effective 2012). adv. reprint service avail. from PSC. **Document type:** *Journal, Academic/Scholarly.* **Description:** Covers the clinical aspects of treating adolescent and children with psychotropic medications. Contains treatment techniques, clinical management, investigative research, and health policy.
Related titles: Online - full text ed.: ISSN 1557-8992. USD 818 to institutions (effective 2012).
Indexed: A01, A03, A08, A22, A26, ASCA, C06, CA, CurCont, E-psyche, E01, E07, EMBASE, ExcerpMed, FoP, H12, H13, I05, ISR, IndMed, Inpharma, JW-P, MEDLINE, NSCI, P02, P03, P10, P20, P22, P24, P25, P30, P35, P48, P53, P54, PQC, PsycInfo, PsycholAb, R10, Reac, SCI, SCOPUS, T02, W07.
—BLDSC (4957.424000), GNLM, IE, Infotrieve, Ingenta. **CCC.**
Published by: Mary Ann Liebert, Inc. Publishers, 140 Huguenot St, 3rd Fl, New Rochelle, NY 10801. TEL 914-740-2100, FAX 914-740-2101, 800-654-3237, info@liebertpub.com. Ed. Harold S Koplewicz TEL 212-308-3118. Adv. contact Harriet I Matysko TEL 914-740-2182.

616.8 618.92 USA ISSN 0883-0738
RJ486 CODEN: JOCNEE
➤ **JOURNAL OF CHILD NEUROLOGY.** Text in English. 1985. m. USD 803, GBP 473 combined subscription to institutions (print & online eds.); USD 787, GBP 464 to institutions (effective 2011). adv. abstr.; bibl.; charts; illus. 80 p./no. 2 cols./p.; back issues avail.; reprint service avail. from PSC. **Document type:** *Journal, Academic/Scholarly.* **Description:** Covers all aspects of nervous system disorders in children, including medical, surgical, pathological, and psychological perspectives.
Related titles: CD-ROM ed.; Online - full text ed.: ISSN 1708-8283. USD 723, GBP 426 to institutions (effective 2011).
Indexed: A01, A03, A08, A20, A22, A36, ASCA, B21, B25, BIOSIS Prev, C03, CA, CABA, CBCARef, CurCont, E-psyche, E01, E03, E12, EMBASE, ERI, ExcerpMed, F08, F11, F12, Faml, GH, H17, ISR, IndMed, Inpharma, JW-N, LT, MEDLINE, MLA-IB, MycolAb, N02, N03, NSA, NSCI, P03, P18, P20, P22, P25, P30, P33, P35, P39, P48, P53, P54, P55, PN&I, PQC, PsycInfo, PsycholAb, R08, R10, RA&MP, RM&VM, RRTA, Reac, SCI, SCOPUS, SoyAb, T02, T05, W07.
—BLDSC (4957.625000), GNLM, IE, Infotrieve, Ingenta, INIST. **CCC.**
Published by: Sage Publications, Inc., 2455 Teller Rd, Thousand Oaks, CA 91320. TEL 805-499-9774, FAX 805-499-0871, info@sagepub.com, http://www.sagepub.com/. Ed. Roger A Brumback. adv.: B&W page USD 1,225; trim 8.125 x 10.875. Circ: 1,413 (paid and controlled).

➤ **JOURNAL OF CHILD PSYCHOLOGY AND PSYCHIATRY.** *see* PSYCHOLOGY

616.8 KOR ISSN 1738-6586
➤ **JOURNAL OF CLINICAL NEUROLOGY.** Text in English. 2005. q. membership. **Document type:** *Journal, Academic/Scholarly.* **Description:** Publishes research articles in neurology, neuroscience, and related fields. Although we are primarily interested in clinical work, experimental or translational research works are also considered if they are related to clinical practice.
Related titles: Online - full text ed.: ISSN 2005-5013. free.
Indexed: P30, SCI, W07.
Published by: Korean Neurological Association/Daehan Sin-gyeong Gwahaghoe, Daeil Bldg. #1111, Insa-dong 43, Jongno-gu, Seoul, 110-741, Korea, S. TEL 82-2-7376530, FAX 82-2-7376535, kna@neuro.or.kr, http://www.neuro.or.kr/. Ed. Dr. Sang-Ahm Lee.

616.8 USA ISSN 0736-0258
QP376.5
➤ **JOURNAL OF CLINICAL NEUROPHYSIOLOGY.** Text in English. 19??. bi-m. USD 1,130 domestic to institutions; USD 1,251 foreign to institutions (effective 2011). adv. bk.rev. charts; illus. index. back issues avail.; reprints avail. **Document type:** *Journal, Academic/Scholarly.* **Description:** Features research articles that cover key concerns in electroencephalography and evoked potentials, clinical neurology, neurosurgery, psychiatry, and experimental research on the central nervous system.
Formerly (until 1984): Journal of the American E E G Society
Related titles: Online - full text ed.: ISSN 1537-1603.
Indexed: A22, ASCA, B21, BDM&CN, BIOBASE, C06, C07, C08, CINAHL, CurCont, E-psyche, EMBASE, ExcerpMed, GenetAb, IABS, ISR, IndMed, Inpharma, MEDLINE, NSA, NSCI, P30, PsycholAb, R10, Reac, SCI, SCOPUS, W07.
—BLDSC (4958.578000), GNLM, IE, Infotrieve, Ingenta, INIST. **CCC.**
Published by: (American Clinical Neurophysiology Society, American Electroencephalographic Society), Lippincott Williams & Wilkins (Subsidiary of: Wolters Kluwer N.V.), 530 Walnut St, Philadelphia, PA 19106. TEL 215-521-8300, FAX 215-521-8902, customerservice@lww.com, http://www.lww.com. Ed. Dr. John S Ebersole TEL 773-834-4702. Pub. Harry Dean. Adv. contact Renee Artuso TEL 516-741-1772. Circ: 1,402.

616.8 GBR ISSN 0967-5868
CODEN: JCNUE6
➤ **JOURNAL OF CLINICAL NEUROSCIENCE.** Text in English. 1963; N.S. 1994. m. EUR 1,528 in Europe to institutions; JPY 164,900 in Japan to institutions; USD 1,359 elsewhere to institutions (effective 2012). adv. bk.rev. back issues avail.; reprints avail. **Document type:** *Journal, Academic/Scholarly.* **Description:** Covers clinical neurosurgery, neurology, and associated neurosciences.
Former titles (until 1994): Clinical and Experimental Neurology (0196-6383); (until 1977): Australian Association of Neurologists Proceedings (0084-7224)
Related titles: Microfilm ed.: N.S. (from PQC); Online - full text ed.: ISSN 1532-2653 (from ScienceDirect).
Indexed: A20, A22, A26, ASCA, B21, BIOBASE, CA, CIN, ChemAb, ChemTitl, E-psyche, E01, EMBASE, ExcerpMed, I05, IABS, IndMed, Inpharma, MEDLINE, NSA, NSCI, P30, R10, RILM, Reac, RefZh, SCI, SCOPUS, T02, W07.
—BLDSC (4958.585000), CASDDS, GNLM, IE, Infotrieve, Ingenta, INIST. **CCC.**
Published by: (Neurosurgical Society of Australasia AUS, Australian and New Zealand Association of Neurologists AUS), Churchill Livingstone (Subsidiary of: Elsevier Health Sciences), The Blvd, Langford Ln, Kidlington, OX5 1GB, United Kingdom. TEL 44-1865-843434, FAX 44-1865-843970, directenquiries@elsevier.com, http://www.elsevierhealth.com/imprint.jsp?iid=9. Ed. Dr. Andrew H Kaye TEL 61-3-93473799. Pub. Gillian Griffith. Adv. contact Sarah Jane Cahill TEL 44-20-74244538. Circ: 708. **Co-sponsors:** Australian Association of Neurologists; Swiss Society of Neurosurgery; Australian and New Zealand Society for Neuropathology.

616.8 USA ISSN 0160-6689
RC321 CODEN: JCLPDE
➤ **JOURNAL OF CLINICAL PSYCHIATRY.** Text in English. 1940. bi-m. USD 156 combined subscription domestic (print & online eds.); USD 207 combined subscription foreign (print & online eds.); USD 45 per issue (effective 2010). adv. bk.rev. charts; illus.; stat. index. Supplement avail.; back issues avail.; reprints avail. **Document type:** *Journal, Academic/Scholarly.* **Description:** Presents original material in the psychiatric, behavioral, and neural sciences, with special emphasis on papers dealing with practical and clinical subjects.
Formerly (until 1978): Diseases of the Nervous System (0012-3714)
Related titles: Audio cassette/tape ed.: Journal of Clinical Psychiatry (Audiograph Series). ISSN 1096-0104. 1997; Microfilm ed.: (from PQC); Online - full text ed.: ISSN 1555-2101. USD 86 (effective 2010).
Indexed: A20, A22, A36, AMHA, ASCA, B21, BRI, CA, CABA, CBRI, CIN, CLFP, ChemAb, ChemTitl, Chicano, CurCont, D01, DBA, DentInd, E-psyche, E12, EMBASE, ExcerpMed, F09, FR, Faml, GH, HRIS, I12, IBR, IBZ, IDIS, INI, ISR, IndMed, Inpharma, JW-P, LT, MEDLINE, N02, N03, NSA, P03, P25, P30, P35, P48, PQC, PsycInfo, PsycholAb, R10, R12, Reac, S02, S03, SCI, SCOPUS, SSCI, SociolAb, T02, T05, ToxAb, VS, W07.
—BLDSC (4958.688000), CASDDS, GNLM, IE, Infotrieve, Ingenta, INIST. **CCC.**
Published by: Physicians Postgraduate Press, Inc., PO Box 752870, Memphis, TN 38175. TEL 901-751-3800, FAX 901-751-3444, permissions@psychiatrist.com. Ed. Dr. Alan J Gelenberg. Pub. John S Shelton. **Subscr. to:** Allen Press Inc., PO Box 1897, Lawrence, KS 66044.

616.89 USA ISSN 0742-1915
RC331
JOURNAL OF CLINICAL PSYCHIATRY MONOGRAPH SERIES. Text in English. 1984. irreg., latest 1997. back issues avail. **Document type:** *Monographic series, Academic/Scholarly.*
Indexed: A22, E-psyche, PsycholAb.
—GNLM, Ingenta, INIST. **CCC.**
Published by: Physicians Postgraduate Press, Inc., PO Box 752870, Memphis, TN 38175. TEL 901-751-3800, FAX 901-751-3444, circulation@psychiatrist.com, http://www.psychiatrist.com.

616.8 616.2 USA ISSN 1550-9389
THE JOURNAL OF CLINICAL SLEEP MEDICINE. Abbreviated title: J C S M. Text in English. 1978. bi-m. USD 75 domestic to individuals; USD 150 foreign to individuals; USD 140 domestic to institutions; USD 300 foreign to institutions; USD 36 per issue (effective 2010). adv. bk.rev. stat.; tr.lit. back issues avail. **Document type:** *Journal, Academic/Scholarly.* **Description:** Provides information on sleep disorders medicine and research.
Former titles (until 2005): A A S M Bulletin; (until 1993): A P S S Newsletter (0897-9375); (until 1986): A S D C Newsletter
Related titles: Online - full text ed.: ISSN 1550-9397.

Indexed: BiolDig, C06, C07, CurCont, E-psyche, EMBASE, ExcerpMed, MEDLINE, NSCI, P30, R10, Reac, SCI, SCOPUS, W07.
—BLDSC (4958.748000), IE. **CCC.**
Published by: The American Academy of Sleep Medicine, 2510 N Frontage Rd, Darien, IL 60561. TEL 630-737-9700, FAX 630-737-9790, publications@aasmnet.org. Ed. Dr. Stuart F Quan. Circ: 10,000.

JOURNAL OF COGNITIVE AND BEHAVIORAL PSYCHOTHERAPIES. *see* PSYCHOLOGY

612.8 153 006.3 USA ISSN 1530-8898
JOURNAL OF COGNITIVE NEUROSCIENCE (ONLINE). Abbreviated title: J O C N. Text in English. 1989. m. USD 915 in US & Canada to institutions (effective 2012). adv. **Document type:** *Journal, Academic/Scholarly.* **Description:** Investigates brain-behavior interaction and promotes lively interchange among the mind sciences.
Media: Online - full text.
—CCC.
Published by: M I T Press, 55 Hayward St, Cambridge, MA 02142. TEL 617-253-2889, FAX 617-577-1545, journals-cs@mit.edu, http://mitpress.mit.edu. Ed. Mark D'Esposito.

JOURNAL OF COGNITIVE REHABILITATION (ONLINE); a publication for the therapist, family and patient. *see* MEDICAL SCIENCES—Physical Medicine And Rehabilitation

JOURNAL OF COMMUNICATION DISORDERS. *see* PSYCHOLOGY

616.8 USA ISSN 0021-9967
QL1 CODEN: JCNEAM
➤ **THE JOURNAL OF COMPARATIVE NEUROLOGY.** Text in English. 1891. 36/yr. GBP 16,133 in United Kingdom to institutions; EUR 20,398 in Europe to institutions; USD 30,860 in United States to institutions; USD 31,364 in Canada & Mexico to institutions; USD 31,616 elsewhere to institutions; GBP 18,557 combined subscription in United Kingdom to institutions (print & online eds.); EUR 23,463 combined subscription in Europe to institutions (print & online eds.); USD 35,489 combined subscription in United States to institutions (print & online eds.); USD 35,993 combined subscription in Canada & Mexico to institutions (print & online eds.); USD 36,245 combined subscription elsewhere to institutions (print & online eds.) (effective 2012). adv. abstr.; bibl.; charts; illus. index. back issues avail.; reprint service avail. from PSC. **Document type:** *Journal, Academic/Scholarly.* **Description:** Focuses is on neuronal communication within systems of neurons, and their relationship to function, development, plasticity, degeneration, and repair.
Former titles (until 1911): The Journal of Comparative Neurology and Psychology (0092-7015); (until 1904): The Journal of Comparative Neurology (0092-7317)
Related titles: Microfiche ed.: (from BHP, PMC, SWZ); Microform ed.: (from PQC); Online - full text ed.: ISSN 1096-9861. GBP 15,747 in United Kingdom to institutions; EUR 19,910 in Europe to institutions; USD 30,860 elsewhere to institutions (effective 2012).
Indexed: A22, A34, A35, A36, A38, ASCA, AgBio, ApicAb, B21, B25, BIOBASE, BIOSIS Prev, CA, CABA, CIN, CRFR, ChemAb, ChemTitl, ChemoAb, CurCont, DentInd, E-psyche, E12, EMBASE, ExcerpMed, FCA, FoVS&M, GH, H16, H17, IABS, IBR, IBZ, ISR, IndMed, IndVet, Inpharma, MEDLINE, MycolAb, N02, N03, N04, N05, NSA, NSCI, P03, P30, P32, P33, P37, P40, PN&I, PsycInfo, R07, R08, R10, RA&MP, Reac, RefZh, S13, S16, SAA, SCI, SCOPUS, TriticAb, VS, W07, W08, WildRev, Z01.
—BLDSC (4962.000000), CASDDS, GNLM, IE, Ingenta, INIST, Linda Hall. **CCC.**
Published by: John Wiley & Sons, Inc., 111 River St, Hoboken, NJ 07030. TEL 201-748-6000, FAX 201-748-6088, info@wiley.com, http://www.wiley.com/WileyCDA/. Ed. Clifford B Saper. Adv. contact Kim Thompkins TEL 212-850-6921. **Subscr. outside the Americas to:** John Wiley & Sons Ltd., The Atrium, Southern Gate, Chichester, West Sussex PO19 8SQ, United Kingdom. TEL 44-1243-779777, 800-243407, FAX 44-1243-775878, cs-journals@wiley.com.

➤ **JOURNAL OF COMPARATIVE PHYSIOLOGY A;** sensory, neural, and behavioral physiology. *see* BIOLOGY—Physiology

006.32 USA ISSN 0929-5313
QP356 CODEN: JCNEFR
➤ **JOURNAL OF COMPUTATIONAL NEUROSCIENCE.** Text in English. 1994. bi-m. EUR 1,027, USD 1,067 combined subscription to institutions (print & online eds.) (effective 2012). adv. back issues avail.; reprint service avail. from PSC. **Document type:** *Journal, Academic/Scholarly.* **Description:** Publishes original papers describing theoretical and experimental work relevant to computations in the brain and nervous system.
Related titles: Online - full text ed.: ISSN 1573-6873 (from IngentaConnect).
Indexed: A22, A26, ASCA, B&BAb, B19, B21, B25, BIOBASE, BIOSIS Prev, BibLing, BioEngAb, CA, CCMJ, CMCI, CurCont, E-psyche, E01, EMBASE, ExcerpMed, I05, IABS, ISR, IndMed, Inpharma, Inspec, MEDLINE, MSN, MathR, MycolAb, NSA, NSCI, P03, P20, P22, P25, P30, P48, P49, P54, PQC, PsycInfo, PsycholAb, SCI, SCOPUS, T02, W07.
—BLDSC (4963.490000), AskIEEE, GNLM, IE, Infotrieve, Ingenta. **CCC.**
Published by: Springer New York LLC (Subsidiary of: Springer Science+Business Media), 233 Spring St, New York, NY 10013. TEL 212-460-1500, FAX 212-460-1575, service-ny@springer.com. Eds. Alain Destexhe, Jonathan D Victor.

➤ **JOURNAL OF CONSCIOUSNESS STUDIES;** controversies in science & the humanities. *see* PSYCHOLOGY

➤ **JOURNAL OF CONSULTING AND CLINICAL PSYCHOLOGY.** *see* PSYCHOLOGY

➤ **JOURNAL OF CONTEMPORARY PSYCHOTHERAPY;** on the cutting edge of modern developments in psychotherapy. *see* PSYCHOLOGY

➤ **JOURNAL OF CREATIVITY IN MENTAL HEALTH.** *see* PSYCHOLOGY

616.8 USA ISSN 2153-5884
▼ **JOURNAL OF CULTURAL NEUROSCIENCE.** Text in English. forthcoming 2011 (Jan.). q. USD 900 (effective 2010). **Document type:** *Journal, Academic/Scholarly.*
Media: Online - full text.
Published by: Kaiser Peer Publishing, PO Box 734, Churchville, NY 14428. TEL 585-393-1464, davidkaiser@spiritualneuroscience.org, http://brainandcosmos.com/info.htm.

618.97 GBR ISSN 1351-8372
➤ **THE JOURNAL OF DEMENTIA CARE;** for all who work with people with dementia. Text in English. 1993. bi-m. GBP 55 domestic to individuals; GBP 71 domestic to institutions; GBP 43 domestic to students; GBP 95 in Europe; GBP 110 elsewhere (effective 2009). adv. **Document type:** *Journal, Trade.* **Description:** Provides practical information, research, and networking for professionals working with people with dementia.
Indexed: B28, C06, C07, C08, CINAHL, E-psyche, SCOPUS.
—BLDSC (4968.230000), IE, Ingenta. **CCC.**
Published by: Hawker Publications Ltd., Culvert House, Culvert Rd, London, SW11 5DH, United Kingdom. TEL 44-20-77202108, FAX 44-20-74983023, suec@hawkerpublications.com. Eds. Sue Benson, Dr. Richard Hawkins. Adv. contact Caroline Bowern TEL 44-20-77202108. B&W page GBP 720, color page GBP 1,105; trim 210 x 298. Circ: 4,000. **Subscr. to:** ESCO Business Services Ltd., Trinity House, Sculpins Ln, Wethersfield, Braintree, Essex CM7 4AY, United Kingdom. TEL 44-1371-810433, FAX 44-1371-851808, enquiries@esco.co.uk, http://www.esco.co.uk.

616.85 USA ISSN 1933-3196
RC489.E98
➤ **JOURNAL OF E M D R PRACTICE AND RESEARCH.** (Eye Movement Desensitization and Reprocessing) Text in English. 2007 (Aug.). q. USD 100 domestic to individuals; USD 140 foreign to individuals; USD 320 domestic to institutions; USD 360 foreign to institutions; USD 150 combined subscription domestic to individuals; USD 210 combined subscription foreign to individuals; USD 400 combined subscription domestic to institutions; USD 450 combined subscription foreign to institutions (effective 2009). **Document type:** *Journal, Academic/Scholarly.* **Description:** Carries research and theoretical articles about EMDR and their application to clinical practice.
Related titles: Online - full text ed.: ISSN 1933-320X. 2007 (Aug). USD 80 domestic to individuals; USD 120 foreign to individuals; USD 295 domestic to institutions; USD 335 foreign to institutions (effective 2009) (from IngentaConnect).
Indexed: A01, CA, P03, P20, P48, P54, PQC, PsycInfo, T02.
—CCC.
Published by: Springer Publishing Company, 11 W 42nd St, 15th Fl, New York, NY 10036. TEL 212-431-4370, FAX 212-941-7842. Ed. Louise Maxfield.

616.8 USA ISSN 1095-0680
RC485 CODEN: JOUEFA
➤ **THE JOURNAL OF ELECTROCONVULSIVE THERAPY.** Short title: E C T. Variant title: The Journal of E C T. Text in English. 1985. q. USD 884 domestic to institutions; USD 1,068 foreign to institutions (effective 2011). adv. bk.rev. charts; illus. index. back issues avail.; reprints avail. **Document type:** *Journal, Academic/Scholarly.* **Description:** Covers all aspects of contemporary electroconvulsive therapy, reporting on major clinical and research developments worldwide.
Formerly (until 1998): Convulsive Therapy (0749-8055)
Related titles: Online - full text ed.: ISSN 1533-4112.
Indexed: A20, A22, ASCA, B21, C06, C07, CurCont, E-psyche, EMBASE, ExcerpMed, FR, FamI, H13, IPsyAb, IndMed, Inpharma, JW-P, MEDLINE, NSA, P02, P03, P10, P20, P30, P35, P48, P53, P54, PQC, PsycInfo, PsycholAb, R10, Reac, SCI, SCOPUS, SSCI, W07.
—BLDSC (4973.095900), GNLM, IE, Infotrieve, Ingenta, INIST. **CCC.**
Published by: (International Society for Neurostimulation), Lippincott Williams & Wilkins (Subsidiary of: Wolters Kluwer N.V.), Two Commerce Sq, 2001 Market St, Philadelphia, PA 19103. TEL 215-521-8300, FAX 215-521-8902, customerservice@lww.com, http://www.lww.com. Ed. Vaughn McCall. Pub. Terry Materese. Adv. contact Renee Artuso TEL 516-741-1772. Circ: 597.

616.89 USA ISSN 1063-4266
RJ499.A1 CODEN: JEBDFC
➤ **JOURNAL OF EMOTIONAL AND BEHAVIORAL DISORDERS.** Short title: J E B D. Text in English. 1993. q. USD 180, GBP 106 combined subscription to institutions (print & online eds.); USD 176, GBP 104 to institutions (effective 2011). adv. abstr.; illus. 64 p./no.; back issues avail.; reprint service avail. from PSC. **Document type:** *Journal, Academic/Scholarly.* **Description:** Covers the diagnosis and treatment of emotional and behavioral disorders of young people, from the research and practice perspectives.
Related titles: Microfilm ed.: (from PQC); Online - full text ed.: ISSN 1538-4799. USD 162, GBP 95 to institutions (effective 2011).
Indexed: A01, A02, A03, A08, A22, A25, A26, ASCA, ASSIA, B04, BRD, C06, C07, C08, C11, C28, CA, CINAHL, CJA, CurCont, DIP, E-psyche, E01, E02, E03, E07, E08, ECER, ERA, ERI, ERIC, EdA, EdI, F09, FamI, G08, G09, H04, H12, I05, IBR, IBZ, Inpharma, M01, M02, MLA-IB, P03, P04, P10, P18, P20, P24, P25, P26, P30, P43, P48, P53, P54, P55, PQC, PsycInfo, PsycholAb, S02, S03, S08, S09, S20, S21, SCOPUS, SOPODA, SSCI, SociolAb, T02, W03, W05, W07.
—BLDSC (4977.470000), IE, Ingenta. **CCC.**
Published by: Sage Publications, Inc., 2455 Teller Rd, Thousand Oaks, CA 91320. TEL 805-499-9774, 800-818-7243, FAX 805-499-0871, 800-583-2665, info@sagepub.com, http://www.sagepub.com. Eds. Douglas Cheney, Krista Kutash. adv.: B&W page USD 400. Circ: 1,100 (paid and free).

616.8 BRA ISSN 1676-2649
➤ **JOURNAL OF EPILEPSY AND CLINICAL NEUROPHYSIOLOGY.** Text in English, Portuguese, Spanish; Summaries in English, Portuguese. 1988. q. USD 70 to non-members; USD 120 foreign to non-members. adv. reprints avail. **Document type:** *Journal, Academic/Scholarly.*
Former titles (until 2002): Brazilian Journal of Epilepsy and Clinical Neurophysiology (0104-9275); (until 1995): Liga Brasileira de Epilepsia. Jornal (0103-3212)
Related titles: Online - full text ed.: free (effective 2011).
Indexed: E-psyche, EMBASE, ExcerpMed, R10, Reac, SCOPUS.
Published by: Liga Brasileira de Epilepsia, Av Ipiranga, 6690, Sala 322, Porto Alegre, RGS 90610-000, Brazil. TEL 55-51-3394936, FAX 55-51-3394936. Ed. Dr. Jaderson Costa da Costa. R&P Magda Lahorgue Nunes. Adv. contact Nurma Pereira. Circ: 700 (controlled).

➤ **JOURNAL OF ESTHETIC AND RESTORATIVE DENTISTRY.** *see* MEDICAL SCIENCES—Dentistry

616.8 USA ISSN 2153-4756
▼ **JOURNAL OF EVIDENCE-BASED NEUROMODULATION.** Text in English. forthcoming 2011 (Jan.). q. USD 900 (effective 2010). **Document type:** *Journal, Academic/Scholarly.*
Media: Online - full text.
Published by: Kaiser Peer Publishing, PO Box 734, Churchville, NY 14428. TEL 585-393-1464, davidkaiser@spiritualneuroscience.org, http://brainandcosmos.com/info.htm.

616.8 NZL ISSN 1179-0695
➤ **JOURNAL OF EXPERIMENTAL NEUROSCIENCE.** Text in English. 2008. irreg. free (effective 2011). **Document type:** *Journal, Academic/Scholarly.*
Media: Online - full text.
—CCC.
Published by: Libertas Academica Ltd., PO Box 300-874, Mairangi Bay, Auckland, 0751, New Zealand. TEL 64-9-4763930, FAX 64-9-3531397, editorial@la-press.com. Ed. Raphael Pinaud.

➤ **JOURNAL OF FAMILY PSYCHOTHERAPY;** the official journal of the International Family Therapy Association. *see* PSYCHOLOGY

306.85 GBR ISSN 0163-4445
RC488.5
➤ **JOURNAL OF FAMILY THERAPY.** Abbreviated title: J F T. Text in English. 1979. q. GBP 315 in United Kingdom to institutions; EUR 400 in Europe to institutions; USD 573 in the Americas to institutions; USD 667 elsewhere to institutions; GBP 363 combined subscription in United Kingdom to institutions (print & online eds.); EUR 461 combined subscription in Europe to institutions (print & online eds.); USD 659 combined subscription in the Americas to institutions (print & online eds.); USD 768 combined subscription elsewhere to institutions (print & online eds.) (effective 2012). adv. bk.rev. illus. index. back issues avail.; reprint service avail. from PSC. **Document type:** *Journal, Academic/Scholarly.* **Description:** Develops the understanding and treatment of human relationships constituted in systems such as couples, families, professional networks, and wider groups, by publishing articles on theory, research, clinical practice and training.
Related titles: Online - full text ed.: ISSN 1467-6427. GBP 315 in United Kingdom to institutions; EUR 400 in Europe to institutions; USD 573 in the Americas to institutions; USD 667 elsewhere to institutions (effective 2012) (from IngentaConnect).
Indexed: A01, A03, A08, A20, A22, A26, ASCA, ASSIA, C06, C07, CA, CurCont, E-psyche, E01, ESPM, F09, FR, FamI, P03, P30, P43, PsycInfo, PsycholAb, RiskAb, S02, S03, S21, SCOPUS, SFSA, SOPODA, SSA, SSCI, SociolAb, T02, W07.
—BLDSC (4983.740000), GNLM, IE, Infotrieve, Ingenta, INIST. **CCC.**
Published by: (Association for Family Therapy and Systemic Practice in the U K), Wiley-Blackwell Publishing Ltd. (Subsidiary of: John Wiley & Sons, Inc.), 9600 Garsington Rd, Oxford, OX4 2DQ, United Kingdom. TEL 44-1865-776868, FAX 44-1865-714591, customerservices@blackwellpublishing.com. Ed. Mark Rivett. Adv. contact Craig Pickett TEL 44-1865-476267. B&W page GBP 445, B&W page USD 823; 112 x 190. Circ: 2,200.

616.89 614 GBR ISSN 1478-9957
➤ **THE JOURNAL OF FORENSIC PSYCHIATRY & PSYCHOLOGY (ONLINE).** Text in English. 2000. bi-m. GBP 594 in United Kingdom to institutions; EUR 783, USD 978 to institutions (effective 2012). adv. back issues avail. **Document type:** *Journal, Academic/Scholarly.* **Description:** Publishes in-depth case studies, current research and short articles on mental health, crime and the law.
Formerly (until 2003): Journal of Forensic Psychiatry (Online) (1469-9478)
Media: Online - full text (from IngentaConnect). **Related titles:** ◆ Print ed.: The Journal of Forensic Psychiatry & Psychology (Print). ISSN 1478-9949.
—BLDSC (4984.597100). **CCC.**
Published by: Routledge (Subsidiary of: Taylor & Francis Group), 4 Park Sq, Milton Park, Abingdon, Oxon OX14 4RN, United Kingdom. TEL 44-20-70176000, FAX 44-20-70176336, subscriptions@tandf.co.uk, http://www.routledge.com. Ed. Conor Duggan. Adv. contact Linda Hann TEL 44-1344-779945. **Subscr. to:** Taylor & Francis Ltd., Journals Customer Service, Sheepen Pl, Colchester, Essex CO3 3LP, United Kingdom.

616.89 614 GBR ISSN 1478-9949
CODEN: JFPPBJ
➤ **THE JOURNAL OF FORENSIC PSYCHIATRY & PSYCHOLOGY (PRINT).** Text in English. 1990. bi-m. GBP 659 combined subscription in United Kingdom to institutions (print & online eds.); EUR 870, USD 1,086 combined subscription to institutions (print & online eds.) (effective 2012). adv. 248 p./no. 1 cols./p.; back issues avail.; reprint service avail. from PSC. **Document type:** *Journal, Academic/Scholarly.* **Description:** Publishes in-depth case studies, current research and short articles on mental health, crime and the law.
Formerly (until 2003): Journal of Forensic Psychiatry (Print) (0958-5184)
Related titles: ◆ Online - full text ed.: The Journal of Forensic Psychiatry & Psychology (Online). ISSN 1478-9957.
Indexed: A01, A03, A08, A20, A22, ASCA, ASSIA, AddicA, CA, CJA, CJPI, CurCont, E-psyche, E01, EMBASE, ExcerpMed, FR, FamI, I02, IBSS, L03, P03, P30, P43, PQC, PsycInfo, PsycholAb, R02, R10, Reac, S02, S03, SCOPUS, SSCI, T02, W07.
—GNLM, IE, Infotrieve, Ingenta, INIST. **CCC.**
Published by: Routledge (Subsidiary of: Taylor & Francis Group), 4 Park Sq, Milton Park, Abingdon, Oxon OX14 4RN, United Kingdom. TEL 44-20-70176000, FAX 44-20-70176336, subscriptions@tandf.co.uk, http://www.routledge.com. Ed. Conor Duggan. Adv. contact Linda Hann TEL 44-1344-779945. **Subscr. to:** Taylor & Francis Ltd., Journals Customer Service, Sheepen Pl, Colchester, Essex CO3 3LP, United Kingdom. TEL 44-20-70175544, FAX 44-20-70175198, tf.enquiries@tfinforma.com.

616.8 306.4 USA ISSN 1573-3602
JOURNAL OF GAMBLING STUDIES (ONLINE). Text in English. 2002. q. EUR 1,170, USD 1,236 to institutions (effective 2012). **Document type:** *Journal, Academic/Scholarly.* **Description:** Contains wide range of attendant and resultant problems, including alcoholism, suicide, crime, and a number of other mental health concerns.
Media: Online - full text (from IngentaConnect).
Indexed: CA, H&TI.
—CCC.

Published by: Springer New York LLC (Subsidiary of: Springer Science+Business Media), 233 Spring St, New York, NY 10013. TEL 212-460-1500, FAX 212-460-1575, service-ny@springer.com. Ed. Jon E Grant.

JOURNAL OF GERIATRIC PSYCHIATRY AND NEUROLOGY. *see* GERONTOLOGY AND GERIATRICS

616.857 ITA ISSN 1129-2369
RC392 CODEN: JHPOAT

➤ **THE JOURNAL OF HEADACHE AND PAIN.** Text in English. 2000. 3/yr. free (effective 2011). back issues avail.; reprint service avail. from PSC. **Document type:** *Journal, Academic/Scholarly.* **Description:** Dedicated to researchers involved in all aspects of headache and pain, including theory, methodology, clinical practice and care.

Related titles: ◆ Online - full text ed.: The Journal of Headache and Pain Online. ISSN 1129-2377; Supplement(s): The Journal of Headache and Pain. Supplement. ISSN 1972-9065. 2000.

Indexed: A01, A03, A08, A22, A26, Agr, B21, BIOBASE, C06, C07, C08, CA, CINAHL, E01, E08, EMBASE, ExcerpMed, G08, H11, H12, I05, IABS, MEDLINE, NSA, NSCI, P02, P03, P20, P22, P24, P30, P48, P54, PQC, PsycInfo, R10, Reac, S09, SCI, SCOPUS, T02, W07.

—BLDSC (4996.673000), IE, Infotrieve, Ingenta, INIST. **CCC.**

Published by: Springer Italia Srl (Subsidiary of: Springer Science+Business Media), Via Decembrio 28, Milan, 20137, Italy. TEL 39-02-54259722, FAX 39-02-55193360, springer@springer.it. Ed. Paolo Martelletti. **Subscr. in the Americas to:** Springer New York LLC, Journal Fulfillment, PO Box 2485, Secaucus, NJ 07096. TEL 201-348-4033, 800-777-4643, FAX 201-348-4505, journals-ny@springer.com, http://www.springer.com; **Subscr. to:** Springer Distribution Center, Kundenservice Zeitschriften, Haberstr 7, Heidelberg 69126, Germany. TEL 49-6221-345-0, FAX 49-6221-345-4229, subscriptions@springer.com, http://link.springer.de.

616.857 DEU ISSN 1129-2377

➤ **THE JOURNAL OF HEADACHE AND PAIN ONLINE.** Text in English. 2000. 3/yr. free base vol(s). (effective 2011). bk.rev. 64 p./no.; back issues avail.; reprints avail. **Document type:** *Journal, Academic/Scholarly.* **Description:** Publishes original papers, short and rapid communications, case reports, review articles and letters pertinent to the various aspects of headache and pain.

Media: Online - full text (from IngentaConnect). **Related titles:** ◆ Print ed.: The Journal of Headache and Pain. ISSN 1129-2369.

—CCC.

Published by: SpringerOpen (Subsidiary of: Springer Science+Business Media), Tiergartenstr 17, Heidelberg, 69121, Germany. info@springeropen.com, http://www.springeropen.com.

616.8 GBR ISSN 0219-6352
QP351 CODEN: JINODT

➤ **JOURNAL OF INTEGRATIVE NEUROSCIENCE.** Abbreviated title: J I N. Text in English. 2002. q. SGD 872, USD 532, EUR 454 combined subscription to institutions (print & online eds.) (effective 2012). adv. back issues avail. **Document type:** *Journal, Academic/Scholarly.* **Description:** Contains articles containing research reports and communications concerned with all aspects of integrative neuroscience, biophysics, molecular biology, cognition, functional brain dynamics, and physiology.

Related titles: Online - full text ed.: ISSN 1757-448X. SGD 793, USD 484, EUR 413 to institutions (effective 2012).

Indexed: A01, A02, A03, A08, A22, B&BAb, B19, B21, B25, BIOSIS Prev, BioEngAb, CA, ChemoAb, E01, EMBASE, ExcerpMed, MEDLINE, MycolAb, NSA, NSCI, P30, R10, Reac, SCI, SCOPUS, T02, W07.

—BLDSC (5007.538425), IE, Ingenta. **CCC.**

Published by: Imperial College Press (Subsidiary of: World Scientific Publishing Co. Pte. Ltd.), 57 Shelton St, Covent Garden, London, WC2H 9HE, United Kingdom. TEL 44-20-78360888, FAX 44-20-78362020, edit@icpress.co.uk, http://www.icpress.co.uk/. Ed. Roman R Poznanski. **Subscr. to:** World Scientific Publishing Co. Pte. Ltd. **Dist. by:** World Scientific Publishing Ltd.; World Scientific Publishing Co., Inc., 27 Warren St, Suite 401-402, Hackensack, NJ 07601. TEL 201-487-9655, 800-227-7562, FAX 201-487-9656, 888-977-2665, wspc@wspc.com.

616.8588 GBR ISSN 1366-8250

➤ **JOURNAL OF INTELLECTUAL AND DEVELOPMENTAL DISABILITY.** Abbreviated title: J I D D. Text in English. 1970. q. GBP 380, EUR 550, USD 690 combined subscription to institutions (print & online eds.); GBP 765, EUR 1,110, USD 1,385 combined subscription to corporations (print & online eds.) (effective 2010). bk.rev. charts; illus. index. back issues avail.; reprint service avail. from PSC. **Document type:** *Journal, Academic/Scholarly.* **Description:** Brings out qualitative and quantitative research papers, literature reviews, conceptual articles, brief reports, case reports, data briefs, and opinions and perspectives.

Former titles (until 1996): Australia and New Zealand Journal of Developmental Disabilities (0726-3864); (until 1982): Australian Journal of Developmental Disabilities (0159-9011); (until 1980): Australian Journal of Mental Retardation (0045-0634)

Related titles: Microfilm ed.: (from PQC); Online - full text ed.: ISSN 1469-9532 (from IngentaConnect).

Indexed: A01, A02, A03, A08, A20, A22, AEI, AMED, ASSIA, AusPAIS, C06, C07, C08, C11, C28, CA, CDA, CINAHL, CPE, CurCont, E-psyche, E01, E03, ECER, EMBASE, ERI, ERIC, ERO, ExcerpMed, F09, FamI, H04, H13, IndMed, L&LBA, MEDLINE, MRefA, P02, P03, P04, P10, P12, P18, P20, P25, P30, P43, P48, P53, P54, PQC, PsycInfo, PsycholAb, R10, Reac, RehabLit, S02, S03, SCOPUS, SOPODA, SSCI, T02, W07.

—IE, Infotrieve, Ingenta. **CCC.**

Published by: (Australian Society for the Study of Intellectual Disability AUS), Informa Healthcare (Subsidiary of: T & F Informa plc), Telephone House, 69-77 Paul St, London, EC2A 4LQ, United Kingdom. TEL 44-20-70175000, FAX 44-20-70176792, healthcare.enquiries@informa.com. Eds. Ian Dempsey, Susan Balandin. Adv. contact Per Sonnerfeldt. Circ: 1,400. **Subscr. in N. America to:** Taylor & Francis Inc., Customer Services Dept, 325 Chestnut St, 8th Fl, Philadelphia, PA 19106. TEL 215-625-8900, 800-354-1420, FAX 215-625-8914, customerservice@taylorandfrancis.com; **Subscr. outside N. America to:** Taylor & Francis Ltd., Journals Customer Service, Sheepen Pl, Colchester, Essex CO3 3LP, United Kingdom. TEL 44-20-70175544, FAX 44-20-70175198.

616.858 GBR ISSN 0964-2633
RC321 CODEN: JIDREN

➤ **JOURNAL OF INTELLECTUAL DISABILITY RESEARCH.** Abbreviated title: J I D R. Text in English. 1957. m. GBP 753 in United Kingdom to institutions; EUR 956 in Europe to institutions; USD 1,388 in the Americas to institutions; USD 1,619 elsewhere to institutions; GBP 867 combined subscription in United Kingdom to institutions (print & online eds.); EUR 1,100 combined subscription in Europe to institutions (print & online eds.); USD 1,597 combined subscription in the Americas to institutions (print & online eds.); USD 1,863 combined subscription elsewhere to institutions (print & online eds.) (effective 2012). adv. bk.rev. abstr.; bibl.; charts; illus. index. back issues avail.; reprint service avail. from PSC. **Document type:** *Journal, Academic/Scholarly.* **Description:** Devoted exclusively to the scientific study of intellectual disability and publishes papers reporting original observations in this field.

Formerly (until 1992): Journal of Mental Deficiency Research (0022-264X)

Related titles: Microform ed.: (from PQC); Online - full text ed.: ISSN 1365-2788. GBP 753 in United Kingdom to institutions; EUR 956 in Europe to institutions; USD 1,388 in the Americas to institutions; USD 1,619 elsewhere to institutions (effective 2012) (from IngentaConnect); Supplement(s): Journal of Intellectual Disability Research. Supplement. ISSN 1351-0886.

Indexed: A01, A02, A03, A08, A20, A22, A26, AMED, AMHA, ASCA, ASSIA, B21, B25, B28, B29, BAS, BDM&CN, BIOSIS Prev, BibInd, C06, C07, C08, C11, CA, CDA, CINAHL, CPE, ChemAb, CurCont, DentInd, E-psyche, E01, E03, E07, ECER, EMBASE, ERA, ERI, ERIC, ExcerpMed, F09, FR, FamI, H04, H12, HospAb, INI, ISR, IndMed, Inpharma, L&LBA, MEA&I, MEDLINE, MycolAb, NSA, P02, P03, P30, P34, P43, P48, PQC, PsycInfo, PsycholAb, R10, Reac, S02, S03, S21, SCOPUS, SOPODA, SSCI, SociolAb, T02, W07.

—BLDSC (5007.538440), GNLM, IE, Infotrieve, Ingenta, INIST. **CCC.**

Published by: (International Association for the Scientific Study of Intellectual Disability, Mencap), Wiley-Blackwell Publishing Ltd. (Subsidiary of: John Wiley & Sons, Inc.), 9600 Garsington Rd, Oxford, OX4 2DQ, United Kingdom. TEL 44-1865-776868, FAX 44-1865-714591, customerservices@blackwellpublishing.com. Ed. A J Holland. Adv. contact Joanna Baker TEL 44-1865-476271.

➤ **JOURNAL OF INTERPROFESSIONAL CARE.** *see* MEDICAL SCIENCES

616.8 511 DEU ISSN 2190-8567

▼ ➤ **JOURNAL OF MATHEMATICAL NEUROSCIENCE.** Text in English. 2011. irreg. free (effective 2011). **Document type:** *Journal, Academic/Scholarly.* **Description:** Publishes research articles on the mathematical modeling and analysis of all areas of neuroscience.

Media: Online - full text.

Indexed: A01.

Published by: SpringerOpen (Subsidiary of: Springer Science+Business Media), Tiergartenstr 17, Heidelberg, 69121, Germany. info@springeropen.com, http://www.springeropen.com. Eds. Oliver Faugeras, Stephen Coombes.

616.8 GBR ISSN 0963-8237
CODEN: JMEHEQ

➤ **JOURNAL OF MENTAL HEALTH.** Text in English. 1992. bi-m. GBP 935, EUR 1,340, USD 1,675 combined subscription to institutions (print & online eds.); GBP 1,870, EUR 2,680, USD 3,350 combined subscription to corporations (print & online eds.) (effective 2010). adv. back issues avail.; reprint service avail. from PSC. **Document type:** *Journal, Academic/Scholarly.* **Description:** Presents papers of direct relevance to clinical practice including all aspects of mental health work, elderly care, and addiction. Includes topics concerning work with offenders, learning difficulties, psychiatric rehabilitation, and primary care.

Related titles: Microfiche ed.; Online - full text ed.: ISSN 1360-0567 (from IngentaConnect).

Indexed: A01, A02, A03, A08, A20, A22, ASSIA, B28, C06, C07, C08, C11, CA, CINAHL, CurCont, E-psyche, E01, EMBASE, ExcerpMed, F09, FR, H04, H13, MEDLINE, P02, P03, P10, P12, P20, P24, P25, P30, P34, P43, P48, P53, P54, PAIS, PQC, PhilInd, PsycholAb, R10, Reac, S02, S03, SCOPUS, SOPODA, SSA, SSCI, SociolAb, T02, W07.

—GNLM, IE, Infotrieve, Ingenta, INIST. **CCC.**

Published by: Informa Healthcare (Subsidiary of: T & F Informa plc), Telephone House, 69-77 Paul St, London, EC2A 4LQ, United Kingdom. TEL 44-20-70175000, healthcare.enquiries@informa.com, http://www.tandf.co.uk/journals/. Adv. contact Per Sonnerfeldt. **Subscr. in N. America to:** Taylor & Francis Inc., Customer Services Dept, 325 Chestnut St, 8th Fl, Philadelphia, PA 19106. TEL 215-625-8900, 800-354-1420, FAX 215-625-2940, customerservice@taylorandfrancis.com; **Subscr. outside N. America to:** Taylor & Francis Ltd., Journals Customer Service, Sheepen Pl, Colchester, Essex CO3 3LP, United Kingdom. TEL 44-20-70175544, FAX 44-20-70175198, tf.enquiries@tfinforma.com.

616.8 GBR ISSN 1466-2817

➤ **JOURNAL OF MENTAL HEALTH LAW.** Text in English. 1999 (Feb.). s-a. GBP 40 to individuals; GBP 65 to institutions (effective 2009). back issues avail.; reprint service avail. from WSH. **Document type:** *Journal, Academic/Scholarly.* **Description:** Focuses on developments within the area of mental health law.

Related titles: Online - full text ed.

—BLDSC (5017.687500). **CCC.**

Published by: (Northumbria University, School of Law), Northumbria Law Press, Enterprise Unit, School of Law, Northumbria University, City Campus E, Newcastle Upon Tyne, NE1 8ST, United Kingdom. TEL 44-191-2437587, FAX 44-191-2437506, nlp@northumbria.ac.uk. Ed. John Horne TEL 44-191-2274649.

362.2 USA ISSN 1931-5864
RC451.4.M47

➤ **JOURNAL OF MENTAL HEALTH RESEARCH IN INTELLECTUAL DISABILITIES.** Text in English. 2008. q. GBP 164 combined subscription in United Kingdom to institutions (print & online eds.); EUR 254, USD 320 combined subscription to institutions (print & online eds.) (effective 2012). adv. bk.rev. reprint service avail. from PSC. **Document type:** *Journal, Academic/Scholarly.* **Description:** Reports original scientific and scholarly contributions to advance knowledge about mental health issues among persons with intellectual disabilities and related developmental disabilities, especially autism spectrum disorders and genetic phenotypes.

Related titles: Online - full text ed.: ISSN 1931-5872. GBP 148 in United Kingdom to institutions; EUR 229, USD 288 to institutions (effective 2012).

Indexed: A01, A22, CA, E01, P03, P30, P48, P50, PQC, PsycInfo, T02.

—BLDSC (5017.688505), IE. **CCC.**

Published by: (National Association for the Dually Diagnosed (N A D D)), Taylor & Francis Inc. (Subsidiary of: Taylor & Francis Group), 325 Chestnut St, Ste 800, Philadelphia, PA 19106. TEL 215-625-2940, 800-354-1420, orders@taylorandfrancis.com, http://www.taylorandfrancis.com. Ed. Johannes Rojahn TEL 703-993-4241. Adv. contact Linda Hann TEL 44-1344-779945.

312.2032 GBR ISSN 1755-6228
RA790.A1

THE JOURNAL OF MENTAL HEALTH, TRAINING, EDUCATION AND PRACTICE; issues for workforce development. Text in English. 2006. q. EUR 689 combined subscription in Europe (print & online eds.); USD 889 combined subscription in the Americas (print & online eds.); GBP 529 combined subscription in the UK & elsewhere (print & online eds.); AUD 999 combined subscription in Australasia (print & online eds.) (effective 2012). adv. back issues avail. **Document type:** *Journal, Academic/Scholarly.* **Description:** Addresses the critical workforce issues in mental health services.

Formerly (until Sep.2007): The Journal of Mental Health Workforce Development (1750-0699)

Related titles: Online - full text ed.: ISSN 2042-8707.

Indexed: B01, B07, B28, CA, T02.

—BLDSC (5017.688530), IE. **CCC.**

Published by: Pier Professional Ltd. (Subsidiary of: Emerald Group Publishing Ltd.), Ste N4, The Old Market, Upper Market St, Hove, BN3 1AS, United Kingdom. TEL 44-1273-783720, FAX 44-1273-783723, info@pierprofessional.com. Eds. Christina Pond, Di Bailey, Ian Baguley, Peter Ryan. adv.: B&W page GBP 350; 160 x 245.

616.8 USA ISSN 0895-8696
QP356.2 CODEN: JMNEES

➤ **JOURNAL OF MOLECULAR NEUROSCIENCE.** Abbreviated title: J M N. Text in English. 1989. 9/yr. EUR 1,305, USD 1,591 combined subscription to institutions (print & online eds.) (effective 2012). adv. bk.rev. illus. index. 120 p./no.; back issues avail.; reprint service avail. from PSC. **Document type:** *Journal, Academic/Scholarly.* **Description:** Covers a broad range of subjects for molecular studies of neural genes through actions of the gene products to diseases caused by defects in particular genes.

Related titles: Online - full text ed.: ISSN 1559-1166 (from IngentaConnect).

Indexed: A22, A26, A29, A34, A35, A36, A38, ASCA, ASFA, AgBio, B20, B21, B25, B27, BIOBASE, BIOSIS Prev, C25, C30, C33, CABA, CIN, ChemAb, ChemTitl, ChemoAb, CurCont, D01, E-psyche, E01, E12, EMBASE, ESPM, ExcerpMed, F08, F11, F12, GH, H12, H16, H17, I05, I10, IABS, ISR, IndMed, IndVet, Inpharma, MEDLINE, MycolAb, N02, N03, N04, N05, NSA, NSCI, O01, P20, P22, P25, P30, P32, P33, P39, P40, P48, P54, PGegResA, PQC, R07, R08, R10, R12, RA&MP, Reac, S13, S16, SCI, SCOPUS, T05, VS, ViroIAbstr, W07, W10.

—BLDSC (5020.717000), CASDDS, GNLM, IE, Infotrieve, Ingenta, INIST. **CCC.**

Published by: Humana Press, Inc. (Subsidiary of: Springer Science+Business Media), 999 Riverview Dr, Ste 208, Totowa, NJ 07512. TEL 973-256-1699, FAX 973-256-8341, humana@humanapr.com, http://humanapress.com/journals.pasp. Ed. Ilana Gozes. Pub. Thomas B. Lanigan Jr. R&P Wendy A. Warren. Adv. contacts John Chasse, Thomas B. Lanigan Jr. **Subscr. to:** Maruzen Co., Ltd., 3-10 Nihonbashi, 2-Chome, Chuo-ku, Tokyo 103, Japan. TEL 81-3-32723884, FAX 81-3-32723923, journal@maruzen.co.jp, http://www.maruzen.co.jp.

➤ **THE JOURNAL OF MUSCULOSKELETAL AND NEURONAL INTERACTIONS.** *see* MEDICAL SCIENCES—Orthopedics And Traumatology

616.8 USA ISSN 1939-0637
R857.N34

▼ ➤ **JOURNAL OF NANONEUROSCIENCE.** Text and summaries in English. 2009 (Mar.). s-a. USD 780; USD 1,580 combined subscription (print & online eds.) (effective 2010). adv. back issues avail. **Document type:** *Journal, Academic/Scholarly.* **Description:** Brings out articles, reviews, commentary on the state of the art knowledge in scientific community, researchers, health planners, health care providers, policy makers, environmentalists, biologists, chemists, and physicist of medical science.

Related titles: Online - full text ed.: ISSN 1939-0653. USD 1,380 (effective 2010) (from IngentaConnect).

Indexed: B&BAb, B19, B21, EMBASE, ExcerpMed, NSA, P30, SCOPUS.

Published by: American Scientific Publishers, 26650 The Old Rd, Ste 208, Valencia, CA 91381. TEL 661-799-7200, FAX 661-254-1207, order@aspbs.com. Ed. Dr. Hari Shanker Sharma TEL 46-18-6119208. **Subscr. to:** 25650 N Lewis Way, Stevenson Ranch, CA 91381.

616.8 USA ISSN 0022-3018
RC321 CODEN: JNMDAN

➤ **JOURNAL OF NERVOUS AND MENTAL DISEASE.** Text in English. 1874. m. USD 753 domestic to institutions; USD 895 foreign to institutions (effective 2011). adv. bk.rev. bibl.; illus. index. back issues avail.; reprints avail. **Document type:** *Journal, Academic/Scholarly.* **Description:** Provides articles which covers theory, etiology, therapy, social impact of illness, and research methods in the field of human behavior.

Formerly (until 1876): The Chicago Journal of Nervous and Mental Disease (1060-1694)

Related titles: Online - full text ed.: ISSN 1539-736X.

Indexed: A01, A03, A08, A20, A21, A22, A26, A36, ABS&EES, AC&P, AHCMS, AIM, ASCA, AddicA, B25, BAS, BIOSIS Prev, C06, C07, C08, C28, CA, CABA, CDA, CINAHL, CLFP, ChPerI, ChemAb, Chicano, CurCont, DBA, DentInd, DokArb, E-psyche, E12, ECER, EMBASE, ExcerpMed, F09, FR, FamI, G08, GH, H11, H12, H13, IBR, IBZ, INI, IPARL, IPsyAb, ISR, IndMed, Inpharma, JW-P, LT, MEDLINE, MLA, MLA-IB, MycolAb, N02, N03, NSCI, P02, P03, P10, P20, P30, P33, P35, P39, P48, P53, P54, PQC, PsycInfo, PsycholAb, R08, R10, R12, RI-1, RRTA, Reac, S02, S03, S21, SCI, SCOPUS, SSCI, T02, T05, V&AA, W07, W09.

—BLDSC (5021.400000), GNLM, IE, Infotrieve, Ingenta, INIST. **CCC.**

Published by: Lippincott Williams & Wilkins (Subsidiary of: Wolters Kluwer N.V.), Two Commerce Sq, 2001 Market St, Philadelphia, PA 19103. TEL 215-521-8300, FAX 215-521-8902, customerservice@lww.com, http://www.lww.com. Ed. Dr. Eugene B Brody. Pub. Terry Materese.

616.8 AUT
QP364.5 CODEN: JNPSEJ
➤ **JOURNAL OF NEURAL TRANSMISSION**; basic neurosciences and genetics, Parkinson's Disease and allied conditions, Alzheimer's Disease and related disorders, biological psychiatry, biological child and adolescent psychiatry. Text in English. 1950. m. EUR 4,025, USD 4,793 combined subscription to institutions (print & online eds.) (effective 2012). adv. charts; illus.; abstr. index. back issues avail.; reprint service avail. from PSC. **Document type:** *Journal, Academic/Scholarly.* **Description:** Publishes research in neurological disorders, including Parkinson's and Alzheimer's diseases.
Formed by the merger of (1989-19??): Journal of Neural Transmission. Parkinson's Disease and Dementia Section (0936-3076); (1950-19??): Journal of Neural Transmission. General Section (0300-9564); Which was formerly (until 1972): Journal of Neuro-Visceral Relations (0022-3026); (until 1967): Acta Neurovegetativa (0375-9245)
Related titles: Microform ed.: (from PQC); Online - full text ed.: ISSN 1435-1463 (from IngentaConnect).
Indexed: A01, A03, A08, A20, A22, A26, A34, A35, A36, ASCA, AgBio, B21, B25, BIOBASE, BIOSIS Prev, BP, C30, CA, CABA, CTA, ChemAb, ChemTitl, CurCont, DBA, E-psyche, E01, E08, E12, EMBASE, ESPM, ExcerpMed, F08, F11, F12, GH, H12, IABS, IBR, IBZ, INIS AtomInd, ISR, IndMed, IndVet, Inpharma, MEDLINE, MycolAb, N02, N03, N05, NSA, NSCI, P03, P20, P22, P30, P32, P35, P37, P48, P54, PQC, PsycInfo, R10, R12, RA&MP, Reac, S09, SCI, SCOPUS, SoyAb, T02, T05, THA, ToxAb, VS, W07, WildRev.
—CASDDS, GNLM, IE, Ingenta, INIST. **CCC.**
Published by: Springer Wien (Subsidiary of: Springer Science+Business Media), Sachsenplatz 4-6, Vienna, W 1201, Austria. TEL 43-1-33024150, FAX 43-1-3302426, journals@springer.at, http://www.springer.at. Ed. Dr. Peter Riederer. Adv. contact Irene Hofmann. B&W page EUR 1,290; 170 x 230. Circ: 800 (paid). **Subscr. in the Americas to:** Springer New York LLC, Journal Fulfillment, PO Box 2485, Secaucus, NJ 07096. TEL 800-777-4643, 201-348-4033, FAX 201-348-4505, journals-ny@springer.com, http://www.springer.com; **Subscr. to:** Springer Distribution Center, Kundenservice Zeitschriften, Haberstr 7, Heidelberg 69126, Germany. TEL 49-6221-3454303, FAX 49-6221-3454229, subscriptions@springer.com.

616.8 AUT ISSN 0303-6995
QP356.3 CODEN: JNTSD4
➤ **JOURNAL OF NEURAL TRANSMISSION. SUPPLEMENT.** Text in English. 1952. irreg., latest vol.68, 2004. price varies. adv. abstr. reprints avail. **Document type:** *Monographic series, Academic/Scholarly.* **Description:** Publishes selected papers from conferences in applied and clinical research in neurological diseases, such as Parkinson's and Alzheimer's.
Former titles (until 1974): Journal of Neuro-Visceral Relations. Supplement (0075-4323); (until 1969): Acta Neurovegetativa. Supplement (0365-513X)
Related titles: Microform ed.: (from PQC).
Indexed: A22, ASCA, B25, BIOBASE, BIOSIS Prev, CIN, ChemAb, ChemTitl, CurCont, E-psyche, EMBASE, ExcerpMed, IABS, INIS AtomInd, ISR, IndMed, Inpharma, MEDLINE, MycolAb, NSCI, P30, P35, R10, Reac, SCI, SCOPUS, W07.
—BLDSC (5021.425000), CASDDS, IE, Ingenta, INIST. **CCC.**
Published by: Springer Wien (Subsidiary of: Springer Science+Business Media), Sachsenplatz 4-6, Vienna, W 1201, Austria. TEL 43-1-3302415-0, FAX 43-1-330242665. Ed. Dr. Peter Riederer. R&P Angela Foessl TEL 43-1-3302415517. Adv. contact Michael Katzenberger TEL 43-1-3302415220. B&W page EUR 1,000; 170 x 250. **Subscr. in N. America to:** Springer New York LLC, Journal Fulfillment, PO Box 2485, Secaucus, NJ 07096. TEL 800-777-4643, 201-348-4033, FAX 201-348-4505, journals-ny@springer.com.

➤ **JOURNAL OF NEURO-OPHTHALMOLOGY.** *see* MEDICAL SCIENCES—Ophthalmology And Optometry

➤ **JOURNAL OF NEUROCHEMISTRY.** *see* BIOLOGY—Biochemistry

616.8 USA ISSN 1932-1481
RC346
➤ **JOURNAL OF NEURODEGENERATION & REGENERATION.** Text in English. 2008. q. USD 298 combined subscription domestic to individuals (print & online eds.); USD 323 combined subscription in Canada to individuals (print & online eds.); USD 363 combined subscription elsewhere to individuals (print & online eds.); USD 398 combined subscription domestic to institutions (print & online eds.); USD 423 combined subscription in Canada to institutions (print & online eds.); USD 463 combined subscription elsewhere to institutions (print & online eds.) (effective 2010). adv. reprints avail. **Document type:** *Journal, Academic/Scholarly.* **Description:** Covers clinical new and ongoing research being conducted in this critical field, research that will lead to better diagnosis, more effective treatments and ultimately, perhaps, cures.
Related titles: Online - full text ed.
Indexed: P30.
—CCC.
Published by: Weston Medical Publishing, LLC, 470 Boston Post Rd, Weston, MA 02493. TEL 781-899-2702, 800-743-7206, FAX 781-899-4900, subscription@pnpco.com, brenda_devito@pnpco.com. Pub. Richard A DeVito Jr.

616.8 USA ISSN 1866-1947
RC321
▼ **JOURNAL OF NEURODEVELOPMENTAL DISORDERS.** Text in English. 2009. q. USD 552 combined subscription to institutions (print & online eds.) (effective 2011). back issues avail.; reprint service avail. from PSC. **Document type:** *Journal, Academic/Scholarly.* **Description:** Contains research across a number of disciplines, including neurobiology, genetics, cognitive neuroscience and psychology.
Related titles: Online - full text ed.: ISSN 1866-1956 (from IngentaConnect).
Indexed: A22, B25, BIOSIS Prev, CurCont, E01, MycolAb, NSCI, P03, P30, PsycInfo, SCI, SCOPUS, W07.
—IE. **CCC.**

Published by: Springer New York LLC (Subsidiary of: Springer Science+Business Media), 233 Spring St, New York, NY 10013. TEL 212-460-1500, FAX 212-460-1575, service@springer-ny.com, http://www.springer.com. Ed. Joseph Piven.

616.8 616.4 GBR ISSN 0953-8194
QP356.4 CODEN: JOUNE2
➤ **JOURNAL OF NEUROENDOCRINOLOGY**; from molecular to translational neurobiology. Text in English. 1989. m. GBP 1,776 in United Kingdom to institutions; EUR 2,256 in Europe to institutions; USD 3,284 in the Americas to institutions; USD 3,830 elsewhere to institutions; GBP 2,043 combined subscription in United Kingdom to institutions (print & online eds.); EUR 2,595 combined subscription in Europe to institutions (print & online eds.); USD 3,777 combined subscription in the Americas to institutions (print & online eds.); USD 4,405 combined subscription elsewhere to institutions (print & online eds.) (effective 2012). adv. bk.rev. bibl.; illus. index. back issues avail.; reprint service avail. from PSC. **Document type:** *Journal, Academic/Scholarly.* **Description:** Integrates the fields of endocrinology and neuroscience. Covers nonvertebrate, vertebrate and clinical endocrinology.
Related titles: Microform ed.: (from PQC); Online - full text ed.: ISSN 1365-2826. 1998. GBP 1,776 in United Kingdom to institutions; EUR 2,256 in Europe to institutions; USD 3,284 in the Americas to institutions; USD 3,830 elsewhere to institutions (effective 2012) (from IngentaConnect).
Indexed: A01, A03, A08, A22, A26, A34, A35, A36, A38, ASCA, AgBio, B21, B25, BIOBASE, BIOSIS Prev, C33, CA, CABA, CIN, CTA, ChemAb, ChemTitl, ChemoAb, CurCont, D01, E-psyche, E01, E12, EMBASE, ExcerpMed, GH, H12, I05, IABS, ISR, IndMed, IndVet, Inpharma, LT, MEDLINE, MycolAb, N02, N03, N04, NSA, NSCI, P03, P30, P37, PN&I, PsycInfo, PsycholAb, R10, R13, RRTA, Reac, RefZh, S13, S16, SCI, SCOPUS, SoyAb, T02, VS, W07.
—BLDSC (5021.543000), CASDDS, GNLM, IE, Infotrieve, Ingenta, INIST. **CCC.**
Published by: (British Society for Neuroendocrinology USA, European Neuroendocrine Association NLD), Wiley-Blackwell Publishing Ltd. (Subsidiary of: John Wiley & Sons, Inc.), 9600 Garsington Rd, Oxford, OX4 2DQ, United Kingdom. TEL 44-1865-776868, FAX 44-1865-714591, customerservices@blackwellpublishing.com. Ed. David R Grattan TEL 64-3-4797442. **Co-sponsor:** British Neuroendocrine Group.

615.82 GBR ISSN 1743-0003
RC386.6
➤ **JOURNAL OF NEUROENGINEERING AND REHABILITATION.** Abbreviated title: J N E R. Text in English. 2005. irreg. free (effective 2010). adv. back issues avail. **Document type:** *Journal, Academic/Scholarly.* **Description:** Aims to foster the publication of research work that results from cross-fertilization of the fields of neuroscience, biomedical engineering, and physical medicine & rehabilitation.
Media: Online - full text.
Indexed: A01, A26, B19, C06, C07, CA, EMBASE, ExcerpMed, I05, MEDLINE, NSA, NSCI, P30, PEI, R09, SCI, SCOPUS, T02, W07.
—CCC.
Published by: BioMed Central Ltd. (Subsidiary of: Springer Science+Business Media), 236 Gray's Inn Rd, London, WC1X 8HB, United Kingdom. TEL 44-20-31922000, FAX 44-20-31922010, info@biomedcentral.com, http://www.biomedcentral.com. Ed. Paolo Bonato. Adv. contact Natasha Bailey TEL 44-20-31922231.

616.8 USA ISSN 0167-7063
QP356.22 CODEN: JLNEDK
➤ **JOURNAL OF NEUROGENETICS.** Text in English. 1983. q. GBP 1,105, EUR 1,210, USD 1,515 combined subscription to institutions (print & online eds.); GBP 2,235, EUR 2,445, USD 3,055 combined subscription to corporations (print & online eds.) (effective 2010). back issues avail.; reprint service avail. from PSC. **Document type:** *Journal, Academic/Scholarly.* **Description:** Publishes papers in the broad field of neurogenetics, covering studies of genes and genetic variants that influence neural development and function.
Related titles: CD-ROM ed.; Microform ed.; Online - full text ed.: ISSN 1563-5260 (from IngentaConnect).
Indexed: A01, A03, A08, A22, AMED, ASCA, ASFA, B21, B25, B26, BIOBASE, BIOSIS Prev, CA, ChemAb, E-psyche, E01, EMBASE, EntAb, ExcerpMed, GenetAb, IABS, ISR, IndMed, Inpharma, MEDLINE, MycolAb, NSA, NSCI, P30, R10, Reac, S01, SCI, SCOPUS, T02, W07.
—CASDDS, GNLM, IE, Infotrieve, Ingenta, INIST. **CCC.**
Published by: Informa Healthcare (Subsidiary of: T & F Informa plc), 325 Chestnut St, Ste 800, Philadelphia, PA 19106. TEL 800-354-1420, FAX 215-625-2940, healthcare.enquiries@informa.com, http://www.informahealthcare.com, http://www.tandf.co.uk/journals/. Ed. Chun-Fang Wu. **Subscr. outside N. America to:** Taylor & Francis Ltd., Journals Customer Service, Sheepen Pl, Colchester, Essex CO3 3LP, United Kingdom. TEL 44-20-70175544, FAX 44-20-70175198, tf.enquiries@tfinforma.com.

616.8 616.07548 USA ISSN 1051-2284
RC78.7.D53 CODEN: JNERET
➤ **JOURNAL OF NEUROIMAGING.** Abbreviated title: J O N. Text in English. 1991. q. GBP 565 in United Kingdom to institutions; EUR 718 in Europe to institutions; USD 872 in the Americas to institutions; USD 1,105 elsewhere to institutions; GBP 650 combined subscription in United Kingdom to institutions (print & online eds.); EUR 826 combined subscription in Europe to institutions (print & online eds.); USD 1,003 combined subscription in the Americas to institutions (print & online eds.); USD 1,271 combined subscription elsewhere to institutions (print & online eds.) (effective 2012). adv. bk.rev. abstr.; charts; illus.; stat. index. 96 p./no. 2 cols./p.; back issues avail.; reprint service avail. from PSC. **Document type:** *Journal, Academic/Scholarly.* **Description:** Includes coverage of MRI, CT, SPECT, PET, neurosonology, transcranial doppler, and carotid ultrasound, for specialists who rely on neuroimaging.
Related titles: Microform ed.: (from PQC); Online - full text ed.: ISSN 1552-6569. GBP 565 in United Kingdom to institutions; EUR 718 in Europe to institutions; USD 872 in the Americas to institutions; USD 1,105 elsewhere to institutions (effective 2012) (from IngentaConnect).
Indexed: A01, A03, A08, A22, A26, ASCA, B&BAb, B19, B21, BIOBASE, BioEngAb, C06, C07, CA, CTA, CurCont, E-psyche, E01, E08, EMBASE, ExcerpMed, G08, H11, H12, I05, IABS, IndMed, Inpharma, MEDLINE, NSA, NSCI, P30, P35, R10, Reac, S09, SCI, SCOPUS, T02, W07.
—BLDSC (5021.548000), GNLM, IE, Infotrieve, Ingenta, INIST. **CCC.**

Published by: (American Society of Neuroimaging), Wiley-Blackwell Publishing, Inc. (Subsidiary of: Wiley-Blackwell Publishing Ltd.), 111 River St, Hoboken, NJ 07030. TEL 201-748-6000, FAX 201-748-6088, info@wiley.com. Ed. Joseph C Masdeu. Adv. contact Stephen Donohue TEL 781-388-8511.

616.8 616.97 NLD ISSN 0165-5728
QP356.47 CODEN: JNRIDW
➤ **JOURNAL OF NEUROIMMUNOLOGY.** Text in English. 1981. 24/yr. EUR 5,496 in Europe to institutions; JPY 730,500 in Japan to institutions; USD 6,152 elsewhere to institutions (effective 2012). adv. charts; illus.; abstr. back issues avail.; reprints avail. **Document type:** *Journal, Academic/Scholarly.* **Description:** Publishes both basic research and clinical problems in neuroimmunology and related neuroscientific disciplines.
Incorporates (1991-1997): Advances in Neuroimmunology (0960-5428)
Related titles: Microform ed.: (from PQC); Online - full text ed.: ISSN 1872-8421 (from IngentaConnect, ScienceDirect); Supplement(s): ISSN 0169-5088.
Indexed: A01, A03, A08, A22, A26, A34, A36, A38, AIDS Ab, AIDS&CR, ASCA, B21, B25, BIOBASE, BIOSIS Prev, C30, C33, CA, CABA, ChemAb, ChemTitl, CurCont, E-psyche, E12, EMBASE, ExcerpMed, F08, F11, F12, GH, H17, I05, IABS, ISR, ImmunAb, IndMed, IndVet, Inpharma, MEDLINE, MycolAb, N02, N03, NSA, NSCI, P03, P30, P32, P33, P35, P39, P40, PN&I, PsycInfo, PsycholAb, R08, R10, RA&MP, Reac, S12, SCI, SCOPUS, T02, T05, VS, W07.
—BLDSC (5021.550000), CASDDS, GNLM, IE, Infotrieve, Ingenta, INIST. **CCC.**
Published by: (International Society for Neuroimmunology), Elsevier BV (Subsidiary of: Elsevier Science & Technology), Radarweg 29, PO Box 211, Amsterdam, 1000 AE, Netherlands. TEL 31-20-4853911, FAX 31-20-4852457, JournalsCustomerServiceEMEA@elsevier.com, http://www.elsevier.nl. Ed. Dr. Cedric S Raine.

616.8 GBR ISSN 1742-2094
RC363
➤ **JOURNAL OF NEUROINFLAMMATION.** Abbreviated title: J N I. Text in English. 2004. irreg. free (effective 2011). adv. back issues avail. **Document type:** *Journal, Academic/Scholarly.* **Description:** Focuses on innate immunological responses of the central nervous system, involving microglia, astrocytes, cytokines, chemokines, and related molecular processes.
Media: Online - full text.
Indexed: A01, A26, A34, A35, A36, B25, BIOSIS Prev, C06, C07, CA, CABA, CurCont, E12, EMBASE, ExcerpMed, F08, GH, H17, I05, IndVet, MEDLINE, MycolAb, N02, NSA, NSCI, P30, P33, P39, PN&I, R08, R10, RA&MP, RM&VM, Reac, SCI, SCOPUS, T02, T05, VS, W07.
—CCC.
Published by: BioMed Central Ltd. (Subsidiary of: Springer Science+Business Media), 236 Gray's Inn Rd, London, WC1X 8HB, United Kingdom. TEL 44-20-31922000, FAX 44-20-31922010, info@biomedcentral.com, http://www.biomedcentral.com. Eds. Robert E Mrak, Sue T Griffin. Adv. contact Natasha Bailey TEL 44-20-31922231.

▼ ➤ **JOURNAL OF NEUROINTERVENTIONAL SURGERY.** *see* MEDICAL SCIENCES—Surgery

616.8 GBR ISSN 0911-6044
➤ **JOURNAL OF NEUROLINGUISTICS.** Text in English. 1985. 6/yr. EUR 840 in Europe to institutions; JPY 111,400 in Japan to institutions; USD 939 elsewhere to institutions (effective 2012). back issues avail.; reprints avail. **Document type:** *Journal, Academic/Scholarly.* **Description:** Provides an international forum for the integration of the language sciences and the neurosciences.
Related titles: Microfilm ed.: (from PQC); Online - full text ed.: ISSN 1873-8052 (from IngentaConnect, ScienceDirect).
Indexed: A01, A03, A08, A20, A22, A26, ASCA, B21, BibLing, CA, CMM, CommAb, E-psyche, EMBASE, ERA, ExcerpMed, I05, L&LBA, L11, MLA-IB, NSA, NSCI, P03, P30, PsycInfo, PsycholAb, RASB, S20, SCI, SCOPUS, SOPODA, SSCI, T02, W07.
—BLDSC (5021.553000), GNLM, IE, Infotrieve, Ingenta, INIST. **CCC.**
Published by: Pergamon (Subsidiary of: Elsevier Science & Technology), The Blvd, Langford Ln, East Park, Kidlington, Oxford OX5 1GB, United Kingdom. TEL 44-1865-843000, FAX 44-1865-843010, JournalsCustomerServiceEMEA@elsevier.com. Ed. H Cohen. **Subscr. to:** Elsevier BV, Radarweg 29, PO Box 211, Amsterdam 1000 AE, Netherlands. TEL 31-20-4853757, FAX 31-20-4853432, http://www.elsevier.nl.

616.8 USA ISSN 1557-0576
➤ **JOURNAL OF NEUROLOGIC PHYSICAL THERAPY.** Abbreviated title: J N P T. Text in English. 1977. q. USD 242 domestic to institutions; USD 328.99 foreign to institutions (effective 2011). adv. back issues avail.; reprints avail. **Document type:** *Journal, Academic/Scholarly.* **Description:** Presents articles that contribute to the development and effective use of neurologic physical therapy. Types of articles include research, systematic reviews, case reports, and special interest papers.
Formerly (until 2003): Neurology Report (1085-049X)
Related titles: Online - full text ed.: ISSN 1557-0584.
Indexed: C06, C07, C08, CA, CINAHL, EMBASE, ExcerpMed, MEDLINE, P20, P22, P24, P26, P30, P48, P54, PQC, R10, Reac, SCOPUS, T02.
—BLDSC (5021.553250), IE, Ingenta. **CCC.**
Published by: (American Physical Therapy Association, Section on Neurology), Lippincott Williams & Wilkins (Subsidiary of: Wolters Kluwer N.V.), Two Commerce Sq, 2001 Market St, Philadelphia, PA 19103. TEL 215-521-8300, FAX 215-521-8902, customerservice@lww.com, http://www.lww.com. Ed. Edelle Field-Fote TEL 305-243-7119. Pub. Paul Gee. Adv. contact Pat Wendelken. Circ: 3,851.

616.8 TUR
➤ **JOURNAL OF NEUROLOGICAL SCIENCES (ONLINE).** Text in Turkish, English. 1996. q. free (effective 2011). **Document type:** *Journal, Academic/Scholarly.* **Description:** Publishes both experimental and clinical neuroscience articles.
Media: Online - full text.
Published by: Ege University Press, c/o Prof. Nezih Oktar, Ege University Hospital, Faculty of Medicine, Department of Neurosurgery, Bornova, Izmir, 35100, Turkey. TEL 90-532-6125939. Ed. Nezih Oktar.

616.8 DEU ISSN 0340-5354
CODEN: JNRYA9

➤ **JOURNAL OF NEUROLOGY/ZEITSCHRIFT FUER NEUROLOGIE**; official journal of the European Neurological Society. Text in English. 1891. m. EUR 3,267, USD 3,915 combined subscription to institutions (print & online eds.) (effective 2012). adv. bk.rev. abstr.; bibl. index. back issues avail.; reprint service avail. from PSC. **Document type:** *Journal, Academic/Scholarly.* **Description:** Provides a source for original investigations in clinical neurology, and related basic research.
Former titles (until 1974): Zeitschrift fuer Neurologie (0012-1037); (until 1970): Deutsche Zeitschrift fuer Nervenheilkunde (0367-004X)
Related titles: Microfiche ed.: (from BHP); Microform ed.: (from PQC); Online - full text ed.: ISSN 1432-1459 (from IngentaConnect); ◆ Supplement(s): Journal of Neurology. Supplement. ISSN 0939-1517.
Indexed: A01, A03, A08, A20, A22, A26, A36, ASCA, Agr, B21, B25, BIOSIS Prev, CA, CABA, ChemAb, CurCont, DentInd, E-psyche, E01, E08, E12, EMBASE, ExcerpMed, FR, G08, GH, H11, H12, I05, IBR, IBZ, ISR, IndMed, Inpharma, JW-N, MEDLINE, MycolAb, N02, N03, NSA, NSCI, P20, P22, P30, P33, P35, P39, P48, P54, PN&I, PQC, R08, R10, R12, RM&VM, Reac, S09, SCI, SCOPUS, T02, T05, W07.
—BLDSC (5021.584000), CASDDS, GNLM, IE, Infotrieve, Ingenta, INIST. **CCC.**
Published by: (European Neurological Society), Dr. Dietrich Steinkopff Verlag (Subsidiary of: Springer Science+Business Media), Tiergartenstr 17, Heidelberg, 69121, Germany. TEL 49-6221-4878821, FAX 49-6221-4878830, info.steinkopff@springer.com, http://www.steinkopff.com. Ed. Dr. T Brandt TEL 49-89-70952570. adv.: B&W page EUR 1,400, color page EUR 2,480; trim 210 x 279. Circ: 3,500 (paid and controlled). **Subscr. in the Americas to:** Springer New York LLC, Journal Fulfillment, PO Box 2485, Secaucus, NJ 07096. TEL 800-777-4643, 201-348-4033, FAX 201-348-4505, journals-ny@springer.com; **Subscr. to:** Springer Distribution Center, Kundenservice Zeitschriften, Haberstr 7, Heidelberg 69126, Germany. TEL 49-6221-3454303, FAX 49-6221-3454229.
Co-sponsor: Deutsche Gesellschaft fuer Neurologie.

616.8 USA ISSN 2155-9562

▼ ➤ **JOURNAL OF NEUROLOGY & NEUROPHYSIOLOGY.** Text in English. 2010 (Oct.). bi-m. free (effective 2011). **Document type:** *Journal, Academic/Scholarly.* **Description:** Provides research on the mechanism and treatment of diseases of the human nervous system, neurology, neurophysiology, and neuroscience.
Media: Online - full text.
Published by: Omics Publishing Group, 5716 Corse Ave, Ste 110, Westlake, Los Angeles, CA 91362. TEL 650-268-9744, 800-216-6499, info@omicsonline.com, http://www.omicsonline.com.

616.8 ESP ISSN 2171-6625

▼ **JOURNAL OF NEUROLOGY AND NEUROSCIENCE.** Text in English. 2010. bi-m. price varies. back issues avail. **Document type:** *Journal, Academic/Scholarly.* **Description:** Considers articles concerned with any aspect of clinical neurosciences such as neurology, psyciatry and neurosurgery, as well as basic research on neuroscience.
Media: Online - full text.
Indexed: A01.
Published by: Internet Medical Publishing info@imedpub.com, http://imedpubjournals.ning.com/. Ed. Jesus Porta-Etessam.

616.8 GBR ISSN 0022-3050
RC321 CODEN: JNNPAV

➤ **JOURNAL OF NEUROLOGY, NEUROSURGERY AND PSYCHIATRY**; an international peer-reviewed journal for health professionals and researchers in all areas of neurology and neurosurgery. Abbreviated title: J N N P. Text in English. 1921. m. GBP 688 to institutions; GBP 853 combined subscription to institutions small FTE (print & online eds.) (effective 2011); subscr. includes Practical Neurology and Journal of NeuroInterventional Surgery. adv. bk.rev. abstr.; bibl.; illus. index. back issues avail.; reprints avail. **Document type:** *Journal, Academic/Scholarly.* **Description:** Focuses on clinical neurology, neurosurgery, neuropsychology, neuropsychiatry, and closely related experimental work.
Former titles (until 1944): Journal of Neurology and Psychiatry (0368-329X); (until 1938): Journal of Neurology and Psychopathology (0266-8637)
Related titles: CD-ROM ed.; Microform ed.: (from PQC); Online - full text ed.: J N N P Online. ISSN 1468-330X. 1997. GBP 677 to institutions small FTE (effective 2011); ◆ Supplement(s): Practical Neurology. ISSN 1474-7758; ◆ Neurology In Practice. ISSN 1473-7086.
Indexed: A01, A03, A08, A20, A22, A26, A36, AMED, ASCA, B21, B25, BDM&CN, BIOBASE, BIOSIS Prev, C06, C07, C08, CA, CABA, CINAHL, ChemAb, CurCont, DentInd, DiabCont, DokArb, E-psyche, E01, E08, E12, EMBASE, ESPM, ExcerpMed, FR, G08, GH, H11, H12, H17, I05, IABS, INI, ISR, IndMed, Inpharma, JW-N, JW-P, LT, MEDLINE, MycolAb, N02, N03, NSA, NSCI, P03, P20, P22, P24, P25, P26, P30, P33, P35, P39, P48, P54, PN&I, PQC, PsycInfo, PsycholAb, R08, R10, R12, RILM, RM&VM, RRTA, Reac, S09, SCI, SCOPUS, T02, T05, ToxAb, W07, W10.
—BLDSC (5021.600000), CASDDS, GNLM, IE, Infotrieve, Ingenta, INIST. **CCC.**
Published by: B M J Group, BMA House, Tavistock Sq, London, WC1H 9JR, United Kingdom. TEL 44-20-73836373, FAX 44-20-73836668, http://group.bmj.com. Ed. Matthew Kiernan. Pub. Janet O'Flaherty TEL 44-20-73836154. Adv. contact Nick Gray TEL 44-20-73836386. Circ: 2,175. **Subscr. to:** PO Box 299, London WC1H 9TD, United Kingdom. TEL 44-20-73836270, FAX 44-20-73836402, support@bmjgroup.com.

616.8 CAN ISSN 1923-2845

▼ ➤ **JOURNAL OF NEUROLOGY RESEARCH.** Text in English. 2011. bi-m. **Document type:** *Journal, Academic/Scholarly.*
Related titles: Online - full text ed.: ISSN 1923-2853. free (effective 2011).
Published by: Elmer Press, 8485 Rue Outaouais, Brossard, Montreal, PQ J4Y 3E2, Canada. TEL 514-467-3868, FAX 450-812-3126, http://www.elmerpress.com/.

616.8 DEU ISSN 0939-1517
CODEN: JNSUE

JOURNAL OF NEUROLOGY. SUPPLEMENT. Text in German. 1985. irreg. price varies. **Document type:** *Monographic series, Academic/Scholarly.*
Related titles: ◆ Supplement to: Journal of Neurology. ISSN 0340-5354.
Indexed: E-psyche, SCOPUS.
—INIST. **CCC.**
Published by: Springer (Subsidiary of: Springer Science+Business Media), Tiergartenstr 17, Heidelberg, 69121, Germany. TEL 49-6221-4870, FAX 49-6221-345229, subscriptions@springer.com, http://www.springer.com.

616.8 658 USA ISSN 2151-3252

▼ ➤ **JOURNAL OF NEUROMARKETING.** Text in English. forthcoming 2011 (Jan.). q. USD 900 (effective 2011). **Document type:** *Journal, Academic/Scholarly.* **Description:** Features neuromarketing research and data, including the use of neurophysiological signals to determine interest in products, advertisements, and individuals.
Media: Online - full text.
Published by: Kaiser Peer Publishing, PO Box 734, Churchville, NY 14428. TEL 585-393-1464, davidkaiser@spiritualneuroscience.org, http://brainandcosmos.com/info.htm.

616.8 616.96 USA ISSN 2090-2344

▼ ➤ **JOURNAL OF NEUROPARASITOLOGY.** Text in English. 2010. q. EUR 300 (effective 2010). **Document type:** *Journal, Academic/Scholarly.*
Related titles: Online - full text ed.: ISSN 2090-2352. free (effective 2011).
Indexed: A01, A34, A36, P33, T02, T05.
Published by: Ashdin Publishing, 147-29 182nd St, Springfield Gardens, NY 11413. info@ashdin.com. Eds. David C Spray, Herbert B Tanowitz.

616.8 USA ISSN 0022-3069
RC321 CODEN: JNENAD

➤ **JOURNAL OF NEUROPATHOLOGY AND EXPERIMENTAL NEUROLOGY.** Abbreviated title: J N E N. Text in English. 1942. m. USD 526 domestic to institutions; USD 580 foreign to institutions (effective 2011). bk.rev. abstr.; bibl.; charts; illus. cum.index: vol.1-15 (1942-1956); vol.16-25 (1957-1966). back issues avail.; reprints avail. **Document type:** *Journal, Academic/Scholarly.* **Description:** Brings out articles on neuropathology and experimental neurology, book reviews, letters and association news.
Related titles: Microform ed.: (from PQC); Online - full text ed.: ISSN 1554-6578.
Indexed: A22, A34, A35, A36, ASCA, ASFA, AgBio, B21, B25, BDM&CN, BIOBASE, BIOSIS Prev, CABA, CIN, ChemAb, ChemTitl, CurCont, E-psyche, E12, EMBASE, ESPM, ExcerpMed, GH, IABS, IBR, IBZ, ISR, IndMed, IndVet, Inpharma, JW-N, MEDLINE, MycolAb, N02, N03, NSA, NSCI, P03, P20, P22, P26, P30, P33, P39, P48, P54, PQC, PsycInfo, R08, R10, RM&VM, Reac, SCI, SCOPUS, T05, THA, VS, VirolAbstr, W07.
—BLDSC (5021.700000), CASDDS, GNLM, IE, Infotrieve, Ingenta, INIST. **CCC.**
Published by: (American Association of Neuropathologists, Inc.), Lippincott Williams & Wilkins (Subsidiary of: Wolters Kluwer N.V.), Two Commerce Sq, 2001 Market St, Philadelphia, PA 19103. TEL 215-521-8300, FAX 215-521-8902, customerservice@lww.com, http://www.lww.com. Ed. Raymond A Sobel TEL 650-852-3279. Circ: 740.

➤ **JOURNAL OF NEUROPHYSIOLOGY.** *see* BIOLOGY—Physiology

616.8 USA ISSN 2150-2773

▼ **JOURNAL OF NEUROPLASTICITY AND NEUROMODULATION.** Text in English. 2011 (Feb.). q. USD 900 (effective 2011). **Document type:** *Journal, Academic/Scholarly.* **Description:** Publishes new research and clinical studies on brain function changes in response to experience and maturation. Studies include brain-based operant conditioning, energy disruption or entrainment techniques, and other neuromodulatory technologies.
Media: Online - full text.
Published by: Kaiser Peer Publishing, PO Box 734, Churchville, NY 14428. TEL 585-393-1464, davidkaiser@spiritualneuroscience.org, http://brainandcosmos.com/info.htm.

616.8 USA ISSN 0895-0172
RC321 CODEN: JNCNE7

➤ **THE JOURNAL OF NEUROPSYCHIATRY AND CLINICAL NEUROSCIENCES.** Text in English. 1989. q. USD 208 combined subscription domestic to individuals (print & online eds.); USD 313 combined subscription foreign to individuals (print & online eds.); USD 459 combined subscription domestic to institutions (print & online eds.); USD 496 combined subscription foreign to institutions (print & online eds.) (effective 2011). adv. bk.rev. abstr.; bibl.; charts; illus.; stat. index. Supplement avail.; back issues avail.; reprints avail. **Document type:** *Journal, Academic/Scholarly.* **Description:** Designed to develop diagnosis and treatment for patients with neuropsychiatric disorders.
Related titles: Microform ed.: (from PQC); Online - full text ed.: ISSN 1545-7222. USD 187 to individuals (effective 2011).
Indexed: A20, A22, ASCA, B21, CIN, ChemAb, ChemTitl, CurCont, E-psyche, EMBASE, ExcerpMed, FR, ISR, IndMed, Inpharma, JW-P, MEDLINE, NSA, NSCI, P03, P20, P22, P25, P30, P35, P48, P54, PQC, PsycInfo, PsycholAb, R10, Reac, SCI, SCOPUS, SWR&A, W07.
—BLDSC (5022.040000), CASDDS, GNLM, IE, Infotrieve, Ingenta, INIST. **CCC.**
Published by: (American Neuropsychiatric Association), American Psychiatric Publishing, Inc., 1000 Wilson Blvd, Ste 1825, Arlington, VA 22209. TEL 703-907-7888, 800-368-5777, FAX 703-907-1092, appi@psych.org, http://www.appi.org. Eds. Dr. Stuart C Yudofsky, Michael D Roy. Adv. contact Valentin Torres TEL 212-904-0375. **Subscr. to:** PO Box 97250, Washington, DC 20090.

616.8 150 GBR ISSN 1748-6645
QP360

➤ **JOURNAL OF NEUROPSYCHOLOGY.** Text in English. 2007 (Mar.). s-a. GBP 158 in United Kingdom to institutions; EUR 213 in Europe to institutions; USD 264 elsewhere to institutions; GBP 193 combined subscription in United Kingdom to institutions (print & online eds.); EUR 260 combined subscription in Europe to institutions (print & online eds.); USD 323 combined subscription elsewhere to institutions (print & online eds.) (effective 2012). adv. back issues avail.; reprint service avail. from PSC. **Document type:** *Journal, Academic/Scholarly.* **Description:** Covers topics that reflect the multidisciplinary character of the field and include clinical and research studies with neurological, psychiatric, and psychological patient populations in all age groups using different methodologies including single-case and group studies, pharmacology, neurophysiology and (functional) neuroimaging.
Related titles: Online - full text ed.: ISSN 1748-6653. GBP 168 in United Kingdom to institutions; EUR 226 in Europe to institutions; USD 280 elsewhere to institutions (effective 2012).
Indexed: A01, A22, CA, CurCont, E01, EMBASE, ExcerpMed, L&LBA, MEDLINE, P03, P30, PsycInfo, R10, Reac, SCI, SCOPUS, SSCI, T02, W07.
—BLDSC (5022.045000), IE, Ingenta. **CCC.**
Published by: (The British Psychological Society), John Wiley & Sons Ltd. (Subsidiary of: John Wiley & Sons, Inc.), 9600 Garsington Rd, Oxford, OX4 2DQ, United Kingdom. TEL 44-1865-776868, FAX 44-1865-714591, customer@wiley.co.uk, http://www.wiley.com. Ed. Edward de Haan. adv.: page GBP 220; trim 174 x 247.

616.8 USA ISSN 0270-6474
QP351 CODEN: JNRSDS

➤ **THE JOURNAL OF NEUROSCIENCE.** Text in English. 1981. w. USD 1,155 combined subscription domestic to non-members (print & online eds.); USD 1,361 combined subscription foreign to non-members (print & online eds.); free to members (effective 2010). illus. Index. back issues avail.; reprints avail. **Document type:** *Journal, Academic/Scholarly.* **Description:** Offers readers rapid access to the most exciting advances occuring across the full spectrum of modern neuroscience.
Related titles: Microfiche ed.: (from PQC); Microfilm ed.: (from PQC); Online - full text ed.: ISSN 1529-2401.
Indexed: A01, A03, A08, A20, A22, A34, A35, A36, A38, ASCA, ASFA, AgBio, AnBeAb, B&AI, B04, B10, B21, B25, BIOBASE, BIOSIS Prev, C33, CA, CABA, CRFR, ChemAb, ChemTitl, ChemoAb, CompAb, CurCont, DentInd, E-psyche, E12, EMBASE, ESPM, ExcerpMed, F08, F11, F12, GH, H16, H17, IABS, IBR, IBZ, ISR, IndMed, IndVet, Inpharma, JW-P, MEDLINE, MycolAb, N02, N03, N05, NSA, NSCI, P03, P30, P32, P33, P37, PsycInfo, PsycholAb, R07, R08, R10, RA&MP, RILM, RM&VM, Reac, S12, S13, S16, SCI, SCOPUS, T02, THA, ToxAb, VS, VirolAbstr, W07, W08, W10.
—BLDSC (5022.075000), CASDDS, GNLM, IE, Infotrieve, Ingenta, INIST. **CCC.**
Published by: Society for Neuroscience, 1121 14th St, NW, Ste 1010, Washington, DC 20005. TEL 202-962-4000, FAX 202-962-4941, info@sfn.org, http://www.sfn.org. Ed. John H R Maunsell.

616.89 NGA

➤ **JOURNAL OF NEUROSCIENCE AND BEHAVIORAL HEALTH.** Text in English. m. free (effective 2010). adv. **Document type:** *Journal, Academic/Scholarly.*
Media: Online - full text.
Published by: Academic Journals, PO Box 73023, Victoria Island, Lagos, Nigeria. service@academicjournals.org. Eds. Dr. Amado F Hernandez, Bechan Sharma, Seter Siziya.

616.8 NLD ISSN 0165-0270
CODEN: JNMEDT

➤ **JOURNAL OF NEUROSCIENCE METHODS.** Text in English. 1979. 18/yr. EUR 5,112 in Europe to institutions; JPY 678,700 in Japan to institutions; USD 5,718 elsewhere to institutions (effective 2012). adv. charts; abstr.; bibl.; illus. back issues avail.; reprints avail. **Document type:** *Journal, Academic/Scholarly.* **Description:** Publishes research papers and critical reviews addressing new methods or significant developments of recognized methods.
Related titles: Microform ed.: (from PQC); Online - full text ed.: ISSN 1872-678X (from IngentaConnect, ScienceDirect).
Indexed: A01, A03, A08, A22, A26, A34, A35, A36, A37, A38, ASCA, AgBio, B&BAb, B19, B21, B25, BIOBASE, BIOSIS Prev, CA, CABA, CIN, CMCI, CTA, ChemAb, ChemTitl, CurCont, E-psyche, E12, EMBASE, ExcerpMed, GH, I05, IABS, ISR, IndMed, IndVet, Inpharma, Inspec, MEDLINE, MycolAb, N02, N03, N04, N05, NSA, NSCI, NucAcAb, P30, P37, PN&I, R07, R10, RILM, Reac, S12, S13, S16, SCI, SCOPUS, T02, VS, W07.
—BLDSC (5022.080000), AskIEEE, CASDDS, GNLM, IE, Infotrieve, Ingenta, INIST. **CCC.**
Published by: Elsevier BV (Subsidiary of: Elsevier Science & Technology), Radarweg 29, PO Box 211, Amsterdam, 1000 AE, Netherlands. TEL 31-20-4853911, FAX 31-20-4852457, JournalsCustomerServiceEMEA@elsevier.com, http://www.elsevier.nl. Eds. Greg A Gerhardt, Vincenzo Crunelli.

616.8 USA ISSN 0360-4012
QP351 CODEN: JNREDK

➤ **JOURNAL OF NEUROSCIENCE RESEARCH.** Abbreviated title: J N R. Text in English. 1975. 16/yr. GBP 7,370 in United Kingdom to institutions; EUR 9,319 in Europe to institutions; USD 14,108 in United States to institutions; USD 14,332 in Canada & Mexico to institutions; USD 14,444 elsewhere to institutions; GBP 8,478 combined subscription in United Kingdom to institutions (print & online eds.); EUR 10,719 combined subscription in Europe to institutions (print & online eds.); USD 16,225 combined subscription in United States to institutions (print & online eds.); USD 16,449 combined subscription in Canada & Mexico to institutions (print & online eds.); USD 16,561 combined subscription elsewhere to institutions (print & online eds.) (effective 2012). adv. bk.rev. charts; illus. index. back issues avail.; reprint service avail. from PSC. **Document type:** *Journal, Academic/Scholarly.* **Description:** Concerned with basic research reports on molecular, cellular, and subcellular aspects of the neurosciences.
Related titles: Microform ed.: (from PQC); Online - full text ed.: ISSN 1097-4547. GBP 7,199 in United Kingdom to institutions; EUR 9,102 in Europe to institutions; USD 14,108 elsewhere to institutions (effective 2012).
Indexed: A20, A22, A34, A35, A36, A38, ASCA, AgBio, AnBeAb, B21, B25, BIOBASE, BIOSIS Prev, C30, C33, CABA, CTA, ChemAb, ChemTitl, ChemoAb, CurCont, D01, E-psyche, EMBASE, ESPM, ExcerpMed, GH, H16, IABS, ISR, IndMed, IndVet, Inpharma, MEDLINE, MycolAb, N02, N03, N04, N05, NSA, NSCI, P03, P30, P32, P37, P40, PsycInfo, R10, RA&MP, Reac, S13, S16, SCI, SCOPUS, T05, THA, ToxAb, VS, W07, WildRev.
—BLDSC (5022.090000), CASDDS, GNLM, IE, Infotrieve, Ingenta, INIST. **CCC.**
Published by: John Wiley & Sons, Inc., 111 River St, Hoboken, NJ 07030. TEL 201-748-6000, FAX 201-748-6088, info@wiley.com, http://www.wiley.com/WileyCDA/. Ed. Jean de Vellis. Pub., Adv. contact Kim Thompkins TEL 212-850-6921. **Subscr. outside the Americas to:** John Wiley & Sons Ltd., The Atrium, Southern Gate, Chichester, West Sussex PO19 8SQ, United Kingdom. TEL 44-1243-779777, 800-243407, FAX 44-1243-775878, cs-journals@wiley.com.

616.8 IND ISSN 0976-3147
▼ **JOURNAL OF NEUROSCIENCES IN RURAL PRACTICE.** Text in English. 2010. s-a. **Document type:** *Journal, Academic/Scholarly.*
Related titles: Online - full text ed.: ISSN 0976-3155. free (effective 2011).
Indexed: A01, P10, P48, P53, P54, PQC.
—**CCC.**
Published by: Medknow Publications and Media Pvt. Ltd., B-9, Kanara Business Ctr, Off Link Rd, Ghatkopar (E), Mumbai, Maharastra 400 075, India. TEL 91-22-66491818, FAX 91-22-66491817, journals@medknow.com, http://www.medknow.com. Ed. Amit Agrawal.

616.8 USA ISSN 0022-3085
RD1 CODEN: JONSAC
➤ **JOURNAL OF NEUROSURGERY.** Text in English. 1944. m. USD 875 combined subscription domestic to institutions (print & online eds.); USD 985 combined subscription foreign to institutions (print & online eds.) (effective 2010); subscr. includes Journal of Neurosurgery: Spine, Journal of Neurosurgery: Pediatrics. adv. bk.rev. bibl.; charts; illus. cum.index covering 50 vols. back issues avail.; reprints avail. **Document type:** *Journal, Academic/Scholarly.* **Description:** Presents medical articles relating to neurosurgery and allied specialties.
Related titles: CD-ROM ed.; Microform ed.: (from PQC); Online - full text ed.: ISSN 1933-0693; ◆ Supplement(s): Journal of Neurosurgery: Spine. ISSN 1547-5654; ◆ Journal of Neurosurgery: Pediatrics. ISSN 1933-0707.
Indexed: A20, A22, AIM, ASCA, B&BAb, B21, B25, BIOBASE, BIOSIS Prev, CIN, ChemAb, ChemTitl, CurCont, DentInd, E-psyche, EMBASE, ExcerpMed, IABS, INI, INIS AtomInd, ISR, IndMed, Inpharma, JW-N, MEDLINE, MycolAb, NSCI, P30, P35, R10, Reac, SCI, SCOPUS, W07.
—BLDSC (5022.100000), CASDDS, GNLM, IE, Infotrieve, Ingenta, INIST. **CCC.**
Published by: American Association of Neurological Surgeons, 5550 Meadowbrook Dr, Rolling Meadows, IL 60008. TEL 847-378-0500, FAX 847-378-0600, info@aans.org, http://www.aans.org. Ed. Dr. John A Jane TEL 434-924-5503. Adv. contact Greg Pessagno TEL 443-512-8899 ext 109. Circ: 9,270.

616.8 USA ISSN 1933-0707
JOURNAL OF NEUROSURGERY: PEDIATRICS. Text in English. 1944. m. includes with subscr. to Journal of Neurosurgery, Journal of Neurosurgery: Spine. adv. back issues avail.; reprints avail. **Document type:** *Journal, Academic/Scholarly.* **Description:** Devoted to the publication of original works relating primarily to neurosurgery, including studies in clinical neurophysiology, organic neurology, ophthalmology, radiology, pathology, and molecular biology.
Supersedes in part (in 2004): Journal of Neurosurgery (0022-3085)
Related titles: Online - full text ed.: ISSN 1933-0715; ◆ Supplement to: Journal of Neurosurgery. ISSN 0022-3085.
Indexed: BIOBASE, C06, C07, CurCont, EMBASE, ExcerpMed, IABS, MEDLINE, P30, R10, Reac, SCI, SCOPUS, W07.
—BLDSC (5022.120000), INIST.
Published by: American Association of Neurological Surgeons, 5550 Meadowbrook Dr, Rolling Meadows, IL 60008. TEL 847-378-0500, FAX 847-378-0600, info@aans.org, http://www.aans.org. Ed. Dr. John A Jane TEL 434-924-5503. Adv. contact Greg Pessagno TEL 443-512-8899 ext 109.

JOURNAL OF NEUROSURGERY: SPINE. *see* MEDICAL SCIENCES—Surgery

JOURNAL OF NEUROSURGICAL SCIENCES; a journal on neurosurgery. *see* MEDICAL SCIENCES—Surgery

616.8 USA ISSN 2150-2757
▼ ➤ **JOURNAL OF NEUROTHERAPY (CHURCHVILLE).** Text in English. forthcoming 2011. q. **Document type:** *Journal, Academic/Scholarly.* **Description:** Covers advances in neuromodulatory therapies.
Media: Online - full content.
Published by: Kaiser Peer Publishing, PO Box 734, Churchville, NY 14428. TEL 585-393-1464, davidkaiser@spiritualneuroscience.org.

616.8 USA ISSN 1087-4208
CODEN: JNOEA2
JOURNAL OF NEUROTHERAPY (PHILADELPHIA). Text in English. 1995. q. GBP 354 combined subscription in United Kingdom to institutions (print & online eds.); EUR 459, USD 466 combined subscription to institutions (print & online eds.) (effective 2012). adv. reprint service avail. from PSC. **Document type:** *Journal, Academic/Scholarly.* **Description:** Provides an integrated multi-disciplinary perspective on clinically relevant research, treatment, and public policy for neurotherapy.
Related titles: Online - full text ed.: ISSN 1530-017X. GBP 318 in United Kingdom to institutions; EUR 413, USD 419 to institutions (effective 2012).
Indexed: A01, A03, A22, ASSIA, B&BAb, B19, B21, C06, C07, C08, CA, CINAHL, E-psyche, E01, EMBASE, ExcerpMed, Inspec, NSA, P03, P30, P48, PQC, PsycInfo, PsycholAb, R10, Reac, S02, S03, SCOPUS, SWR&A, T02.
—BLDSC (5022.260000), IE, Ingenta. **CCC.**
Published by: (International Society for Neuronal Regulation), Routledge (Subsidiary of: Taylor & Francis Group), 325 Chestnut St, Ste 800, Philadelphia, PA 19106. TEL 215-625-8900, 800-354-1420, FAX 215-625-8914, journals@routledge.com, http://www.routledge.com. Ed. Johanne Levesque. adv.: B&W page USD 750, color page USD 1,000; trim 4.375 x 7.125. Circ: 546 (paid).

JOURNAL OF NEUROTRAUMA. *see* MEDICAL SCIENCES—Orthopedics And Traumatology

616.8 USA ISSN 1355-0284
RC359.5 CODEN: JNVIFK
➤ **JOURNAL OF NEUROVIROLOGY.** Text in English. 1995. bi-m. EUR 837, USD 1,030 combined subscription to institutions (print & online eds.) (effective 2012). adv. back issues avail.; reprint service avail. from PSC. **Document type:** *Journal, Academic/Scholarly.* **Description:** Studies neurotropic viruses and viral infections of the nervous system.
Related titles: Online - full text ed.: ISSN 1538-2443 (from IngentaConnect).
Indexed: A01, A03, A08, A22, A34, A35, A36, AIDS&CR, ASCA, AgBio, B21, B25, BIOSIS Prev, CA, CABA, ChemAb, ChemTitl, CurCont, E-psyche, E01, E12, EMBASE, ExcerpMed, F08, GH, IndMed, IndVet, Inpharma, MEDLINE, MycolAb, N02, N03, NSA, NSCI, P03, P30, P33, P35, P39, PN&I, PsycInfo, R08, R10, R12, RA&MP, RM&VM, Reac, SCI, SCOPUS, T02, T05, TAR, TriticAb, VS, ViroIAbstr, W07.
—CASDDS, GNLM, IE, Infotrieve, Ingenta, INIST. **CCC.**
Published by: Springer New York LLC (Subsidiary of: Springer Science+Business Media), 233 Spring St, New York, NY 10013. TEL 212-460-1500, FAX 212-460-1575, journals@springer-ny.com. Ed. Kamel Khalili.

616.8 616.027 USA ISSN 2151-3260
▼ ➤ **JOURNAL OF NORMATIVE ELECTROENCEPHALOGRAPHY.** Text in English. forthcoming 2011 (Jan.). q. USD 900 (effective 2011). **Document type:** *Journal, Academic/Scholarly.* **Description:** Focuses on findings in normative EEG analysis, methodology, and technology.
Media: Online - full text.
Published by: Kaiser Peer Publishing, PO Box 734, Churchville, NY 14428. TEL 585-393-1464, davidkaiser@spiritualneuroscience.org, http://brainandcosmos.com/info.htm.

616.8 USA ISSN 0022-3298
RZ460
➤ **THE JOURNAL OF ORGONOMY.** Text in English. 1967. s-a. USD 49.95 domestic; USD 64.95 foreign; USD 59.95 combined subscription domestic (print & online eds.); USD 74.95 combined subscription foreign (print & online eds.) (effective 2010). bk.rev. bibl.; charts; illus.; stat. index, cum.index: 1967-1995. back issues avail.; reprints avail. **Document type:** *Journal, Academic/Scholarly.* **Description:** Devoted to the study of orgone energy functions in living and nonliving nature, based on the discoveries of Wilhelm Reich.
Related titles: Online - full text ed.: USD 29.95 (effective 2010) (from PQC).
Indexed: E-psyche, MLA-IB.
—Ingenta.
Published by: American College of Orgonomy, PO Box 490, Princeton, NJ 08542. TEL 732-821-1144, FAX 732-821-0174, aco@orgonomy.orgaco@orgonomy.org. Ed. Charles Konia.

616.89 CAN ISSN 0834-4825
CODEN: JORMEI
JOURNAL OF ORTHOMOLECULAR MEDICINE. Text in English. 1968. q. CAD 79 domestic; USD 70 in United States; USD 100 elsewhere (effective 2011). adv. bk.rev. bibl.; charts; illus. back issues avail.; reprints avail. **Document type:** *Journal, Academic/Scholarly.* **Description:** Publishes editorials, clinician's letters, short communications, original research, brief reports, case reports/series, synthesis papers, review articles, viewpoints/opinion pieces, and educational articles. Covers orthomolecular medicine for practitioners, scholars, and students.
Former titles (until 1985): Journal of Orthomolecular Psychiatry (0317-0209); (until 1973): Orthomolecular Psychiatry (0317-0217); (until 1971): Schizophrenia (0036-6129); (until 1969): Journal of Schizophrenia (0449-3109)
Related titles: Microform ed.: (from PQC); Online - full text ed.
Indexed: A04, A20, A22, AMED, C05, CA, ChemAb, E-psyche, EMBASE, ExcerpMed, MEA&I, P03, PsycholAb, R10, Reac, SCOPUS, T02.
—BLDSC (5027.600000), CASDDS, GNLM, IE, Infotrieve, Ingenta, INIST. **CCC.**
Published by: (Canadian Society for Orthomolecular Medicine, International Society for Orthomolecular Medicine), International Schizophrenia Foundation, 16 Florence Ave., Toronto, ON M2N 1E9, Canada. TEL 416-733-2117, FAX 416-733-2352, centre@orthomed.org, http://www.orthomed.org/isom/isom.html. Ed. Jonathan E. Prousky. Circ: 1,400.

616 USA ISSN 1526-5900
RB127 CODEN: JPOAB5
➤ **THE JOURNAL OF PAIN.** Text in English. 1992. m. USD 599 in United States to institutions; USD 750 elsewhere to institutions (effective 2012). adv. back issues avail.; reprints avail. **Document type:** *Journal, Academic/Scholarly.* **Description:** Features scholarly discussion of issues of interest to practitioners and researchers in the field of pain management. Publishes hypotheses on basic scientific and clinical topics and critiques of those hypotheses.
Former titles (until 2000): Pain Forum (1082-3174); (until 1995): A P S Journal (1058-9139)
Related titles: Online - full text ed.: ISSN 1528-8447. 2000 (from ScienceDirect).
Indexed: A20, A22, A26, ASCA, C06, C07, C08, CA, CINAHL, CurCont, E-psyche, E01, EMBASE, ExcerpMed, H12, I05, Inpharma, MEDLINE, NSCI, P03, P30, P35, PsycInfo, PsycholAb, R10, Reac, SCI, SCOPUS, T02, W07.
—BLDSC (5027.785000), GNLM, IE, Ingenta. **CCC.**
Published by: (American Pain Society), Churchill Livingstone (Subsidiary of: Elsevier Health Sciences), 1600 John F Kennedy Blvd, Ste 1800, Philadelphia, PA 19103. TEL 215-239-3900, 800-523-1649, FAX 215-239-3990, JournalsOnlineSupport-usa@elsevier.com, http://www.us.elsevierhealth.com. Ed. Mark P Jensen. Pub. Jane Grochowski TEL 215-239-3714.

616.88 USA ISSN 0885-3924
RB127
➤ **JOURNAL OF PAIN AND SYMPTOM MANAGEMENT.** Text in English. 1982. m. USD 1,110 in United States to institutions; USD 1,235 elsewhere to institutions (effective 2012). adv. bk.rev. index. Supplement avail.; back issues avail.; reprints avail. **Document type:** *Journal, Academic/Scholarly.* **Description:** Provides a forum for the publication of the clinical research and practices related to the relief of illness burden among patients afflicted with serious or life-threatening illness.
Formerly (until 1986): P R N Forum (0743-345X)
Related titles: Microform ed.: (from PQC); Online - full text ed.: ISSN 1873-6513 (from IngentaConnect, ScienceDirect).
Indexed: A01, A03, A08, A20, A22, A26, AMED, ASCA, ASG, ASSIA, B28, BIOBASE, C06, C07, C08, CA, CDA, CINAHL, CurCont, DBA, E-psyche, EMBASE, ExcerpMed, FR, FamI, H12, I05, IABS, IDIS, INI, IndMed, Inpharma, MEDLINE, NSCI, NurAb, P03, P30, P35, PsycInfo, PsycholAb, R10, Reac, SCI, SCOPUS, SociolAb, T02, W07.
—BLDSC (5027.790000), GNLM, IE, Infotrieve, Ingenta, INIST. **CCC.**
Published by: (University Of Wisconsin At Madison, Department of Anesthesiology, American Academy of Hospice & Palliative Medicine), Elsevier Inc. (Subsidiary of: Elsevier Science & Technology), 1600 John F Kennedy Blvd, Philadelphia, PA 19103. TEL 215-239-3900, FAX 215-238-7883, JournalCustomerService-usa@elsevier.com, http://www.elsevier.com. Ed. Dr. Russell K Portenoy TEL 212-844-1460. Pub. Jane Grochowski TEL 215-239-3714. Circ: 4,450.

616.83 NLD ISSN 1877-7171
▼ **JOURNAL OF PARKINSON'S DISEASE.** Text in English. 2011. q. USD 776 combined subscription in North America to institutions (print & online eds.); EUR 555 combined subscription elsewhere to institutions (print & online eds.) (effective 2012). **Document type:** *Journal, Academic/Scholarly.* **Description:** Provides a forum for research in basic science, translational research and clinical medicine that will expedite the fundamental understanding and improve the treatment of Parkinson's disease.
Related titles: Online - full text ed.: ISSN 1877-718X.
Published by: I O S Press, Nieuwe Hemweg 6B, Amsterdam, 1013 BG, Netherlands. TEL 31-20-6883355, FAX 31-20-6870019, info@iospress.nl, http://www.iospress.nl. Eds. J William Langston, Patrik Brundin.

616.853 618.92 NLD ISSN 2146-457X
▼ ➤ **JOURNAL OF PEDIATRIC EPILEPSY.** Text in English. 2011. q. USD 376 combined subscription in North America (print & online eds.); EUR 270 combined subscription elsewhere (print & online eds.) (effective 2012). bk.rev. **Document type:** *Journal, Academic/Scholarly.* **Description:** Covers all topics related to epilepsy and seizure disorders in childhood.
Related titles: Online - full text ed.: ISSN 2146-4588.
Published by: (World Society of Child Science TUR), I O S Press, Nieuwe Hemweg 6B, Amsterdam, 1013 BG, Netherlands. TEL 31-20-6883355, FAX 31-20-6870019, info@iospress.nl, http://www.iospress.nl. Eds. Howard P Goodkin, Husein Caksen.

➤ **JOURNAL OF PEDIATRIC NEUROLOGY.** *see* MEDICAL SCIENCES—Pediatrics

616.8 618.92 IND ISSN 1817-1745
➤ **JOURNAL OF PEDIATRIC NEUROSCIENCES.** Text in English. 2006. s-a. INR 1,000 domestic; USD 100 foreign; INR 1,200 combined subscription domestic (print & online eds.); USD 120 combined subscription foreign (print & online eds.) (effective 2011). adv. **Document type:** *Journal, Academic/Scholarly.*
Related titles: Online - full text ed.: ISSN 1998-3948. INR 800 domestic; USD 80 foreign (effective 2011).
Indexed: A26, C06, C07, CA, E08, EMBASE, ExcerpMed, G08, H11, H12, I05, P10, P30, P48, P53, P54, PQC, R10, Reac, S09, SCOPUS, T02.
—IE. **CCC.**
Published by: (Indian Society for Pediatric Neurosurgery), Medknow Publications and Media Pvt. Ltd., B-9, Kanara Business Ctr, Off Link Rd, Ghatkopar (E), Mumbai, Maharastra 400 075, India. TEL 91-22-66491816, FAX 91-22-66491817, http://www.medknow.com.

➤ **THE JOURNAL OF PHYSIOLOGY.** *see* BIOLOGY—Physiology

612.8 FRA ISSN 0928-4257
QP1 CODEN: JHYSEM
➤ **JOURNAL OF PHYSIOLOGY (PARIS).** Text in English. 1899. 6/yr. EUR 828 in Europe to institutions; JPY 109,500 in Japan to institutions; USD 922 elsewhere to institutions (effective 2012). bk.rev. illus. index. back issues avail.; reprints avail. **Document type:** *Journal, Academic/Scholarly.* **Description:** Covers all aspects of neurobiology relevant to a better understanding of behavior and cognition and the integrative functions of the brain, with a focus on functional imaging, development and plasticity, cellular neurobiology, systems, behavioral and neuromuscular physiology, endocrinology, and cognition.
Formerly (until 1992): Journal de Physiologie (0021-7948)
Related titles: Microform ed.: (from PQC); Online - full text ed.: ISSN 1769-7115 (from IngentaConnect, ScienceDirect).
Indexed: A01, A03, A08, A20, A22, A26, A29, ASCA, ASFA, ApicAb, B20, B21, B25, BIOBASE, BIOSIS Prev, CA, CIN, CRFR, ChemAb, ChemTitl, DentInd, E-psyche, EMBASE, ESPM, ErgAb, ExcerpMed, H&SSA, I05, I10, IABS, ISR, IndMed, Inpharma, MEDLINE, MycolAb, NSCI, P30, PsycholAb, R10, Reac, SCI, SCOPUS, T02, ViroIAbstr, W07, WildRev.
—BLDSC (5039.020000), CASDDS, GNLM, IE, Infotrieve, Ingenta, INIST. **CCC.**
Published by: Elsevier Masson (Subsidiary of: Elsevier Health Sciences), 62 Rue Camille Desmoulins, Issy les Moulineaux, Cedex 92442, France. TEL 33-1-71165500, FAX 33-1-71165600, infos@elsevier-masson.fr, http://www.elsevier-masson.fr. Ed. Y Fregnac. Circ: 850.

616.8 USA ISSN 0742-3098
QP188.P55 CODEN: JPRSE9
➤ **JOURNAL OF PINEAL RESEARCH**; molecular, biological, physiological and clinical aspects of melatonin. Text in English. 1984. 8/yr. GBP 1,064 in United Kingdom to institutions; EUR 1,351 in Europe to institutions; USD 1,786 in the Americas to institutions; USD 2,084 elsewhere to institutions; GBP 1,171 combined subscription in United Kingdom to institutions (print & online eds.); EUR 1,487 combined subscription in Europe to institutions (print & online eds.); USD 1,965 combined subscription in the Americas to institutions (print & online eds.); USD 2,293 combined subscription elsewhere to institutions (print & online eds.) (effective 2010). adv. charts; illus. back issues avail.; reprint service avail. from PSC. **Document type:** *Journal, Academic/Scholarly.* **Description:** Forum for the original scientific results of basic, applied, and clinical research involving any aspect of the pineal gland or its hormonal products in all vertebrate species.
Related titles: Online - full text ed.: ISSN 1600-079X. GBP 1,064 in United Kingdom to institutions; EUR 1,351 in Europe to institutions; USD 1,786 in the Americas to institutions; USD 2,084 elsewhere to institutions (effective 2010) (from IngentaConnect).
Indexed: A01, A03, A08, A22, A26, A34, A35, A36, A38, ASCA, AgBio, B21, B25, BIOSIS Prev, C25, C30, C33, CA, CABA, CIN, ChemAb, ChemTitl, CurCont, D01, E-psyche, E01, E12, EMBASE, ExcerpMed, FCA, GH, H12, H16, H17, ISR, IndMed, IndVet, Inpharma, MEDLINE, MycolAb, N02, N03, N04, NSA, NSCI, O01, P03, P30, P32, P33, P35, P37, P39, P40, PGrRegA, PN&I, PsycInfo, R08, R10, R11, RA&MP, RM&VM, Reac, S17, SCI, SCOPUS, T02, T05, TAR, TriticAb, VS, W07, W10, Z01.

M

—BLDSC (5040.329000), CASDDS, GNLM, IE, Infotrieve, Ingenta, INIST. **CCC.**
Published by: Wiley-Blackwell Publishing, Inc. (Subsidiary of: Wiley-Blackwell Publishing Ltd.), Commerce Pl, 350 Main St, Malden, MA 02148. TEL 781-388-8200, FAX 781-388-8210, info@wiley.com, http://www.wiley.com/WileyCDA/. Ed. Russell J Reiter.

➤ **JOURNAL OF POLICY AND PRACTICE IN INTELLECTUAL DISABILITIES.** *see* HANDICAPPED

➤ **THE JOURNAL OF PRIMARY PREVENTION.** *see* PSYCHOLOGY

616.8 GBR ISSN 1351-0126
RC440 CODEN: JPMNE3

➤ **JOURNAL OF PSYCHIATRIC AND MENTAL HEALTH NURSING**; an international journal for researchers and practioners. Text in English. 1994. 10/yr. GBP 845 in United Kingdom to institutions; EUR 1,072 in Europe to institutions; USD 1,558 in the Americas to institutions; USD 1,821 elsewhere to institutions; GBP 973 combined subscription in United Kingdom to institutions (print & online eds.); EUR 1,233 combined subscription in Europe to institutions (print & online eds.); USD 1,792 combined subscription in the Americas to institutions (print & online eds.); USD 2,094 combined subscription elsewhere to institutions (print & online eds.) (effective 2012). adv. bk.rev. bibl.; illus. index. back issues avail.; reprint service avail. from PSC. **Document type:** *Journal, Academic/Scholarly.* **Description:** Publishes original articles that integrate the knowledge and practice of psychiatric and mental-health nursing.
Related titles: Microform ed.: (from PQC); ◆ Online - full text ed.: Journal of Psychiatric and Mental Health Nursing Online. ISSN 1365-2850.
Indexed: A01, A02, A03, A08, A20, A22, A26, ASG, B28, C06, C07, C08, C11, CA, CINAHL, CurCont, E-psyche, E01, EMBASE, ExcerpMed, F09, H04, H12, INI, MEDLINE, P03, P30, P34, PsycInfo, PsycholAb, R10, Reac, S02, S03, SCI, SCOPUS, SSCI, T02, W07.
—BLDSC (5043.140000), GNLM, IE, Infotrieve, Ingenta. **CCC.**
Published by: Wiley-Blackwell Publishing Ltd. (Subsidiary of: John Wiley & Sons, Inc.), 9600 Garsington Rd, Oxford, OX4 2DQ, United Kingdom. TEL 44-1865-776868, FAX 44-1865-714591, customerservices@blackwellpublishing.com. Ed. Dawn Freshwater. Adv. contact Joanna Baker TEL 44-1865-476271.

616.8 GBR ISSN 1365-2850

➤ **JOURNAL OF PSYCHIATRIC AND MENTAL HEALTH NURSING ONLINE.** Text in English. 1999. 10/yr. GBP 845 in United Kingdom to institutions; EUR 1,072 in Europe to institutions; USD 1,558 in the Americas to institutions; USD 1,821 elsewhere to institutions (effective 2012). adv. back issues avail. **Document type:** *Journal, Academic/Scholarly.* **Description:** Provides an international forum for the publication of original contributions that lead to the advancement of psychiatric and mental health nursing practice.
Media: Online - full text (from IngentaConnect). **Related titles:** Microform ed.: (from PQC); ◆ Print ed.: Journal of Psychiatric and Mental Health Nursing. ISSN 1351-0126.
—**CCC.**
Published by: Wiley-Blackwell Publishing Ltd. (Subsidiary of: John Wiley & Sons, Inc.), 9600 Garsington Rd, Oxford, OX4 2DQ, United Kingdom. TEL 44-1865-776868, FAX 44-1865-714591, customerservices@blackwellpublishing.com, http://www.wiley.com/. Ed. Dawn Freshwater. Adv. contact Joanna Baker TEL 44-1865-476271.

362.2 GBR ISSN 1742-6464
RC321

JOURNAL OF PSYCHIATRIC INTENSIVE CARE; psychiatric intensive care and low secure units. Text in English. s-a. GBP 192, USD 355 to institutions; GBP 199, USD 368 combined subscription to institutions (print & online eds.) (effective 2012). reprint service avail. from PSC. **Document type:** *Journal, Academic/Scholarly.* **Description:** Covers issues affecting the care and treatment of people with severe mental disorder or behavioral functioning.
Related titles: Online - full text ed.: ISSN 1742-2206. GBP 160, USD 296 to institutions (effective 2012).
Indexed: A22, B21, C06, C07, E01, NSA, P03, P20, P25, P48, P54, PQC, PsycInfo.
—BLDSC (5043.175000), IE. **CCC.**
Published by: (The National Association of Psychiatric Intensive Care Units), Cambridge University Press, The Edinburgh Bldg, Shaftesbury Rd, Cambridge, CB2 8RU, United Kingdom. TEL 44-1223-312393, FAX 44-1223-315052, journals@cambridge.org. Eds. Jim Laidlaw, Roland Dix. **Subscr. to:** Cambridge University Press, 100 Brook Hill Dr, W Nyack, NY 10994. TEL 845-353-7500, 800-872-7423, FAX 845-353-4141, journals_subscriptions@cup.org.

616.8 USA ISSN 1527-4160
RC321 CODEN: JPPOBI

➤ **JOURNAL OF PSYCHIATRIC PRACTICE.** Text in English. 1995. bi-m. USD 449 domestic to institutions; USD 528 foreign to institutions (effective 2011). adv. **Document type:** *Journal, Academic/Scholarly.* **Description:** For psychiatrists, psychologists, nurses, and social workers responsible for managing psychiatric patients. Offers readable, reliable coverage on clinically applicable topics.
Formerly (until 2000): Journal of Practical Psychiatry and Behavioral Health (1076-5417)
Related titles: Online - full text ed.: ISSN 1538-1145.
Indexed: A20, C06, C07, C08, CINAHL, CurCont, E-psyche, EMBASE, ExcerpMed, MEDLINE, P03, P30, PsycInfo, PsycholAb, R10, Reac, SCI, SCOPUS, W07.
—BLDSC (5043.220000), GNLM, IE, Infotrieve, Ingenta. **CCC.**
Published by: Lippincott Williams & Wilkins (Subsidiary of: Wolters Kluwer N.V.), 530 Walnut St, Philadelphia, PA 19106. TEL 215-521-8300, FAX 215-521-8902, customerservice@lww.com, http://www.lww.com. Ed. Dr. John M Oldham. Pub. Maria M McMichael. Adv. contact Ray Thibodeau. B&W page USD 800; trim 8.125 x 10.875. Circ: 13,229 (paid and controlled).

616.89 GBR ISSN 0022-3956
RC321 CODEN: JPYRA3

➤ **JOURNAL OF PSYCHIATRIC RESEARCH.** Text in English. 1961. 16/yr. EUR 2,357 in Europe to institutions; JPY 312,900 in Japan to institutions; USD 2,636 elsewhere to institutions (effective 2012). bk.rev. charts; illus. index. back issues avail.; reprints avail. **Document type:** *Journal, Academic/Scholarly.* **Description:** Covers the latest developments in psychiatry and cognate disciplines.
Related titles: Microfilm ed.: (from PQC); Online - full text ed.: ISSN 1879-1379 (from IngentaConnect, ScienceDirect).
Indexed: A01, A03, A08, A20, A22, A26, ASCA, ASSIA, B21, B25, BAS, BIOBASE, BIOSIS Prev, CA, CIS, ChemAb, CurCont, DentInd, E-psyche, EMBASE, ExcerpMed, FR, FamI, GenetAb, HospLI, I05, IABS, ISR, IndMed, Inpharma, JW-P, MEA&I, MEDLINE, MycolAb, NSA, P03, P30, P35, PsycInfo, PsycholAb, R10, Reac, SCI, SCOPUS, SOPODA, SSCI, SociolAb, T02, W07.
—BLDSC (5043.250000), CASDDS, GNLM, IE, Infotrieve, Ingenta, INIST. **CCC.**
Published by: Pergamon (Subsidiary of: Elsevier Science & Technology), The Blvd, Langford Ln, East Park, Kidlington, Oxford OX5 1GB, United Kingdom. TEL 44-1865-843000, FAX 44-1865-843010, JournalsCustomerServiceEMEA@elsevier.com. Eds. Dr. Alan F. Schatzberg, Dr. Florian Holsboer. **Subscr. to:** Elsevier BV, Radarweg 29, PO Box 211, Amsterdam 1000 AE, Netherlands. TEL 31-20-4853757, FAX 31-20-4853432, http://www.elsevier.nl.

616.8 USA ISSN 1090-1248
RC321

➤ **JOURNAL OF PSYCHIATRY**; a journal of advances in psychiatry. Text in English. 1996. m. USD 9.99 (effective 2010). **Document type:** *Journal, Academic/Scholarly.*
Media: Online - full text.
Published by: Current Clinical Strategies Publishing Inc., 27071 Cabot Rd, Ste 126, Laguna Hills, CA 92653. TEL 949-348-8404, 800-331-8227, FAX 909-744-8071, 800-965-9420, info@ccspublishing.com, http://www.ccspublishing.com/ccs/.

➤ **JOURNAL OF PSYCHIATRY AND LAW.** *see* LAW

616.8 CAN ISSN 1180-4882
RC321 CODEN: JPNEEF

➤ **JOURNAL OF PSYCHIATRY AND NEUROSCIENCE/REVUE DE PSYCHIATRIE ET DE NEUROSCIENCE.** Abbreviated title: J P N. Text in English, French. 1976. bi-m. CAD 113 domestic to individuals; CAD 161 domestic to institutions; USD 161 foreign to institutions; CAD 40 per issue domestic; USD 40 per issue foreign (effective 2004). adv. bk.rev. index. back issues avail. **Document type:** *Journal, Academic/Scholarly.* **Description:** Publishes original research articles and review papers in clinical psychiatry (adult and child) neuroscience related to major psychiatric disorders, and neurodegenerative diseases.
Formerly: Psychiatric Journal of the University of Ottawa (0702-8466)
Related titles: Online - full text ed.: ISSN 1488-2434. free (effective 2011).
Indexed: A01, A02, A03, A08, A20, A22, A26, ASCA, B21, B25, BIOSIS Prev, C03, C05, C06, C07, C08, C11, CA, CBCARef, CDA, CINAHL, CPerI, CurCont, E-psyche, E08, EMBASE, ExcerpMed, FamI, G08, H04, H11, H12, I05, ISR, IndMed, MEDLINE, MycolAb, NSA, NSCI, P03, P10, P20, P22, P24, P25, P26, P30, P43, P48, P53, P54, PQC, PsycInfo, PsycholAb, R10, Reac, S09, SCI, SCOPUS, SSCI, SociolAb, T02, W07.
—BLDSC (5043.261000), GNLM, IE, Ingenta, INIST. **CCC.**
Published by: (Canadian College of Neuropsychopharmacology), Canadian Medical Association/Association Medicale Canadienne, 1867 Alta Vista Dr, Ottawa, ON K1G 3Y6, Canada. TEL 613-731-8610, 888-855-2555, FAX 613-236-8864, pubs@cma.ca. Eds. Dr. Russell Joffe, Dr. Simon Young. Pub. Glenda Proctor. R&P Janis Murrey. Adv. contact Beverley Kirkpatrick. B&W page CAD 1,500, color page CAD 2,700; trim 10.88 x 8.13. Circ: 5,000.

362.2 150 USA ISSN 2150-7937
RA790.A1

JOURNAL OF PSYCHIATRY, PSYCHOLOGY AND MENTAL HEALTH. Text in English. 2007. s-a. free (effective 2009). **Document type:** *Journal, Academic/Scholarly.*
Media: Online - full content.
Published by: Scientific Journals International (Subsidiary of: Global Commerce & Communication, Inc), 1407 33rd St S, Saint Cloud, MN 56301. TEL 320-217-6019, info@scientificjournals.org.

JOURNAL OF PSYCHOACTIVE DRUGS; a multidisciplinary forum. *see* DRUG ABUSE AND ALCOHOLISM

JOURNAL OF PSYCHOSOCIAL NURSING AND MENTAL HEALTH SERVICES. *see* MEDICAL SCIENCES—Nurses And Nursing

JOURNAL OF PSYCHOSOMATIC OBSTETRICS AND GYNECOLOGY. *see* MEDICAL SCIENCES—Obstetrics And Gynecology

616.08 USA ISSN 0022-3999
RC52 CODEN: JPCRAT

➤ **JOURNAL OF PSYCHOSOMATIC RESEARCH.** Text in English. 1956. m. USD 2,689 in United States to institutions; USD 3,057 elsewhere to institutions (effective 2012). adv. bk.rev. bibl.; charts. index. back issues avail.; reprints avail. **Document type:** *Journal, Academic/Scholarly.* **Description:** Covers all aspects of the relationships between psychology and medicine.
Related titles: Microfilm ed.: (from PQC); Online - full text ed.: ISSN 1879-1360 (from IngentaConnect, ScienceDirect).
Indexed: A01, A03, A08, A20, A22, A26, A36, AIDS Ab, AMHA, ASCA, ASSIA, B21, B25, BDM&CN, BIOSIS Prev, C06, C07, CA, CABA, ChemAb, CurCont, D01, DIP, DentInd, DokArb, E-psyche, EMBASE, ExcerpMed, F09, FR, FamI, G10, GH, GenetAb, HEA, I05, IBR, IBZ, INI, ISR, IndMed, Inpharma, LT, MEA&I, MEDLINE, MLA-IB, MycolAb, N02, N03, NSA, P03, P30, P33, P35, PsycInfo, PsycholAb, R08, R10, R12, RRTA, Reac, S02, S03, SCI, SCOPUS, SOPODA, SSCI, SociolAb, T02, T05, W07, W09, W10.
—BLDSC (5043.480000), CASDDS, GNLM, IE, Infotrieve, Ingenta, INIST. **CCC.**
Published by: (European Association for Consultation-Liaison Psychiatry and Psychosomatics GBR), Elsevier Inc. (Subsidiary of: Elsevier Science & Technology), 1600 John F Kennedy Blvd, Philadelphia, PA 19103. TEL 215-239-3900, FAX 215-238-7883, JournalCustomerService-usa@elsevier.com. Ed. Dr. F Creed.

616.891 USA ISSN 1053-0479
RC475 CODEN: JPINEH

➤ **JOURNAL OF PSYCHOTHERAPY INTEGRATION.** Text in English. 1991. q. USD 98 domestic to individuals; USD 125 foreign to individuals; USD 667 domestic to institutions; USD 712 foreign to institutions (effective 2011). adv. bk.rev. back issues avail.; reprint service avail. from PSC. **Document type:** *Journal, Academic/Scholarly.* **Description:** Takes a multimodal approach to the study of psychotherapy and behavior change.
Related titles: Online - full text ed.: ISSN 1573-3696 (from IngentaConnect, ScienceDirect).
Indexed: A22, ASCA, ASSIA, C06, C07, E-psyche, E01, EMBASE, ExcerpMed, P03, P30, PsycInfo, PsycholAb, R10, Reac, SCOPUS, SociolAb.
—BLDSC (5043.483300), GNLM, IE, Infotrieve, Ingenta. **CCC.**
Published by: American Psychological Association, 750 First St, NE, Washington, DC 20002. TEL 202-336-5500, 800-374-2721, journals@apa.org. Ed. Dr. Jerry Gold. Adv. contact Doug Constant TEL 202-336-5574. Circ: 700.

➤ **JOURNAL OF PUBLIC MENTAL HEALTH**; the art, science and politics of creating a mentally healthy society. *see* PUBLIC HEALTH AND SAFETY

616.8 USA ISSN 0887-8250
TX546 CODEN: JSSDEO

➤ **JOURNAL OF SENSORY STUDIES.** Text in English. 1986. bi-m. GBP 287 in United Kingdom to institutions; EUR 364 in Europe to institutions; USD 559 elsewhere to institutions; GBP 330 combined subscription in United Kingdom to institutions (print & online eds.); EUR 419 combined subscription in Europe to institutions (print & online eds.); USD 644 combined subscription elsewhere to institutions (print & online eds.) (effective 2012). adv. bk.rev. abstr.; bibl.; charts; illus.; stat. back issues avail.; reprint service avail. from PSC. **Document type:** *Journal, Academic/Scholarly.* **Description:** Promotes the technical and practical advancement of sensory science, publishing a broad spectrum of papers, including observational and experimental studies in the application of sensory evaluation to the food, medical, agricultural, biological, pharmaceutical, cosmetic, consumer, and materials industries.
Related titles: Online - full text ed.: ISSN 1745-459X. GBP 287 in United Kingdom to institutions; EUR 364 in Europe to institutions; USD 559 elsewhere to institutions (effective 2012) (from IngentaConnect).
Indexed: A01, A22, A26, A34, A36, A38, ASFA, Agr, B21, C25, CA, CABA, ChemoAb, CurCont, D01, E-psyche, E01, E12, F05, F06, F07, F10, FCA, FS&TA, GH, H16, ISR, IndVet, MaizeAb, N02, N03, NSA, O01, OR, P03, P30, P32, P37, P38, P40, PGegResA, PGrRegA, PHN&I, PN&I, PsycInfo, PsycholAb, R11, R12, RA&MP, S12, S17, SCI, SCOPUS, SoyAb, T02, T05, TAR, TriticAb, VITIS, VS, W07, W11.
—BLDSC (5063.600000), CASDDS, IE, Infotrieve, Ingenta, INIST. **CCC.**
Published by: (The Society of Sensory Professionals), Wiley-Blackwell Publishing, Inc. (Subsidiary of: Wiley-Blackwell Publishing Ltd.), 111 River St, Hoboken, NJ 07030. TEL 201-748-6000, FAX 201-748-6088, info@wiley.com. Eds. Edgar Chambers IV, Harry T Lawless.

➤ **JOURNAL OF SPINAL CORD MEDICINE.** *see* MEDICAL SCIENCES—Physical Medicine And Rehabilitation

➤ **JOURNAL OF SYSTEMIC THERAPIES.** *see* PSYCHOLOGY

616.8 GBR ISSN 0964-704X
RC338 CODEN: JHNEFS

➤ **JOURNAL OF THE HISTORY OF THE NEUROSCIENCES**; basic and clinical perspectives. Abbreviated title: J H N. Text in English. 1992. q. GBP 350 combined subscription in United Kingdom to institutions (print & online eds.); EUR 464, USD 582 combined subscription to institutions (print & online eds.) (effective 2012). adv. back issues avail.; reprint service avail. from PSC. **Document type:** *Journal, Academic/Scholarly.* **Description:** Contains surveys and examines trends in the study of the neurosciences.
Related titles: Online - full text ed.: ISSN 1744-5213. GBP 315 in United Kingdom to institutions; EUR 417, USD 524 to institutions (effective 2012) (from IngentaConnect).
Indexed: A01, A03, A08, A20, A22, CA, E-psyche, E01, EMBASE, ExcerpMed, HistAb, IndMed, MEDLINE, P03, P20, P22, P30, P43, P48, P54, PQC, PsycInfo, PsycholAb, SCI, SCOPUS, T02, W07.
—GNLM, IE, Infotrieve, Ingenta. **CCC.**
Published by: (International Society for the History of the Neurosciences USA), Psychology Press (Subsidiary of: Taylor & Francis Ltd.), 27 Church Rd, Hove, E Sussex BN3 2FA, United Kingdom. TEL 44-20-70176000, FAX 44-20-70176717, info@psypress.co.uk, http://www.psypress.com. Eds. M Macmillan, P J Koehler, S Finger. **Subscr. in Europe to:** Taylor & Francis Ltd., Journals Customer Service, Sheepen Pl, Colchester, Essex CO3 3LP, United Kingdom. TEL 44-20-70175544, FAX 44-20-70175198, tf.enquiries@tfinforma.com; **Subscr. in N. America:** Taylor & Francis Inc. **Co-sponsors:** World Federation of Neurology/Federation Mondiale de Neurologie; European Club for the History of Neurology.

616.8 NLD ISSN 0022-510X
RC321 CODEN: JNSCAG

➤ **JOURNAL OF THE NEUROLOGICAL SCIENCES.** Text and summaries in English, French, German, Spanish. 1964. 24/yr. EUR 4,302 in Europe to institutions; JPY 572,000 in Japan to institutions; USD 4,811 elsewhere to institutions (effective 2012). adv. bk.rev. bibl.; charts; illus. Index. back issues avail.; reprints avail. **Document type:** *Journal, Academic/Scholarly.* **Description:** Provides a medium for the publication of studies on the interface between clinical neurology and the basic sciences.
Related titles: Microform ed.: (from PQC); Online - full text ed.: ISSN 1878-5883 (from IngentaConnect, ScienceDirect).
Indexed: A01, A03, A08, A20, A22, A26, ASCA, B21, B25, BDM&CN, BIOBASE, BIOSIS Prev, CA, CIN, ChemAb, ChemTitl, CurCont, E-psyche, EMBASE, ExcerpMed, FR, I05, IABS, IBR, IBZ, INI, ISR, IndMed, Inpharma, JW-N, MEDLINE, MycolAb, NSA, NSCI, P03, P30, P35, PsycInfo, PsycholAb, R10, Reac, SCI, SCOPUS, T02, W07.
—BLDSC (5021.560000), CASDDS, GNLM, IE, Infotrieve, Ingenta, INIST. **CCC.**
Published by: (World Federation of Neurology/Federation Mondiale de Neurologie GBR), Elsevier BV (Subsidiary of: Elsevier Science & Technology), Radarweg 29, PO Box 211, Amsterdam, 1000 AE, Netherlands. TEL 31-20-4853911, FAX 31-20-4852457, JournalsCustomerServiceEMEA@elsevier.com, http://www.elsevier.nl. Ed. Dr. Robert P Lisak. **Subscr. in the Americas to:** Elsevier, Subscription Customer Service, 6277 Sea Harbor Dr, Orlando, FL 32887-4800. TEL 407-345-4020, 877-839-7126, FAX 407-363-1354.

616.8 USA ISSN 1085-9489
RC409 CODEN: JPNSFO
➤ **JOURNAL OF THE PERIPHERAL NERVOUS SYSTEM.** Abbreviated title: J P N S. Text in English. 1996. q. GBP 352 in United Kingdom to institutions; EUR 448 in Europe to institutions; USD 452 in the Americas to institutions; USD 689 elsewhere to institutions; GBP 405 combined subscription in United Kingdom to institutions (print & online eds.); EUR 516 combined subscription in Europe to institutions (print & online eds.); USD 520 combined subscription in the Americas to institutions (print & online eds.); USD 793 combined subscription elsewhere to institutions (print & online eds.) (effective 2012). bk.rev. index, cum.index. back issues avail.; reprints avail. **Document type:** *Journal, Academic/Scholarly.* **Description:** Publishes papers encompassing all topics relevant to peripheral nerves, linking molecular biology and medicine to clinical neuroscience.
Related titles: Online - full text ed.: ISSN 1529-8027. GBP 352 in United Kingdom to institutions; EUR 448 in Europe to institutions; USD 452 in the Americas to institutions; USD 689 elsewhere to institutions (effective 2012) (from IngentaConnect).
Indexed: A01, A02, A03, A08, A20, A22, A26, B21, C06, C07, C08, C11, CA, CINAHL, CurCont, E-psyche, E01, EMBASE, ExcerpMed, H04, H12, I05, IndMed, Inpharma, MEDLINE, NSA, NSCI, P30, P35, R10, Reac, SCI, SCOPUS, T02, W07.
—BLDSC (5073.711000), CASDDS, IE, Infotrieve, Ingenta. **CCC.**
Published by: (Peripheral Nerve Society), Wiley-Blackwell Publishing, Inc. (Subsidiary of: Wiley-Blackwell Publishing Ltd.), 111 River St, Hoboken, NJ 07030. TEL 201-748-6000, FAX 201-748-6088, info@wiley.com. Ed. David R Cornblath TEL 410-955-2229. Adv. contact Stephen Donohue TEL 781-388-8511.

616.8 USA ISSN 1544-2896
➤ **JOURNAL OF UNDERGRADUATE NEUROSCIENCE EDUCATION.** Abbreviated title: J U N E. Text in English. 2002. s-a. free (effective 2011). back issues avail. **Document type:** *Journal, Academic/Scholarly.* **Description:** Serves as a mechanism for faculty to exchange information regarding topics such as laboratory exercises, new media, curricular considerations, and teaching methods.
Media: Online - full text.
Indexed: P03, P30, PsycInfo, SCOPUS.
Published by: Davidson College, Faculty for Undergraduate Neuroscience, PO Box 7118, Davidson, NC 28035. TEL 704-894-2338, FAX 704-894-2512, http://www.funfaculty.org. Ed. Gary Dunbar TEL 989-774-3282.

616.8 USA ISSN 1941-5893
JOURNAL OF VASCULAR AND INTERVENTIONAL NEUROLOGY. Text in English. 2008. q. **Document type:** *Journal, Academic/Scholarly.* **Description:** Promotes the dissemination of new information relating to neurovascular medicine, including diagnosis, treatment, prevention and rehabilitation.
Related titles: Online - full text ed.: free (effective 2011).
Indexed: P30.
Published by: Zeenat Qureshi Stroke Research Center, 420 Delawae St, SE, Minneapolis, MN 55455. TEL 612-626-1866, FAX 612-625-7950. Ed. Adnan I Qureshi.

JOURNAL OF VESTIBULAR RESEARCH: EQUILIBRIUM AND ORIENTATION; an international journal of experimental and clinical vestibular science. *see* BIOLOGY—Physiology

616.8982 CAN ISSN 1188-9136
JOURNAL ON DEVELOPMENTAL DISABILITIES/JOURNAL SUR LES HANDICAPS DU DEVELOPPEMENT. Text in English, French. 1990. s-a.
Formerly (until 1991): BrOADD Perspectives (1196-2623)
Indexed: E-psyche, P03, P25, P48, PQC, PsycInfo, PsycholAb.
—BLDSC (4969.290450).
Published by: Ontario Association on Developmental Disabilities/ L'Association Ontarienne Sur les Handicaps du Developpement, 100 College St, Room 511, Toronto, ON M5G 1L5, Canada. TEL 416-946-3680, FAX 416-946-3680, oadd@interlog.com, http://www.interlog.com/~oadd/.

JOURNAL WATCH NEUROLOGY. *see* MEDICAL SCIENCES—Abstracting, Bibliographies, Statistics

JOURNAL WATCH PSYCHIATRY. *see* MEDICAL SCIENCES—Abstracting, Bibliographies, Statistics

JURISPRUDENTIE VERPLICHTE GEESTELIJKE GEZONDHEIDSZORG. *see* LAW

616.8 150 USA ISSN 2152-1530
▼ **K B M JOURNAL OF COGNITIVE SCIENCE.** Text in English. 2010 (Apr.). q. free. **Document type:** *Journal, Academic/Scholarly.* **Description:** Features theoretical and experimental papers on the empirical and theoretical work on cognitive science, psychology, linguistics and neuroscience.
Media: Online - full text.
Published by: K B M Scientific Publishing, Ltd, 971 Pepperwood Dr, Fayetteville, NC 28331-9331. TEL 910-672-1114, info@kbm-scientific-publishing.org.

616.8 617 JPN ISSN 0918-1172
KAGAWA NO SHINKEI GEKA DANWAKAI KAISHI/KAGAWA COLLOQUIUM ON NEUROSURGERY. JOURNAL. Text in Japanese. 1985. a.
Indexed: E-psyche.
Published by: Kagawa No Shinkei Geka Danwakai, Kagawa Ika Daigaku No Shinkei Gekagaku Kyoshitsu, 1750-1 Ikedo, Kita-gun, Miki-cho, Kagawa-ken 761-0700, Japan.

616.8 JPN ISSN 0288-9617
➤ **KANAGAWA-KEN SEISHIN IGAKKAISHI/KANAGAWA ASSOCIATION OF PSYCHIATRY. JOURNAL.** Text in Japanese. 1959. a. JPY 3,000 (effective 2003). adv. back issues avail. **Document type:** *Academic/Scholarly.*
Indexed: E-psyche.
Published by: Kanagawa Association of Psychiatry, c/o Department of Psychiatry, University School of Medicine, Yokohama, 3-9 Fukura, Kanazawa-ku, Yokohama-shi, Kanagawa-ken 236-0004, Japan. TEL 81-45-787-2667, FAX 81-45-783-2540. Ed. Kenji Kosaka. R&P Saeko Fujikake. Adv. contact Eizo Iseki. Circ: 2,000.

616.8 FIN ISSN 1797-0474
KEHITYSVAMMALIITTO. SELVITYKSIA. Text in Finnish. 2007. irreg. back issues avail. **Document type:** *Monographic series, Academic/Scholarly.*
Formed by the merger of (2004-2005): Kotunet (Online) (1795-1917); (2003-2006): Kotu-Raportteja (Print) (1459-3629); Which was formerly (1988-2002): Valtakunnallisen Tutkimus- ja Kokeiluyksikon. Monisteita (0785-367X)
Media: Online - full content.
Published by: Kehitysvammaliitto Ry/Finnish Association on Intellectual and Developmental Disabilities, Viljatie 4 A, Helsinki, 00700, Finland. TEL 358-9-348090, FAX 358-9-3853398, kvl@kvl.fi.

DIE KERBE; Forum fuer Sozialpsychiatrie. *see* SOCIAL SERVICES AND WELFARE

THE KEY. *see* EDUCATION—Special Education And Rehabilitation

616.8 CHE ISSN 1662-4874
RA790.A1 CODEN: BIBPBI
➤ **KEY ISSUES IN MENTAL HEALTH.** Text in English, French, German. 1917. irreg., latest vol.175, 2009. price varies. back issues avail.; reprints avail. **Document type:** *Monographic series, Academic/Scholarly.*
Former titles (until 200?): Bibliotheca Psychiatrica (0067-8147); (until 1970): Bibliotheca Psychiatrica et Neurologica (0366-256X); (until 1948): Abhandlungen aus der Neurologie, Psychiatrie, Psychologie und Ihren Grenzgebieten (1016-2747)
Related titles: Online - full text ed.: ISSN 1662-4882.
Indexed: ASCA, ChemAb, IndMed, P30, SCOPUS.
—BLDSC (2019.390000), GNLM, IE, Infotrieve, INIST. **CCC.**
Published by: S. Karger AG, Allschwilerstr 10, Basel, 4055, Switzerland. TEL 41-61-3061111, FAX 41-61-3061234, karger@karger.ch, http://www.karger.ch. Eds. A Reicher-Rossier, M Steiner.

616.8 AUT ISSN 0934-1420
➤ **KEY TOPICS IN BRAIN RESEARCH.** Text in English. 1988. irreg., latest 1999. price varies. **Document type:** *Monographic series, Academic/Scholarly.*
Published by: Springer Wien (Subsidiary of: Springer Science+Business Media), Sachsenplatz 4-6, Vienna, W 1201, Austria. TEL 43-1-3302415-0, FAX 43-1-330242665, books@springer.at, http://www.springer.at. Eds. A Carlsson, Dr. Peter Riederer. R&P Angela Foessl TEL 43-1-3302415517. **Subscr. to:** Springer New York LLC, 233 Spring St, New York, NY 10013. TEL 800-777-4643, FAX 201-348-4505.

616.8 JPN ISSN 1344-9699
➤ **KINOTEKI NO SHINKEI GEKA/FUNCTIONAL NEUROSURGERY.** Text in English, Japanese. 1987. s-a. membership. adv. back issues avail. **Document type:** *Journal, Academic/Scholarly.*
Indexed: E-psyche.
—BLDSC (5097.053200).
Published by: Nihon Teii Kinow Shimkei Geka Gakkai/Japan Society for Stereotactic and Functional Neurosurgery, Department of Neurosurgery, Nihon University School of Medicine, 30-1, Oyaguchi Kamimachi, Itabashi-ku, Tokyo, 173-8610, Japan. TEL 81-3-39728111 ext 2481, FAX 81-3-35540425, teii@med.nihon-u.ac.jp. Ed., R&P, Adv. contact Yoichi Katayama.

616.8 TUR ISSN 1302-0099
➤ **KLINIK PSIKIYATRI DERGISI.** Text in Turkish. 1998. q. GBP 30 (effective 2010). **Document type:** *Journal, Academic/Scholarly.* **Description:** Contains psychiatry, clinical psychology, psychopharmacology and psychiatric interest of neurology in the fields of experimental and clinical studies. It also includes reviews, case reports, short reports and letters to the editor.
Related titles: Online - full text ed.: free (effective 2010).
Indexed: A01, CA, P03, PsycInfo, T02.
Address: Sedat Simavi sok. 86/A Blok No.13, Ankara, Turkey. klinikpsikiyatri@cty.com.tr. Eds. Nevzat Yuksel, Rasit Tukel, Simavi Vahip.

616.8 TUR ISSN 1017-7833
RM315
➤ **KLINIK PSIKOFARMAKOLOJI BULTENI/BULLETIN OF CLINICAL PSYCHOPHARMACOLOGY.** Text in Turkish, English; Summaries in Turkish, English. 1991. q. free (effective 2009). Index. back issues avail. **Document type:** *Journal, Academic/Scholarly.* **Description:** Primarily focusing on psychopharmacology, biological psychiatry and biological aspects of psychiatry.
Related titles: Online - full text ed.: ISSN 1302-9657. free (effective 2011).
Indexed: A01, A22, A36, BIOBASE, CA, CABA, E-psyche, EMBASE, ExcerpMed, GH, I12, IABS, N02, N03, P03, P10, P20, P25, P48, P53, P54, PQC, PsycInfo, PsycholAb, R10, R12, Reac, SCI, SCOPUS, T02, T05, W07.
—BLDSC (5099.287700), IE, Ingenta.
Published by: Yerkure Tanitim ve Yayincilik Hizmetleri A.S., Siracevizler Cad 43/3, Sisli, Istanbul, 34381, Turkey. TEL 90-212-2194900, FAX 90-212-2305009, yerkure@yerkure.com.tr, http://www.kure.com.tr. Ed. Mesut Cetin. Adv. contact Kure Hetisim Grubu. Circ: 3,000.

621.3 DEU ISSN 1434-0275
RC348 CODEN: KNEUFG
➤ **KLINISCHE NEUROPHYSIOLOGIE**; Zeitschrift fuer Funktionsdiagnostik des Nervensystems. Text in German; Summaries in English, German. 1970. q. EUR 269 to institutions; EUR 380 combined subscription to institutions (print & online eds.); EUR 83 newsstand/cover (effective 2011). adv. bk.rev. abstr.; bibl.; charts; illus.; stat. index. back issues avail.; reprints avail. **Document type:** *Journal, Academic/Scholarly.*
Formerly: E E G - E M G (0012-7590)
Related titles: Microform ed.: (from PQC); Online - full text ed.: ISSN 1439-4081. EUR 367 to institutions (effective 2011).
Indexed: A22, ASCA, CurCont, E-psyche, EMBASE, ExcerpMed, IndMed, NSCI, P03, P30, PsycInfo, R10, Reac, SCI, SCOPUS, W07.
—BLDSC (5099.453000), GNLM, IE, Infotrieve, Ingenta, INIST. **CCC.**
Published by: Georg Thieme Verlag, Ruedigerstr 14, Stuttgart, 70469, Germany. TEL 49-711-8931421, FAX 49-711-8931410, leser.service@thieme.de, kunden.service@thieme.de. Ed. R Dengler. R&P Peter Eich. Adv. contact Andreas Schweiger TEL 49-711-8931245. Circ: 1,100 (paid).

616.8 DEU
KOERPERBEHINDERTENFOERDERUNG NECKAR-ALB. SCHRIFTENREIHE. Text in German. irreg., latest 2006. price varies. **Document type:** *Monographic series, Academic/Scholarly.*
Published by: (Koerperbehindertenfoerderung Neckar-Alb), Attempto Verlag, Dischingerweg 5, Tuebingen, 72070, Germany. TEL 49-7071-97970, FAX 49-7071-979711, info@attempto-verlag.de, http://www.narr.de.

KOMINIKEISYON SYOIGAIGAKU/JAPANESE JOURNAL OF COMMUNICATION DISORDERS. *see* MEDICAL SCIENCES—Otorhinolaryngology

616.853 CHE
KONTAKTE; Zeitung fuer Epilepsie-Betroffene. Text in German. 1986. 2/yr. CHF 15 (effective 2003). **Document type:** *Journal, Consumer.*
Indexed: E-psyche.
Published by: epi-suisse, Seefeldstr 84, Zurich, 8034, Switzerland. TEL 41-43-4886880, FAX 41-43-4886881, info@epi-suisse.ch, http://www.epi-suisse.ch. Ed. Margret Becker. Circ: 900.

616.8 KOR ISSN 2005-3711
➤ **KOREAN NEUROSURGICAL SOCIETY. JOURNAL.** Text in English. m. membership. **Document type:** *Journal, Academic/Scholarly.*
Formerly (until 2005): Daehan Sin'gyeong Oe'gwa Hag'hoeji (1225-8245)
Related titles: Online - full text ed.: ISSN 1598-7876.
Indexed: EMBASE, P30, R10, Reac, SCI, SCOPUS, W07.
—BLDSC (3510.307500), IE.
Published by: Korean Neurosurgical Society, c/o Kyeong-Seok Lee, #402 Posco the # Office Bldg, 151 Sunhwa-dong, Jung-gu, Seoul, 100-130, Korea, S. TEL 82-2-525-7552, FAX 82-2-525-7554, http://www.neurosurgery.or.kr/. Ed. Dr. Jung Yul Park.

616.8 JPN ISSN 1348-4818
KOUJI NOU KINOU KENKYUU/HIGHER BRAIN FUNCTION RESEARCH. Text in Japanese; Summaries in English, Japanese. 1981. q. **Document type:** *Journal, Academic/Scholarly.*
Formerly (until 2000): Shitsugosho Kenkyu (0285-9513)
Related titles: Online - full text ed.: ISSN 1880-6554.
Indexed: B21, E-psyche, NSA.
Published by: Nihon Kouji Nou Kinou Shougai Gakkai/Japan Society for Higher Brain Dysfunction, Edogawa Hospital, 2-24-18 Higashikoiwa, Edogawa-ku, Tokyo, 133-0052, Japan. TEL 81-3-36731557, FAX 81-3-36731512, jsa1977@sepia.ocn.ne.jp, http://www.higherbrain.gr.jp/.

KWALITEIT EN VEILIGHEID. *see* PUBLIC HEALTH AND SAFETY

616.89 JPN ISSN 0023-6144
CODEN: KSSIAC
KYUSHU NEURO-PSYCHIATRY/KYUSHU SHINKEI SEISHIN IGAKU. Text in Japanese; Summaries in English. 1954. q. JPY 5,000. adv. bk.rev. bibl.; charts; stat. index. **Document type:** *Proceedings, Academic/Scholarly.*
Media: Duplicated (not offset). **Related titles:** Microfilm ed.: (from PQC).
Indexed: A22, CIS, ChemAb, E-psyche, INIS AtomInd, PsycholAb.
—CASDDS, GNLM.
Published by: Kyushu Association of Neuro-Psychiatry/Kyushu Seishin Shinkei Gakkai, c/o Department of Neuro-Psychiatry Faculty of Medicine, Kyushu University, Maidashi, Higashi-ku, Fukuoka-shi, 812-0054, Japan. TEL 81-92-642-5620, FAX 81-92-642-5644. Ed., Pub., Adv. contact Nobutada Tashiro. Circ: 1,100 (controlled).

616.8 DEU ISSN 0944-405X
RC423.A1 CODEN: LOINEW
L.O.G.O.S. INTERDISZIPLINAER. Text in English. 1994. 4/yr. EUR 82 in Europe to institutions; JPY 11,200 in Japan to institutions; USD 103 elsewhere to institutions (effective 2010). adv. **Document type:** *Journal, Academic/Scholarly.*
Indexed: CPEI, E-psyche, RILM, SCOPUS.
—GNLM, IE. **CCC.**
Published by: Urban und Fischer Verlag (Subsidiary of: Elsevier GmbH), Loebdergraben 14a, Jena, 07743, Germany. TEL 49-3641-626430, FAX 49-3641-626432, journals@urbanfischer.de, http://www.urbanundfischer.de. Eds. Karen Elger, Thomas Bosch. Circ: 3,450 (paid and controlled). **Non-German speaking countries subscr. to:** Nature Publishing Group, Brunel Rd, Houndmills, Basingstoke, Hamps RG21 6XS, United Kingdom. TEL 44-1256-302629, FAX 44-1256-476117, NatureReviews@nature.com

616.8 GBR ISSN 1474-4422
CODEN: LNAEAM
➤ **THE LANCET NEUROLOGY.** Text in English. 2002. m. EUR 1,472 in Europe to institutions; JPY 188,300 in Japan to institutions; USD 1,579 elsewhere to institutions (effective 2012). back issues avail. **Document type:** *Journal, Academic/Scholarly.* **Description:** Contains articles, viewpoints, news, and reviews in neurology.
Related titles: Online - full text ed.: ISSN 1474-4465 (from IngentaConnect, ScienceDirect); ◆ Regional ed(s).: The Lancet Neurology (Italian Edition). ISSN 1828-6607.
Indexed: A01, A03, A08, A26, B21, CA, CurCont, EMBASE, ExcerpMed, I05, JW-N, MEDLINE, NSA, NSCI, P03, P20, P22, P24, P30, P48, P54, PQC, PsycInfo, R10, Reac, SCI, SCOPUS, T02, W07.
—BLDSC (5146.084000), IE, Ingenta. **CCC.**
Published by: The Lancet Publishing Group (Subsidiary of: Elsevier Health Sciences), 32 Jamestown Rd, London, NW1 7BY, United Kingdom. TEL 44-1865-843077, FAX 44-1865-843970, custserv@lancet.com, http://www.thelancet.com. Ed. Helen Frankish.

616.8 ITA ISSN 1828-6607
➤ **THE LANCET NEUROLOGY (ITALIAN EDITION).** Text in Multiple languages. 2006. q. **Document type:** *Journal, Academic/Scholarly.*
Related titles: ◆ Regional ed(s).: The Lancet Neurology. ISSN 1474-4422.
Published by: Elsevier Masson (Subsidiary of: Elsevier Health Sciences), Via Paleocapa 7, Milan, 20121, Italy. TEL 39-02-881841, FAX 39-02-88184302, info@masson.it, http://www.masson.it.

616.8 PRT ISSN 1647-8150
▼ **THE LANCET NEUROLOGY (PORTUGUESE EDITION).** Text in English. 2010. bi-m. **Document type:** *Journal, Academic/Scholarly.*
Published by: Publisaude Edicoes Medicas, Alameda Antonio Sergio, Edificio Amadeu S Cardoso, Miraflores, Alges, 1495-132, Portugal. TEL 351-214-135032, FAX 351-214-135007, http://publisaude.pai.pt.

616.89 NLD ISSN 1879-5749
LANDELIJKE STICHTING ZELFBESCHADIGING. NIEUWSBRIEF. Text in Dutch. 200?. irreg. (1-2/yr.). **Document type:** *Newsletter, Trade.*
Published by: Landelijke Stichting Zelfbeschadiging, Postbus 140, Utrecht, 3500 AC, Netherlands. TEL 31-30-2311473, stichting@zelfbeschadiging.nl, http://www.zelfbeschadiging.nl.

616.8 GBR ISSN 1357-650X
QP385.5 CODEN: LATEFV
LATERALITY; asymmetries of body, brain and cognition. Text in English. 1996. bi-m. GBP 571 combined subscription in United Kingdom to institutions (print & online eds.); EUR 757, USD 951 combined subscription to institutions (print & online eds.) (effective 2012). back issues avail.; reprint service avail. from PSC. **Document type:** *Journal, Academic/Scholarly.* **Description:** Features high quality research concerned with all aspects of lateralisation.
Related titles: Online - full text ed.: ISSN 1464-0678. GBP 514 in United Kingdom to institutions; EUR 681, USD 856 to institutions (effective 2012) (from IngentaConnect).
Indexed: A01, A03, A08, A20, A22, ASSIA, B21, CA, CurCont, E-psyche, E01, EMBASE, ErgAb, ExcerpMed, IPsyAb, L&LBA, L11, MEDLINE, NSA, P03, P30, P43, PsycInfo, PsycholAb, R09, R10, Reac, SCOPUS, SD, SOPODA, SSCI, T02, W07, Z01.
—IE, Infotrieve, Ingenta, INIST. **CCC.**
Published by: Psychology Press (Subsidiary of: Taylor & Francis Ltd.), 27 Church Rd, Hove, E Sussex BN3 2FA, United Kingdom. TEL 44-20-70176000, FAX 44-20-70176717, info@psypress.co.uk, http://www.psypress.com. Eds. Chris McManus, Giorgio Vallortigara, Mike Nicholls.

LAW AND MENTAL DISABILITY. *see* LAW

616.8 AUT ISSN 1608-8964
LEADING OPINIONS. NEUROLOGIE UND PSYCHIATRIE. Text in German. 2000. 5/yr. adv. **Document type:** *Journal, Academic/Scholarly.*
Related titles: Online - full text ed.: ISSN 1991-2781. 2003.
Published by: Universimed Verlags- und Service GmbH, Markgraf-Rueidiger-Str 8, Vienna, 1150, Austria. TEL 43-1-87679560, FAX 43-1-876795620, office@universimed.com, http://www.universimed.com. Ed. Friederike Hoerandl. Adv. contact Sabine Baeckert. Circ: 3,450 (controlled).

155.67 USA ISSN 1549-5485
➤ **LEARNING & MEMORY (ONLINE).** Text in English. 1994. m. USD 550 to institutions (effective 2010). adv. back issues avail. **Document type:** *Journal, Academic/Scholarly.* **Description:** provides a forum for these investigations in the form of research papers and review articles.
Media: Online - full text.
—CCC.
Published by: Cold Spring Harbor Laboratory Press, 500 Sunnyside Blvd, Woodbury, NY 11797. TEL 516-422-4101, 800-843-4388, FAX 516-422-4097, cshpress@cshl.edu, http://www.cshlpress.com. Ed. John H Byrne.

➤ **LEBENSWELTEN BEHINDERTER MENSCHEN.** *see* HANDICAPPED

616.853 ITA ISSN 0394-560X
LEGA ITALIANA CONTRO L'EPILESSIA. BOLLETTINO. Text in Italian. 1973. q. adv. bk.rev. **Document type:** *Bulletin, Trade.* **Description:** Focuses on epilepsy.
Indexed: A22, E-psyche, EMBASE, ExcerpMed, R10, Reac, SCOPUS.
—BLDSC (2227.150000), GNLM, IE, Ingenta.
Published by: Lega Italiana contro l'Epilessia (L I C E), Via di Rudini 8, Milan, 20142, Italy. TEL 39-02-7718150, FAX 39-02-7718183, http://www.lice.it. Ed. Maria Paola Canevini.

616.8 DEU ISSN 1867-6057
LEIPZIG SERIES IN BRAIN COGNITION AND LANGUAGE. Text in English, German. 2008. irreg., latest vol.22, 2010. price varies. **Document type:** *Monographic series, Academic/Scholarly.*
Published by: Leipziger Universitaetsverlag GmbH, Oststr 41, Leipzig, 04317, Germany. TEL 49-341-9900440, FAX 49-341-9900440, info@univerlag-leipzig.de.

616.8 FRA ISSN 1276-9339
➤ **LA LETTRE DU NEUROLOGUE.** Text in French. 1997. bi-m. EUR 114 in Europe to individuals; EUR 114 DOM-TOM to individuals; EUR 114 in Africa to individuals; EUR 126 elsewhere to individuals; EUR 138 in Europe to institutions; EUR 138 DOM-TOM to institutions; EUR 138 in Africa to institutions; EUR 150 elsewhere to institutions (effective 2009). Supplement avail. **Document type:** *Academic/Scholarly.*
Indexed: E-psyche.
—INIST.
Published by: Edimark S.A.S., 2 Rue Sainte-Marie, Courbevoie, Cedex 92418, France. TEL 33-1-41458000, FAX 33-1-41458025, contact@edimark.fr. Ed. P Amarenco. Pub. Claudie Damour Terrasson.

616.8 FRA ISSN 1774-0789
LA LETTRE DU PSYCHIATRE. Text in French. 2005. bi-m. EUR 96 in Europe to individuals; EUR 96 DOM-TOM to individuals; EUR 96 in Africa to individuals; EUR 108 elsewhere to individuals; EUR 114 in Europe to institutions; EUR 114 DOM-TOM to institutions; EUR 114 in Africa to institutions; EUR 126 elsewhere to institutions (effective 2009). **Document type:** *Newsletter, Consumer.*
—INIST.
Published by: Edimark S.A.S., 2 Rue Sainte-Marie, Courbevoie, Cedex 92418, France. TEL 39-1-41458000, FAX 33-1-41458025, contact@edimark.fr.

LIDWINA. *see* SOCIAL SERVICES AND WELFARE

616.858843 USA ISSN 1059-6593
LIFE-LINE. Text in English. 1991. q. USD 35 membership (effective 2006). **Document type:** *Newsletter.*
Published by: National Hydrocephalus Foundation, c/o Debbi Fields, Ex Dir, 12413 Centralia Rd, PO Box 490248, Lakewood, CA 90715-1653. TEL 562-402-3523, 888-857-3434, FAX 562-924-6666, hydrobrat@earthlink.net, http://www.nhfonline.org.

616.858 362.3 PRT ISSN 0873-6243
LIGA. Text in Portuguese. 1998. q. **Document type:** *Magazine, Consumer.*
Published by: Liga Portuguesa de Deficientes Motores, Rua do Sitio ao Casalinho da Ajuda, Lisbon, 1349-011, Portugal. TEL 351-21-3616910, FAX 351-21-3648639, lpdmcrs@lpdm-crs.pt, http://www.lpdm-crs.rcts.pt.

616.8 CHN ISSN 1005-3220
LINCHUANG JINGSHEN YIXUE ZAZHI/JOURNAL OF CLINICAL PSYCHOLOGICAL MEDICINE. Text in Chinese. 1991. bi-m. USD 24.60 (effective 2009). **Document type:** *Journal, Academic/Scholarly.*
Related titles: Online - full text ed.
—BLDSC (4958.689500), East View, IE, Ingenta.
Published by: Nanjing Yike Daxue, Naoke Xueyuan, 264, Guangzhou Road, Nanjing, 210029, China. TEL 86-25-3700011 ext 6109, FAX 86-25-719457. Ed. Shu-tao Di. **Dist. by:** China International Book Trading Corp, 35 Chegongzhuang Xilu, Haidian District, PO Box 399, Beijing 100044, China. TEL 86-10-68412045, FAX 86-10-68412023, cibtc@mail.cibtc.com.cn, http://www.cibtc.com.cn.

616.8 CHN ISSN 1009-5934
LINCHUANG SHENJING DIANSHENGLIXUE ZAZHI/JOURNAL OF CLINICAL ELECTRONEUROPHYSIOLOGY. Text in Chinese. 1992. q. USD 28.20 (effective 2009). **Document type:** *Journal, Academic/Scholarly.*
Formerly (until 2001): Linchuang Naodianxue Zazhi/Journal of Clinical Electroencephalology (1005-9091)
Related titles: Online - full text ed.
—East View.
Published by: Guiyang Yixueyuan/Guiyang Medical College, 28, Guiyi Jie, Guiyang, 550004, China. **Dist. by:** China International Book Trading Corp, 35 Chegongzhuang Xilu, Haidian District, PO Box 399, Beijing 100044, China. TEL 86-10-68412045, FAX 86-10-68412023, cibtc@mail.cibtc.com.cn, http://www.cibtc.com.cn.

616.8 CHN ISSN 1004-1648
LINCHUANG SHENJINGBINGXUE ZAZHI/JOURNAL OF CLINICAL NEUROLOGY. Text in Chinese. 1988. bi-m. USD 31.20 (effective 2009). **Document type:** *Journal, Academic/Scholarly.*
Related titles: Online - full text ed.
Indexed: EMBASE, ExcerpMed, RefZh, SCOPUS.
—BLDSC (4958.574000), East View.
Published by: Nanjing Yike Daxue Fushunao Keyiyuan, 264 Guangzhou Road, Nanjing, 210029, China. TEL 86-25-3700011 ext 6108, FAX 86-25-3719457. **Dist. by:** China International Book Trading Corp, 35 Chegongzhuang Xilu, Haidian District, PO Box 399, Beijing 100044, China. TEL 86-10-68412045, FAX 86-10-68412023, cibtc@mail.cibtc.com.cn, http://www.cibtc.com.cn.

616.8 CAN ISSN 1924-4401
LINK (EDMONTON). Text in English. 200?. s-a. free to members (effective 2010). back issues avail. **Document type:** *Newsletter, Trade.*
Formerly (until 2006): Registered Psychiatric Nurses Association of Alberta. Link (1703-7794)
Related titles: Online - full text ed.
Published by: College of Registered Psychiatric Nurses of Alberta, 201, 9711 - 45 Ave, Edmonton, AB T6E 5V8, Canada. TEL 780-434-7666, 877-234-7666, FAX 780-436-4165, crpna@crpna.ab.ca.

616.8 USA
LINKAGE (BALTIMORE). Text in English. 1991. q. free. **Document type:** *Newsletter, Government.* **Description:** Keeps mental health professionals, consumers and state employees up-to-date on specific mental health issues within the state system and on general mental health issues.
Indexed: E-psyche.
Published by: Department of Health and Mental Hygiene, 201 Preston St, Rm 416A, Baltimore, MD 21201. TEL 410-767-6629, FAX 410-333-5402. Ed., R&P Jean Smith. Circ: 20,000.

LITI DINGXIANG HE GONGNENGXING SHENJING WAIKE ZAZHI/CHINESE JOURNAL OF STEREOTACTIC AND FUNCTIONAL NEUROSURGERY. *see* MEDICAL SCIENCES—Surgery

616.8 618.97 DNK ISSN 1904-3856
LIVET MED DEMENS. Text in Danish. 1991. q. DKK 200 to individual members; DKK 500 to institutional members (effective 2010). **Document type:** *Magazine, Consumer.*
Former titles (until 2010): Demens (1604-1968); (until 2004): Magasin om Alzheimer og andre Demenssygdomme (1603-0605); (until 2001): Alzheimerforeningen. Magasin (1398-5922); (until 1997): Nyt fra Alzheimerforeningen (0908-0929)
Related titles: Online - full text ed.: ISSN 1904-3864. 2004.
Published by: Alzheimerforeningen, Sankt Lukas Vej 7 A, Hellerup, 2900, Denmark. TEL 45-39-400488, FAX 45-39-619669, post@alzheimer.dk. Ed. Nis Peter Nissen. Circ: 6,800.

LIVING IN THE SPECTRUM: AUTISM & ASPERGER'S. *see* PSYCHOLOGY

616.834 USA
LIVING M S MAGAZINE. (Multiple Sclerosis) Text in English. 1997. w. free. **Document type:** *Magazine, Consumer.* **Description:** Dedicated to showcasing the varied talents of people around the world who have or know someone who has Multiple Sclerosis.
Formerly: M S Reality Bytes
Media: Online - full text.
Published by: M S World, Inc. msworld@msworld.org. Ed. Kathy Alberts.

616.855 SWE ISSN 1102-500X
LOGOPEDNYTT. Text in Swedish. 1979. 8/yr. SEK 500 (effective 2004). adv.
Formerly (until vol.3, 1979): Logopedmeddelande
Indexed: E-psyche.
Published by: Svenska Logopedfoerbundet (SLOF)/Swedish Association of Logopedists, PO Box 760, Nacka, 13124, Sweden. TEL 46-8-4662400, FAX 46-8-4662413. Eds. Camille Bjoernram, Elvira Berg. Adv. contact Caroline Kejneman TEL 46-8-4662411. page SEK 7,840; 180 x 258.

616.8 GBR ISSN 2044-2785
THE LONDON SCHOOL OF ECONOMICS AND POLITICAL SCIENCE. BRAIN, SELF & SOCIETY. WORKING PAPERS. Text in English. 2007. irreg., latest no.3, 2008. free (effective 2010). back issues avail. **Document type:** *Monographic series, Academic/Scholarly.*
Media: Online - full text.
Published by: London School of Economics and Political Science, Centre for the Study of B I O S, Rm V1100, Tower 2, 11th Fl, Houghton St, London, WC2A 2AE, United Kingdom. TEL 44-20-79556998, FAX 44-20-78523791, bios@lse.ac.uk, http://www.lse.ac.uk/collections/BIOS/.

616.83 USA
THE M D A / A L S NEWSLETTER. (Amyotrophic Lateral Sclerosis) Text in English. 1996. m. free to individual members (effective 2003). illus.; maps. reprints avail. **Description:** Covers research, lifestyle articles, caregiving issues, profiles.
Formerly (until 2002): The A L S Newsletter
Published by: Muscular Dystrophy Association, Inc., 3300 E Sunrise Dr, Tucson, AZ 85718. TEL 520-529-2000, FAX 520-529-5383, http://www.mda.org. Ed., R&P Carol Sowell TEL 520-529-2000. Pub. Robert Ross. Circ: 20,000 (paid and controlled).

616.8 USA
M D N G NEUROLOGY. (Medical Doctor Net Guide) Text in English. 2002. 8/yr. USD 75; free to qualified personnel (effective 2009). back issues avail. **Document type:** *Handbook/Manual/Guide, Trade.*
Supersedes in part (in 2001): M D Net Guide
Related titles: Online - full text ed.
Published by: Intellisphere, LLC (Subsidiary of: MultiMedia Healthcare Inc.), Office Center at Princeton Meadows, 666 Plainsboro Rd, Bldg 300, Plainsboro, NJ 08536. TEL 609-716-7777, FAX 609-716-4747, info@mdnetguide.com.

616.89 NLD ISSN 0024-8576
➤ **M G V.** (Maandblad Geestelijke Volksgezondheid) Text in Dutch. 1946. 11/yr. EUR 78.50 to individuals; EUR 169.50 to institutions; EUR 35.50 to students (effective 2008). adv. bk.rev. index. **Document type:** *Academic/Scholarly.*
Formerly (until 1969): Maandblad voor de Geestelijke Volksgezondheid (0925-7039)
Related titles: Online - full text ed.
Indexed: A22, E-psyche.
—BLDSC (5318.930000), GNLM, IE, Infotrieve, Ingenta.
Published by: Trimbos Instituut, De Costakade 45, Postbus 725, Utrecht, 3500 AS, Netherlands. TEL 31-30-2971119, FAX 31-30-2971111, info@trimbos.nl, http://www.trimbos.nl. Ed. David J Bos. adv.: B&W page EUR 605; 174 x 248.

616.834 CAN ISSN 0315-1131
M S CANADA. (Multiple Sclerosis) Text in English. 1974. q. CAD 15 membership (effective 2006). bk.rev. **Document type:** *Newsletter.* **Description:** Provides information on M S research, how to cope with multiple sclerosis, and activities of the Society.
Related titles: Online - full text ed.: free.
Indexed: E-psyche.
Published by: Multiple Sclerosis Society of Canada, 250 Bloor St E, Ste 700, North Tower, Toronto, ON M4W 3R8, Canada. TEL 416-922-6065, FAX 416-967-3044. Ed. Cindy K DesGrosseilliers. Circ: 27,000.

616.834 USA
M S EXCHANGE. (Multiple Sclerosis) Text in English. 4/yr. free (effective 2011). **Document type:** *Newsletter, Academic/Scholarly.*
Published by: Delaware Media Group, 66 S. Maple Ave, Ridgewood, NJ 07450. TEL 201-612-7676, FAX 201-612-8282, info@delmedgroup.com, http://www.delmedgroup.com. Ed. Linda Peckel. Pubs. Frank M Marino, Joseph J D'Onofrio.

362.196834 GBR ISSN 1478-467X
M S IN FOCUS. (Multiple Sclerosis) Text in English. 2003. s-a. free (effective 2009). back issues avail. **Document type:** *Magazine, Consumer.* **Description:** Provides people with MS, their carers, healthcare professionals and support groups will find the following areas of MS in focus invaluable: rehabilitation; quality of life and lifestyle; treatments; MS society projects and programmes; and the activities of the global MS community.
Related titles: Online - full text ed.; German ed.; Spanish ed.
Published by: Multiple Sclerosis International Federation, 3rd Fl Skyline House, 200 Union St, London, SE1 0LX, United Kingdom. TEL 44-20-76201911, FAX 44-20-76201922, info@msif.org. Ed. Michele Messmer Uccelli.

616.834 CAN ISSN 0707-0934
M S ONTARIO. (Multiple Sclerosis) Text in English. 1977. q. CAD 15 membership (effective 2006). adv. bk.rev. **Document type:** *Newsletter.*
Related titles: Online - full text ed.: free (effective 2006); French ed.: S P Ontario. ISSN 1495-107X.
Indexed: E-psyche.
Published by: (Multiple Sclerosis Society of Canada, Ontario Division), Multiple Sclerosis Society of Canada, 250 Bloor St E, Ste 700, North Tower, Toronto, ON M4W 3R8, Canada. TEL 416-922-6065, FAX 416-967-3044, info@mssociety.ca. Ed. Cindy K DesGrosseilliers. Circ: 8,000.

616.834 USA ISSN 0738-3967
M S QUARTERLY REPORT. Variant title: M S Q R. Text in English. q. free to members NARCOMS Patient Registry; USD 90 to individuals in the US, Canada & Puerto Rico; USD 140 elsewhere to individuals; USD 130 to institutions in the US, Canada & Puerto Rico; USD 180 elsewhere to institutions (effective 2006). adv. back issues avail. **Document type:** *Newsletter.* **Description:** Dedicated to examining research and quality-of-life issues pertinent to people with multiple sclerosis.
Formerly (until 1981): M S Quarterly (0195-2285)
Indexed: C06, C07, C08, CINAHL.
—CCC.
Published by: United Spinal Organization, 75-20 Astoria Blvd, Jackson Heights, NY 11370. TEL 718-803-3782, FAX 718-803-0414, info@unitedspinal.org, http://www.unitedspinal.org. Ed. Denise Campagnolo. Adv. contact Amy S Reuter TEL 856-768-9360. B&W page USD 900; trim 8.5 x 11. Circ: 29,000 (paid). **Subscr. to:** PO Box 465, Hanover, PA 17331. TEL 717-632-3535, FAX 717-633-8920, pubsvc@tsp.sheridan.com.

616.89 JOR ISSN 1016-8923
AL MAGALLAH AL-'ARABIYYAH LI-L-TIBB AL-NAFSI/ARAB JOURNAL OF PSYCHIATRY. Text in English, Arabic. 1989. m. **Description:** Consists original scientific reports, review articles, and articles describing the clinical practice of Psychiatry will be of interest for publication in AJP.
Indexed: P03, PsycInfo, PsycholAb.
—BLDSC (1583.239700), IE, Ingenta.
Published by: Ittihad Al-aatibba Aal-nafsaniyin Al-arab/The Arab Federation of Psychiatrists, P O Box 5370, Amman, 11183, Jordan. TEL 00962-6-4624650, FAX 00962-6-4623571, takriti@nol.com.jo, http://www.arabpsynet.com/Journals/AJP/index-ajp.htm.

616.8 FRA ISSN 1289-7590
LA MAISON JAUNE. Text in French. 1998. irreg. back issues avail. **Document type:** *Monographic series, Consumer.*
Published by: Editions Eres, 33 Av. Marcel Dassault, Toulouse, 31500, France. TEL 33-5-61751576, FAX 33-5-61735289, eres@edition-eres.com.

616.8 150 IRN ISSN 1735-4315
➤ **MAJALLAH-I RAVANPIZISHKI VA RAVANSHINASI-I BALINI-I IRAN/IRANIAN JOURNAL OF PSYCHIATRY AND CLINICAL PSYCHOLOGY.** Text in Persian, Modern; Summaries in English. 1994 (Jul.). q. IRR 16,000, USD 16 (effective 2011). abstr. back issues avail.; reprints avail. **Document type:** *Journal, Academic/Scholarly.*
Formerly (until 1994): Andishah va Raftar (1024-0047)
Related titles: Online - full text ed.
Indexed: PsycInfo.
Published by: Danishgah-i Ulum-i Pizishki-i Tihran/Tehran University of Medical Sciences, Tehran Psychiatric Institute, Mental Health Research Center, Shahid Mansuri St., Niayesh St., Sattarkhan Ave., PO Box 14565-441, Tehran, 1443813444, Iran. TEL 98-21-66506853, FAX 98-21-66506853. Ed. Amir Shabani.

616.8 DEU ISSN 0949-121X
MANAGEMENT OF PAIN. Text in German. 1995. irreg. **Document type:** *Monographic series, Academic/Scholarly.*
Published by: Arcis Verlag GmbH, Wendelsteinstr 2, Munich, 85579, Germany. TEL 49-89-605996, FAX 49-89-603279, info@arcis-verlag.de, http://www.arcis-verlag.de.

616.8 USA ISSN 0882-3634
MARKER. Text in English. 1967. 2/yr. free. bk.rev. back issues avail. **Document type:** *Magazine, Consumer.* **Description:** Covers national and local news and events relevant to patients with Huntington's disease and their families. Includes medical and scientific research updates.
Formerly (until 198?): Committee to Combat Huntington's Disease Newsletter (0882-3642)
Indexed: E-psyche.
Published by: Huntington's Disease Society of America, 158 West 29th St, 7th Fl, New York, NY 10001-5300. TEL 212-239-3430, FAX 212-243-2443, hdsainfo@hdsa.org, http://www.hdsa.org/. Ed. Amy Schoenberg. Circ: 60,000.

616.89 GBR ISSN 0076-5465
MAUDSLEY MONOGRAPHS. Text in English. 1955. irreg., latest 2008. price varies. back issues avail. **Document type:** *Monographic series, Academic/Scholarly.*
Related titles: Online - full text ed.
Indexed: E-psyche.
—BLDSC (5413.271000), IE, Ingenta.
Published by: (University of London, Institute of Psychiatry), Routledge (Subsidiary of: Taylor & Francis Group), 4 Park Sq, Milton Park, Abingdon, Oxon OX14 4RN, United Kingdom. TEL 44-20-70176000, FAX 44-20-70176336, subscriptions@tandf.co.uk, http://www.routledge.com. Ed. A S David.

MEALEY'S LITIGATION REPORT: WELDING RODS. *see* LAW—Civil Law

616.89 USA ISSN 2158-1770
MEDICAL PSYCHIATRY. Text in English. 1994. irreg. back issues avail. **Document type:** *Monographic series, Trade.* **Description:** Provides information about psychiatrical treatments.
Related titles: Online - full text ed.
—BLDSC (5531.365000).
Published by: Informa Healthcare (Subsidiary of: T & F Informa plc), 52 Vanderbilt Ave, New York, NY 10017. TEL 212-520-2777, healthcare.enquiries@informa.com, http://www.informahealthcare.com.

616.8 DEU
MEDICAL TRIBUNE NEUROLOGIE - PSYCHIATRIE. Text in German. 2007. bi-m. adv. **Document type:** *Journal, Trade.*
Published by: Medical Tribune Verlagsgesellschaft mbH, Unter den Eichen 5, Wiesbaden, 65195, Germany. TEL 49-611-97460, FAX 49-611-9746303, online@medical-tribune.de, http://www.medical-tribune.de. adv.: B&W page EUR 2,570, color page EUR 3,350. Circ: 7,500 (controlled).

616.89 ITA ISSN 0025-7893
CODEN: MDPSAC
MEDICINA PSICOSOMATICA; rivista di medicina psicosomatica, psicologia clinica e psicoterapia. Text in Italian; Summaries in English, French, Italian. 1956. q. EUR 54.43 (effective 2008). adv. bk.rev. abstr.; bibl.; charts. index. **Document type:** *Journal, Academic/Scholarly.*
Related titles: Online - full text ed.
Indexed: A22, E-psyche, P03, P30, PsycInfo, PsycholAb.
—BLDSC (5533.650000), GNLM, IE, Ingenta, INIST.
Published by: (Societa Italiana Medicina Psicosomatica), Societa Editrice Universo, Via Giovanni Battista Morgagni 1, Rome, RM 00161, Italy. TEL 39-06-44231171, FAX 39-06-4402033, amministrazione@seu-roma.it, http://www.seuroma.com.

616.8 USA ISSN 1543-5024
➤ **MEDICINE AND SOCIETY.** Text in English. 1988. irreg., latest vol.13, 2006. price varies. back issues avail. **Document type:** *Monographic series, Academic/Scholarly.* **Description:** Discusses psychotherapy past and present in the US and Europe.
Related titles: Online - full text ed.
Indexed: E-psyche.
—BLDSC (5534.006900).
Published by: University of California Press, Book Series, 2120 Berkeley Way, Berkeley, CA 94704. TEL 510-642-4247, FAX 510-643-7127, foundation@ucpress.edu. **Subscr. to:** California - Princeton Fulfillment Services, Inc., 1445 Lower Ferry Rd, Ewing, NJ 08618. TEL 609-883-1759, 800-777-4726, FAX 800-999-1958, orders@cpfsinc.com.

616.8 BGR ISSN 1311-6584
➤ **MEDITSINSKI PREGLED. NEVROLOGIIA I PSICHIATRIIA.** Text in Bulgarian; Summaries in Bulgarian, English. 1970. q. BGL 14 domestic; USD 40 foreign (effective 2005). adv. bk.rev. abstr.; bibl.; illus. index. 48 p./no.; back issues avail. **Document type:** *Journal, Academic/Scholarly.* **Description:** Publishes original articles and abstracts of foreign publications in the fields of neurology and psychiatry; covers mental health services, as well as social problems related to mental disorders.
Formerly: Nervni i Psikhichni Zaboliavaniia (0204-5052)
Indexed: ABSML, E-psyche.
—BLDSC (0124.050000).
Published by: Meditsinski Universitet - Sofia, Tsentralna Meditsinska Biblioteka, Tsentur za Informatsiia po Meditsina/Medical University - Sofia, Central Medical Library, Medical Information Center, 1 Sv Georgi Sofiiski ul, Sofia, 1431, Bulgaria. TEL 359-2-9522342, FAX 359-2-9522393, lydia@medun.acad.bg, http://www.medun.acad.bg/cmb_htm/cmb1_home_bg.htm. Ed. Dr. A Aleksiev. R&P, Adv. contact Lydia Tacheva. B&W page USD 50, color page USD 150; trim 160 x 110. Circ: 350.

616.8 NLD ISSN 1566-7898
MEDIUM. Variant title: Myalgische Encephalomyelitis Medium. Text in Dutch. 1988. q. adv. **Document type:** *Magazine, Consumer.*
Published by: M E-C V S Stichting Nederland, Noordse Bosje 16, Hilversum, 1211 BG, Netherlands. TEL 31-35-6211290, FAX 31-35-6211219, info@me-cvs-stichting.nl. adv.: B&W page EUR 703, color page EUR 1,439; trim 210 x 297. Circ: 5,000 (controlled).

616.89 USA ISSN 1532-043X
➤ **MEDSCAPE MENTAL HEALTH.** Text in English. 1996. w. **Document type:** *Journal, Academic/Scholarly.* **Description:** Provides clinicians with information for recognizing and managing psychiatric illnesses.
Media: Online - full text.
Indexed: E-psyche.
Published by: WebMD Medscape Health Network, 224 W 30th St, New York, NY 10001. TEL 888-506-6098.

616.8521 362 FRA ISSN 1763-5985
MEMOIRES. Text in French. 1997. q. EUR 20 (effective 2008). back issues avail. **Document type:** *Journal, Consumer.*
Published by: Association Primo Levi, 107 Av. Parmentier, Paris, 75011, France. TEL 33-1-43148850, FAX 33-1-43140828, primolevi@primolevi.asso.fr.

616.89 USA ISSN 0025-9284
RC321 CODEN: BMCLA4
➤ **MENNINGER CLINIC. BULLETIN**; a journal for the mental health professions. Text in English. 1936. q. USD 85 combined subscription domestic to individuals (print & online eds.); USD 120 combined subscription foreign to individuals (print & online eds.); USD 435 combined subscription domestic to institutions (print & online eds.); USD 480 combined subscription foreign to institutions (print & online eds.) (effective 2011). bk.rev. bibl.; charts; illus. index. back issues avail.; reprints avail. **Document type:** *Journal, Academic/Scholarly.* **Description:** Contains articles on psychiatry, psychology, psychoanalysis, child psychiatry, neuropsychology, clinical research, and related subjects, as well as clinical reports and brief communications.
Related titles: Microform ed.: (from PQC); Online - full text ed.: ISSN 1943-2828.
Indexed: A01, A02, A03, A08, A20, A22, AC&P, ASCA, ASSIA, C11, CA, CPLI, CurCont, E-psyche, E01, EMBASE, ExcerpMed, FR, FamI, H04, HospLI, INI, IndMed, MEA&I, MEDLINE, MLA-IB, P03, P20, P22, P25, P30, P43, P48, P54, PCI, PQC, PsycInfo, PsycholAb, R10, Reac, S02, S03, SCOPUS, SOPODA, SSCI, SWR&A, SociolAb, T02, W07.
—BLDSC (2612.200000), GNLM, IE, Infotrieve, Ingenta, INIST. **CCC.**
Published by: (Menninger Foundation), Guilford Publications, Inc., 72 Spring St, 4th Fl, New York, NY 10012. TEL 800-365-7006, FAX 212-966-6708, info@guilford.com. Ed. Dr. W. Walter Menninger. R&P Kathy Kuehl. Adv. contact Marian Robinson. Circ: 600 (paid).

616.89 USA ISSN 0025-9292
RC321 CODEN: MNPVB
MENNINGER PERSPECTIVE. Text in English. 1970. q. illus. reprints avail. **Document type:** *Magazine, Consumer.* **Description:** Articles related to mental health, mental illness, and Menninger programs.
Formerly: Menninger Quarterly
Related titles: Microform ed.: (from PQC).
Indexed: A22, C06, C07, C08, CINAHL, E-psyche, IMI, P30, PsycholAb.
—GNLM, Ingenta.
Published by: Menninger Foundation, 2801 Gessner Dr., Houston, TX 77080-2503. TEL 785-350-5000, 800-288-3930, FAX 785-273-0797. Circ: 66,000 (controlled).

616.8 IND ISSN 0973-1229
➤ **MENS SANA MONOGRAPHS.** Text in English. 2003. a. INR 700 domestic to individuals (print or online ed.); USD 70 foreign to individuals (print or online ed.); INR 900 domestic to institutions (print or online ed.); USD 90 foreign to institutions (print or online ed.); INR 1,200 domestic to individuals (print & online eds.); USD 120 foreign to individuals (print & online eds.); INR 2,000 domestic to institutions (print & online eds.); USD 200 foreign to institutions (print & online eds.) (effective 2011). adv. **Document type:** *Monographic series, Academic/Scholarly.* **Description:** Devoted to the understanding of medicine, mental health, man and their matrix. It attempts to give in-depth understanding of psychiatric, biomedical, psychological and philosophical consequences of social disorders issues and current events.
Related titles: Online - full text ed.: ISSN 1998-4014.
Indexed: A01, A26, CA, I05, P10, P30, P48, P53, P54, PQC, SCOPUS, T02.
—IE. **CCC.**
Published by: (Mens Sana Research Foundation), Medknow Publications and Media Pvt. Ltd., B-9, Kanara Business Ctr, Off Link Rd, Ghatkopar (E), Mumbai, Maharastra 400 075, India. TEL 91-22-66491816, FAX 91-22-66491817, http://www.medknow.com. Ed. Ajai R Singh.

➤ **MENTAL DISABILITY LAW: CIVIL AND CRIMINAL.** *see* LAW

➤ **MENTAL HEALTH & AGING.** *see* GERONTOLOGY AND GERIATRICS

362.2 371.92 GBR ISSN 1743-6885
MENTAL HEALTH AND LEARNING DISABILITIES RESEARCH AND PRACTICE. Text in English. 2004. s-a. back issues avail. **Document type:** *Journal, Academic/Scholarly.* **Description:** Covers articles relating to mental health or learning disability research, service or educational developments.
Related titles: Online - full text ed.: free (effective 2009).
—BLDSC (5678.580350).
Published by: (South West Yorkshire Mental Health N H S Trust), University of Huddersfield, Queensgate, Huddersfield, HD1 3DH, United Kingdom. TEL 44-1484-422288, FAX 44-1484-450408, international.office@hud.ac.uk, http://www.hud.ac.uk/. **Co-publisher:** South West Yorkshire Mental Health N H S Trust.

MENTAL HEALTH AND SPECIALIST CARE SERVICES; U K Market Report (Year). *see* BUSINESS AND ECONOMICS—Production Of Goods And Services

MENTAL HEALTH AND SUBSTANCE USE; dual diagnosis. *see* DRUG ABUSE AND ALCOHOLISM

616.89 USA ISSN 1552-9096
MENTAL HEALTH BUSINESS WEEK. Text in English. 2004. w. USD 2,295 in US & Canada; USD 2,495 elsewhere; USD 2,525 combined subscription in US & Canada (print & online eds.); USD 2,755 combined subscription elsewhere (print & online eds.) (effective 2008). back issues avail. **Document type:** *Newsletter, Trade.*
Related titles: E-mail ed.; Online - full text ed.: ISSN 1552-910X. USD 2,295 combined subscription (online & email eds.); single user (effective 2008).
Indexed: A15, ABIn, B16, H13, P10, P20, P21, P48, P51, P53, P54, PQC.
Published by: NewsRx, 2727 Paces Ferry Rd SE, Ste 2-440, Atlanta, GA 30339. TEL 770-435-8286, 800-726-4550, FAX 770-435-6800, pressrelease@newsrx.com, http://www.newsrx.com. Pub. Susan Hasty TEL 770-507-7777.

616.8 150 GBR ISSN 1756-834X
➤ **MENTAL HEALTH IN FAMILY MEDICINE.** Text in English. 2003 (June). q. GBP 195 combined subscription (print & online eds.) (effective 2009). adv. abstr.; charts; illus. a.index. back issues avail.; reprints avail. **Document type:** *Journal, Academic/Scholarly.* **Description:** Focuses on research, education, development and delivery of mental health in primary care; as well as the results or original research, innovative techniques and best practice, providing a multidisciplinary forum for professionals in health, social and voluntary care.
Formerly (until 2008): Primary Care Mental Health (1476-4717)
Related titles: Online - full text ed.: ISSN 1756-8358 (from IngentaConnect).
Indexed: A01, A03, A08, A22, B28, C06, C07, C08, CA, CINAHL, E01, EMBASE, ExcerpMed, P43, SCOPUS, T02.
—BLDSC (5678.583510), IE, Ingenta. **CCC.**
Published by: (World Organization of Family Doctors), Radcliffe Publishing Ltd., 18 Marcham Rd, Abingdon, Oxon OX14 1AA, United Kingdom. TEL 44-1235-528820, FAX 44-1235-528830, contact.us@radcliffemed.com. Ed. Gabriel Ivbijaro TEL 44-20-84307712. adv.: B&W page GBP 400; trim 210 x 297. Circ: 2,500.

616.8 344.041 USA ISSN 0889-017X
KF2910.P75
MENTAL HEALTH LAW NEWS. Text in English. 1986. m. looseleaf. USD 79 (effective 2005). 6 p./no. 1 cols./p.; back issues avail. **Document type:** *Newsletter, Trade.* **Description:** Provides case law summaries on mental health malpractice, commitment, appropriate treatment, consent and patient danger to community.
Indexed: E-psyche.
Published by: Interwood Publications, 3 Interweed Pl, Cincinnati, OH 45220. TEL 207-865-9800. Ed., Pub. Frank J Bardack. R&P Frank Bardack.

616.8 344.041 USA ISSN 1551-5133
MENTAL HEALTH LAW WEEKLY. Text in English. 2004. w. USD 2,295 in US & Canada; USD 2,495 elsewhere; USD 2,525 combined subscription in US & Canada (print & online eds.); USD 2,755 combined subscription elsewhere (print & online eds.) (effective 2008). back issues avail. **Document type:** *Newsletter, Trade.*
Related titles: E-mail ed.; Online - full text ed.: ISSN 1551-5141. USD 2,295 combined subscription (online & email eds.); single user (effective 2008).
Indexed: L10, P10, P21, P48, P53, P54, PQC.
Published by: NewsRx, 2727 Paces Ferry Rd SE, Ste 2-440, Atlanta, GA 30339. TEL 770-435-8286, 800-726-4550, FAX 770-435-6800, pressrelease@newsrx.com, http://www.newsrx.com. Pub. Susan Hasty TEL 770-507-7777.

616.858 AUS ISSN 1838-6075
▼ **MENTAL HEALTH LIAISON.** Text in English. 2010. s-a. **Document type:** *Journal, Academic/Scholarly.* **Description:** Aims to provide a forum to publish original research and scholarly papers about the complex speciality of mental health consultation liaison nursing.
Related titles: Online - full text ed.: free (effective 2011).
Published by: Mental Health Consultation Liaison Nurses Association, PO Box 8122, Blacktown, NSW 2148, Australia. Ed. Scott Brunero.

616.8 AUS
MENTAL HEALTH MATTERS. Text in English. 1974. q. free to members (effective 2007). adv. bk.rev. back issues avail. **Document type:** *Newsletter, Trade.*
Former titles (until 1993): N S W A M H News; (until 1986): New South Wales Association for Mental Health. Newsletter (0813-1724); (until 1983): New South Wales Association for Mental Health. News Letter (0155-1205); (until 1979): Mental Health Newsletter (0811-9384); (until 1978): New South Wales Association for Mental Health. News Letter (0811-9376)
Indexed: E-psyche.
Published by: New South Wales Association for Mental Health, Level 5, 80 William St, East Sydney, NSW 2011, Australia. TEL 61-2-93396000, FAX 61-2-93396066, info@mentalhealth.asn.au, http://www.mentalhealth.asn.au. Circ: 500 (controlled).

362.2 NZL ISSN 1178-4997
MENTAL HEALTH NEWSLETTER. Text in English. 2001. q.
Formerly (until 2007): Mental Health Directorate Newsletter (1176-001X)
Related titles: Online - full text ed.: ISSN 1177-9101.
Published by: New Zealand Ministry of Health, Box 5013, Wellington, New Zealand. TEL 64-4-4962000, FAX 64-4-4962340, emailmoh@moh.govt.nz, http://moh.govt.nz.

616.8 GBR ISSN 2043-7501
➤ **MENTAL HEALTH NURSING (ONLINE).** Abbreviated title: M H N. Text in English. 2008. bi-m. free to members (effective 2010). **Document type:** *Journal, Academic/Scholarly.* **Description:** Covers all aspects of mental health nursing in United Kingdom, from education and practice to current news and resource reviews.
Media: Online - full text.
Indexed: P24.
Published by: (Mental Health Nurse's Association), Ten Alps Publishing (Subsidiary of: Ten Alps Group), Commonwealth House, One New Oxford St, London, WC1A 1NU, United Kingdom. TEL 44-20-78782311, FAX 44-20-78782483, info@tenalps.com, http://www.tenalps.com.

616.8 GBR ISSN 1465-8720
RC440
MENTAL HEALTH PRACTICE. Text in English. 1998. 10/yr. GBP 200 in Europe to institutions; GBP 225 elsewhere to institutions (effective 2011). adv. back issues avail. **Document type:** *Journal, Academic/Scholarly.* **Description:** Provides up-to-date information on developments in mental health nursing.
Related titles: Online - full text ed.: GBP 200 to institutions (effective 2011).
Indexed: A01, A02, A03, A08, A26, B28, C06, C07, C08, C11, CA, CINAHL, E-psyche, E08, G08, H04, H11, H12, I05, P20, P24, P34, P48, P54, PQC, S02, S03, S09, T02.
—BLDSC (5678.583750), IE, Ingenta. **CCC.**
Published by: (Royal College of Nursing), R C N Publishing Co. (Subsidiary of: B M J Group), The Heights, 59-65 Lowlands Rd, Harrow, Middx HA1 3AW, United Kingdom. TEL 44-20-84231066, FAX 44-20-84239196, advertising@rcnpublishing.co.uk, http://www.rcnpublishing.co.uk. Eds. Colin Parish, Jean Gray. Adv. contact Neil Hobson TEL 44-20-88723123. page GBP 2,299; trim 216 x 279. Circ: 11,643.

616.89 NLD ISSN 1385-4933
MENTAL HEALTH REFORMS. Text in English. 1996-2003; resumed 2007. irreg. free (effective 2009).
Indexed: SCOPUS.
Published by: Global Initiative on Psychiatry, PO Box 1282, Hilversum, 1200 BG, Netherlands. TEL 31-35-6838727, FAX 31-35-6833646, info@gip-global.org, http://www.gip-global.org. Ed. Ellen Mercer.

360 150 GBR ISSN 1361-9322
RA790.7.G7
THE MENTAL HEALTH REVIEW JOURNAL. Text in English. 1996. q. EUR 689 combined subscription in Europe (print & online eds.); USD 889 combined subscription in the Americas (print & online eds.); GBP 529 combined subscription in the UK & elsewhere (print & online eds.); AUD 999 combined subscription in Australasia (print & online eds.) (effective 2012). adv. back issues avail. **Document type:** *Journal, Academic/Scholarly.* **Description:** Offers readers a medium between policy issues and innovative practice in mental health services.
Related titles: Online - full text ed.: ISSN 2042-8758.
Indexed: A01, B28, C06, C07, C08, CA, CINAHL, E-psyche, P02, P10, P12, P16, P24, P25, P48, P53, P54, PQC, PsycInfo, S02, S03, SWR&A, T02.
—BLDSC (5678.584800), IE, Ingenta. **CCC.**
Published by: (Sainsbury Centre for Mental Health, University of London King's College, Centre for Mental Health Services Development), Pier Professional Ltd. (Subsidiary of: Emerald Group Publishing Ltd.), Ste N4, The Old Market, Upper Market St, Hove, BN3 1AS, United Kingdom. TEL 44-1273-783720, FAX 44-1273-783723, info@pierprofessional.com. Eds. Chiara Samele, Ian Shaw, Mark Freestone. adv.: B&W page GBP 350; 160 x 245.

616.890 GBR ISSN 1474-5186
RA790
MENTAL HEALTH TODAY. Text in English. 1997. m. GBP 35 combined subscription to individuals (print & online eds.); GBP 95 combined subscription to institutions (print & online eds.) (effective 2010). adv. **Document type:** *Magazine, Trade.* **Description:** Keeps you up to date with developments in policy and practice. Its aim is to showcase the diversity of evidence-based best practice in the statutory, voluntary and independent sectors across the UK.
Formerly (until 2001): Mental Health & Learning Disabilities Care (1466-8785); (until 1999): Mental Health Care (1368-1230)
Related titles: Online - full text ed.: GBP 25 to individuals; GBP 75 to institutions (effective 2010).
Indexed: B28, C06, C07, C08, CINAHL, E-psyche, EMBASE, ExcerpMed, F09, MEDLINE, P19, P20, P22, P24, P25, P30, P48, P54, PQC, R10, Reac, SCOPUS.
—BLDSC (5678.589200), IE, Infotrieve, Ingenta. **CCC.**
Published by: Pavilion Publishing, Richmond Hous, Richmond Rd., Brighton, East Sussex BN2 3RL, United Kingdom. TEL 44-844-8805061, 44-1273-623222, FAX 44-844-8805062, info@pavpub.com.

MENTAL HEALTH WEEKLY; news for policy and program decision-makers. *see* PSYCHOLOGY

616.8 USA ISSN 1543-6616
MENTAL HEALTH WEEKLY DIGEST. Text in English. 2003. w. USD 2,295 in US & Canada; USD 2,495 elsewhere; USD 2,525 combined subscription in US & Canada (print & online eds.); USD 2,755 combined subscription elsewhere (print & online eds.) (effective 2008). back issues avail. **Document type:** *Newsletter, Trade.* **Description:** Reports on latest research in depression, schizophrenia, paranoia, and other major mental conditions, including drug development, risk factors and therapies.
Related titles: E-mail ed.; Online - full text ed.: ISSN 1543-6608. USD 2,295 combined subscription (online & email eds.); single user (effective 2008).
Indexed: A26, B02, B15, B17, B18, E08, G04, G08, H11, H12, I05, I07, S09, S23.
—CIS.
Published by: NewsRx, 2727 Paces Ferry Rd SE, Ste 2-440, Atlanta, GA 30339. TEL 770-435-8286, 800-726-4550, FAX 770-435-6800, pressrelease@newsrx.com. Pub. Susan Hasty TEL 770-507-7777.

362.2 ITA ISSN 2036-7465
RA790.A1
▼ ➤ **MENTAL ILLNESS.** Text in English. 2009. irreg. free (effective 2011). **Document type:** *Journal, Academic/Scholarly.*
Media: Online - full text.
Published by: Pagepress, Via Giuseppe Belli 4, Pavia, 27100, Italy. TEL 39-0382-1751762, FAX 39-0382-1750481. Ed. Jens Reimer.

362.2 CAN ISSN 1910-3255
MENTAL ILLNESS FOUNDATION. ACTIVITY REPORT. Text in English. 2003. a. **Document type:** *Report, Trade.*
Media: Online - full text. **Related titles:** French ed.: Fondation des Maladies Mentales. Rapport d'Activites. ISSN 1910-3263.
Published by: Mental Illness Foundation/Fondation des Maladies Mentales, 401-2120 Sherbrooke St E, Montreal, PQ H2K 1C3, Canada. TEL 514-529-5354, FAX 514-529-9877, info@fmm-mif.ca.

THE MENTAL LEXICON. *see* LINGUISTICS

616.8 EGY ISSN 1110-1334
MENTAL PEACE/MAGALLAT AL-NAFS AL-MOTMA'ENNA. Text in Arabic. 1984. 3/yr. **Document type:** *Journal, Academic/Scholarly.*
Published by: World Islamic Association for Mental Health, Gamal Madi Abou El-Azayem Hospital, Nasr City, PO Box 8180, Cairo, 11371, Egypt. http://www.geocities.com/wiamh2001/index.html. Ed. Dr. Farouk El Sendiony.

362.2 616.890 HUN ISSN 1419-8126
MENTALHIGIENE ES PSZICHOSZOMATIKA/JOURNAL OF MENTAL HEALTH AND PSYCHOSOMATICS. Text in Hungarian. 1989. q. EUR 63, USD 84 combined subscription (print & online eds.) (effective 2011). 100 p./no.; **Document type:** *Journal, Academic/Scholarly.*
Formerly (until 1998): Vegeken (0865-7661)
Related titles: Online - full text ed.: ISSN 1786-3759. EUR 54, USD 71 (effective 2011).
Indexed: P03, PsycInfo, PsycholAb, SCOPUS.
—BLDSC (5678.704000), Ingenta.
Published by: Akademiai Kiado Rt. (Subsidiary of: Wolters Kluwer N.V.), Prielle Kornelia u 19/D, Budapest, 1117, Hungary. TEL 36-1-4648222, FAX 36-1-4648221, journals@akkrt.hu. Ed. Maria Kopp.

616.891 ITA ISSN 2037-2752
▼ **MENTE E CURA.** Text in Multiple languages. 2009. s-a. EUR 10 per issue (effective 2010). **Document type:** *Journal, Trade.*
Published by: (Istituto Romano di Psicoterapia Psicodinamica Integrata (I R P P I)), Alpes Italia, Via Cipro 77, Rome, 00136, Italy. info@alpesitalia.it, http://www.alpesitalia.it.

616.8 AUS ISSN 1838-9619
▼ ➤ **MIDDLE EAST JOURNAL OF PSYCHIATRY AND ALZHEIMERS.** Abbreviated title: M E- J P A. Text in English. 2010. 3/yr. adv. **Document type:** *Journal, Academic/Scholarly.* **Description:** Publishes original clinical and educational research of interest to psychiatrists, geriatricians, primary care physicians, practicing clinicians, residents, and others involved in, services for health related problems in older people.
Related titles: Online - full text ed.: ISSN 1838-9627. free (effective 2011).
Published by: Medi+World International, 11 Colston Ave, Sherbrooke, VIC 3789, Australia. TEL 61-3-90059847, FAX 61-3-90125857, admin@mediworld.com.au, http://www.mediworld.com.au. Ed. Abdul Abyad. Pub., Adv. contact Lesley Pocock.

362.2 616.89 FIN ISSN 0303-2558
MIELENTERVEYS/MENTAL HEALTH. Text in Finnish. 1961. bi-m. EUR 42; EUR 21 to students (effective 2004). adv. bk.rev. back issues avail. **Document type:** *Magazine, Trade.*
Indexed: E-psyche.
Published by: Suomen Mielenterveysseura/Finnish Association for Mental Health, Maistraatinportti 4 A, Helsinki, 00240, Finland. TEL 358-9-615516, FAX 358-9-61551770. Ed. Kristina Salonen. Circ: 15,000.

616.8 DEU ISSN 0946-7122
MIGRAENE MAGAZIN. Text in German. 1995. 4/yr. EUR 5.50 newsstand/cover (effective 2007). adv. **Document type:** *Magazine, Trade.*
Published by: MigraeneLiga e.V., Westerwaldstr 1, Ginsheim-Gustavsburg, 65462, Germany. TEL 49-6144-2211, FAX 49-6144-31908, info@migraeneliga-deutschland.de. adv.: B&W page EUR 1,100, color page EUR 1,560. Circ: 10,000 (controlled).

616.857 GBR ISSN 0544-1153
MIGRAINE NEWS. Text in English. 1967. 3/yr. membership donation. bk.rev. **Document type:** *Journal, Trade.* **Description:** Designed to keep migraine sufferers to date with the latest advances in treatment and migraine research.
Indexed: E-psyche.
—**CCC.**
Published by: Migraine Trust, 55-56 Russell Sq, London, WC1B 4HP, United Kingdom. TEL 44-20-74626601, FAX 44-20-74362880, info@migrainetrust.org. Ed. Alli Anthony TEL 44-20-74626605.

616.8 GBR ISSN 2042-468X
▼ ➤ **MIND & BRAIN, THE JOURNAL OF PSYCHIATRY.** Text in English. 2010 (Jun.). s-a. free (effective 2010). back issues avail.; reprints avail. **Document type:** *Journal, Academic/Scholarly.* **Description:** Brings out research, review articles, correspondence on the latest advances in the diagnosis and treatment of mental illness.
Related titles: Online - full text ed.: ISSN 2042-4698.
Indexed: A01, P30.
Published by: San Lucas Medical Ltd., 11-12 Freetrade House, Lowther Rd, Stanmore, Middlesex HA7 1EP, United Kingdom. TEL 44-20-32869384, editor@slm-journals.com, http://www.sanlucasmedical.com.

➤ **MIND, BRAIN, AND EDUCATION.** *see* EDUCATION

616.89 323.4 USA ISSN 1537-5013
MIND FREEDOM JOURNAL; human rights in mental health. Text in English. 1988. biennial. USD 20; USD 20 foreign. adv. bk.rev.; video rev.; film rev. illus. 64 p./no.; back issues avail. **Document type:** *Journal, Consumer.* **Description:** News of human rights in mental health, especially alternatives to forced psychiatric procedures.
Formerly (until Apr. 2001): Dendron News (1073-7138)
Related titles: Diskette ed.; Online - full text ed.: ISSN 1553-7714.
Indexed: E-psyche.
Address: 454 Willamette St, Ste 216, Box 11284, Eugene, OR 97440-3484. TEL 541-345-9106, FAX 541-345-3737. Ed. David Oaks. Pub. Ron Unger. Adv. contacts Coquille Houshour, Matt Morrissey. page USD 250. Circ: 20,000.

▼ **MINDFULNESS.** *see* PSYCHOLOGY

362.2 NZL ISSN 1178-2587
MINDNET.ORG.NZ. Text in English. 2004. irreg. free. back issues avail. **Document type:** *Newsletter, Trade.* **Description:** Keeps you up-to-date with the latest in mental health promotion in Aotearoa New Zealand. Articles generally focus on research, policy, good practice, evidence and events.
Media: Online - full text.
Published by: Mental Health Foundation of New Zealand, PO Box 10051, Dominion Rd, Auckland, 1446, New Zealand. TEL 64-9-3007010, FAX 64-9-3007020, communications@mentalhealth.org.nz, http://www.mentalhealth.org.nz.

616.8 ITA ISSN 0391-1772
➤ **MINERVA PSICHIATRICA;** a journal on psychiatry, psychology and psychopharmacology. Text in Italian; Summaries in English, Italian. 1960. q. USD 240 combined subscription in the European Union to institutions (print & online eds.); USD 255 combined subscription elsewhere to institutions (print & online eds.) (effective 2011). adv. bk.rev. bibl.; charts; illus. index. **Document type:** *Journal, Academic/Scholarly.* **Description:** Covers clinical psychiatry, clinical psychology, social psychiatry, neuropsychiatry and psychopharmacology.
Former titles (until 1976): Minerva Psichiatrica e Psicologica (0374-9320); (until 1972): Minerva Medicopsicologica (0026-4865)
Related titles: Microform ed.: (from PQC); Online - full text ed.: ISSN 1827-1731. 2005.
Indexed: A22, E-psyche, EMBASE, ExcerpMed, FR, IndMed, P03, P30, PsycInfo, PsycholAb, R10, Reac, SCOPUS.
—BLDSC (5794.465000), GNLM, IE, Ingenta, INIST. **CCC.**
Published by: Edizioni Minerva Medica, Corso Bramante 83-85, Turin, 10126, Italy. TEL 39-011-678282, FAX 39-011-674502, journals.dept@minervamedica.it, http://www.minervamedica.it. Ed. M De Vanna. Pub. Alberto Oliaro. Circ: 3,000 (paid).

616.8 DEU ISSN 0946-7211
RD1 CODEN: MINUED
➤ **MINIMALLY INVASIVE NEUROSURGERY.** Text in English. 1958. bi-m. EUR 648 to institutions; EUR 862 combined subscription to institutions (print & online eds.); EUR 125 per issue (effective 2011). adv. bk.rev. illus. reprints avail. **Document type:** *Journal, Academic/Scholarly.* **Description:** Devoted to minimally invasive neuosurgery. Includes operative procedures, clinical advances and all new technological developments.
Formerly (until 1994): Neurochirurgia (0028-3819)
Related titles: Microform ed.: (from PQC); Online - full text ed.: ISSN 1439-2291. EUR 830 to institutions (effective 2011).
Indexed: A01, A03, A08, A22, ASCA, BDM&CN, CA, CurCont, DentInd, E-psyche, EMBASE, ExcerpMed, IBR, IBZ, INI, ISR, IndMed, Inpharma, MEDLINE, NSCI, P30, R10, Reac, SCI, SCOPUS, T02, W07.
—BLDSC (5797.711000), GNLM, IE, Infotrieve, Ingenta, INIST. **CCC.**
Published by: Georg Thieme Verlag, Ruedigerstr 14, Stuttgart, 70469, Germany. TEL 49-711-8931421, FAX 49-711-8931410, leser.service@thieme.de, http://www.thieme-connect.de. Ed. N Hopf. adv.: B&W page EUR 1,040, color page EUR 2,135. Circ: 700 (paid and controlled). **Subscr. to:** Thieme Medical Publishers, 333 Seventh Ave, New York, NY 10001. TEL 212-760-0888, 800-782-3488, FAX 212-947-1112, custserv@thieme.com, http://www.thieme.com/journals.

616.8 CHE ISSN 1662-2685
RC483 CODEN: MPPPBK
➤ **MODERN TRENDS IN PHARMACOPSYCHIATRY.** Text in English. 1968. irreg., latest vol.27, 2010. price varies. reprints avail. **Document type:** *Monographic series, Academic/Scholarly.* **Description:** Information on the development, evaluation and use of drugs and selected therapeutic interventions in psychiatric practice and research.
Formerly: Modern Problems of Pharmacopsychiatry (0077-0094)
Related titles: Online - full text ed.: ISSN 1662-4505.
Indexed: A22, CIN, ChemAb, ChemTitl, E-psyche, EMBASE, ExcerpMed, FoP, IndMed, MycolAb, P30, PsycholAb, R10, Reac, SCOPUS.
—CASDDS, GNLM, IE, Infotrieve, INIST. **CCC.**
Published by: S. Karger AG, Allschwilerstr 10, Basel, 4055, Switzerland. TEL 41-61-3061111, FAX 41-61-3061234, karger@karger.ch, http://www.karger.ch. Ed. B Leonard.

616.8 USA ISSN 1044-7431
QP356.2 CODEN: MOCNED
➤ **MOLECULAR AND CELLULAR NEUROSCIENCE.** Short title: M C N. Text in English. 1990. m. EUR 1,652 in Europe to institutions; JPY 172,600 in Japan to institutions; USD 1,306 elsewhere to institutions (effective 2012). adv. back issues avail.; reprints avail. **Document type:** *Journal, Academic/Scholarly.* **Description:** Focuses on synaptic maintenance and organization, neuron-glia communication and regenerative neurobiology.
Related titles: Online - full text ed.: ISSN 1095-9327 (from IngentaConnect, ScienceDirect).
Indexed: A01, A03, A08, A22, A26, A29, ASCA, B20, B21, B25, B27, BIOSIS Prev, C33, CA, ChemAb, ChemTitl, CurCont, E-psyche, E01, EMBASE, ESPM, ExcerpMed, I05, I10, ISR, IndMed, Inpharma, MEDLINE, MycolAb, NSA, NSCI, P30, R10, Reac, S01, SCI, SCOPUS, T02, VirolAbstr, W07.
—BLDSC (5900.760700), CASDDS, GNLM, IE, Infotrieve, Ingenta, INIST, Linda Hall. **CCC.**
Published by: Academic Press (Subsidiary of: Elsevier Science & Technology), 3251 Riverport Ln, Maryland Heights, MO 63043. TEL 314-447-8010, FAX 314-447-8030, JournalCustomerService-usa@elsevier.com, http://www.elsevierdirect.com/imprint.jsp?iid=5. Eds. J Surmeier, M Baehr, O Isacson TEL 617-855-3243.

616.8 GBR ISSN 2040-2392
RC553.A88
▼ ➤ **MOLECULAR AUTISM.** Text in English. 2009. irreg. free (effective 2011). adv. **Document type:** *Journal, Academic/Scholarly.* **Description:** Provides access to clinical research into the molecular basis of autism and related neurodevelopmental conditions.
Media: Online - full text.
Indexed: A01, A26, E08, H11, H12, I05, P30.
Published by: BioMed Central Ltd. (Subsidiary of: Springer Science+Business Media), 236 Gray's Inn Rd, London, WC1X 8HB, United Kingdom. TEL 44-20-31922000, FAX 44-20-31922010, info@biomedcentral.com, http://www.biomedcentral.com. Eds. Daniel Buxbaum, Simon Baron-Cohen.

616.8 GBR ISSN 1756-6606
QP376
➤ **MOLECULAR BRAIN.** Text in English. 2008. irreg. free (effective 2011). adv. back issues avail. **Document type:** *Journal, Academic/Scholarly.* **Description:** Encompasses all aspects of studies on the nervous system at the molecular, cellular, and system level.
Media: Online - full text.
Indexed: A01, A26, CA, E08, EMBASE, ExcerpMed, H12, I05, MEDLINE, NSA, P03, P30, PsycInfo, S09, SCOPUS, T02.
—Linda Hall. **CCC.**

Published by: BioMed Central Ltd. (Subsidiary of: Springer Science+Business Media), 236 Gray's Inn Rd, London, WC1X 8HB, United Kingdom. TEL 44-20-31922000, FAX 44-20-31922010, info@biomedcentral.com, http://www.biomedcentral.com. Eds. Bong-Kiun Kaang, Kei Cho, Xiao-Jiang Li.

➤ **MOLECULAR NEUROBIOLOGY**; a review journal. *see* BIOLOGY—Biochemistry

616.8 GBR ISSN 1750-1326
QP356.2
➤ **MOLECULAR NEURODEGENERATION.** Text in English. 2006 (Jun.). irreg. free (effective 2011). adv. back issues avail. **Document type:** *Journal, Academic/Scholarly.* **Description:** Covers all aspects of neurodegeneration research at the molecular and cellular levels.
Media: Online - full text.
Indexed: A01, A26, B25, BIOSIS Prev, CA, EMBASE, ExcerpMed, I05, MycolAb, NSA, NSCI, P03, P30, PsycInfo, SCI, SCOPUS, T02, W07.
—**CCC.**
Published by: BioMed Central Ltd. (Subsidiary of: Springer Science+Business Media), 236 Gray's Inn Rd, London, WC1X 8HB, United Kingdom. TEL 44-20-31922000, FAX 44-20-31922010, info@biomedcentral.com, http://www.biomedcentral.com. Eds. Guojun Bu, Huaxi Xu.

616.8 611.01816 GBR ISSN 1359-4184
RC521 CODEN: MOPSFQ
➤ **MOLECULAR PSYCHIATRY.** Abbreviated title: M P. Text in English. 1996. m. EUR 1,918 in Europe to institutions; USD 2,415 in the Americas to institutions; JPY 327,900 in Japan to institutions; GBP 1,239 to institutions in the UK & elsewhere (effective 2011). adv. bk.rev. charts; illus.; stat. index. back issues avail.; reprints avail. **Document type:** *Journal, Academic/Scholarly.* **Description:** Explains key issues in psychiatry and related fields. Brings out pre-clinical and clinical research.
Related titles: Online - full text ed.: ISSN 1476-5578. 1997.
Indexed: A01, A02, A03, A08, A22, A26, A36, B21, B25, BIOSIS Prev, CA, CABA, CIN, ChemAb, ChemTitl, CurCont, E-psyche, E01, E12, EMBASE, ESPM, ExcerpMed, FR, FoP, GH, H12, I05, INI, ISR, IndMed, Inpharma, JW-P, MEDLINE, MycolAb, N02, N03, NSA, NSCI, P03, P20, P22, P25, P30, P33, P35, P39, P43, P48, P54, PQC, PsycInfo, PsycholAb, R07, R10, Reac, S13, SCI, SCOPUS, T02, T05, ToxAb, VS, W07.
—BLDSC (5900.826600), CASDDS, GNLM, IE, Infotrieve, Ingenta, INIST. **CCC.**
Published by: Nature Publishing Group (Subsidiary of: Macmillan Publishers Ltd.), The MacMillan Bldg, 4 Crinan St, London, N1 9XW, United Kingdom. TEL 44-20-78334000, FAX 44-20-78334640. Ed. Dr. Julio Licinio TEL 61-2-61252550. Pub. Stephanie Diment. Adv. contact Ben Harkinson TEL 617-475-9222. **Subscr. to:** Brunel Rd, Houndmills, Basingstoke, Hamps RG21 6XS, United Kingdom. TEL 44-1256-329242, FAX 44-1256-812358, subscriptions@nature.com.

616.834 USA ISSN 1940-3410
RC377
MOMENTUM (NEW YORK). Text in English. 1983. q. USD 30 (effective 2009). adv. bk.rev. illus. 72 p./no. 2 cols./p.; **Document type:** *Magazine, Consumer.* **Description:** Publishes for people with MS and their families, health professionals, counselors and others interested in solving the problems of living with the chronic disease. Also covers disability rights and reports on current research in the field.
Formerly (until 2008): Inside M S (0739-9774); Which incorporated (in 1983): Focus on Research; M S Messenger; National Multiple Sclerosis Society. Annual Report; Patient Service News
Media: Large Type (14 pt.). **Related titles:** Online - full text ed.
Indexed: A01, A02, A03, A08, A26, C06, C07, C08, C11, CA, CINAHL, E-psyche, E08, G06, G07, G08, H03, H04, H11, H12, H13, HlthInd, I05, I07, M01, M02, P02, P10, P19, P20, P24, P34, PQC, RehabLit, S09, S23, T02.
Published by: National Multiple Sclerosis Society, 733 Third Ave, New York, NY 10017-3288. TEL 212-986-3240, FAX 212-986-7981, editor@nmss.org, http://www.nmss.org. Ed. Martha King. R&P Gary Sullivan. Adv. contact William Rosen. B&W page USD 15,275, color page USD 23,031; trim 8.25 x 10.81. Circ: 497,703 (controlled).

616.89 ESP ISSN 0214-4220
CODEN: MONDE4
MONOGRAFIAS DE PSIQUIATRIA. Text in Spanish. 1989. 6/yr. EUR 64.90 (effective 2009). **Document type:** *Journal, Academic/Scholarly.*
Indexed: E-psyche, SCOPUS.
—GNLM. **CCC.**
Published by: Grupo Aula Medica S.A., C Isabel Colbrand, 10 Nave 78, Planta 2a, Madrid, 28050, Spain. TEL 34-91-3586478, FAX 34-91-3589979, informacion@grupoaulamedica.com. Ed. J.L. Ayusso Gutierrez.

616.894 USA ISSN 0077-0620
➤ **MONOGRAPH SERIES ON SCHIZOPHRENIA.** Text in English. 1950. irreg. price varies. back issues avail. **Document type:** *Monographic series, Academic/Scholarly.*
Indexed: E-psyche.
Published by: International Universities Press, Inc., 59 Boston Post Rd, Box 1524, PO Box 389, Madison, CT 06443. TEL 203-245-4000, FAX 203-245-0775, info@iup.com.

616.8 USA ISSN 0077-0671
B3 CODEN: MGGPBE
MONOGRAPHIEN AUS DEM GESAMTGEBIETE DER PSYCHIATRIE/ PSYCHIATRY SERIES. Text in English, German. 1970. irreg., latest vol.116, 2008. price varies. reprints avail. **Document type:** *Monographic series, Academic/Scholarly.*
Supersedes in part (in 1970): Monographien aus dem Gesamtgebiete der Neurologie und Psychiatrie (0376-0464)
Indexed: CA, E-psyche, IndMed, P30, PsycholAb.
—CASDDS, GNLM, Infotrieve, INIST. **CCC.**
Published by: Springer New York LLC (Subsidiary of: Springer Science+Business Media), 233 Spring St, New York, NY 10013. TEL 212-460-1500, FAX 212-460-1575, service-ny@springer.com. Eds. Franz Muller-Spahn, Heinrich Sauer, Henning Sab.

616.89 RUS ISSN 0135-2652
MOSKOVSKII PSIKHOTERAPEVTICHESKII ZHURNAL. Text in Russian. q. USD 99.95 in United States.
Indexed: E-psyche.
—East View.
Published by: Tsentr Psikhologii i Psikhoterapii, Yaroslavskaya ul 13, k 536, Moscow, 129366, Russian Federation. TEL 7-095-2290716. **Dist. by:** East View Information Services, 10601 Wayzata Blvd, Minneapolis, MN 55305. TEL 952-252-1201, 800-477-1005, FAX 952-252-1202, info@eastview.com, http://www.eastview.com.

MOTOR CONTROL. *see* MEDICAL SCIENCES—Physical Medicine And Rehabilitation

616.8 FRA ISSN 0245-5919
MOTRICITE CEREBRALE; readaptation, neurologie du developpement. Text in French. 1980. 4/yr. EUR 169 in Europe to institutions; EUR 128.31 in France to institutions; JPY 26,200 in Japan to institutions; USD 220 elsewhere to institutions (effective 2012). **Document type:** *Journal, Academic/Scholarly.* **Description:** Deals with the physiopathologic aspects of the neurology of development, and with motor or cerebral handicapped people.
Related titles: Microform ed.: (from PQC); Online - full text ed.: (from ScienceDirect).
Indexed: E-psyche, FR, SCOPUS.
—GNLM, INIST. **CCC.**
Published by: (Cercle de Documentation et d'Information pour la Reeducation des Infirmes Moteurs Cerebraux), Elsevier Masson (Subsidiary of: Elsevier Health Sciences), 62 Rue Camille Desmoulins, Issy les Moulineaux, Cedex 92442, France. TEL 33-1-71165500, infos@elsevier-masson.fr. Ed. M Le Metayer. Circ: 1,800. **Subscr. to:** Societe de Periodiques Specialises, BP 22, Vineuil Cedex 41354, France. TEL 33-2-54504612, FAX 33-2-54504611.

616.8 FRA ISSN 1963-1596
LE MOUVEMENT PSYCHANALITIQUE. COLLECTION. Text in French. 1998. irreg. **Document type:** *Monographic series, Academic/ Scholarly.*
Formerly (until 2007): Le Mouvement Psychanalitique (1289-0812)
Published by: L' Harmattan, 5 Rue de l'Ecole Polytechnique, Paris, 75005, France. TEL 33-1-43257651, FAX 33-1-43258203, http://www.editions-harmattan.fr.

616.8 USA ISSN 0885-3185
CODEN: MOVDEA
➤ **MOVEMENT DISORDERS.** Text in English. 1986. 16/yr. GBP 1,058 in United Kingdom to institutions; EUR 1,337 in Europe to institutions; USD 1,736 in United States to institutions; USD 1,960 in Canada & Mexico to institutions; USD 2,072 elsewhere to institutions; GBP 1,219 combined subscription in United Kingdom to institutions (print & online eds.); EUR 1,539 combined subscription in Europe to institutions (print & online eds.); USD 1,996 combined subscription in United States to institutions (print & online eds.); USD 2,220 combined subscription in Canada & Mexico to institutions (print & online eds.); USD 2,332 combined subscription elsewhere to institutions (print & online eds.) (effective 2012). adv. bk.rev.; video rev. charts; illus. index. back issues avail.; reprint service avail. from PSC. **Document type:** *Journal, Academic/Scholarly.* **Description:** Publishes original manuscripts covering diagnosis, therapeutics, pharmacology, biochemistry, physiology, etiology, genetics, and epidemiology of movement disorders; subjects include the etiology, diagnosis, management, and basic science of parkinsonism, chorea, tremors, dystonia, myoclonus, tics, tardive dyskinesia, spasticity, and ataxia.
Related titles: Online - full text ed.: ISSN 1531-8257. GBP 887 in United Kingdom to institutions; EUR 1,120 in Europe to institutions; USD 1,736 elsewhere to institutions (effective 2012); Supplement(s):.
Indexed: A20, A22, ASCA, B21, BIOBASE, C06, C07, CurCont, E-psyche, EMBASE, ExcerpMed, FR, IABS, INI, ISR, IndMed, Inpharma, JW-N, MEDLINE, NRN, NSA, NSCI, P30, P35, RILM, SCI, SCOPUS, T02, W07.
—BLDSC (5980.317200), GNLM, IE, Ingenta, INIST. **CCC.**
Published by: (Movement Disorder Society), John Wiley & Sons, Inc., 111 River St, Hoboken, NJ 07030. TEL 201-748-6000, FAX 201-748-6088, info@wiley.com, http://www.wiley.com/WileyCDA/. Eds. C Warren Olanow TEL 212-241-8435, Jose A Obeso TEL 34-948-194700 ext 2038. **Subscr. to:** John Wiley & Sons Ltd.

616.834 GBR ISSN 1352-4585
RC377 CODEN: MUSCFZ
➤ **MULTIPLE SCLEROSIS**; clinical and laboratory research. Text in English. 1995. m. USD 1,814, GBP 981 combined subscription to institutions (print & online eds.); USD 1,778, GBP 961 to institutions (effective 2011). adv. back issues avail.; reprint service avail. from PSC. **Document type:** *Journal, Academic/Scholarly.* **Description:** Covers the aetiology and pathogenesis of demyelinating and inflammatory diseases of the central nervous system.
Related titles: Online - full text ed.: ISSN 1477-0970. USD 1,633, GBP 883 to institutions (effective 2011); Supplement(s): Multiple Sclerosis. Supplement. ISSN 1361-2433.
Indexed: A01, A03, A08, A20, A22, AIDS&CR, B21, B25, BIOSIS Prev, CA, CIN, ChemAb, ChemTitl, CurCont, E-psyche, E01, EMBASE, ExcerpMed, ISR, ImmunAb, IndMed, Inpharma, MEDLINE, MycolAb, NSA, NSCI, P19, P20, P22, P30, P35, P48, P54, PQC, R10, Reac, SCI, SCOPUS, T02, VirolAbstr, W07.
—BLDSC (5983.195000), CASDDS, GNLM, IE, Infotrieve, Ingenta, INIST. **CCC.**
Published by: Sage Publications Ltd. (Subsidiary of: Sage Publications, Inc.), 1 Oliver's Yard, 55 City Rd, London, EC1Y 1SP, United Kingdom. TEL 44-20-73248500, FAX 44-20-73248600, info@sagepub.co.uk, http://www.uk.sagepub.com/home.nav. Ed. Alan J Thompson.

616.834 USA ISSN 2090-2654
▼ ➤ **MULTIPLE SCLEROSIS INTERNATIONAL.** Text in English. 2010. q. USD 195 (effective 2011). **Document type:** *Journal, Academic/ Scholarly.* **Description:** Publishes original research articles, review articles, and clinical studies related to all aspects of multiple sclerosis.
Related titles: Online - full text ed.: ISSN 2090-2662. free (effective 2011).
Indexed: A01, T02.
Published by: Hindawi Publishing Corporation, 410 Park Ave, 15th Fl, PMB 287, New York, NY 10022. FAX 866-446-3294, hindawi@hindawi.com.

616.834 CAN ISSN 1719-699X
MULTIPLE SCLEROSIS SOCIETY OF CANADA. ALBERTA DIVISION. CONSOLIDATED ANNUAL REPORT. Text in English. a. **Document type:** *Report, Trade.*
Published by: Multiple Sclerosis Society of Canada, Alberta Division (Subsidiary of: Multiple Sclerosis Society of Canada), Victory Centre, 11203 - 70 St, Edmonton, AB T5B 1T1, Canada. TEL 780-463-1190, 800-268-7582, FAX 780-463-7298, info.alberta@mssociety.ca, http://www.mssociety.ca/alberta/default.htm.

616.834 NZL ISSN 1176-4473
MULTIPLE SCLEROSIS SOCIETY OF NEW ZEALAND INFORMATION SERIES. Key Title: M S N Z Information Series. Text in English. 2003. irreg. **Document type:** *Monographic series, Consumer.*
Related titles: Online - full text ed.: ISSN 1178-4261.
Published by: Multiple Sclerosis Society of New Zealand, PO Box 2627, Wellington, 6140, New Zealand. TEL 64-4-4994677, FAX 64-4-4994675, info@msnz.org.nz.

MUSIK-, TANZ- UND KUNSTTHERAPIE; Zeitschrift fuer kuenstlerische Therapien im Bildungs-, Sozial- und Gesundheitswesen. *see* MEDICAL SCIENCES

616.858 USA
N A M I ADVOCATE. Text in English. 1979. 6/yr. free membership. adv. bk.rev. **Document type:** *Newsletter.*
Formerly: N A M I News
Indexed: E-psyche.
Published by: National Alliance for the Mentally Ill, 2107 Wilson Blvd, Ste 300, Arlington, VA 22201-3042. TEL 703-524-7600, 703-516-7227 (TDD), 800-950-6264, FAX 703-524-9094, info@nami.org. Ed. Frieda Eastman. Circ: 80.

616.857 USA ISSN 1521-2106
N H F HEAD LINES. Text in English. 1970. bi-m. USD 25 (effective 2007). bk.rev. back issues avail. **Document type:** *Newsletter.* **Description:** Presents research and information on headache causes and treatments.
Former titles: National Headache Foundation Newsletter; National Migraine Foundation Newsletter
Related titles: Online - full text ed.: USD 20 (effective 2006).
Indexed: C06, C07, C08, CHNI, CINAHL, E-psyche.
Published by: National Headache Foundation, 820 N Orleans Ste 217, Chicago, IL 60610. TEL 888-643-5552, FAX 312-640-9049, http://www.headaches.org. Ed. Lesley Reed. R&P Suzanne Simons. Circ: 45,000 (paid and controlled).

616.8 USA ISSN 0161-1607
RC981
N H R C REPORT. Text in English. 1960. irreg.
Former titles (until 1974): Naval Health Research Center. Abstracts of Completed Research (0164-0518); (until 1973): Navy Medical Neuropsychiatric Research Unit. Abstracts of Completed Research (0162-9425)
Published by: U.S. Naval Health Research Center, PO Box 85122, San Diego, CA 92186-5122. TEL 619-553-8400, FAX 619-553-9389, http://www.nhrc.navy.mil/. **Subscr. to:** U.S. Department of Commerce, National Technical Information Service, 5301 Shawnee Rd, Alexandria, VA 22312. TEL 800-553-6847, FAX 703-321-8547, orders@ntis.fedworld.gov, http://www.ntis.gov/ordering.htm.

616.8 USA ISSN 1933-9607
N N I JOURNAL. (Nevada Neuroscience Institute) Text in English. 2005. 3/yr. adv. back issues avail. **Document type:** *Journal, Academic/ Scholarly.* **Description:** Provides neurosurgeons, neurologists and internists the latest in original research and case studies in neuroscience.
Related titles: Online - full text ed.: ISSN 1940-4468.
Published by: N N I Research Foundation, 3059 S Maryland Pky, Ste 101, Las Vegas, NV 89109. TEL 702-851-5413, FAX 702-851-5412, KMalone@nnrf.net.

616.8 155.67 FRA ISSN 1627-4830
N P G - NEUROLOGIE PSYCHIATRIE GERONTOLOGIE. Text in French. 2001. bi-m. EUR 137 in Europe to institutions; EUR 115.57 in France to institutions; JPY 21,900 in Japan to institutions; USD 178 elsewhere to institutions (effective 2012). **Document type:** *Journal, Academic/Scholarly.*
Related titles: Online - full text ed.: (from ScienceDirect).
Indexed: P03, PsycInfo, SCOPUS.
—BLDSC (6180.498805). **CCC.**
Published by: Elsevier Masson (Subsidiary of: Elsevier Health Sciences), 62 Rue Camille Desmoulins, Issy les Moulineaux, Cedex 92442, France. TEL 33-1-71165500, infos@elsevier-masson.fr. Ed. Christophe Trivalle.

616.83 NLD ISSN 1879-5722
DE NACHTWACHT. Text in Dutch. q. EUR 20 (effective 2010).
Published by: Stichting Restless Legs, Marterlaan 13, Wageningen, 6705 CK, Netherlands. TEL 31-900-7574636, http://www.stichting-restless=legs.org. Ed. Joke Jaarsma.

616.8 CHN ISSN 1006-351X
NAO YU SHENJING JIBING ZAZHI/JOURNAL OF BRAIN AND NERVOUS DISEASE. Text in Chinese. 1993. bi-m. USD 21.60 (effective 2009). **Document type:** *Journal, Academic/Scholarly.*
Related titles: Online - full text ed.
—BLDSC (4954.285000).
Published by: Hebei Yike Daxue, Di-2 Yiyuan, 215, Heping Xilu, Shijiazhuang, 050000, China. TEL 86-311-7222451. **Dist. by:** China International Book Trading Corp, 35 Chegongzhuang Xilu, Haidian District, PO Box 399, Beijing 100044, China. TEL 86-10-68412045, FAX 86-10-68412023, cibtc@mail.cibtc.com.cn, http://www.cibtc.com.cn.

616.8 362.2 USA ISSN 0738-9159
NATIONAL COUNCIL NEWS. Text in English. 1977. m. USD 25. adv. bk.rev. **Document type:** *Newsletter.* **Description:** Covers issues of interest to mental health care professionals and reports Council activities.
Indexed: E-psyche.
Published by: National Community Mental Healthcare Council, 12300 Twinbrook Parkway, Ste 320, Rockville, MD 20852. TEL 301-984-6200. Ed. Joanne Petro. Circ: 3,000.

616.89 NLD ISSN 1573-8140
NATIONALE MONITOR GEESTELIJKE GEZONDHEID. Text in Dutch. 2002. a. EUR 22.50 (effective 2009).
Published by: (Bureau N M G), Trimbos Instituut, De Costakade 45, Postbus 725, Utrecht, 3500 AS, Netherlands. TEL 31-30-2971100, FAX 31-30-2971111, info@trimbos.nl, http://www.trimbos.nl. Eds. Corine de Ruiter, Dr. Hedda van 't Land.

616.89 CAN ISSN 1923-9890
▼ **NATURALLY AUTISTIC**; showcasing the strength and talent of the global austic community. Text in English. 2010. q. CAD 47.95 domestic; CAD 51.95 in United States; CAD 67.95 elsewhere (effective 2011). adv. **Document type:** *Magazine, Trade.*
Description: Aims to support the natural development of autistic people by providing education and training to autistic individuals, their families, and the community at large.
Published by: Naturally Autistic Press, PO Box 1658, Gilbson, BC V0N 1V0, Canada. contact@naturallyautistic.com.

616.8 USA ISSN 1097-6256
QP351 CODEN: NANEFN
➤ **NATURE NEUROSCIENCE.** Abbreviated title: N N. Text in English. 1998. m. EUR 3,214 in Europe to institutions; USD 4,048 in the Americas to institutions; GBP 2,077 to institutions in the UK & elsewhere (effective 2011). adv. Supplement avail.; back issues avail.; reprints avail. **Document type:** *Journal, Academic/Scholarly.*
Description: Publishes papers of the highest quality and significance in all areas of neuroscience, psychophysics, computational modeling and diseases of the nervous system.
Related titles: Online - full text ed.: ISSN 1546-1726.
Indexed: A01, A02, A03, A08, A20, A22, A26, AnBeAb, B21, B25, BIOSIS Prev, C33, CA, CTA, ChemAb, ChemoAb, CurCont, E-psyche, EMBASE, ESPM, EntAb, ExcerpMed, GenetAb, H12, HGA, I05, ISR, IndMed, Inspec, JW-P, MEDLINE, MycolAb, NSA, NSCI, NucAcAb, P03, P20, P22, P25, P30, P43, P48, P54, PQC, PsycInfo, PsycholAb, R10, RILM, Reac, S06, SCI, SCOPUS, T02, ToxAb, VirolAbstr, W07.
—CASDDS, GNLM, IE, Ingenta, INIST. **CCC.**
Published by: Nature Publishing Group (Subsidiary of: Macmillan Publishers Ltd.), 75 Varick St, 9th Fl, New York, NY 10013. TEL 212-726-9200, FAX 212-696-9006, subscriptions@nature.com. Ed. Kalyani Narasimhan. Adv. contact Andy Douglas TEL 44-20-78434975. **Subscr. in the Americas to:** PO Box 5161, Brentwood, TN 37024-5161. TEL 615-850-5315, 800-524-0384, FAX 615-377-0525; **Subscr. to:** Nature Publishing Group, Brunel Rd, Houndmills, Basingstoke, Hamps RG21 6XS, United Kingdom. TEL 44-1256-329242, FAX 44-1256-812358, subscriptions@nature.com.

616.8 GBR ISSN 1759-4758
NATURE REVIEWS NEUROLOGY. Text in English. 2005. m. EUR 1,224 in Europe to institutions; USD 1,257 in the Americas to institutions; GBP 741 to institutions in the UK & elsewhere (effective 2011). adv. back issues avail.; reprints avail. **Document type:** *Journal, Academic/Scholarly.*
Formerly (until 2009): Nature Clinical Practice Neurology (1745-834X)
Related titles: Online - full text ed.: ISSN 1759-4766.
Indexed: A01, A26, B21, CA, CurCont, EMBASE, ExcerpMed, H12, I05, MEDLINE, NSA, NSCI, P30, R10, Reac, SCI, SCOPUS, T02, W07.
—IE, Ingenta. **CCC.**
Published by: Nature Publishing Group (Subsidiary of: Macmillan Publishers Ltd.), The MacMillan Bldg, 4 Crinan St, London, N1 9XW, United Kingdom. TEL 44-20-78334000, FAX 44-20-78334640, NatureReviews@nature.com. Eds. Heather Wood, Dr. Philip Campbell. Adv. contact Andy Douglas TEL 44-22-78434975. **Subscr. to:** Brunel Rd, Houndmills, Basingstoke, Hamps RG21 6XS, United Kingdom. TEL 44-1256-329242, FAX 44-1256-812358, subscriptions@nature.com.

616.8 GBR ISSN 1471-003X
CODEN: NRNAAN
➤ **NATURE REVIEWS. NEUROSCIENCE.** Text in English. 2000 (Oct.). m. EUR 3,214 in Europe to institutions; USD 4,048 in the Americas to institutions; GBP 2,077 to institutions in the UK & elsewhere (effective 2011). adv. back issues avail.; reprints avail. **Document type:** *Journal, Academic/Scholarly.* **Description:** Covers the breadth and depth of modern neuroscience by providing an authoritative, accessible, topical, and engaging first port of call for scientists who are interested in all aspects of neuroscience, from molecules to the mind.
Related titles: Online - full text ed.: ISSN 1471-0048.
Indexed: A01, A02, A03, A08, A22, A26, B21, BIOBASE, C33, CA, CTA, ChemoAb, EMBASE, ExcerpMed, GenetAb, H12, I05, IABS, MEDLINE, NSA, NucAcAb, P03, P20, P22, P25, P30, P43, P48, P54, PQC, PsycInfo, PsycholAb, SCOPUS, T02, VITIS.
—BLDSC (6047.235000), IE, Ingenta, INIST. **CCC.**
Published by: Nature Publishing Group (Subsidiary of: Macmillan Publishers Ltd.), The MacMillan Bldg, 4 Crinan St, London, N1 9XW, United Kingdom. TEL 44-20-78334000, FAX 44-20-78334640, NatureReviews@nature.com. Ed. Claudia Wiedemann. Pub. Stephanie Diment. Adv. contact Andy Douglas TEL 44-22-78434975. **Subscr. elsewhere to:** Brunel Rd, Houndmills, Basingstoke, Hamps RG21 6XS, United Kingdom. TEL 44-1256-329242, FAX 44-1256-812358, subscriptions@nature.com; **Subscr. in N. & S. America to:** Nature Publishing Group.

616.8 NLD
NEDERLANDSE RETT SYNDROOM VERENIGING. NIEUWSBRIEF. Text in Dutch. 1992. s-a. **Document type:** *Newsletter, Consumer.*
Former titles (until 2010): Rett Syndroom Nieuws (1877-0967); (until 2008): Rett Syndroom. Nieuwsbrief (1387-3881)
Published by: Nederlandse Rett Syndroom Vereniging, Postbus 85037, Utrecht, 3508 AA, Netherlands. TEL 31-6-53281592, FAX 31-84-7189177, info@rett.nl, http://www.rett.nl. Ed. Mirjam Rensick.

NEIROFIZIOLOGIYA/NEUROPHYSIOLOGY. *see* BIOLOGY—Physiology

616.8 NPL ISSN 1813-1948
NEPAL JOURNAL OF NEUROSCIENCE. Text in English. 2004. s-a.
Description: It aims at providing a medium for scientific discussion in the field of neuroscience or other information of interest to the specialists dealing with the diseases of the nervous system.
Related titles: Online - full text ed.: ISSN 1813-1956. free (effective 2010).
Indexed: A36, CABA, F08, GH, H17, P33, P39, PN&I, R08, R12, RM&VM, T05.
Published by: Neuroscience Publishing Group, PO Box 8974, Kathmandu, COC 085, Nepal. neurosurg@healthnet.org.np.

616.8 USA ISSN 2150-6817
▼ **THE NERVE**; the neuroanatomy of homosexuality. Text in English. 2009. 3/yr. back issues avail. **Document type:** *Journal, Academic/Scholarly.*
Related titles: Online - full text ed.
Published by: Boston University, The Mind and Brain Society, One Silber Way, Boston, MA 02215. TEL 617-353-2000.

616.8 DEU ISSN 0028-2804
RC346 CODEN: NERVAF
➤ **DER NERVENARZT**; Monatsschrift fuer alle Gebiete nervenaerztlicher Forschung und Praxis. (Includes: Deutsche Gesellschaft fuer Neurologie. Mitteilungsblatt and Gesellschaft Oesterreichischer Nervenaerzte und Psychiater) Text in German. 1928. m. EUR 524, USD 577 combined subscription to institutions (print & online eds.) (effective 2012). adv. bk.rev. charts; illus. index. back issues avail.; reprint service avail. from PSC. **Document type:** *Journal, Academic/Scholarly.* **Description:** Covers neurology, psychiatry, neurosurgery, and psychotherapy.
Related titles: Microform ed.: (from PQC); Online - full text ed.: ISSN 1433-0407 (from IngentaConnect).
Indexed: A01, A03, A08, A20, A22, A26, ASCA, B25, BIOSIS Prev, CA, ChemAb, CurCont, DBA, E-psyche, E01, EMBASE, ExcerpMed, FR, GJP, I05, INI, ISR, IndMed, Inpharma, MEDLINE, MycolAb, NSCI, P03, P30, P35, PsycInfo, PsycholAb, R10, RILM, Reac, S02, S03, SCI, SCOPUS, T02, W07.
—BLDSC (6076.500000), GNLM, IE, Infotrieve, Ingenta, INIST. **CCC.**
Published by: (Deutschen Gesellschaft fuer Psychiatrie, Psychotherapie und Nervenheilkunde), Springer (Subsidiary of: Springer Science+Business Media), Tiergartenstr 17, Heidelberg, 69121, Germany. TEL 49-6221-4870, FAX 49-6221-345229. Eds. Dr. T Brandt, Dr. W Hacke. Adv. contact Stephan Kroeck TEL 49-30-827875739. Circ: 11,800 (paid and controlled). **Subscr. in the Americas to:** Springer New York LLC, Journal Fulfillment, PO Box 2485, Secaucus, NJ 07096. TEL 800-777-4643, 201-348-4033, FAX 201-348-4505, journals-ny@springer.com, http://www.springer.com; **Subscr. to:** Springer Distribution Center, Kundenservice Zeitschriften, Haberstr 7, Heidelberg 69126, Germany. TEL 49-6221-3454303, FAX 49-6221-3454229, subscriptions@springer.com.

616.8 DEU ISSN 0722-1541
➤ **NERVENHEILKUNDE**; Zeitschrift fuer interdisziplinaere Fortbildung. Text in German. 1982. 12/yr. EUR 160 in Europe to individuals; EUR 264 in Europe to institutions; EUR 80 to students; EUR 28 newsstand/cover (effective 2011). adv. **Document type:** *Journal, Academic/Scholarly.*
Indexed: A20, A22, ASCA, E-psyche, EMBASE, ExcerpMed, Inpharma, NSCI, P03, PsycInfo, PsycholAb, R10, Reac, SCI, SCOPUS, W07.
—BLDSC (6076.520000), GNLM, IE, Ingenta. **CCC.**
Published by: Schattauer GmbH, Hoelderlinstr 3, Stuttgart, 70174, Germany. TEL 49-711-229870, FAX 49-711-2298750, info@schattauer.de, http://www.schattauer.com. Eds. D Soyka, M Spitzer. Adv. contact Nicole Doerr. Circ: 29,551 (paid and controlled). **Subscr. to:** CSJ, Postfach 140220, Munich 80452, Germany. TEL 49-89-20959129, schattauer@csj.de.

616.8 FRA ISSN 0988-4068
NERVURE; journal de psychiatrie. Text in French. 1988. irreg. EUR 45 domestic; EUR 75 foreign (effective 2010). **Document type:** *Journal, Trade.*
Related titles: Supplement(s): Le Journal de Nervure. ISSN 1244-703X.
Indexed: FR.
—Infotrieve. **CCC.**
Published by: Maxmed, 54, boulevard La-Tour-Maubourg, Paris, F-75007, France. TEL 33-1-4550-2308, FAX 33-1-4555-6080. Ed. Francois Caroli.

616.8 GBR ISSN 0954-898X
QA76.87 CODEN: NEWKEB
➤ **NETWORK (LONDON, 1990)**; computation in neural systems. Text in English. 1990. q. GBP 455, EUR 655, USD 825 combined subscription to institutions (print & online eds.); GBP 915, EUR 1,315, USD 1,645 combined subscription to corporations (print & online eds.) (effective 2010). adv. bk.rev. illus. index. back issues avail.; reprint service avail. from PSC. **Document type:** *Journal, Academic/Scholarly.* **Description:** Subject coverage includes experimental neuroscience; physics; computer science; applied mathematics and engineering; proposing, analyzing, simulating and designing models with the aim of synthesizing the biological results.
Related titles: Microfiche ed.: USD 439 in the Americas; GBP 224 elsewhere (effective 2004); Online - full text ed.: ISSN 1361-6536 (from IngentaConnect).
Indexed: A01, A03, A08, A22, A28, APA, ASCA, ASFA, B21, BrCerAb, C&ISA, C10, CA, CA/WCA, CCMJ, CIA, CMCI, CerAb, CivEngAb, CompAb, CompLI, CorrAb, CurCont, E&CAJ, E01, E11, EEA, EMA, EMBASE, ESPM, EnvEAb, ExcerpMed, H15, ISR, IndMed, Inspec, M&TEA, M09, MBF, MEDLINE, METADEX, MSN, MathR, NSA, NSCI, P03, P30, PsycInfo, RefZh, SCI, SCOPUS, SolStAb, T02, T04, W07, WAA, Z02.
—AskIEEE, GNLM, IE, Infotrieve, Ingenta, INIST, Linda Hall. **CCC.**
Published by: Informa Healthcare (Subsidiary of: T & F Informa plc), Telephone House, 69-77 Paul St, London, EC2A 4LQ, United Kingdom. TEL 44-20-70175000, FAX 44-20-70176792, healthcare.enquiries@informa.com. Ed. Geoffrey J Goodhill. Adv. contact Per Sonnerfeldt. **Subscr. in N America to:** Taylor & Francis Inc., Customer Services Dept, 325 Chestnut St, 8th Fl, Philadelphia, PA 19106. TEL 215-625-8900, 800-354-1420, FAX 215-625-8914, customerservice@taylorandfrancis.com; **Subscr. outside N America to:** Taylor & Francis Ltd., Journals Customer Service, Sheepen Pl, Colchester, Essex CO3 3LP, United Kingdom. TEL 44-20-70175544, FAX 44-20-70175198, tf.enquiries@tfinforma.com.

➤ **NEURAL COMPUTATION.** *see* COMPUTERS—Artificial Intelligence

616.8 GBR ISSN 1749-8104
QP363.5
➤ **NEURAL DEVELOPMENT.** Text in English. 2006. irreg. free (effective 2011). adv. back issues avail. **Document type:** *Journal, Academic/Scholarly.* **Description:** Covers all aspects of research that use molecular, cellular, physiological or behavioral methods to provide novel insights into the mechanisms that underlie the formation of the nervous system.
Media: Online - full text.
Indexed: A01, A26, B25, BIOSIS Prev, CA, EMBASE, ExcerpMed, I05, MEDLINE, MycolAb, NSA, NSCI, P03, P30, PsycInfo, R10, Reac, SCI, SCOPUS, T02, W07.
—**CCC.**
Published by: BioMed Central Ltd. (Subsidiary of: Springer Science+Business Media), 236 Gray's Inn Rd, London, WC1X 8HB, United Kingdom. TEL 44-20-31922000, FAX 44-20-31922010, info@biomedcentral.com, http://www.biomedcentral.com. Eds. Andrew Lumsden, Bill Harris, Joshua Sanes.

➤ **NEURAL NETWORK WORLD**; international journal on non-standard computing and artificial intelligence. *see* COMPUTERS—Artificial Intelligence

➤ **NEURAL NETWORKS.** *see* COMPUTERS—Artificial Intelligence

616.8 USA ISSN 2090-5904
CODEN: JNPLEW
➤ **NEURAL PLASTICITY.** Text in English. 1989. irreg. USD 295 (effective 2011). **Document type:** *Journal, Academic/Scholarly.* **Description:** Publishes full research papers, short communications, commentary, and review articles concerning all aspects of neural plasticity, with special attention to its functional significance as reflected in behavior.
Former titles: Journal of Neuroplasticity; (until 1998): Journal of Neural Transplantation and Plasticity (0792-8483); (until 1991): Journal of Neural Transplantation (1352-237X)
Related titles: Online - full text ed.: ISSN 1687-5443. free (effective 2011).
Indexed: A01, A26, APA, ASCA, ASFA, B21, B25, BIOSIS Prev, C&ISA, CA, CorrAb, E&CAJ, E-psyche, EEA, EMBASE, ESPM, EnvEAb, ExcerpMed, H11, I05, IndMed, Inpharma, MycolAb, NSA, NSCI, P03, P30, PsycInfo, PsycholAb, R10, Reac, SCI, SCOPUS, SolStAb, T02, W07, WAA.
—BLDSC (6081.281015), GNLM, IE.
Published by: Hindawi Publishing Corporation, 410 Park Ave, 15th Fl, PMB 287, New York, NY 10022. FAX 215-893-4392, 866-446-3294, info@hindawi.com.

➤ **NEURAL PROCESSING LETTERS.** *see* COMPUTERS—Artificial Intelligence

616.8 CHN ISSN 1673-5374
➤ **NEURAL REGENERATION RESEARCH.** Text in English. 2006. m. **Document type:** *Journal, Academic/Scholarly.* **Description:** Focuses on topics related to the influences of neural stem cells, neuroengineering and traditional Chinese medicine with respect to neuroregeneration.
Related titles: Online - full text ed.: ISSN 1876-7958.
Indexed: A28, APA, B25, BIOSIS Prev, BrCerAb, C&ISA, CA/WCA, CIA, CerAb, CivEngAb, CorrAb, E&CAJ, E11, EEA, EMA, EMBASE, ExcerpMed, H15, M&TEA, M09, MBF, METADEX, MycolAb, NSCI, SCI, SCOPUS, SolStAb, T02, T04, W07, WAA.
—BLDSC (6081.281025), IE, Linda Hall. **CCC.**
Published by: (Zhongguo Kangxia Yixueyuan/Chinese Association of Rehabilitation Medicine), Neural Regeneration Research, PO Box 1234, Shenyang, Liaoning 110004, China. TEL 86-24-23381085, FAX 86-24-23394178. Ed. Qunyuan Xu.

616.8 GBR ISSN 2042-1001
▼ ➤ **NEURAL SYSTEMS & CIRCUITS.** Text in English. 2011. irreg. free (effective 2011). **Document type:** *Journal, Academic/Scholarly.*
Description: Contains research on how individual neurons interact at the network level to perform interesting computations.
Media: Online - full text.
Indexed: A01, A26, H12, I05.
Published by: BioMed Central Ltd. (Subsidiary of: Springer Science+Business Media), 236 Gray's Inn Rd, London, WC1X 8HB, United Kingdom. TEL 44-20-31922000, FAX 44-20-31922010, info@biomedcentral.com, http://www.biomedcentral.com. Eds. Peter Latham, Venkatesh Murthy.

616.8 DEU ISSN 0932-4607
NEURO DATE AKTUELL. Text in German. 1987. 9/yr. EUR 40 domestic (effective 2010). adv. **Document type:** *Magazine, Trade.*
Published by: Westermayer Verlags GmbH, Fuchswinkel 2, Pentenried, 82349, Germany. TEL 49-89-2722028, FAX 49-89-2730058, mail@westermayer-verlag.de. Ed. Dr. Benno Huhn. Adv. contact Reinhilde Bossema-Collien. page EUR 1,980; trim 184 x 267. Circ: 6,600 (paid and controlled).

616.8 DEU ISSN 1435-5515
NEURO-DEPESCHE. Text in German. 1998. 10/yr. EUR 60 (effective 2010). adv. **Document type:** *Journal, Academic/Scholarly.*
Published by: Gesellschaft fuer Medizinische Information, Paul-Wassermann-Str 15, Munich, 81829, Germany. TEL 49-89-4366300, FAX 49-89-436630210, info@gfi.online.de. Ed. Joerg Lellwitz.

616.8 SVK ISSN 1337-8767
NEURO MAGAZIN. Text in Slovak. 2008. q. **Document type:** *Magazine, Trade.*
Published by: MedMedia, s.r.o. herda@medmedia.sk. Ed. Sona Jurikova.

617.7 GBR ISSN 0165-8107
RE725
➤ **NEURO-OPHTHALMOLOGY.** Text in English. 1980. bi-m. GBP 535, EUR 710, USD 890 combined subscription to institutions (print & online eds.); GBP 1,070, EUR 1,415, USD 1,775 combined subscription to corporations (print & online eds.) (effective 2010). adv. bk.rev. index. back issues avail.; reprint service avail. from PSC.
Document type: *Journal, Academic/Scholarly.* **Description:** Contains review articles, research papers and short communications on diagnostic methods in neuro-ophthalmology, the visual and oculo-motor systems, the pupil, neuro-ophthalmic aspects of the orbit, migraine, and ocular manifestations of neurological diseases.
Related titles: Microform ed.; Online - full text ed.: ISSN 1744-506X (from IngentaConnect).
Indexed: A01, A03, A08, A22, B21, CA, E-psyche, E01, EMBASE, ExcerpMed, IBR, IBZ, ISR, ImmunAb, Inpharma, NSA, NSCI, P30, R10, Reac, SCI, SCOPUS, T02, W07.
—GNLM, IE, Infotrieve, Ingenta. **CCC.**
Published by: Informa Healthcare (Subsidiary of: T & F Informa plc), Telephone House, 69-77 Paul St, London, EC2A 4LQ, United Kingdom. TEL 44-20-70175000, FAX 44-20-70176792, healthcare.enquiries@informa.com. Eds. Gordon Plant, Walter Jay. **Subscr. in N. America to:** Taylor & Francis Inc., Customer Services Dept, 325 Chestnut St, 8th Fl, Philadelphia, PA 19106. TEL 215-625-8900, 800-354-1420, FAX 215-625-8914, customerservice@taylorandfrancis.com; **Subscr. outside N. America to:** Taylor & Francis Ltd., Journals Customer Service, Sheepen Pl, Colchester, Essex CO3 3LP, United Kingdom. TEL 44-20-70175544, FAX 44-20-70175198, tf.enquiries@tfinforma.com.

616.8 DEU ISSN 1860-1243
NEURO-PSYCHIATRISCHE ZEITUNG. Abbreviated title: NPZ. Text in German. 2004. 6/yr. adv. **Document type:** *Magazine, Trade.*

Published by: abcverlag GmbH, Waldhofer Str 19, Heidelberg, 69123, Germany. TEL 49-6221-75704100, FAX 49-6221-75704109, info@abcverlag.de. Ed. Ulrich van Elst. Adv. contact Harald Garms. Circ: 7,838 (controlled).

616.891 GBR ISSN 1529-4145
RC500 CODEN: NEURCK
➤ **NEURO-PSYCHOANALYSIS**; an interdisciplinary journal for psychoanalysis and the neurosciences. Text in English. 1999. s-a. GBP 60 to individuals; GBP 120 to institutions (effective 2010). adv. bk.rev. back issues avail. **Document type:** *Journal, Academic/ Scholarly.* **Description:** Presents original contributions from the newly converging fields of neuroscience and psychoanalysis.
Related titles: Online - full text ed.: ISSN 2044-3978.
Indexed: E-psyche, P03, PsycInfo, PsycholAb.
—BLDSC (6081.544000), IE, Ingenta.
Published by: (Karnac Books), International Neuro-Psychoanalysis Centre, 13 Prowse Pl, London, NW1 9PN, United Kingdom. TEL 44-20-74826999, FAX 44-20-72844030, admin@neuro-psa.org, http://www.neuro-psa.org.uk/npsa/. Eds. Oliver Turnbull, Yoram Yovell. Adv. contact Fernando Marques. B&W page GBP 200; 150 x 220.

616.834 CAN ISSN 1494-8745
➤ **NEURO TRANSMISSION (ENGLISH EDITION).** Text in English. 2000. q. **Document type:** *Journal, Academic/Scholarly.*
Related titles: French ed.: Neuro Transmission (French Edition). ISSN 1494-8753.
Published by: Parkhurst Publishing, 400 McGill St, 3rd Fl, Montreal, PQ H2Y 2G1, Canada. TEL 514-397-8833, FAX 514-397-0228, contact@parkpub.com, http://www.parkpub.com. Ed. Dr. Pierre Duquette.

616.8 611 TUR ISSN 1303-1783
➤ **NEUROANATOMY**; an annual journal of clinical neuroanatomy. Text in English. 2002 (Dec.). a. free (effective 2009). adv. **Document type:** *Journal, Academic/Scholarly.* **Description:** Publishes articles related to clinical neuroanatomy.
Related titles: Online - full text ed.: ISSN 1303-1775. free (effective 2011).
Indexed: EMBASE, ExcerpMed, R10, Reac, SCOPUS.
—BLDSC (6081.289875), IE.
Published by: M. Mustafa Aldur, c/o M. Mustafa Aldur, Faculty of Medicine, Department of Anatomy, Hacettepe University, Ankara, 06100, Turkey. TEL 90-312-3052466, FAX 90-312-4785200, mustafa@aldur.net. Ed., Pub., R&P, Adv. contact Dr. Mustafa M Aldur. Circ: 1,200 (controlled).

616.8 BRA ISSN 0028-3800
RC321 CODEN: NURBAX
➤ **NEUROBIOLOGIA**; revista de neurologia psiquiatria e neurocirurgia. Text and summaries in English, Portuguese. 1938. q. adv. bk.rev. abstr.; bibl.; charts; illus. index. back issues avail. **Document type:** *Journal, Academic/Scholarly.*
Related titles: Online - full text ed.: ISSN 1807-9865. 2004.
Indexed: E-psyche, IBR, IBZ, P30, PsycholAb.
—GNLM.
Published by: (Universidade Federal de Pernambuco, Departamento de Neuropsiquiatria), Sociedade Editora da Revista Neurobiologia, Caixa Postal 3890, Recife, PE 50040-970, Brazil. FAX 55-81-21268539. Ed. Othon Bastos.

616.8 USA ISSN 1568-2625
NEUROBIOLOGICAL FOUNDATION OF ABERRANT BEHAVIORS. Text in English. 2000. irreg., latest vol.7, 2003. price varies. back issues avail. **Document type:** *Monographic series, Academic/ Scholarly.* **Description:** Aims to serve the growing community of neuroscientists and research psychiatrists who are engaged in the study of aberrant behavior and psychopathology.
Published by: Springer New York LLC (Subsidiary of: Springer Science+Business Media), 233 Spring St, New York, NY 10013. TEL 212-460-1500, FAX 212-460-1575, service-ny@springer.com. Ed. Michael S Myslobodsky.

616.8 570 MEX
R21 CODEN: BEMBA2
NEUROBIOLOGICAL RESEARCH. Text in English. 1942. q. USD 50 (effective 2000). bk.rev. **Document type:** *Journal, Academic/ Scholarly.*
Former titles (until 1997): Boletin de Estudios Medicos y Biologicos (0067-9666); Instituto de Estudios Medicos y Biologicos. Boletin (0366-1695); (until 1994): Laboratorio de Estudios Medicos y Biologicos. Boletin (0020-3858)
Indexed: C01, CIN, ChemAb, ChemTitl, E-psyche, EMBASE, ExcerpMed, IBR, IBZ, IndMed, MEDLINE, P30, R10, Reac, SCOPUS.
—CASDDS, GNLM, Linda Hall.
Published by: Universidad Nacional Autonoma de Mexico, Instituto de Investigaciones Biomedicas, Centro de Neurobiologia, Apartado Postal 70-228, Cuidad Universitaria, Mexico, DF, 04510, Mexico. TEL 52-5-6223838, FAX 52-5-6223839, cavaro@servidor.unam.mx. Eds. Dr. Alfonso Escobar, Flavio Mena.

NEUROBIOLOGY OF AGING; age-related phenomena, neurodegeneration and neuropathology. *see* BIOLOGY—Physiology

612.8 573.8 USA ISSN 0969-9961
RC346 CODEN: NUDIEM
➤ **NEUROBIOLOGY OF DISEASE.** Text in English. 1994. m. EUR 956 in Europe to institutions; JPY 99,900 in Japan to institutions; USD 724 elsewhere to institutions (effective 2012). adv. bk.rev. bibl.; illus. index. back issues avail.; reprints avail. **Document type:** *Journal, Academic/Scholarly.* **Description:** Provides a forum for the publication of research papers on molecular and cellular definitions of disease mechanisms, the neural systems and underpinning behavioral disorders, the genetics of inherited neurological and psychiatric diseases.
Related titles: Microform ed.: (from PQC); Online - full text ed.: ISSN 1095-953X (from IngentaConnect, ScienceDirect).
Indexed: A01, A03, A08, A22, A26, A34, A35, A36, A38, ASCA, AgBio, B21, B25, BIOSIS Prev, BP, CA, CABA, CIN, ChemAb, ChemTitl, CurCont, E-psyche, E01, E12, EMBASE, ExcerpMed, GH, I05, ISR, IndMed, IndVet, Inpharma, MEDLINE, MycolAb, N02, N03, N04, N05, NSA, NSCI, P30, P32, P33, PsycholAb, R07, R08, R10, R13, RA&MP, Reac, S13, S16, SCI, SCOPUS, T02, T05, VS, W07, W10.
—BLDSC (6081.311250), CASDDS, GNLM, IE, Infotrieve, Ingenta, INIST, Linda Hall. **CCC.**

Published by: Academic Press (Subsidiary of: Elsevier Science & Technology), 3251 Riverport Ln, Maryland Heights, MO 63043. TEL 314-447-8010, FAX 314-447-8030, JournalCustomerService-usa@elsevier.com, http://www.elsevierdirect.com/imprint.jsp?iid=5. Eds. T Greenamyre TEL 412-648-9793, S Gilman TEL 734-936-1808. Adv. contact Tino DeCarlo TEL 212-633-3815.

616.8 156 USA ISSN 1074-7427
QP406 CODEN: NLMEFR
➤ **NEUROBIOLOGY OF LEARNING AND MEMORY.** Text in English. 1968. 8/yr. EUR 2,042 in Europe to institutions; JPY 213,100 in Japan to institutions; USD 1,533 elsewhere to institutions (effective 2012). adv. abstr.; charts; illus.; stat. index. back issues avail.; reprints avail. **Document type:** *Journal, Academic/Scholarly.* **Description:** Features papers in all areas of neurally oriented behavioral research and emphasizes the areas of neural plasticity and of mechanisms of learning and memory.
Former titles (until 1995): Behavioral and Neural Biology (0163-1047); (until 1979): Behavioral Biology (0091-6773); (until 1972): Communications in Behavioral Biology. Part A. Original Articles (0588-8042)
Related titles: Online - full text ed.: ISSN 1095-9564 (from IngentaConnect, ScienceDirect).
Indexed: A01, A03, A08, A22, A26, ASCA, AbAn, AnBeAb, B&AI, B10, B21, B25, BIOBASE, BIOSIS Prev, BibInd, CA, CIN, ChemAb, ChemTitl, ChemoAb, CurCont, DentInd, E-psyche, E01, EMBASE, ExcerpMed, FR, I05, IABS, ISR, IndMed, Inpharma, MEDLINE, MycolAb, NSA, NSCI, P03, P10, P12, P30, P48, P53, P54, P56, PQC, PsycInfo, PsycholAb, R10, RASB, Reac, S01, SCI, SCOPUS, SSCI, T02, THA, W07, WildRev.
—BLDSC (6081.311300), CASDDS, GNLM, IE, Infotrieve, Ingenta, INIST. **CCC.**
Published by: Academic Press (Subsidiary of: Elsevier Science & Technology), 3251 Riverport Ln, Maryland Heights, MO 63043. TEL 314-447-8010, FAX 314-447-8030, JournalCustomerService-usa@elsevier.com, http://www.elsevierdirect.com/imprint.jsp?iid=5. Ed. P E Gold TEL 217-244-0673. Adv. contact Tino DeCarlo TEL 212-633-3815.

616.8 GBR ISSN 1355-4794
QP360 CODEN: NROCF5
➤ **NEUROCASE.** Text in English. 1995. bi-m. GBP 657 combined subscription in United Kingdom to institutions (print & online eds.); EUR 866, USD 1,086 combined subscription to institutions (print & online eds.) (effective 2012). adv. bk.rev. 88 p./no.; back issues avail.; reprint service avail. from PSC. **Document type:** *Journal, Academic/ Scholarly.* **Description:** Features both adult and child case studies in neuropsychology, neuropsychiatry, and behavioral neurology.
Related titles: CD-ROM ed.: ISSN 1362-4970; Online - full text ed.: ISSN 1465-3656. GBP 592 in United Kingdom to institutions; EUR 780, USD 978 to institutions (effective 2012) (from IngentaConnect).
Indexed: A01, A20, A22, C06, C07, C08, CA, CINAHL, CurCont, E-psyche, E01, EMBASE, ExcerpMed, Inpharma, L&LBA, MEDLINE, NSCI, P03, P20, P22, P24, P25, P30, P48, P54, PQC, PsycInfo, PsycholAb, R10, Reac, SCI, SCOPUS, T02, W07.
—GNLM, IE, Infotrieve, Ingenta, INIST. **CCC.**
Published by: Psychology Press (Subsidiary of: Taylor & Francis Ltd.), 27 Church Rd, Hove, E Sussex BN3 2FA, United Kingdom. TEL 44-20-70176000, FAX 44-20-70176717, info@psypress.co.uk, http://www.psypress.com. Eds. Bruce L Miller, Hans J Markowitsch. Adv. contact Linda Hann TEL 44-1344-779945. **Subscr. in Europe to:** Taylor & Francis Ltd., Journals Customer Service, Sheepen Pl, Colchester, Essex CO3 3LP, United Kingdom. TEL 44-20-70175544, FAX 44-20-70175198, subscriptions@tandf.co.uk, http://www.tandf.co.uk/journals; **Subscr. in N. America to:** Taylor & Francis Inc., Customer Services Dept, 325 Chestnut St, 8th Fl, Philadelphia, PA 19106. TEL 215-625-8900, 800-354-1420, FAX 215-625-2940.

618 RUS ISSN 1819-7124
NEUROCHEMICAL JOURNAL. Text in English. s-a. EUR 777, USD 939 combined subscription to institutions (print & online eds.) (effective 2012). **Document type:** *Journal, Academic/Scholarly.* **Description:** Provides a source for communication on the latest findings in all areas of contemporary neurochemistry and other fields of relevance (including molecular biology, biochemistry, physiology, neuroimmunology, pharmacology) in order to expand understanding of the functions of nervous system.
Related titles: Online - full text ed.: ISSN 1819-7132 (from IngentaConnect).
Indexed: A22, A26, E01, E08, NSCI, S09, SCI, SCOPUS, W07.
—East View, IE. **CCC.**
Published by: M A I K Nauka - Interperiodica (Subsidiary of: Pleiades Publishing, Inc.), Profsoyuznaya ul 90, Moscow, 117997, Russian Federation. TEL 7-095-3347420, FAX 7-095-3360666, compmg@maik.rssi.ru, http://www.maik.ru. Ed. Armen A Galoyan.

618 USA ISSN 0364-3190
QP356.3 CODEN: NEREDZ
➤ **NEUROCHEMICAL RESEARCH.** Text in English. 1976. m. EUR 2,925, USD 3,045 combined subscription to institutions (print & online eds.) (effective 2012). adv. back issues avail.; reprint service avail. from PSC. **Document type:** *Journal, Academic/Scholarly.* **Description:** Covers all aspects of studies that use neurochemical methodology in research on nervous system structure and function.
Related titles: Microfilm ed.: (from PQC); Online - full text ed.: ISSN 1573-6903 (from IngentaConnect).
Indexed: A01, A03, A08, A22, A26, A34, A35, A36, A38, ASCA, ASFA, AgBio, B21, B25, B27, BIOBASE, BIOSIS Prev, BP, BibLing, C30, C33, CA, CABA, CIN, ChemAb, ChemTitl, ChemoAb, CurCont, D01, DentInd, E-psyche, E01, E12, EMBASE, ESPM, ExcerpMed, F08, F11, F12, GH, H16, I05, IABS, IBR, IBZ, ISR, IndMed, IndVet, Inpharma, MEDLINE, MaizeAb, MycolAb, N02, N03, N04, N05, NSA, NSCI, P15, P20, P22, P30, P32, P33, P35, P37, P40, P48, P52, P54, P56, PQC, R07, R08, R10, R12, R13, RA&MP, Reac, RefZh, S17, SCI, SCOPUS, SoyAb, T02, T05, THA, ToxAb, VITIS, VS, W07, W10.
—BLDSC (6081.312000), CASDDS, GNLM, IE, Infotrieve, Ingenta, INIST. **CCC.**
Published by: Springer New York LLC (Subsidiary of: Springer Science+Business Media), 233 Spring St, New York, NY 10013. TEL 212-460-1500, FAX 212-460-1575, service-ny@springer.com, http://www.springer.com/. Eds. Abel Lajtha, Kazuhiro Ikenaka.

616.8 540 GBR ISSN 0197-0186
QP356.3 CODEN: NEUIDS
➤ **NEUROCHEMISTRY INTERNATIONAL**; the journal for the publication of cellular and molecular aspects of neurochemistry. Text in English. 1980. 16/yr. EUR 2,129 in Europe to institutions; JPY 282,900 in Japan to institutions; USD 2,383 elsewhere to institutions (effective 2012). back issues avail. **Document type:** *Journal, Academic/ Scholarly.* **Description:** Contains papers concerned with the metabolism and function of the nervous system.
Related titles: Microfilm ed.: (from PQC); Online - full text ed.: ISSN 1872-9754 (from IngentaConnect, ScienceDirect); Supplement(s): Neurochemistry International. Supplement. ISSN 1359-5032.
Indexed: A01, A03, A08, A22, A26, A34, A35, A36, A38, ASCA, AgBio, ApicAb, B21, B25, B27, BIOBASE, BIOSIS Prev, BP, C30, C33, CA, CABA, CIN, CTA, ChemAb, ChemTitl, ChemoAb, CurCont, D01, E-psyche, E12, EMBASE, ESPM, ExcerpMed, F08, F11, F12, GH, H16, I05, IABS, IPsyAb, ISR, IndMed, IndVet, Inpharma, MEDLINE, MycolAb, N02, N03, NSA, NSCI, P03, P30, P33, P35, P37, P39, PHN&I, PN&I, PsycholAb, R07, R08, R10, RA&MP, RM&VM, Reac, RefZh, SCI, SCOPUS, SoyAb, T02, T05, ToxAb, VS, W07, W10.
—BLDSC (6081.317000), CASDDS, GNLM, IE, Infotrieve, Ingenta, INIST. **CCC.**
Published by: Elsevier Ltd (Subsidiary of: Elsevier Science & Technology), The Blvd, Langford Ln, Kidlington, Oxford, OX5 1GB, United Kingdom. TEL 44-1865-843000, FAX 44-1865-843010, journalscustomerserviceemea@elsevier.com. Eds. E Sylvester Vizi TEL 36-1-2109421, Roger F Butterworth TEL 514-281-2444 ext 5759. **Subscr. to:** Elsevier BV, Radarweg 29, PO Box 211, Amsterdam 1000 AE, Netherlands. TEL 31-20-4853757, FAX 31-20-4853432, http://www.elsevier.nl.

➤ **NEUROCHIRURGIE.** *see* MEDICAL SCIENCES—Surgery

616.8 617 ESP ISSN 1130-1473
NEUROCIRUGIA/NEUROSURGERY. Text in Spanish, English, Portuguese. 196?-197?; resumed 1989. bi-m. back issues avail.; reprints avail. **Document type:** *Journal, Academic/Scholarly.* **Description:** Covers all fields related to the neurological sciences.
Formerly (until 1989): Neurocirugia Luso-Espanola (1131-3722)
Related titles: Online - full text ed.: 2005. free (effective 2011).
Indexed: A36, CA, CABA, E-psyche, E12, EMBASE, ExcerpMed, GH, H17, MEDLINE, NSCI, P30, P33, PN&I, R10, Reac, SCI, SCOPUS, T02, T05, W07.
—BLDSC (6081.352000). **CCC.**
Published by: Sociedad Espanola de Neurocirugia, Avenida de Pontejos 29-C, atico, Santander, 39005, Spain. TEL 34-94-2392030, http://www.senec.org/. Eds. Dr. Izquierdo, Dr. Diez Lobato. Pub. Dr. Izquierdo. Circ: 1,000.

615.82 USA ISSN 2151-6987
RC489.B53
NEUROCONNECTIONS. Text in English. 2007. q. free to members (effective 2009). adv. back issues avail. **Document type:** *Newsletter, Trade.* **Description:** Promotes excellence in clinical practice, educational applications, and research in applied neuroscience in order to better understand and enhance brain function.
Formerly (until 2007): I S N R Newsletter
Related titles: Online - full text ed.: ISSN 2151-6995. free (effective 2009).
Published by: (Association for Applied Psychophysiology and Biofeedback), International Society for Neurofeedback and Research, 1925 Francisco Blvd E #12, San Rafael, CA 94901. TEL 415-485-1344, 800-488-3867, FAX 415-485-1348, office@isnr.org. Eds. Merlyn Hurd, Roger H Riss.

616.8 GBR ISSN 1758-2024
▼ ➤ **NEURODEGENERATIVE DISEASE MANAGEMENT.** Text in English. 2011. bi-m. GBP 695 combined subscription domestic to institutions (print & online eds.); USD 1,220 combined subscription in North America to institutions (print & online eds.); JPY 129,000 combined subscription in Japan to institutions (print & online eds.); EUR 975 combined subscription elsewhere to institutions (print & online eds.) (effective 2011). adv. **Document type:** *Journal, Academic/Scholarly.* **Description:** Provides guidance to the multidisciplinary disease management community regarding the most effective treatment strategies and the implications of cuttingedge research as it emerges.
Related titles: Online - full text ed.: ISSN 1758-2032. 2011. GBP 615 domestic to institutions; USD 1,080 in North America to institutions; JPY 115,000 in Japan to institutions; EUR 865 elsewhere to institutions (effective 2011).
—**CCC.**
Published by: Future Medicine Ltd. (Subsidiary of: Future Science Ltd.), Unitec House, 2 Albert Pl, London, N3 1QB, United Kingdom. TEL 44-20-83716080, FAX 44-20-83716099, info@futuremedicine.com, http://www.futuremedicine.com/. Ed. Elisa Manzotti TEL 44-20-83716090. Pub. David Hughes. Adv. contact Simon Boisseau TEL 44-208-3716083.

➤ **NEURODEGENERATIVE DISEASES.** *see* MEDICAL SCIENCES—Gastroenterology

➤ **NEUROENDOCRINOLOGY**; international journal for basic and clinical studies on neuroendocrine relationships. *see* MEDICAL SCIENCES—Endocrinology

616.8 SWE ISSN 0172-780X
CODEN: NLETDU
➤ **NEUROENDOCRINOLOGY LETTERS.** Text in English. 1979. bi-m. USD 260 to individuals; USD 435 to individuals Includes supplements; USD 435 to institutions; USD 535 to institutions Includes supplements (effective 2005). adv. bk.rev. illus. back issues avail.; reprints avail. **Document type:** *Journal, Academic/Scholarly.* **Description:** Covers the fields of neuroendocrinology and related areas, including immunological, psychological, oncological and other aspects in normal and pathological physiology.
Related titles: Online - full text ed.
Indexed: A20, A22, ASCA, B21, BIOBASE, CIN, ChemAb, ChemTitl, E-psyche, EMBASE, ExcerpMed, IABS, ISR, MEDLINE, NSA, NSCI, P30, R10, Reac, SCI, SCOPUS, W07.
—BLDSC (6081.371000), CASDDS, GNLM, IE, Infotrieve, Ingenta, INIST. **CCC.**
Published by: Maghira & Maas Publications, PO Box 26132, Stockholm, 10041, Sweden. TEL 46-8-6115565, FAX 46-8-86640771, editor@nel.edu. Ed. Dr. Peter Fedor-Freybergh TEL 41-13553207.

M

616.8 CHE ISSN 0251-5350
RC346 CODEN: NEEPD3

➤ **NEUROEPIDEMIOLOGY.** Text in English. 1982. 8/yr. CHF 3,036, EUR 2,426, USD 2,976 to institutions; CHF 3,332, EUR 2,664, USD 3,262 combined subscription to institutions (print & online eds.) (effective 2012). adv. illus. index. back issues avail. **Document type:** *Journal, Academic/Scholarly.* **Description:** Devoted to descriptive analytical and experimental studies in the epidemiology of neurologic disease.
Related titles: Microform ed.: (from PQC); Online - full text ed.: ISSN 1423-0208. CHF 2,968, EUR 2,374, USD 2,882 to institutions (effective 2012).
Indexed: A22, A36, ASCA, B21, B25, BIOSIS Prev, CA, CABA, CurCont, E-psyche, E01, E12, EMBASE, ESPM, ExcerpMed, GH, H&SSA, H17, INI, ISR, IndMed, Inpharma, MEDLINE, MycolAb, N02, N03, NRN, NSA, NSCI, P03, P20, P22, P25, P26, P30, P33, P35, P39, P48, P50, P54, PN&I, PQC, PsycInfo, PsycholAb, R08, R10, R12, RM&VM, Reac, SCI, SCOPUS, SoyAb, T02, T05, ToxAb, VITIS, VirolAbstr, W07.
—BLDSC (6081.371200), GNLM, IE, Infotrieve, Ingenta, INIST. **CCC.**
Published by: S. Karger AG, Allschwilerstr 10, Basel, 4055, Switzerland. TEL 41-61-3061111, FAX 41-61-3061234, karger@karger.ch, http://www.karger.ch. Ed. V L Feigin. adv.: page CHF 173,000; trim 210 x 280. Circ: 800.

616.8 NLD ISSN 1874-5490

➤ **NEUROETHICS.** Text in English. 2008. 3/yr. EUR 287 combined subscription (print & online eds) (effective 2011). reprint service avail. from PSC. **Document type:** *Journal, Academic/Scholarly.* **Description:** Covers studies in neuroethics and related issues in the sciences of the mind. Focuses on the ethical issues posed by new technologies developed via neuroscience, such as psychopharmaceuticals.
Related titles: Online - full text ed.: ISSN 1874-5504. 2008 (from IngentaConnect).
Indexed: A22, A26, CurCont, E01, E08, EMBASE, ExcerpMed, H12, P03, PsycInfo, S09, SCI, SCOPUS, SSCI, W07.
—IE. **CCC.**
Published by: Springer Netherlands (Subsidiary of: Springer Science+Business Media), Van Godewijckstraat 30, Dordrecht, 3311 GX, Netherlands. TEL 31-78-6576050, FAX 31-78-6576474. Ed. Neil Levy.

616.8 FRA ISSN 1298-5708

NEUROFIBROMATOSES. Text in French. 1999. q.
Indexed: RefZh.
Published by: Association Neurofibromatoses et Recklinghausen, 34 Vieux Chemin de Grenade, Blagnac, 31700, France. TEL 33-561-300337, ass.neurofibromatoses@wanadoo.fr, http://www.anrfrance.org/accueil/.

616.8 DEU ISSN 0947-0875
CODEN: NRFMFO

NEUROFORUM. Text in German. 1995. q. EUR 200, USD 272 to institutions (effective 2012). reprint service avail. from PSC. **Document type:** *Journal, Academic/Scholarly.*
Related titles: Online - full text ed.: ISSN 1868-856X.
Indexed: E-psyche, EMBASE, ExcerpMed, R10, Reac, SCI, SCOPUS, W07.
—CASDDS, GNLM. **CCC.**
Published by: Spektrum Akademischer Verlag GmbH (Subsidiary of: Springer Science+Business Media), Slevogtstr 3-5, Heidelberg, 69126, Germany. TEL 49-6221-91260, FAX 49-6221-9126370, m.barth@elsevier.com, http://www.spektrumverlag.com. Ed. Helmut Kettenmann. Adv. contact Bernd Beutel.

NEUROGENETICS. *see* BIOLOGY—Genetics

616.8 DEU ISSN 1613-0146

NEUROGERIATRIE. Text in German. 2004. q. EUR 96; EUR 28 newsstand/cover (effective 2010). adv. **Document type:** *Journal, Academic/Scholarly.*
Related titles: Online - full text ed.: ISSN 1869-6996.
Published by: Hippocampus Verlag KG, Bismarckstr 8, Bad Honnef, 53604, Germany. TEL 49-2224-919480, FAX 49-2224-919482, verlag@hippocampus.de. Eds. Dr. H Durwen, Dr. P Calabrese. Adv. contact Brigitte Buelau. Circ: 4,700 (paid and controlled).

616.8 USA ISSN 1941-8744

▼ **NEUROHOSPITALIST.** Text in English. 2010 (Feb.). s-a. USD 369, GBP 217 combined subscription to institutions (print & online eds.); USD 362, GBP 213 to institutions (effective 2011). **Document type:** *Journal, Academic/Scholarly.* **Description:** Addresses the diagnosis and treatment of neurological diseases, including research on general neurology, vascular neurology, movement disorders, neuroinfectious diseases, and epilepsy.
Related titles: Online - full text ed.: ISSN 1941-8752. 2010 (Feb.). USD 332, GBP 195 to institutions (effective 2011).
—IE. **CCC.**
Published by: Sage Publications, Inc., 2455 Teller Rd, Thousand Oaks, CA 91320. TEL 805-499-9774, FAX 805-499-0871, info@sagepub.com, http://www.sagepub.com/. Ed. Vanja Douglas.

616.8 USA ISSN 1053-8119
RC386.6.D52 CODEN: NEIMEF

➤ **NEUROIMAGE.** Text in English. 1992. 20/yr. EUR 3,094 in Europe to institutions; JPY 323,300 in Japan to institutions; USD 2,483 elsewhere to institutions (effective 2012). adv. index. back issues avail.; reprints avail. **Document type:** *Journal, Academic/Scholarly.* **Description:** Focuses on the visualization of all neuroscientific data.
Related titles: Online - full text ed.: ISSN 1095-9572 (from IngentaConnect, ScienceDirect).
Indexed: A01, A03, A08, A20, A22, A26, A28, APA, ASCA, B&BAb, B19, B21, B25, BIOSIS Prev, BioEngAb, BrCerAb, C&ISA, CA, CA/WCA, CIA, CerAb, ChemAb, CivEngAb, CorrAb, CurCont, E&CAJ, E-psyche, E01, E11, EEA, EMA, EMBASE, ESPM, EnvEAb, ExcerpMed, GenetAb, H15, I05, ISR, IndMed, Inpharma, M&TEA, M09, MBF, MEDLINE, METADEX, MycolAb, NSA, NSCI, P03, P30, P34, PsycInfo, R10, RILM, Reac, SCI, SCOPUS, SolStAb, T02, T04, W07, WAA.
—BLDSC (6081.372200), GNLM, IE, Infotrieve, Ingenta. **CCC.**
Published by: Academic Press (Subsidiary of: Elsevier Science & Technology), 3251 Riverport Ln, Maryland Heights, MO 63043. TEL 314-447-8010, FAX 314-447-8030, JournalCustomerService-usa@elsevier.com, http://www.elsevierdirect.com/imprint.jsp?iid=5. Ed. Paul Fletcher. Adv. contact Tino DeCarlo TEL 212-633-3815.

➤ **NEUROIMMUNOMODULATION.** *see* MEDICAL SCIENCES—Allergology And Immunology

➤ **NEUROINFORMATICS.** *see* BIOLOGY—Physiology

➤ **NEUROINTERVENTION.** *see* MEDICAL SCIENCES—Radiology And Nuclear Medicine

616.8 DEU

NEUROKOGNITION (TUEBINGEN). Text in German. 2002. irreg., latest vol.3, 2002. price varies. **Document type:** *Monographic series, Academic/Scholarly.*
Published by: Stauffenburg Verlag, Postfach 2525, Tuebingen, 72015, Germany. TEL 49-7071-97300, FAX 49-7071-973030, info@stauffenburg.de.

616.8 DEU ISSN 0933-2715

NEUROLINGUISTIK; Zeitschrift fuer Aphasieforschung und -therapie. Text in German. 1987. s-a. EUR 32 to individuals; EUR 40 to institutions (effective 2003). **Document type:** *Journal, Academic/Scholarly.*
Indexed: MLA-IB.
Published by: HochschulVerlag GmbH, Appuhnstr 20, Hamburg, 22609, Germany. TEL 31-70-3278371, FAX 31-70-3278381, post@hochschulverlag.com. Ed. Gerhard Blanken.

616.8 DEU ISSN 1616-2455

➤ **DER NEUROLOGE UND PSYCHIATER.** Text in German. 1998. m. EUR 81, USD 103 to institutions (effective 2012). adv. **Document type:** *Journal, Academic/Scholarly.*
Former titles (until 2001): Neuro Praxisinformation (1435-0009); Neuro Nachrichten
Indexed: A26, E-psyche.
—CCC.
Published by: Med.Komm - Verlag fuer medizinische Kommunikation (Subsidiary of: Springer Science+Business Media), Neumarkter Str 43, Munich, 81673, Germany. TEL 49-89-43721362, FAX 49-89-43721360, knorre@medkomm.de, http://www.medkomm.de. Ed. Dr. Monika von Berg. Adv. contact Barbara Kanters. B&W page EUR 2,030, color page EUR 3,170; trim 174 x 230. Circ: 10,550 (paid and controlled). **Subscr. to:** Springer Distribution Center, Kundenservice Zeitschriften, Haberstr 7, Heidelberg 69126, Germany. TEL 49-6221-3454303, FAX 49-6221-3454229, subscriptions@springer.com.

616.8 ESP ISSN 0213-4853
RC346 CODEN: NERLEN

➤ **NEUROLOGIA.** Text in Spanish; Summaries in English. 1986. 10/yr. adv. back issues avail.; reprints avail. **Document type:** *Journal, Academic/Scholarly.* **Description:** Covers the investigative research of the Society and accredited clinics throughout the country.
Related titles: CD-ROM ed.: ISSN 1697-1264. 1999; Online - full text ed.: ISSN 1578-1968. 1998 (from ScienceDirect); ◆ Supplement(s): Neurologia. Suplementos. ISSN 1695-5374.
Indexed: A01, A20, A22, E-psyche, EMBASE, ExcerpMed, F03, F04, IME, IndMed, MEDLINE, NSCI, P30, R10, Reac, SCI, SCOPUS, T02, W07.
—BLDSC (6081.374900), GNLM, IE, Infotrieve, Ingenta, INIST. **CCC.**
Published by: (Sociedad Espanola de Neurologia), Elsevier Doyma (Subsidiary of: Elsevier Health Sciences), Traversa de Gracia 17-21, Barcelona, 08021, Spain. TEL 34-932-418800, FAX 34-932-419020, editorial@elsevier.com. Circ: 2,100.

616.8 SVK ISSN 1336-8621

➤ **NEUROLOGIA.** Text in Slovak. 2006. 3/yr. EUR 9 (effective 2009). **Document type:** *Journal, Academic/Scholarly.*
Published by: Samedi s.r.o., Racianska 20, Bratislava, 839 27, Slovakia. TEL 421-2-55645901, FAX 421-2-55645902, samedi@samedi.sk. Ed. Eva Ochabova.

616.8 ESP ISSN 1853-0028

▼ **NEUROLOGIA ARGENTINA.** Text in Spanish. 2009. q. **Document type:** *Journal, Academic/Scholarly.*
Related titles: Online - full text ed.: (from ScienceDirect).
Indexed: SCOPUS.
Published by: (Sociedad Neurologica Argentina ARG), Elsevier Doyma (Subsidiary of: Elsevier Health Sciences), Traversa de Gracia 17-21, Barcelona, 08021, Spain. TEL 34-932-418800, FAX 34-932-419020, doyma@doyma.es, http://www.doyma.es. Ed. Rau Rey.

616.89 HRV ISSN 0353-8842
CODEN: NECRFZ

➤ **NEUROLOGIA CROATICA;** journal of clinical neurosciences. Text in Croatian, English. 1953. q. HRK 200 domestic to institutions; USD 50 foreign to institutions (effective 2011). adv. bk.rev. illus. reprints avail. **Document type:** *Journal, Academic/Scholarly.* **Description:** Covers advances in neurological and neurosurgical research.
Former titles (until 1991): Neurologija (0350-9559); (until 1977): Neuropsihijatrija (0047-9438)
Related titles: Microform ed.: (from PQC); ◆ Supplement(s): Neurologia Croatica. Supplement. ISSN 1331-5196.
Indexed: ASCA, DentInd, E-psyche, EMBASE, ExcerpMed, IndMed, NSCI, P30, PsycholAb, R10, Reac, SCI, SCOPUS, W07.
—BLDSC (6081.377000), CASDDS, GNLM, IE, Infotrieve, Ingenta.
Published by: (Hrvatsko Neurolosko Drustvo/Croatian Neurosurgical Society), Klinicki Bolnicki Centar Zagreb, Klinika za Neurologiju/ Zagreb University Hospital, Department of Neurology, Kispaticeva 12, Zagreb, 10000, Croatia. TEL 385-1-2388176, FAX 385-1-2388176, kbc-zagreb@kbc-zagreb.hr, http://www.kbc-zagreb.hr. Ed. S Hajnsek. Circ: 800.

616.89 HRV ISSN 1331-5196

NEUROLOGIA CROATICA. SUPPLEMENT. Text in Croatian, English. 1994. irreg., latest vol.51, 2002. bk.rev. **Document type:** *Journal, Academic/Scholarly.*
Related titles: ◆ Supplement to: Neurologia Croatica. ISSN 0353-8842.
Published by: Klinicki Bolnicki Centar Zagreb, Klinika za Neurologiju/ Zagreb University Hospital, Department of Neurology, Kispaticeva 12, Zagreb, 10000, Croatia. kbc-zagreb@kbc-zagreb.hr, http://www.kbc-zagreb.hr. Ed. Niko Zurak. Adv. contact Vlatka Ivankovic.

616.8 POL ISSN 0028-3843
RC321 CODEN: NNPOBE

NEUROLOGIA I NEUROCHIRURGIA POLSKA/POLISH JOURNAL OF NEUROLOGY AND NEUROSURGERY. Text in Polish, English; Summaries in English, Russian. 1951. bi-m. EUR 78 foreign (effective 2005). adv. bk.rev. bibl.; illus.; stat. index, cum.index. **Document type:** *Journal, Academic/Scholarly.*
Supersedes in part (in 1967): Neurologia, Neurochirurgia i Psychiatria Polska (1233-2410)
Related titles: Online - full text ed.: ISSN 1897-4260.
Indexed: A22, ChemAb, DentInd, DokArb, E-psyche, EMBASE, ExcerpMed, IndMed, MEDLINE, P30, R10, Reac, SCI, SCOPUS, W07.
—BLDSC (6081.380000), CASDDS, GNLM, IE, Infotrieve, Ingenta, INIST.
Published by: (Polskie Towarzystwo Neurologiczne/Polish Neurological Society, Polskie Towarzystwo Neurochirurgow), Termedia sp. z o.o./Termedia Publishing House, ul Wenedow 9/1, Poznan, 61614, Poland. TEL 48-61-8227781, FAX 48-61-8227781, termedia@termedia.pl. Ed. Dr. Andrzej Szczudlik. Circ: 1,800.

616.8 POL

NEUROLOGIA I PSYCHIATRIA. Text in Polish. q. PLZ 60 domestic (effective 2005). **Document type:** *Journal.*
Published by: Agencja Wydawniczo-Reklamowa, ul Wadowicka 8a, Krakow, 30415, Poland. medicus@medicus.com.pl, http://www.medicus.com.pl.

616.89 617.4 JPN
RD593 CODEN: NMCHBN

➤ **NEUROLOGIA MEDICO-CHIRURGICA.** Text in English. 1959. m. adv. **Document type:** *Journal, Academic/Scholarly.*
Formed by the merger of (1974-1978): Neurologia Medico-Chirurgica. Part I; (1976-1978): Shinkei Geka/Neurologia Medico-Chirurgica. Part II (0387-2572); Both of which superseded in part (1959-1973): Neurologia Medico-Chirurgica (0470-8105)
Related titles: Online - full text ed.: ISSN 1349-8029. 2000. free (effective 2011).
Indexed: B21, DentInd, E-psyche, EMBASE, ExcerpMed, INI, INIS AtomInd, IndMed, MEDLINE, NSA, NSCI, P30, R10, Reac, SCI, SCOPUS, W07.
—BLDSC (6081.390000), IE, Ingenta, INIST. **CCC.**
Published by: Japan Neurosurgical Society/Nihon No Shinkei Geka Gakkai, Ishikawa Bldg. 4/F, 5-25-16 Hongo, Bunkyo-ku, Tokyo, 113-0033, Japan. TEL 81-3-38126226, FAX 81-3-38122090, jns@ss.iij4u.or.jp.

616.8 MEX ISSN 0028-3851

NEUROLOGIA, NEUROCIRUGIA Y PSIQUIATRIA. Text in Spanish. 1951. q. MXN 50 newsstand/cover (effective 2005). back issues avail. **Document type:** *Journal, Academic/Scholarly.*
Formerly (until 1959): Archivos Mexicanos de Neurologia y Psiquiatria (0518-3707); Which was formed by the merger of: Archivos de Neurologia y Psiquiatria de Mexico; Revista Mexicana de Psiquiatria, Neurologia y Neurocirugia
Related titles: Online - full text ed.
Indexed: A01, C01, CA, EMBASE, ExcerpMed, P30, SCOPUS, T02.
Published by: Sociedad Mexicana de Neurologia y Psiquiatria, A.C., Calle de Miami No 47, Col. Napoles, Mexico, D.F., 03810, Mexico. TEL 52-55-56873831, smnp@prodigy.net.mx. Ed. Jose de Jesus Almanza Munoz.

616.8 POL ISSN 1642-316X

NEUROLOGIA PRAKTYCZNA. Text in Polish. 2001. q. PLZ 72 domestic (effective 2005). **Document type:** *Journal, Academic/Scholarly.*
Published by: Wydawnictwo Czelej Sp. z o.o., ul Czeremchowa 21, Lublin, 20807, Poland. TEL 48-81-7437766, FAX 48-81-5347788, wydawnictwo@czelej.com.pl, http://www.czelej.com.pl.

616.8 SVK ISSN 1335-9592

➤ **NEUROLOGIA PRE PRAX.** Text in Slovak. 2002. bi-m. EUR 18 (effective 2010). **Document type:** *Journal, Academic/Scholarly.*
Published by: Solen, s.r.o., Uprkova 23, Bratislava, 811 04, Slovakia. TEL 421-2-54650649, FAX 421-2-54651384, solen@solen.sk. Ed. Jana Repiska.

616.8 ESP ISSN 1695-5374

NEUROLOGIA. SUPLEMENTOS. Text in Spanish. 2003. s-a. **Document type:** *Journal, Academic/Scholarly.*
Related titles: Online - full text ed.: ISSN 1886-9254. 2005; ◆ Supplement to: Neurologia. ISSN 0213-4853.
Indexed: SCOPUS.
—CCC.
Published by: Elsevier Doyma (Subsidiary of: Elsevier Health Sciences), Traversa de Gracia 17-21, Barcelona, 08021, Spain. TEL 34-932-418800, FAX 34-932-419020, editorial@elsevier.com, http://www.elsevier.es/.

616.8 USA ISSN 0733-8619
RC321

➤ **NEUROLOGIC CLINICS.** Text in English. 1983. q. USD 441 in United States to institutions; USD 530 elsewhere to institutions (effective 2012). adv. back issues avail.; reprints avail. **Document type:** *Journal, Academic/Scholarly.* **Description:** Each issue covers a neurologic disease in detail.
Related titles: Microform ed.: (from PQC); Online - full text ed.: ISSN 1557-9875 (from IngentaConnect, ScienceDirect).
Indexed: A20, A22, ASCA, B21, C06, C07, C08, CINAHL, CurCont, E-psyche, EMBASE, ExcerpMed, IndMed, Inpharma, MEDLINE, NSA, NSCI, P03, P30, PsycInfo, PsycholAb, R10, Reac, SCI, SCOPUS, W07.
—BLDSC (6081.441000), GNLM, IE, Infotrieve, Ingenta, INIST. **CCC.**
Published by: W.B. Saunders Co. (Subsidiary of: Elsevier Health Sciences), Elsevier, Health Sciences Division, Order Fulfillment, 3251 Riverport Ln, Maryland Heights, MO 63043. TEL 314-872-8370, 800-325-4177, FAX 314-432-1380, JournalCustomerService-usa@elsevier.com, http://www.us.elsevierhealth.com. Adv. contact John Marmero TEL 212-633-3657.

616.8 USA ISSN 1942-4043

THE NEUROLOGICAL BULLETIN. Text in English. 2008 (Sep.). q. free (effective 2010). **Document type:** *Bulletin, Academic/Scholarly.* **Description:** Publishes original investigations, case reports and case series, therapeutic trials, and timely reviews, written by students, residents, or fellows, with faculty as possible co-authors or mentors.
Media: Online - full text.
Published by: University of Massachusetts Medical School, Department of Neurology, 55 Lake Ave N, Worcester, MA 01655. TEL 508-856-8989, publicaffairs@umassmed.edu, http://www.umassmed.edu/som/dept/neuro/default.aspx. Ed. William Schwartz.

616.8 GBR ISSN 0161-6412
RC321 CODEN: NRESDZ

➤ **NEUROLOGICAL RESEARCH**; a journal of progress in neurosurgery, neurology and neurosciences. Text in English. 1979. 10/yr. GBP 1,308 combined subscription to institutions (print & online eds.); USD 2,173 combined subscription in United States to institutions (print & online eds.) (effective 2012). adv. bk.rev. abstr.; illus.; pat. Index. 120 p./no. 2 cols./p.; back issues avail.; reprint service avail. from PSC. **Document type:** *Journal, Academic/Scholarly.* **Description:** Covers basic and clinical research in neurosurgery, neuro-oncology, neuroradiology, neuropathology and other aspects of neurological research.

Related titles: Microfilm ed.: 1979 (from PQC); Online - full text ed.: ISSN 1743-1328. 2001. GBP 1,176 to institutions; USD 1,955 in United States to institutions (effective 2012) (from IngentaConnect).

Indexed: A20, A22, ASCA, B21, B25, BIOBASE, BIOSIS Prev, CA, CIN, ChemAb, ChemTitl, CurCont, E-psyche, EMBASE, ESPM, ExcerpMed, IABS, IBR, IBZ, IndMed, Inpharma, MEDLINE, MycolAb, NSA, NSCI, P20, P22, P26, P30, P35, P48, P54, PQC, R10, RILM, Reac, SCI, SCOPUS, T02, Telegen, ToxAb, W07.

—BLDSC (6081.442000), CASDDS, GNLM, IE, Infotrieve, Ingenta, INIST. **CCC.**

Published by: Maney Publishing, Ste 1C, Joseph's Well, Hanover Walk, Leeds, W Yorks LS3 1AB, United Kingdom. TEL 44-113-2432800, FAX 44-113-3868178, maney@maney.co.uk. Ed. Manuel Dujovny. **Subscr. in N America to:** Maney Publishing, 875 Massachusetts Ave, 7th Fl, Cambridge, MA 02139. TEL 866-297-5154, FAX 617-354-6875, maney@maneyusa.com.

610 ITA ISSN 1590-1874
RC321 CODEN: IJNSD3

➤ **NEUROLOGICAL SCIENCES.** Text in English. 1980. bi-m. EUR 253, USD 303 combined subscription to institutions (print & online eds.) (effective 2012). adv. bk.rev. reprint service avail. from PSC. **Document type:** *Journal, Academic/Scholarly.* **Description:** Provides a medium for the communication of results and ideas in the field of neuroscience.

Formerly (until 1999): The Italian Journal of Neurological Sciences (0392-0461)

Related titles: Microform ed.: (from PQC); Online - full text ed.: ISSN 1590-3478 (from IngentaConnect).

Indexed: A01, A02, A03, A08, A20, A22, A26, ASCA, B21, B25, BIOSIS Prev, C06, C07, C08, C11, CA, CINAHL, CurCont, E-psyche, E01, EMBASE, ExcerpMed, H04, H12, I05, ISR, IndMed, Inpharma, MEDLINE, MycolAb, NSA, NSCI, P03, P19, P20, P22, P25, P30, P35, P43, P48, P54, PQC, PsycInfo, PsycholAb, R10, Reac, SCI, SCOPUS, T02, W07.

—BLDSC (6081.444000), CASDDS, GNLM, IE, Infotrieve, Ingenta, INIST. **CCC.**

Published by: (Societa Italiana di Neurologia), Springer Italia Srl (Subsidiary of: Springer Science+Business Media), Via Decembrio 28, Milan, 20137, Italy. TEL 39-02-54259722, FAX 39-02-55193360, springer@springer.it. Ed. Dr. Giuliano Avanzini. Circ: 2,100. **Subscr. in the Americas to:** Springer New York LLC, Journal Fulfillment, PO Box 2485, Secaucus, NJ 07096. TEL 800-777-4643, 201-348-4033, FAX 201-348-4505, journals-ny@springer.com, http://www.springer.com; **Subscr. to:** Springer Distribution Center, Kundenservice Zeitschriften, Haberstr 7, Heidelberg 69126, Germany. TEL 49-6221-3454303, FAX 49-6221-3454229, subscriptions@springer.com, http://link.springer.de. **Co-sponsor:** Societa Italiana di Neurofisiologia Clinica.

➤ **NEUROLOGICAL SURGERY/NO SHINKEI GEKA.** *see* MEDICAL SCIENCES—Surgery

616.8 FRA ISSN 2100-9511

NEUROLOGIE.COM. Text in French. 2008. m. (10/yr.). EUR 368 combined subscription domestic to institutions (print & online eds.); EUR 408 combined subscription in the European Union to institutions (print & online eds.); EUR 428 combined subscription elsewhere to institutions (print & online eds.) (effective 2011). **Document type:** *Journal, Academic/Scholarly.*

Related titles: Online - full text ed.: ISSN 2102-6041.

Published by: John Libbey Eurotext, 127 Av. de la Republique, Montrouge, 92120, France. TEL 33-1-46730660, FAX 33-1-40840999, contact@jle.com, http://www.john-libbey-eurotext.fr. Ed. Pierre Amarenco.

616.8 FRA ISSN 1772-8002

NEUROLOGIE PRATIQUE. Text in French. 2005. m. **Document type:** *Newsletter, Trade.*

Published by: L E N Medical - Axis Sante, 15 Rue des Sablons, Paris, 75116, France. TEL 33-1-47553131, FAX 33-1-47553132, info@len-medical.fr, http://www.len-medical.fr.

616.8 CZE ISSN 1213-1814

NEUROLOGIE PRO PRAXI. Text in Czech. 2000. bi-m. CZK 480; CZK 80 per issue (effective 2010). **Document type:** *Journal, Academic/Scholarly.*

Related titles: Online - full text ed.: ISSN 1803-5280.

Published by: Solen s.r.o., Lazecka 297/51, Olomouc 51, 779 00, Czech Republic. TEL 420-582-396038, FAX 420-582-396099, solen@solen.cz, http://www.solen.cz. Ed. Zdenka Bartakova. Circ: 1,500.

616.8 DEU ISSN 0947-2177
CODEN: NEREF3

➤ **NEUROLOGIE UND REHABILITATION**; Neuroprotektion - Neuroplastizitaet - Neurologische Langzeittherapie. Text in German. 1995. bi-m. EUR 133; EUR 28 newsstand/cover (effective 2010). adv. **Document type:** *Journal, Academic/Scholarly.*

Related titles: Online - full text ed.: ISSN 1869-7003.

Indexed: A22, E-psyche, EMBASE, ExcerpMed, R10, Reac, SCOPUS.

—BLDSC (6081.455000), GNLM, IE, Ingenta. **CCC.**

Published by: (Deutsche Gesellschaft fuer Neurologische Rehabilitation), Hippocampus Verlag KG, Bismarckstr 8, Bad Honnef, 53604, Germany. TEL 49-2224-919480, FAX 49-2224-919482, verlag@hippocampus.de. Eds. Dr. C Weiler, Dr. P Buelau, Dr. P Schoenle. Adv. contact Brigitte Buelau. Circ: 3,800 (paid and controlled).

616.8 FRA ISSN 1287-9118

NEUROLOGIES. Text in French. 1998. m. **Document type:** *Journal, Trade.*

Published by: Expressions Groupe, 2 Rue de la Roquette, Cour de Mai, Paris, 75011, France. TEL 33-1-49292929, FAX 33-1-49292919, contact@expressions-sante.fr.

616.8 USA ISSN 1074-7931
RC346 CODEN: NROLFW

➤ **THE NEUROLOGIST.** Text in English. 1995. bi-m. USD 577 domestic to institutions; USD 733 foreign to institutions (effective 2011). adv. back issues avail.; reprints avail. **Document type:** *Journal, Academic/Scholarly.* **Description:** Brings out articles on topics of current interest to physicians treating patients with neurological diseases.

Related titles: Online - full text ed.: USD 351 domestic for academice site license; USD 396 foreign for academice site license; USD 391.50 domestic for corporate site license; USD 436.50 foreign for corporate site license (effective 2002).

Indexed: E-psyche, EMBASE, ExcerpMed, JW-N, MEDLINE, NSCI, P30, R10, Reac, SCI, SCOPUS, W07.

—BLDSC (6081.463500), GNLM, IE, Infotrieve, Ingenta. **CCC.**

Published by: Lippincott Williams & Wilkins (Subsidiary of: Wolters Kluwer N.V.), 530 Walnut St, Philadelphia, PA 19106. TEL 215-521-8300, FAX 215-521-8902, customerservice@lww.com, http://www.lww.com. Ed. Dr. Barney J Stern TEL 410-328-3372. Pub. Harry Dean. Adv. contact Michelle Smith TEL 646-674-6537. Circ: 312.

616.8 USA ISSN 0028-3878
RC321 CODEN: NEURAI

➤ **NEUROLOGY.** Text in English. 1951. 24/yr. USD 1,138 domestic to institutions; USD 1,284 foreign to institutions (effective 2011). adv. bk.rev. bibl.; charts; illus. Index. back issues avail.; reprints avail. **Document type:** *Journal, Academic/Scholarly.* **Description:** Provides reports, discussions, case findings and clinical findings on current research and developments in neurology. Covers neurological symptoms of diseases, diagnostic methods and treatments.

Related titles: E-mail ed.; Microform ed.: (from PQC); Online - full text ed.: ISSN 1526-632X. USD 764.40 domestic academic site license; USD 764.40 foreign academic site license; USD 852.60 domestic corporate site license; USD 852.60 foreign corporate site license (effective 2002); Supplement(s): Neurology (Spanish Edition). ISSN 1666-5791.

Indexed: A20, A22, A26, A34, A36, AIDS Ab, AIM, AMED, ASCA, AddicA, B21, B25, BDM&CN, BIOBASE, BIOSIS Prev, BibInd, C06, C07, C08, C13, CABA, CIN, CINAHL, ChemAb, ChemTitl, CurCont, D01, DentInd, DiabCont, E-psyche, E12, EMBASE, ESPM, ExcerpMed, F08, F11, F12, FR, G08, GH, H11, H12, H16, H17, IABS, IDIS, INI, ISR, IndMed, IndVet, Inpharma, JW, JW-EM, JW-N, JW-P, JW-WH, LT, MEDLINE, MLA-IB, MycolAb, N02, N03, N04, NSA, NSCI, P03, P30, P32, P33, P35, P39, PN&I, PsycInfo, PsycholAb, R07, R08, R10, R12, RA&MP, RILM, RM&VM, RRTA, Reac, S13, S16, SCI, SCOPUS, SOPODA, SoyAb, T05, ToxAb, VS, ViroIAbstr, W07, W10, W11, YAE&RB.

—BLDSC (6081.500000), CASDDS, GNLM, IE, Infotrieve, Ingenta, INIST. **CCC.**

Published by: (American Academy of Neurology), Lippincott Williams & Wilkins (Subsidiary of: Wolters Kluwer N.V.), 530 Walnut St, Philadelphia, PA 19106. TEL 215-521-8300, FAX 215-521-8902, customerservice@lww.com, http://www.lww.com. Ed. Robert A Gross TEL 651-695-2782.

616.8 USA ISSN 2154-4506

▼ **NEUROLOGY (GLENDALE).** Text in English. 2010 (June). s-m. USD 399.89 domestic; USD 431.72 in Canada; USD 479.72 elsewhere (effective 2011). **Document type:** *Journal, Trade.*

Media: Audio CD. **Related titles:** Online - full text ed.: USD 359.72 (effective 2011).

Published by: Audio-Digest Foundation, 1577 E Chevy Chase Dr, Glendale, CA 91206. TEL 818-240-7500, FAX 818-240-7379, marmstrong@audiodigest.org.

616.8 USA ISSN 0741-4234
RC346

NEUROLOGY ALERT. Text in English. 1982. m. USD 319 combined subscription (print & online eds.); USD 53 per issue (effective 2010). index. 8 p./no.; reprints avail. **Document type:** *Newsletter, Trade.* **Description:** Contains abstracts of developments in neurology combined with expert physician commentary.

Related titles: Audio cassette/tape ed.; Online - full text ed.; Polish Translation: Nowosci Neurologiczne. ISSN 1641-6279.

Indexed: A01, A26, E-psyche, E08, G08, H11, H12, I05, P20, P48, P54, PQC, S09.

—CCC.

Published by: A H C Media LLC (Subsidiary of: Thomson Corporation, Healthcare Information Group), 3525 Piedmont Rd, NE, Bldg 6, Ste 400, Atlanta, GA 30305. TEL 404-262-7436, 800-688-2421, FAX 404-262-7837, 800-284-3291, customerservice@ahcmedia.com, http://www.ahcmedia.com/. Eds. Dr. Fred Plum, M Flint Beal, Matthew Fink. Pub. Brenda L Mooney TEL 404-262-5403. **Subscr. to:** PO Box 105109, Atlanta, GA 30348. TEL 404-262-5476, FAX 404-262-5560.

616.8 MYS ISSN 1823-6138
RC346

NEUROLOGY ASIA. Text in English. 1996. s-a. **Document type:** *Journal, Academic/Scholarly.* **Description:** Publishes the results of study and research in neurology, especially Asian neurology, the medical sciences applied to neurological diseases occurring primarily in Asia and aspects of diseases peculiar to Asia.

Formerly: Neurological Journal of South East Asia (1394-780X)

Related titles: Online - full text ed.: free (effective 2011).

Indexed: A01, CA, EMBASE, ExcerpMed, SCI, SCOPUS, T02, W07.

Published by: Association of South East Asian Nations, Neurological Association, c/o Neurology Laboratory, University Malaya Medical Centre, Kuala Lumpur, 59100, Malaysia. Ed. Chong Tin Tan.

NEUROLOGY CODING ALERT; the practical monthly adviser for ethically optimizing coding, reimbursement and efficiency for neurology practices. *see* INSURANCE

616.8 IND ISSN 0028-3886
RC321

➤ **NEUROLOGY INDIA.** Text in English. 1952. bi-m. INR 1,500 domestic to individuals; USD 120 foreign to individuals; INR 2,500 domestic to institutions; USD 250 foreign to institutions; INR 1,800 combined subscription domestic to individuals (print & online eds.); USD 145 combined subscription foreign to individuals (print & online eds.); INR 3,000 combined subscription domestic to institutions (print & online eds.); USD 300 combined subscription foreign to institutions (print & online eds.) (effective 2011). adv. bk.rev. bibl.; illus. cum.index. reprint service avail. from IRC. **Document type:** *Journal, Academic/Scholarly.*

Related titles: CD-ROM ed.; Online - full text ed.: ISSN 1998-4022. INR 1,200 domestic to individuals; USD 95 foreign to individuals; INR 2,000 domestic to institutions; USD 200 foreign to institutions (effective 2011).

Indexed: A01, A03, A08, A20, A26, A36, ASCA, C06, C07, CA, CABA, ChemAb, D01, E-psyche, E08, E12, EMBASE, ExcerpMed, ExtraMED, G08, GH, H11, H12, H17, I05, IndMed, MEDLINE, N02, N03, NSCI, P10, P20, P22, P30, P33, P39, P48, P53, P54, PN&I, PQC, R07, R08, R10, R12, R13, RA&MP, RM&VM, Reac, S09, SCI, SCOPUS, T02, T05, W07.

—GNLM, IE, Ingenta. **CCC.**

Published by: (Neurological Society of India), Medknow Publications and Media Pvt. Ltd., B-9, Kanara Business Ctr, Off Link Rd, Ghatkopar (E), Mumbai, Maharastra 400 075, India. TEL 91-22-66491816, FAX 91-22-66491817, http://www.medknow.com. Ed. Dr. J M K Murthy.

616.8 ITA ISSN 2035-8385

▼ **NEUROLOGY INTERNATIONAL.** Text in Italian. 2009. q. **Document type:** *Journal, Academic/Scholarly.*

Related titles: Online - full text ed.: ISSN 2035-8377. free (effective 2011).

Indexed: EMBASE, SCOPUS.

Published by: Pagepress, Via Giuseppe Belli 4, Pavia, 27100, Italy. TEL 39-0382-1751762, FAX 39-0382-1750481. Ed. Michael A Meyer.

616.8 USA ISSN 1933-1266

➤ **NEUROLOGY, NEUROPHYSIOLOGY AND NEUROSCIENCE.** Abbreviated title: N N N. Text in English. 1996. irreg. free (effective 2011). back issues avail. **Document type:** *Journal, Academic/Scholarly.*

Former titles (until 2006): Neurology & Clinical Neurophysiology (Online) (1526-8748); (until 2000): Journal of Contemporary Neurology (Online) (1081-1818)

Media: Online - full text.

Indexed: EMBASE, ExcerpMed, MEDLINE, P30, R10, Reac, SCOPUS.

—Infotrieve.

Published by: American Academy of Clinical Neurophysiology, Department of Psychiatry, University of Michigan Health System, 1500 E Medical Ctr Dr, SPC 5295, Ann Arbor, MI 48109. TEL 734-936-8269, FAX 734-936-9761, theaacn.org@aetherdataworks.com, http://www.theaacn.org. Ed. Bruce Fisch.

616.8 NLD ISSN 2211-1689

▼ **NEUROLOGY NEWS INTERNATIONAL.** Text in Dutch. 2010. bi-m. adv. **Document type:** *Magazine, Trade.* **Description:** Covers the latest developments in research in neurology.

Published by: Van Zuiden Communications B.V., Postbus 2122, Alphen aan den Rijn, 2400 CC, Netherlands. TEL 31-172-476191, FAX 31-172-471882, zuiden@zuidencomm.nl, http://www.zuidencomm.nl. Circ: 36,000.

616.8 USA ISSN 1553-3271
RC346

NEUROLOGY NOW. Text in English. 2005 (Spr.). bi-m. USD 49 domestic to institutions (effective 2011). adv. back issues avail.; reprints avail. **Document type:** *Magazine, Trade.*

Related titles: Online - full text ed.: ISSN 1553-328X.

—CCC.

Published by: (American Academy of Neurology), Lippincott Williams & Wilkins (Subsidiary of: Wolters Kluwer N.V.), 530 Walnut St, Philadelphia, PA 19106. TEL 215-521-8300, FAX 215-521-8902, customerservice@lww.com, http://www.lww.com. Ed. Robin L Brey.

616.8 USA ISSN 2090-1852

▼ ➤ **NEUROLOGY RESEARCH INTERNATIONAL.** Text in English. 2009. irreg. USD 195 (effective 2011). **Document type:** *Journal, Academic/Scholarly.* **Description:** Publishes original research articles, review articles, case reports, and clinical studies in all areas of neurology.

Related titles: Online - full text ed.: ISSN 2090-1860. free (effective 2011).

Indexed: A01, P30, T02.

Published by: Hindawi Publishing Corporation, 410 Park Ave, 15th Fl, PMB 287, New York, NY 10022. FAX 215-893-4392, 866-446-3294, info@hindawi.com.

616.8 NZL ISSN 1178-6159

NEUROLOGY RESEARCH REVIEW. Text in English. 2007. q. free to qualified personnel (effective 2009). back issues avail. **Document type:** *Journal, Academic/Scholarly.*

Media: Online - full text.

Published by: Research Review Ltd., N Shore Mail Centre, PO Box 100116, Auckland, New Zealand. TEL 64-9-4102277, info@researchreview.co.nz.

616.8 USA ISSN 1075-4598

➤ **NEUROLOGY REVIEWS**; clinical trends & news in neurology. Text in English. 1993. m. USD 100 domestic to medical residents; USD 130 domestic; USD 155 foreign; free to qualified personnel (effective 2008). adv. abstr.; charts; illus. back issues avail.; reprints avail. **Document type:** *Journal, Academic/Scholarly.* **Description:** Covers innovative and emerging news in neurology and neuroscience, with a focus on practical approaches to treating Parkinson's disease, epilepsy, headache, stroke, multiple sclerosis, Alzheimer's disease and other neurologic disorders.

Formerly: Neurology Reviews for the Primary Care Physician (1077-4556)

Indexed: A01, E-psyche, Inpharma, T02.

—CCC.

Published by: Quadrant HealthCom, 7 Century Dr, Ste 302, Parsippany, NJ 07054. TEL 973-206-3434, FAX 973-206-9378, sales@pulmonaryreviews.com, http://www.quadranthealth.com. Ed. Colby K Stong TEL 973-206-2341. Adv. contact Kathleen Corbett TEL 973-206-8022. Circ: 18,700 (paid).

616.8 USA ISSN 1533-7006

NEUROLOGY TODAY. Text in English. 2001. 24/yr. USD 399 domestic to institutions; USD 520 foreign to institutions (effective 2011). adv. back issues avail.; reprints avail. **Document type:** *Newspaper, Academic/Scholarly.* **Description:** Provides news to keep up to date on the practical issues of stroke, Alzheimer's disease, epilepsy, Parkinson's disease, sleep disorders, multiple sclerosis, and other disorders of the brain and nervous system.

Related titles: Online - full text ed.: ISSN 1548-7822.

Indexed: C06, C07.

—BLDSC (6081.503200). **CCC.**

Published by: (American Academy of Neurology), Lippincott Williams & Wilkins (Subsidiary of: Wolters Kluwer N.V.), 333 7th Ave, 19th Fl, New York, NY 10001. TEL 646-674-6545, FAX 646-674-6500, customerservice@lww.com, http://www.lww.com. Eds. Fay Jarosh Ellis, Dr. Steve P Ringel. Pub. Harry Dean.

616.8 NLD

DE NEUROLOOG. Text in Dutch. 1994. 6/m. adv. **Document type:** *Magazine, Trade.*
Published by: Benecke, Arena Boulevard 61-75, Amsterdam, 1101 DL, Netherlands. TEL 31-20-7150600, FAX 31-20-6918446. Pub. Wijnand van Djik. Adv. contact Linda van Iwaarden. color page EUR 2,740; 210 x 297. Circ: 1,250.

NEUROMETHODS. see BIOLOGY—Physiology

616.8 USA ISSN 1094-7159 CODEN: NROMFZ

➤ **NEUROMODULATION**; technology at the neural interface. Text in English. 1998. q. GBP 350 in United Kingdom to institutions; EUR 443 in Europe to institutions; USD 455 in the Americas to institutions; USD 684 elsewhere to institutions; GBP 403 combined subscription in United Kingdom to institutions (print & online eds.); EUR 509 combined subscription in Europe to institutions (print & online eds.); USD 524 combined subscription in the Americas to institutions (print & online eds.); USD 787 combined subscription elsewhere to institutions (print & online eds.) (effective 2012). adv. abstr. back issues avail.; reprints avail. **Document type:** *Journal, Academic/ Scholarly.* **Description:** Disseminates scientific and clinical information relevant to the field of neuromodulation.
Related titles: Microform ed.; Online - full text ed.: ISSN 1525-1403. GBP 350 in United Kingdom to institutions; EUR 443 in Europe to institutions; USD 455 in the Americas to institutions; USD 684 elsewhere to institutions (effective 2012) (from IngentaConnect).
Indexed: A01, A03, A08, A22, A26, B21, CA, E-psyche, E01, EMBASE, ExcerpMed, NSA, NSCI, P30, R10, Reac, S01, SCI, SCOPUS, T02, W07.
—BLDSC (6081.504100), IE, Infotrieve, Ingenta. **CCC.**
Published by: (International Neuromodulation Society, International Functional Electrical Stimulation Society), Wiley-Blackwell Publishing, Inc. (Subsidiary of: Wiley-Blackwell Publishing Ltd.), 111 River St, Hoboken, NJ 07030. TEL 201-748-6000, FAX 201-748-6088, info@wiley.com. Ed. Robert Levy. Adv. contact Karl Franz TEL 781-388-8470.

616.8 615.1 USA ISSN 1535-1084
RC347 CODEN: NMEEAN

➤ **NEUROMOLECULAR MEDICINE.** Text in English. 2002. q. EUR 667, USD 813 combined subscription to institutions (print & online eds.) (effective 2012). bk.rev. illus. back issues avail.; reprint service avail. from PSC. **Document type:** *Journal, Academic/Scholarly.* **Description:** Covers the molecular and biochemical basis of neurological disorders.
Related titles: Online - full text ed.: ISSN 1559-1174 (from IngentaConnect).
Indexed: A22, B21, B25, BIOBASE, BIOSIS Prev, C33, CTA, ChemAb, ChemoAb, E01, EMBASE, ExcerpMed, IABS, MEDLINE, MycolAb, NSA, NSCI, P03, P20, P22, P25, P30, P48, P54, PQC, PsycInfo, R10, Reac, SCI, SCOPUS, W07.
—BLDSC (6081.504300), IE, Ingenta. **CCC.**
Published by: Humana Press, Inc. (Subsidiary of: Springer Science+Business Media), 999 Riverview Dr, Ste 208, Totowa, NJ 07512. TEL 973-256-1699, FAX 973-256-8341, humana@humanapr.com, http://humanapress.com/journals.pasp. Ed. Mark Mattson. Pub. Thomas B. Lanigan Jr. R&P Wendy A. Warren. Adv. contacts John Chasse, Thomas B. Lanigan Jr.

616.8 GBR ISSN 0960-8966
RC925.A1 CODEN: NEDIEC

➤ **NEUROMUSCULAR DISORDERS.** Text in English. 1991. 12/yr. EUR 1,254 in Europe to institutions; JPY 165,500 in Japan to institutions; USD 1,399 elsewhere to institutions (effective 2012). index. back issues avail. **Document type:** *Journal, Academic/Scholarly.* **Description:** Covers all aspects of neuromuscular disorders in childhood and adult life.
Related titles: Microfilm ed.: (from PQC); Online - full text ed.: ISSN 1873-2364 (from IngentaConnect, ScienceDirect).
Indexed: A01, A03, A08, A22, A26, AMED, ASCA, B21, BIOBASE, CA, CurCont, E-psyche, EMBASE, ExcerpMed, I05, IABS, ISR, IndMed, Inpharma, MEDLINE, NSA, NSCI, P30, P35, R10, Reac, SCI, SCOPUS, T02, W07.
—BLDSC (6081.504850), GNLM, IE, Infotrieve, Ingenta. **CCC.**
Published by: Elsevier Ltd (Subsidiary of: Elsevier Science & Technology), The Blvd, Langford Ln, Kidlington, Oxford, OX5 1GB, United Kingdom. TEL 44-1865-843000, FAX 44-1865-843010, journalscustomerserviceemea@elsevier.com. Ed. Dr. Victor Dubowitz TEL 44-20-83833295. **Subscr. to:** Elsevier BV, Radarweg 29, PO Box 211, Amsterdam 1000 AE, Netherlands. TEL 31-20-4853757, FAX 31-20-4853432, http://www.elsevier.nl.

616.8 USA ISSN 0896-6273
QP356.2 CODEN: NERNET

➤ **NEURON.** Text in English. 1988. s-m. EUR 1,844 in Europe to institutions; JPY 192,600 in Japan to institutions; USD 1,423 in US & Canada to institutions; USD 1,603 elsewhere to institutions (effective 2012). bk.rev. abstr. back issues avail. **Document type:** *Journal, Academic/Scholarly.* **Description:** Publishes research articles in molecular, cellular and developmental neurobiology, and also research work in systems (including visual, auditory, motor and limbic systems), neuro-imaging, learning, memory, and behavior and other cognitive studies.
Related titles: Online - full text ed.: ISSN 1097-4199. USD 179 to individuals (effective 2008) (from IngentaConnect, ScienceDirect).
Indexed: A01, A03, A08, A20, A22, A26, ASCA, B21, B25, BIOBASE, BIOSIS Prev, C33, CA, CIN, CTA, ChemAb, ChemTitl, ChemoAb, CurCont, E-psyche, EMBASE, ExcerpMed, GenetAb, I05, IABS, INIS AtomInd, ISR, IndMed, Inpharma, JW-N, MEDLINE, MycolAb, NSA, NSCI, P30, R10, Reac, SCI, SCOPUS, T02, W07, WildRev.
—BLDSC (6081.504900), CASDDS, GNLM, IE, Infotrieve, Ingenta, INIST. **CCC.**
Published by: Cell Press (Subsidiary of: Elsevier Science & Technology), 600 Technology Sq, Cambridge, MA 02139. TEL 617-661-7057, FAX 617-661-7061, celleditor@cell.com. Ed. Katja Brose. Adv. contact Jim Secretario TEL 212-462-1928. Circ: 1,734. **Subscr. to:** 11830 Westline Industrial Dr, St. Louis, MO 63146. TEL 314-579-2880, 866-314-2355, FAX 314-523-5170, subs@cell.com.

616.8 GBR ISSN 1741-0533

➤ **NEURON GLIA BIOLOGY (ONLINE).** Text in English. 2003. q. GBP 320, USD 540 to institutions (effective 2012). adv. **Document type:** *Journal, Academic/Scholarly.* **Description:** Offers an expanded scope that bridges what have traditionally been regarded as separate scientific disciplines.
Media: Online - full text.
—**CCC.**
Published by: Cambridge University Press, The Edinburgh Bldg, Shaftesbury Rd, Cambridge, CB2 8RU, United Kingdom. TEL 44-1223-326070, FAX 44-1223-325150, journals@cambridge.org. Ed. R Douglas Fields.

616.8 DEU

NEURONAL; Das Journal fuer den neurologischen Patienten. Text in German. 2005. 2/yr. adv. **Document type:** *Magazine, Consumer.*
Published by: G F M K GmbH & Co. KG Verlagsgesellschaft, Gezelinallee 37-39, Leverkusen, 51375, Germany. TEL 49-214-310570, FAX 49-214-3105719, info@gfmk.de, http://www.gfmk.de. Circ: 29,425 (paid and controlled).

616.8 FRA ISSN 1626-5734

NEURONALE. Text in French. 2001. bi-m. **Document type:** *Journal, Trade.*
Published by: L E N Medical - Axis Sante, 15 Rue des Sablons, Paris, 75116, France. TEL 33-1-47553131, FAX 33-1-47553132, info@len-medical.fr, http://www.len-medical.fr.

NEUROPAEDIATRIE IN KLINIK UND PRAXIS. see MEDICAL SCIENCES—Pediatrics

616.8 AUS ISSN 0919-6544
RC347

➤ **NEUROPATHOLOGY.** Text in English. 1980. q. GBP 622 in United Kingdom to institutions; EUR 789 in Europe to institutions; USD 1,009 in the Americas to institutions; USD 1,216 elsewhere to institutions; GBP 715 combined subscription in United Kingdom to institutions (print & online eds.); EUR 908 combined subscription in Europe to institutions (print & online eds.); USD 1,160 combined subscription in the Americas to institutions (print & online eds.); USD 1,400 combined subscription elsewhere to institutions (print & online eds.) (effective 2012). adv. back issues avail.; reprint service avail. from PSC. **Document type:** *Journal, Academic/Scholarly.* **Description:** Explores all aspects of clinical and experimental neuropathology and related areas.
Supersedes in part (in 1992): Shinkei Byorigaku (0286-3626)
Related titles: Online - full text ed.: ISSN 1440-1789. GBP 622 in United Kingdom to institutions; EUR 789 in Europe to institutions; USD 1,009 in the Americas to institutions; USD 1,216 elsewhere to institutions (effective 2012) (from IngentaConnect).
Indexed: A01, A03, A08, A22, A26, ASCA, B21, BIOBASE, CA, E-psyche, E01, EMBASE, ExcerpMed, H12, IABS, IndMed, MEDLINE, NSA, NSCI, P03, P30, PsycInfo, PsycholAb, R10, Reac, SCI, SCOPUS, T02, W07.
—BLDSC (6081.513800), IE, Infotrieve, Ingenta. **CCC.**
Published by: (Japanese Society of Neuropathology JPN), Wiley-Blackwell Publishing Asia (Subsidiary of: Wiley-Blackwell Publishing Ltd.), 155 Cremorne St, Richmond, VIC 3121, Australia. TEL 61-3-92743100, FAX 61-3-92743101, subs@blackwellpublishingasia.com, http://www.wiley.com/WileyCDA/. Ed. Hitoshi Takahashi. adv.: B&W page AUD 1,200, color page AUD 2,500; trim 210 x 275. **Subscr. to:** PO Box 378, Carlton South, VIC 3053, Australia.

616.8 GBR ISSN 0305-1846
RC346 CODEN: NANEDL

➤ **NEUROPATHOLOGY AND APPLIED NEUROBIOLOGY.** Text in English. 1974. bi-m. GBP 1,455 in United Kingdom to institutions; EUR 1,847 in Europe to institutions; USD 2,689 in the Americas to institutions; USD 3,135 elsewhere to institutions; GBP 1,673 combined subscription in United Kingdom to institutions (print & online eds.); EUR 2,125 combined subscription in Europe to institutions (print & online eds.); USD 3,093 combined subscription in the Americas to institutions (print & online eds.); USD 3,606 combined subscription elsewhere to institutions (print & online eds.) (effective 2012). adv. bk.rev. bibl.; charts; illus. index. back issues avail.; reprint service avail. from PSC. **Document type:** *Journal, Academic/ Scholarly.* **Description:** Publishes papers on a range of neuropathological topics extending from experimental and molecular neuroscience to clinical papers dealing with the basic applied neurobiological aspects of human and veterinary disease.
Related titles: Microform ed.: (from PQC); Online - full text ed.: ISSN 1365-2990. 1999. GBP 1,455 in United Kingdom to institutions; EUR 1,847 in Europe to institutions; USD 2,689 in the Americas to institutions; USD 3,135 elsewhere to institutions (effective 2012) (from IngentaConnect); ◆ Supplement(s): Neuropathology and Applied Neurobiology. Supplement. ISSN 1359-1940.
Indexed: A01, A02, A03, A08, A22, A26, ASCA, B21, B25, BIOBASE, BIOSIS Prev, C11, CA, CIN, ChemAb, ChemTitl, CurCont, E-psyche, E01, EMBASE, ExcerpMed, H04, H12, IABS, ISR, IndMed, Inpharma, MEDLINE, MycolAb, NSA, NSCI, P30, R10, Reac, SAA, SCI, SCOPUS, T02, THA, W07.
—BLDSC (6081.514000), CASDDS, GNLM, IE, Infotrieve, Ingenta, INIST. **CCC.**
Published by: (British Neuropathological Society), Wiley-Blackwell Publishing Ltd. (Subsidiary of: John Wiley & Sons, Inc.), 9600 Garsington Rd, Oxford, OX4 2DQ, United Kingdom. TEL 44-1865-776868, FAX 44-1865-714591, customerservices@blackwellpublishing.com. Ed. Dr. Stephen S Wharton.

616.8 GBR ISSN 1359-1940

NEUROPATHOLOGY AND APPLIED NEUROBIOLOGY. SUPPLEMENT. Text in English. 1995. irreg. includes with subscr. to Neuropathology and Applied Neurobiology. reprints avail. **Document type:** *Journal, Academic/Scholarly.*
Related titles: ◆ Supplement to: Neuropathology and Applied Neurobiology. ISSN 0305-1846.
—Infotrieve, INIST.
Published by: Wiley-Blackwell Publishing Ltd. (Subsidiary of: John Wiley & Sons, Inc.), 9600 Garsington Rd, Oxford, OX4 2DQ, United Kingdom. TEL 44-1865-776868, FAX 44-1865-714591, customerservices@blackwellpublishing.com, http://www.wiley.com/.

NEUROPEDIATRICS; journal of pediatric neurobiology, neurology and neurosurgery. see MEDICAL SCIENCES—Pediatrics

NEUROPHARMACOLOGY. see PHARMACY AND PHARMACOLOGY

616.8 FRA ISSN 0987-7053
QP351 CODEN: NCLIE4

➤ **NEUROPHYSIOLOGIE CLINIQUE/CLINICAL NEUROPHYSIOLOGY.** Text in French, English. 1970. 6/yr. EUR 441 in Europe to institutions; EUR 429.97 in France to institutions; JPY 57,000 in Japan to institutions; USD 551 elsewhere to institutions (effective 2010). adv. bk.rev. illus. index. reprints avail. **Document type:** *Journal, Academic/Scholarly.* **Description:** Covers the field of neurophysiology, electroencephalography, electromyography, evoked potentials and other investigative approaches in neurology and psychiatry.
Formerly (until 1988): Revue d'Electroencephalographie et de Neurophysiologie Clinique (0370-4475)
Related titles: Microform ed.: (from PQC); Online - full text ed.: ISSN 1769-7131 (from IngentaConnect, ScienceDirect).
Indexed: A01, A03, A08, A22, A26, ASCA, B21, B25, BDM&CN, BIOSIS Prev, CA, CurCont, E-psyche, EMBASE, ExcerpMed, I05, IndMed, Inpharma, MEDLINE, MycolAb, NSA, NSCI, P30, R10, Reac, SCI, SCOPUS, T02, W07.
—BLDSC (6081.517800), GNLM, IE, Infotrieve, Ingenta, INIST. **CCC.**
Published by: (Societe de Neurophysiologie Clinique de Langue Francaise), Elsevier Masson (Subsidiary of: Elsevier Health Sciences), 62 Rue Camille Desmoulins, Issy les Moulineaux, Cedex 92442, France. TEL 33-1-71165500, FAX 33-1-71165600, infos@elsevier-masson.fr. Ed. Jean-Michel Guerit. Circ: 3,000.

➤ **DAS NEUROPHYSIOLOGIE - LABOR.** see MEDICAL SCIENCES—Cardiovascular Diseases

616.8 USA ISSN 0090-2977
QP361 CODEN: NPHYBI

➤ **NEUROPHYSIOLOGY.** Text in English. 1969. 5/yr. EUR 4,221, USD 4,367 combined subscription to institutions (print & online eds.) (effective 2012). adv. back issues avail.; reprint service avail. from PSC. **Document type:** *Journal, Academic/Scholarly.* **Description:** Covers studies on molecular, cellular, and systemic neurophysiology, functional neuromorphology, neuropharmacology, and neurochemistry.
Related titles: Online - full text ed.: ISSN 1573-9007 (from IngentaConnect); ◆ Translation of: Neirofiziologiya. ISSN 0028-2561.
Indexed: A01, A03, A08, A22, A26, Agr, B21, B25, BIOSIS Prev, BibLing, CA, E01, EMBASE, ExcerpMed, I05, IndMed, MycolAb, NSA, P15, P20, P24, P25, P30, P48, P52, P54, P56, PQC, PsycholAb, R10, Reac, SCI, SCOPUS, T02, W07.
—BLDSC (0416.260000), East View, GNLM, IE, Infotrieve, Ingenta, INIST. **CCC.**
Published by: Springer New York LLC (Subsidiary of: Springer Science+Business Media), 233 Spring St, New York, NY 10013. TEL 212-460-1500, FAX 212-460-1575, service-ny@springer.com, http://www.springer.com. Eds. D A Vasilenko, P G Kostyuk.

616.8 NLD ISSN 1387-5817

NEUROPRAXIS. Text in Dutch. 1997. bi-m. EUR 137, USD 206 combined subscription to institutions (print & online eds.) (effective 2009). adv. **Document type:** *Journal, Trade.*
Related titles: Online - full text ed.: ISSN 1876-5785.
Indexed: A22, E01.
Published by: Bohn Stafleu van Loghum B.V. (Subsidiary of: Springer Science+Business Media), Postbus 246, Houten, 3990 GA, Netherlands. TEL 31-30-6383872, FAX 31-30-6383991, boekhandels@bsl.nl, http://www.bsl.nl. Eds. Dr. B Kreukels, Dr. B van Dien. Circ: 1,340.

616.89 FRA ISSN 1633-5767

NEUROPSY NEWS. Text in French. 1995. m.
Formerly (until 2002): Neuro-psy (0296-3981)
Indexed: FR, SCOPUS.
—INIST. **CCC.**
Published by: Editions L' Interligne, 140 rue Jules Guesde, Levallois-Perret Cedex, 92593, France. TEL 33-1-41407500, http://www.neuropsy.fr/.

616.8 GBR ISSN 1178-2021

➤ **NEUROPSYCHIATRIC DISEASE AND TREATMENT (ONLINE).** Text in English. irreg. free (effective 2011). back issues avail. **Document type:** *Journal, Academic/Scholarly.* **Description:** Covers clinical therapeutics and pharmacology, including clinical or pre-clinical studies on a range of neuropsychiatric and neurological disorders.
Media: Online - full text.
Published by: (International Neuropsychiatric Association CAN), Dove Medical Press Ltd., Beechfield House, Winterton Way, Macclesfield, SK11 0JL, United Kingdom. TEL 44-1625-509130, FAX 44-1625-617933. Ed. Roger M Pinder.

616.8 DEU ISSN 0948-6259

➤ **NEUROPSYCHIATRIE.** Text in German. 1985. q. EUR 88; EUR 24 newsstand/cover (effective 2011). adv. abstr. back issues avail.; reprints avail. **Document type:** *Journal, Academic/Scholarly.*
Indexed: A20, ASCA, E-psyche, EMBASE, ExcerpMed, MEDLINE, NSCI, P30, R10, Reac, SCOPUS.
—BLDSC (6081.535700), IE, Ingenta. **CCC.**
Published by: Dustri-Verlag Dr. Karl Feistle, Bajuwarenring 4, Oberhaching, 82041, Germany. TEL 49-89-6138610, FAX 49-89-6135412, info@dustri.de, http://www.dustri.de. Ed., Adv. contact Ullrich Meise. Circ: 1,500.

➤ **NEUROPSYCHIATRIE DE L'ENFANCE ET DE L'ADOLESCENCE.** see MEDICAL SCIENCES—Pediatrics

616.89 GBR ISSN 1758-2008

▼ ➤ **NEUROPSYCHIATRY.** Text in English. forthcoming 2011. 3/yr. GBP 695 combined subscription domestic to institutions (print & online eds.); USD 1,220 combined subscription in North America to institutions (print & online eds.); JPY 129,000 combined subscription in Japan to institutions (print & online eds.); EUR 975 combined subscription elsewhere to institutions (print & online eds.) (effective 2011). adv. **Document type:** *Journal, Academic/Scholarly.* **Description:** Provides a key resource for all physicians and healthcare practitioners who are striving to provide the best possible care for their patients.
Related titles: Online - full text ed.: ISSN 1758-2016. forthcoming. GBP 615 domestic to institutions; USD 1,080 in North America to institutions; JPY 115,000 in Japan to institutions; EUR 865 elsewhere to institutions (effective 2011).
—**CCC.**

Published by: Future Medicine Ltd. (Subsidiary of: Future Science Ltd.), Unitec House, 2 Albert Pl, London, N3 1QB, United Kingdom. TEL 44-20-83716080, FAX 44-20-83716099, info@futuremedicine.com. Ed. Elisa Manzotti TEL 44-20-83716090. Pub. David Hughes. Adv. contact Simon Boisseau TEL 44-208-3716083.

616.8 USA ISSN 1534-7141
NEUROPSYCHIATRY REVIEWS; reporting the latest news in biological psychiatry. Text in English. 2000. m. adv. back issues avail.; reprints avail. **Document type:** *Journal, Trade.* **Description:** Covers new research and emerging trends in neuropsychiatry and neuroscience with an emphasis on practical approaches to diagnosis and treatment.
Related titles: Online - full text ed.
Indexed: A01, T02.
Published by: Quadrant HealthCom, 7 Century Dr, Ste 302, Parsippany, NJ 07054. TEL 973-206-3434, FAX 973-206-9378, sales@pulmonaryreviews.com, http://www.qhc.com. Eds. Colby K Stong TEL 973-206-2341, Glenn S Williams TEL 973-206-2343, Charles B Nemeroff. adv.: B&W page USD 5,840, color page USD 7,700; bleed 11.125 x 13.75. Circ: 40,000.

612.8 CHE ISSN 0302-282X
QP351 CODEN: NPBYAL
➤ **NEUROPSYCHOBIOLOGY**; international journal of experimental and clinical research in biological psychiatry, pharmacopsychiatry, biological psychology, pharmacopsychology and pharmacoelectroencephalography. Text in English. 8/yr. (in 2 vols.). CHF 2,848, EUR 2,276, USD 2,794 to institutions; CHF 3,126, EUR 2,498, USD 3,062 combined subscription to institutions (print & online eds.) (effective 2012). adv. bk.rev. abstr. index. back issues avail. **Document type:** *Journal, Academic/Scholarly.*
Incorporates: International Pharmacopsychiatry (0020-8272)
Related titles: Microform ed.: (from PQC); Online - full text ed.: ISSN 1423-0224. CHF 2,780, EUR 2,224, USD 2,700 to institutions (effective 2012).
Indexed: A01, A03, A08, A20, A22, A36, ASCA, B21, B25, BIOSIS Prev, CA, CABA, CIN, ChemAb, ChemTitl, CurCont, DBA, DentInd, E-psyche, E01, E12, EMBASE, ESPM, ExcerpMed, F08, FR, FoP, GH, IBR, IBZ, IPsyAb, ISR, IndMed, Inpharma, MEDLINE, MycolAb, N02, N03, NSA, NSCI, P03, P15, P20, P22, P25, P26, P30, P32, P35, P43, P48, P52, P54, P56, PQC, PsycInfo, PsycholAb, R10, R12, RA&MP, Reac, SCI, SCOPUS, T02, T05, TAR, ToxAb, W07.
—BLDSC (6081.545000), CASDDS, GNLM, IE, Infotrieve, Ingenta, INIST. **CCC.**
Published by: (International Pharmaco-EEG Group), S. Karger AG, Allschwilerstr 10, Basel, 4055, Switzerland. TEL 41-61-3061111, FAX 41-61-3061234, karger@karger.ch, http://www.karger.ch. Ed. W Strik. adv.: page USD 1,815; trim 210 x 280. Circ: 800.

616.8 GBR ISSN 0028-3932
RC321 CODEN: NUPSA6
➤ **NEUROPSYCHOLOGIA.** Text in English, French, German; Summaries in French, German. 1963. 14/yr. (plus special issue). EUR 3,438 in Europe to institutions; JPY 456,300 in Japan to institutions; USD 3,844 elsewhere to institutions (effective 2012). bk.rev. charts; illus. index. back issues avail.; reprints avail. **Document type:** *Journal, Academic/Scholarly.* **Description:** Promotes the study of human behavior from a neurological point of view, and integrates clinical, general, and experimental contributions to the field.
Related titles: Microfilm ed.: (from PQC); Online - full text ed.: ISSN 1873-3514 (from IngentaConnect, ScienceDirect).
Indexed: A01, A03, A08, A20, A22, A26, AMED, ASCA, AgeL, B21, B25, BAS, BDM&CN, BIOBASE, BIOSIS Prev, BibInd, CA, CurCont, DentInd, E-psyche, EMBASE, ExcerpMed, FR, I05, IABS, IBR, IBZ, ISR, IndMed, Inpharma, L&LBA, MEDLINE, MLA-IB, MycolAb, NSA, NSCI, P03, P30, PsycInfo, PsycholAb, R10, RILM, Reac, SCI, SCOPUS, SOPODA, SSCI, T02, W07, YAE&RB.
—BLDSC (6081.550000), GNLM, IE, Infotrieve, Ingenta, INIST. **CCC.**
Published by: Pergamon (Subsidiary of: Elsevier Science & Technology), The Blvd, Langford Ln, East Park, Kidlington, Oxford OX5 1GB, United Kingdom. TEL 44-1865-843000, FAX 44-1865-843010, JournalsCustomerServiceEMEA@elsevier.com. Ed. A R Mayes TEL 44-161-2752579. **Subscr. to:** Elsevier BV, Radarweg 29, PO Box 211, Amsterdam 1000 AE, Netherlands. TEL 31-20-4853757, FAX 31-20-4853432, http://www.elsevier.nl.

616.8 GBR ISSN 0960-2011
RC387.5 CODEN: NREHE3
➤ **NEUROPSYCHOLOGICAL REHABILITATION.** Text in English. 1991. bi-m. GBP 656 combined subscription in United Kingdom to institutions (print & online eds.); EUR 866, USD 1,086 combined subscription to institutions (print & online eds.) (effective 2012). adv. cum.index. back issues avail.; reprint service avail. from PSC. **Document type:** *Journal, Academic/Scholarly.* **Description:** Provides an international forum for well-designed and properly evaluated intervention strategies, surveys, and observational procedures that are clinically relevant and may also back up theoretical arguments or models.
Related titles: Online - full text ed.: ISSN 1464-0694. GBP 591 in United Kingdom to institutions; EUR 780, USD 978 to institutions (effective 2012) (from IngentaConnect).
Indexed: A01, A03, A08, A22, AMED, ASCA, ASSIA, B21, C06, C07, CA, E-psyche, E01, EMBASE, ExcerpMed, FR, L&LBA, MEDLINE, MLA-IB, NSA, NSCI, P03, P20, P22, P30, P43, P48, P54, PQC, PsycInfo, PsycholAb, R09, R10, Reac, SCI, SCOPUS, SD, SOPODA, T02, W07.
—GNLM, IE, Infotrieve, Ingenta, INIST. **CCC.**
Published by: Psychology Press (Subsidiary of: Taylor & Francis Ltd.), 27 Church Rd, Hove, E Sussex BN3 2FA, United Kingdom. TEL 44-20-70176000, FAX 44-20-70176717, http://www.psypress.com. Ed. Barbara A Wilson. Adv. contact Linda Hann TEL 44-1344-779945. **Subscr. addr. in N America:** Taylor & Francis Inc., Customer Services Dept, 325 Chestnut St, 8th Fl, Philadelphia, PA 19106. TEL 800-354-1420, FAX 215-625-2940; **Subscr. addr. outside N America:** Taylor & Francis Ltd., Journals Customer Service, Sheepen Pl, Colchester, Essex CO3 3LP, United Kingdom. TEL 44-20-70175544, FAX 44-20-70175198, subscriptions@tandf.co.uk, http://www.tandf.co.uk/journals.

616.8 ITA ISSN 1970-321X
NEUROPSYCHOLOGICAL TRENDS. Text in English. 2007. s-a. **Document type:** *Journal, Academic/Scholarly.* **Description:** Aims to encourage debate on current topics about neuropsychology and neuroscience, be a home for research in the field and introduce discussion on methodology.
Related titles: Online - full text ed.: ISSN 1970-3201. free (effective 2011).
Indexed: P03, PsycInfo.
Published by: Edizioni Universitarie di Lettere Economia Diritto (L E D), Via Cervignano 4, Milan, Italy. TEL 39-02-59902055, FAX 39-02-55193636, led@lededizioni.com, http://www.lededizioni.com. Eds. Alberto Granato, Michela Balconi, Salvatore Campanella.

616.8 150 USA ISSN 0894-4105
QP360 CODEN: NEUPEG
➤ **NEUROPSYCHOLOGY.** Text in English. 1987. bi-m. USD 167 domestic to individuals; USD 199 foreign to individuals; USD 415 domestic to institutions; USD 472 foreign to institutions (effective 2011). adv. illus. back issues avail.; reprint service avail. from PSC. **Document type:** *Journal, Academic/Scholarly.* **Description:** Features interdisciplinary contributions on assessment, treatment, and rehabilitation in clinical neuropsychology, focusing on neuropsychological measurement techniques and psychosocial adjustment of the impaired patient.
Related titles: Online - full text ed.: ISSN 1931-1559 (from ScienceDirect).
Indexed: A20, A22, AMED, ASCA, AgeL, B21, C06, C07, CurCont, E-psyche, EMBASE, ExcerpMed, FR, IndMed, L&LBA, MEDLINE, MLA-IB, NSA, NSCI, P03, P30, PsycInfo, PsycholAb, R10, RASB, Reac, SCI, SCOPUS, SOPODA, SSCI, W07.
—BLDSC (6081.553000), GNLM, IE, Infotrieve, Ingenta, INIST. **CCC.**
Published by: (Philadelphia Clinical Neuropsychology Group), American Psychological Association, 750 First St, NE, Washington, DC 20002. TEL 202-336-5500, 800-374-2721, FAX 202-336-5997, journals@apa.org. Ed. Stephen M Rao. Adv. contact Doug Constant TEL 202-336-5574. Circ: 3,100.

153.4 616.8 NLD ISSN 0927-0116
➤ **NEUROPSYCHOLOGY AND COGNITION.** Text in English. 1989. irreg., latest vol.25, 2004. price varies. back issues avail. **Document type:** *Monographic series, Academic/Scholarly.*
Indexed: E-psyche.
—BLDSC (6081.553300), IE, Ingenta.
Published by: Springer Netherlands (Subsidiary of: Springer Science+Business Media), Van Godewijckstraat 30, Dordrecht, 3311 GX, Netherlands. TEL 31-78-6576050, FAX 31-78-6576474. Ed. R Malatesha Joshi.

➤ **NEUROPSYCHOLOGY, DEVELOPMENT AND COGNITION. SECTION A: JOURNAL OF CLINICAL AND EXPERIMENTAL NEUROPSYCHOLOGY.** *see* PSYCHOLOGY

➤ **NEUROPSYCHOLOGY, DEVELOPMENT AND COGNITION. SECTION B: AGING, NEUROPSYCHOLOGY AND COGNITION**; a journal on normal and dysfunctional development. *see* PSYCHOLOGY

➤ **NEUROPSYCHOLOGY, DEVELOPMENT, AND COGNITION. SECTION C: CHILD NEUROPSYCHOLOGY**; a journal on normal and abnormal development in childhood and adolescence. *see* PSYCHOLOGY

➤ **NEUROPSYCHOLOGY, DEVELOPMENT AND COGNITION. SECTION D: THE CLINICAL NEUROPSYCHOLOGIST.** *see* PSYCHOLOGY

616.8 USA ISSN 1040-7308
QP360 CODEN: NERVEJ
➤ **NEUROPSYCHOLOGY REVIEW.** Text in English. 1989. q. EUR 1,001, USD 1,070 combined subscription to institutions (print & online eds.) (effective 2012). adv. back issues avail.; reprint service avail. from PSC. **Document type:** *Journal, Academic/Scholarly.* **Description:** Covers papers in all aspects of neuroscience contributing to a mechanistic understanding of human neuropsychology in normal and clinical populations.
Related titles: Microfilm ed.: (from PQC); Online - full text ed.: ISSN 1573-6660 (from IngentaConnect).
Indexed: A01, A03, A08, A20, A22, A26, ASCA, B21, BIOSIS Prev, BibInd, BibLing, CA, E-psyche, E01, EMBASE, ExcerpMed, H12, I05, IndMed, MEDLINE, MycolAb, NSA, NSCI, P03, P10, P12, P20, P22, P25, P30, P48, P53, P54, PQC, PsycInfo, PsycholAb, R10, Reac, SCI, SCOPUS, SSCI, SWR&A, T02, W07.
—BLDSC (6081.553600), GNLM, IE, Infotrieve, Ingenta. **CCC.**
Published by: Springer New York LLC (Subsidiary of: Springer Science+Business Media), 233 Spring St, New York, NY 10013. TEL 212-460-1500, FAX 212-460-1575, service-ny@springer.com, http://www.springer.com/. Ed. Edith V Sullivan.

616.8 GBR ISSN 0893-133X
RM315 CODEN: NEROEW
➤ **NEUROPSYCHOPHARMACOLOGY.** Abbreviated title: N P P. Text in English. 1987. m. EUR 2,453 in Europe to institutions; USD 2,846 in the Americas to institutions; JPY 419,300 in Japan to institutions; GBP 1,583 to institutions in the UK & elsewhere (effective 2011). adv. back issues avail.; reprints avail. **Document type:** *Journal, Academic/Scholarly.* **Description:** Focuses upon clinical and basic science contributions that advance our understanding of the brain and behaviour.
Related titles: Online - full text ed.: ISSN 1740-634X (from IngentaConnect).
Indexed: A01, A03, A08, A20, A22, ASCA, B21, B25, BIOBASE, BIOSIS Prev, CA, CIN, ChemAb, ChemTitl, CurCont, DBA, E-psyche, E01, EMBASE, ESPM, ExcerpMed, FoP, IABS, ISR, IndMed, Inpharma, JW-P, MEDLINE, MycolAb, NSA, NSCI, P03, P20, P22, P25, P30, P35, P48, P54, PQC, PsycInfo, PsycholAb, S01, SCI, SCOPUS, T02, W07.
—BLDSC (6081.555500), CASDDS, GNLM, IE, Infotrieve, Ingenta, INIST. **CCC.**
Published by: (American College of Neuropsychopharmacology USA), Nature Publishing Group (Subsidiary of: Macmillan Publishers Ltd.), The MacMillan Bldg, 4 Crinan St, London, N1 9XW, United Kingdom. TEL 44-20-78334000, FAX 44-20-78334640. Ed. Dr. James H Meador-Woodruff. Adv. contact Ben Harkinson TEL 617-475-9222. **Subscr. to:** Brunel Rd, Houndmills, Basingstoke, Hamps RG21 6XS, United Kingdom. TEL 44-1256-329242, FAX 44-1256-812358, subscriptions@nature.com.

➤ **NEUROQUANTOLOGY**; an interdisciplinary journal of neuroscience and quantum physics. *see* PHYSICS

➤ **THE NEURORADIOLOGY JOURNAL.** *see* MEDICAL SCIENCES—Radiology And Nuclear Medicine

616.8 DEU ISSN 1611-6496
▼ **NEUROREHA.** Text in German. 2009 (Nov.). 4/yr. EUR 99 to institutions; EUR 275 combined subscription to institutions (print & online eds.) (effective 2011). **Document type:** *Journal, Academic/Scholarly.*
Related titles: Online - full text ed.: ISSN 1611-7654, 2009 (Nov.). EUR 265 to institutions (effective 2011).
Published by: Georg Thieme Verlag, Ruedigerstr 14, Stuttgart, 70469, Germany. TEL 49-711-8931421, FAX 49-711-8931410, leser.service@thieme.de.

616.8 NLD ISSN 1053-8135
RC350.4 CODEN: NRORFG
➤ **NEUROREHABILITATION**; an interdisciplinary journal. Text in English. 1991. 8/yr. USD 1,132 combined subscription in North America (print & online eds.); EUR 810 combined subscription elsewhere (print & online eds.) (effective 2012). bk.rev. back issues avail. **Document type:** *Journal, Academic/Scholarly.* **Description:** Provides multidisciplinary rehabilitation teams with current clinical information for treating patients who are mentally or physically handicapped because of acquired or congenital neurologic disability.
Related titles: Microform ed.: (from PQC); Online - full text ed.: ISSN 1878-6448 (from IngentaConnect).
Indexed: A01, A03, A08, A22, AMED, ASCA, B21, C06, C07, C08, CA, CINAHL, CurCont, E-psyche, E01, EMBASE, ExcerpMed, FamI, MEDLINE, NSA, P03, P30, PsycInfo, PsycholAb, R09, R10, Reac, SCOPUS, SSCI, T02, W07.
—BLDSC (6081.558400), GNLM, IE, Infotrieve, Ingenta. **CCC.**
Published by: I O S Press, Nieuwe Hemweg 6B, Amsterdam, 1013 BG, Netherlands. TEL 31-20-6883355, FAX 31-20-6870019, info@iospress.nl. Eds. Jeffrey S Kreutzer TEL 804-828-9055, Nathan D Zasler TEL 804-346-1803. **Subscr. to:** I O S Press, Inc, 4502 Rachael Manor Dr, Fairfax, VA 22032-3631. sales@iospress.com; Globe Publication Pvt. Ltd., C-62 Inderpuri, New Delhi 100 012, India. TEL 91-11-579-3211, 91-11-579-3212, FAX 91-11-579-8876, custserve@globepub.com, http://www.globepub.com; Kinokuniya Co Ltd., Shinjuku 3-chome, Shinjuku-ku, Tokyo 160-0022, Japan. FAX 81-3-3439-1094, journal@kinokuniya.co.jp, http://www.kinokuniya.co.jp.

616.8 USA ISSN 1545-9683
CODEN: JNRHFV
➤ **NEUROREHABILITATION AND NEURAL REPAIR.** Text in English. 1987. 9/yr. USD 1,393, GBP 819 combined subscription to institutions (print & online eds.); USD 1,365, GBP 803 to institutions (effective 2011). adv. bk.rev. back issues avail.; reprint service avail. from PSC. **Document type:** *Journal, Academic/Scholarly.* **Description:** Deals with neurologic rehabilitation, neural repair and restoration of functions.
Formerly (until 1998): Journal of Neurologic Rehabilitation (0888-4390)
Related titles: Online - full text ed.: ISSN 1552-6844. USD 1,254, GBP 737 to institutions (effective 2011).
Indexed: A22, A26, AMED, ASCA, B21, BIOBASE, C06, C07, C08, CA, CINAHL, E-psyche, E01, E08, EMBASE, ExcerpMed, G08, H11, H12, I05, IABS, MEDLINE, NSA, NSCI, P03, P30, PEI, PsycInfo, PsycholAb, R10, Reac, S09, SCI, SCOPUS, T02, W07.
—BLDSC (6081.558450), GNLM, IE, Ingenta. **CCC.**
Published by: (American Society of Neurorehabilitation), Sage Publications, Inc., 2455 Teller Rd, Thousand Oaks, CA 91320. TEL 805-499-9774, FAX 805-499-0871, info@sagepub.com. Ed. Bruce H Dobkin. adv.: B&W page USD 510, color page USD 860; trim 8.5 x 11. Circ: 1,232 (paid). **Subscr. overseas to:** Sage Publications Ltd., 1 Oliver's Yard, 55 City Rd, London EC1Y 1SP, United Kingdom. TEL 44-207-3248701; FAX 44-207-3248733, subscription@sagepub.co.uk.

616.8 USA ISSN 0959-4965
RC321 CODEN: NERPEZ
➤ **NEUROREPORT**; for rapid communication of neuroscience research. Text in English. 1990. 18/yr. USD 4,599 domestic to institutions; USD 4,815 foreign to institutions (effective 2011). adv. back issues avail.; reprints avail. **Document type:** *Magazine, Academic/Scholarly.* **Description:** Encompasses all the major fields of neuroscience while still reflecting the specialization in each given field.
Related titles: CD-ROM ed.; Online - full text ed.: ISSN 1473-558X. USD 3,463.20 domestic academic site license; USD 3,463.20 foreign academic site license; USD 3,862.80 domestic corporate site license; USD 3,862.80 foreign corporate site license (effective 2002).
Indexed: A20, A22, A29, A35, A36, ASCA, AgBio, AgrForAb, AnBeAb, B&BAb, B19, B20, B21, B25, BIOBASE, BIOSIS Prev, CABA, CIN, CTA, ChemAb, ChemTitl, ChemoAb, CurCont, E-psyche, E01, E12, EMBASE, ESPM, ExcerpMed, F08, F12, GH, H16, IABS, ISR, IndMed, Inpharma, MEDLINE, MaizeAb, MycolAb, N02, N03, NSA, NSCI, P03, P30, P33, P35, PsycInfo, PsycholAb, R07, R08, R10, RA&MP, RASB, RM&VM, Reac, SCI, SCOPUS, SoyAb, T05, ToxAb, VS, VirolAbstr, W07.
—BLDSC (6081.558500), CASDDS, GNLM, IE, Infotrieve, Ingenta, INIST. **CCC.**
Published by: Lippincott Williams & Wilkins (Subsidiary of: Wolters Kluwer N.V.), 530 Walnut St, Philadelphia, PA 19106. TEL 215-521-8300, FAX 215-521-8902, customerservice@lww.com, http://www.lww.com. Ed. Giorgio Gabella. Pub. Phil Daly.

616.8 GBR ISSN 0306-4522
QP351 CODEN: NRSCDN
➤ **NEUROSCIENCE.** Text in English. 1976. 28/yr. EUR 9,612 in Europe to institutions; JPY 1,277,300 in Japan to institutions; USD 10,754 elsewhere to institutions (effective 2012). adv. bk.rev. illus.; stat. index. back issues avail. **Document type:** *Journal, Academic/Scholarly.* **Description:** Presents original research on any aspect of the scientific study of the nervous system.
Related titles: Microfilm ed.: (from PQC); Online - full text ed.: ISSN 1873-7544 (from IngentaConnect, ScienceDirect); ◆ Supplement(s): I B R O News. ISSN 0361-0713.

Indexed: A01, A03, A08, A22, A26, A34, A35, A36, A38, ASCA, AgBio, AnBeAb, ApicAb, B21, B25, BIOBASE, BIOSIS Prev, BP, C30, C33, CA, CABA, CIN, CMCI, CRFR, CTA, ChemAb, ChemTitl, ChemoAb, CurCont, D01, DBA, DentInd, E-psyche, E12, EMBASE, ESPM, ExcerpMed, F08, F11, F12, GH, H16, H17, I05, IABS, ISR, IndMed, IndVet, Inpharma, MEDLINE, MycolAb, N02, N03, N04, NSA, NSCI, P30, P33, P37, P39, PGrRegA, PN&I, R07, R08, R10, R13, RA&MP, RM&VM, Reac, RefZh, S12, S13, SCI, SCOPUS, SoyAb, T02, T05, THA, Telegen, ToxAb, VS, W07, W10, WildRev.
—BLDSC (6081.559000), CASDDS, GNLM, IE, Infotrieve, Ingenta, INIST. **CCC.**
Published by: (International Brain Research Organization FRA), Pergamon (Subsidiary of: Elsevier Science & Technology), The Blvd, Langford Ln, East Park, Kidlington, Oxford OX5 1GB, United Kingdom. TEL 44-1865-843000, FAX 44-1865-843010, JournalsCustomerServiceEMEA@elsevier.com. Ed. Dr. O P Ottersen. **Subscr. to:** Elsevier BV, Radarweg 29, PO Box 211, Amsterdam 1000 AE, Netherlands. TEL 31-20-4853757, FAX 31-20-4853432.

616.8 USA ISSN 0097-0549
RC331 CODEN: NBHPBT
➤ **NEUROSCIENCE AND BEHAVIORAL PHYSIOLOGY.** Text in English. 1967. 9/yr. EUR 2,655, USD 2,752 combined subscription to institutions (print & online eds.) (effective 2012). adv. back issues avail.; reprint service avail. from PSC. **Document type:** *Journal, Academic/Scholarly.* **Description:** Contains translations of papers selected from top Russian journals describing significant results of studies on the nervous system.
Formerly (until 1972): Neuroscience Translations (0028-3959)
Related titles: Microform ed.: (from PMC, PQC); Online - full text ed.: ISSN 1573-899X (from IngentaConnect).
Indexed: A22, A26, AnBeAb, B21, BibLing, CA, ChemAb, ChemoAb, E-psyche, E01, E08, EMBASE, ESPM, ExcerpMed, G08, H11, I05, IndMed, MEDLINE, NSA, P03, P20, P22, P25, P30, P48, P54, PEI, PQC, PsycInfo, PsycholAb, R10, Reac, S09, SCOPUS, T02, THA, ToxAb.
—BLDSC (6081.560000), East View, GNLM, IE, Infotrieve, Ingenta, INIST, Linda Hall. **CCC.**
Published by: Springer New York LLC (Subsidiary of: Springer Science+Business Media), 233 Spring St, New York, NY 10013. TEL 212-460-1500, FAX 212-460-1575, service-ny@springer.com, http://www.springer.com. Ed. Charles D Woody.

616.8 GBR ISSN 0149-7634
QP360 CODEN: NBREDE
➤ **NEUROSCIENCE & BIOBEHAVIORAL REVIEWS.** Text in English. 1977. 8/yr. EUR 2,325 in Europe to institutions; JPY 308,700 in Japan to institutions; USD 2,599 elsewhere to institutions (effective 2012). bk.rev. index. back issues avail.; reprints avail. **Document type:** *Journal, Academic/Scholarly.* **Description:** Covers anatomy, biochemistry, embryology, endocrinology, genetics, pharmacology, physiology and all aspects of biological sciences related to the problems of the nervous system.
Formerly (until 1978): Biobehavioral Reviews (0147-7552)
Related titles: Microfilm ed.: (from PQC); Online - full text ed.: ISSN 1873-7528 (from IngentaConnect, ScienceDirect).
Indexed: A01, A03, A08, A20, A22, A26, A34, A35, A36, A38, ASCA, ASFA, AgBio, AnBeAb, B21, BIOBASE, BIOSIS Prev, BibInd, CA, CABA, CIN, ChemAb, ChemTitl, ChemoAb, CurCont, DentInd, E-psyche, E12, EMBASE, ESPM, ExcerpMed, FR, GH, H17, I05, IABS, IBR, IBZ, ISR, IndMed, IndVet, Inpharma, MEDLINE, MycolAb, N02, N03, N04, NSA, NSCI, P03, P30, P33, PsycInfo, PsycholAb, R10, Reac, S12, SCI, SCOPUS, T02, THA, ToxAb, VS, W07.
—BLDSC (6081.561000), CASDDS, GNLM, IE, Infotrieve, Ingenta, INIST. **CCC.**
Published by: (International Behavioral Neuroscience Society USA), Pergamon (Subsidiary of: Elsevier Science & Technology), The Blvd, Langford Ln, East Park, Kidlington, Oxford OX5 1GB, United Kingdom. TEL 44-1865-843000, FAX 44-1865-843010, JournalsCustomerServiceEMEA@elsevier.com. Eds. Linda J Porrino, Dr. Verity J. Brown. **Subscr. to:** Elsevier BV, Radarweg 29, PO Box 211, Amsterdam 1000 AE, Netherlands. TEL 31-20-4853757, FAX 31-20-4853432, http://www.elsevier.nl.

616.8 USA ISSN 2158-2912
▼ ➤ **NEUROSCIENCE & MEDICINE.** Text in English. 2010. q. **Document type:** *Journal, Academic/Scholarly.* **Description:** Aims to keep a record of the state-of-the-art research and to promote study, research and improvement within its various specialties.
Related titles: Online - full text ed.: ISSN 2158-2947. free (effective 2011).
Published by: Scientific Research Publishing, Inc., PO Box 54821, Irvine, CA 92619. TEL 408-329-4591, service@scirp.org. Ed. Thomas Muller.

616.8 GBR ISSN 2230-3561
▼ ➤ **NEUROSCIENCE AND NEUROECONOMICS.** Text in English. forthcoming 2011. irreg. free (effective 2011). **Document type:** *Journal, Academic/Scholarly.* **Description:** Focuses on the identification of brain structures and measurement of neural activity related to behavior, behavioral predictions, and decision making in health and disease.
Media: Online - full text.
—CCC.
Published by: Dove Medical Press Ltd., Beechfield House, Winterton Way, Macclesfield, SK11 0JL, United Kingdom. TEL 44-1625-509130, FAX 44-1625-617933. Ed. Dr. Annabel Chen.

616.8 CHN ISSN 1673-7067
➤ **NEUROSCIENCE BULLETIN/SHENJING KEXUE TONGBAO (YINWEN BAN).** Text in English. 1985. bi-m. EUR 613, USD 820 combined subscription to institutions (print & online eds.) (effective 2012). adv. back issues avail. **Document type:** *Journal, Academic/Scholarly.*
Former titles (until 2004): Zhongguo Shenjing Kexue Zazhi/Chinese Journal of Neuroscience (1008-0872); (until 1997): Chinese Journal of Physiological Science (0258-6428)
Related titles: Online - full text ed.: ISSN 1995-8218.
Indexed: A22, A26, E-psyche, E01, E08, EMBASE, ExcerpMed, H12, MEDLINE, P30, R10, Reac, S09, SCOPUS.
—BLDSC (6081.561100), East View, IE, Ingenta. **CCC.**
Published by: Zhongguo Kexueyuan Shanghai Shengming Kexue Yanjiuyuan, 319, Yueyang Rd., Rm.405, Bldg.31B, Shanghai, 200031, China. TEL 86-21-54922863, FAX 86-21-54922833. Ed. Dr. Changlin Lu. Pub., Adv. contact Bin Wei. **Dist. by:** Springer, Haber Str 7, Heidelberg 69126, Germany. subscriptions@springer.com, http://www.springer.de; Springer New York LLC, Journal Fulfillment, PO Box 2485, Secaucus, NJ 07096. TEL 212-460-1500, FAX 201-348-4505, journals-ny@springer.com. **Co-publisher:** Springer.

616.8 616.027 USA ISSN 1556-4010
RC386.6.D52
➤ **NEUROSCIENCE IMAGING.** Text in English. 2005. q. USD 295 to institutions; USD 442 combined subscription to institutions (print & online eds.) (effective 2012). **Document type:** *Journal, Academic/Scholarly.* **Description:** Focuses on advances in imaging and mapping strategies to study the brain's structure, function and the relationship between both, from the whole brain to the molecular and cellular tissue level in order to improve the understanding of normal and disease processes.
Related titles: Online - full text ed.: USD 295 to institutions (effective 2012).
Indexed: EMBASE, ExcerpMed, P03, PsycInfo, SCOPUS.
Published by: Nova Science Publishers, Inc., 400 Oser Ave, Ste 1600, Hauppauge, NY 11788. TEL 631-231-7269, FAX 631-231-8175, main@novapublishers.com. Ed. B Schaller.

616.8 IRL ISSN 0304-3940
QP351 CODEN: NELED5
➤ **NEUROSCIENCE LETTERS.** Text in English. 1975. 57/yr. EUR 8,236 in Europe to institutions; JPY 1,094,100 in Japan to institutions; USD 9,211 elsewhere to institutions (effective 2012). bibl.; charts; illus.; abstr. reprints avail. **Document type:** *Report, Academic/Scholarly.* **Description:** Publishes short reports in all areas in the fields of neuroanatomy, neurochemistry, neuroendocrinology, neuropharmacology, and neurobiology.
Related titles: Microform ed.: (from PQC); Online - full text ed.: ISSN 1872-7972 (from IngentaConnect, ScienceDirect); ◆ Supplement(s): Neuroscience Letters. Supplement. ISSN 0167-6253.
Indexed: A01, A03, A08, A20, A22, A26, A34, A35, A36, A38, ASCA, AgBio, AgrForAb, ApicAb, B21, B25, BIOBASE, BIOSIS Prev, BP, C25, C30, C33, CA, CABA, CIN, CTA, ChemAb, ChemTitl, ChemoAb, CurCont, D01, DentInd, E-psyche, E12, EMBASE, ESPM, ExcerpMed, F08, F11, F12, GH, H16, I05, IABS, IBR, IBZ, ISR, IndMed, IndVet, Inpharma, LT, MEDLINE, MycolAb, N02, N03, N04, N05, NSA, NSCI, P30, P32, P33, P35, P37, P39, P40, PN&I, R07, R08, R10, R11, R12, RA&MP, RILM, RM&VM, RRTA, Reac, RefZh, S12, S13, SCI, SCOPUS, SoyAb, T02, T05, THA, ToxAb, VS, VirolAbstr, W07, W10.
—BLDSC (6081.562000), CASDDS, GNLM, IE, Infotrieve, Ingenta, INIST. **CCC.**
Published by: Elsevier Ireland Ltd (Subsidiary of: Elsevier Science & Technology), Elsevier House, Brookvale Plaza, E. Park, Shannon, Co. Clare, Ireland. TEL 353-61-709600, FAX 353-61-709100. Ed. S G Waxman. R&P Annette Moloney. **Subscr. to:** Elsevier BV, Radarweg 29, PO Box 211, Amsterdam 1000 AE, Netherlands. TEL 31-20-4853757, FAX 31-20-4853432, JournalsCustomerServiceEMEA@elsevier.com, http://www.elsevier.nl.

616.8 IRL ISSN 0167-6253
RC321 CODEN: NLSUE2
NEUROSCIENCE LETTERS. SUPPLEMENT. Text in English. 1978. irreg., latest vol.55, 2000.
Related titles: Online - full text ed.: ISSN 1872-8316; ◆ Supplement to: Neuroscience Letters. ISSN 0304-3940.
Indexed: A22, EMBASE, ExcerpMed, MEDLINE, P30, SCOPUS.
—BLDSC (6081.563000), INIST. **CCC.**
Published by: Elsevier Ireland Ltd (Subsidiary of: Elsevier Science & Technology), Elsevier House, Brookvale Plaza, E. Park, Shannon, Co. Clare, Ireland.

616.8 USA ISSN 1086-9956
RC321 CODEN: NENEFH
➤ **NEUROSCIENCE-NET.** Text in English. 1996. irreg. back issues avail. **Document type:** *Journal, Academic/Scholarly.* **Description:** Devoted to publishing research in basic and clinical neuroscience.
Media: Online - full text.
Published by: Scientific Design and Information, Inc., 165 Cervantes Rd, Redwood City, CA 94062. TEL 650-366-1644, FAX 650-367-9630. Ed. John E Johnson Jr.

616.8 USA
NEUROSCIENCE QUARTERLY. Text in English. 1970. q. free to members (effective 2010). back issues avail. **Document type:** *Newsletter, Trade.* **Description:** Provides coverage of SfN news, efforts, events, and other issues important to the neuroscience community.
Formerly: Neuroscience Newsletter (0278-3738)
Related titles: Online - full text ed.: free (effective 2010).
Indexed: E-psyche.
—CCC.
Published by: Society for Neuroscience, 1121 14th St, NW, Ste 1010, Washington, DC 20005. TEL 202-962-4000, FAX 202-962-4941, info@sfn.org.

616.8 IRL ISSN 0168-0102
RC337 CODEN: NERADN
➤ **NEUROSCIENCE RESEARCH.** Text and summaries in English. 1984. 12/yr. EUR 1,644 in Europe to institutions; JPY 218,200 in Japan to institutions; USD 1,838 elsewhere to institutions (effective 2012). index. **Document type:** *Journal, Academic/Scholarly.* **Description:** Covers all fields of neuroscience, from the molecular to behavioral levels.
Related titles: Microform ed.: (from PQC); Online - full text ed.: ISSN 1872-8111 (from IngentaConnect, ScienceDirect); Supplement(s): ISSN 0921-8696.
Indexed: A01, A03, A08, A20, A22, A26, ASCA, ASFA, ApicAb, B21, B25, BIOBASE, BIOSIS Prev, CA, CIN, ChemAb, ChemTitl, CurCont, DBA, E-psyche, EMBASE, ExcerpMed, I05, IABS, IPsyAb, ISR, IndMed, Inpharma, MEDLINE, MycolAb, NSA, NSCI, P03, P30, PsycInfo, PsycholAb, R10, RILM, Reac, SCI, SCOPUS, T02, W07.
—BLDSC (6081.563600), CASDDS, GNLM, IE, Infotrieve, Ingenta, INIST. **CCC.**
Published by: (Japan Neuroscience Society JPN), Elsevier Ireland Ltd (Subsidiary of: Elsevier Science & Technology), Elsevier House, Brookvale Plaza, E. Park, Shannon, Co. Clare, Ireland. TEL 353-61-709600, FAX 353-61-709100. Ed. Dr. T Tsumoto TEL 81-6-6879-3664. R&P Annette Moloney. **Subscr. to:** Elsevier BV, Radarweg 29, PO Box 211, Amsterdam 1000 AE, Netherlands. TEL 31-20-4853757, FAX 31-20-4853432, JournalsCustomerServiceEMEA@elsevier.com, http://www.elsevier.nl.

616.8 IND ISSN 0976-8866
▼ ➤ **NEUROSCIENCE RESEARCH LETTERS.** Text in English. 2010. s-a. USD 425 (effective 2011). **Document type:** *Journal, Academic/Scholarly.* **Description:** Publishes all the latest research articles, reviews and letters in all areas of neuroscience research.
Related titles: Online - full text ed.: ISSN 0976-8874. free (effective 2011).
Published by: Bioinfo Publications, 49/F-72, Vighnahar Complex, Front of Overseas Bank, Sector 12, Kharghar, Navi Mumbai, 410 210, India. TEL 91-22-27743967, FAX 91-22-66736413, editor@bioinfo.in, subscription@bioinfo.in. Ed. Dr. Virendra S Gomase.

616.89 SAU ISSN 1319-6138
NEUROSCIENCES. Text in English. 1996. q. **Document type:** *Journal, Academic/Scholarly.*
Indexed: BIOBASE, EMBASE, ExcerpMed, IABS, MEDLINE, NSCI, P30, R10, Reac, SCI, SCOPUS, W07.
—BLDSC (6081.564600).
Published by: Armed Forces Hospital, PO Box 7897, Riyadh, 11159, Saudi Arabia. TEL 00966-1-4777714, FAX 00966-1-4761810, info@smj.org.sa. Eds. Basim A Yaqub, Saleh M Al-Deeb. Adv. contact Ghada Al-Ahmed.

616.8 IND ISSN 0971-8230
NEUROSCIENCES TODAY. Text in English. 1997. q. **Document type:** *Journal, Academic/Scholarly.*
Published by: C M P Medica (Subsidiary of: C M P Medica Ltd.), Sagar Tech Plz A 615-617, 6th Fl, Andheri Kurla Rd, Saki Naka Jct, Andheri E, Mumbai, 400 072, India. TEL 91-22-66122600, FAX 91-22-66122626, info.india@ubm.com, http://www.ubmindia.in/cmp-medica.asp.

616.8 USA ISSN 1073-8584
RC321 CODEN: NROSFJ
➤ **THE NEUROSCIENTIST;** reviews at the interface of basic and clinical neurosciences. Text in English. 1995. bi-m. USD 1,223, GBP 720 combined subscription to institutions (print & online eds.); USD 1,199, GBP 706 to institutions (effective 2011). adv. 88 p./no. 2 cols./p.; back issues avail.; reprint service avail. from PSC. **Document type:** *Journal, Academic/Scholarly.* **Description:** Reviews laboratory and clinical research in the related fields of neurology, neurobiology, and psychiatry.
Related titles: Online - full text ed.: ISSN 1089-4098. 1995. USD 1,101, GBP 648 to institutions (effective 2011).
Indexed: A01, A03, A08, A22, A26, B07, B21, BIOBASE, BIOSIS Prev, CA, CIN, CTA, ChemAb, ChemTitl, CurCont, E-psyche, E01, E08, EMBASE, ExcerpMed, G08, H04, I05, IABS, MEDLINE, MycolAb, NSA, NSCI, P03, P30, PsycInfo, R10, Reac, S09, SCI, SCOPUS, T02, V02, W07.
—BLDSC (6081.578500), CASDDS, GNLM, IE, Infotrieve, Ingenta. **CCC.**
Published by: Sage Publications, Inc., 2455 Teller Rd, Thousand Oaks, CA 91320. TEL 805-499-9774, 800-818-7243, FAX 805-499-0871, 800-583-2665, info@sagepub.com. Ed. Stephen G Waxman. adv.: B&W page USD 645, color page USD 1,025; bleed 8.5 x 11.125. Circ: 845 (paid). **Subscr. outside the Americas to:** Sage Publications Ltd., 1 Oliver's Yard, 55 City Rd, London EC1Y 1SP, United Kingdom. TEL 44-20-73248701, FAX 44-20-73248733, subscription@sagepub.co.uk.

➤ **NEUROSONOLOGY/SHINKEI CHOONPA IGAKU.** *see* MEDICAL SCIENCES—Radiology And Nuclear Medicine

616.8 USA ISSN 0148-396X
RD593
➤ **NEUROSURGERY (BALTIMORE).** Text in English. 1977. m. USD 934 domestic to institutions; USD 1,272 foreign to institutions (effective 2011). adv. bk.rev. abstr.; bibl.; charts; illus. Index. back issues avail. **Document type:** *Journal, Academic/Scholarly.* **Description:** Explains techniques and devices, plus pertinent research in neuroscience.
Related titles: CD-ROM ed.: ISSN 1081-1281; Online - full text ed.: ISSN 1524-4040. USD 551.20 domestic academic site license; USD 677.20 foreign academic site license; USD 614.80 domestic corporate site license; USD 740.80 foreign corporate site license (effective 2002).
Indexed: A20, A22, A36, B&BAb, B25, BDM&CN, BIOSIS Prev, CABA, CurCont, DentInd, E-psyche, E12, EMBASE, ExcerpMed, FR, GH, H17, INI, ISR, IndMed, Inpharma, JW-N, LT, MEDLINE, MycolAb, N02, N03, NSCI, P30, P33, P35, P37, R08, R10, R13, RM&VM, RRTA, Reac, SCI, SCOPUS, T05, W07.
—BLDSC (6081.582000), GNLM, IE, Infotrieve, Ingenta, INIST. **CCC.**
Published by: (Congress of Neurological Surgeons), Lippincott Williams & Wilkins (Subsidiary of: Wolters Kluwer N.V.), 530 Walnut St, Philadelphia, PA 19106. TEL 215-521-8300, FAX 215-521-8902, customerservice@lww.com, http://www.lww.com. Ed. Nelson M Oyesiku.

➤ **NEUROSURGERY CLINICS OF NORTH AMERICA.** *see* MEDICAL SCIENCES—Surgery

➤ **NEUROSURGERY CODING ALERT;** the practical adviser for ethically optimizing coding, reimbursement and efficiency for neurosurgery practices. *see* INSURANCE

616.8 USA ISSN 1092-0684
➤ **NEUROSURGICAL FOCUS.** Text in English. 1996. m. free (effective 2011). adv. back issues avail. **Document type:** *Journal, Academic/Scholarly.* **Description:** Provides rapid publication of original contributions. Each issue is devoted to the exploration of a topic of interest to neurosurgeons.
Media: Online - full text. **Related titles:** CD-ROM ed.
Indexed: A20, CurCont, E-psyche, EMBASE, ExcerpMed, MEDLINE, NSCI, P30, R10, Reac, SCI, SCOPUS, W07.
—CCC.
Published by: American Association of Neurological Surgeons, 5550 Meadowbrook Dr, Rolling Meadows, IL 60008. TEL 847-378-0500, FAX 847-378-0600, info@aans.org, http://www.aans.org. Ed. Dr. John A Jane TEL 434-924-5503. Adv. contact Greg Pessagno TEL 443-512-8899 ext 109.

➤ **NEUROSURGICAL REVIEW.** *see* MEDICAL SCIENCES—Surgery

616.8 617 ARG ISSN 1850-4485

NEUROTARGET; revista de neurocirugía funcional, estereotaxia, radiocirugía y dolor. Text in Spanish. 2006. 3/yr. USD 80 combined subscription domestic to individuals (print & online eds.); USD 170 combined subscription in the Americas to individuals (print & online eds.); USD 250 combined subscription elsewhere to individuals (print & online eds.); USD 120 combined subscription domestic to institutions (print & online eds.); USD 250 combined subscription in the Americas to institutions (print & online eds.); USD 350 combined subscription elsewhere to institutions (print & online eds.) (effective 2010). back issues avail. **Document type:** *Journal, Academic/Scholarly.*
Related titles: Online - full text ed.
Address: Juncal 2222, 1o. Piso, Buenos Aires, C1125ABD, Argentina. TEL 54-11-60091360, FAX 54-11-60091361, http://www.neurotarget.com/. Ed. Juan Pablo Puente.

616.8 USA ISSN 1933-7213
RC346

➤ **NEUROTHERAPEUTICS.** Text in English. 2004 (Jan.). q. EUR 427, USD 524 combined subscription to institutions (print & online eds.) (effective 2012). adv. back issues avail.; reprints avail. **Document type:** *Journal, Academic/Scholarly.* **Description:** Provides reviews focused on a single topic relating to the treatment of disorders of the nervous system.
Formerly (until 2007): NeuroRx (1545-5343)
Related titles: Online - full text ed.: ISSN 1878-7479 (from IngentaConnect).
Indexed: A26, CA, CurCont, EMBASE, ExcerpMed, I05, MEDLINE, NSCI, P03, P30, PsycInfo, R10, Reac, SCI, SCOPUS, T02, W07.
—BLDSC (6081.585300), IE, Ingenta. **CCC.**
Published by: (American Society for Experimental Neurotherapeutics), Springer New York LLC (Subsidiary of: Springer Science+Business Media), 233 Spring St, New York, NY 10013. TEL 212-460-1500, FAX 212-460-1575, journals-ny@springer.com.

616.8 USA ISSN 1029-8428
RC347.5 CODEN: NURRFI

➤ **NEUROTOXICITY RESEARCH.** Text in English. 1999. 8/yr. EUR 616, USD 832 combined subscription to institutions (print & online eds.) (effective 2012). back issues avail.; reprint service avail. from PSC. **Document type:** *Journal, Academic/Scholarly.* **Description:** Contains papers reporting on both basic and clinical research on classical neurotoxins and mechanisms associated with neurodegeneration, apoptosis, nerve regeneration, and neurotrophic actions.
Related titles: Online - full text ed.: ISSN 1476-3524 (from IngentaConnect).
Indexed: A01, A22, B21, BIOBASE, CA, E01, EMBASE, ESPM, ExcerpMed, IABS, MEDLINE, NSA, NSCI, P30, R10, Reac, SCI, SCOPUS, T02, ToxAb, W07.
—BLDSC (6081.585700), IE, Infotrieve, Ingenta. **CCC.**
Published by: (Neurotoxicity Society), Springer New York LLC (Subsidiary of: Springer Science+Business Media), 233 Spring St, New York, NY 10013. TEL 212-460-1500, FAX 212-460-1575, service-ny@springer.com, http://www.springer.com. Ed. Richard M Kostrzewa.

616.8 NLD ISSN 0161-813X
RC321 CODEN: NRTXDN

➤ **NEUROTOXICOLOGY.** Variant title: Journal of Neurotoxicology. Text in English. 1979. 6/yr. EUR 506 in Europe to institutions; JPY 67,100 in Japan to institutions; USD 566 elsewhere to institutions (effective 2012). adv. bk.rev. abstr.; bibl.; charts; illus. index. Supplement avail.; back issues avail. **Document type:** *Journal, Academic/Scholarly.* **Description:** Publishes original research reports and brief communications relating to neurotoxicology.
Related titles: Online - full text ed.: ISSN 1872-9711 (from IngentaConnect, ScienceDirect).
Indexed: A01, A03, A08, A20, A22, A26, A34, A35, A36, A38, ASFA, AgBio, Agr, B21, B25, BIOBASE, BIOSIS Prev, BP, C30, CA, CABA, ChemAb, CurCont, D01, E-psyche, E04, E05, E12, EMBASE, ESPM, ExcerpMed, F08, F11, F12, FS&TA, GH, H17, I05, IABS, INIS AtomInd, ISR, IndMed, IndVet, Inpharma, LT, MEDLINE, MaizeAb, MycolAb, N02, N03, N04, N05, NSA, NSCI, OR, P30, P32, P33, P37, P39, P40, PGegResA, PGrRegA, R07, R08, R10, R12, R13, RA&MP, RM&VM, RRTA, Reac, S13, S16, SCI, SCOPUS, SoyAb, T02, T05, ToxAb, VS, W07, W10.
—BLDSC (6081.585800), CASDDS, GNLM, IE, Infotrieve, Ingenta, INIST. **CCC.**
Published by: Elsevier BV (Subsidiary of: Elsevier Science & Technology), Radarweg 29, PO Box 211, Amsterdam, 1000 AE, Netherlands. TEL 31-20-4853911, FAX 31-20-4852457, JournalsCustomerServiceEMEA@elsevier.com, http://www.elsevier.nl. Ed. Dr. Joan S Cranmer. **Subscr. to:** Radarweg 29, PO Box 211, Amsterdam 1000 AE, Netherlands. TEL 31-20-4853757, FAX 31-20-4853432.

616.8 USA ISSN 0892-0362
RA1224 CODEN: NETEEC

➤ **NEUROTOXICOLOGY AND TERATOLOGY.** Text in English. 1979. bi-m. EUR 2,061 in Europe to institutions; JPY 273,500 in Japan to institutions; USD 2,306 elsewhere to institutions (effective 2012). adv. illus.; abstr. index. back issues avail.; reprints avail. **Document type:** *Journal, Academic/Scholarly.* **Description:** Brings out studies that cover the developmental and adult neurotoxicity of pesticides, drugs of abuse, pharmaceuticals, solvents, heavy metals, organometals, and general industrial-use compounds etc.
Former titles (until 1987): Neurobehavioral Toxicology and Teratology (0275-1380); (until 1981): Neurobehavioral Toxicology (0191-3581)
Related titles: Microfilm ed.: (from PQC); Online - full text ed.: ISSN 1872-9738 (from IngentaConnect, ScienceDirect).
Indexed: A01, A03, A08, A22, A26, A34, A36, A38, ASCA, AddicA, B21, B25, BIOBASE, BIOSIS Prev, C25, C33, CA, CABA, CIN, ChemAb, ChemTitl, CurCont, D01, DentInd, E-psyche, E04, E05, E12, EMBASE, ESPM, EnvAb, EnvInd, ExcerpMed, GH, H&SSA, H16, I05, IABS, IPsyAb, ISR, IndMed, Inpharma, MEDLINE, MaizeAb, MycolAb, N02, N03, N04, N05, NRN, NSA, NSCI, P03, P30, P32, P33, P37, P39, P40, PsycInfo, PsycholAb, R07, R08, R10, R12, R13, RA&MP, RM&VM, Reac, S02, S03, S13, S16, SCI, SCOPUS, SoyAb, T02, T05, THA, ToxAb, VS, W07, W10.
—BLDSC (6081.586500), CASDDS, GNLM, IE, Infotrieve, Ingenta, INIST. **CCC.**
Published by: (Behavioral Toxicology Society, Neurobehavioral Teratology Society), Elsevier Inc. (Subsidiary of: Elsevier Science & Technology), 1600 John F Kennedy Blvd, Philadelphia, PA 19103. TEL 215-239-3900, FAX 215-238-7883, JournalCustomerService-usa@elsevier.com. Ed. Jane Adams TEL 617-287-6347. Adv. contact Janine Castle TEL 44-1865-843844.

616.8 DEU ISSN 1436-123X

NEUROTRANSMITTER. Text in German. 1992. m. EUR 204, USD 244 to institutions (effective 2012). adv. **Document type:** *Journal, Academic/Scholarly.*
Indexed: A26, E-psyche.
—IE. **CCC.**
Published by: Urban und Vogel Medien und Medizin Verlagsgesellschaft mbH (Subsidiary of: Springer Science+Business Media), Neumarkter Str 43, Munich, 81673, Germany. TEL 49-89-4372-1411, FAX 49-89-4372-1410, verlag@urban-vogel.de. Ed. Claudia Maeck. Adv. contact Peter Urban. B&W page EUR 2,400, color page EUR 3,930; trim 174 x 237. Circ: 11,700 (paid). **Subscr. to:** Springer Distribution Center, Kundenservice Zeitschriften, Haberstr 7, Heidelberg 69126, Germany. TEL 49-6221-3454303, FAX 49-6221-3454229, subscriptions@springer.com.

616.8 RUS ISSN 1560-9545

NEVROLOGICHESKII ZHURNAL/JOURNAL OF NEUROLOGY. Text in Russian; Summaries in English. 1996. bi-m. USD 231 foreign (effective 2005). adv. Website rev. abstr. reprints avail. **Document type:** *Journal, Academic/Scholarly.* **Description:** Covers practical neurology, and trends and advances in the diagnosis and treatment of nervous diseases.
Indexed: A22, E-psyche, RefZh.
—BLDSC (0124.025000), East View, IE, Ingenta.
Published by: Izdatel'stvo Meditsina/Meditsina Publishers, ul B Pirogovskaya, d 2, str 5, Moscow, 119435, Russian Federation. TEL 7-095-2483324, meditsina@mtu-net.ru, http://www.medlit.ru. Ed. Nikolai N Yakhno. Pub. A M Stochik. R&P I Izmailova. Adv. contact O A Fadeeva TEL 7-095-923-51-40. Circ: 1,500. **Dist. by:** East View Information Services, 10601 Wayzata Blvd, Minneapolis, MN 55305. TEL 952-252-1201, 800-477-1005, FAX 952-252-1202, info@eastview.com, http://www.eastview.com.

616.8 NOR ISSN 1500-8347

NEVROPSYKOLOGI. Text in Norwegian. 1998. s-a. NOK 300 membership (effective 2007). 24 p./no.; back issues avail. **Document type:** *Newsletter, Trade.*
Related titles: Online - full text ed.
Published by: Norsk Nevropsykologi Forening/Norwegian Neuropsychological Association, c/o Norsk Psykologforening, PO Box 419, Sentrum, Oslo, 0103, Norway. TEL 47-23-103130, sekretariat@nevropsykologi.org, http://www.nevropsykologi.org. Ed. Maria Stylianou Korsnes.

616.8 USA

NEW MEDICAL THERAPIES BRIEFS. ALZHEIMER'S DISEASE. Text in English. 19??. irreg. free (effective 2009). **Document type:** *Newsletter, Trade.*
Media: Online - full content.
Published by: CenterWatch (Subsidiary of: Jobson Medical Information LLC.), 100 N Washington St, Ste 301, Boston, MA 02114. TEL 617-948-5100, 866-219-3440, customerservice@centerwatch.com.

362.25 USA

NEW MEDICAL THERAPIES BRIEFS. DEPRESSION. Text in English. 200?. irreg. free (effective 2009). **Document type:** *Newsletter, Trade.*
Media: Online - full content.
Published by: CenterWatch (Subsidiary of: Jobson Medical Information LLC.), 100 N Washington St, Ste 301, Boston, MA 02114. TEL 617-948-5100, 866-219-3440, customerservice@centerwatch.com.

616.833005 USA

NEW MEDICAL THERAPIES BRIEFS. PARKINSON'S DISEASE. Text in English. 200?. irreg. free (effective 2009). **Document type:** *Newsletter, Trade.*
Media: Online - full content.
Published by: CenterWatch (Subsidiary of: Jobson Medical Information LLC.), 100 N Washington St, Ste 301, Boston, MA 02114. TEL 617-948-5100, 866-219-3440, customerservice@centerwatch.com.

616.89 USA

THE NEW MESSAGE. Text in English. 1971. q. USD 8 domestic; USD 11 in Canada; USD 14 elsewhere (effective 2007). 12 p./no.; **Document type:** *Newsletter, Consumer.* **Description:** Offers people seeking emotional health and wellness stories, articles and information relating to the 12-step Emotions Anonymous Program.
Former titles: Message (St. Paul); Carrying the E A Message (1072-3765)
Related titles: E-mail ed.: USD 5 (effective 2002).
Indexed: E-psyche.
Published by: Emotions Anonymous, PO Box 4245, St. Paul, MN 55104-0245. TEL 651-647-9712, FAX 651-647-1593. Circ: 800 (paid).

NEW YORK (STATE). COMMISSION ON QUALITY OF CARE FOR THE MENTALLY DISABLED. ANNUAL REPORT. *see* HEALTH FACILITIES AND ADMINISTRATION

616.8 CAN

NEWSLINK. Text in English. 1986. q. looseleaf. membership. adv. back issues avail. **Document type:** *Newsletter.* **Description:** Studies ALS research, fundraising and coping mechanisms and services for families with the disease.
Formerly: Communique (Vancouver)
Related titles: Diskette ed.
Indexed: E-psyche.
Published by: Amyotrophic Lateral Sclerosis Society of B.C., 1600 W 6th Ave, Ste 119, Vancouver, BC V6J 1R3, Canada. TEL 604-685-0737, FAX 604-685-0725. Ed. Sue Lewis-H'alloran. R&P, Adv. contact Judy Bonds. Circ: 6,000.

NEWSLINK (WASHINGTON). *see* PSYCHOLOGY

616.8 RUS ISSN 1028-8554

NEZAVISIMYI PSIKHIATRICHESKII ZHURNAL. Text in Russian. 1991. q. USD 122 in United States (effective 2004). **Document type:** *Journal, Academic/Scholarly.*
Indexed: RefZh.
—East View.
Published by: (Nezavisimaya Psikhiatricheskaya Assotsiatsiya/Independent Psychiatric Association), Izdatel'stvo Folium, Dmitrovskoe shosse 58, Moscow, 127238, Russian Federation. TEL 7-095-4825590, 7-095-4825544, info@folium.ru. **Dist. by:** East View Information Services, 10601 Wayzata Blvd, Minneapolis, MN 55305. TEL 952-252-1201, 800-477-1005, FAX 952-252-1202, info@eastview.com, http://www.eastview.com.

NIGERIAN JOURNAL OF CLINICAL AND COUNSELLING PSYCHOLOGY. *see* PSYCHOLOGY

362.29 JPN ISSN 1340-5829

NIHON ARUKORU SEISHIN IGAKU ZASSHI/JAPANESE JOURNAL OF PSYCHIATRIC RESEARCH ON ALCOHOL. Text in Japanese. 1994. s-a. membership.
Published by: (Nihon Arukoru Seishin Igakukai/Japanese Society of Psychiatric Research on Alcohol), Seiwa Shoten Co. Ltd., 2-5 Kamitakaido, 1-chome, Suginami-ku, Tokyo, 168-0074, Japan. TEL 81-3-33290031, FAX 81-3-53747186, http://www.seiwa-pb.co.jp.

NIHON NOU SHINKEI GEKA GAKKAI SOUKAI SHOUROKUSHUU (CD-ROM)/JAPAN NEUROSURGICAL SOCIETY. ABSTRACTS OF THE ANNUAL MEETING (CD-ROM). *see* MEDICAL SCIENCES—Abstracting, Bibliographies, Statistics

NIHON SEKIZUI SHOUGAI IGAKKAI ZASSHI/JAPAN MEDICAL SOCIETY OF PARAPLEGIA. JOURNAL. *see* MEDICAL SCIENCES—Orthopedics And Traumatology

615.78 JPN ISSN 1340-2544

NIHON SHINKEI SEISHIN YAKURIGAKU ZASSHI/JAPANESE JOURNAL OF PSYCHOPHARMACOLOGY. Text in Japanese. 1981. bi-m. **Document type:** *Journal, Academic/Scholarly.*
Formerly (until 1993): Yakubutsu, Seishin, Kodo (0285-5313)
Indexed: A22, B21, B25, BIOSIS Prev, EMBASE, ESPM, ExcerpMed, MEDLINE, MycolAb, NSA, P30, R10, Reac, SCOPUS, ToxAb.
—BLDSC (4656.641900), IE, Infotrieve.
Published by: Nihon Shinkei Seishin Yakuri Gakkai/Japanese Society of Neuropsychophamacology, 3-39-22 Showa-machi, Maebashi, 371-8511, Japan. TEL 81-27-220-8180, FAX 81-27-220-8192, van@bcasj.or.jp, http://www.onyx.dti.ne.jp/~jsnp/.

616.8 153 NLD ISSN 1872-1427

NIJMEGEN C N S; proceedings of the Cognitive Neuroscience Master of the Radboud University. Text in Dutch. 2006. s-a.
Related titles: Online - full text ed.: ISSN 1872-1435.
Published by: (Radboud University Nijmegen, F.C. Donders Centre for Cognitive Neuroimaging), Radboud Universiteit Nijmegen, Postbus 9102, Nijmegen, 6500 HC, Netherlands. info@communicatie.ru.nl. Eds. Han Langeslag, Maren Urner.

616.8 006.3 JPN ISSN 1341-7924

NINCHI KAGAKU/COGNITIVE STUDIES. Text in Japanese. 1994. q. **Document type:** *Journal, Academic/Scholarly.*
Related titles: Online - full text ed.
Indexed: P03, PsycInfo.
—BLDSC (3292.891000).
Published by: Nihon Ninchi Kagakukai/Japanese Cognitive Science Society, 1-5-1 Chofugaoka, University of Electro-Communications, Department of Systems Engineering, Chofu, Tokyo 182-8585, Japan. TEL 81-42-443-5820, jcss@jcss.gr.jp.

NO NO KAGAKU/BRAIN SCIENCE. *see* PHARMACY AND PHARMACOLOGY

NO SHINKEI GEKA SOKUHO/NEUROSURGERY LETTERS. *see* MEDICAL SCIENCES—Surgery

NO SOTCHU NO GEKA/SURGERY FOR CEREBRAL STROKE. *see* MEDICAL SCIENCES—Surgery

616.8 JPN ISSN 0029-0831
CODEN: NTHAA7

NO TO HATTATSU/BRAIN AND DEVELOPMENT. Text in Japanese; Summaries in English. 1969. bi-m. JPY 9,173; JPY 1,456 newsstand/cover (effective 2004). adv. bk.rev. abstr. Index. **Document type:** *Journal, Academic/Scholarly.*
Related titles: ♦ English ed.: Brain & Development. ISSN 0387-7604.
Indexed: A22, AMHA, B25, BDM&CN, BIOSIS Prev, ChemAb, DentInd, E-psyche, EMBASE, ExcerpMed, F09, INI, ISR, IndMed, MEDLINE, MycolAb, P30, R10, Reac, SCOPUS.
—BLDSC (6113.969000), CASDDS, GNLM, IE, Infotrieve, Ingenta. **CCC.**
Published by: (Nihon Shoni Shinkei Gakkai/Japanese Society of Child Neurology), Shindan to Chiryosha, Sanno Grand Bldg. 4F, 2-14-2 Nagata-cho, Chiyoda-ku, Tokyo, 100-0014, Japan. TEL 81-3-35802770, FAX 81-3-35802776, eigyobu@shindan.co.jp. Ed. Yukuo Konishi. Circ: 4,000.

616.8 618.97 USA ISSN 1949-484X
HV689

▼ ➤ **NON-PHARMACOLOGICAL THERAPIES IN DEMENTIA.** Text in English. 2010 (Jan.). q. USD 245 to institutions; USD 367 combined subscription to institutions (effective 2012). **Document type:** *Journal, Academic/Scholarly.* **Description:** Includes research on the efficacy of all kinds of non-pharmacological treatments proposed in dementia care.
Related titles: Online - full text ed.: USD 245 to institutions (effective 2012).
Published by: Nova Science Publishers, Inc., 400 Oser Ave, Ste 1600, Hauppauge, NY 11788. TEL 631-231-7269, FAX 631-231-8175, journals@novapublishers.com.

616.8 ITA ISSN 1590-0711

NOOS; aggiornamenti in psichiatria. Text in Italian. 1995. 3/yr. **Document type:** *Journal, Academic/Scholarly.*
Related titles: Online - full text ed.
Published by: Il Pensiero Scientifico Editore, Via Bradano 3-C, Rome, 00199, Italy. TEL 39-06-862821, FAX 39-06-86282250, http://www.pensiero.it. Ed. Alberto Siracusano.

616.89 GBR ISSN 0803-9488

➤ **NORDIC JOURNAL OF PSYCHIATRY.** Text in English, Multiple languages; Summaries in English. 1947. bi-m. GBP 170, EUR 230, USD 290 combined subscription to institutions (print & online eds.); GBP 350, EUR 460, USD 580 combined subscription to corporations (print & online eds.) (effective 2010). adv. bk.rev. index. back issues avail.; reprint service avail. from PSC. **Document type:** *Journal, Academic/Scholarly.* **Description:** Addressed to clinical psychiatrists and their co-workers as well as researchers.
Former titles (until 1992): Nordisk Psykiatrisk Tidsskrift (0029-1455); (until 1959): Nordisk Psykiatrisk Medlemsblad (0909-7252)

Related titles: Online - full text ed.: ISSN 1502-4725 (from IngentaConnect); ◆ Supplement(s): Nordic Journal of Psychiatry. Supplement. ISSN 0803-9496.
Indexed: A01, A03, A08, A20, A22, ASCA, AddicA, CA, CurCont, E-psyche, E01, EMBASE, ExcerpMed, F09, Faml, IBR, IBZ, MEDLINE, P03, P30, P43, PCI, PsycInfo, PsycholAb, R10, Reac, S02, S03, SCI, SCOPUS, SSCI, T02, W07.
—BLDSC (6117.927050), GNLM, IE, Infotrieve, Ingenta. **CCC.**
Published by: (Joint Committee of the Nordic Psychiatric Associations NOR), Informa Healthcare (Subsidiary of: T & F Informa plc), Telephone House, 69-77 Paul St, London, EC2A 4LQ, United Kingdom. TEL 44-20-70175000, FAX 44-20-70176792, healthcare.enquiries@informa.com. Ed. Hasse Karlsson TEL 358-40-5195247. Adv. contact Per Sonnerfeldt. **Subscr. in N. America to:** Taylor & Francis Inc., Customer Services Dept, 325 Chestnut St, 8th Fl, Philadelphia, PA 19106. TEL 215-625-8900, 800-354-1420, FAX 215-625-8914, customerservice@taylorandfrancis.com; **Subscr. outside N. America to:** Taylor & Francis Ltd., Journals Customer Service, Sheepen Pl, Colchester, Essex CO3 3LP, United Kingdom. TEL 44-20-70175544, FAX 44-20-70175198, tf.enquiries@tfinforma.com.

616.89 SWE ISSN 0803-9496
NORDIC JOURNAL OF PSYCHIATRY. SUPPLEMENT. Text in Norwegian. 1974. irreg., latest vol.44, 2001. price varies. adv. reprint service avail. from PSC. **Document type:** *Monographic series, Academic/Scholarly.*
Formerly (until 1992): Nordisk Psykiatrisk Tidsskrift. Supplement (0346-8852)
Related titles: ◆ Supplement to: Nordic Journal of Psychiatry. ISSN 0803-9488.
Indexed: E-psyche, IBR, IBZ, SCOPUS.
—BLDSC (6117.927060), IE, Ingenta. **CCC.**
Published by: (Joint Committee of the Nordic Psychiatric Associations NOR), Taylor & Francis A B (Subsidiary of: Taylor & Francis Group), PO Box 3255, Stockholm, 10365, Sweden. TEL 46-8-4408040, FAX 46-8-4408050.

616.89 TUR ISSN 1300-0667
CODEN: NOPAB
➤ **NOROPSIKIYATRI ARSIVI/ARCHIVES OF NEUROPSYCHIATRY.** Text in Turkish. 1964. q. free to qualified personnel (effective 2009). adv. **Document type:** *Journal, Academic/Scholarly.* **Description:** Publishes research articles in psychiatry, neurology, neurosurgery and clinical psychology. In addition, reviews, editorial views, letter to the editor and case reports are also published.
Related titles: Online - full text ed.: free (effective 2011).
Indexed: A01, A26, C06, C07, CA, E-psyche, E08, EMBASE, ExcerpMed, H12, I05, P03, P25, P48, PQC, PsycInfo, R10, Reac, S09, SCI, SCOPUS, T02, W07.
—BLDSC (6133.437000), IE.
Published by: (Turk Noropsikiyatri Dernegi/Turkish Association of Neuropsychiatry), Galenos Yayincilik, Barbaros Bulvari, Salim Aktas Is Hani, No. 85 D:3, Besiktas, Istanbul, 80690, Turkey. TEL 90-212-2369054, FAX 90-212-2369052, info@galenos.com.tr, http://www.galenos.com.tr. Ed., R&P Dr. Mustafa Sercan TEL 90-212-5436565. Adv. contact Noropsikiyatri Dernegi. B&W page TRY 150, color page TRY 200.

616.8 ESP ISSN 1578-4940
NORTE DE SALUD MENTAL. Text in Multiple languages. 1997. 3/yr. **Document type:** *Journal, Academic/Scholarly.*
Formerly (until 2000): G O Z E. Gogo Osasunaren Zientzietarako Erakundea (1577-3051)
Related titles: Online - full text ed.: free (effective 2011).
Indexed: SCOPUS.
Published by: Osasun Mentalaren Elkartea/Asociacion de Salud Mental, Apdo Correos 12, Erandio, Vizcaya, Spain.

616.858 USA ISSN 1536-4771
KFN7765.A29
NORTH CAROLINA MENTAL HEALTH, DEVELOPMENTAL DISABILITIES AND SUBSTANCE ABUSE LAWS. Text in English. 1996. a., latest 2006. USD 32 (effective 2008). 596 p./no.; Supplement avail. **Document type:** *Handbook/Manual/Guide, Trade.* **Description:** Provides an ideal volume for mental health, social service, and health care professionals, as well as attorneys who specialize in topics related to these issues.
Indexed: E-psyche.
Published by: Michie Company (Subsidiary of: LexisNexis North America), 701 E Water St, Charlottesville, VA 22902. TEL 434-972-7600, 800-446-3410, FAX 434-972-7677, customer.support@lexisnexis.com, http://www.michie.com.

616.8 JPN ISSN 0912-0726
RC388.5
NOSOTCHU/JAPANESE JOURNAL OF STROKE. Text in Japanese. 1979. bi-m. **Document type:** *Journal, Academic/Scholarly.*
Indexed: INIS AtomInd.
Published by: Nihon Nosotchu Gakkai/Japan Stroke Society, 35 Shinanomachi, Shinjuku-ku, Keio University School of Medicine, Department of Neurology, Tokyo, 160-8582, Japan. TEL 86-3-33531211 ext 62742, FAX 81-3-33543128, jssoffice@jsts.gr.jp, http://www.jsts.gr.jp/.

616.8 616.15 JPN ISSN 1341-8440
NOU TO JONKAN/BRAIN AND CIRCULATION. Text in Japanese. 1996. 3/yr. (Jan., May & Sep.). JPY 6,615 (effective 2005). **Document type:** *Journal, Academic/Scholarly.*
Indexed: E-psyche.
Published by: Medikaru Rebyusha/Medical Review Co., Ltd., 1-7-3 Hirano-Machi, Chuo-ku, Yoshida Bldg., Osaka-shi, 541-0046, Japan. TEL 81-6-62231468, FAX 81-6-62231245.

616.89 CAN ISSN 1199-7699
NUTRITION & MENTAL HEALTH. Text in English. 1974. q. USD 35 domestic; USD 40 foreign (effective 1999). bk.rev. reprints avail. **Document type:** *Newsletter.*
Former titles (until 1993): Health and Nutrition Update (0831-8530); Huxley Institute - C S F Newsletter (0318-8272); Incorporates: Schizophrenics Anonymous International. Bulletin (0048-9360)
Indexed: E-psyche.
Published by: Canadian Schizophrenia Foundation, 16 Florence Ave, Toronto, ON M2N 1E9, Canada. TEL 416-733-2117, FAX 416-733-2352, centre@orthomed.org, http://www.orthomed.org. Ed. Steven Carter. Circ: 1,000.

612.39 GBR ISSN 1476-8305
NUTRITIONAL NEUROSCIENCE (ONLINE). Text in English. 1998. bi-m. GBP 617 to institutions; USD 883 in United States to institutions (effective 2012). **Document type:** *Journal, Academic/Scholarly.* **Description:** Reports both basic and clinical research in the field of nutrition that relates to the central and peripheral nervous system.
Media: Online - full text (from IngentaConnect).
—BLDSC (6190.375000). **CCC.**
Published by: Maney Publishing, Ste 1C, Joseph's Well, Hanover Walk, Leeds, W Yorks LS3 1AB, United Kingdom. TEL 44-113-2432800, FAX 44-113-3868178, maney@maney.co.uk. Ed. Chandan Prasad. **Subscr. in N. America to:** Maney Publishing, 875 Massachusetts Ave, 7th Fl, Cambridge, MA 02139. TEL 866-297-5154, FAX 617-354-6875, maney@maneyusa.com.

O M; Zeitschrift fuer Orthomolekulare Medizin. (Orthomolekulare Medizin) *see* NUTRITION AND DIETETICS

150 361.3 610 USA ISSN 0164-212X
RC487 CODEN: OTMHDX
➤ **OCCUPATIONAL THERAPY IN MENTAL HEALTH**; a journal of psychosocial practice and research. Abbreviated title: O T M H. Text in English. 1980. q. GBP 518 combined subscription in United Kingdom to institutions (print & online eds.); EUR 670, USD 675 combined subscription to institutions (print & online eds.) (effective 2012). adv. bk.rev. bibl. 120 p./no. 1 cols./p.; back issues avail.; reprint service avail. from PSC. **Document type:** *Journal, Academic/ Scholarly.* **Description:** Provides current material specifically for occupational therapists in mental health clinics, psychiatric hospitals, mental health programs, hospitals, and other settings.
Related titles: Microfiche ed.: (from PQC); Microform ed.; Online - full text ed.: ISSN 1541-3101. GBP 466 in United Kingdom to institutions; EUR 603, USD 607 to institutions (effective 2012).
Indexed: A01, A03, A22, AHCMS, AMED, AMHA, ASSIA, BehAb, C06, C07, C08, CA, CDA, CINAHL, CPLI, E-psyche, E01, ECER, Faml, P48, P50, PC&CA, PQC, PsycholAb, RehabLit, S02, S03, SCOPUS, SD, SWR&A, T02.
—BLDSC (6231.260000), GNLM, IE, Infotrieve, Ingenta, INIST. **CCC.**
Published by: Routledge (Subsidiary of: Taylor & Francis Group), 325 Chestnut St, Ste 800, Philadelphia, PA 19106. TEL 215-625-8900, 800-354-1420, FAX 215-625-8914, journals@routledge.com, http://www.routledge.com. Eds. Marie-Louise Blount, Mary Donohue. adv.: B&W page USD 315, color page USD 550; trim 4.375 x 7.125. Circ: 507 (paid).

616.853 AUT ISSN 1683-6936
OESTERREICHISCHE SEKTION DER INTERNATIONALEN LIGA GEGEN EPILEPSIE. MITTEILUNGEN. Text in German. 2001. q. **Document type:** *Bulletin, Academic/Scholarly.*
Related titles: Online - full text ed.: ISSN 1813-0151.
Published by: (Oesterreichische Sektion der Internationalen Liga gegen Epilepsie), Krause & Pachernegg GmbH, Mozartgasse 10, Gablitz, 3003, Austria. TEL 43-2231-612580, FAX 43-2231-6125810, k_u_p@eunet.at, http://www.kup.at/verlag.htm.

362.3 NLD
OKEE-KRANT; de duidelijkste krant voor jou. Text in Dutch. 1993. 10/yr. EUR 35 to individuals; EUR 60 to institutions (effective 2008). adv. illus. back issues avail. **Document type:** *Consumer.* **Description:** Covers all ways in which persons with mental disabilities can live as independently and productively as possible.
Formerly: Okee (1382-354X)
Related titles: Audio cassette/tape ed.
Indexed: E-psyche.
Published by: Eenvoudig Communiceren, Postbus 10208, Amsterdam, 1001 EE, Netherlands. TEL 31-20-5206070, FAX 31-20-5206061, info@eenvoudigcommuniceren.nl, http://www.eenvoudigcommuniceren.nl.

618.976 GBR ISSN 1463-6662
OLD AGE PSYCHIATRIST. Text in English. 1995. q. **Document type:** *Newsletter, Trade.*
—CCC.
Published by: Royal College of Psychiatrists, Faculty of the Psychiatry of Old Age, 17 Belgrave Sq, London, SW1X 8PG, United Kingdom. TEL 44-20-72352351, FAX 44-20-72451231, rcpsych@rcpsych.ac.uk, http://www.rcpsych.ac.uk/college/faculties/oldage.aspx.

612 USA ISSN 1077-0747
ON THE BRAIN. Text in English. 1992. 3/yr. back issues avail. **Document type:** *Newsletter, Consumer.* **Description:** Focuses on topics in neuroscience.
Related titles: Online - full text ed.: free (effective 2010).
—CCC.
Published by: Harvard Mahoney Neuroscience Institute, Harvard Medical School, Gordon Hall, 25 Shattuck St, Rm 001, Boston, MA 02115. hmni@hms.harvard.edu. Eds. Ann Marie Menting, Karin Kiewra.

616.89 NLD ISSN 2210-3694
OPEN GEEST. Text in Dutch. 1994. q. EUR 16 membership (effective 2010).
Published by: Vereniging Anoiksis, Gansstraat 67 a, Utrecht, 3582 EC, Netherlands. TEL 31-30-2546113. Eds. Niels van Spaandonk, Stan van Heerebeek. Circ: 2,000 (controlled).

616.89 USA ISSN 2161-7325
▼ ➤ **OPEN JOURNAL OF PSYCHIATRY.** Text in English. 2011. q. USD 117 (effective 2011). **Document type:** *Journal, Academic/Scholarly.* **Description:** Provide a platform for scientists and academicians all over the world to promote, share, and discuss various new issues and developments in different areas of psychiatry.
Related titles: Online - full text ed.: ISSN 2161-7333. free (effective 2011).
Published by: Scientific Research Publishing, Inc., PO Box 54821, Irvine, CA 92619. service@scirp.org. Ed. Gjumrakch Aliev.

➤ **THE OPEN NEUROENDOCRINOLOGY JOURNAL.** *see* MEDICAL SCIENCES—Endocrinology

616.8 616.07 NLD ISSN 1874-4400
➤ **THE OPEN NEUROIMAGING JOURNAL.** Text in English. 2007. irreg. free (effective 2011). **Document type:** *Journal, Academic/Scholarly.*
Media: Online - full text.
Indexed: A01, A28, APA, BrCerAb, C&ISA, CA/WCA, CIA, CerAb, CivEngAb, CorrAb, E&CAJ, E11, EEA, EMA, ESPM, H15, M&TEA, M09, MBF, METADEX, P30, SolStAb, T04, WAA.
Published by: Bentham Open (Subsidiary of: Bentham Science Publishers Ltd.), PO Box 294, Bussum, AG 1400, Netherlands. TEL 31-35-6923800, FAX 31-35-6980150, subscriptions@bentham.org. Ed. Michael Schocke.

616.8 NLD ISSN 1874-205X
RC321
➤ **THE OPEN NEUROLOGY JOURNAL.** Text in English. 2007. irreg. free (effective 2011). **Document type:** *Journal, Academic/Scholarly.* **Description:** Covers all areas of neurology and neurological disorders.
Media: Online - full text.
Indexed: A01, EMBASE, NSA, P30, SCOPUS.
Published by: Bentham Open (Subsidiary of: Bentham Science Publishers Ltd.), PO Box 294, Bussum, AG 1400, Netherlands. TEL 31-35-6923800, FAX 31-35-6980150, subscriptions@bentham.org. Ed. George Perry.

616.8 NLD ISSN 1876-5238
RM315
➤ **THE OPEN NEUROPSYCHOPHARMACOLOGY JOURNAL.** Text in English. 2008. irreg. free (effective 2011). **Document type:** *Journal, Academic/Scholarly.*
Media: Online - full text.
Indexed: EMBASE, ExcerpMed, NSA, P30, SCOPUS.
Published by: Bentham Open (Subsidiary of: Bentham Science Publishers Ltd.), PO Box 294, Bussum, AG 1400, Netherlands. TEL 31-35-6923800, FAX 31-35-6980150, subscriptions@bentham.org.

616.8 NLD ISSN 1874-0820
RC321
➤ **THE OPEN NEUROSCIENCE JOURNAL.** Text in English. 2007. irreg. free (effective 2011). **Document type:** *Journal, Academic/Scholarly.* **Description:** Covers all major areas of neuroscience.
Media: Online - full text.
Indexed: A01, CA, NSA, P30, T02.
Published by: Bentham Open (Subsidiary of: Bentham Science Publishers Ltd.), PO Box 294, Bussum, AG 1400, Netherlands. TEL 31-35-6923800, FAX 31-35-6980150, subscriptions@bentham.org. Ed. Geoffrey Burnstock.

616.8 617 NLD ISSN 1876-5297
RD593
➤ **THE OPEN NEUROSURGERY JOURNAL.** Text in English. 2008. irreg. free (effective 2011). **Document type:** *Journal, Academic/ Scholarly.*
Media: Online - full text.
Indexed: NSA.
Published by: Bentham Open (Subsidiary of: Bentham Science Publishers Ltd.), PO Box 294, Bussum, AG 1400, Netherlands. TEL 31-35-6923800, FAX 31-35-6980150, subscriptions@bentham.org. Ed. G I Jallo.

616.8 NLD ISSN 1876-3863
RB127
➤ **THE OPEN PAIN JOURNAL.** Text in English. 2008. irreg. free (effective 2011). **Document type:** *Journal, Academic/Scholarly.*
Media: Online - full text.
Indexed: A01, EMBASE, NSA, P30, SCOPUS.
Published by: Bentham Open (Subsidiary of: Bentham Science Publishers Ltd.), PO Box 294, Bussum, AG 1400, Netherlands. TEL 31-35-6923800, FAX 31-35-6980150, subscriptions@bentham.org. Ed. Ru-Rong Ji.

616.8 NLD ISSN 1874-3544
RC321
➤ **THE OPEN PSYCHIATRY JOURNAL.** Text in English. 2007. irreg. free (effective 2011). **Document type:** *Journal, Academic/Scholarly.* **Description:** Covers all areas of pre-clinical and clinical research in psychiatry.
Media: Online - full text.
Indexed: A01, CA, ESPM, P03, P30, PsycInfo, SSciA, T02.
Published by: Bentham Open (Subsidiary of: Bentham Science Publishers Ltd.), PO Box 294, Bussum, AG 1400, Netherlands. TEL 31-35-6923800, FAX 31-35-6980150, subscriptions@bentham.org. Ed. F Gerard Moeller.

616.8 NLD ISSN 1874-6209
QP425
➤ **THE OPEN SLEEP JOURNAL.** Text in Italian. 2007. irreg. free (effective 2011). **Document type:** *Journal, Academic/Scholarly.* **Description:** Covers all areas of experimental and clinical research on sleep and sleep disorders plus research on wakefulness, dreaming, circadian rhythms and vigilance.
Media: Online - full text.
Indexed: A01, NSA, P30.
Published by: Bentham Open (Subsidiary of: Bentham Science Publishers Ltd.), PO Box 294, Bussum, AG 1400, Netherlands. TEL 31-35-6923800, FAX 31-35-6980150, subscriptions@bentham.org. Ed. Pasquale Montagna.

616.83 362.2 GBR ISSN 0265-511X
HV3008 G7 O66
OPENMIND; the mental health magazine. Text in English. 1983. bi-m. GBP 29 domestic to individuals; GBP 46 domestic to institutions; GBP 17 domestic to members; GBP 22 domestic to students; GBP 50 in Europe; GBP 57 elsewhere (effective 2009). adv. bk.rev.; film rev.; play rev. illus.; tr.lit. index. back issues avail. **Document type:** *Magazine, Consumer.* **Description:** Aims to give people who use mental health services and the people who provide them with an open space to share ideas, inspire one another, complain, express opinions and even share the odd joke or two.
Formed by the merger of (1974-1982): Information Bulletin - Mind (0306-0527); (1973-1982): Mind Out (0305-4128); Which was formerly (until 1973): Mind and Mental Health Magazine (0300-8266); (until 1971): Mental Health (0025-9632); Which was formed by the 1940 merger of: Mental Hygiene; Mental Welfare
Indexed: A22, B28, C06, C07, C08, CINAHL, E-psyche.
—BLDSC (6266.325000), IE, Ingenta. **CCC.**
Published by: Mind - The Mental Health Charity, 15-19 Broadway, Stratford, London, E15 4BQ, United Kingdom. TEL 44-20-85192122, FAX 44-20-85221725, contact@mind.org.uk.

150.198 615.856 USA ISSN 1054-075X
RZ460
ORGONOMIC FUNCTIONALISM; a journal devoted to the work of Wilhelm Reich. Text in English. 1989. a. USD 18.95 (effective 1999).
Indexed: E-psyche.

Published by: Wilhelm Reich Infant Trust, Orgonon, Box 687, Rangeley, ME 04970. TEL 207-864-3443. Eds. Chester M Raphael, Dr. Mary Boyd Higgins. Circ: 200.

ORTHOPEDIC, NEUROLOGICAL AND CHIROPRACTIC PHYSICAL EXAMINATIONS: TECHNIQUE AND SIGNIFICANCE. *see* MEDICAL SCIENCES—Orthopedics And Traumatology

618.9289 NOR ISSN 1891-0904
OSLO UNIVERSITETSSYKEHUS. ULLEVAAL, KLINIKK FOR PSYKISK HELSE - BARN OG UNGDOM. MONOGRAFISERIEN. Text in Norwegian. 1980. irreg. price varies. back issues avail. **Document type:** *Monographic series, Academic/Scholarly.*
Former titles (until 2009): Universitetet i Oslo. Sogn Senter for Barne- og Ungdomspsykiatri. Monografiserien (1504-2537); (until 2001): Universitetet i Oslo. Senter for Barne- og Ungdomspsykiatri. Monografiserien (1502-7511); (until 2000): Universitetet i Oslo. Statens Senter for Barne- og Ungdomspsykiatri. Monografiserien (0808-3991); (until 1994): Universitetet i Oslo. Barnepsykiatrisk Klinikk. Monografiserien (0333-175X)
Published by: Oslo Universitetssykehus, Senter for Psykisk Helse Barn og Ungdom, Kirkeveien 166, Bygning 2, Ullevaal Sykehus, Oslo, 0424, Norway. TEL 47-915-02770, post@oslouniversitetssykehus.no, http://www.oslouniversitetssykehus.no.

616.8 DNK ISSN 1397-0577
OUTSIDEREN; ser phykiatrien indefra. Text in Danish. 1996. 6/yr. DKK 195 to individuals; DKK 375 to institutions (effective 2009). back issues avail. **Document type:** *Magazine, Consumer.*
Address: Bragesgade 10,1, Copenhagen N, Denmark. TEL 45-35-397124, FAX 45-35-397123, http://www.outsideren.dk.

616.89 CAN ISSN 1914-8291
OXYGENE FAMILLES ET SANTE MENTALE. Text in French. 1983. q. **Document type:** *Magazine, Consumer.*
Formerly (until 2006): Association Lavalloise de Parents pour le Bien-Etre Mental. Bulletin (0840-5530)
Related titles: Online - full text ed.: free.
Published by: Association Lavalloise de Parents pour le Bien-Etre Mental, 1800 Bd. le Corbusier, Bureau 134, Laval, PQ H7S 2K1, Canada. TEL 450-688-0541, FAX 450-688-7061, info@alpabem.qc.ca.

616.8 FRA ISSN 2107-691X
▼ **OXYMORON**; revue psychanalytique et interdisciplinaire. Text in French. 2010. irreg.
Media: Online - full text.
Published by: Universite Nice Sophia Antipolis, Service Commun de la Documentation, 28, Ave. Valrose, Parc Valrose, BP 2053, Nice Cedex 2, 06101, France. http://revel.unice.fr/index.php.

616.891 AUS ISSN 1833-1661
P A C F A ENEWS. Text in English. 2004. bi-m. free (effective 2009). adv. back issues avail. **Document type:** *Newsletter, Consumer.*
Media: Online - full text.
Published by: Psychotherapy and Counselling Federation of Australia, 290 Park St, Fitzroy North, VIC 3068, Australia. TEL 61-3-94863077, FAX 61-3-94863933, admin@pacfa.org.au. adv.: page AUD 440; 20 x 27.

616.8 AUS ISSN 1832-3650
P A R C UPDATE. (Primary Australian Resource Centre) Text in English. 2002. q. **Document type:** *Newsletter, Consumer.*
Published by: Primary Mental Health Care Australian Resource Centre, Department of General Practice, Flinders University, PO Box 2100, Adelaide, SA 5001, Australia. parc@flinders.edu.au, http://www.parc.net.au.

616.8 USA ISSN 1548-7059
P C C C N S CAPSULES; from the Primary Care Companion to the Journal of Clinical Psychiatry. (Primary Care Companion Central Nervous System) Text in English. 2003 (Oct.). irreg., latest 2003. **Document type:** *Monographic series, Academic/Scholarly.*
Related titles: Online - full text ed.
Published by: Physicians Postgraduate Press, Inc., PO Box 752870, Memphis, TN 38175. TEL 901-751-3800, FAX 901-751-3444, circulation@psychiatrist.com. Eds. Larry Culpepper, Margaret D Weiss.

616.8 USA
P D F NEWSLETTER. Text in English. 1968. q. bk.rev. **Document type:** *Newsletter, Trade.* **Description:** Publishes reports on scientific research and discoveries, treatments and therapies, commentary from physicians, and insight from Parkinson's specialists.
Formerly (until 1999): U P F Newsletter
Indexed: E-psyche.
Published by: Parkinson's Disease Foundation, 1359 Broadway, Ste 1509, New York, NY 10018. TEL 212-923-4700, FAX 212-923-4778, info@pdf.org.

616.8 USA ISSN 1546-3443
RM315
P D R DRUG GUIDE FOR MENTAL HEALTH PROFESSIONALS. (Physicians' Desk Reference) Variant title: Drug Guide for Mental Health Professionals. Text in English. 2002. irreg., latest 3rd ed. USD 39.95 per issue (effective 2008). **Document type:** *Monographic series, Trade.* **Description:** Covers topics on psychotropics, substances that can be abused, as well as common medications that are prescribed for patients for their other medical conditions.
Published by: Thomson P D R, Five Paragon Dr, Montvale, NJ 07645. TEL 888-227-6469, FAX 201-722-2680, TH.customerservice@thomson.com, http://www.pdr.net.

P N. *see* HANDICAPPED—Physically Impaired

616.89 DEU ISSN 0937-2032
➤ **P P M P.** (Psychotherapie Psychosomatik Medizinische Psychologie) Text in German; Summaries in English, German. 1951. 12/yr. EUR 192 to institutions; EUR 269 combined subscription to institutions (print & online eds.); EUR 28 newsstand/cover (effective 2011). adv. bk.rev. abstr.; bibl.; charts; illus. index. back issues avail.; reprints avail. **Document type:** *Journal, Academic/Scholarly.*
Former titles (until 1988): Psychotherapie Psychosomatik Medizinische Psychologie (0173-7937); Psychotherapie und Medizinische Psychologie (0302-8984); Zeitschrift fuer Psychotherapie und Medizinische Psychologie (0044-3417)
Related titles: Microform ed.: (from PQC); Online - full text ed.: ISSN 1439-1058. EUR 259 to institutions (effective 2011).
Indexed: A20, A22, ASCA, CurCont, E-psyche, EMBASE, ExcerpMed, F09, FR, GJP, IndMed, MEDLINE, MLA-IB, P03, P30, PsycInfo, PsycholAb, R10, RILM, Reac, S02, S03, SCOPUS, SSCI, W07.
—BLDSC (6946.558250), GNLM, IE, Infotrieve, Ingenta, INIST. **CCC.**
Published by: (Allgemeine Aerztliche Gesellschaft fuer Psychotherapie), Georg Thieme Verlag, Ruedigerstr 14, Stuttgart, 70469, Germany. TEL 49-711-8931421, FAX 49-711-8931410, kunden.service@thieme.de. Ed. Dr. Bernhard Strauss. R&P Peter Eich. Adv. contact Andreas Schweiger TEL 49-711-8931245. Circ: 1,700 (paid). **Co-sponsor:** Oesterreichische Aerzte-Gesellschaft fuer Psychotherapie.

616.8521 USA ISSN 1050-1835
P T S D RESEARCH QUARTERLY. (Post-Traumatic Stress Disorder) Text in English. 1990. q. bibl.; abstr. **Document type:** *Government.* **Description:** Contains review articles on specific topics related to PTSD, written by guest experts.
Related titles: Online - full content ed.: free.
Published by: National Center for Post Traumatic Stress Disorder (Subsidiary of: U.S. Department of Veterans Affairs), VA Medical and Regional Office Center (116D), 215 N Main St, White River Junction, VT 05009-0001. TEL 802-296-5132, FAX 802-296-5135, ptsd@dartmouth.edu. Ed. Dr. Matthew J Friedman. **Subscr. to:** U.S. Government Printing Office, Superintendent of Documents, PO Box 371954, Pittsburgh, PA 15250. TEL 202-512-1800, FAX 202-512-2250, orders@gpo.gov, http://www.access.gpo.gov.

616.835 362.43 DNK ISSN 0901-7798
P T U NYT. (Polio-, Trafik- of Ulykkesskadede) Text in Danish. 1985. bi-m. DKK 225 (effective 2009). adv. 48 p./no.; **Document type:** *Magazine, Consumer.*
Formerly (until 1986): Polio-Nyt (0900-5587)
Related titles: Online - full text ed.: 2008.
Indexed: E-psyche.
Published by: Landsforeningen af Polio- Trafik og Ulykkesskadede, Fjeldhammervej 8, Roedovre, 2610, Denmark. TEL 45-36-739000, FAX 45-36-739001, ptu@ptu.dk, http://www.ptu.dk. Eds. Vivian Olesen, Philip Rendtorff. Circ: 7,000.

616.8 NLD ISSN 0304-3959
RB127 CODEN: PAINDB
➤ **PAIN.** Text in Dutch. 1975. 21/yr. EUR 1,140 in Europe to institutions; JPY 151,600 in Japan to institutions; USD 1,278 elsewhere to institutions (effective 2012). adv. bk.rev. abstr. back issues avail.; reprints avail. **Document type:** *Journal, Academic/Scholarly.* **Description:** Provides a forum for information about the nature, mechanism and treatment of pain.
Related titles: Microform ed.: (from PQC); Online - full text ed.: ISSN 1872-6623 (from IngentaConnect, ScienceDirect); Supplement(s): Pain. Supplement. ISSN 0167-6482. 1981.
Indexed: A01, A03, A08, A20, A22, A26, AIDS Ab, AMED, ASCA, B25, B28, BIOBASE, BIOSIS Prev, C06, C07, CA, CIN, ChPerl, ChemAb, ChemTitl, CurCont, DBA, DentInd, E-psyche, EMBASE, ExcerpMed, FR, FamI, H12, I05, IABS, IBR, IBZ, IDIS, INI, ISR, IndMed, Inpharma, MEDLINE, MycolAb, NSCI, P03, P30, P35, PsycInfo, PsycholAb, R10, Reac, SCI, SCOPUS, T02, THA, W07.
—BLDSC (6333.795000), CASDDS, GNLM, IE, Infotrieve, Ingenta, INIST. **CCC.**
Published by: (International Association for the Study of Pain USA), Elsevier BV (Subsidiary of: Elsevier Science & Technology), Radarweg 29, PO Box 211, Amsterdam, 1000 AE, Netherlands. TEL 31-20-4853911, FAX 31-20-4852457, JournalsCustomerServiceEMEA@elsevier.com, http://www.elsevier.nl. Ed. Dr. Allan I Basbaum.

616.994 USA ISSN 1531-6394
RC73
PAIN & CENTRAL NERVOUS SYSTEM WEEK. Text in English. 2000. w. USD 2,295 in US & Canada; USD 2,495 elsewhere; USD 2,525 combined subscription in US & Canada (print & online eds.); USD 2,755 combined subscription elsewhere (print & online eds.) (effective 2008). back issues avail. **Document type:** *Newsletter, Trade.* **Description:** Centers on all pain related issues, its medicine, and the central nervous system.
Formed by the merger of (1998-2000): Neurological Diseases & Disorders Weekly (1535-2730); (1999-2000): Pain Weekly (1535-2692)
Related titles: E-mail ed.; Online - full text ed.: ISSN 1532-4672. USD 2,295 combined subscription (online & email eds.); single user (effective 2008).
Indexed: A26, CWI, G08, H11, H12, H13, I05, M06, P10, P19, P20, P48, P53, P54, PQC.
—CIS.
Published by: NewsRx, 2727 Paces Ferry Rd SE, Ste 2-440, Atlanta, GA 30339. TEL 770-435-8286, 800-726-4550, FAX 770-435-6800, pressrelease@newsrx.com, http://www.newsrx.com. Pub. Susan Hasty TEL 770-507-7777.

616.8 CHE ISSN 0255-3910
RB128 CODEN: RCSHA8
➤ **PAIN AND HEADACHE.** Text in English. 1967. irreg., latest vol.15, 2007. price varies. reprints avail. **Document type:** *Monographic series, Academic/Scholarly.* **Description:** The latest in understanding and controlling pain.
Formerly: Research and Clinical Studies in Headache (0080-1453)
Related titles: Online - full text ed.: ISSN 1662-2820.
Indexed: ChemAb, E-psyche, IndMed, P30, SCOPUS.
—CASDDS, GNLM, IE, Infotrieve, Ingenta, INIST. **CCC.**
Published by: S. Karger AG, Allschwilerstr 10, Basel, 4055, Switzerland. TEL 41-61-3061111, FAX 41-61-3061234, karger@karger.ch, http://www.karger.ch. Ed. H Reichmann.

➤ **THE PAIN CLINIC.** *see* MEDICAL SCIENCES—Anaesthesiology

616.0472 USA ISSN 1083-0707
PAIN. CLINICAL UPDATES. Text in English. 1993. q. **Document type:** *Newsletter, Trade.* **Description:** Aims to provide accurate and timely information about pain therapy.
—BLDSC (6333.796300).
Published by: International Association for the Study of Pain, 909 NE 43rd St, Ste 306, Seattle, WA 98105-6020. TEL 206-547-6409, FAX 206-547-1703, iaspdesk@iasp-pain.org.

616.8 AUT ISSN 1681-1232
PAIN MEDICINE. Text in English. 2002. bi-m.
Related titles: Online - full text ed.: ISSN 1681-1240.
Indexed: SCOPUS.
—CCC.
Published by: V I C E R Publishing, PO Box 14, Vienna, A-1097, Austria. TEL 43-676-9568085, FAX 43-676-9568086, vicer@vicer.org, http://www.vicer.org.

616.8 USA ISSN 1526-2375
CODEN: PMAEAP
PAIN MEDICINE. Text in English. 2000. m. GBP 618 in United Kingdom to institutions; EUR 786 in Europe to institutions; USD 841 in the Americas to institutions; USD 1,212 elsewhere to institutions; GBP 712 combined subscription in United Kingdom to institutions (print & online eds.); EUR 905 combined subscription in Europe to institutions (print & online eds.); USD 967 combined subscription in the Americas to institutions (print & online eds.); USD 1,394 combined subscription elsewhere to institutions (print & online eds.) (effective 2012). adv. back issues avail.; reprints avail. **Document type:** *Journal, Academic/Scholarly.* **Description:** Presents multi-disciplinary information dedicated to the pain clinician, teacher and researcher.
Related titles: Online - full text ed.: ISSN 1526-4637. GBP 618 in United Kingdom to institutions; EUR 786 in Europe to institutions; USD 841 in the Americas to institutions; USD 1,212 elsewhere to institutions (effective 2012) (from IngentaConnect).
Indexed: A01, A03, A08, A20, A22, A26, B21, C06, C07, C08, CA, CINAHL, CurCont, E01, EMBASE, ESPM, ExcerpMed, H&SSA, H12, Inpharma, MEDLINE, P03, P30, P35, PsycInfo, PsycholAb, R09, R10, Reac, RefZh, RiskAb, SCI, SCOPUS, SD, T02, W07.
—BLDSC (6333.806000), IE, Infotrieve, Ingenta. **CCC.**
Published by: (American Academy of Pain Medicine), Wiley-Blackwell Publishing, Inc. (Subsidiary of: Wiley-Blackwell Publishing Ltd.), 111 River St, Hoboken, NJ 07030. TEL 201-748-6000, FAX 201-748-6088, info@wiley.com. Ed. Dr. Rollin M Gallagher TEL 215-823-5800 ext 3399. Adv. contact Karl Franz TEL 781-388-8470.

616.8 USA ISSN 1530-7085
RB127
PAIN PRACTICE. Text in English. 2001. bi-m. GBP 350 in United Kingdom to institutions; EUR 443 in Europe to institutions; USD 463 in the Americas to institutions; USD 684 elsewhere to institutions; GBP 404 combined subscription in United Kingdom to institutions (print & online eds.); EUR 510 combined subscription in Europe to institutions (print & online eds.); USD 532 combined subscription in the Americas to institutions (print & online eds.); USD 787 combined subscription elsewhere to institutions (print & online eds.) (effective 2012). adv. back issues avail.; reprints avail. **Document type:** *Journal, Academic/Scholarly.* **Description:** Provides a comprehensive means of surveying developments in the various areas of importance to pain practitioners.
Related titles: Online - full text ed.: ISSN 1533-2500. 2001. GBP 350 in United Kingdom to institutions; EUR 443 in Europe to institutions; USD 463 in the Americas to institutions; USD 684 elsewhere to institutions (effective 2012) (from IngentaConnect).
Indexed: A01, A03, A08, A22, A26, C06, C07, CA, E01, EMBASE, ExcerpMed, MEDLINE, P03, P30, P43, PsycInfo, PsycholAb, R10, Reac, RefZh, SCOPUS, T02.
—IE, Infotrieve, Ingenta. **CCC.**
Published by: (World Institute of Pain), Wiley-Blackwell Publishing, Inc. (Subsidiary of: Wiley-Blackwell Publishing Ltd.), 111 River St, Hoboken, NJ 07030. TEL 201-748-6000, FAX 201-748-6088, info@wiley.com. Ed. Craig Hartrick. Adv. contact Karl Franz TEL 781-388-8470.

612.88 616.047 CAN ISSN 1203-6765
RB127
➤ **PAIN RESEARCH & MANAGEMENT.** Text in English. 1996. q. CAD 95 domestic to individuals; USD 95 in United States to individuals; USD 120 elsewhere to individuals; CAD 125 domestic to institutions; USD 125 in United States to institutions; USD 160 elsewhere to institutions (effective 2005). adv. bk.rev. back issues avail. **Document type:** *Journal, Academic/Scholarly.* **Description:** Researches basic science and clinical aspects of pain and pain management.
Related titles: Online - full text ed.: ISSN 1918-1523.
Indexed: C03, C06, C07, CBCARef, EMBASE, ExcerpMed, MEDLINE, P03, P20, P22, P25, P30, P48, P54, PQC, PsycInfo, PsycholAb, R10, Reac, SCI, SCOPUS, W07.
—BLDSC (6333.813000), IE, Ingenta. **CCC.**
Published by: (Canadian Pain Society), Pulsus Group Inc., 2902 S Sheridan Way, Oakville, ON L6J 7L6, Canada. TEL 905-829-4770, FAX 905-829-4799, pulsus@pulsus.com. Ed. Dr. Harold Merskey TEL 519-679-1045. Pub. Robert B Kalina. Adv. contact Lisa Robb. B&W page CAD 2,325, color page CAD 4,100; trim 10 x 7. Circ: 18,000 (controlled).

616.8 USA ISSN 2090-1542
▼ ➤ **PAIN RESEARCH AND TREATMENT.** Text in English. 2009. irreg. USD 195 (effective 2011). **Document type:** *Journal, Academic/Scholarly.* **Description:** Publishes original research articles, review articles, case reports, and clinical studies in all aspects of pain and pain management.
Related titles: Online - full text ed.: ISSN 2090-1550. free (effective 2011).
Indexed: A01, T02.
Published by: Hindawi Publishing Corporation, 410 Park Ave, 15th Fl, PMB 287, New York, NY 10022. FAX 215-893-4392, 866-446-3294, info@hindawi.com.

616.8 PAK ISSN 1726-8710
RA790.A1
PAKISTAN PSYCHIATRIC SOCIETY. JOURNAL. Abbreviated title: J P P S. Text in English. 2003. q. **Document type:** *Journal, Academic/Scholarly.* **Description:** Dedicated to encourage and facilitate research at all levels and in all fields of psychiatry.
Related titles: Online - full text ed.: free (effective 2011).
Indexed: A01, T02.
Published by: Pakistan Psychiatric Society, c/o Dept of Psychiatry, Hamdard University Hospital, Taj Medical Complex, M.A.Jinnah Rd, Karachi, Pakistan. TEL 92-21-4534210, FAX 92-21-4311316.

616.8 SAU ISSN 1319-6995
PAN ARAB JOURNAL OF NEUROSURGERY. Text in English. 1997. s-a. **Document type:** *Journal, Academic/Scholarly.*
Indexed: EMBASE, R10, SCOPUS.
Published by: Pan Arab Neurosurgical Society, Riyadh Military Hospital, P O Box 7897, Riyadh, 11159, Saudi Arabia. TEL 966-1-4777714 ext 25443, FAX 966-1-4768273, http://www.panarabneurosurgery.org.sa.

616.83 NLD ISSN 1382-0230
PAPAVER. Text in Dutch. 1977. bi-m. EUR 30 membership (effective 2010). adv. **Document type:** *Magazine, Trade.*
Published by: Parkinson Vereniging, Postbus 46, Bunnik, 3980 CA, Netherlands. TEL 31-30-6561369, info@parkinson-vereniging.nl. Ed. Louise van der Valk. adv.: B&W page EUR 1,298, color page EUR 1,800; trim 210 x 297. Circ: 10,054.

616.833 GBR
THE PARKINSON. Text in English. 1969. q. free to members (effective 2009). adv. bk.rev.; software rev.; Website rev. 32 p./no.; **Document type:** *Magazine, Trade.* **Description:** Covers matters of interest to people with Parkinson's disease.
Related titles: Audio cassette/tape ed.
Published by: Parkinson's Disease Society of the United Kingdom, 215 Vauxhall Bridge Rd, London, SW1V 1EJ, United Kingdom. TEL 44-20-79318080, FAX 44-20-72339908, enquiries@parkinsons.org.uk.

616.833 SWE ISSN 1104-2435
PARKINSON-JOURNALEN. Text in Swedish. 1993. q. SEK 200 membership (effective 2004). **Document type:** *Journal.*
Indexed: E-psyche.
Published by: Svenska Parkinsonfoerbundet/Swedish Parkinson's Disease Association, Nybrokajen 7, Stockholm, 11848, Sweden. TEL 46-8-6119331, FAX 46-8-6119332, parkinsonforbundet@telia.se. Ed. Mareta Hagstrand.

616.8 CAN
PARKINSON POST. Text in English. q. CAD 25 to members (effective 2000). adv. back issues avail. **Document type:** *Newsletter.* **Description:** Advises readers of events, new chapters and support groups, where to get help.
Former titles: Parkinson Network (0824-7315); (until 1984): Parkinson Foundation of Canada. Bulletin (0711-236X)
Related titles: French ed.: ISSN 0845-4299.
Indexed: E-psyche.
Published by: Parkinson Foundation of Canada, 4211 Yonge St Ste 316, Toronto, ON M2P 2A9, Canada. TEL 416-227-9700, 800-565-3000, FAX 416-227-9600. Ed. Trevor Williams. Adv. contact Mara Busca. Circ: 15,000 (paid).

616.8 USA ISSN 0898-7378
PARKINSON REPORT. Text in English. 1957. q. free. charts; illus. **Document type:** *Newsletter.* **Description:** Written for people affected by Parkinson's disease and explores various areas of the research.
Formerly: National Parkinson Foundation. Newsletter
Related titles: Online - full content ed.
Indexed: B21, BiolDig, E-psyche, NSA.
Published by: National Parkinson Foundation, Inc., 1501 N W Ninth Ave/Bob Hope Rd, Miami, FL 33136-1494. TEL 305-243-6666, 800-327-4545, FAX 305-243-5595, contact@parkinson.org. Ed. Dr. Juan Sanchez Ramos.

616.8 NZL ISSN 1177-0635
THE PARKINSONIAN. Text in English. 1982. q. free to members (effective 2010). back issues avail. **Document type:** *Magazine, Trade.* **Description:** Contains news and research, a fact sheet, carer's corner and news from the divisions, as well as relevant information on Parkinson.
Related titles: Online - full text ed.: ISSN 1179-7290. free (effective 2010).
Published by: Parkinsons New Zealand, Level 3, James Smith Bldg, 55 Cuba St, Manners St, PO Box 11067, Wellington, 6142, New Zealand. TEL 64-4-4722796, FAX 64-4-4722162, info@parkinsons.org.nz.

616.8 GBR ISSN 1353-8020
RC382 CODEN: PRDIFO
➤ **PARKINSONISM & RELATED DISORDERS.** Text in English. 1995. 10/yr. EUR 826 in Europe to institutions; JPY 98,400 in Japan to institutions; USD 924 elsewhere to institutions (effective 2012). back issues avail. **Document type:** *Journal, Academic/Scholarly.* **Description:** Features basic and clinical research that contributes to the understanding, diagnosis, and treatment of all neurodegenerative syndromes, in which Parkinsonism, essential tremor, and related disorders play a part.
Related titles: Microform ed.: (from PQC); Online - full text ed.: ISSN 1873-5126 (from IngentaConnect, ScienceDirect).
Indexed: A01, A03, A08, A26, B21, C06, C07, CA, CurCont, E-psyche, EMBASE, ExcerpMed, I05, Inpharma, MEDLINE, NSA, NSCI, P03, P30, P35, PsycInfo, PsycholAb, R10, Reac, SCI, SCOPUS, T02, W07.
—BLDSC (6406.787000), GNLM, IE, Infotrieve, Ingenta. **CCC.**
Published by: Elsevier Ltd (Subsidiary of: Elsevier Science & Technology), The Blvd, Langford Ln, Kidlington, Oxford, OX5 1GB, United Kingdom. TEL 44-1865-843000, FAX 44-1865-843010, journalscustomerserviceemea@elsevier.com. Eds. R F Pfeiffer TEL 901-448-5209, Z K Wszolek TEL 904-953-7228. **Subscr. to:** Elsevier BV, Radarweg 29, PO Box 211, Amsterdam 1000 AE, Netherlands. TEL 31-20-4853757, FAX 31-20-4853432, http://www.elsevier.nl.

616.8 USA ISSN 2042-0080
RC382
▼ ➤ **PARKINSON'S DISEASE.** Text in English. 2010. irreg. free (effective 2011). **Document type:** *Journal, Academic/Scholarly.*
Media: Online - full text.
Indexed: A01, A26, C06, C07, E08, H11, H12, I05, NSA, P30, T02.
Published by: Sage - Hindawi Access to Research, 410 Park Ave, 15th Fl, 287 PMB, New York, NY 10022. FAX 866-446-3294.

➤ **PEDIATRIC NEUROLOGY.** *see* MEDICAL SCIENCES—Pediatrics

616.8 CHE ISSN 1016-2291
RD593 CODEN: PDNEEV
➤ **PEDIATRIC NEUROSURGERY.** Text in English. bi-m. CHF 1,736, EUR 1,387, USD 1,706.50 to institutions; CHF 1,905, EUR 1,522, USD 1,870.50 combined subscription to institutions (print & online eds.) (effective 2012). adv. bk.rev. back issues avail. **Document type:** *Journal, Academic/Scholarly.* **Description:** Features new information and observations in pedriatric neurosurgery and the allied fields of neuroradiology and neuropathology as they relate to the etiology of neurologic diseases and the operative care of affected patients.
Formerly (until 1991): Pediatric Neuroscience (0255-7975); Which supersedes in part (in 1985): Child's Brain (0302-2803)
Related titles: Microform ed.: (from PQC); Online - full text ed.: ISSN 1423-0305. CHF 1,685, EUR 1,348, USD 1,636 to institutions (effective 2012).
Indexed: A01, A03, A08, A22, ASCA, B21, B25, BIOSIS Prev, CA, CurCont, E-psyche, E01, EMBASE, ExcerpMed, H13, IBR, IBZ, ISR, IndMed, Inpharma, MEDLINE, MycolAb, NSA, NSCI, P02, P10, P20, P22, P30, P35, P48, P53, P54, PQC, R10, Reac, SCI, SCOPUS, T02, W07.
—BLDSC (6417.604700), CASDDS, GNLM, IE, Infotrieve, Ingenta, INIST. **CCC.**
Published by: (International Society for Paediatric Neurosurgery), S. Karger AG, Allschwilerstr 10, Basel, 4055, Switzerland. TEL 41-61-3061111, FAX 41-61-3061234, karger@karger.ch, http://www.karger.ch. Ed. D M Frim. R&P Tatjana Sepin. adv.: page CHF 2,600; trim 210 x 280. Circ: 900 (controlled).

➤ **PENNSYLVANIA MESSAGE.** *see* EDUCATION—Special Education And Rehabilitation

616.891 DEU ISSN 1433-6308
PERSOENLICHKEITSSTOERUNGEN - THEORIE UND THERAPIE. Abbreviated title: P T T. Text in German. 1997. q. EUR 98 to individuals; EUR 138 to institutions; EUR 56 to students; EUR 32 newsstand/cover (effective 2011). adv. **Document type:** *Journal, Academic/Scholarly.*
Indexed: E-psyche, P03, PsycInfo, PsycholAb.
—BLDSC (6428.017200). **CCC.**
Published by: Schattauer GmbH, Hoelderlinstr 3, Stuttgart, 70174, Germany. TEL 49-711-229870, FAX 49-711-2298750, info@schattauer.de, http://www.schattauer.com. Ed. Birgit Lang. Adv. contact Nicole Doerr. Circ: 2,150 (paid and controlled). **Subscr. to:** CSJ, Postfach 140220, Munich 80452, Germany. TEL 49-89-20959129, schattauer@csj.de.

616.8 ITA ISSN 1124-9099
PERSONALITA - DIPENDENZE. Text in Italian. 1994. 3/yr. EUR 70 domestic (effective 2010). **Document type:** *Journal, Academic/Scholarly.*
Indexed: E-psyche.
Published by: Enrico Mucchi Editore, Via Emilia Est 1527, Modena, 41100, Italy. TEL 39-059-374094, FAX 39-059-282628, info@mucchieditore.it, http://www.mucchieditore.it. **Co-sponsors:** Societa di Studio per i Disturbi di Personalita, IRET; Federazione Italiana Operatori Tossicodipendenze.

362.2 GBR ISSN 1932-8621
RC554
PERSONALITY AND MENTAL HEALTH; multidisciplinary studies from personality dysfunction to criminal behaviour. Text in English. 2007 (Apr.). q. GBP 261 in United Kingdom to institutions; EUR 304 in Europe to institutions; USD 371 elsewhere to institutions (effective 2012). adv. back issues avail. **Document type:** *Journal, Academic/Scholarly.* **Description:** Provides an authoritative source of information for researchers, practitioners and policy makers working in the field of personality and mental health.
Related titles: Online - full text ed.: GBP 261 in United Kingdom to institutions; EUR 304 in Europe to institutions; USD 371 elsewhere to institutions (effective 2012); Print ed.: ISSN 1932-863X. 2007 (Apr.). free to institutions.
Indexed: ASSIA, C06, CurCont, P03, P30, PsycInfo, SCOPUS, SSCI, W07.
—IE. **CCC.**
Published by: (Personality Disorder Institute), John Wiley & Sons Ltd. (Subsidiary of: John Wiley & Sons, Inc.), 1-7 Oldlands Way, PO Box 808, Bognor Regis, West Sussex PO21 9FF, United Kingdom. TEL 44-1865-778315, FAX 44-1243-843232, cs-journals@wiley.com, http://eu.wiley.com/WileyCDA/. Eds. Kate Davidson, Kenneth R Silk, Roger Mulder. **Subscr. to:** 1-7 Oldlands Way, PO Box 809, Bognor Regis, West Sussex PO21 9FG, United Kingdom. TEL 44-1865-778054, cs-agency@wiley.com.

PERSPECTIVES IN PSYCHIATRIC CARE; journal for advanced practice psychiatric nurses. *see* MEDICAL SCIENCES—Nurses And Nursing

371.9142 612 USA ISSN 1940-7777
➤ **PERSPECTIVES ON NEUROPHYSIOLOGY AND NEUROGENIC SPEECH AND LANGUAGE DISORDERS (ONLINE).** Text in English. 1991. q. USD 55 to individuals; USD 85 to institutions; free to members (effective 2009). adv. back issues avail. **Document type:** *Journal, Academic/Scholarly.* **Description:** Focuses on promoting, interpreting, and disseminating information that is relevant to neurogenic communication disorders and to serve as a conduit for the exchange of information and ideas among division affiliates.
Former titles: Perspectives on Neurophysiology and Neurogenic Speech and Language Disorders (Print) (1940-7769); (until 2002): American Speech-Language-Hearing Association. Special Interest Divisions. Division 2. Neurophysiology and Neurogenic Speech and Language Disorders (Print)
Media: Online - full text.
Indexed: C06, C07, P30.
Published by: American Speech-Language-Hearing Association, 2200 Research Blvd, Rockville, MD 20850. TEL 301-296-5700, FAX 301-296-8580, actioncenter@asha.org, http://www.asha.org/. Ed. Katherine Ross. Adv. contact Pamela J Leppin.

616.89 FRA ISSN 0031-6032
PERSPECTIVES PSYCHIATRIQUES. Text in French. 1963. 4/yr. EUR 117.53 combined subscription domestic (print & online eds.); EUR 174.34 combined subscription in the European Union (print & online eds.); EUR 196 combined subscription elsewhere (print & online eds.) (effective 2012). adv. bk.rev. **Document type:** *Journal, Academic/Scholarly.* **Description:** Presents multidisciplinary discussion and opinion on new methods of treatment and comprehension of mental illness.
Related titles: Online - full text ed.
Indexed: E-psyche, FR, PsycholAb, S02, S03.
—GNLM, INIST.
Published by: (Groupe d'Etudes de Psychiatrie Psychologie et Sciences Sociales), E D P Sciences, 17 Ave du Hoggar, Parc d'Activites de Courtaboeuf, BP 112, Cedex A, Les Ulis, F-91944, France. TEL 33-1-69187575, FAX 33-1-69860678, http://www.edpsciences.org. Circ: 2,500.

618.97 DEU ISSN 1863-5172
PFLEGEN: DEMENZ. Text in German. 2006. 4/yr. EUR 64; EUR 9 newsstand/cover (effective 2011). adv. **Document type:** *Journal, Academic/Scholarly.*
Related titles: Special ed(s).: Pflegen: Demenz - Materialpaket. ISSN 1863-5806. 2006.
Published by: Erhard Friedrich Verlag GmbH, Im Brande 17, Seelze, 30926, Germany. TEL 49-511-400040, FAX 49-511-40004170, info@friedrich-verlag.de, http://www.friedrich-verlag.de. Adv. contact Bianca Kraft.

616.89023105 DEU ISSN 2190-4596
▼ **PFLEGEN: PSYCHOSOZIAL.** Text in German. 2010. 4/yr. EUR 58; EUR 20 newsstand/cover (effective 2011). **Document type:** *Journal, Academic/Scholarly.*
Published by: Erhard Friedrich Verlag GmbH, Im Brande 17, Seelze, 30926, Germany. TEL 49-511-400040, FAX 49-511-40004170, info@friedrich-verlag.de, http://www.friedrich-verlag.de.

616.89 DEU ISSN 0176-3679
RM315 CODEN: PHRMEZ
➤ **PHARMACOPSYCHIATRY;** clinical pharmacology, psychiatry, psychology, neurophysiology, neurobiology, gerontopsychiatry. Text in English. 1968. bi-m. EUR 512 to institutions; EUR 642 combined subscription to institutions (print & online eds.); EUR 84 newsstand/cover (effective 2011). adv. bibl.; charts; illus.; stat. index. reprints avail. **Document type:** *Journal, Academic/Scholarly.*
Former titles: Pharmacopsychiatria (0720-4280); (until 1980): Pharmakopsychiatrie - Neuro-Psychopharmakologie (0031-7098)
Related titles: Microfiche ed.; Microfilm ed.: (from PQC); Online - full text ed.: ISSN 1439-0795. EUR 619 to institutions (effective 2011); ♦ Supplement(s): Pharmacopsychiatry. Supplement. ISSN 0936-9589.
Indexed: A01, A03, A08, A20, A22, ASCA, B25, BIOSIS Prev, CA, ChemAb, ChemTitl, CurCont, DBA, DentInd, E-psyche, EMBASE, ExcerpMed, FR, FoP, GJP, IBR, IBZ, ISR, IndMed, Inpharma, MEDLINE, MycolAb, NSCI, P03, P30, P35, PsycInfo, PsycholAb, R10, Reac, SCI, SCOPUS, T02, W07.
—BLDSC (6447.087950), CASDDS, GNLM, IE, Infotrieve, Ingenta, INIST, Linda Hall. **CCC.**
Published by: (Arbeitsgemeinschaft Neuropsychopharmakologie und Pharmakopsychiatrie), Georg Thieme Verlag, Ruedigerstr 14, Stuttgart, 70469, Germany. TEL 49-711-8931421, FAX 49-711-8931410, leser.service@thieme.de, http://www.thieme-connect.de. Ed. Dr. Walter E. Mueller. R&P Alessandra Kreibaum. adv.: B&W page EUR 1,010, color page EUR 2,105. Circ: 1,000 (paid and controlled). **Subscr. to:** Thieme Medical Publishers, 333 Seventh Ave, New York, NY 10001. custserv@thieme.com, http://www.thieme.com/journals.

616.89 DEU ISSN 0936-9589
PHARMACOPSYCHIATRY. SUPPLEMENT. Text in German. 1982. irreg. price varies. **Document type:** *Monographic series, Academic/Scholarly.*
Formerly (until 198?): Pharmacopsychiatria. Special Issue (0722-2807)
Related titles: Online - full text ed.; ♦ Supplement to: Pharmacopsychiatry. ISSN 0176-3679.
Indexed: E-psyche.
—Infotrieve, INIST. **CCC.**
Published by: Georg Thieme Verlag, Ruedigerstr 14, Stuttgart, 70469, Germany. TEL 49-711-8931421, FAX 49-711-8931410, leser.service@thieme.de, http://www.thieme.de.

PHILOSOPHY, PSYCHIATRY & PSYCHOLOGY. *see* PHILOSOPHY

PHYSIOLOGICAL RESEARCH. *see* BIOLOGY—Physiology

PHYSIOLOGY & BEHAVIOR. *see* BIOLOGY—Physiology

616.8 NLD ISSN 1574-2660
PIJN INFO. Text in Dutch. 2004. irreg. (4-6/yr.). EUR 161.70 per vol. (effective 2008).
Published by: Bohn Stafleu van Loghum B.V. (Subsidiary of: Springer Science+Business Media), Postbus 246, Houten, 3990 GA, Netherlands. TEL 31-30-6383872, FAX 31-30-6383991, boekhandels@bsl.nl, http://www.bsl.nl. Ed. Dr. B J P Crul.

616.836 MEX ISSN 1665-3254
PLASTICIDAD Y RESTAURACION NEUROLOGICA. Text in Spanish. 2003. s-a. back issues avail. **Document type:** *Journal, Academic/Scholarly.*
Related titles: Online - full text ed.
Indexed: C01, EMBASE, ExcerpMed, SCOPUS.
Published by: Asociacion Internacional en pro de la Plasticidad Cerebral, A.C., Cumbres de Acultzingo No. 83-202, Col. Vertiz Narvarte, Mexico, D.F., 03020, Mexico. TEL 52-55-55795831, FAX 52-55-55906858, http://www.plasticidadcerebral.com/. Ed. Adrian Poblano.

616.8 150 USA ISSN 1934-9785
RJ505.P6
PLAY THERAPY. Text in English. 1992. q. free to members (effective 2011). adv. **Document type:** *Magazine, Trade.* **Description:** Focuses on therapeutic aspects of play, and features information on research, techniques and resources for therapists.
Formerly (until 2006): Association for Play Therapy. Newsletter
Related titles: Online - full text ed.: free (effective 2011).
Published by: Association for Play Therapy, Inc., 3198 Willow Ave, Ste 110, Clovis, CA 93612. TEL 559zzzzh294-2128, FAX 559zzzzh294-2129, info@a4pt.org. Ed. Bill Burns TEL 559-294-2128 ext 6. Adv. contact Amber Moya TEL 559-294-2128.

616.89 NLD ISSN 1380-8095
PLUS MINUS. Text in Dutch. 1987. q. EUR 26 membership (effective 2010). bk.rev. back issues avail. **Document type:** *Newspaper, Consumer.*
Indexed: E-psyche.
Published by: Vereniging voor Manisch Depressieven en Betrokkenen, Kaap Hoorndreef 56-C, Utrecht, 3563 AV, Netherlands. TEL 31-30-2803030, FAX 31-30-2802880, vmdb@nsmd.nl.

616.89 ITA ISSN 1591-0598
RC321
POL.IT PSYCHIATRY ONLINE ITALIA. Text in Italian, English. 1995. m. **Document type:** *Journal, Consumer.*
Media: Online - full text.
Published by: Associazione Psychiatry Online Italia, Via Provana Di Leyni 13, Genoa, Italy. http://www.psychiatryonline.it/, http://www.pol-it.org/.

616.8 POL ISSN 1734-5251
➤ **POLSKI PRZEGLAD NEUROLOGICZNY.** Text in Polish. 2005. q. PLZ 66 to individuals; PLZ 132 to institutions (effective 2011). **Document type:** *Journal, Academic/Scholarly.*
Related titles: Online - full text ed.: ISSN 1734-9745.

Published by: (Polskie Towarzystwo Neurologiczne/Polish Neurological Society), Wydawnictwo Via Medica, ul Swietokrzyska 73, Gdansk, 80180, Poland. TEL 48-58-3209494, FAX 48-58-3209460, redakcja@viamedica.pl, http://www.viamedica.pl. Ed. Ryszard Podemski.

616.8 GBR ISSN 1474-7758
RC346 CODEN: PNREBG
➤ **PRACTICAL NEUROLOGY**; an international peer-reviewed journal that keeps health professionals and others up to date in all areas of neurology. Text in English. 2001. bi-m. GBP 521, EUR 703, USD 1,016 to institutions; GBP 646, EUR 872, USD 1,260 combined subscription to institutions (print & online eds.) (effective 2009); included with subscr. to: Journal of Neurology, Neurosurgery, and Psychiatry. adv. back issues avail. **Document type:** *Journal, Academic/Scholarly.* **Description:** Designed for everyone who sees neurological patients and who wants to keep up to date, and safe, in managing them.
Incorporates (2001-2005): Neurology in Practice (1473-7086)
Related titles: Online - full text ed.: ISSN 1474-7766. GBP 560, EUR 756, USD 1,092 to institutions (effective 2009); ◆ Supplement to: Journal of Neurology, Neurosurgery and Psychiatry. ISSN 0022-3050.
Indexed: A01, A03, A08, A22, A26, B21, BIOBASE, C06, C07, C08, CA, CINAHL, E01, EMBASE, ExcerpMed, IABS, JW-N, MEDLINE, NSA, P30, R10, Reac, SCOPUS, T02.
—BLDSC (6595.150000), IE, Ingenta, INIST. **CCC.**
Published by: B M J Group, BMA House, Tavistock Sq, London, WC1H 9JR, United Kingdom. TEL 44-20-73836373, FAX 44-20-73836668, http://group.bmj.com. Ed. Charles Warlow. Adv. contact Euan Currer TEL 44-20-73836181. B&W page GBP 955, color page GBP 1,690; trim 210 x 280. Circ: 2,890. **Subscr. to:** PO Box 299, London WC1H 9TD, United Kingdom. TEL 44-20-73836270, FAX 44-20-73836402, support@bmjgroup.com.

616.8 USA ISSN 2151-3791
PRACTICE MATTERS (PHILADELPHIA); journal of modern psychoanalytic treatment technique. Text in English. 2005. irreg. free (effective 2009). **Document type:** *Journal, Academic/Scholarly.*
Published by: Philadelphia School of Psychoanalysis, 313 S 16th St, Philadelphia, PA 19102. TEL 215-732-8244, FAX 215-732-8454, info@psptraining.com, http://www.psptraining.com. Ed. Raymond Gourley.

616.8 FRA ISSN 1878-7762
▼ **PRATIQUE NEUROLOGIQUE - F M C.** (Formation Medicale Continue) Text in French. 2010. q. EUR 457 in Europe to institutions; EUR 405.48 in France to institutions; JPY 75,900 in Japan to institutions; USD 608 elsewhere to institutions (effective 2012). **Document type:** *Journal, Academic/Scholarly.*
Related titles: Online - full text ed.: ISSN 1878-7770 (from ScienceDirect); ◆ Supplement(s): Pratique Neurologique - F M C. Hors-Serie. ISSN 2211-0828.
Indexed: SCOPUS.
—CCC.
Published by: Elsevier Masson (Subsidiary of: Elsevier Health Sciences), 62 Rue Camille Desmoulins, Issy les Moulineaux, Cedex 92442, France. TEL 33-1-71165500, FAX 33-1-71165600, infos@elsevier-masson.fr, http://www.elsevier-masson.fr.

616.8 FRA ISSN 2211-0828
PRATIQUE NEUROLOGIQUE - F M C. HORS-SERIE. (Formation Medicale Continue) Text in French. 200?. irreg., latest 2010. **Document type:** *Monographic series, Academic/Scholarly.*
Related titles: ◆ Supplement to: Pratique Neurologique - F M C. ISSN 1878-7762.
Published by: Elsevier Masson (Subsidiary of: Elsevier Health Sciences), 62 Rue Camille Desmoulins, Issy les Moulineaux, Cedex 92442, France. TEL 33-1-71165500, FAX 33-1-71165600, infos@elsevier-masson.fr, http://www.elsevier-masson.fr.

616.89 150 DEU ISSN 0032-7034
RJ499.A1 CODEN: PKIKAZ
➤ **PRAXIS DER KINDERPSYCHOLOGIE UND KINDERPSYCHIATRIE**; Ergebnisse aus Psychoanalyse, Psychologie und Familientherapie. Text in German; Summaries in English, German. 1952. 10/yr. EUR 74 domestic; EUR 148 foreign; EUR 47 to students; EUR 13.90 newsstand/cover (effective 2011). adv. bk.rev. abstr.; illus.; stat. index. reprints avail. **Document type:** *Journal, Academic/Scholarly.*
Indexed: A20, A22, CurCont, DIP, E-psyche, EMBASE, ExcerpMed, F09, GJP, IBR, IBZ, INI, IndMed, MEDLINE, P03, P30, PsycInfo, PsycholAb, R10, RILM, Reac, S02, S03, SCOPUS, SSCI, W07.
—BLDSC (6603.171400), GNLM, IE, Infotrieve, Ingenta, INIST. **CCC.**
Published by: Vandenhoeck und Ruprecht, Theaterstr 13, Goettingen, 37073, Germany. TEL 49-551-508440, FAX 49-551-5084422, info@v-r.de. Ed. Kay Niebank. Circ: 2,000 (paid and controlled).

616.89 USA ISSN 2155-7772
➤ **PRIMARY CARE COMPANION TO C N S DISORDERS.** (Central Nervous System) Variant title: Primary Care Companion to CNS Disorders. Text in English. 1999. bi-m. USD 30 per issue domestic to individuals (effective 2010). adv. back issues avail. **Document type:** *Journal, Academic/Scholarly.* **Description:** Strives to bring together knowledge in medicine and psychiatry to improve paient care.
Formerly (until Sep.2010): Primary Care Companion to the Journal of Clinical Psychiatry (1523-5998)
Related titles: Audio CD ed.: 2001; Online - full text ed.: ISSN 2155-7780. free (effective 2011).
Indexed: A39, C06, C07, C27, C29, D03, D04, E13, EMBASE, ExcerpMed, P30, R10, R14, Reac, S14, S15, S18, SCOPUS.
—BLDSC (6612.908205), IE. **CCC.**
Published by: Physicians Postgraduate Press, Inc., PO Box 752870, Memphis, TN 38175. TEL 901-751-3800, FAX 901-751-3444, http://www.allenpress.com.

616.8 USA ISSN 1082-6319
RC321 CODEN: PPRSC5
➤ **PRIMARY PSYCHIATRY.** Text in English. 1994. m. USD 120 (effective 2010). adv. bk.rev. back issues avail. **Document type:** *Journal, Academic/Scholarly.*
Related titles: Online - full text ed.
Indexed: A01, C06, C07, CA, E-psyche, EMBASE, ExcerpMed, P03, P30, PsycInfo, PsycholAb, R10, Reac, SCOPUS, T02.
—BLDSC (6612.912500), IE, Ingenta, INIST. **CCC.**
Published by: M B L Communications, 333 Hudson St, 7th fl, New York, NY 10013. TEL 212-328-0800, FAX 212-328-0600, primepsych@aol.com, http://www.mblcommunications.com. Ed. Dr. Norman Sussman TEL 212-328-0800 ext 220. Pub. Darren Brodeur TEL 212-328-0800 ext 227. Circ: 65,500.

599.8 FRA ISSN 1279-8304
PRIMATOLOGIE. Text in Multiple languages. 1998. a.
Indexed: P30.
Published by: (Societe Francophone de Primatologie), Centre National de la Recherche Scientifique, Institut de Neurosciences Cognitives, 31 Ch. Joseph Aiguier, Marseille, Cedex 20 13402, France. TEL 33-4-91164306, FAX 33-4-91714938.

616.853 USA
PROFILES IN SEIZURE MANAGEMENT; physician series. Text in English. irreg. (every few months). free (effective 2005).
Related titles: Online - full text ed.
Published by: Princeton Media Associates (Subsidiary of: H M P Communications, LLC), 300 Rike Dr, Ste A, Englishtown, NJ 07726. TEL 609-371-1137, FAX 609-371-2733, info@princetoncme.com.

616.8 612.821 NLD ISSN 0079-6123
QP376 CODEN: PBRRA4
➤ **PROGRESS IN BRAIN RESEARCH.** Text in English. 1963. irreg., latest vol.168, 2008. price varies. back issues avail. **Document type:** *Monographic series, Academic/Scholarly.* **Description:** Documents advances in the research of brain physiology.
Related titles: Online - full text ed.: ISSN 1875-7855. 200?.
Indexed: A22, ASCA, B21, BIOSIS Prev, CIN, CTA, ChemAb, ChemTitl, ChemoAb, DentInd, E-psyche, EMBASE, ExcerpMed, ISR, IndMed, MEDLINE, MycolAb, NSA, P30, R10, Reac, SCI, SCOPUS, W07, WildRev.
—BLDSC (6866.400000), CASDDS, GNLM, IE, Infotrieve, Ingenta, INIST. **CCC.**
Published by: Elsevier BV (Subsidiary of: Elsevier Science & Technology), Radarweg 29, PO Box 211, Amsterdam, 1000 AE, Netherlands. TEL 31-20-4853911, FAX 31-20-4852457, JournalsCustomerServiceEMEA@elsevier.com, http://www.elsevier.nl.

➤ **PROGRESS IN NEURO-PSYCHOPHARMACOLOGY & BIOLOGICAL PSYCHIATRY.** *see* PHARMACY AND PHARMACOLOGY

➤ **PROGRESS IN NEUROBIOLOGY.** *see* BIOLOGY—Physiology

616.8 USA
PROGRESS IN NEUROINFORMATICS RESEARCH. Text in English. ceased 19??; resumed 2000. irreg., latest 2000. price varies. adv. back issues avail. **Document type:** *Monographic series, Academic/Scholarly.* **Description:** Contains sophisticated and powerful information technology we are creating plays an ever more prominent role in facilitating interaction and cooperation in everyday life.
Related titles: Online - full text ed.
Indexed: E-psyche.
Published by: Psychology Press (Subsidiary of: Taylor & Francis Inc.), 325 Chestnut St, Ste 800, Philadelphia, PA 19106. TEL 800-354-1420, FAX 215-625-2940, orders@taylorandfrancis.com, http://www.psypress.com. Adv. contact Linda Hann TEL 44-1344-779945.

617.48 CHE ISSN 0079-6492
➤ **PROGRESS IN NEUROLOGICAL SURGERY.** Text in English. 1966. irreg., latest vol.24, 2009. price varies. reprints avail. **Document type:** *Monographic series, Academic/Scholarly.* **Description:** Contains critical distillations of developments of central importance to the theory and practice of neurological surgery.
Related titles: Online - full text ed.: ISSN 1662-3924.
Indexed: ChemAb, E-psyche, EMBASE, ExcerpMed, IndMed, MEDLINE, P30, R10, Reac, SCOPUS.
—GNLM, IE, Ingenta, INIST. **CCC.**
Published by: S. Karger AG, Allschwilerstr 10, Basel, 4055, Switzerland. TEL 41-61-3061111, FAX 41-61-3061234, karger@karger.ch, http://www.karger.ch. Ed. L D Lunsford.

616.8 GBR ISSN 1367-7543
PROGRESS IN NEUROLOGY AND PSYCHIATRY. Text in English. 1997. 9/yr. GBP 97 in United Kingdom to institutions; EUR 125 in Europe to institutions; USD 204 elsewhere to institutions; GBP 112 combined subscription in United Kingdom to institutions (print & online eds.); EUR 144 combined subscription in Europe to institutions (print & online eds.); USD 235 combined subscription elsewhere to institutions (print & online eds.) (effective 2012). adv. back issues avail.; reprint service avail. from PSC. **Document type:** *Journal, Academic/Scholarly.*
Related titles: Online - full text ed.: ISSN 1931-227X. GBP 97 in United Kingdom to institutions; EUR 125 in Europe to institutions; USD 204 elsewhere to institutions (effective 2012).
Indexed: C06, EMBASE, ExcerpMed, SCOPUS.
—BLDSC (6870.345000), IE, Ingenta. **CCC.**
Published by: A & M Publishing Ltd. (Subsidiary of: John Wiley & Sons Ltd.), The Atrium, Southern Gate, Chichester, PO19 8SQ, United Kingdom. http://www.escriber.com/. Pub. Tim Dean. Adv. contact Steve Ripsher TEL 44-1243-770159.

616.8 615.1 GBR ISSN 1748-2321
RM315
PROGRESS IN NEUROTHERAPEUTICS AND NEUROPSYCHOPHARMACOLOGY. Text in English. 2006 (Jan.). a. GBP 95, USD 175 to institutions; GBP 114, USD 212 combined subscription to institutions print & online eds. (effective 2008). back issues avail.; reprint service avail. from PSC. **Document type:** *Journal, Academic/Scholarly.* **Description:** Provides readers with updates of recent clinical trial results, impacts of trials on guidelines and evidence-based practice, advances in trial methodologies, and the evolution of biomarkers in trials.
Related titles: Online - full text ed.: ISSN 1748-233X. GBP 95, USD 175 to institutions (effective 2008).
Indexed: A22, B21, E01, EMBASE, ExcerpMed, NSA, P20, P48, P54, PQC, SCOPUS.
—BLDSC (6870.380250), IE. **CCC.**
Published by: Cambridge University Press, The Edinburgh Bldg, Shaftesbury Rd, Cambridge, CB2 8RU, United Kingdom. TEL 44-1223-312393, FAX 44-1223-315052, journals@cambridge.org, http://www.cambridge.org/uk. R&P Linda Nicol TEL 44-1223-325702. Adv. contact Rebecca Roberts TEL 44-1223-325083.

616.8 BRA ISSN 1679-9887
PSICANALISE & BARROCO EM REVISTA. Text in Multiple languages. 2002. s-a. free (effective 2011). **Document type:** *Journal, Academic/Scholarly.*
Media: Online - full text.
Published by: Universidade Federal de Juiz de Fora, Editora, Rua Jose Lourenco Kelmer s/n, Campus Universitario, Juiz de Fora, MG, Brazil. TEL 55-32-21023800, http://www.ufjf.br. Ed. Denise Maurano Mello.

616.8 ITA ISSN 1591-1209
PSICHE DONNA. Text in Italian. 2000. 3/yr. adv. **Document type:** *Journal, Academic/Scholarly.*
Published by: C I C Edizioni Internazionali, Corso Trieste 42, Rome, 00198, Italy. TEL 39-06-8412673, FAX 39-06-8412688, info@gruppocic.it. Ed. Emilia Costa. adv.: B&W page EUR 1,239.50, color page EUR 1,704.31; 210 x 280.

616.89 ITA ISSN 1129-0846
PSICHIATRI OGGI. Text in Italian. 1999. bi-m. adv. **Document type:** *Magazine, Trade.* **Description:** Contains original articles and case reports on psychiatric diseases and correlated matters addressed to Italian psychiatrists.
Related titles: Online - full text ed.: ISSN 1971-3738. 2007.
Indexed: RefZh.
Published by: C I C Edizioni Internazionali, Corso Trieste 42, Rome, 00198, Italy. TEL 39-06-8412673, FAX 39-06-8412688, info@gruppocic.it, http://www.gruppocic.it.

616.89 ITA ISSN 0393-361X
PSICHIATRIA DELL'INFANZIA E DELL'ADOLESCENZA. Text in Italian; Summaries in English. 1907. q. EUR 60 domestic to individuals; EUR 75 foreign to individuals; EUR 105 domestic to institutions; EUR 115 foreign to institutions (effective 2009). adv. bk.rev. charts; illus.; stat.; tr.lit. index, cum.index. **Document type:** *Journal, Academic/Scholarly.* **Description:** Encompasses all branches of psychiatry, from neonatal age to late adolescence. Comprises original research, synthetic reviews, case histories, field research, magazine reviews and more.
Former titles (until 1983): Neuropsichiatria Infantile (0028-3924); (until 1968): Infanzia Anormale (0393-3679); (until 1909): Associazione Romana per la Cura Medico - Pedagogica dei Fanciulli Anormali e Deficienti Poveri (1124-691X)
Indexed: A22, E-psyche, FR, IBR, IBZ, PsycholAb, SCOPUS.
—BLDSC (6945.843000), IE, Ingenta, INIST.
Published by: (Universita degli Studi di Roma "La Sapienza", Istituto di Neuropsichiatria Infantile), Edizioni Borla Srl, Via delle Fornaci 50, Rome, RM 00165, Italy. TEL 39-06-39376728, FAX 39-06-39376620, borla@edizioni-borla.it, http://www.edizioni-borla.it. Circ: 3,000.

616.8 ITA ISSN 1127-395X
PSICHIATRIA DI CONSULTAZIONE. Text in Italian; Summaries in Italian, English. 1998. q. EUR 50 domestic; EUR 70 foreign (effective 2008). adv. **Document type:** *Magazine, Trade.* **Description:** Contains original articles and case reports on psychiatric diseases and correlated matters addressed at Italian psychiatrists.
Related titles: Online - full text ed.: ISSN 1971-1417.
Published by: C I C Edizioni Internazionali, Corso Trieste 42, Rome, 00198, Italy. TEL 39-06-8412673, FAX 39-06-8412688, info@gruppocic.it, http://www.gruppocic.it.

616.8 150.19 ITA ISSN 1724-4919
➤ **PSICHIATRIA E PSICOTERAPIA (ROME)/ANALYTIC PSYCHOTHERAPY AND PSYCHOPATHOLOGY.** Text in English, Italian. 1982. q. EUR 31 to individuals; EUR 42 to institutions (effective 2008). adv. bk.rev. charts; illus.; stat. 96 p./no.; back issues avail.; reprints avail. **Document type:** *Journal, Academic/Scholarly.* **Description:** Features research papers by doctors worldwide in the field of analytical psychotherapy and psychopathology. Includes articles on psychiatric rehabilitation, neuroscience, psychiatry and culture.
Formerly (until 2003): Psichiatria e Psicoterapia Analitica (0393-9774)
Indexed: A22, A26, E-psyche, I05, P03, PsycInfo, PsycholAb, RefZh, S02, S03.
—GNLM, IE, Ingenta.
Published by: (Associazione Italiana Lotta allo Stigma (A I L A S)), Giovanni Fioriti Editore, Via Archimede 179, Rome, 00197, Italy. TEL 39-06-8072063, FAX 39-06-80664609, info@fioriti.it, http://www.fioriti.it. Circ: 3,000 (paid).

616.8 ITA ISSN 1973-3283
PSICHIATRIA E TERRITORIO. Text in Italian; Summaries in English. 1984. q. **Document type:** *Journal, Trade.* **Description:** Presents the experiences of psychiatric staff in general hospital and therapeutic community situations.
Indexed: E-psyche.
Published by: (Centro Studi Psichiatria e Territorio), Teseo Ricerche Editore, Corso Italia 108, Pisa, 56125, Italy. TEL 39-050-501040, FAX 39-050-502434.

616.8 ITA ISSN 0555-5299
PSICHIATRIA GENERALE E DELL'ETA EVOLUTIVA. Text in Italian. q. **Document type:** *Journal, Academic/Scholarly.*
Indexed: DIP, E-psyche, IBR, IBZ, PsycholAb, RefZh, S02, S03.
Published by: Editrice la Garangola, Via E dalla Costa 6, Padua, 35129, Italy. TEL 39-049-8075557, FAX 39-049-7806580, info@garangola.it, http://www.garangola.it.

616.8 ITA ISSN 1828-0803
PSICOANALISI CORPOREA. Text in Italian. 2006. a. EUR 60 (effective 2009). **Document type:** *Journal, Academic/Scholarly.*
Published by: Fabrizio Serra Editore (Subsidiary of: Accademia Editoriale), c/o Accademia Editoriale, Via Santa Bibbiana 28, Pisa, 56127, Italy. TEL 39-050-542332, FAX 39-050-574888, accademiaeditoriale@accademiaeditoriale.it, http://www.libraweb.net.

616.8 ITA ISSN 1591-2795
PSICOANALISI FORENSE. Text in Italian. 2000. a. EUR 60 combined subscription domestic to institutions; EUR 150 combined subscription foreign to institutions (effective 2009). **Document type:** *Journal, Academic/Scholarly.*
Related titles: Online - full text ed.: ISSN 1724-0603.
Published by: Fabrizio Serra Editore (Subsidiary of: Accademia Editoriale), c/o Accademia Editoriale, Via Santa Bibbiana 28, Pisa, 56127, Italy. TEL 39-050-542332, FAX 39-050-574888, accademiaeditoriale@accademiaeditoriale.it, http://www.libraweb.net.

616.891 ARG ISSN 1668-3870
PSICOANALISIS: AYER Y HOY. Text in Spanish. 2004. s-a. **Document type:** *Journal, Academic/Scholarly.*
Media: Online - full text.
Published by: Asociacion Escuela Argentina de Psicoterapia para Graduados, Julian Alvarez 1933, Buenos Aires, CDHA1425, Argentina. TEL 54-11-48661602, http://www.aeapg.org.ar.

PSICOFARMACOLOGIA. *see* PHARMACY AND PHARMACOLOGY

PSICOMOTRICITA; terapia, prevenzione, formazione. *see* PSYCHOLOGY

616.89 ESP ISSN 0211-5549
CODEN: PSICE3
➤ **PSICOPATOLOGIA.** Text in Spanish. 1981. q. back issues avail.; reprints avail. **Document type:** *Journal, Academic/Scholarly.*
Related titles: Online - full text ed.
Indexed: A22, E-psyche, PsycholAb, S02, S03.
—BLDSC (6945.864000), GNLM, IE, Ingenta. **CCC.**
Published by: (Instituto de Psiquiatras de Lengua Espanola), Promolibro, Psyli.com, C/San Juan de la Cruz 9, Valencia, 46009, Spain. TEL 34-96-3662017, FAX 34-96-3665132, info@psyli.com, http://www.psyli.com. Ed. Francisco Alonso Hernandez. **Co-sponsor:** Asociacion Espanola de Psiquiatria y Psicopatologia.

➤ **PSICOTECH.** *see* PSYCHOLOGY

➤ **PSICOTERAPIA COGNITIVA E COMPORTAMENTALE.** *see* PSYCHOLOGY

616.891 001.3 ITA ISSN 0394-2864
PSICOTERAPIA E SCIENZE UMANE. Text in Italian. 1967. q. EUR 69 combined subscription domestic to institutions (print & online eds.); EUR 114 combined subscription foreign to institutions (print & online eds.) (effective 2009). **Document type:** *Journal, Academic/Scholarly.*
Related titles: Online - full text ed.: ISSN 1972-5043.
Indexed: DIP, E-psyche, IBR, IBSS, IBZ, P03, PhilInd, PsycInfo, PsycholAb, SCOPUS, SociolAb.
Published by: Franco Angeli Edizioni, Viale Monza 106, Milan, 20127, Italy. TEL 39-02-2837141, FAX 39-02-26144793, redazioni@francoangeli.it, http://www.francoangeli.it.

616.89 ITA ISSN 1721-0135
PSICOTERAPIA PSICOANALITICA. Text in Italian. 1994. s-a. EUR 45 domestic to individuals; EUR 50 foreign to individuals; EUR 70 domestic to institutions; EUR 80 foreign to institutions (effective 2009). **Document type:** *Journal, Academic/Scholarly.*
Indexed: E-psyche, P03, PsycInfo.
Published by: Edizioni Borla Srl, Via delle Fornaci 50, Rome, RM 00165, Italy. TEL 39-06-39376728, FAX 39-06-39376620, borla@edizioni-borla.it, http://www.edizioni-borla.it.

150 616.891 ITA ISSN 1828-5198
PSICOTERAPIA, PSICOTERAPIE; la lettera della psicoterapia italiana. Text in Italian. 2000. s-a. EUR 18 domestic to institutions; EUR 27.50 foreign to institutions (effective 2009). **Document type:** *Journal, Academic/Scholarly.*
Published by: (Federazione Italiana Associazioni di Psicoterapia), Franco Angeli Edizioni, Viale Monza 106, Milan, 20127, Italy. TEL 39-02-2837141, FAX 39-02-26144793, redazioni@francoangeli.it, http://www.francoangeli.it.

616.89 ROM ISSN 1841-4877
PSIHIATRU.RO. Text in Romanian. 2005. q. ROL 90 (effective 2011). adv. **Document type:** *Magazine, Trade.*
Related titles: Online - full text ed.: ISSN 2066-821X. 2009.
Published by: Versa Puls Media, s.r.l., Calea Rahovei 266-268, corp 1, etaj 2, Bucharest, 050912, Romania. TEL 40-31-4254040, FAX 40-31-4254041, office@pulsmedia.ro. Ed. Dr. Catalina Tudose. Adv. contact George Pavel. Circ: 1,000 (paid).

616.8 SRB ISSN 0350-2538
CODEN: AZMZB7
➤ **PSIHIJATRIJA DANAS/PSYCHIATRY TODAY.** Text in English, Serbian. 1969. q. USD 30 foreign to individuals; USD 60 foreign to institutions (effective 2011). adv. bk.rev. **Document type:** *Journal, Academic/Scholarly.* **Description:** Contains review papers, research articles, general articles, brief communications, congress calendar.
Formerly: Zavod za Mentalno Zdravlje. Anali (0350-1442)
Indexed: A22, B25, BIOSIS Prev, E-psyche, MycolAb, P03, PsycInfo, PsycholAb, S02, S03, YAE&RB.
—BLDSC (6945.873000), IE, Ingenta.
Published by: (Udruzenje Psihijatara Srbije/Serbian Psychiatric Association), Institut za Mentalno Zdravlje/Institute for Mental Health, Palmoticeva 37, Belgrade, 11000. imz@imh.org.rs. Ed. Dusica Lecic-Tosevski. Circ: 700.

616.8 TUR ISSN 1309-0658
▼ ➤ **PSIKIYATRIDE GUNCEL YAKLASIMLAR/CURRENT APPROACHES IN PSYCHIATRY**; psikiyatrik egitim ve guncelleme dergisi / a journal of psychiatric education and update. Text in English, Turkish. 2009. a. free (effective 2009). cum.index. back issues avail. **Document type:** *Journal, Academic/Scholarly.*
Related titles: Online - full text ed.: ISSN 1309-0674. free (effective 2011).
Indexed: A01, P20, P48, P54, PQC, PsycInfo, SCOPUS, T02.
Address: Cukurova University, Faculty of Medicine, Department of Psychiatry, Balcali, Adana 01330, Turkey. TEL 90-506-5321792, FAX 90-322-3386505, http://cukurovatip.cu.edu.tr/psikiyatri. Ed. Lut Tamam.

616.89 MEX ISSN 0187-4543
PSIQIATRIA. Text in Spanish. 1968. 3/yr.
Indexed: C01, P03, PsycholAb.
Published by: Asociacion Psiquiatrica Mexicana, Periferico Sur No. 4194, Desp. 101, Col. Jardines del Pedregal, Mexico, DF 01900, Mexico. TEL 52-56-525576, FAX 52-56-525516, apm@mercanet.com.mx. Ed. Hector Ortega Soto.

150 COL ISSN 0121-8913
PSIQUE. Text in Spanish. 1991. s-a. USD 7 newsstand/cover (effective 2000). **Document type:** *Journal, Academic/Scholarly.*
Published by: Universidad de Antioquia, Facultad de Ciencias Sociales y Humanas, Apod. Aereo 1226, Medellin, ANT, Colombia. TEL 57-4-210-5763, FAX 57-4-210-5764, cspsique@antares.udea.edu.co.

150 BRA ISSN 1677-3179
PSIQUE. Text in Portuguese. 2002. m. BRL 94.80 (effective 2006). **Document type:** *Journal, Academic/Scholarly.*
Published by: Editora Escala Ltda., Av Prof Ida Kolb, 551, Casa Verde, Sao Paulo, 02518-000, Brazil. TEL 55-11-38552100, FAX 55-11-38579643, escala@escala.com.br, http://www.escala.com.br.

616.89 ARG ISSN 1851-8729
PSIQUIATRIA. Text in Spanish. 2008. q. **Document type:** *Journal, Academic/Scholarly.*
Published by: Sciens Editorial, Scalabrini Ortiz 3183 2o. A, Buenos Aires, Argentina. TEL 54-11-48028775, 54-11-48028775, info@sciens.com.ar, http://www.sciens.com.ar/.

616.8 ESP ISSN 1134-5934
PSIQUIATRIA BIOLOGICA. Text in Spanish. 1994. bi-m. EUR 137.66 combined subscription to individuals print & online eds.; EUR 399.02 combined subscription to institutions print & online eds. (effective 2009). back issues avail. **Document type:** *Journal, Academic/Scholarly.*
Related titles: CD-ROM ed.: ISSN 1696-9138. 2002; Online - full text ed.: ISSN 1578-8962. 1997. EUR 87.79 (effective 2009).
Indexed: E-psyche, EMBASE, ExcerpMed, R10, Reac.
—**CCC.**
Published by: (Sociedad Espanola de Psiquiatria Biologica), Elsevier Doyma (Subsidiary of: Elsevier Health Sciences), Traversa de Gracia 17-21, Barcelona, 08021, Spain. TEL 34-932-418800, FAX 34-932-419020, editorial@elsevier.com. Ed. Julio Vallejo Ruilabe. Circ: 1,000.

616.8 BRA ISSN 0104-7787
CODEN: PSBIFL
➤ **PSIQUIATRIA BIOLOGICA.** Text in Portuguese, Spanish; Summaries in English, Portuguese, Spanish. 1993. q. BRL 48, USD 80 (effective 2004). bk.rev. abstr.; bibl.; charts; illus. back issues avail. **Document type:** *Journal, Academic/Scholarly.* **Description:** Presents studies in clinical psychiatry. Biological psychiatry.
Indexed: C01, ChemAb, E-psyche, SCOPUS.
—BLDSC (6945.933000), IE, Ingenta, INIST.
Published by: Associacao Brasileira de Psiquiatria Biologica, Rua do Ouro 686, Serra, Belo Horizonte, MG 30220-000, Brazil. TEL 55-31-223-2389, FAX 55-31-223-2197. Eds. Carlos Roberto Hojaij, Delcir da Costa. R&P, Adv. contact Julia da Costa. Circ: 5,000 (paid and controlled).

616.8 PRT ISSN 1646-9941
PSIQUIATRIA BIOLOGICA (PORTUGUESE EDITION). Text in Portuguese. 2006. bi-m. **Document type:** *Journal, Trade.*
Published by: (Sociedad Espanola de Psiquiatria Biologica ESP), Medicografica Edicoes Medicas, Rua Camilo Castelo Branco 23-5, Lisbon, 1150-083, Portugal. geral@medicografica.pt, http://www.medicografica.pt.

616.89 MEX ISSN 0188-736X
PSIQUIS. Text in Spanish. 1992. bi-m. back issues avail. **Document type:** *Bulletin, Consumer.*
Indexed: C01.
Published by: Hospital Psiquiatrico Fray Bernardino Alvarez, Ave San Buenaventura s-n, Esq Nino de Jesus, Tlalpan, 14000, Mexico. TEL 52-55-55731500. Ed. Jesus Gutierrez Aguilar.

616.89 GRC ISSN 1105-2333
PSUHIATRIKE/PSYCHIATRIKI. Text in English, Greek. 1990. q. bk.rev. **Document type:** *Journal, Academic/Scholarly.*
Indexed: P03, PsycInfo, PsycholAb.
Published by: Ellenike Psuhiatrike Etaireia/Hellenic Psychiatric Association, 11 Papadiamantopoulou Str., Athens, 11528, Greece. TEL 30-210-7291389, FAX 30-210-7289321, psych@psych.gr, http://www.psych.gr. Ed. George N. Christodoulou.

616.81 DEU ISSN 0949-1619
➤ **PSYCH. PFLEGE HEUTE**; Fachzeitschrift fuer die psychiatrische Pflege. Variant title: Psychiatrische Pflege Heute. Text in German. 1995. bi-m. EUR 92 to institutions; EUR 123 combined subscription to institutions (print & online eds.); EUR 30 newsstand/cover (effective 2011). adv. back issues avail.; reprints avail. **Document type:** *Journal, Academic/Scholarly.*
Related titles: Online - full text ed.: ISSN 1439-0213. EUR 118 to institutions (effective 2011).
Indexed: A22, E-psyche.
—GNLM, IE, Infotrieve. **CCC.**
Published by: Georg Thieme Verlag, Ruedigerstr 14, Stuttgart, 70469, Germany. TEL 49-711-8931421, FAX 49-711-8931410, kunden.service@thieme.de. Ed. Hilde Schaedle Deiniger. Pub. Albrecht Hauff. R&P Peter Eich. Adv. contact Manfred Marggraf. color page EUR 2,390, B&W page EUR 1,280; 175 x 250. Circ: 1,900 (paid).

616.8 FRA ISSN 1767-3143
PSYCHANALYSE, MEDECINE ET SOCIETE. Text in French. 2004. irreg. back issues avail. **Document type:** *Monographic series, Academic/Scholarly.*
Published by: L' Harmattan, 5 Rue de l'Ecole Polytechnique, Paris, 75005, France. TEL 33-1-43257651, FAX 33-1-43258203.

616.89 NLD ISSN 1385-4585
PSYCHE EN GELOOF. Text in Dutch. 1990. q. EUR 35 to individuals; EUR 55 to institutions (effective 2008). adv. bk.rev.
Indexed: A21, P03, PsycInfo, PsycholAb.
Published by: Christelijke Vereniging voor Psychiaters, Psychologen en Psychotherapeuten, c/o A T Hegger, Jan Luykenstraat 23, Utrecht, 3521 VB, Netherlands. at.hegger@worldonline.nl. adv.: page EUR 200; trim 195 x 250. Circ: 450.

616.89 NLD
DE PSYCHIATER (BELGIUM EDITION). Text in Dutch. 2008. 4/yr. adv. **Document type:** *Magazine, Trade.*
Published by: Benecke, Arena Boulevard 61-75, Amsterdam, 1101 DL, Netherlands. TEL 31-20-7150600, FAX 31-20-6918446. Pub. Wijnand van Djik. Adv. contact Linda van Iwaarden. color page EUR 2,961; 210 x 297. Circ: 1,000.

616.89 NLD
DE PSYCHIATER (DUTCH EDITION). Text in Dutch. 1994. 10/yr. adv. **Document type:** *Magazine, Trade.*
Published by: Benecke, Arena Boulevard 61-75, Amsterdam, 1101 DL, Netherlands. TEL 31-20-7150600, FAX 31-20-6918446. Pub. Wijnand van Djik. Adv. contact Linda van Iwaarden. color page EUR 2,961; 210 x 297. Circ: 3,000.

616.8 POL ISSN 1732-9841
➤ **PSYCHIATRIA/PSYCHIATRY.** Text in Polish. 2004. q. EUR 39 to individuals; EUR 59 to institutions (effective 2011). **Document type:** *Journal, Academic/Scholarly.*
Related titles: Online - full content ed.: ISSN 1733-4594.
Indexed: EMBASE, ExcerpMed, SCOPUS.
Published by: Wydawnictwo Via Medica, ul Swietokrzyska 73, Gdansk, 80180, Poland. TEL 48-58-3209494, FAX 48-58-3209460, redakcja@viamedica.pl, http://www.viamedica.pl. Ed. Jerzy Landowski.

616.89 HRV ISSN 0353-5053
CODEN: PSYDEI
PSYCHIATRIA DANUBINA. Text in Croatian. 1989. q. EUR 50 to individuals; EUR 75 to institutions (effective 2005). **Document type:** *Journal, Academic/Scholarly.*
Indexed: A26, E-psyche, EMBASE, ExcerpMed, MEDLINE, P03, P30, PsycInfo, PsycholAb, R10, RILM, Reac, SCI, SCOPUS, SSA, SSCI, SociolAb, W07.
—BLDSC (6946.124000), GNLM, IE, Ingenta.
Published by: (Sveuciliste u Zagrebu, Medicinski Fakultet), Medicinska Naklada Co., Cankarova 13, PP 525, Zagreb, 10000, Croatia. TEL 385-1-3779444, FAX 385-1-3779450, marketing@medicinskanaklada.hr, http://www.medicinskanaklada.hr.

616.8 FIN ISSN 0079-7227
RC321 CODEN: PSFNBI
PSYCHIATRIA FENNICA/FINNISH PSYCHIATRY. Text mainly in English. 1970. a. price varies. adv. bk.rev. **Document type:** *Academic/Scholarly.*
Related titles: Supplement(s): ISSN 0358-5697. 1976.
Indexed: E-psyche, P03, PsycholAb.
—BLDSC (6946.160000), GNLM, IE, Ingenta, INIST.
Published by: (Foundation for Psychiatric Research in Finland), Psychiatria Fennica, Fredrikinkatu 71 A 4, Helsinki, 00100, Finland. TEL 358-9-47706699, FAX 358-9-47706611. Ed. J K Lonnqvist. R&P, Adv. contact Ani Ostamo TEL 358-9-494-077. Circ: 1,600.

616.8 FIN ISSN 0359-1034
CODEN: MPFEE8
PSYCHIATRIA FENNICA. MONOGRAPHS/PSYCHIATRIA FENNICAN MONOGRAFIASARJA. Text in English, Finnish. 1970. irreg. price varies. **Document type:** *Monographic series, Academic/Scholarly.*
Former titles (until 1977): Psychiatria Fennica. Monographs from (0355-7707); (until 1976): Helsinki University Central Hospital. Psychiatric Clinic. Monographs (0073-1722)
Indexed: E-psyche, PsycholAb.
Published by: Psychiatria Fennica, Fredrikinkatu 71 A 4, Helsinki, 00100, Finland. TEL 358-9-47706699, FAX 358-9-47706611. Circ: 900.

616.8 FIN ISSN 0359-3207
PSYCHIATRIA FENNICA. REPORTS. Key Title: Reports of Psychiatria Fennica. Text mainly in Finnish. 1970. irreg. price varies.
Former titles (until 1979): Psychiatria Fennica. Julkaisusarja (0355-7693); (until 1976): Helsingin Yliopisto Keskussairaala. Psykiatrian Klinikka. Julkaisusarja (0073-1730)
Indexed: E-psyche, PsycholAb.
—INIST.
Published by: (Foundation for Psychiatric Research in Finland), Psychiatria Fennica, Fredrikinkatu 71 A 4, Helsinki, 00100, Finland. FAX 358-9-409663. Ed. Marti Heikkinen. R&P, Adv. contact Ani Ostamo TEL 358-9-494-077. Circ: 400.

616.89 HUN ISSN 0237-7896
CODEN: PSHUFJ
PSYCHIATRIA HUNGARICA. Text in Hungarian. 1986. q. **Document type:** *Journal, Academic/Scholarly.*
Indexed: A22, EMBASE, ExcerpMed, MEDLINE, P03, P30, PsycInfo, R10, Reac, SCOPUS.
—BLDSC (6946.185000), IE, Ingenta.
Published by: Magyar Pszichologiai Tarsasag, PO Box 41, Budapest, 1281, Hungary. TEL 36-1-2006533, FAX 36-1-2750000, http://www.mpt.iif.hu.

616.89 POL ISSN 0033-2674
CODEN: PSPOB3
➤ **PSYCHIATRIA POLSKA.** Text in Polish; Summaries in English, French, German, Russian. 1923. bi-m. EUR 50 foreign (effective 2008). adv. bk.rev. abstr.; bibl.; illus. index. 150 p./no. 1 cols./p.; Supplement avail.; back issues avail. **Document type:** *Journal, Academic/Scholarly.* **Description:** Publishes research, clinical experimental reports and theoretical papers in the field of psychiatry.
Supersedes in part (in 1967): Neurologia, Neurochirurgia i Psychiatria Polska (1233-2410)
Related titles: Online - full text ed.
Indexed: A22, BibInd, CA, ChemAb, E-psyche, EMBASE, ExcerpMed, F09, INI, IndMed, MEDLINE, P03, P30, PsycInfo, PsycholAb, R10, Reac, S02, S03, SCI, SCOPUS, T02, W07.
—BLDSC (6946.210000), GNLM, IE, Infotrieve, Ingenta, INIST.
Published by: Polskie Towarzystwo Psychiatryczne, ul Jana Sobieskiego 9, Warsaw, 02957, Poland. Ed., Pub., R&P, Adv. contact Jerzy W Aleksandrowicz. page PLZ 1,600. Circ: 1,500. **Dist. by:** Ars Polona, Obroncow 25, Warsaw 03933, Poland. TEL 48-22-5098609, FAX 48-22-5098610, arspolona@arspolona.com.pl, http://www.arspolona.com.pl.

616.89 SVK ISSN 1335-9584
➤ **PSYCHIATRIA PRE PRAX.** Text in Slovak. 2002. bi-m. EUR 18 (effective 2010). **Document type:** *Journal, Academic/Scholarly.*
Published by: Solen, s.r.o., Uprkova 23, Bratislava, 811 04, Slovakia. TEL 421-2-54650649, FAX 421-2-54651384, solen@solen.sk. Ed. Jana Repiska.

616.8 SVK ISSN 1335-423X
➤ **PSYCHIATRIA, PSYCHOTERAPIA, PSYCHOSOMATIKA.** Text in Slovak. 1994. q. EUR 63.40 in Europe; EUR 72 elsewhere (effective 2011). **Document type:** *Journal, Academic/Scholarly.*
Related titles: Online - full text ed.
Indexed: A22.
—IE.
Published by: (Psychiatricka Nemocnica Philippa Pinela), Slovak Academic Press Ltd., Nam Slobody 6, PO Box 57, Bratislava, 81005, Slovakia. TEL 421-2-55421729, FAX 421-2-55565862, sap@sappress.sk, http://www.sappress.sk. Ed. Pavel Cernak. **Dist. by:** Slovart G.T.G. s.r.o., Krupinska 4, PO Box 152, Bratislava 85299, Slovakia. TEL 421-2-63839472, FAX 421-2-63839485, info@slovart-gtg.sk, http://www.slovart-gtg.sk.

616.89 USA ISSN 0048-5713
RC321 CODEN: PSANCS
➤ **PSYCHIATRIC ANNALS**; a journal of continuing psychiatric education. Text in English. 1971. m. USD 229 combined subscription to individuals (print & online eds.); USD 379 combined subscription to institutions (print & online eds.); USD 39 per issue (effective 2010). bk.rev. illus. index. reprints avail. **Document type:** *Journal, Academic/Scholarly.* **Description:** Provides a thorough, multi-authored look at a single topic in psychiatry.
Related titles: Microform ed.: (from PQC); Online - full text ed.: ISSN 1938-2456.
Indexed: A20, A22, AMHA, ASCA, CA, Chicano, CurCont, E-psyche, Faml, H04, IBR, IBZ, MEA&I, P02, P03, P10, P12, P20, P22, P25, P26, P30, P48, P53, P54, PQC, PsycInfo, PsycholAb, RILM, S02, S03, SCOPUS, SSCI, T02, W07.
—BLDSC (6946.212000), GNLM, IE, Infotrieve, Ingenta. **CCC.**
Published by: Slack, Inc., 6900 Grove Rd, Thorofare, NJ 08086. TEL 856-848-1000, FAX 856-848-6091, customerservice@slackinc.com, http://www.slackinc.com. Ed. Dr. Jan Fawcett. Adv. contact Kara Datz TEL 856-848-1000 ext 549.

616.89 USA ISSN 0193-953X
RC321
➤ **PSYCHIATRIC CLINICS OF NORTH AMERICA.** Text in English. 1978. q. USD 473 in United States to institutions; USD 589 elsewhere to institutions (effective 2012). adv. bibl.; illus. index, cum.index. back issues avail.; reprints avail. **Document type:** *Journal, Academic/ Scholarly.* **Description:** Updates you on the latest trends in patient management and provides a sound basis for choosing treatment options.
Related titles: Online - full text ed.: ISSN 1558-3147 (from ScienceDirect); Spanish Translation: Clinicas Psiquiatricas de Norteamerica. ISSN 1885-9062.
Indexed: A20, A22, AMHA, ASCA, C06, C07, C08, CINAHL, CurCont, E-psyche, EMBASE, ExcerpMed, F09, FR, Faml, IndMed, Inpharma, MEDLINE, P03, P30, PsycInfo, PsycholAb, S02, S03, SCOPUS, SSCI, W07.
—BLDSC (6946.212500), GNLM, IE, Infotrieve, Ingenta, INIST. **CCC.**
Published by: W.B. Saunders Co. (Subsidiary of: Elsevier Health Sciences), Elsevier, Health Sciences Division, Order Fulfillment, 3251 Riverport Ln, Maryland Heights, MO 63043. TEL 314-872-8370, 800-325-4177, FAX 314-432-1380, JournalCustomerService-usa@elsevier.com, http://www.us.elsevierhealth.com. Adv. contact Don Scholz TEL 215-239-3537.

➤ **PSYCHIATRIC GENETICS.** *see* BIOLOGY—Genetics

616.89 USA ISSN 0033-2704
RC321
PSYCHIATRIC NEWS. Text in English. 1948. s-m. USD 111 combined subscription domestic to individuals (print & online eds.); USD 167 combined subscription foreign to individuals (print & online eds.); USD 111 combined subscription domestic to institutions (print & online eds.); USD 199 combined subscription foreign to institutions (print & online eds.) (effective 2011). adv. bk.rev. stat. back issues avail.; reprints avail. **Document type:** *Newspaper, Academic/Scholarly.* **Description:** Covers clinical and research news pertinent to the field of psychiatry.
Formerly (until 1966): American Psychiatric Association. Newsletter
Related titles: Microform ed.: (from PQC); Online - full text ed.: ISSN 1559-1255. USD 101 to individuals (effective 2011).
Indexed: A22, AC&P, E-psyche, IPARL, P20, P25, P30, P48, P54, PQC, SWR&A.
—BLDSC (6946.215000), GNLM, IE, Infotrieve. **CCC.**
Published by: (American Psychiatric Association), American Psychiatric Publishing, Inc., 1000 Wilson Blvd, Ste 1825, Arlington, VA 22209. TEL 703-907-7860, 800-368-5777, appi@psych.org, http://www.appi.org. Ed. James P Krajeski. Adv. contact Valentin Torres TEL 212-904-0375. Circ: 31,375. **Subscr. to:** PO Box 97250, Washington, DC 20090.

616.89 USA ISSN 0033-2720
RC321 CODEN: PSQUAP
➤ **PSYCHIATRIC QUARTERLY.** Text in English. 1927. q. EUR 1,026, USD 1,068 combined subscription to institutions (print & online eds.) (effective 2012). adv. back issues avail.; reprint service avail. from PSC. **Document type:** *Journal, Academic/Scholarly.* **Description:** Brings out research, theoretical papers, and review articles on the assessment, treatment, and rehabilitation of persons with psychiatric disabilities.
Formerly (until 1927): State Hospital Quarterly
Related titles: Microform ed.: (from PQC); Online - full text ed.: ISSN 1573-6709 (from IngentaConnect).
Indexed: A01, A03, A08, A22, A26, AHCMS, AMHA, ASCA, ASSIA, B21, B25, BIOSIS Prev, BibLing, CA, CMHR, Chicano, CurCont, E-psyche, E01, EMBASE, ExcerpMed, FR, Faml, H12, HospLI, IPsyAb, IndMed, MEDLINE, MLA-IB, MycolAb, NSA, P03, P10, P12, P20, P22, P25, P30, P43, P48, P53, P54, PCI, PQC, PsycInfo, PsycholAb, R10, Reac, S02, S03, SCOPUS, SOPODA, SSCI, SociolAb, T02, W07.
—BLDSC (6946.240000), GNLM, IE, Infotrieve, Ingenta, INIST. **CCC.**
Published by: Springer New York LLC (Subsidiary of: Springer Science+Business Media), 233 Spring St, New York, NY 10013. TEL 212-460-1500, FAX 212-460-1575, service-ny@springer.com, http://www.springer.com/. Ed. Jeffrey Borenstein.

616.89 362.2 USA ISSN 1095-158X
RC439.5
➤ **PSYCHIATRIC REHABILITATION JOURNAL.** Abbreviated title: P R J. Text in English. 1995. q. USD 250 domestic to institutions; USD 270 foreign to institutions; USD 310 combined subscription domestic to institutions (print & online eds.); USD 330 combined subscription foreign to institutions (print & online eds.) (effective 2011). adv. bk.rev. back issues avail.; reprints avail. **Document type:** *Journal, Academic/ Scholarly.* **Description:** Provides information relevant to the rehabilitation of persons with severe psychiatric disability. Publishes papers from mental health and rehabilitation professionals, consumers and family members.
Formed by the merger of (1976-1995): Psychosocial Rehabilitation Journal (0147-5622); (1991-1995): Innovations and Research (1062-7553)
Related titles: Microfilm ed.; Online - full text ed.: ISSN 1559-3126. USD 250 to institutions (effective 2011).
Indexed: A01, A02, A03, A08, A20, A22, AMED, AMHA, ASCA, C06, C07, C08, CA, CINAHL, CJA, CMHR, CurCont, E-psyche, EMBASE, ExcerpMed, Faml, H13, IndMed, M01, M02, MEDLINE, NurAb, P03, P10, P19, P20, P22, P24, P25, P26, P30, P34, P53, P54, PQC, PsycInfo, PsycholAb, R09, R10, RILM, Reac, RehabLit, S02, S03, SCOPUS, SOPODA, SSCI, SWR&A, SociolAb, T02, W07.
—BLDSC (6946.240400), IE, Infotrieve, Ingenta. **CCC.**
Published by: Boston University, Sargent College of Health and Rehabilitation Sciences, PO Box 1831, Birmingham, AL 35201. TEL 205-995-1567, 800-633-4931, FAX 205-995-1588, psyrehab@bu.edu. Eds. Judity A Cook, Kenneth J. Gill, William A Anthony. **Co-sponsor:** U.S. Psychiatric Rehabilitation Association.

616.89 USA ISSN 1075-2730
RC443.A1 CODEN: PSSEFQ
➤ **PSYCHIATRIC SERVICES.** Text in English. 1950. m. USD 119 combined subscription domestic to individuals (print & online eds.); USD 178 combined subscription foreign to individuals (print & online eds.); USD 246 combined subscription domestic to institutions (print & online eds.); USD 354 combined subscription foreign to institutions (print & online eds.) (effective 2011). adv. bk.rev.; video rev. charts; illus.; stat. index. back issues avail.; reprints avail. **Document type:** *Journal, Academic/Scholarly.* **Description:** Designed for mental health professionals and others concerned with treatment and services for persons with mental illnesses and mental disabilities.
Former titles (until 1994): Hospital and Community Psychiatry (0022-1597); (until 1966): Mental Hospitals (0096-5502); (until 1951): A P A Mental Hospital Service Bulletin
Related titles: Microform ed.: (from MIM, PQC); Online - full text ed.: ISSN 1557-9700. USD 107 to individuals (effective 2011).
Indexed: A20, A22, AHCMS, AMED, ASCA, C06, C07, C08, C28, CA, CINAHL, CLFP, ChPerI, Chicano, CurCont, E-psyche, EMBASE, ExcerpMed, F09, FR, Faml, HospLI, INI, IPsyAb, ISR, IndMed, Inpharma, JW-P, JW-WH, MEDLINE, MRD, P03, P10, P12, P20, P21, P22, P24, P25, P30, P34, P35, P48, P53, P54, PC&CA, PQC, PsycInfo, PsycholAb, R10, RILM, Reac, S02, S03, SCI, SCOPUS, SSCI, SWR&A, T02, V&AA, W07.
—BLDSC (6946.242300), GNLM, IE, Infotrieve, Ingenta, INIST. **CCC.**
Published by: (American Psychiatric Association), American Psychiatric Publishing, Inc., 1000 Wilson Blvd, Ste 1825, Arlington, VA 22209. TEL 703-907-7884, 800-368-5777, FAX 703-907-1095, appi@psych.org, http://www.appi.org. Ed. Howard H Goldman. Adv. contact Valentin Torres TEL 212-904-0375. **Subscr. to:** PO Box 97250, Washington, DC 20090.

616.89 USA ISSN 0893-2905
RC321
➤ **PSYCHIATRIC TIMES.** Text in English. 1985. m. free to qualified personnel (effective 2010). adv. bk.rev. back issues avail. **Document type:** *Journal, Academic/Scholarly.* **Description:** Features interest to psychiatrists, mental health professionals and others in healthcare professions.
Related titles: Online - full text ed.
Indexed: A01, A02, A03, A08, A26, ASG, B04, BRD, C06, C07, C08, CA, CINAHL, E-psyche, E08, G08, H04, H11, H12, I05, P19, P24, P27, P30, P34, P48, P54, PQC, S02, S03, S09, SCOPUS, SSAI, SSAb, SSI, T02, W03, W05.
—BLDSC (6946.242600), CIS. **CCC.**
Published by: C M P Medica LLC (Subsidiary of: United Business Media Limited), 535 Connecticut Ave, Ste 300, Norwalk, CT 06854. TEL 203-523-7000, FAX 203-662-6420, http://www.ubmmedica.com/. Ed. James L Knoll. Pub., Adv. contact Cindy Flaum.

616.89 CZE ISSN 1211-7579
➤ **PSYCHIATRIE.** Text in French. 1983. q. CZK 350 (effective 2009). adv. **Document type:** *Journal, Academic/Scholarly.*
Related titles: Online - full text ed.: ISSN 1212-6845.
Indexed: A22, E-psyche, EMBASE, ExcerpMed, R10, Reac, SCOPUS.
—BLDSC (6946.242900), IE, Ingenta.
Published by: Tigis s. r. o., Havlovickeho 16, Prague 4, 152 00, Czech Republic. TEL 420-2-51813192, FAX 420-2-51681217, info@tigis.cz. Ed. Cyril Hoeschl.

616.89 DEU ISSN 1614-4864
DIE PSYCHIATRIE; Grundlagen und Perspektiven. Text in German. 2004. 4/yr. EUR 128 to individuals; EUR 204 to institutions; EUR 64 to students; EUR 34 newsstand/cover (effective 2011). adv. **Document type:** *Journal, Academic/Scholarly.*
Indexed: P03, P30, PsycInfo, PsycholAb.
—BLDSC (6946.242950), IE. **CCC.**
Published by: Schattauer GmbH, Hoelderlinstr 3, Stuttgart, 70174, Germany. TEL 49-711-229870, FAX 49-711-2298750, info@schattauer.de, http://www.schattauer.com. Ed. W Gaebel. Adv. contact Nicole Doerr. Circ: 2,400 (paid and controlled).

LA PSYCHIATRIE DE L'ENFANT. *see* MEDICAL SCIENCES—Pediatrics

616.8 FRA ISSN 0755-9755
➤ **PSYCHIATRIE FRANCAISE.** Text in French. 1968. q. EUR 80 domestic; EUR 105 foreign; EUR 55 to students (effective 2008). **Document type:** *Journal, Academic/Scholarly.*
Indexed: A22, FR.
—BLDSC (6946.243600), IE, Ingenta, INIST.
Published by: (Syndicat des Psychiatres Francais), Impact Performance, 2 place du General Koenig, Paris, 75017, France. TEL 33-1-4574-4224, FAX 33-1-4574-6737. Ed. Yves Manela.

616.89 CZE ISSN 1213-0508
➤ **PSYCHIATRIE PRO PRAXI.** Text in Czech. 2000. bi-m. CZK 480; CZK 80 per issue (effective 2010). **Document type:** *Journal, Academic/ Scholarly.*
Related titles: Online - full text ed.: ISSN 1803-5272.
Published by: Solen s.r.o., Lazecka 297/51, Olomouc 51, 779 00, Czech Republic. TEL 420-582-396038, FAX 420-582-396099, solen@solen.cz, http://www.solen.cz. Ed. Iva Dankova. Circ: 1,500.

616.8 FRA ISSN 1639-8319
PSYCHIATRIE, SCIENCES HUMAINES, NEUROSCIENCES. Variant title: P S N. Text in French. 2003. q. EUR 197, USD 238 combined subscription to institutions (print & online eds.) (effective 2012). reprint service avail. from PSC. **Document type:** *Journal, Academic/ Scholarly.*
Related titles: Online - full text ed.: ISSN 1955-2351 (from IngentaConnect).
Indexed: A22, A26, E01, E08, EMBASE, FR, S09, SCI, SCOPUS, W07.
—IE, INIST. **CCC.**
Published by: Springer France (Subsidiary of: Springer Science+Business Media), 22 Rue de Palestro, Paris, 75002, France. TEL 33-1-53009860, FAX 33-1-53009861, sylvie.kamara@springer.com. Eds. Bernard Granger, Luigi Grosso.

616.891 AUT ISSN 1614-7189
➤ **PSYCHIATRIE UND PSYCHOTHERAPIE.** Text in German. 2005. 4/yr. EUR 98, USD 130 combined subscription to institutions (print & online eds.) (effective 2012). adv. reprint service avail. from PSC. **Document type:** *Journal, Academic/Scholarly.*
Related titles: Online - full text ed.: ISSN 1864-581X (from IngentaConnect).
Indexed: A22, A26, E01.
—IE. **CCC.**
Published by: Springer Wien (Subsidiary of: Springer Science+Business Media), Sachsenplatz 4-6, Vienna, W 1201, Austria. TEL 43-1-33024150, FAX 43-1-3302426, journals@springer.at, http://www.springer.at. Eds. Hans Peter Kapfhammer, Wolfgang Fleischhacker. Adv. contact Elise Haidenthaller. color page EUR 2,430; trim 210 x 297. Circ: 1,500 (paid). **Subscr. to:** Springer Distribution Center, Kundenservice Zeitschriften, Haberstr 7, Heidelberg 69126, Germany. TEL 49-6221-3454303, FAX 49-6221-3454229, subscriptions@springer.com.

616.89 DEU ISSN 1611-7867
PSYCHIATRIE UND PSYCHOTHERAPIE UP2DATE. Text in German. 2007. bi-m. EUR 152 to institutions; EUR 209 combined subscription to institutions (print & online eds.); EUR 43 newsstand/cover (effective 2011). adv. **Document type:** *Journal, Academic/Scholarly.*
Related titles: Online - full text ed.: ISSN 1863-7175. 2007. EUR 200 to institutions (effective 2011).
—IE. **CCC.**
Published by: Georg Thieme Verlag, Ruedigerstr 14, Stuttgart, 70469, Germany. TEL 49-711-8931421, FAX 49-711-8931410, leser.service@thieme.de. Ed. Fritz Hohagen. Adv. contact Andreas Schweiger TEL 49-711-8931245.

616.8 DEU ISSN 2191-7140
▼ ➤ **PSYCHIATRISCHE FORSCHUNG.** Text in German. 2011. irreg. free (effective 2011). **Document type:** *Journal, Academic/Scholarly.*
Published by: Universitaet Regensburg, Klinik und Poliklinik fuer Psychiatrie, Psychosomatik und Psychotherapie, Universitaetstr 84, Regensburg, 93053, Germany.

616.8 DEU ISSN 0303-4259
RC321
➤ **PSYCHIATRISCHE PRAXIS.** Text in German; Summaries in English, German. 1974. 8/yr. EUR 199 to institutions; EUR 279 combined subscription to institutions (print & online eds.); EUR 37 newsstand/ cover (effective 2011). adv. bk.rev. bibl.; charts; illus. index. back issues avail.; reprints avail. **Document type:** *Journal, Academic/ Scholarly.*
Related titles: Online - full text ed.: ISSN 1439-0876. EUR 269 to institutions (effective 2011); ◆ Supplement(s): Psychiatrische Praxis. Supplement. ISSN 0934-3008.
Indexed: A20, A22, ASCA, CurCont, E-psyche, EMBASE, ExcerpMed, F09, FR, GJP, INI, IndMed, MEDLINE, P03, P30, PsycInfo, PsycholAb, R10, Reac, S02, S03, SCOPUS, SSCI, W07.
—BLDSC (6946.258000), GNLM, IE, Infotrieve, Ingenta, INIST. **CCC.**
Published by: Georg Thieme Verlag, Ruedigerstr 14, Stuttgart, 70469, Germany. TEL 49-711-8931421, FAX 49-711-8931410, leser.service@thieme.de, http://www.thieme-connect.de. Ed. Steffi Riedel-Heller. Adv. contact Andreas Schweiger TEL 49-711-8931245. color page EUR 2,365, B&W page EUR 1,240; 175 x 250. Circ: 2,000 (paid).

616.8 DEU ISSN 0934-3008
➤ **PSYCHIATRISCHE PRAXIS. SUPPLEMENT.** Text in German. 1987. irreg. price varies. back issues avail.; reprints avail. **Document type:** *Monographic series, Academic/Scholarly.*
Related titles: Online - full text ed.; ◆ Supplement to: Psychiatrische Praxis. ISSN 0303-4259.
Indexed: E-psyche, EMBASE, ExcerpMed, SCOPUS.
Published by: Georg Thieme Verlag, Ruedigerstr 14, Stuttgart, 70469, Germany. TEL 49-711-8931421, FAX 49-711-8931410, leser.service@thieme.de, http://www.thieme.de.

616.89 615.85 NLD ISSN 1877-1858
PSYCHIATRISCHE REHABILITATIE. Text in Dutch. 2008. biennial. EUR 34.90 per vol. (effective 2011).
Published by: Uitgeverij S W P, Postbus 257, Amsterdam, 1000 AG, Netherlands. TEL 31-20-3307200, FAX 31-20-3308040, http://www.swpbook.com.

616.8 GBR ISSN 1758-3209
CODEN: PBULE5
➤ **THE PSYCHIATRIST.** Text in English. 1971. m. GBP 99 combined subscription to institutions (print & online eds.); USD 159 combined subscription in United States to institutions (print & online eds.) (effective 2012). bk.rev. back issues avail.; reprints avail. **Document type:** *Journal, Academic/Scholarly.* **Description:** Covers developments in psychiatric practice and service provision, including articles on audit and education in psychiatry, correspondence column, and reports of organizational developments.
Former titles (until 2010): The Psychiatric Bulletin (0955-6036); (until 1988): Royal College of Psychiatrists. Bulletin (0140-0789); (until 1978): Royal College of Psychiatrists. News and Notes
Related titles: Online - full text ed.: ISSN 1758-3217. 2000. GBP 82 to institutions; USD 128 in United States to institutions (effective 2012).
Indexed: A22, AC&P, ASSIA, AddicA, E-psyche, EMBASE, ERA, ExcerpMed, HospAb, P03, P30, PsycInfo, PsycholAb, R10, Reac, S20, S21, SCOPUS, SOPODA, SociolAb.
—BLDSC (6946.258100), GNLM, IE, Infotrieve, Ingenta. **CCC.**
Published by: Royal College of Psychiatrists, 17 Belgrave Sq, London, SW1X 8PG, United Kingdom. TEL 44-20-72352351, FAX 44-20-72451231, rcpsych@rcpsych.ac.uk, http://www.rcpsych.ac.uk/. Ed. Patricia Casey. Circ: 13,450. **Subscr. in N. America to:** Maney Publishing, 875 Massachusetts Ave, 7th Fl, Cambridge, MA 02139. TEL 866-297-5154, FAX 617-354-6875, maney@maneyusa.com; **Subscr. outside N. America to:** Maney Publishing, Ste 1C, Joseph's Well, Hanover Walk, Leeds, W Yorks LS3 1AB, United Kingdom. TEL 44-113-2432800, FAX 44-113-3868178, subscriptions@maney.co.uk, http://www.maney.co.uk.

616.8 GBR ISSN 1476-1793
PSYCHIATRY (ABINGDON). Text in English. 2002 (Mar.). m. EUR 462 in Europe to institutions; JPY 69,200 in Japan to institutions; USD 589 elsewhere to institutions (effective 2010). adv. back issues avail. **Document type:** *Journal, Trade.* **Description:** Provides review articles that will be useful in day-to-day clinical practice and enhancing psychiatric training.
Related titles: Online - full text ed.: ISSN 1878-7592.
Indexed: CA, EMBASE, ExcerpMed, P30, SCOPUS, T02.
—BLDSC (6946.258200), IE, Ingenta. **CCC.**
Published by: The Medicine Publishing Company (Subsidiary of: Elsevier Ltd), The Boulevard, Langford Ln, Kidlington, Oxford, OX5 1GB, United Kingdom. TEL 44-1865-843154, FAX 44-1865-843965, JournalsCustomerServiceEMEA@elsevier.com, http://www.medicinepublishing.co.uk. Eds. Dr. Andre Tylee, Dr. George George Szmukler. Adv. contact Ellie Ostime TEL 44-20-74244971.

616.89 USA ISSN 0033-2747
RC321 CODEN: PSYCAB
➤ **PSYCHIATRY (NEW YORK)**; interpersonal and biological processes. Text in English. 1938. q. USD 110 combined subscription domestic to individuals (print & online eds.); USD 145 combined subscription foreign to individuals (print & online eds.); USD 535 combined subscription domestic to institutions (print & online eds.); USD 580 combined subscription foreign to institutions (print & online eds.) (effective 2011). adv. bk.rev. index, cum.index: 1938-1967, 1968-1977. 112 p./no.; back issues avail.; reprints avail. **Document type:** *Journal, Academic/Scholarly.* **Description:** Contains new and controversial issues in psychiatry and related social and biological science disciplines.
Related titles: Microform ed.: (from MIM, PQC); Online - full text ed.: ISSN 1943-281X.
Indexed: A01, A02, A03, A08, A20, A22, A26, ABS&EES, AC&P, AMHA, ASSIA, AbAn, AmH&L, B04, B25, BAS, BIOSIS Prev, BRD, C06, C07, C08, C11, CA, CDA, CINAHL, Chicano, CurCont, DIP, E-psyche, E01, E08, EMBASE, ExcerpMed, F09, FR, FamI, G08, H04, H09, H11, H12, H13, HospLI, I05, IBR, IBZ, INI, ISR, IndMed, MEA&I, MEDLINE, MLA-IB, MycolAb, P02, P03, P10, P12, P20, P22, P24, P25, P26, P27, P30, P43, P48, P53, P54, PCI, PQC, PsycInfo, PsycholAb, R10, Reac, S02, S03, S05, S09, SCI, SCOPUS, SOPODA, SSAI, SSAb, SSCI, SSI, SWR&A, SociolAb, T02, W03, W07.
—BLDSC (6946.260000), GNLM, IE, Infotrieve, Ingenta, INIST. **CCC.**
Published by: (Washington School of Psychiatry), Guilford Publications, Inc., 72 Spring St, 4th Fl, New York, NY 10012. TEL 800-365-7006, FAX 212-966-6708, info@guilford.com. Ed. Dr. Robert Ursano. R&P Kathy Kuehl. Adv. contact Marian Robinson. Circ: 1,100 (paid).

616.89 USA ISSN 1555-5194
RC321
➤ **PSYCHIATRY (ONLINE).** Text in English. 2004. m. free (effective 2010). adv. back issues avail. **Document type:** *Journal, Academic/Scholarly.* **Description:** Designed to provide psychiatrists with up-to-date information on the latest treatment options, new techniques, and practice management issues to improve their daily practice in a reader-friendly format.
Media: Online - full text.
Published by: Matrix Medical Communications, LLC, 1595 Paoli Pike, Ste 103, West Chester, PA 19380. TEL 484-266-0702, 866-325-9907, FAX 484-266-0726, editorial@matrixmedcom.com, http://www.matrixmedcom.com. Ed. Amir H Kalali. Pub. Robert L Dougherty TEL 610-325-9905 ext 12.

616.89 USA ISSN 1559-5625
▼ **PSYCHIATRY ALERTS N O S.** (Not Otherwise Specified) Text in English. 2009. m. USD 89 domestic; USD 97.50 in Canada; USD 107.50 elsewhere; USD 141 to institutions (effective 2009). back issues avail. **Document type:** *Newsletter, Trade.*
Related titles: Online - full text ed.: ISSN 1559-5641.
Published by: M.J. Powers & Co. Publishers, 65 Madison Ave, Morristown, NJ 07960. TEL 973-898-1200, FAX 973-898-1201, psych@alertpubs.com.

616.8 AUS ISSN 1323-1316
RC321 CODEN: PCNEFP
➤ **PSYCHIATRY AND CLINICAL NEUROSCIENCES.** Text in English. 1933. bi-m. GBP 969 in United Kingdom to institutions; EUR 1,231 in Europe to institutions; USD 1,567 in the Americas to institutions; USD 1,900 elsewhere to institutions; GBP 1,116 combined subscription in United Kingdom to institutions (print & online eds.); EUR 1,417 combined subscription in Europe to institutions (print & online eds.); USD 1,802 combined subscription in the Americas to institutions (print & online eds.); USD 2,185 combined subscription elsewhere to institutions (print & online eds.) (effective 2012). abstr. back issues avail.; reprint service avail. from PSC. **Document type:** *Journal, Academic/Scholarly.* **Description:** Provides original resarch and reviews in all fields of psychiatry and related areas of the neurosciences.
Former titles (until 1994): Japanese Journal of Psychiatry and Neurology (0912-2036); (until 1985): Folia Psychiatrica et Neurologica Japonica (0015-5721)
Related titles: Online - full text ed.: ISSN 1440-1819. GBP 969 in United Kingdom to institutions; EUR 1,231 in Europe to institutions; USD 1,567 in the Americas to institutions; USD 1,900 elsewhere to institutions (effective 2012) (from IngentaConnect); Japanese ed.: ISSN 1341-0695.
Indexed: A01, A03, A08, A20, A22, A26, ASCA, B21, CA, ChemAb, ChemTitl, CurCont, E-psyche, E01, EMBASE, ExcerpMed, FR, GeoRef, H12, I05, INI, IndMed, Inpharma, MEDLINE, NSA, NSCI, P03, P30, P35, P43, PsycInfo, PsycholAb, R10, Reac, S02, S03, SCI, SCOPUS, SOPODA, T02, W07.
—BLDSC (6946.260550), CASDDS, GNLM, IE, Infotrieve, Ingenta, INIST. **CCC.**
Published by: (The Japanese Society of Psychiatry and Neurology JPN), Wiley-Blackwell Publishing Asia (Subsidiary of: Wiley-Blackwell Publishing Ltd.), 155 Cremorne St, Richmond, VIC 3121, Australia. TEL 61-3-92743100, FAX 61-3-92743101, subs@blackwellpublishingasia.com, http://www.wiley.com/WileyCDA/. Eds. Hiroshi Kurita, Masatoshi Takeda.

➤ **PSYCHIATRY DRUG ALERTS.** *see* PHARMACY AND PHARMACOLOGY

616.8 KOR ISSN 1738-3684
➤ **PSYCHIATRY INVESTIGATION.** Text in English. 2004. q.
Description: Covers all disciplines and research areas relevant to the pathophysiology and management of whole neuropsychiatric disorders and symptoms, as well as researches related to cross cultural psychiatry and ethnic issues in psychiatry.
Related titles: Online - full text ed.
Indexed: EMBASE, ExcerpMed, P30, R10, Reac, SCI, SCOPUS, W07.
—BLDSC (6946.263450), IE, Ingenta.
Published by: Taehan Sin'gyong Chongsin Uihakhoe/Korean Neuropsychiatric Association, RN. 522, G-five Central Plaza 1685-8, Seocho-dong, Seocho-gu, Seoul, 137-882, Korea, S. TEL 82-2-5376171, FAX 82-2-5376174, http://www.knpa.or.kr/. Ed. Chan-Hyung Kim.

616.89 USA ISSN 2162-1950
PSYCHIATRY ISSUE BRIEFS. Text in English. 2004. m. free (effective 2011). back issues avail. **Document type:** *Journal, Academic/Scholarly.* **Description:** Includes all aspects of psychiatry, and to have a special focus on outreach to providers of behavioral health services, and to consumers of these services and their family members.
Formerly (until 2011): C M H S R Issue Brief (2162-173X)
Media: Online - full text.
Published by: University of Massachusetts Medical School, Department of Psychiatry, 55 Lake Ave N, Rm S7-823, Worcester, MA 01655. TEL 508-856-6580, psychiatry@umassmed.edu, http://www.umassmed.edu/psychiatry/index.aspx. Ed. Kathleen Biebel TEL 508-856-8717.

616.89 GBR ISSN 1359-7620
➤ **PSYCHIATRY ON-LINE.** Variant title: International Forum for Psychiatry. Text in English. 1994. m. free (effective 2009). bk.rev.; film rev.; software rev.; video rev.; Website rev. back issues avail. **Document type:** *Journal, Academic/Scholarly.* **Description:** Features case reports, audit, treatment protocols and review papers and research.
Media: Online - full text.
Indexed: E-psyche, SCOPUS.
—**CCC.**
Published by: Priory Lodge Education Ltd., 2 Cornflower Way, Moreton, Wirral CH46 1SV, United Kingdom. Ed. Dr. Ben Green.

616.8 340.6 GBR ISSN 1321-8719
K16 CODEN: PPLAFQ
➤ **PSYCHIATRY PSYCHOLOGY AND LAW.** Text in English. 1993. 3/yr. GBP 200 combined subscription in United Kingdom to institutions (print & online eds.); EUR 303, AUD 310, USD 382 combined subscription to institutions (print & online eds.) (effective 2012). adv. 100 p./no.; back issues avail.; reprint service avail. from PSC,WSH. **Document type:** *Journal, Academic/Scholarly.* **Description:** Presents articles on topics relevant to forensic issues in psychiatry and psychology.
Related titles: Online - full text ed.: ISSN 1934-1687. 2002. GBP 180 in United Kingdom to institutions; EUR 272, AUD 279, USD 344 to institutions (effective 2012) (from IngentaConnect).
Indexed: A01, A11, A22, A26, ASSIA, CA, CJA, CLI, E-psyche, E01, E08, G08, I05, LRI, P03, PsycInfo, PsycholAb, S02, S03, S09, SCOPUS, SSCI, T02, W07.
—BLDSC (6946.263650), GNLM, IE, Ingenta. **CCC.**
Published by: (Australian and New Zealand Association of Psychiatry, Psychology and Law AUS), Routledge (Subsidiary of: Taylor & Francis Group), 4 Park Sq, Milton Park, Abingdon, Oxon OX14 4RN, United Kingdom. TEL 44-20-70176000, FAX 44-20-70176336, subscriptions@tandf.co.uk, http://www.routledge.com. Ed. Ian Freckelton. Adv. contact Linda Hann TEL 44-1344-779945. **Subscr. to:** Taylor & Francis Ltd., Journals Customer Service, Sheepen Pl, Colchester, Essex CO3 3LP, United Kingdom. TEL 44-20-70175544, FAX 44-20-70175198.

616.8 IRL ISSN 0165-1781
RC321 CODEN: PSRSDR
➤ **PSYCHIATRY RESEARCH.** Text in English. 1979. 15/yr. EUR 3,407 in Europe to institutions; JPY 452,600 in Japan to institutions; USD 3,810 elsewhere to institutions (effective 2012). illus. back issues avail.; reprints avail. **Document type:** *Journal, Academic/Scholarly.* **Description:** Publishes research in biochemical, physiological, genetic, psychological and social determinants of behavior, assessment of subjective states, evaluations of somatic and non-somatic psychiatric treatments, and relevant clinically related basic studies from fields such as neuropharmacology and neurochemistry.
Related titles: Microform ed.: (from PQC); Online - full text ed.: ISSN 1872-7123 (from IngentaConnect, ScienceDirect).
Indexed: A01, A03, A08, A20, A22, A26, A36, ASCA, B25, BIOBASE, BIOSIS Prev, CA, CABA, CIN, ChemAb, ChemTitl, CurCont, DBA, E-psyche, E12, EMBASE, ExcerpMed, F09, FR, FamI, GH, I05, IABS, INI, IPsyAb, ISR, IndMed, Inpharma, MEDLINE, MycolAb, N02, N03, P03, P30, P33, P35, P39, PsycInfo, PsycholAb, R07, R10, R12, RA&MP, Reac, S02, S03, SCI, SCOPUS, SSCI, T02, T05, W07, W11.
—BLDSC (6946.263700), CASDDS, GNLM, IE, Infotrieve, Ingenta, INIST. **CCC.**
Published by: Elsevier Ireland Ltd (Subsidiary of: Elsevier Science & Technology), Elsevier House, Brookvale Plaza, E. Park, Shannon, Co. Clare, Ireland. TEL 353-61-709600, FAX 353-61-709100. Ed. Dr. Monte S Buchsbaum. R&P Annette Moloney. **Subscr. to:** Elsevier BV, Radarweg 29, PO Box 211, Amsterdam 1000 AE, Netherlands. TEL 31-20-4853757, FAX 31-20-4853432, JournalsCustomerServiceEMEA@elsevier.com, http://www.elsevier.nl.

616.8 USA ISSN 1939-5949
RA790.A1
PSYCHIATRY RESEARCH JOURNAL. Text in English. 2008 (Jan.). q. USD 295 to institutions; USD 442 combined subscription to institutions (print & online eds.) (effective 2012). **Document type:** *Journal, Academic/Scholarly.* **Description:** Presents the latest research in the field of psychiatry, dealing with the prevention, assessment, diagnosis, treatment, and rehabilitation of the mind and mental illness.
Related titles: Online - full text ed.: USD 295 to institutions (effective 2012).
Published by: Nova Science Publishers, Inc., 400 Oser Ave, Ste 1600, Hauppauge, NY 11788. TEL 631-231-7269, FAX 631-231-8175, main@novapublishers.com.

616.8 IRL ISSN 0925-4927
➤ **PSYCHIATRY RESEARCH: NEUROIMAGING.** Text in English. 1990. 9/yr. EUR 1,336 in Europe to institutions; JPY 177,800 in Japan to institutions; USD 1,496 elsewhere to institutions (effective 2012). back issues avail. **Document type:** *Journal, Academic/Scholarly.* **Description:** Publishes manuscripts on positron emission tomography, MRI, computerized electroencephalographic topography and other imaging techniques, results in psychiatric disorders, dementias, and the effects of behavioral tasks and pharmacological treatments.
Related titles: Online - full text ed.: ISSN 1872-7506 (from IngentaConnect, ScienceDirect).
Indexed: A01, A03, A08, A26, ASCA, B21, B25, BIOBASE, BIOSIS Prev, CA, ChemAb, CurCont, DBA, E-psyche, EMBASE, ExcerpMed, FR, I05, IABS, ISR, IndMed, Inpharma, MycolAb, NSA, NSCI, P03, P35, PsycInfo, PsycholAb, R10, RILM, Reac, SCI, SCOPUS, T02, W07.
—BLDSC (6946.263705), IE, Ingenta, INIST. **CCC.**
Published by: Elsevier Ireland Ltd (Subsidiary of: Elsevier Science & Technology), Elsevier House, Brookvale Plaza, E. Park, Shannon, Co. Clare, Ireland. TEL 353-61-709600, FAX 353-61-709100. Eds. Dr. K. Maurer, Dr. Monte S Buchsbaum, T Dierks. R&P Annette Moloney. **Subscr. to:** Elsevier BV, Radarweg 29, PO Box 211, Amsterdam 1000 AE, Netherlands. TEL 31-20-4853757, FAX 31-20-4853432, JournalsCustomerServiceEMEA@elsevier.com, http://www.elsevier.nl.

616.89 NZL ISSN 1178-6183
PSYCHIATRY RESEARCH REVIEW. Text in English. 2007. bi-m. free to qualified personnel (effective 2009). back issues avail. **Document type:** *Journal, Academic/Scholarly.*
Media: Online - full text.
Published by: Research Review Ltd., N Shore Mail Centre, PO Box 100116, Auckland, New Zealand. TEL 64-9-4102277, info@researchreview.co.nz.

616.891 DEU ISSN 1861-4183
PSYCHO-LOGIK; Jahrbuch fuer Psychotherapie, Philosophie und Kultur. Text in German. 2006. a. EUR 26 (effective 2010). **Document type:** *Journal, Academic/Scholarly.* **Description:** Provides an open forum for the current contexts between psychotherapy, psychology and philosophy, for their cultural situation both in practical and scientific respects.
Published by: Verlag Karl Alber, Hermann-Herder-Str 4, Freiburg, 79104, Germany. TEL 49-761-2717436, FAX 49-761-2717212, info@verlag-alber.de.

PSYCHO-ONCOLOGY; journal of the psychological, social and behavioral dimensions of cancer. *see* MEDICAL SCIENCES—Oncology

PSYCHOANALYSE EN CULTUUR/PSYCHOANALYSIS AND CULTURE. *see* PSYCHOLOGY

PSYCHOANALYTIC PSYCHOLOGY. *see* PSYCHOLOGY

616.8 DEU ISSN 0945-7542
BF173.A2
➤ **PSYCHOANALYTISCHE BLAETTER.** Text in German. 1994. irreg., latest vol.29, 2009. price varies. **Document type:** *Monographic series, Academic/Scholarly.*
Indexed: E-psyche.
Published by: Vandenhoeck und Ruprecht, Theaterstr 13, Goettingen, 37073, Germany. TEL 49-551-508440, FAX 49-551-5084422, info@v-r.de. Circ: 1,600.

616.891 FRA ISSN 0245-9744
RC489.P7
PSYCHODRAME. Text in French. 1973. q. **Document type:** *Journal, Academic/Scholarly.*
Formerly (until 1981): Societe d'Etudes du Psychodrame Pratique et Theorique (0245-9752).
Indexed: FR.
—INIST.
Published by: Societe d'Etudes du Psychodrame Pratique et Theorique, 9 rue Brezin, Paris, 75014, France. http://www.asso-sept.org.

616.8 GBR ISSN 1475-3626
PSYCHODYNAMIC PRACTICE (ONLINE). Text in English. 2000. q. GBP 339 in United Kingdom to institutions; EUR 444, USD 560 to institutions (effective 2012). **Document type:** *Journal, Academic/Scholarly.*
Formerly (until 2002): Psychodynamic Counselling (Online) (1470-1057)
Media: Online - full text (from IngentaConnect). **Related titles:** ◆ Print ed.: Psychodynamic Practice (Print). ISSN 1475-3634.
Indexed: S21.
—BLDSC (6946.277250). **CCC.**
Published by: Routledge (Subsidiary of: Taylor & Francis Group), 4 Park Square, Milton Park, Abingdon, Oxon OX14 4RN, United Kingdom. TEL 44-1235-828600, FAX 44-1235-829000, info@routledge.co.uk, http://www.routledge.com/journals/.

616.8 GBR ISSN 1475-3634
CODEN: PPSRC7
➤ **PSYCHODYNAMIC PRACTICE (PRINT)**; individuals, groups and organisations. Text in English. 1994. q. GBP 376 combined subscription in United Kingdom to institutions (print & online eds.); EUR 493, USD 622 combined subscription to institutions (print & online eds.) (effective 2012). adv. back issues avail.; reprint service avail. from PSC. **Document type:** *Journal, Academic/Scholarly.* **Description:** Explores the application of psychodynamic ideas through different occupational settings, techniques and theories.
Formerly (until 2002): Psychodynamic Counselling (Print) (1353-3339)
Related titles: ◆ Online - full text ed.: Psychodynamic Practice (Online). ISSN 1475-3626.
Indexed: A01, A03, A08, A22, ASSIA, B21, CA, E-psyche, E01, E17, ESPM, P03, P30, P43, PsycInfo, PsycholAb, S02, S03, S21, SCOPUS, SOPODA, SociolAb, T02.
—BLDSC (6946.277250), GNLM, IE, Ingenta. **CCC.**
Published by: Routledge (Subsidiary of: Taylor & Francis Group), 4 Park Sq, Milton Park, Abingdon, Oxon OX14 4RN, United Kingdom. TEL 44-20-70176000, FAX 44-20-70176336, subscriptions@tandf.co.uk, http://www.routledge.com. Ed. Nick Barwick TEL 44-1264-357976. Adv. contact Linda Hann TEL 44-1344-779945. **Subscr. to:** Taylor & Francis Ltd., Journals Customer Service, Sheepen Pl, Colchester, Essex CO3 3LP, United Kingdom. TEL 44-20-70175544, FAX 44-20-70175198, tf.enquiries@tfinforma.com.

➤ **PSYCHOGERIATRIA POLSKA/POLISH JOURNAL OF GERIATRIC PSYCHIATRY.** *see* GERONTOLOGY AND GERIATRICS

616.89 GBR ISSN 0033-2917
RC321 CODEN: PSMDCO
➤ **PSYCHOLOGICAL MEDICINE.** Text in English. 1970. m. GBP 791, USD 1,463 to institutions; GBP 842, USD 1,558 combined subscription to institutions (print & online eds.) (effective 2012). adv. bk.rev. charts; illus. index. back issues avail.; reprint service avail. from PSC. **Document type:** *Journal, Academic/Scholarly.*
Description: Contains original research in clinical psychiatry and the basic sciences relating to it.
Related titles: CD-ROM ed.; Microfilm ed.: (from PQC); Online - full text ed.: ISSN 1469-8978. GBP 635, USD 1,175 to institutions (effective 2012).
Indexed: A01, A03, A08, A20, A22, A36, AHCMS, AMHA, ASCA, ASG, ASSIA, AgeL, B21, C06, C07, CA, CABA, CTA, ChemAb, ChemoAb, CurCont, DIP, DokArb, E-psyche, E01, E12, EMBASE, ESPM, ExcerpMed, F09, FR, FamI, GH, H&SSA, H13, IBR, IBZ, INI, ISR, IndMed, Inpharma, JW-P, LT, MEA&I, MEDLINE, N02, N03, NSA, NSCI, P02, P03, P10, P12, P20, P22, P24, P25, P30, P34, P35, P48, P53, P54, PQC, PsycInfo, PsycholAb, R10, R12, RA&MP, RRTA, Reac, RiskAb, S02, S03, SCI, SCOPUS, SSCI, T02, T05, THA, W07.
—BLDSC (6946.450000), CASDDS, GNLM, IE, Infotrieve, Ingenta, INIST. **CCC.**
Published by: Cambridge University Press, The Edinburgh Bldg, Shaftesbury Rd, Cambridge, CB2 8RU, United Kingdom. TEL 44-1223-312393, FAX 44-1223-315052, journals@cambridge.org, http://www.cambridge.org/uk. Eds. Kenneth S Kendler, Robin M Murray. R&P Linda Nicol TEL 44-1223-325702. Adv. contact Rebecca Roberts TEL 44-1223-325083. B&W page GBP 545, B&W page USD 1,035, color page GBP 1,385, color page USD 2,630. Circ: 1,400. **Subscr. to:** Cambridge University Press, 32 Ave of the Americas, New York, NY 10013. TEL 212-337-5000, FAX 212-691-3239, journals_subscriptions@cup.org.

616.8 150 FRA ISSN 1291-0600
PSYCHOLOGIE DE L'INTERACTION. Text in French. 1996. irreg. EUR 49 domestic; EUR 55 foreign (effective 2008). **Document type:** *Journal, Academic/Scholarly.*
Formerly (until 1997): Interaction et Cognitions (1270-2048)
Published by: L' Harmattan, 5 Rue de l'Ecole Polytechnique, Paris, 75005, France. TEL 33-1-43257651, FAX 33-1-43258203.

616.8 150 FRA ISSN 1760-1703
PSYCHOLOGIE ET NEUROPSYCHIATRIE DU VIEILLISSEMENT. Text in French. 2003. q. EUR 326 combined subscription domestic to institutions (print & online eds.); EUR 342 combined subscription in the European Union to institutions (print & online eds.); EUR 350 combined subscription elsewhere to institutions (print & online eds.) (effective 2011). **Document type:** *Journal, Academic/Scholarly.*
Description: Aims to bring neurologists, psychiatricians, geriatricians and psychologists high quality information to enable them to make decisions in full possession of the facts.
Related titles: Online - full text ed.: ISSN 1950-6988.
Indexed: A22, EMBASE, ExcerpMed, FR, MEDLINE, P03, P30, PsycInfo, PsycholAb, R10, Reac, SCI, SCOPUS, W07.
—BLDSC (6946.532070), IE, Ingenta, INIST. **CCC.**
Published by: John Libbey Eurotext, 127 Av. de la Republique, Montrouge, 92120, France. TEL 33-1-46730660, FAX 33-1-40840999, contact@jle.com, http://www.john-libbey-eurotext.fr. Ed. Christian Derouesne.

PSYCHOLOGY & BEHAVIORAL SCIENCES COLLECTION. *see* PSYCHOLOGY—Abstracting, Bibliographies, Statistics

PSYCHOLOGY & NEUROSCIENCE. *see* PSYCHOLOGY

PSYCHOLOGY & PSYCHIATRY JOURNAL. *see* PSYCHOLOGY

PSYCHOLOGY & PSYCHOTHERAPY; theory, research & practice. *see* PSYCHOLOGY

616.8 GBR ISSN 1179-1578
➤ **PSYCHOLOGY RESEARCH AND BEHAVIOR MANAGEMENT.** Text in English. 2008. irreg. free (effective 2011). **Document type:** *Journal, Academic/Scholarly.* **Description:** Focuses on the science of psychology and its application in behavior management to develop improved outcomes in the clinical, educational, sports and business arenas.
Media: Online - full text.
Indexed: SCOPUS.
—CCC.
Published by: Dove Medical Press Ltd., Beechfield House, Winterton Way, Macclesfield, SK11 0JL, United Kingdom. TEL 44-1625-509130, FAX 44-1625-617933. Ed. Igor Elman.

616.8 DEU ISSN 1611-9991
➤ **PSYCHONEURO**; Psychiatrie - Neurologie - Psychotherapie. Text in German. 1975. m. EUR 87 to institutions; EUR 54 to students; EUR 18 newsstand/cover (effective 2009). adv. bk.rev. abstr. **Document type:** *Journal, Academic/Scholarly.*
Formerly (until 2003): Psycho (0340-7845)
Related titles: Online - full text ed.: ISSN 1439-1813.
Indexed: A22, E-psyche, EMBASE, ExcerpMed, R10, Reac, SCOPUS.
—BLDSC (6946.540250), GNLM, IE, Ingenta. **CCC.**
Published by: Georg Thieme Verlag, Ruedigerstr 14, Stuttgart, 70469, Germany. TEL 49-711-8931421, FAX 49-711-8931410, kunden.service@thieme.de, http://www.thieme.de. Ed. Katrin Wolf. Adv. contact Thomas Bruemmer. B&W page EUR 2,500, color page EUR 3,925. Circ: 9,010 (paid and controlled).

616.8 616.4 GBR ISSN 0306-4530
QP356.45 CODEN: PSYCDE
➤ **PSYCHONEUROENDOCRINOLOGY.** Text in English. 1975. 10/yr. EUR 2,171 in Europe to institutions; JPY 288,200 in Japan to institutions; USD 2,429 elsewhere to institutions (effective 2012). bk.rev. charts; illus.; stat. index. back issues avail. **Document type:** *Journal, Academic/Scholarly.* **Description:** Addresses multidisciplinary issues in psychiatry, psychology, neurology, and endocrinology.
Related titles: Microfilm ed.: (from PQC); Online - full text ed.: ISSN 1873-3360 (from IngentaConnect, ScienceDirect).
Indexed: A01, A03, A08, A20, A22, A26, A34, A36, A38, ASCA, B21, B25, BIOBASE, BIOSIS Prev, CA, CABA, CIN, ChemAb, ChemTitl, CurCont, D01, DBA, E-psyche, EMBASE, ExcerpMed, FR, GH, GeoRef, I05, IABS, ISR, IndMed, IndVet, Inpharma, LT, MEDLINE, MycolAb, N02, N03, N04, NSA, NSCI, P03, P30, P35, PN&I, PsycInfo, PsycholAb, R10, RILM, RRTA, Reac, SCI, SCOPUS, T02, T05, THA, VS, W07.
—BLDSC (6946.540300), CASDDS, GNLM, IE, Infotrieve, Ingenta, INIST. **CCC.**
Published by: (International Society of Psychoneuroendocrinology USA), Pergamon (Subsidiary of: Elsevier Science & Technology), The Blvd, Langford Ln, East Park, Kidlington, Oxford OX5 1GB, United Kingdom. TEL 44-1865-843000, FAX 44-1865-843010, JournalsCustomerServiceEMEA@elsevier.com. Eds. Dr. Ned H Kalin TEL 608-263-2281, Dr. Robert Dantzer. **Subscr. to:** Elsevier BV, Radarweg 29, PO Box 211, Amsterdam 1000 AE, Netherlands. TEL 31-20-4853757, FAX 31-20-4853432, http://www.elsevier.nl.

616.8 POL ISSN 1429-8538
➤ **PSYCHOONKOLOGIA.** Text in Polish. 1997. s-a. **Document type:** *Journal, Academic/Scholarly.* **Description:** Devoted to psychological aspects of oncological diseases.
Related titles: Online - full text ed.: ISSN 1644-4116.
Indexed: C06, C07, E-psyche.
—BLDSC (6946.543275), IE.
Published by: (Polskie Towarzystwo Psychoonkologiczne), Wydawnictwo Via Medica, ul Swietokrzyska 73, Gdansk, 80180, Poland. FAX 48-58-3209460, redakcja@viamedica.pl, http://www.viamedica.pl. Ed. Mikolaj Majkowicz.

616.89 SEN ISSN 0033-314X
RC321 CODEN: PSAFB3
➤ **PSYCHOPATHOLOGIE AFRICAINE**; sciences sociales et psychiatrie en Afrique. Text and summaries in English, French. 1965. 3/yr. XAF 15,000 in Africa to individuals; XAF 25,000 elsewhere to individuals; XAF 24,000 in Africa to institutions; XAF 36,000 elsewhere to institutions (effective 2002). adv. bk.rev. charts. index. **Document type:** *Journal, Academic/Scholarly.* **Description:** Seeks to collect and make known works related to psychiatry, psychopathology and mental health in sub-Saharan Africa.
Related titles: CD-ROM ed.; Microfiche ed.
Indexed: A20, ASD, E-psyche, ExtraMED, FR, PsycholAb, S02, S03.
—GNLM, INIST.
Published by: Societe de Psychopathologie et d'Hygiene Mentale de Dakar, BP 5097, Dakar - Fann, Senegal. TEL 221-824-9888, FAX 221-824-9888, psyfann@ucad.refer.sn. Ed. Daouda Sow. Circ: 11,250. **Dist. by:** Librairies aux 4 Vents, Rue Felix Faure, BP 1820, Dakar, Senegal; Librairie Clairafrique, Pl de l'Independence, Rue Sadiniery, BP 1820, Dakar, Senegal; Le Tiers Mythe, 21 rue Cujas, Paris 75005, France; Presence Africaine, 25 bis rue des Ecoles, Paris 75005, France; Librairie Lipsy, 25 rue des Ecoles, Paris 75005, France; Librairie Thierry Garnier.

616.89 CHE ISSN 0254-4962
RC321 CODEN: PSYHEU
➤ **PSYCHOPATHOLOGY**; international journal of descriptive and experimental psychopathology, phenomenology, and psychiatric diagnosis. Text in English. 1968. bi-m. CHF 1,736, EUR 1,387, USD 1,706.50 to institutions; CHF 1,905, EUR 1,522, USD 1,870.50 combined subscription to institutions (print & online eds.) (effective 2012). adv. bk.rev. index. back issues avail. **Document type:** *Journal, Academic/Scholarly.* **Description:** Publishes studies designed to increase the reliability and precision of explanatory concepts applied in descriptive psychopathology, phenomenology, and clinical diagnostics.
Formerly (until vol.17, 1984): Psychiatria Clinica (0033-264X)
Related titles: Microform ed.; Online - full text ed.: ISSN 1423-033X. 199?. CHF 1,685, EUR 1,348, USD 1,636 to institutions (effective 2012).
Indexed: A01, A03, A08, A20, A22, ASCA, ASD, B21, B25, BIOSIS Prev, CA, CJPI, CurCont, DIP, DentInd, E-psyche, E01, EMBASE, ExcerpMed, FR, FamI, IBR, IBZ, INI, IPsyAb, ISR, IndMed, Inpharma, MEDLINE, MycolAb, NSA, P03, P20, P22, P25, P26, P30, P35, P48, P54, PQC, PsycInfo, PsycholAb, R10, RILM, Reac, S02, S03, SCI, SCOPUS, SSCI, T02, W07.
—BLDSC (6946.543700), CASDDS, GNLM, IE, Infotrieve, Ingenta, INIST. **CCC.**
Published by: S. Karger AG, Allschwilerstr 10, Basel, 4055, Switzerland. TEL 41-61-3061111, FAX 41-61-3061234, karger@karger.ch, http://www.karger.ch. Eds. C Mundt, H Akiskal. R&P Tatjana Sepin. adv.: page CHF 1,730; trim 210 x 280. Circ: 800.

616.89 615 USA ISSN 1936-9255
PSYCHOPHARM REVIEW. Text in English. 1966. m. USD 556 domestic to institutions; USD 600 foreign to institutions (effective 2011). adv. bk.rev. back issues avail. **Document type:** *Newsletter, Academic/Scholarly.* **Description:** Provides advice for recognizing and treating virtually all types of psychiatric disorders.
Formerly (until 2007): International Drug Therapy Newsletter (0020-6571)
Related titles: Online - full text ed.
Indexed: A01, A22, E-psyche, EMBASE, I12, Inpharma, P30, P35, SCOPUS, T02.
—GNLM, IE. **CCC.**
Published by: Lippincott Williams & Wilkins (Subsidiary of: Wolters Kluwer N.V.), 530 Walnut St, Philadelphia, PA 19106. TEL 215-521-8300, FAX 215-521-8902, customerservice@lww.com. Ed. Dr. Philip G Janicak.

PSYCHOPHARMA. *see* PHARMACY AND PHARMACOLOGY

PSYCHOPHARMACOLOGY. *see* PHARMACY AND PHARMACOLOGY

PSYCHOPHARMACOLOGY BULLETIN. *see* PHARMACY AND PHARMACOLOGY

PSYCHOPHARMACOLOGY EDUCATIONAL UPDATE. *see* PHARMACY AND PHARMACOLOGY

PSYCHOPHARMACOLOGY UPDATE. *see* PHARMACY AND PHARMACOLOGY

612.8 USA ISSN 0048-5772
QP351 CODEN: PSPHAF
➤ **PSYCHOPHYSIOLOGY**; an international journal. Text in English. 1964. bi-m. GBP 498 in United Kingdom to institutions; EUR 630 in Europe to institutions; USD 630 in the Americas to institutions; USD 973 elsewhere to institutions; GBP 573 combined subscription in United Kingdom to institutions (print & online eds.); EUR 726 combined subscription in Europe to institutions (print & online eds.); USD 726 combined subscription in the Americas to institutions (print & online eds.); USD 1,119 combined subscription elsewhere to institutions (print & online eds.) (effective 2012). adv. bk.rev. abstr.; charts; illus. index. back issues avail.; reprint service avail. from PSC. **Document type:** *Journal, Academic/Scholarly.* **Description:** Concerns the relationships between human autonomic and central nervous system behavior on the one hand and cognitive performance, personality and emotions on the other. Studies effects of stress, individual differences, aging, anxiety, and psychosomatic and psychiatric disease.
Formerly: Psychophysiology Newsletter
Related titles: Microfilm ed.: (from PQC); Online - full text ed.: ISSN 1469-8986. GBP 498 in United Kingdom to institutions; EUR 630 in Europe to institutions; USD 630 in the Americas to institutions; USD 973 elsewhere to institutions (effective 2012) (from IngentaConnect).
Indexed: A01, A03, A08, A20, A22, A26, ASCA, B21, B25, BDM&CN, BIOSIS Prev, CA, CIS, CMCI, CurCont, DIP, E-psyche, E01, EMBASE, ErgAb, ExcerpMed, FR, FamI, H12, H13, IBR, IBZ, ISR, IndMed, Inpharma, MEDLINE, MycolAb, NSA, NSCI, P03, P10, P12, P20, P30, P35, P43, P48, P52, P53, P54, P56, PQC, PsycInfo, PsycholAb, R09, R10, RASB, RILM, Reac, S02, S03, SCI, SCOPUS, SD, SOPODA, SSCI, T02, THA, VITIS, W07.
—BLDSC (6946.552000), GNLM, IE, Infotrieve, Ingenta, INIST. **CCC.**
Published by: (Society for Psychophysiological Research), Wiley-Blackwell Publishing, Inc. (Subsidiary of: Wiley-Blackwell Publishing Ltd.), 111 River St, Hoboken, NJ 07030. TEL 201-748-6000, FAX 201-748-6088, info@wiley.com, http://www.wiley.com/WileyCDA/. Ed. Dr. Robert F Simons. Adv. contact Kristin McCarthy TEL 201-748-7683.

362.26 GBR ISSN 1752-2439
▼ ➤ **PSYCHOSIS**; psychological, social and integrative approaches. Text in English. 2009. s-a. GBP 201 combined subscription in United Kingdom to institutions (print & online eds.); EUR 314, USD 393 combined subscription to institutions (print & online eds.) (effective 2012). adv. reprints avail. **Document type:** *Journal, Academic/Scholarly.* **Description:** Publishes papers on both quantitative research and qualitative research.
Related titles: Online - full text ed.: ISSN 1752-2447. GBP 181 in United Kingdom to institutions; EUR 283, USD 354 to institutions (effective 2012).
Indexed: A01, CA, PQC, PsycInfo, T02.
—CCC.
Published by: (International Society for the Psychological Treatment of the Schizophrenias and Other Psychoses GRC), Routledge (Subsidiary of: Taylor & Francis Group), 4 Park Sq, Milton Park, Abingdon, Oxon OX14 4RN, United Kingdom. TEL 44-20-70176000, FAX 44-20-70176336, subscriptions@tandf.co.uk, http://www.routledge.com. Ed. Dr. John Read. Adv. contact Linda Hann TEL 44-1344-779945. **Subscr. to:** Taylor & Francis Ltd., Journals Customer Service, Sheepen Pl, Colchester, Essex CO3 3LP, United Kingdom. TEL 44-20-70175544, FAX 44-20-70175198.

➤ **PSYCHOSOCIALE ONCOLOGIE.** *see* MEDICAL SCIENCES—Oncology

616.89 USA ISSN 0033-3174
CODEN: PSMEAP
➤ **PSYCHOSOMATIC MEDICINE.** Text in English. 1938. 9/yr. USD 1,101 domestic to institutions; USD 1,251 foreign to institutions (effective 2011). adv. bk.rev. illus. Index. back issues avail.; reprints avail. **Document type:** *Journal, Academic/Scholarly.* **Description:** Presents research and clinical studies concerning psychosomatic disorders.
Related titles: CD-ROM ed.; Microfilm ed.: (from RPI); Online - full text ed.: ISSN 1534-7796.
Indexed: A20, A22, A36, AIDS Ab, ASCA, ASSIA, B21, B25, B28, BIOSIS Prev, C06, C07, CABA, ChemAb, ChemTitl, CurCont, E-psyche, E12, EMBASE, ExcerpMed, F09, FamI, GH, H13, IBR, IBZ, INI, ISR, IndMed, Inpharma, JW-P, LT, MEDLINE, MS&D, MycolAb, N02, N03, NSA, P02, P03, P10, P20, P24, P30, P35, P48, P53, P54, PQC, PsycInfo, PsycholAb, R10, R12, RRTA, Reac, S02, S03, SCI, SCOPUS, SOPODA, SSCI, SociolAb, T05, VS, W07, W10, W11.
—BLDSC (6946.555000), CASDDS, GNLM, IE, Infotrieve, Ingenta, INIST. **CCC.**
Published by: (American Psychosomatic Society), Lippincott Williams & Wilkins (Subsidiary of: Wolters Kluwer N.V.), 530 Walnut St, Philadelphia, PA 19106. TEL 215-521-8300, FAX 215-521-8902, customerservice@lww.com, http://www.lww.com. Ed. David S Sheps. Pub. Terry Materese. Adv. contact Miriam Terron-Elder TEL 646-674-6538. B&W page USD 970, color page USD 2,090; trim 8.125 x 10.875. Circ: 1,387.

616.89 USA ISSN 0033-3182
RC49 CODEN: PSYCBC
➤ **PSYCHOSOMATICS**; the journal of consultation and liaison psychiatry. Text in English. 1960. bi-m. USD 497 in United States to institutions; USD 539 elsewhere to institutions (effective 2012). adv. bk.rev. abstr.; bibl.; charts; illus.; stat. index. back issues avail.; reprints avail. **Document type:** *Journal, Academic/Scholarly.* **Description:** Designed to help readers in the clinical care of patients with medical and psychiatric comorbidity.
Related titles: Microform ed.: (from PQC); Online - full text ed.: ISSN 1545-7206. USD 199 to individuals (effective 2011) (from ScienceDirect).
Indexed: A20, A22, A34, A36, AMHA, ASCA, B21, CABA, ChemAb, ChemTitl, CurCont, E-psyche, E12, EMBASE, ExcerpMed, F09, FR, FamI, GH, H17, IBR, IBZ, INI, ISR, IndMed, Inpharma, JW-P, JW-WH, MEDLINE, N02, N03, N04, NSA, P03, P20, P22, P24, P25, P26, P30, P33, P35, P48, P54, PQC, PsycInfo, PsycholAb, R10, R12, RA&MP, Reac, S02, S03, SCI, SCOPUS, SSCI, SWR&A, T05, VS, W07.
—BLDSC (6946.557000), CASDDS, GNLM, IE, Infotrieve, Ingenta, INIST. **CCC.**

Published by: (Academy of Psychosomatic Medicine), American Psychiatric Publishing, Inc., 1000 Wilson Blvd, Ste 1825, Arlington, VA 22209. TEL 703-907-7888, 800-368-5777, FAX 703-907-1092, appi@psych.org. Eds. Theodore A Stern, Michael D Roy. Adv. contact Valentin Torres TEL 212-904-0375. **Subscr. to:** PO Box 97250, Washington, DC 20090.

616.8 DEU ISSN 1866-1912
PSYCHOSOZIALE INTERVENTIONEN ZUR PRAEVENTION UND THERAPIE DER DEMENZ. Text in German. 2008. irreg., latest vol.3, 2009. price varies. **Document type:** *Monographic series, Academic/Scholarly.*
Published by: Logos Verlag Berlin, Comeniushof, Gubener Str 47, Berlin, 10243, Germany. TEL 49-30-42851090, FAX 49-30-42851092, redaktion@logos-verlag.de. Ed. Johannes Pantel.

616.8 360 DEU ISSN 0930-4177
PSYCHOSOZIALE UMSCHAU. Text in German. 1985. q. EUR 27 domestic; EUR 32 foreign; EUR 22 to students; EUR 8 newsstand/cover (effective 2008). adv. **Document type:** *Journal, Academic/Scholarly.*
Indexed: E-psyche.
Published by: (Dachverband Psychosoziale Hilfsvereinigungen), Psychiatrie Verlag GmbH, Thomas-Mann-Str 49a, Bonn, 53111, Germany. TEL 49-228-725340, FAX 49-228-7253420, verlag@psychiatrie.de, http://www.psychiatrie.de. Ed. Karin Koch. Adv. contact Cornelia Brodmann. page EUR 850; trim 180 x 259. Circ: 6,250 (paid and controlled).

616.8 150 POL ISSN 0239-4170
➤ **PSYCHOTERAPIA.** Text in Polish; Summaries in English. 1972. q. PLZ 40 domestic; PLZ 15 per issue domestic (effective 2004). bk.rev. abstr.; bibl.; illus. 90 p./no. 1 cols./p.; back issues avail. **Document type:** *Journal, Academic/Scholarly.* **Description:** Publishes clinical, theoretical, and experimental papers and case reports on psychotherapy and clinical psychology.
Indexed: EMBASE, ExcerpMed, R10, Reac, SCOPUS.
Published by: Polskie Towarzystwo Psychiatryczne, ul Jana Sobieskiego 9, Warsaw, 02957, Poland. TEL 48-12-6331203, FAX 48-12-6334067, psych@kom-red-wyd-ptp.com.pl. Ed. Kazimierz Bierzynski. Pub., R&P Jerzy W Aleksandrowicz. Adv. contact Magdalena Sikora.

616.89 DEU ISSN 0935-6185
➤ **PSYCHOTHERAPEUT;** Fachzeitschrift fuer Aerzte und Psychologen in der Praxis und Klinik. Text in German. 1956. bi-m. EUR 222, USD 262 combined subscription to institutions (print & online eds.) (effective 2012). adv. bk.rev. bibl.; charts; illus. back issues avail.; reprint service avail. from PSC. **Document type:** *Journal, Academic/Scholarly.* **Description:** Seeks to promote discussion of different approaches and psychotherapeutic schools.
Former titles: Praxis der Psychotherapie und Psychosomatik (0171-791X); Praxis der Psychotherapie (0032-7077)
Related titles: Microform ed.: (from PQC); Online - full text ed.: ISSN 1432-2080 (from IngentaConnect).
Indexed: A20, A22, A26, ASCA, ChemAb, CurCont, E-psyche, E01, MLA-IB, P03, P30, PsycInfo, PsycholAb, RILM, SCOPUS, SSCI, W07.
—BLDSC (6946.558210), GNLM, IE, Infotrieve, Ingenta, INIST. **CCC.**
Published by: Springer (Subsidiary of: Springer Science+Business Media), Tiergartenstr 17, Heidelberg, 69121, Germany. TEL 49-6221-4870, FAX 49-6221-345229. Eds. J Eckert, M Cierpka. Adv. contact Stephan Kroeck TEL 49-30-827875739. B&W page EUR 1,490, color page EUR 2,680. Circ: 2,400 (paid and controlled). **Subscr. in the Americas to:** Springer New York LLC, Journal Fulfillment, PO Box 2485, Secaucus, NJ 07096. TEL 800-777-4643, 201-348-4033, FAX 201-348-4505, journals-ny@springer.com, http://www.springer.com; **Subscr. to:** Springer Distribution Center, Kundenservice Zeitschriften, Haberstr 7, Heidelberg 69126, Germany. TEL 49-6221-3454303, FAX 49-6221-3454229, subscriptions@springer.com.

616.89 DEU ISSN 1438-7026
RC475
➤ **PSYCHOTHERAPIE IM DIALOG.** Abbreviated title: P i D. Text in German. 2000. q. EUR 110 to institutions; EUR 153 combined subscription to institutions (print & online eds.); EUR 32 newsstand/cover (effective 2011). adv. **Document type:** *Journal, Academic/Scholarly.*
Related titles: Online - full text ed.: ISSN 1439-913X. EUR 148 to institutions (effective 2011).
Indexed: A22.
—IE, Infotrieve. **CCC.**
Published by: Georg Thieme Verlag, Ruedigerstr 14, Stuttgart, 70469, Germany. TEL 49-711-8931421, FAX 49-711-8931410, kunden.service@thieme.de. Ed. Dr. Andrea Dinger-Broda. Adv. contact Andreas Schweiger TEL 49-711-8931245. Circ: 3,800 (paid and controlled).

616.891 GBR ISSN 1476-9263
RC480.5
PSYCHOTHERAPY AND POLITICS INTERNATIONAL. Text in English. 2003. 3/yr. GBP 149 in United Kingdom to institutions; EUR 189 in Europe to institutions; USD 291 elsewhere to institutions; GBP 171 combined subscription in United Kingdom to institutions (print & online eds.); EUR 218 combined subscription in Europe to institutions (print & online eds.); USD 335 combined subscription elsewhere to institutions (print & online eds.) (effective 2012). adv. back issues avail.; reprint service avail. from PSC. **Document type:** *Journal, Academic/Scholarly.* **Description:** Explores the manifold connections and interactions between politics and psychotherapy, both in theory and in practice. It focuses on the application to political problematics of thinking that originates in the field of psychotherapy, and equally on the application within the field of psychotherapy of political concepts and values.
Related titles: Online - full text ed.: ISSN 1556-9195. 2006. GBP 149 in United Kingdom to institutions; EUR 189 in Europe to institutions; USD 291 elsewhere to institutions (effective 2012).
Indexed: A01, C06, C07, CA, P42, PSA, T02.
—BLDSC (6946.558800), IE, Ingenta. **CCC.**
Published by: John Wiley & Sons Ltd. (Subsidiary of: John Wiley & Sons, Inc.), 1-7 Oldlands Way, PO Box 808, Bognor Regis, West Sussex PO21 9FF, United Kingdom. TEL 44-1865-778315, FAX 44-1243-843232, cs-journals@wiley.com, http://eu.wiley.com/WileyCDA/. Ed. Nick Totton. **Subscr. to:** 1-7 Oldlands Way, PO Box 809, Bognor Regis, West Sussex PO21 9FG, United Kingdom. TEL 44-1865-778054, cs-agency@wiley.com.

616.89 CHE ISSN 0033-3190
RC49 CODEN: PSPSBF
➤ **PSYCHOTHERAPY AND PSYCHOSOMATICS.** Text in English. 1953. bi-m. CHF 1,543, EUR 1,233, USD 1,519.50 to institutions; CHF 1,692, EUR 1,352, USD 1,663.50 combined subscription to institutions (print & online eds.) (effective 2012). adv. bk.rev. charts; illus.; bibl. index. back issues avail. **Document type:** *Journal, Academic/Scholarly.* **Description:** Provides comprehensive coverage of the latest original research in psychotherapy and psychosomatics.
Former titles (until 1965): Acta Psychotherapeutica et Psychosomatica (0365-5822); (until 1960): Acta Psychotherapeutica, Psychosomatica et Orthopaedagogica (0365-5679)
Related titles: Microform ed.; Online - full text ed.: ISSN 1423-0348. 199?. CHF 1,492, EUR 1,194, USD 1,449 to institutions (effective 2012).
Indexed: A01, A03, A08, A20, A22, A29, AMHA, ASCA, ASD, B20, B21, B25, BIOSIS Prev, C06, C07, CA, CTA, ChemAb, ChemoAb, CurCont, DentInd, E-psyche, E01, EMBASE, ESPM, ExcerpMed, F09, FR, FamI, I10, IPsyAb, ISR, IndMed, Inpharma, JW-P, MEDLINE, MycolAb, NSA, P03, P20, P22, P24, P25, P26, P30, P35, P48, P54, PQC, PsycInfo, PsycholAb, R10, Reac, SCI, SCOPUS, SSCI, T02, VirolAbstr, W07.
—BLDSC (6946.559000), GNLM, IE, Infotrieve, Ingenta, INIST. **CCC.**
Published by: (International Federation for Medical Psychotherapy), S. Karger AG, Allschwilerstr 10, Basel, 4055, Switzerland. TEL 41-61-3061111, FAX 41-61-3061234, karger@karger.ch, http://www.karger.ch. Ed. G.A. Fava. R&P Tatjana Sepin. adv.: page CHF 1,815; trim 210 x 280. Circ: 1,050.

616.89 DEU ISSN 1439-8931
PSYCHOTRAUMATOLOGIE. Text in German. 2001. q. **Document type:** *Journal, Academic/Scholarly.*
Media: Online - full content. **Related titles:** Online - full text ed.
—CCC.
Published by: Roland Asanger Verlag GmbH, Boedldorf 3, Kroening, 84178, Germany. TEL 49-8744-7262, FAX 49-8744-967755, verlag@asanger.de, http://www.asanger.de.

PSYCSCAN: LEARNING DISORDERS AND MENTAL RETARDATION (ONLINE). *see* PSYCHOLOGY—Abstracting, Bibliographies, Statistics

PSYCSCAN: NEUROPSYCHOLOGY (ONLINE). *see* MEDICAL SCIENCES—Abstracting, Bibliographies, Statistics

PSYCSCAN: PSYCHOPHARMACOLOGY. *see* PHARMACY AND PHARMACOLOGY—Abstracting, Bibliographies, Statistics

616.8 615.3 NLD ISSN 1872-1559
PSYFAR; praktische nascholing over psychofarmacologie. Text in Dutch. 2006. q. EUR 375 (effective 2009). adv.
Related titles: Online - full text ed.: ISSN 1876-3758.
Published by: Prelum Uitgevers, Postbus 545, Houten, 3990 GH, Netherlands. TEL 31-30-6355060, FAX 31-30-6355069, info@prelum.nl, http://www.prelum.nl. Ed. Dr. P Moleman. adv.: B&W page EUR 895, color page EUR 2,150; trim 210 x 297. Circ: 1,835.

PSYKISK HAELSA/MENTAL HEALTH. *see* PSYCHOLOGY

PSYKOANALYTISK TID/SKRIFT. *see* PSYCHOLOGY

616.8 ITA ISSN 0393-0645
QUADERNI ITALIANI DI PSICHIATRIA. Text in Italian. 1981. 4/yr. EUR 370 in Europe to institutions; JPY 49,900 in Japan to institutions; USD 522 elsewhere to institutions (effective 2012). adv. **Document type:** *Journal, Academic/Scholarly.*
Related titles: Online - full text ed.: (from ScienceDirect).
Indexed: B25, BIOSIS Prev, E-psyche, EMBASE, ExcerpMed, MycolAb, SCOPUS.
—CCC.
Published by: (Societa Italiana di Psichiatria), Elsevier Masson (Subsidiary of: Elsevier Health Sciences), Via Paleocapa 7, Milan, 20121, Italy. TEL 39-02-881841, FAX 39-02-88184302, info@masson.it, http://www.masson.it. Eds. Eugenio Borgna, Vittorino Andreoli. Circ: 2,000.

QUADRANT. *see* PSYCHOLOGY

616.858 USA
QUALITY OF CARE AND ADVOCACY. Text in English. 1980. q. bk.rev. **Document type:** *Government.*
Formerly (until 2006): Quality of Care
Indexed: E-psyche.
Published by: New York State Commission on Quality of Care and Advocacy for Persons with Disabilities, 401 State St, Schenectady, NY 12305-2397. FAX 800-624-4143, webmaster@cqcapd.state.ny.us. Ed. Marcus A Gigliotti. R&P Marcus A Gigliotti. Circ: 13,000 (controlled).

616.89 USA ISSN 1087-1578
QUEST (TUCSON). Text in English. 1950. q. USD 15 domestic; USD 24 foreign; free to qualified personnel (effective 2010). bk.rev. illus. 72 p./no.; back issues avail.; reprints avail. **Document type:** *Magazine, Trade.* **Description:** Presents profiles, instructive articles, research and association news, resource listings, and helpful articles of special interest to those with neuromuscular diseases and their families.
Former titles (until 1994): M D A Reports (1061-4370); (until 1992): M D A Newsmagazine (8750-2321); (until 1984): M D A News - Muscular Dystrophy Association (0279-0742); (until 1975): Muscular Dystrophy News (0027-3759)
Related titles: Online - full text ed.: free (effective 2010).
Indexed: A26, CA, CHNI, E-psyche, E07, G08, H11, H12, I05, M01, M02, RehabLit, T02.
Published by: Muscular Dystrophy Association, Inc., 3300 E Sunrise Dr, Tucson, AZ 85718. TEL 520-529-2000, FAX 520-529-5383, publications@mdausa.org, http://www.mda.org. Adv. contact Maureen Tuncer TEL 727-578-2734. Circ: 130,000.

616.8 150 NOR ISSN 1503-2361
R O S - INFO. (Raadgivning om Spiseforstyrrelser) Text in Norwegian. 1990. q. NOK 200 to individual members; NOK 500 to institutional members; NOK 100 to students (effective 2003). **Description:** Information on anorexia and bulimia.
Formerly (until 2002): A B F - nytt (0803-088X)
Published by: Raadgiving om Spiseforstyrrelser (ROS), PO Box 36, Bergen, 5003, Norway. TEL 47-55-326260, FAX 47-55-325701, adm@nettros.no.

RADIOSURGERY. *see* MEDICAL SCIENCES—Surgery

616.89 CHL ISSN 0718-4875
RE-CORTERS PSICONALITICOS. Text in Spanish. 2005. q.
Media: Online - full text.
Published by: Universidad de Santiago de Chile, Escuela de Psicologia, Ave Ecuador 3650, Estacion Central, Santiago, Chile. TEL 56-2-7761986, http://web.usach.cl/psicologia/.

616.8 USA
RE-LEARNING TIMES. Text in English. q. **Document type:** *Newsletter.* **Description:** Resource for anyone interested in ABI, long-term care, or supported living.
Published by: Learning Services Corporation, 707 Morehead Ave, Durham, NC 27707. TEL 888-419-9955 ext. 12. Circ: 10,000.

READING AND WRITING; an interdisciplinary journal. *see* LINGUISTICS

616.834 USA ISSN 1079-4220
REAL LIVING WITH MULTIPLE SCLEROSIS. Text in English. 1993. bi-m. USD 229 domestic to institutions; USD 322 foreign to institutions (effective 2011). adv. back issues avail. **Document type:** *Journal, Academic/Scholarly.* **Description:** Provides people with MS and their families information on how to cope with the clinical and personal consequences of this disease.
Related titles: Online - full text ed.
Indexed: A01, A26, C06, C07, E-psyche, G08, H11, H12, I05, P48, PQC, T02.
—CCC.
Published by: Lippincott Williams & Wilkins (Subsidiary of: Wolters Kluwer N.V.), 351 W Camden St, Baltimore, MD 21201. TEL 410-528-4088, FAX 410-528-4312, customerservice@lww.com. Ed. Dr. Aaron E Miller.

616.8 610.73 USA
A REASON FOR HOPE. Text in English. 1987. 3/yr. free. bk.rev. back issues avail. **Document type:** *Magazine, Consumer.*
Formerly: Link (Calabasas Hills)
Indexed: E-psyche.
Published by: Amyotrophic Lateral Sclerosis Association, 27001 Agoura Rd, Ste 150, Calabasas Hills, CA 91301-5104. TEL 818-880-9007, FAX 818-880-9006, alsinfo@alsa-national.org, http://www.alsa.org. Circ: 80,000.

616.8 NLD ISSN 1574-8898
RM315
➤ **RECENT PATENTS ON C N S DRUG DISCOVERY.** (Central Nervous System) Text in English. 2006. 3/yr. USD 1,000 to institutions (print or online ed.) (effective 2012). adv. back issues avail.; reprints avail. **Document type:** *Journal, Academic/Scholarly.* **Description:** Publishes review articles on recent patents in the field of CNS drug discovery e.g. on novel bioactive compounds, analogs & targets.
Related titles: Online - full text ed.: (from IngentaConnect).
Indexed: A01, A28, A36, APA, B&BAb, B19, B21, BrCerAb, C&ISA, C33, CA, CA/WCA, CABA, CIA, CerAb, CivEngAb, CorrAb, E&CAJ, E11, E12, EEA, EMA, EMBASE, ESPM, EnvEAb, ExcerpMed, GH, H15, M&TEA, M09, MBF, MEDLINE, METADEX, N02, N03, NSA, P30, RA&MP, SCOPUS, SolStAb, T02, T04, WAA.
—IE, Ingenta, Linda Hall. **CCC.**
Published by: Bentham Science Publishers Ltd., PO Box 294, Bussum, 1400 AG, Netherlands. TEL 31-35-6923800, FAX 31-35-6980150, sales@bentham.org. Ed. Vincenzo Di Marzo. **Subscr. to:** Bentham Science Publishers Ltd., c/o Richard E Morrissey, PO Box 446, Oak Park, IL 60301. TEL 312-413-5867, FAX 312-996-7107, subscriptions@bentham.org.

616.8 612.015 USA
➤ **THE RECEPTORS.** Text in English. 1983. irreg., latest 2009. price varies. illus. back issues avail. **Document type:** *Monographic series, Academic/Scholarly.* **Description:** Explores the biochemistry and physiology of the various neuroreceptors and how pharmacological compounds affect them.
Related titles: Online - full text ed.
Published by: Humana Press, Inc. (Subsidiary of: Springer Science+Business Media), 233 Spring St, New York, NY 10013. TEL 212-460-1500, FAX 212-460-1575, service-ny@springer.com. Ed. K A Neve.

➤ **RECHT & PSYCHIATRIE.** *see* PSYCHOLOGY

616.89 ARG ISSN 1851-3425
REDES Y PARADIGMAS. Text in Spanish. 2007. a.
Published by: Fundacion Prosam, Rodriguez Pena, 1046, Buenos Aires, C1020ADV, Argentina. TEL 54-11-49644560, prosam@prosam.org.ar, http://www.prosam.org.ar/. Ed. Ruth Melnistzky.

REFERATIVNYI SBORNIK. PSIKHIATRIYA. NOVOSTI NAUKI I TEKHNIKI. *see* MEDICAL SCIENCES—Abstracting, Bibliographies, Statistics

616.834 SWE ISSN 1651-5471
REFLEX. Text in Swedish. 1954. s-m. SEK 250; free membership (effective 2002). adv. bk.rev. illus.; stat. **Description:** Deals with subjects concerned with neurological disease and disability.
Former titles (until 2002): Handikapp - Reflex (0348-8071); (until 1979): M S-Brevet (0345-8199)
Related titles: Audio cassette/tape ed.
Indexed: E-psyche.
Published by: Neurologiskt Handikappades Riksfoerbund/Swedish Association of Neurologically Disabled, PO Box 3284, Stockholm, 10365, Sweden. TEL 46-8-677-70-10, FAX 46-8-24-13-15. Ed. Thomas Ejderhov. Adv. contact Gerdt Lindzen. Circ: 15,000.

616.8 DEU ISSN 1611-2822
REGENSBURGER PSYCHIATRISCHE SCHRIFTEN. Text in German. 2003. irreg., latest vol.3, 2004. price varies. **Document type:** *Monographic series, Academic/Scholarly.*
Published by: Shaker Verlag GmbH, Kaiserstr 100, Herzogenrath, 52134, Germany. TEL 49-2407-95960, FAX 49-2407-95969, info@shaker.de.

616.89 NLD ISSN 1570-6303
REHABILITATIE. Text in Dutch. 1992. q. EUR 49 to individuals; EUR 74 to institutions; EUR 39 to students (effective 2009). adv. bk.rev. abstr.; charts; illus. index. back issues avail. **Document type:** *Magazine, Academic/Scholarly.* **Description:** Includes information on ambulatory and residental care for people who are dependent on psychiatric care.
Formerly (until 2006): Passage (0927-2658); Which incorporated (1989-1994): Forum (Rotterdam) (0925-0735)
Indexed: E-psyche.

—IE, Infotrieve.
Published by: Uitgeverij S W P, Postbus 257, Amsterdam, 1000 AG, Netherlands. TEL 31-20-3307200, FAX 31-20-3308040, swp@swpbook.com, http://www.swpbook.com. Eds. Annette Plooy, Marianne Bassant. adv.: B&W page EUR 475, color page EUR 1,125. Circ: 1,250 (paid).

REHABILITATION COUNSELING BULLETIN. *see* HANDICAPPED

616.8 DEU
REIHE ZENTRALES NERVENSYSTEM. Text in German. 2007. irreg., latest vol.3, 2009. price varies. **Document type:** *Monographic series, Academic/Scholarly.*
Published by: Hippocampus Verlag KG, Bismarckstr 8, Bad Honnef, 53604, Germany. TEL 49-2224-919480, FAX 49-2224-919482, verlag@hippocampus.de.

362 USA ISSN 1528-509X
REINTEGRATION TODAY. Text in English. 2000. q. free. **Document type:** *Magazine, Consumer.* **Description:** Provides an information resource and community forum for people interested in all aspects of severe mental illness, particularly the process of recovery and reintegration back into society.
Published by: Center for Reintegration, Inc., 609 72nd St, Fl 1, North Bergen, NJ 07047. TEL 201-869-2333, FAX 201-869-2123, reintegration@reintegration.com.

IL REO E IL FOLLE. *see* CRIMINOLOGY AND LAW ENFORCEMENT

REPORT ON EMOTIONAL & BEHAVIORAL DISORDERS IN YOUTH. *see* PSYCHOLOGY

616.8 AUS ISSN 1832-8385
RESEARCH BULLETIN. Text in English. 2005. s-a. free to members (effective 2009). back issues avail. **Document type:** *Bulletin, Trade.* **Description:** Highlights the various issues that affect the lives of the people with mental illness.
Formerly (until 2006): Research Report
Related titles: Online - full text ed.
Published by: Sane Australia, PO Box 226, South Melbourne, VIC 3205, Australia. TEL 61-3-96825933, FAX 61-3-96825944, info@sane.org.

616.8 USA ISSN 1750-9467
RESEARCH IN AUTISM SPECTRUM DISORDERS. Abbreviated title: R A S D. Text in English. 2007. q. EUR 334 in Europe to institutions; JPY 46,500 in Japan to institutions; USD 396 elsewhere to institutions (effective 2012). adv. back issues avail.; reprints avail. **Document type:** *Journal, Academic/Scholarly.* **Description:** Includes diagnosis, incidence and prevalence, methods of evaluating treatment effects, educational, pharmacological, and psychological interventions across the life span.
Related titles: Online - full text ed.: ISSN 1878-0237 (from ScienceDirect).
Indexed: B21, CA, CurCont, EMBASE, ERIC, ExcerpMed, NSA, P03, P30, PsycInfo, SCOPUS, SSCI, T02, W07.
—IE, Ingenta. **CCC.**
Published by: Elsevier Inc. (Subsidiary of: Elsevier Science & Technology), 1600 John F Kennedy Blvd, Philadelphia, PA 19103. TEL 215-239-3900, FAX 215-238-7883, JournalCustomerService-usa@elsevier.com. Ed. Johnny L. Matson. Adv. contact Janine Castle TEL 44-1865-843844.

616.8 GBR ISSN 0891-4222
HV1570.5.U65 CODEN: RDDIEF
➤ **RESEARCH IN DEVELOPMENTAL DISABILITIES.** Text in English. 1987. 6/yr. EUR 759 in Europe to institutions; JPY 100,400 in Japan to institutions; USD 847 elsewhere to institutions (effective 2012). back issues avail. **Document type:** *Journal, Academic/Scholarly.* **Description:** Designed to original behavioral research and theory of severe and pervasive developmental disabilities.
Formed by the merger of (1980-1986): Applied Research in Mental Retardation (0270-3092); (1981-1986): Analysis and Intervention in Developmental Disabilities (0270-4684)
Related titles: Microfilm ed.: (from PQC); Online - full text ed.: ISSN 1873-3379 (from IngentaConnect, ScienceDirect).
Indexed: A01, A03, A08, A20, A22, A26, AMED, ASCA, ASSIA, B25, BIOSIS Prev, BRD, C06, C07, CA, CPE, ChPerI, CurCont, DentInd, E-psyche, E02, E03, ECER, EMBASE, ERA, ERI, ERIC, EdA, EdI, ExcerpMed, F09, FR, FamI, I05, INI, IndMed, M12, MEDLINE, MycolAb, P03, P30, PsycInfo, PsycholAb, R10, Reac, S02, S03, S20, S21, SCOPUS, SSCI, T02, V05, W03, W07, YAE&RB.
—BLDSC (7738.450000), GNLM, IE, Infotrieve, Ingenta, INIST. **CCC.**
Published by: Pergamon (Subsidiary of: Elsevier Science & Technology), The Blvd, Langford Ln, East Park, Kidlington, Oxford OX5 1GB, United Kingdom. TEL 44-1865-843000, FAX 44-1865-843010, JournalsCustomerServiceEMEA@elsevier.com. Ed. Johnny L Matson. **Subscr. to:** Elsevier BV, Radarweg 29, PO Box 211, Amsterdam 1000 AE, Netherlands. TEL 31-20-4853757, FAX 31-20-4853432, http://www.elsevier.nl.

616.8 USA ISSN 1816-4943
➤ **RESEARCH JOURNAL OF PARASITOLOGY.** Text in English. 2006. q. **Document type:** *Journal, Academic/Scholarly.* **Description:** Contains papers on all aspects of parasitology and host-parasite relationships, ranging from the latest discoveries in biochemical and molecular biology to ecology and epidemiology in the context of the medical, veterinary and biological sciences.
Related titles: Online - full text ed.
Indexed: A01, A29, A34, A35, A36, AgBio, AgrForAb, AnBeAb, B21, B23, BP, C30, CA, CABA, E12, E17, EMBASE, ESPM, EntAb, ExcerpMed, F08, F11, F12, GH, H16, H17, IndVet, N04, O01, OR, OceAb, P32, P33, P39, P40, R07, R08, R12, R13, RA&MP, SCOPUS, T02, T05, TAR, VS, Z01.
Published by: Academic Journals Inc., 224, 5th Ave, No 2218, New York, NY 10001. FAX 888-777-8532, support@scialert.com, http://www.academicjournalsinc.com/.

616.8 NLD ISSN 0922-6028
CODEN: RNNEEL
➤ **RESTORATIVE NEUROLOGY AND NEUROSCIENCE.** Text in English. 1989. bi-m. USD 1,534 combined subscription in North America (print & online eds.); EUR 1,095 combined subscription elsewhere (print & online eds.) (effective 2012). bk.rev. back issues avail. **Document type:** *Journal, Academic/Scholarly.* **Description:** Publishes papers from an interdisciplinary perspective on the plasticity and response of the nervous system to accidental or experimental injuries, or transplantation.
Related titles: Microform ed.: (from PQC); Online - full text ed.: ISSN 1878-3627 (from IngentaConnect).
Indexed: A01, A03, A08, A20, A22, ASCA, B21, BIOBASE, CA, CIN, ChemAb, ChemTitl, E-psyche, E01, EMBASE, ExcerpMed, IABS, ISR, Inpharma, MEDLINE, NSA, NSCI, P03, P30, PsycInfo, PsycholAb, R10, Reac, SCI, SCOPUS, T02, W07.
—BLDSC (7777.865100), CASDDS, GNLM, IE, Infotrieve, Ingenta, INIST. **CCC.**
Published by: I O S Press, Nieuwe Hemweg 6B, Amsterdam, 1013 BG, Netherlands. TEL 31-20-6883355, FAX 31-20-6870019, info@iospress.nl. Ed. Dr. Bernhard A Sabel TEL 49-391-6721800. **Subscr. to:** I O S Press, Inc, 4502 Rachael Manor Dr, Fairfax, VA 22032-3631. sales@iospress.com; Globe Publication Pvt. Ltd., C-62 Inderpuri, New Delhi 100 012, India. TEL 91-11-579-3211, 91-11-579-3212, FAX 91-11-579-8876, custserve@globepub.com, http://www.globepub.com; Kinokuniya Co Ltd., Shinjuku 3-chome, Shinjuku-ku, Tokyo 160-0022, Japan. FAX 81-3-3439-1094, journal@kinokuniya.co.jp, http://www.kinokuniya.co.jp.

616.8 618 AUS
RETT SYNDROME ASSOCIATION OF AUSTRALIA. NEWSLETTER. Text in English. 1989. q. looseleaf. **Document type:** *Newsletter.*
Indexed: E-psyche.
Published by: Rett Syndrome Association of Australia, c/o Telethon Institute for Child Health Research, PO Box 855, West Perth, W.A. 6872, Australia. TEL 61-8-94897790, FAX 61-8-94897700, rett@ichr.uwa.edu.au, http://aussierett.ichr.uwa.edu.au/.

616.89 362.2 SWE ISSN 0283-7587
REVANSCH!. Text in Swedish. 1980. s-m. SEK 150 (effective 2007). adv. **Document type:** *Magazine, Consumer.*
Formerly (until 1985): R S M H - Information - Revansch (0280-0187)
Indexed: E-psyche.
Published by: Riksfoerbundet foer Social och Mental Haelsa, Instrumentvaegen 10, Haegersten, 12653, Sweden. TEL 46-8-7723360, FAX 46-8-7723361, rsmh@rsmh.see. adv.: page SEK 4,850.

REVIEW OF EXISTENTIAL PSYCHOLOGY AND PSYCHIATRY. *see* PSYCHOLOGY

616.8 USA
RC321
REVIEW OF PSYCHIATRY SERIES. Text in English. 1982. irreg., latest vol.24, 2005. price varies. back issues avail. **Document type:** *Monographic series, Academic/Scholarly.*
Former titles (until 1998): Review of Psychiatry (1041-5882); (until 1988): Psychiatry Update (0736-1866); (until 1983): Psychiatry (0734-8436)
Indexed: A22.
—BLDSC (7794.160900). **CCC.**
Published by: American Psychiatric Publishing, Inc., 1000 Wilson Blvd, Ste 1825, Arlington, VA 22209. TEL 703-907-7322, 800-368-5777, FAX 703-907-1091, appi@psych.org.

REVIEWS IN ANALGESIA; an international journal. *see* MEDICAL SCIENCES—Anaesthesiology

616.8 USA ISSN 1545-2913
REVIEWS IN NEUROLOGICAL DISEASES. Text in English. 2004 (Win.). q. USD 1,250 to individuals; USD 2,500 to institutions (effective 2009). back issues avail. **Document type:** *Journal, Academic/Scholarly.*
Related titles: Online - full text ed.: ISSN 1949-4378.
Indexed: EMBASE, ExcerpMed, MEDLINE, P30, R10, Reac, SCOPUS.
—BLDSC (7793.547500), IE, Ingenta.
Published by: MedReviews, Llc, 1370 Broadway, Ste 900, New York, NY 10018. TEL 212-971-4036, FAX 212-971-4047, sblack@medreviews.com.

616.8 DEU ISSN 0334-1763
RC321 CODEN: RNEUEO
➤ **REVIEWS IN THE NEUROSCIENCES.** Text in English. 1986. bi-m. EUR 534, USD 801 to institutions; EUR 615, USD 923 combined subscription to institutions (print & online eds.) (effective 2012). adv. back issues avail. **Document type:** *Journal, Academic/Scholarly.* **Description:** Provides a forum in which those working in the neurosciences can find critical evaluations of selective topics.
Related titles: Online - full text ed.: ISSN 2191-0200. EUR 534, USD 801 to institutions (effective 2012).
Indexed: A20, A22, ASCA, BIOSIS Prev, E-psyche, EMBASE, ExcerpMed, IndMed, MEDLINE, MycolAb, NSCI, P03, P30, PsycInfo, R10, Reac, SCI, SCOPUS, W07.
—BLDSC (7793.571000), CASDDS, GNLM, IE, Infotrieve, Ingenta.
Published by: Walter de Gruyter GmbH & Co. KG, Genthiner Str 13, Berlin, 10785, Germany. TEL 49-30-260050, FAX 49-30-26005251, info@degruyter.com, http://www.degruyter.de. Ed. J P Huston. Circ: 1,000.

➤ **REVIEWS OF OCULOMOTOR RESEARCH.** *see* MEDICAL SCIENCES—Ophthalmology And Optometry

616.8 ARG ISSN 1668-9151
REVISTA ARGENTINA DE NEUROCIRUGIA. Text in Spanish, English, Portuguese. 1984. q. back issues avail. **Document type:** *Journal, Academic/Scholarly.*
Related titles: Online - full text ed.: ISSN 1850-1532. 2005. free (effective 2011) (from SciELO).
Published by: Asociacion Argentina de Neurocirugia, Ave Callao 441 8o. F, Buenos Aires, C1022AAE, Argentina. TEL 54-11-43715631, FAX 54-11-43721256, rev.neurocirugia@aanc.org.ar, http://www.aanc.org.ar/. Circ: 600.

616.8 ARG ISSN 1668-5415
REVISTA ARGENTINA DE NEUROPSICOLOGIA. Text in Spanish. 2003. s-a. **Document type:** *Journal, Academic/Scholarly.*
Media: Online - full text.
Published by: Sociedad de Neuropsicologia de Argentina, Malabia 2478, 3o 26, Buenos Aires, C1425EZJ, Argentina. TEL 54-11-48316584, http://www.sonepsa.com.ar.

616.8 150 ARG ISSN 0325-2434
REVISTA ARGENTINA DE PSIQUIATRIA Y PSICOLOGIA DE LA INFANCIA Y DE LA ADOLESCENCIA. Text in Spanish. 1970. s-a. **Document type:** *Journal, Academic/Scholarly.*
Published by: Asociacion Argentina de Psiquiatria y Psicologia de la Infancia y de la Adolescencia (A S A P P I A), Soler 4417, Buenos Aires, 1425, Argentina. asappia@intramed.net.ar.

REVISTA BRASILEIRA DE ANALISE TRANSACIONAL. *see* PSYCHOLOGY

616.8 BRA ISSN 0101-8469
RC346 CODEN: RBNEES
REVISTA BRASILEIRA DE NEUROLOGIA. Text in Portuguese; Summaries in English, Portuguese. 1949. bi-m. adv. charts; illus. **Document type:** *Journal, Academic/Scholarly.* **Description:** Presents studies in clinical neurology.
Formerly (until 1982): Jornal Brasileiro de Neurologia (0021-7514)
Indexed: A22, C01, ChemAb, E-psyche, EMBASE, ExcerpMed, IBR, IBZ, IndMed, P03, P30, PsycInfo, PsycholAb, R10, Reac, SCOPUS.
—GNLM, Ingenta, INIST.
Published by: (Universidade Federal do Rio de Janeiro, Instituto de Neurologia), Editora Cientifica Nacional Ltda. (E C N), Rua da Gloria 366, 3o Andar, Gloria, Rio de Janeiro, RJ 20241-180, Brazil. ecn@rj.sol.com.br. Circ: 4,000.

616.8 BRA ISSN 1414-0365
➤ **REVISTA BRASILEIRA DE NEUROLOGIA E PSIQUIATRIA.** Summaries in English, Portuguese; Text in Portuguese. 1996. q. bk.rev. abstr.; bibl. back issues avail. **Document type:** *Journal, Academic/Scholarly.*
Indexed: C01, E-psyche, EMBASE, ExcerpMed, R10, Reac, SCOPUS.
—Ingenta.
Published by: (Colegio Brasileiro de Neuropsicofarmacologia), Editora Cientifica Nacional Ltda. (E C N), Rua da Gloria 366, 3o Andar, Gloria, Rio de Janeiro, RJ 20241-180, Brazil. ecn@rj.sol.com.br.

616.8 BRA ISSN 0104-5393
REVISTA BRASILEIRA DE PSICODRAMA. Text in Portuguese. 1990. s-a. BRL 60 (effective 2006). **Document type:** *Journal, Academic/Scholarly.*
Published by: Federacao Brasileira de Psicodrama (F E B R A P), Rua Cardoso de Almeida 23, 6o Andar, Perdizes, Sao Paulo, 05013-000, Brazil. TEL 55-11-38733467, FAX 55-11-36733674, http://febrap.org.br. Ed. Devanir Merengue.

616.8 BRA ISSN 1516-8530
REVISTA BRASILEIRA DE PSICOTERAPIA. Text in Portuguese. 1999. 3/yr. BRL 75 (effective 2006). **Document type:** *Journal, Academic/Scholarly.*
Published by: Centro de Estudos Luis Guedes, Rua Ramiro Barcelos 2350, sala 2218, Porto Alegre, RS 90035-903, Brazil. TEL 55-51-33305655, FAX 55-51-33307738, celg@hcpa.ufrgs.br, http://www.ufrgs.br/psiq/celg.html.

616.89 BRA ISSN 1516-4446
➤ **REVISTA BRASILEIRA DE PSIQUIATRIA.** Text in Portuguese; Summaries in English, Spanish. 1967. q. USD 100 (effective 2006). adv. bk.rev. bibl.; charts; stat. **Document type:** *Journal, Academic/Scholarly.* **Description:** Papers on psychiatry and correlated disciplines of general interest to mental health professionals from Brazil and other Latin American countries.
Former titles (until 1998): Associacao Brasileira de Psiquiatria e Asociacion Psiquiatrica de la America Latina. Revista (0102-7646); (until 1985): Associacao Brasileira de Psiquiatria Revista (0101-5311); (until 1972): Revista Brasileira de Psiquiatria (0375-071X)
Related titles: Online - full text ed.: ISSN 1809-452X. free (effective 2011).
Indexed: A01, A20, A22, B25, BIOSIS Prev, CA, CurCont, E-psyche, EMBASE, ExcerpMed, F03, F04, IndMed, MEDLINE, MycolAb, P03, P30, PsycInfo, PsycholAb, R10, Reac, S02, S03, SCI, SCOPUS, SSCI, T02, W07.
—GNLM, IE, Ingenta.
Published by: Associacao Brasileira de Psiquiatria, Rua Pedro de Toledo 967, casa 1, Vl Clementino, Sao Paulo, SP 04039-032, Brazil. TEL 55-11-50816799, FAX 55-11-55796210. Eds. Euripides C Miguel, Jair de Jesu Mari. Circ: 5,000. **Co-sponsor:** Associacao Psiquiatrica da America Latina.

616.8 BRA ISSN 1808-5687
REVISTA BRASILEIRA DE TERAPIAS COGNITIVAS/BRAZILIAN JOURNAL OF COGNITIVE THERAPIES. Text in Portuguese; Abstracts in Portuguese, English. 2005. s-a. **Document type:** *Journal, Academic/Scholarly.*
Published by: Sociedade Brasileira de Terapias Cognitivas, Rua Ramiro Barcelos 1450, Sala 403, Rio Branco, Porto Alegre, RS 90035-002, Brazil. sbtc@sbtc.org.br, http://www.sbtc.org.br.

616.853 CHL ISSN 0717-5337
REVISTA CHILENA DE EPILEPSIA. Text in Spanish. 2000. q. **Document type:** *Journal, Academic/Scholarly.*
Related titles: Online - full text ed.: USD 35 (effective 2005).
Published by: Sociedad de Epileptologia de Chile contacto@epilepsiadechile.com, http://www.epilepsiadechile.com.

616.8 CHL ISSN 0718-4190
REVISTA CHILENA DE MEDICINA DEL SUENO. Text in Spanish. 2006. a. **Document type:** *Monographic series, Academic/Scholarly.*
Published by: Sociedad Chilena de Medicina del Sueno, Feijoa 9621, La Florida, Santiago, Chile. TEL 56-2-7690239, FAX 56-2-2972302, contacto@sochimes.cl, http://www.sochimes.cl/. Ed. Julia Santin.

REVISTA CHILENA DE NEUROCIRUGIA. *see* MEDICAL SCIENCES—Surgery

616.8 150 CHL ISSN 0718-0551
REVISTA CHILENA DE NEUROPSICOLOGIA. Text in Spanish. 2006. s-a. **Document type:** *Journal, Academic/Scholarly.*
Related titles: Online - full text ed.: ISSN 0718-4913. 2006.
Published by: Universidad Mayor, Facultad de Psicologia, Av Alemania, Temuco, 0281, Chile. TEL 56-2-3281000, http://www.umayor.cl.

616.8 CHL ISSN 0034-7388
RC321
REVISTA CHILENA DE NEUROPSIQUIATRIA. Text in Spanish. 1978. q. adv. bk.rev. abstr.; bibl.; charts; illus.; stat. reprint service avail. from IRC. **Document type:** *Journal, Academic/Scholarly.*
Related titles: Online - full text ed.: ISSN 0717-9227. 2002. free (effective 2011) (from SciELO).
Indexed: ChemAb, E-psyche, IBR, IBZ, IndMed, PsycholAb, R10, Reac, SCOPUS.
Published by: Sociedad de Neurologia, Psiquiatria y Neurocirugia de Chile, Carlos Silva 1292, Depto 22, Providencia, Santiago, Chile. TEL 56-2-2342460, secretariagral@123.cl, http://www.sonepsyn.cl. Ed. Hernan Silva. Circ: 1,000.

616.89 CHL ISSN 0718-3798
REVISTA CHILENA DE PSIQUIATRIA Y NEUROLOGIA DE LA INFANCIA Y LA ADOLESCENCIA. Text in Spanish. 1990. 3/yr. back issues avail. **Document type:** *Journal, Academic/Scholarly.*

Former titles (until 2006): Sociedad de Psiquiatria y Neurologia de la Infancia y Adolescencia. Revista (0718-1698); (until 2004): Sociedad de Psiquiatria y Neurologia de la Infancia y Adolescencia. Boletin (0717-1331)
Related titles: Online - full text ed.
Published by: Sociedad de Psiquiatria y Neurologia de la Infancia y Adolescencia, Esmeralda, 678 Of. 203, Santiago, Chile. TEL 56-2-6320884, sopnia@sopnia.com. Ed. Freyna Fernandez K.

616.89 COL ISSN 0034-7450
CODEN: RCPSBR
REVISTA COLOMBIANA DE PSIQUIATRIA. Text in Spanish. 1964. q. COP 120,000 domestic; USD 120 foreign (effective 2011). adv. bk.rev. abstr.; charts; illus. index. back issues avail. **Document type:** *Journal, Academic/Scholarly.*
Related titles: Online - full text ed.: free (effective 2011) (from SciELO).
Indexed: A26, C01, CA, E-psyche, F04, I04, I05, P03, P30, PsycInfo, PsycholAb, S02, S03, T02.
—GNLM.
Published by: Sociedad Colombiana de Psiquiatria, Carrera 18 No. 84-87 Ofic 403, PO Box 203, Bogota, CUND, Colombia. TEL 57-1-2561148, FAX 57-1-6162706, revista@psiquiatria.org.co, http://www.psiquiatria.org.co/. Ed. Carlos Gomez Restrepo. Circ: 1,500.

616.8 PER ISSN 0034-8597
REVISTA DE NEURO-PSIQUIATRIA. Text in Spanish; Summaries in English, French, German. 1938. q. USD 80 foreign (effective 2007). adv. bk.rev. abstr.; charts; illus. index. **Document type:** *Journal, Academic/Scholarly.*
Related titles: Online - full text ed.: ISSN 1609-7394. 1991.
Indexed: C01, E-psyche, IBR, IBZ, IndMed, P30, PsycholAb.
—GNLM.
Published by: Propaceb, Editora de Publicaciones s.r.l., Casilla 1589, Lima, 100, Peru. FAX 51-1-4385479. Eds. Javier Mariategui, Luis Trelles.

616.8 ARG ISSN 1514-3716
RD593
REVISTA DE NEUROCIRUGIA. Text in Spanish. 1998. q. back issues avail. **Document type:** *Journal, Academic/Scholarly.*
Related titles: Online - full text ed.: free (effective 2011).
Published by: Sociedad de Neurocirugia de la Plata, Servicio de Neurocirugia H. Rossi, Calle 37 No. 183, La Plata, 1900, Argentina. cegagliardi@intramed.net.ar, http://www.rneurocirugia.com/. Ed. Carlos E Gagliardi.

618.8 ESP ISSN 0210-0010
➤ **REVISTA DE NEUROLOGIA.** Text in Spanish. 1973. bi-m. EUR 300 domestic to institutions; EUR 325 in the European Union to institutions; EUR 350 elsewhere to institutions (effective 2008). adv. bk.rev. **Document type:** *Journal, Academic/Scholarly.*
Related titles: Online - full text ed.: ISSN 1576-6578. 199?; Supplement(s): Suplementos de Revista de Neurologia. ISSN 1576-6411. 199?.
Indexed: A20, A22, E-psyche, EMBASE, ExcerpMed, F09, IME, INI, IndMed, MEDLINE, NSCI, P30, R10, Reac, SCI, SCOPUS, W07.
—BLDSC (7868.355000), GNLM, IE, Infotrieve, Ingenta, INIST. **CCC.**
Published by: Viguera Editores, Plaza Tetuan 7, Barcelona, 08010, Spain. TEL 34-932-478188, FAX 34-932-317250, editor@revneurol.com, http://www.revneurol.com. Circ: 10,000.

618.8 ESP ISSN 1576-1185
REVISTA DE NEUROLOGIA CLINICA. Text in Spanish. 2000. q. **Document type:** *Journal, Academic/Scholarly.*
—CCC.
Published by: Viguera Editores, Plaza Tetuan 7, Barcelona, 08010, Spain. TEL 34-932-478188, FAX 34-932-317250, editor@revneurol.com, http://www.revneurol.com.

REVISTA DE PSICOANALISIS (MADRID). *see* PSYCHOLOGY

616.8 ESP ISSN 1697-1892
REVISTA DE PSICOGERIATRIA. Text in Spanish. 2001. 4/yr. EUR 50 to individuals; EUR 76 to institutions; EUR 38 to students (effective 2007). **Document type:** *Journal, Academic/Scholarly.*
Indexed: SCOPUS, ToxAb.
Published by: (Sociedad Espanola de Gerontopsiquiatria y Psicogeriatria), Aran Ediciones, Castello 128, 1o, Madrid, 28006, Spain. TEL 34-91-7820030, FAX 34-91-5615787, edita@grupoaran.com, http://www.grupoaran.com.

616.89 ESP ISSN 1695-8691
REVISTA DE PSICOPATOLOGIA Y SALUD MENTAL DEL NINO Y DEL ADOLESCENTE. Text in Spanish. 2003. s-a. EUR 20 domestic; EUR 28 elsewhere (effective 2009). back issues avail. **Document type:** *Journal, Academic/Scholarly.*
Published by: Fundacio Orienta, C Vidal i Borraquer, 28, Sant Boi de Llobregat, Barcelona, 08830, Spain. TEL 34-93-6358810, FAX 34-93-6303457, orienta@fundacioorienta.com. Ed. Alfons Icart.

616.85 URY ISSN 0255-8327
REVISTA DE PSICOTERAPIA PSICOANALITICA. Text in Spanish. 1983. irreg. back issues avail. **Document type:** *Journal, Academic/Scholarly.*
Published by: Asociacion Uruguaya de Psicoterapia Psicoanalitica, Canelones, 2208, Montevideo, 11200, Uruguay. TEL 598-2-4084985, FAX 598-2-4022066, contacto@audepp.org.

REVISTA DE PSICOTERAPIA Y PSICOSOMATICA. *see* PSYCHOLOGY

616.89 CHL ISSN 0716-1220
REVISTA DE PSIQUIATRIA CLINICA. Text in Spanish. 1936. a. **Document type:** *Journal, Academic/Scholarly.*
Former titles (until 1957): Revista de Psiquiatria (0370-6834); (until 1951): Revista de Psiquiatria y Disciplinas Conexas (0716-436X)
Published by: Universidad de Chile, Departamento de Psiquiatria y Salud Mental, Ave de la Paz, 1003, Santiago, 70010, Chile. TEL 56-2-9788601, http://www.uchile.cl/. Ed. Julio Pallavicini Gonzalez.

616.89 BRA ISSN 0101-6083
CODEN: RPCLF2
➤ **REVISTA DE PSIQUIATRIA CLINICA.** Text in Portuguese. 1962. bi-m. adv. bk.rev. back issues avail. **Document type:** *Journal, Academic/Scholarly.*
Formerly (until 1973): Universidade de Sao Paulo. Faculdade de Medicina. Hospital das Clinicas. Clinica Psiquiatrica. Boletim (0102-2814)
Related titles: Online - full text ed.: ISSN 1806-938X. free (effective 2011).
Indexed: C01, E-psyche, EMBASE, ExcerpMed, R10, Reac, SCI, SCOPUS, W07.
—BLDSC (7870.203000), IE.
Published by: (Universidade de Sao Paulo, Faculdade de Medicina, Instituto de Psiquiatria), Lemos Editorial & Graficos Ltda., Rua Rui Barbosa, 70, B Vista, Sao Paulo, SP 01326-010, Brazil. TEL 55-11-251-4300, FAX 55-11-251-4300, lemospl@netpoint.com.br, http://www.lemos.com.br. Ed. Dr. Wagner Farid Gattaz.

616.89 PRT ISSN 0873-612X
REVISTA DE PSIQUIATRIA CONSILIAR E DE LIGACAO. Text in Portuguese. 1995. irreg.
Published by: Grupo Portugues de Psiquiatria Consiliar Ligacao e Psicossomatica, Hospital do Sobral Cid Ceira, Coimbra, 3000, Portugal. Ed. Dr. Celia Franco.

616.89 BRA ISSN 0101-8108
REVISTA DE PSIQUIATRIA DO RIO GRANDE DO SUL. Text in Portuguese. 1979. 3/yr. BRL 40 (effective 2004).
Related titles: CD-ROM ed.: BRL 10; Online - full text ed.: free (effective 2011).
Indexed: C01, EMBASE, ExcerpMed, P03, PsycInfo, PsycholAb, R10, Reac, SCOPUS.
Published by: Sociedade de Psiquiatria do Rio Grande do Sul, Av. Ipiranga, 5311, Sala 202, Porto Alegre, RS 90610-001, Brazil. TEL 55-51-33364846, FAX 55-51-33396277, http://www.sprs.og.br/. Eds. Cesar Luis de Souza Brito, Jaco Zaslavsky.

616.8 618.92 ESP ISSN 1130-9512
REVISTA DE PSIQUIATRIA INFANTO-JUVENIL. Text in Spanish. 1983. q. free to members. back issues avail. **Document type:** *Journal, Academic/Scholarly.*
Former titles (until 1990): Revista de Neuropsiquiatria Infanto-Juvenil (0214-6428); (until 1987): Revista de Neuropsiquiatria Infantil (0213-4985)
Indexed: E-psyche, P03, PsycholAb.
—GNLM.
Published by: Asociacion Espanola de Psiquiatria del Nino y el Adolescente, Espronceda No. 6 2o. B, Naval de Mora la Mata, Caceres, 10300, Spain. http://www.aepij.com. Ed. Luid Martin Recuero.

616.89 ESP ISSN 1888-9891
REVISTA DE PSIQUIATRIA Y SALUD MENTAL. Text in Spanish. 2008. q. EUR 84.21 combined subscription to individuals; EUR 213.20 combined subscription to institutions (effective 2009). back issues avail. **Document type:** *Journal, Academic/Scholarly.*
Related titles: Online - full text ed.: ISSN 1989-4600. 2008 (from ScienceDirect).
Indexed: CA, CurCont, EMBASE, ExcerpMed, SCOPUS, SSCI, T02, W07.
—CCC.
Published by: Elsevier Doyma (Subsidiary of: Elsevier Health Sciences), Traversa de Gracia 17-21, Barcelona, 08021, Spain. TEL 34-932-418800, FAX 34-932-419020, editorial@elsevier.com. Ed. Julio Vallejo Ruilabe. Circ: 2,000.

616.8 ECU ISSN 1019-8113
➤ **REVISTA ECUATORIANA DE NEUROLOGIA.** Text in Spanish; Summaries in English, Spanish. 1992. 3/yr. USD 35 domestic; USD 50 foreign (effective 2002). adv. bk.rev. **Document type:** *Journal, Academic/Scholarly.*
Indexed: A22, ASCA, C01, E-psyche, EMBASE, ExcerpMed, NSCI, R10, Reac, SCI, SCOPUS, W07.
—BLDSC (7852.810000), GNLM, IE, Ingenta.
Published by: Sociedad Ecuatoriana de Neurologia, Apdo (09-01) 3734, Guayaquil, Ecuador. FAX 593-4285790. Ed. Dr. Oscar H Del Brutto. adv.: B&W page USD 200, color page USD 1,000. Circ: 1,000.

616.89 ESP ISSN 1137-3148
REVISTA ELECTRONICA DE PSIQUIATRIA. Key Title: Psiquiatria.com. Text in Spanish. 1997. q. free to qualified personnel (effective 2010). back issues avail. **Document type:** *Journal, Academic/Scholarly.* **Description:** Publishes papers on psychiatry research.
Media: Online - full text.
Published by: InterSalud, Apdo de Correos 227, Palmova, Mallorca, 07181, Spain. info@intersalud.es, http://www.intersalud.es/.

REVISTA ESPANOLA DE NEUROPSICOLOGIA. *see* PSYCHOLOGY

616.8 GTM ISSN 1818-1023
BF1
REVISTA INTERNACIONAL DE PSICOLOGIA. Text in Spanish. 2000. s-a. free (effective 2011). **Document type:** *Journal, Academic/Scholarly.*
Media: Online - full text.
Published by: Instituto de la Familia

616.8 MEX ISSN 0188-9842
P37 CODEN: RLPLF5
REVISTA LATINA DE PENSAMIENTO Y LENGUAJE. Text in Spanish. s-a. USD 50 to individuals; USD 100 to libraries (effective 2004).
Indexed: PsycholAb, SCOPUS.
Published by: (Sociedad Latinoamericana de Neuropsicologia ESP), Sociedad Iberoamericana de Pensamiento y Lenguaje, c/o Victor Manuel Alcaraz, Instituto de Neurociencias, Rayo 2611, Col. Jardines del Bosque, Guadalajara, Jal, Mexico. TEL 52-33-36477776. Ed. Victor Manuel Alcaraz.

616.89 ESP ISSN 1699-4620
REVISTA LATINA DE TERAPIA GESTALT. Text in Multiple languages. 2004. a. back issues avail. **Document type:** *Journal, Academic/Scholarly.*
Media: Online - full text.
Published by: Asociacion Vasca de Terapia Gestalt/Euskalherriko Gestalt Terapia Elkargoa, Isabel II Ave de 18-1o A, San Sebastian, Donosia 20011, Spain. TEL 34-943-457738, zimentarric@euskalnet.net/. Ed. Patxi Sansinenea.

616.8 MEX ISSN 2007-0799
▼ ➤ **REVISTA LATINOAMERICANA DE MEDICINA CONDUCTUAL/ LATIN AMERICAN JOURNAL OF BEHAVIORAL MEDICINE.** Text in English, Spanish. 2011. s-a. MXN 380 domestic to individuals; USD 35 foreign to individuals; MXN 760 domestic to institutions; USD 70 foreign to institutions; MXN 150, USD 17 per issue (effective 2011). adv. bk.rev. abstr.; bibl.; charts; illus.; stat. back issues avail. **Document type:** *Journal, Academic/Scholarly.* **Description:** Publishes original research on health psychology, public health, behavioral medicine, positive psychology, and different approaches to generate knowledge on how to improve and promote health in humans, following different scientific techniques.
Related titles: Online - full text ed.
Published by: Sociedad Mexicana de Analisis de la Conducta/Mexican Society of Behavior Analysis, Calle Zaragoza 91-2, Deleg. Tlalpan, Mexico City, DF 14268, Mexico. TEL 52-777-3179988, http://www.smac.org.mx/. Ed. Rocio Hernandez-Pozo. Pub. Teresa Rojas. Adv. contact Rosendo Hernandez Castro. Circ: 350.

616.8 BRA ISSN 1415-4714
REVISTA LATINOAMERICANA DE PSICOPATOLOGIA FUNDAMENTAL. Text in Portuguese, Spanish. 2008. irreg. free (effective 2011).
Media: Online - full text.
Indexed: A01, C01, CJPI, P20, P25, P48, P54, PQC, SCOPUS, SSCI, T02, W07.
Published by: Associacao Universitaria de Pesquisa em Psicopatologia Fundamental, Rua Tupi 397, cj 104, Sao Paulo, 01233-001, Brazil.

616.8 MEX ISSN 1665-5044
RC321
REVISTA MEXICANA DE NEUROCIENCIA. Text in Spanish. 2000. bi-m. free membership (effective 2006). back issues avail. **Document type:** *Journal, Academic/Scholarly.*
Related titles: Online - full text ed.
Indexed: A01, CA, EMBASE, ExcerpMed, SCOPUS, T02.
Published by: Academia Mexicana de Neurologia, San Francisco, 1384 Torre B 7o Piso, Col. del Valle, Mexico, D.F., 03100, Mexico. TEL 52-55-55759312, FAX 52-55-55599833, revmexneurociencia@yahoo.com. Ed. Lilia Nunez Orozco.

616.8 ARG ISSN 0325-0938
REVISTA NEUROLOGICA ARGENTINA. Text in Spanish; Summaries in Spanish, English. 1936. 3/yr. back issues avail.
Formerly (until 1974): Revista Neurologica de Buenos Aires (0370-6494)
Related titles: Online - full text ed.: ISSN 1515-3347. 1999.
Indexed: EMBASE, ExcerpMed, P30, R10, Reac, SCOPUS.
—BLDSC (7868.360000), GNLM. **CCC.**
Published by: Sociedad Neurologica Argentina, Thames 2127, Buenos Aires, Argentina. TEL 54-11-47735850, sociedadneurologica@ciudad.com.ar. Ed. Ricardo Allegri. Circ: 2,000.

616.8 PER ISSN 1561-3178
REVISTA PERUANA DE NEUROLOGIA. Text in Spanish. 1995. 3/yr. USD 60 to individuals; USD 80 to institutions (effective 2005). **Document type:** *Journal, Academic/Scholarly.*
Related titles: Online - full text ed.: ISSN 1609-7157.
Published by: Sociedad Peruana de Neurologia, Av Javier Prado este Cdra 27, San Borja, Lima, Peru. TEL 51-1-4670293, FAX 51-1-4361113, spn2000@latinmail.com.

616.8 PER ISSN 2079-0058
▼ **REVISTA PERUANA DE PSIQUIATRIA.** Text in Spanish. 2010. s-a. **Document type:** *Journal, Academic/Scholarly.*
Published by: Asociacion Psiquiatrica Peruana, Ave Angamos Oeste, 387, Ofic. 203, Miraflores, Lima, Peru. TEL 51-1-4473739, app@speedy,com.pe, http://www.app.org.pe/index.htm.

616.8 PER ISSN 0255-7967
REVISTA PERUANA DE PSIQUIATRIA HERMILIO VALDIZAN. Text in Spanish. 1983. q. **Document type:** *Journal, Academic/Scholarly.*
Published by: Hospital Hermilio Valdizan, Carretera Central Km 3.5, Santa Anita, Lima, Peru. TEL 51-1-4942410, nodohvaldizan@minsa.gob.pe, http://www.minsa.gob.pe.

▼ **REVISTA PORTUGUESA DE ENFERMAGEM DE SAUDE MENTAL.** *see* MEDICAL SCIENCES—Nurses And Nursing

616.8 PRT ISSN 1645-0078
REVISTA PORTUGUESA DE GRUPANALISE. Text in Portuguese. 2000. irreg. **Document type:** *Magazine, Trade.*
Related titles: Online - full text ed.: GrupanaliseOnline.pt.
Published by: Sociedade Portuguesa de Grupanalise, Rua Jose Carlos Barreiros 25, Lisbon, 1000-087, Portugal. http://www.grupanalise.pt.

616.8 ROM ISSN 1843-0783
➤ **REVISTA ROMANA DE NEUROLOGIE.** Text in Romanian. 2002. q. **Document type:** *Journal, Academic/Scholarly.*
Formerly (until 2002): Societatea de Neurologie din Romania. Revista (1583-4603)
Related titles: English Translation: Romanian Journal of Neurology. ISSN 1843-8148. 2007.
Indexed: A01, CA, EMBASE, SCOPUS, T02.
Published by: Societatea de Neurologie din Romania/Romanian Society of Neurology, 169 Splaiul Independentei, District 5, Bucharest, Romania. FAX 40-21-3128102, http://www.neurology.ro. Ed. Ovidiu Bajenaru.

616.853 URY ISSN 1510-7701
REVISTA URUGUAYA DE EPILEPSIA. Text in Spanish. 1984. irreg. **Document type:** *Journal, Academic/Scholarly.*
Formally: liga Uruguaya Contra la Epilepsia (0797-1052)
Published by: Liga Uruguaya Contra la Epilepsia (L U C E), Ciudadela 1217, Montevideo, 11600, Uruguay. TEL 598-2-9159625, FAX 598-2-4808423, ligaepi@montevideo.com.uy.

616.8 FRA ISSN 2101-6739
CODEN: RNURER
➤ **REVUE DE NEUROPSYCHOLOGIE NEUROSCIENCES COGNITIVES ET CLINIQUES.** Text in French. 1991. 4/yr. EUR 225 combined subscription domestic to institutions; EUR 241 combined subscription in Europe to institutions; EUR 249 combined subscription elsewhere to institutions (effective 2010). adv. bk.rev. **Document type:** *Journal, Academic/Scholarly.*
Formerly (until 2008): Revue de Neuropsychologie (1155-4452)
Related titles: Online - full text ed.: ISSN 2102-6025.
Indexed: A20, A22, ASCA, E-psyche, FR, P03, PsycInfo, PsycholAb, SCOPUS, SOPODA.

—BLDSC (7937.880000), IE, Ingenta, INIST.
Published by: (Societe de Neuropsychologie de Langue Francaise), John Libbey Eurotext, 127 Av. de la Republique, Montrouge, 92120, France. TEL 33-1-46730660, FAX 33-1-40840999, contact@jle.com, http://www.john-libbey-eurotext.fr. Ed. Francis Eustache.

➤ **REVUE EUROPEENE DE PSYCHOLOGIE APPLIQUEE/EUROPEAN REVIEW OF APPLIED PSYCHOLOGY.** *see* PSYCHOLOGY

616.8 FRA ISSN 1289-2130
REVUE FRANCAISE DE PSYCHIATRIE ET PSYCHOLOGIE MEDICALE. Text in French. 1996. m. (10/yr.). **Document type:** *Journal, Trade.*
Indexed: FR, RefZh.
—BLDSC (7904.253050), IE, Ingenta, INIST.
Published by: M F Groupe, 8 Rue Tronchet, Paris, 75008, France. TEL 33-1-140071121, FAX 33-1-140071094, http://www.mfgroupe.com. Circ: 6,000.

616.08 FRA ISSN 1164-4796
➤ **REVUE FRANCAISE DE PSYCHOSOMATIQUE.** Text in French; Abstracts in French, English. 1991. s-a. EUR 64 foreign to institutions (effective 2012). reprint service avail. from SCH. **Document type:** *Journal, Academic/Scholarly.*
Related titles: Online - full text ed.: ISSN 2105-2603.
Indexed: E-psyche, P03, PsycInfo, SCOPUS.
—GNLM, INIST.
Published by: (Institut de Psychosomatique), Presses Universitaires de France, 6 Avenue Reille, Paris, 75685, France. TEL 33-1-58103161, FAX 33-1-45897530, revues@puf.com, http://www.puf.com. Ed. Marina Papageorgiou.

616.8588 CAN
RC569.7.R48
➤ **REVUE FRANCOPHONE DE LA DEFICIENCE INTELLECTUELLE (ONLINE).** Text in French; Summaries in English, French. 1989. d. free (effective 2010). bibl. Index. **Document type:** *Journal, Academic/Scholarly.* **Description:** Publishes research results in intellectual disability and make exchanges between researchers, practisings and professionnals easier.
Formerly: Revue Francophone de la Deficience Intellectuelle (Print) (0847-5733)
Indexed: A22, FR, P03, PsycInfo, PsycholAb.
—IE, Ingenta, INIST. **CCC.**
Published by: Revue Francophone de la Deficience Intellectuelle, Universite du Quebec a Rimouski, Campus de Levis, Departement des Sciences de l'Education, 1595, boulevard Alphonse-Desjardins, Levis, PQ G6V 0A6, Canada. TEL 418-833-8800 ext 3283, FAX 418-838-6973, rfdi@rfdi.org, http://www.rfdi.org/. Pub., R&P, Adv. contact Hubert Gascon.

616.891 FRA ISSN 1967-2055
REVUE LACANIENNE. Text in French. 2008. q. EUR 65 domestic to individuals; EUR 75 domestic to institutions; EUR 80 foreign (effective 2011). back issues avail. **Document type:** *Journal, Academic/Scholarly.*
Related titles: Online - full text ed.: ISSN 2109-9553.
Published by: (Association Lacanienne Internationale), Editions Eres, 33 Av. Marcel Dassault, Toulouse, 31500, France. TEL 33-5-61751576, FAX 33-5-61735289.

616.8 FRA ISSN 0035-3787
CODEN: RENEAM
➤ **REVUE NEUROLOGIQUE.** Text in French; Summaries in English. 1893. 10/yr. EUR 457 in Europe to institutions; EUR 405.48 in France to institutions; JPY 75,900 in Japan to institutions; USD 608 elsewhere to institutions (effective 2012). adv. bk.rev. abstr.; illus. index. reprints avail. **Document type:** *Journal, Academic/Scholarly.* **Description:** Publishes the works of the society, and French and foreign articles.
Related titles: Microfilm ed.: (from BHP); Microform ed.: (from BHP, PQC); Online - full text ed.: (from ScienceDirect).
Indexed: A20, A22, A36, ASCA, B25, BDM&CN, BIOSIS Prev, CABA, CISA, ChemAb, CurCont, E-psyche, E12, EMBASE, ExcerpMed, GH, H17, IBR, IBZ, ISR, IndMed, Inpharma, JW-N, MEDLINE, MycolAb, N02, N03, NSCI, P03, P30, P33, P35, P39, PN&I, PsycInfo, PsycholAb, R07, R08, R10, R12, RILM, RM&VM, Reac, SCI, SCOPUS, T05, W07, W10.
—BLDSC (7937.750000), GNLM, IE, Infotrieve, Ingenta, INIST. **CCC.**
Published by: (Societe Francaise de Neurologie), Elsevier Masson (Subsidiary of: Elsevier Health Sciences), 62 Rue Camille Desmoulins, Issy les Moulineaux, Cedex 92442, France. TEL 33-1-71165500, infos@elsevier-masson.fr. Ed. Christine Tranchant. Circ: 3,000.

616.8 150 ITA ISSN 1722-6155
RICERCA DI SENSO; analisi esistenziale e logoterapia frankliana. Text in Italian. 1999. 3/yr. EUR 31.80 to individuals; EUR 42.80 domestic to institutions; EUR 55 foreign to institutions (effective 2008). **Document type:** *Journal, Academic/Scholarly.*
Formerly (until 2002): Attualita in Logoterapia (1723-7378)
Published by: Edizioni Erickson, Via Praga 5, Settore E, Gardolo, TN 38100, Italy. TEL 39-0461-950690, FAX 39-0461-950698, info@erickson.it. Ed. Eugenio Fizzotti.

616.891 ITA ISSN 1592-8543
RICERCA IN PSICOTERAPIA. Text in Italian; Summaries in Italian, English. 1998. 3/yr. bibl.; illus. **Document type:** *Academic/Scholarly.*
Related titles: Online - full text ed.: ISSN 2038-0046.
Indexed: EMBASE, ExcerpMed, P03, PsycInfo, PsycholAb, R10, Reac, SCOPUS.
Published by: Edizioni La Vita Felice, Via Tadino 52, Milan, 20129, Italy. TEL 39-02-29524600, FAX 39-02-29401896, lavitafelice@iol.it.

616.8 ITA ISSN 1827-4625
RICERCA PSICOANALITICA. Text in Italian. 1990. a. **Document type:** *Journal, Academic/Scholarly.*
Related titles: Online - full text ed.: ISSN 2037-7851.
Published by: Franco Angeli Edizioni, Viale Monza 106, Milan, 20127, Italy. TEL 39-02-2837141, FAX 39-02-26144793, redazioni@francoangeli.it, http://www.francoangeli.it.

616.8 ITA ISSN 1724-8922
RICERCHE IN PSICHIATRIA. Text in Italian. 2004. 3/yr. EUR 50 domestic; EUR 80 foreign (effective 2007). **Document type:** *Journal, Academic/Scholarly.*
Related titles: Online - full text ed.: ISSN 1971-1891. 2003.
Indexed: SCOPUS.
—BLDSC (7966.431000).
Published by: C I C Edizioni Internazionali, Corso Trieste 42, Rome, 00198, Italy. TEL 39-06-8412673, FAX 39-06-8412688, info@gruppocic.it, http://www.gruppocic.it. Ed. Pier Luigi Scapicchio.

616.8047547 JPN ISSN 0485-1447
CODEN: RINOAC
RINSHO NOHA/CLINICAL ELECTROENCEPHALOGRAPHY. Text in Japanese. 1959. m. JPY 27,000 (effective 2005). **Document type:** *Journal, Academic/Scholarly.*
Indexed: INIS AtomInd.
Published by: Nagai Shoten Co. Ltd., 21-15 Fukushima 8-chome, Fukushima-ku, Osaka-shi, 553-0003, Japan. TEL 81-6-64521881, FAX 81-6-64521882, info@nagaishoten.co.jp.

616.89 JPN ISSN 0300-032X
RINSHO SEISHIN IGAKU/JAPANESE JOURNAL OF CLINICAL PSYCHIATRY. Text in Japanese. 1972. m. JPY 45,360 (effective 2003). **Document type:** *Journal, Academic/Scholarly.*
Indexed: INIS AtomInd.
—BLDSC (4651.417000).
Published by: ArcMedium, 7-1 Sanbancho, Chiyoda-ku, Asahi Sanbancho #406, Tokyo, 102-0075, Japan. TEL 81-3-52100821, FAX 81-3-52100824, arc21@arcmedium.co.jp, http://www.arcmedium.co.jp/index.html.

616.8 JPN ISSN 0009-918X
RC346
➤ **RINSHO SHINKEIGAKU/CLINICAL NEUROLOGY.** Text in Japanese; Summaries in English. 1960. m. JPY 13,000 (effective 2001). adv. charts; illus. index. **Document type:** *Journal, Academic/Scholarly.*
Related titles: Online - full text ed.: ISSN 1882-0654.
Indexed: A22, DentInd, E-psyche, EMBASE, ExcerpMed, INI, INIS AtomInd, IndMed, MEDLINE, P30, R10, Reac, SCOPUS.
—BLDSC (3286.309000), GNLM, IE, Infotrieve, Ingenta, INIST.
Published by: Japanese Society of Neurology/Nihon Shinkei Gakkai, Ichimaru Bldg, 2-31-21 Yushima, Bunkyo-ku, Tokyo, 113-0034, Japan. TEL 81-3-3815-1080, FAX 81-3-3815-1931, desk@neurology-jp.org. Ed. Nobuo Yanagisawa. Circ: 6,895.

616.8 JPN ISSN 1345-9171
RINSHO SHINRIGAKU/JAPANESE JOURNAL OF CLINICAL PSYCHOLOGY. Text in Japanese. 2000. bi-m. JPY 10,080; JPY 1,680 newsstand/cover (effective 2008). **Document type:** *Journal, Academic/Scholarly.*
—BLDSC (7971.693000).
Published by: Kongo Shuppan, 1-5-16 Suido, Bunkyo-ku, Tokyo, 112-0005, Japan. TEL 81-3-38156661, FAX 81-3-38186848, kongo@kongoshuppan.co.jp, http://kongoshuppan.co.jp.

616.89 ITA ISSN 0035-6484
CODEN: RPSID3
RIVISTA DI PSICHIATRIA. Text in Italian; Abstracts in English. 1966. bi-m. EUR 130 domestic to institutions; EUR 200 foreign to institutions (effective 2009). adv. bk.rev. charts; illus. index. 64 p./no.; **Document type:** *Journal, Academic/Scholarly.*
Related titles: Online - full text ed.: ISSN 2038-2502; Supplement(s): Psicosi. ISSN 1827-4463. 1992.
Indexed: A22, E-psyche, EMBASE, ExcerpMed, MEDLINE, P03, P30, PsycInfo, PsycholAb, R10, Reac, RefZh, S02, S03, SCI, SCOPUS, SSCI, W07.
—BLDSC (7992.731000), GNLM, IE, Ingenta.
Published by: Il Pensiero Scientifico Editore, Via Bradano 3-C, Rome, 00199, Italy. TEL 39-06-862821, FAX 39-06-86282250, pensiero@pensiero.it, http://www.pensiero.it.

616.8 ITA ISSN 1594-5111
RIVISTA DI PSICOSINTESI TERAPEUTICA. Abstracts in English; Text in Italian. 1984. s-a. EUR 22 domestic; EUR 30 foreign; free to members (effective 2009). **Document type:** *Journal, Academic/Scholarly.*
Formerly (until 1999): Psicosintesi (1827-4293)
Published by: Societa Italiana di Psicosintesi Terapeutica (S I P T), Via San Domenico 14, Florence, 50133, Italy.

150 616.891 ITA ISSN 1825-5442
RIVISTA DI PSICOTERAPIA RELAZIONALE. Text in Italian. 1983. s-a. EUR 33 combined subscription domestic to institutions; EUR 54 combined subscription foreign to institutions (effective 2009). **Document type:** *Journal, Academic/Scholarly.*
Formerly (until 1994): Attraverso lo Specchio (1825-5795)
Related titles: Online - full text ed.: ISSN 1971-8454. 1995.
Published by: (Federazione Italiana Associazioni di Psicoterapia), Franco Angeli Edizioni, Viale Monza 106, Milan, 20127, Italy. TEL 39-02-2837141, FAX 39-02-26144793, redazioni@francoangeli.it, http://www.francoangeli.it.

RIVISTA ITALIANA DI ANALISI TRANSAZIONALE E METODOLOGIE PSICOTERAPEUTICHE. *see* PSYCHOLOGY

616.8 ITA
CODEN: RNBLAC
RIVISTA ITALIANA DI NEUROBIOLOGIA. Text in Italian; Summaries in English. 1955. q. adv. bibl.; charts; illus. index. **Document type:** *Journal, Academic/Scholarly.*
Formerly (until 1984): Rivista di Neurobiologia (0035-6336)
Indexed: A22, ChemAb, DentInd, E-psyche, EMBASE, ExcerpMed, IndMed, P30, R10, Reac, SCOPUS.
—BLDSC (7991.380000), GNLM, IE, Ingenta.
Published by: (Scienze Neurologiche Ospedaliere (S N O)), Arti Grafiche del Liri, Via Napoli 85, Isola del Liri, FR 03036, Italy. TEL 39-0776-808036, FAX 39-0776-800723. Ed. Marino Benvenuti.

616.8 ITA ISSN 1129-6437
CODEN: RSFMA
RIVISTA SPERIMENTALE DI FRENIATRIA; la rivista della salute mentale. Text in Italian; Summaries in English, French. 1875. 3/yr. EUR 63 combined subscription domestic to institutions; EUR 92 combined subscription foreign to institutions (effective 2009). adv. bk.rev. **Document type:** *Journal, Academic/Scholarly.*
Former titles (until 1997): Rivista Sperimentale di Freniatria e Medicina Legale delle Alienazioni Mentali (0370-7261); (until 1895): Rivista Sperimentale di Freniatria e di Medicina Legale (1125-3991)
Related titles: Online - full text ed.: ISSN 1972-5582.
Indexed: ChemAb, E-psyche, IndMed, P03, P30, PsycInfo, PsycholAb, S02, S03.
—GNLM.
Published by: Franco Angeli Edizioni, Viale Monza 106, Milan, 20127, Italy. TEL 39-02-2837141, FAX 39-02-26144793, redazioni@francoangeli.it, http://www.francoangeli.it.

616.8 ROM ISSN 1453-4134
CODEN: RRNPEE
ROMANIAN JOURNAL OF NEUROLOGY: SERIE DE NEUROLOGIE ET PSYCHIATRIE. Text in English, French, German, Russian; Summaries in English. 1964. 2/yr. bk.rev. charts; illus. index. **Document type:** *Journal, Academic/Scholarly.*
Former titles (until 1995): Revue Roumaine de Neurologie et Psychiatrie (1017-5644); (until 1990): Revue Roumaine de Medecine. Neurologie et Psychiatrie (0259-6326); Which supersedes in part (in 1975): Revue Roumaine de Medecine (0303-822X); Which was formed by the 1974 merger of: Revue Roumaine de Medecine Interne (0035-3973); Revue Roumaine d'Endocrinologie (0035-4015); Revue Roumaine de Neurologie et de Psychiatrie (0301-7303)
Indexed: E-psyche, IndMed, P30, PsycholAb, SCOPUS.
—BLDSC (8019.638400), GNLM, IE, Ingenta, INIST.
Published by: (Academia de Stiinte Medicale), Editura Academiei Romane/Publishing House of the Romanian Academy, Calea 13 Septembrie 13, Sector 5, Bucharest, 050711, Romania. TEL 40-21-3188146, FAX 40-21-3182444, edacad@ear.ro, http://www.ear.ro. Ed. Vlad Voiculescu. Circ: 700. **Dist. by:** Rodipet S.A., Piata Presei Libere 1, sector 1, PO Box 33-57, Bucharest 3, Romania. TEL 40-21-2224126, 40-21-2226407, rodipet@rodipet.ro.

616.8 617 ROM ISSN 1220-8841
➤ **ROMANIAN NEUROSURGERY.** Text in English. 1992. q. USD 250 (effective 2011). abstr. back issues avail. **Document type:** *Journal, Academic/Scholarly.* **Description:** Publishes clinical and research papers on neurology and neurosurgery, including ophthalmology, radiology, pathology, physiology, anatomy, medical computing technology, and more.
Related titles: Online - full text ed.: 2007. free (effective 2011).
Indexed: E-psyche.
Published by: Romanian Society of Neurosurgery, 1st NeuroSurgery Department, Bagdasar Arseni Clinical Emergency Hospital, Sos Berceni, No.10-12, Bucharest, Romania. http://www.rsn.ro/. Ed. Dr. Stefan M. Iencean.

616.834 NLD ISSN 1574-9215
RONDOM M S. Text in Dutch. 1988. 3/yr.
Formerly (until 2005): Stichting Vrienden MS Research. Nieuwsbrief (0928-3196)
Published by: Stichting MS Research, Krimkade 20 b, 1e etage, Postbus 200, Voorschoten, 2250 AE, Netherlands. TEL 31-71-5600500, FAX 31-71-5600501, info@msresearch.nl, http://www.msresearch.nl. Ed. Dorinda Roos.

RONEN SEISHIN IGAKU ZASSHI/JAPANESE JOURNAL OF GERIATRIC PSYCHIATRY. *see* GERONTOLOGY AND GERIATRICS

616.89 RUS ISSN 1560-957X
ROSSIISKII PSIKHYATRICHESKII ZHURNAL/RUSSIAN JOURNAL OF PSYCHIATRY. Text in Russian; Summaries in English. 1997. bi-m. USD 221 foreign (effective 2005). adv. bk.rev.; Website rev. abstr.; bibl.; illus. back issues avail.; reprints avail. **Document type:** *Journal, Academic/Scholarly.* **Description:** Covers issues relevant to experimental, clinical and preventive psychiatry, as well as management of psychiatric services.
Related titles: Fax ed.
Indexed: RefZh.
—BLDSC (0154.059258).
Published by: Izdatel'stvo Meditsina/Meditsina Publishers, ul B Pirogovskaya, d 2, str 5, Moscow, 119435, Russian Federation. TEL 7-095-2483324, meditsina@mtu-net.ru, http://www.medlit.ru. Ed., R&P Tatiana B Dmitrieva. Pub. A M Stochik. Adv. contact O A Fadeeva TEL 7-095-923-51-40. Circ: 500. **Dist. by:** East View Information Services, 10601 Wayzata Blvd, Minneapolis, MN 55305. TEL 952-252-1201, 800-477-1005, FAX 952-252-1202, info@eastview.com, http://www.eastview.com.

616.8 GBR
ROYAL COLLEGE OF PSYCHIATRISTS. COLLEGE REPORTS. Text in English. 198?. irreg., latest vol.153, 2009. price varies. back issues avail. **Document type:** *Monographic series, Academic/Scholarly.*
Formerly (until 2007): Royal College of Psychiatrists. Council Report (1460-0986)
Related titles: Online - full text ed.: free.
Indexed: E-psyche.
—**CCC.**
Published by: Royal College of Psychiatrists, 17 Belgrave Sq, London, SW1X 8PG, United Kingdom. TEL 44-20-72352351, FAX 44-20-72451231, rcpsych@rcpsych.ac.uk.

616.8 NLD ISSN 1574-3071
RUDOLF MAGNUS BULLETIN. Text in English. 2002. irreg., latest vol.43, 2009.
Published by: Rudolf Magnus Institute of Neuroscience, Stratenum Bldg, Room STR5.203, Universiteitsweg 100, Utrecht, 3584 CG, Netherlands. TEL 31-30-2533624, FAX 31-30-2538155, http://www.rudolfmagnus.nl.

616.8 ESP ISSN 1138-011X
S D. REVISTA MEDICA INTERNACIONAL SOBRE LA SINDROME DE DOWN (CATALAN EDITION)/S D. INTERNATIONAL MEDICAL REVIEW ON DOWN SYNDROME. Text in Catalan; Abstracts in English. 1986. 3/yr. free (effective 2009). back issues avail. **Document type:** *Journal, Academic/Scholarly.*
Formerly (until 1996): Sindrome de Down (1138-2058)
Related titles: Spanish ed.: S D. Revista Medica Internacional sobre el Sindrome de Down (Spanish Edition). ISSN 1138-2074. 1997.
Indexed: EMBASE, ExcerpMed, R10, Reac.
Published by: Fundacio Catalana Sindrome de Down, C/ Comte Borrell 201-203, entresuelo, Barcelona, 08029, Spain. TEL 34-93-2157423, FAX 34-93-2157699, general@fcsd.org. Circ: 12,000 (free).

S L D EXPERIENCE. (Severe Learning Difficulties) *see* EDUCATION—Special Education And Rehabilitation

S M A D ELECTRONICAL JOURNAL MENTAL HEALTH, ALCOHOL AND DRUGS (ENGLISH EDITION). (Saude Mental Alcool e Drogas) *see* DRUG ABUSE AND ALCOHOLISM

S M A D REVISTA ELECTRONICA EN SALUD MENTAL, ALCOHOL Y DROGAS (SPANISH EDITION). (Saude Mental Alcool e Drogas) *see* DRUG ABUSE AND ALCOHOLISM

S M A D REVISTA ELECTRONICA SAUDE MENTAL ALCOOL E DROGAS. (Saude Mental Alcool e Drogas) *see* DRUG ABUSE AND ALCOHOLISM

S P I N Z NEWS. *see* PUBLIC HEALTH AND SAFETY

616.8 ITA
➤ **SAGGI - CHILD DEVELOPMENT DISABILITIES.** Text in Italian; Summaries in English. 1975. q. adv. bk.rev. cum.index: 1975-1994. **Document type:** *Monographic series, Academic/Scholarly.* **Description:** Covers infant neuropsychology and psychopedagogic rehabilitation.
Formerly (until 2000): Saggi (0390-5179)
Indexed: ASCA, E-psyche, PsycholAb, SCOPUS.
Published by: (Istituto Scientifico "Eugenio Medea"/Scientific Institute "Eugenio Medea"), Ghedini Libraio in Milano Srl, Via del Laghetto 7, Milan, 20122, Italy. TEL 39-02-76023988, FAX 39-02-781150, info@ghedini.it.

616.8 617 JPN ISSN 0385-0943
SAITAMA-KEN NO SHINKEI GEKAIKAI KAIHO/SAITAMA NEUROSURGICAL ASSOCIATION. BULLETIN. Text in Japanese. 1974. s-a. JPY 4,000 to members. **Document type:** *Bulletin.*
Indexed: E-psyche.
Published by: Saitamaken No Shinkei Gekaikai, 5-1 Naka-cho 3-chome, Urawa-shi, Saitama-ken 336-0007, Japan. Eds. Fujio Mizoguchi, Takao Ishibashi.

616.89 MEX ISSN 0185-3325
RA790.A1 CODEN: SAMEF5
➤ **SALUD MENTAL.** Text in English, Spanish. 1978. bi-m. MXN 800 domestic; USD 150 foreign to institutions (effective 2011). adv. bk.rev. bibl.; illus.; abstr. cum.index. Supplement avail.; back issues avail. **Document type:** *Journal, Academic/Scholarly.* **Description:** Covers research in neurosciences, clinical psychiatry, epidemiology, mental health, psychopharmacology, history of psychiatry, problems of ethics, drug addiction and neuropsychology.
Related titles: CD-ROM ed.; Online - full text ed.: free (effective 2011).
Indexed: A01, A20, A22, ASCA, C01, CA, CurCont, E-psyche, IndMed, Inpharma, P03, P30, PsycInfo, PsycholAb, R10, Reac, S02, S03, SCOPUS, SSCI, T02, W07.
—BLDSC (8071.770000), GNLM, IE, Ingenta.
Published by: (Instituto Nacional de Psiquiatria Ramon de la Fuente Muniz), Editorial Laser S.A. de C.V., Lago Alberto 442-7, Col Anahuac, Deleg. Miguel Hidalgo, Mexico City, DF 11320, Mexico. TEL 52-5-2600250, FAX 52-5-2600048. Ed. Dr. Hector Perez Rincon.

➤ **SAMIKSHA.** *see* PSYCHOLOGY

616.8 FRA ISSN 1273-7208
SANTE MENTALE. Text in French. 1995. m. EUR 67 to individuals; EUR 83 to institutions; EUR 54 to students (effective 2008). **Document type:** *Magazine.*
Published by: Acte Presse, 12 rue du Petit Thouars, Paris, 75003, France. TEL 33-1-42775277, FAX 33-1-42775237, smentale@club-internet.fr. Pub. Antoine Lolivier. Adv. contact Beatrice Bertelli.

616.8 FRA ISSN 1634-3298
SAVOIRS ET CLINIQUE. Text in French. 2002. 2/yr. EUR 30 domestic; EUR 45 foreign (effective 2011). back issues avail. **Document type:** *Journal, Academic/Scholarly.*
Formerly (until 2002): Carnets de Lille (1286-1405)
Related titles: Online - full text ed.: ISSN 1776-2871.
Indexed: SCOPUS.
Published by: Editions Eres, 33 Av. Marcel Dassault, Toulouse, 31500, France. TEL 33-5-61751576, FAX 33-5-61735289, eres@edition-eres.com. Ed. Franze Kaltenbeck TEL 33-1-43313677. Circ: 1,000.

616.891 DNK ISSN 0106-2301
RC500
➤ **SCANDINAVIAN PSYCHOANALYTIC REVIEW.** Text in English. 1978. s-a. DKK 445, EUR 58 (effective 2011). bk.rev. back issues avail.; reprints avail. **Document type:** *Journal, Academic/Scholarly.*
Related titles: Online - full text ed.: ISSN 1600-0803. 1999.
Indexed: A01, A03, A08, A20, ASCA, CA, E-psyche, EMBASE, ExcerpMed, P03, P43, PsycInfo, PsycholAb, R10, Reac, S02, S03, SCOPUS.
—BLDSC (8087.572800), GNLM, IE, Ingenta, INIST. **CCC.**
Published by: (Psycho-Analytical Societies in Denmark, Finland, Norway and Sweden), Syddansk Universitetsforlag/University Press of Southern Denmark, Campusvej 55, Odense M, 5230, Denmark. TEL 45-66-157999, FAX 45-66-158126, press@forlag.sdu.dk, http://www.universitypress.dk. Eds. Judy Gammelgaard, Susanne Lunn.

616.89 GBR ISSN 0586-7614
RC514 CODEN: SCZBB3
➤ **SCHIZOPHRENIA BULLETIN.** Text in English. 1969. bi-m. GBP 267 in United Kingdom to institutions; EUR 399 in Europe to institutions; USD 399 in US & Canada to institutions; GBP 267 elsewhere to institutions; GBP 292 combined subscription in United Kingdom to institutions (print & online eds.); EUR 436 combined subscription in Europe to institutions (print & online eds.); USD 436 combined subscription in US & Canada to institutions (print & online eds.); GBP 292 combined subscription elsewhere to institutions (print & online eds.) (effective 2012). adv. abstr.; bibl.; charts; illus.; stat. back issues avail.; reprint service avail. from PSC. **Document type:** *Journal, Academic/Scholarly.*
Related titles: Microform ed.: (from MIM, PQC); Online - full text ed.: ISSN 1745-1701. GBP 233 in United Kingdom to institutions; EUR 348 in Europe to institutions; USD 348 in US & Canada to institutions; GBP 233 elsewhere to institutions (effective 2012) (from IngentaConnect, ScienceDirect).
Indexed: A20, A22, AMHA, ASCA, AddicA, B21, B25, BIOBASE, BIOSIS Prev, C06, C07, CurCont, DIP, E-psyche, E01, ECER, EMBASE, ExcerpMed, F09, FR, Faml, IABS, IBR, IBZ, INI, ISR, IUSGP, IndMed, Inpharma, JW-P, MEDLINE, MycolAb, NSA, NSCI, P03, P20, P22, P24, P25, P26, P30, P35, P48, P54, PQC, PsycInfo, PsycholAb, R10, Reac, SCI, SCOPUS, SSCI, W07.
—BLDSC (8089.400000), GNLM, IE, Infotrieve, Ingenta, INIST. **CCC.**
Published by: (Maryland Psychiatric Research Centre USA), Oxford University Press, Great Clarendon St, Oxford, OX2 6DP, United Kingdom. TEL 44-1865-556767, FAX 44-1865-556646, enquiry@oup.co.uk, http://www.oxfordjournals.org. Ed. William t Carpenter. adv.: B&W page USD 1,296, color page USD 2,160; trim 8.25 x 10.875. Circ: 1,300 (paid).

362.2 CAN ISSN 1198-4104
SCHIZOPHRENIA DIGEST; inspiration and information. Text in English. 1994. bi-m. CAD 19.95 (effective 2003). adv. **Document type:** *Magazine, Consumer.* **Description:** Dedicated to bringing hope, dignity and support to persons with schizophrenia and their families.
Related titles: Regional ed(s).: Schizophrenia Digest (U.S. Edition). ISSN 1559-4114.
—CCC.
Published by: Magpie Publishing Inc., 176 Catherine St, Fort Erie, ON L2A 2J5, Canada. TEL 905-994-0302, 888-834-5537, FAX 905-994-0304. Ed. William McDermott. Pub. William McPhee. adv.: page CAD 6,000; trim 8.375 x 10.875. Circ: 25,000 (paid and controlled).

362.26 616.8982 JPN ISSN 1345-8639
SCHIZOPHRENIA FRONTIER. Text in Japanese. 2000. q. JPY 5,716 (effective 2005). **Document type:** *Journal, Academic/Scholarly.*
—BLDSC (8089.415000).
Published by: Medikaru Rebyusha/Medical Review Co., Ltd., 1-7-3 Hirano-Machi, Chuo-ku, Yoshida Bldg., Osaka-shi, 541-0046, Japan. TEL 81-6-62231468, FAX 81-6-62231245.

616.8 NLD ISSN 0920-9964
RC514 CODEN: SCRSEH
➤ **SCHIZOPHRENIA RESEARCH.** Text in English. 1988. 27/yr. EUR 4,983 in Europe to institutions; JPY 661,700 in Japan to institutions; USD 5,575 elsewhere to institutions (effective 2012). bk.rev. reprints avail. **Document type:** *Journal, Academic/Scholarly.* **Description:** Presents new international research that contributes to the understanding of schizophrenic disorders.
Related titles: Microform ed.: (from PQC); Online - full text ed.: ISSN 1573-2509 (from IngentaConnect, ScienceDirect).
Indexed: A01, A03, A08, A20, A22, A26, ASCA, AddicA, B25, BIOSIS Prev, C06, C07, CA, CurCont, E-psyche, EMBASE, ExcerpMed, F09, FR, Faml, I05, INI, IPsyAb, ISR, IndMed, Inpharma, JW-P, MEDLINE, MycolAb, NSCI, P03, P30, P34, P35, PsycInfo, PsycholAb, R10, Reac, S02, S03, SCI, SCOPUS, SSCI, T02, W07.
—BLDSC (8089.440000), GNLM, IE, Infotrieve, Ingenta, INIST. **CCC.**
Published by: Elsevier BV (Subsidiary of: Elsevier Science & Technology), Radarweg 29, PO Box 211, Amsterdam, 1000 AE, Netherlands. TEL 31-20-4853911, FAX 31-20-4852457, JournalsCustomerServiceEMEA@elsevier.com, http://www.elsevier.nl. Eds. H A Nasrallah, L E DeLisi.

616.8 USA ISSN 2090-2085
▼ **SCHIZOPHRENIA RESEARCH AND TREATMENT.** Text in English. 2009. q. USD 195 (effective 2011). **Document type:** *Journal, Academic/Scholarly.* **Description:** Publishes original research articles, review articles, and clinical studies related to all aspects of schizophrenia.
Related titles: Online - full text ed.: ISSN 2090-2093. free (effective 2011).
Indexed: A01.
Published by: Hindawi Publishing Corporation, 410 Park Ave, 15th Fl, PMB 287, New York, NY 10022. FAX 215-893-4392, 866-446-3294, hindawi@hindawi.com, info@hindawi.com.

SCHMERZTHERAPIE. *see* MEDICAL SCIENCES

616.89 CHE ISSN 0258-7661
CODEN: SANNAW
➤ **SCHWEIZER ARCHIV FUER NEUROLOGIE UND PSYCHIATRIE.** Text in English, French, German, Italian. 1917. 8/yr. CHF 96; CHF 20 newsstand/cover (effective 2009). adv. bk.rev. charts; illus. index per vol. reprints avail. **Document type:** *Journal, Academic/Scholarly.*
Former titles (until 1985): Schweizer Archiv fuer Neurologie, Neurochirurgie und Psychiatrie (0036-7273); (until 1959): Schweizer Archiv fuer Neurologie und Psychiatrie (0370-8373)
Related titles: Online - full text ed.: ISSN 1661-3686. free (effective 2011).
Indexed: A20, ChemAb, E-psyche, EMBASE, ExcerpMed, IndMed, P03, P30, PsycInfo, PsycholAb, R10, Reac, RefZh, S02, S03, SCOPUS, SSCI.
—BLDSC (1643.185000), CASDDS, GNLM, IE, Infotrieve, Ingenta, INIST. **CCC.**
Published by: (Schweizerische Neurologische Gesellschaft), Schwabe und Co. AG, Steinentorstr 13, Basel, 4010, Switzerland. TEL 41-61-2789565, FAX 41-61-2789566, verlag@schwabe.ch, http://www.schwabe.ch. Eds. Dr. A.J. Steck, Dr. D Hell, Dr. F Ferrero, Dr. J Bogousslavsky. Circ: 2,500. **Co-sponsor:** Schweizerische Gesellschaft fuer Psychiatrie.

616.8 370 FRA ISSN 0755-9593
LES SCIENCES DE L'EDUCATION POUR L'ERE NOUVELLE. Text in French. 1966. q. EUR 40 to individuals; EUR 60 to institutions; EUR 30 to students; EUR 14 per issue (effective 2010). **Document type:** *Journal, Academic/Scholarly.*
Formerly (until 1967): Pour l'Ere Nouvelle (0477-8413)
Indexed: CA, FR, L&LBA, RILM, S02, S03, SCOPUS, SD, SSA, SociolAb, T02.
—INIST.
Published by: Universite de Caen, Laboratoire de Psychopedagogie, Esplanade de la Paix, Caen, 14000, France. http://www.unicaen.fr.

616.8 USA ISSN 1555-2284
SCIENTIFIC AMERICAN MIND. Text in English. 1988. bi-m. USD 19.95 domestic; CAD 30 in Canada; USD 30 foreign (effective 2009). adv. back issues avail. **Document type:** *Magazine, Consumer.* **Description:** Covers various topics related to the brain, thoughts, medical and psychological issues.
Supersedes in part (in 2004): Scientific American. Special Edition (1551-2991); Which was formerly (until 200?): Scientific American Presents (1524-0223); (until 1998): Scientific American. Special Issue (1048-0943)
Related titles: Online - full text ed.: USD 4.95 per issue (effective 2009).
Indexed: A01, A03, A08, BiolDig, CA, M02, P43.
—BLDSC (8175.150000), IE, INIST. **CCC.**
Published by: Scientific American, Inc., 75 Varick St, 9th Fl, New York, NY 10013. TEL 212-451-8200, experts@sciam.com. Adv. contact Bruce Brandfon TEL 212-451-8561.

THE SCIENTIFIC REVIEW OF MENTAL HEALTH PRACTICE. *see* PSYCHOLOGY

THE SCRIPT. *see* PSYCHOLOGY

616.8 NLD ISSN 1872-9282
SCRIPT NEUROLOGIE. Text in Dutch. 2006. q. adv.
Published by: Van Zuiden Communications B.V., Postbus 2122, Alphen aan den Rijn, 2400 CC, Netherlands. TEL 31-172-476191, FAX 31-172-471882, zuiden@zuidencomm.nl, http://www.zuidencomm.nl. Eds. Dr. C Franke, Dr. J J Jaspers. adv.: page EUR 2,380; trim 210 x 297. Circ: 1,150 (controlled).

616.831 AUS ISSN 1329-0940
SECRETARIAT. Text in English. 1996. bi-m.
Published by: Alzheimer's Association of Australia Inc., PO Box 108, Higgins, ACT 2615, Australia. TEL 61-2-6254-4233, FAX 61-2-6254-2522, secretariat@alzheimers.org.au.

616.8 JPN ISSN 0915-065X
SEISHIN HOKEN KENKYU/JOURNAL OF MENTAL HEALTH. Text in Japanese. 1953. a. **Document type:** *Journal, Academic/Scholarly.*
Supersedes in part (in 1986): Seishin Eisei Kenkyu/Journal of Mental Health (0559-3158); Which incorporated (1953-1981): Seishin Eisei Shiryo/Annual Report on Mental Health (0454-2010)
Indexed: P03, PsycInfo, PsycholAb.
—BLDSC (5017.680000).
Published by: Seishin Hoken Kenkyujo, Kokuritsu Seishin, Shinkei Senta/National Institute of Mental Health, National Center of Neurology and Psychiatry, 4-1-1 Ogawahigashi-cho Kodaira, Tokyo, 187-8553, Japan. TEL 81-42-3412711, FAX 81-42-3461944, http://www.ncnp-k.go.jp/.

616.8 JPN ISSN 0488-1281
SEISHIN IGAKU/CLINICAL PSYCHIATRY. Text in Japanese; Summaries in English. 1959. m. JPY 30,600; JPY 39,800 combined subscription (print & online eds.) (effective 2010).
Related titles: Online - full text ed.: ISSN 1882-126X.
Indexed: E-psyche, INIS AtomInd, Inpharma, P03, P30, PsycholAb, RefZh, S02, S03.
—BLDSC (3286.340000), GNLM.
Published by: Igaku Shoin Ltd., 1-28-36 Hongo, Bunkyo-ku, Tokyo, 113-8719, Japan. TEL 81-3-3817-5600, FAX 81-3-3815-7791, info@igaku-shoin.co.jp. Circ: 6,000.

616.8 JPN ISSN 0080-8547
SEISHIN IGAKU KENKYUJO GYOSEKISHU/SEISHIN IGAKU INSTITUTE OF PSYCHIATRY. BULLETIN. Text in Japanese; Abstracts and contents page in English. 1954. a. free. reprints avail. **Document type:** *Bulletin, Academic/Scholarly.*
Indexed: E-psyche, P30.
—GNLM.
Published by: Seishin Igaku Kenkyujo/Institute of Clinical Psychiatry, 4-11-11 Komone, Itabashi-ku, Tokyo, 173-0037, Japan. TEL 81-3-39562136, FAX 81-3-39569644.

616.8 610.73 JPN ISSN 1343-2761
SEISHIN KANGO/PSYCHIATRIC MENTAL HEALTH NURSING. Text in Japanese. 1998. bi-m. JPY 7,380; JPY 12,500 combined subscription (print & online eds.) (effective 2010). **Document type:** *Journal, Academic/Scholarly.*
Related titles: Online - full content ed.: ISSN 1347-8370.
Published by: Igaku Shoin Ltd., 1-28-36 Hongo, Bunkyo-ku, Tokyo, 113-8719, Japan. TEL 81-3-3817-5600, FAX 81-3-3815-7791, info@igaku-shoin.co.jp.

616.891 JPN ISSN 0916-8710
SEISHIN RYOHO/JAPANESE JOURNAL OF PSYCHOTHERAPY. Text in Japanese. 1975. bi-m. JPY 1,850 per issue (effective 2001). bk.rev. **Document type:** *Academic/Scholarly.*
Formerly (until 1992): Kikan Seishin Ryoho (0386-9660)
Indexed: E-psyche.
Published by: Kongo Shuppan, 1-5-16 Suido, Bunkyo-ku, Tokyo, 112-0005, Japan. TEL 81-3-3815-6661, FAX 81-3-3818-6848, kongo@kongoshuppan.co.jp, http://kongoshuppan.co.jp. Ed. Haruo Tanaka.

616.8 JPN ISSN 0033-2658
RC321 CODEN: SSHZAS
SEISHIN SHINKEIGAKU ZASSHI/PSYCHIATRIA ET NEUROLOGIA JAPONICA. Text in Japanese; Summaries in English, Japanese. 1962. m. free to members. adv. bibl.; charts; illus. Index. **Document type:** *Journal, Academic/Scholarly.*
Indexed: B25, BIOSIS Prev, ChemAb, E-psyche, EMBASE, ExcerpMed, F09, INI, INIS AtomInd, IndMed, Inpharma, MEDLINE, MycolAb, P30, R10, Reac, SCOPUS.
—BLDSC (6946.130000), GNLM, INIST. **CCC.**
Published by: Nihon Seishin Shinkei Gakkai/Japanese Society of Psychiatry and Neurology, 5-25-18 Hongo, Bunkyo-ku, Tokyo, 113-0033, Japan. TEL 81-3-38142991, FAX 81-3-38142992, info@jspn.or.jp, http://www.jspn.or.jp/5shi.html.

616.8 JPN ISSN 1347-4790
SEISHINKA/PSYCHIATRY. Text in Japanese. 2002. m. JPY 2,625 (effective 2003). **Document type:** *Journal, Academic/Scholarly.*
Published by: Kagaku-Hyoronsha Co. Ltd., 2-10-8, Kana Tomiyama-cho, Chiyoda-ku, Tokyo, 101-8531, Japan. TEL 81-3-32527741, FAX 81-3-32525952, http://www.kahyo.com/index.html.

616.89 JPN ISSN 0912-1862
SEISHINKA CHIRYOGAKU/JAPANESE JOURNAL OF PSYCHIATRIC TREATMENT. Text in Japanese. 1986. m. **Document type:** *Journal, Academic/Scholarly.*
—BLDSC (4658.230000).
Published by: Seiwa Shoten Co. Ltd., 2-5 Kamitakaido, 1-chome, Suginami-ku, Tokyo, 168-0074, Japan.

616.8 GBR ISSN 1059-1311
RC372.A1 CODEN: SEIZE7
➤ **SEIZURE - EUROPEAN JOURNAL OF EPILEPSY.** Text in English. 1992. 10/yr. EUR 1,125 in Europe to institutions; JPY 121,300 in Japan to institutions; USD 998 elsewhere to institutions (effective 2012). back issues avail.; reprint service avail. from PSC. **Document type:** *Journal, Academic/Scholarly.* **Description:** Provides an interdisciplinary forum for original research in all aspects of epilepsy, including the basic sciences, differential diagnosis and epidemiology of seizures, treatment and management of epilepsy, and related social issues.
Related titles: Online - full text ed.: ISSN 1532-2688. USD 811 to institutions (effective 2009) (from ScienceDirect).
Indexed: A20, A22, A26, ASCA, C06, C07, CA, CurCont, E-psyche, E01, EMBASE, ExcerpMed, I05, INI, IPsyAb, ISR, IndMed, Inpharma, MEDLINE, NSCI, P03, P30, P35, PsycInfo, PsycholAb, R10, Reac, SCI, SCOPUS, T02, W07.
—BLDSC (8229.100000), GNLM, IE, Infotrieve, Ingenta, INIST. **CCC.**
Published by: Elsevier Ltd (Subsidiary of: Elsevier Science & Technology), The Blvd, Langford Ln, Kidlington, Oxford, OX5 1GB, United Kingdom. TEL 44-1865-843000, FAX 44-1865-843010, customerserviceau@elsevier.com, http://www.elsevier.com. Eds. A P Aldenkamp, P A J M Boon. Adv. contact Luis Portero TEL 212-633-3970.

616.8 USA ISSN 0271-8235
CODEN: SEMNEP

➤ **SEMINARS IN NEUROLOGY.** Text in English. 1980. 5/yr. USD 721 domestic to institutions; USD 736 foreign to institutions; USD 873 combined subscription domestic to institutions (print & online eds.); USD 902 combined subscription foreign to institutions (print & online eds.) (effective 2011). abstr.; bibl.; charts; illus.; stat. index. reprints avail. **Document type:** *Journal, Academic/Scholarly.* **Description:** Areas of coverage include multiple sclerosis, central nervous system infections, muscular dystrophy, neuro-immunology, spinal disorders, strokes, epilepsy, motor neuron diseases, movement disorders, higher cortical function, neuro-genetics and neuro-opthamology.
Related titles: Microform ed.: (from PQC); Online - full text ed.: ISSN 1098-9021. USD 848 domestic to institutions; USD 862 foreign to institutions (effective 2011).
Indexed: A01, A03, A08, A20, A22, A36, ASCA, BIOSIS Prev, CA, CABA, CurCont, E-psyche, E01, E12, EMBASE, ExcerpMed, GH, H17, IndMed, Inpharma, MEDLINE, MLA-IB, MycolAb, N02, N03, NSCI, P30, P33, P39, PN&I, R08, R10, Reac, SCI, SCOPUS, T02, T05, W07.
—BLDSC (8239.455550), GNLM, IE, Infotrieve, Ingenta, INIST. **CCC.**
Published by: Thieme Medical Publishers (Subsidiary of: Georg Thieme Verlag), 333 Seventh Ave, New York, NY 10001. TEL 212-760-0888, 800-782-3488, FAX 212-947-1112, info@thieme.com, http://www.thieme.com. Ed. Dr. Karen L Roos TEL 317-278-6785. Adv. contact James C Cunningham TEL 201-767-4170. Circ: 2,675.

616.8 618.92 USA ISSN 1071-9091
RJ486 CODEN: SPNEFD

SEMINARS IN PEDIATRIC NEUROLOGY. Text in English. 1994. q. USD 397 in United States to institutions; USD 493 elsewhere to institutions (effective 2012). adv. back issues avail.; reprints avail. **Document type:** *Journal, Academic/Scholarly.* **Description:** Covers topics of current importance in the field of pediatric neurology.
Related titles: Online - full text ed.: ISSN 1558-0776 (from ScienceDirect).
Indexed: A26, C06, C07, C08, CA, CINAHL, CurCont, E-psyche, EMBASE, ExcerpMed, H12, I05, INI, IndMed, MEDLINE, P30, R10, Reac, SCI, SCOPUS, T02, W07.
—BLDSC (8239.456785), GNLM, IE, Infotrieve, Ingenta. **CCC.**
Published by: W.B. Saunders Co. (Subsidiary of: Elsevier Health Sciences), Elsevier, Health Sciences Division, Order Fulfillment, 3251 Riverport Ln, Maryland Heights, MO 63043. TEL 314-872-8370, 800-325-4177, FAX 314-432-1380, JournalCustomerService-usa@elsevier.com, http://www.us.elsevierhealth.com. Ed. Dr. John B Bodensteiner. Pub. Virginia Prada Lopez. Adv. contact John Marmero TEL 212-633-3657.

616.8 RUS ISSN 0235-0092
QP431 CODEN: SESIE6

➤ **SENSORNYE SISTEMY.** Text in Russian. 1987. q. **Document type:** *Journal, Academic/Scholarly.*
Indexed: B25, BIOSIS Prev, MycolAb, RefZh, Z01.
—East View, INIST, Linda Hall. **CCC.**
Published by: M A I K Nauka - Interperiodica (Subsidiary of: Pleiades Publishing, Inc.), Profsoyuznaya ul 90, Moscow, 117997, Russian Federation. TEL 7-095-3347420, FAX 7-095-3360666, compmg@maik.ru. Ed. M A Ostrovskii.

616.89 NLD ISSN 1574-9037

SERIES IN ANXIETY AND RELATED DISORDERS. Text in English. 2004. irreg. price varies. **Document type:** *Monographic series, Academic/Scholarly.* **Description:** Reflects upon the full spectrum of anxiety disorders and their current emphasis in the field of psychology from a clinical perspective.
Published by: Springer Netherlands (Subsidiary of: Springer Science+Business Media), Van Godewijckstraat 30, Dordrecht, 3311 GX, Netherlands. TEL 31-78-6576050, FAX 31-78-6576474. Ed. Martin M Antony.

SEX OFFENDER LAW REPORT. *see* LAW—Criminal Law

616.8 CHN ISSN 1009-7201

SHANDONG JINGSHEN YIXUE/JOURNAL OF PSYCHIATRY. Text in Chinese. 1988. bi-m. CNY 6 newsstand/cover (effective 2008). **Document type:** *Journal, Academic/Scholarly.*
Related titles: Online - full text ed.
—BLDSC (8254.588525).
Published by: Shandong Sheng Jingshen Weisheng Zhongxin, 49, Wenhua Dong Lu, Ji'nan, 250014, China. TEL 86-531-86336672, FAX 86-531-88932855, sdmhc@sdmhc.com, http://www.sdmhc.com. Ed. Chuan-hua Lu.

616.8 CHN ISSN 1002-0829

SHANGHAI JINGSHEN YIXUE/SHANGHAI ARCHIVES OF PSYCHIATRY. Text in Chinese. 1959. bi-m. USD 24.60 (effective 2009). adv. **Document type:** *Journal, Academic/Scholarly.* **Description:** Provides up-to-date coverage of psychiatry in China and around the world.
Related titles: Online - full text ed.
Indexed: E-psyche.
—BLDSC (8254.589076).
Published by: Shanghai Shi Jingshen Weisheng Zhongxin/Shanghai Mental Health Centre, 600 Wanping Nanlu, Shanghai, 200030, China. TEL 86-21-64387250 ext 3296. Ed. Wenwei Yan. Adv. contact Keliang Zhan. page USD 900. Circ: 5,300. **Dist. by:** China International Book Trading Corp, 35 Chegongzhuang Xilu, Haidian District, PO Box 399, Beijing 100044, China. TEL 86-10-68412045, FAX 86-10-68412023, cibtc@mail.cibtc.com.cn, http://www.cibtc.com.cn.

616.8 CHN ISSN 1009-6574

SHENGJINGJIBING YU JINGSHEN WEISHENG/NERVOUS DISEASES AND MENTAL HYGIENE. Text in Chinese. 2001. bi-m. USD 21.60 (effective 2009). **Document type:** *Journal, Academic/Scholarly.*
Related titles: Online - full content ed.; Online - full text ed.
—East View.
Published by: Qiqiha'er Yixueyuan, 249, Heping Lu, Qiqiha'er, 161042, China. TEL 86-452-6713982, http://www.qqhrmc.net.cn/. **Dist. by:** China International Book Trading Corp, 35 Chegongzhuang Xilu, Haidian District, PO Box 399, Beijing 100044, China. TEL 86-10-68412045, FAX 86-10-68412023, cibtc@mail.cibtc.com.cn, http://www.cibtc.com.cn.

616.8 CHN ISSN 1000-7547
CODEN: SJZHAZ

SHENJING JIEPOUXUE ZAZHI/CHINESE JOURNAL OF NEUROANATOMY. Text in Chinese; Abstracts in Chinese, English. 1985. bi-m. CNY 84, USD 35.40 (effective 2009). **Document type:** *Journal, Academic/Scholarly.*
Related titles: Online - full text ed.
Indexed: A36, B&BAb, B19, B21, CABA, E12, ESPM, F08, F11, F12, GH, N02, N03, NSA, NucAcAb, RA&MP, SoyAb, T05, ToxAb, VS.
—BLDSC (8256.418000), East View.
Published by: Zhongguo Jiepou Xuehui/Chinese Society for Anatomical Sciences, no.17, W. Changle Rd., Xi'an, 710032, China. **Dist. by:** China International Book Trading Corp, 35 Chegongzhuang Xilu, Haidian District, PO Box 399, Beijing 100044, China. TEL 86-10-68412045, FAX 86-10-68412023, cibtc@mail.cibtc.com.cn, http://www.cibtc.com.cn.

SHENJING SUNSHANG YU GONGNENG CHONGJIAN/NEURAL INJURY AND FUNCTIONAL RECONSTRUCTION. *see* MEDICAL SCIENCES—Physical Medicine And Rehabilitation

616.8 CHN

SHIJIE HEXIN YIXUE QIKAN WENZHAI (SHENGJINGBINGXUE FENCE)/DIGEST OF THE WORLD CORE MEDICAL JOURNALS (CLINICAL NEUROLOGY). Text in Chinese. 2004. bi-m. **Document type:** *Journal, Academic/Scholarly.*
Supersedes in part (in 2005): Shijie Zuixin Yixue Xinxi Wenzhai/Digest of the World Latest Medical Information (1671-3141)
Related titles: Online - full text ed.
—East View.
Published by: Shijie Tushu Chuban Xi'an Gongsi, 17, Nandajie, Xi'an, 710001, China. TEL 86-29-87265319, FAX 86-29-87265318, wzg1995@163.com, http://wuzhigang.bookonline.com.cn/. **Dist. by:** China International Book Trading Corp, 35 Chegongzhuang Xilu, Haidian District, PO Box 399, Beijing 100044, China. TEL 86-10-68412045, FAX 86-10-68412023, cibtc@mail.cibtc.com.cn, http://www.cibtc.com.cn.

616.8 617.7 JPN ISSN 0389-5610

SHINKEI GAISHO/NEUROTRAUMATOLOGY. Variant title: Nihon Shinkei Gaisho Gakkai Koenshu. Text in Japanese; Summaries in English. 1979. a. membership. back issues avail. **Document type:** *Journal, Academic/Scholarly.*
Indexed: E-psyche, INIS AtomInd.
Published by: Nihon Shinkei Gaisho Gakkai/Japan Society of Neurotraumatology, Jikei University School of Medicine, Department of Neurosurgery, 3-25-8 Nishishinbashi, Minatoku, Tokyo, 105-8461, Japan. TEL 81-3-34331111 ext 3460, FAX 81-3-34596412, neurotrauma@jikei.ac.jp, http://www.neurotraumatology.jp/. Circ: 1,000.

SHINKEI GANKA/NEURO-OPHTHALMOLOGY JAPAN. *see* MEDICAL SCIENCES—Ophthalmology And Optometry

616.8 JPN ISSN 0037-3796

SHINKEI KAGAKU/JAPANESE NEUROCHEMICAL SOCIETY. BULLETIN. Text in Japanese. 1962. s-a. price varies. adv. bk.rev. bibl. **Document type:** *Journal, Academic/Scholarly.*
Formerly: Nerve Chemistry
Indexed: ChemAb, E-psyche.
—**CCC.**
Published by: Nihon Shinkei Kagakkai/Japanese Society for Neurochemistry, 35 Shinaimachi, Shinjuku-ku, Shinanomachi Rengakan, Tokyo, 160-0016, Japan. TEL 81-3-53617107, FAX 81-3-53617091, jsn@imic.or.jp, http://wwwsoc.nii.ac.jp/jsn/v. Circ: 1,500.

616.8 616.97 JPN ISSN 0918-936X

SHINKEI MEN'EKIGAKU/NEUROIMMUNOLOGY. Text in Japanese. 1993. s-a. Index. **Document type:** *Journal, Academic/Scholarly.*
—BLDSC (6081.372700). **CCC.**
Published by: Nihon Shinkei Men'eki Gakkai/Japanese Society for Neuroimmunology, National Institute for Longevity Science, 36-3, Gengo, Morioka, Obu, Aichi 474-8511, Japan. web@neuroimmunology.jp, http://www.neuroimmunology.jp/top.html.

616.8 JPN ISSN 0386-9709

SHINKEI NAIKA/NEUROLOGICAL MEDICINE. Text in Japanese. 1974. m. JPY 2,625 (effective 2003). **Document type:** *Journal, Academic/Scholarly.*
Indexed: INIS AtomInd.
—BLDSC (6081.441500).
Published by: Kagaku-Hyoronsha Co. Ltd., 2-10-8, Kana Tomiyama-cho, Chiyoda-ku, Tokyo, 101-8531, Japan. TEL 81-3-32527741, FAX 81-3-32525952, http://www.kahyo.com/index.html.

616.8 JPN ISSN 0911-1085

SHINKEI SHINRIGAKU/JAPANESE JOURNAL OF NEUROPSYCHOLOGY. Text in Japanese. 1985. s-a. **Document type:** *Journal, Academic/Scholarly.*
—BLDSC (4656.641000).
Published by: Nihon Shinkei Shinri Gakkai/Neuropsychology Association of Japan, 8-1, Kawada-cho, Shinjyuku-ku, Department of Neurology, Tokyo Women's Medical University, Tokyo, 162-8666, Japan. TEL 81-3-3353-8111 Ext 26211.

616.8 JPN ISSN 1342-9892

SHINRYO NAIKA/PSYCHOSOMATIC MEDICINE. Text in Japanese. 1997. q. JPY 2,625 (effective 2003). **Document type:** *Journal, Academic/Scholarly.*
Published by: Kagaku-Hyoronsha Co. Ltd., 2-10-8, Kana Tomiyama-cho, Chiyoda-ku, Tokyo, 101-8531, Japan. TEL 81-3-32527741, FAX 81-3-32525952, http://www.kahyo.com/index.html.

616.8 JPN ISSN 0385-0307
CODEN: SHIGD4

SHINSHIN IGAKU/JAPANESE JOURNAL OF PSYCHOSOMATIC MEDICINE. Text in Japanese; Summaries in English. 1961. m. JPY 20,480, JPY 1,680 (effective 2007). **Document type:** *Journal, Academic/Scholarly.*
Formerly (until 1975): Seishin Shintai Igaku (0559-3182)
Related titles: Online - full text ed.
Indexed: E-psyche, SCOPUS.
—BLDSC (4658.340000), GNLM. **CCC.**
Published by: (Japanese Society of Psychosomatic Medicine), Miwa-Shoten Ltd., 6-17-9 Hongo, Bunkyo-ku, Hongou Tsuna Bldg. 4F, Tokyo, 113-0033, Japan. TEL 81-3-38167796, FAX 81-3-38167756, info@miwapubl.com, http://www.miwapubl.com/. Circ: 4,500.

616.8 618.92 JPN ISSN 0387-8023
CODEN: SHONDL

SHONI NO NOSHINKEI/NERVOUS SYSTEM IN CHILDREN. Text in Japanese. 1978. bi-m. **Document type:** *Journal, Academic/Scholarly.*
Indexed: INIS AtomInd.
Published by: Nibon Shoni Shinkei Gekagaku Kenkyukai/Japanese Society for Pediatric Neurosurgery, Jikei University School of Medicine, Department of Neurosurgery, 3-25-8 Nishi-Shinbashi, Minato-Ku, Tokyo, 105-8461, Japan. TEL 81-3-34381160, FAX 81-3-34381161, jspn-gakkai@umin.ac.jp, http://jpn-spn.umin.jp/.

616.85 616.89 NLD ISSN 1872-4396

SILHOUET. Variant title: NedKAD/Silhouet. Text in Dutch. 2005. q. EUR 39 (effective 2009).
Supersedes in part (in 2006): Silhouet/Vizier (1871-2630); Which was formed by the merger of (2002-2005): Silhouet (1572-3291); Which was formerly (until 2004): Tijdschrift over Angst en Depressie (1570-1328); (1969-2005): Vizier (Driebergen-Rijsenburg, 2003) (1871-2649); Which was formerly (until 2003): Fobie-Vizier (0166-7149)
Related titles: Online - full text ed.: EUR 16 (effective 2009).
Published by: Jan van Ingen Schenau, Ed. & Pub., Korte Voren 1, Lochem, 7241 HR, Netherlands. TEL 31-573-880019, uitgever@silhouet-online.nl. Ed. Katja Pereira.

616.858842 ITA ISSN 1122-147X

SINDROME DOWN NOTIZIE. Text in Italian. 1981. 3/yr. free (effective 2009). bk.rev. bibl. 80 p./no.; back issues avail. **Document type:** *Magazine, Consumer.* **Description:** Covers medical, educational, and social aspects of Down's Syndrome. For families, doctors, psychologists, social workers and teachers.
Indexed: E-psyche.
Published by: Associazione Italiana delle Persone Down (A I P D), Viale delle Milizie 106, Rome, 00192, Italy. TEL 39-06-3723909, FAX 39-06-3722510, http://www.aipd.it. Circ: 5,000.

616.89 ESP ISSN 1130-1538

SISO SAUDE. Variant title: Boletin Oficial de la Asociacion Gallega de Salud Mental. Text in Spanish. 1982. q. back issues avail. **Document type:** *Journal, Academic/Scholarly.*
Formerly (until 1984): Inter-nos (1130-152X)
Published by: Asociacion Galega de Saude Mental, Apdo de Correos 2059, Santiago de Compostela, Coruna, Spain. siso@chez.com. Ed. David Simon Lorga.

616.8 USA ISSN 1550-9109

➤ **SLEEP (ONLINE).** Text in English. m. free to members; USD 225 to non-member individuals; USD 425 to non-member institutions (effective 2011). adv. abstr. Supplement avail.; back issues avail. **Document type:** *Journal, Academic/Scholarly.* **Description:** Publishes original findings and analysis related to sleep disorders, medical dysfunctions during sleep, clinical investigations, therapeutic trials, physiologic events, anatomic structures and molecular components underlying normal and abnormal sleep, psychological and psychophysiologic research, and the pharmacology of sleep.
Media: Online - full text.
—**CCC.**
Published by: Associated Professional Sleep Societies, Llc, 2510 N. Frontage Rd., Darien, IL 60561. TEL 630-737-9700, FAX 630-737-9790, subscriptions@aasmnet.org, http://www.aasmnet.org. Ed. Dr. David F. Dinges. **Co-sponsors:** Sleep Research Society; The American Academy of Sleep Medicine.

616.2 DEU ISSN 1520-9512
RC547 CODEN: SBLRB8

➤ **SLEEP AND BREATHING;** international journal of the science and practice of sleep medicine. Text in English. 1997. q. EUR 402, USD 514 combined subscription to institutions (print & online eds.) (effective 2012). abstr. reprint service avail. from PSC. **Document type:** *Journal, Academic/Scholarly.* **Description:** Discusses the newest clinical research in sleep medicine, covering topics related to the diagnosis and treatment of sleep disordered breathing, including upper airway resistance syndrome and sleep apnea.
Related titles: Online - full text ed.: ISSN 1522-1709 (from IngentaConnect).
Indexed: A22, A26, Agr, B21, CA, CurCont, E-psyche, E01, EMBASE, ExcerpMed, MEDLINE, NSA, P20, P22, P25, P27, P30, P48, P54, PQC, R10, Reac, SCI, SCOPUS, T02, W07.
—BLDSC (8309.445000), IE, Infotrieve, Ingenta, INIST. **CCC.**
Published by: Springer (Subsidiary of: Springer Science+Business Media), Tiergartenstr 17, Heidelberg, 69121, Germany. TEL 49-6221-4870, FAX 49-6221-345229, subscriptions@springer.com. Eds. K P Strohl, N C Netzer.

616.89 TUR ISSN 1302-1192
QP425

➤ **SLEEP AND HYPNOSIS;** an international journal of sleep, dream and hypnosis. Text in English. 1999. s-a. EUR 40 domestic to individuals; EUR 105 to individuals Europe, Asia & Africa; EUR 120 elsewhere to individuals; EUR 100 domestic to institutions; EUR 210 to institutions Europe, Asia & Africa; EUR 220 elsewhere to institutions; EUR 45 newsstand/cover (effective 2008). Index. back issues avail. **Document type:** *Journal, Academic/Scholarly.* **Description:** A multidisciplinary journal covering sleep, dream, and hypnosis research interests.
Related titles: Online - full text ed.: EUR 150 (effective 2008).
Indexed: A01, C06, C07, C08, CA, CINAHL, P03, P20, P24, P25, P30, P48, P54, PQC, PsycInfo, PsycholAb, R10, Reac, SCOPUS, T02.
—BLDSC (8309.445500), IE, Ingenta.
Published by: Yerkure Tanitim ve Yayincilik Hizmetleri A.S., Siracevizler Cad 43/3, Sisli, Istanbul, 34381, Turkey. TEL 90-212-2194900, FAX 90-212-2305009, yerkure@yerkure.com.tr, http://www.kure.com.tr. Ed. Mehmet Yucel Agargun. Pub., R&P Nuket Dilmen Korkmaz.

616.8 USA ISSN 2090-3545

▼ ➤ **SLEEP DISORDERS.** Text in English. 2011. USD 195 (effective 2011). **Document type:** *Journal, Academic/Scholarly.* **Description:** Publishes original research articles, review articles, and clinical studies related to all aspects of sleep disorders.
Related titles: Online - full text ed.: ISSN 2090-3553. 2011. free (effective 2011).
Published by: Hindawi Publishing Corporation, 410 Park Ave, 15th Fl, PMB 287, New York, NY 10022. FAX 215-893-4392, 866-446-3294, info@hindawi.com.

616.8 NLD ISSN 1389-9457
RC547 CODEN: SMLEAB
➤ **SLEEP MEDICINE.** Text in Dutch. 2000. 10/yr. EUR 579 in Europe to institutions; JPY 76,700 in Japan to institutions; USD 645 elsewhere to institutions (effective 2012). adv. bk.rev. illus.; abstr. reprints avail. **Document type:** *Journal, Academic/Scholarly.* **Description:** Examines all human aspects of sleep, integrating the various disciplines involved in sleep medicine.
Related titles: Online - full text ed.: ISSN 1878-5506 (from IngentaConnect, ScienceDirect).
Indexed: A01, A03, A08, A26, B21, C06, C07, CA, D02, E-psyche, EMBASE, ExcerpMed, I05, JW-N, MEDLINE, NSA, NSCI, P03, P30, PsycInfo, R10, Reac, SCI, SCOPUS, T02, W07.
—BLDSC (8309.452000), IE, Infotrieve, Ingenta. **CCC.**
Published by: Elsevier BV (Subsidiary of: Elsevier Science & Technology), Radarweg 29, PO Box 211, Amsterdam, 1000 AE, Netherlands. TEL 31-20-4853911, FAX 31-20-4852457, JournalsCustomerServiceEMEA@elsevier.com, http://www.elsevier.nl. Ed. Sudhansu Chokroverty.

616.8 USA ISSN 1556-407X
RC547
SLEEP MEDICINE CLINICS. Text in English. 2006 (Jan.). q. USD 346 in United States to institutions; USD 381 elsewhere to institutions (effective 2012). adv. back issues avail.; reprints avail. **Document type:** *Journal, Academic/Scholarly.* **Description:** Provides a forum for invited, topical reviews in this rapidly growing field and incudes topics such as obstructive sleep apnea, insomnia, and parasomnias.
Related titles: Online - full text ed.: ISSN 1556-4088. 2006 (from ScienceDirect); Supplement(s): Sleep Medicine Clinics: Continuing Medical Education Supplements. ISSN 1559-7806. 2006 (Feb.).
Indexed: EMBASE, ExcerpMed, P03, P30, PsycInfo, SCOPUS.
—BLDSC (8309.454000), IE. **CCC.**
Published by: W.B. Saunders Co. (Subsidiary of: Elsevier Health Sciences), Elsevier, Health Sciences Division, Order Fulfillment, 3251 Riverport Ln, Maryland Heights, MO 63043. TEL 314-872-8370, 800-325-4177, FAX 314-432-1380, JournalCustomerService-usa@elsevier.com, http://www.us.elsevierhealth.com.

616.8 FRA ISSN 1087-0792
CODEN: SMREFC
➤ **SLEEP MEDICINE REVIEWS.** Text in English. 1997. 6/yr. EUR 723 in Europe to institutions; JPY 77,500 in Japan to institutions; USD 653 elsewhere to institutions (effective 2012). **Document type:** *Journal, Academic/Scholarly.* **Description:** Provides in-depth and up-to-date reviews of sleep disorders, including their aetiology, diagnosis, treatment and implications for related conditions at an individual and public health level.
Related titles: Online - full text ed.: ISSN 1532-2955 (from ScienceDirect).
Indexed: A22, A26, B21, C06, C07, CA, E-psyche, E01, EMBASE, ExcerpMed, I05, MEDLINE, NSA, NSCI, P03, P30, PsycInfo, R10, Reac, SCI, SCOPUS, T02, W07.
—BLDSC (8309.455000), IE, Infotrieve, Ingenta. **CCC.**
Published by: Elsevier Masson (Subsidiary of: Elsevier Health Sciences), 62 Rue Camille Desmoulins, Issy les Moulineaux, Cedex 92442, France. TEL 33-1-71165500, FAX 33-1-71165600, infos@elsevier-masson.fr, http://www.elsevier-masson.fr. Eds. J. Krieger, M. Vitiello.

➤ **SMART LIFE NEWS.** *see* PHARMACY AND PHARMACOLOGY

616.8 302 GBR ISSN 1749-5024
SOCIAL COGNITIVE AND AFFECTIVE NEUROSCIENCE (ONLINE). Abbreviated title: S C A N. Text in English. 2006 (Summer). 5/yr. GBP 132 in United Kingdom to institutions; EUR 197 in Europe to institutions; USD 262 in US & Canada to institutions; GBP 132 elsewhere to institutions (effective 2012). back issues avail. **Document type:** *Journal, Academic/Scholarly.* **Description:** Provides a home for human and animal research that uses neuroscience techniques to understand the social and emotional aspects of the human mind and human behavior.
Media: Online - full text (from IngentaConnect).
Indexed: SCOPUS.
—**CCC.**
Published by: Oxford University Press, Great Clarendon St, Oxford, OX2 6DP, United Kingdom. TEL 44-1865-556767, FAX 44-1865-556646, enquiry@oup.co.uk, http://www.oxfordjournals.org. Ed. Dr. Matthew D Lieberman.

616.8 301 GBR ISSN 1747-0919
QP360.5
SOCIAL NEUROSCIENCE. Text in English. 2006. bi-m. GBP 287 combined subscription in United Kingdom to institutions (print & online eds.); EUR 401, USD 500 combined subscription to institutions (print & online eds.) (effective 2012). back issues avail.; reprint service avail. from PSC. **Document type:** *Journal, Academic/Scholarly.* **Description:** Aims to explain the psychological and neural basis of social and emotional behaviors in humans, as well as understand the neural system in the development and maintenance of social behaviors.
Related titles: Online - full text ed.: ISSN 1747-0927. 2006. GBP 259 in United Kingdom to institutions; EUR 361, USD 450 to institutions (effective 2012).
Indexed: A01, A20, A22, CA, E01, EMBASE, ExcerpMed, MEDLINE, NSCI, P03, P30, P48, P50, PQC, PsycInfo, R10, Reac, SCI, SCOPUS, T02, W07.
—IE, Ingenta, INIST. **CCC.**
Published by: Psychology Press (Subsidiary of: Taylor & Francis Ltd.), 27 Church Rd, Hove, E Sussex BN3 2FA, United Kingdom. TEL 44-20-70176000, FAX 44-20-70176717, info@psypress.co.uk, http://www.psypress.com. Ed. Jean Decety. Adv. contact Linda Hann TEL 44-1344-779945.

616.89 DEU ISSN 0933-7954
RC321 CODEN: SPPEEM
➤ **SOCIAL PSYCHIATRY AND PSYCHIATRIC EPIDEMIOLOGY;** the international journal for research in social and genetic epidemiology and mental health services. Text in English. 1966. m. EUR 2,669, USD 2,544 combined subscription to institutions (print & online eds.) (effective 2012). adv. abstr.; bibl. index. back issues avail.; reprint service avail. from PSC. **Document type:** *Journal, Academic/Scholarly.* **Description:** Concerned with the effects of social conditions on behavior, and the relationship between psychiatric disorders and the social environment.
Formerly (until 1988): Social Psychiatry (0037-7813)
Related titles: Microform ed.: (from PQC); Online - full text ed.: ISSN 1433-9285 (from IngentaConnect).
Indexed: A01, A03, A08, A20, A22, A26, A34, A36, ASCA, AbAn, C06, C07, CA, CABA, ChPerI, Chicano, CurCont, E-psyche, E01, E08, E12, EMBASE, ESPM, ExcerpMed, F09, FR, FamI, GH, H12, IBR, IBZ, INI, IPsyAb, IndMed, LT, MEDLINE, N02, N03, P03, P10, P12, P20, P22, P25, P30, P34, P43, P48, P50, P52, P53, P54, PQC, PsycInfo, PsycholAb, R07, R10, R12, RASB, RRTA, Reac, RiskAb, S02, S03, S09, SCI, SCOPUS, SSCI, T02, T05, VS, W07, W11.
—BLDSC (8318.145700), GNLM, IE, Infotrieve, Ingenta, INIST. **CCC.**
Published by: Dr. Dietrich Steinkopff Verlag (Subsidiary of: Springer Science+Business Media), Tiergartenstr 17, Heidelberg, 69121, Germany. TEL 49-6221-4878821, FAX 49-6221-4878830, info.steinkopff@springer.com, http://www.steinkopff.com. Ed. P Bebbington. R&P Dr. Maria Magdalene Nabbe. adv.: color page EUR 1,780, B&W page EUR 740; trim 210 x 277. Circ: 330 (paid and controlled). **Subscr. in the Americas to:** Springer New York LLC, Journal Fulfillment, PO Box 2485, Secaucus, NJ 07096. TEL 800-777-4643, 201-348-4033, FAX 201-348-4505, journals-ny@springer.com; **Subscr. to:** Springer Distribution Center, Kundenservice Zeitschriften, Haberstr 7, Heidelberg 69126, Germany. TEL 49-6221-3454303, FAX 49-6221-3454229, subscriptions@springer.com.

362.20425 NLD ISSN 1386-3541
SOCIALE PSYCHIATRIE. Text in Dutch. 1994. q. EUR 29 (effective 2008).
Related titles: Online - full text ed.: ISSN 1875-6573.
—Infotrieve.
Published by: Nederlandse Vereniging van Sociaal Psychiatrisch Verpleegkundigen, Postbus 3135, Utrecht, 3502 GC, Netherlands. administratie@nvspv.nl.

616.8 ARG ISSN 1514-089X
SOCIEDAD ARGENTINA DE PSICOANALISIS. REVISTA. Text in Spanish. 1998. a. **Document type:** *Journal, Academic/Scholarly.*
Published by: Sociedad Argentina de Psicoanalisis, Arcos 1521, Buenos Aires, C1426BGI, Argentina. TEL 54-11-47847584.

616.8 COL ISSN 0120-0445
SOCIEDAD COLOMBIANA DE PSICOANALISIS. REVISTA. Text in Spanish. 1976. s-a. **Document type:** *Journal, Academic/Scholarly.*
Indexed: F04, T02.
Published by: Sociedad Colombiana de Psicoanalisis, Av 13 No 86-56, Bogota, Colombia. TEL 57-1-2676224.

SOCIEDADE PSICANALITICA DE PORTO ALEGRE. REVISTA DE PSICANALISE. *see* PSYCHOLOGY

616.8 USA ISSN 2156-8693
▼ ➤ **SOCIETY AND MENTAL HEALTH.** Text in English. forthcoming 2011 (Mar.). 3/yr. USD 250, GBP 147 combined subscription to institutions (print & online eds.); USD 245, GBP 144 to institutions (effective 2011). **Document type:** *Journal, Academic/Scholarly.* **Description:** Publishes original articles that apply sociological concepts and methods to the understanding of the social origins of mental health and illness, the social consequences for persons with mental illness, and the organization and financing of mental health services and care.
Related titles: Online - full text ed.: ISSN 2156-8731. forthcoming. USD 225, GBP 132 to institutions (effective 2011).
—**CCC.**
Published by: (American Sociological Association, Section on Sociology of Mental Health), Sage Publications, Inc., 2455 Teller Rd, Thousand Oaks, CA 91320. TEL 805-499-9774, FAX 805-499-0871, info@sagepub.com, http://www.sagepub.com. Ed. William R. Avison.

616.8 HRV ISSN 0303-7908
CODEN: SPSIDE
SOCIJALNA PSIHIJATRIJA. Text in Croatian. 1973. q. HRK 100 to individuals; HRK 200 to institutions (effective 2003). **Document type:** *Journal, Academic/Scholarly.*
Indexed: EMBASE, ExcerpMed, P03, PsycInfo, PsycholAb, R10, Reac, S02, S03, SCOPUS.
—BLDSC (8319.551000).
Published by: Akademija Medicinskih Znanosti Hrvatske, Subiceva 29, Zagreb, 10000, Croatia. amzh@zg.hinet.hr, http://www.amzh.hr. Ed. Ljubomir Hotujac.

616.8 SWE ISSN 2000-9011
▼ ➤ **SOCIOAFFECTIVE NEUROSCIENCE & PSYCHOLOGY.** Text in English. 2011. free (effective 2011). **Document type:** *Journal, Academic/Scholarly.* **Description:** Contains research on the central nervous system and its complex relationship with the surrounding social environment.
Media: Online - full text.
Published by: Co-Action Publishing, Ripvaegen 7, Jaerfaella, 17564, Sweden. TEL 46-18-4951150, FAX 46-18-4951138, info@co-action.net, http://www.co-action.net. Ed. Harold Mouras.

➤ **SOCIOLOGY OF HEALTH AND ILLNESS;** a journal of medical sociology. *see* SOCIOLOGY

616.8 ITA ISSN 1121-0664
IL SOGNO DELLA FARFALLA; journal of psychiatry and psychotherapy. Text in Italian. 1992. q. EUR 52 domestic; EUR 90 foreign (effective 2009). 96 p./no.; **Document type:** *Journal, Academic/Scholarly.*
Indexed: E-psyche, P03, PsycInfo.
Published by: Nuove Edizioni Romane, Piazza Santa Cecilia 18, Rome, 00153, Italy. TEL 39-06-5881064, FAX 39-06-5818091.

SOINS PSYCHIATRIE; la revue de tous les acteurs du soin et sante mentale. *see* MEDICAL SCIENCES—Nurses And Nursing

SOMATOSENSORY AND MOTOR RESEARCH. *see* BIOLOGY—Physiology

616.89 RUS ISSN 0869-4893
➤ **SOTSYAL'NAYA I KLINICHESKAYA PSIKHYATRIYA.** Text in Russian. 1991. q. USD 99.95 in United States. bk.rev. abstr.; bibl.; illus. 112 p./no. 2 cols./p.; **Document type:** *Journal, Academic/Scholarly.*
Indexed: RefZh.
—BLDSC (0166.276500), East View, Ingenta.
Published by: Rossiiskoe Obshchestvo Psikhyatrov, Poteshnaya ul 3, Moscow, 107258, Russian Federation. TEL 7-095-9637663, FAX 7-095-1621003, krasnov@mtu-net.ru, http://www.mtu-net.ru/niip. Ed. I Ya Gurovich. Circ: 3,000 (paid). **Dist. by:** East View Information Services, 10601 Wayzata Blvd, Minneapolis, MN 55305. TEL 952-252-1201, 800-477-1005, FAX 952-252-1202, info@eastview.com, http://www.eastview.com.

616.8 ZAF ISSN 1608-9685
➤ **SOUTH AFRICAN JOURNAL OF PSYCHIATRY.** Text in English. 3/yr. USD 20 foreign (effective 2003). back issues avail. **Document type:** *Journal, Academic/Scholarly.* **Description:** Publishes clinical and experimental articles on all aspects of psychiatric medicine and other topics in psychiatry.
Related titles: ◆ Supplement to: S A M J South African Medical Journal. ISSN 0256-9574.
Indexed: A01, A26, A36, CABA, D01, EMBASE, ExcerpMed, FR, GH, H12, I05, ISAP, N02, N03, R07, R10, R12, Reac, SCI, SCOPUS, SSCI, T05, W07.
—BLDSC (8070.507100), IE, Ingenta, INIST. **CCC.**
Published by: South African Medical Association, Block F Castle Walk Corporate Park, Nossob St, Erasmuskloof X3, Pretoria 7430, South Africa. TEL 27-12-4812000, FAX 27-12-4812100, publishing@samedical.org, http://www.samedical.org. R&P Peter Roberts. **Subscr. to:** PO Box 74789, Lynnwood Ridge, Pretoria 0040, South Africa.

606.89 USA ISSN 1047-6334
SOUTHERN CALIFORNIA PSYCHIATRIST. Text in English. 1955. m. (11/yr.). USD 30 (effective 2007). adv. bk.rev.; film rev. **Document type:** *Newsletter.*
Formerly (until Aug. 1988): Southern California Psychiatric Society. Newsletter
Indexed: E-psyche.
Published by: Southern California Psychiatric Society, 2999 Overland Ave, Ste 208, Los Angeles, CA 90064-4243. scps2999@earthlink.net. Ed. Dr. Nancy Rosser. R&P, Adv. contact Mindi Thelen TEL 310-815-3650. Circ: 1,350.

616.8 DEU ISSN 0937-2628
SOZIALE PSYCHIATRIE. Text in German. 1977. q. EUR 34; EUR 10 newsstand/cover (effective 2008). adv. bk.rev. back issues avail. **Document type:** *Journal, Academic/Scholarly.*
Formerly (until 1989): D G S P Rundbrief
Indexed: E-psyche.
—**CCC.**
Published by: Deutsche Gesellschaft fuer Soziale Psychiatrie e.V., Zeltinger Str 9, Cologne, 50969, Germany. TEL 49-221-511002, FAX 49-221-529903, dgsp@psychiatrie.de, http://www.psychiatrie.de/website/index.php?/f,11955,12000/. Ed. Michaela Hoffmann. adv.: B&W page EUR 670. Circ: 4,600 (paid and controlled).

SOZIALPSYCHIATRISCHE INFORMATIONEN. *see* PSYCHOLOGY

616.837 CAN ISSN 1922-9445
THE SPIN. Text in English. 1957. q. free to members (effective 2010). bk.rev. **Document type:** *Newsletter, Trade.*
Formerly (until 2009): Paragraphic (0048-2935)
Indexed: E-psyche.
Published by: British Columbia Paraplegic Association, 780 SW Marine Dr, Vancouver, BC V6P 5Y7, Canada. TEL 604-324-3611, 877-324-3611, FAX 604-326-1229, info@bcpara.org, http://www.bcpara.org.

616.837 617.3 GBR ISSN 1362-4393
RC406.P3 CODEN: SPCOFM
➤ **SPINAL CORD.** Abbreviated title: S C. Text in English; Summaries in French, German. 1963. m. EUR 706 in Europe to institutions; USD 837 in the Americas to institutions; JPY 120,600 in Japan to institutions; GBP 456 to institutions in the UK & elsewhere (effective 2011). adv. bk.rev. abstr.; charts; illus.; stat. index. back issues avail.; reprints avail. **Document type:** *Journal, Academic/Scholarly.* **Description:** Expresses as a multi-disciplinary forum for basic science, clinical and applied studies, psychology and epidemiology of spinal disorders.
Formerly (until 1996): Paraplegia (0031-1758)
Related titles: Online - full text ed.: ISSN 1476-5624.
Indexed: A01, A02, A03, A08, A20, A22, A29, AMED, ASCA, B20, B21, B25, BIOSIS Prev, C06, C07, C08, C11, CA, CINAHL, CurCont, E-psyche, E01, EMBASE, ESPM, ExcerpMed, FR, H04, I10, INI, IndMed, Inpharma, MEDLINE, MycolAb, NSA, NSCI, P20, P22, P24, P30, P35, P48, P54, PQC, R09, R10, Reac, SCI, SCOPUS, SD, T02, ViroIAbstr, W07.
—BLDSC (8413.885000), GNLM, IE, Infotrieve, Ingenta, INIST. **CCC.**
Published by: (International Spinal Cord Society), Nature Publishing Group (Subsidiary of: Macmillan Publishers Ltd.), The MacMillan Bldg, 4 Crinan St, London, N1 9XW, United Kingdom. TEL 44-20-78334000, FAX 44-20-78334640. Ed. J J Wyndaele TEL 32-3-8213047. Adv. contact Ben Harkinson TEL 617-475-9222. **Subscr. to:** Brunel Rd, Houndmills, Basingstoke, Hamps RG21 6XS, United Kingdom. TEL 44-1256-329242, FAX 44-1256-812358, subscriptions@nature.com.

➤ **STANDARDS FOR BEHAVIORAL HEALTH CARE.** *see* SOCIAL SERVICES AND WELFARE

➤ **DE STEM VAN DE OUDERS.** *see* HANDICAPPED

➤ **STEREOTACTIC AND FUNCTIONAL NEUROSURGERY.** *see* MEDICAL SCIENCES—Surgery

616.83 NLD ISSN 1879-4319
STICHTING GILLES DE LA TOURETTE. NIEUWSBRIEF. Text in Dutch. 199?. q. EUR 19.50 membership (effective 2010). **Document type:** *Newsletter, Consumer.*
Formerly (until 2009): Tourette Gazet (1568-4792)
Published by: Stichting Gilles de la Tourette, Postbus 925, Rhoon, 3160 AC, Netherlands. info@tourette.nl, http://www.tourette.nl.

STRABISMUS (LONDON). *see* MEDICAL SCIENCES—Ophthalmology And Optometry

616.8 GBR ISSN 1532-2998
STRESS AND HEALTH (ONLINE). Text in English. 1997. 5/yr. GBP 545 in United Kingdom to institutions; EUR 688 in Europe to institutions; USD 1,066 elsewhere to institutions (effective 2012). **Document type:** *Journal, Academic/Scholarly.*
Formerly (until 2001): Stress Medicine (Online) (1099-1700)
Media: Online - full text (from IngentaConnect). **Related titles:** Microform ed.: (from PQC); ◆ Print ed.: Stress and Health (Print). ISSN 1532-3005.
Indexed: SCOPUS.
—BLDSC (8474.128680). **CCC.**
Published by: John Wiley & Sons Ltd. (Subsidiary of: John Wiley & Sons, Inc.), The Atrium, Southern Gate, Chichester, West Sussex PO19 8SQ, United Kingdom. TEL 44-1243-779777, FAX 44-1243-775878, cs-journals@wiley.com, http://eu.wiley.com/WileyCDA/.

616.8 GBR ISSN 1532-3005
R726.5 CODEN: STMEEZ
➤ **STRESS AND HEALTH (PRINT).** Text in English. 1985. 5/yr. GBP 545 in United Kingdom to institutions; EUR 688 in Europe to institutions; USD 1,066 elsewhere to institutions; GBP 628 combined subscription in United Kingdom to institutions (print & online eds.); EUR 792 combined subscription in Europe to institutions (print & online eds.); USD 1,226 combined subscription elsewhere to institutions (print & online eds.) (effective 2012). adv. back issues avail.; reprint service avail. from PSC. **Document type:** *Journal, Academic/Scholarly.*
Description: Provides a forum for the discussion of all aspects of stress that affect the individual in both health and disease.
Formerly (until 2001): Stress Medicine (Print) (0748-8386)
Related titles: Microform ed.: (from PQC); ◆ Online - full text ed.: Stress and Health (Online). ISSN 1532-2998.
Indexed: A01, A03, A08, A20, A22, ASCA, B21, B25, B28, BIOSIS Prev, C06, C07, C08, CA, CINAHL, CurCont, E-psyche, EMBASE, ESPM, ExcerpMed, FR, FamI, H&SSA, H13, IPsyAb, Inpharma, MycolAb, NSA, P02, P03, P10, P20, P30, P47, P48, P53, P54, PEI, PQC, PsycInfo, PsycholAb, R09, R10, Reac, RiskAb, S02, S03, SCI, SCOPUS, SD, SOPODA, SSCI, SociolAb, T02, THA, W07.
—GNLM, IE, Ingenta, INIST. **CCC.**
Published by: (International Society for the Investigation of Stress USA), John Wiley & Sons Ltd. (Subsidiary of: John Wiley & Sons, Inc.), 1-7 Oldlands Way, PO Box 808, Bognor Regis, West Sussex PO21 9FF, United Kingdom. TEL 44-1865-778315, FAX 44-1243-843232, cs-journals@wiley.com, http://eu.wiley.com/WileyCDA/. Ed. Cary L Cooper. **Subscr. in the Americas to:** John Wiley & Sons, Inc., 111 River St, Hoboken, NJ 07030. subinfo@wiley.com; **Subscr. to:** 1-7 Oldlands Way, PO Box 809, Bognor Regis, West Sussex PO21 9FG, United Kingdom. TEL 44-1865-778054, cs-agency@wiley.com.

➤ **STRESSFORSKNINGSRAPPORTER/STRESS RESEARCH REPORTS.** *see* PSYCHOLOGY

616.8 USA ISSN 2042-0056
RC388.5
▼ **STROKE RESEARCH AND TREATMENT.** Text in English. 2010. irreg. free (effective 2011). **Document type:** *Journal, Academic/Scholarly.*
Media: Online - full text.
Indexed: A01, A26, B19, C06, C07, CTA, E08, H12, I05, NSA, P30, T02.
Published by: Sage - Hindawi Access to Research, 410 Park Ave, 15th Fl, 287 PMB, New York, NY 10022. FAX 866-446-3294.

616.8 SWE ISSN 1100-3278
STUDIA PSYCHOLOGICA CLINICA UPSALIENSIA. Text in English. 1989. irreg., latest vol.3, 1993. price varies. **Document type:** *Monographic series, Academic/Scholarly.*
Related titles: ◆ Series of: Acta Universitatis Upsaliensis. ISSN 0346-5462.
Published by: Uppsala Universitet, Acta Universitatis Upsaliensis/ University Publications from Uppsala, PO Box 256, Uppsala, 75105, Sweden. TEL 46-18-4716804, FAX 46-18-4716804, acta@ub.uu.se, http://www.ub.uu.se/upu/auu/index.html. Ed. Bengt Landgren. **Dist. by:** Almqvist & Wiksell International.

616.89 DEU ISSN 1435-6503
STUDIEN ZUR PSYCHIATRIEFORSCHUNG. Text in German. 1991. irreg., latest vol.16, 2009. price varies. **Document type:** *Monographic series, Academic/Scholarly.*
Published by: Verlag Dr. Kovac, Leverkusenstr 13, Hamburg, 22761, Germany. TEL 49-40-3988800, FAX 49-40-39888055, info@verlagdrkovac.de.

616.898 DEU ISSN 1435-6317
STUDIEN ZUR SCHIZOPHRENIEFORSCHUNG. Text in German. 1992. irreg., latest vol.11, 2007. price varies. **Document type:** *Monographic series, Academic/Scholarly.*
Published by: Verlag Dr. Kovac, Leverkusenstr 13, Hamburg, 22761, Germany. TEL 49-40-3988800, FAX 49-40-39888055, info@verlagdrkovac.de.

616.8 ITA ISSN 1972-4241
STUDIES DI GESTALT THERAPY. Text in English. 1992. s-a. **Document type:** *Journal, Academic/Scholarly.*
Published by: Istituto di Gestalt H C C, Via San Sebastiano 38, Syracuse, 96100, Italy. TEL 39-0931-465668, FAX 39-0931-483646, studies@gestalt.it, http://www.gestalt.it. Eds. Dan Bloom, Frank Staemmler, Margherita Spagnuolo Lobb.

616.8526 GBR
STUDIES IN EATING DISORDERS: AN INTERNATIONAL SERIES. Text in English. 1998. irreg., latest vol.2, 1998. price varies. **Document type:** *Monographic series, Academic/Scholarly.* **Description:** Each issue contains contributions relating to a specific topic. Includes coverage of issues faced by practicing therapists in the treatment of eating disorders, and a survey of modern approaches to the prevention of eating disorders.
Indexed: E-psyche.
Published by: Athlone Press Ltd., 1 Park Dr, London, NW11 7SG, United Kingdom. TEL 44-20-8458-0888, FAX 44-20-8458-8115. Ed. Tristan Palmer. Pub. Brian Southam. R&P Doris Southam.

152.1 NLD ISSN 0926-907X
➤ **STUDIES IN VISUAL INFORMATION PROCESSING.** Text in English. 1990. irreg., latest vol.6, 1995. price varies. back issues avail. **Document type:** *Monographic series, Academic/Scholarly.*
Description: Publishes research in a variety of studies dealing with the acquisition, processing, and utilization of visual information.
Related titles: Online - full text ed.
Indexed: E-psyche.
—BLDSC (8491.846600). **CCC.**
Published by: Elsevier BV, North-Holland (Subsidiary of: Elsevier Science & Technology), Sara Burgerhartstraat 25, Amsterdam, 1055 KV, Netherlands. TEL 31-20-4853911, FAX 31-20-4852457, JournalsCustomerServiceEMEA@elsevier.com, http://www.elsevier.com. Eds. Gery d'Ydewalle, Rudolf Groner. **Subscr. to:** Elsevier BV, Radarweg 29, PO Box 211, Amsterdam 1000 AE, Netherlands. TEL 31-20-4853757, FAX 31-20-4853432.

616.8 GBR ISSN 1873-3964
STUDIES ON NEUROPSYCHOLOGY, DEVELOPMENT AND COGNITION. Text in English. 1998. irreg., latest 2008. price varies. back issues avail. **Document type:** *Magazine, Academic/Scholarly.*
Description: Provides state-of-the-art overviews of key areas of interest to a range of clinicians, professionals, researchers, instructors, and students working in clinical neuropsychology, neurology, rehabilitation, and related fields.
Published by: Psychology Press (Subsidiary of: Taylor & Francis Ltd.), 27 Church Rd, Hove, E Sussex BN3 2FA, United Kingdom. TEL 44-20-70176000, FAX 44-20-70176717, info@psypress.co.uk. Ed. Linas A Bieliauskas.

SUICIDE AND LIFE-THREATENING BEHAVIOR. *see* PSYCHOLOGY

362.2072 NOR ISSN 1501-6994
➤ **SUICIDOLOGI.** Text in Norwegian. 1996. 3/yr. back issues avail. **Document type:** *Journal, Academic/Scholarly.*
Formerly (until 1999): Nytt i Suicidologi (0808-2227)
Related titles: Online - full text ed.: free (effective 2011).
Published by: Universitetet i Oslo, Medisinske Fakultet. Seksjon for Selvmordsforskning og -Forebygging/University of Oslo. Medical Faculty. Suicide Research and Prevention Unit, Sognsvannsvn. 21, Bygning 12, Oslo, 0320, Norway. TEL 47-22-923473, FAX 47-22-923958, kirsti.amundson@medisin.uio.no, http://www.med.uio.no/ipsy/ssff/index.html. Ed. Lars Mehlum.

616.8 AUT ISSN 2078-5488
▼ **SUICIDOLOGY ONLINE.** Text in English. 2010. irreg. free (effective 2011). **Document type:** *Journal, Academic/Scholarly.*
Media: Online - full text.
Published by: Medizinische Universitaet Wien, Waehringer Guertel 18-20, Vienna, 1090, Austria. TEL 43-1-404003071, FAX 43-1-4866803. Ed. Nestor D Kapusta.

616.8 360 DEU ISSN 0173-458X
➤ **SUIZIDPROPHYLAXE.** Text in German; Abstracts in English. 1973. q. adv. bk.rev. back issues avail. **Document type:** *Journal, Academic/Scholarly.*
Indexed: DIP, E-psyche, IBR, IBZ.
—GNLM.
Published by: (German Association of Suicide Prevention), S. Roderer Verlag, In der Obern Au 12, Regensburg, 93055, Germany. TEL 49-941-7992270, FAX 49-941-795198, info@roderer-verlag.de, http://roderer-verlag.de. Circ: 1,000.

616.891 362.82 SWE ISSN 1100-3421
SVENSK FAMILJETERAPI. Variant title: S F T. Text in Swedish. 1988. q. **Document type:** *Journal, Trade.*
Indexed: E-psyche.
Published by: Svenska Foereningen foer Familjeterapi/Swedish Association for Family Therapy, c/o Marie Fornemam, Bronsaaldersvaegen 11, Oestersund, 83161, Sweden. TEL 46-7-7673187, marie.forneman@sftt.se, http://www.sfft.se.

616.8 USA ISSN 0887-4476
QP364 CODEN: SYNAET
➤ **SYNAPSE (NEW YORK).** Text in English. 1987. m. GBP 2,934 in United Kingdom to institutions; EUR 3,711 in Europe to institutions; USD 5,500 in United States to institutions; USD 5,668 in Canada & Mexico to institutions; USD 5,752 elsewhere to institutions; GBP 3,376 combined subscription in United Kingdom to institutions (print & online eds.); EUR 4,270 combined subscription in Europe to institutions (print & online eds.); USD 6,326 combined subscription in United States to institutions (print & online eds.); USD 6,494 combined subscription in Canada & Mexico to institutions (print & online eds.); USD 6,578 combined subscription elsewhere to institutions (print & online eds.) (effective 2012). adv. back issues avail.; reprint service avail. from PSC. **Document type:** *Journal, Academic/Scholarly.* **Description:** Embraces new basic and clinical research pertaining to all aspects of synaptic structure and function, including attention to practical clinical consideration.
Related titles: Microform ed.: (from PQC); Online - full text ed.: ISSN 1098-2396. GBP 2,805 in United Kingdom to institutions; EUR 3,548 in Europe to institutions; USD 5,500 elsewhere to institutions (effective 2012).
Indexed: A22, B21, B25, BIOBASE, BIOSIS Prev, C33, CIN, CTA, ChemAb, ChemTitl, CurCont, E-psyche, EMBASE, ExcerpMed, IABS, ISR, IndMed, Inpharma, MEDLINE, MycolAb, NSA, NSCI, P03, P30, PsycInfo, R10, Reac, SCI, SCOPUS, W07.
—BLDSC (8585.880200), CASDDS, GNLM, IE, Infotrieve, Ingenta, INIST. **CCC.**
Published by: John Wiley & Sons, Inc., 111 River St, Hoboken, NJ 07030. TEL 201-748-6000, FAX 201-748-6088, info@wiley.com, http://www.wiley.com/WileyCDA/. Ed. John E Johnson Jr. TEL 650-366-1644. **Subscr. outside the Americas to:** John Wiley & Sons Ltd., The Atrium, Southern Gate, Chichester, West Sussex PO19 8SQ, United Kingdom. TEL 44-1243-779777, 800-243407, FAX 44-1243-775878, cs-journals@wiley.com.

➤ **SYSTEM UBW;** Zeitschrift fuer klassische Psychoanalyse. *see* PSYCHOLOGY

616.8 KOR ISSN 1015-4817
QP351
TAEHAN SIN'GYONG CHONGSIN UIHAK HOEJI/KOREAN NEUROPSYCHIATRIC ASSOCIATION. JOURNAL. Text in Korean; Summaries in English. 1962. bi-m. free. adv. **Document type:** *Journal, Academic/Scholarly.*
Formerly: Neuro-Psychiatry
Indexed: E-psyche.
Published by: Taehan Sin'gyong Chongsin Uihakhoe/Korean Neuropsychiatric Association, RN. 522, G-five Central Plaza 1685-8, Seocho-dong, Seocho-gu, Seoul, 137-882, Korea, S. TEL 82-2-5376171, FAX 82-2-5376174, kpa3355@kornet.net.

616.89 UKR
TAVRICHESKII ZHURNAL PSIKHIATRII/ACTA PSYCHIATRICA, PSYCHOTERAPEUTICA ET ETOLOGICA TAVRICA. Text in Russian. 1997. q. USD 176 foreign (effective 2007). adv. **Document type:** *Journal, Academic/Scholarly.* **Description:** Examines problems of psychiatry, psychotherapy, neurophysiology, ethology and psychology.
Published by: Krymskaya Respublikanskaya Assotsyatsiya Psikhyatrov, Psikhoterapevtov i Psikhologov, ul R Lyuksemburg 27, Simferopol, Ukraine. TEL 380-65-255380, FAX 380-65-273806. Ed. Dr. Nikolai Verbenko. adv.: page USD 200. Circ: 1,000. **Dist. by:** East View Information Services, 10601 Wayzata Blvd, Minneapolis, MN 55305. TEL 952-252-1201, 800-477-1005, FAX 952-252-1202, info@eastview.com, http://www.eastview.com.

616.853 JPN ISSN 0912-0890
CODEN: TENKDV
TENKAN KENKYU. Text in English, Japanese. 1983. s-a. free to members. **Document type:** *Journal, Academic/Scholarly.*
Related titles: Online - full content ed.: ISSN 1347-5509; Online - full text ed.
Indexed: EMBASE, ExcerpMed, INIS AtomInd, R10, Reac, SCOPUS.
—BLDSC (4804.900000), IE, Ingenta. **CCC.**
Published by: Nihon Tenkan Gakkai/Japan Epilepsy Society, 4-6-15 Ogawahigashi-cho Kodaira, Tokyo, 187-0031, Japan. jessec@szec.hosp.go.jp, http://square.umin.ac.jp/jes/.

616.8 ITA ISSN 1974-725X
TEORIA E CLINICA PSICOANALITICA DEL CAMPO FREUDIANO. Text in Italian. 2001. irreg. **Document type:** *Journal, Academic/Scholarly.*
Published by: Franco Angeli Edizioni, Viale Monza 106, Milan, 20127, Italy. TEL 39-02-2837141, FAX 39-02-26144793, redazioni@francoangeli.it, http://www.francoangeli.it.

616.8 USA ISSN 1941-6652
RC321
TEXAS NEUROSCIENCE REVIEW. Text in English. 2007. a. **Document type:** *Journal, Academic/Scholarly.*
Related titles: Online - full text ed.: ISSN 1941-6660.
Published by: University of Texas Press, Journals Division, 2100 Comal, Austin, TX 78722. journals@uts.cc.utexas.edu, http://www.utexas.edu/utpress/journals/journals.html.

616.8 AUT ISSN 0254-7902
TEXTE; psychoanalyse, aesthetik, kulturkritik. Text in German. 1980. q. EUR 60; EUR 18 newsstand/cover (effective 2005). adv. **Document type:** *Journal, Academic/Scholarly.*
Indexed: E-psyche.
Published by: Passagen Verlag GmbH, Walfischgasse 15-14, Vienna, W 1010, Austria. TEL 43-1-5137761, FAX 43-1-5126327, office@passagen.at. Ed., R&P Peter Engelmann. Adv. contact Thomas Szanto. **Subscr. to:** Springer Distribution Center, Kundenservice Zeitschriften, Haberstr 7, Heidelberg 69126, Germany. TEL 49-6221-3454303, FAX 49-6221-3454229, subscriptions@springer.com.

616.8 GBR ISSN 1756-2856
RC346
➤ **THERAPEUTIC ADVANCES IN NEUROLOGICAL DISORDERS.** Text in English. 2008. bi-m. USD 1,071, GBP 579 combined subscription to institutions (print & online eds.); USD 1,050, GBP 567 to institutions (effective 2011). adv. back issues avail.; reprint service avail. from PSC. **Document type:** *Journal, Academic/Scholarly.* **Description:** Aims to cover all areas of neurological disorders from pre-clinical experimental findings to clinical research.
Related titles: Online - full text ed.: ISSN 1756-2864. 2008. USD 964, GBP 521 to institutions (effective 2011).
Indexed: A22, B21, E01, EMBASE, ExcerpMed, NSA, P30, SCOPUS.
—IE. **CCC.**
Published by: Sage Publications Ltd. (Subsidiary of: Sage Publications, Inc.), 1 Oliver's Yard, 55 City Rd, London, EC1Y 1SP, United Kingdom. TEL 44-20-73248500, FAX 44-20-73248600, info@sagepub.co.uk, http://www.uk.sagepub.com/home.nav. Ed. Ralf Gold.

▼ ➤ **THERAPEUTIC ADVANCES IN PSYCHOPHARMACOLOGY.** *see* PHARMACY AND PHARMACOLOGY

616.8 AUS ISSN 1327-9491
➤ **THERAPEUTIC GUIDELINES. NEUROLOGY.** Text in English. 1997. irreg. (every 3-4 yrs.), latest 2007, version 3. AUD 30 per issue to students; AUD 39 per issue (effective 2008). **Document type:** *Handbook/Manual/Guide, Academic/Scholarly.* **Description:** Provides up-to-date recommendations for drug therapy in treating and managing neurologic conditions and disorders and, when appropriate, alternative approaches to overall patient management.
Formerly: Neurology Guidelines
Related titles: CD-ROM ed.; Online - full text ed.; ◆ Series of: e T G Complete. ISSN 1447-1868.
Indexed: E-psyche.
Published by: Therapeutic Guidelines Ltd., Ground Flr, 23-47 Villiers St, North Melbourne, VIC 3051, Australia. TEL 61-3-93291566, 800-061-260, FAX 61-3-93265632, sales@tg.com.au, http://www.tg.com.au. Eds. Dr. Alice Glover, Dr. Michael Kingsford. Circ: 18,000.

616.8 AUS ISSN 1441-5178
➤ **THERAPEUTIC GUIDELINES. PSYCHOTROPIC.** Text in English. 1989. irreg., latest 2003, version 5. AUD 39 newsstand/cover; AUD 33 newsstand/cover to students (effective 2008). **Document type:** *Handbook/Manual/Guide, Academic/Scholarly.* **Description:** Contains concrete recommendations for rational therapy of psychotropic disease and, where necessary, justifies the choice.
Formerly (until 1995): Psychotropic Drug Guidelines (1039-1568)
Related titles: CD-ROM ed.; Online - full text ed.; ◆ Series of: e T G Complete. ISSN 1447-1868.
Indexed: E-psyche.
Published by: Therapeutic Guidelines Ltd., Ground Flr, 23-47 Villiers St, North Melbourne, VIC 3051, Australia. TEL 61-3-93291566, 800-061-260, FAX 61-3-93265632, sales@tg.com.au, http://www.tg.com.au. Eds. Dr. Alice Glover, Dr. Michael Kingsford. Circ: 18,000. **Co-sponsor:** Victorian Drug Usage Advisory Committee.

616.8 CHE ISSN 0250-4952
THERAPIE FAMILIALE. Text in French. 1980. q. CHF 89 to individuals; CHF 185 to institutions; CHF 80 to students (effective 2007). back issues avail. **Document type:** *Journal, Academic/Scholarly.*
Related titles: Online - full text ed.
Indexed: A22, E-psyche, FR, P03, P25, P48, PQC, PsycInfo, PsycholAb, S02, S03, SCOPUS, SSCI, W07.
—BLDSC (8814.754000), IE, Ingenta, INIST. **CCC.**
Published by: Editions Medecine et Hygiene, Chemin de la Mousse 46, CP 475, Chene-Bourg 4, 1225, Switzerland. TEL 41-22-7029311, FAX 41-22-7029355, abonnements@medhyg.ch, http://www.medhyg.ch.

616.8 DEU ISSN 1616-9646
THIEME REFRESHER NEUROLOGIE. Text in German. 2006. irreg. **Document type:** *Monographic series, Academic/Scholarly.*
Published by: Georg Thieme Verlag, Ruedigerstr 14, Stuttgart, 70469, Germany. TEL 49-711-8931421, FAX 49-711-8931410, leser.service@thieme.de, http://www.thieme.de.

616.891 NOR ISSN 1504-3142
TIDSSKRIFT FOR KOGNITIV TERAPI. Text in Norwegian. 2000. q. NOK 400 membership (effective 2011). **Document type:** *Magazine, Trade.*
Formerly (until 2004): Kognitiv Terapi i Norge (1502-3567)
Related titles: Online - full text ed.: ISSN 1890-4106. 2006.

Published by: Norsk Forening for Kognitiv Terapi, Forskningsinstituttet, Modum Bad, Vikersund, 3370, Norway. TEL 47-32-749862, FAX 47-32-749868, post@kognitiv.no. Ed. Arne Repaal.

616.8 NOR ISSN 1503-6707
TIDSSKRIFT FOR PSYKISK HELSEARBEID. Text in Norwegian, Swedish, Danish. 2004. q. NOK 399 to individuals; NOK 699 to institutions; NOK 290 to students (effective 2010). back issues avail. **Document type:** *Journal, Academic/Scholarly.*
Related titles: Online - full text ed.: ISSN 1504-3010. NOK 799 (effective 2010).
Published by: Universitetsforlaget AS/Scandinavian University Press (Subsidiary of: Aschehoug & Co.), Sehesteds Gate 3, P O Box 508, Sentrum, Oslo, 0105, Norway. TEL 47-24-147500, FAX 47-24-147501, post@universitetsforlaget.no, http://www.universitetsforlaget.no. Ed. Anders J Andersen. Circ: 1,500.

616.8 NLD ISSN 1567-3499
TIJDSCHRIFT GEESTELIJKE VERZORGING. Text in Dutch. 4/yr. EUR 27 (effective 2008). adv. **Document type:** *Journal, Trade.*
Former titles (until 1999): Geestelijke Verzorging (1384-9468); (until 1996): Vereniging van Geestelijke Verzorgers in Zorginstellingen. Rondzendbrief (1384-9697); (until 1993): Vereniging van Geestelijke Verzorgers in Ziekenguizen. Rondzendbrief (1384-9689)
Published by: Vereniging van Geestelijke Verzorgers in Zorginstellingen, Postbus 9025, Ede, 6710 HN, Netherlands. TEL 31-318-433876, FAX 31-318-418507, info@vgvz.nl. Ed. Hendrik Nieuwenhuis. adv.: page EUR 205; trim 175 x 250. Circ: 1,100.

616.83 362.4 NLD ISSN 1871-6172
TIJDSCHRIFT VOOR ARTSEN VOOR VERSTANDELIJK GEHANDICAPTEN. Key Title: T A V G. Text in Dutch. 1982. q. EUR 30 (effective 2009). adv.
Former titles (until 2004): T V A Z. Tijdschrift van de Vereniging van Artsen in de Swakzinnigenzorg (1385-724X); (until 1985): N V A Z Bulletin (1385-7231)
Published by: Nederlandse Vereniging van Artsen voor Verstandelijk Gehandicapten, BTC Kantoor 201, Postbus 545, Enschede, 7500 AM, Netherlands. TEL 31-878-759338, secretariaat@nvavg.nl. Ed. G Nijdam.

TIJDSCHRIFT VOOR CLIENTGERICHTE PSYCHOTHERAPIE. *see* PSYCHOLOGY

616.8
➤ **TIJDSCHRIFT VOOR NEUROLOGIE EN NEUROCHIRURGIE/ JOURNAL OF NEUROLOGY & NEUROSURGERY.** Text in Dutch. 8/yr. **Document type:** *Journal, Trade.*
Published by: Ariez Medical Publishing, Kruislaan 419, Amsterdam, 1098 VA, Netherlands. TEL 31-20-5612070, FAX 31-20-5612051, info@ariezmp.nl, http://www.ariezmp.nl.

616.8 618.92 BEL ISSN 0771-9825
TIJDSCHRIFT VOOR ORTHOPEDAGOGIEK, KINDERPSYCHIATRIE EN KLINISCHE KINDERPSYCHOLOGIE. Abbreviated title: T O K K. Text in Dutch. 1975. q. EUR 30 (effective 2005). **Document type:** *Journal, Academic/Scholarly.*
Formerly (until 1981): Tijdschrift voor Orthopedagogiek en Kinderpsychiatrie (0771-9779)
—IE.
Published by: Uitgeverij Acco, Brusselsestraat 153, Leuven, 3000, Belgium. TEL 32-16-628000, FAX 32-16-628001, uitgeverij@acco.be, http://www.acco.be.

616.89 NLD ISSN 0303-7339
CODEN: TPSYB3
TIJDSCHRIFT VOOR PSYCHIATRIE. Variant title: Psychiatrie. Text in Dutch; Summaries in English. 1969. m. EUR 121; EUR 45 to students; EUR 17 newsstand/cover (effective 2008). adv. bk.rev. illus. index. **Document type:** *Journal, Academic/Scholarly.*
Incorporates: Tijdschrift voor Psychiatrie. Boeken (0922-0712); Formerly (until 1972): Nederlands Tijdschrift voor Psychiatrie (0028-2197)
Related titles: Online - full text ed.: ISSN 1875-7456.
Indexed: A22, AC&P, E-psyche, EMBASE, ExcerpMed, MEDLINE, P03, P30, PsycInfo, PsycholAb, R10, Reac, S02, S03, SCOPUS.
—BLDSC (8844.180000), GNLM, IE, Infotrieve, Ingenta.
Published by: (Nederlandse Vereniging voor Psychiatrie), De Tijdstroom Uitgeverij, Janskerkhof 26, Utrecht, 3500 AT, Netherlands. TEL 31-30-2364450, info@tijdstroom.nl, http://www.tijdstroom.nl. Circ: 3,800. **Co-sponsor:** Vereniging van Vlaamse Zenuwartsen.

616.89 NLD ISSN 1382-516X
TIJDSCHRIFT VOOR PSYCHOANALYSE. Text in Dutch. 1995. 4/yr. EUR 69 domestic to individuals; EUR 81 foreign to individuals; EUR 104 domestic to institutions; EUR 117 foreign to institutions; EUR 36 to students (effective 2009). adv. back issues avail. **Document type:** *Journal, Academic/Scholarly.* **Description:** Publishes original studies in psychoanalysis and psychoanalytical psychotherapy, including theoretical and practical subjects.
Indexed: E-psyche.
Published by: (Stichting Tijdschrift voor Psychoanalyse), Boom Uitgevers Amsterdam, Prinsengracht 747-751, Amsterdam, 1017 JX, Netherlands. TEL 31-20-6226107, FAX 31-20-6253327, info@uitgeverijboom.nl, http://www.uitgeverijboom.nl. Ed. Michel Thys. Adv. contact Michiel Klaasen TEL 31-20-5200122. page EUR 385; trim 130 x 200. Circ: 1,050.

616.89 NLD ISSN 0165-1188
TIJDSCHRIFT VOOR PSYCHOTHERAPIE. Text in Dutch. 1975. 6/yr. EUR 152, USD 228 combined subscription to institutions (print & online eds.) (effective 2009). adv. **Document type:** *Journal, Trade.*
Related titles: Online - full text ed.: ISSN 1876-5637.
Indexed: A22, BibInd, E-psyche, E01, P03, PsycholAb, S02, S03, SCOPUS.
—BLDSC (8844.250000), IE, Infotrieve, Ingenta.
Published by: Bohn Stafleu van Loghum B.V. (Subsidiary of: Springer Science+Business Media), Postbus 246, Houten, 3990 GA, Netherlands. TEL 31-30-6383830, FAX 31-30-6383999, boekhandels@bsl.nl, http://www.bsl.nl. Ed. R J Takens. adv.: B&W page EUR 983; trim 158 x 240. Circ: 1,600.

615.8 NLD ISSN 1871-5052
TIJDSCHRIFT VOOR VAKTHERAPIE. Text in Dutch. 2006. q. EUR 60 domestic to individuals; EUR 62 foreign to individuals; EUR 82 domestic to institutions; EUR 84 foreign to institutions (effective 2009). adv. **Document type:** *Journal, Trade.*
Formed by the merger of (1982-2005): Tijdschrift voor Kreatieve Therapie (0169-6912); (1995-2005): Tijdschrift voor Psychomotorische Therapie (1382-3221)
Published by: Federatie voor Vaktherapeutische Beroepen, Fivelingo 253, Utrecht, 3524 BN, Netherlands. TEL 31-30-2800432, info@vaktherapie.nl, http://www.vaktherapie.nl. Eds. Channa de Kruijf, Jolanda van Rijssen, Winneke Rauh. adv.: page EUR 375. Circ: 2,200.

362.2 GBR ISSN 1359-5474
RC394.L37
➤ **THE TIZARD LEARNING DISABILITY REVIEW.** Text in English. 1996. 5/yr. (q. until 2011). EUR 689 combined subscription in Europe (print & online eds.); USD 889 combined subscription in the Americas (print & online eds.); GBP 529 combined subscription in the UK & elsewhere (print & online eds.); AUD 999 combined subscription in Australasia (print & online eds.) (effective 2012). adv. back issues avail. **Document type:** *Journal, Academic/Scholarly.* **Description:** Essential source of information for all those who work in the field of learning disability.
Related titles: Online - full text ed.: ISSN 2042-8782 (from IngentaConnect).
Indexed: A09, A10, B28, B29, C06, C07, C08, CA, CINAHL, CPE, E-psyche, E03, ERA, ERI, P02, P10, P16, P19, P24, P48, P53, P54, PAIS, PQC, S11, S20, S21, SCOPUS, SOPODA, SociolAb, T02, V03, V04.
—BLDSC (8859.316000), IE, Ingenta. **CCC.**
Published by: (University of Kent, Tizard Centre), Pier Professional Ltd. (Subsidiary of: Emerald Group Publishing Ltd.), Ste N4, The Old Market, Upper Market St, Hove, BN3 1AS, United Kingdom. TEL 44-1273-783720, FAX 44-1273-783723, info@pierprofessional.com. Ed. Jim Mansell. Adv. contact Paul Somerville TEL 44-1273-783724. B&W page GBP 350; 160 x 245.

616.8 JPN
TOKYO-TO SHINKEI KAGAKU SOGO KENKYUJO NENPO/TOKYO METROPOLITAN INSTITUTE FOR NEUROSCIENCES. ANNUAL REPORT. Text in Japanese. 1972. a.
Indexed: E-psyche.
Published by: Tokyo-to Shinkei Kagaku Sogo Kenkyujo/Tokyo Metropolitan Institute for Neurosciences, 2-6 Musashidai, Fuchu-shi, Tokyo-to 183-0042, Japan.

617.48 NLD ISSN 0924-6169
➤ **TOPICS IN NEUROSURGERY.** Text in English. 1988. irreg., latest vol.8, 1988. price varies. **Document type:** *Monographic series, Academic/Scholarly.*
Indexed: E-psyche.
Published by: Springer Netherlands (Subsidiary of: Springer Science+Business Media), Van Godewijckstraat 30, Dordrecht, 3311 GX, Netherlands. TEL 31-78-6576050, FAX 31-78-6576474.

616.8 NLD ISSN 0897-3946
➤ **TOPICS IN THE NEUROSCIENCES.** Text in English. 1986. irreg., latest vol.9, 1990. price varies. **Document type:** *Monographic series, Academic/Scholarly.*
Indexed: E-psyche.
Published by: Springer Netherlands (Subsidiary of: Springer Science+Business Media), Van Godewijckstraat 30, Dordrecht, 3311 GX, Netherlands. TEL 31-78-6576050, FAX 31-78-6576474.

616.89 FRA ISSN 0040-9375
BF173.A2
TOPIQUE; revue Freudienne. Text in French. 1967. q. EUR 80 domestic; EUR 100 foreign (effective 2009). **Document type:** *Journal, Academic/Scholarly.* **Description:** Scope is to offer a place where theoretical reflection and clinical experience in psychoanalysis may enrich each other and confront their conflictual borders.
Formerly (until 1968): L' Inconscient (0536-6186)
Related titles: Online - full content ed.
Indexed: A22, DIP, E-psyche, FR, IBR, IBZ, MLA-IB, P03, PsycInfo, PsycholAb, SCOPUS.
—IE, Infotrieve, INIST. **CCC.**
Published by: Editions L' Esprit du Temps, 115 Rue Anatole France, B P 107, Le Bouscat, 33491 Cedex, France. TEL 33-5-56028419, FAX 33-5-56029131, info@lespritdutemps.com.

TORANSUPASONARU SHINRIGAKU/SEISHIN IGAKU/JAPANESE JOURNAL OF TRANSPERSONAL PSYCHOLOGY/PSYCHIATRY. *see* PSYCHOLOGY

TRANSACTIONAL ANALYSIS JOURNAL. *see* PSYCHOLOGY

599.97 GBR ISSN 1363-4615
RC321 CODEN: TRPSFM
➤ **TRANSCULTURAL PSYCHIATRY.** Text in English. 1956. 5/yr. USD 890, GBP 481 combined subscription to institutions (print & online eds.); USD 872, GBP 471 to institutions (effective 2011). adv. bk.rev. abstr.; bibl.; charts. index. cum.index: 1956-1972. back issues avail.; reprint service avail. from PSC. **Document type:** *Journal, Academic/Scholarly.* **Description:** Provides a channel of communication for psychiatrists and social scientists around the world concerned with the relationship between culture and mental health.
Former titles (until 1997): Transcultural Psychiatric Research Review (0041-1108); (until 1969): Transcultural Psychiatric Research Review and Newsletter (0315-4386); (until 1963): Transcultural Research in Mental Health Problems. Review and Newsletter (0315-4394); (until 1959): Transcultural Research in Mental Health Problems. Newsletter (0315-4416)
Related titles: Microfilm ed.: (from PQC); Online - full text ed.: ISSN 1461-7471. USD 801, GBP 433 to institutions (effective 2011).
Indexed: A01, A03, A08, A20, A22, AnthLit, B07, B21, C06, C07, C08, CA, CINAHL, CurCont, DIP, E-psyche, E01, EMBASE, ExcerpMed, FR, H04, I14, IBR, IBZ, IndMed, MEDLINE, NSA, P03, P30, PsycInfo, PsycholAb, R10, Reac, S02, S03, SCOPUS, SSCI, SociolAb, T02, V02, W07.
—BLDSC (9020.580620), GNLM, IE, Infotrieve, Ingenta, INIST. **CCC.**
Published by: (McGill University, Division of Social and Transcultural Psychiatry CAN), Sage Publications Ltd. (Subsidiary of: Sage Publications, Inc.), 1 Oliver's Yard, 55 City Rd, London, EC1Y 1SP, United Kingdom. TEL 44-20-73248500, FAX 44-20-73248600, info@sagepub.co.uk, http://www.uk.sagepub.com/home.nav. Ed. Laurence J Kirmayer. adv.: B&W page GBP 400; 130 x 205. **Subscr. in the Americas to:** Sage Publications, Inc., 2455 Teller Rd, Thousand Oaks, CA 91320. TEL 805-499-9774, FAX 805-499-0871, journals@sagepub.com.

616.8 POL ISSN 2081-3856
▼ ➤ **TRANSLATIONAL NEUROSCIENCE.** Text in English. 2010. 4/yr. EUR 298, USD 366 combined subscription to institutions (print & online eds.) (effective 2012). **Document type:** *Journal, Academic/Scholarly.* **Description:** Contains research from all fields of neuroscience, as well as from related disciplines of neurology, psychiatry and neurosurgery.
Related titles: Online - full text ed.: ISSN 2081-6936. 2010.
Indexed: P30.
Published by: Versita, ul Druga Poprzeczna, 9, Warsaw, 00-951, Poland. TEL 48-22-7015015, FAX 48-22-4335126, info@versita.com, http://www.versita.com. Ed. Goran Simic. **Co-publisher:** Springer.

616.8 611.01816 GBR ISSN 2158-3188
▼ ➤ **TRANSLATIONAL PSYCHIATRY.** Text in English. 2011. free (effective 2011). **Document type:** *Journal, Academic/Scholarly.* **Description:** Explores and researches all areas of psychiatry and neuroscience.
Media: Online - full text.
—**CCC.**
Published by: Nature Publishing Group (Subsidiary of: Macmillan Publishers Ltd.), The MacMillan Bldg, 4 Crinan St, London, N1 9XW, United Kingdom. TEL 44-20-78334000, FAX 44-20-78334640, NatureReviews@nature.com. Ed. Dr. Julio Licinio TEL 61-2-61252550.

616.8 USA ISSN 1868-4483
▼ ➤ **TRANSLATIONAL STROKE RESEARCH.** Text in English. 2010 (Mar.). 4/yr. USD 418 combined subscription to institutions (print & online eds.) (effective 2011). **Document type:** *Journal, Academic/Scholarly.* **Description:** Provides a forum for the dissemination of original research on strokes and in stroke related areas.
Related titles: Online - full text ed.: ISSN 1868-601X. 2010 (from IngentaConnect).
Indexed: A26, H12, P30, SCOPUS.
—**CCC.**
Published by: Springer New York LLC (Subsidiary of: Springer Science+Business Media), 233 Spring St, New York, NY 10013. TEL 212-460-1500, FAX 212-460-1575, journals-ny@springer.com. Ed. John H Zhang.

616.8 ESP ISSN 1888-6116
R71
TRAUMA. Text in Spanish. 1990. q. back issues avail. **Document type:** *Journal, Academic/Scholarly.*
Formerly (until 2008): Mapfre Medicina (1130-5665)
Related titles: Online - full text ed.: 1996. free (effective 2011); Supplement(s): Mapfre Medicina. Suplemento. ISSN 1133-5602. 1991.
Indexed: EMBASE, ExcerpMed, R10, Reac, SCOPUS.
—BLDSC (5369.318355). **CCC.**
Published by: Fundacion Mapfre, Paseo de Recoletos, 23, Madrid, 28004, Spain. TEL 34-91-5812353, FAX 34-91-5816070, fundacion.informacion@mafre.com, http://www.fundacionmapfre.com. Ed. Francisco De la Gala Sanzhez.

616.8 344.041 USA
TRAUMATIC BRAIN INJURY; evaluation and litigation. Text in English. 1994. irreg., latest 2006. USD 129 per issue (effective 2008). 643 p./no.; **Document type:** *Magazine, Trade.* **Description:** Covers the medical and neuropsychological analysis of brain injury, including its causes and effects; the process of case investigation, including evaluation of liability and damages; and trial techniques, including settlement considerations.
Related titles: Online - full text ed.
Indexed: E-psyche.
Published by: Michie Company (Subsidiary of: LexisNexis North America), 701 E Water St, Charlottesville, VA 22902. TEL 434-972-7600, 800-446-3410, FAX 434-972-7677, customer.support@lexisnexis.com, http://www.michie.com. Eds. Dr. Eileen McNamara, Richard W Petrocelli, Dr. Thomas J Guilmette.

616.8 USA ISSN 1087-3104
TRAUMATIC STRESS POINTS NEWSLETTER. Abbreviated title: Traumatic StressPoints. Text in English. 1985. q. free to members. adv. bk.rev. **Document type:** *Newsletter, Trade.* **Description:** Contains news and opinions about the traumatic stress field, ISTSS activities, activities of related organizations, resources and feature articles on topics of interest.
Related titles: Online - full content ed.; Spanish ed.: Puntos de Estres Traumatico. 2005.
Indexed: E-psyche.
Published by: International Society for Traumatic Stress Studies, 60 Revere Dr, Ste 500, Northbrook, IL 60062. TEL 847-480-9028, FAX 847-480-9282, istss@istss.org, http://www.istss.org. Ed. Edward Varra. Circ: 2,500 (paid).

616.8 150 FRA ISSN 1620-5340
TRAVAILLER; revue internationale de psychopathologie et de psychodynamique du travail. Text in French. 1998. s-a. EUR 25 (effective 2008). **Document type:** *Journal, Academic/Scholarly.*
Related titles: Online - full content ed.
Indexed: SCOPUS.
—INIST.
Published by: (Conservatoire National des Arts et Metiers), Martin Media, 10, avenue Victor Hugo, Revigny-sur-Ornain, 55800, France.

TRENDS IN COGNITIVE SCIENCES. *see* PSYCHOLOGY

616.8 GBR ISSN 0166-2236
QP351 CODEN: TNSCDR
➤ **TRENDS IN NEUROSCIENCES.** Text in English. 1978. m. EUR 1,827 in Europe to institutions; JPY 253,400 in Japan to institutions; USD 2,043 elsewhere to institutions (effective 2012). adv. bk.rev.; software rev. illus. index. back issues avail.; reprints avail. **Document type:** *Journal, Academic/Scholarly.* **Description:** For research workers, teachers and students concerned with the structure and function of the brain and with the biological substrates of behavior.
Related titles: Microform ed.: (from PQC); Online - full text ed.: ISSN 1878-108X (from IngentaConnect, ScienceDirect); ◆ Supplement(s): Neurotoxins. ISSN 1357-7115.

Indexed: A01, A02, A03, A08, A20, A22, A26, A29, ASCA, ASFA, AnBeAb, B04, B20, B21, BIOBASE, BIOSIS Prev, BRD, C33, CA, CTA, ChemAb, CurCont, E-psyche, E08, EMBASE, ESPM, ExcerpMed, G03, G08, GSA, GSI, H11, H12, H13, I05, I10, IABS, IBR, IBZ, ISR, IndMed, Inpharma, JW-N, MEDLINE, MycolAb, NSA, NSCI, P02, P03, P10, P12, P20, P30, P48, P53, P54, PQC, PsycInfo, PsycholAb, R10, RILM, Reac, S09, SCI, SCOPUS, T02, Telegen, ViroIAbstr, W03, W07.
—BLDSC (9049.667000), CASDDS, IE, Infotrieve, Ingenta, INIST. **CCC.**
Published by: Elsevier Ltd., Trends Journals (Subsidiary of: Elsevier Science & Technology), 84 Theobald's Rd, London, WC1X 8RR, United Kingdom. TEL 44-20-76114000, FAX 44-20-76114485, JournalsCustomerServiceEMEA@elsevier.com, http://www.elsevier.com. Ed. Sian Lewis. Adv. contact James Kenney TEL 44-20-74244216.

616.8 TUR ISSN 1301-062X
TURK NOROLOJI DERGISI/TURKISH JOURNAL OF NEUROLOGY. Text in Turkish, English. 1995. q. **Document type:** *Journal, Academic/Scholarly.*
Related titles: Online - full text ed.: free (effective 2011).
Indexed: A01, C06, SCOPUS, T02.
Published by: Turk Noroloji Dernegi/Turkish Neurological Society, Mesrutiyet Caddesi 48/7, Ankara, 06650, Turkey. TEL 90-312-4355992, FAX 90-312-4316090.

616.8 TUR ISSN 1019-5157
TURK NOROSIRURJI DERGISI. Text in Turkish. 1990. q. **Document type:** *Journal, Academic/Scholarly.* **Description:** Covers latest developments in the field of neurosurgery by providing articles that discuss advances in clinical practice and neuroscience research of value for the practicing neurosurgeon and resident.
Related titles: Online - full text ed.: free (effective 2010); ◆ English ed.: Turkish Neurosurgery. ISSN 1019-5149.
Published by: Turk Norosirurji Dernegi/Turkish Neurosurgical Society, Turk Norosirurji Dernegi Merkezi, Taskent Caddesi 13/4, Bahcelievler, Ankara, 06500, Turkey. TEL 90-312-2126408, FAX 90-312-2154626, dergi@turknorosirurji.org.tr, http://www.turknorosirurji.org.tr/. Ed. Hakan Caner.

616.89 TUR ISSN 1300-2163
TURK PSIKIYATRI DERGISI. Variant title: Turkish Journal of Psychiatry. Text in Multiple languages. 1990. q. **Document type:** *Journal, Academic/Scholarly.*
Related titles: Online - full text ed.: free (effective 2011).
Indexed: A22, CA, CurCont, EMBASE, ExcerpMed, MEDLINE, P03, P20, P22, P30, P54, PsycInfo, PsycholAb, R10, Reac, SCOPUS, SSCI, T02, W07.
—BLDSC (9072.181700), IE, Ingenta.
Published by: Turkiye Sinir ve Ruh Sagligi Dernegi, Yenisehir, P K 401, Ankara, 06442, Turkey. TEL 90-312-4282040, FAX 90-312-4277822, info@bayt.com.tr. Ed. Aylin Ulusahin.

616.8 TUR ISSN 1019-5149
CODEN: TUNEE
➤ **TURKISH NEUROSURGERY.** Text in English. 1990. q. bk.rev. **Document type:** *Journal, Academic/Scholarly.* **Description:** Covers latest developments in the field of neurosurgery by providing articles that discuss advances in clinical practice and neuroscience research of value for the practicing neurosurgeon and resident.
Related titles: Online - full text ed.: free (effective 2010); ◆ Turkish ed.: Turk Norosirurji Dergisi. ISSN 1019-5157.
Indexed: E-psyche, EMBASE, ExcerpMed, MEDLINE, P30, R10, Reac, SCI, SCOPUS, W07.
—GNLM, IE, Ingenta.
Published by: Turk Norosirurji Dernegi/Turkish Neurosurgical Society, Turk Norosirurji Dernegi Merkezi, Taskent Caddesi 13/4, Bahcelievler, Ankara, 06500, Turkey. TEL 90-312-2126408, FAX 90-312-2154626, dergi@turknorosirurji.org.tr, http://www.turknorosirurji.org.tr/. Ed. Hakan Caner. Circ: 450.

616.858 USA
U.S. CONGRESS: MENTAL HEALTH; legal updates, children & youth updates, federal agencies, state reports, studies on state mental health systems. Text in English. 1972 (vol.11). irreg. (several/mo.). USD 350.
Formerly: U.S. Congress: Mental Health, Mental Retardation
Indexed: E-psyche.
Published by: National Association of State Mental Health Program Directors, 66 Canal Center Plaza, Ste 302, Alexandria, VA 22314-1591. TEL 703-739-9333, FAX 703-548-9517, http://www.nasmhpd.org. Ed. Harry Schnibbe. Circ: 135.

616.8005 GBR ISSN 1758-4000
➤ **U S NEUROLOGY.** (United States) Text in English. 200?. (May). s-a. EUR 80 combined subscription in Europe to individuals (print & online eds.); USD 100 combined subscription in United States to individuals (print & online eds.); EUR 180 combined subscription in Europe to institutions (print & online eds.); USD 225 combined subscription in United States to institutions (print & online eds.) (effective 2009). back issues avail. **Document type:** *Journal, Trade.* **Description:** Focuses on latest developments within the neurological field from a scientific and clinical perspectives.
Former titles (until 2008): U S Neurological Disease (1752-816X); (until 2006): U S Neurology Review
Related titles: Online - full text ed.: U S Neurology (Online). ISSN 1758-4019. EUR 70 in Europe to individuals; USD 85 in United States to individuals; EUR 170 in Europe to institutions; USD 210 in United States to institutions (effective 2009).
Published by: Touch Briefings (Subsidiary of: Touch Group plc), Saffron House, 6-10 Kirby St, London, EC1N 8TS, United Kingdom. TEL 44-20-74525600, FAX 44-20-74525606, info@touchbriefings.com, http://www.touchbriefings.com/.

362.2 SWE ISSN 1652-7380
UNIK. Text in Swedish. 2004. bi-m. SEK 200 (effective 2005). adv. **Document type:** *Magazine, Trade.*
Formed by the merger of (1966-2004): F U B -Kontakt (0345-3790); (1976-2004): Steget (0348-5072)
Published by: Riksfoerbundet foer Utvecklingsstoerda Barn, Ungdomer och Vuxna, Gaevlegatan 18 C, PO Box 6436, Stockholm, 11382, Sweden. TEL 46-8-50886600, FAX 46-8-50886666, fub@fub.se. Adv. contact Pia Sandberg TEL 46-8-6001817. page SEK 10,500; 210 x 297. Circ: 23,000.

616.8 DEU ISSN 1437-7810
UNIVERSITAET LANDAU. NEUROWISSENSCHAFTLICHES SEMINAR. Text in German. 1999. irreg., latest vol.3, 1999. price varies. **Document type:** *Monographic series, Academic/Scholarly.*
Published by: Verlag Dr. Kovac, Leverkusenstr 13, Hamburg, 22761, Germany. TEL 49-40-3988800, FAX 49-40-39888055, info@verlagdrkovac.de. Ed. Monika Pritzel.

616.6 617.7 USA ISSN 1066-4130
V H L FAMILY FORUM. (Von Hippel-Lindau Disease) Text in English; Summaries in French, Italian, Spanish. 1993. q. USD 35 domestic; USD 50 foreign (effective 2007). adv. Website rev.; bk.rev. 16 p./no.; back issues avail.; reprints avail. **Document type:** *Newsletter, Consumer.* **Description:** Enables physicians, patients and family members to exchange information on all aspects of the disease.
Related titles: Audio cassette/tape ed.; Online - full text ed.
Indexed: E-psyche.
Published by: V H L Family Alliance, 2001 Beacon St, Ste 208, Boston, MA 02135-8712. TEL 617-277-5667, FAX 858-712-8712. Ed., Pub., Adv. contact Joyce Wilcox Graff. R&P Joyce W Graff TEL 617-232-5946. Circ: 5,500.

616.8 CHE ISSN 1016-6262
RC489.B4
➤ **VERHALTENSTHERAPIE**; Praxis - Forschung - Perspektiven. Text in German. 1991. q. CHF 246, EUR 159, USD 266 to institutions; CHF 318, EUR 209, USD 341 combined subscription to institutions (print & online eds.) (effective 2012). adv. **Document type:** *Journal, Academic/Scholarly.*
Related titles: Microform ed.: (from PQC); Online - full text ed.: ISSN 1423-0402. CHF 212, EUR 146, USD 219 to institutions (effective 2012).
Indexed: A22, ASCA, BibInd, CurCont, E-psyche, E01, EMBASE, ExcerpMed, P03, PsycInfo, PsycholAb, R10, Reac, SCI, SCOPUS, SSCI, T02, W07.
—BLDSC (9156.600000), GNLM, IE, Infotrieve, Ingenta. **CCC.**
Published by: S. Karger AG, Allschwilerstr 10, Basel, 4055, Switzerland. TEL 41-61-3061111, FAX 41-61-3061234, karger@karger.ch, http://www.karger.ch. Eds. F Hohagen, U Ehlert. R&P Tatjana Sepin. adv.: B&W page EUR 2,300; trim 210 x 297. Circ: 4,000 (paid and controlled).

616.8 DEU ISSN 1865-9985
VERHALTENSTHERAPIE UND VERHALTENSMEDIZIN. Text in English, German. 1979. q. EUR 38; EUR 11 per issue (effective 2011). adv. **Document type:** *Journal, Academic/Scholarly.* **Description:** Contains specific and summary articles on the crucial questions concerning behavioural therapy.
Formerly (until 1997): Verhaltensmodifikation und Verhaltensmedizin (1013-1973)
Indexed: DIP, E-psyche, IBR, IBZ, P03, PsycInfo, PsycholAb.
—BLDSC (9156.650000), GNLM.
Published by: Pabst Science Publishers, Am Eichengrund 28, Lengerich, 49525, Germany. TEL 49-5484-97234, FAX 49-5484-550, pabst@pabst-publishers.com, http://www.pabst-publishers.de. Ed. Hans Reinecker. Circ: 2,420 (paid and controlled).

616.8 ARG ISSN 0327-6139
VERTEX; revista argentina de psiquiatria. Text in Multiple languages. 1990. q. USD 75. **Document type:** *Journal, Academic/Scholarly.*
Indexed: C01, EMBASE, ExcerpMed, MEDLINE, P30, R10, Reac, SCOPUS.
Published by: Polemos Sociedad Anonima, Moreno 1785, 5o Piso, Buenos Aires, 1093, Argentina. TEL 54-11-43835291, FAX 54-11-43432464, editorial@polemos.com.ar, http://www.editorialpolemos.com.ar. Circ: 2,500.

616.8 SVN ISSN 1318-5764
VICEVERSA; Slovenske psihiatricne piblikacije. Text in Slovenian. 1992. s-a. **Document type:** *Journal, Academic/Scholarly.*
—BLDSC (9232.258700).
Published by: Psihiatricna Klinika Ljubljana, Studenec 48, Ljubljana, 1260, Slovenia. TEL 386-1-5872100, FAX 386-1-5284618, info@psih-klinika.si, http://www.psih-klinika.si.

616.8 IRL ISSN 2009-0781
THE VIDEO JOURNAL OF PSYCHIATRY. Text in English. 2007. irreg. **Document type:** *Journal, Academic/Scholarly.*
Media: Online - full text.
Published by: (Royal College of Surgeons in Ireland, Department of Psychiatry), CVSLearning, Room 12 Arts Block Annex, NUIM, Maynooth, Co. Kildare, Ireland. TEL 353-1-7086391.

616.858 362.3 GBR ISSN 1358-6076
VIEWPOINT (LONDON, 1995). Text in English. 1995. bi-m. GBP 15 (effective 2007). adv. bk.rev. illus. reprints avail. **Document type:** *Magazine, Consumer.* **Description:** Publishes features, news items and reports on services and campaigns about issues concerning people with learning disabilities. Aimed at parents, caregivers and health professionals, and people with learning disabilities.
Formed by the 1995 merger of: Gatepost; (1990-1995): M E N C A P News (0963-7117); Which was formerly (until 1992): M E N C A P News and Parents Voice; Which Incorporated: Parents Voice (0031-1936)
Related titles: CD-ROM ed.: Viewpoint (CD-ROM). GBP 25; free people with a learning disability (effective 2007); Supplement(s): Pulse (London).
Indexed: B28, E-psyche, ECER.
Published by: Royal Society for Mentally Handicapped Children and Adults, Mencap Centre, Royal Society For Mentally Handicapped Children &, 123 Golden Ln, London, EC1Y 0RT, United Kingdom. TEL 44-20-7454-0454, FAX 44-20-7454-9193. Ed. Peter Mookram. Circ: 5,500.

616.858 USA ISSN 1546-8844
KFV2765.A29
VIRGINIA MENTAL HEALTH, MENTAL RETARDATION, SUBSTANCE ABUSE AND RELATED LAW ANNOTATED. Text in English. 19??. a. USD 45 combined subscription (print & CD-ROM eds.) (effective 2008). 559 p./no.; **Document type:** *Journal, Trade.* **Description:** Contains a range of statutes selected from the official Code of Virginia and brings together the relevant law in the areas of mental health, mental retardation and substance abuse in an easy-to-use format.
Related titles: CD-ROM ed.
Indexed: E-psyche.
Published by: Michie Company (Subsidiary of: LexisNexis North America), 701 E Water St, Charlottesville, VA 22902. TEL 434-972-7600, 800-446-3410, FAX 434-972-7677, customer.support@lexisnexis.com, http://www.michie.com.

616.8 GBR ISSN 0952-5238
QP474 CODEN: VNEUEY
➤ **VISUAL NEUROSCIENCE.** Text in English. 1988. bi-m. GBP 886, USD 1,498 to institutions; GBP 956, USD 1,618 combined subscription to institutions (print & online eds.) (effective 2012). adv. bk.rev. back issues avail.; reprint service avail. from PSC. **Document type:** *Journal, Academic/Scholarly.* **Description:** Contains theoretical and research-based articles on the neural mechanisms of vision, with primary emphasis on retinal and brain mechanisms underlying visually guided behavior and visual perception in both vertebrate and invertebrate species.
Related titles: Online - full text ed.: ISSN 1469-8714. GBP 794, USD 1,338 to institutions (effective 2012).
Indexed: A20, A22, ASCA, ApicAb, B21, B25, BIOBASE, BIOSIS Prev, CA, CurCont, E-psyche, E01, EMBASE, ExcerpMed, FR, IABS, ISR, IndMed, Inpharma, MEDLINE, MycolAb, NSA, NSCI, P03, P20, P22, P25, P30, P48, P54, PQC, PsycInfo, PsycholAb, R10, Reac, SCI, SCOPUS, T02, W07, Z01.
—BLDSC (9241.296000), GNLM, IE, Infotrieve, Ingenta, INIST. **CCC.**
Published by: Cambridge University Press, The Edinburgh Bldg, Shaftesbury Rd, Cambridge, CB2 8RU, United Kingdom. TEL 44-1223-312393, FAX 44-1223-315052, journals@cambridge.org, http://www.cambridge.org/uk. Ed. Benjamin E Reese. R&P Linda Nicol TEL 44-1223-325702. Adv. contact Rebecca Roberts TEL 44-1223-325083. page GBP 465, page USD 885. Circ: 600. **Subscr. to:** Cambridge University Press, 32 Ave of the Americas, New York, NY 10013. TEL 212-337-5000, FAX 212-691-3239, journals_subscriptions@cup.org.

616.8 NLD ISSN 2212-0300
VIZIER (DRIEBERGEN-RIJSENBURG, 2008). Text in Dutch. 2005. q. **Document type:** *Magazine, Consumer.*
Supersedes in part (in 2006): Silhouet/Vizier (1871-2630); Which was formed by the merger of (2004-2005): Silhouet (1572-3291); Which was formerly (2002-2004): Tijdschrift over Angst en Depressie (1570-1328); (2003-2005): Vizier (Driebergen-Rijsenburg, 2003) (1871-2649); Which was formerly (1969-2003): Fobie-Vizier (0166-7149)
Published by: Angst, Dwang en Fobie Stichting, Hoofdstraat 122, Driegergen, 3972 LD, Netherlands. FAX 31-343-531737, info@adfstichting.nl, http://www.adfstichting.nl.

LA VOIX DES PARENTS. *see* HANDICAPPED

616.89 GBR
W P A SERIES. EVIDENCE AND EXPERIENCE IN PSYCHIATRY. (World Psychiatry Association) Text in English. 1999. irreg., latest 2009, 3rd ed. price varies. adv. back issues avail. **Document type:** *Monographic series, Academic/Scholarly.* **Description:** Aims to provide a critical overview of the research evidence concerning the diagnosis and management of the most prevalent mental disorders and a survey of the relevant clinical experience in the various regions of the world.
Published by: John Wiley & Sons Ltd. (Subsidiary of: John Wiley & Sons, Inc.), 1-7 Oldlands Way, PO Box 808, Bognor Regis, West Sussex PO21 9FF, United Kingdom. TEL 44-1865-778315, FAX 44-1243-843232, cs-journals@wiley.com. Eds. Helen Herrman, Mario Maj, Norman Sartorius. **Subscr. to:** 1-7 Oldlands Way, PO Box 809, Bognor Regis, West Sussex PO21 9FG, United Kingdom. TEL 44-1865-778054, cs-agency@wiley.com.

362 344.0412 NLD ISSN 1877-475X
DE WET B O P Z. (Bijzondere Opnemingen in Psychiatrische Ziekenhuizen) Text in Dutch. 1995. irreg., latest vol.7, 2008. EUR 41.51 per vol. (effective 2011).
Published by: Sdu Uitgevers bv, Postbus 20025, The Hague, 2500 EA, Netherlands. TEL 31-70-3789911, FAX 31-70-3854321, sdu@sdu.nl, http://www.sdu.nl/.

616.8 POL ISSN 1505-7429
WIADOMOSCI PSYCHIATRYCZNE. Text in Polish; Summaries in English. 1998. q. PLZ 60 to institutions (effective 2009). bk.rev. **Document type:** *Journal, Academic/Scholarly.*
Indexed: EMBASE, ExcerpMed, SCOPUS.
—BLDSC (9315.290000), IE.
Published by: Wydawnictwo Medyczne Urban i Partner, ul Marii Sklodowskiej-Curie 55-61, Wroclaw, 50950, Poland. TEL 48-71-3285487, FAX 48-71-3284391, http://www.urbanpartner.pl. Ed. Irena Zaucha-Nowotarska. Circ: 1,000.

616.8 DEU ISSN 1611-4272
WIRTSCHAFTSMAGAZIN FUER DEN NERVENARZT. Text in German. 1996. bi-m. EUR 22.50 (effective 2011). adv. **Document type:** *Magazine, Trade.*
Formerly (until 2000): Wirtschaftsbrief fuer den Nervenarzt (1439-2976)
Published by: W P V- Wirtschafts- und Praxisverlag GmbH, Otto-Hahn-Str 7, Koeln, 50997, Germany. TEL 49-2236-376711, FAX 49-2236-37692530, info@wpv.de. Adv. contact Isabelle Becker TEL 49-2236-376711. Circ: 4,869 (controlled).

WORD FROM WASHINGTON (WASHINGTON, D.C.). *see* HANDICAPPED

616.89 CHE ISSN 0084-1609
WORLD CONGRESS OF PSYCHIATRY. PROCEEDINGS. Text in English. 1950. irreg., latest 2005. price varies. **Document type:** *Proceedings, Academic/Scholarly.*
Indexed: E-psyche.
Published by: World Psychiatric Association, 2 ch du Petit-Bel-Air, Chene-Bourg, 1225, Switzerland. TEL 41-22-3055730, FAX 41-22-3055735, wpasecretariat@wpanet.org, http://www.wpanet.org.

616.8 GBR ISSN 1562-2975
RC321
➤ **THE WORLD JOURNAL OF BIOLOGICAL PSYCHIATRY.** Text in English. 2001. q. GBP 590, EUR 700, USD 870 combined subscription to institutions (print & online eds.); GBP 1,180, EUR 1,400, USD 1,740 combined subscription to corporations (print & online eds.) (effective 2010). adv. back issues avail.; reprint service avail. from PSC. **Document type:** *Journal, Academic/Scholarly.* **Description:** Aims to increase the worldwide communication of knowledge in clinical and basic research on biological psychiatry.
Related titles: Online - full text ed.: ISSN 1814-1412 (from IngentaConnect); Supplement(s): ISSN 1750-953X.

Indexed: A01, A22, CA, CurCont, E01, EMBASE, ExcerpMed, Inpharma, MEDLINE, NSCI, P30, P35, PsycInfo, R10, Reac, SCI, SCOPUS, T02, W07.
—BLDSC (9356.073250), IE, Ingenta. **CCC.**
Published by: Informa Healthcare (Subsidiary of: T & F Informa plc), Telephone House, 69-77 Paul St, London, EC2A 4LQ, United Kingdom. TEL 44-20-70175000, FAX 44-20-70176792, healthcare.enquiries@informa.com. Ed. Siegfried Kasper TEL 43-1-404003568. Adv. contact Per Sonnerfeldt. **Subscr. in N. America to:** Taylor & Francis Inc., Customer Services Dept, 325 Chestnut St, 8th Fl, Philadelphia, PA 19106. TEL 215-625-8900, 800-354-1420, FAX 215-625-8914, customerservice@taylorandfrancis.com; **Subscr. outside N. America to:** Taylor & Francis Ltd., Journals Customer Service, Sheepen Pl, Colchester, Essex CO3 3LP, United Kingdom. TEL 44-20-70175544, FAX 44-20-70175198, tf.enquiries@tfinforma.com.

616.8 USA ISSN 2162-2000
▼ **WORLD JOURNAL OF NEUROSCIENCE.** Abbreviated title: W J N S. Text in English. 2011. q. USD 156 (effective 2011). **Document type:** *Journal, Academic/Scholarly.* **Description:** Provides a platform for scientists and academicians all over the world to promote, share, and discuss various new issues and developments in different areas of Neuroscience.
Related titles: Online - full text ed.: ISSN 2162-2019. free (effective 2011).
Published by: Scientific Research Publishing, Inc., PO Box 54821, Irvine, CA 92619. service@scirp.org. Ed. Gjumrakch Aliev.

WORLD NEUROSURGERY. *see* MEDICAL SCIENCES—Surgery

616.89 ITA ISSN 1723-8617
RA790.A1
➤ **WORLD PSYCHIATRY.** Text in English. 2002. 3/yr. **Document type:** *Journal, Academic/Scholarly.*
Indexed: CurCont, EMBASE, ExcerpMed, P30, R10, Reac, SCI, SCOPUS, SSCI, W07.
—**CCC.**
Published by: (World Psychiatric Association CHE), Elsevier Masson (Subsidiary of: Elsevier Health Sciences), Via Paleocapa 7, Milan, 20121, Italy. TEL 39-02-881841, FAX 39-02-88184302, info@masson.it, http://www.masson.it. Ed. Mario Maj.

616.8 CHN ISSN 1671-3710
XINLI KEXUE JINZHAN/ADVANCES IN PSYCHOLOGICAL SCIENCE. Text in Chinese. 1983. bi-m. USD 53.40 (effective 2009). **Document type:** *Journal, Academic/Scholarly.*
Formerly (until 2001): Xinlixue Dongtai (1004-8529)
Related titles: Online - full text ed.
Published by: Zhongguo Kexueyuan Xinlin Yanjiuso, Dewai Beishatan, Beijing, 100101, China. TEL 86-10-64850861. **Dist. by:** China International Book Trading Corp, 35 Chegongzhuang Xilu, Haidian District, PO Box 399, Beijing 100044, China. TEL 86-10-68412045, FAX 86-10-68412023, cibtc@mail.cibtc.com.cn, http://www.cibtc.com.cn.

616.8 150 CHN ISSN 2095-1159
XINLI YANJIU/PSYCHOLOGICAL RESEARCH. Text in Chinese. 1993. bi-m. **Document type:** *Journal, Academic/Scholarly.*
Formerly (until 2007): Xinli Shijie/Mind World (1005-510X)
Published by: Henan Daxue/Henan University, Minglun Jie, Kaifeng, 475001, China. TEL 86-378-2869137, FAX 86-378-2869137, http://www.henu.edu.cn.

616.8 CHN ISSN 1005-7064
XINLI YU JIANKANG/PSYCHOLOGY AND HEALTH. Text in Chinese. 1994. m. USD 49.20 (effective 2009). **Document type:** *Journal, Academic/Scholarly.*
Published by: Zhongguo Xinli Weisheng Xiehui/Chinese Association for Mental Health, 5 An Kang Lane, De Sheng Men Wai, Beijing, 100088, China. TEL 86-10-82085385, FAX 86-10-62359838, camh@163bj.com. **Dist. by:** China International Book Trading Corp, 35 Chegongzhuang Xilu, Haidian District, PO Box 399, Beijing 100044, China. TEL 86-10-68412045, FAX 86-10-68412023, cibtc@mail.cibtc.com.cn, http://www.cibtc.com.cn.

616.8 CHN ISSN 1672-013X
XINLING SHIJIE/MIND WORLD. Text in Chinese. 2001. m. **Document type:** *Magazine, Consumer.*
Formerly (until 2002): Xinling Xiao Muwu (1009-573X)
Published by: Zhongguo Jiating Yisheng Zazhishe/China Family Doctors Magazine Press, 77, Tiyu Xi Lu Guangli Lu, Dongzhou Dasha B23-26, Tianhe-qu, Guangzhou, China. http://www.jtys.cn/.

616.8 617 USA ISSN 0513-5117
RC329
YEAR BOOK OF NEUROLOGY AND NEUROSURGERY. Text in English. 1902. a. USD 217 in United States to institutions; USD 235 elsewhere to institutions (effective 2012). adv. **Document type:** *Yearbook, Academic/Scholarly.* **Description:** Presents abstracts of pertinent literature with commentary by leading experts in the field.
Supersedes in part (in 1969): The Year Book of Neurology, Psychiatry, and Neurosurgery; Which was formerly: Year Book of Neurology and Psychiatry; (until 1950): Year Book of Neurology, Psychiatry, and Neurosurgery (0364-5126); Which superseded in part (in 1945): Year Book of Neurology, Psychiatry and Endocrinology (0887-3941); Which was formerly (until 1934): Year Book of Neurology and Psychiatry
Related titles: CD-ROM ed.; Online - full text ed.
Indexed: A22, E-psyche.
—BLDSC (9414.627000), GNLM. **CCC.**
Published by: Mosby, Inc. (Subsidiary of: Elsevier Health Sciences), 1600 John F. Kennedy Blvd, Ste 1800, Philadelphia, PA 19103. TEL 215-239-3900, 800-523-1649, FAX 215-239-3990, elspcs@elsevier.com, http://www.us.elsevierhealth.com. Eds. Dr. Ashok Verma, Dr. Scott Gibbs.

616.89 USA ISSN 0084-3970
RC329
YEAR BOOK OF PSYCHIATRY AND APPLIED MENTAL HEALTH. Text in English. 1946. a. USD 239 in United States to institutions; USD 259 elsewhere to institutions (effective 2012). adv. illus. **Document type:** *Yearbook, Academic/Scholarly.* **Description:** Presents abstracts of the pertinent literature with commentary by leading experts in the field.
Supersedes in part (in 1970): The Year Book of Neurology, Psychiatry, and Neurosurgery (0364-5126); Which superseded in part (in 1946): The Year Book of Neurology, Psychiatry and Endocrinology (0887-3941); Which was formerly (until 1934): Year Book of Neurology and Psychiatry
Related titles: CD-ROM ed.; Online - full text ed.
Indexed: A22, E-psyche.
—BLDSC (9415.700000), GNLM. **CCC.**
Published by: Mosby, Inc. (Subsidiary of: Elsevier Health Sciences), 1600 John F. Kennedy Blvd, Ste 1800, Philadelphia, PA 19103. TEL 215-239-3900, 800-523-1649, FAX 215-239-3990, elspcs@elsevier.com, http://www.us.elsevierhealth.com. Ed. Dr. John A Talbott.

616.8 USA ISSN 1946-3200
RJ506.H9
▼ **THE YEAR IN A D H D.** (Attention Deficit and Hyperactivity Disorder) Text in English. 2009. a. USD 99 per issue (effective 2009). **Document type:** *Yearbook, Academic/Scholarly.* **Description:** Collection of current advances in ADHD research.
Related titles: Online - full text ed.: ISSN 1946-3219. USD 24.75 per issue (effective 2009).
Published by: Current Medicine Group LLC (Subsidiary of: Springer Science+Business Media), 400 Market St, Ste 700, Philadelphia, PA 19106. TEL 215-574-2266, FAX 215-574-2225, info@phl.cursci.com, http://www.current-medicine.com.

616.8 USA ISSN 1476-2544
THE YEAR IN NEUROLOGY (YEAR). Text in English. 2001. irreg., latest 2008. 352 p./no.; **Document type:** *Academic/Scholarly.* **Description:** Provides expert commentary on over 150 recent papers selected from the world's leading journals in neurology.
Indexed: P20, P22, P48, P54, PQC.
—**CCC.**
Published by: (New York Academy of Sciences), Wiley-Blackwell Publishing, Inc. (Subsidiary of: Wiley-Blackwell Publishing Ltd.), 111 River St, Hoboken, NJ 07030. TEL 201-748-6000, FAX 201-748-6088, info@wiley.com.

616.8 GBR ISSN 1477-8122
THE YEAR IN SCHIZOPHRENIA. Text in English. 2007 (Jun.). a. USD 99.95 per issue in US & Canada; GBP 59.99 per issue elsewhere (effective 2009). **Document type:** *Journal, Academic/Scholarly.* **Description:** Provides insights on recent advances and present an overview of current thinking.
—BLDSC (9371.628780). **CCC.**
Published by: Clinical Publishing (Subsidiary of: Atlas Medical Publishing Ltd), Oxford Centre for Innovation, Mill St, Oxford, OX2 0JX, United Kingdom. TEL 44-1865-811116, FAX 44-1865-251550, info@clinicalpublishing.co.uk. Eds. G Thaker, W T Carpenter. **Dist. by:** Marston Book Services Ltd., Unit 160, Milton Park, Abingdon, Oxfordshire OX14 4SD, United Kingdom. TEL 44-1235-465500, FAX 44-1235-465555, trade.orders@marston.co.uk, http://www.marston.co.uk/.

616.8 TUR ISSN 1300-8773
RC321
YENI SYMPOSIUM; a journal of psychiatry, neurology and behavioral sciences. Text in Turkish. 1963. q. **Document type:** *Journal, Academic/Scholarly.*
Related titles: Online - full text ed.: ISSN 1304-4591. 2001. free (effective 2011).
Indexed: A01, CA, EMBASE, ExcerpMed, P03, PsycInfo, PsycholAb, R10, Reac, SCOPUS, T02.
Published by: Istanbul Universitesi, Cerrahpasa Tip Fakultesi/Istanbul University, Cerrahpasa Medical Faculty, Cerrahpafla Tip Fakultesi Psikiyatri A.D., Cerrahpafla, P K 34303, Istanbul, 34303, Turkey. TEL 90-212-4143360, FAX 90-212-2401603, ctfedit@istanbul.edu.tr, doksat@tnn.net. Ed. Ertugrul Goksoy.

616.8 JPN ISSN 0513-5710
R97 CODEN: YOAMAQ
➤ **YONAGO ACTA MEDICA.** Text in English. 1954. q. free (effective 2007). back issues avail. **Document type:** *Journal, Academic/Scholarly.* **Description:** Contains research by faculty members.
Related titles: Online - full text ed.: ISSN 1346-8049. 1996.
Indexed: A34, A36, B25, BIOSIS Prev, CABA, CIN, ChemAb, E12, EMBASE, ExcerpMed, GH, H17, INIS AtomInd, IndMed, IndVet, MycolAb, N02, N03, P30, P33, PHN&I, R10, Reac, S13, S16, SCI, SCOPUS, VS, W07.
—BLDSC (9421.000000), CASDDS, GNLM, INIST. **CCC.**
Published by: Tottori Daigaku, Igakubu/Tottori University, Faculty of Medicine, 86 Nishi-cho, Yonago, Tottori 683-8503, Japan. TEL 81-859-386861, FAX 81-859-386869. Ed. Eisaku Ohama. Pub. Takao Inoue. R&P Mr. Isao Shimizu. Circ: 620 (controlled).

616.8 362.7 GBR ISSN 1361-9403
YOUNGMINDS MAGAZINE. Text in English. 1989. bi-m. GBP 32 per issue; free to members (effective 2009). adv. bk.rev.; film rev.; play rev.; Website rev. stat. 36 p./no.; back issues avail. **Document type:** *Magazine, Trade.* **Description:** News-focused magazine committed to covering children's mental health and dedicated to reaching such a broad range of professionals working with children and young people.
Formerly (until 1996): Young Minds Newsletter (1361-939X)
Indexed: E-psyche.
—BLDSC (9421.451383). **CCC.**
Published by: YoungMinds, 48-50 St John St, London, EC1M 4DG, United Kingdom. TEL 44-20-73368445, FAX 44-20-73368446, magazine@youngminds.org.uk. Ed. Derre Hayes.

616.8 DEU ISSN 1439-2623
Z N S & SCHMERZ. (Zentrales Nerven System) Text in German. 1999. q. EUR 58; EUR 15 newsstand/cover (effective 2006). adv. **Document type:** *Magazine, Trade.*
Published by: m d m - Verlag fuer Medizinische Publikationen, Bremsen 4, Leichlingen, 42799, Germany. TEL 49-2175-1691230, FAX 49-2175-1691231, info@mdmverlag.de. adv.: B&W page EUR 2,510, color page EUR 3,590. Circ: 10,500 (paid and controlled).

150 POL ISSN 0324-8526
RJ499.A1
ZAGADNIENIA WYCHOWAWCZE A ZDROWIE PSYCHICZNE. Text in Polish; Summaries in English, Russian. 1968. bi-m. USD 15. bibl.
Formerly (until 1973): Zagadnienia Wychowawcze w Aspekcie Zdrowia Psychicznego (0324-8690)
Indexed: E-psyche.
Published by: Polskie Towarzystwo Higieny Psychicznej/Polish Mental Hygiene Society, ul Targowa 59, lok 16, Warsaw, 03729, Poland. TEL 48-22-8186599, FAX 48-22-8180549, pthp@tlen.pl, http://www.pthp.org.pl.

614.58 POL ISSN 0044-2003
➤ **ZDROWIE PSYCHICZNE.** Text in Polish; Summaries in English, Russian. 1961. q. bk.rev. bibl. index. **Document type:** *Journal, Academic/Scholarly.*
Indexed: E-psyche.
Published by: Polskie Towarzystwo Higieny Psychicznej/Polish Mental Hygiene Society, ul Targowa 59, lok 16, Warsaw, 03729, Poland. TEL 48-22-8186599, FAX 48-22-8180549, pthp@tlen.pl, http://www.pthp.org.pl.

616.853 DEU ISSN 1617-6782
RC372.A1
➤ **ZEITSCHRIFT FUER EPILEPTOLOGIE.** Text in German. 2003. q. EUR 435, USD 436 combined subscription to institutions (print & online eds.) (effective 2012). adv. reprint service avail. from PSC. **Document type:** *Journal, Academic/Scholarly.*
Related titles: Online - full text ed.: ISSN 1610-0646 (from IngentaConnect).
Indexed: A22, A26, E01, EMBASE, ExcerpMed, R10, Reac, SCOPUS.
—IE, Ingenta. **CCC.**
Published by: Dr. Dietrich Steinkopff Verlag (Subsidiary of: Springer Science+Business Media), Tiergartenstr 17, Heidelberg, 69121, Germany. TEL 49-6221-4878821, FAX 49-6221-4878830, info.steinkopff@springer.com, http://www.steinkopff.com. Eds. Dr. Bernhard Steinhoff, Dr. Ruediger Koehling. adv.: B&W page EUR 1,775, color page EUR 2,815; trim 210 x 279. Circ: 1,800 (paid and controlled). **Subscr. to:** Springer Distribution Center, Kundenservice Zeitschriften, Haberstr 7, Heidelberg 69126, Germany. TEL 49-6221-3454303, FAX 49-6221-3454229, subscriptions@springer.com.

616.89 CHE ISSN 1422-4917
➤ **ZEITSCHRIFT FUER KINDER- UND JUGENDPSYCHIATRIE UND PSYCHOTHERAPIE.** Text in German. 1907. q. CHF 389 domestic to institutions; EUR 259 in Europe to institutions (effective 2011). adv. 64 p./no.; **Document type:** *Journal, Academic/Scholarly.*
Former titles (until 1996): Zeitschrift fuer Kinder- und Jugendpsychiatrie (0301-6811); (until 1973): Jahrbuch fuer Jugendpsychiatrie und Ihre Grenzgebiete (0448-1534); (until 1956): Zeitschrift fuer Kinderforschung (0932-1403); (until 1923): Zeitschrift fuer Kinderforschung mit Besonderer Beruecksichtigung der Paedagogischen Pathologie (1011-2456)
Related titles: Online - full text ed.: ISSN 1664-2880.
Indexed: A20, A22, ASCA, CurCont, DIP, E-psyche, EMBASE, ExcerpMed, F09, IBR, IBZ, IndMed, MEDLINE, P03, P30, PCI, PsycInfo, PsycholAb, R10, Reac, S02, S03, SCOPUS, SSCI, W07.
—BLDSC (9467.490000), GNLM, IE, Infotrieve, Ingenta, INIST. **CCC.**
Published by: Verlag Hans Huber AG (Subsidiary of: Hogrefe Verlag GmbH & Co. KG), Laenggassstr 76, Bern 9, 3000, Switzerland. TEL 41-31-3004500, FAX 41-31-3004590, verlag@hanshuber.com, http://www.hanshuber.com. Ed. G Lehmkuhl. Circ: 1,600 (paid and controlled).

616.8 CHE ISSN 1661-4747
BF3 CODEN: ZKPPAP
➤ **ZEITSCHRIFT FUER PSYCHIATRIE, PSYCHOLOGIE UND PSYCHOTHERAPIE.** Text in German. 1951. q. CHF 284, EUR 189 to institutions (effective 2011). adv. bk.rev. index. **Document type:** *Journal, Academic/Scholarly.*
Former titles (until 2006): Zeitschrift fuer Klinische Psychologie, Psychiatrie und Psychotherapie (1431-8172); (until 1996): Zeitschrift fuer Klinische Psychologie, Psychopathologie und Psychotherapie (0723-6557); (until 1983): Zeitschrift fuer Klinische Psychologie und Psychotherapie (0300-869X); (until 1971): Jahrbuch fuer Psychologie, Psychotherapie und Medizinische Anthropologie (0021-4000); (until 1960): Jahrbuch fuer Psychologie und Psychotherapie (0340-3467)
Related titles: Online - full text ed.: ISSN 1664-2929.
Indexed: A20, A22, ASCA, CIS, CurCont, DIP, E-psyche, EMBASE, ExcerpMed, GJP, IBR, IBZ, IndMed, P03, P30, PsycInfo, PsycholAb, R10, Reac, S02, S03, SCOPUS, SOPODA, SSCI, SociolAb, W07.
—BLDSC (9485.030000), GNLM, IE, Infotrieve, Ingenta, INIST. **CCC.**
Published by: (Goerres-Gesellschaft DEU), Verlag Hans Huber AG (Subsidiary of: Hogrefe Verlag GmbH & Co. KG), Laenggassstr 76, Bern 9, 3000, Switzerland. TEL 41-31-3004500, FAX 41-31-3004590, verlag@hanshuber.com, http://verlag.hanshuber.com. Ed. Dr. Franz Petermann. Circ: 500 (paid and controlled).

150.195 616.8917 DEU ISSN 0169-3395
ZEITSCHRIFT FUER PSYCHOANALYTISCHE THEORIE UND PRAXIS. Text in German. 1986. 4/yr. EUR 78; EUR 28 newsstand/cover. **Document type:** *Journal, Academic/Scholarly.*
Indexed: A22, DIP, IBR, IBZ, P03, PsycInfo, PsycholAb, RILM.
—BLDSC (9485.050000), IE, Ingenta.
Published by: Stroemfeld Verlag GmbH, Holzhausenstr 4, Frankfurt Am Main, 60322, Germany. TEL 49-69-9552260, FAX 49-69-95522624, info@stroemfeld.de, http://www.stroemfeld.de.

616.89 DEU ISSN 1438-3608
CODEN: ZPPSB2
➤ **ZEITSCHRIFT FUER PSYCHOSOMATISCHE MEDIZIN UND PSYCHOTHERAPIE.** Text in German; Summaries in English, German. 1954. q. EUR 99 to individuals; EUR 198 to institutions; EUR 81 to students; EUR 28.90 newsstand/cover (effective 2011). adv. bk.rev. abstr. index. **Document type:** *Journal, Academic/Scholarly.*
Former titles (until 1999): Zeitschrift fuer Psychosomatische Medizin und Psychoanalyse (0340-5613); (until 1967): Zeitschrift fuer Psycho-Somatische Medizin (0375-5355)
Related titles: Online - full text ed.
Indexed: A20, A22, ASCA, CERDIC, CurCont, DIP, E-psyche, EMBASE, ExcerpMed, FR, GJP, IBR, IBZ, ISR, IndMed, Inpharma, MEDLINE, P03, P30, PsycInfo, PsycholAb, R10, Reac, SCI, SCOPUS, SSCI, W07.
—BLDSC (9485.280000), GNLM, IE, Infotrieve, Ingenta, INIST. **CCC.**
Published by: Vandenhoeck und Ruprecht, Theaterstr 13, Goettingen, 37073, Germany. TEL 49-551-508440, FAX 49-551-5084422, info@v-r.de. Ed. Gabriele Witte-Lakemann. Circ: 1,900 (paid and controlled).

616.8 CHN ISSN 1003-2754
ZHONGFENG YU SHENJING JIBING ZAZHI/JOURNAL OF APOPLEXY AND NERVOUS DISEASES. Text in Chinese. 1984 (Mar.). bi-m. USD 42.60 (effective 2009). back issues avail. **Document type:** *Journal, Academic/Scholarly.*
Related titles: Online - full content ed.; Online - full text ed.
—East View.
Published by: (Jilin Daxue/Jilin University), Zhongfeng yu Shenjing Jibing Zazhi, 1, Xinmin Dajie, Changchun, 130021, China. Ed. Mingli Rao.

616.8 CHN ISSN 1008-0678
ZHONGGUO LINCHUANG SHENJING KEXUE/CHINESE JOURNAL OF CLINICAL NEUROSCIENCES. Text in Chinese. 1993. bi-m. USD 37.20 (effective 2009).
Related titles: Online - full text ed.
—BLDSC (3180.302600), East View.
Published by: Fudan Daxue Shenjingbingxue Yanjiusuo, 12, Wulumuqi Zhong Lu, Shanghai, 200040, China.

616.8 CHN ISSN 1005-3611
ZHONGGUO LINCHUANG XINLIXUE ZAZHI/CHINESE JOURNAL OF CLINICAL PSYCHOLOGY. Text in Chinese. 1993. q. USD 31.20 (effective 2009). **Document type:** *Journal, Academic/Scholarly.*
Related titles: Online - full text ed.
Indexed: A22, P03, PsycInfo, PsycholAb, S02, S03.
—BLDSC (3180.304000), East View, IE, Ingenta.
Published by: Zhongguo Xinli Weisheng Xiehui/Chinese Association for Mental Health, 5 An Kang Lane, De Sheng Men Wai, Beijing, 100088, China. TEL 86-10-82085385, FAX 86-10-62359838, camh@163bj.com. **Dist. by:** China International Book Trading Corp, 35 Chegongzhuang Xilu, Haidian District, PO Box 399, Beijing 100044, China. TEL 86-10-68412045, FAX 86-10-68412023, cibtc@mail.cibtc.com.cn, http://www.cibtc.com.cn.

616.8 CHN ISSN 1002-0152
ZHONGGUO SHENJING JINGSHEN JIBING ZAZHI/CHINESE JOURNAL OF NERVOUS AND MENTAL DISEASES. Text in Chinese; Abstracts and contents page in Chinese, English. 1975. m. CNY 156; CNY 13 per issue (effective 2010). **Document type:** *Journal, Academic/Scholarly.*
Former titles (until 1982): Shenjing Jingshen Jibing Zazhi/Journal of Nervous and Mental Diseases (1000-2464); (until 1978): Xinyixue: Shenjing Jitong Jibing Fukan
Related titles: Online - full text ed.: (from WanFang Data Corp.).
—BLDSC (3180.435000), IE.
Published by: Zhongshan Daxue, Zhongshan Yixueyuan/Sun Yat-Sen University, Zhongshan School of Medicine, 74, Zhongshan Er-Lu, Guangzhou, 510089, China. TEL 86-20-87333686, FAX 86-20-87331494, http://zssom.sysu.edu.cn/. Eds. Jinsheng Zeng, Kaida Jiang, Liangfu Zhou, Ruxun Huang.

616.8 CHN ISSN 1006-2963
ZHONGGUO SHENJING MIANYIXUE HE SHENJINGBINGXUE ZAZHI/CHINESE JOURNAL OF NEUROIMMUNOLOGY AND NEUROLOGY. Text in Chinese. 1994. bi-m. USD 37.20 (effective 2009). **Document type:** *Journal, Academic/Scholarly.*
Related titles: Online - full text ed.
—East View.
Address: 1, Dongdan Dahua Lu, Beijing, 100730, China. TEL 86-10-65132266 ext 3872, FAX 86-10-65242081. Ed. Xian-Hao Xu. **Dist. by:** China International Book Trading Corp, 35 Chegongzhuang Xilu, Haidian District, PO Box 399, Beijing 100044, China. TEL 86-10-68412045, FAX 86-10-68412023, cibtc@mail.cibtc.com.cn, http://www.cibtc.com.cn.

616.8 CHN ISSN 1673-5110
ZHONGGUO SHIYONG SHENJING JIBING ZAZHI/CHINESE JOURNAL OF PRACTICAL NERVOUS DISEASES. Text in Chinese. 1998. bi-m. USD 40.20 (effective 2009). **Document type:** *Journal, Academic/Scholarly.*
Formerly (until 2006): Shiyong Shenjing Jibing Zazhi/Journal of Practical Nervous Diseases (1672-9218)
Published by: Zhongzhou Daxue, 2, Jingba Lu, Zhengzhou, 450014, China. TEL 86-371-63974256.

ZHONGGUO WEI QINXI SHENJING WAIKE ZAZHI/CHINESE JOURNAL OF MINIMALLY INVASIVE NEUROSURGERY. *see* MEDICAL SCIENCES—Surgery

616.8 CHN ISSN 1006-7884
CODEN: CHSCA
ZHONGHUA JINGSHENKE ZAZHI/CHINESE JOURNAL OF PSYCHIATRY. Text in Chinese. 1955-1960; resumed 1996. q. USD 29.20 (effective 2009). **Document type:** *Journal, Academic/Scholarly.*
Supersedes in part (1955-1960): Zhonghua Shenjing-Jingshenke Zazhi (0412-4057)
Related titles: CD-ROM ed.; Online - full text ed.
Indexed: A22, E-psyche, ExtraMED, IndMed, SCOPUS.
—BLDSC (3180.605000), East View, GNLM, IE, Ingenta.
Published by: Zhonghua Yixuehui Zazhishe/Chinese Medical Association Publishing House, 42 Dongsi Xidajie, Beijing, 100710, China. **Dist. by:** China International Book Trading Corp, 35 Chegongzhuang Xilu, Haidian District, PO Box 399, Beijing 100044, China. TEL 86-10-68412045, FAX 86-10-68412023, cibtc@mail.cibtc.com.cn, http://www.cibtc.com.cn.

616.8 CHN ISSN 1671-2897
ZHONGHUA SHENJING WAIKE JIBING YANJIU ZAZHI/CHINESE JOURNAL OF NEUROSURGICAL DISEASE RESEARCH. Text in Chinese. 2001. bi-m. CNY 18 newsstand/cover (effective 2006). **Document type:** *Journal, Academic/Scholarly.*
Related titles: Online - full text ed.
Published by: Di-4 Junyi Daxue, Di-1 Fushu Yiyuan, 127, Changdong Xi Lu, Xi'an, 710032, China.

ZHONGHUA SHENJING WAIKE ZAZHI/CHINESE JOURNAL OF NEUROSURGERY. *see* MEDICAL SCIENCES—Surgery

616.8 CHN ISSN 1671-8925
ZHONGHUA SHENJING YIXUE ZAZHI/CHINESE JOURNAL OF NEUROMEDICINE. Text in Chinese. 2002. m. **Document type:** *Journal, Academic/Scholarly.*
Related titles: Online - full text ed.
—BLDSC (9512.839940).
Published by: Nanfang Yike Daxue Zhujiang Yiyuan, 253 Middle Gongye Rd., Guangzhou, 510282, China. TEL 86-20-61643273, FAX 86-20-61643272, http://www.zjyy.com.cn/. Ed. Ru-xiang Xu. **Co-sponsor:** Zhonghua Yixuehui/Chinese Medical Association.

616.8 CHN ISSN 1006-7876
➤ **ZHONGHUA SHENJINGKE ZAZHI/CHINESE JOURNAL OF NEUROLOGY.** Text in Chinese. 1955-1966; resumed 1978. bi-m. USD 80.40 (effective 2009). 80 p./no.; **Document type:** *Journal, Academic/Scholarly.*
Supersedes in part (1955-1966): Chung-Hua Shen Ching Ching Shen K'o Tsa Chih/Chinese Journal of Neurology and Psychiatry (0412-4057)
Related titles: CD-ROM ed.; Online - full content ed.; Online - full text ed.
Indexed: A22, EMBASE, ExcerpMed, P30, R10, Reac, SCOPUS.
—BLDSC (3180.435900), East View, IE, Ingenta.
Published by: Zhonghua Yixuehui Zazhishe/Chinese Medical Association Publishing House, 42 Dongsi Xidajie, Beijing, 100710, China. Eds. Li Peng, Xiuhua Chen, Yalin Bao. **Dist. by:** China International Book Trading Corp, 35 Chegongzhuang Xilu, Haidian District, PO Box 399, Beijing 100044, China. TEL 86-10-68412045, FAX 86-10-68412023, cibtc@mail.cibtc.com.cn, http://www.cibtc.com.cn.

616.8 CHN ISSN 1674-6554
ZHONGHUA XINGWEI YIXUE YU NAOKEXUE ZAZHI/CHINESE JOURNAL OF BEHAVIORAL MEDICINE AND BRAIN SCIENCE. Text in Chinese. m.
Formerly (until 2009): Zhongguo Xingwei Yixue Kexue/Chinese Journal of Behavioral Medical Science (1005-8559)
Related titles: Online - full text ed.
Indexed: B21, VirolAbstr.
—BLDSC (9512.840920).
Published by: Jining Yixueyuan/Jining Medical University, 45 Jianshe S. Rd., Jining, 272013, China. TEL 86-537-2400106, FAX 86-537-2400106, http://www.jnmc.edu.cn/. Ed. Zhi-yin Yang. **Co-sponsor:** Zhonghua Yixuehui/Chinese Medical Association.

616.8 RUS ISSN 1997-7298
RC321 CODEN: ZNPIAP
➤ **ZHURNAL NEVROLOGII I PSIKHIATRII IMENI S.S. KORSAKOVA/ JOURNAL OF NEUROLOGY AND PSYCHIATRY. S.S. KORSAKOV.** Text in Russian; Summaries in English. 1901. m. USD 472 in North America (effective 2010). adv. bk.rev. bibl.; charts; illus. index. reprints avail. **Document type:** *Journal, Academic/Scholarly.* **Description:** Disseminates medical aid to patients by publishing original scientific investigations in etiology and pathogenesis, including the prevention and treatment of neurological and mental diseases.
Formerly (until 1993): Zhurnal Nevropatologii i Psikhiatrii im. S.S. Korsakova (0044-4588)
Related titles: Online - full text ed.
Indexed: A20, ASCA, B25, BDM&CN, BIOSIS Prev, ChemAb, CurCont, DBA, DentInd, E-psyche, EMBASE, ExcerpMed, F09, FR, IndMed, Inpharma, MEDLINE, MycolAb, P30, PsycholAb, R10, Reac, RefZh, S02, S03, SCI, SCOPUS, W07.
—CASDDS, East View, GNLM, IE, Infotrieve, INIST. **CCC.**
Published by: (Nauchnoe Obshchestvo Nevrologov i Psikhiatrov), Media Sfera, Dmitrovskoe shosse 46, korp 2, etazh 4, P.O. Box 54, Moscow, 127238, Russian Federation. TEL 7-095-4824329, FAX 7-095-4824312, podpiska@mediasphera.ru, http://mediasphera.ru. Ed. E I Gusev. Circ: 4,000 (paid). **Dist. by:** East View Information Services, 10601 Wayzata Blvd, Minneapolis, MN 55305. TEL 952-252-1201, 800-477-1005, FAX 952-252-1202, info@eastview.com, http://www.eastview.com.

➤ **ZHURNAL VOPROSY NEIROKHIRURGII IM. N.N. BURDENKO/ JOURNAL OF NEUROSURGICAL PROBLEMS.** *see* MEDICAL SCIENCES—Surgery

➤ **ZHURNAL VYSSHEI NERVNOI DEYATEL'NOSTI.** *see* BIOLOGY—Physiology

616.8 CHN ISSN 1007-0478
ZUZHONG YU SHENJING JIBING/STROKE AND NERVOUS DISEASES. Text in Chinese. 1994. bi-m. USD 24.60 (effective 2009). **Document type:** *Journal, Academic/Scholarly.*
Related titles: Online - full text ed.
—East View.
Published by: Wuhan Daxue Remin Yiyuan, 5, Wuchangziyang Road, Wuhan, 430060, China. TEL 86-27-88041919 ext 8839, http://www.hbsti.ac.cn/. Ed. Qing-xing Ceng. **Dist. by:** China International Book Trading Corp, 35 Chegongzhuang Xilu, Haidian District, PO Box 399, Beijing 100044, China. TEL 86-10-68412045, FAX 86-10-68412023, cibtc@mail.cibtc.com.cn, http://www.cibtc.com.cn.

MEDICAL SCIENCES—Radiology And Nuclear Medicine

615.842 USA ISSN 2160-4754
A C R BULLETIN. Text in English. 1945. 10/yr. USD 90 to non-members; free to members (effective 2011). illus. back issues avail. **Document type:** *Bulletin, Trade.* **Description:** Provides organization news and member information, and examines current socio-economic issues in radiology.
Former titles (until 1996): American College of Radiology. Bulletin (2160-4738); (until 1992): A C R Bulletin (0098-6070); (until 1969): American College of Radiology. Bulletin (0098-6100); (until 1958): American College of Radiology. Monthly Newsletter
Related titles: Online - full text ed.: ISSN 2160-4789. free (effective 2011).
Indexed: C06, MCR.
Published by: American College of Radiology, 1891 Preston White Dr, Reston, VA 20191. TEL 703-648-8900, 800-347-7748, FAX 703-620-4730, info@acr.org.

616.07 USA ISSN 0498-3564
RB1
A F I P LETTER. Text in English. 1951. bi-m. **Document type:** *Newsletter, Trade.* **Description:** Publishes information on policies, activities and programs relevant to the military and civilian pathology community.
Published by: Armed Forces Institute of Pathology, 6825 16th St, N W, Washington, DC 20306-6000. TEL 202-782-2115, FAX 202-782-9376. Eds. Bonnie L Casey, Christopher C Kelly, Jacquelyn B Flowers.

615.842 USA
A H R A LINK. Text in English. 1982. m. membership. back issues avail. **Document type:** *Newsletter.*
Formerly: A H R A Announcement
Published by: American Healthcare Radiology Administrators, 490b Boston Post Rd., Ste. 101, Sudbury, MA 01776-3365. publications@ahraonline.org, http://www.ahraonline.org. Ed., R&P Holly Vietzke. Circ: 4,000.

616.075 618 USA
A I U M SOUND WAVES; news from the assosiation for medical ultrasound. Variant title: A I U M Sound Waves Weekly. Text in English. 1985. w. free to members (effective 2010). adv. 8 p./no.; back issues avail. **Document type:** *Newsletter, Trade.* **Description:** Keeps members and ultrasound professionals up-to-date on A.I.U.M. activities, as well as on news and legislation that can affect the field. Provides educational opportunities to practitioners.
Formerly (until Nov.1999): A I U M Reporter
Related titles: Online - full content ed.
Published by: American Institute for Ultrasound in Medicine, 14750 Sweitzer Ln, Ste 100, Laurel, MD 20707. TEL 301-498-4100, 800-638-5352, FAX 301-498-4450, publications@aium.org. Circ: 8,200 (paid).

615.842 CHL ISSN 0717-4055
R895.A1
A L A S B I M N JOURNAL; revista de medicina nuclear. (Asociacion Latinoamericana de Sociedades de Biologia y Medicina Nuclear) Text in Spanish. 1998. q. free (effective 2011). back issues avail. **Document type:** *Journal, Academic/Scholarly.*
Media: Online - full text.
Published by: A L A S B I M N, Servicio de Medicina Nuclear. Clinica Las Condes, La Fontecilla 441, Santiago de Chile, Chile. edalasmn@cybercenter.cl. Ed. Ismael Mena.

616.842 USA ISSN 0161-3863
A S R T SCANNER. Text in English. 1968. bi-m. free to members (effective 2010). adv. **Document type:** *Magazine, Trade.* **Description:** Provides news about the society and the radiologic technology profession.
Related titles: Online - full text ed.
Indexed: A26, C06, C07, C08, CINAHL, H12, I05.
—**CCC.**
Published by: American Society of Radiologic Technologists, 15000 Central Ave, SE, Albuquerque, NM 87123. TEL 505-298-4500, 800-444-2778, FAX 505-298-5063, memberservices@asrt.org. Ed. D D Wolohan. Adv. contact JoAnne Quirindongo TEL 505-298-4500 ext 1317.

ABDOMINAL IMAGING. *see* MEDICAL SCIENCES—Gastroenterology

615.842 NLD ISSN 1076-6332
RC78.A1 CODEN: ARADFX
➤ **ACADEMIC RADIOLOGY.** Text in English. 1994. 12/yr. USD 414 in United States to institutions; USD 449 elsewhere to institutions (effective 2012). adv. stat. **Document type:** *Journal, Academic/Scholarly.* **Description:** Publishes articles describing original investigations in new radiologic techniques and technologies; covers other clinical, theoretical, and ethical issues.
Related titles: Online - full text ed.: ISSN 1878-4046 (from IngentaConnect, ScienceDirect).
Indexed: A22, A26, B&BAb, B19, BioEngAb, C06, C07, CA, CurCont, EMBASE, ExcerpMed, I05, IIL, INI, IndMed, Inpharma, Inspec, MEDLINE, P30, R10, Reac, SCI, SCOPUS, T02, W07.
—BLDSC (0570.514240), GNLM, IE, Infotrieve, Ingenta, INIST. **CCC.**
Published by: (Association of University Radiologists USA), Elsevier BV (Subsidiary of: Elsevier Science & Technology), Radarweg 29, PO Box 211, Amsterdam, 1000 AE, Netherlands. TEL 31-20-4853911, FAX 31-20-4852457, JournalsCustomerServiceEMEA@elsevier.com, http://www.elsevier.nl. Ed. Dr. Stanley Baum. **Subscr. to:** Elsevier, Subscription Customer Service, 6277 Sea Harbor Dr, Orlando, FL 32887-4800. TEL 407-345-4000, 800-654-2452, FAX 407-363-9661. **Co-sponsors:** Society of Chairmen of Academic Radiology Departments; American Association of Academic Chief Residents in Radiology; Association of Program Directors in Radiology.

615.842 GBR ISSN 0284-1851
CODEN: ACRAE3
➤ **ACTA RADIOLOGICA.** Text in English. 1963. 10/yr. USD 1,848 combined subscription in North America to institutions (print & online eds.); EUR 1,504 combined subscription in Europe to institutions (print & online eds.); GBP 1,052 combined subscription to institutions in the UK & elsewhere (print & online eds.) (effective 2012). adv. bk.rev. bibl.; charts; illus. index, cum.index. back issues avail.; reprints avail. **Document type:** *Journal, Academic/Scholarly.* **Description:** Aims to the publication of research articles on diagnostic and interventional radiology, clinical radiology, experimental investigations in animals, and all other research related to imaging procedures.
Formerly (until 1987): Acta Radiologica. Diagnosis (0567-8056); Which superseded in part (in 1963): Acta Radiologica (0001-6926)
Related titles: Online - full text ed.: ISSN 1600-0455. USD 1,663 in North America to institutions; EUR 1,354 in Europe to institutions; GBP 947 to institutions in the UK & elsewhere (effective 2012) (from IngentaConnect).
Indexed: A01, A03, A08, A22, A26, ASCA, B&BAb, B19, B21, C06, C07, CA, CMCI, CPEI, CTA, ChemAb, CurCont, DBA, DentInd, E01, EMBASE, ESPM, EngInd, ExcerpMed, FR, IIL, INIS AtomInd, ISR, IndMed, Inpharma, Inspec, Kidney, MEDLINE, NSA, P30, P35, R10, Reac, SCI, SCOPUS, T02, TM, ToxAb, W07.
—CASDDS, GNLM, IE, Infotrieve, Ingenta, INIST. **CCC.**
Published by: (Societies of Medical Radiology in Denmark, Finland, Iceland, Norway and Sweden DNK), Royal Society of Medicine Press Ltd., 1 Wimpole St, London, W1G 0AE, United Kingdom. TEL 44-20-72902921, FAX 44-20-72902929, publishing@rsm.ac.uk, http://www.rsm.ac.uk/. Ed. Arnulf Skjennald. **Subscr. in N. America to:** Taylor & Francis Inc.; **Subscr. outside N. Amemrica to:** Taylor & Francis Ltd.; **Subscr. to:** Portland Customer Services, Commerce Way, Colchester CO2 8HP, United Kingdom. TEL 44-1206-796351, FAX 44-1206-799331, sales@portland-services.com, http://www.portlandpress.com.

616 USA ISSN 1535-9883
ADVANCE FOR IMAGING AND RADIATION THERAPY PROFESSIONALS. Text in English. 1988. bi-w. free to qualified personnel (effective 2008). adv. back issues avail.; reprints avail. **Document type:** *Magazine, Trade.* **Description:** Features information on imaging and radiation therapy.
Former titles (until 2001): Advance for Radiologic Science Professionals (1074-231X); (until 1990): Advance for Radiologic Technologists (1042-2498)

Related titles: Online - full text ed.: free to qualified personnel (effective 2008).
Published by: Merion Publications, Inc., 2900 Horizon Dr, PO Box 61556, King of Prussia, PA 19406. TEL 610-278-1400, 800-355-5627, FAX 610-278-1421, advance@merion.com, http://www.advanceweb.com. Ed. Joseph Jalkiewicz. Adv. contact Cynthia Caramanico. B&W page USD 3,759, color page USD 4,559; trim 8.125 x 10.5. Circ: 67,700.

▼ **ADVANCES IN BIOMEDICAL SPECTROSCOPY.** *see* CHEMISTRY—Analytical Chemistry

ADVANCES IN X-RAY ANALYSIS (CD-ROM). *see* PHYSICS

616.07 FIN ISSN 1235-1970
QH543.5.A1 CODEN: AARAEN
ALARA. Text in Finnish. 1992. q. EUR 36 domestic; EUR 46 In Scandinavia and Baltic countries; EUR 49 in Europe; EUR 51 elsewhere (effective 2005). adv. **Document type:** *Magazine.*
Indexed: INIS Atomlnd.
Published by: (Sateilyturvakeskus/Radiation and Nuclear Safety Authority Finland), Stellatum Oy, Tyopajankatu 6 A, Helsinki, 00580, Finland. TEL 358-9-8689700, FAX 358-9-86897070, subscriptions@stellatum.fi, http://www.stellatum.fi. Ed. Jorma Sandberg. Adv. contact Pirjo Nyman TEL 358-9-86897027. B&W page EUR 1,000, color page EUR 1,200; 186 x 274. Circ: 2,000.

615.842 USA ISSN 1073-0214
AMERICAN BOARD OF NUCLEAR MEDICINE. INFORMATION POLICIES AND PROCEDURES. Text in English. 1975. a. **Document type:** *Catalog.* **Description:** Information on requirements for certifying examination in nuclear medicine.
Published by: American Board of Nuclear Medicine, 900 Veteran Ave, Los Angeles, CA 90024. TEL 310-825-6787, FAX 310-794-4821, http://www.abnm.org. Ed. William H Blahd. Circ: 1,500.

616.07 USA ISSN 1546-1440
R895.A1
AMERICAN COLLEGE OF RADIOLOGY. JOURNAL. Abbreviated title: J A C R. Text in English. 2004. m. USD 275 in United States to institutions; USD 298 elsewhere to institutions (effective 2012). adv. back issues avail.; reprints avail. **Document type:** *Journal, Academic/Scholarly.* **Description:** Provides radiological practitioners "how to" articles with practical tips on managing every aspect of their practices from organization and management to technology needs and patient service.
Related titles: Online - full text ed.: ISSN 1558-349X (from ScienceDirect).
Indexed: B&BAb, B19, B21, BioEngAb, C06, C07, CA, EMBASE, ESPM, ExcerpMed, G08, H&SSA, H11, H12, I05, MEDLINE, P30, R10, Reac, SCOPUS, T02.
—IE, Ingenta. **CCC.**
Published by: (American College of Radiology), Elsevier Inc. (Subsidiary of: Elsevier Science & Technology), 1600 John F Kennedy Blvd, Philadelphia, PA 19103. TEL 215-239-3900, FAX 215-238-7883, JournalCustomerService-usa@elsevier.com, http://www.elsevier.com. Ed. Bruce Hillman. Adv. contact Bob Heiman TEL 856-673-4000.

615.842 USA ISSN 0195-6108
RC349.R3
➤ **AMERICAN JOURNAL OF NEURORADIOLOGY.** Variant title: A J N R. Text in English. 1980. 10/yr. USD 380 combined subscription domestic to institutions (print & online eds.); USD 440 combined subscription foreign to institutions (print & online eds.) (effective 2011). adv. bk.rev. back issues avail. **Document type:** *Journal, Academic/Scholarly.* **Description:** Publishes original clinical articles on imaging diagnosis of the central nervous system, including the spine, for radiologists, neuroradiologists, neurosurgeons, and neurologists.
Related titles: CD-ROM ed.; Online - full text ed.: ISSN 1936-959X. USD 310 (effective 2011).
Indexed: A20, A22, ASCA, B&BAb, B19, B21, B25, BIOSIS Prev, CTA, CurCont, DentInd, EMBASE, ExcerpMed, IBR, IBZ, IIL, INI, ISR, IndMed, Inpharma, JW-N, MEDLINE, MycolAb, NSA, NSCI, P30, P35, R10, RILM, Reac, SCI, SCOPUS, TM, W07.
—BLDSC (0828.400000), GNLM, IE, Infotrieve, Ingenta, INIST. **CCC.**
Published by: American Society of Neuroradiology, 2210 Midwest Rd, Ste 207, Oak Brook, IL 60523-8205. TEL 630-574-0220, FAX 630-574-0661, jgantenberg@asnr.org.

616.07 USA ISSN 2160-8407
▼ **AMERICAN JOURNAL OF NUCLEAR MEDICINE AND MOLECULAR IMAGING.** Text in English. 2011. free (effective 2011). **Document type:** *Journal, Academic/Scholarly.*
Media: Online - full text.
Published by: E-Century Publishing Corporation, 40 White Oaks Ln, Madison, WI 53711. TEL 608-230-6435, FAX 608-230-6435, info@e-century.org, http://www.e-century.org/. Ed. Belinda Salo.

615.842 USA ISSN 0361-803X
RM845 CODEN: AJROAM
➤ **AMERICAN JOURNAL OF ROENTGENOLOGY.** Abbreviated title: A J R. Text in English. 1906. m. USD 486 domestic to institutions; USD 556 foreign to institutions; USD 350 combined subscription domestic to non-members (print & online eds.); USD 441 combined subscription in Canada to non-members (print & online eds.); USD 420 combined subscription elsewhere to non-members (print & online eds.); USD 295 combined subscription domestic to members (print & online eds.); USD 350 combined subscription foreign to members (print & online eds.); USD 560 combined subscription domestic to institutions (print & online eds.); USD 663.60 combined subscription in Canada to institutions (print & online eds.); USD 630 combined subscription elsewhere to institutions (print & online eds.) (effective 2009). adv. bk.rev. abstr.; bibl.; illus. cum.index every 5 yrs. back issues avail. **Document type:** *Journal, Academic/Scholarly.* **Description:** Contains original articles on all aspects of general and diagnostic radiology, covering all current modalities, including MRI.
Former titles (until 1976): American Journal of Roentgenology, Radium Therapy and Nuclear Medicine (0002-9580); (until 1952): American Journal of Roentgenology and Radium Therapy (0092-5632); (until 1923): American Journal of Roentgenology (0092-5381); (until 1913): American Quarterly of Roentgenology
Related titles: Online - full text ed.: ISSN 1546-3141. USD 260 to individuals; USD 425 to institutions (effective 2009).
Indexed: A20, A22, A34, A36, AIDS Ab, AIM, ASCA, B&BAb, B19, B21, BDM&CN, BIOBASE, C06, C07, CABA, CISA, CTA, ChemAb, CurCont, D01, DBA, DentInd, E12, EMBASE, ESPM, ExcerpMed, FR, GH, H17, IABS, IBR, IBZ, IDIS, IIL, ISR, IndMed, IndVet, Inpharma, JW, JW-EM, Kidney, LT, MEDLINE, MLA-IB, MS&D, N02, N03, NSA, P30, P33, P39, PN&I, R08, R10, R12, RA&MP, RM&VM, RRTA, Reac, SCI, SCOPUS, T05, TAR, TM, ToxAb, VS, W07.
—BLDSC (0836.980000), CASDDS, GNLM, IE, Infotrieve, Ingenta, INIST. **CCC.**
Published by: American Roentgen Ray Society, 44211 Slatestone Ct, Leesburg, VA 20176. TEL 703-729-3353, 800-703-2777, FAX 703-729-4839, http://www.arrs.org. Ed. Thomas H Berquist. Adv. contact Denell Deavers. B&W page USD 2,285, color page USD 3,894; trim 8.75 x 10.875. Circ: 23,285. **Subscr. to:** 1891 Preston White Dr, Reston, VA 20191. TEL 703-649-8900, 800-347-7748, FAX 703-264-2093, subscribe@arrs.org.

616.0757 GBR ISSN 1748-7005
AMERICAN JOURNAL OF ROENTGENOLOGY (CHINESE SELECTED ARTICLES EDITION). Text in Chinese. 2005. q. **Document type:** *Journal, Academic/Scholarly.*
Published by: (American Roentgen Ray Society USA), Wiley-Blackwell Publishing Ltd. (Subsidiary of: John Wiley & Sons, Inc.), 9600 Garsington Rd, Oxford, OX4 2DQ, United Kingdom. TEL 44-1865-776868, FAX 44-1865-714591, customerservices@blackwellpublishing.com, http://www.wiley.com/WileyCDA/.

616.07 MEX ISSN 1665-2118
ANALES DE RADIOLOGIA DE MEXICO. Text in Spanish. 2002. q. MXN 770 domestic; USD 85 foreign (effective 2005). back issues avail. **Document type:** *Journal, Academic/Scholarly.*
Related titles: Online - full text ed.
Indexed: A01, CA, T02.
Published by: Sociedad Mexicana de Radiologia e Imagen, A.C., Coahuila No 35, Mexico, D.F., 06700, Mexico. TEL 52-55-55745250, smrianales@servimed.com.mx, http://www.smri.org.mx/. Ed. Guadalupe Guerrero Avendano.

615.842 AUT ISSN 1011-2529
ANIMAL PRODUCTION AND HEALTH NEWSLETTER. Text in English. 1976. s-a. free. **Document type:** *Newsletter, Academic/Scholarly.*
Published by: International Atomic Energy Agency/Agence Internationale de l'Energie Atomique, Wagramer Str 5, Postfach 100, Vienna, W 1400, Austria. TEL 43-1-2600-0, FAX 43-1-2600-7, sales.publications@iaea.org, http://www.iaea.org. Circ: 1,230. **Co-sponsor:** Food and Agriculture Organization of the United Nations.

616.07 JPN ISSN 0914-7187
R895.A1 CODEN: ANMEEX
ANNALS OF NUCLEAR MEDICINE. Text in English. 1987. q. EUR 368, USD 490 combined subscription to institutions (print & online eds.) (effective 2012). reprint service avail. from PSC. **Document type:** *Journal, Academic/Scholarly.* **Description:** Publishes papers concerned with clinical application of radioisotopes and related subjects.
Related titles: Online - full text ed.: ISSN 1864-6433 (from IngentaConnect).
Indexed: A22, A26, B&BAb, B19, B21, C06, C07, CIN, CTA, ChemAb, ChemTitl, CurCont, E01, E08, EMBASE, ExcerpMed, INIS Atomlnd, IndMed, Inpharma, MEDLINE, NSA, P10, P20, P22, P24, P30, P35, P48, P53, P54, PQC, R10, Reac, S09, SCI, SCOPUS, W07.
—BLDSC (1043.175000), CASDDS, GNLM, IE, Infotrieve, Ingenta. **CCC.**
Published by: (Japanese Society of Nuclear Medicine/Nihon Kaku Igakkai), Springer Japan KK (Subsidiary of: Springer Science+Business Media), No 2 Funato Bldg, 1-11-11 Kudan-kita, Chiyoda-ku, Tokyo, 102-0073, Japan. TEL 81-3-68317000, FAX 81-3-68317001, orders@springer.jp, http://www.springer.jp. Ed. Hiroshi Matsuda.

APPLIED RADIATION AND ISOTOPES. *see* PHYSICS—Nuclear Physics

615.842 USA ISSN 0160-9963
RM845
➤ **APPLIED RADIOLOGY;** the journal of practical medical imaging and management. Text in English. 1972. m. free to members (effective 2011). adv. charts; illus.; tr.lit. cum.index. back issues avail. **Document type:** *Journal, Academic/Scholarly.*
Former titles: Applied Radiology and Nuclear Medicine (0099-2364); Applied Radiology (0044-8451)
Related titles: Online - full text ed.
Indexed: A22, A26, C06, C07, C08, CINAHL, E08, EMBASE, ExcerpMed, H12, HospLI, I05, P20, P24, P30, P48, P52, P54, PQC, R10, Reac, S09, SCOPUS.
—BLDSC (1576.570000), GNLM, IE, Infotrieve, Ingenta.
Published by: Anderson Publishing Ltd., 180 Glenside Ave, Scotch Plains, NJ 07076. TEL 908-301-1995, FAX 908-301-1997, info@appliedradiology.com. Ed. Dr. Stuart E Mirvis. Adv. contact Kieran N Anderson TEL 908-337-3366.

615.842 IND ISSN 0972-2688
ASIAN OCEANIAN JOURNAL OF RADIOLOGY. Text in English. 1996. q. **Document type:** *Journal, Academic/Scholarly.*
Indexed: EMBASE, ExcerpMed, SCOPUS.
—BLDSC (1742.704200).
Published by: Diwanchand Satyapal Aggarwal X-ray Clinic, 10-B, Kasturba Gandhi Marg, New Delhi, 110 001, India. TEL 91-11-43707700, FAX 91-11-23713308, info@dcaimaging.org, http://www.dcaimaging.org/. Ed. Dr. Sudarshan K Aggarwal.

615.842 ARG ISSN 1852-5857
▼ **ASOCIACION ARGENTINA DE BIOLOGIA Y MEDICINA NUCLEAR.** Text in Spanish. 2009. 3/yr. **Document type:** *Journal, Academic/Scholarly.*
Address: Luis Saenz Pena 250, Piso 6 Ofic. A, Buenos Aires, 1110, Argentina. http://www.aabymn.org.ar/.

ASSOCIACAO BRASILEIRA DE RADIOLOGIA ODONTOLOGICA. REVISTA. *see* MEDICAL SCIENCES—Dentistry

616.075 AUS
AUSTRALASIAN JOURNAL OF ULTRASOUND MEDICINE. Text in English. 19??. q. AUD 220. **Document type:** *Journal, Academic/Scholarly.*
Former titles (until 2009): Ultrasound Bulletin; (until 2001): Australasian Society for Ultrasound in Medicine Bulletin (1441-6891); (until 1998): Australasian Society for Ultrasound in Medicine. Newsletter; (until 1990): Australian Society for Ultrasound in Medicine. Newsletter (0725-3001); (until 1979): Australian Society for Ultrasound in Medicine and Biology. Newsletter
Published by: (Australasian Society for Ultrasound in Medicine), Minnis Communications, 4/16 Maple Grove, Toorak, VIC 3142, Australia. TEL 61-3-98245241, FAX 61-3-98245247, minnis@minniscomms.com.au, http://www.minniscomms.com.au. Ed. George Condous.

AUSTRALIAN AND NEW ZEALAND NUCLEAR MEDICINE. *see* MEDICAL SCIENCES

616.07 GBR ISSN 2044-5113
▼ **B J R NEWS.** Text in English. 2011. bi-m. free to members (effective 2011). **Document type:** *Magazine, Trade.*
Published by: The British Institute of Radiology, 36 Portland Pl, London, W1B 1AT, United Kingdom. TEL 44-20-73071400, FAX 44-20-73071414, admin@bir.org.uk, http://www.bir.org.uk.

615.842 GBR ISSN 0961-2653
B J R SUPPLEMENT. (British Journals of Radiology) Text in English. 1947. irreg., latest vol.81, 2008. back issues avail. **Document type:** *Journal, Trade.*
Formerly (until 1989): British Journal of Radiology. Supplement (0306-8854)
Related titles: ◆ Supplement to: British Journal of Radiology. ISSN 0007-1285.
Indexed: EMBASE, ExcerpMed, IndMed, MEDLINE, P30, R10, Reac, SCOPUS.
—BLDSC (2324.000000), INIST. **CCC.**
Published by: British Institute of Radiology, 36 Portland Pl, London, W1B 1AT, United Kingdom. TEL 44-20-73071400, FAX 44-20-73071414, admin@bir.org.uk, http://www.bir.org.uk.

615 GBR ISSN 1471-2342
RC1 CODEN: BMIMA3
➤ **B M C MEDICAL IMAGING.** (BioMed Central) Text in English. 2001 (Nov.). irreg. free (effective 2011). adv. back issues avail.; reprints avail. **Document type:** *Journal, Academic/Scholarly.* **Description:** Covers original research articles in the use, development, and evaluation of imaging techniques to diagnose and manage disease.
Media: Online - full text.
Indexed: A26, A39, B19, BioEngAb, C27, C29, CA, D03, D04, E13, EMBASE, ExcerpMed, I05, MEDLINE, P20, P22, P30, PQC, R14, S14, S15, S18, SCOPUS, T02.
—Infotrieve. **CCC.**
Published by: BioMed Central Ltd. (Subsidiary of: Springer Science+Business Media), 236 Gray's Inn Rd, London, WC1X 8HB, United Kingdom. TEL 44-20-31922000, FAX 44-20-31922010, info@biomedcentral.com. Ed. Dr. Melissa Norton. Adv. contact Natasha Bailey TEL 44-20-31922231.

616.07 GBR ISSN 1756-6649
R895.A1 CODEN: BNMMBV
➤ **B M C MEDICAL PHYSICS.** (BioMed Central) Text in English. 2001 (Aug.). irreg. free (effective 2011). adv. back issues avail.; reprints avail. **Document type:** *Journal, Academic/Scholarly.* **Description:** Covers all aspects of medical physics, including radiobiology, radiation therapy, nuclear medicine, ultrasound, imaging, photomedicine and physiological measurement.
Formerly (until 2008): B M C Nuclear Medicine (1471-2385)
Media: Online - full text.
Indexed: A01, A26, B19, CA, I05, P20, P22, P30, P48, P54, PQC, R10, Reac, SCOPUS, T02.
—Infotrieve. **CCC.**
Published by: BioMed Central Ltd. (Subsidiary of: Springer Science+Business Media), 236 Gray's Inn Rd, London, WC1X 8HB, United Kingdom. TEL 44-20-31922000, FAX 44-20-31922010, info@biomedcentral.com. Ed. Dr. Melissa Norton. Adv. contact Natasha Bailey TEL 44-20-31922231.

616.07 TUR ISSN 1300-6487
BILGISAYARLI TOMOGRAFI BULTENI/BULLETIN OF COMPUTED TOMOGRAPHY. Text in Turkish. 1990 (Mar.). s-a. **Document type:** *Bulletin, Academic/Scholarly.*
Related titles: Online - full text ed.
Published by: Cerrahpasa Medical Faculty, Department of Radiology, Aksaray - Istanbul, 3430, Turkey. ctfrad@istanbul.edu.tr. Ed. Dr. Oktay Cokyuksel.

BIOELECTROMAGNETICS. *see* BIOLOGY—Biophysics

616.07 MYS ISSN 1823-5530
RM845
➤ **BIOMEDICAL IMAGING AND INTERVENTION JOURNAL;** a multidisciplinary open access online journal. Abbreviated title: Biij. Text in English. 2005. q. free (effective 2011). **Document type:** *Journal, Academic/Scholarly.* **Description:** Designed to meet the challenges of biomedical imaging and intervention facing the allied sciences community by providing a new avenue for discussion and exchange of viewpoints.
Media: Online - full content.
Indexed: A01, EMBASE, ExcerpMed, Inspec, SCOPUS, T02.
Published by: University of Malaya, Faculty of Medicine, Department of Biomedical Imaging (Radiology), Kuala Lumpur, 50603, Malaysia. TEL 60-3-79502091, FAX 60-3-79581973, editor@biij.org. Eds. Dr. Basri JJ Abdullah, Kwan-Hoong Ng. R&P, Adv. contact Dr. Basri JJ Abdullah.

615.842 GBR ISSN 0007-1285
QC1 CODEN: BJRAAP
➤ **BRITISH JOURNAL OF RADIOLOGY.** Abbreviated title: B J R. Text in English. 1928. m. GBP 705, USD 1,304 combined subscription to institutions (print & online eds.) (effective 2010). adv. bk.rev. abstr.; charts; illus.; stat. index. back issues avail. **Document type:** *Journal, Academic/Scholarly.* **Description:** Presents research covering the spectrum of radiological disciplines, including radio-diagnosis and therapy, nuclear medicine, ultrasound, NMR, radiobiology, radiation protection, and hyperthermia.

Formed by the merger of (1924-1928): British Journal of Radiology. Roentgen Society Section; Which was formerly (1904-1924): Roentgen Society. Journal; (1924-1928): British Journal of Radiology. B I R Section; Which was formerly (until 1924): British Journal of Radiology. B A R P Section; (until 1915): British Association of Radiology and Physiotherapy. Archives of Radiology and Electrotherapy; (until 1897): Roentgen Society of London. Archives of the Roentgen Ray; (until 1896): Archives of Skiagraphy; (until 18??): Archives of Clinical Skiagraphy
Related titles: Online - full text ed.: ISSN 1748-880X. 2001. GBP 670, USD 1,239 (effective 2010) (from IngentaConnect); ◆ Supplement(s): B J R Supplement. ISSN 0961-2653.
Indexed: A01, A03, A08, A20, A22, A34, A36, AIM, ASCA, B21, C06, C07, CA, CABA, CIN, CISA, CMCI, CTA, ChemAb, ChemTitl, CurCont, DBA, DentInd, DokArb, E12, EMBASE, ESPM, ExcerpMed, FR, GH, H17, IIL, ISR, IndMed, Inpharma, Inspec, MEDLINE, N02, N03, N04, NSA, P30, P33, P35, P39, R10, RM&VM, Reac, SCI, SCOPUS, T02, T05, TM, ToxAb, W07.
—BLDSC (2323.000000), AskIEEE, CASDDS, GNLM, IE, Infotrieve, Ingenta, INIST. **CCC.**
Published by: British Institute of Radiology, 36 Portland Pl, London, W1B 1AT, United Kingdom. TEL 44-20-73071400, FAX 44-20-73071414, admin@bir.org.uk, http://www.bir.org.uk. adv.: B&W page GBP 950, color page GBP 1,260; trim 210 x 297.

616.07 GBR ISSN 1750-2519
C M E JOURNAL. RADIOLOGY UPDATE. (Continuing Medical Education) Text in English. 1999. irreg., latest 2008. GBP 45 per vol. domestic to individuals; GBP 60 per vol. foreign to individuals; GBP 60 per vol. domestic to institutions; GBP 90 per vol. foreign to institutions (effective 2010). back issues avail. **Document type:** *Journal, Academic/Scholarly.* **Description:** Designed to meet the continuing education needs of practicing professionals.
Formerly (until 2005): C M E Journal. Radiology (1466-8386)
Related titles: Online - full text ed.: GBP 30 per vol. (effective 2010).
Indexed: EMBASE, ExcerpMed, SCOPUS.
—BLDSC (7238.650000), IE, Ingenta. **CCC.**
Published by: Rila Publications Ltd., 73 Newman St, London, W1A 4PG, United Kingdom. TEL 44-20-76311299, FAX 44-20-75807166, admin@rila.co.uk. Eds. Dr. Jane Adam TEL 44-20-8725-2933, Stephen Davies.

C M I G EXTRA: CASES. (Computerized Medical Imaging and Graphics) *see* MEDICAL SCIENCES—Computer Applications

616.07 JPN
C Y R I C ANNUAL REPORT. (Cyclotron Radioisotope Center) Text in English. 1980. a. 225 p./no.; **Document type:** *Yearbook, Academic/Scholarly.*
Published by: Tohoku University, Cyclotron Radioisotope Center/Tohoku Daigaku Saikurotoron Rajio Aisotopu Senta, Aoba, Aramaki, Aoba-ku, Sendai-shi, Miyagi-ken 981-0945, Japan. TEL 81-22-217-7800, FAX 81-22-217-3485, http://www.cyric.tohoku.ac.jp. Ed. H Orihara.

615.842 CAN ISSN 1203-9209
CANADIAN ASSOCIATION OF RADIOLOGISTS. FORUM. Text in English. bi-m.
Related titles: Online - full text ed.
Indexed: C03, CBCARef, P48, P52, PQC.
Published by: Canadian Association of Radiologists, 1740 Cote Vertu St, Saint-Laurent, PQ H4L 2A4, Canada.

615.842 USA ISSN 0846-5371
CODEN: JCARAU
➤ **CANADIAN ASSOCIATION OF RADIOLOGISTS JOURNAL/ ASSOCIATION CANADIENNE DES RADIOLOGISTES. JOURNAL.** Text in English, French. 1949. 4/yr. USD 245 elsewhere to institutions (effective 2012). adv. bk.rev. illus. index. back issues avail.; reprints avail. **Document type:** *Journal, Academic/Scholarly.* **Description:** Reports on the most recent advances in the field of radiology, including equipment, technique and procedures.
Formerly (until 1985): Canadian Association of Radiologists. Journal (0008-2902)
Related titles: Microfilm ed.: (from PQC); Online - full text ed.: ISSN 1488-2361. 1994. free (effective 2009) (from ScienceDirect).
Indexed: A01, A02, A03, A08, A22, A39, ASCA, B&BAb, B19, C03, C05, C06, C07, C08, C11, C27, C29, CA, CBCARef, CINAHL, ChemAb, CurCont, D03, D04, E13, EMBASE, ExcerpMed, H04, IIL, INIS AtomInd, ISR, IndMed, Inpharma, MEDLINE, P10, P20, P22, P24, P30, P48, P52, P53, P54, PQC, R10, R14, Reac, S14, S15, S18, SCI, SCOPUS, T02, W07.
—BLDSC (4722.500000), CASDDS, CIS, GNLM, IE, Ingenta, INIST. **CCC.**
Published by: (Canadian Association of Radiologists CAN), Elsevier Inc. (Subsidiary of: Elsevier Science & Technology), 360 Park Ave S, New York, NY 10010. TEL 212-633-3100, FAX 212-633-3140, JournalCustomerService-usa@elsevier.com. Ed. Peter L Munk. adv.: B&W page CAD 790, color page CAD 1,590; trim 10.88 x 8.13. Circ: 1,800.

616.07 CAN ISSN 1923-0931
▼ **THE CANADIAN JOURNAL OF MEDICAL SONOGRAPHY.** Text in English. 2010. s-a. free to members (effective 2010). adv. **Document type:** *Journal, Academic/Scholarly.* **Description:** Promotes the level of professional standards of practice for Sonographers in Canada.
Related titles: Online - full text ed.
Indexed: A01.
Published by: (Canadian Society of Diagnostic Medical Sonographers), Andrew John Publishing Inc., 115 King St W, Ste 220, Dundas, ON L9H 1V1, Canada. TEL 905-628-4309, FAX 905-628-6847, 866-849-1266, info@andrewjohnpublishing.com. Ed. Kathleen Foran. Adv. contact John Birkby.

CANCER RADIOTHERAPIE. *see* MEDICAL SCIENCES—Oncology

616.07 616.1 USA ISSN 0174-1551
CODEN: CAIRDG
➤ **CARDIOVASCULAR AND INTERVENTIONAL RADIOLOGY.** Text in English. 1977. bi-m. EUR 1,108, USD 1,139 combined subscription to institutions (print & online eds.) (effective 2012). adv. bk.rev. back issues avail.; reprint service avail. from PSC. **Document type:** *Journal, Academic/Scholarly.* **Description:** Examines developments in the diagnostic techniques of this specialty from all over the world.
Formerly (until 1980): Cardiovascular Radiology (0342-7196)
Related titles: Microform ed.: (from PQC); Online - full text ed.: ISSN 1432-086X (from IngentaConnect).
Indexed: A22, A26, ASCA, C06, C07, CA, CurCont, E01, EMBASE, ExcerpMed, FR, FS&TA, H12, IIL, IndMed, Inpharma, Kidney, MEDLINE, P20, P22, P24, P30, P35, P48, P54, PQC, R10, Reac, SCI, T02, W07.
—BLDSC (3051.438000), GNLM, IE, Infotrieve, Ingenta, INIST. **CCC.**
Published by: (Cardiovascular and Interventional Radiological Society of Europe AUT), Springer New York LLC (Subsidiary of: Springer Science+Business Media), 233 Spring St, New York, NY 10013. TEL 212-460-1500, service-ny@springer.com. Ed. Dierk Vorwerk.
Co-sponsors: Japanese Society of Angiography and Interventional Radiology; Cardiovascular and Interventional Radiological Society of Europe.

➤ **CARDIOVASCULAR REVASCULARIZATION MEDICINE.** *see* MEDICAL SCIENCES—Cardiovascular Diseases

616.07 GBR ISSN 1476-7120
➤ **CARDIOVASCULAR ULTRASOUND.** Text in English. 2003. irreg. free (effective 2011). adv. back issues avail.; reprints avail. **Document type:** *Journal, Academic/Scholarly.*
Media: Online - full text.
Indexed: A01, A02, A03, A08, A26, B19, C06, C07, CA, CurCont, EMBASE, ExcerpMed, I05, MEDLINE, P20, P22, P30, P48, P54, PQC, R10, Reac, SCI, SCOPUS, T02, W07.
—**CCC.**
Published by: BioMed Central Ltd. (Subsidiary of: Springer Science+Business Media), 236 Gray's Inn Rd, London, WC1X 8HB, United Kingdom. TEL 44-20-31922000, FAX 44-20-31922010, info@biomedcentral.com, http://www.biomedcentral.com. Ed. Eugenio Picano. Adv. contact Natasha Bailey TEL 44-20-31922231.

616.07 USA ISSN 2090-6862
▼ ➤ **CASE REPORTS IN RADIOLOGY.** Text in English. 2011. **Document type:** *Journal, Academic/Scholarly.* **Description:** Publishes case reports in all areas of radiology.
Related titles: Online - full text ed.: ISSN 2090-6870. 2011. free (effective 2011).
Published by: Hindawi Publishing Corporation, 410 Park Ave, 15th Fl, PMB 287, New York, NY 10022. FAX 215-893-4392, 866-446-3294, info@hindawi.com.

616.07 USA ISSN 1930-1871
CATEGORICAL COURSE SYLLABUS. Text in English. 1993. a. USD 173 per issue to non-members; USD 45 per issue to members (effective 2009). adv. back issues avail. **Document type:** *Monographic series, Academic/Scholarly.* **Description:** Aims to provide an understanding of ultrasound imaging techniques and indications for appropriate use in the wide spectrum of diseases and disorders affecting the gastrointestinal tract, the genitourinary tract, thyroid, parathyroid, scrotum, breast, vascular and musculoskeletal systems.
Published by: American Roentgen Ray Society, 1891 Preston White Dr, Reston, VA 20191. TEL 800-227-5463, FAX 703-729-5913, info@arrs.org, http://www.arrs.org.

615.84 CZE ISSN 1210-7883
CODEN: CRADEK
➤ **CESKA RADIOLOGIE.** Text in Czech, Slovak; Summaries in Czech, English. 1946. 6/yr. CZK 560 (effective 2010). adv. bk.rev. **Document type:** *Journal, Academic/Scholarly.*
Former titles: Ceskoslovenska Radiologie (0069-2344); Ceskoslovenska Roentgenologie
Related titles: Online - full text ed.
Indexed: DentInd, EMBASE, ExcerpMed, INIS AtomInd, IndMed, P30, R10, Reac, SCOPUS.
—GNLM, INIST. **CCC.**
Published by: (Ceska Radiologicka Spolecnost J.E. Purkyne/Czech Radiological Society, Ceska Neuroradiologicka Spolecnost J.E. Purkyne, Ceska Spolecnost Intervencni Radiologie J.E. Purkyne), Nakladatelske Stredisko C L S J.E. Purkyne, Sokolska 31, Prague, 12026, Czech Republic. TEL 420-2-24266223, FAX 420-2-24266212, nts@cls.cz, http://www.cls.cz. Ed. Dr. Jiri Ferda. adv.: B&W page CZK 25,100, color page CZK 35,000; 245 x 167. Circ: 1,200.

➤ **CHEMICAL SOCIETY OF JAPAN. SYMPOSIUM ON PHYSICAL AND CHEMICAL ASPECTS OF ULTRASOUND. PROCEEDINGS/ONPA NO BUSSEI TO KAGAKU TORONKAI KOEN RONBUNSHU.** *see* CHEMISTRY

616.075 JPN ISSN 1346-1176
➤ **CHOUOMPA IGAKU.** Text in Japanese. 1974. q. **Document type:** *Journal, Academic/Scholarly.*
Supersedes in part (in 2000): Journal of Medical Ultrasonics (Tokyo, 1997) (1344-1388); Which was formerly (until 1997): Choonpa Igaku/Japanese Journal of Medical Ultrasonics (0287-0592)
Related titles: ◆ English ed.: Journal of Medical Ultrasonics. ISSN 1346-4523.
—BLDSC (5017.091000).
Published by: Nihon Chouompa Gakkai/Japan Society of Ultrasonics in Medicine, Crocevia Hongo 3F, Hongo 3-23-1, Bunkyo-ku, Tokyo, 113 0033, Japan. TEL 81-3-38135540, FAX 81-3-38167644, http://wwwsoc.nii.ac.jp/jsum/index-e.html.

616.075 JPN ISSN 1881-4506
CHOUOMPA KENSA GIJUTSU/JAPANESE JOURNAL OF MEDICAL ULTRASOUND TECHNOLOGY. Text in Japanese. 1976. bi-m. (6-7/yr.). membership. **Document type:** *Journal, Academic/Scholarly.*
Indexed: B&BAb.
Published by: Nihon Choonpa Igau Kensa Kenkyukai/Japan Society of Sonographers, 4-4-19, Takadanobaba, Shinjuku, Tokyo, 169-0075, Japan. TEL 86-3-53488628, FAX 86-3-53488629, jimukyoku@jss.org.

616.07 CHN ISSN 1674-8034
▼ ➤ **CIGONGZHEN CHENGXIANG/CHINESE JOURNAL OF MAGNETIC RESONANCE IMAGING.** Text in Chinese; Abstracts in Chinese, English. 2010. bi-m. CNY 96, USD 96; CNY 16 per issue (effective 2010 & 2011). **Document type:** *Journal, Academic/Scholarly.* **Description:** Publishes papers on basic researches, clinical applications, technology progress, review articles, and other information related to magnetic resonance imaging. Includes sections on: Overseas papers, editorials, and clinical articles.
Related titles: Online - full text ed.
Indexed: A29, B&BAb, B19, B20, B21, ESPM, NSA.
Published by: Cigongzhen Chengxiang Bianjibu, Rm.518t, no.6, Zuoanmennei Dajie, Chongwen District, Beijing, 100061, China. TEL 86-10-67113815, FAX 86-10-67113815. Ed. Jianping Dai. Circ: 8,000.

615.8 USA ISSN 0899-7071
RC78.7.T6 CODEN: CLIMEB
➤ **CLINICAL IMAGING.** Text in English. 1977. bi-m. USD 1,171 in United States to institutions; USD 1,326 elsewhere to institutions (effective 2012). adv. bk.rev. abstr.; charts; illus. index. back issues avail.; reprints avail. **Document type:** *Journal, Academic/Scholarly.* **Description:** Provides information for radiologists, radiology residents, and radiologic technologists. Covers new technology, new applications, and important issues concerning all diagnostic imaging methods.
Former titles (until 1989): C T: The Journal of Computed Tomography (0149-936X); (until 1978): Computed Axial Tomography (0145-7616)
Related titles: Microform ed.: (from PQC); Online - full text ed.: ISSN 1873-4499 (from IngentaConnect, ScienceDirect).
Indexed: A01, A03, A08, A22, A26, ASCA, B&BAb, B19, B21, BioEngAb, CA, CPEI, CompC, CompD, CurCont, EMBASE, EngInd, ExcerpMed, G08, I05, IIL, ISR, IndMed, Inpharma, MEDLINE, P30, R10, Reac, SCI, SCOPUS, T02, W07.
—BLDSC (3286.290600), GNLM, IE, Infotrieve, Ingenta, INIST. **CCC.**
Published by: Elsevier Inc. (Subsidiary of: Elsevier Science & Technology), 1600 John F Kennedy Blvd, Philadelphia, PA 19103. TEL 215-239-3900, FAX 215-238-7883, JournalCustomerService-usa@elsevier.com, http://www.elsevier.com. Ed. Dr. Joseph P Whalen. Adv. contact John Marmero Jr. TEL 212-633-3657.

616.842 GBR ISSN 0961-9275
➤ **CLINICAL M R I;** the practical journal of M R, incorporating Developments in M R. (Magnetic Resonance Imaging) Variant title: Clinical Magnetic Resonance Imaging. Text in English. 1991. q. GBP 50 domestic; USD 75 foreign; GBP 30 to MRRA members (effective 2000). adv. charts; illus. back issues avail. **Document type:** *Journal, Academic/Scholarly.* **Description:** Describes the practice of medical Magnetic Resonance Imaging (MRI), as well as developments and advances in MRI.
Incorporates (1994-1996): Developments in Magnetic Resonance (1369-9504)
Indexed: EMBASE, ExcerpMed, R10, Reac, SCOPUS.
—BLDSC (3286.306500), IE, Ingenta. **CCC.**
Published by: (Magnetic Resonance Radiologist's Association), Clinical Press, Redland Green Farm, Redland, Bristol BS6 7HF, United Kingdom. TEL 44-117-942-0256. Ed. Dr. Simon Blease. R&P Dr. Paul Goddard. Adv. contact Clive Booth. B&W page GBP 1,050, color page GBP 1,650. Circ: 2,500.

615.842 DEU ISSN 1869-1439
CODEN: KLNEFX
➤ **CLINICAL NEURORADIOLOGY.** Text in German, English. 1991. q. EUR 227, USD 269 combined subscription to institutions (print & online eds.) (effective 2012). adv. back issues avail.; reprint service avail. from PSC. **Document type:** *Journal, Academic/Scholarly.*
Formerly (until 2006): Klinische Neuroradiologie (0939-7116)
Related titles: Online - full text ed.: ISSN 1869-1447 (from IngentaConnect).
Indexed: A22, A26, B21, CA, E-psyche, E01, EMBASE, ExcerpMed, MEDLINE, NSA, P30, R10, Reac, SCI, SCOPUS, T02, W07.
—GNLM, IE, Infotrieve, Ingenta. **CCC.**
Published by: (Deutsche, Oesterreichische und Schweizerische Gesellschaft fuer Neuroradiologie), Urban und Vogel Medien und Medizin Verlagsgesellschaft mbH (Subsidiary of: Springer Science+Business Media), Neumarkter Str 43, Munich, 81673, Germany. TEL 49-89-4372-1411, FAX 49-89-4372-1410, verlag@urban-vogel.de, http://www.urban-vogel.de. Ed. L Solymosi. Adv. contacts Renate Senfft, Sibylle Schurr TEL 49-89-43721353. B&W page EUR 1,300, color page EUR 2,400; trim 174 x 240. Circ: 1,100. **Subscr. to:** Springer Distribution Center, Kundenservice Zeitschriften, Haberstr 7, Heidelberg 69126, Germany. TEL 49-6221-3454303, FAX 49-6221-3454229, subscriptions@springer.com.

615.842 USA ISSN 0363-9762
R895.A1 CODEN: CNMEDK
➤ **CLINICAL NUCLEAR MEDICINE.** Text in English. 1976. m. USD 831 domestic to institutions; USD 1,015 foreign to institutions (effective 2011). adv. illus. Index. back issues avail.; reprints avail. **Document type:** *Journal, Academic/Scholarly.* **Description:** Provides information on nuclear medicine that can be readily applied to clinical situations. Ensures dissemination of data on current developments that affect all aspects of the specialty.
Related titles: Microform ed.: (from PQC); Online - full text ed.: ISSN 1536-0229. USD 520 domestic academic site license; USD 584 foreign academic site license; USD 580 domestic corporate site license; USD 644 foreign corporate site license (effective 2002).
Indexed: A22, ASCA, CurCont, DentInd, EMBASE, ExcerpMed, IBR, IBZ, IDIS, IIL, ISR, IndMed, Inpharma, MEDLINE, P30, P35, R10, Reac, SCI, SCOPUS, W07.
—BLDSC (3286.314000), GNLM, IE, Infotrieve, Ingenta, INIST. **CCC.**
Published by: Lippincott Williams & Wilkins (Subsidiary of: Wolters Kluwer N.V.), 333 7th Ave, 19th Fl, New York, NY 10001. TEL 646-674-6300, FAX 646-674-6500, customerservice@lww.com, http://www.lww.com. Ed. Dr. Sheldon Baum. Pub. Matthew Jozwiak. Circ: 655.

615.842 616.99 GBR ISSN 0009-9260
R895.A1 CODEN: CLRAAG
➤ **CLINICAL RADIOLOGY.** Text in English. 1949. m. EUR 1,070 in Europe to institutions; JPY 115,500 in Japan to institutions; USD 1,003 elsewhere to institutions (effective 2012). adv. bk.rev. index, cum.index: 1970-1979. 2 cols./p.; back issues avail.; reprints avail. **Document type:** *Journal, Academic/Scholarly.* **Description:** Features original research, editorials, review articles and case reports on all aspects of diagnostic imaging, including radiography, nuclear medicine, computed tomography, magnetic resonance imaging, ultrasonography, digital radiology and interventional radiology.
Formerly (until 1960): Faculty of Radiologists. Journal (0368-2242)
Related titles: Microform ed.: (from PQC); Online - full text ed.: ISSN 1365-229X. 1997. USD 862 to institutions (effective 2009) (from IngentaConnect, ScienceDirect); Supplement(s): Clinical Radiology. Supplement. ISSN 1361-6714. 1996.
Indexed: A01, A03, A08, A22, A26, A36, A37, ASCA, B&BAb, B19, B20, B21, BIOBASE, BioEngAb, C06, C07, CA, CABA, CISA, CTA, CurCont, DentInd, E01, EMBASE, ESPM, ExcerpMed, FR, GH, H17, I05, IABS, IIL, INIS AtomInd, ISR, IndMed, Inpharma, Inspec, MEDLINE, N02, N03, P30, P33, P35, P39, R10, RM&VM, Reac, SCI, SCOPUS, T02, T05, ToxAb, VirolAbstr, W07.
—BLDSC (3286.350000), GNLM, IE, Infotrieve, Ingenta, INIST. **CCC.**

Published by: (Royal College of Radiologists), W.B. Saunders Co. Ltd. (Subsidiary of: Elsevier Health Sciences), 32 Jamestown Rd, Camden, London, NW1 7BY, United Kingdom. TEL 44-20-74244200, FAX 44-20-74832293, elsols@elsevier.com. Ed. R F Bury.

➤ **COMPUTERIZED MEDICAL IMAGING AND GRAPHICS.** *see* MEDICAL SCIENCES—Computer Applications

538.66 USA ISSN 1546-6086
QC762
CONCEPTS IN MAGNETIC RESONANCE. PART A. Text in English. 2003. bi-m. GBP 819 in United Kingdom to institutions; EUR 1,035 in Europe to institutions; USD 1,395 in United States to institutions; USD 1,535 in Canada & Mexico to institutions; USD 1,605 elsewhere to institutions; GBP 891 combined subscription in United Kingdom to institutions (print & online eds.); EUR 1,126 combined subscription in Europe to institutions (print & online eds.); USD 1,535 combined subscription in United States to institutions (print & online eds.); USD 1,675 combined subscription in Canada & Mexico to institutions (print & online eds.); USD 1,745 combined subscription elsewhere to institutions (print & online eds.) (effective 2010). adv. back issues avail.; reprint service avail. from PSC. **Document type:** *Journal, Academic/Scholarly.* **Description:** Focuses on the lore of magnetic resonance in an understandable presentations for practitioners. Provides a forum for researchers to discuss fundamental aspects of magnetic resonance.
Supersedes in part (in 2003): Concepts in Magnetic Resonance (1043-7347)
Related titles: Online - full text ed.: ISSN 1552-5023. GBP 712 in United Kingdom to institutions; EUR 900 in Europe to institutions; USD 1,395 elsewhere to institutions (effective 2010).
Indexed: B&BAb, B19, BioEngAb, CCI, CurCont, ISR, Inspec, P30, SCI, SCOPUS, W07.
—BLDSC (3399.413420), IE, Ingenta. **CCC.**
Published by: John Wiley & Sons, Inc., 111 River St, Hoboken, NJ 07030. TEL 201-748-6000, FAX 201-748-6088, info@wiley.com, http://www.wiley.com/WileyCDA/. Ed. Daniel D Traficante. Pub., Adv. contact Kim Thompkins TEL 212-850-6921.

538.36 USA ISSN 1552-5031
QC762 CODEN: CMAEEM
➤ **CONCEPTS IN MAGNETIC RESONANCE. PART B: MAGNETIC RESONANCE ENGINEERING.** Text in English. 1989. q. USD 1,395 domestic to institutions; USD 1,535 in Canada & Mexico to institutions; GBP 819 in United Kingdom to institutions; EUR 1,035 in Europe to institutions; USD 1,605 elsewhere to institutions; USD 1,535 combined subscription domestic to institutions (print & online eds.); USD 1,675 combined subscription in Canada & Mexico to institutions (print & online eds.); GBP 891 combined subscription in United Kingdom to institutions (print & online eds.); EUR 1,126 combined subscription in Europe to institutions (print & online eds.); USD 1,745 combined subscription elsewhere to institutions (print & online eds.) (effective 2010); subscr. includes Concepts in Magnetic Resonance. Part A. adv. bk.rev. charts. index, cum.index every 5 yrs. back issues avail.; reprint service avail. from PSC. **Document type:** *Journal, Academic/Scholarly.* **Description:** Devoted to the publication of original investigations concerned with the hardware and software of the engineering and physics aspects of magnetic resonance instrumentation.
Supersedes in part (in 2003): Concepts in Magnetic Resonance (1043-7347)
Related titles: Online - full text ed.: Concepts in Magnetic Resonance. Part B: Magnetic Resonance Engineering (Online). ISSN 1552-504X. USD 1,395, GBP 761, EUR 872 to institutions (effective 2010).
Indexed: ASCA, B&BAb, B19, BioEngAb, CCI, CIN, ChemAb, ChemTitl, CurCont, Inspec, P30, SCI, SCOPUS, W07.
—BLDSC (3399.413430), CASDDS, IE, Infotrieve, Ingenta. **CCC.**
Published by: John Wiley & Sons, Inc., 111 River St, Hoboken, NJ 07030. TEL 201-748-6000, FAX 201-748-6088, info@wiley.com, http://www.wiley.com/WileyCDA/. **Subscr. to:** John Wiley & Sons Ltd.

616.07 USA ISSN 0149-9009
CODEN: CDRAEW
CONTEMPORARY DIAGNOSTIC RADIOLOGY. Abbreviated title: C D R. Text in English. 19??. bi-w. USD 756 domestic to institutions; USD 870 foreign to institutions (effective 2011). back issues avail. **Document type:** *Newsletter, Academic/Scholarly.* **Description:** Features articles on current topics in radiology with optional category or C.M.E. credits.
Formerly (until 1978): Radiologic Science Update
Related titles: Online - full text ed.: ISSN 1938-1395. 19??. USD 409.50 domestic for academic site license; USD 409.50 foreign for academic site license; USD 456.75 domestic for corporate site license; USD 456.75 foreign for corporate site license (effective 2002).
—IE. **CCC.**
Published by: Lippincott Williams & Wilkins (Subsidiary of: Wolters Kluwer N.V.), 530 Walnut St, Philadelphia, PA 19106. TEL 215-521-8300, FAX 215-521-8902, customerservice@lww.com, http://www.lwwnewsletters.com. Ed. Robert E Campbell.

616.07 GBR ISSN 1555-4309
RC78.7.C65 CODEN: CMMICO
CONTRAST MEDIA & MOLECULAR IMAGING. Abbreviated title: C M M I. Text in English. 2006 (Feb.). bi-m. GBP 438 domestic to institutions (print or online ed.); USD 554 in Europe to institutions (print or online ed.); USD 859 elsewhere to institutions (print or online ed.); USD 482 combined subscription domestic to institutions (print & online eds.); USD 610 combined subscription in Europe to institutions (print & online eds.); USD 945 combined subscription elsewhere to institutions (print & online eds.) (effective 2009); subscr. price varies per number of full time employees. adv. back issues avail.; reprint service avail. from PSC. **Document type:** *Journal, Academic/Scholarly.* **Description:** Provides an international forum for the expeditious publication of original scientific papers, reviews, highlights, surveys, and letters to the editors in the booming areas of contrast media and molecular imaging.
Related titles: Online - full text ed.: ISSN 1555-4317. 2006.
Indexed: B&BAb, B19, B21, C33, CTA, CurCont, EMBASE, ExcerpMed, MEDLINE, NSA, P30, R10, Reac, SCI, SCOPUS, W07.
—IE, Ingenta. **CCC.**
Published by: John Wiley & Sons Ltd. (Subsidiary of: John Wiley & Sons, Inc.), 1-7 Oldlands Way, PO Box 808, Bognor Regis, West Sussex PO21 9FF, United Kingdom. TEL 44-1865-778315, FAX 44-1243-843232, cs-journals@wiley.com, http://eu.wiley.com/WileyCDA/. Eds. Robert N Muller, Silvio Aime. **Subscr. to:** 1-7 Oldlands Way, PO Box 809, Bognor Regis, West Sussex PO21 9FG, United Kingdom. TEL 44-1865-778054, cs-agency@wiley.com.

616.842 ITA ISSN 2036-3176
▼ ➤ **CRITICAL ULTRASOUND JOURNAL.** Text in English. 2009 (Oct.). 3/yr. EUR 240, USD 324 combined subscription to institutions (print & online eds.) (effective 2011). reprint service avail. from PSC. **Document type:** *Journal, Academic/Scholarly.* **Description:** Provides information for clinicians using point-of-care ultrasound in any environment or setting.
Related titles: Online - full text ed.: ISSN 2036-7902. 2009.
Indexed: P30, SCOPUS.
—CCC.
Published by: (World Interactive Network Focused On Critical UltraSound (WINFOCUS)), Springer Italia Srl (Subsidiary of: Springer Science+Business Media), Via Decembrio 28, Milan, 20137, Italy. TEL 39-02-54259722, FAX 39-02-55193360, springer@springer.it. Ed. Michael Blaivas.

➤ **CURRENT CARDIOVASCULAR IMAGING REPORTS.** *see* MEDICAL SCIENCES—Cardiovascular Diseases

616.07 NLD ISSN 1573-4056
RC78.7.D53
➤ **CURRENT MEDICAL IMAGING REVIEWS.** Text in English. 2005 (Jan.). q. USD 480 to institutions (print or online ed.) (effective 2012). adv. back issues avail.; reprints avail. **Document type:** *Journal, Academic/Scholarly.* **Description:** Publishes reviews on all the latest advances on medical imaging. All relevant areas are covered by the journal, including advances in the diagnosis, instrumentation and therapeutic applications related to all modern medical imaging techniques.
Related titles: Online - full text ed.: ISSN 1875-6603 (from IngentaConnect).
Indexed: A01, B&BAb, B19, CA, CurCont, EMBASE, ExcerpMed, P30, SCI, SCOPUS, T02, W07.
—BLDSC (3500.255000), IE, Ingenta. **CCC.**
Published by: Bentham Science Publishers Ltd., PO Box 294, Bussum, 1400 AG, Netherlands. TEL 31-35-6923800, FAX 31-35-6980150, sales@bentham.org, http://www.bentham.org. Ed. E Edmund Kim TEL 713-794-1052. **Subscr. to:** Bentham Science Publishers Ltd., c/o Richard E Morrissy, PO Box 446, Oak Park, IL 60301. TEL 312-413-5867, FAX 312-996-7107, subscriptions@bentham.org.

615.842 NLD ISSN 2211-5552
▼ ➤ **CURRENT MOLECULAR IMAGING.** Text in English. forthcoming 2012. s-a. USD 360 to institutions (print or online ed.) (effective 2012). adv. **Document type:** *Journal, Academic/Scholarly.* **Description:** Covers all aspects of experimental and clinical research in molecular imaging.
Related titles: Online - full text ed.: ISSN 2211-5544. forthcoming.
Published by: Bentham Science Publishers Ltd., PO Box 294, Bussum, 1400 AG, Netherlands. TEL 31-35-6923800, FAX 31-35-6980150, sales@bentham.org, http://www.bentham.org. Ed. Abass Alavi. **Subscr. to:** Bentham Science Publishers Ltd., c/o Richard E Morrissy, PO Box 446, Oak Park, IL 60301. TEL 312-413-5867, FAX 312-996-7107, subscriptions@bentham.org.

615.842 USA ISSN 0363-0188
R895.A1 CODEN: CPDRDS
➤ **CURRENT PROBLEMS IN DIAGNOSTIC RADIOLOGY.** Abbreviated title: C P D R. Text in English. 1971. bi-m. USD 284 in United States to institutions; USD 332 elsewhere to institutions (effective 2012). adv. bibl.; illus. cum.index. back issues avail.; reprints avail. **Document type:** *Journal, Academic/Scholarly.* **Description:** Provides monographic clinical reviews written by and intended for practitioners.
Formerly (until 1976): Current Problems in Radiology (0045-9399)
Related titles: Microform ed.: (from PQC); Online - full text ed.: ISSN 1535-6302 (from ScienceDirect).
Indexed: A22, A26, C06, C07, CA, EMBASE, ExcerpMed, I05, IndMed, MEDLINE, P30, R10, Reac, SCOPUS, T02.
—BLDSC (3501.380000), GNLM, IE, Infotrieve, Ingenta. **CCC.**
Published by: Mosby, Inc. (Subsidiary of: Elsevier Health Sciences), 1600 John F. Kennedy Blvd, Ste 1800, Philadelphia, PA 19103. TEL 215-239-3900, 800-523-1649, FAX 215-239-3990, elspcs@elsevier.com, http://www.us.elsevierhealth.com. Ed. Dr. Eric J. Stern. Adv. contact Georgia Nikolaros TEL 212-633-3686.

616.07 USA
CURRENT PROTOCOLS IN MAGNETIC RESONANCE IMAGING. Text in English. 2001. base vol. plus q. updates. looseleaf. USD 495 to individuals base vols. & updates (effective 2010). adv. back issues avail.; reprints avail. **Document type:** *Journal, Academic/Scholarly.* **Description:** Provides the tools needed for acquiring images in any part of the body for any disease condition.
Related titles: CD-ROM ed.; Online - full content ed.
Published by: John Wiley & Sons, Inc., 111 River St, Hoboken, NJ 07030. TEL 201-748-6000, FAX 201-748-6088, info@wiley.com, http://www.wiley.com/WileyCDA/.

615.842 KOR ISSN 1226-2854
DAEHAN BANGSA'SEON GI'SUL HAGHOEJI/KOREAN SOCIETY OF RADIOLOGICAL SCIENCE. JOURNAL. Text in Korean. 1978. s-a. membership. **Document type:** *Journal, Academic/Scholarly.* **Description:** Covers radiological science and technology.
Indexed: INIS AtomInd.
Published by: Daehan Bangsa'seon Gi'sul Haghoe/Korean Society of Radiological Science, Korea University, Department of Radiological Technology, 136-703 Jeongneung-dong, Seongbuk-Gu, Seoul, Korea, S. TEL 82-2-9402820, FAX 82-2-9179074, ksrs@iksrs.or.kr, http://www.iksrs.or.kr/.

615.8 KOR ISSN 1738-2637
DAEHAN YEONGSANG UI HAGHOEJI. Text in Korean; Summaries in English. 1960. bi-m. membership. **Document type:** *Journal, Academic/Scholarly.*
Former titles (until 2004): Daehan Bangsaseon Yihag Hoeji/Korean Radiological Society. Journal (0301-2867); (until 1960): Taehak Pangsason ui Hakhoe Chi
Indexed: INIS AtomInd.
Published by: Korean Society of Radiology, 69, Yangjaecheon-gil, Seocho-gu, Seoul, 137-891, Korea, S. TEL 82-2-5788003, FAX 82-2-5297113, office@radiology.or.kr, http://www.radiology.or.kr/. Ed. Dr. Kyung Soo Lee. Circ: 500.

615.8 JPN ISSN 0914-8663
DANSO EIZO KENKYUKAI ZASSHI/JAPANESE JOURNAL OF TOMOGRAPHY. Text in Japanese; Summaries in English. 1973. 2/yr. (1-3 issues/yr.). **Document type:** *Journal, Academic/Scholarly.*
Related titles: Online - full text ed.
Indexed: INIS AtomInd.
—CCC.
Published by: Danso Eizo Kenkyukai/Japanese Association of Tomography, Nihon University School of Medicine, Department of Radiology, 30-1 Oyaguchi Itabashi, Tokyo, 173-8610, Japan. TEL 81-3-39728111 ext 2553, FAX 81-3-39582454, danso@med.nihon-u.ac.jp, http://www.med.nihon-u.ac.jp/department/radiology/h-ikyoku.htm.

615.842 GBR ISSN 0250-832X
CODEN: DREAC6
➤ **DENTOMAXILLOFACIAL RADIOLOGY.** Text in English. 1971. 8/yr. GBP 160 to individuals; GBP 435 to institutions (effective 2009). adv. charts; illus.; stat. back issues avail.; reprints avail. **Document type:** *Journal, Academic/Scholarly.* **Description:** Contains research papers on radiology of the "lower third," together with clinical reports that illustrate specific uses of diagnostic imaging.
Related titles: Microform ed.: (from PQC); Online - full text ed.: ISSN 1476-542X. 1997; ◆ Supplement(s): Dentomaxillofacial Radiology. Supplement. ISSN 0349-490X.
Indexed: A22, ASCA, CA, CurCont, D02, E01, EMBASE, ExcerpMed, Inpharma, MEDLINE, P30, R10, Reac, SCI, SCOPUS, T02, W07.
—BLDSC (3553.561000), GNLM, IE, Infotrieve, Ingenta. **CCC.**
Published by: (International Association of Dento-Maxillo-Facial Radiology ZAF), British Institute of Radiology, 36 Portland Pl, London, W1B 1AT, United Kingdom. TEL 44-20-73071400, FAX 44-20-73071414, admin@bir.org.uk, http://www.bir.org.uk. Ed. Sharon L Brooks.

615.842 GBR ISSN 0349-490X
DENTOMAXILLOFACIAL RADIOLOGY. SUPPLEMENT. Text in English. irreg. price varies. **Document type:** *Monographic series, Academic/Scholarly.*
Related titles: ◆ Supplement to: Dentomaxillofacial Radiology. ISSN 0250-832X.
Indexed: P30.
Published by: (International Association of Dento-Maxillo-Facial Radiology ZAF), British Institute of Radiology, 36 Portland Pl, London, W1B 1AT, United Kingdom. TEL 44-20-73071400, FAX 44-20-73071414, admin@bir.org.uk, http://www.bir.org.uk.

615.849 NLD ISSN 0167-9074
CODEN: DNMDDS
➤ **DEVELOPMENTS IN NUCLEAR MEDICINE.** Text in English. 1981. irreg., latest vol.34, 2002. price varies. **Document type:** *Monographic series, Academic/Scholarly.*
Indexed: A22, CIN, ChemAb, ChemTitl.
—BLDSC (3579.085430), CASDDS, IE, Ingenta. **CCC.**
Published by: Springer Netherlands (Subsidiary of: Springer Science+Business Media), Van Godewijckstraat 30, Dordrecht, 3311 GX, Netherlands. TEL 31-78-6576050, FAX 31-78-6576474. Ed. Peter H Cox.

616.07 TUR ISSN 1305-3825
R895.A1
➤ **DIAGNOSTIC AND INTERVENTIONAL RADIOLOGY/TANISAL VE GIRIMSEL RADYOLOJI DERGISI.** Text in English. 1994. q. **Document type:** *Journal, Academic/Scholarly.* **Description:** Publishes original articles, reviews, technical notes, pictorial essays, case reports, and letters to the editor. It is a medium for disseminating scientific information based on research, clinical experience, and observations pertaining to diagnostic and interventional radiology.
Formerly (until 2004): Tanisal ve Girisimsel Radyoloji (1300-4360)
Related titles: Online - full text ed.: ISSN 1305-3612. free (effective 2011).
Indexed: C06, C07, EMBASE, ExcerpMed, MEDLINE, P30, R10, Reac, SCI, SCOPUS, W07.
Published by: Turkish Society of Radiology, Hosdere Cad., Guzelkent Sok., Cankaya Evleri F/2, Ankara, 06540, Turkey. TEL 90-312-4423653, FAX 90-312-4423654, info@dirjournal.org. Ed. Dr. Okan Akhan.

616.07 USA ISSN 1551-6091
DIAGNOSTIC & INVASIVE CARDIOLOGY. Text in English. 1961. bi-m. free domestic to qualified personnel; USD 90 in Canada; USD 120 elsewhere (effective 2011). adv. back issues avail. **Document type:** *Magazine, Trade.* **Description:** Keeps users and buyers of cardiology and critical care technology apprised of the latest technology and information.
Supersedes in part (in 2002): M E E N Cardiology - Critical Care Technology; Which superseded in part (in 2000): Medical Electronics and Equipment News (0361-4174); Which was formerly (until 197?): Medical Electronics News (0025-7230)
—IE.
Published by: Reilly Communications Group, 16 E Schaumburg Rd, Schaumburg, IL 60194. TEL 847-882-0631, FAX 847-519-0166, info@rcgpubs.com, http://www.reillycomm.com. Ed. Dave Fornell TEL 847-954-7962. Pub. Sean Reilly TEL 847-954-7960. Adv. contact Stephanie A Ellis TEL 847-954-7959.

616.0754 USA ISSN 0194-2514
RC78.7.D53
DIAGNOSTIC IMAGING. Text in English. 1979. m. free to qualified personnel (effective 2010). adv. bk.rev. back issues avail.; reprints avail. **Document type:** *Journal, Trade.* **Description:** Designed for professionals in the field of radiology, nuclear medicine, and ultrasound imaging.
Related titles: Microform ed.: (from PQC); Online - full text ed.
Indexed: A22, A26, B&BAb, DentInd, G08, H11, H12, I05, ISR, P24, P26, P30, P48, P52, P54, PQC, SCOPUS, T02, TM, VirolAbstr.
—BLDSC (3579.658050), CIS, GNLM, IE, Infotrieve, Ingenta. **CCC.**
Published by: C M P Medica LLC (Subsidiary of: United Business Media Limited), 535 Connecticut Ave, Ste 300, Norwalk, CT 06854. TEL 203-523-7000, FAX 203-662-6420, http://www.ubmmedica.com/. Pub., Adv. contact Beth Scholz TEL 215-297-9327.

616.0754 USA
DIAGNOSTIC IMAGING ASIA PACIFIC. Text in English. 19??. q. free to qualified personnel (effective 2010). adv. back issues avail.
Document type: *Magazine, Trade.* **Description:** Provides Asia Pacific medical imaging professionals with job-critical information on radiology practice.
Related titles: Online - full text ed.
Published by: C M P Medica LLC (Subsidiary of: United Business Media Limited), 535 Connecticut Ave, Ste 300, Norwalk, CT 06854. TEL 203-523-7000, FAX 203-662-6420, http://www.ubmmedica.com/. Ed. Philip Ward. Pub., Adv. contact Beth Scholz TEL 215-297-9327.

616.0754 USA ISSN 1461-0051
DIAGNOSTIC IMAGING EUROPE. Text in English. 1985. 8/yr. free to qualified personnel (effective 2010). adv. **Document type:** *Magazine, Trade.*
Formerly (until 1995): Diagnostic Imaging International (0898-2473)
Related titles: Online - full text ed.
Indexed: A15, A22, ABIn, H13, P10, P20, P51, P53, P54, PQC, TM.
—GNLM, Infotrieve. **CCC.**
Published by: C M P Medica LLC (Subsidiary of: United Business Media Limited), 535 Connecticut Ave, Ste 300, Norwalk, CT 06854. TEL 203-523-7000, FAX 203-662-6420, http://www.ubmmedica.com/. Ed. Philip Ward. Pub., Adv. contact Beth Scholz TEL 215-297-9327.

616.07 USA ISSN 1541-2458
DIAGNOSTIC IMAGING INTELLIGENCE REPORT. Text in English. 2002 (May). m. USD 504 combined subscription in US & Canada (print & online eds.); USD 604 combined subscription elsewhere (print & online eds.) (effective 2009). **Document type:** *Newsletter, Trade.* **Description:** Contains concise, up-to-date analysis that helps the managers and directors of medical imaging facilities make informed, cost-effective choices in this rapidly changing (yet extremely lucrative) field and better understand the underlying political, economic and social drivers which will shape the U.S. market.
Related titles: Online - full text ed.: USD 47 per issue (effective 2008).
—CCC.
Published by: Institute of Management & Administration, Inc., One Washington Park, Ste 1300, Newark, NJ 07102. TEL 973-718-4700, FAX 973-622-0595, subserve@ioma.com, http://www.ioma.com. Ed. Kim Scott.

616.075 618 IND ISSN 0973-614X
➤ **DONALD SCHOOL JOURNAL OF ULTRASOUND IN OBSTETRICS AND GYNECOLOGY.** Text in English. 2007 (Mar.). q. INR 3,000 domestic to individuals; USD 180 foreign to individuals; INR 4,500 domestic to institutions; USD 250 foreign to institutions (effective 2011). adv. bk.rev. illus. back issues avail. **Document type:** *Journal, Academic/Scholarly.* **Description:** Contains articles and case reports on all aspects of ultrasound in obstetrics and gynecology.
Related titles: Online - full text ed.: ISSN 0975-1912.
Indexed: A01, P20, P48, P54, PQC.
Published by: Jaypee Brothers Medical Publishers Pvt. Ltd., 4838/24, Ansari Rd, Daryaganj, New Delhi, 110 002, India. TEL 91-11-43574357, FAX 91-11-43574314, jaypee@jaypeebrothers.com, http://www.jaypeebrothers.com. Eds. Asim Kurjak, Frank A Chervenak. Adv. contact Abhinav Kumar.

616.075 FRA ISSN 1633-0315
E G E O. (Echographie Gynecologique Echographie Obstetricale) Text in French. 1991. m. bk.rev. **Document type:** *Journal, Academic/Scholarly.*
Supersedes in part: L U S (1169-3827); Which was formerly (until 1992): Journal Francais d'Echographie
Related titles: CD-ROM ed.
Published by: Centre Francophone de Formation en Echographie, 25 Av Amedee Bollee, Kilometre Delta, Nimes, 30900, France. TEL 33-4-66680483, FAX 33-4-66642953, contact@ultrason.com. Circ: 2,500.

618 DEU ISSN 2191-219X
▼➤ **E J N M M I RESEARCH.** (European Journal of Nuclear Medicine and Molecular Imaging) Text in English. 2011. irreg. free (effective 2011). **Document type:** *Journal, Academic/Scholarly.* **Description:** Focuses on new basic, translational and clinical research in the field of nuclear medicine and molecular imaging.
Media: Online - full text.
Published by: SpringerOpen (Subsidiary of: Springer Science+Business Media), Tiergartenstr 17, Heidelberg, 69121, Germany. info@springeropen.com, http://www.springeropen.com. Ed. Angelika Bischof Delaloye.

616.0747 571.4 FRA ISSN 1627-3699
E R R S - E U R A D O S NEWSLETTER. (European Late Effects Project - European Radiation Dosimetry - European Radiation Research Society) Key Title: E U L E P. Newsletter. Text in English. 2000. s-a. **Document type:** *Newsletter, Academic/Scholarly.* **Description:** Features scientific works in progress in the areas of radiobiology, ionising radiation dosimetry and radiation protection.
Media: Online - full text.
Published by: Institut de Radioprotection et de Surete Nucleaire, Direction de la.Radioprotection de l'Homme, Service de Dosimetrie, BP 17, Fontenay-aux-Roses, Cedex 92262, France. TEL 33-1-58359121, FAX 33-1-46544610, pihetp@wanadoo.fr.

615.842 539.2 EGY ISSN 1110-0303
➤ **EGYPTIAN JOURNAL OF RADIATION SCIENCES & APPLICATIONS/AL-MAGALLAT AL-MISRIYYAT LIL-'ULUM AL-IS'AA'IYYAT WA TATBIQATIHAA.** Text in Arabic, English. 1984. s-a. USD 77 (effective 2003). charts; illus.; stat. reprint service avail. from IRC. **Document type:** *Journal, Academic/Scholarly.*
Indexed: INIS AtomInd.
Published by: (National Centre for Radiation Research & Technology), National Information and Documentation Centre (NIDOC), Tahrir St., Dokki, Awqaf P.O., Giza, Egypt. TEL 20-2-3371696, FAX 20-2-3371746. Ed. A Z El-Bahey. Circ: 1,000.

616.07 ITA ISSN 1121-8800
EIDO ELECTA; Mediterranean journal of radiology and imaging. Text in English, Italian; Summaries in English, French, Italian. 1989. q. **Document type:** *Journal, Academic/Scholarly.* **Description:** Covers radiotherapy, radiobiology, and nuclear medicine.
Related titles: Online - full text ed.
Published by: Universita degli Studi di Palermo, Piazza Marina 61, Palermo, 90133, Italy. TEL 39-091-334139, FAX 39-091-6110448. Ed. Adelfio Elioi Cardinale.

616.07 JPN ISSN 1346-1362
EIZO JOHO INDUSTRIAL/MONTHLY JOURNAL OF IMAGING AND INFORMATION TECHNOLOGY. Text in Japanese. 1969. m. JPY 16,800 (effective 2007).
Supersedes in part (in 2000): Eizo Joho Medikaru/Image Technology & Information Display (0389-214X)
Published by: Sangyo Kaihatsu Kiko Kabushiki Gaisha/Sangyo Kaihatsukiko Inc., 1-1 Kanda-Izumi-cho, Chiyoda-ku, Tokyo, 101-0024, Japan. TEL 81-3-38617051, FAX 81-3-56877744.

616.07 JPN ISSN 1346-1354
EIZO JOHO MEDICAL/MONTHLY JOURNAL OF MEDICAL IMAGING AND INFORMATION. Text in Japanese; Summaries in English, Japanese. 1969. m. JPY 21,600 (effective 2007). **Document type:** *Journal, Academic/Scholarly.*
Supersedes in part (in 2000): Eizo Joho Medikaru (0389-214X)
Indexed: INIS AtomInd.
Published by: Sangyo Kaihatsu Kiko Kabushiki Gaisha/Sangyo Kaihatsukiko Inc., 1-1 Kanda-Izumi-cho, Chiyoda-ku, Tokyo, 101-0024, Japan. TEL 81-3-38617051, FAX 81-3-56877744. Ed. Tsuneyoshi Sakamaki. Pub. Hiroshi Wakebe. Circ: 15,000.

616.842 DEU ISSN 1070-3004
RA645.5 CODEN: EMRAFG
➤ **EMERGENCY RADIOLOGY**; a journal of practical imaging. Text in German. 1988. bi-m. EUR 519, USD 623 combined subscription to institutions (print & online eds.) (effective 2012). adv. bk.rev. reprint service avail. from PSC. **Document type:** *Journal, Academic/Scholarly.* **Description:** Original articles for radiologists and emergency medicine physicians treating acutely ill and injured patients. Articles deal with "first contact" decisions that need to be made immediately to optimize diagnostic accuracy and patient outcome. Emphasizes plain film procedures, but includes all imaging modalities.
Related titles: Microfiche ed.; Online - full text ed.: ISSN 1438-1435 (from IngentaConnect).
Indexed: A01, A03, A08, A22, A26, C06, C07, CA, E01, EMBASE, ExcerpMed, JW-EM, MEDLINE, P20, P22, P24, P30, P48, P54, PQC, R10, Reac, SCOPUS, T02.
—BLDSC (3733.197500), GNLM, IE, Infotrieve, Ingenta. **CCC.**
Published by: (American Society of Emergency Radiology USA), Springer (Subsidiary of: Springer Science+Business Media), Tiergartenstr 17, Heidelberg, 69121, Germany. TEL 49-6221-4870, FAX 49-6221-345229. Ed. Ronald J. Zagoria. Adv. contact Stephan Kroeck TEL 49-30-827875739. Circ: 1,329 (paid). **Subscr. in the Americas to:** Springer New York LLC, Journal Fulfillment, PO Box 2485, Secaucus, NJ 07096. TEL 800-777-4643, 201-348-4033, FAX 201-348-4505, journals-ny@springer.com, http://www.springer.com; **Subscr. to:** Springer Distribution Center, Kundenservice Zeitschriften, Haberstr 7, Heidelberg 69126, Germany. TEL 49-6221-3454303, FAX 49-6221-3454229, subscriptions@springer.com.

616.07 616.3 FRA ISSN 1879-8527
➤ **ENCYCLOPEDIE MEDICO-CHIRURGICALE. RADIOLOGIE ET IMAGERIE MEDICALE. ABDOMINALE - DIGESTIVE.** Cover title: Traite de Radiodiagnostic: Appareil Digestif. Variant title: Encyclopedie Medico-Chirurgicale. Traite de Radiodiagnostic: Abdominal Digestif. Text in French. 1954. 4 base vols. plus q. updates. EUR 757.62 (effective 2003). bibl.; charts; illus. **Document type:** *Academic/Scholarly.* **Description:** Offers radiologists and gastroenterologists using radiologic techniques to diagnose gastroenterological disorders and diseases an up-to-date, comprehensive reference.
Formerly (until 2009): Encyclopedie Medico-Chirurgicale. Traite de Radiodiagnostic: Appareil Digestif (0246-0610)
Related titles: Online - full text ed.
—INIST. **CCC.**
Published by: Elsevier Masson (Subsidiary of: Elsevier Health Sciences), 62 Rue Camille Desmoulins, Issy les Moulineaux, Cedex 92442, France. TEL 33-1-71165500, FAX 33-1-71165600, infos@elsevier-masson.fr.

616.07 616.2 FRA ISSN 1879-8535
➤ **ENCYCLOPEDIE MEDICO-CHIRURGICALE. RADIOLOGIE ET IMAGERIE MEDICALE. CARDIOVASCULAIRE - THORACIQUE - CERVICALE.** Cover title: Traite de Radiodiagnostic: Coeur - Poumon. Variant title: Encyclopedie Medico-Chirurgicale. Traite de Radiodiagnostic: Thorax. Text in French. 1950. 4 base vols. plus q. updates. EUR 757.62 (effective 2003). bibl.; charts; illus. **Document type:** *Academic/Scholarly.* **Description:** Offers radiologists, cardiologists, and pulmonary specialists a comprehensive, up-to-date reference for diagnosing and treating various diseases and disorders.
Former titles (until 2009): Encyclopedie Medico-Chirurgicale. Traite de Radiodiagnostic: Coeur - Poumon (1169-7768); (until 1991): Encyclopedie Medico-Chirurgicale. Radiodiagnostic: Tome 3, Appareil Cardio-vasculaire, Appareil Pulmonaire (0246-0602); (until 1977): Encyclopedie Medico-Chirurgicale. Radiodiagnostic: Tome 3, Appareil Cardio-vasculaire, Appareil Respiratoire, Larynx (0246-1013)
Related titles: Online - full text ed.
—INIST. **CCC.**
Published by: Elsevier Masson (Subsidiary of: Elsevier Health Sciences), 62 Rue Camille Desmoulins, Issy les Moulineaux, Cedex 92442, France. TEL 33-1-71165500, FAX 33-1-71165600, infos@elsevier-masson.fr.

616.07 616.6 618.1 FRA ISSN 1879-8543
➤ **ENCYCLOPEDIE MEDICO-CHIRURGICALE. RADIOLOGIE ET IMAGERIE MEDICALE. GENITO-URINAIRE - GYNECO-OBSTETRICALE - MAMMAIRE.** Cover title: Traite de Radiodiagnostic: Urologie - Gynecologie. Text in French. 1963. 3 base vols. plus q. updates. EUR 782 (effective 2009). bibl.; charts; illus. **Document type:** *Journal, Academic/Scholarly.* **Description:** Offers radiologists, as well as urologists and gynecologists using radiology a comprehensive, up-to-date reference for diagnosing various disorders.
Former titles (until 2009): Encyclopedie Medico-Chirurgicale. Traite de Radiodiagnostic: Urologie - Gynecologie (1241-8218); (until 1991): Encyclopedie Medico-Chirurgicale. Radiodiagnostic, 5: Appareil Urinaire - Appareil Genital (1154-2926); (until 1987): Encyclopedie Medico-Chirurgicale. Radiodiagnostic, Tome 5: Appareil Genito-urinaire-obstetrique (1154-2918); (until 1983): Encyclopedie Medico-Chirurgicale. Radiodiagnostic, Tome 5: Urologie, Gynecologie (0246-0629); (until 1977): Encyclopedie Medico-Chirurgicale. Radiodiagnostic, Tome 5: Appareil Genito-urinaire, Obstetrique (0246-1021)
—INIST. **CCC.**
Published by: Elsevier Masson (Subsidiary of: Elsevier Health Sciences), 62 Rue Camille Desmoulins, Issy les Moulineaux, Cedex 92442, France. TEL 33-1-71165500, FAX 33-1-71165600, infos@elsevier-masson.fr, http://www.elsevier-masson.fr.

616.07 FRA ISSN 1879-8551
➤ **ENCYCLOPEDIE MEDICO-CHIRURGICALE. RADIOLOGIE ET IMAGERIE MEDICALE. MUSCULOSQUELETTIQUE - NEUROLOGIQUE - MAXILLOFACIALE.** Cover title: Traite de Radiodiagnostic: Squelette Normal - Neuroradiologie - Appareil Locomoteur. Text in French. 1976. 7 base vols. plus q. updates. EUR 1,325.83 (effective 2003). bibl.; charts; illus. **Document type:** *Academic/Scholarly.* **Description:** Provides radiologists, neuroradiologists, rheumatologists, and orthopedists with a comprehensive, up-to-date reference to diagnose disorders in their areas of specialty.
Former titles (until 2009): Encyclopedie Medico-Chirurgicale. Traite de Radiodiagnostic: Squelette Normal - Neuroradiologie - Appareil Locomoteur (1257-5143); (until 1994): Encyclopedie Medico-Chirurgicale. Radiodiagnostic, Tomes 1 et 2: Squelette Normal, Neuroradiologie, Appareil Locomoteur (1246-9602); (until 1991): Encyclopedie Medico-Chirurgicale. Tomes 1 et 2: Neuroradiologie, Appareil Locomoteur (1155-1933); (until 1990): Encyclopedie Medico-Chirurgicale. Radiodiagnostic, Tomes 1 et 2, Squelette, Neuro-radiologie (0246-0599); Which was formed by the merger of (1956-1976): Encyclopedie Medico-Chirurgicale. Radiodiagnostic, Tome 1: Squelette Normal (0246-0998); (1953-1976): Encyclopedie Medico-Chirurgicale. Radiodiagnostic, Tome 2: Squelette Pathologique, Encephale, Moelle (0246-1005)
Related titles: Online - full text ed.
—INIST. **CCC.**
Published by: Elsevier Masson (Subsidiary of: Elsevier Health Sciences), 62 Rue Camille Desmoulins, Issy les Moulineaux, Cedex 92442, France. TEL 33-1-71165500, FAX 33-1-71165600, infos@elsevier-masson.fr.

616.07 FRA ISSN 1879-8497
➤ **ENCYCLOPEDIE MEDICO-CHIRURGICALE. RADIOLOGIE ET IMAGERIE MEDICALE. PRINCIPES ET TECHNIQUES - RADIOPROTECTION.** Variant title: Encyclopedie Medico-Chirurgicale. Traite de Radiodiagnostic: Principes et Techniques d'Imagerie. Text in French. base vol. plus a. updates. EUR 189.40 (effective 2003). bibl.; charts; illus. **Document type:** *Academic/Scholarly.* **Description:** Offers radiologists a comprehensive reference on principles and techniques in their field.
Formerly (until 2009): Encyclopedie Medico-Chirurgicale. Traite de Radiodiagnostic: Principes et Techniques (1624-5865)
Related titles: Online - full text ed.
—CCC.
Published by: Elsevier Masson (Subsidiary of: Elsevier Health Sciences), 62 Rue Camille Desmoulins, Issy les Moulineaux, Cedex 92442, France. TEL 33-1-71165500, FAX 33-1-71165600, infos@elsevier-masson.fr.

615.842 616.07 USA ISSN 1941-3610
ENTERPRISE IMAGING & THERAPEUTIC RADIOLOGY MANAGEMENT. Text in English. 1991. m. free to qualified personnel (effective 2008). adv. back issues avail.; reprints avail. **Document type:** *Magazine, Trade.* **Description:** Designed for medical imaging, therapeutic radiology and cardiology decision-makers.
Former titles (until 2007): Advance for Imaging and Oncology Administrators (1536-1349); (until 2001): Advance for Administrators in Radiology and Radiation Oncology (1096-6285); (until 199?): Advance for Administrators in Radiology
Related titles: Online - full text ed.: free to qualified personnel (effective 2008).
Published by: Merion Publications, Inc., 2900 Horizon Dr, PO Box 61556, King of Prussia, PA 19406. TEL 610-278-1400, 800-355-5627, FAX 610-278-1421, advance@merion.com, http://www.advanceweb.com. Ed. Sharon Breske. Adv. contact Cynthia Caramanico. B&W page USD 4,967, color page USD 6,017; trim 8.375 x 10.5. Circ: 25,006.

616.07 GBR ISSN 1750-1911
CODEN: EPIGC7
▼➤ **EPIGENOMICS.** Text in English. 2009. bi-m. GBP 695 combined subscription domestic (print & online eds.); USD 1,220 combined subscription in North America (print & online eds.); JPY 129,000 combined subscription in Japan (print & online eds.); EUR 975 combined subscription elsewhere (print & online eds.) (effective 2011). adv. back issues avail.; reprints avail. **Document type:** *Journal, Academic/Scholarly.* **Description:** Provides access to a broad range of technologies for the support of drug development and commercialization by patient stratification and drug response prediction.
Related titles: Online - full text ed.: ISSN 1750-192X. GBP 615 domestic to institutions; USD 1,080 in North America to institutions; JPY 115,000 in Japan to institutions; EUR 865 elsewhere to institutions (effective 2011) (from IngentaConnect).
Indexed: A26, B&BAb, B19, B21, BIOSIS Prev, C33, CTA, E08, H12, I05, ImmunAb, NSA, NucAcAb, P20, P30, P48, P54, PQC, SCI, SCOPUS, W07.
—CCC.
Published by: Future Medicine Ltd. (Subsidiary of: Future Science Ltd.), Unitec House, 2 Albert Pl, London, N3 1QB, United Kingdom. TEL 44-20-83716080, FAX 44-20-83716099, info@futuremedicine.com. Ed. Elisa Manzotti TEL 44-20-83716090. Pub. David Hughes. Adv. contact Simon Boisseau TEL 44-208-3716083. Circ: 200.

➤ **EUROPEAN HEART JOURNAL CARDIOVASCULAR IMAGING.** *see* MEDICAL SCIENCES—Cardiovascular Diseases

618 DEU ISSN 1619-7070
CODEN: EJNMD9

➤ **EUROPEAN JOURNAL OF NUCLEAR MEDICINE AND MOLECULAR IMAGING.** Text in English. 1976. m. EUR 2,288, USD 2,780 combined subscription to institutions (print & online eds.) (effective 2012). adv. reprint service avail. from PSC. **Document type:** *Journal, Academic/Scholarly.* **Description:** Covers developments in nuclear medicine, including original articles on diagnosis, therapy with 'open' radionuclides, in-vitro radiobiological and radiation protection.

Formerly (until 2002): European Journal of Nuclear Medicine (0340-6997)

Related titles: Microfiche ed.: (from PQC); Online - full text ed.: ISSN 1619-7089 (from IngentaConnect).

Indexed: A01, A02, A03, A08, A20, A22, A26, ASCA, B&BAb, B07, B19, B21, BioEngAb, C11, CA, CIN, ChemAb, ChemTitl, CurCont, E01, EMBASE, ESPM, ExcerpMed, FR, H04, H12, INI, INIS AtomInd, ISR, IndMed, Inpharma, Inspec, Kidney, MEDLINE, NSA, P20, P22, P24, P30, P35, P48, P52, P54, PQC, R10, Reac, RefZh, SCI, SCOPUS, T02, TM, W07.

—BLDSC (3829.731850), AskIEEE, CASDDS, GNLM, IE, Ingenta, INIST. **CCC.**

Published by: (European Association of Nuclear Medicine), Springer (Subsidiary of: Springer Science+Business Media), Tiergartenstr 17, Heidelberg, 69121, Germany. TEL 49-6221-4870, FAX 49-6221-345229. Ed. Ignasi Carrio. adv.: B&W page EUR 1,480, color page EUR 2,520. Circ: 3,400 (paid and controlled). **Subscr. in the Americas to:** Springer New York LLC, Journal Fulfillment, PO Box 2485, Secaucus, NJ 07096. TEL 800-777-4643, 201-348-4033, FAX 201-348-4505, journals-ny@springer.com, http://www.springer.com; **Subscr. to:** Springer Distribution Center, Kundenservice Zeitschriften, Haberstr 7, Heidelberg 69126, Germany. TEL 49-6221-3454303, FAX 49-6221-3454229, subscriptions@springer.com.

616.07 GBR ISSN 1756-1175

EUROPEAN JOURNAL OF RADIOGRAPHY. Text in English. 2008. q. EUR 440 in Europe to institutions; JPY 72,500 in Japan to institutions; USD 647 elsewhere to institutions (effective 2011). adv. back issues avail.; reprints avail. **Document type:** *Journal, Academic/Scholarly.* **Description:** Covers all aspects of diagnostic imaging, radiotherapy, nuclear medicine and related research.

Related titles: Online - full text ed.

Indexed: CA, EMBASE, ExcerpMed, SCOPUS, T02.

—IE. **CCC.**

Published by: (The Euro-Med Congress for Radiographers MLT), Elsevier Ltd (Subsidiary of: Elsevier Science & Technology), The Blvd, Langford Ln, Kidlington, Oxford, OX5 1GB, United Kingdom. TEL 44-1865-843434, FAX 44-1865-843970, journalscustomerserviceemea@elsevier.com. Ed. Ms. D Pronk Larive.

615.842 IRL ISSN 0720-048X
R895.A1 CODEN: EJRADR

➤ **EUROPEAN JOURNAL OF RADIOLOGY.** Text in English. 1980. 12/yr. EUR 2,182 in Europe to institutions; JPY 289,600 in Japan to institutions; USD 2,441 elsewhere to institutions (effective 2012). adv. bk.rev. charts; illus. index. back issues avail.; reprints avail. **Document type:** *Journal, Academic/Scholarly.* **Description:** Serves as a medium for the exchange of information on the use of radiological and allied imaging and interventional techniques, including information on socio-economics and departmental management.

Incorporates (1987-1989): Journal of Medical Imaging (0920-5497)

Related titles: Online - full text ed.: ISSN 1872-7727 (from IngentaConnect, ScienceDirect).

Indexed: A01, A03, A08, A20, A22, A26, A34, A36, AIDS Ab, ASCA, AgrForAb, BIOBASE, C06, C07, CA, CABA, CPEI, ChemAb, CurCont, DentInd, E12, EMBASE, EngInd, ExcerpMed, F08, FR, GH, H17, I05, IABS, IIL, INIS AtomInd, IndMed, IndVet, Inpharma, MEDLINE, N02, N03, P30, P33, P37, P39, PN&I, R10, RM&VM, Reac, SCI, SCOPUS, T02, T05, VS, W07.

—BLDSC (3829.738050), CASDDS, GNLM, IE, Infotrieve, Ingenta, INIST. **CCC.**

Published by: (Netherlands Society of Radiology), Elsevier Ireland Ltd (Subsidiary of: Elsevier Science & Technology), Elsevier House, Brookvale Plaza, E. Park, Shannon, Co. Clare, Ireland. TEL 353-61-709600, FAX 353-61-709100. Ed. Dr. H Imhof. R&P Annette Moloney. Circ: 1,500. **Subscr. to:** Elsevier BV, Radarweg 29, PO Box 211, Amsterdam 1000 AE, Netherlands. JournalsCustomerServiceEMEA@elsevier.com, http://www.elsevier.nl.

616.07 USA ISSN 1571-4675
RA895.A1

EUROPEAN JOURNAL OF RADIOLOGY EXTRA. Text in English. 2003. m. Included with subscr. to European Journal of Radiology. back issues avail. **Document type:** *Journal, Academic/Scholarly.*

Media: Online - full text (from IngentaConnect, ScienceDirect).

Indexed: A26, CA, I05, SCOPUS, T02.

—BLDSC (3829.738060), IE, Ingenta. **CCC.**

Published by: Elsevier Science Publishing Co., Inc. (New York), 360 Park Ave S, Flr. 11, New York, NY 10010. TEL 212-989-5800, 212-370-5520, FAX 212-633-3990, http://www.elsevier.com. Ed. H Imhof.

616.075 IRL ISSN 0929-8266
R857.U48 CODEN: EJULE8

➤ **EUROPEAN JOURNAL OF ULTRASOUND.** Text in English. 1994. bi-m. EUR 413 in Europe to institutions; JPY 54,800 in Japan to institutions; USD 242 elsewhere to institutions (effective 2002). bk.rev. back issues avail. **Document type:** *Journal, Academic/Scholarly.* **Description:** Serves as a forum for the European scientific and clinical community working with ultrasound in the fields of medicine and biology.

Related titles: Online - full text ed.: (from IngentaConnect).

Indexed: A01, A03, A08, A26, B&BAb, BioEngAb, CA, I05, INI, IndMed, Inspec, P30, SCOPUS.

—GNLM, IE, Infotrieve, Ingenta, INIST. **CCC.**

Published by: (European Federation of Societies for Ultrasound in Medicine and Biology), Elsevier Ireland Ltd (Subsidiary of: Elsevier Science & Technology), Elsevier House, Brookvale Plaza, E. Park, Shannon, Co. Clare, Ireland. TEL 353-61-709600, FAX 353-61-709100. Ed. J M Thijssen. R&P Annette Moloney. **Subscr. to:** Elsevier BV, Radarweg 29, PO Box 211, Amsterdam 1000 AE, Netherlands. TEL 31-20-4853757, FAX 31-20-4853432, JournalsCustomerServiceEMEA@elsevier.com, http://www.elsevier.nl.

615.842 DEU ISSN 0938-7994
R895.A1 CODEN: EURAE3

➤ **EUROPEAN RADIOLOGY**; journal of the European Congress of Radiology. Text in English. 1991. m. EUR 1,397, USD 1,690 combined subscription to institutions (print & online eds.) (effective 2012). adv. reprint service avail. from PSC. **Document type:** *Journal, Academic/Scholarly.* **Description:** Covers all aspects of diagnostic and interventional radiology.

Incorporates (1995-2008): European Radiology. Supplements (1613-3749); (1989-1992): Diagnostic and Interventional Radiology (0998-433X)

Related titles: Online - full text ed.: ISSN 1432-1084 (from IngentaConnect); ◆ Supplement(s): European Radiology. Supplements. ISSN 1613-3749.

Indexed: A01, A03, A08, A22, A26, ASCA, B&BAb, B19, B21, BioEngAb, C06, C07, CA, CurCont, E01, EMBASE, ExcerpMed, H12, IIL, INI, INIS AtomInd, ISR, IndMed, Inpharma, MEDLINE, P20, P22, P24, P30, P35, P48, P54, PQC, R10, Reac, RefZh, SCI, SCOPUS, T02, TM, W07.

—BLDSC (3829.847300), GNLM, IE, Infotrieve, Ingenta, INIST. **CCC.**

Published by: (European Association of Radiology), Springer (Subsidiary of: Springer Science+Business Media), Tiergartenstr 17, Heidelberg, 69121, Germany. TEL 49-6221-4870, FAX 49-6221-345229. Ed. Dr. Adrian K Dixon. adv.: B&W page EUR 2,290, color page EUR 3,590. Circ: 4,500 (paid and controlled). **Subscr. in the Americas to:** Springer New York LLC, Journal Fulfillment, PO Box 2485, Secaucus, NJ 07096. TEL 800-777-4643, 201-348-4033, FAX 201-348-4505, journals-ny@springer.com, http://www.springer.com; **Subscr. to:** Springer Distribution Center, Kundenservice Zeitschriften, Haberstr 7, Heidelberg 69126, Germany. TEL 49-6221-3454303, FAX 49-6221-3454229, subscriptions@springer.com.

➤ **EXCERPTA MEDICA. SECTION 14: RADIOLOGY.** *see* MEDICAL SCIENCES—Abstracting, Bibliographies, Statistics

➤ **EXCERPTA MEDICA. SECTION 23: NUCLEAR MEDICINE.** *see* MEDICAL SCIENCES—Abstracting, Bibliographies, Statistics

616.842 JPN ISSN 0914-790X

FACIAL NERVE RESEARCH. Text in Multiple languages. 1981. a. JPY 8,000 membership (effective 2007). **Document type:** *Journal, Academic/Scholarly.*

Indexed: INIS AtomInd.

—GNLM.

Published by: Japan Society of Facial Nerve Research/Nihon Ganmen Shinkei Kenkyukai, Keio University, School of Medicine, Department of Otorhinolaryngology, 35 Shinanomachi, Shinjuku-ku, Tokyo, 160-8582, Japan. fnradmin@fnr.jp, http://www.fnr.jp/index.php.

FANGSHE MIANYIXUE ZAZHI/JOURNAL OF RADIOIMMUNOLOGY. *see* MEDICAL SCIENCES—Allergology And Immunology

616.07 CHN ISSN 1000-0313

FANGSHEXUE SHIJIAN/RADIOLOGIC PRACTICE. Text in Chinese. 1986. m. CNY 120; CNY 10 per issue (effective 2010). **Document type:** *Journal, Academic/Scholarly.*

Related titles: Online - full text ed.

—East View.

Published by: Huazhong Keji Daxue Tongji Yixueyuan/Huazhong University of Science and Technology, Tongji Medical College, 1095 Jiefang Dadao, Wuhan, 430030, China. TEL 86-27-83662875, FAX 86-27-83662887, http://www.tjmu.edu.cn/. **Dist. by:** China International Book Trading Corp, 35 Chegongzhuang Xilu, Haidian District, PO Box 399, Beijing 100044, China. TEL 86-10-68412045, FAX 86-10-68412023, cibtc@mail.cibtc.com.cn, http://www.cibtc.com.cn.

615.8 FRA ISSN 0181-9801

FEUILLETS DE RADIOLOGIE. Text in French. 1961. 6/yr. EUR 314 in Europe to institutions; EUR 270.32 in France to institutions; JPY 48,500 in Japan to institutions; USD 408 elsewhere to institutions (effective 2012). reprints avail. **Document type:** *Journal, Academic/Scholarly.* **Description:** For help in the preparation of university examinations and the competitive exams of French radiology hospitals.

Related titles: Microform ed.: (from PQC); Online - full text ed.: (from ScienceDirect).

Indexed: A22, EMBASE, ExcerpMed, FR, INIS AtomInd, R10, Reac, SCI, SCOPUS, W07.

—BLDSC (3914.133000), GNLM, IE, Ingenta, INIST. **CCC.**

Published by: Elsevier Masson (Subsidiary of: Elsevier Health Sciences), 62 Rue Camille Desmoulins, Issy les Moulineaux, Cedex 92442, France. TEL 33-1-71165500, infos@elsevier-masson.fr. Ed. Jean-Michel Tubiana. Circ: 4,000. **Subscr. to:** Societe de Periodiques Specialises, BP 22, Vineuil Cedex 41354, France. TEL 33-2-54504612, FAX 33-2-54504611.

615 616.9 CHE ISSN 0071-9676
CODEN: FRTOA7

➤ **FRONTIERS OF RADIATION THERAPY AND ONCOLOGY.** Text in English. 1968. irreg., latest vol.43, 2011. price varies. reprints avail. **Document type:** *Monographic series, Academic/Scholarly.* **Description:** Covers developments in the treatment of cancer with radiation therapy.

Related titles: Online - full text ed.: ISSN 1662-3789.

Indexed: A22, ASCA, BIOSIS Prev, C06, C07, ChemAb, DentInd, EMBASE, ExcerpMed, IndMed, MEDLINE, MycolAb, P30, R10, Reac, SCI, SCOPUS, W07.

—BLDSC (4042.060000), CASDDS, IE, Infotrieve, Ingenta, INIST. **CCC.**

Published by: S. Karger AG, Allschwilerstr 10, Basel, 4055, Switzerland. TEL 41-61-3061111, FAX 41-61-3061234, karger@karger.ch, http://www.karger.ch. Eds. J L Meyer, W Hinkelbein.

➤ **FUSHE FANGHU TONGXUE/RADIATION PROTECTION BULLETIN.** *see* PHYSICS—Nuclear Physics

615.842 NLD ISSN 2212-263X
CODEN: GAMMDV

➤ **GAMMA NIEUWS.** Text in Dutch. 1950. m. (11/yr.). EUR 98.40 membership (effective 2009). adv. bk.rev. illus. **Document type:** *Journal, Academic/Scholarly.*

Supersedes in part (in 2007): Gamma (0016-4380)

Indexed: CIN, ChemAb, ChemTitl.

—CASDDS.

Published by: Nederlandse Vereniging Medische Beeldvorming en Radiotherapie, Catharijnesingel 73, Utrecht, 3511 GM, Netherlands. TEL 31-30-2318842, FAX 31-30-2321362, info@nvmbr.nl. adv.: B&W page EUR 1,595, color page EUR 2,910; trim 210 x 297. Circ: 3,500 (controlled).

616.07 JPN ISSN 0285-0524
CODEN: GASHDC

GAZO SHINDAN/JAPANESE JOURNAL OF DIAGNOSTIC IMAGING. Text in Japanese. 1981. m. JPY 27,720 (effective 2005). **Document type:** *Journal, Academic/Scholarly.*

Indexed: INIS AtomInd.

Published by: Shujunsha Co. Ltd., 3-5-1 Kanda-Nishikicho, Chiyoda-ku, Tokyo, 101-0054, Japan. TEL 81-3-52810551, FAX 81-3-52810550, info@shujunsha.co.jp.

616.0757 GEO ISSN 1512-0031

GEORGIAN JOURNAL OF RADIOLOGY. Text in Russian, English, Georgian. q. 100 p./no. 2 cols./p.; **Document type:** *Journal, Academic/Scholarly.*

Published by: (Georgian Association of Radiology), Georgian Academy of Sciences, Institute of Radiology and Interventional Diagnostics, 13 Tevdore Mgvdeli str, Tbilsi, 380012, Georgia. TEL 995-32-940289, FAX 995-32-344923, radiag@access.sanet.ge.

616.075 636.089 ITA ISSN 1827-1987

GEOSPATIAL HEALTH. Text in English, Italian. 2006. s-a. **Document type:** *Journal, Academic/Scholarly.* **Description:** Focuses on all aspects of the application of geographic information systems, remote sensing and other spatial analysis tools in human and veterinary health.

Related titles: Online - full text ed.: ISSN 1970-7096.

Indexed: A34, A35, A36, A38, AgBio, AgrForAb, CABA, D01, E12, EMBASE, ExcerpMed, F08, F12, G11, GH, H17, I11, IndVet, MEDLINE, N02, N03, P30, P33, P37, P39, R07, R08, R10, R12, Reac, S13, S16, SCI, SCOPUS, T05, VS, W07, W11.

Published by: (Global Network for Geospatial Health), Universita degli Studi di Napoli "Federico II", Facolta di Medicina Veterinaria, Via della Veterinaria 1, Naples, NA 80137, Italy. Ed. Robert Bergquist.

616.07 CHN ISSN 1006-446X

GUANGDONG WEILIANG YUANSU KEXUE/GUANGDONG TRACE ELEMENTS SCIENCE. Text in Chinese. 1994. m. CNY 10, USD 4.20 per issue (effective 2003). **Document type:** *Journal, Academic/Scholarly.*

Related titles: Online - full text ed.

—BLDSC (4223.858320), IE, Ingenta.

Published by: Guangdong-sheng Kexue Jishu Qingbao Yanjiusuo, 100, Xianlie Zhong Lu, Guangzhou, 510070, China. TEL 86-20-87668123, FAX 86-20-87785344. **Dist. by:** China International Book Trading Corp, 35 Chegongzhuang Xilu, Haidian District, PO Box 399, Beijing 100044, China. TEL 86-10-68412045, FAX 86-10-68412023, cibtc@mail.cibtc.com.cn, http://www.cibtc.com.cn. **Co-sponsor:** Guangzhou Diqu Guangdong Weiliang Yuansu Yu Jiankang Yanjiuhui.

615.842 CHN ISSN 1674-1897

➤ **GUOJI YIXUE FANGSHEXUE ZAZHI/INTERNATIONAL JOURNAL OF MEDICAL RADIOLOGY.** Text in Chinese. 1978. bi-m. CNY 90; CNY 15 per issue (effective 2009). **Document type:** *Journal, Academic/Scholarly.*

Formerly (until 2008): Guowai Yixue (Linchuang Fangshexue Fence)/ Foreign Medical Sciences (Clinical Radiology) (1001-1021)

Related titles: Online - full text ed.

—East View.

Published by: Tianjin Yixue Keji Qingbao Yanjiusuo/Tianjin Medical Science and Technology Information Institute, 96-D, Guizhou Lu, Heping-qu, Tianjin, 300070, China. TEL 86-22-23337512, FAX 86-22-23337508, http://www.tjmic.ac.cn/. **Dist. by:** China International Book Trading Corp, 35 Chegongzhuang Xilu, Haidian District, PO Box 399, Beijing 100044, China. TEL 86-10-68412045, FAX 86-10-68412023, cibtc@mail.cibtc.com.cn, http://www.cibtc.com.cn.

616.07 CHN ISSN 1001-098X

GUOWAI YIXUE (FANGSHE YIXUE HEYIXUE FENCE)/FOREIGN MEDICAL SCIENCES (RADIOLOGY & NUCLEAR MEDICINE). Text in Chinese. 1977. bi-m. CNY 36 domestic; USD 17.40 foreign (effective 2005). **Document type:** *Academic/Scholarly.*

Related titles: Online - full text ed.

Indexed: INIS AtomInd.

—East View.

Published by: Zhongguo Yixue Kexueyuan, Fangshe Yixue Yanjiusuo, 238, Baidi, Tianjin, 300192, China. **Dist. by:** China International Book Trading Corp, 35 Chegongzhuang Xilu, Haidian District, PO Box 399, Beijing 100044, China. TEL 86-10-68412045, FAX 86-10-68412023, cibtc@mail.cibtc.com.cn, http://www.cibtc.com.cn.

616.07 DEU ISSN 1975-129X

HAEGUIHAG BUNJA YEONGSANG/NUCLEAR MEDICINE AND MOLECULAR IMAGING. Text in Korean. 1967. 4/yr. EUR 480 combined subscription to institutions (print & online eds.) (effective 2010). **Document type:** *Journal, Academic/Scholarly.*

Former titles (until 2006): Daehan Haeg Yihag Hoeji (1225-6714); (until 1984): Taehan Haek Uihakhoe Chapchi (0378-8725)

Related titles: Online - full content ed.: ISSN 1869-3482.

Indexed: INIS AtomInd.

Published by: (Daehan Haeg Yihaghoe/Korean Society of Nuclear Medicine KOR), Springer (Subsidiary of: Springer Science+Business Media), Tiergartenstr 17, Heidelberg, 69121, Germany. TEL 49-6221-4870, FAX 49-6221-345229, subscriptions@springer.com. Ed. Myung-Hee Sohn.

616.07 USA ISSN 1546-0002
HEALTH IMAGING & I T. (Information Technology) Text in English. 2003. m. free to qualified personnel (effective 2010). adv. back issues avail. **Document type:** *Magazine, Trade.* **Description:** Provides practical and technical insight for radiology, cardiology, administrative and IT executives charged with implementing image and information management solutions across the healthcare enterprise.
Related titles: Online - full text ed.: ISSN 1937-853X. free (effective 2010).
Published by: Trimed Media Group, Inc., 235 Promenade St, Ste 455, Providence, RI 02908. TEL 401-383-5660, FAX 401-383-3896, sales@trimedmedia.com, http://www.trimedmedia.com. Ed. Lisa Fratt. Pub. Jack Spears TEL 410-383-5660 ext 202.

612.014 USA
HEALTH PHYSICS NEWS. Text in English. 1959. m. membership. adv. back issues avail. **Document type:** *Newsletter, Trade.* **Description:** Alerts members to society events, news, and activities, both past and planned.
Formerly (until Dec. 2002): Health Physics Society. Newsletter (0073-1498)
Published by: Health Physics Society, 1313 Dolley Madison Blvd, Ste 402, McLean, VA 22101. TEL 703-790-1745, FAX 703-790-2672, hps@BurkInc.com, http://www.hps.org. Ed. Genevieve S Roessler. Adv. contact Sharon Hebl. Circ: 7,000.

612.014 JPN ISSN 1348-3765
HIROSHIMA DAIGAKU GEMBAKU HOUSHASEN IKAGAKU KENKYUUJO NEMPOU/HIROSHIMA UNIVERSITY. RESEARCH INSTITUTE FOR RADIATION BIOLOGY AND MEDICINE. PROCEEDINGS. Text in English, Japanese. 1960. a. **Document type:** *Proceedings, Academic/Scholarly.*
Formerly: Hiroshima Daigaku Gembaku Hoshano Igaku Kenkyujo Nempo/Hiroshima University. Research Institute for Nuclear Medicine and Biology. Proceedings (0073-232X)
Indexed: INIS AtomInd.
—BLDSC (6789.390000).
Published by: Hiroshima Daigaku, Genbaku Hoshano Kenkyujo/ Hiroshima University, Research Institute for Radiation Biology and Medicine, 1-2-3 Kasumi, Hiroshima, 734-8553, Japan. TEL 81-82-2575555, FAX 81-82-2558339, http://www.rbm.hiroshima-u.ac.jp/index-j.html. Circ: 450 (controlled).

615.842 JPN
HOIKEN SHINPOJUMU SHIRIZU/N I R S SYMPOSIUM. PROCEEDINGS. Text in Japanese; Summaries in English. 1962. a. **Document type:** *Proceedings.*
Published by: Kagaku Gijutsucho, Hoshasen Igaku Sogo Kenkyujo/ Science and Technology Agency, National Institute of Radiological Sciences, 4-9-1, Anagawa, Inage-ku, Chiba, 263-8555, Japan. TEL 81-43-2063025, FAX 81-43-2064061, kokusai@nirs.go.jp, http://www.nirs.go.jp/.

615.842 JPN ISSN 0912-0327
HOKKAIDO HOSHASEN GIJUTSU ZASSHI/JOURNAL OF HOKKAIDO RADIOLOGICAL TECHNOLOGY. Text in Japanese; Summaries in English. 1945. a. membership. adv. **Document type:** *Journal, Academic/Scholarly.*
Formerly: Hokkaido X-sen Kaishi
Published by: Nihon Hoshasen Gijutsu Gakkai, Hokkaido Bukai/ Japanese Society of Radiological Technology, Hokkaido Branch, Niiyo Plaza, 88 Nakagyo-ku, Kyoto, 604, Japan. TEL 81-75-8012238, FAX 81-75-8221041, http://www.dobukai.org/index.htm. Circ: 1,500 (controlled).

616.0757 NOR ISSN 0332-9410
➤ **HOLD PUSTEN.** Text in Norwegian. 1974. 9/yr. NOK 550 domestic; NOK 685 foreign (effective 2011). adv. back issues avail. **Document type:** *Magazine, Academic/Scholarly.*
Related titles: Online - full text ed.: ISSN 1890-8330. 2006.
—CCC.
Published by: Norsk Radiografforbund/The Norwegian Radiography Society, Raadhusgata 4, Oslo, 0151, Norway. TEL 47-23-100470, FAX 47-23-100480, nrf@radiograf.no, http://www.radiograf.no. Ed. Tone Stidahl. Adv. contact Ellinor Da Gunnerud TEL 47-23-100471.

615.842 HKG ISSN 1029-5097
➤ **HONG KONG COLLEGE OF RADIOLOGISTS. JOURNAL.** Text in English. q. HKD 400 domestic; USD 100 foreign (effective 2008). **Document type:** *Journal, Academic/Scholarly.* **Description:** Covers diagnostic imaging, clinical oncology, and nuclear medicine. Includes articles and papers on radiological protection, quality assurance, audit in radiology, and radiological education issues.
Related titles: Online - full text ed.
Indexed: EMBASE, ExcerpMed, R10, Reac.
—BLDSC (4758.557000). **CCC.**
Published by: (Hong Kong College of Radiologists), Hong Kong Academy of Medicine Press, Rm.901, 9/F, HKAM Bldg., 99 Wong Hunk Hang Rd., Aberdeen, Hong Kong. TEL 852-28718822, FAX 852-25159061, hkampress@hkam.org.hk.

615.842 JPN
HOSHANO CHOSA KENKYU HOKOKUSHO/NATIONAL INSTITUTE OF RADIOLOGICAL SCIENCES. SURVEY REPORT. Text in Japanese. a. **Document type:** *Government.*
Published by: Kagaku Gijutsucho, Hoshasen Igaku Sogo Kenkyujo/ Science and Technology Agency, National Institute of Radiological Sciences, 9-1 Anagawa 4-chome, Inage-ku, Chiba-shi, 263-0024, Japan. http://www.nirs.go.jp/. Ed. Tohru Kawai.

615.842 JPN ISSN 0439-5948
R895.A1 CODEN: HISKBI
HOSHASEN IGAKU SOGO KENKYUJO NENPO. Text in English. 1957. a. **Document type:** *Corporate.*
Related titles: Online - full content ed.; English ed.: National Institute of Radiological Sciences. Annual Report. ISSN 0439-5956. 1961.
Published by: Kagaku Gijutsucho, Hoshasen Igaku Sogo Kenkyujo/ Science and Technology Agency, National Institute of Radiological Sciences, 4-9-1, Anagawa, Inage-ku, Chiba, 263-8555, Japan. TEL 81-43-2063025, FAX 81-43-2064061, kokusai@nirs.go.jp. Circ: 1,400.

616.07 JPN ISSN 0441-2540
R895.A1 CODEN: HOKAAN
HOSHASEN KAGAKU (CHIBA)/RADIOLOGICAL SCIENCES. Text in Japanese. 1958. m. JPY 12,600 (effective 2006). **Document type:** *Journal, Academic/Scholarly.*
Formerly (until 1968): Hoiken Nyusu
Indexed: INIS AtomInd.
—CASDDS.
Published by: Kagaku Gijutsucho, Hoshasen Igaku Sogo Kenkyujo/ Science and Technology Agency, National Institute of Radiological Sciences, 4-9-1 Anagawa, Inage-ku, Chiba, 263-8555, Japan. TEL 86-43-2063026, FAX 86-43-2064062, info@nirs.go.jp. **Subscr. to:** Jitsugyo-koho Co.,Ltd., 1-7-8 Kudan-kita,Chiyoda-ku, Tokyo 102-0073, Japan. TEL 86-3-32650951, FAX 86-3-32650952, j-k@jitsugyo-koho.co.jp, http://www.jitsugyo-koho.co.jp/.

616.842 JPN
HOSHASEN RIYO KENKYUKAI HOKOKUSHO, IGAKU RIYO GURUPU/RESEARCH REPORT OF UTILIZATION OF RADIATION BY MEDICAL USER'S GROUP. Text in Japanese. a. JPY 7,000 (effective 2003). **Document type:** *Yearbook, Academic/Scholarly.*
Published by: Nihon Genshiryoku Sangyo Kaigi/Japan Atomic Industrial Forum, Daiishi-Chojiya Bldg, 1-2-13 shiba-Diamon, Minato-ku, Tokyo, 105-8605, Japan. TEL 81-3-57770750, FAX 81-3-57770760, http://www.jaif.or.jp.

616.07 USA ISSN 1095-7863
QC785.5
I E E E NUCLEAR SCIENCE SYMPOSIUM CONFERENCE RECORD. (Institute of Electrical and Electronics Engineers) Text in English. 19??. a. adv. back issues avail. **Document type:** *Proceedings, Trade.*
Former titles (until 1996): I E E E Nuclear Science Symposium and Medical Imaging Conference Record (1091-0026); (until 1995): I E E E Conference Record - Nuclear Science Symposium & Medical Imaging Conference (1082-3654); (until 1993): I E E E Nuclear Science Symposium and Medical Imaging Conference. Conference Record (1078-8840); (until 1991): I E E E Nuclear Science Symposium Conference Record; (until 1990): I E E E Nuclear Science Symposium. Papers
Related titles: CD-ROM ed.; Online - full text ed.
Indexed: EngInd, P30, SCOPUS.
—CCC.
Published by: I E E E, 445 Hoes Ln, Piscataway, NJ 08855. contactcenter@ieee.org, http://www.ieee.org.

615.842 USA ISSN 0278-0062
RC78.A1 CODEN: ITMID4
I E E E TRANSACTIONS ON MEDICAL IMAGING. (Institute of Electrical and Electronics Engineers) Text in English. 1982. m. USD 1,627; USD 2,035 combined subscription (print & online eds.) (effective 2012). adv. back issues avail.; reprints avail. **Document type:** *Journal, Academic/Scholarly.* **Description:** Explores ultrasonics, x-ray imaging and tomography, image processing by computers, microwave and nuclear magnetic resonance imaging.
Related titles: CD-ROM ed.; Microfiche ed.; Online - full text ed.: ISSN 1558-254X. USD 1,480 (effective 2012).
Indexed: A01, A02, A03, A08, A22, A26, A28, APA, ASCA, B&BAb, B01, B06, B07, B09, B19, B21, BioEngAb, BrCerAb, C&ISA, CA, CA/WCA, CIA, CMCI, CPEI, CerAb, CivEngAb, CorrAb, CurCont, E&CAJ, E08, E11, EEA, EMA, EMBASE, ESPM, EngInd, EnvEAb, ErgAb, ExcerpMed, FR, G01, G08, H15, I05, INIS AtomInd, ISMEC, ISR, IndMed, Inpharma, Inspec, M&TEA, M05, M06, M09, MBF, MEDLINE, METADEX, P30, RefZh, S01, S09, SCI, SCOPUS, SolStAb, T02, T04, TM, W07, WAA.
—BLDSC (4363.204500), AskIEEE, GNLM, IE, Infotrieve, Ingenta, INIST, Linda Hall. **CCC.**
Published by: I E E E, 445 Hoes Ln, Piscataway, NJ 08854. TEL 732-981-0060, 800-678-4333, FAX 732-562-6380, contactcenter@ieee.org, http://www.ieee.org. Eds. Milan Sonka, Dawn Melley. **Co-sponsors:** I E E E Acoustics, Speech, and Signal Processing Society; Ultrasonics, Ferroelectrics and Frequency Control Society; Nuclear and Plasma Sciences Society; Engineering in Medicine and Biology Society.

616.07 JPN ISSN 1340-4520
CODEN: IVRAFL
I V R INTERVENTIONAL RADIOLOGY. Text in Japanese. 1986. q. **Document type:** *Journal, Academic/Scholarly.*
Formerly (until 1993): Nihon Kekkan Zoei, Interventional Radiology Kenkyukai Zasshi/J S A I R. Japanese Society of Angiography and Interventional Radiology (0912-280X)
Indexed: INIS AtomInd.
Published by: Nihon Kekkanzouei Intabenshonaru Rajioroji Gakkai/ Japanese Society of Angiography and Interventional Radiology, 1-9-4 Motojuku, Higashi Matsuyama, Saitama 355-0063, Japan. TEL 81-493-354250, FAX 81-493-354236, office@jsair.org.

616.842 JPN ISSN 0915-308X
IBARAKI KAKU IGAKU/IBARAKI JOURNAL OF NUCLEAR MEDICINE. Text in Japanese. 1989. s-a.
Published by: Ibarakiken Rinsho Kaku Igaku Kenkyukai/Ibaraki Association of Clinical Nuclear Medicine, Tsukuba Daigaku Fuzoku Byoin Kaku Igakushitsu, 1-1 Amakubo 2-chome, Tsukuba-shi, Ibaraki-ken 305-0005, Japan.

615.84 JPN ISSN 1345-5354
IGAKU BUTSURI/JAPANESE JOURNAL OF MEDICAL PHYSICS. Variant title: Japan Society of Medical Physics. Official Journal. Nihon Igaku Butsuri Gakkai Kikanshi. Text in English, Japanese. 1981. q.
Former titles (until 2000): Hoshasen Igaku Butsuri/Japanese Journal of Medical Physics (0918-8010); (until 1992): Nippon Igaku Hoshasen Gakkai Butsuri Bukaishi (0288-5506)
Indexed: EMBASE, ExcerpMed, INIS AtomInd, MEDLINE, P30, R10, Reac, SCOPUS.
—BLDSC (4656.240000).
Published by: Nihon Igaku Butsuri Gakkai/Japanese Society of Medical Physics, c/o Division of Medical Physics, NIRS, Anagawa 4-9-1, Inage-ku, Chiba, 263-8555, Japan. jsmp@jsmp.org, http://www.jsmp.org.

616.07543 ESP ISSN 2171-3669
▼ **IMAGEN DIAGNOSTICA.** Text in Multiple languages. 2010. s-a. **Document type:** *Journal, Academic/Scholarly.*
Related titles: Online - full text ed.: ISSN 2171-9705 (from ScienceDirect).
Indexed: SCOPUS.
—CCC.
Published by: (Asociacion Catalana de Tecnicos Especialistas en Imagen para el Diagnostico), Elsevier Doyma (Subsidiary of: Elsevier Health Sciences), Traversa de Gracia 17-21, Barcelona, 08021, Spain. TEL 34-932-418800, FAX 34-932-419020, doyma@doyma.es, http://www.doyma.es. Ed. Francesc Torres.

616.075 GBR ISSN 0965-6812
RC78.7.D53 CODEN: IAGIEC
➤ **IMAGING;** an international journal of clinico-radiological practice. Text in English. 1989. q. GBP 180, USD 333 combined subscription to institutions (print & online eds.) (effective 2010). **Document type:** *Journal, Academic/Scholarly.* **Description:** Provides the latest information on the integrated role of imaging modalities in diagnostic problem solving.
Formerly (until 1992): Current Imaging (0952-0619)
Related titles: Online - full text ed.: ISSN 1748-8818. GBP 150, USD 277 to institutions (effective 2010) (from IngentaConnect).
Indexed: A01, B19, CA, EMBASE, ExcerpMed, R10, Reac, SCOPUS, T02.
—BLDSC (4368.996447), GNLM, IE, Ingenta. **CCC.**
Published by: British Institute of Radiology, 36 Portland Pl, London, W1B 1AT, United Kingdom. TEL 44-20-73071400, FAX 44-20-73071414, admin@bir.org.uk, http://www.bir.org.uk. Ed. S Ostlere.

615.842 USA
IMAGING & RADIOLOGY PRODUCT COMPARISON SYSTEM. Variant title: Healthcare Product Comparison System: Imaging and Radiology Edition. Text in English. m. looseleaf. back issues avail.; reprints avail. **Document type:** *Journal, Trade.* **Description:** Covers hospital-based or freestanding radiology facilities, from MRI units to ultrasonic scanners and cardiac catheterization systems.
Formerly (until 1985): Diagnostic Imaging & Radiology Product Comparison System
Related titles: CD-ROM ed.
Published by: Emergency Care Research Institute, 5200 Butler Pike, Plymouth Meeting, PA 19462. TEL 610-825-6000, FAX 610-834-1275, info@ecri.org, http://www.ecri.org.

616.07 DEU ISSN 1433-3317
➤ **IMAGING DECISIONS M R I.** (Magnetic Resonance Imaging) Text in English. 1997. q. GBP 59 in United Kingdom to institutions; EUR 75 in Europe to institutions; USD 110 in the Americas to institutions; USD 128 elsewhere to institutions; GBP 65 combined subscription in United Kingdom to institutions (print & online eds.); EUR 82 combined subscription in Europe to institutions (print & online eds.); USD 121 combined subscription in the Americas to institutions (print & online eds.); USD 140 combined subscription elsewhere to institutions (print & online eds.) (effective 2010). reprint service avail. from PSC. **Document type:** *Journal, Academic/Scholarly.* **Description:** Presents clinical research related to the optimization of imaging strategies in the diagnosis, follow up and treatment of diseases with the use of computed tomography, magnetic resonance imaging, ultrasonography, conventional X-rays, and nuclear medicine.
Related titles: Online - full text ed.: ISSN 1617-0830. GBP 59 in United Kingdom to institutions; EUR 75 in Europe to institutions; USD 110 in the Americas to institutions; USD 128 elsewhere to institutions (effective 2010) (from IngentaConnect).
Indexed: A01, A03, A08, A22, A26, B&BAb, B19, B21, BioEngAb, C06, C07, CA, E01, EMBASE, ExcerpMed, P30, R10, Reac, SCOPUS, T02.
—IE, Ingenta. **CCC.**
Published by: Wiley-Blackwell Verlag GmbH (Subsidiary of: Wiley-Blackwell Publishing Ltd.), Kurfuerstendamm 57, Berlin, 10707, Germany. TEL 49-30-3279-0665, FAX 49-30-3279-0677, verlag@blackwell.de, http://www.blackwell.de. Ed. Dr. N Hosten.

616.07 USA
IMAGING ECONOMICS. Text in English. 1988. m. free domestic to qualified personnel (effective 2011). adv. back issues avail. **Document type:** *Journal, Trade.* **Description:** Concerns medical radiology and treatment through the use of nuclear medicine.
Incorporates (1986-2009): Medical Imaging (1073-1202); Former titles: Decisions in Imaging Economics (1043-1012); (until 1989): Decisions in Technology Economics (0898-6096)
Related titles: Online - full text ed.
Indexed: H01.
—CCC.
Published by: Allied Healthcare Group (Subsidiary of: Ascend Media), 6100 Ctr Dr, Ste 1020, Los Angeles, CA 90045. TEL 310-642-4400, FAX 310-641-4444, http://www.alliedhealthjournals.com. Ed. Marianne Matthews TEL 212-684-1155. Pub., Adv. contact Joanne Melton TEL 212-533-6450.

616.07 GBR ISSN 1755-5191
▼ ➤ **IMAGING IN MEDICINE.** Text in English. 2009. bi-m. GBP 695 combined subscription domestic (print & online eds.); USD 1,220 combined subscription in North America (print & online eds.); JPY 129,000 combined subscription in Japan (print & online eds.); EUR 975 combined subscription elsewhere (print & online eds.) (effective 2011). adv. back issues avail.; reprints avail. **Document type:** *Journal, Academic/Scholarly.* **Description:** Provides a forum for research updates on recent developments in the field of imaging in medicine.
Related titles: Online - full text ed.: ISSN 1755-5205. GBP 615 domestic to institutions; USD 1,080 in North America to institutions; JPY 115,000 in Japan to institutions; EUR 865 elsewhere to institutions (effective 2011) (from IngentaConnect).
Indexed: A26, B&BAb, E08, H12, I05, P20, P30, P48, P54, PQC, SCOPUS.
—CCC.
Published by: Future Medicine Ltd. (Subsidiary of: Future Science Ltd.), Unitec House, 2 Albert Pl, London, N3 1QB, United Kingdom. TEL 44-20-83716080, FAX 44-20-83716099, info@futuremedicine.com. Eds. Charlotte Barker, Elisa Manzotti TEL 44-20-83716090. Pub. David Hughes. Circ: 200.

615.842 USA ISSN 1936-2234
IN PRACTICE (LEESBURG). Text in English. 2007. q. free to members (effective 2007). adv. **Document type:** *Journal, Trade.* **Description:** Features information about services and products for radiology practices.
Formerly (until 200?): A R R S Memo (1070-2423)
Published by: American Roentgen Ray Society, 44211 Slatestone Ct, Leesburg, VA 20176. TEL 703-729-3353, 800-703-2777, FAX 703-729-4839, http://www.arrs.org. Pub. G Rebecca Haines. Adv. contact Dennell Deavers. B&W page USD 1,075, color page USD 1,875; trim 8.375 x 10.875. Circ: 18,668 (paid).

INDIAN ACADEMY OF ORAL MEDICINE AND RADIOLOGY. JOURNAL. *see* MEDICAL SCIENCES—Dentistry

615.842 IND ISSN 0971-3026
R895.A1 CODEN: IJRAAY
INDIAN JOURNAL OF RADIOLOGY AND IMAGING. NEW SERIES. Text in English. 1946; N.S. 1991. q. INR 1,500 domestic to individuals; USD 150 foreign to individuals; INR 3,000 domestic to institutions; USD 250 foreign to institutions; INR 1,800 combined subscription domestic to individuals (print & online eds.); USD 180 combined subscription foreign to individuals (print & online eds.); INR 3,600 combined subscription domestic to institutions (print & online eds.); USD 300 combined subscription foreign to institutions (print & online eds.) (effective 2011). bk.rev. abstr.; bibl.; charts; illus.; stat. index. **Document type:** *Journal, Academic/Scholarly.*
Former titles (until 1991): Indian Journal of Radiology & Imaging (0970-2016); (until 1984): Indian Journal of Radiology (0019-560X)
Related titles: CD-ROM ed.; Online - full text ed.: ISSN 1998-3808. INR 1,200 domestic to individuals; USD 120 foreign to individuals; INR 2,400 domestic to institutions; USD 200 foreign to institutions (effective 2011).
Indexed: A01, A26, A36, C06, C07, CA, CABA, EMBASE, ExcerpMed, ExtraMED, GH, H12, H17, I05, INIS AtomInd, P30, P33, P39, R10, RM&VM, Reac, SCOPUS, T02, T05.
—BLDSC (4421.010000), IE, Ingenta. **CCC.**
Published by: Medknow Publications and Media Pvt. Ltd., B-9, Kanara Business Ctr, Off Link Rd, Ghatkopar (E), Mumbai, Maharastra 400 075, India. TEL 91-22-66491816, FAX 91-22-66491817, http://www.medknow.com.

616.07 JPN ISSN 0913-8919
INNERVISION. Text in Japanese. m. USD 21,500 (effective 2005). **Document type:** *Journal, Academic/Scholarly.*
Indexed: INIS AtomInd.
—CCC.
Published by: Innervision Co., 3-15-1 Hongo Bunkyo, Tokyo, 113-0033, Japan. TEL 81-3-38183502, FAX 81-3-38183522, info@innervision.co.jp, http://www.innervision.co.jp/.

616.7 530 GBR ISSN 1468-7232
➤ **INSTITUTE OF PHYSICS AND ENGINEERING IN MEDICINE. REPORT.** Text in English. 19??. irreg., latest 2009. price varies. back issues avail. **Document type:** *Monographic series, Academic/Scholarly.*
Former titles (until 1997): Institution of Physics and Engineering in Medicine and Biology. Report (1369-4073); (until Aug.1996): Institute of Physical Sciences in Medicine. Report (0951-6514); (until Sep.1985): Hospital Physicists' Association. Conference Report Series
Published by: Institute of Physics and Engineering in Medicine, Fairmount House, 230 Tadcaster Rd, York, YO24 1ES, United Kingdom. TEL 44-1904-610821, FAX 44-1904-612279, office@ipem.ac.uk.

613.6 GBR ISSN 0146-6453
RA1231.R2 CODEN: ANICD6
➤ **INTERNATIONAL COMMISSION ON RADIOLOGICAL PROTECTION. ANNALS.** Key Title: Annals of the I C R P. Text in English. 1959. 6/yr. EUR 518 in Europe to institutions; JPY 68,800 in Japan to institutions; USD 579 elsewhere to institutions (effective 2012). back issues avail. **Document type:** *Journal, Academic/Scholarly.* **Description:** Covers topics in the field of radiation protection for members of the medical professions and other interested groups.
Formerly (until 1977): I C R P Publication (0074-2740)
Related titles: Microfilm ed.: (from PQC); Online - full text ed.: ISSN 1872-969X (from IngentaConnect, ScienceDirect).
Indexed: A01, A03, A08, A22, A26, AESIS, B21, B25, BIOSIS Prev, CA, CISA, EIA, EMBASE, EnerInd, EngInd, ExcerpMed, GeoRef, I05, INIS AtomInd, IndMed, Inspec, MEDLINE, MycolAb, P30, R10, Reac, S01, SCOPUS, T02.
—BLDSC (1026.600000), CASDDS, GNLM, IE, Infotrieve, Ingenta, INIST, Linda Hall. **CCC.**
Published by: (International Commission on Radiological Protection SWE), Pergamon (Subsidiary of: Elsevier Science & Technology), The Blvd, Langford Ln, East Park, Kidlington, Oxford OX5 1GB, United Kingdom. TEL 44-1865-843000, FAX 44-1865-843010, JournalsCustomerServiceEMEA@elsevier.com. Ed. C H Clement. **Subscr. to:** Elsevier BV, Radarweg 29, PO Box 211, Amsterdam 1000 AE, Netherlands. TEL 31-20-4853757, FAX 31-20-4853432, http://www.elsevier.nl.

615.84 612.014 USA ISSN 0074-3933
INTERNATIONAL CONGRESS OF RADIOLOGY. REPORTS. Text in English. 19??. biennial. **Document type:** *Proceedings, Academic/Scholarly.*
Published by: International Society of Radiology, 7910 Wordmont Ave, Ste 400, Bethesda, MD 20814. TEL 301-657-2652, FAX 301-907-8768, director@intsocradiology.org, http://www.isradiology.org.

616.07 DEU ISSN 1861-6410
➤ **INTERNATIONAL JOURNAL OF COMPUTER ASSISTED RADIOLOGY AND SURGERY.** Text in English. 2006. 2/yr. EUR 530, USD 645 combined subscription to institutions (print & online eds.) (effective 2012). reprint service avail. from PSC. **Document type:** *Journal, Academic/Scholarly.* **Description:** Focuses on research and development areas relating to digital imaging methods and computer-assisted diagnostic and therapeutic workflows that match and enhance the skill levels of health care professionals.
Related titles: Online - full text ed.: ISSN 1861-6429 (from IngentaConnect).
Indexed: A22, A26, CurCont, E01, EMBASE, ExcerpMed, MEDLINE, P30, SCI, SCOPUS, W07.
—IE, Ingenta. **CCC.**
Published by: Springer (Subsidiary of: Springer Science+Business Media), Tiergartenstr 17, Heidelberg, 69121, Germany. TEL 49-6221-4870, FAX 49-6221-345229, subscriptions@springer.com. Eds. H U Lemke, M W Vannier.

➤ **INTERNATIONAL JOURNAL OF LOW RADIATION.** *see* ENVIRONMENTAL STUDIES

616.07 GBR ISSN 1749-8023
INTERNATIONAL JOURNAL OF MAGNETIC RESONANCE IMAGING. Text in English. 2006. q. GBP 272; GBP 43 per issue; free to members (effective 2010). **Document type:** *Journal, Academic/Scholarly.* **Description:** Devoted to the prompt publication of original research articles, technological and instrumental notes, case reports, short communications, educational papers and the state-of-the-art reviews dealing with all aspects of development and application of magnetic resonance imaging in basic and clinical sciences.
Related titles: Online - full text ed.: ISSN 1749-8031.
Published by: World Academic Union (World Academic Press), 113 Academic House, Mill Lane, Wavertree Technology Park, Liverpool, L13 4AH, United Kingdom. TEL 44-870-7779498, journals@worldacademicunion.com, http://www.worldacademicunion.com/. Ed. Qiyong Gong.

INTERNATIONAL JOURNAL OF MICROWAVE AND WIRELESS TECHNOLOGIES. *see* ENGINEERING—Electrical Engineering

615.842 USA ISSN 2090-1712
▼ ➤ **INTERNATIONAL JOURNAL OF MOLECULAR IMAGING.** Text in English. 2009. irreg. USD 195 (effective 2011). **Document type:** *Journal, Academic/Scholarly.* **Description:** Publishes original research articles, review articles, case reports, and clinical studies in all areas of molecular imaging.
Related titles: Online - full text ed.: ISSN 2090-1720. free (effective 2011).
Indexed: A01, P30, P52, T02.
Published by: Hindawi Publishing Corporation, 410 Park Ave, 15th Fl, PMB 287, New York, NY 10022. FAX 215-893-4392, 866-446-3294, info@hindawi.com.

616.0757 USA ISSN 0360-3016
RC271.R3 CODEN: IOBPD3
➤ **INTERNATIONAL JOURNAL OF RADIATION: ONCOLOGY - BIOLOGY - PHYSICS.** Abbreviated title: I J R O B P. Text in English. 1976. 15/yr. USD 3,866 in United States to institutions; USD 4,178 elsewhere to institutions (effective 2012). adv. back issues avail.; reprints avail. **Document type:** *Journal, Academic/Scholarly.* **Description:** Provides articles linking new research and technologies to clinical applications.
Related titles: Microfilm ed.: (from PQC); Online - full text ed.: ISSN 1879-355X (from IngentaConnect, ScienceDirect); Supplement(s): International Journal of Radiation: Oncology - Biology - Physics. Supplement. ISSN 0145-1464. 1976; A S T R O Meeting Supplement. 1975.
Indexed: A01, A03, A08, A20, A22, A26, AHCMS, ASCA, B&BAb, B19, B21, B25, BIOBASE, BIOSIS Prev, BPRC&P, BioEngAb, C06, C07, CA, CIN, CPEI, ChemAb, ChemTitl, CurCont, DentInd, EMBASE, ESPM, EngInd, ExcerpMed, FR, G10, I05, IABS, IIL, INI, INIS AtomInd, ISR, IndMed, Inpharma, Inspec, MEDLINE, MS&D, MycolAb, P30, P35, R10, Reac, SCI, SCOPUS, T02, THA, ToxAb, W07.
—BLDSC (4542.523000), AskIEEE, CASDDS, GNLM, IE, Infotrieve, Ingenta, INIST. **CCC.**
Published by: (American Society for Radiation Oncology), Elsevier Inc. (Subsidiary of: Elsevier Science & Technology), 1600 John F Kennedy Blvd, Philadelphia, PA 19103. TEL 215-239-3900, FAX 215-238-7883, JournalCustomerService-usa@elsevier.com, http://www.elsevier.com. Ed. Dr. James D Cox TEL 713-792-6014. Adv. contact Georgia Nikolaros TEL 212-633-3686. Circ: 7,100.

616.07 IND ISSN 0972-9976
➤ **INTERNATIONAL JOURNAL OF TOMOGRAPHY & STATISTICS.** Text in English. 2003. 3/yr. USD 975 combined subscription to institutions in SAARC Countries & Africa (print & online eds.); USD 1,100 combined subscription in the Americas to institutions; EUR 1,000 combined subscription elsewhere to institutions (effective 2011). **Document type:** *Journal, Academic/Scholarly.* **Description:** Contains research articles, and studies that describe the latest research and developments in computerized tomography and statistics.
Related titles: Online - full text ed.: ISSN 0973-7294. USD 475 to institutions in SAARC Countries & Africa; USD 550 in the Americas to institutions; EUR 500 elsewhere to institutions (effective 2010).
Indexed: A01, A26, CA, CCMJ, I05, MSN, MathR, S06, SCOPUS, T02, Z02.
Published by: Centre for Environment, Social and Economic Research Publications, PO Box 113, Roorkee, Uttarakhand 247 667, India. ceserres@ceser.res.in, http://www.ceser.res.in.

616.07543 IND ISSN 0976-0423
▼ ➤ **INTERNATIONAL JOURNAL OF ULTRASOUND & APPLIED TECHNOLOGIES IN PERIOPERATIVE CARE.** Text in English. 2010 (Apr.). 3/yr. INR 3,000 domestic to individuals; USD 180 foreign to individuals; INR 4,500 domestic to institutions; USD 260 foreign to institutions (effective 2010). adv. bk.rev. abstr.; illus. Index. back issues avail. **Document type:** *Journal, Academic/Scholarly.* **Description:** Covers the use of ultrasound and other technological advances in the perioperative case with aims to publish articles arising out of original research, specialized topic, review articles, editorials and description of new ultrasound techniques and technologies. In addition, journal includes pictorial reviews, letters to the editor, book reviews, and notices of meetings and courses.
Related titles: Online - full text ed.: ISSN 0976-2302.
Published by: Jaypee Brothers Medical Publishers Pvt. Ltd., 4838/24, Ansari Rd, Daryaganj, New Delhi, 110 002, India. TEL 91-11-43574357, FAX 91-11-43574314, jaypee@jaypeebrothers.com, http://www.jaypeebrothers.com. Ed. Atul Gaur. Pub. Rohit Gorawara. R&P Chetna Malhotra. Adv. contact Rakesh Sheoran TEL 91-997-1020680. Circ: 1,200.

616.07 USA ISSN 1524-6965
INTERNATIONAL SOCIETY FOR MAGNETIC RESONANCE IN MEDICINE. SCIENTIFIC MEETING AND EXHIBITION. PROCEEDINGS. Text in English. 1993. a. free to members (effective 2011). back issues avail. **Document type:** *Proceedings, Academic/Scholarly.*
Formerly (until 1994): Society of Magnetic Resonance in Medicine. Proceedings (1065-9889)
Related titles: CD-ROM ed.: ISSN 1545-4436; Online - full text ed.: ISSN 1545-4428. 1982.
Indexed: P30.
Published by: International Society for Magnetic Resonance in Medicine, 2030 Addison St, 7th Flr, Berkeley, CA 94704. TEL 510-841-1899, FAX 510-841-2340, info@ismrm.org.

616.07 681 USA ISSN 1945-7928
INTERNATIONAL SYMPOSIUM ON BIOMEDICAL IMAGING. PROCEEDINGS. Text in English. 2002. a. adv. back issues avail.; reprints avail. **Document type:** *Proceedings, Academic/Scholarly.*
Related titles: CD-ROM ed.: ISSN 1945-7936; Online - full text ed.: ISSN 1945-8452.
Indexed: P30.
—CCC.
Published by: I E E E, 445 Hoes Ln, Piscataway, NJ 08854. TEL 732-981-0060, 800-678-4333, FAX 732-562-6380, customer.service@ieee.org, http://www.ieee.org.

616.07 USA ISSN 1539-4638
➤ **THE INTERNET JOURNAL OF NUCLEAR MEDICINE.** Text in English. 2002. s-a. free (effective 2011). adv. **Document type:** *Journal, Academic/Scholarly.*
Media: Online - full text.
Indexed: A01, A02, A03, A08, A26, A39, C27, C29, CA, D03, D04, E13, G08, H11, H12, I05, R14, S14, S15, S18, T02.
Published by: Internet Scientific Publications, Llc., 23 Rippling Creek Dr, Sugar Land, TX 77479. TEL 832-443-1193, FAX 281-240-1533, wenker@ispub.com. Ed. Surjit S. Wadhwa.

616.07 USA ISSN 1528-8404
R895.A1
➤ **THE INTERNET JOURNAL OF RADIOLOGY.** Text in English. 2000. s-a. free (effective 2011). adv. bk.rev. back issues avail. **Document type:** *Journal, Academic/Scholarly.* **Description:** Provides information from the fields of radiology and nuclear medicine; contains original articles, reviews, case reports, streaming slide shows, streaming videos, letters to the editor, press releases, and meeting information.
Media: Online - full text.
Indexed: A01, A02, A03, A08, A26, C06, C07, CA, G08, H11, H12, I05, RefZh, T02.
Published by: Internet Scientific Publications, Llc., 23 Rippling Creek Dr, Sugar Land, TX 77479. TEL 832-443-1193, FAX 281-240-1533, wenker@ispub.com. Ed. Sumer K Sethi.

616.0757 ITA ISSN 1123-9344
RC349.R3 CODEN: INEUFS
➤ **INTERVENTIONAL NEURORADIOLOGY.** Text in English. 1995. q. EUR 190 domestic; EUR 220 in Europe; EUR 258 elsewhere (effective 2008). adv. bk.rev. abstr. back issues avail. **Document type:** *Journal, Academic/Scholarly.* **Description:** Examines peritherapeutic neuroradiology, surgical procedures and related neurosciences.
Related titles: CD-ROM ed.; Diskette ed.; Fax ed.
Indexed: A01, CA, EMBASE, ExcerpMed, NSCI, R10, Reac, SCI, SCOPUS, T02, W07.
—BLDSC (4557.471854), IE, Ingenta.
Published by: (Associazione Italiana di Neuroradiologian), Centauro SRL, Via del Pratello 8, Bologna, 40122, Italy. TEL 39-051-227634, FAX 39-051-220099, adriana.dallocca@centauro.it, http://www.centauro.it. Ed. Pierre L Lasjaunias. Pub. Dr. Marco Leonardi. R&P Adriana Dall'Occa. Adv. contact Gerardo Dall'Occa. Circ: 1,900.

615.842 USA ISSN 0020-9996
RC78 CODEN: INVRAV
➤ **INVESTIGATIVE RADIOLOGY**; a journal of clinical and laboratory research. Text in English. 1966. m. USD 1,330 domestic to institutions; USD 1,665 foreign to institutions (effective 2011). adv. illus. Index. back issues avail.; reprints avail. **Document type:** *Journal, Academic/Scholarly.* **Description:** Brings out clinical and laboratory investigations in diagnostic imaging, the diagnostic use of radioactive isotopes, computed tomography, positron emission tomography, positron emission tomography, magnetic resonance imaging etc.
Formerly: Journal of Investigative Radiology
Related titles: Microform ed.: (from PQC); Online - full text ed.: ISSN 1536-0210. USD 436 to individuals (effective 2011).
Indexed: A20, A22, ASCA, B25, BIOSIS Prev, CIN, ChemAb, ChemTitl, CurCont, DBA, EMBASE, ExcerpMed, HospLI, IIL, ISR, IndMed, Inpharma, MEDLINE, MycolAb, P30, P35, R10, Reac, SCI, SCOPUS, W07.
—BLDSC (4560.350000), CASDDS, GNLM, IE, Infotrieve, Ingenta, INIST. **CCC.**
Published by: Lippincott Williams & Wilkins (Subsidiary of: Wolters Kluwer N.V.), Two Commerce Sq, 2001 Market St, Philadelphia, PA 19103. TEL 215-521-8300, FAX 215-521-8902, customerservice@lww.com, http://www.lww.com. Ed. Dr. Val M Runge. Pub. Matthew Jozwiak. Circ: 238.

616.07 IRN ISSN 1681-2824
THE IRANIAN JOURNAL OF NUCLEAR MEDICINE/MAJALLAH-I PIZISHKI-I HASTAH'I IRAN. Text in English, Persian, Modern. 1993. s-a. **Document type:** *Journal, Academic/Scholarly.* **Description:** Covers basic and clinical nuclear medicine sciences and relevant applications.
Related titles: Online - full text ed.
Indexed: A01, CA, EMBASE, ExcerpMed, INIS AtomInd, Inspec, P20, P48, P54, PQC, R10, Reac, SCOPUS, T02.
Published by: Tehran University of Medical Sciences Publications, Central Library & Documents Center, Poursina St, Tehran, 14174, Iran. TEL 98-21-6112743, FAX 98-21-6404377, http://diglib.tums.ac.ir/pub/journals.asp. Ed. Mohsen Saghari.

615.842 IRN ISSN 1728-4554
IRANIAN JOURNAL OF RADIATION RESEARCH. Text in English. 2003. q. IRR 20,000 domestic to individuals; USD 50 foreign to individuals; IRR 40,000 domestic to institutions; USD 80 foreign to institutions (effective 2005). **Description:** Provides a forum for the exchange of essential information, not only with specialists working in their own field, but with the entire radiation research community.
Related titles: Online - full text ed.: ISSN 1728-4562.
Indexed: EMBASE, ExcerpMed, INIS AtomInd, P20, P48, P54, PQC, R10, Reac, SCI, SCOPUS, W07.
—BLDSC (4567.529400), IE.
Published by: Novin Medical Radiation Institute, PO Box 14665/599, Tehran, i, Iran. TEL 98-21-8086783, FAX 98-21-8086782, info@ijrr.com. Ed. Hossein Mozharani.

616.07 IRN ISSN 1735-1065
RM845
IRANIAN JOURNAL OF RADIOLOGY. Text in English. 2003. q. **Document type:** *Journal, Academic/Scholarly.* **Description:** Dedicated primarily to the topics relevant to radiology and allied sciences of the developing countries,which have been neglected or have received little attention in the Western medical literature.
Related titles: Online - full text ed.
Indexed: A01, A34, A36, CA, CABA, EMBASE, ExcerpMed, GH, H17, IndVet, P20, P33, P48, P54, PQC, R10, Reac, SCI, SCOPUS, T02, T05, VS, W07.
Published by: Tehran University of Medical Sciences Publications, Central Library & Documents Center, Poursina St, Tehran, 14174, Iran. TEL 98-21-6112743, FAX 98-21-6404377, http://diglib.tums.ac.ir/pub/journals.asp. Ed. Karim Vessal.

616.07 JPN ISSN 0918-5658
IRYO HOSHASEN BOGO NEWSLETTER/NEWSLETTER ON RADIOLOGICAL PROTECTION IN MEDICINE. Text in Japanese. 1991. 3/yr. **Document type:** *Journal, Academic/Scholarly.*
Formerly (until 1992): Kyogikai Nyusu Reta (0917-3056)
Published by: Iryo Hoshasen Bogo Renraku Kyogikai/Japan Association on Radiological Protection in Medicine, Japan Radioisotope Association, 2-28-45 Honkomagome 2-chome, Bunkyo-ku, Tokyo, 113-0021, Japan. TEL 81-3-59786433, FAX 81-3-59786434, http://www.fujita-hu.ac.jp/~ssuzuki/bougo/bougo_index.html.

615.842 EGY ISSN 0021-1907
CODEN: ISRRAC
ISOTOPE AND RADIATION RESEARCH/BUHUTH AL-NAZA'IR WA-AL-ISH'A'. Text in English, French; Summaries in Arabic. 1968. s-a. USD 20 (effective 2003). adv. bk.rev. **Document type:** *Bulletin, Academic/Scholarly.*
Indexed: CIN, ChemAb, ChemTitl, INIS AtomInd, Inspec.
—BLDSC (4583.325000), AskIEEE, CASDDS.
Published by: Middle Eastern Regional Radioisotope Centre for the Arab Countries (M E R R C A C), 3 Sh. Malaeb el Gamaa, Dokki, Cairo, 11321, Egypt. TEL 20-2-3370588, FAX 20-2-3371082, merrcac@yahoo.com, http://www.merrcac.com. Ed. Mahmoud Mukhtar. Circ: 500.

615 JPN ISSN 1880-4977
IYO GAZO JOHO GAKKAI ZASSHI (ONLINE)/JAPANESE JOURNAL OF MEDICAL IMAGING AND INFORMATION SCIENCES. Text in Japanese. 2004. 5/yr. **Document type:** *Journal, Academic/Scholarly.*
Media: Online - full text.
Published by: Iyo Gazo Joho Gakkai/Japan Society of Medical Imaging and Information Sciences, Nangoya University, School of Medicine, School of Health Sciences, 65 Tsuruma-Cho, Showa-Ku, Nagoya, 466-8550, Japan. mii-office@fjt.info.gifu-u.ac.jp, http://www.mii-sci.jp/.

616 JPN ISSN 0918-399X
J A S T R O NEWSLETTER. Text in Japanese. 1988. q. JPY 12,000 membership (effective 2006). **Document type:** *Newsletter, Academic/Scholarly.*
—**CCC.**
Published by: Nihon Hoshasen Shuyo Gakkai/Japanese Society for Therapeutic Radiology and Oncology, 4F Natsume Bldg., 2-18-6 Yushima, Bunkyo-Ku, Tokyo, 113-0034, Japan. TEL 81-3-38182176, FAX 81-3-38182209, http://www.jastro.jp/.

615.8 BEL ISSN 1780-2393
J B R - B T R. (Journal Belge de Radiologie - Belgisch Tijdschrift voor Radiologie) Text in French, Dutch; Summaries in English, German, Russian. 1907. bi-m. EUR 175 domestic; EUR 200 foreign (effective 2011). adv. bk.rev. abstr.; bibl. index. **Document type:** *Journal, Academic/Scholarly.*
Former titles (until 1999): Journal Belge de Radiologie (0302-7430); (until 1923): Journal de Radiologie (0302-7449); (until 1908): Journal Belge de Radiologie (0021-7646)
Indexed: A22, EMBASE, ExcerpMed, IndMed, Inspec, MEDLINE, P30, R10, Reac, SCI, SCOPUS, W07.
—BLDSC (4663.438700), IE, Infotrieve, Ingenta, INIST.
Published by: (Societe Royale Belge de Radiologie/Koninklijke Belgische Vereniging voor Radiologie), Acta Medica Belgica, Avenue Winston Churchill 11/30, Brussels, 1180, Belgium. TEL 32-2-3745158, FAX 32-2-3749628, amb@skynet.be, http://www.ulb.ac.be/medecine/loce/amb.htm. Circ: 800.

615.842 616.99 JPN ISSN 1867-1071
CODEN: RAMEER
➤ **JAPANESE JOURNAL OF RADIOLOGY.** Text in Japanese. 1983. 10/yr. EUR 455, USD 546 combined subscription to institutions (print & online eds.) (effective 2012). adv. reprint service avail. from PSC. **Document type:** *Journal, Academic/Scholarly.* **Description:** Provides a forum for the publication of papers documenting recent advances and new developments in the field of radiology in medicine and biology.
Formerly (until 2009): Radiation Medicine (0288-2043)
Related titles: Online - full text ed.: ISSN 1867-108X (from IngentaConnect).
Indexed: A22, A26, C06, C07, E01, EMBASE, ExcerpMed, INIS AtomInd, IndMed, MEDLINE, P20, P22, P24, P30, P48, P54, PQC, R10, Reac, SCI, SCOPUS, W07.
—BLDSC (7227.975000), CASDDS, GNLM, IE, Infotrieve, Ingenta. **CCC.**
Published by: (Nihon Igaku Hoshasen Gakkai/Japan Radiological Society), Springer Japan KK (Subsidiary of: Springer Science+Business Media), No 2 Funato Bldg, 1-11-11 Kudan-kita, Chiyoda-ku, Tokyo, 102-0073, Japan. TEL 81-3-68317000, FAX 81-3-68317001, orders@springer.jp, http://www.springer.jp. Eds. Atsushi Kubo, Osamu Matsui. Circ: 1,500.

615.842 JPN ISSN 1040-9564
CODEN: JOJAEA
➤ **JAPANESE SOCIETY FOR THERAPEUTIC RADIATION AND ONCOLOGY. JOURNAL.** Text in Japanese; Summaries in English. 1989. 4/yr. JPY 12,000 membership (effective 2006). abstr. back issues avail. **Document type:** *Journal, Academic/Scholarly.* **Description:** Reports research focusing on clinical radiation therapy, combined with surgery, chemotherapy and hyperthermia, and on radiation physics and radiation biology.
Related titles: Online - full content ed.
Indexed: EMBASE, ExcerpMed, INIS AtomInd, R10, Reac, SCOPUS.
—BLDSC (4809.575000), GNLM, IE. **CCC.**
Published by: Nihon Hoshasen Shuyo Gakkai/Japanese Society for Therapeutic Radiology and Oncology, 4F Natsume Bldg., 2-18-6 Yushima, Bunkyo-Ku, Tokyo, 113-0034, Japan. TEL 81-3-38182176, FAX 81-3-38182209, http://www.jastro.jp/.

615.84 AUT ISSN 1684-8209
JATROS RADIOLOGIE. Text in German. 2002. 4/yr. EUR 18 (effective 2007). adv. **Document type:** *Journal, Academic/Scholarly.*
Related titles: Online - full text ed.: ISSN 1991-9204.
Published by: Universimed Verlags- und Service GmbH, Markgraf-Ruediger-Str 8, Vienna, 1150, Austria. TEL 43-1-87679560, FAX 43-1-876795620, office@universimed.com, http://www.universimed.com. Ed. Christian Fexa. Adv. contact Christian Gallei. Circ: 1,500 (paid).

615.84 CHN ISSN 1008-794X
JIERU FANGSHEXUE ZAZHI/JOURNAL OF INTERVENTIONAL RADIOLOGY. Text in Chinese. 1992. bi-m. USD 74.40 (effective 2009). **Document type:** *Journal, Academic/Scholarly.*
Related titles: Online - full text ed.
Indexed: A28, APA, BrCerAb, C&ISA, CA/WCA, CIA, CerAb, CivEngAb, CorrAb, E&CAJ, E11, EEA, EMA, EMBASE, ESPM, EnvEAb, ExcerpMed, H15, INIS AtomInd, M&TEA, M09, MBF, METADEX, R10, Reac, RefZh, SolStAb, T04, WAA.
—BLDSC (4668.910150), East View, Linda Hall.
Published by: Shanghai-shi Yixuehui/Shanghai Medical Association, No. 17, Lane 1220, Huashan Lu, Shanghai, 200052, China. **Dist. by:** China International Book Trading Corp, 35 Chegongzhuang Xilu, Haidian District, PO Box 399, Beijing 100044, China. TEL 86-10-68412045, FAX 86-10-68412023, cibtc@mail.cibtc.com.cn, http://www.cibtc.com.cn.

615.842 JPN
JIKI KYOMEI IGAKKAI PUROGURAMU/SOCIETY OF MAGNETIC RESONANCE IN MEDICINE. PROCEEDINGS OF ANNUAL CONFERENCE. Text in Japanese; Summaries in English. a. **Document type:** *Proceedings, Academic/Scholarly.*
Published by: Nihon Jiki Kyomei Igakkai/Japanese Society of Magnetic Resonance in Medicine, Gotanda Park Side Bldg 4F, 5-24-9 Higashi-gotanda Shinagawa-ku, Tokyo, 141-0022, Japan. TEL 81-3-34438622, FAX 81-3-34438733, http://www.jsmrm.jp/.

615.842 FRA ISSN 0221-0363
➤ **JOURNAL DE RADIOLOGIE;** revue d'imagerie medicale, diagnostique et therapeutique. Text in French; Summaries in English. 1914. m. EUR 657 in Europe to institutions; EUR 469.15 in France to institutions; JPY 99,800 in Japan to institutions; USD 854 elsewhere to institutions (effective 2012). adv. bk.rev. abstr.; illus. index. reprints avail. **Document type:** *Journal, Academic/Scholarly.* **Description:** Discusses radiodiagnosis and new methods of investigation. Reports on international congresses of radiology and on the section meetings of the society.
Incorporates (1980-1999): Journal d'Echographie et de Medecine Ultrasonore (0245-5552); Formerly (until 1978): Journal de Radiologie, d'Electrologie et de Medecine Nucleaire (0368-3966)
Related titles: Microform ed.: (from PQC); Online - full text ed.: (from ScienceDirect).
Indexed: A22, A36, ASCA, CABA, ChemAb, CurCont, DentInd, EMBASE, ExcerpMed, FR, GH, H17, INI, INIS AtomInd, IndMed, Inpharma, MEDLINE, N02, N03, P30, P33, R10, RM&VM, Reac, SCI, SCOPUS, T05, W07.
—BLDSC (5043.972000), GNLM, IE, Infotrieve, Ingenta, INIST, Linda Hall. **CCC.**
Published by: (Societe Francaise de Radiologie et Conseil des Enseignants en Radiologie de France), Elsevier Masson (Subsidiary of: Elsevier Health Sciences), 62 Rue Camille Desmoulins, Issy les Moulineaux, Cedex 92442, France. TEL 33-1-71165500, infos@elsevier-masson.fr. Ed. Patrice Taourel. Circ: 5,000.

616.075 FRA ISSN 1771-4745
JOURNAL D'ECHOGRAPHIE EN RADIOLOGIE. Text in French. 1991. m. EUR 290 (effective 2006). **Document type:** *Journal, Academic/Scholarly.*
Supersedes in part (in 2004): L U S. Litterature Ultra-sonore (1169-3827)
Published by: Centre Francophone de Formation en Echographie, 25 Av Amedee Bollee, Kilometre Delta, Nimes, 30900, France. TEL 33-4-66680483, FAX 33-4-66642953, contact@ultrason.com.

JOURNAL OF CARDIOVASCULAR COMPUTED TOMOGRAPHY. *see* MEDICAL SCIENCES—Cardiovascular Diseases

616.07 IND ISSN 2156-7514
▼ **JOURNAL OF CLINICAL IMAGING SCIENCE.** Text in English. 2010. irreg. **Document type:** *Journal, Academic/Scholarly.*
Related titles: Online - full text ed.: ISSN 2156-5597. free (effective 2011).
Indexed: A01, A26, I05.
—**CCC.**
Published by: Medknow Publications and Media Pvt. Ltd., B-9, Kanara Business Ctr, Off Link Rd, Ghatkopar (E), Mumbai, Maharastra 400 075, India. TEL 91-22-66491818, FAX 91-22-66491817, journals@medknow.com, http://www.medknow.com. Ed. Vikram S Dogra.

JOURNAL OF CLINICAL ONCOLOGY. *see* MEDICAL SCIENCES—Oncology

616.07 USA ISSN 0091-2751
RM862.7 CODEN: JCULDD
JOURNAL OF CLINICAL ULTRASOUND. Abbreviated title: J C U. Text in English. 1973. 9/yr. GBP 891 in United Kingdom to institutions; EUR 1,127 in Europe to institutions; USD 1,757 in United States to institutions; USD 1,883 in Canada & Mexico to institutions; USD 1,946 elsewhere to institutions; GBP 1,026 combined subscription in United Kingdom to institutions (print & online eds.); EUR 1,297 combined subscription in Europe to institutions (print & online eds.); USD 2,020 combined subscription in United States to institutions (print & online eds.); USD 2,146 combined subscription in Canada & Mexico to institutions (print & online eds.); USD 2,209 combined subscription elsewhere to institutions (print & online eds.) (effective 2012). bk.rev. abstr.; charts; illus.; stat. index. back issues avail.; reprint service avail. from PSC. **Document type:** *Journal, Trade.* **Description:** Covers current uses of ultrasound in evaluating disorders affecting the central nervous system, fetus and placenta, gastrointestinal system, reproductive system, urinary system.
Related titles: Microform ed.: (from PQC); Online - full text ed.: ISSN 1097-0096. GBP 897 in United Kingdom to institutions; EUR 1,135 in Europe to institutions; USD 1,757 elsewhere to institutions (effective 2012).
Indexed: A22, ASCA, AcoustA, B&BAb, B19, B21, BDM&CN, BioEngAb, CurCont, DentInd, DokArb, EMBASE, ExcerpMed, FR, IIL, ISR, IndMed, Inpharma, Inspec, MEDLINE, P30, R10, Reac, SCI, SCOPUS, T02, W07.
—BLDSC (4958.791000), GNLM, IE, Infotrieve, Ingenta, INIST. **CCC.**
Published by: John Wiley & Sons, Inc., 111 River St, Hoboken, NJ 07030. TEL 201-748-6000, FAX 201-748-6088, info@wiley.com, http://www.wiley.com/WileyCDA/. Ed. Bruno D Fornage. Pub. Kim Thompkins TEL 212-850-6921. Circ: 1,524. **Subscr. outside the Americas to:** John Wiley & Sons Ltd., The Atrium, Southern Gate, Chichester, West Sussex PO19 8SQ, United Kingdom. TEL 44-1243-779777, FAX 44-1243-775878, cs-journals@wiley.com.

615.842 USA ISSN 0363-8715
RC78.7.T6 CODEN: JCATD5
➤ **JOURNAL OF COMPUTER ASSISTED TOMOGRAPHY.** Abbreviated title: J C A T. Text in English. 1977. bi-m. USD 1,408 domestic to institutions; USD 1,468 foreign to institutions (effective 2011). adv. bk.rev. index. back issues avail.; reprints avail. **Document type:** *Journal, Academic/Scholarly.* **Description:** Provides clinical and research developments in computer-based diagnostic imaging.
Related titles: Microform ed.: (from PQC); Online - full text ed.: ISSN 1532-3145. USD 917.80 domestic academic site license; USD 917.80 foreign academic site license; USD 1,023.70 domestic corporate site license; USD 1,023.70 foreign corporate site license (effective 2002).
Indexed: A22, A36, ASCA, B&BAb, B19, B21, BDM&CN, BIOBASE, CABA, CTA, CurCont, DentInd, EMBASE, ExcerpMed, GH, H17, IABS, IBR, IBZ, IIL, ISR, IndMed, Inpharma, Inspec, Kidney, MEDLINE, N02, N03, NSA, P30, P33, PN&I, R10, RM&VM, Reac, SCI, SCOPUS, T05, TM, W07.
—BLDSC (4963.650000), AskIEEE, GNLM, IE, Infotrieve, Ingenta, INIST. **CCC.**
Published by: Lippincott Williams & Wilkins (Subsidiary of: Wolters Kluwer N.V.), 333 7th Ave, 19th Fl, New York, NY 10001. TEL 646-674-6300, FAX 646-674-6500, customerservice@lww.com, http://www.lww.com. Ed. Dr. Allen D Elster. Pub. Matthew Jozwiak. Circ: 778.

616.07 POL ISSN 1689-832X
JOURNAL OF CONTEMPORARY BRACHYTHERAPY. Text in English. q. PLZ 40 domestic; EUR 20 in Europe; USD 40 elsewhere (effective 2010). **Document type:** *Journal, Academic/Scholarly.* **Description:** Covers clinical brachytherapy, combined modality treatment, advances in radiobiology, hyperthermia and tumour biology, as well as physical aspects relevant to brachytherapy, particularly in the field of imaging, dosimetry and radiation therapy planning.
Related titles: Online - full text ed.: ISSN 2081-2841.
Published by: Termedia sp. z o.o./Termedia Publishing House, ul Wenedow 9/1, Poznan, 61614, Poland. TEL 48-61-8227781, FAX 48-61-8227781, termedia@termedia.pl, http://www.termedia.pl. Ed. Janusz Skowronek.

616.07 USA ISSN 8756-4793
RC78.7.U4 J68
➤ **JOURNAL OF DIAGNOSTIC MEDICAL SONOGRAPHY.** Text in English. 1985. bi-m. USD 657, GBP 387 combined subscription to institutions (print & online eds.); USD 644, GBP 379 to institutions (effective 2011). adv. illus. index. 56 p./no. 2 cols./p.; back issues avail.; reprint service avail. from PSC. **Document type:** *Journal, Academic/Scholarly.*
Related titles: Microform ed.; Online - full text ed.: ISSN 1552-5430. USD 591, GBP 348 to institutions (effective 2011).
Indexed: A22, A26, B&BAb, B07, B19, C06, C07, C08, CA, CINAHL, E01, E08, EMBASE, ExcerpMed, G08, H04, H11, H12, I05, P24, P48, PQC, S09, SCOPUS, T02, V02.
—GNLM, IE, Infotrieve, Ingenta, INIST. **CCC.**
Published by: (Society of Diagnostic Medical Sonography), Sage Publications, Inc., 2455 Teller Rd, Thousand Oaks, CA 91320. TEL 805-499-9774, FAX 805-499-0871, info@sagepub.com. Ed. Michelle Bierig. adv.: B&W page USD 1,750, color page USD 2,365; trim 8.125 x 10.875. Circ: 16,000 (paid). **Subscr. overseas to:** Sage Publications Ltd., 1 Oliver's Yard, 55 City Rd, London EC1Y 1SP, United Kingdom. TEL 44-207-3248701, FAX 44-207-3248733, subscription@sagepub.co.uk.

616.842 USA ISSN 0897-1889
CODEN: JDIMEW
➤ **JOURNAL OF DIGITAL IMAGING.** Abbreviated title: J D I. Text in English. 1988 (Nov.). bi-m. EUR 923, USD 951 combined subscription to institutions (print & online eds.) (effective 2012). adv. index. back issues avail.; reprint service avail. from PSC. **Document type:** *Journal, Academic/Scholarly.* **Description:** Presents the practicing radiologist with information to enhance in the understanding, selection, and use of computer applications in everyday practice.
Related titles: Online - full text ed.: ISSN 1618-727X (from IngentaConnect).
Indexed: A22, A26, ASCA, B&BAb, B19, B21, C06, C07, C08, C10, CA, CINAHL, CMCI, CPEI, CompLI, CurCont, E01, EMBASE, EngInd, ExcerpMed, H12, IIL, INI, ISR, IndMed, Inpharma, Inspec, MEDLINE, NSA, P20, P22, P24, P30, P48, P52, P54, PQC, SCI, SCOPUS, T02, W07.
—BLDSC (4969.610000), GNLM, IE, Infotrieve, Ingenta. **CCC.**
Published by: (Society for Computer Applications in Radiology), Springer New York LLC (Subsidiary of: Springer Science+Business Media), 233 Spring St, New York, NY 10013. TEL 212-460-1500, FAX 212-460-1575, service-ny@springer.com. Ed. Janice Honeyman-Buck TEL 352-273-7594. adv.: B&W page USD 710, color page USD 1,810; trim 10 x 7. Circ: 1,527.

616.07 USA ISSN 1053-1807
RC78.7.N83 CODEN: JMRIFR
➤ **JOURNAL OF MAGNETIC RESONANCE IMAGING.** Abbreviated title: J M R I. Text in English. 1990. m. GBP 1,256 in United Kingdom to institutions; EUR 1,588 in Europe to institutions; USD 2,207 in United States to institutions; USD 2,459 elsewhere to institutions; GBP 1,446 combined subscription in United Kingdom to institutions (print & online eds.); EUR 1,829 combined subscription in Europe to institutions (print & online eds.); USD 2,539 combined subscription in United States to institutions (print & online eds.); USD 2,791 combined subscription elsewhere to institutions (print & online eds.) (effective 2012). adv. back issues avail.; reprint service avail. from PSC. **Document type:** *Journal, Academic/Scholarly.* **Description:** Focuses on research in techniques and equipment, and clinical applications of the noninvasive diagnostic procedure.
Related titles: Online - full text ed.: ISSN 1522-2586. GBP 1,127 in United Kingdom to institutions; EUR 1,425 in Europe to institutions; USD 2,207 elsewhere to institutions (effective 2012).
Indexed: A22, ASCA, B&BAb, B19, B21, BioEngAb, C06, C07, CurCont, EMBASE, ExcerpMed, IIL, ISR, IndMed, Inpharma, Inspec, MEDLINE, NSA, P30, R10, Reac, SCI, SCOPUS, T02, W07.
—BLDSC (5010.791000), GNLM, IE, Ingenta. **CCC.**
Published by: (International Society for Magnetic Resonance in Medicine), John Wiley & Sons, Inc., 111 River St, Hoboken, NJ 07030. TEL 201-748-6000, FAX 201-748-6088, info@wiley.com, http://www.wiley.com/WileyCDA/. Ed. C Leon Partain. Pub. Kim Thompkins TEL 212-850-6921. Adv. contact Stephen Donohue TEL 781-388-8511. Circ: 1,010. **Subscr. outside the Americas to:** John Wiley & Sons Ltd.

615.842 AUS ISSN 1754-9477
R895.A1 CODEN: AURDAW
➤ **JOURNAL OF MEDICAL IMAGING AND RADIATION ONCOLOGY.** Text in English. 1957. bi-m. GBP 416 in United Kingdom to institutions; EUR 528 in Europe to institutions; USD 675 in the Americas to institutions; USD 815 elsewhere to institutions; GBP 479 combined subscription in United Kingdom to institutions (print & online eds.); EUR 608 combined subscription in Europe to institutions (print & online eds.); USD 776 combined subscription in the Americas to institutions (print & online eds.); USD 938 combined subscription elsewhere to institutions (print & online eds.) (effective 2012). adv. bk.rev. charts; illus. cum.index. back issues avail.; reprint service avail. from PSC. **Document type:** *Journal, Academic/Scholarly.* **Description:** Discusses various aspects of clinical radiology.
Former titles (until 2008): Australasian Radiology (0004-8461); (until 1966): College of Radiologists of Australasia. Journal (0374-8545)
Related titles: Microform ed.: (from PQC); Online - full text ed.: ISSN 1754-9485. GBP 416 in United Kingdom to institutions; EUR 528 in Europe to institutions; USD 675 in the Americas to institutions; USD 815 elsewhere to institutions (effective 2012) (from IngentaConnect).
Indexed: A01, A02, A03, A08, A11, A22, A26, B21, C06, C07, C11, CA, CTA, ChemAb, DentInd, E01, EMBASE, ESPM, ExcerpMed, H&SSA, H04, H12, IIL, INIS AtomInd, IndMed, MEDLINE, P30, R10, Reac, SCI, SCOPUS, T02, ToxAb, W07.
—BLDSC (5017.072080), GNLM, IE, Infotrieve, Ingenta, INIST. **CCC.**
Published by: (Royal Australian and New Zealand College of Radiologists), Wiley-Blackwell Publishing Asia (Subsidiary of: Wiley-Blackwell Publishing Ltd.), 155 Cremorne St, Richmond, VIC 3121, Australia. TEL 61-3-92743100, FAX 61-3-92743101, subs@blackwellpublishingasia.com, http://www.wiley.com/WileyCDA/. Ed. David Ball. adv.: B&W page AUD 1,012, color page AUD 2,057; trim 210 x 275. Circ: 2,550. **Subscr. to:** PO Box 378, Carlton South, VIC 3053, Australia.

615.842 USA ISSN 1939-8654
➤ **JOURNAL OF MEDICAL IMAGING AND RADIATION SCIENCES/ JOURNAL DE L'IMAGERIE MEDICALE ET DES SCIENCES DE LA RADIATION.** Abbreviated title: J M I R S. Text in English, French. 1943. q. USD 156 in United States to institutions; USD 156 elsewhere to institutions (effective 2012). adv. bk.rev. charts; illus.; stat. index, cum.index. back issues avail.; reprints avail. **Document type:** *Journal, Academic/Scholarly.* **Description:** Brings out articles on research, new technology and techniques, professional practices, technologists' viewpoints as well as relevant book reviews.
Former titles (until 2008): Canadian Journal of Medical Radiation Technology (0820-5930); (until 1987): Canadian Journal of Radiography, Radiotherapy, Nuclear Medicine (0319-4434); (until 1974): Canadian Journal of Radiography, Radiotherapy, Nucleography (0015-4938); (until 1970): Focal Spot (0319-4426)
Related titles: Microform ed.: (from PQC); Online - full text ed.: ISSN 1876-7982 (from ScienceDirect).
Indexed: C06, C07, C08, CA, CINAHL, EMBASE, ExcerpMed, P30, SCOPUS, T02.
—BLDSC (5017.072900), GNLM, IE, Infotrieve, Ingenta. **CCC.**
Published by: (Canadian Association of Medical Radiation Technologists/ Association Canadienne des Technologues en Radiation Medicale CAN), Elsevier Inc. (Subsidiary of: Elsevier Science & Technology), 1600 John F Kennedy Blvd, Philadelphia, PA 19103. TEL 215-239-3900, FAX 215-238-7883, JournalCustomerService-usa@elsevier.com, http://www.elsevier.com. Ed. John French. Adv. contact Janine Castle TEL 44-1865-843844. Circ: 10,730.

616.07 HKG ISSN 0929-6441
R857.U48 CODEN: JMEUEV
JOURNAL OF MEDICAL ULTRASOUND. Text in English. 1993. q. EUR 210 in Europe to institutions; JPY 32,700 in Japan to institutions; USD 277 elsewhere to institutions (effective 2012). **Document type:** *Journal, Academic/Scholarly.* **Description:** Covers basic, experimental, and clinical sciences in the use of medical ultrasound. Includes original articles, case reports, brief communications, review articles, association news and announcements of meetings.
Related titles: Online - full text ed.: ISSN 2212-1552 (from ScienceDirect).
Indexed: B&BAb, B19, B21, BioEngAb, CA, EMBASE, ExcerpMed, P30, R10, Reac, SCOPUS, T02.
—BLDSC (5017.093000), IE, Ingenta. **CCC.**
Published by: (Society of Ultrasound in Medicine of the Republic of China TWN), Excerpta Medica Asia Ltd. (Subsidiary of: Elsevier Health Sciences), 17-F 8 Commercial Tower, 9 Sun Yip St, Chai Wan, Hong Kong. TEL 852-2965-1300, FAX 852-2976-0778, http://asia.elsevierhealth.com/pharma/. R&P Sindy Fok TEL 852-2965-1366. Circ: 4,800.

JOURNAL OF NEUROIMAGING. *see* MEDICAL SCIENCES—Psychiatry And Neurology

615.842 FRA ISSN 0150-9861
CODEN: JNEUD3
➤ **JOURNAL OF NEURORADIOLOGY/JOURNAL DE NEURORADIOLOGIE.** Text in English, French. 1974. 5/yr. EUR 433 in Europe to institutions; EUR 359.45 in France to institutions; JPY 65,900 in Japan to institutions; USD 563 elsewhere to institutions (effective 2012). adv. bk.rev. illus. reprints avail. **Document type:** *Journal, Academic/Scholarly.* **Description:** Covers all subjects common to neurology, neurosurgery, and general radiology.
Formerly (until Mar. 1978): Journal de Neuroradiologie (0335-0800)
Related titles: Microform ed.: (from PQC); Online - full text ed.: (from ScienceDirect).
Indexed: A22, ASCA, B21, B25, BDM&CN, BIOSIS Prev, CurCont, EMBASE, ExcerpMed, IndMed, Inpharma, MEDLINE, MycolAb, NSA, NSCI, P30, R10, Reac, SCI, SCOPUS, W07.
—BLDSC (5022.072000), GNLM, IE, Infotrieve, Ingenta, INIST. **CCC.**
Published by: (Societe Francaise de Neuroradiologie), Elsevier Masson (Subsidiary of: Elsevier Health Sciences), 62 Rue Camille Desmoulins, Issy les Moulineaux, Cedex 92442, France. TEL 33-1-71165500, infos@elsevier-masson.fr. Ed. Xavier Leclerc. Circ: 1,000.

616.07 539.2 JPN ISSN 1345-4749
JOURNAL OF NUCLEAR AND RADIOCHEMICAL SCIENCES. Text in English. 2000. a. **Document type:** *Journal, Academic/Scholarly.* **Description:** Covers all aspects of nuclear and radiochemistry and related fields.
Related titles: Online - full text ed.: 2000. free (effective 2011).
Indexed: A39, C27, C29, D03, D04, E13, INIS AtomInd, R14, S14, S15, S18.
—BLDSC (5022.848500).
Published by: Japan Society of Nuclear and Radiochemical Sciences, c/o JAERI, 2-4 Shirakata Shirane, Tokai, 319-1195, Japan. FAX 81-29-2826723, office@radiochem.org. Ed. Hisaaki Kudo.

616.1 USA ISSN 1071-3581
RC683.5.R33 CODEN: JNCAE2
➤ **JOURNAL OF NUCLEAR CARDIOLOGY.** Text in English. 1994. 6/yr. EUR 405, USD 607 combined subscription to institutions (print & online eds.) (effective 2012). adv. Supplement avail.; reprint service avail. from PSC. **Document type:** *Journal, Academic/Scholarly.* **Description:** Addresses all aspects of nuclear cardiology, including interpretation, diagnosis, radiopharmaceuticals, and imaging equipment.
Related titles: Online - full text ed.: ISSN 1532-6551 (from IngentaConnect).
Indexed: A22, A26, ASCA, C06, C07, CA, CurCont, E01, EMBASE, ExcerpMed, I05, ISR, IndMed, Inpharma, MEDLINE, P20, P22, P24, P30, P48, P54, PQC, R10, Reac, SCI, SCOPUS, T02, W07.
—BLDSC (5022.870000), GNLM, IE, Infotrieve, Ingenta, INIST. **CCC.**
Published by: (American Society of Nuclear Cardiology (ASNC)), Springer New York LLC (Subsidiary of: Springer Science+Business Media), 233 Spring St, New York, NY 10013. TEL 212-460-1500, FAX 212-460-1575, journals-ny@springer.com. Ed. George Beller. adv.: B&W page USD 1,330; trim 8.125 x 10.875. Circ: 6,499 (paid).

615.842 USA ISSN 0161-5505
RM845 CODEN: JNMEAQ
➤ **THE JOURNAL OF NUCLEAR MEDICINE.** Text in English. 1960. m. USD 268 combined subscription in US & Canada to individuals (print & online eds.); USD 369 combined subscription elsewhere to individuals (print & online eds.); USD 586 combined subscription in US & Canada to institutions (print & online eds.); USD 688 combined subscription elsewhere to institutions (print & online eds.); USD 58 per issue (effective 2011). adv. bk.rev. abstr.; bibl.; charts; illus. Index. 200 p./no.; back issues avail.; reprints avail. **Document type:** *Journal, Academic/Scholarly.* **Description:** Publishes papers in a wide range of areas in nuclear medicine and allied disciplines.
Incorporates: S N M Newsline; Former titles (until 1978): J N M (0097-9031); (until 1973): Journal of Nuclear Medicine (0097-9058)
Related titles: Microform ed.: (from PQC); Online - full text ed.: ISSN 1535-5667. USD 268 to individuals; USD 586 to institutions (effective 2011).
Indexed: A20, A22, A34, A35, A38, ASCA, AgBio, B&BAb, B19, B25, B27, BAS, BIOSIS Prev, CABA, ChemAb, ChemTitl, CurCont, EMBASE, ExcerpMed, FR, IDIS, IIL, INIS AtomInd, ISR, IndMed, IndVet, Inpharma, Inspec, Kidney, MEDLINE, MycolAb, P20, P22, P24, P26, P30, P35, P48, P52, P54, PQC, R10, Reac, SCI, SCOPUS, TM, VS, W07.
—BLDSC (5023.300000), AskIEEE, CASDDS, GNLM, IE, Ingenta, INIST. **CCC.**
Published by: Society of Nuclear Medicine, 1850 Samuel Morse Dr, Reston, VA 20190. TEL 703-708-9000, FAX 703-708-9015, Feedback@snm.org, http://www.snm.org. Eds. David Geffen, Dr. Heinrich R Schelbert.

616.07 USA ISSN 2155-9619
▼ ➤ **JOURNAL OF NUCLEAR MEDICINE & RADIATION THERAPY.** Text in English. 2010 (Oct.). bi-m. free (effective 2011). **Document type:** *Journal, Academic/Scholarly.* **Description:** Features medical research on nuclear medicine, molecular imaging, variant radiation therapies, precautions and radiation protection measures, involvement of risks and benefits in curing diseases and performing surgeries.
Media: Online - full text.
Published by: Omics Publishing Group, 5716 Corse Ave, Ste 110, Westlake, Los Angeles, CA 91362. TEL 650-268-9744, 800-216-6499, info@omicsonline.com, http://www.omicsonline.com.

615.8 USA ISSN 0091-4916
R895.A1 CODEN: JNMTB4
➤ **JOURNAL OF NUCLEAR MEDICINE TECHNOLOGY.** Abbreviated title: J N M T. Text in English. 1973. q. USD 117 combined subscription in US & Canada to individuals (print & online eds.); USD 126 combined subscription elsewhere to individuals (print & online eds.); USD 198 combined subscription in US & Canada to institutions (print & online eds.); USD 213 combined subscription elsewhere to institutions (print & online eds.); USD 58 per issue (effective 2011). adv. bk.rev. charts; illus. index. 75 p./no.; back issues avail.; reprints avail. **Document type:** *Journal, Academic/Scholarly.* **Description:** Focuses entirely on the technology crucial to nuclear medicine.
Related titles: Microform ed.: (from PQC); Online - full text ed.: ISSN 1535-5675. USD 117 to individuals; USD 198 to institutions (effective 2011).
Indexed: A22, B&BAb, B19, C06, C07, C08, CIN, CINAHL, ChemAb, ChemTitl, EMBASE, ExcerpMed, FR, IndMed, Inspec, MEDLINE, P20, P22, P24, P26, P30, P48, P52, P54, PQC, R10, Reac, SCOPUS.
—BLDSC (5023.340000), AskIEEE, CASDDS, GNLM, IE, Infotrieve, Ingenta, INIST. **CCC.**
Published by: Society of Nuclear Medicine, 1850 Samuel Morse Dr, Reston, VA 20190. TEL 703-708-9000, FAX 703-708-9015, Feedback@snm.org, http://www.snm.org. Ed. Frances L Neagley.

▼ ➤ **JOURNAL OF PEDIATRIC NEURORADIOLOGY.** *see* MEDICAL SCIENCES—Pediatrics

615 JPN ISSN 0449-3060
QH652.A1 CODEN: JRARAX
➤ **JOURNAL OF RADIATION RESEARCH.** Text in English. 1960. q. JPY 8,000, USD 95 to members. adv. bk.rev. **Document type:** *Journal, Academic/Scholarly.* **Description:** Publishes original articles in the field of radiation research, including studies in radiation physics, chemistry, biology, radioecology and medicine.
Formerly: Japan Radiation Research Society. Journal
Related titles: Online - full text ed.: ISSN 1349-9157. free (effective 2011).
Indexed: A22, A34, A35, A36, A38, A39, ASCA, ASFA, AgBio, AgrForAb, B21, B25, BIOSIS Prev, BPRC&P, C06, C07, C08, C25, C27, C29, C30, CABA, CIN, CINAHL, CTA, ChemAb, ChemTitl, ChemoAb, CurCont, D03, D04, DentInd, E12, E13, EMBASE, ESPM, ExcerpMed, F08, F11, F12, FCA, GH, H&SSA, H16, INIS AtomInd, ISR, IndMed, IndVet, Inpharma, Inspec, MEDLINE, MycolAb, N02, N03, N05, NSA, O01, P30, P32, P40, R07, R10, R11, R14, RA&MP, Reac, RiskAb, S13, S14, S15, S16, S17, S18, SCI, SCOPUS, SoyAb, T05, ToxAb, VS, W07, W10, W11.
—BLDSC (5043.800000), AskIEEE, CASDDS, GNLM, IE, Infotrieve, Ingenta, INIST, Linda Hall.
Published by: Japan Radiation Research Society, 4-9-1 Anagawa, Inage-ku, Chiba-shi, 263-0024, Japan. Ed. Mitsuo Ikenaga. Circ: 1,500. **Dist. by:** Business Center for Academic Societies Japan, 5-16-19 Honkomagome, Bunkyo-ku, Tokyo 113-0021, Japan. TEL 81-3-58145811.

➤ **JOURNAL OF RADIOLOGICAL PROTECTION.** *see* ENERGY—Nuclear Energy

616.07 USA ISSN 1943-0922
JOURNAL OF RADIOLOGY CASE REPORTS. Text in English. 2007. m. free (effective 2011). **Document type:** *Journal, Academic/Scholarly.*
Media: Online - full text.
Indexed: SCOPUS.
Published by: EduRad, 1228 Quilliams Rd, Cleveland Heights, OH 44121. journals@edurad.org, http://www.edurad.org. Ed. Roland Talanow.

JOURNAL OF RADIOLOGY NURSING. *see* MEDICAL SCIENCES—Nurses And Nursing

616.07 GBR ISSN 1460-3969
RC78
➤ **JOURNAL OF RADIOTHERAPY IN PRACTICE.** Text in English. 1999. q. GBP 255, USD 482 to institutions; GBP 265, USD 495 combined subscription to institutions (print & online eds.) (effective 2012). adv. back issues avail.; reprint service avail. from PSC. **Document type:** *Journal, Academic/Scholarly.* **Description:** Covers all of the current modalities specific to clinical oncology and radiotherapy. It also aims to encourage technical evaluations and case studies as well as equipment reviews that will be of interest to an international radiotherapy market.
Related titles: Online - full text ed.: ISSN 1467-1131. GBP 218, USD 422 to institutions (effective 2012).
Indexed: A22, C06, C07, E01, EMBASE, ExcerpMed, P20, P24, P30, P48, P52, P54, PQC, R10, Reac, SCOPUS.
—BLDSC (5044.700000), IE, Ingenta. **CCC.**
Published by: Cambridge University Press, The Edinburgh Bldg, Shaftesbury Rd, Cambridge, CB2 8RU, United Kingdom. TEL 44-1223-312393, FAX 44-1223-315052, journals@cambridge.org, http://www.cambridge.org/uk. Ed. Angela Duxbury. R&P Linda Nicol TEL 44-1223-325702. Adv. contact Rebecca Roberts TEL 44-1223-325083. B&W page GBP 425, B&W page USD 805, color page GBP 915, color page USD 1,735. **Subscr. in N. American to:** Cambridge University Press, 32 Ave of the Americas, New York, NY 10013. TEL 212-337-5000, FAX 212-691-3239, journals_subscriptions@cup.org

616.07 USA ISSN 2156-213X
▼ ➤ **JOURNAL OF SURGICAL RADIOLOGY.** Text in English. 2010. q. USD 18 per issue (effective 2010). adv. abstr.; bibl.; charts; illus.; stat. Index. back issues avail.; reprints avail. **Document type:** *Journal, Academic/Scholarly.* **Description:** Brings out scientific research, critical reviews, case reports, statistical compilations, descriptions of innovative methods or procedures, clinical studies, technological advances, and editorials in all areas of surgery and radiology.
Related titles: Online - full text ed.: ISSN 2156-4566. free (effective 2010).
Indexed: A01.
Published by: Surgisphere Corporation, 4706 Carmen Ln, Durham, NC 27707. TEL 888-837-8499, http://www.surgisphere.com. Ed. Cynthia Shortell. Pub., Adv. contact Sapan Desai. R&Ps Mark Shapiro, Sapan Desai. Circ: 24,000. **Dist. by:** Catalyst Publishers, 18 Moreland Ave., Staten Island, NY 10305. TEL 718-980-4734, editors@CatalystPublishers.com, http://www.catalystpublishers.com/.

900 USA ISSN 0883-5993
CODEN: JTIME8
➤ **JOURNAL OF THORACIC IMAGING.** Abbreviated title: J T I. Text in English. 1985. q. USD 692 domestic to institutions; USD 826 foreign to institutions (effective 2011). adv. illus. index. back issues avail.; reprints avail. **Document type:** *Journal, Academic/Scholarly.* **Description:** Provides information on all aspects of the use of imaging techniques in the diagnosis of chest disease.
Related titles: Microform ed.; Online - full text ed.: ISSN 1536-0237. USD 436.80 domestic academic site license; USD 486.80 foreign academic site license (effective 2002); USD 487.20 domestic corporate site license; USD 537.20 foreign corporate site license (effective 2002).
Indexed: A22, ASCA, C06, C07, CurCont, EMBASE, ExcerpMed, IIL, INIS AtomInd, IndMed, Inpharma, MEDLINE, P30, R10, Reac, SCI, SCOPUS, W07.
—BLDSC (5069.120000), GNLM, IE, Infotrieve, Ingenta, INIST. **CCC.**

Published by: (Society of Thoracic Radiology), Lippincott Williams & Wilkins (Subsidiary of: Wolters Kluwer N.V.), 333 7th Ave, 19th Fl, New York, NY 10001. TEL 646-674-6300, FAX 646-674-6500, customerservice@lww.com, http://www.lww.com. Ed. Phillip M Boiselle TEL 617-667-1636. Pub. Matthew Jozwiak. Adv. contact Miriam Terron-Elder TEL 646-674-6538. Circ: 849. **Co-sponsor:** Japanese Society of Thoracic Radiology.

615.842 ITA ISSN 1971-3495
R857.U48
JOURNAL OF ULTRASOUND. Text in Multiple languages. 1990. 4/yr. EUR 415 in Europe to institutions; JPY 65,700 in Japan to institutions; USD 622 elsewhere to institutions (effective 2012). adv. back issues avail.; reprints avail. **Document type:** *Journal, Academic/Scholarly.*
Description: Disseminates the results of clinical research and stimulates scientific cooperation within the field.
Former titles (until 2006): Giornale Italiano di Ecografia (1971-3509); (until 1998): Giornale Italiano di Ultrasonologia (1120-3846)
Related titles: Online - full text ed.: (from ScienceDirect).
Indexed: CA, EMBASE, ExcerpMed, R10, Reac, SCOPUS, T02.
—BLDSC (5071.454800), GNLM, IE. **CCC.**
Published by: (Societa Italiana di Ultrasonologia in Medicina e Biologia), Elsevier Masson (Subsidiary of: Elsevier Health Sciences), Via Paleocapa 7, Milan, 20121, Italy. TEL 39-02-881841, FAX 39-02-88184302, info@masson.it, http://www.masson.it. Circ: 3,000.

616.07 534 USA ISSN 0278-4297
CODEN: JUMEDA
➤ **JOURNAL OF ULTRASOUND IN MEDICINE.** Abbreviated title: J U M. Text in English. 1982. m. USD 450 combined subscription domestic to institutions (print & online eds.); USD 495 combined subscription in Canada & Mexico to institutions (print & online eds.); USD 510 combined subscription elsewhere to institutions (print & online eds.) (effective 2010). adv. bk.rev. abstr.; bibl.; charts; illus. index. back issues avail.; reprints avail. **Document type:** *Journal, Academic/Scholarly.* **Description:** Contains basic and clinical aspects of ultrasound, advances in the field, appropriate techniques and equipment modifications.
Related titles: Microform ed.: (from PQC); Online - full text ed.: ISSN 1550-9613. USD 50 (effective 2010).
Indexed: A22, A34, A35, A36, A38, ASCA, B&BAb, B19, C06, C07, CABA, CPEI, CurCont, D01, DentInd, EMBASE, EngInd, ExcerpMed, FR, GH, H17, IBR, IBZ, IIL, ISR, IndMed, IndVet, Inpharma, MEDLINE, N02, N03, P30, P33, P37, R10, R12, RM&VM, Reac, SCI, SCOPUS, T05, TM, VS, W07.
—BLDSC (5071.455000), GNLM, IE, Infotrieve, Ingenta, INIST. **CCC.**
Published by: American Institute for Ultrasound in Medicine, 14750 Sweitzer Ln, Ste 100, Laurel, MD 20707. TEL 301-498-4100, 800-638-5352, FAX 301-498-4450, publications@aium.org, http://www.aium.org. Ed. Dr. Beryl R Benacerraf. Circ: 8,500.

615.842 USA ISSN 1051-0443
RD33.55 CODEN: JVIRE3
➤ **JOURNAL OF VASCULAR AND INTERVENTIONAL RADIOLOGY.** Abbreviated title: J V I R(Journal of Vascular and Interventional Radiology). Text in English. 1990. m. USD 641 in United States to institutions; USD 662 elsewhere to institutions (effective 2012). adv. bk.rev. back issues avail.; reprints avail. **Document type:** *Journal, Academic/Scholarly.* **Description:** Covers all aspects of medical, minimally-invasive, radiological, pathological, and socioeconomic issues of importance to vascular and interventional radiologists.
Related titles: Microform ed.: (from PQC); Online - full text ed.: ISSN 1535-7732 (from ScienceDirect).
Indexed: A22, ASCA, B&BAb, B19, C06, C07, CA, CurCont, EMBASE, ExcerpMed, IIL, ISR, IndMed, Inpharma, MEDLINE, P30, P35, R10, Reac, SCI, SCOPUS, T02, W07.
—BLDSC (5072.263000), GNLM, IE, Infotrieve, Ingenta, INIST. **CCC.**
Published by: (Society of Cardiovascular and Interventional Radiology), Elsevier Inc. (Subsidiary of: Elsevier Science & Technology), 1600 John F Kennedy Blvd, Philadelphia, PA 19103. TEL 215-239-3900, FAX 215-238-7883, JournalCustomerService-usa@elsevier.com, http://www.elsevier.com. Ed. Albert A Nemcek. Adv. contact Michael Targowski TEL 212-633-3693. Circ: 5,010.

615.842 CAN ISSN 0022-7439
K V P NEWS. Text in English. 1964. q. membership. adv. charts; illus. **Document type:** *Newsletter.*
Media: Duplicated (not offset).
Published by: Manitoba Association of Medical Radiation Technologists Inc., 215 819 Sargent Ave, Winnipeg, MB R3E 0B9, Canada. TEL 204-774-5346. Ed. L Wills. Circ: 800.

615.8 JPN ISSN 0022-7854
CODEN: KAIGBZ
KAKU IGAKU/JAPANESE JOURNAL OF NUCLEAR MEDICINE. Variant title: Nihon Kaku Igakkai Kikanshi. Text in Japanese; Summaries in English, Japanese. 1964. 12/yr. Subscr. incld. with membership. adv. abstr.; charts; illus. Index. **Document type:** *Journal, Academic/Scholarly.*
Indexed: A22, B25, BIOSIS Prev, CIN, ChemAb, ChemTitl, EMBASE, ExcerpMed, INIS AtomInd, IndMed, Inspec, JTA, MEDLINE, MycolAb, P30, R10, Reac, SCOPUS.
—CASDDS, GNLM, IE, Infotrieve, Ingenta. **CCC.**
Published by: Nihon Kaku Igakkai/Japanese Society of Nuclear Medicine, c/o Japan Radioisotope Association, 2-28-45 Honkomagome, Bunkyo-ku, Tokyo, 113-0021, Japan. TEL 81-3-39470976, FAX 81-3-39472535, jsnm@mtj.biglobe.ne.jp, http://www.jsnm.org/index.html. Ed. Dr. S Hashimoto.

615.842 JPN ISSN 0912-4195
KAKU IGAKU GAZO SHINDAN/IMAGING DIAGNOSIS IN NUCLEAR MEDICINE. Text in Japanese. 1986. 3/yr.
Published by: Hokuriku Kaku Igaku Kanfarensu/Hokuriku Nuclear Medicine Conference, c/o Kanazawa University, Cancer Research Institute, 13-1, Takara-machi, Kanazawa, Ishikawa 920-0934, Japan.

615.8 JPN ISSN 0289-100X
CODEN: KIGIEM
KAKU IGAKU GIJUTSU/JAPANESE JOURNAL OF NUCLEAR MEDICINE TECHNOLOGY. Text in Japanese. 1981. q.
Indexed: ChemAb, ChemTitl, INIS AtomInd.
—CASDDS. **CCC.**
Published by: Nihon Kaku Igaku Gijutsu Gakkai/Japanese Society of Nuclear Medicine Technology, Asupekku Tenmabashi 403, Tenma 1-18-19, kita-ku, Osaka, 530-0043, Japan. jsnmt-office@umin.ac.jp, http://www.jsnmt.umin.ne.jp/.

615.8 JPN ISSN 0910-2213
KAKU IGAKU SHOREI KENTOKAI SHOREISHU/MEETING ON CASE OF NUCLEAR MEDICINE. PROCEEDINGS. Text in Japanese. 1979. q. **Document type:** *Proceedings, Academic/Scholarly.*
Published by: Nihon Mejifijikkusu K.K./Japan Mediphysics Co., Ltd., 9-8 Roku-Tanji-cho, Nishinomiya-shi, Hyogo-ken 662-0918, Japan. http://www.nmp.co.jp/.

616.07 JPN ISSN 1882-5087
KAN TAN SUI GAZOU/HEPATO-BILIARY-PANCREATIC IMAGING. Text in Japanese. 1999. bi-m. JPY 21,420; JPY 27,900 combined subscription (effective 2010). **Document type:** *Journal, Academic/Scholarly.*
Formerly (until 2008): Shokaki Gazo/Journal of Gastroenterological Imaging (1344-3399)
Related titles: Online - full text ed.: ISSN 1882-5095.
Published by: Igaku Shoin Ltd., 1-28-36 Hongo, Bunkyo-ku, Tokyo, 113-8719, Japan. TEL 81-3-3817-5600, FAX 81-3-3815-7791, info@igaku-shoin.co.jp.

616.075 JPN
KISO GIJUTSU KENKYU BUKAI SHIRYO/TECHNICAL REPORT OF MEDICAL ULTRASOUND ENGINEERING. Text in English, Japanese. 1986. irreg. free. **Document type:** *Proceedings.*
Published by: Nihon Choonpa Igakkai/Japan Society of Ultrasonic Medicine, 23-1 Hongo 3-chome, Bunkyo-ku, Tokyo, 113-0033, Japan. Ed. Iwaki Akiyama.

616.07 JPN
KONICA MINOLTA MEDICAL NETWORK/KONICA X-RAY PHOTOGRAPHIC REVIEW. Text in Japanese. 1950. bi-m. **Document type:** *Trade.*
Former titles (until 2004): Konica Medical Network (1346-7123); (until 2001): Konika X-rei Shashin Kenkyu (0914-871X); (until 1987): Sakura X-rei Shashin Kenkyu/Sakura X-ray Photographic Review (0386-4537)
Related titles: Online - full text ed.
Published by: Konica Minolta, 1-6-1 Marunouchi, Chiyoda-ku, Tokyo, 100-0005, Japan.

616.07 KOR ISSN 1229-6929
KOREAN JOURNAL OF RADIOLOGY. Text in English. 2000. q. KRW 10,000 domestic; USD 20 foreign (effective 2009). back issues avail. **Document type:** *Journal, Academic/Scholarly.* **Description:** Covers clinical radiology and allied sciences, containing original studies, review articles, pictorial essays, perspectives, and case reports.
Related titles: Online - full content ed.: ISSN 2005-8330. 2002. free (effective 2011).
Indexed: CurCont, EMBASE, ExcerpMed, INIS AtomInd, MEDLINE, P30, R10, Reac, SCI, SCOPUS, W07.
—BLDSC (5113.574550), IE, Ingenta.
Published by: Korean Society of Radiology, 69, Yangjaecheon-gil, Seocho-gu, Seoul, 137-891, Korea, S. TEL 82-2-5788003, FAX 82-2-5297113, office@radiology.or.kr, http://www.radiology.or.kr/. Ed. Dr. Kyung Soo Lee.

616.07 CHN ISSN 1008-6978
LINCHUANG CHAOSHENG YIXUE ZAZHI/JOURNAL OF ULTRASOUND IN CLINICAL MEDICINE. Text in Chinese. 1988. m. CNY 12 newsstand/cover (effective 2006). **Document type:** *Journal, Academic/Scholarly.*
Related titles: Online - full text ed.
—BLDSC (5220.196000).
Published by: Chongqing Yike Daxue Di-2 Linchuang Xueyuan/Second Clinical College of Chongqing Medical University, 74, Linjiang Lu, Chongqing, 400010, China. TEL 86-23-63811304, FAX 86-23-63811304. Ed. Hao Yang.

616.07 CHN ISSN 1001-9324
LINCHUANG FANGSHEXUE ZAZHI/JOURNAL OF CLINICAL RADIOLOGY. Text in Chinese. 1982. m. USD 74.40 (effective 2009). **Document type:** *Journal, Academic/Scholarly.*
Related titles: Online - full text ed.
—East View.
Published by: Hubei Sheng Huangshi Shi Yixue Keji Qingbaosuo, 23-22, Hangzhou Lu, Huangshi, 435000, China. TEL 86-714-6222015, FAX 86-714-6260655. **Dist. by:** China International Book Trading Corp, 35 Chegongzhuang Xilu, Haidian District, PO Box 399, Beijing 100044, China. TEL 86-10-68412045, FAX 86-10-68412023, cibtc@mail.cibtc.com.cn, http://www.cibtc.com.cn.

616 USA ISSN 1059-2156
LIPPINCOTT'S REVIEWS. RADIOLOGY. Text in English. 1992. irreg. **Document type:** *Monographic series, Academic/Scholarly.*
—CCC.
Published by: Lippincott Williams & Wilkins (Subsidiary of: Wolters Kluwer N.V.), 530 Walnut St, Philadelphia, PA 19106. TEL 215-521-8300, FAX 215-521-8902, customerservice@lww.com, http://www.lww.com.

615.845 616.07 USA
CODEN: MEEQA
M E E N IMAGING TECHNOLOGY NEWS. (Medical Electronics and Equipment News) Text in English. 1961. 9/yr. free domestic to qualified personnel; USD 120 in Canada; USD 150 elsewhere (effective 2011). adv. bk.rev. abstr.; charts; illus.; stat.; tr.lit. back issues avail. **Document type:** *Magazine, Trade.* **Description:** Keeps users and buyers of medical imaging technology and services apprised of the latest technology available.
Supersedes in part (in 2000): Medical Electronics and Equipment News (0361-4174); Which was formerly (until 197?): Medical Electronics News (0025-7230)
—GNLM, IE.
Published by: Reilly Communications Group, 16 E Schaumburg Rd, Schaumburg, IL 60194. TEL 847-882-0631, FAX 847-519-0166, info@rcgpubs.com, http://www.reillycomm.com. Ed. Dave Fornell TEL 847-954-7962. Pub. Sean Reilly TEL 847-954-7960. Adv. contact Stephanie A Ellis TEL 847-954-7959.

615.842 USA ISSN 0730-725X
RC78.7.N83 CODEN: MRIMDQ
➤ **MAGNETIC RESONANCE IMAGING.** Abbreviated title: M R I. Text in English. 1982. 10/yr. USD 2,119 in United States to institutions; USD 2,381 elsewhere to institutions (effective 2012). adv. bk.rev. back issues avail.; reprints avail. **Document type:** *Journal, Academic/Scholarly.* **Description:** Covers all aspects of physical, life, and clinical science investigations as they relate to the development and use of magnetic resonance imaging.
Incorporates (1982-1992): Reviews of Magnetic Resonance in Medicine (0883-8291)
Related titles: Microfilm ed.: (from PQC); Online - full text ed.: ISSN 1873-5894 (from IngentaConnect, ScienceDirect).
Indexed: A01, A03, A08, A20, A22, A26, A34, A36, A37, A38, ASCA, B&BAb, B19, B21, BIOBASE, BioEngAb, C25, C30, CA, CABA, CIN, ChemAb, ChemTitl, CurCont, D01, E12, EMBASE, ExcerpMed, FS&TA, GH, H16, I05, I11, IABS, INIS AtomInd, ISR, IndMed, Inpharma, Inspec, MEDLINE, N02, N03, NSA, P30, P32, P33, P39, P40, PHN&I, R10, Reac, S01, S13, S16, S17, SCI, SCOPUS, SoyAb, T02, T05, TM, TriticAb, VS, W07.
—BLDSC (5337.795000), AskIEEE, CASDDS, GNLM, IE, Infotrieve, Ingenta, INIST. **CCC.**
Published by: Elsevier Inc. (Subsidiary of: Elsevier Science & Technology), 1600 John F Kennedy Blvd, Philadelphia, PA 19103. TEL 215-239-3900, FAX 215-238-7883, JournalCustomerService-usa@elsevier.com, http://www.elsevier.com. Ed. Dr. John C Gore TEL 615-322-7889. Pub. Herb Niemirow TEL 212-633-3141. Adv. contact Pat Hampton TEL 212-633-3181.

M

616.842 USA ISSN 1064-9689
RC78.7.N83 CODEN: MRIAFQ
MAGNETIC RESONANCE IMAGING CLINICS OF NORTH AMERICA. Spine title: M R I Clinics. Text in English. 1993. q. USD 501 in United States to institutions; USD 628 elsewhere to institutions (effective 2012). adv. back issues avail.; reprints avail. **Document type:** *Journal, Academic/Scholarly.* **Description:** Focuses on a single topic relevant to your MRI practice, from imaging of the shoulder to the latest advances in genitourinary MR imaging.
Related titles: Microform ed.: (from PQC); Online - full text ed.: ISSN 1557-9786 (from ScienceDirect); Supplement(s): Continuing Medical Education Supplement to Magnetic Resonance Imaging Clinics of North America. ISSN 1557-8178. USD 138 (effective 2000).
Indexed: A22, C06, C07, C08, CINAHL, CurCont, EMBASE, ExcerpMed, IIL, INI, IndMed, MEDLINE, P30, R10, Reac, SCI, SCOPUS, SD, W07.
—BLDSC (5337.796000), GNLM, IE, Infotrieve, Ingenta. **CCC.**
Published by: W.B. Saunders Co. (Subsidiary of: Elsevier Health Sciences), Elsevier, Health Sciences Division, Order Fulfillment, 3251 Riverport Ln, Maryland Heights, MO 63043. TEL 314-872-8370, 800-325-4177, FAX 314-432-1380, JournalCustomerService-usa@elsevier.com, http://www.us.elsevierhealth.com. Adv. contact John Marmero TEL 212-633-3657.

616.07 JPN ISSN 1347-3182
RC78.7N83 CODEN: MRMSCT
MAGNETIC RESONANCE IN MEDICAL SCIENCES. Text in English. 2002. q. **Document type:** *Journal, Academic/Scholarly.*
Related titles: Online - full content ed.; Online - full text ed.: ISSN 1880-2206.
Indexed: B&BAb, B19, B21, EMBASE, ExcerpMed, MEDLINE, NSA, P30, R10, Reac, SCOPUS.
—BLDSC (5337.797500). **CCC.**
Published by: Nihon Jiki Kyomei Igakkai/Japanese Society of Magnetic Resonance in Medicine, Gotanda Park Side Bldg 4F, 5-24-9 Higashi-gotanda Shinagawa-ku, Tokyo, 141-0022, Japan. TEL 81-3-34438622, FAX 81-3-34438733, http://www.jsmrm.jp/.

615.842 USA ISSN 0740-3194
RC78.7.N83 CODEN: MRMEEN
➤ **MAGNETIC RESONANCE IN MEDICINE.** Text in English. 1984. m. GBP 1,514 in United Kingdom to institutions; EUR 1,915 in Europe to institutions; USD 2,714 in United States to institutions; USD 2,966 elsewhere to institutions; GBP 1,743 combined subscription in United Kingdom to institutions (print & online eds.); EUR 2,204 combined subscription in Europe to institutions (print & online eds.); USD 3,121 combined subscription in United States to institutions (print & online eds.); USD 3,373 combined subscription elsewhere to institutions (print & online eds.) (effective 2012). adv. index. back issues avail.; reprint service avail. from PSC. **Document type:** *Journal, Academic/Scholarly.* **Description:** Publishes original investigations concerned with all aspects of the development and use of nuclear magnetic resonance and electron paramagnetic resonance techniques for medical applications.
Related titles: CD-ROM ed.; Online - full text ed.: ISSN 1522-2594. GBP 1,385 in United Kingdom to institutions; EUR 1,752 in Europe to institutions; USD 2,714 elsewhere to institutions (effective 2012).
Indexed: A22, ASCA, B&BAb, B19, B21, B25, BIOSIS Prev, BioEngAb, CIN, ChemAb, ChemTitl, CurCont, EMBASE, ExcerpMed, IIL, INIS AtomInd, ISR, IndMed, Inpharma, Inspec, MEDLINE, MycolAb, P30, R10, Reac, SCI, SCOPUS, T02, TM, W07.
—BLDSC (5337.798000), AskIEEE, CASDDS, GNLM, IE, Infotrieve, Ingenta, INIST. **CCC.**
Published by: (International Society of Magnetic Resonance), John Wiley & Sons, Inc., 111 River St, Hoboken, NJ 07030. TEL 201-748-6000, FAX 201-748-6088, info@wiley.com, http://www.wiley.com/WileyCDA/. Ed. Michael B Smith. Adv. contact Stephen Donohue TEL 781-388-8511. Circ: 766. **Subscr. outside the Americas to:** John Wiley & Sons Ltd., The Atrium, Southern Gate, Chichester, West Sussex PO19 8SQ, United Kingdom. TEL 44-1243-779777, 800-243407, FAX 44-1243-775878, cs-journals@wiley.com.

615.842 NZL ISSN 1178-623X
RC78.A1
➤ **MAGNETIC RESONANCE INSIGHTS.** Text in English. 2008. irreg. free (effective 2011). **Document type:** *Journal, Academic/Scholarly.*
Media: Online - full text.
Indexed: A01, P30, T02.
—CCC.
Published by: Libertas Academica Ltd., PO Box 302-624, North Harbour, Auckland, 1330, New Zealand. TEL 64-21-662617, FAX 64-21-740006, editorial@la-press.com. Ed. Sendhil Velan.

➤ **MAGNETIC RESONANCE MATERIALS IN PHYSICS, BIOLOGY AND MEDICINE.** *see* PHYSICS—Nuclear Physics

615.842 HUN ISSN 0025-0287
RM845 CODEN: MARAAF
MAGYAR RADIOLOGIA/JOURNAL OF HUNGARIAN RADIOLOGY. Text in Hungarian, English. 1949. 6/yr. adv. bk.rev. bibl. index. **Document type:** *Journal, Academic/Scholarly.* **Description:** Devoted to all fields of clinical radiology and allied sciences. Publishes scientific papers and informs members of the society about news and events.
Indexed: ChemAb, IndMed, P30.
—GNLM, INIST.

Published by: Magyar Radiologusok Tarsasaga/Society of Hungarian Radiologists, Pf 188, Miskolc, 3501, Hungary. TEL 36-46-321211, FAX 36-46-351018, radiologia@doki.net, http://www.socrad.hu. Ed. Bela Lombay. Circ: 700.

616.07 FRA ISSN 1960-1824
MANIP INFO; le magazine des manipulateurs radio. Variant title: Manipulateurs Info. Text in French. 2007. m. EUR 60 to qualified personnel; EUR 40 to students (effective 2008). **Document type:** *Magazine, Trade.*
Published by: B O M Presse Sarl, 3 Rue Paul Valery, Le Soler, 66270, France. TEL 33-9-62249917, 33-9-62249917.

616.07575 FRA ISSN 0928-1258
R895.A1 CODEN: MNIMEX
➤ **MEDECINE NUCLEAIRE**; imagerie fonctionelle et metabolique. Text in French; Summaries in English, French. 1967. 12/yr. EUR 228 in Europe to institutions; EUR 206.66 in France to institutions; JPY 51,000 in Japan to institutions; USD 300 elsewhere to institutions (effective 2012). adv. **Document type:** *Journal, Academic/Scholarly.* **Description:** Emphasizes current nuclear medicine practices in vivo, including clinical practice, methodology and instrumentation, signal processing, and fundamental and applied biophysics.
Former titles (until 1993): Journal de Medecine Nucleaire et Biophysique (0992-3039); (until 1988): Journal de Biophysique et de Biomecanique (0766-5717); (until 1985): Journal de Biophysique et Medecine Nucleaire (0243-3354); (until 1980): Journal Francais de Biophysique et Medecine Nucleaire (0399-0435); Annales de Physique Biologique et Medicale (0029-0793)
Related titles: Online - full text ed.: (from IngentaConnect, ScienceDirect).
Indexed: A22, ASCA, ChemAb, EMBASE, ExcerpMed, INIS AtomInd, ISR, Inspec, R10, Reac, SCI, SCOPUS, W07.
—BLDSC (5487.920000), AskIEEE, CASDDS, GNLM, IE, Infotrieve, Ingenta, INIST. **CCC.**
Published by: (Societe Francaise de Biophysique et Medecine Nucleaire), Elsevier Masson (Subsidiary of: Elsevier Health Sciences), 62 Rue Camille Desmoulins, Issy les Moulineaux, Cedex 92442, France. TEL 33-1-71165500, FAX 33-1-71165600, infos@elsevier-masson.fr, http://www.elsevier-masson.fr. Ed. J-L Baulieu.

615.842 NLD
MEDICA MUNDI; a review of modern healthcare solutions. Text in German. 1951. s-a. **Document type:** *Magazine, Trade.*
Former titles (until 2001): Kontraste (0942-7112); (until 1992): Roentgenstrahlen (0485-3547)
Published by: Philips Healthcare, PO Box 10000, Best, 5680 DA, Netherlands. TEL 49-7031-4632254, FAX 49-40-417353, michel.rodzynek@philips.com, http://www.healthcare.philips.com.

615 USA ISSN 0958-3947
QC795.32.R3 CODEN: MEDOEJ
➤ **MEDICAL DOSIMETRY.** Text in English. 1984. q. USD 599 in United States to institutions; USD 667 elsewhere to institutions (effective 2012). adv. back issues avail.; reprints avail. **Document type:** *Journal, Academic/Scholarly.* **Description:** Features contributions and review articles by medical dosimetrists, oncologists, physicists, and radiation therapy technologists on clinical applications and techniques of external beam, interstitial, intracavitary and intraluminal irradiation in cancer management.
Former titles (until 1987): American Association of Medical Dosimetrists. Journal (0739-0211); (until 198?): Treatment planning; American Association of Medical Dosimetrists. Newsletter
Related titles: Microfilm ed.: (from PQC); Online - full text ed.: ISSN 1873-4022 (from IngentaConnect, ScienceDirect).
Indexed: A01, A03, A08, A22, CA, CurCont, EMBASE, ExcerpMed, INI, IndMed, Inspec, MEDLINE, P30, R10, Reac, SCI, SCOPUS, T02, W07.
—BLDSC (5527.130000), GNLM, IE, Infotrieve, Ingenta, INIST. **CCC.**
Published by: (American Association of Medical Dosimetrists), Elsevier Inc. (Subsidiary of: Elsevier Science & Technology), 1600 John F Kennedy Blvd, Philadelphia, PA 19103. TEL 215-239-3900, FAX 215-238-7883, JournalCustomerService-usa@elsevier.com, http://www.elsevier.com. Ed. Lon Marsh. Adv. contact Gene Conselyea TEL 732-970-0220. Circ: 2,135.

616.07 NLD ISSN 1361-8415
R857.O6 CODEN: MIAECY
➤ **MEDICAL IMAGE ANALYSIS.** Text in English. 1996. 6/yr. EUR 938 in Europe to institutions; JPY 124,500 in Japan to institutions; USD 1,051 elsewhere to institutions (effective 2012). back issues avail. **Document type:** *Journal, Academic/Scholarly.* **Description:** Provides a forum for the dissemination of new research results in the field of medical image analysis, with special emphasis on efforts related to the application of computer vision, virtual reality and robotics to medical imaging problems.
Related titles: Online - full text ed.: ISSN 1361-8423 (from IngentaConnect, ScienceDirect).
Indexed: A01, A03, A08, A22, A26, B&BAb, B19, B21, BioEngAb, CA, CPEI, CurCont, E01, EMBASE, EngInd, ExcerpMed, I05, ISR, IndMed, Inspec, MEDLINE, P30, R10, Reac, SCI, SCOPUS, T02, W07.
—BLDSC (5527.537000), IE, Infotrieve, Ingenta. **CCC.**
Published by: Elsevier BV (Subsidiary of: Elsevier Science & Technology), Radarweg 29, PO Box 211, Amsterdam, 1000 AE, Netherlands. TEL 31-20-4853911, FAX 31-20-4852457, JournalsCustomerServiceEMEA@elsevier.com, http://www.elsevier.nl. Eds. Dr. James Duncan, Dr. Nicholas Ayache.

➤ **MEDICAL IMAGING BUSINESS WEEK.** *see* BUSINESS AND ECONOMICS

615.842 616.07 GBR
MEDICAL IMAGING HORIZONS. Text in English. 19??. a. adv.
Published by: Quasar International Communications Ltd. (Subsidiary of: Sterling Publishing Group Plc.), Brunel House, 55-57 North Wharf Rd, London, W2 1LA, United Kingdom. TEL 44-20-79159660, FAX 44-20-77242089, Info@SPGmedia.com. adv.: color page GBP 7,900, B&W page GBP 6,600.

616.07 USA ISSN 1551-5168
MEDICAL IMAGING LAW WEEKLY. Text in English. 2004. w. USD 2,295 in US & Canada; USD 2,495 elsewhere; USD 2,525 combined subscription in US & Canada (print & online eds.); USD 2,755 combined subscription elsewhere (print & online eds.) (effective 2008). back issues avail. **Document type:** *Newsletter, Trade.*
Related titles: E-mail ed.; Online - full text ed.: ISSN 1551-515X. USD 2,295 combined subscription (online & email eds.); single user (effective 2008).
Indexed: L10, P10, P21, P48, P53, P54, PQC.
Published by: NewsRx, 2727 Paces Ferry Rd SE, Ste 2-440, Atlanta, GA 30339. TEL 770-435-8286, 800-726-4550, FAX 770-435-6800, pressrelease@newsrx.com. Pub. Susan Hasty TEL 770-507-7777.

615 JPN ISSN 0288-450X
➤ **MEDICAL IMAGING TECHNOLOGY.** Text in English, Japanese. 1983. 6/yr. free to members. adv. **Document type:** *Journal, Academic/Scholarly.* **Description:** Covers all kinds of medical image processing and pattern recognition technologies, including images of conventional X-ray, ultrasound, CT, MRI, nuclear medicine, endoscopy, microscopy, histology, cytology, telemedicine and more.
Related titles: Online - full text ed.
Indexed: A22, B&BAb, INIS AtomInd, Inspec.
—BLDSC (5527.542000), AskIEEE, IE, Ingenta. **CCC.**
Published by: Nihon Iyo Gazo Kogakkai/Japanese Society of Medical Imaging Technology, c/o Quantum, YU Bldg, 3F, 3-19-6, Hongou, Bunkyo-ku, Tokyo, 113-0033, Japan. TEL 81-3-5684-1636, FAX 81-3-5684-1650, QYP06453@nifty.ne.jp, http://www.jamit.jp/index-j.html.

615.9 USA ISSN 1552-9355
MEDICAL IMAGING WEEK. Text in English. 2004. w. USD 2,295 in US & Canada; USD 2,495 elsewhere; USD 2,525 combined subscription in US & Canada (print & online eds.); USD 2,755 combined subscription elsewhere (print & online eds.) (effective 2008). back issues avail. **Document type:** *Newsletter, Trade.*
Related titles: E-mail ed.; Online - full text ed.: ISSN 1552-9363. USD 2,295 combined subscription (online & email eds.); single user (effective 2008).
Indexed: H13, P10, P20, P21, P24, P48, P53, P54, PQC.
Published by: NewsRx, 2727 Paces Ferry Rd SE, Ste 2-440, Atlanta, GA 30339. TEL 770-435-8286, 800-726-4550, FAX 770-435-6800, pressrelease@newsrx.com, http://www.newsrx.com. Pub. Susan Hasty TEL 770-507-7777.

615.842 USA ISSN 0942-5373
CODEN: MERAED
MEDICAL RADIOLOGY. Text in English. 1963. irreg., latest 2010. price varies. reprints avail. **Document type:** *Monographic series, Academic/Scholarly.*
Formerly (until 1985): Handbuch der Medizinischen Radiologie (0085-1396)
—CCC.
Published by: Springer New York LLC (Subsidiary of: Springer Science+Business Media), 233 Spring St, New York, NY 10013. TEL 212-460-1500, FAX 212-460-1575, service-ny@springer.com.

610 USA
MEDICAL TESTS SOURCEBOOK. Text in English. 1999. irreg., latest 3rd ed. USD 84 3rd ed. (effective 2008). charts. Index. **Document type:** *Magazine, Consumer.* **Description:** Basic consumer health information about medical tests.
Published by: Omnigraphics, Inc., PO Box 31-1640, Detroit, MI 48231. TEL 313-961-1340, 800-234-1340, FAX 313-961-1383, 800-875-1340, info@omnigraphics.com. Eds. Joyce Brennfleck Shannon, Karen Bellenir.

616.075 ROM ISSN 1844-4172
RC78.7.U4
MEDICAL ULTRASONOGRAPHY; an international journal of clinical imaging. Text in English. 1999. q. **Description:** Aims to promote ultrasound diagnosis by publishing papers that deal with fundamental and clinical research, scientific reviews, clinical case reports, records of progress in ultrasound physics or in the field of medical technology and equipment, as well as methodological and educational papers.
Formerly (until 2008): Revista Romana de Ultrasonografie (1454-5829)
Related titles: Online - full text ed.: ISSN 2066-8643.
Indexed: A01, MEDLINE, P20, P22, P24, P30, P48, P52, P54, PQC, T02.
—BLDSC (5532.082000), IE.
Published by: Societatea Romana de Ultrasonografie in Medicina si Biologie/Romanian Society for Ultrasonography in Medicine and Biology, 3rd Medical Clinic, Str Croitorilor no. 19-21, Cluj-Napoca, Romania. TEL 40-264-534241, FAX 40-264-534241, inabotar@yahoo.com, http://www.srumb.ro. Eds. Radu I Badea, Sorin M Dudea, Petru A Mircea.

615.842 NLD ISSN 0025-7664
CODEN: MEMUAA
➤ **MEDICAMUNDI.** Text in English; Summaries in English, French, German, Spanish. 1955. 3/yr. free to qualified personnel. adv. charts; illus.; stat. index. **Document type:** *Journal, Academic/Scholarly.* **Description:** Covers modern diagnostic imaging.
Related titles: Online - full text ed.: ISSN 1611-4191.
Indexed: A22, ChemAb, EMBASE, ExcerpMed, INIS AtomInd, IndMed, Inspec, P30, R10, Reac, SCOPUS.
—BLDSC (5532.300000), AskIEEE, CASDDS, GNLM, IE, Infotrieve, Ingenta.
Published by: Philips Healthcare, PO Box 10000, Best, 5680 DA, Netherlands. TEL 49-7031-4632254. Ed. E O'Lionaird. Circ: 12,000 (controlled).

615.842 RUS ISSN 1024-6177
RM845 CODEN: MRRBE5
MEDITSINSKAYA RADIOLOGIYA I RADIATSIONNAYA BEZOPASNOST'. Text in Russian; Summaries in English. 1956. bi-m. EUR 96 foreign (effective 2007). bk.rev. index. **Document type:** *Journal, Academic/Scholarly.* **Description:** Publishes papers devoted to pathogenesis, clinical picture, prevention and treatment of radiation injuries in man. Includes information on radiological conferences and congresses held in Russia and abroad.
Formerly: Meditsinskaya Radiologiya (0025-8334)
Indexed: ASFA, C&ISA, CIN, ChemAb, ChemTitl, DBA, DentInd, E&CAJ, INIS AtomInd, IndMed, Inspec, P30, RefZh, SCOPUS, SolStAb.
—AskIEEE, CASDDS, East View, GNLM, INIST. **CCC.**
Published by: (Akademiya Meditsinskikh Nauk Rossii/Russian Academy of Medical Sciences), Izdatel'stvo Radekon, Kashirskoe shosse 24, Moscow, 115478, Russian Federation. TEL 7-095-1118375, FAX 7-095-3241670. Ed. G A Zedgenidze.

616.075 POL ISSN 1429-4966
MEDYCYNA PRAKTYCZNA. ULTRASONOGRAFIA. Text in Polish. 1997. q. PLZ 80 (effective 2000).
Published by: Medycyna Praktyczna, ul Krakowska 41, Krakow, 31066, Poland. TEL 48-12-4305520, FAX 48-12-4305536, listy@mp.pl, http://www.mp.pl. Ed. Aleksandra Plichta.

616.9897 UKR
CODEN: IJRMF7
MEZHDUNARODNYI ZHURNAL RADIATSIONNOI MEDITSINY. Text in Russian. 1999. q. bk.rev.; film rev.; software rev. bibl.; illus. **Document type:** *Journal, Academic/Scholarly.* **Description:** Examines the mechanisms of radiation injuries development, the dose-effect relationship; assesses the risk of stochastic and deterministic effects as well as improvement of population protection against chronic internal and external irradiation (i.e. aftermath of Chernobyl accident).
Related titles: English ed.: International Journal of Radiation Medicine. ISSN 1562-1154.
Indexed: INIS AtomInd.
Published by: (Assotsiatsiya Vrachi Chernobylya/Doctors of Chernobyl Association), Morion LLC, pr-kt M Bazhana, 10A, Kyiv, 02140, Ukraine. public@morion.kiev.ua, http://www.morion.kiev.ua. Ed., Pub. Angelina I Nyagu. Circ: 3,000 (controlled).

615.842 USA ISSN 1536-1632
CODEN: CPIMF6
➤ **MOLECULAR IMAGING AND BIOLOGY.** Text in Dutch, English. 1998. bi-m. EUR 582, USD 728 combined subscription to institutions (print & online eds.) (effective 2012). back issues avail.; reprint service avail. from PSC. **Document type:** *Journal, Academic/Scholarly.* **Description:** Provides a forum for the presentation of the latest research on clinical applications of positron imaging.
Formerly (until 2002): Clinical Positron Imaging (1095-0397)
Related titles: Online - full text ed.: ISSN 1860-2002 (from IngentaConnect).
Indexed: A01, A03, A08, A22, A26, Agr, B&BAb, B19, B21, BioEngAb, CA, CurCont, E01, EMBASE, ExcerpMed, MEDLINE, P20, P22, P24, P30, P48, P52, P54, P56, PQC, R10, Reac, S01, SCI, SCOPUS, T02, W07.
—BLDSC (5900.817670), IE, Infotrieve, Ingenta. **CCC.**
Published by: (Academy of Molecular Imaging, Institute for Clinical Positron Emission Tomography (PET) NLD, Society for Molecular Imaging), Springer New York LLC (Subsidiary of: Springer Science+Business Media), 233 Spring St, New York, NY 10013. TEL 212-460-1500, service-ny@springer.com, http://www.springer.com/. Ed. Jorge R Barrio TEL 310-267-2917.

616.07 USA ISSN 1941-0549
MOLECULAR IMAGING INSIGHT; bridging the science of molecular imaging and clinical practice. Text in English. 2007. q. adv. back issues avail. **Document type:** *Magazine, Trade.*
Related titles: CD-ROM ed.: ISSN 1937-8548; Online - full text ed.: ISSN 1937-8556. free (effective 2010).
Published by: Trimed Media Group, Inc., 235 Promenade St, Ste 455, Providence, RI 02908. TEL 401-383-5660, FAX 401-383-3896, sales@trimedmedia.com, http://www.trimedmedia.com. Ed. Johannes Czernin. Pub. Jack Spears TEL 401-383-5660 ext 202. Adv. contact Scott Andersen TEL 401-383-5660 ext 210.

615.842 GBR ISSN 0952-3480
QC762 CODEN: NMRBEF
➤ **N M R IN BIOMEDICINE.** (Nuclear Magnetic Resonance) Text in English. 1988. 10/yr. GBP 1,305 in United Kingdom to institutions; EUR 1,650 in Europe to institutions; USD 2,557 elsewhere to institutions; GBP 1,501 combined subscription in United Kingdom to institutions (print & online eds.); EUR 1,898 combined subscription in Europe to institutions (print & online eds.); USD 2,941 combined subscription elsewhere to institutions (print & online eds.) (effective 2011). adv. back issues avail.; reprint service avail. from PSC. **Document type:** *Journal, Academic/Scholarly.* **Description:** Presents original papers in which nuclear magnetic resonance spectroscopy is used for investigating basic biochemical and clinical problems.
Related titles: Microform ed.: (from PQC); Online - full text ed.: ISSN 1099-1492. 1997. GBP 1,305 in United Kingdom to institutions; EUR 1,650 in Europe to institutions; USD 2,557 elsewhere to institutions (effective 2011).
Indexed: A22, ASCA, B&BAb, B19, B21, B27, BIOBASE, BioEngAb, CIN, CPEI, ChemAb, ChemTitl, CurCont, EMBASE, EngInd, ExcerpMed, IABS, ISR, IndMed, Inpharma, Inspec, MEDLINE, P30, R10, Reac, SCI, SCOPUS, T02, W07.
—AskIEEE, CASDDS, GNLM, IE, Infotrieve, Ingenta, INIST. **CCC.**
Published by: John Wiley & Sons Ltd. (Subsidiary of: John Wiley & Sons, Inc.), 1-7 Oldlands Way, PO Box 808, Bognor Regis, West Sussex PO21 9FF, United Kingdom. TEL 44-1865-778315, FAX 44-1243-843232, cs-journals@wiley.com, http://www.wiley.com/WileyCDA/. Ed. John R Griffiths TEL 44-1223-404460. **Subscr. in the Americas to:** John Wiley & Sons, Inc., 111 River St, Hoboken, NJ 07030. TEL 201-748-6645, subinfo@wiley.com; **Subscr. to:** 1-7 Oldlands Way, PO Box 809, Bognor Regis, West Sussex PO21 9FG, United Kingdom. TEL 44-1865-778054, cs-agency@wiley.com.

616.07 571.95 570 GBR ISSN 1743-5390
➤ **NANOTOXICOLOGY.** Text in English. 2007. q. GBP 495, EUR 715, USD 895 to institutions; GBP 925, EUR 1,330, USD 1,660 to corporations (effective 2010). back issues avail.; reprint service avail. from PSC. **Document type:** *Journal, Academic/Scholarly.* **Description:** Addresses research into the interactions between nano-structured materials and living matter.
Related titles: Online - full text ed.: ISSN 1743-5404; Cumulative ed(s).: 2005.
Indexed: A01, B21, B25, B27, BIOSIS Prev, CA, CurCont, EMBASE, ESPM, EnvEAb, MEDLINE, P30, SCI, SCOPUS, T02, W07.
—BLDSC (6015.335549), IE, Linda Hall. **CCC.**
Published by: Informa Healthcare (Subsidiary of: T & F Informa plc), Telephone House, 69-77 Paul St, London, EC2A 4LQ, United Kingdom. TEL 44-20-70175000, FAX 44-20-70176792, healthcare.enquiries@informa.com. Ed. Vicki Stone. **Subscr. in N America to:** Taylor & Francis Inc., Customer Services Dept, 325 Chestnut St, 8th Fl, Philadelphia, PA 19106. TEL 215-625-8900, 800-354-1420, FAX 215-625-8914, customerservice@taylorandfrancis.com; **Subscr. outside N America to:** Taylor & Francis Ltd., Journals Customer Service, Sheepen Pl, Colchester, Essex CO3 3LP, United Kingdom. TEL 44-20-70175544, FAX 44-20-70175198, tf.enquiries@tfinforma.com.

616.842 USA ISSN 1052-5149
CODEN: NCNAEO
➤ **NEUROIMAGING CLINICS OF NORTH AMERICA.** Text in English. 1991. q. USD 436 in United States to institutions; USD 546 elsewhere to institutions (effective 2012). adv. index. back issues avail.; reprints avail. **Document type:** *Journal, Academic/Scholarly.* **Description:** Focuses on a single topic in neuroimaging and provides a sound basis for choosing treatment options.
Related titles: Microform ed.: (from PQC); Online - full text ed.: ISSN 1557-9867 (from ScienceDirect); Supplement(s): Continuing Medical Education Supplement to Neuroimaging Clinics of North America. ISSN 1557-8186. USD 138 (effective 2000).
Indexed: A22, B21, C06, C07, C08, CINAHL, E-psyche, EMBASE, ExcerpMed, IIL, IndMed, MEDLINE, NSA, NSCI, P30, R10, Reac, SCI, SCOPUS, W07.
—BLDSC (6081.372400), GNLM, IE, Infotrieve, Ingenta. **CCC.**
Published by: W.B. Saunders Co. (Subsidiary of: Elsevier Health Sciences), Elsevier, Health Sciences Division, Order Fulfillment, 3251 Riverport Ln, Maryland Heights, MO 63043. TEL 314-872-8370, 800-325-4177, FAX 314-432-1380, JournalCustomerService-usa@elsevier.com, http://www.us.elsevierhealth.com. Adv. contact John Marmero TEL 212-633-3657.

616.07 616.8 KOR ISSN 2093-9043
➤ **NEUROINTERVENTION.** Text in English, Korean. 2006. s-a. adv. abstr.; bibl. back issues avail. **Document type:** *Journal, Academic/Scholarly.* **Description:** Publishes full-length original papers, reviews, pictorial essays, technical notes, case reports, and letters to the editor. Covers the research in and the practice of neurovascular diseases, including observational studies, clinical trials, epidemiology, health services and outcomes studies, and advances in applied (translational) and basic research.
Formerly (until 2010): Sin'gyeong Jungjae Chi'lyo Uihag/ Neurointervention (1975-5643)
Related titles: Online - full text ed.
Published by: Korean Society of Interventional Neuroradiology/Daehan Sin-gyeong Jungjae Chiryo Uihakoe, Department of Radiology, Kyung-Hee University Hospital at Gandong, 149 Sangil-dong, Gangdong-gu, Seoul, 134-090, Korea, S. TEL 82-2-4406186, FAX 82-2-4406932. Ed. Dr. Chang-Woo Ryu. Pub. Dr. Yong Sun Kim.

615.842 DEU ISSN 0028-3940
RC349.R3
➤ **NEURORADIOLOGY;** a journal devoted to neuroimaging and interventional neuroradiology. Text in English. 1970. m. EUR 1,732, USD 2,071 combined subscription to institutions (print & online eds.) (effective 2012). adv. charts. back issues avail.; reprint service avail. from PSC. **Document type:** *Journal, Academic/Scholarly.* **Description:** Covers the diagnosis and treatment of the central nervous system, using plain X-rays, computed tomography, angiography, pneumoencephalography and isotope studies, spinal radiographs, myelography, and spinal vascular studies.
Related titles: Microform ed.: (from PQC); Online - full text ed.: ISSN 1432-1920 (from IngentaConnect).
Indexed: A01, A03, A08, A22, A26, ASCA, B&BAb, B19, B21, BDM&CN, BioEngAb, C06, C07, CA, CurCont, DentInd, E01, EMBASE, ESPM, ExcerpMed, H12, H13, IIL, INIS AtomInd, ISR, IndMed, Inpharma, Kidney, MEDLINE, NSA, NSCI, P02, P10, P20, P22, P24, P30, P35, P48, P52, P53, P54, PQC, R10, Reac, SCI, SCOPUS, T02, TM, ToxAb, W07.
—BLDSC (6081.558000), GNLM, IE, Infotrieve, Ingenta, INIST. **CCC.**
Published by: (European Society of Neuroradiology), Springer (Subsidiary of: Springer Science+Business Media), Tiergartenstr 17, Heidelberg, 69121, Germany. TEL 49-6221-4870, FAX 49-6221-345229. Ed. Dr. James V Byrne. adv.: B&W page EUR 1,390, color page EUR 2,430. Circ: 1,300 (paid and controlled). **Subscr. in the Americas to:** Springer New York LLC, Journal Fulfillment, PO Box 2485, Secaucus, NJ 07096. TEL 800-777-4643, 201-348-4033, FAX 201-348-4505, journals-ny@springer.com, http://www.springer.com; **Subscr. to:** Springer Distribution Center, Kundenservice Zeitschriften, Haberstr 7, Heidelberg 69126, Germany. TEL 49-6221-3454303, FAX 49-6221-3454229, subscriptions@springer.com. **Co-sponsor:** Japanese Neuroradiological Society.

615.842 616.8 ITA ISSN 1971-4009
➤ **THE NEURORADIOLOGY JOURNAL.** Text in Italian, English; Summaries in English, Italian. 1988. bi-m. EUR 190 domestic; EUR 220 in Europe; EUR 258 elsewhere (effective 2008). adv. bk.rev. abstr. 120 p./no.; back issues avail. **Document type:** *Journal, Academic/Scholarly.* **Description:** In June of 2006, this Italian journal evolved into the official journal of important scientific societies from 13 different countries.
Formerly (until 2006): Rivista di Neuroradiologia (1120-9976)
Related titles: CD-ROM ed.; Diskette ed.; Fax ed.
Indexed: A20, ASCA, C06, C07, CA, E-psyche, EMBASE, ExcerpMed, R10, Reac, SCOPUS, T02.
—BLDSC (6081.558200), GNLM, IE, Ingenta.
Published by: (Societa Italiana di Neuroradiologia), Centauro SRL, Via del Pratello 8, Bologna, 40122, Italy. TEL 39-051-227634, FAX 39-051-220099, adriana.dallocca@centauro.it, http://www.centauro.it. Ed. Dr. Marco Leonardi. R&P Adriana Dall'Occa. Adv. contact Gerardo Dall'Occa. Circ: 1,900.

616.07 JPN ISSN 0917-074X
NEUROSONOLOGY/SHINKEI CHOONPA IGAKU. Text in Japanese. 3/yr. **Document type:** *Journal, Academic/Scholarly.*
Related titles: Online - full text ed.
Published by: Nihon Nou-Shinkei Chouompa Gakkai/Japan Academy of Neurosonology, National Cardiovascular Center Research Institute, Department of Vascular Physiology, 5-7-1 Fujishirodai, Suita, Osaka 565-8565, Japan. TEL 81-6-48637051, FAX 81-6-48637052, meiyo-socho@mti.biglobe.ne.jp, http://wwwsoc.nii.ac.jp/jan/index.html.

616.07 JPN ISSN 0289-0925
CODEN: NGIZEY
NIHON GAZO IGAKU ZASSHI/JAPANESE JOURNAL OF MEDICAL IMAGING. Text in Japanese. 1982. q.
Indexed: INIS AtomInd.
Published by: Nihon Rinsho Gazo Igaku Kenkyukai/Japanese Society of Medical Imaging, 9-1-7, Akasaka, Minato-ku, 483 Shuwa Residential Hotel, Tokyo, 107-0052, Japan. TEL 81-3-34050529, FAX 81-3-34050239.

616.07 JPN ISSN 0914-9457
CODEN: NJKZEV
NIHON JIKI KYOMEI IGAKKAI ZASSHI. Text in Japanese. 1981. q. **Document type:** *Journal, Academic/Scholarly.*
Formerly (until 1987): N M R Igaku/Journal of Nuclear Magnetic Resonance Medicine (0286-1364)
Related titles: Online - full content ed.
Indexed: INIS AtomInd.
—BLDSC (4656.070000). **CCC.**
Published by: Nihon Jiki Kyomei Igakkai/Japanese Society of Magnetic Resonance in Medicine, Gotanda Park Side Bldg 4F, 5-24-9 Higashi-gotanda Shinagawa-ku, Tokyo, 141-0022, Japan. TEL 81-3-34438622, FAX 81-3-34438733.

NIHON SEIKEI GEKA CHOONPA KENKYUKAI KAISHI/JAPANESE SOCIETY OF ORTHOPEDIC ULTRASONICS. JOURNAL. *see* MEDICAL SCIENCES—Orthopedics And Traumatology

616.07 618.92 JPN ISSN 0918-8487
CODEN: NSHZEB
NIHON SHONI HOSHASEN GAKKAI ZASSHI/JAPANESE SOCIETY OF PEDIATRIC RADIOLOGY. JOURNAL. Text in Japanese. 1990. s-a. **Document type:** *Journal.*
Indexed: INIS AtomInd.
—CCC.
Published by: Nihon Shoni Hoshasen Gakkai/Japanese Society of Pediatric Radiology, c/o Department of Radiology, Dokkyo University School of Medicine, 88 Kitakobayashi, Mibu-cho, Shimotsuga-gun, Tochigi, 321-0293, Japan. TEL 81-282-871171, FAX 81-282-864940, radiology@dokkyomed.ac.jp, http://www.jspr.jp/. Ed. Eiichi Kohda.

615.8 JPN ISSN 0048-0428
CODEN: NHGZAR
NIPPON IGAKU HOSHASEN GAKKAI ZASSHI/NIPPON ACTA RADIOLOGICA. Text in Japanese; Abstracts and contents page in English. 1940. m. adv. bk.rev. illus. **Document type:** *Journal, Academic/Scholarly.*
Related titles: Online - full text ed.: ISSN 1347-7951.
Indexed: A22, B25, BIOSIS Prev, ChemAb, EMBASE, ExcerpMed, INIS AtomInd, IndMed, JTA, MEDLINE, MycolAb, P30, R10, Reac, SCOPUS.
—BLDSC (6113.254000), CASDDS, GNLM, IE, Infotrieve, Ingenta, INIST.
Published by: Nihon Igaku Hoshasen Gakkai/Japan Radiological Society, JRS Publication Department, 3F NP-II Bldg., 5-1-16 Hongo, Bunkyo-ku, Tokyo, 113-0033, Japan. TEL 81-3-38143077, FAX 81-3-56844075, office@radiology.or.jp, http://www.radiology.or.jp/. Circ: 6,000.

612.014 USA ISSN 0969-8051
R895.A1 CODEN: NMBIEO
➤ **NUCLEAR MEDICINE AND BIOLOGY.** Text in English. 1973. 8/yr. USD 2,160 in United States to institutions; USD 2,431 elsewhere to institutions (effective 2012). adv. back issues avail.; reprints avail. **Document type:** *Journal, Academic/Scholarly.* **Description:** Addresses all aspects of radiopharmaceutical science: synthesis, in vitro and ex vivo studies, in vivo biodistribution by dissection or imaging, radiopharmacology, radiopharmacy, and translational clinical studies of targeted radiotracers.
Former titles (until 1993): International Journal of Radiation Applications and Instrumentation. Part B: Nuclear Medicine and Biology (0883-2897); (until 1986): International Journal of Nuclear Medicine and Biology (0047-0740)
Related titles: Microfilm ed.: (from PQC); Online - full text ed.: ISSN 1872-9614 (from IngentaConnect, ScienceDirect).
Indexed: A01, A03, A08, A22, A26, A34, A36, A37, ASCA, B&BAb, B19, B21, B25, BIOBASE, BIOSIS Prev, C25, C33, CA, CABA, CIN, CTA, ChemAb, ChemTitl, CurCont, DBA, EMBASE, ExcerpMed, GH, I05, IABS, INIS AtomInd, ISR, IndMed, IndVet, Inpharma, Inspec, MEDLINE, MycolAb, N02, N03, NSA, NucAcAb, P30, P33, PN&I, R10, RM&VM, Reac, SCI, SCOPUS, T02, T05, VS, W07.
—BLDSC (6180.920500), CASDDS, GNLM, IE, Infotrieve, Ingenta, INIST, Linda Hall. **CCC.**
Published by: (Society of Radiopharmaceutical Sciences), Elsevier Inc. (Subsidiary of: Elsevier Science & Technology), 1600 John F Kennedy Blvd, Philadelphia, PA 19103. TEL 215-239-3900, FAX 215-238-7883, JournalCustomerService-usa@elsevier.com, http://www.elsevier.com. Ed. William C Eckelman. Pub. Herb Niemirow TEL 212-633-3141. Adv. contact Pat Hampton TEL 212-633-3181.

615.8 USA ISSN 0143-3636
R895.A1 CODEN: NMCODC
➤ **NUCLEAR MEDICINE COMMUNICATIONS.** Text in English. 1980. m. USD 2,266 domestic to institutions; USD 2,437 foreign to institutions (effective 2011). adv. bk.rev. index. back issues avail.; reprints avail. **Document type:** *Journal, Academic/Scholarly.* **Description:** Brings out research and clinical work in all areas of nuclear medicine.
Related titles: Online - full text ed.: ISSN 1473-5628. USD 1,579.50 domestic academic site license; USD 1,579.50 foreign academic site license; USD 1,761.75 foreign corporate site license (effective 2002).
Indexed: A22, ASCA, BIOBASE, ChemAb, ChemTitl, CurCont, E01, EMBASE, ExcerpMed, FR, IABS, IndMed, Inpharma, MEDLINE, MycolAb, P30, P35, R10, Reac, SCI, SCOPUS, W07.
—BLDSC (6180.923000), CASDDS, GNLM, IE, Infotrieve, Ingenta, INIST. **CCC.**
Published by: (British Nuclear Medicine Society GBR), Lippincott Williams & Wilkins (Subsidiary of: Wolters Kluwer N.V.), 530 Walnut St, Philadelphia, PA 19106. TEL 215-521-8300, FAX 215-521-8902, customerservice@lww.com, http://www.lww.com. Ed. A AL-Nahhas. Pub. Phil Daly. Adv. contact Miriam Terron-Elder TEL 646-674-6538. Circ: 765.

616.07 POL ISSN 1506-9680
CODEN: NMRUAY
➤ **NUCLEAR MEDICINE REVIEW.** Text in English. 1998. s-a. EUR 23 to individuals; EUR 47 to institutions (effective 2011). bk.rev. **Document type:** *Journal, Academic/Scholarly.* **Description:** Publishes original and experimental scientific papers, together with reviews of books and news about symposia and congresses.
Related titles: Online - full text ed.: ISSN 1644-4345.
Indexed: C06, C07, CA, EMBASE, ExcerpMed, INIS AtomInd, MEDLINE, P30, R10, Reac, SCOPUS, T02.
—BLDSC (6180.924500), IE.
Published by: (Polskie Towarzystwo Medycyny Nuklearnej/Polish Society of Nuclear Medicine), Wydawnictwo Via Medica, ul Swietokrzyska 73, Gdansk, 80180, Poland. TEL 48-58-3209494, FAX 48-58-3209460, redakcja@viamedica.pl, http://www.viamedica.pl. Ed. Julian Liniecki.

615.8 DEU ISSN 0029-5566
R895.A1 CODEN: NMIMAX
➤ **NUKLEARMEDIZIN/NUCLEAR MEDICINE.** Text in English, French, German. 1956. 6/yr. EUR 231 to individuals; EUR 465 to institutions; EUR 75 to students; EUR 56 newsstand/cover (effective 2011). adv. bk.rev. abstr.; bibl.; charts; illus. index. **Document type:** *Journal, Academic/Scholarly.* **Description:** Original material covering experimental and clinical research with radionuclides, radionuclide imaging, new concepts of functional imaging, case reports.
Formerly (until 1959): Zeitschrift fuer Medizinische Isotopenforschung und Deren Grenzgebiete (0514-2687)
Related titles: Online - full text ed.
Indexed: A20, A22, ASCA, ChemAb, ChemTitl, CurCont, EMBASE, ExcerpMed, FR, IBR, IBZ, INIS AtomInd, ISR, IndMed, Inpharma, MEDLINE, P30, P35, R10, Reac, SCI, SCOPUS, TM, W07.
—BLDSC (6184.453000), CASDDS, GNLM, IE, Infotrieve, Ingenta, INIST. **CCC.**
Published by: (German, Austrian and Swiss Societies of Nuclear Medicine), Schattauer GmbH, Hoelderlinstr 3, Stuttgart, 70174, Germany. TEL 49-711-229870, FAX 49-711-2298750, info@schattauer.de, http://www.schattauer.com. Ed. O Schober. Adv. contact Christian Matthe. Circ: 2,350 (paid and controlled). **Subscr. to:** CSJ, Postfach 140220, Munich 80452, Germany. TEL 49-89-20959129, schattauer@csj.de.

615.842 DEU ISSN 0723-7065
CODEN: NKLZD8
➤ **DER NUKLEARMEDIZINER.** Text in German; Summaries in English. 1977. 4/yr. EUR 189 to institutions; EUR 254 combined subscription to institutions (print & online eds.); EUR 54 newsstand/cover (effective 2011). adv. **Document type:** *Journal, Academic/Scholarly.*
Related titles: Online - full text ed.: ISSN 1439-5800. EUR 245 to institutions (effective 2011).
Indexed: IBR, IBZ, INIS AtomInd, TM.
—BLDSC (6184.485000), CASDDS, GNLM, IE, Ingenta. **CCC.**
Published by: (Berufsverband Deutscher Nuklearmediziner), Georg Thieme Verlag, Ruedigerstr 14, Stuttgart, 70469, Germany. TEL 49-711-8931421, FAX 49-711-8931410, kunden.service@thieme.de. Ed. Dr. Klaus Hahn. Adv. contact Irmgard Mayer TEL 49-711-8931469. Circ: 1,370 (paid).

➤ **OBSERVATOIRE NATIONAL DE LA RADIOTHERAPIE.** *see* MEDICAL SCIENCES—Oncology

616.842 AUT
OE R G MITTEILUNGEN. Text in German. q. bk.rev. **Document type:** *Journal, Academic/Scholarly.*
Published by: Oesterreichische Roentgengesellschaft, Alserstr. 4, Vienna, 1090, Austria. TEL 43-1-405138321, FAX 43-1-405188323, skonstantinou@medacad.org, http://www.oerg.at.

616.07 JPN
OOSAKAFU HOSHASEN GISHIKAI DAIHOGI KAIHO/OSAKA ASSOCIATION OF RADIOLOGIC TECHNOLOGISTS. NEWSLETTER. Text in Japanese. 1979. bi-m. membership. **Document type:** *Journal, Academic/Scholarly.*
Published by: Oosakafu Hoshasen Gishikai/Osaka Association of Radiological Technologists, 1-4-12, Fukuoka, Chuo-ku, Osaka, 540-0028, Japan. TEL 81-6-69451414, FAX 81-6-69451410, osaka@daihougi.ne.jp, http://www.daihougi.ne.jp/.

615.842 616.12 NLD ISSN 1876-5386
RC683.5.I42
➤ **THE OPEN CARDIOVASCULAR IMAGING JOURNAL.** Text in English. 2008. irreg. free (effective 2011). **Document type:** *Journal, Academic/Scholarly.*
Media: Online - full text.
Indexed: A01.
Published by: Bentham Open (Subsidiary of: Bentham Science Publishers Ltd.), PO Box 294, Bussum, AG 1400, Netherlands. TEL 31-35-6923800, FAX 31-35-6980150, subscriptions@bentham.org.

616.075 NLD ISSN 1874-7698
QC762
➤ **THE OPEN MAGNETIC RESONANCE JOURNAL.** Text in English. 2008. irreg. free (effective 2011). **Document type:** *Journal, Academic/Scholarly.*
Media: Online - full text.
Indexed: A01, A28, A39, APA, BrCerAb, C&ISA, C27, C29, CA/WCA, CIA, CerAb, CivEngAb, CorrAb, D03, D04, E&CAJ, E11, E13, EEA, EMA, ESPM, H15, M&TEA, M09, MBF, METADEX, NSA, P30, R14, S14, S15, S18, SolStAb, T04, WAA.
Published by: Bentham Open (Subsidiary of: Bentham Science Publishers Ltd.), PO Box 294, Bussum, AG 1400, Netherlands. TEL 31-35-6923800, FAX 31-35-6980150, subscriptions@bentham.org. Ed. J L G Fierro.

616.07 NLD ISSN 1874-3471
R857.O6
➤ **THE OPEN MEDICAL IMAGING JOURNAL.** Text in English. 2007. irreg. free (effective 2011). **Document type:** *Journal, Academic/Scholarly.* **Description:** Covers all areas of medical imaging and nuclear medicine.
Media: Online - full text.
Indexed: A01, A28, APA, B19, BrCerAb, C&ISA, CA, CA/WCA, CIA, CerAb, CivEngAb, CorrAb, E&CAJ, E11, EEA, EMA, ESPM, H15, M&TEA, M09, MBF, METADEX, NSA, SolStAb, T02, T04, WAA.
Published by: Bentham Open (Subsidiary of: Bentham Science Publishers Ltd.), PO Box 294, Bussum, AG 1400, Netherlands. TEL 31-35-6923800, FAX 31-35-6980150, subscriptions@bentham.org. Eds. Christopher W Tyler, Jean Maublant.

➤ **THE OPEN NEUROIMAGING JOURNAL.** *see* MEDICAL SCIENCES—Psychiatry And Neurology

616.07 NLD ISSN 1876-388X
R895.A1
➤ **THE OPEN NUCLEAR MEDICINE JOURNAL.** Text in English. 2008. irreg. free (effective 2011). **Document type:** *Journal, Academic/Scholarly.*
Media: Online - full text.
Indexed: A01, P30.

M

Published by: Bentham Open (Subsidiary of: Bentham Science Publishers Ltd.), PO Box 294, Bussum, AG 1400, Netherlands. TEL 31-35-6923800, FAX 31-35-6980150, subscriptions@bentham.org. Ed. Helmut F Sinzinger.

➤ **ORAL RADIOLOGY.** *see* MEDICAL SCIENCES—Dentistry

616.07 USA ISSN 1556-8598
P E T CLINICS. (Positron Emission Tomography) Text in English. 2006 (Jan.). q. USD 279 in United States to institutions; USD 312 elsewhere to institutions (effective 2012). adv. back issues avail.; reprints avail. **Document type:** *Journal, Academic/Scholarly.* **Description:** Examines pet's effectiveness in cancer diagnosis and staging as well as exploring pet's usefulness in the areas of dementia, myocardial viability, and other conditions.
Related titles: Online - full text ed.: (from ScienceDirect); Supplement(s): P E T Clinics: Continuing Medical Education Supplement. ISSN 1559-7814.
Indexed: EMBASE, ExcerpMed, P30, SCOPUS.
—BLDSC (6428.816000). **CCC.**
Published by: W.B. Saunders Co. (Subsidiary of: Elsevier Health Sciences), Elsevier, Health Sciences Division, Order Fulfillment, 3251 Riverport Ln, Maryland Heights, MO 63043. TEL 314-872-8370, 800-325-4177, FAX 314-432-1380, JournalCustomerService-usa@elsevier.com, http://www.us.elsevierhealth.com. Adv. contact John Marmero TEL 212-633-3657.

616.07 PAK ISSN 1607-2006
PAKISTAN JOURNAL OF RADIOLOGY. Text in English. 1990. q.
Indexed: INIS AtomInd.
Published by: Radiological Society of Pakistan, c/o Dr Khawja Khurshid, Department of Radiology, Mayo Hospital, Lahore, Pakistan. TEL 92-42-7322126, info@radiologypakistan.org, http://www.radiologypakistan.org. Ed. M A Siddiqui.

618.92 615.842 DEU ISSN 0301-0449
RJ51.R3 CODEN: PDRYA5
➤ **PEDIATRIC RADIOLOGY**; roentgenology, nuclear medicine, ultrasonics, CT, MRI. Text in English. 1973. m. EUR 2,045, USD 2,500 combined subscription to institutions (print & online eds.) (effective 2012). adv. back issues avail.; reprint service avail. from PSC. **Document type:** *Journal, Academic/Scholarly.* **Description:** Reports on the progress and results from all areas of pediatric radiology and related fields.
Related titles: Microform ed.: (from PQC); Online - full text ed.: ISSN 1432-1998 (from IngentaConnect).
Indexed: A01, A03, A08, A22, A26, A29, ASCA, B&BAb, B19, B20, B21, BDM&CN, C06, C07, CA, ChemAb, CurCont, DentInd, E01, E08, EMBASE, ESPM, ExcerpMed, FR, G08, H&SSA, H11, I05, I10, IIL, INI, INIS AtomInd, ISR, IndMed, Inpharma, MEDLINE, NSA, P20, P22, P30, P35, P48, P52, P54, PQC, R10, Reac, S09, SCI, SCOPUS, T02, VirolAbstr, W07.
—BLDSC (6417.606000), GNLM, IE, Infotrieve, Ingenta, INIST. **CCC.**
Published by: (European Society of Pediatric Radiology), Springer (Subsidiary of: Springer Science+Business Media), Tiergartenstr 17, Heidelberg, 69121, Germany. TEL 49-6221-4870, FAX 49-6221-345229. adv.: B&W page EUR 1,390, color page EUR 2,430. Circ: 1,800 (paid and controlled). **Subscr. in the Americas to:** Springer New York LLC, Journal Fulfillment, PO Box 2485, Secaucus, NJ 07096. TEL 800-777-4643, 201-348-4033, FAX 201-348-4505, journals-ny@springer.com, http://www.springer.com; **Subscr. to:** Springer Distribution Center, Kundenservice Zeitschriften, Haberstr 7, Heidelberg 69126, Germany. TEL 49-6221-3454303, FAX 49-6221-3454229, subscriptions@springer.com.

617.05 USA ISSN 1557-8550
PHOTOMEDICINE AND LASER SURGERY (ONLINE). Text in English. 1990. m. USD 1,425 to institutions (effective 2012). adv. **Document type:** *Journal, Academic/Scholarly.* **Description:** Provides techniques and research in phototherapy, low level laser therapy (LLLT), and laser medicine and surgery.
Formerly (until 2004): Journal of Clinical Laser Medicine and Surgery (Online) (1557-8089)
Media: Online - full text.
—BLDSC (6474.304400). **CCC.**
Published by: (North American Association for Laser Therapy, International Society for Laser Surgery and Medicine), Mary Ann Liebert, Inc. Publishers, 140 Huguenot St, 3rd Fl, New Rochelle, NY 10801. TEL 914-740-2100, FAX 914-740-2101, 800-654-3237, info@liebertpub.com. Ed. Raymond J Lanzafame TEL 585-266-2150.

616.07 POL ISSN 1733-134X
➤ **POLISH JOURNAL OF RADIOLOGY.** Text in Polish, English. 1926. q. EUR 65 (effective 2007). adv. illus. **Document type:** *Journal, Academic/Scholarly.*
Former titles (until 2002): Polski Przeglad Radiologii (0860-1089); (until 1983): Polski Przeglad Radiologii i Medycyny Nuclearnej (0137-7183); (until 1961): Polski Przeglad Radiologiczny (1505-2680)
Related titles: Online - full text ed.: 2000.
Indexed: EMBASE, ExcerpMed, INIS AtomInd, P30, R10, Reac, SCOPUS.
—BLDSC (6543.671800), GNLM, IE, Ingenta, INIST.
Published by: Polskie Lekarskie Towarzystwo Radiologiczne/Polish Medical Society of Radiology, Zaklad Radiologii i Radioterapii Pediatrycznej AM w Warszawie, ul Marszalkowska 24, Warsaw, 00576, Poland. TEL 48-22-6285219, FAX 48-22-6214155, http://www.polradiologia.org. Ed. Jerzy Walecki. adv.: B&W page USD 700, color page USD 900.

▼➤ **PRACTICAL RADIATION ONCOLOGY.** *see* MEDICAL SCIENCES—Oncology

➤ **PRIVATE HOSPITAL HEALTHCARE EUROPE. I T & COMMUNICATIONS AND RADIOLOGY & IMAGING.** *see* HEALTH FACILITIES AND ADMINISTRATION

616.07 POL ISSN 0860-3405
CODEN: PMNUE6
PROBLEMY MEDYCYNY NUKLEARNEJ. Text in English, Polish. 1987. s-a.
Indexed: INIS AtomInd.
—BLDSC (6617.952790).
Published by: Polskie Towarzystwo Medycyny Nuklearnej/Polish Society of Nuclear Medicine, Zaklad Medycyny Nuklearnej AM, ul. Banacha 1A, Warsaw, 02-097, Poland. http://www.ptmn.pl.

PROGRESS IN NUCLEAR MAGNETIC RESONANCE SPECTROSCOPY. *see* CHEMISTRY—Analytical Chemistry

612.014 ITA ISSN 1824-4785
R61 CODEN: JNMSD3
➤ **THE QUARTERLY JOURNAL OF NUCLEAR MEDICINE AND MOLECULAR IMAGING.** Text and summaries in English. 1957. bi-m. EUR 275 combined subscription in the European Union to institutions (print & online eds.); EUR 305 combined subscription elsewhere to institutions (print & online eds.) (effective 2011). adv. bk.rev. bibl.; charts; illus. index. reprints avail. **Document type:** *Journal, Academic/Scholarly.* **Description:** Covers clinical and experimental topics on nuclear medicine.
Former titles (until 2004): The Quarterly Journal of Nuclear Medicine (1125-0135); (until 1995): The Journal of Nuclear Biology and Medicine (1121-1075); (until 1991): Journal of Nuclear Medicine and Allied Sciences (0392-0208); (until 1977): Journal of Nuclear Biology and Medicine (0368-3249); Which superseded in part in 1966: Minerva Nucleare (0369-0288)
Related titles: Microform ed.: (from PQC); Online - full text ed.: ISSN 1827-1936. 2005.
Indexed: CISA, ChemAb, EMBASE, ExcerpMed, INIS AtomInd, ISR, IndMed, Inpharma, Inspec, MEDLINE, P20, P22, P24, P26, P30, P35, P48, P52, P54, PQC, R10, Reac, SCOPUS.
—CASDDS, GNLM, IE, Infotrieve, Ingenta, INIST. **CCC.**
Published by: (Italian Association of Nuclear Medicine), Edizioni Minerva Medica, Corso Bramante 83-85, Turin, 10126, Italy. TEL 39-011-678282, FAX 39-011-674502, journals.dept@minervamedica.it. Ed. G Lucignani. Pub. Alberto Oliaro. Circ: 3,000 (paid). **Co-sponsor:** International Association of Radiopharmacology.

615.842 USA
R B M A BULLETIN; progress through sharing. Text in English. 1988 (vol.23, no.11). m. USD 100 domestic to non-members; USD 110 foreign to non-members (effective 2000). adv. bk.rev. **Document type:** *Bulletin.*
Published by: Radiology Business Management Association, 8001 Irvine Center Dr., Ste. 1060, Irvine, CA 92618-2986. TEL 888-224-7262. Ed. Sharon Urch.

616.07 JPN
R E R F UPDATE (ONLINE ENGLISH EDITION). Text in English. a.
Media: Online - full content. **Related titles:** ◆ Japanese ed.: R E R F Update (Online Japanese Edition).
Published by: Radiation Effects Research Foundation/Hoshasen Eiksho Kenkyujo, 5-2 Hijiyama Park, Minami-ku, Hiroshima-shi, Hiroshima-ken 732-0815, Japan. TEL 81-82-2613131, FAX 81-82-2637279, pub-info@rerf.jp. Ed. Donald A Pierce. Pub. Burton G Bennett. R&P Fumie Maruyama TEL 81-82-2619917.

616.07 JPN
R E R F UPDATE (ONLINE JAPANESE EDITION). Text in Japanese. a. **Document type:** *Academic/Scholarly.*
Media: Online - full content. **Related titles:** ◆ English ed.: R E R F Update (Online English Edition).
Published by: Radiation Effects Research Foundation/Hoshasen Eiksho Kenkyujo, 5-2 Hijiyama Park, Minami-ku, Hiroshima-shi, Hiroshima-ken 732-0815, Japan. TEL 81-82-2613131, FAX 81-82-2637279, pub-info@rerf.jp. Ed. Donald A Pierce. Pub. Burton G Bennett. R&P Fumie Maruyama TEL 81-82-2619917.

615.842 USA
R R S NEWS. Text in English. 19??. 3/yr. looseleaf. free to members (effective 2010). back issues avail. **Document type:** *Newsletter, Trade.*
Related titles: Online - full text ed.
Published by: Radiation Research Society, 810 E 10th St, Lawrence, KS 66044 . TEL 800-627-0326, FAX 785-843-6153, info@radres.org, http://www.radres.org/. Ed. Bruce Kimler.

616.07 USA ISSN 1546-346X
R S N A NEWS. (Radiological Society of North America) Text in English. 19??. m. USD 20 to non-members; USD 10 to members (effective 2009). back issues avail.; reprints avail. **Document type:** *Newsletter, Trade.* **Description:** Aims to promote and develop the highest standards of radiology and related sciences through education and research.
Related titles: Online - full content ed.: free (effective 2009).
Published by: Radiological Society of North America, Inc., 820 Jorie Blvd, Oak Brook, IL 60523. TEL 630-571-2670, 800-381-6660, FAX 630-571-7837, membership@rsna.org. Ed. Bruce L McClennan.

615.842 USA ISSN 1041-2182
RC78.7.D53
R T IMAGE; the nation's comprhensive newsmagazine for administrators, educators and radiologic science professionals. (Radiologic Technology) Text in English. 1988. w. free to qualified personnel. bk.rev. charts; illus. **Document type:** *Magazine, Trade.* **Description:** Contains items of interest to radiology managers and radiologic science professionals in all modalities and in hospitals, free-standing centers, and schools.
Indexed: C06.
Published by: Valley Forge Publishing Group, 2570 Blvd of the Generals, Ste 220, Norristown, PA 19403. TEL 800-983-7737, info@valleyforgepress.com, http://www.valleyforgepress.com. Eds. Tom Schaffner, Tom Schaffner. Circ: 65,000.

615.842 GBR ISSN 0264-6412
RAD MAGAZINE; for medical imaging and radiotherapy professionals. Text in English. 1975. m. adv. bk.rev.; software rev.; video rev. **Document type:** *Magazine, Trade.* **Description:** Contains product news, personnel appointments, group meeting reports, and exhibition and conference reviews.
Formed by the 1975 merger of: Consultant Radiologist; Radiotherapist —**CCC.**
Published by: Kingsmoor Publications Ltd., PO Box 7861, Braintree, Essex CM7 4YZ, United Kingdom. TEL 44-1371-812960, FAX 44-1371-812969. Adv. contact David Roberts.

616.07 JPN
RADIATION EFFECTS RESEARCH FOUNDATION. ANNUAL REPORT/ HOSHASEN EIKYO KENKYUSHO NENPO. Text in English, Japanese. 1975. a. **Document type:** *Corporate.*
Published by: Radiation Effects Research Foundation/Hoshasen Eiksho Kenkyujo, 5-2 Hijiyama Park, Minami-ku, Hiroshima-shi, Hiroshima-ken 732-0815, Japan. TEL 81-82-2613131, FAX 81-82-2637279, pub-info@rerf.jp, http://www.rerf.jp/. Ed. Sheldon Wolff. Pub. Shigenobu Nagataki. R&P Reiko Sasaki.

616.07 JPN
RADIATION EFFECTS RESEARCH FOUNDATION. COMMENTARY AND REVIEW SERIES/HOSHASEN EIKYO KENKYUSHO KAISETSU SOSETSU SHU. Text in English; Summaries in English, Japanese. 1989. irreg. **Document type:** *Monographic series, Academic/Scholarly.*
Published by: Radiation Effects Research Foundation/Hoshasen Eiksho Kenkyujo, 5-2 Hijiyama Park, Minami-ku, Hiroshima-shi, Hiroshima-ken 732-0815, Japan. TEL 81-82-2613131, FAX 81-82-2637279, pub-info@rerf.jp, http://www.rerf.jp/. Ed. Donald A Pierce. Pub. Burton G Bennett. R&P Fumie Maruyama TEL 81-82-2619917.

616.07 JPN
RADIATION EFFECTS RESEARCH FOUNDATION NEWSLETTER/ HOEIKEN NYUZU RETA. Text in Japanese. 1975. bi-m. free. **Document type:** *Newsletter.*
Published by: Radiation Effects Research Foundation/Hoshasen Eiksho Kenkyujo, 5-2 Hijiyama Park, Minami-ku, Hiroshima-shi, Hiroshima-ken 732-0815, Japan. TEL 81-82-2613131, FAX 81-82-2637279, pub-info@rerf.jp, http://www.rerf.jp/. Ed. Donald A Pierce. Pub. Burton G Bennett. R&P Fumie Maruyama TEL 81-82-2619917.

615.842 USA
RADIATION ONCOLOGY NEWS. Text in English. 1986. q. free to members. bibl.; tr.lit. back issues avail. **Document type:** *Newsletter.*
Formerly (until vol.4, 1990): S R O A Newsletter
Published by: Society for Radiation Oncology Administrators, 5272 River Rd, Ste 630, Bethesda, MD 20816. TEL 301-718-6510, 866-458-7762, FAX 301-656-0989, sroa@paimgmt.com, http://www.sroa.org. Ed., R&P Jeanne Jendra. Circ: 275.

615.842 616.992 USA ISSN 1084-1911
➤ **RADIATION THERAPIST**; the journal of the radiation oncology sciences. Text in English. 1992. s-a. USD 35 domestic to individuals; USD 65 foreign to individuals; USD 40 domestic to institutions; USD 70 foreign to institutions; free to members (effective 2010). adv. bk.rev. illus. index. back issues avail. **Document type:** *Journal, Academic/Scholarly.* **Description:** Covers specific radiation therapy techniques, anatomy, disease processes, patient positioning, equipment protocols, radiation safety, radiation protection and basic patient care.
Related titles: Online - full text ed.: free to members (effective 2010).
Indexed: A26, C06, C07, C08, CA, CINAHL, H12, I05, T02.
—BLDSC (7228.016000). **CCC.**
Published by: American Society of Radiologic Technologists, 15000 Central Ave, SE, Albuquerque, NM 87123. TEL 505-298-4500, 800-444-2778, FAX 505-298-5063, memberservices@asrt.org. Adv. contact JoAnne Quirindongo TEL 505-298-4500 ext 1317.

615.832 RUS ISSN 0869-8031
QH652.A1 CODEN: RBIREJ
RADIATSIONNAYA BIOLOGIYA, RADIOEKOLOGIYA. Text in Russian. 1961. bi-m. RUR 930 for 6 mos. domestic (effective 2004). bk.rev. index. **Document type:** *Journal, Academic/Scholarly.*
Formerly (until no.4, 1993): Radiobiologiya (0033-8192)
Indexed: B21, B25, BIOSIS Prev, CIN, ChemAb, ChemTitl, EMBASE, ESPM, ExcerpMed, INIS AtomInd, IndMed, Inspec, MEDLINE, MycolAb, P30, R10, Reac, RefZh, SCOPUS, ToxAb.
—AskIEEE, CASDDS, GNLM, Infotrieve, INIST, Linda Hall. **CCC.**
Published by: (Rossiiskaya Akademiya Nauk, Otdelenie Biokhimii, Biofiziki i Khimii Fiziologicheski Aktivnykh Soedinenii), Izdatel'stvo Nauka, Profsoyuznaya ul 90, Moscow, 117864, Russian Federation. TEL 7-095-3347151, FAX 7-095-4202220, secret@naukaran.ru, http://www.naukaran.ru.

615.832 ESP
RADIOBIOLOGY. Text in Spanish. 2001. s-a. free (effective 2009). back issues avail. **Document type:** *Journal, Academic/Scholarly.*
Media: Online - full text.
Published by: Universidad de Malaga, Departamento de Radiologia y Medicina Fisica, Campus de Teatinos, Malaga, 29071, Spain. TEL 34-95-2131578, FAX 34-95-2131630, http://www.uma.es/. Ed. Miguel Ruiz Gamez.

615.842 AUS ISSN 0033-8273
CODEN: RDGRAJ
THE RADIOGRAPHER. Text in English. 1948. 3/yr. free to members (effective 2008). adv. bk.rev. abstr.; illus. index. **Document type:** *Journal, Academic/Scholarly.*
Related titles: Online - full text ed.
Indexed: ChemAb, INIS AtomInd, Inspec, RefZh.
—BLDSC (7236.850000), AskIEEE, CASDDS, IE, Ingenta.
Published by: Australian Institute of Radiography, c/o E.M. Hughes Sec., PO Box 1169, Collingwood, VIC 3066, Australia. TEL 61-3-94193336, FAX 61-3-94160783, air@a-i-r.com/au, http://www.a-i-r.com.au. Ed. Rob Davidson. Adv. contact Bill Minnis TEL 61-3-98245241. page AUD 550; trim 210 x 297. Circ: 4,000.

615.842 USA ISSN 0271-5333
RC78.A1
➤ **RADIOGRAPHICS.** Text in English. 1981. bi-m. USD 255 (effective 2011). adv. abstr.; illus.; maps. back issues avail.; reprints avail. **Document type:** *Journal, Academic/Scholarly.* **Description:** Through extensive use of high-quality, detailed radiologic images and top quality articles, this journal delivers the very best.
Related titles: Microform ed.: (from PQC); Online - full text ed.: ISSN 1527-1323. 1996. free to members (effective 2011).
Indexed: A20, A22, ASCA, B&BAb, B19, B21, BioEngAb, C06, C07, CMCI, CurCont, EMBASE, ExcerpMed, IIL, ISR, IndMed, Inpharma, MEDLINE, P30, R10, Reac, SCI, SCOPUS, W07.
—BLDSC (7236.900000), GNLM, IE, Infotrieve, Ingenta, INIST. **CCC.**
Published by: Radiological Society of North America, Inc., 820 Jorie Blvd, Oak Brook, IL 60523. TEL 630-571-2670, FAX 630-571-7837, membership@rsna.org, http://www.rsna.org. Ed. William W Olmsted TEL 301-657-2221. Adv. contact Jim Drew TEL 630-571-7819.

615.842 GBR ISSN 1078-8174
➤ **RADIOGRAPHY.** Text in English. 1995. q. EUR 443 in Europe to institutions; JPY 47,700 in Japan to institutions; USD 413 elsewhere to institutions (effective 2012). adv. back issues avail.; reprints avail. **Document type:** *Journal, Academic/Scholarly.* **Description:** Publishes clinical and scientific papers on all aspects of diagnostic imaging.
Related titles: Online - full text ed.: ISSN 1532-2831. USD 355 to institutions (effective 2009) (from ScienceDirect).

Indexed: A22, A26, B&BAb, B19, B21, BioEngAb, C06, C07, C08, CA, CINAHL, E01, EMBASE, ESPM, ExcerpMed, H12, I05, INIS AtomInd, R10, Reac, SCOPUS, T02, ToxAb.
—BLDSC (7237.001000), GNLM, IE, Ingenta. **CCC.**
Published by: (Society of Radiographers), W.B. Saunders Co. Ltd. (Subsidiary of: Elsevier Health Sciences), 32 Jamestown Rd, Camden, London, NW1 7BY, United Kingdom. TEL 44-20-74244200, FAX 44-20-74832293, elsols@elsevier.com. Ed. Richard Price.

➤ **RADIOKHIMIYA.** *see* CHEMISTRY—Physical Chemistry

616.07 POL ISSN 1732-6281
RADIOLOG.PL. Text in Polish. 2001. d. free. **Document type:** *Trade.*
Media: Online - full content.
Published by: Open Medical Network, ul Bronikowskiego 3/2, Warsaw, 02796, Poland. TEL 48-22-8940630, FAX 48-22-6483409, redakcja@openmedicalnetwork.com, http://www.openmedicalnetwork.com. Ed., Pub. Lukasz Bialek.

615.842 DEU ISSN 0033-832X
RC78.A1 CODEN: RDLGBC
➤ **DER RADIOLOGE;** Zeitschrift fuer diagnostische und interventionelle Radiologie, Radioonkologie, Nuklearmedizin. Text in German; Summaries in English. 1961. m. EUR 618, USD 703 combined subscription to institutions (print & online eds.) (effective 2012). adv. bk.rev. charts; illus. index. back issues avail.; reprint service avail. from PSC. **Document type:** *Journal, Academic/Scholarly.* **Description:** Discusses diagnostic techniques in the field of radiology.
Related titles: Microform ed.: (from PQC); Online - full text ed.: ISSN 1432-2102 (from IngentaConnect).
Indexed: A20, A22, A26, ASCA, CMCI, CurCont, DentInd, E01, EMBASE, ExcerpMed, FR, IBR, IBZ, INIS AtomInd, ISR, IndMed, Inpharma, MEDLINE, P30, R10, Reac, SCI, SCOPUS, T02, TM, W07.
—BLDSC (7237.700000), GNLM, IE, Infotrieve, Ingenta, INIST, Linda Hall. **CCC.**
Published by: (Arbeitsgemeinschaft Berufsverbaende Medizinische Radiologie), Springer (Subsidiary of: Springer Science+Business Media), Tiergartenstr 17, Heidelberg, 69121, Germany. TEL 49-6221-4870, FAX 49-6221-345229. Ed. M Reiser. Adv. contact Stephan Kroeck TEL 49-30-827875739. Circ: 3,000 (paid and controlled). **Subscr. in the Americas to:** Springer New York LLC, Journal Fulfillment, PO Box 2485, Secaucus, NJ 07096. TEL 800-777-4643, 201-348-4033, FAX 201-348-4505, journals-ny@springer.com, http://www.springer.com; **Subscr. to:** Springer Distribution Center, Kundenservice Zeitschriften, Haberstr 7, Heidelberg 69126, Germany. TEL 49-6221-3454303, FAX 49-6221-3454229, subscriptions@springer.com.

615.842 ESP ISSN 0033-8338
➤ **RADIOLOGIA.** Text in Spanish. 1912. 10/yr. EUR 157.51 to individuals print & online eds.; EUR 398.75 to institutions print & online eds. (effective 2009). bk.rev. abstr.; bibl.; charts; illus.; stat. index. back issues avail.; reprints avail. **Document type:** *Journal, Academic/Scholarly.*
Related titles: Online - full text ed.: ISSN 1578-178X. 1996. EUR 131.21 (effective 2009) (from ScienceDirect).
Indexed: A22, EMBASE, ExcerpMed, FR, IME, INIS AtomInd, MEDLINE, P30, R10, Reac, SCOPUS.
—BLDSC (7237.730000), IE, Ingenta, INIST. **CCC.**
Published by: (Sociedad Espanola de Radiologia y Electrologia Medicas y de Medicina Nuclear), Elsevier Doyma (Subsidiary of: Elsevier Health Sciences), Traversa de Gracia 17-21, Barcelona, 08021, Spain. TEL 34-932-418800, FAX 34-932-419020, editorial@elsevier.com. Ed. J. M. Garcia Santos. Circ: 4,500.

616.07 ESP ISSN 1698-1049
RADIOLOGIA ABDOMINAL. Text in Spanish. 2004. 3/yr. 12 p./no.; back issues avail. **Document type:** *Journal, Trade.*
Published by: Ediciones Mayo S.A., Calle Aribau 185-187, 2a Planta, Barcelona, 08021, Spain. TEL 34-93-2090255, FAX 34-93-2020643, edmayo@ediciones.mayo.es, http://www.edicionesmayo.es. Circ: 3,000.

615.842 BRA ISSN 0100-3984
➤ **RADIOLOGIA BRASILEIRA.** Text in Portuguese. 1958. 6/yr. adv. **Document type:** *Journal, Academic/Scholarly.* **Description:** Publishes original works in radiology, ultrasonography, nuclear medicine, radiotherapy, magnetic resonance and tomography.
Related titles: Online - full text ed.: free (effective 2011).
Indexed: CA, INIS AtomInd, SCOPUS, T02.
Published by: Colegio Brasileiro de Radiologia, Departamento da Associacao Medica Brasileira, Av Paulista 491, 13o Andar, Sao Paulo, SP 01311-909, Brazil. TEL 55-11-32854022, FAX 55-11-32851690.

615.842 ITA ISSN 0033-8362
RM845
➤ **LA RADIOLOGIA MEDICA.** Text in Italian; Summaries in English, Italian. 1914. 8/yr. EUR 533, USD 686 combined subscription to institutions (print & online eds.) (effective 2012). bk.rev. bibl.; charts; illus. index. reprint service avail. from PSC. **Document type:** *Journal, Academic/Scholarly.* **Description:** Covers imaging diagnostics and radiotherapy.
Former titles (until 1979): Minerva Radiologica (0026-4962); (until 1967): Minerva Radiologica, Fisioterapica e Radio - Biologica (0544-2656); (until 1962): Minerva Fisioterapica e Radiobiologica (0368-9719); (until 1960): Minerva Fisioterapica (0369-0202)
Related titles: Microform ed.: (from PQC); Online - full text ed.: ISSN 1826-6983. 2006 (from IngentaConnect).
Indexed: A22, A26, B&BAb, B19, B21, CTA, ChemAb, CurCont, DentInd, E01, EMBASE, ESPM, ExcerpMed, H&SSA, INIS AtomInd, IndMed, MEDLINE, P30, R10, Reac, SCI, SCOPUS, W07.
—BLDSC (7237.800000), GNLM, IE, Infotrieve, Ingenta, INIST. **CCC.**
Published by: (Societa Italiana di Radiologia Medica), Springer Italia Srl (Subsidiary of: Springer Science+Business Media), Via Decembrio 28, Milan, 20137, Italy. TEL 39-02-54259722, FAX 39-02-55193360, springer@springer.it. Ed. Roberto Pozzi Mucelli. Circ: 7,000.

615.842 USA ISSN 0033-8389
RM846 CODEN: RCNAAU
➤ **RADIOLOGIC CLINICS OF NORTH AMERICA.** Text in English. 1963. bi-m. USD 610 in United States to institutions; USD 766 elsewhere to institutions (effective 2012). adv. illus. back issues avail.; reprints avail. **Document type:** *Journal, Academic/Scholarly.* **Description:** Experts in the field provide information on current, practical information on the diagnosis of conditions affecting the entire body. Focuses on a single topic relevant to your imaging practice, from imaging of the acute patient using ultrasound to the latest advances in PET imaging for cancer detection and staging.
Related titles: Microform ed.: (from MIM, PQC); Online - full text ed.: ISSN 1557-8275 (from ScienceDirect); Supplement(s): Continuing Medical Education Supplement to Radiologic Clinics of North America. USD 176 (effective 2000).
Indexed: A22, AIM, ASCA, C06, C07, C08, CINAHL, CurCont, DentInd, EMBASE, ExcerpMed, FR, IIL, INI, INIS AtomInd, ISR, IndMed, Inpharma, MEDLINE, P30, R10, Reac, SCI, SCOPUS, W07.
—BLDSC (7237.830000), GNLM, IE, Infotrieve, Ingenta, INIST. **CCC.**
Published by: W.B. Saunders Co. (Subsidiary of: Elsevier Health Sciences), Elsevier, Health Sciences Division, Order Fulfillment, 3251 Riverport Ln, Maryland Heights, MO 63043. TEL 314-872-8370, 800-325-4177, FAX 314-432-1380, JournalCustomerService-usa@elsevier.com, http://www.us.elsevierhealth.com. Adv. contact John Marmero TEL 212-633-3657.

615.842 USA ISSN 0033-8397
RC78 CODEN: RATIB3
➤ **RADIOLOGIC TECHNOLOGY.** Text in English. 1929. bi-m. USD 70 domestic to individuals; USD 105 foreign to individuals; USD 75 domestic to institutions; USD 113 foreign to institutions; free to members (effective 2010). adv. bk.rev. illus. cum.index. back issues avail. **Document type:** *Journal, Academic/Scholarly.*
Formerly (until 1963): X-Ray Technician
Related titles: Online - full text ed.: ISSN 1943-5657. free to members (effective 2010).
Indexed: A22, A25, A26, B19, C06, C07, C08, CA, CINAHL, ChemAb, E08, EMBASE, ExcerpMed, G06, G07, G08, H11, H12, HospLI, I05, INI, IndMed, MEDLINE, P30, R10, Reac, S08, S09, SCOPUS, T02.
—BLDSC (7237.850000), GNLM, IE, Infotrieve, Ingenta, INIST. **CCC.**
Published by: American Society of Radiologic Technologists, 15000 Central Ave, SE, Albuquerque, NM 87123. TEL 505-298-4500, 800-444-2778, FAX 505-298-5063, memberservices@asrt.org, https://www.asrt.org. Adv. contact JoAnne Quirindongo TEL 505-298-4500 ext 1317.

616.07 JPN ISSN 1865-0333
➤ **RADIOLOGICAL PHYSICS AND TECHNOLOGY.** Text in English. 2008. 2/yr. EUR 130, USD 173 combined subscription to institutions (print & online eds.) (effective 2012). reprint service avail. from PSC. **Document type:** *Journal, Academic/Scholarly.*
Related titles: Online - full text ed.: ISSN 1865-0341. 2008.
Indexed: A22, A26, E01, E08, EMBASE, ExcerpMed, MEDLINE, P30, S09, SCOPUS.
—IE. **CCC.**
Published by: Springer Japan KK (Subsidiary of: Springer Science+Business Media), No 2 Funato Bldg, 1-11-11 Kudan-kita, Chiyoda-ku, Tokyo, 102-0073, Japan. TEL 81-3-68317000, FAX 81-3-68317001, orders@springer.jp, http://www.springer.jp. Ed. Kunio Doi.

616.07 DEU
RADIOLOGIE TECHNIK UND I T SYSTEME. Text in German. a. adv. **Document type:** *Directory, Trade.*
Published by: P N Verlag Dr. Wolf Zimmermann, Leitenberg 5, Finning, 86923, Germany. TEL 49-8806-95770, FAX 49-8806-957711, ktm@pn-verlag.de, http://www.pn-verlag.de. adv.: B&W page EUR 2,890, color page EUR 4,180. Circ: 11,000 (controlled).

616.842 DEU ISSN 2192-0230
RADIOLOGIE-TECHNOLOGIE. Text in German. 1988. 4/yr. EUR 14.60; EUR 3.90 newsstand/cover (effective 2011). adv. **Document type:** *Journal, Trade.*
Formerly (until 2011): Radiologie Assistent (0935-1779)
—GNLM.
Published by: Max Schmidt-Roemhild KG, Mengstr 16, Luebeck, 23552, Germany. TEL 49-451-703101, FAX 49-451-7031253, info@schmidt-roemhild.de, http://www.beleke.de/unternehmen/verlage/schmidtroemhild/index.html. Circ: 2,843 (paid and controlled).

615.842 DEU ISSN 1616-0681
➤ **RADIOLOGIE UP2DATE.** Text in German. 2001. 4/yr. EUR 159 to institutions; EUR 217 combined subscription to institutions (print & online eds.); EUR 50 newsstand/cover (effective 2011). adv. **Document type:** *Journal, Academic/Scholarly.*
Related titles: Online - full text ed.: ISSN 1617-8300. EUR 209 to institutions (effective 2011).
Indexed: INIS AtomInd.
—BLDSC (7237.993000), IE, Infotrieve. **CCC.**
Published by: Georg Thieme Verlag, Ruedigerstr 14, Stuttgart, 70469, Germany. TEL 49-711-8931421, FAX 49-711-8931410, leser.service@thieme.de. Ed. Dr. Ulrich Moedder. adv.: B&W page EUR 1,490, color page EUR 2,600. Circ: 3,400 (paid and controlled).

615.842 USA ISSN 0033-8419
RC78
➤ **RADIOLOGY.** Text in English. 1923. m. USD 495 to institutions (effective 2009). adv. bk.rev. abstr.; charts; illus. index, cum.index every 3 yrs. 308 p./no. 3 cols./p.; back issues avail.; reprints avail. **Document type:** *Journal, Academic/Scholarly.* **Description:** Covers clinical and other investigations relating to radiology and its allied sciences.
Related titles: Microform ed.: (from PQC); Online - full text ed.: ISSN 1527-1315.
Indexed: A20, A22, A36, AIM, B&BAb, B19, B21, B25, BDM&CN, BIOBASE, BIOSIS Prev, BioEngAb, C06, C07, C13, CABA, CIN, CISA, CTA, Cadscan, ChemAb, ChemTitl, CurCont, D01, DBA, DentInd, EMBASE, ExcerpMed, FR, G08, G10, GH, H11, H12, IABS, IDIS, IIL, INI, INIS AtomInd, ISR, IndMed, Inpharma, Inspec, JW, JW-EM, JW-G, Kidney, LeadAb, MEDLINE, MS&D, MycolAb, N02, N03, NSA, P30, P33, P35, R10, RM&VM, Reac, SCI, SCOPUS, T05, TM, VS, W07, Zincscan.
—BLDSC (7238.000000), AskIEEE, CASDDS, GNLM, IE, Infotrieve, Ingenta, INIST. **CCC.**
Published by: Radiological Society of North America, Inc., 820 Jorie Blvd, Oak Brook, IL 60523. TEL 630-571-7819, 800-381-6660, FAX 630-571-7837, membership@rsna.org, http://www.rsna.org. Adv. contact Jim Drew TEL 630-571-7819. B&W page USD 3,480; trim 8.25 x 10.875.

615.842 616.99 SVN ISSN 1318-2099
CODEN: RONCEM
➤ **RADIOLOGY AND ONCOLOGY.** Text in English, Slovenian. 1964. q. EUR 50 foreign to individuals; EUR 100 foreign to institutions (effective 2011). adv. bk.rev. abstr.; bibl.; charts; illus. 80 p./no. 2 cols./p.; back issues avail. **Document type:** *Journal, Academic/Scholarly.* **Description:** Covers radiology, radiotherapy, oncology, nuclear medicine, radiophysics, radiobiology and radiation protection.
Formerly (until vol.25, 1991): Radiologia Iugoslavica (0485-893X)
Related titles: Online - full text ed.: ISSN 1581-3207. 1998. free (effective 2011).
Indexed: CA, CIN, ChemAb, ChemTitl, EMBASE, ExcerpMed, R10, Reac, RefZh, SCI, SCOPUS, T02, W07.
—BLDSC (7238.120000), CASDDS, GNLM, IE, Ingenta, Linda Hall.
Published by: Onkoloski Institut Ljubljana/Institute of Oncology Ljubljana, Zaloska 2, Ljubljana, 1000, Slovenia. TEL 386-1-4314225, FAX 386-1-4314180, mzakelj@onko-i.si, http://www.onko-i.si. Ed. Gregor Sersa. adv.: B&W page USD 250, color page USD 500; trim 17 x 24. Circ: 700.

616.07 USA ISSN 1930-0433
R895.A1
➤ **RADIOLOGY CASE REPORTS.** Text in English. 2006. q. free (effective 2011). **Document type:** *Report, Academic/Scholarly.* **Description:** Publishes case reports that feature radiologic imaging.
Media: Online - full text.
Published by: University of Washington, Odegaard Undergraduate Library, Ground Fl, 022 Odegaard, Seattle, WA 98195. TEL 206-543-9198, FAX 206-221-4890, uwvic@u.washington.edu, http://www.washington.edu.

➤ **RADIOLOGY CODING ALERT;** the practical adviser for ethically optimizing coding reimbursement and efficiency in radiology practices. *see* INSURANCE

616.07 JPN ISSN 1344-316X
RADIOLOGY FRONTIER. Text in Japanese. 1998. q. JPY 8,380 (effective 2005). **Document type:** *Journal, Academic/Scholarly.*
Published by: Medikaru Rebyusha/Medical Review Co., Ltd., 1-7-3 Hirano-Machi, Chuo-ku, Yoshida Bldg., Osaka-shi, 541-0046, Japan. TEL 81-6-62231468, FAX 81-6-62231245.

RADIOLOGY MANAGEMENT. *see* HEALTH FACILITIES AND ADMINISTRATION

616.0757 GBR ISSN 1461-4650
➤ **RADIOLOGY NOW.** Text in English. 1982. 3/yr. back issues avail. **Document type:** *Journal, Academic/Scholarly.* **Description:** Includes advances in radiology and radiological techniques.
Indexed: EMBASE, ExcerpMed, R10, Reac, SCOPUS.
Published by: Franklin Scientific Projects International, 516 Wandsworth Rd, London, SW8 3JX, United Kingdom. TEL 44-20-7501-4085, FAX 44-20-7720-3525. Circ: 3,500.

616.07 USA ISSN 2090-1941
▼ ➤ **RADIOLOGY RESEARCH AND PRACTICE.** Text in English. 2009. q. USD 195 (effective 2011). **Document type:** *Journal, Academic/Scholarly.* **Description:** Publishes original research articles, review articles, and clinical studies in all areas of radiology.
Related titles: Online - full text ed.: ISSN 2090-195X. free (effective 2011).
Indexed: A01.
Published by: Hindawi Publishing Corporation, 410 Park Ave, 15th Fl, PMB 287, New York, NY 10022. FAX 215-893-4392, 866-446-3294, hindawi@hindawi.com.

615.842 USA ISSN 1539-0101
RADIOLOGY TODAY. Text in English. 2000. m. free domestic to qualified personnel; USD 50 in Canada; USD 95 elsewhere; USD 5 per issue (effective 2010). adv. back issues avail.; reprints avail. **Document type:** *Journal, Trade.* **Description:** Presents professional and technological developments for the radiologic science community.
Related titles: Online - full text ed.: free (effective 2010).
Indexed: C06, C07.
Published by: Great Valley Publishing Company, Inc., 3801 Schuylkill Rd, Spring City, PA 19475. TEL 610-948-9500, 800-278-4400, FAX 610-948-4202, Sales@gvpub.com, http://www.gvpub.com. Ed. Jim Knaub. Pub., Adv. contact Mara E Honicker. Circ: 40,000.

616.07 SRB ISSN 0354-1452
RADIOLOSKI ARHIV SRBIJE/RADIOLOGICAL ARCHIVES OF SERBIA. Text in Serbian, English. 1992. s-a. CSD 600 domestic to individuals; CSD 1,200 domestic to institutions; EUR 20 foreign (effective 2005).
Indexed: EMBASE, ExcerpMed, SCOPUS.
Published by: Srpsko Lekarsko Drustvo/Serbian Medical Association, George Washington St, 19, Belgrade, 11000. TEL 381-11-3234450, FAX 381-11-3246090, sld@eunet.yu, http://www.sld.org.yu. Ed. Petar Bosnakovic.

615.842 DEU ISSN 1866-1033
RADIOPRAXIS. Text in German. 2008. 4/yr. EUR 69 to institutions; EUR 102 combined subscription to institutions (print & online eds.); EUR 22 newsstand/cover (effective 2011). **Document type:** *Journal, Academic/Scholarly.*
Related titles: Online - full text ed.: ISSN 1866-1041. 2008. EUR 102 to institutions (effective 2011).
—**CCC.**
Published by: Georg Thieme Verlag, Ruedigerstr 14, Stuttgart, 70469, Germany. TEL 49-711-8931421, FAX 49-711-8931410, leser.service@thieme.de.

615.842 IRL ISSN 0167-8140
RC254.A1 CODEN: RAONDT
➤ **RADIOTHERAPY & ONCOLOGY.** Text in English. 1984. 12/yr. EUR 2,796 in Europe to institutions; JPY 371,100 in Japan to institutions; USD 3,126 elsewhere to institutions (effective 2012). adv. index. reprints avail. **Document type:** *Journal, Academic/Scholarly.* **Description:** Covers areas of interest relating to radiation oncology.
Related titles: Microform ed.: (from PQC); Online - full text ed.: ISSN 1879-0887 (from IngentaConnect, ScienceDirect).

Indexed: A01, A03, A08, A22, A26, ASCA, ASFA, B21, B25, BIOBASE, BIOSIS Prev, CA, CIN, ChemAb, ChemTitl, CurCont, EMBASE, ESPM, ExcerpMed, G10, I05, IABS, IBR, IBZ, INIS AtomInd, ISR, IndMed, Inpharma, Inspec, MEDLINE, MS&D, MycolAb, P30, P35, R10, Reac, SCI, SCOPUS, T02, ToxAb, W07.
—BLDSC (7240.790000), AskIEEE, CASDDS, GNLM, IE, Infotrieve, Ingenta, INIST. **CCC.**
Published by: (European Society for Therapeutic Radiology and Oncology), Elsevier Ireland Ltd (Subsidiary of: Elsevier Science & Technology), Elsevier House, Brookvale Plaza, E. Park, Shannon, Co. Clare, Ireland. TEL 353-61-709600, FAX 353-61-709100, nlinfo@elsevier.nl, http://www.elsevier.nl. Ed. Dr. J Overgaard. Pub. Dr. Peter W Harrison. Adv. contact Samantha Cimurs TEL 44-1865-843258. B&W page USD 1,520, color page USD 3,285; trim 8.25 x 11. Circ: 3,813 (paid); 96 (free). **Subscr. to:** Elsevier BV, Radarweg 29, PO Box 211, Amsterdam 1000 AE, Netherlands. TEL 31-20-4853757, FAX 31-20-4853432, http://www.elsevier.nl.

➤ **REFERATIVNYI SBORNIK. LUCHEVAYA DIAGNOSTIKA. NOVOSTI NAUKI I TEKHNIKI.** *see* MEDICAL SCIENCES—Abstracting, Bibliographies, Statistics

➤ **REFERATOVY VYBER Z RADIODIAGNOSTIKY (ONLINE)/ ABSTRACTS OF RADIOLOGY.** *see* MEDICAL SCIENCES—Abstracting, Bibliographies, Statistics

616 615 BGR ISSN 0486-400X
CODEN: RENRAR
RENTGENOLOGIA I RADIOLOGIA. Text in Bulgarian; Summaries in Russian, English. 1962. q. BGL 16; USD 52 foreign (effective 2002). **Document type:** *Journal.* **Description:** Publishes original articles, surveys, reports, problems relating to radiation protection, scientific news, etc.
Indexed: ABSML, ChemAb, EMBASE, ExcerpMed, INIS AtomInd, R10, Reac, SCOPUS.
—CASDDS, GNLM, INIST.
Published by: (Bulgaria. Ministerstvo na Narodnoto Zdrave), Bulgarska Asotsiatsia po Radiologia/Bulgarian Association of Radiology, 6 Damian Gruev Blvd, Sofia, 1303, Bulgaria. TEL 359-2-9877201, ldiankov@uheg.medicalnet-bg.org, http://www.medun.acad.bg/bar/bar-evnt.htm. Ed. Ljubomir A Diankov. Circ: 620. **Dist. by:** Hemus, 6 Rouski Blvd., Sofia 1000, Bulgaria; **Dist. by:** Sofia Books, ul Silivria 16, Sofia 1404, Bulgaria. TEL 359-2-9586257, info@sofiabooks-bg.com, http://www.sofiabooks-bg.com. **Co-sponsor:** Nauchno Druzhestvo po Rentgenologia i Radiologia.

615 GBR ISSN 1179-1586
RC78.7.D53
➤ **REPORTS IN MEDICAL IMAGING.** Text in English. 2008. irreg. free (effective 2011). **Document type:** *Journal, Academic/Scholarly.*
Media: Online - full text.
Indexed: SCOPUS.
—CCC.
Published by: Dove Medical Press Ltd., Beechfield House, Winterton Way, Macclesfield, SK11 0JL, United Kingdom. TEL 44-1625-509130, FAX 44-1625-617933. Ed. Tarik F Massoud.

616.07 GBR ISSN 2230-228X
▼ ➤ **RESEARCH AND REPORTS IN NUCLEAR MEDICINE.** Text in English. 2011. irreg. free (effective 2011). **Document type:** *Journal, Academic/Scholarly.* **Description:** Publishes research, reports, reviews and commentaries on all areas of nuclear medicine.
Media: Online - full text.
—CCC.
Published by: Dove Medical Press Ltd., Beechfield House, Winterton Way, Macclesfield, SK11 0JL, United Kingdom. TEL 44-1625-509130, FAX 44-1625-617933. Ed. Dr. Isis Gayed.

616.07 USA ISSN 1819-348X
➤ **RESEARCH JOURNAL OF RADIOLOGY.** Text in English. 2006. q. **Document type:** *Journal, Academic/Scholarly.*
Related titles: Online - full text ed.: ISSN 2154-3887.
Indexed: A01, CA, T02.
Published by: Academic Journals Inc., 224, 5th Ave, No 2218, New York, NY 10001. FAX 888-777-8532, support@scialert.com.

612.014 ARG ISSN 0048-7619
REVISTA ARGENTINA DE RADIOLOGIA. Text in Spanish; Summaries in Spanish, English. 1937. 3/yr. adv. abstr.; illus. index. **Document type:** *Journal, Academic/Scholarly.*
Formerly (until 1938): Roentgen (0329-0298)
Related titles: Online - full text ed.: ISSN 1852-9992 (from SciELO).
Indexed: INIS AtomInd.
Published by: Sociedad Argentina de Radiologia, Arenales 1985, Planta Baja, Buenos Aires, C1124AAC, Argentina. TEL 54-11-48155444, secretaria@sar.org.ar, http://www.sar.org.ar. Ed. Matilde Buzzi. Circ: 2,200.

616.075 BRA ISSN 1679-8953
REVISTA BRASILEIRA DE ULTRA - SONOGRAFIA. Abbreviated title: R B U S. Text in Portuguese. 1994. s-a. **Document type:** *Journal, Academic/Scholarly.*
Published by: Sociedade Brasileira de Ultra - Sonografia (S B U S), Rua Teodoro Sampaio 352, Conj 53/54, Pinheiros, Sao Paulo, 05406-000, Brazil. TEL 55-11-30816049, http://www.sbus.org.br.

615.842 CHL ISSN 0717-201X
REVISTA CHILENA DE RADIOLOGIA. Text in Spanish. 1995. q. CLP 25,000 domestic; USD 40 foreign. back issues avail. **Document type:** *Journal, Academic/Scholarly.*
Related titles: Online - full text ed.: ISSN 0717-9308. 2002. free (effective 2011) (from SciELO).
Indexed: INIS AtomInd, SCOPUS.
Published by: (Sociedad Chilena de Radiologia), Publimpacto, Ave. Alejandro Fleming 8796, Las Condes, Santiago, Chile. TEL 56-2-2112854, FAX 56-2-6781397, pulimpacto@netline.cl. Ed. Jose D Arce.

616.07 CHL ISSN 0717-3695
REVISTA CHILENA DE ULTRASONOGRAFIA. Text in Spanish. 1998. q. back issues avail. **Document type:** *Journal, Academic/Scholarly.*
Media: Online - full text.
Published by: Sociedad Chilena de Ultrasonografia en Medicina y Biologia, Ave. Alejandro Fleming 8796, Las Condes, Santiago, Chile. TEL 56-2-2112854, ultrasonografia@netline.cl, http://www.ultrasonografia.cl/. Ed. Patricio Gana.

616.842 BRA
REVISTA DA IMAGEM (ONLINE). Text in Portuguese; Summaries in English, Portuguese. 1978. q. **Document type:** *Journal, Academic/Scholarly.* **Description:** Covers imaging methods for medical diagnosis, research, and clinical applications.
Formerly (until 2007): Revista da Imagem (Print) (0100-9699)
Indexed: INIS AtomInd.
Published by: Sociedade Paulista de Radiologia, Av. Paulista 491, Cjs 41/42, Sao Paulo, SP 01311-000, Brazil. TEL 55-11-32843988, FAX 55-11-32843152.

615.842 ESP ISSN 0212-6982
➤ **REVISTA ESPANOLA DE MEDICINA NUCLEAR.** Text in Spanish. 1982. bi-m. EUR 96.52 combined subscription to individuals print & online eds.; EUR 244.36 combined subscription to institutions print & online eds. (effective 2009). back issues avail.; reprints avail. **Document type:** *Journal, Academic/Scholarly.*
Incorporates (in 1977): Medicina Nuclear (0212-6974)
Related titles: Online - full text ed.: ISSN 1578-200X. 1996. EUR 80.40 (effective 2009) (from ScienceDirect).
Indexed: A22, EMBASE, ExcerpMed, IndMed, MEDLINE, P30, R10, Reac, SCI, SCOPUS, W07.
—BLDSC (7854.109000), IE, Infotrieve, Ingenta, INIST. **CCC.**
Published by: (Sociedad Espanola de Medicina Nuclear), Elsevier Doyma (Subsidiary of: Elsevier Health Sciences), Traversa de Gracia 17-21, Barcelona, 08021, Spain. TEL 34-932-418800, FAX 34-932-419020, editorial@elsevier.com. Ed. J M Freire Macias. Circ: 850. **Co-sponsor:** Asociacion Latinoamericana de Sociedades de Biologia y Medicina Nuclear.

616.07 ESP ISSN 1697-2139
REVISTA ESPANOLA DE ULTRASONIDOS EN OBSTETRICIA Y GINECOLOGIA. Text in Spanish. 2002. q. **Document type:** *Magazine, Trade.*
Media: CD-ROM.
Published by: Sociedad Espanola de Ginecologia y Obstetricia, Paseo de la Habana 190, Madrid, 28036, Spain. TEL 34-91-3509816, FAX 34-91-3509818, http://www.sego.es.

616.075 MEX ISSN 0370-6486
REVISTA MEXICANA DE RADIOLOGIA. Text in Spanish; Summaries in English. 1947. q. bk.rev. abstr.; bibl.; illus.; tr.lit. back issues avail. **Document type:** *Journal, Academic/Scholarly.* **Description:** Provides clinical and research papers to professionals in the fields of radiology and nuclear medicine.
Related titles: Online - full text ed.
Indexed: A01, A20, C01.
—INIST.
Published by: (Federacion Mexicana de Radiologia y Images), Intersistemas S.A. de C.V., Aguiar y Seijas 75, Lomas de Chapultepec, Mexico City, DF 11000, Mexico. TEL 52-55-55202073, FAX 52-55-55403764, http://www.intersistemas.com.mx. **Subscr. to:** Federacion Mexicana de Radiologia y Images, Coahuila 35, Col. Roma, Mexico City, D F 06700, Mexico. TEL 525-584-7715, FAX 525-574-5374, tmri@compuserve.com, http://www.tmri.org.mx.

616.07 PER ISSN 1810-8415
REVISTA PERUANA DE RADIOLOGIA. Text in Spanish. 1997. irreg. **Document type:** *Journal, Academic/Scholarly.*
Related titles: Online - full text ed.: ISSN 1810-8423.
Published by: Sociedad Peruana de Radiologia, Av Jose Pardo 138, Of 603, Miraflores, Lima, Peru. TEL 51-1-4459753, http://www.sopr.org.

616.07 JPN ISSN 0911-1069
RINSHO GAZO/CLINICAL IMAGIOLOGY. Text in Japanese. 1985. m. JPY 35,070 (effective 2007). **Document type:** *Journal, Academic/Scholarly.*
Published by: Medical View Co. Ltd./Mejikaru Byusha, 2-30 Ichigaya-Honmura-cho, Shinjuku-ku, Tokyo, 162-0845, Japan. TEL 81-3-52282050, FAX 81-3-52282059, http://www.medicalview.co.jp.

615.842 JPN ISSN 0009-9252
CODEN: JJCRA
RINSHO HOSHASEN/JAPANESE JOURNAL OF CLINICAL RADIOLOGY. Variant title: Clinical Radiology. Text in Japanese; Summaries in English. 1956. m. JPY 39,690 (effective 2007). abstr.; charts; illus. Index. **Document type:** *Journal, Academic/Scholarly.*
Indexed: A22, DentInd, EMBASE, ExcerpMed, INIS AtomInd, ISR, IndMed, P30, R10, Reac, SCOPUS.
—BLDSC (4651.430000), GNLM, IE, Infotrieve, Ingenta.
Published by: Kanehara Shuppan/Kanehara & Co. Ltd., 2-31-14 Yushima, Bunkyo-ku, Tokyo, 113-8687, Japan. TEL 81-3-38117184, FAX 81-3-38130288, http://www.kanehara-shuppan.co.jp/. Circ: 4,700.

615.842 DEU ISSN 1438-9029
CODEN: RFGVEF
➤ **ROEFO. FORTSCHRITTE AUF DEM GEBIET DER ROENTGENSTRAHLEN UND DER BILDGEBENDEN VERFAHREN.** Text in German; Summaries in English, German. 1949. m. EUR 579 to institutions; EUR 766 combined subscription to institutions (print & online eds.); EUR 61 newsstand/cover (effective 2011). adv. bk.rev. abstr.; bibl.; charts; illus.; stat. index. reprints avail. **Document type:** *Journal, Academic/Scholarly.*
Former titles (until 1996): RoeFo. Fortschritte auf dem Gebiete der Roentgenstrahlen und der Neuen Bildgebenden Verfahren (0936-6652); (until 1989): RoeFo. Fortschritte auf dem Gebiete der Roentgenstrahlen und der Nuklearmedizin (0340-1618); (until 1975): Fortschritte auf dem Gebiete der Roentgenstrahlen und der Nuklearmedizin (0015-8151); (until 1956): Fortschritte auf dem Gebiete der Roentgenstrahlen vereinigt mit Roentgenpraxis (0367-2239); Which was formed by the merger of (1897-1949): Fortschritte auf dem Gebiete der Roentgenstrahlen (0367-2220); &: Roentgenpraxis (0370-6613); Incorporates (1991-1999): Aktuelle Radiologie (0939-267X); Which was formed by the merger of (1948-1990): Roentgen-Blaetter (0300-8592); (1984-1990): Digitale Bilddiagnostik (0724-7591); Which was formerly (1981-1983): Computertomographie (0720-0501)
Related titles: Microform ed.: (from PQC); Online - full text ed.: ISSN 1438-9010. EUR 739 to institutions (effective 2011).
Indexed: A20, A22, CISA, ChemAb, CurCont, DentInd, EMBASE, ExcerpMed, FR, INIS AtomInd, ISR, IndMed, Inpharma, Inspec, MEDLINE, P30, R10, Reac, SCI, SCOPUS, TM, W07.
—BLDSC (8019.170000), CASDDS, GNLM, IE, Infotrieve, Ingenta, INIST. **CCC.**
Published by: (Deutsche Roentgengesellschaft), Georg Thieme Verlag, Ruedigerstr 14, Stuttgart, 70469, Germany. TEL 49-711-8931421, FAX 49-711-8931410, leser.service@thieme.de. Ed. G Adam. R&P Michael Wachinger. Adv. contact Irmgard Mayer TEL 49-711-8931469. B&W page EUR 2,440, color page EUR 3,580. Circ: 7,300 (paid). **Co-sponsor:** Oesterreichische Roentgengesellschaft.

615.842 DEU ISSN 0035-7820
CODEN: RGPXB2
ROENTGENPRAXIS. Text in German. 1947. 4/yr. EUR 110 in Europe to institutions; JPY 15,100 in Japan to institutions; USD 139 elsewhere to institutions (effective 2009). adv. bk.rev. charts; illus. index. **Document type:** *Journal, Academic/Scholarly.* **Description:** Examines the various aspects of radiology and nuclear medicine.
Supersedes in part (in 1963): Roentgen- und Laboratoriumspraxis (0370-5994); Which was formerly (until 1950): Roentgenphotographie, Medizinische Photographie und Medizinische Laboratoriumspraxis (0176-6287); (until 1948): Roentgenphotographie und Medizinische Photographie (0176-652X)
Related titles: Online - full text ed.: (from ScienceDirect).
Indexed: A22, A26, CA, ChemAb, DentInd, EMBASE, ExcerpMed, I05, IBR, IBZ, INIS AtomInd, IndMed, Inspec, MEDLINE, P30, R10, Reac, SCOPUS, T02, TM.
—BLDSC (8021.700000), GNLM, IE, Infotrieve, Ingenta, INIST. **CCC.**
Published by: Urban und Fischer Verlag (Subsidiary of: Elsevier GmbH), Loebdergraben 14a, Jena, 07743, Germany. TEL 49-3641-626430, FAX 49-3641-626432, http://www.urbanundfischer.de. Eds. Hans-Juergen Brambs, Werner Bautz. R&P Kerstin Schumann TEL 49-3641-626444. adv.: B&W page EUR 1,135, color page EUR 2,035; trim 210 x 280. Circ: 2,950 (paid and controlled). **Subscr. in non-German speaking countries to:** Nature Publishing Group, Brunel Rd, Houndmills, Basingstoke, Hamps RG21 6XS, United Kingdom. TEL 44-1256-302629, FAX 44-1256-476117

616.07 USA ISSN 1543-0448
S D M S SOUND NEWS. (Society of Diagnostic Medical Sonography) Text in English. 1999 (Sept.). m. free to members (effective 2003).
Published by: Society of Diagnostic Medical Sonography, 2745 N Dallas Pkwy, Ste. 350, Plano, TX 75093-4706. TEL 214-473-8057, 800-229-9506, FAX 214-473-8563, http://www.sdms.org.

612 USA ISSN 0739-9529
R895.A1 CODEN: SIRAE5
➤ **SEMINARS IN INTERVENTIONAL RADIOLOGY.** Text in English. 1984. q. USD 575 domestic to institutions; USD 587 foreign to institutions; USD 697 combined subscription domestic to institutions (print & online eds.); USD 723 combined subscription foreign to institutions (print & online eds.) (effective 2011). abstr.; bibl.; illus. reprints avail. **Document type:** *Journal, Academic/Scholarly.* **Description:** Provides comprehensive coverage of areas such as cardio-vascular imaging, oncologic interventional radiology, abdominal interventional radiology, ultrasound, MRI imaging, sonography, pediatric radiology, musculoskeletal radiology, metallic stents, renal intervention, angiography, neurointerventions, and CT fluoroscopy along with other areas.
Related titles: Online - full text ed.: ISSN 1098-8963. USD 677 domestic to institutions; USD 691 foreign to institutions (effective 2011).
Indexed: A01, A03, A08, A22, ASCA, CA, FR, IIL, Inpharma, P30, SCOPUS, T02.
—BLDSC (8239.453000), GNLM, IE, Infotrieve, Ingenta, INIST. **CCC.**
Published by: Thieme Medical Publishers (Subsidiary of: Georg Thieme Verlag), 333 Seventh Ave, New York, NY 10001. TEL 212-760-0888, 800-782-3488, FAX 212-947-1112, info@thieme.com. Ed. Brian Funaki TEL 773-702-1306. Adv. contact James C Cunningham TEL 201-767-4170. Circ: 1,285.

616.075 USA ISSN 1089-7860
RC925.A1 CODEN: SMRAFY
➤ **SEMINARS IN MUSCULOSKELETAL RADIOLOGY.** Text in English. 1997. 5/yr. USD 461 domestic to institutions; USD 476 foreign to institutions; USD 567 combined subscription domestic to institutions (print & online eds.); USD 596 combined subscription foreign to institutions (print & online eds.) (effective 2011). reprints avail. **Document type:** *Journal, Academic/Scholarly.* **Description:** Devoted to musculoskeletal and associated imaging techniques and also covers advanced imaging techniques of metabolic bone disease and other areas like the foot and ankle, wrist, spine and other extremities.
Related titles: Online - full text ed.: ISSN 1098-898X. USD 542 domestic to institutions; USD 556 foreign to institutions (effective 2011).
Indexed: A01, A03, A08, C06, C07, CA, CurCont, EMBASE, ExcerpMed, IndMed, MEDLINE, P30, R10, Reac, SCI, SCOPUS, T02, W07.
—BLDSC (8239.455050), GNLM, IE, Infotrieve, Ingenta, INIST. **CCC.**
Published by: Thieme Medical Publishers (Subsidiary of: Georg Thieme Verlag), 333 Seventh Ave, New York, NY 10001. TEL 212-760-0888, 800-782-3488, FAX 212-947-1112, info@thieme.com. Eds. Lawrence White TEL 416-586-5231, Marco Zanetti TEL 41-44-3863303. Adv. contact James C Cunningham TEL 201-767-4170. Circ: 1,029.

616.07575 USA ISSN 0001-2998
CODEN: SMNMAB
➤ **SEMINARS IN NUCLEAR MEDICINE.** Text in English. 1971. q. USD 513 in United States to institutions; USD 631 elsewhere to institutions (effective 2012). adv. abstr.; bibl.; charts; illus. back issues avail.; reprints avail. **Document type:** *Journal, Academic/Scholarly.* **Description:** Contains original articles written by invited experts and is devoted to one topic in the field of nuclear medicine.
Related titles: Online - full text ed.: ISSN 1558-4623 (from ScienceDirect).
Indexed: A22, A26, ASCA, B21, BIOSIS Prev, BioEngAb, C06, C07, CA, CTA, ChemAb, ChemoAb, CurCont, EMBASE, ExcerpMed, FR, I05, IDIS, IIL, ISR, IndMed, Inpharma, Inspec, MEDLINE, MycolAb, NSA, P30, R10, Reac, SCI, SCOPUS, T02, W07.
—BLDSC (8239.456000), CASDDS, GNLM, IE, Infotrieve, Ingenta, INIST. **CCC.**
Published by: W.B. Saunders Co. (Subsidiary of: Elsevier Health Sciences), Elsevier, Health Sciences Division, Order Fulfillment, 3251 Riverport Ln, Maryland Heights, MO 63043. TEL 314-872-8370, 800-325-4177, FAX 314-432-1380, JournalCustomerService-usa@elsevier.com, http://www.us.elsevierhealth.com. Eds. Leonard M Freeman, Dr. M Donald Blaufox. Pub. Mary Heffner TEL 212-633-3953. Circ: 1,055.

➤ **SEMINARS IN ONCOLOGY NURSING.** *see* MEDICAL SCIENCES—Nurses And Nursing

➤ **SEMINARS IN RADIATION ONCOLOGY.** *see* MEDICAL SCIENCES—Oncology

615.842 USA ISSN 0037-198X
RC78 CODEN: SEROAF
➤ **SEMINARS IN ROENTGENOLOGY.** Text in English. 1966. q. USD 500 in United States to institutions; USD 633 elsewhere to institutions (effective 2012). adv. bibl.; charts; illus. back issues avail.; reprints avail. **Document type:** *Journal, Academic/Scholarly.* **Description:** Designed for the practicing radiologist, each issue covers a single topic of current importance and the clinical, pathological, and roentgenologic aspects are emphasized.
Related titles: Online - full text ed.: ISSN 1558-4658 (from ScienceDirect).
Indexed: A22, A26, ASCA, B21, BDM&CN, BIOSIS Prev, C06, C07, C08, CINAHL, CurCont, DentInd, EMBASE, ExcerpMed, FR, H12, I05, IIL, ISR, IndMed, Inpharma, MEDLINE, MycolAb, P30, R10, Reac, SCI, SCOPUS, T02, W07.
—BLDSC (8239.460000), GNLM, IE, Infotrieve, Ingenta, INIST. **CCC.**
Published by: W.B. Saunders Co. (Subsidiary of: Elsevier Health Sciences), Elsevier, Health Sciences Division, Order Fulfillment, 3251 Riverport Ln, Maryland Heights, MO 63043. TEL 314-872-8370, 800-325-4177, FAX 314-432-1380, JournalCustomerService-usa@elsevier.com, http://www.us.elsevierhealth.com. Ed. Jannette Collins. Pub. Mary Heffner TEL 212-633-3953. Adv. contact John Marmero TEL 212-633-3657. Circ: 520.

615.842 USA ISSN 0887-2171
RC78.7.U4 CODEN: SEULDO
➤ **SEMINARS IN ULTRASOUND, C T AND M R I.** (Computerized Tomography and Magnetic Resonance) Text in English. 1980. bi-m. USD 501 in United States to institutions; USD 659 elsewhere to institutions (effective 2012). bibl.; charts; illus. index. back issues avail.; reprints avail. **Document type:** *Journal, Academic/Scholarly.* **Description:** Focuses on new concepts and research findings for physicians involved in the performance and interpretation of ultrasound.
Formerly (until 1984): Seminars in Ultrasound (0194-1720)
Related titles: Online - full text ed.: ISSN 1558-5034 (from ScienceDirect).
Indexed: A22, A26, ASCA, B&BAb, B19, BIOSIS Prev, BioEngAb, C06, C07, C08, CINAHL, CurCont, EMBASE, ExcerpMed, H12, I05, IIL, IndMed, Inpharma, MEDLINE, MycolAb, P30, R10, Reac, SCI, SCOPUS, T02, W07.
—BLDSC (8239.485500), GNLM, IE, Infotrieve, Ingenta, INIST. **CCC.**
Published by: W.B. Saunders Co. (Subsidiary of: Elsevier Health Sciences), Elsevier, Health Sciences Division, Order Fulfillment, 3251 Riverport Ln, Maryland Heights, MO 63043. TEL 314-872-8370, 800-325-4177, FAX 314-432-1380, JournalCustomerService-usa@elsevier.com, http://www.us.elsevierhealth.com. Eds. Dr. Howard Raymond, Dr. Joel D Schwartz. Pub. Mary Heffner TEL 212-633-3953. Circ: 900.

616.842 NLD ISSN 0167-465X
➤ **SERIES IN RADIOLOGY.** Text in English. 1979. irreg., latest vol.25, 1995. price varies. **Document type:** *Monographic series, Academic/Scholarly.*
—BLDSC (8250.200500). **CCC.**
Published by: Springer Netherlands (Subsidiary of: Springer Science+Business Media), Van Godewijckstraat 30, Dordrecht, 3311 GX, Netherlands. TEL 31-78-6576050, FAX 31-78-6576474.

615.842 NZL ISSN 1170-9758
SHADOWS. Text in English. 1958. q. NZD 200 membership (effective 2009). adv. bk.rev. **Document type:** *Journal, Trade.* **Description:** Covers new technologies and techniques in radiology in New Zealand. Issues of importance to New Zealand MRTs are also discussed.
Published by: New Zealand Institute of Medical Radiation Technology, St Heliers, PO Box. 25668, Auckland 5, New Zealand. TEL 64-9-3793059, FAX 64-9-3793029, nzimrt@nzimrt.co.nz, http://www.nzimrt.co.nz/. Ed., R&P Coralie Christie. Circ: 800.

SHIKA HOSHASEN/DENTAL RADIOLOGY. *see* MEDICAL SCIENCES—Dentistry

616.07 CHN ISSN 1002-1671
SHIYONG FANGSHEXUE ZAZHI/PRACTICAL RADIOLOGY. Text in Chinese. 1985. bi-m. USD 74.40 (effective 2009). **Document type:** *Journal, Academic/Scholarly.*
Related titles: Online - full text ed.
Indexed: A28, APA, B&BAb, B19, B21, BrCerAb, C&ISA, CA/WCA, CIA, CerAb, CivEngAb, CorrAb, E&CAJ, E11, EEA, EMA, ESPM, EnvEAb, H15, M&TEA, M09, MBF, METADEX, NSA, SolStAb, T04, WAA.
—BLDSC (8267.297883), East View, Linda Hall.
Published by: Xi'an Shi Weishengju, 20, Huancheng Nanlu Xi-duan, 6/F, No.605, Hailian Building, Xi'an, 710068, China. TEL 86-29-82122004, FAX 86-29-82122003. **Dist. by:** China International Book Trading Corp, 35 Chegongzhuang Xilu, Haidian District, PO Box 399, Beijing 100044, China. TEL 86-10-68412045, FAX 86-10-68412023, cibtc@mail.cibtc.com.cn, http://www.cibtc.com.cn.

616.07 CHN ISSN 1009-6817
SHIYONG YIXUE YINGXIANG ZAZHI/JOURNAL OF PRACTICAL MEDICAL IMAGING. Text in Chinese. 2000. bi-m. CNY 10 newsstand/cover (effective 2006). **Document type:** *Journal, Academic/Scholarly.*
Related titles: Online - full text ed.
Published by: Shanxi Sheng Renmin Yiyuan, 99, Shuangtasi Jie, Taiyuan, 030012, China. TEL 86-351-4960098.

618 DEU ISSN 0364-2348
RC78.A1
➤ **SKELETAL RADIOLOGY**; journal of radiology, pathology and orthopedics. Text in English. 1976. m. EUR 1,509, USD 1,863 combined subscription to institutions (print & online eds.) (effective 2012). adv. bk.rev. charts; illus. index. back issues avail.; reprint service avail. from PSC. **Document type:** *Journal, Academic/Scholarly.* **Description:** Covers the anatomical, pathological, physiological, clinical, metabolic, and epidemiological aspects of the many entities affecting the skeleton.
Related titles: Microfilm ed.: (from PQC); Online - full text ed.: ISSN 1432-2161 (from IngentaConnect).
Indexed: A01, A03, A08, A22, A26, ASCA, B21, BDM&CN, CA, CTA, CurCont, DentInd, E01, EMBASE, ExcerpMed, IIL, INI, INIS AtomInd, ISR, IndMed, Inpharma, MEDLINE, P20, P22, P24, P30, P48, P54, PQC, R10, Reac, SCI, SCOPUS, T02, TM, W07.
—BLDSC (8295.200000), GNLM, IE, Infotrieve, Ingenta, INIST. **CCC.**
Published by: (International Skeletal Society), Springer (Subsidiary of: Springer Science+Business Media), Tiergartenstr 17, Heidelberg, 69121, Germany. TEL 49-6221-4870, FAX 49-6221-345229. Eds. Dr. Iain W McCall, Dr. Jeremy J Kaye. Adv. contact Stephan Kroeck TEL 49-30-827875739. B&W page EUR 1,390, color page EUR 2,430. Circ: 1,500 (paid and controlled). **Subscr. in the Americas to:** Springer New York LLC, Journal Fulfillment, PO Box 2485, Secaucus, NJ 07096. TEL 800-777-4643, 201-348-4033, FAX 201-348-4505, journals-ny@springer.com, http://www.springer.com; **Subscr. to:** Springer Distribution Center, Kundenservice Zeitschriften, Haberstr 7, Heidelberg 69126, Germany. TEL 49-6221-3454303, FAX 49-6221-3454229, subscriptions@springer.com.

➤ **SOLID STATE NUCLEAR MAGNETIC RESONANCE.** *see* CHEMISTRY—Analytical Chemistry

616.075 RUS
SONOACE-INTERNATIONAL. Text in Russian. s-a. free to qualified personnel (effective 2004). **Document type:** *Journal.*
Published by: Medison - ZAO Mediace, Timiryazevskaya 1, Moscow, 127422, Russian Federation. TEL 7-095-7857220, FAX 7-095-2111755, info@medison.ru, http://www.medison.ru. Ed. Nikolai V Viktorov. Circ: 3,000.

616.07 ZAF ISSN 1027-202X
SOUTH AFRICAN JOURNAL OF RADIOLOGY. Text in English. 1996. q. **Document type:** *Journal, Academic/Scholarly.*
Related titles: Online - full text ed.: ISSN 2078-6778. free (effective 2011).
Indexed: A26, H12, I05.
—CCC.
Published by: South African Medical Association, Block F Castle Walk Corporate Park, Nossob St, Erasmuskloof X3, Pretoria 7430, South Africa. TEL 27-12-4812000, FAX 27-12-4812100, publishing@samedical.org, http://www.samedical.org. Ed. Jan Lotz. **Subscr. to:** PO Box 74789, Lynnwood Ridge, Pretoria 0040, South Africa.

616.07 ZAF ISSN 0258-0241
RC78.A1 CODEN: SARAEH
THE SOUTH AFRICAN RADIOGRAPHER. Text in English. 1959. s-a. bk.rev.
Indexed: A01, INIS AtomInd, T02.
Published by: Society of Radiographers of South Africa, PO Box 6014, Roggebaai, 8012, South Africa. TEL 27-21-4194857, FAX 27-21-4212566, sorsa.admin@iafrica.com, http://www.sorsa.org.za/. Ed. Leonie Munro.

616.07572 AUS ISSN 1321-3075
SPECTRUM (COLLINGWOOD). Text in English. 1994. 10/yr. free to members (effective 2008). adv. back issues avail. **Document type:** *Newsletter, Academic/Scholarly.*
Former titles (until 1993): N S W Radiography Newsletter; (until 1987): New South Wales. Australian Institute of Radiography. Newsletter; (until 1982): New South Wales. Australasian Institute of Radiography. Newsletter; (until 1981): New South Wales. Australian Institute of Radiography. Newsletter
Published by: Australian Institute of Radiography, c/o E.M. Hughes Sec., PO Box 1169, Collingwood, VIC 3066, Australia. TEL 61-3-94193336, FAX 61-3-94160783, air@a-i-r.com/au, http://www.a-i-r.com.au. Ed., Adv. contact Bill Minnis TEL 61-3-98245241. page AUD 550; trim 210 x 297.

616.07 USA
RC78.7.D53
STANDARDS FOR DIAGNOSTIC IMAGING SERVICES. Text in English. 2007. a. USD 130 per issue (effective 2011). **Document type:** *Handbook/Manual/Guide, Trade.*
Published by: Joint Commission on Accreditation of Healthcare Organizations, 1515 W. 22nd St, Ste 1300W, Oak Brook, IL 60523. TEL 630-268-7400, feedback@jcrinc.com feedback@jcrinc.com, http://www.jointcommission.org/.

STATENS STRAALSKYDDSINSTITUT. S S I-RAPPORT. *see* PUBLIC ADMINISTRATION

615.842 DEU ISSN 0179-7158
CODEN: STONE4
➤ **STRAHLENTHERAPIE UND ONKOLOGIE**; Zeitschrift fuer Radiologie, Strahlenbiologie, Strahlenphysik. Text and summaries in English, German. 1912. m. EUR 511, USD 673 combined subscription to institutions (print & online eds.) (effective 2012). adv. bk.rev. bibl.; charts; illus. index, cum.index: vols.1-125 (in 5 vols.). back issues avail.; reprint service avail. from PSC. **Document type:** *Journal, Academic/Scholarly.*
Formerly (until 1986): Strahlentherapie (0039-2073)
Related titles: Microform ed.: (from PMC); Online - full text ed.: ISSN 1439-099X (from IngentaConnect); Supplement(s): Strahlentherapie und Onkologie. Supplement. ISSN 1436-7874. 19??.
Indexed: A20, A22, A26, ASCA, B25, BIOSIS Prev, CA, ChemAb, CurCont, E01, EMBASE, ExcerpMed, IBR, IBZ, INI, INIS AtomInd, ISR, IndMed, Inpharma, MEDLINE, MycolAb, P20, P22, P24, P30, P35, P48, P50, P54, PQC, R10, Reac, SCI, SCOPUS, T02, TM, W07.
—BLDSC (8470.010000), CASDDS, GNLM, IE, Infotrieve, Ingenta, INIST. **CCC.**
Published by: (Deutsche Roentgen Gesellschaft, Deutsche Gesellschaft fuer Radioonkologie), Urban und Vogel Medien und Medizin Verlagsgesellschaft mbH (Subsidiary of: Springer Science+Business Media), Neumarkter Str 43, Munich, 81673, Germany. TEL 49-89-4372-1411, FAX 49-89-4372-1410, verlag@urban-vogel.de. Ed. Dr. Elisabeth Renatus. Adv. contact Renate Senfft. B&W page EUR 1,620, color page EUR 2,870; trim 174 x 240. Circ: 2,500 (paid and controlled). **Subscr. to:** Springer Distribution Center, Kundenservice Zeitschriften, Haberstr 7, Heidelberg 69126, Germany. TEL 49-6221-3454303, FAX 49-6221-3454229, subscriptions@springer.com. **Co-sponsors:** Deutsche Gesellschaft fuer Medizinische Physik; Deutsche und Oesterreichische Gesellsch; Arbeitsgemeinschaft Radioonkologie (ARO) der Deutschen Krebsgesellschaft.

➤ **SURGICAL AND RADIOLOGIC ANATOMY**; journal of clinical anatomy. *see* MEDICAL SCIENCES

615.842 GBR ISSN 1360-5518
CODEN: RATOEO
➤ **SYNERGY**; imaging and therapy practice. Text in English. 1988. m. free to members (effective 2009). adv. bk.rev.; Website rev. charts; illus. index. back issues avail.; reprints avail. **Document type:** *Magazine, Academic/Scholarly.* **Description:** Reports original clinical and scientific research in all aspects of the field.
Formerly (until 1995): Radiography Today (0954-8211); Which was formed by the merger of (1935-1988): Radiography (0033-8281); (1979-1988): Radiography News (0144-5510)
Related titles: Online - full text ed.
Indexed: A22, C06, C07, C08, CA, CINAHL, IndMed, P24, P30, P48, P52, PQC, SCOPUS, T02.
—BLDSC (8585.934600), GNLM, IE, Ingenta.
Published by: (Society of Radiographers), A.F.L. Deeson Publishing Ltd., Ewell House, Graveney Rd, Faversham, Kent ME13 8UP, United Kingdom. TEL 44-1795-535468, FAX 44-1795-535469, enquiries@deeson.co.uk, http://www.deeson.co.uk. Ed. Rachel Deeson.

615.842 539 USA
SYNTHESIS AND APPLICATIONS OF ISOTOPICALLY LABELLED COMPOUNDS. Variant title: International Symposium on Synthesis and Applications of Isotopically Labelled Compounds. Proceedings. Text in English. 1983. a., latest 2007. adv. **Document type:** *Proceedings, Academic/Scholarly.*
Published by: John Wiley & Sons, Inc., 111 River St, Hoboken, NJ 07030. TEL 201-748-6000, FAX 201-748-6088, info@wiley.com, http://www.wiley.com/WileyCDA/.

616.07 ITA ISSN 1971-0690
TABLOID RADIOLOGIA. Text in Italian. 2006. m. **Document type:** *Magazine, Trade.*
Published by: Griffin Srl, Via Airoldi 11, Carimate, Como 22060, Italy. TEL 39-031-789085, FAX 39-031-790743, redazione@griffineditore.it, http://www.griffineditore.it.

616.07 KOR ISSN 0301-4029
TAEHAN PANGSASON UIHAKHOE CHAPCHI. Text in Korean. 1964. irreg. membership. **Document type:** *Journal, Academic/Scholarly.*
Published by: Korean Society of Radiology, 69, Yangjaecheon-gil, Seocho-gu, Seoul, 137-891, Korea, S. TEL 82-2-5788003, FAX 82-2-5297113, office@radiology.or.kr, http://www.radiology.or.kr/.

616.07 USA ISSN 1089-2516
CODEN: TVIRFC
TECHNIQUES IN VASCULAR AND INTERVENTIONAL RADIOLOGY. Text in English. 1998. q. USD 364 in United States to institutions; USD 446 elsewhere to institutions (effective 2012). adv. illus. back issues avail.; reprints avail. **Document type:** *Journal, Academic/Scholarly.* **Description:** Presentations in each issue focus on a single clinical technique or problem. Illustrations and a descriptive narrative outline the steps of a particular procedure of interest to interventional surgeons and radiologists.
Related titles: Online - full text ed.: ISSN 1557-9808 (from ScienceDirect).
Indexed: A26, C06, C07, CA, EMBASE, ExcerpMed, I05, MEDLINE, P30, R10, Reac, SCOPUS, T02.
—BLDSC (8745.407000), IE, Infotrieve, Ingenta. **CCC.**
Published by: W.B. Saunders Co. (Subsidiary of: Elsevier Health Sciences), Elsevier, Health Sciences Division, Order Fulfillment, 3251 Riverport Ln, Maryland Heights, MO 63043. TEL 314-872-8370, 800-325-4177, FAX 314-432-1380, JournalCustomerService-usa@elsevier.com, http://www.us.elsevierhealth.com. Ed. Mahmood K Razavi. Pub. Herb Niemirow TEL 212-633-3141. Adv. contact Michael Targowski TEL 212-633-3693.

THYROBULLETIN. *see* MEDICAL SCIENCES—Endocrinology

615.8 NLD ISSN 1381-4842
CODEN: VNGTD6
➤ **TIJDSCHRIFT VOOR NUCLEAIRE GENEESKUNDE.** Text in Dutch; Text occasionally in English; Summaries in English. 1995. q. EUR 45 (effective 2011). adv. bk.rev. abstr. **Document type:** *Journal, Academic/Scholarly.* **Description:** Reports on developments in nuclear medicine and related subjects.
Formed by the merger of (1978-1995): Vangnet (0921-2574); (1979-1995): N G B (Nucleair Geneeskundig Bulletin) (0169-1279); Which incorporates: Nederlandse Vereniging voor Nucleaire Geneeskunde. Mededelingen
—CASDDS.
Published by: (Nederlandse Vereniging Medische Beeldvorming en Radiotherapie, Stichting ter Bevordering van de Nucleaire Geneeskunde), Uitgeverij Kloosterhof Acquisitie Services, Napoleonsweg 128a, Neer, 6086 AJ, Netherlands. TEL 31-475-597151, FAX 31-475-597153, info@kloosterhof.nl, http://www.kloosterhof.nl. Ed. Lioe-Fee de Geus-Oei. adv.: B&W page EUR 1,050, color page EUR 1,455; bleed 210 x 297. Circ: 1,500 (paid). **Co-sponsors:** Nederlandse Vereniging voor Nucleaire Geneeskunde; Belgisch Genootschap voor Nucleaire Geneeskunde (BGNG); Vereniging voor Medisch-Nucleair (VANG).

616 USA ISSN 0899-3459
CODEN: TMRIEY
➤ **TOPICS IN MAGNETIC RESONANCE IMAGING.** Abbreviated title: T M R I. Text in English. 1988. bi-m. USD 207 domestic to institutions; USD 207 foreign to institutions (effective 2011). adv. illus. index. back issues avail.; reprints avail. **Document type:** *Journal, Academic/Scholarly.* **Description:** Discusses clinical applications of MRI to the entire body, including the brain, spine, extracranial organs, and the musculoskeletal system.
Related titles: Microform ed.; Online - full text ed.: ISSN 1536-1004. 2001. USD 429 domestic for academic site license; USD 479 foreign for academic site license; USD 478.50 domestic for corporate site license; USD 528.50 foreign for corporate site license (effective 2002).
Indexed: A22, ASCA, C06, C07, EMBASE, ExcerpMed, ISR, IndMed, Inpharma, Inspec, MEDLINE, P30, R10, Reac, SCOPUS.
—BLDSC (8867.459300), GNLM, IE, Infotrieve, Ingenta. **CCC.**
Published by: Lippincott Williams & Wilkins (Subsidiary of: Wolters Kluwer N.V.), 333 7th Ave, 19th Fl, New York, NY 10001. TEL 646-674-6300, FAX 646-674-6500, customerservice@lww.com, http://www.lww.com. Ed. Scott W Atlas. Pub. Matthew Jozwiak. Adv. contact Miriam Terron-Elder TEL 646-674-6538. Circ: 232.

615.842 USA ISSN 1073-0206
TRACERS. Text in English. 1985. a. back issues avail. **Document type:** *Newsletter.* **Description:** Information regarding specialty of nuclear medicine and certification.
Published by: American Board of Nuclear Medicine, 900 Veteran Ave, Los Angeles, CA 90024. TEL 310-825-6787, FAX 310-794-4821. Ed. William H Blahd. Circ: 3,900.

616.07 TUR ISSN 1304-1495
CODEN: NTIPER
TURKISH JOURNAL OF NUCLEAR MEDICINE/TURK NUKLEER TIP DERGISI. Text in English, Turkish. 1991. q. **Document type:** *Journal, Academic/Scholarly.* **Description:** Publishes original articles, case reports, images, and letters to the editor in the field of nuclear medicine.
Formerly (until 2002): Nukleer Tip (1300-0004)
Related titles: Online - full text ed.: free (effective 2009).
Indexed: INIS AtomInd.
Published by: Turkiye Nukleer Tip Dernegi/Turkish Society of Nuclear Medicine, Cinnah Caddesi Pilot Sok No. 10/12, Cankaya - Ankara, 06690, Turkey. tjnm@tsnm.org, dernekmerkezi@tsnm.org, http://www.tsnm.org/. Ed. Hatice Durak.

616.07 UKR ISSN 1027-3204
CODEN: URZHEF
➤ **UKRAINS'KYI RADIOLOHICHNYI ZHURNAL.** Text in Ukrainian; Abstracts in English, Russian; Contents page in English, Ukrainian. 1993. q. USD 30 for 2 yrs. domestic; USD 50 foreign (effective 2007). adv. 120 p./no. 2 cols./p.; **Document type:** *Journal, Academic/Scholarly.* **Description:** Includes articles on diagnostic and therapeutic radiology, radiation oncology, radiobiology, and radiation protection, including related problems at Chernobyl.
Related titles: Online - full text ed.: Ukrainian Journal of Radiology. ISSN 1684-1573. 2000.
Indexed: INIS AtomInd.
Published by: Instytut Medychnoi Radiolohii im. S.P. Hryhor'eva/ Hryhor'ev Institute of Medical Radiology, vul Pushkins'ka 82, Kharkiv, 61024, Ukraine. TEL 380-572-7041065, FAX 380-572-7000500, imr@ukr.net. Ed. Mykola I Pylypenko. Adv. contact Dr. Natalia Mitryayeva. page USD 100. Circ: 1,000 (paid).

616.075 LTU ISSN 1392-2114
QC244
ULTRAGARSAS/ULTRASOUND. Text in Russian; Summaries in English, Lithuanian. 1969. q. USD 10 per issue foreign (effective 2006). **Document type:** *Journal, Academic/Scholarly.* **Description:** Publishes papers in the following fields: ultrasonic imaging and non-destructive testing, ultrasonic transducers, ultrasonic measurements, physical acoustics, medical and biological ultrasound, room acoustics, noise and vibrations, signal processing.
Formerly: Nauchnye Trudy. Vysshie Uchebnye Zavedeniia Litovskoi SSR. Ultrazvuk (0369-6367)
Indexed: Inspec, RefZh.
—BLDSC (9082.781000).
Published by: Kauno Technologijos Universitetas/Kaunas University of Technology, K Donelaicio g 73, Kaunas, 44029, Lithuania. TEL 370-37-300000, FAX 370-37-324144, rastine@ktu.lt. Ed. Rymantas Kazys. Circ: 500.

616.07 500 USA ISSN 0161-7346
RC78.7.U4 CODEN: ULIMD4
➤ **ULTRASONIC IMAGING**; an international journal. Text in English. 1979. q. index. back issues avail. **Document type:** *Journal, Academic/Scholarly.* **Description:** Covers the development and application of ultrasonic techniques, with emphasis on medical diagnosis.
Related titles: Online - full text ed.: ISSN 1096-0910 (from IngentaConnect).
Indexed: A22, ASCA, C06, C07, C08, CINAHL, CurCont, E01, EMBASE, ExcerpMed, ISR, IndMed, Inspec, MEDLINE, P30, R10, Reac, SCI, SCOPUS, W07.
—BLDSC (9082.787000), AskIEEE, GNLM, IE, Infotrieve, Ingenta, INIST. **CCC.**
Published by: Dynamedia, Inc., 2 Fulham Court, Silver Spring, MD 20902. TEL 800-468-4680.

616.075 ARG
ULTRASONIDO. Text in Spanish. 1996. bi-m. **Document type:** *Magazine, Trade.*
Formerly: Sociedad Argentina de Ultrasonografia en Medicina y Biologia. Revista (0328-6924)
Published by: Sociedad Argentina de Ultrasonografia en Medicina y Biologia, Av Cordoba 744 PB 2, Buenos Aires, 1054, Argentina. TEL 54-11-43949043, info@saumb.org.ar.

616.07 POL
➤ **ULTRASONOGRAFIA.** Text in Polish. 1991. irreg., latest vol.26. price varies. **Document type:** *Academic/Scholarly.*
Formerly (until 1998): Ultrasonografia Polska (0867-3845)
Published by: Polskie Towarzystwo Ultrasonograficzne, c/o Zaklad Diagnostyki Obrazowej, Woj. Szpital Brodnowski, ul Kondratowicza 8, Warsaw, 03242, Poland. TEL 48-22-6740038, usgptu@usgptu.waw.pl, http://www.usgptu.waw.pl. Eds. Wieslaw Jakubovski, Zbigniew Kalina.

616.842 GBR ISSN 1742-271X
RC78.7.U4
ULTRASOUND. Text in English. 1978. q. USD 369 combined subscription in North America to institutions (print & online eds.); EUR 241 combined subscription in Europe to institutions (print & online eds.); GBP 211 combined subscription to institutions in the UK & elsewhere (print & online eds.) (effective 2012). adv. bk.rev. bibl.; charts; illus.; stat.; tr.lit. back issues avail.; reprint service avail. from PSC. **Document type:** *Journal, Academic/Scholarly.* **Description:** Analyzes current developments in ultrasound for members. Provides review articles.
Formerly (until 2004): B M U S Bulletin (0966-1905)
Related titles: Online - full text ed.: ISSN 1743-1344. USD 332 in North America to institutions; EUR 217 in Europe to institutions; GBP 190 to institutions in the UK & elsewhere (effective 2012) (from IngentaConnect).
Indexed: B&BAb, B19, C06, C07, C08, CA, CINAHL, P30, SCOPUS, T02.
—BLDSC (9082.810350), IE, Ingenta. **CCC.**
Published by: (British Medical Ultrasound Society), Royal Society of Medicine Press Ltd., 1 Wimpole St, London, W1G 0AE, United Kingdom. TEL 44-20-72902921, FAX 44-20-72902929, publishing@rsm.ac.uk, http://www.rsmpress.co.uk. Ed. Hazel Edwards. **Subscr. to:** Portland Customer Services, Commerce Way, Colchester CO2 8HP, United Kingdom. TEL 44-1206-796351, FAX 44-1206-799331, sales@portland-services.com, http://www.portlandpress.com.

616.075 USA ISSN 1556-858X
ULTRASOUND CLINICS. Text in English. 2006 (Jan.). q. USD 279 in United States to institutions; USD 312 elsewhere to institutions (effective 2012). adv. back issues avail.; reprints avail. **Document type:** *Journal, Academic/Scholarly.* **Description:** Covers the latest developments and advances in the field. Includes clinical reviews on topics relevant to radiologists, coverage of state-of-the-art applications, color images and feature articles that discuss the use of ultrasound in a range of medical fields.
Related titles: Online - full text ed.: (from ScienceDirect); Supplement(s): Ultrasound Clinics: Continuing Medical Education Supplement. ISSN 1559-7792.
Indexed: EMBASE, ExcerpMed, P30, SCOPUS.
—BLDSC (9082.812800), IE. **CCC.**
Published by: W.B. Saunders Co. (Subsidiary of: Elsevier Health Sciences), Elsevier, Health Sciences Division, Order Fulfillment, 3251 Riverport Ln, Maryland Heights, MO 63043. TEL 314-872-8370, 800-325-4177, FAX 314-432-1380, JournalCustomerService-usa@elsevier.com, http://www.us.elsevierhealth.com.

ULTRASOUND IN OBSTETRICS AND GYNECOLOGY. *see* MEDICAL SCIENCES—Obstetrics And Gynecology

615.842 USA ISSN 0894-8771
RC78.7.U4 CODEN: ULQUEZ
➤ **ULTRASOUND QUARTERLY.** Text in English. 1982. q. USD 585 domestic to institutions; USD 684 foreign to institutions (effective 2011). adv. charts; illus. back issues avail.; reprints avail. **Document type:** *Journal, Academic/Scholarly.* **Description:** Brings out reviews of a variety of topics including trans-vaginal ultrasonography, detection of fetal anomalies, color doppler flow imaging, pediatric ultrasonography, and breast sonography.
Formerly (until 1989): Ultrasound Annual (0888-8264)
Related titles: Online - full text ed.: ISSN 1536-0253.
Indexed: C06, C07, C08, CINAHL, EMBASE, ExcerpMed, MEDLINE, P30, R10, Reac, SCOPUS.
—BLDSC (9082.815550), GNLM, IE, Infotrieve, Ingenta, INIST. **CCC.**
Published by: (Society of Radiologists in Ultrasound), Lippincott Williams & Wilkins (Subsidiary of: Wolters Kluwer N.V.), 333 7th Ave, 19th Fl, New York, NY 10001. TEL 646-674-6300, FAX 646-674-6500, customerservice@lww.com, http://www.lww.com. Ed. Philip W Ralls TEL 323-226-7207. Pub. Matt Jozwiak. Adv. contact Michelle Smith TEL 646-674-6537. Circ: 909.

➤ **UNIVERSITY OF TEXAS. M.D. ANDERSON CANCER CENTER. RESEARCH REPORT.** *see* MEDICAL SCIENCES—Oncology

615.842 RUS ISSN 0042-4676
CODEN: VRRAAT
➤ **VESTNIK RENTGENOLOGII I RADIOLOGII/ANNALS OF ROENTGENOLOGY AND RADIOLOGY.** Text in Russian; Summaries in English. 1920. bi-m. USD 209 foreign (effective 2005). adv. bk.rev. bibl. index. **Document type:** *Journal, Academic/Scholarly.* **Description:** Publishes original papers devoted to elaboration on new methods of X-ray examination and updating the existing ones, their clinical use, problems of computer diagnosis in roentgenology, and more.
Indexed: C&ISA, ChemAb, DentInd, E&CAJ, EMBASE, ExcerpMed, INIS AtomInd, IndMed, MEDLINE, P30, R10, Reac, RefZh, SCOPUS, SolStAb.
—East View, GNLM, INIST. **CCC.**
Published by: Nauchnoe Obshchestvo Rentgenologov i Radiologov, Cherepkovskaya 3-ya ul 15a, k 4, Moscow, 121552, Russian Federation. TEL 7-095-4146314. Ed. A P Savchenko. Adv. contact L N Druzhinina. **Dist. by:** East View Information Services, 10601 Wayzata Blvd, Minneapolis, MN 55305. TEL 952-252-1201, 800-477-1005, FAX 952-252-1202, info@eastview.com, http://www.eastview.com.

615.84 612.014 USA
VIEWBOX. Text in English. 1979. 4/yr. free to members (effective 2010). back issues avail. **Document type:** *Journal, Academic/Scholarly.* **Description:** Reports on the activities of the College, viewpoints of our members, and current legislative matters.
Formerly: American Osteopathic College of Radiology. Newsletter (0065-9576)
Related titles: Online - full text ed.
Published by: American Osteopathic College of Radiology, 119 E 2nd St, Milan, MO 63556. TEL 660-265-4011, 800-258-2627, FAX 660-265-3494, pam@aocr.org. Ed. Frederick E White. Circ: 400.

615.842 CAN ISSN 1711-1439
THE VIEWBOX. Text in English. 1979. 4/yr. adv.
Former titles (until 2003): College of Medical Radiation Technologists and Therapists of Alberta. Journal (1707-097X); (until 2002): A A M R T Journal (1482-5082); (until 1994): Alberta Association of Medical Radiation Technologists. Journal (0833-3106)
Published by: Alberta Association of Medical Radiation Technologists, No 600, Centre 104, 5241 Calgary Trail, Edmonton, AB T6H 5G8, Canada. TEL 780-487-6130, FAX 780-432-9106, info@acmdtt.com. adv.: page CAD 575.

616.07575 IND ISSN 1450-1147
➤ **WORLD JOURNAL OF NUCLEAR MEDICINE.** Text in English. 2002. q. INR 5,000 domestic to institutions; USD 200 foreign to institutions (effective 2011). adv. **Document type:** *Journal, Academic/Scholarly.*
Related titles: Online - full content ed.: ISSN 1607-3312. INR 4,000 domestic to institutions; USD 160 foreign to institutions (effective 2011).
Indexed: INIS AtomInd.
—BLDSC (9356.073600), IE, Ingenta. **CCC.**
Published by: Medknow Publications and Media Pvt. Ltd., B-9, Kanara Business Ctr, Off Link Rd, Ghatkopar (E), Mumbai, Maharastra 400 075, India. TEL 91-22-66491818, FAX 91-22-66491817, http://www.medknow.com. Ed. Ajit Kumar Padhy. adv.: B&W page USD 1,250; 210 x 277.

616.07 CHN ISSN 1949-8470
▼ ➤ **WORLD JOURNAL OF RADIOLOGY.** Text in English. 2009. m. free (effective 2011). **Document type:** *Journal, Academic/Scholarly.* **Description:** Features research on radiology, including radiation oncology, radiologic physics, neuroradiology, nuclear radiology, pediatric radiology, vascular/interventional radiology, and medical imaging.
Media: Online - full text.
Indexed: P30.
Published by: Beijing Baishideng BioMed Scientific Co., Ltd (Subsidiary of: Baishideng Publishing Group Co., Limited), Rm 903, Bldg D, Ocean International Center, 62 Dongsihuan Zhonglu, Chaoyang District, Beijing, 100025, China. TEL 86-10-85381892, FAX 86-10-85381893, baishideng@wjgnet.com.

616.07 CHN ISSN 1006-7035
XIANDAI YIYONG YINGXIANGXUE/MODERN MEDICAL IMAGELOGY. Text in Chinese. 1992. bi-m. USD 20.40 (effective 2009). **Document type:** *Journal, Academic/Scholarly.*
Related titles: Online - full text ed.
—East View.
Published by: Xiandai Yiyong Yingxiangxue Zazhishe, Nan Er Huang Lu Xi-duan, Yanghehuayuan, Xi'an, 710068, China. TEL 86-29-85225982, FAX 86-29-85225979. **Dist. by:** China International Book Trading Corp, 35 Chegongzhuang Xilu, Haidian District, PO Box 399, Beijing 100044, China. TEL 86-10-68412045, FAX 86-10-68412023, cibtc@mail.cibtc.com.cn, http://www.cibtc.com.cn.

616.07 HKG ISSN 1028-1460
XIANGGANG FANGSHE JISHI ZAZHI/HONG KONG RADIOGRAPHERS JOURNAL. Text in Chinese, English. 1999. s-a. **Document type:** *Journal, Trade.*
Indexed: C06, C07, C08, CINAHL.
—BLDSC (4326.406850).
Published by: Xianggang Fangshe Jishi Xuehui/Hong Kong Radiographers' Association, c/o Department of Radiology, Tuen Mun Hospital, Hung Hom, New Territories, Hong Kong.

615.84 USA ISSN 0098-1672
RC78 CODEN: YBDRE3
YEAR BOOK OF DIAGNOSTIC RADIOLOGY. Text in English. 1932. a. USD 217 in United States to institutions; USD 235 elsewhere to institutions (effective 2012). adv. illus. reprints avail. **Document type:** *Yearbook, Academic/Scholarly.* **Description:** Presents abstracts of pertinent literature with commentary by leading experts in the field.
Formerly (until 1975): The Year Book of Radiology (0084-3989)
Related titles: CD-ROM ed.; Online - full text ed.
Indexed: A22.
—BLDSC (9411.629000), GNLM. **CCC.**
Published by: Mosby, Inc. (Subsidiary of: Elsevier Health Sciences), 1600 John F. Kennedy Blvd, Ste 1800, Philadelphia, PA 19103. TEL 215-239-3900, 800-523-1649, FAX 215-239-3990, elspcs@elsevier.com, http://www.us.elsevierhealth.com. Ed. Dr. Anne G Osborne.

615.8 USA ISSN 0084-3903
RC93.A1 CODEN: YNUMAH
YEAR BOOK OF NUCLEAR MEDICINE. Text in English. 1966. a. adv. illus. reprints avail. **Document type:** *Yearbook, Academic/Scholarly.* **Description:** Presents abstracts of pertinent literature with commentary by leading experts in the field.
Related titles: CD-ROM ed.; Online - full text ed.
—BLDSC (9414.645000), GNLM. **CCC.**
Published by: Mosby, Inc. (Subsidiary of: Elsevier Health Sciences), 1600 John F. Kennedy Blvd, Ste 1800, Philadelphia, PA 19103. TEL 215-239-3900, 800-523-1649, FAX 215-239-3990, elspcs@elsevier.com, http://www.us.elsevierhealth.com.

616.0757 GBR ISSN 1746-1065
THE YEAR IN RADIOLOGY. Text in English. 2005. a. USD 99.95 per issue in US & Canada; GBP 59.99 per issue elsewhere (effective 2009). **Document type:** *Yearbook, Trade.* **Description:** Covers topics such as emergency CT imaging, CT angiography and perfusion CT, gynecologic and genitourinary imaging, with additional sections dedicated to scanning protocols and contrast media.
Indexed: P22, PQC.
—BLDSC (9371.628705). **CCC.**
Published by: Clinical Publishing (Subsidiary of: Atlas Medical Publishing Ltd), Oxford Centre for Innovation, Mill St, Oxford, OX2 OJX, United Kingdom. TEL 44-1865-811116, FAX 44-1865-251550, info@clinicalpublishing.co.uk. Eds. E Teasdale, R White, S Saini. **Dist. by:** Marston Book Services Ltd., Unit 160, Milton Park, Abingdon, Oxfordshire OX14 4SD, United Kingdom. TEL 44-1235-465500, FAX 44-1235-465555, trade.orders@marston.co.uk, http://www.marston.co.uk/.

616.0757 CHN ISSN 1005-8001
YINGXIANG ZHENDUAN YU JIERU FANGSHEXUE/JOURNAL OF DIAGNOSTIC IMAGING AND INTERVENTIONAL RADIOLOGY. Text in English. 1992. q. USD 37.20 (effective 2009). **Document type:** *Journal, Academic/Scholarly.*
Related titles: Online - full text ed.
Indexed: INIS AtomInd.
—East View.
Address: 58, Zhongshan Erlu, Guangzhou, 510080, China. **Dist. by:** China International Book Trading Corp, 35 Chegongzhuang Xilu, Haidian District, PO Box 399, Beijing 100044, China. TEL 86-10-68412045, FAX 86-10-68412023, cibtc@mail.cibtc.com.cn, http://www.cibtc.com.cn.

616.07 CHN ISSN 1006-9011
YIXUE YINGXIANGXUE ZAZHI/JOURNAL OF MEDICAL IMAGING. Text in Chinese. 1990. q. USD 62.40 (effective 2009). **Document type:** *Journal, Academic/Scholarly.*
Related titles: Online - full text ed.
Indexed: A28, APA, BrCerAb, C&ISA, CA/WCA, CIA, CerAb, CivEngAb, CorrAb, E&CAJ, E11, EEA, EMA, ESPM, EnvEAb, H15, M&TEA, M09, MBF, METADEX, RefZh, SolStAb, T04, WAA.
—East View.
Address: No.37,Jingsi Weijiu Rd., Jinan, 250021, China. Eds. Bin Zhao, Le-bin Wu.

ZARIN'S RADIOLOGY LIABILITY ALERT. *see* LAW

615.842 DEU ISSN 0722-5067
ZEITSCHRIFT FUER CHEMOTHERAPIE. Text in German. 1980. 6/yr. EUR 36 domestic to individuals; EUR 66 domestic to institutions; EUR 27 domestic to students; EUR 48 foreign (effective 2010). back issues avail. **Document type:** *Journal, Academic/Scholarly.*
—GNLM.
Address: c/o Prof. Hartmut Lode, Eichenallee 36A, Berlin, 14050, Germany. TEL 49-30-3125059, FAX 49-30-3124742. Ed. Dr. Ralf Stahlmann TEL 49-30-84451770. Pub. Hartmut Lode.

616.075 CHN ISSN 1002-0101
R857.U48 CODEN: ZCYZEE
➤ **ZHONGGUO CHAOSHENG YIXUE ZAZHI/CHINESE JOURNAL OF ULTRASOUND IN MEDICINE.** Text in Chinese; Summaries in English. 1985. m. USD 96 (effective 2009). bk.rev. illus. **Document type:** *Journal, Academic/Scholarly.* **Description:** Discusses issues of interest to ultrasound radiologists in all areas of medicine.
Related titles: Online - full content ed.; Online - full text ed.
Indexed: B25, BIOSIS Prev, MycolAb.
—BLDSC (3180.687000), East View.
Published by: Zhongguo Chaosheng Zhenduan Qingbao Zhongxin/Chinese Information Center of Ultrasound Diagnosis, Xiaoying Lu 9-hao, Chaoyang-qu, PO Box 9770, Beijing, 100101, China. TEL 86-10-64941874, FAX 86-10-64941996. Ed., R&P Wanxue Guo TEL 86-1-64902637. Adv. contact Jianxun Wang. **Dist. overseas by:** China International Book Trading Corp, 35 Chegongzhuang Xilu, Haidian District, PO Box 399, Beijing 100044, China. TEL 86-10-68412045, FAX 86-10-68412023, cibtc@mail.cibtc.com.cn, http://www.cibtc.com.cn.

616.0757 CHN ISSN 1004-714X
ZHONGGUO FUSHE WEISHENG/CHINESE JOURNAL OF RADIOLOGICAL HEALTH. Text in Chinese. 1992. q. USD 24.80 (effective 2009). **Document type:** *Journal, Academic/Scholarly.*
Related titles: Online - full text ed.
Indexed: INIS AtomInd.
—East View.
Address: 89, Jingshi Lu, Jinan, 250062, China. TEL 86-531-2919955, FAX 86-531-2929959. **Dist. by:** China International Book Trading Corp, 35 Chegongzhuang Xilu, Haidian District, PO Box 399, Beijing 100044, China. TEL 86-10-68412045, FAX 86-10-68412023, cibtc@mail.cibtc.com.cn, http://www.cibtc.com.cn.

616.07 CHN ISSN 1672-8475
ZHONGGUO JIERU YINGXIANG YU ZHILIAOXUE/CHINESE JOURNAL OF INTERVENTIONAL IMAGING AND THERAPY. Text in Chinese. 2004. bi-m. USD 42.60 (effective 2009). **Document type:** *Journal, Academic/Scholarly.*
Related titles: Online - full text ed.
Indexed: EMBASE, ExcerpMed, R10, Reac, RefZh, SCOPUS.
—BLDSC (9512.737532), East View.
Address: Luozhuang Nanli Hongjialiyuan 1-301, Beijing, 100088, China. TEL 86-10-82050373, FAX 86-10-82050374.

616.07 CHN ISSN 1008-1062
ZHONGGUO LINCHUANG YIXUE YINGXIANG ZAZHI/JOURNAL OF CHINA CLINIC MEDICAL IMAGING. Text in Chinese. 1990. m. USD 49.20 (effective 2009). **Document type:** *Journal, Academic/Scholarly.*
Formerly (until 1997): Linchuang Yixue Yingxiang Zazhi/Journal of Clinical Medical Imaging (1005-0604)
Related titles: Online - full text ed.
Indexed: A28, APA, B&BAb, B19, B21, BrCerAb, C&ISA, CA/WCA, CIA, CerAb, CivEngAb, CorrAb, E&CAJ, E11, EEA, EMA, ESPM, EnvEAb, H15, Inspec, M&TEA, M09, MBF, METADEX, NSA, RefZh, SolStAb, T04, WAA.
—East View, Linda Hall.
Address: 36, Sanhao St, Heping District, Shenyang, 110004, China. TEL 86-24-23925069.

ZHONGGUO TISHIXUE YU TUXIANG FENXI/CHINESE JOURNAL OF STEREOLOGY AND IMAGE ANALYSIS. *see* PHOTOGRAPHY

616.07 CHN ISSN 1000-8209
ZHONGGUO YIXUE WENZHAI (FANGSHE ZHENDUAN)/CHINESE MEDICAL DIGEST (RADIOLOGICAL DIAGNOSIS). Text in Chinese. 1987. q. USD 14.40 (effective 2009). **Document type:** *Journal, Academic/Scholarly.*
—East View.
Published by: Huazhong Keji Daxue Tongji Yixueyuan/Huazhong University of Science and Technology, Tongji Medical College, 13, Hangkong Lu, Wuhan, 430030, China. TEL 86-27-83657957. **Dist. by:** China International Book Trading Corp, 35 Chegongzhuang Xilu, Haidian District, PO Box 399, Beijing 100044, China. TEL 86-10-68412045, FAX 86-10-68412023, cibtc@mail.cibtc.com.cn, http://www.cibtc.com.cn.

615.842 CHN ISSN 1003-3289
ZHONGGUO YIXUE YINGXIANG JISHU/CHINESE JOURNAL OF MEDICAL IMAGING TECHNOLOGY. Text in Chinese. 1985. m. USD 87.60 (effective 2009). adv. back issues avail. **Document type:** *Journal, Academic/Scholarly.* **Description:** Contains research papers on the new developments of medical equipments in the field of medical imaging technology.
Related titles: Online - full text ed.
Indexed: EMBASE, ExcerpMed, Inspec, RefZh, SCOPUS.
—BLDSC (9512.831430), East View.
Address: Zhichun Lu, Luozhuang Nan Li Hongjialiyuan 1-0301, Beijing, 100088, China. TEL 86-10-82050373, FAX 86-10-82050374. **Dist. by:** China International Book Trading Corp, 35 Chegongzhuang Xilu, Haidian District, PO Box 399, Beijing 100044, China. TEL 86-10-68412045, FAX 86-10-68412023, cibtc@mail.cibtc.com.cn, http://www.cibtc.com.cn.

616.07 CHN ISSN 1005-5185
ZHONGGUO YIXUE YINGXIANGXUE ZAZHI/CHINESE JOURNAL OF MEDICAL IMAGING. Text in Chinese. 1993. bi-m. USD 40.20 (effective 2009). **Document type:** *Journal, Academic/Scholarly.*
Related titles: Online - full text ed.
—BLDSC (9512.831440), East View.
Published by: Zhongguo Yixue Yingxiang Jishu Yanjiuhui/Chinese Association of Medical Imaging Technology, 28, Fuxing Lu, Beijing, 100853, China. TEL 86-10-66939381, FAX 86-10-68131142.

616.075 CHN ISSN 1004-4477
➤ **ZHONGHUA CHAOSHENG YINGXIANGXUE ZAZHI/CHINESE JOURNAL OF ULTRASONOGRAPHY.** Text in Chinese; Abstracts in English. 1992. m. adv. 56 p./no.; **Document type:** *Journal, Academic/Scholarly.* **Description:** Covers new developments in theories and applications of ultrasonic diagnosis.
Related titles: CD-ROM ed.; Online - full text ed.
—BLDSC (9512.837050), East View, IE.
Published by: Hebei Yike Daxue/Hebei Medical University, 361 Zhongshan Donglu, Shijiazhuang, Hebei 050017, China. TEL 86-311-86266994, FAX 86-311-86059153. Ed. Yun Zhang. adv.: B&W page CNY 6,000, color page CNY 12,000. Circ: 12,000. **Dist. overseas by:** China International Book Trading Corp, 35 Chegongzhuang Xilu, Haidian District, PO Box 399, Beijing 100044, China. **Co-sponsor:** Zhonghua Yixuehui/Chinese Medical Association.

616.07 CHN ISSN 0254-5098
CODEN: ZFYZDY
ZHONGHUA FANGSHE YIXUE YU FANGHU ZAZHI/CHINESE JOURNAL OF RADIOLOGICAL MEDICINE AND PROTECTION. Text in Chinese. 1981. bi-m. USD 40.20 (effective 2009). **Document type:** *Journal, Academic/Scholarly.*
Related titles: Online - full text ed.
Indexed: INIS AtomInd.
—BLDSC (3180.650000), East View.
Address: 2, Dewai Xinkang Jie, Beijing, 100088, China. eoj@mail.nrmpin.ac.cn. **Dist. by:** China International Book Trading Corp, 35 Chegongzhuang Xilu, Haidian District, PO Box 399, Beijing 100044, China. TEL 86-10-68412045, FAX 86-10-68412023, cibtc@mail.cibtc.com.cn, http://www.cibtc.com.cn.

ZHONGHUA FANGSHE ZHONGLIUXUE ZAZHI/CHINESE JOURNAL OF RADIATION ONCOLOGY. *see* MEDICAL SCIENCES—Oncology

616.07 CHN ISSN 1005-1201
➤ **ZHONGHUA FANGSHEXUE ZAZHI/CHINESE JOURNAL OF RADIOLOGY.** Text in Chinese. 1953. m. USD 106.80 (effective 2009). adv. 96 p./no.; **Document type:** *Journal, Academic/Scholarly.*
Related titles: Online - full content ed.; Online - full text ed.
Indexed: EMBASE, ExcerpMed, INIS AtomInd, P30, R10, Reac, RefZh.
—BLDSC (3180.670000), East View.
Published by: Zhonghua Yixuehui Zazhishe/Chinese Medical Association Publishing House, 42 Dongsi Xidajie, Beijing, 100710, China. TEL 86-10-65265604. Ed. Yuji Gao. adv.: page USD 1,700; 200 x 290. Circ: 30,000 (paid); 100 (controlled). **Co-sponsor:** Chinese Medical Association.

616.07 CHN ISSN 0253-9780
CODEN: CITCDE
ZHONGHUA HEYIXUE ZAZHI/CHINESE JOURNAL OF NUCLEAR MEDICINE. Text in Chinese. 1981. bi-m. USD 43.80 (effective 2009). **Document type:** *Journal, Academic/Scholarly.*
Related titles: Online - full text ed.
Indexed: A22, INIS AtomInd.
—BLDSC (3180.437000), IE, Ingenta.
Address: 23, Daluokong, Wuxi, 214002, China. TEL 86-510-2731904, FAX 86-510-2715010. **Dist. by:** China International Book Trading Corp, 35 Chegongzhuang Xilu, Haidian District, PO Box 399, Beijing 100044, China. TEL 86-10-68412045, FAX 86-10-68412023, cibtc@mail.cibtc.com.cn, http://www.cibtc.com.cn.

616.07 TWN ISSN 1018-8940
ZHONGHUA MINGUO FANGSHEXIAN YIXUE ZAZHI/CHINESE JOURNAL OF RADIOLOGY. Text in Chinese. bi-m. **Document type:** *Journal, Academic/Scholarly.*
Indexed: A22, EMBASE, ExcerpMed, P30, R10, Reac, SCOPUS.
—BLDSC (3180.671000), IE, Ingenta.
Published by: Zhonghua Minguo Fangshexian Xuehui/Radiological Society of the R.O.C., 201, Shih-Pai Rd., Sec. 2, Taipei, 100, Taiwan. TEL 886-2-28769035, FAX 886-2-28769036.

616.07 CHN ISSN 1672-6448
ZHONGHUA YIXUE CHAOSHENG ZAZHI/CHINESE JOURNAL OF MEDICAL ULTRASOUND (ELECTRONIC VERSION). Text in Chinese. 2004. bi-m. CNY 28 newsstand/cover (effective 2006).
Media: CD-ROM. **Related titles:** Online - full text ed.
Indexed: A28, APA, B&BAb, B19, B21, BrCerAb, C&ISA, CA/WCA, CIA, CTA, CerAb, CivEngAb, CorrAb, E&CAJ, E11, EEA, EMA, ESPM, EnvEAb, H15, M&TEA, M09, MBF, METADEX, NSA, SolStAb, T04, WAA.
—East View.
Published by: Zhonghua Yixuehui/Chinese Medical Association, 42 Dong Si Xi Dajie, Beijing, 100710, China. cmj@cma.org.cn, http://www.cmj.org.

MEDICAL SCIENCES—Respiratory Diseases

616.2 USA ISSN 0893-8520
CODEN: AATIEN
A A R C TIMES. Text in English. 1977. m. USD 102.50 to members; USD 50 student members (effective 2007). adv. reprints avail. **Description:** Presents news and features for the cardiorespiratory care profession.
Formerly: A A R Times (0195-1777)
Related titles: Microfilm ed.: (from PQC).
Indexed: A22, C06, C07, C28, CA, CINAHL, P30, T02.
—BLDSC (0537.535500), IE, Ingenta. **CCC.**
Published by: American Association for Respiratory Care, 9425 N MacArthur Blvd, Suite 100, Irving, TX 75063-4706. TEL 972-243-2272, FAX 972-484-2720, info@aarc.org. Circ: 37,000.

616.2 USA ISSN 0892-8916
A T S NEWS. Text in English. 197?. m. free to members (effective 2009). cum.index. **Document type:** *Newsletter.* **Description:** Features reports on ATS assemblies, committees, chapters, international activities, educational offerings, statements and guidelines.
Former titles (until 1986): American Thoracic Society. News (0162-251X); Which superseded (in 1975): A T S News
Related titles: Online - full text ed.: free (effective 2009).
—CCC.
Published by: American Thoracic Society, 61 Broadway, New York, NY 10006. TEL 212-315-8600, FAX 212-315-6498. Ed. Suzy Logan TEL 212-315-8631.

615.64 USA ISSN 1096-6307
ADVANCE FOR MANAGERS OF RESPIRATORY CARE. Text in English. 1992. 10/yr. free to qualified personnel (effective 2008). adv. bk.rev.; software rev.; video rev. charts; illus.; tr.lit. index. back issues avail.; reprints avail. **Document type:** *Magazine, Trade.* **Description:** Covers workplace trends, products and market research for the decision-makers in respiratory care.
Related titles: Online - full text ed.: free (effective 2008).
Published by: Merion Publications, Inc., 2900 Horizon Dr, PO Box 61556, King of Prussia, PA 19406. TEL 610-278-1400, 800-355-5627, FAX 610-278-1421, advance@merion.com, http://www.advanceweb.com. Ed. Sharlene George. Pub. Ann Kielinski. Adv. contact Cynthia Caramanico. B&W page USD 4,135, color page USD 4,935; trim 8.375 x 10.5. Circ: 20,510.

615 USA ISSN 1074-2301
ADVANCE FOR RESPIRATORY CARE PRACTITIONERS; providing strategies in respiratory care and sleep medicine. Text in English. 1988. 27/yr. free to qualified personnel (effective 2008). adv. back issues avail.; reprints avail. **Document type:** *Magazine, Trade.* **Description:** Provides strategies in respiratory care and sleep medicine.
Formerly (until 19??): Advance for Respiratory Therapists (1041-1445)
Related titles: Online - full text ed.: free to qualified personnel (effective 2008).
Published by: Merion Publications, Inc., 2900 Horizon Dr, PO Box 61556, King of Prussia, PA 19406. TEL 610-278-1400, 800-355-5627, FAX 610-278-1421, advance@merion.com, http://www.advanceweb.com. Ed. Vern Enge. Adv. contact Cynthia Caramanico. B&W page USD 2,882, color page USD 3,682; trim 8.375 x 10.5. Circ: 45,239.

616.2 ITA ISSN 1971-9299
AGEING LUNG. Text in Multiple languages. 2007. q. **Document type:** *Journal, Academic/Scholarly.*
Published by: Primula Multimedia, Via G Ravizza 22 B, Pisa, 56121, Italy. TEL 39-050-965242, FAX 39-050-3163810, info@primulaedizioni.it, http://www.primulaedizioni.it.

616.2 TUR ISSN 1302-8715
AKCIGER ARSIVI/ARCHIVES OF PULMONOLOGY. Text in Turkish. 4/yr. **Document type:** *Journal, Academic/Scholarly.*
Related titles: Online - full text ed.: free (effective 2009).
Indexed: A01, CA, T02.
Published by: Turkiye Klinikleri, Turkocagi Caddesi No.30, Balgat, Ankara, 06520, Turkey. TEL 90-312-2865656, FAX 90-312-2865656, yaziisleri@turkiyeklinikleri.com, info@turkiyeklinikleri.com, http://www.turkiyeklinikleri.com. Ed. Mehmet Karadag.

ALERGIA, ASMA E INMUNOLOGIA PEDIATRICAS. *see* MEDICAL SCIENCES—Allergology And Immunology

ALLERGI I PRAKSIS. *see* MEDICAL SCIENCES—Allergology And Immunology

ALLERGY & ASTHMA ADVOCATE (ONLINE); a seasonal guide for relief. *see* MEDICAL SCIENCES—Allergology And Immunology

ALLERGY & ASTHMA TODAY. *see* MEDICAL SCIENCES—Allergology And Immunology

▼ **ALLERGY, ASTHMA & IMMUNOLOGY RESEARCH.** *see* MEDICAL SCIENCES—Allergology And Immunology

616.2 USA ISSN 1073-449X
RC306 CODEN: AJCMED
➤ **AMERICAN JOURNAL OF RESPIRATORY AND CRITICAL CARE MEDICINE.** Abbreviated title: A J R C C M. Text in English. 1917. s-m. USD 290 in North America to individuals; USD 360 elsewhere to individuals; USD 630 in North America to institutions; USD 675 elsewhere to institutions; free to members (effective 2009). adv. bk.rev. abstr.; bibl.; charts; illus.; stat. index, cum.index. back issues avail.; reprints avail. **Document type:** *Journal, Academic/Scholarly.* **Description:** Focuses on human biology and disease, as well as animal studies that contribute to the understanding of pathophysiology and treatment of diseases that affect the respiratory system and crtically ill patients.
Former titles (until 1994): The American Review of Respiratory Disease (0003-0805); (until 1959): American Review of Tuberculosis and Pulmonary Diseases (0096-039X); (until 1955): American Review of Tuberculosis (0096-0381)
Related titles: Microform ed.: (from PMC, PQC); Online - full text ed.: ISSN 1535-4970.
Indexed: A20, A22, A26, A34, A35, A36, AIDS Ab, AIIM, AIM, AMED, ASCA, AgBio, B20, B21, B25, BA, BIOBASE, BIOSIS Prev, BiolDig, C06, C07, C08, CABA, CINAHL, CISA, ChemAb, Chicano, CurCont, D01, DBA, DentInd, E12, EIA, EMBASE, ESPM, EnerInd, ExcerpMed, FR, G08, GH, GeoRef, H&SSA, H11, H12, H17, HospLI, I12, IABS, IDIS, INI, ISR, IndMed, IndVet, Inpharma, JW, JW-EM, JW-ID, LT, MEDLINE, MycolAb, N02, N03, P20, P22, P24, P30, P32, P33, P35, P37, P39, P48, P50, P54, PEI, PN&I, PQC, PollutAb, R08, R10, R12, RA&MP, RILM, RM&VM, RRTA, Reac, S12, S13, S16, SCI, SCOPUS, SoyAb, T05, THA, TM, ToxAb, VS, VirolAbstr, W07, W10, W11.
—BLDSC (0836.590000), CASDDS, GNLM, IE, Infotrieve, Ingenta, INIST. **CCC.**
Published by: (American Lung Association), American Thoracic Society, 61 Broadway, New York, NY 10006. TEL 212-315-8625, FAX 212-315-8613, http://www.thoracic.org. Ed. Edward Abraham. Adv. contact Kevin Dunn TEL 201-767-4170. B&W page USD 2,445, color page USD 4,245; trim 8.325 x 10.875. Circ: 18,500. **Subscr. to:** PO Box 9016, New York, NY 10087. TEL 212-315-8687, FAX 212-315-8689, atsjournals@thoracic.org.

616.2 USA ISSN 1044-1549
QP121.A1 CODEN: AJRBEL
➤ **AMERICAN JOURNAL OF RESPIRATORY CELL AND MOLECULAR BIOLOGY.** Abbreviated title: A J R C M B. Text in English. 1989. m. USD 215 in US & Canada to individuals includes mexico; USD 250 elsewhere to individuals; USD 270 in US & Canada to institutions includes mexico; USD 315 elsewhere to institutions; free to members (effective 2009). adv. back issues avail.; reprints avail. **Document type:** *Journal, Academic/Scholarly.* **Description:** Contains papers that report significant and original observations in the area of pulmonary biology.
Related titles: Online - full text ed.: ISSN 1535-4989.

Indexed: A22, ASCA, B25, B27, BIOBASE, BIOSIS Prev, C33, CIN, ChemAb, ChemTitl, CurCont, EMBASE, ExcerpMed, IABS, INIS AtomInd, ISR, IndMed, Inpharma, MEDLINE, MycolAb, P15, P20, P22, P26, P30, P48, P52, P54, P56, PQC, R10, Reac, SCI, SCOPUS, THA, W07.
—BLDSC (0836.600000), CASDDS, GNLM, IE, Infotrieve, Ingenta, INIST. **CCC.**
Published by: American Thoracic Society, 61 Broadway, New York, NY 10006. TEL 212-315-8619, FAX 212-315-8616, http://www.thoracic.org. Ed. Kenneth B Adler. Adv. contact Kevin Dunn TEL 201-767-4170. B&W page USD 1,105, color page USD 2,255; trim 8.325 x 10.875. Circ: 8,500. **Subscr. to:** PO Box 9016, New York, NY 10087. TEL 212-315-8687, FAX 212-315-8689, atsjournals@thoraic.org.

616.2 GBR ISSN 2042-4701
▼ **THE ANNALS OF RESPIRATORY MEDICINE.** Text in English. 2010. q. free (effective 2010). back issues avail. **Document type:** *Journal, Academic/Scholarly.* **Description:** Covers all aspects of respiratory medicine.
Media: Online - full text.
Indexed: A01, P20, P54.
Published by: San Lucas Medical Ltd., 11-12 Freetrade House, Lowther Rd, Stanmore, Middlesex HA7 1EP, United Kingdom. TEL 44-20-32869384, editor@slm-journals.com, http://www.sanlucasmedical.com. Eds. Oneal Ayson, Jim Jones. Pub. Nahida Zaman TEL 44-20-70960728.

ANNALS OF THORACIC MEDICINE. *see* MEDICAL SCIENCES—Internal Medicine

616.2 JPN
ANNUAL REVIEW KOKYUKI/ANNUAL REVIEW. RESPIRATORY ORGAN. Text in Japanese. 1988. a. JPY 8,200 per issue (effective 2007). adv. **Document type:** *Academic/Scholarly.*
Published by: Chugai Igakusha, 62 Yarai-cho, Shinjuku-ku, Tokyo, 162-0805, Japan. TEL 81-3-32682701, FAX 81-3-32682722, http://www.chugaiigaku.jp/.

APPLIED CARDIOPULMONARY PATHOPHYSIOLOGY; the interface between laboratory and clinical practice. *see* BIOLOGY—Physiology

616.2 ESP ISSN 0300-2896
RC731 CODEN: ARBRDA
ARCHIVOS DE BRONCONEUMOLOGIA. Text in Spanish; Summaries in English. 1964. m. (11/yr.). EUR 269 in Europe to institutions; JPY 43,900 in Japan to institutions; USD 417 elsewhere to institutions (effective 2010). bk.rev. reprints avail. **Document type:** *Journal, Academic/Scholarly.* **Description:** Covers broncho-pneumology, respiratory immunology, biochemical studies of secretions, and pulmonary surgery.
Related titles: Online - full text ed.: ISSN 1579-2129. 1998. EUR 87.71 (effective 2009) (from ScienceDirect).
Indexed: A22, CurCont, EMBASE, ExcerpMed, FR, IME, INI, IndMed, Inpharma, MEDLINE, P30, P35, R10, Reac, SCI, SCOPUS, W07.
—BLDSC (1654.890000), GNLM, Infotrieve, INIST. **CCC.**
Published by: (Sociedad Espanola de Neumologia y Cirugia Toracica), Elsevier Doyma (Subsidiary of: Elsevier Health Sciences), Traversa de Gracia 17-21, Barcelona, 08021, Spain. TEL 34-932-418800, FAX 34-932-419020, doyma@doyma.es, http://www.doyma.es. Ed. J Ruiz Manzano. Adv. contact Anna Pahissa. Circ: 3,100.

616.2 PRT ISSN 1646-0324
ARQUIVOS DE BRONCOPNEUMOLOGIA. Text in Portuguese. 2004. irreg. **Document type:** *Journal, Trade.*
Published by: Medicografica Edicoes Medicas, Rua Camilo Castelo Branco 23-5, Lisbon, 1150-083, Portugal. geral@medicografica.pt, http://www.medicografica.pt.

616.238 NZL ISSN 1175-4141
ASTHMA AND RESPIRATORY NEWS. Text in English. 2000 (Sep.). q. 8 p./no.; **Document type:** *Newsletter, Consumer.* **Description:** Provides the latest news and research on respiratory-tract diseases.
Formed by the merger of: Respiratory News; (1989-2000): Asthma New Zealand (1170-1846)
Related titles: Online - full text ed.: free.
Published by: Asthma and Respiratory Foundation of New Zealand, Level 1, Panama House, 22 Panama St, PO Box 1459, Wellington, 6140, New Zealand. TEL 64-4-4994592, FAX 64-4-4994594, info@asthmafoundation.org.nz. Ed. Kerry Hines. Circ: 12,000.

616.238 AUS
ASTHMA FOUNDATION OF NEW SOUTH WALES. ANNUAL REPORT. Text in English. 1962. a. back issues avail. **Document type:** *Corporate.* **Description:** Provides information on activities conducted, the upcoming challenges and plan of action by the Asthma Foundation of NSW for every calendar year.
Formerly (until 1963): Asthma Foundation of New South Wales. Report of Directors
Related titles: Online - full text ed.: free (effective 2008).
Published by: Asthma Foundation of New South Wales, Level 3, 486 Pacific Hwy, St Leonards, NSW 2065, Australia. TEL 61-2-99063233, FAX 61-2-99064493, ask@asthmansw.org.au. Ed. Lauren Errington.

616.2 JPN ISSN 1347-4650
ASTHMA FRONTIER. Text in Japanese. 2002. a. JPY 2,940 newsstand/cover (effective 2006). **Document type:** *Journal, Academic/Scholarly.*
Published by: Iyaku Journal-sha/Medicine & Drug Journal Co., Ltd., Highness Awajimachi Bldg. 21/F, 3-1-5 Awajimachih, Chuo-Ku, Osaka, 541-0047, Japan. TEL 81-6-62027280, FAX 81-6-62025295, ij-main@iyaku-j.com, http://www.iyaku-j.com/.

616.23 AUS ISSN 1442-7583
ASTHMA MATTERS. Text in English. 1964. q. donation. bk.rev. back issues avail. **Document type:** *Newsletter, Consumer.* **Description:** Features articles on triggers, medications and research reports related to asthma.
Formerly (until 1998): Asthma Welfarer (0044-9776)
Related titles: Online - full text ed.
Published by: Asthma Foundation of New South Wales, Level 3, 486 Pacific Hwy, St Leonards, NSW 2065, Australia. TEL 61-2-99063233, FAX 61-2-99064493, ask@asthmansw.org.au. Ed. Lauren Errington. Circ: 5,000.

616.238 616.97 UKR
➤ **ASTMA TA ALERHIYA/ASTHMA AND ALLERGY/ASTMA I ALLERGIYA.** Text in Ukrainian, Russian. 2002. q. **Document type:** *Journal, Academic/Scholarly.*
Related titles: Online - full text ed.
Published by: (Asotsiatsiya Spetsialistiv po Problemam Bronkhial'noi Astmy i Alerhii Ukrainy), Akademiya Medychnykh Nauk Ukrainy, Instytut Ftyziatrii i Pul'monolohii im. F.H. Yanovs'koho, vul N. Amosova, 10, Kyiv, 03680, Ukraine. TEL 380-44-2750402, FAX 380-44-2752118, admin@ifp.kiev.ua. Ed. L A Yashina.

616.2 DEU ISSN 0341-3055
CODEN: ATLUDF
➤ **ATEMWEGS- UND LUNGENKRANKHEITEN.** Text in German. 1975. m. EUR 170; EUR 16 newsstand/cover (effective 2011). adv. abstr. **Document type:** *Journal, Academic/Scholarly.*
Indexed: A22, CIN, ChemAb, ChemTitl, DBA, DokArb, EMBASE, ExcerpMed, IBR, IBZ, ISR, Inpharma, R10, Reac, RefZh, SCOPUS.
—BLDSC (1765.856000), CASDDS, GNLM, IE, Infotrieve, Ingenta. **CCC.**
Published by: Dustri-Verlag Dr. Karl Feistle, Bajuwarenring 4, Oberhaching, 82041, Germany. TEL 49-89-6138610, FAX 49-89-6135412, info@dustri.de, http://www.dustri.de. Ed. Eugen Heilmaier. R&P Renate Lehmann. Adv. contact Christian Grassl. Circ: 3,800 (paid and controlled).

➤ **AUSTRALIA. BUREAU OF STATISTICS. DEATHS DUE TO DISEASES AND CANCERS OF THE RESPIRATORY SYSTEM, AUSTRALIA (ONLINE).** *see* MEDICAL SCIENCES—Abstracting, Bibliographies, Statistics

➤ **AUSTRALIA. BUREAU OF STATISTICS. NATIONAL HEALTH SURVEY: ASTHMA AND OTHER RESPIRATORY CONDITIONS, AUSTRALIA (ONLINE).** *see* MEDICAL SCIENCES—Abstracting, Bibliographies, Statistics

616.2 GBR ISSN 1471-2466
RC1 CODEN: BPMMBB
➤ **B M C PULMONARY MEDICINE.** (BioMed Central) Text in English. 2001 (Sep.). irreg. free (effective 2011). adv. back issues avail.; reprints avail. **Document type:** *Journal, Academic/Scholarly.* **Description:** Publishes original research articles in all aspects of the prevention, diagnosis and management of pulmonary and associated disorders, as well as related molecular genetics, pathophysiology, and epidemiology.
Media: Online - full text.
Indexed: A26, A34, A36, C06, C07, CA, CABA, E12, EMBASE, ExcerpMed, GH, H17, I05, IndVet, MEDLINE, N02, N03, OGFA, P20, P22, P30, P33, P37, PQC, R08, R10, R12, RA&MP, RM&VM, Reac, SCOPUS, T02, T05, VS.
—Infotrieve. **CCC.**
Published by: BioMed Central Ltd. (Subsidiary of: Springer Science+Business Media), 236 Gray's Inn Rd, London, WC1X 8HB, United Kingdom. TEL 44-20-31922000, FAX 44-20-31922010, info@biomedcentral.com. Ed. Dr. Melissa Norton. Adv. contact Natasha Bailey TEL 44-20-31922231.

616.2 362.18 GBR ISSN 1810-6838
➤ **BREATHE**; continuing medical education for respiratory professionals. Text in English. 2004. q. GBP 104 to institutions; USD 107 in United States to institutions (effective 2012). **Document type:** *Journal, Academic/Scholarly.* **Description:** Introduces basic concepts and state-of-the-art methods. It is essential reading for those exploring continued education in respiratory medicine.
Related titles: Online - full text ed.: ISSN 2073-4735.
Indexed: C06, C07, SCOPUS.
—BLDSC (2277.494645), IE, Ingenta. **CCC.**
Published by: Maney Publishing, Ste 1C, Joseph's Well, Hanover Walk, Leeds, W Yorks LS3 1AB, United Kingdom. TEL 44-113-2432800, FAX 44-113-3868178, maney@maney.co.uk, http://www.maney.co.uk. Ed. A K Simonds. **Subscr. in N America to:** Maney Publishing, 875 Massachusetts Ave, 7th Fl, Cambridge, MA 02139. TEL 866-297-5154, FAX 617-354-6875, maney@maneyusa.com.

616.2 USA
BREATHE (BIRMINGHAM). Text in English. q. free (effective 2005). **Document type:** *Newsletter, Consumer.*
Formerly: Update, Southern Air
Published by: American Lung Association of Alabama, 3125 Independence Dr, Ste 325, Birmingham, AL 35209. TEL 205-933-8821, FAX 205-930-1717. Circ: 7,000 (paid and controlled).

616.2 USA
BREATHE WELL. Text in English. 19??. q. **Document type:** *Magazine, Trade.* **Description:** Designed for those who need the latest information on allergy, asthma, chronic bronchitis, emphysema, pneumonia, smoking risks, flu, and many other topics.
Published by: Jobson Medical Group (Subsidiary of: Jobson Publishing LLC), 100 Ave of the Americas, New York, NY 10013. TEL 212-274-7000, FAX 212-431-0500, http://www.jmihealth.com.

616.2 USA ISSN 1940-493X
BREATHING; your guide to living well. Text in English. 2008 (Mar.). q. free to qualified personnel; USD 20 per issue (effective 2008). adv. **Document type:** *Magazine, Consumer.*
Published by: Academy of Certified Case Managers, 256 Post Rd East, Westport, CT 06880. TEL 203-454-1333, FAX 203-454-1344, Info@academyccm.org, http://www.academyccm.org. Ed. Wolfe Gary. Pub. Howard Mason. adv.: page USD 2,950;.

THE BRITISH JOURNAL OF PRIMARY CARE NURSING. RESPIRATORY DISEASES AND ALLERGY. *see* MEDICAL SCIENCES—Nurses And Nursing

616.2 JPN ISSN 1342-436X
CODEN: BUKOFC
BUNSHI KOKYUKIBYO/RESPIRATORY MOLECULAR MEDICINE. Text in Japanese. 1997. bi-m. JPY 2,100 (effective 2005). **Document type:** *Journal, Academic/Scholarly.*
—BLDSC (2930.656000).
Published by: Sentan Igaku-sha, 1-9-7 Higashi-Nihonbashi, Chuo-ku, Tokyo, 103-0004, Japan. TEL 81-3-58202100, FAX 81-3-58202501, book@sentan.com, http://www.sentan.com/.

616.2 GBR ISSN 1995-5111
THE BUYER'S GUIDE TO RESPIRATORY CARE PRODUCTS. Text in English. 1995. a. free to members (effective 2009). back issues avail. **Document type:** *Directory, Trade.* **Description:** Provides comprehensive overview of the available devices and materials that are of use in respiratory field.
Former titles (until 2007): The Buyer's Guide (1563-0129); (until 1999): The Buyer's Inspiration (1024-3992)
Related titles: Online - full text ed.
—CCC.
Published by: (European Respiratory Society CHE), E R S Journals Ltd., 442 Glossop Rd, Sheffield, S10 2PX, United Kingdom. TEL 44-114-2672860, FAX 44-114-2665064, info@ersj.org.uk, http://www.ersjournals.com/.

616.2 USA ISSN 1541-2555
C O P D; journal of chronic obstructive pulmonary disease. Text in English. 2004. q. (in 1 vol., 4 nos./vol.). GBP 955, EUR 1,265, USD 1,585 combined subscription to institutions (print & online eds.); GBP 1,910, EUR 2,530, USD 3,165 combined subscription to corporations (print & online eds.) (effective 2010). adv. back issues avail.; reprint service avail. from PSC. **Document type:** *Journal, Academic/Scholarly.* **Description:** Publishes a wide range of original research, reviews, case studies, and conference proceedings to promote advances in the pathophysiology, diagnosis, management, and control of lung and airway disease and inflammation - providing a unique forum for the discussion, design, and evaluation of more efficient and effective strategies in patient care.
Related titles: Online - full text ed.: ISSN 1541-2563 (from IngentaConnect).
Indexed: A01, A22, B21, CA, CurCont, E01, EMBASE, ExcerpMed, ImmunAb, MEDLINE, P30, P35, R10, Reac, RefZh, SCI, SCOPUS, T02, W07.
—BLDSC (3465.850000), IE, Ingenta, Linda Hall. **CCC.**
Published by: Informa Healthcare (Subsidiary of: T & F Informa plc), 52 Vanderbilt Ave, New York, NY 10017. TEL 212-262-8230, FAX 212-262-8234, healthcare.enquiries@informa.com, http://www.informahealthcare.com. Ed. Dr. James D Crapo. Adv. contact Daniel Wallen. **Subscr. outside N. America to:** Taylor & Francis Ltd.

615.64 CAN ISSN 1205-9838
RM161 CODEN: CJRTFU
➤ **CANADIAN JOURNAL OF RESPIRATORY THERAPY/REVUE CANADIENNE DE LA THERAPIE RESPIRATOIRE.** Short title: C J R T - R C T R. Text in English, French. 1965. 5/yr. CAD 37 domestic to institutions (effective 1999); CAD 15 newsstand/cover; USD 37 newsstand/cover foreign to institutions (effective 1999). adv. bk.rev. charts; illus.; stat.; bibl. back issues avail.; reprints avail. **Document type:** *Journal, Academic/Scholarly.* **Description:** Official publication of Canadian Society of Respiratory Therapists. Contains feature articles, new product news, history, editorials and abstracts.
Former titles (1985-1996): Registered Respiratory Therapist (0831-2478); (1971-1985): Respiratory Technology (0319-1494); (1965-1971): Canadian Inhalation Therapy (0008-3852)
Related titles: Online - full text ed.
Indexed: C03, C06, C07, C08, CBCARef, CINAHL, EMBASE, ExcerpMed, P20, P24, P48, P54, PQC, R10, Reac, SCOPUS.
—CIS, GNLM. **CCC.**
Published by: Canadian Society of Respiratory Therapists, 1785 Alta Vista Dr Ste 102, Ottawa, ON K1G 3Y6, Canada. TEL 613-731-3164, FAX 613-521-4314. Ed. Norman Tiffin. R&P Marie Claire Bedard. Adv. contact Beverley Kirkpatrick. B&W page CAD 1,060, color page CAD 1,650; trim 10.88 x 8.38. Circ: 2,900.

615.64 CAN ISSN 1198-2241
CODEN: CRJOFV
➤ **CANADIAN RESPIRATORY JOURNAL.** Text in English, French. q. CAD 170 domestic to individuals; USD 170 in United States to individuals; USD 210 elsewhere to individuals; CAD 220 domestic to institutions; USD 220 in United States to institutions; USD 260 elsewhere to institutions (effective 2005). adv. bk.rev. **Document type:** *Journal, Academic/Scholarly.* **Description:** Publishes original research in all areas of respiratory research and therapy, reviews, case reports, letters to the editor, industry news, meeting announcements and reports.
Related titles: Online - full text ed.: ISSN 1916-7245.
Indexed: EMBASE, ExcerpMed, IndMed, MEDLINE, P30, R10, Reac, SCI, SCOPUS, W07.
—BLDSC (3044.615000), GNLM, IE, Infotrieve, Ingenta, INIST. **CCC.**
Published by: (Canadian Thoracic Society), Pulsus Group Inc., 2902 S Sheridan Way, Oakville, ON L6J 7L6, Canada. TEL 905-829-4770, FAX 905-829-4799, pulsus@pulsus.com. Ed. Dr. N R Anthonisen TEL 204-787-2562. Pub. Robert B Kalina. Adv. contact Lisa Robb. B&W page CAD 2,445. Circ: 15,500.

616.238 616.97 KOR ISSN 1226-8739
CEONSIGMIC ALREREU'GI/JOURNAL OF ASTHMA, ALLERGY AND CLINICAL IMMUNOLOGY. Text in Korean. 1981. q. **Document type:** *Journal, Academic/Scholarly.*
Formerly (until 1998): Allerugi (1015-6372)
Published by: Korean Academy of Asthma, Allergy and Clinical Immunology/Daehan Cheonsig Allereugi Hakoe, Rm. 1705, Keumho Palace Bldg., 327-2 Changsin-dong, Jongno-gu, Seoul, 110-540, Korea, S. TEL 82-2-7470528, FAX 82-2-36762847, korall@chol.com, http://www.allergy.or.kr/.

616.2 NLD ISSN 1877-7635
CFCENTRAAL. Text in Dutch. 1969. q. EUR 15 (effective 2009). adv. 2 p./no. 2 cols./p.; **Document type:** *Journal, Academic/Scholarly.*
Former titles (until 2009): Nederlandse Cystic Fibrosis Stichting. C F Nieuws (0925-1944); (until 1989): Nederlandse Cystic Fibrosis Stichting. Bericht (0925-1952)
Published by: Nederlandse Cystic Fibrosis Stichting, Dr A Schweitzerweg 3, Baarn, 3744 MG, Netherlands. TEL 31-35-6479257, FAX 31-35-6479489, info@ncfs.nl, http://www.ncfs.nl.

616.246 PAK ISSN 0528-7944
➤ **THE CHALLENGE.** Text in English. 1959. q. PKR 60, USD 16. adv. bk.rev. charts; stat.; bibl.; illus. **Document type:** *Journal, Academic/Scholarly.* **Description:** Covers news, views and new methods relating to global TB control.
Related titles: CD-ROM ed.; Online - full text ed.
Indexed: Acal, ExtraMED, IndMed.
—GNLM.
Published by: Pakistan Anti-Tuberculosis Association, Block No. 55, Rm. 8, Secretariat, Karachi, Pakistan. TEL 92-21-5688011. Adv. contact M Z Baig. Circ: 2,000.

616.2 616.12 USA ISSN 0012-3692
RC705 CODEN: CHETBF
➤ **CHEST**; the cardiopulmonary and critical care journal. Text in English. 1935. m. USD 240 combined subscription to institutions (print & online eds.); USD 25 per issue; free to members (effective 2009). adv. bk.rev. bibl.; illus. s-a. index. back issues avail.; reprints avail. **Document type:** *Journal, Academic/Scholarly.* **Description:** Features original manuscripts dealing with continuing medical education in the medical or surgical aspects of pulmonary and cardiologic diseases.
Formerly (until 1970): Diseases of the Chest (0096-0217)
Related titles: CD-ROM ed.; Microform ed.: (from PQC); Online - full text ed.: ISSN 1931-3543. USD 216 to institutions (effective 2009); ◆ Italian ed.: Chest (Italian Edition). ISSN 1970-4917; Ed.: Chest (Spanish Edition). ISSN 1578-0023.
Indexed: A01, A02, A03, A08, A20, A22, A25, A26, A34, A36, AIDS Ab, AIIM, AIM, AMED, ASCA, B25, BA, BIOBASE, BIOSIS Prev, C06, C07, C08, C11, CA, CABA, CIN, CINAHL, CISA, ChemAb, ChemTitl, CurCont, DentInd, DokArb, E08, E12, EMBASE, ExcerpMed, F08, FR, G08, GH, H04, H11, H12, H17, I05, I12, IABS, IDIS, INI, INIS AtomInd, ISR, IndMed, IndVet, Inpharma, JW, JW-EM, JW-ID, Kidney, LT, M06, MEDLINE, MycolAb, N02, N03, P19, P20, P22, P24, P30, P33, P34, P35, P37, P39, P48, P50, P54, PN&I, PQC, R08, R10, R12, R13, RA&MP, RILM, RM&VM, RRTA, Reac, S08, S09, S13, S16, SAA, SCI, SCOPUS, SoyAb, T02, T05, THA, TM, VS, W07, W10, W11.
—BLDSC (3172.530000), CASDDS, GNLM, IE, Infotrieve, Ingenta, INIST. **CCC.**
Published by: American College of Chest Physicians, 3300 Dundee Rd, Northbrook, IL 60062. TEL 847-498-1400, 800-343-2227, FAX 847-498-5460, accp@chestnet.org, http://www.chestnet.org. Ed. Richard S Irwin. Pub. Alvin Lever. adv.: B&W page USD 2,230, color page USD 4,080; trim 8 x 10.75. Circ: 20,460 (paid).

616.2 ITA ISSN 1970-4917
➤ **CHEST (ITALIAN EDITION).** Text in Italian. 1999. q. **Document type:** *Journal, Academic/Scholarly.*
Related titles: Online - full text ed.: ISSN 1970-4941. 2002; ◆ English ed.: Chest. ISSN 0012-3692.
Published by: Midia Srl, Via Santa Maddalena 1, Monza, 20052, Italy. TEL 39-039-2304440, FAX 39-039-2304442, http://www.mediaonline.it.

616.2 ITA ISSN 2039-4772
▼ ➤ **CHEST DISEASE REPORTS.** Text in English. 2010. irreg. free (effective 2011). **Document type:** *Journal, Academic/Scholarly.*
Media: Online - full text.
Published by: Pagepress, Via Giuseppe Belli 4, Pavia, 27100, Italy. TEL 39-0382-1751762, FAX 39-0382-1750481, http://www.pagepress.org. Ed. Charles F Bellows.

616.2 GBR ISSN 1471-5260
➤ **CHEST MEDICINE ON-LINE.** Text in English. 1997. m. free (effective 2009). bk.rev.; software rev.; video rev. **Document type:** *Journal, Academic/Scholarly.* **Description:** Features case reports, audits, treatments, protocols, review papers and research on chest problems.
Media: Online - full text.
Published by: Priory Lodge Education Ltd., 2 Cornflower Way, Moreton, Wirral CH46 1SV, United Kingdom. Ed. Dr. Peter Davies.

616.1 616.2 617.6 USA ISSN 1558-6200
CHEST PHYSICIAN. Text in English. 2006 (Jan.). m. USD 209 in US & Canada to institutions; USD 209 elsewhere to institutions (effective 2012). back issues avail.; reprints avail. **Document type:** *Newspaper, Trade.* **Description:** Deals with the major issues facing cardiopulmonary and critical care physicians. Includes clinical content, meeting coverage, expert commentary and clinical trial results, plus reporting on the business and politics affecting specialists in diseases of the chest.
Related titles: Online - full text ed.
—CCC.
Published by: (American College of Chest Physicians), International Medical News Group (Subsidiary of: Elsevier Health Sciences), 5635 Fishers Ln, Ste 6000, Rockville, MD 20852. TEL 240-221-4500, FAX 240-221-4400, m.altier@elsevier.com. Ed. Terry Rudd TEL 240-221-2465. Pub. Alan J Imhoff TEL 973-290-8216. Circ: 17,000. **Subscr. to:** Elsevier, Subscription Customer Service, 60 Columbia Rd, Bldg B, Morristown, NJ 07960. TEL 973-290-8200, FAX 973-290-8250, http://www.elsevier.com/.

616.24 SRB ISSN 0354-4265
CHILDREN'S PULMONOLOGY. Text in English. 1993. s-a. **Document type:** *Journal, Academic/Scholarly.*
Indexed: EMBASE, ExcerpMed, R10, Reac, SCOPUS.
Published by: Institut za Plucne Bolesti, Instituski put 4, Stremska Kamenica, 21204. TEL 381-21-27077, FAX 381-21-27960, Dusan.Bozic@ipb-ild.ac.yu, http://www.ipb-ild.ac.yu.

616.2 GBR ISSN 1479-9723
RC731
➤ **CHRONIC RESPIRATORY DISEASE.** Abbreviated title: C R D. Text in English. 2004. q. USD 572, GBP 310 combined subscription to institutions (print & online eds.); USD 561, GBP 304 to institutions (effective 2011). adv. back issues avail.; reprint service avail. from PSC. **Document type:** *Journal, Academic/Scholarly.* **Description:** Publishes research papers and original articles that have immediate relevance to clinical practice and its multi-disciplinary perspective reflects the nature of modern treatment.
Related titles: Online - full text ed.: ISSN 1479-9731. USD 515, GBP 279 to institutions (effective 2011).
Indexed: A22, B21, CA, E01, EMBASE, ESPM, ExcerpMed, H&SSA, MEDLINE, P20, P22, P30, P48, P54, PQC, R10, Reac, RiskAb, SCOPUS, T02.
—BLDSC (3184.940000), IE, Ingenta. **CCC.**
Published by: Sage Publications Ltd. (Subsidiary of: Sage Publications, Inc.), 1 Oliver's Yard, 55 City Rd, London, EC1Y 1SP, United Kingdom. TEL 44-20-73248500, FAX 44-20-73248600, info@sagepub.co.uk, http://www.uk.sagepub.com/home.nav. Eds. Carolyn Rochester, Mike Morgan, Sally Singh. adv.: B&W page GBP 450; 180 x 250.

616.2 USA ISSN 1542-2771
CLINICAL DIALOGUES; antibiotic-resistant respiratory tract bacteria. Text in English. 2002 (Dec.). q.
Published by: Veritas Institute for Medical Education, Inc., 611 Rt. 46 W., 3rd Fl., Hasbrouck Heights, NJ 07604. TEL 201-727-1115, FAX 201-727-1529, http://www.veritasime.com.

616.2 NZL ISSN 1179-5484
RC666
➤ **CLINICAL MEDICINE INSIGHTS: CIRCULATORY, RESPIRATORY AND PULMONARY MEDICINE.** Abbreviated title: C M I C R P. Text in English. 2007. irreg. free (effective 2011). **Document type:** *Journal, Academic/Scholarly.* **Description:** Covers all aspects of the prevention, diagnosis and management of all associated disorders in addition to related genetic, pathophysiological and epidemiological topics.
Formerly (until 2010): Clinical Medicine: Circulatory, Respiratory and Pulmonary Medicine (1178-1157)
Media: Online - full text.
Indexed: A01, C06, C07, EMBASE, ExcerpMed, P30, SCOPUS, T02.
—CCC.
Published by: Libertas Academica Ltd., PO Box 300-874, Mairangi Bay, Auckland, 0751, New Zealand. TEL 64-9-4763930, FAX 64-9-3531397, enquiries@la-press.com. Ed. Hussein D Foda.

616.2 USA ISSN 1068-0640
RC756 CODEN: CPMEF2
CLINICAL PULMONARY MEDICINE. Text in English. 1994. bi-m. USD 510 domestic to institutions; USD 610 foreign to institutions (effective 2011). adv. back issues avail.; reprints avail. **Document type:** *Journal, Academic/Scholarly.* **Description:** Provides a forum for the discussion of new knowledge in the field of pulmonary medicine that is of interest and relevance to the practitioner.
Related titles: Online - full text ed.: ISSN 1536-5956.
Indexed: A36, BA, CABA, E12, EMBASE, ExcerpMed, GH, H17, LT, N02, N03, P20, P30, P33, P37, P39, PHN&I, R10, RA&MP, RM&VM, RRTA, Reac, SCOPUS, T05, VS.
—BLDSC (3286.347000), GNLM, IE, Infotrieve, Ingenta. **CCC.**
Published by: Lippincott Williams & Wilkins (Subsidiary of: Wolters Kluwer N.V.), Two Commerce Sq, 2001 Market St, Philadelphia, PA 19103. TEL 215-521-8300, FAX 215-521-8902, customerservice@lww.com, http://www.lww.com. Ed. Dr. Michael S Niederman TEL 516-663-4876. Adv. contact Michelle Smith TEL 646-674-6537. Circ: 286.

616.2 USA ISSN 1752-6981
➤ **THE CLINICAL RESPIRATORY JOURNAL.** Text in English. 2007. q. GBP 239 combined subscription in United Kingdom to institutions (print & online eds.); EUR 303 combined subscription in Europe to institutions (print & online eds.); USD 439 combined subscription in the Americas to institutions (print & online eds.); USD 466 combined subscription elsewhere to institutions (print & online eds.) (effective 2012). back issues avail. **Document type:** *Journal, Academic/Scholarly.* **Description:** Provides a rapid-response forum for publishing clinical research in all areas of respiratory medicine from clinical lung disease to basic research relevant to the clinic.
Related titles: Online - full text ed.: ISSN 1752-699X. GBP 208 in United Kingdom to institutions; EUR 263 in Europe to institutions; USD 382 in the Americas to institutions; USD 405 elsewhere to institutions (effective 2012).
Indexed: A01, A22, CA, E01, EMBASE, ExcerpMed, MEDLINE, P30, R10, Reac, SCI, SCOPUS, T02, W07.
—IE. **CCC.**
Published by: (The Nordic Respiratory Academy DNK), Wiley-Blackwell Publishing, Inc. (Subsidiary of: Wiley-Blackwell Publishing Ltd.), Commerce Pl, 350 Main St, Malden, MA 02148. TEL 781-388-8200, FAX 781-388-8210, info@wiley.com, http://www.wiley.com/WileyCDA/. Ed. Vibeke Backer.

616.2 USA ISSN 0272-5231
RC941
➤ **CLINICS IN CHEST MEDICINE.** Text in English. 1980. q. USD 475 in United States to institutions; USD 583 elsewhere to institutions (effective 2012). adv. back issues avail.; reprints avail. **Document type:** *Journal, Academic/Scholarly.* **Description:** Delivers practical advice from the specialty covered with a fresh perspective on problems and controversies.
Related titles: Online - full text ed.: ISSN 1557-8216 (from ScienceDirect).
Indexed: A20, A22, ASCA, C06, C07, C08, CINAHL, CurCont, DokArb, EMBASE, ExcerpMed, FR, ISR, IndMed, Inpharma, MEDLINE, P30, R10, Reac, SCI, SCOPUS, W07.
—BLDSC (3286.545000), GNLM, IE, Infotrieve, Ingenta, INIST. **CCC.**
Published by: W.B. Saunders Co. (Subsidiary of: Elsevier Health Sciences), Elsevier, Health Sciences Division, Order Fulfillment, 3251 Riverport Ln, Maryland Heights, MO 63043. TEL 314-872-8370, 800-325-4177, FAX 314-432-1380, JournalCustomerService-usa@elsevier.com, http://www.us.elsevierhealth.com. Adv. contact Don Scholz TEL 215-239-3537.

616.2 USA ISSN 1098-8319
RC583
COPING WITH ALLERGIES AND ASTHMA. Text in English. 1998. 5/yr. USD 13.95 domestic; USD 20 foreign (effective 2007). adv. reprints avail. **Document type:** *Magazine, Consumer.* **Description:** Targets those fighting asthma and/or allergies, allergists and immunologists, pulmonologists, and support groups. Challenges readers to develop a positive proactive approach and improve their quality of life by becoming allergy and asthma fighters, rather than sufferers. Provides readers with treatment options, offering practical "how-to" information as well as personal accounts.
Published by: Media America, Inc., PO Box 682268, Franklin, TN 37068. TEL 615-790-2400, FAX 615-794-0179. Ed. Laura Shipp. Pub. Michael D Holt. R&P Marsha Moore TEL 615-790-2400 ext 27. Adv. contact Paula K Chadwell. B&W page USD 5,040, color page USD 6,615; trim 8.125 x 10.875. Circ: 50,000 (paid and controlled).

616.2 GBR ISSN 1745-9974
RC756
➤ **COUGH.** Text in English. 2005. irreg. free (effective 2011). adv. back issues avail.; reprints avail. **Document type:** *Journal, Academic/Scholarly.* **Description:** Encompasses the scientific and clinical aspects of both acute and chronic cough.
Media: Online - full text.
Indexed: A01, A26, CA, I05, P30, SCOPUS, T02.
—CCC.
Published by: BioMed Central Ltd. (Subsidiary of: Springer Science+Business Media), 236 Gray's Inn Rd, London, WC1X 8HB, United Kingdom. TEL 44-20-31922000, FAX 44-20-31922010, info@biomedcentral.com, http://www.biomedcentral.com. Eds. Kian Fan Chung, Rubaiyat Haque. Adv. contact Natasha Bailey TEL 44-20-31922231.

➤ **CURRENT ALLERGY & ASTHMA REPORTS.** *see* MEDICAL SCIENCES—Allergology And Immunology

016.2 GBR ISSN 1361-6706
CODEN: CMLRFF
➤ **CURRENT MEDICAL LITERATURE. RESPIRATORY MEDICINE.** Text in English. 1987. q. GBP 60 to individuals; GBP 130 to institutions; free to qualified personnel (effective 2009). back issues avail. **Document type:** *Journal, Academic/Scholarly.* **Description:** Aims to provide physicians and allied healthcare professionals with rapid access to expert commentary and analysis on key topics in respiratory medicine.
Formerly (until 1993): Current Medical Literature. Reversible Obstructive Airways Disease (0950-8724)
Related titles: Online - full text ed.: ISSN 1759-8192; French ed.: Current Medical Literature: Medecine Respiratoire. 2001.
Indexed: A01, A03, A08, CA, T02.
—CCC.
Published by: Remedica Medical Education and Publishing Ltd., Commonwealth House, 1 New Oxford St, London, WC1A 1NU, United Kingdom. TEL 44-20-77592999, FAX 44-20-77592951, info@remedica.com, http://www.remedica.com. Ed. Emma Beagley.

616.7 USA ISSN 1070-5287
RC705 CODEN: COPMFY
CURRENT OPINION IN PULMONARY MEDICINE. Text in English. 1995. bi-m. USD 1,018 domestic to institutions; USD 1,094 foreign to institutions (effective 2011). adv. bibl.; illus. back issues avail.; reprints avail. **Document type:** *Journal, Academic/Scholarly.* **Description:** Covers key subjects, spanning topics such as asthma, obstructive, occupational, and environmental diseases, infectious diseases, disorders of pulmonary circulation, neoplasms of the lung, sleep and respiratory neurobiology, and cystic fibrosis.
Related titles: Online - full text ed.: ISSN 1531-6971. USD 266 to individuals (effective 2011); Optical Disk - DVD ed.: Current Opinion in Pulmonary Medicine, with Evaluated MEDLINE. ISSN 1080-8108; ◆ Czech Translation: Current Opinion in Pulmonary Medicine (Czech and Slovak Edition). ISSN 1214-4738.
Indexed: A22, A34, A36, BA, C06, C07, C08, CABA, CINAHL, CurCont, E01, E12, EMBASE, ExcerpMed, F08, GH, H17, IndMed, IndVet, Inpharma, MEDLINE, N02, N03, P30, P33, P35, P37, P39, R08, R10, RM&VM, Reac, SCI, SCOPUS, SoyAb, T05, VS, W07.
—BLDSC (3500.777200), IE, Infotrieve, Ingenta, INIST. **CCC.**
Published by: Lippincott Williams & Wilkins (Subsidiary of: Wolters Kluwer N.V.), 530 Walnut St, Philadelphia, PA 19106. TEL 215-521-8300, FAX 215-521-8902, customerservice@lww.com, http://www.lww.com. Ed. Om P Sharma. Pub. Ian Burgess. Circ: 405.

616.7 CZE ISSN 1214-4738
CURRENT OPINION IN PULMONARY MEDICINE (CZECH AND SLOVAK EDITION). Text in Czech. 2004. 3/yr. **Document type:** *Journal, Academic/Scholarly.*
Related titles: Online - full text ed.: ISSN 1803-893X; ◆ Translation of: Current Opinion in Pulmonary Medicine. ISSN 1070-5287.
Published by: Medical Tribune CZ, s.r.o., Na Morani 5, Prague 2, 12800, Czech Republic. TEL 420-224-916916, FAX 420-224-922436, info@medical-tribune.cz, http://www.tribune.cz. Ed. Jaroslav Horejsi.

616.995 USA ISSN 1819-3366
➤ **CURRENT RESEARCH IN TUBERCULOSIS.** Text in English. 2006. q. **Document type:** *Journal, Academic/Scholarly.* **Description:** Includes articles on clinical, epidemiological, public health and social aspects of tuberculosis.
Related titles: Online - full text ed.: ISSN 2152-3363. free (effective 2010).
Indexed: A01, A36, B20, B21, CA, CABA, CTA, E12, EMBASE, ESPM, ExcerpMed, GH, ImmunAb, NSA, SCOPUS, T02, T05.
Published by: Academic Journals Inc., 224, 5th Ave, No 2218, New York, NY 10001. FAX 888-777-8532, support@scialert.com, http://www.academicjournalsinc.com/.

616.2 NLD ISSN 1573-398X
RC705
➤ **CURRENT RESPIRATORY MEDICINE REVIEWS.** Text in English. 2005 (Jan.). bi-m. USD 710 to institutions (print or online ed.) (effective 2012). adv. back issues avail.; reprints avail. **Document type:** *Journal, Academic/Scholarly.* **Description:** Publishes frontier reviews on all the latest advances on respiratory diseases and its related areas such as pharmacology, pathogenesis, clinical care, and therapy.
Related titles: Online - full text ed.: ISSN 1875-6387 (from IngentaConnect).
Indexed: A01, B21, C06, C07, CA, EMBASE, ExcerpMed, ImmunAb, P30, R10, Reac, SCOPUS, T02.
—IE, Ingenta. **CCC.**
Published by: Bentham Science Publishers Ltd., PO Box 294, Bussum, 1400 AG, Netherlands. TEL 31-35-6923800, FAX 31-35-6980150, sales@bentham.org, http://www.bentham.org. Ed. Joseph Varon. **Subscr. to:** Bentham Science Publishers Ltd., c/o Richard E Morrissy, PO Box 446, Oak Park, IL 60301. TEL 312-413-5867, FAX 312-996-7107, subscriptions@bentham.org.

616.2 USA ISSN 1542-1007
RC591
CURRENT REVIEW OF ASTHMA. Text in English. 2003. a., latest 2003. USD 79.95 per issue (effective 2010). back issues avail. **Document type:** *Handbook/Manual/Guide, Academic/Scholarly.* **Description:** Comprises up-to-date information related to the field of asthma diagnosis and treatment.
Published by: Current Medicine Group LLC (Subsidiary of: Springer Science+Business Media), 400 Market St, Ste 700, Philadelphia, PA 19106. TEL 215-574-2266, FAX 215-574-2225, service-ny@springer.com, http://www.current-medicine.com/. Ed. Michael A. Kaliner.

616.2 AUS ISSN 1833-0584
CYSTIC FIBROSIS RESEARCH TODAY. Text in English. 2004. m. free (effective 2008). adv. back issues avail. **Document type:** *Journal, Consumer.* **Description:** Contains the latest research about cystic fibrosis, including details on symptoms, genetics, treatment, information.
Media: Online - full text.
Published by: Research Today Publications ad@researchtoday.net, http://www.researchtoday.net.

616.2 PRT ISSN 1647-7391
▼ **D P O C DOENCA PULMONAR OBSTRUCTIVA CRONICA.** Text in Portuguese. 2010. a. **Document type:** *Journal, Academic/Scholarly.*
Published by: Permanyer Portugal, Avenida Duque d'Avila 92, Lisbon, 1050-084, Portugal. TEL 351-213-156081, FAX 351-213-304296, permanyer.portugal@permanyer.com.

616.2 AUT ISSN 1609-2961
CODEN: DAIIAV
➤ **DIFFICULT AIRWAY.** Text in English. 2000. q. USD 75 domestic; USD 115 foreign; USD 35 newsstand/cover (effective 2001). adv. back issues avail. **Document type:** *Journal, Academic/Scholarly.* **Description:** Publishes articles, case reports, reviews, and letters that aim to improve communication in understanding difficult airway management.
Related titles: Online - full text ed.: ISSN 1609-297X.
Indexed: SCOPUS.
Published by: V I C E R Publishing, PO Box 14, Vienna, A-1097, Austria. TEL 43-676-9568085, FAX 43-676-9568086, vicer@vicer.org, http://www.vicer.org. Ed., R&P Roland Hofbauer. adv.: B&W page USD 1,700, color page USD 2,200. Circ: 1,000 (paid and controlled).

616.2 JPN
DOUBLE - BARRED CROSS/FUKUJUJI. Text in Japanese. 1955. bi-m. free. adv. bk.rev. charts; illus.; stat. 32 p./no.;
Formerly: Red Double-Barred Cross (0016-2531)
Published by: Japan Anti-Tuberculosis Association/Kekkaku Yobokai, 1-3-12 Misaki-cho, Chiyoda-ku, Tokyo, 101-0061, Japan. TEL 81-3-3292-9211, FAX 81-3-3292-9208. Ed., Pub. Mutsuo Sato. Circ: 18,000.

616.2 EGY ISSN 1687-8426
THE EGYPTIAN JOURNAL OF BRONCHOLOGY. Text in English. 2007. s-a. **Document type:** *Journal, Academic/Scholarly.*
Published by: Egyptian Scientific Society of Bronchology (E S S B), 14 El Khalil St, Lebanon Sq, El Mohandessin, Giza, Egypt. TEL 202-302-3642, FAX 202-302-7672, info@essbronchology.com, http://www.essbronchology.com/index.html. Ed. Dr. Tarek Safwat.

616.2 EGY ISSN 0422-7638
RC731
THE EGYPTIAN JOURNAL OF CHEST DISEASES AND TUBERCULOSIS. Text in English. 1952. s-a. free to members. **Document type:** *Journal, Academic/Scholarly.*
Published by: Egyptian Society of Chest Diseases and Tuberculosis, Dar El-Hekma, 42 Qasr El-Aini Str, Cairo, Egypt. TEL 20-2-2847821, FAX 20-2-2847822. Ed. Dr. Muhammad Awadh Tag-El-Din.

616.2 FRA ISSN 1155-195X
➤ **ENCYCLOPEDIE MEDICO-CHIRURGICALE. PNEUMOLOGIE.** Cover title: Traite de Pneumologie. Variant title: Encyclopedie Medico-Chirurgicale, Instantanes Medicaux. Pneumologie. Text in French. 2004. 4 base vols. plus q. updates. EUR 902 (effective 2006). bibl.; charts; illus. **Document type:** *Academic/Scholarly.* **Description:** Provides specialists in diagnosing and treating respiratory-tract diseases with a comprehensive and up-to-date reference.
Formerly (until 1991): Encyclopedie Medico-Chirurgicale. Poumon, Plevre, Mediastin (0246-036X)
Related titles: Online - full text ed.
—INIST.
Published by: Elsevier Masson (Subsidiary of: Elsevier Health Sciences), 62 Rue Camille Desmoulins, Issy les Moulineaux, Cedex 92442, France. TEL 33-1-71165500, FAX 33-1-71165600, infos@elsevier-masson.fr.

➤ **ENCYCLOPEDIE MEDICO-CHIRURGICALE. RADIOLOGIE ET IMAGERIE MEDICALE. CARDIOVASCULAIRE - THORACIQUE - CERVICALE.** *see* MEDICAL SCIENCES—Radiology And Nuclear Medicine

616.2 PER ISSN 1027-2674
ENFERMEDADES DEL TORAX. Text in Spanish. 1956. 3/yr. **Document type:** *Journal, Academic/Scholarly.*
Former titles (until 1995): Sociedad Peruana de Tisiologia, Neumologia y Enfermedades del Torax. Revista (0069-2166); (until 1991): Revista Peruana de Tuberculosis y Enfermedades Respiratorias (0375-1295)
Published by: Sociedad Peruana de Tisiologia, Neumologia y Enfermedades del Torax, Domingo Casanova 116, Lima, Peru. TEL 51-1-4409701.

616.2 GBR ISSN 1754-5552
➤ **EUROPEAN RESPIRATORY DISEASE.** Text in English. 2006. s-a. EUR 80 combined subscription in Europe to individuals (print & online eds.); USD 100 combined subscription in United States to individuals (print & online eds.); EUR 180 combined subscription in Europe to institutions (print & online eds.); USD 225 combined subscription in United States to institutions (print & online eds.); free to qualified personnel (effective 2009). adv. back issues avail. **Document type:** *Journal, Academic/Scholarly.* **Description:** Brings together the industry's key opinion leaders and leading companies to create a platform that deliver the most salient research and showcase the latest products to the respiratory community.
Related titles: Online - full text ed.: ISSN 1754-5560. EUR 70 in Europe to individuals; EUR 85 in United States to individuals; EUR 170 in Europe to institutions; EUR 210 in United States to institutions (effective 2009).
Published by: Touch Briefings (Subsidiary of: Touch Group plc), Saffron House, 6-10 Kirby St, London, EC1N 8TS, United Kingdom. TEL 44-20-74525600, FAX 44-20-74525606, info@touchbriefings.com, http://www.touchbriefings.com/.

616.2 CHE ISSN 0903-1936
CODEN: ERJOEI
➤ **THE EUROPEAN RESPIRATORY JOURNAL.** Text in English; Summaries in French. 1988. m. GBP 794 combined subscription to institutions (print & online eds.); USD 1,508 combined subscription in United States to institutions (print & online eds.) (effective 2012). adv. bk.rev. illus. index. reprints avail. **Document type:** *Journal, Academic/Scholarly.* **Description:** Features cutting edge clinical and experimental work in the field of respiratory medicine.
Formed by the merger of (1980-1988): European Journal of Respiratory Diseases (0106-4339); Which was formed by the merger of (19??-1980): Acta Tuberculosa et Pneumologica Belgica (0001-7078); Which was formerly (until 1959): Acta Tuberculosea Belgica (0365-7299); (until 1948): Revue Belge de la Tuberculose; (1925-1980): Scandinavian Journal of Respiratory Diseases (0036-5572); Which was formerly (until 1966): Acta Tuberculosea et Pneumologica Scandinavica (0365-7531); (until 1962): Acta Tuberculosea Scandinavica (0365-7574); (1965-1988): Clinical Respiratory Physiology (0272-7587); Which was formerly (until 1980): Bulletin Europeen de Physiopathologie Respiratoire (0395-3890); (until 1976): Bulletin de Physio-Pathologie Respiratoire (0007-439X)
Related titles: Online - full text ed.: ISSN 1399-3003. GBP 673 to institutions; USD 1,278 in United States to institutions (effective 2012); ◆ Supplement(s): European Respiratory Journal. Supplement. ISSN 0904-1850.
Indexed: A22, A34, A36, A37, AESIS, AMED, ASCA, B21, B25, BA, BIOBASE, BIOSIS Prev, CABA, CIN, CISA, ChemAb, ChemTitl, CurCont, D01, DBA, DentInd, DokArb, E01, E12, EMBASE, ESPM, ExcerpMed, F08, F11, F12, FR, GH, GeoRef, H&SSA, H17, IABS, INI, ISR, IndMed, IndVet, Inpharma, LT, MEDLINE, MycolAb, N02, N03, P30, P33, P35, P37, P39, PHN&I, PN&I, R08, R10, R12, RA&MP, RM&VM, RRTA, Reac, SCI, SCOPUS, T05, THA, TriticAb, VS, W07, W10.
—BLDSC (3829.924200), CASDDS, GNLM, IE, Infotrieve, Ingenta, INIST. **CCC.**
Published by: European Respiratory Society, 4 Ave Sainte-Luce, Lausanne, 1003, Switzerland. TEL 41-21-2130101, FAX 41-21-2130100, info@ersnet.org, http://www.ersnet.org. Eds. Anh Tuan Dinh-Xuan, Vito Brusasco. adv.: B&W page GBP 940, color page GBP 1,700; trim 210 x 280. Circ: 5,500. **Subscr. in N America to:** Maney Publishing, 875 Massachusetts Ave, 7th Fl, Cambridge, MA 02139. TEL 866-297-5154, FAX 617-354-6875, maney@maneyusa.com; **Subscr. outside N America to:** Maney Publishing, Ste 1C, Joseph's Well, Hanover Walk, Leeds, W Yorks LS3 1AB, United Kingdom. TEL 44-113-3868168, FAX 44-113-2486983, subscriptions@maney.co.uk.

616.2 CHE ISSN 0904-1850
CODEN: ERJSEU
EUROPEAN RESPIRATORY JOURNAL. SUPPLEMENT. Text in English. 1934. irreg. price varies. adv. reprints avail. **Document type:** *Monographic series, Academic/Scholarly.*
Former titles (until 1987): European Journal of Respiratory Diseases. Supplementum (0106-4347); (until 1979): Scandinavian Journal of Respiratory Diseases. Supplementum (0080-6730); (until 1965): Acta Tuberculosea et Pneumologica Scandinavica. Supplementum (0365-7612); (until 1961): Acta Tuberculosea Scandinavica. Supplementum (0365-7604)
Related titles: ◆ Supplement to: The European Respiratory Journal. ISSN 0903-1936.
Indexed: EMBASE, ExcerpMed, ISR, IndMed, Inpharma, MEDLINE, P30, P35, R10, Reac, SCOPUS.
—CASDDS, INIST. **CCC.**
Published by: European Respiratory Society, 4 Ave Sainte-Luce, Lausanne, 1003, Switzerland. TEL 41-21-2130101, FAX 41-21-2130100, info@ersnet.org, http://www.ersnet.org.

616.2 CHE ISSN 1025-448X
EUROPEAN RESPIRATORY MONOGRAPH. Text in English. 1996. 3/yr. USD 40 per issue in North America; GBP 25 per issue elsewhere (effective 2004). **Document type:** *Monographic series, Academic/Scholarly.*
Indexed: SCOPUS.
—BLDSC (3829.924300), IE, Ingenta. **CCC.**
Published by: European Respiratory Society, 4 Ave Sainte-Luce, Lausanne, 1003, Switzerland. TEL 41-21-2130101, FAX 41-21-2130100, info@ersnet.org. Ed. Emiel F M Wouters. **Subscr. in N America to:** Maney Publishing, 875 Massachusetts Ave, 7th Fl, Cambridge, MA 02139. TEL 866-297-5154, FAX 617-354-6875, maney@maneyusa.com; **Subscr. outside N America to:** Maney Publishing, Ste 1C, Joseph's Well, Hanover Walk, Leeds, W Yorks LS3 1AB, United Kingdom. TEL 44-113-3868168, FAX 44-113-2486983, subscriptions@maney.co.uk.

616.2 CHE ISSN 0905-9180
CODEN: EREWEH
➤ **EUROPEAN RESPIRATORY REVIEW.** Text in English. 1991. q. bk.rev. reprints avail. **Document type:** *Journal, Academic/Scholarly.* **Description:** Publishes state-of-the-art reviews on current topical issues in respiratory medicine.
Related titles: Online - full text ed.: ISSN 1600-0617. free (effective 2011).
Indexed: A22, BIOBASE, EMBASE, ExcerpMed, IABS, Inpharma, MEDLINE, P30, R10, Reac, SCOPUS.
—BLDSC (3829.924400), GNLM, IE, Infotrieve, Ingenta. **CCC.**
Published by: European Respiratory Society, 4 Ave Sainte-Luce, Lausanne, 1003, Switzerland. TEL 41-21-2130101, FAX 41-21-2130100, info@ersnet.org, http://www.ersnet.org. Ed. Marc Humbert. Circ: 2,500. **Subscr. in N America to:** Maney Publishing, 875 Massachusetts Ave, 7th Fl, Cambridge, MA 02139. TEL 866-297-5154, FAX 617-354-6875, maney@maneyusa.com; **Subscr. outside N America to:** Maney Publishing, Ste 1C, Joseph's Well, Hanover Walk, Leeds, W Yorks LS3 1AB, United Kingdom. TEL 44-113-3868168, FAX 44-113-2486983, subscriptions@maney.co.uk.

➤ **EXCERPTA MEDICA. SECTION 15: CHEST DISEASES, THORACIC SURGERY AND TUBERCULOSIS.** *see* MEDICAL SCIENCES—Abstracting, Bibliographies, Statistics

616.2 GBR ISSN 0190-2148
QP121.A1 CODEN: EXLRDA
➤ **EXPERIMENTAL LUNG RESEARCH.** Text in English. 1980. 10/yr. GBP 1,890, EUR 2,475, USD 3,100 combined subscription to institutions (print & online eds.); GBP 3,780, EUR 4,960, USD 6,195 combined subscription to corporations (print & online eds.) (effective 2010). adv. back issues avail.; reprint service avail. from PSC. **Document type:** *Journal, Academic/Scholarly.* **Description:** Brings out articles in all fields of respiratory tract anatomy, biology, developmental biology, toxicology, and pathology.
Related titles: Online - full text ed.: ISSN 1521-0499 (from IngentaConnect).
Indexed: A01, A02, A03, A08, A22, A34, A35, A36, A38, ASCA, B21, B25, BA, BIOBASE, BIOSIS Prev, C11, CA, CABA, CIN, ChemAb, ChemTitl, CurCont, E01, E12, EMBASE, ExcerpMed, GH, H04, H16, IABS, ISR, IndMed, IndVet, Inpharma, MEDLINE, MycolAb, N02, N03, P30, P33, R08, R10, RA&MP, Reac, SCI, SCOPUS, T02, T05, THA, VS, W07, W10.
—CASDDS, GNLM, IE, Infotrieve, Ingenta, INIST. **CCC.**
Published by: Informa Healthcare (Subsidiary of: T & F Informa plc), Telephone House, 69-77 Paul St, London, EC2A 4LQ, United Kingdom. TEL 44-20-70175000, FAX 44-20-70176792, healthcare.enquiries@informa.com. Ed. Mark Giembycz. Adv. contact Per Sonnerfeldt. **Subscr. in N. America to:** Taylor & Francis Inc., Customer Services Dept, 325 Chestnut St, 8th Fl, Philadelphia, PA 19106. TEL 215-625-8900, 800-354-1420, FAX 215-625-8914, customerservice@taylorandfrancis.com; **Subscr. to:** Taylor & Francis Ltd., Journals Customer Service, Sheepen Pl, Colchester, Essex CO3 3LP, United Kingdom. TEL 44-20-70175544, FAX 44-20-70175198, tf.enquiries@tfinforma.com.

616.2 GBR ISSN 1747-6348
➤ **EXPERT REVIEW OF RESPIRATORY MEDICINE.** Text in English. 2007. bi-m. GBP 695 combined subscription domestic to institutions (print & online eds.); USD 1,220 combined subscription in North America to institutions (print & online eds.); JPY 129,000 combined subscription in Japan to institutions (print & online eds.); EUR 975 combined subscription elsewhere to institutions (print & online eds.) (effective 2011). adv. back issues avail.; reprints avail. **Document type:** *Journal, Academic/Scholarly.* **Description:** Addresses scientific, commercial and policy issues in pulmonary medicine including news and views, commentary and analysis, reports from the conference circuit, as well as full review articles.
Related titles: Online - full text ed.: ISSN 1747-6356. 2007. GBP 615 domestic to institutions; USD 1,080 in North America to institutions; JPY 115,500 in Japan to institutions; EUR 865 elsewhere to institutions (effective 2011) (from IngentaConnect).
Indexed: A26, E08, EMBASE, ExcerpMed, H11, H12, I05, MEDLINE, P20, P30, P48, P50, P54, PQC, SCOPUS.
—BLDSC (9830.066000), IE. **CCC.**
Published by: Expert Reviews Ltd. (Subsidiary of: Future Science Ltd.), Unitec House, 2 Albert Pl, London, N3 1QB, United Kingdom. TEL 44-20-83716080, FAX 44-20-83716099, info@expert-reviews.com. Ed. Elisa Manzotti TEL 44-20-83716090. Pub. David Hughes. Adv. contact Simon Boisseau. Circ: 350.

616.2 FRA ISSN 2108-1735
▼ **F L A M INFOS.** (France Lymphangioleiomyomatose) Text in French. 2010. q. **Document type:** *Newsletter, Consumer.*
Published by: Association France Lymphangioleiomyomatose (F L A M), 9 Rue des Pommiers, Saint Benoit, 86280, France. TEL 33-5-49570000, cy.durand@wanadoo.fr.

616.2 USA
FOCUS JOURNAL FOR RESPIRATORY CARE & SLEEP MEDICINE. Text in English. q. free to qualified personnel. adv. **Document type:** *Journal, Trade.* **Description:** Contains clinical articles in respiratory care and sleep medicine as well as editorial dealing with aspects of management, departmental administration and education.
Related titles: Online - full content ed.
Indexed: A25.
Published by: FOCUS Publications, Inc., 22 S. Parsonage St., Rhinebeck, NY 12572. TEL 845-876-2936, 800-661-5690, FAX 845-876-2940, http://www.foocus.com/. Pub., Adv. contact Bob Miglino. B&W page USD 2,560, color page USD 2,820.

FORSKNING FOER HAELSA. *see* MEDICAL SCIENCES—Cardiovascular Diseases

616.2 VEN ISSN 0798-3719
FOUNDATION. INTERNATIONAL SEMINAR THE RESPIRATORY PULSE. SCIENTIFIC REVIEW. Key Title: Scientific Review. Foundation. International Seminar the Respiratory Pulse. Text in English, Spanish. 1992. a. **Document type:** *Proceedings, Academic/Scholarly.* **Description:** Includes articles related to respiratory system and different human organs related.
Published by: Fundacion Seminario Internacional "El Pulso Respiratorio", Ed. Caribana Apto. 43, Cruce Avda. Universitaria y P. Los Ilustres, Valle Abajo, Caracas, DF 1040, Venezuela. therespiratorypulse@yahoo.com, http://www.the-respiratory-pulse.org.ve. Ed. Dr. Americo Gonzalez Bogen.

GIORNALE EUROPEO DI AEROBIOLOGIA. *see* MEDICAL SCIENCES—Allergology And Immunology

616.2 ITA ISSN 1127-0810
CODEN: GIMTB4
GIORNALE ITALIANO DELLE MALATTIE DEL TORACE/ITALIAN JOURNAL OF CHEST DISEASES. Abbreviated title: G I M T. Text in English, Italian. 1946. bi-m. EUR 47 in Europe to institutions; EUR 53 elsewhere to institutions (effective 2009). adv. bk.rev. charts; illus.; stat. index. back issues avail. **Document type:** *Journal, Academic/Scholarly.* **Description:** News, research papers and surveys on the study of chest diseases.
Former titles (until 1998): Giornale Italiano delle Malattie del Torace (0017-0437); (until 1965): Giornale Italiano della Tubercolosi e delle Malattie del Torace (0367-4622); (until 1956): Giornale Italiano della Tubercolosi (0367-4495)
Related titles: Supplement(s): Giornale Italiano delle Malattie del Torace. Supplemento. ISSN 0374-7913.
Indexed: A22, ChemAb, EMBASE, ExcerpMed, IndMed, P30, R10, Reac, SCOPUS.
—BLDSC (4178.220000), CASDDS, GNLM, INIST.
Published by: Mattioli 1885 SpA, Via Coduro 1, Fidenza, PR 43036, Italy. TEL 39-0524-84547, FAX 39-0524-84751, http://www.mattioli1885.com. Ed. Roberto Cogo. Circ: 10,000.

616.2 CHN ISSN 1001-1064
➤ **GUOWAI YIXUE (HUXI XITONG FENCE)/FOREIGN MEDICAL SCIENCES (RESPIRATORY SYSTEMS).** Text in Chinese. 1981. q. CNY 30 domestic; USD 40.80 foreign (effective 2005). adv. 56 p./no.; **Document type:** *Journal, Academic/Scholarly.* **Description:** Covers the latest development in the field of respiratory diseases.
Related titles: Online - full text ed.
Published by: Weishengbu, Yixue Qingbao Guanli Weiyuanhui, 361 Zhongshan Lu, Shijiazhuang, 050017, China. TEL 81-311-6266873, FAX 81-311-6266518. adv.: B&W page CNY 5,000, color page CNY 7,000. Circ: 9,000. **Dist. overseas by:** China International Book Trading Corp, 35 Chegongzhuang Xilu, Haidian District, PO Box 399, Beijing 100044, China. TEL 86-10-68412045, FAX 86-10-68412023, cibtc@mail.cibtc.com.cn, http://www.cibtc.com.cn.

616.2 USA ISSN 1542-8184
HEALTH MONITOR ALLERGIES & ASTHMA. Variant title: Allergies & Asthma Health Monitor. Text in English. 1993. q. free. adv. **Document type:** *Magazine, Consumer.*
Formerly (until 1993): Respiratory Health Monitor (1067-9324)
Published by: Data Centrum Communications, Inc., 650 From Rd, 2nd Fl, Paramus, NJ 07652. TEL 201-391-1911, FAX 201-225-1440, info@healthmonitor.com, http://www.healthmonitor.com.

616.2 FIN ISSN 1455-528X
HENGITYS JA TERVEYS RY. VUOSIKIRJA. Text in English, Finnish, Swedish. 1972. a. free. **Document type:** *Yearbook, Academic/ Scholarly.*
Formerly (until 1997): Tuberculosis and Respiratory Diseases Yearbook (0355-5011)
Published by: Hengitys ja Terveys ry/Finnish Lung Health Association, Sibeliuksenkatu 11 A 1, Helsinki, 00250, Finland. TEL 358-9-4542120, FAX 358-9-4541210, http://www/filha.fi. Circ: 2,000.

HOFFMAN HEART INSTITUTE OF CONNECTICUT. JOURNAL. *see* MEDICAL SCIENCES—Cardiovascular Diseases

616.2 JPN ISSN 1346-3837
QR180
HOKKAIDO UNIVERSITY. INSTITUTE FOR GENETIC MEDICINE. COLLECTED PAPERS. Text in Japanese; Summaries in English, Japanese. 1953. a.
Former titles (until 1998): Hokkaido University. Institute of Immunological Science. Collected Papers (0910-5026); (until 1979): Hokkaido Daigaku Men'eki Kagaku Kenkyujo Kiyo (0385-504X); (until 1974): Kekkaku No Kenkyu (0075-5354)
Published by: Hokkaido University, Institute for Genetic Medicine, North 15, West 7, Sapporo, 060, Japan. Ed. Ken Ichi Yamamoto. Circ: 300.

616.2 ITA ISSN 1973-9664
HOT TOPICS IN RESPIRATORY MEDICINE. Text in Multiple languages. 2007. 3/yr. **Document type:** *Monographic series, Academic/ Scholarly.*
Related titles: Online - full text ed.: ISSN 2036-0886.
Indexed: A01, EMBASE, SCOPUS.
Published by: F B Communication, Via Mascherella 19, Modena, 41121, Italy. TEL 39-059-4270122, FAX 39-059-4279368, info@fbcommunication.org. Eds. Chritopher P Cannon, Sergio Dalla Volta.

616.2 ESP ISSN 2173-0415
▼ **HOY EN RESPIRATORIO.** Text in Spanish. 2011. 3/yr. **Document type:** *Journal, Academic/Scholarly.*
Published by: Jarpyo Editores S.A., Ave de la Concha Espina, No. 9 Dcha., Madrid, 28016, Spain. TEL 34-91-3144338, editorial@jarpyo.es, http://www.jarpyo.es. Ed. Jose Antonio Quintano Jimenez. Circ: 25,000.

616.2 NLD ISSN 1878-8777
HYP. Text in Dutch. 1986. 5/yr. **Document type:** *Newsletter, Consumer.*
Formerly (until 2009): Hyperbulletin (0920-7090)
Published by: Nederlandse Hyperventilatie Stichting, Postbus 74386, Amsterdam, 1070 BJ, Netherlands. TEL 31-20-6628876, FAX 31-20-6761301, nhs.hyperventilatie@wxs.nl, http://www.hyperventilatie.org.

616.2 FIN ISSN 1458-5871
HYVA HENGITYS. Text in Finnish. 1961. 6/yr. EUR 30 (effective 2005). adv. **Document type:** *Magazine, Trade.*
Formerly (until 2001): Silmu (0782-3266); Which incorporated (1945-1985): Jousi (0047-2948)
Published by: Hengitysliitto Heli ry/Pulmonary Association Heli, Oltermannintie 8, PO Box 40, Helsinki, 00621, Finland. TEL 358-9-7527511, FAX 358-9-75275170. Ed. Pertti Paakkinen TEL 358-9-75275134. adv.: B&W page EUR 1,430, color page EUR 2,140; 210 x 297. Circ: 7,000.

616.2 USA ISSN 2090-5769
▼ ➤ **I S R N PULMONOLOGY.** (International Scholarly Research Network) Text in English. 2011. **Document type:** *Journal, Academic/ Scholarly.* **Description:** Publishes original research articles, review articles, and clinical studies in all areas of pulmonology.
Related titles: Online - full text ed.: ISSN 2090-5777. 2011. free (effective 2011).
Published by: Hindawi Publishing Corporation, 410 Park Ave, 15th Fl, PMB 287, New York, NY 10022. FAX 215-893-4392, 866-446-3294, info@hindawi.com.

616.2 378 USA
I U NEWSLETTER. Text in English. 1979. q. free (effective 2007). **Document type:** *Newsletter.* **Description:** Highlights current events at the college and in the field of respiratory care.
Formerly: C C H S News (Print)
Media: Online - full text.
Published by: California College for Health Services, 5295 S. Commerce Dr, Salt Lake Cty, UT 84107-4724. TEL 800-497-7157, FAX 888-724-6652, cchsinfo@cchs.edu. Ed. Cheryl Latif. Pub., R&P Scott Croydon. Circ: 8,000.

616.2 IND ISSN 0019-5707
RC306 CODEN: IJTBAD
➤ **INDIAN JOURNAL OF TUBERCULOSIS.** Text in English. 1953. q. INR 800 domestic; USD 30 SAARC; USD 35 South East Asian & Eastern Countries; USD 40 elsewhere (effective 2011). bk.rev. abstr.; bibl.; charts; illus.; stat. index, cum.index. back issues avail. **Document type:** *Journal, Academic/Scholarly.* **Description:** Contains scientific articles of high quality contributed by authors from all over the world, specially India. Subjects covered include clinical, epidemiological, public health and social aspects of tuberculosis. It also includes interesting case reports on patients suffering from pulmonary, extra-pulmonary tuberculosis as well as other respiratory diseases.
Related titles: Online - full text ed.: free (effective 2011).
Indexed: ChemAb, EMBASE, ExcerpMed, MEDLINE, P30, R10, Reac, SCOPUS.
—BLDSC (4421.700000), GNLM, IE, Ingenta.
Published by: Tuberculosis Association of India, 3 Red Cross Rd, New Delhi, 110 001, India. TEL 91-11-23715217, FAX 91-11-23711303, tbassnindia@yahoo.co.in. Eds. D Behera, Lalit Kant, R K Srivastava.

616.2 MEX ISSN 0187-7585
➤ **INSTITUTO NACIONAL DE ENFERMEDADES RESPIRATORIAS. REVISTA.** Short title: Revista I N E R. Text in Spanish; Summaries in English, Spanish. 1988. q. MXN 350 domestic; USD 75 in Latin America; USD 85 in United States; USD 95 elsewhere (effective 2007). adv. bk.rev. illus.; stat. back issues avail. **Document type:** *Journal, Academic/Scholarly.* **Description:** Contains original articles, research reports, review articles, clinical cases and notices related to the pathology of the respiratory tract.
Related titles: CD-ROM ed.; Online - full text ed.
Indexed: C01, EMBASE, ExcerpMed, R10, Reac, SCOPUS.
—BLDSC (7819.937500).
Published by: Instituto Nacional de Enfermedades Respiratorias, Calzada de Tlalpan 4502, Colonia Seccion XVI, Mexico City, DF 14080, Mexico. TEL 52-56-664539, http://portal.iner.gob.mx. Circ: 6,000.

616.2 GBR ISSN 1747-1273
INTERNATIONAL JOURNAL OF RESPIRATORY CARE. Text in English. 2005. s-a. GBP 25 in Europe to individuals; GBP 30 elsewhere to individuals; GBP 50 in Europe to institutions; GBP 65 elsewhere to institutions (effective 2009). adv. back issues avail.; reprints avail. **Document type:** *Journal, Academic/Scholarly.* **Description:** Aims to meet the interests and information needs of respiratory care physicians and sleep specialists.
Indexed: EMBASE, ExcerpMed, R10, Reac, SCOPUS.
Published by: Greycoat Publishing Ltd., 106 Earl's Court Rd, Kensington, London, W8 6EG, United Kingdom. TEL 44-20-79376233, FAX 44-20-79370933, mail@greycoatpublishing.co.uk. Eds. Emiel Wouters, Guy Wallis. Adv. contact Robert Sloan.

616.246 FRA ISSN 1027-3719
RC306 CODEN: IJTDFO
➤ **INTERNATIONAL JOURNAL OF TUBERCULOSIS AND LUNG DISEASE.** Abbreviated title: I J T L D. Text in English; Summaries in French, Spanish. 1997. m. adv. Supplement avail. **Document type:** *Journal, Academic/Scholarly.* **Description:** Aims to encourage continuing education of physicians and other health personnel. Contains the most up-to-date information in the field of tuberculosis and lung health. Includes original articles and commissioned reviews on clinical, biological and epidemiological research. Also covers implementation and assessment of field projects and action programs for tuberculosis control and the promotion of lung health.
Related titles: Online - full text ed.: ISSN 1815-7920 (from IngentaConnect).
Indexed: A22, A34, A35, A36, A37, AIDS&CR, AgBio, B20, B21, BA, CA, CABA, CurCont, D01, DBA, E04, E05, E12, EMBASE, ESPM, ExcerpMed, F08, GH, H&SSA, H17, INI, ISR, IndMed, IndVet, Inpharma, LT, MEDLINE, N02, N03, P30, P33, P35, P37, P39, R08, R10, R12, RM&VM, RRTA, Reac, RiskAb, S13, S16, SCI, SCOPUS, SoyAb, T02, T05, TAR, ToxAb, VS, ViroIAbstr, W07, W11.
—BLDSC (4542.696180), GNLM, IE, Infotrieve, Ingenta, INIST. **CCC.**
Published by: International Union against Tuberculosis and Lung Disease (I U A T L D)/Union Internationale contre la Tuberculose et les Maladies Respiratoires, 68 Bd Saint-Michel, Paris, 75006, France. TEL 33-1-44320360, FAX 33-1-43299087, union@iuatld.org, http://www.iuatld.org.

616.2 613.62 620 AUS ISSN 0892-6298
R11
➤ **INTERNATIONAL SOCIETY FOR RESPIRATORY PROTECTION. JOURNAL.** Abbreviated title: J I S R P. Variant title: Journal of the I S R P. Text in English. 1983. q. free to members (effective 2009). **Document type:** *Journal, Academic/Scholarly.* **Description:** Contains technical papers on original work and new treatments of previous research also publishes solicited and unsolicited review articles on topics related to respiratory protection, including but not limited to program administration, implementation, and training.
Related titles: Online - full content ed.
—BLDSC (4802.508000), IE, Ingenta.
Published by: International Society for Respiratory Protection, Private Bag 1001, Mona Vale, NSW 2103, Australia. info@isrp.com.au. Ed. Ziqing Zhuang TEL 412-386-4055.

616.2 USA ISSN 1531-2984
RC702
➤ **THE INTERNET JOURNAL OF PULMONARY MEDICINE.** Text in English. 1997. s-a. free (effective 2011). adv. bk.rev. back issues avail. **Document type:** *Journal, Academic/Scholarly.* **Description:** Contains information from the fields of pulmonary medicine and respiratory diseases, including original articles, reviews, case reports, streaming slide shows, streaming videos, letters to the editor, press releases, and meeting information.
Media: Online - full text.
Indexed: A01, A02, A03, A08, A26, C06, C07, CA, EMBASE, G08, H11, H12, I05, SCOPUS, T02.
Published by: Internet Scientific Publications, Llc., 23 Rippling Creek Dr, Sugar Land, TX 77479. TEL 832-443-1193, FAX 281-240-1533, wenker@ispub.com. Ed. Armando Huaringa.

616.2 BRA ISSN 1806-3713
➤ **JORNAL BRASILEIRO DE PNEUMOLOGIA.** Text in English, Portuguese, Spanish; Summaries in English, Portuguese. 1974. bi-m. adv. bk.rev. 80 p./no.; **Document type:** *Journal, Academic/Scholarly.* **Description:** Publishes original research on pneumology and relates specialties.
Formerly: Jornal de Pneumologia (0102-3586)
Related titles: Online - full text ed.: ISSN 1806-3756. 2004. free (effective 2011).
Indexed: A34, A35, A36, AgBio, C01, CA, CABA, D01, E12, EMBASE, ExcerpMed, GH, H17, IndVet, MEDLINE, N02, N03, P30, P33, P37, P39, PN&I, R08, R10, R12, R13, RM&VM, Reac, SCI, SCOPUS, T02, T05, VS, W07, W10.
—BLDSC (4674.677505), GNLM.
Published by: Sociedade Brasileira de Pneumologia e Tisiologia, Avenida Bandeirantes 3900, Ribeirao Preto, SP 14048-900, Brazil. TEL 55-16-39666562. Ed., R&P Thais Helena A T Queluz. Adv. contact Mr Katayama TEL 55-11-5711719. Circ: 4,000 (paid and controlled).

616.2 USA ISSN 1941-2711
CODEN: JAEMEP
➤ **JOURNAL OF AEROSOL MEDICINE AND PULMONARY DRUG DELIVERY.** Text in English. 1988. bi-m. USD 1,663 domestic to institutions; USD 2,051 foreign to institutions; USD 1,943 combined subscription domestic to institutions (print & online eds.); USD 2,391 combined subscription foreign to institutions (print & online eds.) (effective 2012). adv. reprint service avail. from PSC. **Document type:** *Journal, Academic/Scholarly.* **Description:** Contains original articles and reviews that apply aerosols to the delivery of medication and the investigation for physiologic, pharmacologic, and toxicologic phenomena in the lung.
Formerly (until 2008): Journal of Aerosol Medicine (0894-2684)
Related titles: Online - full text ed.: ISSN 1941-2703. USD 1,741 to institutions (effective 2012).
Indexed: A01, A03, A08, A22, A26, A29, ASCA, B&BAb, B20, B21, CA, CurCont, E01, E07, EMBASE, ESPM, ExcerpMed, H12, I10, Inpharma, MEDLINE, P20, P22, P30, P48, P54, PQC, Reac, SCI, SCOPUS, T02, ViroIAbstr, W07.
—BLDSC (4919.054500), GNLM, IE, Infotrieve, Ingenta, INIST. **CCC.**
Published by: Mary Ann Liebert, Inc. Publishers, 140 Huguenot St, 3rd Fl, New Rochelle, NY 10801. TEL 914-740-2100, FAX 914-740-2101, 800-654-3237, info@liebertpub.com. Ed. Gerald C Smaldone TEL 631-444-3869. Adv. contact Harriet I Matysko TEL 914-740-2182.

616.97 USA ISSN 0277-0903
RC591 CODEN: JOUADU
➤ **JOURNAL OF ASTHMA.** Text in English. 19??. 10/yr. GBP 1,610, EUR 2,120, USD 2,650 combined subscription to institutions (print & online eds.); GBP 3,225, EUR 4,240, USD 5,260 combined subscription to corporations (print & online eds.) (effective 2010). adv. bk.rev. bibl.; charts; illus.; stat. index, cum. index: 1963-1965. back issues avail.; reprint service avail. from PSC. **Document type:** *Journal, Academic/Scholarly.* **Description:** Provides information on new developments in the understanding and management of asthma.
Former titles (until 1981): Journal of Asthma Research (0021-9134); (until 1963): Children's Asthma Research Institute and Hospital. Journal
Related titles: Microfilm ed.; Online - full text ed.: ISSN 1532-4303 (from IngentaConnect).
Indexed: A01, A02, A03, A08, A20, A22, A34, A36, ASCA, B21, C11, CA, CABA, ChemAb, CurCont, D01, DentInd, E-psyche, E01, E12, EMBASE, ExcerpMed, F08, GH, H04, ImmunAb, IndMed, Inpharma, LT, MEDLINE, N02, N03, NRN, OR, P03, P30, P33, P35, P37, P39, P43, PsycInfo, PsycholAb, R08, R10, R11, R12, RILM, RM&VM, RRTA, Reac, SCI, SCOPUS, SoyAb, T02, T05, THA, W07, W10, W11.
—BLDSC (4947.295000), CASDDS, GNLM, IE, Infotrieve, Ingenta, INIST. **CCC.**
Published by: (Association for the Care of Asthma), Informa Healthcare (Subsidiary of: T & F Informa plc), 52 Vanderbilt Ave, New York, NY 10017. TEL 212-262-8230, FAX 212-262-8234, healthcare.enquiries@informa.com, http://www.informahealthcare.com. Ed. Jonathan A Bernstein. Adv. contact Daniel Wallen. **Subscr. outside N. America to:** Taylor & Francis Ltd.

616.2 USA ISSN 1944-6586
CODEN: JBROF2
➤ **JOURNAL OF BRONCHOLOGY & INTERVENTIONAL PULMONOLOGY.** Text in English. 1994. q. USD 511 domestic to institutions; USD 625 foreign to institutions (effective 2011). adv. charts; illus. **Document type:** *Journal, Academic/Scholarly.* **Description:** Examines all aspects of the prevention, diagnosis and treatment of disorders affecting the respiratory system.
Formerly (until 2008): Journal of Bronchology (1070-8030)
Related titles: Online - full text ed.: ISSN 1948-8270.
Indexed: A36, CABA, EMBASE, ExcerpMed, GH, P33, R10, RM&VM, Reac, SCOPUS.
—BLDSC (4954.553000), GNLM, IE, Infotrieve, Ingenta. **CCC.**
Published by: (World Association for Bronchology), Lippincott Williams & Wilkins (Subsidiary of: Wolters Kluwer N.V.), 530 Walnut St, Philadelphia, PA 19106. TEL 215-521-8300, FAX 215-521-8902, customerservice@lww.com, http://www.lww.com. Ed. Dr. Atul C Mehta. adv.: B&W page USD 785, color page USD 1,895. Circ: 1,049 (paid). **Subscr. to:** PO Box 1620, Hagerstown, MD 21741. TEL 301-223-2300, 800-638-3030, FAX 301-223-2365. **Co-sponsor:** American Association for Bronchology.

616.2 USA
THE JOURNAL OF C O P D MANAGEMENT. (Chronic Obstructive Pulmonary Disease) Text in English. 200?. q. **Document type:** *Journal, Trade.* **Description:** Helps to keep pulmonologists, critical care physicians, nurse practitioners, physician assistants, and primary care physicians abreast of the latest developments in treating and managing patients with COPD.
Published by: Jobson Medical Group (Subsidiary of: Jobson Publishing LLC), 100 Ave of the Americas, New York, NY 10013. TEL 212-274-7000, FAX 212-431-0500, http://www.jmihealth.com.

JOURNAL OF CHEMOTHERAPY. *see* MEDICAL SCIENCES—Oncology

THE JOURNAL OF CLINICAL SLEEP MEDICINE. *see* MEDICAL SCIENCES—Psychiatry And Neurology

616.2 USA
➤ **THE JOURNAL OF RESPIRATORY DISEASES (ONLINE).** Text in English. m. **Document type:** *Journal, Academic/Scholarly.* **Description:** Provides practical information about diagnosis and treatment pertaining to the respiratory system, both as a site of primary disease and as a complication of other clinical problems.
Media: Online - full text.

Published by: C M P Medica LLC (Subsidiary of: United Business Media Limited), 535 Connecticut Ave, Ste 300, Norwalk, CT 06854. TEL 203-523-7000, FAX 203-662-6420, http://www.cmpmedica.com. Ed. Dr. Sarah C Williams TEL 203-523-7098.

➤ **KAREI IGAKU KENKYUSHO ZASSHI.** see MEDICAL SCIENCES—Communicable Diseases

616.246 JPN ISSN 0022-9776 CODEN: KEKKAG

KEKKAKU/TUBERCULOSIS. Text in Japanese; Abstracts in English. 1923. m. adv. abstr.; bibl.; charts; illus. index. **Document type:** *Academic/Scholarly.* **Description:** Publishes articles which are devoted to understanding and improving studies in tuberculosis and related fields, including original reports, reviews, case reports and short reports.
Indexed: CIN, ChemAb, ChemTitl, EMBASE, ExcerpMed, INI, INIS AtomInd, IndMed, Inpharma, MEDLINE, P30, R10, Reac, SCOPUS.
—BLDSC (5089.250000), CASDDS, GNLM, INIST. **CCC.**
Published by: Japanese Society for Tuberculosis, c/o Research Institute of Tuberculosis, Matsuyama 3-chome, Kiyose-shi, Tokyo-to 204-0022, Japan. TEL 81-424-92-2091, FAX 81-424-91-8315. Ed. Nobukatsu Ishikawa. Circ: 3,000. **Subscr. to:** Tonggang Shudian, Export Dept, Rm 106 NKB Azeria Bldg, 7-7 Shinogawa-Machi, Shinjuku-ku, Tokyo 162-0814, Japan. TEL 81-3-3269-2131, FAX 81-3-3269-8655.

616.2 JPN ISSN 0287-2137

KIKANSHIGAKU/JAPAN SOCIETY FOR RESPIRATORY ENDOSCOPY. JOURNAL. Text in Japanese. 1979. q. JPY 10,000 membership (effective 2005). back issues avail. **Document type:** *Journal, Academic/Scholarly.*
Indexed: INIS AtomInd.
—BLDSC (4806.300000). **CCC.**
Published by: Nihon Kokyuuki Naishikyou Gakkai/Japan Society for Respiratory Endoscopy, 1005, Ichigaya Tokyu Bldg., 4-2-1 Kudankita, Chiyoda-ku, Tokyo, 102-0073, Japan. TEL 81-3-32383011, FAX 81-3-32383012, office@jsre.org, http://www.jsre.org/.

616.2 JPN ISSN 0286-9314 CODEN: KOKUDH

KOKYU/RESPIRATION RESEARCH. Text in Japanese; Summaries in English, Japanese. 1982. m. JPY 26,460 per issue (effective 2006). **Document type:** *Journal, Academic/Scholarly.*
Indexed: CIN, ChemAb, ChemTitl, INIS AtomInd, Inpharma.
—BLDSC (7777.651000), CASDDS, GNLM.
Published by: Resupireshon Risachi Fandeshon/Respiration Research Foundation, Kagaku-Kaikan 4F, 1-5, Kanda-Surugadai, Chiyoda-ku, Tokyo, 101-0062, Japan. TEL 81-3-32576931, FAX 81-3-32576933, KGK02345@nifty.ne.jp, http://homepage2.nifty.com/rrf/.

616.2 JPN ISSN 0452-3458 CODEN: KOJUA9

KOKYU TO JUNKAN/RESPIRATION AND CIRCULATION. Text in Japanese; Summaries in English. 1953. m. JPY 31,800; JPY 41,400 combined subscription (print & online eds.) (effective 2010). **Document type:** *Journal, Academic/Scholarly.*
Related titles: Online - full text ed.
Indexed: ChemAb, ChemTitl, EMBASE, ExcerpMed, INIS AtomInd, IndMed, Inpharma, P30, R10, Reac, SCOPUS.
—CASDDS, GNLM, INIST.
Published by: Igaku Shoin Ltd., 1-28-36 Hongo, Bunkyo-ku, Tokyo, 113-8719, Japan. TEL 81-3-3817-5600, FAX 81-3-3815-7791, info@igaku-shoin.co.jp. Circ: 4,500.

616.2 JPN ISSN 1347-7285

KOKYUUKI KEA/RESPIRATORY CARE. Text in Japanese. 2003. m. (bi-m until vol.2, no.1, 2004). JPY 20,412; JPY 1,890 newsstand/cover (effective 2007). Supplement avail. **Document type:** *Journal, Academic/Scholarly.*
Published by: Medicus Shuppan/Medicus Publishing Inc., 18-24 Hiroshiba-cho, Suita-shi, Osaka-fu 564-8580, Japan. TEL 81-6-63856911, FAX 81-6-63856873, http://www.medica.co.jp/.

616.2 JPN ISSN 1347-0051

KOKYUUKIKA/RESPIRATORY MEDICINE. Text in Japanese. 2002. m. JPY 2,625 (effective 2003). **Document type:** *Journal, Academic/Scholarly.*
Published by: Kagaku-Hyoronsha Co. Ltd., 2-10-8, Kana Tomiyama-cho, Chiyoda-ku, Tokyo, 101-8531, Japan. TEL 81-3-32527741, FAX 81-3-32525952, http://www.kahyo.com/index.html.

616.241 DEU

KOMPAKT PNEUMOLOGIE. Text in German. 2002. 6/yr. adv. **Document type:** *Journal, Trade.*
Published by: Biermann Verlag GmbH, Otto-Hahn-Str 7, Cologne, 50997, Germany. TEL 49-2236-3760, FAX 49-2236-376999, info@biermann.net, http://www.biermann-verlag.de. Ed. Birgit Grodotzki. Adv. contact Michael Kesten.

616.2 FRA ISSN 1292-5977

➤ **LA LETTRE DU PNEUMOLOGUE.** Text in French. 1998. bi-m. EUR 96 in Europe to individuals; EUR 96 DOM-TOM to individuals; EUR 96 in Africa to individuals; EUR 108 elsewhere to individuals; EUR 114 in Europe to institutions; EUR 114 DOM-TOM to institutions; EUR 114 in Africa to institutions; EUR 126 elsewhere to institutions (effective 2009). **Document type:** *Academic/Scholarly.*
—INIST.
Published by: Edimark S.A.S., 2 Rue Sainte-Marie, Courbevoie, Cedex 92418, France. TEL 33-1-41458000, FAX 33-1-41458025, contact@edimark.fr. Ed. Philippe Godard. Pub. Claudie Damour-Terrasson.

➤ **LIPID EDUCATION SERVICE NEWS BRIEFS.** see MEDICAL SCIENCES—Cardiovascular Diseases

616.24 NLD ISSN 2210-4011

▼ **LONGFIBROSEPATIENTENVERENIGING. INFORMATIEBLAD.** Cover title: Over Leven met Longfibrose. Text in Dutch. 2009. bi-m. **Document type:** *Newsletter, Consumer.*
Published by: Belangenvereniging Longfibrosepatienten Nederland, c/o Academisch Ziekenhuis Maastricht, Secretariaat Longziekten, Postbus 5800, Maastricht, 6202 AZ, Netherlands. TEL 31-43-3619266, longfibrosevereniging@home.nl.

616.238 NLD ISSN 2211-8241

LONGWIJZER. Text in Dutch. 1961. bi-m. EUR 24 membership (effective 2011). adv. **Document type:** *Magazine, Consumer.*
Former titles (until 2011): Luchtwijzer (1574-1893); (until 2005): Contrastma (0166-3992)
Published by: Astma Fonds, Postbus 627, Amersfoort, 3800 AP, Netherlands. TEL 31-33-4341212, FAX 31-33-4341299, info@astmafonds.nl, http://www.astmafonds.nl.

616.2 USA ISSN 0341-2040
QP121 CODEN: LUNGD9

➤ **LUNG**; an international journal on lungs, airways and breathing. Text in English. 1903. bi-m. (in 1 vol., 6 nos./vol.). EUR 697, USD 731 combined subscription to institutions (print & online eds.) (effective 2012). adv. back issues avail.; reprint service avail. from PSC. **Document type:** *Journal, Academic/Scholarly.* **Description:** Brings out articles, reviews and editorials on all aspects of the healthy and diseased lungs, of the airways, and of breathing.
Former titles (until 1976): Pneumonologie (0033-4073); (Until 1970): Beitraege zur Klinik und Erforschung der Tuberkulose und der Lungenkrankheiten (0300-9696); (Until 1965): Beitraege zur Klinik der Tuberkulose und Spezifischen Tuberkulose-Forschung (0366-0966); (Until 1908): Beitraege zur Klinik der Tuberkulose (0179-616X)
Related titles: Microform ed.: (from PQC); Online - full text ed.: ISSN 1432-1750 (from IngentaConnect).
Indexed: A01, A02, A03, A08, A22, A26, A29, A34, A36, ASCA, Agr, B20, B21, B25, BIOSIS Prev, C06, C07, C08, C11, CA, CABA, CIN, CINAHL, CISA, ChemAb, ChemTitl, CurCont, DBA, E01, E08, E12, EMBASE, ESPM, ExcerpMed, G08, GH, H&SSA, H04, H11, H12, H13, I05, I10, IBR, IBZ, ISR, IndMed, Inpharma, MEDLINE, MycolAb, N02, N03, P02, P10, P19, P20, P22, P24, P30, P33, P35, P39, P48, P53, P54, PQC, R10, R12, R13, RM&VM, Reac, S09, SCI, SCOPUS, T02, T05, VirolAbstr, W07.
—BLDSC (5307.160000), CASDDS, GNLM, IE, Infotrieve, Ingenta, INIST. **CCC.**
Published by: Springer New York LLC (Subsidiary of: Springer Science+Business Media), 233 Spring St, New York, NY 10013. TEL 212-460-1500, FAX 212-460-1575, service-ny@springer.com, http://www.springer.com/. **Subscr. outside the Americas to:** Springer Distribution Center, Kundenservice Zeitschriften, Haberstr 7, Heidelberg 69126, Germany. TEL 49-6221-3454303, FAX 49-6221-3454229; **Subscr. to:** Journal Fulfillment, PO Box 2485, Secaucus, NJ 07096. TEL 201-348-4033, FAX 201-348-4505.

➤ **LUNG BIOLOGY IN HEALTH AND DISEASE.** see BIOLOGY—Physiology

616.2 USA ISSN 1542-1961
RC756

LUNG DISORDERS. Text in English. 2002. a. USD 19.95 per issue (effective 2010). **Document type:** *Monographic series, Academic/Scholarly.*
Published by: (Johns Hopkins Medical Institutions), Medletter Associates, 6 Trowbridge Dr, Bethel, CT 06801. Ed. Simeon Margolis.

616.2 IND ISSN 0970-2113
QP121

➤ **LUNG INDIA.** Text in English. 1982. q. INR 1,000 domestic to individuals; USD 100 foreign to individuals; INR 2,000 domestic to institutions; USD 250 foreign to institutions; INR 1,200 combined subscription domestic to individuals (print & online eds.); USD 120 combined subscription foreign to individuals (print & online eds.); INR 2,400 combined subscription domestic to institutions (print & online eds.); USD 300 combined subscription foreign to institutions (print & online eds.) (effective 2011). adv. bk.rev. abstr. **Document type:** *Journal, Academic/Scholarly.* **Description:** Covers respiratory medicine including immunology, intensive care, sleep medicine, thoracic surgery, thoracic imaging, occupational health, and related subjects.
Related titles: Online - full text ed.: ISSN 0974-598X. INR 800 domestic to individuals; USD 80 foreign to individuals; INR 1,600 domestic to institutions; USD 200 foreign to institutions (effective 2011).
Indexed: A01, A26, CA, E08, EMBASE, ExcerpMed, H11, H12, I05, P10, P30, P48, P53, P54, PQC, S09, SCOPUS, T02.
—**CCC.**
Published by: (Indian Chest Society), Medknow Publications and Media Pvt. Ltd., B-9, Kanara Business Ctr, Off Link Rd, Ghatkopar (E), Mumbai, Maharastra 400 075, India. TEL 91-22-66491816, FAX 91-22-66491817, http://www.medknow.com. Ed. Virendra Singh.

616.2 SWE ISSN 2000-5237

▼ **LUNG & ALLERGI FORUM.** Text in Swedish. 2010. q. adv. **Document type:** *Magazine, Trade.*
Related titles: Online - full text ed.
Published by: (Svensk Lungmedicinsk Foerening, Svenska Foereningen foer Allergologi), Mediahuset i Goeteborg AB, Marieholmsgatan 10 C, Goeteborg, 41502, Sweden. TEL 46-31-7071930, FAX 46-31-848642, http://www.mediahuset.se. Eds. Alf Tunsaeter, Lennart Hansson. Adv. contact Dan Johansson TEL 46-31-7072448. page SEK 26,000; 210 x 297.

616.2 JPN ISSN 0919-5742 CODEN: LUPEFF

THE LUNG PERSPECTIVES. Text in Japanese. 1993. q. JPY 8,400 (effective 2005). **Document type:** *Journal, Academic/Scholarly.*
Indexed: CIN, ChemAb, ChemTitl.
—BLDSC (5307.275000), CASDDS.
Published by: Medikaru Rebyusha/Medical Review Co., Ltd., 1-7-3 Hirano-Machi, Chuo-ku, Yoshida Bldg., Osaka-shi, 541-0046, Japan. TEL 81-6-62231468, FAX 81-6-62231245.

616.2 JPN

MEDICAL CONFERENCE SERIES. Text in Japanese. 1961. a. JPY 2,835 newsstand/cover (effective 2001). 50 p./no.; **Document type:** *Proceedings.*
Published by: Japan Anti-Tuberculosis Association/Kekkaku Yobokai, 1-3-12 Misaki-cho, Chiyoda-ku, Tokyo, 101-0061, Japan. TEL 81-3-3292-9211, FAX 81-3-3292-9208, jata@jatahq.org, http://www.jatahq.org. Pub. Toru Mori. Circ: 15,000.

616.246 HUN ISSN 0238-2571

MEDICINA THORACALIS. Text in Hungarian; Summaries in English, German, Russian. 1945. m. adv. bk.rev. charts; illus. index. **Document type:** *Journal, Academic/Scholarly.*
Former titles (until 1989): Pneumonologia Hungarica (0133-1728); (until 1976): Tuberkulozis es Tudobetegsegek (0041-3887); (until 1961): Tuberkulozis (0324-4326); (until 1957): Tuberkulozis Keredsei (0324-427X); (until 1949): Pneumonologia Danubiana (0324-4229)
Indexed: IndMed, P30, SCOPUS.
—GNLM.
Published by: Magyar Tudogyogyasz Tarsasag, Munkacsy M u 70, Torokbalint, 2045, Hungary. TEL 36-62-270315, tudogyogyasz@doki.net, http://www.tudogyogyasz.hu. Circ: 1,200.

616.2 USA

➤ **MEDSCAPE RESPIRATORY CARE.** Text in English. 1997. 6/yr. **Document type:** *Journal, Academic/Scholarly.* **Description:** Provides both primary care physicians and specialists with information for the prevention, diagnosis, and management of respiratory diseases.
Media: Online - full text.
Published by: WebMD Medscape Health Network, 224 W 30th St, New York, NY 10001. TEL 888-506-6098, medscapecustomersupport@webmd.net, http://www.medscape.com.

616.2 USA

MEDSCI UPDATE. Text in English. 1982. m. free. **Document type:** *Newsletter, Trade.* **Description:** Provides information to physicians about the Center's clinical and research programs in allergic, respiratory, and immune system disorders.
Related titles: Online - full content ed.
Published by: National Jewish Medical and Research Center, Office of Professional Education, 1400 Jackson St M317, Denver, CO 80206. TEL 303-398-1000, FAX 303-270-2226, proed@njc.org, http://www.nationaljewish.org/professionals/pro-ed/index.aspx. Circ: 26,000 (controlled).

616.2 ITA ISSN 0026-4954

➤ **MINERVA PNEUMOLOGICA**; a journal on diseases of the respiratory system. Text in Italian; Summaries in English, Italian. 1962. q. EUR 240 combined subscription in the European Union to institutions (print & online eds.); EUR 265 combined subscription elsewhere to institutions (print & online eds.) (effective 2011). bibl.; charts; illus. index. **Document type:** *Journal, Academic/Scholarly.* **Description:** Covers pathophysiology and clinical medicine of the diseases of the respiratory system.
Related titles: Microform ed.: (from PQC); Online - full text ed.: ISSN 1827-1723. 2005.
Indexed: A22, EMBASE, ExcerpMed, R10, Reac, SCOPUS.
—BLDSC (5794.450000), GNLM, IE, Ingenta, INIST. **CCC.**
Published by: Edizioni Minerva Medica, Corso Bramante 83-85, Turin, 10126, Italy. TEL 39-011-678282, FAX 39-011-674502, journals.dept@minervamedica.it, http://www.minervamedica.it. Ed. O Orlandi. Pub. Alberto Oliaro. Circ: 2,900 (paid).

616.2 ITA ISSN 1122-0643 CODEN: MACDE

➤ **MONALDI ARCHIVES FOR CHEST DISEASE.** (Published in two series: the pulmonary series is published bi-monthly and the cardiology series quarterly.) Text and summaries in English. 1945. 10/yr. adv. bk.rev. **Document type:** *Journal, Academic/Scholarly.* **Description:** Publishes original work, editorials, and reviews on matters of clinical respiratory medicine and rehabilitation.
Former titles (until 1992): Archivio Monaldi per le Malattie del Torace (1120-0391); (until 1986): Archivio Monaldi per la Tisiologia e le Malattie dell'Apparato Respiratorio (0004-0185); (until 1969): Archivio di Tisiologia e delle Malattie dell'Apparato Respiratorio (0365-7426); (until 1954): Archivio di Tisiologia (0390-7376)
Indexed: ChemAb, DentInd, EMBASE, ExcerpMed, INI, IndMed, MEDLINE, P30, R10, Reac, SCOPUS.
—BLDSC (5901.590800), CASDDS, GNLM, IE, Ingenta, INIST.
Published by: (Fondazione Salvatore Maugeri), PI-ME Editrice, Via Vigentina 136, Pavia, 27100, Italy. TEL 39-0382-572169, FAX 39-0382-572102, tipografia@pime-editrice.it. Circ: 3,500.

➤ **MOOK: HAIGAN NO RINSHO/CLINICS OF LUNG CANCER: EPIDEMIOLOGY, DETECTION, DIAGNOSES, TREATMENTS.** see MEDICAL SCIENCES—Oncology

➤ **MUCOSAL IMMUNOLOGY UPDATE.** see MEDICAL SCIENCES—Allergology And Immunology

616.2 ITA ISSN 1828-695X

MULTIDISCIPLINARY RESPIRATORY MEDICINE. Text in English, Italian. 2006. q.
Indexed: EMBASE, ExcerpMed, SCI, SCOPUS, W07.
—BLDSC (5983.090600), IE.
Published by: (Associazione Scientifica Interdisciplinare per lo Studio delle Malatite Respiratorie (A I M A R)), Novamedia, Via Monsignor Cavigioli 10, Borgomanero, NO 28021, Italy. TEL 39-0322-846549, FAX 39-0322-843222.

616.246 614 IND

N T I BULLETIN. Text in English. 1964. s-a. bk.rev. abstr.; bibl.; illus. back issues avail. **Document type:** *Bulletin, Academic/Scholarly.* **Description:** Contains original research articles, field reports, TB programmes, and discussions on current problems in the field.
Former titles (until 1993): N T I Newsletter; (until 197?): National Tuberculosis Institute. Newsletter (0377-4937); (until 1974): N T I Newsletter (0047-9136)
Published by: National Tuberculosis Institute, 8 Bellary Rd, Bangalore, Karnataka 560 003, India. TEL 91-80-23441192, FAX 91-80-32440952, ntiindia@blr.vsnl.net.in, http://ntiindia.kar.nic.in.

NATIONAL CENTRE FOR OCCUPATIONAL HEALTH. ANNUAL REPORT. see OCCUPATIONAL HEALTH AND SAFETY

616.2 USA

NEW DIRECTIONS (DENVER). Text in English. 1986. q. free. **Document type:** *Newsletter.* **Description:** Assistance for patients coping with respiratory and immune system problems.
Formerly: Lung Line Letter
Related titles: Online - full content ed.
Published by: National Jewish Medical and Research Center, Public Affairs Department, 1400 Jackson St, Denver, CO 80206. TEL 303-388-4461, allstetterw@njc.org, http://www.nationaljewish.org. Ed. William Allstetter. Circ: 200,000 (controlled).

616.2 USA

NEW MEDICAL THERAPIES BRIEFS. CHRONIC OBSTRUCTIVE PULMONARY DISEASE. Abbreviated title: N M T Briefs. C O P D. Text in English. 200?. irreg. free (effective 2009). **Document type:** *Newsletter, Trade.*
Media: Online - full content.
Published by: CenterWatch (Subsidiary of: Jobson Medical Information LLC.), 100 N Washington St, Ste 301, Boston, MA 02114. TEL 617-948-5100, 866-219-3440, customerservice@centerwatch.com.

NEW MEDICAL THERAPIES BRIEFS. LUNG CANCER. see MEDICAL SCIENCES—Oncology

616.2 JPN ISSN 0029-0645
➤ **NIHON KIKAN SHOKUDOKA GAKKAI KAIHO/JAPAN BRONCHO-ESOPHAGOLOGICAL SOCIETY. JOURNAL.** Text in Japanese, English; Summaries in English. 1950. bi-m. JPY 12,000 membership (effective 2005). adv. bk.rev. abstr. cum.index. back issues avail. **Document type:** *Journal, Academic/Scholarly.* **Description:** Reports on branchoesophagological from basic and clinical points of view.
Related titles: Online - full text ed.
Indexed: INIS AtomInd.
—BLDSC (4804.700000). **CCC.**
Published by: Nihon Kikan Shokudoka Gakkai/Japan Broncho-Esophagological Society, Hakuo Bldg, 2-3-10 Koraku, Bunkyo-ku, Tokyo, 112-0004, Japan. TEL 81-3-38183030, FAX 81-3-38152810. Ed., R&P Tomoyuki Yoshida. adv.: B&W page JPY 60,000; trim 250 x 170. Circ: 3,700.

616.2 JPN ISSN 1343-3490
CODEN: NKYZA2
NIHON KOKYUKI GAKKAI ZASSHI/JAPANESE RESPIRATORY SOCIETY. JOURNAL. Text in Japanese; Summaries in English, Japanese. 1963. m. **Document type:** *Journal, Academic/Scholarly.*
Formerly (until 1998): Nihon Kyobu Shikkan Gakkai Zasshi/Japanese Journal of Thoracic Diseases (0301-1542)
Related titles: Online - full text ed.: ISSN 1345-9538.
Indexed: A22, EMBASE, ExcerpMed, INIS AtomInd, IndMed, MEDLINE, P30, R10, Reac, SCOPUS.
—BLDSC (4809.412000), GNLM, IE, Infotrieve, Ingenta, INIST. **CCC.**
Published by: Nihon Kokyuki Gakkai/Japanese Respiratory Society, Shibata Bldg., 2F, 2-6-4 Uchikanda, Chiyoda-ku, Tokyo, 101-0047, Japan.

NIHON KOKYUKI GEKA GAKKAI ZASSHI/JAPANESE ASSOCIATION FOR CHEST SURGERY. JOURNAL. *see* MEDICAL SCIENCES—Surgery

616.2 POL ISSN 1231-3025
NOWA KLINIKA. Text in Polish. 1994. m. PLZ 60 domestic; EUR 180 foreign (effective 2005). **Document type:** *Journal, Academic/Scholarly.*
Published by: Wydawnictwo Medyczne Agama, ul Poligonowa 2/37, Warsaw, 04051, Poland. klinika@klinika.com.pl, http://www.klinika.com.pl. Ed. H Batura-Gabryel. **Dist. by:** Ars Polona, Obroncow 25, Warsaw 03933, Poland. TEL 48-22-5098609, FAX 48-22-5098610, arspolona@arspolona.com.pl, http://www.arspolona.com.pl.

616.2 ITA ISSN 2038-5404
NUOVI ORIZZONTI. Text in Italian. 2008. irreg. **Document type:** *Monographic series, Academic/Scholarly.*
Published by: Associazione Italiana Pneumologi Ospedalieri (A I P O), Via Antonio da Recanate 2, Milan, 20124, Italy. TEL 39-02-3659035, FAX 39-02-3659036, aiposegreteria@aiporicerche.it, http://www.aiponet.it.

O E D A NEWSLETTER. *see* OCCUPATIONAL HEALTH AND SAFETY

O P A PRATIQUE. (O R L, Pneumo, Allergo) *see* MEDICAL SCIENCES—Otorhinolaryngology

616.2 CAN
ONTARIO THORACIC REVIEWS. Text in English. 1985. 3/yr. free to members. adv. **Document type:** *Journal, Trade.* **Description:** Covers advances in treatment and prevention of respiratory disease.
Published by: Ontario Thoracic Society, 573 King St E, Toronto, ON M5A 4L3, Canada. TEL 416-864-9911, FAX 416-864-9916. Ed. Dr. Robert Hyland. R&P Sheila Bussmann. Circ: 6,000.

THE OPEN LUNG CANCER JOURNAL. *see* MEDICAL SCIENCES—Oncology

616.2 NLD ISSN 1874-3064
RC731
➤ **THE OPEN RESPIRATORY MEDICINE JOURNAL.** Text in English. 2007. irreg. free (effective 2011). **Document type:** *Journal, Academic/Scholarly.* **Description:** Covers all areas of experimental and clinical research in respiratory medicine.
Media: Online - full text.
Indexed: A01, CA, EMBASE, ESPM, P30, SCOPUS, T02.
Published by: Bentham Open (Subsidiary of: Bentham Science Publishers Ltd.), PO Box 294, Bussum, AG 1400, Netherlands. TEL 31-35-6923800, FAX 31-35-6980150, subscriptions@bentham.org. Ed. Christian Domingo.

616.2 GBR ISSN 1526-0542
CODEN: PRRAEZ
PAEDIATRIC RESPIRATORY REVIEWS. Abbreviated title: P R R. Text in English. 2000 (Mar.). q. EUR 382 in Europe to institutions; JPY 41,100 in Japan to institutions; USD 351 elsewhere to institutions (effective 2012). adv. back issues avail.; reprints avail. **Document type:** *Journal, Academic/Scholarly.* **Description:** Contributes to the continuing medical and professional development of pediatricians specializing in the diagnosis, treatment, and management of respiratory disease.
Related titles: Online - full text ed.: ISSN 1526-0550. USD 293 to institutions (effective 2009) (from ScienceDirect).
Indexed: A22, A26, CA, CurCont, E01, EMBASE, ExcerpMed, I05, MEDLINE, P30, R10, Reac, SCI, SCOPUS, T02, W07.
—BLDSC (6333.399970), IE, Infotrieve, Ingenta. **CCC.**
Published by: Elsevier Ltd (Subsidiary of: Elsevier Science & Technology), The Blvd, Langford Ln, Kidlington, Oxford, OX5 1GB, United Kingdom. TEL 44-1865-843000, FAX 44-1865-843010, customerserviceau@elsevier.com. Ed. E Eber.

PEDIATRIC PULMONOLOGY. *see* MEDICAL SCIENCES—Pediatrics

616.2 DEU ISSN 1865-5467
PNEUMO NEWS. Text in German. 2007. bi-m. EUR 73, USD 88 to institutions (effective 2011). adv. **Document type:** *Journal, Academic/Scholarly.*
—**CCC.**
Published by: Urban und Vogel Medien und Medizin Verlagsgesellschaft mbH (Subsidiary of: Springer Science+Business Media), Neumarkter Str 43, Munich, 81673, Germany. TEL 49-89-4372-1411, FAX 49-89-4372-1410, verlag@urban-vogel.de. Ed. Dr. Dirk Einecke. Adv. contact Ines Spankau. B&W page EUR 1,550, color page EUR 2,600; trim 174 x 237. Circ: 3,500 (paid).

616.2 DEU ISSN 1613-5636
➤ **DER PNEUMOLOGE.** Text in German. 2004. 6/yr. EUR 282, USD 319 combined subscription to institutions (print & online eds.) (effective 2012). adv. reprint service avail. from PSC. **Document type:** *Journal, Academic/Scholarly.*
Related titles: Online - full text ed.: ISSN 1613-6055 (from IngentaConnect).
Indexed: A22, A26, E01, EMBASE, SCOPUS.
—BLDSC (6541.111500), IE, Ingenta. **CCC.**
Published by: Springer (Subsidiary of: Springer Science+Business Media), Tiergartenstr 17, Heidelberg, 69121, Germany. TEL 49-6221-4870, FAX 49-6221-345229, subscriptions@springer.com, http://www.springer.com. Circ: 2,400 (paid and controlled).

616.241 PRT ISSN 1646-9445
PNEUMOLOGIA HOJE. Text in Portuguese. 2008. irreg. **Document type:** *Journal, Academic/Scholarly.*
Published by: Sociedade Portuguesa de Pneumologia, Rua Ivone Silva 6 (Edificio Arcis), Lisbon, 1069-130, Portugal. TEL 351-21-7962074, FAX 351-21-7962075, http://www.sppneumologia.pt.

616.2 BGR ISSN 0324-1491
CODEN: PNFTD3
➤ **PNEUMOLOGIA I FTIZIATRIA/PNEUMOLOGY AND PHTYSIATRY.** Text in Bulgarian; Summaries in Bulgarian, English. 1964. 3/yr. free (effective 2005). adv. abstr.; bibl. 64 p./no.; **Document type:** *Journal, Academic/Scholarly.* **Description:** Publishes original articles on lung diseases with emphasis on tuberculosis.
Formerly: Ftiziatria
Indexed: ABSML, CISA.
—GNLM, INIST.
Published by: Meditsinski Universitet - Sofia, Tsentralna Meditsinska Biblioteka, Tsentur za Informatsiia po Meditsina/Medical University - Sofia, Central Medical Library, Medical Information Center, 1 Sv Georgi Sofiiski ul, Sofia, 1431, Bulgaria. TEL 359-2-9522342, FAX 359-2-9522393, lydia@medun.acad.bg, http://www.medun.acad.bg/cmb_htm/cmb1_home_bg.htm. Ed. Dr. P Nikolova. Circ: 300. **Co-sponsor:** Nauchno Druzhestvo po Pneumologia i Ftiziatria.

616.2 618.92 ITA
PNEUMOLOGIA PEDIATRICA. Text in Italian. 1996. q. free (effective 2008). **Document type:** *Journal, Academic/Scholarly.*
Published by: (Societa Italiana per le Malattie Respiratorie (S I M R I)), Primula Multimedia, Via G Ravizza 22 B, Pisa, 56121, Italy. TEL 39-050-965242, FAX 39-050-3163810, info@primulaedizioni.it, http://www.primulaedizioni.it.

616.2 DEU ISSN 0934-8387
RC756 CODEN: PNEMEC
➤ **PNEUMOLOGIE.** Text in German; Summaries in English, German. 1945. m. EUR 269 to institutions; EUR 370 combined subscription to institutions (print & online eds.); EUR 37 newsstand/cover (effective 2011). adv. bk.rev. charts; illus.; stat. index. back issues avail.; reprints avail. **Document type:** *Journal, Academic/Scholarly.*
Former titles (until 1989): Praxis und Klinik der Pneumologie (0342-7498); (until 1977): Praxis der Pneumologie (0032-7069); (until 1964): Tuberkulosearzt (0372-2449)
Related titles: Microfilm ed.: (from PQC); Online - full text ed.: ISSN 1438-8790. EUR 359 to institutions (effective 2011).
Indexed: A22, CISA, ChemAb, DBA, DentInd, EMBASE, ExcerpMed, INI, IndMed, MEDLINE, P30, R10, Reac, SCOPUS.
—BLDSC (6541.113200), CASDDS, GNLM, IE, Infotrieve, Ingenta, INIST. **CCC.**
Published by: (Deutsche Gesellschaft fuer Pneumologie), Georg Thieme Verlag, Ruedigerstr 14, Stuttgart, 70469, Germany. TEL 49-711-8931421, FAX 49-711-8931410, leser.service@thieme.de. Adv. contact Andreas Schweiger TEL 49-711-8931245. Circ: 3,500 (paid and controlled).

616.2 AUT
PNEUMOLOGISCH. Text in German. 6/yr. adv. **Document type:** *Magazine, Trade.*
Published by: Medizin Medien Austria GmbH, Wiedner Hauptstr 120-124, Vienna, 1050, Austria. TEL 43-1-54600, FAX 43-1-54600710, office@medizin-medien.at, http://www.medical-tribune.at. Adv. contact Martina Osterbauer. color page EUR 2,900; trim 210 x 297. Circ: 12,000 (controlled).

616.2 GRC ISSN 1105-848X
PNEUMON. Text in Greek, English. 1988. q.
Related titles: Online - full text ed.: ISSN 1791-4914. free (effective 2011).
Indexed: EMBASE, SCOPUS.
Published by: Hellenic Bronchologic Society, Sotiria Hospital, 152 Mesogion Av, Athens, 11527, Greece. Ed. Demosthenes Bouros.

616.2 POL ISSN 0867-7077
CODEN: PAPKE4
➤ **PNEUMONOLOGIA I ALERGOLOGIA POLSKA.** Text in Polish; Summaries in English. 1926. bi-m. PLZ 198 domestic to institutions; EUR 45 foreign to institutions (effective 2011). adv. bk.rev. abstr.; illus.; stat. **Document type:** *Journal, Academic/Scholarly.* **Description:** Discusses diseases of the lungs, epidemiology, physiology of respiration and clinical pneumonology, allergic diseases of the respiratory system.
Former titles (until 1991): Pneumonologia Polska (0376-4761); (until 1975): Gruzlica i Choroby Pluc (0017-4955); (until 1961): Gruzlica (0367-5149)
Related titles: Online - full text ed.
Indexed: A22, ChemAb, ChemTitl, DokArb, EMBASE, ExcerpMed, IndMed, MEDLINE, P30, R10, Reac, SCOPUS.
—BLDSC (6541.112200), CASDDS, GNLM, IE, Infotrieve, Ingenta, INIST.
Published by: (Polskie Towarzystwo Ftizjopneumonologiczne/Polish Society of Phtysiopneumonology), Wydawnictwo Via Medica, ul Swietokrzyska 73, Gdansk, 80180, Poland. TEL 48-58-3209494, FAX 48-58-3209460, redakcja@viamedica.pl, http://www.viamedica.pl. Ed. Monika Szturmowicz. Circ: 1,100. **Co-sponsors:** Instytut Gruzlicy i Chorob Pluc; Polskie Towarzystwo Alergologiczne/Polish Society of Allergology.

616.2 ITA ISSN 1970-4925
PNEUMORAMA. Text in Italian. 1995. q. **Document type:** *Magazine, Consumer.*
Related titles: Online - full text ed.: ISSN 1970-4933. 2002.
Published by: Midia Srl, Via Santa Maddalena 1, Monza, 20052, Italy. TEL 39-039-2304440, FAX 39-039-2304442, http://www.mediaonline.it.

616.2 ESP ISSN 1576-1959
PREVENCION DEL TABAQUISMO. Text in Spanish. 1994. q. free (effective 2009). back issues avail. **Document type:** *Magazine, Trade.*
Published by: Ediciones Ergon S.A., C/ Arboleda 1, Majadahonda, Madrid, Madrid 28220, Spain. TEL 34-91-6362930, FAX 34-91-6362931, ergon@ergon.es, http://www.ergon.es. Circ: 7,000.

616.2 ITA ISSN 1723-7319
CODEN: LCTMAU
PREVENZIONE RESPIRATORIA. Text in Italian. 1930. q. EUR 20 domestic (effective 2008). adv. bk.rev. bibl.; charts; illus.; stat. index, cum.index: 1943-1944. **Document type:** *Bulletin, Academic/Scholarly.* **Description:** Covers the study and research of tuberculosis and respiratory diseases.
Former titles (until 2000): Lotta Contro la Tubercolosi e le Malattie Polmonari Sociali (0368-7546); (until 1972): Lotta contro la Tubercolosi (0024-6638)
Indexed: CISA, ChemAb, IndMed, P30, SCOPUS.
—GNLM, IE, Ingenta, INIST.
Published by: Federazione Italiana contro le Malattie Polmonari Sociali e la Tubercolosi, Via Giovanni da Procida 7-D, Rome, 00162, Italy. federazione@quibisoft.it. Circ: 3,000.

616.238 GBR ISSN 1471-4418
PRIMARY CARE RESPIRATORY JOURNAL. Abbreviated title: G P I A G. Text in English. 6/yr. **Document type:** *Journal, Academic/Scholarly.* **Description:** Publishes original research papers, reviews, discussion papers and letters relating to all aspects of repiratory conditions in primary care.
Formerly (until 2000): Asthma in General Practice (0968-039X)
Related titles: Online - full text ed.: ISSN 1475-1534. 2001. free (effective 2011).
Indexed: A26, C06, C07, CA, EMBASE, ExcerpMed, I05, MEDLINE, P30, R10, Reac, SCOPUS, T02.
—BLDSC (6612.908442), IE, Ingenta. **CCC.**
Published by: General Practice Airways Group (G P I A G), Smith House, Waterbeck, Lockerbie, DG11 3EY, United Kingdom. Ed. Mark Levy.

616.246 RUS ISSN 1728-2993
CODEN: PRTUAX
PROBLEMY TUBERKULEZA I BOLEZNEI LEGKIKH/PROBLEMS OF TUBERCULOSIS; ezhemesyachnyi nauchno-prakticheskii zhurnal. Text in Russian; Summaries in English. 1923. bi-m. USD 205 foreign (effective 2005). adv. bk.rev. index. **Document type:** *Journal, Academic/Scholarly.* **Description:** Deals with problems of epidemiology and organization of tuberculosis control, as well as prophylaxis, clinical diagnosis and treatment of tuberculosis. Includes data on the theoretical and practical achievements in phthisis and pulmonology.
Formerly (until 2003): Problemy Tuberkuleza (0032-9533)
Indexed: A22, ASFA, CIN, ChemAb, ChemTitl, DentInd, DokArb, EMBASE, ExcerpMed, IndMed, MEDLINE, P30, R10, Reac, SCOPUS.
—BLDSC (0133.841000), CASDDS, East View, GNLM, IE, Infotrieve, Ingenta, INIST. **CCC.**
Published by: (Ministerstvo Zdravookhraneniya Rossiiskoi Federatsii, Rossiiskoe Obshchestvo Ftiziatrov), Izdatel'stvo Meditsina/Meditsina Publishers, ul B Pirogovskaya, d 2, str 5, Moscow, 119435, Russian Federation. TEL 7-095-2483324, meditsina@mtu-net.ru, http://www.medlit.ru. Ed. Mikhail I Perel'man. Pub. A M Stochik. R&P G Postnikova. Adv. contact O A Fadeeva TEL 7-095-923-51-40. Circ: 1,550. **Dist. by:** East View Information Services, 10601 Wayzata Blvd, Minneapolis, MN 55305. TEL 952-252-1201, 800-477-1005, FAX 952-252-1202, info@eastview.com, http://www.eastview.com.

616.2 CHE ISSN 1422-2140
CODEN: PRRRAE
➤ **PROGRESS IN RESPIRATORY RESEARCH.** Text in English. 1963. irreg., latest vol.40, 2011. price varies. reprints avail. **Document type:** *Monographic series, Academic/Scholarly.* **Description:** Surveys of new knowledge on normal and impaired respiratory function.
Formerly: Progress in Respiration Research (0079-6751)
Related titles: Online - full text ed.: ISSN 1662-3932.
Indexed: A22, ChemAb, IndMed, SCOPUS.
—BLDSC (6924.525540), CASDDS, GNLM, IE, Ingenta, INIST. **CCC.**
Published by: S. Karger AG, Allschwilerstr 10, Basel, 4055, Switzerland. TEL 41-61-3061111, FAX 41-61-3061234, karger@karger.ch, http://www.karger.ch. Ed. C T Bolliger.

616.2 IND ISSN 0973-3809
PULMON; the journal of respiratory sciences. Text in English. 1999. 3/yr. adv. **Document type:** *Journal, Trade.*
Published by: Academy of Pulmonary and Critical Care Medicine, Institute of Chest Diseases, Calicut Medical College, Kozhikode, Kerala 673 008, India. TEL 91-495-2357951.

616.2 IND ISSN 2045-8932
▼ **PULMONARY CIRCULATION.** Text in English. 2009. q. INR 500 domestic to individuals; USD 50 foreign to individuals; INR 1,000 domestic to institutions; USD 100 foreign to institutions (effective 2011). adv. **Document type:** *Journal, Academic/Scholarly.*
Related titles: Online - full text ed.: ISSN 2045-8940. INR 400 domestic to individuals; USD 40 foreign to individuals; INR 800 domestic to institutions; USD 80 foreign to institutions (effective 2011).
Indexed: A01.
Published by: (Pulmonary Vascular Research Institute), Medknow Publications and Media Pvt. Ltd., B-9, Kanara Business Ctr, Off Link Rd, Ghatkopar (E), Mumbai, Maharastra 400 075, India. TEL 91-22-66491816, FAX 91-22-66491817, http://www.medknow.com.

616.2 USA ISSN 2090-1836
▼ ➤ **PULMONARY MEDICINE.** Text in English. 2009. irreg. USD 195 (effective 2011). **Document type:** *Journal, Academic/Scholarly.* **Description:** Publishes original research articles, review articles, case reports, and clinical studies in all areas of pulmonary medicine.
Related titles: Online - full text ed.: ISSN 2090-1844. free (effective 2011).
Indexed: A01, T02.
Published by: Hindawi Publishing Corporation, 410 Park Ave, 15th Fl, PMB 287, New York, NY 10022. FAX 215-893-4392, 866-446-3294, info@hindawi.com.

616.2 USA
➤ **PULMONARY PERSPECTIVES.** Text in English. 19??. q. adv. back issues avail. **Document type:** *Journal, Academic/Scholarly.* **Description:** Contains brief articles with editorial commentary for practicing physicians in the chest disciplines.
Related titles: Online - full content ed.: ISSN 1559-6400.
Published by: American College of Chest Physicians, 3300 Dundee Rd, Northbrook, IL 60062. TEL 847-498-1400, 800-343-2227, FAX 847-498-5460, accp@chestnet.org. Circ: 16,000.

616.2 GBR ISSN 1094-5539
RM388 CODEN: PPTHFJ
➤ **PULMONARY PHARMACOLOGY AND THERAPEUTICS.** Text in English. 1988. bi-m. EUR 965 in Europe to institutions; JPY 104,100 in Japan to institutions; USD 858 elsewhere to institutions (effective 2012). adv. bk.rev. reprint service avail. from PSC. **Document type:** *Journal, Academic/Scholarly.* **Description:** Concerned with lung pharmacology from molecular to clinical aspects.
Formerly (until 1997): Pulmonary Pharmacology (0952-0600)
Related titles: Online - full text ed.: ISSN 1522-9629. USD 740 to institutions (effective 2009) (from IngentaConnect, ScienceDirect).
Indexed: A01, A03, A08, A22, A26, B25, BIOSIS Prev, C33, CA, CIN, ChemAb, ChemTitl, DBA, E01, EMBASE, ExcerpMed, I05, IndMed, MEDLINE, MycolAb, P30, R10, Reac, SCI, SCOPUS, T02, W07.
—BLDSC (7156.978500), CASDDS, GNLM, IE, Infotrieve, Ingenta. **CCC.**
Published by: Academic Press (Subsidiary of: Elsevier Science & Technology), 32 Jamestown Rd, Camden, London, NW1 7BY, United Kingdom. TEL 44-20-74244200, FAX 44-20-74832293, corporatesales@elsevier.com. Ed. Dr. Clive Page TEL 44-20-78486096.

616.2 USA ISSN 1086-4423
RC756
PULMONARY REVIEWS; trends in pulmonary and critical care medicine. Text in English. 1996. m. USD 48 domestic to medical residents; USD 60 domestic; USD 75 foreign; free to qualified personnel (effective 2008). adv. abstr.; charts; illus. back issues avail.; reprints avail. **Document type:** *Journal, Trade.* **Description:** Provides physicians with information on disorders that affect the lungs and respiratory tract.
Related titles: Online - full text ed.
Indexed: A01, T02.
—CCC.
Published by: Quadrant HealthCom, 7 Century Dr, Ste 302, Parsippany, NJ 07054. TEL 973-206-3434, FAX 973-206-9378, sales@pulmonaryreviews.com, http://www.quadranthealth.com. Ed. Adriene Marshall TEL 973-206-2345. Pub. Susan M Levey TEL 973-206-8951. Adv. contact Kathleen Corbett TEL 973-206-8022. Circ: 13,500 (paid).

616.2 RUS ISSN 0869-0189
➤ **PULMONOLOGY.** Text in Russian; Abstracts and contents page in English. 1991. bi-m. RUR 462 to individuals; RUR 1,386 to institutions; RUR 77 per issue to individuals; RUR 231 per issue to institutions (effective 2003). adv. bibl.; charts; illus.; stat. 128 p./no.; back issues avail. **Document type:** *Journal, Academic/Scholarly.* **Description:** Publishes experimental and clinical works on all aspects of respiratory medicine. Includes original studies, lectures, reviews and data on pharmacological products.
Related titles: Online - full text ed.
Indexed: RefZh.
—BLDSC (0135.165200).
Published by: Nauchno-Prakticheskii Zhurnal Pul'monologiya, Pulmonology Institute, 32/61, 11-th Parkovaya St, Moscow, 105077, Russian Federation. Ed. Alexander G Chuchalin. Adv. contact Dimitry Soldatov. color page USD 1,200. Circ: 2,000. **outside of Russia:** M K - Periodica, ul Gilyarovskogo 39, Moscow 129110, Russian Federation. TEL 7-095-2845008, FAX 7-095-2813798, info@periodicals.ru, http://www.mkniga.ru; **Dist. by:** Agentsiya Rospechat, Pr-t Marshala Zhukova 4, Moscow 128837, Russian Federation. **Co-sponsors:** Vserossiiskoye Nauchnoe Obshchestvo Pul'monologov/Russian Pneumological Scientific Society; Ministerstvo Zdravookhraneniya Rossiiskoi Federatsii/Ministry of Public Health of Russian Federation.

➤ **PULMONOLOGY CODING ALERT**; the practical adviser for ethically optimizing coding reimbursement and efficiency in pulmonology practices. *see* INSURANCE

616.2 USA ISSN 1040-6050
RM161
R T; for decision makers in respiratory care. Variant title: R T Magazine. Text in English. 1988. m. free domestic to qualified personnel (effective 2011). adv. back issues avail. **Document type:** *Magazine, Trade.* **Description:** Features literature reviews of clinical topics, articles on respiratory care department management, legislative and regulatory news, case reports, profiles of outstanding facilities and practitioners, and departments containing news, industry news, and new product information.
Related titles: Online - full text ed.
Indexed: A26, C06, C07, C08, CA, CINAHL, H12, I05, T02.
—IE, Ingenta. **CCC.**
Published by: Allied Healthcare Group (Subsidiary of: Ascend Media), 6100 Ctr Dr, Ste 1020, Los Angeles, CA 90045. TEL 310-642-4400, FAX 310-641-4444, cagulnek@ascendmedia.com, http://www.alliedhealthjournals.com. Ed. Marian Benjamin TEL 310-642-4400 ext 264. Pub. Darren Sextro TEL 913-894-6923. Adv. contact Dave Jeans TEL 303-856-3067. Circ: 20,000 (controlled).

616.2 ITA ISSN 0033-9563
RASSEGNA DI PATOLOGIA DELL'APPARATO RESPIRATORIO. Text in Italian. 1951. bi-m. adv. bk.rev. bibl.; charts; illus. index. **Document type:** *Journal, Academic/Scholarly.*
Indexed: ChemAb, EMBASE, ExcerpMed, R10, Reac, SCOPUS.
—GNLM.
Published by: (Associazione Italiana Pneumologi Ospedalieri (A I P O)), Pacini Editore SpA, Via A Gherardesca 1, Ospedaletto, PI 56121, Italy. TEL 39-050-313011, FAX 39-050-3130300, pacini.editore@pacinieditore.it, http://www.pacinieditore.it. Ed. Andrea Rossi.

616.2 ARG ISSN 0326-9116
RESPIRACION; revista de enfermedades respiratorias y tuberculosis. Text in Spanish. 1986. q.
Published by: Fundacion Ayuda al Enfermo Respiratorio, Avda. Sarsfield Velez, 405, Buenos Aires, 1281, Argentina. TEL 54-11-44318374, FAX 54-11-44333742. Ed. Luis Julio Gonzalez Montaner.

617.54 616.995 CHE ISSN 0025-7931
RC705 CODEN: RESPBD
➤ **RESPIRATION (ENGLISH EDITION)**; international journal of thoracic medicine. Text in English. 1944. 8/yr. CHF 2,500, EUR 1,996, USD 2,469 to institutions; CHF 2,740, EUR 2,188, USD 2,703 combined subscription to institutions (print & online eds.) (effective 2012). adv. charts; illus. back issues avail. **Document type:** *Journal, Academic/Scholarly.* **Description:** Provides the results of both clinical and experimental investigations on all aspects of the respiratory system in health and disease.
Former titles (until 1968): Medicina Thoracalis (0368-9220); (until 1962): Schweizerische Zeitschrift fuer Tuberkulose und Pneumonologie (0371-4985); (until 1956): Schweizerische Zeitschrift fuer Tuberkulose (1421-5659)
Related titles: Microform ed.; Online - full text ed.: ISSN 1423-0356. 1997. CHF 2,398, EUR 1,918, USD 2,328 to institutions (effective 2012).
Indexed: A01, A03, A08, A22, A36, AMED, ASCA, C06, C07, CA, CABA, CIN, CISA, ChemAb, ChemTitl, CurCont, DokArb, E01, E12, EMBASE, ExcerpMed, FR, GH, H13, H17, IBR, IBZ, ISR, IndMed, Inpharma, MEDLINE, N02, N03, P02, P10, P16, P20, P22, P24, P30, P33, P35, P48, P53, P54, PQC, R08, R10, RA&MP, RM&VM, Reac, SCI, SCOPUS, SoyAb, T02, T05, THA, VS, W07, W10.
—BLDSC (7777.620000), CASDDS, GNLM, IE, Infotrieve, Ingenta, INIST. **CCC.**
Published by: S. Karger AG, Allschwilerstr 10, Basel, 4055, Switzerland. TEL 41-61-3061111, FAX 41-61-3061234, karger@karger.ch, http://www.karger.ch. Ed. C T Bolliger. R&P Tatjana Sepin. Adv. contact Tom Maurer. page CHF 1,730; trim 210 x 280. Circ: 1,100.

617.54 ESP ISSN 1133-8261
RESPIRATION (SPANISH EDITION); revista internacional de enfermedades. Text in Spanish. 1994. bi-m. EUR 100 (effective 2009). back issues avail. **Document type:** *Journal, Academic/Scholarly.*
Published by: Grupo Aula Medica S.A., C Isabel Colbrand, 10 Nave 78, Planta 2a, Madrid, 28050, Spain. TEL 34-91-3586478, FAX 34-91-3589979, informacion@grupoaulamedica.com. Ed. C. T. Bolliger.

616.2 USA
RESPIRATORY & SLEEP MANAGEMENT. Text in English. 2006. m. free domestic; USD 189 foreign (effective 2011). **Document type:** *Magazine, Trade.*
Formerly (until 2009): Respiratory Management (1932-7927)
Published by: 1105 Media Inc., 16261 Laguna Canyon Rd, Irvine, CA 92618. info@1105media.com, http://www.1105media.com. Ed. David Kopf TEL 949-265-1561. Pub. Karen Cavallo TEL 760-779-5595. Adv. contact Caroline Stover TEL 323-605-4398.

615.64 USA ISSN 0020-1324
CODEN: RECACP
➤ **RESPIRATORY CARE**; the science journal of the American Association for Respiratory Care. Text in English, Italian, Japanese. 1956. m. USD 89.95 domestic; USD 109 foreign (effective 2010). adv. bk.rev. abstr. index. reprints avail. **Description:** Disseminates information, viewpoints, and questions about respiratory disease, research, clinical and laboratory practice, education, and patient care science. Includes original research, conference proceedings and clinical practice guidelines.
Formerly (until 1971): Inhalation Therapy
Related titles: Microform ed.: (from PQC); Online - full text ed.: ISSN 1943-3654 (from IngentaConnect).
Indexed: A22, A26, C06, C07, C08, CA, CINAHL, CurCont, EMBASE, ExcerpMed, FR, H12, HospLI, I05, IndMed, MEDLINE, NurAb, P30, R10, Reac, SCI, SCOPUS, T02, THA, W07.
—BLDSC (7777.660000), GNLM, IE, Infotrieve, Ingenta, INIST. **CCC.**
Published by: (American Association for Respiratory Care), Daedalus Enterprises, Inc., 9425 North MacArthur Blvd, Suite 100, Irving, TX 75063. TEL 972-243-2272, FAX 972-484-2720. Ed. Dean R Hess. Circ: 38,000.

616.2 USA
RESPIRATORY CARE EDUCATION ANNUAL. Text in English. a. **Description:** Promotes best practices and research in respiratory care education.
Published by: American Association for Respiratory Care, 9425 N MacArthur Blvd, Suite 100, Irving, TX 75063-4706. TEL 972-243-2272, FAX 972-484-2720, info@aarc.org.

616.2 GBR ISSN 0262-7043
RESPIRATORY DISEASE IN PRACTICE. Text in English. 1982-2005; resumed 2010. q. adv. bk.rev. **Document type:** *Journal, Academic/Scholarly.*
—BLDSC (7777.661000), IE, Ingenta. **CCC.**
Published by: Hayward Medical Communications Ltd. (Subsidiary of: Hayward Group plc), The Pines, Fordham Rd, Newmarket, CB8 7LG, United Kingdom. TEL 44-1638-723560, FAX 44-1638-723561, http://www.hayward.co.uk. Ed. Dr. Phillip Ind. Circ: 14,000. **Subscr. to:** Rosemary House, Lanwades Park, Kentford, Near, Newmarket, Suffolk CB8 7PW, United Kingdom. TEL 44-1638-751515, FAX 44-1638-751517.

616.246 KEN
RESPIRATORY DISEASES RESEARCH CENTRE. ANNUAL REPORT. Text in English. 1974. a. free. back issues avail. **Document type:** *Corporate.*
Former titles: Kenya Tuberculosis and Respiratory Diseases Research Center. Annual Report (1015-0072); Kenya Tuberculosis Investigation Centre. Annual Report; Supersedes in part: East African Tuberculosis Investigation Centre. Annual Report
Published by: Kenya Medical Research Institute, Kenya Tuberculosis & Respiratory Diseases Research Centre, PO Box 47855, Nairobi, Kenya. Circ: 200.

616.2 GBR ISSN 0954-6111
RC731 CODEN: RMEDEY
➤ **RESPIRATORY MEDICINE.** Text in English. 1907. m. EUR 1,171 in Europe to institutions; JPY 126,700 in Japan to institutions; USD 1,073 elsewhere to institutions (effective 2012). adv. bk.rev. charts; illus.; stat. index. back issues avail.; reprint service avail. from PSC. **Document type:** *Journal, Academic/Scholarly.* **Description:** Provides an international forum for new information of relevance to the physician working in the field of respiratory medicine.
Former titles (until 1989): British Journal of Diseases of the Chest (0007-0971); (until 1959): British Journal of Tuberculosis and Diseases of the Chest (0366-0869); (until 1943): British Journal of Tuberculosis (0366-0850)
Related titles: Microform ed.: (from PQC); Online - full text ed.: ISSN 1532-3064. USD 916 to institutions (effective 2009) (from ScienceDirect); ◆ Supplement(s): Respiratory Medicine C M E. ISSN 1755-0017.
Indexed: A22, A26, A29, A34, A35, A36, AIDS Ab, AMED, ASCA, AgBio, B20, B21, C06, C07, C08, CA, CABA, CINAHL, CISA, ChemAb, CurCont, DBA, E01, E12, EMBASE, ESPM, ExcerpMed, F08, FR, GH, H12, H17, I05, I10, IBR, IBZ, INI, ISR, IndMed, IndVet, Inpharma, LT, MEDLINE, N02, N03, P30, P33, P35, PN&I, R07, R08, R10, R12, RA&MP, RM&VM, RRTA, Reac, SCI, SCOPUS, T02, T05, THA, TriticAb, VS, VirolAbstr, W07, W10.
—BLDSC (7777.661900), CASDDS, GNLM, IE, Infotrieve, Ingenta, INIST. **CCC.**
Published by: Elsevier Ltd (Subsidiary of: Elsevier Science & Technology), The Blvd, Langford Ln, Kidlington, Oxford, OX5 1GB, United Kingdom. TEL 44-1865-843000, FAX 44-1865-843010, customerserviceau@elsevier.com. Ed. J C Virchow.

616.2 GBR ISSN 1755-0017
➤ **RESPIRATORY MEDICINE C M E.** Text in English. 2005. q. free (effective 2009). reprints avail. **Document type:** *Journal, Academic/Scholarly.* **Description:** Contains case reports which have an important educational value but cannot be published in the printed journal due to lack of space.
Formerly (until 2008): Respiratory Medicine Extra (1744-9049)
Media: Online - full text (from ScienceDirect). **Related titles:** ◆ Supplement to: Respiratory Medicine. ISSN 0954-6111.
Indexed: CA, EMBASE, ExcerpMed, R10, Reac, SCOPUS, T02.
—IE, Ingenta. **CCC.**
Published by: Elsevier Ltd (Subsidiary of: Elsevier Science & Technology), The Blvd, Langford Ln, Kidlington, Oxford, OX5 1GB, United Kingdom. TEL 44-1865-843000, FAX 44-1865-843010, customerserviceau@elsevier.com, http://www.elsevier.com. Ed. B Yawn.

616.2 GBR ISSN 1745-0454
RESPIRATORY MEDICINE: C O P D UPDATE. (Chronic Obstructive Pulmonary Disease) Text in English. 2005. q. EUR 317 in Europe to institutions; JPY 40,600 in Japan to institutions; USD 359 elsewhere to institutions (effective 2010). adv. back issues avail.; reprints avail. **Document type:** *Journal, Academic/Scholarly.* **Description:** Provides information for researchers and clinicians abreast of the latest developments in the field of COPD research.
Related titles: Online - full text ed.: ISSN 1878-0806. USD 342 to institutions (effective 2009).
Indexed: A26, CA, EMBASE, ExcerpMed, I05, Inpharma, P35, R10, Reac, SCOPUS, T02.
—BLDSC (7777.661910), IE, Ingenta. **CCC.**
Published by: Elsevier Ltd (Subsidiary of: Elsevier Science & Technology), The Blvd, Langford Ln, Kidlington, Oxford, OX5 1GB, United Kingdom. TEL 44-1865-843000, FAX 44-1865-843010, customerserviceau@elsevier.com, http://www.elsevier.com. Ed. John Hurst.

616.2 NLD ISSN 2211-1980
▼ **RESPIRATORY NEWS INTERNATIONAL.** Text in Dutch. 2010. bi-m. adv. **Document type:** *Magazine, Trade.*
Published by: Van Zuiden Communications B.V., Postbus 2122, Alphen aan den Rijn, 2400 CC, Netherlands. TEL 31-172-476191, FAX 31-172-471882, info@vanzuidencommunications.nl, http://www.zuidencomm.nl. Circ: 1,690.

RESPIRATORY PHARMACOLOGY AND PHARMACOTHERAPY. *see* PHARMACY AND PHARMACOLOGY

RESPIRATORY PHYSIOLOGY & NEUROBIOLOGY. *see* BIOLOGY—Physiology

616.2 GBR ISSN 1465-993X
➤ **RESPIRATORY RESEARCH (ONLINE).** Text in English. 2000. irreg. free (effective 2011). adv. back issues avail.; reprints avail. **Document type:** *Journal, Academic/Scholarly.* **Description:** Aims to ensure that researchers and clinicians have easy access to the latest mechanism-defining research and analysis, particularly in the areas of genetics, biochemistry and cell biology.
Media: Online - full text.
Indexed: CurCont, SCI, W07.
—CCC.
Published by: BioMed Central Ltd. (Subsidiary of: Springer Science+Business Media), 236 Gray's Inn Rd, London, WC1X 8HB, United Kingdom. TEL 44-20-31922000, FAX 44-20-31922010, info@biomedcentral.com, http://www.biomedcentral.com. Eds. Jan Lotvall, Reynold A Panettieri. Adv. contact Natasha Bailey TEL 44-20-31922231.

616.2 NZL ISSN 1178-6205
RESPIRATORY RESEARCH REVIEW. Text in English. 2006. m. free to qualified personnel (effective 2009). back issues avail.
Media: Online - full text.
Published by: Research Review Ltd., N Shore Mail Centre, PO Box 100116, Auckland, New Zealand. TEL 64-9-4102277, info@researchreview.co.nz.

616.2 USA ISSN 1543-6659
RM161
RESPIRATORY THERAPEUTICS WEEK. Text in English. 2003. w. USD 2,295 in US & Canada; USD 2,495 elsewhere; USD 2,525 combined subscription in US & Canada (print & online eds.); USD 2,755 combined subscription elsewhere (print & online eds.) (effective 2008). back issues avail. **Document type:** *Newsletter, Trade.*
Related titles: E-mail ed.; Online - full text ed.: ISSN 1543-6640. USD 2,295 combined subscription (online & email eds.); single user (effective 2008).
Indexed: A26, E08, G08, H11, H12, I05, S09.
—CIS.
Published by: NewsRx, 2727 Paces Ferry Rd SE, Ste 2-440, Atlanta, GA 30339. TEL 770-435-8286, 800-726-4550, FAX 770-435-6800, pressrelease@newsrx.com. Ed. Carol Kohn. Pub. Susan Hasty TEL 770-507-7777.

616.2 USA ISSN 2152-355X
RESPIRATORY THERAPY; the journal of pulmonary technique. Text in English. 2005. bi-m. USD 80 domestic; USD 110 foreign (effective 2010). adv. back issues avail. **Document type:** *Journal, Academic/Scholarly.* **Description:** 'Contains information about all aspects of respiratory therapy as actively practiced in a variety of clinical venues and modalities.
Related titles: Online - full text ed.: free (effective 2010).
Published by: Goldstein and Associates, Inc., 10940 Wilshire Blvd, Ste 600, Los Angeles, CA 90024. TEL 310-443-4109, FAX 310-443-4110. Ed. Les Plesko. Pub. Steve Goldstein.

616.2 AUS ISSN 1323-7799
CODEN: RSPIFB
➤ **RESPIROLOGY.** Text in English. 1996. 6/yr. GBP 524 in United Kingdom to institutions; EUR 666 in Europe to institutions; USD 850 in the Americas to institutions; USD 1,027 elsewhere to institutions; GBP 604 combined subscription in United Kingdom to institutions (print & online eds.); EUR 767 combined subscription in Europe to institutions (print & online eds.); USD 978 combined subscription in the Americas to institutions (print & online eds.); USD 1,181 combined subscription elsewhere to institutions (print & online eds.) (effective 2012). adv. back issues avail.; reprint service avail. from PSC. **Document type:** *Journal, Academic/Scholarly.* **Description:** Publishes articles of scientific excellence in clinical and experimental respiratory biology and disease, and related fields of research.
Related titles: Online - full text ed.: ISSN 1440-1843. GBP 524 in United Kingdom to institutions; EUR 666 in Europe to institutions; USD 850 in the Americas to institutions; USD 1,027 elsewhere to institutions (effective 2012) (from IngentaConnect).
Indexed: A01, A03, A08, A20, A22, A26, A34, A36, BA, CA, CABA, CurCont, E01, E12, EMBASE, ExcerpMed, F08, GH, H12, H17, IndMed, IndVet, Inpharma, LT, MEDLINE, N02, N03, OR, P30, P33, P35, P37, P39, PN&I, R08, R10, R12, RA&MP, RM&VM, RRTA, Reac, S13, S16, SCI, SCOPUS, T02, T05, VS, W07, W10.
—BLDSC (7777.666000), GNLM, IE, Infotrieve, Ingenta. **CCC.**
Published by: (Asian Pacific Society of Respirology JPN), Wiley-Blackwell Publishing Asia (Subsidiary of: Wiley-Blackwell Publishing Ltd.), 155 Cremorne St, Richmond, VIC 3121, Australia. TEL 61-3-92743100, FAX 61-3-92743101, subs@blackwellpublishingasia.com, http://www.wiley.com/WileyCDA/. Ed. Philip J Thompson. Adv. contact Kathryn O'Brien. B&W page AUD 1,012, color page AUD 2,057; trim 210 x 275. **Subscr. to:** PO Box 378, Carlton South, VIC 3053, Australia.

616.2 615.8 IRL ISSN 0300-9572
RC86 CODEN: RSUSBS
➤ **RESUSCITATION.** Text in English. 1972. 12/yr. EUR 1,663 in Europe to institutions; JPY 220,100 in Japan to institutions; USD 1,860 elsewhere to institutions (effective 2012). adv. bk.rev. charts; illus. index. reprints avail. **Document type:** *Journal, Academic/Scholarly.* **Description:** Covers the etiology, pathophysiology, diagnosis and treatment of acute diseases.
Related titles: Microform ed.: (from PQC); Online - full text ed.: ISSN 1873-1570 (from IngentaConnect, ScienceDirect).
Indexed: A01, A03, A08, A22, A26, ASCA, C06, C07, CA, CIN, ChemAb, ChemTitl, CurCont, EMBASE, ExcerpMed, FR, I05, IBR, IBZ, INI, ISR, IndMed, Inpharma, JW-EM, MEDLINE, P30, P35, R10, Reac, SCI, SCOPUS, T02, W07.
—BLDSC (7785.420000), CASDDS, GNLM, IE, Infotrieve, Ingenta, INIST. **CCC.**
Published by: (European Resuscitation Council), Elsevier Ireland Ltd (Subsidiary of: Elsevier Science & Technology), Elsevier House, Brookvale Plaza, E. Park, Shannon, Co. Clare, Ireland. TEL 353-61-709600, FAX 353-61-709100, nlinfo@elsevier.nl, http://www.elsevier.nl. Eds. Jerry Nolan, Mike Parr, Dr. Peter J F Baskett. **Subscr. to:** Elsevier BV, Radarweg 29, PO Box 211, Amsterdam 1000 AE, Netherlands. TEL 31-20-4853757, FAX 31-20-4853432, http://www.elsevier.nl.

611.2 ARG ISSN 1666-4000
REVISTA ARGENTINA DE MEDICINA RESPIRATORIA. Text in Spanish. 2001. 3/yr. back issues avail. **Document type:** *Journal, Academic/Scholarly.*
Related titles: Online - full text ed.: ISSN 1852-236X. 2008.
Published by: Asociacion Argentina de Medicina Respiratoria, Division Neumonologia Hospital Clinicas, Cordoba 2351 7o Piso, Buenos Aires, 1120, Argentina. TEL 54-11-59508931, revista@ramr.org, http://www.ramr.org.ar/. Ed. Carlos M Luna.

616.995 ARG ISSN 0327-1595
REVISTA ARGENTINA DEL TORAX. Text in Spanish. 1935. q. back issues avail. **Document type:** *Journal, Academic/Scholarly.*
Former titles (until 1987): Revista Argentina de Tuberculosis, Enfermedades Pulmonares y Salud Publica (0325-9307); (until 1955): Revista Argentina de Tuberculosis (0301-5270)
Indexed: C01.
—INIST.
Published by: Liga Argentina contra la Tuberculosis, Uriarte 2477, Buenos Aires, 1425, Argentina. TEL 54-11-47774447, FAX 54-11-47774691, lalat@netizen.com.ar. Ed. Jorge Pilheu.

616.2 CHL ISSN 0717-5698
REVISTA CHILENA DE ENFERMEDADES RESPIRATORIAS. Text in Spanish. 1991. q. back issues avail. **Document type:** *Journal, Academic/Scholarly.*
Related titles: Online - full text ed.: ISSN 0717-7348. 2002. free (effective 2011).
Indexed: SCOPUS.
Published by: Sociedad Chilena de Enfermedades Respiratorias, Santa Magdalena No. 75, Of. 701, Providencia, Santiago, Chile. TEL 56-2-324729, FAX 56-2-443811, info@serchile.cl.

616.2 COL ISSN 0121-5426
REVISTA COLOMBIANA DE NEUMOLOGIA. Text in Spanish. 1989. q. **Document type:** *Journal, Academic/Scholarly.*
Published by: Sociedad Colombiana de Neumologia, Tisiologia y Enfermedades del Torax, Carretera 22 No 85-94, Of 609, Bogota, Colombia. Ed. Guillermo Ortiz Ruiz.

616.2 PRT ISSN 1647-7944
▼ **REVISTA DE MEDICINA RESPIRATORIA.** Text in Portuguese. 2011. q. **Document type:** *Magazine, Trade.*
Published by: Publicacoes Ciencia e Vida, Praca Cid, Odivelas, 2675-639, Portugal. TEL 351-214-020750.

616.2 ESP ISSN 1576-9895
▼ **REVISTA DE PATOLOGIA RESPIRATORIA.** Text in Spanish. 2010. q. **Document type:** *Journal, Academic/Scholarly.*
—**CCC.**
Published by: (Sociedad Madrilena de Neumologia y Cirugia Toracica), Elsevier Doyma (Subsidiary of: Elsevier Health Sciences), Traversa de Gracia 17-21, Barcelona, 08021, Spain. TEL 34-932-418800, FAX 34-932-419020, doyma@doyma.es, http://www.doyma.es. Ed. Emilio Mayayo.

616.2 ESP ISSN 1889-7347
REVISTA ESPANOLA DE PATOLOGIA TORACICA. Text in Spanish. 1989. 3/yr. free (effective 2008). back issues avail. **Document type:** *Journal, Academic/Scholarly.*
Formerly (until 2009): Neumosur (0214-6266)
Related titles: Online - full text ed.: ISSN 1989-8398. 1989.
Published by: Asociacion de Nuemologos del Sur, Virgen de la Cinta 21, Edif. Presidente B2 11o. C, Sevilla, 41011, Spain. TEL 34-954-282737, FAX 34-954-276080, neumosur@neumosur.net. Ed. Javier Alvarez Gutierrez.

616.2 PRT ISSN 0873-2159
REVISTA PORTUGUESA DE PNEUMOLOGIA. Text in Multiple languages. 1980. bi-m. EUR 446 in Europe to institutions; JPY 49,500 in Japan to institutions; USD 598 elsewhere to institutions (effective 2012). **Document type:** *Journal, Academic/Scholarly.* **Description:** Its aim is to publish scientific work which is either directly or indirectly related to the respiratory system.
Formerly (until 1994): Sociedade Portuguesa de Patologia Respiratoria. Arquivos (0870-6646)
Related titles: Online - full text ed.: free (effective 2011).
Indexed: EMBASE, ExcerpMed, MEDLINE, P30, R10, Reac, SCI, SCOPUS, W07.
—BLDSC (7870.015500). **CCC.**
Published by: Sociedade Portuguesa de Pneumologia, Rua Rodrigues Sampaio 112, 2o Dir B, Lisbon, 1150-281, Portugal. sppneumologia@mail.telepac.pt, http://www.sppneumologia.pt. Ed. Renato Sotto-Mayor. Circ: 2,000.

616.2 616.1 FRA ISSN 0761-8417
CODEN: RPCLEZ
REVUE DE PNEUMOLOGIE CLINIQUE; le poumon et le coeur. Text in French; Summaries in English. 1945. 6/yr. EUR 292 in Europe to institutions; EUR 230.17 in France to institutions; JPY 46,600 in Japan to institutions; USD 380 elsewhere to institutions (effective 2012). adv. bk.rev. abstr.; bibl.; charts; illus.; stat. index. reprints avail. **Document type:** *Journal, Academic/Scholarly.* **Description:** Devoted to the pathology and therapy of afflictions of the respiratory tract.
Formerly: Poumon et le Coeur (0032-5821)
Related titles: Microform ed.: (from PQC); Online - full text ed.: (from ScienceDirect).
Indexed: A22, CISA, ChemAb, DentInd, DokArb, EMBASE, ExcerpMed, IndMed, MEDLINE, P30, R10, Reac, SCI, SCOPUS, W07.
—BLDSC (7942.535000), CASDDS, GNLM, IE, Infotrieve, Ingenta, INIST. **CCC.**
Published by: Elsevier Masson (Subsidiary of: Elsevier Health Sciences), 62 Rue Camille Desmoulins, Issy les Moulineaux, Cedex 92442, France. TEL 33-1-71165500, infos@elsevier-masson.fr. Ed. Jacques Lacronique. Circ: 1,500.

616.2 FRA ISSN 0761-8425
CODEN: RMREEY
➤ **REVUE DES MALADIES RESPIRATOIRES.** Text in French. 1893. 10/yr. EUR 371 in Europe to institutions; EUR 297.75 in France to institutions; JPY 59,600 in Japan to institutions; USD 482 elsewhere to institutions (effective 2012). adv. bk.rev. abstr.; illus. index. reprints avail. **Document type:** *Journal, Academic/Scholarly.* **Description:** Publishes original articles on clinical and laboratory work in the field of respiratory diseases.
Former titles (until 1983): Revue Francaise des Maladies Respiratoires (0301-0279); (until 1973): Revue de Tuberculose et de Pneumologie (0035-1792)
Related titles: Microfilm ed.; Online - full text ed.: ISSN 1776-2588 (from ScienceDirect).
Indexed: A20, A22, A29, ASCA, B20, B21, CISA, ChemAb, CurCont, DokArb, EMBASE, ESPM, ExcerpMed, FR, H&SSA, I10, INI, ImmunAb, IndMed, Inpharma, MEDLINE, P30, P35, R10, Reac, SCI, SCOPUS, VirolAbstr, W07.
—BLDSC (7926.824000), CASDDS, GNLM, IE, Infotrieve, Ingenta, INIST. **CCC.**
Published by: (Societe de Pneumologie de Langue Francaise), Elsevier Masson (Subsidiary of: Elsevier Health Sciences), 62 Rue Camille Desmoulins, Issy les Moulineaux, Cedex 92442, France. TEL 33-1-71165500, infos@elsevier-masson.fr. Circ: 3,000. **Co-sponsor:** Comite National de Defense Contre la Tuberculose.

616.2 FRA ISSN 1877-1203
▼ ➤ **REVUE DES MALADIES RESPIRATOIRES ACTUALITES.** Text in French. 2009. 5/yr. EUR 298 domestic to institutions; EUR 371 in Europe to institutions (except France); JPY 44,500 in Japan to institutions; USD 482 elsewhere to institutions (effective 2011). **Document type:** *Journal, Academic/Scholarly.*
Media: Online - full text (from ScienceDirect). **Related titles:** Online - full text ed.: ISSN 1877-122X.
Indexed: EMBASE, SCOPUS.
—IE. **CCC.**
Published by: Elsevier Masson (Subsidiary of: Elsevier Health Sciences), 62 Rue Camille Desmoulins, Issy les Moulineaux, Cedex 92442, France. TEL 33-1-71165500, FAX 33-1-71165600, infos@elsevier-masson.fr, http://www.elsevier-masson.fr. Ed. Nicolas Roche.

616.2 ITA ISSN 0302-4717
RIVISTA DI PATOLOGIA E CLINICA DELLA TUBERCOLOSI E DI PNEUMOLOGIA. Text in Italian; Summaries in English, French. 1927. bi-m. adv. bk.rev. abstr. index, cum.index. **Document type:** *Journal, Academic/Scholarly.*
Formerly (until 1971): Rivista di Patologia e Clinica della Tubercolosi (0035-6425)
Indexed: P30.
—GNLM, INIST.
Published by: Associazione Emilia Romagna Contro la Tubercolosi e le Malattie Polmonarie Sociali, Via Giovanni Brugnoli, 5, Bologna, BO 40122, Italy. Ed. Enrico Fasano.

616.995 616.9 NPL ISSN 1818-9741
➤ **S A A R C**; journal of tuberculosis, lung diseases and HIV/AIDS. (South Asian Association for Regional Cooperation) Text in English. 2004. s-a. **Document type:** *Journal, Academic/Scholarly.* **Description:** Publishes original articles, review articles, short reports and other communications related to TB, Lung diseases and HIV/AIDS.
Related titles: Online - full text ed.
Published by: S A A R C Tuberculosis and HIV/AIDS Centre, Thimi, Bhaktapur, P O Box 9517, Kathmandu, Nepal. TEL 977-1-6631048, 977-1-6632601, FAX 977-1-6634379, saarctb@mos.com.np, http://www.saarctb.com.np. Eds. V S Salhotra, Kashi Kant Jha.

616.2 ZAF ISSN 0081-2501
S A N T A ANNUAL REPORT. Text in English. 1949. a. free. **Document type:** *Corporate.* **Description:** Features SANTA's financial statements, review of the year's activities, history of investments made, as well as the present status of TB containment.
Published by: South African National Tuberculosis Association/Suid-Afrikaanse Nasionale Tuberkulose Vereniging, Private Bag X10030, Edenvale, 1610, South Africa. TEL 27-11-454-0260, FAX 27-11-454-0096, santa@santa.org.za, http://www.santa.org.za. Ed. Eve Stubbs. R&P Jacqui van Rensburg. Circ: 2,000.

616.246 ZAF
S A N T A T B AND HEALTH NEWS. Text in English. 1953. q. donation. adv. charts; illus.; stat. **Document type:** *Newsletter.* **Description:** Informs readers of news and events involving the association, and discusses issues relating to tuberculosis in South Africa.
Formerly (until vol.33, no.9, 1994): S.A.N.T.A. T B News (0036-0872)
Published by: South African National Tuberculosis Association/Suid-Afrikaanse Nasionale Tuberkulose Vereniging, Private Bag X10030, Edenvale, 1610, South Africa. TEL 27-11-454-0260, FAX 27-11-454-0096, santa@santa.org.za, http://www.santa.org.za. Ed. Eve Stubbs. R&P, Adv. contact Jacqui van Rensburg. Circ: 9,000.

616.99 616.2 ITA ISSN 1124-0490
CODEN: SVDDF2
➤ **SARCOIDOSIS VASCULITIS AND DIFFUSE LUNG DISEASES.** Text in Italian. 1983. s-a. EUR 85 in Europe to institutions; EUR 93 elsewhere to institutions (effective 2008). bk.rev. index. Supplement avail. **Document type:** *Journal, Academic/Scholarly.* **Description:** Publishes editorials, original clinical works and case reports, news, scientific notes, and letters to the editor.
Formerly (until 1995): Sarcoidosis (0393-1447)
Indexed: A22, ASCA, CurCont, EMBASE, ExcerpMed, ISR, IndMed, Inpharma, MEDLINE, P30, P35, R10, Reac, SCI, SCOPUS, W07.
—BLDSC (8076.025300), GNLM, IE, Infotrieve, Ingenta.
Published by: (World Association of Sarcoidosis and Other Granulomatous Disorders), Mattioli 1885 SpA, Via Coduro 1, Fidenza, PR 43036, Italy. TEL 39-0524-84547, FAX 39-0524-84751, http://www.mattioli1885.com. Ed. C Saltini. Circ: 5,000.

616.2 NLD ISSN 1875-7782
SCRIPT PULMONOLOGIE. Text in Dutch. 2008. q. adv.
Published by: Van Zuiden Communications B.V., Postbus 2122, Alphen aan den Rijn, 2400 CC, Netherlands. TEL 31-172-476191, FAX 31-172-471882, zuiden@zuidencomm.nl, http://www.zuidencomm.nl. Eds. Dr. J J Jaspers, Marcel Levi. Circ: 850 (controlled).

616.24 573.25 USA
A SECOND WIND NEWSLETTER. Text in English. m. free to members (effective 2005). **Document type:** *Newsletter.*
Formerly (until 2005): Texas Advocate
Published by: American Lung Association of Texas, 5926 Balcones Dr, Ste 100, Austin, TX 78731. TEL 512-467-6753, FAX 512-467-7621, info@texaslung.org. Ed. Linda Nichols. Pub. Yvette Freeman. Circ: 6,000 (controlled and free).

616.2 USA ISSN 1069-3424
RC306 CODEN: SRCCEX
➤ **SEMINARS IN RESPIRATORY AND CRITICAL CARE MEDICINE**; pulmonology, critical care, allergy and immunology, infections. Text in English. 1979. bi-m. USD 649 domestic to institutions; USD 667 foreign to institutions; USD 794 combined subscription domestic to institutions (print & online eds.); USD 819 combined subscription foreign to institutions (print & online eds.) (effective 2011). adv. index. reprints avail. **Document type:** *Journal, Academic/Scholarly.* **Description:** Provides comprehensive coverage of respiratory and pulmonary disorders and focuses on new diagnostic and therapeutic procedures, laboratory studies, genetic breakthroughs, pathology, clinical features and management as related to such areas asthma and other lung diseases, critical care management, cystic fibrosis, lung and heart transplantation, pulmonary pathogens, and pleural disease as well as many other related disorders.
Formerly (until 1994): Seminars in Respiratory Medicine (0192-9755)
Related titles: Microform ed.: (from PQC); Online - full text ed.: ISSN 1098-9048. USD 764 domestic to institutions; USD 771 foreign to institutions (effective 2011).
Indexed: A01, A03, A08, A22, A35, A36, ASCA, AgBio, C06, C07, CA, CABA, E01, E12, EMBASE, ExcerpMed, FR, GH, H17, ISR, Inpharma, MEDLINE, N02, P30, P32, P33, P37, P40, PN&I, R08, R10, R12, R13, RM&VM, Reac, SCI, SCOPUS, T02, T05, THA, VS, W07.
—BLDSC (8239.457750), GNLM, IE, Infotrieve, Ingenta, INIST. **CCC.**
Published by: Thieme Medical Publishers (Subsidiary of: Georg Thieme Verlag), 333 Seventh Ave, New York, NY 10001. TEL 212-760-0888, 800-782-3488, FAX 212-947-1112, info@thieme.com. Ed. Dr. Joseph P Lynch III TEL 310-825-5988. Adv. contact James C Cunningham TEL 201-767-4170. Circ: 2,312 (paid).

616.2 TUR
SOLUNUM DERGISI/RESPIRATORY JOURNAL/TURKEY RESPIRATORY JOURNAL. Text in Turkish. q. EUR 40 (effective 2010). **Document type:** *Journal, Academic/Scholarly.* **Description:** Covers respiratory-related research papers, case reports, reviews, letters to the editor.
Related titles: Online - full text ed.: free (effective 2009).
Published by: Turkiye Solunum Arastirmalari Dernegi, Kocamustafa Pasa Cad, Esmer Ismerkezi No.118/2, Cerrahpasa, Istanbul, 34303, Turkey. TEL 90-212-6322717, FAX 90-212-5295868, akarabece@probiz.com.tr, info@solunum.org.tr. Ed. Mecit Suerdem.

616.24 NLD ISSN 2210-2078
SPREEKUUR LONGZIEKTEN. Text in Dutch. 1998. q. free to qualified personnel (effective 2010). adv. **Document type:** *Journal, Trade.*
Formerly (until 2010): Longartsen Vademecum (1387-6848)

Published by: Bohn Stafleu van Loghum B.V. (Subsidiary of: Springer Science+Business Media), Postbus 246, Houten, 3990 GA, Netherlands. TEL 31-30-6383872, FAX 31-30-6383991, boekhandels@bsl.nl, http://www.bsl.nl. adv.: color page EUR 3,434; trim 210 x 297. Circ: 487.

616.2 CZE ISSN 1213-810X
STUDIA PNEUMOLOGICA ET PHTHISEOLOGICA. Text in Czech. 1952. bi-m. **Document type:** *Journal, Academic/Scholarly.*
Supersedes (in 1993): Studia Pneumologica et Phtiseologica Cechoslovaca (0371-2222); Which was formerly (until 1970): Rozhledy v Tuberkuloze a Nemocech Plicnich (0035-936X)
Indexed: A36, CABA, E12, GH, LT, N02, N03, P33, R12, RM&VM, SCOPUS, T05, W10, W11.
—INIST. **CCC.**
Published by: Ceska Pneumologicka a Ftizeologicka Spolecnost, c/o Prof Milos Pesek, CSc, Klinika TRN, FN Plzen, Dr E Benese 13, Plzen, 30599, Czech Republic. pesek@fnplzen.cz, http://www.pneumologie.cz.

616.2 IRN ISSN 1735-0344
RC731
TANAFFOS/RESPIRATION; journal of respiratory disease, thoracic surgery, intensive care and tubeculosis. Text in English, Iranian. 2001. q. **Document type:** *Journal, Academic/Scholarly.*
Related titles: Online - full text ed.: free (effective 2011).
Indexed: A34, A36, CABA, E12, EMBASE, ExcerpMed, GH, H17, IndVet, N02, N03, P33, P37, R10, R12, RM&VM, Reac, S13, S16, SCOPUS, T05, VS, W11.
Published by: Shaheed Beheshti Medical University, Medical Sciences and Health Services, Shaheed Bahonar Ave, Darabad, Tehran, 19569, Iran. TEL 98-21-2282111, FAX 98-21-2285777. Ed. Mohammad Reza Masjedi.

616.2 USA ISSN 8756-8616
TECHNOLOGY FOR RESPIRATORY THERAPY. Text in English. 1980. m. **Document type:** *Newsletter, Trade.* **Description:** Contains technology-related information for respiratory specialists.
Formerly (until 1984): Health Devices Update: Respiratory Therapy
Related titles: Online - full text ed.
—CCC.
Published by: Emergency Care Research Institute, 5200 Butler Pike, Plymouth Meeting, PA 19462. TEL 610-825-6000, FAX 610-834-1275, info@ecri.org, http://www.ecri.org.

616.2 NLD ISSN 0040-2125
TEGEN DE TUBERCULOSE. Text in Dutch. 1904. 3/yr. free (effective 2009). adv. bk.rev. illus. **Document type:** *Journal, Academic/Scholarly.*
Indexed: P30.
Published by: Koninklijke Nederlandse Centrale Vereniging Tuberculosefonds, PO Box 146, The Hague, 2501 CC, Netherlands. TEL 31-70-4167222, FAX 31-70-3584004, info@kncvtbc.nl, http://www.kncvtbc.nl.

616.2 GBR ISSN 1753-4658
RC731
➤ **THERAPEUTIC ADVANCES IN RESPIRATORY DISEASE.** Text in English. 2007 (Jun.). bi-m. USD 1,071, GBP 579 combined subscription to institutions (print & online eds.); USD 1,050, GBP 567 to institutions (effective 2011). adv. back issues avail.; reprint service avail. from PSC. **Document type:** *Journal, Academic/Scholarly.* **Description:** Includes emerging therapies for chronic obstructive pulmonary disorder, asthma, pulmonary hypertension and the exacerbations caused by infections and smoking.
Related titles: Online - full text ed.: ISSN 1753-4666. USD 964, GBP 521 to institutions (effective 2011).
Indexed: A22, E01, EMBASE, ExcerpMed, MEDLINE, P30, R10, Reac, SCOPUS.
—BLDSC (8814.642630), IE. **CCC.**
Published by: Sage Publications Ltd. (Subsidiary of: Sage Publications, Inc.), 1 Oliver's Yard, 55 City Rd, London, EC1Y 1SP, United Kingdom. TEL 44-20-73248500, FAX 44-20-73248600, info@sagepub.co.uk, http://www.uk.sagepub.com/home.nav. adv.: B&W page GBP 400; 180 x 250.

616.2 AUS ISSN 1441-516X
➤ **THERAPEUTIC GUIDELINES. RESPIRATORY.** Text in English. 1994. irreg. (every 3-4 yrs.), latest 2005, version 3. AUD 30 per issue to students; AUD 39 per issue (effective 2008). back issues avail. **Document type:** *Handbook/Manual/Guide, Academic/Scholarly.* **Description:** Provides concrete recommendations for rational therapy of respiratory disease and, where necessary, justifies the choice of therapy.
Formerly (until 1999): Respiratory Drug Guidelines
Related titles: CD-ROM ed.; Online - full text ed.; ◆ Series of: e T G Complete. ISSN 1447-1868.
Published by: Therapeutic Guidelines Ltd., Ground Flr, 23-47 Villiers St, North Melbourne, VIC 3051, Australia. TEL 61-3-93291566, 800-061-260, FAX 61-3-93265632, sales@tg.com.au, http://www.tg.com.au. Eds. Dr. Alice Glover, Dr. Michael Kingsford. Circ: 18,000.

616.2 DEU ISSN 1616-9662
THIEME REFRESHER PNEUMOLOGIE. Text in German. 2003. irreg. **Document type:** *Monographic series, Academic/Scholarly.*
Published by: Georg Thieme Verlag, Ruedigerstr 14, Stuttgart, 70469, Germany. TEL 49-711-8931421, FAX 49-711-8931410, leser.service@thieme.de, http://www.thieme.de.

THORACIC SURGERY NEWS. *see* MEDICAL SCIENCES—Surgery

610 GBR ISSN 0040-6376
RC941 CODEN: THORA7
➤ **THORAX**; an international journal of respiratory medicine. Text in English. 1946. m. GBP 528 to institutions; GBP 659 combined subscription to institutions small FTE (print & online eds.) (effective 2011). adv. bk.rev. charts; illus. index. back issues avail.; reprints avail. **Document type:** *Journal, Academic/Scholarly.* **Description:** Covers respiratory medicine with clinical and experimental research articles from various disciplines, including pathology, immunology and surgery.
Related titles: CD-ROM ed.; Microform ed.: (from PQC); Online - full text ed.: eThorax. ISSN 1468-3296. GBP 542 to institutions small FTE (effective 2011).
Indexed: A01, A03, A08, A20, A22, A26, A34, A35, A36, AIDS Ab, AMED, ASCA, AddicA, AgBio, B21, B25, BA, BIOBASE, BIOSIS Prev, C06, C07, CA, CABA, CISA, CTA, ChemAb, ChemoAb, CurCont, D01, DentInd, DokArb, E01, E08, E12, EMBASE, ESPM, ExcerpMed, F08, FR, G08, GH, H11, H12, H17, I05, IABS, IBR, IBZ, IDIS, INI, ISR, ImmunAb, IndMed, IndVet, Inpharma, MEDLINE, MycolAb, N02, N03, P20, P22, P30, P33, P35, P38, P48, P50, P54, PQC, R08, R10, R12, R13, RM&VM, Reac, S09, S12, SCI, SCOPUS, T02, T05, THA, ToxAb, VITIS, VS, W07, W10, W11.
—BLDSC (8820.250000), CASDDS, GNLM, IE, Infotrieve, Ingenta, INIST. **CCC.**
Published by: (British Medical Association, British Thoracic Society), B M J Group, BMA House, Tavistock Sq, London, WC1H 9JR, United Kingdom. TEL 44-20-73836373, FAX 44-20-73836668, http://group.bmj.com. Ed. Andy Bush. Pub. Allison Lang TEL 44-20-73836212. Adv. contact Nick Gray TEL 44-20-73836386. Circ: 4,165. **Subscr. to:** PO Box 299, London WC1H 9TD, United Kingdom. TEL 44-20-73836270, FAX 44-20-73836402, support@bmjgroup.com.

616.2 URY ISSN 0049-4143
TORAX. Text in Spanish; Summaries in English. 1930. q. UYP 15, USD 20 (effective 2005). adv. bibl.; charts; illus. index.
Formerly (until 1952): Revista de Tuberculosis del Uruguay (0797-7808)
Indexed: C01, IndMed, P30, SCOPUS.
—GNLM. **CCC.**
Published by: Sociedad de Tisiologia y Enfermedades del Torax de Uruguay, Ave 18 de Julio, 2175, 2do Piso, Montevideo, 11700, Uruguay. TEL 598-2-309-0297, FAX 598-2-4014775. Ed. Dante Tomalino. **Co-sponsor:** Sociedad de Cardiologia.

616.2 GBR
▼ **TREATMENT STRATEGIES. RESPIRATORY.** Text in English. 2011. a. free to qualified personnel (effective 2011). adv. reprints avail. **Document type:** *Academic/Scholarly.* **Description:** Provides clinicians with information on the latest developments in the respiratory field with emphasis on both therapeutic and technological aspects.
Related titles: Online - full text ed.: ISSN 2046-5823. free (effective 2011).
Published by: Cambridge Research Centre, Coppergate House, 16 Brune St, London, E1 7NJ, United Kingdom. TEL 44-20-79538490, FAX 44-20-80430691, info@treatmentstrategies.co.uk. Ed. Rachel Holcroft.

616.246 GBR ISSN 1472-9792
RC306 CODEN: TUBECU
➤ **TUBERCULOSIS.** Text in English. 1992. bi-m. EUR 1,114 in Europe to institutions; JPY 120,300 in Japan to institutions; USD 1,017 elsewhere to institutions (effective 2012). adv. abstr.; bibl.; illus. index. Supplement avail.; back issues avail.; reprints avail. **Document type:** *Journal, Academic/Scholarly.* **Description:** Publishes primary articles and commissioned reviews on both research and clinical work in tuberculosis and other lung diseases.
Formerly (until 2001): Tubercle and Lung Disease (0962-8479); Which was formed by the merger of (1919-1992): Tubercle (0041-3879); (1986-1992): International Union against Tuberculosis and Lung Disease. Bulletin (1011-789X); Which was formerly (1924-1986): International Union against Tuberculosis. Bulletin (0074-9249)
Related titles: Online - full text ed.: ISSN 1873-281X (from ScienceDirect).
Indexed: A22, A26, A29, A34, A35, A36, ASCA, AgBio, B20, B21, B25, BIOBASE, BIOSIS Prev, C25, CA, CABA, ChemAb, CurCont, DBA, E01, E12, EMBASE, ESPM, ExcerpMed, GH, I05, I10, IABS, ISR, IndMed, IndVet, Inpharma, MEDLINE, MycolAb, N02, P30, P32, P33, P35, P37, P38, P40, PN&I, R10, R12, R13, RM&VM, Reac, SCI, SCOPUS, T02, T05, TAR, THA, VS, VirolAbstr, W07, W11.
—BLDSC (9068.125000), GNLM, IE, Infotrieve, Ingenta, INIST. **CCC.**
Published by: Churchill Livingstone (Subsidiary of: Elsevier Health Sciences), The Blvd, Langford Ln, Kidlington, OX5 1GB, United Kingdom. TEL 44-1865-843434, FAX 44-1865-843970, directenquiries@elsevier.com, http://www.elsevierhealth.com/imprint.jsp?iid=9. Eds. Douglas Young, Patrick J Brennan. Adv. contact Emma Steel TEL 44-207-4244221. Circ: 192.

616.2 KOR ISSN 1738-3536
TUBERCULOSIS AND RESPIRATORY DISEASES. Text in Korean. 1954. m. KRW 50,000 (effective 2009). **Document type:** *Journal, Academic/Scholarly.*
Formerly (until 2004): Kyorhaek Mich' Hohupki Chirhwan (0378-0066)
Related titles: Online - full text ed.
Indexed: A22, EMBASE, ExcerpMed, R10, Reac, SCOPUS.
—BLDSC (9068.135000), IE, Ingenta.
Published by: Taehan Kyorhaek Hyophoe/Korean Academy of Tuberculosis and Respiratory Diseases, 14 Woomyundong, Sochogu, Seoul, 137-140, Korea, S. TEL 82-2-5753825, FAX 82-2-5256683, katrd@lungkorea.com.

616.246 CAN ISSN 1498-525X
RC314
TUBERCULOSIS DRUG RESISTANCE IN CANADA. Text in English. 1998. a.
Published by: Health Canada, Tuberculosis Prevention and Control, Population and Public Health Branch, Building 6, A.L. 0603B, Tunney's Pasture, Ottawa, ON K1A 0K9, Canada. TEL 613-941-0238, FAX 613-946-3902.

TUBERCULOSIS IN CANADA/CANADA. STATISTIQUE CANADA. LA STATISTIQUE DE LA TUBERCULOSE, VOLUME 2: INSTALLATIONS, SERVICES ET FINANCE DES ETABLISSEMENTS. *see* PUBLIC HEALTH AND SAFETY

616.995 USA ISSN 2090-150X
▼ ➤ **TUBERCULOSIS RESEARCH AND TREATMENT.** Text in English. 2009. irreg. USD 395 (effective 2011). **Document type:** *Journal, Academic/Scholarly.* **Description:** Publishes original research articles, review articles, case reports, and clinical studies related to all aspects of tuberculosis.
Related titles: Online - full text ed.: ISSN 2090-1518. free (effective 2011).
Indexed: A01, T02.
Published by: Hindawi Publishing Corporation, 410 Park Ave, 15th Fl, PMB 287, New York, NY 10022. FAX 215-893-4392, 866-446-3294, info@hindawi.com.

616.995 USA ISSN 1543-6632
TUBERCULOSIS WEEK. Text in English. 2003. w. USD 2,295 in US & Canada; USD 2,495 elsewhere; USD 2,525 combined subscription in US & Canada (print & online eds.); USD 2,755 combined subscription elsewhere (print & online eds.) (effective 2008). back issues avail. **Document type:** *Newsletter, Trade.* **Description:** Contains news and information on research into the pathology, epidemiology and treatment of tuberculosis, including reports from the CDC and WHO.
Related titles: E-mail ed.; Online - full text ed.: ISSN 1543-6624. USD 2,295 combined subscription (online & email eds.); single user (effective 2008).
Indexed: A26, E08, G08, H11, H12, I05, S09.
Published by: NewsRx, 2727 Paces Ferry Rd SE, Ste 2-440, Atlanta, GA 30339. TEL 770-435-8286, 800-726-4550, FAX 770-435-6800, pressrelease@newsrx.com. Pub. Susan Hasty TEL 770-507-7777.

616.2 TUR ISSN 1302-7786
TURKISH RESPIRATORY JOURNAL. Text in English. 2000. 3/yr. **Document type:** *Journal, Academic/Scholarly.* **Description:** Aims to promote scientific eminence in clinical and experimental work dealing with the whole field of pulmonary medicine and related fields including cell biology, epidemiology, immunology, pathophysiology, thoracic imaging, paediatric pneumology, occupational medicine, intensive care, sleep medicine and thoracic surgery. It also publishes original investigations, reviews, case reports and letters.
Related titles: Online - full text ed.
Published by: Turkish Thoracic Society, Ankara University, School of Medicine, Department of Chest Diseases, Cebeci - Ankara, Turkey. TEL 90-312-5956582, FAX 90-312-3190046, toraks@toraks.org.tr, http://www.toraks.org.tr/en/public.php. Eds. Dilsad Mungan, Emel Kurt.

616.246 614 USA
RC313
U.S. CENTERS FOR DISEASE CONTROL. REPORTED TUBERCULOSIS IN THE UNITED STATES. Text in English. 1974. a. charts; illus. back issues avail. **Document type:** *Government.* **Description:** Covers basic facts, ways of spreading about tuberculosis. Contains the information which shows the difference between latent TB infection and TB disease.
Former titles (until 1993): U.S. Centers for Disease Control. Tuberculosis Statistics in the United States; (until 1987): U.S. Centers for Disease Control. Tuberculosis in the United States (0149-2616); (until 1985): U.S. Centers for Disease Control. Tuberculosis Statistics. States and Cities (0146-7298)
Related titles: Online - full text ed.: free (effective 2010).
Published by: U.S. Department of Health and Human Services, Centers for Disease Control and Prevention, 1600 Clifton Rd, Atlanta, GA 30333. TEL 800-232-4636, cdcinfo@cdc.gov.

616.2 GBR ISSN 1753-4089
U S RESPIRATORY DISEASE. (United States) Text in English. 2006 (Jul.). s-a. EUR 80 combined subscription in Europe to individuals (print & online eds.); USD 100 combined subscription in United States to individuals (print & online eds.); EUR 180 combined subscription in Europe to institutions (print & online eds.); USD 225 combined subscription in United States to institutions (print & online eds.) (effective 2009). back issues avail. **Document type:** *Journal, Trade.* **Description:** Brings together the industry's opinion leaders and companies to create a platform to deliver the research and showcase the latest products to the respiratory community.
Related titles: Online - full text ed.: ISSN 1753-4097. EUR 70 in Europe to individuals; USD 85 in United States to individuals; EUR 170 in Europe to institutions; USD 210 in United States to individuals (effective 2009).
—CCC.
Published by: Touch Briefings (Subsidiary of: Touch Group plc), Saffron House, 6-10 Kirby St, London, EC1N 8TS, United Kingdom. TEL 44-20-74525600, FAX 44-20-74525606, info@touchbriefings.com, http://www.touchbriefings.com/.

616.24 UKR
➤ **UKRAINS'KYI PUL'MONOLOHICHNYI ZHURNAL/UKRAINIAN JOURNAL OF PULMONOLOGY/UKRAINSKII PUL'MONOLOGICHESKII ZHURNAL.** Text in Ukrainian, Russian. 1993. q. **Document type:** *Journal, Academic/Scholarly.*
Related titles: Online - full text ed.
Published by: Akademiya Medychnykh Nauk Ukrainy, Instytut Ftyziatrii i Pul'monolohii im. F.H. Yanovs'koho, vul N. Amosova, 10, Kyiv, 03680, Ukraine. TEL 380-44-2750402, FAX 380-44-2752118, admin@ifp.kiev.ua. Ed. Yurii Feshchenko TEL 380-44-5291284.

616.246 FRA ISSN 1727-7914
RC306
UNION NEWSLETTER (ENGLISH EDITION). Text in English. 1991. 3/yr. **Document type:** *Newsletter, Trade.*
Former titles (until 2002): I U A T L D. Newsletter (English Edition) (1562-174X); (until 1998): International Union against Tuberculosis and Lung Disease. Newsletter (1021-7754)
Related titles: Online - full text ed.: ISSN 1728-5879; ◆ Spanish ed.: Union Newsletter (Spanish Edition). ISSN 1727-7930; ◆ French ed.: Union Newsletter (French Edition). ISSN 1727-7922.
Published by: International Union against Tuberculosis and Lung Disease (I U A T L D)/Union Internationale contre la Tuberculose et les Maladies Respiratoires, 68 Bd Saint-Michel, Paris, 75006, France. TEL 33-1-44320360, FAX 33-1-43299087, union@iuatld.org, http://www.iuatld.org.

616.246 FRA ISSN 1727-7922
UNION NEWSLETTER (FRENCH EDITION). Text in French. 1991. 3/yr. **Document type:** *Newsletter, Trade.*
Former titles (until 2002): Union Internationale contre la Tuberculose et les Maladies Respiratoires. Newsletter (1562-1758); (until 1999): I U A T L D Newsletter (French Edition) (1019-4924)
Related titles: Online - full text ed.: ISSN 1728-5887; ◆ Spanish ed.: Union Newsletter (Spanish Edition). ISSN 1727-7930; ◆ English ed.: Union Newsletter (English Edition). ISSN 1727-7914.
Published by: International Union against Tuberculosis and Lung Disease (I U A T L D)/Union Internationale contre la Tuberculose et les Maladies Respiratoires, 68 Bd Saint-Michel, Paris, 75006, France. TEL 33-1-44320360, FAX 33-1-43299087, union@iuatld.org, http://www.iuatld.org.

616.246 FRA ISSN 1727-7930
UNION NEWSLETTER (SPANISH EDITION). Text in Spanish. 1991. 3/yr. **Document type:** *Newsletter, Trade.*

Former titles (until 2002): Union Internacional contra la Tubercolosis & Enfermedades Respiratorias. Newsletter (1562-1766); (until 1998): I U A T L D Newsletter (Spanish Edition) (1019-9853)
Related titles: Online - full text ed.: ISSN 1728-5895. 2003; ◆ French ed.: Union Newsletter (French Edition). ISSN 1727-7922; ◆ English ed.: Union Newsletter (English Edition). ISSN 1727-7914.
Published by: International Union against Tuberculosis and Lung Disease (I U A T L D)/Union Internationale contre la Tuberculose et les Maladies Respiratoires, 68 Bd Saint-Michel, Paris, 75006, France. TEL 33-1-44320360, FAX 33-1-43299087, union@iuatld.org, http://www.iuatld.org.

616.2 USA
UPDATE (BIRMINGHAM). Text in English. q. free.
Published by: American Lung Association of Alabama, 3125 Independence Dr., Ste. 325, Birmingham, AL 35209-4177. TEL 205-933-8821, FAX 205-930-1717, http://www.alabamalung.org.

616.2 FRA ISSN 1961-3210
VAINCRE. Text in French. 1966. q. free to members. **Document type:** *Magazine, Consumer.* **Description:** Focuses on research and finding a cure for cystic phibrosis. Also offers support to those afflicted with the disease.
Former titles (until 2007): La Mucoviscidose (0243-7589); (until 1979): Association Francaise de Lutte contre la Mucoviscidose. Bulletin (0243-7570)
Published by: Association Vaincre la Mucoviscidose, 181 Rue Tolbiac, Paris, 75013, France. TEL 33-1-40789191, FAX 33-1-45808644, http://www.vaincrelamuco.org.

616.2 USA
VOICE FOUNDATION. NEWSLETTER. Text in English. 3/yr. USD 50 membership (effective 2007). **Document type:** *Newsletter, Consumer.*
Published by: Voice Foundation, 1721 Pine St, Philadelphia, PA 19103. TEL 215-735-7999, FAX 215-735-9293, office@voicefoundation.org, http://www.voicefoundation.org. Ed. Charlotte Cathcart.

616.2 USA ISSN 8756-3452
RC705
YEAR BOOK OF PULMONARY DISEASE. Text in English. 1986. a. USD 217 in United States to institutions; USD 235 elsewhere to institutions (effective 2012). adv. illus. **Document type:** *Yearbook, Academic/Scholarly.* **Description:** Presents abstracts of pertinent literature with commentary by leading experts in the field.
Related titles: CD-ROM ed.; Online - full text ed.
—GNLM. **CCC.**
Published by: Mosby, Inc. (Subsidiary of: Elsevier Health Sciences), 1600 John F. Kennedy Blvd, Ste 1800, Philadelphia, PA 19103. TEL 215-239-3900, 800-523-1649, FAX 215-239-3990, elspcs@elsevier.com, http://www.us.elsevierhealth.com. Ed. James Barker.

616.2 GBR ISSN 1477-8114
RC731
THE YEAR IN RESPIRATORY MEDICINE (YEAR). Text in English. 2003. a. USD 99.95 per issue in US & Canada; GBP 59.99 per issue elsewhere (effective 2009). 312 p./no.; **Document type:** *Journal, Academic/Scholarly.* **Description:** Provides clinical guidance for all those working in the field of respiratory disease.
Indexed: P20, P22, P48, P54, PQC.
—**CCC.**
Published by: Clinical Publishing (Subsidiary of: Atlas Medical Publishing Ltd), Oxford Centre for Innovation, Mill St, Oxford, OX2 0JX, United Kingdom. TEL 44-1865-811116, FAX 44-1865-251550, info@clinicalpublishing.co.uk. **Dist. by:** Marston Book Services Ltd., Unit 160, Milton Park, Abingdon, Oxfordshire OX14 4SD, United Kingdom. TEL 44-1235-465500, FAX 44-1235-465555, trade.orders@marston.co.uk, http://www.marston.co.uk/.

616.23 JPN ISSN 0914-7683
ZENSOKU/ASTHMA. Text in Japanese. 1988. 4/yr. JPY 6,856 (effective 2005). **Document type:** *Journal, Academic/Scholarly.*
Published by: Medikaru Rebyusha/Medical Review Co., Ltd., 1-7-3 Hirano-Machi, Chuo-ku, Yoshida Bldg., Osaka-shi, 541-0046, Japan. TEL 81-6-62231468, FAX 81-6-62231245.

616.2 - CHN ISSN 1000-6621
RA644.T7
➤ **ZHONGGUO FANGLAO TONGXUN/CHINESE JOURNAL OF ANTITUBERCULOSIS.** Text in Chinese. 1948. m. CNY 120, USD 120; CNY 10 per issue (effective 2011). back issues avail. **Document type:** *Journal, Academic/Scholarly.* **Description:** Covers the newest strategy, results in research and developments in tuberculosis control in China and aboard.
Former titles (until 1990): Zhongguo Fanglao Tongxun/Chinese Antituberculosis Association. Bulletin; (until 1966): Zhongguo Fanglao Zazhi; (until 1960): Zhongguo Fanglao; Which incorporated (1953-1959): Zhonghua Jiehe Bingke Zazhi; (until 1957): Fanglao Tongxun
Related titles: Online - full text ed.
—BLDSC (9512.732705), East View.
Published by: Zhongguo Fanglao Xiehui/Chinese Anti-Tuberculosis Association, 42, Dongsi Xidajie, Dongcheng District, Beijing, 100710, China. http://www.cata1933.cn/newEbiz1/EbizPortalFG/portal/html/index.html. Ed. Xiexiu Wang. Circ: 4,500.

616.99424 CHN ISSN 1009-3419
CODEN: ZFZHAG
➤ **ZHONGGUO FEIYAN ZAZHI/CHINESE JOURNAL OF LUNG CANCER.** Text in Chinese. 1998 (Jul.). bi-m. CNY 120 domestic; USD 120 foreign; CNY 10, USD 5 newsstand/cover (effective 2010). adv. abstr.; charts. back issues avail. **Document type:** *Journal, Academic/Scholarly.* **Description:** Publishes original laboratory and clinical investigations related to lung cancer.
Related titles: Online - full text ed.: ISSN 1999-6187. free (effective 2011).
Indexed: A34, A36, B&BAb, B19, B20, B21, C06, C07, CA, CABA, E12, EMBASE, ESPM, ExcerpMed, GH, ImmunAb, MEDLINE, N02, N03, NucAcAb, OGFA, P30, P33, R08, R10, RA&MP, Reac, SCOPUS, T02, T05, VS, VirolAbstr.
—BLDSC (3180.369100), IE, Ingenta.
Published by: (Tianjin Yike Daxue Zongyiyuan/Tianjin Medical University General Hospital, Zhongguo Kangai Xiehui/Chinese Anticancer Association, Zhongguo Fanglao Xuehui/Chinese Antituberculosis Association), Zhongguo Feiyan Zazhi Bianji Weiyuanhui/Editorial Board of the Chinese Journal of Lung Cancer, no.228, Nanjing Rd., Tianjin, 300020, China. TEL 86-22-27219219, FAX 86-22-27219052. Ed. Qinghua Zhou. adv.: B&W page CNY 3,000, color page CNY 8,000; trim 210 x 297. Circ: 3,000 (paid).

616.2 CHN ISSN 1671-6205
ZHONGGUO HUXI YU WEIZHONG JIANHU ZAZHI/CHINESE JOURNAL OF RESPIRATORY AND CRITICAL CARE MEDICINE. Text in Chinese. 2002. bi-m. USD 27.60 (effective 2009). **Document type:** *Journal, Academic/Scholarly.*
Related titles: Online - full text ed.
Indexed: A29, A36, B&BAb, B19, B20, B21, CABA, D01, E12, ESPM, F08, F11, F12, GH, H16, I10, ImmunAb, N02, N03, P33, R08, R12, RA&MP, RM&VM, T05, VS, VirolAbstr.
—BLDSC (9512.737490), East View.
Published by: Sichuan Daxue, Huaxi Linchuang Yixueyuan, Huaxi Yiyuan/Sichuan University, West China Medical School, West China Hospital, 37, Guoxuexiang, Chengdu, 610041, China.

616.995 CHN ISSN 1001-0939
➤ **ZHONGHUA JIEHE HE HUXI ZAZHI/CHINESE JOURNAL OF TUBERCULOSIS AND RESPIRATORY DISEASES.** Text in Chinese. 1978. m. USD 87.60 (effective 2009). abstr.; charts; illus. 64 p./no.; **Document type:** *Journal, Academic/Scholarly.*
Formerly (until 1986): Zhonghua Jiehe he Huxiji Jibing Zazhi (0253-2689)
Related titles: ◆ CD-ROM ed.: Chinese Academic Journals Full-Text Database. Medicine & Hygiene; Online - full text ed.; 1998.
Indexed: B25, BIOSIS Prev, EMBASE, ExcerpMed, IndMed, MEDLINE, MycolAb, P30, R10, Reac, SCOPUS.
—BLDSC (3180.682000), East View.
Published by: Zhonghua Yixuehui Zazhishe/Chinese Medical Association Publishing House, 42 Dongsi Xidajie, Beijing, 100710, China. TEL 86-10-651222268, FAX 86-10-65273365, http://www.medline.org.cn/. Ed. Nanshan Zhong. **Dist. by:** China International Book Trading Corp, 35 Chegongzhuang Xilu, Haidian District, PO Box 399, Beijing 100044, China. TEL 86-10-68412045, FAX 86-10-68412023, cibtc@mail.cibtc.com.cn, http://www.cibtc.com.cn.

MEDICAL SCIENCES—Rheumatology

616.7 FRA ISSN 1958-3303
A N D A R INFOS. Variant title: Association National de Defense contre l'Arthrite Rhumatoide Infos. Text in French. 200?. s-a. **Document type:** *Newsletter.*
Published by: Association Nationale de Defense contre l'Arthrite Rhumatoide (A N D A R), 7 Rue des Calquieres, Clermont l'Herault, 34800, France. TEL 33-4-67885312, FAX 33-4-67885986, andar@polyarthrite-andar.com, http://www.polyarthrite-andar.com.

616.7 PRT
ACTA REUMATICA PORTUGUESA. Text in English. 2001. q. **Document type:** *Journal, Academic/Scholarly.*
Published by: (Sociedade Reumatologica Portuguesa), Publisaude Edicoes Medicas, Alameda Antonio Sergio, Edificio Amadeu S Cardoso, Miraflores, Alges, 1495-132, Portugal. TEL 351-214-135032, FAX 351-214-135007, http://publisaude.pai.pt. Ed. Lucia Costa.

616.742 PRT ISSN 0303-464X
CODEN: ARUPB
ACTA REUMATOLOGICA PORTUGUESA. Text in Portuguese; Summaries in English, Portuguese. 1973. q. adv. bk.rev. abstr.; bibl.; charts; illus.; stat. **Document type:** *Journal, Academic/Scholarly.*
Indexed: CA, EMBASE, ExcerpMed, MEDLINE, P30, R10, Reac, RefZh, SCI, SCOPUS, T02, W07.
—BLDSC (0662.561000), GNLM.
Published by: Instituto Portugues de Reumatologia, Rua de Dona Estefania 187-189, Lisbon, 1000-154, Portugal. TEL 351-21-3552570, FAX 351-21-3552578, http://www.ipr.pt.

616.7 BEL ISSN 0378-9497
ACTA RHUMATOLOGICA BELGICA. Text in French. 1977. q. **Document type:** *Journal, Academic/Scholarly.*
Indexed: P30, SCOPUS.
—INIST.
Published by: Societe Royale Belge de Rhumatologie/Koninklijke Belgische Vereniging van Reumatologie, Avenue Circulaire 138A, Brussels, 1180, Belgium. TEL 32-2-3723643, FAX 32-2-3754813, http://www.kbvr.be.

616.742 FRA ISSN 0065-1818
L'ACTUALITE RHUMATOLOGIQUE. Text in French. 1964. a. EUR 80.75 per issue (effective 2009). **Document type:** *Journal, Academic/Scholarly.*
—GNLM, INIST. **CCC.**
Published by: (Hopital Lariboisiere, Centre Viggo Petersen), Elsevier Masson (Subsidiary of: Elsevier Health Sciences), 62 Rue Camille Desmoulins, Issy les Moulineaux, Cedex 92442, France. TEL 33-1-71165500, FAX 33-1-71165600, infos@elsevier-masson.fr.

616.72 DEU ISSN 0341-051X
RC933.A1 CODEN: AKRHDB
➤ **AKTUELLE RHEUMATOLOGIE.** Text in German; Summaries in English, German. 1976. bi-m. EUR 229 to institutions; EUR 305 combined subscription to institutions (print & online eds.); EUR 46 newsstand/cover (effective 2011). adv. abstr.; illus. index. reprints avail. **Document type:** *Journal, Academic/Scholarly.*
Related titles: Online - full text ed.: ISSN 1438-9940. EUR 295 to institutions (effective 2011); Supplement(s): Aktuelle Rheumatologie. Supplement. ISSN 1433-7940. 1994.
Indexed: A22, A29, ASCA, B20, B21, B25, BIOSIS Prev, CTA, EMBASE, ESPM, ExcerpMed, I10, ImmunAb, Inpharma, MycolAb, R10, Reac, SCI, SCOPUS, W07.
—BLDSC (0785.873000), GNLM, IE, Infotrieve, Ingenta, INIST. **CCC.**
Published by: Georg Thieme Verlag, Ruedigerstr 14, Stuttgart, 70469, Germany. TEL 49-711-8931421, FAX 49-711-8931410, leser.service@thieme.de. Ed. Daniela Erhard. Adv. contact Christine Volpp TEL 49-711-8931603. Circ: 3,000 (paid).

616.7 GBR ISSN 1350-6129
QP552.A45 CODEN: AIJIET
➤ **AMYLOID;** the journal of protein folding disorders. Text in English. 1994. q. GBP 640, EUR 970, USD 1,210 combined subscription to institutions (print & online eds.); GBP 1,335, EUR 2,025, USD 2,530 combined subscription to corporations (print & online eds.) (effective 2010). adv. back issues avail.; reprint service avail. from PSC. **Document type:** *Journal, Academic/Scholarly.* **Description:** Offers a broad range of topics reflecting the multi-disciplinary nature of amyloid studies.
Related titles: Online - full text ed.: ISSN 1744-2818 (from IngentaConnect).
Indexed: A01, A03, A08, A22, ASCA, B21, B25, B27, BIOSIS Prev, CA, CIN, ChemTitl, CurCont, E-psyche, E01, EMBASE, ExcerpMed, ISR, ImmunAb, IndMed, Inpharma, MEDLINE, NSA, NSCI, P20, P22, P30, P48, P54, PQC, R10, Reac, SCI, SCOPUS, T02, W07.
—CASDDS, GNLM, IE, Infotrieve, Ingenta. **CCC.**
Published by: (International Society of Amyloidosis), Informa Healthcare (Subsidiary of: T & F Informa plc), Telephone House, 69-77 Paul St, London, EC2A 4LQ, United Kingdom. TEL 44-20-70175000, FAX 44-20-70176792, healthcare.enquiries@informa.com, http://informahealthcare.com/. Ed. Alan S Cohen. Adv. contact Per Sonnerfeldt. **Subscr. in N America to:** Taylor & Francis Inc., Customer Services Dept, 325 Chestnut St, 8th Fl, Philadelphia, PA 19106. TEL 215-625-8900, 800-354-1420, FAX 215-625-8914, customerservice@taylorandfrancis.com; **Subscr. outside N America to:** Taylor & Francis Ltd., Journals Customer Service, Sheepen Pl, Colchester, Essex CO3 3LP, United Kingdom. TEL 44-20-70175544, FAX 44-20-70175198, tf.enquiries@tfinforma.com.

616.742 GBR ISSN 0003-4967
CODEN: ARDIAO
➤ **ANNALS OF THE RHEUMATIC DISEASES;** an international peer-reviewed journal for health professionals and researchers in the rheumatic diseases. Abbreviated title: A R D. Text in English. 1935. m. GBP 660 to institutions; GBP 815 combined subscription to institutions small FTE (print & online eds.) (effective 2011). adv. bk.rev. charts; illus. index. back issues avail.; reprints avail. **Document type:** *Journal, Academic/Scholarly.* **Description:** Features articles on all aspects of rheumatology and disorders of connective tissue.
Former titles (until 1939): The Rheumatic Diseases; (until 1938): Reports on Chronic Rheumatic Diseases
Related titles: CD-ROM ed.; Microform ed.: (from PQC); Online - full text ed.: A R D Online. ISSN 1468-2060. GBP 659 to institutions small FTE (effective 2011).
Indexed: A20, A22, A26, A34, A36, AIIM, AMED, ASCA, B21, B25, BIOBASE, BIOSIS Prev, C06, C07, CABA, CIN, CISA, CTA, ChemAb, ChemTitl, CurCont, D01, DBA, DentInd, E01, E08, E12, EMBASE, ExcerpMed, F08, F11, F12, FR, G06, G07, G08, GH, H11, H12, I05, IABS, IDIS, ISR, ImmunAb, IndMed, IndVet, Inpharma, Kidney, MEDLINE, MS&D, MycolAb, N02, N03, P20, P22, P26, P30, P33, P35, P39, P48, P54, PQC, R08, R10, R12, RA&MP, RM&VM, Reac, RefZh, S09, SCI, SCOPUS, SoyAb, T05, VS, W07.
—BLDSC (1043.800000), CASDDS, GNLM, IE, Infotrieve, Ingenta, INIST. **CCC.**
Published by: (E U L A R. European League Against Rheumatism CHE), B M J Group, BMA House, Tavistock Sq, London, WC1H 9JR, United Kingdom. TEL 44-20-73836373, FAX 44-20-73836668, http://group.bmj.com. Ed. Tore K Kvien. Pub. Christiane Notarmarco TEL 44-20-78747096. Adv. contact Nick Gray TEL 44-20-73836386. Circ: 11,815. **Subscr. to:** PO Box 299, London WC1H 9TD, United Kingdom. TEL 44-20-73836270, FAX 44-20-73836402, support@bmjgroup.com.

➤ **ARCHIVIO DI ORTOPEDIA E REUMATOLOGIA.** *see* MEDICAL SCIENCES—Orthopedics And Traumatology

616.7 JPN ISSN 1348-270X
ARTHRITIS/UNDOUKI SHIKKAN TO ENSHOU. Text in Japanese. 2003. 3/yr. (Apr., Aug. & Dec.). USD 6,930 (effective 2005). **Document type:** *Journal, Academic/Scholarly.*
Published by: Medikaru Rebyusha/Medical Review Co., Ltd., 1-7-3 Hirano-Machi, Chuo-ku, Yoshida Bldg., Osaka-shi, 541-0046, Japan. TEL 81-6-62231468, FAX 81-6-62231245.

616.7 USA ISSN 2090-1984
▼ **ARTHRITIS.** Text in English. 2009. q. USD 195 (effective 2011). **Document type:** *Journal, Academic/Scholarly.*
Related titles: Online - full text ed.: ISSN 2090-1992. free (effective 2011).
Indexed: A01.
Published by: Hindawi Publishing Corporation, 410 Park Ave, 15th Fl, PMB 287, New York, NY 10022. FAX 215-893-4392, 866-446-3294, hindawi@hindawi.com.

616.7 USA ISSN 1542-3425
ARTHRITIS ADVISOR; advise and information from a world leader in bone and joint care. Text in English. 2002 (Dec.). m. USD 39 combined subscription domestic (print & online eds.); USD 49 combined subscription in Canada (print & online eds.); USD 59 combined subscription elsewhere (print & online eds.) (effective 2010). back issues avail. **Document type:** *Newsletter, Consumer.* **Description:** Covers information and treatment alternatives for who suffers from any kind of joint, muscle, or bone pain.
Related titles: Online - full text ed.: Arthritis - Advisor.com.
Published by: Belvoir Media Group, LLC, PO Box 5656, Norwalk, CT 06856. TEL 203-857-3100, 800-424-7887, FAX 203-857-3103, customer_service@belvoir.com, http://www.belvoir.com. Ed. Brian Donley. **Subscr. to:** Palm Coast Data, LLC, PO Box 420235, Palm Coast, FL 32142. TEL 800-829-2506, http://www.palmcoastdata.com.

616.742 USA ISSN 0004-3591
RC927.A1 CODEN: ARHEAW
➤ **ARTHRITIS & RHEUMATISM.** Text in English. 1958. m. GBP 1,038 in United Kingdom to institutions; EUR 1,311 in Europe to institutions; USD 1,528 in United States to institutions; USD 1,864 in Canada & Mexico to institutions; USD 2,032 elsewhere to institutions; GBP 1,196 combined subscription in United Kingdom to institutions (print & online eds.); EUR 1,512 combined subscription in Europe to institutions (print & online eds.); USD 1,758 combined subscription in United States to institutions (print & online eds.); USD 2,094 combined subscription in Canada & Mexico to institutions (print & online eds.); USD 2,262 combined subscription elsewhere to institutions (print & online eds.) (effective 2012). adv. bk.rev. bibl.; charts; illus. back issues avail.; reprint service avail. from PSC. **Document type:** *Journal, Academic/Scholarly.* **Description:** Covers all aspects of inflammatory disease.
Incorporates (1988-2000): Arthritis Care and Research (0893-7524)
Related titles: Microform ed.: (from PQC); Online - full text ed.: ISSN 1529-0131. GBP 781 in United Kingdom to institutions; EUR 986 in Europe to institutions; USD 1,528 elsewhere to institutions (effective 2012); ◆ Includes: Arthritis Care and Research. ISSN 0893-7524.
Indexed: A01, A03, A08, A20, A22, A26, A35, A36, AIM, ASCA, AbAn, AgBio, B21, B25, BIOBASE, BIOSIS Prev, C06, C07, C08, CA, CABA, CIN, CINAHL, CISA, CTA, ChemAb, ChemTitl, CurCont, DBA, DentInd, E12, EMBASE, ESPM, ExcerpMed, F09, FR, FamI, G08, GH, H11, H12, I12, IABS, IBR, IBZ, IDIS, INI, ISR, IndMed, Inpharma, JW, JW-D, Kidney, MEDLINE, MS&D, MycolAb, N02, N03, P03, P30, P32, P33, P35, P39, P40, PN&I, PsycholAb, R08, R10, RA&MP, RM&VM, Reac, SCI, SCOPUS, T02, T05, THA, ToxAb, VITIS, VS, W07.
—BLDSC (1733.800000), CASDDS, GNLM, IE, Infotrieve, Ingenta, INIST. **CCC.**
Published by: (American College of Rheumatology), John Wiley & Sons, Inc., 111 River St, Hoboken, NJ 07030. TEL 201-748-6000, FAX 201-748-6088, info@wiley.com, http://www.wiley.com/WileyCDA/. Ed. Michael D Lockshin. Pub. Kim Thompkins TEL 212-850-6921. Circ: 9,900. **Subscr. to:** John Wiley & Sons Ltd.

616.7 USA ISSN 1537-2960
RC927
ARTHRITIS & RHEUMATOLOGY; an internet resource guide. Text in English. 2002. a. USD 24.95 newsstand/cover (effective 2005).
Published by: eMedguides.com, 15 Roszel Rd., Princeton, NJ 08540. TEL 609-520-2001, 800-230-1481, FAX 609-520-2023, http://www.emedguides.com. Ed. Daniel E Furst.

616.7 USA ISSN 2151-464X
➤ **ARTHRITIS CARE & RESEARCH.** Abbreviated title: A C & R. Text in English. 1999. m. adv. back issues avail.; reprints avail. **Document type:** *Journal, Academic/Scholarly.* **Description:** Covers topics such as practice studies, clinical problems, practice guidelines, health care economics, health care policy, educational, social, and public health issues, and future trends in rheumatology practice.
Related titles: Online - full text ed.: ISSN 2151-4658. free to members (effective 2010).
Indexed: B25, BIOSIS Prev, C06, C07, C08, CINAHL, CurCont, MEDLINE, P30, SCI, W07.
—CCC.
Published by: (American College of Rheumatology), John Wiley & Sons, Inc., 111 River St, Hoboken, NJ 07030. FAX 201-748-6088, info@wiley.com, http://www.wiley.com/WileyCDA/. Eds. Edward H Yelin, Patricia P Katz. Adv. contact Valentin Torres TEL 212-904-0375.

616.7 USA ISSN 0191-2836
ARTHRITIS FOUNDATION. ANNUAL REPORT. Text in English. 1948. a. free (effective 2009). **Document type:** *Report, Trade.* **Description:** Designed for the prevention, control and cure of Arthritis and related diseases.
Formerly (until 1965): Arthritis Foundation. Interim Report
Related titles: Online - full text ed.
Published by: Arthritis Foundation, PO Box 7669, Atlanta, GA 30357. TEL 404-872-7100, 800-283-7800, atmail@arthritis.org, http://www.arthritis.org. Ed. Kelly Donahue.

616.722 USA ISSN 1067-9421
ARTHRITIS HEALTH MONITOR. Text in English. 1994. m. free. **Document type:** *Magazine, Consumer.*
Published by: Data Centrum Communications, Inc., 650 From Rd, 2nd Fl, Paramus, NJ 07652. TEL 201-391-1911, FAX 201-225-1440, info@healthmonitor.com, http://www.healthmonitor.com.

616.7 USA
ARTHRITIS HOTLINE. Text in English. 1993. 3/yr. USD 12 (effective 2000). back issues avail. **Document type:** *Newsletter, Consumer.* **Description:** Keeps patients, family members, and medical professionals informed on recent advances in arthritis and related conditions.
Address: 8230 Walnut Hill, 11, Dallas, TX 75231. TEL 214-363-2812, FAX 214-692-8591. Ed., R&P Dr. Scott Zashin. Adv. contact Terri Groom. Circ: 1,000.

616.742 CAN ISSN 0820-9006
ARTHRITIS NEWS. Text in English. 1979. q. USD 14.95 domestic; USD 25.50 foreign. adv. bk.rev. **Document type:** *Magazine, Consumer.* **Description:** Provides articles on arthritis, its treatment, the latest research and coping strategies.
Formerly: C.A.R. Scope (0068-8258)
Related titles: French ed.: Arthro Express. ISSN 1198-7669.
Published by: Maclean Hunter Ltd., Maclean Hunter Bldg, 777 Bay St, Ste 405, Toronto, ON M5W 1A7, Canada. Circ: 20,000 (paid).

616.742 USA ISSN 1530-1524
ARTHRITIS SELF-MANAGEMENT. Text in English. 2000. bi-m. USD 9.97 domestic; USD 36 foreign (effective 2009). Index. 40 p./no.; back issues avail. **Document type:** *Magazine, Consumer.* **Description:** Provides how-to information for people with arthritis.
Published by: R.A. Rapaport Publishing, Inc., 150 W 22nd St, Ste 800, New York, NY 10011. TEL 212-989-0200, FAX 212-989-4786. **Subscr. to:** PO Box 56052, Boulder, CO 80321.

616.7 AUS ISSN 1833-0991
ARTHRITIS SERIES. Text in English. 2005. irreg., latest vol.5, 2007. price varies. back issues avail. **Document type:** *Monographic series, Academic/Scholarly.* **Description:** Contains articles that highlight the impact of osteoarthritis in Australia.
Related titles: Online - full text ed.: free (effective 2008).
Published by: Australian Institute of Health and Welfare, GPO Box 570, Canberra, ACT 2601, Australia. TEL 61-2-62441000, FAX 61-2-62441299, info@aihw.gov.au.

616.7 USA ISSN 0890-1120
RC933.A1
ARTHRITIS TODAY; the magazine for help and hope. Text in English. 1980. bi-m. USD 12.95 domestic; USD 18.95 in Canada; USD 20.95 elsewhere; free to members (effective 2009). adv. illus. back issues avail.; reprints avail. **Document type:** *Magazine, Consumer.* **Description:** Provides the people suffering from arthritis hope and help in a wide variety of areas.
Formerly (until 1987): The National Arthritis News (0882-9705)
Related titles: Online - full text ed.
Indexed: A22, A26, C06, C07, C08, C11, CHNI, CINAHL, E08, G08, H03, H11, H12, H13, HlthInd, I05, M01, M02, P02, P10, P20, P48, P53, P54, PQC, S09, T02.
—BLDSC (1733.877900).
Published by: Arthritis Foundation, PO Box 7669, Atlanta, GA 30357. TEL 404-872-7100, 800-283-7800, arthritisfoundation@arthritis.org, http://www.arthritis.org. Adv. contact Paige Elliott TEL 404-965-7602. B&W page USD 24,230, color page USD 34,745. **Subscr. to:** PO Box 581, Mt. Morris, IL 61054.

616.742 GBR ISSN 0969-7039
ARTHRITIS TODAY. Text in English. 1965. q. donation. charts; illus. **Document type:** *Journal, Consumer.* **Description:** Covers the reviews of ARC-funded research and its progress, along with advice for coping with arthritis from day-to-day.
Formerly (until 1992): Arthritis Research Today (0960-4499)
Related titles: Online - full text ed.
—BLDSC (1733.878000), IE, Ingenta.
Published by: Arthritis Research Campaign, Copeman House, St. Mary's Ct, St. Mary's Gate, Chesterfield, Derbys S41 7TD, United Kingdom. TEL 44-1246-558033, FAX 44-1246-558007, info@arc.org.uk. Circ: 125,000.

616.72 DEU ISSN 0176-5167
ARTHRITIS UND RHEUMA. Text in German. 1973. bi-m. EUR 126 to individuals; EUR 195 to institutions; EUR 63 to students; EUR 34 newsstand/cover (effective 2011). adv. **Document type:** *Journal, Academic/Scholarly.*
Formerly (until 1984): Rheumamedizin (0173-0517)
—IE.
Published by: Schattauer GmbH, Hoelderlinstr 3, Stuttgart, 70174, Germany. TEL 49-711-229870, FAX 49-711-2298750, info@schattauer.de, http://www.schattauer.com. Ed. Claudia Stein. Adv. contact Christoph Brocker. Circ: 7,513 (paid and controlled).

616.7 ESP ISSN 1577-3566
➤ **ASOCIACION ESPANOLA DE REUMATOLOGIA. SEMINARIOS.** Abstracts in Spanish, English; Text in Spanish. 2000. bi-m. EUR 97.87 combined subscription to individuals; EUR 247.78 combined subscription to institutions (effective 2009). adv. abstr.; bibl.; illus.; stat. back issues avail. **Document type:** *Journal, Academic/Scholarly.*
Related titles: Online - full text ed.: EUR 73.09 (effective 2009) (from ScienceDirect).
Indexed: A36, B21, CTA, EMBASE, ExcerpMed, R10, Reac, SCOPUS.
—CCC.
Published by: (Sociedad Espanola de Reumatologia), Elsevier Doyma (Subsidiary of: Elsevier Health Sciences), Traversa de Gracia 17-21, Barcelona, 08021, Spain. TEL 34-932-418800, FAX 34-932-419020, editorial@elsevier.com. Ed. A. Olive Marquez. Circ: 1,600.

616.742 DEU ISSN 0340-0719
BERUFSVERBAND DEUTSCHER RHEUMATOLOGEN. MITTEILUNGEN. Text in German. 1972. 8/yr. **Document type:** *Journal, Trade.*
—CCC.
Published by: Berufsverband Deutscher Rheumatologen, Lindenstr 2, Bad Aibling, 83043, Germany. TEL 49-8061-90580, FAX 49-8061-37921, info@bdrh.de, http://www.bdrh.de.

616.7 GBR
CODEN: BBPRFF
➤ **BEST PRACTICE & RESEARCH: CLINICAL RHEUMATOLOGY.** Text in English. 1975. bi-m. EUR 548 in Europe to institutions; JPY 58,900 in Japan to institutions; USD 484 elsewhere to institutions (effective 2012). adv. back issues avail. **Document type:** *Journal, Academic/Scholarly.* **Description:** Designed to keep the clinician or trainee informed of the latest developments and current recommended practice in the rapidly advancing fields of musculoskeletal conditions and science.
Former titles (until 2001): Bailliere's Best Practice & Research: Clinical Rheumatology (1521-6942); (until 1999): Bailliere's Clinical Rheumatology (0950-3579); Which superseded in part (in 1987): Clinics in Rheumatic Diseases (0307-742X)
Related titles: Online - full text ed.: ISSN 1532-1770 (from ScienceDirect).
Indexed: A22, A26, ASCA, B&BAb, B19, B21, C06, C07, CTA, CurCont, E01, EMBASE, ExcerpMed, FR, I05, ISR, ImmunAb, IndMed, Inpharma, MEDLINE, P30, R10, Reac, SCI, SCOPUS, T02, W07.
—BLDSC (1942.327831), CASDDS, GNLM, IE, Infotrieve, Ingenta, INIST. **CCC.**
Published by: Bailliere Tindall (Subsidiary of: Elsevier Health Sciences), The Blvd, Langford Ln, Kidlington, Oxford OX5 1GB, United Kingdom. TEL 44-1865-843000, FAX 44-1865-843010, directenquiries@elsevier.com. Ed. Dr. A D Woolf.

616.7 FRA ISSN 1959-285X
BOUGE TON RHUMATISME. Text in French. 1994. irreg. **Document type:** *Newsletter, Consumer.*
Formerly (until 2006): Association Francaise de Lutte Antirhumatismale. Journal (1259-6094)
Published by: Association Francaise de Lutte Antirhumatismale (A F L A R), 2 Rue Bourgon, Paris, 75013, France. TEL 33-1-45803000.

616.7 GBR ISSN 1367-8922
➤ **C P D RHEUMATOLOGY.** (Continuing Professional Development) Text in English. 1999. irreg., latest 2003. GBP 45 per vol. domestic to individuals; GBP 60 per vol. foreign to individuals; GBP 60 per vol. domestic to institutions; GBP 90 per vol. foreign to institutions (effective 2010). back issues avail. **Document type:** *Journal, Academic/Scholarly.*
Related titles: Online - full text ed.: GBP 30 per vol. (effective 2010).
Indexed: SCOPUS.
—CCC.
Published by: Rila Publications Ltd., 73 Newman St, London, W1A 4PG, United Kingdom. TEL 44-20-76311299, FAX 44-20-75807166, admin@rila.co.uk. Ed. Dr. Neil Hopkinson TEL 44-120-2704134.

616.7 CAN ISSN 1196-9679
RC927
CANADIAN RHEUMATOLOGY ASSOCIATION. JOURNAL. Text in English. 1999. 3/yr. free (effective 2005). back issues avail. **Description:** Articles range from discussions on diagnosis and management of rheumatic disease to case studies and updates on various CRA initiatives.
Formerly (until 1993): Canadian Rheumatism Association. Journal (1196-9660)
Related titles: Online - full text ed.; French ed.: Societe Canadienne de Rhumatologie. Journal. ISSN 1196-9687.
Published by: (Canadian Rheumatology Association/Societe Canadienne de Rhumatologie), S T A Communications Inc., 955 Blvd St Jean, Ste 306, Pointe Claire, PQ H9R 5K3, Canada. TEL 514-695-7623, FAX 514-695-8554. Pub. Paul F Brand.

616.7 USA ISSN 1947-6035
QM567
▼ ➤ **CARTILAGE.** Text in English. 2010 (Jan.). q. USD 317, GBP 187 combined subscription to institutions (print & online eds.); USD 311, GBP 183 to institutions (effective 2011). **Document type:** *Journal, Academic/Scholarly.* **Description:** Publishes articles related to the musculoskeletal system with particular attention to cartilage repair, development, function, degeneration, transplantation, and rehabilitation.
Related titles: Online - full text ed.: ISSN 1947-6043. USD 285, GBP 168 to institutions (effective 2011).
Indexed: A22, B21, CTA, E01, P30.
—CCC.
Published by: (International Cartilage Repair Society CHE), Sage Publications, Inc., 2455 Teller Rd, Thousand Oaks, CA 91320. TEL 805-499-9774, FAX 805-499-0871, info@sagepub.com. Ed. Roy D Altman.

616.7 CZE ISSN 1210-7905
CODEN: CRVMEG
➤ **CESKA REVMATOLOGIE/CZECH RHEUMATOLOGY.** Text in Czech, Slovak; Summaries in Czech, English. 1923. q. CZK 440, EUR 26.40 (effective 2010). adv. **Document type:** *Journal, Academic/Scholarly.* **Description:** Publishes novelties in the diagnosis and treatment of rheumatic diseases. Focuses on pharmacotherapy of rheumatic diseases and surgical treatment.
Supersedes in part (in 1993): Fysiatricky a Reumatologicky Vestnik (0072-0038)
Related titles: Online - full text ed.
Indexed: A01, EMBASE, ExcerpMed, R10, Reac, SCOPUS.
—BLDSC (3120.319000), CASDDS, GNLM. **CCC.**
Published by: (Ceska Lekarska Spolecnost J.E. Purkyne/Czech Medical Association), Nakladatelske Stredisko C L S J.E. Purkyne, Sokolska 31, Prague, 12026, Czech Republic. nts@cls.cz. Ed. Jiri Vencovsky. adv.: B&W page CZK 29,300, color page CZK 41,200; 244 x 166. Circ: 850.

616.7 JPN ISSN 0916-6033
CHUBU RYUMACHI/CHUBU RHEUMATISM ASSOCIATION. JOURNAL. Text in Japanese. 1970. s-a. **Document type:** *Journal, Academic/Scholarly.*
Formerly (until 1989): Tokai Ryumachi (0286-0309)
Published by: Chubu Ryumachi Gakkai/Chubu Rheumatism Association, Aichi Medical University,, Karimata 21, Yazako Nagakute, Aichi-gun, Aichi, 480-1195, Japan. TEL 86-561-623311, FAX 86-561-634707.

616.7 ITA ISSN 0392-856X
RC927.A1 CODEN: CERHDP
➤ **CLINICAL AND EXPERIMENTAL RHEUMATOLOGY.** Text in English. 1983. bi-m. EUR 185 combined subscription in Europe to individuals (print & online eds.); EUR 215 combined subscription elsewhere to institutions (print & online eds.) (effective 2011). Supplement avail.; back issues avail. **Document type:** *Journal, Academic/Scholarly.*
Related titles: Online - full text ed.: ISSN 1593-098X. EUR 60 (effective 2007).
Indexed: A22, ASCA, BIOBASE, CurCont, EMBASE, ExcerpMed, IABS, ISR, IndMed, Inpharma, Kidney, MEDLINE, MS&D, P30, P35, R10, Reac, SCI, SCOPUS, W07.
—BLDSC (3286.252700), CASDDS, GNLM, IE, Infotrieve, Ingenta, INIST.
Published by: Pacini Editore SpA, Via A Gherardesca 1, Ospedaletto, PI 56121, Italy. TEL 39-050-313011, FAX 39-050-3130300, pacini.editore@pacinieditore.it, http://www.pacinimedicina.it.

616.742 GBR ISSN 0770-3198
RC927 CODEN: CLRHD6
➤ **CLINICAL RHEUMATOLOGY.** Text in English. 1946. bi-m. EUR 1,313, USD 1,347 combined subscription to institutions (print & online eds.) (effective 2012). adv. abstr.; illus. Supplement avail.; reprint service avail. from PSC. **Document type:** *Journal, Academic/Scholarly.*
Formerly (until 1982): Acta Rhumatologica (0250-4642)
Related titles: Online - full text ed.: ISSN 1434-9949 (from IngentaConnect).
Indexed: A01, A03, A08, A20, A22, A26, A34, A36, AMED, ASCA, Agr, BIOBASE, CA, CABA, ChemAb, CurCont, D01, E01, E12, EMBASE, ExcerpMed, F08, F11, F12, GH, H12, H16, H17, IABS, IndMed, IndVet, Inpharma, MEDLINE, N02, N03, P20, P22, P30, P33, P35, P39, P48, P54, PQC, R08, R10, R12, R13, RA&MP, RM&VM, Reac, SCI, SCOPUS, T02, T05, VS, W07.
—BLDSC (3286.374600), CASDDS, GNLM, IE, Infotrieve, Ingenta, INIST. **CCC.**
Published by: (Association Royale des Societes Scientifiques Medicales Belges/Koninklijke Vereniging van de Belgische Medische Wetenschappelijke Genootschappen BEL), Springer U K (Subsidiary of: Springer Science+Business Media), Ashbourne House, The Guildway, Old Portsmouth Rd, Guildford, Surrey GU3 1LP, United Kingdom. TEL 44-1483-734433, FAX 44-1483-734411, postmaster@svl.co.uk. Ed. Paul Davis. **Subscr. in the Americas to:** Springer New York LLC, Journal Fulfillment, PO Box 2485, Secaucus, NJ 07096. TEL 800-777-4643, 201-348-4033, FAX 201-348-4505, journals-ny@springer.com, http://www.springer.com; **Subscr. to:** Springer Distribution Center, Kundenservice Zeitschriften, Haberstr 7, Heidelberg 69126, Germany. TEL 49-6221-3454303, FAX 49-6221-3454229, subscriptions@springer.com.

616.748 CAN ISSN 0828-301X
CONNECTIONS. Text in English. 1984. q. free. bk.rev. illus. back issues avail. **Document type:** *Newsletter.* **Description:** Covers research news, fund raising, client profiles and disability issues.
Related titles: French ed.: Connexions.
Published by: Muscular Dystrophy Association of Canada, 2345 Yonge St, 9th Fl, Toronto, ON M4P 2E5, Canada. TEL 416-488-0030, FAX 416-488-7523. Ed. M W Thompson. Circ: 16,000 (controlled).

616.7 USA
RC927
CURRENT DIAGNOSIS & TREATMENT IN RHEUMATOLOGY. Text in English. 2004. biennial, latest 2006, 2nd ed. USD 70.95 per issue (effective 2010). **Document type:** *Monographic series, Trade.*
Formerly: Current Rheumatology Diagnosis and Treatment (1547-8998)
Published by: McGraw-Hill Education (Subsidiary of: McGraw-Hill Companies, Inc.), 148 Princeton-Hightstown Rd, Hightstown, NJ 08520. TEL 609-426-5793, FAX 609-426-7917, customer.service@mcgraw-hill.com, http://www.mheducation.com/.

016.7 GBR ISSN 0261-3360
CODEN: CLRMDL
➤ **CURRENT MEDICAL LITERATURE. RHEUMATOLOGY.** Text in English. 1982. q. GBP 60 to individuals; GBP 130 to institutions; free to qualified personnel (effective 2009). back issues avail. **Document type:** *Journal, Academic/Scholarly.* **Description:** Aims to provide physicians and allied healthcare professionals with rapid access to expert commentary and analysis on key topics in rheumatology.
Related titles: Online - full text ed.: ISSN 1759-8206; ◆ Polish Translation: Przeglad Pismiennictwa Zagranicznego. Reumatologia. ISSN 1895-2356.
Indexed: A01, A03, A08, CA, T02.
—CCC.
Published by: Remedica Medical Education and Publishing Ltd., Commonwealth House, 1 New Oxford St, London, WC1A 1NU, United Kingdom. TEL 44-20-77592999, FAX 44-20-77592951, info@remedica.com, http://www.remedica.com. Ed. Nicola Seymour.

616.7 USA ISSN 1040-8711
RC925.A1 CODEN: CORHES
CURRENT OPINION IN RHEUMATOLOGY. Text in English. 1989. bi-m. USD 1,018 domestic to institutions; USD 1,094 foreign to institutions (effective 2011). adv. bibl.; illus. back issues avail.; reprints avail. **Document type:** *Journal, Academic/Scholarly.* **Description:** Covers key subjects, spanning topics such as rheumatoid arthritis, vasculitis syndromes, epidemiology and health-related services, crystal deposition diseases, spondyloarthropathies, osteoarthritis, and pediatric and heritable disorders.
Related titles: Online - full text ed.: ISSN 1531-6963. USD 249 to individuals (effective 2011); Optical Disk - DVD ed.: Current Opinion in Rheumatology, with Evaluated MEDLINE. ISSN 1080-8175. 1995.
Indexed: A20, A22, B21, BIOBASE, BIOSIS Prev, C06, C07, C08, CIN, CINAHL, CTA, ChemAb, ChemTitl, ChemoAb, CurCont, E01, EMBASE, ExcerpMed, IABS, ISR, ImmunAb, IndMed, Inpharma, MEDLINE, MycolAb, NSA, P30, P35, R10, Reac, SCI, SCOPUS, W07.
—BLDSC (3500.778000), CASDDS, GNLM, IE, Infotrieve, Ingenta, INIST. **CCC.**
Published by: Lippincott Williams & Wilkins (Subsidiary of: Wolters Kluwer N.V.), 530 Walnut St, Philadelphia, PA 19106. TEL 215-521-8300, FAX 215-521-8902, customerservice@lww.com, http://www.lww.com. Ed. Gary S Hoffman. Pub. Ian Burgess. Circ: 1,351.

CURRENT REVIEWS IN MUSCULOSKELETAL MEDICINE. *see* MEDICAL SCIENCES—Orthopedics And Traumatology

616.723 USA ISSN 1534-6307
RC927
➤ **CURRENT RHEUMATOLOGY REPORTS (ONLINE).** Text in English. 1999. bi-m. EUR 954, USD 1,270 to institutions (effective 2012). back issues avail. **Document type:** *Journal, Academic/Scholarly.* **Description:** Provides views of experts on advances in the rheumatology field.
Media: Online - full text.
—CCC.
Published by: Current Medicine Group LLC (Subsidiary of: Springer Science+Business Media), 400 Market St, Ste 700, Philadelphia, PA 19106. TEL 215-574-2266, FAX 215-574-2225, service-ny@springer.com, http://www.current-medicine.com/. Ed. Bruce Cronstein.

616.7 NLD ISSN 1573-3971
➤ **CURRENT RHEUMATOLOGY REVIEWS.** Text in English. 2005 (Jan.). q. USD 480 to institutions (print or online ed.) (effective 2012). adv. back issues avail.; reprints avail. **Document type:** *Journal, Academic/Scholarly.* **Description:** Publishes frontier reviews on all the latest advances on rheumatology and its related areas such as pharmacology, pathogenesis, epidemiology, clinical care, and therapy.
Related titles: Online - full text ed.: ISSN 1875-6360 (from IngentaConnect).
Indexed: A01, B21, CA, CTA, EMBASE, ExcerpMed, ImmunAb, P30, R10, Reac, SCOPUS, T02.
—IE, Ingenta. **CCC.**
Published by: Bentham Science Publishers Ltd., PO Box 294, Bussum, 1400 AG, Netherlands. TEL 31-35-6923800, FAX 31-35-6980150, sales@bentham.org, http://www.bentham.org. Ed. Swamy Venuturupalli. **Subscr. to:** Bentham Science Publishers Ltd., c/o Richard E Morrissy, PO Box 446, Oak Park, IL 60301. TEL 312-413-5867, FAX 312-996-7107, subscriptions@bentham.org.

616.742 DEU ISSN 0340-0662
DEUTSCHE GESELLSCHAFT FUER RHEUMATOLOGIE. MITTEILUNGEN. Text in German. 1971. 8/yr. **Document type:** *Journal, Trade.*
—CCC.
Published by: Deutsche Gesellschaft fuer Rheumatologie, Luisenstr 41, Berlin, 10117, Germany. TEL 49-30-24048470, FAX 49-30-24048479, info@dgrh.de, http://dgrh.de.

616.7 FRA ISSN 1960-8004
ECHORHUMATO. Variant title: Echo Rhumato. Text in French. 2007. q. **Document type:** *Journal.*
Published by: Mediquid, 122 Rue d'Aguesseau, Boulogne-Billancourt, 92641, France. TEL 33-1-55389182, http://www.mediquid.fr.

616.7 EGY ISSN 1110-1164
THE EGYPTIAN RHEUMATOLOGIST. Text in English. 1979. s-a. **Document type:** *Journal, Academic/Scholarly.*
Related titles: Online - full text ed.: (from ScienceDirect).
—CCC.
Published by: (The Egyptian Society for Joint Diseases and Arthritis), Cairo University, Faculty of Medicine, Egyptian Society for Joint Diseases & Arthritis, Department of Rheumatology & Rehabilitation, Giza, Egypt. Ed. Dr. Basel Zorqani.

616.7 EGY ISSN 1110-161X
EGYPTIAN RHEUMATOLOGY AND REHABILITATION. Text in English. 1972. q. EGP 50 to non-members; EGP 30 to members (effective 2003). **Document type:** *Journal, Academic/Scholarly.*
Supersedes in part (in 1972): Egyptian Association of Physical Medicine and Rehabilitation. Journal (0253-9667)
Published by: Egyptian Society for Rheumatology and Rehabilitation, 6 Lofty El-Sayed Str., El-Demerdash Station, Staff member housing of Ain-Shams University, Bldg.6, Abbasiya, Cairo, Egypt. TEL 20-2-4856957, rheumasociety@yahoo.com. Ed. Dr. Naglaa Gadallah.

616.7 617.3 FRA ISSN 1286-935X
➤ **ENCYCLOPEDIE MEDICO-CHIRURGICALE. APARATO LOCOMOTOR.** Text in Spanish. 1998. 6 base vols. plus q. updates. EUR 1,124.42 (effective 2003). bibl.; illus. **Document type:** *Academic/Scholarly.* **Description:** Offers an up-to-date reference in topics concerning locomotor dysfunctions.
Related titles: ◆ French ed.: Encyclopedie Medico-Chirurgicale. Appareil Locomoteur. ISSN 0246-0521.
—CCC.
Published by: Elsevier Masson (Subsidiary of: Elsevier Health Sciences), 62 Rue Camille Desmoulins, Issy les Moulineaux, Cedex 92442, France. TEL 33-1-71165500, FAX 33-1-71165600, infos@elsevier-masson.fr, http://www.elsevier-masson.fr.

616.7 617.3 FRA ISSN 0246-0521
➤ **ENCYCLOPEDIE MEDICO-CHIRURGICALE. APPAREIL LOCOMOTEUR**; vers le retour a la motricite. Cover title: Traite d'Appareil Locomoteur. Variant title: Encyclopedie Medico-Chirurgicale, Instantanes Medicaux. Appareil Locomoteur. Receuil de l'Encyclopedie Medico-Chirurgicale. Appareil Locomoteur. Text in French. 1961. 7 base vols. plus q. updates. EUR 1,311.83 (effective 2003). bibl.; illus. **Document type:** *Academic/Scholarly.* **Description:** Offers an up-to-date reference in topics concerning rheumatology.
Formed by the merger of (1937-1960): Encyclopedie Medico-Chirurgicale. Os, Articulations, Fractures, Luxations (0246-0645); (1938-1960): Encyclopedie Medico-Chirurgicale. Pathologie des Membres (0246-0718)
Related titles: ◆ Spanish ed.: Encyclopedie Medico-Chirurgicale. Aparato Locomotor. ISSN 1286-935X.
—INIST.
Published by: Elsevier Masson (Subsidiary of: Elsevier Health Sciences), 62 Rue Camille Desmoulins, Issy les Moulineaux, Cedex 92442, France. TEL 33-1-71165500, FAX 33-1-71165600, infos@elsevier-masson.fr.

➤ **ENCYCLOPEDIE MEDICO-CHIRURGICALE. RADIOLOGIE ET IMAGERIE MEDICALE. MUSCULOSQUELETTIQUE - NEUROLOGIQUE - MAXILLOFACIALE.** *see* MEDICAL SCIENCES—Radiology And Nuclear Medicine

➤ **EXCERPTA MEDICA. SECTION 31: ARTHRITIS AND RHEUMATISM.** *see* MEDICAL SCIENCES—Abstracting, Bibliographies, Statistics

616.7 USA ISSN 1936-6884
RC927.3
FIBROMYALGIA AWARE. Text in English. 200?. 3/yr. USD 35 membership (effective 2007). **Document type:** *Magazine, Consumer.* **Description:** Features news and support information for people and families of those diagnosed with fibromyalgia.
Published by: National Fibromyalgia Association, 2200 N Glassell St, Ste A, Orange, CA 92865. TEL 714-921-0150, FAX 714-921-6920, http://www.fmaware.org.

616.74 USA
FIBROMYALGIA HEALTH LETTER. Text in English. 1998. bi-m. **Document type:** *Newsletter.* **Description:** Provides information, advice and research news about fibromyalgia, the second-most commonly diagnosed musculoskeletal disorder.
Formerly (until 1999): Fibromyalgia Wellness Letter (1522-3825)
Published by: Arthritis Foundation, PO Box 7669, Atlanta, GA 30357. TEL 404-965-7888, 404-872-7100, 800-283-7800, atmail@arthritis.org, http://www.arthritis.org.

616.7 USA ISSN 1554-7884
FIBROMYALGIA NETWORK; journal for fibromyalgia syndrome/chronic fatigue syndrome patients. Text in English. 1988. q. USD 28 domestic membership; USD 30 in Canada membership; USD 33 elsewhere membership (effective 2007). bk.rev. 20 p./no. 3 cols./p.; back issues avail. **Document type:** *Newsletter, Consumer.* **Description:** Provides information for patients and physicians on fibromyalgia syndrome (FMS) and chronic fatigue syndrome (CFS), major disabling, chronic conditions characterized by multiple areas of pain plus fatigue.
Address: PO Box 31750, Tucson, AZ 85751-1750. TEL 520-290-5508, 800-853-2929, FAX 520-290-5550, inquiry@fmnetnews.com. Circ: 40,000.

616.7 CHE
FORUM R. Text in French, German, Italian. q. CHF 12.30 (effective 2007). adv. **Document type:** *Newsletter, Consumer.*
Published by: Rheumaliga Schweiz, Josefstr 92, Zurich, 8005, Switzerland. TEL 41-44-4874000, FAX 41-44-4874019, info@rheumaliga.ch, http://www.rheumaliga.ch. Ed. Andre Aeschlimann. adv.: B&W page CHF 2,200, color page CHF 2,860; trim 210 x 297. Circ: 35,000 (controlled).

616.7 ITA ISSN 1129-8731
GIORNALE ITALIANO DI MALATTIE REUMATICHE. Abbreviated title: G I M a R. Text in Italian. 1999. s-a. EUR 47 in Europe to institutions; EUR 53 elsewhere to institutions (effective 2009). **Document type:** *Journal, Academic/Scholarly.*
Published by: Mattioli 1885 SpA, Via Coduro 1, Fidenza, PR 43036, Italy. TEL 39-0524-84547, FAX 39-0524-84751, http://www.mattioli1885.com. Eds. Fausto Salaffi, Alessandro Ciocci. Circ: 20,000.

616.742 GBR ISSN 1741-833X
HANDS ON. Text in English. 1959; N.S. 1985; N.S. 1994. 3/yr. free (effective 2009). back issues avail. **Document type:** *Journal, Academic/Scholarly.* **Description:** Intended to provide succinct and practical advice for general practitioners and hospital doctors about the diagnosis and management of common rheumatic conditions.
Formerly (until 2003): Rheumatic Disease: In Practice (Series 4) (1469-3089); (until 2000): Reports on Rheumatic Diseases. Series 3. Practical Problems (1351-4873); (until 1994): Reports on Rheumatic Diseases. Series 2. Practical Problems (1351-3060); Which superseded in part: Reports on Rheumatic Diseases (0957-0381); Which superseded (in 1985): Rheumatic Diseases Report; Which was formerly (until 1983): Reports on Rheumatic Diseases (0048-7279)
Related titles: Online - full text ed.
—BLDSC (4262.045750), IE, Ingenta.
Published by: Arthritis Research Campaign, Copeman House, St. Mary's Ct, St. Mary's Gate, Chesterfield, Derbys S41 7TD, United Kingdom. TEL 44-1246-558033, FAX 44-1246-558007, info@arc.org.uk. Circ: 40,000.

616.7 CAN ISSN 1710-4300
L'I A L A EN ACTION!. (Institut de l'Appareil Locomoteur et de l'Arthrite) Text in French. 2003. irreg. **Document type:** *Newsletter, Trade.*
Media: Online - full text. **Related titles:** English ed.: I M H A on the Move!. ISSN 1710-4297.
Published by: Canadian Institutes of Health Research, Institute of Musculoskeletal Health and Arthritis/Instituts de Recherche en Sante au Canada, Institut de l'Appareil Locomoteur et de l'Arthrite (I R S C - I A L A), Rm 6230, Medical Sciences Building, 1 King's College Circle, Toronto, ON M5S 1A8, Canada. TEL 416-978-4220, FAX 416-978-3954, info@cihr-irsc.gc.ca, http://www.cihr-irsc.gc.ca/imha-iala.html.

616.7 USA ISSN 2090-5467
▼ ➤ **I S R N RHEUMATOLOGY.** (International Scholarly Research Network) Text in English. 2011. q. **Document type:** *Journal, Academic/Scholarly.*
Related titles: Online - full text ed.: ISSN 2090-5475. free (effective 2011).
Published by: Hindawi Publishing Corporation, 410 Park Ave, 15th Fl, PMB 287, New York, NY 10022. FAX 215-893-4392, 866-446-3294, hindawi@hindawi.com.

616.7 NLD ISSN 2210-3511
IN BALANS. Text in Dutch. 199?. q. EUR 15 (effective 2010). **Document type:** *Magazine, Consumer.*
Published by: Nederlandse Paget Patienten Vereniging, Rhijdstraat 27, Baexem, 6095 BJ, Netherlands. TEL 31-475-451619, info@paget.nl, http://www.paget.nl. Eds. J Eikelboom, W Blom.

616.7 NLD ISSN 1381-7434
IN BEWEGING. Text in Dutch. 1979. m. EUR 19.35 (effective 2010). adv. **Document type:** *Magazine, Consumer.*
Published by: Reumapatientenbond, Postbus 1370, Amersfoort, 3800 BJ, Netherlands. TEL 31-33-4616364, FAX 31-33-4651200, info@reumabond.nl, http://www.reumabond.nl. adv.: B&W page EUR 1,055, color page EUR 1,791; trim 210 x 297. Circ: 17,000.

616.7 IND ISSN 0973-3698
INDIAN JOURNAL OF RHEUMATOLOGY. Text in English. 1982. q. **Document type:** *Journal, Academic/Scholarly.*
Formerly (until 1982): Indian Rheumatology Association. Journal (0971-5045)
Related titles: Online - full text ed.: (from ScienceDirect).
Indexed: EMBASE, ExcerpMed, R10, Reac, SCOPUS, T02.
—CCC.
Published by: Indian Rheumatology Association, c/o Dr Binoy J Paul, Secretary IRA, Golf Link Road, Chevayur PO, Calicut, Kerala 673 017, India. TEL 91-495-2354876, secretary.ira@gmail.com. Ed. S Shankar TEL 91-20-26332781.

616.742 PRT ISSN 1645-6009
INSTITUTO PORTUGUES DE REUMATOLOGIA. JORNAL. Text in Portuguese. 2002. q. **Document type:** *Journal, Academic/Scholarly.*
Published by: (Instituto Portugues de Reumatologia), Revisfarma Edicoes Medicas Lda., Alameda Antonio Sergio, Edificio Amadeu S Cardoso 22, Miraflores Alges, Alges, 1495-132, Portugal. http://revisfarma.pai.pt.

616.7 GBR ISSN 1478-856X
➤ **INTERNATIONAL JOURNAL OF ADVANCES IN RHEUMATOLOGY.** Text in English. 2003. q. GBP 100 to individuals; GBP 130 to institutions; free to qualified personnel (effective 2009). back issues avail. **Document type:** *Journal, Academic/Scholarly.* **Description:** Provides rapid access for busy physicians to a critical and clinically relevant review of the developments that will have most impact on their day-to-day practice.
Related titles: Online - full text ed.: ISSN 2040-3895.
Indexed: A01, T02.
—BLDSC (4541.574000), IE, Ingenta. **CCC.**
Published by: Remedica Medical Education and Publishing Ltd., Commonwealth House, 1 New Oxford St, London, WC1A 1NU, United Kingdom. TEL 44-20-77592999, FAX 44-20-77592951, info@remedica.com, http://www.remedica.com. Ed. Scott Millar. Pub. Simon Kirsch.

616.7 GBR ISSN 1758-4272
➤ **INTERNATIONAL JOURNAL OF CLINICAL RHEUMATOLOGY.** Text in English. 2006. bi-m. GBP 695 combined subscription domestic (print & online eds.); USD 1,220 combined subscription in North America (print & online eds.); JPY 129,000 combined subscription in Japan (print & online eds.); EUR 975 combined subscription elsewhere (print & online eds.) (effective 2011). adv. back issues avail.; reprints avail. **Document type:** *Journal, Academic/Scholarly.* **Description:** Covers key advances in the field of clinical rheumatology reported and analyzed by international experts.
Formerly (until 2009): Future Rheumatology (Print) (1746-0816)
Related titles: Online - full text ed.: ISSN 1758-4280. GBP 615 domestic to institutions; USD 1,080 in North America to institutions; JPY 115,000 in Japan to institutions; EUR 865 elsewhere to institutions (effective 2011) (from IngentaConnect).
Indexed: A26, B21, CA, CTA, E08, EMBASE, ExcerpMed, H11, H12, I05, ImmunAb, P20, P30, P48, P54, PQC, SCOPUS.
—BLDSC (4060.620700), IE, Ingenta. **CCC.**

Published by: Future Medicine Ltd. (Subsidiary of: Future Science Ltd.), Unitec House, 2 Albert Pl, London, N3 1QB, United Kingdom. TEL 44-20-83716080, FAX 44-20-83716099, info@futuremedicine.com. Eds. Christine Forder, Elisa Manzotti TEL 44-20-83716090. Pub. David Hughes. Circ: 420.

616.7 AUS ISSN 1756-1841
RC297

➤ **INTERNATIONAL JOURNAL OF RHEUMATIC DISEASES.** Text in English. 1997. 3/yr. GBP 257 in United Kingdom to institutions; EUR 325 in Europe to institutions; USD 414 in the Americas to institutions; USD 501 elsewhere to institutions; GBP 296 combined subscription in United Kingdom to institutions (print & online eds.); EUR 375 combined subscription in Europe to institutions (print & online eds.); USD 476 combined subscription in the Americas to institutions (print & online eds.); USD 576 combined subscription elsewhere to institutions (print & online eds.) (effective 2012). reprint service avail. from PSC. **Document type:** *Journal, Academic/Scholarly.* **Description:** Contains original articles on clinical or experimental research pertinent to the rheumatic diseases, work on connective tissue diseases and other immune and allergic disorders.
Formerly (until 2008): A P L A R Journal of Rheumatology (0219-0494)
Related titles: Online - full text ed.: ISSN 1756-185X. GBP 257 in United Kingdom to institutions; EUR 325 in Europe to institutions; USD 414 in the Americas to institutions; USD 501 elsewhere to institutions (effective 2012) (from IngentaConnect).
Indexed: A01, A03, A08, A22, A26, B21, CA, CTA, E01, EMBASE, ExcerpMed, ImmunAb, MEDLINE, P30, R10, Reac, SCI, SCOPUS, T02, W07.
—BLDSC (1568.617500), IE, Ingenta. **CCC.**
Published by: (Asia Pacific League of Associations for Rheumatology SGP), Wiley-Blackwell Publishing Asia (Subsidiary of: Wiley-Blackwell Publishing Ltd.), 155 Cremorne St, Richmond, VIC 3121, Australia. TEL 61-3-92743100, FAX 61-3-92743101, subs@blackwellpublishingasia.com, http://www.wiley.com/WileyCDA/. Ed. C S Lau. **Subscr. to:** PO Box 378, Carlton South, VIC 3053, Australia. subscriptions@blacksci-asia.com.au.

616.7 USA ISSN 1687-9260

➤ **INTERNATIONAL JOURNAL OF RHEUMATOLOGY.** Text in English. 2008. irreg. USD 295 (effective 2011). **Document type:** *Journal, Academic/Scholarly.* **Description:** Publishes original research articles as well as review articles in all areas of rheumatology.
Related titles: Online - full text ed.: ISSN 1687-9279. 2008. free (effective 2011).
Indexed: A01, A36, B21, CA, GH, ImmunAb, P30, T02.
Published by: Hindawi Publishing Corporation, 410 Park Ave, 15th Fl, PMB 287, New York, NY 10022. FAX 215-893-4392, 866-446-3294, orders@hindawi.com.

616.7 USA ISSN 1528-8412
RC927

➤ **THE INTERNET JOURNAL OF RHEUMATOLOGY.** Text in English. 2002. s-a. free (effective 2011). adv. bk.rev. back issues avail. **Document type:** *Journal, Academic/Scholarly.* **Description:** Provides information from the field of rheumatology; contains original articles, reviews, case reports, streaming slide shows, streaming videos, letters to the editor, press releases and meeting information.
Media: Online - full text.
Indexed: A01, A02, A03, A08, A26, C06, CA, G08, H11, H12, I05, T02.
Published by: Internet Scientific Publications, Llc., 23 Rippling Creek Dr, Sugar Land, TX 77479. TEL 832-443-1193, FAX 281-240-1533, wenker@ispub.com. Ed. Dr. Bradley J. Bloom.

616.7 USA ISSN 1076-1608
CODEN: JCRHFM

➤ **JOURNAL OF CLINICAL RHEUMATOLOGY**; practical reports on rheumatic & musculoskeletal diseases. Abbreviated title: J C R. Text in English. 1995. 8/yr. USD 654 domestic to institutions; USD 684 foreign to institutions (effective 2011). adv. back issues avail.; reprints avail. **Document type:** *Journal, Academic/Scholarly.* **Description:** Contains information on patient care in a clinically oriented format.
Related titles: Online - full text ed.: ISSN 1536-7355. USD 325 domestic for academic site license; USD 325 foreign for academic site license; USD 362.50 domestic for corporate site license; USD 362.50 foreign for corporate site license (effective 2002).
Indexed: A20, C06, C07, CurCont, EMBASE, ExcerpMed, Inpharma, MEDLINE, P30, P35, R10, Reac, SCI, SCOPUS, W07.
—GNLM, IE, Infotrieve, Ingenta, INIST. **CCC.**
Published by: Lippincott Williams & Wilkins (Subsidiary of: Wolters Kluwer N.V.), Two Commerce Sq, 2001 Market St, Philadelphia, PA 19103. TEL 215-521-8300, FAX 215-521-8902, customerservice@lww.com, http://www.lww.com. Ed. Dr. H Ralph Schumacher TEL 215-823-4480. Pub. Jason Pointe. Adv. contact Bethann H Sands TEL 215-521-8399. Circ: 672.

616.7 GBR ISSN 2043-0248

▼➤ **THE JOURNAL OF CLINICAL RHEUMATOLOGY AND MUSCULOSKELETAL MEDICINE.** Abbreviated title: J C R M M. Text in English. 2010. s-a. free (effective 2011). back issues avail. **Document type:** *Journal, Academic/Scholarly.* **Description:** Covers clinical and experimental aspects of rheumatic diseases and musculoskeletal disorders.
Related titles: Online - full text ed.: ISSN 2043-0256.
Published by: San Lucas Medical Ltd., 11-12 Freetrade House, Lowther Rd, Stanmore, Middlesex HA7 1EP, United Kingdom. TEL 44-20-32869384, support@sanlucasmedical.com, http://www.sanlucasmedical.com. Ed. Oneal Ayson.

➤ **THE JOURNAL OF MUSCULOSKELETAL MEDICINE.** *see* MEDICAL SCIENCES—Orthopedics And Traumatology

➤ **JOURNAL OF MUSCULOSKELETAL PAIN**; innovations in research, theory & clinical practice. *see* MEDICAL SCIENCES—Orthopedics And Traumatology

➤ **JOURNAL OF MUSCULOSKELETAL RESEARCH.** *see* MEDICAL SCIENCES—Orthopedics And Traumatology

616.7 USA ISSN 1944-0421

▼ **JOURNAL OF PROLOTHERAPY.** Abbreviated title: J O P. Text in English. 2009 (Feb.). q. USD 100 combined subscription (print & online eds.); USD 25 combined subscription per issue (print & online eds.) (effective 2010). adv. **Document type:** *Journal, Academic/Scholarly.* **Description:** Provides readers with new information on Prolotherapy. Serves as a forum for physicians and patients alike to tell their stories.
Related titles: Online - full text ed.: ISSN 1944-043X. 2009 (Feb.).
Published by: Beulah Land Press, 715 Lake St, Ste 400, Oak Park, IL 60301. TEL 708-848-5011, FAX 708-848-0978, http://www.benuts.com. Ed. Ross A Hauser.

616.742 CAN ISSN 0315-162X
RC927 CODEN: JRHUA9

➤ **JOURNAL OF RHEUMATOLOGY.** Text in English. 1974. m. CAD 260 domestic to individuals (print & online eds.); USD 260 foreign to individuals (print & online eds.); CAD 445 domestic to institutions (print & online eds.); USD 445 foreign to institutions (print & online eds.); CAD 125 domestic to students (print & online eds.); USD 125 foreign to students (print & online eds.) (effective 2009). adv. bk.rev. index. back issues avail. **Document type:** *Journal, Academic/Scholarly.* **Description:** Includes original research on rheumatology and related fields. Covers case studies, editorials on new therapies, epidemiology, economics and ethics.
Related titles: Microform ed.: (from PQC); Online - full text ed.: ISSN 1499-2752. 2001; Supplement(s): Journal of Rheumatology. Supplement. ISSN 0380-0903.
Indexed: A20, A22, A36, ASCA, B25, BIOBASE, BIOSIS Prev, C06, C07, C08, CABA, CIN, CINAHL, ChPerl, ChemAb, ChemTitl, CurCont, D01, DBA, DentInd, DokArb, E12, EMBASE, ExcerpMed, F09, FR, GH, I12, IABS, IDIS, INI, ISR, IndMed, Inpharma, JW-D, Kidney, MEDLINE, MS&D, MycolAb, N02, N03, P30, P33, P35, P39, R08, R10, R12, RM&VM, Reac, RefZh, SCI, SCOPUS, SoyAb, T05, W07.
—BLDSC (5052.070000), CASDDS, GNLM, IE, Infotrieve, Ingenta, INIST. **CCC.**
Published by: Journal of Rheumatology Publishing Co. Ltd., 365 Bloor East, Ste 901, Toronto, ON M4W 3L4, Canada. TEL 416-967-5155, FAX 416-967-7556. Ed. Dr. Duncan A Gordon TEL 416-967-5155. Adv. contact Peter Palmer. Circ: 3,500. **Subscr. in US to:** Allen Press Inc., PO Box 1897, Lawrence, KS 66044.

616.742 NZL ISSN 1175-8953

JUICE. Text in English. 1973 (Oct.). q. NZD 35 membership (effective 2008). adv. index. back issues avail. **Document type:** *Newsletter, Consumer.* **Description:** Covers arthritis care, management and news.
Former titles (until 2002): Arthritis News (1171-8986); (until 1983): Arthritis & Rheumatism Foundation of New Zealand. Newsletter
Published by: Arthritis Foundation of N Z Inc., PO Box 10-020, Wellington, New Zealand. TEL 64-4-4721427, FAX 64-4-4727066. Ed. Angela Satherley. adv.: page NZD 550. Circ: 15,000.

KANSETSUKYO/ARTHROSCOPY. *see* MEDICAL SCIENCES—Orthopedics And Traumatology

616.7 617.3 JPN ISSN 0915-1125

KOTSU KANSETSU JINTAI/JOURNAL OF MUSCULOSKELETAL SYSTEM. Text in Japanese. 1988. m. JPY 34,020 per issue (effective 2007). **Document type:** *Journal, Academic/Scholarly.*
Published by: ArcMedium, 7-1 Sanbancho, Chiyoda-ku, Asahi Sanbancho #406, Tokyo, 102-0075, Japan. TEL 81-3-52100821, FAX 81-3-52100824, arc21@arcmedium.co.jp, http://www.arcmedium.co.jp/index.html.

616.7 FRA ISSN 0761-5027

➤ **LA LETTRE DU RHUMATOLOGUE.** Text in French. 1983. m. EUR 114 in Europe to individuals; EUR 114 DOM-TOM to individuals; EUR 114 in Africa to individuals; EUR 126 elsewhere to individuals; EUR 138 in Europe to institutions; EUR 138 DOM-TOM to institutions; EUR 138 in Africa to institutions; EUR 150 elsewhere to institutions (effective 2009). Supplement avail. **Document type:** *Academic/Scholarly.*
—INIST. **CCC.**
Published by: Edimark S.A.S., 2 Rue Sainte-Marie, Courbevoie, Cedex 92418, France. TEL 33-1-41458000, FAX 33-1-41458025, contact@edimark.fr. Ed. B Combe. Pub. Claudie Damour-Terrasson.

616.7 PRT

▼ **LIGACOES.** Text in Portuguese. 2009. bi-m. **Document type:** *Magazine, Trade.*
Published by: Sociedade Reumatologica Portuguesa, Av de Berlim 33B, Lisbon, 1800-033, Portugal. TEL 351-21-3534395, FAX 351-21-3159780, info@spreumatologia.pt, www.spreumatologia.pt.

LOOSE CONNECTIONS. *see* SOCIAL SERVICES AND WELFARE

616.7 GBR ISSN 0961-2033
RC924.5.L85 CODEN: LUPUES

➤ **LUPUS.** Text in English. 1991. 14/yr. USD 1,761, GBP 952 combined subscription to institutions (print & online eds.); USD 1,726, GBP 933 to institutions (effective 2011). adv. back issues avail.; reprint service avail. from PSC. **Document type:** *Journal, Academic/Scholarly.* **Description:** Comprehensive information on all aspects of lupus care and research.
Related titles: Online - full text ed.: ISSN 1477-0962. USD 1,585, GBP 857 to institutions (effective 2011).
Indexed: A01, A03, A08, A22, AIDS&CR, ASCA, B21, B25, BIOBASE, BIOSIS Prev, CA, CIN, ChemAb, ChemTitl, CurCont, E01, EMBASE, ExcerpMed, IABS, ISR, ImmunAb, IndMed, Inpharma, MEDLINE, MycolAb, P19, P20, P22, P30, P35, P48, P54, PQC, R10, Reac, SCI, SCOPUS, T02, W07.
—BLDSC (5307.422000), CASDDS, GNLM, IE, Infotrieve, Ingenta, INIST. **CCC.**
Published by: Sage Publications Ltd. (Subsidiary of: Sage Publications, Inc.), 1 Oliver's Yard, 55 City Rd, London, EC1Y 1SP, United Kingdom. TEL 44-20-73248500, FAX 44-20-73248600, info@sagepub.co.uk, http://www.uk.sagepub.com/home.nav. Ed. Graham R V Hughes.

616.7 USA

LUPUS BEACON. Text in English. 1984. 5/yr. USD 20 domestic; USD 22 in Canada & Mexico; USD 26 elsewhere (effective 2002). bk.rev. back issues avail. **Document type:** *Newsletter, Trade.* **Description:** Educational and medical news for patients with systemic lupus erythematosus.
Formerly: L E Beacon
Published by: L.E. Support Club, 8039 Nova Ct, N, Charleston, SC 29420. TEL 843-764-1769, hbmesic@knology.net. Ed., R&P Harriet B Mesic. Circ: 1,500.

616.7 AUS

LUPUS LINKS. Text in English. 19??. 5/yr. free to members (effective 2009). bk.rev. **Document type:** *Newsletter, Consumer.* **Description:** Features news and educational articles from the association, a self-help organization for sufferers of systemic lupus erythematosus and related diseases.
Formerly (until 2005): Lupus Association of New South Wales. Newsletter (1033-2480)
Published by: Lupus Association of New South Wales Inc., PO Box 89, North Ryde, NSW 1670, Australia. TEL 61-2-98786055, FAX 61-2-98786049, info@lupusnsw.org.au.

616.77 USA ISSN 0732-0280

LUPUS NEWS. Text in English. 1979. q. USD 25 domestic; USD 35 foreign (effective 2000). bk.rev. illus. reprints avail. **Document type:** *Newsletter, Consumer.* **Description:** Addresses the many facets of systemic lupus erythematosus - physical, emotional, psychological.
Published by: Lupus Foundation of America, Inc., 2000 L St NW, Ste. 710, Washington, DC 20036-4916. TEL 301-670-9292, FAX 301-670-9486, lupusinfo@lupus.org. Ed., R&P, Adv. contact Jenny Allan. Circ: 55,000.

616.7 USA ISSN 1547-1780

LUPUS NOW. Text in English. 2003 (Fall). 3/yr. USD 25 domestic to non-members; USD 35 foreign to non-members; free to members (effective 2007). adv. 48 p./no.; **Document type:** *Magazine, Consumer.* **Description:** Provides lifestyle and wellness information along with treatment news, summaries of scientific meetings, and new drug developments.
Published by: Lupus Foundation of America, Inc., 2000 L St. NW Ste. 710, Washington, DC 20036. TEL 202-349-1155, FAX 202-349-1156, lupusinfo@lupus.org, http://www.lupus.org. Ed. Jenny Allan. adv.: B&W page USD 4,300, color page USD 5,500; trim 8.375 x 10.875. Circ: 45,000 (paid).

616.7 HUN ISSN 0139-4495

MAGYAR REUMATOLOGIA. Text in Hungarian; Summaries in English. 1960. q. adv. bk.rev. **Document type:** *Journal, Academic/Scholarly.*
Formerly (until 1980): Rheumatologia, Balneologia, Allergologia (0035-4554)
Indexed: ChemAb, P30, SCOPUS.
—GNLM, INIST.
Published by: Magyar Reumatologusok Egyesulete, Uromi ut 56, Budapest, 1023, Hungary. titkarsag@mre.hu, http://www.mre.hu.

616.742 GBR

MATHILDA AND TERENCE KENNEDY INSTITUTE OF RHEUMATOLOGY TRUST. ANNUAL REPORT. Text in English. 1967. a. free. **Document type:** *Corporate.*
Formerly (until 2001): Mathilda and Terence Kennedy Institute of Rheumatology. Annual Report
Published by: Mathilda and Terence Kennedy Institute of Rheumatology Trust, 1 Aspenlea Rd, London, W6 8LH, United Kingdom. TEL 44-181-383-4444, FAX 44-181-383-4499, kir-enquiries-dl@ic.ac.uk. Circ: 1,000 (controlled).

616.7 DEU ISSN 0341-5112

MOBIL; das Rheuma-Magazin. Text in German. 1975. bi-m. EUR 3.20 newsstand/cover (effective 2010). adv. **Document type:** *Magazine, Consumer.*
—GNLM. **CCC.**
Published by: (Deutsche Rheuma-Liga e.V.), W D V Gesellschaft fuer Medien & Kommunikation mbH & Co. OHG, Siemensstr 6, Bad Homburg, 61352, Germany. adv.: B&W page EUR 4,250, color page EUR 5,950; trim 215 x 280. Circ: 189,500 (controlled).

616.7 JPN ISSN 1439-7595

➤ **MODERN RHEUMATOLOGY.** Text in English. 1958. bi-m. EUR 260, USD 306 combined subscription to institutions (print & online eds.) (effective 2012). adv. back issues avail.; reprint service avail. from PSC. **Document type:** *Journal, Academic/Scholarly.* **Description:** Publishes current Japanese research in rheumatology and associated areas (pathology, physiology, clinical immunology).
Formerly (until 1999): Japanese Journal of Rheumatology (0169-1163); Which superseded in part (in 1986): Ryumachi (0300-9157)
Related titles: Online - full text ed.: ISSN 1439-7609 (from IngentaConnect).
Indexed: A01, A03, A08, A22, A26, B21, BIOBASE, CA, E01, EMBASE, ExcerpMed, H12, H13, IABS, ImmunAb, Inpharma, MEDLINE, P02, P10, P20, P22, P30, P48, P53, P54, PQC, R10, Reac, SCI, SCOPUS, T02, W07.
—BLDSC (5895.300000), GNLM, IE, Infotrieve, Ingenta, INIST. **CCC.**
Published by: (Nihon Ryumachi Gakkai/Japan College of Rheumatology), Springer Japan KK (Subsidiary of: Springer Science+Business Media), No 2 Funato Bldg, 1-11-11 Kudan-kita, Chiyoda-ku, Tokyo, 102-0073, Japan. TEL 81-3-68317000, FAX 81-3-68317001, orders@springer.jp, http://www.springer.jp. Ed. Tsuneyo Mimori. Circ: 7,000. **Subscr. in the Americas to:** Springer New York LLC, Journal Fulfillment, PO Box 2485, Secaucus, NJ 07096. TEL 800-777-4643, 201-348-4033, FAX 201-348-4505, journals-ny@springer.com, http://www.springer.com; **Subscr. to:** Springer Distribution Center, Kundenservice Zeitschriften, Haberstr 7, Heidelberg 69126, Germany. TEL 49-6221-3454303, FAX 49-6221-3454229, subscriptions@springer.com.

616.7 DEU ISSN 1861-2105

MORBUS-BECHTEREW-JOURNAL. Text in German. 1980. q. EUR 36 membership (effective 2009). bk.rev. charts; illus. cum.index: 1980-1999. 100 p./no. 2 cols./p.; back issues avail. **Document type:** *Journal, Trade.*
Formerly (until 2003): Bechterew-Brief
Published by: Deutsche Vereinigung Morbus Bechterew, Metzgergasse 16, Schweinfurt, 97421, Germany. TEL 49-9721-22033, FAX 49-9721-22955, dvmb@bechterew.de. Ed. Ernst Feldtkeller. R&P, Adv. contact Ludwig Hammel. Circ: 18,000 (controlled).

616.7 GBR ISSN 1478-2189
RC925.A1

MUSCULOSKELETAL CARE. Text in English. 2003. q. GBP 183 in United Kingdom to institutions; EUR 232 in Europe to institutions; USD 358 elsewhere to institutions; GBP 210 combined subscription in United Kingdom to institutions (print & online eds.); EUR 267 combined subscription in Europe to institutions (print & online eds.); USD 412 combined subscription elsewhere to institutions (print & online eds.) (effective 2012). adv. back issues avail.; reprint service avail. from PSC. **Document type:** *Journal, Academic/Scholarly.* **Description:** Objectives are to inform, appraise and disseminate evidence-based practice; support and develop collaborative working; and to debate multi-professional issues.
Related titles: Online - full text ed.: ISSN 1557-0681. GBP 183 in United Kingdom to institutions; EUR 232 in Europe to institutions; USD 358 elsewhere to institutions (effective 2012).
Indexed: A01, B28, C06, C07, CA, EMBASE, ExcerpMed, MEDLINE, P30, R10, Reac, SCOPUS, T02.
—BLDSC (5986.531500), IE, Ingenta. **CCC.**

Published by: John Wiley & Sons Ltd. (Subsidiary of: John Wiley & Sons, Inc.), 1-7 Oldlands Way, PO Box 808, Bognor Regis, West Sussex PO21 9FF, United Kingdom. TEL 44-1865-778315, FAX 44-1243-843232, cs-journals@wiley.com, http://eu.wiley.com/WileyCDA/. Ed. Sarah Ryan. **Subscr. to:** 1-7 Oldlands Way, PO Box 809, Bognor Regis, West Sussex PO21 9FG, United Kingdom. TEL 44-1865-778054, cs-agency@wiley.com.

616.7 GBR ISSN 1759-4790
NATURE REVIEWS RHEUMATOLOGY. Text in English. 2005. m. EUR 1,244 in Europe to institutions; USD 1,257 in the Americas to institutions; GBP 741 to institutions in the UK & elsewhere (effective 2011). adv. back issues avail.; reprints avail. **Document type:** *Journal, Academic/Scholarly.*
Formerly (until 2009): Nature Clinical Practice Rheumatology (1745-8382)
Related titles: Online - full text ed.: ISSN 1759-4804.
Indexed: A01, A26, CA, CurCont, EMBASE, ExcerpMed, H12, I05, MEDLINE, P30, R10, Reac, SCI, SCOPUS, T02, W07.
—BLDSC (6046.280225), IE. **CCC.**
Published by: Nature Publishing Group (Subsidiary of: Macmillan Publishers Ltd.), The MacMillan Bldg, 4 Crinan St, London, N1 9XW, United Kingdom. TEL 44-20-78334000, FAX 44-20-78334640, NatureReviews@nature.com. Eds. Jennifer Buckland, Dr. Philip Campbell. Adv. contact Andy Douglas TEL 44-22-78434975. **Subscr. to:** Brunel Rd, Houndmills, Basingstoke, Hamps RG21 6XS, United Kingdom. TEL 44-1256-329242, FAX 44-1256-812358, subscriptions@nature.com.

616.7 NLD ISSN 1572-1698
NEDERLANDS TIJDSCHRIFT VOOR REUMATOLOGIE. Text in Dutch. 2001. q. EUR 60 (effective 2009). **Document type:** *Journal, Academic/Scholarly.*
Published by: (Nederlandse Vereniging van Reumatologie), DCHG Medische Communicatie, Zijlweg 70, Haarlem, 2013 DK, Netherlands. TEL 31-23-5514888, FAX 31-23-5515522, info@dchg.nl, http://www.dchg.nl. Ed. Dr. W F Lems. Pub. H Groen.

616.7 NLD ISSN 0924-4506
NEW CLINICAL APPLICATIONS. RHEUMATOLOGY. Text in English. 1989. irreg., latest vol.2, 1989. price varies. **Document type:** *Monographic series, Academic/Scholarly.*
Published by: Springer Netherlands (Subsidiary of: Springer Science+Business Media), Van Godewijckstraat 30, Dordrecht, 3311 GX, Netherlands. TEL 31-78-6576050, FAX 31-78-6576474.

616.7 USA ISSN 1543-4516
NEW DEVELOPMENTS IN RHEUMATIC DISEASES. Text in English. 2003 (Spr.). q.
Related titles: Online - full text ed.: ISSN 1543-4524.
Published by: Physicians & Scientists Publishing Co., PO Box 435, Glenview, IL 60025. TEL 847-559-0605, FAX 847-559-0699, info@medpub.com, http://www.medpub.com.

616.7 JPN ISSN 0287-3214
NIHON RYUMACHI KANSETSU GEKA GAKKAI ZASSHI/JAPANESE JOURNAL OF RHEUMATISM AND JOINT SURGERY. Text in English, Japanese. 1973. q. membership. **Document type:** *Journal, Academic/Scholarly.*
Formerly (until 1980): Ryumachi Geka/Japanese Research Association for Joint Surgery. Proceedings (0303-7975)
Indexed: INIS AtomInd.
Published by: Nihon Ryumachi Kansetsu Geka Gakkai/Japanese Society of Rheumatism and Joint Surgery, Shiga University of Medical Science, Department of Orthopedic Surgery, Seta Tsukinowa-cho, Otsu, Shiga 520-2192, Japan. TEL 81-77-5481172, FAX 81-77-5482254, rimakan@belle.shiga-med.ac.jp, http://www.rimakan.jp/.

616.7 JPN
NIHON RYUMACHI KANSETSU GEKA GEKKAI/JAPANESE SOCIETY OF RHEUMATISM AND JOINT SURGERY. CONGRESS. Text in English, Japanese. 1984. a. **Document type:** *Journal, Academic/Scholarly.*
Published by: Nihon Ryumachi Kansetsu Geka Gakkai/Japanese Society of Rheumatism and Joint Surgery, Shiga University of Medical Science, Department of Orthopedic Surgery, Seta Tsukinowa-cho, Otsu, Shiga 520-2192, Japan. TEL 81-77-5481172, FAX 81-77-5482254, rimakan@belle.shiga-med.ac.jp, http://www.rimakan.jp/.

NIHON SEKITSUI SEKIZUIBYOU GAKKAI ZASSHI/JAPAN SPINE RESEARCH SOCIETY. JOURNAL. *see* MEDICAL SCIENCES—Orthopedics And Traumatology

616.7 NOR ISSN 1892-090X
▼ **NORSK RHEUMABULLETIN.** Text in Norwegian. 2010. q. adv. **Document type:** *Magazine, Trade.*
Related titles: Online - full text ed.
Published by: Norsk Revmatologisk Forening, Legenes Hus, PO Box 1152, Sentrum, Oslo, 0107, Norway. http://www.legeforeningen.no/nrf. Ed. Erik Roedervang.

616.7 AUS
ON THE MOVE. Text in English. 1983. q. free to members (effective 2007). adv. bk.rev. back issues avail. **Document type:** *Magazine, Consumer.* **Description:** News of foundation activities, information on self-help courses, researches on arthritis and treatments.
Former titles: Arthritis Action (1039-284X); Arthritis News
Published by: Arthritis Foundation of South Australia, Unit 1, 202 Glen Osmond Rd, Fullarton, SA 5063, Australia. TEL 61-8-83795711, info@arthritissa.org.au, http://www.arthritissa.org.au. Circ: 8,000.

616.7 GBR ISSN 1179-156X
RC927
▼ ➤ **OPEN ACCESS RHEUMATOLOGY: RESEARCH AND REVIEWS.** Text in English. 2009. irreg. free (effective 2011). **Document type:** *Journal, Academic/Scholarly.* **Description:** Covers all aspects of clinical and experimental rheumatology in the clinic and laboratory.
Media: Online - full text.
Indexed: EMBASE, SCOPUS.
—**CCC.**
Published by: Dove Medical Press Ltd., Beechfield House, Winterton Way, Macclesfield, SK11 0JL, United Kingdom. TEL 44-1625-509130, FAX 44-1625-617933. Ed. Chuan-Ju Liu.

616.7 NLD ISSN 1876-5394
RC933.A1
➤ **THE OPEN ARTHRITIS JOURNAL.** Text in English. 2008. irreg. free (effective 2011). **Document type:** *Journal, Academic/Scholarly.*
Media: Online - full text.
Indexed: CTA.
Published by: Bentham Open (Subsidiary of: Bentham Science Publishers Ltd.), PO Box 294, Bussum, AG 1400, Netherlands. TEL 31-35-6923800, FAX 31-35-6980150, subscriptions@bentham.org.

616.7 NLD ISSN 1874-3129
RC927
➤ **THE OPEN RHEUMATOLOGY JOURNAL.** Text in English. 2007. irreg. free (effective 2011). **Document type:** *Journal, Academic/Scholarly.* **Description:** Aims to provide the most complete and reliable source of information on current developments in rheumatology.
Media: Online - full text.
Indexed: A01, CA, CTA, EMBASE, P30, SCOPUS, T02.
Published by: Bentham Open (Subsidiary of: Bentham Science Publishers Ltd.), PO Box 294, Bussum, AG 1400, Netherlands. TEL 31-35-6923800, FAX 31-35-6980150, subscriptions@bentham.org. Ed. Cornelis L Verweij.

616.7 GBR ISSN 1063-4584
CODEN: OSCAEO
➤ **OSTEOARTHRITIS AND CARTILAGE.** Text in English. 1993. m. EUR 1,040 in Europe to institutions; JPY 112,100 in Japan to institutions; USD 975 elsewhere to institutions (effective 2012). adv. back issues avail.; reprint service avail. from PSC. **Document type:** *Journal, Academic/Scholarly.* **Description:** Publishes original articles on clinical, laboratory, and therapeutic research in osteoarthritis and related concerns, including cartilage, collagen, and orthopedics.
Related titles: Online - full text ed.: ISSN 1522-9653. USD 822 to institutions (effective 2009) (from ScienceDirect).
Indexed: A22, A26, AMED, ASCA, C06, C07, CA, CurCont, E01, EMBASE, ExcerpMed, I05, ISR, IndMed, Inpharma, MEDLINE, P30, P35, R10, Reac, SCI, SCOPUS, T02, W07.
—BLDSC (6303.858870), GNLM, IE, Infotrieve, Ingenta, INIST. **CCC.**
Published by: (International Cartilage Repair Society CHE, Osteoarthritis Research Society International USA), Elsevier Ltd (Subsidiary of: Elsevier Science & Technology), The Blvd, Langford Ln, Kidlington, Oxford, OX5 1GB, United Kingdom. TEL 44-1865-843000, FAX 44-1865-843010, customerserviceau@elsevier.com. Ed. S Lohmander.

616.7 NLD ISSN 1568-4318
OSTEOPOROSE JOURNAAL. Text in Dutch. 2000. q. **Document type:** *Journal, Trade.*
Published by: (Interdisciplinaire Werkgroep Osteoporose), DCHG Medische Communicatie, Zijlweg 70, Haarlem, 2013 DK, Netherlands. TEL 31-23-5514888, FAX 31-23-5515522, info@dchg.nl, http://www.dchg.nl.

616.7 DEU ISSN 1867-6332
OSTEOPOROSE UND RHEUMA AKTUELL; das Fachmagazin fuer Aerztinnen und Aerzte. Text in German. 1998. 4/yr. adv. **Document type:** *Magazine, Trade.*
Formerly (until 2003): Rheuma Aktuell (1436-6347)
Published by: m d m - Verlag fuer Medizinische Publikationen, Bremsen 4, Leichlingen, 42799, Germany. TEL 49-2175-1691230, FAX 49-2175-1691231, info@mdmverlag.de, http://www.mdmverlag.de. Circ: 10,000 (paid and controlled).

616.716 CAN ISSN 1480-3119
OSTEOPOROSIS UPDATE. Text in English. 1988. q. free. **Document type:** *Newsletter, Consumer.*
Formerly (until 1997): Osteoporosis (1192-3423)
Related titles: Online - full content ed.; French ed.: Point sur L'Osteoporose. ISSN 1480-3127. 1988.
—**CCC.**
Published by: (Osteoporosis Canada), Parkhurst Publishing, 400 McGill St, 3rd Fl, Montreal, PQ H2Y 2G1, Canada. TEL 514-397-8833, FAX 514-397-0228, contact@parkpub.com, http://www.parkpub.com.

616.7 TUR ISSN 1308-6324
OSTEOPOROZ DUNYASINDAN/FROM THE OSTEOPOROSIS WORLD/OSTEOPOROSIS WORLD. Text in Turkish. 3/yr. **Document type:** *Journal, Academic/Scholarly.* **Description:** Publishes original research papers of the scientific and clinical values specifically on osteoporosis, on an international level. Additionally, reviews on basic developments in education, editorial short notes, case reports, original views, letters from the fields of physical medicine, rheumatology, rehabilitation, gynaecology containing experiences and comments as well as social subjects are published.
Related titles: Online - full text ed.: free (effective 2010); English ed.
Published by: (Turkish Osteoporosis Association), Istanbul Universitesi, Cerrahpasa Tip Fakultesi, Fiziksel Tip ve Rehabilitasyon Anabilim Daly, Aksaray - Istanbul, Turkey. TEL 90-212-4143000, FAX 90-212-41422697, osteopdunya@osteoporoz.org.tr. Ed. Dr. Merih Sarydoean.

616.7 ESP ISSN 1696-5981
PATOLOGIA DEL APARATO LOCOMOTOR. Text in Spanish. 2003. q. back issues avail. **Document type:** *Journal, Academic/Scholarly.*
Indexed: R10, Reac, SCOPUS.
Published by: Fundacion Mapfre, Paseo de Recoletos, 23, Madrid, 28004, Spain. TEL 34-91-5812353, FAX 34-91-5816070, fundacion.informacion@mafre.com, http://www.fundacionmapfre.com. Ed. Francisco De la Gala Sanzhez.

616.7 618.92 USA ISSN 1546-0096
➤ **PEDIATRIC RHEUMATOLOGY ONLINE JOURNAL.** Text in English. 2003. bi-m. free (effective 2011). **Document type:** *Journal, Academic/Scholarly.* **Description:** Covers all aspects of clinical and basic research related to pediatric rheumatology and allied subjects.
Media: Online - full text.
Indexed: A01, A26, CA, CurCont, EMBASE, ExcerpMed, H12, I05, P30, R10, Reac, SCI, SCOPUS, T02, W07.
—**CCC.**
Published by: University of Chicago Hospitals, Office of Public Affairs, 5841 S Maryland Ave, Chicago, IL 60637. TEL 773-702-1000, http://www.uchospitals.edu. Eds. Alberto Martini, Charles H. Spencer.

616.722 FRA ISSN 1958-1017
POLYARTHRITE INFOS. Text in French. 1989. q. **Document type:** *Journal.* **Description:** For arthritis sufferers.
Published by: Association Francaise des Polyarthritiques, 53 Rue Compans, Esc. 46, Paris, 75019, France. TEL 33-1-40030200, FAX 33-1-40030209, afp@nerim.net, http://www.polyarthrite.org.

PRACTICAL GASTROENTEROLOGY; for the busy gastroenterologist. *see* MEDICAL SCIENCES—Gastroenterology

616.7 ITA ISSN 1974-2800
PROGRESSI IN REUMATOLOGIA CLINICA. Text in Italian. 2007. irreg. **Document type:** *Monographic series, Academic/Scholarly.*
Published by: Edizioni Medico Scientifiche, Via Riviera 39, Pavia, 27100, Italy. TEL 39-0382-526253, FAX 39-0382-423120, edint@edimes@tin.it.

616.7 617.3 FRA ISSN 0997-7503
RACHIS; revue de pathologie vertebrale. Text in French. 1989. bi-m. EUR 75 to individuals; EUR 130 to institutions (effective 2010). adv. bk.rev. charts; illus. index. **Document type:** *Journal, Academic/Scholarly.*
Indexed: FR.
—BLDSC (7225.976000), IE, Ingenta, INIST.
Published by: Le Rachis, 47 rue Le Corbusier, Boulogne Billancourt, 92100, France. TEL 33-6-19717639, contact@le-rachis.com. Ed., Pub. P Antonietti. Circ: 4,000.

616.7 FRA ISSN 1960-1980
REALITES EN RHUMATOLOGIE. Text in French. 2007. m. EUR 48 domestic to qualified personnel; EUR 38 domestic to students; EUR 61 foreign (effective 2008). **Document type:** *Journal, Trade.*
Published by: Performances Medicales, 91 Av. de la Republique, Paris, 75011, France. TEL 33-1-47006714, FAX 33-1-47006999.

REFERATOVY VYBER Z REVMATOLOGIE (ONLINE)/ABSTRACTS OF RHEUMATOLOGY. *see* MEDICAL SCIENCES—Abstracting, Bibliographies, Statistics

616.742 CZE ISSN 1211-2658
CODEN: FYRVAX
➤ **REHABILITACE A FYZIKALNI LEKARSTVI/REHABILITATION AND PHYSICAL MEDICINE.** Text in Czech, Slovak; Summaries in Czech, English. 1923. q. CZK 388, EUR 16.80 (effective 2010). adv. bk.rev. **Document type:** *Journal, Academic/Scholarly.* **Description:** Covers the whole field of medical, vocational and social rehabilitation, physical medicine, physiotherapy and ergotherapy as well as orthotics, prosthetics and all disciplines associated with the rehabilitation process.
Supersedes in part (in 1993): Fysiatricky a Reumatologicky Vestnik (0072-0038)
Related titles: Online - full text ed.
Indexed: A01, IndMed, P30, R10, Reac, SCOPUS.
—CASDDS, GNLM.
Published by: (Ceska Lekarska Spolecnost J.E. Purkyne/Czech Medical Association), Nakladatelske Stredisko C L S J.E. Purkyne, Sokolska 31, Prague, 12026, Czech Republic. nts@cls.cz. Ed. Jan Vacek. adv.: B&W page CZK 23,200, color page CZK 36,400; 245 x 167. Circ: 2,400.

616.7 SWE ISSN 2000-2246
REUMA BULLETINEN. Text in Swedish. 2001. q. adv. **Document type:** *Magazine, Trade.*
Related titles: Online - full text ed.
Published by: (Svensk Reumatologisk Foerening), Mediahuset i Goeteborg AB, Marieholmsgatan 10 C, Goeteborg, 41502, Sweden. TEL 46-31-7071930, FAX 46-31-848642, http://www.mediahuset.se. Ed. Tomas Brenell. Adv. contact Olla Lundblad. Circ: 1,500.

616.742 SWE ISSN 2000-5202
REUMATIKERVAERLDEN. Text in Swedish. 1949. bi-m. SEK 250 (effective 2010). adv. bk.rev. back issues avail. **Document type:** *Magazine, Consumer.*
Former titles (until 2010): Reumatikertidningen (1104-0696); (until 1994): Reuma (0034-6209)
Related titles: Audio cassette/tape ed.; Online - full text ed.
Published by: Reumatikerfoerbundet/Swedish National Association Against Rheumatism, Alstroemergatan 39, PO Box 12851, Stockholm, 11298, Sweden. TEL 46-8-50580500, FAX 46-8-50580550, info@reumatikerforbundet.org, http://www.reumatikerforbundet.org. Ed. Madeleine Baeck TEL 46-8-55606441. Adv. contact Gun Hammar TEL 46-8-218105. Circ: 53,000; 54,900 (controlled).

616.7 ITA ISSN 0048-7449
REUMATISMO. Text in Italian. 1949. 4/yr. free to members; EUR 35 to non-members (effective 2009). adv. bk.rev. illus. Supplement avail.; back issues avail. **Document type:** *Journal, Academic/Scholarly.*
Indexed: A22, ChemAb, EMBASE, ExcerpMed, IndMed, Inpharma, MEDLINE, P30, R10, Reac, SCOPUS.
—BLDSC (7785.544100), GNLM, IE, Infotrieve, Ingenta, INIST.
Published by: (Societa Italiana di Reumatologia (S I R)), Edizioni Medico Scientifiche, Via Riviera 39, Pavia, 27100, Italy. TEL 39-0382-526253, FAX 39-0382-423120, edint@edimes@tin.it.

616.7 HRV ISSN 0374-1338
REUMATIZAM. Text in Croatian; Summaries in English. 1954. bi-m. adv. bk.rev. index. back issues avail.
Indexed: EMBASE, ExcerpMed, IndMed, MEDLINE, P30, R10, Reac, SCOPUS.
—GNLM, INIST.
Published by: Hrvatsko Reumatolosko Drustvo/Croatian Rheumatological Society, Vinogradska 29, Zagreb, 10000, Croatia. Ed. Ivo Jajic. Circ: 1,000. **Subscr. to:** Jurjevska 25-I, Zagreb 41000, Croatia.

616.742 POL ISSN 0034-6233
CODEN: RMTOA2
➤ **REUMATOLOGIA/RHEUMATOLOGY.** Text in Polish; Summaries in English. 1963. q. PLZ 72 domestic (effective 2010). adv. bk.rev. bibl.; charts; illus. index. 110 p./no. 1 cols./p.; back issues avail. **Document type:** *Journal, Academic/Scholarly.* **Description:** Publishes original and clinical reports, review papers, case reports, conference reports and announcements.
Related titles: Online - full text ed.
Indexed: A22, B25, BIOSIS Prev, ChemAb, DentInd, IndMed, MycolAb, P30, R10, Reac, SCOPUS.
—BLDSC (7785.548000), CASDDS, GNLM, IE, Infotrieve, Ingenta, INIST.

Published by: (Instytut Reumatologii/Institute of Rheumatology), Termedia sp. z o.o./Termedia Publishing House, ul Wenedow 9/1, Poznan, 61614, Poland. TEL 48-61-8227781, FAX 48-61-8227781, termedia@termedia.pl. Ed. Jacek Pazdur. Circ: 1,000 (paid).
Co-sponsor: Polskie Towarzystwo Reumatologiczne/Polish Rheumatological Society.

616.7 PRT ISSN 1646-6454
REUMATOLOGIA CLINICA. Text in Portuguese. 2007. q. **Document type:** *Journal, Academic/Scholarly.*
Published by: Medicografica Edicoes Medicas, Rua Camilo Castelo Branco 23-5, Lisbon, 1150-083, Portugal. geral@medicografica.pt, http://www.medicografica.pt.

616.7 ESP ISSN 1699-258X
RC927
REUMATOLOGIA CLINICA. Text in Spanish. 2005. s-a. EUR 150.23 to individuals; EUR 380.34 to institutions (effective 2009). back issues avail. **Document type:** *Journal, Academic/Scholarly.*
Formed by the merger of: Revista Mexicna de Reumatologia (0186-8969); (1974-2005); Revista Espanola de Reumatologia (0304-4815)
Related titles: Online - full text ed.: ISSN 1885-1398 (from ScienceDirect); Supplement(s): ISSN 1886-3604.
Indexed: A01, A22, CA, EMBASE, ExcerpMed, MycolAb, P30, R10, Reac, SCOPUS, T02.
—BLDSC (7785.548500), IE, Ingenta, INIST. **CCC.**
Published by: (Sociedad Espanola de Reumatologia), Elsevier Doyma (Subsidiary of: Elsevier Health Sciences), Traversa de Gracia 17-21, Barcelona, 08021, Spain. TEL 34-932-418800, FAX 34-932-419020, editorial@elsevier.com, http://www.elsevier.es/. Ed. Janitzia Vazquez-Mellado.

616.7 ITA ISSN 0391-8963
IL REUMATOLOGO. Text in Italian; Summaries in English. 1980. q. adv. **Document type:** *Newsletter, Trade.*
Indexed: RefZh.
Published by: C I C Edizioni Internazionali, Corso Trieste 42, Rome, 00198, Italy. TEL 39-06-8412673, FAX 39-06-8412688, info@gruppocic.it, http://www.gruppocic.it.

616.7 617.06 NLD ISSN 2211-615X
▼ **REVALIDATIE - REUMATOLOGIE MAGAZINE.** Text in Dutch. 2011. 3/yr. **Document type:** *Magazine, Trade.*
Published by: Reade, Centrum voor Revalidatie en Reumatologie, Postbus 58271, Amsterdam, 1040 HG, Netherlands. TEL 31-20-6071607, info@reade.nl, http://www.reade.nl. Ed. Karlijn Haantjes. Circ: 6,000.

616.7 BRA ISSN 0482-5004
RC927 CODEN: RBREBM
➤ **REVISTA BRASILEIRA DE REUMATOLOGIA/BRAZILIAN JOURNAL OF RHEUMATOLOGY.** Text in Portuguese; Summaries in English. 1957. bi-m. abstr. **Document type:** *Journal, Academic/Scholarly.*
Related titles: Online - full text ed.: ISSN 1809-4570. 2005. free (effective 2011).
Indexed: C01, ChemAb, EMBASE, ExcerpMed, MEDLINE, P30, R10, Reac, SCOPUS.
—BLDSC (7845.700000), CASDDS.
Published by: Sociedade Brasileira de Reumatologia/Brazilian Society of Rheumatology, Avenida Brigadeiro Luiz Antonio 2466, Sao Paulo, SP 01402-000, Brazil. Eds. Lais V Lage, Roger A Levy.

616.7 COL ISSN 0121-8123
➤ **REVISTA COLOMBIANA DE REUMATOLOGIA.** Text in Spanish, English. 1993. q. **Document type:** *Journal, Academic/Scholarly.*
Related titles: Online - full text ed.: free (effective 2011) (from SciELO).
Published by: Asociacion Colombiana de Reumatologia, Calle 94, No 15-32, Oficina 603, Bogota, Colombia. TEL 57-1-6350840, FAX 57-1-6215145. Ed. Jose Felix Restrepo Suarez.

616.7 CUB ISSN 1606-5581
REVISTA CUBANA DE REUMATOLOGIA. Text in Spanish. 1999. s-a. back issues avail. **Document type:** *Journal, Academic/Scholarly.*
Related titles: Online - full content ed.: ISSN 1817-5996.
Published by: Sociedad Cubana de Reumatologia, Calle 216 entre 13 y 15, Siboney Playa, Habana, Cuba. TEL 53-7-339086, editorial@cimeq.sld.cu. Ed. Gil Alberto Reyes Llerena.

616.7 PER ISSN 1728-5860
REVISTA PERUANA DE REUMATOLOGIA. Text in Spanish. 1995. 3/yr. **Document type:** *Journal, Academic/Scholarly.*
Related titles: Online - full text ed.: ISSN 1609-7181.
Published by: Sociedad Peruana de Reumatologia, Av Jose Pardo 138, Of 1206, Miraflores, Lima, Peru. TEL 51-1-4461323, FAX 51-1-4461323, socreuma@terra.com.pe.

616.742 NOR ISSN 1891-4403
▼ **REVMARAPPORTEN.** Text in Norwegian. 2009. a. **Document type:** *Report, Consumer.*
Related titles: Online - full text ed.
Published by: Norsk Revmatiker Forbund/Norwegian Rheumatism Association, PO Box 2653, Solli, Oslo, 0203, Norway. TEL 47-22-547600, FAX 47-22-431251, post@revmatiker.no.

616.742 NOR ISSN 0800-5575
REVMATIKEREN. Text in Norwegian. 1951. 6/yr. adv. back issues avail. **Document type:** *Magazine, Trade.*
Related titles: Online - full text ed.
Published by: Norsk Revmatiker Forbund/Norwegian Rheumatism Association, PO Box 2653, Solli, Oslo, 0203, Norway. TEL 47-22-547600, FAX 47-22-431251, post@revmatiker.no. Ed. Randi Alsnes. Adv. contact Per Sletholt TEL 47-23-302130. Circ: 38,000.

616.7 615.533 BGR ISSN 1310-0505
➤ **REVMATOLOGIIA.** Text in Bulgarian; Summaries in Bulgarian, English. 1993. q. free (effective 2005). adv. bk.rev. abstr.; bibl.; illus. index. 56 p./no. 2 cols./p.; back issues avail. **Document type:** *Journal, Academic/Scholarly.* **Description:** Presents original articles in the field of rheumatology and related diseases for medical researchers and practitioners.
Indexed: ABSML, EMBASE, ExcerpMed, R10, Reac.

Published by: Meditsinski Universitet - Sofia, Tsentralna Meditsinska Biblioteka, Tsentur za Informatsiia po Meditsina/Medical University - Sofia, Central Medical Library, Medical Information Center, 1 Sv Georgi Sofiiski ul, Sofia, 1431, Bulgaria. TEL 359-2-9522342, FAX 359-2-9522393, lydia@medun.acad.bg, http://www.medun.acad.bg/cmb_htm/cmb1_home_bg.htm. Ed. Dr. J Sheitanov. adv.: B&W page USD 70, color page USD 170; trim 230 x 170. Circ: 300.
Co-sponsor: Bulgarsko Nauchno Druzhestvo po Revmatologiia.

616.742 FRA ISSN 1169-8330
CODEN: RRMOA2
REVUE DU RHUMATISME (FRENCH EDITION). Text in French. 1933. bi-m. EUR 547 in Europe to institutions; EUR 492.65 in France to institutions; JPY 67,100 in Japan to institutions; USD 711 elsewhere to institutions (effective 2012). adv. bk.rev. abstr.; bibl.; charts; illus. index. reprints avail. **Document type:** *Journal, Academic/Scholarly.* **Description:** Publishes original articles, editorials, general reviews, clinical cases, and letters to the editor concerning joint, bone and spine diseases and all the latest advances in the specialty.
Supersedes in part (in 1993): Revue du Rhumatisme et des Maladies Osteoarticulaires (0035-2659); Which was formerly (until 1946): Revue du Rhumatisme (0301-8474)
Related titles: Microform ed.: (from PQC); Online - full text ed.: ISSN 1768-3130. 2002 (from IngentaConnect, ScienceDirect).
Indexed: A01, A03, A08, A22, A26, CA, CISA, ChemAb, FR, I05, ISR, IndMed, P30, SCOPUS, T02.
—BLDSC (7945.590000), CASDDS, GNLM, IE, Infotrieve, Ingenta, INIST. **CCC.**
Published by: (Societe Francaise de Rhumatologie), Elsevier Masson (Subsidiary of: Elsevier Health Sciences), 62 Rue Camille Desmoulins, Issy les Moulineaux, Cedex 92442, France. TEL 33-1-71165500, FAX 33-1-71165600, infos@elsevier-masson.fr. Ed. Marie-Christophe Boissier. Circ: 5,000.

616.7 FRA ISSN 1878-6227
REVUE DU RHUMATISME. MONOGRAPHIES. Text in French. q. EUR 493 domestic to institutions; EUR 547 in Europe to institutions (except France); JPY 67,100 in Japan to institutions; USD 711 elsewhere to institutions (effective 2011). **Document type:** *Monographic series, Academic/Scholarly.*
Related titles: Online - full text ed.: ISSN 2212-0920 (from ScienceDirect).
Indexed: EMBASE, SCOPUS, T02.
—**CCC.**
Published by: (Societe Francaise de Rhumatologie), Elsevier Masson (Subsidiary of: Elsevier Health Sciences), 62 Rue Camille Desmoulins, Issy les Moulineaux, Cedex 92442, France. TEL 33-1-71165500, FAX 33-1-71165600, infos@elsevier-masson.fr, http://www.elsevier-masson.fr.

616.7 ESP ISSN 0211-7274
RHEUMA. Text in Spanish. bi-m. back issues avail.; reprints avail. **Document type:** *Journal, Trade.*
Published by: Jarpyo Editores S.A., Antonio Lopez Aguado 4, Madrid, 28029, Spain. TEL 34-91-3144338, FAX 34-91-3144499, editorial@jarpyo.es, http://www.jarpyo.es. Ed. Juan Torres.

616.7 USA ISSN 0889-857X
RC927 CODEN: RDCAEK
➤ **RHEUMATIC DISEASES CLINICS OF NORTH AMERICA.** Text in English. 1987. q. USD 501 in United States to institutions; USD 619 elsewhere to institutions (effective 2012). adv. index. back issues avail.; reprints avail. **Document type:** *Journal, Academic/Scholarly.* **Description:** Experts in the field provide information on current, practical information on the diagnosis and treatment of conditions affecting joints and connective tissue. Focuses on a single topic relevant to your rheumatology practice, from immunology to the latest treatment advances for rheumatoid arthritis.
Supersedes in part (in 1987): Clinics in Rheumatic Diseases (0307-742X)
Related titles: Online - full text ed.: ISSN 1558-3163 (from ScienceDirect).
Indexed: A22, A36, ASCA, BIOSIS Prev, C06, C07, C08, CABA, CINAHL, CurCont, EMBASE, ExcerpMed, GH, INI, ISR, IndMed, Inpharma, MEDLINE, MycolAb, N02, N03, P30, R10, Reac, SCI, SCOPUS, W07.
—BLDSC (7960.618000), CASDDS, GNLM, IE, Infotrieve, Ingenta, INIST. **CCC.**
Published by: W.B. Saunders Co. (Subsidiary of: Elsevier Health Sciences), Elsevier, Health Sciences Division, Order Fulfillment, 3251 Riverport Ln, Maryland Heights, MO 63043. TEL 314-872-8370, 800-325-4177, FAX 314-432-1380, JournalCustomerService-usa@elsevier.com, http://www.us.elsevierhealth.com. Adv. contact John Marmero TEL 212-633-3657.

616.7 SVK ISSN 1210-1931
CODEN: RHEUE
➤ **RHEUMATOLOGIA.** Text in Slovak. 1987. 4/yr. EUR 91.40 in Europe; EUR 100 elsewhere (effective 2011). **Document type:** *Journal, Academic/Scholarly.*
Indexed: EMBASE, ExcerpMed.
—BLDSC (7960.719000), GNLM, IE, Ingenta.
Published by: (Narodny Ustav Reumatickych Chorob Piestany), Slovak Academic Press Ltd., Nam Slobody 6, PO Box 57, Bratislava, 81005, Slovakia. TEL 421-2-55421729, FAX 421-2-55565862, sap@sappress.sk, http://www.sappress.sk. Ed. Tibor Urbanek. **Dist. by:** Slovart G.T.G. s.r.o., Krupinska 4, PO Box 152, Bratislava 85299, Slovakia. TEL 421-2-63839472, FAX 421-2-63839485, info@slovart-gtg.sk, http://www.slovart-gtg.sk.

616.7 USA ISSN 1931-3268
THE RHEUMATOLOGIST. Text in English. 2006 (Nov.). m. GBP 69 in United Kingdom to institutions; EUR 87 in Europe to institutions; USD 136 elsewhere to institutions (effective 2012). adv. **Document type:** *Journal, Academic/Scholarly.* **Description:** Designed to provide current news and information to rheumatology and rheumatologist health professionals. Carries information on general research topics and clinical trends in rheumatology.
Related titles: Online - full text ed.: ISSN 1931-3209.
—**CCC.**
Published by: (American College of Rheumatology, Association of Rheumatology Health Professionals), John Wiley & Sons, Inc., 111 River St, Hoboken, NJ 07030. TEL 201-748-6000, FAX 201-748-6088, info@wiley.com. Eds. Dawn Antoline, Lisa Dionne. Pub. Vickie Thaw.

616.742 CHE ISSN 0080-2727
RC927.A1 CODEN: RHEUBD
➤ **RHEUMATOLOGY;** the interdisciplinary concept. Text in English. 1966. irreg., latest vol.18, 1996. price varies. reprints avail. **Document type:** *Monographic series, Academic/Scholarly.*
Related titles: Online - full text ed.: ISSN 1662-3959.
Indexed: A22, ChemAb, IndMed, P30, SCOPUS.
—BLDSC (7960.730000), CASDDS, GNLM, INIST. **CCC.**
Published by: S. Karger AG, Allschwilerstr 10, Basel, 4055, Switzerland. TEL 41-61-3061111, FAX 41-61-3061234, karger@karger.ch, http://www.karger.ch. Ed. F Hiepe.

616.742 GBR ISSN 1462-0332
RHEUMATOLOGY (ONLINE). Text in English. m. GBP 569 in United Kingdom to institutions; EUR 856 in Europe to institutions; USD 1,139 in US & Canada to institutions; GBP 569 elsewhere to institutions (effective 2012). **Document type:** *Journal, Academic/Scholarly.*
Formerly (until 1999): British Journal of Rheumatology (Online Edition) (1460-2172)
Media: Online - full text (from IngentaConnect). **Related titles:** Microform ed.: (from PQC); ◆ Print ed.: Rheumatology (Print). ISSN 1462-0324.
—**CCC.**
Published by: Oxford University Press, Great Clarendon St, Oxford, OX2 6DP, United Kingdom. TEL 44-1865-556767, FAX 44-1865-556646, jnl.orders@oup.co.uk, http://www.oxfordjournals.org.

616.742 GBR ISSN 1462-0324
RC925.A1 CODEN: RUMAFK
➤ **RHEUMATOLOGY (PRINT).** Text in English. 1952. m. GBP 673 in United Kingdom to institutions; EUR 1,012 in Europe to institutions; USD 1,348 in US & Canada to institutions; GBP 673 elsewhere to institutions; GBP 734 combined subscription in United Kingdom to institutions (print & online eds.); EUR 1,104 combined subscription in Europe to institutions (print & online eds.); USD 1,470 combined subscription in US & Canada to institutions (print & online eds.); GBP 734 combined subscription elsewhere to institutions (print & online eds.) (effective 2012). adv. bk.rev. bibl.; illus. index. 132 p./no.; Supplement avail.; back issues avail.; reprint service avail. from PSC. **Document type:** *Journal, Academic/Scholarly.* **Description:** Devoted to clinical and laboratory rheumatology, treatment therapy, immunology, and new-drug developments worldwide.
Former titles (until 1999): British Journal of Rheumatology (Print) (0263-7103); (until 1983): Rheumatology and Rehabilitation (0300-3396); (until 1973): Rheumatology and Physical Medicine (0003-4908); (until 1970): Annals of Physical Medicine (0365-5547)
Related titles: Microform ed.: (from PQC); ◆ Online - full text ed.: Rheumatology (Online). ISSN 1462-0332.
Indexed: A01, A03, A08, A20, A22, AIIM, AIM, AMED, ASCA, B21, B25, BIOBASE, BIOSIS Prev, BiolDig, C06, C07, CA, CIN, CTA, ChemAb, ChemTitl, CurCont, DBA, DentInd, E01, EMBASE, ExcerpMed, FR, H13, I12, IABS, ISR, ImmunAb, IndMed, Inpharma, MEDLINE, MS&D, MycolAb, P10, P20, P22, P24, P30, P35, P48, P53, P54, PQC, R10, Reac, SCI, SCOPUS, T02, W07.
—BLDSC (7960.731900), CASDDS, GNLM, IE, Infotrieve, Ingenta, INIST. **CCC.**
Published by: (British Society of Rheumatology), Oxford University Press, Great Clarendon St, Oxford, OX2 6DP, United Kingdom. TEL 44-1865-556767, FAX 44-1865-556646, enquiry@oup.co.uk, http://www.oxfordjournals.org.

616.7 DEU ISSN 0172-8172
CODEN: RHINDE
➤ **RHEUMATOLOGY INTERNATIONAL;** clinical and experimental investigations. Text in English. 1981. 8/yr. EUR 2,192, USD 2,870 combined subscription to institutions (print & online eds.) (effective 2012). adv. back issues avail.; reprint service avail. from PSC. **Document type:** *Journal, Academic/Scholarly.* **Description:** Reflects world-wide progress in the research, diagnosis, and treatment of various rheumatic diseases.
Related titles: Microform ed.: (from PQC); Online - full text ed.: ISSN 1437-160X (from IngentaConnect).
Indexed: A01, A03, A08, A20, A22, A26, A36, A37, ASCA, B25, BIOSIS Prev, CA, CABA, ChemAb, ChemTitl, CurCont, DentInd, E01, E12, EMBASE, ExcerpMed, F08, F11, F12, GH, H12, ISR, IndMed, Inpharma, MEDLINE, MycolAb, N02, N03, P20, P22, P30, P32, P33, P35, P39, P48, P54, PQC, R08, R10, R12, RA&MP, RM&VM, Reac, S12, SCI, SCOPUS, T02, T05, W07.
—BLDSC (7960.738300), CASDDS, GNLM, IE, Infotrieve, Ingenta, INIST. **CCC.**
Published by: Springer (Subsidiary of: Springer Science+Business Media), Tiergartenstr 17, Heidelberg, 69121, Germany. TEL 49-6221-4870, FAX 49-6221-345229. Ed. E-M Lemmel. **Subscr. in the Americas to:** Springer New York LLC, Journal Fulfillment, PO Box 2485, Secaucus, NJ 07096. TEL 800-777-4643, 201-348-4033, FAX 201-348-4505, journals-ny@springer.com, http://www.springer.com; **Subscr. to:** Springer Distribution Center, Kundenservice Zeitschriften, Haberstr 7, Heidelberg 69126, Germany. TEL 49-6221-3454303, FAX 49-6221-3454229, subscriptions@springer.com.

616.7 USA ISSN 1541-9800
RHEUMATOLOGY NEWS. Text in English. 2002. m. USD 114 in United States to institutions; USD 182 elsewhere to institutions (effective 2012). adv. back issues avail.; reprints avail. **Document type:** *Newspaper, Trade.* **Description:** Provides the practicing specialist with timely and relevant news and commentary about clinical developments in the field and about the impact of health care policy on the specialty and the physician's practice.
Related titles: Online - full text ed.
—**CCC.**
Published by: International Medical News Group (Subsidiary of: Elsevier Health Sciences), 5635 Fishers Ln, Ste 6000, Rockville, MD 20852. TEL 877-710-3982, FAX 240-221-4400, m.altier@elsevier.com, http://www.imng.com. Ed. Mary Jo M. Dales. Pub. Alan J Imhoff TEL 973-290-8216. Circ: 9,210. **Subscr. to:** Elsevier, Subscription Customer Service, 60 Columbia Rd, Bldg B, Morristown, NJ 07960. TEL 973-290-8200, FAX 973-290-8250, http://www.elsevier.com/.

616.7 USA ISSN 1876-1143
RHEUMATOLOGY NEWS INTERNATIONAL. Text in English. 2008. 6/yr. USD 173 (effective 2011). **Document type:** *Newspaper, Trade.*
Related titles: Online - full text ed.: ISSN 1876-1151.

Published by: International Medical News Group (Subsidiary of: Elsevier Health Sciences), 5635 Fishers Ln, Ste 6000, Rockville, MD 20852. TEL 877-710-3982, http://www.imng.com. Ed. Mary Jo M Dales TEL 240-221-2470. Pub. Alan J Imhoff TEL 973-290-8216.

616.7 ITA ISSN 2036-7511
▼ **RHEUMATOLOGY REPORTS.** Text in English. 2009. irreg. **Document type:** *Journal, Academic/Scholarly.* **Description:** Publishes experimental and clinical papers about any rheumatological condition, musculoskeletal medicine and surgery.
Related titles: Online - full text ed.: ISSN 2036-752X. free (effective 2011).
Indexed: A01, EMBASE, SCOPUS, T02.
Published by: Pagepress, Via Giuseppe Belli 4, Pavia, 27100, Italy. TEL 39-0382-1751762, FAX 39-0382-1750481. Ed. Robert J Petrella.

616.7 ITA ISSN 2035-8245
▼ **RHEUMATOLOGY REVIEWS.** Text in English. 2009. irreg.
Related titles: Online - full text ed.: ISSN 2035-8156.
Published by: Pagepress, Via Giuseppe Belli 4, Pavia, 27100, Italy. TEL 39-0382-1751762, FAX 39-0382-1750481, http://www.pagepress.org.

616.7 FRA ISSN 0249-7581
RHUMATOLOGIE. Text in French. 1949. 8/yr. adv. bk.rev. **Document type:** *Journal, Trade.*
Indexed: A22, B25, BIOSIS Prev, FR, Inpharma, MycolAb, P30, SCOPUS.
—BLDSC (7963.400000), GNLM, IE, Infotrieve, Ingenta, INIST. **CCC.**
Published by: Meditions Carline (Subsidiary of: Groupe Meditions), 1-3 rue du Depart, Paris, 75014, France. TEL 33-1-40640075, FAX 33-1-43222699, carline@groupemeditions.com.

616.7 FRA ISSN 0295-5261
RHUMATOLOGIE PRATIQUE. Text in French. 1986. bi-m. (5/yr). **Document type:** *Newspaper, Trade.*
Published by: L E N Medical - Axis Sante, 15 Rue des Sablons, Paris, 75116, France. TEL 33-1-47553131, FAX 33-1-47553132, info@len-medical.fr, http://www.len-medical.fr.

616.7 FRA ISSN 1771-0081
RHUMATOS; pratique quotidienne en rhumatologie. Text in French. 2004. m. (10/yr). **Document type:** *Journal, Trade.*
Published by: Expressions Groupe, 2 Rue de la Roquette, Cour de Mai, Paris, 75011, France. TEL 33-1-49292929, FAX 33-1-49292919, contact@expressions-sante.fr.

616.7 JPN ISSN 0914-8760
RINSHOU RYUUMACHI/CLINICAL RHEUMATOLOGY AND RELATED RESEARCH. Text in Japanese. 1988. a. **Document type:** *Journal, Academic/Scholarly.*
—BLDSC (3286.374700). **CCC.**
Published by: Kansai Ryuumachi Gakkai/Japanese Society for Clinical Rheumatology and Related Research, c/o Kinki University School of Medicine, Department of Orthopaedic Surgery, 377-2, Ohno-Higashi, Osaka-Sayama, Osaka 589-8511, Japan. TEL 81-72-3660221 ext 3212, FAX 81-72-3660206, cra@med.kindai.ac.jp, http://www.j-cra.com.

616.99105 615.82 TUR ISSN 1300-0691
➤ **ROMATOLOJI VE TIBBI REHABILITASYON DERGISI/JOURNAL OF RHEUMATOLOGY AND MEDICAL REHABILITATION.** Text and summaries in English, Turkish. 1990. q. looseleaf. adv. bk.rev. back issues avail. **Document type:** *Journal, Academic/Scholarly.* **Description:** Contains original articles and case reports are published in topics related with rheumatology, physical medicine, sports medicine and medical rehabilitation of all kinds.
Indexed: EMBASE, ExcerpMed, R10, Reac, SCOPUS.
—IE, Ingenta.
Published by: Turk Tibbi Rehabilitasyon Kurumu Dernegi/Turkish Society of Rehabilitational Medicine, Hacettepe Universitesi, Tip Fakultesi, Hacettepe - Ankara, 06100, Turkey. TEL 90-312-3094142, FAX 90-312-3105769, hufftr@tr-net.net.tr. Ed., Pub., R&P, Adv. contact Zafer Hascelik. B&W page USD 200, color page USD 300; trim 210 x 290. Circ: 500 (paid); 250 (controlled).

616.742 NLD ISSN 1566-6018
ROND REUMA. Text in Dutch. 1960. q. EUR 10 (effective 2009). adv. **Document type:** *Journal, Academic/Scholarly.* **Description:** Contains general (non-medical) information on activities against rheumatism.
Former titles (until 1999): Reuma Nu (1385-7169); (until 1996): Reuma Bulletin (0034-6217)
Published by: Nationaal Reumafonds, Postbus 59091, Amsterdam, 1040 KB, Netherlands. TEL 31-20-5896464, FAX 31-20-5896444, info@reumafonds.nl, http://www.reumafonds.nl. Circ: 60,000.

616.7 JPN ISSN 0915-227X
RYUMACHIKA/RHEUMATOLOGY. Text in Japanese. 1989. m. JPY 2,625 (effective 2003). **Document type:** *Journal, Academic/Scholarly.*
Published by: Kagaku-Hyoronsha Co. Ltd., 2-10-8, Kana Tomiyama-cho, Chiyoda-ku, Tokyo, 101-8531, Japan. TEL 81-3-32527741, FAX 81-3-32525952, http://www.kahyo.com/index.html.

616.742 GBR ISSN 0300-9742
RC927 CODEN: SJRHAT
➤ **SCANDINAVIAN JOURNAL OF RHEUMATOLOGY.** Text in English. 1955. bi-m. GBP 250, EUR 330, USD 415 combined subscription to institutions (print & online eds.); GBP 500, EUR 660, USD 830 combined subscription to corporations (print & online eds.) (effective 2010). adv. back issues avail.; reprint service avail. from PSC. **Document type:** *Journal, Academic/Scholarly.* **Description:** Covers clinical and experimental aspects of rheumatic diseases.
Formerly (until 1972): Acta Rheumatologica Scandinavica (0001-6934)
Related titles: Online - full text ed.: ISSN 1502-7732. 1998 (from IngentaConnect); ◆ Supplement(s): Scandinavian Journal of Rheumatology. Supplement. ISSN 0301-3847.
Indexed: A01, A03, A08, A22, A36, ASCA, B21, B25, BIOBASE, BIOSIS Prev, C06, C07, CA, CABA, CTA, ChemAb, ChemoAb, CurCont, D01, DBA, DentInd, E01, E12, EMBASE, EnerRA, ExcerpMed, GH, IABS, IBR, IBZ, ISR, ImmunAb, IndMed, Inpharma, MEDLINE, MS&D, MycolAb, N02, N03, NSA, P30, P33, P35, P39, R08, R10, Reac, SCI, SCOPUS, T02, T05, THA, W07.
—BLDSC (8087.546000), CASDDS, GNLM, IE, Infotrieve, Ingenta, INIST. **CCC.**
Published by: (Scandinavian Society for Rheumatology NOR), Informa Healthcare (Subsidiary of: T & F Informa plc), Telephone House, 69-77 Paul St, London, EC2A 4LQ, United Kingdom. TEL 44-20-70175000, FAX 44-20-70176792, healthcare.enquiries@informa.com. Ed. Kristian Stengaard-Pedersen. Adv. contact Per Sonnerfeldt. **Subscr. in N. America to:** Taylor & Francis Inc., Customer Services Dept, 325 Chestnut St, 8th Fl, Philadelphia, PA 19106. TEL 215-625-8900, 800-354-1420, FAX 215-625-8914, customerservice@taylorandfrancis.com; **Subscr. outside N. America to:** Taylor & Francis Ltd., Journals Customer Service, Sheepen Pl, Colchester, Essex CO3 3LP, United Kingdom. TEL 44-20-70175544, FAX 44-20-70175198, tf.enquiries@tfinforma.com.

617.742 SWE ISSN 0301-3847
RC927 CODEN: SJRSAS
➤ **SCANDINAVIAN JOURNAL OF RHEUMATOLOGY. SUPPLEMENT.** Text in English. 1958. irreg., latest 2000. price varies. reprint service avail. from PSC. **Document type:** *Monographic series, Academic/Scholarly.*
Formerly (until 1973): Acta Rheumatologica Scandinavica. Supplementum (0065-163X)
Related titles: Online - full text ed.: ISSN 1502-7740. 1999; ◆ Supplement to: Scandinavian Journal of Rheumatology. ISSN 0300-9742.
Indexed: A01, A03, A08, A22, AMED, EMBASE, ExcerpMed, IndMed, Inpharma, MEDLINE, P30, P35, R10, Reac, SCOPUS, T02.
—BLDSC (8087.546300), CASDDS, IE, Infotrieve, Ingenta, INIST. **CCC.**
Published by: (Scandinavian Society for Rheumatology NOR), Taylor & Francis A B (Subsidiary of: Taylor & Francis Group), PO Box 3255, Stockholm, 10365, Sweden. TEL 46-8-4408040, FAX 46-8-4408050.

616.7 NLD ISSN 1871-4463
SCRIPT REUMATOLOGIE. Text in Dutch. 2005. q. adv.
Published by: Van Zuiden Communications B.V., Postbus 2122, Alphen aan den Rijn, 2400 CC, Netherlands. TEL 31-172-476191, FAX 31-172-471882, zuiden@zuidencomm.nl, http://www.zuidencomm.nl. Eds. Dr. A den Broeder, Dr. J J Jaspers. Circ: 450 (controlled).

616.7 USA ISSN 0049-0172
RC933.A1 CODEN: SAHRBF
➤ **SEMINARS IN ARTHRITIS AND RHEUMATISM.** Text in English. 1971. bi-m. USD 578 in United States to institutions; USD 704 elsewhere to institutions (effective 2012). adv. bibl.; charts; illus. index. back issues avail.; reprints avail. **Document type:** *Journal, Academic/Scholarly.* **Description:** Provides a broad interpretation of the field, including aspects of general medicine and orthopedics. Focusing on topics in rheumatology and have interest to rheumatologists, internal medicine specialists, orthopedic surgeons, immunologists and specialists in bone and marrow metabolism.
Related titles: Online - full text ed.: ISSN 1532-866X (from ScienceDirect).
Indexed: A22, A26, ASCA, BIOSIS Prev, C06, C07, C08, CIN, CINAHL, ChemAb, ChemTitl, CurCont, DentInd, E01, EMBASE, ExcerpMed, H12, I05, ISR, IndMed, Inpharma, MEDLINE, MS&D, MycolAb, P30, R10, Reac, SCI, SCOPUS, T02, W07.
—BLDSC (8239.448000), CASDDS, GNLM, IE, Infotrieve, Ingenta, INIST. **CCC.**
Published by: W.B. Saunders Co. (Subsidiary of: Elsevier Health Sciences), Elsevier, Health Sciences Division, Order Fulfillment, 3251 Riverport Ln, Maryland Heights, MO 63043. TEL 314-872-8370, 800-325-4177, FAX 314-432-1380, JournalCustomerService-usa@elsevier.com, http://www.us.elsevierhealth.com. Ed. Marc C Hochberg TEL 410-706-6474. Pubs. Ali Gavenda TEL 215-239-6112, Pamela Poppalardo TEL 212-633-3911.

616.7 PRT
SOCIEDADE REUMATOLOGICA PORTUGUESA. BOLETIM INFORRMATIVO. Abbreviated title: S R P B I. Text in Portuguese. 2007. 3/yr. **Document type:** *Bulletin, Trade.*
Published by: Sociedade Reumatologica Portuguesa, Av de Berlim 33B, Lisbon, 1800-033, Portugal. TEL 351-21-3534395, FAX 351-21-3159780, info@spreumatologia.pt, www.spreumatologia.pt.

616.7 USA ISSN 1531-4111
SPINELINE; the clinical and news magazine for spine care professionals. Text in English. 2000. bi-m. free membership. adv. **Document type:** *Magazine, Trade.* **Description:** Contains multidisciplinary medical and scientific education, review and commentary on recent research, and aims to assist caregivers in providing high-quality, cost effective care. Provides practical, timely information concerning economic, medicolegal and policy issues; and serves to promote the policies, products, and professional activities of the association.
Published by: North American Spine Society, 22 Calendar Ct., Suite 200, LaGrange, IL 60525. Ed. Dr. Eeric Truumees. adv.: B&W page USD 1,105, color page USD 1,325; trim 8.5 x 11. Circ: 4,454 (paid).

616.74 NLD ISSN 2210-2086
SPREEKUUR REUMATOLOGIE. Text in Dutch. 1998. 4/yr. free to qualified personnel (effective 2010). adv. **Document type:** *Journal, Trade.*
Formerly (until 2010): Reumatologen Vademecum (1389-2681)
Published by: Bohn Stafleu van Loghum B.V. (Subsidiary of: Springer Science+Business Media), Postbus 246, Houten, 3990 GA, Netherlands. TEL 31-30-6383872, FAX 31-30-6383991, boekhandels@bsl.nl, http://www.bsl.nl. adv.: color page EUR 3,434; trim 210 x 297. Circ: 309.

616.7 NLD ISSN 2211-2820
'T STEUNTJE. Text in Dutch. 199?. bi-m.
Published by: Reuma Patienten Vereniging Arnhem e.o., Oranjestraat 19, Duiven, 6921 ZH, Netherlands. TEL 31-316-263824, secretariaat@reuma-arnhem.nl, http://www.reuma-arnhem.nl.

616.742 GBR ISSN 1759-7846
TOPICAL REVIEWS. Variant title: Reports on the Rheumatic Diseases. Text in English. 1959; N.S. 1985; N.S. 1994. 3/yr. free (effective 2009). back issues avail. **Document type:** *Journal, Academic/Scholarly.* **Description:** Offers advice on the diagnosis and treatment of common problems, topical research findings, and theories. Aimed at physicians and other health care professionals.
Former titles (until 2003): Rheumatic Disease Topical Reviews (1469-3097); (until 2000): Reports on Rheumatic Diseases. Series 3. Topical Reviews (1351-4881); (until 1994): Reports on Rheumatic Diseases. Series 2. Topical Reviews (1351-3508); Which superseded in part: Reports on Rheumatic Diseases (0957-0381); Which superseded (in 1985): Rheumatic Diseases Report; (in 1983): Reports on Rheumatic Diseases (0048-7279)
Related titles: Online - full text ed.
—BLDSC (8867.406800), GNLM.
Published by: Arthritis Research Campaign, Copeman House, St. Mary's Ct, St. Mary's Gate, Chesterfield, Derbys S41 7TD, United Kingdom. TEL 44-1246-558033, FAX 44-1246-558007, info@arc.org.uk.

616.742 TUR ISSN 1309-0291
➤ **TURK ROMATOLOJI DERGISI/TURKISH JOURNAL OF RHEUMATOLOGY.** Text in Turkish. 1947. q. **Document type:** *Journal, Academic/Scholarly.* **Description:** Publishes original work on all aspects of rheumatology and disorders of connective tissue.
Formerly: Romatizma (1300-5286)
Related titles: Online - full text ed.: ISSN 1309-0283. free (effective 2011); English ed.
Indexed: A01, A26, C06, C07, CA, EMBASE, H12, I05, R10, Reac, SCI, SCOPUS, T02, W07.
Published by: (Turkish League against Rheumatism (T L A R)), A V E S Yayincilik, Kizilelma cad.5/3, Findikzade - Istanbul, 34096, Turkey. TEL 90-212-5890053, FAX 90-212-5890094, info@avesyayincilik.com. Ed. Deniz Evcik.

616.7 UKR
UKRAINS'KYI REVMATOLOHICHNYI ZHURNAL. Text in Ukrainian, Russian; Abstracts and contents page in English. 2000. q. **Document type:** *Journal.*
Related titles: Online - full text ed.
Published by: Morion LLC, pr-kt M Bazhana, 10A, Kyiv, 02140, Ukraine. public@morion.kiev.ua, http://www.morion.kiev.ua. Ed. V M Kovalenko.

616.7 DEU
WIR IN HESSEN; Ihr hessisches Rheumamagazin. Text in German. 2/yr. adv. **Document type:** *Magazine, Consumer.*
Published by: (Rheuma-Liga Hessen e.V.), G F M K GmbH & Co. KG Verlagsgesellschaft, Gezelinallee 37-39, Leverkusen, 51375, Germany. TEL 49-214-310570, FAX 49-214-3105719, info@gfmk.de, http://www.gfmk.de. Ed. Christian Feldhaus. Adv. contact Lydia Schubert TEL 49-214-310570. Circ: 10,000 (controlled).

WIRTSCHAFTSTIP FUER ORTHOPAEDEN - RHEUMATOLOGEN. *see* MEDICAL SCIENCES—Orthopedics And Traumatology

616.716 GBR ISSN 1742-3090
RC931.O73
THE YEAR IN OSTEOPOROSIS. Text in English. 2004. a., latest vol.2, 2006. USD 99.95 per issue in US & Canada; GBP 59.99 per issue elsewhere (effective 2009). **Document type:** *Journal, Academic/Scholarly.* **Description:** Provides doctors, in particular rheumatologists, gynaecologists, general hospital physicians and GPs with an overview of the latest clinical research.
Related titles: Online - full text ed.
Indexed: P20, P22, P48, P54, PQC.
—BLDSC (9371.628630). **CCC.**
Published by: Clinical Publishing (Subsidiary of: Atlas Medical Publishing Ltd), Oxford Centre for Innovation, Mill St, Oxford, OX2 0JX, United Kingdom. TEL 44-1865-811116, FAX 44-1865-251550, info@clinicalpublishing.co.uk. Eds. A D Woolf, J D Adachi, K Akesson. **Dist. by:** Marston Book Services Ltd., Unit 160, Milton Park, Abingdon, Oxfordshire OX14 4SD, United Kingdom. TEL 44-1235-465500, FAX 44-1235-465555, trade.orders@marston.co.uk/, http://www.marston.co.uk/.

616.7 GBR ISSN 1476-2188
RC927
THE YEAR IN RHEUMATIC DISORDERS. Text in English. 2001. a., latest 2007. USD 99.95 per issue in US & Canada; GBP 59.99 per issue elsewhere (effective 2009). 280 p./no.; **Document type:** *Journal, Academic/Scholarly.* **Description:** Provides authoritative overview of recent developments in the treatment of rheumatic diseases.
Indexed: P20, P22, P54, PQC.
—CCC.
Published by: Clinical Publishing (Subsidiary of: Atlas Medical Publishing Ltd), Oxford Centre for Innovation, Mill St, Oxford, OX2 0JX, United Kingdom. TEL 44-1865-811116, FAX 44-1865-251550, info@clinicalpublishing.co.uk. Eds. H Capell, R Madhok. **Dist. by:** Marston Book Services Ltd., Unit 160, Milton Park, Abingdon, Oxfordshire OX14 4SD, United Kingdom. TEL 44-1235-465500, FAX 44-1235-465555, trade.orders@marston.co.uk, http://www.marston.co.uk/.

616.742 DEU ISSN 0340-1855
CODEN: ZRHMBQ
➤ **ZEITSCHRIFT FUER RHEUMATOLOGIE.** Text and summaries in English, German. 1938. bi-m. EUR 1,041, USD 833 combined subscription to institutions (print & online eds.) (effective 2012). adv. bk.rev. abstr.; bibl.; charts; illus.; pat. back issues avail.; reprint service avail. from PSC. **Document type:** *Journal, Academic/Scholarly.*
Formerly (until 1974): Zeitschrift fuer Rheumaforschung (0044-345X)
Related titles: Microform ed.: (from PQC); Online - full text ed.: ISSN 1435-1250 (from IngentaConnect); Supplement(s): Zeitschrift fuer Rheumatologie. Supplement. ISSN 0941-8466.
Indexed: A20, A22, A26, A36, ASCA, B25, BIOSIS Prev, CA, CABA, CIN, ChemAb, ChemTitl, CurCont, D01, DBA, DentInd, E01, EMBASE, ExcerpMed, FR, GH, IBR, IBZ, INI, ISR, IndMed, Inpharma, MEDLINE, MycolAb, N02, N03, P30, P33, P39, R08, R10, RILM, RM&VM, Reac, SCI, SCOPUS, T02, W07.
—BLDSC (9485.455000), CASDDS, GNLM, IE, Infotrieve, Ingenta, INIST. **CCC.**
Published by: Springer (Subsidiary of: Springer Science+Business Media), Tiergartenstr 17, Heidelberg, 69121, Germany. TEL 49-6221-4870, FAX 49-6221-345229, subscriptions@springer.com. Ed. W L Gross. adv.: B&W page EUR 900, color page EUR 1,940. Circ: 1,600 (paid and controlled). **Subscr. in the Americas to:** Springer New York LLC, Journal Fulfillment, PO Box 2485, Secaucus,

NJ 07096. TEL 800-777-4643, 201-348-4033, FAX 201-348-4505, journals-ny@springer.com. **Co-sponsors:** Deutsche Gesellschaft fuer Rheumatologie; Oesterreichische Gesellschaft fuer Rheumatologie; Gesellschaft fuer Psychosomatik in der Rheumatologie; Berufsverband Deutscher Rheumatologen; Schweizerische Gesellschaft fuer Rheumatologie.

616.7 CHN ISSN 1007-7480
ZHONGHUA FENGSHIBINGXUE ZAZHI/CHINESE JOURNAL OF RHEUMATOLOGY. Text in Chinese. 1997. m. USD 62.40 (effective 2009). **Document type:** *Journal, Academic/Scholarly.* **Description:** Reports on the leading clinical experiments and studies with a theoretical basis. Contains editorials, original articles, reviews, lectures, clinical studies, clinicopathological discussions, academic trends in China and abroad, case reporting, technical exchanges, and other columns.
Related titles: Online - full text ed.
—East View.
Published by: Zhonghua Yixuehui/Chinese Medical Association, 23 Donghuamen, Taiyuan, Shanxi 030013, China. TEL 86-351-3580185, FAX 86-351-3173607. Circ: 15,500 (paid); 200 (controlled). **Dist. by:** China International Book Trading Corp, 35 Chegongzhuang Xilu, Haidian District, PO Box 399, Beijing 100044, China. TEL 86-10-68412045, FAX 86-10-68412023, cibtc@mail.cibtc.com.cn, http://www.cibtc.com.cn.

MEDICAL SCIENCES—Sports Medicine

A C S M'S HEALTH & FITNESS JOURNAL. *see* PHYSICAL FITNESS AND HYGIENE

A S M A NEWS. *see* SPORTS AND GAMES

612.044 617.1027 CZE ISSN 1212-1428
➤ **ACTA UNIVERSITATIS CAROLINAE. KINANTHROPOLOGICA.** Text in Czech. 1965. 2/yr. EUR 40 (effective 2009). **Document type:** *Journal, Academic/Scholarly.* **Description:** Covers sport science, psychology, pedagogy, physiology, sports medicine, biomechanics.
Formerly (until 1995): Acta Universitatis Carolinae: Gymnica (0323-0511)
Indexed: SD.
Published by: (Univerzita Karlova v Praze, Fakulta Telesne Vychovy a Sportu), Nakladatelstvi Karolinum, Ovocny trh 3/5, Prague 1, 11636, Czech Republic. TEL 420-224491275, FAX 420-224212041, cupress@cuni.cz, http://cupress.cuni.cz. Ed. Antonin Rychtecki. Circ: 250.

617.1 JPN ISSN 1340-3141
ADVANCES IN EXERCISE AND SPORTS PHYSIOLOGY. Text in Japanese, English. 1994. q.
Indexed: CA, R09, SD, T02.
—BLDSC (0706.035000), IE, Ingenta.
Published by: University of Tsukuba, Institute of Health and Exercise Physiology, Japan Society of Exercise and Sports Physiology, 1-1-1 Tennodai, Ibaraki-Ken, Tsukuba-Shi, 305-8574, Japan. http://www.taiiku.tsukuba.ac.jp/english/index.html.

617.1 USA ISSN 1056-9677
AMERICAN COLLEGE OF SPORTS MEDICINE. CERTIFIED NEWS. Text in English. 3/yr. free with a valid ACSM Certification (effective 2005). **Document type:** *Newsletter.* **Description:** Provides continuing education credits (CECs) and information to those certified by ACSM.
Published by: (Certification Committee), American College of Sports Medicine, PO Box 1440, Indianapolis, IN 46206. TEL 508-233-4832, FAX 508-233-5298.

617 USA ISSN 0363-5465
RC1200 CODEN: AJSMDO
➤ **AMERICAN JOURNAL OF SPORTS MEDICINE.** Text in English. 1972. m. USD 867, GBP 511 to institutions; USD 885, GBP 521 combined subscription to institutions (print & online eds.) (effective 2012). adv. illus. cum.index: 1972-1996. back issues avail.; reprint service avail. from PSC. **Document type:** *Journal, Academic/Scholarly.* **Description:** Presents original scientific research directed to orthopaedic surgeons specializing in sports medicine.
Formerly (until 1976): Journal of Sports Medicine (0090-4201)
Related titles: CD-ROM ed.; Microfilm ed.: (from PQC); Microform ed.; Online - full text ed.: ISSN 1552-3365. USD 797, GBP 469 to institutions (effective 2012).
Indexed: A01, A02, A03, A08, A20, A22, A25, A26, A36, AMED, ASCA, AbAn, B04, B21, B25, BIOSIS Prev, BRD, C06, C07, C08, C12, CA, CABA, CINAHL, CurCont, E01, E02, E03, E07, E08, EMBASE, ERI, ESPM, EdA, EdI, ExcerpMed, FR, FoSS&M, G03, G05, G06, G07, G08, GH, GSA, GSI, H&SSA, H01, H02, H04, H11, H12, H13, HlthInd, I05, ISR, IndMed, Inpharma, JW, LT, M01, M02, M06, MEDLINE, MycolAb, NRN, P02, P10, P13, P15, P16, P20, P24, P26, P30, P33, P35, P48, P53, P54, PEI, PQC, R09, R10, RRTA, Reac, S06, S08, S09, S23, SCI, SCOPUS, SD, SportS, T02, T05, W03, W07, W11.
—BLDSC (0838.400000), GNLM, IE, Infotrieve, Ingenta, INIST. **CCC.**
Published by: (American Orthopaedic Society for Sports Medicine), Sage Publications, Inc., 2455 Teller Rd, Thousand Oaks, CA 91320. TEL 800-818-7243, FAX 800-583-2665, info@sagepub.com, http://www.sagepub.com/. Ed. Dr. Bruce Reider. **Subscr. outside the Americas to:** Sage Publications Ltd., 1 Oliver's Yard, 55 City Rd, London EC1Y 1SP, United Kingdom. TEL 44-207-3248701, FAX 44-207-3248733, subscription@sagepub.co.uk.

617.1 USA
➤ **AMERICAN MEDICAL ATHLETIC ASSOCIATION. JOURNAL.** Variant title: A M A A Journal. Text in English. 2002. 3/yr. free to members (effective 2010). back issues avail. **Document type:** *Journal, Academic/Scholarly.* **Description:** Publishes original papers related to the medical aspects of sports, exercise, and fitness. Our goal is to assist physicians and other health care professionals in caring for active patients, in encouraging sedentary patients to become active, and in improving personal fitness/training programs readers use for all patients.
Media: Online - full text.
Published by: American Medical Athletic Association, 4405 East-West Hwy, Ste 405, Bethesda, MD 20814. TEL 301-913-9517, 800-776-2732, FAX 301-913-9520, amaa@americanrunning.org. Ed. Steven Jonas.

617.103 USA
AMERICAN PHYSICAL THERAPY ASSOCIATION. SPORTS PHYSICAL THERAPY SECTION. NEWSLETTER. Text in English. 19??. q.
Published by: American Physical Therapy Association, Orthopedic Section, 2920 E Ave S, Ste 200, La Crosse, WI 54601. TEL 608-788-3982, 800-444-3982, FAX 608-788-3965, tdeflorian@orthopt.org, http://www.orthopt.org.

617.1 JPN ISSN 0918-0257
AOMORIKEN SUPOTSU IGAKU KENKYUKAISHI/AOMORI SOCIETY OF SPORTS MEDICINE. JOURNAL. Text in Japanese. 1989. s-a. abstr.; bibl.; charts; illus.; stat. back issues avail. **Document type:** *Proceedings, Academic/Scholarly.*
Formerly: Aomoriken Supotsu Igaku Kenkyukai Koenshu
—CCC.
Published by: Aomoriken Supotsu Igaku Kenkyukai/Aomori Society of Sports Medicine, c/o Mr Yoshihisa Okamura, Hirosaki Daigaku Igakubu Seikei Geka Kyoshitsu, 5 Zaifu-cho, Hirosaki-shi, Aomori-ken 036-8216, Japan.

612.044 CAN ISSN 1715-5312
CODEN: CJAPEY
➤ **APPLIED PHYSIOLOGY, NUTRITION AND METABOLISM/ PHYSIOLOGIE APPLIQUEE, NUTRITION ET METABOLISME.** Text in English, French. 1976. bi-m. CAD 645 to institutions; CAD 810 combined subscription to institutions (print & online eds.) (effective 2011). adv. bk.rev. abstr.; bibl.; charts; stat.; illus. Index. back issues avail.; reprints avail. **Document type:** *Journal, Academic/Scholarly.* **Description:** Focuses on both basic and applied research articles that examine the relationship between the biological sciences and physical activity, health, and fitness.
Former titles (until 2006): Canadian Journal of Applied Physiology (1066-7814); (until 1993): Canadian Journal of Sport Sciences (0833-1235); (until 1987): Canadian Journal of Applied Sport Science (0700-3978)
Related titles: Microfiche ed.: (from MML); Microform ed.: (from MML); Online - full text ed.: ISSN 1715-5320. CAD 540 to institutions (effective 2011) (from IngentaConnect).
Indexed: A01, A02, A03, A08, A22, A26, A34, A35, A36, A37, A38, AMED, ASCA, AgBio, B21, C03, C06, C07, C08, CA, CABA, CBCARef, CBPI, CIN, CINAHL, ChemAb, ChemTitl, CurCont, D01, DIP, E-psyche, E08, E12, EMBASE, ESPM, ErgAb, ExcerpMed, FR, FoSS&M, GH, H&SSA, H12, H16, I05, IBR, IBZ, IndMed, LT, MEDLINE, N02, N03, N04, P03, P30, P48, PEI, PN&I, PQC, PsycholAb, R09, R10, R12, RA&MP, RRTA, Reac, S02, S03, S12, SCI, SCOPUS, SD, SoyAb, SportS, T02, T05, VS, W07, W11.
—BLDSC (1576.482500), CASDDS, GNLM, IE, Infotrieve, Ingenta, INIST. **CCC.**
Published by: (Canadian Society for Exercise Physiology, National Research Council Canada (N R C)/Conseil National de Recherches Canada (C N R C)), N R C Research Press, 1200 Montreal Rd, Bldg M-55, Ottawa, ON K1A 0R6, Canada. TEL 613-993-9084, 800-668-1222, FAX 613-952-7656, pubs@nrc-cnrc.gc.ca, http://pubs.nrc-cnrc.gc.ca. Ed. Dr. Terry Graham. Circ: 965 (paid and free).
Co-sponsor: Canadian Society for Clinical Nutrition.

617.1 ESP ISSN 0212-8799
RC1200 CODEN: AMDEFG
ARCHIVOS DE MEDICINA DEL DEPORTE. Text in Spanish; Summaries in English, French, Spanish. 1984. bi-m. EUR 150 domestic to institutions; EUR 160 in Europe to institutions; EUR 200 elsewhere to institutions (effective 2009). adv. bk.rev. abstr.; bibl.; charts; illus.; mkt. index. 80 p./no.; back issues avail. **Document type:** *Journal, Academic/Scholarly.*
Related titles: CD-ROM ed.: 1984; Online - full text ed.: 1984.
Indexed: IndMed, SCOPUS, SD.
—CCC.
Published by: (Federacion Espanola de Medicina del Deporte (F E M E D E)), Nexus Medica Editores, C/ Passeig d'Amunt 38, Barcelona, 08024, Spain. TEL 34-93-5510260, FAX 34-93-2136672, redaccion@nexusmedica.com, http://www.nexusediciones.com.

613.711 USA ISSN 1942-5864
RD97
▼➤ **ATHLETIC TRAINING & SPORTS HEALTH CARE**; the journal for the practicing clinician. Text mainly in English. 2009 (Jan.). bi-m. USD 79 to individuals; USD 259 to institutions (effective 2009). adv. **Document type:** *Journal, Academic/Scholarly.* **Description:** Provides a forum for the dissemination of contemporary athletic training and sports health care information and guidance to clinicians involved in a variety of allied health professions.
Related titles: Online - full text ed.: ISSN 1942-5872.
Indexed: C06, P24, P48, PQC, R09, SD, T02.
Published by: Slack, Inc., 6900 Grove Rd, Thorofare, NJ 08086. TEL 856-848-1000, 800-257-8290, FAX 856-848-6091, customerservice@slackinc.com, http://www.slackinc.com. Ed. Thomas W Kaminski. adv.: B&W page USD 1,555; trim 8.125 x 10.875. Circ: 100 (paid).

613.711 USA ISSN 1947-380X
GV201
➤ **ATHLETIC TRAINING EDUCATION JOURNAL.** Abbreviated title: A T E J. Text in English. 2006. q. free (effective 2011). back issues avail. **Document type:** *Journal, Academic/Scholarly.* **Description:** Serves as an interface between the theory and practice of athletic training education by providing a forum for scholars, educators, and clinicians to share critical and significant concepts, original research, and innovative ideas.
Media: Online - full text.
Indexed: C06, C07.
Published by: National Athletic Trainers Association, Inc., Brigham Young University, 276 SFH, Provo, UT 84602. TEL 801-422-3181, membership@nata.org, http://www.nata.org/. Ed. William A Pitney.

➤ **AVANCES EN TRAUMATOLOGIA, CIRUGIA, REHABILITACION, MEDICINA PREVENTIVA Y DEPORTIVA.** *see* MEDICAL SCIENCES—Surgery

617.1027 DEU ISSN 1613-0863
BEWEGUNGSTHERAPIE UND GESUNDHEITSSPORT; Praevention, Sporttherapie und Rehabilitation in Wissenschaft und Praxis. Abbreviated title: B & G. Text in German. 1985. bi-m. EUR 39.90 to institutions; EUR 103 combined subscription to institutions; EUR 9 newsstand/cover (effective 2011). adv. **Document type:** *Journal, Academic/Scholarly.*
Former titles (until 2004): Gesundheitssport und Sporttherapie (0939-0626); (until 1990): Sporttherapie in Theorie und Praxis (0930-1348)
Related titles: Online - full text ed.: ISSN 1613-3269. EUR 103 to institutions (effective 2011).
—BLDSC (1947.292100), IE. **CCC.**
Published by: Hippokrates Verlag in MVS Medizinverlage Stuttgart GmbH & Co.KG (Subsidiary of: Georg Thieme Verlag), Oswald-Hesse-Str 50, Stuttgart, 70469, Germany. TEL 49-711-89310, FAX 49-711-8931706, kunden.service@thieme.de, http://www.hippokrates.de. Eds. Gerhard Huber, Klaus Schuele. Adv. contact Kathrin Thomas. Circ: 4,000 (paid and controlled).

612.044 POL ISSN 0860-021X
➤ **BIOLOGY OF SPORT**; a quarterly journal of sport and exercise sciences. Text in English. 1984. q. **Document type:** *Journal, Academic/Scholarly.* **Description:** Publishes reports of methodological and experimental work on science of sport, natural sciences, medicine and pharmacology, technical sciences, biocybernetics and applications of statistics and psychology, with priority for inter-disciplinary papers.
Related titles: Online - full text ed.: free (effective 2011).
Indexed: A36, C06, C07, CA, CABA, FoSS&M, GH, LT, N02, N03, P30, PEI, SCI, SCOPUS, SD, T02, W07.
—BLDSC (2087.247000), IE, Infotrieve, Ingenta.
Published by: Instytut Sportu/Institute of Sport, ul Trylogoo 2/16, Warsaw, 01-982, Poland. TEL 48-22-8340812, FAX 48-22-8350977, insp@insp.waw.pl, http://www.insp.pl. Ed. Ryszard Grucza. **Dist. by:** Ars Polona, Obroncow 25, Warsaw 03933, Poland. TEL 48-22-5098609, FAX 48-22-5098610, arspolona@arspolona.com.pl, http://www.arspolona.com.pl.

617.1 BRA ISSN 1981-6324
RA781
BRAZILIAN JOURNAL OF BIOMOTRICITY. Text in Portuguese, English. 2007. q. free (effective 2011). **Document type:** *Journal, Academic/Scholarly.*
Media: Online - full text.
Indexed: P20, P24, P48, P54, PQC.
Published by: Marco Machado marcomachado@brjb.com.br, http://www.brjb.com.br. Ed. Marco Machado.

617 GBR ISSN 0306-3674
RC1200 CODEN: BJSMDZ
➤ **BRITISH JOURNAL OF SPORTS MEDICINE**; an international peer-reviewed journal of sport and exercise medicine. Abbreviated title: B J S M. Text in English. 1965. m. GBP 520 to institutions; GBP 654 combined subscription to institutions small FTE (print & online eds.) (effective 2011). adv. bk.rev. illus.; stat. Supplement avail.; back issues avail.; reprints avail. **Document type:** *Journal, Academic/Scholarly.* **Description:** Covers management of injuries and physiotherapy, physiological evaluations of sports performance, psychology, nutrition, and the role of medical personnel.
Formerly (until 1968): British Association of Sport and Medicine. Bulletin (0306-3690)
Related titles: Microform ed.: (from PQC); Online - full text ed.: B J S M Online. ISSN 1473-0480. 2000. GBP 521 to institutions small FTE (effective 2011).
Indexed: A01, A03, A08, A22, A26, A36, AMED, ASCA, AgrForAb, B21, C06, C07, C08, CA, CABA, CINAHL, CurCont, D01, E01, E08, E12, EMBASE, ESPM, ErgAb, ExcerpMed, F08, FoSS&M, G08, GH, GeoRef, H&SSA, H11, H12, H13, H16, I05, I11, INI, ISR, IndMed, Inpharma, LT, MEDLINE, N02, N03, NRN, P10, P20, P22, P24, P26, P30, P33, P35, P48, P53, P54, PEI, PQC, R10, R12, RA&MP, RM&VM, RRTA, Reac, S09, S12, S13, SCI, SCOPUS, SD, SportS, T02, T05, W07, W10, W11.
—BLDSC (2324.900000), CASDDS, GNLM, IE, Infotrieve, Ingenta, INIST. **CCC.**
Published by: (British Association of Sport and Exercise Medicine), B M J Group, BMA House, Tavistock Sq, London, WC1H 9JR, United Kingdom. TEL 44-20-73836373, FAX 44-20-73836668, http://group.bmj.com. Ed. Karim Khan. Pub. Janet O'Flaherty TEL 44-20-73836154. Adv. contact Nick Gray TEL 44-20-73836386. Circ: 2,250. **Subscr. to:** PO Box 299, London WC1H 9TD, United Kingdom. TEL 44-20-73836270, FAX 44-20-73836402, support@bmjgroup.com.

▼➤ **CARTILAGE.** *see* MEDICAL SCIENCES—Rheumatology

617.1 USA ISSN 1050-642X
RC1200 CODEN: CJSMED
➤ **CLINICAL JOURNAL OF SPORT MEDICINE.** Abbreviated title: C J S M. Text in English. 1972. bi-m. USD 655 domestic to institutions; USD 847.80 foreign to institutions (effective 2011). adv. bk.rev. charts; illus. back issues avail.; reprints avail. **Document type:** *Journal, Academic/Scholarly.* **Description:** Features original research articles, clinical reviews, case reports, new techniques and procedures in physical examination, exercise testing, diagnostic imaging, and other developments relevant to the clinical practice of sports medicine.
Former titles (until 1991): Canadian Academy of Sport Medicine Review (0831-2893); (until 1986): Canadian Academy of Sport Medicine Newsletter (0715-3422); (until 1980): Canadian Academy of Sport Medicine Journal (0715-3414)
Related titles: Online - full text ed.: ISSN 1536-3724.
Indexed: A01, A03, A08, A22, ASCA, B21, C06, C07, C08, CA, CINAHL, CurCont, EMBASE, ESPM, ExcerpMed, FoSS&M, H&SSA, ISR, IndMed, Inpharma, MEDLINE, P30, PEI, R09, R10, Reac, RiskAb, SCI, SCOPUS, SD, SportS, T02, W07.
—BLDSC (3286.294300), GNLM, IE, Infotrieve, Ingenta. **CCC.**
Published by: (Canadian Academy of Sport Medicine CAN), Lippincott Williams & Wilkins (Subsidiary of: Wolters Kluwer N.V.), 530 Walnut St, Philadelphia, PA 19106. TEL 215-521-8300, FAX 215-521-8902, customerservice@lww.com, http://www.lww.com. Ed. Willem Meeuwisse TEL 403-220-8947. Pub. Sandy Kasko. adv.: B&W page USD 1,330, color page USD 2,775; trim 7.75 x 10.125. Circ: 1,378.
Co-sponsor: American Medical Society for Sports Medicine.

617 USA ISSN 0278-5919
RC1200
➤ **CLINICS IN SPORTS MEDICINE.** Text in English. 1982. q. USD 466 in United States to institutions; USD 563 elsewhere to institutions (effective 2012). adv. back issues avail.; reprints avail. **Document type:** *Journal, Academic/Scholarly.* **Description:** Focuses on a single topic relevant to sports medicine and orthopedic surgery practice, from foot and ankle injuries to returning athletes to competition.

Related titles: Microform ed.: (from PQC); Online - full text ed.: ISSN 1556-228X (from ScienceDirect); ◆ Spanish Translation: Clinicas de Medicina Deportiva de Norteamerica. ISSN 1138-5111.
Indexed: A20, A22, AMED, ASCA, B21, C06, C07, C08, CA, CINAHL, CurCont, DentInd, E-psyche, EMBASE, ESPM, ExcerpMed, FR, FoSS&M, H&SSA, INI, ISR, IndMed, Inpharma, MEDLINE, P30, PEI, R09, SCI, SCOPUS, SD, SportS, T02, W07.
—BLDSC (3286.595500), GNLM, IE, Infotrieve, Ingenta, INIST. **CCC.**
Published by: W.B. Saunders Co. (Subsidiary of: Elsevier Health Sciences), Elsevier, Health Sciences Division, Order Fulfillment, 3251 Riverport Ln, Maryland Heights, MO 63043. TEL 314-872-8370, 800-325-4177, FAX 314-432-1380, JournalCustomerService-usa@elsevier.com, http://www.us.elsevierhealth.com. Adv. contact John Marmero TEL 212-633-3657.

617.1 ESP
CONGRESO EUROPEO DE MEDICINA DEL DEPORTE. RESUMEN DE COMUNICACIONES. Text in Spanish. a. EUR 30 (effective 2009). **Document type:** *Proceedings, Academic/Scholarly.*
Published by: Federacion Espanola de Medicina del Deporte (F E M E D E), Apartado de Correos 1207, Pamplona, Navarra 31080, Spain. TEL 34-948-267706, FAX 34-948-171431, fedeme@fedeme.es, http://www.fedeme.es.

617.1 ESP
CONGRESO NACIONAL DE FEMEDE. LIBRO DE ACTAS. Text in Spanish. a. **Document type:** *Proceedings, Academic/Scholarly.*
Published by: Federacion Espanola de Medicina del Deporte (F E M E D E), Apartado de Correos 1207, Pamplona, Navarra 31080, Spain. TEL 34-948-267706, FAX 34-948-174325, fedeme@arrakis.es, http://www.fedeme.es.

CULTURA, CIENCIA Y DEPORTE. *see* SPORTS AND GAMES

617.1 USA ISSN 1069-5842
RC1200
CURRENT REVIEW OF SPORTS MEDICINE. Text in English. 1994. irreg., latest 1998. reprints avail. **Document type:** *Monographic series, Academic/Scholarly.*
—GNLM.
Published by: Current Medicine Group LLC (Subsidiary of: Springer Science+Business Media), 400 Market St, Ste 700, Philadelphia, PA 19106. TEL 215-574-2266, 800-427-1796, FAX 215-574-2225, info_phl@currentmedicinegroup.com. Eds. John Lombardo, Robert J Johnston.

617.1 USA ISSN 1537-890X
RC1200
CURRENT SPORTS MEDICINE REPORTS. Text in English. 2002 (Feb.). bi-m. USD 535 domestic to institutions; USD 608 foreign to institutions (effective 2011). adv. back issues avail.; reprints avail. **Document type:** *Journal, Academic/Scholarly.* **Description:** Aims to translate the research and advances in the field into information physicians can use in caring for their patients.
Related titles: Online - full text ed.: ISSN 1537-8918.
Indexed: A20, A22, A26, C06, C07, CA, E01, E08, EMBASE, ExcerpMed, FoSS&M, H12, MEDLINE, P30, R09, R10, Reac, S09, SCI, SCOPUS, SD, T02, W07.
—BLDSC (3504.036420), IE, Ingenta. **CCC.**
Published by: (American College of Sports Medicine), Lippincott Williams & Wilkins (Subsidiary of: Wolters Kluwer N.V.), 530 Walnut St, Philadelphia, PA 19106. TEL 215-521-8300, FAX 215-521-8902, customerservice@lww.com, http://www.lww.com. Ed. William O Roberts. Pub. David Myers. Circ: 184.

617.1027 796.6 FRA ISSN 1957-2492
CYCLOTOURISME SANTE. Text in French. 2007. irreg. **Document type:** *Magazine, Consumer.*
Published by: Federation Francaise de Cyclotourisme (F F C T), 12 rue Louis Bertrand, Ivry-sur-Seine, 94207 Cedex, France. TEL 33-1-56208888, FAX 33-1-56208899, http://www.ffct.org.

617.1 DNK ISSN 1397-4211
DANSK SPORTSMEDICIN. Text in Danish. 1981. q. DKK 250 (effective 2008). adv. bk.rev. **Document type:** *Magazine, Trade.*
Formerly (until 1997): D I M S Bulletin (0108-7320)
Published by: Dansk Idraetsmedicinsk Selskab, c/o Gorm H. Rasmussen, Terp Skovvej 82, Hoejbjerg, 8270, Denmark. http://www.dansksportsmedicin.dk. Ed. Kristian Thorborg. Adv. contact Gorm H Rasmussen. page DKK 7,200; 210 x 297. Circ: 2,100.

617.102 DEU ISSN 0344-5925
CODEN: DZSPD8
DEUTSCHE ZEITSCHRIFT FUER SPORTMEDIZIN. Text in German. 1949. 11/yr. EUR 64.90 domestic; EUR 90.90 foreign (effective 2010). adv. **Document type:** *Journal, Trade.*
Former titles (until 1978): Sportarzt und Sportmedizin (0371-3059); (until 1964): Der Sportarzt (0340-5583)
Indexed: A22, B25, BIOSIS Prev, CIN, ChemAb, ChemTitl, DIP, FoSS&M, IBR, IBZ, MycolAb, P30, SCI, SCOPUS, SD, SportS, W07.
—CASDDS, GNLM, IE, Infotrieve. **CCC.**
Published by: (Deutsche Gesellschaft fuer Sportmedizin und Praevention/German Society of Sports Medicine and Prevention, Verein zur Foerderung der Sportmedizin Hannover e.V.), Sueddeutscher Verlag GmbH, Hultscheiner Str 8, Munich, 81677, Germany. FAX 49-89-21837213, http://www.sueddeutsche.de. Pub. Dieter Boening. adv.: B&W page EUR 2,020, color page EUR 3,310. Circ: 15,500.

EUROPEAN JOURNAL OF SPORT SCIENCE. *see* SPORTS AND GAMES

613.7 USA ISSN 0091-6331
RC1200 CODEN: ESSRB8
➤ **EXERCISE AND SPORT SCIENCES REVIEWS.** Text in English. 1973. q. USD 305 domestic to institutions; USD 329 foreign to institutions (effective 2011). adv. charts; illus. back issues avail.; reprints avail. **Document type:** *Journal, Academic/Scholarly.* **Description:** Provides reviews of the contemporary scientific, medical, and research-based topics emerging in the field of sports medicine and exercise science.
Related titles: Online - full text ed.: ISSN 1538-3008.
Indexed: A22, AMED, ASCA, B21, BIOBASE, BIOSIS Prev, C06, C07, CA, EMBASE, ESPM, ExcerpMed, FoSS&M, H&SSA, IABS, ISR, IndMed, MEDLINE, MycolAb, P30, PEI, R10, Reac, RiskAb, SCI, SCOPUS, SD, SportS, T02, W07.
—BLDSC (3836.233000), CASDDS, GNLM, IE, Infotrieve, Ingenta, INIST. **CCC.**
Published by: (American College of Sports Medicine), Lippincott Williams & Wilkins (Subsidiary of: Wolters Kluwer N.V.), 530 Walnut St, Philadelphia, PA 19106. TEL 215-521-8300, FAX 215-521-8902, customerservice@lww.com, http://www.lww.com. Ed. Priscilla M Clarkson. Pub. Terry Materese. Circ: 12,944.

616.07 612.7 DEU ISSN 1077-5552
QP301 CODEN: EIREFY
➤ **EXERCISE IMMUNOLOGY REVIEW.** Text in English. 1994. a. free to members (effective 2010). abstr. back issues avail.; reprints avail. **Document type:** *Journal, Academic/Scholarly.* **Description:** Committed to developing and enriching knowledge in all aspects of immunology that relate to sport, exercise, and regular physical activity.
Related titles: Online - full text ed.
Indexed: B21, C06, C07, C08, CINAHL, CurCont, EMBASE, ExcerpMed, FoSS&M, IBR, IBZ, ImmunAb, IndMed, MEDLINE, P30, PEI, R10, Reac, SCI, SCOPUS, SD, W07.
—BLDSC (3836.235700), GNLM, IE, Infotrieve, Ingenta. **CCC.**
Published by: Verein zur Foerderung der Sportmedizin/Association for the Advancement of Sports Medicine, c/o Prof. Dr. Hinnak Northoff, Institute of Clinical & Experimental Transfusion Medicine, University of Tuebingen, Otfried-Muller-Str. 4/1, Tubingen, D-72076, Germany. TEL 49-7071-2981601, FAX 49-7071-295240. Ed. Hinnak Northoff. Circ: 550 (paid). **Co-sponsors:** Deutsche Gesellschaft fuer Sportmedizin und Praevention/German Society of Sports Medicine and Prevention; International Society of Exercise and Immunology.

➤ **EXERCISE STANDARDS AND MALPRACTICE REPORTER.** *see* LAW

617.1 ESP
F E M E D E. BOLETIN. (Federacion Espanola de Medicina del Deporte) Text in Spanish. a. free. back issues avail. **Document type:** *Bulletin, Trade.*
Related titles: Online - full text ed.
Published by: Federacion Espanola de Medicina del Deporte (F E M E D E), Apartado de Correos 1207, Pamplona, Navarra 31080, Spain. TEL 34-948-267706, FAX 34-948-171431, fedeme@fedeme.es, http://www.fedeme.es.

FOOT & ANKLE INTERNATIONAL. *see* MEDICAL SCIENCES—Orthopedics And Traumatology

FUJIAN TIYU KEJI/FUJIAN SPORTS SCIENCE AND TECHNOLOGY. *see* SPORTS AND GAMES

610 ITA ISSN 1722-8530
GIORNALE ITALIANO DI PSICOLOGIA DELLO SPORT. Text in Italian. 1985. 4/yr. free to members. **Document type:** *Journal, Academic/Scholarly.*
Formerly (until 1999): Movimento (0393-9405)
Indexed: PsycholAb, SD.
Published by: (Associazione Italiana Psicologia dello Sport (A I P S)), Calzetti e Mariucci Editori, Via del Sottopasso 7, Localita Ferriera, Torgiano, PG 06089, Italy. http://www.calzetti-mariucci.it.

617 ESP ISSN 1132-2462
HABILIDAD MOTRIZ. Text in Spanish. 1992. s-a. **Document type:** *Magazine, Trade.*
Published by: Colegio Oficial de Profesores y Licenciados en Educacion Fisica (C O P L E F), Andalucia, C/ Carbonell y Morand 9, Cordoba, 14001, Spain. colefandalucia@wanadoo.es, http://www.colefandalucia.com.

617.1 IND ISSN 0973-340X
INDIAN JOURNAL OF SLEEP MEDICINE. Text in English. 2006. q. INR 1,500 combined subscription domestic to individuals (print & online eds.); USD 150 combined subscription foreign to individuals (print & online eds.); INR 2,000 combined subscription domestic to institutions (print & online eds.); USD 200 combined subscription foreign to institutions (print & online eds.) (effective 2011). **Document type:** *Journal, Academic/Scholarly.* **Description:** Deals with sleep disorders and related fields including anatomy, biochemistry, pathology, pharmacology and physiology.
Related titles: Online - full text ed.: ISSN 0974-0155.
Published by: The Indian Sleep Disorders Association, Rm No 404, Ward 32, 3rd Fl, Casualty Block, Safdarjang Hospital, New Delhi, 110 010, India. TEL 91-11-26190958, jcsuri@rediffmail.com, http://www.isda.in. Eds. M K Sen, J C Suri. **Subscr. to:** Indianjournals.com, Divan Enterprises, B-9, Local Shopping Complex, A-Block, Naraina Vihar, Ring Rd, New Delhi 110 028, India. TEL 91-11-25770411, FAX 91-11-25778876, info@indianjournals.com, http://www.indianjournals.com.

613.78 ESP ISSN 1988-8198
INSTITUTO DE POSTUROLOGIA Y PODOPOSTUROLOGIA. REVISTA. Text in Spanish. 2008. bi-m.
Media: Online - full text.
Published by: Instituto de Posturologia y Podoposturologia, C Girona, 56 1er Piso, Barcelona, 08009, Spain. TEL 34-93-2652476, revista@institutodeposturologia.com. Ed. Ignasi Beltran.

INTERNATIONAL JOURNAL OF APPLIED SPORTS SCIENCES. *see* SPORTS AND GAMES

617.1 USA ISSN 2157-7277
RC1200 CODEN: ATTOF5
➤ **INTERNATIONAL JOURNAL OF ATHLETIC THERAPY & TRAINING;** the professional journal of certified athletic trainers and athletic therapists. Text in English. 1996. bi-m. USD 290 domestic to institutions; USD 305 foreign to institutions; USD 342 combined subscription domestic to institutions (print & online eds.); USD 357 combined subscription foreign to institutions (print & online eds.) (effective 2012). illus. Index. back issues avail.; reprint service avail. from PSC. **Document type:** *Journal, Academic/Scholarly.* **Description:** Designed to provide insights into professional practice issues, highlight sports health care techniques, share experiential knowledge and provide practical applications of current research.
Formerly (until 2011): Athletic Therapy Today (1078-7895)
Related titles: Online - full text ed.: ISSN 2157-7285. USD 290 to institutions (effective 2012).
Indexed: A01, A02, A03, A08, A20, A22, AMED, C06, C07, C08, CA, CINAHL, DIP, ESPM, FoSS&M, H&SSA, IBR, IBZ, P30, PEI, R09, SCI, SCOPUS, SD, T02, W07.
—BLDSC (4542.109500), IE, Ingenta. **CCC.**
Published by: Human Kinetics, 1607 N Market St, Champaign, IL 61820. TEL 800-747-4457, FAX 217-351-2674, info@hkusa.com, http://www.humankinetics.com. Ed. Gary Wilkerson. R&P Martha Gullo TEL 217-403-7534. Adv. contact Amy Bleich TEL 217-403-7803.

➤ **INTERNATIONAL JOURNAL OF SPORT AND HEALTH SCIENCE.** *see* PHYSICAL FITNESS AND HYGIENE

➤ **INTERNATIONAL JOURNAL OF SPORT NUTRITION & EXERCISE METABOLISM.** *see* NUTRITION AND DIETETICS

616.8 ITA ISSN 0047-0767
GV706.4 CODEN: ISPYAN
➤ **INTERNATIONAL JOURNAL OF SPORT PSYCHOLOGY.** Text in English. 1970. q. USD 100 to individuals; USD 140 to institutions (effective 2008). adv. bk.rev. reprints avail. **Document type:** *Journal, Academic/Scholarly.* **Description:** Covers sports medicine.
Related titles: Online - full text ed.: (from SWZ).
Indexed: A20, A22, A36, AMED, ASCA, CA, CABA, CurCont, DIP, E-psyche, E12, ESPM, FoSS&M, GH, IBR, IBZ, LT, P03, P30, PEI, PsycInfo, PsycholAb, R12, RRTA, RiskAb, SCI, SCOPUS, SD, SSCI, SportS, T02, W07, W11.
—BLDSC (4542.681000), IE, Infotrieve, Ingenta.
Published by: (International Society of Sports Psychology), Edizioni Luigi Pozzi s.r.l., Via Panama 68, Rome, 00198, Italy. TEL 39-06-8553548, FAX 39-06-8554105, edizioni_pozzi@tin.it. Eds. Jean Fournier, Keith Davids. Circ: 1,500.

610 DEU ISSN 0172-4622
RC1200 CODEN: IJSMDA
➤ **INTERNATIONAL JOURNAL OF SPORTS MEDICINE.** Text in English. 1980. 12/yr. EUR 679 to institutions; EUR 870 combined subscription to institutions (print & online eds.); EUR 78 per issue (effective 2011). adv. bk.rev. abstr.; bibl.; charts; illus. reprints avail. **Document type:** *Journal, Academic/Scholarly.* **Description:** Provides a forum for the publication of papers dealing with basic or applied information that will advance the field of sports medicine and exercise science.
Related titles: Online - full text ed.: ISSN 1439-3964. EUR 839 to institutions (effective 2011); ◆ Supplement(s): International Journal of Sports Medicine. Supplement. ISSN 0943-917X.
Indexed: A01, A03, A08, A20, A22, A34, A36, A37, AMED, ASCA, ASG, B25, BIOSIS Prev, C06, C07, C08, CA, CABA, CIN, CINAHL, ChemAb, ChemTitl, CurCont, D01, DokArb, E12, EMBASE, ExcerpMed, FoSS&M, GH, ISR, IndMed, IndVet, Inpharma, LT, MEDLINE, MycolAb, N02, N03, N04, NRN, P30, P35, PEI, R09, R10, R12, RA&MP, RRTA, Reac, S13, S16, SCI, SCOPUS, SD, SportS, T02, T05, VS, W07.
—BLDSC (4542.681300), CASDDS, GNLM, IE, Infotrieve, Ingenta, INIST. **CCC.**
Published by: Georg Thieme Verlag, Ruedigerstr 14, Stuttgart, 70469, Germany. TEL 49-711-8931421, FAX 49-711-8931410, leser.service@thieme.de, kunden.service@thieme.de. Eds. G M Atkinson, H Appell. adv.: B&W page EUR 1,210, color page EUR 2,320. Circ: 1,350 (paid and controlled). **Subscr. to:** Thieme Medical Publishers, 333 Seventh Ave, New York, NY 10001. TEL 212-760-0888, 800-782-3488, FAX 212-947-1112, custserv@thieme.com, http://www.thieme.com/journals.

610 DEU ISSN 0943-917X
INTERNATIONAL JOURNAL OF SPORTS MEDICINE. SUPPLEMENT. Text in English. 1982. irreg., latest 2005. EUR 77 per issue (effective 2009). **Document type:** *Monographic series, Academic/Scholarly.*
Related titles: Online - full text ed.; ◆ Supplement to: International Journal of Sports Medicine. ISSN 0172-4622.
Indexed: EMBASE, ExcerpMed, SCOPUS.
—Infotrieve, INIST.
Published by: Georg Thieme Verlag, Ruedigerstr 14, Stuttgart, 70469, Germany. TEL 49-711-8931421, FAX 49-711-8931410, kunden.service@thieme.de. Ed. H Appell.

INTERNATIONAL REVIEW OF SPORT AND EXERCISE PSYCHOLOGY. *see* PSYCHOLOGY

617.1 ZAF ISSN 1528-3356
RC1200
➤ **INTERNATIONAL SPORTMED JOURNAL.** Text in English. 2000. q. USD 50 to individuals; USD 150 to institutions (effective 2005). **Document type:** *Journal, Academic/Scholarly.* **Description:** Publishes articles focused on the prevention, treatment, and rehabilitation of sport injuries and chronic disease states.
Media: Online - full content. **Related titles:** Online - full text ed.
Indexed: A01, A03, A08, C06, C07, C08, CA, CINAHL, FoSS&M, PEI, R09, SCI, SCOPUS, SD, T02, W07.
Published by: International Federation of Sports Medicine/Federation International de Medecine du Sport, c/o UCT/MRC Research Unit for Exercise Science and Sports Medicine, University of Cape Town, Boundary Rd., Newlands, 7700, South Africa. TEL 927-21-6504579, FAX 927-21-6866213, http://www.fims.org. Ed. Dr. Martin P. Schwellnus. R&P Ms. Yvonne Blomkamp.

➤ **INTERNATIONAL SYMPOSIUM ON SAFETY IN ICE HOCKEY. PAPERS.** *see* SPORTS AND GAMES

617.1 USA ISSN 2155-6695
▼ ➤ **THE INTERNET JOURNAL OF SPORTS MEDICINE.** Text in English. forthcoming 2011. s-a. free (effective 2011). **Document type:** *Journal, Trade.*
Media: Online - full text.
Indexed: A01.
Published by: Internet Scientific Publications, Llc., 23 Rippling Creek Dr, Sugar Land, TX 77479. TEL 832-443-1193, FAX 281-240-1533, wenker@ispub.com, hersche@netway.at. Ed. Dr. Prakash Adhikari.

617 613 NLD ISSN 0959-3020
RM727.I76 CODEN: IESCEE
➤ **ISOKINETICS AND EXERCISE SCIENCE.** Text in English. 1991-1996; resumed 1997. q. USD 666 combined subscription in North America (print & online eds.); EUR 475 combined subscription elsewhere (print & online eds.) (effective 2012). illus. back issues avail. **Document type:** *Journal, Academic/Scholarly.* **Description:** Meets the needs of the contemporary exercise scientist and medical practitioner through a consolidated focus on the field of isokinetics.
Related titles: Microform ed.: (from PQC); Online - full text ed.: ISSN 1878-5913 (from IngentaConnect).
Indexed: A01, A02, A03, A08, A22, AMED, ASCA, B25, BIOSIS Prev, C06, C07, C08, CA, CINAHL, E01, EMBASE, ExcerpMed, FoSS&M, H04, MycolAb, P30, PEI, R09, R10, Reac, SCI, SCOPUS, SD, T02, W07.

—BLDSC (4583.269000), IE, Infotrieve, Ingenta, INIST. **CCC.**
Published by: I O S Press, Nieuwe Hemweg 6B, Amsterdam, 1013 BG, Netherlands. TEL 31-20-6883355, FAX 31-20-6870019, info@iospress.nl. Ed. Zeevi Dvir TEL 972-3-640-9019. **Subscr. to:** I O S Press, Inc, 4502 Rachael Manor Dr, Fairfax, VA 22032-3631. sales@iospress.com; Globe Publication Pvt. Ltd., C-62 Inderpuri, New Delhi 100 012, India. TEL 91-11-579-3211, 91-11-579-3212, FAX 91-11-579-8876, custserve@globepub.com, http://www.globepub.com; Kinokuniya Co Ltd., Shinjuku 3-chome, Shinjuku-ku, Tokyo 160-0022, Japan. FAX 81-3-3439-1094, journal@kinokuniya.co.jp, http://www.kinokuniya.co.jp.

617.1 NLD ISSN 2210-6294
JAARBOEK SPORTGENEESKUNDE. Text in Dutch. 2008. a.
Published by: (Vereniging voor Sportgeneeskunde), Arko Sports Media (Subsidiary of: Arko Uitgeverij BV), Postbus 393, Nieuwegein, 3430 AJ, Netherlands. TEL 31-30-7073000, FAX 31-30-6052618, sport@arko.nl, http://www.arko.nl.

617.1 FRA ISSN 0762-915X
CODEN: JTSOAQ
JOURNAL DE TRAUMATOLOGIE DU SPORT. Text in French. 1983. 4/yr. EUR 212 in Europe to institutions; EUR 182.17 in France to institutions; JPY 32,600 in Japan to institutions; USD 276 elsewhere to institutions (effective 2012). **Document type:** *Journal, Academic/Scholarly.* **Description:** For all specialists concerned with bone, visceral, urological, and neurological traumatology, and reconstructive surgery, and for intensive care anaesthesists.
Related titles: Online - full text ed.: (from ScienceDirect).
Indexed: A22, B21, EMBASE, ESPM, ExcerpMed, H&SSA, PEI, R10, Reac, RiskAb, SCOPUS, SD.
—BLDSC (5070.525100), GNLM, IE, Ingenta, INIST. **CCC.**
Published by: Elsevier Masson (Subsidiary of: Elsevier Health Sciences), 62 Rue Camille Desmoulins, Issy les Moulineaux, Cedex 92442, France. TEL 33-1-71165500, infos@elsevier-masson.fr. Ed. J Rodineau. Circ: 2,100.

617.1 USA ISSN 1041-3200
GV706.4
➤ **JOURNAL OF APPLIED SPORT PSYCHOLOGY.** Variant title: Applied Sport Psychology. Text in English. 1989. q. GBP 300 combined subscription in United Kingdom to institutions (print & online eds.); EUR 333, USD 416 combined subscription to institutions (print & online eds.) (effective 2012). adv. back issues avail.; reprint service avail. from PSC. **Document type:** *Journal, Academic/Scholarly.* **Description:** Promotes quality research in the field of sport psychology.
Related titles: Online - full text ed.: ISSN 1533-1571. GBP 269 in United Kingdom to institutions; EUR 300, USD 374 to institutions (effective 2012) (from IngentaConnect).
Indexed: A01, A03, A08, A20, A22, A36, ASCA, C06, C07, CA, CABA, CurCont, E-psyche, E01, FoSS&M, GH, LT, MResA, N02, N03, P03, P30, PEI, PsycInfo, PsycholAb, R09, R12, RRTA, S02, S03, SCI, SCOPUS, SD, SSCI, T02, W07, W11.
—IE, Infotrieve, Ingenta. **CCC.**
Published by: (Association for Applied Sport Psychology), Routledge (Subsidiary of: Taylor & Francis Group), 325 Chestnut St, Ste 800, Philadelphia, PA 19106. TEL 800-354-1420, FAX 215-625-2940, journals@routledge.com, http://www.routledge.com. Ed. Daniel A Weigand. Adv. contact Linda Hann TEL 44-1344-779945.

796 USA ISSN 1062-6050
RC1200 CODEN: JATTEJ
➤ **JOURNAL OF ATHLETIC TRAINING.** Abbreviated title: J A T. Text in English. 1956. q. USD 112 combined subscription to individuals (print & online eds.); USD 245 combined subscription domestic to institutions (print & online eds.); USD 278 combined subscription foreign to institutions (print & online eds.) (effective 2010). adv. bk.rev. bibl.; illus. cum.index. back issues avail.; reprints avail. **Document type:** *Journal, Academic/Scholarly.* **Description:** Features information essential to athletic trainers.
Former titles (until 1992): Athletic Training (0160-8320); (until 1972): National Athletic Trainers Association. Journal (0027-8718)
Related titles: Microfiche ed.: (from PQC); Online - full text ed.: ISSN 1938-162X. free (effective 2011).
Indexed: A01, A02, A03, A08, A22, A25, A26, AMED, ASCA, B25, BIOSIS Prev, C06, C07, C08, CA, CINAHL, CurCont, E01, E03, E07, E08, E09, EMBASE, ERI, ExcerpMed, FoSS&M, G08, H12, H13, I05, MEDLINE, MycolAb, P02, P03, P04, P07, P10, P18, P19, P20, P22, P24, P25, P30, P48, P53, P54, P55, PEI, PQC, PsycInfo, PsycholAb, R09, R10, RASB, Reac, S08, S09, SCI, SCOPUS, SD, SPI, SportS, T02, W07.
—BLDSC (4947.850000), IE, Infotrieve, Ingenta.
Published by: National Athletic Trainers Association, Inc., 2952 N Stemmons Fwy, Dallas, TX 75247. membership@nata.org, http://www.nata.org/. Ed. Christopher D Ingersoll.

➤ **JOURNAL OF BACK AND MUSCULOSKELETAL REHABILITATION.** *see* MEDICAL SCIENCES—Orthopedics And Traumatology

➤ **JOURNAL OF CONTEMPORARY ATHLETICS.** *see* SPORTS AND GAMES

617.1 SGP ISSN 1728-869X
RA781
➤ **JOURNAL OF EXERCISE SCIENCE AND FITNESS.** Text in English. 1995. s-a. EUR 158 in Europe to institutions; JPY 25,000 in Japan to institutions; USD 200 elsewhere to institutions (effective 2012). 100 p./no.; back issues avail. **Document type:** *Journal, Academic/Scholarly.*
Formerly (until 2003): The Hong Kong Journal of Sports Medicine and Sports Science (1027-7323)
Related titles: Online - full text ed.: (from ScienceDirect).
Indexed: C06, C07, C08, CA, CINAHL, PEI, R09, SCI, SCOPUS, SD, T02, W07.
—**CCC.**
Published by: (Hong Kong Association of Sports Medicine & Sports Science HKG), Elsevier (Singapore) Pte Ltd (Subsidiary of: Elsevier Health Sciences), 3 Killiney Rd, #08-01 Winsland House, Singapore, 239519, Singapore. TEL 65-6349-0222, FAX 65-337-2230, http://asia.elsevierhealth.com/home/index.asp. Ed., Adv. contact Frank Fu.

617.1 ESP ISSN 1988-5202
JOURNAL OF HUMAN SPORT AND EXERCISE. Text in English, Spanish. 2006. s-a. free (effective 2011). **Document type:** *Journal, Academic/Scholarly.*
Media: Online - full text.
Indexed: A35, A36, CA, CABA, D01, GH, LT, N02, N03, R12, RRTA, SD, T02, T05, TAR.
Published by: Universidad de Alicante, Carr. San Vicente del Raspeig s-n, Alicante, 03690, Spain. TEL 34-96-5903400, FAX 34-96-5903464, http://www.ua.es/, http://publicaciones.ua.es/. Ed. Jose Perez Turpin.

JOURNAL OF IMAGERY RESEARCH IN SPORT AND PHYSICAL ACTIVITY. *see* PSYCHOLOGY

THE JOURNAL OF MUSCULOSKELETAL MEDICINE. *see* MEDICAL SCIENCES—Orthopedics And Traumatology

JOURNAL OF MUSCULOSKELETAL RESEARCH. *see* MEDICAL SCIENCES—Orthopedics And Traumatology

617 615.82 USA ISSN 0190-6011
RD701 CODEN: JOSPDV
➤ **JOURNAL OF ORTHOPAEDIC AND SPORTS PHYSICAL THERAPY.** Abbreviated title: J O S P T. Text in English. 1979. m. USD 190 combined subscription domestic to individuals (print & online eds.); USD 230 combined subscription in Canada to individuals (print & online eds.); USD 275 combined subscription elsewhere to individuals (print & online eds.); USD 330 combined subscription domestic to institutions (print & online eds.); USD 375 combined subscription in Canada to institutions (print & online eds.); USD 425 combined subscription elsewhere to institutions (print & online eds.); USD 20 per issue domestic; USD 30 per issue foreign (effective 2009). adv. bk.rev. illus. Index. back issues avail.; reprints avail. **Document type:** *Journal, Academic/Scholarly.* **Description:** Features clinical developments in sports medicine for practicing physical therapists, athletic trainers and orthopedic surgeons.
Related titles: Online - full text ed.: ISSN 1938-1344.
Indexed: A20, A22, AMED, ASCA, C06, C07, C08, CA, CINAHL, CurCont, EMBASE, ExcerpMed, FoSS&M, ISR, IndMed, Inpharma, MEDLINE, P30, PEI, R09, R10, Reac, RehabLit, SCI, SCOPUS, SD, SportS, T02, W07.
—BLDSC (5027.660000), GNLM, IE, Infotrieve, Ingenta, INIST. **CCC.**
Published by: American Physical Therapy Association, Orthopedic Section, 1111 N Fairfax St, Ste 100, Alexandria, VA 22314. FAX 703-836-2210, 877-766-3450, tdeflorian@orthopt.org, http://www.orthopt.org. Ed. Guy G Simoneau. Pub. Edith Holmes. Adv. contact Tony Calamaro TEL 610-449-3490. B&W page USD 1,480, color page USD 2,730; trim 8 x 10.5. Circ: 23,500 (paid).

➤ **JOURNAL OF PHYSICAL EDUCATION AND SPORT MANAGEMENT.** *see* PHYSICAL FITNESS AND HYGIENE

617.1 AUS ISSN 1440-2440
GV557 CODEN: JSMSF6
➤ **JOURNAL OF SCIENCE AND MEDICINE IN SPORT.** Abbreviated title: J S A M S. Text in English. 1961. 6/yr. EUR 313 in Europe to institutions; JPY 44,300 in Japan to institutions; USD 412 elsewhere to institutions (effective 2012). adv. bk.rev. charts; illus.; stat. back issues avail. **Document type:** *Journal, Academic/Scholarly.* **Description:** Focuses on sports science and medicine.
Formerly (until Dec.1997): Australian Journal of Science and Medicine in Sport (0813-6289); Which was formed by the 1983 merger of: Australian Journal of Sport Sciences (0725-4679); Australian Journal of Sports Medicine and Exercise Sciences (0811-6377); Which was formerly (until 1982): Australian Journal of Sports Medicine (0045-0650)
Related titles: Online - full text ed.: ISSN 1878-1861 (from ScienceDirect).
Indexed: A22, A26, A36, AMED, AbAn, B21, C06, C07, CA, CABA, EMBASE, ESPM, ErgAb, ExcerpMed, FoSS&M, GH, GeotechAb, H&SSA, H13, I05, IndMed, Inpharma, LT, MEDLINE, N02, N03, NRN, P03, P10, P20, P22, P30, P48, P53, P54, PEI, PQC, PsycInfo, R12, RRTA, SCI, SCOPUS, SD, SportS, T02, T05, W07, W11.
—BLDSC (5054.840000), GNLM, IE, Infotrieve, Ingenta. **CCC.**
Published by: (Sports Medicine Australia), Elsevier Australia (Subsidiary of: Elsevier Health Sciences), Level 12, Tower 1, 475 Victoria Ave, Chatswood, NSW 2067, Australia. TEL 61-2-94228500, 800-263-951, FAX 61-2-94228501, 800-170-160, customerserviceau@elsevier.com, http://www.elsevier.com.au/. Ed. Gregory Kolt.

➤ **JOURNAL OF SMOOTH MUSCLE RESEARCH/NIHON HEIKATSUKIN GAKKAI KIKANSHI.** *see* MEDICAL SCIENCES

➤ **JOURNAL OF SPORT AND EXERCISE PSYCHOLOGY.** *see* PSYCHOLOGY

617.1 USA ISSN 2152-0704
GV706.4
▼ ➤ **JOURNAL OF SPORT PSYCHOLOGY IN ACTION.** Text in English. 2010. 3/yr. GBP 128 combined subscription in United Kingdom to institutions (print & online eds.); EUR 168, USD 212 combined subscription to institutions (print & online eds.) (effective 2012). **Document type:** *Journal, Academic/Scholarly.* **Description:** Designed to promote the application of scientific knowledge to the practice of sport, exercise, and health psychology.
Related titles: Online - full text ed.: ISSN 2152-0712. GBP 115 in United Kingdom to institutions; EUR 152, USD 191 to institutions (effective 2012).
Indexed: SD, T02.
—**CCC.**
Published by: (Association for Applied Sport Psychology), Routledge (Subsidiary of: Taylor & Francis Group), 325 Chestnut St, Ste 800, Philadelphia, PA 19106. TEL 215-625-8900, 800-354-1420, FAX 215-625-8914, journals@routledge.com, http://www.routledge.com. Ed. Melissa A Chase.

617.1 USA ISSN 1056-6716
RD97 CODEN: JSRHEV
➤ **JOURNAL OF SPORT REHABILITATION.** Abbreviated title: J S R. Text in English. 1992. q. USD 368 domestic to institutions; USD 378 foreign to institutions; USD 426 combined subscription domestic to institutions (print & online eds.); USD 436 combined subscription foreign to institutions (print & online eds.) (effective 2012). adv. bk.rev. abstr.; bibl.; charts; stat.; illus. index. back issues avail.; reprint service avail. from PSC. **Document type:** *Journal, Academic/Scholarly.* **Description:** Investigates the process of rehabilitation of sport and exercise injuries regardless of age, gender, athletic ability, level of fitness or health status of the participant.
Related titles: Online - full text ed.: ISSN 1543-3072. USD 368 to institutions (effective 2012).
Indexed: A01, A02, A03, A08, A22, A25, A26, AMED, ASCA, B21, BRD, C06, C07, C08, CA, CINAHL, CurCont, DIP, E-psyche, E08, EMBASE, ESPM, ExcerpMed, FoSS&M, G03, G08, GSA, GSI, H&SSA, H12, I05, IBR, IBZ, Inpharma, MEDLINE, P03, P30, PEI, PsycInfo, PsycholAb, R09, R10, Reac, S08, S09, SCI, SCOPUS, SD, T02, W03, W07.
—BLDSC (5066.189000), GNLM, IE, Infotrieve, Ingenta. **CCC.**
Published by: Human Kinetics, 1607 N Market St, Champaign, IL 61820. TEL 800-747-4457, FAX 217-351-2674, info@hkusa.com, http://www.humankinetics.com. Ed. Carl G Mattacola. Pub. Rainer Martens. R&P Martha Gullo TEL 217-403-7534. Adv. contact Amy Bleich TEL 217-403-7803.

617 IND
JOURNAL OF SPORT TRAUMATOLOGY & ALLIED SPORTS SCIENCES. Text in English. 19??. a. INR 150 per issue to individuals; INR 300 per issue to institutions (effective 2011). **Document type:** *Journal, Academic/Scholarly.*
Published by: (Indian Association of Sports Medicine), Guru Nanak Dev University Press, c/o Ajaib Singh Brar, Amritsar, 143 005, India. TEL 91-183-2258802, vc@gndu.ac.in, http://www.gndu.ac.in/.

610 613.7 ITA ISSN 0022-4707
RC1200 CODEN: JMPFA3
➤ **THE JOURNAL OF SPORTS MEDICINE AND PHYSICAL FITNESS;** a journal on applied physiology, biomechanics, preventive medicine, sports medicine and traumatology, sports psychology. Text in English. 1961. q. EUR 270 combined subscription in the European Union to institutions (print & online eds.); EUR 295 combined subscription elsewhere to institutions (print & online eds.) (effective 2011). adv. bk.rev. bibl.; charts; illus. index. back issues avail.; reprints avail. **Document type:** *Journal, Academic/Scholarly.*
Related titles: Microform ed.: (from SWZ); Online - full text ed.: ISSN 1827-1928. 2005.
Indexed: A20, A22, A34, A36, AMED, ASCA, B21, C06, C07, C08, CABA, CIN, CINAHL, CTA, ChemAb, ChemTitl, CurCont, D01, EMBASE, ExcerpMed, FR, FoSS&M, GH, IndMed, Inpharma, LT, MEA&I, MEDLINE, N02, N03, N04, NRN, P02, P18, P19, P20, P22, P24, P26, P30, P48, P50, P53, P54, P55, PEI, PQC, R12, RRTA, RefZh, S12, SCI, SCOPUS, SD, SportS, T05, VS, W07.
—BLDSC (5066.200000), CASDDS, GNLM, IE, Infotrieve, Ingenta, INIST. **CCC.**
Published by: Edizioni Minerva Medica, Corso Bramante 83-85, Turin, 10126, Italy. TEL 39-011-678282, FAX 39-011-674502, journals.dept@minervamedica.it, http://www.minervamedica.it. Circ: 5,000 (paid).

617.1 TUR ISSN 1303-2968
RC1200
➤ **JOURNAL OF SPORTS SCIENCE AND MEDICINE.** Text in English. 2002. q. free (effective 2010). **Document type:** *Journal, Academic/Scholarly.*
Related titles: Online - full text ed.: free (effective 2011).
Indexed: A01, A02, A03, A08, A26, CA, FoSS&M, H11, I05, P30, PEI, R09, S23, SCI, SCOPUS, SD, T02, W07.
Address: c/o Hakan Gur, MD, PhD, Department of Sports Medicine, Medical Faculty of Uludag University, Bursa, 16059, Turkey. TEL 90-224-4428196, FAX 90-224-4428727, hakan@uludag.edu.tr. Ed. Hakan Gur.

➤ **JOURNAL OF SPORTS SCIENCES.** *see* SPORTS AND GAMES

➤ **JOURNAL OF SPORTS THERAPY;** tri-annual review of sports therapy theory and practice. *see* MEDICAL SCIENCES—Physical Medicine And Rehabilitation

617 ITA ISSN 2038-727X
CODEN: EJSTBJ
JOURNAL OF SPORTS TRAUMATOLOGY. Text and summaries in English, Italian. 1979-2004; resumed 2010. q. EUR 130, EUR 144 combined subscription domestic (print & online eds.) (effective 2011). **Document type:** *Journal, Academic/Scholarly.* **Description:** Contains original studies on experimental and clinical research. Includes case reports, short communications, interviews and conferences.
Former titles (until 2004): European Journal of Sports Traumatology and Related Research (1592-3894); (until 2001): Journal of Sports Traumatology and Related Research (1120-3137); (until 1990): Italian Journal of Sports Traumatology (0391-4089)
Related titles: Online - full text ed.: ISSN 2038-7288.
Indexed: ASCA, B21, ESPM, H&SSA, PEI, SCOPUS, SD, SportS.
—GNLM, IE, Ingenta, INIST.
Published by: Editrice Kurtis s.r.l., Via Luigi Zoja 30, Milan, 20153, Italy. TEL 39-02-48202740, FAX 39-02-48201219, info@kurtis.it, http://www.kurtis.it. Ed. Piero Volpi.

617.1 USA ISSN 1064-8011
GV711
➤ **JOURNAL OF STRENGTH AND CONDITIONING RESEARCH.** Abbreviated title: J S C R. Text in English. 1987. 9/yr. USD 531 domestic to institutions; USD 558 foreign to institutions (effective 2011). adv. charts; illus. Index. 120 p./no.; back issues avail.; reprints avail. **Document type:** *Journal, Academic/Scholarly.* **Description:** Features applied sport science and conditioning papers.
Formerly (until 1993): The Journal of Applied Sport Science Research (1557-6345)
Related titles: Online - full text ed.: ISSN 1533-4287.
Indexed: A01, A03, A20, A22, A25, A26, ASCA, B04, BRD, C06, C07, C08, CA, CINAHL, DIP, E01, E08, EMBASE, ErgAb, ExcerpMed, FoSS&M, G03, G08, GSA, GSI, H12, I05, IBR, IBZ, MEDLINE, P19, P20, P22, P24, P26, P30, P48, P50, P54, PEI, PQC, R09, R10, Reac, S08, S09, SCI, SCOPUS, SD, SportS, T02, W03, W07.
—BLDSC (5066.873700), IE, Infotrieve, Ingenta. **CCC.**

Published by: (National Strength and Conditioning Association), Lippincott Williams & Wilkins (Subsidiary of: Wolters Kluwer N.V.), 530 Walnut St, Philadelphia, PA 19106. TEL 215-521-8300, FAX 215-521-8902, customerservice@lww.com, http://www.lww.com. Ed. William J Kraemer. Pub. Terry Materese. Adv. contact Bob Williams TEL 215-521-8394. B&W page USD 1,780, color page USD 3,580; trim 8.5 x 11. Circ: 27,671.

➤ **JUOKSIJA.** *see* PHYSICAL FITNESS AND HYGIENE

617.1 DEU ISSN 0942-2056
RD561 CODEN: KSSAEQ
➤ **KNEE SURGERY, SPORTS TRAUMATOLOGY, ARTHROSCOPY.** Text in English. 1993. 8/yr. EUR 1,929, USD 2,296 combined subscription to institutions (print & online eds.) (effective 2012). adv. back issues avail.; reprint service avail. from PSC. **Document type:** *Journal, Academic/Scholarly.* **Description:** Covers various aspects of knee surgery, arthroscopy and sports traumatology.
Related titles: Microform ed.: (from PQC); Online - full text ed.: ISSN 1433-7347 (from IngentaConnect).
Indexed: A01, A03, A08, A22, A26, B&BAb, B19, B21, BioEngAb, C06, C07, CA, CurCont, E01, EMBASE, ExcerpMed, FoSS&M, ISR, IndMed, MEDLINE, P20, P22, P24, P30, P48, P54, PEI, PQC, R09, R10, Reac, SCI, SCOPUS, SD, T02, W07.
—BLDSC (5099.864200), IE, Infotrieve, Ingenta. **CCC.**
Published by: (European Society of Sports Traumatology, Knee Surgery and Arthroscopy LUX), Springer (Subsidiary of: Springer Science+Business Media), Tiergartenstr 17, Heidelberg, 69121, Germany. TEL 49-6221-4870, FAX 49-6221-345229. Eds. Dr. Jon Karlsson, Rene Verdonk. adv.: B&W page EUR 1,230, color page EUR 2,270. Circ: 1,800 (paid and controlled). **Subscr. in the Americas to:** Springer New York LLC, Journal Fulfillment, PO Box 2485, Secaucus, NJ 07096. TEL 800-777-4643, 201-348-4033, FAX 201-348-4505, journals-ny@springer.com, http://www.springer.com; **Subscr. to:** Springer Distribution Center, Kundenservice Zeitschriften, Haberstr 7, Heidelberg 69126, Germany. TEL 49-6221-3454303, FAX 49-6221-3454229, subscriptions@springer.com.

617.1 FIN ISSN 0357-2498
LIIKUNNAN JA KANSANTERVEYDEN EDISTAMISSAATIO. JULKAISUJA/LIKES RESEARCH REPORTS ON SPORT AND HEALTH/RESEARCH REPORTS ON SPORT AND HEALTH. Text in English, Finnish. 1975. irreg. price varies. **Document type:** *Monographic series, Academic/Scholarly.*
Published by: Liikunnan ja Kansanterveyden Edistamissaatio/Research Institute of Physical Culture and Health, Uimahalli, Yliopistonkatu, Jyvaskyla, 40100, Finland. TEL 359-14-2601572. Ed. Eino Havakselta.

613.7 USA ISSN 1947-1068
M B M (SAN FRANCISCO). (Mind - Body Management) Text in English. 2008. m. free (effective 2009). back issues avail. **Document type:** *Newsletter, Consumer.* **Description:** Provides information about fitness and nutrition coniderations in our body.
Media: Online - full content.
Published by: Leigh M. Goodwin, Pub., 1040 Bush St, 117, San Francisco, CA 94109. TEL 415-699-1463, LEIGH@LeighGoodwin.com, http://leighgoodwin.com.

617.1 FRA ISSN 1279-1334
MEDECINS DU SPORT; la revue du medecin de terrain. Text in French. 1996. m. **Document type:** *Journal, Trade.*
Published by: Expressions Groupe, 2 Rue de la Roquette, Cour de Mai, Paris, 75011, France. TEL 33-1-49292929, FAX 33-1-49292919, contact@expressions-sante.fr.

617.102 ITA ISSN 0025-7826
➤ **MEDICINA DELLO SPORT**; a journal on sports medicine. Text and summaries in English, Italian, Spanish. 1947. q. EUR 240 combined subscription in the European Union to institutions print & online eds.; EUR 265 combined subscription elsewhere to institutions print & online eds. (effective 2011). adv. bk.rev. bibl.; charts; illus. index. **Document type:** *Journal, Academic/Scholarly.* **Description:** A journal on sports medicine.
Related titles: Online - full text ed.: ISSN 1827-1863. 2005.
Indexed: ASCA, B25, BIOSIS Prev, ChemAb, FoSS&M, IndMed, MycolAb, P30, R10, Reac, SCI, SCOPUS, SD, SportS, W07.
—BLDSC (5533.700000), GNLM, IE, Infotrieve, Ingenta, INIST.
Published by: (Federazione Medico-Sportiva Italiana), Edizioni Minerva Medica, Corso Bramante 83-85, Turin, 10126, Italy. TEL 39-011-678282, FAX 39-011-674502, journals.dept@minervamedica.it, http://www.minervamedica.it. Circ: 6,000.

617.1 POL ISSN 1429-0022
MEDICINA SPORTIVA. Text in Polish. 1997. q. EUR 99 foreign (effective 2005). **Document type:** *Journal, Academic/Scholarly.*
Related titles: Online - full text ed.: ISSN 1734-2260. free (effective 2011).
Indexed: A22, A26, CA, H12, I05, SD, T02.
—BLDSC (5533.710000), IE, Ingenta.
Published by: (Akademia Wychowanie Fizycznego im. Bronislawa Czecha w Krakowie), Medicina Sportiva, ul Wolodyjowskiego 16, Krakow, 31980, Poland. Ed. Zbigniew Szygula. **Dist. by:** Ars Polona, Obroncow 25, Warsaw 03933, Poland. TEL 48-22-5098609, FAX 48-22-5098610, arspolona@arspolona.com.pl, http://www.arspolona.com.pl.

617.102 USA ISSN 0195-9131
RC1200 CODEN: MSPEDA
➤ **MEDICINE AND SCIENCE IN SPORTS AND EXERCISE.** Abbreviated title: M S S E. Text in English. 1969. m. USD 949 domestic to institutions; USD 1,105 foreign to institutions (effective 2011). adv. bk.rev. abstr.; bibl.; charts; illus. Index. back issues avail.; reprints avail. **Document type:** *Journal, Academic/Scholarly.* **Description:** Covers research in sports medicine topics for exercise physiologists, physiatrists, physical therapists and athletic trainers.
Formerly (until 1980): Medicine and Science in Sports (0025-7990)
Related titles: Microfilm ed.: (from PQC); Online - full text ed.: ISSN 1530-0315.
Indexed: A01, A03, A08, A20, A22, A26, A34, A35, A36, A37, A38, AMED, ASCA, ASG, AbAn, AgBio, B04, B25, BIOBASE, BIOSIS Prev, BRD, C06, C07, C08, C25, CA, CABA, CIN, CINAHL, ChemAb, ChemTitl, CurCont, D01, E-psyche, E02, E03, E07, E08, E12, EMBASE, ERI, EdA, EdI, ExcerpMed, FR, FoSS&M, G03, G08, GH, GSA, GSI, GeoRef, H11, H12, H16, I05, IABS, ISR, IndMed, IndVet, Inpharma, LT, MEDLINE, MycolAb, N02, N03, N04, P03, P30, P35, PEI, PN&I, PsycholAb, R09, R10, R12, RA&MP, RASB, RRTA, Reac, S04, S09, S12, S13, S16, SCI, SCOPUS, SD, SoyAb, SportS, T02, T05, TAR, VS, W03, W05, W07, W11, WSA.
—BLDSC (5534.006700), CASDDS, GNLM, IE, Infotrieve, Ingenta, INIST. **CCC.**
Published by: (American College of Sports Medicine), Lippincott Williams & Wilkins (Subsidiary of: Wolters Kluwer N.V.), 530 Walnut St, Philadelphia, PA 19106. TEL 215-521-8300, FAX 215-521-8902, customerservice@lww.com, http://www.lww.com. Ed. Andrew J Young TEL 508-233-5141. Pub. David Myers. adv.: B&W page USD 1,845, color page USD 3,420; trim 8.125 x 10.875. Circ: 13,517.

617.1027 USA ISSN 1567-2352
➤ **MEDICINE AND SCIENCE IN TENNIS.** Text in English. 2000. 3/yr. USD 175 to non-members; free to members (effective 2010). **Document type:** *Journal, Academic/Scholarly.*
Formerly (until 1999): Sports Medicine & Science in Tennis (1567-2492)
Related titles: Online - full content ed.
Indexed: SD.
Published by: Society for Tennis Medicine and Science, 1927 Bridgepointe Pkwy, Unit L117, San Mateo, CA 94404. office@stms.nl. Ed. Javier Maquirriain. Circ: 2,400 (controlled).

617.102 CHE ISSN 0254-5020
CODEN: MSPOB4
➤ **MEDICINE AND SPORT SCIENCE.** Text in English. 1968. irreg., latest vol.55, 2010. price varies. back issues avail.; reprints avail. **Document type:** *Monographic series, Academic/Scholarly.* **Description:** Provides information on the development of sports medicine as a dynamic scientific discipline.
Formerly: Medicine and Sport (0076-6070)
Related titles: Online - full text ed.: ISSN 1662-2812.
Indexed: A22, ChemAb, EMBASE, ExcerpMed, IndMed, MEDLINE, P30, R10, Reac, SCOPUS.
—BLDSC (5534.007300), CASDDS, IE, Ingenta, INIST. **CCC.**
Published by: S. Karger AG, Allschwilerstr 10, Basel, 4055, Switzerland. TEL 41-61-3061111, FAX 41-61-3061234, karger@karger.ch, http://www.karger.ch. Eds. A P Hills, J Borms, M Hebbelinck.

➤ **MEDSCAPE ORTHOPEDICS & SPORTS MEDICINE.** *see* MEDICAL SCIENCES—Orthopedics And Traumatology

617.1 POL ISSN 1232-406X
MEDYCYNA SPORTOWA. Text in Polish. 1986. q.
Indexed: CA, SD, T02.
Published by: MedSportPress, ul Marymoncka 34 skr. 23, Warsaw, 01813, Poland. TEL 48-22-8346772, FAX 48-22-8340431, nauka@medsport.pl, http://www.medsport.pl.

617.1027 CRI ISSN 1659-097X
QP303
MHSALUD; revista en ciencias del movimiento humano. Text in Spanish. 2004. q. free (effective 2011). back issues avail. **Document type:** *Journal, Academic/Scholarly.*
Media: Online - full text.
Published by: Universidad Nacional, Escuela de Ciencias del Deporte, Apdo Postal 1000, Heredia, Costa Rica. mhsalud@una.ac.cr. Ed. Andrea Mora Campos.

MODERN ATHLETE & COACH. *see* SPORTS AND GAMES—Outdoor Life

MOTOR CONTROL. *see* MEDICAL SCIENCES—Physical Medicine And Rehabilitation

617.1 BRA ISSN 1677-7360
MOVIMENTO E PERCEPCAO; revista do curso de educacao fisica C R E U P I. (Centro Regional Universitario Espirito Santo do Pinhal) Text in Portuguese. 2002. s-a. **Document type:** *Journal, Academic/Scholarly.*
Related titles: Online - full text ed.: ISSN 1679-8678.
Published by: Centro Regional Universitario Espirito Santo do Pinhal, Av Helio Vergueiro Leite s/n, Espirito Santo do Pinhal, SP 13990-000, Brazil. Ed. Odilon Jose Roble.

617.1027 USA ISSN 1079-5022
RC1200
N C A A SPORTS MEDICINE HANDBOOK. Text in English. 1981. a., latest 19th ed.
Related titles: Online - full text ed.
Published by: National Collegiate Athletic Association, 700 W Washington St, PO Box 6222, Indianapolis, IN 46206. TEL 317-917-6222, FAX 317-917-6888, esummers@ncaa.org, http://www.ncaa.org/.

613.711 AUS ISSN 1832-5548
NETWORK MAGAZINE. Text in English. 1988. q. free to members (effective 2008). adv. back issues avail. **Document type:** *Magazine, Consumer.* **Description:** Provides information, ideas and advice for those working in the fitness industry.
Former titles (until 1999): Network (1322-3399); (until 1992): Network News
Related titles: Online - full text ed.: free to members (effective 2008).
Indexed: B06, SD.
Published by: Australian Fitness Network, PO Box 1606, Crows Nest, NSW 1585, Australia. TEL 61-2-84247200, FAX 61-2-94376511, info@fitnessnetwork.com.au. Ed. Oli Kitchingman TEL 61-2-84247286. adv.: page AUD 2,625; trim 210 x 297. Circ: 12,000.

617.1 NZL ISSN 0110-6384
RC1200
➤ **NEW ZEALAND JOURNAL OF SPORTS MEDICINE.** Text in English. 1969. q. free membership. bk.rev. **Document type:** *Journal, Academic/Scholarly.* **Description:** Covers all aspects of sports medicine amd sports science research.
Formerly (until 1973): Sports Medicine Bulletin
Indexed: A22, CA, INZP, Inpharma, R09, SD, T02.
—BLDSC (6095.100000), IE, Ingenta. **CCC.**
Published by: Sports Medicine New Zealand, Inc., 40 Logan Park Dr, P.O. Box 6398, Dunedin, New Zealand. TEL 64-3-4777887, FAX 64-3-4777882, smnznat@xtra.co.nz. Circ: 1,000 (controlled).

➤ **NIHON SEIKEI GEKA SUPOTSU IGAKKAISHI/JAPANESE JOURNAL OF ORTHOPEDIC SPORTS MEDICINE.** *see* MEDICAL SCIENCES—Orthopedics And Traumatology

617.1027 BEL
OLYMPIC HEALTH NEWS. Text in French. q. illus. **Document type:** *Newsletter, Trade.*
Related titles: Dutch ed.
Published by: Comite Olympique et Interfederal Belge/Belgian Olympic and Interfederal Committee, Av de Bouchout 9, Brussels, 1020, Belgium. TEL 32-2-474-5150, FAX 32-2-479-4656, info@olympic.org, http://www.olympic.be. Ed., R&P Guido de Bondt.

617.1 USA ISSN 1060-1872
RD97 CODEN: OTSMA7
➤ **OPERATIVE TECHNIQUES IN SPORTS MEDICINE.** Text in English. 1993. q. USD 553 in United States to institutions; USD 682 elsewhere to institutions (effective 2012). illus. back issues avail.; reprints avail. **Document type:** *Journal, Academic/Scholarly.* **Description:** Focuses on a single clinical condition, offering several different management approaches.
Related titles: Online - full text ed.: ISSN 1557-9794 (from ScienceDirect).
Indexed: A26, C06, C07, C08, CINAHL, EMBASE, ExcerpMed, FoSS&M, H12, I05, P30, PEI, R09, R10, Reac, SCI, SCOPUS, SD, T02, W07.
—BLDSC (6269.382500), GNLM, IE, Infotrieve, Ingenta. **CCC.**
Published by: W.B. Saunders Co. (Subsidiary of: Elsevier Health Sciences), Elsevier, Health Sciences Division, Order Fulfillment, 3251 Riverport Ln, Maryland Heights, MO 63043. TEL 314-872-8370, 800-325-4177, FAX 314-432-1380, JournalCustomerService-usa@elsevier.com, http://www.us.elsevierhealth.com. Eds. Dr. David Drez Jr., Dr. Jesse C DeLee. Pub. Jason Miller.

617.1 ZAF ISSN 0377-8576
PAIDONOMIA. Text in Multiple languages. 1973. 3/yr. **Document type:** *Journal, Academic/Scholarly.*
Indexed: ISAP.
Published by: University of Zululand, Private Bag X1001, KwaDlangezwa, KwaZulu-Natal, 3886, South Africa. TEL 27-35-9026000, FAX 27-35-7933735, http://www.uzulu.ac.za.

PEDIATRIC EXERCISE SCIENCE. *see* MEDICAL SCIENCES—Pediatrics

617.102 GBR ISSN 1466-853X
RM695 CODEN: PTSHB4
➤ **PHYSICAL THERAPY IN SPORT.** Text in English. 1978. q. EUR 307 in Europe to institutions; JPY 33,100 in Japan to institutions; USD 274 elsewhere to institutions (effective 2012). adv. bk.rev. abstr. 48 p./no. 2 cols./p.; back issues avail.; reprints avail. **Document type:** *Journal, Academic/Scholarly.* **Description:** Features articles indispensable for the day-to-day practices and continuing professional development of all healthcare professionals involved in sports medicine.
Formerly (until 2000): Physiotherapy in Sport (0954-0741)
Related titles: Online - full text ed.: ISSN 1873-1600 (from ScienceDirect).
Indexed: A26, AMED, C06, C07, C08, CINAHL, EMBASE, ExcerpMed, FoSS&M, H12, I05, MEDLINE, P30, PEI, R10, Reac, SCI, SCOPUS, SD, T02, W07.
—BLDSC (6476.350650), IE, Ingenta. **CCC.**
Published by: (Association of Chartered Physiotherapists in Sports Medicine), Churchill Livingstone (Subsidiary of: Elsevier Health Sciences), The Blvd, Langford Ln, Kidlington, OX5 1GB, United Kingdom. TEL 44-1865-843434, FAX 44-1865-843970, directenquiries@elsevier.com, http://www.elsevierhealth.com/imprint.jsp?iid=9. Ed. Zoe Hudson. Adv. contact Emma Steel TEL 44-207-4244221. Circ: 896.

610 617.102 USA ISSN 0091-3847
➤ **THE PHYSICIAN AND SPORTSMEDICINE.** Text in English. 1973. q. USD 89 domestic to individuals; USD 229 foreign to individuals; USD 289 domestic to institutions; USD 389 foreign to institutions; USD 129 combined subscription domestic to individuals (print & online eds.); USD 269 combined subscription foreign to individuals (print & online eds.) (effective 2010). adv. bk.rev. illus. cum.index: 1973-1986. reprints avail. **Document type:** *Journal, Academic/Scholarly.* **Description:** Serves health care professionals in the medical aspects of sports, exercise and fitness.
Related titles: Online - full text ed.: USD 69 (effective 2010).
Indexed: A20, A22, A25, A26, AMED, ASCA, B02, B04, B15, B17, B18, B21, BRD, BusI, C06, C07, C08, CA, CINAHL, E03, E07, E08, EMBASE, ERI, ESPM, ExcerpMed, FR, FoSS&M, G03, G04, G06, G07, G08, GSA, GSI, H&SSA, H11, H12, H13, HlthInd, I05, Inpharma, M06, MEDLINE, NRN, P02, P10, P13, P18, P20, P24, P26, P30, P48, P53, P54, PEI, PQC, S08, S09, SCI, SCOPUS, SD, SportS, T&II, W03, W07.
—BLDSC (6476.357000), CIS, GNLM, IE, Infotrieve, Ingenta, INIST. **CCC.**
Published by: J T E Multimedia, LLC, 1235 Westlakes Dr, Ste 320, Berwyn, PA 19312. TEL 610-889-3730, FAX 866-297-3168, support@postgradmed.com, http://www.jtemultimedia.com/. Ed. Nicholas A DiNubile.

617.1 CHE ISSN 1424-3814
PLUSPORT NEWS. Text and summaries in French, German. 1962. 4/yr. CHF 22 (effective 2007). adv. bk.rev. **Document type:** *Magazine, Trade.*
Former titles (until 2000): Behindertensport (1422-0210); (until 1978): Invalidensport (0020-9880)
Published by: Schweizerischer Verband fuer Behindertensport, Chriesbaumstr 6, Volketswil, 8604, Switzerland. TEL 41-44-9084500, FAX 41-44-9084501. Ed. Fabrice Mueller. Adv. contact Heidi Kloimstein. page CHF 1,120; trim 185 x 260. Circ: 9,500 (paid and controlled).

PSYCHOLOGY AND SOCIOLOGY OF SPORT: CURRENT SELECTED RESEARCH. *see* PSYCHOLOGY

QUEST (CHAMPAIGN). *see* EDUCATION—Teaching Methods And Curriculum

R I C Y D E - REVISTA INTERNACIONAL DE CIENCIAS DEL DEPORTE/R I C Y D E - INTERNATIONAL JOURNAL OF SPORT SCIENCE. *see* SPORTS AND GAMES

M

617.1 USA ISSN 1543-8627
RC1200 CODEN: RSMECF
➤ **RESEARCH IN SPORTS MEDICINE**; an international journal. Text in English. 1988. q. GBP 828 combined subscription in United Kingdom to institutions (print & online eds.); EUR 855, USD 1,072 combined subscription to institutions (print & online eds.) (effective 2012). adv. reprint service avail. from PSC. **Document type:** *Journal, Academic/Scholarly.* **Description:** Covers major aspects of sports medicine and sports science - prevention, management, and rehabilitation of sports, exercise and physical activity related injuries, and occupational problems.
Former titles (until 2003): Sports Medicine, Training and Rehabilitation (1057-8315); (until 1991): Sports Training, Medicine and Rehabilitation (0893-102X)
Related titles: CD-ROM ed.: 1995; Microform ed.; Online - full text ed.: ISSN 1543-8635. GBP 745 in United Kingdom to institutions; EUR 770, USD 965 to institutions (effective 2012) (from IngentaConnect).
Indexed: A01, A03, A08, A22, A36, AMED, B21, C06, C07, C08, CA, CABA, CINAHL, E01, EMBASE, ESPM, ExcerpMed, FoSS&M, GH, H&SSA, LT, MEDLINE, N02, N03, P30, PEI, R09, R10, R12, RRTA, Reac, SCI, SCOPUS, SD, SoyAb, T02, T05, W07.
—GNLM, IE, Ingenta. **CCC.**
Published by: Taylor & Francis Inc. (Subsidiary of: Taylor & Francis Group), 325 Chestnut St, Ste 800, Philadelphia, PA 19106. TEL 215-625-2940, 800-354-1420, orders@taylorandfrancis.com, http://www.taylorandfrancis.com. Ed. Youlian Hong. Adv. contact Linda Hann TEL 44-1344-779945.

617.1 616.86 ITA ISSN 0370-7466
RESEARCH ON STEROIDS. Text in English. 1964. irreg. **Document type:** *Proceedings, Academic/Scholarly.*
Indexed: P30.
—CCC.
Published by: Societa Editrice Universo, Via Giovanni Battista Morgagni 1, Rome, RM 00161, Italy. TEL 39-06-44231171, FAX 39-06-4402033, amministrazione@seu-roma.it, http://www.seuroma.com.

617.1 ESP ISSN 1888-7546
REVISTA ANDALUZA DE MEDICINA DEL DEPORTE. Text in Spanish. 2001. 3/yr. **Document type:** *Journal, Academic/Scholarly.*
Former titles (until 2007): M D (1698-9775); (until 2004): D M D. Documentacion en Medicina del Deporte (1577-8223)
Indexed: SCOPUS.
Published by: Elsevier Doyma (Subsidiary of: Elsevier Health Sciences), Traversa de Gracia 17-21, Barcelona, 08021, Spain. TEL 34-932-418800, FAX 34-932-419020, editorial@elsevier.com. Ed. Grigoletto Da Silva.

617.1 ARG ISSN 0328-1256
REVISTA ARGENTINA DE ARTROSCOPIA. Text in Spanish. 1994. q. **Document type:** *Journal, Academic/Scholarly.*
Published by: Asociacion Argentina de Artroscopia, Montevideo 1546, 1er Piso, Buenos Aires, 1018, Argentina. aaartroscopia@gmail.com, http://www.artroscopia.com.ar.

617.1 BRA
REVISTA BRASILEIRA DE CIENCIA E MOVIMENTO. Text in Multiple languages. 1987. bi-m. **Document type:** *Journal, Academic/Scholarly.*
Published by: Universidade Catolica de Brasilia, Campus Universitario, QS 07, Lote 01, Aguas Claras, Taguatinga, DF 71966-700, Brazil. TEL 55-61-33569139, FAX 55-61-33563010, nfranca@pos.ucb.br, http://www.ucb.br.

617.1 BRA ISSN 1517-8692
REVISTA BRASILEIRA DE MEDICINA DO ESPORTE/BRAZILIAN JOURNAL OF SPORTS MEDICINE. Text in Portuguese; Abstracts in English, Portuguese. 1995. bi-m. BRL 80 to individuals; BRL 240 to institutions; BRL 160 renewals to institutions (effective 2005).
Formerly: Revista Brasileira de Medicina Esportiva
Related titles: Online - full text ed.: ISSN 1806-9940. 2002. free (effective 2011).
Indexed: A36, AgrForAb, C01, CA, CABA, D01, F08, FoSS&M, GH, LT, N02, N03, PEI, R12, RRTA, S12, SCI, SCOPUS, SD, SoyAb, T02, T05, VS, W07.
Published by: (Sociedade Brasileira de Medicina do Esporte), Redprint Editora Ltda., Rua Domingos de Morais 2777 - 13o, Sao Paulo, SP, 04035-001, Brazil. TEL 55-11-5724813, FAX 55-11-5711719, redprint@uol.com.br. Ed. Antonio Claudio Lucas da Nobrega.

REVISTA DE PSICOLOGIA DEL DEPORTE. *see* PSYCHOLOGY

617.1027 ESP ISSN 1577-0354
RC1200
REVISTA INTERNACIONAL DE MEDICINA Y CIENCIAS DE LA ACTIVIDAD FISICA Y DEL DEPORTE/INTERNATIONAL JOURNAL OF MEDICINE AND SCIENCE OF PHYSICAL ACTIVITY AND SPORT. Text in Spanish. 2000. q. free (effective 2011). back issues avail. **Document type:** *Journal, Academic/Scholarly.*
Media: Online - full text.
Indexed: A36, CABA, GH, LT, N02, N03, R12, RRTA, SCI, SCOPUS, T05, W07, W11.
Published by: Red Iris, Edif. Bronce, Plaza de Manuel Gomez Moreno, s-n 2a planta, Madrid, 28020, Spain. TEL 34-91-2127625, FAX 34-91-5566864, infoiris@rediris.es, http://www.rediris.es/. Ed. Maria del Mar Artigao Castillo.

617.1 613.7 BEL ISSN 0247-106X
S T A P S. (Sciences et Techniques des Activites Physiques et Sportives) Text in French; Summaries in Italian, German, English, Spanish. 1980. q. EUR 100 domestic to institutions; EUR 100 in France to institutions; EUR 110 elsewhere to institutions; EUR 69 domestic to individuals; EUR 69 in France to individuals; EUR 79 elsewhere to individuals; EUR 50 domestic to members; EUR 50 in France to members; EUR 60 elsewhere to members (effective 2011). 80 p./no.; back issues avail. **Document type:** *Journal, Academic/Scholarly.*
Related titles: Online - full text ed.: ISSN 1782-1568.
Indexed: CABA, FR, GH, LT, R12, RRTA, SCOPUS, SD, T05, W11.
—INIST.
Published by: (Association Francophone pour la Recherche en Activites Physiques et Sportives (A F R A P S) FRA), De Boeck Universite (Subsidiary of: Editis), Fond Jean-Paques 4, Louvain-la-Neuve, 1348, Belgium. TEL 32-10-482511, info@superieur.deboeck.com.

617.1 USA ISSN 0905-7188
RC1200 CODEN: SMSSEO
➤ **SCANDINAVIAN JOURNAL OF MEDICINE & SCIENCE IN SPORTS.** Text in English. 1979. bi-m. GBP 477 in United Kingdom to institutions; EUR 607 in Europe to institutions; USD 804 in the Americas to institutions; USD 935 elsewhere to institutions; GBP 550 combined subscription in United Kingdom to institutions (print & online eds.); EUR 698 combined subscription in Europe to institutions (print & online eds.); USD 925 combined subscription in the Americas to institutions (print & online eds.); USD 1,076 combined subscription elsewhere to institutions (print & online eds.) (effective 2012). back issues avail.; reprint service avail. from PSC. **Document type:** *Journal, Academic/Scholarly.* **Description:** Publishes original articles in the fields of traumatology and orthopedics, physiology, biomechanics, and cardiology, as well as sociological, pedagogic, historical and philosophical contributions to the study of sports.
Formerly (until 1990): Scandinavian Journal of Sports Sciences (0357-5632)
Related titles: Online - full text ed.: ISSN 1600-0838. GBP 477 in United Kingdom to institutions; EUR 607 in Europe to institutions; USD 804 in the Americas to institutions; USD 935 elsewhere to institutions (effective 2012) (from IngentaConnect).
Indexed: A01, A02, A03, A08, A20, A22, A26, A36, AMED, ASCA, B21, B25, BIOSIS Prev, C06, C07, C08, CA, CABA, CINAHL, CurCont, E01, E04, E05, EMBASE, ESPM, ExcerpMed, FR, FoSS&M, GH, H&SSA, H04, H12, H13, ISR, IndMed, Inpharma, LT, MEDLINE, MycolAb, N02, N03, P03, P10, P20, P30, P35, P48, P53, P54, PEI, PQC, PsycInfo, PsycholAb, R09, R10, R12, RRTA, Reac, S12, SCI, SCOPUS, SD, SOPODA, SociolAb, SportS, T02, T05, W07.
—BLDSC (8087.517400), GNLM, IE, Infotrieve, Ingenta, INIST. **CCC.**
Published by: (Scandinavian Foundation of Medical Science in Sports DNK), Wiley-Blackwell Publishing, Inc. (Subsidiary of: Wiley-Blackwell Publishing Ltd.), Commerce Pl, 350 Main St, Malden, MA 02148. TEL 781-388-8200, FAX 781-388-8210, info@wiley.com, http://www.wiley.com/WileyCDA/. Ed. Michael Kjaer.

617.102 CHE ISSN 1422-0644
RC1200
SCHWEIZERISCHE ZEITSCHRIFT FUER SPORTMEDIZIN UND SPORTTRAUMATOLOGIE/REVUE SUISSE POUR MEDECINE ET TRAUMATOLOGIE DE SPORTS/RIVISTA SVIZZERA PER MEDICINA E TRAUMATOLOGIA DELLO SPORT. Text in French, German, Italian; Summaries in English, French. 1953. 4/yr. CHF 55 domestic; CHF 75 foreign; CHF 16 newsstand/cover (effective 2003). adv. bk.rev. bibl.; charts; illus. index. **Document type:** *Journal, Academic/Scholarly.*
Former titles (until 1996): Sport (1022-6699); (until 1993): Schweizerische Zeitschrift fuer Sportmedizin (0036-7885)
Indexed: A22, AMED, ChemAb, IBR, IBZ, IndMed, P30, SCOPUS, SD, SportS.
—BLDSC (8123.485000), GNLM, IE, Infotrieve, Ingenta, INIST. **CCC.**
Published by: (Schweizerische Gesellschaft fuer Sportmedizin), Paul Haupt AG, Falkenplatz 14, Bern, 3001, Switzerland. TEL 41-31-3012434, FAX 41-31-3015469, druckerei@haupt.ch, http://www.haupt.ch.

617.1 FRA ISSN 0765-1597
GV557 CODEN: SCSPED
➤ **SCIENCE & SPORTS.** Text in French; Summaries in English, French. 1986. 6/yr. EUR 392 in Europe to institutions; EUR 358.47 in France to institutions; JPY 48,200 in Japan to institutions; USD 510 elsewhere to institutions (effective 2012). **Document type:** *Journal, Academic/Scholarly.* **Description:** Covers central topics related to sports medicine, connected with internal medicine, traumatology, psychology, physiology, biochemistry, biomechanics or technology. Includes original articles, letters to the editor and technical notes.
Related titles: Online - full text ed.: (from IngentaConnect, ScienceDirect).
Indexed: A01, A03, A08, A22, A26, A36, AMED, ASCA, B25, BIOSIS Prev, CA, CABA, EMBASE, ExcerpMed, FoSS&M, GH, I05, LT, MycolAb, N02, N03, P30, PEI, RRTA, SCI, SCOPUS, SD, T02, T05, W07.
—BLDSC (8142.998000), CASDDS, GNLM, IE, Infotrieve, Ingenta, INIST. **CCC.**
Published by: (Societe Francaise de Medecine du Sport), Elsevier Masson (Subsidiary of: Elsevier Health Sciences), 62 Rue Camille Desmoulins, Issy les Moulineaux, Cedex 92442, France. TEL 33-1-71165500, FAX 33-1-71165600, infos@elsevier-masson.fr. Ed. Pierre Pesquies. Circ: 2,000.

617.1 FRA ISSN 1378-1863
SCIENCE & MOTRICITE. Text in French. 1987. 4/yr. EUR 99, EUR 134 combined subscription (print & online eds.) (effective 2012). back issues avail. **Document type:** *Journal, Academic/Scholarly.*
Formerly (until 2002): Science & Motricite (France) (0984-2586)
Related titles: Online - full text ed.: ISSN 1782-1541. EUR 52 in the European Union; EUR 65 elsewhere (effective 2011).
Indexed: FR, SCOPUS, SD.
—BLDSC (8142.978000), IE, Ingenta, INIST.
Published by: (Association des Chercheurs en Activites Physiques et Sportives), E D P Sciences, 17 Ave du Hoggar, Parc d'Activites de Courtaboeuf, BP 112, Cedex A, Les Ulis, F-91944, France. TEL 33-1-69187575, FAX 33-1-69860678, http://www.edpsciences.org.

SEKEI SAIGAI GEKA/ORTHOPAEDIC SURGERY AND TRAUMATOLOGY. *see* MEDICAL SCIENCES—Orthopedics And Traumatology

617.1 ESP ISSN 0214-8927
➤ **SELECCION**; revista espanola e iberoamericana de medicina de la educacion fisica y el deporte. Text in Spanish. 1989. bi-m. EUR 40 domestic; EUR 56 in Europe; EUR 64 elsewhere (effective 2008). adv. charts. **Document type:** *Journal, Academic/Scholarly.* **Description:** Offers original clinical and applied research articles, as well as reviews in the field of sports medicine.
Indexed: A36, CABA, E12, EMBASE, ExcerpMed, GH, LT, N02, N03, R10, RRTA, Reac, SCOPUS.
—INIST.
Published by: (Asociacion Espanola de Escuelas de Medicina de la Educacion Fisica y el Deporte), Alpe Editores S.A., C Pedro Rico, 27, Madrid, 28029, Spain. TEL 34-91-7338892, FAX 34-91-3159652, alpeeditores@sistelcom.com, http://www.alpeeditores.com/. Ed. Fernando Santonja. Pub. Angeles Alvarez. Adv. contact Ana Jurado. color page EUR 10,000; trim 280 x 210. Circ: 4,000 (controlled).

➤ **SOCIOLOGY OF SPORT JOURNAL.** *see* SOCIOLOGY

➤ **SOMATICS**; magazine - journal of the mind - body arts and sciences. *see* PHYSICAL FITNESS AND HYGIENE

617.1 ZAF ISSN 1015-5163
➤ **SOUTH AFRICAN JOURNAL OF SPORTS MEDICINE.** Abbreviated title: S A J S M. Text in English. 1984. q. adv. illus. **Document type:** *Journal, Academic/Scholarly.* **Description:** Examines clinical and experimental topics in all areas of sports medicine.
(until 1989): S A Sports Medicine Association. Journal (0259-4870); (until 1986): S A Journal of Sports Medicine (0257-9308)
Related titles: Online - full text ed.: free (effective 2011).
Indexed: A26, A36, CABA, E12, GH, H12, I05, ISAP, LT, N02, N03, R12, RRTA, T05, W11.
Published by: (South African Medical Association), Health and Medical Publishing Group, 21 Dreyer St, Claremont, 7700, South Africa. TEL 27-21-6578200, FAX 27-21-6834509, http://www.hmpg.co.za. Ed. Mike Lambert.

617.102 TUR ISSN 1300-0551
➤ **SPOR HEKIMLIGI DERGISI/TURKISH JOURNAL OF SPORTS MEDICINE.** Text in Turkish; Summaries in English. 1966. q. free to institutions (effective 2009). adv. bk.rev. abstr. **Document type:** *Journal, Academic/Scholarly.* **Description:** Covers physiological, cardiologic, biochemical, and anthropometric aspects of sports medicine, as well as orthopedic, traumatological and physical therapy and rehabilitation.
Related titles: Online - full text ed.: free (effective 2009).
Indexed: SportS.
Published by: (Turkish Association of Sports Medicine), Ege University Press, PK 24, Bornova - Izmir, Turkey. TEL 90-232-3902380, FAX 90-232-3438053, cem@med.sdu.edu.tr. Ed. Oguz Karamyzrak. Circ: 350.

617.1027 616.12 ITA ISSN 1591-1195
SPORT CARDIOLOGY. Text in Italian; Summaries in English. 1984. s-a. free to members. adv. **Document type:** *Journal, Academic/Scholarly.*
Formerly (until 2000): International Journal of Sport Cardiology (0393-6066)
Indexed: SCOPUS.
Published by: (Societa Italiana di Cardiologia dello Sport), C I C Edizioni Internazionali, Corso Trieste 42, Rome, 00198, Italy. TEL 39-06-8412673, FAX 39-06-8412688, info@gruppocic.it, http://www.gruppocic.it.

617.1 ITA ISSN 0392-9647
SPORT & MEDICINA. Text in Italian. 1984. bi-m. EUR 34 (effective 2008). adv. bk.rev. cum.index. back issues avail.; reprints avail. **Document type:** *Magazine, Consumer.* **Description:** Features articles in fields of sports and medicine. Includes articles on pharmaceutical aids and physical fitness.
Indexed: SD.
Published by: Edi. Ermes Srl, Viale Enrico Forlanini 65, Milan, MI 20134, Italy. TEL 39-02-7021121, FAX 39-02-70211283, eeinfo@eenet.it. Circ: 15,000.

613.711 617.1027 NLD ISSN 1874-6659
CODEN: GESPBS
➤ **SPORT & GENEESKUNDE**; the Flemish/Dutch journal of sports medicine. Text in Dutch; Abstracts in English. 1968. bi-m. EUR 75; EUR 35 to students; EUR 17.50 newsstand/cover (effective 2009). adv. bk.rev. illus.; stat.; abstr. 40 p./no. 2 cols./p.; back issues avail. **Document type:** *Journal, Academic/Scholarly.*
Formerly (until 2007): Geneeskunde en Sport (0016-6448)
Indexed: A22, CA, P30, SCOPUS, SD, T02.
—GNLM, IE, Infotrieve.
Published by: (Vereniging voor Sportgeneeskunde), Arko Sports Media (Subsidiary of: Arko Uitgeverij BV), Postbus 393, Nieuwegein, 3430 AJ, Netherlands. TEL 31-30-6004780, FAX 31-30-6052618, info@arko.nl, http://www.arko.nl. Ed. Dr. J L Tol. adv.: page EUR 1,840; trim 210 x 280.

617.1 AUS ISSN 1032-5662
SPORT HEALTH. Text in English. 1983. q. AUD 35 domestic; AUD 50 foreign (effective 2007). adv. bk.rev.; video rev. charts; illus.; stat. index. back issues avail. **Document type:** *Magazine, Trade.* **Description:** Devoted to all areas of medicine and science in sport and physical activity.
Indexed: A22, SD, SportS.
—BLDSC (8419.622000), IE, Ingenta.
Published by: Sports Medicine Australia, 3-5 Cheney Pl, PO Box 78, Mitchell, ACT 2911, Australia. TEL 61-2-62419344, FAX 61-2-62411611, smanat@sma.org.au. Eds. John Prchard, Kerry Mummery. Adv. contact Nathan Kruger. Circ: 5,000 (paid and controlled).

617.1 FRA ISSN 0993-1252
SPORT MED'. Text in French. 1988. 10/yr. adv. bk.rev. **Document type:** *Journal, Trade.*
Related titles: Supplement(s): Profession Kine - La Reeducation Pratique. 1990.
Indexed: SD.
Published by: Meditions Carline (Subsidiary of: Groupe Meditions), 1-3 rue du Depart, Paris, 75014, France. TEL 33-1-40640075, FAX 33-1-43222699, carline@groupemeditions.com.

617.1 DEU ISSN 0949-328X
SPORT-ORTHOPADIE - SPORT-TRAUMATOLOGIE. Text in German, English. 1984. 4/yr. EUR 141 in Europe to institutions; EUR 141 to institutions in Germany, Austria and Switzerland; JPY 19,700 in Japan to institutions; USD 182 elsewhere to institutions (effective 2012). adv. **Document type:** *Journal, Academic/Scholarly.*
Former titles (until 1995): Praktische Sport-Traumatologie, -Medizin (0949-3271); (until 1992): Praktische Sport-Traumatologie und Sportmedizin (0177-0438)
Related titles: Online - full text ed.: ISSN 1876-4339 (from ScienceDirect).
Indexed: CA, PEI, SCOPUS, T02.
—BLDSC (8419.825250), GNLM, IE. **CCC.**

Published by: (Gesellschaft fuer Orthopaedisch-Traumatologische Sportmedizin), Urban und Fischer Verlag (Subsidiary of: Elsevier GmbH), Loebdergraben 14a, Jena, 07743, Germany. TEL 49-3641-626430, FAX 49-3641-626432, info@urbanfischer.de, http://www.urbanundfischer.de. Ed. Martin Engelhardt. Adv. contact Eva Kraemer TEL 49-89-5383704. B&W page EUR 2,210, color page EUR 3,530; trim 175 x 240. Circ: 5,500 (paid and controlled). **Non-German speaking countries subscr. to:** Nature Publishing Group, Brunel Rd, Houndmills, Basingstoke, Hamps RG21 6XS, United Kingdom. TEL 44-1256-302629, FAX 44-1256-476117, subscriptions@nature.com

SPORT SCIENCES FOR HEALTH. *see* PHYSICAL FITNESS AND HYGIENE

SPORT SCIENCES INTERNATIONAL. *see* SPORTS AND GAMES

617.1027 AUT ISSN 1867-1977
➤ **SPORT- UND PRAEVENTIVMEDIZIN.** Text in German. 1970. q. EUR 229, USD 343 combined subscription to institutions (print & online eds.) (effective 2012). adv. **Document type:** *Journal, Academic/Scholarly.*
Formerly (until 2008): Oesterreichisches Journal fuer Sportmedizin (1012-3156)
Related titles: Online - full text ed.: ISSN 1867-1985. 1999.
Indexed: A22.
—IE. **CCC.**
Published by: (Oesterreichisches Institut fuer Sportmedizin), Springer Wien (Subsidiary of: Springer Science+Business Media), Sachsenplatz 4-6, Vienna, W 1201, Austria. TEL 43-1-33024150, FAX 43-1-3302426, journals@springer.at, http://www.springer.at. Ed. Norbert Bachl. Adv. contact Gabriele Popernitsch. color page EUR 3,350; trim 210 x 297. Circ: 18,000 (paid and controlled).

➤ **SPORTDISCUS WITH FULL TEXT.** *see* SPORTS AND GAMES—Abstracting, Bibliographies, Statistics

617.1 GBR ISSN 1744-9383
SPORTEX DYNAMICS; the publication for professionals seeking sporting excellence. Text in English. 2004. q. GBP 59 to individuals; GBP 175 to libraries (effective 2009). adv. back issues avail. **Document type:** *Magazine, Trade.* **Description:** Focuses on all aspects that affect performance including biomechanical analysis, injury prevention, manual therapies and assessment and strength and conditioning.
Supersedes in part (in 2004): SportEX Health (1471-8154)
Related titles: Online - full text ed.: GBP 50 (effective 2009).
Indexed: C06, C07, C08, CA, CINAHL, R09, SD, T02.
—BLDSC (8419.803710). **CCC.**
Published by: Centor Publishing, 88 Nelson Rd, Wimbledon, SW19 1HX, United Kingdom. TEL 44-845-6521906, FAX 44-845-6521907, info@sportex.net. Ed. Bob Bramah. Pub. Tor Davies. Adv. contact Paul Harris.

SPORTEX HEALTH. *see* PHYSICAL FITNESS AND HYGIENE

617.1 GBR ISSN 1471-8138
SPORTEX MEDICINE. Text in English. 1999. q. GBP 59 to individuals; GBP 175 to libraries (effective 2009). adv. back issues avail. **Document type:** *Magazine, Trade.* **Description:** Focuses on the diagnosis and rehabilitation of musculoskeletal injuries occuring in sport.
Related titles: Online - full text ed.: GBP 50 (effective 2009).
Indexed: AMED, C06, C07, C08, CA, CINAHL, R09, SD, T02.
—BLDSC (8419.803750), IE, Ingenta. **CCC.**
Published by: Centor Publishing, 88 Nelson Rd, Wimbledon, SW19 1HX, United Kingdom. TEL 44-845-6521906, FAX 44-845-6521907, info@sportex.net. Ed. Lynn Booth. Pub. Tor Davies. Adv. contact Paul Harris.

617.1027 USA ISSN 1941-7381
RC1200
▼ ➤ **SPORTS HEALTH**; a multidisciplinary approach. Text in English. 2009 (Jan.). bi-m. USD 358, GBP 211 combined subscription to institutions (print & online eds.); USD 351, GBP 207 to institutions (effective 2011). **Document type:** *Journal, Academic/Scholarly.* **Description:** Publishes review articles, didactic features, and original research dealing with a broad range of sports medicine.
Related titles: Online - full text ed.: ISSN 1941-0921. 2009. USD 322, GBP 190 to institutions (effective 2011).
Indexed: A22, A36, CABA, D01, E01, E12, GH, LT, N02, N03, P30, P33, SD.
—**CCC.**
Published by: Sage Publications, Inc., 2455 Teller Rd, Thousand Oaks, CA 91320. TEL 805-499-9774, 800-818-7243, FAX 805-499-0871, 800-583-2665, info@sagepub.com. Ed. Dr. Edward M Wojtys.

610 NZL ISSN 0112-1642
CODEN: SPMEE7
➤ **SPORTS MEDICINE.** Text in English. 1984. m. price varies based on the number of users. abstr.; bibl.; illus. back issues avail.; reprints avail. **Document type:** *Journal, Academic/Scholarly.* **Description:** Provides comprehensive reviews of the latest research in applied medicine and science in sport and exercise.
Related titles: Online - full text ed.: ISSN 1179-2035 (from IngentaConnect).
Indexed: A01, A02, A03, A08, A20, A22, A26, A29, A36, AMED, ASCA, B20, B21, BiolDig, C06, C07, C08, CA, CABA, CINAHL, CTA, CurCont, D01, E01, E08, EMBASE, ESPM, ErgAb, ExcerpMed, FR, FoSS&M, GH, H&SSA, H12, I05, I10, ISR, IndMed, Inpharma, LT, MEDLINE, N02, N03, NRN, P03, P20, P22, P24, P30, P35, P54, PEI, PQC, PsycInfo, R09, R10, RRTA, Reac, S09, SCI, SCOPUS, SD, SoyAb, SportS, T02, VirolAbstr, W07.
—BLDSC (8419.837340), CASDDS, GNLM, IE, Infotrieve, Ingenta, INIST. **CCC.**
Published by: Adis International Ltd. (Subsidiary of: Wolters Kluwer N.V.), 41 Centorian Dr, Mairangi Bay, Private Bag 65901, Auckland, 1311, New Zealand. TEL 64-9-4770700, FAX 64-9-4770764, journals@adis.com, http://www.adisonline.info/. Ed. Jeremy N Shanahan. **Subscr. in the Americas to:** Adis International Inc.

➤ **SPORTS MEDICINE AND ARTHROSCOPY REVIEW.** *see* MEDICAL SCIENCES—Orthopedics And Traumatology

617.1 GBR ISSN 0952-4630
SPORTS MEDICINE BULLETIN. Text in English. 1980. m. GBP 48 in United Kingdom to individuals; GBP 55 to individuals rest of Europe; GBP 60 rest of world to individuals; GBP 60 in United Kingdom to institutions; GBP 65 to institutions rest of Europe; GBP 75 rest of world to institutions (effective 2000). adv. back issues avail. **Document type:** *Bibliography.* **Description:** Contains details of articles on all aspects of sports medicine and exercise science.
—GNLM.
Published by: National Sports Medicine Institute, Medical College of St Bartholomew's Hospital, Charterhouse Sq, London, EC1M 6BQ, United Kingdom. TEL 44-20-7251-0583, FAX 44-20-7251-0774, enquiry@nsmi.org.uk, http://www.nsmi.org.uk. Adv. contact Kathryn Walter.

617.1 613.7 USA
SPORTS MEDICINE BULLETIN (ONLINE). Text in English. 1966. q. free to members. **Document type:** *Newsletter, Trade.* **Description:** Informs members about ACSM issues, upcoming events, future plans and member news.
Formerly: Sports Medicine Bulletin (Print) (0746-9306)
Media: Online - full content.
Indexed: R09, SD, T02.
Published by: American College of Sports Medicine, PO Box 1440, Indianapolis, IN 46206. TEL 508-233-4832, FAX 508-233-5298, pub2acsm@acsm.org. Circ: 20,000.

617.1027 NZL ISSN 1179-8203
▼ **SPORTS MEDICINE RESEARCH REVIEW.** Text in English. 2010. m. free to qualified personnel (effective 2010). back issues avail. **Document type:** *Journal, Academic/Scholarly.*
Media: Online - full text.
Published by: Research Review Ltd., N Shore Mail Centre, PO Box 100116, Auckland, New Zealand. TEL 64-9-4102277, FAX 64-9-5248653, info@researchreview.co.nz.

SPORTS MEDICINE STANDARDS & MALPRACTICE REPORTER. *see* LAW

617.1 USA
SPORTS MEDICINE UPDATE. Text in English. bi-m. free to members. **Document type:** *Newsletter, Trade.* **Description:** Covers society news, member benefits, available resources, and developments within the orthopaedic sports medicine community.
Related titles: Online - full content ed.
Indexed: SD.
Published by: American Orthopaedic Society for Sports Medicine, 6300 N River Rd, Ste 500, Rosemont, IL 60018. TEL 847-292-4905, aossm@aossm.org, http://www.aossm.org.

SPORTS TRAINERS DIGEST. *see* SPORTS AND GAMES

STRATEGIES (RESTON); a journal for physical and sport educators. *see* EDUCATION—Teaching Methods And Curriculum

SUID-AFRIKAANSE TYDSKRIF VIR NAVORSING IN SPORT, LIGGAAMLIKE OPVOEDKUNDE EN ONTSPANNING/SOUTH AFRICAN JOURNAL FOR RESEARCH IN SPORT, PHYSICAL EDUCATION AND RECREATION. *see* PHYSICAL FITNESS AND HYGIENE

617.1 SWE ISSN 1103-7652
SVENSK IDROTTSMEDICIN. Text in Swedish. 1981. q. adv. **Document type:** *Magazine, Consumer.*
Formerly (until 1993): Idrottsmedicin (0280-5820)
Related titles: Online - full text ed.
Published by: Svensk Idrottsmedicinsk Foerening/Swedish Society of Sports Medicin, c/o Karin Henriksson Larsen, Gymnastik och Idrottshoegskolan, PO Box 5626, Stockholm, 11486, Sweden. TEL 46-8-55010200, FAX 46-8-55010409, kansli@svenskidrottsmedicin.se. Ed. Anna Nylen. Circ: 2,000.

TAIRYOKU KAGAKU/JAPANESE JOURNAL OF PHYSICAL FITNESS AND SPORTS MEDICINE. *see* PHYSICAL FITNESS AND HYGIENE

TENNISPRO MAGAZINE; the international magazine for PTR tennis teachers and coaches. *see* SPORTS AND GAMES—Ball Games

THERMOLOGY INTERNATIONAL. *see* PHYSICS—Heat

613.7 CHN ISSN 1006-1207
➤ **TIYU KEYAN/SPORTS SCIENCE RESEARCH.** Text in Chinese. 1962. q. USD 31.20 (effective 2009). **Document type:** *Journal, Academic/Scholarly.*
Related titles: Online - full text ed.
Indexed: PEI.
—BLDSC (8419.839546), East View, IE, Ingenta.
Published by: Shanghai Research Institute of Sports Science, 87 Wuxing Rd, Shanghai, 200030, China. Eds. Bishuang Situ, Guosheng Wei. Pub. Wenyu Chen.

➤ **DER UNFALLCHIRURG.** *see* MEDICAL SCIENCES—Orthopedics And Traumatology

613.711 GBR ISSN 2045-7308
▼ **WOMEN'S HOME WORKOUTS**; everything you ever wanted to know about home gym training and more..!. Text in English. 2010. a. **Document type:** *Consumer.*
Published by: Wild Bunch Media Ltd., 4th Fl, 26-28 Hammersmith Grove, London, W6 7BA, United Kingdom. TEL 44-20-88341650.

617.1 USA ISSN 0162-0908
RC1200
YEAR BOOK OF SPORTS MEDICINE. Text in English. 1979. a. USD 217 in United States to institutions; USD 235 elsewhere to institutions (effective 2012). adv. illus. reprints avail. **Document type:** *Yearbook, Academic/Scholarly.* **Description:** Presents abstracts of the pertinent literature with commentary by leading experts in the field.
Related titles: CD-ROM ed.; Online - full text ed.
Indexed: AMED.
—BLDSC (9416.417000), GNLM. **CCC.**
Published by: (American College of Sports Medicine), Mosby, Inc. (Subsidiary of: Elsevier Health Sciences), 1600 John F. Kennedy Blvd, Ste 1800, Philadelphia, PA 19103. TEL 215-239-3900, 800-523-1649, FAX 215-239-3990, elspcs@elsevier.com, http://www.us.elsevierhealth.com. Ed. Dr. Roy J Shephard.

617.1 CHN ISSN 1000-6710
ZHONGGUO YUNDONG YIXUE ZAZHI/CHINESE JOURNAL OF SPORTS MEDICAL SCIENCE. Text in Chinese. 1982. bi-m. USD 40.20 (effective 2009). **Document type:** *Journal, Academic/Scholarly.*
Related titles: Online - full content ed.; Online - full text ed.
Indexed: A22, A36, B21, CABA, E12, ESPM, GH, H&SSA, LT, N02, N03, PEI, R12, RA&MP, RRTA, SD, SoyAb, T05, VS.
—BLDSC (3180.676800), East View, IE, Ingenta.
Published by: (Zhongguo Tiyu Kexue Xuehui/China Sports Science Society), Zhongguo Tiyubao Yezongshe, 4, Tiyuguan Lu, Ximen, Beijing, 100061, China. TEL 86-10-67192754, FAX 86-10-67192755, http://www.sportsol.com.cn/. **Dist. by:** China International Book Trading Corp, 35 Chegongzhuang Xilu, Haidian District, PO Box 399, Beijing 100044, China. TEL 86-10-68412045, FAX 86-10-68412023, cibtc@mail.cibtc.com.cn, http://www.cibtc.com.cn. **Co-sponsor:** Yundong Yixue Xuehui/Sports Medical Science Association.

MEDICAL SCIENCES—Surgery

617.95 USA
A A A A S F NEWSLETTER. Text in English. s-a. free membership (effective 2007). adv. back issues avail. **Document type:** *Newsletter.* **Description:** Covers topics of interest to member plastic surgeons, specifically concerning ambulatory surgery facilities.
Formerly: Plastic Surgery Accreditation News (1066-8128)
Published by: American Association for Accreditation of Ambulatory Surgery Facilities, 5101 Washington St, Ste #2F, P O Box 9500, Gurnee, IL 60031. TEL 888-545-5222, FAX 847-775-1985, info@aaaasf.org. Ed. Robert Hamas. Adv. contact Edward Stygar. Circ: 500 (controlled).

617 NLD ISSN 1877-6906
▼ **A A T S DAILY NEWS.** Text in English. 2009. d. (during Annual Meeting). adv. **Document type:** *Newspaper, Trade.*
Related titles: Online - full text ed.: ISSN 1877-6914.
Published by: (American Association for Thoracic Surgery USA), Elsevier BV (Subsidiary of: Elsevier Science & Technology), Radarweg 29, PO Box 211, Amsterdam, 1000 AE, Netherlands. TEL 31-20-4853911, FAX 31-20-4852457, http://www.elsevier.com.

617 USA ISSN 0001-0790
A C O S NEWS. Text in English. 1962. m. free to members (effective 2011). adv. abstr. back issues avail. **Document type:** *Newsletter, Trade.*
Related titles: Online - full text ed.: free (effective 2011).
Published by: American College of Osteopathic Surgeons, 123 N Henry St, Alexandria, VA 22314. TEL 703-684-0416, 800-888-1312, FAX 703-684-3280, info@theacos.org.

617 AUS ISSN 1445-1433
CODEN: ANZJA7
➤ **A N Z JOURNAL OF SURGERY.** (Australia and New Zealand) Text in English. 1928. m. GBP 1,009 in United Kingdom to institutions; EUR 1,282 in Europe to institutions; USD 1,636 in the Americas to institutions; USD 1,977 elsewhere to institutions; GBP 1,160 combined subscription in United Kingdom to institutions (print & online eds.); EUR 1,475 combined subscription in Europe to institutions (print & online eds.); USD 1,882 combined subscription in the Americas to institutions (print & online eds.); USD 2,274 combined subscription elsewhere to institutions (print & online eds.) (effective 2012). adv. bk.rev. bibl.; illus. Index. back issues avail.; reprint service avail. from PSC. **Document type:** *Journal, Academic/Scholarly.* **Description:** Covers original contributions related to clinical practice and research in all fields of surgery and related disciplines.
Former titles (until 2000): Australian and New Zeland Journal of Surgery (0004-8682); (until 1931): College of Surgeons of Australasia. Journal
Related titles: Online - full text ed.: ISSN 1445-2197. GBP 1,009 in United Kingdom to institutions; EUR 1,282 in Europe to institutions; USD 1,636 in the Americas to institutions; USD 1,977 elsewhere to institutions (effective 2012) (from IngentaConnect).
Indexed: A01, A02, A03, A08, A20, A22, A26, A36, ASCA, B&BAb, C11, CA, CABA, CurCont, D01, DentInd, E01, E12, EMBASE, ExcerpMed, GH, H04, H12, H13, H17, INI, INIS AtomInd, ISR, IndMed, Inpharma, LT, MEDLINE, N02, N03, P02, P10, P20, P30, P33, P35, P48, P53, P54, PQC, R10, R12, R13, RM&VM, RRTA, Reac, SCI, SCOPUS, T02, T05, W07.
—BLDSC (1566.878000), GNLM, IE, Infotrieve, Ingenta, INIST. **CCC.**
Published by: (Royal Australasian College of Surgeons), Wiley-Blackwell Publishing Asia (Subsidiary of: Wiley-Blackwell Publishing Ltd.), 155 Cremorne St, Richmond, VIC 3121, Australia. TEL 61-3-92743100, FAX 61-3-92743101, melbourne@wiley.com, http://www.wiley.com/WileyCDA/. Eds. I Gough, P H Chapuis, John C Hall. adv.: B&W page AUD 1,012, color page AUD 2,057; trim 275 x 210. Circ: 6,300.

617 618.92 PAK ISSN 2218-8185
▼ **A P S P JOURNAL OF CASE REPORTS.** (Association of Paediatric Surgeons of Pakistan) Text in English. 2010. s-a. free (effective 2011). **Document type:** *Journal, Academic/Scholarly.*
Media: Online - full text.
Published by: Association of Paediatric Surgeons of Pakistan, Depatrment of Paediatric Surgery, National Institute of Child Health, Rafiquee Shaheed Road, Karachi, Pakistan. Ed. Jamshed Akhtar.

617 USA ISSN 0196-4615
➤ **ABDOMINAL SURGERY.** Variant title: Abdominal Surgery. Text in English. 1959. s-a. free (effective 2010). adv. bk.rev. abstr.; charts; illus.; stat. index. back issues avail. **Document type:** *Journal, Academic/Scholarly.*
Formerly (until 1965): Journal of Abdominal Surgery (0021-8421)
Related titles: Online - full text ed.
Indexed: P30.
—GNLM, INIST.
Published by: American Society of Abdominal Surgeons, 824 Main St, 2nd Fl, Ste 1, Melrose, MA 02176. TEL 781-665-6102, FAX 781-665-4127, office@abdominalsurg.org. Ed. Louis F Alfano.

➤ **ACADEMIE NATIONALE DE CHIRURGIE DENTAIRE. BULLETIN.** *see* MEDICAL SCIENCES—Dentistry

617 FRA ISSN 1634-0647
RD32
➤ **ACADEMIE NATIONALE DE CHIRURGIE. E-MEMOIRES.** Text in French. 2002. irreg. free (effective 2011). **Document type:** *Journal, Academic/Scholarly.*
Media: Online - full text.
—**CCC.**
Published by: Academie Nationale de Chirurgie, Les Cordeliers, 15 rue de l'Ecole de Medecine, Paris, 75006, France. TEL 33-01-43540232, FAX 33-01-43293444, ac.chirurgie@bhdc.jussieu.fr. Ed. Jacques Poilleux.

➤ **ACOUSTIC NEUROMA ASSOCIATION NOTES.** see MEDICAL SCIENCES—Otorhinolaryngology

617.95 CZE ISSN 0001-5423
➤ **ACTA CHIRURGIAE PLASTICAE**; international journal of plastic surgery. Text in English; Summaries in Czech, English. 1959. q. CZK 480, EUR 26.40 (effective 2010). adv. bk.rev. charts; illus. index. **Document type:** *Journal, Academic/Scholarly.* **Description:** Publishes clinical, experimental and theoretical work from the field of plastic, reconstructive and aesthetic surgery.
Related titles: Online - full text ed.
Indexed: A22, B&BAb, DentInd, EMBASE, ExcerpMed, IndMed, MEDLINE, P30, R10, Reac, SCOPUS.
—BLDSC (0611.100000), Infotrieve, INIST.
Published by: (Ceska Lekarska Spolecnost J.E. Purkyne/Czech Medical Association), Nakladatelske Stredisko C L S J.E. Purkyne, Sokolska 31, Prague, 12026, Czech Republic. nts@cls.cz. Ed. M Malinova. adv.: B&W page CZK 21,100, color page CZK 31,600; 245 x 167. Circ: 550.

617 BEL ISSN 1784-3421
CODEN: ACBEAX
➤ **ACTA CHIRURGICA BELGICA.** Text in English. 1901. 6/yr. EUR 110 domestic; EUR 130 foreign (effective 2011). adv. bk.rev. charts; illus. index. **Document type:** *Journal, Academic/Scholarly.*
Formerly (until 1997): Acta Chirurgica Belgica (Bilingual Edition) (0001-5458)
Related titles: ◆ Supplement(s): Acta Chirurgica Belgica. Supplementum. ISSN 0515-2763.
Indexed: A20, A22, A34, A36, ASCA, CABA, CISA, ChemAb, CurCont, DentInd, E12, EMBASE, ExcerpMed, FR, GH, H17, IndMed, IndVet, Inpharma, LT, MEDLINE, N02, N03, P30, P33, P35, R08, R10, R12, RM&VM, RRTA, Reac, RefZh, SCI, SCOPUS, T05, VS, W07.
—BLDSC (0611.130000), CASDDS, GNLM, IE, Infotrieve, Ingenta, INIST. **CCC.**
Published by: (Association Royale des Societes Scientifiques Medicales Belges/Koninklijke Vereniging van de Belgische Medische Wetenschappelijke Genootschappen), Acta Medica Belgica, Avenue Winston Churchill 11/30, Brussels, 1180, Belgium. TEL 32-2-3745158, FAX 32-2-3749628, http://www.ulb.ac.be/medecine/loce/amb.htm.

617 BEL ISSN 0515-2763
CODEN: ACBSA7
ACTA CHIRURGICA BELGICA. SUPPLEMENTUM. Text in English. 1950. irreg. price varies. **Document type:** *Monographic series, Academic/Scholarly.*
Related titles: ◆ Supplement to: Acta Chirurgica Belgica. ISSN 1784-3421.
—INIST.
Published by: Acta Medica Belgica, Avenue Winston Churchill 11/30, Brussels, 1180, Belgium.

617 SRB ISSN 0354-950X
ACTA CHIRURGICA IUGOSLAVICA. Text in English; Abstracts in Serbian. 1950. q. adv. bk.rev. **Document type:** *Journal, Academic/Scholarly.*
Former titles (until 1994): Acta Chirurgica Iugoslavica (0001-5474); (until 1952): Acta Chirurgica (0353-9792)
Related titles: Online - full text ed.: free (effective 2011); Supplement(s): Acta Chirurgica Iugoslavica. Supplementum. ISSN 0353-3425.
Indexed: A22, CA, EMBASE, ExcerpMed, IndMed, MEDLINE, P30, R10, Reac, SCOPUS, T02.
—BLDSC (0611.150000), GNLM, IE, Ingenta.
Published by: Udruzenje Hirurga Jugoslavije/Association of Yugoslav Surgeons, Klinicki Centar Srbije, Institut za Bolesti Digestivnog Sistema, Pasterova 2, Belgrade. TEL 381-11-3618444, actayu@eunet.yu. Ed. Dr. Miroslav Milicevic.

617 ITA ISSN 0393-6376
ACTA CHIRURGICA MEDITERRANEA. Text in English, Italian. 1960. bi-m. EUR 100 domestic; EUR 120 foreign (effective 2011). adv. abstr.; bibl.; illus.; stat. index. **Document type:** *Journal, Academic/Scholarly.* **Description:** Clinical cases in the surgical field are reviewed and discussed.
Formerly: Archivio Siciliano di Medicina e Chirurgia (Sezione Chirurgica)
Indexed: A36, CABA, E12, GH, N02, N03, RA&MP, RefZh.
Published by: (Societa Siciliana di Chirurgia), Carbone Editore, Via Quintino Sella 68, Palermo, PA 90139, Italy. TEL 39-91-321273, FAX 39-91-321782, info@carboneeditore.com, http://carboneeditore.com. Ed. Antonino Pennino. Circ: 6,000.

617 BRA ISSN 0102-8650
ACTA CIRURGICA BRASILEIRA. Text in Portuguese. 1986. bi-m. BRL 120 (effective 2007). back issues avail. **Document type:** *Journal, Academic/Scholarly.*
Related titles: Online - full text ed.: ISSN 1678-2674. free (effective 2011); ◆ Supplement(s): Acta Cirurgica Brasileira. Suplemento. ISSN 0102-9592.
Indexed: A34, A36, C01, CABA, D01, E12, EMBASE, ExcerpMed, F08, F11, F12, GH, H16, H17, INIS AtomInd, IndVet, MEDLINE, N02, N03, P30, P33, P39, PN&I, R10, RA&MP, Reac, SCI, SCOPUS, SoyAb, T05, VS, W07, W10.
—BLDSC (0611.508000), IE.
Published by: Sociedade Brasileira para o Desenvolvimento da Pesquisa em Cirurgia/Brazilian Society for the Development of Research in Surgery, Al Rio Claro 179, 14 Andar, Sao Paulo, SP 01332-010, Brazil. Ed. Alberto Goldenberg.

617 BRA ISSN 0102-9592
ACTA CIRURGICA BRASILEIRA. SUPLEMENTO. Text in Portuguese. 1986. a. back issues avail. **Document type:** *Academic/Scholarly.*
Related titles: ◆ Supplement to: Acta Cirurgica Brasileira. ISSN 0102-8650.
Published by: Sociedade Brasileira para o Desenvolvimento da Pesquisa em Cirurgia/Brazilian Society for the Development of Research in Surgery, Al Rio Claro 179, 14 Andar, Sao Paulo, SP 01332-010, Brazil. http://www.scielo.br. Ed. Alberto Goldenberg.

616 AUT ISSN 0001-6268
RD593 CODEN: ACNUA5
➤ **ACTA NEUROCHIRURGICA**; the European journal of neurosurgery. Text in English. 1950. m. EUR 4,629, USD 5,401 combined subscription to institutions (print & online eds.) (effective 2012). adv. abstr. back issues avail.; reprint service avail. from PSC. **Document type:** *Journal, Academic/Scholarly.* **Description:** Papers dealing with clinical neurosurgery - diagnosis and diagnostic techniques, operative surgery and results, postoperative treatment, and research work in neurosciences.
Related titles: Microfilm ed.: (from PQC); Online - full text ed.: ISSN 0942-0940 (from IngentaConnect); ◆ Supplement(s): Acta Neurochirurgica. Supplementum. ISSN 0065-1419.
Indexed: A01, A03, A08, A20, A22, A26, A29, ASCA, B20, B21, B25, BDM&CN, BIOSIS Prev, CA, CurCont, E-psyche, E01, EMBASE, ESPM, ExcerpMed, FR, H12, INI, INIS AtomInd, ISR, IndMed, Inpharma, MEDLINE, MycolAb, NSA, NSCI, P20, P22, P30, P35, P48, P54, PQC, R10, Reac, SCI, SCOPUS, T02, W07.
—BLDSC (0639.850000), GNLM, IE, Infotrieve, Ingenta, INIST. **CCC.**
Published by: Springer Wien (Subsidiary of: Springer Science+Business Media), Sachsenplatz 4-6, Vienna, W 1201, Austria. TEL 43-1-33024150, FAX 43-1-3302426, journals@springer.at, springer@springer.at, http://www.springer.at. Ed. Nicolas de Tribolet. Adv. contact Irene Hofmann. color page EUR 2,360, B&W page EUR 1,310; 170 x 250. Circ: 1,500 (paid). **Subscr. in the Americas to:** Springer New York LLC, Journal Fulfillment, PO Box 2485, Secaucus, NJ 07096. TEL 201-348-4033, 800-777-4643, FAX 201-348-4505, journals-ny@springer.com; **Subscr. to:** Springer Distribution Center, Kundenservice Zeitschriften, Haberstr 7, Heidelberg 69126, Germany. TEL 49-6221-3454303, FAX 49-6221-3454229, subscriptions@springer.com.

➤ **ACTA NEUROCHIRURGICA. SUPPLEMENTUM.** see MEDICAL SCIENCES—Psychiatry And Neurology

617 ITA ISSN 0392-3088
ACTA PHONIATRICA LATINA. Text in Italian. 1978. q. back issues avail. **Document type:** *Journal, Academic/Scholarly.*
Indexed: L&LBA, NBA, RILM, SOPODA.
—BLDSC (0648.600000), IE, Ingenta.
Published by: Editrice la Garangola, Via E dalla Costa 6, Padua, 35129, Italy. TEL 39-049-8075557, FAX 39-049-7806580, info@garangola.it, http://www.garangola.it.

617.3 ESP ISSN 1576-0332
➤ **LA ACTUALIDAD EN CIRUGIA ORAL Y MAXILOFACIAL.** Text in Spanish. 1999. q. EUR 39 (effective 2007). adv. abstr.; bibl.; illus.; stat. back issues avail. **Document type:** *Journal, Academic/Scholarly.*
Related titles: Online - full text ed.
—CCC.
Published by: (Sociedad Espanola de Cirugia Oral y Maxilofacial (S E C O M)), Aran Ediciones, Castello 128, 1o, Madrid, 28006, Spain. TEL 34-91-7820030, FAX 34-91-5615787, edita@grupoaran.com, http://www.grupoaran.com. Ed. E Gomez Garcia. Pub. Jose Jimenez Marquez. R&P Maria Dolores Linares TEL 34-91-7820035. Circ: 10,000.

➤ **ACTUALIZACIONES EN CIRUGIA ORTOPEDICA Y TRAUMATOLOGIA.** see MEDICAL SCIENCES—Orthopedics And Traumatology

➤ **ADVANCES AND TECHNICAL STANDARDS IN NEUROSURGERY.** see MEDICAL SCIENCES—Psychiatry And Neurology

➤ **ADVANCES IN CHRONIC KIDNEY DISEASE.** see MEDICAL SCIENCES—Urology And Nephrology

617.082 USA ISSN 0065-3411
RD1
ADVANCES IN SURGERY. Text in English. 1965. a. USD 202 in United States to institutions; USD 219 elsewhere to institutions (effective 2012). adv. illus. back issues avail.; reprints avail. **Document type:** *Journal, Academic/Scholarly.* **Description:** Presents a collection of original, fully referenced review articles in selected clinical topics important in all areas of surgery.
Related titles: Microfilm ed.: (from PQC); Online - full text ed.: ISSN 1878-0555 (from ScienceDirect).
Indexed: A22, A26, EMBASE, ExcerpMed, I05, IndMed, MEDLINE, P30, R10, Reac, SCOPUS.
—BLDSC (0711.595000), GNLM, IE, Infotrieve, Ingenta, INIST. **CCC.**
Published by: Mosby, Inc. (Subsidiary of: Elsevier Health Sciences), 1600 John F. Kennedy Blvd, Ste 1800, Philadelphia, PA 19103. TEL 215-239-3900, 800-523-1649, FAX 215-239-3990, elspcs@elsevier.com, http://www.us.elsevierhealth.com. Ed. Dr. John L Cameron.

617.95 USA ISSN 0364-216X
RD119
➤ **AESTHETIC PLASTIC SURGERY.** Text in English. 1977. bi-m. (in 1 vol., 6 nos./vol.). EUR 799, USD 848 combined subscription to institutions (print & online eds.) (effective 2012). adv. back issues avail.; reprint service avail. from PSC. **Document type:** *Journal, Academic/Scholarly.* **Description:** Devoted to the aesthetic surgery of the entire body surface, including facial surgery, body surgery, and extremity surgery. Provides a forum for original articles dealing with techniques advancing the art of aesthetic plastic surgery.
Related titles: Microform ed.: (from PQC); Online - full text ed.: ISSN 1432-5241 (from IngentaConnect).
Indexed: A20, A22, A26, ASCA, B&BAb, B19, B20, B21, CA, CurCont, E01, E08, EMBASE, ESPM, ExcerpMed, FR, H12, I05, IndMed, Inpharma, JW-D, MEDLINE, MS&D, P20, P22, P30, P48, P54, PQC, R10, Reac, S09, SCI, SCOPUS, T02, W07.
—BLDSC (0730.380000), GNLM, IE, Infotrieve, Ingenta, INIST. **CCC.**
Published by: Springer New York LLC (Subsidiary of: Springer Science+Business Media), 233 Spring St, New York, NY 10013. TEL 212-460-1500, 800-777-4643, journals@springer-ny.com. Ed. Dr. Thomas M Biggs. **Subscr. outside the Americas to:** Springer Distribution Center, Kundenservice Zeitschriften, Haberstr 7, Heidelberg 69126, Germany. TEL 49-6221-3454303, FAX 49-6221-3454229, subscriptions@springer.com; **Subscr. to:** Journal Fulfillment, PO Box 2485, Secaucus, NJ 07096. TEL 201-348-4033, FAX 201-348-4505. **Co-sponsors:** Lipoplasty Society of North America; International Society of Aesthetic Plastic Surgery.

617.95 USA ISSN 1090-820X
➤ **AESTHETIC SURGERY JOURNAL.** Abbreviated title: A S J. Text in English. 1988. 8/yr. USD 387, GBP 227 to institutions; USD 395, GBP 232 combined subscription to institutions (print & online eds.) (effective 2012). adv. back issues avail.; reprint service avail. from PSC. **Document type:** *Journal, Academic/Scholarly.* **Description:** Covers topics of current interest to keep practitioners of aesthetic plastic surgery up-to-date with the changing trends and developments in the field.
Former titles (until 1997): Aesthetic Surgery Quarterly (1084-0761); (until 1995): Aesthetic Surgery
Related titles: Online - full text ed.: ISSN 1527-330X. USD 336, GBP 209 to institutions (effective 2012).
Indexed: A22, A26, C06, C07, CA, E01, EMBASE, ExcerpMed, I05, MEDLINE, P30, SCOPUS, T02.
—BLDSC (0730.384000), IE, Ingenta. **CCC.**
Published by: (The Rhinoplasty Society, American Society for Aesthetic Plastic Surgery, Inc.), Sage Publications, Inc., 2455 Teller Rd, Thousand Oaks, CA 91320. TEL 800-818-7243, FAX 800-583-2665, info@sagepub.com, http://www.sagepub.com. Ed. Dr. Foad Nahai.

➤ **AFRICAN JOURNAL OF PAEDIATRIC SURGERY.** see MEDICAL SCIENCES—Pediatrics

617 DEU ISSN 1611-6437
ALLGEMEINE UND VISZERALCHIRURGIE UP2DATE. Text in German. 2007. bi-m. EUR 172 to institutions; EUR 232 combined subscription to institutions (print & online eds.); EUR 35 newsstand/cover (effective 2011). adv. **Document type:** *Journal, Academic/Scholarly.*
Related titles: Online - full text ed.: ISSN 1611-6461. EUR 224 to institutions (effective 2011).
—IE. **CCC.**
Published by: Georg Thieme Verlag, Ruedigerstr 14, Stuttgart, 70469, Germany. TEL 49-711-8931421, FAX 49-711-8931410, leser.service@thieme.de. Eds. Dr. Hans-Peter Bruch, Heinz Becker. Adv. contact Christine Volpp TEL 49-711-8931603. Circ: 2,500 (paid and controlled).

617.95 DEU ISSN 1612-4375
AMBULANTE CHIRURGIE. Text in German. 1996. bi-m. EUR 109, USD 142 to institutions (effective 2010). adv. **Document type:** *Magazine, Trade.*
Formerly (until 2003): Der Niedergelassene Chirurg (1432-783X)
—CCC.
Published by: Urban und Vogel Medien und Medizin Verlagsgesellschaft mbH (Subsidiary of: Springer Science+Business Media), Neumarkter Str 43, Munich, 81673, Germany. TEL 49-89-4372-1411, FAX 49-89-4372-1410, verlag@urban-vogel.de. Ed. Claudia Maeck. Adv. contact Kornelia Echsel. B&W page EUR 2,000, color page EUR 3,300; trim 174 x 237. Circ: 6,193 (paid and controlled).

617 USA ISSN 0002-8045
RD1
AMERICAN COLLEGE OF SURGEONS. BULLETIN. Text in English. 1916. m. free (effective 2005). charts; illus. index. back issues avail.; reprints avail. **Document type:** *Bulletin.*
Related titles: Microform ed.: (from PQC).
Indexed: A22, C06, C07, C08, CINAHL, ChemAb, EMBASE, ExcerpMed, INI, L09, MCR, MEDLINE, P30, R10, Reac, SCOPUS.
—BLDSC (2386.540000), GNLM, IE, Infotrieve, Ingenta. **CCC.**
Published by: American College of Surgeons, Communications Department, 633 N Saint Clair St, Chicago, IL 60611-3211. TEL 312-202-5000, FAX 312-202-5001, http://www.facs.org. Ed. Stephen J Regnier. R&P Linn Meyer TEL 312-202-5311. Circ: 67,850 (controlled).

617 USA ISSN 1072-7515
RD1 CODEN: JACSEX
➤ **AMERICAN COLLEGE OF SURGEONS. JOURNAL.** Abbreviated title: J A C S. Text in English. 1905. m. USD 436 in United States to institutions; USD 750 elsewhere to institutions (effective 2012). adv. bk.rev. bibl.; charts; illus. s-a. index. back issues avail.; reprints avail. **Document type:** *Journal, Academic/Scholarly.* **Description:** Aims to provide its readership the retrieval of information relevant to surgeons. Brings out contributions on all aspects of surgery.
Formerly (until 1994): Surgery, Gynecology and Obstetrics (0039-6087); Incorporates (1950-2001): Surgical Forum (0071-8041); (1913-1993): International Abstracts of Surgery (1087-4712)
Related titles: Microform ed.: (from PMC, PQC); Online - full text ed.: ISSN 1879-1190 (from IngentaConnect, ScienceDirect).
Indexed: A01, A03, A08, A20, A22, A26, A36, AIM, ASCA, BIOBASE, C06, C07, CA, CABA, ChemAb, CurCont, D01, DentInd, E12, EMBASE, ExcerpMed, FR, GH, H16, H17, HospLI, I05, IABS, IDIS, INI, ISR, IndMed, Inpharma, JW-EM, Kidney, MEDLINE, MLA-IB, MS&D, N02, N03, P30, P33, P35, P48, PQC, R10, R12, Reac, S02, S03, SCI, SCOPUS, T02, T05, VITIS, VS, W07.
—BLDSC (4685.784000), CASDDS, GNLM, IE, Infotrieve, Ingenta, INIST. **CCC.**
Published by: (American College of Surgeons), Elsevier Inc. (Subsidiary of: Elsevier Science & Technology), 1600 John F Kennedy Blvd, Philadelphia, PA 19103. TEL 215-239-3900, FAX 215-238-7883, JournalCustomerService-usa@elsevier.com, http://www.elsevier.com. Ed. Timothy J Eberlein. Circ: 54,952.

617 USA ISSN 0094-1999
AMERICAN COLLEGE OF SURGEONS. YEARBOOK. Text in English. 1953. irreg.
Formerly (until 1971): American College of Surgeons. Directory (0094-159X)
Published by: American College of Surgeons, Communications Department, 633 N Saint Clair St, Chicago, IL 60611-3211. TEL 312-202-5000, FAX 312-202-5001, http://www.facs.org.

617.95 USA ISSN 0748-8068
➤ **AMERICAN JOURNAL OF COSMETIC SURGERY.** Abbreviated title: A J C S. Text in English. 1984. q. free to members (effective 2010). adv. bk.rev. back issues avail.; reprints avail. **Document type:** *Journal, Academic/Scholarly.* **Description:** Covers thought, experience, opinion, technique, research, legal aspects, patient relations, office protocol and any other subject relating to cosmetic surgery.
Indexed: JW-D.
—GNLM, IE, Infotrieve.
Published by: American Academy of Cosmetic Surgery, 737 N Michigan Ave, Ste 2100, Chicago, IL 60611. FAX 312-981-6787, info@cosmeticsurgery.org. adv.: B&W page USD 900, color page USD 1,725. Circ: 8,500.

617 USA ISSN 0002-9610
RD1 CODEN: AJSUAB
➤ **THE AMERICAN JOURNAL OF SURGERY.** Abbreviated title: A J S. Text in English. 1890. m. USD 452 in US & Canada to institutions; USD 785 elsewhere to institutions (effective 2012). adv. bk.rev. bibl.; charts; illus. back issues avail.; reprints avail. **Document type:** *Journal, Academic/Scholarly.* **Description:** Focuses for the general surgeon who performs abdominal, cancer, vascular, head and neck, breast, colorectal, and other forms of surgery.
Former titles (until 1905): American Surgery and Gynecology (0271-6402); (until 1900): American Journal of Surgery and Gynecology
Related titles: CD-ROM ed.; Microform ed.: (from PMC, RPI); Online - full text ed.: ISSN 1879-1883 (from IngentaConnect, ScienceDirect).
Indexed: A01, A03, A08, A20, A22, A26, A34, A36, AIIM, AIM, ASCA, BIOBASE, C06, C07, CIN, CABA, CIN, CISA, ChemAb, ChemTitl, CurCont, D01, DentInd, E08, EMBASE, ExcerpMed, FR, G08, GH, H11, H12, H17, I05, IABS, IDIS, INI, ISR, IndMed, IndVet, Inpharma, Kidney, LT, MEDLINE, MS&D, N02, N03, P30, P33, P35, R10, RA&MP, RRTA, Reac, S09, S12, SCI, SCOPUS, SoyAb, T02, T05, VS, W07.
—BLDSC (0838.500000), CASDDS, GNLM, IE, Infotrieve, Ingenta, INIST. **CCC.**
Published by: (Southwestern Surgical Congress), Elsevier Inc. (Subsidiary of: Elsevier Science & Technology), 1600 John F Kennedy Blvd, Philadelphia, PA 19103. TEL 215-239-3900, FAX 215-238-7883, JournalCustomerService-usa@elsevier.com, http://www.elsevier.com. Ed. Kirby I Bland TEL 205-975-2194. Pub. David Dionne TEL 212-633-3912.

➤ **AMERICAN JOURNAL OF SURGICAL PATHOLOGY.** *see* MEDICAL SCIENCES

617 USA ISSN 1600-6135
RD129.5 CODEN: AJTMBR
➤ **AMERICAN JOURNAL OF TRANSPLANTATION.** Abbreviated title: A J T(American Journal of Transplantation). Text in English. 2001 (May). m. GBP 1,378 in United Kingdom to institutions; EUR 1,751 in Europe to institutions; USD 2,317 in the Americas to institutions; USD 2,700 elsewhere to institutions; GBP 1,585 combined subscription in United Kingdom to institutions (print & online eds.); EUR 2,013 combined subscription in Europe to institutions (print & online eds.); USD 2,664 combined subscription in the Americas to institutions (print & online eds.); USD 3,106 combined subscription elsewhere to institutions (print & online eds.) (effective 2012). adv. back issues avail.; reprint service avail. from PSC. **Document type:** *Journal, Academic/Scholarly.* **Description:** Aims to the rapid publication of new high quality data in organ and tissue transplantation and the related sciences.
Related titles: ◆ Online - full text ed.: American Journal of Transplantation (Online). ISSN 1600-6143; ◆ Supplement(s): American Journal of Transplantation. Supplement (Print). ISSN 1601-2577.
Indexed: A01, A02, A03, A08, A22, A26, A36, AIDS&CR, B21, BIOBASE, CA, CABA, CTA, CurCont, D01, E01, E12, EMBASE, ESPM, ExcerpMed, GH, H12, H16, H17, IABS, ImmunAb, Inpharma, LT, MEDLINE, N02, N03, P30, P33, P34, P35, P37, P39, R08, R10, RA&MP, RM&VM, RRTA, Reac, RiskAb, SCI, SCOPUS, T02, T05, VS, VirolAbstr, W07, W11.
—BLDSC (0838.850000), IE, Infotrieve, Ingenta, INIST. **CCC.**
Published by: (American Society of Transplant Surgeons, American Society of Transplantation), Wiley-Blackwell Publishing, Inc. (Subsidiary of: Wiley-Blackwell Publishing Ltd.), Commerce Pl, 350 Main St, Malden, MA 02148. TEL 781-388-8200, FAX 781-388-8210, info@wiley.com, http://www.wiley.com/WileyCDA/. Ed. Philip F Halloran. Circ: 3,300 (paid).

617 USA ISSN 1600-6143
➤ **AMERICAN JOURNAL OF TRANSPLANTATION (ONLINE).** Text in English. 2001 (May). m. GBP 1,378 in United Kingdom to institutions; EUR 1,751 in Europe to institutions; USD 2,317 in the Americas to institutions; USD 2,700 elsewhere to institutions (effective 2012). **Document type:** *Journal, Academic/Scholarly.*
Media: Online - full text (from IngentaConnect). **Related titles:** ◆ Print ed.: American Journal of Transplantation. ISSN 1600-6135.
—CCC.
Published by: (American Society of Transplant Surgeons, American Society of Transplantation), Wiley-Blackwell Publishing, Inc. (Subsidiary of: Wiley-Blackwell Publishing Ltd.), Commerce Pl, 350 Main St, Malden, MA 02148. TEL 781-388-8200, FAX 781-388-8210, info@wiley.com, http://www.wiley.com/WileyCDA/. Ed. Philip F Halloran.

617 USA ISSN 1601-2577
➤ **AMERICAN JOURNAL OF TRANSPLANTATION. SUPPLEMENT (PRINT).** Text in English. 2001. irreg. includes with subscr. to American Journal of Transplantation. back issues avail. **Document type:** *Monographic series, Academic/Scholarly.*
Related titles: Online - full text ed.: American Journal of Transplantation. Supplement (Online). ISSN 1602-1363; ◆ Supplement to: American Journal of Transplantation. ISSN 1600-6135.
—CCC.
Published by: Wiley-Blackwell Publishing, Inc. (Subsidiary of: Wiley-Blackwell Publishing Ltd.), Commerce Pl, 350 Main St, Malden, MA 02148. TEL 781-388-8200, FAX 781-388-8210, info@wiley.com, http://www.wiley.com/WileyCDA/. Ed. Philip F Halloran.

617 USA ISSN 0003-1348
RD1 CODEN: AMSUAW
➤ **AMERICAN SURGEON.** Text in English. 1932. m. USD 250 to individuals; USD 370 to institutions; USD 45 per issue domestic; USD 60 per issue foreign; free to members (effective 2010). adv. illus.; abstr. index. 100 p./no. 2 cols./p.; back issues avail.; reprints avail. **Document type:** *Journal, Academic/Scholarly.*
Formerly (until 1951): Southern Surgeon
Related titles: Online - full text ed.: ISSN 1555-9823 (from IngentaConnect).
Indexed: A01, A02, A03, A08, A20, A22, A29, A34, A36, A37, ASCA, B20, B21, C06, C07, C11, CA, CABA, ChemAb, CurCont, D01, E12, EMBASE, ESPM, ExcerpMed, FR, GH, H04, H13, H17, HospLI, I10, INI, INIS AtomInd, ISR, IndMed, IndVet, Inpharma, M01, M02, MEDLINE, MS&D, N02, N03, P10, P19, P20, P22, P24, P26, P30, P33, P35, P39, P48, P53, P54, PN&I, PQC, R08, R10, R12, RA&MP, RM&VM, Reac, S13, S16, SAA, SCI, SCOPUS, T02, T05, VS, VirolAbstr, W07.
—BLDSC (0857.750000), GNLM, IE, Infotrieve, Ingenta, INIST. **CCC.**
Published by: Southeastern Surgical Congress, 115 Samaritan Dr, #200, Cumming, GA 30040. TEL 678-965-2422, 800-558-8958, FAX 678-965-2278, sesc@sesc.org, http://www.sesc.org. Ed. Dr. J David Richardson TEL 502-852-5452. Circ: 3,250. **Co-sponsor:** American College of Surgeons - Southern California Chapter and the Midwest Surgical Association.

617 USA ISSN 1546-3222
RC941 CODEN: PATSBB
➤ **AMERICAN THORACIC SOCIETY. PROCEEDINGS.** Abbreviated title: P A T S. Text in English. 2004. irreg. free to members (effective 2009); subscr. includes American Journal of Respiratory and Critical Care Medicine and American Journal of Respiratory Cell and Molecular Biology subscribers. adv. **Document type:** *Proceedings, Academic/Scholarly.*
Related titles: Online - full text ed.: ISSN 1943-5665. free (effective 2011).
Indexed: A36, B&BAb, BA, BIOBASE, C06, C07, CABA, E12, EMBASE, ExcerpMed, F08, GH, IABS, Inpharma, MEDLINE, N02, N03, P30, P33, P35, R10, R12, RM&VM, Reac, SCOPUS, T05, VS.
—BLDSC (6636.450000), IE, Ingenta, INIST. **CCC.**
Published by: American Thoracic Society, 61 Broadway, New York, NY 10006. TEL 212-315-8625, FAX 212-315-8613, http://www.thoracic.org. Ed. Alan R Leff. Adv. contact Kevin Dunn TEL 201-767-4170.

617 ESP ISSN 1130-2542
ANALES DE CIRUGIA VASCULAR. Text in Spanish. 1988. bi-m. EUR 133.76 to individuals; EUR 338.64 to institutions (effective 2009). **Document type:** *Journal, Academic/Scholarly.*
Related titles: Online - full text ed.: ISSN 1989-0842. 2007 (from ScienceDirect); ◆ English ed.: Annals of Vascular Surgery. ISSN 0890-5096.
Indexed: SCOPUS.
—CCC.
Published by: Elsevier Doyma (Subsidiary of: Elsevier Health Sciences), Traversa de Gracia 17-21, Barcelona, 08021, Spain. TEL 34-932-418800, FAX 34-932-419020, editorial@elsevier.com, http://www.elsevier.es/. Ed. Manuel Miralles. Circ: 800.

ANALES DE PATOLOGIA VASCULAR. *see* MEDICAL SCIENCES—Cardiovascular Diseases

ANESTEZIOLOGIYA I REANIMATOLOGIYA/ANESTHESIOLOGY AND INTENSIVE CARE. *see* MEDICAL SCIENCES—Anaesthesiology

617 RUS ISSN 1027-6661
ANGIOLOGIYA I SOSUDISTAYA KHIRURGIYA/ANGIOLOGY AND VASCULAR SURGERY. Text in Russian, English. 1995. q. USD 214 foreign (effective 2006). **Document type:** *Journal, Academic/Scholarly.* **Description:** Explores a broad range of subjects pertaining to heart and vascular diseases.
Indexed: EMBASE, ExcerpMed, MEDLINE, P30, R10, Reac, RefZh, SCOPUS.
—BLDSC (0006.607000). **CCC.**
Published by: Rossiiskoe Obshchestvo Angiologov i Sosudistykh Khirurgov/Russian Society of Angiogitst & Vascular Surgeons, ul Bol'shaya Pirogovskaya, d. 2/6, Moscow, 119881, Russian Federation. TEL 7-095-2365558, FAX 7-095-2484845, postmaster@angiolsurgery.org, http://www.angiolsurgery.org. Ed. Anatolii Pokrovskii. **Dist. by:** East View Information Services, 10601 Wayzata Blvd, Minneapolis, MN 55305. TEL 952-252-1201, 800-477-1005, FAX 952-252-1202, info@eastview.com, http://www.eastview.com.

617 618.1 FIN ISSN 0355-9874
ANNALES CHIRURGIAE ET GYNAECOLOGIAE. SUPPLEMENTUM. Text in English. 1946. irreg.
Formerly (until 1975): Annales Chirurgiae et Gynaecologiae Fenniae. Supplementum (0066-2038)
Indexed: EMBASE, ExcerpMed, MEDLINE, P30, R10, Reac, SCOPUS.
—BLDSC (0970.517000), IE, Ingenta, INIST. **CCC.**
Published by: Finnish Medical Society Duodecim, Kalevankatu 11 A, PO Box 713, Helsinki, 00101, Finland. TEL 358-9-618851, FAX 358-9-61885200, annakaisa.tavast@duodecim.fi.

617.95 FRA ISSN 0294-1260
CODEN: ACESE
ANNALES DE CHIRURGIE PLASTIQUE ESTHETIQUE. Variant title: Annales de Chirurgie Plastique et Esthetique. Text in French; Summaries in English. 1956. 6/yr. EUR 495 in Europe to institutions; EUR 478.94 in France to institutions; JPY 69,900 in Japan to institutions; USD 644 elsewhere to institutions (effective 2012). adv. abstr.; charts; illus. **Document type:** *Journal, Academic/Scholarly.* **Description:** Dedicated to all fields of cosmetic, plastic and reconstructive surgery, whether reconstructive surgery after a traumatism, carried out after a malformation, or motivated by psychological troubles in the patient's life. Also publishes editorials, original articles, technical notes, clinical facts, surgical news, general reviews, news in brief, and letters to the editor.
Formerly (until 1983): Annales de Chirurgie Plastique (0003-3960)
Related titles: Online - full text ed.: ISSN 1768-319X (from IngentaConnect, ScienceDirect).
Indexed: A01, A03, A08, A20, A22, A26, CA, ChemAb, EMBASE, ExcerpMed, FR, I05, IndMed, MEDLINE, MS&D, P30, R10, Reac, SCI, SCOPUS, T02, W07.
—BLDSC (0970.541000), GNLM, IE, Infotrieve, Ingenta, INIST. **CCC.**
Published by: Elsevier Masson (Subsidiary of: Elsevier Health Sciences), 62 Rue Camille Desmoulins, Issy les Moulineaux, Cedex 92442, France. TEL 33-1-71165500, FAX 33-1-71165600, infos@elsevier-masson.fr. Ed. Jean-Luc Cariou. Circ: 3,000.

617 FRA ISSN 0299-2213
➤ **ANNALES DE CHIRURGIE VASCULAIRE.** Text in French. 1986. bi-m. EUR 388 in Europe to institutions; EUR 358.47 in France to institutions; JPY 86,800 in Japan to institutions; USD 525 elsewhere to institutions (effective 2012). **Document type:** *Journal, Academic/Scholarly.*
Related titles: Online - full text ed.: (from ScienceDirect).
—INIST. **CCC.**
Published by: Elsevier Masson (Subsidiary of: Elsevier Health Sciences), 62 Rue Camille Desmoulins, Issy les Moulineaux, Cedex 92442, France. TEL 33-1-71165500, infos@elsevier-masson.fr, http://www.elsevier-masson.fr. Eds. E Kieffer, R Berguer.

617 ITA ISSN 0003-469X
CODEN: AICHAL
➤ **ANNALI ITALIANI DI CHIRURGIA.** Text in Italian, English; Abstracts in English. 1922. bi-m. adv. bk.rev. abstr.; charts; illus. index. back issues avail. **Document type:** *Journal, Academic/Scholarly.*
Related titles: Fax ed.
Indexed: A22, ChemAb, DentInd, EMBASE, ExcerpMed, IndMed, MEDLINE, P30, R10, Reac, SCI, SCOPUS, W07.
—BLDSC (1014.300000), GNLM, IE, Infotrieve, Ingenta, INIST.
Published by: Edizioni Luigi Pozzi s.r.l., Via Panama 68, Rome, 00198, Italy. TEL 39-06-8553548, FAX 39-06-8554105, edizioni_pozzi@tin.it. Ed. Nicola Picardi. Circ: 3,000.

617.95 USA ISSN 0148-7043
RD118.AL CODEN: APCSD4
➤ **ANNALS OF PLASTIC SURGERY.** Text in English. 1978. m. USD 994 domestic to institutions; USD 1,259 foreign to institutions (effective 2011). adv. bk.rev. abstr.; charts; illus.; stat. index. back issues avail.; reprints avail. **Document type:** *Journal, Academic/Scholarly.* **Description:** Provides a forum for current scientific and clinical advances in the field and a sounding board for ideas and perspectives on its future.
Related titles: Online - full text ed.: ISSN 1536-3708.
Indexed: A20, A22, A34, A36, ASCA, C33, CABA, CurCont, D01, DentInd, EMBASE, ExcerpMed, FR, GH, IBR, IBZ, ISR, IndMed, IndVet, Inpharma, JW-D, MEDLINE, MS&D, MaizeAb, N02, N03, P30, P33, P35, R08, R10, R12, RM&VM, Reac, SCI, SCOPUS, T05, VS, W07.
—BLDSC (1043.525000), CIS, GNLM, IE, Infotrieve, Ingenta, INIST. **CCC.**
Published by: Lippincott Williams & Wilkins (Subsidiary of: Wolters Kluwer N.V.), 530 Walnut St, Philadelphia, PA 19106. TEL 215-521-8300, FAX 215-521-8902, customerservice@lww.com, http://www.lww.com. Ed. William C Lineaweaver. Pub. Nancy Megley. Circ: 915.

617 USA ISSN 0003-4932
RD1 CODEN: ANSUA5
➤ **ANNALS OF SURGERY.** Text in English. 1885. m. USD 916 domestic to institutions; USD 1,204 foreign to institutions (effective 2011). adv. bk.rev. illus. index. back issues avail.; reprints avail. **Document type:** *Journal, Academic/Scholarly.* **Description:** Provides the international medical community with information on significant contributions to the advancement of surgical science and practice.
Related titles: Microform ed.: (from PMC, PQC); Online - full text ed.: ISSN 1528-1140. USD 553.80 domestic academic site license; USD 671.80 foreign academic site license; USD 617.70 domestic corporate site license; USD 735.70 foreign corporate site license (effective 2002).
Indexed: A20, A22, A35, A36, AHCMS, AIIM, AIM, ASCA, AgBio, CA, CABA, ChemAb, CurCont, D01, E12, EMBASE, ExcerpMed, F08, FR, G08, GH, H11, H12, HospLI, IBR, IBZ, IDIS, ISR, IndMed, Inpharma, JW, JW-EM, Kidney, LT, MEDLINE, MS&D, N02, N03, P30, P33, P35, R10, R12, R13, RA&MP, RM&VM, RRTA, Reac, S12, SCI, SCOPUS, SoyAb, T05, VS, W07.
—BLDSC (1044.500000), CASDDS, GNLM, IE, Infotrieve, Ingenta, INIST. **CCC.**
Published by: (American Surgical Association), Lippincott Williams & Wilkins (Subsidiary of: Wolters Kluwer N.V.), Two Commerce Sq, 2001 Market St, Philadelphia, PA 19103. TEL 215-521-8300, FAX 215-521-8902, customerservice@lww.com, http://www.lww.com. Ed. Dr. Layton F Rikkers. Pub. Jason Pointe. Adv. contact Ronna Ekhouse TEL 215-521-8404. Circ: 3,547. **Co-sponsors:** Philadelphia Academy of Surgery; Southern Surgical Association; New York Surgical Society.

617 GBR ISSN 1750-1164
RD1
➤ **ANNALS OF SURGICAL INNOVATION AND RESEARCH.** Text in English. 2006. irreg. free (effective 2011). adv. back issues avail. **Document type:** *Journal, Academic/Scholarly.* **Description:** Covers all aspects of research in surgery related disciplines.
Media: Online - full text.
Indexed: A01, A26, CA, H12, I05, P30, T02.
—CCC.
Published by: BioMed Central Ltd. (Subsidiary of: Springer Science+Business Media), 236 Gray's Inn Rd, London, WC1X 8HB, United Kingdom. TEL 44-20-31922000, FAX 44-20-31922010, info@biomedcentral.com, http://www.biomedcentral.com. Eds. James Becker, Michael Gagner. Adv. contact Natasha Bailey TEL 44-20-31922231.

617 USA ISSN 1068-9265
CODEN: ASONF4
➤ **ANNALS OF SURGICAL ONCOLOGY.** Text in English. 1994. m. EUR 1,150, USD 1,223 combined subscription to institutions (print & online eds.) (effective 2012). adv. charts; illus. reprint service avail. from PSC. **Document type:** *Journal, Academic/Scholarly.* **Description:** Presents significant developments involving multidisciplinary cancer care and research, for practicing surgeons in all specialties.
Related titles: Microform ed.: (from PQC); Online - full text ed.: ISSN 1534-4681 (from IngentaConnect).
Indexed: A20, A22, A26, ASCA, B21, CurCont, E01, EMBASE, ExcerpMed, ISR, IndMed, Inpharma, MEDLINE, OGFA, P20, P22, P30, P35, P48, P54, PQC, R10, Reac, SCI, SCOPUS, W07.
—BLDSC (1044.550000), GNLM, IE, Infotrieve, Ingenta, INIST. **CCC.**
Published by: (Society of Surgical Oncology), Springer New York LLC (Subsidiary of: Springer Science+Business Media), 233 Spring St, New York, NY 10013. TEL 212-460-1500, journals@springer-ny.com, http://www.springer.com/. Ed. Charles M Balch. Pub. Yvonne Chan. adv.: B&W page USD 1,490; trim 8.25 x 11. Circ: 2,200 (paid).

617.54 JPN ISSN 1341-1098
RD597
ANNALS OF THORACIC AND CARDIOVASCULAR SURGERY. Text in English. 1995. bi-m. **Document type:** *Journal, Academic/Scholarly.*
Formerly (until 1995): Rinsho Kyobu Geka - Japanese Annals of Thoracic Surgery (0389-7893)
Indexed: EMBASE, ExcerpMed, IndMed, MEDLINE, P30, R10, Reac, SCI, SCOPUS, W07.
—BLDSC (1044.700000), GNLM, IE, Infotrieve, Ingenta.

Published by: (Association of Thoracic and Cardiovascular Surgeons of Asia), Medikaru Toribyun/Medical Tribune Inc., Nibankcho TS Bldg, 2-1 Nibancho, Chiyoda-ku, Tokyo, 102-0084, Japan. TEL 81-3-32397217, FAX 81-3-32399375, http://www.medical-tribune.co.jp/. Ed. Dr. Yukiyasu Sezai.

617.54 USA ISSN 0003-4975
CODEN: ATHSAK

➤ **THE ANNALS OF THORACIC SURGERY.** Abbreviated title: A T S. Text in English. 1965. m. USD 714 in United States to institutions; USD 825 elsewhere to institutions (effective 2012). adv. bk.rev. charts; illus.; abstr. index. back issues avail.; reprints avail. **Document type:** *Journal, Academic/Scholarly.* **Description:** Provides coverage of recent progress in chest and cardiovascular surgery and related fields.
Related titles: Microform ed.: (from PQC); Online - full text ed.: ISSN 1552-6259 (from IngentaConnect, ScienceDirect).
Indexed: A20, A22, A26, A36, AIIM, AIM, ASCA, CA, CABA, CurCont, EMBASE, ExcerpMed, G08, GH, H11, H12, H17, IBR, IBZ, IDIS, INI, ISR, IndMed, Inpharma, Kidney, MEDLINE, N02, N03, P30, P33, P35, PN&I, R08, R10, RM&VM, Reac, SCI, SCOPUS, T02, T05, VS, W07.
—BLDSC (1044.750000), GNLM, IE, Infotrieve, Ingenta, INIST. **CCC.**
Published by: (Society of Thoracic Surgeons), Elsevier Inc. (Subsidiary of: Elsevier Science & Technology), 1600 John F Kennedy Blvd, Philadelphia, PA 19103. TEL 215-239-3900, FAX 215-238-7883, JournalCustomerService-usa@elsevier.com, http://www.elsevier.com. Ed. Dr. L Henry Edmunds Jr. TEL 215-662-2092. Adv. contact Michael Targowski TEL 212-633-3693. Circ: 7,050. **Co-sponsor:** Southern Thoracic Surgical Association.

617 POL ISSN 1425-9524
CODEN: ANTRF6

ANNALS OF TRANSPLANTATION. Text in English. 1996. q. USD 103 foreign (effective 2006). **Document type:** *Journal, Academic/Scholarly.*
Indexed: EMBASE, ExcerpMed, MEDLINE, P30, R10, Reac, SCI, SCOPUS, W07.
—BLDSC (1044.900000), IE, Infotrieve, Ingenta.
Published by: (Polish Transplantation Society), Medical University of Warsaw, Institute of Transplantation Sciences, Ul Nowogrodzka 59, Warszawa, 02005, Poland. TEL 48-22-6285363, FAX 48-22-6288987. **Dist. by:** Ars Polona, Obroncow 25, Warsaw 03933, Poland. TEL 48-22-5098609, FAX 48-22-5098610, arspolona@arspolona.com.pl, http://www.arspolona.com.pl.

617 616.1 USA ISSN 0890-5096
RD598.5 CODEN: AVSUEV

➤ **ANNALS OF VASCULAR SURGERY.** Text in English. 1986. 8/yr. USD 924 in United States to institutions; USD 972 elsewhere to institutions (effective 2012). adv. back issues avail.; reprints avail. **Document type:** *Journal, Academic/Scholarly.* **Description:** Covers clinical and experimental work in vascular surgery. Contains research articles, basic science research, surgical notes and techniques, reviews and case reports.
Related titles: Online - full text ed.: ISSN 1615-5947 (from IngentaConnect, ScienceDirect); ◆ Spanish ed.: Anales de Cirugia Vascular. ISSN 1130-2542.
Indexed: A22, A26, ASCA, CurCont, E01, EMBASE, ExcerpMed, H12, ISR, IndMed, Inpharma, MEDLINE, P20, P22, P30, P35, P48, P54, PQC, R10, Reac, SCI, SCOPUS, W07.
—BLDSC (1045.350000), GNLM, IE, Infotrieve, Ingenta, INIST. **CCC.**
Published by: (Vascular Interventional Advances), Elsevier Inc. (Subsidiary of: Elsevier Science & Technology), 1600 John F Kennedy Blvd, Philadelphia, PA 19103. TEL 215-239-3900, FAX 215-238-7883, JournalCustomerService-usa@elsevier.com, http://www.elsevier.com. Eds. O Goeau-Brissonniere, Ramon Berguer. Circ: 1,205.

617 RUS

ANNALY KHIRURGICHESKOI GEPATOLOGII/ANNALS OF SURGICAL HEPATOLOGY. Text in Russian. 1998. q. USD 154 foreign (effective 2004). **Document type:** *Journal, Academic/Scholarly.* **Description:** Covers topical problems of liver, biliary tracts and pancreas surgery.
Published by: Assotsiatsiya Khirurgov-Gepatologov, Kolomenskii pr-zd 4, Klinich b-tsa 7, Moscow, 115446, Russian Federation. Ed. E I Gal'perin. **Dist. by:** East View Information Services, 10601 Wayzata Blvd, Minneapolis, MN 55305. TEL 952-252-1201, 800-477-1005, FAX 952-252-1202, info@eastview.com, http://www.eastview.com.

617 RUS ISSN 1560-9502

ANNALY KHIRURGII. Text in Russian. 1996. bi-m. USD 294 foreign (effective 2005). **Document type:** *Journal, Academic/Scholarly.* **Description:** Provides information about modern advances in practically all branches of surgery as well as major surgical centers in Russia and abroad.
Indexed: RefZh.
—BLDSC (0006.759000), East View.
Published by: Izdatel'stvo Meditsina/Meditsina Publishers, ul B Pirogovskaya, d 2, str 5, Moscow, 119435, Russian Federation. TEL 7-095-2483324, meditsina@mtu-net.ru, http://www.medlit.ru. Ed. Leo A Bockeria. **Dist. by:** East View Information Services, 10601 Wayzata Blvd, Minneapolis, MN 55305. TEL 952-252-1201, 800-477-1005, FAX 952-252-1202, info@eastview.com, http://www.eastview.com.

ANTI-AGING & COSMETIC SURGERY MAGAZINE: MEN'S GUIDE. *see* BEAUTY CULTURE

617 IND ISSN 0003-5998
R97 CODEN: ANTIA8

THE ANTISEPTIC; monthly journal of medicine and surgery. Text in English. 1904. m. INR 540; INR 45 per issue (effective 2011). bk.rev. abstr.; bibl.; illus. index. back issues avail.; reprints avail. **Document type:** *Journal, Trade.*
Indexed: ChemAb, IndMed, P30.
—GNLM.
Published by: Professional Publications Ltd., Satya Sai Nagar, P O Box 2, Madurai, Tamil Nadu 625 003, India. TEL 91-452-2673701, FAX 91-452-2674602. **Subscr. to:** I N S I O Scientific Books & Periodicals.

617.95 USA ISSN 1521-2491
RD118.A1

➤ **ARCHIVES OF FACIAL PLASTIC SURGERY.** Text in English. 1999. bi-m. USD 440 domestic to institutions; USD 550 in the Americas to institutions; EUR 445 in Europe to institutions; GBP 377 elsewhere to institutions (effective 2012). adv. back issues avail.; reprints avail. **Document type:** *Journal, Academic/Scholarly.* **Description:** Provides facial plastic surgeons with essential information that help to enhance their patient's health.
Related titles: Online - full text ed.: ISSN 1538-3660. free to members (effective 2012).
Indexed: A20, A22, B&BAb, B19, B21, BioEngAb, CurCont, EMBASE, ExcerpMed, H13, IndMed, JW-D, MEDLINE, P02, P10, P20, P22, P24, P30, P48, P53, P54, PQC, R10, Reac, SCI, SCOPUS, W07.
—BLDSC (1634.278050), IE, Infotrieve, Ingenta. **CCC.**
Published by: American Medical Association, 515 N State St, Chicago, IL 60654. TEL 312-464-4200, 800-621-8335, FAX 312-464-4142, journalsales@ama-assn.org, http://www.ama-assn.org. Eds. Dr. Wayne F Larrabee Jr., Dr. Catherine D DeAngelis. **Subscr. in the Americas to:** PO Box 10946, Chicago, IL 60654. TEL 312-670-7827, 800-262-2350, ama-subs@ama-assn.org; **Subscr. outside the Americas to:** American Medical Association, J A M A and Archive Journals.

617 USA ISSN 0004-0010
RD1 CODEN: ARSUAX

➤ **ARCHIVES OF SURGERY.** Text in English. 1920. m. USD 670 domestic to institutions; USD 838 in the Americas to institutions; EUR 678 in Europe to institutions; GBP 575 elsewhere to institutions (effective 2012). bk.rev. charts; illus. Index. back issues avail.; reprints avail. **Document type:** *Journal, Academic/Scholarly.* **Description:** Provides clinical and basic science information to assist the surgeon in optimizing patient care as well as promotes the art and science of surgery.
Former titles (until 1960): A M A Archives of Surgery (0096-6908); (until 1950): Archives of Surgery (0272-5533)
Related titles: Microform ed.: (from PMC, PQC); Online - full text ed.: ISSN 1538-3644. free to members (effective 2012).
Indexed: A20, A22, A36, AIIM, AIM, ASCA, B&BAb, B21, CABA, CIN, CISA, CTA, ChemAb, ChemTitl, CurCont, DentInd, E12, EMBASE, ExcerpMed, FR, G08, GH, H11, H12, H13, IDIS, INI, ISR, IndMed, Inpharma, JW, MEDLINE, MS&D, N02, N03, P02, P10, P20, P22, P24, P30, P33, P48, P53, P54, PQC, R10, R12, RM&VM, Reac, SCI, SCOPUS, SoyAb, T05, VS, W07.
—BLDSC (1643.200000), CASDDS, GNLM, IE, Ingenta, INIST. **CCC.**
Published by: American Medical Association, 515 N State St, Chicago, IL 60654. TEL 312-464-4200, 800-621-8335, FAX 312-464-4142, journalsales@ama-assn.org, http://www.ama-assn.org. Eds. Julie Ann Freischlag, Dr. Catherine D DeAngelis. **Subscr. in the Americas to:** PO Box 10946, Chicago, IL 60654. TEL 312-670-7827, 800-262-2350, ama-subs@ama-assn.org; **Subscr. outside the Americas to:** American Medical Association, J A M A and Archive Journals.

➤ **ARQUIVOS BRASILEIROS DE CIRURGIA DIGESTIVA.** *see* MEDICAL SCIENCES—Gastroenterology

617 PRT ISSN 0872-2226
CODEN: APCIFA

ARQUIVOS PORTUGUESES DE CIRURGIA. Text in English, Portuguese. 1990. q. EUR 20 (effective 2005). **Document type:** *Journal, Academic/Scholarly.*
Published by: Associacao de Estudantes da Faculdade de Medicina do Porto (A E F M U P), Alameda Prof. H. Montiero, Piso 1, Oporto, 4200-319, Portugal. aefmup@aefmup.up.pt, http://www.ae.med.up.pt/aefmup/. Ed. Amarante Junior. Adv. contact Fernando Araujo. Circ: 2,500. **Co-sponsor:** Hospital de S. Joao, Faculdade de Medicina do Porto.

ARTHROSCOPY: THE JOURNAL OF ARTHROSCOPY AND RELATED SURGERY. *see* MEDICAL SCIENCES—Orthopedics And Traumatology

ARTIFICIAL ORGANS; replacement, recovery, and regeneration. *see* MEDICAL SCIENCES—Experimental Medicine, Laboratory Technique

617 ITA ISSN 1591-1489

ARTROSCOPIA. Text in Italian, English. 1997. 3/yr. EUR 78 in Europe to institutions; EUR 88 elsewhere to institutions (effective 2008). **Document type:** *Journal, Academic/Scholarly.*
Formerly (until 2000): Manuali Tascabili di Terapia Medica (1126-0327)
Indexed: SCOPUS.
Published by: Societa Italiana di Artroscopia (S I A), CP 3180, Bologna Ponente, Bologna, 40131, Italy. TEL 39-051-380748, FAX 39-051-3764173, segreteria@siaonline.it, http://www.siaonline.it. Circ: 10,000.

617 GBR ISSN 1758-5902

▼ ➤ **ASIAN JOURNAL OF ENDOSCOPIC SURGERY.** Text in English. 2009. 3/yr. **Document type:** *Journal, Academic/Scholarly.* **Description:** Publishes recent research in the fields of endoscopic surgery.
Related titles: ◆ Online - full text ed.: Asian Journal of Endoscopic Surgery (Online). ISSN 1758-5910.
Indexed: A22, E01.
Published by: (Japan Society for Endoscopic Surgery JPN, Asia Endosurgery Task Force JPN), Wiley-Blackwell Publishing Ltd. (Subsidiary of: John Wiley & Sons, Inc.), 9600 Garsington Rd, Oxford, OX4 2DQ, United Kingdom. TEL 44-1865-776868, FAX 44-1865-714591, cs-agency@wiley.com, http://www.wiley.com/. Ed. Masaki Kitajima.

617 GBR ISSN 1758-5910

▼ ➤ **ASIAN JOURNAL OF ENDOSCOPIC SURGERY (ONLINE).** Text in English. 2009. 4/yr. GBP 995 domestic to institutions; EUR 850 in Europe to institutions; USD 630 elsewhere to institutions (effective 2012). **Document type:** *Journal, Academic/Scholarly.* **Description:** Publishes recent research in the fields of endoscopic surgery.
Media: Online - full text. **Related titles:** ◆ Print ed.: Asian Journal of Endoscopic Surgery. ISSN 1758-5902.
Published by: (Japan Society for Endoscopic Surgery JPN, Asia Endosurgery Task Force JPN), Wiley-Blackwell Publishing Ltd. (Subsidiary of: John Wiley & Sons, Inc.), 9600 Garsington Rd, Oxford, OX4 2DQ, United Kingdom. TEL 44-1865-776868, FAX 44-1865-714591, customerservices@blackwellpublishing.com, http://onlinelibrary.wiley.com/. Ed. Masaki Kitajima.

➤ **ASIAN JOURNAL OF ORAL AND MAXILLOFACIAL SURGERY.** *see* MEDICAL SCIENCES—Dentistry

617 HKG ISSN 1015-9584
RD1 CODEN: AJSUEF

➤ **ASIAN JOURNAL OF SURGERY.** Text in English. 1978. 4/yr. EUR 249 in Europe to institutions; JPY 39,200 in Japan to institutions; USD 333 elsewhere to institutions (effective 2012). adv. 120 p./no.; **Document type:** *Journal, Academic/Scholarly.*
Formerly (until 1989): Southeast Asian Journal of Surgery (0258-3186)
Indexed: A34, A36, B&BAb, B21, BioEngAb, CA, CABA, CurCont, D01, E12, EMBASE, ExcerpMed, GH, H17, IndVet, MEDLINE, N02, N03, P30, P33, R08, R10, R12, RM&VM, Reac, SCI, SCOPUS, T02, T05, VS, W07.
—BLDSC (1742.578000), GNLM, IE, Infotrieve, Ingenta. **CCC.**
Published by: (Asian Surgical Association CHN), Elsevier (Singapore) Pte Ltd, Hong Kong Branch (Subsidiary of: Elsevier Health Sciences), 1601, 16/F, Leighton Centre, 77 Leighton Rd., Causeway Bay, Hong Kong. TEL 852-2965-1300, FAX 852-2976-0778, asiajournals@elsevier.com, http://asia.elsevierhealth.com/. Ed. P H Lee. adv.: B&W page USD 2,000, color page USD 4,000. Circ: 1,800 (controlled).

617 ZMB

ASSOCIATION OF SURGEONS OF EAST AFRICA. NEWSLETTER. Text in English. a. **Document type:** *Newsletter, Academic/Scholarly.*
Media: Online - full text.
Published by: Association of Surgeons of East Africa, Woodlands, PO Box 320159, Lusaka, Zambia. TEL 260-1-230710, FAX 260-1-250753, editor_ecajs@yahoo.com. Ed. Nyengo Mkandawire.

617 USA ISSN 1558-4267

ATLAS OF THE HAND CLINICS (ONLINE). Text in English. 1996. s-a. adv. back issues avail.; reprints avail. **Document type:** *Journal, Academic/Scholarly.* **Description:** Delivers practical advice from experts in each specialty covered with a fresh perspective on problems and controversies.
Media: Online - full text.
—CCC.
Published by: W.B. Saunders Co. (Subsidiary of: Elsevier Health Sciences), Elsevier, Health Sciences Division, Order Fulfillment, 3251 Riverport Ln, Maryland Heights, MO 63043. TEL 314-872-8370, 800-325-4177, FAX 314-432-1380, JournalCustomerService-usa@elsevier.com, http://www.us.elsevierhealth.com.

ATLAS OF THE ORAL AND MAXILLOFACIAL SURGERY CLINICS OF NORTH AMERICA. *see* MEDICAL SCIENCES—Dentistry

ATROSKOPIA I CHIRURGIA STAWOW/ARTHROSCOPY AND JOINT SURGERY. *see* MEDICAL SCIENCES—Orthopedics And Traumatology

616.21 USA ISSN 1047-6954

➤ **AUDIO-DIGEST GENERAL SURGERY.** Text in English. 1954. s-m. USD 449.81 domestic; USD 479.72 in Canada; USD 527.72 elsewhere (effective 2010). back issues avail. **Document type:** *Journal, Academic/Scholarly.*
Formerly (until 1990): Audio-Digest Surgery (0271-1273)
Media: Audio cassette/tape. **Related titles:** Audio CD ed.: USD 399.89 domestic; USD 431.72 in Canada; USD 479.72 elsewhere (effective 2010); Online - full text ed.: USD 359.72 (effective 2010).
Published by: Audio-Digest Foundation (Subsidiary of: California Medical Association), 1577 E Chevy Chase Dr, Glendale, CA 91206. TEL 818-240-7500, 800-423-2308, FAX 818-240-7379.

617 616 ESP ISSN 0214-4077

AVANCES EN TRAUMATOLOGIA, CIRUGIA, REHABILITACION, MEDICINA PREVENTIVA Y DEPORTIVA. Text in Spanish. 1971. q. **Document type:** *Journal, Trade.*
Former titles (until 1985): Avances en Traumatologia, Cirugia y Rehabilitacion (0214-4085); (until 1984): Traumatologia, Cirugia y Rehabilitacion (0210-041X)
Published by: Publicaciones Nacionales Tecnicas y Extranjeras (PUNTEX), Padilla 323, Barcelona, 08025, Spain. TEL 34-934-462820, FAX 34-934-462064, puntex@puntex.es, http://www.puntex.es. Circ: 6,000.

617 GBR ISSN 1471-2482
RD1 CODEN: BSMUBM

➤ **B M C SURGERY.** (BioMed Central) Text in English. 2001 (May). irreg. free (effective 2011). adv. back issues avail. **Document type:** *Journal, Academic/Scholarly.* **Description:** Publishes original research articles in surgical research, training, and practice.
Media: Online - full text.
Indexed: A26, C06, C07, CA, EMBASE, ExcerpMed, I05, MEDLINE, P20, P22, P30, R10, Reac, SCOPUS, T02.
—Infotrieve. **CCC.**
Published by: BioMed Central Ltd. (Subsidiary of: Springer Science+Business Media), 236 Gray's Inn Rd, London, WC1X 8HB, United Kingdom. TEL 44-20-31922000, FAX 44-20-31922010, info@biomedcentral.com. Ed. Dr. Melissa Norton. Adv. contact Natasha Bailey TEL 44-20-31922231.

617 ESP ISSN 1989-9769

BALEAR QUIRURGICA. Text in Spanish. 2008. q. back issues avail. **Document type:** *Magazine, Consumer.*
Media: Online - full text.
Published by: Sociedad Balear de Cirugia, C San Miguel 46, Escalera Der. Piso 1o., Palma de Mallorca, 07002, Spain. TEL 34-971-213808, FAX 34-91-213775.

617 BGD ISSN 1015-0870

➤ **BANGLADESH COLLEGE OF PHYSICIANS AND SURGEONS. JOURNAL.** Text in English. 1978. 3/yr. IRR 300 domestic; USD 30 foreign; IRR 100, USD 10 per issue (effective 2010). back issues avail.; reprints avail. **Document type:** *Journal, Academic/Scholarly.*
Related titles: Online - full text ed.: free (effective 2011).
Indexed: A01.
Published by: Bangladesh College of Physicians and Surgeons, 69 Shaheed Tajuddin Sarani, Mohakhali, Dhaka, 1212, Bangladesh. Ed., Pub., R&P Quazi Tarikul Islam.

617 CHE ISSN 1013-7459
CODEN: BBCHEL

BASLER BEITRAEGE ZUR CHIRURGIE; Aktuelle Entwicklungen und neue Verfahren aus der chirurgischen Praxis kompakt vermittelt. Text in German. 1989. irreg., latest vol.10, 1998. price varies. abstr.; bibl.; charts. **Document type:** *Monographic series, Academic/Scholarly.* **Description:** Discusses developments in surgery and its techniques.

—GNLM.
Published by: (Universitaet Basel), Schwabe und Co. AG, Steinentorstr 13, Basel, 4010, Switzerland. TEL 41-61-2789565, FAX 41-61-2789566, TELEX CH-962652, verlag@schwabe.ch, http://www.schwabe.ch. Eds. M Duerig, U Laffer.

617.95 NZL ISSN 1177-1232
BEAUTIFUL YOU. Text in English. 2005. s-a. adv. **Document type:** *Magazine, Consumer.*
Published by: You Enterprises, PO Box 90 693, Auckland Mail Centre, Auckland, New Zealand. TEL 64-9-3060921, FAX 64-9-3060922. Ed. Vanessa Green. adv.: page NZD 6,000; trim 210 x 297. Circ: 10,000.

BEYOND CHANGE; information regarding obesity and obesity surgery. *see* MEDICAL SCIENCES

BLOOD & MARROW TRANSPLANT NEWSLETTER. *see* MEDICAL SCIENCES—Experimental Medicine, Laboratory Technique

BLOOD AND MARROW TRANSPLANTATION REVIEWS. *see* MEDICAL SCIENCES—Experimental Medicine, Laboratory Technique

617 646.72 USA
BLOOM; Colorado's guide to beauty and cosmetic enhancement. Text in English. 2005 (Dec.). 3/w. (Winter, Spring & Summer). USD 9.95 (effective 2005). adv. **Document type:** *Magazine, Consumer.* **Description:** Provides information on cosmetic enhancement, related products and services and doctors in Colorado.
Published by: Bloom Media, LLC., 3421 W. 23rd Ave., Denver, CO 80211. TEL 970-366-4318. Pub. Zac Folk TEL 970-366-4318 ext 901. Adv. contact Richard Bradbury TEL 970-366-4318 ext 902.

617.95 GBR ISSN 1475-665X
BODY LANGUAGE. Abbreviated title: B L. Text in English. 1999 (Feb.). q. GBP 45 in Europe; GBP 12 per issue in Europe (effective 2009). adv. back issues avail.; reprints avail. **Document type:** *Magazine, Consumer.* **Description:** Provides independent information on all procedures and treatments as well as news and views of modern cosmetic surgery products and techniques.
Published by: New Millennium Publishing Ltd., 69 Grand Parade, Brighton, E Sussex BN2 9TS, United Kingdom. TEL 44-1273-606799, http://www.newmillenniumpublishing.com. Ed., Pub. David Williams. Circ: 8,000.

617 MEX
BOLETIN INFORMATIVO. Text in Spanish. m. back issues avail.
Related titles: Online - full text ed.
Published by: Asociacion Mexicana de Cirugia General, A.C., Adolfo Prieto 1649, 4o. Piso, Desp. 401 y 404, Mexico, D.F., 03100, Mexico. TEL 52-55-343581, FAX 52-55-244958, asomexcg@aol.com, http://www.amcg.org.mx/.

BONE MARROW TRANSPLANTATION. *see* MEDICAL SCIENCES—Experimental Medicine, Laboratory Technique

BONE MARROW TRANSPLANTATION. SUPPLEMENT. *see* MEDICAL SCIENCES—Experimental Medicine, Laboratory Technique

617.6 GBR ISSN 1356-3807
BRITISH DENTAL NURSES' JOURNAL. Text in English. 1942. q. GBP 120 domestic to non-members; GBP 150 foreign to non-members; free to members (effective 2009). adv. bk.rev. illus. **Document type:** *Journal, Academic/Scholarly.* **Description:** Contains articles on scientific, dental or other relevant issues, news items or dates of forthcoming events.
Former titles (until 1994): British Dental Surgery Assistant (0007-0629); (until 1957): British Dental Nurses Journal
Indexed: CA, D02, DentInd, P30, SCOPUS, T02.
—GNLM. **CCC.**
Published by: British Association of Dental Nurses, Rm 200, Hillhouse International Business Centre, PO Box 4, Thornton-Cleveleys, FY5 4QD, United Kingdom. TEL 44-1253-338360, admin@badn.org.uk. Ed. Pam Swain. Adv. contact Ed Hunt TEL 44-1689-899177. page GBP 900.

617 GBR ISSN 0268-8697
RD593 CODEN: BJNEEL
➤ **BRITISH JOURNAL OF NEUROSURGERY.** Text in English. 1987. bi-m. GBP 955, EUR 1,375, USD 1,720 combined subscription to institutions (print & online eds.); GBP 1,905, EUR 2,750, USD 3,440 combined subscription to corporations (print & online eds.) (effective 2010). adv. bk.rev. abstr. index. back issues avail.; reprint service avail. from PSC. **Document type:** *Journal, Academic/Scholarly.* **Description:** Covers all aspects of case assessment and surgical practice, as well as wide-ranging research, with an emphasis on clinical rather than experimental material.
Related titles: Microfiche ed.; Online - full text ed.: ISSN 1360-046X (from IngentaConnect).
Indexed: A01, A02, A03, A08, A22, ASCA, B21, C11, CA, CurCont, E01, EMBASE, ExcerpMed, H04, H13, IndMed, Inpharma, MEDLINE, NSA, NSCI, P02, P10, P20, P30, P35, P48, P53, P54, PQC, R10, Reac, SCI, SCOPUS, T02, V&AA, W07.
—GNLM, IE, Infotrieve, Ingenta, INIST. **CCC.**
Published by: Informa Healthcare (Subsidiary of: T & F Informa plc), Telephone House, 69-77 Paul St, London, EC2A 4LQ, United Kingdom. healthcare.enquiries@informa.com, http://www.tandf.co.uk/journals/. Ed. Paul Eldridge. Adv. contact Per Sonnerfeldt. **Subscr. in N America to:** Taylor & Francis Inc., Customer Services Dept, 325 Chestnut St, 8th Fl, Philadelphia, PA 19106. TEL 215-625-8900, 800-354-1420, FAX 215-625-8914, customerservice@taylorandfrancis.com; **Subscr. outside N. America to:** Taylor & Francis Ltd., Journals Customer Service, Sheepen Pl, Colchester, Essex CO3 3LP, United Kingdom. TEL 44-20-70175544, FAX 44-20-70175198, tf.enquiries@tfinforma.com.

617.3 GBR ISSN 0266-4356
➤ **BRITISH JOURNAL OF ORAL AND MAXILLOFACIAL SURGERY.** Text in English. 1963. 8/yr. EUR 809 in Europe to institutions; JPY 87,500 in Japan to institutions; USD 762 elsewhere to institutions (effective 2012). adv. bk.rev. charts; illus. index. back issues avail.; reprints avail. **Document type:** *Journal, Academic/Scholarly.* **Description:** Provides contemporary information on developments within the scope of oral and maxillofacial surgery.
Formerly (until 1984): British Journal of Oral Surgery (0007-117X)
Related titles: Microform ed.: (from PQC); Online - full text ed.: ISSN 1532-1940 (from ScienceDirect).
Indexed: A22, A26, ASCA, B&BAb, B21, CA, CTA, CTD, CurCont, D02, DentAb, DentInd, E01, EMBASE, ExcerpMed, FR, I05, ISR, IndMed, Inpharma, MEDLINE, MycolAb, P30, R10, Reac, SCI, SCOPUS, T02, W07.
—BLDSC (2314.200000), GNLM, IE, Infotrieve, Ingenta, INIST. **CCC.**
Published by: (British Association of Oral and Maxillofacial Surgeons), Churchill Livingstone (Subsidiary of: Elsevier Health Sciences), The Blvd, Langford Ln, Kidlington, OX5 1GB, United Kingdom. TEL 44-1865-843434, FAX 44-1865-843970, directenquiries@elsevier.com, http://www.elsevierhealth.com/imprint.jsp?iid=9. Ed. Peter Brennan. Pub. Gillian Griffith. Adv. contact Sarah Jane Cahill TEL 44-20-74244538. Circ: 1,583.

617 GBR ISSN 0007-1323
RD1 CODEN: BJSUAM
➤ **BRITISH JOURNAL OF SURGERY.** Abbreviated title: B J S. Text in English. 1913. m. GBP 451 in United Kingdom to institutions; EUR 659 in Europe to institutions; USD 674 elsewhere to institutions; GBP 519 combined subscription in United Kingdom to institutions (print & online eds.); EUR 758 combined subscription in Europe to institutions (print & online eds.); USD 776 combined subscription elsewhere to institutions (print & online eds.) (effective 2012). adv. bk.rev. abstr.; illus. index. back issues avail.; reprint service avail. from PSC. **Document type:** *Journal, Academic/Scholarly.* **Description:** Publishes original papers and reviews covering the latest techniques, treatment, and advances in surgery. Includes abstracts of the Surgical Research and the Vascular Societies.
Incorporates (1991-2002): The European Journal of Surgery (1102-4151); Which was formerly (until 1991): Acta Chirurgica (1102-1101); Which incorporated (1986-1994): Theoretical Surgery (0179-8669); (until 1991): Acta Chirurgica Scandinavica (0001-5482); Which incorporated (1980-1991): Netherlands Journal of Surgery (0167-2487); Which was formerly (until 1980): Archivum Chirurgicum Neerlandicum (0004-0657)
Related titles: CD-ROM ed.; Microform ed.: (from PQC); Online - full text ed.: ISSN 1365-2168. GBP 451 in United Kingdom to institutions; EUR 659 in Europe to institutions; USD 674 elsewhere to institutions (effective 2012) (from IngentaConnect); Supplement(s): British Journal of Surgery. Supplement. ISSN 1355-7688.
Indexed: A01, A02, A03, A08, A22, A26, A36, AIIM, AIM, ASCA, ASG, BIOBASE, C05, CA, CABA, ChemAb, CurCont, D01, DBA, DentInd, DokArb, E01, EMBASE, ExcerpMed, FR, G08, GH, H04, H11, H12, H17, IABS, INI, ISR, IndMed, Inpharma, JW, JW-G, Kidney, MEDLINE, MS&D, N02, N03, P30, P33, P35, R10, Reac, SAA, SCI, SCOPUS, SoyAb, T02, T05, VS, W07.
—GNLM, IE, Infotrieve, Ingenta, INIST. **CCC.**
Published by: (Surgery Research Society), John Wiley & Sons Ltd. (Subsidiary of: John Wiley & Sons, Inc.), 1-7 Oldlands Way, PO Box 808, Bognor Regis, West Sussex PO21 9FF, United Kingdom. TEL 44-1865-778315, FAX 44-1243-843232, cs-journals@wiley.com, http://eu.wiley.com/WileyCDA/. Ed. J A Murie. **Subscr. to:** 1-7 Oldlands Way, PO Box 809, Bognor Regis, West Sussex PO21 9FG, United Kingdom. TEL 44-1865-778054, cs-agency@wiley.com.

617 FRA ISSN 1621-224X
BRULURES. Text in French. 2000. q. EUR 50 (effective 2009).
—INIST. **CCC.**
Published by: Societe Francaise d'Etude et de Traitement des Brulures, Domus Medica, 79 rue de Tocqueville, Paris, 75017, France. contact@sfetb.org.

C I N N REPORT. *see* MEDICAL SCIENCES—Psychiatry And Neurology

CANADIAN ASSOCIATION FOR ENTEROSTOMAL THERAPY. THE LINK. *see* MEDICAL SCIENCES—Gastroenterology

CANADIAN JOURNAL OF CARDIOLOGY. *see* MEDICAL SCIENCES—Cardiovascular Diseases

617.95 CAN ISSN 1195-2199
CANADIAN JOURNAL OF PLASTIC SURGERY. Text in English. 1993. bi-m. CAD 95 domestic to individuals; USD 95 in United States to individuals; USD 120 elsewhere to individuals; CAD 125 domestic to institutions; USD 125 in United States to institutions; USD 160 elsewhere to institutions (effective 2005). adv. **Document type:** *Journal, Academic/Scholarly.*
Related titles: Online - full content ed.; Online - full text ed.
Indexed: C03, CBCARef, P30, P48, PQC, SCI, SCOPUS, W07.
—BLDSC (3034.520000), GNLM, IE, Infotrieve, Ingenta. **CCC.**
Published by: Pulsus Group Inc., 2902 S Sheridan Way, Oakville, ON L6J 7L6, Canada. TEL 905-829-4770, FAX 905-829-4799, pulsus@pulsus.com. Ed. Dr. Peter E Wyshynski TEL 519-746-1132. Pub. Robert B Kalina. adv.: B&W page CAD 1,530, color page CAD 2,840; trim 10.88 x 8.13. Circ: 5,200.

617 CAN ISSN 0008-428X
CODEN: CJSUAX
➤ **CANADIAN JOURNAL OF SURGERY/JOURNAL CANADIEN DE CHIRURGIE.** Short title: C J S - J C C. Text in English, French. 1957. bi-m. CAD 119 domestic to individuals; USD 119 foreign to individuals; CAD 182 domestic to institutions; USD 194 foreign to institutions; CAD 20 domestic to students & residents; CAD 40 per issue domestic; USD 40 per issue foreign (effective 2005). adv. bk.rev. bibl.; charts; illus. index. back issues avail.; reprints avail. **Document type:** *Journal, Academic/Scholarly.* **Description:** Contains original research, review articles, continuing education, news for surgeons.
Related titles: Microform ed.: (from PQC); Online - full text ed.: ISSN 1488-2310.
Indexed: A01, A02, A03, A08, A20, A22, A26, A36, ASCA, C03, C05, C06, C07, C08, C11, CA, CABA, CBCARef, CINAHL, CPerl, ChemAb, CurCont, D01, DentInd, E08, EMBASE, ExcerpMed, G08, GH, H04, H11, H12, H17, I05, ISR, IndMed, Inpharma, LT, MEDLINE, N02, N03, NRN, P19, P20, P22, P24, P30, P33, P35, P48, P54, PQC, R08, R10, R12, RA&MP, RM&VM, RRTA, Reac, S09, SCI, SCOPUS, SD, T02, T05, W07, W11.
—BLDSC (3035.800000), CIS, GNLM, IE, Infotrieve, Ingenta, INIST. **CCC.**
Published by: Canadian Medical Association/Association Medicale Canadienne, 1867 Alta Vista Dr, Ottawa, ON K1G 3Y6, Canada. TEL 613-731-8610, 888-855-2555, FAX 613-523-3282, pubs@cma.ca. Eds. Dr. Garth Warnock, Dr. James Waddell. Pub. Glenda Proctor. R&P Janis Murrey. Adv. contact Beverley Kirkpatrick. B&W page CAD 1,300, color page CAD 2,725; trim 10.88 x 8.13. Circ: 2,900.

➤ **CANADIAN OPERATING ROOM NURSING JOURNAL.** *see* MEDICAL SCIENCES—Nurses And Nursing

617 616.1 USA ISSN 1072-9798
CARDIAC SURGERY. Text in English. 1992. irreg. price varies. back issues avail. **Document type:** *Monographic series, Academic/Scholarly.* **Description:** Provides treatment information to cardiac Surgeons.
—CCC.
Published by: Springer New York LLC (Subsidiary of: Springer Science+Business Media), 233 Spring St, New York, NY 10013. TEL 212-460-1500, FAX 212-460-1575, service-ny@springer.com.

CARDIOVASCULAR MED-SURG. *see* MEDICAL SCIENCES—Cardiovascular Diseases

▼ **CARTILAGE.** *see* MEDICAL SCIENCES—Rheumatology

617 USA ISSN 2090-6900
▼ ➤ **CASE REPORTS IN SURGERY.** Text in English. 2011. **Document type:** *Journal, Academic/Scholarly.* **Description:** Publishes case reports in all areas of surgery.
Related titles: Online - full text ed.: ISSN 2090-6919. 2011. free (effective 2011).
Published by: Hindawi Publishing Corporation, 410 Park Ave, 15th Fl, PMB 287, New York, NY 10022. FAX 215-893-4392, 866-446-3294, info@hindawi.com.

617 USA ISSN 2090-6943
▼ ➤ **CASE REPORTS IN TRANSPLANTATION.** Text in English. 2011. **Document type:** *Journal, Academic/Scholarly.* **Description:** Publishes case reports in all areas of transplantation.
Related titles: Online - full text ed.: ISSN 2090-6951. 2011. free (effective 2011).
Published by: Hindawi Publishing Corporation, 410 Park Ave, 15th Fl, PMB 287, New York, NY 10022. FAX 215-893-4392, 866-446-3294, info@hindawi.com.

➤ **CATARACT AND CORNEA.** *see* MEDICAL SCIENCES—Ophthalmology And Optometry

➤ **CENTRAL EUROPEAN NEUROSURGERY.** *see* MEDICAL SCIENCES—Psychiatry And Neurology

617 TUR ISSN 1308-0709
CERRAHI SANATLAR DERGISI/JOURNAL OF SURGICAL ARTS. Text in Turkish, English. 2008. irreg. free (effective 2011). **Document type:** *Journal, Academic/Scholarly.*
Media: Online - full text.
Address: PK 113, Sakarya, 54100, Turkey. TEL 90-532-3163580. Ed. Osman Nuri Dilek.

CESKA A SLOVENSKA NEUROLOGIE A NEUROCHIRURGIE. *see* MEDICAL SCIENCES—Psychiatry And Neurology

617.554 GBR ISSN 2045-0826
CHARTER STOMA CARE. Text in English. 1999. q. free (effective 2010). adv. back issues avail. **Document type:** *Journal, Trade.*
Formerly (until 2004): Charter (1466-3708)
Related titles: Online - full text ed.: free (effective 2010).
—CCC.
Published by: Hayward Medical Communications Ltd. (Subsidiary of: Hayward Group plc), 8-10 Dryden St, Covent Garden, London, WC2E 9NA, United Kingdom. TEL 44-20-72404493, FAX 44-20-72404479, edit@hayward.co.uk, http://www.hayward.co.uk. Eds. Tina Lightfoot, Elaine Bennett. Pub. Keena McKilen.

CHEST PHYSICIAN. *see* MEDICAL SCIENCES—Respiratory Diseases

CHINA MEDICAL ABSTRACTS (SURGERY). *see* MEDICAL SCIENCES—Abstracting, Bibliographies, Statistics

617 DEU ISSN 0009-4722
➤ **DER CHIRURG**; Zeitschrift fuer alle Gebiete der operativen Medizin. Text in German. 1928. m. EUR 563, USD 623 combined subscription to institutions (print & online eds.) (effective 2012). adv. bk.rev. abstr.; bibl.; charts; illus. index. back issues avail.; reprint service avail. from PSC. **Document type:** *Journal, Academic/Scholarly.* **Description:** Covers all aspects of surgery and related fields of medicine.
Related titles: Microform ed.: (from PQC); Online - full text ed.: ISSN 1433-0385 (from IngentaConnect).
Indexed: A01, A03, A08, A22, A26, A36, ASCA, CA, CABA, ChemAb, CurCont, DBA, DokArb, E01, EMBASE, ExcerpMed, GH, H17, INI, ISR, IndMed, Inpharma, MEDLINE, N02, N03, P30, P33, P35, R08, R10, R12, RM&VM, Reac, SCI, SCOPUS, T02, T05, W07.
—BLDSC (3181.150000), GNLM, IE, Infotrieve, Ingenta, INIST. **CCC.**
Published by: (Berufsverband der Deutschen Chirurgen e.V.), Springer (Subsidiary of: Springer Science+Business Media), Tiergartenstr 17, Heidelberg, 69121, Germany. TEL 49-6221-4870, FAX 49-6221-345229. Eds. Joerg-Ruediger Siewert, Joachim Jaehne, Volker Schumpelick. Adv. contact Stephan Kroeck TEL 49-30-827875739. Circ: 6,500 (paid and controlled). **Subscr. in the Americas to:** Springer New York LLC, Journal Fulfillment, PO Box 2485, Secaucus, NJ 07096. TEL 800-777-4643, 201-348-4033, FAX 201-348-4505, journals-ny@springer.com, http://www.springer.com; **Subscr. to:** Springer Distribution Center, Kundenservice Zeitschriften, Haberstr 7, Heidelberg 69126, Germany. TEL 49-6221-3454303, FAX 49-6221-3454229, subscriptions@springer.com. **Co-sponsor:** Deutsche Gesellschaft fuer Chirurgie.

617 POL ISSN 1732-629X
CHIRURG.PL. Text in Polish. 2002. d. free. **Document type:** *Trade.*
Media: Online - full content.
Published by: Open Medical Network, ul Bronikowskiego 3/2, Warsaw, 02796, Poland. TEL 48-22-8940630, FAX 48-22-6483409, redakcja@openmedicalnetwork.com, http://www.openmedicalnetwork.com. Ed., Pub. Lukasz Bialek.

617 ROM ISSN 1221-9118
CODEN: RCOCDA
CHIRURGIA. Text in Romanian; Summaries in English, French, German, Russian. 1952. bi-m. adv. bk.rev. abstr.; charts; illus. **Document type:** *Journal, Academic/Scholarly.*
Supersedes in part (in 1990): Revista de Chirurgie, Oncologie, Radiologie, O.R.L., Oftalmologie, Stomatologie, Chirurgia (0377-5003); Formerly (until 1975): Chirurgia (0009-4730)
Related titles: Online - full text ed.: ISSN 1842-368X.
Indexed: ChemAb, EMBASE, ExcerpMed, IndMed, MEDLINE, P30, R10, Reac, SCI, SCOPUS, W07.
—GNLM, INIST.

Published by: (Societatea Romana de Chirurgie), Asociatia Medicala Romana/Romanian Medical Association, Str Ionel Perlea 10, Sector 1, Bucharest, 70754, Romania. amr@medica.ro, http://www.medica.ro. **Subscr. to:** ILEXIM, Str. 13 Decembrie 3, PO Box 136-137, Bucharest 70116, Romania.

617 ITA ISSN 0394-9508
➤ **CHIRURGIA**; a journal on surgery. Text in Italian; Summaries in English. 1988. bi-m. EUR 255 combined subscription in the European Union to institutions print & online eds.; EUR 280 combined subscription elsewhere to institutions print & online eds. (effective 2011). adv. bk.rev. bibl.; charts; illus. back issues avail. **Document type:** *Journal, Academic/Scholarly.* **Description:** Original articles on topics of a clinical, experimental, cultural or historical nature.
Related titles: Online - full text ed.: ISSN 1827-1782. 2005.
Indexed: EMBASE, ExcerpMed, R10, Reac.
—BLDSC (3181.183000), GNLM, IE, Ingenta. **CCC.**
Published by: (Societa Italiana di Chirurgia), Edizioni Minerva Medica, Corso Bramante 83-85, Turin, 10126, Italy. TEL 39-011-678282, FAX 39-011-674502, journals.dept@minervamedica.it, http://www.minervamedica.it. Ed. Giuseppe Pezzuoli. Pub. Alberto Oliaro. Circ: 5,000 (paid).

616 ITA ISSN 0392-0771
➤ **CHIRURGIA DEL PIEDE**; a journal on physiopathology and surgery of the foot. Text and summaries in English, Italian. 1977. 3/yr. EUR 240 combined subscription in the European Union to institutions print & online eds.; EUR 265 combined subscription elsewhere to institutions print & online eds. (effective 2011). adv. **Document type:** *Journal, Academic/Scholarly.* **Description:** Covers the anatomy, physiology, pathology and clinical medicine of the foot.
Formerly: Rivista di Chirurgia del Piede
Related titles: Online - full text ed.: ISSN 1827-1790. 2005.
Indexed: A22, AMED, SCOPUS.
—BLDSC (3181.360000), IE, Ingenta, INIST.
Published by: Edizioni Minerva Medica, Corso Bramante 83-85, Turin, 10126, Italy. TEL 39-011-678282, FAX 39-011-674502, journals.dept@minervamedica.it, http://www.minervamedica.it. Ed. Giacomo Pisani. Pub. Alberto Oliaro. Adv. contact F Filippo. Circ: 2,000 (paid).

617 POL ISSN 1507-5524
➤ **CHIRURGIA POLSKA.** Text in English. 1999. q. EUR 21 to individuals; EUR 30 to institutions (effective 2011). **Document type:** *Journal, Academic/Scholarly.* **Description:** Aims to establish a suitable platform for exchanging opinions and presenting recent achievements in Polish surgery.
Related titles: Online - full text ed.: ISSN 1644-3349.
Indexed: A01, A22, CA, EMBASE, ExcerpMed, R10, Reac, SCOPUS, T02.
—BLDSC (3181.415000), IE, Ingenta.
Published by: (Polsko-Niemieckie Towarzystwo Chirurgow Naczyniowych), Wydawnictwo Via Medica, ul Swietokrzyska 73, Gdansk, 80180, Poland. TEL 48-58-3209494, FAX 48-58-3209460, redakcja@viamedica.pl, http://www.viamedica.pl. Ed. Krzysztof Ziaja.

617 FRA ISSN 1297-3203
RD559 CODEN: CMAIFZ
CHIRURGIE DE LA MAIN. Text in English, French. 2000. 6/yr. EUR 332 in Europe to institutions; EUR 264.45 in France to institutions; JPY 35,900 in Japan to institutions; USD 432 elsewhere to institutions (effective 2012). **Document type:** *Journal, Academic/Scholarly.* **Description:** Aims to be the French-language platform devoted to the hand and upper limbs.
Formed by the merger of (1996-2000): Main (1262-3601); (1990-2000): Annales de Chirurgie de la Main et du Membre Superieur (1153-2424); Which was formerly (1982-1989): Annales de Chirurgie de la Main (0753-9053)
Related titles: Online - full text ed.: ISSN 1769-6666. 2001 (from IngentaConnect, ScienceDirect).
Indexed: A01, A03, A08, A22, A26, CA, EMBASE, ExcerpMed, FR, I05, IBR, IBZ, IndMed, MEDLINE, P30, R10, Reac, SCI, SCOPUS, T02, W07.
—BLDSC (3181.466000), GNLM, IE, Infotrieve, Ingenta, INIST. **CCC.**
Published by: (Societes de Chirurgie de la Main), Elsevier Masson (Subsidiary of: Elsevier Health Sciences), 62 Rue Camille Desmoulins, Issy les Moulineaux, Cedex 92442, France. TEL 33-1-71165500, FAX 33-1-71165600, infos@elsevier-masson.fr. Ed. Thierry Dubert. Circ: 4,000. **Co-sponsors:** Societe Belge de Chirurgie de la Main; Societe Francaise de Chirurgie de la Main; Groupe d'Etude de la Main.

617 FRA ISSN 1960-1719
CHIRURGIENS DE FRANCE. Text in French. 2007. q. EUR 40 to non-members (effective 2008). back issues avail. **Document type:** *Journal, Trade.*
Related titles: Online - full text ed.: free.
Published by: Union des Chirurgiens de France, 9 Rue Ernest Cresson, Paris, 75014, France. TEL 33-1-45424040, FAX 33-1-45423721, ucdf@orange.fr.

617 DEU ISSN 1615-5378
CHIRURGISCHE ALLGEMEINE. Text in German. 2000. 10/yr. EUR 96 domestic; EUR 98 foreign; EUR 10 newsstand/cover (effective 2009). adv. **Document type:** *Magazine, Trade.*
—**CCC.**
Published by: Dr. R. Kaden Verlag GmbH & Co. KG, Ringstr 19 B, Heidelberg, 69115, Germany. TEL 49-6221-1377600, FAX 49-6221-29910, kaden@kaden-verlag.de, http://www.kaden-verlag.de. adv.: B&W page EUR 2,050, color page EUR 3,295; trim 198 x 250. Circ: 7,200 (paid).

617 DEU ISSN 0009-4846
CODEN: CHPXBE
CHIRURGISCHE PRAXIS; die Zeitschrift fuer den Chirurgen. Text in German. 1957. 4/yr. EUR 175 (effective 2010). bk.rev. abstr.; charts; illus. index, cum.index every 5 yrs. **Document type:** *Journal, Academic/Scholarly.* **Description:** Articles about orthopedic, internal and plastic surgery, featuring new techniques. Includes questions and answers, detailed photographs.
Related titles: Microfilm ed.: (from PQC).
Indexed: A22, SCOPUS.
—BLDSC (3181.472000), GNLM, IE, Infotrieve. **CCC.**
Published by: Hans Marseille Verlag GmbH, Buerkleinstr 12, Munich, 80538, Germany. TEL 49-89-227988, FAX 49-89-2904643, marseille-verlag@t-online.de. Ed. Dr. A Holzgreve. Circ: 5,000.

617 616.7 CHN ISSN 1009-4237
CHUANGSHANG WAIKE ZAZHI/JOURNAL OF TRAUMATIC SURGERY. Text in Chinese. 1999. bi-m. CNY 10 newsstand/cover (effective 2006). **Document type:** *Journal, Academic/Scholarly.*
Related titles: Online - full text ed.
—BLDSC (5070.522000), IE, Ingenta.
Published by: Di-3 Junyi Daxue, Yezhan Waike Yanjiusuo/Third Military Medical University, Research Institute of Surgery, Daping Changjiangzhi Lu, Chongqing, 400042, China. TEL 86-23-68706804, FAX 86-23-68705417.

617 JPN
CHUBU GEKA GAKKAI SOKAIGO/CHUBU SURGICAL SOCIETY. PROCEEDINGS OF ANNUAL MEETING. Text in Japanese. 1965. a. **Document type:** *Proceedings, Academic/Scholarly.*
Published by: Chubu Geka Gakkai, Nagoya University, 1st Surgical Unit, 65 Tsuruma-cho, Showa-ku, Nagoya-shi, Aichi-ken 466-0065, Japan. TEL 86-52-7442219, FAX 86-52-7442230.

617 616.3 ESP ISSN 1576-2025
CIRUGEST ARCHIVOS DE CIRUGIA GENERAL Y DIGESTIVA. Text in Spanish. 1998. a. back issues avail. **Document type:** *Monographic series, Academic/Scholarly.*
Related titles: Online - full text ed.
Published by: Cirugest, Monforte de Lemos, Galicia, Spain. TEL 34-982-410902. Ed. M. Fuentes Sorrivas.

617 URY ISSN 0009-7381
CODEN: CRGUAT
CIRUGIA DEL URUGUAY. Abbreviated title: C U. Contents page in English, Spanish. 1920. bi-m. adv. abstr.; bibl.; illus. index. Supplement avail. **Document type:** *Journal, Academic/Scholarly.*
Former titles (until 1969): Revista de Cirugia del Uruguay (0797-3403); (until 1965): Sociedad de Cirugia del Uruguay. Boletines (0366-3159); (until 1942): Sociedad de Cirugia Montevideo. Boletin
Related titles: Online - full text ed.: ISSN 1688-1281. 1997.
Indexed: C01, INIS AtomInd, P30, SCOPUS.
Published by: Sociedad de Cirugia del Uruguay, Canelones 2280, Montevideo, 11200, Uruguay. TEL 598-2-4026820, FAX 598-2-4030532, scu@cirugia-uy.com, http://www.cirugia-uy.com.
Co-sponsor: Congresos Uruguayos de Cirugia.

617 ESP ISSN 0009-739X
CODEN: CRESAD
CIRUGIA ESPANOLA. Text in English, French, Spanish; Abstracts in English. 1946. m. EUR 138.21 combined subscription to individuals print & online eds.; EUR 349.88 combined subscription to institutions print & online eds. (effective 2009). bk.rev. abstr.; bibl.; illus.; charts. index. **Document type:** *Journal, Academic/Scholarly.*
Formerly (until 1969): Cirugia, Ginecologia y Urologia (0412-5878)
Related titles: Online - full text ed.: ISSN 1578-147X. 1996. EUR 115 (effective 2009) (from ScienceDirect).
Indexed: ChemAb, EMBASE, ExcerpMed, IME, MEDLINE, P30, R10, Reac, SCI, SCOPUS, W07.
—CASDDS, GNLM, INIST. **CCC.**
Published by: (Asociacion Espanola de Cirujanos), Elsevier Doyma (Subsidiary of: Elsevier Health Sciences), Traversa de Gracia 17-21, Barcelona, 08021, Spain. TEL 34-932-418800, FAX 34-932-419020, doyma@doyma.es, http://www.doyma.es. Ed. J L Balibrea Cantero. Adv. contact Juan Esteva de Sagrera. Circ: 3,850.

617 ESP ISSN 1137-0882
CIRUGIA MAYOR AMBULATORIA. Text in Spanish. 1996. q. EUR 59 domestic; USD 100 foreign (effective 2007). **Document type:** *Journal, Academic/Scholarly.*
Related titles: Online - full text ed.
Published by: (Asociacion Espanola de Cirugia Mayor Ambulatoria), Aran Ediciones, Castello 128, 1o, Madrid, 28006, Spain. TEL 34-91-7820030, FAX 34-91-5615787, edita@grupoaran.com, http://www.grupoaran.com.

617 618.92 ESP ISSN 0214-1221
CIRUGIA PEDIATRICA. Text in Multiple languages. 1988. q. free to members (effective 2009). **Document type:** *Journal, Academic/Scholarly.*
Indexed: EMBASE, ExcerpMed, IndMed, MEDLINE, P30, R10, Reac, SCOPUS.
—BLDSC (3267.605000), GNLM, IE, Infotrieve, Ingenta. **CCC.**
Published by: Ediciones Ergon S.A., C/ Arboleda 1, Majadahonda, Madrid, Madrid 28220, Spain. TEL 34-91-6362930, FAX 34-91-6362931, ergon@ergon.es, http://www.ergon.es. Ed. J Bregante Ucedo. Circ: 1,000.

617.952 MEX ISSN 1405-0625
CIRUGIA PLASTICA. Text in Spanish. 1991. 3/yr. MXN 350 domestic; USD 75 in Latin America; USD 85 in US & Canada; USD 95 elsewhere (effective 2007).
Related titles: Online - full text ed.
Published by: Asociacion Mexicana de Cirugia Plastica, Estetica y Reconstructiva, A.C., Flamencos No 74, Col San Jose Insurgentes, Mexico, D.F., 03900, Mexico. TEL 52-55-56154910, FAX 52-55-56154911, amcper@cirugiaplastica.org.mx, http://www.cirugiaplastica.org.mx/. Ed. Jose Luis Romero Zarate.

617.95 ESP ISSN 0376-7892
RD118.A1
CIRUGIA PLASTICA IBERO LATINOAMERICANA. Text in Spanish, English, Portuguese. 1975. q. adv. bk.rev. charts; illus. cum.index: 1968-1998. reprints avail. **Document type:** *Journal, Academic/Scholarly.*
Formed by the merger of (1953-1975): Revista Latinoamericana de Cirugia Plastica (0034-9755); (1968-1975): Revista Espanola de Cirugia Plastica (0034-9364)
Related titles: Diskette ed.; Microform ed.: (from PQC); Online - full text ed.: free (effective 2011).
Indexed: A22, CA, IME, P30, SCOPUS, T02.
—GNLM, IE, Ingenta. **CCC.**
Published by: Sociedad Espanola de Cirugia Plastica Reparadora y Estetica, Calle Villanueva 11, 3a Planta, Madrid, 28001, Spain. TEL 34-91-5765995, FAX 34-91-4315153, info@secpre.org, http://www.secpre.com. Circ: 1,000. **Co-sponsor:** Federacion Ibero Latinoamericana de Cirugia Plastica.

617.95 URY ISSN 0797-4884
CIRUGIA PLASTICA URUGUAYA. Text in Spanish; Summaries in English, Spanish. 1959. q. **Document type:** *Journal, Academic/Scholarly.*
Former titles (until 1966): Revista de Cirugia Plastica del Uruguay (0797-4124); (until 19621): Cirugia Plastica Uruguaya (0009-7403)
Published by: (Sociedad de Cirugia Plastica del Uruguay), Universidad de la Republica, Hospital de Clinicas "Dr. Manuel Quintela", Universidad de la Republica, Avda. Italia s-n, Montevideo, Uruguay.

617 MEX ISSN 0009-7411
RD1
CIRUGIA Y CIRUJANOS. Text in Spanish. 1933. bi-m. MXN 450 domestic; USD 85 in Latin America; USD 95 in US & Canada; USD 105 elsewhere (effective 2007). adv. bk.rev. abstr.; bibl.; illus. back issues avail. **Document type:** *Journal, Academic/Scholarly.* **Description:** Publishes surgical and medical articles.
Related titles: Online - full text ed.: free (effective 2011).
Indexed: C01, CA, ChemAb, EMBASE, ExcerpMed, IndMed, MEDLINE, P30, R10, Reac, SCI, SCOPUS, T02, W07.
—GNLM.
Published by: Academia Mexicana de Cirugia/Mexican Academy of Surgery, Ave. Cuauhtemoc No 330, Col. Doctores, Mexico, D.F., 06725, Mexico. TEL 52-55-55880458, FAX 52-55-57610574, acameci@servimed.com.mx, http://www.amc.org.mx/. Ed. Alejandro Reyes Fuentes. Adv. contact Francisco Tenorio Gonzalez. Circ: 3,000.

617.522 USA ISSN 1055-6656
RD525 CODEN: CPJOEG
➤ **CLEFT PALATE - CRANIOFACIAL JOURNAL.** Abbreviated title: C P C J. Text in English. 1964. bi-m. USD 335 combined subscription domestic to institutions (print & online eds.); USD 383 combined subscription foreign to institutions (print & online eds.) (effective 2010). bk.rev. abstr.; charts; illus.; stat. cum.index: 1964-1988. back issues avail. **Document type:** *Journal, Academic/Scholarly.* **Description:** Covers all clinical and research activities in cleft palate and other craniofacial anomalies.
Formerly (until 1999): Cleft Palate Journal (0009-8701); Which incorporated (1968-1984): Cranio - Facial, Cleft Palate Bibliography (0090-1431); Cleft Palate Journal superseded (in 1964): Cleft Palate Bulletin (0578-4840); Which was formerly (1951-1954): Cleft Palate Newsletter
Related titles: Microform ed.: (from MIM); Online - full text ed.: ISSN 1545-1569. USD 327 to institutions (effective 2010).
Indexed: A20, A22, ASCA, C03, C06, C07, C08, CA, CBCARef, CDA, CINAHL, ChPerl, CurCont, D02, DentInd, E01, EMBASE, ExcerpMed, FR, ISR, IndMed, Inpharma, L&LBA, MEDLINE, P03, P20, P22, P24, P25, P30, P48, P54, PQC, PsycholAb, R10, Reac, RehabLit, S21, SCI, SCOPUS, SOPODA, T02.
—BLDSC (3278.559800), GNLM, IE, Infotrieve, Ingenta, INIST. **CCC.**
Published by: (American Cleft Palate - Craniofacial Association), Allen Press Inc., PO Box 7075, Lawrence, KS 66044. TEL 785-843-1235, FAX 785-843-1274, info@allenpress.com, http://www.allenpress.com/. Ed. Arshad R Muzaffar TEL 573-882-2275. Adv. contact Onkar S Sandal TEL 785-843-1234 ext 218. Circ: 3,100.

➤ **CLINICAL NEUROLOGY AND NEUROSURGERY.** *see* MEDICAL SCIENCES—Psychiatry And Neurology

➤ **CLINICAL NEUROSURGERY.** *see* MEDICAL SCIENCES—Psychiatry And Neurology

617 USA ISSN 0902-0063
CODEN: CLTRED
➤ **CLINICAL TRANSPLANTATION.** Text in English. 1987. bi-m. GBP 869 in United Kingdom to institutions; EUR 1,103 in Europe to institutions; USD 1,455 in the Americas to institutions; USD 1,701 elsewhere to institutions; GBP 999 combined subscription in United Kingdom to institutions (print & online eds.); EUR 1,268 combined subscription in Europe to institutions (print & online eds.); USD 1,673 combined subscription in the Americas to institutions (print & online eds.); USD 1,956 combined subscription elsewhere to institutions (print & online eds.) (effective 2012). adv. bk.rev. back issues avail.; reprint service avail. from PSC. **Document type:** *Journal, Academic/Scholarly.* **Description:** For surgeons of all major and subspecialities; clinical immunologists; cryobiologists; hematologists; gastroenterologists; pulmonologists; nephrologists; cardiologists; and endocrinologists, and sociologists, psychologists and research workers.
Related titles: Online - full text ed.: ISSN 1399-0012. 1999. GBP 869 in United Kingdom to institutions; EUR 1,103 in Europe to institutions; USD 1,455 in the Americas to institutions; USD 1,701 elsewhere to institutions (effective 2012) (from IngentaConnect); Supplement(s): Clinical Transplantation. Supplement. ISSN 1399-6738. 1999.
Indexed: A01, A03, A08, A22, A26, A36, A37, ASCA, B21, BIOBASE, CA, CABA, CurCont, E01, E12, EMBASE, ExcerpMed, FR, GH, H12, H17, IABS, IDIS, ISR, ImmunAb, IndMed, Inpharma, LT, MEDLINE, N02, N03, OR, P30, P33, P35, P39, R08, R10, R12, RA&MP, RM&VM, RRTA, Reac, SCI, SCOPUS, T02, T05, W07.
—BLDSC (3286.399780), GNLM, IE, Infotrieve, Ingenta, INIST. **CCC.**
Published by: Wiley-Blackwell Publishing, Inc. (Subsidiary of: Wiley-Blackwell Publishing Ltd.), Commerce Pl, 350 Main St, Malden, MA 02148. TEL 781-388-8200, FAX 781-388-8210, info@wiley.com, http://www.wiley.com/WileyCDA/. Ed. David E R Sutherland.

617 USA ISSN 0890-9016
RD120.7
CLINICAL TRANSPLANTS. Text in English. 1985. a., latest vol.45, 2005. **Document type:** *Journal, Academic/Scholarly.*
Formerly (until 1986): Clinical Kidney Transplants (0883-914X)
Indexed: A22, EMBASE, ExcerpMed, MEDLINE, P30, R10, Reac, SCOPUS.
—BLDSC (3286.399790), IE, Infotrieve, Ingenta. **CCC.**
Published by: University of California, Los Angeles, Department of Pathology & Laboratory Medicine. Immunogenetics Center, 1000 Veterans Ave, Los Angeles, CA 90095. TEL 310-825-7651, FAX 310-206-3216, http://www.pathology.ucla.edu/.

CLINICAL UPDATE. *see* MEDICAL SCIENCES—Oncology

617 USA ISSN 1531-0043
CODEN: CCRSC9
➤ **CLINICS IN COLON & RECTAL SURGERY.** Text in English. 1988. q. USD 524 domestic to institutions; USD 536 foreign to institutions; USD 663 combined subscription domestic to institutions (print & online eds.); USD 639 combined subscription foreign to institutions (print & online eds.) (effective 2011). adv. index. reprints avail. **Document type:** *Journal, Academic/Scholarly.* **Description:** Publishes topic-specific issues on diseases of the small bowel, colon, rectum, and anus.

Formerly (until 2001): Perspectives in Colon & Rectal Surgery (0894-8054)
Related titles: Online - full text ed.: ISSN 1530-9681. USD 617 domestic to institutions; USD 631 foreign to institutions (effective 2011).
Indexed: P30, SCOPUS, T02.
—BLDSC (3286.545200), GNLM, IE, Infotrieve. **CCC.**
Published by: Thieme Medical Publishers (Subsidiary of: Georg Thieme Verlag), 333 Seventh Ave, New York, NY 10001. TEL 212-760-0888, 800-782-3488, FAX 212-947-1112, info@thieme.com. Ed. Dr. David E. Beck TEL 504-842-4060. Adv. contact James C Cunningham TEL 201-767-4170. Circ: 695.

617 USA ISSN 0094-1298
➤ **CLINICS IN PLASTIC SURGERY.** Text in English. 1974. q. USD 617 in United States to institutions; USD 721 elsewhere to institutions (effective 2012). adv. back issues avail.; reprints avail. **Document type:** *Journal, Academic/Scholarly.* **Description:** Provides updates on the latest trends in patient management; keeps up to date on the newest advances; and provides a sound basis for choosing treatment options.
Related titles: Microform ed.; Online - full text ed.: ISSN 1558-0504 (from ScienceDirect); Translation: Clinicas de Cirugia Plastica. ISSN 0328-2961.
Indexed: A20, A22, ASCA, CurCont, DentInd, EMBASE, ExcerpMed, FR, INI, ISR, IndMed, Inpharma, MEDLINE, MS&D, P30, R10, Reac, SCI, SCOPUS, W07.
—BLDSC (3286.590000), GNLM, IE, Infotrieve, Ingenta, INIST. **CCC.**
Published by: W.B. Saunders Co. (Subsidiary of: Elsevier Health Sciences), Elsevier, Health Sciences Division, Order Fulfillment, 3251 Riverport Ln, Maryland Heights, MO 63043. TEL 314-872-8370, 800-325-4177, FAX 314-432-1380, JournalCustomerService-usa@elsevier.com, http://www.us.elsevierhealth.com. Adv. contact John Marmero TEL 212-633-3657.

617 GBR ISSN 1467-0100
RF305 CODEN: CIIOAQ
➤ **COCHLEAR IMPLANTS INTERNATIONAL.** Text in English. 2000. q. GBP 336 combined subscription to institutions (print & online eds.); USD 657 combined subscription in United States to institutions (print & online eds.) (effective 2012). adv. bk.rev. back issues avail.; reprint service avail. from PSC. **Document type:** *Journal, Academic/Scholarly.* **Description:** Aimed at all those involved with cochlear implants: surgery, pre- and post-operative care, research or manufacture of the implants themselves.
Related titles: Online - full text ed.: ISSN 1556-9152. GBP 305 to institutions; USD 596 in United States to institutions (effective 2012) (from IngentaConnect).
Indexed: A01, C06, C07, CA, EMBASE, ExcerpMed, L&LBA, MEDLINE, P03, P30, PsycInfo, R10, Reac, SCOPUS, T02.
—BLDSC (3292.724200), IE, Ingenta. **CCC.**
Published by: (British Cochlear Implant Group), Maney Publishing, Ste 1C, Joseph's Well, Hanover Walk, Leeds, W Yorks LS3 1AB, United Kingdom. TEL 44-113-2432800, FAX 44-113-3868178, maney@maney.co.uk. Ed. John Graham. **Dist. by:** Turpin Distribution Services Ltd., Pegasus Dr, Stratton Business Park, Biggleswade, Bedfordshire SG18 8QB, United Kingdom. TEL 44-1767-604800, FAX 44-1767-601640, custserv@turpin-distribution.com, http://www.turpin-distribution.com/.

➤ **COCUK CERRAHISI DERGISI/PEDIATRIC SURGERY.** *see* MEDICAL SCIENCES—Pediatrics

617 ARG ISSN 1667-9121
COLECCION TRABAJOS DISTINGUIDOS. SERIE CIRUGIA. Text in Spanish. 2002. 6/yr. back issues avail. **Document type:** *Journal, Academic/Scholarly.*
Media: Online - full text.
Published by: Sociedad Iberoamericana de Informacion Cientifica (S I I C), Ave Belgrano 430, Buenos Aires, C1092AAR, Argentina. TEL 54-11-43424901, FAX 54-11-43313305, atencionallector@siicsalud.com, http://www.siicsalud.com. Ed. Rafael Bernal Castro.

617 BRA ISSN 0100-6991
RD1 CODEN: RCBCFF
➤ **COLEGIO BRASILEIRO DE CIRURGIOES. REVISTA.** Text in Portuguese; Abstracts in English. 1944. bi-m. BRL 180 domestic; USD 180 foreign (effective 2006). adv. bk.rev. back issues avail. **Document type:** *Journal, Academic/Scholarly.* **Description:** Aims at divulging scientific works in the field of surgery.
Related titles: Online - full text ed.: ISSN 1809-4546. 2005. free (effective 2011).
Indexed: C01, EMBASE, MEDLINE, P30, SCOPUS.
Published by: Colegio Brasileiro de Cirurgioes, Rua Visconde de Silva, 52 Andar 3, Rio De Janeiro, RJ 22271-090, Brazil. TEL 55-21-25379164, FAX 55-21-22862595, publicacao@cbc.org.br. Ed. Guilherme Pinto Bravo Neto. Circ: 7,000.

617 BRA ISSN 1808-1851
COLUNA/COLUMNA. Text in Multiple languages. 2004. q. **Document type:** *Journal, Academic/Scholarly.* **Description:** Aims to contribute to the improvement and development of the practice, research and teaching of the themes related to the spinal column in Brazil and in Latin America.
Related titles: Online - full text ed.: ISSN 2177-014X. free (effective 2011).
Indexed: SCOPUS.
Published by: Sociedade Brasileira de Coluna, Al Lorena 1304, Cj 1406-1407, Sao Paulo, SP 01424-001, Brazil. TEL 55-11-30886616.

617.02854 GBR ISSN 1092-9088
CODEN: CAISFL
➤ **COMPUTER AIDED SURGERY.** Text in English. 1995. bi-m. GBP 400, EUR 440, USD 640 combined subscription to institutions (print & online eds.); GBP 800, EUR 880, USD 1,280 combined subscription to corporations (print & online eds.) (effective 2010). adv. back issues avail.; reprint service avail. from PSC. **Document type:** *Journal, Academic/Scholarly.* **Description:** Covers all aspects of surgery performed in conjunction with imaging, and includes the latest applications in neurosurgery, orthopedics, and other surgical subspecialties.
Formerly (until 1997): Journal of Image Guided Surgery (1078-7844)
Related titles: Online - full text ed.: ISSN 1097-0150.
Indexed: A22, B&BAb, B19, B21, BioEngAb, CA, CurCont, E01, EMBASE, ErgAb, ExcerpMed, INI, IndMed, MEDLINE, P30, SCI, SCOPUS, T02, TM, W07.
—GNLM, IE, Infotrieve, Ingenta. **CCC.**

Published by: Informa Healthcare (Subsidiary of: T & F Informa plc), Telephone House, 69-77 Paul St, London, EC2A 4LQ, United Kingdom. TEL 44-20-70175000, FAX 44-20-70176792, healthcare.enquiries@informa.com. Ed. Dr. Richard D Bucholz. Adv. contact Per Sonnerfeldt. **Subscr. in N. America to:** Taylor & Francis Inc., Customer Services Dept, 325 Chestnut St, 8th Fl, Philadelphia, PA 19106. TEL 215-625-8900, 800-354-1420, FAX 215-625-8914, customerservice@taylorandfrancis.com; **Subscr. outside N. America to:** Taylor & Francis Ltd., Journals Customer Service, Sheepen Pl, Colchester, Essex CO3 3LP, United Kingdom. TEL 44-20-70175544, FAX 44-20-70175198, tf.enquiries@tfinforma.com.

617 USA ISSN 1935-1526
CONGRESS QUARTERLY. Text in English. 2000 (Winter). q. USD 195 domestic to institutions; USD 261 foreign to institutions (effective 2011). adv. back issues avail. **Document type:** *Magazine, Academic/Scholarly.* **Description:** Covers malpractice and liability crisis issues, government regulations and reimbursement, practice management topics and other issues that are reshaping neurosurgery.
Formerly (until 2006): Neurosurgery News (1525-819X)
Related titles: Online - full text ed.: free (effective 2010).
—**CCC.**
Published by: (Congress of Neurological Surgeons), Lippincott Williams & Wilkins (Subsidiary of: Wolters Kluwer N.V.), 530 Walnut St, Philadelphia, PA 19106. TEL 215-521-8300, FAX 215-521-8902, customerservice@lww.com. Eds. James S Harrop, Jamie S Ullman. Pub. Carole Pippin. Circ: 6,478.

617 616.8 USA ISSN 0163-2108
CODEN: CNEUET
CONTEMPORARY NEUROSURGERY. Text in English. 1979. bi-w. USD 703 domestic to institutions; USD 698 foreign to institutions (effective 2011). back issues avail. **Document type:** *Newsletter, Academic/Scholarly.* **Description:** Features articles on current topics in neurosurgery with optional category or C.M.E. credits.
Related titles: Online - full text ed.: USD 448.50 domestic for academic site license; USD 448.50 foreign for academic site license; USD 500.25 foreign for corporate site license (effective 2002).
Indexed: E-psyche.
—BLDSC (3425.195300), IE, Ingenta. **CCC.**
Published by: Lippincott Williams & Wilkins (Subsidiary of: Wolters Kluwer N.V.), 530 Walnut St, Philadelphia, PA 19106. TEL 215-521-8300, FAX 215-521-8902, customerservice@lww.com, http://www.lwwnewsletters.com. Ed. Dr. Ali Krisht.

617.95 USA ISSN 1527-4268
CONTEMPORARY SPINE SURGERY. Abbreviated title: C S S. Text in English. 2000. m. USD 520.98 domestic to institutions; USD 675.58 foreign to institutions (effective 2011). back issues avail. **Document type:** *Newsletter, Trade.* **Description:** Provides information on a single topic of importance in spine surgery.
Related titles: Online - full text ed.: ISSN 2161-1181.
—IE. **CCC.**
Published by: Lippincott Williams & Wilkins (Subsidiary of: Wolters Kluwer N.V.), 530 Walnut St, Philadelphia, PA 19106. TEL 215-521-8300, FAX 215-521-8902, customerservice@lww.com. Ed. Dr. Gunnar B Andersson.

617 USA ISSN 0045-8341
RD1 CODEN: CSGYA
➤ **CONTEMPORARY SURGERY.** Text in English. 1972. m. adv. bk.rev. bibl.; charts; illus. index. 60 p./no.; back issues avail.; reprints avail. **Document type:** *Journal, Academic/Scholarly.* **Description:** Contains clinical information which covers the developments and techniques in surgery.
Related titles: Microform ed.: (from PQC); Online - full text ed.
Indexed: A22, A26, H11, I05, P20, P30, P48, P54, PQC.
—GNLM, Ingenta. **CCC.**
Published by: Dowden Health Media, Inc (Subsidiary of: Lebhar-Friedman, Inc.), 110 Summit Ave, Montvale, NJ 07645. TEL 201-740-6100, FAX 201-391-2778, customerservice@dowdenhealth.com, http://www.dowdenhealth.com. Ed. Dr. K Craig Kent. Pub. Aviva Belsky TEL 201-740-6141. Adv. contact Maria Walsh TEL 201-740-6190.

617 GBR
▼ ➤ **CORE SURGERY JOURNAL.** Text in English. 2010. bi-m. USD 319 to institutions; USD 519 combined subscription to institutions (print & online eds.) (effective 2011). back issues avail. **Document type:** *Journal, Academic/Scholarly.* **Description:** Delivers practical and informative articles on topics in each of the surgical specialties in order to maximise learning and understanding. Contains articles which highlight non-clinical aspects of a surgical career with material to ensure progression as a surgical trainee.
Related titles: Online - full text ed.: ISSN 2046-0198. GBP 419 to institutions (effective 2011).
Published by: 123Doc Education, 72 Harley St, London, W1G 7HG, United Kingdom. TEL 44-20-72534363, FAX 44-20-76081387, sales@123library.org, http://www.123doc.com/. Ed. D P Forward.

330 646.72 USA ISSN 1932-7692
RD119
COSMETIC SURGERY PRODUCTS. Text in English. 2004. irreg. USD 4,600 per issue (print or online ed.) (effective 2008). **Document type:** *Report, Trade.* **Description:** Analyzes the US cosmetic surgery product industry, presents historical demand data for the years 1997, 2002 and 2007, and forecasts for 2012 and 2017 by procedure, product and raw material.
Related titles: Online - full text ed.
Published by: The Freedonia Group, Inc., 767 Beta Dr, Cleveland, OH 44143. TEL 440-684-9600, 800-927-5900, FAX 440-646-0484, info@freedoniagroup.com.

617.95 USA ISSN 1094-6810
COSMETIC SURGERY TIMES; a magazine for the innovative cosmetic surgery practice. Text in English. 1997. 10/yr. USD 95 domestic; USD 140 in Canada & Mexico; USD 185 elsewhere; USD 17 newsstand/cover domestic; USD 20 newsstand/cover in Canada & Mexico; USD 26 newsstand/cover elsewhere (effective 2011). adv. tr.lit. back issues avail.; reprints avail. **Document type:** *Magazine, Trade.* **Description:** Covers cosmetic surgery, research, and meetings for dermatology surgeons, plastic surgeons, facial plastic surgeons, oculoplastic surgeons, and oromaxillofacial surgeons.
Related titles: Online - full text ed.: ISSN 1559-8993.
Indexed: A26, B01, B06, B07, B09, E08, G08, H01, H11, H12, I05, M01, M02, P20, P48, P54, PQC, S09, T02.
—**CCC.**

Published by: Advanstar Communications, Inc., 6200 Canoga Ave, 2nd Fl, Woodland Hills, CA 91367. TEL 818-593-5000, FAX 818-593-5020, info@advanstar.com, http://www.advanstar.com. Ed. Amyl Stankiewicz.

617 FRA ISSN 1628-8319
LE COURRIER DE LA TRANSPLANTATION. Text in French. 2001. q. EUR 75 in Europe to individuals; EUR 75 DOM-TOM to individuals; EUR 75 in Africa to individuals; EUR 87 elsewhere to individuals; EUR 96 in Europe to institutions; EUR 96 DOM-TOM to institutions; EUR 96 in Africa to institutions; EUR 108 elsewhere to institutions (effective 2009). back issues avail. **Document type:** *Journal, Academic/Scholarly.*
—INIST.
Published by: Edimark S.A.S., 2 Rue Sainte-Marie, Courbevoie, Cedex 92418, France. TEL 33-1-46676300, FAX 33-1-46676310, contact@edimark.fr.

617 USA ISSN 1943-3875
➤ **CRANIAL MAXILLOFACIAL TRAUMA & RECONSTRUCTION.** Text in English. 2008. q. USD 437 domestic to institutions; USD 449 foreign to institutions; USD 534 combined subscription domestic to institutions (print & online eds.); USD 560 combined subscription foreign to institutions (print & online eds.) (effective 2011). adv. reprints avail. **Document type:** *Journal, Academic/Scholarly.* **Description:** Publishes primary and review articles covering all aspects of surgery of the head, face and jaw.
Related titles: Online - full text ed.: ISSN 1943-3883. 2008. USD 514 domestic to institutions; USD 528 foreign to institutions (effective 2011).
—IE. **CCC.**
Published by: (A O Foundation CHE), Thieme Medical Publishers (Subsidiary of: Georg Thieme Verlag), 333 Seventh Ave, New York, NY 10001. TEL 212-760-0888, 800-782-3488, FAX 212-947-1112, info@thieme.com. Ed. Paul N Manson TEL 410-955-9470. Adv. contact Sergio Cardoso. Circ: 2,400.

617 ESP ISSN 1134-7872
CUADERNOS DE ARTROSCOPIA. Text in Spanish. 1993. s-a. back issues avail. **Document type:** *Journal, Academic/Scholarly.*
Indexed: SCOPUS.
Published by: Asociacion Espanola de Artroscopia, C Fernandez de la Hoz, 61 Entro 1, Madrid, 28003, Spain. TEL 34-91-5360814, FAX 34-91-5360607, aea@aeartroscopia.com, http://www.servitel.es/aeartroscopia. Ed. A. Perez-Caballer.

617 CHL ISSN 0716-7040
CUADERNOS DE CIRUGIA. Text in Spanish. 1987. a. back issues avail. **Document type:** *Monographic series, Academic/Scholarly.*
Related titles: Online - full text ed.
Published by: Universidad Austral de Chile, Instituto de Cirugia, Campus Isla Teja, Casilla 567, Valdivia, Chile. cirugia@uach.cl, http://mingaonline.uach.cl/scielo/. Ed. Carlos Carcamo Ibaceta.

617 USA ISSN 2151-6030
CURRENT DIAGNOSIS & TREATMENT, SURGERY. Text in English. 1980. irreg., latest 2009, 13th ed. 1426 p./no.; **Document type:** *Monographic series, Academic/Scholarly.*
Formerly (until 2010): Current Surgical Diagnosis & Treatment (0894-2277)
Related titles: CD-ROM ed.: USD 74.95 per issue (effective 2010); Online - full text ed.: ISSN 2151-6049.
Published by: McGraw-Hill Education (Subsidiary of: McGraw-Hill Companies, Inc.), 148 Princeton-Hightstown Rd, Hightstown, NJ 08520. TEL 609-426-5793, FAX 609-426-7917, customer.service@mcgraw-hill.com, http://www.mheducation.com/.

617 USA ISSN 1553-8370
CURRENT ESSENTIALS OF SURGERY. Text in English. 2005. irreg. USD 39.95 per issue (effective 2008).
Published by: McGraw-Hill Companies, Inc., 2 Penn Plz, New York, NY 10121. TEL 212-512-2000, FAX 212-904-4209, customer.service@mcgraw-hill.com, http://www.mcgraw-hill.com.

CURRENT OPINION IN OTOLARYNGOLOGY & HEAD AND NECK SURGERY. *see* MEDICAL SCIENCES—Otorhinolaryngology

617 USA ISSN 0011-3840
RD1 CODEN: CPSUA
➤ **CURRENT PROBLEMS IN SURGERY.** Abbreviated title: C P S. Text in English. 1964. m. USD 369 in United States to institutions; USD 429 elsewhere to institutions (effective 2012). adv. charts; illus. cum.index. back issues avail.; reprints avail. **Document type:** *Journal, Academic/Scholarly.* **Description:** Provides current fully referenced information to practicing surgeons.
Related titles: Microfilm ed.: (from PQC); Online - full text ed.: ISSN 1535-6337 (from ScienceDirect).
Indexed: A22, A26, AIM, ASCA, CurCont, DentInd, EMBASE, ExcerpMed, I05, ISR, IndMed, Inpharma, MEDLINE, P30, R10, Reac, SCI, SCOPUS, T02, W07.
—BLDSC (3501.450000), GNLM, IE, Infotrieve, Ingenta, INIST. **CCC.**
Published by: Mosby, Inc. (Subsidiary of: Elsevier Health Sciences), 1600 John F. Kennedy Blvd, Ste 1800, Philadelphia, PA 19103. TEL 215-239-3900, 800-523-1649, FAX 215-239-3990, elspcs@elsevier.com, http://www.us.elsevierhealth.com. Ed. Stanley W Ashley. Adv. contact Kevin Edmonds TEL 215-239-3804.

617 USA ISSN 2153-5396
▼ **CURRENT PROCEDURES: SURGERY.** Variant title: Lange Current Procedures: Surgery. Text in English. 2010 (Jun.). triennial. USD 99 per issue (effective 2010). **Document type:** *Academic/Scholarly.* **Description:** Guide for the most up-to-date standards and procedures for surgery.
Published by: McGraw-Hill Companies, Inc., 2 Penn Plz, New York, NY 10121. TEL 212-512-2000, FAX 212-904-4209, customer.service@mcgraw-hill.com, http://www.mcgraw-hill.com.

617 USA ISSN 0835-3689
RD1
CURRENT SURGICAL THERAPY. Text in English. 1985. irreg., latest 2007, 9th ed. price varies. **Document type:** *Monographic series, Academic/Scholarly.* **Description:** Contains advice on the selection and implementation of the latest treatments for surgical disease.
Related titles: Online - full text ed.
—**CCC.**
Published by: Mosby, Inc. (Subsidiary of: Elsevier Health Sciences), 1600 John F. Kennedy Blvd, Ste 1800, Philadelphia, PA 19103. TEL 215-239-3900, 800-523-1649, FAX 215-239-3990, elspcs@elsevier.com, http://www.us.elsevierhealth.com.

M

CURRENT TECHNIQUES IN ARTHROSCOPY. *see* MEDICAL SCIENCES—Orthopedics And Traumatology

CURRENT TECHNIQUES IN NEUROSURGERY. *see* MEDICAL SCIENCES—Psychiatry And Neurology

617 USA ISSN 1540-7004
CURRENT TECHNIQUES IN SURGICAL PROFILES. Text in English. 2002. q.
Published by: Lawrence DellaCorte Publications, 101 E. 52nd St., 28th Fl., New York, NY 10022. TEL 212-751-2806.

DACHANG-GANGMENBING WAIKE ZAZHI/JOURNAL OF COLOPROCTOLOGICAL SURGERY. *see* MEDICAL SCIENCES

617 TUR ISSN 1301-1839
DAMAR CERRAHI DERGISI/TURKISH JOURNAL OF VASCULAR SURGERY. Text in Turkish; Summaries in English, Turkish. 1992. 3/yr. membership. adv. back issues avail. **Document type:** *Journal, Academic/Scholarly.* **Description:** Covers vascular surgery, diseases and treatment.
Related titles: Online - full text ed.: free (effective 2009).
Published by: Ulusal Vaskuler Cerrahi Dernegi/National Association of Vascular Surgery, Golgeli Sokak 27/13 GOP, Ankara, Turkey. TEL 90-312-4474399, FAX 90-312-4367264, uvcd@uvcd.org.tr, info@turkiyeklinikleri.com. Ed. Dr. Ufuk Demirkilic. Circ: 500.

617 ITA ISSN 1594-3984
DAY SURGERY. Text in Italian, English. 1998. q. EUR 78 in Europe to institutions; EUR 88 elsewhere to institutions (effective 2008). **Document type:** *Journal, Academic/Scholarly.* **Description:** Official publication of Societa Italiana di Chirurgia Ambulatoriale e Day Surgery, it aims at providing the latest information to surgeons, anesthesiologists and all those involved in the operation of Day Surgery centers.
Formerly (until 2001): Giornale Italiano di Medicina Congressuale (1127-0802)
Published by: (Societa Italiana di Chirurgia Ambulatoriale e Day Surgery), Mattioli 1885 SpA, Via Coduro 1, Fidenza, PR 43036, Italy. TEL 39-0524-84547, FAX 39-0524-84751, http://www.mattioli1885.com. Ed. Luciano Corbellini. Circ: 5,000.

DENTOMAXILLOFACIAL RADIOLOGY. *see* MEDICAL SCIENCES—Radiology And Nuclear Medicine

DENTOMAXILLOFACIAL RADIOLOGY. SUPPLEMENT. *see* MEDICAL SCIENCES—Radiology And Nuclear Medicine

617 USA ISSN 1076-0512
CODEN: DESUFE
➤ **DERMATOLOGIC SURGERY.** Text in English. 1975. m. GBP 465 combined subscription in United Kingdom to institutions (print & online eds.); EUR 573 combined subscription in Europe to institutions (print & online eds.); USD 814 combined subscription in the Americas to institutions (print & online eds.); USD 887 combined subscription elsewhere to institutions (print & online eds.) (effective 2012). adv. bk.rev. Index. back issues avail.; reprint service avail. from PSC. **Document type:** *Journal, Academic/Scholarly.* **Description:** Publishes information on new research, methods and instruments used in performing all types of cutaneous surgery.
Former titles (until 1995): Journal of Dermatologic Surgery and Oncology (0148-0812); (until 1977): Journal of Dermatologic Surgery (0097-9716)
Related titles: Microform ed.: (from PQC); Online - full text ed.: ISSN 1524-4725. GBP 394 in United Kingdom to institutions; EUR 500 in Europe to institutions; USD 708 in the Americas to institutions; USD 772 elsewhere to institutions (effective 2012) (from IngentaConnect).
Indexed: A01, A03, A08, A20, A22, A26, ASCA, BIOBASE, C33, CA, CurCont, DentInd, E01, EMBASE, ExcerpMed, FR, H12, IABS, ISR, IndMed, Inpharma, JW-D, MEDLINE, MS&D, P30, P35, R10, Reac, SCI, SCOPUS, T02, W07.
—BLDSC (3555.140000), GNLM, IE, Infotrieve, Ingenta, INIST. **CCC.**
Published by: (American Society of Dermatologic Surgery), Wiley-Blackwell Publishing, Inc. (Subsidiary of: Wiley-Blackwell Publishing Ltd.), 111 River St, Hoboken, NJ 07030. TEL 201-748-6000, FAX 201-748-6088, info@wiley.com. Ed. William P Coleman. Adv. contact Karl Franz TEL 781-388-8470. **Co-sponsors:** American College of Mohs Micrographic Surgery and Cutaneous Oncology; International Society for Dermatologic Surgery; International Society of Cosmetic; International Society of Hair Restoration Surgery; North American Society of Phlebology.

617 RUS ISSN 1560-9510
DETSKAYA KHIRURGIYA. Text in Russian; Summaries in English. 1997. bi-m. USD 144 foreign (effective 2005). adv. Website rev.; bk.rev. abstr.; bibl.; illus. back issues avail. **Document type:** *Journal, Academic/Scholarly.* **Description:** Provides experimental and clinical data for pediatric surgical treatment, anesthesiology. Also examines management.
Related titles: Fax ed.
Indexed: RefZh.
—BLDSC (0053.130800).
Published by: Izdatel'stvo Meditsina/Meditsina Publishers, ul B Pirogovskaya, d 2, str 5, Moscow, 119435, Russian Federation. TEL 7-095-2483324, meditsina@mtu-net.ru, http://www.medlit.ru. Ed. Yurii F Isakov. Pub. A M Stochik. R&P Yu Isakov. Adv. contact O A Fadeeva TEL 7-095-923-51-40. Circ: 500. **Dist. by:** M K - Periodica, ul Gilyarovskogo 39, Moscow 129110, Russian Federation. TEL 7-095-2845008, FAX 7-095-2813798, info@periodicals.ru, http://www.mkniga.ru.

617 DEU ISSN 0942-2854
DEUTSCHE GESELLSCHAFT FUER CHIRURGIE. KONGRESS. Text in German. 1872. a. **Document type:** *Monographic series, Academic/Scholarly.*
Formerly (until 1990): Deutsche Gesellschaft fuer Chirurgie. Verhandlungen (0173-0541)
Indexed: P30, SCOPUS.
—**CCC.**
Published by: Deutsche Gesellschaft fuer Chirurgie, Luisenstr 58-59, Berlin, 10117, Germany. TEL 49-30-28876290, FAX 49-30-28876299, DGChirurgie@t-online.de, http://www.dgch.de.

617 DEU ISSN 0723-709X
DEUTSCHE GESELLSCHAFT FUER CHIRURGIE. MITTEILUNGEN. Text in German. 1972. 4/yr. EUR 96 to institutions; EUR 28 newsstand/cover (effective 2011). adv. **Document type:** *Journal, Academic/Scholarly.*
Published by: (Deutsche Gesellschaft fuer Chirurgie), Georg Thieme Verlag, Ruedigerstr 14, Stuttgart, 70469, Germany. TEL 49-711-8931421, FAX 49-711-8931410, kunden.service@thieme.de. Adv. contact Christine Volpp TEL 49-711-8931603. Circ: 6,800 (paid and controlled).

617 NLD ISSN 0167-5079
DEVELOPMENTS IN SURGERY. Text in English. 1979. irreg., latest vol.11, 1991. price varies. **Document type:** *Monographic series, Academic/Scholarly.*
Published by: Springer Netherlands (Subsidiary of: Springer Science+Business Media), Van Godewijckstraat 30, Dordrecht, 3311 GX, Netherlands. TEL 31-78-6576050, FAX 31-78-6576474.

617 616.3 CHE ISSN 0253-4886
RD540 CODEN: DSIUAN
➤ **DIGESTIVE SURGERY.** Text in English. 1984. bi-m. CHF 2,488, EUR 1,989, USD 2,436.50 to institutions; CHF 2,732, EUR 2,184, USD 2,673.50 combined subscription to institutions (print & online eds.) (effective 2012). adv. illus. index. back issues avail. **Document type:** *Journal, Academic/Scholarly.* **Description:** Answers the complete information needs of surgeons concerned with diseases of the alimentary tract. Keeps the specialist aware of advances in all fields contributing to improvements in the diagnosis and treatment of gastrointestinal disease.
Incorporates: Surgical Gastroenterology
Related titles: Microform ed.: (from PQC); Online - full text ed.: ISSN 1421-9883. CHF 2,437, EUR 1,950, USD 2,366 to institutions (effective 2012).
Indexed: A01, A03, A08, A20, A22, ASCA, CA, CurCont, E01, EMBASE, ExcerpMed, INI, IndMed, Inpharma, MEDLINE, P20, P22, P30, P35, P48, P54, PQC, R10, Reac, SCI, SCOPUS, T02, W07.
—BLDSC (3588.346900), GNLM, IE, Infotrieve, Ingenta, INIST. **CCC.**
Published by: (Collegium Internationale Chirurgiae Digestivae), S. Karger AG, Allschwilerstr 10, Basel, 4055, Switzerland. TEL 41-61-3061111, FAX 41-61-3061234, karger@karger.ch, http://www.karger.ch. Eds. J. P. Neoptolemos, M W Buechler. adv.: page CHF 1,895; trim 210 x 280. Circ: 2,400.

617 USA ISSN 0012-3706
CODEN: DICRAG
➤ **DISEASES OF THE COLON AND RECTUM.** Abbreviated title: D C & R. Text in English. 1958. m. USD 848 domestic to institutions; USD 1,055 foreign to institutions (effective 2011). adv. illus. index. back issues avail.; reprints avail. **Document type:** *Journal, Academic/Scholarly.* **Description:** Designed for colorectal surgeons and gastroenterologists for the transfer of both medical and surgical knowledge and information in this field.
Related titles: Microfilm ed.: (from PQC); Online - full text ed.: ISSN 1530-0358 (from IngentaConnect); ◆ Spanish ed.: Diseases of the Colon Rectum (Spanish Edition). ISSN 0329-0883.
Indexed: A22, A26, A36, ASCA, Agr, BIOBASE, CA, CABA, ChemAb, CurCont, D01, DentInd, E01, E12, EMBASE, ExcerpMed, FR, GH, H12, HospLI, IABS, INI, ISR, IndMed, Inpharma, JW-G, MEDLINE, N02, N03, NRN, P20, P22, P30, P33, P35, P48, P54, PQC, R10, RM&VM, Reac, SCI, SCOPUS, T05, THA, VS, W07.
—BLDSC (3598.200000), CIS, GNLM, IE, Infotrieve, Ingenta, INIST. **CCC.**
Published by: (American Society of Colon and Rectal Surgeons), Lippincott Williams & Wilkins (Subsidiary of: Wolters Kluwer N.V.), 333 7th Ave, 19th Fl, New York, NY 10001. TEL 212-886-1200, FAX 212-886-1205, customerservice@lww.com, http://www.lww.com. Eds. Julio Garcia-Aguilar, Thomas E Read, Robert D Madoff. Circ: 3,265.

617 ARG ISSN 0329-0883
DISEASES OF THE COLON RECTUM (SPANISH EDITION). Text in Spanish. 1997. q. **Document type:** *Journal, Trade.*
Related titles: ◆ English ed.: Diseases of the Colon and Rectum. ISSN 0012-3706.
Published by: Waverly Hispanica, S.A., Padre Vanini, 380 Esp. Alsina, Florida, Buenos Aires, B1602EEF, Argentina. TEL 54-11-47613339, FAX 54-11-47610763.

617 SWE ISSN 1654-0980
DONATIONSRAADET REKOMMENDERAR. Text in Swedish. 2007. irreg., latest vol.1, 2007. free. **Document type:** *Monographic series, Trade.*
Related titles: Online - full text ed.
Published by: Donationsraadet/The Swedish Council for Organ and Tissue Donation, c/o Socialstyrelsen, Raalambsvaegen 3, Stockholm, 10630, Sweden. TEL 46-8-55553000, info@donationsradet.se.

617.5 NLD ISSN 1572-3054
DONORVOORLICHTING COMMUNICATIEF. Key Title: D V Communicatief. Text in Dutch. 2001. 3/yr. **Document type:** *Journal, Trade.*
Formerly (until 2003): S D V Communicatief (1570-4416)
Published by: N I G Z-Donorvoorlichting, De Bleek 13, Postbus 500, Woerden, 3440 AM, Netherlands. TEL 31-348-437650, FAX 31-348-437666, info@donorvoorlichting.nl, http://www.donorvoorlichting.nl.

E J V E S EXTRA. (European Journal of Vascular and Endovascular Surgery) *see* MEDICAL SCIENCES—Cardiovascular Diseases

617 ZMB ISSN 1024-297X
RD1
➤ **EAST AND CENTRAL AFRICAN JOURNAL OF SURGERY.** Text and summaries in English. 1978. a. GBP 10 in Africa to individuals; GBP 20 elsewhere to institutions (effective 2007). adv. bk.rev. cum.index. back issues avail. **Document type:** *Journal, Academic/Scholarly.* **Description:** Publishes original papers on surgery with special relevance for Africa.
Supersedes (in 1994): Association of Surgeons of East Africa. Proceedings (0253-8466)
Related titles: Online - full text ed.: free (effective 2011).
Indexed: A01, A36, CABA, E12, F08, F12, GH, H17, N02, N03, P33, P39, R08, R12, RM&VM, T02, T05.
—GNLM.
Published by: Association of Surgeons of East Africa, Woodlands, PO Box 320159, Lusaka, Zambia. TEL 260-1-230710, FAX 260-1-250753, editor_ecajs@yahoo.com, http://www.asea.org.mz. Ed. I Kakande. R&P John E Jellis. Circ: 800.

617 EGY ISSN 1110-1121
➤ **THE EGYPTIAN JOURNAL OF SURGERY/MAGALLAT AL-GIRAAHAT AL-MISRIYYAT/MAJALLAT AL-JIRAAHAT AL-MISRIYYAT.** Text in English. 1982. q. EGP 60 to individuals; EGP 100 to institutions. **Document type:** *Journal, Academic/Scholarly.*
Related titles: Online - full text ed.: ISSN 1687-7624.
Published by: Egyptian Society of Surgeons, 14 El-Khalil St, Mohandessen, Giza, 12411, Egypt. TEL 20-2-3023642, FAX 20-2-302762, info@ess-eg.org. Ed. Dr. Medhat Mussttafa Sabet.

617 GBR
THE ELECTRONIC JOURNAL OF HAND SURGERY. Text in English. 1996. irreg. **Document type:** *Journal, Academic/Scholarly.*
Media: Online - full content.
Published by: St. James's University Hospital, Department of Plastic, Reconstructive and Hand Surgery, Leeds, LS9 7TF, United Kingdom. TEL 44-113-2065265, FAX 44-113-2066423, ssjspk@leeds.ac.uk.

617 616.025 CAN ISSN 1195-0897
EMERGENCY PRODUCT BUYER. Text in English. 1986. bi-m. USD 35; CAD 45 foreign. adv. bk.rev. abstr.; charts; illus.; stat.; tr.lit. back issues avail. **Document type:** *Newsletter, Trade.* **Description:** Provides a source of continuing medical, business education and professional news for ambulance officers, paramedics, emergency physicians and nurses, and EMS management and training officers in Canada.
Former titles: Emergency Prehospital Medicine (0836-7272); (until 1987): Canadian Journal of Prehospital Medicine (0829-5603)
Published by: C M E Communications, Inc., 20854 Dalton Rd, P O Box 507, Sutton W., ON L0E 1L0, Canada. TEL 416-722-9839, FAX 416-722-9687. Ed. Michael Roschette. Adv. contact John W Moir. Circ: 6,200.

ENCYCLOPEDIE MEDICO-CHIRURGICALE. ANESTESIA - RIANIMAZIONE. *see* MEDICAL SCIENCES—Anaesthesiology

ENCYCLOPEDIE MEDICO-CHIRURGICALE. ANESTHESIE - REANIMATION. *see* MEDICAL SCIENCES—Anaesthesiology

617.5 FRA ISSN 1634-7080
ENCYCLOPEDIE MEDICO-CHIRURGICALE. CIRUGIA GENERAL. Text in Spanish. 2002. a. **Document type:** *Journal, Academic/Scholarly.*
—**CCC.**
Published by: Elsevier Masson (Subsidiary of: Elsevier Health Sciences), 62 Rue Camille Desmoulins, Issy les Moulineaux, Cedex 92442, France. TEL 33-1-71165500, FAX 33-1-71165600, infos@elsevier-masson.fr, http://www.elsevier-masson.fr.

617.5 616.3 FRA ISSN 0246-0424
➤ **ENCYCLOPEDIE MEDICO-CHIRURGICALE. TECHNIQUES CHIRURGICALES. APPAREIL DIGESTIF.** Cover title: Techniques Chirurgicales - Appareil Digestif. Variant title: Encyclopedie Medico-Chirurgicale. Techniques Chirurgicales. Abdominal & Digestif. Text in French. 1964. 3 base vols. plus q. updates. EUR 1,024.07 (effective 2003). bibl.; charts; illus. **Document type:** *Academic/Scholarly.* **Description:** Provides an up-to-date reference to topics concerning GI-tract and abdominal surgery.
Related titles: Online - full text ed.; ◆ Italian ed.: Encyclopedie Medico-Chirurgicale. Tecniche Chirurgiche. Chirurgia Addominale. ISSN 1283-0798.
—INIST.
Published by: Elsevier Masson (Subsidiary of: Elsevier Health Sciences), 62 Rue Camille Desmoulins, Issy les Moulineaux, Cedex 92442, France. TEL 33-1-71165500, FAX 33-1-71165600, infos@elsevier-masson.fr.

617.5 616.13 FRA ISSN 0246-0459
➤ **ENCYCLOPEDIE MEDICO-CHIRURGICALE. TECHNIQUES CHIRURGICALES. CHIRURGIE VASCULAIRE.** Cover title: Techniques Chirurgicales - Chirurgie Vasculaire. Variant title: Encyclopedie Medico-Chirurgicale, Instantanes Medicaux. Techniques Chirurgicales - Chirurgie Vasculaire. Text in French. 1966. 2 base vols. plus q. updates. EUR 682.71 (effective 2003). bibl.; charts; illus. **Document type:** *Academic/Scholarly.* **Description:** Provides an up-to-date reference tool for topics in vascular surgery.
Related titles: Online - full text ed.; ◆ Italian ed.: Encyclopedie Medico-Chirurgicale. Tecniche Chirurgiche. Chirurgia Vascolare. ISSN 1283-0801.
—INIST.
Published by: Elsevier Masson (Subsidiary of: Elsevier Health Sciences), 62 Rue Camille Desmoulins, Issy les Moulineaux, Cedex 92442, France. TEL 33-1-71165500, FAX 33-1-71165600, infos@elsevier-masson.fr.

617 618 FRA ISSN 1624-5857
➤ **ENCYCLOPEDIE MEDICO-CHIRURGICALE. TECHNIQUES CHIRURGICALES. GYNECOLOGIE.** Text in French. 1966. base vol. plus a. updates. EUR 341.36 (effective 2003). bibl.; charts; illus. **Document type:** *Academic/Scholarly.* **Description:** Provides ob-gyns with a comprehensive reference on surgical techniques.
Supersedes in part (in 1997): Encyclopedie Medico-Chirurgicale. Traite de Techniques Chirurgicales - Urologie - Gynecologie (0246-0432)
Related titles: Online - full text ed.
—INIST.
Published by: Elsevier Masson (Subsidiary of: Elsevier Health Sciences), 62 Rue Camille Desmoulins, Issy les Moulineaux, Cedex 92442, France. TEL 33-1-71165500, FAX 33-1-71165600, infos@elsevier-masson.fr.

617.1 FRA ISSN 0246-0467
➤ **ENCYCLOPEDIE MEDICO-CHIRURGICALE. TECHNIQUES CHIRURGICALES. ORTHOPEDIE - TRAUMATOLOGIE.** Cover title: Traite de Techniques Chirurgicales - Orthopedie - Traumatologie. Text in French. 1966. 4 base vols. plus q. updates. EUR 1,365.42 (effective 2003). bibl.; charts; illus. **Document type:** *Academic/Scholarly.* **Description:** Offers orthopedic surgeons a comprehensive, up-to-date reference.
Related titles: Online - full text ed.
—INIST.
Published by: Elsevier Masson (Subsidiary of: Elsevier Health Sciences), 62 Rue Camille Desmoulins, Issy les Moulineaux, Cedex 92442, France. TEL 33-1-71165500, FAX 33-1-71165600, infos@elsevier-masson.fr.

617.5 616.21 FRA ISSN 1624-5849
ENCYCLOPEDIE MEDICO-CHIRURGICALE. TECHNIQUES CHIRURGICALES. TETE ET COU. Cover title: Techniques Chirgicales. Tete et Cou. Text in French. 2 base vols. plus a. updates. EUR 682.71 (effective 2003). bibl.; charts; illus. **Document type:** *Academic/Scholarly.* **Description:** Provides an up-to-date reference for surgeons in otolaryngology.
Supersedes in part (in 1991): Encyclopedie Medico-Chirurgicale. Techniques Chirurgicales. Cou et Tete (1155-570X)
Related titles: Online - full text ed.; ◆ Italian ed.: Encyclopedie Medico-Chirurgicale. Tecniche Chirurgiche. Chirurgia O R L e Cervico-facciale. ISSN 1292-3036.
—INIST.
Published by: Elsevier Masson (Subsidiary of: Elsevier Health Sciences), 62 Rue Camille Desmoulins, Issy les Moulineaux, Cedex 92442, France. TEL 33-1-71165500, FAX 33-1-71165600, infos@elsevier-masson.fr.

617.5 616.21 FRA ISSN 1241-8226
➤ **ENCYCLOPEDIE MEDICO-CHIRURGICALE. TECHNIQUES CHIRURGICALES. THORAX.** Cover title: Techniques Chirurgicales. Thorax. Variant title: Encyclopedie Medico-Chirurgicale, Instantanes Medicaux. Techniques Chirurgicales - Thorax. Text in French. 2 base vols. plus q. updates. EUR 682.71 (effective 2003). bibl.; charts; illus. **Document type:** *Academic/Scholarly.* **Description:** Presents surgeons in otorhinolaryngology with an up-to-date reference on thoracic surgery.
Supersedes in part (in 1991): Encyclopedie Medico-Chirurgicale. Techniques Chirurgicales. Cou - Thorax (1155-570X)
Related titles: Online - full text ed.; ◆ Italian ed.: Encyclopedie Medico-Chirurgicale. Tecniche Chirurgiche. Torace. ISSN 1288-3336.
—INIST.
Published by: Elsevier Masson (Subsidiary of: Elsevier Health Sciences), 62 Rue Camille Desmoulins, Issy les Moulineaux, Cedex 92442, France. TEL 33-1-71165500, FAX 33-1-71165600, infos@elsevier-masson.fr.

617 616.6 FRA ISSN 1283-0879
➤ **ENCYCLOPEDIE MEDICO-CHIRURGICALE. TECHNIQUES CHIRURGICALES. UROLOGIE.** Cover title: Traite de Techniques Chirurgicales - Urologie. Text in French. 1966. 2 base vols. plus q. updates. EUR 682.71 (effective 2003). bibl.; charts; illus. **Document type:** *Academic/Scholarly.* **Description:** Offers urologists a comprehensive, up-to-date reference on surgical techniques.
Supersedes in part (in 1997): Encyclopedie Medico-Chirurgicale. Techniques Chirurgicales - Urologie - Gynecologie
Related titles: Online - full text ed.
Published by: Elsevier Masson (Subsidiary of: Elsevier Health Sciences), 62 Rue Camille Desmoulins, Issy les Moulineaux, Cedex 92442, France. TEL 33-1-71165500, FAX 33-1-71165600, infos@elsevier-masson.fr.

617.5 616.3 FRA ISSN 1282-9129
ENCYCLOPEDIE MEDICO-CHIRURGICALE. TECNICAS QUIRURGICAS. APARATO DIGESTIVO. Text in Spanish. 2000. q. **Document type:** *Journal, Academic/Scholarly.*
Published by: Elsevier Masson (Subsidiary of: Elsevier Health Sciences), 62 Rue Camille Desmoulins, Issy les Moulineaux, Cedex 92442, France. TEL 33-1-71165500, FAX 33-1-71165600, infos@elsevier-masson.fr, http://www.elsevier-masson.fr.

617.5 616.3 FRA ISSN 1283-0798
➤ **ENCYCLOPEDIE MEDICO-CHIRURGICALE. TECNICHE CHIRURGICHE. CHIRURGIA ADDOMINALE.** Variant title: Tecniche Chirurgiche Addominale. Text in Italian. 1998. 3 base vols. plus s-a. updates. EUR 1,036.07 (effective 2003). bibl.; charts; illus. **Document type:** *Academic/Scholarly.* **Description:** Provides an up-to-date reference on topics in abdominal and GI-tract surgery.
Related titles: ◆ French ed.: Encyclopedie Medico-Chirurgicale. Techniques Chirurgicales. Appareil Digestif. ISSN 0246-0424.
Published by: Elsevier Masson (Subsidiary of: Elsevier Health Sciences), 62 Rue Camille Desmoulins, Issy les Moulineaux, Cedex 92442, France. TEL 33-1-71165500, FAX 33-1-71165600, infos@elsevier-masson.fr, http://www.elsevier-masson.fr.

617.5 616.21 FRA ISSN 1292-3036
ENCYCLOPEDIE MEDICO-CHIRURGICALE. TECNICHE CHIRURGICHE. CHIRURGIA O R L E CERVICO-FACCIALE. (Oto-Rhino-Laryngologia) Cover title: Tecniche Chirurgiche. Chirurgia O R L e Cervico-Facciale. Text in Italian. 1998. 2 base vols. plus a. updates. EUR 690.71 (effective 2003). bibl.; charts; illus. **Document type:** *Academic/Scholarly.* **Description:** Provides an up-to-date source for topics in otorhinolaryngologic surgery.
Related titles: ◆ French ed.: Encyclopedie Medico-Chirurgicale. Techniques Chirurgicales. Tete et Cou. ISSN 1624-5849.
Published by: Elsevier Masson (Subsidiary of: Elsevier Health Sciences), 62 Rue Camille Desmoulins, Issy les Moulineaux, Cedex 92442, France. TEL 33-1-71165500, FAX 33-1-71165600, infos@elsevier-masson.fr, http://www.elsevier-masson.fr.

617.5 616.13 FRA ISSN 1283-0801
➤ **ENCYCLOPEDIE MEDICO-CHIRURGICALE. TECNICHE CHIRURGICHE. CHIRURGIA VASCOLARE.** Cover title: Tecniche Chirurgiche. Chirurgia Vascolare. Text in Italian. 1998. 2 base vols. plus updates 4/yr. EUR 690.71 (effective 2003). bibl.; charts; illus. **Document type:** *Academic/Scholarly.* **Description:** Provides an up-to-date reference tool for topics in vascular surgery.
Related titles: ◆ French ed.: Encyclopedie Medico-Chirurgicale. Techniques Chirurgicales. Chirurgie Vasculaire. ISSN 0246-0459.
Published by: Elsevier Masson (Subsidiary of: Elsevier Health Sciences), 62 Rue Camille Desmoulins, Issy les Moulineaux, Cedex 92442, France. TEL 33-1-71165500, FAX 33-1-71165600, infos@elsevier-masson.fr, http://www.elsevier-masson.fr.

617.5 616.21 FRA ISSN 1288-3336
➤ **ENCYCLOPEDIE MEDICO-CHIRURGICALE. TECNICHE CHIRURGICHE. TORACE.** Cover title: Tecniche Chirurgicale. Torace. Text in Italian. 1989. base vol. plus a. updates. EUR 345.36 (effective 2003). bibl.; charts; illus. **Document type:** *Academic/Scholarly.* **Description:** Presents surgeons in otorhinolaryngology with an up-to-date reference on topics on surgery of the thorax.
Related titles: ◆ French ed.: Encyclopedie Medico-Chirurgicale. Techniques Chirurgicales. Thorax. ISSN 1241-8226.
Published by: Elsevier Masson (Subsidiary of: Elsevier Health Sciences), 62 Rue Camille Desmoulins, Issy les Moulineaux, Cedex 92442, France. TEL 33-1-71165500, FAX 33-1-71165600, infos@elsevier-masson.fr, http://www.elsevier-masson.fr.

617 RUS ISSN 1025-7209
➤ **ENDOSKOPICHESKAYA KHIRURGIYA.** Text in Russian. 1995. bi-m. USD 225 in North America (effective 2010). bibl.; charts; illus. reprints avail. **Document type:** *Journal, Academic/Scholarly.*
Related titles: Online - full content ed.
Indexed: RefZh.
—East View.
Published by: (Rossiiskaya Assotsyatsiya Endoskopicheskoi Khirurgii), Media Sfera, Dmitrovskoe shosse 46, korp 2, etazh 4, P.O. Box 54, Moscow, 127238, Russian Federation. TEL 7-095-4824329, FAX 7-095-4824312, podpiska@mediasphera.ru, http://mediasphera.ru. Ed. Sergey I Yemelyanov. Circ: 2,000 (paid). **Dist. by:** East View Information Services, 10601 Wayzata Blvd, Minneapolis, MN 55305. TEL 952-252-1201, 800-477-1005, FAX 952-252-1202, info@eastview.com, http://www.eastview.com.

617.95 CZE ISSN 1802-0402
ESTETIKA. Text in Czech. 2006. 10/yr. CZK 790 (effective 2010). adv. **Document type:** *Magazine, Trade.*
Published by: Vydavatelstvi Fine Tech s.r.o., Branicka 514/140, Prague 4, 147 00, Czech Republic. Ed. Hana Profousova. Adv. contact Miloslava Mikulova.

617 616.1 FRA ISSN 1774-024X
➤ **EUROINTERVENTION.** Text in English. 2005. q. **Document type:** *Journal, Academic/Scholarly.* **Description:** Aims to create a forum of high quality research and education in the field of percutaneous and surgical cardiovascular interventions.
Related titles: Online - full text ed.: ISSN 1969-6213.
Indexed: EMBASE, ExcerpMed, MEDLINE, P30, R10, Reac, SCOPUS.
—BLDSC (3829.268905), INIST. **CCC.**
Published by: Europa Edition, 5 Rue Saint-Pantaleon, Toulouse, 31015, France. FAX 33-5-34452646. Ed. Patrick W Serruys.

617 DEU ISSN 0939-7248
CODEN: EPSUEX
➤ **EUROPEAN JOURNAL OF PEDIATRIC SURGERY.** Text in German. 1991. bi-m. EUR 418 to institutions; EUR 577 combined subscription to institutions (print & online eds.); EUR 79 newsstand/cover (effective 2011). adv. bk.rev. abstr.; illus. index. reprints avail. **Document type:** *Journal, Academic/Scholarly.* **Description:** Aims to integrate and coordinate all endeavors in pediatric surgery and related disciplines in accordance with European standards, to widen the scope and variety of published papers in the specialty and to provide a European forum for pediatric surgery and specialties.
Formed by the merger of (1964-1991): Zeitschrift fuer Kinderchirurgie (0174-3082); Which was formerly (until 1981): Zeitschrift fuer Kinderchirurgie und Grenzgebiete (0044-2909); (1960-1991): Chirurgie Pediatrique (0180-5738); Which was formerly (until 1978): Annales de Chirurgie Infantile (0003-3952)
Related titles: Microform ed.: (from PQC); Online - full text ed.: ISSN 1439-359X. EUR 555 (effective 2011); ◆ Supplement(s): European Journal of Pediatric Surgery. Supplement. ISSN 0939-6764.
Indexed: A01, A03, A08, A20, A22, A34, A36, ASCA, BDM&CN, C06, C07, CA, CABA, CurCont, D01, DentInd, EMBASE, ExcerpMed, F08, GH, H17, IBR, IBZ, ISR, IndMed, IndVet, Inpharma, MEDLINE, N02, N03, N04, P30, P33, P35, R10, RA&MP, RM&VM, Reac, SCI, SCOPUS, T02, T05, VS, W07, W10.
—BLDSC (3829.733450), GNLM, IE, Infotrieve, Ingenta, INIST. **CCC.**
Published by: Georg Thieme Verlag, Ruedigerstr 14, Stuttgart, 70469, Germany. TEL 49-711-8931421, FAX 49-711-8931410, kunden.service@thieme.de, http://www.thieme.de. Eds. A M Holschneider, Y Revillon. Circ: 1,720 (paid and controlled). **Subscr. to:** Thieme Medical Publishers, 333 Seventh Ave, New York, NY 10001. http://www.thieme.com/journals.

617 DEU ISSN 0939-6764
EUROPEAN JOURNAL OF PEDIATRIC SURGERY. SUPPLEMENT. Text in German. 1966. irreg. **Document type:** *Monographic series, Academic/Scholarly.*
Former titles (until 1991): Zeitschrift fuer Kinderchirurgie. Supplement (0932-5654); (until 1981): Zeitschrift fuer Kinderchirurgie und Grenzgebiete (0932-5638)
Related titles: ◆ Supplement to: European Journal of Pediatric Surgery. ISSN 0939-7248.
Indexed: EMBASE, ExcerpMed, RefZh, SCOPUS.
—INIST.
Published by: Hippokrates Verlag in MVS Medizinverlage Stuttgart GmbH & Co.KG (Subsidiary of: Georg Thieme Verlag), Oswald-Hesse-Str 50, Stuttgart, 70469, Germany. TEL 49-711-89310, FAX 49-711-8931706, kunden.service@thieme.de, http://www.medizinverlage.de. Ed. Guenther Buck.

617.95 DEU ISSN 0930-343X
RD118.A1
➤ **EUROPEAN JOURNAL OF PLASTIC SURGERY.** Text in English. 1966. 8/yr. EUR 1,134, USD 1,363 combined subscription to institutions (print & online eds.) (effective 2012). adv. back issues avail.; reprint service avail. from PSC. **Document type:** *Journal, Academic/Scholarly.* **Description:** Covers developments in microsurgery, tissue expansion, craniofacial surgery, and the spin-offs of these techniques into the areas of trauma, the treatment of malignancy, and aesthetic surgery.
Former titles (until 1986): Chirurgia Plastica (0340-5664); (until 1971): Chirurgia Plastica et Reconstructiva (0340-5656)
Related titles: Microform ed.: (from PQC); Online - full text ed.: ISSN 1435-0130 (from IngentaConnect).
Indexed: A01, A03, A08, A22, A26, ASCA, CA, E01, EMBASE, ExcerpMed, Inpharma, MS&D, P30, R10, Reac, SCOPUS, T02.
—BLDSC (3829.736300), GNLM, IE, Infotrieve, Ingenta, INIST. **CCC.**
Published by: (European Association of Plastic Surgeons), Springer (Subsidiary of: Springer Science+Business Media), Tiergartenstr 17, Heidelberg, 69121, Germany. TEL 49-6221-4870, FAX 49-6221-345229. Ed. Dr. Ian T Jackson. adv.: B&W page EUR 880, color page EUR 1,920. Circ: 1,000 (paid and controlled). **Subscr. in the Americas to:** Springer New York LLC, Journal Fulfillment, PO Box 2485, Secaucus, NJ 07096. TEL 800-777-4643, 201-348-4033, FAX 201-348-4505, journals-ny@springer.com, http://www.springer.com; **Subscr. to:** Springer Distribution Center, Kundenservice Zeitschriften, Haberstr 7, Heidelberg 69126, Germany. TEL 49-6221-3454303, FAX 49-6221-3454229, subscriptions@springer.com. **Co-sponsors:** Association of German Plastic Surgeons; Belgian Society for Plastic, Reconstructive and Aesthetic Surgery; Austrian Society for Plastic and Reconstructive Surgery.

➤ **EUROPEAN JOURNAL OF VASCULAR AND ENDOVASCULAR SURGERY.** *see* MEDICAL SCIENCES—Cardiovascular Diseases

617 ITA
EUROPEAN SOCIETY FOR SURGICAL RESEARCH. CONGRESS PROCEEDINGS. (Supplement to: European Surgical Research) Text in English. 1979 (14th ed.). irreg., latest vol.41, 2006. price varies. **Document type:** *Proceedings, Academic/Scholarly.*
Published by: (European Society for Surgical Research SWE), Medimond S.r.l., Via Maserati 5, Bologna, Italy. TEL 39-051-4151123, FAX 39-051-370529, monduzzi@monduzzi.com, http://www.medimond.com.

617 DEU ISSN 0940-6719
RD533 CODEN: ESJOEP
➤ **EUROPEAN SPINE JOURNAL.** Text in English. 1992. 10/yr. EUR 2,193, USD 2,643 combined subscription to institutions (print & online eds.) (effective 2012). adv. reprint service avail. from PSC. **Document type:** *Journal, Academic/Scholarly.* **Description:** Devoted to spine surgery and all related disciplines, including functional and surgical anatomy, biomechanics and pathophysiology, neurology, as well as basic sciences, diagnostic procedures and alternative methods.
Related titles: Online - full text ed.: ISSN 1432-0932 (from IngentaConnect).
Indexed: A01, A03, A08, A20, A22, A26, AMED, B21, C06, C07, CA, CTA, CurCont, E-psyche, E01, EMBASE, ExcerpMed, H12, IndMed, Inpharma, MEDLINE, P20, P22, P30, P35, P48, P54, PQC, R10, Reac, SCI, SCOPUS, T02, W07.
—BLDSC (3830.232200), GNLM, IE, Infotrieve, Ingenta, INIST. **CCC.**
Published by: (European Spine Society), Springer (Subsidiary of: Springer Science+Business Media), Tiergartenstr 17, Heidelberg, 69121, Germany. TEL 49-6221-4870, FAX 49-6221-345229. Ed. Dr. Max Aebi. adv.: B&W page EUR 1,010, color page EUR 2,050. Circ: 1,100 (paid and controlled). **Subscr. in the Americas to:** Springer New York LLC, Journal Fulfillment, PO Box 2485, Secaucus, NJ 07096. TEL 800-777-4643, 201-348-4033, FAX 201-348-4505, journals-ny@springer.com, http://www.springer.com; **Subscr. to:** Springer Distribution Center, Kundenservice Zeitschriften, Haberstr 7, Heidelberg 69126, Germany. TEL 49-6221-3454303, FAX 49-6221-3454229, subscriptions@springer.com.

617 AUT ISSN 1682-8631
CODEN: ACAUB9
➤ **EUROPEAN SURGERY.** Text in German, English; Summaries in English. 1968. bi-m. EUR 562, USD 737 combined subscription to institutions (print & online eds.) (effective 2012). adv. reprint service avail. from PSC. **Document type:** *Journal, Academic/Scholarly.*
Formerly (until 2002): Acta Chirurgica Austriaca (0001-544X)
Related titles: ◆ Online - full text ed.: European Surgery Online. ISSN 1682-4016; Supplement(s): European Surgery. Supplement. ISSN 1682-1769. 2002.
Indexed: A01, A02, A03, A22, A26, ASCA, E01, EMBASE, ExcerpMed, IBR, IBZ, INIS AtomInd, SCI, SCOPUS, W07.
—BLDSC (3830.234900), GNLM, IE, Ingenta, INIST. **CCC.**
Published by: (Oesterreichische Gesellschaft fuer Chirurgie), Springer Wien (Subsidiary of: Springer Science+Business Media), Sachsenplatz 4-6, Vienna, W 1201, Austria. TEL 43-1-33024150, FAX 43-1-3302426, journals@springer.at, http://www.springer.at. Ed. Dr. Franz Martin Riegler. Adv. contact Gabriele Popernitsch. color page EUR 3,130; trim 210 x 297. Circ: 1,500. **Subscr. to:** Springer Distribution Center, Kundenservice Zeitschriften, Haberstr 7, Heidelberg 69126, Germany. TEL 49-6221-3454303, FAX 49-6221-3454229, subscriptions@springer.com; **Subscr. to:** Springer New York LLC, Journal Fulfillment, PO Box 2485, Secaucus, NJ 07096. TEL 201-348-4033, FAX 201-348-4505, journals-ny@springer.com, http://www.springer.com.

617 AUT ISSN 1682-4016
➤ **EUROPEAN SURGERY ONLINE.** Text in German. 1997. 6/yr. **Document type:** *Academic/Scholarly.*
Formerly (until 2002): Acta Chirurgica Austriaca Online (1563-2563)
Media: Online - full text (from IngentaConnect). **Related titles:** ◆ Print ed.: European Surgery. ISSN 1682-8631.
Indexed: SCOPUS.
—CCC.
Published by: Springer Wien (Subsidiary of: Springer Science+Business Media), Sachsenplatz 4-6, Vienna, W 1201, Austria. TEL 43-1-33024150, FAX 43-1-3302426, journals@springer.at, http://www.springer.at.

617 CHE ISSN 0014-312X
RD29 CODEN: EUSRBM
➤ **EUROPEAN SURGICAL RESEARCH;** clinical and experimental surgery. Text in English. 1969. 8/yr. CHF 2,558, EUR 2,044, USD 2,512 to institutions; CHF 2,808, EUR 2,244, USD 2,754 combined subscription to institutions (print & online eds.) (effective 2012). adv. back issues avail. **Document type:** *Journal, Academic/Scholarly.* **Description:** Features original clinical and experimental papers and short technical notes in various fields of operative medicine. Coverage includes surgery, surgical pathophysiology, drug usage, and new surgical techniques.
Related titles: Microform ed.; Online - full text ed.: ISSN 1421-9921. CHF 2,490, EUR 1,992, USD 2,418 to institutions (effective 2012).
Indexed: A01, A02, A03, A08, A22, ASCA, B25, BIOSIS Prev, CA, CIN, ChemAb, ChemTitl, CurCont, E01, EMBASE, ExcerpMed, ISR, IndMed, Inpharma, MEDLINE, MycolAb, P30, R10, Reac, SCI, SCOPUS, T02, W07.
—BLDSC (3830.235000), CASDDS, GNLM, IE, Infotrieve, Ingenta, INIST. **CCC.**
Published by: S. Karger AG, Allschwilerstr 10, Basel, 4055, Switzerland. TEL 41-61-3061111, FAX 41-61-3061234, karger@karger.ch, http://www.karger.ch. Ed. O Kempski. adv.: page CHF 1,730; trim 210 x 280. Circ: 1,600.

617.4 USA ISSN 1663-7976
➤ **EVIDENCE-BASED SPINE-CARE JOURNAL.** Abbreviated title: E B S J. Variant title: Evidence-Based Spine-Care Surgery. Text in English. 2005. q. USD 456 domestic to institutions; USD 465 foreign to institutions; USD 559 combined subscription domestic to institutions (print & online eds.); USD 569 combined subscription foreign to institutions (print & online eds.) (effective 2011). reprints avail. **Document type:** *Journal, Academic/Scholarly.* **Description:** Focuses on comparative studies of effectiveness and seeks to stimulate further areas of high quality spine-related research.
Formerly (until 2009): Evidence-Based Spine Surgery (1867-2302)

Related titles: Online - full text ed.: ISSN 1867-2310. 2005. USD 538 domestic to institutions; USD 549 foreign to institutions (effective 2011).
—CCC.
Published by: Thieme Medical Publishers (Subsidiary of: Georg Thieme Verlag), 333 Seventh Ave, New York, NY 10001. TEL 212-760-0888, 800-782-3488, FAX 212-947-1112, info@thieme.com.

➤ **EXCERPTA MEDICA. SECTION 18: CARDIOVASCULAR DISEASES AND CARDIOVASCULAR SURGERY.** *see* MEDICAL SCIENCES—Abstracting, Bibliographies, Statistics

➤ **EXCERPTA MEDICA. SECTION 33: ORTHOPEDIC SURGERY.** *see* MEDICAL SCIENCES—Abstracting, Bibliographies, Statistics

➤ **EXCERPTA MEDICA. SECTION 7: PEDIATRICS AND PEDIATRIC SURGERY.** *see* MEDICAL SCIENCES—Abstracting, Bibliographies, Statistics

➤ **EXCERPTA MEDICA. SECTION 8: NEUROLOGY AND NEUROSURGERY.** *see* MEDICAL SCIENCES—Abstracting, Bibliographies, Statistics

➤ **EXCERPTA MEDICA. SECTION 9: SURGERY.** *see* MEDICAL SCIENCES—Abstracting, Bibliographies, Statistics

➤ **EXTRACTA ORTHOPAEDICA.** *see* MEDICAL SCIENCES—Abstracting, Bibliographies, Statistics

617 USA ISSN 1559-6990
F A S A UPDATE. (Federated Ambulatory Surgery Association) Text in English. 1984. bi-m. USD 125 to non-members; free to members (effective 2007). **Document type:** *Newsletter, Trade.*
Published by: Federated Ambulatory Surgery Association, 1012 Cameron St, Alexandria, VA 22314-2427. TEL 703-836-8808, FAX 703-549-0976, FASA@fasa.org, http://www.fasa.org.

617.63 DEU ISSN 1864-4279
FACE; international magazine of orofacial esthetics. Text in German. 2007. 4/yr. EUR 44 (effective 2011). adv. **Document type:** *Magazine, Trade.*
Published by: Oemus Media AG, Holbeinstr 29, Leipzig, 04229, Germany. TEL 49-341-484740, FAX 49-341-48474290, info@oemus-media.de. Ed. Heike Isbaner. Pub. Torsten Oemus. Adv. contact Steffi Katharina Goldmann. Circ: 4,000 (controlled).

617.95 USA ISSN 0736-6825
CODEN: FPSUEA
➤ **FACIAL PLASTIC SURGERY**; international quarterly monographs. Text in English. 1983. s-m. USD 664 domestic to institutions; USD 682 foreign to institutions; USD 811 combined subscription domestic to institutions (print & online eds.); USD 850 combined subscription foreign to institutions (print & online eds.) (effective 2011). adv. **Document type:** *Journal, Academic/Scholarly.* **Description:** Covering areas of aesthetic and reconstructive plastic surgery as it relates to the head, neck, and face.
Formerly (until 1983): Seminars in Facial Plastic Surgery
Related titles: Microfilm ed.; Online - full text ed.: ISSN 1098-8793. USD 781 domestic; USD 802 foreign (effective 2011).
Indexed: A01, A03, A08, A22, C33, CA, CurCont, EMBASE, ExcerpMed, MEDLINE, P30, R10, Reac, SCI, SCOPUS, T02, W07.
—BLDSC (3863.421000), GNLM, IE, Infotrieve, Ingenta, INIST. **CCC.**
Published by: Thieme Medical Publishers (Subsidiary of: Georg Thieme Verlag), 333 Seventh Ave, New York, NY 10001. TEL 212-760-0888, 800-782-3488, FAX 212-947-1112, info@thieme.com, http://www.thieme.com. Eds. Anthony P Sclafani TEL 212-979-4200, Ralf Siegert TEL 49-236-1542550. Adv. contact James C Cunningham TEL 201-767-4170. Circ: 1,240.

617.5 USA ISSN 1064-7406
CODEN: FPSCBL
FACIAL PLASTIC SURGERY CLINICS OF NORTH AMERICA. Text in English. 1993. q. USD 459 in United States to institutions; USD 550 elsewhere to institutions (effective 2012). adv. illus. back issues avail.; reprints avail. **Document type:** *Journal, Academic/Scholarly.* **Description:** Focuses on a single topic relevant to facial plastic surgery practice, including rhinoplasty, skin resurfacing, hair transplantation, Botox, facelifts, browlifts, and blepharoplasty.
Related titles: Microform ed.: (from PQC); Online - full text ed.: ISSN 1558-1926 (from ScienceDirect).
Indexed: EMBASE, ExcerpMed, MEDLINE, P30, R10, Reac, SCOPUS.
—BLDSC (3863.421700), GNLM, IE, Infotrieve, Ingenta. **CCC.**
Published by: W.B. Saunders Co. (Subsidiary of: Elsevier Health Sciences), Elsevier, Health Sciences Division, Order Fulfillment, 3251 Riverport Ln, Maryland Heights, MO 63043. TEL 314-872-8370, 800-325-4177, FAX 314-432-1380, JournalCustomerService-usa@elsevier.com, http://www.us.elsevierhealth.com. Adv. contact John Marmero TEL 212-633-3657.

617.5 USA ISSN 2151-8378
CODEN: JPSOCY
➤ **FEMALE PELVIC MEDICINE AND RECONSTRUCTIVE SURGERY.** Text in English. 1995. bi-m. USD 822 domestic to institutions; USD 934 foreign to institutions (effective 2011). adv. back issues avail. **Document type:** *Journal, Academic/Scholarly.* **Description:** Publishes original articles, reviews and case reports covering all areas of the surgical treatment of pelvic disease, including diagnosis, pre- and post-operative care, surgical complications, imaging and critical care of pelvic surgery patients.
Former titles (until 2010): Journal of Pelvic Medicine and Surgery (1542-5983); (until 2003): Journal of Pelvic Surgery (1077-2847)
Related titles: Online - full text ed.: ISSN 2154-4212. USD 365.30 domestic for academic site license; USD 381.30 foreign for academic site license; USD 407.45 domestic for corporate site license; USD 423.45 foreign for corporate site license (effective 2002).
Indexed: A01, A03, A08, EMBASE, ExcerpMed, P30, R10, Reac, SCOPUS.
—BLDSC (3905.168400), GNLM, IE, Ingenta. **CCC.**
Published by: Lippincott Williams & Wilkins (Subsidiary of: Wolters Kluwer N.V.), 530 Walnut St, Philadelphia, PA 19106. TEL 215-521-8300, FAX 215-521-8902, customerservice@lww.com, http://www.lww.com. Ed. Dr. Alfred E Bent. Pubs. Maria M McMichael, Marjorie Spraycar TEL 410-321-5031. R&P Margaret Becker. Adv. contacts Ray Thibodeau, Ray Thibodeau. B&W page USD 1,330, color page USD 1,445; trim 8.125 x 11. Circ: 1,500 (paid). **Subscr. to:** PO Box 1620, Hagerstown, MD 21741. TEL 301-223-2300, 800-638-3030, FAX 301-223-2365.

617 USA ISSN 0742-9819
FOCUS ON SURGICAL EDUCATION. Text in English. 1983. q. free to members (effective 2005). **Document type:** *Newsletter, Trade.*
—Infotrieve.
Published by: Association for Surgical Education, Southern Illinois University School of Medicine, Department of Surgery, P O Box 19655, Springfield, IL 62794-9655. http://www.surgicaleducation.com/educlear/index.htm. Ed. Susan Kepner.

617 NLD ISSN 1874-6799
FOCUS OP CHIRURGIE. Text in Dutch. 2006. q.
Published by: P C C - Pharmaceutical Communications Company, PO Box 51, Almere-Haven, 1300 AB, Netherlands. TEL 31-36-5230880, FAX 31-36-5230859, info@pcc.nl.

617 GBR ISSN 1268-7731
RD563 CODEN: FASUF8
➤ **FOOT AND ANKLE SURGERY.** Text in English. 1994. 4/yr. EUR 549 in Europe to institutions; JPY 72,700 in Japan to institutions; USD 611 elsewhere to institutions (effective 2012). **Document type:** *Journal, Academic/Scholarly.* **Description:** Presents a broad approach to foot and ankle disorders, from basic to clinical management. Explores trauma and chronic diseases in both children and adults.
Formerly (until 1996): European Journal of Foot and Ankle Surgery (1122-8660)
Related titles: Online - full text ed.: ISSN 1460-9584 (from IngentaConnect, ScienceDirect).
Indexed: A01, A03, A08, A22, A26, C06, C07, CA, E01, EMBASE, ExcerpMed, I05, MEDLINE, P30, R10, Reac, SCOPUS, T02.
—BLDSC (3984.875000), IE, Infotrieve, Ingenta, INIST. **CCC.**
Published by: (European Foot and Ankle Society), Elsevier Ltd (Subsidiary of: Elsevier Science & Technology), The Blvd, Langford Ln, Kidlington, Oxford, OX5 1GB, United Kingdom. TEL 44-1865-843000, FAX 44-1865-843010, journalscustomerserviceemea@elsevier.com. Eds. Michael M Stephens, Sandro Giannini, Tom W Smith. Circ: 1,500.

617 TWN
➤ **FORMOSAN JOURNAL OF SURGERY.** Text in Chinese, English. 1968. bi-m. TWD 200 (effective 2001). illus. back issues avail. **Document type:** *Journal, Academic/Scholarly.* **Description:** Publishes scholarly research in all clinical and experimental areas of surgery and related fields.
Formerly (until 1999): Surgical Association R O C. Journal (1011-6788)
Indexed: SCOPUS.
Published by: Surgical Association, c/o National Taiwan University Hospital, Dept of Surgery, No 7, Chung-Shan Rd, Taipei, 100, Taiwan. TEL 886-2-2397-0800 ext 5640, 886-2-2356-2120, FAX 886-2-2393-0877. Ed. Chun-Jean Lee. Pub. Shen-Long Howng. Circ: 5,000. **Co-sponsors:** Association of Thoracic and Cardiovascular Surgeons of Asia; Surgical Society of Gastroenterology R O C; Transplantation Society of Taiwan, R O C; Chinese Association of Pediatric Surgeons; Chinese Association of Endocrine Surgeons.

➤ **FOUNDATIONS OF NEUROLOGICAL SURGERY.** *see* MEDICAL SCIENCES—Psychiatry And Neurology

617 CHN ISSN 1003-5591
FUBU WAIKE/JOURNAL OF ABDOMINAL SURGERY. Text in Chinese. 1988. bi-m. USD 22.80 (effective 2009). **Document type:** *Journal, Academic/Scholarly.*
Related titles: Online - full text ed.
Published by: Zhonghua Yixuehui, Wuhan Fenhui, 155, Hankou Shengli Jie, Wuhan, 430014, China. TEL 86-27-82789737, FAX 86-10-82856411. **Dist. by:** China International Book Trading Corp, 35 Chegongzhuang Xilu, Haidian District, PO Box 399, Beijing 100044, China. TEL 86-10-68412045, FAX 86-10-68412023, cibtc@mail.cibtc.com.cn, http://www.cibtc.com.cn.

617 CHN ISSN 1009-6612
FUQIANGJING WAIKE ZAZHI/JOURNAL OF LAPAROSCOPIC SURGERY. Text in Chinese. 1996. m. CNY 36; CNY 6 per issue (effective 2009). **Document type:** *Journal, Academic/Scholarly.*
Related titles: Online - full text ed.
Published by: Shandong Daxue Qilu Yiyuan/Shandong University Qilu Hospital, 107, Wenhua Xi Lu, Ji'nan, 250012, China. TEL 86-531-86920598, http://www.qiluhospital.com/.

G E C O. COLLECTION. (Groupe d'Etude pour la Chirurgie Osseuse) *see* MEDICAL SCIENCES—Orthopedics And Traumatology

G M S CURRENT POSTERS IN OTORHINOLARYNGOLOGY, HEAD AND NECK SURGERY. (German Medical Science) *see* MEDICAL SCIENCES—Otorhinolaryngology

617.6 DEU ISSN 1862-4006
➤ **G M S THORACIC SURGICAL SCIENCE.** (German Medical Science) Text in English, German. 2004. irreg. free (effective 2011). **Document type:** *Journal, Academic/Scholarly.* **Description:** Covers all aspects and scientific interests of thoracic surgery not involving cardiac surgery.
Formerly (until 2005): Thoracic Surgical Science (1614-9777)
Media: Online - full text.
Indexed: A01, C06, P30, T02.
—CCC.
Published by: (Die Deutsche Gesellschaft fuer Thoraxchirurgie/German Society for Thoracic Surgery), Arbeitsgemeinschaft der Wissenschaftlichen Medizinischen Fachgesellschaften/Association of the Scientific Medical Societies in Germany, Ubierstr 20, Duesseldorf, 40223, Germany. TEL 49-211-312828, FAX 49-211-316819, awmf@awmf.org, http://www.awmf.org.

617.95 JPN ISSN 0389-4045
CODEN: GGHOEL
GAKU GANMEN HOTETSU/JAPANESE ACADEMY OF MAXILLOFACIAL PROSTHETICS. JOURNAL. Text in Japanese. 1978. a. **Document type:** *Journal, Academic/Scholarly.*
Indexed: INIS AtomInd.
—CCC.
Published by: Nihon Gaku Ganmen Hotetsu Kenkyukai/Japanese Academy of Maxillofacial Prosthetics, 2-4-11 Fukagawa Kotoku, Tokyo, 135-0033, Japan. TEL 81-3-56201953, FAX 81-3-56201960, max-service@onebridge.co.jp, http://square.umin.ac.jp/jamfp/.

GANDAN WAIKE ZAZHI/JOURNAL OF HEPATOBILIARY SURGERY. *see* MEDICAL SCIENCES—Gastroenterology

616.1 DEU ISSN 0948-7034
➤ **GEFAESSCHIRURGIE**; Zeitschrift fuer vaskulaere und endovaskulaere Chirurgie. Text in German. 1996. 6/yr. EUR 374, USD 309 combined subscription to institutions (print & online eds.) (effective 2012). adv. back issues avail.; reprint service avail. from PSC. **Document type:** *Journal, Academic/Scholarly.* **Description:** Supplies information on current developments in vascular surgery with a view to supporting continuing professional education.
Related titles: Online - full text ed.: ISSN 1434-3932 (from IngentaConnect).
Indexed: A22, A26, E01, EMBASE, ExcerpMed, R10, Reac, SCI, SCOPUS, W07.
—BLDSC (4095.788000), GNLM, IE, Infotrieve, Ingenta. **CCC.**
Published by: (Deutsche Gesellschaft fuer Gefaesschirurgie), Springer (Subsidiary of: Springer Science+Business Media), Tiergartenstr 17, Heidelberg, 69121, Germany. TEL 49-6221-4870, FAX 49-6221-345229. Circ: 1,900 (paid and controlled). **Subscr. in the Americas to:** Springer New York LLC, Journal Fulfillment, PO Box 2485, Secaucus, NJ 07096. TEL 800-777-4643, 201-348-4033, FAX 201-348-4505, journals-ny@springer.com, http://www.springer.com; **Subscr. to:** Springer Distribution Center, Kundenservice Zeitschriften, Haberstr 7, Heidelberg 69126, Germany. TEL 49-6221-3454303, FAX 49-6221-3454229, subscriptions@springer.com. **Co-sponsors:** Schweizerische Gesellschaft fuer Gefaesschirurgie; Oesterreichische Gesellschaft fuer Gefaesschirurgie.

617 JPN ISSN 0016-593X
GEKA/SURGERY. Text in Japanese. 1937. 13/yr. JPY 37,800 domestic; JPY 48,000 foreign (effective 2007). adv. charts; illus. Index. **Document type:** *Journal, Academic/Scholarly.*
Indexed: INIS AtomInd.
—BLDSC (8548.130000).
Published by: Nankodo Co. Ltd., 3-42-6 Hongo, Bunkyo-ku, Tokyo, 113-8410, Japan. TEL 81-3-38117140, FAX 81-3-38117265, http://www.nankodo.co.jp/. Circ: 6,000.

617 JPN ISSN 0433-2644
CODEN: GECYA8
GEKA CHIRYO/SURGICAL THERAPY. Text in Japanese. 1959. m. USD 354 (effective 2000).
Indexed: INIS AtomInd, P30.
—CASDDS, GNLM, INIST.
Published by: Nagai Shoten Co. Ltd., 21-15 Fukushima 8-chome, Fukushima-ku, Osaka-shi, 553-0003, Japan. Ed. Tadao Nagai.

GEKA SHUDANKAI SHOROKUSHU/TOKYO SURGICAL SOCIETY. ABSTRACTS. *see* MEDICAL SCIENCES—Abstracting, Bibliographies, Statistics

617 JPN ISSN 0389-5564
CODEN: GTEIDA
GEKA TO TAISHA EIYO/JAPANESE JOURNAL OF SURGICAL METABOLISM AND NUTRITION. Text in Japanese; Summaries in English, Japanese. 1968. 5/yr. free to members (effective 2007). **Document type:** *Journal, Academic/Scholarly.*
Formerly (until 1981): Jutsugo Taisha Kenkyukaishi (0389-5556)
Indexed: CIN, ChemAb, ChemTitl.
—BLDSC (4658.863000), CASDDS.
Published by: Jutsugo Taisha Kenkyukai/Japanese Society for Surgical Metabolism and Nutrition, c/o Kagoshima University Hospital, Department of Pediatric Surgery, 8-35-1 Sakuragaoka, Kagoshima, 890-8520, Japan. TEL 81-99-2755441, FAX 81-99-2752628, mimuray@m.u-tokyo.ac.jp.

GENERAL SURGERY CODING ALERT; your practical adviser for ethically optimizing coding reimbursement and efficiency in general surgery practices. *see* INSURANCE

617 USA ISSN 1099-4122
GENERAL SURGERY NEWS. Text in English. 1972. m. USD 70 domestic; USD 90 foreign; USD 7 per issue domestic; USD 10 per issue foreign; free to qualified personnel (effective 2010). adv. back issues avail. **Document type:** *Newspaper, Trade.* **Description:** Features meeting coverage, analysis of journal articles, educational reviews, and information on new drugs and products.
Former titles (until 1997): General Surgery and Laparoscopy News (1065-7088); (until 1991): General Surgery News; (until 1989): Surgical Practice News (0273-7655); (until 1980): Journal of Surgical Practice (0161-9721); (until 1977): Surgical Team (0091-6277)
Related titles: Online - full text ed.
Indexed: P30.
—CCC.
Published by: McMahon Group, 545 W 45th St, 8th Fl, New York, NY 10036. TEL 212-957-5300, FAX 212-957-7230, info@mcmahongroup.com, http://www.mcmahongroup.com. Ed. Kevin Horty TEL 212-957-5300 ext 262. Pub. Raymond E McMahon. Adv. contact Michael Enright TEL 212-957-5300 ext 272. Circ: 38,262.

617.54 JPN ISSN 1863-6705
CODEN: NKZAAY
GENERAL THORACIC AND CARDIOVASCULAR SURGERY. Text in English. 1953. m. EUR 299, USD 364 combined subscription to institutions (print & online eds.) (effective 2012). reprint service avail. from PSC. **Document type:** *Journal, Academic/Scholarly.*
Former titles: The Japanese Journal of Thoracic and Cardiovascular Surgery (1344-4964); (until 1998): Nihon Kyobu Geka Gakkai Zasshi / Japanese Association for Thoracic Surgery. Journal (0369-4739)
Related titles: Online - full text ed.: ISSN 1863-6713 (from IngentaConnect).
Indexed: A22, A26, E01, E08, EMBASE, ExcerpMed, INIS AtomInd, IndMed, MEDLINE, P30, R10, Reac, RefZh, S09, SCOPUS.
—BLDSC (4111.525000), GNLM, IE, Infotrieve, Ingenta, INIST. **CCC.**
Published by: (Japanese Association for Thoracic Surgery), Springer Japan KK (Subsidiary of: Springer Science+Business Media), No 2 Funato Bldg, 1-11-11 Kudan-kita, Chiyoda-ku, Tokyo, 102-0073, Japan. TEL 81-3-68317000, FAX 81-3-68317001, orders@springer.jp, http://www.springer.jp. Ed. Shinichiro Miyoshi.

617.95 618.97 USA ISSN 2151-4585
▼ ➤ **GERIATRIC ORTHOPAEDIC SURGERY & REHABILITATION.** Text in English. 2010 (Mar.). bi-m. USD 510, GBP 300 combined subscription to institutions (print & online eds.); USD 500, GBP 294 to institutions (effective 2011). **Document type:** *Journal, Academic/Scholarly.* **Description:** Provides clinical information concerning musculoskeletal conditions affecting the aging population.

Related titles: Online - full text ed.: ISSN 2151-4593. 2010. USD 459, GBP 270 to institutions (effective 2011).
—CCC.
Published by: Sage Publications, Inc., 2455 Teller Rd, Thousand Oaks, CA 91320. Ed. Dr. Stephen L Kates.

616 ITA ISSN 0391-9005
IL GIORNALE DI CHIRURGIA. Text in Italian; Summaries in English. 1980. 10/yr. EUR 80 domestic; USD 110 foreign (effective 2008). adv. **Document type:** *Journal, Academic/Scholarly.*
Related titles: Online - full text ed.: ISSN 1971-145X.
Indexed: A22, EMBASE, ExcerpMed, IndMed, MEDLINE, P30, R10, Reac, RefZh, SCOPUS.
—BLDSC (4177.350000), GNLM, IE, Infotrieve, Ingenta, INIST. **CCC.**
Published by: (Societa Italiana di Ricerche in Chirurgia), C I C Edizioni Internazionali, Corso Trieste 42, Rome, 00198, Italy. TEL 39-06-8412673, FAX 39-06-8412688, info@gruppocic.it, http://www.gruppocic.it. adv.: B&W page EUR 1,239.50, color page EUR 1,704.31; 210 x 280.

617 RUS ISSN 0236-2791
CODEN: GSKHEV
GRUDNAYA I SERDECHNO-SOSUDISTAYA KHIRURGIYA/CHEST AND CARDIOVASCULAR SURGERY. Text in Russian; Summaries in English. 1959. bi-m. USD 174 foreign (effective 2005). adv. bk.rev.; Website rev. bibl. index. reprints avail. **Document type:** *Journal, Academic/Scholarly.* **Description:** Publishes original articles, reviews on new trends in the field of chest and cardiovascular surgery and related subjects.
Formerly: Grudnaya Khirurgiya (0017-4866)
Indexed: IndMed, P30, RefZh.
—East View, GNLM, INIST. **CCC.**
Published by: Izdatel'stvo Meditsina/Meditsina Publishers, ul B Pirogovskaya, d 2, str 5, Moscow, 119435, Russian Federation. TEL 7-095-2483324, meditsina@mtu-net.ru, http://www.medlit.ru. Ed. Viktor S Savel'ev. Pub. A M Stochik. R&P T Ivanova. Adv. contact O A Fadeeva TEL 7-095-923-51-40. Circ: 700. **Dist. by:** M K - Periodica, ul Gilyarovskogo 39, Moscow 129110, Russian Federation. TEL 7-095-2845008, FAX 7-095-2813798, info@periodicals.ru, http://www.mkniga.ru.

617 CHN ISSN 1000-6877
GUOWAI YIXUE (WAIKEXUE FENCE)/FOREIGN MEDICAL SCIENCES (SURGERY). Text in Chinese. 1974. bi-m. **Document type:** *Journal, Academic/Scholarly.*
Related titles: Online - full text ed.
Published by: Beijing Youyi Yiyuan, 95, Yongan Lu, Beijing, 100050, China. TEL 86-10-63014411 ext 3570, FAX 86-10-63015633. **Dist. by:** China International Book Trading Corp, 35 Chegongzhuang Xilu, Haidian District, PO Box 399, Beijing 100044, China. TEL 86-10-68412045, FAX 86-10-68412023, cibtc@mail.cibtc.com.cn, http://www.cibtc.com.cn.

618.1 DEU ISSN 1613-2076
RG104
➤ **GYNECOLOGICAL SURGERY**; endoscopy, imaging, and allied techniques. Text in English. 2004. 4/yr. EUR 709, USD 949 combined subscription to institutions (print & online eds.) (effective 2012). reprint service avail. from PSC. **Document type:** *Journal, Academic/Scholarly.* **Description:** Provides a forum for the description and discussion of various aspects of interventional endoscopy and ultrasound as integral elements of surgical practice.
Related titles: Online - full text ed.: ISSN 1613-2084 (from IngentaConnect).
Indexed: A22, A26, E01, EMBASE, ExcerpMed, P30, R10, Reac, SCOPUS.
—BLDSC (4233.735500), IE, Ingenta. **CCC.**
Published by: Springer (Subsidiary of: Springer Science+Business Media), Tiergartenstr 17, Heidelberg, 69121, Germany. TEL 49-6221-4870, FAX 49-6221-345229, subscriptions@springer.com. Ed. Ivo L Brosens.

617 USA ISSN 0894-8569
RD546 CODEN: HPBSE9
➤ **H P B SURGERY**; a world journal of hepatic, pancreatic, and biliary surgery. Text in English. 1988. irreg. USD 195 (effective 2011). **Document type:** *Journal, Academic/Scholarly.* **Description:** Covers important developments in the field of HPB surgery and associated disciplines.
Related titles: Online - full text ed.: ISSN 1607-8462. free (effective 2011).
Indexed: A01, A22, CA, IndMed, P30, SCOPUS, T02.
—GNLM, IE, Infotrieve, Ingenta. **CCC.**
Published by: Hindawi Publishing Corporation, 410 Park Ave, 15th Fl, PMB 287, New York, NY 10022. FAX 215-893-4392, 866-446-3294, info@hindawi.com.

617 USA ISSN 1556-3316
➤ **H S S JOURNAL.** (Hospital for Special Surgery) Text in English. 1975. s-a. EUR 422, USD 515 combined subscription to institutions (print & online eds.) (effective 2012). back issues avail.; reprint service avail. from PSC. **Document type:** *Journal, Academic/Scholarly.* **Description:** Brings out articles that offer contributions to the advancement of the knowledge of musculoskeletal diseases and encourages submission of manuscripts from all musculoskeletal disciplines.
Formerly (until 2005): Hospital for Special Surgery. Journal (0362-0727)
Related titles: Online - full text ed.: ISSN 1556-3324 (from IngentaConnect).
Indexed: A22, A26, E01, P20, P24, P30, P48, P54, PQC, SCOPUS.
—BLDSC (4335.344650), IE, Ingenta. **CCC.**
Published by: (Hospital for Special Surgery), Springer New York LLC (Subsidiary of: Springer Science+Business Media), 233 Spring St, New York, NY 10013. TEL 212-460-1500, FAX 212-460-1575, service-ny@springer.com. Ed. Charles N Cornell.

➤ **HAMAMATSU SEIKEI GEKA KIYO/HAMAMATSU UNIVERSITY. ANNUAL OF ORTHOPAEDIC SURGERY.** *see* MEDICAL SCIENCES—Orthopedics And Traumatology

617 USA ISSN 1558-9447
➤ **HAND (NEW YORK).** Text in English. 2006. q. EUR 478, USD 573 combined subscription to institutions (print & online eds.) (effective 2012). back issues avail.; reprint service avail. from PSC. **Document type:** *Journal, Academic/Scholarly.* **Description:** Features articles written by clinicians worldwide presenting current research and clinical work in the field of hand surgery.
Related titles: Online - full text ed.: ISSN 1558-9455 (from IngentaConnect).
Indexed: A22, A26, E01, P30, SCOPUS.
—IE, Ingenta. **CCC.**
Published by: (American Association for Hand Surgery), Springer New York LLC (Subsidiary of: Springer Science+Business Media), 233 Spring St, New York, NY 10013. TEL 212-460-1500, FAX 212-460-1575, service-ny@springer.com. Ed. Michael Neumeister.

617 SGP ISSN 0218-8104
RD559
➤ **HAND SURGERY.** Abbreviated title: H S. Text in English. 1996. 3/yr. SGD 580, USD 363, EUR 293 combined subscription to institutions (print & online eds.) (effective 2012). adv. back issues avail. **Document type:** *Journal, Academic/Scholarly.* **Description:** Covers injury and disease of the hand and upper limb and related research in scientific articles, including case reports, articles on surgical techniques, letters to the Editor, and information regarding meetings and education programmes.
Related titles: Online - full text ed.: ISSN 1793-6535. SGD 527, USD 330, EUR 266 to institutions (effective 2012).
Indexed: A01, A03, A08, A22, B21, CA, CTA, E01, EMBASE, ExcerpMed, IndMed, MEDLINE, P30, R10, Reac, SCOPUS, T02.
—BLDSC (4241.595500), IE, Ingenta. **CCC.**
Published by: (Asia-Pacific Federation of Societies for Surgery of the Hand), World Scientific Publishing Co. Pte. Ltd., 5 Toh Tuck Link, Singapore, 596224, Singapore. TEL 65-6466-5775, FAX 65-6467-7667, wspc@wspc.com.sg, http://www.worldscientific.com. Ed. A Minami TEL 81-11-7065933. **Dist. by:** World Scientific Publishing Co., Inc., 27 Warren St, Ste 401-402, Hackensack, NJ 07601. TEL 201-487-9655, 800-227-7562, FAX 201-487-9656, 888-977-2665, wspc@wspc.com; World Scientific Publishing Ltd., 57 Shelton St, London WC2H 9HE, United Kingdom. TEL 44-207-8360888, FAX 44-207-8362020, sales@wspc.co.uk.

617.95 DEU ISSN 0722-1819
RD559 CODEN: HMPCD9
HANDCHIRURGIE - MIKROCHIRURGIE - PLASTISCHE CHIRURGIE. Text in German. 1982. bi-m. EUR 299 to institutions; EUR 400 combined subscription to institutions (print & online eds.); EUR 56 newsstand/cover (effective 2011). adv. **Document type:** *Journal, Academic/Scholarly.*
Formed by the merger of (1969-1982): Handchirurgie (0046-6794); (1977-1982): Zeitschrift fuer Plastische Chirurgie (0342-7978)
Related titles: Online - full text ed.: EUR 387 to institutions (effective 2011).
Indexed: A22, CurCont, DentInd, EMBASE, ExcerpMed, IndMed, MEDLINE, P30, R10, Reac, SCI, SCOPUS, W07.
—BLDSC (4254.577000), GNLM, IE, Infotrieve, Ingenta, INIST. **CCC.**
Published by: Hippokrates Verlag in MVS Medizinverlage Stuttgart GmbH & Co.KG (Subsidiary of: Georg Thieme Verlag), Oswald-Hesse-Str 50, Stuttgart, 70469, Germany. TEL 49-711-89310, FAX 49-711-8931706, kunden.service@thieme.de, http://www.medizinverlage.de. Eds. U Lanz, W Schneider. Adv. contact Christine Volpp. **Co-sponsors:** Deutschsprachige Arbeitsgemeinschaft fuer Handchirurgie; Deutschsprachige Arbeitsgemeinschaft fuer Mikrochirurgie der Peripheren Nerven; Oesterreichischen; Deutsche Gesellschaft fuer Handchirurgie; Verein der Deutschen Plastischen Chirurgie.

617 CHN ISSN 1009-5187
HANGKONG JUNYI/FLIGHT SURGEON. Text in Chinese. 1957. bi-m. USD 24.60 (effective 2009). **Document type:** *Journal, Academic/Scholarly.*
Related titles: Online - full text ed.
—East View.
Published by: Kongjun Hangkong Yixue Yanjiusuo, 28, Fucheng Lu, Beijing, 100036, China. **Dist. by:** China International Book Trading Corp, 35 Chegongzhuang Xilu, Haidian District, PO Box 399, Beijing 100044, China. TEL 86-10-68412045, FAX 86-10-68412023, cibtc@mail.cibtc.com.cn, http://www.cibtc.com.cn.

617 USA ISSN 1043-3074
RD523 CODEN: HEANEE
➤ **HEAD & NECK**; journal for the sciences and specialities of the head and neck. Text in English. 1978. m. GBP 1,185 in United Kingdom to institutions; EUR 1,498 in Europe to institutions; USD 2,067 in United States to institutions; USD 2,235 in Canada & Mexico to institutions; USD 2,319 elsewhere to institutions; GBP 1,364 combined subscription in United Kingdom to institutions (print & online eds.); EUR 1,725 combined subscription in Europe to institutions (print & online eds.); USD 2,378 combined subscription in United States to institutions (print & online eds.); USD 2,546 combined subscription in Canada & Mexico to institutions (print & online eds.); USD 2,630 combined subscription elsewhere to institutions (print & online eds.) (effective 2012). adv. bk.rev. abstr.; charts; illus.; stat. index. 90 p./no. 2 cols./p.; back issues avail.; reprint service avail. from PSC. **Document type:** *Journal, Academic/Scholarly.* **Description:** Examines the management and prevention of all diseases in the head and neck area, including benign and malignant tumors, congenital deformities, and trauma.
Formerly (until 1989): Head and Neck Surgery (0148-6403)
Related titles: Microform ed.: (from PQC); Online - full text ed.: ISSN 1097-0347. 1978. GBP 1,056 in United Kingdom to institutions; EUR 1,335 in Europe to institutions; USD 2,067 elsewhere to institutions (effective 2012).
Indexed: A22, ASCA, B21, B25, BIOSIS Prev, CA, CTA, CurCont, EMBASE, ExcerpMed, FR, ISR, IndMed, Inpharma, MEDLINE, MycolAb, NSA, P30, P35, R10, Reac, SCI, SCOPUS, T02, W07.
—BLDSC (4274.608500), GNLM, IE, Infotrieve, Ingenta, INIST. **CCC.**
Published by: John Wiley & Sons, Inc., 111 River St, Hoboken, NJ 07030. TEL 201-748-6000, FAX 201-748-6088, info@wiley.com, http://www.wiley.com/WileyCDA/. Ed. Ehab Y Hanna. Adv. contact Kim Thompkins TEL 212-850-6921. **Subscr. outside the Americas to:** John Wiley & Sons Ltd., The Atrium, Southern Gate, Chichester, West Sussex PO19 8SQ, United Kingdom. TEL 44-1243-779777, 800-243407, FAX 44-1243-775878, cs-journals@wiley.com.

617 ITA ISSN 1970-8254
HELIOS. Text in Italian. 1995. s-a. free (effective 2007). **Document type:** *Journal, Academic/Scholarly.*
Related titles: Online - full text ed.: ISSN 1970-8246. 1999.
Published by: C I C Edizioni Internazionali, Corso Trieste 42, Rome, 00198, Italy. TEL 39-06-8412673, FAX 39-06-8412688, info@gruppocic.it, http://www.gruppocic.it.

617 AUT
➤ **HELLENIC JOURNAL OF SURGERY.** Text in Greek. 1929. bi-m. EUR 383, USD 515 combined subscription to institutions (print & online eds.) (effective 2012). **Document type:** *Journal, Academic/Scholarly.*
Formerly: Hellenike Cheirougike (0018-0092)
Related titles: Online - full text ed.: ISSN 1868-8845.
Indexed: A22, E01, P30.
—GNLM, IE. **CCC.**
Published by: Springer Wien (Subsidiary of: Springer Science+Business Media), Sachsenplatz 4-6, Vienna, W 1201, Austria. TEL 43-1-33024150, FAX 43-1-3302426, springer@springer.at, http://www.springer.at. Ed. C Karaliotas.

617 FRA ISSN 1265-4906
RD621 CODEN: HERNFW
➤ **HERNIA**; the journal of hernias and abdominal wall surgery. Text in English. 1997. q. EUR 733, USD 863 combined subscription to institutions (print & online eds.) (effective 2012). reprint service avail. from PSC. **Document type:** *Journal, Academic/Scholarly.* **Description:** Promotes research and fundamental studies on groin hernias as well as on surgery of the anterior and postero-lateral walls of the abdominal cavity, diaphragm and perineum.
Related titles: Online - full text ed.: ISSN 1248-9204 (from IngentaConnect).
Indexed: A01, A03, A08, A22, A26, C06, C07, CA, CurCont, E01, EMBASE, ExcerpMed, H12, MEDLINE, P30, P48, PQC, R10, Reac, SCI, SCOPUS, T02, W07.
—BLDSC (4300.154100), IE, Infotrieve, Ingenta, INIST. **CCC.**
Published by: (Groupe de Recherche Europien de la Paroi Abdominale DEU), Springer France (Subsidiary of: Springer Science+Business Media), 22 Rue de Palestro, Paris, 75002, France. TEL 33-1-53009860, FAX 33-1-53009861, sylvie.kamara@springer.com. Eds. R J Fitzgibbons, Dr. V Schumpelick. Adv. contact Stephan Kroeck TEL 49-30-827875739. **Subscr. in Americas to:** Springer New York LLC, Journal Fulfillment, PO Box 2485, Secaucus, NJ 07096. TEL 800-777-4643, 201-348-4033, FAX 201-348-4505, journals-ny@springer.com, http://www.springer.com; **Subscr. to:** Springer Distribution Center, Kundenservice Zeitschriften, Haberstr 7, Heidelberg 69126, Germany. TEL 49-6221-3454303, FAX 49-6221-3454229, subscriptions@springer.com. **Co-sponsor:** American Hernia Society.

617 RUS ISSN 1810-8997
➤ **HIRURGIA POZVONOCHNIKA.** Text in Russian; Summaries in English, Russian. 2004. q. RUR 1,920 domestic to individuals; RUR 2,400 foreign to individuals; RUR 2,600 domestic to institutions; RUR 3,600 foreign to institutions; RUR 480 per issue domestic; RUR 800 per issue foreign (effective 2009). **Document type:** *Journal, Academic/Scholarly.* **Description:** Publishes original clinical and research articles related to spine surgery for Russian speaking specialists in spine medicine, covering new treatment and diagnostic techniques, anesthesiology, neurosurgery, rehabilitation, biomechanics, morphology etc.
Related titles: Online - full text ed.
Indexed: RefZh.
Published by: Novosibirskij Naucno-issledovatel'skij Institut Travmatologii i Ortopedii/The Novosibirsk Scientific Research Institute of Traumatology and Orthopedy, 17 Frunze Str., Novosibirsk, 630091, Russian Federation. TEL 7-383-2011134, FAX 7-383-2245570, niito@niito.ru, http://www.niito.ru/. Ed. Nikolay N. Fomichev. Pub. Olga E. Kostuykova.

617 JPN ISSN 0288-7509
HOKKAIDO GEKA ZASSHI/HOKKAIDO JOURNAL OF SURGERY. Text in Japanese; Summaries in English, Japanese. 1952. s-a. **Document type:** *Journal, Academic/Scholarly.*
Formerly (until 1962): Nippon Geka Gakkai Hokkaido Chihokaishi (0288-7495)
Indexed: INIS AtomInd.
Published by: Hokkaido Geka Gakkai/Hokkaido Surgical Society, Hokkaido Daigaku Igakubu, Nishi 7-chome, Kita 5-jo, Kita-ku, Sapporo-shi, Hokkaido 060, Japan.

617 JPN ISSN 0913-7629
➤ **HOKURIKU GEKA GAKKAI ZASSHI/HOKURIKU JOURNAL OF SURGERY.** Text in Japanese; Summaries in English. 1982. a. JPY 3,000 (effective 2001). reprints avail. **Document type:** *Academic/Scholarly.*
Published by: Hokuriku Geka Gakkai/Hokuriku Surgical Society, Kanazawa University School of Medicine, Department of Surgery, 13-1, Takaramachi, Kanazawa-shi, Ishikawa-ken 920-8641, Japan. TEL 81-76-265-2354, FAX 81-76-222-6833, go@med.kanazawa-u.ac.jp. Ed., R&P Go Watanabe. Circ: 1,000.

➤ **HOSPITAL DENTISTRY & ORAL-MAXILLOFACIAL SURGERY.** *see* MEDICAL SCIENCES—Dentistry

617 MEX
HOSPITAL JUAREZ DE MEXICO. REVISTA. Text in Spanish. 1930. q. MXN 200 domestic; USD 60 foreign (effective 2005). back issues avail. **Document type:** *Journal, Trade.*
Former titles: Revista de Cirugia del Hospital Juarez (0187-5701); Revista de Cirugia (0370-7830)
Related titles: Online - full text ed.
Published by: Sociedad de Cirugia del Hospital Juarez de Mexico, Ave Instituto Politecnico Nacional No 5160, Col. Magdalena de las Salinas, Mexico, D.F., 07760, Mexico. TEL 52-55-5747-7611, hjm@liceaga.facmed.unam.mx, http://www.famed.unam.mx/hjm/. Ed. Gustavo Acosta Altamirano.

617 JPN
HYOGOKEN ZENGEKAIKAI KAISHI/HYOGO ASSOCIATION OF SURGEONS. JOURNAL. Text in Japanese. 1962. irreg. **Document type:** *Journal, Academic/Scholarly.*
Former titles (until 1977): Hyogo-ken Zen Geka Ikai (0385-5325); (until 1976): Hyogo-ken Geka Seikei Geka Ikai/Hyogo Association of Surgeons and Orthopedic Surgeons. Journal; (until 1968): Hyogo-ken Geka Ikai/Hyogo Association of Surgeons. Journal
Published by: Hyogoken Zengeka Ikai/Hyogo Association of Surgeons, 1-30 Nakayamatedori 6-chome, Chuo-ku, Kobe-shi, Hyogo-ken 650-0004, Japan.

617.95 USA ISSN 1942-5023
I S A P S NEWS. Text in English. 2007. 4/yr. free to members (effective 2010). back issues avail. **Document type:** *Newsletter, Trade.*
Description: Provides cutting edge clinical information for plastic surgeons worldwide, including trends, professional development information, conferences, committees and volunteerism.
Related titles: Online - full text ed.: ISSN 1942-5031. free (effective 2010).
Published by: (International Society of Aesthetic Plastic Surgery), Quality Medical Publishing, Inc., 2248 Welsch Industrial Ct, Saint Louis, MO 63146. TEL 314-878-7808, 800-348-7808, FAX 314-878-9937, qmp@qmp.com, http://www.qmp.com. Ed. J Peter Rubin.

I S C T S - WORLD SOCIETY OF CARDIO - THORACIC SURGEONS. ANNUAL MEETING. *see* MEDICAL SCIENCES—Cardiovascular Diseases

617 USA ISSN 2090-5785
▼ ➤ **I S R N SURGERY.** (International Scholarly Research Network) Text in English. 2011. **Document type:** *Journal, Academic/Scholarly.*
Description: Publishes original research articles, review articles, and clinical studies in all areas of surgery, including plastic and reconstructive surgery as well as oral and maxillofacial surgery.
Related titles: Online - full text ed.: ISSN 2090-5793. 2011. free (effective 2011).
Published by: Hindawi Publishing Corporation, 410 Park Ave, 15th Fl, PMB 287, New York, NY 10022. FAX 215-893-4392, 866-446-3294, info@hindawi.com.

617 JPN ISSN 0917-9070
ICHIGE/JUNTENDO UNIVERSITY. CLINICAL SURGERY SOCIETY. JOURNAL. Text in Japanese. 2/yr.
Published by: (Daiichi Geka Rinsho Kenkyukai), Juntendo Daigaku, Igakubu, 1-1 Hongo 2-chome, Bunkyo-ku, Tokyo, 113-0033, Japan.

INDIAN ASSOCIATION OF PEDIATRIC SURGEONS. JOURNAL. *see* MEDICAL SCIENCES—Pediatrics

617 IND ISSN 0971-7927
INDIAN JOURNAL OF OCTOLARYNGOLOGY AND HEAD AND NECK SURGERY. Text in English. 19??. q. **Document type:** *Journal, Academic/Scholarly.*
Indexed: EconLit, GEOBASE, IBSS, JEL.
Published by: Scientific Publishers, 5-A, New Pali Rd, PO Box 91, Jodhpur, Rajasthan 342 001, India. TEL 91-291-2433323, FAX 91-291-2624154, info@scientificpub.com, http://www.scientificpub.com.

617.95 IND ISSN 0970-0358
➤ **INDIAN JOURNAL OF PLASTIC SURGERY.** Text in English. 1967. s-a. INR 2,000 domestic to individuals; USD 200 foreign to individuals; INR 2,400 combined subscription domestic to institutions (print & online eds.); USD 240 combined subscription foreign to institutions (print & online eds.) (effective 2011). adv. bk.rev. abstr.; bibl.; illus. back issues avail.; reprint service avail. from IRC. **Document type:** *Journal, Academic/Scholarly.* **Description:** Deals with topics in plastic surgery.
Related titles: Online - full text ed.: ISSN 1998-376X. free (effective 2011).
Indexed: A01, A03, A08, A26, CA, E08, G08, H11, H12, I05, P10, P20, P30, P48, P53, P54, PQC, S09, SCOPUS, T02.
—IE. **CCC.**
Published by: (Association of Plastic Surgeons of India), Medknow Publications and Media Pvt. Ltd., B-9, Kanara Business Ctr, Off Link Rd, Ghatkopar (E), Mumbai, Maharastra 400 075, India. TEL 91-22-66491816, FAX 91-22-66491818, publishing@medknow.com, http://www.medknow.com. Ed. Dr. Surajit Bhattacharya TEL 91-522-2380550. adv.: B&W page INR 6,000, color page INR 12,500; trim 280 x 210. Circ: 1,200.

617 IND ISSN 0972-2068
RD1 CODEN: IJSUAV
➤ **INDIAN JOURNAL OF SURGERY.** Text in English. 1939. m. EUR 324, USD 389 combined subscription to institutions (print & online eds.) (effective 2012). adv. bk.rev. charts; illus. **Document type:** *Journal, Academic/Scholarly.*
Related titles: Online - full text ed.: ISSN 0973-9793. 2002 (from IngentaConnect).
Indexed: A01, A03, A08, A22, A26, A35, A36, C06, C07, CA, CABA, ChemAb, D01, E08, E12, G08, GH, H11, H12, I05, N02, N03, P10, P20, P30, P33, PQC, S09, SCI, SCOPUS, T02, T05, TAR, W07.
—GNLM, IE. **CCC.**
Published by: (Association of Surgeons in India), Springer (India) Private Ltd. (Subsidiary of: Springer Science+Business Media), 212, Deen Dayal Upadhyaya Marg, 3rd Fl, Gandharva Mahavidyalaya, New Delhi, 110 002, India. TEL 91-11-45755888, FAX 91-11-45755889. Ed. S Shukla. Circ: 10,000. **Subscr. to:** I N S I O Scientific Books & Periodicals, PO Box 7234, Indraprastha HPO, New Delhi 110 002, India. iihm@ap.nic.in, http://iihm.ap.nic.in/.

▼ ➤ **INDIAN JOURNAL OF SURGICAL ONCOLOGY.** *see* MEDICAL SCIENCES—Oncology

➤ **INDIAN JOURNAL OF THORACIC AND CARDIOVASCULAR SURGERY.** *see* MEDICAL SCIENCES—Cardiovascular Diseases

➤ **INNOVATIONS (PHILADELPHIA);** technology and techniques in cardiothoracic and vascular surgery. *see* MEDICAL SCIENCES—Cardiovascular Diseases

617 616.1 GBR ISSN 1569-9293
CODEN: ICTSCH
INTERACTIVE CARDIOVASCULAR AND THORACIC SURGERY. Text in English. 2002. m. GBP 232 in United Kingdom to institutions; EUR 317 in Europe to institutions; USD 388 in US & Canada to institutions; GBP 232 to institutions in the UK & elsewhere (effective 2012). adv. **Document type:** *Journal, Academic/Scholarly.* **Description:** Covers all aspects of surgery of the heart, great vessels, and the chest.
Related titles: Online - full text ed.: ISSN 1569-9285 (from IngentaConnect); ♦ Issued with: European Journal of Cardio-Thoracic Surgery. ISSN 1010-7940.
Indexed: EMBASE, ExcerpMed, MEDLINE, P30, R10, Reac, SCOPUS.
—BLDSC (4531.871920), IE, Ingenta. **CCC.**
Published by: (European Association for Cardio-Thoracic Surgery CHE), Oxford University Press, Great Clarendon St, Oxford, OX2 6DP, United Kingdom. TEL 44-1865-556767, FAX 44-1865-556646, enquiry@oup.co.uk, http://www.oxfordjournals.org. Ed. Ludwig K von Segesser.

INTERNATIONAL JOURNAL OF ANGIOLOGY. *see* MEDICAL SCIENCES—Cardiovascular Diseases

617 DEU ISSN 0179-1958
RC860 CODEN: IJCDE6
➤ **INTERNATIONAL JOURNAL OF COLORECTAL DISEASE;** clinical and molecular gastroenterology and surgery. Text in English. 1986. bi-m. EUR 2,219, USD 2,629 combined subscription to institutions (print & online eds.) (effective 2012). adv. reprint service avail. from PSC. **Document type:** *Journal, Academic/Scholarly.* **Description:** Includes clinical and laboratory research in the field with sections devoted to symposia and reviews of subjects of topical interest.
Related titles: Online - full text ed.: ISSN 1432-1262 (from IngentaConnect).
Indexed: A01, A03, A08, A22, A26, A35, A36, ASCA, AgBio, Agr, B25, BIOSIS Prev, CA, CABA, CurCont, D01, E01, E12, EMBASE, ExcerpMed, F08, FR, GH, H12, H17, IndMed, Inpharma, MEDLINE, MycolAb, N02, N03, P20, P22, P30, P33, P35, P48, P54, PQC, R10, R12, RA&MP, Reac, SCI, SCOPUS, SoyAb, T02, T05, VS, W07.
—BLDSC (4542.172400), GNLM, IE, Infotrieve, Ingenta, INIST. **CCC.**
Published by: (Association of Coloproctology of Great Britain and Ireland GBR), Springer (Subsidiary of: Springer Science+Business Media), Tiergartenstr 17, Heidelberg, 69121, Germany. TEL 49-6221-4870, FAX 49-6221-345229, subscriptions@springer.com. Ed. Dr. H J Buhr. **Subscr. in the Americas to:** Springer New York LLC, Journal Fulfillment, PO Box 2485, Secaucus, NJ 07096. TEL 201-348-4033, FAX 201-348-4505, journals-ny@springer.com; **Subscr. to:** Springer Distribution Center, Kundenservice Zeitschriften, Haberstr 7, Heidelberg 69126, Germany. TEL 49-6221-3454303, FAX 49-6221-345-4229, 49-6221-3454229.

➤ **INTERNATIONAL JOURNAL OF COMPUTER ASSISTED RADIOLOGY AND SURGERY.** *see* MEDICAL SCIENCES—Radiology And Nuclear Medicine

617 IND ISSN 0975-7899
▼ ➤ **INTERNATIONAL JOURNAL OF HEAD AND NECK SURGERY.** Text in English. 2010. 3/yr. INR 3,000 domestic to individuals; USD 180 foreign to individuals; INR 4,500 domestic to institutions; USD 250 foreign to institutions (effective 2010). adv. bk.rev. Index. reprints avail. **Document type:** *Journal, Academic/Scholarly.* **Description:** Provides information on topics related to head/neck cancers and disorders by a multi-disciplinary approach to treat cancer and present it in an evidence based format such as review articles, debates, guest editorials, etc. Combines inputs from otolaryngologist, plastic/oral/maxilofacial/oculoplastic surgeons, prosthodontists and speech therapists.
Related titles: Online - full text ed.: ISSN 0976-0539.
Indexed: A01, P20, PQC.
Published by: Jaypee Brothers Medical Publishers Pvt. Ltd., 4838/24, Ansari Rd, Daryaganj, New Delhi, 110 002, India. TEL 91-11-43574357, FAX 91-11-43574314, jaypee@jaypeebrothers.com, http://www.jaypeebrothers.com. Ed. Chris de Souza. Pub. Rohit Gorawara. R&P Chetna Malhotra. Adv. contact Rakesh Sheoran TEL 91-997-1020680. Circ: 2,500.

➤ **INTERNATIONAL JOURNAL OF MEDICAL ROBOTICS AND COMPUTER ASSISTED SURGERY.** *see* MEDICAL SCIENCES—Experimental Medicine, Laboratory Technique

➤ **INTERNATIONAL JOURNAL OF ORAL AND MAXILLOFACIAL SURGERY.** *see* MEDICAL SCIENCES—Dentistry

617 IRN ISSN 2008-6482
▼ **INTERNATIONAL JOURNAL OF ORGAN TRANSPLANTATION MEDICINE.** Text in English. 2009. q. **Document type:** *Journal, Academic/Scholarly.*
Related titles: Online - full text ed.: ISSN 2008-6490. free (effective 2011).
Published by: Avicenna Organ Transplant Center, Phase #2, Dokohak Rd, Sadra Town, Shiraz, Fars 71994-67985, Iran. http://booali.org. Ed. Seyed Ali Malek-Hosseini.

INTERNATIONAL JOURNAL OF PERIODONTICS & RESTORATIVE DENTISTRY. *see* MEDICAL SCIENCES—Dentistry

617.95 IND ISSN 0973-6042
RD557.5
➤ **INTERNATIONAL JOURNAL OF SHOULDER SURGERY.** Text in English. 2007. q. INR 2,000 domestic; USD 250 foreign; INR 2,400 combined subscription domestic (print & online eds.); USD 300 combined subscription foreign (print & online eds.) (effective 2011). bk.rev. abstr. reprints avail. **Document type:** *Journal, Academic/Scholarly.* **Description:** Covers basic science, diagnostic and therapeutic aspects of disorders of the shoulder girdle.
Related titles: Online - full text ed.: INR 1,600 domestic; USD 200 foreign (effective 2011).
Indexed: A01, A26, CA, I05, P30, P48, P54, T02.
—IE. **CCC.**
Published by: (Cape Shoulder Institute ZAF), Medknow Publications and Media Pvt. Ltd., B-9, Kanara Business Ctr, Off Link Rd, Ghatkopar (E), Mumbai, Maharastra 400 075, India. TEL 91-22-66491816, FAX 91-22-66491817, http://www.medknow.com.

617 GBR ISSN 1743-9191
INTERNATIONAL JOURNAL OF SURGERY. Text in English. 2003. 6/yr. EUR 519 in Europe to institutions; JPY 71,400 in Japan to institutions; USD 681 elsewhere to institutions (effective 2009). back issues avail. **Document type:** *Journal, Academic/Scholarly.* **Description:** Aims to promote continued developments in surgery through the sharing of knowledge and ideas across all surgical specialities.
Formerly (until 2004): Journal of Surgery (1741-6280)
Related titles: Online - full text ed.: ISSN 1743-9159 (from ScienceDirect).
Indexed: A26, C06, C07, CA, EMBASE, I05, MEDLINE, P30, SCOPUS, T02.
—BLDSC (4542.685050), IE, Ingenta. **CCC.**
Published by: Elsevier Ltd (Subsidiary of: Elsevier Science & Technology), The Blvd, Langford Ln, Kidlington, Oxford, OX5 1GB, United Kingdom. TEL 44-1865-843000, FAX 44-1865-843010, journalscustomerserviceemea@elsevier.com. Ed. David Rosin.

617 GBR ISSN 2210-2612
▼ **INTERNATIONAL JOURNAL OF SURGERY CASE REPORTS.** Text in English. 2010 (May). 8/yr. **Document type:** *Journal, Academic/Scholarly.*
Media: Online - full text (from ScienceDirect).
Indexed: T02.
—**CCC.**
Published by: Elsevier Ltd (Subsidiary of: Elsevier Science & Technology), The Blvd, Langford Ln, Kidlington, Oxford, OX5 1GB, United Kingdom. TEL 44-1865-843000, 44-1865-843434, customerserviceau@elsevier.com, http://www.elsevier.com. Ed. David Rosin.

617 616.992 USA ISSN 2090-1402
▼ ➤ **INTERNATIONAL JOURNAL OF SURGICAL ONCOLOGY.** Text in English. 2009. irreg. USD 195 (effective 2011). **Document type:** *Journal, Academic/Scholarly.* **Description:** Publishes original research articles, review articles, case reports, and clinical studies in all areas of surgical oncology.
Related titles: Online - full text ed.: ISSN 2090-1410. free (effective 2011).
Indexed: A01, T02.
Published by: Hindawi Publishing Corporation, 410 Park Ave, 15th Fl, PMB 287, New York, NY 10022. FAX 215-893-4392, 866-446-3294, info@hindawi.com.

617 USA ISSN 1066-8969
CODEN: IJSPFL
➤ **INTERNATIONAL JOURNAL OF SURGICAL PATHOLOGY.** Text in English. 1993. bi-m. USD 889, GBP 523 to institutions; USD 907, GBP 534 combined subscription to institutions (print & online eds.) (effective 2012). adv. bk.rev. back issues avail.; reprint service avail. from PSC. **Document type:** *Journal, Academic/Scholarly.*
Description: Forum for the communication of scientific information in the field of surgical pathology. Includes studies that emphasize diagnostic and prognostic features involving human tissue.
Related titles: Microfiche ed.: (from PQC); Microfilm ed.: (from PQC); Online - full text ed.: ISSN 1940-2465. USD 816, GBP 481 to institutions (effective 2012).
Indexed: A01, A02, A03, A08, A22, A26, BIOBASE, C11, CA, CurCont, E01, E08, EMBASE, ExcerpMed, G08, H04, H11, H12, I05, IABS, Inpharma, MEDLINE, P20, P22, P26, P30, P48, P54, PQC, R10, Reac, S09, SCI, SCOPUS, T02, W07.
—BLDSC (4542.685300), CASDDS, GNLM, IE, Infotrieve, Ingenta. **CCC.**
Published by: (Australasian, Hong Kong, Spanish, Korean Divisions), Sage Publications, Inc., 2455 Teller Rd, Thousand Oaks, CA 91320. TEL 805-499-9774, 800-818-7243, FAX 805-499-0871, 800-583-2665, info@sagepub.com, http://www.sagepub.com/. Ed. Dr. Juan Rosai.

617 618.92 USA ISSN 0885-6265
INTERNATIONAL PEDIATRICS. Text in English. 1984. m. 64 p./no. 2 cols./p.; back issues avail. **Document type:** *Journal, Academic/Scholarly.* **Description:** Provides an international forum for the exchange of information and ideas encompassed in the field of pediatrics, and provides both general pediatricians and specialists with a single source practical reference. Each issue presents a review of some of the most recent developments in pediatrics and addresses rapidly evolving topics.
Formerly (until 1986): Miami Children's Hospital. Journal
Indexed: A22, EMBASE, ExcerpMed, R10, Reac, SCOPUS.
—BLDSC (4544.896500), IE, Ingenta. **CCC.**
Published by: Miami Children's Hospital, 3100 S W 62nd Ave, Miami, FL 33155. TEL 305-666-6511, 800-432-6837.

617 USA ISSN 0020-8868
CODEN: INTSAO
➤ **INTERNATIONAL SURGERY.** Text in English. 1913. q. USD 165 to individuals; USD 220 to institutions (effective 2010). adv. bk.rev. abstr.; illus. index. reprints avail. **Document type:** *Journal, Academic/Scholarly.* **Description:** Publishes original scientific articles covering important clinical observations, surgical techniques, experimental surgery and research.
Formerly (until 1966): International College of Surgeons. Journal (0096-557X); Incorporated in part (1966-1971): International Surgery Bulletin (0097-5621)
Related titles: Microform ed.: 1913 (from PQC); Online - full text ed.: USD 150 to individuals; USD 200 to institutions (effective 2010).
Indexed: A20, A22, ASCA, ChemAb, CurCont, EMBASE, ExcerpMed, FR, HospLI, IBR, IBZ, IndMed, Inpharma, MEDLINE, P30, P35, R10, Reac, SCI, SCOPUS, W07.
—BLDSC (4550.020000), GNLM, IE, Infotrieve, Ingenta, INIST. **CCC.**
Published by: International College of Surgeons, 1516 N Lake Shore Dr, Chicago, IL 60160. TEL 312-642-3555, FAX 312-787-1624, info@icsglobal.com, http://www.icsglobal.org/. Ed. Nadey Hakim. Adv. contact Max C Downham TEL 312-787-1638. Circ: 3,000.

617.95 USA ISSN 1937-8203
➤ **THE INTERNET JOURNAL OF HAND SURGERY.** Text in English. 2007. s-a. free (effective 2011). **Document type:** *Journal, Academic/Scholarly.*
Media: Online - full text.
Indexed: A01, CA, T02.
Published by: Internet Scientific Publications, Llc., 23 Rippling Creek Dr, Sugar Land, TX 77479. TEL 832-443-1193, FAX 281-240-1533, wenker@ispub.com. Ed. Dominic Power.

617.95 USA ISSN 1937-819X
➤ **THE INTERNET JOURNAL OF HEAD AND NECK SURGERY.** Text in English. 2007. 2/yr. free (effective 2011). **Document type:** *Journal, Academic/Scholarly.*
Media: Online - full text.
Indexed: A01, CA, T02.
Published by: Internet Scientific Publications, Llc., 23 Rippling Creek Dr, Sugar Land, TX 77479. TEL 832-443-1193, FAX 281-240-1533, wenker@ispub.com. Ed. Dr. Sandip Kumar Halder.

610 USA ISSN 2155-739X
▼ ➤ **THE INTERNET JOURNAL OF MICROSURGERY.** Text in English. 2010. s-a. free (effective 2011). **Document type:** *Journal, Trade.*
Media: Online - full text.
Indexed: A01.
Published by: Internet Scientific Publications, Llc., 23 Rippling Creek Dr, Sugar Land, TX 77479. TEL 832-443-1193, FAX 281-240-1533, wenker@ispub.com. Ed. Charbel Moussallem.

617.95 USA ISSN 1937-8254
RD768
➤ **THE INTERNET JOURNAL OF MINIMALLY INVASIVE SPINAL TECHNOLOGY.** Text in English. 2007. 2/yr. free (effective 2010). **Document type:** *Journal, Academic/Scholarly.*
Media: Online - full text.
Indexed: A01, CA, T02.

Published by: Internet Scientific Publications, Llc., 23 Rippling Creek Dr, Sugar Land, TX 77479. TEL 832-443-1193, FAX 281-240-1533, wenker@ispub.com. Ed. Dr. John Chui.

617.48 USA ISSN 1528-8285
RD593

➤ **THE INTERNET JOURNAL OF NEUROSURGERY.** Text in English. 2002. s-a. free (effective 2011). bk.rev. back issues avail. **Document type:** *Journal, Academic/Scholarly.* **Description:** Contains information from the field of neurosurgery and spine orthopedic surgery, including original articles, reviews, case reports, streaming slide shows, streaming videos, letters to the editor, press releases, and meeting information.
Media: Online - full text.
Indexed: A01, A02, A03, A08, A26, C06, C07, CA, G08, H11, H12, I05, T02.
Published by: Internet Scientific Publications, Llc., 23 Rippling Creek Dr, Sugar Land, TX 77479. TEL 832-443-1193, FAX 281-240-1533, wenker@ispub.com. Ed. Ehud Mendel.

➤ **THE INTERNET JOURNAL OF ORTHOPEDIC SURGERY.** *see* MEDICAL SCIENCES—Orthopedics And Traumatology

➤ **THE INTERNET JOURNAL OF PERFUSIONISTS.** *see* MEDICAL SCIENCES—Cardiovascular Diseases

617.95 USA ISSN 1528-8293
RD118.A1

➤ **THE INTERNET JOURNAL OF PLASTIC SURGERY.** Text in English. 2001. s-a. free (effective 2011). adv. bk.rev. back issues avail. **Document type:** *Journal, Academic/Scholarly.* **Description:** Provides information from the field of plastic and reconstructive surgery; contains original articles, reviews, case reports, streaming slide shows, streaming videos, letters to the editor, press releases, and meeting information.
Media: Online - full text.
Indexed: A01, A02, A03, A08, A26, C06, C07, CA, G08, H11, H12, I05, T02.
Published by: Internet Scientific Publications, Llc., 23 Rippling Creek Dr, Sugar Land, TX 77479. TEL 832-443-1193, FAX 281-240-1533, wenker@ispub.com. Ed. Howard Langstein.

617.95 USA ISSN 1937-8270

➤ **THE INTERNET JOURNAL OF SPINE SURGERY.** Text in English. 2004. s-a. free (effective 2011). **Document type:** *Journal, Academic/Scholarly.*
Media: Online - full text.
Indexed: A01, A26, CA, G08, H11, H12, I05, T02.
Published by: Internet Scientific Publications, Llc., 23 Rippling Creek Dr, Sugar Land, TX 77479. TEL 832-443-1193, FAX 281-240-1533, wenker@ispub.com. Ed. William Sukovich.

617 USA ISSN 1528-8242
RD1

➤ **THE INTERNET JOURNAL OF SURGERY.** Text in English. 2000. s-a. free (effective 2011). adv. bk.rev. back issues avail. **Document type:** *Journal, Academic/Scholarly.* **Description:** Contains information from the field of surgery, including original articles, reviews, case reports, streaming slide shows, streaming videos, letters to the editor, press releases, and meeting information.
Media: Online - full text.
Indexed: A01, A02, A03, A08, A26, C06, C07, CA, G08, H11, H12, I05, T02.
Published by: Internet Scientific Publications, Llc., 23 Rippling Creek Dr, Sugar Land, TX 77479. TEL 832-443-1193, FAX 281-240-1533, wenker@ispub.com. Ed. Herwig Cerwenka.

617.6 616.1 USA ISSN 1524-0274
RD536

➤ **THE INTERNET JOURNAL OF THORACIC AND CARDIOVASCULAR SURGERY.** Text in English. 1997. s-a. free (effective 2011). adv. bk.rev. back issues avail. **Document type:** *Journal, Academic/Scholarly.* **Description:** Covers the fields of thoracic, cardiac and vascular surgery, including original articles, reviews, case reports, streaming slide shows, streaming videos, letters to the editor, press releases, and meeting information.
Media: Online - full text.
Indexed: A01, A02, A03, A08, A26, C06, C07, C08, CA, CINAHL, G08, H11, H12, I05, T02.
Published by: Internet Scientific Publications, Llc., 23 Rippling Creek Dr, Sugar Land, TX 77479. TEL 832-443-1193, FAX 281-240-1533, wenker@ispub.com, http://www.ispub.com/journals/ijtcvs.htm. Ed. Dr. Juan Sanchez.

➤ **ISSUES IN CLINICAL NEUROSCIENCES.** *see* MEDICAL SCIENCES—Psychiatry And Neurology

617 ITA ISSN 1824-4777
CODEN: GICVFW

➤ **ITALIAN JOURNAL OF VASCULAR AND ENDOVASCULAR SURGERY;** a journal of vascular and endovascular surgery. Text in English, Italian. 1994. q. EUR 240 combined subscription in the European Union to institutions print & online eds.; EUR 265 combined subscription elsewhere to institutions print & online eds. (effective 2011). adv. **Document type:** *Journal, Academic/Scholarly.* **Description:** Covers the topic of vascular surgery.
Formerly (until 2003): Giornale Italiano di Chirurgia Vascolare (1122-8679)
Related titles: Online - full text ed.: ISSN 1827-1847. 2005.
Indexed: EMBASE, ExcerpMed, R10, Reac, SCI, SCOPUS, W07.
—BLDSC (4588.341610), GNLM, IE, Ingenta. **CCC.**
Published by: Edizioni Minerva Medica, Corso Bramante 83-85, Turin, 10126, Italy. TEL 39-011-678282, FAX 39-011-674502, journals.dept@minervamedica.it, http://www.minervamedica.it. Ed. A Stella. Circ: 2,900 (paid).

➤ **JAPANESE JOURNAL OF INTERVENTIONAL CARDIOLOGY.** *see* MEDICAL SCIENCES—Cardiovascular Diseases

617.95 JPN ISSN 0021-5228

JAPANESE JOURNAL OF PLASTIC & RECONSTRUCTIVE SURGERY/ KEISEI GEKA. Text mainly in Japanese; Text occasionally in English. m. JPY 39,660. adv. bk.rev. charts; illus. index. **Document type:** *Academic/Scholarly.*
Indexed: A22, INIS AtomInd, P30, R10, Reac, SCOPUS.
—BLDSC (4658.100000), GNLM, IE, Infotrieve, Ingenta.
Published by: Kokuseido Shuppan K.K./Kokuseido Publishing Co. Ltd., 23-5-202 Hongo 3-chome, Bunkyo-ku, Tokyo, 113-0033, Japan. TEL 81-3-38110995, FAX 81-3-38131866. Ed., R&P Akira Imai. Circ: 3,500.

617 JPN ISSN 0915-9118

JIN ISHOKU KEKKAN GEKA/RENAL TRANSPLANTATION, VASCULAR SURGERY. Text in English, Japanese. 1989. 2/yr. JPY 2,000 (effective 1998). **Document type:** *Journal, Academic/Scholarly.*
Published by: Jin Ishoku Kekkan Geka Kenkyukai/Japanese Society of Renal Transplantation and Vascular Surgery, Women s Medical University, Department of Urology, 8-1 Kawada-cho, Shinjuku-ku, Tokyo, 162-8666, Japan. TEL 81-3-33538111, FAX 81-3-52697353. Ed. Hiroshi Toma.

617 CHN ISSN 1672-2957

JIZHU WAIKE ZAZHI/JOURNAL OF SPINE SURGERY. Text in Chinese. 2003. bi-m. CNY 6.80 newsstand/cover (effective 2006). **Document type:** *Journal, Academic/Scholarly.*
Related titles: Online - full text ed.
Address: c/o Shanghai Changzheng Hospital, 415, Fengyang Lu, Shanghai, 200003, China. TEL 86-21-63610109 ext 8288, FAX 86-21-63720099.

617 BRA ISSN 0103-5118

JORNAL BRASILEIRO DE NEUROCIRURGIA. Text in Portuguese. 1989. q. **Document type:** *Journal, Academic/Scholarly.*
Published by: Academia Brasileira de Neurocirurgia, Rua da Quitanda 159, 10o Andar, Centro, Rio de Janeiro, RJ 20091-000, Brazil. abnc@.org.br, http://www.abnc.org.br.

617 BRA ISSN 1678-3387

JORNAL BRASILEIRO DE TRANSPLANTES. Abbreviated title: J B T. Text in Portuguese. 1998. 3/yr. **Document type:** *Journal, Academic/ Scholarly.*
Published by: Associacao Brasileira de Transplante de Orgaos (A B T O), Avenida Paulista 2001, 17o Andar, Cerqueira Cesar, Sao Paulo, 01311-300, Brazil. TEL 55-11-32623353, FAX 55-11-32893169, abto@abto.org.br, http://www.abto.org.br.

JOURNAL DE CHIRURGIE THORACIQUE ET CARDIO-VASCULAIRE. *see* MEDICAL SCIENCES—Cardiovascular Diseases

617 FRA ISSN 1878-786X
CODEN: JOCHAQ

➤ **JOURNAL DE CHIRURGIE VISCERALE.** Text in English. 1908. 6/yr. EUR 441 in Europe to institutions; EUR 355.53 in France to institutions; JPY 64,800 in Japan to institutions; USD 573 elsewhere to institutions (effective 2012). adv. bk.rev. abstr.; bibl.; illus. index. reprints avail. **Document type:** *Journal, Academic/Scholarly.* **Description:** Provides original articles, and clinical cases on the main surgical specialities. Includes a regular section on experimental surgery and a review of the international publications in surgery.
Formerly (until 2010): Journal de Chirurgie (0021-7697); Incorporates (1947-2006): Annales de Chirurgie (0003-3944); Which incorporated (in 2000): Chirurgie (0001-4001); Which was formerly (until 1969): Academie de Chirurgie. Memoires (0368-8291); (until 1935): Societe Nationale de Chirurgie. Bulletins et Memoires (0366-4503); (until 1923): Societe de Chirurgie de Paris. Bulletins et Memoires (0366-466X); Which was formed by the merger of (1847-1874): Societe de Chirurgie de Paris. Memoires (0150-9659); (1871-1874): Societe de Chirurgie de Paris. Bulletin (0150-9802); Which was formerly (until 1871): Societe Imperiale de Chirurgie de Paris (0150-9675); (1851-1866): Societe de Chirurgie de Paris. Bulletin (0150-9667)
Related titles: Microform ed.: (from PQC); Online - full text ed.: ISSN 1878-7878 (from ScienceDirect); English ed.: Journal of Visceral Surgery. ISSN 1878-7886. 2010.
Indexed: A20, A22, ASCA, CISA, CurCont, EMBASE, ExcerpMed, FR, INI, ISR, IndMed, Inpharma, MEDLINE, P30, R10, Reac, SCI, SCOPUS.
—BLDSC (4958.235000), GNLM, IE, Infotrieve, Ingenta, INIST. **CCC.**
Published by: Elsevier Masson (Subsidiary of: Elsevier Health Sciences), 62 Rue Camille Desmoulins, Issy les Moulineaux, Cedex 92442, France. TEL 33-1-71165500, FAX 33-1-71165600, infos@elsevier-masson.fr, http://www.elsevier-masson.fr. Ed. Francois Lacaine. Circ: 3,500.

617 FRA ISSN 1167-8224

LE JOURNAL DE COELIO-CHIRURGIE/JOURNAL OF COELIO-SURGERY. Text in French. 1992. q. EUR 124 (effective 2009). **Document type:** *Journal, Academic/Scholarly.* **Description:** The aim of the journal is the diffusion of the knowledge of endoscopic surgery and the exchange of information among and practical training of surgeons.
—BLDSC (4958.797500), INIST. **CCC.**
Published by: (Societe Francaise de Chirurgie Endoscopie), S R E C Diffusion, 268 Ave Victor Hugo, Valence, 26000, France. TEL 33-475-783064.

617 DEU ISSN 1867-4305

➤ **JOURNAL FUER AESTHETISCHE CHIRURGIE.** Text in German. 2008. 4/yr. EUR 298, USD 448 combined subscription to institutions (print & online eds.) (effective 2012). reprint service avail. from PSC. **Document type:** *Journal, Academic/Scholarly.*
Related titles: Online - full text ed.: ISSN 1867-4313.
Indexed: A22, E01, SCOPUS.
—IE. **CCC.**
Published by: Springer (Subsidiary of: Springer Science+Business Media), Tiergartenstr 17, Heidelberg, 69121, Germany. TEL 49-6221-4870, FAX 49-6221-345229, subscriptions@springer.com.

617 GBR ISSN 0885-3282
R856.A1 CODEN: JBAPEL

➤ **JOURNAL OF BIOMATERIALS APPLICATIONS.** Abbreviated title: J B A. Text in English. 1986. 8/yr. USD 1,734, GBP 1,020 combined subscription to institutions (print & online eds.); USD 1,699, GBP 1,000 to institutions (effective 2011). adv. back issues avail.; reprint service avail. from PSC. **Document type:** *Journal, Academic/ Scholarly.* **Description:** Covers research and development of biomaterials used in surgical products and medical devices.
Related titles: E-mail ed.; Online - full text ed.: ISSN 1530-8022. USD 1,561, GBP 918 to institutions (effective 2011).
Indexed: A01, A03, A08, A22, A28, APA, ASCA, ASFA, B&BAb, B19, B21, BioEngAb, BrCerAb, C&ISA, CA, CA/WCA, CIA, CIN, CPEI, CerAb, ChemAb, ChemTitl, CivEngAb, CorrAb, E&CAJ, E01, E11, EEA, EMA, EMBASE, ESPM, EngInd, EnvEAb, ExcerpMed, H04, H15, IndMed, M&PBA, M&TEA, M09, MBF, MEDLINE, METADEX, MSCI, P15, P30, P48, P52, P56, PQC, R10, R18, Reac, S01, SCI, SCOPUS, SolStAb, T02, T04, W07, WAA.
—BLDSC (4953.515000), CASDDS, GNLM, IE, Infotrieve, Ingenta, INIST, Linda Hall. **CCC.**
Published by: Sage Publications Ltd. (Subsidiary of: Sage Publications, Inc.), 1 Oliver's Yard, 55 City Rd, London, EC1Y 1SP, United Kingdom. TEL 44-20-73248500, FAX 44-20-73248600, info@sagepub.co.uk, http://www.uk.sagepub.com/home.nav. Ed. Jonathan Knowles. adv.: B&W page GBP 450; 130 x 205.

➤ **JOURNAL OF BONE AND JOINT SURGERY: AMERICAN AND BRITISH VOLUMES ON CD-ROM.** *see* MEDICAL SCIENCES—Orthopedics And Traumatology

➤ **JOURNAL OF BONE AND JOINT SURGERY: BRITISH VOLUME.** *see* MEDICAL SCIENCES—Orthopedics And Traumatology

➤ **JOURNAL OF BONE AND JOINT SURGERY. BRITISH VOLUME. ORTHOPAEDIC PROCEEDINGS.** *see* MEDICAL SCIENCES—Orthopedics And Traumatology

617.6 GBR ISSN 1749-8090
RD536

➤ **JOURNAL OF CARDIOTHORACIC SURGERY.** Text in English. 2006. irreg. free (effective 2011). adv. back issues avail. **Document type:** *Journal, Academic/Scholarly.* **Description:** Covers all aspects of research in the field of cardiothoracic surgery.
Media: Online - full text.
Indexed: A01, A26, C06, C07, CA, CurCont, EMBASE, ExcerpMed, I05, MEDLINE, P30, R10, Reac, SCI, SCOPUS, T02, W07.
—CCC.
Published by: BioMed Central Ltd. (Subsidiary of: Springer Science+Business Media), 236 Gray's Inn Rd, London, WC1X 8HB, United Kingdom. TEL 44-20-31922000, FAX 44-20-31922010, info@biomedcentral.com, http://www.biomedcentral.com. Eds. David Taggart, Vipin Zamvar. Adv. contact Natasha Bailey TEL 44-20-31922231.

➤ **THE JOURNAL OF CARDIOVASCULAR SURGERY;** a journal on cardiac, vascular and thoracic surgery. *see* MEDICAL SCIENCES—Cardiovascular Diseases

➤ **JOURNAL OF CATARACT & REFRACTIVE SURGERY.** *see* MEDICAL SCIENCES—Ophthalmology And Optometry

➤ **JOURNAL OF COSMETIC AND LASER THERAPY (ONLINE).** *see* MEDICAL SCIENCES—Dermatology And Venereology

➤ **JOURNAL OF COSMETIC AND LASER THERAPY (PRINT).** *see* MEDICAL SCIENCES—Dermatology And Venereology

617 GBR ISSN 1010-5182
CODEN: JCMSET

➤ **JOURNAL OF CRANIO-MAXILLOFACIAL SURGERY.** Text in English. 1973. 8/yr. EUR 745 in Europe to institutions; JPY 76,300 in Japan to institutions; USD 700 elsewhere to institutions (effective 2012). adv. illus. index. back issues avail.; reprints avail. **Document type:** *Journal, Academic/Scholarly.* **Description:** Covers all aspects of surgery of the head, face and jaw.
Formerly (until 1987): Journal of Maxillofacial Surgery (0301-0503)
Related titles: Microform ed.: (from PQC); Online - full text ed.: ISSN 1878-4119 (from ScienceDirect).
Indexed: A20, A22, A26, ASCA, CA, CTD, CurCont, D02, DentInd, E01, EMBASE, ExcerpMed, FR, I05, ISR, IndMed, Inpharma, MEDLINE, P30, P35, R10, Reac, SCI, SCOPUS, T02, W07.
—BLDSC (4965.482000), GNLM, IE, Infotrieve, Ingenta, INIST. **CCC.**
Published by: (European Association for Cranio Maxillo-Facial Surgery), Churchill Livingstone (Subsidiary of: Elsevier Health Sciences), The Blvd, Langford Ln, Kidlington, OX5 1GB, United Kingdom. TEL 44-1865-843434, FAX 44-1865-843970, directenquiries@elsevier.com, http://www.elsevierhealth.com/ imprint.jsp?iid=9. Ed. J Wiltfang. R&P Catherine John TEL 212-424-4200. Adv. contact Emma Steel TEL 44-207-4244221. Circ: 1,467.

617.95 USA ISSN 1049-2275
RD523 CODEN: JSURE8

➤ **JOURNAL OF CRANIOFACIAL SURGERY.** Abbreviated title: J C S. Text in English. 1990. bi-m. USD 1,390 domestic to institutions; USD 1,524 foreign to institutions (effective 2011). adv. bk.rev. abstr.; charts; illus.; stat. index. back issues avail.; reprints avail. **Document type:** *Journal, Academic/Scholarly.* **Description:** Features as a forum of communication for all those involved in craniofacial and maxillofacial surgery. Coverage ranges from aspects of craniofacial surgery to the basic science that underlies surgical practice.
Related titles: Microform ed.: (from PQC); Online - full text ed.: ISSN 1536-3732.
Indexed: A22, ASCA, CTD, CurCont, EMBASE, ExcerpMed, ISR, Inpharma, MEDLINE, P30, P35, R10, Reac, SCI, SCOPUS, W07.
—BLDSC (4965.476000), GNLM, IE, Infotrieve, Ingenta. **CCC.**
Published by: (American Association of Pediatric Plastic Surgeons), Lippincott Williams & Wilkins (Subsidiary of: Wolters Kluwer N.V.), 530 Walnut St, Philadelphia, PA 19106. TEL 215-521-8300, FAX 215-521-8902, customerservice@lww.com, http://www.lww.com. Ed. Dr. Mutaz B Habal. Pub. Jason Pointe. **Co-sponsors:** European Society of Craniofacial Surgery; International Society of Craniofacial Surgery.

➤ **JOURNAL OF CRANIOVERTEBRAL JUNCTION AND SPINE.** *see* MEDICAL SCIENCES—Orthopedics And Traumatology

617 IND ISSN 0974-2077

➤ **JOURNAL OF CUTANEOUS AND AESTHETIC SURGERY.** Text in English. 2008. 3/yr. INR 1,000 domestic to individuals; USD 100 foreign to individuals; INR 2,000 domestic to institutions; USD 200 foreign to institutions; INR 1,200 combined subscription domestic to individuals (print & online eds.); USD 120 combined subscription foreign to individuals (print & online eds.); INR 2,400, USD 2,400 combined subscription domestic to institutions (print & online eds.) (effective 2011). adv. **Document type:** *Journal, Academic/Scholarly.* **Description:** Covers all aspects of cutaneous and aesthetic surgery, including cutaneous surgical procedures, lasers, light based treatments, and aesthetic treatments.
Related titles: Online - full text ed.: ISSN 0974-5157. INR 800 domestic to individuals; USD 80 foreign to individuals; INR 1,600 domestic to institutions; USD 160 foreign to institutions (effective 2011).

Indexed: A01, A26, E08, H12, I05, P10, P30, P48, P53, P54, PQC, S09.
—CCC.
Published by: (Association of Cutaneous Surgeons of India), Medknow Publications and Media Pvt. Ltd., B-9, Kanara Business Ctr, Off Link Rd, Ghatkopar (E), Mumbai, Maharastra 400 075, India. TEL 91-22-66491816, FAX 91-22-66491817, http://www.medknow.com. Ed. Venkatram Mysore.

➤ **JOURNAL OF CUTANEOUS MEDICINE AND SURGERY.** *see* MEDICAL SCIENCES—Dermatology And Venereology

617.4 616.1 USA ISSN 1526-6028 CODEN: JENTFI
➤ **JOURNAL OF ENDOVASCULAR THERAPY.** Text in English. 1994. bi-m. USD 305 combined subscription domestic to institutions (print & online eds.); USD 331 combined subscription foreign to institutions (print & online eds.) (effective 2009). adv. bk.rev. charts; illus. **Document type:** *Journal, Academic/Scholarly.* **Description:** Presents interesting, difficult or unusual case reports representing all topics related to international vascular diagnosis and therapy.
Formerly (until 2000): Journal of Endovascular Surgery (1074-6218); Which supersedes (in 1995): Vascular Surgery (Armonk) (1067-5051)
Related titles: Online - full text ed.: ISSN 1545-1550.
Indexed: A22, ASCA, B21, C06, C07, C08, CA, CINAHL, CTA, CurCont, E01, EMBASE, ExcerpMed, ISR, IndMed, Inpharma, MEDLINE, NSA, P20, P22, P24, P30, P35, P48, P54, PQC, R10, Reac, SCI, SCOPUS, T02, W07.
—BLDSC (4978.230000), GNLM, IE, Infotrieve, Ingenta, INIST. **CCC.**
Published by: (International Society for Endovascular Surgery), Allen Press Inc., 810 E 10th St, PO Box 368, Lawrence, KS 66044. pubserv@allenpress.com, http://www.allenpress.com. Adv. contact Onkar S Sandal TEL 785-843-1234 ext 218. B&W page USD 1,150; trim 8.25 x 10.875. Circ: 2,800.

➤ **JOURNAL OF FELINE MEDICINE AND SURGERY.** *see* VETERINARY SCIENCE

617 USA ISSN 1067-2516
RD560 CODEN: JFSUEI
➤ **THE JOURNAL OF FOOT & ANKLE SURGERY.** Abbreviated title: J F A S. Text in English. 1963. bi-m. USD 321 in US & Canada to institutions; USD 405 elsewhere to institutions (effective 2012). back issues avail.; reprints avail. **Document type:** *Journal, Academic/Scholarly.* **Description:** Presents clinical advances in foot surgery to podiatrists and orthopedic foot surgeons.
Former titles (until 1993): Journal of Foot Surgery (0449-2544); (until 1967): American College of Foot Surgeons. Journal (0517-0591)
Related titles: CD-ROM ed.; Online - full text ed.: ISSN 1542-2224 (from ScienceDirect).
Indexed: A22, A26, AMED, C06, C07, C08, CA, CINAHL, CurCont, EMBASE, ExcerpMed, H12, I05, INI, IndMed, MEDLINE, P30, R10, Reac, SCI, SCOPUS, T02, W07.
—BLDSC (4984.572000), GNLM, IE, Infotrieve, Ingenta, INIST. **CCC.**
Published by: (American College of Foot and Ankle Surgeons), W.B. Saunders Co. (Subsidiary of: Elsevier Health Sciences), Elsevier, Health Sciences Division, Order Fulfillment, 3251 Riverport Ln, Maryland Heights, MO 63043. TEL 314-872-8370, 800-325-4177, FAX 314-432-1380, JournalCustomerService-usa@elsevier.com, http://www.us.elsevierhealth.com. Ed. Scot D Malay TEL 215-967-4463. Pub. Chris Baumle TEL 215-239-3731. Adv. contact Danny Wang TEL 212-633-3158. Circ: 6,200.

617 USA ISSN 1091-255X
RC799
➤ **JOURNAL OF GASTROINTESTINAL SURGERY.** Text in English. 1997. m. EUR 474, USD 573 combined subscription to institutions (print & online eds.) (effective 2012). adv. back issues avail.; reprint service avail. from PSC. **Document type:** *Journal, Academic/Scholarly.* **Description:** Designed to furnish the surgeon with the latest developments in gastrointestinal surgery.
Related titles: Online - full text ed.: ISSN 1873-4626.
Indexed: A01, A03, A08, A22, A26, A34, A36, CA, CABA, CurCont, D01, E01, E12, EMBASE, ExcerpMed, GH, H17, I05, IndMed, Inpharma, MEDLINE, N02, N03, P30, P33, P35, P39, R08, R10, RM&VM, Reac, SCI, SCOPUS, T02, T05, VS, W07.
—BLDSC (4987.625000), IE, Infotrieve, Ingenta, INIST. **CCC.**
Published by: (Society for Surgery of the Alimentary Tract, Inc.), Springer New York LLC (Subsidiary of: Springer Science+Business Media), 233 Spring St, New York, NY 10013. TEL 212-460-1500, FAX 212-460-1575, service-ny@springer.com. Ed. John L Cameron. adv.: B&W page USD 1,275; trim 8.25 x 11. Circ: 2,400 (paid).

➤ **JOURNAL OF GYNECOLOGIC SURGERY.** *see* MEDICAL SCIENCES—Obstetrics And Gynecology

▼ ➤ **JOURNAL OF GYNECOLOGICAL ENDOSCOPY AND SURGERY.** *see* MEDICAL SCIENCES—Obstetrics And Gynecology

617.95 IND ISSN 0974-3227
▼ ➤ **JOURNAL OF HAND AND MICROSURGERY.** Text in English. 2009. 2/yr. EUR 129, USD 194 combined subscription to institutions (print & online eds.) (effective 2012). reprint service avail. from PSC. **Document type:** *Journal, Academic/Scholarly.* **Description:** Publishes origina articles, case reports related to the understanding of diseases, diagnosis, and management of the upper extremity disorders, brachial plexus injuries, congenital hand problems, hand trauma, fractures, tumours, burns and reconstructive microsurgery.
Related titles: Online - full text ed.: ISSN 0974-6897. 2009 (from IngentaConnect).
Indexed: A22, E01, SCOPUS.
—IE. **CCC.**
Published by: Springer (India) Private Ltd. (Subsidiary of: Springer Science+Business Media), 212, Deen Dayal Upadhyaya Marg, 3rd Fl, Gandharva Mahavidyalaya, New Delhi, 110 002, India. TEL 91-11-45755888, FAX 91-11-45755889. Ed. Balan Sankaran.

616 USA ISSN 0363-5023
RD559 CODEN: JHSUDV
➤ **JOURNAL OF HAND SURGERY (AMERICAN VOLUME).** Abbreviated title: J H S. Text in English. 1976. 10/yr. USD 692 in United States to institutions; USD 902 elsewhere to institutions (effective 2012). adv. bk.rev. charts; illus. index. back issues avail.; reprints avail. **Document type:** *Journal, Academic/Scholarly.* **Description:** Publishes articles related to the diagnosis, treatment, and pathophysiology of diseases and conditions of the upper extremity; these include both clinical and basic science studies, along with case reports.
Incorporates (2001-2005): American Society for Surgery of the Hand. Journal (1531-0914)
Related titles: CD-ROM ed.: USD 195 per issue to individuals; USD 350 per issue to institutions (effective 2000); Microfilm ed.: 1976 (from PQC); Online - full text ed.: ISSN 1531-6564 (from ScienceDirect); ◆ Regional ed(s).: Journal of Hand Surgery (European Volume). ISSN 1753-1934.
Indexed: A22, A26, ASCA, B21, BDM&CN, CA, CurCont, DokArb, E01, EMBASE, ESPM, ExcerpMed, FR, H&SSA, I05, IndMed, Inpharma, MEDLINE, P20, P22, P30, P48, P54, PQC, R10, Reac, SCI, SCOPUS, T02, W07.
—BLDSC (4996.620000), GNLM, IE, Infotrieve, Ingenta, INIST. **CCC.**
Published by: (American Society for Surgery of the Hand), W.B. Saunders Co. (Subsidiary of: Elsevier Health Sciences), Elsevier, Health Sciences Division, Order Fulfillment, 3251 Riverport Ln, Maryland Heights, MO 63043. TEL 314-872-8370, 800-325-4177, FAX 314-432-1380, JournalCustomerService-usa@elsevier.com, http://www.us.elsevierhealth.com. Ed. Dr. Paul R Manske. Pub. Jason Miller. Adv. contact Nicole Johnson TEL 215-239-3168. Circ: 4,900.

617 GBR ISSN 1753-1934
RD559
➤ **JOURNAL OF HAND SURGERY (EUROPEAN VOLUME).** Text in English. 1969. 9/yr. USD 1,114, GBP 602 combined subscription to institutions (print & online eds.); USD 1,092, GBP 590 to institutions (effective 2011). adv. back issues avail.; reprint service avail. from PSC. **Document type:** *Journal, Academic/Scholarly.* **Description:** Dedicated to the needs of hand, plastic, reconstructive and orthopaedic surgeons.
Former titles (until Feb.2007): Journal of Hand Surgery (British Volume) (0266-7681); (until 1984): Hand (0072-968X)
Related titles: CD-ROM ed.: USD 190 per issue to individuals; USD 350 per issue to institutions (effective 2000); Microform ed.: (from PQC); Online - full text ed.: ISSN 2043-6289. USD 1,003, GBP 542 to institutions (effective 2011); ◆ Regional ed(s).: Journal of Hand Surgery (American Volume). ISSN 0363-5023.
Indexed: A20, A22, A26, ASCA, B21, CA, CTA, CurCont, E01, EMBASE, ExcerpMed, FR, I05, IndMed, Inpharma, MEDLINE, P30, P35, R10, Reac, SCI, SCOPUS, T02, W07.
—BLDSC (4996.623300), GNLM, IE, Ingenta, INIST. **CCC.**
Published by: (Federation of European Societies for Surgery of the Hand HUN, British Society for Surgery of the Hand), Sage Publications Ltd. (Subsidiary of: Sage Publications, Inc.), 1 Oliver's Yard, 55 City Rd, London, EC1Y 1SP, United Kingdom. TEL 44-20-73248500, FAX 44-20-73248600, info@sagepub.co.uk, http://www.uk.sagepub.com/home.nav. Eds. Geoffrey Hooper, Peter Burge, Joseph J Dias.

617 USA ISSN 1053-2498
RD598 CODEN: JHLTES
➤ **THE JOURNAL OF HEART AND LUNG TRANSPLANTATION.** Abbreviated title: J H L T. Text in English. 1981. m. USD 399 in US & Canada to institutions; USD 537 elsewhere to institutions (effective 2012). adv. charts; illus. index. back issues avail.; reprints avail. **Document type:** *Journal, Academic/Scholarly.* **Description:** Presents the latest clinical information on the rapidly evolving field of intrathoracic transplantation, support and replacement.
Former titles (until 1991): Journal of Heart Transplantation (0887-2570); (until 1984): Heart Transplantation (0278-2723)
Related titles: Microfilm ed.: (from PQC); Online - full text ed.: ISSN 1557-3117 (from IngentaConnect, ScienceDirect).
Indexed: A01, A03, A08, A22, A26, A36, ASCA, B25, BIOSIS Prev, CA, CABA, CurCont, EMBASE, ExcerpMed, GH, H17, I05, IDIS, ISR, IndMed, Inpharma, MEDLINE, MycolAb, N02, N03, P30, P33, P35, P39, R08, R10, RM&VM, Reac, SCI, SCOPUS, T02, T05, VS, W07.
—BLDSC (4996.874000), GNLM, IE, Infotrieve, Ingenta, INIST. **CCC.**
Published by: (European Society of Cardiology FRA, International Society for Heart and Lung Transplantation), Elsevier Inc. (Subsidiary of: Elsevier Science & Technology), 1600 John F Kennedy Blvd, Philadelphia, PA 19103. TEL 215-239-3900, FAX 215-238-7883, JournalCustomerService-usa@elsevier.com, http://www.elsevier.com. Ed. Mandeep B Mehra. Pub. Linda Gruner TEL 212-633-3923. Adv. contact Danny Wang TEL 212-633-3158. Circ: 2,260.

617 JPN ISSN 1868-6974
RD546 CODEN: JHBSFA
➤ **JOURNAL OF HEPATO - BILIARY - PANCREATIC SCIENCES.** Text in English. 1993. bi-m. (in 1 vol., 6 nos./vol.). EUR 480, USD 538 combined subscription to institutions (print & online eds.) (effective 2012). reprint service avail. from PSC. **Document type:** *Journal, Academic/Scholarly.* **Description:** Deals with clinical investigations of and basic research on all aspects of the field of hepatic, biliary, and pancreatic surgery. Also presents case studies and descriptions of surgical techniques.
Formerly (until 2010): Journal of Hepato - Biliary - Pancreatic Surgery (0944-1166)
Related titles: Online - full text ed.: ISSN 1868-6982 (from IngentaConnect).
Indexed: A22, A26, CA, CurCont, E01, EMBASE, ExcerpMed, IndMed, MEDLINE, P30, R10, Reac, SCI, SCOPUS, T02, W07.
—BLDSC (4997.670000), GNLM, IE, Infotrieve, Ingenta. **CCC.**
Published by: (Japanese Society of Hepato-Biliary-Pancreatic Surgery), Springer Japan KK (Subsidiary of: Springer Science+Business Media), No 2 Funato Bldg, 1-11-11 Kudan-kita, Chiyoda-ku, Tokyo, 102-0073, Japan. TEL 81-3-68317000, FAX 81-3-68317001, http://www.springer.jp. Ed. Dr. Tadahiro Takada. Adv. contact Stephan Kroeck TEL 49-30-827875739. **Subscr. in the Americas to:** Springer New York LLC, Journal Fulfillment, PO Box 2485, Secaucus, NJ 07096. TEL 201-348-4033, 800-777-4643, FAX 201-348-4505, journals-ny@springer.com, http://www.springer.com; **Subscr. to:** Eastern Book Service, Inc.; Springer Distribution Center, Kundenservice Zeitschriften, Haberstr 7, Heidelberg 69126, Germany. TEL 49-6221-3454303, FAX 49-6221-3454229, subscriptions@springer.com.

617 615 GBR ISSN 1476-9255
RB131
➤ **JOURNAL OF INFLAMMATION.** Text in English. 2004. irreg. free (effective 2011). adv. back issues avail. **Document type:** *Journal, Academic/Scholarly.* **Description:** Covers all aspects of research into inflammation. Includes molecular, cellular, animal and clinical studies, and related aspects of pharmacology, such as anti-inflammatory drug development, trials and therapeutic developments.
Media: Online - full text.
Indexed: A26, A39, B25, BIOSIS Prev, C27, C29, CA, D03, D04, E13, EMBASE, ExcerpMed, I05, MycolAb, P30, R10, R14, Reac, S14, S15, S18, SCI, T02, W07.
—CCC.
Published by: BioMed Central Ltd. (Subsidiary of: Springer Science+Business Media), 236 Gray's Inn Rd, London, WC1X 8HB, United Kingdom. TEL 44-20-31922000, FAX 44-20-31922010, info@biomedcentral.com, http://www.biomedcentral.com. Eds. Dennis Taub, Paul Kirkham. Adv. contact Natasha Bailey TEL 44-20-31922231.

617 GBR ISSN 0894-1939
RD29 CODEN: JISUE5
➤ **JOURNAL OF INVESTIGATIVE SURGERY.** Text in English. 1988. bi-m. adv. reprint service avail. from PSC. **Document type:** *Journal, Academic/Scholarly.* **Description:** Brings out scientific articles for the advancement of surgery, to the ultimate benefit of patient care and rehabilitation.
Related titles: Online - full text ed.: ISSN 1521-0553 (from IngentaConnect).
Indexed: A01, A02, A03, A08, A20, A22, ASCA, C11, CA, CurCont, E01, EMBASE, ExcerpMed, H04, IndMed, Inpharma, L03, MEDLINE, P30, P35, R10, Reac, S01, SCI, SCOPUS, T02, W07.
—GNLM, IE, Infotrieve, Ingenta. **CCC.**
Published by: Informa Healthcare (Subsidiary of: T & F Informa plc), Telephone House, 69-77 Paul St, London, EC2A 4LQ, United Kingdom. TEL 44-20-70175000, FAX 44-20-70176792, healthcare.enquiries@informa.com. Ed. Luis H Toledo-Pereyra. Adv. contact Per Sonnerfeldt. **Subscr. in N. America to:** Taylor & Francis Inc., Customer Services Dept, 325 Chestnut St, 8th Fl, Philadelphia, PA 19106. TEL 215-625-8900, 800-354-1420, FAX 215-625-8914, customerservice@taylorandfrancis.com; **Subscr. to:** Taylor & Francis Ltd., Journals Customer Service, Sheepen Pl, Colchester, Essex CO3 3LP, United Kingdom. TEL 44-20-70175544, FAX 44-20-70175198, tf.enquiries@tfinforma.com.

617 616.7 USA ISSN 1538-8506
➤ **JOURNAL OF KNEE SURGERY.** Text in English. 1988. q. USD 375 domestic to institutions; USD 411 foreign to institutions; USD 461 combined subscription domestic to institutions (print & online eds.); USD 498 combined subscription foreign to institutions (print & online eds.) (effective 2011). adv. 88 p./no. 2 cols./p.; back issues avail.; reprints avail. **Document type:** *Journal, Academic/Scholarly.* **Description:** Provides a forum for practical, clinical information in such areas as arthroscopy, arthroplasty, magnetic resonance imaging, and reconstructive surgery.
Formerly: American Journal of Knee Surgery (0899-7403)
Related titles: Microform ed.: (from PQC); Online - full text ed.: ISSN 1938-2480. USD 441 domestic to institutions; USD 466 foreign to institutions (effective 2011).
Indexed: B&BAb, B19, B21, CA, CTA, EMBASE, ExcerpMed, IndMed, MEDLINE, P20, P22, P30, P48, P54, PQC, R10, Reac, SCOPUS, SD, T02.
—BLDSC (5009.852000), GNLM, IE, Ingenta. **CCC.**
Published by: Thieme Medical Publishers (Subsidiary of: Georg Thieme Verlag), 333 Seventh Ave, New York, NY 10001. TEL 212-584-4662, 800-782-3488, FAX 212-947-1112, custserv@thieme.com, http://www.thieme.com/journals. Ed. Bernard Bach. adv.: B&W page USD 1,450, color page USD 2,890. Circ: 750 (paid).

617 USA ISSN 1092-6429
RD33.53 CODEN: JLSTFO
➤ **JOURNAL OF LAPAROENDOSCOPIC & ADVANCED SURGICAL TECHNIQUES PARTS A & B.** Variant title: Journal of Laparoendoscopic, Videoscopy. Text in English. 1990. 16/yr. USD 2,314 domestic to institutions; USD 2,845 foreign to institutions; USD 2,704 combined subscription domestic to institutions (print & online eds.); USD 3,321 combined subscription foreign to institutions (print & online eds.) (effective 2012). adv. reprint service avail. from PSC. **Document type:** *Journal, Academic/Scholarly.* **Description:** Disseminates information on the surgical techniques that encompass laparoscopy and endoscopy.
Incorporates (in 2004): Pediatric Endosurgery & Innovative Techniques (1092-6410); Which superseded in part (in 1997): Journal of Laparoendoscopic Surgery (1052-3901)
Related titles: Online - full text ed.: ISSN 1557-9034. USD 2,354 to institutions (effective 2012).
Indexed: A01, A03, A08, A22, ASCA, C06, C07, CA, CurCont, E01, EMBASE, ErgAb, ExcerpMed, ISR, IndMed, Inpharma, MEDLINE, P30, R10, Reac, SCI, SCOPUS, T02, W07.
—BLDSC (5010.098500), GNLM, IE, Infotrieve, Ingenta. **CCC.**
Published by: Mary Ann Liebert, Inc. Publishers, 140 Huguenot St, 3rd Fl, New Rochelle, NY 10801. TEL 914-740-2100, FAX 914-740-2101, 800-654-3237, info@liebertpub.com, http://www.liebertpub.com. Ed. C Daniel Smith TEL 904-953-6389.

617 USA ISSN 1050-6934 CODEN: JLEIEM
➤ **JOURNAL OF LONG-TERM EFFECTS OF MEDICAL IMPLANTS.** Text in English. 1991. bi-m. USD 1,072 to institutions; USD 204 per issue (effective 2010). adv. back issues avail.; reprints avail. **Document type:** *Journal, Academic/Scholarly.* **Description:** Aims to understand the mechanisms of failure of pre-clinically tested medical implants during long-term in vivo service, both in appropriate animal models and in humans, and establishes linkage between pre-clinical and clinical studies.
Related titles: Online - full text ed.: ISSN 1940-4379.
Indexed: A28, APA, ASCA, B&BAb, B19, B21, BioEngAb, BrCerAb, C&ISA, CA/WCA, CIA, CIN, CPEI, CTA, CerAb, ChemTitl, CivEngAb, CorrAb, E&CAJ, E11, EEA, EMA, EMBASE, ESPM, EngInd, EnvEAb, ExcerpMed, H&SSA, H15, I12, ISR, Inpharma, M&PBA, M&TEA, M09, MBF, MEDLINE, METADEX, P30, R10, Reac, RiskAb, SCOPUS, SolStAb, T04, ToxAb, WAA.
—BLDSC (5010.560500), CASDDS, GNLM, IE, Infotrieve, Ingenta, Linda Hall. **CCC.**
Published by: Begell House Inc., 50 Cross Hwy, Redding, CT 06896. TEL 203-938-1300, FAX 203-938-1304, orders@begellhouse.com. Ed. Subrata Saha.

617.95 IND ISSN 0972-8279
➤ **JOURNAL OF MAXILLOFACIAL AND ORAL SURGERY.** Text in English. 2002. 4/yr. EUR 188, USD 252 combined subscription to institutions (print & online eds.) (effective 2012). reprint service avail. from PSC. **Document type:** *Journal, Academic/Scholarly.*
Related titles: Online - full text ed.: ISSN 0974-924X.

Indexed: A22, E01, SCOPUS.
—IE. **CCC.**
Published by: Springer (India) Private Ltd. (Subsidiary of: Springer Science+Business Media), 212, Deen Dayal Upadhyaya Marg, 3rd Fl, Gandharva Mahavidyalaya, New Delhi, 110 002, India. TEL 91-11-45755888, FAX 91-11-45755889. Ed. S M Balaji.

617 JPN ISSN 0917-7728
JOURNAL OF MICROWAVE SURGERY. Text in English, Japanese. 1988. a. JPY 3,500 (effective 2005). **Document type:** *Journal, Academic/Scholarly.*
Formerly (until 1991): Maikurowebu Sajeri (0917-1231)
Published by: Medikaru Rebyusha/Medical Review Co., Ltd., 1-7-3 Hirano-Machi, Chuo-ku, Yoshida Bldg., Osaka-shi, 541-0046, Japan. TEL 81-6-62231468, FAX 81-6-62231245.

617 IND ISSN 0972-9941
RC78.7.ES
➤ **JOURNAL OF MINIMAL ACCESS SURGERY.** Abbreviated title: J M A S. Text in English. 2005. q. INR 1,200 domestic to individuals; USD 120 foreign to individuals; INR 2,000 domestic to institutions; USD 200 foreign to institutions; INR 1,500 combined subscription domestic to individuals; USD 145 combined subscription foreign to individuals; INR 2,400 combined subscription domestic to institutions; USD 240 combined subscription foreign to institutions (effective 2011). adv. **Document type:** *Journal, Academic/Scholarly.* **Description:** Publishes articles in the fields of laparoscopic and thoracoscopic surgery, laparoscopic urology and gastrointestinal endoscopy.
Related titles: Online - full text ed.: ISSN 1998-3921. 2005. INR 1,000 domestic to individuals; USD 95 foreign to individuals; INR 1,600 domestic to institutions; USD 160 foreign to institutions (effective 2011).
Indexed: A01, A26, B&BAb, BioEngAb, CA, E08, G08, H11, H12, I05, P10, P20, P30, P48, P53, P54, PQC, S09, SCOPUS, T02.
—Linda Hall. **CCC.**
Published by: (Indian Association of Gastrointestinal Endo Surgeons), Medknow Publications and Media Pvt. Ltd., B-9, Kanara Business Ctr, Off Link Rd, Ghatkopar (E), Mumbai, Maharastra 400 075, India. TEL 91-22-66491816, FAX 91-22-66491817, http://www.medknow.com. Ed. Tehemton E Udwadia.

617 GBR ISSN 1759-8478
RD593
▼ ➤ **JOURNAL OF NEUROINTERVENTIONAL SURGERY.** Text in English. 2009 (Jul.). 2/yr. **Document type:** *Journal, Academic/Scholarly.* **Description:** Dedicated to the needs of interventional neuroradiologists, interventional neurologists, and endovascular neurosurgeons.
Related titles: Online - full text ed.: ISSN 1759-8486. 2009.
Indexed: C06, CurCont, P30, SCI, W07.
—BLDSC (5021.551500), IE. **CCC.**
Published by: (Society of Vascular and Interventional Neurology USA, Society of NeuroInterventional Surgery USA), B M J Group, BMA House, Tavistock Sq, London, WC1H 9JR, United Kingdom. TEL 44-20-73836373, FAX 44-20-73836668, http://group.bmj.com. Ed. Dr. Robert Tarr.

➤ **JOURNAL OF NEUROLOGY, NEUROSURGERY AND PSYCHIATRY**; an international peer-reviewed journal for health professionals and researchers in all areas of neurology and neurosurgery. *see* MEDICAL SCIENCES—Psychiatry And Neurology

➤ **JOURNAL OF NEUROSURGERY.** *see* MEDICAL SCIENCES—Psychiatry And Neurology

617.13 USA ISSN 1547-5654
JOURNAL OF NEUROSURGERY: SPINE. Text in English. 1944. m. includes with subscr. to Journal of Neurosurgery, Journal of Neurosurgery: Pediatrics. adv. **Document type:** *Journal, Academic/Scholarly.* **Description:** Devoted to the publication of original works relating primarily to neurosurgery, including studies in clinical neurophysiology, organic neurology, ophthalmology, radiology, pathology, and molecular biology.
Supersedes in part (in 2004): Journal of Neurosurgery (0022-3085)
Related titles: Online - full text ed.: ISSN 1547-5646. 1999; ◆ Supplement to: Journal of Neurosurgery. ISSN 0022-3085.
Indexed: A20, A22, C06, C07, CurCont, EMBASE, ExcerpMed, Inpharma, MEDLINE, NSCI, P30, P35, R10, Reac, SCI, SCOPUS, W07.
—BLDSC (5022.130000), IE, Ingenta, INIST. **CCC.**
Published by: American Association of Neurological Surgeons, 5550 Meadowbrook Dr, Rolling Meadows, IL 60008. TEL 847-378-0500, FAX 847-378-0600, info@aans.org, http://www.aans.org. Ed. Dr. John A Jane TEL 434-924-5503. Adv. contact Greg Pessagno TEL 443-512-8899 ext 109.

JOURNAL OF NEUROSURGICAL ANESTHESIOLOGY. *see* MEDICAL SCIENCES—Anaesthesiology

617 616.8 ITA ISSN 0390-5616
➤ **JOURNAL OF NEUROSURGICAL SCIENCES**; a journal on neurosurgery. Text in English. 1957. q. EUR 240 combined subscription in the European Union to institutions print & online eds.; EUR 265 combined subscription elsewhere to institutions print & online eds. (effective 2011). adv. bk.rev. bibl.; charts; illus. index. **Document type:** *Journal, Academic/Scholarly.* **Description:** Covers neurosurgery and related subjects.
Incorporates: Journal of Pediatric Neurosciences; Formerly (until 1973): Minerva Neurochirurgica (0026-4881)
Related titles: Microform ed.: (from PQC, RPI); Online - full text ed.: ISSN 1827-1855. 2005.
Indexed: A22, B21, BDM&CN, E-psyche, EMBASE, ExcerpMed, IndMed, MEDLINE, NSA, NSCI, P20, P22, P26, P30, P48, P54, PQC, R10, Reac, RefZh, SCI, SCOPUS, W07.
—BLDSC (5022.250000), GNLM, IE, Infotrieve, Ingenta, INIST. **CCC.**
Published by: (Societa Italiana di Neurochirurgia), Edizioni Minerva Medica, Corso Bramante 83-85, Turin, 10126, Italy. TEL 39-011-678282, FAX 39-011-674502, journals.dept@minervamedica.it, http://www.minervamedica.it. Ed. R M Villani. Pub. Alberto Oliaro. Circ: 3,000 (paid).

617 GBR ISSN 0963-5386
➤ **THE JOURNAL OF ONE-DAY SURGERY.** Text in English. 1991. q. bk.rev. abstr. 28 p./no. 2 cols./p.; Supplement avail.; back issues avail. **Document type:** *Journal, Academic/Scholarly.* **Description:** Covers articles of relevance to day and short-stay surgery.
Indexed: B28, C06, C07, C08, CINAHL.
—BLDSC (5026.314600), IE. **CCC.**
Published by: (British Association of Day Surgery), Newton Mann Ltd., Fourteen Business Centre, 14 Town St, Duffield, DE56 4EH, United Kingdom. TEL 44-1332-843107, FAX 44-845-009-8871, enquiries@newtonmann.co.uk, http://www.newtonmann.co.uk. Ed. Mark Skues.

➤ **JOURNAL OF ORAL AND MAXILLOFACIAL PATHOLOGY.** *see* MEDICAL SCIENCES—Dentistry

➤ **JOURNAL OF ORAL AND MAXILLOFACIAL SURGERY.** *see* MEDICAL SCIENCES—Dentistry

617 USA ISSN 0022-3468
RD137.A1 CODEN: JPDSA3
➤ **JOURNAL OF PEDIATRIC SURGERY.** Abbreviated title: J P S. Text in English. 1966 (Feb.). m. USD 1,028 in United States to institutions; USD 1,197 elsewhere to institutions (effective 2012). adv. bk.rev. abstr.; bibl.; charts; illus. index. back issues avail.; reprints avail. **Document type:** *Journal, Academic/Scholarly.* **Description:** Provide the most current source of information and references in pediatric surgery. Presents improve the surgical care of infants and children, not only through advances in physiology, pathology and surgical techniques, but also by attention to the unique emotional and physical needs of the young patient.
Related titles: Online - full text ed.: ISSN 1531-5037 (from ScienceDirect).
Indexed: A22, A26, A29, A34, A36, A38, ASCA, B20, B21, BDM&CN, CA, CABA, CCIP, CTA, CurCont, D01, DentInd, E01, E12, EMBASE, ESPM, ExcerpMed, F08, FR, GH, H&SSA, H17, I05, INI, ISR, IndMed, Inpharma, LT, MEDLINE, N02, N03, NSA, P30, P33, P35, P39, R10, R12, R13, RA&MP, RM&VM, RRTA, Reac, SCI, SCOPUS, SoyAb, T02, T05, VS, ViroIAbstr, W07, W10.
—BLDSC (5030.275000), GNLM, IE, Infotrieve, Ingenta, INIST. **CCC.**
Published by: (American Academy of Pediatrics, Surgical Section), W.B. Saunders Co. (Subsidiary of: Elsevier Health Sciences), Elsevier, Health Sciences Division, Order Fulfillment, 3251 Riverport Ln, Maryland Heights, MO 63043. TEL 314-872-8370, 800-325-4177, FAX 314-432-1380, JournalCustomerService-usa@elsevier.com, http://www.us.elsevierhealth.com. Ed. Dr. Jay L Grosfield TEL 317-274-5716. Pub. Pat Hogan. Circ: 1,520. **Co-sponsors:** British Association of Paediatric Surgeons; Canadian Association of Paediatric Surgeons, Pacific Association of Pediatric Surgeons; American Pediatric Surgical Association.

➤ **JOURNAL OF PEDIATRIC SURGICAL SPECIALTIES.** *see* MEDICAL SCIENCES—Pediatrics

➤ **JOURNAL OF PERIOPERATIVE PRACTICE.** *see* MEDICAL SCIENCES—Nurses And Nursing

617.95 GBR ISSN 1532-1959
JOURNAL OF PLASTIC, RECONSTRUCTIVE & AESTHETIC SURGERY (ONLINE). Text in English. m. **Document type:** *Journal, Academic/Scholarly.*
Formerly (until 2006): British Journal of Plastic Surgery (Online) (1465-3087)
Media: Online - full text (from ScienceDirect). **Related titles:** Microform ed.: (from PQC); ◆ Print ed.: Journal of Plastic, Reconstructive & Aesthetic Surgery (Print). ISSN 1748-6815.
—CCC.
Published by: Churchill Livingstone (Subsidiary of: Elsevier Health Sciences), Robert Stevenson House, 1-3, Baxter's Pl, Leith Walk, Edinburgh, Midlothian EH1 3AF, United Kingdom. TEL 44-131-5562424, FAX 44-131-5581278, journals@harcourt.com, http://www.harcourthealth.com.

617.95 GBR ISSN 1748-6815
RD118.A1 CODEN: BJPSAZ
➤ **JOURNAL OF PLASTIC, RECONSTRUCTIVE & AESTHETIC SURGERY (PRINT).** Abbreviated title: J P R A S. Text in English. 1948. m. EUR 905 in Europe to institutions; JPY 97,800 in Japan to institutions; USD 805 elsewhere to institutions (effective 2012). adv. bk.rev. abstr.; illus. index. back issues avail.; reprints avail. **Document type:** *Journal, Academic/Scholarly.* **Description:** Discusses techniques and developments in plastic surgery.
Formerly (until 2006): British Journal of Plastic Surgery (Print) (0007-1226)
Related titles: Microform ed.: (from PQC); ◆ Online - full text ed.: Journal of Plastic, Reconstructive & Aesthetic Surgery (Online). ISSN 1532-1959.
Indexed: A20, A22, A26, ASCA, B&BAb, B21, BioEngAb, CA, ChemAb, CurCont, DentInd, E01, EMBASE, ExcerpMed, FR, I05, INI, ISR, IndMed, Inpharma, JW-D, MEDLINE, MLA-IB, MS&D, P30, P35, R10, Reac, SCI, SCOPUS, T02, W07.
—BLDSC (5040.695800), GNLM, IE, Infotrieve, Ingenta, INIST. **CCC.**
Published by: (British Association of Plastic, Reconstructive and Aesthetic Surgeons, British Association of Plastic Surgeons), Churchill Livingstone (Subsidiary of: Elsevier Health Sciences), The Blvd, Langford Ln, Kidlington, OX5 1GB, United Kingdom. TEL 44-1865-843434, FAX 44-1865-843970, directenquiries@elsevier.com, http://www.elsevierhealth.com/imprint.jsp?iid=9. Ed. S Hofer. Pub. Gillian Griffith. Adv. contact David Dunnachie.

617.95 GBR ISSN 2000-656X
CODEN: SJPSEM
➤ **JOURNAL OF PLASTIC SURGERY AND HAND SURGERY.** Text in English. 1967. bi-m. GBP 340, EUR 450, USD 565 combined subscription to institutions (print & online eds.); GBP 685, EUR 1,130, USD 1,130 combined subscription to corporations (print & online eds.) (effective 2010). adv. back issues avail.; reprint service avail. from PSC. **Document type:** *Journal, Academic/Scholarly.* **Description:** Intended to serve as a forum for plastic surgery, hand surgery and related research in Scandinavia. Interest is focused on original articles on basic research and clinical evaluation.
Former titles (until 2010): Scandinavian Journal of Plastic and Reconstructive Surgery and Hand Surgery (0284-4311); (until 1987): Scandinavian Journal of Plastic and Reconstructive Surgery (0036-5556)
Related titles: Online - full text ed.: ISSN 2000-6764. 2002 (from IngentaConnect); ◆ Supplement(s): Scandinavian Journal of Plastic and Reconstructive Surgery and Hand Surgery. Supplement. ISSN 1101-3923.
Indexed: A01, A03, A08, A22, ASCA, CA, CurCont, DentInd, E01, EMBASE, ExcerpMed, IBR, IBZ, ISR, IndMed, Inpharma, MEDLINE, MS&D, P30, R10, Reac, SCI, SCOPUS, T02, W07.
—BLDSC (5040.696000), CASDDS, GNLM, IE, Infotrieve, Ingenta, INIST. **CCC.**
Published by: (Scandinavian Association of Plastic Surgeons NOR), Informa Healthcare (Subsidiary of: T & F Informa plc), Telephone House, 69-77 Paul St, London, EC2A 4LQ, United Kingdom. TEL 44-20-70175000, FAX 44-20-70176792, healthcare.enquiries@informa.com. Eds. Goran Lundborg, Kiyonori Harii, Jan Lija. **Subscr. in N. America to:** Taylor & Francis Inc., Customer Services Dept, 325 Chestnut St, 8th Fl, Philadelphia, PA 19106. TEL 215-625-8900, 800-354-1420, FAX 215-625-8914, customerservice@taylorandfrancis.com; **Subscr. outside N. America to:** Taylor & Francis Ltd., Journals Customer Service, Sheepen Pl, Colchester, Essex CO3 3LP, United Kingdom. TEL 44-20-70175544, FAX 44-20-70175198, tf.enquiries@tfinforma.com.

616 USA ISSN 0743-684X
RD33.6 CODEN: JRMIE2
➤ **JOURNAL OF RECONSTRUCTIVE MICROSURGERY.** Text in English. 1984. 9/yr. USD 907 domestic to institutions; USD 934 foreign to institutions; USD 1,112 combined subscription domestic to institutions (print & online eds.); USD 1,160 combined subscription foreign to institutions (print & online eds.) (effective 2011). adv. illus. reprints avail. **Document type:** *Journal, Academic/Scholarly.* **Description:** publishes original articles containing clinical information of use to the practicing micro-surgeon.
Related titles: Microfilm ed.; Online - full text ed.: ISSN 1098-8947. USD 1,067 domestic to institutions; USD 1,088 foreign to institutions (effective 2011).
Indexed: A01, A03, A08, A22, ASCA, CA, CurCont, EMBASE, ExcerpMed, INI, IndMed, Inpharma, MEDLINE, P30, R10, Reac, SCI, SCOPUS, T02, W07.
—BLDSC (5048.157000), GNLM, IE, Infotrieve, Ingenta, INIST. **CCC.**
Published by: Thieme Medical Publishers (Subsidiary of: Georg Thieme Verlag), 333 Seventh Ave, New York, NY 10001. TEL 212-760-0888, 800-782-3488, FAX 212-947-1112, info@thieme.com, http://www.thieme.com. Ed. Peter C Neligan TEL 206-543-5516. Adv. contact Berish Strauch. Circ: 1,019. **Co-sponsor:** American Society of the Peripheral Nerve.

617.7 USA ISSN 1081-597X
CODEN: JRSUFZ
➤ **JOURNAL OF REFRACTIVE SURGERY.** Text in English. 1985. m. USD 249 combined subscription to individuals (print & online eds.); USD 359 combined subscription to institutions (print & online eds.); USD 48 per issue (effective 2010). bk.rev. abstr.; charts; illus.; stat.; tr.lit. index. back issues avail.; reprints avail. **Document type:** *Journal, Academic/Scholarly.* **Description:** Forum for original research, review, and evaluation of refractive and corneal surgical procedures.
Former titles (until 1995): Journal of Refractive and Corneal Surgery (1081-0803); (until 1994): Refractive & Corneal Surgery (1042-962X); (until 1989): Journal of Refractive Surgery (0883-0444)
Related titles: Online - full text ed.: ISSN 1938-2391.
Indexed: A22, ASCA, CA, CurCont, EMBASE, ExcerpMed, FR, ISR, IndMed, Inpharma, MEDLINE, OphLit, P20, P22, P30, P35, P48, P54, PQC, R10, Reac, SCI, SCOPUS, T02, W07.
—BLDSC (5048.290000), GNLM, IE, Infotrieve, Ingenta, INIST. **CCC.**
Published by: (International Society of Refractive Surgery), Slack, Inc., 6900 Grove Rd, Thorofare, NJ 08086. TEL 856-848-1000, FAX 856-848-6091, customerservice@slackinc.com, http://www.slackinc.com. Eds. Dr. George Waring, Jennifer Kilpatrick. Pubs. John C. Carter, Richard N Roash. Adv. contacts Cherie Pearson, Frank Cassera. **Subscr. in Japan to:** Woodbell Inc., 4-22-11 Kitaka-Sai, Edogawa-ku, Tokyo 134-0081, Japan. **Co-sponsor:** European Refractive Surgery Society.

617 629.892 GBR ISSN 1863-2483
RD73.S785
➤ **JOURNAL OF ROBOTIC SURGERY.** Text in English. 2007. q. EUR 509, USD 616 combined subscription to institutions (print & online eds.) (effective 2012). reprint service avail. from PSC. **Document type:** *Journal, Academic/Scholarly.*
Related titles: Online - full text ed.: ISSN 1863-2491 (from IngentaConnect).
Indexed: A22, A26, E01, E08, H12, P30, S09, SCOPUS.
—IE. **CCC.**
Published by: Springer U K (Subsidiary of: Springer Science+Business Media), Ashbourne House, The Guildway, Old Portsmouth Rd, Guildford, Surrey GU3 1LP, United Kingdom. TEL 44-1483-734433, FAX 44-1483-734411. Ed. Vipul R. Patel. **Dist. in the Americas by:** Springer New York LLC, Journal Fulfillment, PO Box 2485, Secaucus, NJ 07096. TEL 212-460-1500, FAX 201-348-4505.

617.57 USA ISSN 1058-2746
CODEN: JSESBU
➤ **JOURNAL OF SHOULDER AND ELBOW SURGERY.** Text in English. 1992. bi-m. USD 421 in United States to institutions; USD 505 elsewhere to institutions (effective 2012). adv. back issues avail.; reprints avail. **Document type:** *Journal, Academic/Scholarly.* **Description:** Focuses on medical, surgical, and physical techniques for treating injury/disease of the upper extremity, including the shoulder girdle, arm, and elbow.
Related titles: Online - full text ed.: ISSN 1532-6500 (from ScienceDirect).
Indexed: A22, A26, CA, CurCont, E01, EMBASE, ExcerpMed, FoSS&M, I05, ISR, IndMed, MEDLINE, P30, R10, Reac, SCI, SCOPUS, T02, W07.
—BLDSC (5064.435000), GNLM, IE, Infotrieve, Ingenta, INIST. **CCC.**
Published by: (American Shoulder and Elbow Surgeons), Mosby, Inc. (Subsidiary of: Elsevier Health Sciences), 1600 John F. Kennedy Blvd, Ste 1800, Philadelphia, PA 19103. TEL 215-239-3900, 800-523-1649, FAX 215-239-3990, elspcs@elsevier.com, http://www.us.elsevierhealth.com. Ed. William J Mallon. **Co-sponsors:** European Society for Surgery of Shoulder and Elbow; Japan Shoulder Society; South African Shoulder and Elbow Surgeons; Shoulder and Elbow Society of Australia; Brazilian Orthopaedic and Traumatologic Society, Shoulder and Elbow Committee.

➤ **JOURNAL OF SPINAL DISORDERS & TECHNIQUES.** *see* MEDICAL SCIENCES—Orthopedics And Traumatology

617 USA ISSN 1090-1183
➤ **JOURNAL OF SURGERY**; a journal of advances in surgery. Text in English. 1996. m. USD 9.99 (effective 2010). **Document type:** *Journal, Academic/Scholarly.*
Media: Online - full text.

Published by: (National Medical Society), Current Clinical Strategies Publishing Inc., 27071 Cabot Rd, Ste 126, Laguna Hills, CA 92653. TEL 949-348-8404, 800-331-8227, FAX 909-744-8071, 800-965-9420, info@ccspublishing.com, http://www.ccspublishing.com/ccs/.

617 GBR ISSN 2042-8812
▼➤ **JOURNAL OF SURGICAL CASE REPORTS.** Text in English. 2010. irreg. free (effective 2011). **Document type:** *Journal, Academic/Scholarly.*
Media: Online - full text.
Indexed: A26, E08, H11, H12, I05.
Published by: J S C R Publishing Limited Ed. Derek Alderson.

617 USA ISSN 1931-7204
CODEN: CUSUDB
➤ **JOURNAL OF SURGICAL EDUCATION.** Text in English. 1943. bi-m. USD 321 in United States to institutions; USD 444 elsewhere to institutions (effective 2012). adv. illus. index. back issues avail.; reprints avail. **Document type:** *Journal, Academic/Scholarly.* **Description:** Presents reviews on topics in general surgery, the surgical subspecialties, and nonsurgical medicine from the current medical literature, using an abstract/commentary format.
Former titles (until 2007): Current Surgery (0149-7944); (until 1978): Review of Surgery (0034-6780); (until 1962): Quarterly Review of Surgery; Iuntil 1961): Quarterly Review of Surgery, Obstetrics and Gynecology
Related titles: Microfilm ed.: (from PQC); Online - full text ed.: ISSN 1878-7452 (from IngentaConnect, ScienceDirect).
Indexed: A01, A03, A08, A22, A26, CA, ChemAb, CurCont, DentInd, EMBASE, ExcerpMed, I05, IndMed, MEDLINE, P30, R10, Reac, SCI, SCOPUS, T02, W07.
—BLDSC (5067.379000), CASDDS, GNLM, IE, Infotrieve, Ingenta, INIST. **CCC.**
Published by: (Association of Program Directors in Surgery), Elsevier Inc. (Subsidiary of: Elsevier Science & Technology), 1600 John F Kennedy Blvd, Philadelphia, PA 19103. TEL 215-239-3900, FAX 215-238-7883, JournalCustomerService-usa@elsevier.com, http://www.elsevier.com. Ed. Dr. John A Weigelt. Pub. Andrew Berin. Circ: 675.

617 616.994 USA ISSN 0022-4790
RD651 CODEN: JSONAU
➤ **JOURNAL OF SURGICAL ONCOLOGY.** Text in English. 1969. 16/yr. GBP 2,915 in United Kingdom to institutions; EUR 3,686 in Europe to institutions; USD 5,377 in United States to institutions; USD 5,601 in Canada & Mexico to institutions; USD 5,713 elsewhere to institutions; GBP 3,354 combined subscription in United Kingdom to institutions (print & online eds.); EUR 4,241 combined subscription in Europe to institutions (print & online eds.); USD 6,183 combined subscription in United States to institutions (print & online eds.); USD 6,407 combined subscription in Canada & Mexico to institutions (print & online eds.); USD 6,519 combined subscription elsewhere to institutions (print & online eds.) (effective 2012). adv. charts; illus.; stat. index. back issues avail.; reprint service avail. from PSC. **Document type:** *Journal, Academic/Scholarly.* **Description:** Encompasses surgical approaches and presents studies of related topics such as radiotherapy, chemotherapy, and immunotherapy.
Incorporates (1985-2003): Seminars in Surgical Oncology (8756-0437); Which was formerly (until 1985): International Advances in Surgical Oncology (0190-1575)
Related titles: Microform ed.: (from PQC); Online - full text ed.: ISSN 1096-9098. GBP 2,744 in United Kingdom to institutions; EUR 3,469 in Europe to institutions; USD 5,377 elsewhere to institutions (effective 2012); Supplement(s): Journal of Surgical Oncology. Supplement. ISSN 1046-7416.
Indexed: A22, ASCA, B21, CIN, ChemAb, ChemTitl, CurCont, DentInd, EMBASE, ExcerpMed, FR, INI, ISR, IndMed, Inpharma, MEDLINE, MS&D, P30, P35, R10, Reac, RefZh, SCI, SCOPUS, W07.
—BLDSC (5067.380000), CASDDS, GNLM, IE, Infotrieve, Ingenta, INIST. **CCC.**
Published by: John Wiley & Sons, Inc., 111 River St, Hoboken, NJ 07030. TEL 201-748-6000, FAX 201-748-6088, info@wiley.com, http://www.wiley.com/WileyCDA/. Ed. Walley J Temple. Pub. Kim Thompkins TEL 212-850-6921. Adv. contact Lilly Addison TEL 201-748-8716. Circ: 930. **Subscr. outside the Americas to:** John Wiley & Sons Ltd., The Atrium, Southern Gate, Chichester, West Sussex PO19 8SQ, United Kingdom. TEL 44-1243-779777, 800-243407, FAX 44-1243-775878, cs-journals@wiley.com.

617 USA ISSN 0022-4804
RD1 CODEN: JSGRA2
➤ **JOURNAL OF SURGICAL RESEARCH.** Abbreviated title: J S R. Text in English. 1961. 14/yr. USD 2,230 in United States to institutions; USD 2,535 elsewhere to institutions (effective 2012). adv. bk.rev. charts; illus. index. back issues avail.; reprints avail. **Document type:** *Journal, Academic/Scholarly.* **Description:** Features original articles concerned with clinical and laboratory investigations relevant to surgical practice and teaching.
Related titles: Online - full text ed.: ISSN 1095-8673 (from IngentaConnect, ScienceDirect).
Indexed: A01, A03, A08, A22, A26, A34, A35, A36, ASCA, AgrForAb, B25, BIOSIS Prev, BP, CA, CABA, CIN, ChemAb, ChemTitl, CurCont, E01, EMBASE, ExcerpMed, F08, F11, F12, FR, GH, I05, ISR, IndMed, IndVet, Inpharma, MEDLINE, MS&D, MycolAb, N02, N03, OR, P30, P32, P33, P35, PN&I, R10, R12, R13, RA&MP, RM&VM, Reac, SCI, SCOPUS, T02, T05, VS, W07.
—BLDSC (5067.400000), CASDDS, GNLM, IE, Infotrieve, Ingenta, INIST. **CCC.**
Published by: (Association for Academic Surgery), Academic Press (Subsidiary of: Elsevier Science & Technology), 3251 Riverport Ln, Maryland Heights, MO 63043. TEL 314-447-8010, FAX 314-447-8030, JournalCustomerService-usa@elsevier.com, http://www.elsevierdirect.com/imprint.jsp?iid=5. Eds. Dr. D W McFadden, Dr. Wiley W Souba. Adv. contact Tino DeCarlo TEL 212-633-3815.

617 IND ISSN 2006-8808
▼➤ **JOURNAL OF SURGICAL TECHNIQUE AND CASE REPORT.** Text in English. 2009. s-a. INR 1,500, USD 300 domestic (effective 2010). adv. abstr. **Document type:** *Journal, Academic/Scholarly.*
Related titles: Online - full text ed.
Indexed: A01, A26, E08, H12, I05, T02.
—**CCC.**
Published by: Medknow Publications and Media Pvt. Ltd., B-9, Kanara Business Ctr, Off Link Rd, Ghatkopar (E), Mumbai, Maharastra 400 075, India. TEL 91-22-66491816, 91-22-66491818, publishing@medknow.com, http://www.medknow.com. Ed. Isma'ila A. Mungadi. Pub. Dr. D K Sahu. Adv. contact Kaushik Shah.

617 USA ISSN 1536-5018
RD31.5
➤ **JOURNAL OF THE PHILOSOPHY OF SURGERY AND MEDICINE.** Text in English. 2001 (Oct.). s-a. USD 30 per issue (effective 2011). **Document type:** *Journal, Academic/Scholarly.*
Published by: Wyndham Hall Press, 5050 Kerr Rd, Lima, OH 45806. TEL 419-648-9124, FAX 419-648-9124, orders@wyndhamhallpress.com, http://www.wyndhamhallpress.com/.

617 USA ISSN 0022-5223
RD536 CODEN: JTCSAQ
➤ **THE JOURNAL OF THORACIC AND CARDIOVASCULAR SURGERY.** Text in English. 1931. m. USD 869 in United States to institutions; USD 990 elsewhere to institutions (effective 2012). adv. bibl.; illus. s-a. index. back issues avail.; reprints avail. **Document type:** *Journal, Academic/Scholarly.* **Description:** Devoted to conditions of the heart, lungs, chest and great vessels where surgical intervention is indicated.
Formerly (until 1959): Journal of Thoracic Surgery (0096-5588)
Related titles: CD-ROM ed.: ISSN 1085-8687. 199?; Microfilm ed.: (from PQC); Online - full text ed.: ISSN 1097-685X (from ScienceDirect).
Indexed: A22, A26, AIM, ASCA, BIOBASE, CA, CIN, ChemAb, ChemTitl, CurCont, E01, EMBASE, ExcerpMed, G08, H11, H12, IABS, IDIS, ISR, IndMed, Inpharma, JW-C, MEDLINE, P30, P35, R10, Reac, SCI, SCOPUS, T02, W07.
—BLDSC (5069.100000), CASDDS, GNLM, IE, Infotrieve, Ingenta, INIST. **CCC.**
Published by: (American Association for Thoracic Surgery, Western Thoracic Surgical Association), Mosby, Inc. (Subsidiary of: Elsevier Health Sciences), 1600 John F. Kennedy Blvd, Ste 1800, Philadelphia, PA 19103. TEL 215-239-3900, 800-523-1649, FAX 215-239-3990, elspcs@elsevier.com, http://www.us.elsevierhealth.com. Ed. Lawrence H Cohn. **Co-sponsor:** Western Thoracic Surgical Association.

617 USA ISSN 2090-0007
▼➤ **JOURNAL OF TRANSPLANTATION.** Text in English. 2009. irreg. USD 195 (effective 2011). **Document type:** *Journal, Academic/Scholarly.* **Description:** publishes original research articles, review articles, case reports, and clinical studies in all areas of transplantation.
Related titles: Online - full text ed.: ISSN 2090-0015. free (effective 2011).
Indexed: A01, B21, C06, C07, CA, ImmunAb, P30, T02.
Published by: Hindawi Publishing Corporation, 410 Park Ave, 15th Fl, PMB 287, New York, NY 10022. FAX 215-893-4392, 866-446-3294, info@hindawi.com.

617.4 USA ISSN 0741-5214
RD598.5
➤ **JOURNAL OF VASCULAR SURGERY.** Text in English. 1984. m. USD 842 in United States to institutions; USD 965 elsewhere to institutions (effective 2012). adv. bk.rev. s-a. index. back issues avail.; reprints avail. **Document type:** *Journal, Academic/Scholarly.* **Description:** Presents the latest advances in the knowledge of the peripheral vascular system and vascular surgery.
Related titles: CD-ROM ed.: ISSN 1085-875X; Microfilm ed.: (from PQC); Online - full text ed.: ISSN 1097-6809 (from ScienceDirect).
Indexed: A20, A22, A26, ASCA, B25, BIOSIS Prev, CA, CurCont, E01, EMBASE, ExcerpMed, FR, G08, H11, H12, INI, ISR, IndMed, Inpharma, JW-C, MEDLINE, MycolAb, P30, P35, R10, Reac, SCI, SCOPUS, T02, VITIS, W07.
—BLDSC (5072.270000), GNLM, IE, Infotrieve, Ingenta, INIST. **CCC.**
Published by: (Society for Vascular Surgery), Mosby, Inc. (Subsidiary of: Elsevier Health Sciences), 1600 John F. Kennedy Blvd, Ste 1800, Philadelphia, PA 19103. TEL 215-239-3900, 800-523-1649, FAX 215-239-3990, elspcs@elsevier.com, http://www.us.elsevierhealth.com. Eds. Anton N Sidawy, Bruce A Perler. Circ: 7,465 (paid). **Co-sponsor:** International Society for Cardiovascular Surgery, North American Chapter.

617.554 USA ISSN 1071-5754
➤ **JOURNAL OF W O C N.** (Wound, Ostomy and Continence Nursing) Text in English. 1974. bi-m. USD 336.51 domestic to institutions; USD 458 foreign to institutions (effective 2011). adv. charts; illus.; stat. index. back issues avail.; reprints avail. **Document type:** *Journal, Academic/Scholarly.* **Description:** Explores to nursing care and management of patients with abdominal stomas, wounds, pressure ulcers, fistulas, vascular ulcers, and incontinence.
Former titles (until 1994): Journal of E T Nursing (1055-3045); (until 1991): Journal of Enterostomal Therapy (0270-1170); (until 1980): E T Journal (0195-9883)
Related titles: Microfilm ed.: (from PQC); Online - full text ed.: ISSN 1528-3976.
Indexed: A22, A26, C06, C07, C08, CINAHL, CurCont, E01, EMBASE, ExcerpMed, I05, INI, MEDLINE, NurAb, P30, R10, Reac, SCI, SCOPUS, SSCI, W07.
—BLDSC (5072.632700), GNLM, IE, Infotrieve, Ingenta. **CCC.**
Published by: (Wound, Ostomy and Continence Nurses Society), Lippincott Williams & Wilkins (Subsidiary of: Wolters Kluwer N.V.), Two Commerce Sq, 2001 Market St, Philadelphia, PA 19103. TEL 215-521-8300, FAX 215-521-8902, customerservice@lww.com, http://www.lww.com. Ed. Mikel L Gray. Pub. Beth L Guthy. Circ: 5,973.

617 CHN ISSN 1672-5042
JUJIE SHUSHUXUE ZAZHI/JOURNAL OF REGIONAL ANATOMY AND OPERATIVE SURGERY. Text in Chinese. 1992. bi-m. USD 37.20 (effective 2009). **Document type:** *Journal, Academic/Scholarly.*
Related titles: Online - full text ed.
—East View.
Published by: Chongqing Shi Jiepou Xuehui, 30, Gaotanyan, Shapingba-qu, Chongqing, 400038, China. TEL 86-23-68752251, FAX 86-23-68752250. **Dist. by:** China International Book Trading Corp, 35 Chegongzhuang Xilu, Haidian District, PO Box 399, Beijing 100044, China. TEL 86-10-68412045, FAX 86-10-68412023, cibtc@mail.cibtc.com.cn, http://www.cibtc.com.cn.

617 ROM ISSN 1584-9341
RD32
➤ **JURNALUL DE CHIRURGIE/JOURNAL DE CHIRURGIE/JOURNAL OF SURGERY.** Text in Romanian, English, French. 2005. q. free (effective 2011). **Document type:** *Journal, Academic/Scholarly.*
Media: Online - full text.
Indexed: A01, CA, T02.
Published by: Universitatea de Medicina si Farmacia "G T Popa" Iasi/University of Medicine and Pharmacy "G T Popa" Iasi, Bd Independentei 1, Iasi, 700111, Romania. TEL 40-232-267786, FAX 40-232-218272, http://www.umfiasi.ro. Ed. Radu Moldovan.

➤ **KAGAWA NO SHINKEI GEKA DANWAKAI KAISHI/KAGAWA COLLOQUIUM ON NEUROSURGERY. JOURNAL.** *see* MEDICAL SCIENCES—Psychiatry And Neurology

617 JPN ISSN 1346-0498
KAGOSHIMA-KEN RINSHO GEKA GAKKAISHI/KAGOSHIMA SOCIETY FOR CLINICAL SURGERY. JOURNAL. Text in Japanese. 1985. a. **Document type:** *Journal, Academic/Scholarly.*
Formerly (until 1996): Kagoshimaken Rinsho Geka Ikaishi (0913-459X)
Published by: Kagoshimaken Rinsho Geka Ikai/Kagoshima Society for Clinical Surgery, c/o Kagoshima Medical Society, 8-1 Chuo-cho, Kagoshima, 890-0053, Japan. TEL 81-99-2548121, FAX 81-99-2548129.

KAN TAN SUI GAZOU/HEPATO-BILIARY-PANCREATIC IMAGING. *see* MEDICAL SCIENCES—Radiology And Nuclear Medicine

KANSETSU GEKA/JOURNAL OF JOINT SURGERY. *see* MEDICAL SCIENCES—Orthopedics And Traumatology

KANSETSUKYO/ARTHROSCOPY. *see* MEDICAL SCIENCES—Orthopedics And Traumatology

KARDIOCHIRURGIA I TORAKOCHIRURGIA POLSKA. *see* MEDICAL SCIENCES—Cardiovascular Diseases

KEY NOTE MARKET REPORT: COSMETIC SURGERY. *see* BUSINESS AND ECONOMICS—Marketing And Purchasing

617 BGR ISSN 0450-2167
CODEN: KHIGAF
KHIRURGIA. Text in Bulgarian; Summaries in English, Russian. 1948. bi-m. BGL 24; USD 72 foreign (effective 2002). **Document type:** *Journal.*
Indexed: ChemAb, DentInd, EMBASE, ExcerpMed, IndMed, MEDLINE, P30, R10, Reac, SCOPUS.
—CASDDS, GNLM, Infotrieve, INIST.
Published by: (Bulgaria. Ministerstvo na Narodnoto Zdrave), Izdatelstvo Meditsina i Fizkultura, 11 Slaveikov Sq, Sofia, 1080, Bulgaria. TEL 359-2-9884068, FAX 359-2-9871308, medpubl@abv.bg. Ed. N Vasilev. Circ: 1,200. **Co-sponsor:** Nauchno Druzhestvo po Chirurgia.

617 RUS ISSN 0023-1207
CODEN: KHIRAE
➤ **KHIRURGIYA. ZHURNAL IM. N.I. PIROGOVA/SURGERY.** Text in Russian; Summaries in English. 1925. m. USD 450 in North America (effective 2010). adv. bk.rev. index. reprints avail. **Document type:** *Journal, Academic/Scholarly.* **Description:** Discusses general and abdominal surgery, oncology, traumatology, endocrinology, pediatric surgery, problems of chest surgery and anesthesiology.
Related titles: Online - full content ed.
Indexed: A20, A22, ChemAb, DentInd, EMBASE, ExcerpMed, IndMed, MEDLINE, P30, R10, Reac, RefZh, SCOPUS.
—BLDSC (0394.785000), East View, GNLM, IE, Ingenta, INIST. **CCC.**
Published by: (Assotsiatsiya Khirurgov im. N.I. Pirogova), Media Sfera, Dmitrovskoe shosse 46, korp 2, etazh 4, P.O. Box 54, Moscow, 127238, Russian Federation. TEL 7-095-4824329, FAX 7-095-4824312, podpiska@mediasphera.ru, http://mediasphera.ru. Ed. N N Malinovskii. Circ: 3,000 (paid). **Dist. by:** East View Information Services, 10601 Wayzata Blvd, Minneapolis, MN 55305. TEL 952-252-1201, 800-477-1005, FAX 952-252-1202, info@eastview.com, http://www.eastview.com. **Co-sponsor:** Ministerstvo Zdravookhraneniya Rossiiskoi Federatsii/Ministry of Public Health of Russian Federation.

➤ **KIEFERORTHOPAEDIE NACHRICHTEN.** *see* MEDICAL SCIENCES—Dentistry

➤ **KIKAN GANKA SHUJUTSU/JAPANESE SOCIETY OF OPHTHALMIC SURGEONS. JOURNAL.** *see* MEDICAL SCIENCES—Ophthalmology And Optometry

617 UKR ISSN 1727-0847
➤ **KLINICHNA ANATOMIYA TA OPERATYVNA HHIRURHIYA/CLINICAL ANATOMY AND OPERATIVE SURGERY;** naukovo-praktychnyi medychnyi zhurnal. Text in Ukrainian. 2002. q. **Document type:** *Journal, Academic/Scholarly.*
Related titles: Online - full text ed.: ISSN 1993-5897.
Published by: (Naukove Tovarystvo Anatomiv, Histolohiv, Embriolohiv i Topografoanatomiv Ukrainy/Scientific Society of Anatomists, Histologists and Embryologists of Ukraine), Bukovyns'kyi Derzhavnyi Medychnyi Universytet/Bukovinian State Medical University, vul Ryz'ka 3, Chernivtsi, 58022, Ukraine. Ed. Yu T Ahtemiichuk.

617 UKR ISSN 0023-2130
CODEN: KLKHAM
➤ **KLINICHNA KHIRURHIYA.** Text in Ukrainian. 1921. m. bk.rev. abstr.; bibl. index. **Document type:** *Journal, Academic/Scholarly.*
Former titles (until 1993): Klinicheskaya Khirurgiya; (until 1962): Novyi Khirurgicheskii Arkhiv
Indexed: ChemAb, DentInd, EMBASE, ExcerpMed, IndMed, MEDLINE, P30, R10, Reac, SCOPUS.
—BLDSC (0089.258100), CASDDS, East View, GNLM, INIST. **CCC.**
Published by: (Ministerstvo Okhorony Zdorov'ya Ukrainy, Nauchnoe Obshchestvo Khirurgov Ukrainy), Akademiya Medychnykh Nauk Ukrainy, Instytut Khirurhii ta Transplantolohii, vul Heroiv Sevastopolya, 30, Kyiv, 03680, Ukraine. TEL 380-44-4881811, surgery@i.com.ua, http://www.surgery.org.ua. Ed. Serhii Andreeshchev.

➤ **KNEE SURGERY, SPORTS TRAUMATOLOGY, ARTHROSCOPY.** *see* MEDICAL SCIENCES—Sports Medicine

362.19795 JPN ISSN 0916-0094
KONNICHI NO ISHOKU/TRANSPLANTATION NOW. Text in Japanese. 1988. bi-m. JPY 2,000 newsstand/cover (effective 2005). **Document type:** *Journal, Academic/Scholarly.*
—BLDSC (9025.080000).
Published by: Nihon Igakukan, 6F, 5-3-4 Koishikawa,Bunkyo-ku, Tokyo, 112-0002, Japan. TEL 81-3-38688077, FAX 81-3-38688078.

617.3 CHN ISSN 1005-4979
KOUQIANG HEMIAN WAIKE ZAZHI/JOURNAL OF ORAL AND MAXILLOFACIAL SURGERY. Variant title: China Journal of Oral and Maxillofacial Surgery. Text in Chinese. 1991. q. USD 24.60 (effective 2009). **Document type:** *Journal, Academic/Scholarly.*
Related titles: Online - full text ed.
—East View.
Published by: Tongji Daxue, Fushu Tongji Yiyuan, 399, Yanchang Zhonglu, Shanghai, 200072, China. TEL 86-21-56032686 ext 8025, FAX 86-21-51229067. **Dist. by:** China International Book Trading Corp, 35 Chegongzhuang Xilu, Haidian District, PO Box 399, Beijing 100044, China. TEL 86-10-68412045, FAX 86-10-68412023, cibtc@mail.cibtc.com.cn, http://www.cibtc.com.cn.

617.54 JPN ISSN 0021-5252
KYOBU GEKA/JAPANESE JOURNAL OF THORACIC SURGERY. Text in Japanese; Abstracts and contents page in English. 1948. 13/yr. JPY 36,015 domestic; JPY 48,000 foreign; JPY 4,515 newsstand/cover (effective 2007). adv. charts; illus. Index. **Document type:** *Journal, Academic/Scholarly.*
Indexed: EMBASE, ExcerpMed, IndMed, MEDLINE, P30, R10, Reac, SCOPUS.
—BLDSC (4658.900000), GNLM, IE, Infotrieve, Ingenta, INIST.
Published by: Nankodo Co. Ltd., 3-42-6 Hongo, Bunkyo-ku, Tokyo, 113-8410, Japan. TEL 81-3-38117140, FAX 81-3-38117265, http://www.nankodo.co.jp/. Eds. Akira Furuse, Shigefumi Fujimura. Circ: 3,000.

617 DEU ISSN 1435-2443
RD1 CODEN: LASUF6
➤ **LANGENBECKS ARCHIVES OF SURGERY.** Text in English. 1945. bi-m. EUR 1,218, USD 1,485 combined subscription to institutions (print & online eds.) (effective 2012). adv. back issues avail.; reprint service avail. from PSC. **Document type:** *Journal, Academic/Scholarly.* **Description:** Provides an international forum for the controlled results of clinical surgery.
Former titles (until 1998): Langenbecks Archiv fuer Chirurgie (0023-8236); (until 1969): Langenbecks Archiv fuer Klinische Chirurgie (0174-4542); Which was formed by the merger of (1860-1945): Archiv fuer Klinische Chirurgie (0365-3706); (1872-1945): Deutsche Zeitschrift fuer Chirurgie (0367-0023); Incorporates (1916-1975): Bruns' Beitraege fuer Klinische Chirurgie (0007-2680)
Related titles: Microform ed.: (from PQC); Online - full text ed.: ISSN 1435-2451 (from IngentaConnect).
Indexed: A01, A03, A08, A22, A26, ASCA, B25, BIOSIS Prev, CA, ChemAb, CurCont, DentInd, E01, EMBASE, ExcerpMed, H12, IBR, IBZ, INI, ISR, IndMed, Inpharma, MEDLINE, MycolAb, P30, P35, R10, Reac, SCI, SCOPUS, T02, W07.
—BLDSC (5155.680500), GNLM, IE, Infotrieve, Ingenta, INIST. **CCC.**
Published by: (Deutsche Gesellschaft fuer Chirurgie), Springer (Subsidiary of: Springer Science+Business Media), Tiergartenstr 17, Heidelberg, 69121, Germany. TEL 49-6221-4870, FAX 49-6221-345229. Ed. Dr. Hans G Beger. adv.: B&W page EUR 790, color page EUR 1,830. Circ: 500 (paid and controlled). **Subscr. in the Americas to:** Springer New York LLC, Journal Fulfillment, PO Box 2485, Secaucus, NJ 07096. TEL 201-348-4033, 800-777-4643, FAX 201-348-4505, journals-ny@springer.com, http://www.springer.com; **Subscr. to:** Springer Distribution Center, Kundenservice Zeitschriften, Haberstr 7, Heidelberg 69126, Germany. TEL 49-6221-3454303, FAX 49-6221-3454229, subscriptions@springer.com.

617.55 USA ISSN 1553-7080
LAPAROSCOPY TODAY. Text in English. 1992. s-a. free (effective 2010). **Document type:** *Journal, Trade.* **Description:** Contains brief overviews of products and services in minimally invasive surgery.
Former titles (until 2004): Laparoscopy and S L S Report (1540-2460); (until 2002): The S L S Report (1060-9458)
Related titles: Online - full text ed.: free (effective 2010).
Published by: Society of Laparoendoscopic Surgeons, 7330 SW 62nd Pl., Ste. 410, Miami, FL 33143. TEL 305-665-9959, FAX 305-667-4123, info@sls.org.

617 535.58 USA ISSN 0196-8092
R857.L37 CODEN: LSMEDI
➤ **LASERS IN SURGERY AND MEDICINE.** Text in English. 1980. 11/yr. GBP 1,551 in United Kingdom to institutions; EUR 1,959 in Europe to institutions; USD 2,804 in United States to institutions; USD 2,958 in Canada & Mexico to institutions; USD 3,035 elsewhere to institutions; GBP 1,785 combined subscription in United Kingdom to institutions (print & online eds.); EUR 2,255 combined subscription in Europe to institutions (print & online eds.); USD 3,225 combined subscription in United States to institutions (print & online eds.); USD 3,379 combined subscription in Canada & Mexico to institutions (print & online eds.); USD 3,456 combined subscription elsewhere to institutions (print & online eds.) (effective 2012). adv. abstr.; bibl.; charts; illus. index. back issues avail.; reprint service avail. from PSC. **Document type:** *Journal, Academic/Scholarly.* **Description:** Covers all aspects of biomedical applications of lasers. Presents research regarding clinical trials, new therapeutic techniques, laser biophysics and bioengineering, and photobiology.
Related titles: Microform ed.: (from PQC); Online - full text ed.: ISSN 1096-9101. 1996. GBP 1,433 in United Kingdom to institutions; EUR 1,810 in Europe to institutions; USD 2,804 elsewhere to institutions (effective 2012); Supplement(s): Lasers in Surgery and Medicine. Supplement. ISSN 1050-9267. 1989.
Indexed: A22, ASCA, B&BAb, B19, B21, BioEngAb, C06, C07, CurCont, DentInd, EMBASE, ExcerpMed, ISR, IndMed, Inpharma, Inspec, JW-D, MEDLINE, MS&D, P30, R10, Reac, RefZh, SCI, SCOPUS, W07.
—BLDSC (5156.683000), CASDDS, GNLM, IE, Infotrieve, Ingenta, INIST, Linda Hall. **CCC.**
Published by: (American Society for Laser Medicine and Surgery), John Wiley & Sons, Inc., 111 River St, Hoboken, NJ 07030. TEL 201-748-6000, FAX 201-748-6088, info@wiley.com, http://www.wiley.com/WileyCDA/. Ed. J Stuart Nelson. Adv. contact Stephen Donohue TEL 781-388-8511. Circ: 4,126. **Subscr. outside the Americas to:** John Wiley & Sons Ltd.

617 LTU ISSN 1392-0995
➤ **LIETUVOS CHIRURGIJA.** Text in Lithuanian, English. 1993. q. **Document type:** *Journal, Academic/Scholarly.* **Description:** Publishes original papers that contribute to knowledge in the fields of clinical surgery, experimental surgery and related sciences.
Related titles: Online - full text ed.: ISSN 1648-9942.
Published by: (Vilniaus Chirurgu Draugija/Vilnius Surgical Society, Kauno Krasto Chirurgu Draugija/Kaunas Region Surgical Society, Klaipedos Krasto Chirurgu Draugija/Klaipeda Region Surgical Society), Amerikos-Lietuvos Draugystes Medicinos Biblioteka/American-Lithuanian Friendship Medical Library, Zurnalo "Lietuvos Chirurgija" Redakcija, Vilniaus Universitetine Greitosios Pagalbos Ligonine, Siltnamiu g 29, Vilnius, 04130, Lithuania. TEL 370-5-2362037, lietuvoschirurgija2000@yahoo.co.uk. Ed. Raimundas Lunevicius.

➤ **LINCHUANG MINIAO WAIKE ZAZHI/JOURNAL OF CLINICAL UROLOGICAL SURGERY.** *see* MEDICAL SCIENCES—Urology And Nephrology

617 CHN ISSN 1005-6483
LINCHUANG WAIKE ZAZHI/JOURNAL OF CLINICAL SURGERY. Text in Chinese. 1993. m. USD 49.20 (effective 2009). **Document type:** *Journal, Academic/Scholarly.*
Related titles: Online - full text ed.
—BLDSC (4958.790200), East View.
Published by: Zhonghua Yixuehui, Hubei Fenhui/Chinese Medical Association, Hubei Branch, 100, Dingziqiao Road, Wuchang, Wuhan, 460064, China. TEL 86-27-87893476, FAX 86-27-87893470. Ed. Sheng-quan Zou. **Dist. by:** China International Book Trading Corp, 35 Chegongzhuang Xilu, Haidian District, PO Box 399, Beijing 100044, China. TEL 86-10-68412045, FAX 86-10-68412023, cibtc@mail.cibtc.com.cn, http://www.cibtc.com.cn.

617 616.8 CHN ISSN 1008-2425
LITI DINGXIANG HE GONGNENGXING SHENJING WAIKE ZAZHI/CHINESE JOURNAL OF STEREOTACTIC AND FUNCTIONAL NEUROSURGERY. Text in Chinese. 1986. bi-m. USD 31.20 (effective 2009). **Document type:** *Journal, Academic/Scholarly.*
Formerly (until 1999): Gongnengxing he Liti Dingxiang Shenjing Waike Zazhi (1004-3896)
Related titles: Online - full text ed.
—East View.
Published by: Anhui Sheng Liti Dingxiang Shenjing Waike Yanjiusuo, 17, Lujiang Lu, Hefei, 230001, China. TEL 86-551-2282374, FAX 86-551-2283997. **Dist. by:** China International Book Trading Corp, 35 Chegongzhuang Xilu, Haidian District, PO Box 399, Beijing 100044, China. TEL 86-10-68412045, FAX 86-10-68412023, cibtc@mail.cibtc.com.cn, http://www.cibtc.com.cn.

LIVER TRANSPLANTATION. *see* MEDICAL SCIENCES—Gastroenterology

617 DEU ISSN 1865-9659
DER M K G - CHIRURG. (Mund Kiefer Gesichts) Text in German. 2008. 3/yr. EUR 262, USD 317 combined subscription to institutions (print & online eds.) (effective 2012). reprint service avail. from PSC. **Document type:** *Journal, Academic/Scholarly.*
Related titles: Online - full text ed.: ISSN 1865-9667. 2008.
Indexed: A22, A26, E01, E08, S09, SCOPUS.
—IE. **CCC.**
Published by: Springer (Subsidiary of: Springer Science+Business Media), Tiergartenstr 17, Heidelberg, 69121, Germany. TEL 49-6221-4870, FAX 49-6221-345229, orders-hd-individuals@springer.com, http://www.springer.com.

617.95 DEU ISSN 1610-6407
MAGAZIN FUER AESTHETISCHE CHIRURGIE. Variant title: Aesthetische Chirurgie. Text in German, English. 2001. 4/yr. EUR 76; EUR 19 newsstand/cover (effective 2009). adv. **Document type:** *Magazine, Trade.* **Description:** Contains articles and trade information on all aspects of cosmetic surgery.
Published by: (Deutsche Gesellschaft fuer Aesthetische Chirurgie e.V.), m d m - Verlag fuer Medizinische Publikationen, Bremsen 4, Leichlingen, 42799, Germany. TEL 49-2175-1691230, FAX 49-2175-1691231, info@mdmverlag.de. adv.: B&W page EUR 2,410, color page EUR 3,490. Circ: 5,000 (paid and controlled).

617 HUN ISSN 0025-0295
CODEN: MASEAW
MAGYAR SEBESZET/HUNGARIAN JOURNAL OF SURGERY. Text in Hungarian; Abstracts in English. 1947. 6/yr. EUR 208, USD 284 combined subscription (print & online eds.) (effective 2011). adv. bk.rev. bibl.; illus. **Document type:** *Journal, Academic/Scholarly.*
Related titles: Online - full content ed.: ISSN 1789-4301. EUR 176, USD 242 (effective 2011).
Indexed: ChemAb, EMBASE, ExcerpMed, IndMed, MEDLINE, P30, R10, Reac, SCOPUS.
Published by: (Magyar Sebesz Tarsasag/Hungarian Surgical Society), Akademiai Kiado Rt. (Subsidiary of: Wolters Kluwer N.V.), Prielle Kornelia u 19/D, Budapest, 1117, Hungary. TEL 36-1-4648222, FAX 36-1-4648221, journals@akkrt.hu. Ed. Attila Olah.

617 FRA ISSN 0759-2280
RD563 CODEN: MCPEBW
➤ **MEDECINE ET CHIRURGIE DU PIED.** Text in French. 1984. q. EUR 306, USD 337 combined subscription to institutions (print & online eds.) (effective 2012). reprint service avail. from PSC. **Document type:** *Journal, Academic/Scholarly.*
Related titles: Online - full text ed.: ISSN 1765-2855 (from IngentaConnect).
Indexed: A22, A26, E01, R10, Reac, SCI, SCOPUS, W07.
—BLDSC (5487.729300), IE, Ingenta, INIST. **CCC.**
Published by: (Societe Francaise de Medecine et Chirurgie du Pied), Springer France (Subsidiary of: Springer Science+Business Media), 22 Rue de Palestro, Paris, 75002, France. TEL 33-1-53009860, FAX 33-1-53009861, sylvie.kamara@springer.com. Ed. Dr. P H Benamou. Adv. contact Stephan Kroeck TEL 49-30-827875739. Circ: 2,500. **Subscr. in Americas to:** Springer New York LLC, Journal Fulfillment, PO Box 2485, Secaucus, NJ 07096. TEL 800-777-4643, 201-348-4033, FAX 201-348-4505, journals-ny@springer.com, http://www.springer.com; **Subscr. to:** Springer Distribution Center, Kundenservice Zeitschriften, Haberstr 7, Heidelberg 69126, Germany. TEL 49-6221-3454303, FAX 49-6221-3454229, subscriptions@springer.com, http://link.springer.de.

➤ **MEDICAL DEVICES & SURGICAL TECHNOLOGY WEEK.** *see* MEDICAL SCIENCES

617 BGR ISSN 0204-5389
➤ **MEDITSINSKI PREGLED. KHIRURGICHNI ZABOLIAVANIIA.** Variant title: Surgical Diseases. Text in Bulgarian; Summaries in Bulgarian, English. 1970. q. BGL 14 domestic; USD 40 foreign (effective 2005). adv. abstr.; bibl.; illus. index. 48 p./no.; back issues avail. **Document type:** *Journal, Academic/Scholarly.* **Description:** Presents original articles and abstracts of foreign publications on surgery, covering special surgical conditions, operative surgery, and surgical equipment.
Indexed: ABSML.
Published by: Meditsinski Universitet - Sofia, Tsentralna Meditsinska Biblioteka, Tsentur za Informatsiia po Meditsina/Medical University - Sofia, Central Medical Library, Medical Information Center, 1 Sv Georgi Sofiiski ul, Sofia, 1431, Bulgaria. TEL 359-2-9522342, FAX 359-2-9522393, lydia@medun.acad.bg, http://www.medun.acad.bg/cmb_htm/cmb1_home_bg.htm. Ed. Dr. G Zlatarski. R&P, Adv. contact Lydia Tacheva. B&W page USD 50, color page USD 150; trim 160 x 110. Circ: 300.

617 USA ISSN 1092-0811
RD99.A1
➤ **MEDSURG NURSING**; the journal of adult health. Text in English. 1992. bi-m. USD 45 domestic to individuals; USD 75 foreign to individuals; USD 69 domestic to institutions; USD 99 foreign to institutions; USD 15 per issue domestic; USD 19 per issue foreign (effective 2010). adv. back issues avail. **Document type:** *Journal, Academic/Scholarly.*
Related titles: Online - full text ed.
Indexed: A01, A02, A03, A08, A22, A26, C06, C07, C08, C11, CA, CINAHL, E08, EMBASE, ExcerpMed, Faml, G06, G07, G08, H04, H11, H12, I05, INI, MEDLINE, P20, P22, P24, P30, P34, P48, P54, PQC, R10, Reac, S09, SCOPUS, T02.
—BLDSC (5535.589000), IE, Ingenta. **CCC.**
Published by: (Academy of Medical-Surgical Nurses), Jannetti Publications, Inc., E Holly Ave, PO Box 56, Pitman, NJ 08071. TEL 856-256-2300, FAX 856-589-7463, contact@ajj.com, http://www.ajj.com/. Ed. Dottie Roberts. Pub. Anthony J Jannetti.

617 POL ISSN 1428-2712
MEDYCYNA PRAKTYCZNA. CHIRURGIA. Text in Polish. 1997. bi-m. PLZ 80 (effective 2000).
Published by: Medycyna Praktyczna, ul Krakowska 41, Krakow, 31066, Poland. TEL 48-12-4305520, FAX 48-12-4305536, listy@mp.pl, http://www.mp.pl. Ed. Marcin Zielinski.

617 681 USA ISSN 0738-1085
RD33.6
➤ **MICROSURGERY.** Text in English. 1983. 8/yr. GBP 693 in United Kingdom to institutions; EUR 875 in Europe to institutions; USD 1,189 in United States to institutions; USD 1,301 in Canada & Mexico to institutions; USD 1,357 elsewhere to institutions; GBP 798 combined subscription in United Kingdom to institutions (print & online eds.); EUR 1,007 combined subscription in Europe to institutions (print & online eds.); USD 1,368 combined subscription in United States to institutions (print & online eds.); USD 1,480 combined subscription in Canada & Mexico to institutions (print & online eds.); USD 1,536 combined subscription elsewhere to institutions (print & online eds.) (effective 2012). adv. bk.rev. bibl.; charts; illus. index. back issues avail.; reprint service avail. from PSC. **Document type:** *Journal, Academic/Scholarly.* **Description:** Acts as a multidisciplinary forum for original ideas regarding the use of the operating microscope in a variety of areas.
Formed by the merger of (1979-1983): Journal of Microsurgery (0191-3239); (1979-1983): International Journal of Microsurgery (0222-5069)
Related titles: Microform ed.: (from PQC); Online - full text ed.: ISSN 1098-2752. 1996. GBP 607 in United Kingdom to institutions; EUR 767 in Europe to institutions; USD 1,189 elsewhere to institutions (effective 2012).
Indexed: A20, A22, ASCA, B&BAb, B19, B21, B25, BIOSIS Prev, CurCont, EMBASE, ESPM, ExcerpMed, I10, ImmunAb, IndMed, Inpharma, MEDLINE, MycolAb, NSA, P30, R10, Reac, RefZh, SCI, SCOPUS, W07.
—BLDSC (5760.770000), GNLM, IE, Infotrieve, Ingenta, INIST. **CCC.**
Published by: John Wiley & Sons, Inc., 111 River St, Hoboken, NJ 07030. TEL 201-748-6000, FAX 201-748-6088, info@wiley.com, http://www.wiley.com/WileyCDA/. Ed. Feng Zhang. Adv. contact Stephen Donohue TEL 781-388-8511. **Subscr. outside the Americas to:** John Wiley & Sons Ltd., The Atrium, Southern Gate, Chichester, West Sussex PO19 8SQ, United Kingdom. TEL 44-1243-779777, FAX 44-1243-775878, cs-journals@wiley.com.

617 ITA ISSN 0026-4733
➤ **MINERVA CHIRURGICA**; a journal on surgery. Text in Italian; Summaries in English, Italian. 1946. bi-m. EUR 260 combined subscription in the European Union to institutions print & online eds.; EUR 285 combined subscription elsewhere to institutions print & online eds. (effective 2011). adv. bk.rev. bibl.; charts; illus. index. **Document type:** *Journal, Academic/Scholarly.* **Description:** Covers surgical pathophysiology, clinical medicine and therapy.
Related titles: Microform ed.: (from PQC); Online - full text ed.: ISSN 1827-1626; ◆ Supplement(s): Notiziario Chirurgico. ISSN 0392-3584.
Indexed: A22, ChemAb, DentInd, EMBASE, ExcerpMed, IndMed, MEDLINE, P30, R10, Reac, RefZh, SCI, SCOPUS, W07.
—BLDSC (5794.100000), GNLM, IE, Infotrieve, Ingenta, INIST. **CCC.**
Published by: Edizioni Minerva Medica, Corso Bramante 83-85, Turin, 10126, Italy. TEL 39-011-678282, FAX 39-011-674502, journals.dept@minervamedica.it, http://www.minervamedica.it. Ed. P A Giudice. Pub. Alberto Oliaro. Circ: 5,000 (paid).

617 SVK ISSN 1336-6572
➤ **MINIINVAZIVNA CHIRURGIA A ENDOSKOPIA, CHIRURGIA SUCASNOSTI.** Text in Slovak. 1997. q. USD 40 foreign (effective 2009). **Document type:** *Journal, Academic/Scholarly.*
Former titles (until 2005): Slovensky Chirurg; (until 2003): Chirurgicky Spravodaj (1335-2954)
—BLDSC (5797.664000).
Published by: Slovenka Zdravotnicka Univerzita, Chirurgicka Klinika, Nam L Svobodu 1, Banska Bystrica, Slovakia. Ed. Lubonir Marko.

➤ **MINIMALLY INVASIVE NEUROSURGERY.** *see* MEDICAL SCIENCES—Psychiatry And Neurology

M

617 USA ISSN 2090-1445
▼➤ **MINIMALLY INVASIVE SURGERY.** Text in English. 2009. irreg. USD 195 (effective 2011). **Document type:** *Journal, Academic/Scholarly.* **Description:** Publishes original research articles, review articles, case reports, and clinical studies in all areas of minimally invasive surgery.
Related titles: Online - full text ed.: ISSN 2090-1453. free (effective 2011).
Indexed: A01, T02.
Published by: Hindawi Publishing Corporation, 410 Park Ave, 15th Fl, PMB 287, New York, NY 10022. FAX 215-893-4392, 866-446-3294, info@hindawi.com.

617.95 616.1 DEU ISSN 1813-9175
MULTIMEDIA MANUAL OF CARDIOTHORACIC SURGERY. Text in English. 2003. irreg. **Document type:** *Journal, Academic/Scholarly.* **Description:** Provides a dynamic database archive of cardiothoracic surgery techniques and knowledge.
Media: Online - full text.
Address: University Hospital Freiburg, Department of Cardiovascular Surgery, Hugstetter Str 55, Freiburg, 79106, Germany. TEL 49-761-2709086, FAX 49-761-2709087, info@mmcts.org. Ed. Marko Turina.

617 ITA ISSN 2035-5106
CODEN: CHOMA9
➤ **MUSCULOSKELETAL SURGERY.** Variant title: Musculoskelet Surg. Text in Italian, English. 1917. 3/yr. EUR 181, USD 241 combined subscription to institutions (print & online eds.) (effective 2012). adv. bk.rev. abstr.; bibl.; illus. **Document type:** *Journal, Academic/Scholarly.*
Formerly (until 2009): La Chirurgia degli Organi di Movimento (0009-4749)
Related titles: Online - full text ed.: ISSN 2035-5114 (from IngentaConnect).
Indexed: A22, A26, ChemAb, DentInd, E01, E08, EMBASE, ExcerpMed, IBR, IBZ, IndMed, MEDLINE, P30, S09, SCOPUS.
—BLDSC (5986.535500), GNLM, IE, Infotrieve, Ingenta. **CCC.**
Published by: Springer Italia Srl (Subsidiary of: Springer Science+Business Media), Via Decembrio 28, Milan, 20137, Italy. TEL 39-02-54259722, FAX 39-02-55193360, springer@springer.it. Eds. A Giunti, S Giannini. Circ: 3,000.

➤ **NAIBUNPI GEKA/ENDOCRINE SURGERY.** *see* MEDICAL SCIENCES—Endocrinology

➤ **NATIONAL ADULT CARDIAC SURGICAL DATABASE REPORT (YEAR).** *see* MEDICAL SCIENCES—Cardiovascular Diseases

➤ **NATIONAL ADVISORY DENTAL AND CRANIOFACIAL RESEARCH COUNCIL. MINUTES OF MEETING.** *see* MEDICAL SCIENCES—Dentistry

617 CHE ISSN 1660-2110
NEPHRON CLINICAL PRACTICE. Text in English. 1998. m. **Document type:** *Journal, Academic/Scholarly.*
Supersedes in part (in 2002): Nephron (Online) (1423-0186)
Media: Online - full content. **Related titles:** ◆ Print ed.: The Nephron Journals. ISSN 1660-8151.
Indexed: A01, A03, A08, A22, B25, BIOBASE, BIOSIS Prev, CA, CurCont, E01, EMBASE, ExcerpMed, IABS, Inpharma, MycolAb, SCI, SCOPUS, T02, W07.
—**CCC.**
Published by: S. Karger AG, Allschwilerstr 10, Basel, 4055, Switzerland. TEL 41-61-3061111, FAX 41-61-3061234, karger@karger.ch, http://www.karger.ch. Ed. S Powis.

617 CHE ISSN 1660-2129
RC902.A1
➤ **NEPHRON EXPERIMENTAL NEPHROLOGY.** Text in English. 1998. m. **Document type:** *Journal, Academic/Scholarly.* **Description:** Publishes original research and reviews in the area of renal cell and developmental biology and functional genomics.
Formerly (until 2002): Experimental Nephrology (1421-9956)
Media: Online - full text. **Related titles:** ◆ Print ed.: The Nephron Journals. ISSN 1660-8151.
Indexed: A01, A03, A08, A22, B25, BIOBASE, BIOSIS Prev, CA, CurCont, E01, EMBASE, ExcerpMed, IABS, ISR, Inpharma, MycolAb, SCI, SCOPUS, T02, W07.
—IE. **CCC.**
Published by: S. Karger AG, Allschwilerstr 10, Basel, 4055, Switzerland. TEL 41-61-3061111, FAX 41-61-3061234, karger@karger.ch, http://www.karger.ch. Ed. J Hughes.

617.54 MEX ISSN 1405-2938
➤ **NEUMOLOGIA Y CIRUGIA DE TORAX.** Variant title: Revista de Neumologia y Cirugia de Torax. Text in Spanish; Summaries in English. 1939. q. MXN 300 domestic; USD 65 in Latin America; USD 75 in US & Canada; USD 85 elsewhere (effective 2007). bk.rev. bibl.; charts; illus. Index. back issues avail. **Document type:** *Journal, Academic/Scholarly.* **Description:** Includes original articles, research reports, review articles, clinical cases and notices.
Formerly (until 1961): Revista Mexicana de Tubercolosis y Enfermedades del Aparato Respiratorio (0370-6435)
Indexed: IndMed, P30.
Published by: Sociedad Mexicana de Neumologia y Cirugia de Torax, Calle de Amsterdam 124, Interior 303, Col Hipodromo Condensa, Mexico City, 06100, Mexico. TEL 52-52112350, smncyt@prodigy.net.mx, http://www.smnyct.org.mx/. Ed. Jaime Morales Blanhir. Circ: 2,000.

➤ **NEUROBIOLOGIA**; revista de neurologia psiquiatria e neurocirurgia. *see* MEDICAL SCIENCES—Psychiatry And Neurology

617 616.8 FRA ISSN 0028-3770
CODEN: NUREB9
➤ **NEUROCHIRURGIE.** Text in French. 1955. 6/yr. EUR 492 in Europe to institutions; EUR 416.26 in France to institutions; JPY 75,700 in Japan to institutions; USD 640 elsewhere to institutions (effective 2012). adv. bk.rev. illus. index. reprints avail. **Document type:** *Journal, Academic/Scholarly.* **Description:** The scope goes beyond neurosurgery into neuro-anaesthesiology, neuroradiology, electro-encephalography, gamma-encephalography, echo-encephalography, neuro-ophthalmology, oto-neurology, neuro-endocrinology and more.
Related titles: Microform ed.: (from PQC); Online - full text ed.: (from ScienceDirect).
Indexed: A20, A22, B21, CurCont, E-psyche, EMBASE, ExcerpMed, ISR, IndMed, Inpharma, MEDLINE, NSA, NSCI, P30, R10, Reac, SCI, SCOPUS, W07.
—BLDSC (6081.350000), GNLM, IE, Infotrieve, Ingenta, INIST. **CCC.**
Published by: (Societe Francaise de Neurochirurgie), Elsevier Masson (Subsidiary of: Elsevier Health Sciences), 62 Rue Camille Desmoulins, Issy les Moulineaux, Cedex 92442, France. TEL 33-1-71165500, infos@elsevier-masson.fr. Ed. Francoise Lapierre. Circ: 1,500.

➤ **NEUROCIRUGIA/NEUROSURGERY.** *see* MEDICAL SCIENCES—Psychiatry And Neurology

➤ **NEUROLOGIA I NEUROCHIRURGIA POLSKA/POLISH JOURNAL OF NEUROLOGY AND NEUROSURGERY.** *see* MEDICAL SCIENCES—Psychiatry And Neurology

➤ **NEUROLOGIA MEDICO-CHIRURGICA.** *see* MEDICAL SCIENCES—Psychiatry And Neurology

➤ **NEUROLOGICAL RESEARCH**; a journal of progress in neurosurgery, neurology and neurosciences. *see* MEDICAL SCIENCES—Psychiatry And Neurology

617.4 616.8 JPN ISSN 0301-2603
CODEN: NOKGB6
➤ **NEUROLOGICAL SURGERY/NO SHINKEI GEKA.** Text in Japanese; Summaries in English. 1973. m. JPY 31,800; JPY 41,400 combined subscription (print & online eds.) (effective 2010). adv. bk.rev. **Document type:** *Journal, Academic/Scholarly.*
Related titles: Online - full text ed.: ISSN 1882-1251.
Indexed: A22, ASCA, CIN, ChemAb, ChemTitl, DentInd, E-psyche, EMBASE, ExcerpMed, INIS AtomInd, IndMed, MEDLINE, NSCI, P30, R10, Reac, SCOPUS.
—BLDSC (6081.445000), CASDDS, GNLM, IE, Infotrieve, Ingenta, INIST.
Published by: Igaku Shoin Ltd., 1-28-36 Hongo, Bunkyo-ku, Tokyo, 113-8719, Japan. TEL 81-3-3817-5600, FAX 81-3-3815-7791, info@igaku-shoin.co.jp. Circ: 6,000.

➤ **NEUROPEDIATRICS**; journal of pediatric neurobiology, neurology and neurosurgery. *see* MEDICAL SCIENCES—Pediatrics

➤ **NEUROSURGERY (BALTIMORE).** *see* MEDICAL SCIENCES—Psychiatry And Neurology

617 616.8 USA ISSN 1042-3680
CODEN: NCNAFP
➤ **NEUROSURGERY CLINICS OF NORTH AMERICA.** Text in English. 1989. q. USD 492 in United States to institutions; USD 601 elsewhere to institutions (effective 2012). adv. back issues avail.; reprints avail. **Document type:** *Journal, Academic/Scholarly.* **Description:** Each issue addresses a single topic in the diagnosis and therapy of patients with neurological disorders.
Related titles: Microform ed.: (from PQC); Online - full text ed.: ISSN 1558-1349 (from ScienceDirect).
Indexed: A22, ASCA, B21, C06, C07, C08, CINAHL, CurCont, E-psyche, EMBASE, ExcerpMed, INI, IndMed, Inpharma, MEDLINE, NSA, NSCI, P30, R10, Reac, SCI, SCOPUS, W07.
—BLDSC (6081.582500), GNLM, IE, Infotrieve, Ingenta. **CCC.**
Published by: W.B. Saunders Co. (Subsidiary of: Elsevier Health Sciences), Elsevier, Health Sciences Division, Order Fulfillment, 3251 Riverport Ln, Maryland Heights, MO 63043. TEL 314-872-8370, 800-325-4177, FAX 314-432-1380, JournalCustomerService-usa@elsevier.com, http://www.us.elsevierhealth.com.

➤ **NEUROSURGERY CODING ALERT**; the practical adviser for ethically optimizing coding, reimbursement and efficiency for neurosurgery practices. *see* INSURANCE

617 USA ISSN 1050-6438
RD593 CODEN: NEQUEB
➤ **NEUROSURGERY QUARTERLY.** Text in English. 1991. q. USD 578 domestic to institutions; USD 708 foreign to institutions (effective 2011). adv. charts; illus. back issues avail.; reprints avail. **Document type:** *Journal, Academic/Scholarly.* **Description:** Presents comprehensive reviews by international authorities on the surgical management and treatment of neurological disorders.
Related titles: Online - full text ed.: ISSN 1534-4916. USD 351 domestic for academic site license; USD 401 foreign foracademic site license; USD 391.50 domestic for corporate site license; USD 441.50 foreign for corporate site license (effective 2002).
Indexed: ASCA, B21, EMBASE, ExcerpMed, NSA, NSCI, P30, R10, Reac, SCI, SCOPUS, W07.
—BLDSC (6081.582800), GNLM, IE, Infotrieve, Ingenta. **CCC.**
Published by: Lippincott Williams & Wilkins (Subsidiary of: Wolters Kluwer N.V.), 530 Walnut St, Philadelphia, PA 19106. TEL 215-521-8300, FAX 215-521-8902, customerservice@lww.com, http://www.lww.com. Ed. Dr. Donlin M Long TEL 410-614-3536. Pub. Jason Pointe.

➤ **NEUROSURGICAL FOCUS.** *see* MEDICAL SCIENCES—Psychiatry And Neurology

616 DEU ISSN 0344-5607
RD593 CODEN: NSREDV
➤ **NEUROSURGICAL REVIEW.** Text in English. 1978. q. EUR 844, USD 1,019 combined subscription to institutions (print & online eds.) (effective 2012). adv. back issues avail.; reprint service avail. from PSC. **Document type:** *Journal, Academic/Scholarly.* **Description:** Provides a forum for comprehensive reviews on current issues in neurosurgery.
Related titles: Online - full text ed.: ISSN 1437-2320 (from IngentaConnect).
Indexed: A01, A03, A08, A22, A26, ASCA, B21, B25, BIOSIS Prev, CA, DentInd, E-psyche, E01, EMBASE, ExcerpMed, H12, IBR, IBZ, IndMed, Inpharma, MEDLINE, MycolAb, NSA, NSCI, P30, R10, Reac, SCI, SCOPUS, T02, W07.
—BLDSC (6081.585000), GNLM, IE, Infotrieve, Ingenta, INIST. **CCC.**
Published by: Springer (Subsidiary of: Springer Science+Business Media), Tiergartenstr 17, Heidelberg, 69121, Germany. TEL 49-6221-4870, FAX 49-6221-345229. Ed. H Bertalanffy. **Subscr. in the Americas to:** Springer New York LLC, Journal Fulfillment, PO Box 2485, Secaucus, NJ 07096. TEL 201-348-4033, 800-777-4643, FAX 201-348-4505, journals-ny@springer.com, http://www.springer.com; **Subscr. to:** Springer Distribution Center, Kundenservice Zeitschriften, Haberstr 7, Heidelberg 69126, Germany. TEL 49-6221-3454303, FAX 49-6221-3454229, subscriptions@springer.com.

➤ **NEUROTARGET**; revista de neurocirugia funcional, estereotaxia, radiocirugia y dolor. *see* MEDICAL SCIENCES—Psychiatry And Neurology

617.952 USA ISSN 1556-4878
NEW BEAUTY; the magazine about cosmetics enhancement. Text in English. 2005. q. USD 19.95 (effective 2005). adv. **Document type:** *Magazine, Consumer.* **Description:** Covers cosmetic enhancement to the body and mind, including articles on varies techniques, plastic surgery, technologies and mind.
Published by: Sandow Media Corp., 3731 NW 8th Ave, Boca Raton, FL 33431. TEL 561-750-0151, FAX 561-750-0152, sandowinfo@sandowmedia.com, http://www.sandowmedia.com. Pub. Adam I Sandow. adv.: color page USD 11,900; trim 9 x 11.

617 ITA ISSN 2035-6447
▼ **NEW TECHNOLOGIES IN SURGERY.** Text in English. 2009. s-a. **Document type:** *Journal, Trade.*
Published by: Universita degli Studi dell'Insubria, Dipartimento di Scienze Chirurgiche, Ospedale di Circolo, Via Guicciardini 9, Varese, 21100, Italy. TEL 39-0332-393606, FAX 39-0332260260, dipscienzechir@uninsubria.it, http://www.uninsubria.it/uninsubria/dipartimenti/dsc.html.

617.95 USA
▼ **NEW YOU (MIAMI)**; the official magazine of cosmetic surgery. Text in English. 2010 (Jan.). q. USD 10 per issue (effective 2010). adv. **Document type:** *Magazine, Consumer.* **Description:** Covers real procedures and real results, to the doctors who perform them, and to the women, and men, who want to experience them.
Published by: (American Academy of Cosmetic Surgery), Knightsbridge Media, 1335 Lincoln Rd, Miami, FL 33139. TEL 305-590-8550, FAX 305-695-1047. Ed. J P Faber. Pub. Peter Mansfield. adv.: color page USD 22,250; trim 8 x 10.5.

617.6 NGA ISSN 1595-1103
RD27.44.N6
NIGERIAN JOURNAL OF SURGICAL RESEARCH. Text in English. 1999. q. NGN 4,000 domestic; USD 60 foreign (effective 2004). back issues avail. **Document type:** *Journal, Academic/Scholarly.* **Description:** Covers developments and advances in the broad field of surgery and related clinical and basic sciences in Nigeria and the rest of Africa.
Related titles: Online - full text ed.
Indexed: A36, CABA, EMBASE, ExcerpMed, GH, P33, P39, R10, R12, RM&VM, Reac, SCOPUS, T05, W11.
Published by: Surgical Research Society, c/o Ahmadu Bello University, Zaria, Nigeria. Ed. Emmanuel Ameh.

617 JPN ISSN 0916-7927
NIHON ASHI NO GEKA GAKKAI ZASSHI/JAPAN SOCIETY FOR SURGERY OF THE FOOT. JOURNAL. Text in Japanese. 1980. s-a. **Document type:** *Journal, Academic/Scholarly.*
Former titles (until 1992): Nihon Ashi no Geka Kenkyukai Zasshi (0914-9058); (until 1987): Ashi no Geka Kenkyukaishi (0289-8136)
Published by: Nihon Ashi no Geka Kenkyukai/Japanese Society for Surgery of the Foot, 2-16-1Miyamaeku Sugao, Kawasaki, Kanagawa 216-8511, Japan. TEL 81-44-9778111, FAX 81-44-9779651, info@jssf.jp, http://www.jssf.jp/.

617.95 JPN ISSN 0288-2027
NIHON BIYO GEKA GAKKAI KAIHO/JAPAN SOCIETY OF AESTHETIC PLASTIC SURGERY. JOURNAL. Text in Japanese; Summaries in English. 1979. q.
Published by: Nihon Biyo Geka Gakkai/Japan Society of Aesthetic Plastic Surgery, 2-16-7 Kasuga, Bunkyo-ku, Tokyo, 112-0003, Japan. TEL 81-3-56842922, FAX 81-3-38122492, jsaps@sunpla-mcv.com, http://www.jsaps.com/.

617 616.025 JPN ISSN 1340-2242
CODEN: NFKZF4
NIHON FUKUBU KYUKYU IGAKKAI ZASSHI/JOURNAL OF ABDOMINAL EMERGENCY MEDICINE. Text in Japanese; Abstracts in English. 1984. bi-m. membership. **Document type:** *Journal, Academic/Scholarly.*
Formerly (until 1993): Fukubu Kyukyu Shinryo no Shinpo/Progress in Acute Abdominal Medicine (0289-5021)
Related titles: Online - full text ed.: ISSN 1882-4781. 2008.
Indexed: INIS AtomInd.
—BLDSC (6112.497500).
Published by: Nihon Fukubu Kyukyu Igakkai/Japanese Society for Abdominal Emergency Medicine, Teikyo University School of Medicine, Department of Surgery, 2-11-1 Kaga, Itabashi-ku, Tokyo, 173-8605, Japan. TEL 81-3-39641211 ext 1424, FAX 81-3-39616944, http://plaza.umin.ac.jp/~jaem/.

NIHON GEKAKEI RENGO GAKKAISHI/JAPANESE COLLEGE OF SURGEONS. JOURNAL. *see* MEDICAL SCIENCES—Abstracting, Bibliographies, Statistics

362.19795 JPN ISSN 0578-7947
➤ **NIHON ISHOKU GAKKAI ZASSHI/JAPANESE JOURNAL OF TRANSPLANTATION.** Text in Japanese. 1965. bi-m. **Document type:** *Academic/Scholarly.*
Indexed: INIS AtomInd.
Address: c/o Dr. Kikuo Nomoto, Nihon Gakkai Jimu Center, 5-16-9 Honkomagome, Bunkyo-ku, Tokyo, 113-8622, Japan.

617.95 JPN
NIHON KEISEI GEKA GAKKAI GAKUJUTSU SHUKAI/JAPAN SOCIETY OF PLASTIC AND RECONSTRUCTIVE SURGERY. ANNUAL MEETING. Text in English, Japanese. a. **Document type:** *Abstract/Index.*
Published by: Nihon Keisei Geka Gakkai/Japan Society of Plastic and Reconstructive Surgery, 3F Rakuyo Bldg., 519 Waseda-tsurumaki-cho, Shinjuku-ku, Tokyo, 162-0041, Japan. TEL 81-3-52876773, FAX 81-3-52912176, hyamada@shunkosha.com, http://www.jsprs.or.jp/index.htm.

617.95 JPN ISSN 0389-4703
CODEN: NKGKE7
NIHON KEISEI GEKA GAKKAI KAISHI/JAPAN SOCIETY OF PLASTIC AND RECONSTRUCTIVE SURGERY. JOURNAL. Text in Japanese; Summaries in English. 1981. m. membership. **Document type:** *Journal, Academic/Scholarly.*
Indexed: INIS AtomInd.
—BLDSC (4808.060000).
Published by: Nihon Keisei Geka Gakkai/Japan Society of Plastic and Reconstructive Surgery, 3F Rakuyo Bldg., 519 Waseda-tsurumaki-cho, Shinjuku-ku, Tokyo, 162-0041, Japan. TEL 81-3-52876773, FAX 81-3-52912176, hyamada@shunkosha.com, http://www.jsprs.or.jp/index.htm.

617.413 JPN ISSN 0918-6778
NIHON KEKKAN GEKA GAKKAI ZASSHI. Variant title: Japanese Journal of Vascular Surgery. Japanese Society for Vascular Surgery. Official Journal. Text in Japanese. 1992. 7/yr. **Document type:** *Journal.*
Indexed: INIS AtomInd.
Published by: Nihon Kekkan Geka Gakkai/Japanese Society for Vascular Surgery, Nibancho TS Bldg, 2-1 Nibancho, Chiyoda-ku, Tokyo, 102-0084, Japan. TEL 81-3-32397217, FAX 81-3-32399375, jsvs@iva.jp, http://www.jsvs.org/. Ed. Tadahiro Sasajima.

617 JPN ISSN 0919-0945
NIHON KOKYUKI GEKA GAKKAI ZASSHI/JAPANESE ASSOCIATION FOR CHEST SURGERY. JOURNAL. Text in English, Japanese. 1987. bi-m. membership. adv. **Document type:** *Journal, Academic/Scholarly.*
Formerly (until 1992): Kokyuki Geka (0917-4141)
—CCC.
Published by: Nihon Kokyuki Geka Gakkai/Japanese Association for Chest Surgery, Chiyoda-Seimei KyotoOike Bldg. 3F, 200, Takamiya-cho, Nishiiru, Takakura, Oikedori, Nakagyo-ku, Kyoto, 604-0835, Japan. TEL 81-75-2540545, FAX 81-75-2540546. Ed., R&P Hiromi Wada. Adv. contact Yasumasa Monden.

616 JPN ISSN 0916-4936
NIHON MAIKURO SAJARI GAKKAI KAISHI/JAPANESE SOCIETY OF RECONSTRUCTIVE MICROSURGERY. JOURNAL. Text in Japanese; Summaries in English. 1988. s-a. JPY 8,000 (effective 2001). **Document type:** *Journal, Academic/Scholarly.*
—CCC.
Published by: Nihon Maikuro Sajari Gakkai, Keio Daigaku Igakubu Maikuro Sajarishitsu, 35 Shinano-Machi, Shinjuku-ku, Tokyo, 160-8582, Japan. TEL 81-3-3353-1211, FAX 81-3-3226-0989.

617 616.4 JPN ISSN 1344-6703
NIHON NAISHIKYO GEKA GAKKAI ZASSHI/JAPAN SOCIETY FOR ENDOSCOPIC SURGERY. JOURNAL. Text in Japanese. 1996. bi-m. JPY 17,160 (effective 2010). **Document type:** *Journal, Academic/Scholarly.*
Formerly (until 1998): Naishikyo Geka (1341-7266)
Published by: Igaku Shoin Ltd., 1-28-36 Hongo, Bunkyo-ku, Tokyo, 113-8719, Japan. TEL 81-3-3817-5600, FAX 81-3-3815-7791, info@igaku-shoin.co.jp.

NIHON NOU SHINKEI GEKA GAKKAI SOUKAI SHOUROKUSHUU (CD-ROM)/JAPAN NEUROSURGICAL SOCIETY. ABSTRACTS OF THE ANNUAL MEETING (CD-ROM). *see* MEDICAL SCIENCES—Abstracting, Bibliographies, Statistics

617 JPN ISSN 1345-2843
NIHON RINSHO GEKA GAKKAI ZASSHI/JAPAN SURGICAL ASSOCIATION. JOURNAL. Text in English, Japanese. 1937. m. **Document type:** *Journal, Academic/Scholarly.*
Formerly (until 1997): Nihon Rinsho Geka Igakkai Zasshi/Japanese Society for Clinical Surgery. Journal (0386-9776)
—BLDSC (4808.320000).
Published by: Nihon Rinsho Geka Igakkai/Japan Surgical Association, 4-6-9 Iidabashi, Chiyoda-ku, Akasaka Fukugen Bldg. 8F, Tokyo, 102-0072, Japan. TEL 81-3-32621555, http://www.ringe.jp/jsa/index.html. Circ: 16,000.

NIHON RYUMACHI KANSETSU GEKA GAKKAI ZASSHI/JAPANESE JOURNAL OF RHEUMATISM AND JOINT SURGERY. *see* MEDICAL SCIENCES—Rheumatology

NIHON RYUMACHI KANSETSU GEKA GEKKAI/JAPANESE SOCIETY OF RHEUMATISM AND JOINT SURGERY. CONGRESS. *see* MEDICAL SCIENCES—Rheumatology

NIHON SEISHOKU GEKA GAKKAI ZASSHI/JAPAN SOCIETY OF REPRODUCTIVE SURGERY. JOURNAL. *see* MEDICAL SCIENCES—Obstetrics And Gynecology

617 JPN ISSN 0285-1474
RD597 CODEN: NPZAE5
➤ **NIHON SHINZO KEKKAN GEKA GAKKAI ZASSHI/JAPANESE JOURNAL OF CARDIOVASCULAR SURGERY.** Text in Japanese; Abstracts in English. 1948. bi-m. back issues avail. **Document type:** *Journal, Academic/Scholarly.*
Incorporates: Nihon Shinzo Kekkan Geka Gakkai Gakujutsu Sokai Nittei to Endai Shorokushu/Japanese Society for Cardiovascular Surgery. Abstracts of Meeting; Supersedes in part (in1975): Kyobu Geka (0021-5252)
Related titles: Online - full text ed.
Indexed: INIS AtomInd.
—BLDSC (4651.290000). **CCC.**
Published by: Nihon Shinzo Kekkan Geka Gakkai/Japanese Society for Cardiovascular Surgery, Suzuki Bldg. 6/F, 26-9, Hongo 2-chome, Bunkyo-ku, Tokyo, 113-0033, Japan. TEL 81-3-58422301, FAX 81-3-58422302, http://jscvs.umin.ac.jp/. Ed. Shiaki Kawada.

➤ **NIHON SHONI GEKA GAKKAI ZASSHI/JAPANESE SOCIETY OF PEDIATRIC SURGEONS. JOURNAL.** *see* MEDICAL SCIENCES—Pediatrics

617 JPN ISSN 1340-8593
➤ **NIHON SHUJUTSU IGAKKAISHI/JAPANESE ASSOCIATION FOR OPERATIVE MEDICINE. JOURNAL.** Text in Japanese; Summaries in English. 1980. q. JPY 8,000, USD 66 (effective 2003). 120 p./no.; **Document type:** *Academic/Scholarly.*
Formerly (until 1993): Nihon Shujutsubu Igakkaishi - Japanese Association for Operating Room Technology. Journal (0914-4498)
Published by: Nihon Shijutsu Igakkai, c/o Surgical Center, University of Hospital, 7-3-1 Hongo, Bunkyo-ku, Tokyo, 113-0033, Japan. TEL 81-3-5800-8674, FAX 81-3-5689-8217. Ed. Toyoki Kugimiya. Pub. Ooya Shokai. R&P Y Kakehashi. Circ: 1,400.

617 JPN ISSN 0914-594X
NIHON TOGAI GAKU GANMEN GEKA GAKKAISHI/JAPAN SOCIETY OF CRANIO-MAXILLO-FACIAL SURGERY. JOURNAL. Text in Japanese; Summaries in English, Japanese. 1984. a.
Formerly (until 1985): Nihon Gaku Ganmen Geka Gakkai Kaishi/Japan Society of Maxillo-Facial Surgery. Journal (0914-5931)
Published by: Nihon Togai Gaku Ganmen Geka Gakkai/Japan Society of Cranio-Maxillo-Facial Surgery, c/o Shunkosha, 519, Wasedatsurumaki-cho, Shinjuku-ku, Loyang Bldg. 4F, Tokyo, 162-0802, Japan. TEL 81-3-52916231, FAX 81-3-52912176, tougai@shunkosha.com, http://www.jscmfs.org/.

617.95 JPN ISSN 0387-9194
NIPPON BIYO GEKA GAKKAISHI/JAPAN SOCIETY OF AESTHETIC SURGERY. JOURNAL. Text and summaries in English, Japanese. 1962. q. membership. adv. **Document type:** *Journal, Academic/Scholarly.* **Description:** Publishes scientific papers relating to medicine and aesthetic/cosmetic surgery.
Formerly (until 1978): Biyo no Igaku/Cosmetic Medicine (0387-9186)
—BLDSC (4806.005000).
Published by: Nippon Biyo Geka Gakkai/Japan Society of Aesthetic Surgery, 8-10-8 Ginza, Chuo-ku, 6F Ginza 8-10 Bldg, Tokyo, 104-0061, Japan. TEL 81-3-35711270, FAX 81-3-35713116, jsas@mac.com, http://www.jsas.or.jp/. adv.: page JPY 30,000. Circ: 750 (paid); 400 (controlled).

617 JPN ISSN 0301-4894
CODEN: NGGZAK
NIPPON GEKA GAKKAI ZASSHI/JAPAN SURGICAL SOCIETY. JOURNAL. Text in Japanese; Summaries in English, Japanese. 1899. m. membership. **Document type:** *Journal, Academic/Scholarly.*
Formerly (until 1907): Nippon Geka Gakkaishi (0301-4886)
Indexed: ChemAb, ChemTitl, EMBASE, ExcerpMed, FR, INIS AtomInd, IndMed, MEDLINE, P30, R10, Reac, SCOPUS.
—BLDSC (4808.350000), CASDDS, GNLM, INIST.
Published by: Nihon Geka Gakkai/Japan Surgical Society, 8F, World Trade Center Bldg., 2-4-1 Hamamatsu-cho, Minato-ku, Tokyo, 105-6108, Japan. TEL 81-3-57334094, FAX 81-3-54738864, info@jssoc.or.jp. Ed. Morito Monden.

NO SHINKEI GEKA JANARU/JAPANESE JOURNAL OF NEUROSURGERY. *see* PSYCHOLOGY

617.4 616.8 JPN ISSN 0917-1495
NO SHINKEI GEKA SOKUHO/NEUROSURGERY LETTERS. Text in Japanese. 1990. m. JPY 28,356; JPY 2,625 newsstand/cover (effective 2007). **Document type:** *Journal, Academic/Scholarly.*
Indexed: E-psyche.
Published by: Medicus Shuppan/Medicus Publishing Inc., 18-24 Hiroshiba-cho, Suita-shi, Osaka-fu 564-8580, Japan. TEL 81-6-63856911, FAX 81-6-63856873, http://www.medica.co.jp/.

617.3 616.89 JPN ISSN 0914-5508
NO SOTCHU NO GEKA/SURGERY FOR CEREBRAL STROKE. Text in Japanese; Summaries in English. 1973. q. JPY 2,200 per issue. **Document type:** *Journal, Academic/Scholarly.*
Formerly (until 1986): Nosotchu no Geka Kenkyukai Koenshu/Conference of Surgical Treatment of Stroke. Proceedings (0387-8031)
Related titles: Online - full text ed.: ISSN 1880-4683.
Indexed: E-psyche, INIS AtomInd.
—BLDSC (6152.725000). **CCC.**
Published by: Nihon Nousotchuu no Geka Gakkai/Japanese Society on Surgery for Cerebral Stroke, Department of Neurosurgery, Tohoku University School of Medicine, 1-1 Seiryo-machi, Aoba-ku, Sendai City, Miyagi 980-8574, Japan. TEL 81-22-7177230, FAX 81-22-7177233, http://nsg.med.tohoku.ac.jp/jsscs/index.html.

617.9 SWE ISSN 2000-6527
▼ **NYA TRANSPLANTATIONSNYTT**; donation och transplantation. Variant title: Transplantationsnytt. Text in Swedish. 2009. 3/yr. **Document type:** *Magazine, Trade.*
Related titles: Online - full text ed.
Published by: Sahlgrenska Universitetssjukhuset, Enheten foer Transplantation och Leverkirurgi/Sahlgrenska University Hospital, Transplantationscentrum, Bruna Straeket 5, Goeteborg, 41345, Sweden. TEL 46-31-3421000, FAX 46-31-419711, http://www.transplantationscentrum.se/sv/SU/5/Transplantationscentrum_Avd_138/Transplatationscentrum. Ed. Anne FLoden.

O P E NURSING/OPE NASHINGU. (Operating Room) *see* MEDICAL SCIENCES—Nurses And Nursing

617 DEU ISSN 0178-1715
O P JOURNAL; wissenschaftliche, klinische und technische Informationen. (Operations) Text in German. 1985. 3/yr. EUR 60 to institutions; EUR 102 combined subscription to institutions (print & online eds.); EUR 26 newsstand/cover (effective 2011). adv. **Document type:** *Journal, Academic/Scholarly.*
Related titles: Online - full text ed.: ISSN 1439-2496. EUR 102 to institutions (effective 2011).
—GNLM. **CCC.**
Published by: Georg Thieme Verlag, Ruedigerstr 14, Stuttgart, 70469, Germany. TEL 49-711-8931421, FAX 49-711-8931410, leser.service@thieme.de. Eds. Dr. Andreas Wentzensen, Dr. Karl Heinrich Winker. R&P Michael Wachinger.

O R REPORTS. (Operating Room) *see* HEALTH FACILITIES AND ADMINISTRATION—Abstracting, Bibliographies, Statistics

617 USA
O R TODAY; your surgical products & services resource guide. (Operating Room) Text in English. m. free domestic to qualified personnel; USD 30 domestic; USD 55 foreign (effective 2005). **Document type:** *Magazine, Trade.*
Published by: M D Publishing, 18 Eastbrook Bend, #A, Peachtree Cty, GA 30269-1530. TEL 770-632-9040, 800-906-3373, FAX 770-632-9090. Pub. John Krieg.

617 USA ISSN 0960-8923
RD540 CODEN: OBSUEB
➤ **OBESITY SURGERY.** Text in English. 1991. m. EUR 838, USD 1,018 combined subscription to institutions (print & online eds.) (effective 2012). bibl.; abstr.; stat. 150 p./no.; back issues avail.; reprint service avail. from PSC. **Document type:** *Journal, Academic/Scholarly.* **Description:** Aims to provide an interdisciplinary opportunity for publishing and communicating research and techniques for treatment of massive obesity.
Related titles: Online - full text ed.: ISSN 1708-0428 (from IngentaConnect).
Indexed: A20, A22, A26, ASCA, CurCont, E01, EMBASE, ExcerpMed, H12, I05, INI, ISR, IndMed, Inpharma, MEDLINE, P20, P22, P30, P35, P48, P50, P54, PQC, R10, Reac, SCI, SCOPUS, T02, W07.
—BLDSC (6196.953000), GNLM, IE, Infotrieve, Ingenta, INIST. **CCC.**
Published by: (International Federation for the Surgery of Obesity), Springer New York LLC (Subsidiary of: Springer Science+Business Media), 233 Spring St, New York, NY 10013. TEL 212-460-1500, 212—460-1500, service-ny@springer.com, http://www.springer.com/. Eds. Henry Buchwald, Nicola Scopinaro.

➤ **OCULAR SURGERY NEWS (CHINA EDITION).** *see* MEDICAL SCIENCES—Ophthalmology And Optometry

617.7 USA ISSN 2157-8567
➤ **OCULAR SURGERY NEWS (EUROPE EDITION).** Abbreviated title: O S N I E. Text in English. 1990. m. adv. **Document type:** *Journal, Academic/Scholarly.* **Description:** Provides coverage of scientific meetings and developments in all subspecialties in ophthalmology.
Supersedes in part (in 2009): Ocular Surgery News (Europe/Asia-Pacific Edition) (1551-4552)
Related titles: ◆ Regional ed(s).: Ocular Surgery News (Latin America Edition). ISSN 1520-944X; ◆ Ocular Surgery News (China Edition). ISSN 1938-5374; ◆ Ocular Surgery News (India Edition). ISSN 1938-5366; ◆ Ocular Surgery News (Japan Edition). ISSN 1533-0125.
Indexed: A01, P20, P48, P54, PQC.
—CCC.
Published by: Slack, Inc., 6900 Grove Rd, Thorofare, NJ 08086. TEL 856-848-1000, FAX 856-848-6091, customerservice@slackinc.com, http://www.slackinc.com.

➤ **OCULAR SURGERY NEWS (INDIA EDITION).** *see* MEDICAL SCIENCES—Ophthalmology And Optometry

➤ **OCULAR SURGERY NEWS (JAPAN EDITION).** *see* MEDICAL SCIENCES—Ophthalmology And Optometry

➤ **OCULAR SURGERY NEWS (LATIN AMERICA EDITION).** *see* MEDICAL SCIENCES—Ophthalmology And Optometry

617.7 USA ISSN 8750-3085
OCULAR SURGERY NEWS (US EDITION). Text in English. 1983. s-m. USD 429 to individuals; USD 549 to institutions; USD 39 per issue (effective 2010). adv. 100 p./no. 4 cols./p.; reprints avail. **Document type:** *Newspaper, Academic/Scholarly.* **Description:** Provides coverage of scientific meetings and events in ophthalmology as well as current practice management issues.
Formerly (until 1984): I O L & Ocular Surgery News (0745-709X)
Related titles: Online - full text ed.
Indexed: C06, C07, C08, CA, CINAHL, P20, P24, P48, P54, PQC, T02.
—BLDSC (6235.154600), IE, Infotrieve. **CCC.**
Published by: Slack, Inc., 6900 Grove Rd, Thorofare, NJ 08086. TEL 856-848-1000, FAX 856-848-6091, customerservice@slackinc.com, http://www.slackinc.com. Adv. contact Lisa Sabatini TEL 877-307-5255 ext 305.

617 KOR ISSN 1226-0053
OE GWA HAG-HOEJI/KOREAN SURGICAL SOCIETY. JOURNAL. Text in Korean. 1960. m. membership. **Document type:** *Journal, Academic/Scholarly.*
Indexed: P30, SCI.
Published by: Daehan Oe Gwa Hag-hoe/Korean Surgical Society, Rm 5627, 5F Main Bldg, Seoul National University Hospital, 28 Yeongeon-dong, Jongno-gu, Seoul, 110-744, Korea, S. TEL 82-2-7971220, FAX 82-2-7904081.

OFTAL'MOKHIRURGIYA. *see* MEDICAL SCIENCES—Ophthalmology And Optometry

617 NLD ISSN 1879-5188
OK MANAGEMENT. (OperatieKamer) Text in Dutch. 2008. q. EUR 80 domestic; EUR 95 foreign (effective 2010). adv. **Document type:** *Magazine, Trade.*
Published by: (Nederlandse Vereniging Leidinggevenden Operatieafdeling), Y-Publicaties, Postbus 10208, Amsterdam, 1001 EE, Netherlands. TEL 31-20-5206060, FAX 31-20-5206061, info@y-publicaties.nl, http://www.y-publicaties.nl. Pub. Ralf Beekveldt. Circ: 1,500.

617 610.73 NLD ISSN 1872-6712
OK OPERATIONEEL. (OperatieKamer) Text in Dutch. 2006. 6/yr. EUR 59.50 domestic; EUR 75 foreign (effective 2010). adv. **Document type:** *Magazine, Trade.*
Formed by the merger of (2003-2005): OK Magazine (1570-9132); (1977-2006): Operationeel (1380-2917)
Published by: (Landelijke Vereniging van Operatie-Assistenten), Y-Publicaties, Postbus 10208, Amsterdam, 1001 EE, Netherlands. TEL 31-20-5206060, FAX 31-20-5206061, info@y-publicaties.nl, http://www.y-publicaties.nl. Pub. Ralf Beekveldt. adv.: B&W page EUR 2,915, color page EUR 3,875; trim 215 x 285.

617 GBR ISSN 1178-7082
➤ **OPEN ACCESS SURGERY.** Text in English. 2008. irreg. free (effective 2011). **Document type:** *Journal, Academic/Scholarly.* **Description:** Focuses on all aspects of surgical procedures and interventions.
Media: Online - full text.
Indexed: SCOPUS.
—CCC.
Published by: Dove Medical Press Ltd., Beechfield House, Winterton Way, Macclesfield, SK11 0JL, United Kingdom. TEL 44-1625-509130, FAX 44-1625-617933.

617 616.1 NZL ISSN 1179-0652
OPEN JOURNAL OF CARDIOVASCULAR SURGERY. Text in English. 2008. a. free (effective 2011).
Media: Online - full text.
Indexed: C06.
—CCC.
Published by: Libertas Academica Ltd., PO Box 300-874, Mairangi Bay, Auckland, 0751, New Zealand. TEL 64-9-4763930, FAX 64-9-3531397, enquiries@la-press.com. Ed. Hendrick Barner.

THE OPEN NEUROSURGERY JOURNAL. *see* MEDICAL SCIENCES—Psychiatry And Neurology

617 NLD ISSN 1876-9764
➤ **OPEN RECONSTRUCTIVE AND COSMETIC SURGERY.** Text in English. 2008. irreg. free (effective 2011). **Document type:** *Journal, Academic/Scholarly.* **Description:** Covers all areas of plastic and reconstructive surgery.
Formerly (until 2008): The Open Plastic and Reconstructive Surgery Journal (1875-1822)
Media: Online - full text.
Published by: Bentham Open (Subsidiary of: Bentham Science Publishers Ltd.), PO Box 294, Bussum, AG 1400, Netherlands. TEL 31-35-6923800, FAX 31-35-6980150, subscriptions@bentham.org. Eds. Carlo R Bernardino, Darrell Brooks.

617 NLD ISSN 1874-3005
RD1
➤ **THE OPEN SURGERY JOURNAL.** Text in English. 2007. irreg. free (effective 2011). **Document type:** *Journal, Academic/Scholarly.* **Description:** Covers all areas on the practice, education, and research of surgery.
Media: Online - full text.
Indexed: A01, CA, T02.
Published by: Bentham Open (Subsidiary of: Bentham Science Publishers Ltd.), PO Box 294, Bussum, AG 1400, Netherlands. TEL 31-35-6923800, FAX 31-35-6980150, subscriptions@bentham.org. Ed. Jose M Lopez-Novoa.

617 616.992 NLD ISSN 1876-5041
➤ **THE OPEN SURGICAL ONCOLOGY JOURNAL.** Text in English. 2008. irreg. free (effective 2011). **Document type:** *Journal, Academic/Scholarly.*
Media: Online - full text.
Indexed: A01, OGFA.
Published by: Bentham Open (Subsidiary of: Bentham Science Publishers Ltd.), PO Box 294, Bussum, AG 1400, Netherlands. TEL 31-35-6923800, FAX 31-35-6980150, subscriptions@bentham.org. Ed. Giovanni Ramacciato.

617 NLD ISSN 1874-4184
RD120.7
➤ **THE OPEN TRANSPLANTATION JOURNAL.** Text in English. 2007. irreg. free (effective 2011). **Document type:** *Journal, Academic/Scholarly.*
Media: Online - full text.
Indexed: A01.
Published by: Bentham Open (Subsidiary of: Bentham Science Publishers Ltd.), PO Box 294, Bussum, AG 1400, Netherlands. TEL 31-35-6923800, FAX 31-35-6980150, subscriptions@bentham.org. Ed. Atholl Johnston.

617 USA ISSN 1532-365X
OPERATING ROOM RISK MANAGEMENT. Abbreviated title: O R R M. Text in English. 1993. bi-m. looseleaf. **Document type:** *Magazine, Trade.* **Description:** Covers operating room risk management and quality assurance issues.
—CCC.
Published by: Emergency Care Research Institute, 5200 Butler Pike, Plymouth Meeting, PA 19462. TEL 610-825-6000, FAX 610-834-1275, info@ecri.org, http://www.ecri.org. Ed. Andrea Zavod.

THE OPERATING THEATRE JOURNAL. *see* MEDICAL SCIENCES—Anaesthesiology

OPERATIVE TECHNIQUES IN OTOLARYNGOLOGY - HEAD AND NECK SURGERY. *see* MEDICAL SCIENCES—Otorhinolaryngology

617 USA ISSN 1522-2942
OPERATIVE TECHNIQUES IN THORACIC AND CARDIOVASCULAR SURGERY. Text in English. 1998. q. USD 421 in United States to institutions; USD 483 elsewhere to institutions (effective 2012). adv. illus. back issues avail.; reprints avail. **Document type:** *Journal, Academic/Scholarly.* **Description:** Provides a forum for cardiothoracic surgeons to share surgical techniques from around the world.
Formerly (until 1998): Operative Techniques in Cardiac & Thoracic Surgery (1085-5637)
Related titles: Online - full text ed.: ISSN 1532-8627 (from ScienceDirect).
Indexed: A26, CA, EMBASE, ExcerpMed, I05, R10, Reac, SCOPUS, T02.
—BLDSC (6269.382520), IE, Ingenta. **CCC.**
Published by: (American Association for Thoracic Surgery), W.B. Saunders Co. (Subsidiary of: Elsevier Health Sciences), Elsevier, Health Sciences Division, Order Fulfillment, 3251 Riverport Ln, Maryland Heights, MO 63043. TEL 314-872-8370, 800-325-4177, FAX 314-432-1380, JournalCustomerService-usa@elsevier.com, http://www.us.elsevierhealth.com. Ed. Fred A Crawford. Pub. Joshua P Spieler. Adv. contact Betty Ann Gilchrist TEL 203-938-3156. Circ: 1,020.

OPHTHALMIC PLASTIC AND RECONSTRUCTIVE SURGERY. *see* MEDICAL SCIENCES—Ophthalmology And Optometry

617.7 USA ISSN 1542-8877
RE80 CODEN: OSLAF2
➤ **OPHTHALMIC SURGERY, LASERS AND IMAGING.** Text in English. 1968. bi-m. USD 159 combined subscription to individuals (print & online eds.); USD 499 combined subscription to institutions (print & online eds.); USD 78 per issue (effective 2010). adv. bk.rev. charts; illus. 88 p./no. 2 cols./p.; back issues avail.; reprints avail. **Document type:** *Journal, Academic/Scholarly.* **Description:** Covers the entire spectrum of ophthalmic surgery and treatment. Also presents the latest applications for laser surgery as well as potential indications and treatment modalities in regularly featured experimental science articles.
Former titles (until 2003): Ophthalmic Surgery and Lasers (1082-3069); (until 1995): Ophthalmic Surgery (0022-023X); Which superseded (in 1970): Journal of Cryosurgery
Related titles: Microform ed.: (from PQC); Online - full text ed.: ISSN 1938-2375.
Indexed: A22, A29, AMED, ASCA, B&BAb, B20, B21, BioEngAb, CA, CurCont, DentInd, EMBASE, ESPM, ExcerpMed, FR, I10, ISR, IndMed, Inpharma, MEDLINE, MS&D, P16, P20, P22, P26, P30, P35, P48, P53, P54, PQC, R10, Reac, SCI, SCOPUS, T02, VirolAbstr, W07.
—BLDSC (6271.517500), GNLM, IE, Ingenta, INIST. **CCC.**
Published by: (Association for Research in Vision and Ophthalmology, International Society for Imaging in the Eye), Slack, Inc., 6900 Grove Rd, Thorofare, NJ 08086. TEL 856-848-1000, FAX 856-848-6091, customerservice@slackinc.com, http://www.slackinc.com. Ed. Dr. Carmen A Puliafito TEL 617-636-9033.

➤ **OPHTHALMO CHIRURGIE.** *see* MEDICAL SCIENCES—Ophthalmology And Optometry

➤ **OPPORTUNITIES FOR THEATRE STAFF & OTHER SPECIALISTS.** *see* MEDICAL SCIENCES—Nurses And Nursing

➤ **ORAL & MAXILLOFACIAL CODING ALERT.** *see* INSURANCE

➤ **ORAL AND MAXILLOFACIAL SURGERY.** *see* MEDICAL SCIENCES—Otorhinolaryngology

617.6 USA ISSN 1042-3699
CODEN: OMSCAU
ORAL AND MAXILLOFACIAL SURGERY CLINICS OF NORTH AMERICA. Text in English. 1989. q. USD 490 in United States to institutions; USD 583 elsewhere to institutions (effective 2012). adv. back issues avail.; reprints avail. **Document type:** *Journal, Academic/Scholarly.* **Description:** Focuses on a single topic relevant to your oral and maxillofacial surgery practice, from reconstructive procedures to cosmetic techniques, including such topics as dental implants, cleft palate surgery, sleep disorders, lasers, pharmacology, soft tissue flaps, and neoplasms.
Related titles: Microform ed.: (from PQC); Online - full text ed.: ISSN 1558-1365 (from ScienceDirect).
Indexed: A22, C06, C07, EMBASE, ExcerpMed, MEDLINE, P30, R10, Reac, SCOPUS.
—GNLM, IE, Infotrieve, Ingenta. **CCC.**
Published by: W.B. Saunders Co. (Subsidiary of: Elsevier Health Sciences), Elsevier, Health Sciences Division, Order Fulfillment, 3251 Riverport Ln, Maryland Heights, MO 63043. TEL 314-872-8370, 800-325-4177, FAX 314-432-1380, JournalCustomerService-usa@elsevier.com, http://www.us.elsevierhealth.com. Adv. contact John Marmero TEL 212-633-3657.

ORAL SURGERY, ORAL MEDICINE, ORAL PATHOLOGY, ORAL RADIOLOGY AND ENDODONTOLOGY. *see* MEDICAL SCIENCES—Dentistry

ORALCHIRURGIE JOURNAL. *see* MEDICAL SCIENCES—Dentistry

ORBIT. *see* MEDICAL SCIENCES—Ophthalmology And Optometry

617 617.6 ITA
ORDINE PROVINCIALE DEI MEDICI CHIRURGHI E DEGLI ODONTOIATRI. NOTIZIARIO. Text in Italian. 1957. bi-m. free to members. adv. **Document type:** *Newsletter, Trade.*
Formerly: Ordine dei Medici della Provincia di Venezia. Notiziario
Published by: (Ordine Provinciale dei Medici Chirurghi e degli Odontoiatri), Mazzanti Editori Srl, Via delle Industrie 19B, Marghera, VE 30175, Italy. TEL 39-041-5385565, FAX 39-041-2529525, info@mazzantieditori.it, http://www.mazzantieditori.it.

617 ITA ISSN 1828-0595
ORGANS, TISSUES AND CELLS. Text in English. 1997. 3/yr. **Document type:** *Journal, Academic/Scholarly.* **Description:** Publishes articles about organ and tissue donation, sharing and transplantation.
Formerly (until 2006): Organs and Tissues (0265-1254)
—BLDSC (6291.120375).
Published by: (European Transplant Coordinators Organization BEL), Editrice Compositori Srl, Via Stalingrado 97-2, Bologna, 40128, Italy. TEL 39-051-3540111, FAX 39-051-327877, 1865@compositori.it, http://www.compositori.it. Ed. Alessandro Nanni Costa.

ORTHOPAEDIC PRACTICE MANAGEMENT. *see* HEALTH FACILITIES AND ADMINISTRATION

OSTOMY - WOUND MANAGEMENT. *see* MEDICAL SCIENCES—Orthopedics And Traumatology

OTOLARYNGOLOGY - HEAD AND NECK SURGERY. *see* MEDICAL SCIENCES—Otorhinolaryngology

THE OTORHINOLARYNGOLOGIST. *see* MEDICAL SCIENCES—Otorhinolaryngology

OTORINOLARYNGOLOGIA A CHIRURGIA HLAVY A KRKU. *see* MEDICAL SCIENCES—Otorhinolaryngology

617 USA
CODEN: SUFOAX
OWEN H. WANGENSTEEN SURGICAL FORUM. Variant title: Surgical Forum. Text in English. 1950. a. USD 30 (effective 2001). charts; illus. back issues avail. **Document type:** *Proceedings, Abstract/Index.*
Formerly: Forum on Fundamental Surgical Problems (0071-8041)
Related titles: CD-ROM ed.
Indexed: A22, ASCA, CIN, ChemAb, ChemTitl, P30, SCOPUS.
—CASDDS, GNLM, IE, Ingenta, INIST. **CCC.**
Published by: American College of Surgeons, Communications Department, 633 N Saint Clair St, Chicago, IL 60611-3211. TEL 312-202-5000, FAX 312-202-5001, http://www.facs.org. R&P Linn Meyer TEL 312-202-5311. Circ: 2,000.

617 JPN ISSN 1349-645X
P E P A R S. (Perspective Essential Plastic Aesthetic Reconstructive Surgery) Variant title: P E P A R S. Text in Japanese. 2005. a. price varies. **Document type:** *Monographic series, Academic/Scholarly.*
Published by: Zennihon Byoin Shuppankai, 3-16-4 Hongo, Bunkyo-Ku, 7F, Tokyo, 113-0033, Japan. TEL 81-3-56895989, FAX 81-3-56898030, http://www.zenniti.com/.

617 GBR ISSN 1754-9493
RD32
➤ **PATIENT SAFETY IN SURGERY.** Text in English. 2007. irreg. free (effective 2011). adv. back issues avail. **Document type:** *Journal, Academic/Scholarly.* **Description:** Covers all issues related to safety and quality of patient care in surgery and surgical subspecialties.
Media: Online - full text.
Indexed: A01, A26, C06, C07, CA, H12, I05, P30, SCOPUS, T02.
—CCC.
Published by: BioMed Central Ltd. (Subsidiary of: Springer Science+Business Media), 236 Gray's Inn Rd, London, WC1X 8HB, United Kingdom. TEL 44-20-31922000, FAX 44-20-31922010, info@biomedcentral.com, http://www.biomedcentral.com. Eds. Philip F Stahel, Pierre-Alain Clavien. Adv. contact Natasha Bailey TEL 44-20-31922231.

➤ **PEDIATRIA OGGI MEDICA E CHIRURGICA.** *see* MEDICAL SCIENCES—Pediatrics

➤ **PEDIATRIC CARDIOLOGY.** *see* MEDICAL SCIENCES—Cardiovascular Diseases

617 618.92 DEU ISSN 0179-0358
CODEN: PSUIED
➤ **PEDIATRIC SURGERY INTERNATIONAL.** Text in English. m. EUR 2,118, USD 2,615 combined subscription to institutions (print & online eds.) (effective 2012). adv. back issues avail.; reprint service avail. from PSC. **Document type:** *Journal, Academic/Scholarly.* **Description:** Devoted to publishing new and important information from the entire spectrum of pediatric surgery.
Related titles: Microform ed.: (from PQC); Online - full text ed.: ISSN 1437-9813 (from IngentaConnect).
Indexed: A01, A03, A08, A22, A26, A36, ASCA, CA, CABA, CurCont, D01, E01, E08, E12, EMBASE, ExcerpMed, FR, G08, GH, H11, H12, H17, I05, IndMed, Inpharma, MEDLINE, N02, N03, P20, P22, P30, P33, P35, P48, P54, PQC, R10, R12, RA&MP, RM&VM, Reac, S09, SCI, SCOPUS, SoyAb, T02, T05, VS, W07, W10.
—BLDSC (6417.628000), GNLM, IE, Infotrieve, Ingenta, INIST. **CCC.**
Published by: Springer (Subsidiary of: Springer Science+Business Media), Tiergartenstr 17, Heidelberg, 69121, Germany. TEL 49-6221-4870, FAX 49-6221-345229. Eds. Dr. A G Coran, Dr. P Puri. **Subscr. in the Americas to:** Springer New York LLC, Journal Fulfillment, PO Box 2485, Secaucus, NJ 07096. TEL 201-348-4033, 800-777-4643, FAX 201-348-4505, journals-ny@springer.com, http://www.springer.com; **Subscr. to:** Springer Distribution Center, Kundenservice Zeitschriften, Haberstr 7, Heidelberg 69126, Germany. TEL 49-6221-3454303, FAX 49-6221-3454229, subscriptions@springer.com.

617 618.92 PRI ISSN 1089-7739
PEDIATRIC SURGERY UPDATE. Text in English. 1993. m. free. back issues avail. **Document type:** *Newsletter, Trade.* **Description:** Covers current issues and reviews in the practice of pediatric surgery for primary physicians, pediatricians, surgeons, residents, medical students, and other health-related professionals.
Media: Online - full text.
Address: PO Box 10426, Caparra Height Sta, San Juan, 00922-0426, Puerto Rico. TEL 787-786-3495, FAX 787-720-6103. Ed. Dr. Humberto Lugo-Vicente. R&P Dr. Humberto Lugo Vicente.

PEDIATRIC TRANSPLANTATION. *see* MEDICAL SCIENCES—Pediatrics

617 DEU ISSN 1875-2772
▼ **PERIOPERATIVE MEDIZIN;** Zeitschrift fuer Fort- und Weiterbildung. Text in German. 2009. 4/yr. EUR 327 in Europe to institutions; JPY 47,600 in Japan to institutions; USD 390 elsewhere to institutions (effective 2011). adv. **Document type:** *Journal, Academic/Scholarly.*
Related titles: Online - full text ed.
Indexed: CA, EMBASE, ExcerpMed, SCOPUS, T02.
—IE. **CCC.**
Published by: Urban und Fischer Verlag (Subsidiary of: Elsevier GmbH), Karlstr 45, Munich, 80333, Germany. TEL 49-89-53830, FAX 49-89-5383939, journals@urbanfischer.de. Ed. Edmund Neugebauer. Adv. contact Eva Kraemer TEL 49-89-5383704.

617 USA ISSN 1531-0035
➤ **PERSPECTIVES IN VASCULAR SURGERY AND ENDOVASCULAR THERAPY.** Text in English. 1988. q. USD 744, GBP 438 combined subscription to institutions (print & online eds.); USD 729, GBP 429 to institutions (effective 2011). adv. back issues avail.; reprint service avail. from PSC. **Document type:** *Journal, Academic/Scholarly.* **Description:** Devoted exclusively to all aspects of cerebrovascular, cardiovascular, peripheral vascular, and endovascular surgery.
Formerly: Perspectives in Vascular Surgery (0894-8046)
Related titles: Online - full text ed.: ISSN 1521-5768. USD 670, GBP 394 to institutions (effective 2011); ◆ Supplement(s): Vascular Surgery and Endovascular Therapy Outlook. ISSN 1531-0027.
Indexed: A22, C06, C07, CA, E01, EMBASE, ExcerpMed, MEDLINE, P30, R10, Reac, SCOPUS, T02.
—BLDSC (6428.176800), GNLM, IE, Infotrieve, Ingenta, INIST. **CCC.**
Published by: Sage Publications, Inc., 2455 Teller Rd, Thousand Oaks, CA 91320. TEL 805-499-9774, FAX 805-499-0871, info@sagepub.com, http://www.sagepub.com/. Ed. Dr. Peter Gloviczki. adv.: B&W page USD 1,150; trim 8.125 x 10.875. Circ: 1,870 (paid and free).

617.5 ESP ISSN 0212-7709
EL PEU; revista de podologia. Text in Spanish. 1982. q. EUR 70 to institutions (effective 2009). back issues avail. **Document type:** *Journal, Academic/Scholarly.*
Published by: Nexus Medica Editores, C/ Passeig d'Amunt 38, Barcelona, 08024, Spain. TEL 34-93-5510260, FAX 34-93-2136672, redaccion@nexusmedica.com.

617 PHL ISSN 0031-7691
➤ **PHILIPPINE JOURNAL OF SURGICAL SPECIALITIES.** Text in English. 1959. q. PHP 50 to non-members; PHP 40 to members (effective 2001). adv. charts; illus.; stat.; abstr.; bibl. 50 p./no.; back issues avail. **Document type:** *Journal, Academic/Scholarly.*
Formerly (until 1967): Philippine Journal of Surgery and Surgical Specialties (0370-0267)
Related titles: CD-ROM ed.: 1970 (vol.25); Online - full content ed.
Indexed: ChemAb, ExtraMED, IndMed, P30, SCOPUS.
Published by: Philippine College of Surgeons, 3F PCS Bldg, 992 Edsa, Quezon City, Philippines. TEL 632-929-4047, FAX 632-929-2297, pcs@pcs.org.ph, http://www.pcs.org.ph. Ed., Adv. contact Dr. Edgardo R Cortez. Circ: 1,500.

➤ **PHOTOMEDICINE AND LASER SURGERY (ONLINE).** *see* MEDICAL SCIENCES—Radiology And Nuclear Medicine

617.95 USA ISSN 0032-1052
RD118.A1 CODEN: PRSUAS
➤ **PLASTIC AND RECONSTRUCTIVE SURGERY.** Text in English. 1946. m. USD 1,043 domestic to institutions; USD 1,487 foreign to institutions (effective 2011). adv. bk.rev. abstr.; charts; illus. index, cum.index vols.59-72, 1985. back issues avail.; reprints avail. **Document type:** *Journal, Academic/Scholarly.* **Description:** Provides reports on the techniques and follow-up for all areas of plastic and reconstructive surgery, including breast reconstruction, experimental studies, maxillofacial reconstruction etc.
Former titles (until 1963): Plastic and Reconstructive Surgery and the Transplantation Bulletin (0096-8501); (until 1958): Plastic and Reconstructive Surgery (1075-1270)
Related titles: Online - full text ed.: ISSN 1529-4242. USD 639.60 domestic academic site license; USD 752.60 foreign academic site license; USD 713.40 domestic corporate site license; USD 826.40 foreign corporate site license (effective 2002).
Indexed: A20, A22, AIM, ASCA, C33, ChemAb, CurCont, DentInd, EMBASE, ExcerpMed, FR, G10, INI, ISR, IndMed, Inpharma, JW-D, MEDLINE, MS&D, P30, P35, R10, RILM, Reac, SCI, SCOPUS, W07.
—BLDSC (6528.924000), GNLM, IE, Infotrieve, Ingenta, INIST. **CCC.**
Published by: (American Society of Plastic Surgeons), Lippincott Williams & Wilkins (Subsidiary of: Wolters Kluwer N.V.), 351 W Camden St, Baltimore, MD 21201. TEL 410-528-4000, FAX 410-528-4312, customerservice@lww.com, http://www.lww.com. Ed. Rod J Rohrick TEL 214-645-7790. Pub. James R Mulligan. Circ: 10,067.

617.95 USA ISSN 2090-1461
▼➤ **PLASTIC SURGERY INTERNATIONAL.** Text in English. 2009. irreg. USD 195 (effective 2011). **Document type:** *Journal, Academic/ Scholarly.* **Description:** Publishes original research articles, review articles, case reports, and clinical studies in all areas of plastic surgery.
Related titles: Online - full text ed.: ISSN 2090-147X. free (effective 2011).
Indexed: A01, T02.
—IE.
Published by: Hindawi Publishing Corporation, 410 Park Ave, 15th Fl, PMB 287, New York, NY 10022. FAX 215-893-4392, 866-446-3294, info@hindawi.com.

617.95 USA ISSN 1043-4119
PLASTIC SURGERY NEWS. Text in English. 1989. m. USD 75 (effective 2000). adv. **Document type:** *Newsletter.*
Published by: American Society of Plastic Surgeons, 444 E Algonquin Rd, Arlington, IL 60005-4664. TEL 847-228-9900, FAX 847-229-9131, http://www.plasticsurgery.org. Ed., R&P John Everson. Circ: 5,700.

617.95 USA ISSN 1084-1660
PLASTIC SURGERY PRODUCTS. Abbreviated title: P S P. Text in English. 1991. 13/yr. free to qualified personnel (effective 2011). adv. **Document type:** *Magazine, Trade.* **Description:** Offers the latest news in products and services as well as informational articles for plastic surgery professionals.
Related titles: Online - full text ed.
Indexed: A26, H01, H12, I05.
—CCC.
Published by: Allied Healthcare Group (Subsidiary of: Ascend Media), 6100 Ctr Dr, Ste 1020, Los Angeles, CA 90045. TEL 310-642-4400, FAX 310-641-4444, http://www.alliedhealthjournals.com. Ed. Jeffrey Frentzen. Pub. Darren Sextro TEL 913-894-6923. Adv. contact Dave Jeans TEL 303-856-3067. Circ: 12,000.

PLASTIC SURGICAL NURSING. *see* MEDICAL SCIENCES—Nurses And Nursing

617.95 DEU ISSN 1618-6214
PLASTISCHE CHIRURGIE. Text in German. 1994. q. EUR 80; EUR 23 newsstand/cover (effective 2009). adv. **Document type:** *Journal, Academic/Scholarly.*
Formerly (until 2001): Vereinigung der Deutschen Plastischen Chirurgen. Zeitschrift (1436-3682)
—CCC.
Published by: (Vereinigung der Deutschen Plastischen Chirurgen), Dr. R. Kaden Verlag GmbH & Co. KG, Ringstr 19 B, Heidelberg, 69115, Germany. TEL 49-6221-1377600, FAX 49-6221-29910, kaden@kaden-verlag.de, http://www.kaden-verlag.de. Adv. contact Ingo Rosenstock. B&W page EUR 970, color page EUR 2,095; trim 178 x 230. Circ: 1,800 (paid and controlled).

615.534 GBR ISSN 1756-3291
➤ **PODIATRY REVIEW.** Text in English. 1939. bi-m. free to members. adv. bk.rev.; software rev. back issues avail. **Document type:** *Journal, Academic/Scholarly.* **Description:** Contains a diary of events, reports on past events, details of group activities together with articles by members and specialists which are of interest and value to its readership.
Formerly (until 2008): Chiropody Review (0009-4714)
Indexed: C06, C07, C08, CA, CINAHL, T02.
—BLDSC (6541.498090). **CCC.**
Published by: Institute of Chiropodists and Podiatrists, 27 Wright St, Southport, Merseyside, PR9 0TL, United Kingdom. TEL 44-1704-546141, FAX 44-1704-500477, http://www.iocp.org.uk/. Ed., R&P R H S Henry. Adv. contact Jill Burnett Hurst. B&W page GBP 385, color page GBP 495; 175 x 264. Circ: 2,500.

617.585 DEU ISSN 1430-8886
PODOLOGIE. Text in German. 1948. m. EUR 95 (effective 2011). adv. bk.rev. charts; illus. index. **Document type:** *Journal, Academic/ Scholarly.*
Formerly (until 1996): Der Fuss (0427-7783)
Published by: Verlag Neuer Merkur GmbH, Paul-Gerhardt-Allee 46, Munich, 81245, Germany. TEL 49-89-3189050, FAX 49-89-31890538, info@vnmonline.de, http://www.vnmonline.de. Ed. Dr. Angelika Schaller. Pub. Burkhard P. Bierschenck. adv.: B&W page EUR 1,468, color page EUR 2,568. Circ: 5,779 (paid and controlled).

617.585 CHE ISSN 1660-0835
PODOLOGIE SCHWEIZ. Text in French, German. 1943. m. adv. **Document type:** *Magazine, Trade.*
Former titles (until 2000): Der Schweizer Podologe (1422-1314); (until 1980): Schweizer Pedicure (0036-7435)
Published by: Schweizerischer Podologen-Verband, Tribschenstr 7, Luzern, 6002, Switzerland. TEL 41-41-3685800, FAX 41-41-3685859, sekretariat@podologen.ch, http://www.podologen.ch. adv.: page CHF 935; trim 190 x 272. Circ: 900 (paid and controlled).

617 POL ISSN 0032-373X
➤ **POLSKI PRZEGLAD CHIRURGICZNY/POLISH JOURNAL OF SURGERY.** Text in Polish, English. 1922. m. EUR 109 foreign (effective 2011). adv. bk.rev. abstr.; bibl.; charts; illus. index. 100 p./no. 2 cols./p.; **Document type:** *Journal, Academic/Scholarly.*
Related titles: Online - full text ed.: free (effective 2011).
Indexed: ChemAb, DentInd, IndMed, P30, R10, Reac, SCOPUS.
—GNLM, INIST.
Published by: Towarzystwo Chirurgow Polskich, ul. Nowiniarska 1 lok.28, Warsaw, 00235, Poland. TEL 48-22-8317524, FAX 48-22-8317524, biuro@tchp65.pl, http://www.tchp.pl. Circ: 2,100. **Dist. by:** Ars Polona, Obroncow 25, Warsaw 03933, Poland. TEL 48-22-5098609, FAX 48-22-5098610, arspolona@arspolona.com.pl, http://www.arspolona.com.pl.

617 POL ISSN 1643-9279
POSTEPY W CHIRURGII GLOWY I SZYI/ADVANCES IN HEAD AND NECK SURGERY. Text in Polish. 2002. s-a. **Document type:** *Journal, Academic/Scholarly.*
Related titles: Online - full text ed.
—BLDSC (6563.835350).
Published by: (Uniwersytet Medyczny im. Karola Marcinkowskiego w Poznaniu, Katedra i Klinika Otolaryngologii i Onkologii Laryngologicznej), Termedia sp. z o.o./Termedia Publishing House, ul Wenedow 9/1, Poznan, 61614, Poland. TEL 48-61-8227781, termedia@termedia.pl. Ed. Witold Szyfter.

617 USA ISSN 1944-5652
▼ **PRACTICAL MEDICINE AND SURGERY.** Text in English. 2009. q. USD 30 (effective 2010). **Document type:** *Journal, Academic/ Scholarly.* **Description:** Contains content regarding the art and science of medicine.
Media: Online - full text.
Published by: Greentree Publishing, 912 Royer Dr, Charlottesville, VA 22902. TEL 434-242-6068, 877-411-6348, http:// www.greentreepub.com.

PROGRESS IN NEUROLOGICAL SURGERY. *see* MEDICAL SCIENCES—Psychiatry And Neurology

617 CHE ISSN 0079-6824
RD11 CODEN: PSURA2
➤ **PROGRESS IN SURGERY.** Text in English. 1961. irreg., latest vol.25, 1998. price varies. reprints avail. **Document type:** *Monographic series, Academic/Scholarly.*
Indexed: ASCA, ChemAb, ISR, IndMed, P30.
—GNLM, Infotrieve, INIST. **CCC.**
Published by: S. Karger AG, Allschwilerstr 10, Basel, 4055, Switzerland. TEL 41-61-3061111, FAX 41-61-3061234, karger@karger.ch, http://www.karger.ch. Eds. E H Farthmann, M W Buechler.

617.4 USA ISSN 1526-9248
RD129.5 CODEN: PTRRBT
➤ **PROGRESS IN TRANSPLANTATION.** Text in English. 1991. q. free to members (effective 2011). adv. illus. back issues avail.; reprints avail. **Document type:** *Journal, Academic/Scholarly.* **Description:** Provides a professional forum for exchange of the continually changing body of knowledge in transplantation through the publication of original research, case studies, donor management issues, international papers, review articles, clinical practice issues, and policy papers of interest to the various professional disciplines focused on transplantation.
Formerly (until 2000): Journal of Transplant Coordination (0905-9199)
Related titles: Online - full text ed.
Indexed: C06, C07, C08, CA, CINAHL, CurCont, EMBASE, ExcerpMed, INI, IndMed, MEDLINE, P20, P22, P24, P30, P48, P54, PQC, R10, Reac, SCI, SCOPUS, T02, W07.
—BLDSC (6924.608580), GNLM, IE, Infotrieve, Ingenta. **CCC.**
Published by: (North American Transplant Coordinators Organization), InnoVision Communications, 101 Columbia, Aliso Viejo, CA 92656. TEL 949-448-7370, 800-899-1712, FAX 949-362-2049.

362.19795 CHN ISSN 1674-7445
▼➤ **QIGUAN YIZHI/ORGAN TRANSPLANTATION.** Text in Chinese; Abstracts in Chinese, English. 2010. bi-m. CNY 72, USD 72; CNY 12 per issue (effective 2010 & 2011). **Document type:** *Journal, Academic/Scholarly.* **Description:** Provides report on the development of experimental and clinical research in organ transplatation. Its content includes original article (experimental and clinical research), monographic study, review, lecture, technical exchange, case report, academic trends, meeting summary and advertisements of medicine and medical instrument.
Related titles: Online - full text ed.
Indexed: B&BAb, B21, ImmunAb.
Published by: Zhongshan Daxue Fushu Di-3 Yiyuan/The Third Affiliated Hospital of Sun Yat-Sen University, 600, Tianhe Rd., Guangzhou, 510630, China. TEL 86-20-85253160, FAX 86-20-38736410, http://www.zssy.com.cn/. Ed. Gui-hua Chen. Circ: 3,000.

617 CHE ISSN 1024-2651
RADIOSURGERY. Text in English. 1995. irreg., latest vol.6, 2006. price varies. **Document type:** *Monographic series, Academic/Scholarly.* **Description:** Summarizes the most up-to-date information on stereotactic radiosurgery.
Related titles: Online - full text ed.: ISSN 1662-3940.
Indexed: E-psyche, SCOPUS.
—BLDSC (7240.470000), IE, Infotrieve, Ingenta.
Published by: (International Stereotactic Radiosurgery Society), S. Karger AG, Allschwilerstr 10, Basel, 4055, Switzerland. TEL 41-61-3061111, FAX 41-61-3061234, karger@karger.ch, http:// www.karger.ch. Ed. Douglas Kondziolka.

617 ITA ISSN 2037-4038
RASSEGNA MEDICO CHIRURGICA. Text in Italian; Summaries in English. 1946. s-a. abstr.; bibl.; charts; illus. index. **Document type:** *Journal, Academic/Scholarly.*
Former titles (until 1998): Societa Medico-Chirurgica della Provincia di Cremona. Bollettino (1121-1342); (until 1982): Societa Medico-Chirurgica e Ospedali Provincia de Cremona. Bollettino (0391-5999); (until 1975): Societa Medico-Chirurgica di Cremona. Bollettino (0037-8852)
Indexed: IndMed, P30.
Published by: Societa Medico Chirurgica di Cremona, Ordine Provinciale dei Medici Chirurghi ed Odontoiatri di Cremona, Via Palestro 66, Cremona, CR 26100, Italy. TEL 39-0372-35224, FAX 39-0372-27368, http://www.omedcr.it.

617 GBR ISSN 0143-8395
RD1
RECENT ADVANCES IN SURGERY. Text in English. 1928. a. GBP 35 per issue (effective 2009). back issues avail. **Document type:** *Monographic series, Academic/Scholarly.* **Description:** Provides comprehensive up-to-date information for candidates of the MRCS/AFRCS examinations, and forms a useful update of general surgery for candidates of the intercollegiate examination.
Indexed: A22.
—BLDSC (7303.995000), GNLM, IE, Ingenta.
Published by: Royal Society of Medicine Press Ltd., 1 Wimpole St, London, W1G 0AE, United Kingdom. TEL 44-20-72902900, FAX 44-20-72902989, publishing@rsm.ac.uk, http://www.rsm.ac.uk/. Eds. Colin Johnson, Irving Taylor.

617.95 IRL ISSN 1649-9425
REJUVENATE. Text in English. 2007. q. EUR 24.99; EUR 4.95 newsstand/cover (effective 2007). adv. **Document type:** *Magazine, Consumer.*
Published by: Proactive Publications, 88 Lower Baggot St, Dublin, 2, Ireland. TEL 353-1-6110840, FAX 353-1-6110941, http://www.hlaw.ie. Ed. Marie Loftus. adv.: page EUR 2,500. Circ: 30,000.

617 355 CHN ISSN 1000-9736
RENMIN JUNYI/PEOPLE'S MILITARY SURGEON. Text in Chinese. m. USD 49.20 (effective 2009). **Document type:** *Journal, Academic/ Scholarly.*
Related titles: Online - full text ed.
—East View.
Published by: Renmin Junyi Chubanshe, 22, Fuxing Lu Jia 3, Beijing, 100842, China. **Dist. by:** China International Book Trading Corp, 35 Chegongzhuang Xilu, Haidian District, PO Box 399, Beijing 100044, China. TEL 86-10-68412045, FAX 86-10-68412023, cibtc@mail.cibtc.com.cn, http://www.cibtc.com.cn.

617 COL ISSN 0121-7372
REPERTORIO DE MEDICINA Y CIRUGIA. Text in Spanish. 1946. s-a. back issues avail. **Document type:** *Monographic series, Academic/ Scholarly.*
Related titles: Online - full text ed.
Indexed: A36, CABA, GH, LT, N02, N03, R12, T05, TAR.
Published by: Fundacion Universitaria de Ciencias de la Salud, Hospital San Jose, Calle 10 No. 18-75, Bogota, Colombia. TEL 57-1-5998977 ext. 157, publicaciones@fucsalud.edu.co. Ed. Dario Cadena.

RESPIRATION (ENGLISH EDITION); international journal of thoracic medicine. *see* MEDICAL SCIENCES—Respiratory Diseases

617 ARG ISSN 0048-7600
REVISTA ARGENTINA DE CIRUGIA. Text in Spanish. 1960. bi-m. adv. bk.rev. bibl.; charts; illus. index. **Document type:** *Journal, Academic/ Scholarly.*
Indexed: C01, IBR, IBZ, P30.
Published by: Asociacion Argentina de Cirugia, Marcelo T de Alvear 2415, Buenos Aires, 1122, Argentina. TEL 54-11-4822 6489, FAX 54-11-4822 6458, http://www.aac.org.ar. Circ: 3,050.

617 ARG ISSN 0326-2219
REVISTA ARGENTINA DE MASTOLOGIA. Text in Spanish. 1982. q. **Document type:** *Journal, Academic/Scholarly.*
Published by: Sociedad Argentina de Mastologia, Av santa Fe 1206, Piso 2D, Buenos Aires, C1059ABT, Argentina. TEL 54-11-48153844, FAX 54-11-48132796, info@samas.org.ar, http://www.samas.org.ar.

REVISTA ARGENTINA DE NEUROCIRUGIA. *see* MEDICAL SCIENCES—Psychiatry And Neurology

617 ARG ISSN 0328-9206
REVISTA ARGENTINA DE RESIDENTES DE CIRUGIA. Text in Spanish. 1996. 3/yr. back issues avail. **Document type:** *Magazine, Trade.*
Related titles: Online - full text ed.: ISSN 1852-4524. 1996.
Published by: Asociacion Argentina de Medicos Residentes de Cirugia General (A A M R C G), M T de Alvear 2415, Buenos Aires, Argentina. Ed. Jose Ignacio Pitaco.

REVISTA BRASILEIRA DE CIRURGIA CARDIOVASCULAR/ BRAZILIAN JOURNAL OF CARDIOVASCULAR SURGERY. *see* MEDICAL SCIENCES—Cardiovascular Diseases

617 BRA ISSN 0100-2171
REVISTA BRASILEIRA DE CIRURGIA DA CABECA E PESCOCO. Text in Portuguese; Abstracts and contents page in English, Portuguese. 1974. 4/yr. price varies. **Document type:** *Journal, Trade.*
Published by: Sociedade Brasileira de Cirurgia da Cabeca e Pescoco, Rua Rocha 440, 2o Andar, Sao Paulo, SP 01330-000, Brazil. http://www.sbccp.org.br. Ed. Rogerio A Dedivitis.

617 BRA ISSN 0101-9880
RC864
REVISTA BRASILEIRA DE COLOPROCTOLOGIA. Text in Multiple languages. 1981. q. **Document type:** *Journal, Academic/Scholarly.*
Related titles: Online - full text ed.: free (effective 2011).
Indexed: SCOPUS.
Published by: Sociedade Brasileira de Coloproctologia, Avenida Marechal Camara 160/916, Rio de Janeiro, 20020-080, Brazil. TEL 55-21-22408927, FAX 55-21-22205803, sbcp@sbcp.org.br, http://www.sbcp.org.br. Ed. Eduardo de Paula Vieira.

617 BRA ISSN 1678-7137
REVISTA BRASILEIRA DE VIDEOCIRURGIA. Text in Portuguese. 2003. q. **Document type:** *Journal, Academic/Scholarly.*
Related titles: Online - full text ed.: ISSN 1679-1797.
Published by: Sociedade Brasileira de Videocirurgia (S O B R A C I L), Av das Americas 4801, Sala 308, Centro Medico Richet, Barra de Tijuca, Rio de Janeiro, 22631-004, Brazil. sobracil@sobracil.org.br, http://www.sobracil.org.br.

617 CHL ISSN 0379-3893
RD1
REVISTA CHILENA DE CIRUGIA. Text in Spanish. 1949. 3/yr. back issues avail. **Document type:** *Journal, Academic/Scholarly.*
Formerly (until 1976): Sociedad de Cirujanos de Chile. Archivos (0716-3371); Which was formed by the merger of (1931-1948): Sociedad de Cirujanos del Hospital. Archivos (0716-338X); (1922-1948): Sociedad de Cirugia de Chile. Boletin (0716-3398)
Related titles: Online - full text ed.: ISSN 0718-4026. 2006. free (effective 2011) (from SciELO).
Indexed: SCI, SCOPUS, W07.
Published by: Sociedad de Cirujanos de Chile, Roman Diaz 205 Of. 401, Providencia, Santiago, Chile. tangram@terra.cl, http:// www.cirujanosdechile.cl. Ed. Julio Yarmuch Gutierrez.

617 CHL ISSN 0716-4491
REVISTA CHILENA DE NEUROCIRUGIA. Text in Spanish. 1987. quadrennial. **Document type:** *Journal, Academic/Scholarly.*
Related titles: Online - full text ed.
Indexed: A26, G08, I04, I05.
Published by: Sociedad de Neurocirugia de Chile, Esmeralda 678 2o Piso, Santiago, Chile. TEL 56-2-6334149, FAX 56-2-6391085, neurocirugia@tia.cl. Ed. Leonidas Quintana.

617 COL ISSN 0120-856X
REVISTA COLOMBIANA DE CIRUGIA. Text in Spanish. 1986. q. COP 100 domestic; USD 100 foreign (effective 2010). back issues avail. **Document type:** *Journal, Academic/Scholarly.*
Related titles: Online - full text ed.: ISSN 2011-7582. 1986 (from SciELO).
Published by: Asociacion Colombiana de Cirugia, Calle 100 No. 14-63 Ofic 502, Bogota, Colombia. TEL 57-1-2574560, FAX 57-1-6114776, sccirug@colomsat.net.co, http://www.ascolcirugia.com/. Ed. Jose Felix Patino.

617 COL ISSN 0121-2729
REVISTA COLOMBIANA DE CIRUGIA PLASTICA Y RECONSTRUCTIVA. Text in Spanish. 1989. s-a. **Document type:** *Journal, Academic/Scholarly.*

Published by: Sociedad Colombiana de Cirugia Plastica, Estetica, Maxilofacial y de la Mano, Edificio los Hexagonos, Av 15 No 119 A-43, Of 406, Bogota, Colombia. TEL 57-1-2140462, http://www.cirugiaplastica.org.co.

REVISTA CUBANA DE ANGIOLOGIA Y CIRUGIA VASCULAR. *see* MEDICAL SCIENCES—Cardiovascular Diseases

617 CUB ISSN 0034-7493 CODEN: RCBCAA
REVISTA CUBANA DE CIRUGIA. Text in Spanish; Summaries in English, Spanish. 1962. 3/yr. USD 28 in North America; USD 30 in South America; USD 34 elsewhere (effective 2005). bibl.; charts; illus. index. back issues avail. **Document type:** *Journal, Academic/Scholarly.*
Related titles: Online - full text ed.: ISSN 1561-2945. 1995. free (effective 2011).
Indexed: A01, C01, CA, ChemAb, IBR, IBZ, INIS AtomInd, IndMed, SCOPUS, T02.
—INIST.
Published by: Centro Nacional de Informacion de Ciencias Medicas (C N I C M), Calle E No 454, El Vedado, Havana, 10400, Cuba. TEL 537-322004, FAX 537-333063, http://www.sld.cu. Circ: 2,000.
Co-sponsor: Sociedad Cubana de Cirurgia.

617.98 ARG ISSN 0327-7062
REVISTA DE CIRUGIA INFANTIL. Text in Spanish. 1991. q. ARS 60 in Argentina; USD 76 in Latin America; USD 96 elsewhere. back issues avail. **Document type:** *Journal, Academic/Scholarly.*
Published by: Federacion de Sociedades de Cirugia de Pediatria del Cono Sur de America, Sanchez Bustamante 305 PB1, Buenos Aires, 1173, Argentina. TEL 54-11-48654264. Ed. Raul Korman. Circ: 1,500.

616 MEX ISSN 1665-7330
REVISTA DE ESPECIALIDADES MEDICO-QUIRURGICAS. Text in Spanish. 1996. q. back issues avail. **Document type:** *Journal, Government.*
Indexed: C01.
Published by: Centro Medico Nacional 20 de Noviembre - ISSSTE, Ave Coyoacan 525, Esq Felix Cuevas, Del Benito Juarez, Mexico, 03100, Mexico. TEL 52-55-52005003, FAX 52-55-52003590. Ed. Aura Erazo Valle.

REVISTA DE NEUROCIRUGIA. *see* MEDICAL SCIENCES—Psychiatry And Neurology

617.6 ESP ISSN 1130-0558
REVISTA ESPANOLA DE CIRUGIA ORAL Y MAXILOFACIAL. Text in Spanish; Summaries in English. 1979. bi-m. free to qualified personnel (effective 2009). **Document type:** *Journal, Academic/Scholarly.*
Formerly (until 1977): Revista Iberoamericana de Cirugia Oral y Maxilofacial (0210-5926)
Related titles: Online - full text ed.: ISSN 2173-9161. 2010. free (effective 2011) (from ScienceDirect).
Indexed: CA, D02, SCOPUS, T02.
—CCC.
Published by: (Sociedad Espanola de Cirugia Oral y Maxilofacial (S E C O M)), Ediciones Ergon S.A., C/ Arboleda 1, Majadahonda, Madrid, Madrid 28220, Spain. TEL 34-91-6362930, FAX 34-91-6362931, ergon@ergon.es, http://www.ergon.es. Circ: 2,200.

REVISTA ESPANOLA DE CIRUGIA ORTOPEDICA Y TRAUMATOLOGIA. *see* MEDICAL SCIENCES—Orthopedics And Traumatology

617 ESP ISSN 1132-6336
REVISTA ESPANOLA DE TRASPLANTES. Text in Spanish. 1992. q. EUR 70. back issues avail. **Document type:** *Journal, Academic/Scholarly.* **Description:** Publishes research and clinical articles concerning organ transplant surgery.
Published by: (Organizacion Nacional de Trasplantes), Grupo Saned, Capitan Haya 60, 1o, Madrid, 28028, Spain. TEL 34-91-7499500, FAX 34-91-7499501, saned@medynet.com, http://www.gruposaned.com. Ed. Blanca Miranda. Circ: 2,000.

617 GTM ISSN 1022-6834
REVISTA GUATEMALTECA DE CIRUGIA. Text in Spanish. 1992. q. **Document type:** *Journal, Academic/Scholarly.*
Published by: Asociacion de Cirujanos de Guatemala, 12a Calle 1-25, Zona 10, Edificio Geminis 10 Torre Sur Nivel, Of 1309, Guatemala City, Guatemala. TEL 502-23352968, FAX 502-23353591, asocirgua@terra.com.gt, http://www.asocirgua.com.

617 ESP ISSN 1698-8396
REVISTA IBEROAMERICANA DE CIRUGIA DE LA MANO. Text in Spanish. 1973. 3/yr. **Document type:** *Journal, Academic/Scholarly.*
Formerly (until 2000): Revista Espanola de Cirugia de la Mano (0210-2323)
Related titles: Online - full text ed.: ISSN 1698-840X.
Published by: Sociedad Espanola de Cirugia de la Mano (SECMA), Santa Isabel 15, Madrid, 28012, Spain. Ed. Alfredo Quintana Guitian.

617 MEX
REVISTA MEXICANA DE CIRUGIA ENDOSCOPICA. Text in Spanish. 2000. q. MXN 350 domestic; USD 75 in Latin America; USD 85 in US & Canada; USD 95 elsewhere (effective 2007). back issues avail. **Document type:** *Journal, Academic/Scholarly.*
Related titles: Online - full text ed.
Published by: Asociacion Mexicana de Cirugia Endoscopica, Melchor Ocampo 193, Torre C Primer Piso, Desp 101 F, Col. Anzures, Mexic, D.F., 11300, Mexico. TEL 52-55-52602089, FAX 52-55-52602274, amcl@prodigy.net.mx, http://www.amce.com.mx/. Ed. Carlos Melgoza Ortiz.

REVISTA PORTUGUESA DE ESTOMATOLOGIA MEDICINA DENTARIA E CIRURGIA MAXILOFACIAL. *see* MEDICAL SCIENCES—Dentistry

617 VEN ISSN 0378-6420
REVISTA VENEZOLANA DE CIRUGIA. Text in Spanish. 1975. q. **Document type:** *Journal, Academic/Scholarly.*
Former titles (until 1976): Sociedad Venezolana de Cirugia. Revista (0378-6412); (until 1975): Sociedad Venezolana de Cirugia. Boletin
Published by: Sociedad Venezolana de Cirugia, Avda Sucre de los Dos Caminos, Torre Centro Boyaca, Piso 17, Of 173, Caracas, Venezuela. TEL 58-212-2868106, FAX 58-212-2868459, info@svcirugia.org, http://www.svcirugia.org.

617 FRA ISSN 0336-7525
LA REVUE DE CHIRURGIE ESTHETIQUE DE LANGUE FRANCAISE. Text in French; Summaries in English, French. 1975. q. EUR 160 domestic to individuals; EUR 190 foreign to individuals; EUR 320 domestic to institutions; EUR 380 foreign to institutions (effective 2009). adv. bk.rev. bibl. **Document type:** *Journal, Academic/Scholarly.*
Indexed: FR.
—INIST.
Published by: Societe Francaise de Chirurgie Esthetique, 54 av. Lefevre, Le Plessis-Trevise, 94420, France. TEL 33-1-45941664, FAX 33-1-40549972. Ed. Dr. Jacques Bassot.

617.6 FRA ISSN 0035-1768 CODEN: RSCMAL
REVUE DE STOMATOLOGIE ET DE CHIRURGIE MAXILLO-FACIALE. Text in French. 1894. 6/yr. EUR 416 in Europe to institutions; EUR 340.84 in France to institutions; JPY 65,100 in Japan to institutions; USD 541 elsewhere to institutions (effective 2012). adv. bk.rev. illus. index. reprints avail. **Document type:** *Journal, Academic/Scholarly.* **Description:** Presents general reviews on topical subjects, original articles concerning maxillofacial pathology and surgery, and practical notes concerning topical therapeutics or techniques.
Formerly: Revue de Stomatologie
Related titles: Microform ed.: (from PQC); Online - full text ed.: ISSN 1776-257X (from ScienceDirect).
Indexed: A22, CA, CTD, D02, DentInd, EMBASE, ExcerpMed, FR, IndMed, MEDLINE, P30, R10, Reac, SCI, SCOPUS, W07.
—BLDSC (7953.325000), GNLM, IE, Infotrieve, Ingenta, INIST. **CCC.**
Published by: Elsevier Masson (Subsidiary of: Elsevier Health Sciences), 62 Rue Camille Desmoulins, Issy les Moulineaux, Cedex 92442, France. TEL 33-1-71165500, infos@elsevier-masson.fr. Ed. Lotfi B Slama. Circ: 1,600.

617 JPN ISSN 0386-9857 CODEN: RIGEBG
RINSHO GEKA/JOURNAL OF CLINICAL SURGERY. Text in Japanese. 1945. m. JPY 40,160 per issue; JPY 52,200 combined subscription (print & online eds.) (effective 2010). **Document type:** *Journal, Academic/Scholarly.*
Related titles: Online - full text ed.: ISSN 1882-1278.
Indexed: INIS AtomInd, P30.
—BLDSC (4958.790000), CASDDS, GNLM.
Published by: Igaku Shoin Ltd., 1-28-36 Hongo, Bunkyo-ku, Tokyo, 113-8719, Japan. TEL 81-3-3817-5600, FAX 81-3-3815-7791, info@igaku-shoin.co.jp.

617 615.82 ITA ISSN 0080-3243
RIVISTA DI CHIRURGIA DELLA MANO. Text in Italian. 1963. 3/yr. EUR 78 in Europe to institutions; EUR 88 elsewhere to institutions (effective 2009). adv. illus. index, cum.index. **Document type:** *Journal, Academic/Scholarly.*
Former titles (until 2000): Chirurgia e Riabilitazione della Mano e dell'Arto Superiore (1590-0460); (until 1991): Rivista di Chirurgia della Mano
Related titles: Microform ed.: 1962.
Published by: (Societa Italiana di Chirurgia della Mano), Mattioli 1885 SpA, Via Coduro 1, Fidenza, PR 43036, Italy. TEL 39-0524-84547, FAX 39-0524-84751, http://www.mattioli1885.com. Ed. Maurizio Corradi. Circ: 1,500.

ROMANIAN NEUROSURGERY. *see* MEDICAL SCIENCES—Psychiatry And Neurology

617 IDN ISSN 0216-0951
ROPANASURI. Text in Indonesian. 1968. q. **Document type:** *Journal, Academic/Scholarly.*
Indexed: P30.
Published by: Ikatan Ahli Bedah Indonesia, c/o Sekretariat IKABI, Jl. Diponegoro no.71 Bagian Ilmu Bedah, R.S.Cipto Mangunkusumo, Jakarta Pusat, Indonesia. TEL 62-21-3905553, FAX 62-21-3908270, http://www.ikabisurgeon.com/.

617 GBR ISSN 0035-8843
RD1 CODEN: ARCSAF
➤ **ROYAL COLLEGE OF SURGEONS OF ENGLAND. ANNALS.** Text in English. 1947. 8/yr. GBP 210 combined subscription in Europe to institutions (print & online eds.); USD 385 combined subscription in United States to institutions (print & online eds.); GBP 225 combined subscription elsewhere to institutions (print & online eds.) (effective 2012). adv. bk.rev.; Website rev. abstr.; bibl. annual article index. back issues avail. **Document type:** *Journal, Academic/Scholarly.* **Description:** Publishes papers that relate to all branches of surgery.
Related titles: Microform ed.: (from PQC); Online - full text ed.: ISSN 1478-7083. USD 345 in North America to institutions; GBP 185 elsewhere to institutions (effective 2012) (from IngentaConnect); ◆ Supplement(s): Royal College of Surgeons of England. Bulletin. ISSN 1473-6357.
Indexed: A20, A22, ASCA, ChemAb, CurCont, DentInd, EMBASE, ExcerpMed, GeoRef, INI, ISR, IndMed, Inpharma, MEDLINE, NRN, P30, P35, R10, Reac, SCI, SCOPUS, SpeleolAb, THA, W07.
—BLDSC (1031.550000), GNLM, IE, Infotrieve, Ingenta, INIST. **CCC.**
Published by: The Royal College of Surgeons of England, 35-43 Lincoln's Inn Fields, London, WC2A 3PE, United Kingdom. TEL 44-20-74053474, FAX 44-20-78319438, communications@rcseng.ac.uk. Ed. Colin Johnson. Adv. contact Pam Noble TEL 44-1620-823383. **Subscr. to:** Portland Customer Services, Commerce Way, Colchester CO2 8HP, United Kingdom. TEL 44-1206-796351, FAX 44-1206-799331, sales@portland-services.com, http://www.portlandpress.com.

617 GBR ISSN 1473-6357
ROYAL COLLEGE OF SURGEONS OF ENGLAND. BULLETIN. Variant title: R C S Bulletin. Text in English. 19??. m. free with subscr. to Royal College of Surgeons of England. Annals. adv. back issues avail. **Document type:** *Bulletin, Academic/Scholarly.* **Description:** Provides a forum for the debate of current issues of interest in the field of medicine.
Formerly (until 2000): Royal College of Surgeons of England. College and Faculty Bulletin (1358-5304)
Related titles: Online - full text ed.: ISSN 1478-7075. free to members (effective 2009) (from IngentaConnect); ◆ Supplement to: Royal College of Surgeons of England. Annals. ISSN 0035-8843.
—BLDSC (2700.270000), IE, Ingenta, INIST. **CCC.**
Published by: The Royal College of Surgeons of England, 35-43 Lincoln's Inn Fields, London, WC2A 3PE, United Kingdom. TEL 44-20-74053474, FAX 44-20-78319438, chiefexecutive@rcseng.ac.uk. Ed. Mike Parker. Adv. contact Pam Noble TEL 44-1620-823383. B&W page GBP 475, color page GBP 1,250.

617 CZE ISSN 0035-9351
➤ **ROZHLEDY V CHIRURGII/SURGICAL REVIEW.** Text in Czech, Slovak; Summaries in Czech, English. 1922. m. CZK 1,176, EUR 50.40 (effective 2010). adv. bk.rev. **Document type:** *Journal, Academic/Scholarly.* **Description:** Contains original clinical papers and experimental articles. Informs its readers on news from the Czech Surgical Association, publishes book reviews, lectures and brief reports from the literature.
Related titles: Online - full text ed.
Indexed: A22, EMBASE, ExcerpMed, IndMed, MEDLINE, P30, R10, Reac, SCOPUS.
—BLDSC (8033.480000), GNLM, IE, Ingenta, INIST. **CCC.**
Published by: (Ceska Lekarska Spolecnost J.E. Purkyne/Czech Medical Association), Nakladatelske Stredisko C L S J.E. Purkyne, Sokolska 31, Prague, 12026, Czech Republic. nts@cls.cz. Ed. Milos Hajek. adv.: B&W page CZK 28,600, color page CZK 40,200; 250 x 170. Circ: 1,800.

617.95 USA ISSN 1935-9810
S A S JOURNAL. Text in English. 2007 (Mar.). q. USD 1,264 to institutions (effective 2011). **Document type:** *Journal, Academic/Scholarly.* **Description:** Dedicated to promoting the latest advancements in spinal surgery.
Media: Online - full content. **Related titles:** Online - full text ed.: (from ScienceDirect).
Indexed: EMBASE, ExcerpMed, P30, SCOPUS, T02.
—CCC.
Published by: (Spine Arthroplasty Society), Elsevier Inc. (Subsidiary of: Elsevier Science & Technology), 360 Park Ave S, New York, NY 10010. TEL 212-633-3100, 888-437-4636, FAX 212-633-3140, JournalCustomerService-usa@elsevier.com. Ed. Hansen Yuan.

617.95 FRA ISSN 0338-3849 CODEN: CENSE5
L A S O F C O T. CAHIERS D'ENSEIGNEMENT. (Societe Francaise de Chirurgie Orthopedique et Traumatologique) Text in French. 1975. irreg.
Indexed: FR.
—INIST.
Published by: Elsevier Masson (Subsidiary of: Elsevier Health Sciences), 62 Rue Camille Desmoulins, Issy les Moulineaux, Cedex 92442, France. TEL 33-1-71165500, FAX 33-1-71165600, infos@elsevier-masson.fr, http://www.elsevier-masson.fr.

SAGE; excellence in elderly anaesthesia. *see* MEDICAL SCIENCES—Anaesthesiology

SAITAMA-KEN NO SHINKEI GEKAIKAI KAIHO/SAITAMA NEUROSURGICAL ASSOCIATION. BULLETIN. *see* MEDICAL SCIENCES—Psychiatry And Neurology

658 USA ISSN 0190-5066
RD110
SAME-DAY SURGERY. Text in English. 1977. m. USD 499 combined subscription (print & online eds.); USD 83 per issue (effective 2010). bk.rev. back issues avail.; reprints avail. **Document type:** *Newsletter, Trade.* **Description:** Covers news and advice for hospital-based same-day surgery programs, freestanding ambulatory surgery centers, and office-based surgery programs.
Incorporates (1989-1997): Advanced Technology in Surgical Care; Which was formerly (until 199?): Clinical Laser Monthly (0746-469X); (until 1996): Surgery Alert (0748-1942); (until 1995): Same-Day Surgery Manual; (until 1995): Anesthesiology Malpractice Protection Report (1050-8775); Which incorporated (in 1991): Anesthesiology Alert (1040-7774)
Related titles: Microfilm ed.: (from PQC); Online - full text ed.
Indexed: A26, C06, C07, C08, CA, CINAHL, G08, H11, H12, I05, P20, P24, P30, P48, P54, PQC, T02.
—BLDSC (8071.966000), Infotrieve. **CCC.**
Published by: A H C Media LLC (Subsidiary of: Thomson Corporation, Healthcare Information Group), 3525 Piedmont Rd, NE, Bldg 6, Ste 400, Atlanta, GA 30305. TEL 404-262-7436, 800-688-2421, FAX 404-262-7837, 800-284-3291, customerservice@ahcmedia.com, http://www.ahcmedia.com/. Pub. Brenda L Mooney TEL 404-262-5403. **Subscr. to:** PO Box 105109, Atlanta, GA 30348. TEL 404-262-5476, FAX 404-262-5560.

SANFUJINKA SHUJUTSU/GYNECOLOGIC AND OBSTETRIC SURGERY. *see* MEDICAL SCIENCES—Obstetrics And Gynecology

617.54 617.41 GBR ISSN 1401-7431
RC666 CODEN: SCJOFY
➤ **SCANDINAVIAN CARDIOVASCULAR JOURNAL.** Text in English. 1967. bi-m. GBP 325, EUR 430, USD 540 combined subscription to institutions (print & online eds.); GBP 650, EUR 1,075, USD 1,080 combined subscription to corporations (print & online eds.) (effective 2010). adv. back issues avail.; reprint service avail. from PSC. **Document type:** *Journal, Academic/Scholarly.* **Description:** Promotes cardiovascular research that crosses disciplinary boundaries.
Formerly (until 1997): Scandinavian Journal of Thoracic and Cardiovascular Surgery (0036-5580)
Related titles: Online - full text ed.: ISSN 1651-2006 (from IngentaConnect); ◆ Supplement(s): Scandinavian Cardiovascular Journal. Supplementum. ISSN 1401-7458.
Indexed: A01, A03, A08, A22, ASCA, C06, C07, CA, CurCont, E01, EMBASE, ExcerpMed, IBR, IBZ, INI, ISR, IndMed, Inpharma, MEDLINE, P30, P35, R10, Reac, SCI, SCOPUS, T02, W07.
—BLDSC (8087.472600), GNLM, IE, Infotrieve, Ingenta, INIST. **CCC.**
Published by: (Scandinavian Association for Thoracic Surgery FIN), Informa Healthcare (Subsidiary of: T & F Informa plc), Telephone House, 69-77 Paul St, London, EC2A 4LQ, United Kingdom. TEL 44-20-70175000, FAX 44-20-70176792, healthcare.enquiries@informa.com. Eds. Knut Gjesdal, Rolf Ekroth. Adv. contact Per Sonnerfeldt. **Subscr. in N. America to:** Taylor & Francis Inc., Customer Services Dept, 325 Chestnut St, 8th Fl,

Philadelphia, PA 19106. TEL 215-625-8900, 800-354-1420, FAX 215-625-8914, customerservice@taylorandfrancis.com, http://www.taylorandfrancis.com; **Subscr. outside N. America to:** Taylor & Francis Ltd., Journals Customer Service, Sheepen Pl, Colchester, Essex CO3 3LP, United Kingdom. TEL 44-20-70175544, FAX 44-20-70175198, tf.enquiries@tfinforma.com.

617.95 SWE ISSN 1101-3923

➤ **SCANDINAVIAN JOURNAL OF PLASTIC AND RECONSTRUCTIVE SURGERY AND HAND SURGERY. SUPPLEMENT.** Text in English. 1967. irreg., latest vol.27, 1995. **Document type:** *Monographic series, Academic/Scholarly.*
Formerly (until 1990): Scandinavian Journal of Plastic and Reconstructive Surgery. Supplementum (0581-9474)
Related titles: ◆ Supplement to: Journal of Plastic Surgery and Hand Surgery. ISSN 2000-656X.
Indexed: IndMed, P30, SCOPUS.
—INIST. **CCC.**
Published by: (Scandinavian Hand Surgery Foundation NOR), Taylor & Francis A B (Subsidiary of: Taylor & Francis Group), PO Box 3255, Stockholm, 10365, Sweden. TEL 46-8-4408040, FAX 46-8-4408050. **Dist. by:** Almqvist & Wiksell International.

617 618.1 FIN ISSN 1457-4969 CODEN: SJSCBK

➤ **SCANDINAVIAN JOURNAL OF SURGERY.** Text in English. 1919. q. EUR 67 to individuals in Nordic countries; EUR 118 to institutions in Nordic countries; EUR 101 in Europe to individuals; EUR 185 in Europe to institutions; EUR 135 elsewhere to individuals; EUR 202 elsewhere to institutions (effective 2004). adv. bibl.; charts; illus. Supplement avail.; back issues avail. **Document type:** *Journal, Academic/Scholarly.*
Former titles (until 2002): Annales Chirurgiae et Gynaecologiae (0355-9521); (until 1975): Annales Chirurgiae et Gynaecologiae Fenniae (0003-3855); Which superseded in part (in 1945): Acta Societatis Medicorum Fennicae Duodecim. Series B (0365-172X); (in 1930): Acta Societatis Medicorum Fennicae Duodecim (0365-1738)
Related titles: Microform ed.: (from PQC).
Indexed: A22, ASCA, ChemAb, CurCont, EMBASE, ExcerpMed, INI, IndMed, Inpharma, MEDLINE, P30, R10, Reac, RefZh, SCI, SCOPUS, W07.
—BLDSC (8087.549500), CASDDS, GNLM, IE, Ingenta, INIST. **CCC.**
Published by: Suomen Kirurgiyhdistyksen/Finnish Surgical Society, PO Box 49, Helsinki, 00501, Finland. TEL 358-9-3930768, FAX 358-9-3930835, http://www.kirurgiyhdistys.fi. Eds. Hanna T. Aro, Peter J. Roberts. adv.: B&W page EUR 840, color page EUR 1,515. Circ: 2,000. **Co-sponsor:** Scandinavian Surgical Society.

➤ **SCHWEIZER ARCHIV FUER NEUROLOGIE UND PSYCHIATRIE.** *see* MEDICAL SCIENCES—Psychiatry And Neurology

➤ **SEKEI SAIGAI GEKA/ORTHOPAEDIC SURGERY AND TRAUMATOLOGY.** *see* MEDICAL SCIENCES—Orthopedics And Traumatology

617 USA

SELECTED READINGS IN GENERAL SURGERY. Text in English. 1974. m. (11/yr.). USD 799 domestic to institutions; USD 899 foreign to institutions; USD 1,030 combined subscription domestic to institutions (print & CD-ROM eds.); USD 1,140 combined subscription foreign to institutions (print & CD-ROM eds.) (effective 2011). bibl. back issues avail.; reprints avail. **Document type:** *Journal, Academic/Scholarly.* **Description:** Examines the field of general surgery during a five-year period with summaries and editorial commentary, plus self-evaluation test. Continuing medical education credit available.
Related titles: CD-ROM ed.: USD 749 domestic to institutions; USD 849 foreign to institutions (effective 2011); Online - full text ed.: USD 699 to institutions (effective 2011).
Published by: American College of Surgeons, Division of Education, 633 N Saint Clair St, Chicago, IL 60611. TEL 312-202-5438, 800-631-0033, FAX 312-202-5009, postmaster@facs.org, http://www.facs.org/education/index.html. Ed. Lewis Flint.

617.95 USA ISSN 0739-5523

SELECTED READINGS IN PLASTIC SURGERY. Text in English. 1980. 15/yr. USD 300 domestic; USD 350 foreign; USD 40 newsstand/cover domestic; USD 50 newsstand/cover foreign (effective 2005). bibl. **Document type:** *Monographic series.*
—GNLM.
Address: 411 N Washington Ave, Ste 6900, Dallas, TX 75246-1777. TEL 214-824-0154, FAX 214-824-0463, srps@swbell.net, http://www.srps.org. Ed. Jeffrey M Kenkel. R&P Sheri Quisenberry. Circ: 1,500 (controlled).

616.3 USA ISSN 1043-1489 CODEN: SCRSFI

SEMINARS IN COLON AND RECTAL SURGERY. Text in English. 1990. q. USD 358 in United States to institutions; USD 443 elsewhere to institutions (effective 2012). adv. back issues avail.; reprints avail. **Document type:** *Journal, Academic/Scholarly.* **Description:** Offers a comprehensive and coordinated review of a single, timely topic related to the diagnosis and treatment of proctologic diseases. Practical information that serves as a lasting reference for colorectal surgeons, general surgeons, surgeons in training and their colleagues in medicine with an interest in colorectal disorders.
Related titles: Online - full text ed.: ISSN 1558-4585 (from ScienceDirect).
Indexed: A22, C06, C07, C08, CINAHL, EMBASE, ExcerpMed, P30, R10, Reac, SCOPUS.
—BLDSC (8239.448400), GNLM, IE, Infotrieve, Ingenta. **CCC.**
Published by: W.B. Saunders Co. (Subsidiary of: Elsevier Health Sciences), Elsevier, Health Sciences Division, Order Fulfillment, 3251 Riverport Ln, Maryland Heights, MO 63043. TEL 314-872-8370, FAX 314-447-8093, JournalCustomerService-usa@elsevier.com, http://www.us.elsevierhealth.com. Ed. Dr. David J Schoetz Jr. TEL 781-744-8889. Pub. Herb Niemirow TEL 212-633-3141. Adv. contact Jim Pattis TEL 201-767-4170.

618.92 USA ISSN 1055-8586 CODEN: SPSUEH

SEMINARS IN PEDIATRIC SURGERY. Text in English. 1992 (Feb.). q. USD 444 in United States to institutions; USD 558 elsewhere to institutions (effective 2012). adv. back issues avail.; reprints avail. **Document type:** *Journal, Academic/Scholarly.* **Description:** Provides topical coverage of the latest techniques and the newest advances in the surgical care of infants and children.
Related titles: Online - full text ed.: ISSN 1532-9453 (from ScienceDirect).
Indexed: A22, A26, C06, C07, CA, CurCont, EMBASE, ExcerpMed, H11, H12, I05, IndMed, MEDLINE, P30, R10, Reac, SCI, SCOPUS, T02, W07.
—BLDSC (8239.456790), GNLM, IE, Infotrieve, Ingenta. **CCC.**
Published by: W.B. Saunders Co. (Subsidiary of: Elsevier Health Sciences), Elsevier, Health Sciences Division, Order Fulfillment, 3251 Riverport Ln, Maryland Heights, MO 63043. TEL 314-872-8370, 800-325-4177, FAX 314-432-1380, JournalCustomerService-usa@elsevier.com, http://www.us.elsevierhealth.com. Ed. Dr. Jay L Grosfield TEL 317-274-5716. Pub. Pat Hogan. Adv. contact John Marmero TEL 212-633-3657.

SEMINARS IN PERINATOLOGY. *see* MEDICAL SCIENCES—Pediatrics

617 USA ISSN 1535-2188 CODEN: PPSUEI

➤ **SEMINARS IN PLASTIC SURGERY.** Text in English. 1987. q. USD 618 domestic to institutions; USD 630 foreign to institutions; USD 747 combined subscription domestic to institutions (print & online eds.); USD 773 combined subscription foreign to institutions (print & online eds.) (effective 2011). adv. cum.index: vols.1-5. reprints avail. **Document type:** *Journal, Academic/Scholarly.* **Description:** Publishes topic-specific issues covering all areas of aesthetic and reconstructive plastic surgery and includes issues devoted to breast reconstruction, rhinoplasty, lipogenesis and lipoplasty, craniomaxillofacial trauma, and all other major plastic surgery procedures.
Formerly (until 2002): Perspectives in Plastic Surgery (0892-3957)
Related titles: Online - full text ed.: ISSN 1536-0067. USD 727 domestic to institutions; USD 741 foreign to institutions (effective 2011).
Indexed: A01, A03, A08, CA, P30, T02.
—BLDSC (8239.456950), GNLM, IE, Infotrieve. **CCC.**
Published by: Thieme Medical Publishers (Subsidiary of: Georg Thieme Verlag), 333 Seventh Ave, New York, NY 10001. TEL 212-760-0888, 800-782-3488, FAX 212-947-1112, info@thieme.com. Ed. Larry H Hollier TEL 832-822-3190. Adv. contact James C Cunningham TEL 201-767-4170. Circ: 725.

➤ **SEMINARS IN SPINE SURGERY.** *see* MEDICAL SCIENCES—Orthopedics And Traumatology

617.54 616.1 USA ISSN 1043-0679

SEMINARS IN THORACIC AND CARDIOVASCULAR SURGERY. Text in English. 1989. q. USD 479 in United States to institutions; USD 617 elsewhere to institutions (effective 2012). back issues avail.; reprints avail. **Document type:** *Journal, Academic/Scholarly.* **Description:** Topics is explored that present detailed descriptions and sound evaluations of developments in diagnosis and treatment, new techniques, and scientific and technologic advances.
Related titles: Online - full text ed.: ISSN 1532-9488 (from ScienceDirect).
Indexed: A22, C06, C07, CA, EMBASE, ExcerpMed, INI, IndMed, MEDLINE, P30, R10, Reac, SCOPUS, T02.
—BLDSC (8239.475000), GNLM, IE, Infotrieve, Ingenta. **CCC.**
Published by: (American Association for Thoracic Surgery), W.B. Saunders Co. (Subsidiary of: Elsevier Health Sciences), Elsevier, Health Sciences Division, Order Fulfillment, 3251 Riverport Ln, Maryland Heights, MO 63043. TEL 314-872-8370, 800-325-4177, FAX 314-432-1380, JournalCustomerService-usa@elsevier.com, http://www.us.elsevierhealth.com. Eds. David H Adams, Michael A Maddaus, Dr. Timothy J Gardner.

616 USA ISSN 0895-7967
RD598.5 CODEN: SVSUEP

SEMINARS IN VASCULAR SURGERY. Text in English. 1988. q. USD 516 in United States to institutions; USD 638 elsewhere to institutions (effective 2012). back issues avail.; reprints avail. **Document type:** *Journal, Academic/Scholarly.* **Description:** Provides particular clinical problem and features new diagnostic and operative techniques and expands their capabilities and to keep pace with the most rapidly evolving areas of surgery.
Related titles: Online - full text ed.: ISSN 1558-4518 (from ScienceDirect).
Indexed: A22, A26, CA, CurCont, EMBASE, ExcerpMed, H11, H12, I02, I05, IndMed, MEDLINE, P30, R10, Reac, SCI, SCOPUS, T02, W07.
—BLDSC (8239.486500), GNLM, IE, Infotrieve, Ingenta. **CCC.**
Published by: W.B. Saunders Co. (Subsidiary of: Elsevier Health Sciences), Elsevier, Health Sciences Division, Order Fulfillment, 3251 Riverport Ln, Maryland Heights, MO 63043. TEL 314-872-8370, 800-325-4177, FAX 314-432-1380, JournalCustomerService-usa@elsevier.com, http://www.us.elsevierhealth.com. Ed. Dr. Robert B Rutherford. Pub. Josh Spieler. Adv. contact Betty Ann Gilchrist TEL 203-938-3156. Circ: 520.

617 CHN ISSN 1671-2722

SHIYONG SHOUWAIKE ZAZHI/CHINESE JOURNAL OF PRACTICAL HAND SURGERY. Text in English. q. USD 16.40 (effective 2009). **Document type:** *Journal, Academic/Scholarly.*
Related titles: Online - full text ed.
—East View.
Published by: Shenyang Yixueyuan, Fushu Zhongxin Yiyuan/Affiliated Central Hospital of Shenyang Medical College, 5, Nanqi Xilu, Shenyang, 110024, China. TEL 86-24-25704346. **Dist. by:** China International Book Trading Corp, 35 Chegongzhuang Xilu, Haidian District, PO Box 399, Beijing 100044, China. TEL 86-10-68412045, FAX 86-10-68412023, cibtc@mail.cibtc.com.cn, http://www.cibtc.com.cn.

617 JPN ISSN 0385-6313

SHONI GEKA/JAPANESE JOURNAL OF PEDIATRIC SURGERY. Text in Japanese; Summaries in English. 1969. m. JPY 40,900 (effective 2005). **Document type:** *Journal, Academic/Scholarly.*
Supersedes in part (in 1976): Shoni Geka, Naika/Japanese Journal of Pediatric Surgery and Medicine (0387-2386)
Indexed: INIS AtomInd.
—BLDSC (4656.942000).
Published by: Tokyo Igakusha Ltd., 35-4 Hongo 3-chome, Bunkyo-ku, Tokyo, 113-0033, Japan. TEL 81-3-38114119, FAX 81-3-38116135.

617 JPN ISSN 0037-4423

SHUJUTSU/OPERATION. Text in Japanese. 1947. m. JPY 41,055 (effective 2007). bk.rev. cum.index. **Document type:** *Journal, Academic/Scholarly.*
Indexed: IndMed, P30.
—GNLM.
Published by: Kanehara Shuppan/Kanehara & Co. Ltd., 2-31-14 Yushima, Bunkyo-ku, Tokyo, 113-8687, Japan. TEL 81-3-38117184, FAX 81-3-38130288, http://www.kanehara-shuppan.co.jp/. Circ: 9,500.

617 CUB ISSN 1028-4389

SILAC. Text in Spanish. 1993. s-a. **Document type:** *Journal, Academic/Scholarly.*
Published by: Asociacion Medica del Caribe, Calle 18, No. 710 entre 7ma. y 29 A, Playa, Havana, Cuba. TEL 53-7-2051575, FAX 53-7-662075, ameca@ceniai.inf.cu, http://www.ameca.cu/index.php.

617 GBR ISSN 2044-6012

▼ **THE SILVER SCALPEL.** Text in English. 2010. 3/yr. free (effective 2010). adv. **Document type:** *Magazine, Consumer.* **Description:** Aims to develop the interest, educational and career opportunities of all students interested in surgery.
Related titles: Online - full text ed.
Published by: University College London Surgical Society, c/o CSC Reception, UCL Union, 25 Gordon St, London, WC1H 0AY, United Kingdom. editors@uclsurgicalsociety.co.uk. Eds. Christopher Akhunbay-Fudge, Radoslaw Rippel.

SKIN DEEP. *see* BEAUTY CULTURE

617 USA ISSN 1531-5010 CODEN: SBKABK

➤ **SKULL BASE;** an interdisciplinary approach. Text in English. 1991. bi-m. USD 762 domestic to institutions; USD 780 foreign to institutions; USD 927 combined subscription domestic to institutions (print & online eds.); USD 966 combined subscription foreign to institutions (print & online eds.) (effective 2011). adv. reprints avail. **Document type:** *Journal, Academic/Scholarly.* **Description:** Publishes original articles containing clinical and experimental information of use to the practicing skull base surgeon.
Formerly (until 2001): Skull Base Surgery (1052-1453)
Related titles: Online - full text ed.: ISSN 1532-0065. 1990. USD 897 domestic to institutions; USD 918 foreign to institutions (effective 2011).
Indexed: A01, A03, A08, A20, A22, ASCA, CA, CurCont, E01, EMBASE, ExcerpMed, Inpharma, NSCI, P30, R10, Reac, SCI, SCOPUS, T02, W07.
—BLDSC (8308.825000), GNLM, IE, Infotrieve, Ingenta, INIST. **CCC.**
Published by: Thieme Medical Publishers (Subsidiary of: Georg Thieme Verlag), 333 Seventh Ave, New York, NY 10001. TEL 212-760-0888, 800-782-3488, FAX 212-947-1112, info@thieme.com. Eds. Dr. Michael Gleeson, Dr. Robert F Spetzler. Adv. contact James C Cunningham TEL 201-767-4170. Circ: 1,460.

617 USA ISSN 2157-6971

▼ ➤ **SKULL BASE REPORTS.** Text in English. 2011. 2/yr. **Document type:** *Journal, Academic/Scholarly.* **Description:** Contains reports on skull base cases and procedures.
Related titles: Online - full text ed.: ISSN 2157-698X. 2011. free (effective 2011).
Published by: Thieme Medical Publishers (Subsidiary of: Georg Thieme Verlag), 333 Seventh Ave, New York, NY 10001. TEL 212-760-0888, 800-782-3488, FAX 212-947-1112, info@thieme.com. Eds. Dr. Dennis H Kraus, Dr. Michael Gleeson.

617 BRA ISSN 1516-2001

SOCIEDADE BRASILEIRA DE CIRURGIA PLASTICA. REVISTA. Text in Multiple languages. 1986. 3/yr. **Document type:** *Journal, Academic/Scholarly.*
Former titles (until 1995): Sociedade Brasileira de Cirurgia Plastica, Estetica e Reconstructiva. Revista (0104-8643); (until 1992): Sociedade Brasileira de Cirurgia Plastica. Revista (0103-1708)
Published by: Sociedade Brasileira de Cirurgia Plastica, Avenida Pacaembu 746, 11o Andar, Sao Paulo, 01234-000, Brazil. TEL 55-11-38261499, FAX 55-11-38261710, sbcp@cirurgiaplastica.org.br, http://www.cirurgiaplastica.org.br.

616 ITA ISSN 0366-3434

SOCIETA MEDICO-CHIRURGICA DI MODENA. BOLLETTINO. Text in Italian; Summaries in English. 1886. bi-m. **Document type:** *Journal, Academic/Scholarly.*
Formerly (until 1896): La Rassegna di Scienze Mediche (0393-4187)
Published by: Societa Medico-Chirurgica di Modena, Policlinico, Via del Pozzo 71, Modena, MO 41100, Italy. TEL 39-059-4224538.

617 USA ISSN 1086-8089

➤ **SOCIETY OF LAPAROENDOSCOPIC SURGEONS. JOURNAL.** Abbreviated title: J S L S. Text in English. 1997. q. free to members (effective 2010). back issues avail. **Document type:** *Journal, Academic/Scholarly.* **Description:** Contains original articles on basic science and technical topics in all the fields involved with laparoendoscopic surgery.
Related titles: Online - full text ed.: ISSN 1938-3797. free (effective 2010) (from IngentaConnect).
Indexed: A20, CurCont, EMBASE, ExcerpMed, IndMed, MEDLINE, P30, R10, Reac, SCI, SCOPUS, W07.
—BLDSC (4889.800000), IE, Infotrieve, Ingenta.
Published by: Society of Laparoendoscopic Surgeons, 7330 SW 62nd Pl., Ste. 410, Miami, FL 33143. TEL 305-665-9959, FAX 305-667-4123, info@sls.org. Ed. Michael S Kavic.

617 ZAF ISSN 0038-2361 CODEN: SAJSBS

➤ **SOUTH AFRICAN JOURNAL OF SURGERY/SUID-AFRIKAANSE JOERNAAL VIR CHIRURGIE.** Text in Afrikaans, English. 1963. q. adv. bk.rev. bibl.; charts; illus. index. reprints avail. **Document type:** *Journal, Academic/Scholarly.* **Description:** Publishes clinical and research articles in all areas of surgery.
Related titles: Online - full text ed.: ISSN 2078-5151. free (effective 2011).
Indexed: A22, A26, A36, ASCA, CABA, CurCont, EMBASE, ExcerpMed, GH, H12, I05, INIS AtomInd, ISAP, IndMed, Inpharma, MEDLINE, P30, P33, R10, R&VM, Reac, SCI, SCOPUS, T05, W07, W11.
—BLDSC (8340.300000), GNLM, IE, Infotrieve, Ingenta. **CCC.**
Published by: (Association of Surgeons of South Africa), South African Medical Association, Block F Castle Walk Corporate Park, Nossob St, Erasmuskloof X3, Pretoria 7430, South Africa. TEL 27-12-4812000, FAX 27-12-4812100, publishing@samedical.org, http://www.samedical.org. **Subscr. to:** PO Box 74789, Lynnwood Ridge, Pretoria 0040, South Africa.

617 USA ISSN 0891-3633
R15

SOUTHERN SURGICAL ASSOCIATION. TRANSACTIONS. Text in English. 1887. a. **Document type:** *Proceedings, Academic/Scholarly.*
Formerly (until 1916): Southern Surgical and Gynecological Association. Transactions (0891-3625)
Related titles: Microform ed.: (from PQC).
Indexed: P30.
—CCC.
Published by: Southern Surgical Association, c/o Mark Evers, Markey Cancer Ctr, University of Kentucky, 800 Rose ST, CC 140, Lexington, KY 40536. TEL 859-323-6542, FAX 859-323-2074, mark.evers@uky.edu, http://www.southernsurg.org.

SPOR HEKIMLIGI DERGISI/TURKISH JOURNAL OF SPORTS MEDICINE. *see* MEDICAL SCIENCES—Sports Medicine

617 CHE ISSN 1011-6125
RD593 CODEN: SFUNE4

➤ **STEREOTACTIC AND FUNCTIONAL NEUROSURGERY.** Text in English. 1938. bi-m. CHF 1,864, EUR 1,489, USD 1,830.50 to institutions; CHF 2,045, EUR 1,634, USD 2,006.50 combined subscription to institutions (print & online eds.) (effective 2012). adv. bibl.; illus.; charts. index. back issues avail. **Document type:** *Journal, Academic/Scholarly.* **Description:** Provides a single source for the reader to keep abreast of developments in the most rapidly advancing subspecialty within neurosurgery.
Former titles (until 1989): Applied Neurophysiology (0379-2676); (until 1975): Confinia Neurologia (0010-5678)
Related titles: Microform ed.: (from RPI); Online - full text ed.: ISSN 1423-0372. CHF 1,813, EUR 1,450, USD 1,760 to institutions (effective 2012).
Indexed: A22, ASCA, B21, B25, BDM&CN, BIOSIS Prev, CA, CMCI, ChemAb, DentInd, E-psyche, E01, EMBASE, ExcerpMed, ISR, IndMed, MEDLINE, MycolAb, NSA, NSCI, P30, PsycholAb, R10, Reac, SCI, SCOPUS, T02, W07.
—BLDSC (8464.368000), CASDDS, GNLM, IE, Infotrieve, Ingenta, INIST. **CCC.**
Published by: (World and American Society for Stereotactic and Functional Neurosurgery), S. Karger AG, Allschwilerstr 10, Basel, 4055, Switzerland. TEL 41-61-3061111, FAX 41-61-3061234, karger@karger.ch, http://www.karger.ch. Ed. David W. Roberts. R&P Tatjana Sepin. adv.: page CHF 1,815; trim 210 x 280. Circ: 900.

617 NLD ISSN 2210-5883

STNU!. Text in Dutch. 2003. a.
Published by: Stichting Transplantatie Nu, Postbus 2358, Hilversum, 1200 CJ, Netherlands. TEL 31-35-6912668, info@stnu.nl.

STRATEGIES IN TRAUMA AND LIMB RECONSTRUCTION. *see* MEDICAL SCIENCES—Orthopedics And Traumatology

SUIZO/JAPAN PANCREAS SOCIETY. JOURNAL. *see* MEDICAL SCIENCES—Internal Medicine

617 GBR ISSN 1479-666X

➤ **THE SURGEON.** Text in English. 2003 (Feb.). bi-m. EUR 332 in Europe to institutions; JPY 44,000 in Japan to institutions; USD 474 elsewhere to institutions (effective 2012). adv. bk.rev. back issues avail.; reprints avail. **Document type:** *Journal, Academic/Scholarly.* **Description:** Publishes articles from all specialties and aims to educate, entertain, give insight into new surgical techniques and technology, and provide a forum for debate and discussion.
Formed by the merger of (1955-2003): Royal College of Surgeons of Edinburgh. Journal (0035-8835); (1971-2003): Irish Colleges of Physicians and Surgeons. Journal (0374-8405); Which was formerly (1963-1971): Royal College of Surgeons in Ireland. Journal (0035-8827)
Related titles: Online - full text ed.: (from ScienceDirect); Supplement(s): Surgeon News.
Indexed: A01, A03, A08, C06, C07, CA, CurCont, EMBASE, ExcerpMed, MEDLINE, P30, R10, Reac, SCI, SCOPUS, T02, W07.
—BLDSC (8548.120500), IE, Ingenta, INIST. **CCC.**
Published by: (Royal College of Surgeons in Ireland IRL, Royal College of Surgeons of Edinburgh), Elsevier Ltd (Subsidiary of: Elsevier Science & Technology), The Blvd, Langford Ln, Kidlington, Oxford, OX5 1GB, United Kingdom. TEL 44-1865-843434, FAX 44-1865-843970, customerserviceau@elsevier.com, http://www.elsevier.com. Ed. Austin L Leahy.

617 GBR ISSN 0263-9319
RD1

SURGERY. Text in English. 1983. m. EUR 625 in Europe to institutions; JPY 93,700 in Japan to institutions; USD 796 elsewhere to institutions (effective 2012). back issues avail. **Document type:** *Journal, Academic/Scholarly.* **Description:** Comprehensive collection of educational reviews that present the current knowledge and practice of surgery.
Related titles: CD-ROM ed.; Online - full text ed.: ISSN 1878-1764 (from ScienceDirect).
Indexed: CA, EMBASE, ExcerpMed, SCOPUS, T02.
—BLDSC (8548.123600), IE, Infotrieve, Ingenta. **CCC.**
Published by: The Medicine Publishing Company (Subsidiary of: Elsevier Ltd), The Boulevard, Langford Ln, Kidlington, Oxford, OX5 1GB, United Kingdom. TEL 44-1865-843154, FAX 44-1865-843965, JournalsCustomerServiceEMEA@elsevier.com, http://www.medicinepublishing.co.uk. Ed. William E G Thomas. Pub. Melanie Burton. Adv. contact Ellie Ostime TEL 44-20-74244971.

617 USA ISSN 0039-6060
RD1 CODEN: SURGAZ

➤ **SURGERY.** Text in English. 1937. m. USD 703 in United States to institutions; USD 794 elsewhere to institutions (effective 2012). adv. illus. s-a. index. reprints avail. **Document type:** *Journal, Academic/Scholarly.* **Description:** Contains information on developments in clinical and experimental surgery.
Related titles: Microfilm ed.: (from PMC, PQC); Online - full text ed.: ISSN 1532-7361 (from ScienceDirect).
Indexed: A22, A26, A36, AHCMS, AIM, ASCA, B&BAb, B20, B21, B25, BIOBASE, BIOSIS Prev, CA, CABA, CTA, ChemAb, CurCont, E01, EMBASE, ESPM, ExcerpMed, FR, GH, I05, IABS, ISR, ImmunAb, IndMed, Inpharma, Kidney, MEDLINE, MS&D, MycolAb, N02, N03, NSA, P30, P33, R10, RA&MP, Reac, SCI, SCOPUS, T02, T05, VS, W07.
—BLDSC (8548.125000), CASDDS, GNLM, IE, Ingenta, INIST. **CCC.**
Published by: (Society of University Surgeons), Mosby, Inc. (Subsidiary of: Elsevier Health Sciences), 1600 John F. Kennedy Blvd, Ste 1800, Philadelphia, PA 19103. TEL 215-239-3900, 800-523-1649, FAX 215-239-3990, elspcs@elsevier.com, http://www.us.elsevierhealth.com. Eds. A L Warshaw, M G Sarr.
Co-sponsors: Central Surgical Association; American Association of Endocrine Surgeons.

617 USA ISSN 1550-7289

➤ **SURGERY FOR OBESITY AND RELATED DISEASES.** Abbreviated title: S O A R D. Text in English. 2005. bi-m. USD 457 in United States to institutions; USD 482 elsewhere to institutions (effective 2012). adv. back issues avail.; reprints avail. **Document type:** *Journal, Academic/Scholarly.* **Description:** Covers techniques for the treatment of severe obesity and documents the effects of surgically induced weight loss on obesity physiological, psychiatric and social co-morbidities.
Related titles: Online - full text ed.: ISSN 1878-7533 (from ScienceDirect).
Indexed: A26, CA, CurCont, EMBASE, ExcerpMed, I05, MEDLINE, P30, R10, Reac, SCI, SCOPUS, T02, W07.
—BLDSC (8548.162000), IE, Ingenta. **CCC.**
Published by: (American Society for Metabolic and Bariatric Surgery), Elsevier Inc. (Subsidiary of: Elsevier Science & Technology), 1600 John F Kennedy Blvd, Philadelphia, PA 19103. TEL 215-239-3900, FAX 215-238-7883, JournalCustomerService-usa@elsevier.com, http://www.elsevier.com. Ed. Harvey J Sugerman. Adv. contact Janine Castle TEL 44-1865-843844.

617 JPN ISSN 1340-5594

SURGERY FRONTIER. Text in Japanese. 1994. q. JPY 9,144 (effective 2005). **Document type:** *Journal, Academic/Scholarly.*
Published by: Medikaru Rebyusha/Medical Review Co., Ltd., 1-7-3 Hirano-Machi, Chuo-ku, Yoshida Bldg., Osaka-shi, 541-0046, Japan. TEL 81-6-62231468, FAX 81-6-62231245.

617 PAK ISSN 1816-3211

SURGERY JOURNAL. Text in English. 2007. 4/yr. EUR 900 to individuals; EUR 1,200 to institutions; EUR 150 newsstand/cover (effective 2007). **Document type:** *Journal, Academic/Scholarly.*
Related titles: Online - full text ed.: ISSN 1818-7781. free (effective 2007).
Published by: Medwell Journals, ANSInet Bldg, 308-Lasani Town, Sargodha Rd, Faisalabad, 38090, Pakistan. TEL 92-41-5010004, 92-41-5004000, FAX 92-21-5206789, medwellonline@gmail.com, http://www.medwellonline.net.

344.041 617 USA ISSN 1551-5575

SURGERY LITIGATION & LAW WEEKLY. Text in English. 2004. w. USD 300 (effective 2008). back issues avail. **Document type:** *Newsletter, Trade.*
Related titles: E-mail ed.; Online - full text ed.: ISSN 1551-5583. USD 2,595 (effective 2007).
Indexed: L10, P10, P21, P48, P53, P54, PQC.
Published by: NewsRx, 2727 Paces Ferry Rd SE, Ste 2-440, Atlanta, GA 30339. TEL 770-435-8286, 800-726-4550, FAX 770-435-6800, pressrelease@newsrx.com, http://www.newsrx.com. Pub. Susan Hasty TEL 770-507-7777.

617 USA ISSN 1553-6785

SURGERY NEWS. Text in English. 2005. m. free to members (effective 2010). adv. back issues avail. **Document type:** *Newspaper, Trade.* **Description:** Provides coverage of clinical, regulatory, legislative, and financial aspects of surgery and medicine.
Related titles: Online - full text ed.: free (effective 2010).
Published by: (American College of Surgeons), Elsevier Society News Group (Subsidiary of: Elsevier Inc.), 5635 Fishers Ln, Ste 6000, Rockville, MD 20852. TEL 240-221-4500, FAX 240-221-4400, m.branca@elsevier.com, http://www.esng-meded.com. Ed. Lazar J Greenfield.

617 JPN ISSN 0941-1291
CODEN: SUTOE

➤ **SURGERY TODAY;** the Japanese journal of surgery. Text in English. 1899. m. EUR 718, USD 862 combined subscription to institutions (print & online eds.) (effective 2012). bk.rev. 96 p./no.; back issues avail.; reprint service avail. from PSC. **Document type:** *Journal, Academic/Scholarly.* **Description:** Covers recent advances and new developments in all fields of surgery, both clinical and experimental.
Formerly (until 1991): Japanese Journal of Surgery (0047-1909)
Related titles: Online - full text ed.: ISSN 1436-2813 (from IngentaConnect).
Indexed: A01, A03, A08, A22, A26, A34, A36, ASCA, AgrForAb, CA, CABA, ChemAb, CurCont, D01, E01, E12, EMBASE, ExcerpMed, F08, FR, GH, H17, INIS AtomInd, IndMed, IndVet, Inpharma, MEDLINE, N02, N03, P30, P33, P39, R10, RA&MP, RM&VM, Reac, SCI, SCOPUS, SPPI, T02, T05, VS, W07.
—BLDSC (8548.164500), CASDDS, GNLM, IE, Infotrieve, Ingenta, INIST. **CCC.**
Published by: (Japan Surgical Society/Nihon Gan Chiryo Gakkai), Springer Japan KK (Subsidiary of: Springer Science+Business Media), No 2 Funato Bldg, 1-11-11 Kudan-kita, Chiyoda-ku, Tokyo, 102-0073, Japan. TEL 81-3-68317000, FAX 81-3-68317001, http://www.springer.jp. Ed. Yoshihiko Maehara. Circ: 1,500. **Subscr. in the Americas to:** Springer New York LLC, Journal Fulfillment, PO Box 2485, Secaucus, NJ 07096. TEL 800-777-4643, 201-348-4033, FAX 201-348-4505, journals-ny@springer.com, http://www.springer.com; **Subscr. to:** Springer Distribution Center, Kundenservice Zeitschriften, Haberstr 7, Heidelberg 69126, Germany. TEL 49-6221-3454303, FAX 49-6221-3454229, subscriptions@springer.com.

➤ **SURGICAL AND RADIOLOGIC ANATOMY;** journal of clinical anatomy. *see* MEDICAL SCIENCES

617 USA ISSN 0039-6109
RD34 CODEN: SCNAA7

➤ **SURGICAL CLINICS OF NORTH AMERICA.** Text in English. 1912. bi-m. USD 532 in United States to institutions; USD 661 elsewhere to institutions (effective 2012). adv. bibl.; illus. index, cum.index every 3 yrs. back issues avail.; reprints avail. **Document type:** *Journal, Academic/Scholarly.* **Description:** Discusses various surgical techniques and procedures.
Former titles (until 1921): Surgical Clinics of Chicago (0748-6650); (until 1917): Clinics of John B. Murphy at Mercy Hospital, Chicago
Related titles: Microform ed.: (from PQC); Online - full text ed.: ISSN 1558-3171 (from ScienceDirect); ◆ Spanish ed.: Clinicas Quirurgicas de Norteamerica. ISSN 0186-0216.
Indexed: A20, A22, AIM, ASCA, C06, C07, C08, CINAHL, ChemAb, CurCont, EMBASE, ExcerpMed, INI, ISR, IndMed, Inpharma, MEDLINE, P30, R10, Reac, SCI, SCOPUS, W07.
—BLDSC (8548.200000), CASDDS, GNLM, IE, Infotrieve, Ingenta, INIST. **CCC.**
Published by: W.B. Saunders Co. (Subsidiary of: Elsevier Health Sciences), Elsevier, Health Sciences Division, Order Fulfillment, 3251 Riverport Ln, Maryland Heights, MO 63043. TEL 314-872-8370, 800-325-4177, FAX 314-432-1380, JournalCustomerService-usa@elsevier.com.

617 USA ISSN 0930-2794
CODEN: SUREEX

➤ **SURGICAL ENDOSCOPY;** surgical and interventional techniques. Text in English. 1987. m. (in 1 vol., 12 nos./vol.). EUR 1,264, USD 1,302 combined subscription to institutions (print & online eds.) (effective 2012). adv. back issues avail.; reprint service avail. from PSC. **Document type:** *Journal, Academic/Scholarly.* **Description:** Covers surgical aspects of interventional endoscopy, ultrasound and other techniques in the fields of gastroenterology, obstetrics, gynecology, and urology, as well as gastroenterologic, thoracic, traumatic, orthopedic and pediatric surgery.
Related titles: Microform ed.: (from PQC); Online - full text ed.: ISSN 1432-2218 (from IngentaConnect).
Indexed: A01, A03, A08, A20, A22, A26, ASCA, C06, C07, CA, CurCont, E01, EMBASE, ErgAb, ExcerpMed, FR, H12, ISR, IndMed, Inpharma, MEDLINE, P20, P22, P24, P30, P48, P54, PQC, R10, Reac, SCI, SCOPUS, T02, W07.
—BLDSC (8548.215000), GNLM, IE, Infotrieve, Ingenta, INIST. **CCC.**
Published by: (Society of American Gastrointestinal Endoscopic Surgeons, European Association for Endoscopic Surgery), Springer New York LLC (Subsidiary of: Springer Science+Business Media), 233 Spring St, New York, NY 10013. TEL 212-460-1500, FAX 212-460-1575, journals@springer-ny.com, http://www.springer.com/. Eds. Alfred Cuschieri, Mark A Talamini. **Subscr. outside the Americas to:** Springer Distribution Center, Kundenservice Zeitschriften, Haberstr 7, Heidelberg 69126, Germany. TEL 49-6221-3454303, FAX 49-6221-3454229, subscriptions@springer.com; **Subscr. to:** Journal Fulfillment, PO Box 2485, Secaucus, NJ 07096. TEL 201-348-4033, FAX 201-348-4505.

617.22 616.01 USA ISSN 1096-2964
CODEN: SIUNAL

➤ **SURGICAL INFECTIONS.** Text in English. 1998. bi-m. USD 754 domestic to institutions; USD 907 foreign to institutions; USD 882 combined subscription domestic to institutions (print & online eds.); USD 1,061 combined subscription foreign to institutions (print & online eds.) (effective 2012). adv. reprint service avail. from PSC. **Document type:** *Journal, Academic/Scholarly.* **Description:** Provides practicing surgeons, infectious disease specialists, and investigators with comprehensive information on the biology, prevention, and management of post-operative infections.
Related titles: Online - full text ed.: ISSN 1557-8674. USD 798 to institutions (effective 2012).
Indexed: A01, A03, A08, A20, A22, A26, A34, A36, C06, C07, CA, CABA, CurCont, D01, E01, E07, E12, EMBASE, ExcerpMed, GH, H12, H17, I05, LT, MEDLINE, N02, N03, P30, P33, P39, R08, R10, R12, RM&VM, RRTA, Reac, SCI, SCOPUS, T02, T05, VS, W07.
—BLDSC (8548.227000), IE, Infotrieve, Ingenta. **CCC.**
Published by: (Surgical Infection Society), Mary Ann Liebert, Inc. Publishers, 140 Huguenot St, 3rd Fl, New Rochelle, NY 10801. TEL 914-740-2100, FAX 914-740-2101, 800-654-3237, info@liebertpub.com. Ed. Philip S Barie TEL 212-746-5401. Adv. contact Harriet I Matysko TEL 914-740-2182.

617 618 USA ISSN 1553-3506
CODEN: SLSEB6

SURGICAL INNOVATION. Text in English. 1994 (Mar.). q. USD 938, GBP 552 combined subscription to institutions (print & online eds.); USD 919, GBP 541 to institutions (effective 2011). adv. illus. back issues avail.; reprint service avail. from PSC. **Document type:** *Journal, Academic/Scholarly.* **Description:** Each issue focuses on a current application of this minimally invasive surgery; also covers surgical techniques and technological advances.
Formerly (until Dec 2004): Seminars in Laparoscopic Surgery (1071-5517)
Related titles: Online - full text ed.: ISSN 1553-3514. USD 844, GBP 497 to institutions (effective 2011).
Indexed: A22, C06, C07, CA, CurCont, E01, EMBASE, ExcerpMed, IndMed, MEDLINE, P30, R10, Reac, SCI, SCOPUS, T02, W07.
—BLDSC (8548.228000), GNLM, IE, Infotrieve, Ingenta. **CCC.**
Published by: Sage Publications, Inc., 2455 Teller Rd, Thousand Oaks, CA 91320. TEL 805-499-9774, FAX 805-499-0871, info@sagepub.com, http://www.sagepub.com/. Eds. Dr. Adrian E Park, Dr. Lee Swanstrom. adv.: B&W page USD 745, color page USD 1,820; trim 10 x 7. Circ: 1,025.

617 616.3 618 USA ISSN 1530-4515
CODEN: SLENEY

➤ **SURGICAL LAPAROSCOPY, ENDOSCOPY AND PERCUTANEOUS TECHNIQUES.** Text in English. 1991. bi-m. USD 763 domestic to institutions; USD 790 foreign to institutions (effective 2011). adv. charts; illus. back issues avail.; reprints avail. **Document type:** *Journal, Academic/Scholarly.* **Description:** Provides coverage of laparoscopic and endoscopic techniques and procedures, current clinical and basic science research, preoperative and postoperative patient management.
Formerly (until 1999): Surgical Laparoscopy and Endoscopy (1051-7200)
Related titles: Microform ed.: (from PQC); Online - full text ed.: ISSN 1534-4908. USD 259 (effective 2005).
Indexed: A22, ASCA, C06, C07, C08, CINAHL, CurCont, EMBASE, ExcerpMed, ISR, IndMed, Inpharma, MEDLINE, P30, R10, Reac, SCI, SCOPUS, W07.
—BLDSC (8548.234200), GNLM, IE, Infotrieve, Ingenta. **CCC.**
Published by: Lippincott Williams & Wilkins (Subsidiary of: Wolters Kluwer N.V.), 530 Walnut St, Philadelphia, PA 19106. TEL 215-521-8300, FAX 215-521-8902, customerservice@lww.com, http://www.lww.com. Eds. Carol E H Scott-Connor TEL 319-356-0330, Maurice Arregui TEL 317-872-1158. Pub. Jason Pointe. Circ: 475.

617 IND ISSN 2152-7806

▼ **SURGICAL NEUROLOGY INTERNATIONAL.** Text in English. 2010. irreg. free (effective 2011). **Document type:** *Journal, Academic/Scholarly.*
Media: Online - full text.

Indexed: A01, P10, P30, P48, P53, P54, PQC, T02.
—CCC.
Published by: Medknow Publications and Media Pvt. Ltd., B-9, Kanara Business Ctr, Off Link Rd, Ghatkopar (E), Mumbai, Maharastra 400 075, India. TEL 91-22-66491816, 91-22-66491818, journals@medknow.com, http://www.medknow.com.

SURGICAL ONCOLOGY; a review journal of cancer research & management. *see* MEDICAL SCIENCES—Oncology

SURGICAL ONCOLOGY CLINICS OF NORTH AMERICA. *see* MEDICAL SCIENCES—Oncology

617 AUS ISSN 1744-1625
RD1 CODEN: ACSHCR
➤ **SURGICAL PRACTICE.** Text in English. 1997. q. GBP 295 in United Kingdom to institutions; EUR 375 in Europe to institutions; USD 480 in the Americas to institutions; USD 579 elsewhere to institutions; GBP 340 combined subscription in United Kingdom to institutions (print & online eds.); EUR 431 combined subscription in Europe to institutions (print & online eds.); USD 552 combined subscription in the Americas to institutions (print & online eds.); USD 666 combined subscription elsewhere to institutions (print & online eds.) (effective 2012). back issues avail.; reprint service avail. from PSC. **Document type:** *Journal, Academic/Scholarly.* **Description:** Publishes clinical and research papers in all areas of surgery and related disciplines.
Formerly (until 2005): College of Surgeons Hong Kong. Annals (1028-4001)
Related titles: Online - full text ed.: ISSN 1744-1633. GBP 295 in United Kingdom to institutions; EUR 375 in Europe to institutions; USD 480 in the Americas to institutions; USD 579 elsewhere to institutions (effective 2012) (from IngentaConnect).
Indexed: A01, A02, A03, A08, A22, A26, B21, C11, CA, E01, ESPM, H&SSA, H04, H13, P02, P10, P20, P48, P53, P54, PQC, RiskAb, SCI, SCOPUS, T02, W07.
—BLDSC (8548.244500), IE, Infotrieve, Ingenta. **CCC.**
Published by: (College of Surgeons Hong Kong HKG), Wiley-Blackwell Publishing Asia (Subsidiary of: Wiley-Blackwell Publishing Ltd.), 155 Cremorne St, Richmond, VIC 3121, Australia. TEL 61-3-92743100, FAX 61-3-92743101, melbourne@wiley.com, http://www.wiley.com/WileyCDA/. Eds. David TY Lam, Stephen WK Cheng, Paul BS Lai. **Subscr. to:** PO Box 378, Carlton South, VIC 3053, Australia.

617 USA
SURGICAL PRODUCT COMPARISON SYSTEM. Variant title: Healthcare Product Comparison System: Surgical Edition. Text in English. 1987. m. looseleaf. **Document type:** *Journal, Trade.* **Description:** Covers ambulatory surgery facilities, from arthroscopes to operating tables.
Related titles: CD-ROM ed.
Published by: Emergency Care Research Institute, 5200 Butler Pike, Plymouth Meeting, PA 19462. TEL 610-825-6000, FAX 610-834-1275, info@ecri.org, http://www.ecri.org.

616 USA ISSN 0161-1372
RD1
➤ **SURGICAL ROUNDS.** Abbreviated title: S R. Text in English. 1978. m. free to qualified personnel (effective 2008). adv. back issues avail.; reprints avail. **Document type:** *Journal, Trade.* **Description:** Provides timely, practical, well-illustrated, how-to articles of interest to office- and hospital-based surgeons.
Related titles: Microform ed.: (from PQC).
Indexed: A22, A26, C06, C07, C08, CINAHL, H01, P30.
—BLDSC (8548.249000), GNLM, IE, Infotrieve, Ingenta. **CCC.**
Published by: Ascend Media (Subsidiary of: B N P Media), 7015 College Blvd, Ste 600, Overland Park, KS 66211. TEL 913-469-1110, FAX 913-469-0806, info@ascendmedia.com, http://www.ascendmedia.com. Ed. Christina T Loguidice TEL 609-524-9517. Pub. Jerome Manullo TEL 609-524-9519. adv.: B&W page USD 6,350; trim 7.875 x 10.75. Circ: 50,631.

617 USA ISSN 2157-9407
▼ **SURGICAL SCIENCE.** Text in English. 2010. q. **Document type:** *Journal, Academic/Scholarly.*
Related titles: Online - full text ed.: ISSN 2157-9415. free (effective 2011).
Published by: Scientific Research Publishing, Inc., 5005 Paseo Segovia, Irvine, CA 92603. TEL 408-329-4591, http://www.srpublishing.org.

617 ITA ISSN 2038-9582
▼ ➤ **SURGICAL TECHNIQUES DEVELOPMENTS.** Text in English. 2010. irreg. **Document type:** *Journal, Academic/Scholarly.*
Media: Online - full text.
Published by: Pagepress, Via Giuseppe Belli 4, Pavia, 27100, Italy. TEL 39-0382-1751762, FAX 39-0382-1750481.

617 USA ISSN 0164-4238
RD32.3
THE SURGICAL TECHNOLOGIST. Text in English. 1969. m. USD 40 domestic to non-members; USD 55 foreign to non-members; free to members (effective 2011). adv. bk.rev. illus. back issues avail. **Document type:** *Journal, Academic/Scholarly.* **Description:** Emphasis is given to surgical procedures and equipment, legislative-regulatory issues, aseptic techniques and professional development.
Formerly (until 1978): O R Tech (0275-4622)
Indexed: A22, C06, C07, C08, CINAHL, HospLI, P30, SCOPUS.
—BLDSC (8548.259000), IE, Infotrieve, Ingenta.
Published by: Association of Surgical Technologists, Inc., 6 W Dry Creek Cir, Ste 200, Littleton, CO 80120. TEL 303-694-9130, 800-637-7433, FAX 303-694-9169, ast@ast.org, http://www.ast.ogr. Ed. Tom Borak.

617 USA ISSN 1090-3941
RD1
SURGICAL TECHNOLOGY INTERNATIONAL; international developments in surgery and surgical research. Text in English. 1991. a., latest vol.13, 2005. USD 135 per issue (effective 2005). back issues avail. **Document type:** *Magazine, Trade.* **Description:** Presents the latest developments in surgical operative techniques and technnologies.
Indexed: EMBASE, ExcerpMed, MEDLINE, P30, R10, Reac, SCOPUS.
—BLDSC (8548.259500), IE, Ingenta.
Published by: Universal Medical Press, Incorporated, 2443 Fillmore St #229, San Francisco, CA 94115. TEL 415-436-9790, FAX 415-436-9791, info@ump.com, http://www.ump.com. Ed. Dr. Zoltan Szabo.

SURGISTRATEGIES; solutions for outpatient healthcare. *see* HEALTH FACILITIES AND ADMINISTRATION

617 USA
SUTURELINE. Text in English. q. membership. adv.
Published by: American Association of Surgical Physician Assistants, P O Box 867, Bernardsville, NJ 07924. TEL 888-882-2772, FAX 732-805-9582, http://www.aaspa.com. Circ: 500.

617 SWE ISSN 0346-847X
SVENSK KIRURGI. Text in Swedish. 1974; N.S. 1994. bi-m. GBP 21, USD 35 to institutions (effective 2004). **Document type:** *Journal, Academic/Scholarly.*
Published by: Svensk Kirurgisk Forening, PO Box 738, Stockholm, 10135, Sweden. TEL 46-8-4400230, FAX 46-8-222330, kansliet@svenskkirurgi.se. Ed. Martin Bjoerk.

617 CHE ISSN 1661-1381
CODEN: SWSUFX
➤ **SWISS KNIFE.** Text in English, French, German. 1995. q. adv. index. 48 p./no.; Supplement avail. **Document type:** *Journal, Academic/Scholarly.*
Supersedes in part (in 2004): Swiss Surgery (1023-9332); Which was formed by the merger of (1945-1995): Helvetica Chirurgica Acta (0018-0181); Which superseded in part (1934-1944): Helvetica Medica Acta (0018-0203); (1907-1995): Zeitschrift fuer Unfallchirurgie und Versicherungsmedizin (1017-1584); Which was formerly (until 1990): Zeitschrift fuer Unfallchirurgie, Versicherungsmedizin und Berufskrankheiten (0254-6310); (until 1982): Zeitschrift fuer Unfallmedizin und Berufskrankheiten (0044-3603); (until 1935): Schweizerische Zeitschrift fuer Unfallmedizin und Berufskrankheiten (0640-3603); (until 1928): Revue Suisse des Accidents de Travail (1420-2115)
Indexed: A22, CISA, ChemAb, DentInd, FR, IBR, IBZ, INI, IndMed, P30, SCOPUS.
—GNLM, IE, Infotrieve, Ingenta, INIST. **CCC.**
Published by: (Schweizerische Gesellschaft fuer Traumatologie und Versicherunsmedizin), Schweizerische Gesellschaft fuer Chirurgie, Netzibodenstr 34, Postfach 1527, Pratteln, 4133, Switzerland. TEL 41-61-8159660, FAX 41-61-8114775, info@sgc-ssc.ch, http://www.sgc-ssc.ch. adv.: color page CHF 3,019; trim 170 x 261. Circ: 2,000 (controlled).

617.952 KOR ISSN 1015-6402
TAEHAN SONGHYONG OEKWA HAKHOE CHI/KOREAN SOCIETY OF PLASTIC AND RECONSTRUCTIVE SURGERY. JOURNAL. Text in Korean. 1974. bi-m. membership. **Document type:** *Journal, Academic/Scholarly.*
Indexed: B&BAb, B19, B21, BioEngAb, CTA.
Published by: Taehan Songhyong Oekwa Hakhoe/Korean Society of Plastic and Reconstructive Surgery, Seocho World Officetel 1814, Seocho-dong 1355-3 Seocho-ku, Seoul, 137-070, Korea, S. TEL 82-2-34724252, FAX 82-2-34724254, kprs@chollian.net, http://www.plasticsurgery.or.kr/.

617 GBR ISSN 1756-1132
TECHNIC. Text in English. 194?. m. free to members (effective 2009). adv. bk.rev. **Document type:** *Journal, Academic/Scholarly.* **Description:** Provides professional expertise during the patient's stay in hospital.
Former titles (until 2007): Journal of Operating Department Practice (1746-7357); (until 2004): Technic (0954-6014)
Indexed: B28, C06, C07, C08, CINAHL.
—IE, Ingenta.
Published by: (College of Operating Department Practitioners), Ten Alps Publishing (Subsidiary of: Ten Alps Group), Trelawney House, Chestergate, Macclesfield, Cheshire SK11 6DW, United Kingdom. TEL 44-1625-613000, FAX 44-1625-511446, info@tenalpspublishing.com, http://www.tenalpspublishing.com.

617.95 USA ISSN 1536-0644
➤ **TECHNIQUES IN FOOT & ANKLE SURGERY.** Text in English. 2002. q. USD 369 domestic to institutions; USD 458 foreign to institutions (effective 2011). adv. illus. **Document type:** *Journal, Academic/Scholarly.* **Description:** Contains detailed information on the most innovative and successful surgical techniques for the correction of foot and ankle disorders.
Related titles: Online - full text ed.: ISSN 1538-1943. USD 180.70 academic site license; USD 201.55 corporate site license (effective 2002).
Indexed: EMBASE, ExcerpMed, R10, Reac, SCOPUS.
—BLDSC (8745.047500), IE. **CCC.**
Published by: Lippincott Williams & Wilkins (Subsidiary of: Wolters Kluwer N.V.), 530 Walnut St, Philadelphia, PA 19106. TEL 215-521-8300, FAX 215-521-8902, customerservice@lww.com, http://www.lww.com. Eds. Dr. Bruce E Cohen, Dr. Robert B Anderson, Dr. W. Hodges Davis. Adv. contact Renee Artuso TEL 516-741-1772. color page USD 1,790, B&W page USD 952; trim 8.25 x 11. Circ: 1,500 (paid). **Subscr. to:** PO Box 1620, Hagerstown, MD 21741. TEL 301-223-2300, 800-638-3030, FAX 301-223-2365.

617.57059 USA ISSN 1089-3393
CODEN: THUEAW
TECHNIQUES IN HAND & UPPER EXTREMITY SURGERY. Text in English. 1997. q. USD 430 domestic to institutions; USD 500 foreign to institutions (effective 2011). adv. back issues avail.; reprints avail. **Document type:** *Journal, Academic/Scholarly.* **Description:** Covers topics such as arthroscopy, microvascular surgery, plastic surgery, congenital anomalies, tendon and nerve disorders, trauma, and work-related injuries.
Related titles: Online - full text ed.: ISSN 1531-6572. USD 258.70 domestic academic site license; USD 258.70 foreign academic site license; USD 288.55 domestic corporate site licens; USD 288.55 foreign corporate site licens (effective 2002).
Indexed: C06, C07, EMBASE, ExcerpMed, MEDLINE, P30, R10, Reac, SCOPUS.
—BLDSC (8745.101000), IE, Infotrieve, Ingenta. **CCC.**
Published by: Lippincott Williams & Wilkins (Subsidiary of: Wolters Kluwer N.V.), 530 Walnut St, Philadelphia, PA 19106. TEL 215-521-8300, FAX 215-521-8902, customerservice@lww.com, http://www.lww.com. Eds. James R Doyle, Dr. Jesse B Jupiter. Pub. Kevin Anderer. Circ: 854.

617.95 USA ISSN 1536-0636
TECHNIQUES IN KNEE SURGERY. Text in English. 2002. q. USD 369 domestic to institutions; USD 459 foreign to institutions (effective 2011). adv. illus. back issues avail.; reprints avail. **Document type:** *Journal, Academic/Scholarly.* **Description:** Presents details on reconstructive knee surgery techniques and points out the advantages and limitations of new equipment and technology.
Related titles: Online - full text ed.: ISSN 1538-1935. USD 180.70 academic site license; USD 201.55 corporate site license (effective 2002).
Indexed: A01, CA, EMBASE, ExcerpMed, R10, Reac, SCOPUS, T02.
—BLDSC (8745.216300), IE, Ingenta. **CCC.**
Published by: Lippincott Williams & Wilkins (Subsidiary of: Wolters Kluwer N.V.), 530 Walnut St, Philadelphia, PA 19106. TEL 215-521-8300, FAX 215-521-8902, customerservice@lww.com, http://www.lww.com. Pub. Kevin Anderer. Adv. contact Renee Artuso TEL 516-741-1772. Circ: 355.

617 USA ISSN 1523-9896
CODEN: TSESB4
TECHNIQUES IN SHOULDER AND ELBOW SURGERY. Text in English. 2000. q. USD 430 domestic to institutions; USD 500 foreign to institutions (effective 2011). adv. back issues avail.; reprints avail. **Document type:** *Journal, Academic/Scholarly.* **Description:** Contains details of advanced techniques, including the evolution of and rationale for the procedures. Also identifies the pitfalls and possible complications, providing tips for improving surgical results.
Related titles: Online - full text ed.: ISSN 1539-591X. USD 258.70 domestic for academic site license; USD 258.70 foreign for academic site license; USD 288.55 domestic for corporate site license; USD 288.55 foreign for corporate site license (effective 2002).
Indexed: SCOPUS.
—BLDSC (8745.346000), IE, Ingenta. **CCC.**
Published by: Lippincott Williams & Wilkins (Subsidiary of: Wolters Kluwer N.V.), 530 Walnut St, Philadelphia, PA 19106. TEL 215-521-8300, FAX 215-521-8902, customerservice@lww.com, http://www.lww.com. Eds. Dr. Edward Craig, Russell F Warren. Pub. Kevin Anderer. Circ: 897.

617 THA ISSN 0125-6068
CODEN: TJSUDJ
THAI JOURNAL OF SURGERY. Text in English. 1980. q. THB 200 domestic; USD 25 foreign to individuals; USD 30 foreign to institutions. **Document type:** *Journal, Academic/Scholarly.*
Indexed: CA, T02.
—BLDSC (8813.975800), IE, Ingenta.
Published by: Royal College of Surgeons of Thailand, Royal Golden Jubilee Bldg., 2 Soi Soonvijai, New Petchaburi Rd., Bangkok, 10310, Thailand. TEL 662-716-6141 ext 3, FAX 662-716-6144, http://www.surgeons.or.th/index.php.

617 DEU ISSN 0171-6425
RD536 CODEN: TCSUD4
➤ **THE THORACIC AND CARDIOVASCULAR SURGEON.** Text in English. 1952. 8/yr. EUR 516 to institutions; EUR 674 combined subscription to institutions (print & online eds.); EUR 78 per issue (effective 2011). adv. bk.rev. abstr.; bibl.; charts; illus.; stat. index. reprints avail. **Document type:** *Journal, Academic/Scholarly.*
Formerly (until 1978): Thoraxchirurgie - Vaskulaere Chirurgie (0040-6384)
Related titles: Online - full text ed.: ISSN 1439-1902. EUR 649 to institutions (effective 2011); Supplement(s): The Thoracic and Cardiovascular Surgeon. Supplement. ISSN 0946-4778. 19??.
Indexed: A01, A03, A08, A22, ASCA, CA, ChemAb, CurCont, EMBASE, ExcerpMed, IBR, IBZ, ISR, IndMed, Inpharma, MEDLINE, P30, P35, R10, Reac, SCI, SCOPUS, T02, W07.
—BLDSC (8820.240000), CASDDS, GNLM, IE, Infotrieve, Ingenta, INIST. **CCC.**
Published by: (Deutsche Gesellschaft fuer Thorax-, Herz- und Gefaesschirurgie), Georg Thieme Verlag, Ruedigerstr 14, Stuttgart, 70469, Germany. TEL 49-711-8931421, FAX 49-711-8931410, leser.service@thieme.de, http://www.thieme-connect.de. Ed. W P Kloevekorn. adv.: B&W page EUR 1,200, color page EUR 2,295. Circ: 1,600 (paid). **Subscr. to:** Thieme Medical Publishers, 333 Seventh Ave, New York, NY 10001. TEL 212-760-0888, 800-782-3488, FAX 212-947-1112, custserv@thieme.com, http://www.thieme.com/journals.

617 USA ISSN 1547-4127
CODEN: CSCAFT
THORACIC SURGERY CLINICS. Text in English. 1991. q. USD 385 in United States to institutions; USD 487 elsewhere to institutions (effective 2012). adv. index. back issues avail.; reprints avail. **Document type:** *Journal, Academic/Scholarly.* **Description:** Covers a single specific topic in the diagnosis or surgical treatment of lung, heart, and throat diseases in each issue.
Formerly (until 2004): Chest Surgery Clinics of North America (1052-3359)
Related titles: Microform ed.: (from PQC); Online - full text ed.: ISSN 1558-5069 (from ScienceDirect).
Indexed: EMBASE, ExcerpMed, IndMed, MEDLINE, P30, R10, Reac, SCOPUS.
—BLDSC (8820.247000), GNLM, IE, Infotrieve, Ingenta. **CCC.**
Published by: W.B. Saunders Co. (Subsidiary of: Elsevier Health Sciences), Elsevier, Health Sciences Division, Order Fulfillment, 3251 Riverport Ln, Maryland Heights, MO 63043. TEL 314-872-8370, 800-325-4177, FAX 314-432-1380, JournalCustomerService-usa@elsevier.com, http://www.us.elsevierhealth.com.

617.54059 616.2 USA ISSN 1558-0156
THORACIC SURGERY NEWS. Text in English. 2005 (Sept.-Oct.). 10/yr. free to members (effective 2010). adv. back issues avail. **Document type:** *Newspaper, Trade.* **Description:** Contains sections devoted to the news of general thoracic surgery, adult cardiac surgery, transplantation, and congenital heart disease.
Related titles: Online - full text ed.: free (effective 2010).
Published by: (American Association for Thoracic Surgery), Elsevier Society News Group (Subsidiary of: Elsevier Inc.), 5635 Fishers Ln, Ste 6000, Rockville, MD 20852. TEL 240-221-4500, FAX 240-221-4400, m.branca@elsevier.com, http://www.esng-meded.com. Ed. Yolonda L Colson TEL 617-732-6648.

617 ARG ISSN 1852-3188
TOBILLO Y PIE. Text in Spanish. 2008. s-a. **Document type:** *Magazine, Trade.*
Published by: Sociedad Argentina de Medicina y Cirugia del Pie y la Pierna, Vicente Lopez 2nd. Piso, Buenos Aires, C1128ABC, Argentina. TEL 54-11-48012820, FAX 54-11-48017703, secretariasamecipp@yahoo.com.ar, http://www.samecipp.org.ar/.

TOPICS IN NEUROSURGERY. *see* MEDICAL SCIENCES—Psychiatry And Neurology

617 616.21 JPN ISSN 1349-581X
TOUKEIBU GEKA/JAPAN SOCIETY FOR HEAD AND NECK SURGERY. JOURNAL. Text in Japanese. 1991. 3/w. **Document type:** *Journal, Academic/Scholarly.*

—CCC.
Published by: Nihon Toukeibu Geka Gakkai/Japan Society for Head and Neck Surgery, Niigata University School of Medicine, Otolaryngology, Head & Neck Surgery, 1-757 Asahi-machi, Niigata, 951-8510, Japan. TEL 81-25-2272306, FAX 81-25-2270786, otoikyok@med.niigata-u.ac.jp, http://jshns15.umin.jp/.

TRANSPLANT CHRONICLES. *see* MEDICAL SCIENCES—Urology And Nephrology

617.4 USA ISSN 1399-3062
➤ **TRANSPLANT INFECTIOUS DISEASE (ONLINE).** Text in English. 1999. q. GBP 429 in United Kingdom to institutions; EUR 545 in Europe to institutions; USD 719 in the Americas to institutions; USD 840 elsewhere to institutions (effective 2012). adv. **Document type:** *Journal, Academic/Scholarly.*
Media: Online - full text (from IngentaConnect). **Related titles:** ◆ Print ed.: Transplant Infectious Disease (Print). ISSN 1398-2273.
—CCC.
Published by: Wiley-Blackwell Publishing, Inc. (Subsidiary of: Wiley-Blackwell Publishing Ltd.), Commerce Pl, 350 Main St, Malden, MA 02148. TEL 781-388-8200, FAX 781-388-8210, info@wiley.com, http://www.wiley.com/WileyCDA/.

617.4 USA ISSN 1398-2273
CODEN: TIDSFZ
➤ **TRANSPLANT INFECTIOUS DISEASE (PRINT).** Text in English. 1999. q. GBP 429 in United Kingdom to institutions; EUR 545 in Europe to institutions; USD 719 in the Americas to institutions; USD 840 elsewhere to institutions; GBP 493 combined subscription in United Kingdom to institutions (print & online eds.); EUR 628 combined subscription in Europe to institutions (print & online eds.); USD 827 combined subscription in the Americas to institutions (print & online eds.); USD 966 combined subscription elsewhere to institutions (print & online eds.) (effective 2012). adv. back issues avail.; reprint service avail. from PSC. **Document type:** *Journal, Academic/Scholarly.* **Description:** Provides a forum for presenting the most current information on the prevention and treatment of infection complicating organ and bone marrow transplantation.
Related titles: ◆ Online - full text ed.: Transplant Infectious Disease (Online). ISSN 1399-3062; Supplement(s): Transplant Infectious Disease. Supplement. ISSN 1399-6975.
Indexed: A01, A03, A08, A22, A26, A29, A34, A36, B21, BIOBASE, CA, CABA, CurCont, D01, E01, E12, EMBASE, ExcerpMed, GH, H12, H17, IABS, IndVet, LT, MEDLINE, N02, P30, P33, P39, R08, R10, RM&VM, RRTA, Reac, SCI, SCOPUS, T02, T05, VS, VirolAbstr, W07.
—BLDSC (9024.988700), IE, Infotrieve, Ingenta, INIST. **CCC.**
Published by: (Transplantation Society CAN), Wiley-Blackwell Publishing, Inc. (Subsidiary of: Wiley-Blackwell Publishing Ltd.), Commerce Pl, 350 Main St, Malden, MA 02148. TEL 781-388-8200, FAX 781-388-8210, info@wiley.com, http://www.wiley.com/WileyCDA/. Ed. Robert H Rubin.

➤ **TRANSPLANT NURSES JOURNAL.** *see* MEDICAL SCIENCES—Nurses And Nursing

617.95 GBR ISSN 1179-1616
▼ ➤ **TRANSPLANT RESEARCH AND RISK MANAGEMENT.** Text in English. 2009. a. free (effective 2011). back issues avail. **Document type:** *Journal, Academic/Scholarly.* **Description:** Focuses on all aspects of transplantation and risk management to achieve optimal outcomes in the recipient improving survival and quality of life.
Media: Online - full text.
—CCC.
Published by: Dove Medical Press Ltd., Beechfield House, Winterton Way, Macclesfield, SK11 0JL, United Kingdom. TEL 44-1625-509130, FAX 44-1625-617933. Ed. Qing Yi.

617 USA ISSN 0041-1337
QP89 CODEN: TRPLAU
➤ **TRANSPLANTATION.** Text in English. 1953. s-m. USD 1,766 domestic to institutions; USD 2,017 foreign to institutions (effective 2011). adv. bk.rev. illus. Index. back issues avail.; reprints avail. **Document type:** *Journal, Academic/Scholarly.* **Description:** Covers areas such as cell therapy and islet transplantation, clinical transplantation, experimental transplantation, immunobiology and genomics, and xenotransplantation.
Formerly (until 1963): Transplantation Bulletin (0564-1217); Supersedes in part (in 1963): Plastic and Reconstructive Surgery and the Transplantation Bulletin (0096-8501); Which was formerly (until 1958): Plastic and Reconstructive Surgery (1075-1270)
Related titles: Online - full text ed.: ISSN 1534-6080. USD 1,081.60 domestic for academic site license; USD 1,187.60 foreign for academic site license; USD 1,206.40 domestic for corporate site license; USD 1,312.40 foreign for corporate site license (effective 2002).
Indexed: A20, A22, A34, A35, A36, AIDS&CR, ASCA, AgBio, B21, B25, BIOBASE, BIOSIS Prev, CABA, CIN, ChemAb, CurCont, D01, DiabCont, EMBASE, ExcerpMed, F09, FR, GH, IABS, IDIS, ISR, ImmunAb, IndMed, IndVet, Inpharma, JW-G, Kidney, LT, MEDLINE, MS&D, MycolAb, N02, N03, P30, P33, P35, P39, PN&I, R08, R10, RM&VM, Reac, SCI, SCOPUS, T05, Telegen, VS, VirolAbstr, W07.
—BLDSC (9024.990000), CASDDS, GNLM, IE, Infotrieve, Ingenta, INIST, Linda Hall. **CCC.**
Published by: (Transplantation Society CAN), Lippincott Williams & Wilkins (Subsidiary of: Wolters Kluwer N.V.), Two Commerce Sq, 2001 Market St, Philadelphia, PA 19103. TEL 215-521-8300, FAX 215-521-8902, customerservice@lww.com, http://www.lww.com. Pub. Jim Mulligan. Adv. contact Sherry Reed TEL 410-528-4000 ext 8553. Circ: 1,044.

617 DEU ISSN 1612-7587
TRANSPLANTATION AKTUELL. Text in German. 1993. q. EUR 12; EUR 3 newsstand/cover (effective 2011). **Document type:** *Journal, Academic/Scholarly.*
Formerly (until 2001): B D O Blaetter (0941-4231)
Published by: Pabst Science Publishers, Am Eichengrund 28, Lengerich, 49525, Germany. TEL 49-5484-97234, FAX 49-5484-550, pabst@pabst-publishers.com, http://www.pabst-publishers.de.

TRANSPLANTATION INDEX AND REVIEWS. *see* EDUCATION

617 USA ISSN 0041-1345
RD120.7 CODEN: TRPPA8
➤ **TRANSPLANTATION PROCEEDINGS.** Text in English. 1969. 10/yr. USD 983 in North America to institutions; USD 1,289 elsewhere to institutions (effective 2012). adv. bibl.; charts; illus. Index. back issues avail.; reprints avail. **Document type:** *Journal, Academic/Scholarly.* **Description:** Includes reviews and original reports in current problems in transplantation biology and medicine.
Related titles: Microform ed.: (from PQC); Online - full text ed.: ISSN 1873-2623. 199? (from IngentaConnect, ScienceDirect).
Indexed: A01, A03, A08, A20, A22, A26, A34, A35, A36, A38, ASCA, AgBio, AgrForAb, B25, BIOBASE, BIOSIS Prev, CA, CABA, ChemAb, ChemTitl, CurCont, E12, EMBASE, ExcerpMed, F08, F09, FR, GH, H16, H17, I05, IABS, IDIS, INI, ISR, IndMed, IndVet, Inpharma, MEDLINE, MS&D, MycolAb, N02, N03, N04, P30, P33, P35, P39, PN&I, R08, R10, R12, R13, RA&MP, RM&VM, Reac, SCI, SCOPUS, T02, T05, VS, W07, W10, W11.
—BLDSC (9025.100000), CASDDS, GNLM, IE, Infotrieve, Ingenta, INIST. **CCC.**
Published by: (Transplantation Society CAN), Elsevier Inc. (Subsidiary of: Elsevier Science & Technology), 1600 John F Kennedy Blvd, Philadelphia, PA 19103. TEL 215-239-3900, FAX 215-238-7883, JournalCustomerService-usa@elsevier.com, http://www.elsevier.com. Ed. Dr. Barry D Kahan. Adv. contact Danny Wang TEL 212-633-3158.

617 USA ISSN 0955-470X
➤ **TRANSPLANTATION REVIEWS.** Text in English. 1984. q. USD 490 in United States to institutions; USD 604 elsewhere to institutions (effective 2012). back issues avail.; reprints avail. **Document type:** *Journal, Academic/Scholarly.* **Description:** Contains review articles on the latest developments in both clinical and experimental transplantation surgery and features invited articles by authorities in immunology, transplantation medicine and surgery.
Formerly (until 1987): Progress in Transplantation (0266-4852)
Related titles: Online - full text ed.: ISSN 1557-9816 (from ScienceDirect).
Indexed: A26, CA, EMBASE, ExcerpMed, H12, I05, MEDLINE, P30, R10, Reac, SCOPUS, T02.
—BLDSC (9025.220000), GNLM, IE, Infotrieve, Ingenta. **CCC.**
Published by: W.B. Saunders Co. (Subsidiary of: Elsevier Health Sciences), Elsevier, Health Sciences Division, Order Fulfillment, 3251 Riverport Ln, Maryland Heights, MO 63043. TEL 314-872-8370, 800-325-4177, FAX 314-432-1380, JournalCustomerService-usa@elsevier.com, http://www.us.elsevierhealth.com. Ed. Stuart J Knechtle. Pub. Pat Hogan. Adv. contact Danny Wang TEL 212-633-3158.

617 USA ISSN 1941-885X
TRANSPLANTATION UPDATES. Text in English. 2005. q. free (effective 2010). back issues avail. **Document type:** *Newsletter, Trade.* **Description:** Provides clinical and research information which helps to improve knowledge of solid organ transplantation and improve care of transplant patients.
Related titles: Online - full text ed.: ISSN 1941-8868.
Published by: Lippincott Williams & Wilkins (Subsidiary of: Wolters Kluwer N.V.), 333 7th Ave, 19th Fl, New York, NY 10001. TEL 646-674-6525, FAX 646-674-6500, customerservice@lww.com, http://www.lww.com. Ed. Arthur J Matas.

617 DEU ISSN 0946-9648
➤ **TRANSPLANTATIONSMEDIZIN.** Text and summaries in English, German. 1989. q. EUR 32; EUR 10 newsstand/cover (effective 2011). adv. bk.rev. abstr. **Document type:** *Journal, Academic/Scholarly.* **Description:** Contains original articles and case reports on transplantation in surgery, immunology, internal medicine, urology, nephrology.
Formerly (until 1994): Zeitschrift fuer Transplantationsmedizin (0935-1965)
Related titles: Online - full text ed.: free (effective 2011).
Indexed: A22, SCOPUS.
—BLDSC (9025.255000), GNLM, IE, Ingenta. **CCC.**
Published by: (Deutsche Transplantationsgesellschaft), Pabst Science Publishers, Am Eichengrund 28, Lengerich, 49525, Germany. TEL 49-5484-97234, FAX 49-5484-550, pabst@pabst-publishers.com, http://www.pabst-publishers.de. Ed. Arno-E Lison. adv.: B&W page EUR 540. Circ: 1,740 (paid and controlled).

617 TUN ISSN 0330-5961
TUNISIE CHIRURGICALE. Text in French. 1992. q.
—INIST.
Published by: L' Association Tunisienne de Chirurgie, B P 282, Publiposte Ennasr II, Tunis, 2037, Tunisia. TEL 216-71-571492, http://www.atc.org.tn.

TURK GOGUS KALP DAMAR CERRAHISI DERGISI/TURKISH JOURNAL OF THORACIC AND CARDIOVASCULAR SURGERY. *see* MEDICAL SCIENCES—Cardiovascular Diseases

TURK NOROSIRURJI DERGISI. *see* MEDICAL SCIENCES—Psychiatry And Neurology

617.95 TUR ISSN 1300-6878
TURK PLASTIK, REKONSTRUKTIF VE ESTETIK CERRAHI DERGISI/ TURKISH SOCIETY OF PLASTIC RECONSTRUCTIVE AESTHETIC SURGEONS. JOURNAL. Text in Turkish. 1993. s-a. **Document type:** *Journal, Academic/Scholarly.* **Description:** Publishes the scientific work of medical researchers in Plastic Surgery fields including cranio-maxillofacial surgery, orthognathic surgery, microsurgery, hand surgery, trauma surgery, surgery of the congenital anomalies, burns, oncologic surgery, and aesthetic surgery.
Related titles: Online - full text ed.: ISSN 1308-8475. free (effective 2010).
Published by: Turk Plastik, Rekonstruktif ve Estetik Cerrahi, Billur Sokak No.35/3, Kavaklidere - Ankara, 06700, Turkey. TEL 90-312-4272223, FAX 90-312-4275273, ismailkuran@gmail.com.

TURKISH NEUROSURGERY. *see* MEDICAL SCIENCES—Psychiatry And Neurology

617.12 USA ISSN 1077-8268
RD127
U N O S UPDATE. Text in English. 1985. bi-m. free domestic; USD 100 foreign (effective 2006). **Document type:** *Magazine, Trade.* **Description:** Contains news and information of interest to the organ transplant community.
Indexed: P30.
Published by: United Network for Organ Sharing, 700 N 4th St, Richmond, VA 23219. TEL 804-782-4800, FAX 804-782-4817, editor@unos.org.

617.48 UKR ISSN 1810-3154
➤ **UKRAINS'KYI NEIROKHIRURHICHNYI ZHURNAL.** Text in Ukrainian. 2000. q. **Document type:** *Journal, Academic/Scholarly.*
Published by: Akademiya Medychnykh Nauk Ukrainy, Instytut Neirokhirurhii imeni akademika A.P. Romodanova, vul Manuils'kogo 32, Kyiv, 04050, Ukraine. brain@neuro.kiev.ua, http://www.neuro.kiev.ua/win.

617 TUR ISSN 1300-0705
CODEN: UCDEE
➤ **ULUSAL CERRAHI DERGISI/TURKISH JOURNAL OF SURGERY.** Text in Turkish. 1985. q. adv. bk.rev. back issues avail. **Document type:** *Journal, Academic/Scholarly.* **Description:** Publishes research and clinical articles relating to general surgery, including gastrointestinal, endocrine, breast and endoscopic surgery, surgical physiology and surgical oncology.
Related titles: Online - full text ed.: ISSN 1308-8521.
Indexed: A01, CA, SCOPUS, T02.
—GNLM.
Published by: Turkish Surgical Association, Koru Mah. Ihlamur Cad. No.26, Cayyolu - Ankara, 06810, Turkey. TEL 90-312-2419990, FAX 90-312-2419991, turkcer@turkcer.org.tr. Ed. Dr. Sadik Kilicturgay. Adv. contact A. S. Eksel. page USD 500. Circ: 1,000 (controlled).

➤ **ULUSAL TRAVMA VE ACIL CERRAHI DERGISI/TURKISH JOURNAL OF TRAUMA & EMERGENCY SURGERY.** *see* MEDICAL SCIENCES—Orthopedics And Traumatology

617 ITA ISSN 2038-131X
UPDATES IN SURGERY. Text in English. 1947. q. EUR 263, USD 356 combined subscription to institutions (print & online eds.) (effective 2012). bk.rev. index, cum.index. **Document type:** *Journal, Academic/Scholarly.* **Description:** Designed for surgeons, it publishes papers pertaining to a number of surgery-related topics, such as procedures, operative approaches, patient selection and biotechnology issues.
Formerly (until 2010): Chirurgia Italiana (0009-4773)
Related titles: Online - full text ed.: ISSN 2038-3312 (from IngentaConnect).
Indexed: A22, ChemAb, EMBASE, ExcerpMed, IndMed, MEDLINE, P30, R10, Reac, SCOPUS.
—BLDSC (9121.969350), GNLM, IE, Ingenta.
Published by: (Societa Italiana di Chirurgia), Springer Italia Srl (Subsidiary of: Springer Science+Business Media), Via Decembrio 28, Milan, 20137, Italy. TEL 39-02-54259722, FAX 39-02-55193360, springer@springer.it. Eds. Francesco Basile, Lorenzo Capussotti.

VASCULAR. *see* MEDICAL SCIENCES—Cardiovascular Diseases

616 USA ISSN 1538-5744
RD598 CODEN: VASUA9
➤ **VASCULAR AND ENDOVASCULAR SURGERY.** Text in English. 1967. 8/yr. USD 969, GBP 570 combined subscription to institutions (print & online eds.); USD 950, GBP 559 to institutions (effective 2011). adv. 3 cols./p.; back issues avail.; reprint service avail. from PSC. **Document type:** *Journal, Academic/Scholarly.* **Description:** Contains original papers relating to any phase of vascular diseases, operative procedures, clinical or laboratory research and case reports.
Formerly (until 2002): Vascular Surgery (Glen Head) (0042-2835)
Related titles: Online - full text ed.: ISSN 1938-9116. USD 872, GBP 513 to institutions (effective 2011).
Indexed: A01, A03, A08, A22, A26, ASCA, C06, C07, CA, CurCont, E01, E08, EMBASE, ExcerpMed, G08, H11, H12, H13, I05, Inpharma, MEDLINE, P10, P20, P22, P26, P30, P35, P48, P53, P54, PQC, R10, Reac, S09, SCI, SCOPUS, T02, W07.
—BLDSC (9148.730000), GNLM, IE, Ingenta, INIST. **CCC.**
Published by: Sage Publications, Inc., 2455 Teller Rd, Thousand Oaks, CA 91320. TEL 805-499-9774, FAX 805-499-0871, info@sagepub.com, http://www.sagepub.com/. Eds. Dr. Dennis Bandyk, Dr. Peter Gloviczki. adv.: B&W page USD 1,075, color page USD 2,125; trim 8.5 x 11. Circ: 4,303 (paid).

617.413 616.1 USA ISSN 1558-0148
VASCULAR SPECIALIST. Text in English. 2005 (Sept.-Oct.). bi-m. adv. **Document type:** *Newspaper, Trade.* **Description:** Covers the world of medicine with breaking news, on-site medical meeting coverage, and expert perspectives.
Published by: (Society for Vascular Surgery), Elsevier Society News Group (Subsidiary of: Elsevier Inc.), 60 Columbia Rd, Bldg B, Morristown, NJ 07960. TEL 973-290-8200, FAX 973-290-8250. Pub. Alan J Imhoff TEL 973-290-8216. Adv. contact Betty Ann Gilchrist TEL 203-938-3156. B&W page USD 2,780; trim 8.5 x 14.

617 RUS ISSN 0042-4625
CODEN: VKHGAG
➤ **VESTNIK KHIRURGII IM. I.I. GREKOVA/I.I. GREKOV ANNALS OF SURGERY.** Text in Russian; Summaries in English, Russian. 1885. m. USD 270 foreign (effective 2005). adv. bk.rev. illus. index. back issues avail. **Document type:** *Journal, Academic/Scholarly.* **Description:** Carries articles touching on various problems of clinical and experimental surgery, anesthesiology and reanimatology.
Related titles: E-mail ed.; Fax ed.; Online - full text ed.
Indexed: A20, ChemAb, DentInd, DokArb, EMBASE, ExcerpMed, INI, IndMed, MEDLINE, P30, R10, Reac, RefZh, SCOPUS.
—BLDSC (0036.700000), East View, GNLM, INIST. **CCC.**
Published by: Izdatel'stvo Eskulap, Levashovskii pr 12, St Petersburg, 197110, Russian Federation. TEL 7-812-9442434. Ed. F G Uglov. Pub. Catherine Tkalenko. R&P, Adv. contact Alexei Belkin TEL 7-812-235-1719. B&W page USD 600, color page USD 2,000; trim 295 x 210. Circ: 2,000 (paid). **Dist. by:** East View Information Services, 10601 Wayzata Blvd, Minneapolis, MN 55305. TEL 952-252-1201, 800-477-1005, FAX 952-252-1202, info@eastview.com, http://www.eastview.com.

617 RUS ISSN 1814-1471
➤ **VOPROSY REKONSTRUKTIVNOI I PLASTICHESKOI KHIRURGII;** nauchno-prakticheskii zhurnal. Text in Russian. 2001. q. USD 150 in United States (effective 2007). **Document type:** *Journal, Academic/Scholarly.*
Indexed: RefZh.
—BLDSC (0044.394000).

Published by: Rossiiskaya Akademiya Meditsinskikh Nauk, Sibirskoe Otdelenie, Tomskii Nauchnyi Tsentr, Nauchno-Issledovatel'skii Institut Mikrokhirurgii, Moskovskii trakt, 2, Tomsk, 634050, Russian Federation. TEL 7-3822-645378. Ed. V F Baitinger. **Dist. by:** East View Information Services, 10601 Wayzata Blvd, Minneapolis, MN 55305. TEL 952-252-1201, 800-477-1005, FAX 952-252-1202, info@eastview.com, http://www.eastview.com.

617 CHN ISSN 1007-9610
WAIKE LILUN YU SHIJIAN/JOURNAL OF SURGERY CONCEPTS & PRACTICE. Text in Chinese. 1996. bi-m. USD 31.20 (effective 2009). **Document type:** *Journal, Academic/Scholarly.*
Related titles: Online - full text ed.
—East View.
Address: 197, Ruijin Erlu, 14/F, Keji Dalou, Shanghai, 200025, China. TEL 86-21-64370045 ext 611432, FAX 86-21-64374749. **Dist. by:** China International Book Trading Corp, 35 Chegongzhuang Xilu, Haidian District, PO Box 399, Beijing 100044, China. TEL 86-10-68412045, FAX 86-10-68412023, cibtc@mail.cibtc.com.cn, http://www.cibtc.com.cn.

617 GBR ISSN 2045-4384
WELSH SURGICAL SOCIETY. ABSTRACT. PROCEEDINGS. Text in English. 19??. s-a. **Document type:** *Proceedings.*
Published by: Welsh Surgical Society, c/o D T Williams, Ysbyty Gwynedd, Penrhosgarnedd, Bangor, Gwynedd LL57 2PW, United Kingdom. dean.williams2@wales.nhs.uk, http://www.welshsurgeons.com.

617 POL ISSN 1895-4588
➤ **WIDEOCHIRURGIA I INNE TECHNIKI MALO INWAZYJNE/VIDEOSURGERY AND OTHER MINIINVASIVE TECHNIQUES.** Text in Polish, English. 2006. q. PLZ 46 (effective 2010). **Document type:** *Journal, Academic/Scholarly.* **Description:** Serves as a forum for exchange of multidisciplinary experiences in fields such as: surgery, gynaecology, urology, gastroenterology, neurosurgery, ENT surgery, cardiac surgery, anaesthesiology and radiology, as well as other branches of medicine dealing with miniinvasive techniques.
Related titles: Online - full text ed.
Indexed: EMBASE, SCI, SCOPUS, W07.
Published by: Termedia sp. z o.o./Termedia Publishing House, ul Wenedow 9/1, Poznan, 61614, Poland. TEL 48-61-8227781, termedia@termedia.pl, http://www.termedia.pl. Circ: 2,000.

617 GBR
WORLD FOCUS. Text in English. 1972. q. back issues avail. **Document type:** *Newsletter, Trade.*
Former titles (until 2009): World Optometry (1948-5352); (until 1997): Interoptics
Related titles: Online - full text ed.: free (effective 2009).
Published by: World Council of Optometry, 41-42 Craven St, London, WC2N 5NG, United Kingdom. TEL 44-20-78396000, FAX 44-20-78396800, enquiries@worldoptometry.org.

616.12 USA ISSN 2150-1351
▼ ➤ **WORLD JOURNAL FOR PEDIATRIC AND CONGENITAL HEART SURGERY.** Text in English. 2010 (Jan.). q. USD 371, GBP 218 combined subscription to institutions (print & online eds.); USD 364, GBP 214 to institutions (effective 2011). **Document type:** *Journal, Academic/Scholarly.* **Description:** Dedicated to the advancement and dissemination of knowledge pertaining to congenital heart anomalies, and pediatric heart diseases in general.
Related titles: Online - full text ed.: ISSN 2150-136X. USD 334, GBP 196 to institutions (effective 2011).
Indexed: A22, E01.
—IE. **CCC.**
Published by: Sage Publications, Inc., 2455 Teller Rd, Thousand Oaks, CA 91320. TEL 805-499-9774, 800-818-7243, FAX 805-499-0871, 800-583-2665, info@sagepub.com. Ed. Dr. Marshall Jacobs.

617 GBR ISSN 1749-7922
RD1
➤ **WORLD JOURNAL OF EMERGENCY SURGERY.** Text in English. 2006. irreg. free (effective 2011). adv. back issues avail.; reprints avail. **Document type:** *Journal, Academic/Scholarly.* **Description:** Covers all aspects of emergency surgery.
Media: Online - full text.
Indexed: A01, A26, C06, C07, CA, I05, P30, SCOPUS, T02.
—**CCC.**
Published by: (World Society of Emergency Surgery ITA), BioMed Central Ltd. (Subsidiary of: Springer Science+Business Media), 236 Gray's Inn Rd, London, WC1X 8HB, United Kingdom. TEL 44-20-31922000, FAX 44-20-31922010, info@biomedcentral.com, http://www.biomedcentral.com. Eds. Ernest Moore, Fausto Catena.

▼ ➤ **WORLD JOURNAL OF ENDOCRINE SURGERY.** *see* MEDICAL SCIENCES—Endocrinology

▼ ➤ **WORLD JOURNAL OF GASTROINTESTINAL SURGERY.** *see* MEDICAL SCIENCES—Gastroenterology

617 IND ISSN 0974-5092
➤ **WORLD JOURNAL OF LAPAROSCOPIC SURGERY.** Text in English. 2008. 3/yr. INR 3,000 domestic to individuals; USD 180 foreign to individuals; INR 4,500 domestic to institutions; USD 250 foreign to institutions (effective 2010). adv. bk.rev. illus. back issues avail. **Document type:** *Journal, Academic/Scholarly.* **Description:** Dedicated to the dissemination of the technical and scientific exchange of knowledge among various countries in the field of minimal access surgery.
Related titles: Online - full text ed.: ISSN 0975-1955.
Indexed: A01, CA, P20, P48, P54, PQC, T02.
Published by: Jaypee Brothers Medical Publishers Pvt. Ltd., 4838/24, Ansari Rd, Daryaganj, New Delhi, 110 002, India. TEL 91-11-43574357, FAX 91-11-43574314, jaypee@jaypeebrothers.com, http://www.jaypeebrothers.com. Eds. Dr. Jiri Frontek, Dr. R K Mishra. Pub. Jitendar Pal Vij. R&P Chetna Malhotra. adv.: page INR 20,000; trim 7 x 10. Circ: 300 (controlled); 500 (paid).

617 USA ISSN 0364-2313
RD1 CODEN: WJSUDI
➤ **WORLD JOURNAL OF SURGERY.** Text in English. 1936. m. EUR 1,480, USD 1,535 combined subscription to institutions (print & online eds.) (effective 2012). adv. bk.rev. back issues avail.; reprint service avail. from PSC. **Document type:** *Journal, Academic/Scholarly.* **Description:** Provides a forum for the information on major clinical problems in the fields of clinical and experimental surgery, surgical education, and socioeconomic aspects of surgical care.
Supersedes (in 1976): Societe Internationale de Chirurgie. Bulletin (0037-945X); Formerly: Journal International de Chirurgie
Related titles: CD-ROM ed.; Microform ed.: (from PQC); Online - full text ed.: ISSN 1432-2323 (from IngentaConnect).
Indexed: A01, A03, A08, A20, A22, A26, A34, A35, A36, A37, A38, ASCA, AgBio, CA, CABA, ChemAb, CurCont, D01, E01, E12, EMBASE, ExcerpMed, F08, F11, F12, FR, GH, H12, H17, INI, ISR, IndMed, Inpharma, MEDLINE, N02, N03, P20, P22, P30, P33, P34, P35, P39, P48, P54, PQC, R10, R12, RA&MP, RM&VM, Reac, SCI, SCOPUS, T02, T05, VS, W07, W11.
—BLDSC (9356.074300), CASDDS, GNLM, IE, Infotrieve, Ingenta, INIST. **CCC.**
Published by: (International Society of Surgery/Societe Internationale de Chirurgie CHE), Springer New York LLC (Subsidiary of: Springer Science+Business Media), 233 Spring St, New York, NY 10013. TEL 212-460-1500, FAX 212-460-1575, service-ny@springer.com, http://www.springer.com/. Ed. John G Hunter TEL 503-494-0997. **Subscr. outside the Americas to:** Springer Distribution Center, Kundenservice Zeitschriften, Haberstr 7, Heidelberg 69126, Germany. TEL 49-6221-3454303, FAX 49-6221-3454229; **Subscr. to:** Journal Fulfillment, PO Box 2485, Secaucus, NJ 07096. TEL 201-348-4033, FAX 201-348-4505.

➤ **WORLD JOURNAL OF SURGICAL ONCOLOGY.** *see* MEDICAL SCIENCES—Oncology

617 616.8 USA ISSN 1878-8750
CODEN: SGNRAI
➤ **WORLD NEUROSURGERY.** Text in English. 1973. m. USD 1,232 in United States to institutions; USD 1,382 elsewhere to institutions (effective 2012). adv. bk.rev. Index. back issues avail.; reprints avail. **Document type:** *Journal, Academic/Scholarly.* **Description:** Provides neurosurgeons with timely and comprehensive coverage of important clinical and research advances in neurosurgery.
Formerly (until 2010): Surgical Neurology (0090-3019)
Related titles: Microform ed.: (from PQC); Online - full text ed.: ISSN 1878-8769 (from IngentaConnect, ScienceDirect).
Indexed: A01, A03, A08, A20, A22, A26, A28, A36, APA, ASCA, B21, B25, BDM&CN, BIOBASE, BIOSIS Prev, BrCerAb, C&ISA, CA, CA/WCA, CABA, CIA, CerAb, CivEngAb, CorrAb, CurCont, DentInd, E&CAJ, E-psyche, E11, EEA, EMA, EMBASE, ESPM, EnvEAb, ExcerpMed, FR, GH, H15, I05, IABS, INI, ISR, IndMed, Inpharma, M&TEA, M09, MBF, MEDLINE, METADEX, MycolAb, NSA, NSCI, P30, P33, PN&I, R08, R10, R12, Reac, RefZh, SCI, SCOPUS, SolStAb, T02, T04, T05, W07, WAA.
—BLDSC (8548.240000), GNLM, IE, Infotrieve, Ingenta, INIST. **CCC.**
Published by: (World Federation of Neurosurgical Societies CHE), Elsevier Inc. (Subsidiary of: Elsevier Science & Technology), 1600 John F Kennedy Blvd, Philadelphia, PA 19103. TEL 215-239-3900, FAX 215-238-7883, JournalCustomerService-usa@elsevier.com, http://www.elsevier.com. Ed. Michael L J Apuzzo TEL 323-442-3001. Pub. Herb Niemirow TEL 212-633-3141.

617.95 USA ISSN 0908-665X
QR188.8 CODEN: XENOFL
➤ **XENOTRANSPLANTATION.** Text in English. 1994. bi-m. GBP 716 in United Kingdom to institutions; EUR 909 in Europe to institutions; USD 1,203 in the Americas to institutions; USD 1,402 elsewhere to institutions; GBP 824 combined subscription in United Kingdom to institutions (print & online eds.); EUR 1,046 combined subscription in Europe to institutions (print & online eds.); USD 1,384 combined subscription in the Americas to institutions (print & online eds.); USD 1,613 combined subscription elsewhere to institutions (print & online eds.) (effective 2012). adv. reprint service avail. from PSC. **Document type:** *Journal, Academic/Scholarly.* **Description:** Reports new findings in the field of organ and tissue transplantation across species barriers.
Related titles: Online - full text ed.: ISSN 1399-3089. GBP 716 in United Kingdom to institutions; EUR 909 in Europe to institutions; USD 1,203 in the Americas to institutions; USD 1,402 elsewhere to institutions (effective 2012) (from IngentaConnect).
Indexed: A01, A03, A08, A22, A26, A34, A35, A36, A38, AgBio, B21, B25, BIOSIS Prev, CA, CABA, CurCont, E01, E12, EMBASE, ExcerpMed, F08, GH, H12, H17, ISR, ImmunAb, IndMed, IndVet, Inpharma, MEDLINE, MycolAb, N04, P30, P33, P39, PN&I, R08, R10, RM&VM, Reac, SCI, SCOPUS, T02, VS, W07.
—BLDSC (9367.026000), GNLM, IE, Infotrieve, Ingenta. **CCC.**
Published by: (International Xenotransplantation Association CAN), Wiley-Blackwell Publishing, Inc. (Subsidiary of: Wiley-Blackwell Publishing Ltd.), Commerce Pl, 350 Main St, Malden, MA 02148. TEL 781-388-8200, FAX 781-388-8210, info@wiley.com, http://www.wiley.com/WileyCDA/. Ed. Carl Groth. Adv. contact Stephen Donohue TEL 781-388-8511.

➤ **YANKE XIN JINZHAN/RECENT ADVANCES IN OPHTHALMOLOGY.** *see* MEDICAL SCIENCES—Ophthalmology And Optometry

617 USA ISSN 1551-7977
CODEN: YBHSEQ
YEAR BOOK OF HAND AND UPPER LIMB SURGERY. Text in English. 1985. a. USD 217 in United States to institutions; USD 235 elsewhere to institutions (effective 2012). adv. illus. **Document type:** *Yearbook, Academic/Scholarly.* **Description:** Presents abstracts of pertinent literature with commentary by leading experts in the field.
Formerly (until 2004): The Year Book of Hand Surgery (0739-5949)
Related titles: CD-ROM ed.; Online - full text ed.
—BLDSC (9412.865000), GNLM, INIST. **CCC.**
Published by: Mosby, Inc. (Subsidiary of: Elsevier Health Sciences), 1600 John F. Kennedy Blvd, Ste 1800, Philadelphia, PA 19103. TEL 215-239-3900, 800-523-1649, FAX 215-239-3990, elspcs@elsevier.com, http://www.us.elsevierhealth.com. Eds. Amy L Ladd, Dr. Richard A. Berger.

YEAR BOOK OF NEUROLOGY AND NEUROSURGERY. *see* MEDICAL SCIENCES—Psychiatry And Neurology

617.95 USA ISSN 1535-1513
CODEN: YPRSA
YEAR BOOK OF PLASTIC AND AESTHETIC SURGERY. Text in English. 1970. a. USD 217 in United States to institutions; USD 235 elsewhere to institutions (effective 2012). adv. illus. reprints avail. **Document type:** *Yearbook, Academic/Scholarly.* **Description:** Presents abstracts of pertinent literature with commentary by leading experts in the field.
Former titles (until 2002): The Year Book of Plastic, Reconstructive, and Aesthetic Surgery (1040-175X); (until 1989): The Year Book of Plastic and Reconstructive Surgery (0084-3962)
Related titles: CD-ROM ed.; Online - full text ed.
—BLDSC (9415.400000), GNLM. **CCC.**
Published by: Mosby, Inc. (Subsidiary of: Elsevier Health Sciences), 1600 John F. Kennedy Blvd, Ste 1800, Philadelphia, PA 19103. TEL 215-239-3900, 800-523-1649, FAX 215-239-3990, elspcs@elsevier.com, http://www.us.elsevierhealth.com. Ed. Dr. Stephen Miller.

617.005 USA ISSN 0090-3671
RD9
YEAR BOOK OF SURGERY. Text in English. 1901. a. USD 239 in United States to institutions; USD 259 elsewhere to institutions (effective 2012). adv. illus. **Document type:** *Yearbook, Academic/Scholarly.* **Description:** Presents abstracts of pertinent literature with commentary by leading experts in the field.
Former titles (until 1971): The Year Book of General Surgery (0084-3776); (until 1933): General Surgery
Related titles: CD-ROM ed.; Online - full text ed.
—BLDSC (9416.450000), GNLM, INIST. **CCC.**
Published by: Mosby, Inc. (Subsidiary of: Elsevier Health Sciences), 1600 John F. Kennedy Blvd, Ste 1800, Philadelphia, PA 19103. TEL 215-239-3900, 800-523-1649, FAX 215-239-3990, elspcs@elsevier.com, http://www.us.elsevierhealth.com. Ed. Dr. Edward M Copeland III.

YEAR BOOK OF VASCULAR SURGERY. *see* MEDICAL SCIENCES—Cardiovascular Diseases

ZEITSCHRIFT FUER HERZ-, THORAX- UND GEFAESSCHIRURGIE. *see* MEDICAL SCIENCES—Cardiovascular Diseases

ZEITSCHRIFT FUER ORTHOPAEDIE UND UNFALLCHIRURGIE. *see* MEDICAL SCIENCES—Orthopedics And Traumatology

617 DEU ISSN 0044-409X
CODEN: ZECHAU
➤ **ZENTRALBLATT FUER CHIRURGIE.** Text in German. 1874. bi-m. EUR 269 to institutions; EUR 359 combined subscription to institutions (print & online eds.); EUR 49 newsstand/cover (effective 2011). adv. bk.rev. abstr.; charts; illus. index. 80 p./no.; back issues avail. **Document type:** *Journal, Academic/Scholarly.*
Related titles: Microfiche ed.: (from BHP); Online - full text ed.: ISSN 1438-9592. EUR 345 to institutions (effective 2011); Supplement(s): Zentralblatt fuer Chirurgie. Supplement. ISSN 0233-1616. 1969.
Indexed: A20, A22, ASCA, ChemAb, CurCont, DentInd, EMBASE, ExcerpMed, INI, IndMed, Inpharma, MEDLINE, P30, P35, R10, Reac, SCI, SCOPUS, W07.
—BLDSC (9504.700000), GNLM, IE, Infotrieve, Ingenta, INIST. **CCC.**
Published by: (Vereinigung Mittelrheinischer Chirurgen), Johann Ambrosius Barth Verlag in Medizinverlage Heidelberg GmbH & Co. KG, Ruedigerstr 14, Stuttgart, 70469, Germany. TEL 49-711-8931-0, FAX 49-711-8931422, kunden.service@thieme.de. Ed. R T Grundmann. Adv. contact Grit Koeltzsch. B&W page EUR 1,480, color page EUR 2,545; trim 210 x 280. Circ: 2,020 (paid).
Co-sponsors: Thueringische Gesellschaft fuer Chirurgie; Vereinigung der Bayerischen Chirurgen; Saechsische Chirurgenvereinigung.

➤ **ZHEJIANG CHUANGSHANG WAIKE/ZHEJIANG JOURNAL OF TRAUMATIC SURGERY.** *see* MEDICAL SCIENCES—Orthopedics And Traumatology

➤ **ZHONGGUO ER-BI-YANHOU-TOU-JING WAIKE/CHINESE ARCHIVES OF OTOLARYNGOLOGY HEAD AND NECK SURGERY.** *see* MEDICAL SCIENCES—Otorhinolaryngology

➤ **ZHONGGUO GU YU GUANJIE WAIKE/CHINESE BONE AND JOINT SURGERY.** *see* MEDICAL SCIENCES—Orthopedics And Traumatology

617 CHN ISSN 1672-3244
ZHONGGUO KOUQIANG HEMIAN WAIKE ZAZHI/CHINA JOURNAL OF ORAL AND MAXILLOFACIAL SURGERY. Text in Chinese. 2000. bi-m. USD 24.60 (effective 2009). **Document type:** *Journal, Academic/Scholarly.*
Related titles: Online - full text ed.
Indexed: CA, D02, T02.
—East View.
Published by: Shanghai Jiaotong Daxue, Kouqiang Yixueyuan/Shanghai Jiao Tong University, School of Stomatology, 639, Zhizaoju Lu, Shanghai, 200011, China. TEL 86-21-33183312, FAX 86-21-63121780.

617.952 CHN ISSN 1673-7040
ZHONGGUO MEIRONG ZHENGXING WAIKE ZAZHI/CHINESE JOURNAL OF AESTHETIC AND PLASTIC SURGERY. Text in Chinese. 1990. bi-m. USD 62.40 (effective 2009). **Document type:** *Journal, Academic/Scholarly.*
Related titles: Online - full text ed.
Indexed: B&BAb, B19, B21, CTA.
Published by: Liaoning Sheng Renmin Yiyuan, 33, Wenyi Lu, Liaoning, 110016, China. TEL 86-24-24131293, FAX 86-24-24125660.

617 CHN ISSN 1007-9424
ZHONGGUO PU-WAI JICHU YU LINCHUANG ZAZHI/CHINESE JOURNAL OF BASES AND CLINICS IN GENERAL SURGERY. Text in Chinese. 1994. bi-m. USD 62.40 (effective 2009). **Document type:** *Journal, Academic/Scholarly.*
Formerly (until 1998): Pu-wai Jichu yu Linchuang Zazhi/Journal of Bases and Clinics in General Surgery (1006-8295)
Related titles: Online - full text ed.
—East View.
Published by: Sichuan Daxue Huaxi Yiyuan/Sichuan University, West China Hospital, 37 Guoxue Xiang, Wuhou-qu, Chengdu, 610041, China. **Dist. by:** China International Book Trading Corp, 35 Chegongzhuang Xilu, Haidian District, PO Box 399, Beijing 100044, China. TEL 86-10-68412045, FAX 86-10-68412023, cibtc@mail.cibtc.com.cn, http://www.cibtc.com.cn.

617 CHN ISSN 1005-6947
ZHONGGUO PUTONG WAIKE ZAZHI/CHINESE JOURNAL OF GENERAL SURGERY. Text in Chinese. 1992. m. USD 74.40 (effective 2009). **Document type:** *Journal, Academic/Scholarly.*
Related titles: Online - full text ed.
—BLDSC (9512.792660).

Published by: Zhongnan Daxue/Central South University, 87, Xiangya Lu, Changsha, 410008, China. http://www.csu.edu.cn/chinese/. **Dist. by:** China International Book Trading Corp, 35 Chegongzhuang Xilu, Haidian District, PO Box 399, Beijing 100044, China. TEL 86-10-68412045, FAX 86-10-68412023, cibtc@mail.cibtc.com.cn, http://www.cibtc.com.cn.

617 CHN ISSN 1005-2208
➤ **ZHONGGUO SHIYONG WAIKE ZAZHI/CHINESE JOURNAL OF PRACTICAL SURGERY.** Text in Chinese; Abstracts in English. 1981. m. USD 49.20 (effective 2009). adv. **Document type:** *Journal, Academic/Scholarly.* **Description:** Features new developments and methods of practical diagnosis, treatment, and prevention of surgical diseases.
Formerly: Shiyong Waike Zazhi - Journal of Practical Surgery (1001-0831)
Related titles: Online - full text ed.
Indexed: B&BAb, B19, B20, B21, ESPM, ImmunAb, RefZh.
—BLDSC (9512.798850).
Published by: Zhongguo Shiyong Yixue Zazhishe, 9, Nanjing Nan Jie, 5th Fl., Heping-qu, Shenyang, Liaoning 110001, China. Ed. Yong-Feng Liu. adv.: page USD 1,500. Circ: 50,000.

617 616.8 CHN ISSN 1009-122X
ZHONGGUO WEI QINXI SHENJING WAIKE ZAZHI/CHINESE JOURNAL OF MINIMALLY INVASIVE NEUROSURGERY. Text in Chinese. 1996. m. USD 62.40 (effective 2009). **Document type:** *Journal, Academic/Scholarly.*
Related titles: Online - full text ed.
—East View.
Published by: Guangzhou Junqu Guangzhou Zongyiyuan/Guangzhou General Hospital of P L A, 111, Liuhua Lu, Guangzhou, 510010, China. TEL 86-20-61654596, FAX 86-20-36221117.

617 CHN ISSN 1009-6604
ZHONGGUO WEICHUANG WAIKE ZAZHI/CHINESE JOURNAL OF MINIMALLY INVASIVE SURGERY. Text in Chinese. 2001. m. USD 62.40 (effective 2009). **Document type:** *Journal, Academic/Scholarly.*
Related titles: Online - full text ed.
—East View.
Published by: Beijing Daxue Di-3 Yiyuan, 49, Huayuan Bei Lou, Beijing, 100083, China.

617 CHN ISSN 1009-9905
ZHONGGUO XIANDAI PUTONG WAIKE JINZHAN/CHINESE JOURNAL OF CURRENT ADVANCES IN GENERAL SURGERY. Text in Chinese. 1998. bi-m. USD 31.20 (effective 2009). **Document type:** *Journal, Academic/Scholarly.*
Related titles: Online - full text ed.
—East View.
Published by: Shangdon Daxue, Qilu Yiyuan, 107, Wenhua Xilu, Jinan, 250012, China. TEL 86-531-2169203. **Dist. by:** China International Book Trading Corp, 35 Chegongzhuang Xilu, Haidian District, PO Box 399, Beijing 100044, China. TEL 86-10-68412045, FAX 86-10-68412023, cibtc@mail.cibtc.com.cn, http://www.cibtc.com.cn.

617 CHN ISSN 1009-2188
ZHONGGUO XIANDAI SHOUSHUXUE ZAZHI/CHINESE JOURNAL OF MODERN OPERATIVE SURGERY. Text in Chinese. 1996. bi-m. CNY 10 newsstand/cover (effective 2006). **Document type:** *Journal, Academic/Scholarly.*
Related titles: Online - full text ed.
Published by: Zhongnan Daxue, Xiangya Er Yiyuan/Central South University, 2nd Xiangya Hospital, 86, Renmin Zhong Lu, Changsha, 410011, China. TEL 86-731-5524272.

ZHONGGUO XIONGXIN XUEGUAN WAIKE LINCHUANG ZAZHI. *see* MEDICAL SCIENCES—Cardiovascular Diseases

617.95 CHN ISSN 1002-1892
CODEN: ZXCZEH
➤ **ZHONGGUO XIUFU CHONGJIAN WAIKE ZAZHI/CHINESE JOURNAL OF REPARATIVE AND RECONSTRUCTIVE SURGERY.** Text in Chinese; Summaries in English. 1987. bi-m. USD 80.40 (effective 2009). illus. 72 p./no.; **Document type:** *Journal, Academic/Scholarly.* **Description:** Contains original research articles and clinical reviews on reparative and reconstructive surgery. Also covers new instruments, materials and techniques.
Formerly (until 1991): Xiufu Chongjian Waike Zazhi
Related titles: CD-ROM ed.; Online - full text ed.
Indexed: A22, A29, B&BAb, B19, B20, B21, CTA, EMBASE, ESPM, ExcerpMed, I10, ImmunAb, IndMed, MEDLINE, P30, R10, Reac, RefZh, SCOPUS, VirolAbstr.
—BLDSC (3180.674200), East View, GNLM, IE, Infotrieve, Ingenta.
Published by: (Zhongguo Kangfu Yixuehui/Chinese Rehabilitation Medical Association, Xiufu Chongjian Waike Zhuanye Weiyuanhui), Zhongguo Xiufu Chongjian Waike Zazhi Bianjibu, Huaxi Yike Daxue Fushu Diyi Yiyuan Nei, 37 Guoxue Xiang, Chengdu, Sichuan 610041, China. TEL 86-28-5422431, 86-28-5422432, FAX 86-28-5422432. Ed., Pub. Zhiming Yang. R&P, Adv. contact Jun Yu. Circ: 6,000. **Dist. overseas by:** China International Book Trading Corp, 35 Chegongzhuang Xilu, Haidian District, PO Box 399, Beijing 100044, China.

617 CHN ISSN 1007-6948
ZHONGGUO ZHONG-XIYI JIEHE WAIKE ZAZHI/CHINESE JOURNAL OF SURGERY OF INTEGRATED TRADITIONAL CHINESE AND WESTERN MEDICINE. Text in Chinese. 1994. bi-m. USD 27 (effective 2009). **Document type:** *Academic/Scholarly.*
Related titles: Online - full text ed.
—East View.
Published by: Zhongguo Zhong-Xiyi Jiehe Waike Zazhishe, 122, San-Wei Lu, Tianjin, 300100, China. **Dist. by:** China International Book Trading Corp, 35 Chegongzhuang Xilu, Haidian District, PO Box 399, Beijing 100044, China. TEL 86-10-68412045, FAX 86-10-68412023, cibtc@mail.cibtc.com.cn, http://www.cibtc.com.cn.

617 CHN ISSN 1674-4136
ZHONGGUO ZHONGLIU WAIKE ZAZHI/CHINESE JOURNAL OF SURGICAL ONCOLOGY. Text in Chinese. 1982. bi-m.
Formerly (until 2009): Zhongguo Yixue Wenzhai (Waikexue)/China Medical Abstracts (Surgery) (1001-1293)
Related titles: Online - full text ed.
Published by: Jiangsu Sheng Yixue Qingbao Yanjiusuo, 129, Hanzhong Lu, Nanjing, 210029, China. TEL 86-25-4706094. **Co-sponsors:** Zhongguo Yishi Xiehui; Jiangsu Sheng Zhongliu Yiyuan.

617 CHN ISSN 1007-8118
ZHONGHUA GANDAN WAIKE ZAZHI/CHINESE JOURNAL OF HEPATOBILIARY SURGERY. Text in Chinese; Abstracts in English. 1995. m. USD 80.40 (effective 2009). cum.index. 64 p./no.; reprints avail. **Document type:** *Journal, Academic/Scholarly.*
Formerly (until 1998): Gandan Yipi Waike Zazhi
Related titles: Online - full text ed.
Indexed: A22.
—BLDSC (3180.350200), East View, IE, Ingenta.
Published by: Zhonghua Yixueyuan Zhazhishe/Chinese Medical Association Publishing House, Fuxing Road 28, Jiefangjun Zongyiyuan, Beijing, 100853, China. TEL 86-1-68177009, FAX 86-1-68177009, zhgdwkzz@vip.163.com, http://www.cma-cmn.net/. Ed., Pub. Yongxiong Liu. Circ: 5,000.

ZHONGHUA NEIFENMI WAIKE ZAZHI/CHINESE JOURNAL OF ENDOCRINE SURGERY. *see* MEDICAL SCIENCES—Endocrinology

617 CHN ISSN 0254-1785
CODEN: ZQYZEA
ZHONGHUA QIGUAN YIZHI ZAZHI/CHINESE JOURNAL OF ORGAN TRANSPLANTATION. Text in Chinese. 1980. m. USD 56.40 (effective 2009). **Document type:** *Journal, Academic/Scholarly.*
Related titles: Online - full text ed.
—BLDSC (3180.463000), East View.
Published by: Zhonghua Yixuehui, Wuhan Fenhui, 155, Shengli Jie, Wuhan, 430014, China. **Dist. by:** China International Book Trading Corp, 35 Chegongzhuang Xilu, Haidian District, PO Box 399, Beijing 100044, China. TEL 86-10-68412045, FAX 86-10-68412023, cibtc@mail.cibtc.com.cn, http://www.cibtc.com.cn.

ZHONGHUA SHAOSHANG ZAZHI/CHINESE JOURNAL OF BURNS. *see* MEDICAL SCIENCES—Dermatology And Venereology

616.8 CHN ISSN 1001-2346
➤ **ZHONGHUA SHENJING WAIKE ZAZHI/CHINESE JOURNAL OF NEUROSURGERY.** Text in Chinese; Summaries in English. 1985. m. USD 78 (effective 2009). adv. bk.rev. index. 64 p./no.; back issues avail. **Document type:** *Journal, Academic/Scholarly.*
Related titles: CD-ROM ed.; Online - full text ed.
Indexed: E-psyche, ExtraMED.
—East View, GNLM.
Published by: (Beijing Neurosurgical Institute), Zhonghua Yixuehui/Chinese Medical Association, 6, Tiantan Xili, Bejing, 00050, China. TEL 86-10-65113169, FAX 86-10-67054496. Ed. Chungcheng Wang. R&P, Adv. contact Li Li. Circ: 10,000. **Dist. by:** China International Book Trading Corp, 35 Chegongzhuang Xilu, Haidian District, PO Box 399, Beijing 100044, China. TEL 86-10-68412045, FAX 86-10-68412023, cibtc@mail.cibtc.com.cn, http://www.cibtc.com.cn.

617 CHN ISSN 1005-054X
ZHONGHUA SHOUWAIKE ZAZHI/CHINESE JOURNAL OF HAND SURGERY. Text in Chinese. 1985. q. USD 31.20 (effective 2009). **Document type:** *Academic/Scholarly.*
Formerly: Shouwaike Zazhi/ Journal of Hand Surgery (1003-9457)
Related titles: Online - full text ed.
—East View.
Published by: Zhonghua Yixuehui Zazhishe/Chinese Medical Association Publishing House, 42 Dongsi Xidajie, Beijing, 100710, China. **Dist. by:** China International Book Trading Corp, 35 Chegongzhuang Xilu, Haidian District, PO Box 399, Beijing 100044, China. TEL 86-10-68412045, FAX 86-10-68412023, cibtc@mail.cibtc.com.cn, http://www.cibtc.com.cn.

617 CHN ISSN 0529-5815
RD1
ZHONGHUA WAIKE ZAZHI/CHINESE JOURNAL OF SURGERY. Text in Chinese. 1951. s-m. USD 160.80 (effective 2009). **Document type:** *Journal, Academic/Scholarly.*
Related titles: CD-ROM ed.; Online - full text ed.
Indexed: A22, EMBASE, ExcerpMed, ExtraMED, IndMed, MEDLINE, P30, R10, Reac, SCOPUS.
—BLDSC (3180.680000), East View, IE, Infotrieve, Ingenta, INIST.
Published by: Zhonghua Yixuehui Zazhishe/Chinese Medical Association Publishing House, 42 Dongsi Xidajie, Beijing, 100710, China. **Dist. by:** China International Book Trading Corp, 35 Chegongzhuang Xilu, Haidian District, PO Box 399, Beijing 100044, China. TEL 86-10-68412045, FAX 86-10-68412023, cibtc@mail.cibtc.com.cn, http://www.cibtc.com.cn.

617 616.3 CHN ISSN 1671-0274
ZHONGHUA WEI-CHANG WAIKE ZAZHI/CHINESE JOURNAL OF GASTROINTESTINAL SURGERY. Text in Chinese. 1998. bi-m. USD 40.20 (effective 2009). **Document type:** *Journal, Academic/Scholarly.*
Formerly (until 2000): Zhongguo Wei-chang Waike Zazhi (1008-5890)
Related titles: Online - full text ed.
Indexed: EMBASE, ExcerpMed, MEDLINE, P30, R10, Reac, SCOPUS.
—BLDSC (9512.840100), East View.
Published by: Zhongshan Yike Daxue, Fushu Di-1 Yiyuan, 58, Zhongshan Er-Lu, Guangzhou, 510080, China. TEL 86-28-87332200 ext 8662, FAX 86-20-87335945.

ZHONGHUA XIAOER WAIKE ZAZHI/CHINESE JOURNAL OF PEDIATRIC SURGERY. *see* MEDICAL SCIENCES—Pediatrics

ZHONGHUA XIAOHUA WAIKE ZAZHI/CHINESE JOURNAL OF DIGESTIVE SURGERY. *see* MEDICAL SCIENCES—Gastroenterology

617.95 CHN ISSN 1009-4598
CODEN: ZZSZE9
ZHONGHUA ZHENGXING WAIKE ZAZHI/CHINESE JOURNAL OF PLASTIC SURGERY. Text in Chinese. 1985. bi-m. USD 37.20 (effective 2009). adv. bk.rev. back issues avail. **Document type:** *Journal, Academic/Scholarly.*
Supersedes in part (in 1999): Zhonghua Zhengxing Shaoshang Waike Zazhi/Chinese Journal of Plastic Surgery and Burns (1000-7806)
Related titles: CD-ROM ed.; Online - full text ed.
Indexed: EMBASE, ExcerpMed, ExtraMED, IndMed, MEDLINE, P30, R10, Reac, SCOPUS.
—BLDSC (3180.554000), East View, GNLM, IE, Infotrieve, Ingenta.
Published by: Zhonghua Yixuehui/Chinese Medical Association, c/o Zhongguo Yixue Kexueyuan, Zhengxing Shaoshang Waike Yanjiusuo, Ba Da Chu Lu, Beijing, 100041, China. TEL 86-10-88703789, FAX 86-10-68864137. Circ: 6,200. **Dist. overseas by:** China International Book Trading Corp, 35 Chegongzhuang Xilu, Haidian District, PO Box 399, Beijing 100044, China. TEL 86-10-68412045, FAX 86-10-68412023, cibtc@mail.cibtc.com.cn, http://www.cibtc.com.cn.

616.89 RUS ISSN 0042-8817
CODEN: ZVNBDJ
ZHURNAL VOPROSY NEIROKHIRURGII IM. N.N. BURDENKO/JOURNAL OF NEUROSURGICAL PROBLEMS. Text in Russian; Summaries in English. 1937. q. USD 109 foreign (effective 2005). adv. bk.rev. index. **Document type:** *Journal, Academic/Scholarly.* **Description:** Discusses theoretical, practical and organization problems of modern neurosurgery. Informs of the advances in the treatment of neurosurgical diseases of the central, peripheral and vegetative nervous system.
Indexed: ChemAb, EMBASE, ExcerpMed, IndMed, MEDLINE, P30, R10, Reac, RefZh, SCOPUS.
—East View, GNLM, INIST. **CCC.**
Published by: Izdatel'stvo Meditsina/Meditsina Publishers, ul B Pirogovskaya, d 2, str 5, Moscow, 119435, Russian Federation. TEL 7-095-2483324, meditsina@mtu-net.ru, http://www.medlit.ru. Ed. Aleksandr N Konovalov. Pub. A M Stochik. R&P V Ivannikova. Adv. contact O A Fadeeva TEL 7-095-923-51-40. Circ: 750. **Dist. by:** M K - Periodica, ul Gilyarovskogo 39, Moscow 129110, Russian Federation. TEL 7-095-2845008, FAX 7-095-2813798, info@periodicals.ru, http://www.mkniga.ru.

MEDICAL SCIENCES—Urology And Nephrology

616.6 CAN ISSN 1180-4939
A G I R. (Association Generale des Insuffisants Renaux) Text in French. 1980. q. free. back issues avail. **Document type:** *Bulletin, Consumer.*
Related titles: Online - full text ed.
Published by: Association Generale des Insuffisants Renaux (A G I R), Succ. St-Michel, B P 433, Montreal, PQ H2A 3N1, Canada. TEL 514-852-9297, FAX 514-323-1231, jeannine.goyer@agir.qc.ca, http://www.agir.qc.ca.

616.6 USA ISSN 1943-8044
▼ **A S N KIDNEY NEWS.** Text in English. 2009. bi-m. free to members. adv. **Document type:** *Journal, Academic/Scholarly.* **Description:** Examines research findings and policy changes, pinpointing emerging trends in industry, medicine, and training that impact practitioners in kidney health and disease.
Related titles: Online - full text ed.: ISSN 1943-8052.
Published by: American Society of Nephrology, 1725 I St, NW, Ste 510, Washington, DC 20006. TEL 202-416-0940, 202-659-0599, FAX 202-659-0709, email@asn-online.org. Ed. Pascale H Lane. adv.: B&W page USD 3,250; trim 10.5 x 14.5. Circ: 18,000.

616.6 USA ISSN 1088-7350
RC870
A U A NEWS. Text in English. 1987. bi-m. USD 110 to non-members; USD 135 to institutions (effective 2008). adv. **Document type:** *Magazine, Trade.* **Description:** Issues news and developments in urology, including clinical information, case studies, and reports on economic policies and legislation.
Formerly (until 1996): A U A Today (1046-1051)
Related titles: Online - full text ed.: ISSN 1538-8557.
Indexed: A01, CA, P34, T02.
—**CCC.**
Published by: American Urological Association, 1000 Corporate Blvd, Linthicum, MD 21090. TEL 410-689-3700, 866-746-4282, FAX 410-689-3800, publications@auanet.org, http://www.auanet.org. Circ: 11,189.

616.6 ESP ISSN 0210-4806
ACTAS UROLOGICAS ESPANOLAS. Text in Spanish. 1977. bi-m. EUR 290 in Europe to institutions; GBP 251 in United Kingdom to institutions; JPY 38,100 in Japan to institutions; USD 405 elsewhere to institutions (effective 2012). back issues avail. **Document type:** *Journal, Academic/Scholarly.*
Related titles: Online - full text ed.: ISSN 1699-7980. 1999. free (effective 2011) (from ScienceDirect).
Indexed: A22, EMBASE, ExcerpMed, G10, IndMed, MEDLINE, P30, R10, Reac, SCI, SCOPUS, W07.
—BLDSC (0670.418000), IE, Infotrieve, Ingenta, INIST. **CCC.**
Published by: Asociacion Espanola de Urologia, C Oruro 9 Bajo Izq., Madrid, 28016, Spain. TEL 34-91-364-0849, FAX 34-91-366-1298, aeu@aeu.es, http://www.aeu.es/. Ed. Jose Luis Ruiz Cerda.

616.6 FRA ISSN 1168-1098
ACTUALITES NEPHROLOGIQUES JEAN HAMBURGER. Text in French. 1960. irreg. price varies. cum.index: 1960-69. **Document type:** *Monographic series, Academic/Scholarly.*
Formerly (until 1989): Actualites Nephrologiques de l'Hopital Necker (0567-8811)
Indexed: ChemAb.
—INIST.
Published by: (Hopital Necker, Clinique Nephrologique), Editions Flammarion, 87 Quai Panhard et Levassor, Paris, 75647 Cedex 13, France. TEL 33-1-40513100, http://www.flammarion.com. Ed. J P Grunfeld. **U.S. subscr. address:** S.F.P.A., c/o Mr Benech, 14 E 60th St, New York, NY 10022.

616.6 617 USA ISSN 1548-5595
CODEN: ARRTFU
➤ **ADVANCES IN CHRONIC KIDNEY DISEASE.** Text in English. 1994. bi-m. USD 375 in United States to institutions; USD 416 elsewhere to institutions (effective 2012). adv. reprints avail. **Document type:** *Journal, Academic/Scholarly.* **Description:** Reports on advancements in the treatment and care of patients with kidney failure. Contains material also of interest to medical technicians, nurses, and social workers.
Formerly (until 2004): Advances in Renal Replacement Therapy (1073-4449)
Related titles: Online - full text ed.: ISSN 1548-5609 (from ScienceDirect).
Indexed: C06, C07, C08, CINAHL, CurCont, EMBASE, ExcerpMed, INI, IndMed, Inpharma, MEDLINE, P30, R10, Reac, SCI, SCOPUS, W07.
—BLDSC (0703.851000), GNLM, IE, Infotrieve, Ingenta, INIST. **CCC.**
Published by: (National Kidney Foundation, Inc.), W.B. Saunders Co. (Subsidiary of: Elsevier Health Sciences), Independence Sq W, Ste 300, The Curtis Center, Philadelphia, PA 19106-3399. FAX 215-238-8772. Ed. Jerry Yee. adv.: B&W page USD 940; trim 8.25 x 11. Circ: 825 (paid). **Subscr. to:** Elsevier, Subscription Customer Service, 6277 Sea Harbor Dr, Orlando, FL 32887-4800. TEL 800-654-2452, FAX 407-363-9661.

616.1 CAN ISSN 1197-8554
CODEN: APDIFF
ADVANCES IN PERITONEAL DIALYSIS. Text in English. 1989. a., latest vol.20, 2004.
Indexed: EMBASE, ExcerpMed, IndMed, MEDLINE, P30, R10, Reac, SCOPUS.
—IE, Infotrieve, Ingenta, INIST. **CCC.**
Published by: Multimed Inc., 66 Martin St, Milton, ON L9T 2R2, Canada. TEL 905-875-2456, http://www.multi-med.com. Ed. Dr. Ramesh Khanna.

ADVANCES IN REPRODUCTIVE HEALTH CARE. *see* MEDICAL SCIENCES—Obstetrics And Gynecology

616.6 USA ISSN 1687-6369
➤ **ADVANCES IN UROLOGY.** Text in English. 2007. irreg. USD 495 (effective 2011). **Document type:** *Journal, Academic/Scholarly.* **Description:** Covers all aspects of basic and clinical urologic research.
Related titles: Online - full text ed.: ISSN 1687-6377. free (effective 2011).
Indexed: A01, C06, C07, CA, H12, I05, P30, SCOPUS, T02.
—IE.
Published by: Hindawi Publishing Corporation, 410 Park Ave, 15th Fl, PMB 287, New York, NY 10022. FAX 215-893-4392, 866-446-3294, hindawi@hindawi.com. Ed. Richard Santucci.

616.6 FRA ISSN 1110-5704
AFRICAN JOURNAL OF UROLOGY. Text in English. 1995. q. EUR 163, USD 216 combined subscription to institutions (print & online eds.) (effective 2012). back issues avail. **Document type:** *Journal, Academic/Scholarly.*
Related titles: Online - full text ed.: ISSN 1961-9987.
Indexed: A22, E01.
—BLDSC (0732.570000), IE, Ingenta. **CCC.**
Published by: (Pan African Urological Surgeon's Association EGY), Springer France (Subsidiary of: Springer Science+Business Media), 22 Rue de Palestro, Paris, 75002, France. TEL 33-1-53009860, FAX 33-1-53009861, sylvie.kamara@springer.com. Ed. Dr. I M Khalaf.

616.6 EGY ISSN 2090-0910
AFRO ARAB JOURNAL OF VOIDING DYSFUNCTION/MAGALLAT AL-'ARABIYYAT LIL-IDHTRABAT AL-BAWLIYYAT/MAJALLAT AL-'ARABIYYAT LIL-IDHTRABAT AL-BAWLIYYAT. Text in English. 2007. s-a. **Document type:** *Journal, Academic/Scholarly.*
Formerly (until 2009): Pan Arab Journal of Voiding Dysfunction (1687-7896)
Published by: Pan Arab Continence Society, 12 Botrous Ghaly St, Roxy, Heliopolis, Cairo, Egypt. info2006@pacsoffice.org, http://www.pacsoffice.org. Ed. Dr. Hassan Shaker.

616.6 CZE ISSN 1210-955X
➤ **AKTUALITY V NEFROLOGII.** Text in Czech. 1994. irreg. CZK 220 (effective 2009). **Document type:** *Journal, Academic/Scholarly.*
Related titles: Online - full content ed.: ISSN 1213-3248.
Indexed: EMBASE, ExcerpMed, R10, Reac, SCOPUS.
—BLDSC (0785.717000), IE.
Published by: Tigis s. r. o., Havlovickeho 16, Prague 4, 152 00, Czech Republic. TEL 420-2-51813192, FAX 420-2-51681217, info@tigis.cz. Ed. Sylvie Sulkova-Dusilova.

616.6 DEU ISSN 0001-7868
RC870 CODEN: ZURNAV
➤ **AKTUELLE UROLOGIE.** Text in German; Summaries in English, German. 1970. 6/yr. EUR 268 to institutions; EUR 366 combined subscription to institutions (print & online eds.); EUR 56 newsstand/cover (effective 2011). adv. bk.rev. abstr.; illus. index. reprints avail. **Document type:** *Journal, Academic/Scholarly.*
Incorporates (1907-1991): Zeitschrift fuer Urologie und Nephrologie (0044-3611)
Related titles: Online - full text ed.: ISSN 1438-8820. EUR 352 to institutions (effective 2011).
Indexed: A20, A22, ASCA, ChemAb, CurCont, EMBASE, ExcerpMed, IndMed, Inpharma, MEDLINE, P30, R10, Reac, SCI, SCOPUS, W07.
—BLDSC (0785.887000), CASDDS, GNLM, IE, Infotrieve, Ingenta, INIST. **CCC.**
Published by: Georg Thieme Verlag, Ruedigerstr 14, Stuttgart, 70469, Germany. TEL 49-711-8931421, FAX 49-711-8931410, leser.service@thieme.de. Eds. D Jocham, Dr. K Miller. Adv. contact Christine Volpp TEL 49-711-8931603. Circ: 1,800 (paid).

616.6 USA ISSN 0272-6386
CODEN: AJKDDP
➤ **AMERICAN JOURNAL OF KIDNEY DISEASES.** Abbreviated title: A J K D. Text in English. 1981 (Jul.). m. USD 998 in United States to institutions; USD 1,111 elsewhere to institutions (effective 2012). adv. bk.rev. abstr. index. back issues avail.; reprints avail. **Document type:** *Journal, Academic/Scholarly.* **Description:** Includes research papers, position papers and proceedings of National Kidney Foundation scientific symposia.
Related titles: Online - full text ed.: ISSN 1523-6838. suspended (from ScienceDirect).
Indexed: A20, A22, A34, A36, AIIM, ASCA, C06, C07, C08, CA, CABA, CIN, CINAHL, ChemAb, ChemTitl, CurCont, D01, E01, E12, EMBASE, ExcerpMed, F08, F11, F12, FR, GH, H16, IBR, IBZ, IDIS, INI, ISR, IndMed, Inpharma, Kidney, LT, MEDLINE, N02, N03, N04, P30, P33, P35, P37, PHN&I, R08, R10, R12, RA&MP, RM&VM, RRTA, Reac, S12, SCI, SCOPUS, SPPI, SoyAb, T02, T05, THA, W07, W11.
—BLDSC (0826.860000), CASDDS, GNLM, IE, Infotrieve, Ingenta, INIST. **CCC.**
Published by: (National Kidney Foundation, Inc.), W.B. Saunders Co. (Subsidiary of: Elsevier Health Sciences), Elsevier, Health Sciences Division, Order Fulfillment, 3251 Riverport Ln, Maryland Heights, MO 63043. TEL 314-872-8370, 800-325-4177, FAX 314-432-1380, JournalCustomerService-usa@elsevier.com, http://www.us.elsevierhealth.com. Ed. Andrew S Levey. Adv. contact Richard Devanna TEL 201-767-4170. Circ: 3,900.

616.6 CHE ISSN 0250-8095
RC902.A1 CODEN: AJNED9
➤ **AMERICAN JOURNAL OF NEPHROLOGY.** Text in English. 1981. 6/yr. CHF 4,824, EUR 3,856, USD 4,725 to institutions; CHF 5,296, EUR 4,234, USD 5,183 combined subscription to institutions (print & online eds.) (effective 2012). adv. illus. index. back issues avail. **Document type:** *Journal, Academic/Scholarly.* **Description:** Aims to provide the clinical care of adult and pediatric nephrology patients. The editorial scope ranges from studies on the biochemistry and immunology of kidney diseases to new knowledge on such established clinical problems as dialysis, transplantation, and hypertension.
Related titles: Microform ed.: (from PQC); Online - full text ed.: ISSN 1421-9670. CHF 4,722, EUR 3,778, USD 4,584 to institutions (effective 2012).
Indexed: A20, A22, A29, ASCA, B20, B21, B25, BIOSIS Prev, CA, ChemAb, CurCont, DBA, DentInd, E01, EMBASE, ESPM, ExcerpMed, I10, ISR, IndMed, Inpharma, Kidney, MEDLINE, MycolAb, P20, P22, P24, P26, P30, P35, P48, P54, PQC, R10, Reac, SCI, SCOPUS, T02, VirolAbstr, W07.
—BLDSC (0828.370000), CASDDS, GNLM, IE, Infotrieve, Ingenta, INIST. **CCC.**
Published by: S. Karger AG, Allschwilerstr 10, Basel, 4055, Switzerland. TEL 41-61-3061111, FAX 41-61-3061234, karger@karger.ch, http://www.karger.ch. Ed. G Bakris. adv.: page CHF 1,895; trim 210 x 280. Circ: 2,200 (paid and controlled).

➤ **AMERICAN JOURNAL OF PHYSIOLOGY: RENAL PHYSIOLOGY.** *see* BIOLOGY—Physiology

616.6 USA
AMERICAN KIDNEY FUND. ANNUAL REPORT. Text in English. 1971. a. free (effective 2010). back issues avail. **Document type:** *Report, Corporate.* **Description:** Provides a overview of the organization's accomplishments, finances, and major contributors.
Related titles: Online - full text ed.
Published by: American Kidney Fund, 6110 Executive Blvd, Ste 1010, Rockville, MD 20852. TEL 800-638-8299, contributions@kidneyfund.org.

616.6 USA ISSN 1555-9041
RC902.A1
➤ **AMERICAN SOCIETY OF NEPHROLOGY. CLINICAL JOURNAL.** Abbreviated title: C J A S N. Text in English. 2006 (Jan.). m. USD 740 domestic to institutions (print or online ed.); USD 890 foreign to institutions (print or online ed.); USD 320 combined subscription domestic to individuals (print & online eds.); USD 470 combined subscription foreign to individuals (print & online eds.); USD 845 combined subscription domestic to institutions (print & online eds.); USD 995 combined subscription foreign to institutions (print & online eds.); free to members (effective 2010). back issues avail.; reprints avail. **Document type:** *Journal, Academic/Scholarly.* **Description:** Publishes original research in the areas of clinical nephrology, hypertension, organ transplantation and critical care.
Related titles: Online - full text ed.: ISSN 1555-905X. 2006 (Jan.).
Indexed: A22, C06, C07, CurCont, EMBASE, ExcerpMed, Inpharma, MEDLINE, P30, P35, R10, Reac, SCI, SCOPUS, W07.
—BLDSC (3286.294020), IE, Ingenta. **CCC.**
Published by: American Society of Nephrology, 1725 I St, NW, Ste 510, Washington, DC 20006. TEL 202-659-0599, FAX 202-659-0709, email@asn-online.org, http://www.asn-online.org/. Ed. William M Bennett. Adv. contact Qien Porter TEL 201-653-4777 ext 16.

616.6 USA ISSN 1046-6673
RC902 CODEN: JASNEU
➤ **AMERICAN SOCIETY OF NEPHROLOGY. JOURNAL.** Abbreviated title: J A S N. Text in English. 1990. m. USD 1,635 to institutions; USD 510 combined subscription to individuals (print & online eds.); USD 1,735 combined subscription to institutions (print & online eds.); free to members (effective 2011). adv. abstr. back issues avail. **Document type:** *Journal, Academic/Scholarly.* **Description:** Contains original articles for nephrologists and other specialists who study kidney function and renal diseases.
Related titles: Online - full text ed.: ISSN 1533-3450. USD 1,580 to institutions (effective 2011); ◆ Supplement(s): Nephrology Self-Assessment Program. ISSN 1536-836X.
Indexed: A20, A22, A34, A35, A36, A38, ASCA, AgBio, B25, BIOSIS Prev, C06, C07, CABA, CIN, ChemAb, ChemTitl, CurCont, D01, E12, EMBASE, ExcerpMed, GH, H16, ISR, IndMed, Inpharma, Kidney, LT, MEDLINE, MycolAb, N02, N03, N04, N05, P30, P35, R10, R12, RA&MP, RRTA, Reac, S12, S13, S16, SCI, SCOPUS, T05, VS, W07.
—BLDSC (4693.005000), CASDDS, GNLM, IE, Infotrieve, Ingenta, INIST. **CCC.**
Published by: American Society of Nephrology, 1725 I St, NW, Ste 510, Washington, DC 20006. TEL 202-659-0599, FAX 202-659-0709, email@asn-online.org, http://www.asn-online.org/. Ed. Eric G Neilson.

616.6 JPN
ANNUAL REVIEW JINZO/ANNUAL REVIEW. KIDNEY. Text in Japanese. 1988. a. JPY 9,400 per issue (effective 2007). adv. **Document type:** *Academic/Scholarly.*
Published by: Chugai Igakusha, 62 Yarai-cho, Shinjuku-ku, Tokyo, 162-0805, Japan. TEL 81-3-32682701, FAX 81-3-32682722, http://www.chugaiigaku.jp/.

616.6 ESP ISSN 0004-0614
RC870 CODEN: AEURAB
➤ **ARCHIVOS ESPANOLES DE UROLOGIA.** Text in Spanish; Summaries in English. 1944. m. EUR 140 domestic to individuals; EUR 150 in Europe to individuals; EUR 270 elsewhere to individuals; EUR 260 domestic to institutions; EUR 300 in Europe to institutions; EUR 320 elsewhere to institutions (effective 2009). adv. bk.rev. bibl.; charts; illus.; stat.; tr.lit. index. 120 p./no.; back issues avail.; reprints avail. **Document type:** *Journal, Academic/Scholarly.* **Description:** Includes original research and clinical case studies.
Related titles: CD-ROM ed.; Online - full text ed.: ISSN 1576-8260. 2000. free (effective 2011).
Indexed: A22, B25, BIOSIS Prev, ChemAb, EMBASE, ExcerpMed, G10, IME, IndMed, MEDLINE, MycolAb, P30, R10, Reac, RefZh, SCOPUS.
—BLDSC (1654.960000), CASDDS, GNLM, IE, Infotrieve, Ingenta, INIST. **CCC.**
Published by: Iniestares S.A., General Ampudia, 14- Bajo a, Madrid, 28003, Spain. TEL 34-91-5357892, FAX 34-91-5357893, http://www.iniestares.es/. Ed., R&P, Adv. contact Concha Martin Gallego. Circ: 2,000.

616.6 SRB ISSN 0354-7760
➤ **ARCHIVUM UROLOGICUM.** Text in English, Serbian. 1974. q. YUN 600; EUR 100 foreign. adv. bk.rev. 130 p./no. 2 cols./p.; back issues avail. **Document type:** *Journal, Academic/Scholarly.* **Description:** Covers urology, nephrology and surgery.
Formerly: Uroloski Arhiv (0351-093X)
Published by: Uroloska Klinika, Univerzetskog Klinickog Centra, Gen Zdanova 51, Belgrade, 1000. TEL 381-11-656277, FAX 381-11-659460, urologcl@eunet.yu. Ed. Sava Micic. R&P G. Arizanovic. Adv. contact G Arizanovic. B&W page EUR 500, color page EUR 1,500. Circ: 500.

616.6 ESP ISSN 0210-9476
ASOCIACION ESPANOLA DE A T S EN UROLOGIA. REVISTA. Text in Spanish. 1980. q. **Document type:** *Journal, Academic/Scholarly.*
Published by: Asociacion Espanola de Enfermeria en Urologia, Ave Ramon y Cajal, 20, Sevilla, 41005, Spain. TEL 34-954-933800, FAX 34-954-933000, enfuro@enfuro.org, http://www.enfuro.org/.

616.6 USA ISSN 0271-1338
➤ **AUDIO-DIGEST UROLOGY.** Text in English. 1978. s-m. USD 449.81 domestic; USD 479.72 in Canada; USD 527.72 elsewhere (effective 2010). back issues avail. **Document type:** *Journal, Academic/Scholarly.*
Media: Audio cassette/tape. **Related titles:** Audio CD ed.: USD 399.89 domestic; USD 431.72 in Canada; USD 479.72 elsewhere (effective 2010); Online - full text ed.: USD 359.72 (effective 2010).
Published by: Audio-Digest Foundation (Subsidiary of: California Medical Association), 1577 E Chevy Chase Dr, Glendale, CA 91206. TEL 818-240-7500, 800-423-2308, FAX 818-240-7379.

616.6 615.82 AUS ISSN 1448-0131
RC902.A1
➤ **AUSTRALIAN AND NEW ZEALAND CONTINENCE JOURNAL.** Text in English. 1995. q. AUD 75 membership (effective 2008). adv. back issues avail. **Document type:** *Journal, Academic/Scholarly.*
Formerly (until 2002): Australian Continence Journal (1324-2989)
Related titles: Online - full text ed.
Indexed: A11, C06, C07, C08, CA, CINAHL, T02.
—BLDSC (1796.854000).
Published by: (Australian Continence Foundation, New Zealand Continence Association Inc. NZL), Cambridge Publishing (Subsidiary of: Cambridge Media), 128 Northwood St, West Leederville, W.A. 6007, Australia. TEL 61-8-93823911, FAX 61-8-93823187, mail@cambridgmedia.com.au. Ed. Peter Dietz. Adv. contact Simon Henriques TEL 61-8-93823911. page AUD 1,890; 210 x 297. Circ: 2,000.

616.6 BGR ISSN 1312-2517
B A N T A O JOURNAL. (Balkan Cities Association of Nephrology, Dialysis, Transplantation and Artificial Organs) Text in English. 2003. irreg. **Document type:** *Journal, Academic/Scholarly.*
Related titles: Online - full text ed.: free (effective 2011).
Published by: Kidney Foundation, M Drinov 55 St, Varna, 900, Bulgaria. Ed. Goce Spasovski.

616.6 GBR ISSN 1464-410X
RC870
B J U INTERNATIONAL (ONLINE). (British Journal of Urology) Text in English. 1997. 18/yr. GBP 723 in United Kingdom to institutions; EUR 920 in Europe to institutions; USD 1,334 in the Americas to institutions; USD 1,558 elsewhere to institutions (effective 2012). **Document type:** *Journal, Academic/Scholarly.*
Formerly (until 1999): British Journal of Urology (Online) (1365-2176)
Media: Online - full text (from IngentaConnect). **Related titles:** Microform ed.: (from PQC); ◆ Print ed.: B J U International (Print). ISSN 1464-4096.
—**CCC.**
Published by: Wiley-Blackwell Publishing Ltd. (Subsidiary of: John Wiley & Sons, Inc.), 9600 Garsington Rd, Oxford, OX4 2DQ, United Kingdom. TEL 44-1865-776868, FAX 44-1865-714591, customerservices@blackwellpublishing.com, http://www.wiley.com/WileyCDA/.

616.6 GBR ISSN 1464-4096
RC870 CODEN: BJINFO
➤ **B J U INTERNATIONAL (PRINT).** (British Journal of Urology) Text in English. 1929. s-m. (in 2 vols., 9 nos./vol.). GBP 723 in United Kingdom to institutions; EUR 920 in Europe to institutions; USD 1,334 in the Americas to institutions; USD 1,558 elsewhere to institutions; GBP 833 combined subscription in United Kingdom to institutions (print & online eds.); EUR 1,058 combined subscription in Europe to institutions (print & online eds.); USD 1,534 combined subscription in the Americas to institutions (print & online eds.); USD 1,792 combined subscription elsewhere to institutions (print & online eds.) (effective 2012). adv. bk.rev. abstr.; bibl.; illus. index, cum.index. back issues avail.; reprint service avail. from PSC. **Document type:** *Journal, Academic/Scholarly.* **Description:** Aims to provide the very highest standard of research and clinical material for the urological community.
Formerly (until 1999): British Journal of Urology (Print) (0007-1331)
Related titles: Microform ed.: (from PQC); ◆ Online - full text ed.: B J U International (Online). ISSN 1464-410X; ◆ Supplement(s): B J U International. Supplement. ISSN 1465-5101.
Indexed: A01, A03, A08, A20, A22, A26, A29, A34, A36, ASCA, B20, B21, B25, BIOBASE, BIOSIS Prev, CA, CABA, CIN, CTA, ChemAb, ChemTitl, CurCont, D01, E01, E12, EMBASE, ESPM, ExcerpMed, F08, F11, F12, FR, G10, GH, H12, H17, I10, IABS, IBR, IBZ, INI, ISR, IndMed, Inpharma, MEDLINE, MycolAb, N02, N03, NRN, P30, P33, P34, P35, P39, R08, R10, R12, RA&MP, RM&VM, Reac, SAA, SCI, SCOPUS, SoyAb, T02, T05, THA, VS, VirolAbstr, W07, W10.
—BLDSC (2105.758000), CASDDS, GNLM, IE, Infotrieve, Ingenta, INIST. **CCC.**
Published by: (British Association of Urological Surgeons, Urological Society of India IND, Urological Society of Australasia AUS), Wiley-Blackwell Publishing Ltd. (Subsidiary of: John Wiley & Sons, Inc.), 9600 Garsington Rd, Oxford, OX4 2DQ, United Kingdom. TEL 44-1865-776868, FAX 44-1865-714591, customerservices@blackwellpublishing.com, http://www.wiley.com/. Ed. John Fitzpatrick. Adv. contact Neil Chesher TEL 44-1865-476383. Circ: 4,560.

616.6 GBR ISSN 1465-5101
B J U INTERNATIONAL. SUPPLEMENT. Text in English. 1964. irreg. includes with subscr. to B J U International. **Document type:** *Journal, Academic/Scholarly.*
Formerly (until 1999): British Journal of Urology. Supplement (1358-8672)
Related titles: Online - full text ed.; ◆ Supplement to: B J U International (Print). ISSN 1464-4096.
Indexed: EMBASE, ExcerpMed, SCOPUS.
—INIST. **CCC.**
Published by: Wiley-Blackwell Publishing Ltd. (Subsidiary of: John Wiley & Sons, Inc.), 9600 Garsington Rd, Oxford, OX4 2DQ, United Kingdom. TEL 44-1865-776868, FAX 44-1865-714591, customerservices@blackwellpublishing.com, http://www.wiley.com/.

616.6 GBR ISSN 1471-2369
RC1 CODEN: BNMEB7
➤ **B M C NEPHROLOGY.** (BioMed Central) Text in English. 2000 (Oct.). irreg. free (effective 2011). adv. back issues avail.; reprints avail. **Document type:** *Journal, Academic/Scholarly.* **Description:** Publishes original research articles in all aspects of the prevention, diagnosis and management of kidney and associated disorders, as well as related molecular genetics, pathophysiology, and epidemiology.
Media: Online - full text.
Indexed: A26, C06, C07, CA, CTA, EMBASE, ExcerpMed, I05, MEDLINE, P20, P22, P30, R10, Reac, SCI, SCOPUS, T02, W07.
—Infotrieve. **CCC.**
Published by: BioMed Central Ltd. (Subsidiary of: Springer Science+Business Media), 236 Gray's Inn Rd, London, WC1X 8HB, United Kingdom. TEL 44-20-31922000, FAX 44-20-31922010, info@biomedcentral.com. Ed. Dr. Melissa Norton. Adv. contact Natasha Bailey TEL 44-20-31922231.

616.6 GBR ISSN 1471-2490
RC1 CODEN: BUMRCS
➤ **B M C UROLOGY.** (BioMed Central) Text in English. 2001 (Aug.). irreg. free (effective 2011). adv. back issues avail.; reprints avail. **Document type:** *Journal, Academic/Scholarly.* **Description:** Publishes original research articles in all aspects of the prevention, diagnosis and management of urological disorders, as well as related molecular genetics, pathophysiology, and epidemiology.
Media: Online - full text.
Indexed: A26, C06, C07, CA, CTA, EMBASE, ExcerpMed, I05, MEDLINE, P20, P22, P30, R10, Reac, SCOPUS, T02.
—Infotrieve. **CCC.**
Published by: BioMed Central Ltd. (Subsidiary of: Springer Science+Business Media), 236 Gray's Inn Rd, London, WC1X 8HB, United Kingdom. TEL 44-20-31922000, FAX 44-20-31922010, info@biomedcentral.com. Ed. Dr. Melissa Norton. Adv. contact Natasha Bailey TEL 44-20-31922231.

616.6 BGD ISSN 1015-0889
CODEN: BRJOEJ
BANGLADESH RENAL JOURNAL. Text in English. 1982. s-a.
Indexed: EMBASE, ExcerpMed, R10, Reac, SCOPUS.
—BLDSC (1861.726500), IE, Ingenta.
Published by: Bangladesh Renal Association, Bangabandhu Sheikh Mujib Medical University, Dept of Nephrology, Shahbag Ave, Dhaka, 1000, Bangladesh. FAX 880-2-864811, dr.harun@bdcom.com. Ed. Dr. Harun Ur Rashid.

616.6 CAN
BLADDERTALK. Text in English. 1992. q. CAD 35; USD 35 foreign. **Document type:** *Newsletter.* **Description:** Features testimonials by patients, research information, news from urology conferences, coping tips, information on pharmaceuticals.
Formerly (until Sep. 1996): Helpline
Published by: Canadian Interstitial Cystitis Society, 406 S Willingdon Ave, P O Box 28625, Burnaby, BC V5C 6J4, Canada. TEL 250-758-4894, FAX 250-758-3207. Circ: 1,000.

616.6 GBR ISSN 1875-9742
RD571
▼ ➤ **BRITISH JOURNAL OF MEDICAL AND SURGICAL UROLOGY.** Text in English. 2009. bi-m. EUR 411 in Europe to institutions; JPY 68,400 in Japan to institutions; USD 650 elsewhere to institutions (effective 2012). adv. back issues avail.; reprints avail. **Document type:** *Journal, Academic/Scholarly.* **Description:** Publishes original research, commissioned reviews, comment articles and relevant case reports, with the overall aim of being readable, educational and relevant.
Related titles: Online - full text ed.: ISSN 1875-9750 (from ScienceDirect).
Indexed: CA, EMBASE, ExcerpMed, R10, Reac, SCOPUS, T02.
—IE. **CCC.**
Published by: (The British Association of Urological Surgeons (BAUS)), Elsevier Ltd (Subsidiary of: Elsevier Science & Technology), The Blvd, Langford Ln, Kidlington, Oxford, OX5 1GB, United Kingdom. TEL 44-1865-843434, FAX 44-1865-843970, journalscustomerserviceemea@elsevier.com. Ed. Justin Vale.

616.6 GBR ISSN 1365-5604
BRITISH JOURNAL OF RENAL MEDICINE. Abbreviated title: B J R M. Text in English. 1995. q. adv. bk.rev. back issues avail. **Document type:** *Journal, Academic/Scholarly.* **Description:** Provides articles of interest and benefit to all specialties involved in the provision of renal care.
Related titles: Online - full text ed.: ISSN 2045-7839. GBP 60, EUR 80 to individuals; GBP 250, EUR 375 to institutions (effective 2010).
—BLDSC (2324.250000), IE, Ingenta. **CCC.**
Published by: Hayward Medical Communications Ltd. (Subsidiary of: Hayward Group plc), 8-10 Dryden St, Covent Garden, London, WC2E 9NA, United Kingdom. TEL 44-20-72404493, FAX 44-20-72404479, edit@hayward.co.uk, http://www.hayward.co.uk. Ed. Dr. John Bradley.

C A N N T JOURNAL. *see* MEDICAL SCIENCES—Nurses And Nursing

616.6 CAN ISSN 1195-9479
➤ **CANADIAN JOURNAL OF UROLOGY.** Text in English. 1994. bi-m. USD 350 combined subscription to individuals (print & online eds.); USD 500 combined subscription to institutions (print & online eds.) (effective 2010). charts; abstr.; bibl. **Document type:** *Journal, Academic/Scholarly.*
Related titles: Online - full text ed.: USD 175 to individuals; USD 350 to institutions (effective 2010).
Indexed: A20, A26, CurCont, E08, EMBASE, ExcerpMed, H12, IndMed, MEDLINE, P30, R10, Reac, S09, SCI, SCOPUS, W07.
—BLDSC (3036.600000), IE, Ingenta. **CCC.**
Address: 2330 Ward St, Ste 604, St. Laurent, PQ H4M 2V6, Canada. TEL 514-744-1184, FAX 514-744-1138. Ed. Dr. Leonard Gomella.

616.6 CAN ISSN 1911-6470
RC870
➤ **CANADIAN UROLOGICAL ASSOCIATION. JOURNAL/ ASSOCIATION DES UROLOGUES DU CANADA. JOURNAL.** Text in English, French. 2007. irreg. **Document type:** *Journal, Academic/ Scholarly.*
Indexed: A01, A26, C06, C07, CA, CPerI, E08, H12, I05, P30, SCI, SCOPUS, T02, W07.
—BLDSC (3046.094500), IE.
Published by: (Canadian Urological Association/Association des Urologues du Canada), Canadian Medical Association/Association Medicale Canadienne, 1867 Alta Vista Dr, Ottawa, ON K1G 3Y6, Canada. TEL 888-855-2555, FAX 613-236-8864, pubs@cma.ca, http://www.cma.ca.

▼ ➤ **CARDIORENAL MEDICINE.** *see* MEDICAL SCIENCES—Cardiovascular Diseases

616.6 USA ISSN 2090-6641
▼ ➤ **CASE REPORTS IN NEPHROLOGY.** Text in English. 2011. **Document type:** *Journal, Academic/Scholarly.* **Description:** Publishes case reports in all areas of nephrology.
Related titles: Online - full text ed.: ISSN 2090-665X. 2011. free (effective 2011).
Published by: Hindawi Publishing Corporation, 410 Park Ave, 15th Fl, PMB 287, New York, NY 10022. FAX 215-893-4392, 866-446-3294, info@hindawi.com.

616.6 USA ISSN 2090-696X
▼ ➤ **CASE REPORTS IN UROLOGY.** Text in English. 2011. **Document type:** *Journal, Academic/Scholarly.* **Description:** Publishes case reports in all areas of urology.
Related titles: Online - full text ed.: ISSN 2090-6978. 2011. free (effective 2011).
Published by: Hindawi Publishing Corporation, 410 Park Ave, 15th Fl, PMB 287, New York, NY 10022. FAX 215-893-4392, 866-446-3294, info@hindawi.com.

616.6 CZE ISSN 1211-8729
➤ **CESKA UROLOGIE.** Text in Czech. 1997. q. CZK 400; CZK 100 per issue (effective 2010). **Document type:** *Journal, Academic/Scholarly.*
Published by: (Ceska Lekarska Spolecnost J.E. Purkyne, Ceska Urologicka Spolecnost/Czech Medical Association of J.E. Purkyne, Czech Urological Society), Galen, spol. s r.o., Na Belidle 34, Prague 5, 15000, Czech Republic. TEL 420-2-57326178, FAX 420-2-57326170, objednavky@galen.cz, http://www.galen.cz. Ed. Milan Hora.

616.6 JPN ISSN 1342-1751
QP249 CODEN: CENPFV
➤ **CLINICAL AND EXPERIMENTAL NEPHROLOGY.** Text in English. 1997. bi-m. EUR 270, USD 288 combined subscription to institutions (print & online eds.) (effective 2012). 80 p./no.; reprint service avail. from PSC. **Document type:** *Journal, Academic/Scholarly.* **Description:** Covers the biology, physiology of the kidney, and the basic & clinical science of kidney diseases.
Related titles: Online - full text ed.: ISSN 1437-7799 (from IngentaConnect).
Indexed: A01, A03, A08, A22, A26, CA, CurCont, E01, EMBASE, ExcerpMed, H12, MEDLINE, P20, P22, P30, P48, P54, PQC, R10, Reac, SCI, SCOPUS, T02, W07.
—BLDSC (3286.251550), CASDDS, GNLM, IE, Infotrieve, Ingenta. **CCC.**
Published by: (Nihon Jinzo Gakkai/Japanese Society of Nephrology), Springer Japan KK (Subsidiary of: Springer Science+Business Media), No 2 Funato Bldg, 1-11-11 Kudan-kita, Chiyoda-ku, Tokyo, 102-0073, Japan. TEL 81-3-68317000, FAX 81-3-68317001, http://www.springer.jp. Ed. Dr. Genjiro Kimura. Circ: 8,000. **Subscr. in the Americas to:** Springer New York LLC, Journal Fulfillment, PO Box 2485, Secaucus, NJ 07096. TEL 201-348-4033, 800-777-4643, FAX 201-348-4505, journals-ny@springer.com, http://www.springer.com; **Subscr. to:** Springer Distribution Center, Kundenservice Zeitschriften, Haberstr 7, Heidelberg 69126, Germany. TEL 49-6221-3454303, FAX 49-6221-3454229, subscriptions@springer.com.

➤ **CLINICAL GENITOURINARY CANCER (ONLINE).** *see* MEDICAL SCIENCES—Oncology

616.6 NZL ISSN 1179-5611
➤ **CLINICAL MEDICINE INSIGHTS: UROLOGY.** Text in English. 2008. irreg. free (effective 2010). **Document type:** *Journal, Academic/ Scholarly.* **Description:** Covers all aspects of the diagnosis, management and prevention of urology disorders, in addition to related genetic, pathophysiological and epidemiological topics.
Formerly (until 2010): Clinical Medicine: Urology (1178-2188)
Media: Online - full text.
Indexed: C06, C07, P30, T02.
—**CCC.**
Published by: Libertas Academica Ltd., PO Box 300-874, Mairangi Bay, Auckland, 0751, New Zealand. TEL 64-9-4763930, FAX 64-9-3531397, enquiries@la-press.com. Ed. Xiangyi Lu.

616.6 DEU ISSN 0301-0430
CODEN: CLNHBI
➤ **CLINICAL NEPHROLOGY.** Text in English. 1973. m. USD 310 to institutions; USD 365 combined subscription to institutions (print & online eds.) (effective 2011). adv. back issues avail.; reprints avail. **Document type:** *Journal, Academic/Scholarly.*
Related titles: Online - full text ed.: USD 365 to institutions (effective 2011).
Indexed: A22, A34, A36, ASCA, BIOBASE, BP, CA, CABA, CIN, ChemAb, ChemTitl, CurCont, D01, E12, EMBASE, ExcerpMed, GH, H16, H17, IABS, IBR, IBZ, IDIS, INI, ISR, IndMed, Inpharma, Kidney, MEDLINE, N02, N03, P30, P33, P35, P39, PHN&I, R08, R10, R12, R13, RA&MP, RM&VM, Reac, SCI, SCOPUS, SoyAb, T02, T05, VITIS, VS, W07.
—BLDSC (3286.307100), CASDDS, GNLM, IE, Infotrieve, Ingenta, INIST. **CCC.**
Published by: Dustri-Verlag Dr. Karl Feistle, Bajuwarenring 4, Oberhaching, 82041, Germany. TEL 49-89-6138610, FAX 49-89-6135412, info@dustri.de, http://www.dustri.de. Ed. H H Malluche. Adv. contact Joerg Feistle. Circ: 4,900.

616.6 ARG ISSN 1667-9075
COLECCION TRABAJOS DISTINGUIDOS. SERIE UROLOGIA. Text in Spanish. 2003. 6/yr. back issues avail. **Document type:** *Journal, Academic/Scholarly.*
Media: Online - full text.
Published by: Sociedad Iberoamericana de Informacion Cientifica (S I I C), Ave Belgrano 430, Buenos Aires, C1092AAR, Argentina. TEL 54-11-43424901, FAX 54-11-43313305, atencionallector@siicsalud.com, http://www.siicsalud.com. Ed. Rafael Bernal Castro.

616.6 MEX ISSN 0187-4829
RC870
COLEGIO MEXICANO DE UROLOGIA. BOLETIN. Text in Spanish. 1984. quadrennial. back issues avail. **Document type:** *Journal, Academic/Scholarly.*
Related titles: Online - full text ed.
Indexed: A01, C01, CA, T02.
Published by: Colegio Mexicano de Urologia, A.C., Montecito No 38, Torre de Oficinas WTC Piso 33, Ofic 32, Col Napoles, Mexico, D.F., 03819, Mexico. TEL 52-55-54882092, cmunacional@cmu.com.mx. Ed. Jose Luis Lorenzo Monterrubio.

616.6 ARG ISSN 0328-3968
COLPOSCOPIA. Text in Spanish. 1993. 3/yr. **Document type:** *Journal, Academic/Scholarly.*
Formerly (until 1994): Sociedad Argentina de Patologia del Tracto Genital Inferior y Colposcopia. Revista (0328-0349)
Published by: Sociedad Argentina de Patologia del Tracto Genital Inferior y Colposcopia, Posadas 1567, Buenos Aires, Argentina. TEL 54-11-48074099.

616.6 USA ISSN 0278-1700
CODEN: CONHD7
➤ **CONTEMPORARY NEPHROLOGY.** Text in English. 1981. irreg., latest vol.4. back issues avail. **Document type:** *Monographic series, Academic/Scholarly.*
—CASDDS, GNLM. **CCC.**
Published by: Springer New York LLC (Subsidiary of: Springer Science+Business Media), 233 Spring St, New York, NY 10013. TEL 212-460-1500, FAX 212-460-1575, service-ny@springer.com, http://www.springer.com/.

616.6 CHE ISSN 0302-5144
CODEN: CNEPDD
➤ **CONTRIBUTIONS TO NEPHROLOGY.** Text in English. 1975. irreg., latest vol.174, 2011. price varies. reprints avail. **Document type:** *Monographic series, Academic/Scholarly.* **Description:** Explores problems of immediate importance for clinical nephrology.
Related titles: Online - full text ed.: ISSN 1662-2782.
Indexed: A22, ASCA, B21, BIOSIS Prev, CIN, CTA, ChemAb, ChemTitl, EMBASE, ExcerpMed, IndMed, MEDLINE, MycolAb, P30, R10, Reac, SCI, SCOPUS, W07.
—BLDSC (3461.035000), CASDDS, GNLM, IE, Infotrieve, Ingenta, INIST. **CCC.**
Published by: S. Karger AG, Allschwilerstr 10, Basel, 4055, Switzerland. TEL 41-61-3061111, FAX 41-61-3061234, karger@karger.ch, http://www.karger.ch. Ed. Claudio Ronco.

616.6 USA ISSN 1931-7212
CURRENT BLADDER DYSFUNCTION REPORTS. Text in English. 2006 (Sum.). q. reprint service avail. from PSC. **Document type:** *Journal, Academic/Scholarly.*
Related titles: Online - full text ed.: ISSN 1931-7220. USD 1,158 to institutions (effective 2010).
Indexed: A22, A26, E01, E08, P30, S09, SCOPUS.
—IE. **CCC.**
Published by: Current Medicine Group LLC (Subsidiary of: Springer Science+Business Media), 400 Market St, Ste 700, Philadelphia, PA 19106. TEL 215-574-2266, 800-427-1796, FAX 215-574-2225, info@phl.cursci.com, http://www.current-medicine.com.

616.6 USA
➤ **CURRENT CLINICAL UROLOGY.** Text in English. 1999. irreg., latest 2009. price varies. illus. Index. back issues avail.; reprints avail. **Document type:** *Monographic series, Academic/Scholarly.* **Description:** Covers all aspects of urology and related internal medicine and surgery.
Related titles: Online - full text ed.
Published by: Humana Press, Inc. (Subsidiary of: Springer Science+Business Media), 233 Spring St, New York, NY 10013. TEL 212-460-1500, FAX 212-460-1575, service-ny@springer.com. Ed. Eric A Klein.

616.6 USA ISSN 1943-832X
▼ **CURRENT DIAGNOSIS & TREATMENT NEPHROLOGY & HYPERTENSION.** Text in English. 2009 (Jan.). triennial. USD 67.95 per issue (effective 2010). **Document type:** *Monographic series, Academic/Scholarly.*
Published by: McGraw-Hill Companies, Inc., PO Box 182604, Columbus, OH 43272. TEL 877-833-5524, FAX 614-759-3749, customer.service@mcgraw-hill.com, http://www.mcgraw-hill.com.

016.6 GBR ISSN 1357-1532
RC870 CODEN: CMLUEN
➤ **CURRENT MEDICAL LITERATURE. UROLOGY.** Text in English. 1987; N.S. 1995. q. GBP 60 to individuals; GBP 130 to institutions; free to qualified personnel (effective 2009). back issues avail. **Document type:** *Journal, Academic/Scholarly.* **Description:** Aims to provide physicians and allied healthcare professionals with rapid access to expert commentary and analysis on key topics in urology.
Supersedes in part (in 1995): Current Medical Literature. Nephrology and Urology (0951-9629)
Related titles: Online - full text ed.: ISSN 1759-8214; Hungarian Translation: Current Medical Literature. Urologiai Szemle. ISSN 1785-1262. 2003.
Indexed: A01, A03, A08, CA, T02.
—Infotrieve. **CCC.**
Published by: Remedica Medical Education and Publishing Ltd., Commonwealth House, 1 New Oxford St, London, WC1A 1NU, United Kingdom. TEL 44-20-77592999, FAX 44-20-77592951, info@remedica.com, http://www.remedica.com. Ed. Emma Beagley.

610 GBR ISSN 1062-4821
CODEN: CNHYEM
➤ **CURRENT OPINION IN NEPHROLOGY & HYPERTENSION.** Text in English. 1992. bi-m. USD 1,254 domestic to institutions; USD 1,346 foreign to institutions (effective 2011). adv. bibl.; illus. back issues avail.; reprints avail. **Document type:** *Journal, Academic/Scholarly.* **Description:** Presents review articles directed toward clinicians and practicing kidney and hypertension specialists.
Related titles: Online - full text ed.: ISSN 1473-6543. 2000. USD 266 to individuals (effective 2011); Optical Disk - DVD ed.: Current Opinion in Nephrology & Hypertension, with Evaluated MEDLINE. ISSN 1080-8221.
Indexed: A22, BIOBASE, C06, C07, C08, CINAHL, CurCont, E01, EMBASE, ExcerpMed, IABS, ISR, IndMed, Inpharma, MEDLINE, P30, P35, SCI, SCOPUS, W07.
—BLDSC (3500.775830), IE, Infotrieve, Ingenta, INIST. **CCC.**
Published by: Lippincott Williams & Wilkins, Ltd., 250 Waterloo Rd, London, SE1 8RD, United Kingdom. TEL 44-20-79810600, FAX 44-20-79810601, customerservice@lww.com, http://www.lww.com. Ed. Barry M Brenner. Pub. Ian Burgess. adv.: B&W page USD 965, color page USD 1,275; trim 8.125 x 10.875.

616.6 USA ISSN 0963-0643
RC870 CODEN: CUOUEQ
CURRENT OPINION IN UROLOGY. Text in English. 1990. bi-m. USD 1,248 domestic to institutions; USD 1,342 foreign to institutions (effective 2011). adv. bibl.; illus. index. back issues avail.; reprints avail. **Document type:** *Journal, Academic/Scholarly.* **Description:** Covers key subjects such as benign prostatic hyperplasia, robotics, urolithiasis, prostate cancer, female urology, kidney cancer, bladder cancer, reconstructive surgery, pediatric urology and andrology, sexual dysfunction and infertility.
Related titles: Diskette ed.; Online - full text ed.: ISSN 1473-6586. USD 266 to individuals (effective 2011); Optical Disk - DVD ed.: Current Opinion in Urology, with Evaluated MEDLINE. ISSN 1080-8094. 1995.
Indexed: A22, BIOBASE, CurCont, E01, EMBASE, ExcerpMed, IABS, IndMed, MEDLINE, P30, R10, Reac, SCI, SCOPUS, W07.
—BLDSC (3500.779500), GNLM, IE, Infotrieve, Ingenta. **CCC.**
Published by: Lippincott Williams & Wilkins (Subsidiary of: Wolters Kluwer N.V.), 530 Walnut St, Philadelphia, PA 19106. TEL 215-521-8300, FAX 215-521-8902, customerservice@lww.com, http://www.lww.com. Eds. Johannes W Vieweg, Michael Marberger. Pub. Ian Burgess. Circ: 325.

616.6 CHE ISSN 1661-7649
CURRENT UROLOGY. Text in English. 2007. q. CHF 908, EUR 725, USD 896 to institutions; CHF 995, EUR 795, USD 980 combined subscription to institutions (print & online eds.) (effective 2012). adv. **Document type:** *Journal, Academic/Scholarly.*
Related titles: Online - full text ed.: ISSN 1661-7657. CHF 874, EUR 699, USD 849 to institutions (effective 2012).
Indexed: A22, E01, EMBASE, ExcerpMed, R10, Reac, SCOPUS.
—BLDSC (3504.960400), IE. **CCC.**
Published by: S. Karger AG, Allschwilerstr 10, Basel, 4055, Switzerland. TEL 41-61-3061111, FAX 41-61-3061234, karger@karger.ch, http://www.karger.ch. Eds. P Ekman, S Zhao.

616.6 USA ISSN 1527-2737
RC870
CURRENT UROLOGY REPORTS. Text in English. 2000. bi-m. reprint service avail. from PSC. **Document type:** *Journal, Academic/Scholarly.*
Related titles: Online - full text ed.: ISSN 1534-6285. 2000. EUR 870, USD 1,158 to institutions (effective 2010).
Indexed: A22, A26, E01, EMBASE, ExcerpMed, H12, I05, MEDLINE, P30, R10, Reac, SCOPUS.
—BLDSC (3504.960500), IE, Ingenta. **CCC.**
Published by: Current Medicine Group LLC (Subsidiary of: Springer Science+Business Media), 400 Market St, Ste 700, Philadelphia, PA 19106. TEL 215-574-2266, 800-427-1796, FAX 215-574-2225, info@phl.cursci.com, http://www.current-medicine.com. Ed. Mark Soloway.

616.6 KOR ISSN 0494-4747
RC870
DAIHAN BINYOGIGWA HAGHOI JI/KOREAN JOURNAL OF UROLOGY. Text in Korean. 1960. bi-m. membership. **Document type:** *Journal, Academic/Scholarly.*
Related titles: Online - full text ed.
Indexed: R10, Reac, SCOPUS.
—BLDSC (5113.575000), IE.
Published by: Daihan Binyogigwa Haghoi/Korean Urological Association, Rm. 419, 4F, Jungmyung Honeyville Plaza # 965 Dogok-dong, Kangnnam-gu, Seoul, 135-270, Korea, S. TEL 82-2-5738190, FAX 82-2-5738192, urokorea@kornet.net.

616.6 DEU ISSN 0941-0406
DEUTSCHE ARBEITSGEMEINSCHAFT FUER KLINISCHE NEPHROLOGIE. MITTEILUNGEN. Text in German. 197?. a. **Document type:** *Journal, Academic/Scholarly.*
Formerly (until 1993): Arbeitsgemeinschaft fuer Klinische Nephrologie. Mitteilungen (0172-7311)
Indexed: IBR, IBZ.
—GNLM. **CCC.**
Published by: (Deutsche Arbeitsgemeinschaft fuer Klinische Nephrologie e.V.), Vandenhoeck und Ruprecht, Theaterstr 13, Goettingen, 37073, Germany. TEL 49-551-508440, FAX 49-551-5084422, info@v-r.de, http://www.v-r.de.

616.6 DEU ISSN 0178-4625
DEUTSCHE GESELLSCHAFT FUER UROLOGIE. MITTEILUNGEN. Text in German. 1985. q. **Document type:** *Journal, Academic/Scholarly.*
—GNLM.
Published by: Deutsche Gesellschaft fuer Urologie, Uerdinger Str 64, Duesseldorf, 40474, Germany. TEL 49-211-5160960, FAX 49-211-51609660, info@dgu.de, http://www.urologenportal.de. Circ: 4,400.

616.6 NLD ISSN 0167-8205
CODEN: DNEPDO
➤ **DEVELOPMENTS IN NEPHROLOGY.** Text in English. 1981. irreg., latest vol.40, 1999. price varies. back issues avail. **Document type:** *Monographic series, Academic/Scholarly.*
Indexed: CIN, ChemAb, ChemTitl.
—BLDSC (3579.085360), CASDDS. **CCC.**
Published by: Springer Netherlands (Subsidiary of: Springer Science+Business Media), Van Godewijckstraat 30, Dordrecht, 3311 GX, Netherlands. TEL 31-78-6576050, FAX 31-78-6576474.

616.6 610.73 SWE ISSN 1104-4616
DIALAESEN; tidningen foer personal inom transplantation & njursjukvaard i Norden. Text in Swedish. 1993. bi-m. SEK 180 (effective 2006). adv. back issues avail. **Document type:** *Magazine, Academic/Scholarly.* **Description:** For all medical personnel involved with nephrology.
Related titles: Online - full text ed.
Address: Getabacksv. 4, Taaby, 8754, Sweden. info@dialasen.com. Ed. Ulla Winge. Pub., Adv. contact Pia Lundstroem. page SEK 13,900; 215 x 280. Circ: 3,200 (controlled).

616.61 ESP ISSN 1886-2845
DIALISIS Y TRANSPLANTE. Text in Spanish. 1979. q. EUR 67.57 combined subscription to individuals (print & online eds.); EUR 171.05 combined subscription to institutions (print & online eds.) (effective 2009). **Document type:** *Journal, Academic/Scholarly.*
Formerly (until 2003): Sociedad Espanola de Dialisis y Transplante. Revista (0210-3451)
Related titles: Online - full text ed.: ISSN 1886-7278. 2006. EUR 56.28 (effective 2009) (from ScienceDirect).
Indexed: EMBASE, ExcerpMed, SCOPUS.
—**CCC.**
Published by: Elsevier Doyma (Subsidiary of: Elsevier Health Sciences), Traversa de Gracia 17-21, Barcelona, 08021, Spain. TEL 34-932-418800, FAX 34-932-419020, editorial@elsevier.com. Ed. J. Ocharan-Corcuera. Circ: 500.

616.6 DEU ISSN 1434-0704
DIALYSE AKTUELL. Text in German. 1997. 8/yr. EUR 48 to institutions; EUR 102 combined subscription to institutions (print & online eds.); EUR 12 newsstand/cover (effective 2011). adv. **Document type:** *Magazine, Trade.*
Related titles: Online - full text ed.: ISSN 1860-3300. EUR 102 to institutions (effective 2011).
—BLDSC (3579.783200), IE. **CCC.**
Published by: Georg Thieme Verlag, Ruedigerstr 14, Stuttgart, 70469, Germany. TEL 49-711-8931421, FAX 49-711-8931410, kunden.service@thieme.de. Ed. Guenther Buck. Adv. contact Hans-Joachim Scholten. Circ: 8,200 (paid and controlled).

616.61 USA ISSN 0090-2934
CODEN: DITRD2
DIALYSIS & TRANSPLANTATION. Abbreviated title: D & T. Text in English. 1972 (Apr.). m. GBP 69 in United Kingdom to institutions; EUR 87 in Europe to institutions; USD 136 elsewhere to institutions (effective 2012). charts; illus. back issues avail.; reprint service avail. from PSC. **Document type:** *Journal, Trade.* **Description:** Publishes clinical application articles on new techniques and technologies, as well as coverage of pertinent legislative and economic issues.
Related titles: Online - full text ed.: ISSN 1932-6920.
Indexed: A20, A22, A29, A36, ASCA, B&BAb, B19, B20, B21, CABA, CTA, CurCont, D01, E12, EMBASE, ESPM, ExcerpMed, FR, GH, H17, I10, Inpharma, N02, N03, P30, P33, P35, R10, R12, RM&VM, Reac, RefZh, SCI, SCOPUS, T05, VirolAbstr, W07.
—BLDSC (3579.785000), CASDDS, GNLM, IE, Infotrieve, Ingenta, INIST. **CCC.**
Published by: John Wiley & Sons, Inc., 111 River St, Hoboken, NJ 07030. TEL 201-748-6000, FAX 201-748-6088, info@wiley.com, http://www.wiley.com/WileyCDA/.

616.6 DEU ISSN 0940-5623
DIATRA JOURNAL; Fachzeitschrift fuer Nephrologie und Transplantation. Text in German. 1991. q. EUR 19 domestic; EUR 23 foreign (effective 2009). bk.rev. **Document type:** *Journal, Academic/Scholarly.* **Description:** Covers nephrology and transplantation in the areas of medicine, law and social welfare.
Published by: Diatra Verlag GmbH, Postfach 1230, Eltville, 65332, Germany. TEL 49-6123-73478, FAX 49-6123-73287, dj@diatra-verlag.de. Ed. Robert Laube. Adv. contact Gerhard Stroh. Circ: 19,000 (controlled).

616 616.6 CAN ISSN 1486-1410
DIRECTORY OF PARTICIPATING DIALYSIS CENTRES, TRANSPLANT CENTRES AND ORGAN PROCUREMENT ORGANIZATIONS IN CANADA/REPERTOIRE DES CENTRES DE DIALYSE PARTICIPANTS AU CANADA. Text in English, French. 1994. a. **Document type:** *Directory, Trade.*
Related titles: Online - full text ed.: ISSN 1914-0975. 2004.
Published by: (Canadian Institute for Health Information, Canadian Organ Replacement Register), Canadian Institute for Health Information/Institut Canadien d'Information sur la Sante, 377 Dalhousie St, Ste 200, Ottawa, ON K1N 9N8, Canada. TEL 613-241-7860, FAX 613-241-8120, nursing@cihi.ca, http://www.cihi.ca.

616.6 NLD ISSN 1871-2592
E A U - E B U UPDATE SERIES. (European Association of Urology - European Board of Urology) Text in English. 2003. 6/yr. EUR 275 in Europe to institutions; JPY 36,400 in Japan to institutions; USD 308 elsewhere to institutions (effective 2009). **Document type:** *Journal, Academic/Scholarly.* **Description:** Deals with contemporary issues in the key areas within urology.
Formerly (until 2005): E A U Update Series (European Association of Urology) (1570-9124)
Related titles: Online - full text ed.: (from IngentaConnect).
Indexed: A01, A03, A08, A26, CA, EMBASE, ExcerpMed, I05, SCOPUS, T02.
—BLDSC (3647.002950), IE, Ingenta. **CCC.**
Published by: Elsevier BV (Subsidiary of: Elsevier Science & Technology), Radarweg 29, PO Box 211, Amsterdam, 1000 AE, Netherlands. TEL 31-20-4853911, FAX 31-20-4852457, JournalsCustomerServiceEMEA@elsevier.com, http://www.elsevier.nl. Ed. Fritz H Schroeder.

616.6 EGY ISSN 1110-5712
EGYPTIAN JOURNAL OF UROLOGY. Text in English. 1995. s-a. EGP 300 for 100 copies (effective 2003). **Document type:** *Journal, Academic/Scholarly.*
Published by: Egyptian Urological Association, 33 Ramsis St, Marouf Tower (B), Flr 14, Cairo, 11111, Egypt. TEL 202-577-6717, FAX 202-578-0588, http://www.uroegypt.org/?id=172. Ed. Dr. I M Khalaf.

616.6 GRC ISSN 1105-140X
ELLENIKE NEFROLOGIA/HELLENIC NEPHROLOGY. Text in Multiple languages. 1989. q. free to qualified personnel. **Document type:** *Journal, Academic/Scholarly.*
—BLDSC (4285.437500).
Published by: Hellenic Society of Nephrology, 15 Meandrou St, Athens, 11528, Greece. TEL 30-2310-992851, FAX 30-2310-992851.

616.6 FRA ISSN 1762-0945
➤ **ENCYCLOPEDIE MEDICO-CHIRURGICALE. NEPHROLOGIE.** Cover title: Traite de Nephrologie - Urologie. Variant title: Encyclopedie Medico-Chirurgicale, Instantanes Medicaux. Nephrologie - Urologie. Text in French. 1939. 2 base vols. plus q. updates. EUR 451 (effective 2006). bibl.; charts; illus. **Document type:** *Academic/Scholarly.* **Description:** Provides urologists with a comprehensive, up-to-date reference for diagnosing and treating kidney and other urinary-tract diseases, disorders, and conditions.
Supersedes in part (in 2003): Encyclopedie Medico-Chirurgicale. Nephrologie - Urologie (1155-1917); Which was formerly (until 1991): Encyclopedie Medico-Chirurgicale. Rein, Organes Genito-urinaires (0246-0572); (until 1957): Encyclopedie Medico-Chirurgicale. Rein (0246-0742)
Related titles: Online - full text ed.
—IE, INIST.
Published by: Elsevier Masson (Subsidiary of: Elsevier Health Sciences), 62 Rue Camille Desmoulins, Issy les Moulineaux, Cedex 92442, France. TEL 33-1-71165500, FAX 33-1-71165600, infos@elsevier-masson.fr.

➤ **ENCYCLOPEDIE MEDICO-CHIRURGICALE. RADIOLOGIE ET IMAGERIE MEDICALE. GENITO-URINAIRE - GYNECO-OBSTETRICALE - MAMMAIRE.** *see* MEDICAL SCIENCES—Radiology And Nuclear Medicine

➤ **ENCYCLOPEDIE MEDICO-CHIRURGICALE. TECHNIQUES CHIRURGICALES. UROLOGIE.** *see* MEDICAL SCIENCES—Surgery

616.6005 GBR ISSN 1758-3829
EUROPEAN UROLOGICAL REVIEW. Text in English. s-a. adv. back issues avail. **Document type:** *Journal, Trade.* **Description:** Focuses on current trends and future developments in the prevention, diagnosis and treatment of disorders affecting the reproductive organs and the urinary system.
Formerly (until 2008): European Genito-Urinary Disease (1755-1072); Which supersede in part (in 2007): European Renal & Genito-Urinary Disease (1752-9034); Which was formerly (until 2006): European Kidney & Urological Disease
Related titles: Online - full text ed.: ISSN 1758-406X.
Published by: Touch Briefings (Subsidiary of: Touch Group plc), Saffron House, 6-10 Kirby St, London, EC1N 8TS, United Kingdom. TEL 44-20-74525600, FAX 44-20-74525606, info@touchbriefings.com.

616.6 NLD ISSN 0302-2838
RC870 CODEN: EUURAV
➤ **EUROPEAN UROLOGY.** Text in English. 12/yr. EUR 3,817 in Europe to institutions; JPY 506,400 in Japan to institutions; USD 4,269 elsewhere to institutions (effective 2012). abstr. index. back issues avail. **Document type:** *Journal, Academic/Scholarly.* **Description:** Publishes original research articles on a wide range of urological disorders. Covers oncology, impotence, infertility, pediatrics, lithiasis, and endourology.
Related titles: Microform ed.; Online - full text ed.: ISSN 1421-993X. CHF 116 in Europe with print edition; CHF 116 overseas with print edition; USD 90 in United States with print edition (effective 2001) (from IngentaConnect, ScienceDirect); ◆ Regional ed(s).: European Urology (Italian Edition). ISSN 1828-6569; ◆ Supplement(s): European Urology Supplements. ISSN 1569-9056.
Indexed: A01, A03, A08, A22, A26, ASCA, B21, B25, BIOSIS Prev, CA, CTA, ChemAb, CurCont, E01, EMBASE, ExcerpMed, G10, I05, INI, ISR, IndMed, Inpharma, MEDLINE, MycolAb, NRN, P30, P35, R10, Reac, SCI, SCOPUS, T02, W07.
—BLDSC (3830.370500), CASDDS, GNLM, IE, Infotrieve, Ingenta, INIST. **CCC.**
Published by: (European Association of Urology CHE), Elsevier BV (Subsidiary of: Elsevier Science & Technology), Radarweg 29, PO Box 211, Amsterdam, 1000 AE, Netherlands. TEL 31-20-4853911, FAX 31-20-4852457, JournalsCustomerServiceEMEA@elsevier.com, http://www.elsevier.nl. Ed. Francesco Montorsi. **Co-sponsors:** European Society for Urological Oncology and Endocrinology; European Organization for Research and Treatment of Cancer, Genito Urinary Group.

616.6 ITA ISSN 1828-6569
➤ **EUROPEAN UROLOGY (ITALIAN EDITION).** Text in Multiple languages. 2006. 3/yr. **Document type:** *Journal, Academic/Scholarly.*
Related titles: ◆ Regional ed(s).: European Urology. ISSN 0302-2838.
Published by: Elsevier Masson (Subsidiary of: Elsevier Health Sciences), Via Paleocapa 7, Milan, 20121, Italy. TEL 39-02-881841, FAX 39-02-88184302, info@masson.it, http://www.masson.it.

616.6 NLD ISSN 1569-9056
RC870
EUROPEAN UROLOGY SUPPLEMENTS. Text in English. 4/yr. free to members (effective 2009). **Document type:** *Journal, Academic/Scholarly.*
Incorporates (1992-2009): European Urology Update Series (0968-7645)
Related titles: Online - full text ed.: 2002 (from IngentaConnect, ScienceDirect); ◆ Supplement to: European Urology. ISSN 0302-2838.
Indexed: A01, A03, A08, A20, A22, A26, B25, BIOSIS Prev, CA, CurCont, EMBASE, ExcerpMed, I05, Inpharma, MycolAb, P35, R10, Reac, SCI, SCOPUS, T02, W07.
—BLDSC (3830.370520), IE, Ingenta, INIST. **CCC.**
Published by: (European Association of Urology CHE), Elsevier BV (Subsidiary of: Elsevier Science & Technology), Radarweg 29, PO Box 211, Amsterdam, 1000 AE, Netherlands. TEL 31-20-4853911, FAX 31-20-4852457, JournalsCustomerServiceEMEA@elsevier.com, http://www.elsevier.nl. Ed. Francesco Montorsi.

EXCERPTA MEDICA. SECTION 28: UROLOGY AND NEPHROLOGY. *see* MEDICAL SCIENCES—Abstracting, Bibliographies, Statistics

616.6 GBR ISSN 1747-406X
▼ **EXPERT REVIEW OF UROLOGY.** Text in English. forthcoming 2011. 3/yr. ((6x/yr. in 2010)). GBP 290 combined subscription domestic (print & online eds.); USD 555 combined subscription in North America (print & online eds.); JPY 60,500 combined subscription in Japan (print & online eds.); EUR 360 combined subscription elsewhere (print & online eds.) (effective 2009). adv. back issues avail.; reprints avail. **Document type:** *Journal, Academic/Scholarly.*
Related titles: Online - full text ed.: ISSN 1747-4078. forthcoming. GBP 255 domestic; USD 495 in North America; JPY 53,500 in Japan; EUR 320 elsewhere (effective 2009).
Published by: Expert Reviews Ltd. (Subsidiary of: Future Science Ltd.), Unitec House, 2 Albert Pl, London, N3 1QB, United Kingdom. TEL 44-20-83492033, FAX 44-20-83432313, info@expert-reviews.com, http://www.expert-reviews.com/. Ed. Elisa Manzotti TEL 44-20-83716090. Adv. contact Simon Boisseau.

616.6 USA ISSN 1524-7651
FAMILY FOCUS (NEW YORK). Text in English. 1989. q. free to members (effective 2011). 16 p./no.; back issues avail. **Document type:** *Newsletter, Consumer.* **Description:** Information for dialysis and transplant patients and their families.
Related titles: Online - full text ed.
Published by: National Kidney Foundation, Inc., 30 E 33rd St, New York, NY 10016. TEL 212-889-2210, 800-622-9010, FAX 212-689-9261, info@kidney.org.

616.6 USA ISSN 1523-634X
FAMILY UROLOGY. Text in English. 1995. q. adv. **Description:** Provides educational and informational articles and departments to those suffering from urologic diseases as well as their family members. It also covers columns, Q&A, book reviews, treatment updates, and news & notes.
Indexed: P30.
Published by: American Foundation for Urologic Disease, 1128 N. Charles St., Baltimore, MD 21201. TEL 410-468-1800, 800-242-2383, FAX 410-468-1808, kym@afud.org, http://www.afud.org. adv.: B&W page USD 4,550, color page USD 5,950; trim 8.5 x 10.875. Circ: 65,000 (controlled).

616.6 POL ISSN 1899-3338
➤ **FORUM NEFROLOGICZNE.** Text in Polish. 2008. q. PLZ 66 domestic to individuals; PLZ 132 domestic to institutions (effective 2011). **Document type:** *Journal, Academic/Scholarly.*
Related titles: Online - full text ed.: ISSN 1899-4113.
Published by: (Polskie Towarzystwo Nefrologiczne), Wydawnictwo Via Medica, ul Swietokrzyska 73, Gdansk, 80180, Poland. TEL 48-58-3209494, FAX 48-58-3209460, redakcja@viamedica.pl, http://www.viamedica.pl. Ed. Boleslaw Rutkowski.

➤ **GELBE LISTE PHARMINDEX. UROLOGEN.** *see* PHARMACY AND PHARMACOLOGY

616.6 ITA ISSN 0394-9362
➤ **GIORNALE DI TECNICHE NEFROLOGICHE E DIALITICHE.** Text in Italian. 1989. q. EUR 69.50 in Europe to institutions; EUR 87 elsewhere to institutions (effective 2009). bibl.; charts; illus. 48 p./no.; back issues avail.; reprints avail. **Document type:** *Journal, Academic/Scholarly.*
Related titles: Online - full text ed.: ISSN 1724-5974.
—CCC.
Published by: Wichtig Editore Srl, Via Friuli 72, Milan, MI 20135, Italy. TEL 39-02-55195443, FAX 39-02-55195971, info@wichtig-publisher.com. Eds. Dr. Nicola Di Paolo, Dr. Umberto Buoncristiani. Circ: 500 (controlled).

616.6 ITA ISSN 0393-5590
➤ **GIORNALE ITALIANO DI NEFROLOGIA.** Text in Italian; Summaries in English. 1984. bi-m. EUR 179 in Europe to institutions; EUR 217 elsewhere to institutions (effective 2009). abstr.; bibl.; charts; illus. Index. 128 p./no.; back issues avail.; reprints avail. **Document type:** *Journal, Academic/Scholarly.*
Indexed: A22, EMBASE, ExcerpMed, Inpharma, MEDLINE, P30, R10, Reac, RefZh, SCOPUS.
—BLDSC (4178.233000), GNLM, IE, Infotrieve, Ingenta. **CCC.**
Published by: Wichtig Editore Srl, Via Friuli 72, Milan, MI 20135, Italy. TEL 39-02-55195443, FAX 39-02-55195971, info@wichtig-publisher.com. Ed. Giovanni Gambaro. Circ: 2,000 (controlled).

616.6 BRA
GLOSSARIUM UROLOGIA. Text in Portuguese. 2000. a. adv. illus. **Document type:** *Magazine, Trade.*
Published by: Elea Ciencia Editorial Ltda., Rua Barao de Uba 48, Rio de Janeiro, RJ 20260-050, Brazil. TEL 55-21-2932112, FAX 55-21-2937818. Ed., Pub. Luiz Augusto Rodrigues. R&P, Adv. contact Alexandre Augusto Rodrigues. color page BRL 4,375; trim 15 x 21. Circ: 3,000.

616.6 CHN ISSN 1001-4594
GUOWAI YIXUE (MINIAO XITONG FENCE)/FOREIGN MEDICAL SCIENCES (UROLOGIC SYSTEM). Text in English. bi-m. CNY 60 domestic; USD 25.20 foreign (effective 2005). **Document type:** *Journal, Academic/Scholarly.*
Related titles: Online - full text ed.
—East View.
Published by: Zhonghua Yixuehui, Hunan Fenhui, 30, Xiangya Lu, Changsha, 410008, China. TEL 86-731-4472665, FAX 86-731-4822023. **Dist. by:** China International Book Trading Corp, 35 Chegongzhuang Xilu, Haidian District, PO Box 399, Beijing 100044, China. TEL 86-10-68412045, FAX 86-10-68412023, cibtc@mail.cibtc.com.cn, http://www.cibtc.com.cn.

616.6 DEU ISSN 0935-8234
HAEUSLICHE PFLEGE; Organisieren - Betreuen - Kompetent beraten. Text in German. 1992. m. EUR 98 (effective 2010). adv. **Document type:** *Journal, Trade.*
—GNLM.
Published by: Vincentz Verlag, Plathnerstr 4c, Hannover, 30175, Germany. TEL 49-511-9910000, FAX 49-511-9910099, info@vincentz.de, http://www.vincentz.de. Ed. Stefan Neumann. adv.: B&W page EUR 1,430, color page EUR 2,510. Circ: 7,321 (paid and controlled).

616.6 JPN ISSN 0919-5750
HAINYO SHOGAI PURAKUTISU. Text in Japanese. q. JPY 7,240 (effective 2005). **Document type:** *Journal, Academic/Scholarly.*
Published by: Medikaru Rebyusha/Medical Review Co., Ltd., 1-7-3 Hirano-Machi, Chuo-ku, Yoshida Bldg., Osaka-shi, 541-0046, Japan. TEL 81-6-62231468, FAX 81-6-62231245.

616.6 USA ISSN 1935-164X
RC899
HARVARD MEDICAL SCHOOL PERSPECTIVES ON PROSTATE DISEASE. Text in English. 2007. q. USD 99 combined subscription (print & online eds.) (effective 2009). back issues avail. **Document type:** *Journal, Academic/Scholarly.* **Description:** Provides information on how best to treat prostate disease, including prostate cancer, benign prostatic hyperplasia, and prostatitis, as well as erectile dysfunction and low testosterone levels.
Related titles: Online - full text ed.: USD 89 (effective 2009).
Published by: Harvard Health Publications Group (Subsidiary of: Harvard Medical School), 10 Shattuck St, Ste 612, Boston, MA 02115. TEL 877-649-9457, hhp@hms.harvard.edu, http://www.health.harvard.edu. Eds. Suzanne Rose, Anthony L Komaroff, Marc B Garnick.

616.6 JPN ISSN 0914-6180
HINYOKI GEKA/JAPANESE JOURNAL OF UROLOGICAL SURGERY. Text in Japanese. 1988. m. JPY 2.83 newsstand/cover (effective 2007). **Document type:** *Journal, Academic/Scholarly.*
Published by: Igaku Tosho Shuppan Co. Ltd., Tohgane Bldg, 2-28-1 Hongo, Bunkyo-ku, Tokyo, 113-0033, Japan. TEL 81-3-38118210, FAX 81-3-38118236, info@igakutosho.co.jp, http://www.igakutosho.co.jp/.

616.6 JPN ISSN 0018-1994
CODEN: HIKYAJ
HINYOKIKA KIYO/ACTA UROLOGICA JAPONICA. Text in Japanese; Summaries in English. 1955. m. JPY 10,000 (effective 2007). adv. Index. **Document type:** *Journal, Academic/Scholarly.*
Indexed: A22, EMBASE, ExcerpMed, G10, INIS AtomInd, IndMed, Inpharma, MEDLINE, MycolAb, P30, R10, Reac, RefZh, SCOPUS.
—BLDSC (0670.420000), GNLM, IE, Infotrieve, Ingenta, INIST.
Address: Metabo-Okazaki 301, 18, Sannoh-Cho, Shogo-in, Sakyo-ku, Kyoto, 606-8392, Japan. TEL 81-75-7520100, FAX 81-75-7520190. Ed. Osamu Ogawa. Circ: 2,500.

616.6 JPN ISSN 1349-6549
HINYOUKI KEA. Text in Japanese. 1996. m. JPY 20,412; JPY 1,890 newsstand/cover (effective 2007). Supplement avail. **Document type:** *Journal, Academic/Scholarly.*
Formerly (until 2004): Urological Nursing/Uro, Nashingu (1341-8920)
Published by: Medicus Shuppan/Medicus Publishing Inc., 18-24 Hiroshiba-cho, Suita-shi, Osaka-fu 564-8580, Japan. TEL 81-6-63856911, FAX 81-6-63856873, http://www.medica.co.jp/.

HOKKAIDO TOSEKI RYOHO GAKKAI PUROGURAMU ENDAI SHOROKU/HOKKAIDO SOCIETY FOR DIALYSIS THERAPY. PROGRAM AND ABSTRACTS. *see* MEDICAL SCIENCES—Abstracting, Bibliographies, Statistics

616.6 JPN
HOKKAIDO TOSEKI RYOHO GAKKAI SHINPOJUMU/HOKKAIDO SOCIETY FOR DIALYSIS THERAPY. PROCEEDINGS OF SYMPOSIUM. Text in Japanese. 1988. a. **Document type:** *Proceedings, Academic/Scholarly.*
Published by: Hokkaido Toseki Ryoho Gakkai/Hokkaido Society for Dialysis Therapy, 3, Nishi 7-chome, Kita 1-jo, Chuo-ku, Sapporo, Hokkaido 060-0001, Japan. jimu@dotoseki.net, http://www.dotoseki.net/.

616.6 HKG ISSN 1561-5413
RC902.A1
➤ **HONG KONG JOURNAL OF NEPHROLOGY.** Text in English. biennial. EUR 149 in Europe to institutions; JPY 23,600 in Japan to institutions; USD 189 elsewhere to institutions (effective 2012). **Document type:** *Journal, Academic/Scholarly.* **Description:** Promotes research in the field of nephrology and a forum for the discussion of key issues in nephrology for Hong Kong and Southeast Asia. Also serves as a source of communication between nephrologists of Hong Kong and China and the international community.
Related titles: Online - full text ed.: ISSN 1876-4371 (from ScienceDirect).
Indexed: A36, B21, CA, CABA, CTA, E12, EMBASE, ExcerpMed, GH, H17, N02, N03, P33, R10, R12, RA&MP, RM&VM, Reac, SCOPUS, T02, T05, VS.
—BLDSC (4326.385750), IE. **CCC.**
Published by: (Hong Kong Society of Nephrology USA), Elsevier (Singapore) Pte Ltd, Hong Kong Branch (Subsidiary of: Elsevier Health Sciences), 1601, 16/F, Leighton Centre, 77 Leighton Rd., Causeway Bay, Hong Kong. TEL 852-2965-1300, FAX 852-2976-0778, asiajournals@elsevier.com, http://asia.elsevierhealth.com/. Ed. Alex WY Yu.

616.6 USA
I C A UPDATE (ROCKVILLE). Text in English. 1984. q. USD 45 domestic membership; USD 60 foreign membership (effective 2007). **Document type:** *Newsletter.* **Description:** Creates public awareness and provides information about IC research and ICA activities to patients and the medical community.
Published by: Interstitial Cystitis Association, 110 N Washington St, Ste 340, Rockville, MD 20850. TEL 301-610-5300, FAX 301-610-3508, icamail@ichelp.org, http://www.ichelp.org/.

616.6 USA ISSN 2090-5807
▼ ➤ **I S R N UROLOGY.** (International Scholarly Research Network) Text in English. 2011. **Document type:** *Journal, Academic/Scholarly.* **Description:** Publishes original research articles, review articles, and clinical studies in all areas of urology.
Related titles: Online - full text ed.: ISSN 2090-5815. 2011. free (effective 2011).
Published by: Hindawi Publishing Corporation, 410 Park Ave, 15th Fl, PMB 287, New York, NY 10022. FAX 215-893-4392, 866-446-3294, info@hindawi.com.

616.6 USA ISSN 1531-670X
INCONTINENCE PRODUCT SOURCEBOOK. Text in English. 2000. q.
Published by: Kestrel Health Information, Inc., 206 Commerce St, PO Box 189, Hinesburg, VT 05461. TEL 802-482-4000, FAX 802-329-2077, http://www.kestrelhealthinfo.com/. Ed. Catherine Milne. Pub. Jeanne Cunningham TEL 802-482-4000 ext 224.

616.6 ESP ISSN 1888-2633
INCONTINENCIA URINARIA DE IMPACTO. Text in Spanish. 2008. q. **Document type:** *Journal, Trade.*
Published by: Luzan 5 S.A. de Ediciones, Pasaje Virgen de la Alegria 14, Madrid, 28027, Spain. TEL 34-91-4057260, FAX 34-91-4034907, luzan@luzan5.es, http://www.luzan5.es.

616.61 IND ISSN 0971-4065
➤ **INDIAN JOURNAL OF NEPHROLOGY.** Abbreviated title: A J N. Text in English. 1985. q. INR 1,200 domestic; USD 100 foreign to individuals; USD 150 foreign to institutions; INR 1,500 combined subscription domestic; USD 120 combined subscription foreign to individuals; USD 180 combined subscription foreign to institutions (effective 2011). adv. **Document type:** *Journal, Academic/Scholarly.* **Description:** Publishes articles covering all the aspects of laboratory and clinical nephrology. It includes original researches, reviews, editorials, technical notes, symposia proceedings, and Society news.
Related titles: Online - full content ed.: ISSN 1998-3662. free (effective 2011).
Indexed: A01, A26, A34, A36, C06, C07, CA, CABA, EMBASE, ExcerpMed, GH, H12, H17, I05, IndVet, N02, N03, P10, P30, P33, P48, P53, P54, PQC, R08, R10, R11, RA&MP, RM&VM, Reac, SCOPUS, T02, T05, VS.
—IE.
Published by: (Indian Society of Nephrology), Medknow Publications and Media Pvt. Ltd., B-9, Kanara Business Ctr, Off Link Rd, Ghatkopar (E), Mumbai, Maharastra 400 075, India. TEL 91-22-66491816, FAX 91-22-66491817, http://www.medknow.com. Ed. Vinay Sakhuja TEL 91-172-2756731.

616.6 IND ISSN 0970-1591
RC870
➤ **INDIAN JOURNAL OF UROLOGY.** Text in English. 1984. q. INR 1,800 domestic to individuals; USD 150 foreign to individuals; INR 2,400 domestic to institutions; USD 250 foreign to institutions; INR 2,200 combined subscription domestic to individuals (print & online eds.); USD 180 combined subscription foreign to individuals (print & online eds.); INR 2,900 combined subscription domestic to institutions (print & online eds.); USD 300 combined subscription foreign to institutions (print & online eds.) (effective 2011). adv. bk.rev. abstr. reprints avail. **Document type:** *Journal, Academic/Scholarly.* **Description:** Covers urology including oncology, sexual dysfunction, incontinence, endourology, trauma and reconstructive surgery, andrology, transplantation, imaging, pathology. Audience include: Urologists, general surgeons, pediatric surgeons.
Related titles: Online - full text ed.: ISSN 1998-3824. 2005. INR 1,500 domestic to individuals; USD 120 foreign to individuals; INR 2,000 domestic to institutions; USD 200 foreign to institutions (effective 2011).
Indexed: A26, A34, A36, A37, C06, C07, CA, CABA, E08, E12, EMBASE, ExcerpMed, F08, G08, GH, H11, H12, H16, H17, I05, LT, N02, N03, P10, P30, P33, P48, P53, P54, PHN&I, PN&I, PQC, R08, R10, R12, RA&MP, RM&VM, RRTA, Reac, S09, SCOPUS, T02, T05, VS.
—BLDSC (4421.750000), IE, Ingenta. **CCC.**
Published by: (Urological Society of India), Medknow Publications and Media Pvt. Ltd., B-9, Kanara Business Ctr, Off Link Rd, Ghatkopar (E), Mumbai, Maharastra 400 075, India. TEL 91-22-66491816, FAX 91-22-66491817, http://www.medknow.com. Ed. Nitin S Kekre.

616.6 CAN ISSN 1910-8370
INSTRUCTION MANUAL. CHRONIC RENAL FAILURE PATIENTS ON RENAL REPLACEMENT THERAPY (ONLINE). Text in English. 2002. a. **Document type:** *Handbook/Manual/Guide, Consumer.*
Media: Online - full text. **Related titles:** ◆ Print ed.: Instruction Manual. Chronic Renal Failure Patients on Renal Replacement Therapy (Print). ISSN 1498-8100; French ed.: Manuel d'Instructions, Patients en Traitement pour l'Insuffisance Renale Chronique. ISSN 1910-8397.
Published by: Canadian Institute for Health Information/Institut Canadien d'Information sur la Sante, 377 Dalhousie St, Ste 200, Ottawa, ON K1N 9N8, Canada. TEL 613-241-7860, FAX 613-241-8120, nursing@cihi.ca, http://www.cihi.ca.

616.6 CAN ISSN 1498-8100
INSTRUCTION MANUAL. CHRONIC RENAL FAILURE PATIENTS ON RENAL REPLACEMENT THERAPY (PRINT). Text in English. 2001. a. **Document type:** *Handbook/Manual/Guide, Consumer.*
Related titles: ◆ Online - full text ed.: Instruction Manual. Chronic Renal Failure Patients on Renal Replacement Therapy (Online). ISSN 1910-8370; French ed.: Manuel d'Instructions, Patients en Traitement pour l'Insuffisance Renale Chronique. ISSN 1702-8701.
Published by: (Canadian Institute for Health Information, Canadian Organ Replacement Register), Canadian Institute for Health Information/Institut Canadien d'Information sur la Sante, 377 Dalhousie St, Ste 200, Ottawa, ON K1N 9N8, Canada. TEL 613-241-7860, FAX 613-241-8120, nursing@cihi.ca, http://www.cihi.ca.

616.6 BRA ISSN 1677-5538
RC870
➤ **INTERNATIONAL BRAZILIAN JOURNAL OF UROLOGY.** Text in English. 2000. bi-m. **Document type:** *Journal, Academic/Scholarly.*
Formerly (until 2002): Brazilian Journal of Urology (1517-6878)
Related titles: Online - full text ed.: ISSN 1677-6119. 2000. free (effective 2011); Portuguese ed.: Jornal Brasileiro de Urologia. ISSN 0100-0519. 1975.
Indexed: CurCont, EMBASE, ExcerpMed, MEDLINE, P30, R10, Reac, SCI, SCOPUS, W07.
—BLDSC (4537.518000).
Published by: Sociedade Brasileira de Urologia/Brazilian Society of Urology, Rua Bambina 153, Botafogo, Rio de Janeiro, 22251-050, Brazil. TEL 55-21-22464092, FAX 55-21-22464194. Ed. Dr. Francisco Sampaio. Circ: 6,000 (paid).

616.65 GBR ISSN 0105-6263
QP253 CODEN: IJANDP
➤ **INTERNATIONAL JOURNAL OF ANDROLOGY.** Abbreviated title: I J A. Text in English. 1978. bi-m. GBP 612 in United Kingdom to institutions; EUR 915 in Europe to institutions; USD 1,129 in the Americas to institutions; USD 1,321 elsewhere to institutions; GBP 704 combined subscription in United Kingdom to institutions (print & online eds.); EUR 1,053 combined subscription in Europe to institutions (print & online eds.); USD 1,299 combined subscription in the Americas to institutions (print & online eds.); USD 1,519 combined subscription elsewhere to institutions (print & online eds.) (effective 2012). adv. bk.rev. abstr.; bibl.; illus. index. back issues avail.; reprint service avail. from PSC. **Document type:** *Journal, Academic/Scholarly.* **Description:** Aims to promote and integrate basic and clinical research in andrology and to publish new ideas and exciting advances in the field.

Related titles: Microform ed.: (from PQC); Online - full text ed.: ISSN 1365-2605. GBP 612 in United Kingdom to institutions; EUR 915 in Europe to institutions; USD 1,129 in the Americas to institutions; USD 1,321 elsewhere to institutions (effective 2012) (from IngentaConnect); ◆ Supplement(s): International Journal of Andrology. Supplement. ISSN 0106-1607.
Indexed: A01, A02, A03, A08, A22, A26, A34, A35, A36, A38, ASCA, AgBio, Agr, B25, BIOBASE, BIOSIS Prev, C11, CA, CABA, CIN, ChemAb, ChemTitl, CurCont, D01, DentInd, E01, E12, EMBASE, ExcerpMed, Faml, G10, GH, H04, H12, H16, IABS, ISR, IndMed, IndVet, Inpharma, MEDLINE, MycolAb, N02, N03, P30, P32, P33, P35, PGrRegA, PN&I, R07, R08, R10, R13, RA&MP, RM&VM, Reac, SAA, SCI, SCOPUS, SoyAb, T02, T05, THA, VS, W07, W10.
—BLDSC (4542.080000), CASDDS, GNLM, IE, Infotrieve, Ingenta, INIST. **CCC.**
Published by: (European Academy of Andrology), Wiley-Blackwell Publishing Ltd. (Subsidiary of: John Wiley & Sons, Inc.), 9600 Garsington Rd, Oxford, OX4 2DQ, United Kingdom. TEL 44-1865-776868, FAX 44-1865-714591, customerservices@blackwellpublishing.com. Ed. Ewa Rajpert-De Meyts.

616.65 GBR ISSN 0106-1607
CODEN: IJSPDJ
INTERNATIONAL JOURNAL OF ANDROLOGY. SUPPLEMENT. Text in English. 1978. irreg. includes with subscr. to International Journal of Andrology. adv. illus. reprints avail. **Document type:** *Journal, Academic/Scholarly.*
Related titles: Online - full text ed.; ◆ Supplement to: International Journal of Andrology. ISSN 0105-6263.
Indexed: ChemAb, SCOPUS.
—CASDDS, INIST.
Published by: Wiley-Blackwell Publishing Ltd. (Subsidiary of: John Wiley & Sons, Inc.), 9600 Garsington Rd, Oxford, OX4 2DQ, United Kingdom. TEL 44-1865-776868, FAX 44-1865-714591, customerservices@blackwellpublishing.com, http://www.wiley.com/.

616.6 GBR ISSN 0955-9930
RC889 CODEN: IJIRFB
➤ **INTERNATIONAL JOURNAL OF IMPOTENCE RESEARCH;** the journal of sexual medicine. Abbreviated title: I J I R. Text in English. 1989. bi-m. EUR 978 in Europe to institutions; USD 1,229 in the Americas to institutions; JPY 167,100 in Japan to institutions; GBP 632 to institutions in the UK & elsewhere (effective 2011). adv. charts; illus.; stat. back issues avail.; reprints avail. **Document type:** *Journal, Academic/Scholarly.* **Description:** Addresses sexual medicine for both genders as an interdisciplinary field.
Related titles: Online - full text ed.: ISSN 1476-5489. 1997.
Indexed: A01, A02, A03, A08, A22, A26, ASG, CA, CurCont, E01, EMBASE, ExcerpMed, G10, H12, I05, ISR, IndMed, Inpharma, MEDLINE, P20, P22, P30, P35, P48, P54, PQC, R10, Reac, SCI, SCOPUS, T02, W07.
—BLDSC (4542.302700), GNLM, IE, Infotrieve, Ingenta, INIST. **CCC.**
Published by: Nature Publishing Group (Subsidiary of: Macmillan Publishers Ltd.), The MacMillan Bldg, 4 Crinan St, London, N1 9XW, United Kingdom. TEL 44-20-78334000, FAX 44-20-78334640. Ed. Nestor F Gonzalez-Cadavid. Adv. contact Ben Harkinson TEL 617-475-9222. **Subscr. to:** Brunel Rd, Houndmills, Basingstoke, Hamps RG21 6XS, United Kingdom. TEL 44-1256-329242, FAX 44-1256-812358, subscriptions@nature.com.

616.6 USA ISSN 2090-2158
▼ ➤ **INTERNATIONAL JOURNAL OF NEPHROLOGY.** Text in English. 2010. irreg. free (effective 2011). **Document type:** *Journal, Academic/Scholarly.*
Media: Online - full text.
Indexed: A01, P30, T02.
Published by: Sage - Hindawi Access to Research, 410 Park Ave, 15th Fl, 287 PMB, New York, NY 10022. FAX 866-446-3294.

616.6 GBR ISSN 1178-7058
➤ **INTERNATIONAL JOURNAL OF NEPHROLOGY AND RENOVASCULAR DISEASE.** Text in English. 2008. irreg. free (effective 2011). **Document type:** *Journal, Academic/Scholarly.* **Description:** Focuses on the pathophysiology of the kidney and vascular supply.
Media: Online - full text.
Indexed: EMBASE, SCOPUS.
—**CCC.**
Published by: Dove Medical Press Ltd., Beechfield House, Winterton Way, Macclesfield, SK11 0JL, United Kingdom. TEL 44-1625-509130, FAX 44-1625-617933. Ed. Pravin C Singhal.

➤ **INTERNATIONAL JOURNAL OF UROLOGICAL NURSING.** *see* MEDICAL SCIENCES—Nurses And Nursing

616.6 AUS ISSN 0919-8172
RC870 CODEN: IJURF3
➤ **INTERNATIONAL JOURNAL OF UROLOGY.** Text in English. 1994. m. (3 combined). GBP 869 in United Kingdom to institutions; EUR 1,103 in Europe to institutions; USD 1,407 in the Americas to institutions; USD 1,701 elsewhere to institutions; GBP 1,000 combined subscription in United Kingdom to institutions (print & online eds.); EUR 1,269 combined subscription in Europe to institutions (print & online eds.); USD 1,619 combined subscription in the Americas to institutions (print & online eds.); USD 1,957 combined subscription elsewhere to institutions (print & online eds.) (effective 2012). back issues avail.; reprint service avail. from PSC. **Document type:** *Journal, Academic/Scholarly.* **Description:** Covers the latest clinical and experimental developments in the field of urology.
Related titles: Online - full text ed.: ISSN 1442-2042. 1999. GBP 869 in United Kingdom to institutions; EUR 1,103 in Europe to institutions; USD 1,407 in the Americas to institutions; USD 1,701 elsewhere to institutions (effective 2012) (from IngentaConnect).
Indexed: A01, A02, A03, A08, A22, A26, B21, BIOBASE, C11, CA, CTA, CurCont, E01, EMBASE, ExcerpMed, G10, H04, H12, IABS, INIS AtomInd, IndMed, Inpharma, MEDLINE, P30, P35, R10, Reac, SCI, SCOPUS, T02, W07.
—BLDSC (4542.697100), GNLM, IE, Infotrieve, Ingenta, INIST. **CCC.**
Published by: (Japanese Urological Association/Shadan Hojin, Nihon Hinyokika Gakkai JPN), Wiley-Blackwell Publishing Asia (Subsidiary of: Wiley-Blackwell Publishing Ltd.), 155 Cremorne St, Richmond, VIC 3121, Australia. TEL 61-3-92743100, FAX 61-3-92743101, subs@blackwellpublishingasia.com, http://www.wiley.com/WileyCDA/. Ed. Dr. Akihiko Okuyama. Circ: 4,027 (paid).

616.6 GRC
➤ **INTERNATIONAL SATELLITE SYMPOSIUM ON ACUTE RENAL FAILURE. PROCEEDINGS.** Text in Greek. 1960. biennial. price varies. **Document type:** *Proceedings, Academic/Scholarly.*
Formerly: International Congress of Nephrology. Abstracts of Reports and Communications (0074-3771)
Indexed: ChemAb.
Published by: International Society of Nephrology, Commission on Acute Renal Failure, Hippokration General Hospital, 50 Papanastasiou St, Thessaloniki, 543 42, Greece. TEL 30-31-835955, FAX 30-31-861111. Ed. Menelaos Papadimitriou. **Co-sponsors:** Aristotelian University; Hellenic Society of Nephrology.

➤ **INTERNATIONAL UROGYNECOLOGY JOURNAL;** and pelvic floor dysfunction. *see* MEDICAL SCIENCES—Obstetrics And Gynecology

616.6 NLD ISSN 0301-1623
RC902.A1 CODEN: IURNAE
➤ **INTERNATIONAL UROLOGY AND NEPHROLOGY.** Text in English. 1969. q. EUR 1,169, USD 1,186 combined subscription to institutions (print & online eds.) (effective 2012). adv. bk.rev. back issues avail.; reprint service avail. from PSC. **Document type:** *Journal, Academic/Scholarly.* **Description:** Publishes original papers, preliminary reports and reviews which contribute to progress in urological surgery, nephrology and andrology.
Incorporates (1991-2000): Geriatric Nephrology and Urology (0924-8455); Formerly (until 1970): Urology and Nephrology (0042-1162)
Related titles: Online - full text ed.: ISSN 1573-2584 (from IngentaConnect).
Indexed: A22, A26, B21, B25, BIOSIS Prev, BibLing, CTA, ChemAb, CurCont, E01, EMBASE, ExcerpMed, G10, IndMed, MEDLINE, MycolAb, P20, P22, P30, P48, P54, PQC, R10, Reac, SCI, SCOPUS, W07.
—BLDSC (4551.568000), CASDDS, GNLM, IE, Infotrieve, Ingenta, INIST. **CCC.**
Published by: Springer Netherlands (Subsidiary of: Springer Science+Business Media), Van Godewijckstraat 30, Dordrecht, 3311 GX, Netherlands. TEL 31-78-6576050, FAX 31-78-6576474, http://www.springer.com. Ed. Dimitrios G Oreopoulos.

616.6 DEU
RC902.A1
INTERNATIONAL YEARBOOK OF NEPHROLOGY DIALYSIS TRANSPLANTATION. Text in English. 1989. irreg. price varies. back issues avail. **Document type:** *Journal, Academic/Scholarly.*
Formerly (until 1994): International Yearbook of Nephrology (0921-9862)
Indexed: ASCA, ISR.
—BLDSC (4552.334000), GNLM. **CCC.**
Published by: Springer (Subsidiary of: Springer Science+Business Media), Tiergartenstr 17, Heidelberg, 69121, Germany. TEL 49-6221-4870, FAX 49-6221-345229, subscriptions@springer.com, http://www.springer.com. **Subscr. in N. America to:** Springer New York LLC, Journal Fulfillment, PO Box 2485, Secaucus, NJ 07096. TEL 201-348-4033, FAX 201-348-4505.

616.61 USA ISSN 1540-2665
RC1
➤ **THE INTERNET JOURNAL OF NEPHROLOGY.** Text in English. 2003. s-a. free (effective 2011). adv. **Document type:** *Journal, Academic/Scholarly.*
Media: Online - full text.
Indexed: A01, A02, A03, A08, A26, C06, C07, C08, CA, CINAHL, G08, H11, H12, I05, P30, RefZh, T02.
Published by: Internet Scientific Publications, Llc., 23 Rippling Creek Dr, Sugar Land, TX 77479. TEL 832-443-1193, FAX 281-240-1533, wenker@ispub.com. Ed. Edgar V Lerma.

616.6 USA ISSN 1528-8390
RC870
➤ **THE INTERNET JOURNAL OF UROLOGY.** Text in English. 2002. s-a. free (effective 2011). adv. bk.rev. back issues avail. **Document type:** *Journal, Academic/Scholarly.* **Description:** Provides information from the field of urology; contains original articles, reviews, case reports, streaming slide shows, streaming videos, letters to the editor, press releases and meeting information.
Media: Online - full text.
Indexed: A01, A02, A03, A08, A26, C06, C07, CA, G08, H11, H12, I05, T02.
Published by: Internet Scientific Publications, Llc., 23 Rippling Creek Dr, Sugar Land, TX 77479. TEL 832-443-1193, FAX 281-240-1533, wenker@ispub.com. Ed. Dr. Ganesh Gopalakrishnan.

616.6 IRN ISSN 1735-8582
➤ **IRANIAN JOURNAL OF KIDNEY DISEASES.** Text in English. 2007. q. **Document type:** *Journal, Academic/Scholarly.* **Description:** Its objective is to serve as a focal point for debates and exchange of knowledge and experience among researchers in the field of nephrology.
Related titles: Online - full text ed.: ISSN 1735-8604. free (effective 2011).
Indexed: A01, A35, A36, B21, C06, C07, CA, CABA, D01, E12, EMBASE, ExcerpMed, GH, H16, ImmunAb, LT, MEDLINE, N02, N03, P20, P22, P30, P33, P48, P54, PQC, R12, RM&VM, RRTA, SCOPUS, T02, T05, VS.
—IE.
Published by: Iranian Society of Nephrology, Unit 12, no 77, Shahid Tousi St, Dr Gharib St, Keshavarz Blvd, Tehran, 1419783311, Iran. Ed. Mohsen Nafar.

616.6 JPN ISSN 0914-5265
JIN TO KOTSU TAISHA/KIDNEY AND METABOLIC BONE DISEASES. Text in Japanese. 1988. q. JPY 11,900 (effective 2007). **Document type:** *Journal, Academic/Scholarly.*
Published by: Nihon Medikaru Senta/Nihon Medical Center, Inc., Kyowa Bldg., 1-64, Kanda-jinbo-cho, Chiyoda-ku, Tokyo, 101-0051, Japan. TEL 81-3-32913901, FAX 81-3-32913377, http://www.nmckk.co.jp/.

JIN TO TOSEKI/KIDNEY AND DIALYSIS. *see* MEDICAL SCIENCES

616.6 JPN ISSN 0912-0319
JINFUZEN O IKIRU/DIALYSIS AND TRANSPLANT. Text in Japanese. 1974. s-a. JPY 1,000 to individuals for membership; JPY 25,000 to institutions for membership; JPY 50,000 to corporations for membership (effective 2006). **Document type:** *Journal, Academic/Scholarly.*
Published by: Jin Kenkyukai Nihon Jinzou Zaidan./Kidney Foundation, Japan, Iidabashi Delta Bldg. 2F, 2-1-11, Koraku, Bunkyo-ku, Tokyo, 112-0004, Japan. TEL 81-3-38152989, FAX 81-3-38154988.

616.6 JPN ISSN 0911-9752
JINZO/KIDNEY. Text in Japanese. 1978. 3/yr. JPY 10,000 to individuals for membership; JPY 25,000 to institutions for membership; JPY 50,000 to corporations for membership (effective 2006). **Document type:** *Journal, Academic/Scholarly.*
Published by: Jin Kenkyukai Nihon Jinzou Zaidan./Kidney Foundation, Japan, Iidabashi Delta Bldg. 2F, 2-1-11, Koraku, Bunkyo-ku, Tokyo, 112-0004, Japan. TEL 81-3-38152989, FAX 81-3-38154988. Circ: 1,200.

M

616.6 BRA ISSN 0101-2800
CODEN: JBNEDI
JORNAL BRASILEIRO DE NEFROLOGIA. Text in Portuguese, English. 197?. irreg. **Document type:** *Journal, Academic/Scholarly.*
Related titles: Online - full text ed.: ISSN 2175-8239. free (effective 2011).
Indexed: MEDLINE, P30.
Published by: Sociedade Brasileira de Nefrologia, Rua Machado Bittencourt 205, Conj 53, Vila Clementino, Sao Paulo, 04044-000, Brazil. TEL 55-11-55791242, FAX 55-11-55736000, secret@sbn.org.br, http://www.sbn.org.br.

616.6 AUT ISSN 1023-6090
RC870 CODEN: JUURFN
➤ **JOURNAL FUER UROLOGIE UND UROGYNAEKOLOGIE;** Zeitschrift fuer Urologie und Urogynaekologie in Klinik und Praxis. Text in German. 1994. q. EUR 36; EUR 10 newsstand/cover (effective 2005). adv. abstr.; bibl. 32 p./no. 3 cols./p.; back issues avail. **Document type:** *Journal, Academic/Scholarly.* **Description:** Contains research articles on various aspects of urology.
Related titles: Online - full text ed.: ISSN 1680-9424. 2001. free (effective 2011); International ed.: Journal fuer Urologie und Urogynaekologie. Ausgabe Schweiz. ISSN 1607-8071. 1999.
Indexed: SCOPUS.
—BLDSC (5071.875000). **CCC.**
Published by: Krause & Pachernegg GmbH, Mozartgasse 10, Gablitz, 3003, Austria. TEL 43-2231-612580, FAX 43-2231-612510, k_u_p@eunet.at, http://www.kup.at/verlag.htm. Ed. Dr. Franz Fischl. Circ: 1,800 (paid).

➤ **JOURNAL OF ANDROLOGY.** *see* MEDICAL SCIENCES

616.6 USA ISSN 0892-7790
RD572 CODEN: JENDE3
➤ **JOURNAL OF ENDOUROLOGY.** Variant title: Journal of Endourology and Part B, Videourology. (Part A is print issues; Part B: Video Urology is online only.) Text in English. 1987. 18/yr. USD 2,133 domestic to institutions; USD 2,629 foreign to institutions; USD 2,493 combined subscription domestic to institutions (print & online eds.); USD 3,066 combined subscription foreign to institutions (print & online eds.) (effective 2012). adv. reprint service avail. from PSC. **Document type:** *Journal, Academic/Scholarly.* **Description:** Covers invasive techniques and technologies in the diagnosis, treatment, and surgical management of urologic disease to ensure optimal patient care.
Related titles: Online - full text ed.: ISSN 1557-900X. USD 2,213 to institutions (effective 2012); ◆ Supplement(s): Videourology. ISSN 2151-1136.
Indexed: A01, A03, A08, A22, A26, ASCA, B25, BIOSIS Prev, CA, CurCont, E01, E07, EMBASE, ExcerpMed, H12, I05, ISR, IndMed, Inpharma, MEDLINE, MycolAb, P30, P35, R10, Reac, SCI, SCOPUS, T02, W07.
—BLDSC (4978.210000), GNLM, IE, Infotrieve, Ingenta, INIST. **CCC.**
Published by: (Endourological Society), Mary Ann Liebert, Inc. Publishers, 140 Huguenot St, 3rd Fl, New Rochelle, NY 10801. TEL 914-740-2100, FAX 914-740-2101, 800-654-3237, info@liebertpub.com. Eds. Arthur D Smith TEL 718-470-3900, Ralph V Clayman TEL 714-456-3329.

➤ **JOURNAL OF LOWER GENITAL TRACT DISEASE.** *see* MEDICAL SCIENCES—Obstetrics And Gynecology

616.6 ITA ISSN 1121-8428
➤ **JOURNAL OF NEPHROLOGY.** Text in English. 1988. bi-m. EUR 359 in Europe to institutions (print & online eds.); EUR 397 elsewhere to institutions (print & online eds.) (effective 2009). adv. abstr.; bibl.; charts; illus. Index. 64 p./no.; back issues avail.; reprints avail. **Document type:** *Journal, Academic/Scholarly.* **Description:** Publishes original manuscripts dealing with both clinical and laboratory investigations of relevance to the broad fields of nephrology, dialysis and transplantation.
Formerly (until 1992): Journal of Nephrology (1120-3625)
Related titles: Online - full text ed.: ISSN 1724-6059.
Indexed: A20, A36, ASCA, B25, BIOSIS Prev, CABA, CurCont, E12, EMBASE, ExcerpMed, GH, H17, IndMed, Inpharma, Kidney, LT, MEDLINE, MycolAb, N02, N03, P30, P33, P35, P39, R10, RA&MP, RM&VM, Reac, RefZh, S13, S16, S17, SCI, SCOPUS, T05, VS, W07, W11.
—BLDSC (5021.399400), GNLM, IE, Infotrieve, Ingenta. **CCC.**
Published by: Wichtig Editore Srl, Via Friuli 72, Milan, MI 20135, Italy. TEL 39-02-55195443, FAX 39-02-55195971, info@wichtig-publisher.com, http://www.wichtig-publisher.com. Ed. Francesca Mallamaci. Circ: 2,000 (paid); 2,600 (controlled).

616.6 CAN ISSN 1918-025X
JOURNAL OF NEPHROLOGY AND RENAL TRANSPLANTATION. Text in English. 2008. q. **Document type:** *Journal, Academic/Scholarly.*
Related titles: Online - full text ed.: ISSN 1918-0268. free (effective 2011).
Published by: OminiScientia, No 510, 780 Montgomery St, Fredericton, NB E3B 2Y1, Canada. Ed. Ali Ghafari.

616.6 360 USA ISSN 1532-0863
HV687.A2
JOURNAL OF NEPHROLOGY SOCIAL WORK. Abbreviated title: J N S W. Text in English. 1977. a. free to members (effective 2011). **Document type:** *Journal, Academic/Scholarly.* **Description:** Provides the nephrology social work community with a scholarly resource that can be used to inform clinical practice, advance policy and advocacy efforts, and enhance patient care.
Formerly (until 1996): National Kidney Foundation. Council of Nephrology Social Workers. Perspectives
Related titles: Online - full text ed.
Indexed: CA, S02, S03, SCOPUS, SSA, SWR&A, T02.
Published by: National Kidney Foundation, Council of Nephrology Social Workers, 30 E 33rd St, New York, NY 10016. TEL 800-622-9010, http://www.kidney.org/professionals/CNSW/.

616.6 PAK ISSN 1606-9331
JOURNAL OF NEPHROLOGY, UROLOGY, AND TRANSPLANTATION. Text in English. 2000. q.
Indexed: R10, Reac, SCOPUS.
Published by: Sindh Institute of Urology and Transplantation, Dow Medical College, Karachi, 74200, Pakistan. TEL 92-21-9215718, FAX 92-21-9215469, info@siut.org, http://www.siut.org/.

616.6 NLD ISSN 1477-5131
RJ466
➤ **JOURNAL OF PEDIATRIC UROLOGY.** Text in English. 2004. 6/yr. EUR 488 in Europe to institutions; JPY 64,900 in Japan to institutions; USD 546 elsewhere to institutions (effective 2012). **Document type:** *Journal, Academic/Scholarly.* **Description:** Aims to advance and improve the education in pediatric urology and the diffusion of knowledge of new and improved methods of teaching and practising pediatric urology in all its branches.
Related titles: Online - full text ed.: ISSN 1873-4898 (from ScienceDirect).
Indexed: A26, CA, CurCont, EMBASE, ExcerpMed, I05, MEDLINE, P30, R10, Reac, SCI, SCOPUS, T02, W07.
—IE, Ingenta. **CCC.**
Published by: Elsevier BV (Subsidiary of: Elsevier Science & Technology), Radarweg 29, PO Box 211, Amsterdam, 1000 AE, Netherlands. TEL 31-20-4853911, FAX 31-20-4852457, JournalsCustomerServiceEMEA@elsevier.com, http://www.elsevier.nl. Ed. David Frank.

616.6 FRA ISSN 1755-6678
➤ **JOURNAL OF RENAL CARE.** Text in English. 1983. q. GBP 253 in United Kingdom to institutions; EUR 322 in Europe to institutions; USD 505 in the Americas to institutions; USD 546 elsewhere to institutions; GBP 291 combined subscription in United Kingdom to institutions (print & online eds.); EUR 370 combined subscription in Europe to institutions (print & online eds.); USD 581 combined subscription in the Americas to institutions (print & online eds.); USD 629 combined subscription elsewhere to institutions (print & online eds.) (effective 2012). bk.rev. back issues avail.; reprint service avail. from PSC. **Document type:** *Journal, Academic/Scholarly.* **Description:** Covers clinical, research, educational and profession oriented material for nephrology professionals.
Former titles (until 2007): E D T N A - E R C A Journal (1019-083X); (until 1985): E D T N A Journal (0265-3133)
Related titles: Online - full text ed.: ISSN 1755-6686. GBP 253 in United Kingdom to institutions; EUR 322 in Europe to institutions; USD 505 in the Americas to institutions; USD 546 elsewhere to institutions (effective 2012) (from IngentaConnect); French ed.; Greek ed.: 199?; Italian ed.; Spanish ed.; Dutch ed.; German ed.
Indexed: A22, B28, C06, C07, C08, CA, CINAHL, E01, EMBASE, ExcerpMed, INI, MEDLINE, P30, R10, Reac, SCOPUS, T02.
—BLDSC (3661.116725), IE, Infotrieve, Ingenta. **CCC.**
Published by: European Dialysis and Transplant Nurses Association, European Renal Care Association, 24 Rue Chauchat, Paris, 75009, France. TEL 33-1-53858269, FAX 33-1-53858283, info@edtnaerca.org, http://edtna-erca.org. Eds. Ray James, Cordelia Ashwanden. Circ: 4,000. **Subscr. to:** Wiley-Blackwell Publishing Ltd., Journal Customer Services, 9600 Garsington Rd, PO Box 1354, Oxford OX4 2XG, United Kingdom. TEL 44-1865-778315, FAX 44-1865-471775.

➤ **JOURNAL OF RENAL NUTRITION.** *see* NUTRITION AND DIETETICS

616.6 CAN ISSN 1488-5069
JOURNAL OF SEXUAL AND REPRODUCTIVE MEDICINE/JOURNAL DES MALADIES DE LA FONCTION SEXUELLE ET DE LA REPRODUCTION. Text in English. 2001. q. CAD 85 domestic to individuals; USD 85 in United States to individuals; USD 100 elsewhere to individuals; CAD 110 elsewhere to institutions; USD 110 in United States to institutions; USD 120 elsewhere to institutions (effective 2004). **Document type:** *Journal, Academic/Scholarly.*
—BLDSC (5064.045000).
Published by: Pulsus Group Inc., 2902 S Sheridan Way, Oakville, ON L6J 7L6, Canada. TEL 905-829-4770, FAX 905-829-4799, pulsus@pulsus.com. Ed. R W Casey.

616.6 USA ISSN 0022-5347
RC870 CODEN: JOURAA
➤ **THE JOURNAL OF UROLOGY.** Text in English. 1907. m. USD 928 in United States to institutions; USD 1,211 elsewhere to institutions (effective 2012). adv. abstr.; bibl.; illus. Index. back issues avail.; reprints avail. **Document type:** *Journal, Academic/Scholarly.* **Description:** Presents investigative studies on critical areas of research and practice, survey articles providing condensations of the important urology literature worldwide, and practice-oriented reports on significant clinical observations.
Incorporates (1963-1982): Investigation Urology (0021-0005); (1951-1982): Urological Survey (0042-1146); Formerly (until 1921): American Urological Association. Transactions (0894-0398)
Related titles: CD-ROM ed.; Online - full text ed.: ISSN 1527-3792. USD 663 domestic academic site license; USD 820 foreign academic site license; USD 739.50 domestic corporate site license; USD 896.50 foreign corporate site license (effective 2002) (from ScienceDirect); ◆ Spanish Translation: The Journal of Urology (Spanish Edition). ISSN 1133-8245; ◆ Regional ed(s).: The Journal of Urology (Italian Edition). ISSN 1828-6593; ◆ The Journal of Urology (Spanish Edition). ISSN 1133-8245.
Indexed: A20, A22, A26, A29, A34, A36, AIM, ASCA, B20, B21, B25, BIOBASE, BIOSIS Prev, CA, CABA, CIN, CISA, CTA, ChemAb, ChemTitl, CurCont, D01, DBA, E12, EMBASE, ESPM, ExcerpMed, F08, F11, F12, FR, G10, GH, I05, I10, IABS, IBR, IBZ, IDIS, INI, INIS AtomInd, ISR, IndMed, IndVet, Inpharma, Kidney, LT, MEDLINE, MS&D, MycolAb, N02, N03, NRN, P30, P32, P33, P35, P39, P40, PHN&I, R10, R12, RA&MP, RM&VM, RRTA, Reac, S12, SCI, SCOPUS, SoyAb, T02, T05, THA, TM, TriticAb, VS, VirolAbstr, W07, W11.
—BLDSC (5071.900000), CASDDS, GNLM, IE, Infotrieve, Ingenta, INIST. **CCC.**
Published by: (American Urological Association), Elsevier Inc. (Subsidiary of: Elsevier Science & Technology), 1600 John F Kennedy Blvd, Philadelphia, PA 19103. TEL 215-239-3900, FAX 215-238-7883, JournalCustomerService-usa@elsevier.com, http://www.elsevier.com. Ed. William D Steers. Pub. Linda Gruner TEL 212-633-3923. Adv. contact Brian Vishnupad TEL 212-633-3129. Circ: 14,710.

616.6 ITA ISSN 1828-6593
➤ **THE JOURNAL OF UROLOGY (ITALIAN EDITION).** Text in Multiple languages. 2006. q. **Document type:** *Journal, Academic/Scholarly.*
Related titles: ◆ Regional ed(s).: The Journal of Urology. ISSN 0022-5347; ◆ The Journal of Urology (Spanish Edition). ISSN 1133-8245.
Published by: Elsevier Masson (Subsidiary of: Elsevier Health Sciences), Via Paleocapa 7, Milan, 20121, Italy. TEL 39-02-881841, FAX 39-02-88184302, info@masson.it, http://www.masson.it.

➤ **KIDNEY;** a current survey of world literature. *see* MEDICAL SCIENCES—Abstracting, Bibliographies, Statistics

616.6 CHE ISSN 1420-4096
QP249 CODEN: KBPRFC
➤ **KIDNEY AND BLOOD PRESSURE RESEARCH.** Text in French. 1979. bi-m. CHF 2,268, EUR 1,813, USD 2,222.50 to institutions; CHF 2,490, EUR 1,990, USD 2,438.50 combined subscription to institutions (print & online eds.) (effective 2012). adv. bk.rev. illus. index. back issues avail. **Document type:** *Journal, Academic/Scholarly.* **Description:** Comprises both clinical and basic studies at the interface of nephrology and cardiovascular research.
Former titles (until 1996): Renal Physiology and Biochemistry (1011-6524); (until 1989): Renal Physiology (0378-5858)
Related titles: Microfilm ed.; Microform ed.: (from PQC); Online - full text ed.: ISSN 1423-0143. CHF 2,217, EUR 1,774, USD 2,152 to institutions (effective 2012).
Indexed: A01, A03, A08, A22, A29, A34, A35, A36, A38, ASCA, AgBio, B20, B21, B25, BIOSIS Prev, CA, CABA, ChemAb, ChemTitl, CurCont, E01, E12, EMBASE, ESPM, ExcerpMed, GH, I10, ISR, IndMed, Inpharma, MEDLINE, MycolAb, N02, N03, N04, P20, P22, P30, P35, P48, P54, PQC, R10, R12, Reac, SCI, SCOPUS, T02, T05, VirolAbstr, W07.
—BLDSC (5094.207500), CASDDS, GNLM, IE, Infotrieve, Ingenta, INIST. **CCC.**
Published by: (Gesellschaft fuer Nephrologie), S. Karger AG, Allschwilerstr 10, Basel, 4055, Switzerland. TEL 41-61-3061111, FAX 41-61-3061234, karger@karger.ch, http://www.karger.ch. Ed. V Tesar. adv.: page CHF 189,500; trim 210 x 280. Circ: 2,700 (controlled). **Co-sponsors:** Deutsche Hypertonie Gesellschaft; Deutsche Liga zur Bekaempfung des hohen Blutdruckes e.V.

616.6 USA ISSN 1934-8754
KIDNEY DISEASE RESEARCH UPDATES. Text in English. 1999. q. **Document type:** *Newsletter, Trade.*
Supersedes in part (in 2005): Research Updates in Kidney and Urologic Health (1934-8770)
Media: Online - full text.
Published by: National Kidney and Urologic Diseases Information Clearinghouse, 3 Information Way, Bethesda, MD 20892-3580. TEL 800-891-5390, nkudic@info.niddk.nih.gov.

616.6 GBR ISSN 0085-2538
RC902.A1 CODEN: KDYIA5
➤ **KIDNEY INTERNATIONAL.** Abbreviated title: K I. Text in English. 1972. s-m. EUR 2,265 in Europe to institutions; USD 2,168 in the Americas to institutions; JPY 387,000 in Japan to institutions; GBP 1,460 to institutions in the UK & elsewhere (effective 2011). adv. back issues avail.; reprints avail. **Document type:** *Journal, Academic/Scholarly.* **Description:** Aims to inform the renal researcher and the practicing nephrologist on all aspects of renal research.
Related titles: Microform ed.: (from PQC); Online - full text ed.: ISSN 1523-1755. USD 1,409 in the Americas to institutions & Caribbean; GBP 978 elsewhere to institutions (effective 2006); Chinese ed.: Kidney International Selections. Zhongwenban. ISSN 1882-2347; Japanese ed.: Kidney International Selections. Nihongoban. ISSN 1884-2933; ◆ Supplement(s): Kidney International. Supplement. ISSN 0098-6577.
Indexed: A01, A03, A08, A20, A22, A26, A34, A36, A38, AIDS Ab, ASCA, B21, B25, BIOBASE, BIOSIS Prev, C06, C07, C08, CA, CABA, CIN, CINAHL, CTA, ChemAb, ChemTitl, CurCont, D01, DiabCont, E01, E12, EMBASE, ExcerpMed, GH, IABS, ISR, IndMed, IndVet, Inpharma, Kidney, MEDLINE, MycolAb, N02, N03, P20, P22, P24, P30, P35, P48, P54, PQC, R10, R12, RA&MP, Reac, S12, SCI, SCOPUS, T02, T05, THA, VS, W07.
—CASDDS, GNLM, IE, Infotrieve, Ingenta, INIST. **CCC.**
Published by: (International Society of Nephrology USA), Nature Publishing Group (Subsidiary of: Macmillan Publishers Ltd.), The MacMillan Bldg, 4 Crinan St, London, N1 9XW, United Kingdom. TEL 44-20-78334000, FAX 44-20-78334640. Ed. Qais Al-Awqati. Adv. contact Ben Harkinson TEL 617-475-9222. **Subscr. to:** Brunel Rd, Houndmills, Basingstoke, Hamps RG21 6XS, United Kingdom. TEL 44-1256-329242, FAX 44-1256-812358, subscriptions@nature.com.

616.6 SVK ISSN 1336-7579
➤ **KLINICKA UROLOGIA.** Text in Slovak. 2005. 3/yr. EUR 9 (effective 2009). **Document type:** *Journal, Academic/Scholarly.*
Published by: Samedi s.r.o., Racianska 20, Bratislava, 839 27, Slovakia. TEL 421-2-55645901, FAX 421-2-55645902, samedi@samedi.sk. Ed. Danica Paulenova.

616.6 DEU ISSN 1862-2887
KONTINENZ AKTUELL. Text in German. 1996. 3/yr. EUR 12 to non-members; EUR 5 newsstand/cover (effective 2010). adv. **Document type:** *Journal, Academic/Scholarly.*
Formerly (until 2005): G I H Aktuell (1432-363X)
Published by: (Deutsche Kontinenz Gesellschaft e.V.), Bibliomed - Medizinische Verlagsgesellschaft mbH, Postfach 1150, Melsungen, 34201, Germany. TEL 49-5661-73440, FAX 49-5661-8360, info@bibliomed.de. Ed. Dr. Christoph Seif. Adv. contact Sigrid Fecher. Circ: 12,500 (controlled).

616.6 JPN ISSN 0919-5491
KONYOUSANKESSHO TO TSUFU/HYPERURICEMIA AND GOUT. Text in Japanese. 1993. s-a. JPY 3,780 (effective 2005). **Document type:** *Journal, Academic/Scholarly.*
Published by: Medikaru Rebyusha/Medical Review Co., Ltd., 1-7-3 Hirano-Machi, Chuo-ku, Yoshida Bldg., Osaka-shi, 541-0046, Japan. TEL 81-6-62231468, FAX 81-6-62231245.

616.6 ITA ISSN 1120-3471
LETTERA DI UROLOGIA. Text in Italian. 1989. q. free. adv. **Document type:** *Newsletter, Trade.*
Formerly (until 1999): Lettera di Uroginecologia (1120-0456)
Published by: C I C Edizioni Internazionali, Corso Trieste 42, Rome, 00198, Italy. TEL 39-06-8412673, FAX 39-06-8412688, info@gruppocic.it, http://www.gruppocic.it.

616.6 CHN ISSN 1001-1420
LINCHUANG MINIAO WAIKE ZAZHI/JOURNAL OF CLINICAL UROLOGICAL SURGERY. Text in Chinese. 1986. m. USD 68.40 (effective 2009). **Document type:** *Journal, Academic/Scholarly.*
Related titles: Online - full text ed.: (from WanFang Data Corp.).
—East View.
Published by: Huazhong Keji Daxue Tongji Yixueyuan Fushu Xiehe Yiyuan/Tongji Medical University, Union Hospital, 1277, Jiefang Dadao, Wuhan, 430022, China. TEL 86-27-85726126, FAX 86-27-85726126, http://www.whuh.com/. **Dist. by:** China International Book Trading Corp, 35 Chegongzhuang Xilu, Haidian District, PO Box 399, Beijing 100044, China. TEL 86-10-68412045, FAX 86-10-68412023, cibtc@mail.cibtc.com.cn, http://www.cibtc.com.cn.

M P R (UROLOGISTS EDITION). (Monthly Prescribing Reference) *see* PHARMACY AND PHARMACOLOGY

616.6 HUN ISSN 0864-8921
MAGYAR UROLOGIA. Text in Hungarian. 1974. 4/yr. **Document type:** *Journal, Academic/Scholarly.*
Formerly (until 1989): Urologiai es Nephrologiai Szemle (0133-3127)
Indexed: SCOPUS.
—BLDSC (5351.015000), GNLM.
Published by: Magyar Urologiai Tarsasag/Hungarian Society of Urology, c/o Jozsef Kondas, President, Semmelweis University, Dept of Urology, Ulloi ut 78/b, Budapest, 1082, Hungary. magyurol@urol.sote.hu, http://www.magyurol.hu.

616.6 ITA ISSN 0393-2249
CODEN: MINEAT
➤ **MINERVA UROLOGICA E NEFROLOGICA;** a journal on nephrology and urology. Text in Italian; Summaries in English, Italian. 1983. q. EUR 240 combined subscription in the European Union to institutions (print & online eds.); EUR 265 combined subscription elsewhere to institutions (print & online eds.) (effective 2011). adv. bk.rev. bibl.; charts; illus. index. **Document type:** *Journal, Academic/Scholarly.* **Description:** Covers pathophysiology and clinical medicine of renal disease and medical and surgical urology.
Formed by the merger of (1949-1983): Minerva Urologica (0026-4989); (1954-1983): Minerva Nefrologica (0026-4873)
Related titles: Microform ed.: (from PQC); Online - full text ed.: ISSN 1827-1758. 2005.
Indexed: A22, ChemAb, EMBASE, ExcerpMed, IndMed, MEDLINE, P30, R10, Reac, SCOPUS.
—BLDSC (5794.720000), CASDDS, GNLM, IE, Infotrieve, Ingenta, INIST. **CCC.**
Published by: Edizioni Minerva Medica, Corso Bramante 83-85, Turin, 10126, Italy. TEL 39-011-678282, FAX 39-011-674502, journals.dept@minervamedica.it, http://www.minervamedica.it. Circ: 3,000 (paid).

616.61 GBR ISSN 1753-0784
N D T PLUS. (Nephrology Dialysis Transplantation) Text in English. 2007. bi-m. included with subscr. to: Nephrology Dialysis Transplantation. reprint service avail. from PSC. **Document type:** *Journal, Academic/Scholarly.* **Description:** Publishes practical and clinically orientated content and provides a valuable teaching tool to help inform, guide and improve practice and training for nephrologists.
Related titles: Online - full text ed.: ISSN 1753-0792. 2007 (from IngentaConnect); ◆ Supplement to: Nephrology, Dialysis, Transplantation. ISSN 0931-0509.
Indexed: A01, A03, A08, A22, A34, A36, BIOBASE, CABA, D01, E01, E12, EMBASE, ExcerpMed, GH, H17, IABS, N02, N03, N04, P30, P33, P35, P39, R08, R10, RM&VM, Reac, SCOPUS, SoyAb, T02, T05, VS, W10.
—BLDSC (6067.866500), IE, INIST. **CCC.**
Published by: Oxford University Press, Great Clarendon St, Oxford, OX2 6DP, United Kingdom. TEL 44-1865-556767, FAX 44-1865-556646, enquiry@oup.co.uk, http://www.oup.co.uk/. Ed. N Lameire TEL 32-9-3324402.

616.6 JPN ISSN 1346-0005
NAGANO-KEN TOSEKI KENKYUKAISHI/NAGANO PREFECTURAL SOCIETY OF DIALYSIS THERAPY. JOURNAL. Text in English, Japanese; Summaries in English. 1978. a. **Document type:** *Journal, Academic/Scholarly.*
Formerly (until 1996): Naganoken Jinko Toseki Kenkyukaishi (0910-2329)
Published by: Naganoken Jinko Toseki Kenkyukai/Nagano Prefectural Society of Dialysis Therapy, c/o Shinshu University School of Medicine, Division of Artificial Kidney, 3-1-1 Asahi, Matsumoto, 390-8621, Japan.

616.6 USA ISSN 0077-5096
NATIONAL KIDNEY FOUNDATION. ANNUAL REPORT. Text in English. 1957. a. back issues avail. **Document type:** *Report, Consumer.*
Related titles: Online - full text ed.: free (effective 2011).
Published by: National Kidney Foundation, Inc., 30 E 33rd St, New York, NY 10016. TEL 212-889-2210, 800-622-9010, FAX 212-689-9261, info@kidney.org. Ed. Ellie Schlam.

616.6 GBR ISSN 1759-5061
RC902.A1
NATURE REVIEWS NEPHROLOGY. Text in English. 2005. m. EUR 1,224 in Europe to institutions; USD 1,257 in the Americas to institutions; GBP 741 to institutions in the UK & elsewhere (effective 2011). adv. back issues avail.; reprints avail. **Document type:** *Journal, Academic/Scholarly.*
Formerly (until 2009): Nature Clinical Practice Nephrology (1745-8323)
Related titles: Online - full text ed.: ISSN 1759-507X.
Indexed: A01, A26, CA, CurCont, EMBASE, ExcerpMed, H12, I05, MEDLINE, P30, R10, Reac, SCI, SCOPUS, T02, W07.
—BLDSC (6046.280175), IE. **CCC.**
Published by: Nature Publishing Group (Subsidiary of: Macmillan Publishers Ltd.), The MacMillan Bldg, 4 Crinan St, London, N1 9XW, United Kingdom. TEL 44-20-78334000, FAX 44-20-78334640, NatureReviews@nature.com. Eds. Dr. Philip Campbell, Susan Allison. Adv. contact Andy Douglas TEL 44-22-78434975. **Subscr. to:** Brunel Rd, Houndmills, Basingstoke, Hamps RG21 6XS, United Kingdom. TEL 44-1256-329242, FAX 44-1256-812358, subscriptions@nature.com.

616.6 GBR ISSN 1759-4812
➤ **NATURE REVIEWS. UROLOGY.** Text in English. 2004 (Nov.). m. EUR 1,224 in Europe to institutions; USD 1,257 in the Americas to institutions; GBP 741 to institutions in the UK & elsewhere (effective 2011). adv. back issues avail. **Document type:** *Journal, Academic/Scholarly.* **Description:** Features unique content designed to be of real, practical value in making diagnosis and treatment decisions. Sections include editorial and opinion pieces, highlights from the current literature, commentaries on the application of recent research to practical patient care, comprehensive reviews, and in-depth case studies.
Formerly (until 2009): Nature Clinical Practice Urology (1743-4270)
Related titles: Online - full text ed.: ISSN 1759-4820.
Indexed: A26, B21, CA, CTA, CurCont, EMBASE, ExcerpMed, H12, I05, Inpharma, MEDLINE, P30, P35, R10, Reac, SCI, SCOPUS, W07.
—BLDSC (6046.280250), IE, Ingenta. **CCC.**
Published by: Nature Publishing Group (Subsidiary of: Macmillan Publishers Ltd.), The MacMillan Bldg, 4 Crinan St, London, N1 9XW, United Kingdom. TEL 44-20-78334000, FAX 44-20-78334640, NatureReviews@nature.com. Eds. Dr. Philip Campbell, Suzanne Farley. Adv. contact Andy Douglas TEL 44-22-78434975. **Subscr. to:** Brunel Rd, Houndmills, Basingstoke, Hamps RG21 6XS, United Kingdom. TEL 44-1256-329242, FAX 44-1256-812358, subscriptions@nature.com.

616.6 NLD ISSN 0929-0184
CODEN: NTURE
➤ **NEDERLANDS TIJDSCHRIFT VOOR UROLOGIE.** Text in Dutch. 1993. 8/yr. EUR 49.50 to individuals; EUR 63.50 to institutions; EUR 32 to students (effective 2009). adv. **Document type:** *Journal, Academic/Scholarly.* **Description:** Informs urologists and urologists in training of developments in their field and alerts members to association news and forthcoming congresses and symposia.
Indexed: A22, EMBASE, SCOPUS.
—BLDSC (6072.470000), GNLM, IE, Ingenta.
Published by: (Nederlandse Vereniging voor Urologie), Elsevier Gezondheidszorg bv (Subsidiary of: Reed Business bv), Planetenbaan 80-99, Maarssen, 3606 AK, Netherlands. TEL 31-346-577901, FAX 31-346-577371, marketing.gezondheidszorg@reedbusiness.nl, http://www.elseviergezondheidszorg.nl. Ed. H van der Poel. Pub. Paul Emons. adv.: B&W page EUR 1,491, color page EUR 3,085; trim 210 x 297. Circ: 811 (paid and controlled). **Subscr. to:** Elsevier Den Haag, Postbus 16500, The Hague 2500 BM, Netherlands. TEL 31-70-381-9900, FAX 31-70-333-8399.

616.6 ESP ISSN 0211-6995
RC902.A1
➤ **NEFROLOGIA.** Text in Spanish. 1981. 6/yr. EUR 146 to individuals; EUR 198 to institutions (effective 2009). **Document type:** *Journal, Academic/Scholarly.*
Related titles: Online - full text ed.: ISSN 1989-2284; English ed.: ISSN 2013-2514; Supplement(s): Nefrologia. Suplemento. ISSN 1131-4168. 1981.
Indexed: A22, ASCA, CA, CurCont, EMBASE, ExcerpMed, IndMed, Inpharma, MEDLINE, P30, P35, R10, Reac, SCI, SCOPUS, T02, W07.
—BLDSC (6075.150500), GNLM, IE, Infotrieve, Ingenta. **CCC.**
Published by: (Sociedad Espanola de Nefrologia), Pulso Ediciones S.A., Rambla del Celler 117-119, Sant Cugat del Valles, Barcelona, Barcelona 08190, Spain. TEL 34-93-5896264, FAX 34-93-5895077, pulso@pulso.com, http://www.pulso.com/.

616.6 616.132 POL ISSN 1644-485X
➤ **NEFROLOGIA I NADCISNIENIE TETNICZE.** Text in Polish. 2002. bi-m. PLZ 119 domestic to institutions (effective 2011). **Document type:** *Journal, Academic/Scholarly.*
Published by: Wydawnictwo Via Medica, ul Swietokrzyska 73, Gdansk, 80180, Poland. TEL 48-58-3209494, FAX 48-58-3209460, redakcja@viamedica.pl, http://www.viamedica.pl. Ed. Andrzej Ksiazek.

616.6 MEX ISSN 0187-7801
NEFROLOGIA MEXICANA. Text in Spanish. 1980. q. MXN 300 domestic; MXN 60 foreign (effective 2005). back issues avail. **Document type:** *Journal, Academic/Scholarly.*
Related titles: Online - full text ed.
Indexed: C01.
Published by: Sociedad Mexicana de Nefrologia, A.C., Chilpancingo No.51 Piso 4 Desp. 402, Col. Hipodromo Condesa, Mexico D.F., 60110, Mexico. TEL 52-55-56151931, FAX 52-55-55745551, nefromex@infosel.net.mx, http://www.smn.org.mx/. Ed. Manuel Torres Zamora.

616.6 BGR ISSN 0204-6105
NEFROLOGIIA, HEMODIALIZA I TRANSPLANTATSIIA/ NEPHROLOGY, HEMODIALYSIS AND TRANSPLANTATION. Text in Bulgarian; Summaries in Bulgarian, English. 1995. q. free (effective 2005). bk.rev. abstr.; bibl. 56 p./no. 2 cols./p.; **Document type:** *Journal, Academic/Scholarly.* **Description:** Publishes original articles by Bulgarian authors in the fields of nephrology, hemodialysis and kidney transplantation.
Published by: Meditsinski Universitet - Sofia, Tsentralna Meditsinska Biblioteka, Tsentur za Informatsiia po Meditsina/Medical University - Sofia, Central Medical Library, Medical Information Center, 1 Sv Georgi Sofiiski ul, Sofia, 1431, Bulgaria. TEL 359-2-9522342, FAX 359-2-9522393, lydia@medun.acad.bg, http://www.medun.acad.bg/cmb_htm/cmb1_home_bg.htm. Ed. Dr. Z Kiriakov. Circ: 500.

616.6 DEU ISSN 1862-040X
➤ **DER NEPHROLOGE**; Zeitschrift fuer Nephrologie und Hypertensiologie. Text in German. 2006. 4/yr. EUR 274, USD 336 combined subscription to institutions (print & online eds.) (effective 2012). adv. reprint service avail. from PSC. **Document type:** *Journal, Academic/Scholarly.*
Related titles: Online - full text ed.: ISSN 1862-0418 (from IngentaConnect).
Indexed: A22, A26, E01, EMBASE, SCOPUS.
—IE, Ingenta. **CCC.**
Published by: Springer (Subsidiary of: Springer Science+Business Media), Tiergartenstr 17, Heidelberg, 69121, Germany. TEL 49-6221-4870, FAX 49-6221-345229, subscriptions@springer.com. Ed. Danilo Fliser.

616.6 FRA ISSN 1769-7255
RC902 CODEN: NEPHDY
➤ **NEPHROLOGIE & THERAPEUTIQUE.** Text in French. 1883. 7/yr. EUR 191 in Europe to institutions; EUR 165.52 in France to institutions; JPY 23,000 in Japan to institutions; USD 218 elsewhere to institutions (effective 2012). adv. bk.rev. **Document type:** *Journal, Academic/Scholarly.*
Supersedes (in 2005): Nephrologie (0250-4960); Which superseded in part (in 1980): Journal d'Urologie et de Nephrologie (0021-8200); Which was formerly (until 1961): Journal d'Urologie Medicale et Chirurgicale (0368-4679); (until 1912): Annales des Maladies des Organes Genito-Urinaires (0150-9594)
Related titles: Online - full text ed.: ISSN 1872-9177 (from ScienceDirect).
Indexed: A20, A22, A26, ASCA, CA, CIN, ChemAb, ChemTitl, CurCont, EMBASE, ExcerpMed, FR, I05, INI, IndMed, Inpharma, MEDLINE, MycolAb, P30, R10, Reac, SCI, SCOPUS, T02, W07.
—BLDSC (6075.680000), CASDDS, GNLM, IE, Infotrieve, Ingenta, INIST. **CCC.**
Published by: Elsevier Masson (Subsidiary of: Elsevier Health Sciences), 62 Rue Camille Desmoulins, Issy les Moulineaux, Cedex 92442, France. TEL 33-1-71165500, FAX 33-1-71165600, infos@elsevier-masson.fr. Ed. Ziad Massy.

616.6 AUS ISSN 1320-5358
CODEN: NEPHF2
➤ **NEPHROLOGY.** Text in English. 1995. bi-m. GBP 533 in United Kingdom to institutions; EUR 678 in Europe to institutions; USD 863 in the Americas to institutions; USD 1,044 elsewhere to institutions; GBP 613 combined subscription in United Kingdom to institutions (print & online eds.); EUR 780 combined subscription in Europe to institutions (print & online eds.); USD 994 combined subscription in the Americas to institutions (print & online eds.); USD 1,200 combined subscription elsewhere to institutions (print & online eds.) (effective 2012). back issues avail.; reprint service avail. from PSC. **Document type:** *Journal, Academic/Scholarly.* **Description:** Publishes research covering the clinical and experimental aspects of nephrology.
Related titles: Online - full text ed.: ISSN 1440-1797. GBP 533 in United Kingdom to institutions; EUR 678 in Europe to institutions; USD 863 in the Americas to institutions; USD 1,044 elsewhere to institutions (effective 2012) (from IngentaConnect).
Indexed: A01, A03, A08, A22, A26, B21, CA, CIN, CTA, ChemAb, ChemTitl, CurCont, E01, EMBASE, ExcerpMed, H12, Inpharma, MEDLINE, P30, P35, R10, Reac, SCI, SCOPUS, T02, W07.
—BLDSC (6075.684400), CASDDS, GNLM, IE, Infotrieve, Ingenta. **CCC.**
Published by: (Asian Pacific Society of Nephrology), Wiley-Blackwell Publishing Asia (Subsidiary of: Wiley-Blackwell Publishing Ltd.), 155 Cremorne St, Richmond, VIC 3121, Australia. TEL 61-3-92743100, FAX 61-3-92743101, subs@blackwellpublishingasia.com, http://www.wiley.com/WileyCDA/. Ed. David Harris.

616.6 GBR ISSN 0931-0509
CODEN: NDTREA
➤ **NEPHROLOGY, DIALYSIS, TRANSPLANTATION.** Abbreviated title: N D T. Text in English. 1964. m. GBP 721 in United Kingdom to institutions; EUR 1,081 in Europe to institutions; USD 1,441 in US & Canada to institutions; GBP 721 elsewhere to institutions; GBP 786 combined subscription in United Kingdom to institutions (print & online eds.); EUR 1,180 combined subscription in Europe to institutions (print & online eds.); USD 1,572 combined subscription in US & Canada to institutions (print & online eds.); GBP 786 combined subscription elsewhere to institutions (print & online eds.) (effective 2012). adv. bk.rev. 228 p./no.; back issues avail.; reprint service avail. from PSC. **Document type:** *Journal, Academic/Scholarly.* **Description:** Publishes clinical and laboratory investigations of relevance to nephrology, dialysis and transplantation.
Former titles (until 1986): European Dialysis and Transplant Association. Proceedings (0959-9800); (until 1979): Dialysis, Transplantation, Nephrology (0308-9401); (until 1973): European Dialysis and Transplant Association. Proceedings (0071-2736)
Related titles: Online - full text ed.: ISSN 1460-2385. GBP 605 in United Kingdom to institutions; EUR 912 in Europe to institutions; USD 1,216 in US & Canada to institutions; GBP 605 elsewhere to institutions (effective 2012) (from IngentaConnect); Translation: Nephrology, Dialysis, Transplantation (Magyar kiad). ISSN 1787-713X; ◆ Supplement(s): N D T Plus. ISSN 1753-0784.
Indexed: A01, A03, A08, A20, A22, A36, AIDS Ab, ASCA, B&BAb, B21, B25, BIOBASE, BIOSIS Prev, BP, BioEngAb, C30, CA, CABA, CIN, CTA, ChemAb, ChemTitl, CurCont, E01, E12, EMBASE, ExcerpMed, FR, GH, H16, H17, IABS, INI, ISR, ImmunAb, IndMed, Inpharma, Kidney, LT, MEDLINE, MaizeAb, MycolAb, N02, N03, P20, P22, P30, P33, P35, P39, P48, P54, PN&I, PQC, R08, R10, R12, R13, RA&MP, RM&VM, RRTA, Reac, SCI, SCOPUS, SoyAb, T02, T05, VS, W07, W10, W11.
—BLDSC (6075.685300), CASDDS, GNLM, IE, Infotrieve, Ingenta, INIST. **CCC.**
Published by: (European Dialysis and Transplant Association BEL), Oxford University Press, Great Clarendon St, Oxford, OX2 6DP, United Kingdom. TEL 44-1865-556767, FAX 44-1865-556646, enquiry@oup.co.uk, http://www.oxfordjournals.org. Ed. N Lameire TEL 32-9-3324402. **U.S. subscr. to:** Oxford University Press, 2001 Evans Rd, Cary, NC 27513. TEL 919-677-0977 ext 5777, 800-852-7323, FAX 919-677-1714, jnlorders@oup-usa.org, http://www.us.oup.com. **Co-sponsor:** European Renal Association.

616.6 USA ISSN 0896-1263
CODEN: NNISES
➤ **NEPHROLOGY NEWS & ISSUES.** Abbreviated title: N N I. Text in English. 1987 (Feb.). m. USD 55 domestic; USD 65 in Canada; USD 80 elsewhere; USD 4.50 per issue; free to members (effective 2011). adv. bk.rev. illus.; stat. back issues avail. **Document type:** *Journal, Academic/Scholarly.* **Description:** Serves the nephrology and renal care community, including nephrologists, surgeons, nurses, technicians and administrators in transplant centers, private practice, in-hospital and free standing clinics. Reports news and information on new techniques, issues, products, government actions and other developments.
Incorporates: Nephrology News and Issues - Europe
Related titles: Online - full text ed.: ISSN 1944-7493. free (effective 2011).
Indexed: A22, C06, C07, C08, CINAHL, EMBASE, ExcerpMed, F09, INI, MEDLINE, P30, R10, Reac, SCOPUS.
—BLDSC (6075.685600), GNLM, IE, Infotrieve, Ingenta. **CCC.**
Published by: N N & I, Inc., 17797 N Perimeter Dr, Ste D-109, Scottsdale, AZ 85255. TEL 866-944-9619. Adv. contact Phyllis Kehoe TEL 480-342-9620.

➤ **NEPHROLOGY NURSING JOURNAL.** *see* MEDICAL SCIENCES—Nurses And Nursing

616.6 ITA ISSN 2035-8261
▼ **NEPHROLOGY REVIEWS.** Text in English. 2009. irreg. **Document type:** *Journal, Academic/Scholarly.*
Related titles: Online - full text ed.: ISSN 2035-813X. free (effective 2011).
Indexed: A01, T02.
—**CCC.**
Published by: Pagepress, Via Giuseppe Belli 4, Pavia, 27100, Italy. TEL 39-0382-1751762, FAX 39-0382-1750481. Ed. Howard Trachtman.

616.6 USA
NEPHROLOGY ROUNDS. Text in English. 2003. q. free (effective 2004). **Description:** Provide interested physicians throughout the United States and around the world with a unique window on some of the most current information and discussion on important scientific and clinical developments in the field of renal medicine.
Media: Online - full text.
Published by: Brigham and Women's Hospital, 75 Francisc St, Boston, MA 02115. TEL 617-732-6020, FAX 617-582-6010. Eds. Barry Brenner, Joseph Bonventre.

616.6 USA ISSN 1536-836X
NEPHROLOGY SELF-ASSESSMENT PROGRAM. Text in English. 2002. bi-m. free to members (effective 2010). adv. back issues avail.; reprints avail. **Document type:** *Journal, Trade.* **Description:** Helps to clinical nephrologists who seek to renew and refresh their clinical knowledge and diagnostic and therapeutic skills.
Related titles: Online - full text ed.: ISSN 1934-3175; ◆ Supplement to: American Society of Nephrology. Journal. ISSN 1046-6673.
Indexed: P30.
—INIST. **CCC.**
Published by: (American Society of Nephrology), Lippincott Williams & Wilkins (Subsidiary of: Wolters Kluwer N.V.), 530 Walnut St, Philadelphia, PA 19106. TEL 215-521-8300, FAX 215-521-8902, customerservice@lww.com, http://www.lww.com.

616.6 USA ISSN 1940-5960
NEPHROLOGY TIMES. Text in English. 2008. m. USD 267 domestic to institutions; USD 345 foreign to institutions (effective 2011). adv. **Document type:** *Newspaper, Academic/Scholarly.* **Description:** Dedicated to providing timely, authoritative, and engaging coverage of the hot-button issues and emerging controversies that shape practice, including clinical news, research highlights, and policy changes.
Related titles: Online - full text ed.: ISSN 1945-0605.
—**CCC.**
Published by: Lippincott Williams & Wilkins (Subsidiary of: Wolters Kluwer N.V.), 16522 Hunters Green Pky, Hagerstown, MD 21740. TEL 410-528-8572, 800-787-8981, FAX 410-528-4105, customerservice@lww.com, http://www.lww.com. Ed. Michelle Hogan. adv.: B&W page USD 3,100; trim 10.875 x 15. Circ: 9,000 (controlled).

616.6 CHE ISSN 1660-8151
RC902.A1 CODEN: NPRNAY
➤ **THE NEPHRON JOURNALS.** (Consists of three subjournals: Nephron Clinical Practice; Nephron Experimental Nephrology; Nephron Physiology) Text in English. 1964. m. (in 3 vols., 4 nos./vol.). CHF 5,157, EUR 4,122, USD 5,049 to institutions; CHF 5,664, EUR 4,527, USD 5,541 combined subscription to institutions (print & online eds.) (effective 2012). adv. charts; illus. index. back issues avail. **Document type:** *Journal, Academic/Scholarly.* **Description:** Provides extensive coverage to important developments concerning the structure, functions and diseases of the kidneys. Contains practice-oriented findings from many fields, including anatomy, pathophysiology, biochemistry, microbiology, endocrinology, immunology and pharmacology.
Formerly (until 2002): Nephron (0028-2766); Incorporates (1993-2002): Experimental Nephrology (1018-7782)
Related titles: ◆ Online - full content ed.: Nephron Clinical Practice. ISSN 1660-2110; ◆ Online - full text ed.: Nephron Experimental Nephrology. ISSN 1660-2129; Nephron Physiology. ISSN 1660-2137.
Indexed: A22, A35, A36, AIDS Ab, ASCA, AgBio, CA, CABA, CIN, ChemAb, ChemTitl, D01, DentInd, DiabCont, E01, E12, F08, F11, F12, FR, GH, IBR, IBZ, ISR, IndMed, Inpharma, Kidney, MEDLINE, N02, N03, P20, P22, P30, P33, P35, P39, P48, P54, PN&I, PQC, R10, R12, RA&MP, RM&VM, Reac, SCOPUS, SoyAb, T05, VS.
—BLDSC (6075.690500), CASDDS, GNLM, Ingenta, INIST. **CCC.**
Published by: S. Karger AG, Allschwilerstr 10, Basel, 4055, Switzerland. TEL 41-61-3061111, FAX 41-61-3061234, karger@karger.ch, http://www.karger.ch. Ed. L G Fine. adv.: page CHF 1,895; trim 210 x 280. Circ: 2,600.

616.1 USA ISSN 0733-2467
QM401 CODEN: NEUREM
➤ **NEUROUROLOGY AND URODYNAMICS.** Text in English. 1982. 8/yr. GBP 1,538 in United Kingdom to institutions; EUR 1,945 in Europe to institutions; USD 2,868 in United States to institutions; USD 2,966 in Canada & Mexico to institutions; USD 3,015 elsewhere to institutions; GBP 1,770 combined subscription in United Kingdom to institutions (print & online eds.); EUR 2,238 combined subscription in Europe to institutions (print & online eds.); USD 3,298 combined subscription in United States to institutions (print & online eds.); USD 3,396 combined subscription in Canada & Mexico to institutions (print & online eds.); USD 3,445 combined subscription elsewhere to institutions (print & online eds.) (effective 2012). adv. bk.rev. back issues avail.; reprint service avail. from PSC. **Document type:** *Journal, Academic/Scholarly.* **Description:** Provides multidisciplinary coverage of recent developments in the study of the urinary tract function.
Related titles: Microform ed.: (from PQC); Online - full text ed.: ISSN 1520-6777. 1996. GBP 1,463 in United Kingdom to institutions; EUR 1,850 in Europe to institutions; USD 2,868 elsewhere to institutions (effective 2012).
Indexed: A22, ASCA, B21, B25, BIOSIS Prev, CIN, ChemAb, ChemTitl, CurCont, EMBASE, ExcerpMed, ISR, IndMed, Inpharma, MEDLINE, MycolAb, NSA, P30, P35, R10, Reac, RefZh, SCI, SCOPUS, W07.
—BLDSC (6081.589000), CASDDS, GNLM, IE, Infotrieve, Ingenta, INIST. **CCC.**

Published by: John Wiley & Sons, Inc., 111 River St, Hoboken, NJ 07030. TEL 201-748-6000, FAX 201-748-6088, info@wiley.com, http://www.wiley.com/WileyCDA/. Ed. Christopher R Chapple. **Subscr. outside the Americas to:** John Wiley & Sons Ltd., The Atrium, Southern Gate, Chichester, West Sussex PO19 8SQ, United Kingdom. TEL 44-1243-779777, 800-243407, FAX 44-1243-775878, cs-journals@wiley.com.

616.6 NLD ISSN 0924-4999
➤ **NEW CLINICAL APPLICATIONS. DERMATOLOGY.** Text in English. 1986. irreg., latest vol.10, 1989. price varies. **Document type:** *Monographic series, Academic/Scholarly.*
Published by: Springer Netherlands (Subsidiary of: Springer Science+Business Media), Van Godewijckstraat 30, Dordrecht, 3311 GX, Netherlands. TEL 31-78-6576050, FAX 31-78-6576474.

616.6 NLD ISSN 0924-4514
➤ **NEW CLINICAL APPLICATIONS. NEPHROLOGY.** Text in English. 1988. irreg., latest vol.11, 1989. price varies. **Document type:** *Monographic series, Academic/Scholarly.*
Published by: Springer Netherlands (Subsidiary of: Springer Science+Business Media), Van Godewijckstraat 30, Dordrecht, 3311 GX, Netherlands. TEL 31-78-6576050, FAX 31-78-6576474.

616.3445 USA
NEW MEDICAL THERAPIES BRIEFS. CROHN'S DISEASE. Text in English. 200?. irreg. free (effective 2009). **Document type:** *Newsletter, Trade.*
Media: Online - full content.
Published by: CenterWatch (Subsidiary of: Jobson Medical Information LLC.), 100 N Washington St, Ste 301, Boston, MA 02114. TEL 617-948-5100, 866-219-3440, customerservice@centerwatch.com.

616.6 DEU ISSN 1865-8822
DER NIERENPATIENT. Text in German. 1976. 8/yr. EUR 29.20; EUR 4.30 newsstand/cover (effective 2010). adv. bk.rev. **Document type:** *Journal, Academic/Scholarly.* **Description:** Covers nephrology in the areas of medicine, law, social services and welfare for doctors, patients and medical personnel.
Formerly (until 2008): Der Dialysepatient (0724-0252)
Published by: (Dialysepatienten Deutschlands e.V.), Verlag Kirchheim und Co. GmbH, Kaiserstr 41, Mainz, 55116, Germany. TEL 49-6131-960700, FAX 49-6131-9607070, info@kirchheim-verlag.de, http://www.kirchheim-verlag.de. Ed. Angela Monecke. Circ: 17,200 (paid and controlled).

616.6 JPN ISSN 0021-5287
CODEN: NGKZA6
NIHON HINYOKIKA GAKKAI ZASSHI/JAPANESE JOURNAL OF UROLOGY. Text in Japanese; Summaries in English. 1911. m. membership. adv. reprints avail. **Document type:** *Journal, Academic/Scholarly.*
Formerly (until 1927): Nippon Hinyo-Kibyo Gakkai Zasshi
Related titles: Microform ed.: (from PQC).
Indexed: A22, CISA, EMBASE, ExcerpMed, G10, INIS AtomInd, IndMed, MEDLINE, P30, R10, Reac, SCOPUS.
—BLDSC (4659.050000), CASDDS, GNLM, IE, Infotrieve, Ingenta, INIST. **CCC.**
Published by: Nihon Hinyokika Gakkai/Japanese Urological Association, Saito-Building 5F., Yushima 2-17-15, Bunkyo-ku, Tokyo, 113-0034, Japan. TEL 81-3-38147921, FAX 81-3-38144117, jpurol@mb.infoweb.ne.jp, http://www.urol.or.jp/. Circ: 5,500.

616.6 JPN ISSN 0385-2385
CODEN: NJGKAU
NIHON JINZO GAKKAISHI/JAPANESE JOURNAL OF NEPHROLOGY. Text in Japanese. 1959. m. **Document type:** *Journal, Academic/Scholarly.*
Indexed: A22, EMBASE, ExcerpMed, INIS AtomInd, MEDLINE, P30, R10, Reac, SCOPUS.
—BLDSC (4656.640000), IE, Infotrieve, Ingenta, INIST. **CCC.**
Published by: Nihon Jinzo Gakkai/Japanese Society of Nephrology, 7F Tendai Bldg, Tenjin-machi 1, Shinjuku-ku, Tokyo, 104-0031, Japan. TEL 81-3-32698251, FAX 81-3-32698253, office@jsn.or.jp, http://www.jsn.or.jp/.

616.6922 JPN ISSN 1345-8361
NIHON SEI KINO GAKKAI ZASSHI/JAPANESE JOURNAL OF IMPOTENCE RESEARCH. Text in English. 1986. 3/yr. **Document type:** *Journal, Academic/Scholarly.*
Formerly (until 1999): Impotence/Inpotensu Kenkyukaishi (0912-7097)
—BLDSC (6113.020000).
Published by: Nihon Sei Kino Gakkai. Jimukyoku/Japanese Society for Impotence Research, Saitama Medical School, Department of Urology, 38 Morohongo, Moroyama, Saitama 350-0495, Japan. TEL 81-49-2761243, FAX 81-49-295-8004.

616.61 JPN ISSN 1340-3451
NIHON TOSEKI IGAKKAI ZASSHI/JAPANESE SOCIETY OF DIALYSIS THERAPY. JOURNAL. Text in English, Japanese. 1968. m. free to members (effective 2005). **Document type:** *Journal, Academic/Scholarly.*
Former titles (until 1994): Nihon Toseki Ryoho Gakkai Zasshi (0911-5889); (until 1985): Jinko Toseki Kenkyukai Kaishi (0288-7045)
Indexed: INIS AtomInd.
—BLDSC (4809.425000). **CCC.**
Published by: Nihon Toseki Igakkai/Japanese Society for Dialysis Therapy, 2-38-21 Hongo, Bunkyo-ku, Tokyo, 113-0033, Japan. TEL 81-3-58000786, FAX 81-3-58000787.

616.61 JPN ISSN 0914-7136
NIHON TOSEKI IKAI ZASSHI/JOURNAL OF JAPAN CLINICAL DIALYSIS. Text in Japanese. 1985. 3/yr. **Document type:** *Academic/Scholarly.*
Published by: Nihon Toseki Ikai, 15-2 Kanda-Suda-cho 1-chome, Chiyoda-ku, Tokyo, 101-0041, Japan. TEL 81-3-3255-6471, FAX 81-3-3255-6471. Ed. Nobutshi Iida.

616.6 JPN ISSN 0029-0726
NISHI NIHON HINYOKIKA/NISHINIHON JOURNAL OF UROLOGY. Text in Japanese; Summaries in English. 1969. m. JPY 10,000. adv. bk.rev. **Document type:** *Journal, Academic/Scholarly.*
Supersedes in part: Hifu to Hinyo/Dermatology and Urology (0011-9091)
Indexed: A22, INIS AtomInd, SCOPUS.
—BLDSC (6113.604000), GNLM, IE, Ingenta, INIST.
Published by: (Department of Urology), Nihon Hifuka Gakkai Nishinihon Soukai, c/o Japanese Urological Association, Saito-Building 5F. Yushima 2-17-15, Bunkyo-ku, Tokyo, 113-0034, Japan. Circ: 3,000.

616.61060489 DNK ISSN 0108-2388
NYRENYT. Variant title: Nyre Nyt. Text in Danish. 1975. 6/yr. DKK 200 membership (effective 2009). adv. bk.rev. illus. back issues avail. **Document type:** *Magazine, Consumer.*
Formerly (until 1981): Dialyse og Transplantation (0108-2779)
Related titles: Online - full text ed.
Published by: Nyreforeningen/Danish Kidney Association, Herlufsholmvejen 37, Vanloese, 2720, Denmark. TEL 45-43-524252, FAX 45-43-710096, mail@nyeforeningen.dk. Ed. Stig Hedegaard Kristensen TEL 45-86-404006. Circ: 6,000.

616.61 JPN ISSN 0912-6937
➤ **OOSAKA TOSEKI KENKYUKAI KAISHI/OSAKA SOCIETY FOR DIALYSIS THERAPY. JOURNAL.** Text in Japanese. 1983. s-a. JPY 1,000 (effective 1999). adv. **Document type:** *Journal, Academic/Scholarly.*
—**CCC.**
Published by: Oosaka Toseki Kenkyukai/Osaka Society for Dialysis Therapy, Osaka City University, Medical School, Department of Urology, 1-4-3 Asahimachi, Abeno-ku, Osaka, 545-8585, Japan. FAX 81-6-66474426, http://plaza.umin.ac.jp/odm/. Ed., Adv. contact Mitsushige Nishikawa. Pub., R&P Taketoshi Kishimoto. Circ: 3,000.

616.6 GBR ISSN 1179-1551
▼ ➤ **OPEN ACCESS JOURNAL OF UROLOGY.** Text in English. 2009. a. free (effective 2011). back issues avail. **Document type:** *Journal, Academic/Scholarly.* **Description:** Brings out research, reports, editorials, reviews and commentaries on all aspects of adult and pediatric urology in the clinic and laboratory.
Media: Online - full text.
Indexed: EMBASE, SCOPUS.
—**CCC.**
Published by: Dove Medical Press Ltd., Beechfield House, Winterton Way, Macclesfield, SK11 0JL, United Kingdom. TEL 44-1625-509130, FAX 44-1625-617933. Ed. Janet Colli.

616.6 USA ISSN 2160-5440
▼ ➤ **OPEN JOURNAL OF UROLOGY.** Abbreviated title: O J U. Text in English. 2011. q. USD 156 (effective 2011). **Document type:** *Journal, Academic/Scholarly.* **Description:** Provides a platform for researchers and academics all over the world to promote, share, and discuss various new issues and developments in urology related problems.
Related titles: Online - full text ed.: ISSN 2160-5629. free (effective 2011).
Published by: Scientific Research Publishing, Inc., PO Box 54821, Irvine, CA 92619. service@scirp.org.

616.6 NLD ISSN 1874-303X
RC870
➤ **THE OPEN UROLOGY & NEPHROLOGY JOURNAL.** Text in English. 2008. irreg. free (effective 2011). **Document type:** *Journal, Academic/Scholarly.*
Media: Online - full text.
Indexed: A01, CTA.
Published by: Bentham Open (Subsidiary of: Bentham Science Publishers Ltd.), PO Box 294, Bussum, AG 1400, Netherlands. TEL 31-35-6923800, FAX 31-35-6980150, subscriptions@bentham.org. Ed. Tushar Vachharajani.

616.65 CAN ISSN 1486-2018
OUR VOICE. Text in English. 1996. q. free. **Document type:** *Newsletter.*
Related titles: French ed.: Entre - Nous. ISSN 1486-0589.
Published by: (Canadian Prostate Health Council), Parkhurst Publishing, 400 McGill St, 3rd Fl, Montreal, PQ H2Y 2G1, Canada. TEL 514-397-8833, FAX 514-397-0228, contact@parkpub.com, http://www.parkpub.com.

616.6 USA
▼ ➤ **P R E P NEPHROLOGY**; the premier nephrology self-assessment. (Pediatrics Review and Education Program) Text in English. 2009. m. USD 199 to non-members; USD 179 to members (effective 2010). **Document type:** *Journal, Academic/Scholarly.*
Media: Online - full text.
Published by: American Academy of Pediatrics, 141 NW Pt Blvd, Elk Grove Village, IL 60007. TEL 847-434-4000, FAX 847-434-8000, journals@aap.org, http://www.aap.org. Eds. Douglas Silverstein, Tej Mattoo. **Subscr. to:** 72139 Eagle Way, Chicago, IL 60678. TEL 866-843-2271, FAX 847-228-1281.

616.62 DEU ISSN 0174-4860
PATHOGENESE UND KLINIK DER HARNSTEINE. Text in German. 19??. irreg. **Document type:** *Monographic series, Academic/Scholarly.*
—**CCC.**
Published by: Dr. Dietrich Steinkopff Verlag (Subsidiary of: Springer Science+Business Media), Tiergartenstr 17, Heidelberg, 69121, Germany. TEL 49-6221-4878821, FAX 49-6221-4878830, info.steinkopff@springer.com, http://www.steinkopff.com.

616.6 DEU ISSN 0931-041X
RJ278 CODEN: PEDNEF
➤ **PEDIATRIC NEPHROLOGY.** Text in English. 1987. m. EUR 3,756, USD 4,494 combined subscription to institutions (print & online eds.) (effective 2012). adv. reprint service avail. from PSC. **Document type:** *Journal, Academic/Scholarly.* **Description:** Laboratory and clinical research of acute and chronic diseases that affect renal function in children.
Related titles: Online - full text ed.: ISSN 1432-198X (from IngentaConnect).
Indexed: A01, A02, A03, A08, A22, A26, A34, A36, ASCA, B25, BIOSIS Prev, C06, C07, C11, CA, CABA, CurCont, D01, E01, E08, E12, EMBASE, ExcerpMed, FR, G08, GH, H04, H11, H12, H17, I05, ISR, IndMed, IndVet, Inpharma, Kidney, LT, MEDLINE, MycolAb, N02, N03, N05, P20, P22, P24, P30, P33, P35, P39, P48, P54, PQC, R08, R10, R12, R13, RA&MP, RM&VM, RRTA, Reac, S09, SCI, SCOPUS, T02, T05, VS, W07.
—BLDSC (6417.603000), CASDDS, GNLM, IE, Infotrieve, Ingenta, INIST. **CCC.**
Published by: (International Pediatric Nephrology Association), Springer (Subsidiary of: Springer Science+Business Media), Tiergartenstr 17, Heidelberg, 69121, Germany. TEL 49-6221-4870, FAX 49-6221-345229. Ed. Dr. O Mehls. **Subscr. in the Americas to:** Springer New York LLC, Journal Fulfillment, PO Box 2485, Secaucus, NJ 07096. TEL 800-777-4643, 201-348-4033, FAX 201-348-4505, journals-ny@springer.com, http://www.springer.com; **Subscr. to:** Springer Distribution Center, Kundenservice Zeitschriften, Haberstr 7, Heidelberg 69126, Germany. TEL 49-6221-3454303, FAX 49-6221-3454229, subscriptions@springer.com.

616.6 FRA ISSN 1778-3712
RC900
PELVI-PERINEOLOGIE. Text in French. 2006. q. EUR 264, USD 328 combined subscription to institutions (print & online eds.) (effective 2011). reprint service avail. from PSC. **Document type:** *Journal, Academic/Scholarly.*
Related titles: Online - full text ed.: ISSN 1778-3720 (from IngentaConnect).
Indexed: A22, A26, E01, SCI, SCOPUS, W07.
—BLDSC (6418.660000), IE, Ingenta, INIST. **CCC.**
Published by: Springer France (Subsidiary of: Springer Science+Business Media), 22 Rue de Palestro, Paris, 75002, France. TEL 33-1-53009860, FAX 33-1-53009861, sylvie.kamara@springer.com. Ed. Gerard Amarenco.

PERITONEAL DIALYSIS INTERNATIONAL. *see* MEDICAL SCIENCES

616.6 CZE ISSN 1214-178X
POSTGRADUALNI NEFROLOGIE. Text in Czech. 2003. q. **Document type:** *Journal, Academic/Scholarly.*
Related titles: Online - full text ed.
Published by: (Ceska Transplantacni Spolecnost), Medical Tribune CZ, s.r.o., Na Morani 5, Prague 2, 12800, Czech Republic. TEL 420-224-916916, FAX 420-224-922436, info@medical-tribune.cz, http://www.tribune.cz. Ed. D Lipovska. Circ: 700.

616.6 FRA ISSN 1166-7087
➤ **PROGRES EN UROLOGIE.** Text in French. 1991. bi-m. EUR 230 in Europe to institutions; EUR 201.76 in France to institutions; JPY 38,300 in Japan to institutions; USD 312 elsewhere to institutions (effective 2012). adv. **Document type:** *Journal, Academic/Scholarly.* **Description:** Contains one or two review articles, ten original articles, four clinical cases, one surgical technique paper, and an international bibliographical survey.
Related titles: Online - full text ed.: (from ScienceDirect); Supplement(s): Progres en Urologie. Formation Medicale Continue. ISSN 1761-676X.
Indexed: A22, CurCont, EMBASE, ExcerpMed, FR, G10, IndMed, Inpharma, MEDLINE, P30, R10, Reac, SCI, SCOPUS, W07.
—BLDSC (6864.938800), GNLM, IE, Infotrieve, Ingenta, INIST. **CCC.**
Published by: (Association Francaise d'Urologie), Elsevier Masson (Subsidiary of: Elsevier Health Sciences), 62 Rue Camille Desmoulins, Issy les Moulineaux, Cedex 92442, France. TEL 33-1-71165500, FAX 33-1-71165600, infos@elsevier-masson.fr, http://www.elsevier-masson.fr. **Co-sponsors:** Association des Urologues du Quebec; Societe Francaise d'Urologie.

➤ **PROGRESS IN HUMAN REPRODUCTION RESEARCH.** *see* MEDICAL SCIENCES—Obstetrics And Gynecology

616.6 ITA ISSN 1720-030X
PROSTATA NEWS. Text in Italian. 2002. 3/yr. adv. **Document type:** *Journal, Academic/Scholarly.* **Description:** Provides information on the activities of the Associazione per la Ricerca di Base in Urologia.
Published by: (Associazione per la Ricerca di Base in Urologia), C I C Edizioni Internazionali, Corso Trieste 42, Rome, 00198, Italy. TEL 39-06-8412673, FAX 39-06-8412688, info@gruppocic.it, http://www.gruppocic.it. adv.: B&W page EUR 1,681.07, color page EUR 2,114.89; 210 x 290.

616.6 USA ISSN 0270-4137
RC899 CODEN: PRSTDS
➤ **THE PROSTATE.** Text in English. 1980. 16/yr. GBP 2,824 in United Kingdom to institutions; EUR 3,571 in Europe to institutions; USD 5,198 in United States to institutions; USD 5,422 in Canada & Mexico to institutions; USD 5,534 elsewhere to institutions; GBP 3,249 combined subscription in United Kingdom to institutions (print & online eds.); EUR 4,110 combined subscription in Europe to institutions (print & online eds.); USD 5,978 combined subscription in United States to institutions (print & online eds.); USD 6,202 combined subscription in Canada & Mexico to institutions (print & online eds.); USD 6,314 combined subscription elsewhere to institutions (print & online eds.) (effective 2012). bibl.; charts; illus. index. back issues avail.; reprint service avail. from PSC. **Document type:** *Journal, Academic/Scholarly.* **Description:** Presents coverage of clinical, anatomic, embryologic, physiologic, endocrinologic, and biochemical studies.
Related titles: Microform ed.: (from PQC); Online - full text ed.: ISSN 1097-0045. 1996. GBP 2,653 in United Kingdom to institutions; EUR 3,354 in Europe to institutions; USD 5,198 elsewhere to institutions (effective 2012); Supplement(s): The Prostate. Supplement. ISSN 1050-5881. 1981.
Indexed: A20, A22, A34, A35, A36, A38, ASCA, AgBio, B25, BIOSIS Prev, C30, CABA, CIN, ChemAb, ChemTitl, CurCont, D01, E12, EMBASE, ExcerpMed, F08, FR, G10, GH, H16, ISR, IndMed, IndVet, Inpharma, MEDLINE, MycolAb, N02, N03, N04, P30, P33, P35, PGrRegA, R08, R10, RA&MP, Reac, RefZh, SCI, SCOPUS, SoyAb, T05, VS, W07, W10.
—BLDSC (6935.194000), CASDDS, GNLM, IE, Infotrieve, Ingenta, INIST. **CCC.**
Published by: John Wiley & Sons, Inc., 111 River St, Hoboken, NJ 07030. TEL 201-748-6000, FAX 201-748-6088, info@wiley.com, http://www.wiley.com/WileyCDA/. Ed. John T Isaacs. Pub. Kim Thompkins TEL 212-850-6921. Adv. contact Stephen Donohue TEL 781-388-8511. **Subscr. outside the Americas to:** John Wiley & Sons Ltd., The Atrium, Southern Gate, Chichester, West Sussex PO19 8SQ, United Kingdom. TEL 44-1243-779777, 800-243407, FAX 44-1243-775878, cs-journals@wiley.com.

616.6 USA ISSN 1544-2306
RC899
PROSTATE BULLETIN. Text in English. 1998. q. USD 195 domestic; USD 240 in Canada (effective 2003).

Published by: The Johns Hopkins Medical Institutions, James Buchanan Brady Urological Institute, 600 N. Wolfe St., Baltimore, MD 21287-2101. TEL 410-955-8964, http://urology.jhu.edu/. Ed., Pub. Rodney M. Friedman.

▼ **PROSTATE CANCER.** *see* MEDICAL SCIENCES—Oncology

PROSTATE CANCER AND PROSTATIC DISEASES. *see* MEDICAL SCIENCES—Oncology

616.13 USA ISSN 1542-1716
RC899
PROSTATE DISORDERS. Text in English. 1994. a. USD 24.95 per issue (effective 2010). **Document type:** *Journal, Academic/Scholarly.*
Published by: (Johns Hopkins Medical Institutions), Medletter Associates, 6 Trowbridge Dr, Bethel, CT 06801. Ed. Simeon Margolis.

616.65 CAN ISSN 1486-0562
PROSTATE UPDATE. Text in English. 1994. q. **Document type:** *Newsletter.*
Related titles: Online - full content ed.; French ed.: Prostate, Mise a Jour. ISSN 1486-0570.
Published by: (Canadian Prostate Health Council), Parkhurst Publishing, 400 McGill St, 3rd Fl, Montreal, PQ H2Y 2G1, Canada. TEL 514-397-8833, FAX 514-397-0228, contact@parkpub.com, http://www.parkpub.com.

616.13 USA ISSN 1550-9478
RENAL & UROLOGY NEWS; world review for urologists & nephrologists. Abbreviated title: R U N. Text in English. 2002. m. USD 75 domestic; USD 85 in Canada; USD 110 elsewhere; free to qualified personnel (effective 2010). adv. back issues avail. **Document type:** *Journal, Trade.* **Description:** Provides coverage of major urologic and nephrologic conferences as well as important studies in peer-reviewed research journals.
Indexed: A01, A26, G08, H11, H12, I05, P20, P48, P54, PQC.
—CCC.
Published by: Haymarket Media Inc. (Subsidiary of: Haymarket Group Ltd.), 114 W 26th St, 4th Fl, New York, NY 10001. TEL 646-638-6000, custserv@haymarketmedia.com, http://www.haymarket.com. Ed. Jody A Charnow TEL 646-638-6089. Pub. Dominic Barone TEL 646-638-6097. Adv. contact William Canning TEL 646-638-6151. Circ: 16,000.

616.614 USA ISSN 1940-4646
RC902.A1
RENAL BUSINESS TODAY; your practice management resource. Text in English. 2006. m. USD 40 combined subscription domestic; USD 50 combined subscription in Canada; USD 60 combined subscription elsewhere (effective 2008). adv. **Document type:** *Magazine, Trade.* **Description:** Offers information on the latest business and technology trends in renal care, advice, strategic business solutions and related industry features.
Published by: Virgo Publishing, Llc, 3300 N Central Ave, Ste 300, Phoenix, AZ 85012. TEL 480-990-1101, FAX 480-990-0819, jsiefert@vpico.com, http://www.vpico.com. Ed. Keith Chartier. adv.: color page USD 5,040, B&W page USD 3,540; trim 8.125 x 10.875. Circ: 20,001 (paid).

616.6 USA ISSN 0886-022X
RC918.R4 CODEN: REFAE8
➤ **RENAL FAILURE.** Text in English. 1977. 8/yr. GBP 2,405, EUR 3,170, USD 3,965 combined subscription to institutions (print & online eds.); GBP 4,810, EUR 6,340, USD 7,930 combined subscription to corporations (print & online eds.) (effective 2010). adv. back issues avail.; reprint service avail. from PSC. **Document type:** *Journal, Academic/Scholarly.* **Description:** Addresses advances in the fields of chronic renal failure, hypertension, and renal transplantation.
Former titles (until 1987): Uremia Investigation (0740-1353); (until 1984): Clinical and Experimental Dialysis and Apheresis (0276-5497); (until 1981): Journal of Dialysis (0362-8558)
Related titles: Microform ed.: (from RPI); Online - full text ed.: ISSN 1525-6049 (from IngentaConnect).
Indexed: A01, A03, A08, A22, A35, A36, ASCA, AgBio, AgrForAb, B21, B25, BIOSIS Prev, C30, CA, CABA, CIN, CTA, ChemAb, ChemTitl, CurCont, D01, E01, E12, EMBASE, ExcerpMed, F08, F11, F12, GH, H16, H17, ISR, ImmunAb, IndMed, Inpharma, MEDLINE, MycolAb, N02, N03, P30, P32, P33, P35, P39, P40, R08, R10, R12, RA&MP, RM&VM, Reac, RefZh, S12, SCI, SCOPUS, SoyAb, T02, T05, VS, W07.
—BLDSC (7356.869800), CASDDS, GNLM, IE, Infotrieve, Ingenta, INIST. **CCC.**
Published by: Informa Healthcare (Subsidiary of: T & F Informa plc), 52 Vanderbilt Ave, New York, NY 10017. TEL 212-262-8230, FAX 212-262-8234, healthcare.enquiries@informa.com, http://www.informahealthcare.com. Ed. Dr. Kate Rittenhouse-Olson. Adv. contact Daniel Wallen. **Subscr. outside N. America to:** Taylor & Francis Ltd.

616.6 GBR ISSN 2045-7073
▼ **RENAL NEWS.** Text in English. 2010. 3/yr. **Document type:** *Newsletter, Trade.*
Published by: UK Renal Pharmacy Group, 26 Oriental Rd, Woking, Surrey GU22 7AW, United Kingdom. TEL 44-1483-724472, FAX 44-1483-727816, info@renalpharmacy.org.uk, http://www.renalpharmacy.org.uk.

616.6 AUS ISSN 1832-3804
RC902.A1
➤ **RENAL SOCIETY OF AUSTRALASIA JOURNAL.** Abbreviated title: R S A J. Text in English. 2005. 3/yr. free to members (effective 2009). adv. back issues avail. **Document type:** *Journal, Academic/Scholarly.* **Description:** Designed for nephrology nurses and associated professionals to share their ideas and their research to promote evidence-based, high quality care for persons living with renal disease.
Related titles: Online - full text ed.: free (effective 2009).
Indexed: A26, C06, C07, C08, CA, CINAHL, H11, H12, I05, P24, P48, PQC, T02.
Published by: Renal Society of Australasia, PO Box 155, Heidelberg, VIC 3084, Australia. rsaboard@renalsociety.org. Ed. Paul Bennett TEL 61-4-38834706. Adv. contact Lee-Anne Sparkes.

616.6 360 USA ISSN 1532-6195
RENALINK. Text in English. 1977. q. free to members (effective 2011). bibl. **Document type:** *Newsletter, Trade.* **Description:** Covers professional, legislative and regional issues of concern to social workers, nurses, technicians, and dietitians who specialize in working with renal patients.
Incorporates: C N N T Newsletter; C R N News and Briefs Newsletter; Formerly (until 2000): C N S W Newsletter (0164-7032)
Related titles: Online - full text ed.: free to members (effective 2011).
Published by: National Kidney Foundation, Inc., 30 E 33rd St, New York, NY 10016. TEL 212-889-2210, 800-622-9010, FAX 212-689-9261, info@kidney.org.

616.6 USA ISSN 1523-6161
RC870
REVIEWS IN UROLOGY. Text in English. 1999. q. includes with subscr. to Reviews in Cardiovascular Medicine, Reviews in Obstetrics and Gynecology & Reviews in Neurological Diseases. adv. back issues avail. **Document type:** *Journal, Academic/Scholarly.*
Related titles: Online - full text ed.: ISSN 2153-8182.
Indexed: P30.
—BLDSC (7798.075000), IE, Ingenta.
Published by: MedReviews, Llc, 494 Eighth Ave, Ste 1000, New York, NY 10001. TEL 212-201-6860, FAX 212-201-6850, sblack@medreviews.com.

616.6 613.081 ARG ISSN 1669-7618
REVISTA ARGENTINA DE ANDROLOGIA. Text in Spanish. 2005. 3/yr. **Document type:** *Journal, Academic/Scholarly.*
Published by: Sociedad Argentina de Andrologia, Vuelta de Obligado 2490, Buenos Aires, Argentina. TEL 54-11-48661779, http://www.saa.org.ar.

616.6 ARG ISSN 0327-3326
REVISTA ARGENTINA DE UROLOGIA. Text in Spanish. 1932-1988; resumed 1990. q. adv. illus. **Document type:** *Journal, Academic/Scholarly.*
Former titles (until 1988): Revista Argentina de Urologia y Nefrologia (0048-7627); (until 1966): Revista Argentina de Urologia (0325-2531)
Indexed: C01, IndMed, P30, SCOPUS.
—GNLM, INIST.
Published by: Sociedad Argentina de Urologia, Pasaje de la Carcova 3526, Buenos Aires, Argentina. TEL 54-11-49634336, sau@sau-net.org.

616.6 CHL ISSN 0716-0429
REVISTA CHILENA DE UROLOGIA. Text in Spanish. 1925. 3/yr. CLP 15,000 domestic; USD 40 foreign (effective 2005). **Document type:** *Journal, Academic/Scholarly.*
Former titles (until 1945): Sociedad Chilena de Urologia. Revista (0716-5099); (until 1936): Sociedad de Urologia. Revista (0716-5161)
Published by: Sociedad Chilena de Urologia, Avenida General Bustamante 16, Piso 4, Providencia, Santiago, Chile. TEL 56-2-2042464, FAX 56-2-2253951.

616.6 ARG ISSN 0326-3428
REVISTA DE NEFROLOGIA, DIALISIS Y TRANSPLANTE. Text in Spanish. 1980. 3/yr. **Document type:** *Journal, Trade.*
Indexed: C01, EMBASE, R10, SCI, SCOPUS, W07.
Published by: Sociedad Argentina de Nefrologia, Av Pueyrredon 1085, Planta Alta, Buenos Aires, 1118, Argentina. TEL 54-11-49637123, FAX 54-11-49614437, san@san.org.ar, http://www.san.org.ar.

616.6 ESP ISSN 1696-1773
REVISTA DE UROLOGIA. Text in Spanish. 2000. q. **Document type:** *Journal, Academic/Scholarly.*
Formerly (until 2003): Revisiones en Urologia (1576-0901)
Published by: Luzan 5 S.A. de Ediciones, Pasaje Virgen de la Alegria 14, Madrid, 28027, Spain. TEL 34-91-4057260, FAX 34-91-4034907, luzan@luzan5.es, http://www.luzan5.es.

616.6 MEX ISSN 0035-0001
REVISTA MEXICANA DE UROLOGIA. Text in Spanish. 1940. bi-m. MXN 180 domestic; USD 80 foreign (effective 2005). back issues avail. **Document type:** *Journal, Academic/Scholarly.*
Related titles: Online - full text ed.
Indexed: C01, P30, SCOPUS.
Published by: Sociedad Mexicana de Urologia, Edificio Wrold Trade Center, Montecillo No 38 Piso 25, Col. Napoles, Mexico, D.F., 03810, Mexico. TEL 52-55-54883385. Ed. Carlos Murphy Sanchez.

616.6 VEN ISSN 0035-0591
RC870 CODEN: RVURAB
REVISTA VENEZOLANA DE UROLOGIA. Summaries in English, Spanish. 1941. s-a. adv. bk.rev. bibl.; charts; illus.; stat. index. back issues avail.; reprints avail. **Document type:** *Journal, Academic/Scholarly.*
Formerly (until 1960): Revista de Urologia (0370-7725)
Related titles: Microform ed.: 1940 (from PQC); Print ed.
Indexed: ChemAb, IndMed, P30.
—GNLM.
Published by: Sociedad Venezolana de Urologia, Ave Francisco de Miranda Edif Menegrandre, Piso 6 Ofic 6-4, Caracas, Venezuela. TEL 58-212-2853673, FAX 58-212-2856240, http://www.soveuro.org.ve/. Ed. Jose Manuel Pardo. Circ: 2,000.

616.6 JPN ISSN 0385-2393
RINSHO HINYOKIKA/JAPANESE JOURNAL OF CLINICAL UROLOGY. Text in Japanese; Summaries in English. 1946. m. (13/yr.). JPY 41,360; JPY 53,800 combined subscription (print & online eds.) (effective 2010). **Document type:** *Journal, Academic/Scholarly.*
Related titles: Online - full text ed.: ISSN 1882-1332.
Indexed: A22, INIS AtomInd, SCOPUS.
—BLDSC (4651.450000), GNLM, IE, Ingenta, INIST.
Published by: Igaku Shoin Ltd., 1-28-36 Hongo, Bunkyo-ku, Tokyo, 113-8719, Japan. TEL 81-3-3817-5600, FAX 81-3-3815-7791, info@igaku-shoin.co.jp. Circ: 4,000.

616.61 JPN ISSN 0910-5808
RINSHO TOSEKI/JAPANESE JOURNAL OF CLINICAL DIALYSIS. Text in Japanese. 1985. m. JPY 35,490 (effective 2007).
Published by: Nihon Medikaru Senta/Nihon Medical Center, Inc., Kyowa Bldg., 1-64, Kanda-jinbo-cho, Chiyoda-ku, Tokyo, 101-0051, Japan. TEL 81-3-32913901, FAX 81-3-32913377, http://www.nmckk.co.jp/.

616.6 ITA ISSN 1970-8238
S I A ANDRONEWS. (Societa Italiana di Andrologia) Text in Italian. 2000. q. **Document type:** *Journal, Trade.*
Related titles: Online - full text ed.: ISSN 1970-822X.
Published by: (Societa Italiana di Andrologia (S I A)), C I C Edizioni Internazionali, Corso Trieste 42, Rome, 00198, Italy. TEL 39-06-8412673, FAX 39-06-8412688, info@gruppocic.it, http://www.gruppocic.it.

616.6 SAU ISSN 1319-2442
RC902.A1
➤ **SAUDI JOURNAL OF KIDNEY DISEASES AND TRANSPLANTATION.** Text in English. 1990. q. **Document type:** *Journal, Academic/Scholarly.* **Description:** Includes editorial reviews from experts worldwide, original articles, case reports, review articles, practical procedures, letters, and country reports on renal replacement therapy.
Formerly: Saudi Kidney Disease and Transplantation
Related titles: Online - full text ed.: free (effective 2011).
Indexed: A26, E08, EMBASE, ExcerpMed, H11, H12, I05, MEDLINE, P30, R10, Reac, S09, SCOPUS.
—BLDSC (8076.974300), GNLM, IE, Ingenta.
Published by: Saudi Center for Organ Transplantation, Publication Office, P O Box 27049, Riyadh, 11417, Saudi Arabia. TEL 966-1-4451100, FAX 966-1-4453934, TELEX 406310 KIDNEY SJ. Circ: 3,500.

616.6 GBR ISSN 0036-5599
RC870 CODEN: SJUNAS
➤ **SCANDINAVIAN JOURNAL OF UROLOGY AND NEPHROLOGY.** Text in English. 1967. bi-m. GBP 340, EUR 450, USD 565 combined subscription to institutions (print & online eds.); GBP 685, EUR 905, USD 1,130 combined subscription to corporations (print & online eds.) (effective 2010). adv. charts; illus. back issues avail.; reprint service avail. from PSC. **Document type:** *Journal, Academic/Scholarly.* **Description:** Focuses on basic and clinical research work in the two fields of medicine within the five Nordic countries.
Related titles: Online - full text ed.: ISSN 1651-2065 (from IngentaConnect); ◆ Supplement(s): Scandinavian Journal of Urology and Nephrology. Supplement. ISSN 0300-8886.
Indexed: A01, A03, A08, A22, A36, ASCA, B25, BIOBASE, BIOSIS Prev, CA, CABA, CIN, ChemAb, ChemTitl, CurCont, DBA, E01, E12, EMBASE, ExcerpMed, F08, FR, G10, GH, H17, IABS, IBR, IBZ, ISR, IndMed, Inpharma, MEDLINE, MycolAb, N02, N03, P30, P33, P35, PN&I, R10, RA&MP, RM&VM, Reac, SCI, SCOPUS, SoyAb, T02, T05, THA, VS, W07.
—BLDSC (8087.560000), CASDDS, GNLM, IE, Infotrieve, Ingenta, INIST. **CCC.**
Published by: (Scandinavian Association of Urology NOR), Informa Healthcare (Subsidiary of: T & F Informa plc), Telephone House, 69-77 Paul St, London, EC2A 4LQ, United Kingdom. TEL 44-20-70175000, FAX 44-20-70176792, healthcare.enquiries@informa.com. Ed. Jan Adolfsson. Adv. contact Per Sonnerfeldt. **Subscr. in N. America to:** Taylor & Francis Inc., Customer Services Dept, 325 Chestnut St, 8th Fl, Philadelphia, PA 19106. TEL 215-625-8900, 800-354-1420, FAX 215-625-8914, customerservice@taylorandfrancis.com; **Subscr. outside N. America to:** Taylor & Francis Ltd., Journals Customer Service, Sheepen Pl, Colchester, Essex CO3 3LP, United Kingdom. TEL 44-20-70175544, FAX 44-20-70175198, tf.enquiries@tfinforma.com.

616.6 NOR ISSN 0300-8886
RC870 CODEN: SJUNBT
SCANDINAVIAN JOURNAL OF UROLOGY AND NEPHROLOGY. SUPPLEMENT. Text in English. 1968. irreg. price varies. reprint service avail. from PSC. **Document type:** *Monographic series, Academic/Scholarly.*
Related titles: Online - full text ed.: ISSN 1651-2537; ◆ Supplement to: Scandinavian Journal of Urology and Nephrology. ISSN 0036-5599.
Indexed: A01, A03, A08, A22, ChemAb, EMBASE, ExcerpMed, IBR, IBZ, IndMed, MEDLINE, P30, P35, R10, Reac, SCOPUS, T02.
—BLDSC (8087.565000), CASDDS, IE, Infotrieve, Ingenta, INIST. **CCC.**
Published by: Taylor & Francis A S (Subsidiary of: Taylor & Francis Group), Biskop Gunnerusgate 14A, PO Box 12 Posthuset, Oslo, 0051, Norway. TEL 47-23-103460, FAX 47-23-103461, journals@tandf.no, http://www.tandf.co.uk.

616.6 NLD ISSN 1875-7804
SCRIPT UROLOGIE. Text in Dutch. 2008. q. adv.
Published by: Van Zuiden Communications B.V., Postbus 2122, Alphen aan den Rijn, 2400 CC, Netherlands. TEL 31-172-476191, FAX 31-172-471882, zuiden@zuidencomm.nl, http://www.zuidencomm.nl. Eds. Dr. J J Jaspers, Dr. P Venema. Circ: 650 (controlled).

616.6 USA ISSN 0894-0959
➤ **SEMINARS IN DIALYSIS.** Text in English. 1988. bi-m. GBP 515 in United Kingdom to institutions; EUR 652 in Europe to institutions; USD 696 in Canada & Mexico to institutions; USD 664 in the Americas to institutions; USD 1,007 elsewhere to institutions; GBP 592 combined subscription in United Kingdom to institutions (print & online eds.); EUR 751 combined subscription in Europe to institutions (print & online eds.); USD 801 combined subscription in Canada & Mexico to institutions (print & online eds.); USD 764 combined subscription in the Americas to institutions (print & online eds.); USD 1,159 combined subscription elsewhere to institutions (print & online eds.) (effective 2012). adv. back issues avail.; reprint service avail. from PSC. **Document type:** *Journal, Academic/Scholarly.* **Description:** Clinical journal devoted to research and practice of dialysis.
Related titles: Online - full text ed.: ISSN 1525-139X. GBP 515 in United Kingdom to institutions; EUR 652 in Europe to institutions; USD 696 in Canada & Mexico to institutions; USD 664 in the Americas to institutions; USD 1,007 elsewhere to institutions (effective 2012) (from IngentaConnect).
Indexed: A01, A02, A03, A08, A22, A26, ASCA, C06, C07, CA, CurCont, E01, EMBASE, ExcerpMed, ISR, IndMed, Inpharma, MEDLINE, P30, R10, Reac, SCI, SCOPUS, T02, W07.
—BLDSC (8239.448930), GNLM, IE, Infotrieve, Ingenta. **CCC.**
Published by: (American Society of Diagnostic and Interventional Nephrology), Wiley-Blackwell Publishing, Inc. (Subsidiary of: Wiley-Blackwell Publishing Ltd.), 111 River St, Hoboken, NJ 07030. TEL 201-748-6000, FAX 201-748-6088, info@wiley.com. Ed. Dr. Richard A Sherman. Adv. contact Stephen Donohue TEL 781-388-8511.

616.6 USA ISSN 0270-9295
CODEN: SNEPDJ
➤ **SEMINARS IN NEPHROLOGY.** Text in English. 1981 (Mar.). bi-m. USD 463 in United States to institutions; USD 595 elsewhere to institutions (effective 2012). adv. bibl.; charts; illus. index. back issues avail.; reprints avail. **Document type:** *Journal, Academic/Scholarly.* **Description:** Provides a comprehensive and authoritative review of a single timely topic related to clinical nephrology.

Related titles: Online - full text ed.: ISSN 1558-4488 (from ScienceDirect).
Indexed: A22, A34, A36, ASCA, C06, C07, CABA, ChemAb, ChemTitl, CurCont, EMBASE, ExcerpMed, GH, ISR, IndMed, IndVet, Inpharma, MEDLINE, N02, N03, P30, P33, P39, R08, R10, R12, RM&VM, Reac, SCI, SCOPUS, T05, VS, W07, W11.
—BLDSC (8239.455200), CASDDS, GNLM, IE, Infotrieve, Ingenta, INIST. **CCC.**
Published by: W.B. Saunders Co. (Subsidiary of: Elsevier Health Sciences), Elsevier, Health Sciences Division, Order Fulfillment, 3251 Riverport Ln, Maryland Heights, MO 63043. TEL 314-872-8370, 800-325-4177, FAX 314-432-1380, JournalCustomerService-usa@elsevier.com, http://www.us.elsevierhealth.com. Ed. Joseph V Bonventre. Pub. Livia Berardi. Adv. contact Richard Devanna TEL 201-767-4170. Circ: 1,000.

➤ **SEXOLOGIES**; revue europeenne de sante sexuelle - european journal of sexual health. *see* MEDICAL SCIENCES—Obstetrics And Gynecology

617.461059 CHN ISSN 1006-298X
SHENZANGBING YU TOUXI SHENYIZHI ZAZHI/NEPHROSIS - DIALYSIS AND RENAL TRANSPLANTATION. Text in Chinese. 1992. bi-m. USD 31.20 (effective 2009). **Document type:** *Journal, Academic/Scholarly.*
Related titles: Online - full text ed.
—BLDSC (8256.423600), East View.
Published by: Nanjing Daxue, Yixueyuan, 305, Zhongshan Donglu, Nanjing, 210002, China. TEL 86-25-80860040, FAX 86-25-84801992. **Dist. by:** China International Book Trading Corp, 35 Chegongzhuang Xilu, Haidian District, PO Box 399, Beijing 100044, China. TEL 86-10-68412045, FAX 86-10-68412023, cibtc@mail.cibtc.com.cn, http://www.cibtc.com.cn.

616.6 USA ISSN 0892-1245
RC870
SMITH'S GENERAL UROLOGY. Variant title: General Urology. Text in English. 1957. irreg., latest 2007, 17th ed. USD 79.95 (print or online ed.); 17th ed. (effective 2008). **Document type:** *Journal, Academic/Scholarly.*
Related titles: Online - full text ed.
—BLDSC (8311.370000), IE.
Published by: McGraw-Hill Companies, Inc., 1221 Ave of the Americas, 43rd fl, New York, NY 10020. TEL 212-512-2000, customer.service@mcgraw-hill.com, http://www.mcgraw-hill.com. Ed. Emil A Tanagho.

616.6 610.73 ESP ISSN 1139-1375
SOCIEDAD ESPANOLA DE ENFERMERIA NEFROLOGICA. REVISTA. Text in Spanish. 1977. q. **Document type:** *Journal, Academic/Scholarly.*
Former titles (until 1997): B I S E D E N. Boletin Informativo de la Sociedad Espanola de Enfermeria Nefrologica (1131-4710); (until 1983): B I S E A N. Boletin Informativo le la Sociedad Espanola de A T S de Nefrologia (1131-4729)
Related titles: Online - full text ed.: ISSN 2173-9153. 2009. free (effective 2011).
Indexed: A26, C06, C07, C08, CINAHL, I04, I05, SCOPUS.
—**CCC.**
Published by: Sociedad Espanola de Enfermeria Nefrologica, Dr Esquerdo 157, Portal 30C, 1oF, Madrid, 28007, Spain. TEL 34-91-4093737, FAX 34-91-5040977, seden@seden.org.

SONOACE-INTERNATIONAL. *see* MEDICAL SCIENCES—Radiology And Nuclear Medicine

616.6 NLD ISSN 2210-2051
➤ **SPREEKUUR UROLOGIE.** Text in Dutch. 1999. 4/yr. free to qualified personnel (effective 2010). adv. **Document type:** *Journal, Trade.*
Formerly (until 2010): Urologen Vademecum (1389-983X)
Published by: Bohn Stafleu van Loghum B.V. (Subsidiary of: Springer Science+Business Media), Postbus 246, Houten, 3990 GA, Netherlands. TEL 31-30-6383872, FAX 31-30-6383991, boekhandels@bsl.nl, http://www.bsl.nl. adv.: color page EUR 3,434; trim 210 x 297. Circ: 341.

635 GBR
ST PETER'S NEWSLETTER. Text in English. s-a. back issues avail. **Document type:** *Newsletter.* **Description:** Provides information on cure for kidney disease and urological disorders.
Related titles: Online - full text ed.: free (effective 2009).
Published by: (University College London), St. Peter's Trust for Kidney, Bladder & Prostate Research (Subsidiary of: University College London), South House A-5, Royal Free Hospital, Pond St, London, NW3 2QG, United Kingdom. TEL 44-20-74439388, FAX 44-20-74439388, spt@ucl.ac.uk. **Co-sponsor:** H R H The Duchess of Gloucester G C V O.

616.6 USA ISSN 1747-8049
➤ **T S W UROLOGY.** (The Scientific World) Text in English. 1996. a. (updated continuously). USD 99, EUR 89 to individuals; USD 225, EUR 203 to institutions (effective 2010). back issues avail. **Document type:** *Journal, Academic/Scholarly.* **Description:** Publishes original didactic or research articles relevant to physicians and scientists in the area of urology.
Incorporates (2001-2005): Digital Urology Journal
Media: Online - full text.
Published by: The ScientificWorld Ltd. TEL 914-763-0909, information@thescientificworld.com. Ed. Anthony Atala.

616.6 GBR ISSN 1756-2872
RC870
▼ ➤ **THERAPEUTIC ADVANCES IN UROLOGY.** Text in English. 2009 (Mar.). bi-m. USD 1,071, GBP 579 combined subscription to institutions (print & online eds.); USD 1,050, GBP 567 to institutions (effective 2011). back issues avail. **Document type:** *Journal, Academic/Scholarly.* **Description:** Features reviews and original research relating to a range of topics within the area of urology, with a strong focus on emerging pharmacological therapies.
Related titles: Online - full text ed.: ISSN 1756-2880. USD 964, GBP 521 to institutions (effective 2011).
Indexed: A22, E01, EMBASE, SCOPUS.
—**CCC.**
Published by: Sage Publications Ltd. (Subsidiary of: Sage Publications, Inc.), 1 Oliver's Yard, 55 City Rd, London, EC1Y 1SP, United Kingdom. TEL 44-20-73248500, FAX 44-20-73248600, info@sagepub.co.uk, http://www.uk.sagepub.com/home.nav. Ed. Anthony Atala.

616.1 AUS ISSN 1744-9979
CODEN: THAPF4
➤ **THERAPEUTIC APHERESIS AND DIALYSIS.** Text in English. 1997. bi-m. GBP 362 in United Kingdom to institutions; EUR 459 in Europe to institutions; USD 585 in the Americas to institutions; USD 706 elsewhere to institutions; GBP 417 combined subscription in United Kingdom to institutions (print & online eds.); EUR 528 combined subscription in Europe to institutions (print & online eds.); USD 673 combined subscription in the Americas to institutions (print & online eds.); USD 812 combined subscription elsewhere to institutions (print & online eds.) (effective 2012). adv. back issues avail.; reprint service avail. from PSC. **Document type:** *Journal, Academic/Scholarly.* **Description:** Covers the development of new devices and techniques of apheresis in the treatment of severe refractory diseases.
Formerly: Therapeutic Apheresis (1091-6660)
Related titles: Online - full text ed.: ISSN 1744-9987. GBP 362 in United Kingdom to institutions; EUR 459 in Europe to institutions; USD 585 in the Americas to institutions; USD 706 elsewhere to institutions (effective 2012) (from IngentaConnect).
Indexed: A01, A03, A08, A22, A26, B21, CA, ChemAb, CurCont, E01, EMBASE, ESPM, ExcerpMed, H&SSA, H12, INI, IndMed, MEDLINE, P30, R10, Reac, SCI, SCOPUS, T02, W07.
—BLDSC (8814.642670), CASDDS, IE, Infotrieve, Ingenta. **CCC.**
Published by: (International Society for Apheresis JPN), Wiley-Blackwell Publishing Asia (Subsidiary of: Wiley-Blackwell Publishing Ltd.), 155 Cremorne St, Richmond, VIC 3121, Australia. TEL 61-3-92743100, FAX 61-3-92743101, subs@blackwellpublishingasia.com, http://www.wiley.com/WileyCDA/. Eds. Wolfgang Ramlow, Dr. Tadao Akizawa. **Co-sponsors:** Japanese Society for Apherisis; Japanese Society for Dialysis Therapy.

616.6 NLD ISSN 0924-6177
➤ **TOPICS IN RENAL MEDICINE.** Text in English. 1986. irreg., latest vol.10, 1991. price varies. **Document type:** *Monographic series, Academic/Scholarly.*
—**CCC.**
Published by: Springer Netherlands (Subsidiary of: Springer Science+Business Media), Van Godewijckstraat 30, Dordrecht, 3311 GX, Netherlands. TEL 31-78-6576050, FAX 31-78-6576474.

616.6 JPN ISSN 0917-2114
TOSEKI FURONTIA/QUARTERLY JOURNAL OF DIALYSIS. Text in Japanese. 1991. 4/yr. **Document type:** *Journal, Academic/Scholarly.*
Published by: (Fuso Yakuhin Kogyo K.K./Fuso Pharmaceutical Industries, Ltd.), Medikaru Rebyusha/Medical Review Co., Ltd., 1-7-3 Hirano-Machi, Chuo-ku, Yoshida Bldg., Osaka-shi, 541-0046, Japan. TEL 81-6-62231468, FAX 81-6-62231245, http://www.m-review.co.jp/.

616.6 JPN ISSN 1341-1489
TOSEKI KEA; Japanese journal of dialysis & caring. Text in Japanese. 1995. m. JPY 20,412; JPY 1,890 newsstand/cover (effective 2007). Supplement avail. **Document type:** *Journal, Academic/Scholarly.*
Published by: Medicus Shuppan/Medicus Publishing Inc., 18-24 Hiroshiba-cho, Suita-shi, Osaka-fu 564-8580, Japan. TEL 81-6-63856911, FAX 81-6-63856873, http://www.medica.co.jp/.

616.6 617 USA ISSN 1524-7635
TRANSPLANT CHRONICLES. Text in English. 1990. q. free to members (effective 2011). back issues avail. **Document type:** *Newsletter, Consumer.* **Description:** News and information for transplant patients and their families.
Related titles: Online - full text ed.: free (effective 2011).
Published by: National Kidney Foundation, Inc., 30 E 33rd St, New York, NY 10016. TEL 212-889-2210, 800-622-9010, FAX 212-689-9261, info@kidney.org. Ed. Laurel Williams.

616.6 GBR ISSN 2044-3730
TRENDS IN UROLOGY AND MEN'S HEALTH. Text in English. 1996. bi-m. GBP 70 in United Kingdom to institutions; EUR 98 in Europe to institutions; USD 164 elsewhere to institutions; GBP 81 combined subscription in United Kingdom to institutions (print & online eds.); EUR 113 combined subscription in Europe to institutions (print & online eds.); USD 189 combined subscription elsewhere to institutions (print & online eds.) (effective 2012). adv. back issues avail.; reprint service avail. from PSC. **Document type:** *Journal, Academic/Scholarly.* **Description:** Features a wide range of articles covering practical management issues from a primary and secondary care point of view.
Supersedes in part (in 2010): Trends in Urology, Gynaecology & Sexual Health (1362-5306)
Related titles: Online - full text ed.: ISSN 2044-3749. GBP 70 in United Kingdom to institutions; EUR 98 in Europe to institutions; USD 164 elsewhere to institutions (effective 2012).
Indexed: C06.
—BLDSC (9049.688730), IE, Ingenta. **CCC.**
Published by: Wiley-Blackwell Publishing Ltd. (Subsidiary of: John Wiley & Sons, Inc.), 9600 Garsington Rd, Oxford, OX4 2DQ, United Kingdom. TEL 44-1865-776868, FAX 44-1865-714591, customerservices@blackwellpublishing.com, http://www.wiley.com/. Eds. Roger Kirby, John Fitzpatrick.

616.6 TUR ISSN 1300-5804
➤ **TURK UROLOJI DERGISI/TURKISH JOURNAL OF UROLOGY.** Text in Turkish. 1983. a. **Document type:** *Journal, Academic/Scholarly.*
Related titles: Online - full text ed.
Indexed: A01, C06, C07, P20, P22, P48, P54, PQC, SCOPUS, T02.
—BLDSC (9072.196000).
Published by: (Turk Uroloji Dernegi/Turkish Urological Society), Aves Yayincilik, Kizilelma Cad 5/3, Findikazade, Istanbul, 34096, Turkey. TEL 90-212-5890053, FAX 90-212-5890094, info@avesyayincilik.com, http://www.avesyayincilik.com. Ed. Dr. H Murat Tunc.

616.6 ESP ISSN 1133-0414
UNIVERSIDAD COMPLUTENSE. CLINICAS UROLOGICAS. Variant title: Clinicas Urologicas de la Complutense. Text in Spanish. 1993. irreg. price varies. back issues avail. **Document type:** *Monographic series, Academic/Scholarly.* **Description:** Presents monographic issues on urologic topics.
Published by: (Universidad Complutense de Madrid, Facultad de Medicina), Universidad Complutense de Madrid, Servicio de Publicaciones, C/ Obispo Trejo 2, Ciudad Universitaria, Madrid, 28040, Spain. TEL 34-91-3941127, FAX 34-91-3941126, servicio.publicaciones@rect.ucm.es, http://www.ucm.es/publicaciones.

616.6 USA ISSN 1074-8687
RC870
URO-GRAM. Text in English. 1972. bi-m. USD 60 to members. adv. bk.rev. **Document type:** *Newsletter, Trade.* **Description:** Provides urology health care workers with information, news and events of the association as well as items affecting urologic practice in general.
Indexed: C06, C07, C08, CINAHL, P24, P48, PQC.
Published by: Society of Urologic Nurses and Associates, PO Box 56, Pitman, NJ 08071-0056. TEL 856-256-2335, FAX 856-589-7463. Ed., R&P Glenda Wilkinson. Adv. contact Cheryl Underhill. Circ: 2,500.

616.6 DEU ISSN 1432-9026
URO NEWS. Text in German. 1997. bi-m. EUR 122, USD 129 to institutions (effective 2012). adv. **Document type:** *Journal, Academic/Scholarly.*
Indexed: A26.
—IE. **CCC.**
Published by: Urban und Vogel Medien und Medizin Verlagsgesellschaft mbH (Subsidiary of: Springer Science+Business Media), Neumarkter Str 43, Munich, 81673, Germany. TEL 49-89-4372-1411, FAX 49-89-4372-1410, verlag@urban-vogel.de. Ed. Dr. Doris Berger. Adv. contact Paul Berger TEL 49-89-4372-1342. B&W page EUR 2,100, color page EUR 3,350; trim 174 x 237. Circ: 4,500 (paid and controlled). **Subscr. to:** Springer Distribution Center, Kundenservice Zeitschriften, Haberstr 7, Heidelberg 69126, Germany. TEL 49-6221-3454303, FAX 49-6221-3454229, subscriptions@springer.com.

616.61 ESP ISSN 1018-5151
URODINAMICA APLICADA. Text in Spanish. 1989. q. **Document type:** *Journal, Academic/Scholarly.*
Published by: Sociedad Iberoamericana de Neurologia y Uroginecologia, Apdo de Coreso 17, Alicante, 03080, Spain. http://centrourologiaintegrada.com/sinug/index.php. Ed. Jesus Salinas Casado.

616.6 ITA ISSN 2038-8314
➤ **UROGYNAECOLOGIA INTERNATIONAL JOURNAL (ONLINE).** Text in English. 2000. irreg. **Document type:** *Journal, Academic/Scholarly.*
Media: Online - full text.
Published by: Pagepress, Via Giuseppe Belli 4, Pavia, 27100, Italy. TEL 39-0382-1751762, FAX 39-0382-1750481, http://www.pagepress.org.

616.6 DEU ISSN 0340-2592
RC870 CODEN: URGABW
➤ **DER UROLOGE. SECTION A**; Zeitschrift fuer klinische und praktische Urologie. Key Title: Urologe. Ausgabe A. Text in German; Summaries in English, German. 1962. m. EUR 673, USD 750 combined subscription to institutions (print & online eds.) (effective 2012). adv. bk.rev. abstr.; charts; illus. index, cum.index: 1962-1969. back issues avail.; reprint service avail. from PSC. **Document type:** *Journal, Academic/Scholarly.* **Description:** Covers new developments and techniques in urology.
Formerly (until 1970): Urologe (0375-4685); Incorporates (1961-2002): Der Urologe. Section B (0042-1111); Which was formerly (until 1970): Urologische Facharzt (0301-1410)
Related titles: Microform ed.: (from PQC); Online - full text ed.: ISSN 1433-0563 (from IngentaConnect).
Indexed: A22, A26, ASCA, B25, BIOSIS Prev, CurCont, E01, EMBASE, ExcerpMed, FR, G10, IBR, IBZ, ISR, IndMed, Inpharma, MEDLINE, P30, P35, R10, Reac, SCI, SCOPUS, W07.
—GNLM, IE, Infotrieve, Ingenta, INIST. **CCC.**
Published by: (Deutsche Gesellschaft fuer Urologie), Springer (Subsidiary of: Springer Science+Business Media), Tiergartenstr 17, Heidelberg, 69121, Germany. TEL 49-6221-4870, FAX 49-6221-345229. Adv. contact Stephan Kroeck TEL 49-30-827875739. Circ: 6,800 (paid and controlled). **Subscr. in the Americas to:** Springer New York LLC, Journal Fulfillment, PO Box 2485, Secaucus, NJ 07096. TEL 800-777-4643, 201-348-4033, FAX 201-348-4505, journals-ny@springer.com, http://www.springer.com; **Subscr. to:** Springer Distribution Center, Kundenservice Zeitschriften, Haberstr 7, Heidelberg 69126, Germany. TEL 49-6221-3454303, FAX 49-6221-3454229, subscriptions@springer.com.

616.6 ITA ISSN 0391-5603
UROLOGIA/UROLOGY; rivista internazionale di cultura urologica. Text in Italian. 1934. q. adv. bk.rev. charts; illus. index. back issues avail. **Document type:** *Journal, Academic/Scholarly.*
Related titles: Online - full text ed.: ISSN 1724-6075.
Indexed: A01, CA, ChemAb, MEDLINE, P30, RefZh, T02.
—INIST. **CCC.**
Published by: (Society of Urology of Northern Italy), Wichtig Editore Srl, Via Friuli 72, Milan, MI 20135, Italy. TEL 39-02-55195443, FAX 39-02-55195971, info@wichtig-publisher.com, http://www.wichtig-publisher.com. Circ: 1,300 (controlled).

616.6 PRT ISSN 1646-9631
UROLOGIA CLINICA. Text in Portuguese. 2008. q. **Document type:** *Journal, Academic/Scholarly.*
Published by: Medicografica Edicoes Medicas, Rua Camilo Castelo Branco 23-5, Lisbon, 1150-083, Portugal. geral@medicografica.pt, http://www.medicografica.pt.

616.6 BRA ISSN 1413-0351
➤ **UROLOGIA CONTEMPORANEA.** Text and summaries in Portuguese. 1995. q. adv. bk.rev. back issues avail. **Document type:** *Magazine, Academic/Scholarly.*
Related titles: Online - full text ed.
Published by: Sociedade Brasileira de Urologia/Brazilian Society of Urology, Rua Bambina 153, Botafogo, Rio de Janeiro, 22251-050, Brazil. TEL 55-21-22464092, FAX 55-21-22464194, http://www.sbu.org.br.

616.6 CHE ISSN 0042-1138
RC870 CODEN: URINAC
➤ **UROLOGIA INTERNATIONALIS.** Text in English. 1955. 8/yr. (in 2 vols.). CHF 4,352, EUR 3,480, USD 4,254 to institutions; CHF 4,780, EUR 3,822, USD 4,668 combined subscription to institutions (print & online eds.) (effective 2012). adv. bk.rev. bibl.; charts; illus. index. back issues avail. **Document type:** *Journal, Academic/Scholarly.* **Description:** Presents original papers and reports of practice-oriented research into the etiology, pathophysiology and management of diseases of the urinary and urogenital tract.
Incorporates (1987-2000): Acta Urologica Italica (0394-2511)
Related titles: Microform ed.; Online - full text ed.: ISSN 1423-0399. 199?. CHF 4,284, EUR 3,428, USD 4,160 to institutions (effective 2012).

Indexed: A01, A03, A08, A22, ASCA, B25, BIOSIS Prev, CA, CIN, ChemAb, ChemTitl, CurCont, E01, EMBASE, ExcerpMed, G10, IndMed, Inpharma, MEDLINE, MycolAb, P30, P35, R10, Reac, SCI, SCOPUS, T02, W07.
—BLDSC (9124.480000), CASDDS, GNLM, IE, Infotrieve, Ingenta, INIST. **CCC.**
Published by: S. Karger AG, Allschwilerstr 10, Basel, 4055, Switzerland. TEL 41-61-3061111, FAX 41-61-3061234, karger@karger.ch, http://www.karger.ch. Eds. M. Porena, M.P. Wirth. R&P Tatjana Sepin. adv.: page CHF 1,815; trim 210 x 280. Circ: 800.

616.6 POL ISSN 0500-7208 CODEN: URPOAG
UROLOGIA POLSKA/POLISH JOURNAL OF UROLOGY. Text in Polish. 1951. q. **Document type:** *Journal, Academic/Scholarly.*
Indexed: A36, CA, CABA, GH, N02, N03, P20, P30, P33, P48, P54, PQC, T02, T05.
Published by: Polskie Towarzystwo Urologiczne, Klinika Urologii i Rehabilitacji Urologicznej, Uniwersytecki Szpital Kliniczny Nr 2 im. WAM, ul Zeromskiego 113, Lodz, 90549, Poland. TEL 48-42-6393531, FAX 48-42-6368214. Ed. Marek Sosnowski.

616.6 USA ISSN 0094-0143 RC870 CODEN: UCNADW
➤ **UROLOGIC CLINICS OF NORTH AMERICA.** Text in English. 1974. q. USD 519 in United States to institutions; USD 636 elsewhere to institutions (effective 2012). adv. back issues avail.; reprints avail. **Document type:** *Journal, Academic/Scholarly.* **Description:** Focuses on a single topic relevant to your urology practice, including prostate cancer, sexually transmitted diseases, erectile dysfunction, renal cancer, dermatologic issues, fertility issues, ureteroscopy, and laparoscopic surgery.
Related titles: Microform ed.: (from PQC); Online - full text ed.: ISSN 1558-318X (from ScienceDirect); Supplement(s): Continuing Medical Education Supplement to Urologic Clinics of North America. USD 138 (effective 2000).
Indexed: A22, AIM, ASCA, C06, C07, C08, CINAHL, CurCont, DentInd, EMBASE, ExcerpMed, FR, G10, ISR, IndMed, Inpharma, MEDLINE, MycolAb, P30, R10, Reac, SCI, SCOPUS, W07.
—BLDSC (9124.620000), GNLM, IE, Infotrieve, Ingenta, INIST. **CCC.**
Published by: W.B. Saunders Co. (Subsidiary of: Elsevier Health Sciences), Elsevier, Health Sciences Division, Order Fulfillment, 3251 Riverport Ln, Maryland Heights, MO 63043. TEL 314-872-8370, 800-325-4177, FAX 314-432-1380, JournalCustomerService-usa@elsevier.com, http://www.us.elsevierhealth.com.

616.6 USA ISSN 1934-8762
UROLOGIC DISEASES RESEARCH UPDATES. Text in English. 1999. q. **Document type:** *Newsletter, Trade.*
Supersedes in part (in 2005): Research Updates in Kidney and Urologic Health (1934-8770)
Media: Online - full text.
Published by: (National of Institutes of Health, The National Institute of Diabetes and Digestive and Kidney Diseases (N I D D K)), National Kidney and Urologic Diseases Information Clearinghouse, 3 Information Way, Bethesda, MD 20892-3580. TEL 800-891-5390, nkudic@info.niddk.nih.gov.

616.6 610.736 USA ISSN 1053-816X CODEN: URNUES
➤ **UROLOGIC NURSING.** Text in English. 1980. bi-m. USD 42 domestic; USD 72 foreign; USD 15 per issue (effective 2010). adv. back issues avail.; reprints avail. **Document type:** *Journal, Academic/Scholarly.* **Description:** Features clinical articles covering a wide variety of urologic issues and clinical procedures.
Formerly (until 1988): A U A A Journal (0882-9594)
Related titles: Online - full text ed.
Indexed: A01, A02, A03, A08, A22, A26, C06, C07, C08, C11, CA, CINAHL, E08, EMBASE, ExcerpMed, G08, H04, H11, H12, I05, INI, MEDLINE, P20, P22, P24, P30, P48, P54, PQC, R10, Reac, S09, SCOPUS, T02.
—BLDSC (9124.625000), GNLM, IE, Infotrieve, Ingenta. **CCC.**
Published by: (Society of Urologic Nurses and Associates, Inc. (SUNA)), Jannetti Publications, Inc., E Holly Ave, PO Box 56, Pitman, NJ 08071. TEL 856-256-2300, FAX 856-589-7463, contact@ajj.com, http://www.ajj.com/. Pub. Anthony J Jannetti. Adv. contact Susan Iannelli. Circ: 5,000. **Co-sponsor:** Urology Nurses of Canada (UNC).

➤ **UROLOGIC ONCOLOGY**; seminars and original investigations. *see* MEDICAL SCIENCES—Oncology

616.6 DEU ISSN 0300-5623 CODEN: URLRA5
➤ **UROLOGICAL RESEARCH**; a journal of clinical and laboratory investigation in urolithiasis and related areas. Text and summaries in English. 1973. bi-m. EUR 1,370, USD 1,656 combined subscription to institutions (print & online eds.) (effective 2012). adv. charts. index. back issues avail.; reprint service avail. from PSC. **Document type:** *Journal, Academic/Scholarly.* **Description:** Covers research in the fields of clinical medicine, animal experimentation, and laboratory techniques. Contributions are designed to increase understanding of the functions of the genitourinary system in normal and diseased states.
Related titles: Microform ed.: (from PQC); Online - full text ed.: ISSN 1434-0879 (from IngentaConnect).
Indexed: A01, A03, A08, A22, A26, A34, A36, ASCA, Agr, AgrForAb, B25, BIOSIS Prev, CA, CABA, CIN, ChemAb, CurCont, D01, E01, EMBASE, ExcerpMed, F08, F11, F12, GH, H12, H16, ISR, IndMed, Inpharma, MEDLINE, MycolAb, N02, N03, O01, P20, P22, P30, P35, P48, P54, PQC, R10, R12, RA&MP, Reac, S12, SCI, SCOPUS, T02, T05, TAR, VS, W07.
—BLDSC (9124.650000), CASDDS, GNLM, IE, Infotrieve, Ingenta, INIST. **CCC.**
Published by: Springer (Subsidiary of: Springer Science+Business Media), Tiergartenstr 17, Heidelberg, 69121, Germany. TEL 49-6221-4870, FAX 49-6221-345229. Ed. Dr. William G Robertson. **Subscr. in the Americas to:** Springer New York LLC, Journal Fulfillment, PO Box 2485, Secaucus, NJ 07096. TEL 800-777-4643, 201-348-4033, FAX 201-348-4505, journals-ny@springer.com, http://www.springer.com; **Subscr. to:** Springer Distribution Center, Kundenservice Zeitschriften, Haberstr 7, Heidelberg 69126, Germany. TEL 49-6221-3454303, FAX 49-6221-3454229, subscriptions@springer.com.

616.6 GBR ISSN 1879-5226
UROLOGICAL SCIENCE. Text in English. q. EUR 200 in Europe to institutions; JPY 31,500 in Japan to institutions; USD 263 elsewhere to institutions (effective 2012). **Document type:** *Journal, Academic/Scholarly.*
Former titles (until 2010): Taiwan Miniao Keyi Xuehui Zazhi; (until 2002): Zhonghua Minguo Miniao keyi Xuehui Zazhi
Related titles: Online - full text ed.: (from ScienceDirect).
Indexed: B21, ImmunAb, SCOPUS, T02.
—**CCC.**
Published by: (Taiwan Urological Association TWN), Elsevier Ltd (Subsidiary of: Elsevier Science & Technology), The Blvd, Langford Ln, Kidlington, Oxford, OX5 1GB, United Kingdom. TEL 44-1865-843434, FAX 44-1865-843970, journalscustomerserviceemea@elsevier.com. Ed. Alex T L Lin.

616.6 CZE ISSN 1214-2085
➤ **UROLOGICKE LISTY.** Text in Czech. 2003. q. CZK 600 domestic; EUR 24 foreign (effective 2010). **Document type:** *Journal, Academic/Scholarly.* **Description:** Publishes the most current information for urologists, including the guidelines from the the European Urology Association.
Related titles: Online - full text ed.: ISSN 1801-7584.
Published by: Medica Healthworld a.s., Bidlaky 20, Brno, 63900, Czech Republic. TEL 420-533-337311, FAX 420-533-337312, info@mhw.cz, http://www.mhw.cz. Ed. Dalibor Pacik. Circ: 1,000.

616.6 CZE ISSN 1213-1768
➤ **UROLOGIE PRO PRAXI.** Text in Czech. 2001. bi-m. CZK 420; CZK 70 per issue (effective 2010). **Document type:** *Journal, Academic/Scholarly.*
Related titles: Online - full text ed.: ISSN 1803-5299.
Published by: Solen s.r.o., Lazecka 297/51, Olomouc 51, 779 00, Czech Republic. TEL 420-582-396038, FAX 420-582-396099, solen@solen.cz, http://www.solen.cz. Ed. Zdenka Bartakova. Circ: 800.

616.6 AUT ISSN 1561-526X
UROLOGIK; Fachzeitschrift fuer Urologie. Text in German. 1994. bi-m. EUR 28 (effective 2007). adv. **Document type:** *Journal, Academic/Scholarly.*
Published by: Universimed Verlags- und Service GmbH, Markgraf-Ruediger-Str 8, Vienna, 1150, Austria. TEL 43-1-87679560, FAX 43-1-876795620, office@universimed.com, http://www.universimed.com. Ed. Christian Fexa. Adv. contact Heidrun Eberl. Circ: 1,500 (paid).

616.6 DEU ISSN 1439-4871
UROLOGISCHE NACHRICHTEN. Text in German. 1995. m. adv. **Document type:** *Journal, Trade.*
Published by: Biermann Verlag GmbH, Otto-Hahn-Str 7, Cologne, 50997, Germany. TEL 49-2236-3760, FAX 49-2236-376999, info@biermann.net, http://www.biermann-verlag.de. Ed. Markus Schmitz. Adv. contact Daniel Helmers.

616.6 RUS ISSN 1728-2985 CODEN: URNEAA
UROLOGIYA/UROLOGY. Text in Russian; Summaries in English. 1923. bi-m. USD 197 foreign (effective 2005). adv. bk.rev. bibl.; abstr. **Document type:** *Journal, Academic/Scholarly.* **Description:** Reports on the advances of Russian and foreign medicine in the domain of urology and nephrology.
Former titles (until 1999): Urologiya i Nefrologiya (0042-1154); (until 1965): Urologiya (0258-8404)
Indexed: B25, BIOSIS Prev, ChemAb, EMBASE, ExcerpMed, IndMed, MEDLINE, MycolAb, P30, R10, Reac, RefZh, SCOPUS.
—BLDSC (0385.100000), CASDDS, East View, GNLM, INIST. **CCC.**
Published by: Izdatel'stvo Meditsina/Meditsina Publishers, ul B Pirogovskaya, d 2, str 5, Moscow, 119435, Russian Federation. TEL 7-095-2483324, meditsina@mtu-net.ru, http://www.medlit.ru. Ed. Nikolai A Lopatkin. Pub. A M Stochik. R&P L Sladkova. Adv. contact O A Fadeeva TEL 7-095-923-51-40. Circ: 2,000. **Dist. by:** East View Information Services, 10601 Wayzata Blvd, Minneapolis, MN 55305. TEL 952-252-1201, 800-477-1005, FAX 952-252-1202, info@eastview.com, http://www.eastview.com.

616.6 USA ISSN 0090-4295 RC870
➤ **UROLOGY.** Text in English. 1973. m. USD 651 in US & Canada to institutions; USD 909 elsewhere to institutions (effective 2012). adv. bk.rev. abstr.; bibl.; charts; stat. back issues avail.; reprints avail. **Document type:** *Journal, Academic/Scholarly.* **Description:** For hospital based and private practice physicians. Contains original scientific reports, case reports and review updates.
Related titles: Microform ed.; Online - full text ed.: ISSN 1527-9995 (from IngentaConnect, ScienceDirect); Polish ed.: ISSN 1731-0377.
Indexed: A01, A03, A08, A20, A22, A26, A34, A36, ASCA, B23, B25, BIOBASE, BIOSIS Prev, C06, C07, CA, CABA, CurCont, DentInd, E12, EMBASE, ExcerpMed, F08, FR, G10, GH, H16, H17, I05, IABS, ISR, IndMed, Inpharma, LT, MEDLINE, MycolAb, N02, N03, N04, NRN, P30, P33, P35, R08, R10, R12, R13, RA&MP, RILM, RM&VM, RRTA, Reac, SCI, SCOPUS, SoyAb, T02, T05, THA, VS, W07.
—BLDSC (9124.703000), GNLM, IE, Ingenta, INIST. **CCC.**
Published by: (Societe Internationale d'Urologie/International Society of Urology CAN), Excerpta Medica, Inc. (Subsidiary of: Elsevier Health Sciences), 685 US-202, Bridgewater, NJ 08807. TEL 908-547-2100, FAX 908-547-2200, excerptamedica@elsevier.com, http://www.excerptamedica.com/. Ed. Eric A Klein. Pub. Matt Jozwiak. adv.: B&W page USD 2,740, color page USD 4,430; bleed 8.25 x 11. Circ: 5,205.

616.6 IND ISSN 0974-7796
▼ **UROLOGY ANNALS.** Text in English. 2009. 3/yr. INR 1,500 domestic to individuals; USD 150 foreign to individuals; INR 3,000 domestic to institutions; USD 300 foreign to institutions (effective 2011). adv. bk.rev. abstr. **Document type:** *Journal, Academic/Scholarly.* **Description:** Covers genitourinary diseases of male and female including neurourology, pediatric urology, urologic oncology.
Related titles: Online - full text ed.: ISSN 0974-7834. INR 1,200 domestic to individuals; USD 120 foreign to individuals; INR 2,400 domestic to institutions; USD 240 foreign to institutions (effective 2011).
Indexed: A01, A26, CA, E08, H11, H12, I05, P10, P30, P48, P53, P54, PQC, S09, T02.
—**CCC.**
Published by: (Saudi Urological Association SAU), Medknow Publications and Media Pvt. Ltd., B-9, Kanara Business Ctr, Off Link Rd, Ghatkopar (E), Mumbai, Maharastra 400 075, India. TEL 91-22-66491816, FAX 91-22-66491817, http://www.medknow.com.

UROLOGY CODING ALERT; your practical adviser for ethically optimizing coding, payment, and efficiency in urology practices. *see* INSURANCE

616.6 IRN ISSN 1735-1308 RC870
UROLOGY JOURNAL. Text in English. 2003. q. **Document type:** *Journal, Academic/Scholarly.*
Related titles: Online - full text ed.: ISSN 1735-546X. 2004. free (effective 2011).
Indexed: A01, A35, A36, AgBio, C06, C07, CA, CABA, D01, EMBASE, ExcerpMed, F08, GH, H17, MEDLINE, N02, N03, P20, P22, P30, P33, P48, P54, PQC, R10, R12, RA&MP, RM&VM, Reac, SCI, SCOPUS, T02, T05, W07.
—IE.
Published by: (Urology Nephrology Research Center (U N R C)), Shaheed Beheshti Medical University, Medical Sciences and Health Services, Shaheed Bahonar Ave, Darabad, Tehran, 19569, Iran. TEL 98-21-2282111, FAX 98-21-2285777. Ed. Abbas Basiri.

616.6 GBR ISSN 1368-8960
UROLOGY NEWS. Text in English. 1996. bi-m. GBP 17 domestic; GBP 25 in Europe; GBP 40 elsewhere (effective 2009). adv. bk.rev. back issues avail. **Document type:** *Magazine, Trade.* **Description:** Reviews current literature in urology and related fields.
Related titles: Online - full text ed.
—BLDSC (9124.707150). **CCC.**
Published by: Pinpoint Scotland Ltd., 9 Gayfield St, Edinburgh, Scotland EH1 3NT, United Kingdom. TEL 44-131-5574184, FAX 44-131-5574701, info@pinpoint-scotland.com. Ed. Jennifer Fallon TEL 44-131-5574184. Adv. contact Alasdair Grierson TEL 44-131-4788404. Circ: 4,500; 41,000 (controlled).

616.6 USA
UROLOGY NURSES ONLINE. Text in English. irreg. **Description:** Promotes the exchange of information among nurses practicing in urology.
Published by: Digital Urology Journal, 300 Longwood Ave, Hunnewell 3, Boston, MA 02115. FAX 617-355-6587, mail@duj.com. Ed. Mary Kelly.

616.6 USA ISSN 0093-9722 RC870
UROLOGY TIMES; the leading news source for Urologists. Text in English. 1973. m. USD 99 domestic; USD 147 in Canada & Mexico; USD 195 elsewhere; USD 17 newsstand/cover domestic; USD 21 newsstand/cover in Canada & Mexico; USD 25 newsstand/cover elsewhere (effective 2011). adv. back issues avail. **Document type:** *Magazine, Trade.* **Description:** Features news for office-based and hospital-based urologists and osteopathic urologists.
Related titles: Microform ed.: (from PQC); Online - full text ed.: ISSN 2150-7384. free (effective 2011); ◆ Supplement(s): Urology Times: The Urology Times Clinical Edition.
Indexed: A01, A02, A03, A08, A15, A26, ABIn, C06, C07, C08, C11, CINAHL, G08, H03, H04, H11, H12, I05, M01, M02, P19, P26, P34, P48, P51, P54, PQC, PROMT, T02.
—**CCC.**
Published by: Advanstar Communications, Inc., 6200 Canoga Ave, 2nd Fl, Woodland Hills, CA 91367. TEL 818-593-5000, FAX 818-593-5020, info@advanstar.com, http://www.advanstar.com. Ed. Richard R Kerr TEL 440-891-2758. Adv. contact Samantha Armstrong TEL 732-346-3083.

616.6 USA
➤ **UROLOGY TIMES: THE UROLOGY TIMES CLINICAL EDITION.** Text in English. 1989. q. (bi-m. until 2008). adv. charts; illus. Index. back issues avail.; reprints avail. **Document type:** *Journal, Academic/Scholarly.* **Description:** Contains 2-3 articles and departments regarding practical solutions to clinical problems in urology.
Formerly (until Jan.2008): Contemporary Urology (1042-2250)
Related titles: Online - full text ed.; ◆ Supplement to: Urology Times. ISSN 0093-9722.
Indexed: A22, A26, C06, C07, C08, CA, CINAHL, E08, G08, H11, H12, I05, P26, P30, P48, P54, PQC, S09, SCOPUS, T02.
—BLDSC (3425.314500), GNLM, IE, Infotrieve, Ingenta. **CCC.**
Published by: Advanstar Communications, Inc., 6200 Canoga Ave, 2nd Fl, Woodland Hills, CA 91367. TEL 818-593-5000, FAX 818-593-5020, info@advanstar.com, http://www.advanstar.com.

616.6 JPN ISSN 1347-9636
UROLOGY VIEW. Text in Japanese. 2003. bi-m. JPY 17,640 (effective 2007). **Document type:** *Journal, Academic/Scholarly.*
Published by: Medical View Co. Ltd./Mejikaru Byusha, 2-30 Ichigaya-Honmura-cho, Shinjuku-ku, Tokyo, 162-0845, Japan. TEL 81-3-52282050, FAX 81-3-52282059, eigyo@medicalview.co.jp, http://www.medicalview.co.jp.

616.6 NLD ISSN 1877-7384
▼ **UROSCOPE.** Text in Dutch. 2009. q. **Document type:** *Magazine, Trade.*
Published by: Van Zuiden Communications B.V., Postbus 2122, Alphen aan den Rijn, 2400 CC, Netherlands. TEL 31-172-476191, FAX 31-172-471882, zuiden@zuidencomm.nl, http://www.zuidencomm.nl. Ed. Samuel V Yrastorza.

616.6 USA ISSN 1939-4810
➤ **UROTODAY INTERNATIONAL JOURNAL.** Text in English. 2003. irreg., latest 2010. free. **Document type:** *Journal, Academic/Scholarly.* **Description:** Contains reviews and original research papers on all fields of urology.
Media: Online - full text.
Indexed: SCOPUS.
Published by: UroToday Inc., 1802 Fifth St, Berkeley, CA 94710. FAX 510-540-0930, http://www.urotoday.com/.

616.6 GBR ISSN 1758-3969
▼ **US UROLOGY DISEASE.** Text in English. 2009. a. back issues avail. **Document type:** *Report, Trade.* **Description:** Provides an overview of current trends and future developments in the prevention, diagnosis and treatment of disorders affecting the reproductive organs and the urinary system.
Formerly (until 2009): US Genito-Urinary Disease
Media: Online - full text.

Published by: Touch Briefings (Subsidiary of: Touch Group plc), Saffron House, 6-10 Kirby St, London, EC1N 8TS, United Kingdom. TEL 44-20-74525600, FAX 44-20-74525606, info@touchbriefings.com.

V H L FAMILY FORUM. (Von Hippel-Lindau Disease) *see* MEDICAL SCIENCES—Psychiatry And Neurology

616.6 USA ISSN 2151-1136
▼ ➤ **VIDEOUROLOGY.** Variant title: Part B, Videourology. Text in English. 2010. bi-m. USD 1,875 to institutions (effective 2011). **Document type:** *Journal, Trade.* **Description:** Provides surgical and micro-invasive video demonstrations of the latest techniques and technologies used to optimize surgical patient outcome. A companion to the Journal of Endourology.
Media: Online - full content. **Related titles:** ◆ Supplement to: Journal of Endourology. ISSN 0892-7790.
—CCC.
Published by: Mary Ann Liebert, Inc. Publishers, 140 Huguenot St, 3rd Fl, New Rochelle, NY 10801. TEL 914-740-2100, FAX 914-740-2101, info@liebertpub.com.

616.1 DEU ISSN 1616-3850
WIRTSCHAFTSMAGAZIN FUER DEN UROLOGEN. Text in German. 1997. bi-m. EUR 22.50 (effective 2011). adv. **Document type:** *Magazine, Trade.*
Formerly (until 2000): Wirtschaftsbrief fuer den Urologen (1439-2992)
Published by: W P V- Wirtschafts- und Praxisverlag GmbH, Otto-Hahn-Str 7, Koeln, 50997, Germany. TEL 49-2236-376711, FAX 49-2236-37692530, info@wpv.de. Adv. contact Isabelle Becker TEL 49-2236-376711. Circ: 2,703 (controlled).

616.6 DEU ISSN 1866-2900
WIRTSCHAFTSTIP FUER UROLOGEN. Text in German. 1997. m. EUR 21.40 (effective 2008). adv. **Document type:** *Journal, Trade.*
Published by: Aerzte Zeitung Verlagsgesellschaft mbH (Subsidiary of: Springer Science+Business Media), Am Forsthaus Gravenbruch 5, Neu-Isenburg, 63263, Germany. TEL 49-6102-506157, FAX 49-6102-506123, info@aerztezeitung.de, http://www.aerztezeitung.de. adv.: B&W page EUR 1,890, color page EUR 3,120. Circ: 2,765 (controlled).

616.6 DEU ISSN 0724-4983
RC870 CODEN: WJURDJ
➤ **WORLD JOURNAL OF UROLOGY.** Text in English. 1983. bi-m. EUR 1,216, USD 1,481 combined subscription to institutions (print & online eds.) (effective 2012). adv. bk.rev. charts; illus. back issues avail.; reprint service avail. from PSC. **Document type:** *Journal, Academic/Scholarly.* **Description:** Conveys the essential results of urological research and their practical and clinical relevance.
Related titles: Microform ed.: (from PQC); Online - full text ed.: ISSN 1433-8726 (from IngentaConnect).
Indexed: A01, A03, A08, A22, A26, ASCA, Agr, B25, BIOSIS Prev, CA, CurCont, E01, EMBASE, ExcerpMed, G10, H12, INI, ISR, IndMed, Inpharma, MEDLINE, MycolAb, NRN, P20, P22, P30, P35, P48, P54, PQC, R10, Reac, SCI, SCOPUS, T02, W07.
—BLDSC (9356.074500), CASDDS, GNLM, IE, Infotrieve, Ingenta, INIST. CCC.
Published by: (Urological Research Society), Springer (Subsidiary of: Springer Science+Business Media), Tiergartenstr 17, Heidelberg, 69121, Germany. TEL 49-6221-4870, FAX 49-6221-345229. Ed. Dr. M S Steiner. **Subscr. in the Americas to:** Springer New York LLC, Journal Fulfillment, PO Box 2485, Secaucus, NJ 07096. TEL 800-777-4643, 201-348-4033, FAX 201-348-4505, journals-ny@springer.com, http://www.springer.com; **Subscr. to:** Springer Distribution Center, Kundenservice Zeitschriften, Haberstr 7, Heidelberg 69126, Germany. TEL 49-6221-3454303, FAX 49-6221-3454229, subscriptions@springer.com.

616.6 CHN ISSN 1009-8291
CODEN: XMWZBF
XIANDAI MINIAO WAIKE ZAZHI/JOURNAL OF MODERN UROLOGY. Text in Chinese; Abstracts in Chinese, English. 1996. bi-m. CNY 66, USD 66; CNY 11 per issue (effective 2010). adv. **Document type:** *Journal, Academic/Scholarly.*
Related titles: Online - full text ed.
Indexed: RefZh.
Published by: Xi'an Jiaotong Daxue Yixueyuan/Xi'an Jiaotong University College of Medicine, 76, Yanta Xilu Rd., Xi'an, 710061, China. TEL 86-29-82657054, FAX 86-29-82655021, http://www.med.xjtu.edu.cn/. Ed. Ai-ling Hu. Circ: 3,000.

616.6 USA ISSN 0084-4071
YEAR BOOK OF UROLOGY. Text in English. 1922. a. USD 217 in United States to institutions; USD 235 elsewhere to institutions (effective 2012). adv. illus. **Document type:** *Yearbook, Academic/Scholarly.* **Description:** Contains abstracts of the articles that reported the year's breakthrough developments in urology, carefully selected from more than 500 journals worldwide.
Formerly (until 1933): Urology
Related titles: CD-ROM ed.; Online - full text ed.
—GNLM. CCC.
Published by: Mosby, Inc. (Subsidiary of: Elsevier Health Sciences), 1600 John F. Kennedy Blvd, Ste 1800, Philadelphia, PA 19103. TEL 215-239-3900, 800-523-1649, FAX 215-239-3990, elspcs@elsevier.com, http://www.us.elsevierhealth.com. Eds. Dr. Douglas L Coplen Jr., Dr. Gerald L. Andriole Jr.

616.6 GBR ISSN 1742-3082
THE YEAR IN RENAL MEDICINE. Text in English. 2005 (Jan.). a., latest 2005. USD 99.95 per issue in US & Canada; GBP 59.99 per issue elsewhere (effective 2009). 400 p./no.; **Document type:** *Journal, Academic/Scholarly.* **Description:** Covers new developments in nephrology and renal medicine.
Indexed: P20, P22, P48, P54, PQC.
—CCC.
Published by: Clinical Publishing (Subsidiary of: Atlas Medical Publishing Ltd), Oxford Centre for Innovation, Mill St, Oxford, OX2 0JX, United Kingdom. TEL 44-1865-811116, FAX 44-1865-251550, info@clinicalpublishing.co.uk. Ed. J Levy Hammersmith. **Dist. by:** Marston Book Services Ltd., Unit 160, Milton Park, Abingdon, Oxfordshire OX14 4SD, United Kingdom. TEL 44-1235-465500, FAX 44-1235-465555, trade.orders@marston.co.uk, http://www.marston.co.uk/.

616.6 GBR ISSN 1479-5353
RC870
THE YEAR IN UROLOGY. Text in English. 2003. a., latest vol.3, 2006. USD 99.95 per issue in US & Canada; GBP 59.99 per issue elsewhere (effective 2009). 384 p./no.; **Document type:** *Journal, Academic/Scholarly.* **Description:** Focuses on diagnostic and general urology, urological oncology, non-malignant disorders of the lower urinary tract.
Indexed: P20, P22, P54, PQC.
—CCC.
Published by: Clinical Publishing (Subsidiary of: Atlas Medical Publishing Ltd), Oxford Centre for Innovation, Mill St, Oxford, OX2 0JX, United Kingdom. TEL 44-1865-811116, FAX 44-1865-251550, info@clinicalpublishing.co.uk. Eds. H Schwaibold, J L Probert. **Dist. by:** Marston Book Services Ltd., Unit 160, Milton Park, Abingdon, Oxfordshire OX14 4SD, United Kingdom. TEL 44-1235-465500, FAX 44-1235-465555, trade.orders@marston.co.uk, http://www.marston.co.uk/.

616.6 UKR
ZDOROV'YE MUZHCHINY/ZROROV'YA CHOLOVIKA; nauchno-prakticheskii zhurnal. Text in Russian. 2003. q. UAK 60 domestic; USD 75 foreign (effective 2007). **Document type:** *Journal, Academic/Scholarly.*
Published by: (Akademiya Medychnykh Nauk Ukrainy, Instytut Urolohii/Academy of Medical Sciences of Ukraine, Institute of Urology, Assotsiatsiya Seksolohiv i Androlohiv Ukrainy), Vydavnychyi Dim Professional, vul Yuriya Kotsyubyns'kogo 9A, Korpus 2, 8-i etazh, Kyiv, 04053, Ukraine. office@zdr.kiev.ua, http://www.zdr.kiev.ua. Ed. N A Azurkina. **Dist. by:** East View Information Services, 10601 Wayzata Blvd, Minneapolis, MN 55305. TEL 952-252-1201, 800-477-1005, FAX 952-252-1202, info@eastview.com, http://www.eastview.com.

616.6 CHN ISSN 1000-6702
ZHONGHUA MINIAO WAIKE ZAZHI/CHINESE JOURNAL OF UROLOGY. Text in Chinese. 1980. m. USD 68.40 (effective 2009). **Document type:** *Journal, Academic/Scholarly.*
Related titles: Online - full content ed.; Online - full text ed.
—East View.
Published by: Zhonghua Yixuehui/Chinese Medical Association, Dongdan 3 Tiaojia, no.7, Bejing, 100005, China. Ed. Fang-Liu Gu. **Dist. by:** China International Book Trading Corp, 35 Chegongzhuang Xilu, Haidian District, PO Box 399, Beijing 100044, China. TEL 86-10-68412045, FAX 86-10-68412023, cibtc@mail.cibtc.com.cn, http://www.cibtc.com.cn.

MEETINGS AND CONGRESSES

338.476 060 381.1 USA
A A P E X TODAY. (Automotive Aftermarket Products Expo) Text in English. d. adv. **Document type:** *Magazine, Trade.* **Description:** Covers the annual AAPEX in Las Vegas.
Related titles: Online - full text ed.
Published by: Babcox Publications, Inc., 3550 Embassy Pky, Akron, OH 44333. TEL 330-670-1234, FAX 330-670-0874, bbabcox@babcox.com, http://www.babcox.com. Adv. contact Jeff Stankard TEL 330-670-1234 ext 282. B&W page USD 6,250; trim 7.875 x 10.875. Circ: 30,000.

A U M A MESSE-GUIDE DEUTSCHLAND. *see* BUSINESS AND ECONOMICS—Marketing And Purchasing

A U M A TRADE FAIR GUIDE WORLDWIDE. *see* BUSINESS AND ECONOMICS—Marketing And Purchasing

381.1 GBR ISSN 0960-6416
ACCESS ALL AREAS. Text in English. 1992. 10/yr. adv. **Document type:** *Magazine, Trade.* **Description:** Covers the production angle on everything from The Henley Regatta to Glastonbury Festival via the Notting Hill Carnival and the PLASA Show. Provides all the news from the sector together with coverage of all the key events in the British calendar, as well as previewing the relevant exhibitions and checking in with key industry figures to monitor their ambitions and opinions.
—CCC.
Published by: Ocean Media Group Ltd. (Subsidiary of: Trinity Mirror Plc.), 1 Canada Sq, 19th Fl, Canary Wharf, London, E14 5AP, United Kingdom. TEL 44-20-77728300, FAX 44-20-77728599, Pamela.McSweeney@oceanmedia.co.uk, http://www.oceanmedia.co.uk. Ed. Nic Howden TEL 44-20-77728444. Adv. contact Michelle Tayton TEL 44-24-76571174. B&W page GBP 1,911, color page GBP 2,315; trim 240 x 314.

060 CAN
ACTEXPRESS. Text in English. 1989. irreg. price varies. adv. **Document type:** *Proceedings.* **Description:** Proceedings of conferences and meetings on various subjects.
Published by: University of Ottawa Press/Presses de l'Universite d'Ottawa, 542 King Edward, Ottawa, ON K1N 6N5, Canada. TEL 613-562-5246, FAX 613-562-5247. Ed. Vicki Bennett. R&P Martine Beauchesne. Adv. contact Elizabeth Thebaud.

ADVANCE BAND MAGAZINE; the international voice of adult bands. *see* MUSIC

AERZTE ZEITUNG. *see* MEDICAL SCIENCES

ALLESTIRE; politica-tecnica-economia per mostre fiere congressi vetrine negozi stand. *see* BUSINESS AND ECONOMICS

AMERICAN LIBRARY ASSOCIATION. ANNUAL CONFERENCE PROGRAM. *see* LIBRARY AND INFORMATION SCIENCES

011 USA
ANNUAL GUIDE TO EXPOSITION SERVICE. Text in English. a. **Document type:** *Directory.*
Published by: Exposition Service Contractors Association, 2920 N. Green Valley Pkwy., Ste. 414, Henderson, NV 89014-0413. TEL 214-742-9217, FAX 214-741-2519.

330 USA
ASSOCIATION CONVENTIONS & FACILITIES; the source for association meeting planning management. Text in English. 2008. bi-m. USD 60 domestic; USD 105 foreign (effective 2008). adv. **Document type:** *Magazine, Trade.* **Description:** Provides in-depth editorial focus on selection of site, accommodations and transportation, current legislation, conference, seminar,and training facilities, budget and cost controls, and destination reports.
Published by: Coastal Communications Corp., 2700 N Military Trail, Ste 120, Boca Raton, FL 33431-6394. TEL 561-989-0600, FAX 561-989-9509, cccpublisher@att.net. Ed., Pub. Harvey Grotsky. adv.: B&W page USD 7,210, color page USD 8,010; trim 8.125 x 10.875. Circ: 20,500 (controlled).

060 381.1 USA ISSN 1086-8291
ASSOCIATION LEADERSHIP. Text in English. 1987. bi-m. USD 45 to non-members; free to members (effective 2009). adv. back issues avail. **Document type:** *Magazine, Trade.*
Formerly (until 1994): Executive
Related titles: E-mail ed.; Online - full text ed.: free (effective 2009).
Published by: (Texas Society of Association Executives), Naylor LLC, 5950 NW 1st Pl, Gainesville, FL 32607. TEL 800-369-6220, FAX 352-331-3525, http://www.naylor.com. Ed. Lyle Fitzsimmons. Pub. Kathleen Gardner. Adv. contact Rick Jones. B&W page USD 1,549.50, color page USD 2,349.50; trim 8.375 x 10.875.

011 USA ISSN 1042-3141
AS6
ASSOCIATION MEETINGS; conventions, conferences, and exhibitions. Text in English. 1984. 6/yr. USD 51 domestic; USD 59 in Canada; USD 85 elsewhere; free to qualified personnel (effective 2011). adv. charts; illus. **Document type:** *Magazine, Trade.*
Formerly (until 1989): Convention World (8750-1686); Incorporates (1916-198?): World Convention Dates (0043-8383)
Related titles: Online - full text ed.
Indexed: A09, A10, B01, B02, B06, B07, B09, B11, B15, B17, B18, BPI, BRD, G04, G05, G06, G07, G08, H&TI, H06, I05, T02, V03, V04, W01, W02, W03, W05.
—Ingenta. CCC.
Published by: Penton Media, Inc., 11 River Bend Dr South, PO Box 4949, Stamford, CT 06907-0949. TEL 203-358-9900, FAX 203-358-5823, information@penton.com, http://www.pentonmedia.com. Ed. Larry Keltto TEL 507-4552-2136. Circ: 22,000.

011 GBR ISSN 0958-0271
ASSOCIATION MEETINGS INTERNATIONAL. Abbreviated title: A M I. Text in English. 1989. bi-m. GBP 45 domestic; USD 120 foreign; free to qualified personnel (effective 2009). adv. back issues avail. **Document type:** *Magazine, Trade.* **Description:** Provides some slack and room to grow, claims sponsorship expert.
Related titles: Online - full text ed.: free (effective 2009).
Indexed: RASB.
—CCC.
Published by: Conference and Travel Publications Ltd., Kings House, Cantelupe Rd, East Grinstead, West Sussex RH19 3BE, United Kingdom. TEL 44-1342-306700, FAX 44-1342-302547, cat@cat-publications.com. Ed. Rob Spalding. Pub. Stephen Lewis. adv.: color page EUR 9,998. Circ: 9,998.

011 USA
ASSOCIATION OF INTERNATIONAL MEETING PLANNERS. NEWSLETTER. Text in English. m. **Document type:** *Newsletter.*
Published by: Association of International Meeting Planners, 2547 Monroe St, Dearborn, MI 48124-3013. TEL 313-563-0360, FAX 248-669-0636. Ed. Stephen R Castor.

060 520 USA ISSN 1050-3390
CODEN: ASPSFO
ASTRONOMICAL SOCIETY OF THE PACIFIC. CONFERENCE PROCEEDINGS. Variant title: AS P Conference Series. Text in English. 1988. a., latest vol.27, 2004. price varies. back issues avail. **Document type:** *Proceedings, Academic/Scholarly.* **Description:** Provides a comprehensive overview of the latest research in a particular field of astronomy.
Indexed: Inspec.
—BLDSC (1756.200000), IE, Ingenta.
Published by: Astronomical Society of the Pacific, 390 Ashton Ave, San Francisco, CA 94112. TEL 415-337-1100, 800-335-2624, FAX 415-337-5205, service@astrosociety.org. Ed. J Ward Moody TEL 801-422-2111.

764.060 913 USA
AUSTIN MEETING PLANNER & DESTINATION GUIDE. Variant title: Austin Meeting Planner and Destination Guide. Text in English. a. adv. **Document type:** *Guide, Consumer.* **Description:** Details accommodations, meeting facilities, dining, transportation and event services in the Austin area.
Published by: Weaver Publications, Inc., 2420 Alcott St, Denver, CO 80211. TEL 303-458-1211, FAX 303-477-0724, info@weaver-group.com, http://pub.weaver-group.com. Circ: 7,000.

AUSTRALIAN CONFERENCE ON NUCLEAR AND COMPLEMENTARY TECHNIQUES OF ANALYSIS. PROCEEDINGS. *see* CHEMISTRY—Analytical Chemistry

011 USA
B O M A INTERNATIONAL CONVENTION DIRECTORY. Text in English. 1908. a. adv. **Document type:** *Directory.*
Published by: Building Owners and Managers Association International, 1201 New York Ave, N W, Ste 300, Washington, DC 20005. TEL 202-408-2662, FAX 202-371-0181, info@boma.org, http://www.boma.org/. Ed. Patricia Areno. Circ: 5,000.

060 USA
BEST EVENTS BOSTON; special events resource directory. Text in English. 1996. a. free to qualified personnel. adv. **Document type:** *Magazine, Trade.* **Description:** Resource for corporate and social special events with editorial listings, and photos of the people and places used to plan events.
Formerly (until 2010): Agenda Boston
Related titles: Online - full text ed.
Published by: Red 7 Media, LLC, 10 Norden Pl, Norwalk, CT 06855. TEL 203-854-6730, FAX 203-854-6735, http://red7media.com. Pub. Dan Hanover TEL 203-899-8446. adv.: B&W page USD 4,595, color page USD 4,895; trim 8.125 x 10.875. Circ: 43,500 (controlled).

910.2 330 060 USA
▼ **BEST EVENTS CALIFORNIA**; special events resource directory. Text in English. 2010. a. free to qualified personnel. adv. **Document type:** *Magazine, Trade.*
Formed by the 2010 merger of: Agenda Northern California; Agenda Southern California
Related titles: Online - full text ed.
Published by: Red 7 Media, LLC, 10 Norden Pl, Norwalk, CT 06855. TEL 203-854-6730, FAX 203-854-6735, http://red7media.com. Pub. Dan Hanover TEL 203-899-8446. adv.: B&W page USD 4,595, color page USD 4,895; trim 7.625 x 10.375. Circ: 13,800 (controlled).

060 910.2 330 USA
BEST EVENTS CHICAGO; special events resource directory. Text in English. a. free to qualified personnel. adv. **Document type:** *Magazine, Trade.* **Description:** Resource for corporate and social special events with editorial listings, and photos of the people and places used to plan events.
Formerly (until 2010): Agenda Chicago
Related titles: Online - full text ed.
Published by: Red 7 Media, LLC, 10 Norden Pl, Norwalk, CT 06855. TEL 203-854-6730, FAX 203-854-6735, http://red7media.com. Pub. Dan Hanover TEL 203-899-8446. adv.: B&W page USD 4,595, color page USD 4,895; trim 8.125 x 10.875. Circ: 11,750 (controlled).

910.2 330 060 USA
TX911.2
BEST EVENTS NEW YORK; special events resource directory. Text in English. 1989. 5/yr. free to qualified personnel. adv. **Document type:** *Magazine, Trade.* **Description:** Resource for corporate and social special events with editorial listings, and photos of the people and places used to plan events.
Formerly (until 2010): Agenda New York (1045-4969)
Related titles: Online - full text ed.
Published by: Red 7 Media, LLC, 10 Norden Pl, Norwalk, CT 06855. TEL 203-854-6730, FAX 203-854-6735, http://red7media.com. Ed. Rachel Gary. Pub. Sharon Kress. adv.: B&W page USD 5,895, color page USD 6,395; trim 8.125 x 10.875. Circ: 11,500 (controlled).

060 910.2 330 USA
BEST EVENTS WASHINGTON; special events resource directory. Text in English. 1995. a. free to qualified personnel. adv. **Document type:** *Magazine, Trade.* **Description:** Resource for corporate and social special events with editorial listings, and photos of the people and places used to plan events in the Washington, DC area.
Formerly (until 2010): Agenda Washington
Related titles: Online - full text ed.
Published by: Red 7 Media, LLC, 10 Norden Pl, Norwalk, CT 06855. TEL 203-854-6730, FAX 203-854-6735, http://red7media.com. Pub. Dan Hanover TEL 203-899-8446. adv.: B&W page USD 4,595, color page USD 4,895; trim 8.125 x 10.875. Circ: 13,000 (controlled).

381.1 USA
BIZBASH (CHICAGO); events meetings marketing style strategy ideas. Text in English. 2008 (Apr.). 3/yr. free to qualified personnel (effective 2011). adv. **Document type:** *Magazine, Trade.* **Description:** Covers the resources for event & meeting planning, including vendors, supplies and venues in Chicago.
Published by: BizBash Media, 8 W 38th St, 2nd Fl, New York, NY 10018. TEL 646-638-3600, FAX 646-638-3601, info@bizbash.com, http://bizbash.com/. Ed. Chad Kaydo TEL 646-839-6868. Adv. contact Lauren Stonecipher TEL 646-839-6843.

BIZBASH (FLORIDA); events meetings marketing style strategy ideas. *see* BUSINESS AND ECONOMICS

BIZBASH (NEW YORK). *see* BUSINESS AND ECONOMICS

BIZBASH (TORONTO). *see* BUSINESS AND ECONOMICS

381.1 USA
BIZBASH (WASHINGTON D.C.); events meetings marketing style strategy ideas. Text in English. 2007. 3/yr. free to qualified personnel (effective 2011). adv. **Document type:** *Magazine, Trade.* **Description:** Covers the resources for event & meeting planning, including vendors, supplies and venues in the Washington D.C. area.
Published by: BizBash Media, 8 W 38th St, 2nd Fl, New York, NY 10018. TEL 646-638-3600, FAX 646-638-3601, info@bizbash.com, http://bizbash.com/. Ed. Chad Kaydo TEL 646-839-6868. Adv. contact Lauren Stonecipher TEL 646-839-6843.

BLACK MEETINGS & TOURISM. *see* TRAVEL AND TOURISM

011 BWA
BOTSWANA INTERNATIONAL TRADE FAIR. ANNUAL EXHIBITORS' CATALOGUE. Abbreviated title: B I T F Annual Exhibitors' Catalogue. Text in English. 1968. a. free. adv. **Document type:** *Catalog, Government.* **Description:** Profiles exhibitors and their products, both national and international.
Published by: Ministry of Commerce and Industry, Department of Trade and Investment Promotion (T I P A), Private Bag 00367, Gaborone, Botswana. TEL 267-351790, FAX 267-305375. Circ: 10,000.

381.029 GBR
BRITISH CONFERENCE DESTINATIONS DIRECTORY (YEAR). Text in English. 1990. a. adv. **Document type:** *Directory.* **Description:** Lists and describes British conference and convention facilities.
Published by: Eventia, Sixth Fl, Charles House, 148-149 Great Charles St, Birmingham, Warks B3 3HT, United Kingdom. TEL 44-121-212-1400, FAX 44-121-212-3131, info@eventia.org.uk, http://www.bacd.org.uk. Circ: 12,500 (controlled).

381.1 CAN ISSN 1201-4087
BUSINESS EVENTS GUIDE (YEAR)/GUIDE EVENEMENTS D'AFFAIRES. Text in English. 1990. a. CAD 379 includes guide and CD-ROM; CAD 249.95 for guide only; CAD 299 for CD-ROM only. adv. **Document type:** *Directory.* **Description:** Comprehensive listing of show producers, event organizers and meeting planners in Canada.
Formerly: Guide Annuel (Year) Salons Expositions Congres (1193-7076)
Related titles: CD-ROM ed.: USD 199.
Published by: International Press Publications Inc, 90 Nolan Ct, Ste 21, Markham, ON L3R 4L9, Canada. TEL 905-946-9588, FAX 905-946-9590. Ed. Marie Boisvert. Pub. Michel Perrotte. Circ: 10,000.

658 338 GBR
BUSINESS RATIO REPORT: EXHIBITION AND CONFERENCE INDUSTRY. Text in English. 1988. a., latest no.6, 2008, May. GBP 365 per issue (effective 2010). charts; stat. back issues avail. **Document type:** *Report, Trade.* **Description:** Covers companies active in the exhibition and conference industry.
Formerly (until 19??): Business Ratio Report: Exhibition and Conference Organisers (0955-4483)
Published by: Key Note Ltd. (Subsidiary of: Bonnier Business Information), Harlequin House, 5th Fl, 7 High St, Teddington, Richmond upon Thames, TW11 8EE, United Kingdom. TEL 44-845-5040452, FAX 44-845-5040453, sales@keynote.co.uk.

011 DEU ISSN 1869-6260
BUSY. Text in German. 1988. s-a. free. bk.rev. illus. 42 p./no.; back issues avail. **Document type:** *Magazine, Trade.*
Formerly (until 2004): Dortmunder Messebrief (0949-7501)
Published by: Westfalenhallen Dortmund GmbH, Strobelallee 45, Dortmund, 44139, Germany. TEL 49-231-12040, FAX 49-231-1204724, medien@westfalenhallen.de, http://www.westfalenhallen.de.

610 011 CHE ISSN 1010-593X
CALENDAR OF CONGRESSES OF MEDICAL SCIENCES. Text in English, French. 1972. irreg. adv. **Document type:** *Directory, Trade.*
Formerly (until 1982): C I O M S Calendar of International and Regional Congresses of Medical Sciences (0379-8100); Which was formed by the merger of (1952-1972): Calendar of International Congresses of Medical Sciences (0589-915X); (1961-1972): Calendar of Regional Congresses of Medical Sciences (0301-2891)
Published by: Council for International Organizations of Medical Sciences/Conseil des Organisations Internationales des Sciences Medicales, c/o World Health Organization, 20 Ave Appia, Geneva 27, 1211, Switzerland. TEL 41-22-7913467, FAX 41-22-7914286, cioms@who.int, http://www.cioms.ch. Ed. Dr. Zbigniew Bankowski. Circ: 2,000.

340 USA ISSN 0364-0558
KF49.C58
CALENDARS OF THE UNITED STATES HOUSE OF REPRESENTATIVES AND HISTORY OF LEGISLATION. Text in English. 1986. w. (every Monday when Congress is in session). USD 270 (effective 2001). **Document type:** *Government.* **Description:** Contains information concerning the business of the House and the Senate.
Related titles: Online - full text ed.: ISSN 1555-1067.
Published by: U.S. House of Representatives, H-312 US Capital, Washington, DC 20515. TEL 202-224-3121, http://www.house.gov. **Subscr. to:** U.S. Government Printing Office, Superintendent of Documents, PO Box 371954, Pittsburgh, PA 15250.

011 658 CAN
CANADIAN ASSOCIATION OF EXPOSITION MANAGERS. COMMUNIQUE. Text in English. 8/yr. adv. **Document type:** *Newsletter.*
Published by: Canadian Association of Exposition Managers/Association Canadienne des Directeurs d'Expositions, 6900 Airport Rd, Ste 239 A, P O Box 82, Mississauga, ON L4V 1E8, Canada. TEL 905-678-9377, FAX 905-678-9578. Ed., R&P Carol Ann Burrell. Adv. contact Debbie Wilson. page CAD 525. Circ: 400.

011 610 CAN ISSN 1193-6452
CANADIAN DIRECTORY OF HEALTH CARE CONFERENCES/ REPERTOIRE CANADIEN DES CONFERENCES DE SOINS DE SANTE. Text in English. 1991. m. free. **Document type:** *Directory.* **Description:** Lists all Canadian health care conferences currently scheduled to the year 2000. Listings are organized by month and year and include location, theme, sponsoring organization and contact person.
Media: Online - full text.
Published by: Canadian Nurses Association/Association des Infirmieres et Infirmiers du Canada, 50 Driveway, Ottawa, ON K2P 1E2, Canada. TEL 613-237-2133, FAX 613-237-3520.

060 USA ISSN 1946-1925
CENTAUR'S YELL. Text in English. 1987. q.
Related titles: Online - full text ed.: ISSN 1946-1933.
Published by: Delta Lambda Phi National Social Fraternity, National Alumni Association, 2020 Pennsylvania Ave, NW, No 355, Washington, DC 20006. TEL 202-527-9453, 800-587-3728, FAX 202-318-2277, helpdesk@dlp.org, http://sites.dlp.org.

011 USA
CENTER LINES. Text in English. q. free to members. **Document type:** *Newsletter.*
Published by: International Association of Conference Centers, 243 N. Lindbergh Blvd., St. Louis, MO 63141. TEL 314-993-8575, FAX 314-993-8919, ctrlines@iacconline.org, http://www.iacconline.org. Ed., R&P Steven M Smith. Circ: 2,000.

CHRONIQUE O N U. *see* POLITICAL SCIENCE—International Relations

323.4 USA
CIVIL LIBERTIES ALERT. Text in English. 1977. a. free. **Document type:** *Newsletter.* **Description:** National legislative report includes Congressional voting records on selected votes and information about important legislation in the Congress concerning civil liberties.
Published by: American Civil Liberties Union (Washington, DC), 915 15th St NW, Washington, DC 20005-2302. TEL 202-544-1681, FAX 202-546-0738. Ed. Rachel Fischer Alberts. Circ: 5,000.

060 USA
COLORADO MEETINGS & EVENTS. Text in English. 2003. q. free to qualified personnel (effective 2011). adv. back issues avail. **Document type:** *Magazine, Trade.* **Description:** Aimed at meetings and events professionals working in Colorado and includes essential information on a range of topics, from venues and supplier news, to tips, best practices and industry developments.
Related titles: Online - full text ed.: free (effective 2011).
Published by: Tiger Oak Publications, Inc., OneTiger Oak Plz, 900 S Third St, Minneapolis, MN 55415. TEL 612-548-3180, FAX 612-548-3181, customerservice@tigeroak.com, http://www.tigeroak.com. Ed. Beth Buehler TEL 970-349-1168. Adv. contact Bob Haddad TEL 303-617-0548.

CON-TEMPORAL. *see* LITERATURE—Mystery And Detective

060 GBR ISSN 0955-5005
CONFERENCE & ASSOCIATION WORLD. Text in English. 1988. bi-m. **Document type:** *Magazine, Trade.*
Formed by the merger of (1985-1988): Association World (0951-4619); (1979-1988): Conference World (0143-7895); Which was formerly: A C E News
Published by: A C E International, Riverside House, 160 High St, Huntingdon, Cambs PE18 6SG, United Kingdom. TEL 44-1480-457595, FAX 44-1480-412863, http://www.aceinternational.org/.

060 GBR
CONFERENCE CALENDAR (ONLINE). Text in English. 1996. bi-m. GBP 50 single user (effective 2009). adv. back issues avail. **Document type:** *Handbook/Manual/Guide, Trade.* **Description:** Listing of conferences, awards, and exhibitions classified by 120 subject headings with the intent of informing all interested individuals in these kinds of events.
Formerly: Conference Calendar (Print) (1365-6058)
Media: Online - full content.
Published by: Fleming Information Services, 123 Adams Gardens Estate, Brunel Rd, London, SE16 4JH, United Kingdom. TEL 44-20-72379777, FAX 44-20-72379777.

CONFERENCE PAPERS INDEX. *see* MEETINGS AND CONGRESSES—Abstracting, Bibliographies, Statistics

011 CAN ISSN 0841-968X
CONGRES MENSUEL, BULLETIN DE NOUVELLES. Text in English. 1988. m. USD 40 (effective 2000). adv. **Document type:** *Bulletin, Trade.* **Description:** For meeting planners.
Formerly (until 1988): Congres Mensuel (0841-9671)
Related titles: ◆ English ed.: Meetings Monthly, News Bulletin. ISSN 0841-9663.
Published by: Publicom Inc., Place d Armes, C P 365, Montreal, PQ H2Y 3H1, Canada. TEL 514-274-0004, FAX 514-274-5884. Ed., Adv. contact Guy Jonkman. Circ: 6,341.

011 ESP ISSN 0214-8056
CONGRESOS CONVENCIONES E INCENTIVOS. Text in Spanish. 1985. 9/yr. adv. bk.rev. **Document type:** *Directory, Trade.*
Address: Torre de Madrid planta 13-2, Princesa, 1, Madrid, 28008, Spain. TEL 91-548-09-73, FAX 91-5479813. Ed. Maria Angeles Gonzalez. Pub. Jose Luis G Salgado. Adv. contact Fernando Rodriguez San Segundo. Circ: 6,000 (paid); 6,000 (controlled).

CONTROLLED RELEASE NEWSLETTER. *see* CHEMISTRY—Organic Chemistry

011 ITA ISSN 1723-4174
CONVEGNI INCENTIVE & COMUNICAZIONE. Text in Italian. 1987. 7/yr. bk.rev. **Document type:** *Magazine, Trade.*
Formerly (until 1995): Convegni e Comunicazione
Published by: Convegni Srl, Via Ezio Biondi 1, Milan, MI 20154, Italy. TEL 39-02-349921, FAX 39-02-34992290, convegni@convegni.it, http://www.convegni.it. Circ: 13,000.

CONVENE. *see* BUSINESS AND ECONOMICS—Management

011 AUS ISSN 1039-1029
CONVENTION & INCENTIVE MARKETING. Abbreviated title: C I M. Text in English. 1974. m. AUD 99 (effective 2009). adv. back issues avail. **Document type:** *Magazine, Trade.* **Description:** Discusses conferences, exhibitions and incentives throughout Australia, New Zealand and Asia.
Formerly (until 1988): Convention (0312-0821)
Related titles: Online - full text ed.
Published by: Rank Publishing Co., PO Box 189, St Leonards, NSW 1590, Australia. TEL 61-2-94382300, FAX 61-2-94385962. Ed. Louis Allen. Pub. Robert Yeomans. Adv. contact Susan Fordree. Circ: 15,311.

060 USA ISSN 1556-1097
CONVENTION FORUM; serving meeting professionals throughout the southeast. Text in English. 2005. bi-m. USD 35; USD 6 newsstand/cover (effective 2006). adv. **Document type:** *Magazine, Trade.* **Description:** Focuses on destination showcases, state spotlights, sensational sites and cities througout the Southeast. Contains lodging information and destination-specific information about facilities, resources, local attractions and events.
Related titles: Online - full content ed.
Indexed: H&TI, H06, T02.
Published by: Maverick Marketing, LLC, PO Box 700241, St Cloud, FL 34770-0241. Pub. Michelle M Lock. Adv. contacts Debbie Del Gaudio, Michelle M Lock. B&W page USD 2,105, color page USD 2,520; trim 8.375 x 10.875. Circ: 8,600 (controlled).

060 DEU
CONVENTION INTERNATIONAL. Text in German. 1980. bi-m. EUR 35 domestic; EUR 45 foreign (effective 2007). adv. **Document type:** *Magazine, Trade.*
Published by: H.W.G. Verlag und Werbung, Wiedbachstr 50, Neuwied, 56567, Germany. TEL 49-2631-96460, FAX 49-2631-964612, info@hwg-media.de, http://www.hwg-media.de. adv.: B&W page EUR 2,300, color page EUR 3,300. Circ: 9,955 (paid and controlled).

011 CAN ISSN 0226-8922
CONVENTIONS & MEETINGS CANADA. Text in English. 1971. a. adv. back issues avail. **Document type:** *Directory, Trade.* **Description:** Includes information on hotels, motor inns, convention centers and other meeting facilities across Canada.
Published by: Rogers Publishing Ltd./Les Editions Rogers Limitee, One Mount Pleasant Rd, 11th Fl, Toronto, ON M4Y 2Y5, Canada. TEL 416-764-2000, FAX 416-764-3941, http://www.rogerspublishing.ca. Circ: 10,416 (controlled).

011 USA ISSN 1074-0627
CONVENTIONSOUTH. Text in English. 1983. m. USD 18 (effective 2002). adv. 72 p./no. 4 cols./p.; **Document type:** *Magazine, Trade.* **Description:** For people who plan meetings, conferences and conventions that are held in the South. Covers 13 southeastern states. Articles include how-to features, meeting site profiles, and related news items.
Published by: Convention South, PO Box 2267, Gulf Shores, AL 36547. TEL 251-968-5300, FAX 251-968-4532, info@conventionsouth.com. Ed. J Talty O'Connor. Pub. J. Talty O'Connor. R&P Kristen McIntosh. Adv. contact Dianne O'Connor. B&W page USD 3,075, color page USD 3,875; bleed 8.5 x 11. Circ: 16,000 (controlled).

CORPORATE EVENT. *see* BUSINESS AND ECONOMICS

011 GBR ISSN 1756-6312
CORPORATE EVENT SERVICES. Text in English. 1990. a. GBP 50 (effective 2009). **Document type:** *Directory, Trade.* **Description:** Contains information on companies and suppliers operating in the event industry in the UK.
—BLDSC (3472.061285). **CCC.**
Published by: Wilmington Media & Entertainment (Subsidiary of: Wilmington Group Plc), 19 - 21 Christopher St, London, EC2A 2BS, United Kingdom. TEL 44-20-74226800, FAX 44-20-74226822, investorinfo@wilmington.co.uk, http://www.wilmington.co.uk/.

CORPORATE EVENTS GUIDE; your essential guide to event planning. *see* BUSINESS AND ECONOMICS

011 USA
HD2743
CORPORATE MEETING PLANNERS. Text in English. 19??. a. USD 1,299 combined subscription per issue (print & CDROM eds.); USD 500 per issue (effective 2011). **Document type:** *Directory, Trade.* **Description:** Lists more than 12,000 corporate meeting planners who plan off-site meetings for over 11,000 corporations. Arranged alphabetically by state and city, information includes: type of business, addresses and telephone numbers, fax numbers, number of meetings each year, number of attendees, basic geographic destination (including outside USA), and months meetings are held.
Formerly: Nationwide Directory of Corporate Meeting Planners (0735-4444)
Related titles: CD-ROM ed.
Published by: Briefings Media Group, 2807 N Parham Rd, Ste 200, Richmond, VA 23294. TEL 804-762-9600, FAX 804-217-8999, info@briefingsmediagroup.com, http://www.briefingsmediagroup.com.

060 CAN
CORPORATE MEETINGS & EVENTS. Abbreviated title: C M & E. Text in English. bi-m. **Document type:** *Magazine, Trade.* **Description:** Reaches individuals who conceptualize, plan, organize and manage various types of events for Canadian corporations.
Published by: MediaEdge Communications, Llc, 5255 Yonge St, Ste 1000, Toronto, ON M2N 6P4, Canada. TEL 416-512-8186, 866-216-0860, FAX 416-512-8344, info@mediaedge.ca. Ed. Chuck Nervick.

910.09 USA ISSN 0745-1636
HD5260
CORPORATE MEETINGS & INCENTIVES. Text in English. 1980. m. USD 77 domestic; USD 85 in Canada; USD 106 elsewhere; free domestic to qualified personnel (effective 2011). adv. **Document type:** *Magazine, Trade.* **Description:** Articles for senior-level corporate executives and travel agents responsible for selecting sites and destinations for meetings and incentive travel programs.
Related titles: Online - full text ed.
Indexed: A09, A10, B01, B02, B06, B07, B09, B11, B15, B17, B18, BPI, BRD, G04, G06, G07, G08, H&TI, H06, I05, T02, V03, V04, W01, W02, W03, W05.
—CCC.
Published by: Penton Media, Inc., 11 River Bend Dr South, PO Box 4949, Stamford, CT 06907-0949. TEL 203-358-9900, FAX 203-358-5823, information@penton.com, http://www.penton.com. Ed. Barbara Scofidio TEL 978-448-8211. Circ: 34,236.

060 CAN ISSN 1481-594X
CORPORATE TRAVEL MANAGEMENT. Text in English. 1998. q. CAD 19.95 (effective 2003). adv. **Document type:** *Magazine, Trade.* **Description:** Provides information for people who make, enforce and influence business travel policy.
Indexed: A15, ABIn, C03, CBCABus, PQC.
Published by: Rogers Publishing Ltd./Les Editions Rogers Limitee, One Mount Pleasant Rd, 11th Fl, Toronto, ON M4Y 2Y5, Canada. TEL 416-764-2000, FAX 416-764-1740, http://www.rogerspublishing.ca. Ed. Matt Nicholls.

011 USA
COUNCIL OF PROTOCOL EXECUTIVES. DIRECTORY. Text in English. 1989. q. USD 48; USD 58 foreign. **Document type:** *Directory.*
Formerly: Council of Protocol Executives. Newsletter
Published by: Council of Protocol Executives, 101 W 12th St, Ste PHH, New York, NY 10011. TEL 212-633-6934, FAX 212-633-6934. Ed. Edna Fine Greenbauw. Circ: 5,000 (paid).

764.060 USA
DALLAS MEETING PROFESSIONALS GUIDE. Text in English. a. adv. **Document type:** *Guide, Consumer.*
Published by: Weaver Publications, Inc., 2420 Alcott St, Denver, CO 80211. TEL 303-458-1211, FAX 303-477-0724, info@weaver-group.com, http://pub.weaver-group.com. Circ: 8,000.

DAWSONS VENUE SELECTIONS. *see* TRAVEL AND TOURISM

617.6 011 CAN
DENTAL GUIDE (SCARBOROUGH); the CE planner for the dental profession. Text in English. 1993. q. CAD 35; CAD 55 foreign. adv. **Description:** Lists dental conferences, meetings and seminars around the world, with a focus on travel combined with dental education.
Published by: Thomson Healthcare Communications (Subsidiary of: Rogers Publishing Ltd./Les Editions Rogers Limitee), 1120 Birchmount Rd, Ste 200, Scarborough, ON M1K 5G4, Canada. TEL 416-750-8900, FAX 416-751-8126. Ed. Heather Howie. Adv. contact Peter Greenhough. B&W page CAD 1,595, color page CAD 2,685; trim 10.75 x 8.13. Circ: 16,000.

068.492 USA
DESTINATION HOLLAND. Text in English. 1994. 4/yr. free. **Document type:** *Newsletter.*
Formerly: Convention News
Published by: Netherlands Convention Bureau, 355 Lexington Ave, 21st Fl, New York, NY 10017. TEL 213-370-7360, FAX 212-370-9507.

060 GBR ISSN 2044-8201
▼ ➤ **DIAMOND LIGHT SOURCE PROCEEDINGS.** Text in English. 2010. irreg., latest vol.1, 2010. free (effective 2012). **Document type:** *Proceedings, Academic/Scholarly.* **Description:** Covers the proceedings of conferences held at the Diamond Light Source synchrotron radiation facility in the UK.
Media: Online - full text.
Published by: Cambridge University Press, The Edinburgh Bldg, Shaftesbury Rd, Cambridge, CB2 8RU, United Kingdom. TEL 44-1223-312393, FAX 44-1223-315052, information@cambridge.org, http://www.cambridge.org/.

➤ **DOJO DENSENBYO DANWAKAI REPOTO/P S J SOILBORNE DISEASE WORKSHOP REPORT.** *see* AGRICULTURE—Crop Production And Soil

011 USA
E S C A VOICE. Text in English. q. **Document type:** *Newsletter.*
Published by: Exposition Service Contractors Association, 2920 N. Green Valley Pkwy., Ste. 414, Henderson, NV 89014-0413. TEL 214-742-9217, FAX 214-741-2519.

060 DEU ISSN 0175-808X
EUROPAEISCHE HOCHSCHULSCHRIFTEN. REIHE 39: KONGRESSBERICHTE. Text in German. 1984. irreg., latest vol.4, 1991. price varies. **Document type:** *Monographic series, Academic/Scholarly.*
Published by: Peter Lang GmbH (Subsidiary of: Peter Lang Publishing Group), Eschborner Landstr 42-50, Frankfurt Am Main, 60489, Germany. TEL 49-69-7807050, FAX 49-69-78070550, zentrale.frankfurt@peterlang.com, http://www.peterlang.com.

069 CZE ISSN 1802-436X
EUROVELETRHY. Text in Czech. 1994. bi-m. adv. **Document type:** *Magazine, Trade.*
Formerly (until 2007): Ceskomoravske Veletrhy (1801-7045)
Published by: Vaclav Janda, V Zavetri 4, Prague 7, 170 00, Czech Republic. TEL 420-266-791551, euroveletrhy@etelnet.cz.

011 GBR ISSN 1477-738X
EVENT. Text in English. 1992. m. GBP 85 (effective 2009). adv. back issues avail.; reprints avail. **Document type:** *Magazine, Trade.* **Description:** Aimed at the professional exhibition organizer. Covers news, opinions, and the latest products in the exhibition industry.
Incorporates (2002-2008): R S V P the Magazine (1478-5978); Former titles (until 2002): Marketing Event (1368-2407); (until 1997): Exhibition Management (0965-3457)
Related titles: Online - full text ed.
Indexed: A15, ABIn, B01, B02, B06, B07, B08, B09, B15, B17, B18, C12, G04, G06, G07, G08, I05, I07, P48, P51, PQC, S23, T02.
—CCC.
Published by: Haymarket Publishing Ltd. (Subsidiary of: Haymarket Media Group), 174 Hammersmith Rd, London, W6 7JP, United Kingdom. TEL 44-20-82674210, info@haymarket.com, http://www.haymarket.com. Ed. Jeremy King TEL 44-20-82674055. Adv. contacts Victoria Chapman TEL 44-20-82678004, Ian Houghton TEL 44-20-82674140. Circ: 12,319. **Subscr. to:** 12-13 Cranleigh Gardens Industrial Estate, Southall UB1 2DB, United Kingdom. TEL 44-84-51557355, FAX 44-20-86067503, subscriptions@haymarket.com, http://www.haymarketbusinesssubs.com.

381.1 658 USA ISSN 1098-9102
EVENT SOLUTIONS. Text in English. 1996. 12/yr. USD 65 domestic; USD 85 in Canada; USD 125 elsewhere (effective 2008). adv. **Document type:** *Magazine, Trade.* **Description:** Dedicated to providing event solutions to all levels of management in the events industry.
Related titles: Online - full text ed.: ISSN 1945-2055.
Published by: Event Publishing LLC, 5400 S Lakeshore Dr, Ste 101, Tempe, AZ 85283. TEL 480-831-5100, FAX 480-777-2300. Ed. Michelle Glicksman. Pub. John Baragona. adv.: B&W page USD 3,575, color page USD 4,670; bleed 8.375 x 11.125. Circ: 25,000 (paid and controlled).

381.1 DEU
EVENTS (FRANKFURT AM MAIN). Text in German. 1986. 5/yr. EUR 51.63; EUR 9.40 newsstand/cover (effective 2011). adv. **Document type:** *Magazine, Trade.* **Description:** Caters national and international decision makers and planners in the event industry with an optimized print run to avoid wastage. Serves as an essential advertising medium for suppliers in the meetings, incentives and events sector, as well as for convention bureaus, tourist boards, congress and exhibition centers.
Published by: Werbe- und Verlags-Gesellschaft Ruppert mbH, Emil-Hoffmann-Str 13, Cologne, 50996, Germany. TEL 49-2236-3366118, FAX 49-2236-336610. Ed., Pub. Hans Juergen Heinrich. Adv. contact Inga Schade. Circ: 16,275 (paid and controlled).

EXECUTIVE UPDATE. *see* BUSINESS AND ECONOMICS—Management

381.1 659 USA
EXHIBIT CITY NEWS. Text in English. m. USD 48 domestic; USD 79 foreign (effective 2001). adv. back issues avail. **Document type:** *Newspaper, Trade.* **Description:** Covers news and events about the convention and tradeshow industry.
Published by: Mr. Tradeshow Communications, LLC, 4914 Boulder Hwy, Suite 20, Las Vegas, NV 89121. TEL 702-309-8023, FAX 702-309-8027, http://www.exhibitcitynews.com. Pub. Don Svehla. Adv. contact Jonathan Harris.

011 GBR ISSN 0014-4649
EXHIBITION BULLETIN. Text in English. 1948. m. charts; illus. index. **Document type:** *Bulletin, Trade.* **Description:** Provides advance listings of fairs and shows throughout the world, plus services directory.
Indexed: KES.
—BLDSC (3836.250000).
Published by: Tarsus Martex, Commonwealth House, 2 Chalk Hill Rd, Hammersmith, London, W6 8DW, United Kingdom. TEL 44-20-88462700, FAX 44-20-88462801. Ed., R&P Faiza Fareed. Pub. Buzz Carter. Adv. contact Stuart Barnett.

011 GBR ISSN 1366-7556
EXHIBITION BULLETIN YEARBOOK. Text in English. 1997. a.
—BLDSC (3836.260000).
Published by: Tarsus Martex, Commonwealth House, 2 Chalk Hill Rd, Hammersmith, London, W6 8DW, United Kingdom. TEL 44-20-88462700, FAX 44-20-88462801, http://www.e-bulletin.com.

382.029 TWN ISSN 1019-0996
EXHIBITIONS ROUND THE WORLD. Text in English. 1982. a. USD 80 (effective 2001). adv. **Document type:** *Directory.* **Description:** Contains dates, locations, and all other essential data on over 4,000 of the world's major trade exhibitions.
Published by: Interface Global Taiwan Co., Ltd., PO Box 173-12, Taipei, 116, Taiwan. TEL 886-2-23913251, FAX 886-2-2395-2901, tradwind@ms2.hinet.net. Ed. Daniel Foong. Pub., R&P, Adv. contact Donald Shapiro. Circ: 20,000. **Subscr. in U.S. to:** Trade Winds Inc., PO Box 820519, Dallas, TX 75382. TEL 972-699-1188, FAX 972-699-1189, twinds8888@aol.com.

011 CHE
EXPODATA. Text in German. 10/yr. **Document type:** *Trade.*
Published by: Kunzler-Bachmann AG, Geltenwilenstr 8 a, St. Gallen, 9001, Switzerland. TEL 071-235555, FAX 071-236745. Ed. Urs Seiler. Circ: 5,500.

EXPOVISIE. *see* BUSINESS AND ECONOMICS—International Commerce

381.1 CAN
EXPOWORLD.NET. Text in English. 1998. m. free. **Document type:** *Newsletter.* **Description:** Informs subscribers on Internet resources on expositions and trade shows worldwide.
Media: Online - full text.
Published by: ExpoWorld.net Ltd., 78 Tilden Cresc, Toronto, ON M9P 1V7, Canada. TEL 416-244-1168, FAX 416-247-8387. Ed. John Passalacqua.

FAIR NEWS. *see* MUSEUMS AND ART GALLERIES

011 USA
FAIRS AND EXPOS. Text in English. 10/yr. USD 30 to non-members (effective 1998). adv. **Document type:** *Magazine, Trade.*
Formerly: Fairs and Expositions (0194-4649)
Published by: International Association of Fairs and Expositions, PO Box 985, Springfield, MO 65801. TEL 417-862-5771, 800-516-0313, FAX 417-862-0156. Ed. Max Willis. Pub. Lewis Miller. Adv. contact Steve Siever. Circ: 3,500.

FLORIDA OFFICIAL MEETING PLANNERS GUIDE. *see* TRAVEL AND TOURISM

GENETICS SOCIETY OF CANADA BULLETIN. *see* BIOLOGY—Genetics

011 USA
GLOBAL CONNECTIONS. Text in English. 1978. q. USD 29.50 (effective 2001). adv. bk.rev. **Document type:** *Newsletter.* **Description:** Aimed at registered meeting planners, certified destination specialists and certified event planners.
Published by: International Society of Meeting Planners, 1224 N Nokomis N E, Alexandria, MN 56308-5072. TEL 320-763-4919, FAX 320-763-9290, ismp@iami.org, http://www.iami.org/ismp/. Ed., Pub., R&P, Adv. contact Robert Johnson. Circ: 5,000.

GLOBAL PERSPECTIVES IN REAL ESTATE. *see* BUSINESS AND ECONOMICS—International Commerce

011 ARG ISSN 0301-7567
Q101
GUIA DE REUNIONES CIENTIFICAS Y TECNICAS EN LA ARGENTINA. Text in Spanish. 1959. a. free. adv.
Published by: (Argentina. Ministerio de Cultura y Educacion, Argentina. Secretaria de Estado de Ciencia y Tecnologia), Fundacion para la Educacion la Ciencia y la Cultura, Moreno, 431, Buenos Aires, 1091, Argentina. Circ: 4,000.

610 USA
H C E A ASSOCIATION ALERT; The newsletter for the healthcare exhibition & meeting organizer. Text in English. 1998. 2/yr. free to members. 4 p./no. 2 cols./p.; back issues avail. **Document type:** *Newsletter, Trade.* **Description:** Includes critical analysis of association related issues, advocacy for healthcare conventions and exhibitions as an industry, and needs oriented articles.
Published by: Healthcare Convention & Exhibitors Association, 1100 Johnson Ferry Rd, Ste 300, Atlanta, GA 30342. TEL 404-252-3663, FAX 404-252-0774, hcea@assnhq.com. Eds. Jane Boyle TEL 404-252-3663, Mary Anderson. Adv. contact Jane Boyle TEL 404-252-3663. Circ: 4,000 (controlled).

060 610 USA
H C E A DIRECTORY; a directory of healthcare meetings and conventions. Text in English. 2/yr. USD 245 to non-members (effective 2000). 600 p./no. 2 cols./p.; **Document type:** *Directory, Trade.* **Description:** Lists more than 6000 healthcare meetings.
Formerly: H C E A Handbook
Published by: Healthcare Convention & Exhibitors Association, 1100 Johnson Ferry Rd, Ste 300, Atlanta, GA 30342. TEL 404-252-3663, FAX 404-252-0774, hcea@kellencompany.com. R&P Lavay Sheldon. Adv. contact Gretta Hall TEL 404-252-3663. Circ: 1,000 (paid).

060 NLD ISSN 1574-7921
HOLLAND IN CONGRES; vakblad over internationale meetings en congressen in Nederland. Text in Dutch. 1980. s-a. free to qualified personnel (effective 2010). adv. **Document type:** *Magazine, Trade.*
Former titles (until 2005): M I C E. Meetings Incentives Congressen Exhibitions (1570-5331); (until 2002): Congresnieuws (1382-2233)
Published by: Nederlands Bureau voor Toerisme en Congressen, Vlietweg 15, Postbus 458, Leidschendam, 2260 MG, Netherlands. TEL 31-70-3705705, FAX 31-70-3201654, info@holland.com, http://www.holland.com. Eds. Eric Bakermans, Jan Bakker. adv.: B&W page EUR 1,766, color page EUR 2,556; trim 225 x 285. Circ: 5,000 (controlled).

060 DEU
HOPPENSTEDTS TAGUNGSORTE EUROPEAN CONGRESS ORGANIZERS' GUIDE. Text in German. 1955. a. adv. **Document type:** *Directory, Trade.*
Published by: Sutter Verlagsgesellschaft GmbH, Bottroper Str 20, Essen, 45141, Germany. TEL 49-201-8316001, FAX 49-201-8316009, asv@sutter.de, http://www.sutter-verlag.de. adv.: color page EUR 3,010. Circ: 7,218 (paid and controlled).

011 910.202 USA
I A C V B NEWS. Text in English. 25/yr. adv. **Document type:** *Newsletter.* **Description:** Offers trade information on convention and meeting planning,and visitor bureaus for professionals.
Former titles: Crossroads for Meeting Professionals; (until 1995): International Association of Convention and Visitor Bureaus. Newsletter
Published by: International Association of Convention and Visitor Bureaus, 2000 L St, N W, Ste 702, Washington, DC 20036-4990. TEL 202-296-7888, FAX 202-296-7889. Ed. Lorri Lee Ragan. adv.: B&W page USD 1,575, color page USD 1,890; trim 11 x 8.25. Circ: 15,000 (controlled).

011 USA
I A F E DIRECTORY. Text in English. a. USD 85 to non-members (effective 1998). adv. **Document type:** *Directory.*
Published by: International Association of Fairs and Expositions, PO Box 985, Springfield, MO 65801. TEL 417-862-5771, 800-516-0313, FAX 417-862-0156. Ed. Max Willis. Pub. Lewis Miller. Adv. contact Steve Siever. Circ: 3,000.

I C J MICE MAGAZINE. (Incentive Congress Journal) *see* BUSINESS AND ECONOMICS—Marketing And Purchasing

I E E E AUTOTESTCON. (Institute of Electrical and Electronics Engineers) *see* ENGINEERING—Electrical Engineering

060 USA
ILLINOIS MEETINGS & EVENTS. Text in English. 1999. q. free to qualified personnel (effective 2011). adv. back issues avail.
Document type: *Magazine, Trade.* **Description:** Aimed at meetings and events professionals working in Illinois and includes essential information on a range of topics, from venues and supplier news, to tips, best practices and industry developments.
Related titles: Online - full text ed.: free (effective 2011).
Published by: Tiger Oak Publications, Inc., OneTiger Oak Plz, 900 S Third St, Minneapolis, MN 55415. TEL 612-548-3180, FAX 612-548-3181, customerservice@tigeroak.com, http://www.tigeroak.com. Ed. Lauren K Hurley TEL 773-412-2536. Adv. contact Melissa Brownstein TEL 773-909-6354.

INCENTIVE TRAVEL & CORPORATE MEETINGS. *see* TRAVEL AND TOURISM

DIE INFO; Mitteilungen des Bundesverbandes. *see* FORESTS AND FORESTRY

060 CAN ISSN 1198-189X
INFOCONGRES. Text in English. 3/yr. CAD 19.55; CAD 20 foreign (effective 2000).
Published by: Quebec dans le Monde, C P 8503, Sainte Foy, PQ G1V 4N5, Canada. TEL 418-659-5540, FAX 418-659-4143, quebecmonde@total.net, http://www.total.net/~quebecmonde. R&P Denis Turcotte.

610 011 USA
INSIGHT (ATLANTA). Text in English. 2/yr. free to members. 24 p./no. 2 cols./p.; back issues avail. **Document type:** *Magazine, Trade.*
Published by: Healthcare Convention & Exhibitors Association, 1100 Johnson Ferry Rd, Ste 300, Atlanta, GA 30342. TEL 404-252-3663, FAX 404-252-0774, hcea@assnhq.com. Ed. Mary Anderson. Circ: 2,000.

910 900 MEX ISSN 0020-4188
F1402
INSTITUTO PANAMERICANO DE GEOGRAFIA E HISTORIA. BOLETIN AEREO. Text in Spanish. 1955. 3/yr. looseleaf. free. **Document type:** *Proceedings.*
Published by: Instituto Panamericano de Geografia e Historia, Ex-Arzobispado 29, Col Observatorio, Del Miguel Hidalgo, Mexico City, DF 11860, Mexico. TEL 52-55-52775791, FAX 52-55-52716172, info@ipgh.org.mx, http://www.ipgh.org/. **Subscr. to:** IPGH, c/o Depto. de Distribucion y Ventas, Apdo. 18879, Mexico City, DF 11870, Mexico.

011 USA ISSN 1931-9975
INSURANCE AND FINANCIAL MEETINGS MANAGEMENT. Text in English. 1992. bi-m. USD 45 domestic; USD 105 foreign (effective 2008). adv. back issues avail.; reprints avail. **Document type:** *Magazine, Trade.* **Description:** Contains articles and relevant information about meeting and convention destinations, industry activities, motivation and incentive programs, platform speakers, studies on convention practices and related topics.
Former titles: Insurance Meetings Management (1095-9726); (until 199?): Insurance Meetings and Incentive Travel (1078-7666); (until 1994): Insurance Conventions and Incentive Travel (1068-9435)
Published by: Coastal Communications Corp., 2700 N Military Trail, Ste 120, Boca Raton, FL 33431-6394. TEL 561-989-0600, FAX 561-989-9509, cccpublisher@att.net. Ed., Pub. Harvey Grotsky. Circ: 5,017 (controlled).

011 BEL ISSN 0538-6349
INTERNATIONAL CONGRESS CALENDAR. Text in English. 1961. q. EUR 260 (effective 2003). adv. index, cum.index. **Document type:** *Directory, Trade.* **Description:** Provides current information on over 7,000 international events scheduled for the next 15 years.
Indexed: RASB.
—GNLM, INIST, Linda Hall.
Published by: Union of International Associations/Union des Associations Internationales, Rue Washington 40, Brussels, 1050, Belgium. TEL 32-2-6401808, FAX 32-2-6436199, uia@uia.be, http://www.uia.org. Ed. G de Coninck.

011 BEL ISSN 0538-6772
INTERNATIONAL CONGRESS SCIENCE SERIES. Text in English. 1961. irreg., latest vol.12. price varies.
—Linda Hall.
Published by: Union of International Associations/Union des Associations Internationales, Rue Washington 40, Brussels, 1050, Belgium. TEL 32-2-6401808, FAX 32-2-6436199.

060 GBR ISSN 0969-2622
CODEN: ICGSEM
INTERNATIONAL CONGRESS, SYMPOSIUM AND SEMINAR SERIES. Text in English. 1993. irreg.
—Ingenta. **CCC.**
Published by: Parthenon Publishing Group (Subsidiary of: C R C Press, LLC), 23-25 Blades Court, Deodar Road, London, SW15 2NU, United Kingdom. TEL 44-20-8875-0909, FAX 44-20-8871-9996, http://www.parthpub.com/journal.html.

011 PHL ISSN 0074-588X
INTERNATIONAL FEDERATION OF ASIAN AND WESTERN PACIFIC CONTRACTORS' ASSOCIATIONS. PROCEEDINGS OF THE ANNUAL CONVENTION. (Proceedings published by organizing committee) Text in English. a. **Document type:** *Proceedings.*
Published by: International Federation of Asian and Western Pacific Contractors' Associations, Padilla Bldg, 3rd Fl., Ortigas Commercial Center, Emerald Ave., Pasig, Manila, Philippines. TEL 632-631-2782, FAX 632-631-2773, ifawpca@mozcom.com, http://www.ifawpca.org.

INTERNATIONAL SOCIETY OF CITRICULTURE. PROCEEDINGS. *see* AGRICULTURE

011 CAN ISSN 0844-2762
AS6
INTERNATIONAL TRADE FAIRS AND CONFERENCES DIRECTORY (YEAR). Text in English. 1986. a. CAD 149.95. **Document type:** *Directory.* **Description:** Contains essential information on 5,300 trade show events taking place in over 75 countries worldwide.
Published by: International Press Publications Inc, 90 Nolan Ct, Ste 21, Markham, ON L3R 4L9, Canada. TEL 905-946-9588.

INTERNATIONAL TRADESHOW DIRECTORY. *see* BUSINESS AND ECONOMICS—Trade And Industrial Directories

060.688 USA ISSN 1547-0148
TX911.2
JOURNAL OF CONVENTION & EVENT TOURISM. Text in English. 1998. q. GBP 230 combined subscription in United Kingdom to institutions (print & online eds.); EUR 298, USD 306 combined subscription to institutions (print & online eds.) (effective 2012). adv. reprint service avail. from PSC. **Document type:** *Journal, Academic/Scholarly.* **Description:** Offers information about trends and innovations in applied research and management practices.
Formerly (until 2004): Journal of Convention & Exhibition Management (1094-608X)
Related titles: Microform ed.; Online - full text ed.: ISSN 1547-0156. GBP 207 in United Kingdom to institutions; EUR 268, USD 276 to institutions (effective 2012).
Indexed: A01, A03, A10, A22, B01, B07, B09, CA, CABA, E01, GH, H&TI, H06, IBR, IBZ, LT, M&MA, M02, N02, R12, RRTA, RefZh, S02, S03, S13, S16, SCOPUS, SD, SWR&A, T02, TAR, V03, W11.
—BLDSC (4965.262000), IE, Ingenta. **CCC.**
Published by: Routledge (Subsidiary of: Taylor & Francis Group), 325 Chestnut St, Ste 800, Philadelphia, PA 19106. TEL 215-625-8900, 800-354-1420, FAX 215-625-8914, journals@routledge.com, http://www.routledge.com. Ed. Robert R Nelson. adv.: B&W page USD 315, color page USD 550; trim 4.375 x 7.125. Circ: 106 (paid).

JULI-MAGAZIN. *see* POLITICAL SCIENCE—Civil Rights

KEY NOTE MARKET REPORT: EXHIBITIONS & CONFERENCES. *see* BUSINESS AND ECONOMICS—Production Of Goods And Services

910.09 DEU
KOELNER KONGRESS REPORT. Text in German. 1970. s-a. free. adv. **Document type:** *Consumer.*
Related titles: English ed.: Cologne Convention.
Published by: KoelnTourismus/Cologne Tourist Board, Unter Fettenhennen 19, Cologne, 50667, Germany. info@koelntourismus.de, http://www.koeln.de/tourismus/koelntourismus/. Eds. Adrea Vop, Erhard Schlieter. Adv. contact Klaus Odenthal. Circ: 6,000.

011 NLD ISSN 0942-0568
KONCIZE. Text in Esperanto. 1975. bi-w. adv. bk.rev. **Document type:** *Bulletin.* **Description:** Information on Esperanto meetings, travel.
Published by: Nederlandse Esperanto-Jongeren/European Esperanto Youth, Nieuwe Binnenweg 176, Rotterdam, 3015 BJ, Netherlands. TEL 31-6-36141205, ledenadministratie@esperanto-jongeren.nl, http://www.esperanto-jongeren.nl.

499.992 NLD ISSN 0083-3851
PM8201
KONGRESA LIBRO. Text in Esperanto. 1905. a. EUR 6.90 (effective 2010). adv. illus. 100 p./no.; **Document type:** *Proceedings, Trade.* **Description:** Contains program information, background articles and lists of participants.
Published by: Universala Esperanto-Asocio, Nieuwe Binnenweg 176, Rotterdam, 3015 BJ, Netherlands. TEL 31-10-4361044, FAX 31-10-4361751, info@uea.org, http://www.uea.org.

011 DEU
KONGRESS KALENDER MEDIZIN. Text in German. 1961. a. EUR 41.22 (effective 2007). **Document type:** *Catalog, Trade.*
Formerly: Demeter Kongress Kalender Medizin (0933-9760)
—GNLM.
Published by: Spitta Verlag GmbH und Co. KG, Ammonitenstr 1, Balingen, 72336, Germany. TEL 49-7433-9520, FAX 49-7433-952111, kundencenter@spitta.de, http://www.spitta.de.

068.485 SWE ISSN 0348-1433
KUNGLIGA VITTERHETS HISTORIE OCH ANTIKVITETS AKADEMIEN. KONFERENSER. Text in English, German, Swedish. 1977. irreg., latest vol.56, 2003. price varies. back issues avail. **Document type:** *Proceedings, Academic/Scholarly.*
Indexed: RASB.
Published by: Kungliga Vitterhets Historie och Antikvitets Akademien/Royal Academy of Letters, History, and Antiquities, Villagatan 3, PO Box 5622, Stockholm, 11486, Sweden. TEL 46-8-4404280, FAX 46-8-4404290, kansli@vitterhetsakad.se. **Dist. by:** Almqvist & Wiksell International, P O Box 7634, Stockholm 10394, Sweden. TEL 46-8-6136100, FAX 46-8-217050.

793.060 913 USA
LAS VEGAS CONVENTION AND MEETING PLANNERS GUIDE. Text in English. a. adv. **Document type:** *Handbook/Manual/Guide, Trade.* **Description:** Contains charts and amenities listings designed specifically for meeting planners making buying choices.
Published by: Weaver Publications, Inc., 2420 Alcott St, Denver, CO 80211. TEL 303-458-1211, FAX 303-477-0724, info@weaver-group.com, http://www.weaver-group.com. Circ: 7,500.

THE LONDON & U K DATEBOOK. *see* SOCIAL SERVICES AND WELFARE

M + A - MESSEPLANER INTERNATIONAL; schedule for fairs and exhibitions worldwide. *see* BUSINESS AND ECONOMICS—Trade And Industrial Directories

M + A REPORT; das Magazin fuer Messen, Events und Marketing. *see* ADVERTISING AND PUBLIC RELATIONS

011 ITA ISSN 0390-2692
M C MEETING E CONGRESS. Text in Italian. 1973. 8/yr. EUR 150 domestic; EUR 200 foreign (effective 2008). adv. **Document type:** *Magazine, Trade.*
Published by: Ediman Srl, Via Ripamonti 89, Milan, 20139, Italy. TEL 39-02-57311511, FAX 39-02-55231486, http://www.ediman.it. Circ: 11,000.

011 ITA
M I C E. (Meetings Incentives Conferences Events) Text in Italian, English. 8/yr. EUR 70 domestic (effective 2008). **Document type:** *Magazine, Trade.*
Related titles: Online - full text ed.; Supplement(s): M I C E Guide (Year). EUR 30 (effective 2006).
Published by: BE-MA Editrice Srl, Via Teocrito 50, Milan, MI 20128, Italy. TEL 39-02-252071, FAX 39-02-27000692, segreteria@bema.it.

060 AUS ISSN 1446-4691
MACQUARIE UNIVERSITY CALENDAR OF GOVERNANCE, LEGISLATION & RULES. Text in English. 2001. a., latest 2008. back issues avail. **Document type:** *Journal, Academic/Scholarly.*
Supersedes in part (in 2001): Macquarie University Calendar (0810-5049); Which was formerly (until 1984): Macquarie University. Calendar of Macquarie University
Related titles: Online - full text ed.: free (effective 2009).
Published by: Macquarie University, Balaclava Rd, North Ryde, NSW 2109, Australia. TEL 61-2-98507111, FAX 61-2-98507433, mqinfo@mq.edu.au, http://www.mq.edu.au.

MEDICAL EXPRESS REPORTS. *see* MEDICAL SCIENCES

011 USA ISSN 0093-1314
R845
MEDICAL MEETINGS; international guide for health care meeting planners. Text in English. 1973. 8/yr. USD 51 domestic; USD 60 in Canada; USD 85 elsewhere; free domestic to qualified personnel (effective 2011). adv. **Document type:** *Magazine, Trade.*
Description: Directed to medical conference organizers and meetings planners.
Related titles: Online - full text ed.
Indexed: A09, A10, A26, B01, B02, B06, B07, B09, B15, B17, B18, BPI, BRD, G04, G06, G07, G08, H&TI, H01, H06, H11, H12, I05, M06, P21, P48, PQC, RehabLit, T02, V03, V04, W01, W02, W03, W05.
—Ingenta. **CCC.**
Published by: Penton Media, Inc., 11 River Bend Dr South, PO Box 4949, Stamford, CT 06907-0949. TEL 203-358-9900, FAX 203-358-5823, information@penton.com, http://www.pentonmedia.com. Ed. Sue Pelletier TEL 978-448-0377. Circ: 13,100 (controlled).

011 DEU ISSN 0175-3053
MEDIZINISCHE KONGRESSE; national - international. Text in German. 1957. a. EUR 39.50 domestic; EUR 48 in Europe; EUR 60 elsewhere (effective 2005). back issues avail. **Document type:** *Directory, Trade.*
Published by: M, K & K Verlagsgesellschaft mbH, Postfach 400132, Neu-Isenburg, 63246, Germany. TEL 49-69-69500845, FAX 49-69-69500827. Ed., Pub. Ingrid Haack. R&P Dieter Haack. Adv. contact Monika Schmidt. Circ: 32,000.

001 910.09 GBR ISSN 0953-2803
MEETING AND INCENTIVE TRAVEL. Abbreviated title: M & I T. Text in English. 1985. 10/yr. GBP 60 domestic; USD 200 foreign; free to qualified personnel (effective 2009). adv. back issues avail.
Document type: *Magazine, Trade.*
Formerly (until 1987): Venue (0267-7490)
—BLDSC (5536.222490), IE, Ingenta. **CCC.**
Published by: Conference and Travel Publications Ltd., Kings House, Cantelupe Rd, East Grinstead, West Sussex RH19 3BE, United Kingdom. TEL 44-1342-306700, FAX 44-1342-302547, cat@cat-publications.com. Ed. Katherine Simmons. Pub. Stephen Lewis. adv.: color page EUR 7,975. Circ: 18,058.

658.456 USA ISSN 0145-630X
MEETING NEWS; news, info & ideas for better meetings. Text in English. 1977. 18/yr. USD 89 domestic; USD 99 in Canada; USD 205 elsewhere; USD 10 newsstand/cover; free to qualified personnel (effective 2009). adv. Supplement avail. **Document type:** *Magazine, Trade.* **Description:** Provides resources for all levels of managers and buyers responsible for meetings, conventions, trade shows and incentives about events shaping the industry.
Related titles: Online - full text ed.; Supplement(s): The Incentive Travel Buyer's Handbook. ISSN 1941-4277.
Indexed: A09, A10, A15, ABIn, B01, B06, B07, B09, H&TI, H06, Hospl, P34, P48, P51, PAIS, PQC, T02, V03, V04.
—**CCC.**
Published by: Nielsen Business Publications (Subsidiary of: Nielsen Business Media, Inc.), 770 Broadway, New York, NY 10003. TEL 646-654-4500, FAX 646-654-4948, bmcomm@nielsen.com, http://www.nielsenbusinessmedia.com. Ed. Terri Hardin TEL 646-654-7364. adv.: B&W page USD 12,800, color page USD 16,100; trim 9 x 10.875. Circ: 50,100. **Subscr. to:** PO Box 1189, Skokie, IL 60076.

011 USA ISSN 0025-8652
AS6
MEETINGS AND CONVENTIONS. Abbreviated title: M & C. Text in English. 1966. m. (plus annual directory). USD 89 domestic; USD 119 in Canada & Mexico; USD 209 elsewhere; free to qualified personnel (effective 2011). bk.rev. illus.; tr.lit. reprints avail. **Document type:** *Magazine, Trade.* **Description:** Covers industry news, issues and trends, practical how-to features and destination guides for more than 75,000 meeting professionals.
Related titles: Online - full text ed.: USD 41.50 (effective 2011); ◆ Supplement(s): T & E Magazine. ISSN 1934-9521; ◆ Official Meeting Facilities Guide.
Indexed: A12, A13, A15, A17, A22, ABIn, B01, B02, B03, B06, B07, B08, B09, B11, B15, B17, B18, BusI, C12, CWI, E07, G04, G06, G07, G08, H&TI, H06, I05, M01, M02, P06, P07, P34, P48, P51, P53, P54, PQC, T&DA, T&II, T03.
—BLDSC (5312.920000), IE, Ingenta. **CCC.**
Published by: Northstar Travel Media LLC (Subsidiary of: Boston Ventures Management, Inc.), 100 Lighting Way, Secaucus, NJ 07094. TEL 201-902-2000, FAX 201-902-2045, http://www.northstartravelmedia.com/. Ed. Lori Cioffi TEL 201-902-1786.

011 SGP
MEETINGS AND CONVENTIONS ASIA PACIFIC. Text in English. 1993. bi-m. adv. back issues avail. **Document type:** *Magazine, Trade.*
Description: Covers issues related to planning meetings, conventions and exhibitions for key decision-makers in 12 Asia Pacific countries.
Published by: Venture Asia Publishing, 10 Craig Rd, Singapore, 089670, Singapore. TEL 65-223-2911, FAX 65-223-1866. Ed. Raini Hamdi. Pub., R&P Selin Koh. Adv. contact Ms. Elissa Wong. page USD 7,286. Circ: 12,108 (controlled).

MEETINGS & EXPOSITIONS (ONLINE). *see* BUSINESS AND ECONOMICS—Management

011 CAN ISSN 0225-8285
MEETINGS & INCENTIVE TRAVEL. Text in English. 1972. 7/yr. free domestic to qualified personnel; CAD 74 domestic; CAD 93 foreign (effective 2007). adv. **Document type:** *Magazine, Trade.*
Description: Contains news, trends and technologies for corporate and association meeting, convention and incentive travel planners.
Formerly (until 1980): Canadian Sales Meetings and Conventions (0318-1049)
Related titles: Microfiche ed.: (from MML); Microform ed.: (from MML); Online - full text ed.

Indexed: A15, ABIn, B16, C03, CBCABus, CBPI, H&TI, H06, P10, P53, P54, PQC, T02.
—CIS.
Published by: Rogers Publishing Ltd./Les Editions Rogers Limitee, One Mount Pleasant Rd, 11th Fl, Toronto, ON M4Y 2Y5, Canada. TEL 416-764-2000, FAX 416-764-3941, http://www.rogerspublishing.ca. Pub. Stephen Dempsey TEL 416-764-1635. Circ: 12,300.

MEETINGS EAST. *see* TRAVEL AND TOURISM

MEETINGS MIDAMERICA. *see* TRAVEL AND TOURISM

011 CAN ISSN 0841-9663
MEETINGS MONTHLY, NEWS BULLETIN; for Canadian meeting planners. Text in English. 1988. m. USD 40 (effective 2000). adv. bk.rev. back issues avail. **Document type:** *Bulletin, Trade.*
Formerly: Meetings Monthly (0841-9655)
Related titles: ◆ English ed.: Congres Mensuel, Bulletin de Nouvelles. ISSN 0841-968X.
Published by: (Association of Meeting Organizers), Publicom Inc., Place d Armes, C P 365, Montreal, PQ H2Y 3H1, Canada. TEL 514-274-0004, FAX 514-274-5884, TELEX 055-61866. Ed. Guy Jonkman. Circ: 12,703 (controlled).

333.792 AUT ISSN 0047-6641
QC770
MEETINGS ON ATOMIC ENERGY. Text in English. 1969. q. index. **Document type:** *Directory, Trade.*
Related titles: Online - full text ed.
—BLDSC (5536.222500), INIST, Linda Hall. **CCC.**
Published by: International Atomic Energy Agency/Agence Internationale de l'Energie Atomique, Wagramer Str 5, Postfach 100, Vienna, W 1400, Austria. TEL 43-1-2600-22045, FAX 43-1-2600-7, official.mail@iaea.org, http://www.iaea.or.at/worldatom/meeting/moae.html. Ed. Sandra Salvini Plawen. Circ: 1,800.

MEETINGS SOUTH. *see* TRAVEL AND TOURISM

MEETINGS WEST. *see* TRAVEL AND TOURISM

011 AUT
MESSE & EVENT. Text in German. 1981. bi-m. EUR 18 (effective 2005). adv. bk.rev. **Document type:** *Magazine, Trade.*
Formerly: Messemarkt
Published by: N.J. Schmid Verlag, Leberstr 122, Vienna, 1110, Austria. TEL 43-1-74032735, FAX 43-1-74032750, g.milletich@schmid-verlag.at. Ed. Christoph Berndl. Adv. contact Monika Steiner. B&W page EUR 2,260, color page EUR 3,420; trim 180 x 267. Circ: 21,000 (paid and controlled).

MEXICO MEETING & INCENTIVE PLANNER. *see* TRAVEL AND TOURISM

060 NLD ISSN 1574-9487
M!CE TRAVEL!. Text in Dutch. 2005. 5/m. adv. **Document type:** *Magazine, Trade.*
Published by: Reisrevue Groep bv, Stationsplein 3, Hilversum, 1211 EX, Netherlands. TEL 31-35-6728848, FAX 31-35-6728833. Eds. Emma Heuvelmans, Jan Lokhoff.

060 USA
MICHIGAN MEETINGS & EVENTS. Text in English. 19??. q. free to qualified personnel (effective 2011). adv. back issues avail. **Document type:** *Magazine, Trade.* **Description:** Aimed at meetings and events professionals working in Michigan and includes essential information on a range of topics, from venues and supplier news, to tips, best practices and industry developments.
Related titles: Online - full text ed.: free (effective 2011).
Published by: Tiger Oak Publications, Inc., OneTiger Oak Plz, 900 S Third St, Minneapolis, MN 55415. TEL 612-548-3180, FAX 612-548-3181, customerservice@tigeroak.com, http://www.tigeroak.com. Ed. Cathleen Hagan TEL 248-627-3492. Adv. contact Laurie Burger TEL 586-416-4195.

016.5 USA
MIND: THE MEETINGS INDEX (ONLINE). Text in English. irreg. free. **Document type:** *Directory, Trade.* **Description:** Offers free access to locate future conferences, congresses, meetings and symposia.
Media: Online - full text.
Published by: InterDok Corp., 173 Halstead Ave, Box 326, Harrison, NY 10528. TEL 914-835-3506, FAX 914-835-6757, jb@interdok.com.

060 USA
MINNESOTA GROUP & PACKAGE TRAVEL PLANNER. Text in English. 2002. q. adv. **Document type:** *Magazine, Trade.*
Formed by the 2002 merger of: Minnesota Destinations; Minnesota Group Tour Guide
Published by: Tiger Oak Publications, Inc., OneTiger Oak Plz, 900 S Third St, Minneapolis, MN 55415. TEL 612-548-3180, FAX 612-548-3181, http://www.tigeroak.com.

060 USA
MINNESOTA MEETINGS + EVENTS. Text in English. 19??. q. free (effective 2009). adv. back issues avail.; reprints avail. **Document type:** *Magazine, Consumer.* **Description:** Aimed at meetings and events professionals working in Minnesota and includes essential information on a range of topics, from venues and supplier news, to tips, best practices and industry developments.
Published by: Tiger Oak Publications, Inc., OneTiger Oak Plz, 900 S Third St, Minneapolis, MN 55415. TEL 612-548-3180, FAX 612-548-3181, http://www.tigeroak.com. Pub. R Craig Bednar. Adv. contact John Sullivan. color page USD 5,875; trim 8.375 x 10.875. Circ: 6,549.

060 USA
MINNESOTA MEETINGS & EVENTS ANNUAL RESOURCES DIRECTORY. Text in English. 19??. a. adv. **Document type:** *Directory, Trade.* **Description:** Contains information in hospitality industry provider categories such as catering, attractions, speakers, entertainment, transportation companies, destination management companies, and more.
Related titles: Online - full text ed.: free to qualified personnel (effective 2009).
Published by: Tiger Oak Publications, Inc., OneTiger Oak Plz, 900 S Third St, Minneapolis, MN 55415. TEL 612-548-3180, FAX 612-548-3181, http://www.tigeroak.com. adv.: page USD 2,200; bleed 8.375 x 10.875.

060 CAN ISSN 1922-3250
MUSEUMS ASSOCIATION OF SASKATCHEWAN. BOARD & STAFF QUARTERLY REPORT. Text in English. 1975. q. free to members (effective 2010). back issues avail. **Document type:** *Report, Trade.* **Description:** Provides information about the annual general meeting and conference, and updates on other board and staff activities.
Former titles (until 2009): M A S en Masse (1921-8818); (until 2008): Muse News (1915-934X); (until 2007): Museums Association of Saskatchewan. Bulletin (0849-0112); (until 1989): Saskatchewan Museums Association. Bulletin (0828-9417); (until 1984): Liason (0712-9246); (until 1981): Saskatchewan Museums Quarterly (0381-1042)
Related titles: Online - full text ed.: free (effective 2010).
Published by: Museums Association of Saskatchewan, 424 McDonald St, Regina, SK S4N 6E1, Canada. TEL 306-780-9279, 866-568-7386.

011 IND
N A S S D O C RESEARCH INFORMATION SERIES. CONFERENCE ALERT; quarterly calendar. (N A S S D O C Research Information Series) Text in English. 19??. q. INR 25 per issue (effective 2011). **Document type:** *Journal, Academic/Scholarly.* **Description:** Contains a quarterly list of conferences, seminars and training courses in social sciences, and library and information sciences.
Related titles: Duplicated (not offset) ed.
Indexed: RASB.
Published by: (National Social Science Documentation Centre), Indian Council of Social Science Research, JNU Institutional Area, Aruna Asaf Ali Marg, New Delhi, 110 067, India. TEL 91-11-26741849, FAX 91-11-26741836, info@icssr.org.

060 910.2 330 USA
NATIONAL VENUES GUIDE. Text in English. 1998. s-a. USD 49.95 per issue (effective 2011). adv. **Document type:** *Directory, Trade.* **Description:** Focuses solely on venues and venue selection.
Formerly (until 200?): Agenda Venues
Published by: Red 7 Media, LLC, 10 Norden Pl, Norwalk, CT 06855. TEL 203-854-6730, FAX 203-854-6735, http://red7media.com. Pub. Sharon Kress. adv.: B&W page USD 3,495; trim 8.125 x 10.875. Circ: 43,500 (paid).

763.060 763.913 USA
NEW ORLEANS MEETINGS PLANNERS GUIDE. Text in English. a. adv. **Document type:** *Guide, Consumer.* **Description:** Contains information about accommodations, including convention facilities and hotels/motels; dining and reception facilities and attractions which includes arts, festivals, shopping and extensive user-friendly maps.
Published by: Weaver Publications, Inc., 2420 Alcott St, Denver, CO 80211. TEL 303-458-1211, FAX 303-477-0724, info@weaver-group.com. Circ: 5,000.

060 USA
NORTHERN CALIFORNIA MEETINGS AND EVENTS. Text in English. 200?. q. free to qualified personnel (effective 2011). adv. back issues avail. **Document type:** *Magazine, Trade.* **Description:** Includes essential information on a range of topics, from venues and supplier news, to tips, best practices and industry developments.
Related titles: Online - full text ed.: free (effective 2011).
Published by: Tiger Oak Publications, Inc., OneTiger Oak Plz, 900 S Third St, Minneapolis, MN 55415. TEL 612-548-3180, FAX 612-548-3181, customerservice@tigeroak.com, http://www.tigeroak.com. Ed. Janet Fullwood TEL 916-393-1994. Pub. R Craig Bednar.

060 USA
NORTHWEST MEETINGS AND EVENTS. Text in English. 200?. q. free to qualified personnel (effective 2011). adv. back issues avail. **Document type:** *Magazine, Trade.* **Description:** Aimed at meetings and events professionals working in the Northwest and includes essential information on a range of topics, from venues and supplier news, to tips, best practices and industry developments.
Related titles: Online - full text ed.: free (effective 2011).
Published by: Tiger Oak Publications, Inc., OneTiger Oak Plz, 900 S Third St, Minneapolis, MN 55415. TEL 612-548-3180, FAX 612-548-3181, customerservice@tigeroak.com, http://www.tigeroak.com. Ed. Teresa Kenney TEL 206-920-8507. Pub. R Craig Bednar.

647 USA
OFFICIAL MEETING FACILITIES GUIDE. Abbreviated title: O M F G. Text in English. 19??. a. includes with subscr. to Meetings and Conventions. **Document type:** *Directory, Trade.* **Description:** Provides planners the opportunity of viewing desired venues through detailed search options, including geographic information, amenities and name selections. It provides users with the same important information offered through the OMFG and OMFG-I directories which enables them to review and compare meeting facilities, convention centers, CVBs, and destinations efficiently at the time their decisions are being made.
Incorporates (in 200?): Official Meeting Facilities Guide. Europe (1054-3309); Official Meeting Facilities Guide. International; Official Meeting Facilities Guide. North America (1070-4515); Which was formerly (1974-1992): Official Meeting Facilities Guide (0094-5242)
Related titles: Online - full text ed.; ◆ Supplement to: Meetings and Conventions. ISSN 0025-8652.
Published by: Northstar Travel Media LLC (Subsidiary of: Boston Ventures Management, Inc.), 100 Lighting Way, Secaucus, NJ 07094. TEL 201-902-2000, FAX 201-902-2045, http://www.northstartravelmedia.com/.

658.456 USA ISSN 1943-1864
ONE+. Text in English. 1984. m. USD 99 domestic; USD 129 foreign (effective 2009). adv. 128 p./no. 3 cols./p.; back issues avail. **Document type:** *Magazine, Trade.* **Description:** Focuses on all aspects of meetings planning, including site selection and negotiation, food and beverage tips, special events ideas, budgeting and general meetings management.
Former titles (until 2008): The Meeting Professional (1093-5029); (until 1997): Meeting Manager (8750-7218)
Related titles: Online - full text ed.; Supplement(s): Convention Centers; Resorts and Spas; Gaming Venues; Golf Venues.
Indexed: H&TI, T02.
—Ingenta.
Published by: Meeting Professionals International, 3030 Lyndon B. Johnson Fwy, Ste 1700, Dallas, TX 75234. TEL 972-702-3035, FAX 972-702-3096, publications@mpiweb.org. Ed. David R Basler. adv.: color page USD 6,500; trim 10.88 x 8.13. Circ: 32,000 (controlled).

060 USA ISSN 1947-4733
AS6
ONE+ EUROPE, MIDDLE EAST, AND AFRICA; connecting you to the global meeting + event community. Text in English. 2007. bi-m. USD 99 domestic to non-members; USD 129 foreign to non-members; free to members (effective 2009). adv. back issues avail. **Document type:** *Magazine, Trade.*
Formerly (until 2009): Meeting Professional European Digest (1937-8564)
Related titles: Online - full text ed.: ISSN 1947-4741. free (effective 2009).
Published by: Meeting Professionals International, 3030 Lyndon B. Johnson Fwy, Ste 1700, Dallas, TX 75234. TEL 972-702-3000, FAX 972-702-3070, publications@mpiweb.org. Ed. David R Basler. Adv. contact Maria Catalano TEL 32-2-3720017. page USD 3,700; trim 207 x 276.

011 USA
PERSPECTIVES (SILVER SPRING). Text in English. q. free to members. **Document type:** *Newsletter.* **Description:** Contains information about NCBMP activities, member services and latest industry trends.
Formerly: National Coalition of Black Meeting Planners. Newsletter
Related titles: Online - full content ed.
Published by: National Coalition of Black Meeting Planners, 8630 Fenton St, Ste 126, Silver Spring, MD 20910-3803. TEL 202-628-3952, FAX 301-588-0011, ncbmphq@verizon.net, http://www.ncbmp.com. Circ: 2,000.

PHILATELIC EXHIBITOR. *see* PHILATELY

PHYSICIANS' TRAVEL & MEETING GUIDE. *see* TRAVEL AND TOURISM

PREVUE; destination insight for meeting + incentive planners. *see* TRAVEL AND TOURISM

PROCUREMENT.TRAVEL; the source for managaed travel insight. *see* TRAVEL AND TOURISM

060 NLD ISSN 1387-3121
HF5734.5
QUALITY IN MEETINGS. Text in Dutch. 1950. 6/yr. EUR 36 (effective 2009). adv. illus. **Document type:** *Journal, Trade.*
Formerly (until 1997): Congresvisie (1380-3409); Which superseded in part (in 1994): Expo - Congresvisie (0927-7420); Which was formerly (until 1992): Expovisie (0014-5254); (until 1951): Beursklanken voor Handel en Industrie
Indexed: A22.
—IE, Infotrieve.
Published by: Hollandia Publishing BV, Postbus 341, Heerhugowaard, 1700 AH, Netherlands. TEL 31-72-5760500, FAX 31-72-5760505, hp@hollandia.nl. Ed. Edwin Nunnink. Adv. contact Marten Mulder TEL 31-72-5760546. Circ: 7,000.

RAHNAMA-YI SIMINARHA-YI IRAN/DIRECTORY OF SCIENTIFIC MEETINGS HELD IN IRAN. *see* SCIENCES: COMPREHENSIVE WORKS

REJUVENATE. *see* BUSINESS AND ECONOMICS—Management

RELIGIOUS CONFERENCE MANAGER. *see* RELIGIONS AND THEOLOGY

RENDEVENEMENT (FRENCH EDITION). *see* ADVERTISING AND PUBLIC RELATIONS

S C A L A C S. (Southern California Section of American Chemical Society) *see* CHEMISTRY

794.060 913.794 910.2 USA
SAN DIEGO MEETING & CONVENTION PLANNER'S GUIDE. Variant title: San Diego Meeting and Convention Planner's Guide. Text in English. 199?. a. adv. **Document type:** *Handbook/Manual/Guide, Trade.*
Published by: Weaver Publications, Inc., 2420 Alcott St, Denver, CO 80211. TEL 303-458-1211, FAX 303-477-0724, info@weaver-group.com, http://pub.weaver-group.com. Circ: 15,000.

794.060 913.794 USA
SAN FRANCISCO MEETING AND EVENT PLANNER'S GUIDE. Variant title: San Francisco Meeting & Event Planner's Guide. Text in English. 19??. a. adv. **Document type:** *Handbook/Manual/Guide, Trade.*
Formerly: San Francisco Facilities & Services for Conventions, Meetings & Events Directory
Published by: Weaver Publications, Inc., 2420 Alcott St, Denver, CO 80211. TEL 303-458-1211, FAX 303-477-0724, info@weaver-group.com, http://pub.weaver-group.com. Circ: 15,000.

▼ **SCHENCKS EVENTLOCATION GUIDE.** *see* HOTELS AND RESTAURANTS

500 011 USA ISSN 0487-8965
Q101 CODEN: SMETAL
SCIENTIFIC MEETINGS. Text in English. 1957. q. USD 85 in US & Canada; USD 92.50 elsewhere; USD 25 per issue elsewhere (effective 2000). back issues avail.; reprints avail. **Document type:** *Directory.* **Description:** Directory of forthcoming scientific, technical, medical, engineering and management meetings and international conferences.
Related titles: Diskette ed.: USD 125 (effective 2000); Microform ed.: (from PQC).
Indexed: RASB.
—CASDDS, Linda Hall.
Published by: Scientific Meetings Publications, 5214 Soledad Mountain Rd, San Diego, CA 92138. TEL 858-270-2910, FAX 858-270-2910, scimeeting@accessl.net. Ed., Pub., R&P Irving Wasserberg. Circ: 1,200 (paid).

SHANGHAI SHIBO/EXPO 2010 SHANGHAI. *see* BUSINESS AND ECONOMICS

381.1 SGP ISSN 0218-7388
TX911.2
SINGAPORE CONVENTION & EXHIBITION DIRECTORY (YEAR). Text in English. a. USD 50 (effective 2008). adv. **Document type:** *Directory, Trade.* **Description:** Guide to the convention and exhibition facilities and the relevant supporting services available in Singapore.
Published by: Marshall Cavendish Business Information Pty. Ltd. (Subsidiary of: Times Publishing Group), Times Centre, 1 New Industrial Rd, Singapore, 536196, Singapore. TEL 65-6213-9288, FAX 65-6285-0161, bizinfo@sg.marshallcavendish.com, http://www.marshallcavendish.com/.

011 USA
SOCIETY OF GOVERNMENT MEETING PLANNERS. NEWSLETTER. Text in English. m. membership only. adv. **Document type:** *Newsletter.*
Published by: Society of Government Meeting Planners, 6 Clouser Rd, Mechanicsburg, PA 17055-9735. TEL 717-795-7467, FAX 717-795-7552.

616.07 ZAF
➤ **SOUTH AFRICAN SOCIETY OF PATHOLOGISTS. CONGRESS BROCHURE.** Text in Afrikaans, English. a. free. adv. **Document type:** *Proceedings, Academic/Scholarly.*
Published by: South Africa Society of Pathologists, PO Box 2034, Pretoria, 0001, South Africa. TEL 27-12-3283600. Circ: 300.

060 USA
SOUTHERN CALIFORNIA MEETINGS AND EVENTS. Text in English. 200?. q. free to qualified personnel (effective 2011). adv. back issues avail. **Document type:** *Magazine, Trade.* **Description:** Aimed at meetings and events professionals working in Southern California and includes essential information on a range of topics, from venues and supplier news, to tips, best practices and industry developments.
Related titles: Online - full text ed.: free (effective 2011).
Published by: Tiger Oak Publications, Inc., OneTiger Oak Plz, 900 S Third St, Minneapolis, MN 55415. TEL 612-548-3180, FAX 612-548-3181, customerservice@tigeroak.com, http://www.tigeroak.com. Ed. Lauren K Hurley TEL 773-412-2536. Pub. R Craig Bednar.

SUCCESSFUL MEETINGS; the authority on meetings and incentive travel management. *see* BUSINESS AND ECONOMICS—Marketing And Purchasing

381.1 338.4 SGP
T T G - B T M I C E CHINA. Variant title: Travel Trade Gazette - Business Travel Meetings, Incentives, Conferences and Exhibitions China. Text in English. m. free to qualified personnel. **Document type:** *Newspaper, Trade.*
Formerly (until 2003): B T N China
Published by: T T G Asia Media Pte Ltd, 6 Raffles Quay #16-02, Singapore, 048580, Singapore. TEL 65-6395-7575, FAX 65-6536-8639, contact@ttgasia.com, http://www.ttgasiamedia.com/.

060 338.4791 SGP
TX907.5.A78
T T G M I C E; Asia's leading magazine for meetings, incentives, conferences and exhibitions. (Travel Trade Gazette Meetings, Incentives, Conferences and Exhibitions) Variant title: T T G Meetings, Incentives, Conferences and Exhibitions. Text in English. 1992. bi-m. free to qualified personnel. adv. **Document type:** *Magazine, Trade.* **Description:** Covers trends, new products, issues and events relating the incentive and meetings industry in Asia.
Former titles: Incentive & Meetings Asia (0218-849X); (until 1994): Incentive Asia (0218-4435)
Related titles: Online - full text ed.
—CIS.
Published by: T T G Asia Media Pte Ltd, 6 Raffles Quay #16-02, Singapore, 048580, Singapore. TEL 65-6395-7575, FAX 65-6536-8639, contact@ttgasia.com, http://www.ttgasiamedia.com/. Ed. Raini Hamdi. adv.: color page USD 7,969. Circ: 10,808 (controlled).

381.1 SGP
T T G M I C E PLANNER. (Travel Trade Gazette Meetings, Incentives, Conferences and Exhibitions) Text in English. a. free to qualified personnel.
Published by: T T G Asia Media Pte Ltd, 6 Raffles Quay #16-02, Singapore, 048580, Singapore. TEL 65-6395-7575, FAX 65-6536-8639, contact@ttgasia.com, http://www.ttgasiamedia.com/. Circ: 18,000.

011 DEU ISSN 0342-7951
T W/CONVENTION INDUSTRY; the global magazine for meeting, incentive and event professionals. (Tagungs-Wirtschaft) Text in English, German. 1977. 7/yr. EUR 66.50 in Europe; EUR 67.50 elsewhere (effective 2009). adv. tr.lit. back issues avail. **Document type:** *Magazine, Trade.* **Description:** International trade magazine for meeting and incentive professionals.
Related titles: ◆ Supplement(s): T W TagungsRegionen.
Indexed: H&TI, H06, T02.
—BLDSC (9076.748500), IE, Ingenta.
Published by: M + A Verlag fuer Messen, Ausstellungen und Kongresse GmbH (Subsidiary of: Deutscher Fachverlag GmbH), Mainzer Landstr 251, Frankfurt Am Main, 60326, Germany. TEL 49-69-759502, FAX 49-69-75951280, mua@expodatabase.com, http://www.m-averlag.com. Ed. Dirk Mewis. Adv. contact Christine Fuchs. B&W page EUR 4,800, color page EUR 6,150; trim 210 x 275. Circ: 20,280 (paid and controlled).

011 DEU
T W TAGUNGSREGIONEN. Text in German. 1983. 4/yr. EUR 10 newsstand/cover (effective 2006). adv. **Document type:** *Directory, Trade.*
Former titles (until 1993): T W Veranstaltungsplaner; M und A Tagungsplaner; M und A Tagungsplaner Europa (0343-0545)
Related titles: ◆ Supplement to: T W. ISSN 0342-7951.
Published by: M + A Verlag fuer Messen, Ausstellungen und Kongresse GmbH (Subsidiary of: Deutscher Fachverlag GmbH), Mainzer Landstr 251, Frankfurt Am Main, 60326, Germany. TEL 49-69-759502, FAX 49-69-75951280, mua@expodatabase.com, http://www.m-averlag.com. Ed. Bernd Graf. adv.: B&W page EUR 3,660, color page EUR 4,350; trim 205 x 275. Circ: 13,820 (paid and controlled).

060 USA
TEXAS MEETINGS & EVENTS. Text in English. 19??. q. free to qualified personnel (effective 2011). adv. back issues avail. **Document type:** *Magazine, Trade.* **Description:** Aimed at meetings and events professionals working in Texas and includes essential information on a range of topics, from venues and supplier news, to tips, best practices and industry developments.
Related titles: Online - full text ed.: free (effective 2011).
Published by: Tiger Oak Publications, Inc., OneTiger Oak Plz, 900 S Third St, Minneapolis, MN 55415. TEL 612-548-3180, FAX 612-548-3181, customerservice@tigeroak.com, http://www.tigeroak.com. Ed. Robin Fowler TEL 817-598-0058. Pub. R Craig Bednar.

381.1 DEU ISSN 1437-4250
TRADE FAIRS INTERNATIONAL. Text in German. 1999. bi-m. EUR 30.70 domestic; EUR 37 foreign; EUR 7.70 newsstand/cover (effective 2006). adv. **Document type:** *Magazine, Trade.*
Published by: T F I Verlagsgesellschaft mbH, Oberfeld 32, Starnberg, 82319, Germany. TEL 49-8151-277907, FAX 49-8151-277909, Info@tfi-publications.com, http://www.tfi-publications.com. Ed. Peter Borstel. Adv. contact Axel Thunig. B&W page EUR 3,190, color page EUR 3,990. Circ: 12,582 (paid and controlled).

381.1 USA ISSN 1046-4395
T394
TRADE SHOWS WORLDWIDE; an international directory of events, facilities and suppliers. Text in English. 1985. a. USD 520 (effective 2009). back issues avail. **Document type:** *Directory, Trade.* **Description:** Contains detailed entries for over 10,000 scheduled exhibitions, trade shows, association conventions, and similar events.
Formerly (until 1990): Trade Shows and Professional Exhibits Directory (0886-1439)
Related titles: Diskette ed.; Magnetic Tape ed.; Online - full text ed.
Published by: Gale (Subsidiary of: Cengage Learning), 27500 Drake Rd, Farmington Hills, MI 48331. TEL 248-699-4253, 800-877-4253, FAX 877-363-4253, gale.galeord@thomson.com, http://gale.cengage.com. Eds. Charity Anne Dorgan, Martin Connors.

616.994 011 CHE
U I C C INTERNATIONAL CALENDAR OF MEETINGS ON CANCER. (Union Internationale Contre le Cancer) Text in English. biennial. free. **Document type:** *Proceedings, Trade.*
Formerly: U I C C Calendar of International Meetings on Cancer
Published by: International Union Against Cancer, 62 route de Frontenex, Geneva, 1207, Switzerland. TEL 41-22-8091811, FAX 41-22-8091810, info@uicc.ch, http://www.uicc.ch.

U N CHRONICLE. (United Nations) *see* POLITICAL SCIENCE—International Relations

060 910.2 CAN ISSN 1719-9794
VANCOUVER OFFICIAL MEETING PLANNER'S GUIDE. Text in English. 1990. a., latest 2006. **Document type:** *Handbook/Manual/Guide, Consumer.*
Formerly (until 2005): Vancouver Meeting Planner's Guide (0849-3812)
Published by: Weaver Official Publications, 409 Granville, Ste. 523, Vancouver, BC V6C IT2, Canada. TEL 604-697-9114, FAX 604-697-9113, http://www.weaver-group.com. Ed. Steven McKenzie.

011 GBR ISSN 2042-3098
VENUEFINDER.COM. BLUE & GREEN. Text in English. 19??. a. charts; illus. **Document type:** *Directory, Trade.* **Description:** Directed to special-interest and leisure-oriented meeting organizers, from large conferences to small training seminars. Provides a regionalized list of more than 4,500 United Kingdom venues indexed alphabetically with contact names.
Formed by the merger of (2007-2010): Conference Blue & Green. The Green Book (1756-1159); Which was formerly (until 2007): Conference Green Book (0260-2199); (2006-2010): Conference Blue & Green. The Blue Book (1756-1140); Which was formerly (until 2006): Conference Blue Book (0260-2431)
Related titles: CD-ROM ed.: 1996; Online - full text ed.: free (effective 2010).
Published by: U B M Information Ltd. (Subsidiary of: United Business Media Limited), Ludgate House, 245 Blackfriars Rd, London, SE1 9UY, United Kingdom. TEL 44-20-79215000, communications@ubm.com, http://www.ubm.com.

VILLE, CASTELLI E PALAZZI. *see* TRAVEL AND TOURISM

VIRGATS. *see* ETHNIC INTERESTS

VOYAGES ET STRATEGIE; le magazine de la stimulation et du tourisme d'affaires. *see* TRAVEL AND TOURISM

W M W SKRIPTUM; Kongressjournal. (Wiener Medizinische Wochenschrift) *see* MEDICAL SCIENCES

060 381.1 USA
WISCONSIN MEETINGS. Text in English. 2005. s-a. free to qualified personnel (effective 2009). adv. back issues avail. **Document type:** *Magazine, Trade.* **Description:** Aims to help the meeting planners to coordinate corporate events, meetings and trade shows in Wisconsin.
Published by: Nei-Turner Media Group, 93 W Geneva St, PO Box 1080, Williams Bay, WI 53191. TEL 262-245-1000, 800-386-3228, FAX 262-245-2000, info@ntmediagroup.com, http://www.ntmediagroup.com. Ed. Sarah Hoke TEL 800-386-3228 ext 109. Pub. Gary Nei. Adv. contact Louise Andreski TEL 866-873-9133. color page USD 3,060; trim 8.125 x 11.125. Circ: 1,000.

WOLFENBUETTELER BIBLIOTHEKS - INFORMATIONEN. *see* HISTORY

669 011 USA
WORLD MATERIALS CALENDAR (ONLINE). Text in English. 19??. bi-m. **Description:** Lists forthcoming meetings in metals and materials.
Media: Online - full text.
Published by: ProQuest LLC (Bethesda) (Subsidiary of: Cambridge Information Group), 789 E Eisenhower Pky, Ann Arbor, MI 48103. TEL 734-761-4700, FAX 734-997-4222, journals@csa.com.

381.1 CHN ISSN 1674-3598
ZHONGGUO HUIZHAN/CHINA CONFERENCE & EXHIBITION. Text in Chinese. 2000. s-m. CNY 360 (effective 2009). **Document type:** *Magazine, Trade.*
Formerly (until 2002): Zhanlan yu Zhuanye Shichang Xinxi/Exhibition & Marketplace (1009-2358)
Published by: (Zhongguo Xinxi Xiehui), Zhongguo Huizhan Zazhishe, 6, Shuguang Xi Li, Shijian Guoji 5F, Beijing, 100028, China. TEL 86-10-58678316, FAX 86-10-58678326, www.ciia.org.cn/.

1 X 1 IHR PARTNER. *see* AGRICULTURE

MEETINGS AND CONGRESSES—Abstracting, Bibliographies, Statistics

016 GBR ISSN 0959-4906
Z7403
BRITISH LIBRARY. DOCUMENT SUPPLY CENTRE. INDEX OF CONFERENCE PROCEEDINGS. Text in English. 1964. m. (plus a. cumulation). GBP 130 domestic; GBP 160 foreign (effective 2010). cum.index: 1964-1988. back issues avail. **Document type:** *Proceedings, Abstract/Index.* **Description:** Contains information about conferences held worldwide regardless of subject or language.
Former titles (until 1989): British Library. Document Supply Centre. Index of Conference Proceedings Received (0954-2256); (until 1986): British Library. Lending Division. Index of Conference Proceedings Received (0305-5183); (until 1975): British Library. Lending Division. Index of Conference Proceedings Received by the B L L (0300-9971); (until 1973): British Library. Lending Division. Index of Conference Proceedings Received by the N L L (0301-1046)
Related titles: Online - full text ed.
Indexed: AESIS, RASB.
—BLDSC (4377.416550), GNLM, INIST, Linda Hall. **CCC.**
Published by: British Library, Document Supply Centre, Boston Spa, Wetherby, W Yorks LS23 7BQ, United Kingdom. TEL 44-1937-546060, FAX 44-1937-546333, customer-services@bl.uk, http://www.bl.uk/reshelp/atyourdesk/docsupply/about/index.html.

600 500 011 USA ISSN 0162-704X
Z7403
CONFERENCE PAPERS INDEX. Text in English. 1973. bi-m. Index. back issues avail. **Document type:** *Abstract/Index.* **Description:** Lists authors and titles of papers presented at scientific conferences worldwide.
Formerly (until 1978): World Meetings Information Center. Current Programs (0091-0139); Incorporates: Conference Papers Annual Index (0194-0546); Which was formerly: Current Programs Annual Index
Related titles: Online - full text ed.: ISSN 1555-6468.
Indexed: RASB.
—BLDSC (3409.745300), GNLM, INIST, Linda Hall.
Published by: ProQuest LLC (Bethesda) (Subsidiary of: Cambridge Information Group), 789 E Eisenhower Pky, Ann Arbor, MI 48103. TEL 734-761-4700, FAX 734-997-4222, journals@csa.com.

DIRECTORY OF PUBLISHED PROCEEDINGS. SERIES S S H - SOCIAL SCIENCES - HUMANITIES. *see* HUMANITIES: COMPREHENSIVE WORKS—Abstracting, Bibliographies, Statistics

016 DEU ISSN 0933-1905
INTERNATIONALE JAHRESBIBLIOGRAPHIE DER KONGRESSBERICHTE/INTERNATIONAL ANNUAL BIBLIOGRAPHY OF CONGRESS PROCEEDINGS. Short title: I J B K. Text in Multiple languages. 1987. a. (in 3 vols.). EUR 952 (effective 2008). **Document type:** *Bibliography.*
Media: CD-ROM. **Related titles:** Online - full content ed.: ISSN 1865-0295. EUR 952 (effective 2008).
Published by: De Gruyter Saur (Subsidiary of: Walter de Gruyter GmbH & Co. KG), Mies-van-der-Rohe-Str 1, Munich, 80807, Germany. TEL 49-89-769020, FAX 49-89-76902150, wdg-info@degruyter.com.

MEN'S HEALTH

A X M (ONLINE); life is what you make it. *see* HOMOSEXUALITY

612.67 GBR ISSN 1368-5538
CODEN: AGMAF7
➤ **THE AGING MALE.** Text in English. 1998. q. GBP 285, EUR 410, USD 510 combined subscription to institutions (print & online eds.); GBP 560, EUR 815, USD 1,020 combined subscription to corporations (print & online eds.) (effective 2010). adv. bk.rev. illus. back issues avail.; reprint service avail. from PSC. **Document type:** *Journal, Academic/Scholarly.* **Description:** Features research papers as well as review papers and other appropriate educational material.
Related titles: Online - full text ed.: ISSN 1473-0790 (from IngentaConnect).
Indexed: A01, A03, A08, A22, ASG, AgeL, C06, C07, CA, CurCont, E01, EMBASE, ExcerpMed, H13, MEDLINE, P02, P10, P20, P22, P30, P48, P53, P54, PQC, R09, R10, Reac, SCI, SCOPUS, SD, T02, W07.
—IE, Infotrieve, Ingenta. **CCC.**
Published by: (International Society for the Study of the Aging Male), Informa Healthcare (Subsidiary of: T & F Informa plc), Telephone House, 69-77 Paul St, London, EC2A 4LQ, United Kingdom. TEL 44-20-70175000, FAX 44-20-70176792, healthcare.enquiries@informa.com. Ed. Bruno Lunenfeld TEL 44-20-70176379. Adv. contact Per Sonnerfeldt. **Subscr. in N. America to:** Taylor & Francis Inc., Customer Services Dept, 325 Chestnut St, 8th Fl, Philadelphia, PA 19106. TEL 215-625-8900, 800-354-1420, FAX 215-625-8914, customerservice@taylorandfrancis.com; **Subscr. outside N. America to:** Taylor & Francis Ltd., Journals Customer Service, Sheepen Pl, Colchester, Essex CO3 3LP, United Kingdom. TEL 44-20-70175544, FAX 44-20-70175198, tf.enquiries@tfinforma.com.

613.081 USA ISSN 1557-9883
RA777.8
➤ **AMERICAN JOURNAL OF MEN'S HEALTH.** Abbreviated title: A J M H. Text in English. 2007 (Mar.). bi-m. USD 575, GBP 338 to institutions; USD 587, GBP 345 combined subscription to institutions (print & online eds.) (effective 2012). adv. back issues avail.; reprint service avail. from PSC. **Document type:** *Journal, Academic/Scholarly.* **Description:** Contains information regarding men's health and illness. Covers all health, behavioral and social disciplines, including but not limited to medicine, nursing, allied health, public health, health psychology/behavioral medicine, and medical sociology and anthropology.
Related titles: Online - full text ed.: ISSN 1557-9891. 2007. USD 528, GBP 311 to institutions (effective 2012).
Indexed: A20, A22, A36, CABA, CurCont, D01, E01, EMBASE, ESPM, ExcerpMed, GH, LT, MEDLINE, N02, N03, P30, R12, RRTA, RiskAb, SCOPUS, SSCI, T05, W07, W11.
—BLDSC (0828.200000), IE. **CCC.**
Published by: (Men's Health Network), Sage Publications, Inc., 2455 Teller Rd, Thousand Oaks, CA 91320. TEL 800-818-7243, FAX 800-583-2665, info@sagepub.com, http://www.sagepub.com. Ed. Demetrius J Porche.

613.081 613.7 AUS ISSN 1836-0114
AUSTRALIAN MEN'S FITNESS. Abbreviated title: A M F. Text in English. 2008. m. AUD 80 domestic; AUD 100 in New Zealand; AUD 120 elsewhere; AUD 7.95 newsstand/cover (effective 2011). adv. back issues avail. **Document type:** *Magazine, Consumer.* **Description:** Designed for the men who want solid information about getting fit, losing weight, building muscle, eating well, fashion and relationships.
Published by: Odysseus Publishing, PO Box 81, St Leonards, NSW 1590, Australia. TEL 61-2-94391955, FAX 61-2-94391977, info@your-web-domain.com, http://www.odysseus.com.au. Ed. Todd Cole. Adv. contact Rob Brown. Circ: 26,765.

M

613.081 AUT ISSN 1727-0669
RC875
BLICKPUNKT DER MANN; wissenschaftliches Journal fuer Maennergesundheit. Text in German. 2003. q. EUR 36; EUR 10 newsstand/cover (effective 2005). **Document type:** *Journal, Academic/Scholarly.*
Related titles: Online - full text ed.: ISSN 1727-4613. free (effective 2011).
—BLDSC (2111.300020). **CCC.**
Published by: Krause & Pachernegg GmbH, Mozartgasse 10, Gablitz, 3003, Austria. TEL 43-2231-612580, FAX 43-2231-6125810, k_u_p@eunet.at, http://www.kup.at/verlag.htm. Eds. Friedrich Jockenhoevel, Theodor Klotz.

CANADIAN CREATIVE ARTS IN HEALTH, TRAINING AND EDUCATION. *see* MEDICAL SCIENCES

CARERS IN VICTORIA. *see* SOCIAL SERVICES AND WELFARE

613.081 USA
CHROME DOME BULLETIN. Text in English. 1972. s-a. looseleaf. USD 10. bk.rev. **Document type:** *Newsletter.*
Published by: Bald-Headed Men of America, 102 Bald Dr, Morehead City, NC 28557. TEL 252-726-1855, FAX 252-726-6061. Ed. John T Capps. Circ: 15,000.

CONTEMPORARY SEXUALITY; the international resource for educators, researchers and therapists. *see* PSYCHOLOGY

613.081 USA ISSN 1086-1122
EXERCISE & HEALTH; the complete fitness guide for men. Text in English. 1996. q. USD 23.97 (effective 2008). adv. illus. **Document type:** *Magazine, Consumer.*
Published by: Harris Publications, Inc., 1115 Broadway, New York, NY 10010. TEL 212-807-7100, FAX 212-807-1479, comments@harris-pub.com, http://www.harris-pub.com. adv.: B&W page USD 3,146, color page USD 4,235; trim 8 x 10.8.

EXERCISE FOR MEN ONLY. *see* PHYSICAL FITNESS AND HYGIENE

613.081 USA ISSN 1089-1102
RA777.8
HARVARD MEN'S HEALTH WATCH. Variant title: Men's Health Watch. Text in English. 1996. m. USD 28 combined subscription (print & online eds.) (effective 2009). 8 p./no. 3 cols./p.; back issues avail. **Document type:** *Newsletter, Consumer.* **Description:** Focuses on health from men's perspective including new prevention strategies, new diagnostic techniques, new medications and treatments.
Related titles: Online - full text ed.: ISSN 1943-5126. USD 24 (effective 2009).
Indexed: A01, A03, A08, A26, C06, C07, C08, C11, CINAHL, E08, EMBASE, ExcerpMed, G05, G06, G07, G08, G10, H03, H11, H12, I05, I07, M01, M02, M06, MEDLINE, P30, PEI, R10, Reac, S09, S23, SCOPUS, T02.
—BLDSC (4268.275000). **CCC.**
Published by: Harvard Health Publications Group (Subsidiary of: Harvard Medical School), 10 Shattuck St, Ste 612, Boston, MA 02115. TEL 877-649-9457, hhp@hms.harvard.edu, http://www.health.harvard.edu. Eds. Dr. Harvey B Simon, Anthony L Komaroff.

HEALTH AND STRESS; the newsletter of the American Institute of Stress. *see* MEDICAL SCIENCES

HOOFDZAKEN; nieuwsblad over migraine, hoofd- en aangezichtspijnen. *see* MEDICAL SCIENCES—Psychiatry And Neurology

I P S F NEWS BULLETIN. *see* PHARMACY AND PHARMACOLOGY

610 USA ISSN 1532-6306
RA777.8
➤ **INTERNATIONAL JOURNAL OF MEN'S HEALTH.** Text in English. 2002 (Jan). 3/yr. USD 220 domestic to institutions; USD 240 foreign to institutions; USD 250 combined subscription to institutions (print & online eds.) (effective 2010). adv. bk.rev. Index. back issues avail.; reprints avail. **Document type:** *Journal, Academic/Scholarly.* **Description:** Covers all aspects of men's health.
Related titles: Online - full text ed.: ISSN 1933-0278. USD 210 (effective 2010).
Indexed: A01, A03, A08, A26, A36, ASG, ASSIA, C06, C07, C08, CA, CABA, CINAHL, E-psyche, E08, EMBASE, ExcerpMed, Faml, G08, G10, GH, GW, H11, H12, I05, I07, LT, N02, N03, P03, P19, P24, P30, P48, PQC, PsycInfo, PsycholAb, R10, R12, RRTA, Reac, S09, S23, SCOPUS, T02, T05.
—BLDSC (4542.351500), IE, Ingenta. **CCC.**
Published by: Men's Studies Press, PO Box 32, Harriman, TN 37748. TEL 423-369-2375, FAX 423-369-1126, publisher@mensstudies.com. Ed. Miles Groth. Pub. Dr. James A Doyle. adv.: B&W page USD 150; 4.75 x 7.875.

613.081 NLD ISSN 1875-6867
RA777.8
➤ **JOURNAL OF MEN'S HEALTH.** Variant title: J M H G. Text in English. 2004. 4/yr. EUR 643 in Europe to institutions; JPY 85,500 in Japan to institutions; USD 722 elsewhere to institutions (effective 2012). adv. **Document type:** *Journal, Academic/Scholarly.* **Description:** Covers all aspects of men's health and gender medicine.
Formerly (until 2008): The Journal of Men's Health & Gender (Print) (1571-8913)
Related titles: Online - full text ed.: ISSN 1875-6859 (from ScienceDirect).
Indexed: A26, AddicA, CA, CurCont, E08, EMBASE, ExcerpMed, G10, H11, H12, P03, P30, PsycInfo, PsycholAb, R10, Reac, S09, SCI, SCOPUS, SSCI, T02, W07.
—BLDSC (5017.644200), IE, Ingenta, INIST. **CCC.**
Published by: Elsevier BV (Subsidiary of: Elsevier Science & Technology), Radarweg 29, PO Box 211, Amsterdam, 1000 AE, Netherlands. TEL 31-20-4853911, FAX 31-20-4852457, JournalsCustomerServiceEMEA@elsevier.com, http://www.elsevier.nl. Ed. S Meryn. adv.: B&W page EUR 1,161, color page EUR 4,219; trim 210 x 280.

➤ **A K W A MAGAZINE.** *see* PHYSICAL FITNESS AND HYGIENE

➤ **MAENNER.** *see* HOMOSEXUALITY

613.081 DEU
MANNSBILDER; Das Magazin fuer Maenner im Leben. Text in German. 4/yr. adv. **Document type:** *Magazine, Consumer.*
Published by: (Deutsche Gesellschaft fuer Mann und Gesundheit e.V.), Fromm & Fromm GmbH, Achtern Felln 26, Hasloh, 25474, Germany. TEL 49-4106-63070, FAX 49-4106-630715, info@2xfromm.de, http://www.pmi-medien.de. Circ: 50,000 (controlled).

379.8 RUS ISSN 1682-2412
MEN'S FITNESS. Text in Russian. 2001. bi-m. **Document type:** *Magazine, Consumer.*
Published by: S K Press, Marksistkaya 34, str 10, Moscow, 109147, Russian Federation. deliver@skpress.ru, http://www.skpress.ru.

613.7 USA ISSN 1541-2776
GV481
➤ **MEN'S FITNESS.** Abbreviated title: M F. Variant title: Joe Weider's Men's Fitness. Text in English. 1985. 10/yr. USD 15 domestic; USD 25 in Canada; USD 28 elsewhere; USD 9.95 newsstand/cover (effective 2009). adv. bk.rev. illus. reprints avail. **Document type:** *Magazine, Consumer.* **Description:** Designed for the young and success-seeking male demographic.
Former titles (until 2001): Joe Weider's Men's Fitness (0893-4460); (until 1987): Joe Weider's Sports Fitness (0885-0763); (until 1985): Sports Fitness (0887-9052); Joe Weider's Men's Fitness was Incorporated (1995-1998): Joe Weider's Prime Health & Fitness (1083-0952); Which was formerly: Joe Weider's Prime Fitness & Health
Related titles: Online - full text ed.
Indexed: A22, A26, C11, G05, G06, G07, G08, H03, H11, H12, I05, I07, M02, M06, MASUSE, MagInd, PEI, SD, SPI, T02.
—Ingenta.
Published by: A M I - Weider Publications (Subsidiary of: American Media, Inc.), 21100 Erwin St, Woodland Hills, CA 91367. TEL 818-595-0589, 800-998-0731, FAX 818-884-6910, http://www.americanmediainc.com. Ed. Roy S. Johnson. Pub. Jay Goldberg. R&P Anne Byron. adv.: B&W page USD 63,440, color page USD 78,995; trim 7.75 x 10.5. Circ: 700,000 (paid). **Subscr. to:** PO Box 37211, Boone, IA 50037. **Dist. in the UK by:** Comag, Tavistock Rd, W Drayton, Middlesex UB7 7QE, United Kingdom.

613.081 USA ISSN 1531-457X
MEN'S FITNESS EN ESPANOL. Variant title: Joe Weider's Men's Fitness en Espanol. Text in Spanish. 2000. m. USD 26; USD 2.95 newsstand/cover (effective 2001). adv. **Document type:** *Magazine, Consumer.* **Description:** Presents articles and features on the latest in exercise, health sports training and adventures travel.
Published by: Conde Nast Americas, 1101 Brickell Ave 15th Fl, Miami, FL 33131. TEL 305-371-9393, 800-792-5999, FAX 305-371-9392, newsesp@gate.net. Ed. Jose Forteza. Pub. Joe Weider. adv.: color page USD 17,100. Circ: 280,000 (paid).

610 PHL
MEN'S HEALTH; change your life. Text in English. m. PHP 1,230; PHP 120 newsstand/cover (effective 2005). adv. **Document type:** *Magazine, Consumer.* **Description:** Aims to help men take control and take care of their bodies as well as their mental and emotional lives.
Published by: Summit Media, Level 1, Robinsons Galleria, Ortigas Ave, Quezon City, 1100, Philippines. TEL 63-2-6317738, FAX 63-2-6372206, luz.bolos@summitmedia.com.ph, http://www.summitmedia.com.ph. Ed. Jeryc Garcia. Adv. contact Alvin Jimenez.

610 PRT
MEN'S HEALTH. Text in Portuguese. 2001. m. EUR 2.90 newsstand/cover (effective 2005). adv. **Document type:** *Magazine, Consumer.*
Published by: Motorpress Lisboa, SA (Subsidiary of: Gruner + Jahr AG & Co), Rua Policarpio Anjos No. 4, Cruz Quebrada, Dafundo 1495-742, Portugal. TEL 351-21-4154500, FAX 351-21-4154501, buzine@motorpress.pt, http://www.mpl.pt. Ed. Montse Sala. Pub. Isabel Magalhaes. Circ: 30,331.

610 ESP
MEN'S HEALTH. Text in Spanish. 2001. m. adv. **Document type:** *Magazine, Consumer.*
Published by: Motorpress Iberica (Subsidiary of: Gruner + Jahr AG & Co), Ancora 40, Madrid, 28045, Spain. TEL 34-91-3470100, FAX 34-91-3470152, http://www.motorpress-iberica.es. Ed. Alberto Saborido. Circ: 117,000 (paid and controlled).

610 ARG
MEN'S HEALTH. Text in Spanish. m. adv. **Document type:** *Magazine, Consumer.*
Published by: Editorial Televisa Argentina, Av Paseo Colon 275, Piso 10, Buenos Aires, Buenos Aires 1063, Argentina. TEL 54-11-4343-2225, FAX 54-11-4345-0955, http://www.televisa.com.ar.

610 FRA ISSN 1294-971X
MEN'S HEALTH. Text in French. 1999. bi-m. adv. **Document type:** *Magazine, Consumer.*
Related titles: Supplement(s): Coach. ISSN 2107-5255. 2010.
Published by: 1633 SA, 73 Rue Claude Bernard, Paris, 75005, France. TEL 33-1-44397820, FAX 33-1-44397828, lwildblood@1633sa.fr, http://www.1633sa.fr. Ed. Patrick Guerinet. Circ: 83,000 (paid and controlled).

610 DEU ISSN 1432-3818
MEN'S HEALTH; das Magazin fuer Maenner. Text in German. 1996. m. EUR 41; EUR 3.80 newsstand/cover (effective 2007). adv. back issues avail. **Document type:** *Magazine, Consumer.*
Related titles: E-mail ed.; Fax ed.; Online - full text ed.; ◆ Regional ed(s).: Men's Health. ISSN 1054-4836; ◆ Men's Health. ISSN 1356-7438; ◆ Men's Health. ISSN 1027-6874; ◆ Supplement(s): Men's Health Best Fashion.
Published by: Rodale Motor Presse GmbH und Co. KG (Subsidiary of: Motor Presse Stuttgart GmbH & Co. KG), Leuschnerstr 1, Stuttgart, 70174, Germany. TEL 49-711-18201, FAX 49-711-1821779, aglaessing@motorpresse.de, http://www.motorpresse.de. Ed. Frank Hofmann. Pub. Dr. Thomas Garms. R&P Christine Juergensen TEL 49-853-30331. Adv. contact Corinna Stahlke. page EUR 19,500. Circ: 236,203 (paid). **Subscr. to:** P M S GmbH & Co. KG, Postfach 20080, Hamburg, Germany. TEL 49-203-76908-0, FAX 49-203-7690830.

610 USA ISSN 1054-4836
RA777.8 CODEN: MEHEE9
MEN'S HEALTH; tons of useful stuff. Text in English. 1986. 10/yr. USD 24.94 domestic; CAD 39.50 in Canada; USD 49.07 elsewhere; USD 2.22 per issue (effective 2008). adv. illus. back issues avail.; reprints avail. **Document type:** *Magazine, Consumer.* **Description:** Tells men how to look good and how to live better and longer.
Formerly (until 1987): Prevention Magazine's Guide to Men's Health (0886-2346)
Related titles: Online - full text ed.; ◆ Regional ed(s).: Men's Health. ISSN 1356-7438; ◆ Men's Health. ISSN 1027-6874; ◆ Men's Health. ISSN 1432-3818.
Indexed: A01, A02, A03, A08, A11, A22, A26, B04, BRD, C05, C06, C07, C08, C11, C12, CHNI, CINAHL, CPerI, G05, G06, G07, G08, GW, H03, H04, H11, H12, H13, HlthInd, I05, I07, M01, M02, M06, MASUSE, MagInd, P02, P10, P13, P19, P20, P24, P34, P48, P53, P54, PQC, R03, RGAb, RGPR, S04, T02, U01, W03, W05.
—Ingenta.
Published by: Rodale, Inc., 733 Third Ave, 15th Fl, New York, NY 10022. TEL 212-697-2040, FAX 212-682-2237, customer_service@rodale.com, http://www.rodaleinc.com. Ed. David Zinczenko. Pub. Jack Essig TEL 212-573-0244. Adv. contact Elaina Nan Fulgham TEL 212-573-0369. page USD 169.115. Circ: 1,804,949 (paid).

610 GBR ISSN 1356-7438
MEN'S HEALTH; tons of useful stuff. Text in English. 1995. 11/yr. GBP 26 domestic; GBP 70 in Europe; GBP 100 elsewhere; GBP 3.95 newsstand/cover (effective 2009). adv. back issues avail. **Document type:** *Magazine, Consumer.*
Related titles: ◆ Regional ed(s).: Men's Health. ISSN 1054-4836; ◆ Men's Health. ISSN 1027-6874; ◆ Men's Health. ISSN 1432-3818.
—CCC.
Published by: Natmag - Rodale Ltd., 72 Broadwick St, London, W1F 9EP, United Kingdom. TEL 44-20-74395000, FAX 44-20-74396886, natmags@subscription.co.uk, http://www.natmags.co.uk. Ed. Morgan Rees. Pub. Alun Williams. Adv. contact Michael Hand. Circ: 250,094.

613.081 305.31 RUS ISSN 1562-5117
MEN'S HEALTH. Text in Russian. 1998. m. USD 34.20 domestic; USD 119 foreign (effective 2005). adv. **Document type:** *Magazine, Consumer.*
—East View.
Published by: Independent Media (Moscow), 3 Polkovaya Ul, Bldg 1, Moscow, 127018, Russian Federation. TEL 7-095-2323200, FAX 7-095-2321761, podpiska@imedia.ru, http://www.independent-media.ru. Ed. Ilya Bezugly. Pub. Karen Dukess. Adv. contact Arkadi Tsimbler. Circ: 140,000.

613.081 GRC ISSN 1109-8775
MEN'S HEALTH. Text in Greek. 2003 (Nov.). m. adv. **Document type:** *Magazine, Consumer.* **Description:** Provides men with the latest information on health, fitness and nutrition, careers, relationships, fashion and travel.
Published by: Liberis Publications S.A./Ekdoseon Lymperi A.E., Ioannou Metaxa 80, Karelas, Koropi 19400, Greece. TEL 30-210-6688000, FAX 30-210-6688300, info@liberis.gr, http://www.liberis.gr. Ed. Vasilas Vardakas. Adv. contact Katerina Alevizou. Circ: 31,692 (paid).

613.081 SVN ISSN 1580-559X
MEN'S HEALTH. Text in Slovenian. 2001. m. EUR 39.90 (effective 2008). adv. **Document type:** *Magazine, Consumer.*
Published by: Adria Media Ljubljana, Zaloznistvo in Trzenje, d.o.o., Vosnjakova ulica 3, Ljubljana, 1000, Slovenia. TEL 386-1-3000700, FAX 386-1-3000713, info@adriamedia.si, http://www.adriamedia.si. Ed. Matevz Korosec. adv.: page EUR 2,000; trim 210 x 280. Circ: 20,360 (paid and controlled).

613.081 ITA ISSN 1590-3575
MEN'S HEALTH. Text in Italian. 2000. m. EUR 19.90 (effective 2008). **Document type:** *Magazine, Consumer.*
Published by: Arnoldo Mondadori Editore SpA, Via Mondadori 1, Segrate, 20090, Italy. TEL 39-02-66814363, FAX 39-030-3198412, http://www.mondadori.com.

613.081 AUS ISSN 1329-3079
MEN'S HEALTH. Text in English. 1997. m. AUD 79.95 domestic; AUD 89.95 in New Zealand; AUD 139.95 elsewhere (effective 2008). adv. **Document type:** *Magazine, Consumer.* **Description:** Provides advice on fitness, nutrition, sex and relationships, workplace stress, style and grooming, and health tips for men.
Published by: Pacific Magazines Pty Ltd., 35-51 Mitchell St, McMahons Point, NSW 2060, Australia. TEL 61-2-94643300, FAX 61-2-94643375, http://www.pacificmagazines.com.au. Ed. Bruce Ritchie. Adv. contact Paul Bates TEL 61-294643204. page AUD 9,245; bleed 216 x 285. Circ: 70,000. **Subscr. to:** Subscribe Today, GPO Box 4983, Sydney, NSW 2001, Australia. TEL 61-2-82965425, FAX 61-2-92793161, http://www.subscribetoday.com.au.

613.081 HUN ISSN 1785-1238
MEN'S HEALTH. Text in Hungarian. 2003. m. HUF 8,340; HUF 695 newsstand/cover (effective 2006). adv. **Document type:** *Magazine, Consumer.*
Related titles: Optical Disk - DVD ed.: ISSN 1785-3575. 2004.
Published by: Motor-Presse Budapest Lapkiado kft, Hajogyari-sziget 307, Budapest, 1033, Hungary. TEL 36-1-4369244, FAX 36-1-4369248, mpb@motorpresse.hu, http://www.motorpresse.hu. Ed. Gergely Buglya. Pub. Dietmar Metzger. Adv. contact Nora Gyorfi.

613.081 ZAF ISSN 1027-6874
MEN'S HEALTH. Text in English. 1997. m. ZAR 259 (effective 2006). adv. **Document type:** *Magazine, Consumer.*
Related titles: Print ed.: ISSN 1563-5783; ◆ Regional ed(s).: Men's Health. ISSN 1432-3818; ◆ Men's Health. ISSN 1356-7438; ◆ Men's Health. ISSN 1054-4836.
Published by: Touchline Media, PO Box 16368, Vlaeberg, Cape Town 8018, South Africa. TEL 27-21-217810, FAX 27-21-215118, http://www.touchline.co.za. Ed. Andy Ellis. Pub. Andrew Sneddon. adv.: B&W page ZAR 34,300, color page ZAR 42,600; trim 210 x 276. Circ: 90,360.

613.081 NLD ISSN 1388-4190
MEN'S HEALTH. Text in Dutch. 1998. 10/yr. EUR 49.95; EUR 5.35 newsstand/cover (effective 2010). adv. **Document type:** *Magazine, Consumer.*
Published by: Weekbladpers Tijdschriften, Raamgracht 4, Amsterdam, 1011 KK, Netherlands. TEL 31-20-5518711, FAX 31-20-5518638, http://www.weekbladpers.nl. Ed. Ronald Janus. Pub. Femke Leemeijer. Adv. contact Raymond van Kasterop. color page EUR 5,015; trim 215 x 280. Circ: 43,722.

613.081 SRB ISSN 1451-6616
MEN'S HEALTH. Text in Serbian. 2003. m. CSD 2,189 (effective 2008). adv. **Document type:** *Magazine, Consumer.*

Published by: Adria Media Serbia d.o.o., Omladinskih Brigada 88a, Belgrade, 11070. TEL 381-11-2079900, FAX 381-11-2079988, b.rademann@adriamedia.co.yu, http://www.adriamedia.co.yu. Ed. Ivan Radojcic. Adv. contact Miloslav Parezanovic. page EUR 1,750; trim 210 x 280.

613.081 BRA ISSN 1809-4732
MEN'S HEALTH. Text in Portuguese. 2006. m. BRL 10 newsstand/cover (effective 2010). adv. **Document type:** *Magazine, Consumer.*
Published by: Editora Abril, S.A., Avenida das Nacoes Unidas 7221, Pinheiros, Sao Paulo, SP 05425-902, Brazil. TEL 55-11-50872112, FAX 55-11-50872100, abrilsac@abril.com.br, http://www.abril.com.br. adv.: page BRL 63,600; trim 208 x 274. Circ: 122,028 (paid).

613.081 HRV ISSN 1334-7640
MEN'S HEALTH. Text in Croatian. 2004. m. HRK 290 (effective 2011). adv. **Document type:** *Magazine, Consumer.*
Published by: Adria Media Zagreb d.o.o., Radnicka Cesta 39, Zagreb, 10000, Croatia. TEL 385-1-4444800, FAX 385-1-4444801, info@adriamedia.hr.

613.081 GBR ISSN 1756-6843
▼ **MEN'S HEALTH (TRAVEL EDITION).** Text in English. 2011. s-a. **Document type:** *Magazine, Consumer.*
Published by: Natmag - Rodale Ltd., 72 Broadwick St, London, W1F 9EP, United Kingdom. TEL 44-20-74395000, FAX 44-20-74396886.

362 USA ISSN 1527-084X
MEN'S HEALTH ADVISOR; advise and information from a world leader in healthcare. Text in English. 19??. m. USD 39 domestic; USD 49 in Canada; USD 59 elsewhere (effective 2010). back issues avail. **Document type:** *Magazine, Consumer.* **Description:** Discusses important and vital issues facing men concerned about their health.
Related titles: Online - full text ed.
Indexed: A26, E08, G06, G07, G08, H11, H12, I05, S09.
Published by: Belvoir Media Group, LLC, 800 Connecticut Ave, Norwalk, CT 06854. TEL 203-857-3100, 800-424-7887, FAX 203-857-3103, customer_service@belvoir.com, http://www.belvoir.com. **Subscr. to:** Palm Coast Data, LLC, PO Box 420235, Palm Coast, FL 32142. TEL 800-829-2542, http://www.palmcoastdata.com.

645 613.081 ZAF ISSN 1818-2089
MEN'S HEALTH LIVING. Text in English. 2006. bi-m. ZAR 187 (effective 2007). adv. **Document type:** *Magazine, Consumer.*
Published by: Touchline Media, PO Box 16368, Vlaeberg, Cape Town 8018, South Africa. TEL 27-21-4083800, FAX 27-21-4083811, http://www.touchline.co.za. Ed. Piers Buckle TEL 27-21-4083854. Pub. Andrew Sneddon. adv.: color page ZAR 19,200; trim 230 x 260. Circ: 91,849.

613.081 USA ISSN 1559-5536
MEN'S HEALTH MUSCLE. Text in English. 2004. 10/yr. USD 59.97 (effective 2009). back issues avail. **Document type:** *Magazine, Consumer.*
Published by: Rodale, Inc., 33 E Minor St, Emmaus, PA 18098. TEL 610-967-5171, FAX 610-967-8963, customer_service@rodale.com, http://www.rodaleinc.com.

613.081 USA ISSN 1937-5433
MEN'S HEALTH PERSONAL TRAINER. Text in English. 2007 (Sep.). q. USD 45.56 (effective 2009). **Document type:** *Magazine, Consumer.*
Media: Online - full content.
Published by: Rodale, Inc., 33 E Minor St, Emmaus, PA 18098. TEL 610-967-5171, 800-914-9363, FAX 610-967-8963, info@rodale.com, http://www.rodaleinc.com.

613.081 SGP
MEN'S HEALTH SINGAPORE. Text in English. 2003. m. SGD 57.60 (effective 2008). **Document type:** *Magazine, Consumer.*
Published by: S P H Magazines Pte Ltd. (Subsidiary of: Singapore Press Holdings Ltd.), 82 Genting Ln Level 7, Media Centre, Singapore, 349567, Singapore. TEL 65-6319-6319, FAX 65-6319-6345, sphmag@sph.com.sg, http://www.sphmagazines.com.sg/. Circ: 30,000.

613 305.31 USA ISSN 1058-3041
MEN'S WORKOUT. Text in English. 1990. 7/yr. USD 28.97 (effective 2008). adv. **Document type:** *Magazine, Consumer.*
Published by: Harris Publications, Inc., 1115 Broadway, New York, NY 10010. TEL 212-807-7100, FAX 212-807-1479, comments@harris-pub.com, http://www.harris-pub.com. Ed. Michael Catarevas. Pub. Stanley R Harris. adv.: B&W page USD 3,146, color page USD 4,235; trim 8 x 10.8.

MENSTUFF; the national men's resource. *see* MEN'S STUDIES

613.081 USA
MUSCLE ELEGANCE. Text in English. 2000. q. USD 7.95 newsstand/cover domestic; CAD 9.95 newsstand/cover in Canada (effective 2002). adv. **Document type:** *Magazine, Consumer.*
Published by: Muscle Elegance Magazine, Inc., PMB No.409, 13300-56 Cleveland Ave, Ft. Myers, FL 33907. Ed. Denise Masino.

NIHON SEI KINO GAKKAI ZASSHI/JAPANESE JOURNAL OF IMPOTENCE RESEARCH. *see* MEDICAL SCIENCES—Urology And Nephrology

613.081 CAN ISSN 1702-4412
OPTIMALE (ENGLISH EDITION); the magazine for men's sexual health. Text in English. 2002. q. **Document type:** *Magazine, Consumer.*
Related titles: French ed.: Optimale (French Edition). ISSN 1702-4404.
Published by: (Canadian Male Sexual Health Council), Parkhurst Publishing, 400 McGill St, 3rd Fl, Montreal, PQ H2Y 2G1, Canada. TEL 514-397-8833, FAX 514-397-0228, contact@parkpub.com, http://www.parkpub.com.

OTTAWA CITY WOMAN. *see* WOMEN'S HEALTH

OUTLOOK (SEATTLE); reproductive health. *see* PUBLIC HEALTH AND SAFETY

REVISTA ARGENTINA DE ANDROLOGIA. *see* MEDICAL SCIENCES—Urology And Nephrology

613.081 613.04244 ARG ISSN 0326-9825
S A S H. REVISTA ARGENTINA DE SEXUALIDAD HUMANA. (Sociedad Argentina de Sexualidad Humana) Text in Spanish. 1987. q. **Document type:** *Journal, Academic/Scholarly.*
Published by: Sociedad Argentina de Sexualidad Humana, Santos Dumont 3454, 3o, Buenos Aires, 1427, Argentina. info@sasharg.ar, http://www.sasharg.com.ar.

613 CHN
SHISHANG JIANKANG - NANSHI/MEN'S HEALTH. Text in Chinese. 2000. m. CNY 240 (effective 2008). adv. **Document type:** *Magazine, Consumer.*
Published by: Trends Communication Co. Ltd., 22/F Trends Bldg., 9, Guanghua Rd., Beijing, 100020, China. http://www.trends.com.cn/.

613.081 155 USA ISSN 0277-3422
SPRINGER SERIES: FOCUS ON MEN. Text in English. 1980. irreg., latest 2006. price varies. **Document type:** *Monographic series, Academic/Scholarly.* **Description:** Focuses on men's issues from a psychological perspective.
Indexed: E-psyche.
Published by: Springer Publishing Company, 11 W 42nd St, 15th Fl, New York, NY 10036. TEL 212-431-4370, FAX 212-941-7842, contactus@springerpub.com, http://www.springerpub.com. R&P Dorothy Kouwenberg.

TODAY'S HEALTH AND WELLNESS. *see* PHYSICAL FITNESS AND HYGIENE

613.081 DEU ISSN 1612-5177
VITA. Text in German. 2003. 6/yr. adv. **Document type:** *Magazine, Trade.*
Published by: Fromm & Fromm GmbH, Achtern Felln 26, Hasloh, 25474, Germany. TEL 49-4106-63070, FAX 49-4106-630715, info@2xfromm.de, http://www.pmi-medien.de. Adv. contact Romy Demeter. color page EUR 3,450. Circ: 3,250 (controlled).

616.6 CHN ISSN 1008-0848
ZHONGGUO NANKEXUE ZAZHI/CHINESE JOURNAL OF ANDROLOGY. Text in Chinese. 1986. m. USD 56.40 (effective 2009). **Document type:** *Journal, Academic/Scholarly.*
Formerly (until 1997): Nanxingxue Zazhi (1004-3942)
Related titles: Online - full text ed.
Indexed: EMBASE, ExcerpMed, R10, Reac, SCOPUS.
—BLDSC (9512.784355), East View.
Published by: Shanghai Jiaotong Daxue Yixueyuan, Fushu Renji Yiyuan, 145 Shandong Zhong Lu, Shanghai, 200001, China.

613.081 CHN ISSN 1009-3591
ZHONGHUA NANKEXUE/NATIONAL JOURNAL OF ANDROLOGY. Text in Chinese. 1995. m. USD 62.40 (effective 2009). **Document type:** *Journal, Academic/Scholarly.*
Former titles (until 1999): Nanke Xuebao/Acta Andrologica Sinica (1008-3839); Shiyong Nanke Zazhi
Related titles: Online - full text ed.
Indexed: EMBASE, ExcerpMed, G10, MEDLINE, P30, R10, Reac, SCOPUS.
—BLDSC (6026.150300), East View, IE, Ingenta.
Published by: Nanjing Junqu Zongyiyuan, 305, Zhongshan Donglu, Najing, 210002, China. TEL 86-25-80860178, FAX 86-25-84803061. **Dist. by:** China International Book Trading Corp, 35 Chegongzhuang Xilu, Haidian District, PO Box 399, Beijing 100044, China. TEL 86-10-68412045, FAX 86-10-68412023, cibtc@mail.cibtc.com.cn, http://www.cibtc.com.cn.

MEN'S HEALTH—Abstracting, Bibliographies, Statistics

PROQUEST FAMILY HEALTH. *see* MEDICAL SCIENCES—Abstracting, Bibliographies, Statistics

MEN'S INTERESTS

A K; das Schweizer Magazin fuer den schwulen Mann. *see* HOMOSEXUALITY

A V N ONLINE MAGAZINE; adult internet news & webmaster resource. (Adult Video News) *see* COMPUTERS—Internet

051 USA ISSN 1533-5976
ADAM BLACK VIDEO ILLUSTRATED. Text in English. 1994. bi-m. **Document type:** *Magazine, Consumer.*
Published by: Knight Publishing Corporation, 8060 Melrose Ave, Los Angeles, CA 90046. TEL 323-653-8060, FAX 323-655-9452, psi@loop.com. Adv. contact Timothy Connelly.

051 USA
ADAM EROTOMIC. Text in English. q. USD 8.99 per issue (effective 2000). adv. **Document type:** *Magazine, Consumer.*
Published by: Knight Publishing Corporation, 8060 Melrose Ave, Los Angeles, CA 90046. TEL 323-653-8060, FAX 323-655-9452, psi@loop.com. Ed. Jared Rutter. Adv. contact Timothy Connelly.

ADAM GAY VIDEO EROTICA. *see* HOMOSEXUALITY

363.4 USA
ADAM GIRLS INTERNATIONAL TEENZ. Text in English. bi-m. USD 6.99 (effective 2000). **Document type:** *Magazine, Consumer.* **Description:** Contains sexually graphic material.
Formerly: Adam Girls International
Published by: Knight Publishing Corporation, 8060 Melrose Ave, Los Angeles, CA 90046. TEL 323-653-8060, FAX 323-655-9452, psi@loop.com. Ed. Jared Rutter. Adv. contact Timothy Connelly.

305.31 USA
ADAM MAGAZINE. Text in English. 2002 (Jan). bi-m. USD 9.95 domestic; USD 18.95 in Canada; USD 27.95 elsewhere; USD 2.95 newsstand/cover (effective 2002). adv. **Document type:** *Magazine, Consumer.* **Description:** Covers automobiles, personal finance, men's fashion, sports, and trends; also includes sections on fiction, history, and biographies.
Published by: Monarch Services, 4517 Harford Rd, Baltimore, MD 21214. TEL 410-254-9200, FAX 410-254-7115, adameditor@aol.com. Ed. Miguel Bilar.

306 CAN ISSN 1719-5349
ADORABLE AU SUMMUM. Text in French. 2003. m. **Document type:** *Magazine, Consumer.*
Former titles (until 2006): Adorable (1711-6333); (until 2004): Audace (1708-5527)
Published by: Genex Communications Inc., 1134 Grande Allee O, Quebec, PQ G1S 1E5, Canada. TEL 418-687-9810, http://www.genexcommunications.com.

052.081 SRB ISSN 1369-8060
ADRENALIN. Text in English. 1994. m. adv. illus. **Document type:** *Magazine, Consumer.* **Description:** Contains features that appeal to affluent young males and their habits.
Related titles: Italian ed.: ISSN 1747-017X. 1997; Russian ed.; German ed.; French ed.
Published by: Alliance International Media Ltd., Kneginje Zorke 11b, Belgrade, 11000. office@allianceinternationalmedia.com. **Dist. by:** Comag, Tavistock Rd, W Drayton, Middlesex UB7 7QE, United Kingdom. TEL 44-1895-433600, FAX 44-1895-433605.

305.3 NLD ISSN 1877-0924
AKTUEEL MAN. Text in Dutch. 2008. 10/yr. EUR 45; EUR 4.50 newsstand/cover (effective 2011). adv. **Document type:** *Magazine, Consumer.*
Published by: Audax Publishing B.V., Joan Muyskenweg 6-6a, Amsterdam, 1096 CJ, Netherlands. TEL 31-20-5979450, FAX 31-20-5979622, info@publishing.audax.nl, http://www.audax.nl. Ed. Wim Schaap. Circ: 27,742.

363.4 USA ISSN 1083-2459
ALL MAN. Text in English. 1987. bi-m. illus. **Document type:** *Magazine, Consumer.*
Formerly: All Male
Published by: Mavety Media Group, 225 Broadway, Ste 2801, New York, NY 10007-3079. TEL 212-966-8400, FAX 212-966-9366. **Dist. by:** Curtis Circulation Co., 730 River Rd, New Milford, NJ 07646.

305.31 AUS ISSN 1832-6838
ALPHA; it's sport and it's personal. Text in English. 2005. m. AUD 20 domestic; AUD 50 in New Zealand; AUD 2.95 newsstand/cover (effective 2008). adv. back issues avail. **Document type:** *Magazine, Consumer.* **Description:** Covers travel, adventure, health, fitness, fashion, motoring, grooming and more. It is a men's magazine, with a mix of sport and lifestyle.
Indexed: SD.
Published by: News Magazines Pty Ltd., Level 3, 2 Holt St, Surry Hills, NSW 2010, Australia. TEL 61-2-92883000, subscriptions@newsmagazines.com.au, http://www.newsspace.com.au/magazines. Ed. Rob Pegley TEL 61-2-80622093. Adv. contact Vince Lam. page AUD 16,950; trim 228 x 297. Circ: 124,450.

306.7 CAN
AMERICAN CURVES. Text in English. 2002 (Nov.). bi-m. USD 19.99 domestic; USD 39.99 foreign; USD 5.99 newsstand/cover (effective 2004). **Document type:** *Magazine, Consumer.*
Published by: Canusa Products, 5775 Mclaughlin Rd, Mississauga, ON L5R 3P7, Canada. TEL 905-678-7312. Circ: 260,000.

306.775 USA ISSN 1931-0129
TS537
AMERICAN HANDGUNNER TACTICAL ANNUAL. Text in English. a. **Document type:** *Magazine, Consumer.*
Published by: Publishers Development Corp., F M G Publications, 12345 World Trade Dr, San Diego, CA 92128. TEL 858-605-0253, FAX 858-605-0247, http://www.fmgpublications.com.

306.74 USA
THE AMERICAN SEX SCENE: GUIDE TO BORDELLOS. Text in English. m. USD 49.95.
Published by: Qlimax, 313 N York Rd, Hatboro, PA 19040. TEL 800-887-6900, FAX 215-654-1895. Ed. Michael Phoenix.

051 USA
AMERICA'S HORNIEST PEOPLE. Text in English. m. USD 49.95.
Related titles: E-mail ed.
Published by: Qlimax, 313 N York Rd, Hatboro, PA 19040. TEL 800-887-6900, FAX 215-654-1895.

305.31 RUS ISSN 0868-8915
ANDREI. Text in Russian. s-a. USD 85 in United States.
Address: Varshavskoe shosse 128-1, Moscow, 113587, Russian Federation. TEL 7-095-3133320. **Dist. by:** East View Information Services, 10601 Wayzata Blvd, Minneapolis, MN 55305. TEL 952-252-1201, 800-477-1005, FAX 952-252-1202, info@eastview.com, http://www.eastview.com.

ANTHEM (NASHVILLE). *see* MUSIC

051 USA
APOCALIPSTICK. Text in English. irreg. **Description:** Covers everything virtual and virtually everything focusing on issues of importance to men living in Brooklyn.
Media: Online - full text.

052 GBR ISSN 1353-1972
ARENA HOMME PLUS. Text in English. 1994. s-a. GBP 14 domestic; GBP 20 foreign; GBP 7.87 per issue domestic; GBP 12.30 per issue in Europe; GBP 14.20 per issue elsewhere (effective 2009). adv. **Document type:** *Magazine, Consumer.* **Description:** Provides an international forum in which leading photographers and writers can express new ideas and possibilities.
Indexed: D05, SCOPUS.
—IE.
Published by: H. Bauer Publishing Ltd. (Subsidiary of: Bauer Media Group), Mappin House, 4 Winsley St, London, W1W 8HF, United Kingdom. TEL 44-20-71828000, http://www.bauer.co.uk. Ed. Jo Ann Furniss. Adv. contact Miles Dunbar TEL 44-20-72955419. **Subscr. to:** Tower House, Sovereign Park, Market Harborough, Leicestershire LE16 9EF, United Kingdom. TEL 44-1858-438866, subs@greatmagazines.co.uk.

059.927 SAU ISSN 1319-089X
AP95.A6
ARRAJOL. Text in Arabic. 1992. m. adv. illus. **Document type:** *Magazine, Consumer.* **Description:** Contains upscale lifestyle features and topics for Arab men.
Published by: Saudi Research & Publishing Co., P O Box 478, Riyadh, 11411, Saudi Arabia. TEL 966-1-4419933, FAX 966-1-4429555, editorial@majalla.com, http://www.srpc.com/main. adv.: page SAR 20,000; trim 220 x 285. Circ: 32,968 (paid). **Subscr. in U.S. to:** Attache International, 3050 Broadway, Ste 300, Boulder, CO 80304-3154. TEL 303-442-8900.

305.91 USA ISSN 1081-5767
HQ756.6
AT-HOME DAD; men who change diapers change the world. Text in English. 1994. q. adv. illus. reprints avail. **Document type:** *Newsletter, Consumer.* **Description:** Provides connections and resources and articles about at homedads for the two million fathers who stay home with their children.
Related titles: Online - full text ed.
Indexed: GW, P19, P48, PQC.
Address: 61 Brightwood Ave, North Andover, MA 01845.

M

305.31 646.32 SGP
AUGUST MAN. Text in English. m. adv. **Document type:** *Magazine, Consumer.* **Description:** Covers the latest and greatest in travel, business, music, technology, pop culture and motoring.
Published by: C R Media Pte Ltd., Blk 1008 Toa Payoh N #07-11, Singapore, 318996, Singapore. TEL 65-6256-6201, FAX 65-6251-0348, enquiries@crmedia.com.sg, http://www.crmedia.com.sg. adv.: B&W page SGD 5,280, color page SGD 5,940; trim 210 x 276.

779.28 AUS ISSN 0818-3589
AUSTRALIAN HOT TALK. Variant title: Hottalk. Text in English. 1984. 4/yr. AUD 33 (effective 2008). adv. **Document type:** *Magazine, Consumer.* **Description:** Provides a forum for liberated men and women to share their experiences, fantasies and ideas.
Published by: Horwitz Publications Pty. Ltd., Level 4, 55 Chandos St, St Leonards, NSW 2065, Australia. TEL 61-2-89870300, deliaq@horwitz.com.au. Ed. Ian Gerrard.

779.28 AUS ISSN 0158-0655
AUSTRALIAN PENTHOUSE; Australian men's magazine. Text in English. 1979. m. AUD 119.90 (effective 2008). adv. back issues avail. **Document type:** *Magazine, Consumer.*
Published by: Horwitz Publications Pty. Ltd., Level 4, 55 Chandos St, St Leonards, NSW 2065, Australia. TEL 61-2-89870300, deliaq@horwitz.com.au. Ed. Ian Gerrard. Adv. contact Stephen Brandon TEL 61-2-89870320. color page AUD 4,100. Circ: 132,000.

305.31 NLD ISSN 1872-2849
AVANTGARDEMEN. Text in Dutch. 2006. s-a. EUR 6.95 newsstand/cover (effective 2009). adv. **Document type:** *Magazine, Consumer.*
Published by: Audax Publishing B.V., Joan Muyskenweg 6-6a, Amsterdam, 1096 CJ, Netherlands. TEL 31-20-5979450, FAX 31-20-5979622, info@publishing.audax.nl, http://www.audax.nl. adv.: page EUR 4,900; bleed 230 x 300. Circ: 35,000.

AVENUE REPORT; where lifestyle meets luxury. *see* CLOTHING TRADE—Fashions

BACK - TALK MAGAZINE. *see* HOMOSEXUALITY

BASS GUIDE. *see* SPORTS AND GAMES—Outdoor Life

BEAU. *see* HOMOSEXUALITY

▼ **BEEF!;** fuer Maenner mit geschmack. *see* HOME ECONOMICS

779.28 GBR ISSN 1463-9122
BELLY; where fat chicks are cool. Text in English. 1998. 4/yr. GBP 25; USD 15 in United States; GBP 8 in Europe; GBP 10 elsewhere; GBP 7 newsstand/cover (effective 2000). adv. **Document type:** *Magazine, Consumer.* **Description:** Contains nude photo spreads featuring large and voluptuous women.
Published by: R W P, PO Box 1956, London, N19 4NR, United Kingdom. TEL 44-171-607-8899, FAX 44-171-607-8866, info@belly.co.uk, http://www.belly.co.uk.

BEST LIFE. *see* LIFESTYLE

779.28 GBR
BEST OF 50 PLUS. Text in English. bi-m. GBP 4.99 newsstand/cover. adv. **Document type:** *Magazine, Consumer.* **Description:** Publishes a selection of erotic photographs of nude women.
Published by: Fantasy Publications Ltd., 211 Old St, Ground Fl, London, EC1V 9NR, United Kingdom. TEL 44-171-308-5467, FAX 44-20-7308-5075. **Dist. by:** Northern & Shell Distribution, Northern & Shell Tower, 4 Selsdon Way, London E14 9GL, United Kingdom. TEL 44-171-308-5090, FAX 44-171-308-5078.

779.28 GBR ISSN 0955-1808
BEST OF ESCORT. Text in English. s-a. GBP 2.25 newsstand/cover. adv. **Document type:** *Magazine, Consumer.* **Description:** Collects the hottest erotic shots of naked women in the sexiest poses.
Published by: Paul Raymond Publications Ltd., 2 Archer St, London, W1V 8JJ, United Kingdom. TEL 44-20-72928000, FAX 44-20-72928021. **Dist. by:** Comag, Tavistock Rd, W Drayton, Middlesex UB7 7QE, United Kingdom. TEL 44-1895-444055, FAX 44-1895-433602.

779.28 GBR ISSN 0958-448X
BEST OF FIESTA. Text in English. 1990. bi-m. GBP 3.25 newsstand/cover. adv. **Document type:** *Magazine, Consumer.* **Description:** Contains more of the hottest erotic nude shots of gorgeous women.
Published by: Galaxy Publications Ltd., PO Box 312, Galaxy Publications Ltd, Witham, Essex CM8 3SZ, United Kingdom. TEL 44-1376-534500, FAX 44-1376-534536. **Dist. by:** Blackhorse Distribution Ltd., Blackhorse Distribution Ltd, Freebourne Rd, PO Box 1124, Witham, Essex CM8 3XJ, United Kingdom. TEL 44-1376-534530, FAX 44-1376-534531.

052 GBR ISSN 1465-0584
THE BEST OF FORUM. Text in English. 1993. 9/yr. GBP 31 (effective 2009). adv. back issues avail. **Document type:** *Magazine, Consumer.* **Description:** Showcases the best articles from past issues of the UK and US editions of Forum. It is also packed with the juiciest readers' letters old and new.
Published by: Trojan Publishing Ltd., 3rd Fl, 207 Old St, London, EC1V 9NR, United Kingdom. TEL 44-20-76086300, FAX 44-20-76086320, info@trojanpublishing.co.uk, http://www.trojanpublishing.co.uk/. Ed. Elizabeth Coldwell. Adv. contact Louise McMahon TEL 44-20-76086360.

779.28 GBR ISSN 0960-3581
BEST OF MAYFAIR. Text in English. 198?. s-a. GBP 2.95 newsstand/cover. adv. **Document type:** *Magazine, Consumer.* **Description:** Exposes the hidden erotic charms of the sexiest women.
Published by: Paul Raymond Publications Ltd., 2 Archer St, London, W1V 8JJ, United Kingdom. TEL 44-20-72928000, FAX 44-20-72928021. **Dist. by:** Comag, Tavistock Rd, W Drayton, Middlesex UB7 7QE, United Kingdom. TEL 44-1895-444055, FAX 44-1895-433602.

779.28 GBR ISSN 0955-193X
BEST OF MEN ONLY. Text in English. 198?. m. GBP 2.85 newsstand/cover. adv. **Document type:** *Magazine, Consumer.* **Description:** Displays erotic photos of sexy nude women.
Published by: Paul Raymond Publications Ltd., 2 Archer St, London, W1V 8JJ, United Kingdom. TEL 44-20-72928000, FAX 44-20-72928021. **Dist. by:** Comag, Tavistock Rd, W Drayton, Middlesex UB7 7QE, United Kingdom. TEL 44-1895-444055, FAX 44-1895-433602.

779.28 GBR ISSN 0955-1859
BEST OF RAZZLE. Text in English. s-a. GBP 2.25 newsstand/cover. adv. **Document type:** *Magazine, Consumer.* **Description:** Presents the rudest erotic photos of sexy nude women.
Published by: Paul Raymond Publications Ltd., 2 Archer St, London, W1V 8JJ, United Kingdom. TEL 44-20-72928000, FAX 44-20-72928021. **Dist. by:** Comag, Tavistock Rd, W Drayton, Middlesex UB7 7QE, United Kingdom. TEL 44-1895-444055, FAX 44-1895-433602.

306.705 GBR ISSN 1752-3141
BESTA FIESTA. Text in English. 2006. m. **Document type:** *Magazine, Consumer.*
Published by: Galaxy Publications Ltd., PO Box 312, Galaxy Publications Ltd, Witham, Essex CM8 3SZ, United Kingdom. TEL 44-1376-534541, fiesta@fiesta.org, http://www.fiesta.org.

BIG APPLE PARENT. *see* CHILDREN AND YOUTH—About

051 USA ISSN 1083-2467
BIG BUTT. Text in English. 1990. bi-m. USD 59.95 domestic; USD 74.95 in Canada & Mexico; USD 88.95 elsewhere (effective 2003). **Document type:** *Magazine, Consumer.*
Published by: Heat Wave Publications, Inc., 462 Broadway, Ste 4000, New York, NY 10013. TEL 212-966-8400. **Subscr. to:** Jiffy Fulfillment Inc., PO Box 1102, Cranford, NJ 07016-1102. **Dist. by:** Curtis Circulation Co., 730 River Rd, New Milford, NJ 07646.

052 GBR ISSN 1365-358X
THE BIG CHEESE; alternative music mayhem. Text in English. 1996. bi-m. GBP 32.99 domestic; GBP 50.32 in Europe; GBP 44.16 elsewhere; GBP 4.60 per issue (effective 2009). adv. bk.rev.; film rev.; music rev.; video rev. back issues avail. **Document type:** *Magazine, Consumer.* **Description:** Presents various aspects of various lifestyles for young men.
Published by: Big Cheese Publishing, Unit 7 Clarendon Bldg, 25 Horsell Rd, Highbury, London, N5 1XL, United Kingdom. TEL 44-20-76070303. Circ: 17,000 (paid).

646.32 USA ISSN 1944-6667
TR679
BIG MAN MAGAZINE. Text in English. 2008 (Dec.). s-a. USD 6 per issue (effective 2009). **Document type:** *Magazine, Consumer.*
Published by: Kennedy & Torres Inc., 368 Broadway, Ste 503, New York, NY 10013. TEL 212-571-0210. Ed. Toni Torres.

BIRTH OF TRAGEDY MAGAZINE; the fear issue, the God issue, the power issue, the love issue, the sex issue. *see* LITERARY AND POLITICAL REVIEWS

052 GBR ISSN 1364-596X
BIZARRE. Text in English. 1996. m. GBP 41.50 domestic; GBP 57 foreign (effective 2009). adv. back issues avail. **Document type:** *Magazine, Consumer.* **Description:** Cutting-edge men's lifestyle magazine with a bold and bizarre sense of style and humor.
Published by: John Brown Citrus Publishing, 136-142 Bramley Rd, London, W10 6SR, United Kingdom. TEL 44-20-75653000, FAX 44-20-75653060, http://www.johnbrownmedia.com. **Subscr. to:** Bradley Pavilions. **Dist. by:** Comag.; **Dist. in US by:** Eastern News Distributors Inc.

BLACK INCHES. *see* HOMOSEXUALITY

779.28 USA ISSN 2152-7075
▼ **BLACK LINGERIE.** Text in English. 2010. m. USD 24.95 (effective 2010). **Document type:** *Magazine, Consumer.* **Description:** Special edition of Show Magazine.
Related titles: ◆ Special ed. of: Show (Los Angeles). ISSN 1559-9515.
Published by: Cummings Media, 500 Molino St, Ste 111, Los Angeles, CA 90013. TEL 213-402-4634, sean@cummingsmedia.com.

051 USA
BLACK TAIL. Text in English. 1989. m. USD 363.40. illus.
Formerly (until 1991): Mocha
Published by: Tux Magazine, Inc., 462 Broadway, Ste 4000, New York, NY 10013. TEL 212-966-8400. **Dist. by:** Curtis Circulation Co., 730 River Rd, New Milford, NJ 07646.

053.1 DEU ISSN 0945-599X
BLITZ ILLU. Text in German. 1992. w. adv. **Document type:** *Magazine, Consumer.* **Description:** Magazine for young people featuring erotica.
Published by: Pabel-Moewig Verlag KG (Subsidiary of: Bauer Media Group), Karlsruherstr 31, Rastatt, 76437, Germany. TEL 49-7222-130, FAX 49-7222-13218, empfang@vpm.de, http://www.vpm-online.de. Adv. contact Rainer Gross. Circ: 115,000 (paid). **Dist. in UK by:** Powers International Ltd., 100 Rochester Row, London SW1P 1JP, United Kingdom. TEL 44-20-7630-9966, FAX 44-20-7630-9922.

646.32 051 NLD ISSN 1875-1725
BLVD MAN. Variant title: Boulevard Man. Text in Dutch. 1996. q. EUR 18 (effective 2009). adv. **Document type:** *Magazine, Consumer.*
Formerly (until 2006): S Q - Society Quarterly (1569-6510)
Published by: Credits Media BV, Vijzelgracht 21-25, Amsterdam, 1017 HN, Netherlands. TEL 31-20-5302570, FAX 31-20-5302585, creditsmedia@creditsmedia.nl, http://www.creditsmedia.nl. Ed. Pieter Schol. Pub. Eugen van de Pas. Adv. contact Alex Sitompoel. page EUR 4,098; 225 x 300. Circ: 50,000.

808.803538 USA ISSN 1556-0430
BOINK. Text in English. 2005 (Jan.). 4/yr. (during the school year (Sep.-May)). USD 29.95 combined subscription print & online ed.; USD 7.95 newsstand/cover (effective 2007). **Document type:** *Magazine, Consumer.* **Description:** Explores modern sexuality issues for college students.
Related titles: Online - full text ed.
Published by: Boink Publishing, 304 Newbury St, Ste 313, Boston, MA 02115. Ed. Alecia Oleyourryk.

070.489 CHE ISSN 1660-4520
BOLERO MEN. Text in German. 2003. 3/yr. adv. **Document type:** *Magazine, Consumer.*
Related titles: ◆ Supplement to: Bolero. ISSN 1420-3944.
Published by: Bolero Zeitschriftenverlag AG, Giesshuebelstr 62i, Zuerich, 8045, Switzerland. TEL 41-1-4548282, FAX 41-1-4548272, service@boleroweb.ch, http://www.boleroweb.ch. adv.: page CHF 12,500; trim 213 x 275. Circ: 60,000 (controlled).

053.1 DEU
BOND MEN'S MAGAZINE. Text in German. 4/yr. EUR 5 newsstand/cover (effective 2010). adv. **Document type:** *Magazine, Consumer.*

Published by: Maiestas, Sundernstr 21, Melle, 49328, Germany. TEL 49-160-5080352. Eds., Pubs. Catharina van Zwol, Hendrik Birke. Circ: 20,000 (paid and controlled).

BONITA. *see* ETHNIC INTERESTS

305.31 GBR ISSN 1461-6939
BOYS TOYS. Text in English. 1999. m. GBP 45.60 domestic; GBP 90 in Europe; GBP 120 elsewhere (effective 2010). adv. illus. back issues avail. **Document type:** *Magazine, Consumer.* **Description:** Offers single men an investigative journalistic approach to a wealth of lifestyle topics, including gadgets, travel, automobiles, fashion, sports, and health and fitness.
Published by: Freestyle Publications Ltd., Alexander House, Ling Rd, Tower Park, Poole, Dorset BH12 4NZ, United Kingdom. TEL 44-1202-735090, FAX 44-1202-733969. Ed. Tom Perkins. Adv. contact Christian Dickinson.

BRAUT UND BRAEUTIGAM MAGAZIN. *see* WOMEN'S INTERESTS

305.31 SVK ISSN 1336-1457
BREJK. Text in Slovak. 2002. m. EUR 24; EUR 2.20 newsstand/cover (effective 2011). adv. **Document type:** *Magazine, Consumer.*
Related titles: Online - full content ed.: ISSN 1336-3085.
Published by: Spolocnost 7 Plus s.r.o., Panonska cesta 7, Bratislava 5, 85232, Slovakia. TEL 421-2-32153111, FAX 421-2-32153376, predplatne@7plus.sk, http://www.7plus.sk. Ed. Adrian Potancok TEL 421-2-32153275. Circ: 28,000 (paid).

779.28 305.89607305 USA ISSN 1948-2019
▼ **BRICKHOUSE MAGAZINE.** Short title: Brickhouse. Text in English. 2009. m. USD 4.99 per issue (effective 2009). **Document type:** *Magazine, Consumer.* **Description:** Features African-American models and urban culture.
Related titles: Online - full text ed.: ISSN 1948-2027.
Published by: Gemdigi LLC, 2921 Lenox Rd, Ste 113, Atlanta, GA 30324. TEL 678-237-7500, admin@gemdigi.com, http://www.gemdigi.com/.

BRIDE AND GROOM (SHREWSBURY). *see* MATRIMONY

051 CAN
BUBBLEGUM GIRLS. Text in English. 2001. bi-m. CAD 19.99; CAD 6.99 newsstand/cover (effective 2002). adv. **Document type:** *Magazine, Consumer.*
Published by: Black Knight Publishing, Inc., PO Box 83, Vaudreuil-Dorion, PQ J7V 5V8, Canada. Ed. Jay Offman.

051 USA
BUSTY BEAUTIES. Text in English. 1988. m. USD 39.95. adv. back issues avail. **Document type:** *Magazine, Consumer.*
Formerly (until 2004): Hustler Busty Beauties (1059-6798)
Published by: Magna Publishing, 210 Rte 4 E, Ste 211, Paramus, NJ 07652. TEL 201-843-4004, FAX 201-843-8775. adv.: B&W page USD 2,876; trim 10 x 7.38. Circ: 70,000.

059.94511 HUN ISSN 1419-2489
C K M. (Celtudatos Kalandvagyo ferfiak Magazinja) Text in Hungarian. 1998. m. HUF 4,800; HUF 695 newsstand/cover (effective 2011). adv. **Document type:** *Magazine, Consumer.*
Related titles: Online - full text ed.: ISSN 1586-5584. 2000.
Published by: Marquard Media Magyarorszag Kiado Kft. (Subsidiary of: Marquard Media AG), Hajogyari-sziget 213, Budapest, 1033, Hungary. TEL 36-1-5050800, FAX 36-1-5050805, info@marquardmedia.hu, http://www.marquardmedia.hu. Ed. Peter Pantl. Adv. contact Antal Kertesi. Circ: 18,981 (paid).

779.28 POL ISSN 1505-6562
C K M. (Czasopismo Kazdego Mezczyzny) Text in Polish. 1998. m. PLZ 81 (effective 2011). adv. **Document type:** *Magazine, Consumer.*
Published by: Marquard Media Polska Sp. z o.o. (Subsidiary of: Marquard Media AG), ul Wilcza 50/52, Warsaw, 00-679, Poland. TEL 48-22-4211000, FAX 48-22-4211111, info@marquard.pl, http://www.marquard.pl. Ed. Piotr Gontowski. Adv. contact Monika Ruszkowska. Circ: 112,802 (paid).

779.28 SRB ISSN 1451-5970
C K M. Text in Serbian. 2003. m. CSD 1,800; CSD 150 newsstand/cover (effective 2011). adv. **Document type:** *Magazine, Consumer.*
Published by: Color Media International, Temerinska 102, Novi Sad, 21000. TEL 381-21-4897100, FAX 381-21-4897126, milan.sobot@color.rs, http://www.color.rs. Ed. Dasko Milinovic. Adv. contact Goran Radulovic. Circ: 35,000 (paid).

CAFE. *see* GENERAL INTEREST PERIODICALS—Sweden

CATENA. *see* RELIGIONS AND THEOLOGY—Roman Catholic

363.4 USA ISSN 1083-2645
CELEB CONFIDENTIAL. Text in English. a. **Document type:** *Magazine, Consumer.*
Formerly: Celebrity Confidential
Published by: Spotlite Communications, Inc., 462 Broadway, Ste 4000, New York, NY 10013. TEL 212-966-8400. **Dist. by:** Curtis Circulation Co., 730 River Rd, New Milford, NJ 07646.

051 USA ISSN 1075-0819
CELEBRITY SKIN. Text in English. 8/yr. USD 29.95 domestic; USD 39.95 foreign; USD 4.99 newsstand/cover.
Published by: Man's World Publications Inc., 801 Second Ave, New York, NY 10017. TEL 212-661-7878. Ed. Charlie Malloy. **Subscr. to:** PO Box 642, Mt Morris, IL 61054.

051 USA
CELEBRITY SLEUTH. Text in English. 198?. 9/yr. USD 8 per issue. illus.
Published by: Broadcast Communications, Inc., 462 Broadway, Ste 4000, New York, NY 10013. TEL 212-966-8400. **Dist. by:** Curtis Circulation Co., 730 River Rd, New Milford, NJ 07646.

305.31 AUS ISSN 1324-2962
CERTIFIED MALE MAGAZINE. Text in English. 199?. q. AUD 22 domestic; NZD 35 in New Zealand; USD 25 in US & Canada (effective 2001). **Description:** Contains men's stories, men's rights, masculism, men and feminism, the men's movement, men's groups, fathers and fathering, parenting, boy's education, men's health, domestic violence, gender, relationships, family law, divorce, child support and custody, sexuality, discrimination, sex roles, gender politics and many other issues examined from a male perspective.
Published by: Certified Male, GPO Box 1, Springwood, NSW 2777, Australia. TEL 61-4-7511127, FAX 61-4-7515518. Ed. Peter Vogel.

779.28 CZE ISSN 1212-4052
CESKE LOZNICE. Text in Czech. 1999. m. CZK 594; CZK 49.50 newsstand/cover (effective 2009). **Document type:** *Magazine, Consumer.*

Published by: PK 62, a.s., Bohdalecka 6, Prague 10, 101 00, Czech Republic. TEL 420-281-090611, FAX 420-281-090622, pk62@pk62.cz, http://www.pk62.cz. Ed. Petr Stransky.

306.7 CZE
CESKE PANICKY. Text in Czech. 2006. 2/yr. CZK 156; CZK 78 newsstand/cover (effective 2009). **Document type:** *Magazine, Consumer.*
Published by: PK 62, a.s., Bohdalecka 6, Prague 10, 101 00, Czech Republic. TEL 420-281-090611, FAX 420-281-090622, pk62@pk62.cz, http://www.pk62.cz.

CHALLENGE (CONVENT STATION). *see* HOMOSEXUALITY

CHE WANG ZAZHI/CAR PLUS. *see* TRANSPORTATION—Automobiles

051 USA ISSN 1059-7131
CHERI; the all-true sex news magazine. Text in English. 13/yr. USD 29.95 domestic; USD 50 foreign; USD 7.99 newsstand/cover (effective 2000). **Document type:** *Magazine, Consumer.*
Published by: Cheri Magazine, Inc., 801 Second Ave, New York, NY 10017. TEL 212-661-7878. Ed. Ken Kimmel. **Subscr. to:** PO Box 411, Mt Morris, IL 61054.

779.28 USA ISSN 1536-7991
CHERI XXX HARDCORE; maximum penetration. Text in English. 2001 (Jun.). bi-m. USD 15.99 newsstand/cover (effective 2001). adv. **Document type:** *Magazine, Consumer.*
Published by: Cheri Magazine, Inc., 801 Second Ave, New York, NY 10017. TEL 212-661-7878, FAX 212-883-1244.

CHIRON RISING; entertainment for mature men and admirers. *see* HOMOSEXUALITY

CIGAR AFICIONADO; the good life magazine for men. *see* TOBACCO

CIGAR INSIDER (ONLINE). *see* TOBACCO

363.4 USA ISSN 0743-8389
CINEMA BLUE. Text in English. 198?. a. USD 32.95. **Description:** Reviews of x-rated video cassettes.
Published by: Hudson Communications, Inc., 462 Broadway, Ste 4000, New York, NY 10013. TEL 212-966-8400. Ed. Felicia Freedom. **Dist. by:** Flynt Distributing Co., 9171 Wilshire Blvd, Ste 300, Beverly Hills, CA 90210.

363.4 USA
CINEMA BLUE PRESENTS EROTIC STARS. Text in English. 1989. a. USD 19.95. illus.
Published by: Galaxy Publications, Inc., 462 Broadway, Ste 4000, New York, NY 10013. TEL 212-966-8400. **Dist. by:** Flynt Distributing Co., 9171 Wilshire Blvd, Ste 300, Beverly Hills, CA 90210.

363.4 USA
CINEMA BLUE PRESENTS RED-HOT COUPLES. Text in English. 1989. a. USD 19.95. illus.
Published by: Heat Publications, Inc. (Subsidiary of: Mavety Media Group), 462 Broadway, Ste 4000, New York, NY 10013. TEL 212-966-8400. **Dist. by:** Flynt Distributing Co., 9171 Wilshire Blvd, Ste 300, Beverly Hills, CA 90210.

CLEAN SHEETS. *see* LITERATURE

363.4 USA
CLOSE SHAVE. Text in English. 1989. a. illus.
Published by: Vista Publications, Inc., 462 Broadway, Ste 4000, New York, NY 10013. TEL 212-966-8400. **Dist. by:** Curtis Circulation Co., 730 River Rd, New Milford, NJ 07646.

051 USA ISSN 1072-8066
CLUB CONFIDENTIAL. Text in English. 19??. m. free to members (effective 2009). adv. illus. **Document type:** *Magazine, Consumer.* **Description:** Features intimately descriptive articles accompanied by four-color pictorials of today's popular erotica models.
Published by: Paragon Publishing Inc., PO Box 309, Newtown, CT 06470. TEL 203-364-0475, FAX 203-364-0691, advertising@clubmediainc.com, http://www.clubonline.com. adv.: page USD 3,000; bleed 8.25 x 11.125.

051 USA ISSN 0747-0819
CLUB INTERNATIONAL. Text in English. 19??. m. free to members (effective 2009). adv. **Document type:** *Magazine, Consumer.* **Description:** Contains erotic editorial content with pictorial of print and movie models of today's adult entertainment industry.
Published by: Paragon Publishing Inc., PO Box 309, Newtown, CT 06470. TEL 203-364-0475, FAX 203-364-0691, advertising@clubmediainc.com, http://www.clubonline.com. adv.: page USD 6,000; bleed 8.25 x 11.125.

052 GBR ISSN 0955-1816
CLUB INTERNATIONAL. Text in English. 1972. m. GBP 42; GBP 2.60 newsstand/cover. adv. **Document type:** *Magazine, Consumer.* **Description:** Contains erotic nude photos of beautiful women in various poses and positions.
Published by: Paul Raymond Publications Ltd., 2 Archer St, London, W1V 8JJ, United Kingdom. TEL 44-20-72928000. Ed. Robert Swift. Adv. contact Nicola Swift. **Subscr. to:** MRM, PO Box 503, Leicester LE94 0AD, United Kingdom. TEL 44-1858-410510. **Dist. by:** Comag, Tavistock Rd, W Drayton, Middlesex UB7 7QE, United Kingdom. TEL 44-1895-444055, FAX 44-1895-433602.

051 USA ISSN 0747-0827
CLUB MAGAZINE. Text in English. 1974. m. free to members (effective 2009). adv. back issues avail. **Document type:** *Magazine, Consumer.* **Description:** Contains erotically entertaining articles and cartoons and pictorials featuring popular models.
Published by: Paragon Publishing Inc., PO Box 309, Newtown, CT 06470. TEL 203-364-0475, FAX 203-364-0691, advertising@clubmediainc.com, http://www.clubonline.com. adv.: page USD 12,000; bleed 8.25 x 11.125.

306.7 USA
CO - ED MAGAZINE. Text in English. 2005. m. USD 9.95 (effective 2006). adv. **Document type:** *Magazine, Consumer.* **Description:** Covers campus life, sports, music, spring break, fashion, dating for college students.
Related titles: Online - full content ed.
Published by: CORY Publishing L.L.C., 321 Newark St., 5th Fl, Hoboken, NJ 07030. TEL 201-526-0203, FAX 201-526-0207, subscriptions@co-edmagazine.com. Ed. Kirk Miller. Pub. David Allen Liebler. adv.: B&W page USD 12,000, color page USD 13,800; trim 8.25 x 10.875.

305.31 USA
COEXISTENCE. Text in English. 2007. m. USD 30; USD 4.95 newsstand/cover domestic; USD 5.95 newsstand/cover in Canada (effective 2008). adv. illus. **Document type:** *Magazine, Consumer.*
Published by: Coexistence Magazine, 4157 Elm View Dr, Encino, CA 91316. TEL 818-916-3342, 866-611-0456, coexistence@coexistencemag.com, editorial@coexistencemag.com, shake@coexistencemag.com. Ed. Varuzhan VS Shahdzadeh. Pub. Shahdad Shake Kelishadi.

306.7 USA ISSN 2156-4086
▼ **COLLEGE GENTLEMAN.** Text in English. 2010. bi-m. USD 6 (effective 2011). **Document type:** *Magazine, Trade.*
Published by: College Gentleman, Llc., 9115 E Baseline Rd, Ste C-102, Mesa, AZ 85209. TEL 866-606-4116, http://www.collegegentleman.com.

CONSCIENCE; a news journal of prochoice Catholic opinion. *see* RELIGIONS AND THEOLOGY—Roman Catholic

CONTROVERSY; life without it is boring. *see* GENERAL INTEREST PERIODICALS—United States

070.483 DEU ISSN 0935-7475
COUPE; die junge Illustrierte. Text in German. 1985. m. EUR 37.20; EUR 3.10 newsstand/cover (effective 2009). adv. **Document type:** *Magazine, Consumer.* **Description:** Contains leisure and professional interests for young adults along with erotic stories and pictures.
Related titles: Online - full text ed.
Published by: Inter Content KG (Subsidiary of: Heinrich Bauer Verlag), Karlsruher Str 31, Rastatt, 76437, Germany. TEL 49-40-30190, FAX 49-40-301923, online@imckg.de, http://www.vpm.de. adv.: B&W page EUR 8,973, color page EUR 10,835; trim 200 x 269. Circ: 62,637 (paid). **Subscr. to:** V K G Verlagsvertriebs KG, Postfach 112202, Hamburg 20422, Germany. TEL 49-180-5313939, FAX 49-40-30198123, kundenservice@bauerverlag.de.

051 USA
COUPLES. Text in English. m.
Published by: Couples Magazine LLC, 2568 Pine Ridge Rd., W Bloomfield, MI 48324-1955. Ed. Jonathan Shelton.

303.51 USA
CUDDLES. Text in English. 2000. bi-m. USD 35.99; USD 7.99 newsstand/cover (effective 2001). adv. **Document type:** *Magazine, Consumer.*
Published by: Global Publications, 401 Broadway, New York, NY 10013. Ed. Randi Romance.

CURRENTS (CHICAGO); a review of mainstream arts & other issues affecting gay males. *see* HOMOSEXUALITY

CYBERSOCKET WEB MAGAZINE; the leader in gay & lesbian online information. *see* HOMOSEXUALITY

056.1 ESP ISSN 1575-3360
D T - DOWNTOWN. Text in Spanish. 1992. m. (11/yr.). EUR 11.52 (effective 2009). adv. back issues avail. **Document type:** *Magazine, Consumer.*
Formerly (until 1998): Downtown (1575-3352)
Related titles: Online - full text ed.
Published by: Focus Ediciones SL (Subsidiary of: Edipresse Publications SA), Paseo de la Castellana 129, 1o, Madrid, 28046, Spain. TEL 34-91-5973090, FAX 34-91-5972326, camado@focusediciones.com, http://www.focusediciones.com. Ed. Antonio Marquez Coello. Circ: 67,003.

D V MAN. (Damernas Vaerld) *see* CLOTHING TRADE—Fashions

305.31 USA
DADMAG.COM. Text in English. irreg. **Document type:** *Journal, Consumer.* **Description:** Covers fatherhood issues, including topics such as career, relationships, travel, sex, fitness, single parent, and more.
Media: Online - full content.
Published by: DADMAG.com, LLC, 1333 N Kingsbury, Ste 100, Chicago, IL 60622. InfoCenter@Dadmag.com.

305.31 746.9 646.72 CHN
DADUSHI (NANSHI BAN)/METROPOLIS. Text in Chinese. 2000. m. CNY 120 (effective 2009). **Document type:** *Magazine, Consumer.*
Published by: Dadushi Zazhishe/Metropolis Magazine Publishing House, Rm.1604, 345 Xianxia Rd., Shanghai, 200336, China. TEL 86-21-51187981, FAX 86-21-51187975.

808.8 USA
DARK ANGELS. Text in English. m. adv. **Document type:** *Magazine, Consumer.* **Description:** Contains erotic esoterica and esoteric erotica.
Media: Online - full text.
Address: 29 Dracut St., Dorchestr Ctr, MA 02124-3818. TEL 617-789-3908.

052 GBR ISSN 0961-9704
TT490
DAZED & CONFUSED. Text in English. 1990. m. GBP 39 domestic; GBP 49 in Europe; USD 75 in United States; GBP 75 elsewhere; GBP 4 per issue domestic; USD 7 per issue in United States; GBP 10 per issue elsewhere; GBP 3.95, USD 9.95 newsstand/cover (effective 2009). adv. back issues avail. **Document type:** *Magazine, Consumer.* **Description:** Covers all facets of music, fashion, film and celebrities.
Related titles: Online - full text ed.: GBP 20 (effective 2009).
—CCC.
Published by: Waddell Ltd., 112-116 Old St, London, EC1V 9BG, United Kingdom. Ed. Rod Stanley. Pub. Rankin Waddell. Adv. contact Stephen White TEL 44-20-75496832.

305.31 AUS ISSN 1833-7090
DAZED & CONFUSED AUS - NZ. (Australia -New Zealand) Text in English. 2006. bi-m. AUD 7.50 per issue (effective 2007). **Document type:** *Magazine, Consumer.* **Description:** Aimed at young men aged 18-35.
Published by: Paper Tiger Media Group, 56-58 Catherine St, Leichhardt, NSW 2040, Australia. TEL 61-2-9564-4100, FAX 61-2-9564-4150, enquiries@ptmg.com.au, http://www.ptmg.com.au.

306.7 RUS
DEKAMERON. Text in Russian. m. RUR 108 for 6 mos. domestic (effective 2004). **Document type:** *Newspaper, Consumer.*
Published by: Izdatel'stvo S-Info, A-ya 42, Moscow, 125284, Russian Federation. TEL 7-095-7969294, FAX 7-095-2520920, s-info@si.ru. **Subscr. to:** Unicont Enterprises Inc., 1340 Centre St, Ste 209, Newton, MA 02459. TEL 800-763-7475, FAX 617-964-8753, podpiska@unipressa.com.

305.31 305.4 USA
DEPTH; for men and women of generation x. Text in English. 2003. q. USD 18; USD 5.95 newsstand/cover domestic; USD 9.95 newsstand/cover in Canada (effective 2003).
Address: 25 Highland Park Village, Ste 100-512, Dallas, TX 75205. Ed., Pub. Julia Moore.

051 USA ISSN 0740-4921
NX504
DETAILS. Variant title: Details for Men. Text in English. 1982-2000; resumed 2001. 11/yr. USD 7.97 domestic; USD 30 in Canada; USD 42.95 elsewhere (effective 2008). adv. bk.rev.; film rev.; music rev. illus. back issues avail.; reprints avail. **Document type:** *Magazine, Consumer.* **Description:** Designed to introduce styles, which sets the trends and breaks the stories that keep the readers ahead of the crowd.
Related titles: Online - full text ed.
Indexed: G08, I05, MLA-IB.
—CCC.
Published by: Fairchild Publications, Inc. (Subsidiary of: Advance Publications, Inc.), 750 3rd Ave, 3rd Fl, New York, NY 10017. TEL 212-630-4900, FAX 212-630-4919, customerservice@fairchildpub.com, http://www.fairchildpub.com. Ed. Daniel Peres. Pub. Steven DeLuca TEL 212-630-4825. adv.: B&W page USD 39,000, color page USD 58,520; trim 8 x 10.875. Circ: 458,536 (paid).

779.28 DEU
DICKERCHEN HITPARADE. Text in German. bi-m. EUR 20.40; EUR 3.90 newsstand/cover (effective 2007). adv. **Document type:** *Magazine, Consumer.*
Published by: S P N Zeitschriften Verlags GmbH, Waidmannstr 35, Hamburg, 22769, Germany. TEL 49-40-8501039, FAX 49-40-8501126, info@spn-verlag.de.

DIMENSIONS MAGAZINE. *see* WOMEN'S INTERESTS

053.931 NLD ISSN 2211-9876
▼ **DONALD.** Text in Dutch. 2009. q. **Document type:** *Magazine, Consumer.*
Published by: Sanoma Uitgevers B.V., Postbus 1900, Hoofddorp, 2130 JH, Netherlands. TEL 31-23-5566770, FAX 31-23-5565376, http://www.sanomamedia.nl.

DREAMBOYS. *see* HOMOSEXUALITY

▼ **DREAMER.** *see* LIFESTYLE

051 USA
DRILL; for men who serve. Text in English. 2003 (Oct.). bi-m. USD 15; USD 3.50 newsstand/cover (effective 2004). adv. **Document type:** *Magazine, Consumer.* **Description:** Contains information, entertainment, news and features for men in the US military.
Published by: John Brown Publishing Inc., 15 E 32nd St, 8th Fl, New York, NY 10016. TEL 212-931-9800, FAX 212-213-4526, http://www.johnbrownpublishing.com. Ed. Lance Gould. Pub., R&P Duncan Milne. Adv. contact Mario Grande TEL 646-435-7096. color page USD 12,000. Circ: 130,000 (controlled).

779.28 USA ISSN 1521-8686
DUDE. Text in English. 1997. bi-m. USD 36; USD 7.99 newsstand/cover. adv. **Document type:** *Magazine, Consumer.*
Published by: Firestone Publishing, 214 Brazilian Ave., Ste. 300, Palm Beach, FL 33480. TEL 561-659-0121, FAX 561-659-0214.

305.31 USA
DULL MEN'S CLUB. Text in English. m. Free. **Description:** Provides jokes, stories, news and other information geared towards the dull man.
Media: Online - full content.
Published by: National Council of Dull Men info@dullmen.com.

EASYRIDERS. *see* SPORTS AND GAMES—Bicycles And Motorcycles

EDELWEISS MEN. *see* CLOTHING TRADE—Fashions

070.48346 PRT ISSN 0873-3996
EGO. Text in Portuguese. 1996. m. EUR 30 domestic; EUR 63.72 in Europe; EUR 96 rest of world (effective 2005).
Published by: Impala Sociedade Editorial, Rua da Impala 33A, Sao Pedro de Penaferrim, Sintra, 2710-070, Portugal. TEL 351-219-238218, FAX 351-219-238463, assinaturas@impala.pt, http://www.impala.pt. Ed. Antonio Mateus. **Distr. by:** Electroliber, Rua Vasco da Gama 4-A, Sacavem 2865, Portugal. TEL 351-9425394.

306.7 RUS
EGOIST. Text in Russian. m. RUR 81 for 6 mos. domestic (effective 2002). **Document type:** *Newspaper, Consumer.*
Published by: Izdatel'stvo S-Info, A-ya 42, Moscow, 125284, Russian Federation. TEL 7-095-7969294, FAX 7-095-2520920, s-info@si.ru. **Subscr. to:** Unicont Enterprises Inc., 1340 Centre St, Ste 209, Newton, MA 02459. TEL 800-763-7475, FAX 617-964-8753, podpiska@unipressa.com.

ELE E ELA; uma revista para ler a dois. *see* WOMEN'S INTERESTS

EN LA VIDA; voces de lesbians, gays, bisexuales y transgeneros latinos. *see* HOMOSEXUALITY

305.31 GBR ISSN 2044-8171
▼ **ENJOY FOR MEN**; the essential handbook for men. Text in English. 2010. q. **Document type:** *Handbook/Manual/Guide, Trade.*
Related titles: Online - full text ed.: free (effective 2011).
Published by: Enjoy for Men Directory Magazine, Ste 105, 4 Montpelier St, Knightsbridge, SW7 1EE, United Kingdom. TEL 44-208-7780343, FAX 44-208-7613200.

▼ **ENJOY SOHO.** *see* LIFESTYLE

054.1 FRA ISSN 1246-404X
ENTREVUE. Text in French. 1992. m. EUR 27; EUR 3 newsstand/cover (effective 2008). adv. **Document type:** *Magazine, Consumer.*
Formerly (until 1993): Interview (1169-5463)
Published by: Hachette Filipacchi Medias S.A. (Subsidiary of: Lagardere Media), 149/151 Rue Anatole France, Levallois-Perret, 925340, France. TEL 33-1-413462, FAX 33-1-413469, lgardere@interdeco.fr, http://www.lagardere.com.

054.1 FRA ISSN 1261-3800
ENTREVUE HORS SERIE. Text in French. 1995. irreg. EUR 5 newsstand/cover (effective 2007). adv. **Document type:** *Magazine, Consumer.*
Published by: Hachette Filipacchi Medias S.A. (Subsidiary of: Lagardere Media), 149/151 Rue Anatole France, Levallois-Perret, 925340, France. TEL 33-1-413462, FAX 33-1-413469, lgardere@interdeco.fr, http://www.lagardere.com.

053.1 DEU ISSN 0342-1872
ER. Text in German. 1950. m. adv. **Document type:** *Magazine, Consumer.*
Published by: Konrad A. Holtz AG, Gutenbergstr 1, Neudrossenfeld, 95512, Germany. TEL 09203-600-0. Ed. Siegfried Kohl. Circ: 80,000.

305.31 770 USA
EROTIC PHYSIQUE; the photography of body image productions. Text in English. 2000. m. USD 39.95; USD 7.95 newsstand/cover (effective 2001). adv. **Document type:** *Magazine, Consumer.*
Published by: Specialty Productions LLC, Box 4356, Los Angeles, CA 90078-4356. TEL 323-468-1919, http://www.eroticphysique.com.

306.7 GBR ISSN 1477-1594
THE EROTIC REVIEW. Text in English. 1995. q. GBP 25 (effective 2009). adv. illus. **Document type:** *Magazine, Consumer.*
Incorporates (in 2006-2007): SEx (1753-7495); Formerly (until 1997): The Erotic Print Society Review
Published by: Erotic Review Books, 1st Fl., 17 Harwood Rd., London, SW6 4QP, United Kingdom. eps@leadline.co.uk. Circ: 30,000. **Subscr. to:** E R Books, 54 New St., Worcester WR1 2DL, United Kingdom. TEL 44-871-7110134, 800-026-2524, FAX 44-871-5750080, leadline@eroticprints.org.

EROTICA READERS AND WRITERS ASSOCIATION. *see* LITERATURE

808.803538 USA ISSN 1947-5330
▼ **EROTIQUE.** Text in English. 2009. 3/yr. USD 20 (effective 2009). **Document type:** *Journal, Consumer.* **Description:** Features erotic short stores and literature.
Published by: Wapshott Press, PO Box 31513, Los Angeles, CA 90031-0513. TEL 323-226-4979, editor@wapshottpress.com.

052 GBR ISSN 0952-6706
ESCORT. Text in English. 1980. m. GBP 32; GBP 1.90 newsstand/cover (effective 2001). adv. **Document type:** *Magazine, Consumer.*
Published by: Paul Raymond Publications Ltd., 2 Archer St, London, W1V 8JJ, United Kingdom. TEL 44-20-72928000. Ed. James Hundleby. Adv. contact Nicola Swift. **Dist. by:** Comag, Tavistock Rd, W Drayton, Middlesex UB7 7QE, United Kingdom. TEL 44-1895-444055, FAX 44-1895-433602.

306.77 GBR ISSN 1748-7919
ESCORT SWINGMAG.CO.UK. Variant title: Swingmag.co.uk. Text in English. 2005. m. **Document type:** *Magazine, Consumer.*
Related titles: Online - full text ed.
Published by: Paul Raymond Publications Ltd., 2 Archer St, London, W1V 8JJ, United Kingdom. TEL 44-20-72928000, FAX 44-20-72928021.

051 USA ISSN 0194-9535
AP2
ESQUIRE. Text in English. 1933. m. USD 8 (effective 2010); USD 3.99 newsstand/cover (effective 2008). adv. bk.rev.; film rev.; rec.rev. illus. back issues avail.; reprints avail. **Document type:** *Magazine, Consumer.* **Description:** Provides intellectually curious and socially aware men with information on diverse topics from politics and health to fashion and the arts.
Former titles (until 1979): Esquire Fortnightly (0884-5220); (until 1978): Esquire (0014-0791)
Related titles: Microform ed.: (from PQC); Online - full text ed.
Indexed: A01, A02, A03, A08, A11, A22, A25, A26, AES, AcaI, B04, B14, BEL&L, BRD, BRI, C05, C12, CBRI, CLFP, CPerI, E08, F01, F02, G05, G06, G07, G08, G09, HlthInd, I05, I07, M01, M02, M06, MASUSE, MLA-IB, MRD, MagInd, P02, P10, P13, P30, P48, P53, P54, PMR, PQC, R03, R04, R06, RGAb, RGPR, RILM, S08, S09, T02, U01, W03.
—BLDSC (3811.662500), CIS, IE, Infotrieve, Ingenta.
Published by: Hearst Magazines (Subsidiary of: Hearst Corporation), 300 W 57th St, 12th Fl, New York, NY 10019. TEL 212-649-4468, FAX 646-280-1069, HearstMagazines@hearst.com, http://www.hearstcorp.com/magazines/. Ed. David Granger. Pub. Kevin O'Malley. adv.: color page USD 103,960, B&W page USD 69,950; trim 8 x 10.875. Circ: 700,000 (paid).

052 GBR ISSN 0960-5150
ESQUIRE; the sharper read for men. Text in English. 1991. m. GBP 24.99 domestic; GBP 70 in Europe; GBP 75 elsewhere; GBP 4.25 newsstand/cover (effective 2009). adv. **Document type:** *Magazine, Consumer.* **Description:** Covers a diverse range of topics from music to politics, health to fashion, lifestyle tips to inspiring features and beautiful women.
Related titles: Online - full text ed.
—CCC.
Published by: National Magazine Company Ltd., 72 Broadwick St, London, W1F 9EP, United Kingdom. TEL 44-20-74395601, FAX 44-20-7439675, Jane.wynyard@natmags.co.uk. Ed. Jeremy Langmead. Pub. Maria Parviz. Adv. contact Darren Singh. Circ: 52,705. **Subscr. to:** Quality Magazines, Tower House, Sovereign Park, Market Harborough, Leicestershire LE16 9EF, United Kingdom. TEL 44-1858-438844, qualitymagazines@subscription.co.uk, http://www.qualitymagazines.co.uk/. **Dist. by:** Comag, Tavistock Rd, W Drayton, Middlesex UB7 7QE, United Kingdom. TEL 44-1895-433600, FAX 44-1895-433605, hazel.isaacs@comag.co.uk, http://www.comag.co.uk.

056.1 ESP ISSN 1888-1114
ESQUIRE. Text in Spanish. 2007. m. adv. **Document type:** *Magazine, Consumer.*
Published by: Spainmedia Magazines, Almirante 9, 3 izq, Madrid, 28004, Spain. TEL 34-91-2061040, FAX 34-91-2061044, pgil@spain-media.es. Ed. Andres Rodriguez. Adv. contact Carlos Sanchez. page EUR 10,000; trim 200 x 275.

057.86 CZE ISSN 1211-4006
ESQUIRE. Text in Czech. 1996. m. CZK 715 (effective 2009). adv. **Document type:** *Magazine, Consumer.* **Description:** Provides articles and features on items of interest to men including sex, cars, electronics, music and sports.
Published by: Stratosfera s.r.o., Drtinova 8, Prague 5, 150 00, Czech Republic. TEL 420-234-109540, FAX 420-234-109264, online@stratosfera.cz, http://www.stratosfera.cz. Adv. contact Martina Palkoskova. page CZK 213,000; trim 200 x 270. Circ: 21,626 (paid). **Subscr. to:** SEND Predplatne s.r.o., PO Box 141, Prague 4 140 21, Czech Republic. TEL 420-225-985225, FAX 420-225-341425, send@send.cz.

059.9435 TUR ISSN 1300-8099
ESQUIRE. Text in Turkish. 1993. m. USD 20 (effective 2009). **Document type:** *Magazine, Consumer.*
Published by: Merkez Dergi/Merkez Magazine Group, Teyfik Mah., 20 Temmuz Cad., No. 24, Sefakoy, Istanbul, 34295, Turkey. TEL 90-212-4112000, 90-212-4112000, FAX 90-212-3543884.

305.31 053.931 NLD ISSN 0926-8901
ESQUIRE. Text in Dutch. 1991. 8/yr. EUR 36.95; EUR 5.45 newsstand/cover (effective 2009). adv. **Document type:** *Magazine, Consumer.*
Published by: Esquire Media BV, Postbus 93616, Amsterdam, 1090 EC, Netherlands. TEL 31-20-6391996. Ed. Arno Kantelberg. adv.: page EUR 4,750; trim 213 x 275. Circ: 30,792.

646.32 HKG ISSN 1727-5237
ESQUIRE/JUNZI ZAZHI. Text in Chinese. 1988. m. HKD 384 domestic; HKD 1,704 in Southeast Asia; HKD 1,920 elsewhere (effective 2010). adv. **Document type:** *Magazine, Consumer.*
Related titles: Online - full text ed.
Published by: South China Media Limited/Nan-Hua Chuanmei, 3/F., Wah Shing Centre, 5 Fung Yip St., Chai Wan, Hong Kong. TEL 852-2202-5000, FAX 852-2963-0529.

646.32 USA ISSN 1949-6486
TT570
▼ **ESSENTIAL HOMME**; men's style guide. Text in English. 2010. bi-m. USD 14.95 domestic; USD 29.95 foreign; USD 4.99 per issue domestic; USD 5.99 per issue in Canada (effective 2011). adv. back issues avail. **Document type:** *Magazine, Consumer.*
Related titles: Online - full text ed.: ISSN 1949-6494.
Published by: Essential Publications, U.S. Llc, 30 E 37th St, Ste 4B, New York, NY 10016. TEL 646-833-7904, FAX 646-833-7904. Ed. Terry Lu. Pub., Adv. contact Algis Puidokas.

058.81 DNK ISSN 0906-9690
HQ1090.7.D4
EUROMAN. Text in Danish. 1992. m. DKK 387 (effective 2011). adv. **Document type:** *Magazine, Consumer.*
Related titles: Online - full text ed.
Published by: Euroman Publications A/S, Hellerupvej 51, Hellerup, 2900, Denmark. TEL 45-39-457770, FAX 45-39-457780, info@euroman.dk. Circ: 26,482 (controlled).

059.956 JPN
EVENING. Text in Japanese. m. **Document type:** *Magazine, Consumer.*
Published by: Kodansha Ltd., 2-12-21 Otowa, Bunkyo-ku, Tokyo, 112-8001, Japan. TEL 81-3-3946-6201, FAX 81-3-3944-9915, http://www.kodansha.co.jp.

305.31 USA
EVERYTHING FOR MEN. Text in English. 2006 (Jul.). m. USD 36; USD 5 newsstand/cover (effective 2006). **Document type:** *Magazine, Consumer.* **Description:** Covers autos, home, health, travel, online, money, fashion, sports, and entertainment.
Published by: Epic Media Inc., 2049 Century Park E., Ste. 1920, Century City, CA 90067. TEL 310-691-8800, FAX 310-277-4778, http://epicmediainc.com/. Ed. Rob Hill. Circ: 250,000.

EXERCISE FOR MEN ONLY. *see* PHYSICAL FITNESS AND HYGIENE

305.31 USA
EXOTIC MAGAZINE. Text in English. 1993. m. **Document type:** *Magazine, Consumer.*
Published by: X Publishing, 818 SW 3d Ave, No 1324, Portland, OR 97204. TEL 503-241-4317, FAX 503-241-7239, xmag@uswest.net. Ed. Jim Goad. Pub. Frank Faillace. Circ: 120,000.

779.28 CZE ISSN 1211-4480
EXTAZE. Text in Czech. 1991. m. CZK 888; CZK 74 newsstand/cover (effective 2009). **Document type:** *Magazine, Consumer.*
Published by: PK 62, a.s., Bohdalecka 6, Prague 10, 101 00, Czech Republic. TEL 420-281-090611, FAX 420-281-090622, pk62@pk62.cz, http://www.pk62.cz. Ed. Milan Kolar.

EZERMESTER 2000. *see* HOW-TO AND DO-IT-YOURSELF

052 AUS ISSN 1440-3358
F H M (AUSTRALIA). (For Him Magazine) Text in English. 1998. m. AUD 60; AUD 8.50 newsstand/cover (effective 2009). adv. **Document type:** *Magazine, Consumer.* **Description:** Contains a variety of articles, photos and features on girls, music, sports, gadgets and all the best things in life.
Published by: A C P Magazines Ltd. (Subsidiary of: P B L Media Pty Ltd.), 54-58 Park St, Sydney, NSW 2000, Australia. TEL 61-2-92828000, FAX 61-2-91263769. Ed. Ben Smithurst. Adv. contact Nia Llewelyn. Circ: 51,825 (paid and controlled).

054.1 FRA ISSN 1295-9138
F H M (FRANCE). (For Him Magazine) Text in English. 1999. m. EUR 29.90 (effective 2008). adv. **Document type:** *Magazine, Consumer.* **Description:** Covers lifestyle, entertainment and consumer items of interest to men.
Published by: Mondadori France, 1 Rue du Colonel Pierre-Avia, Paris, Cedex 15 75754, France. TEL 33-1-46484848, contact@mondadori.fr, http://www.mondadori.fr. adv.: page EUR 17,200. Circ: 179,901 (paid and controlled).

070.48 DEU ISSN 1860-0026
F H M (GERMANY). (For Him Magazine) Text in German. 2000. m. EUR 4.50 newsstand/cover (effective 2011). adv. **Document type:** *Magazine, Consumer.* **Description:** Features articles and photos on items of interest to men such as women, cars, electronic gadgets, sports and music.
—CCC.
Published by: All Type Media GmbH, Lyonel-Feiniger-Str 28, Munich, 80807, Germany. TEL 49-89-89057870, FAX 49-89-890578727, info@alltypemedia.de.

059.89 GRC
F H M (GREECE). Text in Greek. 2005. m. adv. **Document type:** *Magazine, Consumer.*
Published by: F H M Greece, 80 Michalakopoulou St, Athens, 115 28, Greece. TEL 30-211-3657400, FAX 30-211-3658004. Ed. Nicholaos Piperis. Adv. contact Nikos Tsouanatos. page EUR 7,100.

059.94511 HUN ISSN 1586-4839
F H M (HUNGARY); for him magazine. (Ferfiak Himek Magazinja) Text in Hungarian. 2000. m. HUF 6,672 (effective 2004). adv. 132 p./no.; **Document type:** *Magazine, Consumer.* **Description:** Covers a wide variety of lifestyle and entertainment items of interest to men.
Published by: Sanoma Budapest Kiadoi Rt. (Subsidiary of: Sanoma Magazines Finland Corporation), Bokor Utca 15-19, Budapest, 1037, Hungary. TEL 36-1-4371100, FAX 36-1-2502303, info@sanomabp.hu, http://www.sanoma.hu. Ed. David Hraschek. Adv. contact Katalin Vadady. page HUF 1,200,000; trim 222 x 297. Circ: 53,695 (paid).

059.99221 IDN
F H M (INDONESIA). Text in Indonesian. 2003. m. adv. **Document type:** *Magazine, Consumer.*
Published by: F H M Indonesia, Jalan Biliton 7C, Jakarta, 10350, Indonesia. TEL 62-21-31908982, FAX 62-21-31907064. Ed. Richard Sam Bera. Adv. contact Winda Nugroho. page USD 1,900. Circ: 50,000 (paid).

059.9193 LVA ISSN 1691-094X
F H M (LATVIA). (For Him Magazine) Text in Latvian. 2003. m. LVL 14.68 (effective 2011). adv. **Document type:** *Magazine, Consumer.*
Published by: Izdevnieciba Lilita SIA, Mukusala Business Centre, Mukusalas Str 41B, Riga, 1004, Latvia. TEL 371-67061600, FAX 371-67616050, izdevnieciba@lilita.lv, http://www.lilita.lv. Ed. Sandris Metuzals. Adv. contact Ilze Ozola. Circ: 15,000 (paid).

059.9192 LTU ISSN 1648-9837
F H M (LITHUANIA). (For Him Magazine) Text in Lithuanian. 2004. m. adv. **Document type:** *Magazine, Consumer.*
Published by: UAB Ieva, Laisves pr 60-600, Vilnius, Lithuania. TEL 37-05-2424677, FAX 37-05-2427127. Ed. Aidas Puklevicius. Pub. Victor Tombak. adv.: page EUR 2,172.

059.992 MYS ISSN 1511-3248
F H M (MALAYSIA EDITION). (For Him Magazine) Text in Malay. 1999. m. **Document type:** *Magazine, Consumer.*
Published by: Emap Malaysia, No 18A Jalan Persiaran, Ste 1101, Menara Yayasan Selangor, Petaling Jaya, 46000, Malaysia. TEL 603-7956-1789, FAX 603-7957-6369, bounty@tm.net.my. Ed. M Zulkifli. Pub. Bryan Chew. Circ: 13,737 (paid).

056.1 MEX
F H M (MEXICO). (For Him Magazine) Text in Spanish. 2003. m. adv. **Document type:** *Magazine, Consumer.*
Published by: Grupo Editorial Premiere, Horacio no 804, Colonia Polanco, Mexico DF, 11550, Mexico. TEL 52-55-11011300, FAX 52-55-55528051, reginasb@gepremiere.com, http://www.gepremiere.com. Ed. Jorge Arias. Pub. Eduardo Scheffler. adv.: page USD 5,347. Circ: 55,000 (paid and controlled).

053.931 NLD ISSN 1568-184X
F H M (NETHERLANDS). (For Him Magazine) Text in Dutch. 2003. 10/yr. EUR 45; EUR 5.10 newsstand/cover (effective 2009). adv. **Document type:** *Magazine, Consumer.*
Published by: De Telegraaf Tijdschriftengroep, Postbus 127, Amsterdam, 1000 AC, Netherlands. TEL 31-20-5853279, FAX 31-20-5853176, ttg@telegraaf.nl, http://www.ttg.nl. Eds. Eelko Rol, Robert van den Ham. adv.: page EUR 4,591; trim 222 x 300. Circ: 50,140 (paid and controlled).

058.82 NOR ISSN 1504-0100
F H M (NORWAY). (For Him Magazine) Text in Norwegian. 2004. m. adv. **Document type:** *Magazine, Consumer.*
Published by: Bonnier Publications International AS (Subsidiary of: Bonnier Publications AS), Kirkegata 20, PO Box 433, Sentrum, Oslo, 0103, Norway. TEL 47-22-401200, FAX 47-22-401201. Ed. Stig Jokobsen. Pub. Per Juul. Adv. contact Patrik Ekblom. page NOK 37,500.

052 PHL
F H M (PHILIPPINES). (For Him Magazine) Text in English. 2000. m. PHP 1,275 (effective 2005). adv. **Document type:** *Magazine, Consumer.*
Published by: Summit Media, Level 1, Robinsons Galleria, Ortigas Ave, Quezon City, 1100, Philippines. TEL 63-2-6317738, FAX 63-2-6372206. Ed. Allan Madrilejos. Pub. Denis del Callar. Adv. contact Maiza Mueco. page PHP 106,000. Circ: 130,000 (paid and controlled).

056.9 PRT
F H M (PORTUGAL). (For Him Magazine) Text in Portuguese. 2005. m. EUR 28.84; EUR 3 newsstand/cover (effective 2007). adv. **Document type:** *Magazine, Consumer.*
Published by: Edimpresa Editora Lda., Rua Calvet de Magalhaes 242, Laveiras, Paco de Arcos, 2770-022, Portugal. TEL 351-21-4698000, FAX 351-21-4698501, edimpresa@edimpresa.pt, http://www.edimpresa.pt. Ed. Pedro Mendes. Pub. Goncalo Fonseca. Adv. contact Hugo Rodrigues. page EUR 5,050; trim 220 x 297. Circ: 55,884 (paid).

055.91 ROM ISSN 1583-6517
F H M (ROMANIA). (For Him Magazine) Text in Romanian. 2000. m. ROL 55 (effective 2005). adv. **Document type:** *Magazine, Consumer.* **Description:** Features articles and photos on items of interest to men such as women, cars, electronic gadgets, sports and music.
Published by: Sanoma - Hearst Romania srl, Str Argentina nr 41, sect 1, Bucharest, Romania. TEL 40-21-2307921, FAX 40-21-2305585, office@sanomahearst.ro. Ed. Istvan Lorincz. Pub. Radu Potolea. Adv. contact Cezar Burlan. page EUR 4,600. Circ: 29,537 (paid and controlled).

305.3 RUS
F H M (RUSSIA). (For Him Magazine) Text in Russian. m. adv. **Document type:** *Magazine, Consumer.*
Published by: Independent Media (Moscow), 3 Polkovaya Ul, Bldg 1, Moscow, 127018, Russian Federation. TEL 7-095-2323200, FAX 7-095-2321761, podpiska@imedia.ru, http://www.independent-media.ru. Ed. Dmitri Gubin. Adv. contact Elena Buryakova. page USD 8,600.

052 SGP
F H M (SINGAPORE). (For Him Magazine) Text in English. 1998. m. SGD 72 domestic; SGD 100 Malaysia & Brunei; SGD 190 ASEAN countries; SGD 240 elsewhere (effective 2005). adv. **Document type:** *Magazine, Consumer.*

Published by: MediaCorp Publishing, Caldecott Broadcast Centre, Andrew Road, Singapore, 299939, Singapore. TEL 65-64837118, FAX 65-64812098, subhelp@mediacorppub.com.sg, http://corporate.mediacorpsingapore.com/index.htm. Ed. Henry Rimmer. Adv. contact Jean Pham. page SGD 4,950. Circ: 31,918 (paid).

057.84 SVN
F H M (SLOVENIA). (For Him Magazine) Text in Slovenian. 2004. m. EUR 33 (effective 2007). adv. **Document type:** *Magazine, Consumer.*
Published by: VideoToP d.o.o., Trg Revolucije 2, Maribor, 2000, Slovenia. TEL 386-2-3303300, FAX 386-2-3303311, http://www.videotop.si. Circ: 15,000 (paid).

052 ZAF ISSN 1562-4692
F H M (SOUTH AFRICA). Text in English. 1999. m. adv. **Document type:** *Magazine, Consumer.*
Published by: National Magazines (Subsidiary of: National Media Ltd.), PO Box 1802, Cape Town, 8000, South Africa. Ed. Neil Bierbaum TEL 27-11-3220863. adv.: color page ZAR 21,656. Circ: 58,525.

056.1 ESP
F H M (SPAIN). (For Him Magazine) Text in Spanish. 2004. m. EUR 15.52 (effective 2009). adv. **Document type:** *Magazine, Consumer.*
Published by: Focus Ediciones SL (Subsidiary of: Edipresse Publications SA), Paseo de la Castellana 129, 1o, Madrid, 28046, Spain. TEL 34-91-5973090, FAX 34-91-5972326, camado@focusediciones.com. Ed. Miguel Villamizar. Pub. Isabel Suarez. adv.: page EUR 9,400. Circ: 603,300.

059.951 TWN ISSN 1606-6995
F H M (TAIWAN). (For Him Magazine) Text in Chinese. 2000. m. adv. **Document type:** *Magazine, Consumer.*
Published by: F H M Taiwan Publishing Ltd., Ruei Guang Rd, Ln 188, N 51, 1st Fl, Taipei, Taiwan. TEL 886-2-27971911, FAX 886-2-26964935. Ed. Han Ku. adv.: page TWD 2,941. Circ: 10,000 (paid).

059.95911 THA ISSN 0859-2527
F H M (THAILAND). (For Him Magazine) Text in Thai. 1995. m. THB 100 newsstand/cover (effective 2010). adv. **Document type:** *Magazine, Consumer.*
Published by: Inspire Entertainment Co., 115-66 Moo 12, Soi Ramintra 40, Ramintra Rd, Klong-kum, Bung-kum, Bangkok, 10230, Thailand. TEL 662-508-8100, FAX 662-693-3287, contact@inspire.co.th, http://www.inspire.co.th. Adv. contact Amara Thitithamraksa. Circ: 150,000 (paid).

059.9435 TUR
F H M (TURKEY). (For Him Magazine) Text in Turkish. m. TRY 72 (effective 2009). adv. **Document type:** *Magazine, Consumer.*
Published by: Ciner Gazete Dergi Basim Yayincilik San. ve Tic. A.S., Abdulhakhamit Cad. No.25, Beyoglu / Istanbul, Turkey. TEL 90-216-5546600, cagrimerkezi@cinerabone.com. adv.: page TRY 12,100. Circ: 22,000 (paid and controlled).

305.3 UKR
F H M (UKRAINE). Text in Russian. 2002. m. UAK 10 newsstand/cover (effective 2005). **Document type:** *Magazine, Consumer.*
Published by: Independent Media (Ukraine) (Subsidiary of: Independent Media (Moscow)), vul Pimonenko 13, korp 6a, 3 etazh, Kyiv, 04050, Ukraine. TEL 380-44-2386048, FAX 380-44-2386049. Ed. Timur Dorofeev. Circ: 30,000.

070.48 GBR ISSN 0966-0933
HQ1088
F H M (UNITED KINGDOM). (For Him Magazine) Text in English. 1985. m. GBP 35 domestic; GBP 60 foreign; GBP 3.99 newsstand/cover (effective 2009). adv. bk.rev. illus. back issues avail.; reprints avail. **Document type:** *Magazine, Consumer.* **Description:** Contains stunning pictures of stars, witty articles on sports, travel, relationships, and fashion for the image-conscious man.
Formerly (until 1992): For Him Magazine (0958-0980)
Related titles: Online - full text ed.
—CCC.
Published by: H. Bauer Publishing Ltd. (Subsidiary of: Bauer Media Group), Mappin House, 4 Winsley St, London, W1W 8HF, United Kingdom. TEL 44-20-74361515, FAX 44-20-71828021, http://www.bauer.co.uk. Ed. Sarah Ketterer TEL 44-20-71828028. Adv. contact Liz Jazayeri TEL 44-20-72955384. page GBP 21,000.
Subscr. to: Tower House, Sovereign Park, Market Harborough, Leicestershire LE16 9EF, United Kingdom. TEL 44-1858-438866, subs@greatmagazines.co.uk.

F H M COLLECTIONS. (For Him Magazine) *see* CLOTHING TRADE—Fashions

052 GBR
F Q; the essential dad mag. (Father's Quarterly) Text in English. 2003. bi-m. GBP 16.99; GBP 2.99 newsstand/cover (effective 2009). adv. back issues avail. **Document type:** *Magazine, Consumer.* **Description:** Designed to revolutionise the men's lifestyle market by celebrating parenthood and lifestyle changes that come along with it.
Related titles: Online - full text ed.
Published by: 3 Dimensional Media Ltd., Seymour House, S St, Bromley, Kent, BR1 1RH, United Kingdom. TEL 44-20-84606060, FAX 44-20-84606050, contactus@fqmagazine.co.uk, http://www.3dmg.com/.

808 USA
FAMILY AFFAIRS. Text in English. 1980. m. USD 43.97. adv. back issues avail. **Document type:** *Magazine, Consumer.* **Description:** Erotic literature.
Published by: Letters, Magazine, Inc., 310 Cedar Lane, Box 1314, Teaneck, NJ 07666. TEL 201-836-9177, FAX 201-836-5055. Eds. Jackie Lewis, Lisa Rosen. Pub. Louis Rosen. Adv. contact Allison Reynolds. Circ: 80,000.

363.4 USA
FAMILY HEAT. Text in English. bi-m. USD 21.95.
Published by: Mountainside Press, Inc., 462 Broadway, Ste 4000, New York, NY 10013. TEL 212-966-8400. **Dist. by:** Curtis Circulation Co., 730 River Rd, New Milford, NJ 07646.

051 USA
FAMILY LETTERS. Text in English. m. USD 43.97. adv. **Document type:** *Newsletter, Consumer.*
Published by: Piccolo Publications, Inc., 310 Cedar Lane, Teaneck, NJ 07666. TEL 201-836-9177, FAX 201-836-5055. Eds. Jackie Lewis, Lisa Rosen. Pub. Louis Rosen. Adv. contact Allison Reynolds.

779.28 CZE ISSN 1211-4499
FANTASTIC. Text in Czech. 1991. bi-m. CZK 316 (effective 2009). **Document type:** *Magazine, Consumer.*
Published by: PK 62, a.s., Bohdalecka 6, Prague 10, 101 00, Czech Republic. TEL 420-281-090611, FAX 420-281-090622, pk62@pk62.cz, http://www.pk62.cz. Ed. Milan Kolar.

646.32 NLD ISSN 1574-8979
FANTASTIC MAN. Text in English. 2005. s-a. EUR 20 in Europe; EUR 37 elsewhere (effective 2009). **Document type:** *Magazine, Consumer.*
Published by: Fantastic Man Magazine, Kleine-Gartmanplantsoen 21, Amsterdam, 1017 RP, Netherlands. TEL 31-20-3209032, FAX 31-842-248511, office@fantasticman.com. Eds. Gert Jonkers, Jop van Bennekom.

059.927 LBN
AL-FARES. Text in Arabic. m. LBP 50,000 domestic; USD 150 in US & Canada (effective 2003). adv. illus. 200 p./no.; **Document type:** *Magazine, Consumer.* **Description:** Covers men's interests.
Published by: Dar As-Sayad S.A.L., C/o Said Freiha, Hazmieh, P O Box 1038, Beirut, Lebanon. TEL 961-5-456373, FAX 961-5-452700, contactpr@csi.com, alanwar@alanwar.com, http://www.alanwar.com. Adv. contact Said Freiha. Circ: 68,400.

FATHERING MAGAZINE; the online magazine for men with families. *see* CHILDREN AND YOUTH—About

649 306.8742 USA ISSN 1941-594X
FATHERS PERSPECTIVE. Text in English. 2008. bi-m. USD 16.95 domestic; USD 34.95 foreign (effective 2008). **Document type:** *Magazine, Consumer.*
Related titles: Online - full text ed.: ISSN 1941-5958.
Published by: Dream Publishing, 11523 Edgewater Dr, Cleveland, OH 44102. TEL 216-272-2958. Pub. Gregory Johnson.

305.31 NLD ISSN 1873-3174
FELDERHOF. Text in Dutch. 2006. bi-m. EUR 28.50; EUR 5.25 newsstand/cover (effective 2009). adv. **Document type:** *Magazine, Consumer.*
Published by: Sanoma Uitgevers B.V., Postbus 1900, Hoofddorp, 2130 JH, Netherlands. TEL 31-23-5566770, FAX 31-23-5565376, corporatecommunications@sanomamedia.nl, http://www.sanomamedia.nl. Eds. Marjolein Westerterp, Rik Felderhof. Pub. Sandra Dol. adv.: color page EUR 6,750; trim 230 x 297. Circ: 90,000.

FEMME FATALES; revealing the sexy sirens of film, TV, music & the web. *see* MOTION PICTURES

305.31 USA
FEMME MIRROR. Text in English. 1976. q. USD 36 (effective 2004). adv. bk.rev. **Document type:** *Newsletter.* **Description:** Contains information of interest to heterosexual transvestites and cross-dressers.
Published by: Tri Ess, PO Box 194, Tulare, CA 93275. TEL 713-349-8969. Ed., R&P, Adv. contact Jane Ellen Fairfax. Circ: 1,400.

779.28 FRA ISSN 1959-5484
FEMMES MURES FRUSTREES. Text in French. 2008. irreg. **Document type:** *Magazine, Consumer.*
Published by: C B Media Groupe, 23 Rue Richer, Paris, 75009, France.

059.956 JPN
FENEK. Text in Japanese. m. **Document type:** *Magazine, Consumer.*
Published by: Kodansha Ltd., 2-12-21 Otowa, Bunkyo-ku, Tokyo, 112-8001, Japan. TEL 81-3-3946-6201, FAX 81-3-3944-9915, http://www.kodansha.co.jp.

059.951 CHN ISSN 1673-3789
FENGDU/MAXIM YOUR LIFE. Text in Chinese. 2005. m.
Published by: Beijing Review Publishing Co., 24 Baiwanzhuang Rd, Beijing, 100037, China.

363.4 USA
FETISH LETTERS. Text in English. bi-m. USD 21.95.
Published by: Domino Press, Inc. (Subsidiary of: Mavety Media Group), 462 Broadway, Ste 4000, New York, NY 10013. TEL 212-966-8400. **Dist. by:** Curtis Circulation Co., 730 River Rd, New Milford, NJ 07646.

058.7 SWE ISSN 0283-0647
FIB-AKTUELLT. Text in Swedish. 1962. m. SEK 54.50 per issue (effective 2005). **Document type:** *Consumer.*
Supersedes in part (1983-1985): Stopp, F I B Aktuellt (0281-2118)
Published by: Baltic Press AB, PO Box 4035, Solna, Stockholm, 17104, Sweden. TEL 46-8-7996309.

052 GBR ISSN 0265-1270
FIESTA. Text in English. 1965. m. GBP 26.95; GBP 2.25 newsstand/cover (effective 1999). adv. bk.rev. **Document type:** *Magazine, Consumer.* **Description:** Features erotic nude photography with accompanying features.
Related titles: Online - full text ed.
Published by: Galaxy Publications Ltd., PO Box 312, Galaxy Publications Ltd, Witham, Essex CM8 3SZ, United Kingdom. FAX 44-1376-534536. Ed. Ross Gilfillan. Adv. contact Corrine Franklin. Circ: 170,813. **Dist. by:** Blackhorse Distribution Ltd., Blackhorse Distribution Ltd, Freebourne Rd, PO Box 1124, Witham, Essex CM8 3XJ, United Kingdom. TEL 44-1376-501919, FAX 44-1376-501990.

779.28 GBR ISSN 1358-7617
FIESTA BLACK LABEL. Text in English. 1995. bi-m. GBP 3.95 newsstand/cover. adv. **Document type:** *Magazine, Consumer.* **Description:** Presents hot and heavy erotic photos of nude women in action.
Published by: Galaxy Publications Ltd., PO Box 312, Galaxy Publications Ltd, Witham, Essex CM8 3SZ, United Kingdom. TEL 44-1376-534500, FAX 44-1376-534536. Ed. Ross Gilfillan. **Dist. by:** Blackhorse Distribution Ltd., Blackhorse Distribution Ltd, Freebourne Rd, PO Box 1124, Witham, Essex CM8 3XJ, United Kingdom. TEL 44-1376-534530, FAX 44-1376-534531.

779.28 GBR ISSN 0956-4357
FIESTA READERS' LETTERS. Text in English. 198?. s-a. GBP 3.95 newsstand/cover. adv. **Document type:** *Magazine, Consumer.* **Description:** Contains erotic letters and photos.
Published by: Galaxy Publications Ltd., PO Box 312, Galaxy Publications Ltd, Witham, Essex CM8 3SZ, United Kingdom. TEL 44-1376-534500, FAX 44-1376-534536. **Dist. by:** Blackhorse Distribution Ltd., Blackhorse Distribution Ltd, Freebourne Rd, PO Box 1124, Witham, Essex CM8 3XJ, United Kingdom. TEL 44-1376-534530, FAX 44-1376-534531.

779.28 GBR ISSN 0955-9310
FIESTA READERS' WIVES. Text in English. 198?. s-a. GBP 3.25 newsstand/cover. adv. **Document type:** *Magazine, Consumer.* **Description:** Presents ordinary housewives in a variety of erotic nude and rude poses.
Published by: Galaxy Publications Ltd., PO Box 312, Galaxy Publications Ltd, Witham, Essex CM8 3SZ, United Kingdom. TEL 44-1376-534500, FAX 44-1376-534536. **Dist. by:** Blackhorse Distribution Ltd., Blackhorse Distribution Ltd, Freebourne Rd, PO Box 1124, Witham, Essex CM8 3XJ, United Kingdom. TEL 44-1376-534530, FAX 44-1376-534531.

052 ZAF ISSN 1022-3088
FIRST BITE; the adults' choice. Text in English. 1993. bi-m. ZAR 24; ZAR 5.20 newsstand/cover. illus. **Document type:** *Magazine, Consumer.*
Published by: Viclen Promotions, PO Box 354, Mondeor, Gauteng 2110, South Africa.

779.28 USA ISSN 1948-948X
▼ **FLAVA GIRL MAGAZINE.** Text in English. 2009. q. USD 20 (effective 2009). **Document type:** *Magazine, Consumer.* **Description:** Features models of all nationalities.
Published by: Cassandra Lewis, Ed. & Pub., PO Box 352, Groveland, FL 34736. TEL 407-401-5215, flavagirlmagazine@yahoo.com.

779.28 CZE ISSN 1211-4510
FLIRT. Text in Czech. 1994. m. CZK 358.80; CZK 29.90 newsstand/cover (effective 2009). adv. **Document type:** *Magazine, Consumer.*
Published by: PK 62, a.s., Bohdalecka 6, Prague 10, 101 00, Czech Republic. TEL 420-281-090611, FAX 420-281-090622, pk62@pk62.cz, http://www.pk62.cz. Ed. David Dvorak.

305.31 SVK ISSN 1337-8880
FOR MEN. Text in Slovak. 2008. m. EUR 33 (effective 2011). adv. **Document type:** *Magazine, Consumer.*
Published by: Versa Media, s.r.o., Dohnanyho 16, Bratislava, 82108, Slovakia. TEL 421-2-50200911, FAX 421-2-50200934, pozdena@versamedia.sk. Ed. Rene Decastelo. Adv. contact Stanislav Hruby.

305.3 ITA ISSN 1722-6104
FOR MEN MAGAZINE. Text in Italian. 2003. m. EUR 15 domestic; EUR 43 foreign (effective 2008). **Document type:** *Magazine, Consumer.*
Published by: Cairo Editore (Subsidiary of: Cairo Communication SpA), Via Tucidide 56, Torre 3, Milan, 20134, Italy. TEL 39-02-748111, FAX 39-02-70100102, info@cairocommunication.it, http://www.cairocommunication.it. Ed. Andrea Biavardi.

306.705 GBR ISSN 1746-7527
FOREPLAY. Text in English. 2005. m. **Document type:** *Magazine, Consumer.*
Published by: Paul Raymond Publications Ltd., 2 Archer St, London, W1V 8JJ, United Kingdom. TEL 44-20-72928000, FAX 44-20-72928021, menonly@pr-org.co.uk.

FORMALWORDS. *see* CLOTHING TRADE—Fashions

305.31 CZE ISSN 1801-7355
FORMEN. Text in Czech. 2006. m. CZK 990 (effective 2011). adv. **Document type:** *Magazine, Consumer.*
Published by: Mlada Fronta, Mezi Vodami 1952/9, Prague 4, 14300, Czech Republic. TEL 420-2-25276201, FAX 420-2-25276222, online@mf.cz. Ed. Rene Decastelo. Adv. contact Tatiana Keriova.

052 GBR ISSN 0015-833X
FORUM (LONDON, 1967); the international journal of human relations. Text in English. 1967. m. GBP 36 domestic (effective 2009). adv. bk.rev. illus. index. **Document type:** *Magazine, Consumer.*
Indexed: CPerI, E-psyche, RASB.
Published by: Trojan Publishing Ltd., 3rd Fl, 207 Old St, London, EC1V 9NR, United Kingdom. TEL 44-20-76086300, FAX 44-20-76086320, info@trojanpublishing.co.uk, http://www.trojanpublishing.co.uk/. Ed. Elizabeth Coldwell. Adv. contact Louise McMahon TEL 44-20-76086360. B&W page GBP 2,050, color page GBP 2,250; trim 148 x 210. Circ: 40,000 (paid).

051 USA
FORUM SPECIALS. Text in English. q. USD 5 newsstand/cover. **Document type:** *Magazine, Consumer.*
Published by: General Media Communications, Inc. (Subsidiary of: FriendFinder Networks Inc.), 6800 Broken Sound Pkwy, Ste 100, Boca Raton, FL 33487. TEL 561-912-7000, FAX 561-912-7038, info@ffn.com, http://www.ffn.com. Ed. Kathy Cavanaugh.

051 USA ISSN 1041-9470
FOX MAGAZINE. Text in English. 1984. 13/yr. USD 29.95; USD 8.99 per issue (effective 2009). adv. bk.rev.; film rev. illus. **Document type:** *Magazine, Consumer.*
Published by: Magna Publishing, 210 Rte 4 E, Ste 211, Paramus, NJ 07652. TEL 201-843-4004, FAX 201-843-8775, http://www.magnapublishing.com. Adv. contact Martin Puntus TEL 201-843-4004 ext 113. page USD 1,500; trim 7.875 x 10.875.

646.32 ITA ISSN 1721-2545
FOX UOMO; il mensile a 360 gradi per l'uomo che cambia. Text in Italian. 2002. m. adv. **Document type:** *Magazine, Consumer.* **Description:** Fashion, health, body care, tips to be successful in life and with women.
Published by: Uniline Srl (Subsidiary of: Casa Editrice Universo SpA), Corso di Porta Nuova 3A, Milan, 20121, Italy. TEL 39-02-636751, FAX 39-02-252007333. Circ: 425,000.

053.1 DEU
FREITAG (BADEN-BADEN); die Monatszeitschrift fuer freie Tage. Text in German. 1975. s-m. adv.
Published by: Sonnenverlag GmbH, Lichtentaler Allee 10, Baden-Baden, 76530, Germany. Ed. Helmut Eilers.

052 GBR ISSN 1464-4053
FRONT. Text in English. 1998. m. GBP 36; GBP 3 newsstand/cover (effective 2002). **Document type:** *Magazine, Consumer.* **Description:** Lifestyle and entertainment features and articles geared towards young males and their interests.
Published by: Cabal Communications Ltd., 374 Euston Rd, London, NW1 3BL, United Kingdom. TEL 44-20-75545700, FAX 44-20-73873330, http://uk.sireh.com/c/1/cabal_communications_ltd_london/. **Dist. by:** Comag, Tavistock Rd, W Drayton, Middlesex UB7 7QE, United Kingdom. TEL 44-1895-433676, FAX 44-1895-433602.

779.28 CHE ISSN 1422-7762
FULLSIZE. Text in German. 1995. bi-m. CHF 20, EUR 14 (effective 2002). adv. **Document type:** *Magazine, Consumer.* **Description:** Filled with nude and erotic photos of full figured women.
Published by: Fullsize Neue Medien, Postfach 120, Wallbach, 4323, Switzerland.

FUTURE SEX. *see* SINGLES' INTERESTS AND LIFESTYLES

305.3 646.32 ROM
G Q. Text in Romanian. 2008. m. adv. **Document type:** *Magazine, Consumer.*
Published by: Liberis Publications Romania SRL, Maria Rosetti St, 49 A, sector 2, Bucharest, 020482, Romania. TEL 40-316-900611, FAX 40-316-900615, office@liberis.ro. Ed. Dragos Placinta. Adv. contact Alex Tudose.

305.3 646.32 GBR ISSN 0954-8750
TT570
G Q (BRITISH EDITION). (Gentlemen's Quarterly) Text in English. 1988. m. GBP 47.40 domestic; GBP 80 in Europe; GBP 79 in United States; GBP 119 newsstand/cover elsewhere (effective 2010). adv. illus. back issues avail. **Document type:** *Magazine, Consumer.* **Description:** Where men turn to when they're thinking about food, fashion, sports and women.
Related titles: ◆ Supplement(s): G Q Style. ISSN 1748-2895.
Indexed: SCOPUS.
—CCC.
Published by: Conde Nast Publications Ltd. (Subsidiary of: Advance Publications, Inc.), Vogue House, Hanover Sq, London, W1S 1JU, United Kingdom. TEL 44-20-74999080, FAX 44-20-74951102, newbusiness@condenast.co.uk, http://www.condenast.co.uk. Ed. Dylan Jones.

305.3 646.32 FRA ISSN 1959-7800
G Q (FRENCH EDITION). (Gentlemen's Quarterly) Text in French. 2008. m. EUR 19.95; EUR 3.40 newsstand/cover (effective 2011). adv. **Document type:** *Magazine, Consumer.*
Published by: Publications Conde Nast S.A., 56 A rue du Faubourg Saint-Honore, Paris, 75008, France. TEL 33-1-53436000, FAX 33-1-53436060.

G Q (LISBON). (Gentlemen's Quarterly) *see* CLOTHING TRADE—Fashions

305.3 646.32 ITA ISSN 1129-3780
G Q (MILANO). (Gentlemen's Quarterly) Text in Italian. 1999. m. EUR 18 (effective 2008). **Document type:** *Magazine, Consumer.*
Published by: Edizioni Conde Nast SpA (Subsidiary of: Arnoldo Mondadori Editore SpA), Piazza Castello 27, Milan, MI 20122, Italy. info@condenet.it, http://www.condenast.it.

303.5 646.32 RUS
G Q (MOSCOW). (Gentlemen's Quarterly) Text in Russian. m. **Document type:** *Magazine, Consumer.*
Published by: Conde Nast Russia, Bolshaya Dmitrovka, 11, Moscow, 101999, Russian Federation. TEL 7-095-745-5565, FAX 7-095-745-5770.

305.3 646.32 DEU ISSN 1434-5560
G Q (MUNICH). (Gentlemen's Quarterly) Text in German. 1984. m. EUR 51; EUR 5 newsstand/cover (effective 2011). adv. film rev. **Document type:** *Magazine, Consumer.* **Description:** Lifestyle and fashion magazine for men.
Formerly (until 1997): Maenner Vogue (0177-7246)
Related titles: ◆ English ed.: G Q (New York). ISSN 0016-6979.
—CCC.
Published by: Conde Nast Verlag GmbH, Karlstr 23, Munich, 80333, Germany. TEL 49-89-381040, FAX 49-89-38104230, empfang@condenast.de, http://www.condenast.de. Pub. Wolfgang Winter. Adv. contact Anja Grewe. Circ: 143,788 (paid).

305.3 646.32 USA ISSN 0016-6979
G Q (NEW YORK); gentlemen's quarterly for men. (Gentlemen's Quarterly) Text in English. 1957. m. USD 10 domestic; USD 20 in Canada; USD 58 elsewhere (effective 2009). adv. bk.rev. illus.; mkt. back issues avail.; reprints avail. **Document type:** *Magazine, Consumer.* **Description:** Covers men's style and culture.
Formerly (until 1983): Gentlemen's Quarterly
Related titles: Microform ed.: (from PQC); Online - full text ed.; ◆ German ed.: G Q (Munich). ISSN 1434-5560.
Indexed: A11, A22, ASIP, B04, BRD, G05, G06, G07, G08, G09, I05, IIFP, M01, M02, MagInd, P02, P10, P53, P54, PQC, R03, RGAb, RGPR, RILM, T02, W03, WBA, WMB.
—Ingenta. **CCC.**
Published by: Conde Nast Publications, Inc. (Subsidiary of: Advance Publications, Inc.), 4 Times Sq, 6th Fl, New York, NY 10036. TEL 212-286-2860, FAX 212-286-6905, http://www.condenast.com. Ed. Jim Nelson. Pub. Peter King Hunsinger TEL 212-286-2788. Adv. contact Michael Mueller TEL 212-286-4762. B&W page USD 78,940, color page USD 118,500; trim 8 x 10.875. Circ: 915,173 (paid).

646.32 305.3 ESP ISSN 1134-6884
G Q (SPANISH EDITION). (Gentlemen's Quarterly) Text in Spanish. 1993. 11/yr. EUR 24.75 (effective 2008). adv. back issues avail. **Document type:** *Magazine, Consumer.*
Related titles: Online - full text ed.
Published by: Conde Nast Espana, C Jenner No. 5, Bajo 1, Madrid, 28010, Spain. TEL 34-607-8011715, contacta@condenet.es, http://www.condenet.es. Ed. Natalia Gamero.

305.3 646.32 AUS ISSN 1440-7795
G Q AUSTRALIA. (Gentlemen's Quarterly) Text in English. 1998. m. AUD 39.95 domestic; AUD 60 in New Zealand; AUD 82.50 elsewhere; AUD 8.95 per issue domestic; AUD 9.90 per issue in New Zealand (effective 2008). adv. back issues avail. **Document type:** *Magazine, Consumer.* **Description:** Features grooming tips, fashion details, gritty local stories and celebrity interviews, as well as the latest technology and music reviews to help keep men in the know.
Published by: News Magazines Pty Ltd., 180 Bourke Rd, Alexandria, NSW 2015, Australia. TEL 61-2-93536666, FAX 61-2-93530935, subscriptions@newsmagazines.com.au, http://www.newsspace.com.au/magazines. Ed. Grant Peace. Adv. contact Dennis Michael TEL 61-2-80622928. color page AUD 7,950; trim 220 x 297.

G Q STYLE. (Gentlemen's Quarterly) *see* CLOTHING TRADE—Fashions

746.92 DEU ISSN 1610-4315
G Q STYLE. (Gentlemen's Quarterly) Text in German. 2002. 2/yr. EUR 6.80 newsstand/cover (effective 2011). adv. **Document type:** *Magazine, Consumer.*
Published by: Conde Nast Verlag GmbH, Karlstr 23, Munich, 80333, Germany. TEL 49-89-381040, FAX 49-89-38104230, empfang@condenast.de, http://www.condenast.de. Pub. Wolfgang Winter. Adv. contact Anja Grewe. Circ: 90,000 (paid and controlled).

646.32 AUS ISSN 1838-8426
▼ **G Q STYLE AUSTRALIA.** Text in English. 2011. s-a. includes with subscr. to G Q Australia. **Document type:** *Magazine, Trade.* **Description:** For fashion aficionados and the man who wants to broaden his style horizons.
Published by: News Magazines, 180 Bourke Rd, Alexandria, NSW 2015, Australia. Adv. contact Tamara Cloos.

051 USA
GAB MAGAZINE. Text in English. 1992. w. free. adv. bk.rev. **Document type:** *Newspaper, Consumer.* **Description:** Reviews social and entertainment activities in the Chicago area.
Former titles (until Oct. 1995): Babble Magazine; (until 1993): Gag
Address: 3227 N Sheffield, Chicago, IL 60657. TEL 773-248-4542, FAX 773-477-6382. Ed., Adv. contact Jim Pickett. Pub., R&P Malone Sizelove. page USD 430; trim 10.5 x 8. Circ: 18,000.

056.1 ARG ISSN 1668-4125
GABO. Text in Spanish. 2004. bi-m. ARS 7.90 newsstand/cover (effective 2008).
Published by: Producciones Publiexpress, Magallanes 1346, Buenos Aires, C1288ABB, Argentina. TEL 54-11-43031484, FAX 54-11-43031280, rrhh@publiexpress.com.ar, http://www.publiexpress.com.ar/. Ed. Martin Jimeno. Circ: 13,000.

053.1 DEU
GALA MEN. Text in German. 2/yr. EUR 5 newsstand/cover (effective 2010). adv. **Document type:** *Magazine, Consumer.*
Published by: Gruner + Jahr AG & Co, Am Baumwall 11, Hamburg, 20459, Germany. TEL 49-40-37030, FAX 49-40-37035601, info@gujmedia.de, http://www.guj.de. Adv. contact Jonas Wolf. Circ: 120,000 (paid).

306.705 GBR ISSN 1745-8536
GALAXY HOT LETTERS. Text in English. 200?. m. **Document type:** *Magazine, Consumer.*
Published by: Galaxy Publications Ltd., PO Box 312, Galaxy Publications Ltd, Witham, Essex CM8 3SZ, United Kingdom. TEL 44-1376-534500, FAX 44-1376-534536.

051 USA ISSN 0195-072X
GALLERY. Text in English. 1972. 13/yr. USD 8.99 per issue; free to members (effective 2009). adv. bk.rev.; film rev. illus. **Document type:** *Magazine, Consumer.*
Published by: Magna Publishing, 210 Rte 4 E, Ste 211, Paramus, NJ 07652. TEL 201-843-4004, FAX 201-843-8775, http://www.magnapublishing.com. Adv. contact Martin Puntus TEL 201-843-4004 ext 113. page USD 4,500; trim 7.875 x 10.875. **Subscr. to:** Montcalm Publishing Corp. **Dist. in UK by:** Portman Distribution.

305.31 GBR ISSN 2045-7685
▼ **GAZZETTA;** for the sharpest guys in the room. Variant title: Gaz7etta. Text in English. 2010. w. **Document type:** *Magazine, Trade.* **Description:** Delivers the real deal behind the style, sport, politics, money and entertainment stories of the week.
Published by: Bauer Consumer Media Ltd., Mappin House, 4 Winsley St, London, W1W 8HF, United Kingdom. TEL 44-20-71828000, http://www.bauermedia.co.uk. Ed. Andrew Pemberton.

059.956 JPN
GEKKAN RIKUJYO KYOGI. Text in Japanese. m. **Document type:** *Magazine, Consumer.*
Published by: Kodansha Ltd., 2-12-21 Otowa, Bunkyo-ku, Tokyo, 112-8001, Japan. TEL 81-3-3946-6201, FAX 81-3-3944-9915, http://www.kodansha.co.jp.

GENDER EQUALITY MAGAZINE. *see* WOMEN'S INTERESTS

305.31 USA
GENESIS (PARAMUS). Text in English. 1974. m. **Document type:** *Magazine, Consumer.*
Published by: Magna Publishing, 210 Rte 4 E, Ste 211, Paramus, NJ 07652. TEL 201-843-4004. Circ: 450,000.

055 ITA ISSN 1722-2222
GENTLEMAN. Text in Italian. 1998. m. **Document type:** *Magazine, Consumer.*
Formerly (until 2000): G. Gentleman (1971-4890)
Published by: Classeditori, Via Marco Burigozzo 5, Milan, MI 20122, Italy. TEL 39-02-582191, http://www.classeditori.com.

305.31 BEL ISSN 1783-3086
GENTLEMAN (DUTCH EDITION); xl-magazine voor mannen. Text in Dutch. 2006. bi-m. EUR 26 (effective 2010). adv. **Document type:** *Magazine, Consumer.*
Related titles: ◆ French ed.: Gentleman (French Edition). ISSN 1783-3094.
Published by: Roularta Media Group, Meiboomlaan 33, Roeselare, 8800, Belgium. TEL 32-51-266111, FAX 32-51-266866, info@roularta.be, http://www.roularta.be.

305.31 BEL ISSN 1783-3094
GENTLEMAN (FRENCH EDITION); le magazine xl de l'homme moderne. Text in French. 2006. bi-m. EUR 26 (effective 2010). adv. **Document type:** *Magazine, Consumer.*
Related titles: ◆ Dutch ed.: Gentleman (Dutch Edition). ISSN 1783-3086.
Published by: Roularta Media Group, Meiboomlaan 33, Roeselare, 8800, Belgium. TEL 32-51-266111, FAX 32-51-266866, info@roularta.be, http://www.roularta.be. Circ: 25,417 (paid).

053.931 NLD ISSN 1875-1989
GEORGE. Text in Dutch. 2006. 8/yr. EUR 54.50; EUR 6.95 newsstand/cover (effective 2010). adv. **Document type:** *Magazine, Consumer.*
Published by: Paint It Blue Magazines, Kabelweg 37, 2e etage, Amsterdam, 1014 BA, Netherlands. http://www.paintitblue.nl. Adv. contact Geert Leeftink TEL 31-20-7155253. page EUR 4,500; trim 230 x 300.

305.31 USA ISSN 1550-6614
GIANT (NEW YORK). Text in English. 2004. bi-m. USD 7.97 (effective 2010). adv. back issues avail. **Document type:** *Magazine, Consumer.* **Description:** Covers topics of interest to men, including fashion, entertainment, music and sex.
Related titles: Online - full text ed.: USD 5 (effective 2010).
Indexed: G05, G06, G07, G08, I05.
Published by: Giant Magazine, LLC., PO Box 8392, Red Oak, IA 51591. TEL 212-431-4477, FAX 212-505-3478. Ed. Emil Wilbekin. Pub. Jeff Mazzacano. Adv. contact Reggie Hudson. B&W page USD 24,750, color page USD 27,500; trim 8 x 10.5. Circ: 250,000.

051 USA ISSN 1939-0033
GIRLS AND CORPSES. Text in English. 2007. q. USD 8.95 newsstand/cover (effective 2007). adv. **Document type:** *Magazine, Consumer.*
Address: 11333 Moorpark St, Ste 192, Studio City, CA 91602. Ed., Pub. Robert Steven Rhine.

051 USA ISSN 1060-1422
CODEN: JPOBFC
GIRLS OF OUTLAW BIKER. Text in English. 1990. bi-m. adv. illus. **Document type:** *Magazine, Consumer.*
Published by: Outlaw Biker Enterprises, Inc./Art & Ink, 1000 Seaboard St, Ste C6, Charlotte, NC 28206. TEL 704-333-3331, FAX 704-333-3433, webhead@outlawbiker.com, http://www.outlawbiker.com. Ed. Joy Surles. Pub. Casey Exton. Adv. contact Ken Knabb.

051 USA ISSN 0031-4935
GIRLS OF PENTHOUSE. Text in English. 1969. bi-m. USD 6.99 newsstand/cover (effective 2009). illus. back issues avail. **Document type:** *Magazine, Consumer.* **Description:** Erotic literature.
Indexed: MagInd, PMR.
Published by: General Media Communications, Inc. (Subsidiary of: FriendFinder Networks Inc.), 6800 Broken Sound Pkwy, Ste 100, Boca Raton, FL 33487. TEL 561-912-7000, FAX 561-912-7038, info@ffn.com, http://www.ffn.com. Pub. Marc Bell. Circ: 18,000.

779.28 DEU
DIE GIRLS VON F H M. (For Him Magazine) Text in German. 2008. 4/yr. EUR 5.90 newsstand/cover (effective 2009). adv. **Document type:** *Magazine, Consumer.*
Published by: Mitte Editionen GmbH (Subsidiary of: Egmont Ehapa Verlag GmbH), Wallstr 59, Berlin, 10179, Germany. TEL 49-30-240080, FAX 49-30-24008199, http://www.mitte-editionen.de. Ed. Christian Kallenberg. Adv. contact Stefanie Keck. page EUR 10,000; trim 222 x 300. Circ: 100,000 (paid and controlled).

GLEICHSTELLUNG IN DER PRAXIS. *see* WOMEN'S INTERESTS

059.956 JPN
GOETHE. Text in Japanese. m. JPY 750 newsstand/cover (effective 2008). adv. **Document type:** *Magazine, Consumer.*
Published by: Gentosha Inc., 4-9-7 Sendagaya Shibuya-ku, Tokyo, 151-0051, Japan. TEL 81-3-5411-6211, FAX 81-3-5411-6225, info@gentosha.co.jp.

GOOD VIBES MAGAZINE. *see* LITERATURE

306.770 FRA ISSN 1774-0398
LE GUIDE DU KOKIN; la France et la Belgique libertines. Text in French. 2005. a. EUR 14.90 per issue (effective 2009). **Document type:** *Magazine, Consumer.*
Published by: Editions Prova, BP 2271, Mulhouse, 68068 Cedex, France.

808.803538 USA
H BOMB. Text in English. 2004. 2/yr. USD 7.95 newsstand/cover domestic; USD 8.95 newsstand/cover foreign (effective 2005). adv. **Document type:** *Magazine, Consumer.* **Description:** Contains sex themed articles, nonfiction, fiction, poetry, and art by the students of Harvard University.
Address: c/o Vladimir Djuric, 235 Mather Mail Center, Cambridge, MA 02138. adv.: page USD 900; 8.5 x 11.

305.31 KEN ISSN 1991-1017
H M. (His Magazine) Text in English. 2005. m. KES 1,750 (effective 2006). adv. **Document type:** *Magazine, Consumer.*
Published by: Media 7 Group Kenya Ltd., PO Box 50087, City Square, Nairobi, 00200, Kenya. TEL 254-20-550957, FAX 254-20-551997, info@media7group.com. adv.: B&W page KES 79,750, color page KES 99,750; trim 210 x 276.

051 USA
HAIR TO STAY; the world's only magazine for lovers of natural, hairy women. Text in English. q. USD 40; USD 50 in Canada; USD 70 elsewhere. video rev. illus. **Description:** Publishes erotic photos, drawings, stories, and fantasies.
Published by: Winter Publishing Inc., PO Box 80667, Dartmouth, MA 02748. TEL 508-994-2908. Pub. Pam Winter.

051 USA ISSN 1075-0797
HAWK. Text in English. 1991. 13/yr. USD 37.95; USD 7.99 per issue (effective 2005). adv. **Document type:** *Magazine, Consumer.* **Description:** Targets men in their 20s and 30s, with editorials and articles on fashion, fitness, and music.
Published by: Blue Horizon Media, 801 Second Ave, New York, NY 10017. TEL 212-661-7878, FAX 212-692-9297. Ed. Mario Grillo. adv.: B&W page USD 2,000. Circ: 250,000 (paid).

646.32 746.92 DNK ISSN 1604-7680
HE. Text in English. 2005. 2/yr. USD 9.99 (effective 2007). **Document type:** *Magazine, Consumer.*
Published by: He Magazine, Vimmelskaftet 47, Copenhagen, 1161, Denmark. TEL 45-70-204614, FAX 45-70-201412, info@he-magazine.com, http://www.he-magazine.com. Ed. Bent Lee. Adv. contact Martin Chidekel.

070.48 USA
HEARTLAND U S A (ONLINE). Text in English. 1991. bi-m. adv. bk.rev. **Document type:** *Magazine, Consumer.* **Description:** Features articles of relevance to the tobacco consumers.
Formerly: Heartland U S A (Print)
Media: Online - full text.
Published by: U S T Publishing (Subsidiary of: Babco Associates), 1 Sound Shore Dr, Ste 3, Greenwich, CT 06830.

779.28 DEU
HEAVY RUBBER. Text in German. 4/yr. EUR 77 (effective 2006). adv. **Document type:** *Magazine, Consumer.* **Description:** Covers all aspects of the rubber fetish scene.

Published by: Marquis, Flensburger Str 5, Solingen, 42655, Germany. TEL 49-212-2521051, FAX 49-212-2521060, mail@marquis.de, http://www.marquis.de.

053.1 DEU
HIGH LIFE; Internationaler Lifestyle fuer Maenner. Text in German. 2002. 3/yr. EUR 18; EUR 7 newsstand/cover (effective 2007). adv. **Document type:** *Magazine, Consumer.*
Published by: Klocke Verlag GmbH, Hoefeweg 40, Bielefeld, 33619, Germany. TEL 49-521-911110, FAX 49-521-9111112, info@klocke-verlag.de, http://www.klocke-verlag.de. adv.: B&W page EUR 9,500, color page EUR 12,000; trim 172 x 252. Circ: 89,632 (paid and controlled).

070.48346 USA ISSN 1075-0800
HIGH SOCIETY. Text in English. 1976. m. (13/yr.). illus. **Document type:** *Magazine, Consumer.*
Published by: Crescent Publishing Group, Inc., 801 Second Ave, New York, NY 10017. TEL 212-661-7878, FAX 212-692-9297. **Subscr. to:** High Society, PO Box 316, Mt Morris, IL 61054. TEL 800-877-5389.

646.32 HKG ISSN 1727-2882
HIM. Text in Chinese. 2000. m. HKD 198 domestic; HKD 1,296 in Southeast Asia, includes subscr. to Che Wang Azzhi; HKD 1,536 elsewhere (effective 2010); includes subscr. to Che Wang Zazzhi. adv. **Document type:** *Magazine, Consumer.*
Related titles: Online - full text ed.
Published by: South China Media Limited/Nan-Hua Chuanmei, 3/F., Wah Shing Centre, 5 Fung Yip St., Chai Wan, Hong Kong. TEL 852-2202-5000, FAX 852-2963-0515, http://www.scmedia.com.hk/.

305.3 056.1 USA
HOMBRE (NEW YORK). Text in English, Spanish. 2001. q. USD 9.95 (effective 2002). **Description:** Created for the modern Latino man, it consist of profiles of business, entertainment and sports leaders, features on finance, health and lifestyle, fashions, restaurants and nightclubs, cars, motorcycles, boats and planes.
Published by: H.I.T.Communications, 244 Fifth Ave, #2073, New York, NY 10001. TEL 212-252-2343, FAX 212-591-6401, frhitcom@aol.com.

305.31 646.32 FRA ISSN 1958-3494
HOMMES STREET HOMMES; le 1er magazine nantais dedie aux hommes. Text in French. 2006. q. free. **Document type:** *Magazine, Consumer.*
Published by: Hommes Street Hommesa, 9 Av. Emile-Boissier, Nantes, 44000, France.

HONORBOUND MAGAZINE FOR MEN. *see* RELIGIONS AND THEOLOGY—Protestant

051 USA
HOOTERS; wings - beer - hooters girls - more than an eyeful!. Text in English. 1989. bi-m. USD 13.95 domestic; USD 18.95 in Canada; USD 28.95 elsewhere; USD 4.99 newsstand/cover (effective 2005). adv. **Document type:** *Magazine, Consumer.*
Published by: Hooters Magazine, 1815 The Exchange, Atlanta, GA 30339. TEL 770-951-2040, hooterspr@hooters.com, http://www.hooters.com. Ed., Pub. Darren Hinerman.

808 USA
HOT FAMILY LETTERS. Text in English. 1980. 10/yr. USD 39.97. adv. back issues avail. **Description:** Erotic literature.
Formerly: Hot Letters
Published by: Piccolo Publications, Inc., 310 Cedar Lane, Teaneck, NJ 07666. TEL 201-836-9177, FAX 201-836-5055. Eds. Jackie Lewis, Lisa Rosen. Pub. Louis Rosen. Adv. contact Allison Reynolds. Circ: 65,900.

051 USA ISSN 1524-3265
HOUSE OF ROSES; universal entertainment for men. Text in English. 1998. q. USD 12; USD 4.99 newsstand/cover (effective 2001). bk.rev.; film rev.; music rev.; tel.rev.; video rev.; Website rev. 148 p./no.; **Document type:** *Magazine, Consumer.* **Description:** Contains articles and features of interest to modern men of color.
Published by: House of Roses, Inc., PO Box 93759, Los Angeles, CA 90093. TEL 323-871-0554, joeyb@houseofroses.com. Circ: 110,000 (paid). **Dist. by:** International Publishers Direct, 27500 Riverview Center Blvd, Bonita Springs, FL 34134. TEL 858-320-4563, FAX 858-677-3220.

052 ZAF ISSN 1021-707X
HUSTLER. Variant title: Hustler S.A. Text in English. 1993. m. ZAR 295 (effective 1999). adv. illus. **Document type:** *Magazine, Consumer.*
Published by: J T Publishing, PO Box 17134, Doornfontein, 2028, South Africa. Ed., R&P Charl Pretorius TEL 614-1911. Adv. contact Grant Holder.

052 GBR ISSN 1351-9646
HUSTLER. Text in English. 1997. m. GBP 29; GBP 3.95 newsstand/cover (effective 1999). adv. illus. **Document type:** *Magazine, Consumer.* **Description:** Contains photos depicting women in erotic poses and stories for adult audiences.
Published by: J T Publishing Ltd., 124-132 Clerkenwell Rd, London, EC1R 5DL, United Kingdom. TEL 44-171-713-5151, FAX 44-171-713-1661. Ed. Jeff Zerbst. Pub. Joe Theron. Adv. contact Julie Wright. **Subscr. to:** Dept. S, PO Box 626, London EC1R 5TD, United Kingdom. **Dist. by:** M M C Ltd., Octagon House, White Hart Meadows, Ripley, Woking, Surrey GU23 6HR, United Kingdom. TEL 44-1483-211222, FAX 44-1483-224541.

363.4 USA ISSN 0149-4635
AP2
HUSTLER. Text in English. 1974. 13/yr. USD 39.95; USD 7.99 newsstand/cover (effective 2005). adv. bk.rev.; film rev.; play rev. illus. back issues avail. **Document type:** *Magazine, Consumer.* **Description:** Features erotic pictures of women and stories, along with film and theatre reviews and other items of interest to men.
Published by: L F P, Inc., 8484 Wilshire Blvd., Ste. 900, Beverly Hills, CA 90211. TEL 323-651-5400, FAX 323-651-0651. Pub. Larry Flynt. Adv. contact Allen Maine. page USD 14,185. Circ: 1,000,000 (paid).

779.28 ROM ISSN 1582-7380
HUSTLER. Text in Romanian. 2001. m. adv. **Document type:** *Magazine, Consumer.*
Published by: Geronia Romania, Bd. Unirii nr. 20, bl. 5C, sc. 1, et. 8, ap. 49, sector 4, Bucharest, Romania. TEL 40-21-3356825, FAX 40-21-3355900.

051 USA ISSN 1059-9703
HUSTLER EROTIC VIDEO GUIDE. Text in English. 1985. m. USD 39.95 (effective 1999). adv. film rev. illus. back issues avail.; reprints avail. **Description:** Provides information on adult videos, the lastest technology in adult entertainment and mail order information.
Published by: L F P, Inc., 8484 Wilshire Blvd., Ste. 900, Beverly Hills, CA 90211. TEL 213-651-5400, FAX 213-651-2741. Ed. Michael Albo. Pub. Larry Flynt. adv.: page USD 2,422; trim 10.88 x 8.25. Circ: 60,000.

301.412 USA ISSN 0884-4348
HUSTLER FANTASIES. Text in English. m. adv. **Description:** Contains real erotic letters from real people.
Published by: L F P, Inc., 8484 Wilshire Blvd., Ste. 900, Beverly Hills, CA 90211. TEL 323-651-5400, FAX 213-651-2741. Pub. Larry Flynt. Adv. contact Allen Maine. page USD 300; trim 8.5 x 5.38.

301.412 USA ISSN 0199-5405
HUSTLER HUMOR. Text in English. m. **Document type:** *Magazine, Consumer.*
Published by: Larry Flynt Publications, Inc., 8484 Wilshire Blvd, Ste 900, Beverly Hills, CA 90211. TEL 310-858-7100, FAX 310-274-7985. Ed. Minette Watkins.

779.28 USA
HUSTLER SPECIALS. BEST OF BARELY LEGAL. Text in English. irreg. adv. **Document type:** *Magazine, Consumer.*
Published by: L F P, Inc., 8484 Wilshire Blvd., Ste. 900, Beverly Hills, CA 90211. TEL 323-651-5400, FAX 213-651-2741. Pub. Larry Flynt. Adv. contact Allen Maine.

779.28 USA
HUSTLER SPECIALS. GIRLS OF HUSTLER. Text in English. irreg. adv. **Document type:** *Magazine, Consumer.* **Description:** Features young women in erotic photographs appearing in earlier issues of Husler magazine.
Published by: L F P, Inc., 8484 Wilshire Blvd., Ste. 900, Beverly Hills, CA 90211. TEL 323-651-5400, FAX 213-651-2744. Pub. Larry Flynt. Adv. contact Allen Maine. page USD 2,422; trim 10.88 x 8.25.

779.28 USA ISSN 1521-6586
HUSTLER'S ASIAN FEVER. Text in English. 1999. bi-m. adv. **Document type:** *Magazine, Consumer.* **Description:** Includes erotic photographs of Asian women and women of Asian ancestry.
Published by: L F P, Inc., 8484 Wilshire Blvd., Ste. 900, Beverly Hills, CA 90211. TEL 323-651-5400, FAX 213-651-2741. Ed. Rick Woods. Pub. Larry Flynt. Adv. contact Jeff Sebens. page USD 1,505; trim 10.88 x 8.25. Circ: 100,000.

779.28 USA ISSN 1078-4160
HUSTLER'S BARELY LEGAL. Text in English. 1992. m. (13/yr.). adv. **Document type:** *Magazine, Consumer.* **Description:** Includes photographs of very young women in erotic poses.
Published by: L F P, Inc., 8484 Wilshire Blvd., Ste. 900, Beverly Hills, CA 90211. TEL 323-651-5400, FAX 213-651-2741. Ed. Allan MacDonell. Pub. Larry Flynt. Adv. contact Allen Maine. page USD 5,000; trim 10.88 x 8.25. Circ: 150,000.

779.28 USA ISSN 1521-6578
HUSTLER'S BROWN SUGAR. Text in English. 1999. m. adv. **Document type:** *Magazine, Consumer.* **Description:** Features erotic photographs of brown- and dark-skinned women.
Published by: L F P, Inc., 8484 Wilshire Blvd., Ste. 900, Beverly Hills, CA 90211. TEL 323-651-5400, FAX 213-651-2741. Ed. C B David. Pub. Larry Flynt. Adv. contact Jeff Sebens. page USD 1,505; trim 10.88 x 8.25. Circ: 100,000.

052 GBR ISSN 1461-3735
HUSTLER'S DEBUT. Text in English. 1995. m. GBP 3.95 newsstand/cover; ZAR 29.95 newsstand/cover in South Africa. adv. illus. **Document type:** *Magazine, Consumer.* **Description:** Contains erotic pictures of women for an adult audience.
Incorporates (1995-1997): Hustler's Barely Legal (1352-8092)
Published by: J T Publishing Ltd., 124-132 Clerkenwell Rd, London, EC1R 5DL, United Kingdom. TEL 44-171-713-5151, FAX 44-171-713-1661. Ed. Fiona Overall. Adv. contact Julie Wright. **Dist. by:** M M C Ltd., Octagon House, White Hart Meadows, Ripley, Woking, Surrey GU23 6HR, United Kingdom. TEL 44-1483-211222, FAX 44-1483-224541.

779.28 USA ISSN 1092-9487
HUSTLER'S HOMETOWN GIRLS. Text in English. 1997. m. adv. **Document type:** *Magazine, Consumer.* **Description:** Features erotic photographs of young American small-town women.
Published by: L F P, Inc., 8484 Wilshire Blvd., Ste. 900, Beverly Hills, CA 90211. TEL 323-651-5400, FAX 213-651-2741. Ed. Scott Hunter. Pub. Larry Flynt. Adv. contact Allen Maine. page USD 1,935; trim 10.88 x 8.25. Circ: 125,000.

779.28 USA ISSN 1521-6594
HUSTLER'S HONEY BUNS. Text in English. 1999. bi-m. adv. **Document type:** *Magazine, Consumer.* **Description:** Contains erotic photographs of young women viewed from behind.
Published by: L F P, Inc., 8484 Wilshire Blvd., Ste. 900, Beverly Hills, CA 90211. TEL 323-651-5400, FAX 213-651-2741. Ed. Rick Woods. Pub. Larry Flynt. Adv. contact Jeff Sebens. page USD 1,505; trim 10.88 x 8.25. Circ: 100,000.

779.28 USA
HUSTLER'S JAIL BABES. Text in English. m. **Document type:** *Magazine, Consumer.* **Description:** Includes erotic photographs of young women.
Published by: L F P, Inc., 8484 Wilshire Blvd., Ste. 900, Beverly Hills, CA 90211. TEL 323-651-5400, FAX 213-651-2741. Pub. Larry Flynt. adv.: page USD 1,935.

306.77 USA ISSN 1092-9495
HUSTLER'S LEG WORLD; the world's best leg magazine. Text in English. 1997. m. USD 39.95; USD 7.99 newsstand/cover (effective 2000). adv. film rev.; video rev. bibl.; tr.lit. back issues avail. **Document type:** *Magazine, Consumer.* **Description:** Focuses on foot fetish.
Related titles: Online - full text ed.
Published by: Larry Flynt Publications, Inc., 8484 Wilshire Blvd, Ste 900, Beverly Hills, CA 90211. TEL 213-651-5400, FAX 213-651-2741. Ed. Rick S Hall. Pub. Larry Flynt. Adv. contact Allen Maine. page USD 1,935; trim 10 x 7.38.

779.28 USA
HUSTLER'S SPECIALS. BEST OF BEAVER HUNT. Text in English. adv. **Document type:** *Magazine, Consumer.* **Description:** Contains erotic and sexually explicit photographs of nude women in seductive poses.
Published by: L F P, Inc., 8484 Wilshire Blvd., Ste. 900, Beverly Hills, CA 90211. TEL 323-651-5400, FAX 213-651-2741. Pub. Larry Flynt. Adv. contact Allen Maine. page USD 2,422; trim 10.88 x 8.25.

779.28 USA ISSN 1099-5137
HUSTLER'S TABOO. Text in English. 1998. m. adv. **Document type:** *Magazine, Consumer.* **Description:** Contains erotic photographs featuring women in sedutive poses, covering a variety of sexual fetishes.
Published by: L F P, Inc., 8484 Wilshire Blvd., Ste. 900, Beverly Hills, CA 90211. TEL 323-651-5400, FAX 213-651-2741. Ed. Carlos J Populus. Pub. Larry Flynt. Adv. contact Allen Maine. page USD 1,505; trim 10.88 x 8.25. Circ: 125,000.

IMPETUS. *see* ART

IN UNIFORM - THE MAGAZINE. *see* HOMOSEXUALITY

051 USA
INCITING DESIRE; the zine of desire without boundaries. Text in English. 1990. irreg. USD 4.50 per issue. adv. bk.rev. **Document type:** *Monographic series, Consumer.*
Address: 343 Soquel Ave, Ste 151, Santa Cruz, CA 95062. TEL 408-425-3397. Adv. contact Rhonda Oxley. B&W page USD 150.

305.31 USA
INDY MEN'S MAGAZINE. Text in English. 2002. m. USD 12 (effective 2004). adv. illus. **Document type:** *Magazine, Consumer.*
Address: 8500 Keystone Crossing, Ste 100, Indianapolis, IN 46240. TEL 317-255-3850, FAX 317-254-5944, ashlee@indymensmagazine.com. Ed. Lou Harry. Adv. contact Tom Rothrock. B&W page USD 2,400, color page USD 3,375.

INKED; culture. style. art. *see* ART

INSIDE OUTDOOR. *see* CLOTHING TRADE

INSTITUT POUR L'EGALITE DES FEMMES ET DES HOMMES. RAPPORT D'ACTIVITES. *see* WOMEN'S INTERESTS

051 USA
THE INTERNATIONAL; the magazine of adventure and pleasure for men. Text in English. 1997. m.
Published by: Tomorrow Enterprises, 2228 E 20th St, Oakland, CA 94606. TEL 510-532-6501, FAX 510-536-5886, tonyattomr@aol.com. Circ: 5,000.

305.31 IRL
▼ **IRISH TATLER MAN.** Text in English. 2010. 4/yr. EUR 11.96 (effective 2011). adv. **Document type:** *Magazine, Consumer.*
Published by: Harmonia Ltd., Rosemount House, Dundrum Rd, Dublin, 14, Ireland. TEL 353-1-2405300, FAX 353-1-6619757, fneeson@harmonia.ie. Ed. Alexander Fitzgerald. Adv. contact Dave Burke.

053.931 NLD ISSN 1875-2438
J F K. (John Fitzgerald Kennedy) Text in Dutch. 2006. 7/yr. EUR 30; EUR 4.95 newsstand/cover (effective 2009). adv. **Document type:** *Magazine, Consumer.*
Published by: G M G Media BV, Postbus 267, Amsterdam, 1000 AG, Netherlands. TEL 31-20-3011700, FAX 31-20-3011701, http://www.gmg.nl. adv.: color page EUR 6,950; trim 210 x 274. Circ: 40,000.

646.32 HKG
J MEN. (Jessica) Text in Chinese. m. HKD 192 domestic; HKD 1,152 in Southeast Asia; HKD 1,392 elsewhere (effective 2010). **Document type:** *Magazine, Consumer.*
Related titles: Online - full text ed.
Published by: South China Media Limited/Nan-Hua Chuanmei, 3/F., Wah Shing Centre, 5 Fung Yip St., Chai Wan, Hong Kong. TEL 852-2963-0725, FAX 852-2963-0529, http://www.scmedia.com.hk/.

305.5 305.4 ITA ISSN 1591-1047
JACK. Text in Italian. 2000. m. EUR 23.40 (effective 2009). adv. **Document type:** *Magazine, Consumer.* **Description:** Covers a wide variety of consumer items and topics of interest to men including technology and the Internet.
Published by: Gruner + Jahr (G + J) Mondadori SpA (Subsidiary of: Arnoldo Mondadori Editore SpA), Corso Monforte 54, Milan, 20122, Italy. TEL 39-02-76210206, FAX 39-02-76013439, info@gujm.it. Ed. Jacopo Loredan. Circ: 111,382 (paid).

746.9 NLD
JAMES. Text in Dutch. 2007. 2/yr. EUR 4.95 newsstand/cover (effective 2009). adv. **Document type:** *Magazine, Consumer.*
Published by: Sanoma Men's Magazines, Haaksbergweg 75, Amsterdam (ZO), 1101 BR, Netherlands. TEL 31-20-7518000, FAX 31-20-7518301, sales@smm.nl, http://www.smm.nl. Ed. Jan Heemskerk. adv.: color page EUR 7,500; trim 210 x 275. Circ: 75,000 (controlled).

JOURNAL OF COUPLE & RELATIONSHIP THERAPY. *see* PSYCHOLOGY

779.28 GBR ISSN 1747-1192
THE JOURNAL OF EROTIC PHOTOGRAPHY. Text in English. 2005. q. GBP 35, EUR 70, USD 90 (effective 2006). **Document type:** *Journal, Consumer.* **Description:** Explores the full range of erotic imagery - from the classical nude to the surreal, from the sublime to fetish and bizarre.
Published by: Diverse Publications Ltd., Unit 56, 3 Couthill House, 80 Water Ln, Wilmslow, Cheshire, SK9 5AJ, United Kingdom. TEL 44-870-2409998, FAX 44-1625-535616, diversepublications@yahoo.co.uk.

779.28 051 USA ISSN 1949-1123
▼ **JOUSEUR.** Text in English. 2009 (Dec.). bi-m. USD 12.99 per issue (effective 2009). **Document type:** *Magazine, Consumer.* **Description:** Features models, lifestyles, reviews and entertainment.
Media: Online - full content.
Published by: Andre Wilson, Ed. & Pub., 12342 Villager Ct, Tampa, FL 33625. TEL 813-230-5305, editor@jouseur.com.

051 USA ISSN 0734-4309
JUGGS. Text in English. 198?. m. USD 39.95; USD 55.95 foreign. illus.
Published by: M M Publications, Ltd. (Subsidiary of: Mavety Media Group), 462 Broadway, Ste 4000, New York, NY 10013. TEL 212-966-8400. Ed. Dian Hanson. **Dist. by:** Flynt Distributing Co., 9171 Wilshire Blvd, Ste 300, Beverly Hills, CA 90210.

305.31 305.896 USA ISSN 1090-0365
JUST FOR BLACK MEN; for strong, positive caring brothers. Cover title: For Strong, Positive Black Men. Short title: Black Men. Text in English. 1996. bi-m. USD 18 domestic; USD 24 in Canada; USD 27 elsewhere; USD 4.95 newsstand/cover domestic; CAD 4.99 newsstand/cover in Canada; GBP 2.50 newsstand/cover in United Kingdom (effective 2002). adv. bk.rev. illus. reprints avail. **Document type:** *Magazine, Consumer.* **Description:** Offers African American men news and articles on positive lifestyle, fashion, sports, and health and fitness.
Published by: Black Men Publications, 46 Violet Ave, Poughkeepsie, NY 12601. Ed. Kate Feguson. Pub. John Blassingame. Adv. contact Mitch Herskowitz. **Subscr. to:** PO Box 752, Mt Morris, IL 61054-7920.

KAISERIN; a magazine for boys with problems. *see* HOMOSEXUALITY

KEY NOTE MARKET ASSESSMENT. MEN'S TOILETRIES & FRAGRANCES. *see* BUSINESS AND ECONOMICS—Production Of Goods And Services

305.31 USA ISSN 1536-531X
KING. Text in English. 2001 (Nov.). m. USD 12 domestic; USD 15.60 in Canada; USD 24 elsewhere (effective 2009). adv. **Document type:** *Magazine, Consumer.* **Description:** Covers modern urban men's lifestyle, fashion, music, relationships, sports, automobiles, and more.
Related titles: Online - full text ed.: King-Mag.Com.
Published by: Harris Publications, Inc., 1115 Broadway, New York, NY 10010. TEL 212-807-7100, FAX 212-924-2352, subscriptions@harris-pub.com, http://www.harris-pub.com. Adv. contact Ben Harris.

052 GBR ISSN 0265-1289
KNAVE. Text in English. 1968. m. (13/y). GBP 35.95; GBP 56.95 foreign; GBP 2.60 newsstand/cover; USD 6.99 newsstand/cover in United States (effective 1999). adv. bk.rev. **Document type:** *Magazine, Consumer.* **Description:** Men's leisure interests including erotic photography, features and interviews.
Related titles: Online - full text ed.
Published by: Galaxy Publications Ltd., PO Box 312, Galaxy Publications Ltd, Witham, Essex CM8 3SZ, United Kingdom. TEL 44-1376-534500, FAX 44-1376-534536. Ed. Ruth Davis. Adv. contact Corrine Franklin. B&W page GBP 2,536; trim 210 x 299. Circ: 57,000. **Dist. by:** Blackhorse Distribution Ltd., Blackhorse Distribution Ltd, Freebourne Rd, PO Box 1124, Witham, Essex CM8 3XJ, United Kingdom. TEL 44-1376-501919, FAX 44-1376-501990.

052 GBR ISSN 1365-0734
KNAVE PENPOWER. Text in English. 199?. m. GBP 3.95 newsstand/cover. adv. **Document type:** *Magazine, Consumer.* **Description:** Features shameless sexual scribblings along with erotic nude photos of young women.
Published by: Galaxy Publications Ltd., PO Box 312, Galaxy Publications Ltd, Witham, Essex CM8 3SZ, United Kingdom. TEL 44-1376-534500, FAX 44-1376-534536. Ed. Ross Gilfillan. Adv. contact Corinne Franklin. **Dist. by:** Blackhorse Distribution Ltd., Blackhorse Distribution Ltd, Freebourne Rd, PO Box 1124, Witham, Essex CM8 3XJ, United Kingdom.

305.31 ZAF ISSN 1990-942X
KREW. Text in English. 2006. w. ZAR 550; ZAR 12.95 newsstand/cover (effective 2006). adv. **Document type:** *Magazine, Consumer.*
Published by: Krew Magazine, PO Box 16344, Vlaeberg, South Africa. TEL 27-21-4879400, FAX 27-21-4223210, http://www.krew.com. Ed. Gavin Williams. Pub. Tim Culley. adv.: page ZAR 19,950; trim 220 x 280.

305.31 CHN ISSN 1005-1074
KUASHIJI/ACROSS CENTURIES MEN'S WORLD. Variant title: Transcentury. Text in Chinese. 1993. m. USD 21.60 (effective 2009). **Document type:** *Magazine, Consumer.*
—East View.
Published by: Henan Sheng Shehui Kexueyuan/Henan Academy of Social Science, 50 Wenhua Lu, Zhengzhou, Henan 450002, China. TEL 86-371-3941462, http://www.hnass.com.cn/. **Dist. by:** China International Book Trading Corp, 35 Chegongzhuang Xilu, Haidian District, PO Box 399, Beijing 100044, China. TEL 86-10-68412045, FAX 86-10-68412023, cibtc@mail.cibtc.com.cn, http://www.cibtc.com.cn.

THE LATEST SCOOP. *see* TRANSPORTATION—Automobiles

363.4 USA
LATIN MEN. Text in English. a.
Published by: Heat Publications, Inc. (Subsidiary of: Mavety Media Group), 462 Broadway, Ste 4000, New York, NY 10013. TEL 212-966-8400. **Dist. by:** Curtis Circulation Co., 730 River Rd, New Milford, NJ 07646.

779.28 USA
LEG SEX. Text in English. m. USD 10 newsstand/cover (effective 2004). adv. **Document type:** *Magazine, Consumer.*
Published by: The Score Group, 1629 NW 84th Ave, Miami, FL 33126-1031. TEL 305-662-5959, FAX 305-662-8922, model@scoregroup.com. **Dist. in UK by:** M M C Ltd., Octagon House, White Hart Meadows, Ripley, Woking, Surrey GU23 6HR, United Kingdom. TEL 44-1483-211222, FAX 44-1483-224541.

363.4 USA ISSN 0734-4295
LEG SHOW. Text in English. 1989 (vol.7, no.2). m. USD 59.95; USD 98.95 foreign. illus.
Published by: Leg Glamour, Inc., 462 Broadway, Ste 4000, New York, NY 10013. TEL 212-966-8400. Ed. Dian Hanson. **Dist. by:** Curtis Circulation Co., 730 River Rd, New Milford, NJ 07646.

363.4 USA
LEG SHOW PRESENTS HIGH-HEELED WOMEN. Text in English. 1989 (vol.2, no.2). a. illus.
Published by: Leg Glamour, Inc., 462 Broadway, Ste 4000, New York, NY 10013. TEL 212-966-8400. **Dist. by:** Curtis Circulation Co., 730 River Rd, New Milford, NJ 07646.

305.31 USA
LEG TEASE PRESENTS: CORPORAL. Text in English. 2000. m. USD 42; USD 7.99 newsstand/cover (effective 2001). adv. **Document type:** *Magazine, Consumer.*
Published by: World Media Group, 153 W 27th St, Rm 1005, New York, NY 10001.

LEGEND OF JENNIE LEE. *see* CLUBS

058.7 SWE ISSN 0345-7109
LEKTYR. Text in Swedish. 1923. m. SEK 54.50 per issue (effective 2005). **Document type:** *Consumer.*
Published by: Baltic Press AB, PO Box 4035, Solna, Stockholm, 17104, Sweden. TEL 46-8-7996309.

779.28 CZE ISSN 1211-4472
LEO. Text in Czech. 1990. m. CZK 828; CZK 69 newsstand/cover (effective 2009). **Document type:** *Magazine, Consumer.*
Published by: PK 62, a.s., Bohdalecka 6, Prague 10, 101 00, Czech Republic. TEL 420-281-090611, FAX 420-281-090622, pk62@pk62.cz, http://www.pk62.cz. Ed. Milos Barta.

779.28 CZE ISSN 1211-4537
LEO CTENI. Text in Czech. 1994. q. CZK 160; CZK 13.33 newsstand/cover (effective 2009). **Document type:** *Magazine, Consumer.*
Published by: PK 62, a.s., Bohdalecka 6, Prague 10, 101 00, Czech Republic. TEL 420-281-090611, FAX 420-281-090622, pk62@pk62.cz, http://www.pk62.cz. Ed. Jiri Havelka.

779.28 CZE ISSN 1213-3167
LEO SPECIAL. Text in Czech. 2001. 2/yr. CZK 156; CZK 78 newsstand/cover (effective 2009). **Document type:** *Magazine, Consumer.*
Published by: PK 62, a.s., Bohdalecka 6, Prague 10, 101 00, Czech Republic. TEL 420-281-090611, FAX 420-281-090622, pk62@pk62.cz, http://www.pk62.cz. Ed. Milos Barta.

808 USA ISSN 0279-1250
LETTERS MAGAZINE (TEANECK). Text in English. 1979. m. USD 43.97 (effective 1997). adv. back issues avail. **Document type:** *Magazine, Consumer.* **Description:** Erotic literature.
Published by: Letters, Magazine, Inc., 310 Cedar Lane, Box 1314, Teaneck, NJ 07666. TEL 201-836-9177, FAX 201-836-5055. Eds. Jackie Lewis, Lisa Rosen. Pub. Louis Rosen. Adv. contact Allison Reynolds. Circ: 97,535.

LEVINGS DIVORCE MAGAZINE. *see* LAW—Family And Matrimonial Law

305.31 054 BEL ISSN 1780-0838
LA LIBRE ESSENTIELLE HOMME. Text in French. 2003. bi-m. back issues avail. **Document type:** *Magazine, Consumer.*
Published by: La Libre Belgique S.A., 79 Rue des Francs, Brussels, 1040, Belgium. TEL 32-2-7444444, FAX 32-2-2112832, llb.direction@saipm.com.

051 USA ISSN 1933-236X
LIQUID (NEW YORK, 2006). Text in English. 2006. bi-m. USD 5.99 newsstand/cover (effective 2008). adv. **Document type:** *Magazine, Consumer.* **Description:** A lifestyle magazine devoted to African American men's interests. Includes fashion and accessories, cars, sports, entertainment and business features.
Published by: X M G Publishing, 5 Penn Plaza, 23rd Fl, New York, NY 10001. TEL 718-217-5217, editorial@liquid-mag.com. Ed. Laurence Christina.

306.76 AUS ISSN 1833-5314
THE LITTLE BLACK BOOK. Text in English. 2006. m. **Document type:** *Magazine, Consumer.* **Description:** A guide to the Australian sex industry.
Published by: Nexlinkcorp Pty Ltd, PO Box H-76, Hurlstone Park, NSW 2193, Australia. info@thelittleblackbook.com.au, http://www.thelittleblackbook.com.au. Circ: 30,000.

051 USA ISSN 1094-0456
LIVE YOUNG GIRLS. Text in English. 19??. 10/yr. USD 49.95; USD 7.99 newsstand/cover. **Document type:** *Magazine, Consumer.* **Description:** Features nude scenes of beautiful, provocative young women.
Former titles (until 199?): Live Girls (1074-844X); Live! (New York) (1060-1139)
Published by: Live Periodicals, Inc., 801 Second Ave, New York, NY 10017. TEL 212-661-7878, FAX 212-883-1244. Ed. V Von Webb. **Subscr. to:** PO Box 351, Mt Morris, IL 61054.

LOADED. *see* LEISURE AND RECREATION

659.23 POL ISSN 1734-1566
LOGO. Text in Polish. 2005. m. PLZ 59 domestic; PLZ 197 in United States; PLZ 7.90 newsstand/cover domestic (effective 2011). adv. **Document type:** *Magazine, Consumer.*
Published by: Agora S.A., ul Czerska 8/10, Warsaw, 00732, Poland. TEL 48-22-5556000, FAX 48-22-5554850, pomoc@agora.pl, http://www.agora.pl. Ed. Marek Jackiewicz. Adv. contact Paulina Skorwider. Circ: 97,555.

051 USA ISSN 1529-3254
LOLLYPOPS. Text in English. 1999. q. free to members (effective 2009). adv. **Document type:** *Magazine, Consumer.*
Formerly (until 2000): Gallery Presents Lollypops (1529-0549)
Published by: Magna Publishing, 210 Rte 4 E, Ste 211, Paramus, NJ 07652. TEL 201-843-4004, FAX 201-843-8775, http://www.magnapublishing.com. adv.: page USD 950; trim 7.875 x 10.875.

779.28 USA
LOOKER; babes - sex - stuff. Text in English. 2003 (Mar.). bi-m. USD 10 newsstand/cover (effective 2004). adv. **Document type:** *Magazine, Consumer.* **Description:** Contains features on various men's lifestyle interests as well as photos of topless models.
Published by: The Score Group, 1629 NW 84th Ave, Miami, FL 33126-1031. TEL 305-662-5959, 800-421-0760, FAX 305-662-8922, model@scoregroup.com.

LOVING ALTERNATIVES MAGAZINE. *see* SINGLES' INTERESTS AND LIFESTYLES

LOVING MORE MAGAZINE; new models for relationships. *see* LIFESTYLE

646.32 KOR ISSN 1975-9649
LUEL. Text in Korean. 2007. m. KRW 51,800 (effective 2009). **Document type:** *Magazine, Consumer.*
Related titles: Online - full text ed.
Published by: Hachette Ein*s Media Co., Ltd./A Swe Tteu Negseuteu Mi'dieo., 4, 6, 7 Fl. Pax Tower, 231-13 Nonhyun-dong, Gangnam-gu, Seoul, 135-010, Korea, S. TEL 82-2-21048031, FAX 82-2-21048090, http://www.hemkorea.co.kr/.

051 USA
LUSTY LETTERS. Text in English. 8/yr. USD 4.50 newsstand/cover. adv. **Document type:** *Newsletter, Consumer.*
Published by: Sportomatic Ltd., PO Box 392, White Plains, NY 10602. Ed. Julie Silver. Pub., Adv. contact Wayne Shuster. R&P Diana Sheridan.

058.81 DNK ISSN 1397-6257
M!. Text in Danish. 1997. m. DKK 429 (effective 2009). adv. **Document type:** *Magazine, Consumer.*
Published by: Benjamin Media A/S, Finsensvej 6 D, Frederiksberg, 2000, Denmark. TEL 45-70-220255, FAX 45-70-220056, info@benjamin.dk, http://www.benjamin.dk. Ed. Dennis Christiansen. adv.: color page DKK 45,800; 223 x 297. Circ: 45,799 (controlled).

646.32 USA ISSN 1555-6875
M (THE COLONY). Text in English. 2005. q. **Document type:** *Magazine, Consumer.*
Published by: M. Publications, 6810 Davidson, Ste 305, The Colony, TX 75056. TEL 972-480-5307, FAX 972-742-4722, http://mpublications.com/publishing/index.html.

305.31 GBR ISSN 0954-6898
M 8. Text in English. m. GBP 30 domestic; GBP 55 in Europe; GBP 70 elsewhere; GBP 3.50 newsstand/cover. **Document type:** *Magazine, Consumer.*
Published by: M 8 Magazine, Top Floor, 11 Lynedoch Pl, Glasgow, G3 6AB, United Kingdom. TEL 44-141-3531118, FAX 44-141-3531448. Ed. Jerry Ross. Pub. David Faulds. **Dist. by:** Seymour Distribution Ltd, 86 Newman St, London W1T 3EX, United Kingdom. TEL 44-20-73968000, FAX 44-20-73968002.

M R (NORWALK). (Menswear Retailing) *see* CLOTHING TRADE

643.7 USA ISSN 1556-2336
T1
MAKE; technology on your time. Variant title: O'Reilly Make. Text in English. 2005. q. USD 34.95 combined subscription domestic (print & online eds.); USD 39.95 combined subscription in Canada (print & online eds.); USD 49.95 combined subscription elsewhere (print & online eds.) (effective 2010). adv. illus. back issues avail. **Document type:** *Magazine, Consumer.* **Description:** Brings the do-it-yourself mindset to all the technology in your life. Includes projects, people and stories in every issue.
Related titles: Online - full text ed.
Published by: O'Reilly Media, Inc., 1005 Gravenstein Hwy N, Sebastopol, CA 95472. TEL 707-827-7000, FAX 707-829-0104, http://www.oreilly.com/. Ed. Mark Frauenfelder. Pub. Dale Dougherty.

051 USA
MAN BAG MAGAZINE. Text in English. 1991. a. illus. **Description:** Contains sexual stories, fantasies, confession and satire.
Published by: (Anti-Sculpture League), ArtPolice, Inc., 5045 Abbott Ave S., Minneapolis, MN 55410-2142. TEL 612-824-8903. Eds. Frank Gaard, Stu Mead. Circ: 800.

051 UAE
MAN IN THE GULF. Text in English. q. adv. **Description:** Covers fashion, health, sports, motoring, entertainment, lifestyle, life and relationships, holidays, nightlife, and others.
Published by: Motivate Publishing, PO Box 2331, Dubai, United Arab Emirates. TEL 971-4-824060, FAX 971-4-824436. Ed. Richard Best. Pub. Ian Fairservice. Adv. contact Shawki Abd Elmalik. B&W page USD 1,400, color page USD 2,000. Circ: 15,000.

058.82 NOR ISSN 0807-0164
MANN. Text in Norwegian. 1996. bi-m. NOK 199; NOK 67 newsstand/cover (effective 2009). adv. **Document type:** *Magazine, Consumer.*
Published by: Hjemmet Mortensen AS, Gullhaugveien 1, Nydalen, Oslo, 0441, Norway. TEL 47-22-585000, FAX 47-22-585959, firmapost@hm-media.no, http://www.hm-media.no. Ed. Knut-Christian Moeng. adv.: page NOK 38,900.

052 IND
MAN'S WORLD; for the man in full. Abbreviated title: M W. Text in English. 2000. m. INR 1,200; INR 100 per issue (effective 2011). adv. back issues avail. **Document type:** *Magazine, Consumer.*
Published by: MW.Com India Pvt. Ltd., 3rd Fl, Zainab Villa, Opp: Moti Mahal, 187, Turner Rd, Bandra, Mumbai, 400 050, India. TEL 91-22-61436363.

305.31 ZAF ISSN 1990-7222
MANWEES. Text in Afrikaans. 2006. m. ZAR 210; ZAR 24.95 newsstand/cover (effective 2006). adv. **Document type:** *Magazine, Consumer.*
Published by: MAN-WEES Edms., PO Box 260317, Excom, 2023, South Africa. TEL 27-11-6468070, FAX 27-11-6460855, info@manwees.co.za, http://www.manwees.co.za. Ed. Wilhelm du Plessis. Pub. Mike de Villiers.

779.28 CZE ISSN 1212-4060
MARKYZ. Text in Czech. 1999. bi-m. CZK 534; CZK 89 newsstand/cover (effective 2009). 52 p./no.; **Document type:** *Magazine, Consumer.*
Published by: PK 62, a.s., Bohdalecka 6, Prague 10, 101 00, Czech Republic. TEL 420-281-090611, FAX 420-281-090622, pk62@pk62.cz, http://www.pk62.cz. Ed. Petr Stransky.

779.28 DEU ISSN 1360-5313
MARQUIS; the fetish fantasy magazine. Text in German. 1995. bi-m. EUR 77 (effective 2006). adv. back issues avail. **Document type:** *Magazine, Consumer.* **Description:** Contains articles and photos covering a wide variety of fetishes.
Related titles: English ed.: ISSN 1360-5305. 1995; French ed.: ISSN 1367-4595. 1995.
Address: Flensburger Str 5, Solingen, 42655, Germany. TEL 49-212-2521051, FAX 49-212-2521060, mail@marquis.de, http://www.marquis.de. Ed. Peter W Czernich.

070.483 059.992 790.1 IDN ISSN 0215-1715
AP95.I5
MATRA; Majalan Trend Pria. Text in Indonesian. 1986. m. USD 26. **Description:** Leisure magazine for men.
Published by: Yayasan Bapora, Jl. Warung Buncit Raya Perumahan, Buncit Raya Permai Kav 1, Jakarta, 12550, Indonesia. TEL 021-780-3510, FAX 021-780-1660, TELEX 62797-IA. Ed. Fikri Jufri. adv.: B&W page USD 1,316, color page USD 2,632; trim 257 x 190. Circ: 95,000.

051 USA ISSN 8756-7644
MAX. Text in English. 1985. 9/yr. USD 37.95; USD 47.95 foreign. illus.
Published by: Max Magazine, Inc. (Subsidiary of: Mavety Media Group), 462 Broadway, Ste 4000, New York, NY 10013. TEL 212-966-8400. Ed. Dian Hanson. **Dist. by:** Kable Media Services, Inc, 11 W 42nd St, 28th Fl, New York, NY 10036. TEL 212-768-1000.

MAX. *see* GENERAL INTEREST PERIODICALS—Italy

056.1 MEX
MAX. Text in Spanish. m. MXN 250 (effective 2005). adv. **Document type:** *Magazine, Consumer.*
Published by: Grupo Editorial Premiere, Horacio no 804, Colonia Polanco, Mexico DF, 11550, Mexico. TEL 52-55-11011300, FAX 52-55-55528051, reginasb@gepremiere.com, http://www.gepremiere.com.

052.081 305.31 GBR ISSN 1357-0862
MAXIM. Text in English. 1995. m. GBP 3.60 newsstand/cover (effective 2009). adv. **Document type:** *Magazine, Consumer.* **Description:** Aims to give readers a broader, deeper, more considered range of contents of heady mix of well-written features, all the latest music, film, games and fashion, all delivered in a snappy, smart and informed style.
Related titles: Online - full text ed.; ◆ Regional ed(s).: Maxim (Print). ISSN 1092-9789.
Published by: Dennis Publishing Ltd., 30 Cleveland St, London, W1T 4JD, United Kingdom. TEL 44-20-79076000, FAX 44-20-79076020, reception@dennis.co.uk, http://www.dennis.co.uk/. Adv. contact Jenny Sinnot TEL 44-20-79076808. Circ: 43,542. **Subscr. to:** Bradley Pavillions. **Dist. by:** Seymour Distribution Ltd.

057.811 BGR ISSN 1312-6644
MAXIM. Text in Bulgarian. 2005. m. BGL 4.95 newsstand/cover (effective 2011). adv. **Document type:** *Magazine, Consumer.*
Published by: Attica Media Bulgaria, 14A Charles Darwin Str, Enter B, Fl 3, Sofia, 1113, Bulgaria. TEL 359-2-8703491, FAX 359-2-8704681, administration@atticamedia.bg, http://www.atticamedia.bg.

057.85 POL ISSN 1641-9162
MAXIM. Text in Polish. 2001. m. adv. **Document type:** *Magazine, Consumer.*
Related titles: ◆ Russian ed.: Maxim. ISSN 1682-8976; ◆ Czech ed.: Maxim. ISSN 1214-1569.
Published by: Hachette Filipacchi Polska, Ul. Pruszkowska 17, Warsaw, 02-119, Poland. TEL 48-22-6689083, FAX 48-22-6689183.

305.31 RUS ISSN 1682-8976
MAXIM. Text in Russian. 2002. m. **Document type:** *Magazine, Consumer.*
Related titles: ◆ Polish ed.: Maxim. ISSN 1641-9162; ◆ Czech ed.: Maxim. ISSN 1214-1569.
—East View.
Published by: Hachette Filipacchi, ul Myasnitskaya, d 35, ofis 743, Moscow, 101959, Russian Federation. TEL 7-095-9332256.

305.31 SRB ISSN 1820-5151
MAXIM. Text in Serbian. 2005. m. **Document type:** *Magazine, Consumer.*
Published by: Attica Media Serbia, Kozjacka 2, Beograd. TEL 381-11-2648432, FAX 381-11-2648457, office@atticamedia.rs, http://www.atticamedia.rs. Ed. Lazar Jovanovic. Adv. contact Rajko Adamovic.

394.011 CZE ISSN 1214-1569
MAXIM. Text in Czech. 2003. m. CZK 719 (effective 2010). adv. **Document type:** *Magazine, Consumer.*
Related titles: ◆ Russian ed.: Maxim. ISSN 1682-8976; ◆ Polish ed.: Maxim. ISSN 1641-9162.
Published by: Hachette Filipacchi 2000 s.r.o., Na Zatorce 3, Prague 6, 160 00, Czech Republic. TEL 420-2-33023100, FAX 420-2-33023101, sevitova@hf.cz, http://www.hf.cz. Ed. Pavel Vondracek. Adv. contact Jan Nassir.

059.951 HKG
MAXIM (CHINESE MAINLAND EDITION). Text in Chinese. 2004 (Apr.). m. CNY 20 newsstand/cover (effective 2004). adv. **Document type:** *Magazine, Consumer.*
Published by: South China Morning Post Ltd., 16/F Somerset House, Taikoo Pl, 979 King's Rd, PO Box 47, Quarry Bay, Hong Kong, Hong Kong. TEL 852-25652222, FAX 852-28111048, info@scmp.com, http://www.scmp.com. Ed. Lolita Hu. Pub. Angie Wong. Circ: 140,000 (paid and controlled).

305.31 HKG
MAXIM (HONG KONG EDITION). Text in Chinese. 2004 (Apr.). m. HKD 35 newsstand/cover (effective 2004). adv. **Document type:** *Magazine, Consumer.* **Description:** Covers lifestyle items of interest to young men.
Published by: South China Morning Post Ltd., 16/F Somerset House, Taikoo Pl, 979 King's Rd, PO Box 47, Quarry Bay, Hong Kong, Hong Kong. TEL 852-25652222, FAX 852-28111048, info@scmp.com, http://www.scmp.com. Eds. Jimmy Poon, Lolita Hu. Circ: 40,000 (paid and controlled).

051.081 305.31 USA ISSN 1092-9789
HQ1090.3
MAXIM (PRINT). Text in English. 1997. m. USD 17.97 for 3 yrs. domestic; USD 47.97 in Canada; USD 5.99 newsstand/cover (effective 2009). adv. illus. back issues avail.; reprints avail. **Document type:** *Magazine, Consumer.* **Description:** Contains useful information for men delivered with a sense of humor and style.
Related titles: ◆ Online - full text ed.: Maxim Online; ◆ Regional ed(s).: Maxim. ISSN 1357-0862.
Published by: Dennis Digital, Inc (Subsidiary of: Dennis Publishing, Inc.), 1040 Ave of the Americas, 12th Fl, New York, NY 10018. TEL 212-302-2626, FAX 212-302-2635. Pub. Ben Madden TEL 212-372-3886. Adv. contact Anthony Flaccavento TEL 212-372-8651. B&W page USD 217,578, color page USD 241,756; trim 7.75 x 10.5. Circ: 2,535,884 (paid). **Subscr. to:** Maxim, PO Box 420705, Palm Coast, FL 32142. TEL 800-829-5572.

056.1 MEX ISSN 1657-9119
MAXIM EN ESPANOL; para hombres. Text in Spanish. 2001. m. MXN 297 domestic (effective 2010). adv. **Document type:** *Magazine, Consumer.*
Published by: Editorial Televisa, Vasco de Quiroga 2000, Edificio E, Colonia Santa Fe, Mexico City, DF 01210, Mexico. TEL 52-55-52612761, FAX 52-55-52612704, info@editorialtelevisa.com, http://www.esmas.com/editorialtelevisa/. Circ: 180,000 (paid and controlled).

051.081 USA
MAXIM ONLINE. Text in English. 2000. d. adv. **Document type:** *Magazine, Consumer.* **Description:** Provides interactive features and content of interest to men, including sports, gadgets, photos of women, sex topics, music and fun.
Media: Online - full text. **Related titles:** ◆ Print ed.: Maxim (Print). ISSN 1092-9789.
Published by: Dennis Digital, Inc (Subsidiary of: Dennis Publishing, Inc.), 1040 Ave of the Americas, 12th Fl, New York, NY 10018. TEL 212-302-2626, FAX 212-302-2635, editors@maximmag.com. Pub. Ben Madden TEL 212-372-3886. Adv. contact Anthony Flaccavento TEL 212-372-8651.

051 USA
MAYFAIR. Text in English. m. (13/yr.). USD 6.99 newsstand/cover domestic; USD 7.99 newsstand/cover in Canada (effective 2001). **Document type:** *Magazine, Consumer.*
Published by: Mayfair Glen Publishing, Inc., PO Box 815, Sandy Hook, CT 06482-0815. TEL 203-426-8992, FAX 203-426-9533.

070.48346 GBR ISSN 0025-6161
MAYFAIR. Text in English. 1966. m. (13/yr.). GBP 44; GBP 2.80 newsstand/cover (effective 2005). adv. bk.rev. illus. **Document type:** *Magazine, Consumer.* **Description:** Publishes erotic articles, letters, and photographs of women, along with features on sports, celebrities, and other items of interest to men.
Published by: Paul Raymond Publications Ltd., 2 Archer St, London, W1V 8JJ, United Kingdom. TEL 44-20-72928000, FAX 44-20-72928021. Ed. Steve Shields. Adv. contact Nicola Swift. **Subscr. to:** MRM, PO Box 503, Leicester LE94 0AD, United Kingdom. TEL 44-1858-410510. **Dist. by:** Comag, Tavistock Rd, W Drayton, Middlesex UB7 7QE, United Kingdom. TEL 44-1895-444055, FAX 44-1895-433602.; **Dist. in N. America by:** Curtis Circulation Co., 730 River Rd, New Milford, NJ 07646. TEL 201-634-7400.

051 USA ISSN 0966-5374
MAYFAIR SPECIALS. Text in English. bi-m. **Document type:** *Magazine, Consumer.*
Published by: Mayfair Glen Publishing, Inc., PO Box 815, Sandy Hook, CT 06482-0815. TEL 203-426-8992, FAX 203-426-9533.

306.7 GBR ISSN 1748-7420
MAYFAIR SUMMER SPECIAL (YEAR). Text in English. 2004. a. adv. **Document type:** *Magazine, Consumer.*
Published by: Paul Raymond Publications Ltd., 2 Archer St, London, W1V 8JJ, United Kingdom. TEL 44-20-72928000, FAX 44-20-72928021, menonly@pr-org.co.uk, http://www.sexclub.co.uk.

057.1 RUS
MEDVED'. Text in Russian. 1995. m. USD 189 in United States (effective 2007). adv. bk.rev.; film rev.; play rev.; video rev.; software rev. abstr.; bibl.; illus.; tr.lit. back issues avail. **Document type:** *Magazine, Consumer.* **Description:** Covers broad subjects of interest to men from 18 to 50 years old.
Related titles: Diskette ed.: 1995; Microfilm ed.: 1995.
Address: Bol'shoi Sukharevskii pereulok d 19/2, Moscow, 127051, Russian Federation. TEL 7-095-2072656. Ed. Stanislav Yushkin. Pub. Igor' Svinarenko. adv.: page USD 7,800; trim 285 x 210. Circ: 50,000. **Dist. by:** East View Information Services, 10601 Wayzata Blvd, Minneapolis, MN 55305. TEL 952-252-1201, 800-477-1005, FAX 952-252-1202, info@eastview.com, http://www.eastview.com.

305.31 GRC ISSN 1108-6289
MEN. Text in Greek. 1993. m. EUR 111 domestic; EUR 166 in Europe; EUR 166 in Cyprus & Turkey; EUR 193 elsewhere (effective 2005). adv. **Document type:** *Magazine, Consumer.*
Published by: Special Publications S.A. (Subsidiary of: Lambrakis Press SA), Panepistimiou 18, Athens, 106 72, Greece. TEL 30-1-3686111, FAX 30-1-3634772. **Subscr. to:** 80, Mihalakopoulou St, Athens 115 28, Greece. TEL 30-211-365-9767, FAX 30-211-365-9798.

MEN ARE FROM MARS & WOMEN ARE FROM VENUS. *see* SOCIOLOGY

052 GBR ISSN 0025-9217
MEN ONLY. Text in English. 1935. m. GBP 44 domestic; GBP 48 foreign; GBP 2.60 newsstand/cover (effective 2001). adv. bk.rev.; film rev. **Document type:** *Magazine, Consumer.* **Description:** Contains top-quality glamour photography.
Published by: Paul Raymond Publications Ltd., 2 Archer St, London, W1V 8JJ, United Kingdom. TEL 44-20-72928000. Ed. Rob Swift. Adv. contact Nicola Swift. Circ: 150,000. **Subscr. to:** PO Box 503, Leicester LE94 0AD, United Kingdom. **Dist. by:** Comag, Tavistock Rd, W Drayton, Middlesex UB7 7QE, United Kingdom. TEL 44-1895-444055, FAX 44-1895-433602.

305.31 USA
THE MEN'S BOOK CHICAGO. Abbreviated title: M N C H. Text in English. 2004. s-a. USD 20; USD 5.95 per issue (effective 2009). adv. back issues avail. **Document type:** *Magazine, Consumer.* **Description:** Features from fashion and sports to watches and fine dining for men in Chicago.
Related titles: Online - full text ed.: free (effective 2008).
Published by: Modern Luxury, LLC., 200 W Hubbard St, 8th fl, Chicago, IL 60610. TEL 312-274-2500, FAX 312-274-2501, http://www.modernluxury.com. Ed. Matt Lee. Pub. John Carroll. adv.: color page USD 9,395; trim 10 x 12. Circ: 30,000.

305.31 USA
THE MEN'S BOOK L A. (Los Angeles) Text in English. 2005. a. USD 20; USD 5.95 per issue (effective 2009). adv. back issues avail. **Document type:** *Magazine, Consumer.* **Description:** Features from fashion and sports to watches and fine dining for men in Los Angeles.
Related titles: Online - full text ed.: free (effective 2008).
Published by: Modern Luxury, LLC., 5455 Wilshire Blvd, Ste 1442, Los Angeles, CA 90036. TEL 323-930-9400, FAX 323-930-9401, http://www.modernluxury.com. Eds. Matt Lee, Andrew Myers, Degen Pener. Pub. Alan Klein. adv.: B&W page USD 9,395; trim 10 x 12. Circ: 30,000.

MEN'S CAR. *see* LIFESTYLE

059.956 JPN
MEN'S CLUB DORSO. Text in Japanese. 1999. q. JPY 750 newsstand/cover (effective 2002). adv. **Document type:** *Magazine, Consumer.* **Description:** Contains upmarket fashion and lifestyle information for men in their thirties and forties.
Published by: Hachette Fujingaho Co. Ltd. (Subsidiary of: Hachette Filipacchi Medias S.A.), 2-9-1 Nishi Shinbashi, Minato-ku, Tokyo, 105-0003, Japan. TEL 81-3-3506-6601, FAX 81-3-3506-6606, http://www.hfm.co.jp. Circ: 70,000 (paid).

MEN'S EDGE. *see* PHYSICAL FITNESS AND HYGIENE

MEN'S HEALTH. *see* LIFESTYLE

MEN'S HEALTH. *see* MEN'S HEALTH

MEN'S HEALTH BEST FASHION. *see* CLOTHING TRADE—Fashions

051 USA ISSN 1063-4657
GV191.2
MEN'S JOURNAL. Text in English. 1992. m. USD 11.88 (effective 2009). adv. bk.rev. illus. reprints avail. **Document type:** *Magazine, Consumer.* **Description:** Active men's journal with articles featuring fitness and health, sports, travel and adventure.
Related titles: Online - full text ed.
Indexed: BRI.
Published by: Wenner Media, Inc., 1290 Ave of Americas, New York, NY 10104. TEL 212-484-1616, FAX 212-484-3433. Pub. Matt Mastrangelo TEL 212- 484-3420. adv.: B&W page USD 84,375, color page USD 94,150; trim 8 x 10.875. Circ: 700,000 (paid). **Subscr. to:** PO Box 8248, Red Oak, IA 51591. **Dist. in UK by:** Comag.

305.31 NLD ISSN 1877-1726
MEN'S MIND!. Cover title: What's on a Men's Mind. Text in Dutch. 2004. w. EUR 104; EUR 2 newsstand/cover (effective 2010). adv. **Document type:** *Magazine, Consumer.*
Formerly (until 2008): Woamm! (1573-0247)
Published by: Teampress bv, Postbus 43117, The Hague, 2504 AC, Netherlands. TEL 31-70-3082050, FAX 31-70-3082069, http://www.teampress.nl. adv.: page EUR 2,857.50; trim 215 x 285.

305.3 USA ISSN 1079-6207
MEN'S STYLE. Text in English. 1995. bi-m. USD 23.70 domestic; USD 29.70 in Canada; USD 3.95 newsstand/cover (effective 2000). adv. bk.rev.; film rev.; music rev.; play rev. illus. **Document type:** *Magazine, Consumer.* **Description:** Covers food, movies, music, the arts, relationships, literature and fashion.
Published by: Baio & Company Publishing, NA, Inc, 4 Aurora Dr., # 403, Cranbury, NJ 08512-3285. TEL 732-261-7105, FAX 732-287-0548. Ed., Pub., R&P, Adv. contact Louis J Baio Sr.

646.32 AUS ISSN 1449-6704
MEN'S STYLE AUSTRALIA. Text in English. 2004. bi-m. AUD 49.75 domestic; AUD 77.75 in New Zealand; AUD 97.75 elsewhere; AUD 9.95 newsstand/cover (effective 2008). adv. **Document type:** *Magazine, Consumer.* **Description:** Features technology, gadgets and cars and what a man loves most: music, movies, books, health, humour, sport and sex.
Indexed: G06, G07, G08, I05.
Published by: A C P Magazines Ltd. (Subsidiary of: P B L Media Pty Ltd.), 54-58 Park St, Sydney, NSW 2000, Australia. TEL 61-2-92828000, FAX 61-2-91263769, research@acpaction.com.au. Ed. Peter Holder. Adv. contact Andrew Cook TEL 61-2-92639760. color page AUD 7,725; trim 235 x 297. **Subscr. to:** Magshop, Reply Paid 4967, Sydney, NSW 2001, Australia. TEL 61-2-136116, subs@magstore.com.au, http://shop.magstore.com.au.

646.32 USA ISSN 1556-4096
TT570
MEN'S VOGUE. Text in English. 2005 (Fall). q. **Document type:** *Magazine, Consumer.* **Description:** Covers high-end men's lifestyle, including fashion, travel, food and more.
Indexed: ASIP, G08, I05.
—CCC.
Published by: Conde Nast Publications, Inc. (Subsidiary of: Advance Publications, Inc.), 750 3rd Ave, New York, NY 10017. TEL 212-630-3740, FAX 212-630-5899, talktous@luckymag.com, http://www.condenast.com. Ed. Jay Fielden.

MEN'S WORKOUT. *see* MEN'S HEALTH

052 GBR ISSN 0955-5552
MEN'S WORLD. Text in English. 1988. m. GBP 2.60 newsstand/cover; USD 30 combined subscription per issue domestic (effective 2005). adv. **Document type:** *Magazine, Consumer.*
Published by: Paul Raymond Publications Ltd., 2 Archer St, London, W1V 8JJ, United Kingdom. TEL 44-20-72928000. Ed. Rebecca Eden. Adv. contact Nicola Swift. **Subscr. to:** MRM, PO Box 503, Leicester LE94 0AD, United Kingdom. TEL 44-1858-410510. **Dist. by:** Comag, Tavistock Rd, W Drayton, Middlesex UB7 7QE, United Kingdom. TEL 44-1895-444055, FAX 44-1895-433602.; **Dist. in N. America by:** Curtis Circulation Co., 730 River Rd, New Milford, NJ 07646. TEL 201-634-7400.

305.31 306.7662 USA ISSN 1944-5482
▼ **MENSBOOK JOURNAL.** Text in English. 2009 (Jan.). q. USD 60 (effective 2009). **Document type:** *Magazine, Consumer.*
Published by: 47 West Communications, PO Box 418, Sturbridge, MA 01566.

MENSTUFF; the national men's resource. *see* MEN'S STUDIES

687 LIE
MENSTYLE. Text in German. 1964. 2/yr. EUR 9.80 (effective 2007). adv. **Document type:** *Magazine, Consumer.*
Published by: Neue Verlagsanstalt, In der Fina 18, Schaan, 9494, Liechtenstein. TEL 423-233-4381, FAX 423-233-4382, info@neue-verlagsanstalt.li, http://www.neue-verlagsanstalt.li. Ed. Andrea Greuner. Pub., Adv. contact Rita Quaderer. B&W page EUR 12,990, color page EUR 12,990. Circ: 45,388 (controlled).

305.31 RUS ISSN 1680-5968
MIR RAZVLECHENII. Text in Russian. 2001. m. **Document type:** *Magazine, Consumer.*
Published by: Izdatel'skii Dom L K Press, Bol'shoi Savvinskii per, dom 9, Moscow, 119435, Russian Federation. info@lkpress.ru, http://www.lkpress.ru. Circ: 70,000.

MIXTE. *see* WOMEN'S INTERESTS

MIXTE 100% HOMME. *see* CLOTHING TRADE—Fashions

779.28 USA ISSN 1948-710X
▼ **MODEL FORCE MAGAZINE.** Short title: Force. Text in English. 2009. bi-m. USD 5.99 per issue (effective 2009). **Document type:** *Magazine, Consumer.* **Description:** Features African-American female models.
Published by: Donald C. Evans, Ed. & Pub., 5876 Ridge Dr, Mableton, GA 30126. TEL 678-598-3725, chocolatebottoms@gmail.com.

646.32 CHN ISSN 1674-5299
▼ **MODENG SHENSHI/MR. MODERN.** Text in Chinese. 2009. m. CNY 336 (effective 2009). **Document type:** *Magazine, Consumer.*
Related titles: Online - full text ed.
Published by: Beijing Bierde Guanggao Youxian Gongsi/Beijing Hachette Advertising Co., Ltd. (Subsidiary of: Hachette Filipacchi Medias S.A.), 19, Deguomen wai Dajie, Guoji Dasha 2202, Beijing, 100004, China. Adv. contact Alex Lei TEL 86-21-6133 5199.

646.32 FRA ISSN 1265-0080
MONSIEUR; le magazine de l'homme elegant. Text in French. 1995. bi-m. EUR 28 domestic (effective 2010). back issues avail. **Document type:** *Magazine, Consumer.*
Related titles: ◆ Supplement(s): Monsieur. Hors-Serie. ISSN 1950-3466.
Published by: Montaigne Publications, 72 bd Berthier, Paris, 75017, France. TEL 33-1-47634800, FAX 33-1-47634908, courrier@monsieur.fr.

646.32 FRA ISSN 1950-3466
MONSIEUR. HORS-SERIE. Text in French. 2006. irreg. **Document type:** *Magazine, Consumer.*
Related titles: ◆ Supplement to: Monsieur. ISSN 1265-0080.
Published by: Montaigne Publications, 72 bd Berthier, Paris, 75017, France. TEL 33-1-47634800, FAX 33-1-47634908, courrier@monsieur.fr.

305.89607305 051 USA ISSN 1936-8607
MPOWER PLUS. Text in English. 2007 (May). q. free to qualified personnel (effective 2009). **Document type:** *Magazine, Consumer.* **Description:** A lifestyle publication for urban men, covering topics such as health and fitness, sex and music.
Published by: Regent Entertainment Media Inc., 10990 Wilshire Blvd, Penthouse 1800, Los Angeles, CA 90024. TEL 310-806-4288, FAX 310-806-4268, info@regententertainment.com, http://www.regententertainment.com.

056.1 808 CUB
MUJERES Y MUCHACHA. Text in Spanish. m. USD 48. illus.
Formerly: Romances
Published by: (Federacion de Mujeres Cubanas), Ediciones Cubanas, Obispo 527, Havana, Cuba.

N B A F MAGAZINE. (National Bodybuilding and Fitness) *see* PHYSICAL FITNESS AND HYGIENE

779.28 CZE ISSN 1211-7978
N E I REPORT. (Nezavisla Eroticka Iniciativa) Text in Czech. 1990. fortn. CZK 741; CZK 28.50 newsstand/cover (effective 2009). **Document type:** *Magazine, Consumer.*
Published by: Klarex s.r.o., Jeseniova 49, Prague 3, 130 00, Czech Republic. TEL 420-267-297577, FAX 420-267-097236.

N S MAN. *see* MILITARY

646.32 CHN ISSN 1674-6155
▼ **NANREN FENGSHANG/LEON.** Text in English. 2009. m. **Document type:** *Magazine, Consumer.*
Published by: Zhongguo Qinggongye Chubanshe/China Light Industry Press, 7, Chang'an Jie, Beijing, 100740, China. TEL 86-10-85111729, FAX 86-10-85111730, club@chlip.com.cn, http://www.chlip.com.cn/.

059.951 CHN ISSN 1672-8378
NANRENZHUANG/F H M (BEJING). Text in Chinese. 2004. m. CNY 240 (effective 2008). adv. **Document type:** *Magazine, Consumer.*
Related titles: Online - full text ed.
—East View.
Published by: Trends Communication Co. Ltd., 21/F, Trends Bldg., 9, Guanghua Rd., Beijing, 100020, China. FAX 86-10-65871680, http://www.trends.com.cn/. adv.: page CNY 80,000.

363.4 USA
NASTY LETTERS. Text in English. bi-m. USD 21.95.
Published by: Starlight Press, Inc., 462 Broadway, Ste 4000, New York, NY 10013. TEL 212-966-8400. **Dist. by:** Curtis Circulation Co., 730 River Rd, New Milford, NJ 07646.

NATURAL BODYBUILDING AND FITNESS. *see* PHYSICAL FITNESS AND HYGIENE

NATURAL MUSCLE MAGAZINE. *see* PHYSICAL FITNESS AND HYGIENE

779.28 USA ISSN 1092-728X
NAUGHTY NEIGHBORS; the original amateur magazine. Text in English. 1995. 13/yr. USD 10 newsstand/cover domestic (effective 2004). adv. **Document type:** *Magazine, Consumer.*
Published by: The Score Group, 1629 NW 84th Ave, Miami, FL 33126-1031. TEL 305-662-5959, FAX 305-662-8922, model@scoregroup.com. Ed. John Fox. Adv. contact John Romano. **Subscr. to:** Units 161-167, Block F, Riverside Business Centre,, Haldane Pl, London SW18 4UQ, United Kingdom. **Dist. in UK by:** M M C Ltd., Octagon House, White Hart Meadows, Ripley, Woking, Surrey GU23 6HR, United Kingdom. TEL 44-1483-211731, 44-1483-211222, FAX 44-1483-211731.

NERVE (ONLINE); love, sex, culture. *see* LITERATURE

779.28 DEU ISSN 0943-0970
DAS NEUE WOCHENEND. Text in German. 1948. w. (Wed.). adv. illus. **Document type:** *Magazine, Consumer.*
Formerly (until 1992): Wochenend (0940-0591)
Indexed: RASB.
Published by: Pabel-Moewig Verlag KG (Subsidiary of: Bauer Media Group), Karlsruherstr 31, Rastatt, 76437, Germany. TEL 49-7222-130, FAX 49-7222-13218, empfang@vpm.de, http://www.vpm-online.de. Adv. contact Rainer Gross. B&W page EUR 2,372, color page EUR 4,136; trim 192 x 260. Circ: 65,462 (paid).

NEW MAN (ONLINE); the magazine about becoming men of integrity. *see* RELIGIONS AND THEOLOGY

305.31 USA
NIGHTLYFE. Text in English. 2006 (Jul.). m. USD 11 (effective 2006). adv. **Document type:** *Magazine, Consumer.* **Description:** Covers metropolitan man's entertainment after dark, including clubs, bars, lounges, and restaurants.
Published by: Nightlyfe Inc., 1 Penn Plaza, Ste. 1426, New York, NY 10119. TEL 212-714-4773. Ed. Daniel Peres. Adv. contact Leslie Catchings. B&W page USD 24,449, color page USD 35,500; trim 9 x 10.875. Circ: 300,000.

056.1 ESP ISSN 1576-6136
NOX. Text in Spanish. 2000. s-a. **Document type:** *Magazine, Consumer.*
Published by: Focus Ediciones SL (Subsidiary of: Edipresse Publications SA), Paseo de la Castellana 129, 1o, Madrid, 28046, Spain. TEL 34-91-5973090, FAX 34-91-5972326, camado@focusediciones.com. Ed. Antonio Marquez Coello. Circ: 43,888.

305.31 JOR ISSN 1999-6675
NOX. Text in English. 2006. m. adv. **Document type:** *Magazine, Consumer.*
Published by: Near East Media, PO Box 940166, Amman, 11194, Jordan. TEL 962-6-516-3357, FAX 962 6 516 3267. Ed. Eddie Taylor.

779.28 USA ISSN 1063-8237
NUGGET (PALM BEACH); a feast of fetishes. Text in English. m. USD 57; USD 7.99 newsstand/cover. adv. **Document type:** *Magazine, Consumer.*
Published by: Firestone Publishing, 214 Brazilian Ave., Ste. 300, Palm Beach, FL 33480. TEL 305-557-0071, 800-642-4061, FAX 305-577-6005, dugent@dugent.com, http://www.dugent.com, http://www.sexmags.com.

NUMERO HOMME. *see* CLOTHING TRADE—Fashions

305.31 GBR ISSN 1742-8858
NUTS. Text in English. 2004. w. GBP 76.50 domestic; EUR 120 in Europe (eurozone); GBP 80 in Europe (non-eurozone); USD 160 in United States; GBP 80.81 in Canada; GBP 120 elsewhere; GBP 1.40 newsstand/cover (effective 2008). adv. **Document type:** *Magazine, Consumer.* **Description:** Contains a unique mix of sexy women, gritty real-life stories, sport, news plus complete TV listings.
Published by: I P C ignite! Ltd. (Subsidiary of: I P C Media Ltd.), The Blue Fin Building, 110 Southwark St, London, SE1 0SU, United Kingdom. TEL 44-20-31485000, http://www.ipcmedia.com/about/ignite/. Ed. Dominic Smith TEL 44-20-31486910. Pub. Clair Poteous TEL 44-20-31486776. Adv. contact Oliver Scull TEL 44-20-31486708. page GBP 10,120. Circ: 270,053 (paid). **Dist. by:** MarketForce UK Ltd, The Blue Fin Bldg, 3rd Fl, 110 Southwark St, London SE1 0SU, United Kingdom. TEL 44-20-31483300, FAX 44-20-31488105, salesinnovation@marketforce.co.uk, http://www.marketforce.co.uk/.

646.32 USA ISSN 1931-2784
NYLON GUYS (NEW YORK). Text in English. 2005. q. USD 12 domestic; USD 17 in Canada; USD 27 elsewhere (effective 2008). adv. **Document type:** *Magazine, Consumer.*
Published by: Nylon Holding Inc., 110 Greene St, Ste 607, New York, NY 10012-3838. TEL 212-226-6454, 800-580-8050, FAX 212-226-7738, nylonmag@aol.com, http://www.nylonmag.com. Ed. Marvin Scott Jarrett. adv.: B&W page USD 8,765, color page USD 10,819; trim 8 x 10.5. Circ: 100,000.

779.28 FRA ISSN 1959-5425
NYMPHOS LIBERTINES. Text in French. 2007. bi-m. **Document type:** *Magazine, Consumer.*
Published by: C B Media Groupe, 23 Rue Richer, Paris, 75009, France.

779.28 DEU
O; the art. the fashion. the fantasy. Text in English. 1988. q. **Document type:** *Magazine, Consumer.* **Description:** Presents works of an erotic nature from the worlds of art, fashion and fantasy for members of both sexes.
Published by: Eromedia GmbH, Girardetstrasse 40, Essen, 45131, Germany. TEL 49-201-7269035, FAX 49-201-7269052, eromedia@t-online.de. Ed., Pub. Ronald B Brockmeyer.

305.31 RUS ISSN 1680-5976
O M; om - edinitsa soprotivleniya. Text in Russian. 1995. m. USD 154 foreign (effective 2005). **Document type:** *Magazine, Consumer.* **Description:** Covers life style, fashions, literature, design, new technologies, health matters, mass culture idols, sex and relation between the sexes.
Published by: Izdatel'skii Dom L K Press, Bol'shoi Savvinskii per, dom 9, Moscow, 119435, Russian Federation. info@lkpress.ru, http://www.lkpress.ru. **Dist. by:** East View Information Services, 10601 Wayzata Blvd, Minneapolis, MN 55305. TEL 952-252-1201, 800-477-1005, FAX 952-252-1202, info@eastview.com, http://www.eastview.com.

059.956 JPN
OBRA. Text in Japanese. m. **Document type:** *Magazine, Consumer.*
Published by: Kodansha Ltd., 2-12-21 Otowa, Bunkyo-ku, Tokyo, 112-8001, Japan. TEL 81-3-3946-6201, FAX 81-3-3944-9915, http://www.kodansha.co.jp.

343.4 USA
OFF-BEAT LETTERS. Text in English. bi-m. USD 21.95.
Published by: Opal Press, Inc., 462 Broadway, Ste 4000, New York, NY 10013. TEL 212-966-8400. **Dist. by:** Curtis Circulation Co., 730 River Rd, New Milford, NJ 07646.

L'OFFICIEL HOMMES. *see* CLOTHING TRADE—Fashions

779.28 CZE ISSN 1801-0776
OLDIES. Text in Czech. 2005. 2/yr. CZK 156; CZK 78 newsstand/cover (effective 2009). **Document type:** *Magazine, Consumer.*
Published by: PK 62, a.s., Bohdalecka 6, Prague 10, 101 00, Czech Republic. TEL 420-281-090611, FAX 420-281-090622, pk62@pk62.cz, http://www.pk62.cz.

L'OPTIMUM. *see* CLOTHING TRADE—Fashions

363.4 USA
ORIENTAL DOLLS. Text in English. q.
Published by: Fast Lane Publishing, Inc., 462 Broadway, Ste 4000, New York, NY 10013. TEL 212-966-8400. **Dist. by:** Curtis Circulation Co., 730 River Rd, New Milford, NJ 07646.

051 USA ISSN 1083-768X
ORIENTAL DOLLS PRESENTS: ASIAN HOTTIES. Text in English. 2001. q. USD 19.95; USD 6.99 newsstand/cover (effective 2002). adv. **Document type:** *Magazine, Consumer.*
Published by: Fast Lane Publishing, Inc., 462 Broadway, Ste 4000, New York, NY 10013. TEL 212-966-8400. Ed. Joe Morgan. Pub. Mimi Miyagi.

OUT. *see* HOMOSEXUALITY

305.31 USA ISSN 1934-6271
OUTSIDE'S GO; travel & style for men. Text in English. 2007 (Mar.). q. USD 18 to individuals (effective 2009). adv. illus. back issues avail. **Document type:** *Magazine, Consumer.* **Description:** Designed for men who thrive on active, high-end travel and a commitment to personal style.
Published by: Mariah Media Inc., 400 Market St, Santa Fe, NM 87501. TEL 505-989-7100, 800-678-1131, FAX 505-820-7933, info@outsidego.com. adv.: color page USD 36,500; trim 8 x 10.875. Circ: 25,000 (paid).

363.4 USA
OVER 40. Text in English. 198?. m. USD 59.95. illus.
Published by: Midlife Publications, Inc., 462 Broadway, Ste 4000, New York, NY 10013. TEL 212-966-8400. **Dist. by:** Curtis Circulation Co., 730 River Rd, New Milford, NJ 07646.

363.4 USA
OVER 50. Text in English. 9/yr. USD 44.95.
Published by: Modernismo Publications, Ltd. (Subsidiary of: Mavety Media Group), 225 Broadway, Ste 2801, New York, NY 10007. TEL 212-966-8400. **Dist. by:** Dist. by, Curtis Circulation Co, 730 River Rd, New Milford, NJ 07648-3048.

OYE. *see* ETHNIC INTERESTS

305.31 USA
PANTY GIRLS. Text in English. 2000. m. USD 42; USD 7.99 newsstand/cover (effective 2001). adv. **Document type:** *Magazine, Consumer.*
Published by: Star Publishing, 153 W 27th St, Rm 1005, New York, NY 10001. http://www.pantygirlsonline.com. Ed. Victoria Reeves. Pub. Richard Shore.

605.31 DEU ISSN 1432-8771
PAPS; die Welt der Vaeter. Text in German. 1994. q. EUR 14.60 domestic; EUR 15.40 foreign; EUR 3.75 newsstand/cover (effective 2002). **Document type:** *Magazine, Consumer.* **Description:** Covers all aspects of fatherhood and child rearing.
Published by: (paps e.V.), Velber im OZ Verlag GmbH, Guenterstalstr. 57, Freiburg, 79102, Germany. TEL 49-761-705780, FAX 49-761-7057839, butsch@oz-bpv.de, http://www.oz-verlag.com. Ed. Ralf Ruhl.

PARADIS; un magazine pour l'homme contemporain. *see* LIFESTYLE

051 USA
PARADISE MAGAZINE; for the 90's male. Text in English. 1993. m. USD 3.95 newsstand/cover. adv. illus. **Document type:** *Magazine, Consumer.*
Published by: Paradise Magazine, Inc., PO Box 2116, New York, NY 10116-2116. TEL 212-630-0242. Ed. J Walters.

PARANOID BACHELOR GUY; random verbal violence for the young and jaded. *see* SINGLES' INTERESTS AND LIFESTYLES

PARENTS EXPRESS; the newspaper for Philadelphia area parents. *see* EDUCATION—Teaching Methods And Curriculum

053.1 ARG ISSN 1851-331X
PARTY SEX. Text in Spanish. 2007. bi-m.
Published by: Ideas Vivas Editorial, Paso 192, Avellaneda, Buenos Aires, 1870, Argentina. TEL 54-11-42941476, FAX 54-11-42144436, ideasvivas@infovia.com.ar.

057.1 LVA ISSN 1407-9186
PATRON. Text in Russian. 2000. 10/yr. LVL 11.98 (effective 2011). adv. **Document type:** *Magazine, Consumer.*
Published by: Izdevnieciba Lilita SIA, Mukusala Business Centre, Mukusalas Str 41B, Riga, 1004, Latvia. TEL 371-67061600, FAX 371-67616050, izdevnieciba@lilita.lv, http://www.lilita.lv. Circ: 15,000 (paid).

051 USA ISSN 0090-2020
AP2
PENTHOUSE; the magazine of sex, politics and protest. Text in English. 1969. m. USD 29.95; USD 8.99 per issue (effective 2009). adv. illus. **Document type:** *Magazine, Consumer.* **Description:** Contains erotic photos and stories, as well as life-style articles of interest to men.
Related titles: Online - full text ed.: 1969.
Indexed: A21, A22, ASIP, G06, G07, G08, I05, RI-1, RI-2.
Published by: General Media Communications, Inc. (Subsidiary of: FriendFinder Networks Inc.), 6800 Broken Sound Pkwy, Ste 100, Boca Raton, FL 33487. TEL 561-912-7000, FAX 561-912-7038. Eds. Bob Guccione, Peter Bloch. Pub. Bob Guccione. R&P Bruce Garfunkel. adv.: B&W page USD 36,300, color page USD 40,700. Circ: 980,106.

052 GBR ISSN 0950-0685
PENTHOUSE. Text in English. 1965. m. Please contact publisher for subscr. rates. adv. **Document type:** *Magazine, Consumer.*
Published by: Trojan Publishing Ltd., 3rd Fl, 207 Old St, London, EC1V 9NR, United Kingdom. TEL 44-20-76086300, FAX 44-20-76086320, info@trojanpublishing.co.uk, http://www.trojanpublishing.co.uk/. Circ: 113,000 (paid).

053.1 DEU
PENTHOUSE; das Magazin in dem alles steht. Text in German. 1980-2002; N.S. 2003-2003; N.S. 2005 (Nov.). m. EUR 55.20; EUR 4.60 newsstand/cover (effective 2007). adv. **Document type:** *Magazine, Consumer.*
Published by: Lightspeed Media GmbH, Nymphenburgerstr 70, Munich, 80335, Germany. TEL 49-89-7266960, FAX 49-89-72669655, info@lightspeed-media.de, http://www.lightspeed-media.de. Ed. Markus Boden. Pub. Stefan Masseck. Adv. contact Hendrik Boeing. page EUR 9,900; trim 230 x 300. Circ: 150,000 (paid).

054.1 FRA ISSN 0762-5006
PENTHOUSE. Text in French. 1985. m. **Document type:** *Consumer.*
Published by: Not Too Bad Publishing, 9 allee des Barbanniers, Parc des Barbanniers, Genevilliers, 92238 Cedex, France. TEL 331-4085-7071, FAX 331-4794-3794.

363.47 HKG
PENTHOUSE. Text in Chinese. 1985. m. adv. film rev. **Document type:** *Consumer.*
Published by: Yongder Hall Group, 14-F Aik San Bldg, 14 Westlands Rd, Quarry Bay, Hong Kong, Hong Kong. TEL 852-296-30111, FAX 852-2565-8217. Ed. Wong Ki Lung. Adv. contact Carrie Leung. Circ: 51,684.

779.28 GRC ISSN 1108-8087
PENTHOUSE. Text in Greek. 1999. m. adv. **Document type:** *Magazine, Consumer.*
Published by: Daphne Communications S.A., 26-28 G Averof Str, Athens, 14232, Greece. TEL 30-210-2594100, FAX 30-210-2586740, info@daphne.gr, http://www.daphne.gr. Circ: 12,700 (paid).

779.28 THA ISSN 1685-6465
PENTHOUSE. Text in Thai. 2002. m. adv. **Document type:** *Magazine, Consumer.*
Published by: Pen Publishing Co. Ltd., 281/11 Soi Sriphuen, Rimklongprapa Fungsai Rd, Ladyao, Jatujak, Bangkok, 10900, Thailand. TEL 66-2-58777046, FAX 66-2-9103832.

779.28 HUN ISSN 1786-8890
PENTHOUSE. Text in Hungarian. 2004. m. adv. **Document type:** *Magazine, Consumer.*
Formerly (until 2005): Az Igazi Penthouse (1785-9514)
Published by: Penthouse Hungaria Szolgaltato Kft, Hattyu u 16 IV, em 1, Budapest, 1015, Hungary. TEL 36-1-2253660, FAX 36-1-3740544.

M

051 USA ISSN 1043-0210
HQ1
PENTHOUSE FORUM; the international journal of human relations. Text in English. 1976. 10/yr. USD 29.95; USD 5.50 newsstand/cover (effective 2009). bk.rev. illus. index. back issues avail. **Document type:** *Magazine, Consumer.* **Description:** Allows men and women to share experiences and fantasies. Provides data and entertainment concerning sex and sexuality.
Formerly (until 1988): Forum (0160-2195)
Indexed: A22.
Published by: General Media Communications, Inc. (Subsidiary of: FriendFinder Networks Inc.), 6800 Broken Sound Pkwy, Ste 100, Boca Raton, FL 33487. TEL 561-912-7000, FAX 561-912-7038, info@ffn.com. Circ: 30,000 (paid).

051 USA ISSN 0883-8798
PENTHOUSE LETTERS; the magazine of sexual marvels. Text in English. 1981. m. USD 29.95 domestic; USD 48.95 foreign; USD 6.99 newsstand/cover (effective 2009). bk.rev. illus. back issues avail. **Document type:** *Magazine, Consumer.* **Description:** Features erotic fantasy letters.
Related titles: Online - full text ed.: USD 19.95 (effective 2009).
Published by: General Media Communications, Inc. (Subsidiary of: FriendFinder Networks Inc.), 6800 Broken Sound Pkwy, Ste 100, Boca Raton, FL 33487. TEL 561-912-7000, FAX 561-912-7038, info@ffn.com, http://www.ffn.com. Circ: 96,000.

051 USA ISSN 0274-5143
PENTHOUSE VARIATIONS. Variant title: Variations. Text in English. 1978. m. USD 29.95 domestic; USD 48.95 foreign; USD 5.25 newsstand/cover (effective 2009). adv. film rev.; video rev. 96 p./no. 2 cols./p.; back issues avail. **Document type:** *Magazine, Consumer.* **Description:** Provides interpersonal portraits of America's couples. Offers sexual fact and fiction for entertainment and education.
Related titles: Online - full text ed.: USD 29.95 (effective 2009).
Published by: General Media Communications, Inc. (Subsidiary of: FriendFinder Networks Inc.), 6800 Broken Sound Pkwy, Ste 100, Boca Raton, FL 33487. TEL 561-912-7000, FAX 561-912-7038, info@ffn.com, http://www.ffn.com.

779.28 AUS ISSN 1321-9847
PEOPLE. Text in English. 1990. w. AUD 4.25 newsstand/cover (effective 2008). adv. bk.rev. **Document type:** *Magazine, Consumer.* **Description:** Features nude or semi-nude photos and pictorials of beautiful models and actresses.
Formed by the merger of (1990-1990): New Pix (1321-9901); Which was formerly (until 1990): Pix (1034-7267); (1972-1990): People (1321-9928); Which was formerly (until 1985): People With Pix (1321-991X); (until 1977): People Pix (0310-6896); Which was formed by the merger of (1968-1972): People (0031-4978); (1938-1972): Pix (0032-0390)
Published by: A C P Magazines Ltd. (Subsidiary of: P B L Media Pty Ltd.), 54-58 Park St, Sydney, NSW 2000, Australia. TEL 61-2-92828000, FAX 61-2-91263769. Ed. Martin Vine. Adv. contact Patrick Campbell TEL 61-2-92828369. color page AUD 3,190; trim 210 x 297. Circ: 51,112. **Subscr. to:** Magshop, Reply Paid 4967, Sydney, NSW 2001, Australia. TEL 61-2-136116, subs@magstore.com.au, http://shop.magstore.com.au.

051 USA ISSN 1094-3927
HQ450
PERFECT 10; the connoisseur's magazine. Text in English. 1998. q. USD 23.97 domestic; USD 33.97 in Canada; USD 43.97 elsewhere; USD 6.95 newsstand/cover (effective 2004). adv. **Document type:** *Magazine, Consumer.*
Published by: Perfect 10, Inc., PO Box 3398, Beverly Hills, CA 90212. TEL 818-712-6999, 800-606-6639, 888-338-7897, FAX 310-273-7941. Ed., Pub. Norm Zadeh. Adv. contact Robert Johnson. **Subscr. to:** PO Box 469115, Escondido, CA 92046-9115. **Dist. in UK by:** Comag, Tavistock Rd, W Drayton, Middlesex UB7 7QE, United Kingdom. TEL 44-1895-444055, FAX 44-1895-433602.

779.28 DEU
DAS PFIFF MAGAZIN; jung - frech - aktuell. Text in German. m. EUR 1.95 newsstand/cover (effective 2007). adv. **Document type:** *Magazine, Consumer.*
Published by: S P N Zeitschriften Verlags GmbH, Waidmannstr 35, Hamburg, 22769, Germany. TEL 49-40-8501039, FAX 49-40-8501126, info@spn-verlag.de.

051 USA
PICTORIAL. Text in English. m. USD 52 domestic; USD 70 foreign; USD 5.95 newsstand/cover (effective 1999). adv. back issues avail.
Published by: Players International Publications, 8060 Melrose Ave, Los Angeles, CA 90046. TEL 213-653-8060, FAX 213-655-9452. Adv. contact Tim Connelley. B&W page USD 840, color page USD 1,200; trim 10.88 x 8.13. Circ: 65,000. **Dist. by:** All America Distribution Corp., 8431 Melrose Ave, Los Angeles, CA 90069. TEL 213-651-2650, FAX 213-655-9452.

779.28 AUS ISSN 1033-3258
THE PICTURE. Text in English. 1988. w. AUD 4.25 newsstand/cover (effective 2008). adv. **Document type:** *Magazine, Consumer.* **Description:** Provides a mix of humor and photo spreads of nude women.
Published by: A C P Magazines Ltd. (Subsidiary of: P B L Media Pty Ltd.), 54-58 Park St, Sydney, NSW 2000, Australia. TEL 61-2-92828000, FAX 61-2-91263769. Ed. Shayne Bugden. Adv. contact Patrick Campbell TEL 61-2-92828369. color page AUD 4,400; trim 205 x 275. Circ: 74,476 (paid and controlled). **Subscr. to:** Magshop, Reply Paid 4967, Sydney, NSW 2001, Australia. TEL 61-2-136116, subs@magstore.com.au, http://shop.magstore.com.au.

779.28 AUS ISSN 1449-6666
THE PICTURE PREMIUM. Text in English. 1998. m. AUD 99 domestic; AUD 125 in New Zealand; AUD 150 elsewhere; AUD 9.80 newsstand/cover (effective 2008). adv. **Document type:** *Magazine, Consumer.* **Description:** Contains explicit photos of nude women and humorous articles.
Published by: A C P Magazines Ltd. (Subsidiary of: P B L Media Pty Ltd.), 54-58 Park St, Sydney, NSW 2000, Australia. TEL 61-2-92828000, FAX 61-2-91263769, http://www.acp.com.au. Ed. Boris Mihailovic. Adv. contact Patrick Campbell TEL 61-2-92828369. color page AUD 1,710; trim 200 x 275. **Subscr. to:** Magshop, Reply Paid 4967, Sydney, NSW 2001, Australia. TEL 61-2-136116, subs@magstore.com.au, http://shop.magstore.com.au.

779.28 DEU
PIEP!. Text in German. m. EUR 1.50 newsstand/cover (effective 2003). adv. **Document type:** *Magazine, Consumer.*
Related titles: Online - full text ed.
Published by: Inter Content KG (Subsidiary of: Heinrich Bauer Verlag), Karlsruher Str 31, Rastatt, 76437, Germany. online@imckg.de, http://www.vpm.de. adv.: B&W page EUR 2,682, color page EUR 3,609. Circ: 70,000 (paid and controlled). **Subscr. to:** V K G Verlagsvertriebs KG, Postfach 112202, Hamburg 20422, Germany. TEL 49-180-5313939, FAX 49-40-30198123, kundenservice@bauerverlag.de.

PLANET Q. *see* HOMOSEXUALITY

779.28 SRB ISSN 1451-6950
PLAYBOY. Text in Serbian. 2004. m. adv. **Document type:** *Magazine, Consumer.*
Published by: Attica Media Serbia, Kozjacka 2, Beograd. TEL 381-11-2648432, FAX 381-11-2648457, office@atticamedia.rs, http://www.atticamedia.rs. Ed. Perica Gunjic. Adv. contact Rajko Adamovic.

305.3 ROM ISSN 1454-7538
PLAYBOY (BUCHAREST). Text in Romanian. 1999. m. adv. **Document type:** *Magazine, Consumer.*
Published by: P B R Publishing, Str. Luterana nr. 11, bl. Cinor, Bucharest, Romania. TEL 40-21-3033887, FAX 40-21-3033944.

305.3 HUN ISSN 0865-350X
PLAYBOY (BUDAPEST). Text in Hungarian. 1989. m. HUF 5,940; HUF 895 newsstand/cover (effective 2011). adv. bk.rev. illus. **Document type:** *Magazine, Consumer.*
Published by: Marquard Media Magyarorszag Kiado Kft. (Subsidiary of: Marquard Media AG), Hajogyari-sziget 213, Budapest, 1033, Hungary. TEL 36-1-5050800, FAX 36-1-5050805, info@marquardmedia.hu, http://www.marquardmedia.hu. Ed. Peter Radnai. Adv. contact Antal Kertesi. Circ: 20,046 (paid).

305.3 ARG ISSN 0328-4360
PLAYBOY (BUENOS AIRES). Text in Spanish. 1985. m. bk.rev. illus. **Document type:** *Consumer.*
Published by: Editorial Perfil S.A., Chacabuco 271, Buenos Aires, Buenos Aires 1069, Argentina. TEL 54-11-4341-9000, FAX 54-11-4341-9090, correo@perfil.com.ar, http://www.perfil.com.ar. adv.: B&W page USD 7,490, color page USD 11,660. Circ: 70,000.

305.3 USA ISSN 0032-1478
AP2
PLAYBOY (CHICAGO); entertainment for men. (Also published in 14 overseas editions) Text in English. 1953. m. USD 29.97 domestic; USD 47.05 in Canada; USD 45 elsewhere; USD 6.99 newsstand/cover domestic; GBP 3.50 newsstand/cover in United Kingdom (effective 2005). adv. bk.rev.; film rev.; rec.rev. illus. index, cum.index: 1953-68, 1969-73, 1974-78, 1979-83, 1984-88. reprints avail. **Document type:** *Magazine, Consumer.* **Description:** Features erotic photographs of women. Covers all the interests in men's lives, including fashion, entertainment, music, and sports cars.
Related titles: Braille ed.; Microform ed.: (from BHP, PQC); Online - full text ed.; Supplement(s): Moore's Index to Playboy Magazine. ISSN 1559-4173. 19??.
Indexed: A22, ASIP, BEL&L, G09, I05, IPARL, MLA-IB, MRD, MagInd, P02, P06, P10, P53, P54, PMR, PQC.
—Ingenta.
Published by: Playboy Enterprises, Inc., 680 N Lake Shore Dr, Chicago, IL 60611. TEL 312-751-8000, FAX 312-751-2818, http://www.playboy.com. Eds. James Kamisky, Hugh Hefner, Arthur Kretchmer, Christopher Napolitano. Pubs. Diane M Silberstein, James N Dimonekas, James N. Dimonekas. adv.: B&W page USD 77,190, color page USD 108,090; trim 10.88 x 8.13. Circ: 3,150,000 (paid). **Subscr. to:** PO Box 2007, Harlan, IA 51537-4007. **Dist. in UK by:** Comag, Tavistock Rd, W Drayton, Middlesex UB7 7QE, United Kingdom. TEL 44-1895-444055, FAX 44-1895-433602.

305.3 HRV ISSN 1331-2065
PLAYBOY (CROATIA). Text in Croatian. 1997. m. adv. **Document type:** *Magazine, Consumer.*
Published by: Europapress Holding d.o.o., Slavonska Avenija 4, Zagreb, 10000, Croatia. TEL 385-1-3642146, 385-1-3642145.

305.3 TWN ISSN 1026-7018
PLAYBOY (GUOJI ZHONGWENBAN). Text in Chinese. 1996. m. adv. bk.rev. illus. **Document type:** *Consumer.*
Related titles: Online - full content ed.
Published by: Xieji Wenhua Shiye Gufen Youxian Gongsi/Kings International Multimedia Co., Ltd., 14-F, 88 Sec-1, Hsin-Tai 5th Rd, His-Chin Town, Taipei County, Taiwan. TEL 886-2-2696-8466, FAX 886-2-2696-493, http://www.sayho.com.tw/index.html. Ed. Ann Wang. adv.: B&W page USD 3,157, color page USD 4,341. Circ: 32,000.

305.3 ITA ISSN 1125-6672
PLAYBOY (ITALIAN EDITION). Text in Italian. 1972-199?; resumed 200?. m. bk.rev. illus. **Document type:** *Magazine, Consumer.*
Published by: Play Media Company, Via di Santa Cornelia 5A, Formello, RM 00060, Italy. TEL 39-06-33221250, FAX 39-06-33221235, http://www.playmediacompany.it. Circ: 75,000.

305.3 UKR
PLAYBOY (KIEV). Text in Russian. m. UAK 72.24 for 6 mos. domestic (effective 2004). **Document type:** *Magazine, Consumer.*
Published by: Burda Ukraina, Zhylianskaja ul. 29, Kiev, 01033, Ukraine. TEL 38-044-4908363, FAX 38-044-4908364, zhestkov@burda.ua, http://www.burda.ua.

305.3 MEX
PLAYBOY (MEXICO). Text in Spanish. 1976. m. bk.rev. illus. **Document type:** *Consumer.*
Published by: Editorial Caballero, MARICOPA 57, Col Napoles, Mexico City, DF 03810, Mexico. TEL 52-5-687-6638, FAX 52-5-682-0534. Ed. Perla Carreto. adv.: B&W page USD 4,376, color page USD 6,612. Circ: 100,000.

305.3 RUS
PLAYBOY (MOSCOW). Text in Russian. 1995. m. (11/yr.). RUR 1,320 domestic; RUR 110 newsstand/cover domestic (effective 2004). adv. bk.rev.; music rev.; video rev. bibl.; illus. back issues avail. **Document type:** *Magazine, Consumer.* **Description:** Features erotic pictures of women, along with stories, fashion, entertainment, accessories, travel, interviews with celebrities and related stories.
Published by: Izdatel'skii Dom Burda, ul Pravdy 8, Moscow, 125040, Russian Federation. TEL 7-095-7979849, FAX 7-095-2571196, vertrieb@burda.ru, http://www.burda.ru. adv.: color page USD 7,700. Circ: 105,000 (paid). **Dist. by:** East View Information Services, 10601 Wayzata Blvd, Minneapolis, MN 55305. TEL 952-252-1201, 800-477-1005, FAX 952-252-1202, info@eastview.com, http://www.eastview.com.

305.3 DEU ISSN 0939-8546
PLAYBOY (MUNICH); alles, was Maennern Spass macht. Text in German. 1972. m. EUR 59.40; EUR 4.90 newsstand/cover (effective 2010). adv. **Document type:** *Magazine, Consumer.* **Description:** Covers all areas of interest to men, from leisure activities to beautiful women.
Published by: Playboy Deutschland Publishing GmbH (Subsidiary of: Hubert Burda Media Holding GmbH & Co. KG), Arabellastr 21, Munich, 81925, Germany. TEL 49-89-92500, FAX 49-89-92501220, team@playboy.de. Ed. Florian Boitin. Pub. Juergen Feldmann. Adv. contact Katherine Kreiner. Circ: 209,933 (paid). **Dist. in U.S. by:** G L P International Inc., 153 S Dean St, Englewood, NJ 07631-3513. TEL 201-871-1010, subscribe@glpnews.com.

305.3 POL ISSN 1230-2724
PLAYBOY (POLISH EDITION). Text in Polish. 1992. m. PLZ 99 (effective 2011). adv. bk.rev. illus. **Document type:** *Magazine, Consumer.*
Published by: Marquard Media Polska Sp. z o.o. (Subsidiary of: Marquard Media AG), ul Wilcza 50/52, Warsaw, 00-679, Poland. TEL 48-22-4211000, FAX 48-22-4211111, info@marquard.pl, http://www.marquard.pl. Ed. Marcin Meller. Adv. contact Monika Ruszkowska. Circ: 95,674 (paid).

305.3 CZE ISSN 0862-9374
PLAYBOY (PRAGUE). Text in Czech. 1991. m. CZK 99 newsstand/cover (effective 2011). adv. illus. **Document type:** *Magazine, Consumer.*
Published by: Axel Springer Praha a.s., Rosmarin Business Center, Dilnicka 12, Prague 7, 17000, Czech Republic. TEL 420-2-34692111, FAX 420-2-34692102. Ed. Vladimir Olexa. Adv. contact Petra Kardova. Circ: 45,000. **Subscr. to:** SEND Predplatne s.r.o., PO Box 141, Prague 4 140 21, Czech Republic. TEL 420-225-985225, FAX 420-225-341425, send@send.cz.

305.3 BRA ISSN 0104-1746
PLAYBOY (SAO PAULO). Text in Portuguese. 1978. m. BRL 128; BRL 12 newsstand/cover (effective 2010). adv. bk.rev.; film rev.; music rev.; play rev.; video rev. charts; illus. back issues avail. **Document type:** *Magazine, Consumer.* **Description:** Presents beautiful and famous women of Brazil and the world.
Formerly: Homen
Related titles: Online - full text ed.
Published by: Editora Abril, S.A., Avenida das Nacoes Unidas 7221, Pinheiros, Sao Paulo, SP 05425-902, Brazil. TEL 55-11-50872112, FAX 55-11-50872100, abrilsac@abril.com.br, http://www.abril.com.br. adv.: page USD 115,000; trim 202 x 266. Circ: 192,973 (paid). **Subscr. to:** Rua do Curtume, Rua do Curtume, 769, Sao Paulo, SP 0506-900, Brazil. TEL 55-11-823-9100.

305.3 SVK ISSN 1336-7277
PLAYBOY (SLOVAKIA). Text in Slovak. 2005. m. SKK 120, EUR 3.99 newsstand/cover (effective 2011). adv. **Document type:** *Magazine, Consumer.*
Published by: Mediavision, s.r.o., Sasinkova 5, Bratislava, 81108, Slovakia. TEL 421-2-50227211, FAX 421-2-50227339, redakcia@mediavision.sk, http://www.mediavision.sk. Ed. Milos Scepka. Adv. contact Jan Kulhanek.

305.3 SVN ISSN 1580-6294
PLAYBOY (SLOVENSKA IZDAJA). Text in Slovenian. 2001. m. EUR 49.90 (effective 2008). adv. **Document type:** *Magazine, Consumer.*
Published by: Adria Media Ljubljana, Zaloznistvo in Trzenje, d.o.o., Vosnjakova ulica 3, Ljubljana, 1000, Slovenia. TEL 386-1-3000700, FAX 386-1-3000713, info@adriamedia.si, http://www.adriamedia.si. Ed. Barbara Bizjack. adv.: page EUR 2,000; trim 210 x 280. Circ: 19,800 (paid and controlled).

305.3 BGR ISSN 1312-0069
PLAYBOY (SOFIA). Text in Bulgarian. 2002. m. BGL 4.95 newsstand/cover (effective 2011). adv. **Document type:** *Magazine, Consumer.*
Published by: Attica Media Bulgaria, 14A Charles Darwin Str, Enter B, Fl 3, Sofia, 1113, Bulgaria. TEL 359-2-8703491, FAX 359-2-8704681, administration@atticamedia.bg, http://www.atticamedia.bg.

305.3 ESP ISSN 1576-771X
PLAYBOY (SPAIN). Text in Spanish. 1978. m. bk.rev. illus. **Document type:** *Magazine, Consumer.*
Published by: Grupo Godo, Av Diagonal 477, 5o, Barcelona, 08036, Spain. TEL 34-93-3444100, FAX 34-93-3444250, http://www.grupogodo.com. Circ: 70,000.

305.3 JPN
PLAYBOY (TOKYO). Text in Japanese. 1975. m. adv. bk.rev. illus. **Document type:** *Consumer.*
Published by: Shueisha Inc., 2-5-10 Hitotsubashi, Chiyoda-ku, Tokyo, 101-0003, Japan. TEL 81-3-32306032, FAX 81-3-32646575. Ed. Suzuhito Imai. Circ: 450,000.

PLAYBOY ENTERPRISES. ANNUAL REPORT. *see* BUSINESS AND ECONOMICS—Abstracting, Bibliographies, Statistics

051 746.92 USA ISSN 0744-4885
PLAYBOY FASHION. Text in English. q. **Document type:** *Magazine, Consumer.*
Formerly: Playboy Guide Fashion for Men (0279-7755)
Published by: Playboy Enterprises, Inc., 680 N Lake Shore Dr, Chicago, IL 60611. TEL 312-751-8000, FAX 312-751-2818. Pub. Hugh Hefner.

305.3 NLD ISSN 0168-1184
PLAYBOY NEDERLAND. Text in Dutch. 1983. m. EUR 57; EUR 5.45 newsstand/cover (effective 2009). adv. bk.rev.; video rev. illus. back issues avail. **Document type:** *Magazine, Consumer.* **Description:** Features erotic photographs of beautiful women, along with stories. Discusses lifestyle topics of interest to men who work hard and play hard.
Published by: Sanoma Men's Magazines, Haaksbergweg 75, Amsterdam (ZO), 1101 BR, Netherlands. TEL 31-20-7518000, FAX 31-20-7518301, sales@smm.nl, http://www.smm.nl. adv.: color page EUR 8,490; trim 210 x 280. Circ: 57,456.

051 USA ISSN 1062-225X
PLAYBOY NUDES. Text in English. 1990. a. **Document type:** *Magazine, Consumer.* **Description:** Features erotic photographs portraying nude women.

Published by: Playboy Enterprises, Inc., 680 N Lake Shore Dr, Chicago, IL 60611. TEL 312-751-8000, FAX 312-751-2818. Pub. Hugh Hefner.

051 USA ISSN 1062-2284
PLAYBOY PRESENTS INTERNATIONAL PLAYMATES. Text in English. 1992. a. **Document type:** *Magazine, Consumer.* **Description:** Presents women from all over the world in erotic poses.
Published by: Playboy Enterprises, Inc., 680 N Lake Shore Dr, Chicago, IL 60611. TEL 312-751-8000, FAX 312-751-2818. Pub. Hugh Hefner.

051 USA ISSN 1069-1251
PLAYBOY PRESENTS PLAYBOY'S VIDEO PLAYMATES. Text in English. 1993. a. **Document type:** *Magazine, Consumer.* **Description:** Features women who have appeared in Playboy's erotic videotapes.
Published by: Playboy Enterprises, Inc., 680 N Lake Shore Dr, Chicago, IL 60611. TEL 312-751-8000, FAX 312-751-2818. Pub. Hugh Hefner.

051 USA ISSN 1062-2276
PLAYBOY'S BATHING BEAUTIES. Text in English. 1989. a. **Document type:** *Magazine, Consumer.* **Description:** Presents attractive women in swimsuits.
Published by: Playboy Enterprises, Inc., 680 N Lake Shore Dr, Chicago, IL 60611. TEL 312-751-8000, FAX 312-751-2818. Pub. Hugh Hefner.

051 USA ISSN 1066-5129
PLAYBOY'S BLONDES, BRUNETTES, REDHEADS. Text in English. 1985. a. **Document type:** *Magazine, Consumer.* **Description:** Presents attractive women in erotic poses.
Published by: Playboy Enterprises, Inc., 680 N Lake Shore Dr, Chicago, IL 60611. TEL 312-751-8000, FAX 312-751-2818. Pub. Hugh Hefner.

051 746.92 USA ISSN 1059-4191
PLAYBOY'S BOOK OF LINGERIE. Text in English. bi-m. USD 6.95 newsstand/cover; USD 7.95 newsstand/cover in Canada (effective 2001). **Document type:** *Magazine, Consumer.* **Description:** Contains erotic photographs of women wearing lingerie.
Published by: Playboy Enterprises, Inc., 680 N Lake Shore Dr, Chicago, IL 60611. TEL 312-751-8000, FAX 312-751-2818. Pub. Hugh Hefner. **Dist. in UK by:** Comag, Tavistock Rd, W Drayton, Middlesex UB7 7QE, United Kingdom. TEL 44-1895-444055, FAX 44-1895-433602.

051 USA ISSN 1063-9616
PLAYBOY'S CALENDAR PLAYMATES. Text in English. 1992. a. **Document type:** *Magazine, Consumer.* **Description:** Presents Playboy centerfold models who have appeared in calendars.
Published by: Playboy Enterprises, Inc., 680 N Lake Shore Dr, Chicago, IL 60611. TEL 312-751-8000, FAX 312-751-2818. Pub. Hugh Hefner.

051 USA ISSN 1061-9070
PLAYBOY'S CAREER GIRLS. Text in English. 1992. a. **Document type:** *Magazine, Consumer.* **Description:** Presents career women in erotic poses.
Published by: Playboy Enterprises, Inc., 680 N Lake Shore Dr, Chicago, IL 60611. TEL 312-751-2818, FAX 312-751-2818. Pub. Hugh Hefner.

051 USA ISSN 1062-2268
PLAYBOY'S COLLEGE GIRLS. Text in English. 1983. a. **Document type:** *Magazine, Consumer.* **Description:** Presents college women in erotic poses.
Published by: Playboy Enterprises, Inc., 680 N Lake Shore Dr, Chicago, IL 60611. TEL 312-751-8000, FAX 312-751-2818. Pub. Hugh Hefner.

051 USA ISSN 1062-0494
PLAYBOY'S GIRLS OF SUMMER. Text in English. 1983. a. **Document type:** *Magazine, Consumer.* **Description:** Features erotic photographs of attractive women.
Published by: Playboy Enterprises, Inc., 680 N Lake Shore Dr, Chicago, IL 60611. TEL 312-751-8000, FAX 312-751-2818. Pub. Hugh Hefner.

051 USA ISSN 1061-9089
PLAYBOY'S GIRLS OF THE WORLD. Text in English. 1992. a. **Document type:** *Magazine, Consumer.* **Description:** Features erotic photographs of attractive women from all over the world.
Published by: Playboy Enterprises, Inc., 680 N Lake Shore Dr, Chicago, IL 60611. TEL 312-751-8000, FAX 312-751-2818. Pub. Hugh Hefner.

051 USA ISSN 1068-2295
PLAYBOY'S GIRLS OF WINTER. Text in English. 1984. a. USD 6.95 newsstand/cover; GBP 4.50 newsstand/cover in United Kingdom. **Document type:** *Magazine, Consumer.* **Description:** Features erotic photographs of attractive women.
Published by: Playboy Enterprises, Inc., 680 N Lake Shore Dr, Chicago, IL 60611. TEL 312-751-8000, FAX 312-751-2818. Ed., Pub. Jeff Cohen. **Dist. in UK by:** Comag, Tavistock Rd, W Drayton, Middlesex UB7 7QE, United Kingdom. TEL 44-1895-444055, FAX 44-1895-433602.

051 USA ISSN 1069-224X
PLAYBOY'S GREAT PLAYMATE HUNT. Text in English. 1989. a. **Document type:** *Magazine, Consumer.*
Published by: Playboy Enterprises, Inc., 680 N Lake Shore Dr, Chicago, IL 60611. TEL 312-751-8000, FAX 312-751-2818. Pub. Hugh Hefner.

051 USA ISSN 1061-6640
PLAYBOY'S PLAYMATE REVIEW. Text in English. 1985. a. **Document type:** *Magazine, Consumer.* **Description:** Presents women who have appeared in Playboy centerfolds.
Published by: Playboy Enterprises, Inc., 680 N Lake Shore Dr, Chicago, IL 60611. TEL 312-751-8000, FAX 312-751-2818. Pub. Hugh Hefner.

051 USA ISSN 1091-7276
PLAYBOY'S PLAYMATES IN BED. Text in English. a. USD 6.95 newsstand/cover; GBP 4.50 newsstand/cover in United Kingdom. **Document type:** *Magazine, Consumer.*
Published by: Playboy Enterprises, Inc., 680 N Lake Shore Dr, Chicago, IL 60611. TEL 312-751-8000, FAX 312-751-2818. Ed., Pub. Jeff Cohen. **Dist. in UK by:** Comag, Tavistock Rd, W Drayton, Middlesex UB7 7QE, United Kingdom. TEL 44-1895-444055, FAX 44-1895-433602.

051 USA ISSN 1066-5137
PLAYBOY'S WET & WILD WOMEN. Text in English. 1987. a. **Document type:** *Magazine, Consumer.* **Description:** Presents women in erotic poses.
Published by: Playboy Enterprises, Inc., 680 N Lake Shore Dr, Chicago, IL 60611. TEL 312-751-8000, FAX 312-751-2818. Pub. Hugh Hefner.

646.32 JPN
POPEYE. Text in Japanese. 1976. m. JPY 6,490 (effective 2005). **Document type:** *Magazine, Consumer.*
Published by: Magazine House, Ltd., 3-13-10 Ginza, Chuo-ku, Tokyo, 104-8003, Japan. Ed. Shinichiro Onodera. Circ: 352,000.

051 USA
PORN FREE. Text in English. 1994. q. free. adv. video rev. **Document type:** *Magazine, Consumer.* **Description:** Includes interviews, fiction, humor, art, and news. For heterosexuals.
Published by: Abby Ehmann, Ed. & Pub., PO Box 1365, Stuyvesant Sta, New York, NY 10009. TEL 212-598-4343. Adv. contact Abby Ehmann. B&W page USD 100; trim 10.5 x 8. Circ: 500 (controlled).

306.7 CZE
PORNO ROKU. Text in Czech. 2002. 2/yr. CZK 158; CZK 79 newsstand/cover (effective 2009). **Document type:** *Magazine, Consumer.*
Published by: PK 62, a.s., Bohdalecka 6, Prague 10, 101 00, Czech Republic. TEL 420-281-090611, FAX 420-281-090622, pk62@pk62.cz, http://www.pk62.cz.

779.28 CZE ISSN 1214-8628
PRAVE 18. Text in Czech. 2005. 2/yr. CZK 90; CZK 45 newsstand/cover (effective 2009). **Document type:** *Magazine, Consumer.*
Published by: PK 62, a.s., Bohdalecka 6, Prague 10, 101 00, Czech Republic. TEL 420-281-090611, FAX 420-281-090622, pk62@pk62.cz, http://www.pk62.cz.

305.31 DEU
▼ **PROVOCATEUR**; was Maenner bewegt. Text in German. 2011 (Jun.). bi-m. EUR 25.80 domestic; EUR 31.20 foreign; EUR 4.80 newsstand/cover (effective 2011). adv. **Document type:** *Magazine, Consumer.*
Published by: Meth Media Deutschland GmbH, Mozartstr 51/2.OG, Stuttgart, 70180, Germany. TEL 49-711-32067616, FAX 49-711-32067611. Ed. Simone Mueller. Adv. contact Klaus Baader.

306.7 USA
THE QLIMAX TIMES. Text in English. m. USD 39.95. **Document type:** *Newspaper.*
Published by: Qlimax, 313 N York Rd, Hatboro, PA 19040. TEL 800-887-6900, FAX 215-654-1895.

052 GBR
QUEST. Text in English. 2000. m. USD 85, GBP 60, EUR 105 to qualified personnel (effective 2009). adv. back issues avail. **Document type:** *Magazine, Consumer.* **Description:** Covers a broad range of topics and features of interest to men.
Published by: Blue Sky Brands Ltd., Century Pl, Liptraps Ln, Tunbridge Wells, Kent TN2 3EH, United Kingdom. TEL 44-1892-774888, FAX 44-1892-774889. Ed. Simon Wilkinson.

052 AUS ISSN 1449-650X
RALPH. Text in English. 1997. m. AUD 79.50; AUD 8.25 newsstand/cover (effective 2008). adv. **Document type:** *Magazine, Consumer.* **Description:** Contains articles, photos and features on beautiful women, celebrity interviews, sports, adventure, trivia, fashion, toys, and music reviews.
Related titles: Online - full text ed.
Indexed: A11, T02.
Published by: A C P Magazines Ltd. (Subsidiary of: P B L Media Pty Ltd.), 54-58 Park St, Sydney, NSW 2000, Australia. TEL 61-2-92828000, FAX 61-2-91263769, research@acpaction.com.au, http://www.acp.com.au. Eds. Michael Pickering, Santi Pintado. Adv. contact Amanda Tsolakis. color page AUD 9,425; trim 225 x 297. Circ: 85,063. **Subscr. to:** Magshop.

051 USA ISSN 1541-4671
RAMP; the evolution of man. Text in English. 2002 (Nov.). bi-m. USD 14.97 (effective 2004). adv. illus. **Document type:** *Magazine, Consumer.* **Description:** Provides topical information for men on entertainment, fashion, cars, travel, gear and gadgets, sports, fitness, food and drink, and beautiful women.
Published by: Ramp Media, Inc., 801 Second Ave, New York, NY 10017. TEL 212-986-5100, FAX 646-658-7586, subscribe@rampmag.com. Ed. Les Kovach. Pub. Richard Amann. adv.: B&W page USD 14,280, color page USD 20,400; trim 8.375 x 10.875. Circ: 240,000 (paid). **Subscr. to:** PO Box 403, Mount Morris, IL 61054. TEL 800-490-5648.

052 GBR ISSN 1356-8132
RAVERS. Text in English. 1995. m. GBP 39.95; GBP 2.60 newsstand/cover. **Document type:** *Magazine, Consumer.*
Published by: Galaxy Publications Ltd., PO Box 312, Galaxy Publications Ltd, Witham, Essex CM8 3SZ, United Kingdom. FAX 44-1376-534500. **Dist. by:** Blackhorse Distributors Ltd., Freebourne Rd, PO Box 1124, Witham, Essex CM8 3XY, United Kingdom. TEL 44-1376-501919, FAX 44-1376-501990.

052 GBR ISSN 1357-3624
RAVERS CHRISTMAS SPECIAL. Text in English. 1995. a. **Document type:** *Magazine, Consumer.*
Published by: Galaxy Publications Ltd., PO Box 312, Galaxy Publications Ltd, Witham, Essex CM8 3SZ, United Kingdom. FAX 44-1376-534536.

052 GBR ISSN 1357-3608
RAVERS SUMMER SPECIAL. Text in English. 1995. a. **Document type:** *Magazine, Consumer.*
Published by: Galaxy Publications Ltd., PO Box 312, Galaxy Publications Ltd, Witham, Essex CM8 3SZ, United Kingdom. FAX 44-1376-510680.

052 GBR ISSN 0955-1840
RAZZLE; for hard men. Text in English. m. GBP 32; GBP 1.90 newsstand/cover (effective 2001). back issues avail. **Document type:** *Magazine, Consumer.*
Published by: Paul Raymond Publications Ltd., 2 Archer St, London, W1V 8JJ, United Kingdom. TEL 44-20-72928000, FAX 44-20-72928021. **Subscr. to:** MRM, PO Box 503, Leicester LE94 0AD, United Kingdom. TEL 44-1858-410510. **Dist. by:** Comag, Tavistock Rd, W Drayton, Middlesex UB7 7QE, United Kingdom. TEL 44-1895-444055, FAX 44-1895-433602.

808.803 538 USA ISSN 2162-1071
▼ **RIPE EROTICA MAGAZINE.** Text in English. 2011. m. USD 0.99 per issue (effective 2011). **Document type:** *Magazine, Trade.*
Media: Online - full text.
Published by: Stephen Buck, Ed. & Pub.

306.775 GBR
RITUAL MAGAZINE. Text in English. q. adv.
Address: 2 Lansdowne Row, Berkeley Square, London, W1X 8HL, United Kingdom. FAX 44-20-7493-4935. adv.: B&W page GBP 730, B&W page USD 1,170, color page USD 950, color page GBP 1,520; trim 210 x 297.

306.7 NLD ISSN 1571-9278
DE RODE LANTAARN. Text in Dutch. 2003. q. EUR 16 (effective 2008). adv.
Published by: De Wallenwinkel, Enge Kerksteeg 3, Amsterdam, 1012 GV, Netherlands. TEL 31-20-4207328.

056.9 BRA ISSN 1807-7331
ROMANO. Text in Portuguese. 2004. m. BRL 5.90 newsstand/cover (effective 2006). **Document type:** *Magazine, Consumer.*
Published by: Editora Escala Ltda., Av Prof Ida Kolb, 551, Casa Verde, Sao Paulo, 02518-000, Brazil. TEL 55-11-38552100, FAX 55-11-38579643, escala@escala.com.br, http://www.escala.com.br.

305.42 USA ISSN 1093-894X
THE ROMANTIC; hundreds of tips for fun and creative romance. Text in English. 1996. bi-m. USD 15 domestic; USD 20 foreign (effective 2000). adv. bk.rev. illus. **Document type:** *Newsletter.*
Published by: Sterling Publications, PO Box 1567, Cary, NC 27511-1567. TEL 919-462-0900, 888-476-6268. Ed., Pub., R&P, Adv. contact Michael Webb. Circ: 10,000 (paid).

059.956 JPN
SABRA. Text in Japanese. bi-w. JPY 300 newsstand/cover (effective 2002). adv. **Document type:** *Magazine, Consumer.*
Published by: Shogakukan Inc., 3-1 Hitotsubashi 2-chome, Chiyoda-ku, Tokyo, 101-8001, Japan. TEL 81-3-3230-5211, FAX 81-3-3264-8471, http://www.shogakukan.co.jp.

305.31 RUS ISSN 0869-7604
SAM: ZHURNAL DLYA UMEL'TSEV. Text in Russian. m. —East View.
Published by: Izdatel'skii dom Gefest, B Semenovskaya 40, Moscow, 105023, Russian Federation. TEL 7-095-3662945, FAX 7-095-3662434. Ed. Yu S Stolyarov. **Dist. by:** East View Information Services, 10601 Wayzata Blvd, Minneapolis, MN 55305. TEL 952-252-1201, 800-477-1005, FAX 952-252-1202, info@eastview.com, http://www.eastview.com.

779.28 DEU
ST. PAULI NACHRICHTEN; das Lustblatt Nr.1. Text in German. 1970. m. EUR 3 newsstand/cover (effective 2007). adv. **Document type:** *Magazine, Consumer.* **Description:** Provides a wide variety of erotic photos and stories as well as personal ads.
Published by: S P N Zeitschriften Verlags GmbH, Waidmannstr 35, Hamburg, 22769, Germany. TEL 49-40-8501039, FAX 49-40-8501126, info@spn-verlag.de. adv.: color page EUR 3,900. Circ: 130,000 (controlled).

SAVILE ROW STYLE MAGAZINE. *see* CLOTHING TRADE—Fashions

808.803538 USA
SCARLETT LETTERS; a literary journal of women erotica. Text in English. 1998. bi-m. adv. back issues avail. **Document type:** *Journal, Consumer.* **Description:** Publishes short fiction, poetry, visual art and humor for men.
Media: Online - full text.
Published by: J T's Stockroom, 2140 Hyperion Ave, Los Angeles, CA 90027. TEL 800-755-8697, scarltgrrl@aol.com, http://scaretletters.com/. Ed. Heather Corinna.

779.28 DEU
SCHLUESSELLOCH. Text in German. 1970. w. adv. **Document type:** *Magazine, Consumer.*
Formerly (until 1971): Durchs Schluesselloch
Published by: Pabel-Moewig Verlag KG (Subsidiary of: Bauer Media Group), Karlsruherstr 31, Rastatt, 76437, Germany. TEL 49-7222-130, FAX 49-7222-13218, empfang@vpm.de, http://www.vpm-online.de. Adv. contact Rainer Gross. B&W page EUR 2,372, color page EUR 4,136; 192 x 260. Circ: 92,000 (paid).

301.412 USA ISSN 1073-2438
CODEN: ARRTFU
SCORE (MIAMI). Text in English. 1992. m. (13/yr.). USD 49.95 (effective 1999). adv. bk.rev. **Document type:** *Magazine, Consumer.*
Published by: Quad International, Inc., 4931 S W 75th Ave, Miami, FL 33155-4440. TEL 305-662-5959, FAX 305-662-5952. Ed. Michael T Uwate. Pub., R&P John C Fox. Adv. contact John Romano. color page USD 3,225; trim 10.88 x 8. Circ: 187,221 (paid).

SER PADRES/BEING PARENTS. *see* WOMEN'S INTERESTS

306.7 374 USA
SEX, ETC.; sex education by teens, for teens!. Text in English. 19??. 3/yr. USD 15 (effective 2010). back issues avail. **Document type:** *Magazine, Trade.* **Description:** Provides resources, advocacy, training, and technical assistant in support of balanced, comprehensive sexuality education in the United States.
Related titles: Online - full text ed.
Published by: Network for Family Life Education, Rutgers University, The State University of New Jersey, 41 Gordon Rd, Ste C, Piscataway, NJ 08854. TEL 732-445-7929, FAX 732-445-7970.

779.28 CZE ISSN 1211-4502
SEX KONTAKT MAGAZIN. Text in Czech. 1992. m. CZK 564; CZK 47 newsstand/cover (effective 2009). **Document type:** *Magazine, Consumer.*
Published by: PK 62, a.s., Bohdalecka 6, Prague 10, 101 00, Czech Republic. TEL 420-281-090611, FAX 420-281-090622, pk62@pk62.cz, http://www.pk62.cz. Ed. Zdenek Urban.

779.28 DEU
SEX WOCHE; das junge Magazin. Variant title: Sexwoche. Text in German. w. adv. **Document type:** *Magazine, Consumer.* **Description:** Filled with sexy and erotic photos of nude women.
Published by: Pabel-Moewig Verlag KG (Subsidiary of: Bauer Media Group), Karlsruherstr 31, Rastatt, 76437, Germany. TEL 49-7222-130, FAX 49-7222-13218, empfang@vpm.de, http://www.vpm-online.de. Adv. contact Rainer Gross. B&W page EUR 2,372, color page EUR 4,136; 192 x 260. Circ: 71,000 (paid). **Subscr. to:** G L P International. TEL 201-871-1010, FAX 201-871-0870, info@glpnews.com, http://www.glpnews.com.

306.7 USA ISSN 1933-7426
SEXHERALD. Text in English. 2003. m. **Document type:** *Magazine, Consumer.*
Media: Online - full text.
Address: http://www.sexherald.com.

051 USA
SEXUAL CONFESSIONS. Text in English. bi-m. adv. **Document type:** *Magazine, Consumer.*

Published by: Mavety Media Group, 225 Broadway, Ste 2801, New York, NY 10007-3079. TEL 212-966-8400, FAX 212-966-9366.

306.7 374 USA
SEXUAL INTELLIGENCE. Text in English. 200?. m. free (effective 2010). **Document type:** *Newsletter, Consumer.* **Description:** Features news, media critiques, social commentary, and political insight—all focused on sexuality.
Media: Online - full text.
Address: c/o Dr. Marty Klein, 2439 Birch St. #2, Palo Alto, CA 94306. TEL 650-856-6533, mklein@sexed.org. Ed., Pub. Marty Klein.

▼ **SEXY!.** *see* LIFESTYLE

779.28 DEU
SEXY. Text in English. w. adv. **Document type:** *Magazine, Consumer.* **Description:** Contains erotic stories and nude pictorials filled with beautiful women.
Published by: Pabel-Moewig Verlag KG (Subsidiary of: Bauer Media Group), Karlsruherstr 31, Rastatt, 76437, Germany. TEL 49-7222-130, FAX 49-7222-13218, empfang@vpm.de, http://www.vpm-online.de. Adv. contact Rainer Gross. B&W page EUR 2,372, color page EUR 4,136; trim 192 x 260. Circ: 96,000 (paid).

051 USA
SEXY N Y C. Text in English. 1996. m. USD 2.99 newsstand/cover. adv. illus. **Document type:** *Guide, Consumer.* **Description:** Covers adult entertainment in New York City.
Published by: Paradise Magazine, Inc., PO Box 2116, New York, NY 10116-2116. TEL 212-630-0242. Ed. Linda E Jacobs. Pub. Thomas Barris.

SHADES BEYOND GRAY. *see* LITERATURE

051 USA
SHARPMAN.COM; the ultimate guide to men's living. Text in English. 1998. w.
Media: Online - full content.
Published by: SharpMan Media LLC, 11718 Barrington Ct., No. 702, Los Angeles, CA 90049. http://www.sharpman.com. Ed. Y M Reiss. Circ: 60,000.

305.31 790.1 USA ISSN 1934-7065
SHIMMY MAGAZINE. Text in English. 200?. q. **Document type:** *Magazine, Consumer.*
Published by: Black Graves Media, PO Box 11232, Santa Ana, CA 92711. http://www.blackgraves.com.

646.4 CHN
SHISHANG BASHA - NANSHI/HARPER'S BAZAAR (MEN'S EDITION). Text in Chinese. 2003. m. CNY 200 (effective 2008). **Document type:** *Magazine, Consumer.*
Related titles: Online - full text ed.
Published by: Trends Communication Co. Ltd., 21/F, Trends Bldg., 9, Guanghua Rd., Beijing, 100020, China. TEL 86-10-65872155, http://www.trends.com.cn/.

059.951 CHN ISSN 1673-2553
SHISHANG XIANSHENG/ESQUIRE. Text in Chinese. m. CNY 20 newsstand/cover (effective 2008). adv. **Document type:** *Magazine, Consumer.*
Formerly: Shishang (1005-1988)
—East View.
Published by: Trends Communication Co. Ltd., 24/F, Trends Bldg., 9, Guanghua Rd., Beijing, 100020, China. http://www.trends.com.cn/.

779.28 USA ISSN 1559-9515
SHOW (LOS ANGELES); the art of sexy. Variant title: Show Magazine. Text in English. 2006. q. USD 24.95 (effective 2010). **Document type:** *Magazine, Consumer.* **Description:** Features urban models and show girls.
Related titles: ◆ Special ed(s).: Showcase (Los Angeles). ISSN 2152-9256; ◆ Black Lingerie. ISSN 2152-7075; ◆ The Art of Sexy by Show. ISSN 2152-9264.
Published by: Cummings Media, 500 Molino St, Ste 111, Los Angeles, CA 90013. TEL 213-402-4634, sean@cummingsmedia.com.

779.28 USA ISSN 2152-9256
▼ **SHOWCASE (LOS ANGELES).** Text in English. 2010. bi-m. USD 9.95 per issue (effective 2010). **Document type:** *Magazine, Consumer.* **Description:** Features models from Show Magazine.
Related titles: ◆ Special ed. of: Show (Los Angeles). ISSN 1559-9515.
Published by: Cummings Media, 500 Molino St, Ste 111, Los Angeles, CA 90013. TEL 213-402-4634, sean@cummingsmedia.com.

SKIN TWO. *see* LIFESTYLE

305.31 USA ISSN 1555-4694
SLY; conquer your world. Text in English. 2005. 8/yr. adv. **Document type:** *Magazine, Consumer.* **Description:** Aimed at 40 year old and older men.
Published by: American Media, Inc., 4950 Communication Ave, Ste 100, Boca Raton, FL 33431. TEL 212-743-6527, 800-998-0731, kslivken@amilink.com, http://www.americanmediainc.com. Pubs. Alan Stiles TEL 212-545-4846, Diane Newman TEL 212-545-4846. adv.: B&W page USD 13,775, color page USD 14,500; trim 9 x 10.875.

779.28 USA ISSN 1554-8392
SMOOTH GIRL. Text in English. 2004. 3/yr. USD 4.99 newsstand/cover (effective 2004). adv. back issues avail. **Document type:** *Magazine, Consumer.*
Published by: Star Media, Inc., 212 W 35th St, 2nd Fl, New York, NY 10001-2508. TEL 212-334-4902. Ed. Sean Cummings TEL 212-925-1150 ext 24. Pub. Sandra Vasceannie TEL 212-925-1150 ext 11. adv.: B&W page USD 4,500, color page USD 8,500; trim 8 x 10.75. Circ: 141,605.

305.31 051 USA
SOAK MAGAZINE. Text in English. 2004. bi-m. USD 19.95 domestic; USD 30.95 foreign (effective 2005). adv. **Document type:** *Magazine, Consumer.* **Description:** Features beautiful models, actresses and pop singers. Covers movies, music and trends as well as cars, fashions and gadgets.
Published by: Ad Innovations, Inc., 803 S. Dymond Rd., Libertyville, IL 60048-3029. Adv. contacts Dominic Niro TEL 773-710-7181, Lisa Norling-Christensen TEL 773-255-6229. color page USD 1,922; trim 8.25 x 10.875. Circ: 36,000 (paid). **Subscr. to:** Soak Magazine, Inc., 2407 Oakton St, Ste A, Arlington Heights, IL 60005.

SOPHISTICATED GROOM. *see* MATRIMONY

051 USA ISSN 0894-9751
SPECTATOR (BERKELEY); California's original adult newsmagazine. Text in English. w. USD 39 (effective 2000). adv. illus. reprints avail. **Description:** Includes analyses on sexual matters; a contact magazine for the sexually active adult. Contains calender listings for the San Francisco Bay Area.
Published by: Bold Type, Inc., PO Box 1984, Berkeley, CA 94701-1984. TEL 510-658-3380, FAX 510-658-3326, Layne@spectator.net, http://www.spectator.net. Ed. Layne Winklebleck. Adv. contact Kevinn Minor.

306.7 RUS
SPID-INFO. Text in Russian. m. RUR 198 for 6 mos. domestic (effective 2004). **Document type:** *Newspaper, Consumer.*
Related titles: Online - full content ed.
Published by: Izdatel'stvo S-Info, A-ya 42, Moscow, 125284, Russian Federation. TEL 7-095-7969294, FAX 7-095-2520920, s-info@si.ru. Ed. Andrei Mann. Circ: 2,910,000. **Subscr. to:** Unicont Enterprises Inc., 1340 Centre St, Ste 209, Newton, MA 02459. TEL 800-763-7475, FAX 617-964-8753, podpiska@unipressa.com.

SPORTS ILLUSTRATED (SWIMSUIT EDITION). *see* CLOTHING TRADE—Fashions

SPORTS ILLUSTRATED SWIMSUIT GERMANY. *see* CLOTHING TRADE—Fashions

779.28 DEU
ST. PAULI MAGAZIN. Text in German. bi-m. EUR 15; EUR 3.30 newsstand/cover (effective 2007). adv. **Document type:** *Magazine, Consumer.*
Published by: S P N Zeitschriften Verlags GmbH, Waidmannstr 35, Hamburg, 22769, Germany. TEL 49-40-8501039, FAX 49-40-8501126, info@spn-verlag.de. adv.: color page EUR 3,900. Circ: 100,000 (controlled).

052 ZAF ISSN 1022-3096
STAG SEXUAL FORUM. Text in English. 1993. m. ZAR 5.50 per issue. adv. illus. **Document type:** *Journal, Consumer.*
Published by: Viclen Promotions, PO Box 354, Mondeor, Gauteng 2110, South Africa.

STAND FIRM; God's challenge for today's man. *see* RELIGIONS AND THEOLOGY—Protestant

059.89 GRC ISSN 1107-8588
STATUS. Text in Greek. 1988. m. EUR 40 (effective 2011). adv. **Document type:** *Magazine, Consumer.* **Description:** Contains articles on business, cars, motorbikes, men's fashion, extreme and adventure sports, relationships, sex and current events.
Published by: Liberis Publications S.A./Ekdoseon Lymperi A.E., Ioannou Metaxa 80, Karelas, Koropi 19400, Greece. TEL 30-210-6688000, FAX 30-210-6688300, info@liberis.gr, http://www.liberis.gr. Ed. Kimon Fragakis.

051.081 305.31 USA ISSN 1524-2838
AP2
STUFF; for men. Text in English. 1998. m. adv. illus. **Document type:** *Magazine, Consumer.* **Description:** Provides evidence of why it's a man's world - fast cars, great looking girls, wild stories, easy money, and gadgets.
Published by: Dennis Publishing, Inc., 1040 Ave of the Americas, 22nd Fl, New York, NY 10018. TEL 212-302-2626, FAX 212-302-2635.

STUFF; for men. *see* LIFESTYLE

053.1 DEU
STUFF; Das weltbeste Gadget-Magazin. Text in German. bi-m. EUR 21; EUR 3.90 newsstand/cover (effective 2007). adv. **Document type:** *Magazine, Consumer.*
Published by: MediaVentura Publishing GmbH, Haussmannstr 240, Stuttgart, 70188, Germany. TEL 49-711-99797264, FAX 49-711-99797393. Ed., Pub. Udo Woehrle. Adv. contact Stephan W Brinkmann. page EUR 7,000. Circ: 100,000 (paid and controlled).

056.9 PRT
STUFF. Text in Portuguese. 2006. m. EUR 18.72; EUR 1.95 newsstand/cover (effective 2007). adv. **Document type:** *Magazine, Consumer.*
Published by: Edimpresa Editora Lda., Rua Calvet de Magalhaes 242, Laveiras, Paco de Arcos, 2770-022, Portugal. TEL 351-21-4698000, FAX 351-21-4698501, edimpresa@edimpresa.pt, http://www.edimpresa.pt. Ed. Ana Joaquim. adv.: page EUR 5,000; trim 220 x 297. Circ: 40,033 (paid).

057.86 CZE ISSN 1214-2603
STUFF. Text in Czech. 2003. m. CZK 715 (effective 2009). adv. **Document type:** *Magazine, Consumer.*
Published by: Stratosfera s.r.o., Drtinova 8, Prague 5, 150 00, Czech Republic. TEL 420-234-109540, FAX 420-234-109264, online@stratosfera.cz, http://www.stratosfera.cz. Adv. contact Martina Palkoskova. page CZK 165,000. Circ: 8,754 (paid). **Subscr. to:** SEND Predplatne s.r.o., PO Box 141, Prague 4 140 21, Czech Republic. TEL 420-225-985225, FAX 420-225-341425, send@send.cz, http://www.send.cz.

059.95911 THA ISSN 1686-5332
STUFF. Text in Thai. 2004. m. THB 90 newsstand/cover (effective 2010). adv. **Document type:** *Magazine, Consumer.*
Published by: Inspire Entertainment Co., 115-66 Moo 12, Soi Ramintra 40, Ramintra Rd, Klong-kum, Bung-kum, Bangkok, 10230, Thailand. TEL 662-508-8100, FAX 662-693-3287, contact@inspire.co.th, http://www.inspire.co.th. Adv. contact Witthaya Choenubol. Circ: 100,000 (paid).

305.31 ZAF ISSN 1994-313X
STUFF. Text in English. 2007. bi-m. ZAR 112.28 (effective 2008). adv. **Document type:** *Magazine, Consumer.*
Published by: Avusa Media Limited, 37 Bath Ave, Rosebank, Johannesburg, South Africa. TEL 27-11-2803403. adv.: page ZAR 18,000; trim 220 x 297.

305.31 POL
▼ **STUFF.** Text in Polish. 2010. m. PLZ 4.90 newsstand/cover (effective 2011). adv. **Document type:** *Magazine, Consumer.*
Published by: Ginza Media Group, ul Srodziemnomorska 47, Warsaw, 02-758, Poland. TEL 48-22-2034880, FAX 48-22-6424524. Ed. Marcin Prokop. Adv. contact Malgorzata Karasiewicz. Circ: 50,000 (paid).

305.31 RUS
STUFF. Text in Russian. 2001. 10/yr. RUR 1,010 (effective 2006). adv. **Document type:** *Magazine, Consumer.*
Published by: Izdatel'stvo Otkrytye Sistemy/Open Systems Publications, ul Rustaveli, dom 12A, komn 117, Moscow, 127254, Russian Federation. TEL 7-095-2539206, FAX 7-095-2539204, info@osp.ru, http://www.osp.ru. Circ: 50,000.

STUFF NANO EDITION. *see* LIFESTYLE

305.31 GBR ISSN 1472-2879
SUBJECT MAGAZINE. Text in English. 2001. 3/yr. GBP 5.95 (effective 2001). back issues avail. **Document type:** *Magazine, Consumer.* **Description:** Covers music, pop culture, film, and life style.
Published by: Stable Publications Ltd., PO Box 31959, London, W2 5YA, United Kingdom. TEL 44-20-7792-2444, FAX 44-20-7792-1333, info@subject-magazine.com. Ed. Ross Cottingham.

051 USA ISSN 1069-1723
SWANK. Text in English. 1956. m. USD 52 (effective 2000). adv. **Document type:** *Magazine, Consumer.*
Published by: Magna Publishing, 210 Rte 4 E, Ste 211, Paramus, NJ 07652. Ed. Paul Gambino. R&P Christine Montel. Adv. contact Arnold Held. Circ: 200,000.

051 USA
SWANK'S D-CUP. Text in English. 13/yr. USD 35; USD 6.99 newsstand/cover (effective 1999). **Document type:** *Magazine, Consumer.*
Published by: Magna Publishing, 210 Rte 4 E, Ste 211, Paramus, NJ 07652. TEL 201-843-4004, FAX 201-843-8775.

051 USA
SWANK'S LEG ACTION. Text in English. 13/yr. USD 35; USD 6.99 newsstand/cover (effective 1999). **Document type:** *Magazine, Consumer.*
Published by: Magna Publishing, 210 Rte 4 E, Ste 211, Paramus, NJ 07652. TEL 201-487-6124, FAX 201-487-9360.

051 790.1 USA
SWANK'S LEISURE. Text in English. 11/yr. USD 35; USD 6.99 newsstand/cover (effective 1999). adv. **Document type:** *Magazine, Consumer.*
Published by: Magna Publishing, 210 Rte 4 E, Ste 211, Paramus, NJ 07652. TEL 201-843-4004, FAX 201-843-8775.

T & L GOLF. (Travel & Leisure) *see* SPORTS AND GAMES—Ball Games

059.956 JPN
TARZAN. Text in Japanese. 1986. bi-w. JPY 9,900 (effective 2005). **Document type:** *Magazine, Consumer.* **Description:** Covers fitness and health issues with fashion, travel and lifestyle features.
Published by: Magazine House, Ltd., 3-13-10 Ginza, Chuo-ku, Tokyo, 104-8003, Japan. Circ: 250,000.

TASA-ARVO. *see* WOMEN'S INTERESTS

052 GBR ISSN 1355-1485
TEAZER. Text in English. 1996. m. GBP 2.60 newsstand/cover; USD 6.99 newsstand/cover in United States. adv. **Document type:** *Magazine, Consumer.*
Published by: Galaxy Publications Ltd., PO Box 312, Galaxy Publications Ltd, Witham, Essex CM8 3SZ, United Kingdom. TEL 44-1376-534500, FAX 44-1376-534536. Ed. Ross Gilfillan. Adv. contact Corrinne Berry. **Dist. by:** Blackhorse Distribution Ltd., Blackhorse Distribution Ltd, Freebourne Rd, PO Box 1124, Witham, Essex CM8 3XJ, United Kingdom. TEL 44-1376-534530, FAX 44-1376-534531.

779.28 GBR ISSN 1365-8557
TEAZER JUST 18. Text in English. 1997. m. (13/yr.). GBP 2.60 newsstand/cover. adv. **Document type:** *Magazine, Consumer.* **Description:** Presents young nude women in erotic poses and positions.
Published by: Galaxy Publications Ltd., PO Box 312, Galaxy Publications Ltd, Witham, Essex CM8 3SZ, United Kingdom. TEL 44-1376-534500, FAX 44-1376-534536. **Dist. by:** Blackhorse Distribution Ltd., Blackhorse Distribution Ltd, Freebourne Rd, PO Box 1124, Witham, Essex CM8 3XJ, United Kingdom. TEL 44-1376-534530, FAX 44-1376-534531.

808.803538 USA
THEPOSITION. Text in English. 2000. w. adv. **Document type:** *Magazine, Consumer.* **Description:** Covers all sides of the sexual spectrum by featuring today's headlines, people, politics, and controversies in sex and culture.
Media: Online - full content.
Published by: ThePosition, L.L.C., 233 5th Ave, Ste 2A, New York, NY 10016. TEL 212-689-6337, FAX 212-269-8162, advertise@theposition.com. Ed. Jack Heidenry. Pub. Daniel Gluck.

051 USA ISSN 1935-3480
THIQUE. Text in English. 2007. bi-m. adv. **Document type:** *Magazine, Consumer.* **Description:** Includes entertainment, art, fashion, sports, business, health and technology news and advice for men.
Related titles: Online - full text ed.: ISSN 1935-3707.
Published by: Thique Multimedia Group, PO Box 43745, Baltimore, MD 21236. TEL 410-838-8771. Pub. Lae Cole.

779.28 DNK ISSN 1395-2404
TIDENS KVINDER. Text in Danish. 1994. bi-m. DKK 297 (effective 2008). adv. **Document type:** *Magazine, Consumer.* **Description:** Contains erotic articles and photos on sexual relations between men and women.
Related titles: Online - full text ed.
Published by: Aller International A-S, Marielundsvej 46 E, Herlev, 2730, Denmark. TEL 45-44-858888, FAX 45-44-858887, reception@aller.dk, http://www.aller.dk. Ed. Lene Byriel. Adv. contact Birthe Schleicher. page DKK 21,100; 208 x 280.

052 CAN
HQ1090.7.C2
TORO (ONLINE). Text in English. 2003. 8/yr. free. adv. **Document type:** *Magazine, Consumer.* **Description:** Provides a source for cutting edge information on sports, style, travel, entertainment, sex and popular culture for men.
Formerly (until 2008): Toro (Print) (1709-1314)
Indexed: C03, CBCARef, P48, PQC.
Published by: Black Angus Media Inc., 125 Blake St., Toronto, ON M4J 3E2, Canada. TEL 416-850-4144, FAX 647-439-5521. Ed. Derek Finkle. Pub. Dinah Quattrin.

051 USA
TOTAL MAN. Text in English. s-m. **Document type:** *Newsletter.* **Description:** Deals with men's issues: relationships, parenting, health & fitness, foods, fashion, money, careers, technology, sports and politics.

Media: Online - full text.
Published by: Total Interactive, 409 Lanmark Road, St. Louis, MO 63137. TEL 314-388-9960.

779.28 CHE
TREFFPUNKT; das internationale Sex-Kontakt Magazin. Text in German. 1974. m. adv. **Document type:** *Magazine, Consumer.* **Description:** Contains services and personal listings for those seeking various types of sexual encounters.
Published by: Roluba AG, Postfach 4548, Basel, 4002, Switzerland. TEL 41-61-6911010, FAX 41-61-6911005, info@roluba.ch, http://www.roluba.ch. adv.: B&W page CHF 1,245, color page CHF 1,620; trim 195 x 290.

306.77 FRA ISSN 1771-2688
LA TRIBUNE DU PLAISIR. Text in French. 2007. m. **Document type:** *Magazine, Consumer.*
Published by: Editions Prova, BP 2271, Mulhouse, 68068 Cedex, France. TEL 33-8-99190069.

779.28 GBR ISSN 1366-3631
TWO BLUE COUPLES. Text in English. 1995. bi-m. GBP 3.50 newsstand/cover. adv. **Document type:** *Magazine, Consumer.* **Description:** Presents sexually explicit erotic photos of nude women in action.
Formerly (until 1996): Two Blue Couples Only (1357-3578)
Published by: Galaxy Publications Ltd., PO Box 312, Galaxy Publications Ltd, Witham, Essex CM8 3SZ, United Kingdom. TEL 44-1376-534500, FAX 44-1376-534536. **Dist. by:** Blackhorse Distribution Ltd., Blackhorse Distribution Ltd, Freebourne Rd, PO Box 1124, Witham, Essex CM8 3XJ, United Kingdom. TEL 44-1376-534530, FAX 44-1376-534531.

779.28 POL ISSN 1230-8706
TWOJ WEEKEND. Text in Polish. 1992. fortn. PLZ 2.20 newsstand/cover (effective 2003). adv. **Document type:** *Magazine, Consumer.*
Published by: Wydawnictwo Bauer Sp. z o.o. (Subsidiary of: Bauer Media Group), ul Motorowa 1, Warsaw, 04-035, Poland. TEL 48-22-5170500, FAX 48-22-5170125, kontakt@bauer.pl, http://www.bauer.pl. Adv. contact Katarzyna Jablonska. page PLZ 10,000; trim 215 x 290.

305.31 SAU ISSN 1319-3287
URDU NEWS. Text in Urdu. 1992. m. adv. **Document type:** *Newspaper, Consumer.* **Description:** Focuses on the male lifestyle in the Arab world. It contains articles and information of interest to men, including fashion, automotive news, and others. It's target audience is the adult male population of the Kingdom and the Arab world.
Published by: Saudi Research & Publishing Co., P O Box 478, Riyadh, 11411, Saudi Arabia. TEL 966-1-4419933, FAX 966-1-4429555, editorial@majalla.com, http://www.srpc.com/main. adv.: page SAR 18,600. Circ: 45,260 (paid).

646.32 USA ISSN 1546-0835
V MAN. (Visionaire) Text in English. 2003 (Fall/Win.). s-a. USD 4.95 newsstand/cover domestic; GBP 4.95 newsstand/cover in United Kingdom; EUR 7.95 newsstand/cover Germany & Italy; EUR 8.95 newsstand/cover in France Germany & Italy (effective 2004). adv. **Document type:** *Magazine, Consumer.*
Published by: Visionaire Publishing, 11 Mercer St, New York, NY 10013. TEL 212-274-8959, FAX 212-343-2595, http://www.visionaireworld.com. Eds. Philip Utz, Stephen Gan. Adv. contact Giorgio Pace.

VARLA. *see* LIFESTYLE

051 USA ISSN 0194-6935
VELVET. Text in English. 197?. 13/yr. USD 6.99 newsstand/cover. adv. **Document type:** *Magazine, Consumer.*
Published by: Magna Publishing, 210 Rte 4 E, Ste 211, Paramus, NJ 07652. TEL 201-843-4004, FAX 201-843-8775.

306.7 USA
VENUS OR VIXEN; read some smut!. Text in English. 1996. a. free (effective 2003). **Description:** Offers the finest in erotic fiction, sex related feature articles, book, web and toy reviews, and erotic artwork. It is a pansexual, pro-sexual erotic web zine.
Media: Online - full text.
Address: 815 Washington St, Box No. 3, Oakland, CA 94607. staff@venusorvixen.com, care@venusorvixen.com, http://www.venusorvixon.com. Eds. Cara Bruce, Lisa Montanarelli.

058.82 NOR ISSN 0042-4951
VI MENN. Text in Norwegian. 1951. 18/yr. NOK 379; NOK 46 newsstand/cover (effective 2009). adv. illus. **Document type:** *Magazine, Consumer.*
Incorporates (in 2004): Vi Menn Fotball (1502-8917); Which was formerly (until 2001): Fotball (0333-4341); (until 1950): Norges Fotballforbunds Meddelelsesblad (1500-9866); (1911-1947): Fotball (0808-5471); Incorportes (1979-1981): Sport i Bilder (1501-5548)
Related titles: Online - full text ed.: ISSN 1500-1962.
—CCC.
Published by: Hjemmet Mortensen AS, Gullhaugveien 1, Nydalen, Oslo, 0441, Norway. TEL 47-22-585000, FAX 47-22-585959, firmapost@hm-media.no, http://www.hm-media.no. Ed. Alexander Oysta. adv.: color page NOK 59,500; trim 192 x 260. Circ: 106,736 (paid).

056.9 BRA ISSN 0104-737X
VIP EXAME. Text in Portuguese. 1981. m. BRL 106.56; BRL 9.99 newsstand/cover (effective 2010). adv. **Document type:** *Magazine, Consumer.*
Related titles: ◆ Supplement to: Exame. ISSN 0102-2881.
Published by: Editora Abril, S.A., Avenida das Nacoes Unidas 7221, Pinheiros, Sao Paulo, SP 05425-902, Brazil. TEL 55-11-50872112, FAX 55-11-50872100, abrilsac@abril.com.br, http://www.abril.com.br. adv.: page BRL 63,200; trim 202 x 266. Circ: 61,636 (paid).

VIVE LA DIFFERENCE. *see* ETHNIC INTERESTS

646.32 FRA ISSN 1776-2170
VOGUE HOMMES INTERNATIONAL. Text in French. 1985. s-a. EUR 9 (effective 2011). adv. **Document type:** *Magazine, Consumer.*
Formerly (until 2000): Vogue Hommes International Mode (0982-6084)
Published by: Publications Conde Nast S.A., 56 A rue du Faubourg Saint-Honore, Paris, 75008, France. TEL 33-1-53436000, FAX 33-1-53436060.

305.31 USA ISSN 1522-5585
VOICE MALE. Text in English. 1986. quadrennial. USD 25 membership (effective 2000). bk.rev. illus. **Document type:** *Newsletter, Consumer.* **Description:** Examines topics and issues of interest to men and women who want to read a pro-feminist, male-positive, gay-affirmative perspective. Subjects covered include domestic violence prevention, education against sexism and sexual assault, fathering issues, male health, survivors of childhood abuse, mythopoetics, and support groups.
Formerly (until 1998): Valley Men (1092-4795)
Related titles: Online - full text ed.
Indexed: DYW, GW, P48, PQC.
Published by: Men's Resource Center of Western Massachusetts, 236 N Pleasant St, Amherst, MA 01002. TEL 413-253-9887, wma@mrc-wma.com.

057.1 RUS ISSN 1560-5469
VOT TAK!. Text in Russian. 1998. w. adv. **Document type:** *Magazine, Consumer.*
Published by: Izdatel'skii Dom Burda, ul Pravdy 8, Moscow, 125040, Russian Federation. TEL 7-095-7979849, FAX 7-095-2571196, vertrieb@burda.ru, http://www.burda.ru. adv.: page USD 4,500. Circ: 400,000 (paid and controlled).

305.31 306.7 UKR
VOT TAK!. Text in Russian. w. UAK 56.94 for 6 mos. domestic (effective 2004). **Document type:** *Magazine, Consumer.*
Published by: Burda Ukraina, Zhyljanskaja ul. 29, Kiev, 01033, Ukraine. TEL 38-044-4908363, FAX 38-044-4908364, zhestkov@burda.ua, http://www.burda.ua. Ed. Vitalii Novak TEL 380-44-4908361.

779.28 USA
W W E DIVAS (YEAR). (World Wrestling Entertainment, Inc.) Text in English. irreg., latest 2002. USD 6.99 newsstand/cover (effective 2002). **Document type:** *Magazine, Consumer.*
Published by: World Wrestling Entertainment, Inc., 1241 E Main St, Stamford, CT 06902. TEL 203-352-8600, FAX 203-352-8699. **Subscr. to:** PO Box 485, Mt Morris, IL 61054-8393.

051 USA
WANTED. Text in English. bi-m.
Published by: Metal Hammer Communications, Inc., 462 Broadway, Ste 4000, New York, NY 10013. TEL 212-966-8400. **Dist. by:** Flynt Distributing Co., 9171 Wilshire Blvd, Ste 300, Beverly Hills, CA 90210.

051 BEL
THE WEIRD SIDE EZINE. Text in English. m. adv. bk.rev. **Document type:** *Newsletter.* **Description:** Presents a selection of weird news from around the world.
Media: Online - full text.
Published by: Weird Side Ezine, Nijverheidsstraat 27, Bruges, 8000, Belgium. TEL 32-50-375972. Ed., Pub. Dirk Dupon.

305.31 USA
WHAT NEXT. Text in English. 2006 (Fall). bi-m. **Document type:** *Magazine, Consumer.*
Published by: What's Next Media, 39 W. 37th St., 15th Fl., New York, NY 10018. TEL 646-366-0833. Pub., Adv. contact Mark Gleason TEL 646-366-0833.

WHITE CRANE; a journal of gay wisdom & culture. *see* HOMOSEXUALITY

053.1 AUT
WIENER. Text in German. 1980. m. EUR 21 (effective 2008). adv. **Document type:** *Magazine, Consumer.*
Published by: Wiener Verlags GmbH & Co. KG (Subsidiary of: Styria Medien AG), Geiselbergstr 15, Vienna, 1110, Austria. TEL 43-1-60117249, FAX 43-1-60117350. Ed. Waltraud Hable. Pub. Andre Eckert. Adv. contact Andreas Mandl. page EUR 7,190; trim 210 x 278. Circ: 130,000.

WILDFOWL; the magazine for duck & goose hunters. *see* SPORTS AND GAMES—Outdoor Life

305.31 CAN ISSN 1719-6663
WINNIPEG MEN. Text in English. 2004. q. CAD 12 (effective 2006). **Document type:** *Magazine, Consumer.*
Published by: Studio Publications Inc., 2nd Flr - 70 Albert St, Winnipeg, MB R3B 0E1, Canada. TEL 204-992-3402, FAX 204-475-3003, http://studiopublications.net/. Ed. Lindsay Stewart TEL 204-992-3404. Pub. Glenn Tinley.

808 USA
X FAMILY LETTERS. Text in English. 1980. 10/yr. USD 39.97. adv. back issues avail. **Description:** Erotic literature.
Formerly: X Letters
Published by: Piccolo Publications, Inc., 310 Cedar Lane, Teaneck, NJ 07666. TEL 201-836-9177, FAX 201-836-5055. Eds. Jackie Lewis, Lisa Rosen. Pub. Louis Rosen. Adv. contact Allison Reynolds. Circ: 66,000.

035.31 AUS
X Y: MEN, MASCULINITIES AND GENDER POLITICS. Text in English. 1990. irreg. **Document type:** *Magazine, Consumer.* **Description:** Focuses on men and masculinity and explores personal and social changes.
Media: Online - full text.
Published by: X Y: Men, Masculinities and Gender Politcs, PO Box 473, Blackwood, SA 5051, Australia.

305.31 USA
XES. Text in English. 2001. m. USD 7.99 newsstand/cover (effective 2001). adv. **Document type:** *Magazine, Consumer.*
Published by: Pleasure Time Books, 210 Rte 4 E, Ste 211, Paramus, NJ 07652. http://www.xesmag.com.

051 USA ISSN 1522-0095
YOUNG & PINK. Text in English. 2001. 9/yr. USD 6.99 (effective 2002). adv. **Document type:** *Magazine, Consumer.*
Published by: All Coasts, Inc., 9030 W Sahara Ave, PMB 422, Las Vegas, NV 889117. Ed. Marc Star. Pub. Royce Martine.

059.956 JPN
YOUNG MAGAZINE UPPERS. Text in Japanese. fortn. **Document type:** *Magazine, Consumer.*
Published by: Kodansha Ltd., 2-12-21 Otowa, Bunkyo-ku, Tokyo, 112-8001, Japan. TEL 81-3-3946-6201, FAX 81-3-3944-9915, http://www.kodansha.co.jp.

306.7 USA ISSN 2159-4082
▼ **YUM YUM MAGAZINE.** Text in English. 2010. m. USD 5 per issue (effective 2011). **Document type:** *Magazine, Trade.*
Published by: Yum Yum Magazine, Inc., 12117 Old Credmoor Rd, Raleigh, NC 27613. TEL 919-522-4707.

▼ **ZEUS.** *see* HOMOSEXUALITY

059.95911 THA
ZOO. Text in Thai. w. THB 50 newsstand/cover (effective 2010). adv. **Document type:** *Magazine, Consumer.*
Published by: Inspire Entertainment Co., 115-66 Moo 12, Soi Ramintra 40, Ramintra Rd, Klong-kum, Bung-kum, Bangkok, 10230, Thailand. TEL 662-508-8100, FAX 662-693-3287, contact@inspire.co.th, http://www.inspire.co.th. Adv. contact Kitti Piyamahachot. Circ: 80,000 (paid).

305.31 GBR ISSN 1740-8512
ZOO. Variant title: Zoo Weekly. Text in English. 2004. w. GBP 58 domestic; GBP 80 in Europe & USA; GBP 100 elsewhere (effective 2009). adv. **Document type:** *Magazine, Consumer.* **Description:** Covers sex, sports and humor.
Related titles: Online - full text ed.
Published by: H. Bauer Publishing Ltd. (Subsidiary of: Bauer Media Group), Mappin House, 4 Winsley St, London, W1W 8HF, United Kingdom. TEL 44-20-71828000, http://www.bauer.co.uk. Ed. Natalie Cornish TEL 44-20-71828355. Adv. contact Anu Short TEL 44-20-72956705. page GBP 8,800.

ZOO (AFRIKAANSE EDITION). *see* LIFESTYLE

ZOO (ENGLISH EDITION). *see* LIFESTYLE

305.31 AUS ISSN 1833-3222
ZOO WEEKLY. Text in English. 2006. w. AUD 161; AUD 4.25 newsstand/cover (effective 2008). adv. **Document type:** *Magazine, Consumer.* **Description:** Contains mix of news, sport, gags and girls, combined with its weekly entertainment guide, the couch, will filter and edit the explosion of information and choices confronting young men from today's vast array of media channels.
Published by: A C P Magazines Ltd. (Subsidiary of: P B L Media Pty Ltd.), 54-58 Park St, Sydney, NSW 2000, Australia. TEL 61-2-92828000, FAX 61-2-91263769, research@acpaction.com.au. Ed. Paul Merrill. Adv. contact Ben Cook TEL 61-2-81149483. page AUD 11,255; trim 220 x 300. Circ: 122,000.

2; the only magazine for couples. *see* WOMEN'S INTERESTS

3 V MAGAZINE; complete lifestyle for men. *see* RELIGIONS AND THEOLOGY

MEN'S STUDIES

305.31 USA ISSN 1070-6836
ALADDIN'S WINDOW; the vision of awakened men. Text in English. 1991. q. USD 30 domestic; USD 50 foreign (effective 2000). adv. bk.rev.; film rev. back issues avail. **Document type:** *Newsletter.* **Description:** Covers men's issues as they relate to psychology of evolution and awareness.
Related titles: Magnetic Tape ed.
Published by: J.R. Molloy, PO Box 333, Palo Cedro, CA 96073. TEL 916-474-1385. Ed. Chrom Blackstone. Adv. contact J R Molloy. Circ: 340 (paid).

779.28 USA ISSN 2152-9264
THE ART OF SEXY BY SHOW. Text in English. bi-m. USD 11.95 (effective 2010). **Document type:** *Magazine, Consumer.* **Description:** Special edition of Show Magazine.
Related titles: ◆ Special ed. of: Show (Los Angeles). ISSN 1559-9515.
Published by: Cummings Media, 500 Molino St, Ste 111, Los Angeles, CA 90013. TEL 213-402-4634, sean@cummingsmedia.com.

AT-HOME DAD; men who change diapers change the world. *see* MEN'S INTERESTS

CERTIFIED MALE MAGAZINE. *see* MEN'S INTERESTS

COLUMBIA JOURNAL OF GENDER AND THE LAW. *see* LAW

305.31 USA ISSN 1941-5583
▼ ➤ **CULTURE, SOCIETY AND MASCULINITIES.** Text in English. 2009 (Feb.). s-a. USD 150 domestic to institutions; USD 170 foreign to institutions; USD 165 combined subscription to institutions (print & online eds.) (effective 2010). **Document type:** *Journal, Academic/Scholarly.*
Related titles: Online - full text ed.: ISSN 1941-5591. 2009 (Feb.). USD 120 to institutions (effective 2010).
Indexed: GW, S02, S03, SociolAb, T02.
Published by: Men's Studies Press, PO Box 32, Harriman, TN 37748. TEL 423-369-2375, FAX 423-369-1126, publisher@mensstudies.com. Ed. Diederik F Janssen.

323.4 USA
FATHERS' JOURNAL. Text in English. m. membership. **Description:** Dedicated to preserving the rights of fathers.
Published by: Fathers for Equal Rights of America, PO Box 2272, Southfield, MI 48037. TEL 313-354-3080.

GENDER AND EDUCATION. *see* EDUCATION

GENDER AND HISTORY. *see* HISTORY

GENDER & SOCIETY. *see* SOCIOLOGY

GENDER STUDIES; Interdisziplinaere Schriftenreihe zur Geschlechterforschung. *see* SOCIOLOGY

GENDERCODES; Transkriptionen zwischen Wissen und Geschlecht. *see* WOMEN'S STUDIES

GENUS. *see* WOMEN'S STUDIES

GENUS: GENDER IN MODERN CULTURE. *see* SOCIOLOGY

IPHIS - GENDER STUDIES IN DEN ALTERTUMSWISSENSCHAFTEN; Beitraege zur altertumswissenschaftlichen Genderforschung. *see* SOCIOLOGY

305.31 USA ISSN 1559-1646
E185.86 CODEN: JAAMF6
➤ **JOURNAL OF AFRICAN AMERICAN STUDIES.** Text in English. 1993. q. EUR 392, USD 536 combined subscription to institutions (print & online eds.) (effective 2012). illus. back issues avail.; reprint service avail. from PSC. **Document type:** *Journal, Academic/Scholarly.* **Description:** Aims to serves as a multidisciplinary forum for social scientists engaged in the analysis of the struggles and triumphs of black males.

Former titles (until 2003): Journal of African American Men (1081-1753); (until 1995): Journal of African American Male Studies (1063-4460)
Related titles: Online - full text ed.: ISSN 1936-4741 (from IngentaConnect).
Indexed: A01, A03, A08, A22, A26, AmHI, CA, E01, E08, G08, H07, HEA, I02, I05, IIBP, MLA-IB, R02, S02, S03, S09, SCOPUS, SOPODA, SRRA, SSA, SociolAb, T02.
—BLDSC (4919.987250), IE. **CCC.**
Published by: Springer New York LLC (Subsidiary of: Springer Science+Business Media), 233 Spring St, New York, NY 10013. TEL 212-460-1500, FAX 212-460-1575, journals@springer-ny.com. Ed. Anthony J Lemelle.

305.31 305.89607305 USA ISSN 2155-1189
▼ ➤ **JOURNAL OF BLACK MASCULINITY.** Text in English. 2010 (Sep.). q. USD 19.95 per issue (effective 2011). **Document type:** *Journal, Academic/Scholarly.* **Description:** Provides multidisciplinary analyses of issues and/or perspectives with regard to black masculinities.
Media: Online - full text. **Related titles:** Print ed.: ISSN 2158-9623. USD 109.95; USD 12.95 per issue (effective 2011).
Published by: University of North Carolina at Greensboro, 1400 Spring Garden St, Greensboro, NC 27412 . TEL 336-334-5000, cpgause@uncg.edu, http://www.uncg.edu/.

➤ **JOURNAL OF GENDER STUDIES.** *see* WOMEN'S STUDIES

➤ **JOURNAL OF MEN, MASCULINITIES AND SPIRITUALITY.** *see* RELIGIONS AND THEOLOGY

305.31 USA ISSN 1060-8265
HQ1088
➤ **JOURNAL OF MEN'S STUDIES**; a scholarly journal about men and masculinities . Text in English. 1992. 3/yr. USD 220 domestic to institutions; USD 240 foreign to institutions; USD 250 combined subscription to institutions (print & online eds.) (effective 2010). adv. bk.rev. illus. back issues avail.; reprints avail. **Document type:** *Journal, Academic/Scholarly.* **Description:** Publishes scholarly material in the field of men's studies, recognizing the varied influences of class, culture, race and sexual orientation on defining men's experiences.
Related titles: Online - full text ed.: ISSN 1933-0251. USD 210 (effective 2010).
Indexed: A01, A03, A08, A22, A26, AmHI, B04, BRD, CA, CWI, DYW, E-psyche, E08, FamI, G08, GW, H07, H08, HAb, HumInd, I05, I07, L01, L02, MLA-IB, P03, P10, P25, P27, P30, P43, P48, P53, P54, PQC, PsycInfo, PsycholAb, S02, S03, S09, S11, S23, SD, SFSA, SSAI, SSAb, SSI, SociolAb, T02, V&AA, W01, W02, W03, W05.
—BLDSC (5017.645000), CIS, IE, Ingenta. **CCC.**
Published by: Men's Studies Press, PO Box 32, Harriman, TN 37748. TEL 423-369-2375, FAX 423-369-1126, publisher@mensstudies.com. Ed., Pub. Dr. James A Doyle. adv.: B&W page USD 150. Circ: 390 (paid).

➤ **KIND UND VATER**; Informationen zur aktiven Vaterschaft. *see* CHILDREN AND YOUTH—About

➤ **L S E GENDER INSTITUTE. NEW WORKING PAPER SERIES.** (London School of Economics) *see* WOMEN'S STUDIES

➤ **L S E GENDER INSTITUTE. RESEARCH IN PROGRESS.** (London School of Economics) *see* WOMEN'S STUDIES

305.3 340 USA ISSN 1040-3760
HQ1090
THE LIBERATOR (FOREST LAKE). Text in English. 1968. m. adv. bk.rev. illus. 28 p./no.; back issues avail.; reprints avail. **Document type:** *Magazine, Consumer.* **Description:** Aimed at men who seek equal rights and dignity with women across a broad spectrum of life, including divorce, employment and crime punishment.
Formerly (until 1988): Legal Beagle
Published by: Men's Defense Association, 17854 Lyons St, Forest Lake, MN 55025. info@mensdefense.org, http://www.mensdefense.org/.

305.31 USA ISSN 2161-5020
BF637.C6
MEN (SEATTLE). Text in English. 1977. irreg. USD 3 per issue (effective 2011). **Document type:** *Journal, Trade.* **Description:** Drafts policy statement on the liberation of males and on U.S. veterans' oppression; includes section on men's oppression, counseling men, men and women as allies, and war and violence.
Published by: Rational Island Publishers, PO Box 2081, Main Office Station, Seattle, WA 98111. TEL 206-284-0311, FAX 206-284-8429, litsales@rc.org, http://www.rationalisland.com.

305.31 USA ISSN 1097-184X
HQ1088
➤ **MEN AND MASCULINITIES.** Text in English. 1998. 5/yr. bk.rev. illus. back issues avail.; reprint service avail. from PSC. **Document type:** *Journal, Academic/Scholarly.* **Description:** Presents empirical and theoretical articles that use both interdisciplinary and multidisciplinary approaches, employ diverse methods, and are grounded in current theoretical perspectives within gender studies.
Related titles: Online - full text ed.: ISSN 1552-6828. USD 570, GBP 335 to institutions (effective 2011).
Indexed: A01, A02, A03, A08, A20, A22, B07, CA, CMM, CurCont, E-psyche, E01, H04, I14, IBSS, L01, L02, MLA-IB, P03, P42, PEI, PSA, PsycInfo, PsycholAb, S02, S03, S21, SCOPUS, SSA, SSCI, SociolAb, T02, V02, W07, W09.
—IE, Infotrieve, Ingenta. **CCC.**
Published by: Sage Publications, Inc., 2455 Teller Rd, Thousand Oaks, CA 91320. TEL 805-499-9774, 800-818-7243, FAX 805-499-0871, 800-583-2665, info@sagepub.com. Ed. Michael S Kimmel. **Subscr. outside the Americas to:** Sage Publications Ltd., 1 Oliver's Yard, 55 City Rd, London EC1Y 1SP, United Kingdom. TEL 44-20-73248701, FAX 44-20-73248733, subscription@sagepub.co.uk.

➤ **MEN OF INTEGRITY.** *see* RELIGIONS AND THEOLOGY

➤ **MEN'S JOURNAL.** *see* MEN'S INTERESTS

305.31 613.081 USA
MENSTUFF; the national men's resource. Text in English. 1985. m. free (effective 2010). bk.rev. illus. back issues avail. **Document type:** *Newsletter, Trade.* **Description:** Features information, events listings, resources and reviews concerning a positive change in male roles and relationships.
Former titles (until 1996): Menstuff (Print) (1074-7842); (until 1993): National Men's Resource Calendar; (until 1992): Men's Resource Hotline Calendar; (until 1988): Men's Resource Hotline
Media: Online - full text.
Published by: National Men's Resource Center, PO Box 800, San Anselmo, CA 94979-0800.

N I K K MAGASIN. (Nordisk Institutt for Kundskap om Koenn) *see* SOCIOLOGY

▼ **N I K K. PUBLIKATIONER.** *see* SOCIOLOGY

NAN NU; men, women and gender in China. *see* ASIAN STUDIES

PSYCHOLOGY OF MEN & MASCULINITY. *see* PSYCHOLOGY

QUERELLES - NET. *see* SOCIOLOGY

RACE, GENDER & CLASS; an interdisciplinary journal. *see* ETHNIC INTERESTS

REGENSBURGER BEITRAEGE ZUR GENDER-FORSCHUNG. *see* SOCIOLOGY

STUDIEN INTERDISZIPLINAERE GESCHLECHTERFORSCHUNG. *see* WOMEN'S STUDIES

TODAY'S DADS; taking the needs of children to heart. *see* LAW—Family And Matrimonial Law

305.32 USA ISSN 0886-862X
TRANSITIONS (MINNEAPOLIS). Text in English. 1981. bi-m. USD 30 to non-members; free to members (effective 2010). bk.rev.; film rev. illus. back issues avail.; reprints avail. **Document type:** *Newsletter, Consumer.* **Description:** Looks at the ways sex discrimination affects men.
Related titles: Online - full text ed.
Indexed: DYW, GW, P48, PQC.
Published by: National Coalition of Free Men, PO Box 582023, Minneapolis, MN 55458. TEL 516-482-6378, 888-223-1280, ncfm@ncfm.org, http://www.ncfm.org. Ed. Kevin Young.

305.3 USA
WINGSPAN (NORTH LAKE); journal of the male spirit. Text in English. 1986. q. adv. **Document type:** *Newsletter, Consumer.* **Description:** Covers issues pertaining to male psychology and spirituality, with think pieces from leaders of the men's movement, workshop profiles and extensive listings of nationwide men's events.
Indexed: E-psyche.
Published by: Wingspan, PO Box 265, North Lake, WI 53064. TEL 414-695-8815, charding@tiac.net. Eds. Christopher Harding, Karl Larson. adv.: B&W page USD 1,960. Circ: 25,000.

X Y: MEN, MASCULINITIES AND GENDER POLITICS. *see* MEN'S INTERESTS

MEN'S STUDIES—Abstracting, Bibliographies, Statistics

GENDER STUDIES DATABASE. *see* WOMEN'S STUDIES—Abstracting, Bibliographies, Statistics

METALLURGY

see also METALLURGY—Welding ; MINES AND MINING INDUSTRY

669 BRA ISSN 0104-0898
TN4 CODEN: MABMA5
A B M METALURGIA E MATERIAIS. Text in Portuguese. 1965. m. USD 155 foreign. adv. bk.rev. abstr.; charts; illus.; stat. index, cum.index every 10 yrs. **Document type:** *Journal, Academic/Scholarly.*
Formerly (until Apr. 1992): Metalurgia A B M (0026-0983); Which was formed by the merger of: A B M Boletim; A B M Noticiario
Related titles: Microform ed.: (from PQC).
Indexed: A28, APA, BrCerAb, C&ISA, C01, CA/WCA, CIA, CIN, CPEI, CerAb, ChemAb, ChemTitl, CivEngAb, CorrAb, E&CAJ, E11, EEA, EMA, ESPM, EngInd, EnvEAb, H15, INIS AtomInd, M&TEA, M09, MBF, METADEX, SCOPUS, SolStAb, T04, WAA.
—CASDDS, INIST, Linda Hall.
Published by: Associacao Brasileira de Metalurgia e Materiais, Rua Antonio Comparato 218, Sao Paulo, SP 04605-030, Brazil. TEL 55-11-55344333, FAX 55-11-55344330, http://www.abmbrasil.com.br. Ed. Maria Da Luz Calegari. Adv. contact Fernando Cosme Rizzo Assuncao. Circ: 6,000.

671.732 USA
CODEN: PATCEY
A E S F ANNUAL TECHNICAL CONFERENCE PROCEEDINGS (CD-ROM EDITION). (American Electroplaters and Surface Finishers Society) Text in English. a. USD 325 (effective 2005).
Former titles (until 2000): A E S F Annual Technical Conference Proceedings (Print Edition) (1075-7988); (until 1986): American Electroplaters' Society Annual Technical Conference (0270-2622)
Media: CD-ROM.
—Linda Hall. **CCC.**
Published by: American Electroplaters and Surface Finishers Society, Inc. (AESF), 1 Thomas Circle NW, 10th Fl, Washington, DC 20005. TEL 202-457-8401, FAX 202-530-0659, aesf@aesf.org, http://www.aesf.org.

669.722 DEU ISSN 1745-0330
A P T ALUMINIUM NEWS. Text in English. 4/yr. EUR 39 in Europe; USD 70.60 in North America (effective 2009). adv. **Document type:** *Magazine, Trade.*
Indexed: A28, APA, BrCerAb, C&ISA, CA/WCA, CIA, CerAb, CivEngAb, CorrAb, E&CAJ, E11, EEA, EMA, H15, M&TEA, M09, MBF, METADEX, SolStAb, T04, WAA.
—Linda Hall.
Published by: Giesel Verlag GmbH (Subsidiary of: Schluetersche Verlagsgesellschaft mbH und Co. KG), Rehkamp 3, Isernhagen, 30916, Germany. TEL 49-511-73040, FAX 49-511-7304157, giesel@giesel.de. Ed. John Travis. Adv. contact Stefan Schwichtenberg TEL 49-511-7304142. B&W page EUR 1,550, color page EUR 2,550; trim 180 x 270. Circ: 5,000 (controlled).

667 USA ISSN 1092-230X
ABRASIVE BLAST CLEANING NEWSLETTER. Text in English. q. adv. **Document type:** *Newsletter, Trade.*
—Linda Hall.
Published by: Electronics, Inc., 56790 Magnetic Dr, Mishawaka, IN 46545. TEL 574-256-5001, 800-832-5653, FAX 874-256-5222, shotpeener@shotpeener.com, http://www.electronics-inc.com. adv.: B&W page USD 660, color page USD 990.

669.142 ESP ISSN 1135-4895
ACERO INOXIDABLE. Text in Spanish. 1985. 3/yr. free. **Document type:** *Magazine, Trade.*
Indexed: A28, APA, BrCerAb, C&ISA, CA/WCA, CIA, CerAb, CivEngAb, CorrAb, E&CAJ, E11, EEA, EMA, H15, IECT, M&TEA, M09, MBF, METADEX, SolStAb, T04, WAA.
—CCC.
Published by: Centro para la Investigacion y Desarrollo del Acero Inoxidable (C E D I N O X), Calle Santiago de Compostela 100, Madrid, 28035, Spain. TEL 34-91-3985231, FAX 34-91-3985190, http://www.cedinox.es, http://www.cedinox.es.

669 CHL
TS300 CODEN: SILAD8
ACERO LATINOAMERICANO. Text in Portuguese, Spanish; Summaries in English. 1960. bi-m. USD 105 in the Americas to members; USD 115 elsewhere to members; USD 165 in the Americas to non-members; USD 175 elsewhere to non-members (effective 2002). adv. bk.rev. bibl.; charts; illus. index. reprints avail. **Document type:** *Trade.* **Description:** Provides information about the iron and steel mining and production industry.
Former titles (until Oct. 1996): Siderurgia Latinoamericana (0379-7759); Revista Latinoamericana de Siderurgia (0034-9798); (until 1962): Instituto Latinoamericana del Fierro y Acero. Boletin Informativo
Related titles: Microform ed.: 1960 (from PQC).
Indexed: A22, A28, APA, BrCerAb, C&ISA, C01, CA/WCA, CIA, CerAb, ChemAb, CivEngAb, CorrAb, E&CAJ, E11, EEA, EMA, H15, IBR, IBZ, M&TEA, M09, MBF, METADEX, SolStAb, T04, WAA.
—CASDDS, Linda Hall.
Published by: Instituto Latinoamericano del Fierro y el Acero, Calle Benjamin 2944, 5o piso - Las Condes, Santiago, 9, Chile. TEL 56-2-2330545, FAX 56-2-2330768, ilafa@entelchile.net. Ed. Roberto Lopez. Circ: 1,500.

669 GBR ISSN 1359-6454
TS200 CODEN: ACMAFD
➤ **ACTA MATERIALIA.** Text in English, French, German. 1953. 20/yr. EUR 3,669 in Europe to institutions; JPY 487,400 in Japan to institutions; USD 4,107 elsewhere to institutions (effective 2012). adv. bk.rev. charts; illus.; abstr. index. back issues avail.; reprints avail. **Document type:** *Journal, Academic/Scholarly.* **Description:** Provides a forum for publishing original papers and commissioned overviews which advance the understanding of the relationship between the structure and the properties of materials.
Former titles (until 1996): Acta Metallurgica et Materialia (0956-7151); (until 1990): Acta Metallurgica (0001-6160)
Related titles: Microform ed.: (from PQC); Online - full text ed.: ISSN 1873-2453. EUR 115.26 in Europe to individuals; JPY 14,000 in Japan to individuals; USD 125 elsewhere to individuals (effective 2001) (from IngentaConnect, ScienceDirect).
Indexed: A01, A03, A08, A22, A26, A28, APA, ASCA, ApMecR, BrCerAb, C&ISA, C24, C33, CA, CA/WCA, CEABA, CIA, CIN, CMCI, CPEI, Cadscan, CerAb, ChemAb, ChemTitl, CivEngAb, CorrAb, CurCont, E&CAJ, E11, EEA, EMA, ESPM, EngInd, EnvEAb, F&EA, GeoRef, H15, I05, IBR, IBZ, ISMEC, ISR, Inspec, LeadAb, M&TEA, M09, MBF, METADEX, MSCI, P30, PhysBer, R18, RILM, RefZh, S01, SCI, SCOPUS, SolStAb, SpeleolAb, T02, T04, TM, W07, WAA, Zincscan.
—BLDSC (0629.920000), AskIEEE, CASDDS, IE, Infotrieve, Ingenta, INIST, Linda Hall. **CCC.**
Published by: (Acta Metallurgica, Inc. USA), Pergamon (Subsidiary of: Elsevier Science & Technology), The Blvd, Langford Ln, East Park, Kidlington, Oxford OX5 1GB, United Kingdom. TEL 44-1865-843000, FAX 44-1865-843010, JournalsCustomerServiceEMEA@elsevier.com. Eds. Kazuhiro Hono TEL 81-298-592022, Martin Harmer TEL 610-758-4227, Sungho Jin TEL 858-534-4903. **Subscr. to:** Elsevier BV, Radarweg 29, PO Box 211, Amsterdam 1000 AE, Netherlands. http://www.elsevier.nl.

669 CHN ISSN 1006-7191
TN4 CODEN: AMSIFZ
ACTA METALLURGICA SINICA. Text in English. 1994. q. EUR 229 in Europe to institutions; JPY 33,900 in Japan to institutions; USD 292 elsewhere to institutions (effective 2010). back issues avail. **Document type:** *Journal, Academic/Scholarly.* **Description:** Covers the new progress in materials sciences, including materials physics, physical metallurgy, process metallurgy, mining and ore dressing, testing methods, powder metallurgy, composites, welding and joining, oxidation and corrosion.
Formed by the merger of (1988-1994): Acta Metallurgica Sinica. Series A: Physical Metallurgy and Material Science (1000-9442); (1988-1994): Acta Metallurgica Sinica. Series B: Process Metallurgy and Miscellaneous (1000-9450)
Related titles: Online - full text ed.
Indexed: A28, APA, BrCerAb, C&ISA, CA/WCA, CIA, CIN, CPEI, CerAb, ChemAb, CivEngAb, CorrAb, E&CAJ, E11, EEA, EMA, ESPM, EngInd, EnvEAb, H15, IMMAb, M&TEA, M09, MBF, METADEX, RefZh, SCOPUS, SolStAb, T04, TM, WAA.
—BLDSC (0637.535000), CASDDS, IE, Ingenta, Linda Hall. **CCC.**
Published by: Zhongguo Kexueyuan Jinshu Yanjiusuo/Chinese Academy of Sciences, Institute of Metal Research, 72, Wenhua Lu, Shenyang, Liaoning 110015, China. http://www.imr.ac.cn/index.jsp. Circ: 300. **Dist. by:** Haiyang Chubanshe, International Department, 8 Dahuisi Rd, Haidian District, Beijing 100081, China. TEL 86-10-62179976, FAX 86-10-62173569, oceanpress@china.com, http://www.oceanpress.cn/; China International Book Trading Corp, 35 Chegongzhuang Xilu, Haidian District, PO Box 399, Beijing 100044, China. TEL 86-10-68412045, FAX 86-10-68412023, cibtc@mail.cibtc.com.cn, http://www.cibtc.com.cn.

ACTA POLYTECHNICA SCANDINAVICA. C H. CHEMICAL TECHNOLOGY SERIES. *see* CHEMISTRY

669 FRA ISSN 0996-4207
ACTUALITES; la vie economique et sociale. Text in French. 1949. bi-m. EUR 86 domestic to individuals; EUR 108 foreign to individuals; EUR 43 domestic to students; EUR 54 foreign to students (effective 2009). adv. bk.rev. charts; illus. **Document type:** *Magazine, Trade.*
Former titles (until 1988): Actualite Industrielle Economique et Sociale (0753-700X); (until 1982): Actualites Industrielles Lorraines (0044-6165)
Published by: Union des Industries et Metiers de la Metallurgie, 56 Av. de Wagram, Paris, Cedex 17 75854, France. TEL 33-1-40542144, FAX 33-1-40542257. Circ: 29,000.

ADVANCED COMPOSITES BULLETIN. *see* PLASTICS

669 USA ISSN 1540-1766
ADVANCED METALLIZATION CONFERENCE. PROCEEDINGS. Text in English. 19??. irreg., latest vol.27, 2007. USD 112 per issue to non-members; USD 97 per issue to members (effective 2009). **Document type:** *Proceedings, Academic/Scholarly.* **Description:** Focuses on latest Research and Development and manufacturing results, as well as real-world integration and reliability data on the application of metallization and related technologies for advanced IC devices.
Indexed: Englnd.
—BLDSC (0696.915400). **CCC.**
Published by: Materials Research Society, 506 Keystone Dr, Warrendale, PA 15086. TEL 724-779-3003, FAX 724-779-8313, info@mrs.org, http://www.mrs.org/s_mrs/index.asp.

669.1 HKG ISSN 1816-112X
ADVANCED STEEL CONSTRUCTION. Text in English. 2005. q. **Document type:** *Journal, Trade.*
Published by: Hong Kong Institute of Steel Construction, Hong Kong Polytechnic University, Department of Civil and Structural Engineering, Kowloon, Hong Kong. http://www.hkisc.org.

671.732 UKR ISSN 1810-0384
TN681
ADVANCES IN ELECTROMETALLURGY. Text in English. 1985. q. USD 184 foreign (effective 2005). **Document type:** *Journal, Academic/ Scholarly.* **Description:** Includes electroslag technology (electroslag melting and refining, casting). It is divided into the following main sections: Electroslag technology - Electom beam processes - Plasmaarc technology - Vacuum are remelting and vacuum inducting melting - General problems of special electrometallurgy.
Formerly (until 2002): Advances in Special Electrometallurgy (0267-4009)
Related titles: ◆ Ukrainian ed.: Problemy Spetsial'noi Elektrometallurgii. ISSN 0131-1611; ◆ Translation of: Sovremennaya Elektrometallurgiya. ISSN 0233-7681.
Indexed: A10, A26, A28, APA, BrCerAb, C&ISA, CA/WCA, CIA, CTE, CerAb, CivEngAb, CorrAb, E&CAJ, E08, E11, EEA, EMA, ESPM, EnvEAb, G08, H15, I05, M&TEA, M09, MBF, METADEX, SolStAb, T04, V03, WAA.
—BLDSC (0404.609500), Ingenta. **CCC.**
Published by: (Natsional'na Akademiya Nauk Ukrainy, Instytut Elektrozvaryuvannya im. EO Patona), Paton Publishing House, E.O. Paton Welding Institute, vul Bozhenko, 11, Kyi, 03680, Ukraine. TEL 380-44-2276302, FAX 380-44-2680486, journal@paton.kiev.ua, http://www.nas.gov.ua/pwj/.

669 CAN
ADVANCES IN INDUSTRIAL MATERIALS. Text in English. 1998. irreg. CAD 20 per issue (effective 2004).
Published by: Canadian Institute of Mining, Metallurgy and Petroleum, Metallurgical Society, 3400 de Maisonneuve Blvd W, Ste 1210, Montreal, PQ H3Z 3B8, Canada. TEL 514-939-2710, FAX 514-939-2714, cim@cim.org, http://www.cim.org.

ADVANCES IN MATERIALS SCIENCE AND ENGINEERING. *see* ENGINEERING—Engineering Mechanics And Materials

669 USA ISSN 1561-2635
ADVANCES IN METALLIC ALLOYS. Text in English. 2001. irreg., latest 2011. price varies. back issues avail. **Document type:** *Monographic series, Academic/Scholarly.*
Related titles: Online - full text ed.: ISSN 2154-2341.
Published by: C R C Press, LLC (Subsidiary of: Taylor & Francis Group), 6000 Broken Sound Pky, NW, Ste 300, Boca Raton, FL 33487. TEL 800-272-7737, FAX 800-374-3401, orders@crcpress.com.

671.3705 669 USA ISSN 1546-7724
TN695 CODEN: APMME3
ADVANCES IN POWDER METALLURGY & PARTICULATE MATERIALS. Text in English. 1989. a., latest 2002. USD 950 per issue to non-members; USD 850 per issue to members APMI members; USD 760 per issue to members MPIF members (effective 2011). back issues avail. **Document type:** *Proceedings, Trade.*
Former titles (until 1993): Advances in Powder Metallurgy & Particulate Materials (1065-5824); (until 1992): Advances in Powder Metallurgy (1042-8860)
Related titles: CD-ROM ed.
Indexed: A22, CIN, ChemAb, ChemTitl, Englnd, ISMEC, SCOPUS.
—BLDSC (0710.635000), CASDDS, IE, Ingenta, INIST, Linda Hall. **CCC.**
Published by: Metal Powder Industries Federation, 105 College Rd E, Princeton, NJ 08540. TEL 609-452-7700, FAX 609-987-8523, info@mpif.org.

ADVANCES IN X-RAY ANALYSIS (CD-ROM). *see* PHYSICS

669.1 CHN ISSN 1671-7872
AHNUI GONGYE DAXUE XUEBAO (ZIRAN KEXUE BAN)/ANHUI UNIVERSITY OF TECHNOLOGY. JOURNAL (NATURAL SCIENCE EDITION). Text in Chinese. 1984. q. CNY 20; CNY 5 newsstand/cover (effective 2002). **Document type:** *Journal, Academic/Scholarly.*
Former titles (until 2000): Huadong Yejin Xueyuan Xuebao (1000-2170); (until 1985): Ma'anshan Gangtie Xueyuan Xuebao
Related titles: Online - full content ed.; Online - full text ed.
Indexed: A28, APA, BrCerAb, C&ISA, CA/WCA, CIA, CerAb, CivEngAb, CorrAb, E&CAJ, E11, EEA, EMA, ESPM, EnvEAb, H15, M&TEA, M09, MBF, METADEX, RefZh, SolStAb, T04, WAA.
—BLDSC (4697.960000), IE, Ingenta, Linda Hall.
Published by: Anhui Gongye Daxue/Anhui University of Technology, Hudong Lu #59, Ma'anshan, 243002, China. TEL 86-555-2400613, FAX 86-555-2471263, ZBGZP@ahpu.edu.cn, http://www.ahut.edu.cn.

669 POL ISSN 0867-6631
AKADEMIA GORNICZO-HUTNICZA. ROZPRAWY MONOGRAFIE. Text in Polish. 1994. irreg. **Document type:** *Monographic series, Academic/Scholarly.*
Indexed: A28, APA, BrCerAb, C&ISA, CA/WCA, CIA, CerAb, CivEngAb, CorrAb, E&CAJ, E11, EEA, EMA, GeoRef, H15, M&TEA, M09, MBF, METADEX, RefZh, SolStAb, T04, WAA.
Published by: Akademia Gorniczo-Hutnicza im. Stanislawa Staszica/ University of Mining and Metallurgy, Al Mickiewicza 30, Krakow, 30059, Poland. http://www.agh.edu.pl.

669.722 ITA ISSN 1122-1429
AL - ALLUMINIO E LEGHE/AL - ALUMINIUM AND ITS ALLOYS. Text in English, Italian; Summaries in English, French, Spanish. 1989. m. (11/yr.). adv. **Document type:** *Magazine, Trade.* **Description:** Covers the global aluminum market from an Italian perspective.
Related titles: Online - full text ed.; Supplement(s):.
Indexed: A28, APA, BrCerAb, C&ISA, CA/WCA, CIA, CerAb, CivEngAb, CorrAb, E&CAJ, E11, EEA, EMA, H15, M&TEA, M09, MBF, METADEX, SolStAb, T04, WAA.
—BLDSC (0804.450000), IE, Ingenta, Linda Hall.
Published by: Edimet SpA, Via Corfu 102, Brescia, BS 25124, Italy. TEL 39-030-2421043, FAX 39-030-223802, info@edimet.com, http://www.edimet.com/it. Circ: 6,000.

669 USA ISSN 0002-614X
TA490 CODEN: ALDGAA
➤ **ALLOY DIGEST.** Text in English. 1952. m. looseleaf. USD 693 to non-members; USD 316 to members (effective 2009). abstr.; charts. cum.index: 1952-1999. back issues avail. **Document type:** *Journal, Academic/Scholarly.* **Description:** Featuring graphs, charts and tables, these sheets give facts and figures on composition or characterization, physical and mechanical properties, heat treatment, and machinability.
Related titles: CD-ROM ed.: USD 1,395 to non-members; USD 1,325 to members (effective 2000); Fax ed.; Online - full text ed.; Supplement(s):.
Indexed: A28, APA, BrCerAb, C&ISA, CA/WCA, CIA, CerAb, CivEngAb, CorrAb, E&CAJ, E11, EEA, EMA, H15, M&TEA, M09, MBF, METADEX, SolStAb, T04, WAA.
—Linda Hall. **CCC.**
Published by: A S M International, 9639 Kinsman Rd, Materials Park, OH 44073. TEL 440-338-5151, FAX 440-338-4634, CustomerService@asminternational.org.

669 BEL
ALUGLOBE. Text in English. q. **Document type:** *Magazine, Trade.*
Indexed: APA, C&ISA, CorrAb, E&CAJ, EEA, SolStAb, WAA.
Published by: Norsk Hydro, Hydro Aluminium Group, Roetgenerstrasse 65, Raeren, 4730, Belgium. TEL 32-87-858150, FAX 32-87-858169.

669.722 NLD ISSN 0920-5608
ALUMINIUM; vakblad over aluminium en aluminiumlegeringen. Text in Dutch. 1986. 10/yr. EUR 120 domestic; EUR 140 foreign (effective 2009). adv.
Related titles: ◆ Supplement(s): Aluminiumgids. ISSN 1568-7775.
—BLDSC (0804.075700), IE, Ingenta, Linda Hall.
Published by: Uitgeverij TCM B.V., Postbus 101, Leiden, 2300 AC, Netherlands. TEL 31-71-5144044, FAX 31-71-5131093, info@uitgeverijtcm.nl, http://www.uitgeverijtcm.nl. Ed. M E E Van Beek. Pub. A J Schomagel. adv.: B&W page EUR 1,529, color page EUR 2,204; bleed 210 x 297.

669.722 ITA
ALUMINIUM FINISHING. Text in English. q. back issues avail. **Document type:** *Magazine, Trade.*
Media: Online - full text.
Indexed: APA, C&ISA, CorrAb, E&CAJ, EEA, SolStAb, WAA.
Published by: Interall Srl, Via Marinuzzi 138, Modena, MO 41100, Italy. TEL 39-059-282390, FAX 39-059-280462, interall@tin.it. Ed. Walter Dalla Barba.

669.722 GBR ISSN 1475-455X
CODEN: ALTOEG
ALUMINIUM INTERNATIONAL TODAY; the journal of aluminium production and processing. Text in English. 1989. bi-m. GBP 201 domestic; GBP 219 foreign; free to qualified personnel (effective 2010); includes Furnaces Internatiuonal. adv. reprints avail. **Document type:** *Journal, Trade.* **Description:** Covers aluminum production and processing together with industry news, contracts, products, and economic, market and regional reports.
Formerly (until 2001): Aluminium Today (0955-8209); Incorporates (1982-199?): Aluminium Industry (0268-5280)
Related titles: Online - full text ed.: free (effective 2010); Chinese ed.; Russian ed.; ◆ Supplement(s): Furnaces International. ISSN 1740-6501; Aluminium International Buyer's Directory. ISSN 1759-9482. 1997.
Indexed: A28, APA, B01, B02, B06, B07, B08, B09, B15, B17, B18, BrCerAb, C&ISA, C12, CA/WCA, CIA, CerAb, CivEngAb, CorrAb, E&CAJ, E11, EEA, EMA, ESPM, Englnd, EnvEAb, G04, G06, G07, G08, H15, I05, M&TEA, M01, M02, M09, MBF, METADEX, RefZh, SCOPUS, SolStAb, T02, T04, V02, WAA.
—BLDSC (0806.026500), IE, Ingenta, Linda Hall. **CCC.**
Published by: D M G Business Media Ltd. (Subsidiary of: D M G World Media Ltd.), Equitable House, Lyon Rd, Harrow, Middlesex HA1 2EW, United Kingdom. TEL 44-20-85152080, http://www.dmgworldmedia.com. Ed. Tim Smith TEL 44-1737-855154. adv.: color page GBP 3,320; trim 210 x 297. Circ: 7,400.

669.722 DEU
ALUMINIUM-KURIER NEWS. Text in German. 1995. m. EUR 51.65 domestic; EUR 59.85 foreign; EUR 8 newsstand/cover (effective 2007). adv. **Document type:** *Journal, Trade.*
Published by: P S E Redaktionsservice GmbH, Kirchplatz 8, Geretsried, 82524, Germany. TEL 49-8171-61028, FAX 49-8171-60974, pse-redaktionsservice@t-online.de. Ed. Stefan Elgass. adv.: B&W page EUR 1,990, color page EUR 3,990. Circ: 9,596 (paid and controlled).

669.722 DEU ISSN 0947-4064
ALUMINIUM-LIEFERVERZEICHNIS. Text in German. 19??. a. EUR 16.50 (effective 2008). **Document type:** *Directory, Trade.*
Former titles (until 1994): A L I - Aluminium-Lieferverzeichnis (0944-1573); (until 1992): Aluminum-Lieferverzeichnis (0176-2664)
—Linda Hall.
Published by: Aluminium-Verlag GmbH, Postfach 101262, Duesseldorf, 40003, Germany. TEL 49-211-1591371, FAX 49-211-1591379, info@alu-verlag.de, http://www.alu-verlag.com.

669.722 ZAF
ALUMINIUM NEWS. Text in English. 1994. q. **Document type:** *Newsletter, Trade.*
Published by: (Aluminium Federation of South Africa), Promech Publishing, PO Box 85502, Emmarentia, Johannesburg 2029, South Africa. TEL 27-11-7811401, FAX 27-11-7811403. adv.: B&W page ZAR 2,000, color page ZAR 2,800; trim 210 x 297. Circ: 4,000 (controlled).

669.722 DEU ISSN 1432-5071
ALUMINIUM-PRAXIS. Text in German. 1996. m. EUR 66.50 domestic; EUR 72.50 foreign (effective 2010). adv. **Document type:** *Magazine, Trade.*
Published by: Giesel Verlag GmbH (Subsidiary of: Schluetersche Verlagsgesellschaft mbH und Co. KG), Rehkamp 3, Isernhagen, 30916, Germany. TEL 49-511-73040, FAX 49-511-7304157, giesel@giesel.de, http://www.giesel.de. Circ: 7,978 (paid and controlled).

669.722 SWE ISSN 0282-2628
ALUMINIUM SCANDINAVIA. Text in Swedish. 3/yr.
Indexed: CorrAb, WAA.
Address: Romfartuna, Nortuna Gaard, Box 515, Vaesteras, 725 94, Sweden. TEL 46-21-27040, FAX 46-21-27045.

669.722 GBR ISSN 1465-8240
ALUMINIUM TIMES. Text in English. 1999. 5/yr. GBP 78 domestic; GBP 92 foreign; free to qualified personnel (effective 2009). adv. **Document type:** *Magazine, Trade.* **Description:** Informs readers of the latest trends in the aluminium industry as well as new products and services.
Indexed: A28, APA, BrCerAb, C&ISA, CA/WCA, CIA, CerAb, CivEngAb, CorrAb, E&CAJ, E11, EEA, EMA, H15, M&TEA, M09, MBF, METADEX, SolStAb, T04, WAA.
—Linda Hall. **CCC.**
Published by: Modern Media Communications Ltd, Gresham House, 54 High St, Shoreham by Sea, West Sussex BN43 5DB, United Kingdom. TEL 44-1273-453033, FAX 44-1273-453085, info@mmcpublications.co.uk. Ed., Adv. contact John Clarke. page GBP 1,710, page EUR 2,780, page USD 3,420; trim 210 x 297. Circ: 5,200.

669.722 NLD ISSN 1568-7775
ALUMINIUMGIDS. Text in Dutch. 1997. a. adv.
Related titles: ◆ Supplement to: Aluminium. ISSN 0920-5608.
Published by: Uitgeverij TCM B.V., Postbus 101, Leiden, 2300 AC, Netherlands. TEL 31-71-5144044, FAX 31-71-5131093, info@uitgeverijtcm.nl, http://www.uitgeverijtcm.nl. adv.: color page EUR 1,595. Circ: 7,500.

669.772 USA
ALUMINUM ASSOCIATION. PINK SHEETS; desig. & comp. limits for castings & ingot. Text in English. 19??. every 3 yrs., latest 2009. USD 40 for 3 yrs. to non-members; USD 20 for 3 yrs. to members (effective 2011).
Published by: Aluminum Association, 1525 Wilson Blvd, Ste 600, Arlington, VA 22209. TEL 703-358-2960, FAX 703-358-2961, DBarthel@po.ASM-Intl.org.

669.772 USA
ALUMINUM ASSOCIATION. TEAL SHEETS. Text in English. 19??. triennial, latest 2009. USD 40 for 3 yrs. (effective 2011). **Document type:** *Trade.*
Published by: Aluminum Association, 1525 Wilson Blvd, Ste 600, Arlington, VA 22209. TEL 703-358-2960, FAX 703-358-2961, http://www.aluminum.org/.

669.772 USA
ALUMINUM DESIGN MANUAL. Text in English. 19??. every 5 yrs., latest 2010. USD 295 per issue to non-members for 5 years; USD 250 per issue to members for 5 years (effective 2011). **Document type:** *Handbook/Manual/Guide, Trade.*
Published by: Aluminum Association, 1525 Wilson Blvd, Ste 600, Arlington, VA 22209. TEL 703-358-2960, FAX 703-358-2961.

669.722 USA
ALUMINUM SITUATION. Text in English. 19??. m. USD 460 (effective 2011). **Document type:** *Trade.*
Related titles: Microfiche ed.: (from CIS).
Indexed: SRI.
Published by: Aluminum Association, 1525 Wilson Blvd, Ste 600, Arlington, VA 22209. TEL 703-358-2960, FAX 703-358-2961, http://www.aluminum.org/.

673 USA ISSN 0065-6658
TA480.A6
ALUMINUM STANDARDS AND DATA. Text in English. 1968. triennial, latest 2009. USD 125 for 3 yrs. (effective 2011). **Document type:** *Trade.*
Published by: Aluminum Association, 1525 Wilson Blvd, Ste 600, Arlington, VA 22209. TEL 703-358-2960, FAX 703-358-2961, http://www.aluminum.org/. Circ: 40,000.

673 USA
ALUMINUM STANDARDS AND DATA - METRIC. Text in English. 19??. triennial, latest 2009. USD 125 for 3 yrs. (effective 2011). **Document type:** *Trade.*
Published by: Aluminum Association, 1525 Wilson Blvd, Ste 600, Arlington, VA 22209. TEL 703-358-2960, FAX 703-358-2961, http://www.aluminum.org/. Circ: 40,000.

669.772 USA
ALUMINUM: TECHNOLOGY, APPLICATIONS, AND ENVIRONMENT; a profile of a modern metal. Text in English. 19??. irreg., latest 1998. USD 95 per issue (effective 2011). **Document type:** *Trade.*
Published by: Aluminum Association, 1525 Wilson Blvd, Ste 600, Arlington, VA 22209. TEL 703-358-2960, FAX 703-358-2961, http://www.aluminum.org/.

669 USA
AMERICAN COPPER COUNCIL. NEWSLETTER. Text in English. q. membership. **Document type:** *Newsletter.*
Published by: American Copper Council, 2 South End Ave, No 4C, New York, NY 10280. TEL 212-945-4990.

669.028 671.2 USA
TS200 CODEN: TAFOA6
AMERICAN FOUNDRY SOCIETY. TRANSACTIONS. Text in English. 1896. a. back issues avail.; reprints avail. **Document type:** *Proceedings, Academic/Scholarly.* **Description:** Provides facts and figures on every casting process, and looks at production procedures.
Former titles (until 2000): American Foundrymen's Society. Transactions (0065-8375); (until 1948): American Foundrymen's Association. Transactions; (until 1904): American Foundrymen's Association. Journal
Related titles: CD-ROM ed.; Microform ed.: (from PMC, PQC); Online - full text ed.
Indexed: A22, BCIRA, CIN, ChemAb, ChemTitl, TM.
—CASDDS, IE, Infotrieve, Ingenta, INIST, Linda Hall. **CCC.**
Published by: American Foundry Society, 1695 N Penny Ln, Schaumburg, IL 60173. TEL 847-824-0181, 800-537-4237, FAX 847-824-7848, library@afsinc.org.

AMERICAN METAL MARKET; the world metal information network. *see* BUSINESS AND ECONOMICS—Marketing And Purchasing

AMERICAN METAL MARKET - WEEKLY. *see* BUSINESS AND ECONOMICS—Marketing And Purchasing

669.142 NLD ISSN 1879-7741

▼ **AMERICAN STAINLESS NEWS.** Text in English. 2009. q. USD 75 (effective 2010). adv. **Document type:** *Newspaper, Trade.* **Description:** Presents the latest news and views on technical, market, management and procurement issues to all major industries, such as petrochemicals and chemicals, oil and gas, power generation, marine, engineering and contracting, defense, food and beverage, and aerospace.
Related titles: Online - full text ed.: ISSN 1879-775X.
Published by: K C I Publishing B.V., PO Box 396, Zutphen, 7200 AJ, Netherlands. TEL 31-575-585270, FAX 31-575-511099, kci@kci-world.com, http://www.kci-world.com. Adv. contact Ivan Gane.

ANALYTICA. *see* CHEMISTRY—Analytical Chemistry

ANNUAL BOOK OF A S T M STANDARDS. VOLUME 01.01. STEEL-PIPING, TUBING, FITTINGS. *see* ENGINEERING—Engineering Mechanics And Materials

ANNUAL BOOK OF A S T M STANDARDS. VOLUME 01.02. FERROUS CASTINGS, FERROALLOYS. *see* ENGINEERING—Engineering Mechanics And Materials

ANNUAL BOOK OF A S T M STANDARDS. VOLUME 01.03. STEEL PLATE, SHEET, STRIP, WIRE; STAINLESS STEEL BAR. (American Society for Testing and Materials) *see* ENGINEERING—Engineering Mechanics And Materials

ANNUAL BOOK OF A S T M STANDARDS. VOLUME 01.04. STEEL-STRUCTURAL, REINFORCING, PRESSURE VESSEL; RAILWAY. (American Society for Testing and Materials) *see* ENGINEERING—Engineering Mechanics And Materials

ANNUAL BOOK OF A S T M STANDARDS. VOLUME 01.05. STEEL-BARS, BEARINGS, CHAIN, SPRINGS. (American Society for Testing and Materials) *see* ENGINEERING—Engineering Mechanics And Materials

ANNUAL BOOK OF A S T M STANDARDS. VOLUME 01.06. COATED STEEL PRODUCTS. (American Society for Testing and Materials) *see* ENGINEERING—Engineering Mechanics And Materials

ANNUAL BOOK OF A S T M STANDARDS. VOLUME 01.07. SHIPS AND MARINE TECHNOLOGY. (American Society for Testing and Materials) *see* ENGINEERING—Engineering Mechanics And Materials

ANNUAL BOOK OF A S T M STANDARDS. VOLUME 02.01. COPPER AND COPPER ALLOYS. (American Society for Testing and Materials) *see* ENGINEERING—Engineering Mechanics And Materials

ANNUAL BOOK OF A S T M STANDARDS. VOLUME 02.02. DIE-CAST METALS; ALUMINUM AND MAGNESIUM ALLOYS. (American Society for Testing and Materials) *see* ENGINEERING—Engineering Mechanics And Materials

ANNUAL BOOK OF A S T M STANDARDS. VOLUME 02.04. NONFERROUS METALS-NICKEL, COBALT, LEAD, TIN, ZINC, CADMIUM, PRECIOUS, REACTIVE, REFRACTORY METALS AND ALLOYS; MATERIALS FOR THERMOSTATS, ELECTRICAL HEATING AND RESISTANCE CONTACTS AND CONNECTORS. (American Society for Testing and Materials) *see* ENGINEERING—Engineering Mechanics And Materials

ANNUAL BOOK OF A S T M STANDARDS. VOLUME 02.05. METALLIC AND INORGANIC COATINGS; METAL POWDERS, SINTERED P-M STRUCTURAL PARTS. (American Society for Testing and Materials) *see* ENGINEERING—Engineering Mechanics And Materials

ANNUAL BOOK OF A S T M STANDARDS. VOLUME 03.01. METALS - MECHANICAL TESTING; ELEVATED AND LOW-TEMPERATURE TESTS METALLOGRAPHY. (American Society for Testing and Materials) *see* ENGINEERING—Engineering Mechanics And Materials

ANNUAL BOOK OF A S T M STANDARDS. VOLUME 03.02. WEAR AND EROSION; METAL CORROSION. (American Society for Testing and Materials) *see* ENGINEERING—Engineering Mechanics And Materials

ANNUAL BOOK OF A S T M STANDARDS. VOLUME 03.03. NONDESTRUCTIVE TESTING. (American Society for Testing and Materials) *see* ENGINEERING—Engineering Mechanics And Materials

ANNUAL BOOK OF A S T M STANDARDS. VOLUME 03.05. ANALYTICAL CHEMISTRY FOR METALS, ORES, AND RELATED MATERIALS (I): E32 TO LATEST. (American Society for Testing and Materials) *see* ENGINEERING—Engineering Mechanics And Materials

338.4 JPN

ANNUAL STATISTICS OF MATERIALS PROCESS INDUSTRIES, JAPAN. Text in English. 1984. a. JPY 4,500 newsstand/cover.
Formerly: Foundry Statistics of Japan
Related titles: Japanese ed.
Indexed: APA, C&ISA, CorrAb, E&CAJ, EEA, SolStAb, WAA.
Published by: Materials Process Technology Center/Sokeizai Senta, 5-8 Shibakoen 3-chome, Minato-ku, Tokyo, 105-0011, Japan.

669 USA

ANOPLATE NEWS. Text in English. q. back issues avail. **Document type:** *Newsletter, Trade.*
Indexed: APA, C&ISA, CIA, CorrAb, E&CAJ, EEA, SolStAb, WAA.
Published by: Anoplate Corporation, 459 Pulaski St, Syracuse, NY 13204. TEL 315-471-6143, FAX 315-471-7132, http://www.anoplate.com.

620.162 620.11 GBR ISSN 0003-5599
TA462 CODEN: ACMEBL

➤ **ANTI-CORROSION METHODS AND MATERIALS.** Abbreviated title: A C M M. Text in English. 1954. bi-m. EUR 4,879 combined subscription in Europe (print & online eds.); USD 5,069 combined subscription in the Americas (print & online eds.); GBP 3,509 combined subscription in the UK & elsewhere (print & online eds.); AUD 6,839 combined subscription in Australasia (print & online eds.) (effective 2012). bk.rev. abstr.; bibl.; charts; illus.; tr.lit. index. reprint service avail. from PSC. **Document type:** *Journal, Academic/Scholarly.* **Description:** Covers the materials and technologies employed in corrosion prevention.
Formerly (until 1966): Corrosion Technology (0589-8404)
Related titles: Online - full text ed.: ISSN 1758-4221 (from IngentaConnect).
Indexed: A01, A03, A08, A15, A20, A22, A28, A32, ABIn, AESIS, APA, APIAb, APICat, APIH&E, APIOC, APIPR, APIPS, APITS, ASCA, ASFA, BMT, BrCerAb, BrTechI, C&ISA, CA, CA/WCA, CEA, CEABA, CIA, CIN, CPEI, CTE, Cadscan, CerAb, ChemAb, ChemTitl, CivEngAb, CorrAb, E&CAJ, E01, E11, EEA, EMA, ESPM, EmerIntel, EngInd, EnvEAb, F&EA, FLUIDEX, GasAb, H15, HRIS, ICEA, LeadAb, M&TEA, M09, MBF, METADEX, MSCI, OceAb, P26, P48, P51, P52, P54, PQC, RefZh, SCI, SCOPUS, SWRA, SolStAb, T02, T04, TM, W07, WAA, WSCA, Zincscan.
—BLDSC (1547.450000), CASDDS, IE, Infotrieve, Ingenta, INIST, Linda Hall, PADDS. **CCC.**
Published by: Emerald Group Publishing Ltd., Howard House, Wagon Ln, Bingley, W Yorks BD16 1WA, United Kingdom. TEL 44-1274-777700, FAX 44-1274-785201, information@emeraldinsight.com. Ed. Dr. William M Cox. Pubs. Harry Colson, Nancy Rolph. Circ: 2,880. **Subscr. in N America to:** Emerald Group Publishing Limited, One Mifflin Pl, Ste 400, Harvard Sq, Cambridge, MA 02138. TEL 617-576-5782, 888-309-7810, FAX 617-576-5883.

669 USA ISSN 1059-2997

ANVIL MAGAZINE. Text in English. 1975. m. USD 49.50 domestic; USD 55.50 in Canada; USD 69.50 elsewhere (effective 2000 & 2001). adv. bk.rev. back issues avail. **Document type:** *Journal, Trade.* **Description:** Presents a trade magazine for farriers and blacksmiths.
Formerly (until 1992): Anvil (0890-2534)
Published by: Rob Edwards, Ed & Pub, 2776 Sourdough Flat, Box 1810, Georgetown, CA 95634-1810. TEL 530-333-2142, FAX 530-333-2906. Ed. Timothy S Sebastian. Pub., Adv. contact Rob Edwards. R&P Mimi Clark. Circ: 5,000 (paid).

669 621 ITA ISSN 1973-7238

APPLICAZIONI LASER. Text in Italian. 2004. bi-m. **Document type:** *Magazine, Trade.*
Published by: PubliTec Srl, Via Passo Pordoi 10, Milan, MI 20139, Italy. TEL 39-02-535781, FAX 39-02-56814579, info@publitec.it, http://www.publitec.it.

669 NLD ISSN 0169-4332
TA418.7 CODEN: ASUSEE

➤ **APPLIED SURFACE SCIENCE.** Text in English. 1978. 24/yr. EUR 7,744 in Europe to institutions; JPY 1,027,800 in Japan to institutions; USD 8,665 elsewhere to institutions (effective 2012). bk.rev. cum.index: vols.11-20, 1986. back issues avail. **Document type:** *Journal, Academic/Scholarly.* **Description:** Concerned with the microscopic understanding of the synthesis and behavior of surfaces and interfaces.
Formerly (until 1985): Applications of Surface Science (0378-5963)
Related titles: Microform ed.: (from PQC); Online - full text ed.: ISSN 1873-5584 (from IngentaConnect, ScienceDirect).
Indexed: A01, A03, A08, A20, A22, A26, A28, AESIS, APA, ASCA, BrCerAb, C&ISA, C13, C24, C33, CA, CA/WCA, CCI, CEABA, CIA, CIN, CPEI, Cadscan, CerAb, ChemAb, ChemTitl, CivEngAb, CorrAb, CurCR, CurCont, E&CAJ, E11, EEA, EMA, ESPM, EngInd, EnvEAb, FR, GeoRef, H15, I05, ISMEC, ISR, Inspec, LeadAb, M&TEA, M09, MBF, METADEX, MSCI, P30, PhotoAb, R16, RefZh, S01, SCI, SCOPUS, SolStAb, SpeleolAb, T02, T04, TM, W07, WAA, Zincscan.
—BLDSC (1580.082000), AskIEEE, CASDDS, IE, Infotrieve, Ingenta, INIST, Linda Hall. **CCC.**
Published by: Elsevier BV, North-Holland (Subsidiary of: Elsevier Science & Technology), Sara Burgerhartstraat 25, Amsterdam, 1055 KV, Netherlands. TEL 31-20-4853911, FAX 31-20-4852457, JournalsCustomerServiceEMEA@elsevier.com. Eds. F H P M Habraken, H Kobayashi, R R L Opila. **Subscr. to:** Elsevier BV, Radarweg 29, PO Box 211, Amsterdam 1000 AE, Netherlands. TEL 31-20-4853757, FAX 31-20-4853432.

➤ **ARBEIDSMARKTMONITOR METALEKTRO.** *see* BUSINESS AND ECONOMICS—Labor And Industrial Relations

➤ **ARCHITECT & SPECIFICATOR.** *see* ARCHITECTURE

669 POL ISSN 1897-3310
TS228.99 CODEN: KMSTD6

ARCHIVES OF FOUNDRY ENGINEERING. Text in Polish; Summaries in English, Russian. 1978. q. **Document type:** *Journal, Academic/Scholarly.* **Description:** Original papers on different questions of iron and non-iron metallurgy.
Former titles (until 2007): Archiwum Odlewnictwa (1642-5308); (until 2001): Krzepniecie Metali i Stopow (0208-9386)
Related titles: Online - full text ed.: free (effective 2011).
Indexed: A28, APA, B22, BrCerAb, C&ISA, CA/WCA, CIA, CIN, CerAb, ChemAb, ChemTitl, CivEngAb, CorrAb, E&CAJ, E11, EEA, EMA, H15, M&TEA, M09, MBF, METADEX, SolStAb, T04, WAA.
—CASDDS, Linda Hall.
Published by: Polska Akademia Nauk, Oddzial w Katowicach, Komisja Odlewnictwa/Polish Academy of Sciences, Katowice Branch, Commission of Foundry Engineering, ul Graniczna 32, Katowice, 40018, Poland. TEL 48-32-2561938. **Dist. by:** Ars Polona, Obroncow 25, Warsaw 03933, Poland. TEL 48-22-5098609, FAX 48-22-5098610, arspolona@arspolona.com.pl, http://www.arspolona.com.pl.

ARCHIVES OF MATERIALS SCIENCE AND ENGINEERING. *see* ENGINEERING—Engineering Mechanics And Materials

669 POL ISSN 1733-3490
TN4.P57 CODEN: ARMEER

ARCHIVES OF METALLURGY AND MATERIALS. Text in English. 1956. q. abstr.; charts; illus. **Document type:** *Journal, Academic/Scholarly.*
Former titles (until 2004): Archives of Metallurgy (0860-7052); (until 1987): Archiwum Hutnictwa (0004-0770)
Related titles: Online - full text ed.: free (effective 2011) (from Versita).
Indexed: A22, A28, APA, B22, BrCerAb, C&ISA, CA/WCA, CIA, CIN, CerAb, ChemAb, ChemTitl, CivEngAb, CoppAb, CorrAb, CurCont, E&CAJ, E11, EEA, EMA, GeoRef, H15, IMMAb, Inspec, M&TEA, M09, MBF, METADEX, MSCI, SCI, SCOPUS, SolStAb, SpeleolAb, T04, TM, W07, WAA.
—BLDSC (1637.934400), AskIEEE, CASDDS, IE, Ingenta, INIST, Linda Hall.
Published by: (Polska Akademia Nauk, Komitet Metalurgii), Akademia Gorniczo-Hutnicza im. Stanislawa Staszica/University of Mining and Metallurgy, Al Mickiewicza 30, Krakow, 30059, Poland. TEL 48-12-172666, FAX 48-12-332316, rektorat@uci.agh.edu.pl, http://www.agh.edu.pl. Circ: 510. **Dist. by:** Ars Polona, Obroncow 25, Warsaw 03933, Poland. TEL 48-22-5098609, FAX 48-22-5098610, arspolona@arspolona.com.pl, http://www.arspolona.com.pl.

669 FRA ISSN 0220-3332

ARGUS DES METAUX. Text in French. d. **Document type:** *Newsletter.* **Description:** Daily information, market prices and reports on non-ferrous metals.
Published by: Veron et Cie, 42 Rue d'Antrain, Rennes, 35700, France. TEL 33-2-99853838, FAX 33-2-99853076, contact@metaltribune.com, http://www.metaltribune.com/. Circ: 300 (controlled).

673.722 JPN ISSN 0285-5240

ARUTOPIA. Text in Japanese. 1970. m. **Document type:** *Journal, Academic/Scholarly.*
Indexed: A28, APA, BrCerAb, C&ISA, CA/WCA, CIA, CerAb, CivEngAb, CorrAb, E&CAJ, E11, EEA, EMA, ESPM, EnvEAb, H15, M&TEA, M09, MBF, METADEX, SolStAb, T04, WAA.
—BLDSC (0806.225000), IE, Ingenta, Linda Hall.
Published by: Kallos Publishing Co., Ltd., 1-17-12 Kyobashi, Chuo-ku, Tokyo, 104, Japan. TEL 81-3-3562-5736, FAX 81-3-3561-7080, kallos@kallos.co.jp, http://www.kallos.co.jp/.

671.2 PRT

ASSOCIACAO PORTUGUESA DE FUNDICAO. BOLETIM. Text in Portuguese; Summaries in English, French, Portuguese. 1964. 4/yr. adv. bk.rev.; film rev. stat.; tr.lit. index. **Document type:** *Bulletin.*
Formerly (until 1990): Fundicao (0872-1890)
Related titles: Online - full text ed.
Published by: Associacao Portuguesa de Fundicao/Portuguese Foundry Association, Rua Campo Alegre, 672, 2d Esq, Porto, 4150, Portugal. TEL 355-22-6090675, 355-22-6000764, info@apf.com.pt, http://www.apf.com.pt. Ed. Mr. Malheiro. Circ: 1,000.

669.142 USA

ASSOCIATION OF STEEL DISTRIBUTORS. NEWS AND VIEWS. Text in English. m. membership. **Document type:** *Newsletter.*
Published by: Association of Steel Distributors, 401 N Michigan Ave, Chicago, IL 60611-4267. TEL 312-644-6610, FAX 312-321-6774. Ed., R&P Daniel S Consiglio. Circ: 300 (controlled).

ASU O KIZUKU/CONSTRUCTION TOMORROW. *see* ENGINEERING—Civil Engineering

669.6 DEU

@BLECHNET.COM; Das Magazin. Text in German. 2002. 5/yr. adv. **Document type:** *Magazine, Trade.*
Indexed: TM.
Published by: Vogel Business Media GmbH & Co.KG, Max-Planck-Str 7-9, Wuerzburg, 97064, Germany. TEL 49-931-4180, FAX 49-931-4182750, info@vogel.de, http://www.vogel-media.de. Ed. Ken Fauhy TEL 49-931-4182203. Adv. contact Winfried Burkard TEL 49-931-4182686. B&W page EUR 2,520, color page EUR 3,654. Circ: 11,000 (controlled).

AUSTRALASIAN INSTITUTE OF MINING AND METALLURGY. MONOGRAPH SERIES. *see* MINES AND MINING INDUSTRY

AUSTRALASIAN INSTITUTE OF MINING AND METALLURGY PUBLICATIONS. *see* MINES AND MINING INDUSTRY

669 AUS ISSN 1832-6080

AUSTRALIAN MANUFACTURING TECHNOLOGY. Variant title: A M T Magazine. Text in English. 2002. m. free to qualified personnel (effective 2008). adv. **Document type:** *Magazine, Trade.* **Description:** Focuses on metal machining, cutting, and fabrication.
Related titles: Online - full text ed.: free (effective 2008).
Published by: Australian Manufacturing Technology Institute Ltd., Ste 1, 673 Boronia Rd, Wantirna, VIC 3152, Australia. TEL 61-3-98003666, FAX 61-3-98003436, info@amtil.com.au. Eds. John Leah, Barbara Schulz. Adv. contact Dan Duncan. color page AUD 3,195, B&W page AUD 2,870; trim 210 x 297. Circ: 10,000.

AUSZUEGE AUS DEN EUROPAEISCHEN PATENTANMELDUNGEN. TEIL 1A. CHEMIE UND HUETTENWESEN/EXTRACTS FROM EUROPEAN PATENT APPLICATIONS. PART 1A. CHEMISTRY AND METALLURGY. *see* PATENTS, TRADEMARKS AND COPYRIGHTS—Abstracting, Bibliographies, Statistics

AUSZUEGE AUS DEN EUROPAEISCHEN PATENTSCHRIFTEN. TEIL 1. GRUND- UND ROHSTOFFINDUSTRIE, CHEMIE UND HUETTEN-WESEN, BAUWESEN UND BERGBAU. *see* PATENTS, TRADEMARKS AND COPYRIGHTS—Abstracting, Bibliographies, Statistics

B H M/JOURNAL OF MINING, METALLURGICAL, MATERIALS, GEOTECHNICAL AND PLANT ENGINEERING; Zeitschrift fuer Rohstoffe, Geotechnik, Metallurgie, Werkstoffe, Maschinen- und Anlagentechnik. (Berg- und Huettenmaennische Monatshefte) *see* MINES AND MINING INDUSTRY

669.1 IND

B S P MAGAZINE/ISPAT VIHANGAM. Text in English. 1959. q. free (effective 2011). **Document type:** *Magazine, Government.*
Related titles: Hindi ed.
Published by: Steel Authority of India Ltd., Bhilai Steel Plant, Bhilai, 490 001, India. TEL 91-788-2223587, FAX 91-788-2222890, md_bsp@sail-bhilaisteel.com, https://sail-bhilaisteel.com/index.html.

669 DEU ISSN 0005-3848
CODEN: BBROAB

BAENDER, BLECHE, ROHRE. Text in German. 1959. 8/yr. EUR 115 domestic; EUR 133 foreign (effective 2010). adv. bk.rev. charts; illus. index. **Document type:** *Magazine, Trade.*
Incorporates (1966-1974): D F B O Mitteilungen (0340-3920); Which was formerly (until 1969): Deutsche Forschungsgesellschaft fuer Blechverarbeitung und Oberflaechenbehandlung. Mitteilungen (0720-0951)

M

Indexed: A22, A28, APA, BrCerAb, C&ISA, CA/WCA, CIA, CIN, CISA, Cadscan, CerAb, ChemAb, ChemTitl, CivEngAb, CorrAb, E&CAJ, E11, EEA, EMA, ESPM, EnvEAb, H15, ISMEC, LeadAb, M&TEA, M09, MBF, METADEX, SCOPUS, SolStAb, T04, TM, WAA, Zincscan. —BLDSC (1861.580000), CASDDS, IE, Infotrieve, Ingenta, INIST, Linda Hall. **CCC.**

Published by: Henrich Publikationen GmbH, Talhofstr 24b, Gilching, 82205, Germany. TEL 49-8105-38530, FAX 49-8105-385311, info@verlag.henrich.de, http://www.henrich.de. Ed. Hans-Georg Schaetzl. Adv. contact Thomas Schumann. Circ: 12,632 (controlled).

THE BANNER (GARY). *see* LABOR UNIONS

BANYASZATI ES KOHASZATI LAPOK - BANYASZAT. *see* MINES AND MINING INDUSTRY

669 HUN ISSN 0005-5670
TN4 CODEN: BKLKBX

➤ **BANYASZATI ES KOHASZATI LAPOK - KOHASZAT.** Text in Hungarian; Summaries in English. 1868. bi-m. USD 80 (effective 2001). adv. bk.rev. charts; illus.; pat.; tr.mk. index. 60 p./no.; **Document type:** *Journal, Academic/Scholarly.*

Formerly (until 1968): Kohaszati Lapok (0368-6469); Which supersedes in part (in 1951): Banyaszati es Kohaszati Lapok (0365-9011)

Indexed: A28, APA, ApMecR, BrCerAb, C&ISA, CA/WCA, CIA, CerAb, ChemAb, CivEngAb, CorrAb, E&CAJ, E11, EEA, EMA, ESPM, EnvEAb, H15, M&TEA, M09, MBF, METADEX, PetrolAb, SolStAb, SpeleolAb, T04, TM, WAA. —CASDDS, INIST, Linda Hall.

Published by: Orszagos Magyar Banyaszati es Kohaszati Egyesulet, Fo utca 68, Budapest, 1027, Hungary. ombke@mtesz.hu, http://www.mtesz.hu/tagegy/ombke. Ed., Adv. contact Balazs Vero TEL 36-1-4630537. Circ: 2,000.

669 CHN ISSN 1008-0716

BAOGANG JISHU/BAO-STEEL TECHNOLOGY. Text in Chinese. 1983. bi-m. USD 31.20 (effective 2009). **Document type:** *Journal, Academic/Scholarly.*

Related titles: Online - full text ed.

Indexed: A28, APA, BrCerAb, C&ISA, CA/WCA, CIA, CerAb, CivEngAb, CorrAb, E&CAJ, E11, EEA, EMA, H15, M&TEA, M09, MBF, METADEX, SolStAb, T04, WAA. —BLDSC (1863.114000), East View.

Published by: Baoshan Gangtie Jituan Gongsi/BaoSteel Group Crop., Baogang Zhihui Zhongxin, Shanghai, 201900, China. TEL 81-21-26649250, FAX 81-21-26643977.

669 CHN ISSN 1009-5438

BAOGANG KEJI/SCIENCE & TECHNOLOGY OF BAOTOU STEEL (GROUP) CORPORATION. Text in Chinese. 1974. bi-m. CNY 15 newsstand/cover (effective 2006). **Document type:** *Journal, Academic/Scholarly.*

Related titles: Online - full text ed.

Published by: Baotou Gangtie (Jituan) Youxian Zeren Gongsi, Kunqu Baogang, Hexichang-qu, Huanbao Lou, Baotou, 014010, China. TEL 86-472-2186065, FAX 86-472-2183081.

669 CHN ISSN 1674-3458

BAOSTEEL TECHNICAL RESEARCH. Variant title: Baogang Jishui Yanjiu. Text in English. 2007. q. **Document type:** *Journal, Academic/Scholarly.*

Indexed: A28, APA, BrCerAb, CA/WCA, CIA, CerAb, CivEngAb, E11, EEA, EMA, ESPM, EnvEAb, H15, M&TEA, M09, MBF, METADEX, P52, RefZh, T04. —BLDSC (1863.119000).

Published by: Baosteel Group Corp., 655 Fujin Rd, Baoshan District, Shanghai, 201900, China. TEL 86-21-26648493, FAX 86-21-26643977. Ed. Guoqiang Weng.

669 CHN ISSN 1004-9762

BAOTOU GANGTIE XUEYUAN XUEBAO/BAOTOU UNIVERSITY OF IRON AND STEEL TECHNOLOGY. JOURNAL. Text in Chinese. 1982. q. USD 16.40 (effective 2009). abstr.; charts; illus.; bibl. 96 p./no.; back issues avail. **Document type:** *Journal, Academic/Scholarly.*

Related titles: Online - full text ed.

Published by: Baotou Gangtie Xueyuan/Baotou University of Iron and Steel Tehnology, A-Er-Ding Dajie no.7, Baotou, 014010, China. TEL 86-472-5951610, FAX 86-472-5951628. Circ: 30 (paid); 300 (controlled).

669 GBR ISSN 0964-7686

BASE METALS MONTHLY. Text in English. 1991. m. GBP 1,405 domestic; EUR 2,060 in Europe; USD 2,805 elsewhere (effective 2009). **Document type:** *Bulletin, Trade.* **Description:** Comprehensive research publication covering all the latest market developments and price trends in the base metals market.

—CCC.

Published by: Metal Bulletin Plc. (Subsidiary of: Euromoney Institutional Investor Plc.), Nestor House, Playhouse Yard, London, EC4V 5EX, United Kingdom. TEL 44-20-77797390, FAX 44-20-77797389, help@metalbulletin.com, http://www.metalbulletin.com. Ed. Neil Buxton. Adv. contact Stefano di Nardo TEL 44-20-78275220.

BAYERN METALL. *see* ENGINEERING—Mechanical Engineering

BEIJING KEJI DAXUE XUEBAO. *see* MINES AND MINING INDUSTRY

669.1 CHN

BEIJING UNIVERSITY OF IRON AND STEEL TECHNOLOGY. JOURNAL/BEIJING GANGTIE JISHU DAXUE XUEBAO. Text in Chinese. 1955. q. USD 25. reprints avail.

Published by: Beijing Gangtie Jishu Daxue/Beijing University of Iron and Steel Technology, 30 Xueyuan Lu, Haidian-qu, Beijing, China. Ed. Jinwu Xu.

BERGSMANNEN MED JERNKONTORETS ANNALER. *see* MINES AND MINING INDUSTRY

669 DEU ISSN 0945-0904

BERICHTE AUS DER METALLURGIE. Text in German. 1994. irreg., latest vol.29, 2004. price varies. **Document type:** *Monographic series, Academic/Scholarly.*

Published by: Shaker Verlag GmbH, Kaiserstr 100, Herzogenrath, 52134, Germany. TEL 49-2407-95960, FAX 49-2407-95969, info@shaker.de.

669 USA

BETHLEHEM REVIEW. Text in English. q. **Document type:** *Journal, Trade.*

Published by: Bethlehem Steel Corp, 1170 Eighth Avenue, Bethlehem, PA 18016. TEL 610-694-2424.

BIOMEDICAL MATERIALS (DROITWICH). *see* MEDICAL SCIENCES

669 537.5 BEL ISSN 0379-0401
CODEN: BBIBDW

BISMUTH INSTITUTE. BULLETIN. Text in English. 1973. irreg. (3-4/yr.). free. bk.rev. pat.; tr.lit. cum.index: 1973-1992. back issues avail. **Document type:** *Bulletin.* **Description:** Technical publication reporting advances of permanent interest in metallurgy, electronics, chemistry, medicine, and cosmetics.

Indexed: EIA, EnvAb. —CASDDS, Linda Hall.

Published by: Bismuth Institute - Information Centre, Borgstraat 301, Grimbergen, 1850, Belgium. TEL 32-2-2524747, FAX 32-2-2522775, palmieri@pandora.be. Ed. Yves Palmieri. Circ: 2,000.

669 DEU ISSN 0942-9751

BLECH. Text in German. 1992. 7/yr. EUR 55 domestic; EUR 70 foreign; EUR 15 newsstand/cover (effective 2010). adv. **Document type:** *Magazine, Trade.*

Related titles: Online - full text ed.

Indexed: TM.

Published by: Schluetersche Verlagsgesellschaft mbH und Co. KG, Hans-Boeckler-Allee 7, Hannover, 30173, Germany. TEL 49-511-85500, FAX 49-511-85501100, info@schluetersche.de, http://www.schluetersche.de. Ed. Guenter Koegel. Adv. contact Gabriele Maier. color page EUR 3,553, B&W page EUR 2,533; trim 184 x 260. Circ: 12,823 (paid and controlled).

669 DEU ISSN 1616-3362

BLECH INFORM. Text in German. 2001. 5/yr. EUR 80.50 domestic; EUR 86 foreign; EUR 16.40 newsstand/cover (effective 2011). adv. **Document type:** *Journal, Trade.* **Description:** Covers all aspects of working with sheet metal.

Indexed: RefZh, TM.

Published by: Carl Hanser Verlag GmbH & Co. KG, Kolbergerstr 22, Munich, 81679, Germany. TEL 49-89-998300, FAX 49-89-984809, info@hanser.de. Ed. Thomas Mavidris. Adv. contact Martin Ricchiuti. Circ: 12,671 (paid and controlled).

669 DEU ISSN 0006-4688
CODEN: BRPFBJ

BLECH-ROHRE-PROFILE; internationale Fachzeitschrift fuer die Herstellung und Verarbeitung von Band, Blech, Rohren und Profilen. Text in German. 1970. 9/yr. EUR 124 domestic; EUR 137 in Europe; EUR 183 elsewhere (effective 2011). adv. bk.rev. charts; illus.; mkt.; pat.; tr.lit. **Document type:** *Magazine, Trade.*

Formed by the merger of (1953-1970): Blech (0366-1040); (1962-1970): Rohre und Profile (0723-8347)

Indexed: A22, A28, APA, ApMecR, BrCerAb, C&ISA, CA/WCA, CIA, CIN, CerAb, ChemAb, ChemTitl, CivEngAb, CorrAb, E&CAJ, E11, EEA, EMA, ESPM, EnvEAb, H15, M&TEA, M09, MBF, METADEX, SolStAb, T04, TM, WAA. —BLDSC (2110.630000), CASDDS, IE, Infotrieve, Ingenta, INIST, Linda Hall. **CCC.**

Published by: Meisenbach GmbH, Franz-Ludwig-Str 7a, Bamberg, 96047, Germany. TEL 49-951-8610, FAX 49-951-861158, geschltg@meisenbach.de. Ed. Volker Albrecht. Adv. contact Georg Meisenbach. Circ: 11,506 (paid and controlled).

669 CHL

BOLETIN MERCADOLOGICO I L A F A. Text in Spanish. bi-m. USD 50 to members; USD 60 to non-members (effective 2002).

Published by: Instituto Latinoamericano del Fierro y el Acero, Calle Benjamin 2944, 5o piso - Las Condes, Santiago, 9, Chile. TEL 56-2-2330545, FAX 56-2-2330768, ilafa@entelchile.net, http://www.ilafa.org.

669 SGP

BOOK SERIES ON COMPLEX METAL ALLOYS. Text in English. 2008. irreg., latest vol.2, 2009. price varies. back issues avail. **Document type:** *Monographic series, Academic/Scholarly.*

Published by: World Scientific Publishing Co. Pte. Ltd., 5 Toh Tuck Link, Singapore, 596224, Singapore. TEL 65-6466-5775, FAX 65-6467-7667, wspc@wspc.com.sg, http://www.worldscientific.com. Eds. Esther Belin-Ferre, Jean-Marie Dubois. **Subscr. to:** Farrer Rd, PO Box 128, Singapore 912805, Singapore. sales@wspc.com.sg. **Dist. by:** World Scientific Publishing Ltd., 57 Shelton St, London WC2H 9HE, United Kingdom. TEL 44-207-8360888, FAX 44-207-8362020, sales@wspc.co.uk.; World Scientific Publishing Co., Inc., 27 Warren St, Ste 401-402, Hackensack, NJ 07601. TEL 201-487-9655, 800-227-7562, FAX 201-487-9656, 888-977-2665, wspc@wspc.com.

620.112 SGP

BOOK SERIES ON COMPLEX METALLIC ALLOYS. Text in English. 2008. irreg., latest vol.4, 2010. price varies. back issues avail. **Document type:** *Monographic series, Academic/Scholarly.*

Published by: World Scientific Publishing Co. Pte. Ltd., 5 Toh Tuck Link, Singapore, 596224, Singapore. TEL 65-6466-5775, FAX 65-6467-7667, wspc@wspc.com.sg, http://www.worldscientific.com. Eds. Esther Belin-Ferre, Jean-Marie Dubois. **Dist. by:** World Scientific Publishing Co., Inc., 27 Warren St, Ste 401-402, Hackensack, NJ 07601. TEL 201-487-9655, 800-227-7562, FAX 201-487-9656, 888-977-2665, wspc@wspc.com; World Scientific Publishing Ltd., 57 Shelton St, London WC2H 9HE, United Kingdom. TEL 44-207-8360888, FAX 44-207-8362020, sales@wspc.co.uk.

BOUWEN MET STAAL. *see* BUILDING AND CONSTRUCTION

BRANCHENFUEHRER GALVANOTECHNIK. *see* BUSINESS AND ECONOMICS—Trade And Industrial Directories

BRAZILIAN JOURNAL OF MATERIALS SCIENCE AND ENGINEERING. *see* ENGINEERING—Engineering Mechanics And Materials

BU'SIG GWA BANGSIG/CORROSION AND PROTECTION. *see* ENGINEERING—Engineering Mechanics And Materials

671.2 658.8 GBR ISSN 1473-1134

BUSINESS RATIO REPORT. IRON FOUNDERS (YEAR). Text in English. 1979. a. GBP 365 per issue (effective 2010). charts; stat. back issues avail. **Document type:** *Report, Trade.*

Former titles (until 2000): Business Ratio. Iron Founders (1469-7408); (until 1999): Business Ratio Plus. Iron Founders (1359-6039); (until 1995): Business Ratio Report. Iron Founders (0261-8559)

Published by: Key Note Ltd. (Subsidiary of: Bonnier Business Information), Harlequin House, 5th Fl, 7 High St, Teddington, Richmond upon Thames, TW11 8EE, United Kingdom. TEL 44-845-5040452, FAX 44-845-5040453, sales@keynote.co.uk.

671.2 GBR ISSN 1475-0007

BUSINESS RATIO REPORT. METAL STOCKHOLDERS. Text in English. 2000. a. GBP 365 per issue (effective 2010). charts; stat. back issues avail. **Document type:** *Report, Trade.* **Description:** Covers companies active as metal stockholders.

Formerly (until 2001): Business Ratio. Metal Stockholders (1472-0477); Which was formed by the merger of (1999-2000): Business Ratio. Steel Stockholders (1467-9000); Which was formerly (until 1999): Business Ratio Plus. Steel Stockholders (1358-3689); (until 1994): Business Ratio Report. Steel Stockholders (0267-274X); (1999-2000): Business Ratio. Non-Ferrous Metal Stockholders (1468-3717); Which was formerly (until 1999): Business Ratio Plus. Non-Ferrous Metal Stockholders (1358-4235); (until 1994): Business Ratio Report. Non-Ferrous Metal Stockholders (0267-2731); Business Ratio Report. Steel Stockholders & Business Ratio Report. Non-Ferrous Metal Stockholders superseded in part (in 1985): Business Ratio Reports. Metal Stockholders (0261-9091)

Published by: Key Note Ltd. (Subsidiary of: Bonnier Business Information), Harlequin House, 5th Fl, 7 High St, Teddington, Richmond upon Thames, TW11 8EE, United Kingdom. TEL 44-845-5040452, FAX 44-845-5040453, sales@keynote.co.uk.

671.2 658.8 GBR ISSN 1472-9970

BUSINESS RATIO REPORT. NON-FERROUS FOUNDERS (YEAR). Text in English. 1978. a. GBP 365 per issue (effective 2010). charts; stat. back issues avail. **Document type:** *Report, Trade.*

Former titles (until 2000): Business Ratio. Non-Ferrous Founders (1468-8921); (until 1999): Business Ratio Plus. Non-Ferrous Founders (1357-8812); (until 1994): Business Ratio Report. Non-Ferrous Founders (0261-9164)

Published by: Key Note Ltd. (Subsidiary of: Bonnier Business Information), Harlequin House, 5th Fl, 7 High St, Teddington, Richmond upon Thames, TW11 8EE, United Kingdom. TEL 44-845-5040452, FAX 44-845-5040453, sales@keynote.co.uk.

671.2 GBR ISSN 1473-2637

BUSINESS RATIO REPORT. THE FORGING INDUSTRY. Text in English. 1979. a., latest no.30, 2008, Feb. GBP 365 per issue (effective 2010). charts; stat. back issues avail. **Document type:** *Report, Trade.* **Description:** Covers companies active in the forging industry.

Former titles (until 2001): Business Ratio. The Forging Industry (1469-882X); (until 2000): Business Ratio Plus: The Forging Industry (1358-5126); (until 1995): Business Ratio Report: The Forging Industry (1354-2338); (until 1994): Business Ratio Report. Drop Forgers (0261-7838)

Published by: Key Note Ltd. (Subsidiary of: Bonnier Business Information), Harlequin House, 5th Fl, 7 High St, Teddington, Richmond upon Thames, TW11 8EE, United Kingdom. TEL 44-845-5040452, FAX 44-845-5040453, sales@keynote.co.uk.

669.3 USA

C B S A CAPSULES. Text in English. 1951. m. USD 25 (effective 2000). charts; illus.; stat.; tr.lit. back issues avail. **Document type:** *Newsletter.* **Description:** Includes legislative and regulatory news related to metal industry, management and business news, and news about members.

Published by: Copper & Brass Servicenter Association, 994 Old Eagle School Rd, Ste 1019, Wayne, PA 19087-1802. TEL 610-265-6658, FAX 610-265-3419. Ed. R Franklin Brown Jr. Circ: 165.

C I M DIRECTORY. *see* MINES AND MINING INDUSTRY

C I N D E JOURNAL. *see* ENGINEERING—Engineering Mechanics And Materials

669.1 RUS ISSN 2072-0815

C I S IRON AND STEEL REVIEW. (Commonwealth of Independent States) Text in English. 2007. a.

Related titles: ◆ Supplement to: Chernye Metally. ISSN 0132-0890.

Published by: Izdatel'stvo Ruda i Metally/Ore and Metals Publishers, Leninskii prospekt 6, korpus 1, ofis 622, a/ya 71, Moscow, 119049, Russian Federation. rim@rudmet.ru. Ed. Evgenii Tsiryul'nikov. Circ: 1,000.

669 DEU ISSN 0935-7262

C P & T INTERNATIONAL. (Casting Plant and Technology) Text in English. 1985. q. EUR 110 domestic; EUR 117 foreign (effective 2009). adv. **Document type:** *Magazine, Trade.*

Formerly: C P and T (0177-1469)

Related titles: ◆ Russian Translation: S P + T. Liteinoe Proizvodstvo i Tekhnologiya Liteinogo Dela. ISSN 0934-8069.

Indexed: A28, APA, BrCerAb, C&ISA, CA/WCA, CIA, CerAb, CivEngAb, CorrAb, E&CAJ, E11, EEA, EMA, ESPM, EnvEAb, H15, M&TEA, M09, MBF, METADEX, RefZh, SolStAb, T04, TM, WAA. —BLDSC (3064.085500), IE, Ingenta, Linda Hall. **CCC.**

Published by: (Verein Deutscher Giessereifachleute), Giesserei-Verlag GmbH, Postfach 102532, Duesseldorf, 40016, Germany. TEL 49-211-67070, FAX 49-211-6707517, giesserei@stahleisen.de, http://www.giesserei-verlag.de. adv.: B&W page EUR 2,248, color page EUR 3,046. Circ: 8,357 (paid and controlled).

C R U MONITOR. ALUMINA. (Commodities Research Unit) *see* BUSINESS AND ECONOMICS—Production Of Goods And Services

C R U MONITOR. ALUMINIUM. (Commodities Research Unit) *see* BUSINESS AND ECONOMICS—Production Of Goods And Services

C R U MONITOR. ALUMINIUM PRODUCTS. (Commodities Research Unit) *see* BUSINESS AND ECONOMICS—Production Of Goods And Services

C R U MONITOR. BULK FERROALLOYS. (Commodities Research Unit) *see* BUSINESS AND ECONOMICS—Production Of Goods And Services

C R U MONITOR. COPPER. (Commodities Research Unit) *see* BUSINESS AND ECONOMICS—Production Of Goods And Services

C R U MONITOR. COPPER RAW MATERIALS: CONCENTRATES, BLISTER AND SCRAP. (Commodities Research Unit) *see* BUSINESS AND ECONOMICS—Production Of Goods And Services

C R U MONITOR. COPPER STUDIES. (Commodities Research Unit) *see* BUSINESS AND ECONOMICS—Production Of Goods And Services

C R U MONITOR. LEAD AND ZINC CONCENTRATES. (Commodities Research Unit) *see* BUSINESS AND ECONOMICS—Production Of Goods And Services

C R U MONITOR. NICKEL, CHROME, MOLYBDENUM. (Commodities Research Unit) *see* BUSINESS AND ECONOMICS—Production Of Goods And Services

C R U MONITOR. STEEL. (Commodities Research Unit) *see* BUSINESS AND ECONOMICS—Production Of Goods And Services

C R U MONITOR. STEELMAKING RAW MATERIALS. (Commodities Research Unit) *see* BUSINESS AND ECONOMICS—Production Of Goods And Services

C R U MONITOR. TIN. (Commodities Research Unit) *see* BUSINESS AND ECONOMICS—Production Of Goods And Services

C R U MONITOR. ZINC. (Commodities Research Unit) *see* BUSINESS AND ECONOMICS—Production Of Goods And Services

669.722 FRA ISSN 0990-6908
TN490.A5
CAHIERS D'HISTOIRE DE L'ALUMINIUM. Text in English. 1987. 2/yr. EUR 25 domestic to individual members; EUR 30 domestic to individuals; EUR 40 foreign to individuals (effective 2010). **Document type:** *Journal, Academic/Scholarly.*
Indexed: CorrAb, WAA.
—INIST.
Published by: Institut Pour l'Histoire de l'Aluminium, Immeuble Le Signac, ZAC des Barbanniers, 1 Av. du General de Gaule, Gennevilliers, 92230, France. TEL 33-1-49686400, FAX 33-1-49686410, histalu@histalu.org.

669 TWN ISSN 0379-6906
TA401 CODEN: TLKHAJ
CAILIAO KEXUE/CHINESE JOURNAL OF MATERIALS SCIENCE. Variant title: Materials Science Quarterly. Text in Chinese, English. 1969. q. TWD 400 to non-members; free to members (effective 2004); (foreign $36). reprints avail. **Document type:** *Journal, Academic/Scholarly.*
Indexed: A22, CIN, ChemAb, ChemTitl.
—CASDDS. **CCC.**
Published by: Chinese Society for Materials Science, No.2-1, Lane 81, 300 Tahsueh Road, Hsinchu, 31015, Taiwan. TEL 886-3-5734223, webmaster@twcsms.org, http://www.twcsms.org/. Ed. Sing Tien Wu. Pub. Li Chung Lee. Circ: 1,500.

669 CHN ISSN 1005-0299
TN4
➤ **CAILIAO KEXUE YU GONGYI/MATERIAL SCIENCE AND TECHNOLOGY.** Text in Chinese; Summaries in English. 1982. q. USD 37.20 (effective 2009). **Document type:** *Academic/Scholarly.* **Description:** Covers metal materials and hot working, as well as ceramic materials, semi-conduct materials, polymer and composites materials.
Formerly (until 1993): Jinshu Kexue yu Gongyi (1001-0181)
Related titles: Online - full text ed.
Indexed: A28, APA, BrCerAb, C&ISA, CA/WCA, CIA, CIN, CPEI, CerAb, ChemAb, ChemTitl, CivEngAb, CorrAb, E&CAJ, E11, EEA, EMA, ESPM, EngInd, EnvEAb, H15, M&TEA, M09, MBF, METADEX, SCOPUS, SolStAb, T04, WAA.
—BLDSC (5396.433000), East View, Linda Hall.
Published by: Harbin Gongye Daxue/Harbin Institute of Technology, 92 Xidazhi St, Harbin, Heilongjiang 150001, China. TEL 86-451-6414135, FAX 86-451-6418376, TELEX 87217 HIT CN. Ed. Xuemeng Song. Circ: 2,000.

669 536 CHN ISSN 1009-6264
CODEN: CRXAAK
CAILIAO RECHULI XUEBAO/TRANSACTIONS OF MATERIALS AND HEAT TREATMENT. Text in Chinese; Contents page in English. 1980. q. USD 53.40 (effective 2009). **Document type:** *Journal, Trade.*
Formerly (until 2001): Jinshu Rechuli Xuebao/Transactions of Metal Heat Treatment (0254-587X)
Related titles: Online - full text ed.
Indexed: A28, APA, BrCerAb, C&ISA, C33, CA/WCA, CIA, CPEI, CerAb, CivEngAb, CorrAb, E&CAJ, E11, EEA, EMA, ESPM, EngInd, EnvEAb, H15, M&TEA, M09, MBF, METADEX, SCOPUS, SolStAb, T04, WAA.
—BLDSC (9020.537650), East View, Linda Hall.
Address: No. 18, Xueqing Road, Beijing, 100083, China. TEL 86-10-62914115, FAX 86-10-62935465. Ed. Jing'en Zhou. **Dist. by:** China International Book Trading Corp, 35 Chegongzhuang Xilu, Haidian District, PO Box 399, Beijing 100044, China. TEL 86-10-68412045, FAX 86-10-68412023, cibtc@mail.cibtc.com.cn, http://www.cibtc.com.cn.

669 CHN ISSN 1005-3093
TA401 CODEN: CYXUEV
CAILIAO YANJIU XUEBAO/CHINESE JOURNAL OF MATERIALS RESEARCH. Text in Chinese. 1987. bi-m. USD 53.40 (effective 2009). adv. 112 p./no.; **Document type:** *Journal, Academic/Scholarly.* **Description:** Covers metallic materials, inorganic non-metallic materials, organic polymer materials and composite materials.
Formerly (until 1994): Cailiao Kexue Jinzhan/Materials Science Progress (1000-8500)
Related titles: Online - full text ed.
Indexed: A22, A28, APA, BrCerAb, C&ISA, CA/WCA, CIA, CIN, CPEI, CerAb, ChemAb, ChemTitl, CivEngAb, CorrAb, E&CAJ, E11, EEA, EMA, ESPM, EngInd, EnvEAb, H15, M&TEA, M09, MBF, METADEX, SCOPUS, SolStAb, T04, WAA.
—BLDSC (3180.369800), CASDDS, East View, IE, Ingenta, Linda Hall. **CCC.**
Published by: Zhongguo Kexueyuan Jinshu Yanjiusuo/Chinese Academy of Sciences, Institute of Metal Research, 72, Wenhua Lu, Shenyang, Liaoning 110015, China. TEL 86-24-83978072, FAX 86-24-23971297. **Dist. by:** China International Book Trading Corp, 35 Chegongzhuang Xilu, Haidian District, PO Box 399, Beijing 100044, China. TEL 86-10-68412045, FAX 86-10-68412023, cibtc@mail.cibtc.com.cn, http://www.cibtc.com.cn. **Co-sponsors:** Chinese Materials Research Society; National Natural Science Foundation of China.

669 CHN ISSN 1673-9981
CAILIAO YANJIU YU YINGYONG. Text in Chinese. 1991. q. **Document type:** *Journal, Academic/Scholarly.*
Formerly (until 2007): Guangdong Yousejinshu Xuebao/Journal of Guangdong Non-Ferrous Metals (1003-7837)
Related titles: Online - full text ed.
—BLDSC (2952.457800).
Published by: Guangdong Yousejinshu Yanjiuyuan, 363 Changxing Rd., Tianhe Dist., Guangzhou, 510650, China. TEL 86-20-61086285, FAX 86-20-85231605.

669 CHN ISSN 1671-6620
QE390.2.G65
CAILIAO YU YEJIN XUEBAO/JOURNAL OF MATERIALS AND METALLURGY. Text in Chinese. 2002. q. USD 24.80 (effective 2009). **Document type:** *Journal, Academic/Scholarly.*
Related titles: Online - full text ed.
Indexed: A28, APA, BrCerAb, C&ISA, CA/WCA, CIA, CerAb, CivEngAb, CorrAb, E&CAJ, E11, EEA, EMA, ESPM, EnvEAb, H15, M&TEA, M09, MBF, METADEX, RefZh, SolStAb, T04, WAA.
—BLDSC (5012.233000), IE, Ingenta, Linda Hall.
Published by: Dongbei Daxue/Northeastern University, No.3, Alley 11, Wenhua Rd, PO Box 114, Shenyang, 110004, China. TEL 86-24-83687664, FAX 86-24-23906316, http://www.neu.edu.cn/.

669.722 ARG ISSN 0328-2007
CAMARA ARGENTINA DE LA INDUSTRIA DEL ALUMINIO Y METALES AFINES. REVISTA. Text in Spanish. 1985. irreg. **Document type:** *Magazine, Trade.*
Published by: Camara Argentina de la Industria del Aluminio y Metales Afines, Parana 467, 1er Piso, Of 3 y 4, Buenos Aires, Argentina. http://www.aluminiocaiama.org.

669 CAN ISSN 1701-2031
CANADA. STATISTICS CANADA. PRIMARY METAL INDUSTRIES (ONLINE). Text in English. 1985. a. **Document type:** *Directory, Trade.*
Formerly (until 1997): Primary Metal Industries (Print) (0835-0116); Which was formed by the merger of (1983-1985): Primary Steel, Steel Pipe and Tube Industries and Iron Foundries (0828-9808); Which was formerly (1981-1983): Iron, Steel and Pipe Mills including Foundries (0319-8960); Which was formed by the merger of (1960-1981): Iron and Steel Mills (0575-884X); Which was formerly (1948-1959): Primary Iron and Steel Industry (0700-0235); (1960-1981): Iron Foundries (0527-5458); (1960-1981): Steel Pipe and Tube Mills (0527-6241); Both of which superseded in part (in 1959): Iron Castings Industry (0700-0944); Which was formerly (19??-1948): Iron Castings Industry in Canada (0826-6336); (1984-1985): Non-ferrous Metal Smelting and Refining Industries (0828-9786); Which was formerly (until 1983): Smelting and Refining (0384-4935); (1954-1961): Smelting and Refining Industry (0527-6195); (1984-1985): Non-ferrous Metal Rolling, Casting and Extruding Industries (0828-9964); Which was formerly (1981-1983): Non-ferrous Metal Rolling, Casting, and Extruding (0319-8952); Which was formed by the merger of (1970-1981): Copper and Copper Alloy Rolling, Casting and Extruding (0700-1053); Which was formerly (until 1969): Copper and Alloy Rolling, Casting and Extruding (0527-4982); Which superseded in part (in 1960): Brass and Copper Products Industry (0700-0979); Which was formerly (1930-1949): Brass & Copper Products Industry in Canada (0826-6328); (1960-1981): Aluminum Rolling, Casting and Extruding (0527-477X); Which was formerly (1943-1959): Aluminum Products Industry (0700-0928); (1970-1981): Metal Rolling, Casting and Extruding (0575-898X); Which was formerly (until 1969): Metal Rolling, Casting and Extruding, Not Elsewhere Specified (0825-9143); (until 1960): White Metal Alloys Industry (0384-3831); (until 1949): White Metal Products Industry (0825-9070); (until 194?): White Metal Products Industry in Canada (0825-9089); (until 1944): White Metal Alloys Industry
Media: Online - full content.
Published by: Statistics Canada, Manufacturing, Construction and Energy Division (Subsidiary of: Statistics Canada/Statistique Canada), Ste 1500 Main Bldg Holland Ave, Ottawa, ON K1A OT6, Canada. TEL 613-951-8116, 800-263-1136, infostats@statcan.ca.

669.3 CAN ISSN 0008-3291
CANADIAN COPPER/CUIVRE CANADIEN. Text in English, French. 1960. 3/yr. free (effective 2005). illus. 16 p./no. 3 cols./p.; **Document type:** *Bulletin, Trade.* **Description:** Articles promoting and developing the uses of copper, its alloys and compounds.
Formerly: Canadian Coppermetals
Indexed: A28, APA, BrCerAb, C&ISA, CA/WCA, CIA, CerAb, CivEngAb, CoppAb, CorrAb, E&CAJ, E11, EEA, EMA, H15, M&TEA, M09, MBF, METADEX, RefZh, SolStAb, T04, WAA.
—Linda Hall.
Published by: Canadian Copper and Brass Development Association, 415-49 The Donway W., North York, ON M3C 3M9, Canada. TEL 416-391-5599, FAX 416-391-3823, http://www.coppercanada.ca. Ed., R&P Stephen A W Knapp. Circ: 16,000.

669 GBR ISSN 0008-4433
CODEN: CAMQAU
➤ **CANADIAN METALLURGICAL QUARTERLY.** Text in English. 1977. q. GBP 486 combined subscription to institutions (print & online eds.); USD 768 combined subscription in United States to institutions (print & online eds.) (effective 2012). adv. abstr. back issues avail.; reprint service avail. from PSC. **Document type:** *Journal, Academic/Scholarly.* **Description:** Devoted to the science, practice and technology of metallurgy, including mineral processing, extractive metallurgy, alloy development and metal working.
Related titles: Microfilm ed.: (from PQC); Online - full text ed.: ISSN 1879-1395. GBP 445 to institutions; USD 695 in United States to institutions (effective 2012) (from IngentaConnect).
Indexed: A22, A26, A28, AESIS, APA, ASCA, BCIRA, BrCerAb, C&ISA, C33, CA/WCA, CIA, CIN, CPEI, Cadscan, CerAb, ChemAb, ChemTitl, CivEngAb, CorrAb, CurCont, E&CAJ, E11, EEA, EMA, ESPM, EngInd, EnvEAb, GeoRef, H15, I05, IMMAb, INIS AtomInd, ISR, Inspec, LeadAb, M&TEA, M09, MBF, METADEX, MSCI, RefZh, SCI, SCOPUS, SolStAb, SpeleolAb, T04, TM, W07, WAA, Zincscan.
—BLDSC (3038.800000), AskIEEE, CASDDS, IE, Infotrieve, Ingenta, INIST, Linda Hall. **CCC.**
Published by: (Canadian Institute of Mining, Metallurgy and Petroleum, Metallurgical Society CAN), Maney Publishing, Ste 1C, Joseph's Well, Hanover Walk, Leeds, W Yorks LS3 1AB, United Kingdom. TEL 44-113-2432800, FAX 44-113-3868178, maney@maney.co.uk, http://www.maney.co.uk. Eds. J D Boyd, William Thompson. Circ: 1,200.

➤ **CANADIAN METALWORKING.** *see* MACHINERY

671.2 GBR ISSN 1745-4476
CAST METAL & DIECASTING TIMES. Text in English. 2004. 5/yr. GBP 77 domestic; GBP 91 foreign; free to qualified personnel (effective 2009). adv. **Document type:** *Magazine, Trade.* **Description:** Promotes the supply sector and covers new products, company developments, people and contracts won as well as articles highlighting people and companies.
Formed by the merger of (1999-2004): Cast Metal Times (1465-9123); (1999-2004): Diecasting Times (1467-0240)
Indexed: A28, APA, BrCerAb, C&ISA, CA/WCA, CIA, CerAb, CivEngAb, CorrAb, E&CAJ, E11, EEA, EMA, H15, M&TEA, M09, MBF, METADEX, SolStAb, T04, WAA.
—Linda Hall. **CCC.**
Published by: Modern Media Communications Ltd, Gresham House, 54 High St, Shoreham by Sea, West Sussex BN43 5DB, United Kingdom. TEL 44-1273-453033, FAX 44-1273-453085, info@mmcpublications.co.uk. adv.: page GBP 1,350, page EUR 2,193, page USD 2,700; trim 210 x 297. Circ: 5,000.

671.2 JPN ISSN 0019-2813
CASTING DIGEST/IMONO DAIJESUTO. Text in Japanese. 1949. m. JPY 1,200.
Published by: Nihon Cast Iron Foundry Association/Nihon Imono Kogyokai, 501 Kikai Shinko Kaikan, 3-5-8 Shibakoen, Minato-ku, Tokyo, 105-0011, Japan. Ed. G Kunitomo.

671.2029 USA
TS200 CODEN: CEFWDA
CASTING SOURCE DIRECTORY. Text in English. 1969. a. USD 99 (effective 1999). adv. bk.rev. illus. **Document type:** *Directory.*
Former titles (until 1991): Casting World (0887-9060); (until 1986): Casting Engineering and Foundry World (0273-9607); Which was formed by the merger of: Casting Engineering (0008-7513); Foundry World (0191-1767)
Indexed: BCIRA, Cadscan, LeadAb, Zincscan.
—CASDDS, Linda Hall.
Published by: Continental Communications Inc., PO Box 1919, Bridgeport, CT 06601-1919. Ed. W Troland. Pub. W. Troland. Circ: 76,000.

669 621 IND
CASTING TECHNOLOGY; a complete global publication on ferrous and non-ferrous foundries. Text in English. 19??. bi-m. INR 1,200, USD 175 (effective 2011). adv. back issues avail. **Document type:** *Magazine, Trade.* **Description:** Provides information on application of numerical modelling in SSM automotive brake calliper castings.
Published by: I S R Infomedia Ltd., Merlin Links, 5th Fl, Block 5E & F 166B, S.P. Mukherjee Rd, Kolkata, 700 026, India. TEL 91-33-24658581, FAX 91-33-24653790, isrinfo@eth.net, http://www.isrinfomedia.com.

671.2 NLD ISSN 1877-6809
▼ **CASTINGS AND FORGINGS NEWS.** Cover title: C F N. Text in English. 2009. bi-m. EUR 99 (effective 2010). adv. **Document type:** *Newspaper, Trade.* **Description:** Focuses on the development, manufacture and use of castings and forgings.
Related titles: Online - full text ed.: ISSN 1877-6817.
Published by: K C I Publishing B.V., PO Box 396, Zutphen, 7200 AJ, Netherlands. TEL 31-575-585270, FAX 31-575-511099, kci@kci-world.com, http://www.kci-world.com.

669 GBR ISSN 0965-0253
CASTINGS BUYER; metal casting your engineering needs. Text in English. 1987. s-a. free (effective 2009). back issues avail. **Document type:** *Magazine, Trade.* **Description:** Aims to promote the use of cast components specifically targeted at end users and customers to the foundry industry.
—Linda Hall.
Published by: Institute of Cast Metals Engineers, 47 Birmingham Rd, West Bromwich, W Mids B70 6PY, United Kingdom. TEL 44-121-6016979, FAX 44-121-6016981, info@icme.org.uk. Ed. Lynn Postle TEL 44-121-6016979. Adv. contact Les Rivers TEL 44-1568-797123.

669.1 ESP
CATALOGO SIDERURGICO. Text in Spanish. 1987. biennial. **Document type:** *Catalog, Trade.*
Published by: Acermet Comunicacion, Cea Bermudez 14, Madrid, 28003, Spain. TEL 34-91-5337899, FAX 34-91-5341419, info@acermetal.es, http://www.acermetal.es.

CENTRAL SOUTH UNIVERSITY OF TECHNOLOGY. JOURNAL; science & technology of mining and metallurgy. *see* MINES AND MINING INDUSTRY

669 ESP
CENTRE METAL.LURGIC. MEMORIA. Text in Spanish. 4/yr. **Document type:** *Yearbook, Consumer.*
Published by: Centre Metal.lurgic, Tres Creus 66, Sabadell, Barcelona, 08202, Spain. TEL 34-93-7457810, FAX 34-93-7260995, http://www.centrem.es/. Ed. Pere Font Grasa. Circ: 1,500.

669 ESP
CENTRO NACIONAL DE INVESTIGACIONES METALURGICAS. MEMORIA. Variant title: Memoria CENIM. Text in Spanish. 1995. a. back issues avail. **Document type:** *Monographic series, Academic/Scholarly.*
Published by: Instituto de Estudios Documentales sobre Ciencia y Tecnologia (I E D C Y T), Ciencia y Tecnologia, Joaquin Costa 22, Madrid, 28002, Spain. TEL 34-91-5635482, FAX 34-91-5642644, http://www.cindoc.csic.es.

669 RUS ISSN 0135-5910
CHERNAYA METALLURGIYA. Text in Russian. m.
Indexed: C&ISA, CorrAb, E&CAJ, RASB, RefZh, SolStAb, TM, WAA.
—East View.
Published by: Chermetinformatsiya, Ul Krzhizhanovskogo 14, korp 3, Moscow, 117218, Russian Federation. TEL 7-095-1244909. Ed. A N Ivoditov. **Dist. by:** East View Information Services, 10601 Wayzata Blvd, Minneapolis, MN 55305. TEL 952-252-1201, 800-477-1005, FAX 952-252-1202, info@eastview.com, http://www.eastview.com.

669 RUS
CHERNAYA SOTNYA. Text in Russian. m. USD 99.95 in United States.
Address: B Gruzinskaya 12, kv 57, Moscow, 123242, Russian Federation. TEL 7-095-2053554, FAX 7-095-2840120. Ed. A R Shtil'mark. **US dist. addr.:** East View Information Services, 10601 Wayzata Blvd, Minneapolis, MN 55305. TEL 952-252-1201, 800-477-1005, FAX 952-252-1202, info@eastview.com, http://www.eastview.com.

M

669 RUS ISSN 0132-0890
CHERNYE METALLY/FERROUS METALS. Text in Russian. 1961. m. USD 1,272 foreign (effective 2009). **Document type:** *Journal, Trade.* **Description:** Presents articles on the whole spectrum of the problems, innovations and news of foreign iron and steel industry.
Related titles: ◆ German ed.: Stahl und Eisen. ISSN 0340-4803; ◆ Supplement(s): M P T. Metallurgicheskoe Proizvodstvo i Tekhnologiya Metallurgicheskih Protsessov. ISSN 0934-8077; ◆ S P + T. Liteinoe Proizvodstvo i Tekhnologiya Liteinogo Dela. ISSN 0934-8069; ◆ C I S Iron and Steel Review. ISSN 2072-0815.
Indexed: RefZh.
—East View.
Published by: Izdatel'stvo Ruda i Metally/Ore and Metals Publishers, Leninskii prospekt 6, korpus 1, ofis 622, a/ya 71, Moscow, 119049, Russian Federation. rim@rudmet.ru. Ed. Oleg N Soskovets. Circ: 1,000. **Dist. by:** East View Information Services, 10601 Wayzata Blvd, Minneapolis, MN 55305. TEL 952-252-1201, 800-477-1005, FAX 952-252-1202, info@eastview.com, http://www.eastview.com.

CHIBA KIKINSHI NYUSU. *see* MACHINERY

CHIBAKEN KIKAI KINZOKU SHIKENJO. JIGYO GAIYO/MACHINERY AND METALLURGY RESEARCH INSTITUTE OF CHIBA PREFECTURE. REPORT. *see* MACHINERY

669 CHN ISSN 1672-6421
TS229.5.C6
CHINA FOUNDRY. Text in English. q. USD 40; USD 10 newsstand/cover (effective 2006). **Document type:** *Journal, Academic/Scholarly.*
Indexed: A28, APA, BrCerAb, C&ISA, CA/WCA, CIA, CerAb, CivEngAb, CorrAb, E&CAJ, E11, EEA, EMA, ESPM, EnvEAb, H15, M&TEA, M09, MBF, METADEX, RefZh, SCI, SCOPUS, SolStAb, T04, TM, W07, WAA.
—Linda Hall.
Published by: (Shenyang Research Institute of Foundry), Foundry Journal Agency, 17 Youfeng South Street, Tiexi District, Shenyang, 110022, China. TEL 86-24-25847830, FAX 86-24-25611880, http://www.foundryworld.com/. Ed. Chenguang Ge. Adv. contact Bo Wang.

669.142 TWN ISSN 1015-6070
➤ **CHINA STEEL TECHNICAL REPORT/CHUNG KANG CHI PAO.** Key Title: C S C China Steel Technical Report - Zhonggang Jibao. Text in English. 1987. a. **Document type:** *Report, Academic/Scholarly.* **Description:** Covers steelmaking, new materials and technology. Highlights current technical activities at China Steel, and serves to exchange information with foreign and domestic steelmakers.
Indexed: A28, APA, BrCerAb, C&ISA, CA/WCA, CIA, CerAb, CivEngAb, CorrAb, E&CAJ, E11, EEA, EMA, ESPM, EnvEAb, H15, M&TEA, M09, MBF, METADEX, SolStAb, T04, WAA.
—BLDSC (3180.234639), IE, Ingenta, Linda Hall.
Published by: China Steel Corporation, Technology Division, No 1 Chungkang Rd, Lin Hai Industrial District, Hsiaokang, Kaohsiung, Taiwan. TEL 886-7-8021111, FAX 886-7-7-8022432, TELEX 71108-STLMILL. Ed. Gwo Hua Cheng.

669 CHN ISSN 1004-4493
CODEN: CREFEC
CHINA'S REFRACTORIES. Text in English. 1992. q. USD 76 (effective 2001). adv. bk.rev. 48 p./no.; back issues avail. **Document type:** *Journal, Academic/Scholarly.* **Description:** Provides important news and statistical data on the Chinese refractories market as well as technical and academic discussions.
Indexed: A28, APA, BrCerAb, C&ISA, CA/WCA, CIA, CerAb, CivEngAb, CorrAb, E&CAJ, E11, EEA, EMA, ESPM, EnvEAb, H15, M&TEA, M09, MBF, METADEX, SolStAb, T04, WAA.
—BLDSC (3180.262000), CASDDS, IE, Ingenta, Linda Hall.
Published by: Yejin Bu, Luoyang Naihuo Cailiao Yanjiuyuan/Luoyang Institute of Refractories Research, No 43 Xiyuan Lu, Jianxi-qu Luoyang, Henan, 471039, China. TEL 86-379-4233501 ext 2376, FAX 86-379-4913630, nhcl@public2.lyptt.ha.cn. Ed., Adv. contact Jiehua Liu. Pub. Jinxiang Wang. Circ: 30,000 (paid and controlled).

CHINESE JOURNAL OF REACTIVE POLYMERS. *see* ENGINEERING—Chemical Engineering

669 TWN ISSN 1011-6761
CHUKUNG. Key Title: Zhugong (Gaoxiong). Text in Chinese. 1969. q. TWD 800, USD 70 (effective 2003). adv. bk.rev. **Document type:** *Trade.*
Indexed: A28, APA, BrCerAb, C&ISA, CA/WCA, CIA, CerAb, CivEngAb, CorrAb, E&CAJ, E11, EEA, EMA, ESPM, EnvEAb, H15, M&TEA, M09, MBF, METADEX, SolStAb, T04, TM, WAA.
—BLDSC (3189.654500), IE, Ingenta, Linda Hall.
Published by: Taiwan Foundry Society, 1001 Kaonan Highway, Kaohsiung, Taiwan. TEL 886-7-353-4792, FAX 886-7-352-4989, foundry@seed.net.tw. Ed., Pub. Yung-Ning Pan. R&P, Adv. contact Ingeborg Ouyang TEL 886-7-352-4792. Circ: 650.

671.2 JPN ISSN 0387-0502
CODEN: CTONDV
CHUTANZO, NETSUSHORI/CASTING, FORGING & HEAT TREATMENTS. Text in Japanese. 1947. m. JPY 8,500, USD 49.25. adv. bk.rev. abstr.; bibl.; charts; illus.; mkt.; pat.; stat. index.
Formerly (until Aug. 1978): Casting and Forging (0009-6652)
Indexed: ChemAb.
—CASDDS.
Published by: Nihon Chutanzo Kyokai/Japan Casting & Forging Society, 3-13 Urashima Bldg, Kyobashi, Higashi-ku, Osaka-shi, 540, Japan. Ed. Jun Dodo. Circ: 20,000.

671.2 JPN ISSN 1342-0429
CODEN: CHKOFY
➤ **CHUZO KOGAKU/JAPAN FOUNDRY ENGINEERING SOCIETY. JOURNAL.** Text in Japanese. 1929. m. JPY 12,000 (effective 2003). adv. bk.rev. **Document type:** *Journal, Academic/Scholarly.*
Formerly (until 1996): Imono - Japan Foundrymen's Society. Journal (0021-4396)
Indexed: A28, APA, BCIRA, BrCerAb, C&ISA, CA/WCA, CIA, CIN, CerAb, ChemAb, ChemTitl, CivEngAb, CorrAb, E&CAJ, E11, EEA, EMA, ESPM, EnvEAb, H15, INIS AtomInd, M&TEA, M09, MBF, METADEX, SolStAb, T04, TM, WAA.
—BLDSC (4804.930000), CASDDS, INIST, Linda Hall. **CCC.**
Published by: Nippon Chuzo Kogakukai/Japan Foundry Engineering Society, 8-12-13 Ginza, Chuo-ku, Tokyo, 104-0061, Japan. TEL 81-3-35412758, FAX 81-3-35412750, jfs@jfs.or.jp. Ed., Adv. contact Masahiko Noguchi.

669.142 GBR ISSN 2043-6297
COATED STEELS MARKET TRACKER. Text in English. 1998. m. GBP 1,545, USD 3,085, EUR 2,266 (effective 2010). back issues avail. **Document type:** *Journal, Trade.*
Formerly (until 2009): Coated Steels Monthly (1466-8114)
—**CCC.**
Published by: Metal Bulletin Plc. (Subsidiary of: Euromoney Institutional Investor Plc.), Nestor House, Playhouse Yard, London, EC4V 5EX, United Kingdom. TEL 44-20-77797390, FAX 44-20-77797389, help@metalbulletin.com, http://www.metalbulletin.com.

669.733 GBR
COBALT NEWS (ONLINE). Text in English. 19??. q. free (effective 2009). back issues avail. **Document type:** *Magazine, Trade.* **Description:** Focuses on promotional material on uses for, and development in, cobalt technology supported by items of interest to cobalt producers, uses and all the customers.
Media: Online - full text.
Published by: Cobalt Development Institute, 167 High St, Guildford, Surrey, GU1 3AJ, United Kingdom. TEL 44-1483-578877, FAX 44-1483-573873, info@thecdi.com.

COKE OVEN MANAGERS' ASSOCIATION. YEAR BOOK. *see* MINES AND MINING INDUSTRY

669.142 USA
COLD FINISHED STEEL BAR INSTITUTE. MONTHLY IMPORT ANALYSIS. Text in English. m. membership.
Published by: Cold Finished Steel Bar Institute, 201 Park Washington Court, Falls Church, VA 22046-4527. TEL 703-538-3543, FAX 703-241-5603, info@cfsbi.com, http://www.cfsbi.com/. Ed. Murray J Belman.

COMPONENTI INDUSTRIALI. *see* ENGINEERING—Mechanical Engineering

669 CHE ISSN 1423-1697
CONCAST STANDARD NEWS. Text in English. 1962. s-a. back issues avail. **Document type:** *Journal, Trade.*
Former titles (until 1989): Concast Technology News (0258-0705); (until 1982): Concast News (0573-2166)
Indexed: APA, C&ISA, CorrAb, E&CAJ, EEA, SolStAb, WAA.
Published by: Concast Standard AG, Toedistrasse 9, Zurich, 8027, Switzerland. TEL 41-1-2046511, FAX 41-1-2028122, sales@concast.ch, http://www.concast-standard.com.

THE CONNECTION. *see* BUILDING AND CONSTRUCTION

669 CAN
COPPER (YEAR) VOLUME I: PLENARY LECTURES, ECONOMICS AND APPLICATIONS OF COPPER. Text in English. 1995. irreg. CAD 205 per issue to members; CAD 245 per issue to non-members (effective 2004). **Document type:** *Monographic series, Academic/Scholarly.*
Formerly (until 2004): Copper (Year) Volume I: Plenary Lectures, Economics, Applications and Fabrication of Copper
Published by: Canadian Institute of Mining, Metallurgy and Petroleum, Metallurgical Society, 3400 de Maisonneuve Blvd W, Ste 1210, Montreal, PQ H3Z 3B8, Canada. TEL 514-939-2710, FAX 514-939-2714, cim@cim.org, http://www.cim.org.

669 CAN
COPPER (YEAR) VOLUME II: HEALTH, ENVIRONMENT AND SUSTAINABLE DEVELOPMENT. Text in English. 1995. irreg. CAD 205 per issue to members; CAD 245 per issue to non-members (effective 2004).
Formerly: Copper (Year) Volume II: Mineral Processing and Environment
Published by: Canadian Institute of Mining, Metallurgy and Petroleum, Metallurgical Society, 3400 de Maisonneuve Blvd W, Ste 1210, Montreal, PQ H3Z 3B8, Canada. TEL 514-939-2710, FAX 514-939-2714, cim@cim.org, http://www.cim.org.

669 CAN
COPPER (YEAR) VOLUME III: MINERAL PROCESSING. Text in English. 1995. irreg. CAD 205 per issue to members; CAD 245 per issue to non-members (effective 2004).
Formerly: Copper (Year) Volume III: Electrorefining and Hydrometallurgy of Copper
Published by: Canadian Institute of Mining, Metallurgy and Petroleum, Metallurgical Society, 3400 de Maisonneuve Blvd W, Ste 1210, Montreal, PQ H3Z 3B8, Canada. TEL 514-939-2710, FAX 514-939-2714, cim@cim.org, http://www.cim.org.

669 CAN
COPPER (YEAR) VOLUME IV: PYROMETALLURGY OF COPPER-HERMANN SCHWARZE SYMPOSIUM. BOOK 1, SMELTING OPERATIONS, ANCILLARY OPERATIONS AND FURNANCE INTEGRITY. Text in English. 1995. irreg. CAD 310 per issue to members; CAD 375 per issue to non-members (effective 2004).
Formerly: Copper (Year) Volume IV: Hydrometallurgy of Copper
Published by: Canadian Institute of Mining, Metallurgy and Petroleum, Metallurgical Society, 3400 de Maisonneuve Blvd W, Ste 1210, Montreal, PQ H3Z 3B8, Canada. TEL 514-939-2710, FAX 514-939-2714, cim@cim.org, http://www.cim.org.

669 CAN
➤ **COPPER (YEAR) VOLUME IV: PYROMETALLURGY OF COPPER-HERMANN SCHWARZE SYMPOSIUM. BOOK 2, TECHNOLOGY DEVELOPMENT, PROCESS MODELING AND FUNDAMENTALS.** Text in English. 1995. irreg. CAD 310 per issue to members; CAD 375 per issue to non-members (effective 2005). **Document type:** *Journal, Academic/Scholarly.*
Published by: Canadian Institute of Mining, Metallurgy and Petroleum, Metallurgical Society, 3400 de Maisonneuve Blvd W, Ste 1210, Montreal, PQ H3Z 3B8, Canada. TEL 514-939-2710, FAX 514-939-2714, cim@cim.org, http://www.cim.org.

669 CAN
➤ **COPPER (YEAR) VOLUME V: COPPER ELECTROREFINING AND ELECTROWINNING.** Text in English. irreg. CAD 245 per issue to non-members; CAD 205 per issue to members (effective 2004). **Document type:** *Monographic series, Academic/Scholarly.*
Published by: Canadian Institute of Mining, Metallurgy and Petroleum, Metallurgical Society, 3400 de Maisonneuve Blvd W, Ste 1210, Montreal, PQ H3Z 3B8, Canada. TEL 514-939-2710, FAX 514-939-2714, cim@cim.org, http://www.cim.org.

669 CAN
COPPER (YEAR) VOLUME VI: HYDROMETALLURGY OF COPPER. BOOK 1, LEACHING AND PROCESS DEVELOPMENT. Text in English. irreg. CAD 375 per issue to non-members; CAD 310 per issue to members (effective 2004).
Published by: Canadian Institute of Mining, Metallurgy and Petroleum, Metallurgical Society, 3400 de Maisonneuve Blvd W, Ste 1210, Montreal, PQ H3Z 3B8, Canada. TEL 514-939-2710, FAX 514-939-2714, cim@cim.org, http://www.cim.org.

669 CAN
COPPER (YEAR) VOLUME VI: HYDROMETALLURGY OF COPPER. BOOK 2, MODELING, IMPURITY CONTROL AND SOLVENT EXTRACTION. Text in English. irreg. CAD 375 per issue to non-members; CAD 310 per issue to members (effective 2004).
Published by: Canadian Institute of Mining, Metallurgy and Petroleum, Metallurgical Society, 3400 de Maisonneuve Blvd W, Ste 1210, Montreal, PQ H3Z 3B8, Canada. TEL 514-939-2710, FAX 514-939-2714, cim@cim.org, http://www.cim.org.

669.3 GBR
COPPER DEVELOPMENT ASSOCIATION PUBLICATION. Text in English. irreg., latest vol.47.
Related titles: Online - full content ed.
Published by: Copper Development Association, Verulam Industrial Estate, 224 London Rd, St. Albans, Herts AL1 1AQ, United Kingdom. TEL 44-1727-731200, FAX 44-1727-731216, copperdev@compuserve.com, http://www.cda.org.uk.

▼ **COPPER SURVEY.** *see* MINES AND MINING INDUSTRY

669.3 621 USA ISSN 0730-8299
COPPER TOPICS. Text in English. 1968. q. free. back issues avail. **Document type:** *Newspaper.* **Description:** Cites newsworthy applications of copper, brass and bronze products in the USA.
Indexed: APA, C&ISA, CorrAb, E&CAJ, EEA, SolStAb, WAA.
—Linda Hall.
Published by: Copper Development Association Inc., 260 Madison Ave, New York, NY 10016-2401. TEL 212-251-7211, FAX 212-251-7234. Ed. Ken Geremia. Circ: 35,000 (controlled).

620.11223 541.37 PRT ISSN 0870-1164
TA418.74 CODEN: CPMAEN
CORROSAO E PROTECCAO DE MATERIAIS. Text in Portuguese. 1982. irreg. EUR 22 domestic; EUR 44.30 in Europe; EUR 49.50 elsewhere (effective 2005).
Indexed: A22, A28, APA, BrCerAb, C&ISA, CA/WCA, CIA, CerAb, CivEngAb, CorrAb, E&CAJ, E11, EEA, EMA, H15, M&TEA, M09, MBF, METADEX, SolStAb, T04, WAA.
—BLDSC (3472.800000), IE, Ingenta, Linda Hall.
Published by: Laboratorio de Tratamento de Superficies e Revestimentos, Estrada do Paco do Lumiar, No. 22 Ed. E, Lisbon, 1649-038, Portugal. TEL 351-21-0924649, FAX 351-21-7163796. Ed. Teresa Diamantino. Circ: 3,000.

CORROSION; journal of science and engineering. *see* ENGINEERING—Mechanical Engineering

CORROSION AND COATINGS. *see* PAINTS AND PROTECTIVE COATINGS

669 541.37 USA ISSN 0892-4228
TA418.74
➤ **CORROSION ENGINEERING.** Text in English. 1987. m. USD 3,035 per vol. domestic; USD 3,555 per vol. foreign (effective 2010). back issues avail. **Document type:** *Journal, Academic/Scholarly.* **Description:** Covers corrosion monitoring and testing, corrosion-resistant materials, protective coatings and surface treatment, and cathodic protection.
Indexed: A22.
—BLDSC (3473.585000), IE, Infotrieve, Ingenta, INIST, Linda Hall. **CCC.**
Published by: Allerton Press, Inc. (Subsidiary of: Pleiades Publishing, Inc.), 250 W 57th St, New York, NY 10107. TEL 212-459-0535, FAX 646-424-9695, journals@allertonpress.com. Ed. Toshiaki Ohtsuka. **Subscr. to:** PO Box 830399, Birmingham, AL 35283. TEL 205-995-1567, 800-633-4931, FAX 205-995-1588.

620.162 540 GBR ISSN 1478-422X
TA462 CODEN: CESTBU
➤ **CORROSION ENGINEERING, SCIENCE AND TECHNOLOGY.** Text in English. 1965. bi-m. GBP 874 combined subscription to institutions (print & online eds.); USD 1,532 combined subscription in United States to institutions (print & online eds.) (effective 2012). adv. bk.rev.; software rev. charts; illus. index. 80 p./no.; back issues avail.; reprint service avail. from PSC. **Document type:** *Journal, Academic/Scholarly.* **Description:** Covers all aspects of the theory and practice of corrosion engineering and of corrosion processes and their control.
Formerly (until 2003): British Corrosion Journal (0007-0599)
Related titles: Online - full text ed.: ISSN 1743-2782. GBP 816 to institutions; USD 1,437 in United States to institutions (effective 2012) (from IngentaConnect).
Indexed: A&ATA, A01, A03, A08, A20, A22, A28, ABIPC, ABTICS, AESIS, APA, APIAb, APICat, APIH&E, APIOC, APIPR, APIPS, APITS, ASCA, BCIRA, BrCerAb, BrTechI, C&ISA, C33, CA, CA/WCA, CEA, CEABA, CIA, CIN, CPEI, Cadscan, CerAb, ChemAb, ChemTitl, CivEngAb, CorrAb, E&CAJ, E11, EEA, EMA, ESPM, EngInd, EnvEAb, H15, IPackAb, ISR, Inspec, LeadAb, M&TEA, M09, MBF, METADEX, MSCI, P26, P48, P52, P54, PQC, PetrolAb, RefZh, SCI, SCOPUS, SolStAb, T02, T04, TCEA, TM, W07, WAA, WSCA, Zincscan.
—BLDSC (3473.700000), AskIEEE, CASDDS, IE, Ingenta, INIST, Linda Hall, PADDS. **CCC.**
Published by: (Institute of Materials, Minerals and Mining), Maney Publishing, Ste 1C, Joseph's Well, Hanover Walk, Leeds, W Yorks LS3 1AB, United Kingdom. TEL 44-113-2432800, FAX 44-113-3868178, maney@maney.co.uk, http://www.maney.co.uk. Ed. S B Lyon. Adv. contact Robin Fox TEL 44-20-73060300 ext 231. **Subscr. in N America to:** Maney Publishing, 875 Massachusetts Ave, 7th Fl, Cambridge, MA 02139. TEL 866-297-5154, FAX 617-354-6875, maney@maneyusa.com

➤ **CORROSION MANAGEMENT.** *see* ENGINEERING—Engineering Mechanics And Materials

➤ **CORROSION MANAGEMENT.** *see* ENGINEERING—Engineering Mechanics And Materials

669 016 DEU ISSN 0334-6005
CODEN: CORVE2

➤ **CORROSION REVIEWS.** Text in English. 1972. bi-m. EUR 419, USD 629 to institutions; EUR 484, USD 726 combined subscription to institutions (print & online eds.) (effective 2012). adv. bk.rev. index. back issues avail. **Document type:** *Journal, Academic/Scholarly.* **Description:** Devoted to critical international overviews of specified fields that are key to advancing the understanding and application of corrosion science and engineering in the service of society.
Formerly (until 1985): Reviews on Coatings and Corrosion (0048-7538)
Related titles: Online - full text ed.: ISSN 2191-0316. EUR 419, USD 629 to institutions (effective 2012).
Indexed: A28, APA, ASFA, BrCerAb, C&ISA, C33, CA/WCA, CIA, CIN, CPEI, CerAb, ChemAb, ChemTitl, CivEngAb, CorrAb, E&CAJ, E11, EEA, EMA, ESPM, EngInd, EnvEAb, FLUIDEX, H15, M&TEA, M09, MBF, METADEX, MSCI, RefZh, SCI, SCOPUS, SWRA, SolStAb, T04, W07, WAA.
—CASDDS, IE, INIST, Linda Hall.
Published by: Walter de Gruyter GmbH & Co. KG, Genthiner Str 13, Berlin, 10785, Germany. TEL 49-30-26005176, 49-30-260050, info@degruyter.com, http://www.degruyter.de. Eds. Noam Eliaz, Ron Latanision. Circ: 1,000.

620.112 GBR ISSN 0010-938X
CODEN: CRRSAA

➤ **CORROSION SCIENCE**; the journal on environmental degradation of materials and its control. Text in English. 1961. 12/yr. EUR 3,825 in Europe to institutions; JPY 507,900 in Japan to institutions; USD 4,278 elsewhere to institutions (effective 2012). adv. charts; illus. index. back issues avail. **Document type:** *Journal, Academic/Scholarly.* **Description:** Covers topics including high temperature oxidation, passivity, anodic oxidation, biochemical corrosion, stress corrosion cracking, and corrosion control.
Related titles: Microfilm ed.: (from PQC); Online - full text ed.: (from IngentaConnect, ScienceDirect).
Indexed: A&ATA, A01, A03, A05, A08, A20, A22, A23, A24, A26, A28, A32, ABIPC, APA, APIAb, APICat, APIH&E, APIOC, APIPR, APIPS, APITS, AS&TA, AS&TI, ASCA, ASFA, ApMecR, B04, B13, B21, BMT, BrCerAb, BrTechI, C&ISA, C10, C24, C33, CA, CA/WCA, CEA, CEABA, CIA, CIN, CPEI, CTE, Cadscan, CerAb, ChemAb, ChemTitl, CivEngAb, CoppAb, CorrAb, CurCR, CurCont, E&CAJ, E04, E05, E11, EEA, EMA, ESPM, EnerRev, EngInd, EnvAb, EnvEAb, F&EA, FLUIDEX, H15, I05, IBR, IBZ, ISMEC, ISR, Inspec, LeadAb, M&TEA, M09, MBF, METADEX, MSCI, OceAb, PetrolAb, R16, RefZh, SCI, SCOPUS, SWRA, SolStAb, T02, T04, TCEA, TM, W07, WAA, WSCA, Zincscan.
—BLDSC (3476.500000), AskIEEE, CASDDS, IE, Infotrieve, Ingenta, INIST, Linda Hall, PADDS. **CCC.**
Published by: (Institute of Corrosion), Pergamon (Subsidiary of: Elsevier Science & Technology), The Blvd, Langford Ln, East Park, Kidlington, Oxford OX5 1GB, United Kingdom. TEL 44-1865-843000, FAX 44-1865-843010, JournalsCustomerServiceEMEA@elsevier.com. Ed. G T Burstein. **Subscr. to:** Elsevier BV, Radarweg 29, PO Box 211, Amsterdam 1000 AE, Netherlands. TEL 31-20-4853757, FAX 31-20-4853432, http://www.elsevier.nl.

➤ **CORROSION SCIENCE AND TECHNOLOGY.** *see* ENGINEERING—Engineering Mechanics And Materials

620.162 USA ISSN 1521-4494
CODEN: COTEFU

CORROSION TECHNOLOGY. Text in English. 1989. irreg., latest 2009. price varies. **Document type:** *Monographic series, Academic/Scholarly.*
Related titles: Online - full text ed.: ISSN 2155-4854.
Indexed: GeoRef.
—BLDSC (3477.002000), IE. **CCC.**
Published by: C R C Press, LLC (Subsidiary of: Taylor & Francis Group), 6000 Broken Sound Pky, NW, Ste 300, Boca Raton, FL 33487. TEL 800-272-7737, FAX 800-374-3401, orders@crcpress.com.

669 BRA ISSN 1808-351X

CORTE & CONFORMACAO DE METAIS. Text in Portuguese. 2005. m. free to qualified personnel. **Document type:** *Magazine, Trade.*
Published by: Aranda Editora Tecnica e Cultural, Alamed Olga 315, Perdizes, Sao Paulo, SP 01155-900, Brazil. TEL 55-11-38245300, FAX 55-11-36669585, info@arandanet.com.br, http://www.arandanet.com.br.

D & B INDUSTRIAL GUIDE. *see* BUSINESS AND ECONOMICS—Trade And Industrial Directories

682 DNK ISSN 1602-7213

D S-BLADET. (Dansk Smedemesterforening) Text in Danish. 2002. 15/yr. DKK 400 to members (effective 2009). adv. bk.rev. abstr.; illus.; tr.lit. **Document type:** *Magazine, Trade.* **Description:** Oriented towards the metallic industries, heating, ventilation, sanitary installations, as well as being a member magazine for the Association.
Formerly (2001-2002): DS Haandvaerk og Industri (1602-6977); Which was formed by the merger of (1910-2001): Dansk Smede-Tidende (0011-6483); (199?-2001): DSbladet (1600-8928)
Related titles: Online - full text ed.: 2001.
Published by: D S Haandvaerk og Industri/Danish Blacksmith Association, Magnoliavej 2, Odense SV, 5250, Denmark. TEL 45-66-173333, FAX 45-66-173230, ds@ds-net.dk, http://www.ds-net.dk. Ed. Ole Andersen. adv.: B&W page DKK 8,060, color page DKK 11,260; 185 x 265. Circ: 3,550 (controlled).

669 KOR ISSN 1738-8228
CODEN: TKHCDJ

➤ **DAEHAN GEUMSOG JAE'LYO HAGHOEJI/KOREAN JOURNAL OF METALS AND MATERIALS.** Text in English, Korean. 1963. m. membership. adv. film rev.; software rev. bibl.; illus. **Document type:** *Journal, Academic/Scholarly.* **Description:** Original papers covering metallurgy and materials science.
Former titles (until 2000): Daehan Geumsog Haghoeji/Korean Institute of Metals and Materials. Journal (0253-3847); (until 1976): Geumsog Haghoeji/Korean Institute of Metals. Journal (0454-627X)
Indexed: A28, APA, BrCerAb, C&ISA, CA/WCA, CIA, CerAb, CivEngAb, CorrAb, E&CAJ, E11, EEA, EMA, ESPM, EnvEAb, H15, INIS AtomInd, Inspec, M&TEA, M09, MBF, METADEX, SCI, SCOPUS, SolStAb, T04, TM, W07, WAA.
—BLDSC (4812.320100), AskIEEE, CASDDS, IE, Linda Hall.
Published by: Daehan Geumsog Jae'lyo Haghoe/Korean Institute of Metals and Materials, 6th Fl., 1666-12 Seocho-dong, Seocho-gu, Seoul, 137-881, Korea, S. TEL 82-2-5571071, FAX 82-2-5571080, kim@kim.or.kr. Circ: 2,500.

669 CHN ISSN 1004-5635

DAXING ZHUDUANJIAN/HEAVY CASTING AND FORGING. Text in Chinese. 1979. bi-m. **Document type:** *Magazine, Trade.*
Related titles: Online - full text ed.
Published by: Zhongguo Di-2 Zhongxing Jixie Jituan Gongsi, Daxing Teduanjian Yanjiusuo/China National Erzhong Group Co., 406, Zhujiang Lu, Deyang, 618013, China. TEL 86-838-2340101.

669 CHE ISSN 1012-0386
CODEN: DDAFE7

➤ **DEFECT AND DIFFUSION FORUM.** Key Title: Diffusion and Defect Data. Part A: Defect and Diffusion Forum. Text in English. 1967. 12/yr. EUR 1,056 (effective 2005). index. **Document type:** *Journal, Academic/Scholarly.*
Supersedes in part (in 1988): Diffusion and Defect Data (0377-6883); Which was formerly (until 1974): Diffusion Data (0012-267X)
Indexed: A22, C33, CPEI, ChemAb, EngInd, GeoRef, Inspec, RefZh, SCOPUS, SpeleolAb.
—BLDSC (3584.254000), CASDDS, IE, Ingenta, INIST, Linda Hall.
Published by: Scitec Publications Ltd., Brandrain 6, Uetikon-Zurich, CH-8707, Switzerland. TEL 41-1-9221022, FAX 41-1-9221033, scitec@scitec.ch, http://www.scitech.ch. Eds. David Fisher, Fred Wohlbier, Graeme Murch.

669 ESP ISSN 0210-685X

DEFORMACION METALICA; revista de las tecnicas de fabricacion, acabado y transformacion del fleje, de la chapa, de tubos, perfiles y alambre. Text in Spanish. 1977. m. EUR 120.74 domestic; EUR 143.54 foreign (effective 2010). adv. charts; illus. **Document type:** *Magazine, Trade.* **Description:** Covers manufacturing techniques, finishing and transformation of sheet iron, hoop iron, pipes and tubing, profiles, wires and cables.
Indexed: A&ATA, A28, APA, BrCerAb, C&ISA, CA/WCA, CIA, CerAb, CivEngAb, CorrAb, E&CAJ, E11, EEA, EMA, H15, IECT, M&TEA, M09, MBF, METADEX, SolStAb, T04, WAA.
—BLDSC (3546.292230), IE, Ingenta.
Published by: Reed Business Information SA (Subsidiary of: Reed Business Information International), Zancoeta 9, Bilbao, 48013, Spain. TEL 34-944-285600, FAX 34-944-425116, rbi@rbi.es. Ed. Nuria Martin. Adv. contact Manuel Masip. Circ: 4,000.

620.112 RUS ISSN 1814-4632

➤ **DEFORMATSIYA I RAZRUSHENIE MATERIALOV.** Text in Russian. 2005. m. USD 625 foreign (effective 2005). **Document type:** *Journal, Academic/Scholarly.*
Indexed: RefZh.
Published by: Nauka i Tekhnologii, Stromynskii per, 4/1, Moscow, 107076, Russian Federation. admin@nait.ru, http://www.nait.ru. Ed. Yu K Kovneristyi. **Dist. by:** East View Information Services, 10601 Wayzata Blvd, Minneapolis, MN 55305. TEL 952-252-1201, 800-477-1005, FAX 952-252-1202, info@eastview.com, http://www.eastview.com.

669 621 ITA ISSN 1973-7270

DEFORMAZIONE. Text in Italian. 1993. m. **Document type:** *Magazine, Trade.*
Published by: PubliTec Srl, Via Passo Pordoi 10, Milan, MI 20139, Italy. TEL 39-02-535781, FAX 39-02-56814579, info@publitec.it, http://www.publitec.it.

669.142 JPN ISSN 0011-8389
CODEN: DESEAT

DENKI SEIKO/ELECTRIC FURNACE STEEL. Text in Japanese; Summaries in English. 1925. q. JPY 2,000 (effective 1999). adv. bk.rev. charts; illus. **Document type:** *Academic/Scholarly.*
Related titles: Online - full content ed.; Online - full text ed.
Indexed: A22, A28, APA, BrCerAb, C&ISA, CA/WCA, CIA, CIN, CerAb, ChemAb, ChemTitl, CivEngAb, CorrAb, E&CAJ, E11, EEA, EMA, ESPM, EnvEAb, H15, M&TEA, M09, MBF, METADEX, SolStAb, T04, TM, WAA.
—BLDSC (3551.000000), CASDDS, IE, Ingenta, Linda Hall.
Published by: (Electric Furnace Steel Research Association/Denki Seiko Kenkyukai), Daido Steel Co. Ltd., 2-30 Daido-cho, Minami-ku, Nagoya-shi, Aichi-ken 457-0811, Japan. TEL 81-52-611-9414, FAX 81-52-614-5812. Ed., R&P, Adv. contact Yuzo Ohtakara. Circ: 2,000.

DENNITSA. *see* COLLEGE AND ALUMNI

669.1 338 FRA
HD9510.1

DEVELOPMENTS IN STEELMAKING CAPACITY OF NON-O E C D ECONOMIES/CAPACITES DE PRODUCTION D'ACIER DANS LES PAYS NON O C D E. (Organisation for Economic Cooperation and Development) Text in English, French. 1999. biennial. EUR 130, GBP 101, USD 184, JPY 19,500 per issue (effective 2009). **Description:** Reports on trends in the steelmaking capacity in economies that are not members of the OECD. Examines the current steelmaking capacity of these economies and likely changes projected for the next two years.
Formerly (until 2008): Developments in Steelmaking Capacity of Non-O E C D Countries (1563-0927); Which was formed by the merger of (1995-1998): Les Capacites de Production d'Acier dans les Pays non O C D E (French Edition) (1026-1885); (1995-1998): Steelmaking Capacity of non-O E C D Countries (English Edition)
Related titles: Online - full content ed.: ISSN 1999-1606. EUR 56, USD 72, GBP 37, JPY 7,400 (effective 2005).
Published by: Organisation for Economic Cooperation and Development (O E C D)/Organisation de Cooperation et de Developpement Economiques (O C D E), 2 Rue Andre Pascal, Paris, 75775 Cedex 16, France. TEL 33-1-45248200, FAX 33-1-45248500, http://www.oecd.org. **Dist. in N. America by:** O E C D Turpin North America, PO Box 194, Downingtown, PA 19335-0194. TEL 610-524-5361, 800-456-6323, FAX 610-524-5417, bookscustomer@turpinna.com.

DIE CASTING BUYERS GUIDE. *see* MACHINERY

DIE CASTING ENGINEER. *see* ENGINEERING—Engineering Mechanics And Materials

669 USA ISSN 0745-449X
TS239

DIE CASTING MANAGEMENT. Text in English. 1983. bi-m. USD 35 domestic; USD 84 foreign (effective 2004). adv. 52 p./no.; **Document type:** *Magazine, Trade.*
Indexed: A22, A28, APA, BrCerAb, C&ISA, CA/WCA, CIA, Cadscan, CerAb, CivEngAb, CorrAb, E&CAJ, E11, EEA, EMA, H15, LeadAb, M&TEA, M09, MBF, METADEX, SolStAb, T04, WAA, Zincscan.
—IE, Ingenta, Linda Hall.
Published by: C-K Publishing, Inc., PO Box 247, Wonder Lake, IL 60097-0247. editor@diecastmgmt.com, www.diecastmgmt.com. Ed. Larry Teeman. Pub. Robert Crofts TEL 815-728-0912. Circ: 4,600.

671 USA

DIRECT FROM MIDREX. Text in English. 1974. q. free. charts; illus. **Document type:** *Newsletter, Trade.* **Description:** Presents news, features, and announcements pertaining to direct reduction of iron ore.
Indexed: APA, C&ISA, CIA, CorrAb, E&CAJ, EEA, SolStAb, WAA.
Published by: (Midrex International B.V.), Midrex Direct Reduction Corp., 2725 Water Ridge Pkwy, Charlotte, NC 28217. TEL 704-378-3380, FAX 704-373-1611, info@midrex.com. Circ: 3,000 (controlled).

669.722 DEU ISSN 0932-0938

DIRECTORIES OF THE WORLD ALUMINIUM INDUSTRY. Text in English. irreg., latest vol.3. EUR 803 per vol. in Europe; USD 1,225 per vol. elsewhere. **Document type:** *Directory, Trade.* **Description:** Provides detailed information on alumina production and producers throughout the world.
Published by: Aluminium-Verlag GmbH, Postfach 101262, Duesseldorf, 40003, Germany. TEL 49-211-1591371, FAX 49-211-1591379, info@alu-verlag.de, http://www.alu-verlag.com.

669 ESP

DIRECTORIO DEL METAL. Text in Spanish. a. EUR 89.32 domestic; EUR 117.52 foreign (effective 2010). **Document type:** *Directory.* **Description:** Lists Spanish companies in the fields of metallurgy, welding and surface treatment. Includes contact names, address and size information. Classifies over 1000 products.
Formerly: Anuario del Metal
Published by: Reed Business Information SA (Subsidiary of: Reed Business Information International), Zancoeta 9, Bilbao, 48013, Spain. TEL 34-944-285600, FAX 34-944-425116, rbi@rbi.es, http://www.rbi.es. Ed. Nuria Martin.

669 USA ISSN 0070-5039
TS301

DIRECTORY IRON AND STEEL PLANTS. Text in English. 1917. a. USD 135 to non-members; USD 95 to members (effective 2009). adv. **Document type:** *Directory, Trade.* **Description:** Lists more than 2,000 companies and 17,500 individuals in the iron and steel industry. It contains an alphabetical listing of all major equipment, product and service suppliers to the international iron and steel industry.
Published by: Association for Iron & Steel Technology, 186 Thorn Hill Rd, Warrendale, PA 15086. TEL 724-776-6040, 724-814-3000, FAX 724-814-3001, info@aistech.org, http://www.aistech.org. Ed. Janet Rogowski. Pub. Darlene Fritz. Circ: 8,000.

DIRECTORY OF CONSULTANTS AND TRANSLATORS FOR ENGINEERED MATERIALS. *see* BUSINESS AND ECONOMICS—Trade And Industrial Directories

DIRECTORY OF STEEL FOUNDRIES AND BUYER'S GUIDE. *see* BUSINESS AND ECONOMICS—Trade And Industrial Directories

669 UKR

DONETSKII KRYAZH. Text in Ukrainian. w.
Published by: Donetskii Metallurgich, Ul B Khmel'nitskogo 92, Donetsk, Ukraine. **Dist. by:** East View Information Services, 10601 Wayzata Blvd, Minneapolis, MN 55305. TEL 952-252-1201, 800-477-1005, FAX 952-252-1202, info@eastview.com, http://www.eastview.com.

DOW JONES N E - METALLE AKTUELL. *see* BUSINESS AND ECONOMICS—Economic Situation And Conditions

DOW JONES N E - METALLE PREISMONITOR. *see* BUSINESS AND ECONOMICS—Economic Situation And Conditions

DOW JONES STAHL AKTUELL. *see* BUSINESS AND ECONOMICS—Economic Situation And Conditions

DOW JONES STAHL MONITOR. *see* BUSINESS AND ECONOMICS—Economic Situation And Conditions

671.84 DEU ISSN 0012-5911
CODEN: DRAHA5

DRAHT; internationale Fachzeitschrift fuer die Draht- und Kabelindustrie und alle Bereiche der Drahtverarbeitung. Text in German. 1950. bi-m. EUR 98 domestic; EUR 106 in Europe; EUR 136 elsewhere (effective 2011). adv. bk.rev. illus.; pat. **Document type:** *Magazine, Trade.*
Incorporates (1907-1995): Drahtwelt (0012-592X)
Related titles: ◆ English ed.: Wire. ISSN 0043-5996.
Indexed: A22, Cadscan, ChemAb, Inspec, LeadAb, SCOPUS, TM, Zincscan.
—CASDDS, IE, Infotrieve, INIST, Linda Hall. **CCC.**
Published by: Meisenbach GmbH, Franz-Ludwig-Str 7a, Bamberg, 96047, Germany. TEL 49-951-8610, FAX 49-951-861158, draht@meisenbach.de. Ed. Wolfgang Fili. Adv. contact Georg Meisenbach. Circ: 6,174 (paid and controlled). **Subscr. to:** InTime Services GmbH, Bajuwarenring 14, Oberhaching 82041, Germany.

671.2 DEU ISSN 2190-7099

DRUCKGUSS. Text in German. 2002. 4/yr. adv. **Document type:** *Magazine, Trade.*
Formerly (until 2008): Druckguss-Praxis (1619-2478)
Indexed: TM.
Published by: Fachverlag Schiele und Schoen GmbH, Markgrafenstr 11, Berlin, 10969, Germany. TEL 49-30-2537520, FAX 49-30-2517248, service@schiele-schoen.de, http://www.schiele-schoen.de. Circ: 2,200 (paid and controlled).

671.2 CHN ISSN 1000-3940

DUANYA JISHU/FORGING & STAMPING TECHNOLOGY. Text in Chinese. 1976. bi-m. USD 37.20 (effective 2009). **Document type:** *Magazine, Trade.*
Related titles: Online - full text ed.
Indexed: RefZh.
—East View, Linda Hall.
Published by: Beijing Jidian Yanjiusuo/Beijing Research Institute of Mechanical & Electrical Technology, 18, Xueqing Lu, Beijing, 100083, China. TEL 86-10-62920652, FAX 86-10-62920652. **Dist. by:** China International Book Trading Corp, 35 Chegongzhuang Xilu, Haidian District, PO Box 399, Beijing 100044, China. TEL 86-10-68412045, FAX 86-10-68412023, cibtc@mail.cibtc.com.cn, http://www.cibtc.com.cn.

669 USA ISSN 1079-7580
TN605
E P D CONGRESS. (Extraction and Processing Division) Text in English. 1990. a. GBP 75 per issue in Europe; CAD 119 per issue in Canada; USD 99 per issue elsewhere (effective 2010). back issues avail. **Document type:** *Handbook/Manual/Guide, Trade.* **Description:** Covers new technological developments in process metallurgy.
Related titles: CD-ROM ed.: USD 101; USD 71 to members (effective 2005).
Indexed: ESPM, EnvEAb.
—BLDSC (3793.389000). **CCC.**
Published by: (Minerals, Metals and Materials Society, Extraction and Processing Division), John Wiley & Sons, Inc., 111 River St, Hoboken, NJ 07030. TEL 201-748-6000, FAX 201-748-6088, info@wiley.com, http://www.wiley.com/WileyCDA/. Ed. Edgar E Vidal.

669 CAN
➤ **ECOMATERIALS AND ECOPROCESSES - (COM 2003).** Text in English. irreg. CAD 170 per issue to non-members; CAD 140 per issue to members (effective 2004). **Document type:** *Monographic series, Academic/Scholarly.*
Published by: Canadian Institute of Mining, Metallurgy and Petroleum, Metallurgical Society, 3400 de Maisonneuve Blvd W, Ste 1210, Montreal, PQ H3Z 3B8, Canada. TEL 514-939-2710, FAX 514-939-2714, cim@cim.org, http://www.cim.org.

669 DEU
DIE EISEN, BLECH UND METALL VERARBEITENDE INDUSTRIE, STAHLVERFORMUNG. Text in German. 1952. a. USD 51 (effective 2000). **Document type:** *Directory.*
Related titles: CD-ROM ed.; Online - full text ed.
Published by: Industrieschau-Verlagsgesellschaft mbH, Postfach 100262, Darmstadt, 64202, Germany. TEL 49-6151-3892-0, FAX 49-6151-33164. Ed., R&P Margit Selka. Circ: 10,000. **US subscr. to:** Western Hemisphere Publishing Corp. TEL 503-640-3736, FAX 503-640-2748.

669 RUS ISSN 1684-5781
➤ **ELEKTROMETALLURGIYA.** Text in Russian. 1998. m. USD 1,445 foreign (effective 2005). **Document type:** *Journal, Academic/Scholarly.* **Description:** Covers a broad range of questions related to electrometallurgy, technological and design options in the building or modernization of electric smelting complexes; various electric equipment for the heating and smelting of metal, its operation, etc.
Indexed: RefZh.
—BLDSC (0398.790000).
Published by: Nauka i Tekhnologii, Stromynskii per, 4/1, Moscow, 107076, Russian Federation. admin@nait.ru, http://www.nait.ru. Ed. Yu I Utochkin. **Dist. by:** East View Information Services, 10601 Wayzata Blvd, Minneapolis, MN 55305. TEL 952-252-1201, 800-477-1005, FAX 952-252-1202, info@eastview.com, http://www.eastview.com.

669 621 ITA ISSN 2035-1798
ELEMENTO TUBO. Text in Italian. 2008. q. **Document type:** *Magazine, Trade.*
Published by: PubliTec Srl, Via Passo Pordoi 10, Milan, MI 20139, Italy. TEL 39-02-535781, FAX 39-02-56814579, info@publitec.it, http://www.publitec.it.

620.112 NLD ISSN 1875-9491
ELSEVIER'S CORROSION SCIENCE SERIES. Variant title: Corrosion Series. Text in English. 2008. irreg., latest vol.1, 2008. price varies. **Document type:** *Monographic series, Academic/Scholarly.*
Indexed: SCOPUS.
Published by: Elsevier BV (Subsidiary of: Elsevier Science & Technology), Radarweg 29, PO Box 211, Amsterdam, 1000 AE, Netherlands. TEL 31-20-4853911, FAX 31-20-4852457, JournalsCustomerServiceEMEA@elsevier.com. Ed. G T Burstein.

671.8 GBR
TS270.A1
EQUIP4WIRE.COM. Text in English, French, German, Italian, Spanish. 1951. a. adv. **Document type:** *Directory, Trade.*
Formerly (until 2003): Wire Industry Yearbook (0084-0424)
Related titles: Online - full text ed.
Published by: Mack Brooks Publishing Ltd., Forum Pl, Hatfield, Herts AL10 0RN, United Kingdom. TEL 44-1707276400, FAX 44-1707276641, mail@wireindustry.com. Ed. Adam Schulman. Adv. contact Neil Clayton. Circ: 9,500 (paid).

669.722 BEL
EUROPEAN ALUMINIUM ASSOCIATION. ALUMINIUM QUARTERLY REPORT. Text in English. q.
Published by: European Aluminium Association, Avenue de Broqueville 12, Brussels, 1150, Belgium. TEL 32-2-7756352, FAX 32-2-7790531, eaa@eaa.be, http://www.eaa.net. Ed. Jolanda Bruynel.

620.112 GBR
EUROPEAN FEDERATION OF CORROSION. NEWSLETTER. Text in English. 19??. a. **Document type:** *Newsletter, Academic/Scholarly.* **Description:** Designed for the members of the European federation of corrosion by the Institute of materials, minerals and mining.
Related titles: Online - full text ed.: free (effective 2010).
Published by: (European Federation of Corrosion), Institute of Materials, Minerals and Mining, 1 Carlton House Terr, London, SW1Y 5DB, United Kingdom. TEL 44-20-74517300, FAX 44-20-78391702, http://www.iom3.org/.

620.112 GBR ISSN 1354-5116
EUROPEAN FEDERATION OF CORROSION. PUBLICATIONS. Text in English. 1989. irreg. back issues avail. **Document type:** *Monographic series, Academic/Scholarly.*
Indexed: A28, APA, BrCerAb, C&ISA, CA/WCA, CIA, CerAb, CivEngAb, CorrAb, E&CAJ, E11, EEA, EMA, H15, M&TEA, M09, MBF, METADEX, SolStAb, T04, WAA.
—BLDSC (3829.708000), IE, Ingenta. **CCC.**
Published by: (European Federation of Corrosion), Institute of Materials, Minerals and Mining, 1 Carlton House Terr, London, SW1Y 5DB, United Kingdom. TEL 44-20-74517300, FAX 44-20-78391702, http://www.iom3.org/.

EUROPEAN STEEL REVIEW. *see* BUSINESS AND ECONOMICS—International Commerce

EXTRACTS FROM EUROPEAN PATENT SPECIFICATIONS. PART 1. PRIMARY INDUSTRY, CHEMISTRY AND METALLURGY, FIXED CONSTRUCTIONS, MINING. *see* PATENTS, TRADEMARKS AND COPYRIGHTS—Abstracting, Bibliographies, Statistics

EXTRACTS FROM INTERNATIONAL PATENT APPLICATIONS. PART 1: PRIMARY INDUSTRY, CHEMISTRY AND METALLURGY, FIXED CONTRUCTIONS, MINING. *see* PATENTS, TRADEMARKS AND COPYRIGHTS—Abstracting, Bibliographies, Statistics

669 USA ISSN 1541-2415
F & M; the business of metal manufacturing. (Fabricating & Metalworking) Text in English. 2002. 10/yr. USD 77 domestic; USD 102 in Canada & Mexico; USD 149 elsewhere; free to qualified personnel (effective 2008). adv. Supplement avail.; back issues avail.; reprints avail. **Document type:** *Magazine, Trade.* **Description:** Covers metalforming, welding, metalcutting, tooling and workholding, inspection and safety operations.
Related titles: Online - full text ed.
Indexed: A09, A10, A15, A28, ABIn, APA, B02, B15, B17, B18, BrCerAb, C&ISA, CA/WCA, CIA, CerAb, CivEngAb, CorrAb, E&CAJ, E11, EEA, EMA, ESPM, EnvEAb, G04, G08, H15, H20, I05, M&TEA, M09, MBF, METADEX, P48, P51, P52, PQC, SolStAb, T02, T04, V03, V04, WAA.
—Linda Hall. **CCC.**
Published by: Cygnus Business Media, Inc., 1233 Janesville Ave, PO Box 803, Fort Atkinson, WI 53538. TEL 920-563-6388, 800-547-7377, FAX 920-563-1702, http://www.cygnusb2b.com. Ed. Michael Riley TEL 205-681-3393. Pub. Tony Morrison TEL 866-832-8473. Adv. contacts Adrienne Gallender TEL 888-407-7737, Glen Hobson. page USD 4,913; trim 7.875 x 10.5. Circ: 40,000.

671 USA ISSN 1551-1006
F F JOURNAL; the magazine for today's fabricating & forming technology. (Fabricating & Forming) Text in English. 2004 (May). 6/yr. free to qualified personnel (effective 2007). adv. **Document type:** *Magazine, Trade.* **Description:** Focuses on the latest developments in areas critical to the future of fabricating and forming.
—CCC.
Published by: Trend Publishing Inc., 625 N Michigan Ave, 11th Fl, Chicago, IL 60611-3199. TEL 312-654-2300, FAX 312-654-2323. Ed. Lincoln Brunner. Pub. Michael D'Alexander. Adv. contact James D'Alexander. Circ: 43,000 (controlled).

669 USA
F M A CONNECTIONS. Text in English. bi-m. USD 120 to non-members; free to members. **Document type:** *Newsletter.* **Description:** Covers the metal forming and fabricating industries. Features member news, information on association-sponsored technical conferences and expositions, educational articles on current industry topics.
Former titles (until Jan. 1998): Discover F M A; (until July 1993): F M A News
Published by: Fabricators & Manufacturers Association, International, 833 Featherstone Rd, Rockford, IL 61107. TEL 815-399-8775, 888-394-4362, info@fmanet.org, http://www.fmanet.org. Ed., R&P Christine Zigmont. Pub. John Nandzik. Circ: 2,500.

669 CAN
FAB CANADA. Text in English. 1997. m. CAD 78 domestic; USD 76 in United States; CAD 6.50 per issue domestic (effective 2005). adv. **Document type:** *Magazine, Trade.* **Description:** Dedicated to the welding, fabricating, stamping, robotics and metal supply industries. Delivers a constant flow of shop floor focused editorials, helping readers stay current on new trends and developments in their industry. Reporting on the latest in technology, trade shows and industry events.
Published by: Canadian Industrial Publishing Group, 5100 South Service Rd, Unit 36, Burlington, ON L7L 6A5, Canada. TEL 905-637-2317, FAX 905-634-2776. Ed. Joe Thompson. Pub., Adv. contact Gordon Valley. B&W page CAD 1,725, B&W page USD 1,380; trim 7.75 x 10.25. Circ: 15,810.

669 USA
FABRICATING EQUIPMENT NEWS. Abbreviated title: F E N. Text in English. m. adv. **Document type:** *Magazine, Trade.* **Description:** Provides a comprehensive guide to equipment, safety, legal and technical information as well as a forum for discussion about topics important to the industry.
Published by: Grand View Media Group, Inc. (Subsidiary of: EBSCO Industries, Inc.), 200 Croft St, Ste 1, Birmingham, AL 35242. TEL 888-431-2877, FAX 205-408-3797, webmaster@grandviewmedia.com, http://www.gvmg.com. adv.: color page USD 3,402; trim 7.875 x 10.5.

669 USA ISSN 0888-0301
THE FABRICATOR. Text in English. 1971. m. USD 75 domestic; USD 95 in Canada & Mexico; USD 140 elsewhere; free domestic to qualified personnel (effective 2009). adv. bk.rev. reprints avail. **Document type:** *Magazine, Trade.* **Description:** Disseminates practical design, engineering, and manufacturing technical information about modern metal forming and fabricating techniques, machinery, tooling, and management concepts, emphasizing the fabrication of sheet, coil, tube, pipe, plate, and structural shapes.
Formerly: F M A's Journal of the Fabricator (0192-8066)
Related titles: Online - full text ed.: free; Spanish ed.: Fabricator en Espanol.
Indexed: A28, APA, BMT, BrCerAb, C&ISA, CA/WCA, CADCAM, CIA, CerAb, CivEngAb, CorrAb, E&CAJ, E11, EEA, EMA, ESPM, EnvAb, EnvEAb, H15, M&TEA, M09, MBF, METADEX, SoftBase, SolStAb, T04, WAA.
—BLDSC (3863.147000), IE, Ingenta, Linda Hall.
Published by: (Fabricators & Manufacturers Association, International), F M A Communications, 833 Featherstone Rd, Rockford, IL 61107-6302. TEL 815-399-8700, FAX 815-381-1370, info@thefabricator.com, http://www.fma-communications.com. Ed. Dan Davis. Pub. Edward Youdell. adv.: B&W page USD 9,065, color page USD 10,690; trim 10.5 x 13.325. Circ: 63,000 (controlled).

669 DEU ISSN 0179-3586
DER FAHRZEUG- UND METALL-LACKIERER - DAS LACKIERERHANDWERK; die Fachzeitschrift fuer den Autolackierer. Abbreviated title: F M L. Text in German. 1956. m. EUR 49.50 domestic; EUR 56 foreign; EUR 5.40 newsstand/cover (effective 2008). adv. bk.rev. abstr.; charts; illus.; mkt.; pat.; stat.; tr.lit. index. **Document type:** *Magazine, Trade.*
Formerly (until 1985): Der Fahrzeug- und Metall-Lackierer (0014-6854)
Indexed: RefZh, WSCA.
Published by: Audin Verlag GmbH, Westenriederstr 49, Munich, 80331, Germany. TEL 49-89-2422830, FAX 49-89-24228319, info@audin.de, http://www.audin.de. Ed. Wolfgang Auer. Adv. contact Gabriele Dinnendahl. color page EUR 4,180, B&W page EUR 2,200; trim 185 x 260. Circ: 6,300 (paid and controlled).

674.84 USA ISSN 1085-6730
FASTENER INDUSTRY NEWS. Text in English. 1979. 20/yr. USD 265 in North America; USD 295 elsewhere; USD 295 in North America for print & online eds.; USD 325 elsewhere for print & online eds. (effective 2003). adv. bk.rev. back issues avail. **Document type:** *Newsletter, Trade.* **Description:** Focuses on management, mergers, buyouts, current events in manufacturing and distribution segments of the fastener industry worldwide.
Related titles: Online - full text ed.: USD 245 (effective 2003).
Address: 2207 NE Broadway, Ste 300, Portland, OR 97232-1608. TEL 503-335-0183, FAX 503-335-3451. Ed., R&P John Wolz. Pubs. Ann Bisgyer, John Wolz. Adv. contact Ann Bisgyer.

FEDERATIE GOUD EN ZILVER. JAARBOEK. *see* JEWELRY, CLOCKS AND WATCHES

FEHS - INSTITUT FUER BAUSTOFF-FORSCHUNG. SCHRIFTENREIHE. (Forschungsgemeinschaft Eisenhuettenschlacken) *see* ENVIRONMENTAL STUDIES—Waste Management

669 CHN ISSN 1006-6543
FENMO YEJIN GONGYE/POWDER METALLURGY INDUSTRY. Text in Chinese. 1991. bi-m. USD 31.20 (effective 2009). **Document type:** *Academic/Scholarly.*
Related titles: Online - full text ed.
Indexed: A22.
—BLDSC (6572.095000), East View, IE, Ingenta.
Published by: (Zhongguo Gangxie Fenmo Yejin Xiehui, Zhongguo Jixie Fenmo Yejin Zhuanye Xiehui), Fenmo Yejin Gongye, 76 Xueyuan Nanlu, Beijing, 100081, China. TEL 86-1-62181028, FAX 86-1-62181445. Ed. Honghai Wang.

669 CHN ISSN 1001-3784
TN695
FENMO YEJIN JISHU/POWDER METALLURGY TECHNOLOGY. Text in Chinese. 1982. bi-m. USD 31.20 (effective 2009). **Document type:** *Journal, Academic/Scholarly.*
Related titles: Online - full text ed.
Indexed: A28, APA, BrCerAb, C&ISA, CA/WCA, CIA, CerAb, CivEngAb, CorrAb, E&CAJ, E11, EEA, EMA, ESPM, EngInd, EnvEAb, H15, M&TEA, M09, MBF, METADEX, SCOPUS, SolStAb, T04, WAA.
—BLDSC (6541.078900), East View, IE, Ingenta, Linda Hall.
Address: 11, Songjiazhuang Lu, Yongdingmen wei, Beijing, China. TEL 86-10-67621317, FAX 86-10-67634067.

669 VEN
FERRETARIA/HARDWARE. Text in Spanish. 1973. m. **Document type:** *Trade.* **Description:** Covers information on management and marketing that is of interest to the industrial and trade sector.
Published by: Camara Ferreteria Nacional/National Hardware Chamber, Av Este, 2, No. 215, piso 5, Edif. Camara de Comercio, Los Caobos, Caracas, DF 1050, Venezuela. TEL 571-16-12. Ed. Andreina Salazar. adv.: B&W page USD 750, color page USD 1,000. Circ: 6,000.

669 MEX
FERRETECNIC - F Y T; la revista de la industria ferretera. Text in Spanish. 1963. m. free. adv. bk.rev. back issues avail. **Document type:** *Trade.*
Published by: Publitecnic S.A., Calle 4, no. 188, Apdo. Postal 74-290, Mexico City, DF 09070, Mexico. TEL 52-6852819, FAX 52-6706318. Ed. Fernando Ulacia Esteve. Circ: 10,000 (controlled).

669.1 GBR ISSN 1750-6573
FERRO-ALLOY DIRECTORY (YEAR). Text in English. 2003. a. GBP 407, USD 897, EUR 617 per issue (effective 2010). **Document type:** *Directory, Trade.* **Description:** Provides information about the world's producers and traders of noble, specialty and bulk alloys.
Supersedes in part (in 2003): Ore & Alloys for the Global Steel Industry (1470-143X); Which was formed by the merger of (1992-2000): Iron and Maganease Ore Databook (0967-7925); Which was formerly (until 1992): Iron Ore Databook (0950-2548); (1992-2000): Ferro-Alloy Directory & Databook (0953-721X); Which was formerly (until 1992): Ferro-Alloy Directory (0266-3198)
Published by: Metal Bulletin Plc. (Subsidiary of: Euromoney Institutional Investor Plc.), Nestor House, Playhouse Yard, London, EC4V 5EX, United Kingdom. TEL 44-20-77797390, FAX 44-20-77797389, help@metalbulletin.com, http://www.metalbulletin.com. Adv. contact Stefano di Nardo TEL 44-20-78275220.

669 330 GBR ISSN 2044-8376
FERRO-ALLOYS MARKET TRACKER. Text in English. 1992. m. GBP 1,545, EUR 2,266, USD 3,085 (effective 2011). adv. back issues avail. **Document type:** *Journal, Trade.* **Description:** Looks at the markets for ferro-alloys worldwide.
Formerly (until 2009): Ferro-Alloys Monthly (0967-8204)
Related titles: Online - full text ed.: ISSN 2045-2780.
—CCC.
Published by: Metal Bulletin Plc. (Subsidiary of: Euromoney Institutional Investor Plc.), Nestor House, Playhouse Yard, London, EC4V 5EX, United Kingdom. TEL 44-20-77797999, FAX 44-20-72465200, help@metalbulletin.com, http://www.metalbulletin.com.

669.1 JPN
TN704.J3 CODEN: FERAF5
FERRUM/IRON AND STEEL INSTITUTE OF JAPAN. BULLETIN. Text in Japanese. 1996. m. JPY 24,000; JPY 2,000 newsstand/cover (effective 2003). 80 p./no.; back issues avail. **Document type:** *Bulletin, Trade.*
Formerly: Feramu (1341-688X); Which superseded in part (in 1996): Tetsu to Hagane (0021-1575)
Indexed: A28, APA, BrCerAb, C&ISA, CA/WCA, CIA, CIN, CerAb, ChemAb, ChemTitl, CivEngAb, CorrAb, E&CAJ, E11, EEA, EMA, ESPM, EnvEAb, H15, M&TEA, M09, MBF, METADEX, RefZh, SolStAb, T04, TM, WAA.
—BLDSC (2593.110000), CASDDS, Linda Hall. **CCC.**
Published by: Nippon Tekko Kyokai/Iron and Steel Institute of Japan, Niikura Bldg, 2nd Fl, 2 Kanda-Tsukasacho 2-chome, Chiyoda-ku, Tokyo, 101-0048, Japan. TEL 81-3-52097011, FAX 81-3-32571110, admin@isij.or.jp, http://www.isij.or.jp. Ed. Tatsuhiko Tanaka. Pub. Yasuo Uchinaka. R&P Yoshihiro Kuwabara. Circ: 10,000.

669.1 CHE ISSN 1422-9137
T3
FERRUM; Nachrichten aus der Eisenbibliothek. Text in German. 1954. a. free. bk.rev. back issues avail. **Document type:** *Journal, Academic/Scholarly.* **Description:** Examines the history of technology, in particular iron and steel manufacturing.

Formerly (until 1977): Nachrichten aus der Eisen-Bibliothek der Georg Fischer Aktiengesellschaft (0428-4968)
Indexed: A28, APA, BrCerAb, C&ISA, CA/WCA, CIA, CerAb, CivEngAb, CorrAb, E&CAJ, E11, EEA, EMA, H15, M&TEA, M09, MBF, METADEX, SolStAb, T04, TM, WAA.
—BLDSC (3908.650000).
Published by: Eisenbibliothek, Klostergut Paradies, Schlatt, 8252, Switzerland. TEL 41-52-6312743, FAX 41-52-6312755, eisenbibliothek@georgfischer.com, http://www.eisenbibliothek.ch. Ed. Annette Bouheiry.

669.9 DEU ISSN 0936-8760
FERTIGUNG; Fachmagazin fuer Bearbeitung, Montage, Kontrolle. Text in German. 1973. 9/yr. EUR 118 domestic; EUR 127 foreign; EUR 15 newsstand/cover (effective 2011). adv. bk.rev. illus. index. **Document type:** *Magazine, Trade.* **Description:** Focuses on the development and use of tools, machine tools and production systems as well as their material and data flow systems.
Formerly (until 1989): Moderne Fertigung (0344-7596)
Related titles: ◆ Supplement(s): Werkzeuge. ISSN 0939-5342.
Indexed: RefZh, TM.
Published by: Verlag Moderne Industrie AG & Co. KG, Justus-von-Liebig-Str 1, Landsberg, 86899, Germany. TEL 49-8191-1250, FAX 49-8191-125211, info@mi-verlag.de, http://www.mi-verlag.de. Ed. Wolfgang Pittrich. Adv. contact Helmut Schempp. B&W page EUR 4,070, color page EUR 5,620; trim 178 x 257. Circ: 16,655 (paid and controlled).

671.732 USA ISSN 0015-2358
FINISHERS' MANAGEMENT. Text in English. 1957. m. (10/yr.). USD 35 domestic; USD 45 foreign (effective 2000). adv. bk.rev. charts; illus.; mkt. reprints avail. **Document type:** *Magazine, Trade.* **Description:** Management magazine for job shop owners and captive shop managers in the surface finishing market.
Formerly: Plating Management and Metal Finishers Management
Related titles: Microfilm ed.: (from PQC).
Indexed: APA, C&ISA, CorrAb, E&CAJ, EEA, SolStAb, WAA.
—Linda Hall.
Published by: Publication Management, Inc., 4350 DiPaolo Center, Dearlove Rd, Glenview, IL 60025. TEL 847-699-1700, 847-699-1706, FAX 847-699-1703. Eds., Pubs. Hugh Morgan, Jason Morgan. R&P Hugh Morgan. Adv. contacts Jason Morgan, David Friedman, John McConnel. B&W page USD 2,335, color page USD 4,335. Circ: 11,200.

669 RUS ISSN 0015-3230
TN690 CODEN: FMMTAK
➤ **FIZIKA METALLOV I METALLOVEDENIE.** Text in Russian. 1955. m. RUR 1,500 for 6 mos. domestic; USD 1,287 foreign (effective 2010). adv. index. **Document type:** *Journal, Academic/Scholarly.* **Description:** Presents information on the theory of metals, electrical and magnetic properties, structure, phase, transformation, diffusion, strength and plasticity.
Related titles: Online - full text ed.; ◆ English ed.: Physics of Metals and Metallography. ISSN 0031-918X; ◆ English Translation: Physics of Metals and Metallography. ISSN 0031-918X.
Indexed: ASCA, C&ISA, C33, CIN, Cadscan, ChemAb, ChemTitl, CoppAb, CorrAb, E&CAJ, GeoRef, INIS AtomInd, ISR, Inspec, LeadAb, PhysBer, RefZh, SCOPUS, SolStAb, TM, WAA, Zincscan.
—BLDSC (0389.800000), AskIEEE, CASDDS, East View, INIST, Linda Hall. **CCC.**
Published by: (Rossiiskaya Akademiya Nauk, Ural'skoe Otdelenie), Izdatel'stvo Nauka, Profsoyuznaya ul 90, Moscow, 117864, Russian Federation. TEL 7-095-3347151, FAX 7-095-4202220, secret@naukaran.ru, http://www.naukaran.ru. Ed. V V Ustinov. **Dist. by:** East View Information Services, 10601 Wayzata Blvd, Minneapolis, MN 55305. TEL 952-252-1201, 800-477-1005, FAX 952-252-1202, info@eastview.com, http://www.eastview.com.

620.1 RUS
TA467 CODEN: ZAMEA9
FIZIKOKHIMIYA POVERKHNOSTI I ZASHCHITA MATERIALOV. Text in Russian. 1965. bi-m. USD 381 foreign (effective 2010). index. **Document type:** *Journal, Academic/Scholarly.*
Formerly (until 2009): Zashchita Metallov (0044-1856)
Related titles: ◆ English Translation: Protection of Metals and Physical Chemistry of Surfaces. ISSN 2070-2051.
Indexed: A&ATA, C&ISA, CEABA, ChemAb, CorrAb, E&CAJ, INIS AtomInd, Inspec, RefZh, SCOPUS, SolStAb, TM, WAA, WSCA.
—BLDSC (0390.027500), CASDDS, East View, INIST, Linda Hall. **CCC.**
Published by: (Rossiiskaya Akademiya Nauk/Russian Academy of Sciences), Izdatel'stvo Nauka, Profsoyuznaya ul 90, Moscow, 117864, Russian Federation. TEL 7-095-3347151, FAX 7-095-4202220, secret@naukaran.ru, http://www.naukaran.ru. Ed. Aslan Yu Tsivadze. Circ: 3,175. **Dist. by:** East View Information Services, 10601 Wayzata Blvd, Minneapolis, MN 55305. TEL 952-252-1201, FAX 952-252-1202, info@eastview.com, http://www.eastview.com.

FLUID PHASE EQUILIBRIA. *see* CHEMISTRY—Physical Chemistry

671.2 ITA ISSN 0015-6078
TS200 CODEN: FNDAAR
FONDERIA. Text in English, Italian. 1951. q. EUR 30 domestic; EUR 60 in Europe; EUR 80 elsewhere (effective 2011). adv. bk.rev. charts; illus.; tr.lit. index. **Document type:** *Magazine, Trade.* **Description:** Technical review of Italian foundry industry. Covers metals, metallurgy, casting processes, treatments, foundry items and equipment.
Related titles: Online - full text ed.
Indexed: A28, APA, BCIRA, BrCerAb, C&ISA, CA/WCA, CIA, CerAb, ChemAb, CivEngAb, CorrAb, E&CAJ, E11, EEA, EMA, H15, M&TEA, M09, MBF, METADEX, SolStAb, T04, WAA.
—CASDDS, INIST.
Published by: Tecniche Nuove SpA, Via Eritrea 21, Milan, MI 201, Italy. TEL 39-02-390901, FAX 39-02-7570364, info@tecnichenuove.com. Ed. Loris Cantarelli. Circ: 6,500.

671.2 FRA ISSN 2106-7635
TS200 CODEN: FFAUDJ
▼ **FONDERIE MAGAZINE.** Text in Multiple languages. 2010. m. (10/yr.). EUR 150 in the European Union; EUR 185 elsewhere (effective 2010). adv. bk.rev. abstr.; bibl.; charts; illus. index, cum.index. **Document type:** *Magazine, Trade.* **Description:** Publishes results of studies of CTIF. Features original works of French, as well as foreign engineers, practical advice, industrial projects, information on the professional life of engineers.
Formed by the merger of (200?-2010): Sup'fonderie (1630-5116); Which was formerly (until 200?): Revue des E S F (1143-3477); (19??-1986): Ecole Superieure de Fonderie (0988-9701); (1970-2010): Hommes et Fonderie (0018-4357); Which was formed by the merger of (1958-1969): Technicien de Fonderie (0494-9102); (1968-1969): Association Technique de Fonderie. Revue Mensuelle d'Information (0151-6868); Which was formerly (1948-1967): Association Technique de Fonderie. Bulletin Mensuel d'Information (0366-4708); (1981-2010): Fonderie, Fondeur d'Aujourd'hui (0249-3136); Which was formed by the merger of (1946-1981): Fonderie (0015-6094); (1964-1981): Fondeur d'Aujourd'hui (0015-6116); Which was formerly (1950-1964): Journal d'Informations Techniques des Industries de la Fonderie (0368-2641)
Indexed: A28, APA, BCIRA, BrCerAb, C&ISA, CA/WCA, CIA, CIN, Cadscan, CerAb, ChemAb, ChemTitl, CivEngAb, CorrAb, E&CAJ, E11, EEA, EMA, ESPM, EngInd, EnvEAb, GeoRef, H15, Inspec, LeadAb, M&TEA, M09, MBF, METADEX, RefZh, SCOPUS, SolStAb, SpeleolAb, T04, TM, WAA, Zincscan.
—BLDSC (3976.055000), CASDDS, INIST, Linda Hall. **CCC.**
Published by: Editions Techniques des Industries de la Fonderie, 44 av. de la Division Leclerc, Sevres, 92310, France. TEL 33-1-41146300, FAX 33-1-45341434, contact@etif.fr. Ed. Chantal Couvret. Circ: 1,600.

671.2 FRA ISSN 1775-2523
FONDERIE SOUS PRESSION INTERNATIONAL. Text in French. 1994. bi-m. **Document type:** *Trade.* **Description:** Covers techniques and technologies in diecasting.
Formerly (until 1999): Fonderie sous Pression (1260-3120)
Published by: Europe Metal, 136 Ave. Emile Zola, Boulogne Billancourt, 92100, France. TEL 33-1-46103131, FAX 33-1-46211063, http://www.eurometal.com.

669 USA ISSN 1949-8438
▼ **FORGE (TROY).** Text in English. 2009. q. USD 17 per issue (effective 2009). **Document type:** *Magazine, Trade.* **Description:** Features news and information for the forge industry.
Related titles: Online - full text ed.: ISSN 1949-8446.
Published by: B N P Media, 2401 W Big Beaver Rd, Ste 700, Troy, MI 48084. TEL 248-244-6252, FAX 248-244-6439, portfolio@bnpmedia.com, http://www.bnpmedia.com.

671.2 GBR ISSN 0955-5293
FORGE (YEAR). Text in English. 1908. bi-m. GBP 35.50 in United Kingdom; GBP 52.50 rest of world (effective 2001). adv. bk.rev. bibl.; stat.; tr.lit. **Document type:** *Magazine, Trade.* **Description:** News about farriery and blacksmithing.
Formerly: Farriers Journal
Published by: (National Association Farriers, Blacksmiths and Agricultural Engineers), Farriers' Journal Publishing Co. Ltd., Ave B, Tenth St, NAC Stoneleigh ., Kenilworth, Warks CV8 2LG, United Kingdom. TEL 44-1203-696595, FAX 44-1203-696708. Ed. E Boden. R&P J Webb. Adv. contact P Wodvine. Circ: 4,200.

671.2 USA ISSN 1054-1756
FORGING. Text in English. 1990. bi-m. USD 42 domestic; USD 50 in Canada; USD 67 elsewhere; free in US & Canada to qualified personnel (effective 2011). adv. illus.; tr.lit. **Document type:** *Journal, Trade.*
Related titles: Online - full text ed.
Indexed: A05, A15, A28, ABIn, APA, AS&TA, AS&TI, B01, B02, B03, B06, B07, B09, B11, B15, B17, B18, BRD, BrCerAb, C&ISA, C10, CA/WCA, CIA, CerAb, CivEngAb, CorrAb, E&CAJ, E11, EEA, EMA, ESPM, EnvEAb, G04, G08, H15, I05, M&TEA, M09, MBF, METADEX, P52, PQC, SolStAb, T02, T04, W03, W05, WAA.
—CIS, Linda Hall. **CCC.**
Published by: Penton Media, Inc., 1300 E 9th St, Cleveland, OH 44114. TEL 216-696-7000, FAX 216-696-3432, information@penton.com, http://www.penton.com. Ed. Robert E Brooks TEL 216-931-9450. Circ: 5,000 (controlled).

FORWARD (CHICAGO). *see* BUSINESS AND ECONOMICS—Production Of Goods And Services

671.2 USA ISSN 0360-8999
TS200 CODEN: FNMTBS
FOUNDRY MANAGEMENT & TECHNOLOGY. Text in English. 1892. m. USD 59 domestic; USD 67 in Canada; USD 84 elsewhere; free domestic to qualified personnel (effective 2011). adv. bk.rev. illus.; stat.; tr.lit. reprints avail. **Document type:** *Magazine, Trade.* **Description:** Includes technical developments, foundry management problems and operating practices.
Formerly: Foundry (0015-9034)
Related titles: Microfilm ed.: (from PQC); Online - full text ed.: ISSN 1944-9526.
Indexed: A09, A10, A15, A22, A23, A24, A28, ABIn, APA, B01, B02, B03, B06, B07, B08, B09, B11, B13, B15, B17, B18, B21, BCIRA, BrCerAb, BusI, C&ISA, C12, CA, CA/WCA, CIA, CerAb, CivEngAb, CorrAb, E&CAJ, E11, EEA, EMA, ESPM, EngInd, EnvEAb, ErgAb, G04, G06, G07, G08, H&SSA, H15, I05, M&TEA, M01, M02, M09, MBF, METADEX, P52, PQC, S22, SCOPUS, SRI, SolStAb, T&II, T02, T04, TM, V02, V03, V04, WAA.
—BLDSC (4026.600000), IE, Infotrieve, Ingenta, INIST, Linda Hall. **CCC.**
Published by: Penton Media, Inc., 1300 E 9th St, Cleveland, OH 44114. TEL 216-696-7000, FAX 216-696-3432, information@penton.com, http://www.penton.com. Ed. Robert Brooks TEL 216-931-9450. adv.: B&W page USD 4,400, color page USD 5,450. Circ: 19,500 (controlled).

671.2 GBR ISSN 0266-9994
FOUNDRY PRACTICE; the authoritative magazine for foundry engineers. Text in English. 1932. s-a. free (effective 2009). adv. back issues avail. **Document type:** *Journal, Trade.* **Description:** Aims to keep customers informed of the latest developments in our proprietary products and services and encourage the implementation of best practice.
Formerly (until 1998): Foseco Foundry Practice (0427-0525)
Related titles: Online - full text ed.
Indexed: A28, APA, BrCerAb, C&ISA, CA/WCA, CIA, CerAb, CivEngAb, CorrAb, E&CAJ, E11, EEA, EMA, ESPM, EnvEAb, H15, M&TEA, M09, MBF, METADEX, SolStAb, T04, WAA.
—Linda Hall.
Published by: Foseco International Limited, PO Box 5516, Tamworth, Staffordshire B78 3XQ, United Kingdom. TEL 44-1827-289999, FAX 44-1827-250806, UKCustomerServices@Foseco.com, http://www.foseco.co.uk.

671.2 GBR ISSN 1758-9789
TS200 CODEN: FUTJAD
FOUNDRY TRADE JOURNAL INTERNATIONAL. Text in English. 1902. m. GBP 194 domestic; EUR 275 in Europe; GBP 252 elsewhere (effective 2010). adv. bk.rev.; film rev. abstr.; charts; illus.; mkt.; pat.; stat.; tr.lit. s-a. index. back issues avail.; reprints avail. **Document type:** *Journal, Trade.* **Description:** Contains reports on trade and technical matters in the foundry industry.
Incorporates (1992-2010): Die Casting World (0965-6111); Formerly (until 2008): Foundry Trade Journal (0015-9042); Which incorporated: Iron and Steel Trades Journal and Iron Trade Circular; (1987-2003): The Foundryman (0953-6035); Which was formerly (1957-1987): British Foundryman (0007-0718); Which was formed by the merger of (1946-1956): Institute of British Foundrymen. Journal (0368-2706); (1919-1956): Institute of British Foundrymen. Proceedings (0369-9862); Which was formerly (1907-1919): British Foundrymen's Association. Proceedings; (1992-2000): Foundry International (1368-0277); Which was formerly (1978-1992): Foundry Trade Journal International (0143-6902)
Related titles: Microfilm ed.: (from PQC); Online - full text ed.; ◆ Supplement(s): Foundry Yearbook and Castings Buyers' Directory (Year). ISSN 0264-5319; ◆ Diecasting World. ISSN 0965-6111.
Indexed: A&ATA, A22, A28, APA, B02, B15, B17, B18, BCIRA, BrCerAb, BrTechI, C&ISA, CA/WCA, CIA, CISA, Cadscan, CerAb, ChemAb, CivEngAb, CoppAb, CorrAb, E&CAJ, E11, EEA, EMA, ESPM, EngInd, EnvEAb, ErgAb, G04, G06, G07, G08, H15, I05, LeadAb, M&TEA, M09, MBF, METADEX, RefZh, SCOPUS, SolStAb, T04, TM, WAA, Zincscan.
—BLDSC (4028.012500), CASDDS, IE, Infotrieve, Ingenta, INIST, Linda Hall. **CCC.**
Published by: (Pattern Model and Mouldmakers Association, European Investment Casters' Federation), Institute of Cast Metals Engineers, 47 Birmingham Rd, West Bromwich, W Mids B70 6PY, United Kingdom. TEL 44-121-6016979, FAX 44-121-6016981, info@icme.org.uk, http://www.icme.org.uk. Ed. Lynn Postle TEL 44-121-6016979. Adv. contact Terry Fendley TEL 44-1293-776492. color page GBP 2,449; 185 x 265. Circ: 4,500. **Dist. by:** Turpin Distribution Services Ltd.

FOUNDRY YEARBOOK AND CASTINGS BUYERS' DIRECTORY (YEAR). *see* BUSINESS AND ECONOMICS—Trade And Industrial Directories

669 BRA ISSN 1808-3587
FUNDICAO E SERVICOS. Abbreviated title: F S. Text in Portuguese. 1990. m. free to qualified personnel. adv. bk.rev. back issues avail. **Document type:** *Magazine, Trade.*
Published by: Aranda Editora Tecnica e Cultural, Alamed Olga 315, Perdizes, Sao Paulo, SP 01155-900, Brazil. TEL 55-11-38245300, FAX 55-11-36669585, info@arandanet.com.br, http://www.arandanet.com.br. Ed. Fernanda Nascimento. Pub., Adv. contact Jose Roberto Goncalves. page USD 2,021; 21 x 28. Circ: 8,000.

669 ARG ISSN 0429-8950
CODEN: FUNDBY
FUNDIDOR. Text in Spanish. 1957. 3/yr. free. adv. bk.rev. **Document type:** *Trade.*
Indexed: BCIRA, ChemAb.
—CASDDS.
Published by: Camara de Industriales Fundidores, Adolfo Alsina 1609, 1o piso, Buenos Aires, 1088, Argentina. TEL 54-11-43716840, FAX 54-11-48144407. adv.: B&W page ARS 450; 230 x 160. Circ: 3,000.

669 ESP ISSN 1132-0362
FUNDIDORES. Text in Spanish. 1991. 9/yr. adv. **Document type:** *Magazine, Trade.*
Related titles: Online - full text ed.: free; ◆ Supplement(s): Guia de Fundidores. ISSN 1137-0157.
Indexed: IECT.
Published by: Metal Spain, Hermosilla 38, 1B, Madrid, 28001, Spain. TEL 34-91-5765609, FAX 34-91-5782924, magazine@metalspain.co.

669 JPN ISSN 0532-8799
TP156.P3 CODEN: FOFUA2
FUNTAI OYOBI FUNMATSUYAKIN/JAPAN SOCIETY OF POWDER AND POWDER METALLURGY. Text in Japanese. 1947. irreg. free to members.
Indexed: A28, APA, BrCerAb, C&ISA, C33, CA/WCA, CIA, CPEI, CerAb, ChemAb, CivEngAb, CorrAb, E&CAJ, E11, EEA, EMA, ESPM, EngInd, EnvEAb, H15, INIS AtomInd, ISMEC, Inspec, M&TEA, M09, MBF, METADEX, SCOPUS, SolStAb, T04, WAA.
—BLDSC (4808.070000), Linda Hall. **CCC.**
Published by: Funtai Funmatsu Yakin Kyokai/Japan Society of Powder & Powder Metallurgy, 15 Morimoto-cho, Shimogamo, Sakyo-ku, Kyoto, 606-0805, Japan. TEL 81-75-7213650, FAX 81-75-7213653, funkyo@mbox.kyoto-inet.or.jp.

669 621.402 GBR ISSN 1740-6501
TN672
FURNACES INTERNATIONAL; furnace technology for thermal processing of metals & materials. Text in English. 1929. q. adv. back issues avail. **Document type:** *Magazine, Trade.* **Description:** Magazine for the thermal process and industrial heating of metals and materials.
Incorporates (1978-2003): Metallurgia (0141-8602); Which was formerly (until 1978): Metallurgia and Metal Forming (0368-945X); Which was formed by the merger of (1966 -1971): Metal Forming (0026-0622); Which was formerly (until 1966): Metal Treatment (1756-6851); (until 1965): Metal Treatment and Drop Forging (0369-2280); (1929-1971): Metallurgia (0026-0835); Which incorporated (in 1929): Metallurgical Engineer (0369-2310)
Related titles: Online - full text ed.; Chinese ed.: 2005 (June); ◆ Supplement to: Aluminium International Today. ISSN 1475-455X.
Indexed: A05, A26, A28, APA, AS&TA, AS&TI, B02, B04, B15, B17, B18, BRD, BrCerAb, C&ISA, C10, CA/WCA, CIA, CPEI, CerAb, CivEngAb, CorrAb, E&CAJ, E08, E11, EEA, EMA, EngInd, G04, G06, G07, G08, H15, I05, M&TEA, M09, MBF, METADEX, RefZh, S04, S09, SCOPUS, SolStAb, T04, TM, W03, W05, WAA.
—BLDSC (4059.046000), IE, Ingenta, Linda Hall.
Published by: Quartz Business Media Ltd., Westgate House, 120/130 Station Rd, Redhill, Surrey RH1 1ET, United Kingdom. TEL 44-1737-855000, FAX 44-1737-855475, http://www.quartzltd.co.uk/business. Adv. contact Tony Meyer TEL 44-1276-470182. B&W page GBP 1,300, color page GBP 2,100; trim 210 x 297. Circ: 2,000.

620.11223 CHN ISSN 1002-6495
TA462 CODEN: FKFJED
FUSHI KEXUE YU FANGHU JISHU/CORROSION SCIENCE AND PROTECTION TECHNIQUE. Text in Chinese. 1989. bi-m. USD 40.20 (effective 2009). back issues avail. **Document type:** *Journal, Academic/Scholarly.*
Related titles: Online - full content ed.; Online - full text ed.
Indexed: A22, A28, A32, APA, BrCerAb, C&ISA, CA/WCA, CEABA, CIA, CIN, CerAb, ChemAb, ChemTitl, CivEngAb, CorrAb, E&CAJ, E11, EEA, EMA, ESPM, EnvEAb, FLUIDEX, H15, Inspec, M&TEA, M09, MBF, METADEX, OceAb, RefZh, SCOPUS, SolStAb, T04, WAA.
—BLDSC (3476.605000), AskIEEE, CASDDS, East View, IE, Ingenta, Linda Hall.
Published by: Zhongguo Kexueyuan Jinshu Yanjiusuo/Chinese Academy of Sciences, Institute of Metal Research, 62, Wencui Lu, Shenyang, 110016, China. TEL 86-24-23893476, FAX 86-24-23891320, http://www.imr.ac.cn/index.jsp.

669 AUS
GALVANIZE. Text in English. 1981. q. free to qualified personnel. bk.rev. **Document type:** *Newsletter, Trade.* **Description:** Covers various applications of galvanized steel in structures and locations.
Formerly (until 1981): Galvanizing Report
Related titles: Online - full text ed.: free.
Published by: Galvanizers Association of Australia, Level 5, 124 Exhibition St, Melbourne, VIC 3000, Australia. TEL 61-3-96541266, FAX 61-3-96541136, gaa@gaa.com.au.

671.732 DEU ISSN 0016-4232
TS200 CODEN: GVTKAY
GALVANOTECHNIK; Lackiertechnik, Duennschicht/Plasmatechnik, Mikrosystemtechnik, Umwelttechnik. Text in German. 1902. m. EUR 68.95 domestic; EUR 86.40 foreign; EUR 10 newsstand/cover (effective 2009). adv. bk.rev. abstr.; charts; illus.; pat.; stat.; tr.lit. index. 310 p./no.; **Document type:** *Magazine, Trade.*
Formerly (until 1958): Metallwaren-Industrie und Galvanotechnik (0369-2876)
Related titles: ◆ Supplement(s): Produktion von Leiterplatten und Systemen. ISSN 1436-7505.
Indexed: A22, A28, APA, BrCerAb, C&ISA, CA/WCA, CEABA, CIA, CIN, CPEI, CTE, CerAb, ChemAb, ChemTitl, CivEngAb, CorrAb, E&CAJ, E11, EEA, EMA, ESPM, EngInd, EnvEAb, H15, ISMEC, Inspec, M&TEA, M09, MBF, METADEX, RefZh, SCOPUS, SolStAb, T04, TM, WAA.
—BLDSC (4068.080000), AskIEEE, CASDDS, IE, Infotrieve, Ingenta, INIST, Linda Hall. **CCC.**
Published by: Eugen G. Leuze Verlag, Karlstr 4, Saulgau, 88348, Germany. TEL 49-7581-48010, FAX 49-7581-480110, info@leuze-verlag.de. Ed. Kurt Reichert. Adv. contact Udo Steindl TEL 49-7581-480115. B&W page EUR 1,020, color page EUR 1,500; trim 130 x 200. Circ: 4,266 (paid and controlled).

671.732 ITA ISSN 1121-855X
CODEN: GNFIE8
GALVANOTECNICA E NUOVE FINITURE. Text in Italian. 1950. 5/yr. EUR 70 foreign (effective 2008). adv. bk.rev. abstr.; bibl.; illus. index, cum.index: 1953-1987. **Document type:** *Magazine, Trade.* **Description:** Includes papers on plating, surface finishing and related issues.
Former titles (until 1991): Galvanotecnica e Nuove Finiture (1120-6454); (until 1988): Galvanotecnica e Processi al Plasma (1120-6446); (until 1983): Galvanotecnica (0016-4240)
Indexed: A28, APA, BrCerAb, C&ISA, CA/WCA, CIA, CIN, CerAb, ChemAb, ChemTitl, CivEngAb, CorrAb, E&CAJ, E11, EEA, EMA, ESPM, EnvEAb, H15, M&TEA, M09, MBF, METADEX, RefZh, SolStAb, T04, WAA.
—BLDSC (4068.451500), CASDDS, INIST.
Published by: Associazione Italiana Finiture dei Metalli, Via Renato Fucini 6, Milan, 20133, Italy. Circ: 25,000 (paid).

669 CHN ISSN 1004-7638
GANG TIE FAN TAI/IRON STEEL VANADIUM TITANIUM. Text in Chinese. 1980. q. CNY 13.50 per issue (effective 2008). **Document type:** *Journal, Academic/Scholarly.*
Related titles: Online - full text ed.
Indexed: A28, APA, BrCerAb, C&ISA, CA/WCA, CIA, CerAb, CivEngAb, CorrAb, E&CAJ, E11, EEA, EMA, ESPM, EnvEAb, H15, M&TEA, M09, MBF, METADEX, RefZh, SolStAb, T04, WAA.
—BLDSC (4069.281509).
Published by: Pangang Jituan, Panzhihua Gangtie Yanjiusuo/PanGang Group, Panzhihua Iron & Steel Research Institute, 90, Taoyuan Jie, Panzhihua, 617000, China. TEL 86-812-3380539, FAX 86-812-3380533, dj@panyan.cn, http://www.panyan.cn/.

696 CHN ISSN 1001-2311
GANGGUAN/STEEL PIPE. Text in Chinese; Abstracts in Chinese, English. 1964. bi-m. USD 31.20 (effective 2009). **Document type:** *Journal, Academic/Scholarly.* **Description:** Covers metal materials, research, metal formation process, technology, equipment, computer(CAD) application, highlights of the steel tube-making industry in China and steel tube market, etc.
Related titles: Online - full text ed.
Indexed: A28, APA, BrCerAb, C&ISA, CA/WCA, CIA, CerAb, CivEngAb, CorrAb, E&CAJ, E11, EEA, EMA, ESPM, EnvEAb, H15, M&TEA, M09, MBF, METADEX, RefZh, SolStAb, T04, WAA.
—East View, Linda Hall.
Address: Niushekou, Chengdu, 610066, China. TEL 86-28-84545640, FAX 86-28-84553136. Ed. Haitao Cheng. Circ: 5,000.

669 CHN ISSN 0449-749X
TS300 CODEN: KATIAR
GANGTIE/IRON AND STEEL. Text in Chinese. m. USD 106.80 (effective 2009).
Related titles: Online - full text ed.
Indexed: A22, A28, APA, BrCerAb, C&ISA, CA/WCA, CIA, CIN, CerAb, ChemAb, ChemTitl, CivEngAb, CorrAb, E&CAJ, E11, EEA, EMA, ESPM, EngInd, EnvEAb, H15, M&TEA, M09, MBF, METADEX, SCOPUS, SolStAb, T04, TM, WAA.
—BLDSC (4577.900000), CASDDS, East View, IE, Ingenta, Linda Hall.
Published by: Yejin Gongye Chubanshe, 39 Songzhuyuan Beixiang, Shatan, Beijing, 100009, China. TEL 4015782. Ed. Lu Da.

669.1 CHN ISSN 1001-1447
➤ **GANGTIE YANJIU/RESEARCH ON IRON AND STEEL.** Text in Chinese; Abstracts in Chinese, English. 1973. bi-m. CNY 48, USD 48; CNY 8 per issue (effective 2010). adv. **Document type:** *Journal, Academic/Scholarly.*
Related titles: Online - full text ed.
Indexed: A28, APA, BrCerAb, C&ISA, CA/WCA, CIA, CerAb, CivEngAb, E11, EEA, EMA, ESPM, EnvEAb, H15, M&TEA, M09, MBF, METADEX, T04.
Published by: Wuhan Gangtie Gongsi Gangtie Yanjiusuo, No.28 Yejin Dadao, Qingshan District, Wuhan, 430083, China. TEL 86-27-86487772, FAX 86-27-86487773. Ed. Zhong-jie Yu. Circ: 2,000. **Co-sponsor:** Wuhan Gangtie (Jituan) Gongsi/Wuhan Iron & Steel (Group) Corp.

669 CHN ISSN 1001-0963
GANGTIE YANJIU XUEBAO. Text in Chinese. 1981. m. USD 106.80 (effective 2009). **Document type:** *Journal, Academic/Scholarly.*
Related titles: Online - full text ed.; ◆ English ed.: Journal of Iron and Steel Research International. ISSN 1006-706X.
Indexed: A28, APA, ASFA, BrCerAb, C&ISA, CA/WCA, CIA, CerAb, CivEngAb, CorrAb, E&CAJ, E11, EEA, EMA, ESPM, EnvEAb, H15, Inspec, M&TEA, M09, MBF, METADEX, SCOPUS, SolStAb, T04, TM, WAA.
—BLDSC (5008.330000), East View, Linda Hall.
Address: 76 Xueyuan Nan Lu, Beijing, 100081, China. **Dist. by:** China International Book Trading Corp, 35 Chegongzhuang Xilu, Haidian District, PO Box 399, Beijing 100044, China. TEL 86-10-68412045, FAX 86-10-68412023, cibtc@mail.cibtc.com.cn, http://www.cibtc.com.cn.

669 622 DEU
CODEN: GDMSAX
GESELLSCHAFT FUER BERGBAU, METALLURGIE, ROHSTOFF- UND UMWELTTECHNIK. SCHRIFTENREIHE. Text in English, German. 1951. irreg., latest vol.119, 2009. EUR 40 per vol. (effective 2009). **Document type:** *Monographic series, Academic/Scholarly.*
Former titles (until 1996): Gesellschaft Deutscher Metallhuetten- und Bergleute. Schriftenreihe (0720-1877); (until 1976): G D M B Schriften (0342-1376); (until 1972): Gesellschaft Deutscher Metallhuetten- und Bergleute. Schriften (0433-857X)
Indexed: GeoRef, IMMAb, SpeleolAb, TM.
—CASDDS. **CCC.**
Published by: (Gesellschaft fuer Bergbau, Metallurgie, Rohstoff- und Umwelttechnik), G D M B Geschaeftsstelle, Paul Ernst Str 10, Clausthal-Zellerfeld, 38678, Germany. TEL 49-5323-93720, FAX 49-5323-937937, info@gdmb.de, http://www.gdmb.de.

671.2 DEU ISSN 0016-9765
TS200 CODEN: GIESAS
GIESSEREI; Zeitschrift fuer das gesamte Giessereiwesen. Contents page in English, French. 1914. m. EUR 140 domestic; EUR 218 foreign; EUR 19.50 newsstand/cover (effective 2008). adv. bk.rev. bibl.; charts; illus.; mkt.; pat. index. **Document type:** *Magazine, Trade.*
Incorporates (19??-1990): Giessereitechnik (0016-9803); Which was formerly (until 1955): Metallurgie und Giessereitechnik (0369-0059); Former titles (until 1951): Neue Giesserei (0369-3848); (until 1948): Die Giesserei (0175-1034); Which incorporated (1904-1930): Giesserei-Zeitung (0367-4630); (1880-1944): Giessereipraxis (0175-1042); Which was formerly (until 1935): Zeitschrift fuer die Gesamte Giessereipraxis (0372-8730); (until 1918): Eisen-Zeitung (0367-1410)
Related titles: Microfilm ed.: (from PMC).
Indexed: A22, A28, APA, BCIRA, BrCerAb, C&ISA, CA/WCA, CIA, CIN, CISA, CerAb, ChemAb, ChemTitl, CivEngAb, CorrAb, E&CAJ, E11, EEA, EMA, ESPM, EnvEAb, H15, IBR, IBZ, M&TEA, M09, MBF, METADEX, NumL, RILM, SolStAb, T04, TM, WAA.
—BLDSC (4174.000000), CASDDS, IE, Infotrieve, Ingenta, INIST, Linda Hall. **CCC.**
Published by: (Verein Deutscher Giessereifachleute e.V.), Giesserei-Verlag GmbH, Postfach 102532, Duesseldorf, 40016, Germany. TEL 49-211-67070, FAX 49-211-6707517, giesserei@stahleisen.de, http://www.giesserei-verlag.de. R&P Wilfried Wendt. Adv. contact Juergen Simonis. B&W page EUR 1,664, color page EUR 2,462; trim 174 x 260. Circ: 3,539 (paid and controlled).

671.2 DEU ISSN 0016-9773
GIESSEREI - ERFAHRUNGSAUSTAUSCH. Text in German. 1957. m. EUR 59 domestic; EUR 84 foreign; EUR 8 newsstand/cover (effective 2008). adv. bk.rev. **Document type:** *Magazine, Trade.*
Indexed: TM.
Published by: Giesserei-Verlag GmbH, Postfach 102532, Duesseldorf, 40016, Germany. TEL 49-211-67070, FAX 49-211-6707517, giesserei@stahleisen.de, http://www.giesserei-verlag.de. adv.: B&W page EUR 1,169, color page EUR 1,919; trim 180 x 260. Circ: 3,901 (paid and controlled).

669 DEU
GIESSEREI JAHRBUCH. Text in German. 1954. a. adv. abstr.; pat.; stat. **Document type:** *Yearbook, Trade.*
Formerly (until 1999): Giesserei-Kalender (0340-8175)
Published by: (Verein Deutscher Giessereifachleute), Giesserei-Verlag GmbH, Postfach 102532, Duesseldorf, 40016, Germany. TEL 49-211-67070, FAX 49-211-6707517, giesserei@stahleisen.de, http://www.giesserei-verlag.de. Adv. contact Barbara Keisker. B&W page EUR 778; trim 120 x 170. Circ: 5,000 (paid).

671.2 DEU ISSN 0016-9781
CODEN: GIPXAU
GIESSEREI-PRAXIS. Text in German. 1914. 10/yr. EUR 145.50 domestic; EUR 167 foreign; EUR 13.50 newsstand/cover (effective 2011). adv. bk.rev. abstr.; charts; illus.; mkt.; tr.lit. index. **Document type:** *Magazine, Trade.*
Formerly (until 1952): Giesserei-Praktiker (0367-4592); Which superseded in part (in 1950): Die Giesserei (0175-1034); Which incorporated (1904-1930): Giesserei-Zeitung (0367-4630); (1880-1944): Giessereipraxis (0175-1042); Which was formerly (until 1935): Zeitschrift fuer die Gesamte Giessereipraxis (0372-8730); (until 1918): Eisen-Zeitung (0367-1410)
Indexed: A22, A28, APA, B01, BCIRA, BrCerAb, C&ISA, CA/WCA, CIA, CISA, Cadscan, CerAb, ChemAb, CivEngAb, CorrAb, E&CAJ, E11, EEA, EMA, ESPM, EnvEAb, H15, LeadAb, M&TEA, M09, MBF, METADEX, SolStAb, T04, TM, WAA, Zincscan.
—CASDDS, IE, Infotrieve, Linda Hall. **CCC.**
Published by: Fachverlag Schiele und Schoen GmbH, Markgrafenstr 11, Berlin, 10969, Germany. TEL 49-30-2537520, FAX 49-30-2517248, service@schiele-schoen.de, http://www.schiele-schoen.de. Ed. Hartmut Polzin. Adv. contact Hildegard Thuering TEL 49-30-25375253. Circ: 3,500 (paid and controlled).

671.2 AUT ISSN 0016-979X
CODEN: GIERBQ
GIESSEREI RUNDSCHAU. Text in German. 1954. 6/yr. EUR 56 domestic; EUR 69.50 foreign (effective 2005). adv. bk.rev. bibl.; illus.; pat.; stat.; tr.lit. **Document type:** *Journal, Trade.*
Indexed: A22, BCIRA, CIN, ChemAb, ChemTitl, RefZh, TM.
—BLDSC (4175.050000), CASDDS, IE, Ingenta.
Published by: (Verein Oesterreichischer Giessereifachleute), Verlag Lorenz, Ebendorferstr 10, Vienna, W 1010, Austria. TEL 43-1-40566950, FAX 43-1-4068693, office@verlag-lorenz.at. Ed. Erich Nechtelberger. Adv. contact Irene Esch. B&W page EUR 1,245, color page EUR 2,370; trim 185 x 264. Circ: 1,000 (paid and controlled). **Co-sponsor:** Fachverband der Giessereiindustrie und des Oesterreichischen Giesserei Institutes.

671.2 DEU ISSN 0046-5933
TS200 CODEN: GSFGBY
GIESSEREIFORSCHUNG. Text in German; Contents page in English, French, German. 1949. q. adv. **Document type:** *Journal, Trade.*
Former titles (until 1967): Giesserei, Technisch-Wissenschaftliche Beihefte, Giessereiwesen und Metallkunde (0367-5386); (until 1951): Die Neue Giesserei. Technisch-Wissenschaftliche Beihefte, Metallkunde und Giessereiwesen (0175-1050)
Indexed: A22, A28, APA, BCIRA, BrCerAb, C&ISA, CA/WCA, CIA, CIN, CerAb, ChemAb, ChemTitl, CivEngAb, CorrAb, E&CAJ, E11, EEA, EMA, ESPM, EnvEAb, H15, M&TEA, M09, MBF, METADEX, SolStAb, T04, TM, WAA.
—BLDSC (4175.090000), CASDDS, IE, Infotrieve, Ingenta, INIST, Linda Hall. **CCC.**
Published by: (Verein Deutscher Giessereifachleute e.V.), Giesserei-Verlag GmbH, Postfach 102532, Duesseldorf, 40016, Germany. TEL 49-211-67070, FAX 49-211-6707517, giesserei@stahleisen.de, http://www.giesserei-verlag.de. R&P Wilfried Wendt.

GIJUTSU JOHO MIE. KIKAI KINZOKU HEN/TECHNICAL INFORMATION IN MIE PREFECTURE: MACHINE AND METAL SERIES. see MACHINERY

669 JPN ISSN 1341-3422
TN207
GIJUTSUBU GIJUTSU KENKYU HOKOKU/TECHNOLOGY & RESEARCH REPORT. Text in Japanese. 1969. irreg.
Formerly (until 1993): Kyotsu Shisetsu Gijutsu Kenkyu Hokoku (0911-3398)
Indexed: A28, APA, BrCerAb, C&ISA, CA/WCA, CIA, CerAb, CivEngAb, CorrAb, E&CAJ, E11, EEA, EMA, H15, M&TEA, M09, MBF, METADEX, SolStAb, T04, WAA.
Published by: Tohoku Daigaku, Kinzoku Zairyo Kenkyujo, 2-1-1 Katahira, Aoba-ku, Sendai, 980-8577, Japan.

669 ITA ISSN 0392-3622
IL GIORNALE DELLA SUBFORNITURA. Text in Italian. 1981. 8/yr. EUR 53 domestic; EUR 77 foreign (effective 2009). adv. **Document type:** *Magazine, Trade.*
Published by: Reed Business Information Spa (Subsidiary of: Reed Business Information International), Viale Giulio Richard 1, Milan, 20143, Italy. TEL 39-02-818301, FAX 39-02-81830406, info@reedbusiness.it, http://www.reedbusiness.it. Circ: 10,000.

669 SWE ISSN 0017-0682
CODEN: GJUTAG
GJUTERIET. Text in Swedish. 1911. 8/yr. SEK 475 domestic; SEK 650 foreign (effective 2001). adv. charts; illus. back issues avail. **Document type:** *Magazine, Trade.*
Formerly (until 1915): Gjutmaestaren
Indexed: BCIRA, ChemAb.
—CASDDS, Linda Hall.
Published by: (Svenska Gjuteriforeningen), AB Gjuteriinformation i Joenkoeping, PO Box 2033, Joenkoeping, 55002, Sweden. TEL 46-36-301200, FAX 46-36-166866, info@gjuteriforeningen.se. Ed. Zoltan Tiroler. Adv. contact Fredrik Eckerstroem. Circ: 3,600 (controlled).

669 ITA ISSN 1972-7518
GLOBAL METALWORKING. Text in Multiple languages. 2008. bi-m. EUR 30 domestic; EUR 60 in Europe; EUR 80 elsewhere (effective 2011). **Document type:** *Journal, Trade.*
Published by: Tecniche Nuove SpA, Via Eritrea 21, Milan, MI 201, Italy. TEL 39-02-390901, FAX 39-02-7570364, info@tecnichenuove.com. Ed. Andrea Chan.

GOLD NEWS/NOUVELLES DE L'OR. see MINES AND MINING INDUSTRY

669.22 GBR ISSN 2045-5313
THE GOLDSMITHS' COMPANY TECHNICAL JOURNAL. Text in English. 2005 (Spring). s-a. free (effective 2011). back issues avail. **Document type:** *Journal, Trade.* **Description:** Presents new developments and useful technical information.
Formerly (until 2010): The Goldsmiths' Company Technical Bulletin (1747-4256)
Related titles: CD-ROM ed.: ISSN 1747-4272; Online - full text ed.: ISSN 2045-5321.
Published by: Worshipful Company of Goldsmiths, Goldsmiths' Hall, Foster Ln, London, EC2V 6BN, United Kingdom. TEL 44-20-76067010, FAX 44-20-76061511, the.clerk@thegoldsmiths.co.uk.

GOLDSMITHS' REVIEW. see JEWELRY, CLOCKS AND WATCHES

669 CHN ISSN 1007-4252
GONGNENG CAILIAO YU QIJIAN XUEBAO/JOURNAL OF FUNCTIONAL MATERIALS AND DEVICES. Text in Chinese. 1995. q. CNY 20; CNY 5 per issue. **Document type:** *Journal, Academic/Scholarly.*
Related titles: Online - full text ed.
Indexed: EngInd, Inspec, RefZh, SCOPUS.
—BLDSC (4986.812000), IE, Ingenta.
Published by: Chinese Academy of Sciences, Shanghai Institute of Metallurgy, 865 Chang Ning Rd, Shanghai, 200050, China. Ed. Zou Shichang.

669 546.3 GBR
GOOD PRACTICE (LONDON, 1993). Abbreviated title: I C M M Newsletter. Text in English. 1993. s-a. free. **Document type:** *Newsletter, Trade.* **Description:** Includes news regarding the Council's work on behalf of the mining and metals industry and sustainable development. It also has the latest developments regarding research topics, opinion and industry trends on economic, social and environmental matters.

Former titles: International Council on Mining and Metals. Newsletter (Online); International Council on Metals and the Environment. Newsletter (Print) (1023-4055)
Media: Online - full content.
—Linda Hall.
Published by: International Council on Mining and Metals, 19 Stratford Pl, 3rd Fl, London, W1C 1BQ, United Kingdom. TEL 44-20-72904920, FAX 44-20-72904939, info@icmm.com, http://www.icmm.com.

669 ESP ISSN 1137-0157
GUIA DE FUNDIDORES. Text in Spanish. 1996. irreg. **Document type:** *Directory, Trade.*
Related titles: Online - full text ed.; ◆ Supplement to: Fundidores. ISSN 1132-0362.
Published by: Metal Spain, Hermosilla 38, 1B, Madrid, 28001, Spain. TEL 34-91-5765609, FAX 34-91-5782924, magazine@metalspain.co, http://www.metalspain.com.

669.772 USA
GUIDELINES FOR HANDLING MOLTEN ALUMINUM. Text in English. 19??. every 10 yrs., latest 2002. USD 100 per issue for 10 years (effective 2011). **Document type:** *Trade.*
Published by: Aluminum Association, 1525 Wilson Blvd, Ste 600, Arlington, VA 22209. TEL 703-358-2960, FAX 703-358-2961, http://www.aluminum.org/.

669.2 CHN ISSN 1004-0676
TN410 CODEN: GUIJE7
GUIJINSHU/PRECIOUS METALS. Text in Chinese. 1980. q. USD 20.80 (effective 2009). **Document type:** *Journal, Academic/Scholarly.*
Related titles: Online - full text ed.
Indexed: A22, A28, APA, BrCerAb, C&ISA, C33, CA/WCA, CIA, CerAb, CivEngAb, CorrAb, E&CAJ, E11, EEA, EMA, ESPM, EnvEAb, H15, M&TEA, M09, MBF, METADEX, SCOPUS, SolStAb, T04, WAA.
—BLDSC (6603.915100), East View, IE, Ingenta, Linda Hall.
Published by: Kunming Guijinshu Yanjiusuo/Kunming Institute of Precious Metals, Beier Huanlu, Kunming, 650221, China. TEL 86-871-5132018, FAX 86-871-5133790, http://www.ipm.com.cn/. **Dist. by:** China International Book Trading Corp, 35 Chegongzhuang Xilu, Haidian District, PO Box 399, Beijing 100044, China. TEL 86-10-68412045, FAX 86-10-68412023, cibtc@mail.cibtc.com.cn, http://www.cibtc.com.cn.

GUOCHENG GONGCHENG XUEBAO/CHINESE JOURNAL OF PROCESS ENGINEERING. *see* ENGINEERING—Chemical Engineering

669 DEU ISSN 1867-2493
CODEN: HTMMD5
H T M; journal of heat treatment and materials. (Heat Treatment Materials) Text in German. 1941. bi-m. EUR 402.40 domestic; EUR 407.20 foreign; EUR 81.20 newsstand/cover (effective 2011). adv. bibl.; charts; illus. index. **Document type:** *Journal, Trade.*
Former titles (until 2009): H T M - Haerterie-Technische Mitteilungen (0341-101X); (until 1976): H T M - Haerterie-Technische Mitteilungen (0017-6583)
Indexed: A28, APA, BrCerAb, C&ISA, CA/WCA, CIA, CIN, CPEI, CerAb, ChemAb, ChemTitl, CivEngAb, CorrAb, E&CAJ, E11, EEA, EMA, Englnd, H15, M&TEA, M09, MBF, METADEX, RefZh, SCOPUS, SolStAb, T04, TM, WAA.
—CASDDS, IE, Infotrieve, Ingenta, INIST, Linda Hall. **CCC.**
Published by: (Arbeitsgemeinschaft Waermebehandlung und Werkstoff-Technik e.V.), Carl Hanser Verlag GmbH & Co. KG, Kolbergerstr 22, Munich, 81679, Germany. TEL 49-89-998300, FAX 49-89-984809, info@hanser.de, http://www.hanser.de. Ed. Johann Grosch. Adv. contact Dietmar von der Au. Circ: 1,544 (paid and controlled).

669.1 530 NLD ISSN 1567-2719
➤ **HANDBOOK OF MAGNETIC MATERIALS.** Text in Dutch. 1980. irreg., latest vol.17, 2007. price varies. back issues avail. **Document type:** *Monographic series, Academic/Scholarly.* **Description:** Publishes studies and research with a reference and an overview of the field of magnetism.
Formerly (until 2002): Handbook of Ferromagnetic Materials (1574-9304)
Related titles: Online - full text ed.: ISSN 1875-5216.
Indexed: CIN, ChemAb, ChemTitl, SCOPUS.
—CCC.
Published by: Elsevier BV, North-Holland (Subsidiary of: Elsevier Science & Technology), Sara Burgerhartstraat 25, Amsterdam, 1055 KV, Netherlands. TEL 31-20-4853911, FAX 31-20-4852457, JournalsCustomerServiceEMEA@elsevier.com, http://www.elsevier.com. Ed. K H J Buschow. **Subscr. to:** Elsevier BV, Radarweg 29, PO Box 211, Amsterdam 1000 AE, Netherlands. TEL 31-20-4853757, FAX 31-20-4853432.

➤ **HANDBOOK ON THE PHYSICS AND CHEMISTRY OF RARE EARTHS.** *see* PHYSICS

669.1 DEU ISSN 0440-2014
HANDBUCH DER EUROPAEISCHEN EISEN- UND STAHLWERKE/ HANDBOOK OF THE EUROPEAN IRON AND STEEL WORKS/ MANUEL DES USINES EUROPEENNES DE LA SIDERURGIE. Text in Multiple languages. 1961. irreg. **Document type:** *Trade.*
—BLDSC (4250.439600).
Published by: Montan- und Wirtschaftsverlag GmbH, Postfach 105164, Duesseldorf, 40042, Germany. TEL 49-211-6707518, FAX 49-211-6707578, ulrich.scharfenorth@stahleisen.de, http://www.stahleisen.de.

671.2 KOR ISSN 1598-706X
HAN'GUG JUJO GONG HAGHOEJI/KOREAN FOUNDRYMEN'S SOCIETY. JOURNAL. Text in Korean. 1981. bi-m. membership. **Document type:** *Journal, Academic/Scholarly.*
Formerly (until 2000): Jujo (1017-4516)
Indexed: TM.
—BLDSC (4812.252000).
Published by: Han'gug Jujo Gong Haghoe/Korean Foundrymen's Society, 131 Dangsan-dong 1 St., Yeongdeungpo-gu, Seoul, 150-800, Korea, S. TEL 82-2-20692877, FAX 82-2-20692879, kfs@kfs.or.kr, http://www.kfs.or.kr.

669 USA
HEAT TREATERS CERTIFICATION MANUAL. Text in English. a. USD 69 (effective 2000). **Document type:** *Handbook/Manual/Guide, Trade.*
Published by: Metal Treating Institute, 1550 Roberts Dr, Jacksonville, FL 32250-3222. TEL 904-249-0448, FAX 904-249-0459.

671 USA ISSN 1536-2558
TS209 CODEN: HTPEAR
HEAT TREATING PROGRESS. Abbreviated title: H T P. Text in English. 2000. 7/yr. free to members (effective 2009). adv. back issues avail. **Document type:** *Magazine, Trade.* **Description:** Provides articles on existing and emerging technologies, profiles on new products, industry news and events, technical tips, legislative and business trends, and challenging commentary.
Related titles: Online - full text ed.; ◆ Supplement to: Advanced Materials & Processes. ISSN 0882-7958.
Indexed: A26, A28, APA, B01, B02, B07, B15, B17, B18, BrCerAb, C&ISA, CA, CA/WCA, CIA, CPEI, CerAb, CivEngAb, CorrAb, E&CAJ, E11, EEA, EMA, Englnd, G04, H15, I05, M&TEA, M09, MBF, METADEX, SCOPUS, SolStAb, T04, WAA.
—BLDSC (4276.260000), IE, Ingenta, Linda Hall. **CCC.**
Published by: (A S M Heat Treating Society), A S M International, 9639 Kinsman Rd, Materials Park, OH 44073. TEL 440-338-5151, FAX 440-338-4634, CustomerService@asminternational.org. Ed. Ed Kubel TEL 239-561-9361. Pub. Joseph M Zion TEL 440-338-5151 ext 5226. adv.: B&W page USD 2,879, color page USD 4,139; bleed 8.25 x 11.125.

669 CHN ISSN 1674-5183
HEILONGJIANG YEJIN. Text in Chinese. 1981. q. **Document type:** *Journal, Academic/Scholarly.*
Related titles: Online - full text ed.
Published by: (Heilongjiang Sheng Jinshu Xuehui/Heilongjiang Society of Metallurgy, Heilongjiang Sheng Yejin Yanjiusuo/Heilongjiang Institute of Metallurgy), Heilongjiang Yejin Bianjibu/Editorial Office of Heilongjiang Metallurgy, 32, Wenzhitoudao Jie, Harbin, 150040, China. TEL 86-451-82133636, FAX 86-451-82114920.

HEPHAISTOS; internationale Zeitschrift fuer Metallgestalter. *see* ART

HI-HAKAI KENSA/JAPANESE SOCIETY FOR NON-DESTRUCTIVE INSPECTION. JOURNAL. *see* ENGINEERING—Engineering Mechanics And Materials

669 GBR ISSN 0142-3304
TN600 CODEN: HIMED6
➤ **HISTORICAL METALLURGY.** Text in English. 1963. s-a. GBP 105 to institutions; USD 188 in United States to institutions (effective 2012). bk.rev. cum.index: vols.1-7, vols.8-18. reprint service avail. from PSC. **Document type:** *Journal, Academic/Scholarly.* **Description:** Covers metallurgy from prehistoric times to the present.
Formerly (until 1974): Historical Metallurgy Group. Bulletin (0441-6759)
Indexed: A&ATA, B24, BCIRA, BrArAb, CIN, ChemAb, ChemTitl, FR, NumL.
—BLDSC (4758.360000), CASDDS, Ingenta, INIST, Linda Hall. **CCC.**
Published by: Historical Metallurgy Society Ltd., Science Museum, Exhibition Rd, London, SW7 2DD, United Kingdom. TEL 44-20-79388051, lesley@mcowell.flyer.co.uk, http://www.nmsi.ac.uk. Eds. David Crossley, Dr. Justine Bayley, Sam Murphy. Circ: 500. **Subscr. in N America to:** Maney Publishing, 875 Massachusetts Ave, 7th Fl, Cambridge, MA 02139. TEL 866-297-5154, FAX 617-354-6875, maney@maneyusa.com; **Subscr. outside N America to:** Maney Publishing, Ste 1C, Joseph's Well, Hanover Walk, Leeds, W Yorks LS3 1AB, United Kingdom. TEL 44-113-3868168, FAX 44-113-2486983, subscriptions@maney.co.uk.

669 GBR
HISTORICAL METALLURGY SOCIETY. NEWSLETTER. Text in English. 19??. 3/yr. free to members (effective 2009). back issues avail. **Document type:** *Newsletter, Trade.*
Indexed: BrArAb, NumL.
Published by: Historical Metallurgy Society Ltd., 1, Carlton House Gardens, London, SW1 5DB, United Kingdom. Ed. David Dungworth TEL 44-23-92856783.

THE HOME SHOP MACHINIST. *see* MACHINERY

HONG KONG LINKAGE INDUSTRY DIRECTORY (YEAR). *see* BUSINESS AND ECONOMICS—Trade And Industrial Directories

669 GBR ISSN 1363-0148
HOT DIP GALVANIZING. Abbreviated title: H D G. Text in English. 199?. q. free to qualified personnel (effective 2009). **Document type:** *Magazine, Trade.* **Description:** Provides a review of projects that feature galvanized steel from across Europe.
Related titles: Online - full text ed.
Indexed: A28, APA, BrCerAb, C&ISA, CA/WCA, CIA, CerAb, CivEngAb, CorrAb, E&CAJ, E11, EEA, EMA, ESPM, EnvEAb, H15, M&TEA, M09, MBF, METADEX, SolStAb, T04, WAA.
—Linda Hall.
Published by: Galvanizers Association, Wren's Ct, 56 Victoria Rd, Sutton Coldfield, West Midlands B72 1SY, United Kingdom. TEL 44-121-3558838, FAX 44-121-3558727, ga@hdg.org.uk.

671.2 POL ISSN 1230-3534
TN4 CODEN: WIHUAL
HUTNIK - WIADOMOSCI HUTNICZE. Text in Polish; Summaries in English, German, Russian. 1992. m. EUR 128 foreign (effective 2006). adv. bk.rev. abstr.; illus. index. 48 p./no.; **Document type:** *Magazine, Trade.* **Description:** Covers steel production.
Formed by the merger of (1929-1992): Hutnik (0018-8077); (1945-1992): Wiadomosci Hutnicze (0043-5139)
Indexed: B22, CIN, ChemAb, ChemTitl, IMMAb, RASB, TM.
—CASDDS, IE, INIST, Linda Hall.
Published by: (Stowarzyszenie Inzynierow i Technikow Przemyslu Hutniczego w Polsce), Wydawnictwo SIGMA - N O T Sp. z o.o., ul Ratuszowa 11, PO Box 1004, Warsaw, 00950, Poland. TEL 48-22-8180918, FAX 48-22-6192187, sekretariat@sigma-not.pl, http://www.sigma-not.pl. Ed. Andrzej Wycislik TEL 48-32-2552933. adv.: B&W page PLZ 1,200, color page PLZ 2,000. Circ: 600. **Dist. by:** Ars Polona, Obroncow 25, Warsaw 03933, Poland. TEL 48-22-5098609, FAX 48-22-5098610, arspolona@arspolona.com.pl, http://www.arspolona.com.pl.

669 NLD ISSN 0304-386X
TN688 CODEN: HYDRDA
➤ **HYDROMETALLURGY.** Text in English. 1975. 20/yr. EUR 2,714 in Europe to institutions; JPY 359,900 in Japan to institutions; USD 3,033 elsewhere to institutions (effective 2012). adv. bk.rev. charts; illus.; abstr. index. back issues avail. **Document type:** *Journal, Academic/Scholarly.* **Description:** Brings together studies on novel processes, process design, chemistry, modelling, control, economics and interfaces between unit operations, and provides a forum for discussions on case histories and operational difficulties.
Related titles: Microform ed.: (from PQC); Online - full text ed.: ISSN 1879-1158 (from IngentaConnect, ScienceDirect).
Indexed: A01, A03, A08, A22, A26, A28, AESIS, APA, ASCA, B21, BrCerAb, C&ISA, C33, CA, CA/WCA, CEA, CEABA, CIA, CIN, CPEI, CTE, Cadscan, CerAb, ChemAb, ChemTitl, CivEngAb, CoppAb, CorrAb, CurCont, E&CAJ, E11, EEA, EMA, ESPM, Englnd, EnvEAb, GeoRef, H15, I05, I10, IMMAb, ISMEC, ISR, LeadAb, M&TEA, M09, MBF, METADEX, MSCI, RefZh, S01, SCI, SCOPUS, SolStAb, SpeleolAb, T02, T04, TCEA, W07, WAA, Zincscan.
—BLDSC (4352.153000), CASDDS, IE, Infotrieve, Ingenta, INIST, Linda Hall. **CCC.**
Published by: Elsevier BV (Subsidiary of: Elsevier Science & Technology), Radarweg 29, PO Box 211, Amsterdam, 1000 AE, Netherlands. TEL 31-20-4853911, FAX 31-20-4852457, JournalsCustomerServiceEMEA@elsevier.com, http://www.elsevier.nl. Eds. D M Muir, K Osseo-Asare, N J Welham.

669 IND ISSN 0972-0480
TN645.I4
➤ **I I M METAL NEWS.** Text in English. 1979. q. INR 900 to non-members; free to members (effective 2011). bk.rev. 56 p./no.; **Document type:** *Journal, Academic/Scholarly.* **Description:** Publishes articles for general dissemination of metallurgical knowledge among engineering community.
Related titles: Online - full text ed.
Indexed: A28, APA, BrCerAb, C&ISA, CA/WCA, CIA, CerAb, CivEngAb, CorrAb, E&CAJ, E11, EEA, EMA, ESPM, EnvEAb, H15, M&TEA, M09, MBF, METADEX, SolStAb, T04, TM, WAA.
Published by: Indian Institute of Metals, Metal House, Plot 13/4, Block AQ, Sector V, Salt Lake City, Kolkata, West Bengal 700 091, India. TEL 91-33-23675004, FAX 91-33-23675335, iimmetalnews@yahoo.com.

➤ **I L O METAL TRADES COMMITTEE. REPORT.** (International Labour Organization) *see* BUSINESS AND ECONOMICS—Labor And Industrial Relations

671.3 CHE
I M F NEWS. Text in English. 1972. fortn. free.
Published by: International Metalworkers Federation, 54 bis, Rte. des Acacias, Geneva, 1227, Switzerland. FAX 022-3431510, TELEX 423298-METL-CH.

I M I MONITOR. *see* BUSINESS AND ECONOMICS—Labor And Industrial Relations

669.1 JPN ISSN 0915-1559
TS300 CODEN: IINTEY
➤ **I S I J INTERNATIONAL.** Text in English. 1961. m. JPY 50,000 to non-members; JPY 4,000 newsstand/cover to non-members (effective 2004). adv. abstr.; bibl.; charts; illus.; stat. index, cum.index. 120 p./no.; back issues avail. **Document type:** *Journal, Academic/Scholarly.* **Description:** Provides the core subject matter of iron and steel worldwide. Intended for those concerned with the processing, structure, property, and application of engineering materials.
Formerly: Iron and Steel Institute of Japan. Transactions (0021-1583); Supersedes: Tetsu-To-Hagane Overseas
Related titles: Microfilm ed.; Online - full text ed.: ISSN 1347-5460.
Indexed: A22, A28, AESIS, APA, ASCA, BrCerAb, C&ISA, C33, CA/WCA, CIA, CIN, CPEI, CerAb, ChemAb, ChemTitl, CivEngAb, CorrAb, CurCont, E&CAJ, E11, EEA, EMA, ESPM, Englnd, EnvEAb, GeoRef, H15, IBR, IBZ, INIS AtomInd, ISMEC, ISR, JCT, JTA, M&TEA, M09, MBF, METADEX, MSCI, RefZh, SCI, SCOPUS, SolStAb, T04, TM, W07, WAA.
—BLDSC (4582.963000), CASDDS, IE, Infotrieve, Ingenta, INIST, Linda Hall. **CCC.**
Published by: Nippon Tekko Kyokai/Iron and Steel Institute of Japan, Niikura Bldg, 2nd Fl, 2 Kanda-Tsukasacho 2-chome, Chiyoda-ku, Tokyo, 101-0048, Japan. TEL 81-3-52097011, FAX 81-3-32571110, editol@isij.or.jp, http://www.isij.or.jp. Ed. Shozo Mizoguchi. Pubs. Yasuo Uchinaka, Yoshihiro Kuwabara. adv.: page JPY 150,000. Circ: 1,700.

➤ **I S R I DIGEST.** *see* ENVIRONMENTAL STUDIES—Waste Management

➤ **IBARAKIKEN KOGYO GIJUTSU JOHO. KIKAI KENZOKU HEN/ IBARAKI PREFECTURE INDUSTRIAL RESEARCH INFORMATION: MACHINE AND METAL SECTION.** *see* MACHINERY

669 USA ISSN 1045-5779
CODEN: ICASEQ
INCAST. Text in English. 1988. m. USD 60; USD 90 foreign (effective 1999). adv. bk.rev. back issues avail. **Document type:** *Journal, Trade.* **Description:** Deals with news and technology on the investment casting process of manufacturing metal ports for casters and suppliers of good services.
Indexed: A28, APA, BrCerAb, C&ISA, CA/WCA, CIA, CerAb, CivEngAb, CorrAb, E&CAJ, E11, EEA, EMA, H15, M&TEA, M09, MBF, METADEX, SolStAb, T04, TM, WAA.
—Linda Hall.
Published by: Investment Casting Institute, 8150 N Central Expy, Ste M 1008, Dallas, TX 75206-1602. TEL 214-368-8896, FAX 214-368-8852. Ed., Pub., R&P, Adv. contact Leland Martin. Circ: 1,500.

669 GBR ISSN 2040-6770
▼ **INDIA METALS REPORT.** Text in English. 2009. q. USD 975 (effective 2010). **Document type:** *Report, Trade.* **Description:** Features latest-available data for steel, aluminium and other major globally-traded commodities.
Published by: Business Monitor International Ltd., Senator House, 85 Queen Victoria St, London, EC4V 4AB, United Kingdom. TEL 44-20-72480468, FAX 44-20-72480467, subs@businessmonitor.com, http://www.businessmonitor.com.

669 IND ISSN 0972-9364
INDIA SURFACE FINISHING. Text in English. 199?. q. INR 600; INR 200 per issue (effective 2011). **Document type:** *Journal, Academic/Scholarly.*
Formerly (until 2004): Metal Finishers' Association of India. Transactions (0971-5304)
Indexed: A28, APA, BrCerAb, C&ISA, CA/WCA, CIA, CerAb, CivEngAb, CorrAb, E&CAJ, E11, EEA, EMA, H15, INIS AtomInd, M&TEA, M09, MBF, METADEX, SolStAb, T04, WAA.
—BLDSC (4429.900500), IE, Ingenta, Linda Hall.

Published by: Metal Finishers' Association of India, 203, Atlanta Estate, Vitbhatti, Goregaon Mulund Link Rd, Off .W.E.Hwy, Goregaon (E), Mumbai, 400 063, India. TEL 91-22-28769691, FAX 91-22-28769691, mfaihq@vsnl.net, http://www.mfai.org.

671.2 IND ISSN 0379-5446
TS200 CODEN: IFOJAI
INDIAN FOUNDRY JOURNAL. Text in English. 1955. m. INR 1,500 domestic to non-members; USD 100 SAARC to non-members; USD 125 elsewhere to non-members; INR 125 per issue to non-members; free to members (effective 2011). adv. bk.rev.; film rev. abstr.; bibl.; charts; illus.; pat.; stat. **Document type:** *Journal, Academic/Scholarly.* **Description:** Provides various commercial information, reports news, trends and round-ups of IIF Regions/Chapters activities and technological developments in the Foundry Industry.
Indexed: A28, APA, BCIRA, BrCerAb, C&ISA, CA/WCA, CIA, CIN, Cadscan, CerAb, ChemAb, ChemTitl, CivEngAb, CorrAb, E&CAJ, E11, EEA, EMA, ESPM, EnvEAb, H15, LeadAb, M&TEA, M09, MBF, METADEX, SolStAb, T04, TM, WAA, Zincscan.
—BLDSC (4409.300000), CASDDS, IE, Ingenta, Linda Hall.
Published by: Institute of Indian Foundrymen, Head Office, IIF Center, 335 Rajdanga Main, Rajdanga St, Kolkata, West Bengal 700 078, India. **Subscr. to:** I N S I O Scientific Books & Periodicals, PO Box 7234, Indraprastha HPO, New Delhi 110 002, India.

669 IND ISSN 0972-2815
TN4 CODEN: TIIMA3
➤ **INDIAN INSTITUTE OF METALS. TRANSACTIONS.** Text in English. 1948. bi-m. EUR 517, USD 698 combined subscription to institutions (print & online eds.) (effective 2012). adv. bk.rev. charts; illus. index, cum.index covering 5 yrs. **Document type:** *Journal, Academic/Scholarly.* **Description:** Publishes original research articles that contribute to the advancement of ferrous and non-ferrous process metallurgy, materials engineering, physical, chemical and mechanical metallurgy, welding science and technology, surface engineering and characterisation, materials development, thermodynamics and kinetics, materials modelling and to other allied branches of metallurgy and materials engineering.
Related titles: Online - full text ed.: ISSN 0975-1645 (from IngentaConnect).
Indexed: A&ATA, A22, A28, AESIS, APA, ASCA, CA/WCA, CIA, CIN, CTE, ChemAb, ChemTitl, CivEngAb, CurCont, E01, E11, EEA, EIA, EMA, ESPM, EnerInd, EnvEAb, F&EA, GeoRef, H15, IMMAb, INIS AtomInd, Inspec, MBF, MSCI, SCI, SCOPUS, T04, W07.
—BLDSC (8939.000000), AskIEEE, CASDDS, Ingenta, INIST. **CCC.**
Published by: Indian Institute of Metals, Metal House, Plot 13/4, Block AQ, Sector V, Salt Lake City, Kolkata, West Bengal 700 091, India. TEL 91-33-23675004, FAX 91-33-23675335, iimmetalnews@yahoo.com, jcmarwah@yahoo.com, http://www.iim-india.net. Circ: 4,000. **Subscr. to:** I N S I O Scientific Books & Periodicals, PO Box 7234, Indraprastha HPO, New Delhi 110 002, India. iihm@ap.nic.in, http://iihm.ap.nic.in/. **Co-publisher:** Springer (India) Private Ltd.

➤ **INDIAN JOURNAL OF GEOLOGY.** *see* EARTH SCIENCES—Geology

669.1 MEX ISSN 0188-4301
INDUSTRIA SIDERURGICA EN MEXICO. Text in Spanish. 1981. a. MXN 35 (effective 1999).
Published by: Instituto Nacional de Estadistica, Geografia e Informatica, Secretaria de Programacion y Presupuesto, Prol. Heroe de Nacozari 2301 Sur, Puerta 11, Acceso, Aguascalientes, 20270, Mexico. TEL 52-4-918-1948, FAX 52-4-918-0739. Circ: 2,000.

671.3 USA
INDUSTRIAL DIGEST. Text in English. 1969. m. (plus buyers' guide). adv. illus. back issues avail. **Document type:** *Magazine, Trade.* **Description:** Focuses on metalworking plants manufacturing end-products by means of cutting and-or forming-type machine tools and allied equipment.
Former titles (until 2007): Production Technology News (1543-1924); (until 2003): Metalworking Digest (0026-1009)
Related titles: Online - full text ed.; Supplement(s): Metalworking Digest Literature Review.
Indexed: A09, A10, B01, B02, B03, B06, B07, B09, B15, B17, B18, G04, G06, G07, G08, I05, M02, T02, V03, V04.
—CCC.
Published by: Advantage Business Media, 100 Enterprise Dr, Ste 600, PO Box 912, Rockaway, NJ 07886. TEL 973-920-7000, FAX 973-920-7531, AdvantageCommunications@advantagemedia.com, http://www.advantagebusinessmedia.com. Ed. Rich Stevancsecz TEL 973-920-7059. Pub. Joe May TEL 508-624-4399. adv.: B&W page USD 5,190; trim 8.19 x 11. Circ: 81,000 (controlled).

INDUSTRIAL HEATING; the international journal of thermal technology. *see* ENGINEERING—Industrial Engineering

669.142 FRA ISSN 0256-9868
L'INDUSTRIE SIDERURGIQUE EN (YEAR)/IRON AND STEEL INDUSTRY IN (YEAR). Text in French, English. 1955. a., latest 2008.
Related titles: Online - full text ed.: ISSN 1996-2819. 1994.
Published by: Organisation for Economic Cooperation and Development (O E C D)/Organisation de Cooperation et de Developpement Economiques (O C D E), 2 Rue Andre Pascal, Paris, 75775 Cedex 16, France. TEL 33-1-45248200.

669 DEU
INFOIL NEWSLETTER. Text in English. q. **Document type:** *Newsletter, Trade.*
Related titles: Online - full text ed.
Indexed: APA, C&ISA, CorrAb, E&CAJ, EEA, SolStAb, WAA.
Published by: European Aluminium Foil Association, Am Bonneshof 5, Dusseldorf, 40474, Germany. FAX 49-211-4796408.

669 USA
INFOMET. Text in English. 6/yr. **Document type:** *Journal, Trade.*
Related titles: Spanish ed.; ◆ Supplement to: World Industrial Reporter. ISSN 0043-8561.
Published by: Keller International Publishing Corp., 150 Great Neck Rd, Great Neck, NY 11021. TEL 516-829-9210, FAX 516-824-5414, info@supplychainbrain.com, http://www.supplychainbrain.com.

INLINE (ENGLISH EDITION). *see* BUILDING AND CONSTRUCTION—Hardware

INLINE (FINNISH EDITION). *see* BUILDING AND CONSTRUCTION—Hardware

INLINE (GERMAN EDITION). *see* BUILDING AND CONSTRUCTION—Hardware

INLINE (POLISH EDITION). *see* BUILDING AND CONSTRUCTION—Hardware

INLINE (SWEDISH EDITION). *see* BUILDING AND CONSTRUCTION—Hardware

INORGANIC MATERIALS. *see* CHEMISTRY—Inorganic Chemistry

▼ **INORGANIC MATERIALS: APPLIED RESEARCH.** *see* CHEMISTRY—Inorganic Chemistry

INSIGHT (NORTHAMPTON); non-destructive testing and condition monitoring. *see* ENGINEERING—Engineering Mechanics And Materials

669 DEU ISSN 0943-4631
INSTITUT FUER EISENHUETTENKUNDE. BERICHTE. Text in German. 1993. irreg., latest 2009. price varies. **Document type:** *Monographic series, Academic/Scholarly.*
Indexed: TM.
Published by: Shaker Verlag GmbH, Kaiserstr 100, Herzogenrath, 52134, Germany. TEL 49-2407-95960, FAX 49-2407-95969, info@shaker.de.

669 CAN ISSN 1193-9400
INSTITUTE FOR MICROSTRUCTURAL SCIENCES. ANNUAL ACTIVITIES REPORT. Text in English. a. **Document type:** *Report, Academic/Scholarly.*
—Linda Hall.
Published by: Institute for Microstructural Sciences, Bldg. 50, Montreal Road, Ottawa, ON K1A 0R6, Canada. TEL 613-993-4583, FAX 613-957-8734, http://www.nrc.ca/ims.

INSTITUTE OF MATERIALS, MINERALS AND MINING. TRANSACTIONS. SECTION A: MINING TECHNOLOGY. *see* MINES AND MINING INDUSTRY

INSTITUTE OF MATERIALS, MINERALS AND MINING. TRANSACTIONS. SECTION B: APPLIED EARTH SCIENCE. *see* MINES AND MINING INDUSTRY

INSTITUTE OF MATERIALS, MINERALS AND MINING. TRANSACTIONS. SECTION C: MINERAL PROCESSING & EXTRACTIVE METALLURGY. *see* MINES AND MINING INDUSTRY

669 GBR ISSN 0443-3726
INSTITUTE OF METAL FINISHING. BULLETIN. Text in English. 1951. q. **Document type:** *Bulletin.*
Formerly: E T S Bulletin
Related titles: ◆ Supplement to: Institute of Metal Finishing. Transactions. ISSN 0020-2967.
Published by: Institute of Metal Finishing, Exeter House, 48 Holloway Head, Birmingham, Warks B1 1NG, United Kingdom. TEL 44-121-6227387, FAX 44-121-6666316, exeterhouse@instituteofmetalfinishing.org, http://www.uk-finishing.org.uk.

669 GBR ISSN 0020-2967
TS200.I475 CODEN: TIMFA2
➤ **INSTITUTE OF METAL FINISHING. TRANSACTIONS;** the international journal for surface engineering and coatings. Text in English. 1951. bi-m. GBP 408 combined subscription to institutions (print & online eds.); USD 769 combined subscription in United States to institutions (print & online eds.) (effective 2012). adv. bk.rev. abstr.; charts; illus. back issues avail.; reprint service avail. from PSC. **Document type:** *Journal, Academic/Scholarly.* **Description:** Provides international coverage of all aspects of surface finishing and surface engineering, from fundamental research to in-service applications.
Formerly (until 1954): Electrodepositors' Technical Society. Journal (0368-2056)
Related titles: Online - full text ed.: ISSN 1745-9192. GBP 369 to institutions; USD 695 in United States to institutions (effective 2012) (from IngentaConnect); ◆ Supplement(s): Institute of Metal Finishing. Bulletin. ISSN 0443-3726.
Indexed: A10, A22, A28, APA, ASCA, BrCerAb, C&ISA, C33, CA, CA/WCA, CIA, CISA, CPEI, CTE, CerAb, ChemAb, CivEngAb, CoppAb, CorrAb, CurCont, E&CAJ, E11, EEA, EMA, ESPM, EngInd, EnvEAb, H15, Inspec, M&TEA, M09, MBF, METADEX, MSCI, SCI, SCOPUS, SolStAb, T02, T04, TM, V03, W07, WAA, WSCA.
—BLDSC (8941.000000), CASDDS, IE, Infotrieve, Ingenta, INIST, Linda Hall. **CCC.**
Published by: (Institute of Metal Finishing), Maney Publishing, Ste 1C, Joseph's Well, Hanover Walk, Leeds, W Yorks LS3 1AB, United Kingdom. TEL 44-113-2432800, FAX 44-113-3868178, maney@maney.co.uk, http://www.maney.co.uk. Ed. Dr. Sheelagh Campbell. Adv. contact Robin Fox TEL 44-20-73060300 ext 231. **Subscr. in N America to:** Maney Publishing, 875 Massachusetts Ave, 7th Fl, Cambridge, MA 02139. TEL 866-297-5154, FAX 617-354-6875, maney@maneyusa.com.

669 SWE ISSN 0015-7953
INSTITUTET FOER METALLFORSKNING. FORSKNINGSVERKSAMHETEN. Text in Swedish. 1952. a. free. bibl.; illus. **Document type:** *Corporate.*
Published by: Institutet foer Metallforskning/Swedish Institute for Metals Research, Drottning Kristinas vaeg 48, Stockholm, 11428, Sweden. FAX 46-8-440-45-35. Ed. Staffan Ekelund. Circ: 2,400.

669 SWE ISSN 1403-848X
INSTITUTET FOR METALFARSKNING. FORSKNINGSRAPPORT/ SWEDISH INSTITUTE FOR METALS RESEARCH. RESEARCH REPORT. Text in Swedish. irreg. **Document type:** *Monographic series, Academic/Scholarly.*
Indexed: A28, APA, BrCerAb, C&ISA, CA/WCA, CIA, CerAb, CivEngAb, CorrAb, E&CAJ, E11, EEA, EMA, H15, M&TEA, M09, MBF, METADEX, SolStAb, T04, WAA.
Published by: Institutet foer Metallforskning/Swedish Institute for Metals Research, Drottning Kristinas Vag 48, Stockholm, 114 28, Sweden. TEL 46-8-4404800, FAX 46-8-4404535, info@simr.se, http://www.simr.se.

669 IND
TN1 CODEN: JIMDEQ
➤ **INSTITUTION OF ENGINEERS (INDIA). METALLURGICAL & MATERIALS ENGINEERING DIVISION. JOURNAL.** Text in English. 1983. s-a. INR 600 (effective 2011). adv. charts; illus. index. **Document type:** *Journal, Academic/Scholarly.*
Formerly: Institution of Engineers (India). Metallurgy and Material Science Division. Journal (0257-4411)
Indexed: A28, APA, BrCerAb, C&ISA, CA/WCA, CIA, CIN, CPEI, CerAb, ChemAb, ChemTitl, CivEngAb, CorrAb, E&CAJ, E11, EEA, EMA, ESPM, EngInd, EnvEAb, H15, Inspec, M&TEA, M09, MBF, METADEX, SCOPUS, SolStAb, T04, WAA.
—BLDSC (4794.039500), AskIEEE, CASDDS, IE, Ingenta, INIST, Linda Hall.
Published by: (Metallurgical & Materials Engineering Division), The Institution of Engineers (India), 8 Gokhale Rd, Kolkata, West Bengal 700 020, India. TEL 91-33-40155400, technical@ieindia.org.

➤ **INSTITUTION OF ENGINEERS (INDIA). MINING ENGINEERING DIVISION. JOURNAL.** *see* MINES AND MINING INDUSTRY

➤ **INSTITUTO GEOLOGICO MINERO Y METALURGICO. BOLETIN. SERIE D. ESTUDIOS REGIONALES.** *see* MINES AND MINING INDUSTRY

621.74 ROM ISSN 1453-0392
INSTITUTULUI NATIONAL DE CERCETARE-DEZVOLTARE IN SUDURA. BULETINUL. Text in Romanian. 1997. q.
Indexed: A28, APA, BrCerAb, C&ISA, CA/WCA, CIA, CerAb, CivEngAb, CorrAb, E&CAJ, E11, EEA, EMA, ESPM, EnvEAb, H15, M&TEA, M09, MBF, METADEX, SolStAb, T04, WAA, Weldasearch.
—Linda Hall.
Published by: (Institutul National de Cercetare-Dezvoltare in Sudura si Incercari de Materiale), Editura Sudura S.R.L., Bv Mihai Viteazul 30, 5, Timisoara, 1441, Romania.

669 POL ISSN 0137-9941
TN4 CODEN: PIMZDL
➤ **INSTYTUT METALURGII ZELAZA. PRACE/INSTITUTE OF FERROUS METALLURGY. TRANSACTIONS.** Text in Polish; Summaries in English, Russian. 1949. q. USD 130 foreign (effective 2002). **Document type:** *Academic/Scholarly.* **Description:** Covers production of iron and steel and further processing of steel.
Indexed: B22, ChemAb, IMMAb, TM.
—CASDDS, INIST, Linda Hall.
Published by: Instytut Metalurgii Zelaza, Ul K Miarki 12, Gliwice, 44100, Poland. TEL 48-32-2345200, FAX 48-32-2345300, imz@imz.gliwice.pl. Ed. Adam Schwedler. Circ: 400.

669 POL ISSN 0867-583X
INSTYTUT SPAWALNICTWA. BIULETYN/POLISH CENTRE OF WELDING TECHNOLOGY. JOURNAL. Text in Polish. 1977. q. EUR 127 foreign (effective 2006).
Formerly (until 1991): Instytut Spawalnictwa. Prace (0137-267X)
Indexed: A28, APA, B22, BrCerAb, C&ISA, CA/WCA, CIA, CerAb, CivEngAb, CorrAb, E&CAJ, E11, EEA, EMA, ESPM, EnvEAb, H15, M&TEA, M09, MBF, METADEX, SolStAb, T04, WAA.
—Linda Hall.
Published by: Instytut Spawalnictwa v Gliwicach/Polish Centre of Welding Technology, Bl Czeslawa 16/18, Gliwice, 44-100, Poland. TEL 48-32-2310011, FAX 48-32-2314652, is@is.gliwice.pl, http://www.is.gliwice.pl. **Dist. by:** Ars Polona, Obroncow 25, Warsaw 03933, Poland. TEL 48-22-5098609, FAX 48-22-5098610, arspolona@arspolona.com.pl, http://www.arspolona.com.pl.

INTERFAX. CHINA COMMODITIES DAILY - ENERGY & METALS. *see* BUSINESS AND ECONOMICS—Investments

INTERFAX. RUSSIA METALS & MINING WEEKLY. *see* MINES AND MINING INDUSTRY

540 620.1 GBR ISSN 0966-9795
TN689 CODEN: IERME5
➤ **INTERMETALLICS.** Text in English. 1993. 12/yr. EUR 2,477 in Europe to institutions; JPY 329,100 in Japan to institutions; USD 2,772 elsewhere to institutions (effective 2012). adv. bk.rev. abstr. index. back issues avail. **Document type:** *Journal, Academic/Scholarly.* **Description:** Covers all aspects of ordered chemical compounds between two or more metals, including fundamental chemistry, microstructure, dynamics and stress as well as applications in processing and synthesis, multiphase intermetallic alloys in dentistry, and applications of hard magnetic materials incorporating rare earth metals.
Related titles: Microform ed.: (from PQC); Online - full text ed.: ISSN 1879-0216 (from IngentaConnect, ScienceDirect).
Indexed: A01, A03, A08, A26, A28, APA, ASCA, BrCerAb, C&ISA, C24, C33, CA, CA/WCA, CCI, CIA, CIN, CPEI, CerAb, ChemAb, ChemTitl, CivEngAb, CorrAb, CurCont, E&CAJ, E11, EEA, EMA, ESPM, EngInd, EnvEAb, H15, I05, ISR, Inspec, M&TEA, M09, MBF, METADEX, MSCI, RefZh, SCI, SCOPUS, SolStAb, T02, T04, TM, W07, WAA.
—BLDSC (4534.562000), AskIEEE, CASDDS, IE, Infotrieve, Ingenta, Linda Hall. **CCC.**
Published by: Elsevier Ltd (Subsidiary of: Elsevier Science & Technology), The Blvd, Langford Ln, Kidlington, Oxford, OX5 1GB, United Kingdom. TEL 44-1865-843000, FAX 44-1865-843010. Eds. C T Liu, David Morris, G Sauthoff. **Subscr. to:** Elsevier BV, Radarweg 29, PO Box 211, Amsterdam 1000 AE, Netherlands. TEL 31-20-4853757, FAX 31-20-4853432, JournalsCustomerServiceEMEA@elsevier.com, http://www.elsevier.nl.

669.722 DEU
TS550 CODEN: ALUMAB
INTERNATIONAL ALUMINIUM JOURNAL. Text in English, German. 1919. m. EUR 285 domestic; EUR 289 in Europe; USD 375 elsewhere (effective 2009). adv. bk.rev. abstr.; bibl.; charts; illus.; stat. index. **Document type:** *Magazine, Trade.*
Formerly (until 2008): Aluminium (0002-6689)
Related titles: Online - full text ed.
Indexed: A22, A28, APA, BrCerAb, C&ISA, CA/WCA, CIA, CerAb, ChemAb, CivEngAb, CorrAb, E&CAJ, E11, EEA, EMA, ESPM, EnvEAb, GeoRef, H15, IPackAb, Inspec, M&TEA, M09, MBF, METADEX, PST, SolStAb, SpeleolAb, T04, TM, WAA.
—BLDSC (4535.685500), AskIEEE, CASDDS, IE, Infotrieve, Ingenta, INIST, Linda Hall. **CCC.**
Published by: (Aluminium-Zentrale e.V.), Giesel Verlag GmbH (Subsidiary of: Schluetersche Verlagsgesellschaft mbH und Co. KG), Rehkamp 3, Isernhagen, 30916, Germany. TEL 49-511-73040, FAX 49-511-7304157, giesel@giesel.de, http://www.giesel.de. Ed. Volker Karow. Adv. contact Stefan Schwichtenberg TEL 49-511-7304142. B&W page EUR 1,560, color page EUR 2,565; trim 210 x 297. Circ: 2,279 (paid and controlled).

669.4 GBR
TA480.L4 CODEN: ICLPAY
INTERNATIONAL CONFERENCE ON LEAD. CONFERENCE PROCEEDINGS. Text in English. 1962. triennial. **Document type:** *Proceedings.*
Formerly: International Conference on Lead. Proceedings (0074-316X)
—CASDDS.
Published by: International Lead Association, 17a Welbeck Way, London, W1G 9YJ, United Kingdom. TEL 44-20-74998422, FAX 44-20-74931555, enq@ila-lead.org, http://www.ila-lead.org/. Circ: 1,000.

669 692.1 USA ISSN 0074-6118
INTERNATIONAL FOUNDRY CONGRESS. PAPERS AND COMMUNICATIONS. (Papers published in host countries) Text in English. a. price varies. **Document type:** *Proceedings.*
Formerly: World Foundry Congress
Indexed: ChemAb.
Address: c/o American Foundrymens Society, 505 State St, Des Plaines, IL 60016. TEL 708-824-0181, FAX 708-824-7848.

671.36 GBR ISSN 1749-5148
INTERNATIONAL HEAT TREATMENT AND SURFACE ENGINEERING. Text in English. 2007. q. GBP 220 combined subscription to institutions (print & online eds.); USD 440 combined subscription in United States to institutions (print & online eds.) (effective 2012). adv. reprint service avail. from PSC. **Document type:** *Journal, Academic/Scholarly.* **Description:** Covers topics ranging from science and engineering, analysis and testing to process development and business related issues, supplemented by industry and event news.
Related titles: Online - full text ed.: ISSN 1749-5156. GBP 198 to institutions; USD 396 in United States to institutions (effective 2012) (from IngentaConnect).
Indexed: CPEI, SCOPUS.
—BLDSC (4540.721650), IE. **CCC.**
Published by: (International Federation of Heat Treatment and Surface Engineering, Chinese Heat Treatment Society CHN, Shanghai Jiao Tong University CHN, Institute of Materials, Minerals and Mining), Maney Publishing, Ste 1C, Joseph's Well, Hanover Walk, Leeds, W Yorks LS3 1AB, United Kingdom. TEL 44-113-2432800, FAX 44-113-3868178, maney@maney.co.uk. Eds. Shipu Chen, Tom Bell. **Subscr. in N. America to:** Maney Publishing, 875 Massachusetts Ave, 7th Fl, Cambridge, MA 02139. TEL 866-297-5154, FAX 617-354-6875, maney@maneyusa.com.

338.2 672 BEL
INTERNATIONAL IRON AND STEEL INSTITUTE. SUMMARIES OF CONFERENCE REPORTS. Text in English. 1967. a. free to members; EUR 30 per issue to non-members (effective 2001). charts; illus.; stat. **Document type:** *Proceedings.* **Description:** Includes summaries of conference presentations.
Former titles (until 1998): International Iron and Steel Institute. Annual Conference Report; (until 1996): International Iron and Steel Institute. Report of Conference Proceedings (0074-6630)
Published by: International Iron and Steel Institute, Rue Colonel Bourg 120, Brussels, 1140, Belgium. TEL 32-2-702-8900, FAX 32-2-702-8899.

669 620 GBR ISSN 1364-0461
➤ **THE INTERNATIONAL JOURNAL OF CAST METALS RESEARCH.** Text in English. 1988. bi-m. GBP 410 combined subscription to institutions (print & online eds.); USD 662 combined subscription in United States to institutions (print & online eds.) (effective 2012). adv. charts; illus. back issues avail.; reprint service avail. from PSC. **Document type:** *Journal, Academic/Scholarly.* **Description:** Devoted to the dissemination of information on the science and engineering of cast metals, solidification and casting processes.
Formerly (until 1996): Cast Metals (0953-4962)
Related titles: Online - full text ed.: ISSN 1743-1336. 2004. GBP 371 to institutions; USD 598 in United States to institutions (effective 2012) (from IngentaConnect).
Indexed: A01, A28, APA, BrCerAb, C&ISA, CA, CA/WCA, CIA, CerAb, CivEngAb, CorrAb, CurCont, E&CAJ, E11, EEA, EMA, ESPM, EnvEAb, H15, Inspec, M&TEA, M09, MBF, METADEX, MSCI, SCI, SCOPUS, SolStAb, T02, T04, W07, WAA.
—BLDSC (4542.161300), IE, Infotrieve, Ingenta. **CCC.**
Published by: Maney Publishing, Ste 1C, Joseph's Well, Hanover Walk, Leeds, W Yorks LS3 1AB, United Kingdom. TEL 44-113-2432800, FAX 44-113-3868178, maney@maney.co.uk. Eds. D M Stefanescu, Hideyuki Yasuda, N R Green. **Subscr. in N America to:** Maney Publishing, 875 Massachusetts Ave, 7th Fl, Cambridge, MA 02139. TEL 866-297-5154, FAX 617-354-6875, maney@maneyusa.com.

669 DEU ISSN 1862-5282
CODEN: IJMRFV
INTERNATIONAL JOURNAL OF MATERIALS RESEARCH. Text in German; Summaries in English. 1911. m. EUR 698 combined subscription to individuals (print & online eds.); EUR 1,298 combined subscription to institutions (print & online eds.); EUR 63.90 newsstand/cover (effective 2011). adv. bk.rev. charts; illus.; pat. index. **Document type:** *Journal, Trade.* **Description:** Contains topical and up-to-date coverage of current research progress in the field of materials science.
Former titles (until 2006): Zeitschrift fuer Metallkunde (0044-3093); (until 1948): Metallforschung (0179-4833); (until 1946): Zeitschrift fuer Metallkunde (0179-4841); (until 1919): Internationale Zeitschrift fuer Metallographie (0368-0975)
Related titles: Microform ed.: (from PMC); Online - full text ed.
Indexed: A20, A22, A28, APA, ASCA, ApMecR, BrCerAb, C&ISA, C24, C33, CA/WCA, CCI, CEABA, CIA, CIN, CPEI, CerAb, ChemAb, ChemTitl, CivEngAb, CoppAb, CorrAb, CurCR, CurCont, E&CAJ, E11, EEA, EMA, ESPM, EngInd, EnvEAb, GeoRef, H15, IBR, IBZ, INIS AtomInd, ISMEC, ISR, Inspec, M&TEA, M09, MBF, METADEX, MSCI, R16, SCI, SCOPUS, SolStAb, SpeleolAb, T04, TM, W07, WAA.
—BLDSC (4542.336100), AskIEEE, CASDDS, IE, Infotrieve, Ingenta, INIST, Linda Hall. **CCC.**
Published by: (Deutsche Gesellschaft fuer Materialkunde e.V.), Carl Hanser Verlag GmbH & Co. KG, Kolbergerstr 22, Munich, 81679, Germany. TEL 49-89-998300, FAX 49-89-984809, info@hanser.de. Ed. M Ruehle. Adv. contact Hermann Kleiner. Circ: 800 (paid and controlled).

669 USA ISSN 1939-5981
TS236
➤ **INTERNATIONAL JOURNAL OF METALCASTING.** Abbreviated title: I J M C. Text in English. 2007 (Fall). q. USD 129 in North America to non-members; USD 179 elsewhere to non-members; USD 99 in North America to members; USD 149 elsewhere to members (effective 2010). back issues avail.; reprints avail. **Document type:** *Journal, Academic/Scholarly.* **Description:** Covers the transfer of research and technology for the metalcasting industry.
Related titles: Online - full text ed.
Indexed: A01, A28, APA, BrCerAb, C&ISA, CA, CA/WCA, CIA, CPEI, CerAb, CivEngAb, CorrAb, CurCont, E&CAJ, E11, EEA, EMA, ESPM, EnvEAb, H15, M&TEA, M09, MBF, METADEX, MSCI, SCI, SolStAb, T02, T04, W07, WAA.
—BLDSC (4542.352235), IE.
Published by: American Foundry Society, 1695 N Penny Ln, Schaumburg, IL 60173. TEL 847-824-0181, 800-537-4237, FAX 847-824-7848, library@afsinc.org, http://www.afsinc.org. Ed. Tom Prucha. Pub. Alfred Spada TEL 847-824-0181 ext 281.

➤ **INTERNATIONAL JOURNAL OF MINERAL PROCESSING.** *see* MINES AND MINING INDUSTRY

➤ **INTERNATIONAL JOURNAL OF MINERALS METALLURGY AND MATERIALS.** *see* MINES AND MINING INDUSTRY

➤ **INTERNATIONAL JOURNAL OF MINING, RECLAMATION AND ENVIRONMENT.** *see* MINES AND MINING INDUSTRY

669 621 GBR ISSN 1368-9290
TS247 CODEN: IJNPFU
➤ **INTERNATIONAL JOURNAL OF NON-EQUILIBRIUM PROCESSING.** Text in English. 1984. 4/yr. GBP 179, USD 329 (effective 2010). back issues avail. **Document type:** *Journal, Academic/Scholarly.* **Description:** Covers science and technology of rapid solidification and allied processes and the formation, structure, properties, and application of its products.
Formerly (until 1997): International Journal of Rapid Solidification (0265-0916)
Indexed: A22, A28, APA, ASCA, BrCerAb, C&ISA, CA/WCA, CIA, CIN, CPEI, CerAb, ChemAb, ChemTitl, CivEngAb, CorrAb, E&CAJ, E11, EEA, EMA, EngInd, H15, ISMEC, Inspec, M&TEA, M09, MBF, METADEX, SCOPUS, SolStAb, T04, WAA.
—BLDSC (4542.387500), AskIEEE, CASDDS, IE, Infotrieve, Ingenta, INIST, Linda Hall. **CCC.**
Published by: A B Academic Publishers, The Old Vicarage, Church St, Bicester, Oxon OX26 6AY, United Kingdom. TEL 44-1869-320949, jrnls@abapubl.demon.co.uk.

669 USA ISSN 0888-7462
TN695 CODEN: IPMTEA
INTERNATIONAL JOURNAL OF POWDER METALLURGY. Text in English. 1965. bi-m. USD 85 worldwide to individuals; USD 210 in US & Canada to institutions; USD 235 elsewhere to institutions (effective 2006). adv. bk.rev. abstr.; charts; stat.; pat.; tr.lit. Index. 72 p./no.; back issues avail. **Document type:** *Journal, Trade.* **Description:** Covers research, engineering, production, product, and news of business developments and trends. Features news items and articles on the industry, companies and people.
Incorporates (1972-1996): P - M Technology Newsletter (0734-4805); Which was formerly (until 1982): P - M Technology (0146-972X); Former titles (until 1986): International Journal of Powder Metallurgy and Powder Technology (0361-3488); (until 1974): International Journal of Powder Metallurgy (0020-7535)
Related titles: Microform ed.: (from PQC).
Indexed: A05, A22, A23, A24, A28, APA, AS&TA, AS&TI, ASCA, B04, B13, BrCerAb, C&ISA, C10, C33, CA, CA/WCA, CIA, CIN, CPEI, Cadscan, CerAb, ChemAb, ChemTitl, CivEngAb, CoppAb, CorrAb, CurCont, E&CAJ, E11, EEA, EMA, ESPM, EngInd, EnvEAb, H15, ISR, Inspec, LeadAb, M&TEA, M09, MBF, METADEX, MSCI, RefZh, SCI, SCOPUS, SolStAb, T02, T04, TM, W07, WAA, Zincscan.
—BLDSC (4542.477000), CASDDS, IE, Infotrieve, Ingenta, INIST, Linda Hall. **CCC.**
Published by: (American Powder Metallurgy Institute), A P M I International, 105 College Rd E, Princeton, NJ 08540-6692. TEL 609-452-7700, FAX 609-987-8523, apmi@mpif.org, http://www.mpif.org. Ed. Alan Lawley. Pub. C James Trombino. R&P James Adams. Circ: 3,200 (paid and free).

669 GBR ISSN 0958-0611
TN700 CODEN: IRMME3
➤ **INTERNATIONAL JOURNAL OF REFRACTORY METALS AND HARD MATERIALS.** Abbreviated title: I J R M H M. Text in English. 1982. 6/yr. EUR 1,151 in Europe to institutions; JPY 152,400 in Japan to institutions; USD 1,284 elsewhere to institutions (effective 2012). adv. back issues avail. **Document type:** *Journal, Academic/Scholarly.* **Description:** Features papers concerned with all aspects of the science, technology and application of refractory metals and hard materials.
Formerly (until 1989): International Journal of Refractory and Hard Metals (0263-4368)
Related titles: Microform ed.: (from PQC); Online - full text ed.: (from IngentaConnect, ScienceDirect).
Indexed: A01, A03, A08, A22, A26, A28, APA, ASCA, BrCerAb, C&ISA, C24, C33, CA, CA/WCA, CIA, CIN, CPEI, CTE, CerAb, ChemAb, ChemTitl, CivEngAb, CorrAb, CurCont, E&CAJ, E11, EEA, EMA, ESPM, EngInd, EnvEAb, H15, I05, Inspec, M&TEA, M09, MBF, METADEX, MSCI, P30, RefZh, S01, SCI, SCOPUS, SolStAb, T02, T04, TM, W07, WAA.
—BLDSC (4542.525420), AskIEEE, CASDDS, IE, Ingenta, INIST. **CCC.**
Published by: (International Plansee Society for Powder Metallurgy), Elsevier Ltd (Subsidiary of: Elsevier Science & Technology), The Blvd, Langford Ln, Kidlington, Oxford, OX5 1GB, United Kingdom. TEL 44-1865-843000, FAX 44-1865-843010, journalscustomerserviceemea@elsevier.com. Ed. H M Ortner. **Subscr. to:** Elsevier BV, Radarweg 29, PO Box 211, Amsterdam 1000 AE, Netherlands. TEL 31-20-4853757, FAX 31-20-4853432, http://www.elsevier.nl.

➤ **INTERNATIONAL JOURNAL OF SELF-PROPAGATING HIGH-TEMPERATURE SYNTHESIS.** *see* PHYSICS—Heat

669 USA
INTERNATIONAL MAGNESIUM ASSOCIATION. BUYER'S GUIDE. Text in English. 1992. biennial. free to members (effective 2010). **Document type:** *Directory, Trade.* **Description:** Lists companies offering metallic magnesium products and services.
Related titles: Online - full text ed.
Published by: International Magnesium Association, 1000 N Rand Rd, Ste 214, Wauconda, IL 60084. TEL 847-526-2010, FAX 847-526-3993, info@intlmag.org.

671 USA ISSN 0161-5769
TN799.M2
INTERNATIONAL MAGNESIUM ASSOCIATION. WORLD MAGNESIUM CONFERENCE. PROCEEDINGS. Text in English. 1943. a. USD 300 to non-members; USD 200 to members (effective 2010). back issues avail. **Document type:** *Proceedings, Academic/Scholarly.* **Description:** Provides information about World Magnesium Conference.
Formerly (until 1983): World Magnesium Conference & Exposition. Proceedings
Related titles: CD-ROM ed.: USD 250 to non-members; USD 150 to members (effective 2010).
Published by: International Magnesium Association, 1000 N Rand Rd, Ste 214, Wauconda, IL 60084. TEL 847-526-2010, FAX 847-526-3993, info@intlmag.org.

671.3 CHE ISSN 0074-6983
INTERNATIONAL METALWORKERS' CONGRESS. REPORTS. Text in English. quadrennial. USD 10. **Document type:** *Proceedings.*
Published by: International Metalworkers Federation, 54 bis, Rte. des Acacias, Geneva, 1227, Switzerland. FAX 022-3431510.

671.823 GBR ISSN 1471-6542
INTERNATIONAL SHEET METAL REVIEW. Abbreviated title: I S M R. Text in English. 1999. bi-m. GBP 90 (effective 2009). adv. back issues avail. **Document type:** *Magazine, Trade.*
Published by: T R M G Ltd, Winchester Court, 1 Forum Place, Hatfield, Herts AL10 0RN, United Kingdom. TEL 44-1707-273999, FAX 44-1707-276555, tracey@trmg.co.uk, http://www.trmg.co.uk. Ed. Sara Waddington. Adv. contact Arfan Qureshi. color page GBP 2,908; trim 210 x 297.

669 338.476 GBR ISSN 1369-8605
INTERNATIONAL STEEL REVIEW. Abbreviated title: I S R. Text in English. 1995. m. GBP 1,130 combined subscription domestic (print & online eds.); GBP 1,145 combined subscription foreign (print & online eds.); GBP 225 per issue (effective 2010). back issues avail. **Document type:** *Newsletter, Trade.* **Description:** Covers the domestic steel pricing data for flat and long products in eleven countries across the globe, including - United States, Canada, China, Japan, South Korea, Taiwan, Poland, Czech/Slovak Republics and the main five EU member states - covering 70% of world consumption.
Related titles: Online - full text ed.
Indexed: A28, APA, BrCerAb, C&ISA, CA/WCA, CIA, CerAb, CivEngAb, CorrAb, E&CAJ, E11, EEA, EMA, H15, M&TEA, M09, MBF, METADEX, SolStAb, T04, WAA.
—Linda Hall.
Published by: M E P S (International) Ltd, 263 Glossop Rd, Sheffield, S Yorkshire S10 2GZ, United Kingdom. TEL 44-114-2750570, FAX 44-114-2759808, subs@meps.co.uk.

669 USA
INTERNATIONAL TITANIUM ASSOCIATION. (YEAR) BUYERS GUIDE. Abbreviated title: I T A Buyers Guide. Text in English. a. USD 20 to non-members; free to members (effective 2011). **Document type:** *Directory, Trade.* **Description:** Offers detailed company information on over 100 of the world's leading titanium companies.
Published by: International Titanium Association, 2655 W Midway Blvd, Ste 300, Broomfield, CO 80020. TEL 303-404-2221, FAX 303-404-9111, info@titanium.org.

669 USA
INTERNATIONAL TITANIUM ASSOCIATION. INTERNATIONAL CONFERENCE ON TITANIUM PRODUCTS AND APPLICATIONS. PROCEEDINGS. Text in English. a. USD 245 per issue (effective 2011). **Document type:** *Proceedings, Trade.* **Description:** Contain information on aerospace, industrial and medical applications, new powder metallurgy, processing and heat treating, corrosion technology and applications, and raw materials.
Formerly: Titanium Development Association. International Conference on Titanium Products and Applications. Proceedings
Published by: International Titanium Association, 2655 W Midway Blvd, Ste 300, Broomfield, CO 80020. TEL 303-404-2221, FAX 303-404-9111, info@titanium.org, http://www.titanium.org.

669.1 IND ISSN 0578-7661
IRON & STEEL REVIEW. Text in English. 1957. 14/yr. INR 7,000, USD 650 (effective 2011). adv. bk.rev. back issues avail. **Document type:** *Magazine, Trade.* **Description:** It is a Global Publication on Steel & Heavy Engineering.
Indexed: TM.
Published by: I S R Infomedia Ltd., Merlin Links, 5th Fl, Block 5E & F 166B, S.P. Mukherjee Rd, Kolkata, 700 026, India. TEL 91-33-24658581, FAX 91-33-24653790, isrinfo@eth.net, http://www.isrinfomedia.com.

669.142 USA ISSN 1547-0423
TS300 CODEN: ISTRCO
➤ **IRON & STEEL TECHNOLOGY.** Text in English. 2004. m. USD 155 In US,Canada & Mexico; USD 195 elsewhere; USD 20 per issue In US,Canada & mexico; USD 25 per issue elsewhere; free membership (effective 2011). adv. back issues avail. **Document type:** *Journal, Academic/Scholarly.* **Description:** Covers latest information on breakthroughs and trends in equipment, processes and operating practices in the international iron and steelmaking industry.
Formed by the merger of (1924-2004): A I S E Steel Technology (1528-5855); Which was formerly (until 1999): Iron and Steel Engineer (0021-1559); (1974-2004): Iron and Steelmaker (0275-8687); Which was formerly (until 1980): I and S M (0097-8388)
Related titles: Online - full content ed.
Indexed: A22, A28, APA, BrCerAb, C&ISA, CA/WCA, CIA, CPEI, CerAb, CivEngAb, CorrAb, E&CAJ, E11, EEA, EMA, ESPM, EngInd, EnvEAb, H15, Inspec, M&TEA, M09, MBF, METADEX, SCOPUS, SolStAb, T04, TM, WAA.
—BLDSC (4580.340000), IE, Ingenta, INIST, Linda Hall.
Published by: Association for Iron & Steel Technology, 186 Thorn Hill Rd, Warrendale, PA 15086. TEL 724-814-3000, FAX 724-814-3001, info@aistech.org, http://www.aistech.org.

338.476691 GBR ISSN 1754-4254
IRON & STEEL TODAY. Text in English. 2007. 5/yr. GBP 93 domestic; GBP 103 foreign; free to qualified personnel (effective 2009). adv. **Document type:** *Magazine, Trade.* **Description:** Provides information for managers involved in the purchase of plant, equipment and materials employed within an iron and steelworks or fabrication plant such as rolling mill and stock holder.
—CCC.
Published by: Modern Media Communications Ltd, Gresham House, 54 High St, Shoreham by Sea, West Sussex BN43 5DB, United Kingdom. TEL 44-1273-453033, FAX 44-1273-453085, info@mmcpublications.co.uk. Ed., Adv. contact Paul Binns. page GBP 1,950, page EUR 3,025, page USD 3,900; trim 210 x 297. Circ: 5,000.

669.1 GBR ISSN 0075-0875
IRON AND STEEL WORKS OF THE WORLD (YEAR). Text in English. 1952. biennial. GBP 407, EUR 617, USD 897 per issue (effective 2010). adv. back issues avail. **Document type:** *Directory, Trade.* **Description:** Contains details of the world's producers of iron, raw, rolled and coated steel, as well as key data on iron-ore mining companies and those active in the global seaborne market.
Related titles: CD-ROM ed.: ISSN 1755-5590.
—BLDSC (4580.405700). **CCC.**
Published by: Metal Bulletin Plc. (Subsidiary of: Euromoney Institutional Investor Plc.), Nestor House, Playhouse Yard, London, EC4V 5EX, United Kingdom. TEL 44-20-77797390, FAX 44-20-77797389, help@metalbulletin.com, http://www.metalbulletin.com. Adv. contact Stefano di Nardo TEL 44-20-78275220.

IRONWORKER. *see* LABOR UNIONS

669.1 ZAF ISSN 0019-0594
ISCOR NEWS. Text in English. 1936. bi-m. free. charts; illus.; stat. **Document type:** *Newsletter, Corporate.* **Description:** Covers the latest techniques, productivity improvements and developments in metallurgy, as well as other corporate activities.
Related titles: CD-ROM ed.; Online - full text ed.
Indexed: ISAP.
Published by: (Iscor Limited/Yscor Beperk), Fox Publishing, PO Box 2496, Parklands, Johannesburg 2121, South Africa. TEL 27-11-482-1415, FAX 27-11-482-1415, garys@hq.iscorltd.co.za, gibbs@fox.co.za, http://www.iscorltd.co.za, http://www.aztec.co.za/biz/fox. Ed. Gary N Scallan. Circ: 28,000.

669.142 BGD
ISPAT (CHITTAGONG). Text in Bengali, English. 1973. a. free. adv.
Published by: Chittagong Steel Mills Ltd., PO Box 429, Chittagong, Bangladesh. Circ: 2,500.

669 RUS ISSN 0368-0797
CODEN: IVUMAX
IZVESTIYA VYSSHIKH UCHEBNYKH ZAVEDENII. CHERNAYA METALLURGIYA. Text in Russian. 1958. m. USD 199.95 in United States. **Document type:** *Journal, Academic/Scholarly.*
Indexed: INIS AtomInd, SCOPUS.
—CCC.
Published by: Moskovskii Gosudarstvennyi Institut Stali i Splavov, Leninskii pr-t 4, Moscow, 117936, Russian Federation. TEL 7-095-2361427, FAX 7-095-2361427. Ed. V A Grigorian. **Dist. by:** East View Information Services, 10601 Wayzata Blvd, Minneapolis, MN 55305. TEL 952-252-1201, 800-477-1005, FAX 952-252-1202, info@eastview.com, http://www.eastview.com.

669 RUS ISSN 0021-3438
CODEN: IVUTAK
➤ **IZVESTIYA VYSSHIKH UCHEBNYKH ZAVEDENII. TSVETNAYA METALLURGIYA.** Text in Russian. 1958. bi-m. USD 205 foreign (effective 2005). **Document type:** *Journal, Academic/Scholarly.* **Description:** Publishes original research papers and critical reviews on most aspects of physical metallurgy and material science.
Related titles: ◆ English Translation: Russian Journal of Non-Ferrous Metals. ISSN 1067-8212.
Indexed: A22, C33, CorrAb, RefZh, SCOPUS, WAA.
—BLDSC (0077.960000), East View, IE, Ingenta, INIST, Linda Hall. **CCC.**
Published by: Moskovskii Institut Stali i Splavov/Moscow Institute of Steel and Alloys, Leninskii prospekt 4, Moscow, 119991, Russian Federation. TEL 7-095-2372222, FAX 7-095-2378007, welcome@ir.misis.ru, http://www.ir.misis.ru. **Dist. by:** East View Information Services, 10601 Wayzata Blvd, Minneapolis, MN 55305. TEL 952-252-1201, 800-477-1005, FAX 952-252-1202, info@eastview.com, http://www.eastview.com.

669 JPN ISSN 1348-0669
J F E GIHOU. Text in Japanese. 2003. q. **Document type:** *Journal, Academic/Scholarly.*
Formed by the merger of (1980-2003): Kawasaki Steel Technical Report (0388-9475); (1988-2003): N K K Giho (0915-0536); Which was formerly (1955-1998): Nippon Kokan Giho (0468-2815)
Related titles: ◆ English ed.: J F E Technical Report. ISSN 1348-0677.
—BLDSC (4668.387260), Linda Hall.
Published by: J F E R & D Corp., 1-1 Minamiwatarida-cho, Kawasaki-ku, Kawasaki, 260-0835, Japan. TEL 81-43-2622051, FAX 81-43-2622061, http://www.jfe-rd.co.jp/en/index.html.

669 JPN ISSN 1348-0677
TS300
J F E TECHNICAL REPORT. Text in English. 2003. q. **Document type:** *Journal, Academic/Scholarly.*
Formed by the merger of (1980-2003): Kawasaki Steel Technical Report (0388-9475); (1988-2003): N K K Technical Review (0915-0544); Which was formerly (1963-1988): Nippon Kokan Technical Report Overseas (0546-1731)
Related titles: ◆ Japanese ed.: J F E Gihou. ISSN 1348-0669.
Indexed: A28, APA, BrCerAb, C&ISA, CA/WCA, CIA, CPEI, CerAb, CivEngAb, CorrAb, E&CAJ, E11, EEA, EMA, ESPM, EngInd, EnvEAb, H15, M&TEA, M09, MBF, METADEX, RefZh, SCOPUS, SolStAb, T04, TM, WAA.
—BLDSC (4668.387270), INIST, Linda Hall.
Published by: J F E R & D Corp., 1-1 Minamiwatarida-cho, Kawasaki-ku, Kawasaki, 260-0835, Japan. TEL 81-43-2622051, FAX 81-43-2622061.

669 USA ISSN 1047-4838
TN1 CODEN: JOMMER
➤ **J O M.** (Journal of Metals) Text in English. 1949. m. EUR 303, USD 357 combined subscription to institutions (print & online eds.) (effective 2012). bk.rev.; software rev. illus.; stat. index. back issues avail.; reprint service avail. from PSC. **Document type:** *Journal, Academic/Scholarly.* **Description:** Features articles devoted for the dissemination of original research, presentation of comprehensive technology reviews, as well as examination of cutting-edge industrial technologies in the broad area of materials science and engineering.
Former titles (until 1989): Journal of Metals (0148-6608); (until 1977): J O M (0098-4558); (until 1974): Journal of Metals (0022-2674); Which was formed by the merger of (1934-1949): Metals Technology (0096-5855); (1919-1949): Mining and Metallurgy (0096-7289); Which was formerly (until 1919): American Institute of Mining and Metallurgical Engineers. Bulletin (0376-1916)
Related titles: Microfiche ed.: (from PQC); Online - full text ed.: ISSN 1543-1851 (from IngentaConnect).
Indexed: A05, A15, A20, A22, A23, A24, A26, A28, ABIn, AESIS, APA, AS&TA, AS&TI, ASCA, B04, B10, B13, BCIRA, BRD, BiolDig, BrCerAb, C&ISA, C10, CA, CA/WCA, CEABA, CIA, CPEI, Cadscan, CerAb, ChemAb, CivEngAb, CorrAb, CurCont, E&CAJ, E01, E11, EEA, EMA, ESPM, EngInd, EnvEAb, F&EA, GeoRef, H12, H15, I05, IBR, IBZ, IMMAb, INIS AtomInd, ISMEC, ISR, Inspec, L09, LeadAb, M&TEA, M09, MBF, METADEX, MSCI, P26, P30, P48, P51, P52, P54, PQC, PROMT, RefZh, S04, SCI, SCOPUS, SolStAb, SpeleolAb, T02, T04, TM, W03, W05, W07, WAA, Zincscan.
—BLDSC (4673.254500), AskIEEE, CASDDS, IE, Infotrieve, Ingenta, INIST, Linda Hall. **CCC.**
Published by: (T M S - The Minerals, Metals and Materials Society), Springer New York LLC (Subsidiary of: Springer Science+Business Media), 233 Spring St, New York, NY 10013. TEL 212-460-1500, FAX 212-460-1575, journals@springer-ny.com. Ed. James J Robinson.

➤ **J O T.** (Journal fuer Oberflaechentechnik) *see* MACHINERY

➤ **J S S C BULLETIN.** (Japanese Society of Steel Construction) *see* BUILDING AND CONSTRUCTION

➤ **J S S C JOURNAL OF CONSTRUCTIONAL STEEL.** (Japanese Society of Steel Construction) *see* BUILDING AND CONSTRUCTION

669 KOR ISSN 1738-7507
JAE'LYO MA'DANG/TRENDS IN METALS & MATERIALS ENGINEERING. Text in Multiple languages. 1988. bi-m. **Document type:** *Journal, Academic/Scholarly.*
Formerly (until 1999): Daehan Geumsog Haghoe Hoebo/Korean Institute of Metals and Materials. Bulletin (1225-1550)
Indexed: A28, APA, BrCerAb, C&ISA, CA/WCA, CIA, CerAb, CivEngAb, CorrAb, E&CAJ, E11, EEA, EMA, H15, M&TEA, M09, MBF, METADEX, SolStAb, T04, WAA.
—BLDSC (9049.662000), Linda Hall.
Published by: Daehan Geumsog Jae'lyo Haghoe/Korean Institute of Metals and Materials, POSCO Center 4th Fl (East Wing), 892 Daechi 4-dong, Kangnam-ku, Seoul, 135-777, Korea, S. TEL 82-2-5571071, FAX 82-2-5571080, kim@kim.or.kr.

669 DEU ISSN 0075-2819
TS670 CODEN: JBOFAN
JAHRBUCH OBERFLAECHENTECHNIK (YEAR). Text in German. 1954. a. EUR 54 (effective 2008). adv. **Document type:** *Journal, Trade.*
Indexed: Cadscan, ChemAb, ChemTitl, LeadAb, Zincscan.
—BLDSC (4631.900000), CASDDS, IE, Ingenta. **CCC.**
Published by: Eugen G. Leuze Verlag, Karlstr 4, Saulgau, 88348, Germany. TEL 49-7581-48010, FAX 49-7581-480110, info@leuze-verlag.de, http://www.leuze-verlag.de.

JAHRBUCH SCHWEISSTECHNIK. *see* TECHNOLOGY: COMPREHENSIVE WORKS

672 DEU ISSN 0724-8482
HD9523.1
JAHRBUCH STAHL. Text in German. 1951. a. EUR 40 per issue; EUR 20 per issue to members (effective 2011). adv. abstr.; pat.; stat. **Document type:** *Yearbook, Trade.*
Former titles: Stahleisen Kalender (0081-4180); Taschenbuch fuer die Stahlindustrie
Indexed: GeoRef, SpeleolAb.
—Linda Hall.
Published by: (Stahlinstitut VDEh), Verlag Stahleisen GmbH, Sohnstr 65, Duesseldorf, 40237, Germany. TEL 49-211-67070, FAX 49-211-6707310, stahleisen@stahleisen.de. adv.: B&W page EUR 794, color page EUR 1,364; trim 120 x 170. Circ: 4,032 (paid and controlled).

669 JPN
JAPAN METAL BULLETIN (ONLINE EDITION). Text in English. 1953. w. adv. bk.rev. mkt. back issues avail. **Document type:** *Bulletin, Trade.* **Description:** Covers imports, exports and production of Japanese metal industry.
Formerly: Japan Metal Bulletin (Print Edition) (0021-4523)
Media: Online - full content. **Related titles:** E-mail ed.
Indexed: A28, APA, BrCerAb, C&ISA, CA/WCA, CIA, CerAb, CivEngAb, CorrAb, E&CAJ, E11, EEA, EMA, GeoRef, H15, M&TEA, M09, MBF, METADEX, SolStAb, SpeleolAb, T04, WAA.
Published by: Sangyo Press Co., Ltd./Sangyo Shimbun, 2-4-2 Muromachi Nihonbashi, Chuo-Ku Tokyo,, Tokyo, 103-0022, Japan. TEL 81-3-32412371, FAX 81-3-32415671, masakiyo@sangyo.co.jp. Circ: 10,000.

669 JPN ISSN 0368-444X
CODEN: JSWTAK
JAPAN STEEL WORKS TECHNICAL NEWS. Text in Multiple languages. 1961. irreg. per issue exchange basis.
Published by: Nihon Seikosho/Japan Steel Works, Ltd., 1-12 Yurakucho, Chiyoda-ku, Tokyo, 100-0006, Japan.

671 DNK ISSN 0109-9418
JERN- OG MASKININDUSTRIEN. Text in Danish. 1907. 47/yr. DKK 425 (effective 2010). adv. back issues avail. **Document type:** *Newspaper, Trade.* **Description:** Trade journal for the mechanical engineering world.
Incorporates (in 2002): Dansk Teknisk Tidsskrift (0011-6505); Which was formerly (until 1942): Den Tekniske Forenings Tidsskrift (1924) (0105-6735); Which superseded in part (1907-1923): Teknisk Tidsskrift (0105-6743)
Related titles: Online - full text ed.: ISSN 1903-640X. 200?; ◆ Includes: Proces-Teknik. ISSN 1603-1806.
—Linda Hall.
Published by: Danske Fagmedier, Marielundvej 46 E, Herlev, 2730, Denmark. TEL 45-44-858899, FAX 45-44-858887, info@danskefagmedier.dk, http://www.danskefagmedier.dk. Eds. Jesper Israelsen TEL 45-44-857396, Henrik Fougt TEL 45-44-857385. Adv. contact Soeren Schou-Nielsen TEL 45-44-857377. B&W page DKK 32,300, color page DKK 36,300; 365 x 266. Circ: 23,238.

669.1 SWE ISSN 0347-4283
JERNKONTORETS BERGSHISTORISKA SKRIFTSERIE. Text in English, Swedish. 1930. irreg., latest vol.44, 2005. price varies. back issues avail. **Document type:** *Monographic series, Academic/Scholarly.*
Published by: Jernkontoret/Swedish Steel Producers' Association, PO Box 1721, Stockholm, 11187, Sweden. TEL 46-8-6791700, FAX 46-8-6112089, office@jernkontoret.se.

JERNKONTORETS BERGSHISTORISKA UTSKOTT. H. *see* MINES AND MINING INDUSTRY

669.1 622 SWE ISSN 0280-249X
JERNKONTORETS FORSKNING. SERIE D. Text in English, Swedish. 1969. irreg., latest vol.818, 2006. SEK 300 per issue (effective 2007). back issues avail. **Document type:** *Monographic series, Academic/Scholarly.*
Related titles: Online - full text ed.
Published by: Jernkontoret/Swedish Steel Producers' Association, PO Box 1721, Stockholm, 11187, Sweden. TEL 46-8-6791700, FAX 46-8-6112089, office@jernkontoret.se.

669 CHN
JIANGXI LIGONG DAXUE XUEBAO/JIANGXI UNIVERSITY OF SCIENCE AND TECHNOLOGY. JOURNAL. Text in Chinese. 1980. bi-m. USD 18 (effective 2009). back issues avail. **Document type:** *Journal, Academic/Scholarly.*
Former titles: Nanfang Yejin Xueyuan Xuebao/Southern Institute of Metallurgy. Journal (1007-1229); (until 1989): Jiangxi Yejin Xueyuan Xuebao/Jiangxi Institute of Metallurgy. Journal (1000-226X)
Related titles: Online - full text ed.
Indexed: A28, APA, BrCerAb, C&ISA, CA/WCA, CIA, CerAb, CivEngAb, CorrAb, E&CAJ, E11, EEA, EMA, ESPM, EnvEAb, H15, M&TEA, M09, MBF, METADEX, RefZh, SolStAb, T04, WAA.
—East View, Linda Hall.
Published by: Jiangxi Ligong Daxue, 86, Hongqi Dadao, Ganzhou, Jiangxi 341000, China. TEL 86-797-8240222, FAX 86-797-8312211, http://www.jxust.cn/. Ed. Man Miao Li. **Dist. by:** China International Book Trading Corp, 35 Chegongzhuang Xilu, Haidian District, PO Box 399, Beijing 100044, China. TEL 86-10-68412045, FAX 86-10-68412023, cibtc@mail.cibtc.com.cn, http://www.cibtc.com.cn.

669 CHN
JINSHU CAILIAO YU YEJIN GONGCHENG/METAL MATERIALS AND METALLURGY ENGINEERING. Text in Chinese. 1973. bi-m. USD 24.60 (effective 2009).
Formerly: Hunan Yejin (1005-6084)
Related titles: Online - full text ed.
—East View.
Published by: Hunan Sheng Jinshu Xuehui, 589, Xiangzhang Lu, Changsha, 410014, China. TEL 86-731-5587119 ext 636, FAX 86-731-5172613. **Dist. by:** China International Book Trading Corp, 35 Chegongzhuang Xilu, Haidian District, PO Box 399, Beijing 100044, China. TEL 86-10-68412045, FAX 86-10-68412023, cibtc@mail.cibtc.com.cn, http://www.cibtc.com.cn.

669 CHN ISSN 1674-1641
JINSHU JIAGONG. LENGJIAGONG/M W METAL CUTTING. Text in Chinese. 1950. s-m. **Document type:** *Magazine, Trade.* **Description:** Covers Chinese metalworking manufacturing industry, reports development of Chinese and foreign enterprises, introduces latest technology in manufacturing industry, and provides support for enterprise managers, technicians and sales persons to pick up latest information on market, new products and technology.
Formerly (until 2008): Jixie Gongren. Lengjiagong/Machinist Metal Cutting (1000-7768)
Related titles: Online - full text ed.
Published by: (Jixie Gongye Xinxi Yanjiuyuan), Jinshu Jiagong Zazhishe/Metal Working Magazine Agency, 22, Baiwanzhuang Dajie, Beijing, 100037, China. TEL 86-10-88379790 ext.615.

669 CHN ISSN 1674-165X
JINSHU JIAGONG. REJIAGONG/M W METAL FORMING. Text in Chinese. 1950. s-m. **Document type:** *Magazine, Trade.*
Formerly (until 2008): Jixie Gongren. Rejiagong/Machinist Metal Forming (1000-775X)
Related titles: Online - full text ed.
Published by: (Jixie Gongye Xinxi Yanjiuyuan), Jinshu Jiagong Zazhishe/Metal Working Magazine Agency, 22, Baiwanzhuang Dajie, Beijing, 100037, China.

JINSHU KUANGSHAN/METAL MINE. *see* MINES AND MINING INDUSTRY

JINSHU RECHULI/HEAT TREATMENT OF METALS. *see* ENGINEERING—Engineering Mechanics And Materials

669 CHN ISSN 0412-1961
TN4 CODEN: CHSPA4
➤ **JINSHU XUEBAO/ACTA METALLURGICA SINICA.** Text in Chinese; Abstracts in English. 1956. m. USD 133.20 (effective 2009). back issues avail. **Document type:** *Journal, Academic/Scholarly.* **Description:** Covers research on physical metallurgy, process metallurgy and materials science in China, including mining and ore dressing, oxidation and corrosion, metal working, testing methods and refractories.
Related titles: Online - full text ed.; English ed.: Journal of Metallurgy, Part A & B.
Indexed: A22, A28, APA, BrCerAb, C&ISA, C33, CA/WCA, CEABA, CIA, CIN, CPEI, CerAb, ChemAb, ChemTitl, CivEngAb, CorrAb, CurCont, E&CAJ, E11, EEA, EMA, ESPM, EngInd, EnvEAb, GeoRef, H15, Inspec, M&TEA, M09, MBF, METADEX, MSCI, RefZh, SCI, SCOPUS, SolStAb, SpeleolAb, T04, TM, W07, WAA.
—BLDSC (0637.500000), AskIEEE, CASDDS, East View, IE, Ingenta, INIST, Linda Hall.

Published by: (Zhongguo Kexueyuan Jinshu Yanjiusuo/Chinese Academy of Sciences, Institute of Metal Research), Kexue Chubanshe/Science Press, 16 Donghuang Cheng Genbei Jie, Beijing, 100717, China. TEL 86-10-64000246, FAX 86-10-64030255, http://www.sciencep.com/. Ed. Ke Hun. Circ: 1,200. **Dist. by:** China International Book Trading Corp, 35 Chegongzhuang Xilu, Haidian District, PO Box 399, Beijing 100044, China. TEL 86-10-68412045, FAX 86-10-68412023, cibtc@mail.cibtc.com.cn, http://www.cibtc.com.cn.

669 CHN ISSN 1003-4226
JINSHU ZHIPIN/METAL PRODUCTS. Text in English. 1972. bi-m. CNY 60; CNY 10 per issue (effective 2010). **Document type:** *Magazine, Trade.*
Formerly (until 1978): Gangsi yu Gangsheng
Related titles: Online - full text ed.: (from WanFang Data Corp.).
—BLDSC (4669.110200), IE.
Published by: Zhonggang Jituan Zhengzhou Jinshuzhipin Yanjiuyuan/SinoSteel Zhengzhou Research Institute of Steel Wire Products Co., Ltd., 26, Huagong W. Rd., Zhengzhou Hi-Tech Zone, Zhengzhou, Henan 450001, China. TEL 86-371-67852060, FAX 86-371-67852057, http://www.zrw.cn. Ed. Wei Song.

669 TWN ISSN 0254-5888
TS300 CODEN: CSYLDY
JISHU YU XUNLIAN/TECHNOLOGY & TRAINING. Text in Chinese. 1976. bi-m.
Indexed: A28, APA, BrCerAb, C&ISA, CA/WCA, CIA, CerAb, CivEngAb, CorrAb, E&CAJ, E11, EEA, EMA, ESPM, EnvEAb, H15, M&TEA, M09, MBF, METADEX, SolStAb, T04, WAA.
—BLDSC (4669.205910), Linda Hall.
Published by: Zhongguo Gangtie Gufen Yvouxian Gongsi/China Steel Corporation, 1 Chung Kang Rd, Kaohsiung, 81233, Taiwan. TEL 886-7-8021111, FAX 886-7-8022511, http://www.csc.com.tw.

▼ **JOHN LOTHIAN NEWSLETTER (METALS EDITION).** *see* BUSINESS AND ECONOMICS—Investments

669 USA
JOINING OF ADVANCED AND SPECIALITY MATERIALS. Text in English. 2003. a., latest vol.7, 2005. USD 25 per issue to non-members; USD 20 per issue to members (effective 2009). **Document type:** *Proceedings.* **Description:** Highlights the advancement in joining technologies for both established and emerging engineering materials.
Published by: A S M International, 9639 Kinsman Rd, Materials Park, OH 44073. TEL 440-338-5151, FAX 440-338-4634, CustomerService@asminternational.org.

669 NLD ISSN 0925-8388
TN1 CODEN: JALCEU
➤ **JOURNAL OF ALLOYS AND COMPOUNDS.** Text in English, French, German. 1959. 42/yr. EUR 12,220 in Europe to institutions; JPY 1,620,300 in Japan to institutions; USD 13,728 elsewhere to institutions (effective 2012). adv. bk.rev. bibl.; illus. Index. back issues avail. **Document type:** *Journal, Academic/Scholarly.* **Description:** Provides an international forum where materials scientists, chemists and physicists can present their results both to workers in their own fields and to others active in related areas.
Formerly (until 1991): Journal of the Less-Common Metals (0022-5088)
Related titles: Microform ed.: (from PQC); Online - full text ed.: ISSN 1873-4669 (from IngentaConnect, ScienceDirect).
Indexed: A01, A03, A08, A22, A26, A28, AESIS, APA, ASCA, BrCerAb, C&ISA, C24, C31, C33, CA, CA/WCA, CCI, CEABA, CIA, CIN, CPEI, Cadscan, CerAb, ChemAb, ChemTitl, CivEngAb, CorrAb, CurCR, CurCont, E&CAJ, E11, EEA, EMA, ESPM, EngInd, EnvEAb, GeoRef, H15, I05, ISMEC, ISR, Inspec, LeadAb, M&TEA, M09, MBF, METADEX, MSCI, P30, P34, PhysBer, R16, RefZh, S01, SCI, SCOPUS, SolStAb, SpeleolAb, T02, T04, TM, W07, WAA, Zincscan.
—BLDSC (4927.180000), AskIEEE, CASDDS, IE, Infotrieve, Ingenta, INIST, Linda Hall. **CCC.**
Published by: Elsevier BV (Subsidiary of: Elsevier Science & Technology), Radarweg 29, PO Box 211, Amsterdam, 1000 AE, Netherlands. TEL 31-20-4853911, FAX 31-20-4852457, JournalsCustomerServiceEMEA@elsevier.com, http://www.elsevier.nl. Ed. K H J Buschow. **Subscr. to:** Elsevier, Subscription Customer Service, 6277 Sea Harbor Dr, Orlando, FL 32887-4800. TEL 407-345-4020, 877-839-7126, FAX 407-363-1354.

671.732 USA ISSN 1559-9590
TS670.A1
JOURNAL OF APPLIED SURFACE FINISHING. Text in English. 2006 (Jan.-Mar.). q. USD 275 to non-members; USD 400 to institutions; USD 120 to members (effective 2006). **Document type:** *Journal, Trade.*
Related titles: Online - full text ed.: ISSN 1559-9604.
Published by: American Electroplaters and Surface Finishers Society, Inc. (AESF), 1 Thomas Circle NW, 10th Fl, Washington, DC 20005. TEL 202-457-8401, FAX 202-530-0659, info@aesf.org.

669 GBR ISSN 1466-8858
TA462
➤ **THE JOURNAL OF CORROSION SCIENCE AND ENGINEERING.** Abbreviated title: J C S E. Text in English. 1995. irreg., latest vol.12. free. back issues avail. **Document type:** *Journal, Academic/Scholarly.* **Description:** Contains papers on various aspects of corrosion science, including treatments, inhibition/inhibitors, coatings, and other related subjects.
Media: Online - full content.
Indexed: A28, APA, BrCerAb, C&ISA, CA/WCA, CIA, CerAb, CivEngAb, CorrAb, E&CAJ, E11, EEA, EMA, H15, M&TEA, M09, MBF, METADEX, SCOPUS, SolStAb, T04, WAA.
—CCC.
Published by: University of Manchester, Corrosion and Protection Centre, School of Materials, PO Box 88, Manchester, M60 1QD, United Kingdom. TEL 44-161-2004848, FAX 44-161-2004865, corrosion@manchester.ac.uk, http://www.materials.manchester.ac.uk/research/groups/corrosionandprotection/. Ed. Bob Cottis TEL 44-161-3064843.

669 USA ISSN 1547-7029
TA169.5 CODEN: JFAPBC
➤ **JOURNAL OF FAILURE ANALYSIS AND PREVENTION.** Abbreviated title: J F A P. Text in English. 2001. bi-m. EUR 683, USD 830 combined subscription to institutions (print & online eds.) (effective 2012). adv. back issues avail.; reprint service avail. from PSC. **Document type:** *Journal, Academic/Scholarly.* **Description:** Presents information gathering techniques, technical analysis, and emerging tools that assist failure analysis professionals in determining the cause of failures and eliminating failures in the future.
Formerly (until 2004): Practical Failure Analysis (1529-8159)
Related titles: Online - full text ed.: ISSN 1864-1245 (from IngentaConnect).
Indexed: A01, A22, A26, A28, APA, BrCerAb, C&ISA, CA, CA/WCA, CIA, CPEI, CerAb, CivEngAb, CorrAb, E&CAJ, E01, E11, EEA, EMA, EngInd, H15, I05, M&TEA, M09, MBF, METADEX, P52, SCOPUS, SolStAb, T02, T04, WAA.
—BLDSC (4983.627000), IE, Ingenta, Linda Hall. **CCC.**
Published by: (A S M International, The Materials Information Society), Springer New York LLC (Subsidiary of: Springer Science+Business Media), 233 Spring St, New York, NY 10013. TEL 212-460-1500, FAX 212-460-1575, service-ny@springer.com. Ed. McIntyre Louthan.

669 CHN ISSN 1006-706X
TN693.I7
➤ **JOURNAL OF IRON AND STEEL RESEARCH INTERNATIONAL.** Text in English. s-a. USD 79.80 (effective 2009). **Document type:** *Journal, Academic/Scholarly.*
Related titles: Online - full text ed.: (from ScienceDirect); ◆ Chinese ed.: Gangtie Yanjiu Xuebao. ISSN 1001-0963.
Indexed: A28, APA, ASFA, BrCerAb, C&ISA, CA/WCA, CIA, CerAb, CivEngAb, CorrAb, E&CAJ, E11, EEA, EMA, ESPM, EnvEAb, H15, Inspec, M&TEA, M09, MBF, METADEX, MSCI, SCI, SCOPUS, SolStAb, T04, W07, WAA.
—BLDSC (5008.350000), East View, IE, Ingenta, Linda Hall. **CCC.**
Published by: Gangtie Yanjiu Xuebao, 76 Xueyuan Nan Lu, Beijing, 100081, China. **Subscr. outside China to:** Maney Publishing, China Journal Distribution Services, Hudson Rd, Leeds LS9 7DI, United Kingdom. TEL 44-113-2497481, FAX 44-113-2486983, subscriptions@maney.co.uk.

➤ **JOURNAL OF MATERIALS ENGINEERING AND PERFORMANCE.** *see* ENGINEERING—Engineering Mechanics And Materials

➤ **JOURNAL OF MATERIALS SCIENCE AND ENGINEERING. A.** *see* ENGINEERING—Engineering Mechanics And Materials

➤ **JOURNAL OF MATERIALS SCIENCE AND ENGINEERING. B.** *see* ENGINEERING—Engineering Mechanics And Materials

669 CHN ISSN 1005-0302
CODEN: JSCTEQ
➤ **JOURNAL OF MATERIALS SCIENCE & TECHNOLOGY;** an international journal in the field of materials science. Text in English. 1985. bi-m. USD 1,085 per vol. in US & Canada; USD 1,345 per vol. elsewhere (effective 2006). abstr.; charts; illus. 96 p./no.; back issues avail. **Document type:** *Journal, Academic/Scholarly.* **Description:** Covers metals, inorganic nonmetallic materials, organic polymer materials and composite materials.
Formerly (until 1993): Chinese Journal of Metal Science and Technology (1000-3029)
Related titles: Online - full text ed.: (from ScienceDirect).
Indexed: A28, APA, ASCA, BrCerAb, C&ISA, CA/WCA, CIA, CIN, CPEI, CerAb, ChemAb, ChemTitl, CivEngAb, CorrAb, CurCont, E&CAJ, E11, EEA, EMA, ESPM, EngInd, EnvEAb, H15, ISMEC, Inspec, M&TEA, M09, MBF, METADEX, MSCI, SCI, SCOPUS, SolStAb, T02, T04, TM, W07, WAA.
—BLDSC (5012.252000), CASDDS, IE, Infotrieve, Ingenta, INIST, Linda Hall. **CCC.**
Published by: Zhongguo Kexueyuan Jinshu Yanjiusuo/Chinese Academy of Sciences, Institute of Metal Research, 72, Wenhua Lu, Shenyang, Liaoning 110015, China. TEL 86-24-23843169, FAX 86-24-23891320, http://www.imr.ac.cn/index.jsp. Ed. Zhuangqi Hu.

669 USA ISSN 1687-9465
➤ **JOURNAL OF METALLURGY.** Text in English. irreg. USD 195 (effective 2011). **Document type:** *Journal, Academic/Scholarly.* **Description:** Publishes original research articles as well as review articles in all areas of metallurgy.
Related titles: Online - full text ed.: ISSN 1687-9473. free (effective 2011).
Indexed: C10, CA, P52, T02.
Published by: Hindawi Publishing Corporation, 410 Park Ave, 15th Fl, PMB 287, New York, NY 10022. FAX 215-893-4392, 866-446-3294, info@hindawi.com.

669 IND ISSN 0972-4257
TN1 CODEN: JMMSBS
➤ **JOURNAL OF METALLURGY AND MATERIALS SCIENCE.** (J.Met. Mater. Sc. (ISSN 0972-4257)) Text in English. 1959. q. INR 3,000 (effective 2011). bk.rev. charts; illus.; mkt.; pat.; abstr. 60 p./no. 1 cols./p.; back issues avail.; reprints avail. **Document type:** *Journal, Academic/Scholarly.* **Description:** Contains information from the fields of mines, metals and materials.
Formerly (until 2000): N M L Technical Journal (0027-6839)
Related titles: Online - full text ed.: ISSN 0974-1267. INR 2,000 domestic; USD 200 foreign (effective 2008).
Indexed: A28, APA, BrCerAb, C&ISA, CA/WCA, CIA, CIN, CerAb, ChemAb, ChemTitl, CivEngAb, CorrAb, E&CAJ, E11, EEA, EMA, H15, M&TEA, M09, MBF, METADEX, SolStAb, T04, TM, WAA.
—CASDDS, Ingenta, Linda Hall.
Published by: National Metallurgical Laboratory, P.O. Burmamines, Jamshedpur, Bihar 831 007, India. TEL 91-657-2345000, FAX 91-6572345213, director@nmlindia.org. **Subscr. to:** I N S I O Scientific Books & Periodicals; Indianjournals.com.

➤ **JOURNAL OF MINES, METALS AND FUELS.** *see* MINES AND MINING INDUSTRY

669 SRB ISSN 1450-5339
➤ **JOURNAL OF MINING AND METALLURGY. SECTION B: METALLURGY.** Text in English. 1964. 2/yr. **Document type:** *Journal, Academic/Scholarly.*
Supersedes in part (in 1997): Glasnik Rudarstva i Metalurgije (0354-0545); Which was formerly (until 1990): Tehnicki Fakultet i Institut za Bakar Bor. Zbornik Radova (0351-2150)
Related titles: Online - full text ed.: free (effective 2011).
Indexed: A01, MSCI, RefZh, SCI, SCOPUS, W07.
Published by: Technical Faculty Bor, Vojske Jugoslavije 12, Bor, 19210. TEL 381-30-424547, office@tf.bor.ac.yu, http://www.tf.bor.ac.yu. Ed. Zivan Zivkovic.

➤ **JOURNAL OF NON-DESTRUCTIVE TESTING & EVALUATION.** *see* ENGINEERING—Engineering Mechanics And Materials

669 USA ISSN 1547-7037
TN689 CODEN: JPEDAV
➤ **JOURNAL OF PHASE EQUILIBRIA AND DIFFUSION.** Abbreviated title: J P E D. Text in English. 1991. bi-m. EUR 1,996, USD 2,419 combined subscription to institutions (print & online eds.) (effective 2012). adv. bk.rev. charts; illus. index. back issues avail.; reprint service avail. from PSC. **Document type:** *Journal, Academic/Scholarly.* **Description:** Focuses on the crystallographic, chemical, diffusion, and other kinetic properties of phases.
Formerly (until 2004): Journal of Phase Equilibria (1054-9714); Which was formed by the merger of (1980-1991): Bulletin of Alloy Phase Diagrams (0197-0216); (1985-1991): Journal of Alloy Phase Diagrams (0970-1478)
Related titles: Microform ed.: (from PQC); Online - full text ed.: ISSN 1863-7345 (from IngentaConnect).
Indexed: A01, A22, A26, A28, APA, ASCA, BrCerAb, C&ISA, C33, CA, CA/WCA, CCI, CIA, CIN, CPEI, CerAb, ChemAb, ChemTitl, CivEngAb, CoppAb, CorrAb, CurCont, E&CAJ, E01, E11, EEA, EMA, ESPM, EngInd, EnvEAb, H15, I05, Inspec, M&TEA, M09, MBF, METADEX, MSCI, P16, P48, P52, P53, P54, PQC, RefZh, SCI, SCOPUS, SolStAb, T02, T04, W07, WAA.
—BLDSC (5034.070000), AskIEEE, CASDDS, IE, Infotrieve, Ingenta, INIST, Linda Hall. **CCC.**
Published by: (A S M International), Springer New York LLC (Subsidiary of: Springer Science+Business Media), 233 Spring St, New York, NY 10013. TEL 212-460-1500, FAX 212-460-1575, journals@springer-ny.com, http://www.springer.com. Ed. John F Smith.

669 NLD ISSN 1002-0721
QD172.R2 CODEN: JREAE6
➤ **JOURNAL OF RARE EARTHS.** Text in English. 1990. bi-m. EUR 314 in Europe to institutions; JPY 46,400 in Japan to institutions; USD 401 elsewhere to institutions (effective 2012). **Document type:** *Journal, Academic/Scholarly.* **Description:** International journal that introduces development in rare earth science and technology and its wide range of applications.
Formerly (until 1991): Chinese Rare Earth Society. Journal
Related titles: Online - full text ed.: (from ScienceDirect); Chinese ed.: Zhongguo Xitu Xuebao. ISSN 1000-4343.
Indexed: A28, APA, ASCA, BrCerAb, C&ISA, CA/WCA, CCI, CEABA, CIA, CPEI, CerAb, ChemAb, ChemTitl, CivEngAb, CorrAb, E&CAJ, E11, EEA, EMA, ESPM, EngInd, EnvEAb, GeoRef, H15, Inspec, M&TEA, M09, MBF, METADEX, RefZh, SCI, SCOPUS, SolStAb, SpeleolAb, T04, W07, WAA.
—BLDSC (5046.600000), AskIEEE, East View, IE, Ingenta, Linda Hall. **CCC.**
Published by: (Zhongguo Xitu Xuehui CHN), Elsevier BV (Subsidiary of: Elsevier Science & Technology), Radarweg 29, PO Box 211, Amsterdam, 1000 AE, Netherlands. TEL 31-20-4853911, FAX 31-20-4852457, JournalsCustomerServiceEMEA@elsevier.com, http://www.elsevier.nl. Ed. Xu Guangxian. **Subscr. to:** Kexue Chubanshe, International Sales & Marketing Dept., 16 Donghuangchenggen North St, Beijing 100717, China. TELEX 22313 CPC CN.

669 016 DEU ISSN 0334-8938
TA417.6 CODEN: JMBMEQ
➤ **JOURNAL OF THE MECHANICAL BEHAVIOR OF MATERIALS.** Text in English. 1972. 6/yr. EUR 399, USD 599 to institutions; EUR 459, USD 689 combined subscription to institutions (print & online eds.) (effective 2012). adv. bk.rev. back issues avail. **Document type:** *Journal, Academic/Scholarly.* **Description:** Publishes articles in camera-ready format on original research, short communications and reviews covering all modern engineering materials: metals and alloys, ceramics and glass, polymers and composite materials, wood, elastomers, etc. In addition to regular issues, special issues on specific subjects are often published.
Formerly (until 1989): Reviews on Deformation Behaviour of Materials (0048-7589)
Related titles: Online - full text ed.: ISSN 2191-0243. EUR 399, USD 599 to institutions (effective 2012).
Indexed: A28, APA, ApMecR, BrCerAb, C&ISA, CA/WCA, CIA, CIN, CerAb, ChemAb, ChemTitl, CivEngAb, CorrAb, E&CAJ, E11, EEA, EMA, ESPM, EnvEAb, H15, M&TEA, M09, MBF, METADEX, SCOPUS, SolStAb, T04, WAA.
—BLDSC (5015.810000), CASDDS, IE, Ingenta, INIST, Linda Hall.
Published by: Walter de Gruyter GmbH & Co. KG, Genthiner Str 13, Berlin, 10785, Germany. TEL 49-30-260050, FAX 49-30-26005251, info@degruyter.com, http://www.degruyter.de. Circ: 1,000.

669 JPN
KATAYAMA GIHO/KATAYAMA TECHNICAL REPORT. Text in Japanese. 1981. a.
Published by: Katayama Tekkojo/Katayama Iron Works, Ltd., 2-21 Minami-Okajima 6-chome, Taisho-ku, Osaka-shi, 551-0021, Japan.

669 JPN ISSN 0451-5994
TN773 CODEN: KEIKA6
KEIKINZOKU. Variant title: Japan Institute of Light Metals. Journal. Text in Japanese. 1951. m. subscr. inclds. membership. **Document type:** *Journal, Academic/Scholarly.*
Related titles: Online - full text ed.: ISSN 1880-8018.
Indexed: A22, A28, APA, BrCerAb, C&ISA, CA/WCA, CIA, CPEI, CerAb, CivEngAb, CorrAb, E&CAJ, E11, EEA, EMA, ESPM, EngInd, EnvEAb, GeoRef, H15, INIS AtomInd, ISMEC, Inspec, M&TEA, M09, MBF, METADEX, SCOPUS, SolStAb, T04, WAA.
—BLDSC (4805.200000), IE, Ingenta, INIST, Linda Hall. **CCC.**
Published by: Keikinzoku Gakkai/Japan Institute of Light Metals, Tsukamoto Sozan Bldg., 4-2-15 Ginza, Chuo-ku, Tokyo, 104-0061, Japan. TEL 81-3-35380232, FAX 81-3-35380226, jilm@kt.rim.or.jp, http://www.jilm.or.jp.

671.52 JPN ISSN 0368-5306
TS227.A1 CODEN: KEYOBV
KEIKINZOKU YOSETSU/JOURNAL OF THE LIGHT METAL WELDING & CONSTRUCTION. Text in Japanese. 1963. m. JPY 10,080 (effective 2005). **Document type:** *Journal, Academic/Scholarly.*

Indexed: A22, A28, APA, BrCerAb, C&ISA, CA/WCA, CIA, CPEI, CerAb, CivEngAb, CorrAb, E&CAJ, E11, EEA, EMA, ESPM, EngInd, EnvEAb, H15, M&TEA, M09, MBF, METADEX, SCOPUS, SolStAb, T04, WAA, Weldasearch.
—BLDSC (5010.472000), IE, Ingenta, Linda Hall.
Published by: Keikinzoku Yosetsu Gijutsukai/Japan Light Metal Welding & Construction Association, Keikinzoku Yosetsu Kozo Kyokai Yura Bldg., 3-37-23 Sakumacho Kanda Chiyodaku, Tokyo, 101-0025, Japan. TEL 81-3-38635545, FAX 81-3-38648707, aed06656@nifty.com, http://www.jlwa.or.jp/.

669 666 CHE ISSN 1013-9826
TA401 CODEN: KEMAEY
➤ **KEY ENGINEERING MATERIALS.** Text in English. 1975. 22/yr. EUR 1,716 (effective 2004). abstr.; bibl.; charts; illus. cum.index. **Document type:** *Journal, Academic/Scholarly.* **Description:** Covers the entire range of basic and applied aspects of the synthesis and characterization, modelling, processing and application of advanced engineering materials.
Formerly: Mechanical and Corrosion Properties. Series A. Key Engineering Materials (0252-1059); Which superseded in part: Mechanical and Corrosion Properties (0250-9784); Which was formerly (until 1979): Mechanical Properties (0361-2821)
Indexed: A22, A28, APA, BrCerAb, C&ISA, CA/WCA, CIA, CIN, CPEI, CerAb, ChemAb, ChemTitl, CivEngAb, CorrAb, E&CAJ, E11, EEA, EMA, ESPM, EngInd, EnvEAb, GeoRef, H15, INIS AtomInd, ISMEC, Inspec, M&TEA, M09, MBF, METADEX, P30, RefZh, SCOPUS, SolStAb, T04, TM, VITIS, WAA.
—BLDSC (5091.822720), AskIEEE, CASDDS, IE, Infotrieve, Ingenta, INIST, Linda Hall. **CCC.**
Published by: Trans Tech Publications Ltd., Laubisrutistr 24, Stafa-Zurich, 8712, Switzerland. TEL 41-1-9221022, FAX 41-1-9221033, info@ttp.net, http://www.ttp.ch. Eds. Fred H Wohlbier, Yiu-Wing Mai.

669 JPN ISSN 0910-2205
CODEN: KIDOEP
KIDORUI/RARE EARTHS. Text in English, Japanese; Summaries in English. 1982. s-a. subscr. incld. with membership. **Document type:** *Journal, Academic/Scholarly.*
Indexed: CIN, ChemAb, ChemTitl.
—BLDSC (7291.817000), CASDDS. **CCC.**
Published by: Nihon Kidorui Gakkai/Rare Earth Society of Japan, Osaka Daigaku Kogakubu Oyo Kagakka, 2-1 Yamada-Oka, Suita-shi, Osaka-fu 565-0871, Japan. TEL 81-6-68797352, FAX 81-6-68797354, kidorui@chem.eng.osaka-u.ac.jp, http://kidorui.chem.eng.osaka-u.ac.jp/. Ed. Gin Ya Adachi.

669.722 JPN ISSN 0285-6689
CODEN: KAHKA7
KINKI ARUMINYUMU HYOMEN SHORI KENKYUKAI KAISHI. Text in Japanese. 1965. bi-m. **Document type:** *Journal, Academic/Scholarly.*
Indexed: A28, APA, BrCerAb, C&ISA, CA/WCA, CIA, CerAb, CivEngAb, CorrAb, E&CAJ, E11, EEA, EMA, ESPM, EnvEAb, H15, M&TEA, M09, MBF, METADEX, SolStAb, T04, WAA.
—BLDSC (5096.515000), Linda Hall.
Published by: Kinki Aruminyumu Hyomen Shori Kenkyukai/Aluminium Finishing Society of Kinki, Kinki University School of Science & Engineering, Department of Applied Chemistry, 3-4-1 Kowakae, Higashi, Osaka City, 577-8502, Japan. http://ccpc01.cc.kindai.ac.jp/sci/ouyou/index.html.

669 JPN ISSN 0368-6337
TN600 CODEN: KNZKAI
KINZOKU/MATERIALS SCIENCE & TECHNOLOGY. Text in Japanese. 1931. s-m. JPY 22,680 domestic; JPY 26,000 foreign (effective 2002). **Document type:** *Journal, Academic/Scholarly.* **Description:** Contains regular articles on the history metal physics, techno-literacy, and metal usage in everyday life.
Indexed: A28, APA, BrCerAb, C&ISA, CA/WCA, CIA, CerAb, CivEngAb, CorrAb, E&CAJ, E11, EEA, EMA, H15, INIS AtomInd, M&TEA, M09, MBF, METADEX, RefZh, SolStAb, T04, WAA.
—BLDSC (5396.434570), Linda Hall.
Published by: AGNE Gijutsu Center, Kitamura Bldg, 1-25, Minamiaoyama 5-chome, Minato-ku, Tokyo, 107-0062, Japan. http://www.agne.co.jp/.

669 JPN ISSN 0285-8452
CODEN: KIHKEX
KINZOKU HAKUBUTSUKAN KIYO/METALS MUSEUM. BULLETIN. Text in Multiple languages. a., latest vol.35. price varies. **Document type:** *Monographic series, Academic/Scholarly.*
—Linda Hall. **CCC.**
Published by: Nippon Kinzoku Gakkai, Fuzoku Kinzohu Hakubutsukan/Japan Institute of Metals, Metals Museum, 1-14-32, Ichibancho, Aoba-ku, Sendai 980-8544, Japan. TEL 81-22-2233685, FAX 81-22-2236312, overseas@jim.or.jp, http://wwwsoc.nii.ac.jp/jim/index-j.shtml.

KJEMI. *see* CHEMISTRY

669.142 621 DEU ISSN 0948-0684
KLOECKNER WERKE HEUTE; Maschinenbau, Kunststoff Verarbeitung. Text in German. 1952. q. bk.rev. **Document type:** *Consumer.* **Description:** Staff magazine of Kloeckner-Werke.
Formerly: K W Heute (0937-6186)
Published by: (Kloeckner-Werke AG), Kloeckner Presse und Information GmbH, Kloecknerstr 29, Duisburg, 47057, Germany. TEL 49-203-396-1, FAX 49-203-343695. Circ: 15,000.

669 RUS ISSN 0869-7531
KOMITET ROSSIISKOI FEDERATSII PO METALLURGII. VESTNIK. Text in Russian. m. USD 119.95 in United States.
Indexed: RASB.
—East View.
Published by: Chermetinformatsiya, Ul Krzhizhanovskogo 14, korp 3, Moscow, 117218, Russian Federation. TEL 7-095-2015053, FAX 7-095-2018047. **Dist. by:** East View Information Services, 10601 Wayzata Blvd, Minneapolis, MN 55305. TEL 952-252-1201, 800-477-1005, FAX 952-252-1202, info@eastview.com, http://www.eastview.com.

KOMPLEKSNOE ISPOL'ZOVANIE MINERAL'NOGO SYR'YA/COMPLEX USE OF NATIONAL RESOURCES. *see* MINES AND MINING INDUSTRY

620.112 SWE ISSN 0348-7199
CODEN: RKORD9
KORROSIONSINSTITUTET RAPPORT. Variant title: K I Report. Text in Swedish. irreg.
Indexed: A22, A28, APA, BrCerAb, C&ISA, CA/WCA, CIA, CerAb, CivEngAb, CorrAb, E&CAJ, E11, EEA, EMA, H15, M&TEA, M09, MBF, METADEX, SolStAb, T04, WAA.
—IE, Ingenta, Linda Hall.
Published by: Korrosionsinstitutet, Kraaftriket 23 A, Stockholm, 10405, Sweden. TEL 46-8-6741700, FAX 46-8-6741780, info@corr-institute.se, http://www.corr-institute.se.

620.112 RUS ISSN 1813-7016
➤ **KORROZIYA: MATERIALY, ZASHCHITA.** Text in Russian. 2003. m. USD 629 foreign (effective 2005). **Document type:** *Journal, Academic/Scholarly.* **Description:** Covers general and sectoral problems of corrosion, inhibitors of corrosion, protective coating, methods of investigations and corrosion monitoring, microbe corrosion, history of corrosion investigations.
Indexed: RefZh.
—BLDSC (0092.475000).
Published by: Nauka i Tekhnologii, Stromynskii per, 4/1, Moscow, 107076, Russian Federation. admin@nait.ru, http://www.nait.ru. Ed. A Yu Tsivadze. **Dist. by:** East View Information Services, 10601 Wayzata Blvd, Minneapolis, MN 55305. TEL 952-252-1201, 800-477-1005, FAX 952-252-1202, info@eastview.com, http://www.eastview.com.

669 SVK ISSN 0023-432X
TN4 CODEN: KOMAAW
➤ **KOVOVE MATERIALY/METAL MATERIALS.** Text in Slovak, Czech, English; Summaries in English. 1963. bi-m. USD 83 (effective 2003). adv. bk.rev. charts; illus. index. 72 p./no.; **Document type:** *Journal, Academic/Scholarly.* **Description:** Publishes original works from research of metal structure and structure of metal alloys as well as the results of basic research in physical metallurgy and metallurgical processes of iron and non-iron metals.
Indexed: A28, APA, ASCA, BrCerAb, C&ISA, CA/WCA, CIA, CIN, CIS, Cadscan, CerAb, ChemAb, ChemTitl, CivEngAb, CorrAb, CurCont, E&CAJ, E11, EEA, EMA, ESPM, EnvEAb, H15, INIS AtomInd, Inspec, LeadAb, M&TEA, M09, MBF, METADEX, MSCI, SCI, SCOPUS, SolStAb, T04, W07, WAA, Zincscan.
—BLDSC (5115.120000), AskIEEE, CASDDS, IE, Ingenta, INIST, Linda Hall.
Published by: Slovenska Akademia Vied, Ustav Materialov a Mechaniky Strojov, Racianska 75, Bratislava 3, 83102, Slovakia. TEL 421-2-44254751, FAX 421-2-44253301, ummssimk@savba.sk. Ed. Pavol Sebo. R&P Vladimir Giba. Adv. contact Olga Simkova TEL 421-2-49268214. Circ: 250. **Dist. by:** Slovart G.T.G. s.r.o., Krupinska 4, PO Box 152, Bratislava 85299, Slovakia. TEL 421-2-63839472, FAX 421-2-63839485, http://www.slovart-gtg.sk. **Co-sponsor:** Ustav Fyziki Materialu Akademie Ved Cesky Republiky.

669 551 CHN ISSN 1001-5663
KUANGCHAN YU DIZHI/MINERALS AND GEOLOGY. Text in Chinese. q. USD 31.20 (effective 2009).
Related titles: Online - full text ed.
Indexed: GeoRef, SpeleolAb.
—East View.
Published by: Zhongguo Youse Jinshu Gongye Zonggongsi, Kuangshan Dizhi Yanjiuyuan, Sanlidian, Guilin, Guangxi 541004, China. TEL 443865. Ed. Li Jiazhen.

KUANGYE GONGCHENG/MINING AND METALLURGICAL ENGINEERING. *see* MINES AND MINING INDUSTRY

669 CHN ISSN 1009-0479
AS452.K795
KUNMING YEJIN GAODENG ZHUANKE XUEXIAO XUEBAO/KUNMING METALLURGY COLLEGE. JOURNAL. Text in Chinese. 1985. bi-m. CNY 6 newsstand/cover (effective 2006). **Document type:** *Journal, Academic/Scholarly.*
Related titles: Online - full text ed.
Indexed: ESPM, EnvEAb.
Published by: Kunming Yejin Gaodeng Zhuanke Xuexiao, 388, Xuefu Lu, Kunming, 650033, China. TEL 86-871-6051718, FAX 86-871-6051719.

671 RUS
TS200 CODEN: KSPRAO
KUZNECHNO-SHTAMPOVOCHNOE PROIZVODSTVO. OBRABOTKA MATERIALOV DAVLENIEM. Text in Russian. 1959. m. USD 450 foreign (effective 2004). adv. index. **Document type:** *Journal, Trade.* **Description:** Publishes the latest development of research institutes, carries articles on novel metal forming technology, including precision stamping under superductility conditions.
Formerly (until 2001): Kuznechno-Shtampovochnoe Proizvodstvo (0234-8241)
Indexed: C&ISA, ChemAb, CorrAb, E&CAJ, RefZh, SCOPUS, SolStAb, WAA.
—BLDSC (0093.850000).
Published by: Redaktsiya Zhurnala Kuznechno-Shtampovochnoe Proizvodstvo, Vadkovskii per, dom 18a, komn 309, Moscow, 127055, Russian Federation. TEL 7-095-7249422, FAX 7-095-9789726, http://www.mashinostroyenie.ru. adv.: page MRK 4,000. Circ: 1,100. **Dist. by:** Informnauka Ltd., Ul Usievicha 20, Moscow 125190, Russian Federation. alfimov@viniti.ru.

669 ITA ISSN 0391-5891
CODEN: LAMID6
LAMIERA; rivista tecnica per la deformazione, taglio, tranciatura, finitura e assemblaggio della lamiera. Text in Italian. 1964. m. EUR 60 domestic; EUR 120 in Europe; EUR 140 elsewhere (effective 2011). adv. illus. **Document type:** *Magazine, Trade.* **Description:** Information on the pressing, deformation, cut finishing and assembling of cut metal.
Related titles: Online - full text ed.
Indexed: A22, A28, APA, BrCerAb, C&ISA, CA/WCA, CIA, CerAb, ChemAb, CivEngAb, CorrAb, E&CAJ, E11, EEA, EMA, H15, M&TEA, M09, MBF, METADEX, SolStAb, T04, WAA.
—BLDSC (5144.200000), CASDDS, IE, Ingenta, Linda Hall.
Published by: Tecniche Nuove SpA, Via Eritrea 21, Milan, MI 201, Italy. TEL 39-02-390901, FAX 39-02-7570364, info@tecnichenuove.com. Ed. Fabio Boiocchi. Circ: 7,000.

LEGISVIEWS. *see* PUBLIC ADMINISTRATION

LEXIKON OCELI. *see* BUSINESS AND ECONOMICS—Trade And Industrial Directories

669.142 CHN ISSN 1002-1043
TS300
➤ **LIANGANG/STEELMAKING.** Text in Chinese; Abstracts in Chinese, English. 1985. bi-m. CNY 60, USD 60; CNY 10 per issue (effective 2010). adv.
Related titles: Online - full text ed.
Indexed: A28, APA, BrCerAb, C&ISA, CA/WCA, CIA, CerAb, CivEngAb, E11, EEA, EMA, ESPM, EnvEAb, H15, M&TEA, M09, MBF, METADEX, T04.
—BLDSC (8464.106700), IE.
Published by: Wuhan Gangtie Gongsi Gangtie Yanjiusuo, No.28 Yejin Dadao, Qingshan District, Wuhan, 430083, China. TEL 86-27-86487772, FAX 86-27-86487773. Ed. Zhong-min Xiao. Circ: 3,000. **Co-sponsors:** Zhongguo Jinshu Xuehui/Chinese Society for Metals; Wuhan Gangtie (Jituan) Gongsi/Wuhan Iron & Steel (Group) Corp.

669.1 CHN ISSN 1001-1471
LIANTIE/IRONMAKING. Text in Chinese. 1982. bi-m. USD 24.60 (effective 2009). adv. **Document type:** *Journal, Academic/Scholarly.*
Related titles: Online - full text ed.
—BLDSC (4580.438000), East View.
Published by: Wuhan Gangtie Sheji Yanjiu Zongyuan/W I S D R I Engineering & Research Inc., 12 Yejin Ave., Qingshan District, Wuhan, Hubei 430080, China. Ed. Guoyou Pan. **Dist. overseas by:** China International Book Trading Corp, 35 Chegongzhuang Xilu, Haidian District, PO Box 399, Beijing 100044, China. TEL 86-10-68412045, FAX 86-10-68412023, cibtc@mail.cibtc.com.cn, http://www.cibtc.com.cn.

669 CHN ISSN 1674-1048
➤ **LIAONING KEJI DAXUE XUEBAO/LIAONING UNIVERSITY OF SCIENCE AND TECHNOLOGY LIAONING. JOURNAL.** Text in Chinese. 1979 (Sep). bi-m. back issues avail. **Document type:** *Journal, Academic/Scholarly.*
Former titles (until 2007): Anshan Keji Daxue Xuebao/Anshan University of Science and Technology. Journal (1672-4410); (until 2002): Anshan Gangtie Xueyuan Xuebao/Anshan Institute of Iron and Steel Technology. Journal (1000-1654)
Related titles: Online - full text ed.
Indexed: A28, APA, BrCerAb, C&ISA, CA/WCA, CIA, CerAb, CivEngAb, CorrAb, E&CAJ, E11, EEA, EMA, ESPM, EnvEAb, H15, M&TEA, M09, MBF, METADEX, SolStAb, T04, WAA.
—BLDSC (5186.247600), Linda Hall.
Published by: Liaoning Keji Daxue/Liaoning University of Science and Technology, 185, Qianshan Lu, Gaoxin Jishu Chanye Kaifa-qu, Anshan, 114051, China. TEL 86-412-5929158, FAX 86-412-5929157. Ed. Qiu-bai Sun.

669 USA ISSN 0024-3345
TN1 CODEN: LMAGAL
LIGHT METAL AGE. Text in English. 1943. bi-m. USD 45 (effective 2005). adv. bk.rev. abstr.; bibl.; illus.; pat. index. **Document type:** *Magazine, Trade.*
Related titles: Online - full text ed.
Indexed: A05, A22, A23, A24, A28, APA, AS&TA, AS&TI, B04, B13, BCIRA, BrCerAb, C&ISA, CA/WCA, CIA, CIN, CerAb, ChemAb, ChemTitl, CivEngAb, CorrAb, E&CAJ, E11, EEA, EMA, ESPM, EngInd, EnvEAb, H15, ISR, M&TEA, M09, MBF, METADEX, PROMT, SCOPUS, SolStAb, T04, TM, WAA.
—BLDSC (5210.500000), CASDDS, IE, Infotrieve, Ingenta, INIST, Linda Hall.
Published by: Fellom Publishing, 170 S Spruce Ave, Ste 120, San Francisco, CA 94080. TEL 650-588-8832, FAX 650-588-0901. Ed. Wanda Fellom. Pub. Ann Marie Fellom. Circ: 5,204 (controlled).

669 CAN
LIGHT METALS (YEAR). Text in English. 1996. a. CAD 150 per issue to members; CAD 180 per issue to non-members (effective 2004). **Document type:** *Proceedings.*
Indexed: IMMAb.
Published by: Canadian Institute of Mining, Metallurgy and Petroleum, Metallurgical Society, 3400 de Maisonneuve Blvd W, Ste 1210, Montreal, PQ H3Z 3B8, Canada. TEL 514-939-2710, FAX 514-939-2714, cim@cim.org, http://www.cim.org.

669 USA ISSN 0147-0809
TN773
LIGHT METALS (YEAR). Text in English. 1998. a. CAD 311 per issue in Canada; GBP 195 per issue in Europe; USD 259 per issue elsewhere (effective 2010). back issues avail. **Document type:** *Proceedings, Trade.*
Related titles: CD-ROM ed.
Indexed: A22, EngInd, GeoRef, SCOPUS.
—BLDSC (5211.600000), IE, Ingenta. **CCC.**
Published by: (T M S - The Minerals, Metals and Materials Society), John Wiley & Sons, Inc., 111 River St, Hoboken, NJ 07030. TEL 201-748-6000, FAX 201-748-6088, info@wiley.com. Ed. John Johnson Jr.

669.722 CAN ISSN 0707-8013
LE LINGOT. Text in French. 1936. fortn. free.
Formerly: Kitimat-Kemano Ingot
Published by: Alcan Smelters and Chemicals Ltd., P O Box 1370, Jonquiere, PQ G7S 4K9, Canada. TEL 418-548-1121. Ed. Mathieu Bouchard. Circ: 15,000.

671.2 RUS ISSN 0024-449X
T4 CODEN: LIPRAX
LITEINOE PROIZVODSTVO/JOURNAL OF FOUNDRY. Text in Russian; Contents page in English. 1930. m. USD 282 foreign (effective 2005). adv. abstr.; charts; illus.; stat. index. **Document type:** *Journal, Trade.* **Description:** Covers the experience of advanced plants in technical renovation of operating foundries and deals with the use of low-waste and energy-saving technologies.
Indexed: BCIRA, C&ISA, CIN, ChemAb, ChemTitl, CorrAb, E&CAJ, RefZh, SCOPUS, SolStAb, TM, WAA.
—CASDDS, East View, INIST, Linda Hall. **CCC.**
Published by: (Russia. Rossiiskaya Assotsiatsiya Liteishchikov), Liteinoe Proizvodstvo, Gzhel'sky per, 13a, 2 etazh, komn 40, Moscow, 105120, Russian Federation. Ed. I A Yaskevich. adv.: page MRK 4,000. Circ: 5,700. **Dist. by:** M K - Periodica, ul Gilyarovskogo 39, Moscow 129110, Russian Federation. TEL 7-095-2845008, FAX 7-095-2813798, info@periodicals.ru, http://www.mkniga.ru.

669 RUS ISSN 0302-9069
TS200 CODEN: STTMCO
LITEINOE PROIZVODSTVO, METALLOVEDENIE I OBRABOTKA METALLOV DAVLENIEM. Text in Russian. irreg. illus.

Indexed: ChemAb.
—CCC.
Published by: (Krasnoyarskii Institut Tsvetnykh Metallov), Krasnoyarskoe Knizhnoe Izdatel'stvo, Pr-t Mira 89, Krasnoyarsk, Russian Federation.

669 DEU
LITERATURSCHAU "STAHL UND EISEN" (ONLINE). Text in German. 1964. s-m. EUR 1,900 (effective 2011). **Document type:** *Journal, Trade.* **Description:** Provides technical information, target-group tailored economic news as well as information on training and education, career issues and legal information.
Former titles (until 2011): Literaturschau "Stahl und Eisen" (Print) (0933-8934); (until 1988): Zeitschriften- und Buecherschau "Stahl und Eisen" (0340-4951); (until 1974): Stahl und Eisen (0340-479X)
Media: Online - full text. **Related titles:** Diskette ed.
Indexed: GeoRef, SpeleolAb.
—CCC.
Published by: Verlag Stahleisen GmbH, Sohnstr 65, Duesseldorf, 40237, Germany. TEL 49-211-67070, FAX 49-211-6707310, stahleisen@stahleisen.de, http://www.stahleisen.de.

671.2 SVN ISSN 0024-5135
TS200 CODEN: LIVVA7
LIVARSKI VESTNIK. Text in English; Contents page in Slovenian. 1954. q. EUR 35 foreign (effective 2012). adv. bk.rev.; Website rev. abstr.; bibl.; charts; illus. index. 48 p./no. 2 cols./p.; back issues avail. **Document type:** *Journal, Academic/Scholarly.* **Description:** Covers foundry, founding alloys, mould and core materials, melting and open, and the environment.
Indexed: A28, APA, BrCerAb, C&ISA, CA/WCA, CIA, CerAb, ChemAb, CivEngAb, CorrAb, E&CAJ, E11, EEA, EMA, ESPM, EnvEAb, H15, M&TEA, M09, MBF, METADEX, SolStAb, T04, TM, WAA.
—CASDDS, Linda Hall.
Published by: Drustvo Livarjev Slovenije/Slovenian Foundrymen Society, Lepi pot 6, PO Box 424, Ljubljana, 1001, Slovenia. TEL 386-1-2522488, FAX 386-1-4269934, drustvo.livarjev@siol.net. Ed. Alojz Krizman. Circ: 800.

671.2 HRV ISSN 1330-2132
TS200 CODEN: LJEVAV
LJEVARSTVO/JOURNAL FOR THEORY AND APPLICATION IN FOUNDRY; easopis za teoriju i praksu u ljevarstvu. Text in Croatian. 1954. 3/yr. USD 15.65. adv. bk.rev. charts; illus. cum.index.
Former titles (until 1991): Livarstvo (0352-8936); (until 1986): Ljevarstvo (0024-5402)
Related titles: Online - full text ed.
Indexed: A28, APA, BrCerAb, C&ISA, CA/WCA, CIA, CIN, CerAb, ChemAb, ChemTitl, CivEngAb, CorrAb, E&CAJ, E11, EEA, EMA, H15, M&TEA, M09, MBF, METADEX, SolStAb, T04, WAA.
—CASDDS, Linda Hall.
Published by: Hrvatsko Udruzenje za Ljevarstvo/Croatian Foundry Association, Froudeova 9, Zagreb, 10020, Croatia. TEL 385-1-524339, FAX 385-1-527284. Ed. Ivo Katavic. Circ: 1,300.

M & T - METALLHANDWERK. *see* BUILDING AND CONSTRUCTION

M C GILL DOORWAY MAGAZINE. *see* PLASTICS

669 JPN
M M I J INTERNATIONAL CONFERENCES. PROCEEDINGS. (Mining and Materials Processing Institute of Japan) Text in Japanese. 1985. irreg., latest vol.7, 1991. price varies. **Document type:** *Proceedings, Trade.*
Published by: Shigen Sozai Gakkai/Mining and Materials Processing Institute of Japan, Nogizaka Bldg, 9-6-41 Akasaka, Minato-ku, Tokyo, 107-0052, Japan. TEL 81-3-34020541, FAX 81-3-34031776, info@mmij.or.jp, http://www.mmij.or.jp/.

669 600 DEU ISSN 0026-0797
TS200 CODEN: MOFEAV
M O - METALLOBERFLAECHE; Beschichten von Kunststoff und Metall. Text in German. 1946. 10/yr. EUR 129; EUR 14.90 newsstand/cover (effective 2010). adv. bk.rev. abstr.; illus. **Document type:** *Journal, Trade.*
Indexed: A&ATA, A22, A28, APA, BrCerAb, C&ISA, CA/WCA, CEABA, CIA, CIN, Cadscan, CerAb, ChemAb, ChemTitl, CivEngAb, CorrAb, E&CAJ, E11, EEA, EMA, ESPM, EngInd, EnvEAb, H15, IBR, IBZ, ISMEC, LeadAb, M&TEA, M09, MBF, METADEX, PST, SCOPUS, SolStAb, T04, TM, WAA, WSCA, Zincscan.
—BLDSC (5693.000000), CASDDS, IE, Infotrieve, Ingenta, INIST, Linda Hall. **CCC.**
Published by: I G T Informationsgesellschaft Technik GmbH, Oskar-Maria-Graf-Ring 23, Munich, 81737, Germany. TEL 49-89-6736970, FAX 49-89-67369719, info@igt-verlag.de. Eds. Carsten Blumenstengel, Nadja Gosch. Pub. Lothar Zobel. Adv. contact Dagmar Batschat.

669 DEU ISSN 0935-7254
TN600 CODEN: MMTIEZ
M P T. METALLURGICAL PLANT AND TECHNOLOGY INTERNATIONAL. Text and summaries in English. 1978. bi-m. EUR 199; EUR 38 per issue (effective 2011). adv. index. back issues avail. **Document type:** *Journal, Trade.* **Description:** Covers all aspects from ore preparation to surface treatment. Includes major articles on plant and equipment and many short news items.
Formerly (until 1989): M P T - Metallurgical Plant and Technology (0171-4511)
Related titles: ◆ Russian Translation: M P T. Metallurgicheskoe Proizvodstvo i Tekhnologiya Metallurgicheskih Protsessov. ISSN 0934-8077; Chinese Translation: Yejin Shebei he Jishu. ISSN 0930-1852. 1986.
Indexed: A22, A28, AESIS, APA, BrCerAb, C&ISA, CA/WCA, CIA, CPEI, CerAb, CivEngAb, CorrAb, E&CAJ, E11, EEA, EMA, ESPM, EngInd, EnvEAb, GeoRef, H15, ISMEC, M&TEA, M09, MBF, METADEX, RefZh, SCOPUS, SolStAb, T04, TM, WAA.
—BLDSC (5698.453100), CASDDS, IE, Infotrieve, Ingenta, Linda Hall. **CCC.**
Published by: Verlag Stahleisen GmbH, Sohnstr 65, Duesseldorf, 40237, Germany. TEL 49-211-67070, FAX 49-211-6707310, stahleisen@stahleisen.de, http://www.stahleisen.de. Ed. Arnt Hannewald. Adv. contact Sigrid Klinge. B&W page EUR 3,452, color page EUR 4,250; trim 174 x 260. Circ: 8,935 (controlled).

669 RUS ISSN 0934-8077
M P T. METALLURGICHESKOE PROIZVODSTVO I TEKHNOLOGIYA METALLURGICHESKIH PROTSESSOV. Text in Russian. 1987. s-a. 120 p./no.; **Document type:** *Journal, Trade.* **Description:** Devoted to innovations in the field of metallurgical technologies, equipment and products abroad.
Related titles: ◆ Translation of: M P T. Metallurgical Plant and Technology International. ISSN 0935-7254; ◆ Supplement to: Chernye Metally. ISSN 0132-0890.
Indexed: RefZh.
Published by: Izdatel'stvo Ruda i Metally/Ore and Metals Publishers, Leninskii prospekt 6, korpus 1, ofis 622, a/ya 71, Moscow, 119049, Russian Federation. rim@rudmet.ru. Ed. Evgenii Tsiryul'nikov. Circ: 8,000.

363.7282 GBR
M R W. (Materials Recycling Week) Text in English. 1912. w. GBP 130 domestic; GBP 182 in Europe; GBP 253 elsewhere (effective 2009); subscr. includes Handbook. adv. bk.rev. charts; illus.; mkt.; tr.lit. back issues avail. **Document type:** *Magazine, Trade.* **Description:** Presents information on metallic materials reclamation.
Former titles (until 2008): Materials Recycling Week (1354-8522); (until 1994): Materials Reclamation Weekly (0025-5386); (until 1968): Waste Trade World; (until 1967): Waste Trade World and Iron and Steel Scrap Review; (until 1939): Waste Trade World
Related titles: Microform ed.: (from PQC); Online - full text ed.
Indexed: E04, E05, G02, IPackAb, KES, P&BA, R18, T02, WasteInfo.
—IE, Infotrieve. **CCC.**
Published by: Emap Inform, Greater London House, Hampstead Rd, London, NW1 3EJ, United Kingdom. TEL 44-20-77285000, http://www.emap.com. Ed. Paul Sanderson TEL 44-20-77284531. Adv. contact Ian Wilson TEL 44-20-77284515. page GBP 1,950; trim 210 x 297.

669 USA
M T S TESTING NEWS. Text in English. q.
Published by: M T S Systems Corporation, 14000 Technology Dr, Eden Prairie, MN 55344-2290. TEL 952-937-4000, FAX 952-937-4515, http://www.mts.com/.

669 ZAF
MACHINE TOOL BUYERS GUIDE FOR SOUTHERN AFRICA. Text in English. 1988. a. ZAR 110. **Document type:** *Directory.* **Description:** Intended for users of metalworking machinery.
Published by: George Warman Publications (Pty.) Ltd., Rondebosch, PO Box 705, Cape Town, 7701, South Africa. info@gwarmanpublications.co.za, http://www.gwarmanpublications.co.za. Ed. Abdul Rawoot.

MACHINERY AND STEEL. *see* MACHINERY

MACHINES PRODUCTION. *see* MACHINERY

669.723 USA ISSN 0047-5491
MAGNESIUM MONTHLY REVIEW; comprehensive report for busy people. Text in English. 1971. m. looseleaf. USD 60 in North America; USD 75 elsewhere (effective 2007). bk.rev. index. 9 p./no.; back issues avail. **Document type:** *Newsletter.* **Description:** Covers news, developments, trends and predictions in the field of magnesium for world industry leaders, including production, markets, techniques, and foreign developments.
Related titles: E-mail ed.
Indexed: A28, APA, BrCerAb, C&ISA, CA/WCA, CIA, CerAb, CivEngAb, CorrAb, E&CAJ, E11, EEA, EMA, ESPM, EnvEAb, H15, M&TEA, M09, MBF, METADEX, SolStAb, T04, WAA.
—Linda Hall.
Address: 226 Deer Trace, Prattville, AL 36067-3806. TEL 334-365-9184, FAX 775-637-9192, bobbrown@mindspring.com. Ed. David C Brown. Pub. Robert Brown. Circ: 466 (paid and controlled).

669 USA ISSN 0891-6942
MAGNESIUM NEWSLETTER. Text in English. 1944. w. looseleaf. free to members (effective 2010). **Document type:** *Newsletter, Trade.* **Description:** Contains news item, industry articles and press releases from around the world.
Indexed: A28, APA, BrCerAb, C&ISA, CA/WCA, CIA, CerAb, CivEngAb, CorrAb, E&CAJ, E11, EEA, EMA, H15, M&TEA, M09, MBF, METADEX, SolStAb, T04, WAA.
—Linda Hall.
Published by: International Magnesium Association, 1000 N Rand Rd, Ste 214, Wauconda, IL 60084. TEL 847-526-2010, FAX 847-526-3993, info@intlmag.org, http://www.intlmag.org.

MAGNESIUM RESEARCH (ONLINE). *see* MEDICAL SCIENCES

669 540 DEU ISSN 0792-1241
QD1 CODEN: MGMCE8
➤ **MAIN GROUP METAL CHEMISTRY.** Text in English. 1972. bi-m. EUR 400, USD 600 to institutions; EUR 460, USD 690 combined subscription to institutions (print & online eds.) (effective 2012). adv. bk.rev. index. back issues avail. **Document type:** *Journal, Academic/Scholarly.* **Description:** Instituted for the rapid publication of preliminary communications, new research and review articles within the field of main group metal and semi-metal chemistry.
Former titles (until 1987): Silicon, Germanium, Tin and Lead Compounds (0334-7575); (until 1986): Reviews on Silicon, Germanium, Tin and Lead Compounds (0048-7570)
Related titles: Online - full text ed.: EUR 400, USD 600 to institutions (effective 2012).
Indexed: A01, ASCA, C33, CCI, CIN, ChemAb, ChemTitl, CurCR, CurCont, R16, SCI, SCOPUS, W07.
—BLDSC (5351.850000), CASDDS, IE, Ingenta, INIST, Linda Hall.
Published by: Walter de Gruyter GmbH & Co. KG, Genthiner Str 13, Berlin, 10785, Germany. TEL 49-30-260050, FAX 49-30-26005251, info@degruyter.com, http://www.degruyter.de.

671.2 CAN ISSN 1926-3910
▼ **MANUFACTURING FOR PROFIT.** Text in English. 2010. irreg., latest vol.2, no.2, 2011. back issues avail. **Document type:** *Magazine, Trade.*
Related titles: Online - full text ed.: free (effective 2011).
Published by: S M T C L Canada, 2783 Portland Dr, Oakville, ON L6H 6M6, Canada. TEL 905-829-1579, FAX 905-829-8692, info@smtcl.ca, http://www.smtcl.ca.

MAQUINAS & METAIS. *see* MACHINERY

MAQUINAS E METAIS. *see* MACHINERY

669 DNK ISSN 0905-2151
MASKIN - AKTUELT. Text in Danish. 1950. 8/yr. DKK 334 to individuals; DKK 820 to institutions; DKK 274 to students (effective 2010). adv. bk.rev. bibl.; illus. **Document type:** *Magazine, Trade.* **Description:** Focuses on people and companies in the iron, metal and engineering industry. Provides information on the products and services which form the basis of production, as well as on the political and economic conditions in the industry.
Former titles (until 1989): S M E A (0105-8711); (until 1968): Maskin - Industrien (0036-1658)
Related titles: Online - full text ed.: 2007.
Indexed: ASCA.
Published by: TechMedia A/S, Naverland 35, Glostrup, 2600, Denmark. TEL 45-43-242628, FAX 45-43-242626, info@techmedia.dk. Ed. Helle Friemann Nielsen TEL 45-43-242637. Adv. contact Claus Flyckt Hansen TEL 45-43-242675. B&W page DKK 19,000, color page DKK 22,600; trim 191 x 277. Circ: 8,200 (controlled).

MATERIA/BERGSHANTERINGEN. *see* MINES AND MINING INDUSTRY

669 JPN ISSN 1340-2625
TN4 CODEN: NKZKAU
MATERIA/JAPAN INSTITUTE OF METALS. BULLETIN. Text in Japanese. 1962. m. JPY 21,600 (effective 2000 & 2001). adv. charts. **Document type:** *Bulletin.*
Formerly (until 1994): Nihon Kinzoku Gakkai Kaiho (0021-4426)
Indexed: A28, APA, BrCerAb, C&ISA, CA/WCA, CIA, CerAb, CivEngAb, CorrAb, E&CAJ, E11, EEA, EMA, H15, INIS AtomInd, Inspec, JTA, M&TEA, M09, MBF, METADEX, SolStAb, T04, WAA.
—CASDDS, INIST, Linda Hall. **CCC.**
Published by: Nihon Kinzoku Gakkai/Japan Institute of Metals, 1-14-32 Ichibancho, Aoba-ku, Sendai, Sendai, 980-8544, Japan. TEL 81-22-2233685, FAX 81-22-2236312. Ed. Shuji Hanada. Circ: 10,000.

MATERIALI IN TEHNOLOGIJE/MATERIALS AND TECHNOLOGY. *see* ENGINEERING—Engineering Mechanics And Materials

620.112 DEU ISSN 0947-5117
TA401 CODEN: MTCREQ
➤ **MATERIALS AND CORROSION.** Text in English, German. 1925. m. GBP 1,946 in United Kingdom to institutions; EUR 2,972 in Europe to institutions; USD 3,812 elsewhere to institutions; GBP 2,238 combined subscription in United Kingdom to institutions (print & online eds.); EUR 3,418 combined subscription in Europe to institutions (print & online eds.); USD 4,384 combined subscription elsewhere to institutions (print & online eds.) (effective 2012). adv. bk.rev. abstr.; charts; illus.; pat.; tr.lit. index. reprint service avail. from PSC. **Document type:** *Journal, Academic/Scholarly.* **Description:** Presents papers on all aspects of materials behavior in corrosive environments as well as on corrosion testing and protection.
Former titles (until 1995): Werkstoffe und Korrosion (0043-2822); (until 1950): Archiv fuer Metallkunde (0365-4303); (until 1946): Korrosion und Metallschutz (0368-6191)
Related titles: Online - full text ed.: ISSN 1521-4176. GBP 1,946 in United Kingdom to institutions; EUR 2,972 in Europe to institutions; USD 3,812 elsewhere to institutions (effective 2012).
Indexed: A&ATA, A20, A22, A28, APA, APIAb, APICat, APIH&E, APIOC, APIPR, APIPS, APITS, ASCA, ApMecR, BMT, BrCerAb, C&ISA, C33, CA/WCA, CEABA, CIA, CIN, CPEI, CTE, CerAb, ChemAb, ChemTitl, CivEngAb, CoppAb, CorrAb, CurCont, DokArb, E&CAJ, E11, EEA, EMA, ESPM, EngInd, EnvEAb, H15, INIS AtomInd, ISMEC, ISR, Inspec, M&TEA, M09, MBF, METADEX, MSCI, PetrolAb, RefZh, SCI, SCOPUS, SolStAb, T02, T04, TM, W07, WAA, WSCA.
—BLDSC (9298.000000), AskIEEE, CASDDS, IE, Infotrieve, Ingenta, INIST, Linda Hall, PADDS. **CCC.**
Published by: (Arbeitsgemeinschaft Korrosion - DECHEMA), Wiley - V C H Verlag GmbH & Co. KGaA (Subsidiary of: John Wiley & Sons, Inc.), Postfach 101161, Weinheim, 69451, Germany. TEL 49-6201-606400, FAX 49-6201-606184, info@wiley-vch.de, http://www.wiley-vch.de. adv.: page EUR 2,000. Circ: 751 (paid and controlled). **Subscr. in the Americas to:** John Wiley & Sons, Inc., 111 River St, Hoboken, NJ 07030. TEL 201-748-6645, info@wiley.com, http://www.wiley.com/WileyCDA/; **Subscr. outside Germany, Austria & Switzerland to:** John Wiley & Sons Ltd., The Atrium, Southern Gate, Chichester, West Sussex PO19 8SQ, United Kingdom. TEL 44-1243-779777, FAX 44-1243-775878, cs-agency@wiley.com.

➤ **MATERIALS AT HIGH TEMPERATURES**; materials generation applications. *see* ENGINEERING—Engineering Mechanics And Materials

669 AUS ISSN 1037-7107
TA401 CODEN: MAUSEK
MATERIALS AUSTRALIA; the magazine of engineering materials technology. Abbreviated title: M A. Text in English. 1969. bi-m. AUD 120 domestic; AUD 140 in Asia & the Pacific; AUD 160 elsewhere; free to members (effective 2008). adv. bk.rev. back issues avail. **Document type:** *Magazine, Trade.* **Description:** Offers news on the latest technological developments, case studies, company profiles, news on the people who make up the industry, new products and processes; includes a conference diary featuring an extensive list of Australian and overseas conferences.
Former titles (until 1991): Materials Australasia (0818-3597); (until 1986): Metals Australasia (0156-174X); (until 1977): Metals Australia (0047-6897)
Indexed: A28, AESIS, APA, BrCerAb, C&ISA, CA/WCA, CIA, CerAb, ChemAb, CivEngAb, CorrAb, E&CAJ, E11, EEA, EMA, GeoRef, H15, INIS AtomInd, Inspec, M&TEA, M09, MBF, METADEX, SolStAb, T04, WAA.
—CASDDS, Ingenta, INIST, Linda Hall.
Published by: (Institute of Materials Engineering Australasia Pty. Ltd., Institute of Metals and Materials Australasia Ltd.), Great Southern Press Pty Ltd., GPO Box 4967, Melbourne, VIC 3001, Australia. TEL 61-3-92485100, FAX 61-3-96022708, http://gs-press.com.au. Ed. Zelda Tupicoff. Adv. contact Lucy Nguyen. color page AUD 1,980; trim 210 x 297. Circ: 2,000.

669.95 USA ISSN 1044-5803
TN690 CODEN: MACHEX
➤ **MATERIALS CHARACTERIZATION.** Text in English. 1968. m. EUR 1,284 in Europe to institutions; JPY 170,400 in Japan to institutions; USD 1,442 elsewhere to institutions (effective 2012). adv. bk.rev. bibl.; charts; illus. index. back issues avail.; reprints avail. **Document type:** *Journal, Academic/Scholarly.* **Description:** Focuses on all characterization techniques, including all forms of microscopy (light, electron, acoustic, etc.,) and analysis (especially microanalysis and surface analytical techniques).
Formerly (until 1990): Metallography (0026-0800)
Related titles: Microform ed.: (from PQC); Online - full text ed.: ISSN 1873-4189 (from IngentaConnect, ScienceDirect).
Indexed: A01, A03, A08, A20, A22, A26, A28, APA, ASCA, ApMecR, BrCerAb, C&ISA, C24, C33, CA, CA/WCA, CIA, CIN, CIS, CPEI, Cadscan, CerAb, ChemAb, ChemTitl, CivEngAb, CorrAb, CurCont, E&CAJ, E11, EEA, EMA, ESPM, EngInd, EnvEAb, FR, H15, I05, INIS AtomInd, ISR, Inspec, LeadAb, M&TEA, M09, MBF, METADEX, MSCI, PhysBer, RefZh, S01, SCI, SCOPUS, SolStAb, T02, T04, TM, W07, WAA, Zincscan.
—BLDSC (5394.106500), AskIEEE, CASDDS, IE, Infotrieve, Ingenta, INIST, Linda Hall. **CCC.**
Published by: (International Metallographic Society Inc.), Elsevier Inc. (Subsidiary of: Elsevier Science & Technology), 1600 John F Kennedy Blvd, Philadelphia, PA 19103. TEL 215-239-3900, FAX 215-238-7883, JournalCustomerService-usa@elsevier.com. Eds. Chris Bagnall TEL 724-836-7837, I Baker. Adv. contact Janine Castle TEL 44-1865-843844.

669 CAN
MATERIALS FOR RESOURCE RECOVERY AND TRANSPORT. Text in English. 1998. irreg. CAD 20 per issue (effective 2004).
Published by: Canadian Institute of Mining, Metallurgy and Petroleum, Metallurgical Society, 3400 de Maisonneuve Blvd W, Ste 1210, Montreal, PQ H3Z 3B8, Canada. TEL 514-939-2710, FAX 514-939-2714, cim@cim.org, http://www.cim.org.

669 AUS ISSN 1447-6738
TN1 CODEN: MFOREM
MATERIALS FORUM (CD-ROM). Text in English. 1956. a. AUD 160 domestic; AUD 210 foreign (effective 2008). adv. bk.rev. bibl.; charts; illus. Index. back issues avail. **Document type:** *Monographic series, Academic/Scholarly.* **Description:** Provides details on the structure and properties of engineering materials: metals, ceramics, polymers, and composites.
Former titles (until 2000): Materials Forum (Print) (0883-2900); (until 1986): Metals Forum (0160-7952); (until 1977): Australasian Institute of Metals. Journal (0815-6549); (until 1976): Australian Institute of Metals. Journal (0004-9352)
Media: CD-ROM. **Related titles:** Microform ed.: (from PQC).
Indexed: A22, A28, APA, ASCA, BCIRA, BrCerAb, C&ISA, C33, CA/WCA, CIA, CPEI, Cadscan, CerAb, ChemAb, ChemTitl, CivEngAb, CorrAb, E&CAJ, E11, EEA, EMA, EngInd, H15, IMMAb, INIS AtomInd, ISMEC, ISR, Inspec, LeadAb, M&TEA, M09, MBF, METADEX, SCOPUS, SolStAb, T04, WAA, Zincscan.
—BLDSC (5394.314000), AskIEEE, CASDDS, INIST, Linda Hall. **CCC.**
Published by: Institute of Materials Engineering Australasia Pty. Ltd., 21 Bedford St, Ste 205, North Melbourne, VIC 3051, Australia. TEL 61-3-93267266, FAX 61-3-93267272, imea@materialsaustralia.com.au, http://www.materialsaustralia.com.au. Circ: 1,800.

669 CAN
MATERIALS SOLUTIONS FOR ENVIRONMENTAL PROBLEMS. Text in English. 1997. irreg. CAD 20 per issue (effective 2004).
Published by: Canadian Institute of Mining, Metallurgy and Petroleum, Metallurgical Society, 3400 de Maisonneuve Blvd W, Ste 1210, Montreal, PQ H3Z 3B8, Canada. TEL 514-939-2710, FAX 514-939-2714, cim@cim.org, http://www.cim.org.

669 GBR ISSN 1066-7857
TA401 CODEN: MATTEI
➤ **MATERIALS TECHNOLOGY**; advanced performance materials. Text in English. 1986. 5/yr. GBP 593 combined subscription to institutions (print & online eds.); USD 1,084 combined subscription in United States to institutions (print & online eds.) (effective 2012). adv. bk.rev.; Website rev. abstr.; charts; illus.; stat. index. 66 p./no. 2 cols./p.; back issues avail.; reprint service avail. from PSC. **Document type:** *Journal, Academic/Scholarly.* **Description:** Publishes news, articles, and announcements pertaining to technological advancements and research in the fields of metallurgy, ceramics, polymers, fibers, composites. Also contans market information and updates.
Incorporates (1995-1999): Advanced Performance Materials (0929-1881); Formerly (until 1993): Materials and Processing Report (0887-1949)
Related titles: Microform ed.: (from PQC); Online - full text ed.: ISSN 1753-5557. GBP 541 to institutions; USD 989 in United States to institutions (effective 2012) (from IngentaConnect).
Indexed: A28, APA, BrCerAb, C&ISA, C10, C24, CA, CA/WCA, CEABA, CIA, CPEI, CerAb, CivEngAb, CorrAb, CurCont, E&CAJ, E11, EEA, EMA, ESPM, EngInd, EnvEAb, H15, ICEA, Inspec, M&TEA, M09, MBF, METADEX, MSCI, R18, SCI, SCOPUS, SolStAb, T02, T04, TM, W07, WAA.
—BLDSC (5396.444180), AskIEEE, IE, Infotrieve, Ingenta, Linda Hall. **CCC.**
Published by: Maney Publishing, Ste 1C, Joseph's Well, Hanover Walk, Leeds, W Yorks LS3 1AB, United Kingdom. TEL 44-113-2432800, FAX 44-113-3868178, maney@maney.co.uk. Eds. F H (Sam) Froes, Paul Hogg. **Subscr. in N. America to:** Maney Publishing, 875 Massachusetts Ave, 7th Fl, Cambridge, MA 02139. TEL 866-297-5154, FAX 617-354-6875, maney@maneyusa.com.

669 JPN ISSN 1345-9678
TN4 CODEN: MTJIEY
➤ **MATERIALS TRANSACTIONS.** Text in English. 1960. m. JPY 3,150 domestic; USD 480 foreign; USD 40 newsstand/cover; free to members (effective 2002). **Document type:** *Journal, Academic/Scholarly.*
Former titles (until 2001): Materials Transactions, J I M (0916-1821); (until 1989): Japan Institute of Metals. Transactions (0021-4434)
Related titles: Online - full text ed.: ISSN 1347-5320.
Indexed: A22, A28, APA, ASCA, BrCerAb, C&ISA, C24, C33, CA/WCA, CIA, CPEI, CerAb, ChemAb, ChemTitl, CivEngAb, CorrAb, CurCont, E&CAJ, E11, EEA, EMA, ESPM, EngInd, EnvEAb, GeoRef, H15, IBR, IBZ, INIS AtomInd, ISR, Inspec, JCT, JTA, M&TEA, M09, MBF, METADEX, MSCI, SCI, SCOPUS, SolStAb, SpeleolAb, T04, TM, W07, WAA.
—BLDSC (5396.509000), AskIEEE, CASDDS, IE, Ingenta, INIST, Linda Hall. **CCC.**
Published by: Nihon Kinzoku Gakkai/Japan Institute of Metals, 1-14-32 Ichibancho, Aoba-ku, Sendai, Sendai, 980-8544, Japan. TEL 81-22-2233685, FAX 81-22-2236312, http://wwwsoc.nii.ac.jp/jim/. Ed. Ryuzo Watanabe. Circ: 2,000. **Subscr. in Japan to:** Maruzen Co., Ltd., 3-10 Nihonbashi 2-chome, Chuo-ku, Tokyo 103-0027, Japan. TEL 81-3-3272-0521, FAX 81-3-3272-0693, http://www.maruzen.co.jp. **Dist. outside of Japan by:** Maruzen Co., Ltd., Import & Export Dept, PO Box 5050, Tokyo International, Tokyo 100-3191, Japan. TEL 81-3-32733234, FAX 81-3-32716076, http://www.maruzen.co.jp.

669 GBR ISSN 0967-8638
TN1 CODEN: MORLEE
MATERIALS WORLD. Text in English. 1967-1981 (Dec.); resumed 1993. m. GBP 332 to institutions; USD 572 in United States to institutions (effective 2012). adv. bk.rev.; software rev.; Website rev. charts; illus.; tr.lit. index. 48 p./no.; back issues avail.; reprint service avail. from PSC. **Document type:** *Magazine, Trade.* **Description:** Covers the science, manufacturing technology and use of metals, ceramics, plastics, composite engineering materials and functional materials.
Incorporates (1997-2002): International Mining and Minerals (1461-4715); Which was formed by the merger of (1988-1997): Mining Industry International (0955-2847); Which was formerly (1975-1988): I M M Bulletin (0308-9789); (1904-1975): Institution of Mining and Metallurgy. Bulletin (0376-1770); and of (1969-1997): Mining Technology (0026-5276); Which was formerly (1942-1969): Mining Electrical and Mechanical Engineer (0374-373X); Formed by the merger of (1984-1993): Metals and Materials (0266-7185); Which was formed by the merger of (1973-1984): Metallurgist and Materials Technologist (0306-526X); (1982-1984): Metals Society World (0265-2722); and of (1984-1993): British Ceramic. Transactions and Journal (0266-7606); Which was formerly (1971-1984): British Ceramic Society. Transactions and Journal (0307-7357); Which was formed by the merger of (1939-1971): British Ceramic Society. Transactions (0371-5469); Which was formerly (1917-1939): Ceramic Society. Transactions (0371-5655); (1903-1917): English Ceramic Society. Transactions (0371-6236); (1???-1903): North Staffordshire Ceramic Society. Transactions; and of (1963-1970): British Ceramic Society. Journal (0524-5133); (1976-1993): Plastics and Rubber International (0309-4561); Which was formerly (1976-1976): Plastics and Rubber (0308-311X); Which was formed by the merger of (1968-1976): Plastics and Polymers (0300-3582); Which was formerly (1954-1968): Plastics Institute Transactions and Journal (0369-9943); (1948-1954): Plastics Institute Transactions (0370-0402); (1932-1948): Institute of the Plastics Industry. Transactions (0371-7941); and of (1975-1976): Rubber Industry (0306-9583); Which was formerly (1973-1975): Institute of the Rubber Industry. Journal (0144-106X); (1967-1973): I R I. Journal (0019-0462); Which was formed by the merger of (1954-1967): Institute of the Rubber Industry. Transactions (0534-2880); (1925-1967): Institution of the Rubber Industry. Transactions (0371-7968); Which was formerly (1???-1925): Institution of the Rubber Industry. Yearbook
Related titles: Online - full text ed.
Indexed: A&ATA, A05, A20, A22, A26, A28, ABTICS, APA, AS&TA, AS&TI, ASCA, B02, B03, B11, B15, B17, B18, BCIRA, BrCerAb, C&ISA, CA/WCA, CBNB, CIA, CIN, CPEI, CTE, Cadscan, CerAb, ChemAb, ChemTitl, CivEngAb, CoppAb, CorrAb, CurPA, E&CAJ, E11, EEA, EMA, ESPM, EngInd, EnvEAb, FR, G04, G08, GeoRef, H15, HECAB, I05, IMMAb, ISMEC, Inspec, LeadAb, M&TEA, M09, MBF, METADEX, MSCI, P02, P26, P48, P52, P54, PQC, PST, R18, SCI, SCOPUS, SolStAb, SpeleolAb, T04, W07, WAA, WSCA, Zincscan.
—BLDSC (5396.550000), AskIEEE, CASDDS, IE, Infotrieve, Ingenta, INIST, Linda Hall. **CCC.**
Published by: (Institute of Materials, Minerals and Mining), I O M Communications Ltd. (Subsidiary of: Institute of Materials, Minerals and Mining), 1 Carlton House Terr, London, SW1Y 5DB, United Kingdom. TEL 44-20-74517300, FAX 44-20-78391702. Ed. Katherine Williams TEL 44-20-74517314. Adv. contact James Priest TEL 44-20-76571831. B&W page GBP 1,470; trim 210 x 297. Circ: 18,595. **Subscr. in N America to:** Maney Publishing, 875 Massachusetts Ave, 7th Fl, Cambridge, MA 02139. TEL 866-297-5154, FAX 617-354-6875, maney@maneyusa.com. **Subscr. to:** Maney Publishing, Ste 1C, Joseph's Well, Hanover Walk, Leeds, W Yorks LS3 1AB, United Kingdom. TEL 44-113-2432800, FAX 44-113-3868178, maney@maney.co.uk, http://www.maney.co.uk.

669 DEU ISSN 0933-5137
TA401 CODEN: MATWER
➤ **MATERIALWISSENSCHAFT UND WERKSTOFFTECHNIK/ MATERIALS SCIENCE AND ENGINEERING TECHNOLOGY.** Text in English, German. 1970. m. GBP 1,893 in United Kingdom to institutions; EUR 2,935 in Europe to institutions; USD 3,706 elsewhere to institutions; GBP 2,177 combined subscription in United Kingdom to institutions (print & online eds.); EUR 3,375 combined subscription in Europe to institutions (print & online eds.); USD 4,262 combined subscription elsewhere to institutions (print & online eds.) (effective 2012). bk.rev. abstr.; charts; illus.; tr.lit. index. reprint service avail. from PSC. **Document type:** *Journal, Academic/Scholarly.* **Description:** Provides the fundamental and practical information needed by people concerned with materials development, manufacture and testing in order to choose the material that best suits the purpose at hand.
Formerly (until 1988): Zeitschrift fuer Werkstofftechnik (0049-8688)
Related titles: Online - full text ed.: ISSN 1521-4052. GBP 1,893 in United Kingdom to institutions; EUR 2,935 in Europe to institutions; USD 3,706 elsewhere to institutions (effective 2012).
Indexed: A22, A28, APA, ASCA, BCIRA, BrCerAb, C&ISA, CA/WCA, CEABA, CIA, CPEI, CerAb, ChemAb, ChemTitl, CivEngAb, CoppAb, CorrAb, CurCont, E&CAJ, E11, EEA, EMA, ESPM, EngInd, EnvEAb, H15, INIS AtomInd, Inspec, M&TEA, M09, MBF, METADEX, MSCI, P30, SCI, SCOPUS, SolStAb, T04, TM, W07, WAA.
—BLDSC (5396.640000), CASDDS, IE, Infotrieve, Ingenta, INIST, Linda Hall. **CCC.**
Published by: Wiley - V C H Verlag GmbH & Co. KGaA (Subsidiary of: John Wiley & Sons, Inc.), Postfach 101161, Weinheim, 69451, Germany. TEL 49-6201-606400, FAX 49-6201-606184, info@wiley-vch.de, http://www.wiley-vch.de. Circ: 700. **Subscr. in the Americas to:** John Wiley & Sons, Inc., 111 River St, Hoboken, NJ 07030. TEL 201-748-6645, subinfo@wiley.com; **Subscr. outside Germany, Austria & Switzerland to:** John Wiley & Sons Ltd., The Atrium, Southern Gate, Chichester, West Sussex PO19 8SQ, United Kingdom. TEL 44-1243-779777, FAX 44-1243-775878, cs-agency@wiley.com. **Co-sponsors:** Stahlinstitut VDEh; Deutsche Gesellschaft fur Materialkunde; Deutsche Gesellschaft fuer Chemisches Appartewesen e.V.

669 ITA ISSN 0025-9829
MERCATO METALSIDERURGICO. Text in Italian. 1954. m. free to members. adv. bk.rev. **Document type:** *Bulletin, Trade.* **Description:** Review of markets for and prices of major steel products and non-ferrous metals, ferrous and non-ferrous scrap and hardware.
Published by: Assofermet, Corso Venezia 47-49, Milan, 20121, Italy. TEL 39-02-76008807, FAX 39-02-781027. Ed., R&P Eugenio Turchetti. Circ: 1,800.

671 NLD ISSN 0026-0479
METAAL & TECHNIEK; vakblad voor het midden- en kleinbedrijf in de metaal. Short title: M & T. Text in Dutch. 1955. m. (11/yr.). EUR 99.50 domestic; EUR 112.50 foreign; EUR 49.50 to students (effective 2010). adv. stat. **Document type:** *Trade.* **Description:** Follows the latest developments in methods of production and new products. Also discusses organizational, marketing and economic aspects of the metallurgical industry.
Incorporates (192?-1974): Staal (0038-8823)
Indexed: KES.
Published by: Media Business Press BV, Postbus 8632, Rotterdam, 3009 AP, Netherlands. TEL 31-10-2894075, FAX 31-10-2894076, info@mbp.nl, http://www.mbp.nl/. Ed. Ewald Lohmann. adv.: B&W page EUR 1,900, color page EUR 3,130; trim 230 x 280. Circ: 12,421. **Co-sponsor:** Metaalunie.

672 NLD ISSN 1872-1397
METAALPUNT. Text in Dutch. 2006. 48/yr. free to qualified personnel (effective 2009). adv.
Published by: VakVisie Uitgeverij, Postbus 30, Zutphen, 7200 AA, Netherlands. TEL 31-575-572254, FAX 31-575-573718, info@vakvisie.nl. Ed. Hans Ouwekerk TEL 31-575-570303. Adv. contact Doriena van der Schild TEL 31-575-570303.

METAL. *see* LABOR UNIONS

METAL & STEEL TRADERS OF THE WORLD (YEAR). *see* BUSINESS AND ECONOMICS—Trade And Industrial Directories

METAL ARCHITECTURE. *see* ARCHITECTURE

669 IND ISSN 0972-2238
METAL ASIA; a complete metal magazine. Text in English. 1999. bi-m. INR 3,000, USD 300 (effective 2011). adv. back issues avail. **Document type:** *Magazine, Trade.*
Published by: I S R Infomedia Ltd., Merlin Links, 5th Fl, Block 5E & F 166B, S.P. Mukherjee Rd, Kolkata, 700 026, India. TEL 91-33-24658581, FAX 91-33-24653790, isrinfo@eth.net, http://www.isrinfomedia.com.

METAL BUILDING DEVELOPER. *see* BUILDING AND CONSTRUCTION

669 GBR ISSN 0026-0533
TN1 CODEN: MTBLAX
METAL BULLETIN. Text in English. 1913. w. GBP 1,317 domestic; USD 3,017 in United States; EUR 2,427 in Europe; USD 3,147 elsewhere (effective 2010). adv. mkt.; stat.; tr.lit. index. **Document type:** *Bulletin, Trade.* **Description:** News bulletin for the metals and steel industry worldwide.
Related titles: Online - full text ed.
Indexed: A&ATA, A15, A28, AESIS, APA, B01, B03, BrCerAb, C&ISA, CA/WCA, CIA, CIN, Cadscan, CerAb, ChemAb, ChemTitl, CivEngAb, CoppAb, CorrAb, E&CAJ, E11, EEA, EMA, H15, IMMAb, KES, LeadAb, M&TEA, M09, MBF, METADEX, P06, P51, PROMT, RASB, SolStAb, T04, WAA, Zincscan.
—CASDDS, Linda Hall. **CCC.**
Published by: Metal Bulletin Plc. (Subsidiary of: Euromoney Institutional Investor Plc.), Park House, 3 Park Terr, Worcester Park, Surrey KT4 7HY, United Kingdom. TEL 44-20-78279977, FAX 44-20-78275290, editorial@metalbulletin.com. Circ: 9,000.

669 GBR ISSN 0373-4064
TN1 CODEN: MMBMFQ
METAL BULLETIN MONTHLY. Text in English. 1972. m. GBP 1,117 domestic; EUR 2,147 in Europe; USD 2,727 elsewhere (effective 2010). adv. bk.rev. tr.lit. index. **Document type:** *Magazine, Trade.* **Description:** Covers key commercial and technological developments along the complete length of the ferrous and non-ferrous metal supply chains.
Related titles: Online - full text ed.
Indexed: A&ATA, A15, A22, A28, ABIn, AESIS, APA, B01, B03, B07, BrCerAb, C&ISA, CA/WCA, CIA, Cadscan, CerAb, CivEngAb, CoppAb, CorrAb, E&CAJ, E11, EEA, EMA, ESPM, EnvEAb, GeoRef, H15, IMMAb, KES, LeadAb, M&TEA, M09, MBF, METADEX, P48, P51, P52, PQC, SolStAb, T04, TM, WAA, Zincscan.
—BLDSC (5683.770000), CASDDS, IE, Infotrieve, Ingenta, INIST. **CCC.**
Published by: Metal Bulletin Plc. (Subsidiary of: Euromoney Institutional Investor Plc.), Nestor House, Playhouse Yard, London, EC4V 5EX, United Kingdom. TEL 44-20-77797390, FAX 44-20-77797389, help@metalbulletin.com, http://www.metalbulletin.com. Eds. David Brooks, Scott Robertson. Adv. contact Stefano di Nardo TEL 44-20-78275220.

669 658.8 GBR
METAL BULLETIN'S GUIDE TO THE LONDON METAL EXCHANGE. Text in English. 1976. irreg., latest 2009. GBP 247, USD 397, EUR 187 per issue (effective 2010). adv. **Document type:** *Handbook/ Manual/Guide, Academic/Scholarly.* **Description:** Covers market operations together with historical background and individual chapters devoted to each product traded.
Formerly (until 2009): Wolff's Guide to the London Metal Exchange (0144-5960)
—CCC.

Published by: Metal Bulletin Plc. (Subsidiary of: Euromoney Institutional Investor Plc.), Nestor House, Playhouse Yard, London, EC4V 5EX, United Kingdom. TEL 44-20-77797390, FAX 44-20-77797389, help@metalbulletin.com, http://www.metalbulletin.com. Adv. contact Stefano di Nardo TEL 44-20-78275220. **Co-publisher:** Rudolf Wolff and Co. Ltd.

669.029 GBR ISSN 0955-6540
HD9975.A1
METAL BULLETIN'S INTERNATIONAL SCRAP DIRECTORY (YEAR). Text in English. 1976. a. GBP 407, EUR 617, USD 897 per issue (effective 2010). **Document type:** *Directory, Trade.* **Description:** International directory of companies engaged in trading and physical processing of iron and steel and non-ferrous scrap metals.
Former titles (until 1989): European and North American Scrap Directory (0261-426X); (until 1981): European Scrap Directory (0308-7786)
Published by: Metal Bulletin Plc. (Subsidiary of: Euromoney Institutional Investor Plc.), Nestor House, Playhouse Yard, London, EC4V 5EX, United Kingdom. TEL 44-20-77797390, FAX 44-20-77797389, help@metalbulletin.com, http://www.metalbulletin.com. Adv. contact Stefano di Nardo TEL 44-20-78275220.

669.028 USA ISSN 2160-343X
TS228.99 CODEN: ECSNBK
METAL CASTING DESIGN & PURCHASING. Abbreviated title: M C D P. Text in English. 1969. bi-m. USD 119 in North America; USD 150 elsewhere; USD 7 per issue domestic; USD 12 per issue foreign; free to qualified personnel (effective 2010). adv. back issues avail. **Document type:** *Magazine, Trade.*
Former titles (until 2009): Engineered Casting Solutions (1523-4371); (until 1999): Casting World (0887-9060)
Related titles: Online - full text ed.: free (effective 2010).
Indexed: A10, A28, APA, BrCerAb, C&ISA, CA/WCA, CIA, CPEI, CerAb, CivEngAb, CorrAb, E&CAJ, E11, EEA, EMA, ESPM, EngInd, EnvEAb, H15, M&TEA, M09, MBF, METADEX, SCOPUS, SolStAb, T04, TM, V03, WAA.
—Linda Hall. **CCC.**
Published by: American Foundry Society, 1695 N Penny Ln, Schaumburg, IL 60173. TEL 847-824-0181, FAX 847-824-7848, library@afsinc.org, http://www.afsinc.org. Ed., Pub. Alfred Spada TEL 847-824-0181 ext 281. Circ: 30,000.

671.2 AUS
TS200 CODEN: CSNGAT
METAL CASTING TECHNOLOGIES. Abbreviated title: M C T. Text in English. 1955. q. AUD 99.65 domestic; AUD 125.40 foreign (effective 2009). adv. bk.rev. illus.; pat.; stat. index. back issues avail. **Document type:** *Magazine, Trade.* **Description:** Provides a mixture of news, product information, and technical datas about metal casting technologies.
Incorporates (1994-2000): Metal Asia; Former titles (until 1998): Metal Casting and Surface Finishing; (until 1992): Metals and Castings Australasia; (until 1987): Castings (0008-7521)
Related titles: Microform ed.: (from PQC); Online - full text ed.: free (effective 2009).
Indexed: AESIS, APA, BCIRA, C&ISA, CIA, CISA, ChemAb, CorrAb, E&CAJ, EEA, SolStAb, WAA.
—CASDDS.
Published by: (Australian Foundry Institute), Rala Information Service Pty Ltd., Rear 205 Darling St, PO Box 134, Balmain, NSW 2041, Australia. TEL 61-2-95551944, FAX 61-2-95551496, melinda@rala.com.au. Pub. Barbara Cail. Adv. contact Adam Cail. page AUD 2,148; trim 210 x 297.

669 USA ISSN 0539-4511
TN1
METAL CENTER NEWS. Text in English. 1961. 13/yr. USD 99 domestic; USD 115 in Canada; USD 169 elsewhere (effective 2005). adv. bk.rev. charts; illus.; stat. back issues avail.; reprints avail. **Document type:** *Magazine, Trade.* **Description:** Trade publication that reaches key metal distributors and warehousing operations selling sheet and plate metals, rod, bar and structural piping and tubing, as well as those providing pre-production services such as shearing, grinding and near-net shaping.
Related titles: Online - full text ed.; ◆ Supplement(s): Metal Distribution. ISSN 0098-2210.
Indexed: A09, A10, A12, A13, A15, A17, A22, A28, ABIn, APA, B01, B03, B06, B07, B08, B09, B11, BrCerAb, C&ISA, C12, CA/WCA, CIA, CerAb, CivEngAb, CorrAb, E&CAJ, E11, EEA, EMA, ESPM, EnvEAb, H15, I05, M&TEA, M09, MBF, METADEX, P06, P16, P48, P51, P52, P53, P54, PQC, PROMT, SolStAb, T02, T03, T04, V02, V03, V04, WAA.
—Linda Hall. **CCC.**
Published by: Sackett Media, 1100 Jorie Blvd, Ste 207, Oak Brook, IL 60523. TEL 630-571-1067, FAX 630-572-0689. Ed. Tim Triplett TEL 630-571-1206. Pub. Nancy Hartley. Adv. contacts Jana Bricker TEL 630-572-0702, Karen Leonard TEL 630-572-0670. B&W page USD 3,650, color page USD 5,020; trim 7.88 x 10.75. Circ: 15,200 (controlled).

METAL CONSTRUCTION NEWS. *see* BUILDING AND CONSTRUCTION

381 USA ISSN 0098-2210
HD9506.U6
METAL DISTRIBUTION. Text in English. 1975. a. USD 15. adv. illus. back issues avail.
Related titles: ◆ Supplement to: Metal Center News. ISSN 0539-4511.
Published by: Sackett Media, 1100 Jorie Blvd, Ste 207, Oak Brook, IL 60523. TEL 630-571-1067, FAX 630-572-0689. Ed. Tim Triplett TEL 630-571-1206. Pub. Nancy Hartley. Circ: 11,800.

669 USA ISSN 0026-0576
TS550 CODEN: MEFIA7
METAL FINISHING. Text in English. 1903. m. EUR 252 in Europe to institutions; JPY 33,700 in Japan to institutions; USD 123 in United States to institutions; USD 173 in Canada & Mexico to institutions; USD 284 elsewhere to institutions (effective 2012). adv. bk.rev. abstr.; illus.; mkt.; pat.; tr.lit. Index. Supplement avail.; back issues avail.; reprints avail. **Document type:** *Journal, Trade.* **Description:** Covers technical and practical aspects of finishing metal and plastic products, including waste treatment and pollution control.
Incorporates (1945-1957): Organic Finishing (0096-2112); Formerly (until 1940): Metal Industry (0360-5159); Which superseded (in 1903): Aluminum World and Brass and Copper Industries (0096-901X); Which incorporated: Brass Founder and Finisher and Electro-Platers' Review; Copper and Brass; (1933-1936): Platers' Guide (0096-8331); Which was formerly (until 1933): Brass World (0524-2150)
Related titles: Microfilm ed.: (from PQC); Online - full text ed.: ISSN 1873-4057 (from IngentaConnect, ScienceDirect).
Indexed: A05, A22, A23, A24, A26, A28, APA, AS&TA, AS&TI, B01, B04, B06, B07, B09, B13, BrCerAb, C&ISA, C10, CA, CA/WCA, CIA, CPEI, CTE, Cadscan, CerAb, ChemAb, ChemTitl, CivEngAb, CorrAb, E&CAJ, E11, EEA, EMA, ESPM, EngInd, EnvEAb, H15, I05, IPackAb, ISR, Inspec, LeadAb, M&TEA, M09, MBF, METADEX, PROMT, RefZh, SCOPUS, SolStAb, T02, T04, WAA, WSCA, Zincscan.
—BLDSC (5684.000000), CASDDS, IE, Infotrieve, Ingenta, INIST, Linda Hall. **CCC.**
Published by: Elsevier Inc. (Subsidiary of: Elsevier Science & Technology), 360 Park Ave S, New York, NY 10010. TEL 212-633-3100, FAX 212-633-3140, JournalCustomerService-usa@elsevier.com, http://www.elsevier.com. Ed. Reginald Tucker. Pub. Gregory A Valero. Circ: 24,000.

669.1 GBR ISSN 1741-6167
METAL PRODUCERS OF THE WORLD DIRECTORY (YEAR). Text in English. 2003. biennial. GBP 357, USD 717, EUR 537 per issue; GBP 611, USD 1,291, EUR 923 combined subscription per issue (print & online eds.) (effective 2010). **Document type:** *Directory, Trade.* **Description:** Contains information and contact details for major non-ferrous and ferro-alloy works, smelters and refineries.
Formerly (until 2002): Ore & Alloys for the Global Steel Industry (1470-143X); Which was formed by the merger of (1992-2000): Iron and Manganease Ore Databook (0967-7925); Which was formerly (until 1992): Iron Ore Databook (0950-2548); (1992-2000): Ferro-Alloy Directory & Databook (0953-721X); Which was formerly (until 1992): Ferro-Alloy Directory (0266-3198)
Related titles: CD-ROM ed.: ISSN 1755-9014; Online - full text ed.
Published by: Metal Bulletin Plc. (Subsidiary of: Euromoney Institutional Investor Plc.), Nestor House, Playhouse Yard, London, EC4V 5EX, United Kingdom. TEL 44-20-77797390, FAX 44-20-77797389, help@metalbulletin.com, http://www.metalbulletin.com. Adv. contact Stefano di Nardo TEL 44-20-78275220.

671 USA ISSN 0026-0673
TN4 CODEN: MHTRAN
➤ **METAL SCIENCE AND HEAT TREATMENT.** Text in English. 1959. 5/yr. EUR 4,931, USD 5,068 combined subscription to institutions (print & online eds.) (effective 2012). adv. back issues avail.; reprint service avail. from PSC. **Document type:** *Journal, Academic/Scholarly.* **Description:** Discusses fundamental, practical issues of physical metallurgy, new achievements in heat treatment of alloys, surface engineering, and heat treatment equipment.
Formerly (until 1963): Metal Science and Heat Treatment of Metals
Related titles: Microfilm ed.: (from PQC); Online - full text ed.: ISSN 1573-8973 (from IngentaConnect); ◆ Translation of: Metallovedenie i Termicheskaya Obrabotka Metallov. ISSN 0026-0819.
Indexed: A01, A03, A08, A22, A26, A28, APA, ASCA, BibLing, BrCerAb, C&ISA, C33, CA, CA/WCA, CIA, CPEI, Cadscan, CerAb, ChemAb, ChemTitl, CivEngAb, CorrAb, CurCont, E&CAJ, E01, E11, EEA, EMA, ESPM, EnerRA, EngInd, EnvEAb, H15, ISR, Inspec, LeadAb, M&TEA, M09, MBF, METADEX, MSCI, P52, S01, SCI, SCOPUS, SolStAb, T02, T04, W07, WAA, Zincscan.
—BLDSC (0415.895000), AskIEEE, CASDDS, East View, IE, Infotrieve, Ingenta, INIST, Linda Hall. **CCC.**
Published by: (Russia. Ministerstvo Mashinostroeniya i Aiborostroeniya RUS), Springer New York LLC (Subsidiary of: Springer Science+Business Media), 233 Spring St, New York, NY 10013. TEL 212-460-1500, FAX 212-460-1575, service-ny@springer.com, http://www.springer.com. Ed. L B Skoromnikova.

669 CHN ISSN 1000-6826
METAL WORLD. Text in Chinese. bi-m. USD 21.60 (effective 2009).
Indexed: APA, C&ISA, CorrAb, E&CAJ, EEA, SolStAb, WAA.
—East View.
Published by: (T M S - The Minerals, Metals and Materials Society USA), Chinese Society for Metals, Prof. Zhong Zengyong, 46 Dongsixi Dajie, Beijing, 100711, China. TEL 86-10-65133925, FAX 86-10-65124122.

669 621.9 ESP ISSN 1697-3119
METALES Y METALURGIA. Text in Spanish. 1961. w. EUR 344.83 combined subscription domestic (print & email eds.); EUR 495 combined subscription foreign (print & email eds.) (effective 2009). adv. bk.rev. illus.; stat. **Document type:** *Magazine, Trade.*
Formerly (until 1986): Metales y Maquinas (0210-055X)
Related titles: E-mail ed.: ISSN 1988-9259. 2000.
Indexed: GeoRef, SpeleolAb.
Published by: Tecnipublicaciones Espana, S.L., Avda de Manoteras 44, 3a Planta, Madrid, 28050, Spain. TEL 34-91-2972000, FAX 34-91-2972154, tp@tecnipublicaciones.com.

METALETTER. *see* LABOR UNIONS

669 UKR ISSN 1814-5566
➤ **METALEVI KOSTRUKTSII/METAL CONSTRUCTIONS.** Text in Ukrainian, Russian, English. 1998. q. abstr.; bibl.; charts; illus.; maps; pat. **Document type:** *Journal, Academic/Scholarly.*
Related titles: Online - full text ed.: ISSN 1993-3517.
Published by: Donbass'ka Derzhavna Akademiya Budivnytstva i Arkhitektury/Donbas National Academy of Civil Engineering and Architecture, vul Derzhavina 2, Makeyevka, Donetsk 86123, Ukraine. TEL 380-62-3002938, FAX 380-62-2214159, pc@donnasa.edu.ua, http://www.donnasa.edu.ua. Ed. Evgen Gorokhov.

671 USA ISSN 1040-967X
TS200
METALFORMING. Text in English. 1967. m. USD 25 domestic; USD 175 foreign; free to qualified personnel (effective 2006). adv. charts; illus.; stat.; tr.lit. 84 p./no.; back issues avail.; reprints avail. **Document type:** *Magazine, Trade.* **Description:** Covers industry news and trends, new technologies, equipment and materials in the metal forming and fabricating industries.
Formerly (until 1998): Metal Stamping (0026-069X)
Indexed: A22, A28, APA, BrCerAb, C&ISA, CA/WCA, CIA, CerAb, CivEngAb, CorrAb, E&CAJ, E11, EEA, EMA, ESPM, EnvEAb, H15, M&TEA, M09, MBF, METADEX, SolStAb, T04, TM, WAA.
—BLDSC (5685.230000), IE, Infotrieve, Ingenta, Linda Hall.
Published by: Precision Metalforming Association, 6363 Oak Tree Blvd, Cleveland, OH 44131. TEL 216-901-8800, FAX 216-901-9669, http://www.pma.org. Ed. Brad F Kuvin. Pub. Kathy DeLollis. adv.: B&W page USD 4,675, color page USD 5,700. Circ: 60,000 (free).

669 USA
METALFORMING MEXICO; sirviendo a los que agregan valor a la placa metalica. Text in Spanish. 2004. 3/yr. USD 5.50 per issue (effective 2007). adv. **Document type:** *Magazine, Trade.* **Description:** Keeps you up-to-date with the latest news on metalforming technologies and management solutions.
Published by: Precision Metalforming Association, 6363 Oak Tree Blvd, Cleveland, OH 44131. TEL 216-901-8800, FAX 216-901-9669, metalforming@pma.org, http://www.pma.org. adv.: B&W page USD 1,600, color page USD 1,800; trim 8 x 10.75. Circ: 10,000 (controlled).

669 DEU ISSN 0026-0746
TN3 CODEN: MTLLAF
METALL; internationale Fachzeitschrift fuer Wirtschaft, Technik und Wissenschaft. Text in German; Summaries in English. 192?. 10/yr. EUR 210.30 domestic; EUR 215 foreign; EUR 21 newsstand/cover (effective 2010). adv. bk.rev. abstr.; charts; illus.; mkt.; pat.; tr.lit. index, cum.index. **Document type:** *Magazine, Trade.*
Former titles (until 1947): Metallwissenschaft, Metalltechnik (0368-9581); (until 1929): Metallwirtschaft (0723-502X)
Indexed: A&ATA, A20, A22, A28, APA, BrCerAb, C&ISA, CA/WCA, CEABA, CIA, CIN, CerAb, ChemAb, ChemTitl, CivEngAb, CoppAb, CorrAb, E&CAJ, E11, EEA, EMA, ESPM, EnvEAb, GeoRef, H15, Inspec, KES, M&TEA, M09, MBF, METADEX, SCOPUS, SolStAb, SpeleolAb, T04, TM, WAA.
—BLDSC (5692.000000), CASDDS, IE, Infotrieve, Ingenta, INIST, Linda Hall. **CCC.**
Published by: Giesel Verlag GmbH (Subsidiary of: Schluetersche Verlagsgesellschaft mbH und Co. KG), Rehkamp 3, Isernhagen, 30916, Germany. TEL 49-511-73040, FAX 49-511-7304157, giesel@giesel.de, http://www.giesel.de. Ed. Catrin Kammer. Circ: 2,472 (paid and controlled).

669 CHE
METALL. Text in German. 12/yr. **Document type:** *Trade.*
Published by: Zuerichsee Medien AG, Seestr 86, Staefa, 8712, Switzerland. TEL 01-9285611, FAX 01-9285600. Ed. Fridolin Kretz. Circ: 5,000.

669 AUT
METALL; Fachmagazin fuer die Metallverarbeitende Wirtschaft. Text in German. m. EUR 55 domestic; EUR 80 foreign (effective 2005). adv. bk.rev. illus. **Document type:** *Magazine, Trade.*
Published by: Oesterreichischer Wirtschaftsverlag GmbH (Subsidiary of: Sueddeutscher Verlag GmbH), Wiedner Hauptstr 120-124, Vienna, W 1051, Austria. TEL 43-1-546640, FAX 43-1-54664406, office@wirtschaftsverlag.at, http://www.wirtschaftsverlag.at. Ed. Eberhard Fuchs. Adv. contact Robert Huber. B&W page EUR 2,130, color page EUR 3,045; trim 185 x 255. Circ: 8,400 (paid and controlled).

669.1 DEU
METALL AKTUELL. Text in German. 1976. bi-m. adv. **Document type:** *Magazine, Trade.*
Published by: Fachverband Metall Nordrhein-Westfalen, Ruhrallee 12, Essen, 45138, Germany. TEL 49-201-896470, FAX 49-201-252548, fvm@metallhandwerk-nrw.de, http://www.metallhandwerk-nrw.de.

669 UKR
METALL BYULLETEN'. UKRAINA. Text in Russian. m. USD 1,450 in United States.
Address: Ul Solmenskaya 5, ofis 1005, Kiev, Ukraine. TEL 276-82-72. **Dist. by:** East View Information Services, 10601 Wayzata Blvd, Minneapolis, MN 55305. TEL 952-252-1201, 800-477-1005, FAX 952-252-1202, info@eastview.com, http://www.eastview.com.

669 658 UKR
METALL I LIT'E UKRAINY. Text in Russian. 1994. m.
Address: Khoriva, 41, Kiev, 254071, Ukraine.

669 UKR ISSN 1606-6294
METALL UKRAINY. Text in Russian. w. UAK 900 per month domestic; USD 150 per month foreign (effective 2003).
Related titles: E-mail ed.: 2002. UAK 360 domestic; USD 60 foreign (effective 2003); Online - full content ed.: ISSN 1606-6286. 1997. UAK 720 domestic; USD 120 foreign (effective 2003); English ed.: The Metal Business. ISSN 1606-6316; ◆ Supplement to: Metallurgicheskaya i Gornorudnaya Promyshlennost'. ISSN 0543-5749.
Published by: Delovoi Mir/Business World, P.O. Box 127, Dnepropetrovsk, 49000, Ukraine.

669 GRC ISSN 1105-2430
METALLEIOLOGIKA-METALLOURGIKA HRONIKA/MINING AND METALLURGICAL ANNALS. Text in Multiple languages. 1969. s-a. **Document type:** *Journal, Academic/Scholarly.*
Indexed: A28, APA, BrCerAb, C&ISA, CA/WCA, CIA, CerAb, CivEngAb, CorrAb, E&CAJ, E11, EEA, EMA, H15, M&TEA, M09, MBF, METADEX, SolStAb, T04, WAA.
—Linda Hall.
Published by: Panellinios Syllogos Diplomatouhon Mihanikon Metalleion-Metallourgon Mihanikon/Hellenic Society of Mining and Metallurgical Engineers, Epirou 27, Athens, 10433, Greece.

671 BEL
METALLERIE (FRENCH EDITION); revue professionelle pour l'industrie metalliere. Text in French. 1998. 11/yr. (plus 20 e-mails). EUR 68 (effective 2005). adv. illus.; tr.lit. **Document type:** *Trade.* **Description:** Reports on new products, techniques, equipment and tools, and occupational safety issues in the metalworking industry.
Related titles: Dutch ed.: Metallerie (Dutch Edition). ISSN 1373-8747. 1998.
Published by: Professional Media Group, Torhoutsesteenweg 226 bus 2/6, Zedelgem, B-8210, Belgium. TEL 32-50-240404, FAX 32-50-240445, info@pmgroup.be, http://www.pmgroup.be. adv.: color page EUR 2,575; trim 297 x 210. Circ: 16,000 (controlled).

669 ITA ISSN 1122-1410
METALLI. Text in Italian. bi-m. adv. **Document type:** *Magazine, Trade.* **Description:** Specializing in ferrous and non-ferrous metals, covers metal price trends, R&D, exhibitions and conferences, and management practices of manufacturers and distributors.
Published by: Edimet SpA, Via Corfu 102, Brescia, BS 25124, Italy. TEL 39-030-2421043, FAX 39-030-223802, info@edimet.com, http://www.edimet.com/it. Circ: 4,500 (paid).

671 FIN ISSN 1237-6663
TJ4
METALLITEKNIIKKA. Text in Finnish. 1947. m. EUR 84 (effective 2007). adv. bk.rev. abstr.; bibl.; charts; illus. **Document type:** *Magazine, Trade.* **Description:** Contains information on production technologies and organization in all sectors of the metal industry: metal processing, the machine and component industries, as well as electrotechnical and electronics industries.
Formerly (until 1994): Konepajamies (0023-3277)
Related titles: Online - full text ed.
Indexed: BCIRA.
Published by: (Metalliteollisuuden Keskusliitto), Talentum Media Oyj, Annankatu 34-36, PO Box 920, Helsinki, 00101, Finland. TEL 358-204-4240, FAX 358-204-424130, info@talentum.fi, http://www.talentum.fi. Ed. Mika Hamalainen TEL 358-40-3424303. Adv. contact Marja Saulo TEL 358-20-4424361. color page EUR 4,050; trim 190 x 279. Circ: 9,600.

669 530 UKR ISSN 1024-1809
TN689 CODEN: MANFDD
METALLOFIZIKA I NOVEISHIE TEKHNOLOGII; an international research journal. Text in English, Russian, Ukrainian. 1968. m. EUR 84 in Europe; USD 102 elsewhere (effective 2005). adv. bk.rev. abstr.; bibl. back issues avail. **Document type:** *Journal, Academic/Scholarly.* **Description:** Publishes both theoretical and experimental reviews and original articles in fundamental research and applications of metallic solids and liquids, electronic structure and properties, phase transformations, crystal-lattice defects, physics of strength and plasticity, metallic surfaces and films, amorphous and liquid states for an audience of scientists and engineers working in metal physics and physical metallurgy.
Formerly (until 1994): Metallofizika (0204-3580)
Related titles: E-mail ed.; Fax ed.
Indexed: A28, APA, ASCA, BrCerAb, C&ISA, C33, CA/WCA, CIA, CerAb, ChemAb, ChemTitl, CivEngAb, CorrAb, Djerelo, E&CAJ, E11, EEA, EMA, ESPM, EnvEAb, H15, INIS AtomInd, Inspec, M&TEA, M09, MBF, METADEX, MSCI, PhysBer, RefZh, SCI, SCOPUS, SolStAb, T04, W07, WAA.
—BLDSC (0108.700000), AskIEEE, CASDDS, East View, INIST, Linda Hall. **CCC.**
Published by: Natsional'na Akademiya Nauk Ukrainy, Instytut Metalofizyky/National Academy of Sciences of the Ukraine, Institute of Metal Physics, bulvar Akad Vernadskogo 36, Kyiv, 103142, Ukraine. TEL 380-44-4241221, FAX 380-44-4242561, mfint@imp.kiev.ua, tatar@imp.kiev.ua, http://www.imp.kiev.ua. Ed., R&P A P Shpak. Adv. contact V A Tatarenko.

669 RUS
METALLOSNABZHENIE I SBYT. Text in Russian. bi-m. USD 120 in United States.
Published by: Izdatel'skii Dom Metall-Inform, 3-ya Mytishchinskaya ul 3, Moscow, 129626, Russian Federation. TEL 7-095-2871562, FAX 7-095-2872642. Ed. A G Romanov. **Dist. by:** East View Information Services, 10601 Wayzata Blvd, Minneapolis, MN 55305. TEL 952-252-1201, 800-477-1005, FAX 952-252-1202, info@eastview.com, http://www.eastview.com.

669 RUS ISSN 0026-0819
CODEN: MTOBD3
METALLOVEDENIE I TERMICHESKAYA OBRABOTKA METALLOV. Text in Russian. 1955. m. USD 698 foreign (effective 2004). adv. bk.rev. bibl. index. **Document type:** *Journal, Trade.* **Description:** Covers the state-of-the-art developments of advanced science and engineering in the area of physical metallurgy and metal heat treatment.
Related titles: ◆ English Translation: Metal Science and Heat Treatment. ISSN 0026-0673; Translation:.
Indexed: C&ISA, CIN, ChemAb, ChemTitl, CorrAb, E&CAJ, INIS AtomInd, Inspec, RefZh, SCOPUS, SolStAb, TM, WAA.
—BLDSC (0108.300000), AskIEEE, CASDDS, East View, INIST, Linda Hall. **CCC.**
Published by: (Assotsiatsiya Metallovedov Rossii), Izdatel'stvo Mashinostroenie, Stromynskii per 4, Moscow, 107076, Russian Federation. TEL 7-095-2683858, mashpubl@mashin.ru. Ed. A P Gulyaev. adv.: page MRK 4,000. Circ: 1,300. **Dist. by:** M K - Periodica, ul Gilyarovskogo 39, Moscow 129110, Russian Federation. TEL 7-095-2845008, FAX 7-095-2813798, info@periodicals.ru, http://www.mkniga.ru. **Co-sponsor:** Moskovskaya Assotsiatsiya Metallovedov.

671.2 RUS ISSN 0026-0827
TS300 CODEN: METGA3
METALLURG. Text in Russian. 1956. m. USD 338 foreign (effective 2006). adv. bk.rev. bibl.; charts; illus.; stat. index. **Document type:** *Journal.* **Description:** Covers modernization and development programs; new developments in raw materials, ironmaking, steelmaking, rolling mill technology, pipe and tube making, wire industry; new materials and products; product quality; environmental protection; economics and loabor relations; patents; company profiles.
Related titles: ◆ English Translation: Metallurgist. ISSN 0026-0894.
Indexed: C&ISA, ChemAb, ChemTitl, CorrAb, E&CAJ, RASB, RefZh, SolStAb, TM, WAA.
—CASDDS, East View, INIST, Linda Hall. **CCC.**
Published by: Izdatel'stvo Metallurgizdat, 2-ya Baumanskaya ul, 9/23, Moscow, 105005, Russian Federation. TEL 7-095-5403881, metallurg_izd@mtu-net.ru. Ed. O N Novoselova. Adv. contact E H Ivanova. B&W page USD 600. Circ: 1,600. **Dist. by:** East View Information Services, 10601 Wayzata Blvd, Minneapolis, MN 55305. TEL 952-252-1201, 800-477-1005, FAX 952-252-1202, info@eastview.com, http://www.eastview.com.

669 ITA ISSN 0026-0843
CODEN: MITLAC
LA METALLURGIA ITALIANA. Text in Italian. 1909. 11/yr. free to members. adv. bk.rev. illus. index. **Document type:** *Magazine, Trade.*
Indexed: A22, A28, APA, ApMecR, BrCerAb, C&ISA, CA/WCA, CEABA, CIA, CIN, CPEI, Cadscan, CerAb, ChemAb, ChemTitl, CivEngAb, CoppAb, CorrAb, E&CAJ, E11, EEA, EMA, EngInd, H15, IMMAb, ISMEC, Inspec, M&TEA, M09, MBF, METADEX, MSCI, SCI, SCOPUS, SolStAb, T04, TM, W07, WAA, Zincscan.
—BLDSC (5697.000000), CASDDS, IE, Ingenta, INIST, Linda Hall. **CCC.**
Published by: Associazione Italiana di Metallurgia, Piazzale Rodolfo Morandi, 2, Milan, 20121, Italy. TEL 39-02-76021132, FAX 39-02-76020551, aim@aimnet.it, http://www.metallurgia-italiana.net.

669 USA ISSN 1073-5623
CODEN: MMTAEB
➤ **METALLURGICAL AND MATERIALS TRANSACTIONS A - PHYSICAL METALLURGY AND MATERIALS SCIENCE.** Text and summaries in English; Text in English. 1970. 13/yr. EUR 2,528, USD 3,059 combined subscription to institutions (print & online eds.) (effective 2012). adv. charts; illus.; stat. index. back issues avail.; reprint service avail. from PSC. **Document type:** *Journal, Academic/Scholarly.* **Description:** Focuses on physical metallurgy and materials science, with a special emphasis on relationships among the processing, structure and properties of materials.
Formerly (until 1994): Metallurgical Transactions A - Physical Metallurgy and Materials Science (0360-2133); Which superseded in part (in 1975): Metallurgical Transactions (0026-086X); Which was formed by the merger of (1958-1970): Metallurgical Society of AIME. Transactions (0543-5722); (1961-1970): American Society for Metals. Transactions Quarterly (0097-3912); Which was formerly (until 1961): American Society for Metals. Transactions (0096-7416); (until 1934): American Society for Steel Treating. Transactions (0096-476X); Which was formed by the merger of (1917-1920): Steel Treating Research Society. Proceedings (0099-6009); (1918-1920): American Steel Treaters Society. Journal (0095-8999)
Related titles: Microform ed.: (from PMC, PQC); Online - full text ed.: ISSN 1543-1940 (from IngentaConnect).
Indexed: A05, A22, A26, A28, AESIS, APA, AS&TA, AS&TI, ASCA, BCIRA, BRD, BrCerAb, C&ISA, C10, C33, CA, CA/WCA, CEABA, CIA, CPEI, Cadscan, CerAb, ChemAb, ChemTitl, CivEngAb, CorrAb, CurCont, E&CAJ, E01, E11, EEA, EMA, ESPM, EngInd, EnvEAb, GeoRef, H12, H15, I05, ISR, Inspec, LeadAb, M&TEA, M09, MBF, METADEX, MSCI, P02, P10, P26, P48, P52, P53, P54, PQC, PhysBer, RefZh, S04, S10, SCI, SCOPUS, SolStAb, T02, T04, TM, W03, W05, W07, WAA, Zincscan.
—BLDSC (5698.110000), AskIEEE, CASDDS, IE, Infotrieve, Ingenta, INIST, Linda Hall. **CCC.**
Published by: (The Minerals, Metals & Materials Society), Springer New York LLC (Subsidiary of: Springer Science+Business Media), 233 Spring St, New York, NY 10013. TEL 212-460-1500, FAX 212-460-1575, service-ny@springer.com. Ed. David E Laughlin.

669 620 USA ISSN 1073-5615
TN1 CODEN: MTBSEO
➤ **METALLURGICAL AND MATERIALS TRANSACTIONS B - PROCESS METALLURGY AND MATERIALS PROCESSING SCIENCE.** Text and summaries in English. 1975. bi-m. EUR 1,775, USD 2,151 combined subscription to institutions (print & online eds.) (effective 2012). adv. bk.rev. charts; illus.; stat. index. back issues avail.; reprint service avail. from PSC. **Document type:** *Journal, Academic/Scholarly.* **Description:** Focuses on process metallurgy and materials processing science.
Formerly (until 1994): Metallurgical Transactions B - Process Metallurgy (0360-2141); Which superseded in part (in 1975): Metallurgical Transactions (0026-086X); Which was formed by the merger of (1958-1970): Metallurgical Society of A I M E. Transactions (0543-5722); (1961-1970): A S M Transactions Quarterly (0097-3912); Which was formerly (until 1961): American Society for Metals. Transactions (0096-7416); (untill 1934): American Society for Steel Treating. Transactions (0096-476X); Which was formed by the merger of (1918-1920): American Steel Treaters Society. Journal (0095-8999); (1917-1920): Steel Treating Research Society. Proceedings (0099-6009)
Related titles: Microform ed.: (from PQC); Online - full text ed.: ISSN 1543-1916 (from IngentaConnect).
Indexed: A22, A23, A24, A28, AESIS, APA, ASCA, B13, BrCerAb, C&ISA, C10, C33, CA, CA/WCA, CEABA, CIA, CIN, CPEI, CTE, Cadscan, CerAb, ChemAb, ChemTitl, CivEngAb, CorrAb, CurCont, E&CAJ, E01, E11, EEA, EMA, ESPM, EngInd, EnvEAb, GeoRef, H15, IMMAb, ISR, Inspec, LeadAb, M&TEA, M09, MBF, METADEX, MSCI, P26, P48, P52, P54, PQC, PhysBer, SCI, SCOPUS, SolStAb, T02, T04, TM, W07, WAA, Zincscan.
—BLDSC (5698.115000), AskIEEE, CASDDS, IE, Infotrieve, Ingenta, INIST, Linda Hall. **CCC.**
Published by: (T M S - The Minerals, Metals and Materials Society), Springer New York LLC (Subsidiary of: Springer Science+Business Media), 233 Spring St, New York, NY 10013. TEL 212-460-1500, FAX 212-460-1575, service-ny@springer.com, http://www.springer.com. Ed. David E Laughlin.

669 UKR ISSN 2076-0507
▼ **METALLURGICAL AND MINING INDUSTRY.** Text in English. 2009. bi-m. **Document type:** *Journal, Academic/Scholarly.*
Related titles: Online - full text ed.: ISSN 2078-8312. free (effective 2011); ◆ Russian ed.: Metallurgicheskaya i Gornorudnaya Promyshlennost'. ISSN 0543-5749.
Published by: Nauchno-Issledovatel'skii Institut Ukrmetallurginform/"Ukrmetallurginform"Scientific and Technical Agency", LLC, vul Dzerzhiskoho 23, Dnipropetrovsk, 49027, Ukraine. TEL 380-56-7448166, FAX 380-562-461295, office@metaljournal.com.ua, http://www.metinfo.dp.ua.

669 ITA ISSN 0393-6074
METALLURGICAL SCIENCE & TECHNOLOGY. Text in Italian. 1983. s-a. **Document type:** *Journal, Academic/Scholarly.*
Indexed: A28, APA, BrCerAb, C&ISA, CA/WCA, CIA, CerAb, CivEngAb, CorrAb, E&CAJ, E11, EEA, EMA, ESPM, EnvEAb, H15, M&TEA, M09, MBF, METADEX, RefZh, SolStAb, T04, WAA.
Published by: Teksid Spa, Via Umberto II 3-5, Carmagnola, TO 10122, Italy. http://www.teksidaluminium.com.

669 UKR ISSN 0543-5749
CODEN: MGPNAI
➤ **METALLURGICHESKAYA I GORNORUDNAYA PROMYSHLENNOST'.** Text in Russian; Summaries in English. 1960. bi-m. UAK 2,100 domestic; USD 300 foreign; UAK 350, USD 50 per issue (effective 2009). adv. bk.rev. abstr.; bibl.; charts; illus.; stat.; tr.lit. Index. back issues avail. **Document type:** *Journal, Academic/Scholarly.* **Description:** Covers all stages of metallurgy processes and metal forming from ironmaking to delivery of the products as well as quality assurance and environmental control.
Related titles: CD-ROM ed.: ISSN 2077-0545; ◆ English ed.: Metallurgical and Mining Industry. ISSN 2076-0507; ◆ Supplement(s): Metall Ukrainy. ISSN 1606-6294.
Indexed: C&ISA, ChemAb, ChemTitl, CorrAb, E&CAJ, RefZh, SCOPUS, SolStAb, TM, WAA.
—BLDSC (0109.070000), CASDDS, East View, INIST, Linda Hall. **CCC.**
Published by: Nauchno-Issledovatel'skii Institut Ukrmetallurginform/"Ukrmetallurginform"Scientific and Technical Agency", LLC, vul Dzerzhiskoho 23, Dnipropetrovsk, 49027, Ukraine. TEL 380-56-7448166, FAX 380-562-461295, office@metaljournal.com.ua, http://www.metinfo.dp.ua. Ed., R&P Grinev Anatoliy Fedorovich. Pub. Kanov Gennadiy Lavrentiyevich. Adv. contact Sherstobitova Alena Sergeyevna. B&W page USD 125, color page USD 300. Circ: 500. **Dist. by:** East View Information Services, 10601 Wayzata Blvd, Minneapolis, MN 55305. TEL 952-252-1201, 800-477-1005, FAX 952-252-1202, info@eastview.com, http://www.eastview.com.

669 UKR ISSN 1816-1200
➤ **METALLURGICHESKIE PROTSESSY I OBORUDOVANIE**; mezhdunarodnyi nauchno-tekhnicheskii i proizvodstvennyi zhurnal. Text in Russian. 2005. q. UAK 675 domestic to institutions; UAK 935 foreign to institutions (effective 2011). bk.rev.; software rev. abstr.; bibl.; charts; illus.; maps; mkt.; pat.; stat.; tr.lit. Index. back issues avail. **Document type:** *Journal, Academic/Scholarly.*
Related titles: Online - full text ed.
Indexed: RefZh.
Published by: Technopark DonGTU "Unitech", ul Artema, 58, Donetsk, 83001, Ukraine. TEL 380-62-3485056, FAX 380-62-3049019, m-lab@ukr.net. Ed. Sergey P Yeronko. Pub. Alexei L Sotnikov. Circ: 1,000 (paid).

669 USA ISSN 0026-0894
TS300 CODEN: MTLUA8
➤ **METALLURGIST.** Text in English. 1956. bi-m. EUR 3,953, USD 4,084 combined subscription to institutions (print & online eds.) (effective 2012). adv. illus.; pat. back issues avail.; reprint service avail. from PSC. **Document type:** *Journal, Academic/Scholarly.* **Description:** Publishes original research and reviews on technological achievements, new patents, metallurgical manufacturing, and various innovations and inventions.
Related titles: Microfilm ed.: (from PQC); Online - full text ed.: ISSN 1573-8892 (from IngentaConnect); ◆ Translation of: Metallurg. ISSN 0026-0827.
Indexed: A01, A03, A08, A22, A26, A28, APA, ASCA, BibLing, BrCerAb, C&ISA, CA, CA/WCA, CIA, CPEI, Cadscan, CerAb, CivEngAb, CorrAb, CurCont, E&CAJ, E01, E11, EEA, EMA, ESPM, EngInd, EnvEAb, H15, LeadAb, M&TEA, M09, MBF, METADEX, MSCI, P52, SCI, SCOPUS, SolStAb, T02, T04, W07, WAA, Zincscan.
—BLDSC (0416.000000), East View, IE, Infotrieve, Ingenta, INIST, Linda Hall. **CCC.**
Published by: Springer New York LLC (Subsidiary of: Springer Science+Business Media), 233 Spring St, New York, NY 10013. TEL 212-460-1500, FAX 212-460-1575, service-ny@springer.com, http://www.springer.com. Ed. Olga N Novoselova.

621.9 669 RUS
METALLURGIYA MASHINOSTROENIYA. Text in Russian. bi-m. **Document type:** *Journal, Trade.*
Published by: Liteinoe Proizvodstvo, Gzhel'sky per, 13a, 2 etazh, komn 40, Moscow, 105120, Russian Federation. lp@niit.ru, http://www.foundrymag.ru.

669 POL ISSN 1230-2325
TN600 CODEN: MFOEEH
➤ **METALLURGY AND FOUNDRY ENGINEERING.** Text in English; Summaries in Polish. 1975. q. PLZ 10.50 per issue (effective 2011). illus.; abstr.; bibl. 120 p./no. 1 cols./p.; **Document type:** *Journal, Academic/Scholarly.* **Description:** Disseminates knowledge relating to the metallurgical and foundry engineering or materials science in general.
Formerly (until 1992): Akademia Gorniczo-Hutnicza. im. Stanislawa Staszica. Metalurgia i Odlewnictwo. Kwartalnik (0137-6535)
Indexed: A28, APA, BrCerAb, C&ISA, CA/WCA, CIA, CerAb, ChemAb, CivEngAb, CorrAb, E&CAJ, E11, EEA, EMA, H15, M&TEA, M09, MBF, METADEX, SolStAb, T04, WAA.
—CASDDS, Ingenta, Linda Hall.
Published by: (Akademia Gorniczo-Hutnicza im. Stanislawa Staszica/University of Mining and Metallurgy), Wydawnictwo A G H, al Mickiewicza 30, Krakow, 30059, Poland. TEL 48-12-6173228, FAX 48-12-6364038, wydagh@uci.agh.edu.pl. Ed. Jan Kazanecki. Circ: 120 (paid). **Dist. by:** Ars Polona, Obroncow 25, Warsaw 03933, Poland. TEL 48-22-5098609, FAX 48-22-5098610, arspolona@arspolona.com.pl, http://www.arspolona.com.pl.

669 USA ISSN 0094-5447
TN675.3
METALLURGY - MATERIALS EDUCATION YEARBOOK. Variant title: Materials Education Yearbook for the United States and Abroad. Text in English. 1961. a. USD 45 to non-members; USD 20 to members (effective 2009). **Document type:** *Directory, Trade.* **Description:** Designed to be a reference guide of metallurgy-materials science and engineering for four-year and graduate college programs.
Published by: A S M International, 9639 Kinsman Rd, Materials Park, OH 44073. TEL 440-338-5151, FAX 440-338-4634, CustomerService@asminternational.org.

669 RUS ISSN 0869-5733
CODEN: MEALET
➤ **METALLY.** Text in Russian. 1965. bi-m. USD 341 foreign (effective 2005). **Document type:** *Journal, Academic/Scholarly.* **Description:** Presents original experimental research papers on theory of metallurgy, materials technology and science of metals, non-ferrous, ferrous, rare and other metals and alloys.
Formerly (until 1991): Izvestiya Akademii Nauk SSSR. Metally (0568-5303)
Related titles: Online - full text ed.: ISSN 1555-6255; ◆ English Translation: Russian Metallurgy. ISSN 0036-0295.
Indexed: A22, C&ISA, C33, ChemAb, ChemTitl, CorrAb, E&CAJ, INIS AtomInd, Inspec, RefZh, SCOPUS, SolStAb, TM, WAA.
—BLDSC (0109.250000), CASDDS, East View, IE, Ingenta, INIST, Linda Hall. **CCC.**
Published by: (Rossiiskaya Akademiya Nauk/Russian Academy of Sciences), Izdatel'stvo Nauka, Profsoyuznaya ul 90, Moscow, 117864, Russian Federation. TEL 7-095-3347151, FAX 7-095-4202220, secret@naukaran.ru, http://www.naukaran.ru. **Dist. by:** East View Information Services, 10601 Wayzata Blvd, Minneapolis, MN 55305. TEL 952-252-1201, 800-477-1005, FAX 952-252-1202, info@eastview.com, http://www.eastview.com.

669 RUS
METALLY EVRAZII. Text in Russian. bi-m.

Published by: Natsional'noe Obozrenie Ltd., Slavyanskaya pl 2, ofis 3031, Moscow, 103074, Russian Federation. TEL 7-095-2207016, FAX 7-095-9284852. Ed. E V Shashkov. Dist. by: East View Information Services, 10601 Wayzata Blvd, Minneapolis, MN 55305. TEL 952-252-1201, 800-477-1005, FAX 952-252-1202, info@eastview.com, http://www.eastview.com.

669 USA ISSN 1542-295X
NA4133
METALMAG; education building owners, architects and contractors. Text in English. 2000. 8/yr. USD 36 domestic; USD 64 in Canada; USD 192 elsewhere; USD 5.95 newsstand/cover domestic; USD 7.95 newsstand/cover foreign; free to qualified personnel (effective 2008). adv. back issues avail.; reprints avail. **Document type:** *Magazine, Trade.* **Description:** Educates architects, building owners and contractors about how metal is an attractive, functional and environmentally friendly material for their next project.
Related titles: Online - full text ed.
Published by: Hanley Wood, LLC (Subsidiary of: J.P. Morgan Chase & Co.), 1 Thomas Cir, NW, Ste 600, Washington, DC 20005. TEL 202-452-0800, FAX 202-785-1974, fanton@hanleywood.com, http://www.hanleywood.com. Ed. Jim Schneider. Pub. John Riester. Adv. contact Barrett Hahn TEL 919-402-9300. color page USD 5,850, B&W page USD 3,900; trim 8.375 x 10.875. Circ: 30,600 (controlled).

669 330 USA
METALMECANICA. Text in Spanish, English, Portuguese. 19??. m. adv. back issues avail. **Document type:** *Magazine, Consumer.*
Related titles: Online - full text ed.
Published by: B 2 B Portales, Inc (Subsidiary of: Carvajal International, Inc.), 6505 Blue Lagoon Dr, Ste 430, Miami, FL 33126. TEL 305-448-6875, FAX 305-448-9942, contactenos@b2bportales.com, http://www.b2bportales.com. Ed. Eduardo Tovar.

669 CHE ISSN 2075-4701
▼ ➤ **METALS.** Text in English. 2011. q. free (effective 2011). **Document type:** *Journal, Academic/Scholarly.* **Description:** Contains research on the relationships between the structure, the properties or the functions of all kinds of metals.
Media: Online - full text.
Published by: M D P I AG, Postfach, Basel, 4005, Switzerland. TEL 41-61-6837734, FAX 41-61-3028918, http://www.mdpi.org/. Eds. Hugo Lopez, James Albright.

669 KOR ISSN 1598-9623
TA459 CODEN: MMIECY
➤ **METALS AND MATERIALS INTERNATIONAL.** Text in English. 1995. bi-m. EUR 651, USD 978 combined subscription to institutions (print & online eds.) (effective 2012). reprint service avail. from PSC. **Document type:** *Journal, Academic/Scholarly.* **Description:** Publishes original papers and occasional critical reviews on all aspects of research and technology in materials engineering: physical metallurgy, materials science, and processing of metals and other materials.
Formerly (until 2001): Metals and Materials (1225-9438)
Related titles: Online - full content ed.: ISSN 2005-4149.
Indexed: A22, A28, APA, BrCerAb, C&ISA, CA/WCA, CIA, CerAb, CivEngAb, CorrAb, CurCont, E&CAJ, E01, E11, EEA, EMA, ESPM, EnvEAb, H15, M&TEA, M09, MBF, METADEX, MSCI, P52, SCI, SCOPUS, SolStAb, T04, W07, WAA.
—BLDSC (5699.321500), IE, Ingenta, Linda Hall. **CCC.**
Published by: (Han'gug Bu'sig Haghoe/Corrosion Science Society of Korea, Korean Society for Technology of Plasticity, Materials Research Society of Korea), Daehan Geumsog Jae'lyo Haghoe/ Korean Institute of Metals and Materials, POSCO Center 4th Fl (East Wing), 892 Daechi 4-dong, Kangnam-ku, Seoul, 135-777, Korea, S. TEL 82-2-5571071, FAX 82-2-5571080, kim@kim.or.kr, http://www.kim.or.kr. Ed. Nack J. Kim. **Co-publisher:** Springer Netherlands.

669 HKG ISSN 1024-4654
METALS BULLETIN. Text in Chinese. 1981. bi-m. HKD 170; HKD 30 newsstand/cover. adv. **Document type:** *Bulletin.* **Description:** Provides up-to-date information to designers, engineers, technical management and approved authorities in industrial and scientific establishments related to the metals industry.
Published by: Hong Kong Productivity Council, HKPC Bldg, 78 Tat Chee Ave, Kowloon, Hong Kong. TEL 852-2788-5950, FAX 852-2788-5959. Ed. Vincent Shin. adv.: B&W page HKD 3,400, color page HKD 5,800. Circ: 5,000.

669 658 USA
METALS SOURCING GUIDE. Text in English. 1987. a. **Document type:** *Directory, Trade.* **Description:** Assists buyers in finding new or alternative sources of supplies.
Published by: Reed Business Information (Subsidiary of: Reed Business), 225 Wyman St, Waltham, MA 02451. TEL 781-734-8203, FAX 781-734-8076, corporatecommunications@reedbusiness.com, http://www.reedbusiness.com. Pub. Kathy Doyle TEL 781-734-8201.

669 USA
METALS WATCH. Text in English. q. free. back issues avail. **Document type:** *Magazine, Trade.* **Description:** Presents articles and news about metal industry and related issues.
Media: Online - full text.
Published by: Specialty Steel & Forge, 239 New Rd., # 203, Parsippany, NJ 07054-4274. TEL 973-808-8300, FAX 973-808-4488. Ed. Tom Stundza.

METALSMITH. *see* ARTS AND HANDICRAFTS

669 ROM ISSN 1582-2214
METALUGIA INTERNATIONAL. Text in English. 1999. q. **Document type:** *Journal, Trade.*
Indexed: A28, APA, BrCerAb, C10, CA, CA/WCA, CIA, CerAb, CivEngAb, E11, EEA, EMA, ESPM, EnvEAb, H15, M&TEA, M09, MBF, METADEX, SCI, SCOPUS, T02, T04, W07.
Published by: Editura Stiintifica, Bucharest, Romania.

669 ROM ISSN 0461-9579
METALURGIA (BUCHAREST). Text in Romanian. 1954. m. **Document type:** *Journal, Trade.*
Former titles (until 1963): Metalurgia si Constructia de Masini (0368-8909)
Indexed: A28, APA, BrCerAb, C&ISA, C10, CA, CA/WCA, CIA, CerAb, CivEngAb, CorrAb, E&CAJ, E11, EEA, EMA, ESPM, EnvEAb, H15, M&TEA, M09, MBF, METADEX, SolStAb, T02, T04, TM, WAA.
—BLDSC (5699.780000), INIST, Linda Hall.
Published by: Editura Stiintifica, Bucharest, Romania.

669 ESP ISSN 0026-0991
T4 CODEN: MYELAF
METALURGIA Y ELECTRICIDAD. Text in Spanish. 1937. 10/yr. EUR 81 domestic; EUR 126 foreign (effective 2009). bk.rev. abstr.; bibl.; charts; illus.; tr.lit. index. **Document type:** *Magazine, Trade.*
Indexed: A22, A28, APA, BrCerAb, C&ISA, CA/WCA, CIA, CerAb, ChemAb, CivEngAb, CoppAb, CorrAb, E&CAJ, E11, EEA, EMA, ESPM, EnvEAb, H15, IECT, Inspec, M&TEA, M09, MBF, METADEX, RefZh, SolStAb, T04, WAA.
—BLDSC (5700.000000), AskIEEE, CASDDS, IE, Ingenta, Linda Hall. **CCC.**
Published by: Ediciones Metyel, S.L., Antonio Gonzalez Porras, 35 2o, Madrid, 28019, Spain. TEL 34-91-4690240, FAX 34-91-4690304, meytel.@meytel.com. Ed. Francisco Carmona. Circ: 6,530.

669 643 HRV ISSN 0543-5846
CODEN: METABK
➤ **METALURGIJA/METALLURGY.** Text in Croatian. 1962. q. adv. 84 p./no. 2 cols./p.; **Document type:** *Journal, Academic/Scholarly.* **Description:** Presents scientific and professional papers.
Related titles: CD-ROM ed.: ISSN 1334-2584; Online - full text ed.: ISSN 1334-2576. free (effective 2011).
Indexed: A01, A22, A28, APA, BrCerAb, C&ISA, CA, CA/WCA, CIA, CPEI, CerAb, ChemAb, CivEngAb, CorrAb, E&CAJ, E11, EEA, EMA, ESPM, EngInd, EnvEAb, FLUIDEX, H15, M&TEA, M09, MBF, METADEX, MSCI, RefZh, SCI, SCOPUS, SolStAb, T02, T04, TM, W07, WAA.
—BLDSC (5700.120000), CASDDS, IE, Ingenta, Linda Hall.
Published by: Hrvatsko Metalursko Drustvo/Croatian Metallurgical Society, Berislaviceva 6, Zagreb, 10000, Croatia. TEL 385-1-6198689, FAX 385-1-6198689, golja@siscia.simet.hr. Ed. Ilija Mamuzic. Circ: 600.

669 TUR ISSN 1300-4824
CODEN: METJEG
METALURJI. Text in Turkish, English. 1972. bi-m. **Document type:** *Journal, Academic/Scholarly.*
Related titles: Online - full text ed.
Indexed: INIS AtomInd.
Published by: Turkiye Mimar Muhendisler Odalari Birligi, Metalurji Muhendisleri Odasi, Hatay Sokak 10/9, Kizilay, Ankara, 06650, Turkey. TEL 90-312-4254160, FAX 90-312-4189343, oda@metalurji.org.tr.

669 USA
METALWORKING EQUIPMENT NEWS. Abbreviated title: M E N. Text in English. 1998. m. adv. **Document type:** *Magazine, Trade.* **Description:** Provides helpful and timely information on issues pertinent to the metalworking industry.
Published by: Grand View Media Group, Inc. (Subsidiary of: EBSCO Industries, Inc.), 200 Croft St, Ste 1, Birmingham, AL 35242. TEL 888-431-2877, FAX 205-408-3797, webmaster@grandviewmedia.com, http://www.gvmg.com. adv.: B&W page USD 3,450, color page USD 4,350; trim 7.875 x 10.5.

669 GBR ISSN 0026-1033
TJ1180.A1
METALWORKING PRODUCTION. Abbreviated title: M W P. Text in English. 1910. bi-m. free to qualified personnel (effective 2009). adv. charts; illus.; tr.lit. index. **Document type:** *Magazine, Trade.* **Description:** Provides information for production executives and engineers responsible for purchase of production machine tools and auxiliary equipment.
Former titles (until 1955): The Machinist; (until 1933): American Machinist
Related titles: Microform ed.: (from PQC); Online - full text ed.
Indexed: A05, A09, A10, A15, A22, A28, ABIn, APA, AS&TA, AS&TI, B01, B02, B03, B06, B07, B09, B11, B15, B17, B18, BMT, BRD, BrCerAb, BrTechI, C&ISA, C10, CA/WCA, CIA, CerAb, CivEngAb, CorrAb, E&CAJ, E11, EEA, EMA, ESPM, EnvEAb, G04, G06, G07, G08, H15, I05, Inspec, KES, M&TEA, M09, MBF, METADEX, P16, P48, P51, P52, P53, P54, PQC, RefZh, S04, SCOPUS, SolStAb, T02, T03, T04, V03, V04, W03, W05, WAA.
—BLDSC (5700.250000), CIS, IE, Infotrieve, Ingenta, INIST, Linda Hall. **CCC.**
Published by: Centaur Communications Ltd., St Giles House, 50 Poland St, London, W1F 7AX, United Kingdom. TEL 44-20-79704000, customerservices@centaur.co.uk, http://www.centaur.co.uk/. Ed., Pub. Mike Excell TEL 44-20-79704420. Adv. contact Karl Creamer. page GBP 2,205; trim 210 x 286.

669 CAN ISSN 0383-090X
METALWORKING PRODUCTION & PURCHASING; Canadian publication for production, purchasing & management in metalworking. Text in English. 1974. bi-m. CAD 35 domestic; USD 59.50 in United States; USD 105 elsewhere (effective 2008). adv. **Document type:** *Magazine, Trade.*
Related titles: Online - full text ed.; Supplement(s): Canadian Machine Tool Dealer. ISSN 1719-7139.
Indexed: A15, ABIn, C03, CBCABus, P48, P51, PQC.
—CIS.
Published by: C L B Media, Inc. (Subsidiary of: Canada Law Book Inc.), 240 Edward St, Aurora, ON L4G 3S9, Canada. TEL 905-727-0077, FAX 905-727-0017, http://www.clbmedia.ca. Ed. Jerry Cook TEL 905-713-4388. Pub. Nigel Bishop TEL 905-713-4395. Circ: 19,891 (controlled).

671 USA
METALWORKING TECHNOLOGY UPDATES. Text in English. 1994. s-a. back issues avail. **Document type:** *Newsletter.* **Description:** Focuses on casting technology, foaming technology, powder metallurgy and ceramic materials.
Related titles: Online - full text ed.
Indexed: APA, C&ISA, CIA, CorrAb, E&CAJ, EEA, SolStAb, WAA.
Published by: National Center for Excellence in Metalworking Technology, 199 CTC Dr, Johnstown, PA 15904-1935. TEL 814-269-2731.

669 CAN
METSOC INTERNATIONAL SYMPOSIUM ON METALS AND THE ENVIRONMENT. PROCEEDINGS VOLUME. Text in English. 1998. irreg. CAD 20 per vol. (effective 2004).
Published by: Canadian Institute of Mining, Metallurgy and Petroleum, Metallurgical Society, 3400 de Maisonneuve Blvd W, Ste 1210, Montreal, PQ H3Z 3B8, Canada. TEL 514-939-2710, FAX 514-939-2714, cim@cim.org, http://www.cim.org.

MINERACAO METALURGIA. *see* MINES AND MINING INDUSTRY

669 531.64 USA ISSN 0882-7508
TN496 CODEN: MPERE8
➤ **MINERAL PROCESSING AND EXTRACTIVE METALLURGY REVIEW.** Text in English. 1983. q. GBP 2,516 combined subscription in United Kingdom to institutions (print & online eds.); EUR 2,339, USD 2,937 combined subscription to institutions (print & online eds.) (effective 2012). adv. reprint service avail. from PSC. **Document type:** *Journal, Academic/Scholarly.* **Description:** Publishes papers dealing with applied and theoretical aspects of extractive and process metallurgy and mineral processing.
Formerly (until 1985): Mineral Processing and Technology Review (0735-9632)
Related titles: Microform ed.; Online - full text ed.: ISSN 1547-7401. GBP 2,264 in United Kingdom to institutions; EUR 2,105, USD 2,643 to institutions (effective 2012) (from IngentaConnect).
Indexed: A01, A03, A08, A22, A28, AESIS, APA, BrCerAb, C&ISA, CA, CA/WCA, CIA, CPEI, CerAb, CivEngAb, CorrAb, CurCont, E&CAJ, E01, E11, E14, EEA, EMA, ESPM, EngInd, EnvEAb, GeoRef, H15, IMMAb, M&TEA, M09, MBF, METADEX, MSCI, P26, P52, P54, P56, PQC, S01, SCI, SCOPUS, SolStAb, T02, T04, W07, WAA.
—IE, Infotrieve, Ingenta, INIST, Linda Hall. **CCC.**
Published by: Taylor & Francis Inc. (Subsidiary of: Taylor & Francis Group), 325 Chestnut St, Ste 800, Philadelphia, PA 19106. TEL 215-625-2940, 800-354-1420, orders@taylorandfrancis.com, http://www.taylorandfrancis.com. Ed. S Komar Kawatra. Adv. contact Linda Hann TEL 44-1344-779945.

➤ **MINERALES.** *see* MINES AND MINING INDUSTRY

669 IND ISSN 0378-6366
TN1 CODEN: MMREDC
MINERALS & METALS REVIEW. Text in English. 1948. m. USD 275, EUR 200, INR 3,500 (print or online ed.); USD 325, EUR 250, INR 5,500 combined subscription (print & online eds.) (effective 2011). adv. bk.rev. charts; illus.; stat. back issues avail. **Document type:** *Journal, Academic/Scholarly.*
Formerly (until 1975): Eastern Metals Review; Incorporates: Iron & Steel Newsletter (0970-1788); Minerals Market Reporter (0970-177X); Non-Ferrous Report (0970-163X)
Related titles: Online - full text ed.
Indexed: A28, APA, BrCerAb, C&ISA, CA/WCA, CBNB, CIA, CTE, CerAb, CivEngAb, CorrAb, E&CAJ, E11, EEA, EMA, ESPM, EnvEAb, H15, M&TEA, M09, MBF, METADEX, SolStAb, T04, WAA.
—CASDDS, Linda Hall.
Published by: Asian Industry & Information Services Pvt. Ltd., Feltham House,1st Fl, 10, J.N.Heredia Marg, Ballard Estate, Mumbai, Maharastra 400001, India. TEL 91-22-22660623, FAX 91-22-22660632, contact@mmronline.com.

MINERIA CHILENA. *see* MINES AND MINING INDUSTRY

669 JPN ISSN 0289-6214
CODEN: MRMMED
MINING AND MATERIALS PROCESSING INSTITUTE OF JAPAN. METALLURGICAL REVIEW. Text in English. s-a. **Document type:** *Journal, Trade.*
Indexed: ChemAb, ChemTitl, IMMAb, SCOPUS.
—BLDSC (5698.497000), CASDDS, IE, Ingenta, Linda Hall. **CCC.**
Published by: Shigen Sozai Gakkai/Mining and Materials Processing Institute of Japan, Nogizaka Bldg, 9-6-41 Akasaka, Minato-ku, Tokyo, 107-0052, Japan. TEL 81-3-34020541, FAX 81-3-34031776, info@mmij.or.jp, http://www.mmij.or.jp/.

THE MINING, GEOLOGICAL AND METALLURGICAL INSTITUTE OF INDIA. PROCEEDINGS. *see* MINES AND MINING INDUSTRY

THE MINING, GEOLOGICAL AND METALLURGICAL INSTITUTE OF INDIA. TRANSACTIONS. *see* MINES AND MINING INDUSTRY

669 ZAF ISSN 1012-5299
MINTEK BULLETIN. Text in English. 3/yr. back issues avail.
Indexed: A28, APA, BrCerAb, C&ISA, CA/WCA, CIA, CerAb, CivEngAb, CorrAb, E&CAJ, E11, EEA, EMA, H15, M&TEA, M09, MBF, METADEX, SolStAb, T04, WAA.
Published by: Mintek, 200 Hans Strijdom Dr, Private Bag X3015, Randburg, Gauteng 2125, South Africa. TEL 27-11-709-4111, FAX 27-11-709-4326, http://www.mintek.ac.za.

669 JPN ISSN 0914-5958
MIYAJI GIHO/MIYAJI TECHNICAL REPORT. Text in Japanese; Summaries in English. 1985. a.
Published by: Miyaji Tekkojo/Miyaji Iron Works Co., Ltd., 7-5 Nihonbashi Ohdenma-cho Chuo-ku, Tokyo, 103-0011, Japan. TEL 81-3-3639-2111, FAX 81-3-3639-2279, post@miyaji-iron.com, http://www.miyaji-iron.com/.

671 USA ISSN 0277-9951
MODERN APPLICATIONS NEWS; metalworking ideas for today's job. Abbreviated title: M A N. Text in English. 1967. m. USD 92 domestic; USD 112 in Canada & Mexico; USD 165 elsewhere; free to qualified personnel (effective 2008). adv. illus.; tr.lit. back issues avail.; reprints avail. **Document type:** *Magazine, Trade.*
Former titles (until 1979): Modern Applications News for Design and Manufacturing (0026-7473); Materials Application News for Design and Manufacturing
Related titles: Online - full text ed.
Indexed: A01, A03, A05, A08, A26, A28, APA, AS&TA, AS&TI, B02, B15, B17, B18, BRD, BrCerAb, C&ISA, C10, CA, CA/WCA, CIA, CerAb, CivEngAb, CorrAb, E&CAJ, E11, EEA, EMA, G04, G08, H15, I05, M&TEA, M09, MBF, METADEX, S04, SolStAb, T02, T04, W03, W05, WAA.
—Linda Hall. **CCC.**
Published by: Nelson Publishing, Inc., 2500 Tamiami Trail N, Nokomis, FL 34275. TEL 941-966-9521, FAX 941-966-2590, http://www.nelsonpub.com. Ed. Pete Nofel. Pub. Robert Olree. adv.: B&W page USD 5,675, color page USD 7,040; trim 7.75 x 10.75. Circ: 75,000 (paid).

671.2 USA ISSN 0026-7562
TS200 CODEN: MOCAB5
MODERN CASTING. Text in English. 1921. m. USD 50 in North America; USD 85 elsewhere; USD 30 domestic; USD 10 foreign; free to qualified personnel (effective 2010). adv. bk.rev. charts; illus.; tr.lit. back issues avail.; reprints avail. **Document type:** *Journal, Trade.* **Description:** Contains technology, business practices and news in the metalcasting industry.

M

Former titles (until 1966): Modern Castings and American Foundryman (0096-4662); (until 1955): American Foundryman (0096-9028); (until 1938): American Foundrymen's Association. Bulletin (0099-4979)
Related titles: Microform ed.; Online - full text ed.: free (effective 2010).
Indexed: A05, A10, A15, A22, A23, A24, A28, ABIn, AESIS, APA, AS&TA, AS&TI, B04, B13, BCIRA, BRD, BrCerAb, C&ISA, C10, CA/WCA, CIA, CIN, CerAb, ChemAb, ChemTitl, CivEngAb, CorrAb, E&CAJ, E11, EEA, EMA, ESPM, EngInd, EnvEAb, G06, G07, G08, H15, I05, ISR, Inspec, L09, M&TEA, M09, MBF, METADEX, P26, P48, P51, P52, P54, PQC, S04, SCOPUS, SolStAb, T02, T04, TM, V03, W03, W05, WAA.
—BLDSC (5884.800000), CASDDS, IE, Infotrieve, Ingenta, INIST, Linda Hall. **CCC.**
Published by: American Foundry Society, 1695 N Penny Ln, Schaumburg, IL 60173. TEL 847-824-0181, FAX 847-824-7848, library@afsinc.org, http://www.afsinc.org. Ed., Pub. Alfred Spada TEL 847-824-0181 ext 281.

671 USA ISSN 0026-8127
TS200 CODEN: MOMLAJ
MODERN METALS. Text in English. 1945. 11/yr. USD 120 domestic; USD 140 in Canada; USD 175 elsewhere (effective 2006). adv. charts; illus.; mkt.; tr.lit. back issues avail. **Document type:** *Magazine, Trade.*
Related titles: Online - full text ed.
Indexed: A05, A22, A23, A24, A28, APA, AS&TA, AS&TI, B04, B10, B13, BRD, BrCerAb, C&ISA, C10, CA, CA/WCA, CIA, CerAb, ChemAb, CivEngAb, CoppAb, CorrAb, E&CAJ, E11, EEA, EMA, ESPM, EngInd, EnvEAb, H15, ISR, M&TEA, M09, MBF, METADEX, PST, S04, SCOPUS, SolStAb, T02, T04, W03, W05, WAA.
—IE, Infotrieve, Ingenta, INIST, Linda Hall. **CCC.**
Published by: Trend Publishing Inc., 625 N Michigan Ave, 11th Fl, Chicago, IL 60611-3199. TEL 312-654-2300, FAX 312-654-2323. Ed. Lauren Duensing. Pub. Michael D'Alexander. adv.: B&W page USD 4,600; trim 7.8 x 10.75. Circ: 36,000 (controlled).

MODERN STEEL CONSTRUCTION. *see* BUILDING AND CONSTRUCTION

669 DEU ISSN 1864-3515
MODERNE METALLTECHNIK UND KUNSTSTOFFTECHNIK; das Magazin fuer Ausbildung und Beruf. Text in German. 1987. m. **Document type:** *Magazine, Trade.*
Formerly (until 2007): M - Moderne Metalltechnik (0933-8810)
Published by: Directa Buldt Fachverlag, Luebecker Str 8, Bad Schwartau, 23611, Germany. TEL 49-451-499990, FAX 49-451-4999940, info@directa-verlag.de, http://www.directa-verlag.de.

669 ESP ISSN 1132-0354
MOLDES. Text in Spanish. 1989. 6/yr. adv. **Document type:** *Magazine, Trade.*
Related titles: Online - full text ed.: free.
Indexed: IECT.
Published by: Metal Spain, Hermosilla 38, 1B, Madrid, 28001, Spain. TEL 34-91-5765609, FAX 34-91-5782924, magazine@metalspain.co.

669 GBR
MOLY REVIEW. Text in English. 19??. s-a. free (effective 2009). back issues avail. **Document type:** *Magazine, Trade.* **Description:** Features several short articles of general interest which all have a molybdenum connection.
Formerly (until 2009): International Molybdenum Association Newsletter
Related titles: Online - full text ed.
Indexed: APA, C&ISA, CorrAb, E&CAJ, EEA, SolStAb, WAA.
Published by: International Molybdenum Association, 4 Heathfield Terr, London, W4 4JE, United Kingdom. TEL 44-207-8711580, FAX 44-208-9946067, info@imoa.info, http://www.imoa.org.uk. Eds. James Chater, Nicole Kinsman.

MONUMENTAL BRASS SOCIETY. TRANSACTIONS. *see* ARCHAEOLOGY

672 RUS ISSN 0131-5145
TN730 CODEN: NTMSDL
MOSKOVSKII INSTITUT STALI I SPLAVOV. NAUCHNYE TRUDY. Text in Russian. 1972. irreg. illus. **Document type:** *Journal, Academic/Scholarly.*
Indexed: ChemAb, RASB.
—CASDDS, Linda Hall.
Published by: Moskovskii Institut Stali i Splavov/Moscow Institute of Steel and Alloys, Leninskii prospekt 4, Moscow, 119991, Russian Federation. TEL 7-095-2372222, FAX 7-095-2378007, welcome@ir.misis.ru, http://www.ir.misis.ru.

N A D C A INTERNATIONAL DIE CASTING CONGRESS. TRANSACTIONS. *see* ENGINEERING—Engineering Mechanics And Materials

669 DEU ISSN 0174-4534
N C FERTIGUNG; Fachmagazin fuer Spangebende Metallbearbeitung. (Numeric Control) Text in German. 1980. 10/yr. EUR 80 domestic; EUR 95 foreign; EUR 18 newsstand/cover (effective 2010). adv. **Document type:** *Magazine, Trade.*
Incorporates (1988-1990): C I M (0935-2945)
Related titles: Online - full text ed.
Indexed: TM.
Published by: Schluetersche Verlagsgesellschaft mbH und Co. KG, Hans-Boeckler-Allee 7, Hannover, 30173, Germany. TEL 49-511-85500, FAX 49-511-85501100, info@schluetersche.de, http://www.schluetersche.de. Ed. Helmut Angeli. Adv. contact Gabriele Maier. color page EUR 5,130, B&W page EUR 3,900; trim 188 x 272. Circ: 21,700 (paid and controlled).

620.112 JPN ISSN 1348-141X
N I M S CORROSION DATA SHEETS/BUSSHITSU ZAIRYOU KENKYUU KIKOU FUSHOKU DETA SHITO. Text in English, Japanese. 2002. irreg. price varies. **Document type:** *Monographic series, Academic/Scholarly.*
Indexed: A28, APA, BrCerAb, C&ISA, CA/WCA, CIA, CerAb, CivEngAb, CorrAb, E&CAJ, E11, EEA, EMA, ESPM, EnvEAb, H15, M&TEA, M09, MBF, METADEX, RefZh, SolStAb, T04, WAA.
—Linda Hall.
Published by: National Institute for Materials Science/Busshitsu Zairyou Kenkyuu Kikou, Planning Section of Administration Division, 2-3-54 Nakameguro, Meguro-ku, Tokyo, 153-0061, Japan. TEL 81-3-37192727, FAX 81-3-37192177, inquiry@nims.go.jp, http://www.nims.go.jp.

669 JPN ISSN 1347-3093
N I M S FATIGUE DATA SHEET/BUSSHITSU ZAIRYOU KENKYUU KIKOU HIROU DETA SHITO. Text in English, Japanese. irreg. **Document type:** *Monographic series, Academic/Scholarly.*
Indexed: A28, APA, BrCerAb, C&ISA, CA/WCA, CIA, CerAb, CivEngAb, CorrAb, E&CAJ, E11, EEA, EMA, H15, M&TEA, M09, MBF, METADEX, SolStAb, T04, WAA.
—Linda Hall.
Published by: National Institute for Materials Science/Busshitsu Zairyou Kenkyuu Kikou, Planning Section of Administration Division, 2-3-54 Nakameguro, Meguro-ku, Tokyo, 153-0061, Japan. TEL 81-3-37192727, FAX 81-3-37192177, inquiry@nims.go.jp, http://www.nims.go.jp.

620.112 JPN ISSN 1348-1428
TL953
N I M S SPACE USE MATERIALS STRENGTH DATA SHEET/ BUSSHITSU ZAIRYOU KENKYUU KIKOU UCHUU KANREN ZAIRYOU KYOUDO DETA SHITO. Text in English, Japanese. 2003. irreg. **Document type:** *Monographic series, Academic/Scholarly.*
Indexed: A28, APA, BrCerAb, C&ISA, CA/WCA, CIA, CerAb, CivEngAb, CorrAb, E&CAJ, E11, EEA, EMA, H15, M&TEA, M09, MBF, METADEX, SolStAb, T04, WAA.
—Linda Hall.
Published by: National Institute for Materials Science/Busshitsu Zairyou Kenkyuu Kikou, Planning Section of Administration Division, 2-3-54 Nakameguro, Meguro-ku, Tokyo, 153-0061, Japan. TEL 81-3-37192727, FAX 81-3-37192177, inquiry@nims.go.jp, http://www.nims.go.jp.

669 USA
N O M M A NEWSLETTER. Text in English. bi-m. membership only. **Document type:** *Newsletter, Trade.*
Published by: National Ornamental & Miscellaneous Metals Association, 532 Forest Pkwy, Ste A, Forest Park, GA 30297-6137. TEL 404-363-4009, FAX 404-366-1852, nommainfo@nomma.org, http://www.nomma.org. Ed. Todd Daniel.

669 CHN ISSN 1001-1935
CODEN: NACAEN
NAIHUO CAILIAO. Text in Chinese; Abstracts in Chinese, English. 1966. bi-m. USD 21.60 (effective 2009). adv. bk.rev. abstr.; bibl.; charts; illus.; maps. Index. back issues avail.; reprints avail. **Document type:** *Journal, Academic/Scholarly.* **Description:** Reports new achievements and experiences in the research, production, and application of refractories in China.
Related titles: Online - full text ed.
Indexed: A28, APA, BrCerAb, C&ISA, CA/WCA, CIA, CIN, CerAb, ChemAb, ChemTitl, CivEngAb, CorrAb, E&CAJ, E11, EEA, EMA, ESPM, EngInd, EnvEAb, H15, M&TEA, M09, MBF, METADEX, RefZh, SCOPUS, SolStAb, T04, WAA.
—BLDSC (6015.309800), CASDDS, IE, Ingenta, Linda Hall.
Published by: Yejin Bu, Luoyang Naihuo Cailiao Yanjiuyuan/Luoyang Institute of Refractories Research, No 43 Xiyuan Lu, Jianxi-qu Luoyang, Henan, 471039, China. nhcl@public2.lyptt.ha.cn, http://www.nhcl.com.cn. Ed. Zhengguo Fang. Pub. Jinxiang Wang. Adv. contact Junlan Chai. page USD 1,000; trim 210 x 292. Circ: 8,500.

669 CHN ISSN 1673-7792
NAIHUO YU SHIHUI/REFRACTORIES & LIME. Text in Chinese. m. **Document type:** *Magazine, Trade.*
Formerly (until 2007): Guowai Naihuo Cailiao/Foreign Refractories (1000-7563)
Related titles: Online - full text ed.
Published by: Zhong-Ye Jiao-Nai Gongcheng Jishu Youxian Gongsi/A C R E Coking And Refractory Engineering Consulting Corporation, M C C, 27, Nanshengli Lu, Anshan, 114002, China. TEL 86-412-5510206, FAX 86-412-5531333, http://www.acre.com.cn.

669 JPN
NALK REPORT. Text in English. m. USD 920 (effective 2004). adv. **Document type:** *Bulletin, Newsletter, Trade.*
Indexed: APA, C&ISA, CIA, CorrAb, E&CAJ, EEA, SolStAb, WAA.
Published by: Nalk Corporation, Rm 615 Grand Palace Tamachi, 4-9-18 Shibaura, Minato-ku, Tokyo, 108-0023, Japan. TEL 81-3-3456-4416, FAX 81-3-3456-4417. Pub. Isao Nakada TEL 81-3-3456-5205. Adv. contact Keiko Miyata. Circ: 300 (paid and controlled).

669.2 JPN ISSN 0027-772X
NAMARI TO AEN/LEAD AND ZINC. Text in Japanese. 1964. bi-m. JPY 1,000 (effective 2001). adv. bk.rev. abstr.; charts; illus.; stat. cum.index. **Document type:** *Bulletin, Bibliography.* **Description:** Covers important issues in metallurgy.
Indexed: JTA.
Published by: Japan Lead Zinc Development Association/Nihon Namari Aen Juyo Kenkyukai, Shuwa No 3 Toranomon Bldg, 1-21-8 Toranomon, Minato-ku, Tokyo, 105-0001, Japan. TEL 81-3-3591-0812, FAX 81-3-3503-5796. Ed., Pub., R&P, Adv. contact Kenji Sasaki TEL 81-3-3591-0812. Circ: 1,500 (controlled).

669.142 CHN ISSN 1009-9700
NANFANG JINSHU/SOUTHERN METALS. Text in Chinese. 1980 (Nov.). bi-m. CNY 8 per issue domestic (effective 2011). back issues avail. **Document type:** *Journal, Academic/Scholarly.*
Fomerly (until 2001): Nanfang Gangtie/Iron and Steel of South China (1007-5437)
Related titles: Online - full text ed.
Published by: (Guangdong Sheng Yejin Gongye Zonggongsi), Guangdong Sheng Jinshu Xuehui, Zhongsha Er-Lu #48 Houzuo, Guangzhou, Guangdong 510080, China. TEL 86-20-87654977, FAX 86-20-87654977, http://www.gdpms.com. Ed. Wei Fang Su.

669.722 USA
NATIONAL ASSOCIATION OF ALUMINUM DISTRIBUTORS. TOPICS. Text in English. q. free to qualified personnel. **Document type:** *Newsletter.*
Published by: National Association of Aluminum Distributors, 1900 Arch St, Philadelphia, PA 19103-1498. TEL 215-564-3484, FAX 215-963-9784. Ed. Vaughn Wurst. R&P Joe Koury. Circ: 1,000.

671.2 NLD ISSN 1875-208X
NEDERLANDSE VERANTWOORDELIJKHEIDSTEKENS VANAF 1797. Text in Dutch. 2006. irreg. EUR 77.50 per issue (effective 2010).
Formed by the merger of (2003-2004): Nederlandse Verantwoordelijkheidstekens van 1797 tot 1953 (1571-3717); (2003-2004): Nederlandse Verantwoordelijkheidstekens vanaf 1953 (1571-3725); Both of which superseded in part: Nederlandse Verantwoordelijkheidstekens sinds 1797 (1571-3571)
Published by: Waarborg Holland, Stationsplein 9a, Gouda, 2801 AK, Netherlands. TEL 31-182-589300, FAX http://www.waarborg.nl, info@waarborg.nl.

669 600 JPN ISSN 0288-0490
TN672 CODEN: NESHDF
NETSU SHORI/JAPAN SOCIETY FOR HEAT TREATMENT. JOURNAL. Text in Japanese. 1960. bi-m. JPY 8,000 domestic membership; JPY 9,000 foreign membership (effective 2004). adv. bk.rev. **Document type:** *Journal, Academic/Scholarly.*
Indexed: A22, A28, APA, BrCerAb, C&ISA, CA/WCA, CIA, CIN, CerAb, ChemAb, ChemTitl, CivEngAb, CorrAb, E&CAJ, E11, EEA, EMA, ESPM, EnvEAb, H15, M&TEA, M09, MBF, METADEX, RefZh, SolStAb, T04, WAA.
—BLDSC (4807.500000), CASDDS, IE, Ingenta, Linda Hall. **CCC.**
Published by: Nihon Netsu Shori Gijutsu Kyokai/Japan Society for Heat Treatment, 3-2-10 Kayaba-cho Nihonbashi Chuo-ku, Tokyo, 103-0025, Japan. TEL 81-3-56437866, FAX 81-3-56437867, jsht@aurora.ocn.ne.jp. Ed. Suzuki Tomoo. Circ: 5,000.

669.1 JPN ISSN 0911-8764
NEWS FROM NISSHIN STEEL. Text in English. q. illus. **Description:** Contains news and articles about the company.
Published by: Nisshin Steel Co. Ltd., 4-1 Marunochi 3-chome, Chiyoda-ku, Tokyo, 100-0005, Japan. FAX 81-3-3214-1895.

669 540 GBR ISSN 1357-8421
NICAD (YEAR). Text in English. irreg. **Document type:** *Monographic series, Academic/Scholarly.* **Description:** Provides a detailed review of nickel-cadmium technology, applications and markets.
—BLDSC (6109.845000).
Published by: International Cadmium Association, International Cadium Association, 43 Weymouth St, London, W1N 3LQ, United Kingdom. TEL 44-171-499-8425, FAX 44-171-486-4007.

669.733 CAN
NICKEL - COBALT (YEAR): VOLUME III: PYROMETALLURGICAL OPERATIONS, ENVIRONMENT, VESSEL INTEGRITY. Text in English. 1997. irreg. CAD 20 per issue (effective 2004).
Published by: Canadian Institute of Mining, Metallurgy and Petroleum, Metallurgical Society, 3400 de Maisonneuve Blvd W, Ste 1210, Montreal, PQ H3Z 3B8, Canada. TEL 514-939-2710, FAX 514-939-2714, cim@cim.org, http://www.cim.org.

669 JPN ISSN 0546-126X
NIHON SEIKOSHO GIHO/JAPAN STEEL WORKS TECHNICAL REVIEW. Text in English, Japanese. 1959. s-a.
Published by: Nihon Seikosho/Japan Steel Works, Ltd., 1-12 Yurakucho, Chiyoda-ku, Tokyo, 100-0006, Japan.

669 USA
NIOBIUM UPDATE. Text in English. q.
Published by: Niobium Products Co Inc, 1000 Old Pond Rd, Bridgeville, PA 15017. TEL 412-221-7008.

669 JPN ISSN 0021-4876
HD9510.1 CODEN: NIKGAV
➤ **NIPPON KINZOKU GAKKAISHI/JAPAN INSTITUTE OF METALS. JOURNAL.** Text in Japanese; Abstracts and contents page in English. 1937. m. JPY 96,000 membership (effective 2004). adv. Index. **Document type:** *Journal, Academic/Scholarly.* **Description:** Contains original technical papers.
Related titles: Online - full text ed.
Indexed: A20, A22, A28, APA, ASCA, BrCerAb, C&ISA, C33, CA/WCA, CEABA, CIA, CIN, CPEI, Cadscan, CerAb, ChemAb, ChemTitl, CivEngAb, CorrAb, CurCont, E&CAJ, E11, EEA, EMA, ESPM, EngInd, EnvEAb, H15, INIS AtomInd, ISR, Inspec, JCT, JTA, LeadAb, M&TEA, M09, MBF, METADEX, MSCI, PhysBer, SCI, SCOPUS, SolStAb, T04, TM, W07, WAA, Zincscan.
—BLDSC (4805.250000), AskIEEE, CASDDS, IE, Ingenta, INIST, Linda Hall. **CCC.**
Published by: Nihon Kinzoku Gakkai/Japan Institute of Metals, 1-14-32 Ichibancho, Aoba-ku, Sendai, Sendai, 980-8544, Japan. TEL 81-22-2233685, FAX 81-22-2236312. Circ: 5,000.

669.1 JPN ISSN 0048-0452
NIPPON STEEL NEWS. Text in English. 1970. m. free. illus. **Description:** Focuses on technological innovations, new companies and mergers.
Indexed: A28, APA, BrCerAb, C&ISA, CA/WCA, CIA, CerAb, CivEngAb, CorrAb, E&CAJ, E11, EEA, EMA, ESPM, EnvEAb, H15, M&TEA, M09, MBF, METADEX, SolStAb, T04, WAA.
—Linda Hall.
Published by: Nippon Steel Corporation, 6-3 Ote-Machi 2-chome, Chiyoda-ku, Tokyo, 100-0004, Japan. TEL 03-242-4111, FAX 03-275-9607, TELEX J-22291.

669.1 JPN
NIPPON STEEL REPORT. Text in Japanese. a. **Description:** Presents financial information on the company. Explores business developments, electronics information, new materials, sales, revenue and future management risks.
Published by: Nippon Steel Corporation, 6-3 Ote-Machi 2-chome, Chiyoda-ku, Tokyo, 100-0004, Japan. TEL 03-242-4111, FAX 03-275-5607.

672.05 JPN ISSN 0300-306X
TS300
NIPPON STEEL TECHNICAL REPORT. Text in Japanese. 1972. s-a. free. illus.
Formerly: Nippon Steel Technical Report. Overseas
Related titles: Translation of: Seitetsu Kenkyu.
Indexed: A22, A28, APA, BrCerAb, C&ISA, CA/WCA, CIA, CerAb, CivEngAb, CorrAb, E&CAJ, E11, EEA, EMA, H15, ISMEC, JCT, JOF, JTA, M&TEA, M09, MBF, METADEX, SCOPUS, SolStAb, T04, TM, WAA.
—IE, Ingenta, INIST, Linda Hall.
Published by: Nippon Steel Corporation, 6-3 Ote-Machi 2-chome, Chiyoda-ku, Tokyo, 100-0004, Japan. TEL 03-242-4111.

669.1 JPN
NISSHIN. Text in Japanese. 1990 (Apr., no.434). m. **Document type:** *Newsletter.* **Description:** In-house magazine for company employees.

Published by: Nisshin Steel Co. Ltd., 4-1 Marunochi 3-chome, Chiyoda-ku, Tokyo, 100-0005, Japan. TEL 03-216-5511, FAX 03-214-1895.

669.1 JPN
NISSHIN STEEL. ANNUAL REPORT. Text in English. a. charts; illus.; stat.
Published by: Nisshin Steel Co. Ltd., 4-1 Marunochi 3-chome, Chiyoda-ku, Tokyo, 100-0005, Japan. FAX 81-3-3214-1895, TELEX 222-2788.

NON-DESTRUCTIVE TESTING - AUSTRALIA; a journal of measurement control & testing. *see* ENGINEERING—Engineering Mechanics And Materials

669 RUS
NON-FERROUS METALS. Text in English. 2001. m. **Document type:** *Journal, Trade.* **Description:** Covers economics of non-ferrous metallurgy, heavy non-ferrous metals, and noble metals and alloys.
Related titles: ◆ Translation of: Tsvetnye Metally. ISSN 0372-2929; ◆ Supplement to: Tsvetnye Metally. ISSN 0372-2929.
Published by: Izdatel'stvo Ruda i Metally/Ore and Metals Publishers, Leninskii prospekt 6, korpus 1, ofis 622, a/ya 71, Moscow, 119049, Russian Federation. rim@rudmet.ru. Ed. Aleksandr Putilov. Circ: 500.

669 CAN ISSN 1208-5855
HD9539.A3
NONFERROUS METALS OUTLOOK. Text in English. a.
Related titles: Online - full text ed.: ISSN 1493-745X.
Published by: Natural Resources Canada, Minerals and Metals Sector (Subsidiary of: Natural Resources Canada/Ressources Naturelles Canada), 580 Booth St, Ottawa, ON K1A 0E4, Canada. TEL 613-947-6580, FAX 613-952-7501, info-mms@nrcan.gc.ca, http://www.nrcan.gc.ca/mms/hm_e.htm.

669 622 CHN ISSN 1003-6326
TA479.3 CODEN: TNMCEW
➤ **NONFERROUS METALS SOCIETY OF CHINA. TRANSACTIONS.** Text in English. 1991. bi-m. (q. until 2001). CNY 20 newsstand/cover (effective 2004). abstr. 176 p./no.; **Document type:** *Journal, Academic/Scholarly.* **Description:** Publishes research papers on the latest developments in the fields of nonferrous metals and mining technology.
Related titles: Online - full text ed.: ISSN 2210-3384 (from ScienceDirect); ◆ Chinese ed.: Zhongguo Youse Jinshu Xuebao. ISSN 1004-0609.
Indexed: A28, APA, ASCA, BrCerAb, C&ISA, CA/WCA, CIA, CPEI, CerAb, ChemAb, CivEngAb, CorrAb, E&CAJ, E11, EEA, EMA, ESPM, EngInd, EnvEAb, GeoRef, H15, IMMAb, Inspec, M&TEA, M09, MBF, METADEX, MSCI, RefZh, SCI, SCOPUS, SolStAb, SpeleolAb, T04, TM, W07, WAA.
—BLDSC (8989.500000), AskIEEE, CASDDS, IE, Ingenta, Linda Hall. **CCC.**
Published by: Nonferrous Metals Society of China/Zhongguo Youse Jinshu Xuehui, Central South University of Technology, Changsha, 410083, China. TEL 86-731-8876765, FAX 86-731-8877197, f-ysxb@csut.edu.cn, http://www.csut.edu.cn/~f-ysxb/. Circ: 200 (paid); 500 (controlled).

669.772 USA
NORTH AMERICAN ALUMINUM INDUSTRY PLANT DIRECTORY (ONLINE). Text in English. 19??. a. free (effective 2011). **Document type:** *Directory, Trade.*
Formerly: North American Aluminum Industry Plant Directory (Print)
Media: Online - full text.
Published by: Aluminum Association, 1525 Wilson Blvd, Ste 600, Arlington, VA 22209. TEL 703-358-2960, FAX 703-358-2961, http://www.aluminum.org/.

THE NORTH AMERICAN SCRAP METALS DIRECTORY (CD-ROM). *see* ENVIRONMENTAL STUDIES—Waste Management

THE NORTH AMERICAN SCRAP METALS DIRECTORY (PRINT). *see* ENVIRONMENTAL STUDIES—Waste Management

(YEAR) NORTH CAROLINA METAL PROCESSORS DIRECTORY. *see* MACHINERY

669 RUS
NOVYE ISSLEDOVANIYA V KHIMII, METALLURGII I OBOGASHCHENII. Text in Russian. irreg. illus.
Related titles: Series of: Nauchnye Trudy.
Published by: Sankt-Peterburgskii Gornyi Institut/St. Petersburg Mining Institute, 21-ya Liniya 2, Vasilevskii Ostrov, St Petersburg, 199026, Russian Federation. TEL 7-812-2136078, FAX 7-812-2132613, TELEX 121494.

669 RUS ISSN 0208-1008
NOVYE PROMYSHLENNYE KATALOGI. GORNO-SHAKHTNOE I METALLURGICHESKOE OBORUDOVANIE. Text in Russian. m. USD 345 in United States.
—East View.
Published by: Rossiiskii N.I.I. Problem Transporta, Lubyanskii pr 5, Moscow, 101820, Russian Federation. TEL 7-095-9254609, FAX 7-095-2002203. **Dist. by:** East View Information Services, 10601 Wayzata Blvd, Minneapolis, MN 55305. TEL 952-252-1201, 800-477-1005, FAX 952-252-1202, info@eastview.com, http://www.eastview.com.

669 RUS
NOVYE PROMYSHLENNYE KATALOGI. OBORUDOVANIE DLYA OBRABOTKI I OTDELKI METALLA I DREVESINY. DETALI MASHIN. ROBOTOTEKHNIKA. Text in Russian. m. USD 365 in United States.
Published by: Rossiiskii N.I.I. Problem Transporta, Lubyanskii pr 5, Moscow, 101820, Russian Federation. TEL 7-095-9254609, FAX 7-095-2002202. **Dist. by:** East View Information Services, 10601 Wayzata Blvd, Minneapolis, MN 55305. TEL 952-252-1201, 800-477-1005, FAX 952-252-1202, info@eastview.com, http://www.eastview.com.

669 POL ISSN 0867-2628
CODEN: OBPLAX
➤ **OBROBKA PLASTYCZNA METALI/METAL FORMING.** Text in Polish; Summaries in English. 1959. 5/yr. PLZ 110 domestic; USD 50 foreign (effective 2002). adv. 50 p./no.; back issues avail. **Document type:** *Journal, Academic/Scholarly.* **Description:** Publishes articles about metal forming technology, machines, tools and scientific investigations.
Formerly (until 1990): Obrobka Plastyczna (0472-4313)
Indexed: A01, B22, TM.
—CASDDS, Linda Hall.
Published by: Instytut Obrobki Plastycznej, Ul Jana Pawla II 14, Poznan, 61139, Poland. TEL 48-61-8771081, FAX 48-61-8791682, TELEX 0413480 INOP PL, http://www.inop.poznan.pl. Ed. Boleslaw Kwasniewski. Adv. contact Teresa Zielniewicz. Circ: 300.

669 POL ISSN 1230-7408
CODEN: OCPOAF
OCHRONA POWIETRZA I PROBLEMY ODPADOW. Text in Polish. 1967. bi-m. EUR 74 foreign (effective 2005). **Document type:** *Journal, Academic/Scholarly.*
Formerly (until 1993): Ochrona Powietrza (0137-3714)
Indexed: AgrLib, B22, CIN, ChemAb, ChemTitl, INIS AtomInd.
—CASDDS, Linda Hall.
Published by: (Stowarzyszenie Inzynierow i Technikow Przemyslu Hutniczego w Polsce), Wydawnictwo Naukowo-Techniczne EcoEdycja, ul Warszawska 31, Katowice, 40010, Poland. TEL 48-32-2597911. Ed. Janusz Lutynski. Circ: 2,150. **Dist. by:** Ars Polona, Obroncow 25, Warsaw 03933, Poland. TEL 48-22-5098609, FAX 48-22-5098610, arspolona@arspolona.com.pl, http://www.arspolona.com.pl.

620.11223 POL ISSN 0473-7733
TA418.74 CODEN: OPZKA8
OCHRONA PRZED KOROZJA. Text in Polish. 1957. m. PLZ 422.10 domestic; EUR 251 foreign (effective 2011). adv. 32 p./no.; **Document type:** *Journal, Trade.*
Related titles: Online - full text ed.
Indexed: A28, APA, B22, BrCerAb, C&ISA, CA/WCA, CIA, CerAb, ChemAb, ChemTitl, CivEngAb, CorrAb, E&CAJ, E11, EEA, EMA, H15, M&TEA, M09, MBF, METADEX, SolStAb, T04, WAA, WSCA.
—CASDDS, INIST, Linda Hall.
Published by: (Poland. Stowarzyszenie Inzynierow i Technikow Przemyslu Chemicznego), Wydawnictwo SIGMA - N O T Sp. z o.o., ul Ratuszowa 11, PO Box 1004, Warsaw, 00950, Poland. TEL 48-22-8180918, FAX 48-22-6192187, sekretariat@sigma-not.pl. Ed. Edward Smieszek TEL 48-32-2310224. adv.: B&W page PLZ 1,600, color page PLZ 3,300. Circ: 1,100. **Dist. by:** Ars Polona, Obroncow 25, Warsaw 03933, Poland. TEL 48-22-5098609, FAX 48-22-5098610, arspolona@arspolona.com.pl, http://www.arspolona.com.pl. **Co-sponsor:** Polski Komitet Ochrony przed Korozja NOT.

671.2 POL ISSN 1730-2250
ODLEWNICTWO. NAUKA I PRAKTYKA/JOURNAL OF THE FOUNDRY RESEARCH INSTITUTE. Text in Polish. 1998. bi-m. PLZ 155 domestic; EUR 94 foreign (effective 2005). **Document type:** *Journal, Academic/Scholarly.*
Formerly (until 2003): Instytut Odlewnictwa. Biuletyn (1506-1949)
Indexed: A28, APA, B22, BrCerAb, C&ISA, CA/WCA, CIA, CerAb, CivEngAb, CorrAb, E&CAJ, E11, EEA, EMA, H15, M&TEA, M09, MBF, METADEX, SolStAb, T04, WAA.
—Linda Hall.
Published by: Instytut Odlewnictwa, Zakopianska 73, Krakow, 30418, Poland. TEL 48-12-2618381, FAX 48-12-2660870, iod@iod.krakow.pl, http://www.iod.krakow.pl. **Dist. by:** Ars Polona, Obroncow 25, Warsaw 03933, Poland. TEL 48-22-5098609, FAX 48-22-5098610, arspolona@arspolona.com.pl, http://www.arspolona.com.pl.

669 DEU ISSN 0078-3420
CODEN: ORSMAR
OERLIKON SCHWEISSMITTEILUNGEN. Text in German. 1955. irreg. free. adv. **Document type:** *Bulletin.* **Description:** Technical and scientific information on welding and related fields.
Indexed: BMT, CEABA, CIN, ChemAb, ChemTitl.
—CASDDS.
Published by: Oerlikon Schweisstechnik GmbH, Eisenberg, 67304, Germany. FAX 49-6351-76335. Ed. Helmut Nies. Adv. contact H Bilavski. Circ: 5,000.

620.112 NLD ISSN 1876-5033
➤ **THE OPEN CORROSION JOURNAL.** Text in English. 2008. irreg. free (effective 2011). **Document type:** *Journal, Academic/Scholarly.*
Media: Online - full text.
Indexed: A01.
Published by: Bentham Open (Subsidiary of: Bentham Science Publishers Ltd.), PO Box 294, Bussum, AG 1400, Netherlands. TEL 31-35-6923800, FAX 31-35-6980150, subscriptions@bentham.org.

669 622 NLD ISSN 1874-8414
➤ **THE OPEN MINERAL PROCESSING JOURNAL.** Text in English. 2008. irreg. free (effective 2011). **Document type:** *Journal, Academic/Scholarly.* **Description:** Covers all areas of mineral processing and extractive metallurgy.
Media: Online - full text.
Indexed: E04, E05, ESPM, SSciA.
Published by: Bentham Open (Subsidiary of: Bentham Science Publishers Ltd.), PO Box 294, Bussum, AG 1400, Netherlands. TEL 31-35-6923800, FAX 31-35-6980150, subscriptions@bentham.org. Ed. K Hanumantha Rao.

669 NLD ISSN 1571-9995
CODEN: TOCOEP
OPPERVLAKTETECHNIEKEN. Short title: O T C. O en C. Text in Dutch. 1952. m. (11/yr.). EUR 87.50 (effective 2010). adv. bk.rev. **Document type:** *Magazine, Trade.* **Description:** Covers technical and practical topics for persons in the corrosion coatings industry, including managers, marketing personnel, engineers and developers, and application specialists.
Former titles (until 2003): O en C (1388-6541); (until 1995): OTC (1388-655X); (until 1992): Tijdschrift voor Oppervlaktetechnieken en Corrosiebestrijding (0923-1722); (until 1989): Tijdschrift voor Oppervlaktetechnieken van Materialen (0167-5095); (until 1981): Belgisch - Nederlands Tijdschrift voor Oppervlaktetechnieken van Materialen (0166-2686); (until 1978): Belgisch - Nederlands Tijdschrift voor Oppervlakte Technieken van Metalen (0366-144X); (until 1972): Tijdschrift voor Oppervlakte Technieken van Metalen (0040-7569); (until 1961): Galvano - Techniek (0367-3693); (until 1957): Metallic Bullletin (0461-9382)
Indexed: A22, CISA, ChemAb, ChemTitl, WSCA.
—BLDSC (6272.481000), CASDDS, IE, Infotrieve, Linda Hall.
Published by: Vereniging voor Oppervlaktetechnieken van Materialen/Association for Surface Finishing Techniques, Postbus 2600, Nieuwegein, 3430 GA, Netherlands. TEL 31-30-6300390, FAX 31-30-6300389, info@vom.nl, http://www.vom.nl. Ed. E J D Uittenbroek. Circ: 3,000.

669 GBR ISSN 0969-9929
ORACLE (STAFFORD). Text in English. 1989. q. free to members (effective 2009). bk.rev. abstr. **Document type:** *Newsletter, Trade.* **Description:** Contains technical articles on metallurgy and informs members of coming events and conferences.
Formerly: Oracle Technical Supplement
Published by: Institute of Sheet Metal Engineering, PO Box 2242, Stafford, ST17 0WH, United Kingdom. TEL 44-1785-716886, FAX 44-1785-716886, ismesec@googlemail.com, http://www.isme.org.uk.

669 690 USA ISSN 0191-5940
ORNAMENTAL & MISCELLANEOUS METAL FABRICATOR. Text in English. 1959. bi-m. USD 30 in North America; USD 44 elsewhere (effective 2005). adv. bk.rev. index. back issues avail.; reprints avail. **Document type:** *Magazine, Trade.* **Description:** Covers outstanding work, industry trends, new technology, and small business.
Formerly (until 1977): Ornamental Metal Fabricator
Indexed: A09, A10, A28, APA, BrCerAb, C&ISA, CA/WCA, CIA, CerAb, CivEngAb, CorrAb, E&CAJ, E11, EEA, EMA, H15, M&TEA, M09, MBF, METADEX, SolStAb, T04, V03, V04, WAA.
—Linda Hall.
Published by: National Ornamental & Miscellaneous Metals Association, 532 Forest Pkwy, Ste A, Forest Park, GA 30297-6137. TEL 404-363-4009, FAX 404-366-1852, nommainfo@nomma.org, http://www.nomma.org. Ed., Adv. contact Rachel Squires Bailey. B&W page USD 1,120, color page USD 1,405; trim 8.25 x 11. Circ: 9,000 (paid and free).

669.142 SWE ISSN 0284-3366
OVAKO STEEL A B. TECHNICAL REPORT. Text in English. 1983. irreg.
Formerly (until 1986): S K F Steel A B. Technical Report (0282-9878)
Indexed: A28, APA, BrCerAb, C&ISA, CA/WCA, CIA, CerAb, CivEngAb, CorrAb, E&CAJ, E11, EEA, EMA, H15, M&TEA, M09, MBF, METADEX, SolStAb, T04, WAA.
—Linda Hall.
Published by: Ovako Steel A B, P O Box 5013, Upplands Vaesby, 19405, Sweden. TEL 46-8-6221300, FAX 46-8-6221328, ovako.sverige@skf.com.

671.7 NOR ISSN 0801-9606
OVERFLATE TEKNIKK; overflatebehandling og korrosjonsvern. Text in Norwegian. 1958. s-a. NOK 355 (effective 2007). **Document type:** *Magazine, Trade.*
Former titles (until 1986): Galvano Teknisk Tidsskrift (0046-5372); (until 1969): Norsk Galvano Teknisk Tidsskrift (0332-6616)
Indexed: CISA.
Published by: Overflatenytt AS, PO Box 147, Gjerdrum, 2024, Norway. TEL 47-63-990527. Ed. Erik Bang. Circ: 2,800.

OXIDATION OF METALS. *see* CHEMISTRY—Physical Chemistry

669 NLD ISSN 2210-7142
P B NIEUWS. (Plant Bewerking) Text in Dutch. 2007. 5/yr. EUR 39.95 (effective 2010). adv. **Document type:** *Magazine, Trade.*
Formerly (until 2010): LaserNieuws (1875-1628)
Published by: Uitgeverij de Ruygt, Postbus 2108, Apeldoorn, 7302 EM, Netherlands. TEL 31-55-3601060, FAX 31-55-3600860, info@udr-media.nl, http://www.udr-media.nl. Ed. Eric Weustink. Adv. contact Peter de Ruygt. page EUR 1,995; 185 x 270. Circ: 5,000.

P M E MAGAZINE. *see* INSURANCE

PARTICULATE SCIENCE AND TECHNOLOGY; an international journal. *see* ENGINEERING—Chemical Engineering

669 USA
PERSPECTIVES: STEEL TUBE & PIPE. Text in English. 19??. w. USD 1,395 combined subscription (online & email eds.) (effective 2011). adv. back issues avail. **Document type:** *Newsletter, Trade.* **Description:** Examines market conditions specifically as they relate to the tube and pipe market.
Media: Online - full text. **Related titles:** E-mail ed.
Published by: American Metal Market LLC (Subsidiary of: Metal Bulletin Plc.), 230 Park Ave 5, 6th Fl, New York, NY 10003. TEL 212-213-6202, 800-947-9553, FAX 212-213-6617, subscriptions@amm.com. Adv. contact Mary Connors TEL 646-274-6250.

620.1 669 RUS ISSN 0031-918X
TN690 CODEN: PHMMA6
➤ **PHYSICS OF METALS AND METALLOGRAPHY.** Text in English. 1955. m. EUR 5,541, USD 6,761 combined subscription to institutions (print & online eds.) (effective 2012). adv. bk.rev. bibl.; charts; illus. back issues avail. **Document type:** *Journal, Academic/Scholarly.* **Description:** Contains investigations of the physical properties of metals and alloys, and studies of phenomena occurring during all phases of manufacture.
Related titles: Online - full text ed.: ISSN 1555-6190 (from IngentaConnect); ◆ Russian ed.: Fizika Metallov i Metallovedenie. ISSN 0015-3230; ◆ Translation of: Fizika Metallov i Metallovedenie. ISSN 0015-3230.
Indexed: A22, A26, CPEI, CurCont, E01, EngInd, I05, ISR, Inspec, MSCI, P52, PhysBer, SCI, SCOPUS, W07.
—BLDSC (0416.860000), East View, IE, Infotrieve, Ingenta, INIST, Linda Hall. **CCC.**
Published by: M A I K Nauka - Interperiodica (Subsidiary of: Pleiades Publishing, Inc.), Profsoyuznaya ul 90, Moscow, 117997, Russian Federation. TEL 7-095-3347420, FAX 7-095-3360666, compmg@maik.ru, http://www.maik.ru. Ed. Vladimir V Ustinov. R&P Vladimir I Vasil'ev. Circ: 900. **Dist. outside of the Americas by:** Springer, Haber Str 7, Heidelberg 69126, Germany. TEL 49-6221-3454303, FAX 49-6221-3454229; **Dist. by:** Springer New York LLC, Journal Fulfillment, PO Box 2485, Secaucus, NJ 07096. TEL 212-460-1500, FAX 201-348-4505.

671.732 USA ISSN 0360-3164
TS670 CODEN: PSFMDH
PLATING AND SURFACE FINISHING; electroplating, finishing of metals, organic finishing. Text in English. 1909. m. USD 115 in North America; USD 240 elsewhere; USD 8 per issue (effective 2005). adv. bk.rev. abstr.; bibl.; charts; illus.; pat.; tr.lit. index. reprints avail. **Document type:** *Magazine, Trade.*
Incorporates (1949-1975): A E S Research Report (0361-0411); Former titles (until 1975): Plating (0032-1397); (until 1948): American Electroplaters' Society. Monthly Review (0096-7483)
Related titles: Microform ed.: (from PQC).

Indexed: A05, A20, A22, A23, A24, A28, APA, AS&TA, AS&TI, ASCA, B04, B13, BrCerAb, C&ISA, C10, CA, CA/WCA, CIA, CIN, CTE, Cadscan, CerAb, ChemAb, ChemTitl, CivEngAb, CoppAb, CorrAb, E&CAJ, E11, EEA, EMA, EngInd, H15, ISR, Inspec, LeadAb, M&TEA, M09, MBF, METADEX, RefZh, SCOPUS, SolStAb, T02, T04, WAA, Zincscan.
—BLDSC (6538.050000), AskIEEE, CASDDS, IE, Infotrieve, Ingenta, INIST, Linda Hall. **CCC.**
Published by: American Electroplaters and Surface Finishers Society, Inc. (AESF), 1 Thomas Circle NW, 10th Fl, Washington, DC 20005. TEL 202-457-8401, FAX 202-530-0659, aesf@aesf.org. Ed., Adv. contact Donald Berry. Pub. Jon Bednerik. B&W page USD 2,100, color page USD 3,500. Circ: 7,000 (controlled).

338.476697 GBR ISSN 0268-7305
HD9539.P5
PLATINUM (YEAR). Text in English. 1985. a. free. **Document type:** *Report, Trade.* **Description:** Survey and analysis of the supply and demand for platinum and platinum group metals (palladium, rhodium, ruthenium, iridium) and developments in their markets.
Indexed: GeoRef, RefZh, SpeleolAb.
—BLDSC (6538.180000).
Published by: Johnson Matthey PLC, 40-42 Hatton Garden, London, EC1N 8EE, United Kingdom. TEL 44-20-7269-8000, FAX 44-20-7269-8389, jmpmr@matthey.com, http://www.matthey.com. Ed. A J Cowley. Circ: 16,000.

669.2 GBR ISSN 1471-0676
PLATINUM METALS REVIEW (ONLINE). Text in English. 1998 (Apr). q. free (effective 2011). back issues avail. **Document type:** *Journal, Academic/Scholarly.* **Description:** Aims to stimulate, encourage and support the research of scientists worldwide who are working with the platinum group metals.
Media: Online - full text (from IngentaConnect).
Indexed: CCI, CPEI, CurCont, EngInd, SCI, TM, W07.
—Linda Hall.
Published by: Johnson Matthey PLC, 40-42 Hatton Garden, London, EC1N 8EE, United Kingdom. TEL 44-20-72698400, FAX 44-20-72698433, http://www.matthey.com. Ed. David Jollie.

PLATT'S METALS WEEK. *see* MINES AND MINING INDUSTRY

669 POL ISSN 0324-802X
TN600 CODEN: ZNPHBN
POLITECHNIKA SLASKA. ZESZYTY NAUKOWE. HUTNICTWO. Text in Polish; Summaries in English, Russian. 1971. irreg. price varies.
Indexed: B22, ChemAb.
—BLDSC (9512.327300), CASDDS, Linda Hall.
Published by: Politechnika Slaska, ul Akademicka 5, Gliwice, 44100, Poland. wydawnictwo_mark@polsl.pl. Ed. Stanislaw Serkowski. Circ: 205. **Dist. by:** Ars Polona, Obroncow 25, Warsaw 03933, Poland.

POLYTECHNICAL UNIVERSITY OF BUCHAREST. SCIENTIFIC BULLETIN. SERIES B: CHEMISTRY AND MATERIALS SCIENCE. *see* CHEMISTRY

666 UKR ISSN 0032-4795
TN695 CODEN: PMANAI
➤ **POROSHKOVAYA METALLURGIYA**; vsesoyuznyi nauchno-tekhnicheskii zhurnal. Text in English, Russian, Ukrainian; Summaries in English, Ukrainian. 1961. bi-m. USD 185 foreign (effective 2004). bk.rev. illus. **Document type:** *Journal, Academic/Scholarly.* **Description:** Covers theory and technology of powders preparation; physics of sintering; mechanics of powders compaction; pressure treatment of porous bodics, materials based on powders of metals, high-melting point compounds and ceramics; fundamentals of theory and technology of coatings; heterogeneous equilibria in multicomponent systems; study of structure and properties of multiphase materials, strengthened and reinforced porous and fibrous materials; functional gradient and laminated powder materials.
Related titles: ◆ English Translation: Powder Metallurgy and Metal Ceramics. ISSN 1068-1302.
Indexed: C&ISA, CEABA, CIN, ChemAb, ChemTitl, CoppAb, CorrAb, Djerelo, E&CAJ, FR, INIS AtomInd, Inspec, RefZh, SCOPUS, SolStAb, WAA.
—BLDSC (0130.280000), AskIEEE, CASDDS, East View, INIST, Linda Hall. **CCC.**
Published by: Natsional'na Akademiya Nauk Ukrainy, Instytut Problem Materialoznavstva im. Frantsevicha/National Academy of Sciences of Ukraine, Frantsevich Institute for Problems of Materials Science, vul Krzhizhanivsky 3, Kyiv, 03680, Ukraine. TEL 380-44-4441524, FAX 380-44-4442131, science@materials.kiev.ua. Ed. V I Trefilov. Circ: 400. **Dist. by:** East View Information Services, 10601 Wayzata Blvd, Minneapolis, MN 55305. TEL 952-252-1201, 800-477-1005, FAX 952-252-1202, info@eastview.com, http://www.eastview.com.

669 668.4 666 GBR ISSN 1753-1497
POWDER INJECTION MOULDING INTERNATIONAL. Text in English. 2007. q. GBP 95 (effective 2009). adv. back issues avail. **Document type:** *Magazine, Trade.* **Description:** Covers the metal, ceramic and carbide injection molding industries.
Indexed: A28, APA, BrCerAb, C&ISA, CA/WCA, CIA, CerAb, CivEngAb, CorrAb, E&CAJ, E11, EEA, EMA, ESPM, EnvEAb, H15, M&TEA, M09, MBF, METADEX, SolStAb, T04, WAA.
—BLDSC (6571.927500), IE. **CCC.**
Published by: Inovar Communications Ltd., Dogpole House, Dogpole, Shrewsbury, SY1 1EN, United Kingdom. TEL 44-1743-241289, FAX 44-1743-369660, info@inovar-communications.com, http://www.inovar-events.com/. Ed. Nick Williams. Adv. contact Jon Craxford TEL 44-207-1939749.

671 GBR ISSN 0032-5899
TN695 CODEN: PWMTAU
➤ **POWDER METALLURGY.** Text in English. 1958. q. GBP 632 combined subscription to institutions (print & online eds.); USD 1,106 combined subscription in United States to institutions (print & online eds.) (effective 2012). adv. bk.rev. abstr. index. 96 p./no.; back issues avail.; reprint service avail. from PSC. **Document type:** *Journal, Academic/Scholarly.* **Description:** Provides international coverage of the science and practice of powder metallurgy and particulate engineering.
Related titles: Online - full text ed.: ISSN 1743-2901. GBP 599 to institutions; USD 1,048 in United States to institutions (effective 2012) (from IngentaConnect).
Indexed: A01, A03, A08, A10, A22, A28, ABTICS, APA, ASCA, BrCerAb, C&ISA, C33, CA, CA/WCA, CBNB, CIA, CIN, CPEI, Cadscan, CerAb, ChemAb, ChemTitl, CivEngAb, CoppAb, CorrAb, CurCont, E&CAJ, E11, EEA, EMA, ESPM, EngInd, EnvEAb, H15, ISR, Inspec, LeadAb, M&TEA, M09, MBF, METADEX, MSCI, P26, P48, P52, P54, PQC, RefZh, SCI, SCOPUS, SolStAb, T02, T04, TM, V03, W07, WAA, Zincscan.
—BLDSC (6571.950000), AskIEEE, CASDDS, IE, Infotrieve, Ingenta, INIST, Linda Hall. **CCC.**
Published by: (Institute of Materials, Minerals and Mining), Maney Publishing, Ste 1C, Joseph's Well, Hanover Walk, Leeds, W Yorks LS3 1AB, United Kingdom. TEL 44-113-2432800, FAX 44-113-3868178, maney@maney.co.uk. Ed. J J Dunkley. Adv. contact Robin Fox TEL 44-20-73060300 ext 231. **Subscr. in N America to:** Maney Publishing, 875 Massachusetts Ave, 7th Fl, Cambridge, MA 02139. TEL 866-297-5154, FAX 617-354-6875, maney@maneyusa.com.

671.37 USA ISSN 1068-1302
TN695 CODEN: PMMCEF
➤ **POWDER METALLURGY AND METAL CERAMICS.** Text in English. 1962. 5/yr. EUR 6,272, USD 6,791 combined subscription to institutions (print & online eds.) (effective 2012). adv. back issues avail.; reprint service avail. from PSC. **Document type:** *Journal, Academic/Scholarly.* **Description:** Covers topics of the theory, manufacturing technology, and properties of powder, technology of forming processes, technology of sintering, heat treatment, and thermochemical treatment etc.
Former titles (until 1993): Soviet Powder Metallurgy and Metal Ceramics (0038-5735); (until 1962): Soviet Powder Metallurgy
Related titles: Microfilm ed.: (from PQC); Online - full text ed.: ISSN 1573-9066 (from IngentaConnect); ◆ Translation of: Poroshkovaya Metallurgiya. ISSN 0032-4795.
Indexed: A01, A03, A08, A22, A26, A28, APA, ASCA, BibLing, BrCerAb, C&ISA, C33, CA, CA/WCA, CIA, CIN, CPEI, CerAb, ChemAb, ChemTitl, CivEngAb, CorrAb, CurCont, E&CAJ, E01, E11, EEA, EMA, ESPM, EnerRA, EngInd, EnvEAb, H15, Inspec, M&TEA, M09, MBF, METADEX, MSCI, P52, SCI, SCOPUS, SolStAb, T02, T04, W07, WAA.
—BLDSC (0416.906000), AskIEEE, CASDDS, East View, IE, Infotrieve, Ingenta, INIST, Linda Hall. **CCC.**
Published by: Springer New York LLC (Subsidiary of: Springer Science+Business Media), 233 Spring St, New York, NY 10013. TEL 212-460-1500, FAX 212-460-1575, service-ny@springer.com, http://www.springer.com. Ed. Valeriy Skorokhod.

669 SVK ISSN 1335-8987
POWDER METALLURGY PROGRESS; journal of science and technology of particle materials. Text in English. 2001. q.
Indexed: A28, APA, BrCerAb, C&ISA, CA/WCA, CIA, CerAb, CivEngAb, CorrAb, E&CAJ, E11, EEA, EMA, ESPM, EnvEAb, H15, M&TEA, M09, MBF, METADEX, RefZh, SolStAb, T04, WAA.
—BLDSC (6572.120000), IE, Ingenta, Linda Hall.
Published by: Slovenska Akademia Vied, Ustav Materialoveho Vyskumu/Slovak Academy of Sciences, Institute of Materials Research, Watsonova 47, Kosice, 043 53, Slovakia. TEL 421-55-6338115, FAX 421-55-6337108, imrsas@imrnov.saske.sk. Ed. Marcela Selecka.

PRACA, ZDROWIE, BEZPIECZENSTWO. *see* OCCUPATIONAL HEALTH AND SAFETY

621 USA ISSN 1092-3942
PRACTICAL WELDING TODAY. Abbreviated title: P W T. Text in English. 1997. bi-m. USD 45 domestic; USD 55 in Canada & Mexico; USD 75 elsewhere; free domestic to qualified personnel (effective 2009). adv. reprints avail. **Document type:** *Magazine, Trade.* **Description:** Covers new techniques, products, and managerial issues in the metal welding and joining industries.
Related titles: Online - full text ed.: free.
Indexed: A28, APA, BrCerAb, C&ISA, CA/WCA, CIA, CerAb, CivEngAb, CorrAb, E&CAJ, E11, EEA, EMA, ESPM, EnvEAb, H15, M&TEA, M09, MBF, METADEX, SolStAb, T04, WAA, Weldasearch.
—BLDSC (6596.750000), IE, Ingenta, Linda Hall.
Published by: (Fabricators & Manufacturers Association, International), F M A Communications, 833 Featherstone Rd, Rockford, IL 61107-6302. TEL 815-399-8700, FAX 815-381-1370, info@thefabricator.com. Ed. Dan Davis. Pub. Edward Youdell. adv.: B&W page USD 4,065, color page USD 5,515; trim 8.25 x 10.75. Circ: 35,000 (controlled).

620.112 RUS
PRAKTIKA PROTIVOKORROZIONNOI ZASHCHITY/PRACTICE OF ANTI-CORROSION PROTECTION. Text in Russian. 1996. q.
Published by: Kartek, Leninskii Pr-t 31, str 5, k 120, Moscow, 117292, Russian Federation. TEL 7-095-9554012, 7-095-9554038. Ed. A P Akol'zin.

669 DEU ISSN 0032-678X
TN690 CODEN: PMTLA5
➤ **PRAKTISCHE METALLOGRAPHIE.** Text in English, German. 1964. m. EUR 148 combined subscription to individuals (print & online eds.); EUR 258 combined subscription to institutions (print & online eds.); EUR 14.40 newsstand/cover (effective 2011). adv. bk.rev. abstr.; charts; illus.; mkt. index. **Document type:** *Journal, Academic/Scholarly.*
Related titles: Online - full text ed.
Indexed: A20, A22, A28, APA, BrCerAb, C&ISA, CA/WCA, CEABA, CIA, CIN, CPEI, CerAb, ChemAb, ChemTitl, CivEngAb, CorrAb, CurCont, E&CAJ, E11, EEA, EMA, ESPM, EngInd, EnvEAb, FR, H15, INIS AtomInd, ISMEC, Inspec, M&TEA, M09, MBF, METADEX, MSCI, SCI, SCOPUS, SolStAb, T04, TM, W07, WAA.
—BLDSC (6601.050000), AskIEEE, CASDDS, IE, Infotrieve, Ingenta, INIST, Linda Hall. **CCC.**
Published by: Carl Hanser Verlag GmbH & Co. KG, Kolbergerstr 22, Munich, 81679, Germany. TEL 49-89-998300, FAX 49-89-984809, info@hanser.de. Ed. F Muecklich. Adv. contact Hermann Kleiner. Circ: 1,350 (paid and controlled).

669.2 USA
PRECIOUS METALS (CD-ROM). Text in English. 1976. a. USD 47 (effective 2005).
Formerly (until 2000): Precious Metals (Print) (8756-0917)
Media: CD-ROM.
Indexed: A22.
—CCC.
Published by: International Precious Metals Institute, 4400 Bayou Blvd., Suite 18, Pensacola, FL 32503-1908. TEL 850-476-1156, FAX 850-476-1548, mail@ipmi.org, http://www.impi.org.

621.74 ROM ISSN 1224-452X
PRELUCRARI LA CALD. Text in Romanian. q.
Published by: Intec S.A., 105, Oltenitei Street, sector 4, Bucharest, 75651, Romania. TEL 40-1-3322045, FAX 40-1-3322004, secretariat@intec.ro, http://www.intec.ro.

669 ITA ISSN 1126-1498
PRESSOCOLATA E TECNOLOGIA/P & T - PRESSACOLATA E TECNOLOGIA. Text in English, Italian; Summaries in German, French, Spanish. 1997. q. adv. **Document type:** *Magazine, Trade.* **Description:** Represents the Italian outlook on the international diecasting world; covers issues ranging from production equipment to technologies and products.
Related titles: Online - full text ed.
Indexed: A28, APA, BrCerAb, C&ISA, CA/WCA, CIA, CerAb, CivEngAb, CorrAb, E&CAJ, E11, EEA, EMA, H15, M&TEA, M09, MBF, METADEX, SolStAb, T04, WAA.
Published by: Edimet SpA, Via Corfu 102, Brescia, BS 25124, Italy. TEL 39-030-2421043, FAX 39-030-223802, info@edimet.com, http://www.edimet.com/it. Circ: 5,000.

669 UKR ISSN 0131-1611
TN681 CODEN: PSELEA
PROBLEMY SPETSIAL'NOI ELEKTROMETALLURGII; respublikanskii mezhvedomstvennyi sbornik nauchnykh trudov. Text in Ukrainian. 1975. q. USD 85.
Related titles: ◆ English ed.: Advances in Electrometallurgy. ISSN 1810-0384.
Indexed: CIN, ChemAb, ChemTitl, Djerelo, SCOPUS.
—CASDDS, INIST. **CCC.**
Published by: Natsional'na Akademiya Nauk Ukrainy, Instytut Elektrozvaryuvannya im. EO Patona, Vul Bozhenka 11, Kiev, 252650, Ukraine. TEL 38-22-2683484, FAX 38-22-2275288. Ed. B E Paton. **Dist. by:** East View Information Services, 10601 Wayzata Blvd, Minneapolis, MN 55305. TEL 952-252-1201, 800-477-1005, FAX 952-252-1202, info@eastview.com, http://www.eastview.com.

669 NLD ISSN 1572-4409
➤ **PROCESS METALLURGY.** Text in Dutch. 1978. irreg., latest vol.12, 2002. price varies. **Document type:** *Monographic series, Academic/Scholarly.* **Description:** Discusses techniques of raw-materials extraction and their environmental impact.
Related titles: Online - full text ed.: ISSN 2212-0084.
Indexed: CIN, ChemAb, ChemTitl, IMMAb, SCOPUS, SpeleolAb.
—BLDSC (6849.988700). **CCC.**
Published by: Elsevier BV (Subsidiary of: Elsevier Science & Technology), Radarweg 29, PO Box 211, Amsterdam, 1000 AE, Netherlands. TEL 31-20-4853911, FAX 31-20-4852457, JournalsCustomerServiceEMEA@elsevier.com, http://www.elsevier.nl.

669 RUS ISSN 1684-257X
➤ **PROIZVODSTVO PROKATA.** Text in Russian. 1998. m. USD 1,500 foreign (effective 2005). **Document type:** *Journal, Academic/Scholarly.* **Description:** Presents information about the production and processing of various metals and non-metal materials used in modern equipment. Includes technical information essential for foremen and highly skilled workers.
Indexed: RefZh.
Published by: Nauka i Tekhnologii, Stromynskii per, 4/1, Moscow, 107076, Russian Federation. admin@nait.ru, http://www.nait.ru. **Dist. by:** East View Information Services, 10601 Wayzata Blvd, Minneapolis, MN 55305. TEL 952-252-1201, 800-477-1005, FAX 952-252-1202, info@eastview.com, http://www.eastview.com.

669 RUS ISSN 2070-2051
TA462 CODEN: PMPCBR
➤ **PROTECTION OF METALS AND PHYSICAL CHEMISTRY OF SURFACES.** Text in English. 1964. bi-m. EUR 5,395, USD 4,878 combined subscription to institutions (print & online eds.) (effective 2012). back issues avail. **Document type:** *Journal, Academic/Scholarly.* **Description:** Tackles theoretical and applied problems of corrosion and how to protect metallic materials, along with issues concerning natural, technological, and model media.
Formerly (until 2009): Protection of Metals (0033-1732)
Related titles: Microfilm ed.: (from PQC); Online - full text ed.: ISSN 2070-206X (from IngentaConnect); ◆ Translation of: Fizikokhimiya Poverkhnosti i Zashchita Materialov.
Indexed: A01, A03, A08, A22, A26, A28, APA, ASCA, BibLing, BrCerAb, C&ISA, C33, CA, CA/WCA, CIA, CPEI, CerAb, ChemAb, ChemTitl, CivEngAb, CorrAb, CurCont, E&CAJ, E01, E11, EEA, EMA, ESPM, EnerRA, EngInd, EnvEAb, H15, Inspec, M&TEA, M09, MBF, METADEX, MSCI, P52, SCI, SCOPUS, SolStAb, T02, T04, TM, W07, WAA.
—BLDSC (0420.521000), CASDDS, East View, IE, Infotrieve, Ingenta, INIST, Linda Hall. **CCC.**
Published by: (Rossiiskaya Akademiya Nauk/Russian Academy of Sciences), M A I K Nauka - Interperiodica (Subsidiary of: Pleiades Publishing, Inc.), Profsoyuznaya ul 90, Moscow, 117997, Russian Federation. TEL 7-095-3347420, FAX 7-095-3360666, compmg@maik.ru, http://www.maik.ru. Ed. Aslan Yu Tsivadze. **Dist. in the Americas by:** Springer New York LLC, Journal Fulfillment, PO Box 2485, Secaucus, NJ 07096. TEL 212-460-1500, FAX 201-348-4505; **Dist. outside the Americas by:** Springer, Haber Str 7, Heidelberg 69126, Germany. TEL 49-6221-3454303, FAX 49-6221-3454229.

669 UKR ISSN 0235-5884
TS228.99 CODEN: PRLIET
➤ **PROTSESSY LIT'YA.** Text in Russian; Summaries in Russian, English. 1992. adv. bk.rev. abstr.; bibl.; illus. index. back issues avail. **Document type:** *Academic/Scholarly.* **Description:** Presents articles on metallurgy, manufacture and treatment of metals, hydrodynamics of castings processes, crystallization, structure formation and hardening of alloys, automation, mechanization and computerization of casting processes.
Related titles: Diskette ed.: ◆ English Translation: Casting Processes. ISSN 0964-3281.
Indexed: C&ISA, CorrAb, E&CAJ, RefZh, SolStAb, TM, WAA.
—East View, Linda Hall.

Published by: Natsional'na Akademiya Nauk Ukrainy, Fizyko-Tekhnolohichnyi Instytut Metaliv ta Splaviv/National Academy of Sciences of the Ukraine, Physico-Technological Institute of Metals and Alloys, Pr Vernadskogo 34-1, Kiev, 252680, Ukraine. FAX 380-44-444-1250. **Subscr. to:** Pressa, Khreschatyk 22, Kiev 252001, Ukraine. TEL 380-44-229-7969, FAX 380-44-229-7969.

671.2 363.7 POL ISSN 0033-2275
TS200 CODEN: PRZOAB
PRZEGLAD ODLEWNICTWA. Text in Polish; Summaries in English, German, Russian. 1951. m. looseleaf. USD 35.50. adv. bk.rev. abstr.; charts; illus.; pat.; bibl.; stat.; mkt.; tr.lit. index. 60 p./no. 2 cols./p.; back issues avail. **Description:** Publishes articles about foundry practice, metallurgy, environmental protection and basic theory of someffoundry processes.
Indexed: A28, APA, B22, BCIRA, BrCerAb, C&ISA, CA/WCA, CIA, CISA, CerAb, ChemAb, ChemTitl, CivEngAb, CorrAb, E&CAJ, E11, EEA, EMA, H15, M&TEA, M09, MBF, METADEX, SolStAb, T04, TM, WAA.
—CASDDS, IE, INIST, Linda Hall.
Address: ul. Zakopianska 73, Krakow, 30418, Poland. TEL 48-12-2618241, FAX 48-12-2618247, podlewnictwa@pro.onet.pl. Ed. Jan Marcinkowski. adv.: B&W page PLZ 1,000, color page PLZ 1,400; 210 x 297. Circ: 1,000.

338.476 GBR ISSN 1757-6091
THE QUARTERLY GLOBAL CHROME AND STAINLESS REVIEW. Text in English. 2004. q. GBP 4,230, USD 8,460, EUR 6,225 to non-members; free to members (effective 2010). **Document type:** *Journal, Trade.* **Description:** Covers Stainless Steel, Ferro-Chrome, Nickel, Stainless Steel, Mills, China, Supply and Demand Forecasts, World Production Figures.
Formerly (until 2008): The Quarterly Global Chrome Review (1745-5413)
—CCC.
Published by: Metal Bulletin Plc. (Subsidiary of: Euromoney Institutional Investor Plc.), Nestor House, Playhouse Yard, London, EC4V 5EX, United Kingdom. TEL 44-20-77797390, FAX 44-20-77797389, help@metalbulletin.com, http://www.metalbulletin.com. Adv. contact Stefano di Nardo TEL 44-20-78275220.

672 JPN ISSN 0373-8868
TS300 CODEN: RDKSB9
R & D KOBE SEIKO GIHO/KOBE STEEL ENGINEERING REPORTS/ RESEARCH AND DEVELOPMENT. Text in English, Japanese. 1951. 3/yr.
Former titles (until 1968): Kobe Seiko Giho (0286-9969); (until 1963): Kobe Seiko (0286-9950)
Indexed: A22, A28, APA, BrCerAb, C&ISA, CA/WCA, CIA, CPEI, CerAb, CivEngAb, CorrAb, E&CAJ, E11, EEA, EMA, ESPM, Englnd, EnvEAb, H15, INIS AtomInd, ISMEC, M&TEA, M09, MBF, METADEX, SCOPUS, SolStAb, T04, TM, WAA.
—BLDSC (7714.480000), IE, Ingenta, INIST, Linda Hall.
Published by: Kobe Seikojo/Kobe Steel Ltd., Shinko Bldg., 10-26, Wakinohamacho 2-chome, Chuo-ku, Kobe, Hyogo 651-8585, Japan. TEL 81-78-2615111, FAX 71-78-2614123.

669 622 USA
R I C INSIGHT. Text in English. 1988. m. USD 300 (effective 2000). **Document type:** *Newsletter.* **Description:** Covers current developments and trends in the science and technology of rare earth materials, with emphasis on the application and commercialization of these materials.
Published by: Rare-earth Information Center, Institute for Physical Research and Technology, Iowa State University, 112 Wilhelm Hall, Ames, IA 50011-3020. TEL 515-294-2272, FAX 515-294-3709. Ed. R William McCallum. Circ: 250.

669 622 USA
R I C NEWS. Text in English. 1966. q. free. bk.rev. bibl.; illus. **Document type:** *Newsletter.* **Description:** Emphasizes research and business news in the areas of metallurgy and physics of rare earth metals, alloys, and compounds.
Related titles: Online - full text ed.
Indexed: AESIS.
Published by: Rare-earth Information Center, Institute for Physical Research and Technology, Iowa State University, 112 Wilhelm Hall, Ames, IA 50011-3020. TEL 515-294-2272, FAX 515-294-3709. Ed. R William McCallum. Circ: 3,500.

669 GBR ISSN 0143-4861
R L J: ROSKILL'S LETTER FROM JAPAN. Text in English. 1976. m. GBP 320, USD 640, EUR 560 (effective 2009). index. back issues avail. **Document type:** *Newsletter, Trade.* **Description:** Provides facts and figures on resources, consumption, production, imports and exports in several metals and minerals markets, forecasting future trends.
Published by: Roskill Information Services Ltd., 27a Leopold Rd, London, SW19 7BB, United Kingdom. TEL 44-20-89440066, FAX 44-20-89479568, info@roskill.co.uk, http://www.roskill.co.uk. Circ: 75.

R M Z - MATERIALS AND GEOENVIRONMENT/MATERIALS AND GEOENVIRONMENT; periodical for mining, metallurgy and geology. (Rudarsko Metalurski Zbornik) *see* MINES AND MINING INDUSTRY

669.1 NLD ISSN 1875-032X
R V S AKTUEEL. (Roest Vast Staal Aktueel) Text in Dutch. 2007. bi-m. adv.
Published by: K C I Publishing B.V., PO Box 396, Zutphen, 7200 AJ, Netherlands. TEL 31-5755-85270, FAX 31-5750-11099. Adv. contact Nicole Nagel.

669 USA ISSN 1045-9065
TA800 CODEN: PETCDR
RAPID EXCAVATION AND TUNNELING CONFERENCE PROCEEDINGS. Text in English. 1972. biennial. USD 179 per issue to non-members; USD 139 per issue to members; USD 111 per issue to students (effective 2010). back issues avail. **Document type:** *Proceedings, Trade.*
Formerly (until 1974): North American Rapid Excavation and Tunneling Conference Proceedings (0375-7269)
Related titles: CD-ROM ed.: ISSN 1558-772X.
Indexed: GeoRef, SCOPUS.
—BLDSC (6848.882000), Ingenta. **CCC.**
Published by: Society for Mining, Metallurgy and Exploration, 8307 Shaffer Pkwy, Littleton, CO 80127. TEL 303-948-4200, 800-763-3132, FAX 303-973-3845, cs@smenet.org. Eds. Bill Mariucci, Gary Almeraris. **Co-sponsor:** American Society of Civil Engineers.

669 GBR ISSN 1875-5372
RARE METAL MATERIALS AND ENGINEERING. Text in English. m. back issues avail. **Document type:** *Journal, Academic/Scholarly.* **Description:** Covers the development, production and testing of titanium, refractory metals, noble metals, rare metals, rare earth metals and superconducting materials. Also includes design and fabrication technology of ceramic materials, magnetic materials, nanophase materials, biological materials and advanced materials.
Media: Online - full text (from ScienceDirect). **Related titles:** ◆ Chinese ed.: Xiyou Jinshu Cailiao yu Gongcheng. ISSN 1002-185X.
Indexed: CA, T02.
—BLDSC (7291.826000). **CCC.**
Published by: (Xibei Youse Jinshu Yanjiuyuan/Northwest Institute of Nonferrous Metal Research CHN), Elsevier Ltd (Subsidiary of: Elsevier Science & Technology), The Blvd, Langford Ln, Kidlington, Oxford, OX5 1GB, United Kingdom. TEL 44-1865-843000, FAX 44-1865-843010, customerserviceau@elsevier.com, http://www.elsevier.com.

669 CHN ISSN 1001-0521
TA479.3 CODEN: RARME8
➤ **RARE METALS.** Text in English. 1982. bi-m. EUR 559, USD 840 combined subscription to institutions (print & online eds.) (effective 2012). adv. **Document type:** *Journal, Academic/Scholarly.* **Description:** Devoted to experimental and theoretical developments in metallurgy, characterization and applications of rare metals and alloys, with particular emphasis on advanced materials.
Related titles: Online - full text ed.: ISSN 1867-7185; Chinese ed.: Xiyou Jinshu. ISSN 0258-7076. CNY 60 domestic; USD 60 foreign (effective 2000).
Indexed: A22, A28, APA, BrCerAb, C&ISA, C33, CA/WCA, CIA, CIN, CPEI, CerAb, ChemAb, ChemTitl, CivEngAb, CorrAb, E&CAJ, E01, E11, EEA, EMA, ESPM, Englnd, EnvEAb, GeoRef, H15, IMMAb, M&TEA, M09, MBF, METADEX, MSCI, P52, SCI, SCOPUS, SolStAb, SpeleolAb, T04, TM, W07, WAA.
—BLDSC (7291.829850), CASDDS, IE, Ingenta, Linda Hall. **CCC.**
Published by: Zhongguo Youse Jinshu Xuehui/Chinese Society of Nonferrous Metal, 2 Xinjiekouwai Dajie, Beijing, 100088, China. TEL 86-1-6201-4488, FAX 86-1-6202-5838, TELEX 222204 GRINM CN, xyjsbjb@xinmail.com. Ed., R&P Tu Hailing. Circ: 300 (controlled). **Subscr. outside China to:** Maney Publishing, China Journal Distribution Services, Hudson Rd, Leeds LS9 7DI, United Kingdom. TEL 44-113-2497481, FAX 44-113-2486983, subscriptions@maney.co.uk. **Co-publisher:** Springer.

➤ **REACTIVE AND FUNCTIONAL POLYMERS.** *see* ENGINEERING—Chemical Engineering

669 USA
RECYCLING MAGNET. Text in English. q. **Document type:** *Journal, Trade.*
Published by: Steel Recycling Institute, 680 Andersen Drive, Pittsburgh, PA 15220-2700. TEL 800-876-7274, sri@recycle-steel.org, http://www.recycle-steel.org.

RECYCLING TODAY. *see* ENVIRONMENTAL STUDIES—Waste Management

RECYCLING TODAY EQUIPMENT & SERVICES BUYERS' GUIDE. *see* ENVIRONMENTAL STUDIES—Waste Management

REPERTORIO SIDERURGICO LATINOAMERICANO. *see* BUSINESS AND ECONOMICS—Trade And Industrial Directories

660.6 GBR ISSN 1358-2283
CODEN: REBIFD
RESOURCE AND ENVIRONMENTAL BIOTECHNOLOGY. Text in English. 1988. 4/yr. GBP 139, USD 269 (effective 2010). bk.rev. back issues avail. **Document type:** *Journal, Academic/Scholarly.* **Description:** Use of living organisms and their products in extraction recovery of minerals, oils and other materials.
Formerly (until 1995): Biorecovery (0269-7572)
Indexed: A10, A22, A29, AEBA, ASCA, ASFA, Agr, B&BAb, B20, B21, B25, BIOSIS Prev, BioDAb, BioEngAb, CA, CIN, ChemAb, ChemTitl, E04, E05, EIA, ESPM, EnvAb, GeoRef, I10, IMMAb, MycolAb, SCOPUS, SWRA, T02, V03, VirolAbstr.
—BLDSC (7777.601540), CASDDS, IE, Ingenta, INIST. **CCC.**
Published by: A B Academic Publishers, The Old Vicarage, Church St, Bicester, Oxon OX26 6AY, United Kingdom. TEL 44-1869-320949, jrnls@abapubl.demon.co.uk.

RESURSOZBERIHAYUCHI TEKHNOLOHII VYROBNYTSTVA TA OBROBKY TYSKOM MATERIALIV V MASHYNOBUDUVANNI/ RESOURCE SAVING TECHNOLOGIES FOR PRODUCTION AND PRESSURE SHAPING OF MATERIALS IN MACHINE-BUILDING. *see* MACHINERY

669 ESP ISSN 0034-8570
TN600 CODEN: RMTGAC
REVISTA DE METALURGIA. Text and summaries in English, Spanish. 1965. bi-m. EUR 87.51 domestic; EUR 134.71 foreign (effective 2009). adv. bk.rev. abstr. index. back issues avail. **Document type:** *Journal, Academic/Scholarly.*
Formed by the merger of (1961-1964): Metales No Ferreos (0539-4546); (1951-1964): Ciencia y Tecnica de la Soldadura (0529-7354); (1948-1964): Instituto del Hiero y del Acero (0367-8032)
Related titles: Microfilm ed.; Online - full text ed.: ISSN 1988-4222. free (effective 2011).
Indexed: A20, A22, A28, APA, ASCA, BrCerAb, C&ISA, CA/WCA, CEA, CEABA, CIA, CIN, CPEI, Cadscan, CerAb, ChemAb, ChemTitl, CivEngAb, CorrAb, CurCont, E&CAJ, E11, EEA, EMA, ESPM, Englnd, EnvEAb, GeoRef, H15, IECT, INIS AtomInd, LeadAb, M&TEA, M09, MBF, METADEX, MSCI, RefZh, SCI, SCOPUS, SolStAb, SpeleolAb, T04, TCEA, TM, W07, WAA, Zincscan.
—BLDSC (7865.800000), CASDDS, IE, Infotrieve, Ingenta, INIST, Linda Hall. **CCC.**
Published by: Consejo Superior de Investigaciones Cientificas (C S I C), Departamento de Publicaciones, Vitruvio 8, Madrid, 28006, Spain. publ@csic.es, http://www.publicaciones.csic.es.

669 620.1 VEN ISSN 0255-6952
REVISTA LATINOAMERICANA DE METALURGIA Y MATERIALES. Text in Spanish. q. **Document type:** *Journal, Academic/Scholarly.*
Related titles: Online - full text ed.: free (effective 2011).
Indexed: A01, A28, APA, BrCerAb, C&ISA, C01, CA/WCA, CIA, CerAb, CivEngAb, CorrAb, E&CAJ, E11, EEA, EMA, H15, M&TEA, M09, MBF, METADEX, SCOPUS, SolStAb, T04, WAA.
Published by: Universidad Simon Bolivar, Departamento de Ciencias de los Materiales, Apartado 89000, Caracas, 1080, Venezuela. TEL 58-212-9063387, FAX 58-212-9063388. Ed. Alejandro Mueller.

669 CUB
REVISTA TECNOLOGIA: MINERIA Y METALURGIA. Text in Spanish. s-a. USD 12.
Published by: (Cuba. Ministerio de la Industria Basica), Ediciones Cubanas, Obispo 527, Havana, Cuba. TEL 32-5556-60.

M

669 FRA ISSN 0035-1563
TN2 CODEN: CITMDA
➤ **REVUE DE METALLURGIE.** Cover title: Revue de Metallurgie. Cahiers d'Information Techniques. Text in English, French. 1904. 12/yr. GBP 458, EUR 550, USD 733 combined subscription to institutions (print & online eds.) (effective 2012). bk.rev. abstr.; bibl.; charts; pat. index. **Document type:** *Journal, Academic/Scholarly.*
Incorporates (1904-1992): Revue de Metallurgie. Memoires et Etudes Scientifiques (0245-8292); Which was formerly (until 1980): Revue de Metallurgie. Memoires Scientifiques (0025-9128); Incorporates: Centre de Documentation Siderurgique. Circulaire d'Informations Techniques (0008-963X)
Related titles: Microform ed.: (from PMC); Online - full text ed.: ISSN 1156-3141. GBP 308, EUR 370, USD 493 to institutions (effective 2012).
Indexed: A20, A22, A28, APA, ASCA, ApMecR, BrCerAb, C&ISA, C10, CA, CA/WCA, CIA, CPEI, Cadscan, CerAb, ChemAb, ChemTitl, CivEngAb, CorrAb, CurCont, E&CAJ, E11, EEA, EMA, ESPM, Englnd, EnvEAb, ErgAb, F&EA, FR, GeoRef, H15, INIS AtomInd, ISR, Inspec, LeadAb, M&TEA, M09, MBF, METADEX, MSCI, SCI, SCOPUS, SolStAb, SpeleolAb, T02, T04, TM, W07, WAA, Zincscan.
—AskIEEE, CASDDS, IE, Infotrieve, Ingenta, INIST, Linda Hall. **CCC.**
Published by: (Revue de Metallurgie), E D P Sciences, 17 Ave du Hoggar, Parc d'Activites de Courtaboeuf, BP 112, Cedex A, Les Ulis, F-91944, France. TEL 33-1-69187575, FAX 33-1-69860678, subscribers@edpsciences.org, http://www.edpsciences.org.

671.2 669 FRA
REVUE EUROPE METAL. Text in French. 10/yr.
Published by: Europe Metal, 136 Ave. Emile Zola, Boulogne Billancourt, 92100, France. TEL 33-1-46103131, FAX 33-1-46211063, http://www.eurometal.com.

051 USA ISSN 0192-9569
REYNOLDS REVIEW. Text in English. q. back issues avail. **Document type:** *Newsletter.*
Published by: Reynolds Metals Company, 6601 W Broad St, Richmond, VA 23230. TEL 804-281-2468. Ed. Anne F Waring. Circ: 30,750.

669 AUT
RHI BULLETIN; the journal of refractory innovations. Text in English. 2/yr. free. **Document type:** *Bulletin, Trade.*
Published by: R H I AG, Wienerbergstr 11, Vienna, 1100, Austria. TEL 43-502-136345, FAX 43-502-136745, volkmar.weilguni@rhi-ag.com, http://www.rhi-ag.com.

RINGSIDER. *see* BUSINESS AND ECONOMICS

620.11 DNK ISSN 0907-0079
RISOE INTERNATIONAL SYMPOSIUM ON MATERIALS SCIENCE. PROCEEDINGS. Text in Danish. 1980. a. price varies. **Document type:** *Proceedings, Academic/Scholarly.*
Formerly (until 1991): Risoe International Symposium on Metallurgy and Materials Science. Proceedings (0108-8599)
—BLDSC (6848.966900). **CCC.**
Published by: Risoe D T U, Nationallaboratoriet for Baeredygtigt Energi/Risoe D T U, National Laboratory for Sustainable Energy (Subsidiary of: Danmarks Tekniske Universitet/Technical University of Denmark), Frederiksborgvej 399, Roskilde, 4000, Denmark. TEL 45-46-774677, FAX 45-46-775586, risoe@risoe.dk.

669.142 NLD ISSN 0169-3328
ROESTVAST STAAL. Text in Dutch. 1985. 10/yr. EUR 120 domestic; EUR 140 foreign (effective 2010). adv. **Document type:** *Magazine, Trade.*
Related titles: ◆ Supplement(s): Roestvast Staalgids. ISSN 1568-7910.
—BLDSC (8019.168000), IE.
Published by: Uitgeverij TCM B.V., Postbus 101, Leiden, 2300 AC, Netherlands. TEL 31-71-5144044, FAX 31-71-5131093, info@uitgeverijtcm.nl, http://www.uitgeverijtcm.nl. adv.: B&W page EUR 1,529, color page EUR 2,204; trim 210 x 297. Circ: 4,000.

669.142 NLD ISSN 1568-7910
ROESTVAST STAALGIDS. Text in Dutch. 1984. a. adv.
Related titles: ◆ Supplement to: Roestvast Staal. ISSN 0169-3328.
Published by: Uitgeverij TCM B.V., Postbus 101, Leiden, 2300 AC, Netherlands. TEL 31-71-5144044, FAX 31-71-5131093, info@uitgeverijtcm.nl, http://www.uitgeverijtcm.nl. adv.: color page EUR 2,140. Circ: 75,000.

669 GBR ISSN 0965-7711
ROSKILL'S LITHIUM DIGEST. Text in English. 1991. q. GBP 240, USD 480, EUR 420 (effective 2009). **Document type:** *Newsletter, Trade.* **Description:** Covers recent issues and developments concerning lithium.
Indexed: A28, APA, BrCerAb, C&ISA, CA/WCA, CIA, CerAb, CivEngAb, CorrAb, E&CAJ, E11, EEA, EMA, ESPM, EnvEAb, H15, M&TEA, M09, MBF, METADEX, SolStAb, T04, WAA.
—Linda Hall.
Published by: Roskill Information Services Ltd., 27a Leopold Rd, London, SW19 7BB, United Kingdom. TEL 44-20-89440066, FAX 44-20-89479568, info@roskill.co.uk, http://www.roskill.co.uk.

669 622 SRB ISSN 0350-2627
➤ **RUDARSTVO - GEOLOGIJA - METALURGIJA.** Text in Serbian; Summaries in English. 1950. bi-m. **Document type:** *Journal, Academic/Scholarly.*
Related titles: ◆ Supplement to: Masinstvo. ISSN 0461-2531.
Published by: Savez Inzenjera i Tehnicara Srbije, Kneza Milosa 7, Belgrade, 11000. TEL 381-11-3237363, sits@beotel.yu, http://www.sits.org.yu. Ed. Dejan Milovanovic. Circ: 1,000.

669 671.2 POL ISSN 0035-9696
CODEN: RMNZA5
RUDY I METALE NIEZELAZNE. Text in Polish; Summaries in English, French, German, Russian. 1956. m. PLZ 277.20 domestic; EUR 167 foreign (effective 2011). adv. bk.rev. abstr.; charts; illus.; mkt. index. 52 p./no.; **Document type:** *Journal, Trade.* **Description:** Explores mining, ore geology and dressing, metallurgy of nonferrous metals, and roll mills.

Related titles: Online - full text ed.
Indexed: A28, APA, B22, BrCerAb, C&ISA, CA/WCA, CIA, CerAb, ChemAb, ChemTitl, CivEngAb, CoppAb, CorrAb, E&CAJ, E11, EEA, EMA, ESPM, EnvEAb, GeoRef, H15, IMMAb, M&TEA, M09, MBF, METADEX, SolStAb, SpeleolAb, T04, WAA.
—CASDDS, INIST, Linda Hall.
Published by: (Stowarzyszenie Naukowo-Techniczne Inzynierow i Technikow Metali Niezelaznych, Stowarzyszenie Inzynierow i Technikow Przemyslu Hutniczego w Polsce), Wydawnictwo SIGMA - N O T Sp. z o.o., ul Ratuszowa 11, PO Box 1004, Warsaw, 00950, Poland. TEL 48-22-8180918, FAX 48-22-6192187, sekretariat@sigma-not.pl. Ed. Zbigniew Misiolek TEL 48-32-2551017 ext 278. adv.: B&W page PLZ 1,550, color page PLZ 3,410. Circ: 500. **Dist. by:** Ars Polona, Obroncow 25, Warsaw 03933, Poland. TEL 48-22-5098609, FAX 48-22-5098610, arspolona@arspolona.com.pl, http://www.arspolona.com.pl.

669 USA ISSN 1067-8212
TN758
➤ **RUSSIAN JOURNAL OF NON-FERROUS METALS.** Text in English. 1960. m. EUR 1,446, USD 1,753 combined subscription to institutions (print & online eds.) (effective 2012). charts; illus.; abstr. index. back issues avail. **Document type:** *Journal, Academic/Scholarly.* **Description:** Covers theoretical and applied aspects of production and treatment of non-ferrous metals.
Formerly (until 1992): The Soviet Journal of Non-Ferrous Metals (0038-5484)
Related titles: Online - full text ed.: ISSN 1934-970X; ◆ Translation of: Izvestiya Vysshikh Uchebnykh Zavedenii. Tsvetnaya Metallurgiya. ISSN 0021-3438.
Indexed: A22, A26, ChemAb, E01, E08, GeoRef, MSCI, P52, S09, SCI, W07.
—East View, IE, Infotrieve, Ingenta, INIST, Linda Hall. **CCC.**
Published by: (Moskovskii Institut Stali i Splavov/Moscow Institute of Steel and Alloys RUS), Allerton Press, Inc. (Subsidiary of: Pleiades Publishing, Inc.), 18 W 27th St, New York, NY 10001. TEL 646-424-9686, FAX 646-424-9695, journals@allertonpress.com. Ed. Evgeny A. Levashov.

669 RUS ISSN 0036-0295
TN4 CODEN: RMLYAQ
➤ **RUSSIAN METALLURGY.** Text in English. 1960. bi-m. EUR 3,119, USD 3,804 combined subscription to institutions (print & online eds.) (effective 2012). charts; illus. index. **Document type:** *Journal, Academic/Scholarly.* **Description:** Covers physical chemistry of metal production, metal physics, production processes, ferrous and non-ferrous metals, and alloys.
Former titles (until 1965): Russian Metallurgy and Mining (0485-7372); (until 1963): Russian Metallurgy and Fuels (0485-7364)
Related titles: Online - full text ed.: ISSN 1531-8648 (from IngentaConnect); ◆ Translation of: Metally. ISSN 0869-5733.
Indexed: A22, A26, ASCA, CCMJ, CPEI, Cadscan, E01, I05, Inspec, LeadAb, P52, SCOPUS, Zincscan.
—BLDSC (0420.769000), AskIEEE, East View, IE, Ingenta, INIST, Linda Hall. **CCC.**
Published by: (Rossiiskaya Akademiya Nauk/Russian Academy of Sciences), M A I K Nauka - Interperiodica (Subsidiary of: Pleiades Publishing, Inc.), Profsoyuznaya ul 90, Moscow, 117997, Russian Federation. TEL 7-095-3347420, FAX 7-095-3360666, compmg@maik.ru, http://www.maik.ru. Ed. Oleg A Bannykh. **Dist. in the Americas by:** Springer New York LLC, Journal Fulfillment, PO Box 2485, Secaucus, NJ 07096. TEL 212-460-1500, FAX 201-348-4505; **Dist. outside of the Americas by:** Springer, Haber Str 7, Heidelberg 69126, Germany. TEL 49-6221-3454303, FAX 49-6221-3454229.

669.1 MYS ISSN 0116-9645
S E A I S I NEWSLETTER. Text in English. 1981. m. back issues avail. **Document type:** *Newsletter, Trade.*
Published by: South East Asia Iron & Steel Institute, 2E, 5th Floor, Block 2, Worldwide Business Park, Jalan Tinju 13/50, 40675 Shah Alam, Selangor Darul Ehsan, Malaysia. TEL 603-55191102, FAX 603-55191159, seaisi@seaisi.org, http://www.seaisi.org.

669.1 MYS ISSN 0129-5721
TS300 CODEN: SEQUDV
➤ **S E A I S I QUARTERLY JOURNAL.** Text in English. 1972. q. USD 85 (effective 2000). adv. back issues avail. **Document type:** *Journal, Academic/Scholarly.*
Indexed: A22, A28, AESIS, APA, BCIRA, BrCerAb, C&ISA, CA/WCA, CIA, CIN, CPEI, CerAb, ChemAb, ChemTitl, CivEngAb, CorrAb, E&CAJ, E11, EEA, EMA, ESPM, EngInd, EnvEAb, GeoRef, H15, M&TEA, M09, MBF, METADEX, SCOPUS, SolStAb, T04, TM, WAA.
—BLDSC (8213.725000), CASDDS, IE, Ingenta, Linda Hall.
Published by: South East Asia Iron and Steel Institute, P.O. Box 7094, Snah Alam, Selangor 40702, Malaysia. TEL 60-3-559-1102, FAX 60-3-559-1159. Ed. Takashi Kitamura. R&P, Adv. contact Wah Sum Wong. Circ: 2,000.

669 CHE
S M U V ZEITUNG; Wochenzeitung der Gewerkschaft Industrie, Gewerbe, Dienstleistungen. (Schweizerischer Metall- und Uhrenarbeitnehmer Verband) Text in German. 1973 (vol.72). w. CHF 51 (effective 1999). adv. bk.rev. charts; illus. **Document type:** *Newspaper.*
Published by: Gewerkschaft Industrie Gewerbe Dienstleistungen SMUV/Syndicat de l'Industrie, de la Construction et des Services FTMH, Weltpoststr 20, Postfach 272, Bern 15, 3000, Switzerland. TEL 41-31-3502345, FAX 41-31-3502211. Adv. contact Doris Jossen. B&W page CHF 5,491, color page CHF 7,966; trim 429 x 284. Circ: 51,058.

S N A G NEWSLETTER. *see* ARTS AND HANDICRAFTS

SAFETY! MAGAZINE. *see* ENGINEERING—Chemical Engineering

SCHLEIFEN UND POLIEREN. *see* ENGINEERING—Industrial Engineering

669 DEU ISSN 0933-8330
SCHMIEDE JOURNAL. Text in German. 1988. s-a. EUR 10 (effective 2005). adv. bk.rev. **Document type:** *Magazine, Trade.*
Published by: Industrieverband Massivumformung e.V., Goldene Pforte 1, Hagen, 58093, Germany. TEL 49-2331-95880, FAX 49-2331-51046, cpair@imu.wsm-net.de. Ed. Klaus-Ulrich Schwermer. Adv. contact Uwe Riemeyer TEL 49-202-271690. B&W page EUR 1,950; trim 186 x 270. Circ: 4,375 (paid and controlled).

669 DEU ISSN 1610-0727
SCHRIFTENREIHE DES I M E. Text in German. 2002. irreg., latest vol.24, 2011. price varies. **Document type:** *Monographic series, Academic/Scholarly.*
Published by: (Rheinisch-Westfaelische Technische Hochschule Aachen, IME Metallurgische Prozesstechnik und Metallrecycling), Shaker Verlag GmbH, Kaiserstr 100, Herzogenrath, 52134, Germany. TEL 49-2407-95960, FAX 49-2407-95969, info@shaker.de.

669 666 SRB ISSN 0350-820X
TN695 CODEN: SCSNB4
➤ **SCIENCE OF SINTERING.** Text in English; Summaries in Russian, Serbian. 1969. 3/yr. adv. bk.rev. back issues avail. **Document type:** *Journal, Academic/Scholarly.* **Description:** Provides a suitable medium for the publication of papers on theoretical and experimental studies.
Formerly: Physics of Sintering (0031-9198)
Related titles: Online - full text ed.: free (effective 2011).
Indexed: A22, A28, APA, BrCerAb, C&ISA, CA, CA/WCA, CIA, CerAb, ChemAb, ChemTitl, CivEngAb, CorrAb, E&CAJ, E11, EEA, EMA, ESPM, EnvEAb, H15, INIS AtomInd, Inspec, M&TEA, M09, MBF, METADEX, MSCI, RefZh, SCI, SCOPUS, SolStAb, T02, T04, W07, WAA.
—BLDSC (8164.278000), AskIEEE, CASDDS, IE, Ingenta, INIST, Linda Hall.
Published by: International Institute for the Science of Sintering, c/o ITN SANU, Knez-Mihailova 35/IV, PO Box 315, Belgrade, 11000. TEL 381-11-637367, FAX 381-11-637239, scisint@sanu.ac.yu, http://www.iiss.sanu.ac.yu.

669 USA
SCRAP PRICE BULLETIN. Variant title: Iron Age Scrap Price Bulletin. Text in English. 19??. w. USD 1,095 combined subscription (print, online & email eds.) (effective 2011). adv. **Document type:** *Bulletin, Trade.* **Description:** Features an essential, independent source for weekly ferrous scrap pricing.
Formerly: Iron Age
Related titles: E-mail ed.; Online - full text ed.: USD 1,095 combined subscription (online & email eds.) (effective 2011).
Published by: American Metal Market LLC (Subsidiary of: Metal Bulletin Plc.), 230 Park Ave S, 6th Fl, New York, NY 10003. TEL 212-213-6202, 800-947-9553, FAX 212-213-6617, subscriptions@amm.com, http://www.amm.com. Ed. John Ambrosia TEL 708-784-1043. Adv. contact Mary Connors TEL 646-274-6250.

669 USA
SCRAP TRENDS OUTLOOK. Text in English. 19??. m. USD 995 (effective 2011). adv. **Document type:** *Trade.*
Media: Online - full text.
Published by: American Metal Market LLC (Subsidiary of: Metal Bulletin Plc.), 230 Park Ave S, 6th Fl, New York, NY 10003. TEL 212-213-6202, 800-947-9553, FAX 212-213-6617; subscriptions@amm.com. Adv. contact Mary Connors TEL 646-274-6250.

669 GBR ISSN 1359-6462
TN1 CODEN: SCMAF7
➤ **SCRIPTA MATERIALIA.** Text in English. 1967. 24/yr. EUR 1,784 in Europe to institutions; JPY 236,700 in Japan to institutions; USD 1,993 elsewhere to institutions (effective 2012). bk.rev. bibl.; charts; illus.; stat.; abstr. back issues avail.; reprints avail. **Document type:** *Journal, Academic/Scholarly.* **Description:** Features papers advancing the understanding of the physical properties of materials, including metals, alloys, ceramics, polymers, and glasses.
Incorporates (1992-1999): Nanostructured Materials (0965-9773); Former titles (until 1996): Scripta Metallurgica et Materialia (0956-716X); (until 1990): Scripta Metallurgica (0036-9748)
Related titles: Microfilm ed.: (from PQC); Online - full text ed.: ISSN 1872-8456 (from IngentaConnect, ScienceDirect).
Indexed: A01, A03, A08, A22, A26, A28, APA, ASCA, BrCerAb, C&ISA, C24, C33, CA, CA/WCA, CIA, CIN, CPEI, Cadscan, CerAb, ChemAb, ChemTitl, CivEngAb, CorrAb, CurCont, E&CAJ, E11, EEA, EMA, ESPM, EngInd, EnvEAb, FR, GeoRef, H15, I05, ISMEC, ISR, Inspec, LeadAb, M&TEA, M09, MBF, METADEX, MSCI, P30, PhysBer, RefZh, S01, SCI, SCOPUS, SolStAb, T02, T04, TM, W07, WAA, Zincscan.
—BLDSC (8212.970000), AskIEEE, CASDDS, IE, Infotrieve, Ingenta, INIST, Linda Hall. **CCC.**
Published by: (Acta Metallurgica, Inc. USA), Pergamon (Subsidiary of: Elsevier Science & Technology), The Blvd, Langford Ln, East Park, Kidlington, Oxford OX5 1GB, United Kingdom. TEL 44-1865-843000, FAX 44-1865-843010, JournalsCustomerServiceEMEA@elsevier.com. Eds. Ke Lu, Kevin Hemker TEL 410-516-4489, Subhash Risbud TEL 530-752-0474. Circ: 1,600. **Subscr. to:** Elsevier BV, Radarweg 29, PO Box 211, Amsterdam 1000 AE, Netherlands. TEL 31-20-4853757, FAX 31-20-4853432, http://www.elsevier.nl.

338.476 GBR ISSN 2042-7565
SEAMLESS STEEL TUBE AND PIPE MARKET TRACKER. Text in English. 2005. m. GBP 1,545, USD 3,085, EUR 2,266 (effective 2010). **Document type:** *Journal, Trade.* **Description:** Provides up-to-date prices, market trends and developments in key markets and products across the seamless steel tube and pipe industry.
Formerly (until 2009): Seamless Steel Tube and Pipe Monthly (1749-3757)
—CCC.
Published by: Metal Bulletin Plc. (Subsidiary of: Euromoney Institutional Investor Plc.), Nestor House, Playhouse Yard, London, EC4V 5EX, United Kingdom. TEL 44-20-77797390, FAX 44-20-77797389, help@metalbulletin.com, http://www.metalbulletin.com.

SEARCHER. *see* LABOR UNIONS

669.9 CHN ISSN 1007-2365
SELECTED PAPERS OF ENGINEERING CHEMISTRY AND METALLURGY. Text in Chinese. irreg.
Indexed: A28, APA, BrCerAb, C&ISA, CA/WCA, CIA, CerAb, CivEngAb, CorrAb, E&CAJ, E11, EEA, EMA, H15, M&TEA, M09, MBF, METADEX, SolStAb, T04, WAA.
Published by: (Chinese Academy of Sciences, Institute of Process Engineering), Kexue Chubanshe/Science Press, 16 Donghuang Cheng Genbei Jie, Beijing, 100717, China.

661.0724 BEL ISSN 1024-4204
SELENIUM - TELLURIUM DEVELOPMENT ASSOCIATION. BULLETIN. Text in English. irreg. (3-4/yr.). bibl.; illus. **Document type:** *Bulletin.* **Description:** Promotes knowledge about applications of selenium and tellurium in metallurgy, pharmaceuticals, feed additives, pigments, chemicals and electronics.
Indexed: AESIS.
Published by: Selenium - Tellurium Development Association, Borgtstraat 301, Grimbergen, 1850, Belgium. TEL 32-2-252-1490, FAX 32-2-252-2775, info@stda.be, http://www.stda.be. Ed. Yves Palmieri. Circ: 2,000.

661.0724 BEL
SELENIUM - TELLURIUM DEVELOPMENT ASSOCIATION. SYMPOSIUM PROCEEDINGS. Text in English. 199?. a. USD 135 (effective 2000). **Document type:** *Proceedings.* **Description:** Publishes papers presented at the STDA symposium, all dealing with current vital applications of selenium and tellurium. Reports on state-of-the-art technologies.
Published by: Selenium - Tellurium Development Association, Borgtstraat 301, Grimbergen, 1850, Belgium. TEL 32-2-252-1490, FAX 32-2-252-2775, info@stda.be, http://www.stda.be.

669 CHN ISSN 1004-4620
SHANDONG YEJIN/SHANDONG METALLURGY. Text in Chinese. 1979. bi-m. CNY 7 per issue (effective 2008). **Document type:** *Journal, Academic/Scholarly.*
Related titles: Online - full text ed.
—BLDSC (8254.588598).
Published by: Shandong Jinshu Xuehui/Shandong Society of Metals, 66, East of Jiefang Rd, Jinan, 250014, China. TEL 86-531-88593054, FAX 86-531-88593055.

669 CHN
SHANGHAI IRON AND STEEL RESEARCH INSTITUTE. Text in Chinese. irreg.
Address: 1001 Taihe Rd, Shanghai, 200940, China.

669 CHN ISSN 1001-2125
SHANGHAI JINSHU (YOUSE FENCE). Text in Chinese. 1979. bi-m. **Document type:** *Academic/Scholarly.* **Description:** Publishes original papers on the properties of nonferrous metals and alloys, as well as material producing and measuring techniques.
Formerly (until 1981): Shanghai Yejin
Indexed: ChemAb, ChemTitl.
Published by: Shanghai Youse Jinshu Xiehui/Shanghai Nonferrous Metal Society, PO Box 600 402, Shanghai, 201600, China. TEL 86-21-7822880, FAX 86-21-325739. Ed. Guan Dagao. adv.: B&W page USD 350, color page USD 600. **Dist. overseas by:** China International Book Trading Corp, 35 Chegongzhuang Xilu, Haidian District, PO Box 399, Beijing 100044, China.

669 JPN
SHEET METAL AND FABRICATOR/SHITO METARU; comprehensive news. Text in Japanese. 1991. m. JPY 11,550 (effective 2002). adv. **Document type:** *Bulletin.*
Former titles: Sheet Metal (0918-0699); (until 1992): Machinist - Mashinisuto (0911-7903); (until 1958): World Progress of Production Engineering - Kaigai Kikai Shiryo (0911-789X)
Published by: Machinist Publishing Co. Ltd./Mashinisuto Shuppan K.K., 2-7-3-tyome, Tamagawa Den'encyofu, Setagawa-ku, Tokyo, 158-0085, Japan. TEL 81-3-5483-8251, FAX 81-3-5483-8033, info@machinist.co.jp, http://www.machinist.co.jp/. Ed., R&P Norio Ishikawa. Adv. contact Hiroshi Tozuka. B&W page USD 1,100, color page USD 2,900; trim 100 x 728. Circ: 24,000.

SHIGEN SOZAI/MINING AND MATERIALS PROCESSING INSTITUTE OF JAPAN. JOURNAL. *see* MINES AND MINING INDUSTRY

669.1 CHN ISSN 1672-9587
SHIJIE GANGTIE/WORLD IRON & STEEL. Text in Chinese. 1979. bi-m. **Document type:** *Magazine, Trade.*
Formerly (until 1992): Baogang Qingbao
Address: 655, Fujing Lu, Shanghai, 201900, China. TEL 86-21-26643643, FAX 86-21-26643977.

669 JPN
SHITO METARU SUKURU/SHEET METAL SCHOOL. Text in Japanese. bi-m. JPY 1,500 per issue. **Document type:** *Academic/Scholarly.*
Published by: Amada, 200 Ishida, Isehara-shi, Kanagawa-ken 259-1116, Japan.

671 USA ISSN 1069-2010
SHOT PEENER NEWSLETTER. Text in English. q. **Document type:** *Newsletter.*
Indexed: A28, APA, BrCerAb, C&ISA, CA/WCA, CIA, CerAb, CivEngAb, CorrAb, E&CAJ, E11, EEA, EMA, ESPM, EnvEAb, H15, M&TEA, M09, MBF, METADEX, SolStAb, T04, WAA.
—Linda Hall.
Published by: Electronics, Inc., 56790 Magnetic Dr, Mishawaka, IN 46545. TEL 574-256-5001, 800-832-5653, FAX 874-256-5222, shotpeener@shotpeener.com, http://www.electronics-inc.com.

669.142 BRA
SIDERURGIA BRASILEIRA. RELATORIO DE DIRETORIA. Text in English. 1973. a. free. stat.
Published by: Siderurgia Brasileira S.A., Setor de Autarquias sul, Quadra 2, Bloco E, Brasilia, DF 70070, Brazil. FAX 061-226-5844, TELEX 061-1542. Circ: 5,000.

SILVER INSTITUTE LETTER; information on silver for industry. *see* MINES AND MINING INDUSTRY

SOCIETY FOR MINING, METALLURGY, AND EXPLORATION. TRANSACTIONS. *see* MINES AND MINING INDUSTRY

669 CHE ISSN 1012-0394
CODEN: DDBPE8
➤ **SOLID STATE PHENOMENA.** Key Title: Diffusion and Defect Data. Part B: Solid State Phenomena. Abbreviated title: S S P. Text in English. 1967. 6/yr. USD 576 (effective 2002). **Document type:** *Journal, Academic/Scholarly.*
Supersedes in part (in 1988): Diffusion and Defect Data (0377-6883); Which was formerly (until 1974): Diffusion Data (0012-267X)
Related titles: Online - full text ed.: USD 440 (effective 2002).
Indexed: A22, C33, ChemAb, EngInd, Inspec, RefZh, SCOPUS.
—BLDSC (3584.255000), AskIEEE, CASDDS, IE, Infotrieve, Ingenta, INIST, Linda Hall.
Published by: Scitec Publications Ltd., Brandrain 6, Uetikon-Zurich, CH-8707, Switzerland. TEL 41-1-9221022, FAX 41-1-9221033, scitec@scitec.ch, http://www.scitech.ch.

669 USA
SOURCES (RICHMOND HEIGHTS). Text in English. 1962. a. USD 35. adv. **Document type:** *Directory, Trade.*
Former titles: Sources for Stamping; (until 1979): Metal Stamping Buyer's Guide
Published by: Precision Metalforming Association, 27027 Chardon Rd, Richmond, OH 44143. metalforming@pma.org. Circ: 12,000.

669 GBR ISSN 2040-6835
▼ **SOUTH AFRICA METALS REPORT.** Text in English. 2010. q. USD 975, EUR 695 combined subscription (print & email eds.) (effective 2011). **Document type:** *Report, Trade.* **Description:** Provides industry professionals and strategists, sector analysts, business investors, trade associations and regulatory bodies with independent forecasts and competitive intelligence on the metals and construction industry in South Africa.
Related titles: E-mail ed.
Published by: Business Monitor International Ltd., Senator House, 85 Queen Victoria St, London, EC4V 4AB, United Kingdom. TEL 44-20-72480468, FAX 44-20-72480467, subs@businessmonitor.com.

669 622 ZAF ISSN 0038-223X
TN1 CODEN: JSAMAP
➤ **SOUTH AFRICAN INSTITUTE OF MINING AND METALLURGY. JOURNAL.** Text in English. 1894. bi-m. (plus 1 special issue). USD 140 (effective 2000). adv. bk.rev. bibl.; charts; illus. index, cum.index: vols. 35-54 (July 1935-June 1954). reprints avail. **Document type:** *Journal, Academic/Scholarly.*
Related titles: Microform ed.: (from PMC, PQC).
Indexed: A22, A28, AESIS, APA, ASCA, ApMecR, BrCerAb, C&ISA, CA/WCA, CEA, CEABA, CIA, CIN, CISA, CPEI, Cadscan, CerAb, ChemAb, ChemTitl, CivEngAb, CorrAb, CurCont, E&CAJ, E11, EEA, EIA, EMA, ESPM, EngInd, EnvEAb, ErgAb, GeoRef, H15, HRIS, IMMAb, INIS AtomInd, ISAP, LeadAb, M&TEA, M09, MBF, METADEX, MSCI, RefZh, SCI, SCOPUS, SolStAb, SpeleolAb, T04, TCEA, TM, W07, WAA, Zincscan.
—BLDSC (4901.500000), CASDDS, IE, Ingenta, INIST, Linda Hall. **CCC.**
Published by: South African Institute of Mining and Metallurgy, PO Box 61127, Marshalltown, Johannesburg 2107, South Africa. TEL 27-11-834-1273, FAX 27-11-838-5923, journal@saimm.co.za. Ed. R E Robinson. R&P P Bester. Adv. contact H Isseron. Circ: 3,800.

669 622 ZAF
SOUTH AFRICAN INSTITUTE OF MINING AND METALLURGY. MONOGRAPH SERIES. Text in English. 1978. irreg. price varies. **Document type:** *Monographic series.*
Indexed: IMMAb, SpeleolAb.
Published by: South African Institute of Mining and Metallurgy, PO Box 61127, Marshalltown, Johannesburg 2107, South Africa. TEL 27-11-834-1273, FAX 27-11-838-5923.

671.732 UKR ISSN 0233-7681
TN681
SOVREMENNAYA ELEKTROMETALLURGIYA. Text in Russian; Summaries in English. 1985. q. USD 52 foreign (effective 2005). **Document type:** *Journal, Academic/Scholarly.* **Description:** Presents the results of theoretical and experimental research carried out at the Paton Welding Institute in the field of electrometallurgy.
Related titles: ◆ English Translation: Advances in Electrometallurgy. ISSN 1810-0384.
Indexed: CorrAb, RefZh, TM, WAA.
—East View, Linda Hall. **CCC.**
Published by: (Natsional'na Akademiya Nauk Ukrainy, Instytut Elektrozvaryuvannya im. EO Patona), Paton Publishing House, E.O. Paton Welding Institute, vul Bozhenko, 11, Kyi, 03680, Ukraine. TEL 380-44-2276302, FAX 380-44-2680486, journal@paton.kiev.ua, http://www.nas.gov.ua/pwj/.

669 IND
SPOTLIGHT/PARIKRAMA. Text in English. 19??. fortn. free (effective 2011). **Document type:** *Magazine, Government.*
Related titles: Hindi ed.
Published by: Steel Authority of India Ltd., Bhilai Steel Plant, Bhilai, 490 001, India. TEL 91-788-2223587, FAX 91-788-2222890, md_bsp@sail-bhilaisteel.com, https://sail-bhilaisteel.com/index.html.

669 RUS
SPRAVOCHNIK SNABZHENTSA. Text in Russian. irreg. **Document type:** *Directory.*
Published by: Torgovyi Dom Metallov LTD, Ul Akademika Koroleva 15, Moscow, 129515, Russian Federation. TEL 7-095-2173778, 7-095-2173754, FAX 7-095-2167992.

671 USA ISSN 1532-9585
SPRAYTIME. Text in English. 1992. q. **Document type:** *Newsletter, Trade.*
Indexed: A28, APA, BrCerAb, C&ISA, CA/WCA, CIA, CerAb, CivEngAb, CorrAb, E&CAJ, E11, EEA, EMA, ESPM, EnvEAb, H15, M&TEA, M09, MBF, METADEX, SolStAb, T04, WAA.
—Linda Hall.
Published by: A S M Thermal Spray Society (Subsidiary of: A S M International), 9639 Kinsman Rd, Materials Park, OH 44073-0002. TEL 440-338-5151, 800-368-9800, 800-336-5152, http://www.asm-intl.org/tss.

669.1 DEU ISSN 0340-4803
TS300 CODEN: STEIA3
STAHL UND EISEN; Zeitschrift fuer die Herstellung und Verarbeitung von Eisen und Stahl. Text in German, English; Abstracts in English, German. 1881. m. EUR 222 domestic; EUR 292 foreign; EUR 30 per issue (effective 2011). adv. bk.rev. bibl.; charts; illus.; mkt.; pat.; stat.; tr.lit. index. **Document type:** *Magazine, Trade.*
Incorporates (1964-1974): Klepzig-Fachberichte fuer die Fuehrungskraefte aus Maschinenbau und Huettenwesen (0023-2092)
Related titles: Microform ed.: (from PMC); Online - full text ed.; ◆ Russian ed.: Chernye Metally. ISSN 0132-0890.
Indexed: A20, A22, A23, A24, A28, APA, ASCA, ApMecR, B13, BCIRA, BrCerAb, C&ISA, CA/WCA, CEABA, CIA, CIN, CISA, CerAb, ChemAb, ChemTitl, CivEngAb, CorrAb, CurCont, E&CAJ, E11, EEA, ELLIS, EMA, ESPM, EngInd, EnvEAb, GeoRef, H15, IBR, IBZ, ISR, Inspec, KES, M&TEA, M09, MBF, METADEX, MSCI, RefZh, SCI, SCOPUS, SolStAb, SpeleolAb, T04, TM, TM, W07, WAA.
—BLDSC (8427.000000), AskIEEE, CASDDS, IE, Infotrieve, Ingenta, INIST, Linda Hall. **CCC.**
Published by: (Stahlinstitut VDEh), Verlag Stahleisen GmbH, Sohnstr 65, Duesseldorf, 40237, Germany. TEL 49-211-6707-0, FAX 49-211-6707310, stahleisen@stahleisen.de, http://www.stahleisen.de. Ed. Gerd Krause. Adv. contact Sabine Dudek. B&W page EUR 2,520, color page EUR 6,480; trim 180 x 260. Circ: 4,659 (paid and controlled).

STAHLBAU - NACHRICHTEN. *see* BUILDING AND CONSTRUCTION

DER STAHLFORMENBAUER. *see* ENGINEERING—Industrial Engineering

669.142 DEU ISSN 0178-6571
STAHLMARKT; Informationen aus Stahlindustrie, Stahlhandel und Verarbeitung. Text in German. 1951. m. EUR 99 domestic; EUR 114 foreign; EUR 11 newsstand/cover (effective 2011). adv. bk.rev. illus.; stat. index. **Document type:** *Journal, Trade.*
Former titles (until 1985): Contintentaler Stahlmarkt (0343-3862); (until 1972): Continentaler Eisenhandel (0343-3870)
Related titles: CD-ROM ed.: EUR 29 (effective 2011).
Indexed: ELLIS, KES, RefZh, TM.
—IE, Infotrieve.
Published by: Montan- und Wirtschaftsverlag GmbH, Postfach 105164, Duesseldorf, 40042, Germany. TEL 49-211-67070, FAX 49-211-6707517, http://www.stahleisen.de. Ed. Wiebke Sanders. Adv. contact Ruth Jentsch. B&W page EUR 2,301, color page EUR 3,099; trim 164 x 260. Circ: 6,970 (paid and controlled).

669.1 DEU ISSN 0942-9336
STAHLREPORT; Das BDS-Magazin fuer die Stahldistribution. Text in German. 1946. m. EUR 65; EUR 7 newsstand/cover (effective 2009). adv. **Document type:** *Magazine, Trade.*
Incorporates (19??-1993): Lernen und Leisten (0942-9344); Both Stahlreport and Lernen und Leisten superseded in part (in 1991): Lernen und Leisten, Stahl-Report (0179-4450); Which was formerly (until 1984): Stahl-Report (0340-6040); (until 1976): Lernen und Leisten (0024-1059)
Indexed: RefZh.
Published by: Bundesverband Deutscher Stahlhandel, Max-Planck-Str 1, Duesseldorf, 40237, Germany. TEL 49-211-864970, FAX 49-211-8649722, info-bds@stahlhandel.com. adv.: color page EUR 3,640, B&W page EUR 2,080; trim 192 x 269. Circ: 3,500 (paid and controlled).

669.14 IND ISSN 0971-9482
STAINLESS INDIA. Text in English. 1995. q. free (effective 2011). back issues avail. **Document type:** *Magazine, Trade.*
Related titles: Online - full text ed.: free (effective 2011).
Indexed: A28, APA, BrCerAb, C&ISA, CA/WCA, CIA, CerAb, CivEngAb, CorrAb, E&CAJ, E11, EEA, EMA, H15, M&TEA, M09, MBF, METADEX, SolStAb, T04, WAA.
—Linda Hall.
Published by: Indian Stainless Steel Development Association, c/o Ramesh R Gopal, L-22/4, Ground Fl, DLF Phase-II, Gurgaon, 122 002, India. TEL 91-124-4375501, FAX 91-124-4375509, issdastainless@gmail.com.

669.1 ZAF ISSN 0038-917X
STAINLESS STEEL. Text in English. 1965. every 8 wks. free to members. adv. bk.rev. charts; illus. **Document type:** *Magazine, Trade.* **Description:** Includes technical articles, association news, company profiles, new products.
Indexed: A28, APA, BrCerAb, C&ISA, CA/WCA, CIA, CerAb, CivEngAb, CorrAb, E&CAJ, E11, EEA, EMA, ESPM, EnvEAb, H15, M&TEA, M09, MBF, METADEX, SolStAb, T04, WAA.
—BLDSC (8430.102000).
Published by: Southern Africa Stainless Steel Development Association, PO Box 4479, Rivonia, Gauteng 2128, South Africa. TEL 27-11-861727732, FAX 27-11-866394280, info@sassda.co.za, http://www.sassda.co.za. Ed. Melissa Rowlston. R&P Susan Custers TEL 27-11-781-1401. Circ: 4,000 (controlled).

669.1029 ZAF
STAINLESS STEEL BUYER'S GUIDE (YEAR). Text in English. a. free. adv. **Document type:** *Directory, Trade.* **Description:** Annual directory that provides a list of members, company profiles, products and technical data for the stainless steel industry.
Published by: Southern Africa Stainless Steel Development Association, PO Box 4479, Rivonia, Gauteng 2128, South Africa. TEL 27-11-803-5610, FAX 27-11-803-2011, info@sassda.co.za. Ed. Dorit Israelsohn. Adv. contact Susan Custers TEL 27-11-781-1401. Circ: 2,715 (controlled).

669 GBR ISSN 1742-3511
STAINLESS STEEL DIRECTORY (YEAR). Text in English. 1988. a. GBP 407, EUR 476, USD 675 per issue (effective 2010). **Document type:** *Directory, Trade.* **Description:** Directory of international stainless steel producers and traders.
Formerly (until 2004): Stainless Steel Databook (0953-7228)
Published by: Metal Bulletin Plc. (Subsidiary of: Euromoney Institutional Investor Plc.), Nestor House, Playhouse Yard, London, EC4V 5EX, United Kingdom. TEL 44-20-77797390, FAX 44-20-77797389, help@metalbulletin.com, http://www.metalbulletin.com. Adv. contact Stefano di Nardo TEL 44-20-78275220.

669 GBR ISSN 1478-1824
STAINLESS STEEL FOCUS; the journal for the stainless steel specialist. Text in English. 198?. m. GBP 248 (effective 2009). adv. **Document type:** *Journal, Trade.* **Description:** Provides news and analysis of the markets for stainless steel and the raw materials for stainless steel production - nickel, chrome and stainless steel scrap.
Indexed: A28, APA, BrCerAb, C&ISA, CA/WCA, CIA, CerAb, CivEngAb, CorrAb, E&CAJ, E11, EEA, EMA, ESPM, EnvEAb, H15, M&TEA, M09, MBF, METADEX, SolStAb, T04, WAA.
—Linda Hall.
Published by: Stainless Steel Focus Ltd., Morgan House, Gilbert Dr, Boston, PE21 7TR, United Kingdom. TEL 44-1205-319093, FAX 44-1205-319095, info@stainless-steel-focus.com. Circ: 8,500.

669.142 GBR ISSN 0306-2988
CODEN: SSTID6
STAINLESS STEEL INDUSTRY. Text in English. 1973. bi-m. GBP 175, USD 275, EUR 210 combined subscription (print & online eds.) (effective 2009). adv. bk.rev. back issues avail. **Document type:** *Magazine, Trade.* **Description:** Covers all aspects of stainless steel technology for purchasing officers, design engineers, metallurgists, and other executives.
Related titles: Online - full text ed.: GBP 75, USD 120, EUR 90 (effective 2009).
Indexed: A28, APA, BrCerAb, C&ISA, CA/WCA, CIA, CIN, CerAb, ChemAb, ChemTitl, CivEngAb, CorrAb, E&CAJ, E11, EEA, EMA, H15, M&TEA, M09, MBF, METADEX, RefZh, SolStAb, T04, WAA.
—BLDSC (8430.120000), CASDDS, Linda Hall.
Published by: (British Stainless Steel Association), Modern Metals Publications Ltd., PO Box 1187, Gerrards Cross, Bucks SL9 7YP, United Kingdom. TEL 44-1753-885968, FAX 44-1753-882980, http://www.ssind.mcmail.com. Ed. Frank Russell.

M

669 338.47669142 GBR ISSN 1460-2628
STAINLESS STEEL REVIEW. Abbreviated title: S S R. Text in English. 1997. m. GBP 1,080 combined subscription domestic (print & online eds.); GBP 1,095 combined subscription foreign (print & online eds.); GBP 225 per issue (effective 2010). back issues avail. **Document type:** *Newsletter, Trade.* **Description:** Provides stainless steel price and market information for hot rolled plate (304 and 316), hot rolled coil (304 and 316), cold rolled coil (304,316,409 and 430), plus drawn and peeled bar (304 and 316).
Related titles: Online - full text ed.
Published by: M E P S (International) Ltd, 263 Glossop Rd, Sheffield, S Yorkshire S10 2GZ, United Kingdom. TEL 44-114-2750570, FAX 44-114-2759808, subs@meps.co.uk.

669.142 NLD ISSN 1383-7184
STAINLESS STEEL WORLD; the magazine for stainless steel users, suppliers and fabricators. Text in English; Text occasionally in Dutch, German. 1989. 10/yr. EUR 239 (effective 2009). adv. illus.; tr.lit. **Document type:** *Magazine, Trade.* **Description:** Covers business and technical developments affecting the stainless steels industry worldwide.
Formerly (until vol.7, no.7, 1995): Stainless Steel Europe (0924-5820); Incorporates (in 1995): Titanium World (1383-7192); Which was formerly (1994-1995): Titanium Europe (1380-3506)
Related titles: Online - full text ed.: EUR 239 (effective 2009).
Indexed: A28, APA, BrCerAb, C&ISA, CA/WCA, CEABA, CIA, CerAb, CivEngAb, CorrAb, E&CAJ, E11, EEA, EMA, ESPM, EnvEAb, FR, H15, M&TEA, M09, MBF, METADEX, SolStAb, T04, WAA.
—IE, Infotrieve, INIST, Linda Hall.
Published by: K C I Publishing B.V., PO Box 396, Zutphen, 7200 AJ, Netherlands. TEL 31-575-585270, FAX 31-575-511099, kci@kci-world.com, http://www.kci-world.com. Adv. contact Robert Campo TEL 31-575-585275.

669.142 GBR ISSN 2043-6467
STAINLESS STEELS MARKET TRACKER. Text in English. 1993. m. GBP 1,545, USD 3,085, EUR 2,266 (effective 2010). back issues avail. **Document type:** *Journal, Trade.*
Former titles (until 2009): Stainless Steels Monthly (1478-7261); (until 2002): Nickel and Stainless Steels Monthly (1466-7533); (until 1999): Stainless Steels Monthly (1355-5634); (until 1994): Alloy & Stainless Steels Monthly (1352-3732)
—**CCC.**
Published by: Metal Bulletin Plc. (Subsidiary of: Euromoney Institutional Investor Plc.), Nestor House, Playhouse Yard, London, EC4V 5EX, United Kingdom. TEL 44-20-77797390, FAX 44-20-77797389, help@metalbulletin.com, http://www.metalbulletin.com.

669.1 RUS ISSN 0038-920X
CODEN: STALAQ
STAL'. Text in Russian. 1931. m. USD 551 foreign (effective 2005). adv. bk.rev. charts; illus. index. **Document type:** *Journal, Trade.* **Description:** Deals with ferrous metallurgy.
Related titles: ◆ Partial translation of: Steel in Translation. ISSN 0967-0912.
Indexed: A22, C&ISA, CIN, ChemAb, ChemTitl, CorrAb, E&CAJ, RASB, RefZh, SCOPUS, SolStAb, TM, WAA.
—BLDSC (0166.740000), CASDDS, East View, IE, Ingenta, INIST, Linda Hall. **CCC.**
Published by: (Mezhdunarodnyi Soyuz Metallurgov/International Metallurgists' Union), Izdatel'stvo Intermet Inzhiniring, Staropimenovskii per 8, str 1, pod 2, Moscow, 103006, Russian Federation. TEL 7-095-2999785, FAX 7-095-7559040, stal@imet.ru. Ed. S V Kolpakov. Adv. contact L P Sorkin. Circ: 900. **Dist. by:** East View Information Services, 10601 Wayzata Blvd, Minneapolis, MN 55305. TEL 952-252-1201, 800-477-1005, FAX 952-252-1202, info@eastview.com, http://www.eastview.com.

669 POL ISSN 1895-6408
STAL, METALE & NOWE TECHNOLOGIE. Text in Polish. 2006. bi-m. PLZ 78 domestic (effective 2011). **Document type:** *Magazine, Trade.* **Description:** Contains technical articles related to the production, processing, distribution, assembly and measurement of various types of steel, aluminum, zinc and other nonferrous metals.
Related titles: Online - full text ed.
Published by: Wydawnictwo Elamed, Al Rozdzienskiego 188, Katowice, 40203, Poland. TEL 48-32-2580361, FAX 48-32-2039356, elamed@elamed.com.pl, http://www.elamed.com.pl. Ed. Renata Caputa.

669 621 USA ISSN 1091-2460
STAMPING JOURNAL. Text in English. 1989. m. USD 55 domestic; USD 65 in Canada & Mexico; USD 85 foreign; free domestic to qualified personnel (effective 2009). adv. 3 cols./p.; reprints avail. **Document type:** *Journal, Trade.* **Description:** Disseminates news and information relating to the metal stamping industry. Contains articles and news releases designed to assist owners, managers, manufacturing engineers, supervisors and foremen in the evaluation of new methods and techniques.
Formerly: Stamping Quarterly (1043-5093)
Related titles: Online - full text ed.: free.
Indexed: A28, APA, BrCerAb, C&ISA, CA/WCA, CIA, CerAb, CivEngAb, CorrAb, E&CAJ, E11, EEA, EMA, ESPM, EnvEAb, H15, M&TEA, M09, MBF, METADEX, SolStAb, T04, WAA.
—BLDSC (8430.235200), IE, Ingenta, Linda Hall.
Published by: (Fabricators & Manufacturers Association, International), F M A Communications, 833 Featherstone Rd, Rockford, IL 61107-6302. TEL 815-399-8700, FAX 815-381-1370, info@thefabricator.com. Ed. Kate Bachman. Pub. Edward Youdell. adv.: B&W page USD 3,500, color page USD 4,895; trim 8.25 x 10.75. Circ: 35,000.

671.3 USA ISSN 1056-3784
TN695
STANDARD TEST METHODS FOR METAL POWDERS AND POWDER METALLURGY PRODUCTS (YEAR). Text in English. 19??. a. USD 65 to non-members; USD 55 to members (effective 2008). **Document type:** *Handbook/Manual/Guide, Trade.* **Description:** Contains 38 standards covering terminology and recommended methods of test for metal powders, powder metal and metal injection molded parts, metallic filters, and powder metallurgy equipment.
Related titles: CD-ROM ed.: USD 70 to non-members; USD 60 to members (effective 2008); Online - full text ed.: USD 70 to non-members; USD 60 to members (effective 2008).
Published by: American Powder Metallurgy Institute, 105 College Rd E, Princeton, NJ 08540-6992. TEL 609-452-7700, FAX 609-987-8523, apmi@mpif.org.

669 624 KOR ISSN 1229-9367
TA684
➤ **STEEL & COMPOSITE STRUCTURES**; an international journal. Text in English. 2001. bi-m. USD 108 to individuals (print or online ed.); USD 345 to institutions; USD 155 combined subscription to individuals (print & online eds.); USD 369 combined subscription to institutions (print & online eds.) (effective 2009). **Document type:** *Journal, Academic/Scholarly.* **Description:** Reports research developments in the steel and steel-concrete composite structures, including bucking, stability, fatigue, fracture, fire performance, connections, frames, bridges, plates, shells, composite structural components, hybrid structures, fabrication, maintenance, design code, dynamic, vibration, nonferrous metal structures, and analytical methods.
Related titles: Online - full content ed.: ISSN 1598-6233. USD 325 to institutions (effective 2009).
Indexed: A28, APA, ApMecR, B21, BrCerAb, C&ISA, CA, CA/WCA, CIA, CPEI, CerAb, CivEngAb, CorrAb, CurCont, E&CAJ, E11, EEA, EMA, ESPM, EngInd, EnvEAb, H&SSA, H15, ICEA, M&TEA, M09, MBF, METADEX, MSCI, S&VD, SCI, SCOPUS, SolStAb, T02, T04, W07, WAA.
—BLDSC (8462.240000), IE, Ingenta, Linda Hall.
Published by: Techno-Press, PO Box 33, Yuseong-gu, Daejeon 305-600, Korea, S. TEL 82-42-3508451, FAX 82-42-3508450, technop@chol.com, http://technop.kaist.ac.kr. Ed. Chang-Koon Choi.

➤ **STEEL AUSTRALIA.** *see* BUILDING AND CONSTRUCTION

669.1 IND
STEEL BULLETIN - PANORAMA/STEEL BULLETIN - BHILAI DARSHAN. Alternating issues in English, Hindi. 19??. s-m. free (effective 2011). **Document type:** *Bulletin.*
Published by: Steel Authority of India Ltd., Bhilai Steel Plant, Bhilai, 490 001, India. TEL 91-788-2223587, FAX 91-788-2222890, md_bsp@sail-bhilaisteel.com, https://sail-bhilaisteel.com/index.html.

STEEL CONSTRUCTION. *see* BUILDING AND CONSTRUCTION

STEEL CONSTRUCTION. *see* BUILDING AND CONSTRUCTION

STEEL CONSTRUCTION - DESIGN AND RESEARCH. *see* BUILDING AND CONSTRUCTION

669 USA
STEEL DIGEST. Text in English. 1983. bi-m. free to qualified personnel. back issues avail. **Document type:** *Newsletter.* **Description:** Examines continuous steelmaking process; reports on development and new technologies in international steelmaking industry.
Published by: Techint Technologies, PO Box 5408, Concord, NC 28027-1507. TEL 704-549-4177, FAX 704-549-4178. Ed., R&P John A Vallomy. Circ: 550.

669 DEU ISSN 1866-8453
STEEL GRIPS; journal of steel and related materials. Text in English. 200?. bi-m. EUR 321 domestic; EUR 300 foreign (effective 2010). **Document type:** *Magazine, Trade.* **Description:** Aims to link all those working with steel, at a university, research institute or in a steelworks plant.
Media: Online - full text.
Published by: G R I P S Media GmbH, Eichendorffstr 64, Bad Harzburg, 38667, Germany. TEL 49-5322-54575, FAX 49-5322-54574, c.garbracht@grips-media.info. Ed. Kerstin Garbracht. Adv. contact Clemens Garbracht.

669.1 USA ISSN 0967-0912
TS300 CODEN: STETE6
➤ **STEEL IN TRANSLATION.** Text in English. 1971. m. EUR 2,741, USD 3,313 combined subscription to institutions (print & online eds.) (effective 2012). abstr.; charts; illus. index. back issues avail. **Document type:** *Journal, Academic/Scholarly.* **Description:** Covers technical and scientific developments in all aspects of iron and steelmaking, metalworking and automation of metallurgical processes.
Formerly (until 1992): Steel in the U S S R (0038-9218); Which superseded (in 1971): Stal' in English (0585-0282)
Related titles: Online - full text ed.: ISSN 1935-0988; ◆ Partial Russian translation(s): Stal'. ISSN 0038-920X.
Indexed: A22, A26, ASCA, CPEI, ChemAb, E01, E08, ErgAb, P52, S09, SCOPUS, TM.
—BLDSC (0425.890050), East View, IE, Infotrieve, Ingenta, INIST, Linda Hall. **CCC.**
Published by: Allerton Press, Inc. (Subsidiary of: Pleiades Publishing, Inc.), 18 W 27th St, New York, NY 10001. TEL 646-424-9686, FAX 646-424-9695, journals@allertonpress.com. Eds. Serafim V Kolpakov, Vuli A Grigoryan.

669.142 JPN
STEEL INDUSTRY OF JAPAN (YEAR). Text in English. a., latest 2002. **Document type:** *Yearbook, Trade.*
Indexed: APA, C&ISA, CorrAb, E&CAJ, EEA, SolStAb, WAA.
Published by: Japan Iron and Steel Federation/Nihon Tekko Renmei, Eisei Iinkai, Keidanren Kaikan, 9-4 Ote-Machi 1-chome, Chiyoda-ku, Tokyo, 100-0004, Japan. TEL 81-3-3279-3612, 81-3-3669-4811, FAX 81-3-3664-1457.

669.142 USA ISSN 1063-4339
STEEL INDUSTRY UPDATE. Text in English. m. **Document type:** *Newsletter, Trade.*
Indexed: A28, APA, BrCerAb, C&ISA, CA/WCA, CIA, CerAb, CivEngAb, CorrAb, E&CAJ, E11, EEA, EMA, ESPM, EnvEAb, H15, M&TEA, M09, MBF, METADEX, SolStAb, T04, WAA.
—Linda Hall.
Published by: Locker Associates, 225 Broadway, Ste 2625, New York, NY 10007. TEL 212-962-2980, FAX 212-608-3077, http://www.lockerassociates.com/.

669.142 338 USA ISSN 1942-9002
STEEL MARKET UPDATE. Text in English. 2008. irreg. **Document type:** *Newsletter, Trade.* **Description:** Provides the latest news and updates that impact the steel industry.
Media: Online - full content.
Published by: Paragon Metal Services, 71 Ridgetop Ct, Dawsonville, GA 30534. TEL 706-216-5440, 800-432-3475, FAX 706-216-6270.

STEEL MARKETS DAILY. *see* BUSINESS AND ECONOMICS

669 IND
STEEL METALS & MINERAL INTERNATIONAL. Text in English. 19??. a. INR 7,000, USD 650 per issue (effective 2011). adv. back issues avail. **Document type:** *Magazine, Trade.* **Description:** Provides information on steelmaking raw materials - the recent trends.
Published by: I S R Infomedia Ltd., Merlin Links, 5th Fl, Block 5E & F 166B, S.P. Mukherjee Rd, Kolkata, 700 026, India. TEL 91-33-24658581, FAX 91-33-24653790, israinfo@eth.net.

669.142 USA
STEEL NEWS. Text in English. q. free to members. **Document type:** *Newsletter.*
Contact Owner: A F L - C I O, United Steel Workers, Local 2102, 1414 E Evans St, Pueblo, CO 81004. TEL 719-564-8600, FAX 719-564-7426. Circ: 1,000 (paid and controlled).

669 GBR
STEEL NEWS (LONDON). Text in English. 11/yr.
Address: 9 Albert Embankment, London, SE1 7SN, United Kingdom. TEL 44-71-735-7654, TELEX 916061. Ed. Brian Richards. Circ: 53,000.

669 BEL ISSN 1029-8916
STEEL R T D NEWSLETTER. Text in English. 1998. s-a. **Document type:** *Newsletter, Academic/Scholarly.*
Indexed: C&ISA, CorrAb, E&CAJ, SolStAb, WAA.
—Linda Hall.
Published by: European Commission, Directorate General - Research, PO Box 2201, Luxembourg, 1022, Belgium. FAX 32-2-296-5987, ecsc-steel@cec.eu.int, http://www.cordis.lu/ecsc/home.html.

669.1 DEU ISSN 1611-3683
TS300 CODEN: SRITB9
➤ **STEEL RESEARCH INTERNATIONAL.** Text in English. 1927. m. GBP 934 in United Kingdom to institutions; EUR 1,088 in Europe to institutions; USD 1,598 elsewhere to institutions; GBP 1,074 combined subscription in United Kingdom to institutions (print & online eds.); EUR 1,252 combined subscription in Europe to institutions (print & online eds.); USD 1,838 combined subscription elsewhere to institutions (print & online eds.) (effective 2012). adv. charts; illus. index. reprint service avail. from PSC. **Document type:** *Journal, Academic/Scholarly.* **Description:** Presents fundamental steel research in the fields of process metallurgy, metal working and materials technology.
Incorporates (1817-2006): Scandinavian Journal of Metallurgy (0371-0459); Which superseded in part (in 1977): Jernkontorets Annaler (0021-5902); Former titles (until 2003): Steel Research (0177-4832); (until 1985): Archiv fuer das Eisenhuettenwesen (0003-8962); Berichte des Vereins Deutscher Eisenhuettenleute
Related titles: Online - full content ed.: ISSN 1869-344X. GBP 934 in United Kingdom to institutions; EUR 1,088 in Europe to institutions; USD 1,598 elsewhere to institutions (effective 2012).
Indexed: A01, A03, A08, A22, A28, APA, ASCA, ApMecR, BrCerAb, C&ISA, C33, CA, CA/WCA, CEABA, CIA, CIN, CPEI, CerAb, ChemAb, ChemTitl, CivEngAb, CorrAb, CurCont, E&CAJ, E11, EEA, EMA, ESPM, EngInd, EnvEAb, GeoRef, H15, IBR, IBZ, INIS AtomInd, ISMEC, ISR, Inspec, M&TEA, M09, MBF, METADEX, MSCI, RefZh, S01, SCI, SCOPUS, SolStAb, SpeleolAb, T02, T04, TM, W07, WAA.
—BLDSC (8464.097000), AskIEEE, CASDDS, IE, Ingenta, INIST, Linda Hall. **CCC.**
Published by: (Stahlinstitut VDEh), Wiley - V C H Verlag GmbH & Co. KGaA (Subsidiary of: John Wiley & Sons, Inc.), Postfach 101161, Weinheim, 69451, Germany. TEL 49-6201-606400, FAX 49-6201-606184, info@wiley-vch.de, http://www.wiley-vch.de. Ed. Dorothea Velikonja. adv.: B&W page EUR 1,070; trim 174 x 260. Circ: 1,500 (paid). **Co-sponsor:** Max-Planck-Institut fuer Eisenforschung.

669.142 IND
STEEL SCENARIO. Text in English. 1991. m. INR 500 domestic; USD 50 foreign (effective 2011). **Document type:** *Journal, Trade.*
Published by: Spark Steel and Economy Research Centre Pvt. Ltd., CG-106, Salt Lake City, Kolkata, 700091, India. TEL 91-33-23340043, FAX 91-33-23376290, info@steelscenario.com. Ed. Monoj Chatterjee.

669.1 GBR ISSN 0143-7798
TN1 CODEN: STLTA3
STEEL TIMES INTERNATIONAL. Abbreviated title: S T I. Text in English. 1866. 8/yr. GBP 149 domestic; GBP 213 foreign (effective 2009). adv. bk.rev. back issues avail.; reprints avail. **Document type:** *Journal, Trade.* **Description:** Covers the production cycle from ore processing, through ironmaking, steelmaking, casting and rolling, to finishing and stockholding.
Incorporates (1964-2001): Steel Times (0039-095X); Which incorporated in part (1962-1963): Steel and Coal (0371-3628); Which was formerly (until 1962): Iron & Coal (0140-5101); (until 1961): Iron and Coal Trades Review (0367-732X)
Related titles: Microform ed.: (from PQC); Online - full text ed.; Chinese ed.; Russian ed.
Indexed: A22, A28, APA, B01, B02, B06, B07, B08, B09, B15, B17, B18, BrCerAb, BrTechI, C&ISA, C12, CA/WCA, CIA, CISA, CerAb, ChemAb, CivEngAb, CorrAb, E&CAJ, E11, EEA, EMA, ESPM, EngInd, EnvEAb, F&EA, G04, G06, G07, G08, H15, I05, IMMAb, ISMEC, KES, M&TEA, M01, M02, M09, MBF, METADEX, P34, RefZh, SCOPUS, SolStAb, T02, T04, TM, V02, WAA.
—BLDSC (8464.105300), CASDDS, IE, Infotrieve, Ingenta, INIST, Linda Hall. **CCC.**
Published by: Quartz Business Media Ltd., Westgate House, 120/130 Station Rd, Redhill, Surrey RH1 1ET, United Kingdom. TEL 44-1737-855000, FAX 44-1737-855475, http://www.quartzltd.co.uk/business. Ed. Tim Smith TEL 44-1737-855154. Adv. contact Ken Clark TEL 44-1737-855117. color page GBP 3,460; trim 210 x 297. Circ: 8,000.

669.029 GBR ISSN 1756-946X
STEEL TIMES INTERNATIONAL. BUYERS' GUIDE AND DIRECTORY. Text in English. 1992. a. adv. **Document type:** *Directory, Trade.* **Description:** Contains reference information for iron- and steelmakers worldwide, in addition to a listing of plants and services.
Former titles (until 2008): Iron and Steel International Directory (Year) (1469-2007); (until 1997): Iron and Steel International (0967-4403)
Indexed: Inspec, SCOPUS.
—INIST. **CCC.**
Published by: D M G World Media Ltd. (Subsidiary of: Daily Mail and General Trust PLC), Westgate House, 120/130 Station Rd, Redhill, Surrey RH1 1ET, United Kingdom. TEL 44-1737-855000, FAX 44-1737-855475, info@uk.dmgworldmedia.com, http://www.dmgworldmedia.com.

669 GBR ISSN 2040-2015
STEEL, WEEKLY MARKET TRACKER. Text in English. 1991. m. GBP 3,995 domestic; EUR 5,875 in Europe; USD 7,990 elsewhere (effective 2010). **Document type:** *Magazine, Trade.* **Description:** Delivers global market analysis, key industry statistics and in-depth reviews of regional markets.
Formed by the merger of (1991-2009): Steel Markets Monthly (Print) (0964-7694); (2002-2009): Emerging Steel Markets Monthly (1478-7253); Which was formerly (until 2002): CIS Steel Markets Monthly (1468-5159)
Media: Online - full text.
—CCC.
Published by: Metal Bulletin Plc. (Subsidiary of: Euromoney Institutional Investor Plc.), Nestor House, Playhouse Yard, London, EC4V 5EX, United Kingdom. TEL 44-20-77797390, FAX 44-20-77797389, help@metalbulletin.com, http://www.metalbulletin.com. Ed. Tony Murray. Adv. contact Stefano di Nardo TEL 44-20-78275220.

671.2 DNK ISSN 0039-1549
STOEBERIET. Text in Danish. 1919. 8/yr. **Document type:** *Magazine, Trade.*
Published by: Danmarks Stoeberitekniske Forening/Foundrymens Organization of Denmark, Ladegaardsvej 2, Videbaek, 6920, Denmark. sk@dsf-shs.dk, http://www.dsf-shs.dk.

671.2 NOR ISSN 0039-1824
CODEN: STOEA7
STOEPERITIDENDE. Text in Norwegian. 1935. 6/yr. NOK 170. adv. bk.rev. abstr.; bibl.; charts; illus. **Document type:** *Trade.*
Indexed: BCIRA.
—CASDDS.
Published by: Norges Stoeperitekniske Forening/Norwegian Foundry Technical Association, Postboks 7117 H, Oslo, 0307, Norway. Circ: 800.

STUDIES OF HIGH TEMPERATURE SUPERCONDUCTORS; advances in research and applications. *see* CHEMISTRY—Electrochemistry

669 JPN ISSN 0039-4963
HD9539.A1 CODEN: SKEGA2
SUMITOMO KEIKINZOKU GIHO/SUMITOMO LIGHT METAL TECHNICAL REPORTS. Text in English, Japanese. 1960. a. per issue exchange basis. charts; illus. index. back issues avail. **Document type:** *Bulletin, Academic/Scholarly.* **Description:** Covers the manufacture, application and evaluation of alloys.
Indexed: A22, A28, APA, BrCerAb, C&ISA, CA/WCA, CIA, CIN, CerAb, ChemAb, ChemTitl, CivEngAb, CoppAb, CorrAb, E&CAJ, E11, EEA, EMA, ESPM, EnvEAb, H15, INIS AtomInd, M&TEA, M09, MBF, METADEX, SolStAb, T04, WAA.
—BLDSC (8517.985000), CASDDS, IE, Ingenta, Linda Hall. **CCC.**
Published by: Sumitomo Light Metal Industries Ltd., Research & Development Center/Sumitomo Keikinzoku Kogyo K. K., 3-1-12 Chitose, Minato-ku, Nagoya-shi, Aichi-ken 455-0011, Japan. FAX 81-52-651-8117. Ed., R&P, Adv. contact Shin Tsuchida TEL 81-52-651-2100. Circ: 1,500.

669 JPN ISSN 0371-411X
CODEN: SUKIA6
SUMITOMO KINZOKU/SUMITOMO METALS. Text in Japanese. 1949. q. **Document type:** *Journal, Academic/Scholarly.*
Formerly (until 1952): Fuso Kinzoku (0367-3340)
Indexed: A22, C&ISA, E&CAJ, EngInd, ISMEC, SCOPUS, SolStAb.
—Linda Hall. **CCC.**
Published by: Sumitomo Metal Industries Ltd., 5-33 Kitahama 4-chome, Chuo-ku, Osaka, 541-0041, Japan. TEL 81-6-62205111, FAX 81-6-62230305, http://www.sumitomometals.co.jp/.

669 JPN
SUMITOMO METAL INDUSTRIES. ANNUAL REPORT. Text in English. a.
Published by: Sumitomo Metal Industries Ltd., 5-33 Kitahama 4-chome, Chuo-ku, Osaka, 541-0041, Japan.

669 JPN ISSN 0585-9131
TS300.S8 CODEN: SUSEAY
SUMITOMO SEARCH. Text in English. 1969. irreg.
Indexed: A22, C&ISA, E&CAJ, ISMEC, Inspec, SCOPUS, SolStAb.
—Linda Hall.
Published by: Sumitomo Metal Industries Ltd., 5-33 Kitahama 4-chome, Chuo-ku, Osaka, 541-0041, Japan.

669 ESP ISSN 1575-8400
SUPERFICIES. Text in Spanish. 1999. 5/yr. **Document type:** *Magazine, Trade.*
Related titles: Online - full text ed.: free.
Published by: Metal Spain, Hermosilla 38, 1B, Madrid, 28001, Spain. TEL 34-91-5765609, FAX 34-91-5782924, magazine@metalspain.co.

669 GBR ISSN 0267-0844
TA418.7 CODEN: SUENET
➤ **SURFACE ENGINEERING.** Text in English. 1985. 8/yr. GBP 1,318 combined subscription to institutions (print & online eds.); USD 2,296 combined subscription in United States to institutions (print & online eds.) (effective 2012). adv. bk.rev.; software rev. abstr. 88 p./no.; back issues avail.; reprint service avail. from PSC. **Document type:** *Journal, Academic/Scholarly.* **Description:** Covers developments in processes and techniques of surface engineering and their industrial applications.
Incorporates (in 1986): Surfacing Journal International (0269-2848); Which was formerly (1973-1985): Surfacing Journal (0307-7365)
Related titles: Online - full text ed.: ISSN 1743-2944. GBP 1,248 to institutions; USD 2,170 in United States to institutions (effective 2012) (from IngentaConnect).

Indexed: A01, A03, A08, A20, A22, A28, APA, BCIRA, BrCerAb, C&ISA, C33, CA, CA/WCA, CIA, CIN, CPEI, CTE, CerAb, ChemAb, ChemTitl, CivEngAb, CorrAb, CurCont, E&CAJ, E11, EEA, EMA, ESPM, EngInd, EnvEAb, H15, Inspec, M&TEA, M09, MBF, METADEX, MSCI, RefZh, SCI, SCOPUS, SolStAb, T02, T04, TM, W07, WAA, Weldasearch.
—BLDSC (8547.850000), AskIEEE, CASDDS, IE, Infotrieve, Ingenta, INIST, Linda Hall. **CCC.**
Published by: (Institute of Materials, Minerals and Mining), Maney Publishing, Ste 1C, Joseph's Well, Hanover Walk, Leeds, W Yorks LS3 1AB, United Kingdom. TEL 44-113-2432800, FAX 44-113-3868178, maney@maney.co.uk, http://www.maney.co.uk. Ed. T S Sudarshan. Adv. contact Robin Fox TEL 44-20-73060300 ext 231. **Subscr. in N. America to:** Maney Publishing, 875 Massachusetts Ave, 7th Fl, Cambridge, MA 02139. TEL 866-297-5154, FAX 617-354-6875, maney@maneyusa.com.

669 USA ISSN 1550-2570
➤ **T M S LETTERS.** (The Minerals, Metals and Materials Society) Text in English. 2004. m. free to members (effective 2010). back issues avail. **Document type:** *Newsletter, Trade.*
Media: Online - full text.
Published by: T M S - The Minerals, Metals and Materials Society, 184 Thorn Hill Rd, Warrendale, PA 15086. TEL 724-776-9000, 800-759-4867, FAX 724-776-3770, publications@tms.org.

669 JPN ISSN 0039-8993
TN677.5 CODEN: TAKOAV
TAIKABUTSU/REFRACTORIES. Text in Japanese. 1949. m. JPY 12,000 (effective 2004). adv. charts; illus.; stat. **Document type:** *Bulletin.*
Indexed: A22, A28, APA, BrCerAb, C&ISA, CA/WCA, CIA, CIN, CerAb, ChemAb, ChemTitl, CivEngAb, CorrAb, E&CAJ, E11, EEA, EMA, ESPM, EnvEAb, H15, INIS AtomInd, JTA, M&TEA, M09, MBF, METADEX, SolStAb, T04, WAA.
—BLDSC (8598.515000), CASDDS, IE, Ingenta, INIST, Linda Hall.
Published by: Technical Association of Refractories/Taikabutsu Gijutsu Kyokai, 7-3-13, Ginza, Chuo-ku, Tokyo, 104-0061, Japan. TEL 81-3-35720705, FAX 81-335720175, http://www.tarj.org/. Ed. Yoshio Hattori. Adv. contact Youko Yoshii. Circ: 2,500.

669 CHN ISSN 1001-3741
CODEN: TAJIFD
➤ **TANSU JISHU/CARBON TECHNIQUES.** Text in Chinese; Abstracts in Chinese, English. 1982. bi-m. CNY 90, USD 90; CNY 5 per issue (effective 2010). adv. back issues avail. **Document type:** *Journal, Academic/Scholarly.*
Related titles: Online - full text ed.
Indexed: A22, RefZh.
—BLDSC (3050.995800), IE.
Published by: Zhonggang Jituan Jilin Tansu Gufen Youxian Gongsi/ Sinosteel Jilin Carbon Co., Ltd., No.9 Hadawan St., Jilin City, 132002, China. TEL 86-432-62749715, http://www.jlts.cn/Html/Main.asp. Ed. Zhiyou Xie. Circ: 1,800.

669 622 621.381 BEL ISSN 1019-2026
TA480.T34
TANTALUM-NIOBIUM INTERNATIONAL STUDY CENTER. QUARTERLY BULLETIN. Text in English. 1974. q. free (effective 2005). back issues avail. **Document type:** *Newsletter, Academic/Scholarly.*
Indexed: A28, APA, BrCerAb, C&ISA, CA/WCA, CIA, CerAb, CivEngAb, CorrAb, E&CAJ, E11, EEA, EMA, ESPM, EnvEAb, H15, M&TEA, M09, MBF, METADEX, RefZh, SolStAb, T04, WAA.
—BLDSC (2772.350000), IE, Ingenta, Linda Hall.
Published by: Tantalum-Niobium International Study Center, 40 Rue Washington, Brussels, 1050, Belgium. TEL 32-2-649-5158, FAX 32-2-649-6447. Circ: 1,000.

669 DEU ISSN 0082-1772
TASCHENBUCH DER GIESSEREI-PRAXIS. Text in German. 1952. a. EUR 54.90 (effective 2010). adv. **Document type:** *Directory, Trade.*
Published by: Fachverlag Schiele und Schoen GmbH, Markgrafenstr 11, Berlin, 10969, Germany. TEL 49-30-2537520, FAX 49-30-2517248, service@schiele-schoen.de, http://www.schiele-schoen.de. Ed. Stephan Hasse.

669 DEU
TASCHENBUCH DES METALLHANDELS. Text in German. irreg. price varies. **Document type:** *Journal, Trade.*
Published by: Giesel Verlag GmbH (Subsidiary of: Schluetersche Verlagsgesellschaft mbH und Co. KG), Rehkamp 3, Isernhagen, 30916, Germany. TEL 49-511-73040, FAX 49-511-7304157, giesel@giesel.de, http://www.giesel.de.

669 JPN
TN677.5 CODEN: TAOVD7
TECHNICAL ASSOCIATION OF REFRACTORIES, JAPAN. JOURNAL. Text in English. 1981. q. JPY 40,000 (effective 2004). adv. illus.; charts; stat. **Document type:** *Bulletin.* **Description:** Covers the science and technology of high-temperature materials centering on the field of refractories.
Formerly (until 1999): Taikabutsu Overseas (0285-0028)
Indexed: A28, APA, BrCerAb, C&ISA, CA/WCA, CIA, CRIA, CerAb, CivEngAb, CorrAb, E&CAJ, E11, EEA, EMA, ESPM, EnvEAb, H15, M&TEA, M09, MBF, METADEX, SolStAb, T04, TM, WAA.
—BLDSC (8598.516000), CASDDS, IE, Ingenta, Linda Hall.
Published by: Technical Association of Refractories/Taikabutsu Gijutsu Kyokai, 7-3-13, Ginza, Chuo-ku, Tokyo, 104-0061, Japan. TEL 81-3-35720705, FAX 81-335720175, http://www.tarj.org/. Ed. Kazunori Kijima. Adv. contact Youko Yoshii. Circ: 600.

TECHNIKA. *see* MACHINERY

669 BRA ISSN 2176-1515
TECNOLOGIA EM METALURGIA, MATERIAIS E MINERACAO. Text in Portuguese. 2004. q. **Document type:** *Journal, Academic/Scholarly.*
Formerly (until 2009): Tecnologia em Metalurgia e Materiais (1807-300X)
Related titles: Online - full text ed.: ISSN 2176-1523.
Indexed: A26, A28, APA, BrCerAb, C&ISA, C01, CA, CA/WCA, CIA, CerAb, CivEngAb, CorrAb, E&CAJ, E11, EEA, EMA, ESPM, EnvEAb, H15, I04, I05, M&TEA, M09, MBF, METADEX, SolStAb, T02, T04, WAA.
—BLDSC (8762.800476), IE, Linda Hall.
Published by: Associacao Brasileira de Metalurgia e Materiais, Rua Antonio Comparato 218, Sao Paulo, SP 04605-030, Brazil. TEL 55-11-55344333, FAX 55-11-55344330. Ed. Roberto Ribeiro de Avillez.

669.1 PRT ISSN 0871-5742
TECNOLOGIA QUALIDADE. Text in Portuguese. 1981. q. adv. bk.rev. abstr.; bibl. **Document type:** *Journal, Trade.*
Formerly (until 1988): Soldadura e Construcao Metalica (0870-0710)
Published by: Instituto de Soldadura e Qualidade, Av Prof Dr Cavaco Silva 33, Taguspark, Oeiras, 2740-120, Portugal. TEL 351-21-4228100, FAX 351-21-4228128.

669 ITA ISSN 1128-5842
TECNOLOGIE DEL FILO. Text in Italian. 1983. q. EUR 30 domestic; EUR 60 in Europe; EUR 80 elsewhere (effective 2011). adv. **Document type:** *Magazine, Trade.* **Description:** Technical information on wire, steel wire and new ferrous wire work.
Former titles (until 1999): Tecnologie del Filo. Barra Tubo (1123-8380); (until 1995): Tecnologie del Filo (0392-7954)
Related titles: Online - full text ed.
Indexed: A28, APA, BrCerAb, C&ISA, CA/WCA, CIA, CerAb, CivEngAb, CorrAb, E&CAJ, E11, EEA, EMA, H15, M&TEA, M09, MBF, METADEX, SolStAb, T04, WAA.
—Linda Hall.
Published by: Tecniche Nuove SpA, Via Eritrea 21, Milan, MI 201, Italy. TEL 39-02-390901, FAX 39-02-7570364, info@tecnichenuove.com. Ed. Loris Cantarelli. Circ: 5,000.

669 621 ITA ISSN 0391-1683
TECNOLOGIE MECCANICHE; sistemi per produrre. Text in Italian. 1970. 11/yr. EUR 97 domestic; EUR 144 foreign (effective 2009). **Document type:** *Magazine, Trade.*
—INIST, Linda Hall.
Published by: Reed Business Information Spa (Subsidiary of: Reed Business Information International), Viale Giulio Richard 1, Milan, 20143, Italy. TEL 39-02-818301, FAX 39-02-81830406, info@reedbusiness.it, http://www.reedbusiness.it. Circ: 12,000.

669 PRT ISSN 0870-8444
TECNOMETAL; revista de informacao tecnica. Text in Portuguese. 1979. bi-m. adv.
Indexed: A28, APA, BrCerAb, C&ISA, CA/WCA, CIA, CerAb, CivEngAb, CorrAb, E&CAJ, E11, EEA, EMA, ESPM, EnvEAb, H15, M&TEA, M09, MBF, METADEX, SolStAb, T04, WAA.
—Linda Hall.
Published by: Associacao dos Industriais Metalurgicos e Metalomecanicos do Norte, Rua dos Platanos, 197, Porto, 41004-414, Portugal. TEL 355-226-166860, FAX 355-226-107473, publicacoes@aimmap.pt, http://www.aimmap.pt. Ed. Miguel Bandeira Quaresma. Circ: 2,500.

669 DEU ISSN 1868-7644
TECSCAN JOURNAL. BLECHBEARBEITUNG. Variant title: Blechbearbeitung. Text in German. 1970. 6/yr. EUR 200 (effective 2010). adv. abstr.; bibl.; charts; illus. back issues avail. **Document type:** *Journal, Trade.*
Former titles (until 2009): Informationsdienst F I Z Technik. Blechbearbeitung (1866-8208); (until 2007): V D I Informationsdienst. Blechbearbeitung (0170-9526)
—CCC.
Published by: Fachinformationszentrum Technik e.V., Hanauer Landstr 151-153, Frankfurt Am Main, 60314, Germany. TEL 49-69-4308213, FAX 49-69-4308200, kundenberatung@fiz-technik.de, http://www.fiz-technik.de.

669 621.3 DEU ISSN 1868-7709
TECSCAN JOURNAL. ELEKTRISCH ABTRAGENDE FERTIGUNGSVERFAHREN. Variant title: Elektrisch Abtragende Fertigungsverfahren. Text in German. 1971. q. EUR 170 (effective 2010). adv. abstr.; bibl.; charts; illus. **Document type:** *Journal, Trade.*
Former titles (until 2009): Informationsdienst F I Z Technik. Elektrisch Abtragende Fertigungsverfahren (1866-8100); (until 2007): Informationsdienst Verein Deutscher Ingenieure. Elektrisch Abtragende Fertigungsverfahren (0170-9569); (until 1978): VDI Informationsdienst. Elektrisch Abtragende Fertigungsverfahren (0341-1621); (until 1974): Informationsdienst Neue Fertigungsverfahren. Teil 3: Elektrisch Abtragende Fertigungsverfahren (0341-1575)
—CCC.
Published by: Fachinformationszentrum Technik e.V., Hanauer Landstr 151-153, Frankfurt Am Main, 60314, Germany. TEL 49-69-4308213, FAX 49-69-4308200, kundenberatung@fiz-technik.de, http://www.fiz-technik.de.

669 RUS ISSN 0321-4664
CODEN: TLSPDI
TEKHNOLOGIYA LEGKIKH SPLAVOV; nauchno-tekhnicheskii zhurnal. Text in Russian. 1963. m. USD 507 in United States (effective 2004). **Document type:** *Journal, Trade.*
Indexed: INIS AtomInd, RefZh.
—BLDSC (0180.505000).
Published by: Vserosiiskii Institut Legkikh Splavov, Gorbunova 2, Moscow, 121596, Russian Federation. TEL 7-095-4449214. Ed. A N Khovanov. **Dist. by:** East View Information Services, 10601 Wayzata Blvd, Minneapolis, MN 55305. TEL 952-252-1201, 800-477-1005, FAX 952-252-1202, info@eastview.com, http://www.eastview.com.

669 RUS ISSN 1684-2499
➤ **TEKHNOLOGIYA METALLOV/METAL TECHNOLOGY**; ezhemesyachnyi proizvodstvennyi i nauchno-tekhnicheskii zhurnal. Text in Russian. 1998. m. USD 887 foreign (effective 2005). **Document type:** *Journal, Academic/Scholarly.* **Description:** Presents information about production of metals and non-metal materials used in modern equipment; statistics about Russian and foreign materials, equipment, tools; automation of production processes; safety procedures; ecology.
Indexed: RefZh.
—BLDSC (0180.531500).
Published by: Nauka i Tekhnologii, Stromynskii per, 4/1, Moscow, 107076, Russian Federation. admin@nait.ru, http://www.nait.ru. Ed. S B Maslenkov. **Dist. by:** East View Information Services, 10601 Wayzata Blvd, Minneapolis, MN 55305. TEL 952-252-1201, 800-477-1005, FAX 952-252-1202, info@eastview.com, http://www.eastview.com.

669.1 JPN ISSN 0040-2273
TEKKO RODO EISEI/JOURNAL OF LABOR HYGIENE IN IRON AND STEEL INDUSTRY. Text in Japanese; Contents page in English. 1950. 2/yr. free. bk.rev.
Indexed: CISA.
Published by: (Hygiene Committee), Japan Iron and Steel Federation/ Nihon Tekko Renmei, Eisei Iinkai, Keidanren Kaikan, 9-4 Ote-Machi 1-chome, Chiyoda-ku, Tokyo, 100-0004, Japan. TEL 81-3-3279-3612, FAX 81-3-3245-0144, TELEX 222-4210. Circ: 500.

TEKKOTSU/STEEL FRAME. *see* BUILDING AND CONSTRUCTION

671 DNK ISSN 1901-6352
TEKNOVATION; business-to-business i metal-, plast- og maskinindustrierne. Text in Danish. 2006. 10/yr. free. adv. back issues avail. **Document type:** *Magazine, Trade.*
Related titles: Online - full text ed.
Published by: B2B-Press, Sydvestvej 110,1, Glostrup, 2600, Denmark. TEL 45-46-139000, FAX 45-46-139021. Eds. Adam Estrup TEL 45-20-184669, John Nyberg TEL 45-30-915544. Adv. contact Henrik Bang TEL 45-26-882684. B&W page DKK 28,350, color page DKK 31,350; 266 x 365. Circ: 18,000.

669 CHN ISSN 1003-8620
TA478
TESHU GANG/SPECIAL STEEL. Text in Chinese. 1980. bi-m. USD 42.60 (effective 2009). 64 p./no.; **Document type:** *Trade.*
Related titles: Online - full text ed.
Indexed: A22, A28, APA, BrCerAb, C&ISA, CA/WCA, CIA, CerAb, CivEngAb, CorrAb, E&CAJ, E11, EEA, EMA, ESPM, EnvEAb, H15, M&TEA, M09, MBF, METADEX, SCOPUS, SolStAb, T04, WAA.
—BLDSC (8404.300000), East View, IE, Ingenta.
Published by: (Zhongguo Jinshu Xuehui/Chinese Society for Metals, Teshu Gang Xuehui), Teshu Gang Zazhishe, Dazhi Teshu Gang Gufeng Youxian Gongsi, Gangtie Yanjiusuo, Huangshi, Hubei 435001, China. TEL 86-714-6292102, FAX 86-714-6222610. Ed. Wang Xueyao. **Dist. overseas by:** China International Book Trading Corp, 35 Chegongzhuang Xilu, Haidian District, PO Box 399, Beijing 100044, China.

669 USA
TESTING TECHNOLOGY. Text in English. 1976. m. **Document type:** *Abstract/Index.*
Former titles: Metallography and Testing Digest; Testing and Control Digest
Published by: A S M International, 9639 Kinsman Rd, Materials Park, OH 44073. TEL 440-338-5151, FAX 440-338-4634, CustomerService@asminternational.org, http://asmcommunity.asminternational.org.

669.1 JPN ISSN 0021-1575
TN705 CODEN: TEHAA2
➤ **TETSU TO HAGANE/IRON AND STEEL INSTITUTE OF JAPAN. JOURNAL.** Text in Japanese; Summaries in English. 1915. m. subscr. incld. with membership. adv. abstr. Index. 60 p./no.; back issues avail. **Document type:** *Journal, Academic/Scholarly.*
Indexed: A20, A22, A28, APA, ASCA, BrCerAb, C&ISA, C33, CA/WCA, CIA, CPEI, CerAb, ChemAb, CivEngAb, CorrAb, CurCont, E&CAJ, E11, EEA, EMA, ESPM, EngInd, EnvEAb, H15, INIS AtomInd, ISR, Inspec, JTA, M&TEA, M09, MBF, METADEX, MSCI, RefZh, SCI, SCOPUS, SolStAb, T04, TM, W07, WAA.
—BLDSC (4803.045000), CASDDS, IE, Infotrieve, Ingenta, INIST, Linda Hall. **CCC.**
Published by: Nippon Tekko Kyokai/Iron and Steel Institute of Japan, Niikura Bldg, 2nd Fl, 2 Kanda-Tsukasacho 2-chome, Chiyoda-ku, Tokyo, 101-0048, Japan. TEL 81-3-52097011, FAX 81-3-32571110, editol@isij.or.jp, http://www.isij.or.jp. Ed. Shozo Mizoguchi. Pub. Yasuo Uchinaka. R&P Yoshihiro Kuwabara. Circ: 3,000.

669 CHN ISSN 1001-2249
TS228.99
TEZHONG ZHUZAO JI YOUSE HEJIN/SPECIAL CASTING & NON-FERROUS ALLOYS. Text in Chinese. 1983. bi-m. USD 62.40 (effective 2009).
Related titles: Online - full text ed.
Indexed: A28, APA, BrCerAb, C&ISA, CA/WCA, CIA, CerAb, CivEngAb, CorrAb, E&CAJ, E11, EEA, EMA, ESPM, EngInd, EnvEAb, H15, M&TEA, M09, MBF, METADEX, RefZh, SCOPUS, SolStAb, T04, WAA.
—BLDSC (8813.790140), East View, Linda Hall.
Published by: (Zhongguo Jixie Gongcheng Xuehui/Chinese Society of Mechanical Engineering, Wuhan Jixie Gongyi Yanjiusuo), Guofang Kexue Jishu Daxue/National University of Defense Technology, Wuhan, China.

669 USA ISSN 1052-7877
Z695.1.M55
THESAURUS OF METALLURGICAL TERMS. Text in English. 1968. biennial. **Description:** Controlled vocabulary for effective searching of Materials Information Metadex database.
Published by: ProQuest LLC (Bethesda) (Subsidiary of: Cambridge Information Group), 789 E Eisenhower Pky, Ann Arbor, MI 48103. TEL 734-761-4700, FAX 734-997-4222, journals@csa.com.

THYSSENKRUPP TECHFORUM (ENGLISH EDITION). *see* TECHNOLOGY: COMPREHENSIVE WORKS

THYSSENKRUPP TECHFORUM (GERMANY EDITION). *see* TECHNOLOGY: COMPREHENSIVE WORKS

669 RUS
TITAN. Text in Russian. q. USD 150 in United States.
Published by: Mezhgosudarstvennaya Assotsyatsiya Titan, B Tolmachevskii per 5, Moscow, 109017, Russian Federation. TEL 7-095-4449214. **Dist. by:** East View Information Services, 10601 Wayzata Blvd, Minneapolis, MN 55305. TEL 952-252-1201, 800-477-1005, FAX 952-252-1202, info@eastview.com, http://www.eastview.com. **Co-sponsor:** Vserossiiskii Institut Legkikh Splavov.

669 RUS
TITANIUM. Text in English. q. USD 145 in United States.
Indexed: APA, CorrAb, EEA, SolStAb, WAA.
Published by: Mezhgosudarstvennaya Assotsyatsiya Titan, B Tolmachevskii per 5, Moscow, 109017, Russian Federation. TEL 7-095-4449214. **Dist. by:** East View Information Services, 10601 Wayzata Blvd, Minneapolis, MN 55305. TEL 952-252-1201, 800-477-1005, FAX 952-252-1202, info@eastview.com, http://www.eastview.com. **Co-sponsor:** Vserossiiskii Institut Legkikh Splavov.

669 USA
CODEN: MTITDR
TITANIUM (YEAR): A STATISTICAL REVIEW. Text in English. 19??. a. USD 75 to non-members; free to members (effective 2011).
Document type: *Proceedings, Trade.* **Description:** Compiles titanium statistics obtained from government and trade organization data.
—CASDDS.
Published by: International Titanium Association, 2655 W Midway Blvd, Ste 300, Broomfield, CO 80020. TEL 303-404-2221, FAX 303-404-9111, info@titanium.org.

669 JPN ISSN 1341-1713
TITANIUM JAPAN. Key Title: Chitan. Text in Japanese. q.
Formerly (until 1994): Chitaniumu Jirukniumu (0577-9391)
Indexed: A28, APA, BrCerAb, C&ISA, CA/WCA, CIA, CerAb, CivEngAb, CorrAb, E&CAJ, E11, EEA, EMA, ESPM, EnvEAb, GeoRef, H15, INIS AtomInd, M&TEA, M09, MBF, METADEX, SolStAb, T04, WAA.
—BLDSC (8858.898300), Linda Hall.
Published by: Nihon Chitan Kyokai/Japan Titanium Society, Tokyo, Japan. FAX 81-3-32936187, http://www.titan-japan.com/indexe.htm.

669 USA
TITANIUM NEWS. Text in English. q. free (effective 2011). **Document type:** *Newsletter, Trade.*
Indexed: APA, C&ISA, CorrAb, E&CAJ, EEA, SolStAb, WAA.
Published by: International Titanium Association, 2655 W Midway Blvd, Ste 300, Broomfield, CO 80020. TEL 303-404-2221, FAX 303-404-9111, info@titanium.org, http://www.titanium.org.

669 622 JPN ISSN 0919-4827
CODEN: TDSSA2
TOHOKU DAIGAKU SOZAI KOGAKU KENKYUJO IHO/TOHOKU UNIVERSITY. INSTITUTE FOR ADVANCED MATERIALS PROCESSING. BULLETIN. Text in Japanese; Summaries in English. 1942. s-a. per issue exchange basis. charts; illus.; stat. **Document type:** *Bulletin, Academic/Scholarly.* **Description:** Covers the field of metallurgical, environmental and nuclear chemistry and materials science.
Formerly (until 1993): Tohoku Daigaku Senko Seiren Kenkyujo Iho - Tohoku University. Research Institute of Mineral Dressing and Metallurgy. Bulletin (0040-876X)
Indexed: A28, APA, BrCerAb, C&ISA, CA/WCA, CIA, CIN, CerAb, ChemAb, ChemTitl, CivEngAb, CorrAb, E&CAJ, E11, EEA, EMA, H15, IMMAb, INIS AtomInd, JTA, M&TEA, M09, MBF, METADEX, SolStAb, T04, WAA.
—CASDDS, Linda Hall.
Published by: Tohoku Daigaku, Sozai Kogaku Kenkyujo/Tohoku University, Institute for Advanced Materials Processing, 1-1 Katahira 2-chome, Aoba-ku, Sendai, 980-8577, Japan. TEL 81-22-217-5166, FAX 81-22-217-5211. Ed. Yoshio Waseda. Circ: (controlled).

TOHOKU UNIVERSITY. SCIENCE REPORTS OF THE RESEARCH INSTITUTES. SERIES A: PHYSICS, CHEMISTRY, AND METALLURGY/TOHOKU DAIGAKU KENKYUJO HOKOKU. A-SHU: BUTSURIGAKU, KAGAKU, YAKINGAKU. *see* PHYSICS

669 FRA ISSN 0985-5637
TOLERIE; le magazine du materiel et de la technologie du travail des metaux en feuille. Text in French. 1987. 8/yr. EUR 149.40 domestic; EUR 187.51 foreign (effective 2010). adv. **Description:** Contains information about new products and thematic information on technology used in sheet metal working, such as punching machines, bending machines, lasers, shearing machines.
Published by: Marlau Editions, 16 allee de la Source, Pontault -Combault, 77340, France. TEL 33-01-60280533, FAX 33-01-60287730.

TOMOEGUMI TEKKOJO GIHO/TOMOEGUMI IRON WORKS TECHNICAL REPORT. *see* BUILDING AND CONSTRUCTION

669 CHN ISSN 1009-3842
TONGYE GONGCHENG/COPPER ENGINEERING. Text in Chinese. 1984. q. USD 16.40 (effective 2009). adv. **Document type:** *Journal, Academic/Scholarly.* **Description:** Covers scientific experiments, applications of new technology relating to copper production.
Formerly (until 1999): Jiangxi Tongye Gongcheng/Jiangxi Copper Engineering (1006-4451)
Related titles: Online - full text ed.
Indexed: RefZh.
Published by: Jiangxi Tongye Gongsi, Yejin Dadao, Guixi, Jiangxi 335424, China. TEL 86-701-3357672. Circ: 1,600.

671 FRA ISSN 2108-2804
TN672 CODEN: TRTHA4
TRAITEMENTS & MATERIAUX. Text in French. 1963. 6/yr. EUR 145 domestic; EUR 165 DOM-TOM; EUR 180 foreign (effective 2011). adv. bk.rev. charts; illus. index. **Document type:** *Magazine, Trade.* **Description:** Technical review for engineers and technicians of heat treatment.
Former titles (until 2010): Traitement Thermique et Ingenierie des Surfaces (1779-0107); (until 2002): Traitement Thermique (0041-0950)
Indexed: A22, C&ISA, ChemAb, CorrAb, E&CAJ, INIS AtomInd, SolStAb, WAA.
—CASDDS, IE, Infotrieve, Ingenta, INIST, Linda Hall. **CCC.**
Published by: P Y C Edition, 16-18 Place de la Chapelle, Paris, 75018, France. TEL 33-1-53264800, FAX 33-1-53264801, info@pyc.fr. Ed. Beatrice Becherini. Adv. contact Pierre Pagnard. Circ: 1,750.

669 FRA ISSN 1266-8753
TRAMETAL; revue technique sur le travail des metaux. Text in French. 1995. m. EUR 125 domestic; EUR 200 foreign (effective 2008).
Indexed: RefZh.
Published by: Apt'editions, 2 av. de la Cristallerie, Sevres, Cedex 92316, France. TEL 33-1-46261028, FAX 33-1-46264211. Ed., R&P Robert Eleonore. Pub. Isabelle Rovira. Adv. contact Elisabeth Bartoli. Circ: 10,000.

669 NLD ISSN 0340-4285
QD172.T6 CODEN: TMCHDN
➤ **TRANSITION METAL CHEMISTRY;** an international journal. Text in Dutch. 8/yr. EUR 2,897, USD 3,131 combined subscription to institutions (print & online eds.) (effective 2012). adv. charts; illus. index. reprint service avail. from PSC. **Document type:** *Journal, Academic/Scholarly.* **Description:** Publishes preliminary communications and full-length research papers on the chemistry of the f-group metals.
Related titles: Online - full text ed.: ISSN 1572-901X (from IngentaConnect).
Indexed: A20, A22, A26, ASCA, BibLing, C24, C33, CA, CCI, CPEI, ChemAb, ChemTitl, CurCR, CurCont, E01, EngInd, GeoRef, I05, ISR, P52, R16, RefZh, SCI, SCOPUS, SpeleolAb, T02, W07.
—BLDSC (9020.860000), CASDDS, IE, Infotrieve, Ingenta, INIST, Linda Hall. **CCC.**
Published by: Springer Netherlands (Subsidiary of: Springer Science+Business Media), Van Godewijckstraat 30, Dordrecht, 3311 GX, Netherlands. TEL 31-78-6576050, FAX 31-78-6576474, http://www.springer.com. Ed. Marcus C Durrant.

669 536 ESP ISSN 1132-0346
TRATAMIENTOS TERMICOS. Text in Spanish. 1991. 6/yr. **Document type:** *Magazine, Trade.*
Related titles: Online - full text ed.: free.
Indexed: IECT.
Published by: Metal Spain, Hermosilla 38, 1B, Madrid, 28001, Spain. TEL 34-91-5765609, FAX 34-91-5782924, magazine@metalspain.co.

TRATTAMENTI E FINITURE. *see* PAINTS AND PROTECTIVE COATINGS

620.112 IND ISSN 0972-4826
TRENDS IN CORROSION RESEARCH. Text in English. 2002. a. EUR 134.10 in Europe; JPY 17,852 in Japan; USD 149 elsewhere (effective 2010). **Document type:** *Journal, Academic/Scholarly.* **Description:** Provides a medium for the publication of review articles and original research papers in all aspects of this field and includes both metallic and non-metallic corrosion.
Related titles: CD-ROM ed.
Indexed: A28, APA, CA/WCA, CIA, CivEngAb, E11, EEA, EMA, H15, MBF, T04.
Published by: Research Trends (P) Ltd., T.C. 17 / 250 (3), Chadiyara Rd, Poojapura, Trivandrum, Kerala 695 012, India. TEL 91-471-2344424, FAX 91-471-2344423, info@researchtrends.net.

669 GBR ISSN 1751-5831
TRIBOLOGY (LEEDS); materials, surfaces & interfaces. Text in English. 2007. q. GBP 411 combined subscription to institutions (print & online eds.); USD 761 combined subscription in United States to institutions (print & online eds.) (effective 2012). adv. reprint service avail. from PSC. **Document type:** *Journal, Academic/Scholarly.*
Related titles: Online - full text ed.: ISSN 1751-584X. GBP 372 to institutions; USD 688 in United States to institutions (effective 2012) (from IngentaConnect).
Indexed: A28, APA, APIAb, BrCerAb, C&ISA, CA/WCA, CIA, CPEI, CerAb, CivEngAb, CorrAb, E&CAJ, E11, EEA, EMA, ESPM, EnvEAb, H15, M&TEA, M09, MBF, METADEX, SCOPUS, SolStAb, T04, WAA.
—BLDSC (9050.216975), IE. **CCC.**
Published by: (Institute of Materials, Minerals and Mining), Maney Publishing, Ste 1C, Joseph's Well, Hanover Walk, Leeds, W Yorks LS3 1AB, United Kingdom. TEL 44-113-2432800, FAX 44-113-3868178, maney@maney.co.uk, http://www.maney.co.uk. Ed. Anne Neville. **Subscr. in N. America to:** Maney Publishing, 875 Massachusetts Ave, 7th Fl, Cambridge, MA 02139. TEL 866-297-5154, FAX 617-354-6875, maney@maneyusa.com.

669 FRA ISSN 1624-5326
LA TRIBUNE DE LA SUDERURGIE. Text in French. 1998. w. EUR 236 domestic; EUR 255 foreign (effective 2010). **Document type:** *Newsletter, Trade.*
Supersedes in part (in 1998): La Tribune des Metaux (1167-4849)
Published by: Veron et Cie, 42 Rue d'Antrain, Rennes, 35700, France. TEL 33-2-99853838, FAX 33-2-99853076, contact@metaltribune.com.

669 FRA ISSN 1167-4849
LA TRIBUNE DES METAUX. Text in French. 1992. w. EUR 220 domestic; EUR 235 foreign (effective 2010). **Document type:** *Newsletter, Trade.*
Published by: Veron et Cie, 42 Rue d'Antrain, Rennes, 35700, France. TEL 33-2-99853838, FAX 33-2-99853076, contact@metaltribune.com.

669 RUS ISSN 0372-2929
TN4 CODEN: TVMTAX
TSVETNYE METALLY. Text in Russian. 1926. m. USD 1,227 foreign (effective 2009). adv. bibl.; illus. index. **Document type:** *Journal, Trade.* **Description:** Covers many aspects of non-ferrous metallurgy: heavy non-ferrous metals, rare metals, carbonaceous materials, light alloys, and metal working.
Related titles: ◆ English Translation: Non-Ferrous Metals; ◆ Supplement(s): Non-Ferrous Metals; Alyuminii i Ego Splavy/Lit'e Pod Davleniem i Liteinye Tekhnologii.
Indexed: C&ISA, ChemAb, CorrAb, E&CAJ, IMMAb, INIS AtomInd, RASB, RefZh, SCOPUS, SolStAb, WAA.
—BLDSC (0396.450000), CASDDS, East View, IE, Infotrieve, Linda Hall. **CCC.**
Published by: Izdatel'stvo Ruda i Metally/Ore and Metals Publishers, Leninskii prospekt 6, korpus 1, ofis 622, a/ya 71, Moscow, 119049, Russian Federation. rim@rudmet.ru. Ed. Aleksandr Putilov. adv.: page USD 1,000. Circ: 1,500. **Dist. by:** East View Information Services, 10601 Wayzata Blvd, Minneapolis, MN 55305. TEL 952-252-1201, 800-477-1005, FAX 952-252-1202, info@eastview.com, http://www.eastview.com.

669 621 USA ISSN 1091-2479
TS280
THE TUBE & PIPE JOURNAL. Abbreviated title: T P J. Text in English. 1990. 8/yr. USD 55 domestic; USD 65 in Canada & Mexico; USD 85 elsewhere; free domestic to qualified personnel (effective 2009). adv. reprints avail. **Document type:** *Journal, Trade.* **Description:** Contains news and information relating to the metal tube and pipe producing and fabricating industries. Includes articles and news releases to assist owners, managers, manufacturing engineers, supervisors, and foremen in the evaluation of new methods and techniques.
Formerly (until 1997): Tube and Pipe Quarterly (1051-4120)
Related titles: Online - full text ed.: free.
Indexed: A28, APA, BrCerAb, C&ISA, CA/WCA, CIA, CerAb, CivEngAb, CorrAb, E&CAJ, E11, EEA, EMA, ESPM, EnvEAb, H15, M&TEA, M09, MBF, METADEX, SWRA, SolStAb, T04, WAA.
—BLDSC (9068.057200), IE, Ingenta, Linda Hall.
Published by: (Tube & Pipe Association, International), F M A Communications, 833 Featherstone Rd, Rockford, IL 61107-6302. TEL 815-399-8700, FAX 815-381-1370, info@thefabricator.com. Ed. Dan Davis. Pub. Edward Youdell. adv.: B&W page USD 3,580, color page USD 5,010; trim 8.25 x 10.75. Circ: 31,507 (controlled).
Co-sponsor: Fabricators & Manufacturers Association, International.

669 GBR
U K STEEL EXPORTS. Text in English. 19??. a. GBP 195 per issue (effective 2010). charts; stat. **Document type:** *Report, Trade.* **Description:** Compiles monthly statistics of U.K. exports of iron and steel products to more than 100 countries.
Formerly: U K Exports of Iron and Steel
Published by: I S S B Ltd., 1 Carlton House Ter, London, SW1Y 5DB, United Kingdom. TEL 44-20-73433900, FAX 44-20-73433901, info@issb.co.uk, http://www.issb.co.uk.

669 GBR
U K STEEL IMPORTS. Text in English. 19??. a. GBP 195 per issue (effective 2010). charts; stat. **Document type:** *Report, Trade.* **Description:** Compiles statistics of U.K. imports of iron and steel, by month, from more than 36 nations.
Formerly: U K Imports of Iron and Steel
Published by: I S S B Ltd., 1 Carlton House Ter, London, SW1Y 5DB, United Kingdom. TEL 44-20-73433900, FAX 44-20-73433901, info@issb.co.uk, http://www.issb.co.uk.

671.2 USA ISSN 0041-8048
U S PIPER. Text in English. 1928. s-a. free. illus. **Document type:** *Journal, Trade.*
Indexed: A28, APA, BrCerAb, C&ISA, CA/WCA, CIA, CerAb, CivEngAb, CorrAb, E&CAJ, E11, EEA, EMA, H15, M&TEA, M09, MBF, METADEX, SolStAb, T04, WAA.
—Linda Hall.
Published by: United States Pipe and Foundry Company, PO Box 10406, Birmingham, AL 35202. TEL 205-254-7442, FAX 205-254-7165. Ed., Pub., R&P George J Bogs. Circ: 8,500.

671 DEU
U T F SCIENCE (ONLINE). Text in German. 2000. 4/yr. free (effective 2011). **Document type:** *Magazine, Trade.*
Formerly (until 2009): U T F Science (Print)
Indexed: APA, CorrAb, EEA, SolStAb, WAA.
Published by: Meisenbach GmbH, Franz-Ludwig-Str 7a, Bamberg, 96047, Germany. TEL 49-951-8610, FAX 49-951-861158, info@meisenbach.de, http://www.meisenbach.de. Ed. Volker Albrecht.

669 GBR
UK STEEL ASSOCIATION. ANNUAL REVIEW. Text in English. 19??. a. free (effective 2009). back issues avail. **Document type:** *Journal, Trade.* **Description:** Provides information about UK Steel Association.
Related titles: Online - full text ed.: free (effective 2009).
Published by: UK Steel Association, Broadway House, Tothill St, London, SW1H 9NQ, United Kingdom. TEL 44-20-72227777, FAX 44-20-72222782, steel@eef.org.uk, http://www.eef.org.uk/uksteel/default.htm.

671 621.9 668.4 DEU ISSN 0300-3167
UMFORMTECHNIK. Text in German. 1967. 4/yr. EUR 86 domestic; EUR 89 in Europe; EUR 110 elsewhere (effective 2011). adv. charts; illus. index. **Document type:** *Magazine, Trade.* **Description:** Methods, machines and tooling for sheet-metal forming, forging and rolling processes, parting techniques as well as plastics processing.
Indexed: TM.
—INIST.
Published by: Meisenbach GmbH, Franz-Ludwig-Str 7a, Bamberg, 96047, Germany. TEL 49-951-8610, FAX 49-951-861158, info@meisenbach.de, http://www.meisenbach.de. Ed. Wolfgang Fili. Adv. contact Georg Meisenbach. Circ: 4,401 (paid and controlled).
Subscr. to: InTime Services GmbH, Bajuwarenring 14, Oberhaching 82041, Germany. TEL 49-89-85853553, FAX 449-89-8585362447, meisenbach@intime-media-services.de, http://www.intime-media-services.de.

UNITED STEELWORKERS OF AMERICA. INFORMATION. *see* LABOR UNIONS

UNIVERSIDAD, CIENCIA Y TECNOLOGIA. *see* ENGINEERING

669 ROM ISSN 1453-083X
UNIVERSITATEA "DUNAREA DE JOS" DIN GALATI. ANALELE. FASCICULA IX. METALURGIE SI STIINTA MATERIALELOR/ "DUNAREA DE JOS" UNIVERSITY OF GALATI. ANNALS. FASCICLE IX. METALLURGY AND MATERIAL SCIENCE. Text in Romanian. 1983. a.
Former titles (until 1993): Universitatii "Dunarea de Jos" Galati. Analele. Fascicula IX. Metalurgie (1221-4604); (until 1986): Universitatii din Galati. Analele. Fascicula IX. Metalurgie si Cocserie (1220-0832)
Indexed: A01, A28, APA, BrCerAb, C&ISA, CA/WCA, CIA, CerAb, CivEngAb, CorrAb, E&CAJ, E11, EEA, EMA, ESPM, EnvEAb, H15, M&TEA, M09, MBF, METADEX, SolStAb, T04, WAA.
—Linda Hall.
Published by: Universitatea "Dunarea de Jos" din Galati, Str Domneasca Nr 111, Galati, 6200, Romania. TEL 40-36-460328, FAX 40-36-461353, http://www.ugal.ro.

UNIVERSITY OF CHEMICAL TECHNOLOGY AND METALLURGY. JOURNAL. *see* ENGINEERING—Chemical Engineering

669 HUN ISSN 1219-4255
Q1 CODEN: PTUBDW
UNIVERSITY OF MISKOLC. PUBLICATIONS. SERIES B, METALLURGY. Text in English, German, Russian. 1975. irreg. bibl. index. **Document type:** *Monographic series, Academic/Scholarly.*
Formerly (until 1994): Technical University for Heavy Industry. Publications. Series B, Metallurgy (0324-4679)
Indexed: CIS, CRIA, CRICC, IMMAb, Z02.
—CASDDS, Linda Hall.
Published by: Miskolci Egyetem/University of Miskolc, Miskolc, 3515, Hungary. TEL 36-46-565111, FAX 36-46-367933, http://www.uni-miskolc.hu. Circ: 300.

USPEKHI FIZIKI METALLOV; a research journal. *see* PHYSICS

669.3 NOR ISSN 0807-111X
V F T-AKTUELT. Text in Norwegian. 1920. 10/yr. adv. bk.rev. charts; illus.
Former titles (until 1995): Kobber- og Blikkenslagernytt (0803-7752); (until 1992): Kobber- og Blikkenslagermesteren (0023-2505); (until 1961): Blikkenslagermesteren (0801-5287)

Published by: Ventilasjons- 0g Blikkenslagerbedriftenes Landsforbund, PO Box 5478, Oslo, 0305, Norway. TEL 47-23-08-76-70, FAX 47-22-46-93-05. Ed. Dag Solberg TEL 47-23-08-75-71. Adv. contact Heidi Nygaard. color page NOK 7,800, B&W page NOK 4,600; 185 x 260. Circ: 925.

VAKUUMIST; casopis za vakuumsko znanost, tehniko in tehnologije, vakuumsko metalurgijo, tanke plasti, povrsine in fiziko plazme. *see* PHYSICS

669 AUT ISSN 1025-627X CODEN: RAXRAF
VEITSCH-RADEX RUNDSCHAU. Text in German. 1946. s-a. **Document type:** *Bulletin.*
Formerly (until 1993): Radex Rundschau (0370-3657)
Indexed: CIN, CRIA, CRICC, ChemAb, ChemTitl, GeoRef, SCOPUS, SpeleolAb.
—CASDDS, Ingenta, INIST, Linda Hall. **CCC.**
Published by: Veitsch-Radex GmbH, Magnesitstrasse 2, Leoben, St 8700, Austria. TEL 43-3842-205300. Ed. Bernd Buchberger. Pub. Gunter Karhut.

669 CZE ISSN 0474-8484
TN4 CODEN: SRAHAY
VYSOKA SKOLA BANSKA - TECHNICKA UNIVERZITA OSTRAVA. SBORNIK VEDECKYCH PRACI: RADA HUTNICKA/INSTITUTE OF MINING AND METALLURGY. TRANSACTIONS: METALLURGICAL SERIES. Text in Czech; Summaries in English, German, Russian. 1955. a. price varies. bk.rev. abstr.; bibl.; charts; illus.; stat. index. **Document type:** *Monographic series, Academic/Scholarly.*
Supersedes in part (in 1967): Vysoka Skola Banska v Ostrave. Sbornik Vedeckych Praci (0474-8468)
Indexed: CIN, ChemAb, ChemTitl, CoppAb, F&EA, GeoRef, IMMAb.
—CASDDS, INIST, Linda Hall.
Published by: Vysoka Skola Banska, Technicka Univerzita Ostrava/ Technical University of Ostrava, 17 Listopadu 15, Ostrava, 70833, Czech Republic. TEL 420-597-321111, FAX 420-597-323233, http://www.vsb.cz.

669 THA ISSN 0857-6149
WARASAN LOHA, WATSADU LAE LAE/METALS, MATERIALS AND MINERALS BULLETIN. Text in English, Thai. s-a. USD 5 domestic; USD 25 foreign (effective 2007). **Document type:** *Journal, Academic/ Scholarly.*
Indexed: A28, APA, BrCerAb, C&ISA, CA/WCA, CIA, CerAb, CivEngAb, CorrAb, E&CAJ, E11, EEA, EMA, ESPM, EnvEAb, H15, M&TEA, M09, MBF, METADEX, SolStAb, T04, WAA.
—Linda Hall.
Published by: Chulalongkorn University, Metallurgy and Materials Science Research Institute, Soi Chula 12 Phyathai Rd., Bangkok, 10330, Thailand. TEL 66-2-2184210-12, FAX 66-2-6117586, mladda@chula.ac.th, http://www.material.chula.ac.th/.

669 CAN
WASTE PROCESSING AND RECYCLING IN MINERAL AND METALLURGICAL INDUSTRIES III. Text in English. 1998. irreg. CAD 20 per issue (effective 2004).
Published by: Canadian Institute of Mining, Metallurgy and Petroleum, Metallurgical Society, 3400 de Maisonneuve Blvd W, Ste 1210, Montreal, PQ H3Z 3B8, Canada. TEL 514-939-2710, FAX 514-939-2714, cim@cim.org, http://www.cim.org.

338.476 GBR ISSN 1749-3765
WELDED STEEL TUBE AND PIPE MONTHLY. Text in English. 2004. m. **Document type:** *Journal, Trade.* **Description:** Contains up-to-date prices, market trends and developments in key markets and products within the welded steel tube industry.
Formerly (until 2005): Steel Tube and Pipe Monthly (1743-1883)
—CCC.
Published by: Metal Bulletin Plc. (Subsidiary of: Euromoney Institutional Investor Plc.), Nestor House, Playhouse Yard, London, EC4V 5EX, United Kingdom. TEL 44-20-77797390, FAX 44-20-77797389, help@metalbulletin.com, http://www.metalbulletin.com.

671.3 USA ISSN 0361-6304
TN695
WHO'S WHO IN P M. Text in English. a. USD 95 to non-members; USD 65 to members (effective 2008). adv. **Document type:** *Directory, Trade.* **Description:** It is a reference publication in the powder metallurgy and particulate materials industries.
Formerly: American Powder Metallurgy Institute. Membership Directory and Yearbook
Related titles: CD-ROM ed.: USD 125 domestic to non-members; USD 140 foreign to non-members; USD 30 to members (effective 2008).
—CCC.
Published by: American Powder Metallurgy Institute, 105 College Rd E, Princeton, NJ 08540-6992. TEL 609-452-7700, FAX 609-987-8523, apmi@mpif.org.

671.84 DEU ISSN 0043-5996
TS270.A1
WIRE; international technical journal for the wire and cable industry and all areas of wire processing. Text in English. 1951. 2/yr. EUR 33 domestic; EUR 36 foreign (effective 2011). adv. bk.rev. charts; illus. **Document type:** *Magazine, Trade.* **Description:** Covers the manufacture and processing of wire and cable.
Incorporates (1959-1995): Wireworld (0934-5906); Which was formerly (until 1987): Wireworld International (0043-6046)
Related titles: ◆ German ed.: Draht. ISSN 0012-5911.
Indexed: A22, A28, APA, BrCerAb, C&ISA, CA/WCA, CIA, CerAb, ChemAb, CivEngAb, CoppAb, CorrAb, E&CAJ, E11, EEA, EMA, ESPM, EngInd, EnvEAb, H15, Inspec, M&TEA, M09, MBF, METADEX, SCOPUS, SolStAb, T04, WAA.
—BLDSC (9320.350000), IE, Ingenta, INIST, Linda Hall. **CCC.**
Published by: Meisenbach GmbH, Franz-Ludwig-Str 7a, Bamberg, 96047, Germany. TEL 49-951-8610, FAX 49-951-861158, wire@meisenbach.de, http://www.meisenbach.de. Ed. Joerg Dambock. Adv. contact Georg Meisenbach. Circ: 3,770 (paid and controlled).

671.84 GBR ISSN 0043-6011
TS270.A1 CODEN: WIRIAZ
WIRE INDUSTRY; international monthly journal. Text in English. 1934. m. GBP 95 domestic; GBP 135 foreign (effective 2004). adv. bk.rev. bibl.; charts; illus.; pat. index. **Document type:** *Magazine, Trade.* **Description:** Focuses on wire, cable and related products for readers in 128 countries.
Indexed: A22, A28, APA, BrCerAb, C&ISA, CA/WCA, CIA, CPEI, CerAb, ChemAb, CivEngAb, CoppAb, CorrAb, E&CAJ, E11, EEA, EMA, EngInd, H15, M&TEA, M09, MBF, METADEX, SCOPUS, SolStAb, T04, TM, WAA.
—IE, Infotrieve, Ingenta, INIST, Linda Hall. **CCC.**
Published by: Mack Brooks Publishing Ltd., Forum Pl, Hatfield, Herts AL10 0RN, United Kingdom. TEL 44-1707276400, FAX 44-1707276641. Ed. Adam Schulman. Pub. Dave Tellett. Circ: 11,601.

674.84 USA
WIRE INDUSTRY NEWS. Text in English. 1973. bi-w. USD 275 domestic; USD 325 foreign (effective 2000). **Document type:** *Newsletter.* **Description:** Focuses on management, mergers, buy-outs, current events in the industry, promotions and business conditions.
Published by: C R U International, 6305 Ivy Ln., Ste. 422, Greenbelt, MD 20770-6339. TEL 301-441-8997, FAX 301-441-9091. Ed. Karen Chasez.

WIRE ROPE NEWS AND SLING TECHNOLOGY. *see* PACKAGING

338.2741 GBR ISSN 1463-9327
WORLD GOLD ANALYST. Text in English. 1957. q. GBP 245, USD 400 (effective 2010). adv. back issues avail.; reprints avail. **Document type:** *Magazine, Trade.*
Former titles (until 1998): Mining Journal Gold Service International Quarterly (0952-3553); (until 1987): Mining Journal Quarterly Review of South African Gold Shares (0143-3415)
Related titles: Online - full text ed.
—CCC.
Published by: G F M S World Gold, Hedges House, 153 - 155 Regent St, London, W1B 4JE, United Kingdom. TEL 44-20-74781777, FAX 44-20-74781779, info@gfms.co.uk. Ed. Paul Burton TEL 44-20-74781750.

WORLD MATERIALS CALENDAR (ONLINE). *see* MEETINGS AND CONGRESSES

669 622 DEU ISSN 1613-2394
TN3 CODEN: ERZMAK
WORLD OF METALLURGY - ERZMETALL; journal for exploration, mining, processing, metallurgy, recycling and environmental technology. Text in German, English; Summaries in English. 1904. m. EUR 210 domestic; EUR 230 foreign; EUR 42 per issue (effective 2009). adv. bk.rev.; software rev. abstr.; charts; illus.; mkt.; pat.; stat.; maps. index. 64 p./no.; reprints avail. **Document type:** *Journal, Trade.* **Description:** Journal for exploration, mining, processing, recycling and environmental technology.
Former titles (until 2004): Erzmetall (0044-2658); (until 1969): Zeitschrift fuer Erzbergbau und Metallhuettenwesen (0372-848X); (until 1948): Metall und Erz (1011-4602); Which superseded in part (in 1912): Metallurgie (1011-4599)
Related titles: Online - full text ed.
Indexed: A22, AESIS, CEABA, CIN, CISA, CPEI, Cadscan, ChemAb, ChemTitl, CoppAb, EngInd, F&EA, GeoRef, IBR, IBZ, IMMAb, LeadAb, MinerAb, RefZh, SCOPUS, SpeleolAb, TM, Zincscan.
—BLDSC (9356.671750), CASDDS, IE, Infotrieve, Ingenta, INIST, Linda Hall. **CCC.**
Published by: (Gesellschaft fuer Bergbau, Metallurgie, Rohstoff- und Umwelttechnik), G D M B Geschaeftsstelle, Paul Ernst Str 10, Clausthal-Zellerfeld, 38678, Germany. TEL 49-5323-93720, FAX 49-5323-937937, info@gdmb.de, http://www.gdmb.de. Ed. Juergen Zuchowski. adv.: B&W page EUR 2,240, color page EUR 3,029; trim 180 x 270. Circ: 2,600 (paid and controlled).

WORLD STEEL OUTLOOK. *see* BUSINESS AND ECONOMICS—International Commerce

338.2 672 BEL
WORLDSTEEL NEWSLETTER. Text in English. 1998. irreg. (3-4 times a year). free. charts; illus.; stat. **Document type:** *Newsletter, Trade.* **Description:** Reports on news in the international iron and steel marketplace.
Related titles: Online - full content ed.
Published by: International Iron and Steel Institute, Rue Colonel Bourg 120, Brussels, 1140, Belgium. TEL 32-2-7028900, FAX 32-2-7028899, web@iisi.be. Ed. Fiona Brichaut.

669 CHN ISSN 1008-4371
WUGANG JISHU/WUHAN IRON AND STEEL CORPORATION TECHNOLOGY. Text in Chinese. 1963. bi-m. USD 31.20 (effective 2009). **Document type:** *Journal, Academic/Scholarly.*
Related titles: Online - full text ed.
—East View.
Published by: Wuhan Gangtie (Jituan) Gongsi/Wuhan Iron & Steel (Group) Corp., Gangdu Huayuan, 124-men Zonghe Lou, Gang Jishu Zhongxin Xinxisuo, Wuhan, 430081, China. TEL 86-27-86483102, FAX 86-27-86483107.

669 CHN ISSN 1001-1587
WUJIN KEJI. Text in Chinese. 1973. bi-m. CNY 3 per issue. **Description:** Covers research, technology, management in the field of daily use hardware.
Published by: (China Hardware Association), Shenyang Light Industry Research and Design Institute, 7, Ningshan Donglu, Huanggu-qu, Shenyang, Liaoning 110032, China. TEL 465196. Ed. Hou Zhiguang. Circ: 10,000. **Co-sponsor:** Quanguo Riyong Wujin Gongye Keji Qingbaozhan.

669 CHN ISSN 1671-3818
YEJIN CONGKAN/METALLURGICAL COLLECTIONS. Text in Chinese; Abstracts in Chinese, English. 1978. bi-m. back issues avail. **Document type:** *Journal, Academic/Scholarly.*
Published by: (Guangdong Sheng Jinshu Xuehui), Guangzhou Gangtie Qiyejituan Youxian Gongsi, 1, Fangcun Dadao, Guangzhou, 510381, China. TEL 86-20-81899270, FAX 86-20-81899270.

669.1 CHN ISSN 1000-7571
YEJIN FENXI/METALLURGICAL ANALYSIS. Text in Chinese. 1981. bi-m. USD 62.40 (effective 2009).
Related titles: Online - full text ed.
Indexed: A28, APA, BrCerAb, C&ISA, CA/WCA, CIA, CerAb, CivEngAb, CorrAb, E&CAJ, E11, EEA, EMA, ESPM, EngInd, EnvEAb, GeoRef, H15, M&TEA, M09, MBF, METADEX, SCOPUS, SolStAb, T04, TM, WAA.
—BLDSC (5698.050000), East View, Linda Hall.
Published by: Yejinbu Gangtie Yanjiu Zongyuan/Central Iron and Steel Research Institute, 76 Xueyuan Nanlu, Beijin, 100081, China.

669 CHN ISSN 1001-1617
YEJIN NENGYUAN/ENERGY FOR METALLURGICAL INDUSTRY. Text in Chinese. 1982. bi-m. **Document type:** *Trade.* **Description:** Covers energy economics and management, systematic energy saving techniques, waste heat and energy recovery techniques, and energy conversion technology.
Related titles: Online - full text ed.
Published by: Yejin Bu, Anshan Reneng Yanjiusuo/Ministry of Metallurgical Industry, Anshan Research Institute of Thermo-Energy, 43 Luhua St, Tiedong-qu, Anshan, Liaoning 114004, China. TEL 0412-536495. Ed. Huang Renxiang.

669 CHN ISSN 1001-1269
TN675.5
YEJIN SHEBEI/METALLURGICAL EQUIPMENT. Text in Chinese. 1979. bi-m. USD 24.60 (effective 2009). adv. 64 p./no.; **Document type:** *Academic/Scholarly.* **Description:** Covers the latest development of China's metallurgical equipment.
Related titles: Online - full text ed.
Indexed: A28, APA, BrCerAb, C&ISA, CA/WCA, CIA, CerAb, CivEngAb, CorrAb, E&CAJ, E11, EEA, EMA, ESPM, EnvEAb, H15, M&TEA, M09, MBF, METADEX, SolStAb, T04, WAA.
—BLDSC (5698.181000), East View, Linda Hall.
Published by: Beijing Yejin Shebei Yanjiuyuan/Beijing Research Institute of Metallurgical Equipment, PO Box 9821, Beijing, 100029, China. TEL 86-10-6426-9911, FAX 86-10-6426-8694. Ed. Zhongming Chen. Adv. contact Jin Shun.

669 629.8 CHN ISSN 1000-7059 CODEN: YEZIE5
YEJIN ZIDONGHUA/METALLURGICAL INDUSTRY AUTOMATION. Text in Chinese; Abstracts in Chinese, English. 1976. bi-m. CNY 60, USD 60; CNY 10 newsstand/cover (effective 2008). **Document type:** *Magazine, Trade.* **Description:** Covers the latest developments of theoretical and applied researches in the fields of metallurgical industry automation.
Related titles: Online - full text ed.
Indexed: A28, APA, BrCerAb, C&ISA, CA/WCA, CIA, CerAb, CivEngAb, CorrAb, E&CAJ, E11, EEA, EMA, ESPM, EnvEAb, H15, M&TEA, M09, MBF, METADEX, RefZh, SolStAb, T04, WAA.
—Linda Hall.
Published by: Yejin Zidonghua Zazhishe, 72 S Xisihuan Rd, Beijng, 100071, China. TEL 86-10-63815269, FAX 86-10-63841318. Ed. Liying Shen. Circ: 7,500.

YOUKUANGYE/URANIUM MINING AND METALLURGY. *see* MINES AND MINING INDUSTRY

669 CHN ISSN 1001-0211 CODEN: YSCSAE
YOUSE JINSHU/CHINESE JOURNAL OF NONFERROUS METAL. Text in Chinese. 1980. m. USD 20.80 (effective 2009). adv. bk.rev. **Document type:** *Journal, Academic/Scholarly.* **Description:** Covers the fields of geology, mining, mineral processing, metallurgy, materials science and engineering.
Related titles: Online - full text ed.
Indexed: A28, AESIS, APA, BrCerAb, C&ISA, CA/WCA, CIA, CIN, CerAb, ChemAb, ChemTitl, CivEngAb, CorrAb, E&CAJ, E11, EEA, EMA, GeoRef, H15, M&TEA, M09, MBF, METADEX, RefZh, SolStAb, SpeleolAb, T04, WAA.
—BLDSC (6117.069000), CASDDS, East View, IE, Ingenta, Linda Hall.
Published by: Nonferrous Metals Society of China/Zhongguo Youse Jinshu Xuehui, Central South University of Technology, Changsha, 410083, China. TEL 86-731-8876765, FAX 86-731-8877197. adv.: B&W page USD 1,200, color page USD 1,800. Circ: 12,000.

669 CHN ISSN 1674-9669
➤ **YOUSE JINSHU KEXUE YU GONGCHENG/NONFERROUS METALS SCIENCE AND ENGINEERING.** Text in Chinese; Abstracts in Chinese, English. 1987. bi-m. CNY 60, USD 60; CNY 10 per issue (effective 2011 & 2012). adv. abstr. back issues avail. **Document type:** *Journal, Academic/Scholarly.* **Description:** Features articles on metallurgy, material, mining industry, environment; contains a few advertisements.
Formerly (until 2010): Jiangxi Youse Jinshu/Jiangxi Nonferrous Metals (1005-2712)
Related titles: Online - full text ed.
Published by: Youse Jinshu Kexue yu Gongcheng Bianjibu, 86, Hongqi Ave., Ganzhou, Jiangxi 341000, China. TEL 86-797-8312555, FAX 86-797-8312211. Circ: 1,000. **Co-sponsors:** Jiangxi Youse Jinshu Gongye Gongsi; Jiangxi Sheng Youse Jinshu Xuehui.

669 CHN ISSN 1671-9492
YOUSE JINSHU. XUANKUANG BUFEN/NONFERROUS METALS. Text in Chinese. 1949. bi-m. USD 18 (effective 2009). **Document type:** *Journal, Academic/Scholarly.*
Related titles: Online - full text ed.
Published by: Beijing KuangYe Yanjiu Zongyuan/Beijing General Research Institute of Mining & Metallurgy, Xizhimen Wai, Wenxin Jie #1, Beijing, 100044, China. TEL 86-10-88399431, FAX 86-10-88382109, http://www.bgrimm.com/.

620.11 SWE ISSN 0349-4470
YTFORUM. Text in Swedish. 1980. 8/yr. SEK 480 (effective 2001). adv. 3 cols./p.; **Document type:** *Journal, Trade.*
Published by: Ytforum Foerlag, Fack 462, Linkoeping, 58105, Sweden. TEL 46-13-31-41-75, FAX 46-13-14-38-49. Ed., Pub., Adv. contact Goeran Ekstroem. B&W page SEK 9,000, color page SEK 13,500; trim 185 x 265. Circ: 2,500 (paid and controlled).

669 943.7 CZE ISSN 0139-9810
Z DEJIN HUTNICTVI. Text in Czech; Summaries in English, German. 1972. irreg., latest vol.38, 2008. CZK 150 per vol. (effective 2009). illus.; bibl.
Published by: Narodni Technicke Muzeum, Kostelni 42, Prague 7, 17078, Czech Republic. TEL 420-2-20399101, FAX 420-2-20399200, info@ntm.cz, http://www.ntm.cz.

671.2 JPN ISSN 0919-8423 CODEN: ZAIKFC
ZAIKEN/WASEDA UNIVERSITY. KAGAMI MEMORIAL LABORATORY FOR MATERIALS SCIENCE AND TECHNOLOGY. Text in English. 1950. a. free. adv. **Document type:** *Journal, Academic/Scholarly.*
Former titles (until 1993): Waseda University. Report of Materials Science and Technology (0916-6521); (until 1989): Waseda University. Report of Castings Research Laboratory (0511-1927)
Indexed: ChemAb, GeoRef, IBR, IBZ, RefZh, SpeleolAb.
—BLDSC (9425.920330), CASDDS, Linda Hall.

M

Published by: Waseda University, Kagami Memorials Laboratory for Materials Science and Technology, 2-8-26 Nishi-Waseda, Shinjuku-ku, Tokyo, 162-0051, Japan. TEL 81-3-3203-4782, FAX 81-3-3205-1353. Ed. M Nagumo. Adv. contact I Ohdomari. Circ: 500.

620.112 JPN ISSN 0917-0480
TA418.74 CODEN: ZAKAEP
ZAIRYO TO KANKYO/CORROSION ENGINEERING. Text in Japanese; Summaries in English. 1951. m. adv. bk.rev. charts; illus.; pat. Index. back issues avail. **Document type:** *Journal, Academic/Scholarly.*
Formerly (until vol.40, no.1, 1991): Boshoku Gijutsu (0010-9355)
Indexed: A22, CIN, CPEI, ChemAb, ChemTitl, EngInd, INIS AtomInd, Inspec, JTA, RefZh, SCOPUS.
—BLDSC (3473.600000), CASDDS, IE, Ingenta, INIST, Linda Hall. **CCC.**
Published by: Fushoku Boshoku Kyokai/Japan Society of Corrosion Engineering, 1-33-3 Hongo, Bunkyo-ku, Tokyo Pro. Bldg, 2nd Fl, Tokyo, 113-0033, Japan. TEL 81-3-38151161, FAX 81-3-38151291, jim@jcorr.or.jp. Ed. Katsuhisa Sugimoto. Adv. contact Koji Yamakawa. Circ: 1,200.

669 JPN ISSN 0914-6628
TS300
➤ **ZAIRYO TO PUROSESU/CURRENT ADVANCES IN MATERIALS AND PROCESSES.** Text mainly in Japanese; Text occasionally in English. 1988. irreg. **Document type:** *Journal, Academic/Scholarly.*
Supersedes in part (in 1988): Tetsu to Hagane (0021-1575)
Indexed: A22, TM.
—BLDSC (3494.064250), IE, Ingenta. **CCC.**
Published by: Nippon Tekko Kyokai/Iron and Steel Institute of Japan, Niikura Bldg, 2nd Fl, 2 Kanda-Tsukasacho 2-chome, Chiyoda-ku, Tokyo, 101-0048, Japan. TEL 81-3-52097011, FAX 81-3-32571110, admin@isij.or.jp, editol@isij.or.jp, http://www.isij.or.jp. Ed. Hiroshi Itaya. Pub. Yasuo Uchinaka. R&P Yoshihiro Kuwabara.

➤ **ZAMBIA CONSOLIDATED COPPER MINES LTD. ANNUAL REPORT AND ACCOUNTS.** *see* MINES AND MINING INDUSTRY

669 622 CHN ISSN 1004-0609
TA479.3 CODEN: ZYJXFK
ZHONGGUO YOUSE JINSHU XUEBAO. Text in Chinese. 1990. bi-m. (q. until 2001). USD 159.60 (effective 2009). **Document type:** *Journal, Academic/Scholarly.* **Description:** Publishes research papers on the latest developments in the fields of nonferrous metals and mining technology.
Related titles: Online - full text ed.; ◆ English ed.: Nonferrous Metals Society of China. Transactions. ISSN 1003-6326.
Indexed: A22, A28, APA, BrCerAb, C&ISA, CA/WCA, CIA, CPEI, CerAb, CivEngAb, CorrAb, E&CAJ, E11, EEA, EMA, ESPM, EngInd, EnvEAb, GeoRef, H15, Inspec, M&TEA, M09, MBF, METADEX, RefZh, SCOPUS, SolStAb, T04, WAA.
—BLDSC (3180.436700), AskIEEE, CASDDS, East View, IE, Ingenta, Linda Hall.
Published by: Nonferrous Metals Society of China/Zhongguo Youse Jinshu Xuehui, Central South University of Technology, Changsha, 410083, China. FAX 86-731-8877197, http://www.csut.edu.cn/~f-ysxb/. Circ: 400 (paid); 700 (controlled). **Dist. overseas by:** Allerton Press, Inc., 18 W 27th St, New York, NY 10001. TEL 646-424-9686, FAX 646-424-9695, journals@allertonpress.com, http://www.allertonpress.com.

628.4458 CHN ISSN 1008-9500
ZHONGGUO ZIYUAN ZONGHE LIYONG/CHINA RESOURCES COMPREHENSIVE UTILIZATION. Text in Chinese; Summaries in English. 1982. m. USD 49.20 (effective 2009). adv. 48 p./no.; **Document type:** *Journal, Academic/Scholarly.* **Description:** Covers recycling valuable components from secondary resources.
Former titles (until 1999): Zhongguo Wuzi Zaisheng (1004-0986); Jinshu Zaisheng (1001-4446)
Related titles: Diskette ed.; Online - full content ed.; Online - full text ed.
—East View.
Published by: China Resources Comprehensive Utilization Periodical Office, Bureau of Domestic Trades, Huanghe Nanlu 65, Xuzhou, Jiangsu 221006, China. TEL 86-516-5736600, FAX 86-516-5736119, crcu@pub.xz.jsinfo.net. R&Ps Jun Chen, Zhai Xin TEL 86-516-5736600. Adv. contact Jun Chen. Circ: 5,000. **Dist. by:** China National Publishing and Foreign Trade Co., PO Box 782, Beijing, China.

ZHONGNAN DAXUE XUEBAO (ZIRAN KEXUE BAN)/CENTRAL SOUTH UNIVERSITY. JOURNAL (SCIENCE AND TECHNOLOGY). *see* MINES AND MINING INDUSTRY

681.7669 CHN ISSN 1001-4977
TS228.99 CODEN: ZHUZET
ZHUZAO/FOUNDRY. Text in Chinese. 1952. m. CNY 18 per issue (effective 2011). **Document type:** *Journal, Academic/Scholarly.*
Formerly (until 1983): Zhugong
Related titles: Online - full text ed.
Indexed: A28, APA, BrCerAb, C&ISA, CA/WCA, CIA, CerAb, CivEngAb, CorrAb, E&CAJ, E11, EEA, EMA, EngInd, H15, M&TEA, M09, MBF, METADEX, SCOPUS, SolStAb, T04, TM, WAA.
—BLDSC (4026.010000), East View, Linda Hall.
Published by: Shenyang Zhuzao Yanjiusuo/Shenyang Research Institute of Foundry, 17, Yunfeng Nan Jie, Tiexi-qu, Shenyang, 110022, China. TEL 86-24-25847830.

671.2 CHN ISSN 1000-8365
CODEN: ZHUJEF
ZHUZAO JISHU/FOUNDRY TECHNOLOGY. Text in Chinese. 1979. bi-m. USD 74.40 (effective 2009). adv. abstr.; bibl.; charts; illus.; mkt. back issues avail. **Document type:** *Journal, Academic/Scholarly.* **Description:** Covers casting theory and methods, applied foundry technology research, and energy saving and environment protection of foundry.
Related titles: CD-ROM ed.; Online - full text ed.
Indexed: A28, APA, BrCerAb, C&ISA, CA/WCA, CIA, CIN, CerAb, ChemAb, ChemTitl, CivEngAb, CorrAb, E&CAJ, E11, EEA, EMA, ESPM, EngInd, EnvEAb, H15, M&TEA, M09, MBF, METADEX, SCOPUS, SolStAb, T04, WAA.
—BLDSC (4027.800000), CASDDS, East View, IE, Ingenta.
Published by: Xi'an Shi Zhuzao Xuehui/Xi'an Foundryman's Society, 5, Jinhua Nanlu, Box 608, Xi'an University of Technology, Xi'an, Shaanxi 710048, China. TEL 86-29-82312292, FAX 86-29-83282430, http://www.formarket.net/. adv.: B&W page USD 300, color page USD 600; trim 210 x 2297. **Dist. overseas by:** China International Book Trading Corp, 35 Chegongzhuang Xilu, Haidian District, PO Box 399, Beijing 100044, China. TEL 86-10-68412045, FAX 86-10-68412023, cibtc@mail.cibtc.com.cn, http://www.cibtc.com.cn.

METALLURGY—Abstracting, Bibliographies, Statistics

669.722 016 USA ISSN 1066-0623
Z6679.A47
ALUMINUM INDUSTRY ABSTRACTS; a monthly review of the world's technical literature on aluminum. Text in English. 1968. bi-m. (plus a CD index). USD 1,365 combined subscription (includes a. index on CD-ROM) (effective 2011). abstr. Index. **Document type:** *Abstract/Index.* **Description:** Compendium of information on aluminium and its alloys derived from the business and technical literature published worldwide.
Formerly (until 1991): World Aluminum Abstracts (0002-6697)
—Linda Hall.
Published by: (Aluminum Association), ProQuest LLC (Bethesda) (Subsidiary of: Cambridge Information Group), 7200 Wisconsin Ave, Ste 715, Bethesda, MD 20814. TEL 301-961-6798, 800-843-7751, FAX 301-961-6799, journals@csa.com, service@csa.com. Eds. Eileen De Guire, Kathleen Hickman, Scott Ryan. Circ: 1,100. **Co-sponsors:** European Aluminum Association; Aluminum Development Council; Japan Light Metal Association.

669.021 GBR ISSN 1360-8444
ANNUAL STAINLESS STEEL STATISTICS. Text in English. 1972. a. GBP 500 per issue (print or online ed.); GBP 600 combined subscription per issue (print & online ed.) (effective 2009). **Document type:** *Bulletin.* **Description:** Presents data from diverse sources in a common format for all countries.
Formerly (until 1995): World Stainless Steel Statistics (0141-0806)
Related titles: Online - full text ed.
Published by: World Bureau of Metal Statistics, 27a High St, Ware, Herts SG12 9BA, United Kingdom. TEL 44-1920-461274, FAX 44-1920-464258, enquiries@world-bureau.co.uk. Ed. J L T Davies.

669.1 622 CHL
ANUARIO ESTADISTICO DE LA SIDERURGIA Y MINERIA DE HIERRO EN AMERICA LATINA. Text in Spanish; Index in English. a. USD 95 in the Americas to members; USD 110 elsewhere to members; USD 125 in the Americas to non-members; USD 140 elsewhere to non-members (effective 2002).
Published by: Instituto Latinoamericano del Fierro y el Acero, Calle Benjamin 2944, 5o piso - Las Condes, Santiago, 9, Chile. TEL 56-2-2330545, FAX 56-2-2330768, ilafa@entelchile.net.

AVANCE DE INFORMACION ECONOMICA. INDUSTRIA MINEROMETALURGICA. *see* MINES AND MINING INDUSTRY—Abstracting, Bibliographies, Statistics

C A SELECTS. INORGANIC & ORGANOMETALLIC REACTION MECHANISMS. *see* CHEMISTRY—Abstracting, Bibliographies, Statistics

C A SELECTS. METALLO ENZYMES & METALLO COENZYMES. *see* CHEMISTRY—Abstracting, Bibliographies, Statistics

669.7 016 USA ISSN 0749-7350
CODEN: CSSCEC
C A SELECTS. SELENIUM & TELLURIUM CHEMISTRY. Text in English. 1984. s-w. looseleaf. USD 385 to non-members; USD 115 to members; USD 575 combined subscription to individuals (print & online eds.) (effective 2010). abstr. index. **Document type:** *Abstract/Index.* **Description:** Covers all aspects of selenium and tellurium chemistry.
Incorporates: Selenium and Tellurium Abstracts (0037-1467)
Related titles: Online - full text ed.: USD 380 to non-members; USD 114 to members (effective 2011).
—Linda Hall.
Published by: Chemical Abstracts Service (Subsidiary of: American Chemical Society), 2540 Olentangy River Rd, Columbus, OH 43210-0012. TEL 614-447-3600, FAX 614-447-3713, help@cas.com, http://caselects.cas.org. Circ: 800. **Subscr. to:** PO Box 3012, Columbus, OH 43210. TEL 800-753-4227, FAX 614-447-3751.

669 USA ISSN 0148-2440
CODEN: CSCMDT
C A SELECTS. SILVER CHEMISTRY. Text in English. s-w. USD 385 to non-members; USD 115 to members; USD 575 combined subscription to individuals (print & online eds.) (effective 2011). **Document type:** *Abstract/Index.* **Description:** Covers the chemistry and chemical technology of silver and silver-containing compounds.
Related titles: Online - full text ed.: USD 380 to non-members; USD 114 to members (effective 2011).
Published by: Chemical Abstracts Service (Subsidiary of: American Chemical Society), 2540 Olentangy River Rd, Columbus, OH 43210-0012. TEL 614-447-3600, FAX 614-447-3713, help@cas.com, http://caselects.cas.org. **Subscr. to:** PO Box 3012, Columbus, OH 43210. TEL 800-753-4227, FAX 614-447-3751.

016.669 USA
C S A MATERIALS RESEARCH DATABASE WITH METADEX. Text in English. base vol. plus m. updates. **Document type:** *Database, Abstract/Index.* **Description:** This database brings together in one place the majority of the leading materials science databases, with specialist content on materials science, metallurgy, ceramics, polymers, and composites used in engineering application.
Media: Online - full text.
Published by: ProQuest LLC (Bethesda) (Subsidiary of: Cambridge Information Group), 7200 Wisconsin Ave, Ste 715, Bethesda, MD 20814.

338.4 CAN ISSN 1481-9805
CANADA. STATISTICS CANADA. FABRICATED METAL PRODUCTS INDUSTRIES (ONLINE)/CANADA. STATISTIQUE CANADA. INDUSTRIES DE LA FABRICATION DES PRODUITS METALLIQUES. Text in English, French. 1985. a. CAD 40 domestic; USD 40 foreign (effective 1999). **Document type:** *Government.* **Description:** Provides the number of establishments, number of employees, salaries and wages, cost of materials and fuel, value of shipments and value added.
Formerly (until 199?): Canada. Statistics Canada. Fabricated Metal Products Industries (Print) (0835-0124); Which was formed by the merger of (1927-1985): Wire and Wire Products Industries (0828-9913); Which was formerly (until 1983): Wire and Wire Products Manufacturers (0576-0062); (until 1960): Wire and Wire Goods Industry (0384-479X); (until 1948): Wire and Wire Goods Industry in Canada (0830-1700); Canada. Statistics Canada. Fabricated Metal Products Industries was formed by the merger of (1960-1985): Other Metal Fabricating Industries (0828-9948); Which was formerly (until 1983): Miscellaneous Metal Fabricating Industries (0575-903X); Which was formed by the merger of (1948-1960): Iron Castings Industry (0700-0944); Which was formerly (until 1948): Iron Castings Industry in Canada (0826-6336); (1933-1960): Miscellaneous Non-Ferrous Metal Products Industry (0410-5516); (1930-1960): Brass and Copper Products Industry (0700-0979); Which was formerly (until 1949): Brass & Copper Products Industry in Canada (0826-6328); (194?-1960): Miscellaneous Iron and Steel Products Industry (0700-0987); Which was formerly (until 1948): Miscellaneous Iron and Steel Products Industry in Canada (0826-6344); Canada. Statistics Canada. Fabricated Metal Products Industries was formed by the merger of (194?-1985): Machine Shop Industry (0828-9816); Which was formerly (until 1983): Machine Shops (0384-3963); (until 1960): Machine Shops Industry (0384-3971); (until 1948): Machine Shops Industry in Canada (0826-824X); Canada. Statistics Canada. Fabricated Metal Products Industries was formed by the merger of (1948-1985): Heating Equipment Industry (0828-993X); Which was formerly (until 1983): Heating Equipment Manufacturers (0575-870X); Which superseded in part (in 1960): Boilers and Plate Work Industry (0700-0383); Which was formerly (until 1951): Boilers, Tanks and Plate Work Industry (0833-2061); Heating Equipment Manufacturers superseded in part (in 1959): Heating and Cooking Apparatus Industry (0527-5393); Which was formerly (until 1949): Cooking and Heating Apparatus Industry in Canada; Canada. Statistics Canada. Fabricated Metal Products Industries was formed by the merger of (1981-1985): Power Boilers, Heat Exchanger and Fabricated Structural Metal Products Industries (0828-9956); Which was formerly (until 1983): Fabricated Structural Metal, Boiler and Plate Works (0319-8979); Which was formed by the merger of (1948-1981): Boiler and Plate Works (0527-4842); (1960-1981): Fabricated Structural Metal Industry (0527-5091); Which was formerly (until 1959): Bridge Building and Structural Steel Industry (0700-0421); (until 1949): Bridge and Structural Steel Industry; Canada. Statistics Canada. Fabricated Metal Products Industries was formed by the merger of (1983-1985): Hardware, Tool and Cutlery Industries (0828-9905); Which was formerly (until 1982): Hardware, Tool and Cutlery Manufacturers (0575-8696); (until 1959): Hardware, Tools and Cutlery Industry (0384-3408); (until 1948): Hardware, Tools and Cutlery Industry in Canada; Canada. Statistics Canada. Fabricated Metal Products Industries was formed by the merger of (194?-1985): Ornamental and Architectural Metal Products Industry (0828-9921); Which was formerly (until 1982): Ornamental and Architectural Metal Industry (0527-5997); Which superseded in part (in 1959): Sheet Metal Products Industry (0700-0995); Which was formerly (until 1947): Sheet Metal Products Industry in Canada (0826-6859); Canada. Statistics Canada. Fabricated Metal Products Industries was formed by the merger of (1943-1985): Stamped, Pressed and Coated Metal Products Industries (0828-9794); Which was formerly (until 1984): Metal Stamping, Pressing and Coating Industry (0527-5687); Which superseded in part (in 1960): Aluminum Products Industry (0700-0928)
Related titles: Microform ed.: (from MML); Online - full text ed.
Published by: Statistics Canada, Operations and Integration Division (Subsidiary of: Statistics Canada/Statistique Canada), Circulation Management, 120 Parkdale Ave, Ottawa, ON K1A 0T6, Canada. TEL 613-951-7277, 800-267-6677, FAX 613-951-1584.

669.1 CAN ISSN 0380-7851
CANADA. STATISTICS CANADA. PRIMARY IRON AND STEEL/ CANADA. STATISTIQUE CANADA. FER ET ACIER PRIMAIRE. Text in English, French. 1946. m. CAD 41 domestic; USD 41 foreign (effective 1999). **Document type:** *Government.* **Description:** Provides current data on the Canadian iron and steel industry.
Related titles: Online - full text ed.
Published by: Statistics Canada, Operations and Integration Division (Subsidiary of: Statistics Canada/Statistique Canada), Circulation Management, 120 Parkdale Ave, Ottawa, ON K1A 0T6, Canada. TEL 613-951-7277, 800-267-6677, FAX 613-951-1584.

CORROSION ABSTRACTS. *see* ENGINEERING—Abstracting, Bibliographies, Statistics

338.3 672 BEL
CRUDE STEEL PRODUCTION. Text in English. m. free to members; EUR 250 to non-members (effective 2001). **Description:** Reports on crude steel production worldwide, including comparisons with previous month and previous year.
Related titles: Online - full text ed.
Published by: International Iron and Steel Institute, Rue Colonel Bourg 120, Brussels, 1140, Belgium. TEL 32-2-702-8900, FAX 32-2-702-8899.

669 LUX ISSN 1609-4107
EISEN UND STAHL - JAEHRLICHE STATISTIKEN. Text in English, German, French. 1982. a. **Document type:** *Bulletin, Trade.*
Former titles (until 1996): EUROSTAT. Jern og Stal. Staststisk Arbog (1016-9393); (until 1987): EUROSTAT. Jahrbuch Eisen und Stahl (0256-7806)
Published by: (European Commission, Statistical Office of the European Communities (E U R O S T A T)), European Commission, Office for Official Publications of the European Union, 2 Rue Mercier, Luxembourg, L-2985, Luxembourg. TEL 352-29291, FAX 352-29291, info@publications.europa.eu, http://publications.europa.eu.

ESTADISTICAS DEL COBRE Y OTROS MINERALES ANUARIO. *see* MINES AND MINING INDUSTRY—Abstracting, Bibliographies, Statistics

669.016 DEU ISSN 0721-9679
GIESSEREI-LITERATURSCHAU. Text in German. 1982. m. EUR 200 (effective 2005). bk.rev. **Document type:** *Journal, Trade.*
Description: Comprehensive information about new publications in the field of foundry technology, including related issues such as environmental protection, energy industry, and industrial safety.
Published by: Verein Deutscher Giessereifachleute, Sohnstr 70, Duesseldorf, 40237, Germany. TEL 49-211-6871254, FAX 49-211-6871361, infozentrum@vdg.de, http://www.vdg.de. Circ: 200.

669.22 016 GBR ISSN 1027-8591
TN760 CODEN: GLDBBS
➤ **GOLD BULLETIN.** Text in English. 1968. q. free (effective 2011). bk.rev. abstr.; illus. **Document type:** *Bulletin, Academic/Scholarly.*
Description: Focuses on the latest science, technology and applications of gold. Includes papers on the latest research advances, reviews, conference reports and highlights of patents and scientific literature.
Former titles (until 1996): Gold Bulletin and Gold Patent Digest (1016-5339); (until 1968): Gold Bulletin (0017-1557); Which incorporates (1983-1988): Gold Patent Digest (0258-7262)
Related titles: Online - full text ed.: ISSN 2190-7579. free (effective 2011).
Indexed: A01, A20, A26, A28, A39, AESIS, APA, B02, BrArAb, BrCerAb, C&ISA, C27, C29, CA, CA/WCA, CIA, CIN, CTE, CerAb, ChemAb, ChemTitl, CivEngAb, CorrAb, CurCont, D03, D04, E&CAJ, E11, E13, EEA, EMA, FR, G04, G08, GeoRef, H15, I05, IMMAb, ISAP, Inspec, M&TEA, M09, MBF, METADEX, MSCI, NumL, P30, R14, S14, S15, S18, SCI, SCOPUS, SolStAb, T02, T04, W07, WAA.
—CASDDS, IE, Ingenta, INIST, Linda Hall.
Published by: World Gold Council, 55 Old Broad St, London, EC2M 1RX, United Kingdom. TEL 44-20-78264700, FAX 44-20-78264799, info@gold.org, http://www.gold.org/. Eds. Dr. Christopher W Corti, Richard J Holliday.

669.142 GBR
GUIDE TO THE CLASSIFICATION OF STEEL INDUSTRY PRODUCTS IN THE U.K. CUSTOMS TARIFF AND COMBINED NOMENCLATURE OF THE EUROPEAN UNION (YEAR). Text in English. 19??. a. GBP 60 per issue to non-members; GBP 48 per issue to members (effective 2010). **Document type:** *Directory, Trade.*
Description: Explains the relationship between the UK and EU 8 digit customs tariff by using products of the steel industry as example.
Former titles (until 1994): Guide to the Classification of Steel Industry Products in the U.K. Customs Tariff and E E C Combined Nomenclature; (until 1993): Guide to the Classification of Steel Industry Products in the Customs Tariff of the European Communities; Guide to the Classification of Steel Industry Products in the U K Customs Tariff
Published by: I S S B Ltd., 1 Carlton House Ter, London, SW1Y 5DB, United Kingdom. TEL 44-20-73433900, FAX 44-20-73433901, info@issb.co.uk.

I M M ABSTRACTS. (Institution of Mining and Metallurgy) *see* MINES AND MINING INDUSTRY—Abstracting, Bibliographies, Statistics

INFORMATIONSDIENST F I Z TECHNIK. BESCHICHTEN, BESCHICHTUNGSANLAGEN, OBERFLAECHENBEHANDLUNG. *see* ENGINEERING—Abstracting, Bibliographies, Statistics

INSTYTUT OBROBKI SKRAWANIEM. PRZEGLAD DOKUMENTACYJNY. *see* ENGINEERING—Abstracting, Bibliographies, Statistics

669.1 GBR ISSN 0961-2904
INTERNATIONAL STEEL STATISTICS - AUSTRALIA. Text in English. 1970. a. GBP 195 per issue to non-members; GBP 156 per issue to members (effective 2010). **Document type:** *Report, Trade.*
Description: Covers the production, consumption, and import and export of iron and steel products by quality and market in Australia.
Former titles (until 1990): International Steel Statistics - Australia and New Zealand (0952-5831); (until 1980): International Steel Statistics. Australia
Related titles: Online - full text ed.; Series of: International Steel Statistics Country Books Series.
Published by: I S S B Ltd., 1 Carlton House Ter, London, SW1Y 5DB, United Kingdom. TEL 44-20-73433900, FAX 44-20-73433901, info@issb.co.uk.

669.1 GBR ISSN 0952-584X
INTERNATIONAL STEEL STATISTICS - AUSTRIA. Text in English. 1970. a. GBP 195 per issue to non-members; GBP 156 per issue to members (effective 2010). **Document type:** *Yearbook, Trade.*
Description: Provides information on the production, consumption, import and export of iron and steel products by quality and market in Austria.
Related titles: Online - full text ed.; Series of: International Steel Statistics Country Books Series.
Published by: I S S B Ltd., 1 Carlton House Ter, London, SW1Y 5DB, United Kingdom. TEL 44-20-73433900, FAX 44-20-73433901, info@issb.co.uk.

669.1 GBR ISSN 0952-5858
INTERNATIONAL STEEL STATISTICS - BELGIUM, LUXEMBOURG. Text in English. 1979. a. GBP 195 per issue to non-members; GBP 156 per issue to members (effective 2010). **Document type:** *Yearbook, Trade.* **Description:** Provides information on the consumption, production, and export and import of steel products by quality and market in Belgium and Luxemburg.
Related titles: Online - full text ed.; Series of: International Steel Statistics Country Books Series.
Published by: I S S B Ltd., 1 Carlton House Ter, London, SW1Y 5DB, United Kingdom. TEL 44-20-73433900, FAX 44-20-73433901, info@issb.co.uk.

669.1 GBR ISSN 0952-5866
INTERNATIONAL STEEL STATISTICS - BRAZIL. Text in English. 1970. a. GBP 195 per issue to non-members; GBP 156 per issue to members (effective 2010). **Document type:** *Yearbook, Trade.*
Description: Covers the production, consumption, and import and export of iron and steel products by quality and market in Brazil.
Related titles: Online - full text ed.; Series of: International Steel Statistics Country Books Series.
Published by: I S S B Ltd., 1 Carlton House Ter, London, SW1Y 5DB, United Kingdom. TEL 44-20-73433900, FAX 44-20-73433901, info@issb.co.uk.

669.1 GBR ISSN 0952-5874
INTERNATIONAL STEEL STATISTICS - CANADA. Text in English. 1970. a. GBP 195 per issue to non-members; GBP 156 per issue to members (effective 2010). **Document type:** *Yearbook, Trade.*
Description: Provides information on the production, consumption, and import and export of iron and steel products by quality and market in Canada.
Related titles: Online - full text ed.; Series of: International Steel Statistics Country Books Series.
Published by: I S S B Ltd., 1 Carlton House Ter, London, SW1Y 5DB, United Kingdom. TEL 44-20-73433900, FAX 44-20-73433901, info@issb.co.uk.

669.1 GBR ISSN 1475-5602
INTERNATIONAL STEEL STATISTICS - CHINA. Text in English. 2001. a. GBP 195 per issue to non-members; GBP 156 per issue to members (effective 2010). **Document type:** *Yearbook, Trade.* **Description:** Provides information on the production, consumption, and import and export of iron and steel products by quality and market in China.
Related titles: Online - full text ed.
Published by: I S S B Ltd., 1 Carlton House Ter, London, SW1Y 5DB, United Kingdom. TEL 44-20-73433900, FAX 44-20-73433901, info@issb.co.uk.

669.1 GBR ISSN 0960-2372
INTERNATIONAL STEEL STATISTICS - DENMARK. Text in English. 1979. a. GBP 195 per issue to non-members; GBP 156 per issue to members (effective 2010). **Document type:** *Yearbook, Trade.*
Description: Provides information on the production, consumption, and import and export of iron and steel products by quality and market in Denmark.
Supersedes in part (in 1989): International Steel Statistics - Denmark and Greece (0952-5882); Which was formerly (until 1984): International Steel Statistics. Denmark
Related titles: Online - full text ed.; Series of: International Steel Statistics Country Books Series.
Published by: I S S B Ltd., 1 Carlton House Ter, London, SW1Y 5DB, United Kingdom. TEL 44-20-73433900, FAX 44-20-73433901, info@issb.co.uk.

669.1 GBR ISSN 0952-5890
INTERNATIONAL STEEL STATISTICS - FINLAND. Text in English. 1970. a. GBP 195 per issue to non-members; GBP 156 per issue to members (effective 2010). **Document type:** *Yearbook, Trade.*
Description: Covers the production, consumption, and import and export of iron and steel products by quality and market in Finland.
Related titles: Online - full text ed.; Series of: International Steel Statistics Country Books Series.
Published by: I S S B Ltd., 1 Carlton House Ter, London, SW1Y 5DB, United Kingdom. TEL 44-20-73433900, FAX 44-20-73433901, info@issb.co.uk.

669.1 GBR ISSN 0952-5904
INTERNATIONAL STEEL STATISTICS - FRANCE. Text in English. 1970. a. GBP 195 per issue to non-members; GBP 156 per issue to members (effective 2010). **Document type:** *Yearbook, Trade.*
Description: Provides information on the production, consumption, and import and export of iron and steel products by quality and market in France.
Related titles: Online - full text ed.; Series of: International Steel Statistics Country Books Series.
Published by: I S S B Ltd., 1 Carlton House Ter, London, SW1Y 5DB, United Kingdom. TEL 44-20-73433900, FAX 44-20-73433901, info@issb.co.uk.

669.1 GBR ISSN 1472-5045
INTERNATIONAL STEEL STATISTICS - GERMANY. Text in English. 1970. a. GBP 195 per issue to non-members; GBP 156 per issue to members (effective 2010). **Document type:** *Yearbook, Trade.*
Description: Provides information on the consumption, production, and export and import of iron and steel products by quality and market in Germany.
Former titles (until 1997): International Steel Statistics - Federal Republic of Germany (0952-5912); (until 1981): International Steel Statistics - Germany
Related titles: Online - full text ed.; Series of: International Steel Statistics Country Books Series.
Published by: I S S B Ltd., 1 Carlton House Ter, London, SW1Y 5DB, United Kingdom. TEL 44-20-73433900, FAX 44-20-73433901, info@issb.co.uk.

669.1 GBR ISSN 0960-2380
INTERNATIONAL STEEL STATISTICS - GREECE. Text in English. a. GBP 195 per issue to non-members; GBP 156 per issue to members (effective 2010). **Document type:** *Yearbook, Trade.* **Description:** Provides information on the consumption, production, and export and import of iron and steel products by quality and market in Greece.
Supersedes in part (in 1989): International Steel Statistics. Denmark and Greece (0952-5882); Which was formerly (until 1984): International Steel Statistics. Denmark
Related titles: Online - full text ed.; Series of: International Steel Statistics Country Books Series.
Published by: I S S B Ltd., 1 Carlton House Ter, London, SW1Y 5DB, United Kingdom. TEL 44-20-73433900, FAX 44-20-73433901, info@issb.co.uk.

669.1 GBR ISSN 0952-5920
INTERNATIONAL STEEL STATISTICS - IRISH REPUBLIC. Text in English. 1970. a. GBP 195 per issue to non-members; GBP 156 per issue to members (effective 2010). **Document type:** *Yearbook, Trade.* **Description:** Covers the production, consumption, and import and export of iron and steel products by quality and market in Ireland.
Formerly (until 1980): International Steel Statistics. Irish Republic, New Zealand, Hong Kong
Related titles: Online - full text ed.; Series of: International Steel Statistics Country Books Series.
Published by: I S S B Ltd., 1 Carlton House Ter, London, SW1Y 5DB, United Kingdom. TEL 44-20-73433900, FAX 44-20-73433901, info@issb.co.uk.

669.1 GBR ISSN 0952-5939
INTERNATIONAL STEEL STATISTICS - ITALY. Text in English. 1970. a. GBP 195 per issue to non-members; GBP 156 per issue to members (effective 2010). **Document type:** *Yearbook, Trade.* **Description:** Provides information on the production, consumption, and import and export of iron and steel products by quality and market in Italy.
Related titles: Online - full text ed.; Series of: International Steel Statistics Country Books Series.
Published by: I S S B Ltd., 1 Carlton House Ter, London, SW1Y 5DB, United Kingdom. TEL 44-20-73433900, FAX 44-20-73433901, info@issb.co.uk.

669.1 GBR ISSN 0952-5947
INTERNATIONAL STEEL STATISTICS - JAPAN. Text in English. 1970. a. GBP 195 per issue to non-members; GBP 156 per issue to members (effective 2010). **Document type:** *Yearbook, Trade.* **Description:** Covers the production, consumption, and import and export of iron and steel products by quality and market in Japan.
Related titles: Online - full text ed.; Series of: International Steel Statistics Country Books Series.
Published by: I S S B Ltd., 1 Carlton House Ter, London, SW1Y 5DB, United Kingdom. TEL 44-20-73433900, FAX 44-20-73433901, info@issb.co.uk.

669.1 GBR ISSN 0952-6005
INTERNATIONAL STEEL STATISTICS - NETHERLANDS. Text in English. 1970. a. GBP 195 per issue to non-members; GBP 156 per issue to members (effective 2010). **Document type:** *Yearbook, Trade.* **Description:** Supplies information on the consumption and production, and import and export of iron and steel products by quality and market in the Netherlands.
Related titles: Online - full text ed.; Series of: International Steel Statistics Country Books Series.
Published by: I S S B Ltd., 1 Carlton House Ter, London, SW1Y 5DB, United Kingdom. TEL 44-20-73433900, FAX 44-20-73433901, info@issb.co.uk.

669.1 GBR ISSN 0952-6013
INTERNATIONAL STEEL STATISTICS - NORWAY. Text in English. 1970. a. GBP 195 per issue to non-members; GBP 156 per issue to members (effective 2010). **Document type:** *Yearbook, Trade.*
Description: Covers the production, consumption, and import and export of iron and steel products by quality and market in Norway.
Related titles: Online - full text ed.; Series of: International Steel Statistics Country Books Series.
Published by: I S S B Ltd., 1 Carlton House Ter, London, SW1Y 5DB, United Kingdom. TEL 44-20-73433900, FAX 44-20-73433901, info@issb.co.uk.

669.1021 GBR ISSN 0958-4951
INTERNATIONAL STEEL STATISTICS - PORTUGAL. Text in English. 19??. a. GBP 195 per issue to non-members; GBP 156 per issue to members (effective 2010). **Document type:** *Yearbook, Trade.*
Description: Provides information on the consumption, production, and export and import of iron and steel products by quality and market in Portugal.
Supersedes in part (in 1989): International Steel Statistics - Spain and Portugal (0952-6129); Which was formerly (until 1988): International Steel Statistics - Spain (0954-6472); International Steel Statistics. Spain and Portugal superseded in part (in 1988): International Steel Statistics - Eastern European Countries, Portugal, Turkey, Yugoslavia (0957-2759); Which superseded in part (in 1983): International Steel Statistics - Eastern European Countries, Greece, Turkey, Yugoslavia
Related titles: Online - full text ed.; Series of: International Steel Statistics Country Books Series.
Published by: I S S B Ltd., 1 Carlton House Ter, London, SW1Y 5DB, United Kingdom. TEL 44-20-73433900, FAX 44-20-73433901, info@issb.co.uk.

669.1 GBR ISSN 1474-2489
INTERNATIONAL STEEL STATISTICS - RUSSIA. Text in English. 2001. a. GBP 195 per issue to non-members; GBP 156 per issue to members (effective 2010). **Document type:** *Yearbook, Trade.*
Description: Provides information on the production, consumption, and import and export of iron and steel products by quality and market in Russia.
Related titles: Online - full text ed.
Published by: I S S B Ltd., 1 Carlton House Ter, London, SW1Y 5DB, United Kingdom. TEL 44-20-73433900, FAX 44-20-73433901, info@issb.co.uk.

669.1 GBR ISSN 0952-603X
INTERNATIONAL STEEL STATISTICS - SOUTH KOREA. Text in English. 1970. a. GBP 195 per issue to non-members; GBP 156 per issue to members (effective 2010). **Document type:** *Yearbook, Trade.* **Description:** Provides information on the production, consumption, and import and export of iron and steel products by quality and market in South Korea.
Related titles: Online - full text ed.; Series of: International Steel Statistics Country Books Series.
Published by: I S S B Ltd., 1 Carlton House Ter, London, SW1Y 5DB, United Kingdom. TEL 44-20-73433900, FAX 44-20-73433901, info@issb.co.uk.

669.1021 GBR ISSN 0958-4943
INTERNATIONAL STEEL STATISTICS - SPAIN. Text in English. 1970. a. GBP 195 per issue to non-members; GBP 156 per issue to members (effective 2010). stat. **Document type:** *Yearbook, Trade.*
Description: Covers the production, consumption, and import and export of iron and steel products by quality and market in Spain.
Supersedes in part (in 1989): International Steel Statistics - Spain and Portugal (0952-6129); Which was formerly (until 1988): International Steel Statistics - Spain (0954-6472); International Steel Statistics. Spain and Portugal superseded in part (in 1988): International Steel Statistics - Eastern European Countries, Portugal, Turkey, Yugoslavia (0957-2759); Which superseded in part (in 1983): International Steel Statistics - Eastern European Countries, Greece, Turkey, Yugoslavia
Related titles: Online - full text ed.; Series of: International Steel Statistics Country Books Series.
Published by: I S S B Ltd., 1 Carlton House Ter, London, SW1Y 5DB, United Kingdom. TEL 44-20-73433900, FAX 44-20-73433901, info@issb.co.uk.

310 671 GBR ISSN 0952-6803
INTERNATIONAL STEEL STATISTICS - SUMMARY TABLES. Text in English. 1970. a. GBP 400 per issue to non-members; GBP 320 per issue to members (effective 2010). **Document type:** *Yearbook, Trade.* **Description:** Sets out summary tables for the countries in the International Steel Statistics Country Books Series. Covers production iron and crude steel, imports and exports of finished steel products.
Formerly (until 1979): International Steel Statistics. World Tables

Related titles: Online - full text ed.; Series of: International Steel Statistics Country Books Series.
Published by: I S S B Ltd., 1 Carlton House Ter, London, SW1Y 5DB, United Kingdom. TEL 44-20-73433900, FAX 44-20-73433901, info@issb.co.uk.

669.1 GBR ISSN 0952-6048
INTERNATIONAL STEEL STATISTICS - SWEDEN. Text in English. 1970. a. GBP 195 per issue to non-members; GBP 156 per issue to members (effective 2010). **Document type:** *Yearbook, Trade.* **Description:** Provides information on the production, consumption, and import and export of iron and steel products by quality and market in Sweden.
Related titles: Online - full text ed.; Series of: International Steel Statistics Country Books Series.
Published by: I S S B Ltd., 1 Carlton House Ter, London, SW1Y 5DB, United Kingdom. TEL 44-20-73433900, FAX 44-20-73433901, info@issb.co.uk.

669.1 GBR ISSN 0952-6099
INTERNATIONAL STEEL STATISTICS - SWITZERLAND. Text in English. 1970. a. GBP 195 per issue to non-members; GBP 156 per issue to members (effective 2010). **Document type:** *Yearbook, Trade.* **Description:** Provides information on the consumption, production, and export and import of iron and steel products by quality and market in Switzerland.
Related titles: Online - full text ed.; Series of: International Steel Statistics Country Books Series.
Published by: I S S B Ltd., 1 Carlton House Ter, London, SW1Y 5DB, United Kingdom. TEL 44-20-73433900, FAX 44-20-73433901, info@issb.co.uk.

669.1 GBR ISSN 1356-7896
INTERNATIONAL STEEL STATISTICS - TAIWAN. Text in English. 1994. a. GBP 195 per issue to non-members; GBP 156 per issue to members (effective 2010). **Document type:** *Yearbook, Trade.* **Description:** Provides information on the production, consumption, and import and export of iron and steel products by quality and market in Taiwan.
Related titles: Online - full text ed.; Series of: International Steel Statistics Country Books Series.
Published by: I S S B Ltd., 1 Carlton House Ter, London, SW1Y 5DB, United Kingdom. TEL 44-20-73433900, FAX 44-20-73433901, info@issb.co.uk.

669.1 GBR ISSN 0952-6811
INTERNATIONAL STEEL STATISTICS - U S A. Text in English. 1970. a. GBP 195 per issue to non-members; GBP 156 per issue to members (effective 2010). **Document type:** *Yearbook, Trade.* **Description:** Provides information on the production, consumption, and import and export of iron and steel products by quality and market in the U.S.
Related titles: Online - full text ed.; Series of: International Steel Statistics Country Books Series.
Published by: I S S B Ltd., 1 Carlton House Ter, London, SW1Y 5DB, United Kingdom. TEL 44-20-73433900, FAX 44-20-73433901, info@issb.co.uk.

669.1 GBR ISSN 0307-7608
HD9521.4
INTERNATIONAL STEEL STATISTICS - UNITED KINGDOM. Text in English. 1970. a. GBP 195 per issue to non-members; GBP 156 per issue to members (effective 2010). **Document type:** *Yearbook, Trade.* **Description:** Covers the production, consumption, and import and export of iron and steel products by quality and market in the U.K.
Related titles: Online - full text ed.; Series of: International Steel Statistics Country Books Series.
—Linda Hall.
Published by: I S S B Ltd., 1 Carlton House Ter, London, SW1Y 5DB, United Kingdom. TEL 44-20-73433900, FAX 44-20-73433901, info@issb.co.uk.

314 669 LUX
IRON AND STEEL YEARLY STATISTICS. Text in English. 1977. a. USD 30. **Document type:** *Monographic series.*
Former titles: Iron and Steel Statistical Yearbook; Statistical Office of the European Communities. Iron and Steel. Yearbook
Related titles: Microfiche ed.: (from CIS).
Indexed: IIS.
Published by: (European Commission, Statistical Office of the European Communities (E U R O S T A T)), European Commission, Office for Official Publications of the European Union, 2 Rue Mercier, Luxembourg, L-2985, Luxembourg. **Dist. in the U.S. by:** Bernan Associates, Bernan, 4611-F Assembly Dr., Lanham, MD 20706-4391. TEL 301-459-0056, 800-274-4447.

338.3 672 BEL
IRON PRODUCTION. Text in English. m. free to members; EUR 175 to non-members (effective 2001). **Description:** Reports on iron production worldwide, including output of pig iron and direct reduced iron, and comparisons with previous month and previous year.
Published by: International Iron and Steel Institute, Rue Colonel Bourg 120, Brussels, 1140, Belgium. TEL 32-2-702-8900, FAX 32-2-702-8899, library@iisi.be.

JOURNAL OF MATERIALS SCIENCE & TECHNOLOGY; an international journal in the field of materials science. *see* METALLURGY

KAGAKU GIJUTSU BUNKEN SOKUHO. KINZOKU KOGAKU, KOZAN KOGAKU, CHIKYU NO KAGAKU-HEN/CURRENT BIBLIOGRAPHY ON SCIENCE AND TECHNOLOGY: EARTH SCIENCE, MINING AND METALLURGY. *see* EARTH SCIENCES—Abstracting, Bibliographies, Statistics

669 JPN ISSN 0451-6001
KEIKINZOKU KOGYO TOKEI NENPO/LIGHT METAL STATISTICS IN JAPAN. Variant title: Light Metal Statistics in Japan. Annual Report. Text in English, Japanese. 1950. a. JPY 15,000. bk.rev. stat. **Document type:** *Journal, Trade.*
Indexed: SpeleolAb.
Published by: Japan Aluminium Association, Tsukamoto-Sozan Bldg, 2-15 Ginza 4-chome, Chuo-ku, Tokyo, 104-0061, Japan. TEL 81-3-3538-0221, FAX 81-3-3538-0233. Ed. K Nagakubo. Circ: 1,200.

669 016 HUN ISSN 0231-0708
KOHASZATI ES ONTESZETI SZAKIRODALMI TAJEKOZTATO/ METALLURGY AND FOUNDRY ABSTRACTS. Text in Hungarian. 1949. m. HUF 9,700. abstr. index.
Supersedes (in 1982): Muszaki Lapszemle. Kohaszat, Onteszet - Technical Abstracts. Metallurgy, Foundry (0027-5034)
Published by: Orszagos Muszaki Informacios Kozpont es Konyvtar/ National Technical Information Centre and Library, Muzeum utca 17, PO Box 12, Budapest, 1428, Hungary. Ed. Gabor Libertiny. Circ: 330. **Subscr. to:** Kultura, PO Box 149, Budapest 1389, Hungary.

669.2 PRT ISSN 0023-9577
HD9539.L38
LEAD AND ZINC STATISTICS. Text in English, French. 1961. m. EUR 1,190, USD 1,670 non-member countries companies; EUR 595, USD 835 member countries companies (effective 2009). mkt.; stat.; charts. 68 p./no.; **Document type:** *Bulletin, Abstract/Index.* **Description:** Provides long-term historical coverage of world production and consumption of lead and zinc since 1960, combining detailed annual tables with quarterly and monthly series.
Related titles: Microfiche ed.: (from CIS); Online - full text ed.
Indexed: IIS, RASB.
Published by: International Lead and Zinc Study Group, Rua Almirante Barroso 38 - 5th Fl, 1000 - 013, Lisboa, Portugal. TEL 351-21-3592420, FAX 351-21-3592429, root@ilzsg.org.

671.52 016 DEU ISSN 1433-2213
LITERATURSCHAU: SCHWEISSEN UND VERWANDTE VERFAHREN/ WELDING AND ALLIED PROCESSES. Text in German. 1956. 10/yr. cum. author and keyword index. back issues avail. **Document type:** *Government.* **Description:** Features developments in welding, metallurgy, engineering, weldability of materials, equipment, application, failures, testing.
Former titles (until 1996): Referate: Schweissen und Verwandte Verfahren (0944-9396); (until 1992): Referateorgan Schweissen und Verwandte Verfahren (0340-4749); (until 1971): Selective Abstracting Service: Welding and Allied Processes (0037-1432)
Related titles: Online - full text ed.
Published by: Bundesanstalt fuer Materialforschung und -pruefung, Unter den Eichen 87, Berlin, 12205, Germany. TEL 49-30-81040, FAX 49-30-8112029, info@bam.de, http://www.bam.de. **Co-sponsors:** Fachinformationszentrum Technik e.V.; Deutscher Verband fuer Schweissen und verwandte Verfahren e.V.

016.669 016.638 USA ISSN 1555-8444
MATERIALS BUSINESS FILE. Text in English. 1985. base vol. plus m. updates. **Document type:** *Database, Abstract/Index.* **Description:** Focuses on industry news, international trade data, government regulations and management issues related to the metals and materials industries.
Media: Online - full text.
Published by: ProQuest LLC (Bethesda) (Subsidiary of: Cambridge Information Group), 789 E Eisenhower Pky, Ann Arbor, MI 48103. TEL 734-761-4700, FAX 734-997-4222, info@proquest.com.

669 016 GBR ISSN 0026-0657
TN695
METAL POWDER REPORT. Abbreviated title: M P R. Text in English. 1946. 11/yr. EUR 579 in Europe to institutions; JPY 76,800 in Japan to institutions; USD 648 elsewhere to institutions (effective 2012). adv. bk.rev. abstr.; charts; pat.; tr.lit. index. back issues avail.; reprints avail. **Document type:** *Magazine, Trade.* **Description:** Contains reports the latest developments in worldwide powder production, consolidation, sintering and new powder metallurgy products and their applications.
Related titles: Online - full text ed.: ISSN 1873-4065 (from IngentaConnect, ScienceDirect).
Indexed: A01, A03, A08, A22, A26, A28, APA, BrCerAb, C&ISA, CA, CA/WCA, CIA, CPEI, Cadscan, CerAb, CivEngAb, CoppAb, CorrAb, E&CAJ, E11, EEA, EMA, ESPM, EngInd, EnvEAb, H15, I05, ISMEC, Inspec, LeadAb, M&TEA, M09, MBF, METADEX, S01, SCOPUS, SolStAb, T02, T04, TM, WAA, Zincscan.
—BLDSC (5687.825000), IE, Infotrieve, Ingenta, INIST, Linda Hall. **CCC.**
Published by: Elsevier Advanced Technology (Subsidiary of: Elsevier Science & Technology), The Blvd, Langford Ln, Kidlington, Oxon OX5 1GB, United Kingdom. TEL 44-1865-843434, FAX 44-1865-843970, eatsales@elsevier.co.uk, http://www.elsevier.com. Ed. Richard Felton TEL 44-1865-843670. **Subscr. to:** Elsevier BV, Radarweg 29, PO Box 211, Amsterdam 1000 AE, Netherlands. TEL 31-20-4853757, FAX 31-20-4853432, JournalsCustomerServiceEMEA@elsevier.com, http://www.elsevier.nl.

016.68 USA ISSN 0026-0924
TN1
METALS ABSTRACTS. Text in English. 1968. m. (plus a. cumulative index CD). USD 5,285 combined subscription (12 print issues plus & a. index on CD-ROM); USD 6,435 combined subscription (METADEX combined with Metals Abstracts Index/24 print issues plus a. index on CD-ROM); USD 715 combined subscription (Metals Annual Index in print & on CD-ROM) (effective 2011). Index. reprints avail. **Document type:** *Abstract/Index.* **Description:** Monitors international literature on all aspects of metallurgical science and technology.
Formed by the merger of: Review of Metal Literature (0096-4808); Metallurgical Abstracts (0428-3171)
Related titles: Cumulative ed(s).: Metals Abstracts Annual Cumulation. USD 3,175 combined subscription (print & CD-ROM eds.) (effective 2011).
—BLDSC (5699.250000), Linda Hall. **CCC.**
Published by: ProQuest LLC (Bethesda) (Subsidiary of: Cambridge Information Group), 7200 Wisconsin Ave, Ste 715, Bethesda, MD 20814. TEL 301-961-6798, 800-843-7751, FAX 301-961-6799, journals@csa.com. Circ: 1,500.

016.669 USA ISSN 0026-0932
TN1
METALS ABSTRACTS INDEX. Text in English. 1968. m. (plus a. index CD). USD 2,300 combined subscription (includes Alloys Index & a. index on CD-ROM) (effective 2011). **Document type:** *Abstract/Index.* **Description:** Companion publication of Metals Abstracts containing subject, author and corporate author indexes.
Incorporates (1974-2009): Alloys Index (0094-8233)
—BLDSC (5699.260000). **CCC.**
Published by: ProQuest LLC (Bethesda) (Subsidiary of: Cambridge Information Group), 7200 Wisconsin Ave, Ste 715, Bethesda, MD 20814. TEL 301-961-6798, FAX 301-961-6799, journals@csa.com, http://www.csa.com. Ed. Carole Houk.

669.1 JPN ISSN 0497-1140
MONTHLY REPORT OF THE IRON AND STEEL STATISTICS. Text in English, Japanese. 1977 (vol.20). m. JPY 6,000. stat. **Description:** Provides statistcs on production, supply and demand, exports, imports, raw materials, and labor.
Indexed: AESIS.
Published by: (Economic Research and Statistics Department), Japan Iron and Steel Federation/Nihon Tekko Renmei, Eisei linkai, Keidanren Kaikan, 9-4 Ote-Machi 1-chome, Chiyoda-ku, Tokyo, 100-0004, Japan. TEL 81-3-3279-3610, FAX 81-3-3272-7493.

669 620 DEU ISSN 1436-7505
PRODUKTION VON LEITERPLATTEN UND SYSTEMEN. Variant title: P L U S. Text in German. 1954. m. EUR 68.95 domestic; EUR 86.40 foreign; EUR 10 newsstand/cover (effective 2009). adv. pat.; tr.lit. 180 p./no.; **Document type:** *Magazine, Trade.*
Former titles (until 1999): Galvano-Referate (0344-2241); (until 1959): Archiv fuer Metall-Finisching (0176-1935)
Related titles: ◆ Supplement to: Galvanotechnik. ISSN 0016-4232.
Indexed: A28, APA, BrCerAb, C&ISA, CA/WCA, CIA, CerAb, CivEngAb, CorrAb, E&CAJ, E11, EEA, EMA, H15, M&TEA, M09, MBF, METADEX, RefZh, SolStAb, T04, TM, WAA.
—IE. **CCC.**
Published by: Eugen G. Leuze Verlag, Karlstr 4, Saulgau, 88348, Germany. TEL 49-7581-48010, FAX 49-7581-480110, info@leuze-verlag.de, http://www.leuze-verlag.de. adv.: color page EUR 1,500, B&W page EUR 1,020; trim 130 x 200. Circ: 3,400 (paid).

669.1 ITA ISSN 1826-3658
LA PRODUZIONE DELL'INDUSTRIA SIDERURGICA. Text in Italian. 2003. a. **Document type:** *Government.*
Published by: Istituto Nazionale di Statistica (I S T A T), Via Cesare Balbo 16, Rome, 00184, Italy. TEL 39-06-46731, http://www.istat.it.

PROGRESS IN COAL STEEL AND RELATED SOCIAL RESEARCH; a European journal. *see* MINES AND MINING INDUSTRY—Abstracting, Bibliographies, Statistics

REFERATIVNYI ZHURNAL. EKONOMIKA OTRASLEI METALLURGICHESKOGO I MASHINOSTROITELNOGO KOMPLEKSOV; vypusk svodnogo toma. *see* BUSINESS AND ECONOMICS—Abstracting, Bibliographies, Statistics

016.6201 RUS ISSN 0131-3533
CODEN: RKZKA6
REFERATIVNYI ZHURNAL. KORROZIYA I ZASHCHITA OT KORROZII; otdel'nyi vypusk. Text in Russian. 1968. m. USD 994.80 foreign (effective 2011). **Document type:** *Journal, Abstract/Index.*
Related titles: CD-ROM ed.; Online - full text ed.; ◆ English Translation: Corrosion Control Abstracts. ISSN 0010-9347.
Indexed: ChemAb.
—CASDDS, East View.
Published by: VINITI RAN, ul Usievicha 20, Moscow, 125190, Russian Federation. TEL 7-499-1526113, FAX 7-499-9430060, dir@viniti.ru, http://www.viniti.ru. Ed. Vladimir Bondar. **Dist. by:** Informnauka Ltd., Ul Usievicha 20, Moscow 125190, Russian Federation. alfimov@viniti.ru.

016.669 RUS ISSN 0202-9626
REFERATIVNYI ZHURNAL. METALLOVEDENIE I TERMICHESKAYA OBRABOTKA; vypusk svodnogo toma. Text in Russian. 1959. m. USD 645.60 foreign (effective 2011). **Document type:** *Journal, Abstract/Index.*
Related titles: CD-ROM ed.; Online - full text ed.
—East View.
Published by: VINITI RAN, ul Usievicha 20, Moscow, 125190, Russian Federation. TEL 7-499-1526113, FAX 7-499-9430060, dir@viniti.ru, http://www.viniti.ru. **Dist. by:** Informnauka Ltd., Ul Usievicha 20, Moscow 125190, Russian Federation. alfimov@viniti.ru.

016.669 RUS ISSN 0202-9634
REFERATIVNYI ZHURNAL. METALLURGICHESKAYA TEPLOTEKHNIKA. OBORUDOVANIE, IZMERENIYA, KONTROL I AVTOMATIZATSIYA V METALLURGICHESKOM PROIZVODSTVE; vypusk svodnogo toma. Text in Russian. 1960. m. USD 216 foreign (effective 2011). **Document type:** *Journal, Abstract/Index.*
Related titles: CD-ROM ed.; Online - full text ed.
—East View.
Published by: VINITI RAN, ul Usievicha 20, Moscow, 125190, Russian Federation. TEL 7-499-1526113, FAX 7-499-9430060, dir@viniti.ru, http://www.viniti.ru. **Dist. by:** Informnauka Ltd., Ul Usievicha 20, Moscow 125190, Russian Federation. alfimov@viniti.ru.

016.669 RUS ISSN 0034-2491
CODEN: RZMTA5
REFERATIVNYI ZHURNAL. METALLURGIYA; svodnyi tom. Text in Russian. 1961. m. USD 1,718.40 foreign (effective 2011). abstr.; bibl.; pat. **Document type:** *Journal, Abstract/Index.*
Related titles: CD-ROM ed.; Online - full text ed.
Indexed: ChemAb.
—CASDDS, East View, Linda Hall. **CCC.**
Published by: VINITI RAN, ul Usievicha 20, Moscow, 125190, Russian Federation. TEL 7-499-1526113, FAX 7-499-9430060, dir@viniti.ru, http://www.viniti.ru. Ed. O A Bannykh. Circ: 1,649. **Dist. by:** Informnauka Ltd., Ul Usievicha 20, Moscow 125190, Russian Federation. alfimov@viniti.ru.

016.669 RUS ISSN 0203-5170
REFERATIVNYI ZHURNAL. METALLURGIYA TSVETNYKH METALLOV; vypusk svodnogo toma. Text in Russian. 1959. m. USD 445.20 foreign (effective 2011). **Document type:** *Journal, Abstract/ Index.*
Related titles: CD-ROM ed.; Online - full text ed.
—East View.
Published by: VINITI RAN, ul Usievicha 20, Moscow, 125190, Russian Federation. TEL 7-499-1526113, FAX 7-499-9430060, dir@viniti.ru, http://www.viniti.ru. **Dist. by:** Informnauka Ltd., Ul Usievicha 20, Moscow 125190, Russian Federation. alfimov@viniti.ru.

016.669 RUS
REFERATIVNYI ZHURNAL. POROSHKOVAYA METALLURGIYA. NANOMATERIALY, POKRYTIYA I PLENKI, POLUCHAEMYE FIZIKO-METALLURGICHESKIMI METODAMI; vypusk svodnogo toma. Text in Russian. 1986. m. USD 334.80 foreign (effective 2011). **Document type:** *Journal, Abstract/Index.*
Formerly (until Jan. 2009): Referativnyi Zhurnal. Poroshkovaya Metallurgiya. Pokrytiya i Plenki, Poluchaemye Fiziko-Metallurgicheskimi Metodami (0234-4734)
Related titles: CD-ROM ed.; Online - full text ed.

—East View.
Published by: VINITI RAN, ul Usievicha 20, Moscow, 125190, Russian Federation. TEL 7-499-1526113, FAX 7-499-9430060, dir@viniti.ru, http://www.viniti.ru. **Dist. by:** Informnauka Ltd., Ul Usievicha 20, Moscow 125190, Russian Federation. alfimov@viniti.ru.

016.669 RUS ISSN 0202-9650
REFERATIVNYI ZHURNAL. PROIZVODSTVO CHUGUNA I STALI; vypusk svodnogo toma. Text in Russian. 1958. m. USD 334.80 foreign (effective 2011). **Document type:** *Journal, Abstract/Index.*
Related titles: CD-ROM ed.; Online - full text ed.
—East View.
Published by: VINITI RAN, ul Usievicha 20, Moscow, 125190, Russian Federation. TEL 7-499-1526113, FAX 7-499-9430060, dir@viniti.ru, http://www.viniti.ru. **Dist. by:** Informnauka Ltd., Ul Usievicha 20, Moscow 125190, Russian Federation. alfimov@viniti.ru.

016.669 RUS ISSN 0202-9669
REFERATIVNYI ZHURNAL. PROKATNOYE I VOLOCHIL'NOYE PROIZVODSTVO; vypusk svodnogo toma. Text in Russian. 1960. m. USD 282 foreign (effective 2011). **Document type:** *Journal, Abstract/Index.*
Related titles: CD-ROM ed.; Online - full text ed.
—East View.
Published by: VINITI RAN, ul Usievicha 20, Moscow, 125190, Russian Federation. TEL 7-499-1526113, FAX 7-499-9430060, dir@viniti.ru, http://www.viniti.ru. **Dist. by:** Informnauka Ltd., Ul Usievicha 20, Moscow 125190, Russian Federation. alfimov@viniti.ru.

016.67152 016.316 RUS ISSN 0131-3525
REFERATIVNYI ZHURNAL. SVARKA; otdel'nyi vypusk. Text in Russian. 1965. m. USD 417.60 foreign (effective 2011). **Document type:** *Journal, Abstract/Index.*
Related titles: CD-ROM ed.; Online - full text ed.
—East View.
Published by: VINITI RAN, ul Usievicha 20, Moscow, 125190, Russian Federation. TEL 7-499-1526113, FAX 7-499-9430060, dir@viniti.ru, http://www.viniti.ru. Ed. Oleg Bannykh. **Dist. by:** Informnauka Ltd., Ul Usievicha 20, Moscow 125190, Russian Federation. alfimov@viniti.ru.

016.6712 RUS ISSN 0202-9596
REFERATIVNYI ZHURNAL. TEKHNOLOGIYA I OBORUDOVANIE KUZNECHNO-SHTAMPOVOCHNOGO PROIZVODSTVA; vypusk svodnogo toma. Text in Russian. 1956. m. USD 332.40 foreign (effective 2011). **Document type:** *Journal, Abstract/Index.*
Related titles: CD-ROM ed.; Online - full text ed.
—East View.
Published by: VINITI RAN, ul Usievicha 20, Moscow, 125190, Russian Federation. TEL 7-499-1526113, FAX 7-499-9430060, dir@viniti.ru, http://www.viniti.ru. **Dist. by:** Informnauka Ltd., Ul Usievicha 20, Moscow 125190, Russian Federation. alfimov@viniti.ru.

016.6712 RUS ISSN 0202-960X
REFERATIVNYI ZHURNAL. TEKHNOLOGIYA I OBORUDOVANIE LITEINOGO PROIZVODSTVA; vypusk svodnogo toma. Text in Russian. 1956. m. USD 315.60 foreign (effective 2011). **Document type:** *Journal, Abstract/Index.*
Related titles: CD-ROM ed.; Online - full text ed.
—East View.
Published by: VINITI RAN, ul Usievicha 20, Moscow, 125190, Russian Federation. TEL 7-499-1526113, FAX 7-499-9430060, dir@viniti.ru, http://www.viniti.ru. **Dist. by:** Informnauka Ltd., Ul Usievicha 20, Moscow 125190, Russian Federation. alfimov@viniti.ru.

016.669 RUS ISSN 0202-9677
REFERATIVNYI ZHURNAL. TEORIYA METALLURGICHESKIKH PROTSESSOV; vypusk svodnogo toma. Text in Russian. 1961. m. USD 144 foreign (effective 2011). **Document type:** *Journal, Abstract/Index.*
Related titles: CD-ROM ed.; Online - full text ed.
—East View.
Published by: VINITI RAN, ul Usievicha 20, Moscow, 125190, Russian Federation. TEL 7-499-1526113, FAX 7-499-9430060, dir@viniti.ru, http://www.viniti.ru. **Dist. by:** Informnauka Ltd., Ul Usievicha 20, Moscow 125190, Russian Federation. alfimov@viniti.ru.

669.1 310 IND ISSN 0081-511X
HD9526.I6
STATISTICS FOR IRON AND STEEL INDUSTRY IN INDIA. Text in English. 1964. biennial. price varies. index. **Document type:** *Government.*
Published by: Steel Authority of India Ltd., Ispat Bhavan, Lodi Rd, New Delhi, 110 003, India. TEL 91-11-24367481, FAX 91-11-24367015, sailco@vsnl.com, http://www.sail.co.in/.

669 310 DEU ISSN 0936-9864
STATISTISCHES JAHRBUCH DER STAHLINDUSTRIE. Text in German. 1929. a. EUR 44.90 per issue (effective 2011). **Document type:** *Yearbook, Trade.* **Description:** Reports annually on key indicators of the steel industry last year and the comparison years.
Formerly (until 1989): Statistisches Jahrbuch der Eisen- und Stahlindustrie (0081-5365)
Related titles: CD-ROM ed.; Online - full text ed.
Indexed: GeoRef, SpeleolAb.
Published by: (Wirtschaftsvereinigung Stahlindustrie), Verlag Stahleisen GmbH, Sohnstr 65, Duesseldorf, 40237, Germany. TEL 49-211-67070, FAX 49-211-6707310, stahleisen@stahleisen.de, http://www.stahleisen.de.

338.2 672 BEL ISSN 0771-2871
HD9510.1
STEEL STATISTICAL YEARBOOK (YEAR). Text in English. a. EUR 100 to members Print & online eds.; EUR 200 to non-members Print & online eds. (effective 2001). charts; illus.; stat. **Description:** Presents statistics and information, by country, on crude steel production, casting development, trade figures, consumption, and raw materials.
Incorporates (in 1998): Steel Statistics of Developing Countries (1018-1156)
Related titles: CD-ROM ed.; Diskette ed.: USD 248.
—Linda Hall.
Published by: International Iron and Steel Institute, Rue Colonel Bourg 120, Brussels, 1140, Belgium. TEL 32-2-702-8900, FAX 32-2-702-8899.

669 016 GBR
SURFACE FINISHING; metal finishing database software. Text in English. 1989. bi-m. GBP 295, USD 450 (effective 1998). **Document type:** *Abstract/Index.* **Description:** Summarizes articles from major journals covering electroplating, electroless plating, electroforming, anodizing, conversion coating, etching, and other surface-treatment processes, including P.C.B. processing and effluent treatment.
Formerly: Elbase
Media: CD-ROM.
Published by: M F I S Ltd., PO Box 70, Stevenage, Herts SG1 4DF, United Kingdom. TEL 44-1438-745115, FAX 44-1438-364536. Ed. A T Kuhn.

669 016 GBR
SURFACE FINISHING ABSTRACTS (ONLINE). Text in English. 1959. base vol. plus updates. USD 290 single user (effective 2009). abstr.; pat. index. **Document type:** *Database, Abstract/Index.* **Description:** Details, patents, reports, standards and translations from industrial countries of the world.
Media: Online - full content.
Published by: Finishing Publications Ltd & Metal Finishing Information Services Ltd, PO Box 70, Stevenage, Herts SG1 4DF, United Kingdom. TEL 44-1438-745115, FAX 44-1438-364536, finpubs@compuserve.com, http://finpubs.demonweb.co.uk/index.htm. Ed. Anselm Kuhn.

061.669 DEU ISSN 1868-7679
TECSCAN JOURNAL. KALT- UND WARMMASSIVUMFORMUNG. Variant title: Kalt- und Warmmassivumformung. Text in German. 1970. 4/yr. EUR 170 (effective 2010). adv. abstr.; bibl.; charts; illus. **Document type:** *Journal, Abstract/Index.*
Former titles (until 2009): Informationsdienst F I Z Technik. Kalt- und Warmmassivumformung (1437-451X); (until 1999): Informationsdienst Kaltmassivumformung (0170-9550); (until 1978): V D I Informationsdienst. Kaltmassivumformung (0341-1605); (until 1974): Informationsdienst Umformtechnik. Teil 1: Kaltmassivumformung (0341-1583)
—CCC.
Published by: Fachinformationszentrum Technik e.V., Hanauer Landstr 151-153, Frankfurt Am Main, 60314, Germany. TEL 49-69-4308213, FAX 49-69-4308200, kundenberatung@fiz-technik.de, http://www.fiz-technik.de.

016.669 DEU ISSN 1868-7660
TECSCAN JOURNAL. NEUE FERTIGUNGSVERFAHREN. Variant title: Neue Fertigungsverfahren. Text in German. 1977. bi-m. EUR 200 (effective 2010). adv. abstr.; bibl.; charts; illus. **Document type:** *Journal, Abstract/Index.*
Former titles (until 2009): Informationsdienst F I Z Technik. Neue Fertigungsverfahren (1866-8119); (until 2007): Verein Deutscher Ingenieure Informationsdienst. Neue Fertigungsverfahren (0720-9878); (until 1981): V D I Informationsdienst. Neue Fertigungsverfahren (0170-947X)
—CCC.
Published by: (Verein Deutscher Ingenieure e.V.), Fachinformationszentrum Technik e.V., Hanauer Landstr 151-153, Frankfurt Am Main, 60314, Germany. TEL 49-69-4308213, FAX 49-69-4308200, kundenberatung@fiz-technik.de, http://www.fiz-technik.de.

016.669 DEU ISSN 1868-7695
TECSCAN JOURNAL. SCHMIEDEN UND PRESSEN. Variant title: Schmieden und Pressen. Text in German. 1976. 6/yr. EUR 200 (effective 2010). adv. abstr.; bibl.; charts; illus. **Document type:** *Journal, Abstract/Index.*
Former titles (until 2009): Informationsdienst F I Z Technik. Schmieden und Pressen (1865-4592); (until 2007): Informationsdienst Verein Deutscher Ingenieure. Schmieden und Pressen (0171-3647); (until 1978): V D I Informationsdienst. Schmieden und Pressen (0171-3639)
—CCC.
Published by: Fachinformationszentrum Technik e.V., Hanauer Landstr 151-153, Frankfurt Am Main, 60314, Germany. TEL 49-69-4308213, FAX 49-69-4308200, kundenberatung@fiz-technik.de, http://www.fiz-technik.de.

016.69 DEU ISSN 1868-7628
TECSCAN JOURNAL. STRANGPRESSEN VON METALLEN. Variant title: Strangpressen von Metallen. Text in German. 1977. 3/yr. EUR 140 (effective 2010). adv. abstr.; bibl.; charts; illus. **Document type:** *Journal, Abstract/Index.*
Former titles (until 2009): Informationsdienst F I Z Technik. Strangpressen von Metallen (1866-8224); (until 2007): Informationsdienst Verein Deutscher Ingenieure. Strangpressen von Metallen (0721-7242); (until 1981): V D I Informationsdienst. Strangpressen von Metallen (0170-9488)
—CCC.
Published by: Fachinformationszentrum Technik e.V., Hanauer Landstr 151-153, Frankfurt Am Main, 60314, Germany. TEL 49-69-4308213, FAX 49-69-4308200, kundenberatung@fiz-technik.de, http://www.fiz-technik.de.

669 310 USA ISSN 0049-4828
HD9539.T8
TUNGSTEN STATISTICS. Text in English. 1967. q. USD 25 per issue.
Related titles: Microfiche ed.: (from CIS).
Indexed: IIS.
—CCC.
Published by: (United Nations, Conference on Trade and Development (U N C T A D)), United Nations Publications, 2 United Nations Plaza, Rm DC2-853, New York, NY 10017. TEL 212-963-8302, 800-253-9646, FAX 212-963-3489, publications@un.org, https://unp.un.org.

669.1 338.4 GBR ISSN 0952-5505
U K IRON AND STEEL INDUSTRY. ANNUAL STATISTICS. Text in English. 1918. a. GBP 210 per issue to non-members; GBP 168 per issue to members (effective 2010). stat. back issues avail. **Document type:** *Journal, Trade.* **Description:** Provides UK iron and steel industry with historical comparisons and detailed trade information.
Formerly (until 1970): Iron and Steel. Annual Statistics for the United Kingdom (0075-0867)
Published by: I S S B Ltd., 1 Carlton House Ter, London, SW1Y 5DB, United Kingdom. TEL 44-20-73433900, FAX 44-20-73433901, info@issb.co.uk.

U S SILVER SUMMARY. *see* MINES AND MINING INDUSTRY—Abstracting, Bibliographies, Statistics

669.021 GBR ISSN 0043-8758
HD9539.A1
WORLD METAL STATISTICS. Text in English. 1948. m. GBP 1,975 domestic (print or online eds.); GBP 2,030 in Europe; GBP 2,050 elsewhere (effective 2009). adv. stat. **Document type:** *Bulletin, Trade.* **Description:** Comprehensive statistical guide, updated monthly, including production and consumption of the major non-ferrous metals, listed on a country by country basis.
Formerly (until 1967): World Non-Ferrous Metal Statistics
Related titles: E-mail ed.: GBP 330, USD 660 (effective 2005); Online - full text ed.
Indexed: GeoRef, SpeleolAb.
—CCC.
Published by: World Bureau of Metal Statistics, 27a High St, Ware, Herts SG12 9BA, United Kingdom. TEL 44-1920-461274, FAX 44-1920-464258, enquiries@world-bureau.co.uk.

669.021 GBR ISSN 0266-7355
HD9539.A1
WORLD METAL STATISTICS. YEARBOOK. Text in English. 1984. a. GBP 550 per issue; GBP 650 combined subscription per issue (print & online eds.) (effective 2009). **Document type:** *Yearbook, Corporate.* **Description:** Provides the annual figures for the previous year together with comparisons for the previous years.
Related titles: Online - full text ed.: GBP 545 per issue (effective 2009).
Indexed: CoppAb.
Published by: World Bureau of Metal Statistics, 27a High St, Ware, Herts SG12 9BA, United Kingdom. TEL 44-1920-461274, FAX 44-1920-464258, enquiries@world-bureau.co.uk.

669.021 PRT ISSN 1570-8489
WORLD NICKEL STATISTICS (ONLINE). Text in English. 1991. m. EUR 3,000 to non-members; EUR 2,000 to members (effective 2011). **Document type:** *Bulletin, Trade.*
Formerly (until 2002): World Nickel Statistics (Print) (1022-2561)
Media: Online - full text.
Published by: International Nickel Study Group, Rua Almirante Barroso 38 - 5th, Lisbon, 1000-013, Portugal. TEL 351-213-567030, FAX 351-213-567039, insg@insg.org.

669.23 338.2 USA
HD9536.A1
WORLD SILVER PRODUCTION FORECAST. Variant title: Mine Production of Silver. Text in English. 1973. a. USD 50; USD 55 foreign (effective 1999). stat. back issues avail. **Description:** Covers silver production in 58 countries.
Formerly: World Mine Production of Silver (1044-7482)
Indexed: SRI.
Published by: Silver Institute, 14264, Washington, DC 20044-4264. TEL 202-835-0185, FAX 202-835-0155. Ed. Paul W Bateman.

669 GBR ISSN 1361-8954
WORLD STEEL EXPORTS. Variant title: World Steel Exports - All Qualities. Text in English. 1970. q. GBP 660 to non-members; GBP 528 to members (effective 2010). **Document type:** *Journal, Trade.* **Description:** Covers the details of exports of 34 major steel producing countries collectively accounting for 90% of world steel exports.
Formerly (until 1995): World Trade Steel (0952-5734)
Related titles: Online - full text ed.
Published by: I S S B Ltd., 1 Carlton House Ter, London, SW1Y 5DB, United Kingdom. TEL 44-20-73433900, FAX 44-20-73433901, info@issb.co.uk.

669.142 GBR ISSN 1361-8946
WORLD STEEL EXPORTS - STAINLESS, HIGH SPEED & OTHER ALLOY. Text in English. 1979. q. GBP 475 to non-members for Stainless & Other Alloy; GBP 380 to members for Stainless & Other Alloy; GBP 275 to non-members for High Speed; GBP 220 to members for High Speed (effective 2010). **Document type:** *Journal, Trade.* **Description:** Provides a cumulative (quarterly) look at the export trade of major steel-producing countries in selected alloy products.
Formerly (until 1995): World Trade - Stainless, High Speed & Other Alloy Steel (0952-5742)
Published by: I S S B Ltd., 1 Carlton House Ter, London, SW1Y 5DB, United Kingdom. TEL 44-20-73433900, FAX 44-20-73433901, info@issb.co.uk.

338.2 672 BEL
WORLD STEEL IN FIGURES (YEAR). Text in English. a. free. charts; illus.; stat. **Description:** Contains facts on steel including employment, capital investment expenditure, iron ore production, scrap consumption, consumption of direct reduced iron, and the geographic distribution of steel production and consumption.
Published by: International Iron and Steel Institute, Rue Colonel Bourg 120, Brussels, 1140, Belgium. TEL 32-2-702-8900, FAX 32-2-702-8899.

338.3 672 GBR ISSN 1359-4249
WORLD STEEL STATISTICS MONTHLY. Text in English. 1995. m. GBP 975 to non-members; GBP 780 to members (effective 2010). charts. **Document type:** *Journal, Trade.* **Description:** Provides countrywise statistics on world steel and raw materials production and trade.
Published by: (International Iron and Steel Institute BEL), I S S B Ltd., 1 Carlton House Ter, London, SW1Y 5DB, United Kingdom. TEL 44-20-73433900, FAX 44-20-73433901, info@issb.co.uk.

METALLURGY—Welding

669 DEU ISSN 0943-9358
AACHENER BERICHTE FUEGETECHNIK. Text in German. 1993. irreg., latest 2010. price varies. **Document type:** *Monographic series, Academic/Scholarly.*
Indexed: TM.
Published by: Shaker Verlag GmbH, Kaiserstr 100, Herzogenrath, 52134, Germany. TEL 49-2407-95960, FAX 49-2407-95969, info@shaker.de.

671.52 USA
APPLIED WELDING; advancing your welding performance. Text in English. q.
Media: Online - full text.
Indexed: APA, C&ISA, CIA, CorrAb, E&CAJ, EEA, SolStAb, WAA.
Published by: Miller Electric Manufacturing Co, 1635 W Spencer St, PO Box 1079, Appleton, WI 54912-1079. TEL 920-734-9821, http://www.millerwelds.com.

671.52 AUS ISSN 1039-0642
CODEN: AUWJA7
AUSTRALASIAN WELDING JOURNAL. Abbreviated title: A W J. Text in English. 1957. q. adv. bk.rev. illus. **Document type:** *Journal, Trade.* **Description:** Disseminates information about welding developments, techniques, processes and equipment for the Australian industry.
Former titles (until 1992): Australian Welding Journal (1324-1044); (until 1967): Welding Fabrication and Design (0372-7246); (until 1960): Australian Welding Journal (0005-0431)
Indexed: A28, AESIS, APA, BrCerAb, C&ISA, CA/WCA, CIA, CerAb, CivEngAb, CorrAb, E&CAJ, E11, EEA, EMA, ESPM, EnvEAb, H15, INIS AtomInd, M&TEA, M09, MBF, METADEX, SolStAb, T04, WAA, Weldasearch.
—BLDSC (1796.405000), CASDDS, Ingenta, INIST, Linda Hall.
Published by: Welding Technology Institute of Australia, Unit 50, 8 Ave of the Americas, Newington, NSW 2127, Australia. TEL 61-2-97484443, FAX 61-2-97482858, info@wtia.com.au. Ed. Anne Rorke. Pub. Word Design. Adv. contact Chris Burns TEL 61-2-47394455.

669 UKR ISSN 0005-111X
TK4660.A1 CODEN: AVSVAU
AVTOMATICHESKAYA SVARKA; vsesoyuznyi nauchno-tekhnicheskii i proizvodstvennyi zhurnal. Text in Russian. 1948. m. USD 156 foreign (effective 2005). adv. bk.rev. charts; illus. index. **Document type:** *Journal, Academic/Scholarly.*
Related titles: ◆ English Translation: Paton Welding Journal. ISSN 0957-798X.
Indexed: A22, AcoustA, C&ISA, CIN, ChemAb, ChemTitl, CorrAb, Djerelo, E&CAJ, INIS AtomInd, Inspec, RefZh, SCOPUS, SolStAb, WAA, Weldasearch.
—BLDSC (0002.000000), CASDDS, East View, IE, Ingenta, INIST, Linda Hall. **CCC.**
Published by: (Natsional'na Akademiya Nauk Ukrainy, Instytut Elektrozvaryuvannya im. EO Patona), Paton Publishing House, E.O. Paton Welding Institute, vul Bozhenko, 11, Kyi, 03680, Ukraine. TEL 380-44-2276302, FAX 380-44-2680486, journal@paton.kiev.ua. Circ: 6,000.

671.52 DEU ISSN 1867-4887
BRANDENBURGISCHE TECHNISCHE UNIVERSITAET COTTBUS. LEHRSTUHL FUEGETECHNIK. BERICHTE. Text in German. 2008. irreg., latest vol.2, 2009. price varies. **Document type:** *Monographic series, Academic/Scholarly.*
Published by: (Brandenburgische Technische Universitaet Cottbus, Lehrstuhl Fuegetechnik), Shaker Verlag GmbH, Kaiserstr 100, Herzogenrath, 52134, Germany. TEL 49-2407-95960, FAX 49-2407-95969, info@shaker.de, http://www.shaker.de.

671.52 CHN ISSN 1004-5341
TS227.A1
CHINA WELDING. Text in English. 1992. s-a. USD 39.20 (effective 2009). back issues avail. **Document type:** *Journal, Academic/Scholarly.*
Related titles: Online - full text ed.
Indexed: A28, APA, BrCerAb, C&ISA, CA/WCA, CIA, CPEI, CerAb, CivEngAb, CorrAb, E&CAJ, E11, EEA, EMA, ESPM, EngInd, EnvEAb, H15, M&TEA, M09, MBF, METADEX, RefZh, SCOPUS, SolStAb, T04, TM, WAA, Weldasearch.
—BLDSC (3180.239200), East View, IE, Ingenta, INIST, Linda Hall.
Published by: Harbin Research Institute of Welding, 111 Hexing Rd, Harbin, 150080, China.

671.52 GBR
CONNECT (CAMBRIDGE). Text in English. bi-m. free to members (effective 2009). back issues avail.; reprints avail. **Document type:** *Magazine, Trade.* **Description:** Covers articles & report on opweld project, fatigue testing of pipe connector, laser cladding process for repair, corrosion resistant alloys, structural energy storage.
Related titles: Online - full text ed.: free (effective 2009).
Indexed: Weldasearch.
Published by: T W I - The Welding Institute, Granta Park, Great Abington, Cambridge, CB21 6AL, United Kingdom. TEL 44-1223-899000, FAX 44-1223-892588, twi@twi.co.uk. Ed. Penny Edmundson.

621.791 UKR ISSN 0234-4874
TA492.W4
DIAGNOSTIKA I PROIGNOZIROVANIE RAZRUSHENIYA SVARNYKH KONSTRUKTSII. Text in Russian. 1985. irreg. **Document type:** *Journal, Academic/Scholarly.*
Indexed: C&ISA, CorrAb, E&CAJ, SolStAb, WAA.
—INIST, Linda Hall.
Published by: Natsional'na Akademiya Nauk Ukrainy, Instytut Elektrozvaryuvannya im. EO Patona, Vul Bozhenka 11, Kiev, 252650, Ukraine. TEL 38-22-2683484, FAX 38-22-2275288.

671.52 CHN ISSN 1001-2303
DIANHANJI/ELECTRIC WELDING MACHINE. Text in Chinese; Abstracts in Chinese, English. 1971. m. CNY 120, USD 120 (effective 2009). **Document type:** *Magazine, Trade.* **Description:** Covers the latest developments of theoretical and applied researches in the fields of electric welding machine.
Related titles: Online - full text ed.
Indexed: A28, APA, BrCerAb, C&ISA, CA/WCA, CIA, CerAb, CivEngAb, CorrAb, E&CAJ, E11, EEA, EMA, ESPM, EnvEAb, H15, M&TEA, M09, MBF, METADEX, RefZh, SolStAb, T04, WAA.
Published by: (Chengdu Dianhanji Yanjiusuo), Dianhanji Zazahishe, No.24, Hangtian Rd., Longtan City Industry Concentrate Development Zone, Erduan E 3rd Ring Rd., Chengdu, 610052, China. TEL 86-28-84216671, FAX 86-28-84216654, cddhjzzs@mail.sc.cninfo.net.

621.791 DEU ISSN 0427-8682
FACHBUCHREIHE SCHWEISSTECHNIK. Text in German. 1955. irreg., latest vol.155, 2011. price varies. **Document type:** *Monographic series, Trade.*
—BLDSC (3863.203000), Linda Hall.
Published by: (Deutscher Verband fuer Schweissen und verwandte Verfahren e.V.), D V S Verlag GmbH, Aachener Str 172, Duesseldorf, 40223, Germany. TEL 49-211-15910, FAX 49-211-1591150, verlag@dvs-hg.de, http://www.dvs-verlag.de.

671.52 SWE ISSN 1101-8658
FOGNINGSTEKNIK. Text in Swedish. 1989. bi-m. adv. **Document type:** *Magazine, Trade.*
Published by: Aller Business AB (Subsidiary of: Aller Business AS), Hemvaernsgatan 11, PO Box 6054, Solna, 17106, Sweden. TEL 46-8-56488630, FAX 46-8-897005, info@allerbusiness.se, http://www.allerbusiness.se. Ed. Anna Blomen TEL 46-8-56488641. Adv. contact Mertz Laakso. Circ: 33,000.

671.52 ZAF ISSN 1022-8187
CODEN: FWPJA7
FOUNDRY & HEAT TREATMENT S A. Text in English. 1961; N.S. 1993. bi-m. ZAR 64.98; ZAR 76 in Africa; ZAR 96 elsewhere. adv. bk.rev. charts; illus.; tr.lit. index, cum.index: 1961-1963. reprints avail. **Document type:** *Journal, Trade.*
Former titles (until 1993): F W P Materials Engineering Journal (1021-5999); Founding, Welding, Production Engineering Journal; (until vol.17, no.3, 1977): F.W.P. Journal (0015-9026)
Related titles: Microform ed.: N.S. (from PQC).
Indexed: BCIRA, CIN, ChemAb, ChemTitl, ISAP.
—CASDDS, INIST, Linda Hall.
Published by: (South African Institutes of Foundrymen, Welding and Production Engineers), George Warman Publications (Pty.) Ltd., Rondebosch, PO Box 705, Cape Town, 7701, South Africa. info@gwarmanpublications.co.za, http://www.gwarmanpublications.co.za. Circ: 1,826.

671.52 CHN ISSN 1001-1382
TS227.A1
HANJIE/WELDING & JOINING. Text in Chinese. m. USD 62.40 (effective 2009).
Related titles: Online - full text ed.
Indexed: A22, ASFA, OceAb.
—BLDSC (9289.970000), East View, IE, Ingenta.
Published by: (Chinese Mechanical Engineering Society), Jixie Dianzi Gongye Bu, Harbin Hanjie Yanjiusuo/Ministry of Engineering and Electronic Industry, Harbin Welding Research Institute, 65, Hexing Lu, Harbin, Heilongjiang 150080, China. TEL 36695. Ed. Ren Dacheng.

671.52 CHN ISSN 0253-360X
TS227.A1 CODEN: HHPAD2
HANJIE XUEBAO/CHINA WELDING INSTITUTION. TRANSACTIONS. Text in Chinese; Abstracts in English. 1980. q. USD 80.40 (effective 2009). **Document type:** *Proceedings, Academic/Scholarly.*
Related titles: Online - full text ed.
Indexed: A22, A28, APA, BrCerAb, C&ISA, CA/WCA, CIA, CIN, CPEI, CerAb, ChemAb, ChemTitl, CivEngAb, CorrAb, E&CAJ, E11, EEA, EMA, ESPM, EngInd, EnvEAb, H15, M&TEA, M09, MBF, METADEX, RefZh, SCOPUS, SolStAb, T04, WAA, Weldasearch.
—BLDSC (8912.450000), CASDDS, East View, IE, Ingenta, Linda Hall.
Published by: (Zhongguo Jixie Gongcheng Xuehui/Chinese Society of Mechanical Engineering), Harbin Hanjie Yanjiusuo/Harbin Research Institute of Welding, 111 Hexing Lu, Harbin, Heilongjiang 150080, China. TEL 6336695. Ed. Li Zhaoshan. adv.: page USD 2,000. Circ: 12,000. **Dist. overseas by:** China International Book Trading Corp, 35 Chegongzhuang Xilu, Haidian District, PO Box 399, Beijing 100044, China.

671.52 USA
HAYNES ALLOYS DIGEST. Text in English. 1950. q. free. back issues avail. **Document type:** *Bulletin.* **Description:** Solutions to problems caused by deterioration of equipment from heat and corrosion.
Former titles: Haynes High Performance Alloys Digest; Cabot High Performance Alloys Digest
Published by: Haynes International, Inc., 1020 W Park Ave, Box 9013, Kokomo, IN 46904-9013. TEL 317-456-6000, FAX 317-456-6905, TELEX 27-2280. Circ: 11,000 (controlled).

671.52 FIN ISSN 0437-6056
HITSAUSTEKNIIKKA - SVETSTEKNIK. Text in Finnish. 1949. 6/yr. EUR 55 in Scandinavia; EUR 100 elsewhere; EUR 10 per issue (effective 2005). adv. **Document type:** *Journal, Trade.* **Description:** Aims to provide professionally high quality theoretical and practical information concerning welding technology and its related trades for specialists and non-specialists alike.
Indexed: M09, T04, Weldasearch.
Published by: Suomen Hitsausteknillinen Yhdistys/Welding Society of Finland, Makelankatu 36 A, Helsinki, 00510, Finland. TEL 358-9-7732199, FAX 358-9-7732661, shy@co.inet.fi. Ed. Juha Lukkari. Adv. contact Terttu Lindewald. B&W page EUR 1,100, color page EUR 1,500; 178 x 266. Circ: 5,500 (controlled).

671.52 IND ISSN 0046-9092
CODEN: IWLJAK
INDIAN WELDING JOURNAL. Abbreviated title: I W J. Text in English. 1969. q. free to members (effective 2011). adv. bk.rev. abstr.; bibl.; charts; illus. **Document type:** *Journal, Academic/Scholarly.* **Description:** Promotes knowledge and technology of joining materials.
Indexed: A09, A22, A28, APA, BrCerAb, C&ISA, CA/WCA, CIA, CerAb, ChemAb, CivEngAb, CorrAb, E&CAJ, E11, EEA, EMA, ESPM, EnvEAb, H15, M&TEA, M09, MBF, METADEX, SolStAb, T04, WAA, Weldasearch.
—BLDSC (4431.070000), CASDDS, IE, Ingenta, INIST, Linda Hall.
Published by: Indian Institute of Welding, Mayur Apartments, Flat No. 4B/N, 3A, Dr. U. N. Brahmachari St, Kolkata, 700 017, India. TEL 91-33-22813208, FAX 91-33-22871350, hq@iiwindia.com, http://www.iiwindia.com.

671.52 USA ISSN 1523-7168
INSPECTION TRENDS; the magazine for materials inspection and testing personnel. Abbreviated title: Insp. trends. Text in English. 1998. q. USD 30 domestic to non-members; USD 50 foreign to non-members; USD 20 to members; USD 10 per issue to non-members; USD 7 per issue to members (effective 2011). adv. back issues avail. **Document type:** *Magazine, Trade.* **Description:** Covers inspection and testing of welds and materials, as well as conferences.
Related titles: Online - full text ed.: free (effective 2011).
Published by: American Welding Society, 550 N W LeJeune Rd, Miami, FL 33126. TEL 305-443-9353, 800-443-9353, info@aws.org. Ed. Mary Ruth Johnsen. Pub. Andrew Cullison. Adv. contact Lea Garrigan Badwy. Circ: 18,000 (paid).

671.52 JPN ISSN 0021-4787
TS227.A1 CODEN: YOGAAK
JAPAN WELDING SOCIETY. JOURNAL/YOSETSU GAKKAISHI. Text in English, Japanese. 1926. q. JPY 12,000 (effective 2001). adv. bk.rev. bibl.; charts; illus. **Document type:** *Journal, Academic/Scholarly.*
Indexed: A28, APA, BrCerAb, C&ISA, CA/WCA, CIA, CIN, CPEI, CerAb, ChemAb, ChemTitl, CivEngAb, CorrAb, E&CAJ, E11, EEA, EMA, ESPM, EngInd, EnvEAb, H15, INIS AtomInd, JTA, M&TEA, M09, MBF, METADEX, SCOPUS, SolStAb, T04, WAA, Weldasearch.
—CASDDS, INIST, Linda Hall.
Published by: Japan Welding Society/Yosetsu Gakkai, 1-11 Kanda-Sakuma-cho, Chiyoda-ku, Tokyo, 101-0025, Japan. TEL 81-3-3253-0488, FAX 81-3-3253-3059. Ed. Masabumi Suzuki.

671.52 NLD ISSN 0023-8694
CODEN: LASTAW
LASTECHNIEK. Text in Dutch. 1934. m. adv. index. **Document type:** *Trade.*
Indexed: A22, CIN, CISA, ChemAb, ChemTitl, M09, T04, Weldasearch.
—BLDSC (5157.000000), CASDDS, IE, Infotrieve, Ingenta, INIST, Linda Hall.
Published by: Nederlands Instituut voor Lastechniek/Dutch Welding Institute, Boerhaavelaan 40, Zoetermeer, 2713 HX, Netherlands. TEL 31-88-4008560, FAX 31-79-3531178, info@nil.nl. adv.: B&W page EUR 1,615, color page EUR 2,465; trim 210 x 297. Circ: 3,100.

671.52 USA
M E M C O NEWS. Text in English. 1950. q. free to qualified personnel. **Document type:** *Magazine, Trade.* **Description:** News, features, and photography on contemporary applications of arc welding equipment.
Published by: Miller Electric Manufacturing Co., 1635 W Spencer, Box 1079, Appleton, WI 54911. TEL 920-735-4249, FAX 920-735-4013. Ed. Mike Pankratz. R&P Mike Pankratzt TEL 920-734-9821. Circ: 100,000 (controlled).

671.52 CHN ISSN 1001-4934
MOJU JISHU/DIE AND MOULD TECHNOLOGY. Text in Chinese. 1983. bi-m.
Related titles: Online - full text ed.
—East View.
Published by: (Shanghai Moju Jishu Yanjiusuo), Shanghai Jiaotong Daxue Chubanshe/Shanghai Jiaotong University Press, 951, Fanyu Lu, Xuhui-qu, Shanghai, 200030, China. TEL 86-21-64073126, sjtup@sjtu.edu.cn, http://www.jiaodapress.com.cn/default.asp.

671 JPN ISSN 0387-4508
TS227.A1 CODEN: TRJWD2
OSAKA UNIVERSITY. JOINING & WELDING RESEARCH INSTITUTE. TRANSACTIONS. Text in English. s-a. (2 nos./vol.). back issues avail. **Document type:** *Journal, Academic/Scholarly.*
Indexed: A22, A28, APA, BrCerAb, C&ISA, CA/WCA, CIA, CerAb, CivEngAb, CorrAb, E&CAJ, E11, EEA, EMA, ESPM, EnvEAb, H15, INIS AtomInd, M&TEA, M09, MBF, METADEX, SolStAb, T04, TM, WAA, Weldasearch.
—BLDSC (8975.400000), IE, Ingenta, INIST, Linda Hall.
Published by: Osaka University, Joining and Welding Research Institute, 11-1 Mihogaoka, Ibaraki, Osaka, 567-0047, Japan. TEL 81-6-68775111, FAX 81-6-68798689. Circ: 1,000 (controlled).

671.52 UKR ISSN 0957-798X
PATON WELDING JOURNAL. Text in English. 1986. m. USD 460 foreign (effective 2005). adv. **Document type:** *Journal, Academic/Scholarly.* **Description:** Describes the work carried out at the E O Paton Electric Welding Institute in Kiev in all areas of welding. Reports latest work on the theory and practice of welding processes, arc physics, welding metallurgy, testing and properties of welded structures and joints and assessment of welding equipment.
Supersedes in part (in 1989): Welding International (0950-7116); Which was formed by the merger of (1959-1986): Automatic Welding (0005-108X); (1959-1986): Welding Production (0043-230X)
Related titles: Online - full text ed.; ◆ Translation of: Avtomaticheskaya Svarka. ISSN 0005-111X.
Indexed: M09, T04, Weldasearch.
—BLDSC (0416.679500), AskIEEE, IE, Ingenta, INIST, Linda Hall. **CCC.**
Published by: (Natsional'na Akademiya Nauk Ukrainy, Instytut Elektrozvaryuvannya im. EO Patona), Paton Publishing House, E.O. Paton Welding Institute, vul Bozhenko, 11, Kyi, 03680, Ukraine. TEL 380-44-2276302, FAX 380-44-2680486, journal@paton.kiev.ua. adv.: B&W page USD 150; 170 x 250.

671.52 DEU ISSN 0554-9965
DER PRAKTIKER; Das Magazin fuer Schweisstechnik und Mehr. Text in German. 1948. m. EUR 81; EUR 11 newsstand/cover (effective 2011). adv. **Document type:** *Magazine, Trade.*
Indexed: A22, A28, APA, BrCerAb, C&ISA, CA/WCA, CIA, CerAb, CivEngAb, CorrAb, E&CAJ, E11, EEA, EMA, ESPM, EnvEAb, H15, M&TEA, M09, MBF, METADEX, RefZh, SolStAb, T04, TM, WAA, Weldasearch.
—BLDSC (6599.550000), IE, Infotrieve, INIST, Linda Hall. **CCC.**
Published by: (Deutscher Verband fuer Schweissen und verwandte Verfahren e.V.), D V S Verlag GmbH, Aachener Str 172, Duesseldorf, 40223, Germany. TEL 49-211-15910, FAX 49-211-1591150, verlag@dvs-hg.de, http://www.dvs-verlag.de. Ed. Dietmar Rippegather. Adv. contact Iris Jansen. Circ: 10,109 (paid and controlled).

671.52 POL ISSN 0033-2364
CODEN: PRZAA3
PRZEGLAD SPAWALNICTWA. Text in Polish. 1949. m. USD 90. bk.rev. bibl.; charts; illus. index.
Related titles: Microfilm ed.
Indexed: B22, CIN, CISA, ChemAb, ChemTitl, M09, T04, Weldasearch.
—CASDDS, INIST, Linda Hall.
Published by: (Stowarzyszenie Inzynierow i Technikow Mechanikow Polskich), Oficyna Wydawnicza S I M P Press Ltd., ul Swietokrzyska 14a, Warsaw, 00050, Poland. TEL 48-22-272542. Ed. Jan Pilarczyk. adv.: B&W page USD 1,010. Circ: 1,100. **Dist. by:** Ars Polona, Obroncow 25, Warsaw 03933, Poland.

671.52 USA
R & D FOCUS. (Research and Development) Text in English. 1986. 3/yr. free. charts; illus. **Description:** Covers ongoing cooperative research and development in zinc and lead.
Published by: International Lead Zinc Research Organization, Inc., PO Box 12036, Research Triangle Park, NC 27709-2036. TEL 919-361-4647, FAX 919-361-1957, TELEX 261533. Ed. John A Sharpe III. Circ: 1,100.

671.52 USA
R W M A NEWS. Text in English. 1939. q. free. **Document type:** *Newsletter.* **Description:** Provides information on the resistance welding industry, standards and educational resources.

Published by: Resistance Welder Manufacturers Association, 100 N. 20th St., Ste. 400, Philadelphia, PA 19103-1462. TEL 215-564-3484, FAX 215-963-9785. Circ: 500.

671.52 BRA ISSN 0104-9224
➤ **REVISTA SOLDAGEM & INSPECAO.** Text in Portuguese. 1995. q. **Document type:** *Journal, Academic/Scholarly.*
Related titles: Online - full text ed.: ISSN 1980-6973. 2005. free (effective 2011).
Indexed: A28, APA, BrCerAb, C&ISA, CA/WCA, CIA, CPEI, CerAb, CivEngAb, CorrAb, E&CAJ, E11, EEA, EMA, ESPM, EnvEAb, H15, M&TEA, M09, MBF, METADEX, MSCI, SCI, SCOPUS, SolStAb, T04, W07, WAA, Weldasearch.
—Linda Hall.
Published by: Associacao Brasileira da Soldagem, Rua Dr Guilherme Bannitz 126, Conj 42, Itaim-Bibi, Sao Paulo, 04532-060, Brazil. TEL 55-11-30455040, FAX 55-11-30458578, abs@abs-soldagem.org.br, http://www.abs-soldagem.org.br. Ed. Paulo J Modenesi.

671.52 ITA ISSN 0035-6794
TS227 CODEN: RISAAT
RIVISTA ITALIANA DELLA SALDATURA. Text in Italian. 1949. bi-m. adv. bk.rev. bibl.; charts; illus.; pat. index. **Document type:** *Magazine, Trade.* **Description:** Published by the Italian Institute of Welding, it is aimed at professionals in the field of welding.
Indexed: A28, APA, BrCerAb, C&ISA, CA/WCA, CIA, CISA, CPEI, CerAb, ChemAb, CivEngAb, CorrAb, E&CAJ, E11, EEA, EMA, EngInd, H15, M&TEA, M09, MBF, METADEX, SCOPUS, SolStAb, T04, WAA, Weldasearch.
—CASDDS, INIST, Linda Hall.
Published by: Istituto Italiano della Saldatura, Lungobisagno Istria, 15, Genoa, GE 16141, Italy. TEL 39-010-83411, FAX 39-010-8367780, iis@iis.it, http://www.iis.it.

671.52 ZAF
S A I W FUSION. Text in English. 1994. bi-m. illus. **Document type:** *Magazine, Trade.*
Published by: South African Institute of Welding/Suid-Afrikaanse Instituut vir Sweiwese, PO Box 527, Crown Mines, 2025, South Africa.

671.52 RUS ISSN 0934-8069
S P + T. LITEINOE PROIZVODSTVO I TEKHNOLOGIYA LITEINOGO DELA. Text in Russian. 1987. a. 80 p./no.; **Document type:** *Journal, Trade.* **Description:** Devoted to innovations in the field of casting and foundry technologies, equipment and products abroad.
Related titles: ◆ Translation of: C P & T International. ISSN 0935-7262; ◆ Supplement to: Chernye Metally. ISSN 0132-0890.
Indexed: RefZh.
Published by: Izdatel'stvo Ruda i Metally/Ore and Metals Publishers, Leninskii prospekt 6, korpus 1, ofis 622, a/ya 71, Moscow, 119049, Russian Federation. rim@rudmet.ru. Ed. Evgenii Tsiryul'nikov. Circ: 4,000.

671.52 JPN
SANGYO TOKUSHIN (YOSETUPAN). Text in Japanese. d. JPY 63,000 (effective 2008). **Document type:** *Bulletin, Trade.*
Published by: Sanpo Shuppan K.K./Sanpo Publications, Inc., 1-11 Kanda Sakuma-cho Chiyoda-ku, Tokyo, 101-0025, Japan. sanpo@sanpo-pub.co.jp, http://www.sanpo-pub.co.jp/.

669 DEU ISSN 1616-7376
SCHRIFTENREIHE FUEGETECHNIK MAGDEBURG. Text in German. 2000. irreg., latest 2009. price varies. **Document type:** *Monographic series, Academic/Scholarly.*
Published by: Shaker Verlag GmbH, Kaiserstr 100, Herzogenrath, 52134, Germany. TEL 49-2407-95960, FAX 49-2407-95969, info@shaker.de.

671.52 AUT ISSN 1027-3352
CODEN: SWTEAJ
SCHWEISS- UND PRUEFTECHNIK; oesterreichische Fachzeitschrift fuer Schweissen, Schneiden und Pruefen. Text in German. 1946. m. EUR 60 (effective 2005). bk.rev. back issues avail. **Document type:** *Magazine, Trade.*
Formerly (until 1996): Schweisstechnik (0253-5262)
Indexed: A28, APA, BrCerAb, C&ISA, CA/WCA, CIA, CerAb, ChemAb, ChemTitl, CivEngAb, CorrAb, E&CAJ, E11, EEA, EMA, ESPM, EnvEAb, H15, M&TEA, M09, MBF, METADEX, SolStAb, T04, TM, WAA, Weldasearch.
—CASDDS, INIST, Linda Hall.
Published by: Oesterreichische Gesellschaft fuer Schweisstechnik, Arsenal Objekt 207, Vienna, W 1030, Austria. TEL 43-1-7982168, FAX 43-1-798216836, oegs@aon.at, http://www.oegs.org. Ed. Johann Wasserbauer. Adv. contact Susanne Mesaric. Circ: 1,300.

671.52 DEU ISSN 0036-7184
TS227 CODEN: SCSCA4
SCHWEISSEN UND SCHNEIDEN. Text in German. 1948. bi-m. EUR 156; EUR 16.50 newsstand/cover (effective 2011). adv. bk.rev. bibl.; charts; illus.; pat. index. reprints avail. **Document type:** *Magazine, Trade.*
Incorporates: Schweisstechnik (0036-7192)
Related titles: Microform ed.: (from PQC).
Indexed: A22, A28, APA, ApMecR, BMT, BrCerAb, C&ISA, CA/WCA, CEABA, CIA, CIN, CISA, CerAb, ChemAb, ChemTitl, CivEngAb, CoppAb, CorrAb, DokArb, E&CAJ, E11, EEA, EMA, ESPM, EnvEAb, H15, Inspec, M&TEA, M09, MBF, METADEX, SCOPUS, SolStAb, T04, WAA, Weldasearch.
—CASDDS, IE, Ingenta, INIST, Linda Hall. **CCC.**
Published by: (Deutscher Verband fuer Schweissen und verwandte Verfahren e.V.), D V S Verlag GmbH, Aachener Str 172, Duesseldorf, 40223, Germany. TEL 49-211-15910, FAX 49-211-1591150, verlag@dvs-hg.de, http://www.dvs-verlag.de. Ed. Dietmar Rippegather. Adv. contact Iris Jansen. Circ: 5,295 (paid and controlled).

671.52 DEU ISSN 1612-3441
DER SCHWEISSER; Informationen fuer den Praktiker. Text in German. 2001. bi-m. EUR 21 (effective 2011). adv. **Document type:** *Magazine, Trade.*
Published by: D V S Verlag GmbH, Aachener Str 172, Duesseldorf, 40223, Germany. TEL 49-211-15910, FAX 49-211-1591150, verlag@dvs-hg.de. Circ: 12,000 (controlled).

671.52 CHE ISSN 0036-7206
SCHWEISSTECHNIK/SOUDURE. Text in French, German. 1911. m. adv. charts; illus.; pat. Supplement avail. **Document type:** *Trade.*
Indexed: CISA, ChemAb, Weldasearch.
Published by: (Schweizerischer Verein fuer Schweisstechnik), Technica Verlags AG, Hoehenweg 1, Rupperswil, 5102, Switzerland. TEL 41-62-8893000, FAX 41-62-8893003, verkauf@technica-verlag.ch. Circ: 3,330.

671.52 GBR ISSN 1743-2936
➤ **SCIENCE AND TECHNOLOGY OF WELDING AND JOINING (ONLINE).** Text in English. 1999. 8/yr. GBP 637 to institutions; USD 1,129 in United States to institutions (effective 2012). back issues avail. **Document type:** *Journal, Academic/Scholarly.* **Description:** Examines the science and technology of welding and joining processes for all materials.
Media: Online - full text (from IngentaConnect).
—CCC.
Published by: (Japan Welding Society/Yosetsu Gakkai JPN, Institute of Materials, Minerals and Mining), Maney Publishing, Ste 1C, Joseph's Well, Hanover Walk, Leeds, W Yorks LS3 1AB, United Kingdom. TEL 44-113-2432800, FAX 44-113-3868178, maney@maney.co.uk, http://www.maney.co.uk. Eds. H K D H Bhadeshia, Dr. S R David, T G Debroy. **Subscr. in N. America to:** Maney Publishing, 875 Massachusetts Ave, 7th Fl, Cambridge, MA 02139. TEL 866-297-5154, FAX 617-354-6875, maney@maneyusa.com.

671.52 CAN
SHEET METAL JOURNAL. Text in English. q. free to qualified personnel. **Document type:** *Magazine, Trade.* **Description:** Offers professionals, working in the sheet metal industry, a forum to share information and improve communication.
Published by: Point One Media, #3-2232 Wilgress Rd, Nanaimo, BC V9S 4N4, Canada. TEL 877-755-2762, FAX 250-758-8665, info@pointonemedia.com, http://www.pointonemedia.com. Ed. Lara Perraton. Pub. Joe Perraton.

671.52 ESP ISSN 1130-0280
SOLDADURA Y TECNOLOGIAS DE UNION. Text in Spanish. 1990. bi-m. EUR 72.07 domestic; EUR 94.87 foreign (effective 2010). adv. **Document type:** *Magazine, Trade.* **Description:** Covers soldering and welding techniques, equipment and installations.
Indexed: IECT, Weldasearch.
Published by: Reed Business Information SA (Subsidiary of: Reed Business Information International), Zancoeta 9, Bilbao, 48013, Spain. TEL 34-944-285600, FAX 34-944-425116, rbi@rbi.es. Ed. Nuria Martin. Adv. contact Eduardo Lazaro. Circ: 3,500.

671.52 GBR ISSN 0954-0911
TS610 CODEN: SSMOEO
➤ **SOLDERING & SURFACE MOUNT TECHNOLOGY.** Abbreviated title: S S M T. Text in English. 1981. q. EUR 2,609 combined subscription in Europe (print & online eds.); USD 3,039 combined subscription in the Americas (print & online eds.); GBP 1,879 combined subscription in the UK & elsewhere (print & online eds.); AUD 3,629 combined subscription in Australasia (print & online eds.) (effective 2012). charts; illus. back issues avail.; reprint service avail. from PSC. **Document type:** *Journal, Academic/Scholarly.* **Description:** Provides an independent forum for the critical evaluation and dissemination of research and development, applications, processes and current practices relating to all areas of soldering and surface mount technology.
Formerly (until 1989): Brazing and Soldering (0263-0060)
Related titles: Online - full text ed.: ISSN 1758-6836 (from IngentaConnect).
Indexed: A15, A22, A28, ABIn, APA, B01, B06, B07, B09, BrCerAb, C&ISA, CA, CA/WCA, CIA, CIN, CPEI, Cadscan, CerAb, ChemAb, ChemTitl, CivEngAb, CorrAb, CurCont, E&CAJ, E01, E11, EEA, EMA, ESPM, EmerIntel, EngInd, EnvEAb, H15, Inspec, LeadAb, M&TEA, M09, MBF, METADEX, MSCI, P26, P48, P51, P52, P54, PQC, RefZh, SCI, SCOPUS, SolStAb, T02, T04, TM, W07, WAA, Weldasearch, Zincscan.
—BLDSC (8327.242650), AskIEEE, CASDDS, IE, Infotrieve, Ingenta, INIST, Linda Hall. **CCC.**
Published by: (Surface Mount and Related Technologies (SMART) Group), Emerald Group Publishing Ltd., Howard House, Wagon Ln, Bingley, W Yorks BD16 1WA, United Kingdom. TEL 44-1274-777700, FAX 44-1274-785201, information@emeraldinsight.com. Ed. Martin Goosey. Pub. Harry Colson.

➤ **SOUTH AFRICAN INSTITUTE OF WELDING. NATIONAL REGISTER/SUID-AFRIKAANSE INSTITUUT VIR SWEIWESE. NASIONALE REGISTER.** *see* BUSINESS AND ECONOMICS—Trade And Industrial Directories

671.52 POL ISSN 1732-1425
SPAJANIE METALI I TWORZYW W PRAKTYCE. Text in Polish. 2002. q.
Formerly (until 2004): Zgrzewanie Metali i Tworzyw w Praktyce (1644-4019)
Indexed: B22.
Published by: Wydawnictwo Lektorium, ul Robotnicza 72, Wroclaw, 53608, Poland. TEL 48-71-7985900, FAX 48-71-7985947, info@lektorium.pl, http://www.lektorium.com.

STROJNISKI VESTNIK/JOURNAL OF MECHANICAL ENGINEERING. *see* ENGINEERING—Mechanical Engineering

671.52 ROM ISSN 1453-0384
SUDURA. Text in English, Romanian. 1997. q.
Indexed: A28, APA, BrCerAb, C&ISA, CA/WCA, CIA, CerAb, CivEngAb, CorrAb, E&CAJ, E11, EEA, EMA, H15, M&TEA, M09, MBF, METADEX, SolStAb, T04, WAA, Weldasearch.
—Linda Hall.
Published by: Editura Sudura S.R.L., Bv Mihai Viteazul 30, 5, Timisoara, 1441, Romania. editura.sudura@xnet.ro, http://www.asr.ro/publishing.htm.

671 RUS ISSN 0491-6441
CODEN: SVAPAI
SVAROCHNOE PROIZVODSTVO. Text in Russian. 1930. m. USD 381 foreign (effective 2005). bk.rev. abstr.; bibl.; charts; illus. index. **Document type:** *Journal, Trade.* **Description:** Carries articles on the following major processes: welding, resurfacing, brazing, thermal cutting, spraying and application of metal coating.
Indexed: C&ISA, CIN, CISA, ChemAb, ChemTitl, CorrAb, E&CAJ, Inspec, RefZh, SolStAb, WAA, Weldasearch.
—CASDDS, East View, INIST, Linda Hall. **CCC.**
Published by: Izdatel'stvo Mashinostroenie, Stromynskii per 4, Moscow, 107076, Russian Federation. TEL 7-095-2683858, mashpubl@mashin.ru, http://www.mashin.ru. Ed. V A Kazakov. Circ: 2,000. **Dist. by:** Informnauka Ltd., Ul Usievicha 20, Moscow 125190, Russian Federation. alfimov@viniti.ru.

671.52 NOR ISSN 0804-2489
SVEISEAKTUELT. Text in Norwegian. 1946. bi-m. NOK 50. adv. bk.rev. bibl.; charts; illus. index. **Document type:** *Magazine, Trade.*
Formerly (until 1992): Sveiseteknikk (0039-6427)
Indexed: Weldasearch.
Published by: Norsk Sveiseteknisk Forening, PO Box 242, Lysaker, 1326, Norway. TEL 47-67-838600, FAX 47-67-838601, jga@standard.no, http://www.welderpassport.com. adv.: B&W page NOK 9,000, color page NOK 13,500; 185 x 270.

671.52 SWE ISSN 0341-4248
SVETSAREN; a welding review. Text in German. 1936. 3/yr. free. charts; illus. **Document type:** *Trade.* **Description:** Focuses on technical developments and new applications in welding and cutting as well as presenting new technology and products.
Formerly: Kjelberg - Esab - Schriften (0075-6261)
Related titles: English ed.: Svetsaren (English Edition). ISSN 0346-8577. 1965.
Indexed: ApMecR, ChemAb, Inspec, SCOPUS, Weldasearch.
—IE, Ingenta. **CCC.**
Published by: Esab AB Marketing Communications, Fack 8004, Goeteborg, 40277, Sweden. TEL 46-31-150-90-00, FAX 46-31-509-390. Ed., R&P Lennart Lundberg TEL 46-31-509-000. Circ: 1,600 (controlled).

671.52 SWE ISSN 0039-7091
CODEN: SVTNA5
SVETSEN. Text in Multiple languages. 1941. bi-m. adv. bk.rev. charts; illus. **Document type:** *Magazine, Trade.*
Indexed: A28, APA, BrCerAb, C&ISA, CA/WCA, CIA, CerAb, ChemAb, CivEngAb, CorrAb, E&CAJ, E11, EEA, EMA, ESPM, EnvEAb, H15, M&TEA, M09, MBF, METADEX, SolStAb, T04, WAA, Weldasearch.
—CASDDS, Linda Hall.
Published by: Svetstekniska Foereningen, Box 5073, Stockholm, 10242, Sweden. TEL 46-8-791-29-00, FAX 46-8-679-94-04, svetskom@svets.a.se. Ed., Adv. contact Birgit Lagergren. B&W page SEK 10,800, color page SEK 16,800; trim 172 x 250. Circ: 3,200 (controlled).

671.52 GBR
T W I BULLETIN. Text in English. 1968. bi-m. free to members (effective 2009). **Document type:** *Bulletin.* **Description:** Provides information on welding and joining, engineering, NDT inspection, materials, surfacing, and lifecycle integrity.
Former titles (until 19??): Welding Institute Research Bulletin; B W R A Bulletin
Published by: T W I - The Welding Institute, T W I, Abington Hall, Pampisford Rd, Abington, Cambridge, CB1 6AL, United Kingdom. twi@twi.co.uk, http://www.twi.co.uk.

671.52 DEU ISSN 1614-4783
TECHNISCHE UNIVERSITAET BRAUNSCHWEIG. INSTITUT FUER FUEGE- UND SCHWEISSTECHNIK. FORSCHUNGSBERICHTE. Text in German. 2001. irreg., latest vol.23, 2009. price varies. **Document type:** *Monographic series, Academic/Scholarly.*
Formerly (until 2005): Technische Universitaet Braunschweig. Institut fuer Schweisstechnik. Forschungsberichte (1617-2248)
Published by: Shaker Verlag GmbH, Kaiserstr 100, Herzogenrath, 52134, Germany. TEL 49-2407-95960, FAX 49-2407-95969, info@shaker.de.

TEKHNICHESKAYA DIAGNOSTIKA I NERAZRUSHAYUSHCHII KONTROL'/TECHNICAL DIAGNOSTICS AND NONDESTRUCTIVE TESTING; nauchno-teoreticheskii zhurnal. *see* PHYSICS

671.52 SVN ISSN 0505-0278
VARILNA TEHNIKA. Text in Slovenian. 1952. q. USD 150 foreign (effective 2005). **Document type:** *Journal.*
Indexed: A28, APA, BrCerAb, C&ISA, CA/WCA, CIA, CerAb, CivEngAb, CorrAb, E&CAJ, E11, EEA, EMA, ESPM, EnvEAb, H15, M&TEA, M09, MBF, METADEX, SolStAb, T04, WAA, Weldasearch.
—Linda Hall.
Published by: Institut za Varilstvo, Ptujska cesta 19, Ljubljana, 1000, Slovenia. TEL 386-1-2809400, FAX 386-1-2809422, info@i-var.si, http://www.i-var.si. Ed. Pavel Stular.

671.52 USA
W R C PROGRESS REPORTS. Text in English. 1977. bi-m. free to members (effective 2011). **Document type:** *Report, Trade.*
Indexed: Weldasearch.
Published by: Welding Research Council, PO Box 201547, Shaker Heights, OH 44120. TEL 216-658-3847, FAX 216-658-3854, wrc@forengineers.org, http://www.forengineers.org/wrc/.

671.52 IND ISSN 0970-4477
➤ **W R I JOURNAL.** (Welding Research Institute) Text in English. 19??. q. **Document type:** *Journal, Academic/Scholarly.* **Description:** Contains technical articles, news of forthcoming seminars and conferences, as well as new products in the welding industry.
Formerly (until 1989): W R I Keywords
Indexed: M09, T04, Weldasearch.
—Linda Hall.
Published by: Bharat Heavy Electricals Ltd., Welding Research Institute, BHEL, Tiruchirappalli, Tamil Nadu 620 014, India. TEL 91-431-2520266, FAX 91-431-2520770, wri@bheltry.co.in, http://www.wriindia.com.

671.52 DEU ISSN 1612-3433
TS227.A1
WELDING AND CUTTING. Text in English. 2002. bi-m. EUR 113; EUR 19.50 newsstand/cover (effective 2011). adv. **Document type:** *Magazine, Trade.*
Indexed: A28, APA, BrCerAb, C&ISA, CA/WCA, CIA, CPEI, CerAb, CivEngAb, CorrAb, E&CAJ, E11, EEA, EMA, ESPM, EngInd, EnvEAb, H15, M&TEA, M09, MBF, METADEX, RefZh, SCOPUS, SolStAb, T04, WAA, Weldasearch.
—CCC.
Published by: D V S Verlag GmbH, Aachener Str 172, Duesseldorf, 40223, Germany. TEL 49-211-15910, FAX 49-211-1591150, verlag@dvs-hg.de, http://www.dvs-verlag.de. Ed. Dietmar Rippegather. Adv. contact Iris Jansen. Circ: 10,000 (paid and controlled).

671.52 FRA ISSN 0043-2288
TS227 CODEN: WDWRAI
➤ **WELDING IN THE WORLD/SOUDAGE DANS LE MONDE.** Text in English, French. 1963. bi-m. EUR 446 in the European Union (effective 2010). adv. abstr.; charts; illus. back issues avail. **Document type:** *Journal, Academic/Scholarly.* **Description:** Contains reports, recommendations, addresses and draft standards emanating from commissioned reports and surveys of the IIW, including coverage of processes, metallurgy, testing and inspection, health and safety issues.
Related titles: Microfilm ed.: (from PQC); Online - full text ed.: ISSN 1878-6669.
Indexed: A22, BMT, C&ISA, CIN, CISA, CPEI, ChemAb, ChemTitl, E&CAJ, EngInd, Inspec, M09, MSCI, SCI, SCOPUS, SolStAb, T04, TM, W07, Weldasearch.
—BLDSC (9293.200000), CASDDS, IE, Infotrieve, Ingenta, INIST, Linda Hall. **CCC.**
Published by: International Institute of Welding/Institute International de la Soudure, IIW Secretariat, Villepinte, BP 50362, Roissy CDG, Cedex 95942, France. TEL 33-1-49903615, FAX 33-1-49903680, iiwdoc@wanadoo.fr, http://www.iiw-iis.org. Circ: 900.

671.52 GBR ISSN 0950-7116
TS227.A1 CODEN: WEINEF
WELDING INTERNATIONAL. Text in English. 1987. m. GBP 2,069 combined subscription in United Kingdom to institutions (print & online eds.); EUR 3,147, USD 3,952 combined subscription to institutions (print & online eds.) (effective 2012). adv. bibl.; charts; illus. index. back issues avail.; reprint service avail. from PSC. **Document type:** *Journal, Abstract/Index.* **Description:** Provides translations of complete articles selected from major welding journals of the world.
Formed by the merger of (1959-1986): Automatic Welding (0005-108X); (1959-1986): Welding Production (0043-230X)
Related titles: Online - full text ed.: ISSN 1754-2138. GBP 1,862 in United Kingdom to institutions; EUR 2,832, USD 3,557 to institutions (effective 2012) (from IngentaConnect).
Indexed: A10, A22, A26, A28, APA, BrCerAb, C&ISA, C10, CA, CA/WCA, CIA, CPEI, CerAb, CivEngAb, CorrAb, E&CAJ, E01, E11, EEA, EMA, ESPM, EnvEAb, H15, Inspec, M&TEA, M09, MBF, METADEX, P16, P26, P48, P52, P53, P54, PQC, RefZh, SCOPUS, SolStAb, T02, T04, TM, V03, WAA, Weldasearch.
—BLDSC (9290.670000), AskIEEE, IE, Infotrieve, Ingenta, INIST, Linda Hall. **CCC.**
Published by: (T W I - The Welding Institute), Taylor & Francis Ltd. (Subsidiary of: Taylor & Francis Group), 4 Park Sq, Milton Park, Abingdon, Oxfordshire OX14 4RN, United Kingdom. TEL 44-20-70176000, FAX 44-20-70176336, subscriptions@tandf.co.uk, http://www.taylorandfrancis.com. **Subscr. to:** Journals Customer Service, Sheepen Pl, Colchester, Essex CO3 3LP, United Kingdom. TEL 44-20-70175544, FAX 44-20-70175198, tf.enquiries@tfinforma.com.

671.52 USA ISSN 0043-2296
TS227 CODEN: WEJUA3
➤ **WELDING JOURNAL.** Abbreviated title: W J. Text in English. 1922. m. USD 90 domestic to non-members; USD 130 foreign to non-members; USD 8 per issue to non-members; USD 6 per issue to members (effective 2010). adv. bk.rev. illus.; pat.; tr.lit. index. back issues avail.; reprints avail. **Document type:** *Journal, Trade.* **Description:** Covers news of the welding and metal fabricating industry including the latest products, trends, technology and events.
Former titles (until 1937): American Welding Society Journal (0095-9936); (until 1934): American Welding Society. Journal; (until 1922): American Welding Society. Proceedings
Related titles: Microform ed.: (from PMC, PQC); Online - full text ed.; ◆ Supplement(s): Welding Research. ISSN 0096-7629.
Indexed: A05, A20, A22, A23, A24, A28, AESIS, APA, AS&TA, AS&TI, ASCA, ApMecR, B04, B13, BMT, BRD, BrCerAb, C&ISA, C10, CA, CA/WCA, CADCAM, CIA, CIN, CPEI, CerAb, ChemAb, CivEngAb, CorrAb, CurCont, E&CAJ, E11, EEA, EMA, ESPM, EngInd, EnvEAb, ErgAb, H15, IBR, IBZ, INIS AtomInd, ISR, M&TEA, M09, MBF, METADEX, MSCI, RefZh, RoboAb, S04, SCI, SCOPUS, SolStAb, T02, T04, TM, W03, W05, W07, WAA, Weldasearch.
—BLDSC (9291.000000), CASDDS, IE, Infotrieve, Ingenta, INIST, Linda Hall. **CCC.**
Published by: American Welding Society, 550 N W LeJeune Rd, Miami, FL 33126. TEL 305-443-9353, 800-443-9353, FAX 305-442-7451, info@aws.org. Ed., Pub. Andy Cullison TEL 305-443-9353 ext 249. Adv. contact Frank Wilson TEL 305-443-9353 ext 465.

671.52 USA ISSN 0043-2318
TS227
WELDING RESEARCH ABROAD. Text in English. 1955. 10/yr. free to members (effective 2011). charts; illus.; stat. index. **Document type:** *Journal, Trade.*
Indexed: A22, C&ISA, CPEI, E&CAJ, EngInd, SCOPUS, SolStAb, TM.
—BLDSC (9291.500000), IE, Infotrieve, Ingenta, INIST, Linda Hall.
Published by: Welding Research Council, PO Box 201547, Shaker Heights, OH 44120. TEL 216-658-3847, FAX 216-658-3854, wrc@forengineers.org, http://www.forengineers.org/wrc/.

671.52 USA ISSN 0043-2326
TS227 CODEN: WRCBA2
WELDING RESEARCH COUNCIL. BULLETIN. Text in English. 1949. 10/yr. free to members (effective 2011). charts; illus. **Document type:** *Bulletin, Trade.*
Formerly (until 1961): Welding Research Council. Bulletin Series (0421-2118)
Indexed: A22, C&ISA, CPEI, ChemAb, E&CAJ, EngInd, ISMEC, M09, SCOPUS, SolStAb, T04, TM, Weldasearch.
—BLDSC (9364.585000), CASDDS, IE, Ingenta, INIST, Linda Hall.
Published by: Welding Research Council, PO Box 201547, Shaker Heights, OH 44120. TEL 216-658-3847, FAX 216-658-3854, wrc@forengineers.org, http://www.forengineers.org/wrc/.

671.52 USA ISSN 0511-4381
CODEN: WERNA
WELDING RESEARCH NEWS. Text in English. 1967. q. free to members (effective 2011). **Document type:** *Bulletin, Trade.* **Description:** Highlights articles and items on current developments in welding research.
—BLDSC (9292.200000), INIST, Linda Hall.
Published by: Welding Research Council, PO Box 201547, Shaker Heights, OH 44120. TEL 216-658-3847, FAX 216-658-3854, mprager@forengineers.org, http://www.forengineers.org/wrc/.

671.52 USA ISSN 1545-9691
THE WORLD OF WELDING. Text in English. 1990. q. free (effective 2004). adv. **Document type:** *Newsletter, Trade.*
Related titles: Online - full text ed.
Indexed: A09, A10, A28, APA, BrCerAb, C&ISA, CA/WCA, CIA, CerAb, CivEngAb, CorrAb, E&CAJ, E11, EEA, EMA, ESPM, EnvEAb, H15, M&TEA, M02, M09, MBF, METADEX, SolStAb, T02, T04, V03, V04, WAA, Weldasearch.
—Linda Hall.
Published by: Hobart Institute of Welding Technology, 400 Trade Sq E, Troy, OH 45373. TEL 800-332-9448, FAX 937-332-5200. Ed., R&P, Adv. contact Martha A Baker TEL 937-332-5603. Circ: 8,000.

671.52 JPN ISSN 0288-4771
TS227.A1 CODEN: YGRODU
YOSETSU GAKKAI RONBUNSHU/JAPAN WELDING SOCIETY. QUARTERLY JOURNAL. Text in Japanese. 1983. q. **Document type:** *Journal, Academic/Scholarly.*
Related titles: Online - full text ed.
Indexed: A28, APA, BrCerAb, C&ISA, C33, CA/WCA, CIA, CPEI, CerAb, ChemAb, CivEngAb, CorrAb, E&CAJ, E11, EEA, EMA, ESPM, EngInd, EnvEAb, H15, INIS AtomInd, M&TEA, M09, MBF, METADEX, SCOPUS, SolStAb, T04, TM, WAA, Weldasearch.
—INIST, Linda Hall. **CCC.**
Published by: Yosetsu Gakkai/Japan Welding Society, Sanho Sakuma Bldg, 1-11 Kanda Sakuma-cho, Tokyo, Chiyoda-ku 101-0025, Japan. TEL 81-3-32530488, FAX 81-3-32533059.

671.52 JPN ISSN 0387-0197
YOSETU GIJUTSU/WELDING REVIEW. Text in Japanese. 1953. q. JPY 17,124 (effective 2008). **Document type:** *Magazine, Trade.*
Incorporated (1949-1966): Yosetsukai/Welding World (0372-7793)
Published by: Sanpo Shuppan K.K./Sanpo Publications, Inc., 1-11 Kanda Sakuma-cho Chiyoda-ku, Tokyo, 101-0025, Japan. sanpo@sanpo-pub.co.jp, http://www.sanpo-pub.co.jp/. Ed. Hiroshi Morita.

671.52 JPN
YOSETU NYUSU/WELDING NEWS. Text in Japanese. w. JPY 24,468 (effective 2008). **Document type:** *Trade.*
Published by: Sanpo Shuppan K.K./Sanpo Publications, Inc., 1-11 Kanda Sakuma-cho Chiyoda-ku, Tokyo, 101-0025, Japan. sanpo@sanpo-pub.co.jp.

671.52 HRV ISSN 0044-1902
CODEN: ZAVAA8
ZAVARIVANJE. Text in Croatian; Abstracts and contents page in English, German. 1958. bi-m. USD 70. adv. bk.rev. index.
Indexed: CIN, ChemAb, ChemTitl, Weldasearch.
—CASDDS, Linda Hall.
Published by: Drustvo za Tehniku Zavarivanja Hrvatske, Djure Salaja 1, Zagreb, 41000, Croatia. TELEX 22648 FSB YU. Ed. Goran Vrucimic. Circ: 2,000.

671.52 SVK ISSN 0044-5525
CODEN: ZVARAX
ZVARANIE/WELDING. Text in Czech, Slovak; Summaries in English. 1952. m. EUR 65 (effective 2009). adv. bk.rev. charts; illus.; pat. **Document type:** *Journal, Academic/Scholarly.* **Description:** Scientific and technical publication aimed at welding, brazing/soldering, adhesive bonding, cutting, thermal spraying, heat treatment, quality assurance, testing of materials, hygiene, and work safety.
Indexed: A22, A28, APA, BrCerAb, C&ISA, CA/WCA, CIA, CIN, CISA, CerAb, ChemAb, ChemTitl, CivEngAb, CorrAb, E&CAJ, E11, EEA, EMA, ESPM, EnvEAb, H15, INIS AtomInd, M&TEA, M09, MBF, METADEX, SolStAb, T04, TM, WAA, Weldasearch.
—CASDDS, IE, Ingenta, INIST, Linda Hall.
Published by: Vyskumny Ustav Zvaracsky, Priemyselny Institut SR, Racianska 71, Bratislava, 83259, Slovakia. TEL 421-2-49246475, FAX 421-2-49246296. adv.: color page USD 690. Circ: 1,650. **Dist. by:** Slovart G.T.G. s.r.o., Krupinska 4, PO Box 152, Bratislava 85299, Slovakia. TEL 421-2-63839472, FAX 421-2-63839485, info@slovart-gtg.sk, http://www.slovart-gtg.sk.

METEOROLOGY

551.6 USA ISSN 1949-4335
A C D TALES. (Atmospheric Chemistry Division) Text in English. 1991. irreg. **Document type:** *Monographic series, Trade.*
Published by: National Center for Atmospheric Research, PO Box 3000, Boulder, CO 80307. TEL 303-497-1000, http://www.ncar.ucar.edu.

551.5 USA
A M S UPDATE. Text in English. 1980. m. adv. back issues avail. **Document type:** *Newsletter.* **Description:** Contains news briefs, dates, notes on people, information on grants, and contracts for meteorologists, oceanographers, and hydrologists.
Former titles (until 2003): A M S Newsletter (Online) (1095-1296); (until 1996): A M S Newsletter (Print) (0730-2029)
Media: Online - full text.
—CCC.
Published by: American Meteorological Society, 45 Beacon St, Boston, MA 02108. TEL 617-227-2425, FAX 617-742-8718, amspubs@ametsoc.org, http://www.ametsoc.org.

551.6 USA
ACCLIMATIONS. Text in English. 1998. bi-m. back issues avail. **Document type:** *Newsletter, Government.*
Related titles: Online - full text ed.
Published by: U.S. National Assessment of Potential Consequences of Climate Variability and Change, 400 Virginia Ave, S W, Ste 750, Washington, DC 20024. TEL 202-314-2239, FAX 202-488-8681.

551.6 HUN ISSN 0563-0614
ACTA CLIMATOLOGICA. Variant title: Acta Universitatis Szegediensis: Acta Climatologica et Chorologica. Text in English. 1959. biennial. charts; illus. **Document type:** *Monographic series, Academic/Scholarly.* **Description:** Focuses on general climatology, urban climatology, air pollution, bio- and agrometeorology.
Indexed: M&GPA.
Published by: (Szegedi Tudomanyegyetem, Termeszettudomanyi Kar/University of Szeged, Faculty of Science), Szegedi Tudomanyegyetem/University of Szeged, c/o E Szabo, Exchange Librarian, Dugonics ter 13, PO Box 393, Szeged, 6701, Hungary. TEL 36-62-544009, FAX 36-62-420895, Eneh.Szabo@bibl.u-szeged.hu, http://www.u-szeged.hu. Ed. Janos Unger. Circ: 400.

ACTA GEOGRAPHICA AC GEOLOGICA ET METEOROLOGICA DEBRECINA. *see* GEOGRAPHY

551.5 CHN ISSN 0894-0525
QC851 CODEN: AMTSEZ
➤ **ACTA METEOROLOGICA SINICA.** Text in English. 1987. bi-m. EUR 755, USD 929 combined subscription to institutions (print & online eds.) (effective 2012). adv. bk.rev. illus. Index. 128 p./no.; back issues avail.; reprints avail. **Document type:** *Journal, Academic/Scholarly.* **Description:** Covers variety of topics spanning all areas of atmospheric sciences, focusing on important findings and latest advances of atmospheric sciences in China.
Related titles: Microfiche ed.: (from PQC); Online - full text ed.: ISSN 2191-4788 (from WanFang Data Corp.); ◆ Chinese ed.: Qixiang Xuebao. ISSN 0577-6619.
Indexed: Cadscan, ChemAb, E04, E05, GEOBASE, Inspec, LeadAb, M&GPA, P26, P48, P52, P54, P56, PQC, PhysBer, SCI, SCOPUS, W07, Zincscan.
—BLDSC (0637.710000), IE, Ingenta, INIST. **CCC.**
Published by: Chinese Meteorological Society/Zhongguo Qixiang Xuehui, 46 Zhongguancun Nan Dajie, Haidian District, Beijing, 100081, China. TEL 86-10-68407634, FAX 86-10-58993104. Ed. Zhou Xiuji. R&P Zhou Shijian TEL 86-10-6840-7092. Adv. contact Yu Weiping TEL 86-10-6840-6262. Circ: 300 (paid); 30 (controlled). **Dist. outside mainland China by:** Springer, Haber Str 7, Heidelberg 69126, Germany. TEL 49-6221-3454303, FAX 49-6221-3454229, subscriptions@springer.com, http://www.springer.de. **Co-publisher:** Springer.

551.5 CHN ISSN 0256-1530
QC851
➤ **ADVANCES IN ATMOSPHERIC SCIENCES.** Abstracts and contents page in Chinese; Text in English. 1984. bi-m. EUR 854, USD 1,056 combined subscription to institutions (print & online eds.) (effective 2012). 128 p./no.; reprint service avail. from PSC. **Document type:** *Journal, Academic/Scholarly.* **Description:** Covers the latest achievements and developments in atmospheric sciences, including marine meteorology, meteorology-associated geophysics, and theoretical and practical aspects of these disciplines.
Related titles: ◆ CD-ROM ed.: Chinese Academic Journals Full-Text Database. Science & Engineering, Series A. ISSN 1007-8010; Microform ed.: (from PQC); Online - full text ed.: ISSN 1861-9533; ◆ Chinese ed.: Diqiu Kexue Jinzhan. ISSN 1001-8166.
Indexed: A22, A26, A28, A37, APA, BrCerAb, C&ISA, C25, C30, CA/WCA, CABA, CIA, CerAb, CivEngAb, CorrAb, CurCont, E&CAJ, E01, E11, E12, EEA, EMA, ESPM, EnvEAb, F08, F12, FCA, G11, H15, H16, I05, I11, IBR, IBZ, M&GPA, M&TEA, M09, MBF, METADEX, MaizeAb, N02, P26, P32, P40, P47, P48, P52, P54, P56, PGegResA, PGrRegA, PQC, PollutAb, R11, R12, S13, S16, SCI, SCOPUS, SWRA, SolStAb, T04, TAR, TriticAb, W07, W11, WAA.
—East View, IE, Ingenta, INIST. **CCC.**
Published by: Chinese Academy of Sciences, Institute of Atmospheric Physics, PO Box 9804, Beijing, 100029, China. FAX 86-10-82021254, http://www.iap.ac.cn/. Eds. Da-Lin Zhang, Guoxiong Wu, Huijun Wang. Circ: 1,000. **Dist. outside of China by:** Springer, Haber Str 7, Heidelberg 69126, Germany. TEL 49-6221-3454303, FAX 49-6221-3454229, subscriptions@springer.com; **Dist. by:** Haiyang Chubanshe, International Department, 8 Dahuisi Rd, Haidian District, Beijing 100081, China. TEL 86-10-62179976, FAX 86-10-62173569, oceanpress@china.com, http://www.oceanpress.cn/.

551.5 USA ISSN 1687-9309
➤ **ADVANCES IN METEOROLOGY.** Text in English. 2008. irreg. USD 295 (effective 2011). **Document type:** *Journal, Academic/Scholarly.* **Description:** Publishes original research articles as well as review articles in all areas of meteorology.
Related titles: Online - full text ed.: ISSN 1687-9317. free (effective 2011).
Indexed: A01, CA, M&GPA, P52, P56, T02.
Published by: Hindawi Publishing Corporation, 410 Park Ave, 15th Fl, PMB 287, New York, NY 10022. FAX 215-893-4392, 866-446-3294, orders@hindawi.com.

➤ **ADVANCES IN NATURAL AND TECHNOLOGICAL HAZARDS RESEARCH.** *see* TECHNOLOGY: COMPREHENSIVE WORKS

551.65 JPN ISSN 0448-3723
AEROLOGICAL DATA OF JAPAN/KOSO GEPPO. Text in English. 1947. m. stat.
Media: Duplicated (not offset).
Published by: Kishocho/Japan Meteorological Agency, 1-3-4 Otemachi, Chiyoda-ku, Tokyo, 100-8122, Japan. Circ: (controlled).

AEROSOL AND AIR QUALITY RESEARCH. *see* ENGINEERING—Chemical Engineering

551.6 ROM ISSN 2067-743X
▼ **AERUL SI APA. COMPONENTE ALE MEDIULUI.** Text in Romanian, English. 2010. s-a. **Document type:** *Journal, Academic/Scholarly.*
Related titles: Online - full text ed.: free (effective 2011).
Published by: (Universitatea "Babes-Bolyai", Facultatea de Geografie), Presa Universitara Clujeana/Cluj University Press, 51-st B.P.Hasdeu St, Cluj-Napoca, Romania. TEL 40-264-405352, FAX 40-264-597401, editura@editura.ubbcluj.ro, http://www.editura.ubbcluj.ro.

551.5 SEN ISSN 0065-4248
AGENCE POUR LA SECURITE DE LA NAVIGATION AERIENNE EN AFRIQUE ET A MADAGASCAR. DIRECTION DE L'EXPLOITATION METEOROLOGIQUE. PUBLICATIONS. SERIE 1. Text in French. 1966. irreg. price varies. **Document type:** *Monographic series, Academic/Scholarly.*
Published by: Agence pour la Securite de la Navigation Aerienne en Afrique et a Madagascar, Direction de l'Exploitation Meteorologique, Ave J Jaures, BP 3144, Dakar, Senegal. TEL 221-8695262, FAX 221-8207494, guitteyeama@asecna.org. Pub. Amadou Guitteye.

551.5 SEN ISSN 0084-6015
AGENCE POUR LA SECURITE DE LA NAVIGATION AERIENNE EN AFRIQUE ET A MADAGASCAR. DIRECTION DE L'EXPLOITATION METEOROLOGIQUE. PUBLICATIONS. SERIE 2. Text in French. 1965. irreg. price varies. **Document type:** *Monographic series, Academic/Scholarly.*
Published by: Agence pour la Securite de la Navigation Aerienne en Afrique et a Madagascar, Direction de l'Exploitation Meteorologique, Ave J Jaures, BP 3144, Dakar, Senegal. TEL 221-8695262, FAX 221-8207494, guitteyeama@asecna.org. Pub. Amadou Guitteye.

AGRARMETEOROLOGISCHER MONATSBERICHT FUER BRANDENBURG, SACHSEN-ANHALT, THUERINGEN UND SACHSEN (ONLINE). *see* AGRICULTURE—Crop Production And Soil

AGRARMETEOROLOGISCHER WOCHENBERICHT FUER BRANDENBURG, SACHSEN-ANHALT, THUERINGEN UND SACHSEN (ONLINE). *see* AGRICULTURE—Crop Production And Soil

551.5 630 NLD ISSN 0168-1923
S600
➤ **AGRICULTURAL AND FOREST METEOROLOGY.** Text in English, French, German. 1964. 12/yr. EUR 3,186 in Europe to institutions; JPY 423,600 in Japan to institutions; USD 3,562 elsewhere to institutions (effective 2012). adv. bk.rev. abstr.; bibl.; charts; illus. index. reprints avail. **Document type:** *Journal, Academic/Scholarly.* **Description:** Publishes articles and reviews in the interdisciplinary fields of meteorology and climatology applied to agriculture and forestry.
Formerly (until 1984): Agricultural Meteorology (0002-1571)
Related titles: Microform ed.: (from PQC); Online - full text ed.: ISSN 1873-2240 (from IngentaConnect, ScienceDirect).
Indexed: A01, A03, A08, A22, A26, A28, A33, A34, A35, A36, A37, A38, APA, ASCA, AgBio, Agr, AgrForAb, B25, BA, BIOBASE, BIOSIS Prev, BrCerAb, C&ISA, C25, C30, CA, CA/WCA, CABA, CIA, CIS, CTFA, CerAb, CivEngAb, CorrAb, CurCont, D01, E&CAJ, E04, E05, E11, E12, EEA, EMA, ESPM, EnvAb, EnvEAb, EnvInd, F08, F11, F12, FCA, FR, G11, GEOBASE, GH, GeoRef, H15, H16, I05, I11, IABS, IAOP, IBR, IBZ, ISR, LT, M&GPA, M&TEA, M09, MBF, METADEX, MaizeAb, MycolAb, N02, N04, O01, OR, P32, P38, P40, PGegResA, PGrRegA, PHN&I, PN&I, PlantSci, PollutAb, R07, R11, R12, R13, RA&MP, RRTA, S&MA, S12, S13, S16, S17, SCI, SCOPUS, SSciA, SWRA, SolStAb, SoyAb, SpeleolAb, T02, T04, TAR, TriticAb, VITIS, VS, W07, W10, W11, WAA.
—BLDSC (0742.890000), IE, Infotrieve, Ingenta, INIST, Linda Hall. **CCC.**
Published by: Elsevier BV (Subsidiary of: Elsevier Science & Technology), Radarweg 29, PO Box 211, Amsterdam, 1000 AE, Netherlands. TEL 31-20-4853911, FAX 31-20-4852457, JournalsCustomerServiceEMEA@elsevier.com, http://www.elsevier.nl. Ed. X Lee.

551.5 THA ISSN 0857-2410
AGROMETEOROLOGICAL REPORT. Text in Thai. 1968. m. free. **Document type:** *Government.*
Published by: Ministry of Transport and Communications, Meteorological Department, 4353 Sukhumvit Rd, Bangna, Bangkok, 10260, Thailand. TEL 393-9409, FAX 393-9409. Circ: 250.

551.63 JPN ISSN 0916-5053
AICHIKEN KISHO GEPPO/AICHI PREFECTURE. MONTHLY REPORT OF METEOROLOGY. Text in Japanese. 1926. m.
Published by: Kishocho, Nagoya Chiho Kishodai/Japan Meteorological Agency, Nagoya Local Meteorological Observatory, 2-18 Hiyori-cho, Chikusa-ku, Nagoya-shi, Aichi-ken 464-0039, Japan.

AIR POLLUTION MONITORING AND SAMPLING. *see* ENVIRONMENTAL STUDIES—Pollution

551.5 USA ISSN 0003-0007
QC851 CODEN: BAMIAT
➤ **AMERICAN METEOROLOGICAL SOCIETY. BULLETIN.** Abbreviated title: B A M S. Text in English. 1920. m. USD 130 domestic to non-members; USD 220 foreign to non-members; free to members (effective 2009). adv. bk.rev. abstr.; bibl.; charts; illus.; stat. index. back issues avail.; reprints avail. **Document type:** *Journal, Academic/Scholarly.* **Description:** Presents survey articles, professional and membership news, announcements and American Meteorological Society activities.
Related titles: Microfilm ed.: (from PMC); Online - full text ed.: ISSN 1520-0477. free (effective 2009).
Indexed: A01, A02, A03, A05, A08, A20, A22, A23, A24, A25, A26, A33, A36, A37, ABS&EES, APD, AS&TA, AS&TI, ASCA, ASFA, ApMecR, B04, B10, B13, BRD, BiolDig, C10, C25, C30, CA, CABA, CPEI, ChemAb, CurCont, E01, E04, E05, E08, E12, ESPM, EngInd, EnvAb, EnvInd, F08, F12, FCA, G01, G03, G08, G11, GH, GSA, GSI, GeoRef, I05, I11, IBR, IBZ, INIS AtomInd, ISR, Inspec, L09, LT, M&GPA, MaizeAb, OceAb, P02, P10, P26, P32, P34, P40, P48, P52, P53, P54, P56, PQC, PollutAb, R12, RRTA, RefZh, S01, S04, S08, S09, S10, S13, S16, SCI, SCOPUS, SWRA, SpeleolAb, T02, T05, TAR, TriticAb, VITIS, W03, W05, W07, W11.
—BLDSC (2388.000000), AskIEEE, IE, Infotrieve, Ingenta, INIST, Linda Hall. **CCC.**
Published by: American Meteorological Society, 45 Beacon St, Boston, MA 02108. TEL 617-227-2425, FAX 617-742-8718, amspubs@ametsoc.org. Ed. Jeffrey Rosenfeld. Pub. Keith L Seitter. Adv. contact Kelly G Savoie TEL 617-227-2426 ext 215. B&W page USD 1,125, color page USD 2,575; trim 7.875 x 10.5. **Subscr to.:** Allen Press Inc., PO Box 1897, Lawrence, KS 66044. http://www.allenpress.com.

551.6 USA
➤ **AMERICAN METEOROLOGICAL SOCIETY. HISTORICAL MONOGRAPH SERIES.** Text in English. 1963. irreg., latest vol.13, 2001. price varies. adv. back issues avail. **Document type:** *Monographic series, Academic/Scholarly.* **Description:** Covers the history of weather, weather forecasting, and the science of meteorology from its inception through the present day, with special emphasis on US weather.
Published by: American Meteorological Society, 45 Beacon St, Boston, MA 02108. TEL 617-227-2425, FAX 617-742-8718, amspubs@ametsoc.org. Ed. John S Perry TEL 703-369-1646.

551.5 USA ISSN 0065-9401
CODEN: MMONAL
➤ **AMERICAN METEOROLOGICAL SOCIETY. METEOROLOGICAL MONOGRAPHS.** Text in English. 1947. irreg., latest vol.33. price varies. back issues avail. **Document type:** *Monographic series, Academic/Scholarly.* **Description:** Collections of scientific papers devoted to individual research topics of concern to meteorologists, oceanographers, and hydrologists.
Related titles: Online - full text ed.: ISSN 1943-3646.
Indexed: A22, ChemAb, GeoRef, Inspec, M&GPA, SpeleolAb.
—BLDSC (5709.000000), IE, Ingenta, INIST, Linda Hall. **CCC.**
Published by: American Meteorological Society, 45 Beacon St, Boston, MA 02108. TEL 617-227-2425, FAX 617-742-8718, amspubs@ametsoc.org. Ed. Peter Ray TEL 850-644-1894.

551.5 USA ISSN 8755-9552
AMERICAN WEATHER OBSERVER. Text in English. 1984. m. USD 24.95. adv. index. back issues avail. **Document type:** *Newsletter.* **Description:** For amateur or professional weather observers, weather enthusiasts, or school weather clubs.
Published by: Belvidere Daily Republican Company, 130 S. State St., Ste. 203, Belvidere, IL 61008-3630. TEL 815-544-5665, FAX 815-544-6334. Ed., R&P Steven D Steinke. Pub. Patrick B Mattison. Circ: 2,000 (paid).

555.1 PHL ISSN 0115-5032
ANG TAGAMASID. Text in English, Tagalog. 1973. bi-m. free.
Published by: Philippine Atmospheric, Geophysical and Astronomical Services Administration, 1424 Quezon Ave, Quezon City, 1101, Philippines. Ed. Venus R Valdemoro. Circ: 1,000.

551.5 DEU ISSN 0072-4122
CODEN: ATSTAA
ANNALEN DER METEOROLOGIE. NEUE FOLGE. Text in German. 1873; N.S. 1963. irreg., latest vol.44, 2009. price varies. **Document type:** *Monographic series, Trade.*
Former titles (until 1948): Annalen der Hydrographie und Maritimen Meteorologie (0174-8114); (until 1875): Hydrographische Mittheilungen (0933-6508)
Indexed: ASFA, B21, ESPM, GeoRef, Inspec, M&GPA, SCOPUS.
—CASDDS, Linda Hall. **CCC.**
Published by: Deutscher Wetterdienst, Bibliothek, Kaiserleistr 29-35, Offenbach Am Main, 63067, Germany. TEL 49-69-80620, FAX 49-69-80624484, info@dwd.de, http://www.dwd.de.

551.6 AUS ISSN 1833-2404
ANTARCTIC CLIMATE AND ECOSYSTEMS COOPERATIVE RESEARCH CENTRE. TECHNICAL REPORT. Text in English. 2005. irreg., latest 2006. **Document type:** *Monographic series, Trade.*
Published by: Antarctic Climate and Ecosystems Cooperative Research Centre, Private Bag 80, Hobart, TAS 7001, Australia. TEL 61-3-62267888, FAX 61-3-62262440, enquiries@acecrc.org.au, http://www.acecrc.org.au.

551 JPN
ANTARCTIC METEOROLOGICAL DATA. Text in English. 1963. a.
Published by: Kishocho/Japan Meteorological Agency, 1-3-4 Otemachi, Chiyoda-ku, Tokyo, 100-8122, Japan.

551.5 PRT ISSN 0870-2950
ANUARIO CLIMATOLOGICO. (Since 1977 issued in 3 parts: A: Continente (ISSN 0870-6360); B: Acores (ISSN 0870-6379); C: Madeira (ISSN 0870-6387); 2/01: ISSN's not found in ISDS database.) Text in Portuguese. 1947. a. stat. **Description:** Publishes original papers relating to the study of climatology and climate change.
Published by: Instituto de Meteorologia, Rua C do Aeroporto, Lisbon, 1749-077, Portugal. TEL 351-21-8447000, FAX 351-21-8402370, informacoes@meteo.pt, http://www.meteo.pt/. Circ: 500.

551.5 JPN ISSN 0029-7399
AOMORIKEN KISHO GEPPO/AOMORI PREFECTURE. MONTHLY REPORT OF METEOROLOGY. Text in Japanese. 1951. m. free. bk.rev. charts; stat. **Document type:** *Government.*
Published by: Kishodai, Aomori Chiho Kishodai/Japan Meteorological Agency, Aomori Local Meteorological Observatory, 1-17-19 Hanazono, Aomori-shi, Aomori-ken 030-0966, Japan. http://www.sendai-jma.go.jp/tidai/aomori/. Circ: 340 (controlled).

ARIZONA AGRI-WEEKLY; for week ending. *see* AGRICULTURE

551.5 KOR ISSN 1976-7633
➤ **ASIA-PACIFIC JOURNAL OF ATMOSPHERIC SCIENCES.** Text in Korean, English. 1965. 4/yr. EUR 481, USD 578 combined subscription to institutions (print & online eds.) (effective 2012). **Document type:** *Journal, Academic/Scholarly.*
Formerly (until 2008): Hangug Gisang Haghoeji (1225-0899)
Related titles: Online - full text ed.: ISSN 1976-7951.
Indexed: ESPM, M&GPA, PollutAb, SCI, SCOPUS, W07.
—IE. **CCC.**
Published by: Korean Meteorological Society, Youngdungpo-gu, Shingil-dong 508, Ciwon Bldg 704, Seoul, 150-050, Korea, S. TEL 82-2-8351619, FAX 82-2-8491541, komes@komes.or.kr, http://www.komes.or.kr. **Co-publisher:** Springer.

551.5 ESP ISSN 1696-764X
ASOCIACION METEOROLOGICA ESPANOLA. BOLETIN. Text in Spanish. 1982. s-a. EUR 28 (effective 2008). back issues avail. **Document type:** *Bulletin, Academic/Scholarly.*
Former titles (until 2003): Revista de Meteorologia (0214-4387); (until 1983): A M E. Boletin (0211-3635)
Indexed: M&GPA.
Published by: Asociacion Meteorologica Espanola, C Leonardo Prieto Castro No. 8, Madrid, 28040, Spain. TEL 34-91-5819889, FAX 34-91-5819767, ameinfo@ame-web/prg, http://www.ame-web.org/. Ed. Fernando Aguado Encabo.

551.6 FRA ISSN 0242-4002
ASSOCIATION NATIONALE D'ETUDE ET DE LUTTE CONTRE LES FLEAUX ATMOSPHERIQUES. RAPPORT DE CAMPAGNE. Text in French; Summaries in French. 1952. a. free. bk.rev. charts; illus.; stat. back issues avail. **Document type:** *Bulletin, Corporate.* **Description:** Presents research conducted in the control and relief of natural disasters.
Former titles: Association Nationale de Lutte Contre les Fleaux Atmospheriques. Rapport de Campagne (0373-7349); Association d'Etudes des Moyens de Lutte Contre les Fleaux Atmospheriques. Rapport de Compagne
—INIST.
Published by: Association Nationale d'Etude et de Lutte contre les Fleaux Atmospheriques, 52 rue Alfred Dumeril, Toulouse, 31400, France. TEL 33-5-61520565, FAX 33-5-62267124. Ed. Nicole Dulenc. Pub. Eugene Boyer. Circ: 1,000.

551.5 MEX ISSN 0187-6236
QC851 CODEN: ATMSEF
➤ **ATMOSFERA.** Text in Spanish, English. 1988. q. MXN 300 domestic; USD 60 foreign to individuals; USD 80 foreign to institutions (effective 2011). illus. Index. reprints avail. **Document type:** *Journal, Academic/Scholarly.* **Description:** Includes theoretical and empirical articles on meteorology, atmospheric sciences, climatic change and related fields.
Related titles: Online - full text ed.: free (effective 2011) (from SciELO).
Indexed: A22, ASFA, B21, C01, CurCont, ESPM, GEOBASE, M&GPA, PollutAb, SCI, SCOPUS, W07.
—BLDSC (1767.112900), IE, Ingenta.
Published by: Universidad Nacional Autonoma de Mexico, Centro de Ciencias de la Atmosfera, Circuito Exterior, Ciudad Universitaria, Mexico City, D.F. 04510, Mexico. TEL 52-55-56224074, FAX 52-55-56160789, http://serpiente.dgsca.unam.mx/cca. Ed. Carlos Gay.

551.5 CHE ISSN 2073-4433
▼ ➤ **ATMOSPHERE.** Text in English. 2010 (Jul.). q. free (effective 2011). bk.rev. back issues avail. **Document type:** *Journal, Academic/Scholarly.* **Description:** Publishes reviews, regular research papers, communications and short notes on atmospheric sciences, atmospheric physics and chemistry, air, meteorology, and environmental sciences.
Media: Online - full text.
Published by: M D P I AG, Postfach, Basel, 4005, Switzerland. TEL 41-61-6837734, FAX 41-61-3028918, http://www.mdpi.org/. Ed. Daniela Jacob. Pub. Shu-Kun Lin.

551.51 AUS ISSN 1325-0299
QC869.4.A8
ATMOSPHERE. Text in English. 1982. s-a. free. illus. 12 p./no.; **Document type:** *Government.* **Description:** The newsletter of CSIRO Atmospheric Research.
Former titles (until 1995): D A R Bulletin (1033-2987); (until 1987): CSIRO Division of Atmospheric Research. Newsletter (1033-2979)
Related titles: Online - full text ed.
Published by: C S I R O, 150 Oxford St, PO Box 1139, Collingwood, VIC 3066, Australia. TEL 61-3-96627500, FAX 61-3-96627555, publishing@csiro.au, http://www.publish.csiro.au/.

551.5 551.46 GBR ISSN 0705-5900
QC851 CODEN: ATOCDA
➤ **ATMOSPHERE - OCEAN.** Text in English; Text occasionally in French; Abstracts in English, French. 1963. q. GBP 104 combined subscription in United Kingdom to institutions (print & online eds.); EUR 137, USD 173 combined subscription to institutions (print & online eds.) (effective 2012). charts; illus.; maps. a.index. 90 p./no. 2 cols./p.; back issues avail.; reprint service avail. from PSC. **Document type:** *Journal, Academic/Scholarly.* **Description:** Contains scientific articles and reviews on all aspects of meteorology, oceanography, hydrology, and relevant notes, correspondence.
Supersedes (with vol.16, 1978): Atmosphere (0004-6973)
Related titles: CD-ROM ed.: ISSN 1488-7576. CAD 50 domestic to institutions; CAD 55 foreign to institutions (effective 2009); Online - full text ed.: ISSN 1480-9214. 1998. GBP 94 in United Kingdom to institutions; EUR 124, USD 155 to institutions (effective 2012).
Indexed: A22, A37, ASCA, ASFA, ApMecR, B21, BiolDig, C25, CA, CABA, CMCI, CurCont, E04, E05, E12, ESPM, F08, F12, FR, G11, GEOBASE, GH, GeoRef, I11, ISR, Inspec, M&GPA, OceAb, P33, PGrRegA, PollutAb, R07, R08, R13, RefZh, S13, S16, SCI, SCOPUS, SWRA, T02, W07, W11.
—BLDSC (1767.117000), CASDDS, IE, Infotrieve, Ingenta, INIST, Linda Hall. **CCC.**
Published by: (Canadian Meteorological and Oceanographic Society/ Societe Canadienne de Meteorologie et d'Oceanographie CAN), Routledge (Subsidiary of: Taylor & Francis Group), 4 Park Sq, Milton Park, Abingdon, Oxon OX14 4RN, United Kingdom. TEL 44-20-70176000, FAX 44-20-70176336, subscriptions@tandf.co.uk. Circ: 600 (paid).

551.5 USA ISSN 2160-0414
▼ **ATMOSPHERIC AND CLIMATE SCIENCE.** Text in English. 2011. q. **Document type:** *Journal, Academic/Scholarly.*
Related titles: Online - full text ed.: ISSN 2160-0422. free (effective 2011).
Published by: Scientific Research Publishing, Inc., 5005 Paseo Segovia, Irvine, CA 92603. Ed. Shaocai Yu.

551.5 551.46 CHN ISSN 1674-2834
ATMOSPHERIC AND OCEANIC SCIENCE LETTERS. Text in English. 2008. bi-m. **Document type:** *Journal, Academic/Scholarly.*
Related titles: Online - full text ed.
Published by: Chinese Academy of Sciences, Institute of Atmospheric Physics, PO Box 9804, Beijing, 100029, China. TEL 86-10-82995202, FAX 86-10-82995053, http://www.iap.ac.cn/.

551.5 DEU ISSN 1680-7316
QC879.6 DB .A853
➤ **ATMOSPHERIC CHEMISTRY AND PHYSICS.** Text in English. 24/yr. EUR 1,344 to members; EUR 2,987 to non-members (effective 2009). **Document type:** *Journal, Academic/Scholarly.* **Description:** Publishes studies investigating the Earth's atmosphere and the underlying chemical and physical processes.
Related titles: Online - full text ed.: ISSN 1680-7324. 2002. free (effective 2011).
Indexed: A20, A33, APA, C&ISA, CA, CorrAb, CurCont, E&CAJ, E04, E05, EEA, ESPM, GEOBASE, GeoRef, M&GPA, P52, P56, PollutAb, SCI, SCOPUS, SolStAb, T02, W07, WAA.
—BLDSC (1767.119500). **CCC.**
Published by: (European Geophysical Society), Copernicus GmbH, Bahnhofsallee 1e, Goettingen, 37081, Germany. TEL 49-551-9003390, FAX 49-551-90033970, info@copernicus.org, http://www.copernicus.org.

551.5 DEU ISSN 1680-7367
➤ **ATMOSPHERIC CHEMISTRY AND PHYSICS DISCUSSIONS.** Text in English. irreg. **Document type:** *Journal, Academic/Scholarly.* **Description:** Publishes studies investigating the Earth's atmosphere and the underlying chemical and physical processes.
Related titles: Online - full text ed.: ISSN 1680-7375. free (effective 2011).
Indexed: A33, CA, E04, E05, ESPM, GEOBASE, M&GPA, PollutAb, SCOPUS, SSciA, T02.
—**CCC.**
Published by: (European Geophysical Society), Copernicus GmbH, Bahnhofsallee 1e, Goettingen, 37081, Germany. TEL 49-551-9003390, FAX 49-551-90033970, info@copernicus.org, http://www.copernicus.org.

551.5 DEU ISSN 1867-1381
QC876
➤ **ATMOSPHERIC MEASUREMENT TECHNIQUES.** Text in English. irreg. **Document type:** *Journal, Academic/Scholarly.* **Description:** Provides a forum for research and discussion on advances in remote sensing, in-situ and laboratory measurement techniques involving the Earth's atmosphere.
Related titles: Online - full text ed.: ISSN 1867-8548. free (effective 2011).
Indexed: A01, CurCont, GEOBASE, P52, P56, SCI, T02, W07.
Published by: Copernicus GmbH, Bahnhofsallee 1e, Goettingen, 37081, Germany. TEL 49-551-9003390, FAX 49-551-90033970, info@copernicus.org, http://www.copernicus.org.

551.5 DEU ISSN 1867-8610
QC876
➤ **ATMOSPHERIC MEASUREMENT TECHNIQUES DISCUSSIONS.** Text in English. 2008. irreg. free (effective 2011). **Document type:** *Journal, Academic/Scholarly.*
Media: Online - full text.
Indexed: A01, T02.
Published by: Copernicus GmbH, Bahnhofsallee 1e, Goettingen, 37081, Germany. TEL 49-551-9003390, FAX 49-551-90033970, info@copernicus.org, http://www.copernicus.org.

▼ ➤ **ATMOSPHERIC POLLUTION RESEARCH.** *see* ENVIRONMENTAL STUDIES—Pollution

551.5 NLD ISSN 0169-8095
CODEN: ATREEW
➤ **ATMOSPHERIC RESEARCH.** Text in English, French. 1963. 16/yr. EUR 2,187 in Europe to institutions; JPY 290,500 in Japan to institutions; USD 2,448 elsewhere to institutions (effective 2012). bk.rev. abstr.; bibl.; charts; illus. index. back issues avail.; reprints avail. **Document type:** *Journal, Academic/Scholarly.* **Description:** Publishes scientific papers dealing with the part of the atmosphere where meteorological events occur.
Formerly (until 1986): Journal de Recherches Atmospheriques (0021-7972)
Related titles: Online - full text ed.: ISSN 1873-2895 (from IngentaConnect, ScienceDirect).
Indexed: A01, A03, A08, A22, A26, A28, A33, A37, APA, ASCA, ASFA, AgrForAb, BA, BrCerAb, C&ISA, C25, C30, CA, CA/WCA, CABA, CIA, CIN, CPEI, CerAb, ChemAb, ChemTitl, CivEngAb, CorrAb, CurCont, E&CAJ, E04, E05, E11, E12, EEA, EMA, ESPM, EnerRev, EngInd, EnvAb, EnvEAb, EnvInd, F08, F12, FCA, FR, G11, GEOBASE, GH, GeoRef, H15, H16, I05, I11, IBR, IBZ, ISR, Inspec, M&GPA, M&TEA, M09, MBF, METADEX, MaizeAb, OceAb, P33, PGrRegA, PhysBer, PollutAb, R07, R08, R11, RM&VM, RefZh, S13, S16, SCI, SCOPUS, SWRA, SolStAb, SoyAb, SpeleolAb, T02, T04, T05, W07, WAA.
—BLDSC (1767.470000), AskIEEE, CASDDS, IE, Infotrieve, Ingenta, INIST, Linda Hall. **CCC.**
Published by: Elsevier BV (Subsidiary of: Elsevier Science & Technology), Radarweg 29, PO Box 211, Amsterdam, 1000 AE, Netherlands. TEL 31-20-4853911, FAX 31-20-4852457, JournalsCustomerServiceEMEA@elsevier.com, http://www.elsevier.nl. Ed. A Flossmann.

551.5 GBR ISSN 1530-261X
QC851
➤ **ATMOSPHERIC SCIENCE LETTERS.** Text in English. 2000. q. GBP 220 in United Kingdom to institutions; EUR 277 in Europe to institutions; USD 430 elsewhere to institutions (effective 2012). adv. bk.rev. back issues avail. **Document type:** *Journal, Academic/Scholarly.* **Description:** Covers shorter contributions in the field of atmospheric and closely related sciences. It offers a frame work for scientific debate - providing a platform for discussing scientific issues and techniques. Covers articles of general interest, scientific meetings reports, news and events and an actively edited discussion section.
Media: Online - full text (from IngentaConnect).
Indexed: A22, CA, CurCont, E01, GEOBASE, M&GPA, SCI, SCOPUS, W07.
—BLDSC (1767.480000), IE, Ingenta. **CCC.**
Published by: (Royal Meteorological Society), John Wiley & Sons Ltd. (Subsidiary of: John Wiley & Sons, Inc.), 1-7 Oldlands Way, PO Box 808, Bognor Regis, West Sussex PO21 9FF, United Kingdom. TEL 44-1865-778315, FAX 44-1243-843232, cs-journals@wiley.com, http://eu.wiley.com/WileyCDA/. Ed. Alan Gadian TEL 44-113-3436461. **Subscr. to:** 1-7 Oldlands Way, PO Box 809, Bognor Regis, West Sussex PO21 9FG, United Kingdom. TEL 44-1865-778054, cs-agency@wiley.com.

551.5 AUS ISSN 1838-2525
▼ **AUSTRALIAN LOCAL GOVERNMENT AND CLIMATE CHANGE WORKING PAPER.** Text in English. 2010. a. free (effective 2011). **Document type:** *Monographic series, Government.*
Media: Online - full text.
Published by: Australian Centre of Excellence for Local Government, PO Box 123, Broadway, NSW 2007, Australia. TEL 61-2-95143855, FAX 61-2-95144705, acelg@acelg.org.au.

551.5 AUS ISSN 1836-716X
QC851
➤ **AUSTRALIAN METEOROLOGICAL AND OCEANOGRAPHIC JOURNAL.** Abbreviated title: A M M. Text in English. 1944. q. AUD 43 to individuals (effective 2010). bk.rev. abstr.; charts; illus. Index. back issues avail. **Document type:** *Journal, Academic/Scholarly.* **Description:** Covers meteorology, oceanography, hydrology and related fields with emphasis on the Southern Hemisphere.
Former titles (until 2008): Australian Meteorological Magazine (0004-9743); (until 1951): Weather Development and Research Bulletin (0372-7173); (until 1946): Tropical Weather Research Bulletin; (until 1944): Tropical Research Bulletin
Related titles: Online - full text ed.
Indexed: A22, ASCA, ASFA, CTO, ChemAb, CurCont, ESPM, GEOBASE, GeoRef, ISR, Inspec, M&GPA, OceAb, SCI, SCOPUS, SWRA, W07.
—AskIEEE, Ingenta, INIST, Linda Hall. **CCC.**
Published by: Bureau of Meteorology, GPO Box 1289, Melbourne, VIC 3001, Australia. TEL 61-3-96694000, FAX 61-3-96694699, a.hollis@bom.gov.au. Eds. Blair Trewin, Neville Smith. **Co-sponsor:** Australian Meteorological and Oceanographic Society.

551.5 AUS ISSN 1035-6576
AUSTRALIAN METEOROLOGICAL AND OCEANOGRAPHIC SOCIETY. BULLETIN. Text in English. 1976. bi-m. free to members (effective 2008). adv. bk.rev. back issues avail. **Document type:** *Bulletin, Consumer.* **Description:** Provides articles of interest related to the meteorology or the oceanography of the southern hemisphere.
Former titles (until 1990): Australian Meteorological and Oceanographic Society. Newsletter (1031-0134); (until 1987): Australian Royal Meteorological Society. Newsletter (1030-1828)
Indexed: ASFA, B21, ESPM, M&GPA.
Published by: Australian Meteorological and Oceanographic Society, PO Box 1289, Melbourne, VIC 3001, Australia. FAX 61-3-96694660. Ed. Allyson Williams. Adv. contact W Wright. Circ: 400.

551.5 551 AUT ISSN 0067-2351
AUSTRIA. ZENTRALANSTALT FUER METEOROLOGIE UND GEODYNAMIK. JAHRBUCH. Text in German. 1864. irreg. price varies. back issues avail. **Document type:** *Yearbook, Government.*
Indexed: SpeleolAb.
Published by: Zentralanstalt fuer Meteorologie und Geodynamik, Hohe Warte 38, Vienna, 1190, Austria. TEL 43-1-36026, FAX 43-1-3691233, dion@zamg.ac.at, http://www.zamg.ac.at. Ed. Peter Steinhauser. Circ: 500.

AVALANCHE REVIEW. *see* EARTH SCIENCES

551.5 CUB ISSN 1029-2039
B I V A. (Boletin Informativo de la Vigilancia Atmosferica) Text in Spanish. 1995. m.
Media: Online - full text.
Published by: Ministerio de Ciencia Tecnologica y Medio Ambiente, Instituto de Meteorologia, Apdo. Postal 4279, Havana, 10400, Cuba. TEL 537-8308996, FAX 537-8338010, http://www.met.inf.cu/. Ed. Maria Julio.

551.5 IDN ISSN 0126-0561
QC925.8 .I5
BADAN METEOROLOGI DAN GEOFISIKA. LAPORAN EVALUASI HUJAN DAN PERKIRAAN HUJAN. Text in Indonesian. 1976. m.
Formerly: Pusat Meteorologi dan Geofisika. Laporan Evaluasi Hujan dan Perkiraan Hujan
Published by: Meteorological and Geophysical Institute/Badan Meteorologi dan Geofisika, Jalan Arief Rakhman Hakim 3, Jakarta, Indonesia.

551.63 JPN
BAIU TO TAIFU NO YOSO/BAIU AND TYPHOON PREDICTION. Text in Japanese. a.
Published by: Kishocho, Fukuoka Kanku Kishodai/Japan Meteorological Agency, Fukuoka District Meteorological Observatory, 1-2-36 Ohori, Chuo-ku, Fukuoka-shi, 810-0052, Japan.

551.5 AUS ISSN 1837-2074
BE THE CHANGE. Text in English. 2005. q. free (effective 2010). back issues avail. **Document type:** *Newsletter, Trade.* **Description:** Contains the latest news on global warming, climate change, and carbon planet.
Formerly (until 2007): Carbon Planet Newsletter
Related titles: Online - full text ed.: ISSN 1837-2082.
Published by: Carbon Planet, PO Box 3656, Rundle Mall, SA 5000, Australia. TEL 61-8-82379000, FAX 61-8-82329115, info@carbonplanet.com. Ed. Vivienne Holloway.

551.5 570 NLD ISSN 1877-5284
▼ **BIOMETEOROLOGY.** Text in English. 2009. irreg. price varies. **Document type:** *Monographic series, Academic/Scholarly.*
Published by: Springer Netherlands (Subsidiary of: Springer Science+Business Media), Van Godewijckstraat 30, Dordrecht, 3311 GX, Netherlands. TEL 31-78-6576050, FAX 31-78-6576474, http://www.springer.com. Ed. Glenn McGregor.

570 JPN ISSN 1022-9205
BIOMETEOROLOGY BULLETIN. Text in English. s-a. USD 85 for membership to individuals; USD 150 for membership to institutions in hard-currency countries; USD 75 for membership to institutions in soft-currency countries (effective 2003). adv. **Document type:** *Bulletin, Academic/Scholarly.*
Indexed: M&GPA.
—BLDSC (2087.960000).
Published by: International Society of Biometeorology, c/o Dr Masaaki Shibata, Department of Biometeorology, Yamanashi Institute of Environmental Sciences, Fuji-Yoshida, Yamanashi 403-0005, Japan. TEL 81-555-72-6184, FAX 81-555-72-6205, mshibata@yies.pref.yamanashi.jp, http://www.es.mq.edu.au/ISB/index.htm. Ed., R&P, Adv. contact Dr. Paul J Beggs. Circ: 300 (controlled).

551.5 BRA ISSN 0067-9585
BOLETIM CLIMATOLOGICO. Text in Portuguese. 1960. irreg., latest vol.5, 1984. price varies or avail. on exchange.
Published by: Universidade de Sao Paulo, Instituto Oceanografico, Praca do Oceanografico, 191, Cidade Universitaria, Sao Paulo, SP 05508-900, Brazil. Circ: 100.

551.5 PRT ISSN 0870-4686
BOLETIM METEOROLOGICO. Text in Portuguese. 1948. d. charts; stat. **Document type:** *Bulletin.* **Description:** Charts of isobaric surfaces.
Published by: Instituto de Meteorologia, Rua C do Aeroporto, Lisbon, 1749-077, Portugal. TEL 351-21-8447000, FAX 351-21-8402370, informacoes@meteo.pt, http://www.meteo.pt/.

551.5 630 PRT ISSN 0870-4694
BOLETIM METEOROLOGICO PARA A AGRICULTURA. Text in Portuguese. 1951-1958; resumed. 3/m. charts; illus.; stat. **Document type:** *Bulletin.* **Description:** Meteorological information and its impact on agriculture.
Published by: Instituto de Meteorologia, Rua C do Aeroporto, Lisbon, 1749-077, Portugal. TEL 351-21-8447000, FAX 351-21-8402370, informacoes@meteo.pt, http://www.meteo.pt/.

BOLETIN AGROMETEOROLOGICO DEL CENTRO SUR DE LA PROVINCIA DE BUENOS AIRES. *see* AGRICULTURE

551.6 CHL ISSN 0717-8913
BOLETIN CLIMATICO. Text in Spanish. 1995. m. free (effective 2006). back issues avail. **Document type:** *Bulletin, Trade.*
Media: Online - full text.
Published by: Universidad de Chile, Departamento de Geofisica, Blanco Escalada, 2002, Santiago, Chile. TEL 56-2-6968686, FAX 56-2-6968790, http://met.dgf.uchile.cl/clima. Ed. Juan Quintana.

551.5 ECU
BOLETIN DE ALERTA CLIMATICO/CLIMATE ALERT BULLETIN. Text in English, Spanish. 1990. m. maps; charts; illus.
Formerly (until 2001): E R F E N Boletin (0257-7380)
Related titles: Online - full text ed.
Indexed: ASFA, B21, ESPM.
Published by: (Instituto Oceanografico de la Armada), Comision Permanente del Pacifico Sur, Edificio Inmaral 1er Piso, Av Carlos Julio Arosemena, Km 3, Guayaquil, Ecuador. TEL 593-4-2221-202, FAX 593-4-2221-201.

551.5 CUB ISSN 1029-2047
BOLETIN DE LA VIGILANCIA DEL CLIMA. Text in Spanish. 1997. m.
Media: Online - full text.
Published by: Ministerio de Ciencia Tecnologica y Medio Ambiente, Instituto de Meteorologia, Apdo. Postal 4279, Havana, 10400, Cuba. TEL 537-8308996, FAX 537-8338010, http://www.met.inf.cu/.

551.5 DEU ISSN 0006-7156
QC851
BONNER METEOROLOGISCHE ABHANDLUNGEN. Text in English, German. 1962. irreg., latest vol.62, 2006. price varies. abstr.; charts; illus. **Document type:** *Monographic series, Academic/Scholarly.*
Indexed: M&GPA, SCOPUS.
—Linda Hall.
Published by: (Universitaet Bonn, Meteorologisches Institut), Asgard-Verlag Dr. Werner Hippe GmbH, Einsteinstr 10, St. Augustin, 53757, Germany. TEL 49-2241-31640, FAX 49-2241-316436, service@asgard.de, http://www.asgard.de.

551.5 570 NLD ISSN 0006-8314
QC880 CODEN: BLMEBR
➤ **BOUNDARY-LAYER METEOROLOGY;** an international journal of physical and biological processes in the atmospheric boundary layer. Text in English. 1970. m. EUR 3,240, USD 3,380 combined subscription to institutions (print & online eds.) (effective 2012). bk.rev. illus. index. reprint service avail. from PSC. **Document type:** *Journal, Academic/Scholarly.* **Description:** Publishes papers on the physical and biological processes occurring in the lowest 1000 meters of the Earth's atmosphere.
Related titles: Microform ed.: (from PQC); Online - full text ed.: ISSN 1573-1472 (from IngentaConnect).
Indexed: A01, A03, A08, A22, A26, A28, A33, A37, APA, APD, ASCA, ASFA, Agr, AgrForAb, ApMecR, BibLing, BrCerAb, C&ISA, C25, C30, CA, CA/WCA, CABA, CIA, CMCI, CPEI, CTO, CerAb, CivEngAb, CorrAb, CurCont, E&CAJ, E01, E04, E05, E11, E12, EEA, EMA, ESPM, EnerRev, EngInd, EnvEAb, F08, F12, FCA, FLUIDEX, G11, GEOBASE, GeoRef, H15, H16, I05, I11, IBR, IBZ, ISR, Inspec, M&GPA, M&TEA, M09, MBF, METADEX, MaizeAb, O01, OR, OceAb, P26, P32, P47, P48, P52, P54, P56, PGegResA, PQC, PhysBer, R11, RefZh, S13, S16, SCI, SCOPUS, SWRA, SolStAb, SoyAb, SpeleolAb, T02, T04, TAR, TriticAb, W07, WAA.
—BLDSC (2264.270000), AskIEEE, IE, Infotrieve, Ingenta, INIST, Linda Hall. **CCC.**
Published by: Springer Netherlands (Subsidiary of: Springer Science+Business Media), Van Godewijckstraat 30, Dordrecht, 3311 GX, Netherlands. TEL 31-78-6576050, FAX 31-78-6576474, http://www.springer.com. Eds. John R Garratt, P A Taylor.

551.579 CAN ISSN 0045-303X
BRITISH COLUMBIA SNOW SURVEY BULLETIN. Text in English. 1940. 8/yr.
Media: Online - full text.
—Linda Hall.
Published by: (River Forecast Center), Ministry of the Environment, Lands and Parks, Sta Provincial Government, P O Box 9344, Victoria, BC V8W 9M1, Canada. Ed. David D Gooding.

332.6 USA ISSN 0896-3045
BROWNING NEWSLETTER. Text in English. 1981 (vol.5). m. USD 225 (effective 2005). charts; stat. 8 p./no.; **Document type:** *Newsletter, Consumer.* **Description:** Based on the proposition that the Earth's climate has entered a period of sharp change and that this change in climate is the driving force behind human history. Extensive studies of physical data and phenomena (named for Dr. Iben Browning, a climatologist).
Related titles: E-mail ed.
Indexed: MLA-IB.
Published by: Fraser Management Associates, Inc., 309 S Willard St, Box 494, Burlington, VT 05402. TEL 802-658-0322, FAX 802-658-0260, ellen@fraser.com, http://www.fraser.com. Ed. Evelyn Browning Garriss.

551.5 BGR ISSN 0861-0762
QC851 CODEN: BJMHEP
BULGARIAN JOURNAL OF METEOROLOGY AND HYDROLOGY. Text in English. 1990. q. **Document type:** *Journal, Academic/Scholarly.*
Indexed: GeoRef, M&GPA.
—INIST, Linda Hall.
Published by: Bulgarska Akademiya na Naukite, National Institute of Meteorology and Hydrology, 66 Tsarigradsko Chaussee, Sofia, 1784, Bulgaria. TEL 389-2-9753986, FAX 389-2-9880380, office@meteo.bg, http://www.meteo.bg.

551.509 FRA ISSN 1775-8173
BULLETIN CLIMATIQUE MENSUEL SUD-EST CIGALE. Text in French. 1995. m. **Document type:** *Bulletin, Trade.*
Published by: Meteo France, Direction Interregionale Sud-Est, Division ETO/Climatologie, 2 bd Chateau Double, Aix-en-Provence, 13098 Cedex 02, France.

551.509 FRA ISSN 1775-8149
BULLETIN CLIMATOLOGIQUE MENSUEL. 05 HAUTE ALPES. Text in French. 2005. m. **Document type:** *Bulletin, Trade.*
Published by: Meteo France, Centre Departemental de la Meteorologie. Haute Alpes, Central Parc, Briancon, 05100, France.

551.509 FRA ISSN 1775-8157
BULLETIN CLIMATOLOGIQUE MENSUEL. 34 HERAULT. Text in French. 2005. m. **Document type:** *Bulletin, Trade.*
Published by: Meteo France, Centre Departemental de la Meteorologie. Montpellier, Aeroport de Montpellier Mediterranee, Mauguio, 34134 Cedex, France.

551.509 FRA ISSN 1775-8165
BULLETIN CLIMATOLOGIQUE MENSUEL. 66 PYRENEES-ORIENTALES. Text in French. 2005. m. **Document type:** *Bulletin, Trade.*

Published by: Meteo France, Centre Departemental de Meteorologie. Pyrenees-Orientales, Aeroport de Perpignan-Rivesaltes, Perpignan, 66000, France.

551.509 FRA ISSN 1775-8130
BULLETIN CLIMATOLOGIQUE MENSUEL. 84 VAUCLUSE. Text in French. 2005. m. **Document type:** *Bulletin, Trade.*
Published by: Meteo France, Centre Departemental de la Meteorologie. Vaucluse, 785 Chemin de l'Hermitage, Carpentras, 84200, France.

551.509 FRA ISSN 1774-9298
BULLETIN CLIMATOLOGIQUE MENSUEL. DEUX SEVRES. Text in French. 1969. m. **Document type:** *Bulletin, Trade.*
Formerly (until 2005): Bulletin Climatologique des Deux-Sevres (0335-7791)
Published by: Meteo France, Centre Departemental de Meteorologie. Deux-Sevres, Aerodrome de Niort-Souche, Niort, 79000, France.

551.658 AUS ISSN 1037-3608
QC857.A8
BUREAU OF METEOROLOGY. ANNUAL REPORT. Text in English. 19??. a. **Document type:** *Journal, Trade.*
Former titles (until 1991): Bureau of Meteorology. Annual Review (0728-6899); (until 1981): Bureau of Meteorology (0812-5376); (until 1974): Bureau of Meteorology. Annual Report (0812-5368)
Indexed: M&GPA.
—CCC.
Published by: Bureau of Meteorology, GPO Box 1289, Melbourne, VIC 3001, Australia. TEL 61-3-96694000, FAX 61-3-96694699, webclim@bom.gov.au, http://www.bom.gov.au.

551.68 USA ISSN 1053-1106
QD181.C1 CODEN: CDCOEX
C D I A C COMMUNICATIONS. Text in English. irreg. (1-2/yr.). free. bk.rev. charts; illus. **Document type:** *Newsletter, Government.* **Description:** Communicates information relevant to research and information management in global environmental change, including climate change and global warming.
Indexed: ASCA, GeoRef, SpeleolAb.
Published by: (U.S. Department of Energy, Office of Industrial Technologies), Carbon Dioxide Information Analysis Center, Oak Ridge National Laboratory, Box 2008, MS 6335, Oak Ridge, TN 37831-6335. TEL 865-574-0390, FAX 865-574-2232. Eds. Karen Gibson, Sonja Jones. Circ: 10,000.

551.6 333.79 NOR ISSN 0804-4511
C I C E R O. POLICY NOTE. (Center for International Climate and Environmental Research) Text in English. 1991. irreg. back issues avail. **Document type:** *Monographic series.*
Related titles: Online - full text ed.
Published by: C I C E R O Senter for Klimaforskning/Center for International Climate and Environmental Research, PO Box 1129, Blindern, Oslo, 0318, Norway. TEL 47-22-858750, FAX 47-22-858751, admin@cicero.uio.no.

551.6 333.79 NOR ISSN 0804-4562
C I C E R O. REPORT. (Center for International Climate and Environmental Research) Text in English. 1993. irreg. free. back issues avail. **Document type:** *Monographic series, Academic/Scholarly.*
Related titles: Online - full text ed.
Published by: C I C E R O Senter for Klimaforskning/Center for International Climate and Environmental Research, PO Box 1129, Blindern, Oslo, 0318, Norway. TEL 47-22-858750, FAX 47-22-858751, admin@cicero.uio.no.

551.6 333.79 NOR ISSN 0804-452X
C I C E R O. WORKING PAPER. (Center for International Climate and Environmental Research) Text in English. 1991. irreg. back issues avail. **Document type:** *Monographic series, Academic/Scholarly.*
Related titles: Online - full text ed.
Published by: C I C E R O Senter for Klimaforskning/Center for International Climate and Environmental Research, PO Box 1129, Blindern, Oslo, 0318, Norway. TEL 47-22-858750, FAX 47-22-858751, admin@cicero.uio.no.

551.5 USA
C I S L NEWS. (Computational & Information Systems Laboratory) Text in English. 198?. irreg. free (effective 2009). back issues avail. **Document type:** *Newsletter, Trade.* **Description:** Designed for the users of NCAR scientific computing facilities.
Former titles (until 2005): S C D News; (until 2000): S C D Zine (Online) (1948-2736); (until 1996): S C D Computing News (Print) (1948-2566); (until 1988): S C D Record
Media: Online - full content.
Published by: National Center for Atmospheric Research, PO Box 3000, Boulder, CO 80307. TEL 303-497-1000, http://www.ncar.ucar.edu. Ed. Lynda Lester.

551.6 551.46 CAN ISSN 1195-8898
QC851
C M O S BULLETIN/BULLETIN S C M O. Text in English, French. 1972. bi-m. CAD 100 domestic to institutions; CAD 115 in United States to institutions; CAD 140 elsewhere to institutions (effective 2009). adv. bk.rev. charts; illus. 32 p./no.; back issues avail. **Document type:** *Bulletin, Academic/Scholarly.* **Description:** News of the activities of the Society and of meteorology and oceanography in Canada and around the world. Also includes technical articles and views on applied climatology, operational meteorology and oceanography.
Supersedes (in 1994): Canadian Meteorological and Oceanographic Society. Newsletter (0827-0384)
Related titles: Online - full text ed.
Indexed: M&GPA.
—Linda Hall.
Published by: Canadian Meteorological and Oceanographic Society/ Societe Canadienne de Meteorologie et d'Oceanographie, Station D, PO Box 3211, Ottawa, ON K1P 6H7, Canada. TEL 613-991-4494, FAX 613-990-1617, publications@cmos.ca, http://www.cmos.ca. Ed. Paul-Andre Bolduc. Circ: 1,000 (paid).

551.51 AUS ISSN 1445-6982
C S I R O ATMOSPHERIC RESEARCH TECHNICAL PAPER. (Commonwealth Scientific and Industrial Research Organization) Text in English. 1983. irreg. (approx. 1-3/yr.). free. back issues avail. **Document type:** *Government.* **Description:** Documents scientific achievements from field observations.
Former titles (until 1998): Commonwealth Scientific and Industrial Research Organization. Division of Atmospheric Research. Technical Paper (1998) (1038-2186); (until 1989): Commonwealth Scientific and Industrial Research Organization. Division of Atmospheric Research. Technical Paper (1989) (0811-4625); (until 1983): Commonwealth Scientific and Industrial Research Organization. Division of Atmospheric Physics. Technical Paper (0159-8112); (until 1971): Commonwealth Scientific and Industrial Research Organization. Division of Meteorological Physics. Technical Paper (0069-7516); Commonwealth Scientific and Industrial Research Organization. Section of Meteorological Physics. Technical Paper
Media: Online - full text.
Indexed: ASFA, B21, ESPM, GeoRef, M&GPA.
—IE, INIST, Linda Hall.
Published by: C S I R O, Marine and Atmospheric Research, 107-121 Station St, Aspendale, VIC 3195, Australia. TEL 61-3-92394400, FAX 61-3-92394444, publishing@csiro.au, http://www.publish.csiro.au/.

551.578 ZAF
CAELUM. Text in English, Afrikaans. 1991. base vol. plus irreg. updates. ZAR 70 per vol. (effective 2005). charts; illus.; maps. **Document type:** *Magazine, Government.* **Description:** Offers a history of notable weather events in South Africa since 1500.
Published by: South African Weather Service, Department of Environmental Affairs and Tourism, Private Bag X97, Pretoria, 0001, South Africa. TEL 27-82-233-8686, FAX 27-12-3093989.

551.5 ESP ISSN 0213-3849
S414
CALENDARIO METEOROLOGICO. Text in Spanish. 1943. a. EUR 6 (effective 2002). **Document type:** *Monographic series.*
Formerly (until 1983): Calendario Meteorofenologico (0490-3463)
Indexed: IIMP, SpeleolAb.
Published by: Instituto Nacional de Meteorologia, Ciudad Universitaria, Apartado 285, Madrid, 28070, Spain. http://www.inm.es.

551.6 CAN ISSN 1207-8514
QC985
CANADIAN CLIMATE SUMMARY. Text in English, French. 1979. m.
Formerly (until 1996): Canada. Atmospheric Environment Service. Climatic Perspectives - Perspectives Climatiques (0225-5707); Which incorporated (1963-1983): Canadian Weather Review (0008-5294)
Published by: Environment Canada, Meteorological Service of Canada (Subsidiary of: Environment Canada/Environnement Canada), National Office, Ottawa, ON K1A 0H3, Canada. TEL 819-997-2800, FAX 819-953-2225, climate.service@ec.gc.ca, http://www.ec.gc.ca. **Subscr. to:** Supply and Services Canada.

551.5 USA ISSN 2160-7338
CANADIAN FORECAST EXECUTIVE SUMMARY. Text in English. 200?. q. **Document type:** *Journal, Trade.*
Published by: I H S Global Insight (USA) Inc., 24 Hartwell Ave, Lexington, MA 02421. TEL 781-301-9100, FAX 781-301-9416, info@ihsglobalinsight.com, http://www.ihsglobalinsight.com/.

551.5 551.46 CAN
CANADIAN METEOROLOGICAL AND OCEANOGRAPHIC SOCIETY. ANNUAL CONGRESS PROGRAM AND ABSTRACTS. Text in English; Text occasionally in French. 1967. a., latest vol.38, 2004. CAD 65 to institutions (effective 2009). adv. 150 p./no.; back issues avail. **Document type:** *Journal, Academic/Scholarly.* **Description:** Program for, and abstracts of, papers on all aspects of meteorology and oceanography, presented at yearly CMOS congresses.
Former titles: Canadian Meteorological and Oceanographic Society. Annual Congress (0705-5919); Canadian Meteorological Society. Annual Congress (0068-9254)
Related titles: CD-ROM ed.: 2002.
Published by: Canadian Meteorological and Oceanographic Society/ Societe Canadienne de Meteorologie et d'Oceanographie, Station D, PO Box 3211, Ottawa, ON K1P 6H7, Canada. TEL 613-991-4494, FAX 613-990-1617, publications@cmos.ca, http://www.cmos.ca. Circ: 400 (paid and controlled).

551.6 551.46 CAN ISSN 1181-6163
CANADIAN METEOROLOGICAL AND OCEANOGRAPHIC SOCIETY. ANNUAL REVIEW (YEAR). Text in English, French. 1983. a. CAD 160 (corporate membership) (effective 2009). adv. back issues avail. **Description:** Reports on the Society's activities including budget, financial reports and auditor's reports for the previous fiscal period.
Related titles: Online - full text ed.
Published by: Canadian Meteorological and Oceanographic Society/ Societe Canadienne de Meteorologie et d'Oceanographie, Station D, PO Box 3211, Ottawa, ON K1P 6H7, Canada. TEL 613-991-4494, FAX 613-990-1617, publications@cmos.ca, http://www.cmos.ca. Ed. Paul-Andre Bolduc. R&P Carmen Harvey. Circ: 860.

551.5 GBR ISSN 1750-0680
GE149
CARBON BALANCE AND MANAGEMENT. Text in English. 2006. irreg. free (effective 2011). adv. back issues avail. **Document type:** *Journal, Academic/Scholarly.* **Description:** Covers aspects of the global carbon cycle.
Media: Online - full text.
Indexed: A01, A26, A37, A39, Agr, C27, C29, CA, D03, D04, E13, E17, F12, G02, G11, GeoRef, I05, I11, P30, PGegResA, PollutAb, R14, S12, S13, S14, S15, S16, S18, SCOPUS, T02.
—Linda Hall. **CCC.**
Published by: BioMed Central Ltd. (Subsidiary of: Springer Science+Business Media), 236 Gray's Inn Rd, London, WC1X 8HB, United Kingdom. TEL 44-20-31922000, FAX 44-20-31922010, info@biomedcentral.com, http://www.biomedcentral.com. Eds. Georgii Alexandrov, Robert Dickinson, Takehisa Oikawa.

551.5 USA
CARBON DIOXIDE AND CLIMATE. Text in English. a. free. **Document type:** *Newsletter, Government.*
Published by: U.S. Department of Energy, Carbon Dioxide Research Program, 1000 Independence Ave, S W, Washington, DC 20585. **Dist. by:** U.S. Department of Commerce, National Technical Information Service, 5301 Shawnee Rd, Alexandria, VA 22312. TEL 800-363-2068, subscriptions@ntis.gov.

551.5 CHN ISSN 1671-1742
QC851
CHENGDU XINXI GONGCHENG XUEYUAN XUEBAO/CHENGDU UNIVERSITY OF INFORMATION TECHNOLOGY. JOURNAL. Text in Chinese. 1986. bi-m. CNY 5 newsstand/cover (effective 2006). **Document type:** *Journal, Academic/Scholarly.*
Formerly (until 2000): Chengdu Qixiang Xueyuan Xuebao/Chengdu Meteorological Institute. Journal (1001-5418)
Related titles: Online - full text ed.
Published by: Chengdu Xinxi Gongcheng Xueyuan/Chengdu University of Information Technology, 24, Xuefu Lu Yi-duan, Xinan Hangkonggang Jingji Kaifa-qu, Chengdu, 610225, China. TEL 86-28-85966485.

M

551.65 JPN ISSN 0009-3467
CHIBAKEN KISHO GEPPO/CHIBA PREFECTURE. MONTHLY REPORT OF METEOROLOGY. Text in Japanese. 1933. m. JPY 5,200. charts; stat.
Media: Duplicated (not offset).
Published by: Kishocho, Choshi Chiho Kishodai/Japan Meteorological Agency, Choshi Local Meteorological Observatory, 2-6431 Kawaguchi-cho, Choshi-shi, Chiba-ken 288-0001, Japan.

551.6 537 JPN
CHUGOKU CHIHO DENRYOKU KISHO GAIHO/CHUGOKU DISTRICT. REPORT OF THE POWER AND WEATHER. Text in Japanese. 1942. a.
Published by: Kishocho, Hiroshima Chiho Kishodai/Japan Meteorological Agency, Hiroshima Local Meteorological Observatory, 6-30 Kami-Hatsuchobori, Naka-ku, Hiroshima-shi, 730-0012, Japan.

CIEL ET TERRE. *see* ASTRONOMY

551.5 GBR ISSN 1756-5529
QC902.8
CLIMATE AND DEVELOPMENT. Text in English. 2008. q. GBP 503 combined subscription in United Kingdom to institutions (print & online eds.); EUR 665, USD 831 combined subscription to institutions (print & online eds.) (effective 2012). adv. **Document type:** *Journal, Academic/Scholarly.* **Description:** Provides a forum to communicate research, review and discussion on the interfaces between climate, development and practice.
Related titles: Online - full text ed.: ISSN 1756-5537. GBP 453 in United Kingdom to institutions; EUR 598, USD 755 to institutions (effective 2012) (from IngentaConnect).
Indexed: A26, AgrForAb, B21, BA, C25, C30, CA, CABA, CurCont, E04, E05, E08, E12, ESPM, F08, F12, FCA, G02, GEOBASE, GH, H16, I05, I11, LT, M&GPA, N02, R12, S12, S13, S16, SSCI, SSciA, T02, T05, TAR, W07, W11.
—IE. **CCC.**
Published by: Earthscan Ltd., Dunstan House, 14a St Cross St, London, EC1N 8XA, United Kingdom. TEL 44-20-78411930, FAX 44-20-72421474, earthinfo@earthscan.co.uk. Ed. Richard J T Klein TEL 46-8-6747054. Adv. contact Emma Barnes. **Subscr. to:** Portland Customer Services, Commerce Way, Colchester CO2 8HP, United Kingdom. TEL 44-1206-796351, FAX 44-1206-799331, sales@portland-services.com, http://www.portlandpress.com.

551.6 USA
CLIMATE: ANNUAL REVIEW. Text in English. 19??. a. free (effective 2009). back issues avail.; reprints avail. **Document type:** *Government.* **Description:** Provide information about the global temperatures, and research projects to improve future climate forecasts.
Media: Online - full text.
Published by: U.S. National Climatic Data Center (Subsidiary of: U.S. Department of Commerce), Federal Bldg, 151 Patton Ave, Asheville, NC 28801. TEL 828-271-4800, FAX 828-271-4876, ncdc.info@noaa.gov, http://www.ncdc.noaa.gov. Ed. Mike Changery.

551.5 DEU ISSN 1611-8855
CLIMATE CHANGE. Text in Multiple languages. 2001. irreg. **Document type:** *Monographic series, Academic/Scholarly.*
Related titles: Online - full text ed.: ISSN 1862-4359.
Indexed: GeoRef.
Published by: Umweltbundesamt, Woerlitzer Platz 1, Dessau, 06844, Germany. TEL 49-340-21030, FAX 49-340-21042285, info@umweltbundesamt.de, http://www.umweltbundesamt.de.

551.5 CAN ISSN 0835-3980
CLIMATE CHANGE DIGEST. Text in English. 1984. irreg. free. **Document type:** *Monographic series, Academic/Scholarly.*
Indexed: ASFA, B21, ESPM, SpeleolAb.
—CCC.
Published by: Science Assessment & Integration Branch, Meteorological Service of Canada, 4905 Dufferin St, Downsview, ON M3H 5T4, Canada.

CLIMATE CHANGE MANAGEMENT. *see* ENVIRONMENTAL STUDIES—Pollution

551.657 USA ISSN 1048-6747
QC982
CLIMATE DIAGNOSTICS BULLETIN. Text in English. 1983. m.
Indexed: GeoRef.
—Linda Hall.
Published by: National Centers for Environmental Prediction, 5200 Auth Rd, Camp Springs, MD 20746. http://wwwt.ncep.noaa.gov.

551.6 DEU ISSN 0930-7575
QC981.7.D94 CODEN: CLDYEM
➤ **CLIMATE DYNAMICS;** observational, theoretical and computational research on the climate system. Text in English. 1986. 16/yr. EUR 4,408, USD 5,235 combined subscription to institutions (print & online eds.) (effective 2012). adv. back issues avail.; reprint service avail. from PSC. **Document type:** *Journal, Academic/Scholarly.* **Description:** Focuses on the dynamics of the entire climate system, including atmosphere, ocean, cryosphere, surface biomass and lithosphere.
Related titles: Online - full text ed.: ISSN 1432-0894 (from IngentaConnect).
Indexed: A01, A02, A03, A08, A22, A26, A33, ASCA, ASFA, Agr, CA, CurCont, E01, ESPM, FR, G02, GEOBASE, GeoRef, I05, INIS AtomInd, ISR, Inspec, M&GPA, OceAb, P26, P47, P48, P52, P54, P56, PQC, PollutAb, RefZh, SCI, SCOPUS, SSciA, SWRA, SpeleolAb, T02, W07.
—BLDSC (3279.108000), AskIEEE, IE, Infotrieve, Ingenta, INIST, Linda Hall. **CCC.**

Published by: Springer (Subsidiary of: Springer Science+Business Media), Tiergartenstr 17, Heidelberg, 69121, Germany. TEL 49-6221-4870, FAX 49-6221-345229. Eds. Edwin K Schneider, Elisa Mancini. **Subscr. in the Americas to:** Springer New York LLC, Journal Fulfillment, PO Box 2485, Secaucus, NJ 07096. TEL 201-348-4033, 800-777-4643, FAX 201-348-4505, journals-ny@springer.com, http://www.springer.com; **Subscr. to:** Springer Distribution Center, Kundenservice Zeitschriften, Haberstr 7, Heidelberg 69126, Germany. TEL 49-6221-3454303, FAX 49-6221-3454229, subscriptions@springer.com.

▼ ➤ **CLIMATE LAW.** *see* LAW

551.6 GBR
CLIMATE MONITOR ONLINE. Text in English. 1976 (vol.5). m. free (effective 2009). illus.; maps. back issues avail. **Document type:** *Report, Academic/Scholarly.* **Description:** Contains summaries of global climatic conditions, articles of general interest on climatology, and unique polar temperature information and other data updates.
Former titles (until 1998): Climate Monitor (Print) (0140-458X); (until 1977): Crumb. Climatic Research Unit Monthly Bulletin (0306-1388)
Media: Online - full text.
—CCC.
Published by: University of East Anglia, School of Environmental Sciences. Climatic Research Unit, School of Environmental Sciences, Faculty of Science, Norwich, NR4 7TJ, United Kingdom. TEL 44-1603-592722, FAX 44-1603-507784, cru@uea.ac.uk.

551.6 DEU ISSN 0936-577X
QC851 CODEN: CLREEW
➤ **CLIMATE RESEARCH.** Text in English. 1990. 12/yr. (in 4 vols., 3 nos./vol.). EUR 796 combined subscription (print & online eds.) (effective 2011). **Document type:** *Journal, Academic/Scholarly.* **Description:** Presents original papers, short notes and reviews on basic and applied research devoted to all aspects of climate.
Related titles: ◆ Online - full text ed.: Climate Research Online. ISSN 1616-1572.
Indexed: A22, A33, A34, A35, A36, A37, A38, ASCA, ASFA, B21, B25, BIOSIS Prev, C25, C30, CA, CABA, CurCont, DIP, E04, E05, E12, ESPM, EnvAb, EnvInd, F08, F12, FCA, FLUIDEX, G02, G11, GEOBASE, GH, GeoRef, H16, I11, IBR, IBZ, ISR, IndVet, LT, M&GPA, MaizeAb, MycolAb, N02, O01, P32, P33, P37, P38, P40, PGegResA, PN&I, PollutAb, R07, R08, R11, R12, RRTA, S12, S13, S16, S17, SCI, SCOPUS, SSciA, SoyAb, T02, T05, TAR, TriticAb, VITIS, VS, W07, W08, W11.
—BLDSC (3279.180000), IE, Infotrieve, Ingenta.
Published by: Inter-Research, Nordbuente 23, Oldendorf, 21385, Germany. TEL 49-4132-7127, FAX 49-4132-8883, ir@int-res.com. Eds. Mikhail Semenov, Nils Stenseth.

551.6 DEU ISSN 1616-1572
➤ **CLIMATE RESEARCH ONLINE.** Text in English. 2000. 9/yr. EUR 716 (effective 2011). **Document type:** *Journal, Academic/Scholarly.*
Media: Online - full text. **Related titles:** ◆ Print ed.: Climate Research. ISSN 0936-577X.
—CCC.
Published by: Inter-Research, Nordbuente 23, Oldendorf, 21385, Germany. TEL 49-4132-7127, FAX 49-4132-8883, ir@int-res.com.

551.5 USA
CLIMATE WATCH BRIEF. Text in English. 1992. m. free. adv. **Document type:** *Newsletter.* **Description:** Presents a summary of key climate conditions.
Formerly: Climate Watch
Published by: Global Climate Coalition, 1275 K St N W, Ste 890, Washington, DC 20005-4006. TEL 202-974-5011. Ed. Glenn Kelly. R&P, Adv. contact Eric Holdsworth.

551.65 USA
CLIMATEWIRE. Text in English. 2008. d. adv. back issues avail. **Document type:** *Newspaper, Consumer.* **Description:** Provides information of the debate over climate policy and its effects on business, the environment and society.
Related titles: Online - full text ed.: ISSN 1946-4568.
Published by: Environment and Energy Publishing, LLC, 122 C St, N W, Ste 722, Washington, DC 20001. TEL 202-628-6500, FAX 202-737-5299, pubs@eenews.net. Ed. John Fialka TEL 202-446-0460. Adv. contact Richard Nordin TEL 202-446-0447.

551.5 NLD ISSN 0165-0009
QC981.8.C5 CODEN: CLCHDX
➤ **CLIMATIC CHANGE**; an interdisciplinary, international journal devoted to the description, causes and implications of climatic change. Text in English. 1977. 24/yr. EUR 4,071, USD 4,223 combined subscription to institutions (print & online eds.) (effective 2012). bk.rev. illus. Index. reprint service avail. from PSC. **Document type:** *Journal, Academic/Scholarly.* **Description:** Dedicated to the problem of climatic variability and change, its descriptions, causes, implications and interactions among these.
Related titles: Microform ed.: (from PQC); Online - full text ed.: ISSN 1573-1480 (from IngentaConnect).
Indexed: A&AAb, A01, A02, A03, A08, A20, A22, A26, A33, A34, A35, A36, A37, A38, ASCA, ASFA, Agr, AgrForAb, B21, B23, B25, BA, BIOBASE, BIOSIS Prev, BibLing, C25, C30, CA, CABA, CIN, CPEI, ChemAb, ChemTitl, CurCont, D01, DIP, E01, E04, E05, E08, E11, E12, EIA, ESPM, EnerInd, EnerRev, EngInd, EnvAb, EnvInd, F08, F11, F12, FCA, FR, G02, G08, G11, GEOBASE, GH, GeoRef, H16, HPNRM, I05, I11, IABS, IBR, IBZ, ISR, IndVet, Inspec, LT, M&GPA, MaizeAb, MycolAb, N02, N03, O01, OR, OceAb, P02, P10, P26, P30, P32, P33, P34, P37, P39, P48, P52, P53, P54, P56, PGegResA, PGrRegA, PN&I, PQC, PollutAb, R07, R08, R11, R12, R13, RA&MP, RRTA, RefZh, S09, S10, S12, S13, S16, S17, SCI, SCOPUS, SSciA, SWRA, SoyAb, SpeleolAb, T02, T04, T05, TAR, TriticAb, VS, W07, W08, W10, W11, WildRev.
—BLDSC (3279.250000), AskIEEE, CASDDS, IE, Infotrieve, Ingenta, INIST, Linda Hall. **CCC.**
Published by: Springer Netherlands (Subsidiary of: Springer Science+Business Media), Van Godewijckstraat 30, Dordrecht, 3311 GX, Netherlands. TEL 31-78-6576050, FAX 31-78-6576474, http://www.springer.com.

551.5 BRA ISSN 1980-654X
QC851
CLIMATOLOGIA E ESTUDOS DA PAISAGEM. Abbreviated title: C L I M E P. Text in Portuguese. 2006. s-a. **Document type:** *Journal, Abstract/Index.*
Media: Online - full text.
Indexed: GEOBASE.
Published by: Universidade Estadual Paulista "Julio de Mesquita Filho", Instituto de Geociencias e Ciencias Exatas, Rua 10, 2527, Bairro Santana, Rio Claro, SP 13500-230, Brazil. TEL 55-19-35262200, http://www.rc.unesp.br/igce/.

551.5 GRC ISSN 1011-6109
QC989.G97
CLIMATOLOGICAL BULLETIN. Text in English. 1977. a.
Published by: National Observatory of Athens, Meteorological Institute, PO Box 20048, Athens, 11810, Greece. TEL 30-01-2103490101, FAX 30-01-2103490140, http://www.noa.gr.

551.5 USA
CLIMATOLOGICAL DATA (ONLINE). Abbreviated title: C D. (Issued separately in: 42 states, 6 New England states, Maryland-Delaware, Puerto Rico, Virgin Islands, and Hawaii & Pacific Islands) Text in English. 1890. m. (plus a. update). USD 4 per issue (effective 2009). illus. back issues avail.; reprints avail. **Document type:** *Government.* **Description:** Contains station daily maximum and minimum temperatures and precipitation.
Formerly (until 19??): Climatological Data (Print) (0009-8949)
Media: Online - full content. **Related titles:** Magnetic Tape ed.; Microfiche ed.
Indexed: ABIPC.
Published by: (U.S. Department of Commerce), U.S. National Climatic Data Center (Subsidiary of: U.S. Department of Commerce), Federal Bldg, 151 Patton Ave, Asheville, NC 28801. TEL 828-271-4800, FAX 828-271-4876, ncdc.info@noaa.gov, http://www.ncdc.noaa.gov. Circ: 23,000.

551.6 USA ISSN 0145-0050
QC983
CLIMATOLOGICAL DATA. ALABAMA. Text in English. 1976. m. USD 63; USD 12 per issue (effective 2009). back issues avail. **Document type:** *Government.* **Description:** Contains station daily maximum and minimum temperatures and precipitation, as well as summaries for heating and cooling degree days.
Former titles (until 1976): U.S. Department of Commerce. National Oceanic and Atmospheric Administration. Environmental Data Service. Climatological Data, Alabama; (until 1966): U.S. Weather Bureau. Climatological Data. Alabama
Related titles: Online - full text ed.: USD 42; USD 4 per issue (effective 2009); Supplement(s): Supplemental Climatological Data, Late Reports and Corrections. Alabama.
—Linda Hall.
Published by: U.S. National Climatic Data Center (Subsidiary of: U.S. Department of Commerce), Federal Bldg, 151 Patton Ave, Asheville, NC 28801. TEL 828-271-4800, FAX 828-271-4876, NODC.Services@noaa.gov, http://www.ncdc.noaa.gov.

551.6 USA ISSN 0145-0387
QC983
CLIMATOLOGICAL DATA. ARIZONA. Text in English. 1914. m. USD 63; USD 12 per issue (effective 2009). back issues avail. **Document type:** *Government.* **Description:** Contains station daily maximum and minimum temperatures and precipitation, as well as summaries for heating and cooling degree days.
Former titles (until 1976): U.S. Department of Commerce. National Oceanic and Atmospheric Administration. Environmental Data Service. Climatological Data, Arizona; (until 1966): U.S. Weather Bureau. Climatological Data. Arizona
Related titles: Online - full text ed.: USD 42; USD 4 per issue (effective 2009).
—Linda Hall.
Published by: U.S. National Climatic Data Center (Subsidiary of: U.S. Department of Commerce), Federal Bldg, 151 Patton Ave, Asheville, NC 28801. TEL 828-271-4800, FAX 828-271-4876, NODC.Services@noaa.gov, http://www.ncdc.noaa.gov.

551.6 USA ISSN 0145-0069
QC983
CLIMATOLOGICAL DATA. CALIFORNIA. Text in English. 1897. m. USD 63; USD 12 per issue (effective 2009). back issues avail. **Document type:** *Government.*
Former titles (until 1975): United States. Environmental Data Service. Climatological Data, California; United States. Weather Bureau. Climatological Data, California
Related titles: Online - full text ed.: USD 42; USD 4 per issue (effective 2009); Supplement(s): Supplemental Climatological Data, Late Reports and Corrections. California. ISSN 0730-2746.
—Linda Hall.
Published by: U.S. National Climatic Data Center (Subsidiary of: U.S. Department of Commerce), Federal Bldg, 151 Patton Ave, Asheville, NC 28801. TEL 828-271-4800, FAX 828-271-4876, NODC.Services@noaa.gov, http://www.ncdc.noaa.gov.

551.6 USA ISSN 0145-0506
QC983
CLIMATOLOGICAL DATA. COLORADO. Text in English. 1914. m. USD 63; USD 12 per issue (effective 2009). back issues avail. **Document type:** *Government.* **Description:** Contains station daily maximum and minimum temperatures and precipitation, as well as summaries for heating and cooling degree days.
Former titles (until 1976): U.S. Department of Commerce. National Oceanic and Atmospheric Administration. Environmental Data Service. Climatological Data. Colorado; (until 1966): U.S. Weather Bureau. Climatological Data. Colorado
Related titles: Online - full text ed.: USD 42; USD 4 per issue (effective 2009); Supplement(s): Supplemental Climatological Data, Late Reports and Corrections. Colorado. ISSN 0730-661X.
—Linda Hall.
Published by: U.S. National Climatic Data Center (Subsidiary of: U.S. Department of Commerce), Federal Bldg, 151 Patton Ave, Asheville, NC 28801. TEL 828-271-4800, FAX 828-271-4876, NODC.Services@noaa.gov, http://www.ncdc.noaa.gov.

551.6 USA ISSN 0145-0484
QC983
CLIMATOLOGICAL DATA. FLORIDA. Text in English. 1914. m. USD 63; USD 12 per issue (effective 2009). back issues avail. **Document type:** *Government.* **Description:** Contains station daily maximum and minimum temperatures and precipitation, as well as summaries for heating and cooling degree days.
Former titles (until 1976): U.S. Department of Commerce. National Oceanic and Atmospheric Administration. Environmental Data Service. Climatological Data, Florida; (until 1966): U.S. Weather Bureau. Climatological Data. Florida
Related titles: Online - full text ed.: USD 42; USD 4 per issue (effective 2009); Supplement(s): Supplemental Climatological Data, Late Reports and Corrections. Florida. ISSN 0730-6601.
—Linda Hall.
Published by: U.S. National Climatic Data Center (Subsidiary of: U.S. Department of Commerce), Federal Bldg, 151 Patton Ave, Asheville, NC 28801. TEL 828-271-4800, FAX 828-271-4876, NODC.Services@noaa.gov, http://www.ncdc.noaa.gov.

551.5 IDN ISSN 0009-8957
CLIMATOLOGICAL DATA FOR JAKARTA OBSERVATORY. Text in English. 1956. a. per issue exchange basis.
Published by: Meteorological and Geophysical Institute/Badan Meteorologi dan Geofisika, Jalan Arief Rakhman Hakim 3, Jakarta, Indonesia.

551.6 USA ISSN 0145-0492
QC983
CLIMATOLOGICAL DATA. GEORGIA. Text in English. 1914. m. USD 63; USD 12 per issue (effective 2009). back issues avail. **Document type:** *Government.* **Description:** Contains station daily maximum and minimum temperatures and precipitation, as well as summaries for heating and cooling degree days.
Former titles (until 1976): U.S. Department of Commerce. National Oceanic and Atmospheric Administration. Environmental Data Service. Climatological Data. Georgia; (until 1966): U.S. Weather Bureau. Climatological Data. Georgia
Related titles: Online - full text ed.: USD 42; USD 4 per issue (effective 2009); Supplement(s): Supplemental Climatological Data, Late Reports and Corrections. Georgia. ISSN 0730-2754.
—Linda Hall.
Published by: U.S. National Climatic Data Center (Subsidiary of: U.S. Department of Commerce), Federal Bldg, 151 Patton Ave, Asheville, NC 28801. TEL 828-271-4800, FAX 828-271-4876, NODC.Services@noaa.gov, http://www.ncdc.noaa.gov.

551.6 USA ISSN 0095-4373
QC983
CLIMATOLOGICAL DATA. HAWAII AND PACIFIC. Text in English. 1972. m.
Formed by the merger of (1956-1972): Climatological Data. Pacific (0732-6807); Climatological Data. Hawaii (0094-9507).
—Linda Hall.
Published by: U.S. National Climatic Data Center (Subsidiary of: U.S. Department of Commerce), Federal Bldg, 151 Patton Ave, Asheville, NC 28801. TEL 828-271-4800, FAX 828-271-4876, ncdc.info@noaa.gov, http://www.ncdc.noaa.gov.

551.6 USA ISSN 0145-0514
QC983
CLIMATOLOGICAL DATA. IDAHO. Text in English. 1914. m. USD 63; USD 12 per issue (effective 2009). back issues avail. **Document type:** *Government.* **Description:** Contains station daily maximum and minimum temperatures and precipitation, as well as summaries for heating and cooling degree days.
Former titles (until 1976): U.S. Department of Commerce. National Oceanic and Atmospheric Administration. Environmental Data Service. Climatological Data. Idaho; (until 1966): U.S. Weather Bureau. Climatological Data. Idaho
Related titles: Online - full text ed.: USD 42; USD 4 per issue (effective 2009).
—Linda Hall.
Published by: U.S. National Climatic Data Center (Subsidiary of: U.S. Department of Commerce), Federal Bldg, 151 Patton Ave, Asheville, NC 28801. TEL 828-271-4800, FAX 828-271-4876, NODC.Services@noaa.gov, http://www.ncdc.noaa.gov.

551.6 USA ISSN 0145-0522
QC983
CLIMATOLOGICAL DATA. ILLINOIS. Text in English. 1914. m. USD 63; USD 12 per issue (effective 2009). back issues avail. **Document type:** *Government.* **Description:** Contains station daily maximum and minimum temperatures and precipitation, as well as summaries for heating and cooling degree days.
Former titles (until 1976): U.S. Department of Commerce. National Oceanic and Atmospheric Administration. Environmental Data Service. Climatological Data, Illinois; (until 1966): U.S. Weather Bureau. Climatological Data. Illinois; Climatological Data. Illinois Section
Related titles: Online - full text ed.: USD 42; USD 4 per issue (effective 2009).
—Linda Hall.
Published by: U.S. National Climatic Data Center (Subsidiary of: U.S. Department of Commerce), Federal Bldg, 151 Patton Ave, Asheville, NC 28801. TEL 828-271-4800, FAX 828-271-4876, NODC.Services@noaa.gov, http://www.ncdc.noaa.gov.

551.6 USA ISSN 0145-0530
QC983
CLIMATOLOGICAL DATA. INDIANA. Text in English. 1914. m. USD 63; USD 12 per issue (effective 2009). back issues avail. **Document type:** *Government.* **Description:** Contains station daily maximum and minimum temperatures and precipitation, as well as summaries for heating and cooling degree days.
Former titles (until 1976): U.S. Department of Commerce. National Oceanic and Atmospheric Administration. Environmental Data Service. Climatological Data, Indiana; (until 1966): U.S. Weather Bureau. Climatological Data. Indiana; Climatological Data. Indiana Section
Related titles: Online - full text ed.: USD 42; USD 4 per issue (effective 2009).
—Linda Hall.
Published by: U.S. National Climatic Data Center (Subsidiary of: U.S. Department of Commerce), Federal Bldg, 151 Patton Ave, Asheville, NC 28801. TEL 828-271-4800, FAX 828-271-4876, NODC.Services@noaa.gov, http://www.ncdc.noaa.gov.

551.6 USA ISSN 0145-0468
QC983
CLIMATOLOGICAL DATA. IOWA. Text in English. 1914. m. USD 63; USD 12 per issue (effective 2009). back issues avail. **Document type:** *Government.* **Description:** Contains station daily maximum and minimum temperatures and precipitation, as well as summaries for heating and cooling degree days.
Former titles (until 1976): U.S. Department of Commerce. National Oceanic and Atmospheric Administration. Environmental Data Service. Climatological Data, Iowa; (until 1966): U.S. Weather Bureau. Climatological Data. Iowa
Related titles: Online - full text ed.: USD 42; USD 4 per issue (effective 2009).
—Linda Hall.
Published by: U.S. National Climatic Data Center (Subsidiary of: U.S. Department of Commerce), Federal Bldg, 151 Patton Ave, Asheville, NC 28801. TEL 828-271-4800, FAX 828-271-4876, NODC.Services@noaa.gov, http://www.ncdc.noaa.gov.

551.6 USA ISSN 0145-0433
QC983
CLIMATOLOGICAL DATA. KENTUCKY. Text in English. 1914. m. USD 63; USD 12 per issue (effective 2009). back issues avail. **Document type:** *Government.* **Description:** Contains station daily maximum and minimum temperatures and precipitation, as well as summaries for heating and cooling degree days.
Former titles (until 1976): U.S. Department of Commerce. National Oceanic and Atmospheric Administration. Environmental Data Service. Climatological Data, Kentucky; (until 1966): U.S. Weather Bureau. Climatological Data. Kentucky; Climatological Data. Kentucky Section
Related titles: Online - full text ed.: USD 42; USD 4 per issue (effective 2009); Supplement(s): Supplemental Climatological Data, Late Reports and Corrections. Kentucky. ISSN 0730-2851.
—Linda Hall.
Published by: U.S. National Climatic Data Center (Subsidiary of: U.S. Department of Commerce), Federal Bldg, 151 Patton Ave, Asheville, NC 28801. TEL 828-271-4800, FAX 828-271-4876, NODC.Services@noaa.gov, http://www.ncdc.noaa.gov.

551.6 USA ISSN 0145-0409
QC983
CLIMATOLOGICAL DATA. LOUISIANA. Text in English. 1914. m. USD 63; USD 12 per issue (effective 2009). back issues avail. **Document type:** *Government.* **Description:** Contains station daily maximum and minimum temperatures and precipitation, as well as summaries for heating and cooling degree days.
Former titles (until 1976): U.S. Department of Commerce. National Oceanic and Atmospheric Administration. Environmental Data Service. Climatological Data. Louisiana; (until 1966): U.S. Weather Bureau. Climatological Data. Louisiana
Related titles: Online - full text ed.: USD 42; USD 4 per issue (effective 2009); Supplement(s): Supplemental Climatological Data, Late Reports and Corrections. Louisiana. ISSN 0730-286X.
—Linda Hall.
Published by: U.S. National Climatic Data Center (Subsidiary of: U.S. Department of Commerce), Federal Bldg, 151 Patton Ave, Asheville, NC 28801. TEL 828-271-4800, FAX 828-271-4876, NODC.Services@noaa.gov, http://www.ncdc.noaa.gov.

551.6 USA ISSN 0145-0549
QC983
CLIMATOLOGICAL DATA. MARYLAND AND DELAWARE. Text in English. 1914. m. USD 63; USD 12 per issue (effective 2009). back issues avail. **Document type:** *Government.* **Description:** Contains station daily maximum and minimum temperatures and precipitation, as well as summaries for heating and cooling degree days.
Former titles (until 1976): U.S. Department of Commerce. National Oceanic and Atmospheric Administration. Environmental Data Service. Climatological Data. Maryland and Delaware; (until 1966): U.S. Weather Bureau. Climatological Data. Maryland and Delaware
Related titles: Online - full text ed.: USD 42; USD 4 per issue (effective 2009); Supplement(s): Supplemental Climatological Data, Late Reports and Corrections. Maryland & Delaware. ISSN 0730-2878.
—Linda Hall.
Published by: U.S. National Climatic Data Center (Subsidiary of: U.S. Department of Commerce), Federal Bldg, 151 Patton Ave, Asheville, NC 28801. TEL 828-271-4800, FAX 828-271-4876, NODC.Services@noaa.gov, http://www.ncdc.noaa.gov.

551.6 USA ISSN 0145-0425
QC983
CLIMATOLOGICAL DATA. MISSISSIPPI. Text in English. 1914. m. USD 63; USD 12 per issue (effective 2009). back issues avail. **Document type:** *Government.* **Description:** Contains station daily maximum and minimum temperatures and precipitation, as well as summaries for heating and cooling degree days.
Former titles (until 1976): U.S. Department of Commerce. National Oceanic and Atmospheric Administration. Environmental Data Service. Climatological Data, Mississippi; (until 1966): U.S. Weather Bureau. Climatological Data. Mississippi
Related titles: CD-ROM ed.
—Linda Hall.
Published by: U.S. National Climatic Data Center (Subsidiary of: U.S. Department of Commerce), Federal Bldg, 151 Patton Ave, Asheville, NC 28801. TEL 828-271-4800, FAX 828-271-4876, NODC.Services@noaa.gov, http://www.ncdc.noaa.gov.

551.657 USA ISSN 0364-6068
QC983
CLIMATOLOGICAL DATA. MISSOURI. Text in English. 1976. m. USD 63; USD 12 per issue (effective 2009). back issues avail. **Document type:** *Government.*
Former titles (until 1975): United States. Environmental Data Service. Climatological Data, Missouri; Climatological Data, Missouri
Related titles: Online - full text ed.: USD 42; USD 4 per issue (effective 2009).
—Linda Hall.
Published by: U.S. National Climatic Data Center (Subsidiary of: U.S. Department of Commerce), Federal Bldg, 151 Patton Ave, Asheville, NC 28801. TEL 828-271-4800, FAX 828-271-4876, NODC.Services@noaa.gov, http://www.ncdc.noaa.gov.

551.657 USA ISSN 0364-5312
QC983
CLIMATOLOGICAL DATA. NEVADA. Text in English. 1976. m. USD 63; USD 12 per issue (effective 2009). back issues avail. **Document type:** *Government.*
Former titles (until 1975): United States. Environmental Data Service. Climatological Data, Nevada; United States. Weather Bureau. Climatological Data, Nevada
Related titles: Online - full text ed.: USD 42; USD 4 per issue (effective 2009).
—Linda Hall.
Published by: U.S. National Climatic Data Center (Subsidiary of: U.S. Department of Commerce), Federal Bldg, 151 Patton Ave, Asheville, NC 28801. TEL 828-271-4800, FAX 828-271-4876, NODC.Services@noaa.gov, http://www.ncdc.noaa.gov.

551.6 USA ISSN 0364-5339
QC983
CLIMATOLOGICAL DATA. NEW ENGLAND. Text in English. 1976. m. USD 4 combined subscription per issue (print, online & CD-ROM eds.) (effective 2008). back issues avail. **Document type:** *Government.* **Description:** Features the daily maximum and minimum temperatures and precipitation data of stations in New England.
Related titles: Online - full text ed.
—Linda Hall.
Published by: U.S. National Climatic Data Center (Subsidiary of: U.S. Department of Commerce), Federal Bldg, 151 Patton Ave, Asheville, NC 28801. TEL 828-271-4800, FAX 828-271-4876, NODC.Services@noaa.gov, http://www.ncdc.noaa.gov.

551.657 USA ISSN 0364-5614
QC983
CLIMATOLOGICAL DATA. NEW JERSEY. Text in English. 1976. m. USD 63; USD 12 per issue (effective 2009). back issues avail. **Document type:** *Government.*
Former titles (until 1975): United States. Environmental Data Service. Climatological Data, New Jersey; United States. Weather Bureau. Climatological Data, New Jersey
Related titles: Online - full text ed.: USD 42; USD 4 per issue (effective 2009); Supplement(s): Supplemental Climatological Data, Late Reports and Corrections. New Jersey. ISSN 0730-2762.
—Linda Hall.
Published by: U.S. National Climatic Data Center (Subsidiary of: U.S. Department of Commerce), Federal Bldg, 151 Patton Ave, Asheville, NC 28801. TEL 828-271-4800, FAX 828-271-4876, NODC.Services@noaa.gov, http://www.ncdc.noaa.gov.

551.657 USA ISSN 0364-5606
QC983
CLIMATOLOGICAL DATA. NEW YORK. Text in English. 1976. m. USD 63; USD 12 per issue (effective 2009). back issues avail. **Document type:** *Government.* **Description:** Features the daily maximum and minimum temperatures and precipitation data of stations in New York.
Related titles: Online - full text ed.: USD 42; USD 4 per issue (effective 2009); Supplement(s): Supplemental Climatological Data, Late Reports and Corrections. New York.
—Linda Hall.
Published by: U.S. National Climatic Data Center (Subsidiary of: U.S. Department of Commerce), Federal Bldg, 151 Patton Ave, Asheville, NC 28801. TEL 828-271-4800, FAX 828-271-4876, NODC.Services@noaa.gov, http://www.ncdc.noaa.gov.

551.657 USA ISSN 0364-5584
QC983
CLIMATOLOGICAL DATA. OHIO. Text in English. 1976. m. USD 63; USD 12 per issue (effective 2009). back issues avail. **Document type:** *Government.* **Description:** Features the daily maximum and minimum temperatures and precipitation data of stations in Ohio.
Related titles: Online - full text ed.: USD 42; USD 4 per issue (effective 2009).
—Linda Hall.
Published by: U.S. National Climatic Data Center (Subsidiary of: U.S. Department of Commerce), Federal Bldg, 151 Patton Ave, Asheville, NC 28801. TEL 828-271-4800, FAX 828-271-4876, NODC.Services@noaa.gov, http://www.ncdc.noaa.gov.

551.657 USA ISSN 0364-5843
QC983
CLIMATOLOGICAL DATA. PENNSYLVANIA. Text in English. 1976. m. USD 63; USD 12 per issue (effective 2009). back issues avail. **Document type:** *Government.* **Description:** Features the daily maximum and minimum temperatures and precipitation data of stations in Pennsylvania.
Related titles: Online - full text ed.: USD 42; USD 4 per issue (effective 2009).
—Linda Hall.
Published by: U.S. National Climatic Data Center (Subsidiary of: U.S. Department of Commerce), Federal Bldg, 151 Patton Ave, Asheville, NC 28801. TEL 828-271-4800, FAX 828-271-4876, NODC.Services@noaa.gov, http://www.ncdc.noaa.gov.

551.657 USA ISSN 0364-5010
QC983
CLIMATOLOGICAL DATA. TENNESSEE. Text in English. 1976. m. USD 63; USD 12 per issue (effective 2009). back issues avail. **Document type:** *Government.* **Description:** Features the daily maximum and minimum temperatures and precipitation data of stations in Tennessee.
Related titles: Online - full text ed.: USD 42; USD 4 per issue (effective 2009).
—Linda Hall.
Published by: U.S. National Climatic Data Center (Subsidiary of: U.S. Department of Commerce), Federal Bldg, 151 Patton Ave, Asheville, NC 28801. TEL 828-271-4800, FAX 828-271-4876, NODC.Services@noaa.gov, http://www.ncdc.noaa.gov.

551.657 USA ISSN 0364-5592
QC983
CLIMATOLOGICAL DATA. UTAH. Text in English. 1976. m. USD 63; USD 12 per issue (effective 2009). back issues avail. **Document type:** *Government.* **Description:** Features the daily maximum and minimum temperatures and precipitation data of stations in Utah.
Related titles: Online - full text ed.: USD 42; USD 4 per issue (effective 2009).
—Linda Hall.
Published by: U.S. National Climatic Data Center (Subsidiary of: U.S. Department of Commerce), Federal Bldg, 151 Patton Ave, Asheville, NC 28801. TEL 828-271-4800, FAX 828-271-4876, NODC.Services@noaa.gov, http://www.ncdc.noaa.gov.

551.6 USA ISSN 0364-5630
QC983
CLIMATOLOGICAL DATA. VIRGINIA. Text in English. 1976. m. USD 4 combined subscription per issue (print, online & CD-ROM eds.) (effective 2008). back issues avail. **Document type:** *Government.* **Description:** Features the daily maximum and minimum temperatures and precipitation data of stations in Virginia.
Related titles: CD-ROM ed.; Online - full text ed.; Supplement(s): Supplemental Climatological Data, Late Reports and Corrections. Virginia.
—Linda Hall.
Published by: U.S. National Climatic Data Center (Subsidiary of: U.S. Department of Commerce), Federal Bldg, 151 Patton Ave, Asheville, NC 28801. TEL 828-271-4800, FAX 828-271-4876, NODC.Services@noaa.gov, http://www.ncdc.noaa.gov.

551.6 USA ISSN 0364-5371
QC983
CLIMATOLOGICAL DATA. WEST VIRGINIA. Text in English. 1975. m. USD 63; USD 12 per issue (effective 2009). back issues avail. **Document type:** *Government.*
Former titles (until 1975): United States. Environmental Data Service. Climatological Data, West Virginia; United States. Weather Bureau. Climatological Data, West Virginia
Related titles: Online - full text ed.: USD 42; USD 4 per issue (effective 2009).
—Linda Hall.
Published by: U.S. National Climatic Data Center (Subsidiary of: U.S. Department of Commerce), Federal Bldg, 151 Patton Ave, Asheville, NC 28801. TEL 828-271-4800, FAX 828-271-4876, NODC.Services@noaa.gov, http://www.ncdc.noaa.gov.

551.6 JPN ISSN 0388-0206
CLIMATOLOGICAL NOTES. Text in English. 1969. irreg.
—Linda Hall.
Published by: Tsukuba Daigaku, Chikyu Kagakukei/University of Tsukuba, Institute of Geoscience, 1-1 Tenno-Dai 1-chome, Tsukuba-shi, Ibaraki-ken 305-0006, Japan.

551.5 CAN ISSN 1493-2776
CO2 - CLIMATE REPORT. Text in English. 1983. a. free. **Document type:** *Newsletter.*
Related titles: Online - full text ed.: ISSN 1495-5644.
Published by: Science Assessment & Integration Branch, Meteorological Service of Canada, 4905 Dufferin St, Downsview, ON M3H 5T4, Canada. Ed. Pam Kertland.

555.16 USA ISSN 0195-8259
QC983
COMPARATIVE CLIMATIC DATA FOR THE UNITED STATES. Abbreviated title: C C D. Text in English. 1976. a. back issues avail.; reprints avail. **Document type:** *Government.* **Description:** Details the climatic conditions at major weather observing stations in all 50 states, Puerto Rico and Pacific Islands.
Formerly (until 1978): Comparative Climatic Data (0195-8666)
Related titles: Online - full text ed.: free (effective 2009).
—Linda Hall.
Published by: U.S. National Climatic Data Center (Subsidiary of: U.S. Department of Commerce), Federal Bldg, 151 Patton Ave, Asheville, NC 28801. TEL 828-271-4800, FAX 828-271-4876, ncdc.info@noaa.gov, http://www.ncdc.noaa.gov.

551.5 CHE ISSN 0250-9288
COMPOSITION OF THE W M O. Text in English. q. USD 125 (effective 2001). **Document type:** *Directory.* **Description:** Lists members of the WMO and the composition of W.M.O. constituent bodies, panels, committees and working groups.
Published by: World Meteorological Organization, 7 bis Avenue de la Paix, Case postale 2300, Geneva 2, 1211, Switzerland. TEL 41-22-7308111. **Dist. in U.S. by:** American Meteorological Society, 45 Beacon St, Boston, MA 02108. TEL 617-227-2425.

551.5 363.7 DEU ISSN 1994-0416
GB641
THE CRYOSPHERE. Text in English. 2007. 4/yr. EUR 176; EUR 48 newsstand/cover (effective 2009). **Document type:** *Journal, Academic/Scholarly.* **Description:** Dedicated to the publication and discussion of research articles, short communications and review papers on all aspects of frozen water and ground on Earth and on other planetary bodies.
Related titles: Online - full text ed.: ISSN 1994-0424. free (effective 2011).
Indexed: A01, CABA, CurCont, E12, ESPM, GEOBASE, I11, OceAb, P52, P56, S13, S16, SCI, SCOPUS, SWRA, T02, W07.
Published by: Copernicus GmbH, Bahnhofsallee 1e, Goettingen, 37081, Germany. TEL 49-551-9003390, FAX 49-551-90033970, info@copernicus.org, http://www.copernicus.org. Ed. Jonathan L Bamber.

551.5 363.7 DEU ISSN 1994-0432
➤ **THE CRYOSPHERE DISCUSSIONS.** Text in English. 2007. irreg. **Document type:** *Journal, Academic/Scholarly.*
Related titles: Online - full text ed.: ISSN 1994-0440. free (effective 2011).
Indexed: E04, E05, GEOBASE, SCOPUS, T02.
Published by: Copernicus GmbH, Bahnhofsallee 1e, Goettingen, 37081, Germany. TEL 49-551-9003390, FAX 49-551-90033970, info@copernicus.org, http://www.copernicus.org.

551.5 630 CUB ISSN 0138-6190
CUBA. MINISTERIO DE LA AGRICULTURA. CENTRO DE INFORMACION Y DOCUMENTACION AGROPECUARIO. NOTICIERO AGROPECUARIO. SUPLEMENTO AGROMETEOROLOGICO. Text in Spanish. irreg. **Document type:** *Government.*
Published by: Centro de Informacion y Documentacion Agropecuario, Gaveta Postal 4149, Havana, 4, Cuba.

CZECH AEROSPACE PROCEEDINGS. *see* AERONAUTICS AND SPACE FLIGHT

551.5 551.46 CHE
D B C P TECHNICAL DOCUMENT SERIES. Text in English. irreg.

Published by: (Data Buoy Cooperation Panel FRA), World Meteorological Organization, 7 bis Avenue de la Paix, Case postale 2300, Geneva 2, 1211, Switzerland. TEL 41-22-7308111, FAX 41-22-7308022, http://www.wmo.int.

DAIKIKYU SHINPOJUMU. *see* ASTRONOMY

551.5 USA
QC983

DAILY WEATHER MAPS (WEEKLY SERIES); weekly series. Text in English. 18??. w. USD 75 (print or CD-ROM ed.) (effective 2009). illus. back issues avail.; reprints avail. **Document type:** *Government.* **Description:** Provides relevant meteorological information.
Former titles (until 1996): Daily Weather Maps; (until 1984): United States. National Environmental Satellite, Data, and Information Service. Daily Weather Maps; (until 1983): United States. Environmental Data and Information Service. Daily Weather Maps; (until 1978): United States. Environmental Data Service. Daily Weather Maps (0898-6592); (until 1968): United States. Weather Bureau. Daily Weather Maps
Related titles: CD-ROM ed.; Online - full text ed.: free (effective 2009).
Published by: (National Oceanic and Atmospheric Administration, National Weather Service, Climate Prediction Center), U.S. National Climatic Data Center (Subsidiary of: U.S. Department of Commerce), Federal Bldg, 151 Patton Ave, Asheville, NC 28801. TEL 828-271-4800, FAX 828-271-4876, ncdc.info@noaa.gov, http://www.ncdc.noaa.gov.

551.5 CHN ISSN 1006-9895
DAIQI KEXUE/CHINESE JOURNAL OF ATMOSPHERIC SCIENCE. Text in Chinese, English. 1976. bi-m. USD 133.20 (effective 2009). back issues avail. **Document type:** *Journal, Academic/Scholarly.*
Related titles: Online - full text ed.
Indexed: A22.
—BLDSC (3180.295250), East View, IE, Ingenta, Linda Hall.
Published by: (Zhongguo Kexueyuan Daiqi Wuli Yanjiusuo/Chinese Academy of Sciences, Institute of Atmospheric Physics), Kexue Chubanshe/Science Press, 16 Donghuang Cheng Genbei Jie, Beijing, 100717, China. TEL 86-10-64000246, FAX 86-10-64030255. **Dist. by:** China International Book Trading Corp, 35 Chegongzhuang Xilu, Haidian District, PO Box 399, Beijing 100044, China. TEL 86-10-68412045, FAX 86-10-68412023, cibtc@mail.cibtc.com.cn, http://www.cibtc.com.cn.

551.5 CHN ISSN 1674-7097
CODEN: DKXAAG
DAQI KEXUE XUEBAO/TRANSACTIONS OF ATMOSPHERIC SCIENCES. Text in Chinese. 1978. bi-m. **Document type:** *Journal, Academic/Scholarly.*
Formerly (until 2009): Nanjing Qixiang Xueyuan Xuebao/Nanjing Institute of Meteorology. Journal (1000-2022)
Related titles: Online - full text ed.: (from WanFang Data Corp.).
Indexed: A37, C25, C30, CABA, E12, F08, F12, FCA, G11, GH, H16, I11, M&GPA, P32, P40, PGegResA, R11, S13, S16, TAR, TriticAb.
—BLDSC (4828.677900).
Published by: Nanjing Xinxi Gongcheng Daxue/Nanjing University of Information Science & Technology, 219, Ningliu Rd., Nanjing, Jiangsu Province 210044, China. TEL 86-25-58731158, FAX 86-25-58731520, qks@nuist.edu.cn, http://www.nuist.edu.cn.

551.5 IDN ISSN 0303-1969
DATA-DATA IKLIM DI INDONESIA. Text in English, Indonesian. 1971. a.
Published by: Meteorological and Geophysical Institute/Badan Meteorologi dan Geofisika, Jalan Arief Rakhman Hakim 3, Jakarta, Indonesia.

551.5 GRC ISSN 1012-2389
DELTION ELLENIKES METEOROLOGIKES ETAIREIAS/HELLENIC METEOROLOGICAL SOCIETY. BULLETIN. Text in English, Greek. irreg.
Published by: Ellenike Meteorologike Etaireia/Hellenic Meteorological Society, National Observatory of Athens, Institute of Environmental Research & Sustainable Developmen, PO Box 20048, Athens, 11810, Greece. TEL 30-1-3490122, FAX 30-1-3490113, retalis@env.meteo.noa.gr, nastos@geol.uoa.gr, http://www.meteo.noa.gr.

551.5 DNK ISSN 0905-3263
DENMARK. DANISH METEOROLOGICAL INSTITUTE. SCIENTIFIC REPORT. Variant title: Denmark. Danmarks Meteorologiske Institut. Videnskabelige Rapporter. Text mainly in English; Text occasionally in Danish. 1989. irreg. free (effective 2005). back issues avail. **Document type:** *Monographic series, Academic/Scholarly.*
Related titles: Online - full content ed.: ISSN 1399-1949.
Published by: Danmarks Meteorologiske Institut/Danish Meteorological Institute, Lyngbyvej 100, Copenhagen OE, 2100, Denmark. TEL 45-39-157500, FAX 45-39-271080, epost@dmi.dk.

551.5 DNK ISSN 0906-897X
DENMARK. DANISH METEOROLOGICAL INSTITUTE. TECHNICAL REPORT. Variant title: Denmark. Danmarks Meteorologiske Institut. Tekniske Rapporter. Text mainly in English; Text occasionally in Danish. 1989. irreg. free (effective 2005). back issues avail. **Document type:** *Monographic series, Academic/Scholarly.*
Related titles: Online - full content ed.: ISSN 1399-1388.
—BLDSC (8715.182580).
Published by: Danmarks Meteorologiske Institut/Danish Meteorological Institute, Lyngbyvej 100, Copenhagen OE, 2100, Denmark. TEL 45-39-157500, FAX 45-39-271080, epost@dmi.dk.

551.5 DNK ISSN 1398-490X
DENMARK. DANMARKS METEOROLOGISKE INSTITUT. DANMARKS KLIMACENTER. RAPPORT. Variant title: Danish Meteorological Institute. Danish Climate Centre. Report. Text mainly in English; Text occasionally in Danish. 1998. irreg. back issues avail. **Document type:** *Monographic series, Academic/Scholarly.*
Related titles: Online - full content ed.: ISSN 1399-1957.
Published by: Danmarks Meteorologiske Institut, Danmarks Klimacenter/Danish Meteorological Institute, Danish Climate Centre, Lyngbyvej 200, Copenhagen OE, 2100, Denmark. TEL 45-39-157500, FAX 45-39-271080, epost@dmi.dk. Ed. May-Britt Raarup Bundsgaard.

551.6 537 JPN ISSN 0286-0937
DENRYOKU TO KISHO/POWER AND WEATHER COORDINATING COMMITTEE. ANNUAL REPORT. Text in Japanese. 1953. biennial.
Published by: Denryoku Kisho Renrakukai/Power and Weather Coordination Committee (Subsidiary of: Japan Weather Association/Nihon Kisho Kyokai), Sunshine 60 Bldg. 55 F, 3-1-1 Higashi-Ikebukuro, Toshima-ku, Tokyo, 170-6055, Japan. TEL 81-3-3295-1521, FAX 81-3-3295-7835.

551.5 DEU ISSN 0177-8501
DEUTSCHE METEOROLOGISCHE GESELLSCHAFT. MITTEILUNGEN. Text in German. 1975. q. free to members (effective 2009). **Document type:** *Journal, Trade.*
Indexed: M&GPA.
Published by: Deutsche Meteorologische Gesellschaft, Carl-Heinrich-Becker-Weg 6-10, Berlin, 12165, Germany. TEL 49-30-79708324, FAX 49-30-7919002, sekretariat@dmg-ev.de. Ed. Joerg Rapp. Circ: 1,900 (controlled).

551.5 DEU ISSN 0072-4130
QC857.G3
DEUTSCHER WETTERDIENST. BERICHTE. Text in German. 1953. irreg., latest vol.232, 2008. price varies. **Document type:** *Monographic series, Trade.*
Indexed: GeoRef, M&GPA, SCOPUS, SpeleolAb.
—INIST, Linda Hall.
Published by: Deutscher Wetterdienst, Bibliothek, Kaiserleistr 29-35, Offenbach Am Main, 63067, Germany. TEL 49-69-80620, FAX 49-69-80624484, info@dwd.de, http://www.dwd.de.

551.5 DEU
DEUTSCHER WETTERDIENST. GESCHAEFTSFELD FORSCHUNG UND ENTWICKLUNG. EINZELVEROEFFENTLICHUNGEN. Text in English, German. 1953. irreg., latest vol.119, 2009. price varies. bk.rev. **Document type:** *Monographic series, Academic/Scholarly.* **Description:** Different meteorological topics, mainly on the marine climatological sector.
Former titles: Deutscher Wetterdienst. Geschaeftsfeld Seeschiffahrt. Einzelveroeffentlichungen; Deutscher Wetterdienst. Seewetteramt. Einzelveroeffentlichungen (0072-1603)
Published by: Deutscher Wetterdienst, Geschaeftsfeld Forschung und Entwicklung, Bernhard-Nocht-Str 76, Hamburg, 20359, Germany. TEL 49-40-66901444, FAX 49-40-66901499, ella.kranich-wiers@dwd.de, http://www.dwd.de. Circ: 250.

551.5 DEU ISSN 0433-8251
QC989
DEUTSCHER WETTERDIENST. JAHRESBERICHT. Text in German. 1953. a. **Document type:** *Yearbook, Trade.*
—Linda Hall.
Published by: Deutscher Wetterdienst, Bibliothek, Kaiserleistr 29-35, Offenbach Am Main, 63067, Germany. TEL 49-69-80620, FAX 49-69-80624484, info@dwd.de, http://www.dwd.de. Circ: 1,000 (controlled).

551.6 DEU ISSN 0459-0236
DEUTSCHER WETTERDIENST. LEITFAEDEN FUER DIE AUSBILDUNG. Text in German. 196?. irreg., latest vol.8, 1998. price varies. **Document type:** *Monographic series, Trade.*
Published by: Deutscher Wetterdienst, Bibliothek, Kaiserleistr 29-35, Offenbach Am Main, 63067, Germany. TEL 49-69-80620, FAX 49-69-80624484, info@dwd.de, http://www.dwd.de.

551.63 DEU
QC989.G3
DEUTSCHES METEOROLOGISCHES JAHRBUCH. Text in German. 1953. a. EUR 154 (effective 2009). **Document type:** *Yearbook, Trade.*
Former titles (until 1995): Deutsches Meteorologisches Jahrbuch. Bundesrepublik Deutschland (0724-7125); (until 1980): Deutsches Meteorologisches Jahrbuch. Bundesrepublik (0417-3562); Which was formed by the merger of (1949-1953): Deutsches Meteorologisches Jahrbuch. Britische Zone. Teil 1-3: Taegliche Beobachtungen, Monats- und Jahresergebnisse, Niederschlagsbeobachtungen (0170-2475); (1949-1953): Deutsches Meteorologisches Jahrbuch. US-Zone (0170-2491); (1949-1953): Deutsches Meteorologisches Jahrbuch. Gebiet der Ehemalige Franzoesischen Besatzungszone (0417-3570); (1949-1953): Deutsches Meteorologisches Jahrbuch. Saarland (0417-3589)
—Linda Hall.
Published by: Deutscher Wetterdienst, Bibliothek, Kaiserleistr 29-35, Offenbach Am Main, 63067, Germany. TEL 49-69-80620, FAX 49-69-80624484, info@dwd.de, http://www.dwd.de.

551.5 NLD ISSN 0167-5117
QC851 CODEN: DASCDW
➤ **DEVELOPMENTS IN ATMOSPHERIC SCIENCE.** Text in English. 1974. irreg., latest vol.24, 1999. price varies. back issues avail. **Document type:** *Monographic series, Academic/Scholarly.* **Description:** Reports on current research in all areas of atmospheric science.
Related titles: Online - full text ed.
Indexed: A22, GeoRef, Inspec, M&GPA, SCOPUS, SpeleolAb.
—BLDSC (3579.065000), CASDDS, INIST. **CCC.**
Published by: Elsevier BV (Subsidiary of: Elsevier Science & Technology), Radarweg 29, PO Box 211, Amsterdam, 1000 AE, Netherlands. TEL 31-20-4853911, FAX 31-20-4852457, JournalsCustomerServiceEMEA@elsevier.com, http://www.elsevier.nl.

551.6 DEU ISSN 0043-7085
DIE WITTERUNG IN UEBERSEE. Text in German, English. 1953. m. EUR 41; EUR 6 per issue (effective 2009). charts. back issues avail. **Document type:** *Bulletin, Government.* **Description:** Monthly and annual global climate review of tropical storms, temperature, precipitation and sea level pressure (actual values and departures from normal).
Related titles: Online - full text ed.
Published by: Deutscher Wetterdienst, Abteilung Klimaueberwachung, Postfach 301190, Hamburg, 20203, Germany. http://www.dwd.de. Circ: 230 (paid and controlled).

551.5 551.46 NLD ISSN 0377-0265
GC190.2 CODEN: DAOCDC
➤ **DYNAMICS OF ATMOSPHERES AND OCEANS.** Text mainly in English; Text occasionally in French, German. 1977. 6/yr. EUR 1,362 in Europe to institutions; JPY 181,000 in Japan to institutions; USD 1,526 elsewhere to institutions (effective 2012). adv. bk.rev. abstr.; illus. Index. back issues avail.; reprints avail. **Document type:** *Journal, Academic/Scholarly.* **Description:** Publishes theoretical, numerical, observational and laboratory studies on the fluid dynamics of atmospheres and oceans and their interactions, on related basic dynamical processes, and on climatic and biogeochemical problems in which fluid dynamics play an essential role.
Related titles: Microform ed.: (from PQC); Online - full text ed.: ISSN 1872-6879 (from IngentaConnect, ScienceDirect).
Indexed: A01, A03, A08, A22, A26, A28, APA, ASCA, ASFA, ApMecR, BrCerAb, C&ISA, CA, CA/WCA, CIA, CPEI, CerAb, CivEngAb, CorrAb, CurCont, E&CAJ, E04, E05, E11, EEA, EMA, ESPM, EngInd, EnvAb, EnvEAb, FR, GEOBASE, GeoRef, H15, I05, ISR, Inspec, M&GPA, M&TEA, M09, MBF, METADEX, MSCT, OceAb, PhysBer, RefZh, SCI, SCOPUS, SWRA, SolStAb, T02, T04, W07, WAA.
—BLDSC (3637.143300), AskIEEE, IE, Infotrieve, Ingenta, INIST, Linda Hall. **CCC.**
Published by: Elsevier BV (Subsidiary of: Elsevier Science & Technology), Radarweg 29, PO Box 211, Amsterdam, 1000 AE, Netherlands. TEL 31-20-4853911, FAX 31-20-4852457, JournalsCustomerServiceEMEA@elsevier.com, http://www.elsevier.nl. Ed. A Moore.

551.5 USA
THE E O L OBSERVER; deployment, development, data services. (Earth Observing Laboratory) Text in English. 1990. irreg. free (effective 2009). **Document type:** *Newsletter, Academic/Scholarly.* **Description:** Covers field deployments, instrumentation news, and other items of interest to the atmospheric sciences community.
Formerly (until 2005): A T D Observer (1948-0377)
Media: Online - full text.
Published by: National Center for Atmospheric Research, Earth Observing Laboratory, 1850 Table Mesa Dr, Boulder, CO 80305. TEL 303-497-8801, 303-497-8166, FAX 303-497-8770, wakimoto@ucar.edu, http://www.ncar.ucar.edu.

551.5 ECU
ECUADOR. INSTITUTO NACIONAL DE METEOROLOGIA E HIDROLOGIA. ANUARIO METEOROLOGICO. Text in Spanish. 1959. a. USD 20.40. index. **Document type:** *Government.*
Supersedes: Ecuador. Servicio Nacional de Meteorologia e Hidrologia. Anuario Meteorologico (0070-8941)
Published by: Instituto Nacional de Meteorologia e Hidrologia, Inaquito 700 y Corea, Quito, Ecuador. TEL 593-2-433934.

551.6 ECU
ECUADOR. INSTITUTO NACIONAL DE METEOROLOGIA E HIDROLOGIA. BOLETIN CLIMATOLOGICO. Text in Spanish. 1962. m. **Document type:** *Bulletin, Government.*
Supersedes: Ecuador. Servicio Nacional de Meteorologia e Hidrologia. Boletin Climatologico
Published by: Instituto Nacional de Meteorologia e Hidrologia, Inaquito 700 y Corea, Quito, Ecuador. TEL 593-2-433934.

551.6 SWE ISSN 2000-3919
▼ **EFFEKT**; klimatmagasinet. Text in Swedish. 2009. 5/yr. SEK 340 to individuals; SEK 600 to institutions; SEK 69 per issue (effective 2010). adv. **Document type:** *Magazine, Consumer.*
Published by: Klimatmagasinet Effekt Ekonomisk Foerening, PO Box 17506, Stockholm, 11891, Sweden. Ed. Jesper Weithz TEL 46-709-183499. Adv. contact Daniel Sestrajacic TEL 46-8-55921230. page SEK 10,000; 215 x 280.

551.5 EGY ISSN 1687-1014
EGYPT. METEOROLOGICAL AUTHORITY. METEOROLOGICAL RESEARCH BULLETIN. Text in English; Summaries in Arabic. 1969. s-a. charts.
Published by: Meteorological Authority, Kubri-el-Qubbeh, Cairo, Egypt.

551 JPN ISSN 0916-5061
EHIMEKEN KISHO GEPPO/EHIME PREFECTURE. MONTHLY REPORT OF METEOROLOGY. Text in Japanese. 1903. m.
Published by: Kishocho, Matsuyama Chiho Kishodai/Japan Meteorological Agency, Matsuyama Local Meteorological Observatory, 102 Kita-Mochida-Machi, Matsuyama-shi, Ehime-ken 790-0873, Japan.

551.5 USA
ELECTRONIC JOURNAL OF OPERATIONAL METEOROLOGY. Text in English. 2001. irreg. **Document type:** *Magazine, Trade.*
Media: Online - full text.
Indexed: M&GPA.
Published by: National Weather Association, 228 W Millbrook Rd, Raleigh, NC 27609. TEL 919-845-1546.

551.5 USA ISSN 1559-5404
➤ **ELECTRONIC JOURNAL OF SEVERE STORMS METEREOLOGY.** Abbreviated title: E J S S M. Text in English. 2006. irreg., latest vol.5, no.6, 2010. free (effective 2011). back issues avail. **Document type:** *Journal, Academic/Scholarly.* **Description:** Serves the community of meteorology that is concerned with severe storms, including both convective and nonconvective severe weather.
Media: Online - full text.
Indexed: A01, A39, C27, C29, CA, D03, D04, E13, R14, S14, S15, S18, T02.
Published by: Electronic Journal of Severe Storms Metereology (E J S S M), PO Box 5043, Norman, OK 73070. Ed. Roger Edwards.

➤ **ENERGY & ENVIRONMENT.** *see* ENERGY

551.65 DEU ISSN 1614-0761
EUROPAEISCHER WETTERBERICHT (ONLINE). Text in German. 1876. d. EUR 361.11 (effective 2009). charts; stat. **Document type:** *Trade.*
Former titles (until 2002): Europaeischer Wetterbericht (Print) (0341-2970); (until 1975): Taeglicher Wetterbericht (0039-8926)
Media: Online - full content. **Related titles:** CD-ROM ed.: ISSN 1614-0753. 2002. EUR 61.23 per issue (effective 2005).
Published by: Deutscher Wetterdienst, Bibliothek, Kaiserleistr 29-35, Offenbach Am Main, 63067, Germany. TEL 49-69-80620, FAX 49-69-80624484, info@dwd.de, http://www.dwd.de.

551.5 USA ISSN 1948-0334
EXPLORE THE ATMOSPHERIC SCIENCES. Text in English. 1997. 3/yr. back issues avail. **Document type:** *Newsletter, Consumer.*

Related titles: Online - full text ed.: ISSN 1948-1888.
Published by: National Center for Atmospheric Research, PO Box 3000, Boulder, CO 80307. TEL 303-497-1000, http://www.ncar.ucar.edu.

551.5 USA ISSN 0565-9248
QC869.4.U5
FEDERAL PLAN FOR METEOROLOGICAL SERVICES AND SUPPORTING RESEARCH (YEAR). Text in English. 196?. a.
Related titles: Online - full text ed.: ISSN 1559-6710.
—Linda Hall.
Published by: Federal Coordinator for Meteorological Services and Supporting Research, 8455 Colesville Rd, Ste 1500, Silver Spring, MD 20910. TEL 301-427-2002, ofcm.mail@noaa.gov.

551.5 FIN ISSN 0782-6079
FINNISH METEOROLOGICAL INSTITUTE. REPORTS. Text in English, Finnish. 1986. irreg., latest 2004. price varies. back issues avail. **Document type:** *Monographic series, Government.*
Published by: Ilmatieteen Laitos/Finnish Meteorological Institute, Vuorikatu 24, PO Box 503, Helsinki, 00101, Finland. TEL 358-9-19291, FAX 358-9-179581.

550 RUS
FIZIKA NIZHNEI ATMOSFERY. Text in Russian. 1972. irreg. illus.
Related titles: ◆ Series of: Institut Eksperimental'noi Meteorologii. Trudy. ISSN 0131-4823.
Published by: (Institut Eksperimental'noi Meteorologii), Gidrometeoizdat, Ul Beringa 38, St Petersburg, 199397, Russian Federation.

551 DEU ISSN 0173-1769
FRANKFURTER GEOWISSENSCHAFTEN ARBEITEN. SERIE B. METEOROLOGIE UND GEOPHYSIK. Text in German. 1987. irreg.
Indexed: GeoRef.
Published by: Johann Wolfgang Goethe Universitaet Frankfurt am Main, Fachbereich Geowissenschaften, Bockenheimer Landstr. 133, 6, OG, Frankfurt am Main, 60054, Germany. TEL 49-69-798-28128, FAX 49-69-798-28416, dekanat-geowiss@em.uni-frankfurt.de.

551.6 USA
THE FRONT LINE. Text in English. 1995. bi-m.
Media: Online - full content.
Published by: Front Line, Kennedy High School, Waterbury, CT 06786.

551 JPN ISSN 0912-5639
FUKUI DAIGAKU SEKISETSU KENKYUSHITSU KENKYU HOKOKU/ FUKUI UNIVERSITY. LABORATORY OF SNOW AND ICE. RESEARCH REPORT. Text in Japanese; Summaries in English. 1970. a.
Published by: Fukui Daigaku, Sekisetsu Kenkyushitsu/Fukui University, Laboratory of Snow and Ice, 9-1 Bunkyo 3-chome, Fukui-shi, 910-0017, Japan.

551 JPN
FUKUIKEN KISHO GEPPO/FUKUI PREFECTURE. MONTHLY REPORT OF METEOROLOGY. Text in Japanese. 1968. m.
Published by: Kishocho, Fukui Chiho Kishodai/Japan Meteorological Agency, Fukui Local Meteorological Observatory, 5-2 Toyoshima 2-chome, Fukui-shi, 910-0857, Japan.

551.5 JPN ISSN 0016-2558
FUKUOKA DISTRICT METEOROLOGICAL OBSERVATORY. UNUSUAL METEOROLOGICAL REPORT/FUKUOKA KANKU KISHODAI IJO KISHO HOKOKU. Text in Japanese. 1961. q. free.
Published by: Fukuoka District Meteorological Observatory/Fukuoka Kanku Kishodai, 1-2-36 Ohori, Chuo-ku, Fukuoka-shi, 810-0052, Japan. Circ: 200.

551 JPN
FUKUOKA KANKU KISHO KENKYUKAISHI/FUKUOKA DISTRICT MEETING FOR THE STUDY OF METEOROLOGY. PROCEEDINGS. Text in Japanese. 1947. a. **Document type:** *Proceedings.*
Published by: Kishocho, Fukuoka Kanku Kishodai/Japan Meteorological Agency, Fukuoka District Meteorological Observatory, 1-2-36 Ohori, Chuo-ku, Fukuoka-shi, 810-0052, Japan.

551.5 JPN ISSN 0016-2566
FUKUOKA KANKU KISHODAI GIJUTSU TSUSHIN/FUKUOKA DISTRICT METEOROLOGICAL OBSERVATORY. TECHNICAL TIMES. Text in Japanese. 1955. m. free. bk.rev.
Published by: Kishocho, Fukuoka Kanku Kishodai/Japan Meteorological Agency, Fukuoka District Meteorological Observatory, 1-2-36 Ohori, Chuo-ku, Fukuoka-shi, 810-0052, Japan. Circ: 170.

551.6 JPN
FUKUOKA KANKU KISHODAI YOHO/FUKUOKA METEOROLOGICAL OBSERVATORY. MEMOIRS. Text in Japanese. 1941. a.
Published by: Kishocho, Fukuoka Kanku Kishodai/Japan Meteorological Agency, Fukuoka District Meteorological Observatory, 1-2-36 Ohori, Chuo-ku, Fukuoka-shi, 810-0052, Japan.

551.65 JPN ISSN 0016-2574
FUKUOKAKEN KISHO GEPPO/FUKUOKA PREFECTURE. MONTHLY REPORT OF METEOROLOGY. Text in Japanese. 1890. m. JPY 1,600.
Published by: Kishocho, Fukuoka Kanku Kishodai/Japan Meteorological Agency, Fukuoka District Meteorological Observatory, 1-2-36 Ohori, Chuo-ku, Fukuoka-shi, 810-0052, Japan. Circ: 140.

551 JPN ISSN 0916-5371
FUKUSHIMAKEN KISHO GEPPO/FUKUSHIMA PREFECTURE. MONTHLY REPORT OF METEOROLOGY. Text in Japanese. 1951. m.
Published by: Kishocho, Fukushima Chiho Kishodai/Japan Meteorological Agency, Fukushima Local Meteorological Observatory, 1-9 Matsuki-cho, Fukushima-shi, 960-8018, Japan.

551.6 JPN ISSN 0429-9000
QC993.83
FUNE TO KAIJO KISHO/SHIP AND MARITIME METEOROLOGY. Text in Japanese. 1957. q.
Indexed: JPI.
Published by: Kishocho/Japan Meteorological Agency, 1-3-4 Otemachi, Chiyoda-ku, Tokyo, 100-8122, Japan.

G E W E X NEWS. (Global Energy and Water Cycle Experiment) *see* EARTH SCIENCES—Hydrology

551.6 USA
G H C C FORECAST. (Global Hydrology and Climate Center) Text in English. 1994. m. **Document type:** *Bulletin, Government.*
Related titles: Online - full text ed.
Published by: Global Hydrology and Climate Center, Earth Science Department, 320 Sparkman Dr NW, Huntsville, AL 35805-1912. TEL 256-922-5721, FAX 256-922-5772. Eds. Don Perkey, Tim Miller.

GANHANQU YANJIU/ARID ZONE RESEARCH. *see* EARTH SCIENCES—Geology

551.5 CHN ISSN 1000-0534
GAOYUAN QIXIANG/HIGHLAND METEOROLOGY. Text in English. 1982. q. USD 106.80 (effective 2009). **Document type:** *Journal, Academic/Scholarly.*
Related titles: Online - full text ed.
Indexed: ASFA, M&GPA, OceAb.
—BLDSC (6537.842000), East View.
Published by: (Zhongguo Kexueyuan Lanzhou Gaoyuan Daqi Wuli Yanjiusuo), Kexue Chubanshe/Science Press, 16 Donghuang Cheng Genbei Jie, Beijing, 100717, China. TEL 86-10-64000246, FAX 86-10-64030255, http://www.sciencep.com/. Ed. Zheng-an Qian. **Dist. by:** China International Book Trading Corp, 35 Chegongzhuang Xilu, Haidian District, PO Box 399, Beijing 100044, China. TEL 86-10-68412045, FAX 86-10-68412023, cibtc@mail.cibtc.com.cn, http://www.cibtc.com.cn.

551.6 DEU ISSN 0943-9862
GESCHICHTE DER METEOROLOGIE IN DEUTSCHLAND. Text in German. 1993. irreg., latest vol.8, 2007. **Document type:** *Monographic series, Trade.*
Indexed: M&GPA.
Published by: Deutscher Wetterdienst, Bibliothek, Kaiserleistr 29-35, Offenbach Am Main, 63067, Germany. TEL 49-69-80620, FAX 49-69-80624484, info@dwd.de, http://www.dwd.de.

551.5 630 GHA
GHANA. METEOROLOGICAL DEPARTMENT. AGROMETEOROLOGICAL BULLETIN. Text in English. 1965. m. stat. **Document type:** *Bulletin, Government.*
Published by: Meteorological Department, PO Box 87, Accra, Ghana.

551.5 GHA
GHANA. METEOROLOGICAL DEPARTMENT. CLIMATOLOGICAL NOTES. Text in English. irreg., latest vol.5. price varies. **Document type:** *Government.*
Published by: Meteorological Department, PO Box 87, Accra, Ghana.

551.5 GHA
GHANA. METEOROLOGICAL DEPARTMENT. MONTHLY SUMMARY OF EVAPORATION. Text in English. 1961. m. GHC 500. **Document type:** *Government.*
Published by: Meteorological Department, PO Box 87, Accra, Ghana.

551.5 GHA ISSN 0431-8315
GHANA. METEOROLOGICAL DEPARTMENT. MONTHLY SUMMARY OF RAINFALL. Text in English. 1952. m. GHC 500. **Document type:** *Government.*
Published by: Meteorological Department, PO Box 87, Accra, Ghana.

551.5 GHA ISSN 0431-8323
GHANA. METEOROLOGICAL DEPARTMENT. MONTHLY WEATHER REPORT. Text in English. 1949. m. GHC 500. **Document type:** *Government.*
Published by: Meteorological Department, PO Box 87, Accra, Ghana.

551.5 GHA
GHANA. METEOROLOGICAL DEPARTMENT. PROFESSIONAL NOTES. Text in English. irreg., latest vol.23. price varies. **Document type:** *Government.*
Published by: Meteorological Department, PO Box 87, Accra, Ghana.

551.5 GHA
GHANA. METEOROLOGICAL DEPARTMENT. SUN AND MOON TABLES FOR GHANA. Short title: Sun and Moon Tables for Ghana. Text in English. 1954. a. GHC 500. **Document type:** *Government.*
Published by: Meteorological Department, PO Box 87, Accra, Ghana.

551 JPN ISSN 0916-507X
GIFUKEN KISHO GEPPO/GIFU PREFECTURE. MONTHLY REPORT OF METEOROLOGY. Text in Japanese. 1952. m.
Published by: Kishocho, Gifu Chiho Kishodai/Japan Meteorological Agency, Gifu Local Meteorological Observatory, 6 Kano-Ninomaru, Gifu-shi, 500-8484, Japan.

551.5 USA ISSN 1936-9484
QC981.8.C5
GLOBAL CLIMATE CHANGE (LEXINGTON). Text in English. 200?. q. **Document type:** *Report, Trade.*
Published by: I H S Global Insight (USA) Inc., 24 Hartwell Ave, Lexington, MA 02421. TEL 781-301-9100, FAX 781-301-9416, info@ihsglobalinsight.com, http://www.ihsglobalinsight.com/.

551.5 ITA ISSN 2038-9647
▼ ➤ **GLOBAL METEOROLOGY.** Text in English. 2010. irreg. **Document type:** *Journal, Academic/Scholarly.*
Media: Online - full text.
Published by: Pagepress, Via Giuseppe Belli 4, Pavia, 27100, Italy. TEL 39-0382-1751762, FAX 39-0382-1750481.

➤ **GLOBAL VOLCANISM NETWORK. BULLETIN.** *see* EARTH SCIENCES—Geology

551.5 CHN ISSN 1007-6190
GUANGDONG QIXIANG/GUANGDONG METEOROLOGY. Text in English. 1973. q. CNY 5 newsstand/cover (effective 2005). **Document type:** *Journal, Academic/Scholarly.*
Related titles: Online - full text ed.
Published by: Guangdong-Sheng Sheyingjia Xiehui/Guangdong Meteorological Society, 6, Fujin Lu, Dongshan, 510080, China. TEL 86-20-87672469, FAX 86-20-87623693, http://www.grmc.gov.cn/qxxh/.

551 JPN ISSN 0916-5088
GUNMAKEN KISHO GEPPO/GUNMA PREFECTURE. MONTHLY REPORT OF METEOROLOGY. Text in Japanese. 1900. m.
Published by: Kishocho, Maebashi Chiho Kishodai/Japan Meteorological Agency, Maebashi Local Meteorological Observatory, 20-12 Showa-Machi 3-chome, Maebashi-shi, Gunma-ken 371-0034, Japan.

551.63 630 JPN
GUNMAKEN NOGYO KISHO SAIGAI SOKUHO/GUNMA PREFECTURE. NEWS OF AGRICULTURAL METEOROLOGY DISASTER. Text in Japanese. 1987. irreg. **Document type:** *Government.*
Published by: Gunmaken Prefectural Government, 1-1 Ote-Machi 1-chome, Maebashi-shi, Gunma-ken 371-0026, Japan.

551.6 GUY
GUYANA. HYDROMETEOROLOGICAL SERVICE. ANNUAL CLIMATOLOGICAL DATA SUMMARY. Text in English. 1973. a. GYD 1,000. illus. **Document type:** *Government.*
Indexed: SpeleolAb.
Published by: Ministry of Agriculture, Hydrometeorological Service, Brickdam 18, Stabroek, Georgetown, Guyana. TEL 592-2-72463. Ed. Simon Kemp. Circ: 200.

M

551.63 JPN ISSN 0440-1077
QC994.6
HAKODATE KAIYO KISHODAI. KAIJO KISHO HOKOKU/HAKODATE MARINE OBSERVATORY. MARINE METEOROLOGICAL REPORT. Text in Japanese. 1957. a.
Published by: Kishocho, Hakodate Kaiyo Kishodai/Japan Meteorological Agency, Hakodate Marine Observatory, 3-4-4 Mihara, Hakodate-shi, Hokkaido 041-0806, Japan.

551 JPN ISSN 0438-4172
HAKODATE KAIYO KISHODAI. YOHO/HAKODATE MARINE OBSERVATORY. BULLETIN. Text in English, Japanese. 1944. irreg.
Published by: Kishocho, Hakodate Kaiyo Kishodai/Japan Meteorological Agency, Hakodate Marine Observatory, 3-4-4 Mihara, Hakodate-shi, Hokkaido 041-0806, Japan.

551.5 BGR ISSN 0018-1331
HIDROLOGIJA I METEOROLOGIJA. Summaries in Multiple languages. 1964. bi-m. price varies. reprint service avail. from IRC. **Document type:** *Academic/Scholarly.*
Formerly: Bulgarska Akademiia na Naukite. Institut po Khidrologiia i Meteorologiia. Izvestiia (0068-3876)
Indexed: BSLGeo, GeoRef, M&GPA, SpeleolAb.
Published by: (Bulgarska Akademiya na Naukite/Bulgarian Academy of Sciences, Institut po Khidrologiia i Meteorologiia), Sofiiski Universitet Sv. Kliment Ohridski, Universitetsko Izdatelstvo/Sofia University St. Kliment Ohridski University Press, Akad G Bonchev 6, Sofia, 1113, Bulgaria. Ed. I Marinov. Circ: 500. **Dist. by:** Hemus, 6 Rouski Blvd., Sofia 1000, Bulgaria.

551.6 JPN ISSN 0916-2038
HIROSAKI DAIGAKU RIGAKUBU KANCHI KISHO JIKKENSHITSU HOKOKU/HIROSAKI UNIVERSITY. FACULTY OF SCIENCE. LABORATORY OF COLD REGIONS METEOROLOGY. ANNUAL REPORT. Text in Japanese. 1989. a.
Published by: (Kanchi Kisho Jikkenshitsu), Hirosaki Daigaku, Rikogakubu/Hirosaki University, Faculty of Science & Technology, 1 bunkyo-cho,, Hirosaki, Aomori 036-8224, Japan.

551.6 JPN ISSN 0285-6840
HIROSAKI DAIGAKU RIGAKUBU SETSUGAI KANSOKUJO HOKOKU/ HIRASAKI UNIVERSITY. SNOW AND ICE OBSERVATORY. SCIENCE REPORTS. Text in English, Japanese. 1981. irreg.
Published by: (Setsugai Kansokujo), Hirosaki Daigaku, Rikogakubu/ Hirosaki University, Faculty of Science & Technology, 1 bunkyo-cho,, Hirosaki, Aomori 036-8224, Japan.

551 JPN ISSN 0385-7158
HIROSHIMAKEN KISHO GEPPO/HIROSHIMA PREFECTURE. MONTHLY REPORT OF METEOROLOGY. Text in Japanese. m.
Published by: Kishocho, Hiroshima Chiho Kishodai/Japan Meteorological Agency, Hiroshima Local Meteorological Observatory, 6-30 Kami-Hatsuchobori, Naka-ku, Hiroshima-shi, 730-0012, Japan.

551.5 USA
HISTORICAL CLIMATOLOGY SERIES 5-1. HEATING DEGREE DAYS. Text in English. 1931. m. USD 16 per issue (effective 2008). stat. **Document type:** *Government.* **Description:** Presents up-to-date information on the heating fuel demand on a state-wide basis.
Media: Online - full content.
Published by: (U.S. Department of Commerce), U.S. National Climatic Data Center (Subsidiary of: U.S. Department of Commerce), Federal Bldg, 151 Patton Ave, Asheville, NC 28801. TEL 828-271-4800, FAX 828-271-4876, NODC.Services@noaa.gov, http://www.ncdc.noaa.gov.

551.5 USA
HISTORICAL CLIMATOLOGY SERIES 5-2: COOLING DEGREE DAYS. Text in English. 1931. m. USD 16 per issue (effective 2008). stat. **Document type:** *Government.* **Description:** Features up-to-date information on the cooling fuel demand on a state-wide basis.
Formerly: Historical Climatology Series 5-2: Cooling Degree Days (Print)
Media: Online - full content.
Published by: (U.S. Department of Commerce), U.S. National Climatic Data Center (Subsidiary of: U.S. Department of Commerce), Federal Bldg, 151 Patton Ave, Asheville, NC 28801. TEL 828-271-4800, FAX 828-271-4876, NODC.Services@noaa.gov, http://www.ncdc.noaa.gov.

551.5 USA ISSN 1555-5763
QC855
HISTORY OF METEOROLOGY. Text in English, Spanish, German. 2004. a. free (effective 2011). back issues avail. **Document type:** *Journal, Academic/Scholarly.*
Formerly (until 2005): International Commission on the History of Meteorology. Proceedings (1551-3580)
Media: Online - full text.
Indexed: A39, C27, C29, CA, D03, D04, E13, HistAb, M&GPA, R14, S14, S15, S18, T02.
Published by: International Commission on the History of Meteorology (I C H M) http://www.meteohistory.org.

551 JPN ISSN 0916-5096
HOKKAIDO KISHO GEPPO/HOKKAIDO MONTHLY REPORT OF METEOROLOGY. Text in Japanese. 1865. m.
Published by: Kishocho, Sapporo Kanku Kishodai/Japan Meteorological Agency, Sapporo District Meteorological Observatory, 2, Nishi 18-chome, Kita 2-jo, Chuo-ku, Sapporo-shi, Hokkaido 060, Japan.

551 630 JPN ISSN 0915-6062
HOKKAIDO NO NOGYO KISHO/HOKKAIDO JOURNAL OF AGRICULTURAL METEOROLOGY. Text in Japanese. 1964. a.
Published by: Nihon Nogyo Kisho Gakkai, Hokkaido Shibu/Society of Agricultural Meteorology of Japan, Hokkaido Branch, Hokkaido Daigaku Nogakubu, Nogyo Butsurigaku Kenkyushitsu, Nishi 9-chome, Kita 9-jo, Sapporo-shi, Hokkaido 060, Japan.

551 JPN
HOKKAIDO NO SEPPYO/SNOW AND ICE IN HOKKAIDO. Text in Japanese. 1982. a. membership.

Published by: Nihon Seppyo Gakkai, Hokkaido Shibu/Japanese Society of Snow and Ice, Hokkaido Branch, Hokkaido Daigaku Teion Kagaku Kenkyujo, Nishi 8-chome, Kita 19-jo, Kita-ku, Sapporo-shi, Hokkaido 060, Japan.

551.655 HKG ISSN 1024-4468
QC851
HONG KONG METEOROLOGICAL SOCIETY. BULLETIN. Text in English. 1991. s-a.
Indexed: M&GPA.
Published by: Hong Kong Meteorological Society, c/o Hong Kong Observatory, 134A Nathan Rd, Kowloon, Hong Kong. TEL 852-2926-6640, FAX 852-2375-2645, olee@graduate.hku.hk, http://www.cityu.edu.hk/HKMetS/intro2.htm. Ed. Bill Kyle.

551.5 HKG
HONG KONG OBSERVATORY ALMANAC. Text in Chinese, English. 1984. a., latest 2001. price varies.
Formerly: Royal Observatory Almanac
Published by: Hong Kong Observatory, 134 A Nathan Rd, Kowloon, Hong Kong. TEL 852-29263113, FAX 852-23119448, hkopmo@hko.gov.hk, http://www.hko.gov.hk/. **Subscr. to:** Government Publications Centre, Low Block, Ground Fl, Queensway Government Offices, 66 Queensway, Hong Kong, Hong Kong. TEL 852-2842-8845.

551.5 HKG
HONG KONG OBSERVATORY. DAILY WEATHER CHART. Text in Chinese, English. 1934. d. price varies. charts; stat.
Formerly: Hong Kong. Royal Observatory. Daily Weather Chart
Published by: Hong Kong Observatory, 134 A Nathan Rd, Kowloon, Hong Kong. TEL 852-29263113, FAX 852-23119448, hkopmo@hko.gov.hk, http://www.hko.gov.hk/.

551.5 HKG
HONG KONG OBSERVATORY. HISTORICAL PUBLICATIONS. Text in English. 1884. irreg. price varies.
Formerly: Hong Kong. Royal Observatory. Historical Publications
Published by: Hong Kong Observatory, 134 A Nathan Rd, Kowloon, Hong Kong. TEL 852-29263113, FAX 852-23119448, hkopmo@hko.gov.hk, http://www.hko.gov.hk/.

551.5 HKG
HONG KONG OBSERVATORY. HONG KONG TIDE TABLES. Text in Chinese, English. 1987. a. price varies.
Published by: Hong Kong Observatory, 134 A Nathan Rd, Kowloon, Hong Kong. TEL 852-29263113, FAX 852-23119448, hkopmo@hko.gov.hk, http://www.hko.gov.hk/.

551.5 HKG
HONG KONG OBSERVATORY. MARINE CLIMATOLOGICAL SUMMARY CHARTS FOR THE SOUTH CHINA SEA. Text in English. 1971. a., latest 1990. price varies.
Formerly: Hong Kong. Royal Observatory. Marine Climatological Summary Charts for the South China Sea
Published by: Hong Kong Observatory, 134 A Nathan Rd, Kowloon, Hong Kong. TEL 852-29263113, FAX 852-23119448, hkopmo@hko.gov.hk, http://www.hko.gov.hk/.

551.5 HKG
HONG KONG OBSERVATORY. MONTHLY WEATHER SUMMARY. Text in Chinese, English. 1976. m.
Formerly: Hong Kong. Royal Observatory. Monthly Weather Summary
Indexed: IIS.
Published by: Hong Kong Observatory, 134 A Nathan Rd, Kowloon, Hong Kong. TEL 852-29263113, FAX 852-23119448, hkopmo@hko.gov.hk, http://www.hko.gov.hk/.

551.5 HKG
HONG KONG OBSERVATORY. NEWSLETTER FOR FRIENDS OF OBSERVATORY. Text in Chinese. bi-m. **Document type:** *Newsletter.*
Related titles: Online - full content ed.
Published by: Hong Kong Observatory, 134 A Nathan Rd, Kowloon, Hong Kong. TEL 852-29263113, FAX 852-23119448, hkopmo@hko.gov.hk.

551.5 HKG
HONG KONG OBSERVATORY. NEWSLETTER FOR HONG KONG VOLUNTARY OBSERVATING SHIPS. Text in Chinese, English. a. free. **Document type:** *Newsletter, Government.*
Related titles: Online - full content ed.
Published by: Hong Kong Observatory, 134 A Nathan Rd, Kowloon, Hong Kong. TEL 852-29263113, FAX 852-23119448, hkopmo@hko.gov.hk.

551.5 HKG
HONG KONG OBSERVATORY. NEWSLETTER FOR THE AVIATION COMMUNITY; weather on wings. Text in English. s-a. free. **Document type:** *Newsletter, Trade.*
Media: Online - full content.
Published by: Hong Kong Observatory, 134 A Nathan Rd, Kowloon, Hong Kong. TEL 852-29263113, FAX 852-23119448, mailbox@hko.gov.hk.

551.5 HKG
HONG KONG OBSERVATORY. OCCASIONAL PAPER. Text in Chinese, English. 1950. irreg., latest vol.67, 2001.
Formerly: Hong Kong. Royal Observatory. Occasional Paper (1012-4497)
Published by: Hong Kong Observatory, 134 A Nathan Rd, Kowloon, Hong Kong. TEL 852-29263113, FAX 852-23119448, hkopmo@hko.gov.hk, http://www.hko.gov.hk/.

551.5 HKG
HONG KONG OBSERVATORY. TECHNICAL NOTE. Text in English. 1949. irreg., latest vol.101, 2000. price varies. **Description:** Contains occasional publications of research results carried out by staff of the Observatory that are distributed to other meteorological organizations.
Formerly: Hong Kong. Royal Observatory. Climatological Note
Published by: Hong Kong Observatory, 134 A Nathan Rd, Kowloon, Hong Kong. TEL 852-29263113, FAX 852-23119448, hkopmo@hko.gov.hk, http://www.hko.gov.hk/.

551.5 HKG
HONG KONG OBSERVATORY. TECHNICAL NOTES (LOCAL). Text in Chinese, English. 1961. irreg., latest vol.76, 1999. price varies. **Document type:** *Monographic series, Academic/Scholarly.* **Description:** Contains occasional publications of research results carried out by staff of the Observatory that are distributed mainly to local libraries.
Formerly: Hong Kong. Royal Observatory. Technical Notes (Local)
Indexed: SpeleolAb.
Published by: Hong Kong Observatory, 134 A Nathan Rd, Kowloon, Hong Kong. TEL 852-29263113, FAX 852-23119448, hkopmo@hko.gov.hk, http://www.hko.gov.hk/.

551.5 HKG
HONG KONG OBSERVATORY. TROPICAL CYCLONES (YEAR); tropical cyclone summaries. Text in Chinese, English. 1968. a. price varies.
Formerly (until 1987): Hong Kong. Royal Observatory. Meteorological Results - Part III
Related titles: CD-ROM ed.
Published by: Hong Kong Observatory, 134 A Nathan Rd, Kowloon, Hong Kong. TEL 852-29263113, FAX 852-23119448, hkopmo@hko.gov.hk, http://www.hko.gov.hk/.

551.5 USA ISSN 0364-6076
QC925.1.U8
HOURLY PRECIPITATION DATA. ALABAMA. Text in English. 1965. m. USD 46; USD 7 per issue (effective 2009). back issues avail. **Document type:** *Government.* **Description:** Contains data on the hourly precipitation amounts obtained from recording rain gages and includes an hourly account of precipitation amounts for many locations within Alabama.
Related titles: Online - full text ed.: USD 4 per issue (effective 2009). —Linda Hall.
Published by: (U.S. Department of Commerce), U.S. National Climatic Data Center (Subsidiary of: U.S. Department of Commerce), Federal Bldg, 151 Patton Ave, Asheville, NC 28801. TEL 828-271-4800, FAX 828-271-4876, NODC.Services@noaa.gov, http://www.ncdc.noaa.gov.

551.5 USA ISSN 0364-6084
QC925.1.U8
HOURLY PRECIPITATION DATA. ARIZONA. Text in English. 1965. m. USD 57 domestic; USD 68 foreign; USD 7 per issue (effective 2009). back issues avail. **Document type:** *Government.* **Description:** Provides information about hourly precipitation data for Arizona.
Related titles: Online - full text ed.: USD 4 per issue (effective 2009). —Linda Hall.
Published by: (U.S. Department of Commerce), U.S. National Climatic Data Center (Subsidiary of: U.S. Department of Commerce), Federal Bldg, 151 Patton Ave, Asheville, NC 28801. TEL 828-271-4800, FAX 828-271-4876, NODC.Services@noaa.gov, http://www.ncdc.noaa.gov.

551.5 USA ISSN 0090-2683
QC925.1.U8
HOURLY PRECIPITATION DATA. ARKANSAS. Text in English. 1951. m. USD 57 domestic; USD 68 foreign; USD 7 per issue (effective 2009). back issues avail. **Document type:** *Government.* **Description:** Provides information about hourly precipitation data for Arkansas.
Related titles: Online - full content ed.: USD 4 per issue (effective 2009). —Linda Hall.
Published by: (U.S. Department of Commerce), U.S. National Climatic Data Center (Subsidiary of: U.S. Department of Commerce), Federal Bldg, 151 Patton Ave, Asheville, NC 28801. TEL 828-271-4800, FAX 828-271-4876, NODC.Services@noaa.gov, http://www.ncdc.noaa.gov.

551.5 USA ISSN 0364-6092
QC925.1.U8
HOURLY PRECIPITATION DATA. CALIFORNIA. Text in English. 1965. m. USD 57 domestic; USD 68 foreign; USD 7 per issue (effective 2009). back issues avail. **Document type:** *Government.* **Description:** Provides information about hourly precipitation data for California.
Related titles: Online - full content ed.: USD 4 per issue (effective 2009). —Linda Hall.
Published by: (U.S. Department of Commerce), U.S. National Climatic Data Center (Subsidiary of: U.S. Department of Commerce), Federal Bldg, 151 Patton Ave, Asheville, NC 28801. TEL 828-271-4800, FAX 828-271-4876, NODC.Services@noaa.gov, http://www.ncdc.noaa.gov.

551.5 USA ISSN 0364-6106
QC925.1.U8
HOURLY PRECIPITATION DATA. COLORADO. Text in English. 1965. m. USD 57 domestic; USD 68 foreign; USD 7 per issue (effective 2009). back issues avail. **Document type:** *Government.* **Description:** Contains data on the hourly precipitation amounts obtained from recording rain gages and includes an hourly account of precipitation amounts for many locations within Colorado.
Related titles: Online - full text ed.: USD 4 per issue (effective 2009). —Linda Hall.
Published by: (U.S. Department of Commerce), U.S. National Climatic Data Center (Subsidiary of: U.S. Department of Commerce), Federal Bldg, 151 Patton Ave, Asheville, NC 28801. TEL 828-271-4800, FAX 828-271-4876, NODC.Services@noaa.gov, http://www.ncdc.noaa.gov.

551.5 USA ISSN 0364-6114
QC925.1.U8
HOURLY PRECIPITATION DATA. FLORIDA. Text in English. 1965. m. USD 57 domestic; USD 68 foreign; USD 7 per issue (effective 2009). back issues avail. **Document type:** *Government.* **Description:** Contains data on the hourly precipitation amounts obtained from recording rain gages and includes an hourly account of precipitation amounts for many locations within Florida.
Related titles: Online - full text ed.: USD 4 per issue (effective 2009). —Linda Hall.
Published by: (U.S. Department of Commerce), U.S. National Climatic Data Center (Subsidiary of: U.S. Department of Commerce), Federal Bldg, 151 Patton Ave, Asheville, NC 28801. TEL 828-271-4800, FAX 828-271-4876, NODC.Services@noaa.gov, http://www.ncdc.noaa.gov.

551.5 USA ISSN 0364-6122
QC925.1.U8
HOURLY PRECIPITATION DATA. GEORGIA. Text in English. 1965. m. USD 57 domestic; USD 68 foreign; USD 7 per issue (effective 2009). back issues avail. **Document type:** *Government.* **Description:** Contains data on the hourly precipitation amounts obtained from recording rain gages and includes an hourly account of precipitation amounts for many locations within Georgia.
Related titles: Online - full text ed.: USD 4 per issue (effective 2009). —Linda Hall.
Published by: (U.S. Department of Commerce), U.S. National Climatic Data Center (Subsidiary of: U.S. Department of Commerce), Federal Bldg, 151 Patton Ave, Asheville, NC 28801. TEL 828-271-4800, FAX 828-271-4876, NODC.Services@noaa.gov, http://www.ncdc.noaa.gov.

551.5 USA
HOURLY PRECIPITATION DATA. HAWAII, ALASKA AND PACIFIC ISLANDS. Text in English. 1965. m. USD 57 domestic; USD 68 foreign; USD 7 per issue (effective 2009). back issues avail. **Document type:** *Government.* **Description:** Contains data on the hourly precipitation amounts obtained from recording rain gages and includes an hourly account of precipitation amounts for many locations within Hawaii and Pacific.
Former titles (until 1997): Hourly Precipitation Data. Hawaii and Pacific; (until 1978): Hourly Precipitation Data. Hawaii (0364-6130)
Related titles: Online - full text ed.: USD 4 per issue (effective 2009).
Published by: (U.S. Department of Commerce), U.S. National Climatic Data Center (Subsidiary of: U.S. Department of Commerce), Federal Bldg, 151 Patton Ave, Asheville, NC 28801. TEL 828-271-4800, FAX 828-271-4876, NODC.Services@noaa.gov, http://www.ncdc.noaa.gov.

551.5 USA ISSN 0364-6149
QC925.1.U8
HOURLY PRECIPITATION DATA. IDAHO. Text in English. 1965. m. USD 57 domestic; USD 68 foreign; USD 7 per issue (effective 2009). back issues avail. **Document type:** *Government.* **Description:** Contains data on the hourly precipitation amounts obtained from recording rain gages and includes an hourly account of precipitation amounts for many locations within Idaho.
Related titles: Online - full text ed.: ISSN 1930-9597. USD 4 per issue (effective 2009). —Linda Hall.
Published by: (U.S. Department of Commerce), U.S. National Climatic Data Center (Subsidiary of: U.S. Department of Commerce), Federal Bldg, 151 Patton Ave, Asheville, NC 28801. TEL 828-271-4800, FAX 828-271-4876, NODC.Services@noaa.gov, http://www.ncdc.noaa.gov.

551.5 USA ISSN 0364-6157
QC925.1.U8
HOURLY PRECIPITATION DATA. ILLINOIS. Text in English. 1951. m. USD 57 domestic; USD 68 foreign; USD 7 per issue (effective 2009). back issues avail. **Document type:** *Government.* **Description:** Contains data on the hourly precipitation amounts obtained from recording rain gages and includes an hourly account of precipitation amounts for many locations within Illinois.
Related titles: Online - full text ed.: USD 4 per issue (effective 2009). —Linda Hall.
Published by: (U.S. Department of Commerce), U.S. National Climatic Data Center (Subsidiary of: U.S. Department of Commerce), Federal Bldg, 151 Patton Ave, Asheville, NC 28801. TEL 828-271-4800, FAX 828-271-4876, NODC.Services@noaa.gov, http://www.ncdc.noaa.gov.

551.5 USA ISSN 0364-6165
QC925.1.U8
HOURLY PRECIPITATION DATA. INDIANA. Text in English. 1951. m. USD 57 domestic; USD 68 foreign; USD 7 per issue (effective 2009). back issues avail. **Document type:** *Government.* **Description:** Contains data on the hourly precipitation amounts obtained from recording rain gages and includes an hourly account of precipitation amounts for many locations within Indiana.
Related titles: Online - full text ed.: USD 4 per issue (effective 2009). —Linda Hall.
Published by: (U.S. Department of Commerce), U.S. National Climatic Data Center (Subsidiary of: U.S. Department of Commerce), Federal Bldg, 151 Patton Ave, Asheville, NC 28801. TEL 828-271-4800, FAX 828-271-4876, NODC.Services@noaa.gov, http://www.ncdc.noaa.gov.

551.5 USA ISSN 0364-6173
QC925.1.U8
HOURLY PRECIPITATION DATA. IOWA. Text in English. 1951. m. USD 57 domestic; USD 68 foreign; USD 7 per issue (effective 2009). back issues avail. **Document type:** *Government.* **Description:** Contains data on the hourly precipitation amounts obtained from recording rain gages and includes an hourly account of precipitation amounts for many locations within Iowa.
Related titles: Online - full text ed.: USD 4 per issue (effective 2009). —Linda Hall.
Published by: (U.S. Department of Commerce), U.S. National Climatic Data Center (Subsidiary of: U.S. Department of Commerce), Federal Bldg, 151 Patton Ave, Asheville, NC 28801. TEL 828-271-4800, FAX 828-271-4876, NODC.Services@noaa.gov, http://www.ncdc.noaa.gov.

551.5 USA ISSN 0364-6181
QC925.1.U8
HOURLY PRECIPITATION DATA. KANSAS. Text in English. 1951. m. USD 57 domestic; USD 68 foreign; USD 7 per issue (effective 2009). back issues avail. **Document type:** *Government.* **Description:** Contains data on the hourly precipitation amounts obtained from recording rain gages and includes an hourly account of precipitation amounts for many locations within Kansas.
Related titles: Online - full text ed.: USD 4 per issue (effective 2009). —Linda Hall.
Published by: (U.S. Department of Commerce), U.S. National Climatic Data Center (Subsidiary of: U.S. Department of Commerce), Federal Bldg, 151 Patton Ave, Asheville, NC 28801. TEL 828-271-4800, FAX 828-271-4876, NODC.Services@noaa.gov, http://www.ncdc.noaa.gov.

551.5 USA ISSN 0364-5401
QC925.1 U8
HOURLY PRECIPITATION DATA. KENTUCKY. Text in English. 1951. m. USD 57 domestic; USD 68 foreign; USD 7 per issue (effective 2009). back issues avail. **Document type:** *Government.* **Description:** Contains data on the hourly precipitation amounts obtained from recording rain gages and includes an hourly account of precipitation amounts for many locations within Kentucky.
Related titles: Online - full text ed.: USD 4 per issue (effective 2009). —Linda Hall.

Published by: (U.S. Department of Commerce), U.S. National Climatic Data Center (Subsidiary of: U.S. Department of Commerce), Federal Bldg, 151 Patton Ave, Asheville, NC 28801. TEL 828-271-4800, FAX 828-271-4876, NODC.Services@noaa.gov, http:// www.ncdc.noaa.gov.

551.5 USA ISSN 0364-5398
QC925. 1. U8
HOURLY PRECIPITATION DATA. LOUISIANA. Text in English. 1951. m. USD 57 domestic; USD 68 foreign; USD 7 per issue (effective 2009). back issues avail. **Document type:** *Government.* **Description:** Contains data on the hourly precipitation amounts obtained from recording rain gages and includes an hourly account of precipitation amounts for many locations within Louisiana.
Related titles: Online - full text ed.: USD 4 per issue (effective 2009).
—Linda Hall.
Published by: (U.S. Department of Commerce), U.S. National Climatic Data Center (Subsidiary of: U.S. Department of Commerce), Federal Bldg, 151 Patton Ave, Asheville, NC 28801. TEL 828-271-4800, FAX 828-271-4876, NODC.Services@noaa.gov, http:// www.ncdc.noaa.gov.

551.5 USA ISSN 0364-538X
QC925. 1 U8
HOURLY PRECIPITATION DATA. MARYLAND & DELAWARE. Text in English. 1951. m. USD 57 domestic; USD 68 foreign; USD 7 per issue (effective 2009). back issues avail. **Document type:** *Government.* **Description:** Contains data on the hourly precipitation amounts obtained from recording rain gages and includes an hourly account of precipitation amounts for many locations within Maryland and Delaware.
Related titles: Online - full text ed.: USD 4 per issue (effective 2009).
—Linda Hall.
Published by: (U.S. Department of Commerce), U.S. National Climatic Data Center (Subsidiary of: U.S. Department of Commerce), Federal Bldg, 151 Patton Ave, Asheville, NC 28801. TEL 828-271-4800, FAX 828-271-4876, NODC.Services@noaa.gov, http:// www.ncdc.noaa.gov.

551.5 USA ISSN 0364-6203
QC925.1.U8
HOURLY PRECIPITATION DATA. MICHIGAN. Text in English. 1951. m. USD 57 domestic; USD 68 foreign; USD 7 per issue (effective 2009). back issues avail. **Document type:** *Government.* **Description:** Contains data on the hourly precipitation amounts obtained from recording rain gages and includes an hourly account of precipitation amounts for many locations within Michigan.
Related titles: Online - full text ed.: USD 4 per issue (effective 2009).
—Linda Hall.
Published by: (U.S. Department of Commerce), U.S. National Climatic Data Center (Subsidiary of: U.S. Department of Commerce), Federal Bldg, 151 Patton Ave, Asheville, NC 28801. TEL 828-271-4800, FAX 828-271-4876, ncdc.info@noaa.gov, http://www.ncdc.noaa.gov.

551.5 USA ISSN 0364-6211
HOURLY PRECIPITATION DATA. MINNESOTA. Text in English. 1951. m. USD 57 domestic; USD 68 foreign; USD 7 per issue (effective 2009). back issues avail. **Document type:** *Government.* **Description:** Contains data on the hourly precipitation amounts obtained from recording rain gages and includes an hourly account of precipitation amounts for many locations within Minnesota.
Related titles: Online - full text ed.: USD 4 per issue (effective 2009).
—Linda Hall.
Published by: (U.S. Department of Commerce), U.S. National Climatic Data Center (Subsidiary of: U.S. Department of Commerce), Federal Bldg, 151 Patton Ave, Asheville, NC 28801. TEL 828-271-4800, FAX 828-271-4876, NODC.Services@noaa.gov, http:// www.ncdc.noaa.gov.

551.5 USA ISSN 0364-622X
QC925.1.U8
HOURLY PRECIPITATION DATA. MISSISSIPPI. Text in English. 1951. m. USD 57 domestic; USD 68 foreign; USD 7 per issue (effective 2009). back issues avail. **Document type:** *Government.* **Description:** Contains data on the hourly precipitation amounts obtained from recording rain gages and includes an hourly account of precipitation amounts for many locations within Mississippi.
Related titles: Online - full text ed.: USD 4 per issue (effective 2009).
—Linda Hall.
Published by: (U.S. Department of Commerce), U.S. National Climatic Data Center (Subsidiary of: U.S. Department of Commerce), Federal Bldg, 151 Patton Ave, Asheville, NC 28801. TEL 828-271-4800, FAX 828-271-4876, ncdc.info@noaa.gov, NODC.Services@noaa.gov, http://www.ncdc.noaa.gov.

551.5 USA ISSN 0364-6238
QC925.1.U8
HOURLY PRECIPITATION DATA. MISSOURI. Text in English. 1951. m. USD 57 domestic; USD 68 foreign; USD 7 per issue (effective 2009). back issues avail. **Document type:** *Government.* **Description:** Contains data on the hourly precipitation amounts obtained from recording rain gages and includes an hourly account of precipitation amounts for many locations within Missouri.
Related titles: Online - full text ed.: USD 4 per issue (effective 2009).
—Linda Hall.
Published by: (U.S. Department of Commerce), U.S. National Climatic Data Center (Subsidiary of: U.S. Department of Commerce), Federal Bldg, 151 Patton Ave, Asheville, NC 28801. TEL 828-271-4800, FAX 828-271-4876, NODC.Services@noaa.gov, http:// www.ncdc.noaa.gov.

551.5 USA ISSN 0364-6246
QC925.1.U8
HOURLY PRECIPITATION DATA. MONTANA. Text in English. 1951. m. USD 57 domestic; USD 68 foreign; USD 7 per issue (effective 2009). back issues avail. **Document type:** *Government.* **Description:** Contains data on the hourly precipitation amounts obtained from recording rain gages and includes an hourly account of precipitation amounts for many locations within Montana.
Related titles: Online - full text ed.: USD 4 per issue (effective 2009).
—Linda Hall.
Published by: (U.S. Department of Commerce), U.S. National Climatic Data Center (Subsidiary of: U.S. Department of Commerce), Federal Bldg, 151 Patton Ave, Asheville, NC 28801. TEL 828-271-4800, FAX 828-271-4876, NODC.Services@noaa.gov, http:// www.ncdc.noaa.gov.

551.5 USA ISSN 0364-6254
QC925.1.U8
HOURLY PRECIPITATION DATA. NEBRASKA. Text in English. 1951. m. USD 57 domestic; USD 68 foreign; USD 7 per issue (effective 2009). back issues avail. **Document type:** *Government.* **Description:** Contains data on the hourly precipitation amounts obtained from recording rain gages and includes an hourly account of precipitation amounts for many locations within Nebraska.
Related titles: Online - full text ed.: USD 4 per issue (effective 2009).
—Linda Hall.
Published by: (U.S. Department of Commerce), U.S. National Climatic Data Center (Subsidiary of: U.S. Department of Commerce), Federal Bldg, 151 Patton Ave, Asheville, NC 28801. TEL 828-271-4800, FAX 828-271-4876, NODC.Services@noaa.gov, http:// www.ncdc.noaa.gov.

551.5 USA ISSN 0364-6262
QC925.1.U8
HOURLY PRECIPITATION DATA. NEVADA. Text in English. 1951. m. USD 57 domestic; USD 68 foreign; USD 7 per issue (effective 2009). back issues avail. **Document type:** *Government.* **Description:** Contains data on the hourly precipitation amounts obtained from recording rain gages and includes an hourly account of precipitation amounts for many locations within Nevada.
Related titles: Online - full text ed.: USD 4 per issue (effective 2009).
—Linda Hall.
Published by: (U.S. Department of Commerce), U.S. National Climatic Data Center (Subsidiary of: U.S. Department of Commerce), Federal Bldg, 151 Patton Ave, Asheville, NC 28801. TEL 828-271-4800, FAX 828-271-4876, NODC.Services@noaa.gov, http:// www.ncdc.noaa.gov.

551.5 USA ISSN 0364-6270
QC925.1.U8
HOURLY PRECIPITATION DATA. NEW ENGLAND. Text in English. 1951. m. USD 57 domestic; USD 68 foreign; USD 7 per issue (effective 2009). back issues avail. **Document type:** *Government.* **Description:** Contains data on the hourly precipitation amounts obtained from recording rain gages and includes an hourly account of precipitation amounts for many locations within New England.
Related titles: Online - full text ed.: USD 4 per issue (effective 2009).
—Linda Hall.
Published by: (U.S. Department of Commerce), U.S. National Climatic Data Center (Subsidiary of: U.S. Department of Commerce), Federal Bldg, 151 Patton Ave, Asheville, NC 28801. TEL 828-271-4800, FAX 828-271-4876, NODC.Services@noaa.gov, http:// www.ncdc.noaa.gov.

551.5 USA ISSN 0364-6289
QC925.1.U8
HOURLY PRECIPITATION DATA. NEW JERSEY. Text in English. 1951. m. USD 57 domestic; USD 68 foreign; USD 7 per issue (effective 2009). back issues avail. **Document type:** *Government.* **Description:** Contains data on the hourly precipitation amounts obtained from recording rain gages and includes an hourly account of precipitation amounts for many locations within New Jersey.
Related titles: Online - full text ed.: USD 4 per issue (effective 2009).
—Linda Hall.
Published by: (U.S. Department of Commerce), U.S. National Climatic Data Center (Subsidiary of: U.S. Department of Commerce), Federal Bldg, 151 Patton Ave, Asheville, NC 28801. TEL 828-271-4800, FAX 828-271-4876, NODC.Services@noaa.gov, http:// www.ncdc.noaa.gov.

551.5 USA ISSN 0364-6297
QC925.1.U8
HOURLY PRECIPITATION DATA. NEW MEXICO. Text in English. 1951. m. USD 57 domestic; USD 68 foreign; USD 7 per issue (effective 2009). back issues avail. **Document type:** *Government.* **Description:** Contains data on the hourly precipitation amounts obtained from recording rain gages and includes an hourly account of precipitation amounts for many locations within New Jersey.
Related titles: Online - full text ed.: USD 4 per issue (effective 2009).
—Linda Hall.
Published by: (U.S. Department of Commerce), U.S. National Climatic Data Center (Subsidiary of: U.S. Department of Commerce), Federal Bldg, 151 Patton Ave, Asheville, NC 28801. TEL 828-271-4800, FAX 828-271-4876, NODC.Services@noaa.gov, http:// www.ncdc.noaa.gov.

551.5 USA ISSN 0364-6300
QC925.1.U8
HOURLY PRECIPITATION DATA. NEW YORK. Text in English. 1951. m. USD 57 domestic; USD 68 foreign; USD 7 per issue (effective 2009). back issues avail. **Document type:** *Government.* **Description:** Contains data on the hourly precipitation amounts obtained from recording rain gages and includes an hourly account of precipitation amounts for many locations within New York.
Related titles: Online - full text ed.: USD 4 per issue (effective 2009).
—Linda Hall.
Published by: (U.S. Department of Commerce), U.S. National Climatic Data Center (Subsidiary of: U.S. Department of Commerce), Federal Bldg, 151 Patton Ave, Asheville, NC 28801. TEL 828-271-4800, FAX 828-271-4876, NODC.Services@noaa.gov, http:// www.ncdc.noaa.gov.

551.5 USA ISSN 0364-6319
QC925.1.U8
HOURLY PRECIPITATION DATA. NORTH CAROLINA. Text in English. 1951. m. USD 57 domestic; USD 68 foreign; USD 7 per issue (effective 2009). back issues avail. **Document type:** *Government.* **Description:** Contains data on the hourly precipitation amounts obtained from recording rain gages and includes an hourly account of precipitation amounts for many locations within North Carolina.
Related titles: Online - full text ed.: USD 4 per issue (effective 2009).
—Linda Hall.
Published by: (U.S. Department of Commerce), U.S. National Climatic Data Center (Subsidiary of: U.S. Department of Commerce), Federal Bldg, 151 Patton Ave, Asheville, NC 28801. TEL 828-271-4800, FAX 828-271-4876, NODC.Services@noaa.gov, http:// www.ncdc.noaa.gov.

551.5 USA ISSN 0364-6327
QC925.1.U8
HOURLY PRECIPITATION DATA. NORTH DAKOTA. Text in English. 1951. m. USD 57 domestic; USD 68 foreign; USD 7 per issue (effective 2009). back issues avail. **Document type:** *Government.* **Description:** Contains data on the hourly precipitation amounts obtained from recording rain gages and includes an hourly account of precipitation amounts for many locations within North Dakota.
Related titles: Online - full text ed.: USD 4 per issue (effective 2009).
—Linda Hall.
Published by: (U.S. Department of Commerce), U.S. National Climatic Data Center (Subsidiary of: U.S. Department of Commerce), Federal Bldg, 151 Patton Ave, Asheville, NC 28801. TEL 828-271-4800, FAX 828-271-4876, NODC.Services@noaa.gov, http:// www.ncdc.noaa.gov.

551.5 USA ISSN 0364-6335
QC925.1.U8
HOURLY PRECIPITATION DATA. OHIO. Text in English. 1951. m. USD 57 domestic; USD 68 foreign; USD 7 per issue (effective 2009). back issues avail. **Document type:** *Government.* **Description:** Contains data on the hourly precipitation amounts obtained from recording rain gages and includes an hourly account of precipitation amounts for many locations within Ohio.
Related titles: Online - full text ed.: USD 4 per issue (effective 2009).
—Linda Hall.
Published by: (U.S. Department of Commerce), U.S. National Climatic Data Center (Subsidiary of: U.S. Department of Commerce), Federal Bldg, 151 Patton Ave, Asheville, NC 28801. TEL 828-271-4800, FAX 828-271-4876, NODC.Services@noaa.gov, http:// www.ncdc.noaa.gov.

551.5 USA ISSN 0364-6343
QC925.1.U8
HOURLY PRECIPITATION DATA. OKLAHOMA. Text in English. 1951. m. USD 57 domestic; USD 68 foreign; USD 7 per issue (effective 2009). back issues avail. **Document type:** *Government.* **Description:** Contains data on the hourly precipitation amounts obtained from recording rain gages and includes an hourly account of precipitation amounts for many locations within Oklahoma.
Related titles: Online - full text ed.: USD 4 per issue (effective 2009).
—Linda Hall.
Published by: (U.S. Department of Commerce), U.S. National Climatic Data Center (Subsidiary of: U.S. Department of Commerce), Federal Bldg, 151 Patton Ave, Asheville, NC 28801. TEL 828-271-4800, FAX 828-271-4876, NODC.Services@noaa.gov, http:// www.ncdc.noaa.gov.

551.5 USA ISSN 0364-6351
HOURLY PRECIPITATION DATA. OREGON. Text in English. 1951. m. USD 57 domestic; USD 68 foreign; USD 7 per issue (effective 2009). back issues avail. **Document type:** *Government.* **Description:** Contains data on the hourly precipitation amounts obtained from recording rain gages and includes an hourly account of precipitation amounts for many locations within Oregon.
Related titles: Online - full text ed.: USD 4 per issue (effective 2009).
—Linda Hall.
Published by: (U.S. Department of Commerce), U.S. National Climatic Data Center (Subsidiary of: U.S. Department of Commerce), Federal Bldg, 151 Patton Ave, Asheville, NC 28801. TEL 828-271-4800, FAX 828-271-4876, NODC.Services@noaa.gov, http:// www.ncdc.noaa.gov.

551.5 USA ISSN 0364-619X
QC925.1.U8
HOURLY PRECIPITATION DATA. PENNSYLVANIA. Text in English. 1951. m. USD 57 domestic; USD 68 foreign; USD 7 per issue (effective 2009). back issues avail. **Document type:** *Government.* **Description:** Contains data on the hourly precipitation amounts obtained from recording rain gages and includes an hourly account of precipitation amounts for many locations within Pennsylvania.
Related titles: Online - full text ed.: USD 4 per issue (effective 2009).
—Linda Hall.
Published by: (U.S. Department of Commerce), U.S. National Climatic Data Center (Subsidiary of: U.S. Department of Commerce), Federal Bldg, 151 Patton Ave, Asheville, NC 28801. TEL 828-271-4800, FAX 828-271-4876, ncdc.info@noaa.gov, http://www.ncdc.noaa.gov.

551.5 USA ISSN 1058-5079
HOURLY PRECIPITATION DATA. PUERTO RICO & VIRGIN ISLANDS. Text in English. 1971. m. USD 57 domestic; USD 68 foreign; USD 7 per issue (effective 2009). back issues avail. **Document type:** *Government.*
Formerly (until 1978): Hourly Precipitation Data. Puerto Rico (0090-2691)
Related titles: Online - full text ed.: USD 4 per issue (effective 2009).
—Linda Hall.
Published by: (U.S. Department of Commerce), U.S. National Climatic Data Center (Subsidiary of: U.S. Department of Commerce), Federal Bldg, 151 Patton Ave, Asheville, NC 28801. TEL 828-271-4800, FAX 828-271-4876, NODC.Services@noaa.gov, http:// www.ncdc.noaa.gov.

551.5 USA ISSN 0364-636X
QC925.1.U8
HOURLY PRECIPITATION DATA. SOUTH CAROLINA. Text in English. 1951. m. USD 57 domestic; USD 68 foreign; USD 7 per issue (effective 2009). back issues avail. **Document type:** *Government.* **Description:** Contains data on the hourly precipitation amounts obtained from recording rain gages and includes an hourly account of precipitation amounts for many locations within South Carolina.
Related titles: Online - full text ed.: USD 4 per issue (effective 2009).
—Linda Hall.
Published by: (U.S. Department of Commerce), U.S. National Climatic Data Center (Subsidiary of: U.S. Department of Commerce), Federal Bldg, 151 Patton Ave, Asheville, NC 28801. TEL 828-271-4800, FAX 828-271-4876, NODC.Services@noaa.gov, http:// www.ncdc.noaa.gov.

551.5 USA ISSN 0364-6378
QC925.1.U8
HOURLY PRECIPITATION DATA. SOUTH DAKOTA. Text in English. 1951. m. USD 57 domestic; USD 68 foreign; USD 7 per issue (effective 2009). back issues avail. **Document type:** *Government.* **Description:** Contains data on the hourly precipitation amounts obtained from recording rain gages and includes an hourly account of precipitation amounts for many locations within South Dakota.
Related titles: Online - full text ed.: USD 4 per issue (effective 2009).

—Linda Hall.
Published by: (U.S. Department of Commerce), U.S. National Climatic Data Center (Subsidiary of: U.S. Department of Commerce), Federal Bldg, 151 Patton Ave, Asheville, NC 28801. TEL 828-271-4800, FAX 828-271-4876, NODC.Services@noaa.gov, http://www.ncdc.noaa.gov.

551.5 USA ISSN 0364-6386
QC925.1.U8
HOURLY PRECIPITATION DATA. TENNESSEE. Text in English. 1951. m. USD 57 domestic; USD 68 foreign; USD 7 per issue (effective 2009). back issues avail. **Document type:** *Government.* **Description:** Contains data on the hourly precipitation amounts obtained from recording rain gages and includes an hourly account of precipitation amounts for many locations within Tennessee.
Related titles: Online - full text ed.: USD 4 per issue (effective 2009).
—Linda Hall.
Published by: (U.S. Department of Commerce), U.S. National Climatic Data Center (Subsidiary of: U.S. Department of Commerce), Federal Bldg, 151 Patton Ave, Asheville, NC 28801. TEL 828-271-4800, FAX 828-271-4876, NODC.Services@noaa.gov, http://www.ncdc.noaa.gov.

551.5 USA ISSN 0364-6882
QC925.1.U8
HOURLY PRECIPITATION DATA. TEXAS. Text in English. 1951. m. USD 57 domestic; USD 68 foreign; USD 7 per issue (effective 2009). back issues avail. **Document type:** *Government.* **Description:** Contains data on the hourly precipitation amounts obtained from recording rain gages and includes an hourly account of precipitation amounts for many locations within Texas.
Related titles: Online - full text ed.: USD 4 per issue (effective 2009).
—Linda Hall.
Published by: (U.S. Department of Commerce), U.S. National Climatic Data Center (Subsidiary of: U.S. Department of Commerce), Federal Bldg, 151 Patton Ave, Asheville, NC 28801. TEL 828-271-4800, FAX 828-271-4876, NODC.Services@noaa.gov, http://www.ncdc.noaa.gov.

551.5 USA ISSN 0364-6920
QC925.1.U8
HOURLY PRECIPITATION DATA. UTAH. Text in English. 1951. m. USD 57 domestic; USD 68 foreign; USD 7 per issue (effective 2009). back issues avail. **Document type:** *Government.* **Description:** Contains data on the hourly precipitation amounts obtained from recording rain gages and includes an hourly account of precipitation amounts for many locations within Utah.
Related titles: Online - full text ed.: USD 4 per issue (effective 2009).
—Linda Hall.
Published by: (U.S. Department of Commerce), U.S. National Climatic Data Center (Subsidiary of: U.S. Department of Commerce), Federal Bldg, 151 Patton Ave, Asheville, NC 28801. TEL 828-271-4800, FAX 828-271-4876, NODC.Services@noaa.gov, http://www.ncdc.noaa.gov.

551.5 USA ISSN 0364-6874
QC925.1.U8
HOURLY PRECIPITATION DATA. VIRGINIA. Text in English. 1951. m. USD 57 domestic; USD 68 foreign; USD 7 per issue (effective 2009). back issues avail. **Document type:** *Government.* **Description:** Contains data on the hourly precipitation amounts obtained from recording rain gages and includes an hourly account of precipitation amounts for many locations within Virginia.
Related titles: Online - full text ed.: USD 4 per issue (effective 2009).
—Linda Hall.
Published by: (U.S. Department of Commerce), U.S. National Climatic Data Center (Subsidiary of: U.S. Department of Commerce), Federal Bldg, 151 Patton Ave, Asheville, NC 28801. TEL 828-271-4800, FAX 828-271-4876, NODC.Services@noaa.gov, http://www.ncdc.noaa.gov.

551.5 USA ISSN 0364-6912
QC925.1.U8
HOURLY PRECIPITATION DATA. WASHINGTON. Text in English. 1951. m. USD 57 domestic; USD 68 foreign; USD 7 per issue (effective 2009). back issues avail. **Document type:** *Government.* **Description:** Contains data on the hourly precipitation amounts obtained from recording rain gages and includes an hourly account of precipitation amounts for many locations within Washington.
Related titles: Online - full text ed.: USD 4 per issue (effective 2009).
—Linda Hall.
Published by: (U.S. Department of Commerce), U.S. National Climatic Data Center (Subsidiary of: U.S. Department of Commerce), Federal Bldg, 151 Patton Ave, Asheville, NC 28801. TEL 828-271-4800, FAX 828-271-4876, NODC.Services@noaa.gov, http://www.ncdc.noaa.gov.

551.5 USA ISSN 0364-6904
QC925.1.U8
HOURLY PRECIPITATION DATA. WEST VIRGINIA. Text in English. 1951. m. USD 57 domestic; USD 68 foreign; USD 7 per issue (effective 2009). back issues avail. **Document type:** *Government.* **Description:** Contains data on the hourly precipitation amounts obtained from recording rain gages and includes an hourly account of precipitation amounts for many locations within West Virginia.
Related titles: Online - full text ed.: USD 4 per issue (effective 2009).
—Linda Hall.
Published by: (U.S. Department of Commerce), U.S. National Climatic Data Center (Subsidiary of: U.S. Department of Commerce), Federal Bldg, 151 Patton Ave, Asheville, NC 28801. TEL 828-271-4800, FAX 828-271-4876, NODC.Services@noaa.gov, http://www.ncdc.noaa.gov.

551.5 USA ISSN 0364-6939
QC925.1.U8
HOURLY PRECIPITATION DATA. WISCONSIN. Text in English. 1951. m. USD 57 domestic; USD 68 foreign; USD 7 per issue (effective 2009). back issues avail. **Document type:** *Government.* **Description:** Contains data on the hourly precipitation amounts obtained from recording rain gages and includes an hourly account of precipitation amounts for many locations within Wisconsin.
Related titles: Online - full text ed.: USD 4 per issue (effective 2009).
—Linda Hall.
Published by: (U.S. Department of Commerce), U.S. National Climatic Data Center (Subsidiary of: U.S. Department of Commerce), Federal Bldg, 151 Patton Ave, Asheville, NC 28801. TEL 828-271-4800, FAX 828-271-4876, NODC.Services@noaa.gov, http://www.ncdc.noaa.gov.

551.1 USA ISSN 0364-6890
QC925.1.U8
HOURLY PRECIPITATION DATA. WYOMING. Text in English. 1951. m. USD 57 domestic; USD 68 foreign; USD 7 per issue (effective 2009). back issues avail. **Document type:** *Government.* **Description:** Contains data on the hourly precipitation amounts obtained from recording rain gages and includes an hourly account of precipitation amounts for many locations within Wyoming.
Related titles: Online - full text ed.: USD 4 per issue (effective 2009).
—Linda Hall.
Published by: (U.S. Department of Commerce), U.S. National Climatic Data Center (Subsidiary of: U.S. Department of Commerce), Federal Bldg, 151 Patton Ave, Asheville, NC 28801. TEL 828-271-4800, FAX 828-271-4876, NODC.Services@noaa.gov, http://www.ncdc.noaa.gov.

551.5 HRV ISSN 1330-0083
QC989.C87
HRVATSKI METEOROLOSKI CASOPIS/CROATIAN METEOROLOGICAL JOURNAL. Text in Multiple languages. 1957. a. **Document type:** *Journal.* **Description:** Publishes scientific and professional papers in the field of meteorology and related activities.
Former titles (until 1991): Meteorolosko Drustvo Socijalisticke Republike Hrvatske. Rasprave (1330-1241); (until 1990): Republicki Hidrometeoroloski Zavod Socijalisticke Republike Hrvatske. Rasprave (0352-1079); (until 1981): Republicki Hidrometeoroloski Zavod Socijalisticke Republike Hrvatske. Rasprave i Prikazi (1330-3856); (until 1971): Hidrometeoroloski Zavod Socijalisticke Republike Hrvatske. Rasprave i Prikazi (1330-3848); (until 1963): Hidrometeoroloski Zavod Narodne Republike Hrvatske. Rasprave i Prikazi (0514-1516)
Indexed: GEOBASE, M&GPA, SCOPUS.
Published by: Hrvatsko Meteorolosko Drustvo/Croatian Meteorological Society, c/o Alica Bajic, Gric 3, Zagreb, 10000, Croatia. TEL 385-1-4565682, FAX 385-1-431026, bajic@cirus.dhz.hr.

551 JPN ISSN 0916-5037
HYOGOKEN KISHO GEPPO/HYOGO PREFECTURE. MONTHLY REPORT OF METEOROLOGY. Text in Japanese. m.
Published by: Kobe Kaiyo Kishodai/Kobe Marine Observatory (Subsidiary of: Kishocho/Japan Meteorological Agency), 1-4-3 Wakinohama-Kaigandori, Chuo-ku, Kobe, 651-0073, Japan. Ed. Tuyoshi Nakai.

551.6 GBR ISSN 2045-0311
▼ **I C P SERIES ON CLIMATE CHANGE IMPACTS, ADAPTATION, AND MITIGATION.** Text in English. 2010. irreg., latest vol.1, 2010. price varies. **Document type:** *Monographic series, Academic/Scholarly.*
Published by: Imperial College Press (Subsidiary of: World Scientific Publishing Co. Pte. Ltd.), 57 Shelton St, Covent Garden, London, WC2H 9HE, United Kingdom. TEL 44-20-78360888, FAX 44-20-78362020, edit@icpress.co.uk, http://www.icpress.co.uk/. Eds. Cynthia Rosenzweig, Daniel Hillel. **Dist. by:** World Scientific Publishing Co., Inc., 27 Warren St, Ste 401-402, Hackensack, NJ 07601. TEL 201-487-9655, 800-227-7562, FAX 201-487-9656, 888-977-2665, wspc@wspc.com.

I C R R ANNUAL REPORT. (Institute for Cosmic Ray Research) *see* ASTRONOMY

551 JPN ISSN 0916-5304
IBARAKIKEN KISHO GEPPO/IBARAKI PREFECTURE. MONTHLY REPORT OF METEOROLOGY. Text in Japanese. 1897. m.
Published by: Kishocho, Mito Chiho Kishodai/Japan Meteorological Agency, Mito Local Meteorological Observatory, 4-6 Kane-Machi 1-chome, Mito-shi, Ibaraki-ken 310-0066, Japan.

551.5 HUN ISSN 0324-6329
➤ **IDOJARAS/QUARTERLY JOURNAL OF THE HUNGARIAN METEOROLOGICAL SERVICE**; quarterly journal of the Hungarian Meteorological Service. Text and summaries in English. 1897. q. HUF 16,000 domestic; USD 70 foreign (effective 2003). adv. bk.rev. abstr.; bibl.; charts; illus. 75 p./no. 1 cols./p.; back issues avail. **Document type:** *Journal, Academic/Scholarly.* **Description:** Publishes papers on atmospheric sciences, hydrology and related topics.
Former titles (until 1904): Atmosphaera (0324-6272); (until 1902): Idojaras (0367-7443)
Indexed: GEOBASE, GeoRef, M&GPA, RefZh, SCI, SCOPUS, SpeleolAb, W07.
—INIST, Linda Hall.
Published by: Orszagos Meteorologiai Szolgalat/Hungarian Meteorological Service, Pf 38, Budapest, 1525, Hungary. TEL 36-1-3464801, FAX 36-1-3464809, prager.t@met.hu, http://omsz.met.hu/omsz.html. Ed. Tamas Prager. R&P Ivan Mersich TEL 36-1-3464666. Adv. contact Margit Antal. Circ: 400.

551.5 FIN ISSN 0782-6109
ILMATIETEEN LAITOS. METEOROLOGISIA JULKAISUJA/FINNISH METEOROLOGICAL INSTITUTE. PUBLICATIONS. Text in English, Finnish. 1986. irreg., latest vol.45, 2001. price varies. back issues avail. **Document type:** *Monographic series, Government.*
Indexed: M&GPA.
Published by: Ilmatieteen Laitos/Finnish Meteorological Institute, Vuorikatu 24, PO Box 503, Helsinki, 00101, Finland. TEL 358-9-19291, FAX 358-9-179581.

551.5 IND ISSN 0250-6017
INDIAN INSTITUTE OF TROPICAL METEOROLOGY. ANNUAL REPORT. Text in English, Hindi. 1971. a., latest 2000. back issues avail. **Document type:** *Report, Academic/Scholarly.*
Related titles: Online - full text ed.: free (effective 2011).
Indexed: GeoRef, SpeleolAb.
Published by: Indian Institute of Tropical Meteorology, Dr. Homi Bhabha Rd, Pashan, Pune, Maharashtra 411 008, India. TEL 91-20-25904200, FAX 91-20-2589-3825, lip@tropmet.res.in.

551.5 IND ISSN 0252-1075
INDIAN INSTITUTE OF TROPICAL METEOROLOGY. CONTRIBUTIONS. Key Title: Contributions from the Indian Institute of Tropical Meteorology. Text in English. 1971. irreg., latest vol.126, 2010. back issues avail. **Document type:** *Monographic series, Academic/Scholarly.*
Formerly (until 1980): Indian Institute of Tropical Meteorology. Research Report (0250-6009)
Related titles: Online - full text ed.: free (effective 2011).
Published by: Indian Institute of Tropical Meteorology, Dr. Homi Bhabha Rd, Pashan, Pune, Maharashtra 411 008, India. TEL 91-20-25904200, FAX 91-20-2589-3825, lip@tropmet.res.in.

INDIAN JOURNAL OF RADIO & SPACE PHYSICS. *see* ASTRONOMY

INDIANA. AGRICULTURAL STATISTICS SERVICE. CROP & WEATHER REPORT. *see* AGRICULTURE—Crop Production And Soil

INFORMAZIONI NAUTICHE. *see* TRANSPORTATION—Ships And Shipping

551.5 ZAF
INKANYAMBA: TORNADOES IN SOUTH AFRICA. Text in English. irreg. ZAR 140 per vol. (effective 2001). charts; illus.; stat. Index. **Document type:** *Government.* **Description:** Highlights the relevance and scale of tornadic events in South Africa and give meteorological background and statistical overview of the recorded events.
Published by: South African Weather Service, Department of Environmental Affairs and Tourism, Private Bag X97, Pretoria, 0001, South Africa. TEL 27-82-233-8686, FAX 27-12-3093989, pubenq@weathersa.co.za, http://www.weathersa.co.za. Circ: 150.

551.5 RUS ISSN 0131-4823
INSTITUT EKSPERIMENTAL'NOI METEOROLOGII. TRUDY. Text in Russian. 1977 (vol.16). irreg. price varies. abstr.
Related titles: ◆ Series: Fizika Nizhnei Atmosfery.
Indexed: ChemAb.
Published by: (Institut Eksperimental'noi Meteorologii), Gidrometeoizdat, Ul Beringa 38, St Petersburg, 199397, Russian Federation. Circ: 400.

INSTITUT ROYAL METEOROLOGIQUE DE BELGIQUE. ANNUAIRE: MAGNETISME TERRESTRE/KONINKLIJK METEOROLOGISCH INSTITUUT VAN BELGIE. JAARBOEK: AARDMAGNETISME. *see* EARTH SCIENCES—Geology

551.6 BEL ISSN 0029-7682
QC989.B8
INSTITUT ROYAL METEOROLOGIQUE DE BELGIQUE. BULLETIN MENSUEL: OBSERVATIONS CLIMATOLOGIQUES/KONINKLIJK METEOROLOGISCHE INSTITUUT VAN BELGIE. MAANDBULLETIN: KLIMATOLOGISCHE WAARNEMINGEN. Key Title: Bulletin Mensuel: Observations Climatologiques - Maandbulletin: Klimatologische Waarnemingen. Text in Dutch, French. 1928. m. charts; illus.; stat. **Document type:** *Bulletin, Trade.* **Description:** Discusses meteorological observations.
Former titles (until 1965): Institut Royal Meteorologique de Belgique. Bulletin Mensuel: Climatologie, Rayonnement, Radioactivite, Declinaison Magnetique (0772-358X); (until 1959): Institut Royal Meteorologique de Belgique. Bulletin Mensuel: Apercu Climatologique (0772-3598)
Published by: Institut Royal Meteorologique de Belgique/Koninklijk Meteorologisch Instituut van Belgie, Av Circulaire 3, Brussels, 1180, Belgium. TEL 32-2-373-0502, FAX 32-2-375-1259, http://www.meteo.oma.be. Ed. H Malcorps. Circ: 540.

551.514 523.01 BEL ISSN 0020-2533
INSTITUT ROYAL METEOROLOGIQUE DE BELGIQUE. BULLETIN MENSUEL: OBSERVATIONS IONOSPHERIQUES ET DU RAYONNEMENT COSMIQUE/KONINKLIJK METEOROLOGISCHE INSTITUUT VAN BELGIE. MAANDBULLETIN: WAARNEMINGEN VAN DE IONOSFEER EN DE KOSMISCHE STRALING. Key Title: Bulletin Mensuel: Observations Ionospheriques et du Rayonnement Cosmique - Maandbulletin van de Ionosfeer en de Kosmische Straling. Text in Dutch, French. 1946. m. charts; stat. **Document type:** *Bulletin, Trade.* **Description:** Discusses the ionosphere and cosmic rays.
Formerly (until 1969): Institut Royal Meteorologique de Belgique. Bulletin Mensuel. Observations Ionospherigiques (0524-7799)
Indexed: A28, APA, BrCerAb, C&ISA, CA/WCA, CIA, CerAb, CivEngAb, CorrAb, E&CAJ, E11, EEA, EMA, ESPM, EnvEAb, H15, M&GPA, M&TEA, M09, MBF, METADEX, SolStAb, T04, WAA.
—CCC.
Published by: Institut Royal Meteorologique de Belgique/Koninklijk Meteorologisch Instituut van Belgie, Av Circulaire 3, Brussels, 1180, Belgium. TEL 32-2-373-0502, FAX 32-2-375-1259, http://www.meteo.oma.be. Ed. H Malcorps. Circ: 320.

529 BEL ISSN 0007-5280
INSTITUT ROYAL METEOROLOGIQUE DE BELGIQUE. BULLETIN QUOTIDIEN DU TEMPS/KONINKLIJK METEOROLOGISCH INSTITUUT VAN BELGIE. DAGELIJKS WEERBULLETIN. Cover title: Bulletin Quotidien du Temps - Dagelijks Weerbulletin. Text in Dutch, French. d. charts; stat. **Document type:** *Bulletin, Trade.* **Description:** Reports on daily weather conditions.
Published by: Institut Royal Meteorologique de Belgique/Koninklijk Meteorologisch Instituut van Belgie, Av Circulaire 3, Brussels, 1180, Belgium. TEL 32-2-373-0502, FAX 32-2-375-1259, http://www.meteo.oma.be. Ed. H Malcorps. Circ: 300.

551.514 BEL ISSN 0770-0164
INSTITUT ROYAL METEOROLOGIQUE DE BELGIQUE. BULLETIN TRIMESTRIEL: OBSERVATIONS D'OZONE/KONINKLIJK METEOROLOGISCHE INSTITUUT VAN BELGIE. DRIEMAANDELIJKS BULLETIN: OZON WAARNEMINGEN. Key Title: Bulletin Trimestriel: Observations d'Ozone - Driemaandelijks Bulletin: Ozon Waarnemingen. Text in Dutch, French. 1965. q. charts; stat. **Document type:** *Bulletin, Trade.* **Description:** Reports on atmospheric ozone and its depletion.
Indexed: Inspec.
—AskIEEE.
Published by: Institut Royal Meteorologique de Belgique/Koninklijk Meteorologisch Instituut van Belgie, Av Circulaire 3, Brussels, 1180, Belgium. TEL 32-2-373-0502, FAX 32-2-375-1259, http://www.meteo.oma.be. Ed. H Malcorps. Circ: 190.

551.5 BEL ISSN 0770-0261
QC989.B8
INSTITUT ROYAL METEOROLOGIQUE DE BELGIQUE. MISCELLANEA. SERIE A/KONINKLIJK METEOROLOGISCH INSTITUUT VAN BELGIE. MISCELLANEA. SERIE A. Text in Multiple languages. 1971. irreg. **Document type:** *Journal, Academic/Scholarly.*
Indexed: Inspec.

Published by: Institut Royal Meteorologique de Belgique/Koninklijk Meteorologisch Instituut van Belgie, Av Circulaire 3, Brussels, 1180, Belgium. TEL 32-2-373-0502, FAX 32-2-375-1259, rmi_info@oma.be, http://www.meteo.oma.be.

551.5 BEL ISSN 0770-4615
INSTITUT ROYAL METEOROLOGIQUE DE BELGIQUE. PUBLICATIONS. SERIE B/KONINKLIJK METEOROLOGISCH INSTITUUT VAN BELGIE. PUBLICATIES. REEKS B. Text in English, French, Dutch. 1952. irreg. **Document type:** *Monographic series, Academic/Scholarly.*
Indexed: Inspec.
—Linda Hall.
Published by: Institut Royal Meteorologique de Belgique/Koninklijk Meteorologisch Instituut van Belgie, Av Circulaire 3, Brussels, 1180, Belgium. TEL 32-2-373-0508, FAX 32-2-373-0528, rmi_info@oma.be, http://www.meteo.oma.be.

INSTITUTO MEDICO SUCRE. REVISTA. *see* SCIENCES: COMPREHENSIVE WORKS

551.46 551.5 POL ISSN 0208-4325
INSTYTUT METEOROLOGII I GOSPODARKI WODNEJ. GAZETA OBSERWATORA/JOURNAL OF I M W M OBSERVER. Key Title: Gazeta Obserwatora I M G W. Text in Polish. 1948. 6/yr. USD 36 (effective 2002). bk.rev. charts; illus. cum.index. **Document type:** *Journal, Academic/Scholarly.* **Description:** Articles on meteorology, hydrology, oceanology, water management, hydrotechnics, water quality, methodic, measurements, instruments.
Formerly (until 1973): Gazeta Obserwatora P I H M (0208-4341)
Indexed: AgrLib.
Published by: Instytut Meteorologii i Gospodarki Wodnej/Institute of Meteorology and Water Management, Ul Podlesna 61, Warsaw, 01673, Poland. TEL 48-22-8341651, FAX 48-22-8345466, bointe@imgw.pl. Ed. Stanislaw Salamonik. Pub. Jan Zielinski. R&P Maria Storozynska. Circ: 1,300.

551.5 POL ISSN 0239-6262
QC989.P7 CODEN: MBSMEX
INSTYTUT METEOROLOGII I GOSPODARKI WODNEJ. MATERIALY BADAWCZE. SERIA: METEOROLOGIA/INSTITUTE OF METEOROLOGY AND WATER MANAGEMENT. RESEARCH PAPERS. SERIES: METEOROLOGY. Text in Polish; Summaries in English. 1974. irreg. USD 15 (effective 2002). abstr.; charts; illus. **Document type:** *Monographic series.* **Description:** Articles on meteorology, meteorological elements, observational data, forecastings, measurements, instruments, research works.
Indexed: AgrLib, GeoRef.
Published by: Instytut Meteorologii i Gospodarki Wodnej/Institute of Meteorology and Water Management, Ul Podlesna 61, Warsaw, 01673, Poland. TEL 48-22-8341651, FAX 48-22-8345466, bointe@imgw.pl, Krystyna_Storozynska@imgw.pl. Pub. Jan Zielinski. Adv. contact Maria Storozynska. Circ: 200.

551.5 POL ISSN 0208-6263
CODEN: WIMWDL
INSTYTUT METEOROLOGII I GOSPODARKI WODNEJ. WIADOMOSCI/INSTITUTE OF METEOROLOGY AND WATER MANAGEMENT. REPORTS. Cover title: Wiadomosci Instytutu Meteorologii i Gospodarki Wodnej. Text in Polish; Summaries in English. 1947. q. USD 15 (effective 2002). adv. abstr.; bibl.; charts; illus.; stat. cum.index. **Description:** Articles on meteorology, hydrology, oceanology, water management, water quality, forecastings, methodics measurements.
Former titles (until 1978): Wiadomosci Meteorologii i Gospodarki Wodnej (0137-2653); (until 1974): Wiadomosci Sluzby Hydrologicznej i Meteorologicznej (0043-5171)
Indexed: AgrLib, ESPM, GeoRef, M&GPA, SWRA, SpeleolAb.
—CASDDS, INIST.
Published by: Instytut Meteorologii i Gospodarki Wodnej/Institute of Meteorology and Water Management, Ul Podlesna 61, Warsaw, 01673, Poland. TEL 48-22-8341651, FAX 48-22-8345466, TELEX 814331, bointe@imgw.pl. Ed. Wlodzimierz Meyer. Pub. Jan Zielinski. R&P, Adv. contact Maria Storozynska. Circ: 250.

551.5 CAN ISSN 0074-1663
INTERNATIONAL ASSOCIATION OF METEOROLOGY AND ATMOSPHERIC PHYSICS. REPORT OF PROCEEDINGS OF GENERAL ASSEMBLY. Text in English. 1924. biennial. USD 20. **Document type:** *Proceedings.*
Published by: International Association of Meteorology and Atmospheric Physics, c/o Prof Roland List, Department of Physics, University of Toronto, Toronto, ON M5S 1A7, Canada. TEL 416-978-2982, FAX 416-978-8905. Circ: (controlled).

551.576 CAN ISSN 0074-3011
INTERNATIONAL CONFERENCE ON CLOUD PHYSICS. PROCEEDINGS. (Proceedings published in host countries) Text in English. 1968. irreg., latest 1982, 8th, Aubiere, France. CAD 20. adv. **Document type:** *Proceedings.*
Published by: (International Association of Meteorology and Atmospheric Physics), International Commission on Cloud Physics, c/o Prof R List, University of Toronto, Toronto, ON M5S 1A6, Canada. Circ: 1,500.

551.5 570 DEU ISSN 0020-7128
QH543 CODEN: IJBMAO
➤ **INTERNATIONAL JOURNAL OF BIOMETEOROLOGY;** the description, causes, and implications of climatic change. Text in English. 1957. bi-m. EUR 868, USD 1,048 combined subscription to institutions (print & online eds.) (effective 2012). adv. abstr.; bibl.; charts; illus. index. reprint service avail. from PSC. **Document type:** *Journal, Academic/Scholarly.* **Description:** Covers research in plant, animal, human and general biometeorology in the areas of plant-weather interaction, ecological modeling, animal-weather interaction, and the effects of electric, magnetic and electromagnetic fields on biological functions.
Related titles: Online - full text ed.: ISSN 1432-1254 (from IngentaConnect).
Indexed: A01, A03, A08, A22, A26, A29, A34, A35, A36, A37, A38, ASCA, ASFA, AgBio, Agr, AgrForAb, B20, B21, B25, B27, BIOSIS Prev, C25, C30, CA, CABA, ChemAb, CurCont, D01, E01, E12, EMBASE, ESPM, ExcerpMed, F08, F11, F12, FCA, FR, G11, GH, GeoRef, H16, I05, I10, I11, IBR, IBZ, ISR, IndMed, IndVet, LT, M&GPA, MEDLINE, MaizeAb, MycolAb, N02, N03, N04, O01, P20, P22, P26, P30, P32, P33, P37, P39, P40, P47, P48, P52, P54, P56, PGegResA, PQC, PollutAb, R07, R08, R11, R13, RM&VM, RRTA, RefZh, S13, S16, S17, SCI, SCOPUS, SSciA, SWRA, SoyAb, SpeleolAb, T02, T05, TAR, TriticAb, VITIS, VS, VirolAbstr, W07, W08, W10, WildRev, Z01.
—BLDSC (4542.154000), CASDDS, GNLM, IE, Infotrieve, Ingenta, INIST, Linda Hall. **CCC.**
Published by: (International Society of Biometeorology), Springer (Subsidiary of: Springer Science+Business Media), Tiergartenstr 17, Heidelberg, 69121, Germany. TEL 49-6221-4870, FAX 49-6221-345229. Ed. Scott C Sheridan. Circ: 1,300. **Subscr. in the Americas to:** Springer New York LLC, Journal Fulfillment, PO Box 2485, Secaucus, NJ 07096. TEL 800-777-4643, 201-348-4033, FAX 201-348-4505, journals-ny@springer.com, http://www.springer.com; **Subscr. to:** Springer Distribution Center, Kundenservice Zeitschriften, Haberstr 7, Heidelberg 69126, Germany. TEL 49-6221-3454303, FAX 49-6221-3454229, subscriptions@springer.com.

▼➤ **THE INTERNATIONAL JOURNAL OF CLIMATE CHANGE: IMPACTS AND RESPONSES.** *see* ENVIRONMENTAL STUDIES

551.5 333.714 GBR ISSN 1756-8692
▼➤ **INTERNATIONAL JOURNAL OF CLIMATE CHANGE STRATEGIES AND MANAGEMENT.** Abbreviated title: I J C C S M. Text in English. 2009. 4/yr. EUR 339 combined subscription in Europe (print & online eds.); USD 439 combined subscription in the Americas (print & online eds.); GBP 229 combined subscription in the UK & elsewhere (print & online eds.); AUD 599 combined subscription in Australasia (print & online eds.) (effective 2012). back issues avail.; reprint service avail. from PSC. **Document type:** *Journal, Academic/Scholarly.* **Description:** Addresses the need for disseminating scholarly research, projects and other initiatives, such as new policies, strategies or action plans, which may lead to a better understanding of the subject matter of climate change.
Related titles: Online - full text ed.: ISSN 1756-8706.
Indexed: CurCont, ESPM, GEOBASE, P48, P51, P52, P53, P54, P56, PQC, SSCI, W07.
—CCC.
Published by: Emerald Group Publishing Ltd., Howard House, Wagon Ln, Bingley, W Yorks BD16 1WA, United Kingdom. TEL 44-1274-777700, FAX 44-1274-785201, information@emeraldinsight.com, http://www.emeraldinsight.com. Ed. Walter Leal Filho TEL 49-40-76618056. Pub. Nicola Codner.

551.5 GBR ISSN 0899-8418
QC980 CODEN: IJCLEU
➤ **INTERNATIONAL JOURNAL OF CLIMATOLOGY.** Text in English. 1981. 15/yr. GBP 1,822 in United Kingdom to institutions; EUR 2,302 in Europe to institutions; USD 3,568 elsewhere to institutions; GBP 2,095 combined subscription in United Kingdom to institutions (print & online eds.); EUR 2,647 combined subscription in Europe to institutions (print & online eds.); USD 4,104 combined subscription elsewhere to institutions (print & online eds.) (effective 2012). bk.rev. charts; illus.; maps. index. back issues avail.; reprint service avail. from PSC. **Document type:** *Journal, Academic/Scholarly.* **Description:** Spans the field of climatology, encompassing regional and global studies, local and microclimatological investigations, changes in climate, and applications.
Formerly (until 1989): Journal of Climatology (0196-1748)
Related titles: Microform ed.: (from PQC); Online - full text ed.: ISSN 1097-0088. GBP 1,822 in United Kingdom to institutions; EUR 2,302 in Europe to institutions; USD 3,568 elsewhere to institutions (effective 2012).
Indexed: A20, A22, A33, A34, A36, A37, A38, APD, ASCA, ASFA, AgrForAb, C25, C30, CA, CABA, CIS, CPEI, CurCont, E04, E05, E12, ESPM, EnerRev, EngInd, EnvAb, F08, F12, FCA, FR, G11, GEOBASE, GH, GeoRef, H16, I11, IBR, IBZ, ISR, Inspec, LT, M&GPA, MaizeAb, N02, O01, OceAb, P32, P33, PGegResA, PollutAb, R08, R11, R12, R13, RRTA, RefZh, S12, S13, S16, SCI, SCOPUS, SSciA, SWRA, SoyAb, SpeleolAb, T02, T05, TAR, TriticAb, VS, W07, W11.
—AskIEEE, IE, Infotrieve, Ingenta, INIST, Linda Hall. **CCC.**
Published by: (Royal Meteorological Society), John Wiley & Sons Ltd. (Subsidiary of: John Wiley & Sons, Inc.), 1-7 Oldlands Way, PO Box 808, Bognor Regis, West Sussex PO21 9FF, United Kingdom. TEL 44-1865-778315, FAX 44-1243-843232, cs-journals@wiley.com, http://eu.wiley.com/WileyCDA/. Ed. G R McGregor. **Subscr. in the Americas to:** John Wiley & Sons, Inc., 111 River St, Hoboken, NJ 07030. TEL 201-748-6645, subinfo@wiley.com; **Subscr. to:** 1-7 Oldlands Way, PO Box 809, Bognor Regis, West Sussex PO21 9FG, United Kingdom. TEL 44-1865-778054, cs-agency@wiley.com.

551.5 GBR ISSN 1758-2083
QC981.8.G56
▼➤ **INTERNATIONAL JOURNAL OF GLOBAL WARMING.** Text in English. 2009. 4/yr. EUR 494 to institutions (print or online ed.); EUR 672 combined subscription to institutions (print & online eds.) (effective 2012). bk.rev. abstr.; bibl.; stat.; charts; illus. **Document type:** *Journal, Academic/Scholarly.* **Description:** Seeks to unite all disciplines involved in the understanding of and response to global warming and its impacts through solutions.
Related titles: Online - full text ed.: ISSN 1758-2091 (from IngentaConnect).
Indexed: A26, E08, ESPM, SCI, SSciA, W07.
—IE. **CCC.**
Published by: Inderscience Publishers, PO Box 735, Olney, Bucks MK46 5WB, United Kingdom. TEL 44-1234-240519, FAX 44-1234-240515, editorial@inderscience.com. Ed. Dr. Ibrahim Dincer. **Subscr. to:** World Trade Centre Bldg, 29 Rte de Pre-Bois, Case Postale 856, Geneva 15 1215, Switzerland. FAX 41-22-7910885, subs@inderscience.com.

551.5 GBR ISSN 1748-2992
QC851
➤ **THE INTERNATIONAL JOURNAL OF METEOROLOGY.** Abbreviated title: I J Met. Text in English. 1975. 10/yr. GBP 40, EUR 68, USD 92 to individuals; GBP 100 domestic to institutions; GBP 111 in Europe to institutions; GBP 121 elsewhere to institutions (effective 2010). adv. bk.rev. illus.; abstr.; tr.lit. index. 40 p./no.; back issues avail.; reprints avail. **Document type:** *Journal, Academic/Scholarly.* **Description:** Aims to document the research TORRO carried out on British tornadoes and other severe weather.
Formerly (until Sep.2005): Journal of Meteorology (0307-5966)
Related titles: Online - full text ed.
Indexed: A22, ASFA, CABA, E12, GEOBASE, I11, Inspec, M&GPA, RefZh, S13, S16, SCOPUS, TAR.
—BLDSC (4542.352250), IE, Infotrieve, Ingenta, Linda Hall.
Published by: (Tornado & Storm Research Organisation), Artetech Publishing Co., Thelwall, PO Box 972, Warrington, WA4 9DP, United Kingdom. TEL 44-7813-075509, FAX 44-870-7061858. Ed. Samantha J A Hall. adv.: B&W page GBP 200, color page GBP 400; 130 x 180.

▼➤ **INTERNATIONAL JOURNAL OF OCEAN AND CLIMATE SYSTEMS.** *see* EARTH SCIENCES—Oceanography

551.46 GBR ISSN 1029-1725
INTERNATIONAL W O C E NEWSLETTER. (World Ocean Circulation Experiment) Text in English. 1985. q. free (effective 2009). adv. back issues avail. **Document type:** *Newsletter, Trade.* **Description:** Reports the results concerned with project management and with observations, theory, and models of the ocean.
Formerly (until 1995): World Ocean Circulation Experiment. Newsletter (1357-6984)
Related titles: Online - full text ed.: ISSN 1564-8060.
Indexed: GeoRef.
Published by: World Ocean Circulation Experiment International Project Office, Southampton Oceanography Centre, Empress Dock, Southampton, Hants SO14 3ZH, United Kingdom. TEL 44-23-80596666, woceipo@soc.soton.ac.uk, http://www.noc.soton.ac.uk/OTHERS/woceipo/.

550 JPN ISSN 0389-8237
QC973.4.I6
IONOSPHERIC DATA AT SHOWA STATION (ANTARCTICA). Text in Japanese. a. stat. **Document type:** *Academic/Scholarly.*
Published by: National Institute of Information and Communications Technology/Jouhou Tsuushin Kenkyuu Kikou, 4-2-1 Nukui-Kitamachi, Koganei, Tokyo 184-8795, Japan. TEL 81-42-3277516, http://www.nict.go.jp.

551.514 JPN ISSN 0021-0382
QC803.J3
IONOSPHERIC DATA IN JAPAN/DENRISO GEPPO. Text in English. 1950. m. free. charts; stat. **Document type:** *Government.*
Published by: National Institute of Information and Communications Technology/Jouhou Tsuushin Kenkyuu Kikou, 4-2-1 Nukui-Kitamachi, Koganei, Tokyo 184-8795, Japan. TEL 81-42-3277516, http://www.nict.go.jp. Circ: 250.

551.5 ISR ISSN 0026-1122
➤ **ISRAEL METEOROLOGICAL SOCIETY/METEOROLOGIA B'YISRA'EL.** Text in Hebrew. 1963. irreg. USD 10 (effective 2001). bk.rev. charts; illus. **Document type:** *Monographic series, Academic/Scholarly.* **Description:** Papers on meteorology, climatology, and their applications.
Indexed: IHP, M&GPA.
Address: P O Box 25, Bet-dagan, Israel. TEL 972-3-9682165, FAX 972-3-9682126, http://ims.huji.ac.il/Main_eng.htm. Ed. Dr. Baruch Ziv. Circ: 300.

551.51 ITA ISSN 0075-1936
ISTITUTO DI FISICA DELL'ATMOSFERA, ROME. PUBBLICAZIONI SCIENTIFICHE. Text in English, Italian. 1962. irreg. price varies. **Document type:** *Monographic series.*
Published by: Consiglio Nazionale delle Ricerche, Istituto di Scienze dell'Atmosfera e del Clima, Via Piero Gobetti 101, Bologna, 40129, Italy. TEL 39-051-6399619, FAX 39-051-6399658, direttore@isac.cnr.it, http://www.isac.cnr.it. Ed. Alberto Mugnai. R&P Franco Vivona TEL 39-6-59293027.

551.5 630 551.4 ITA
➤ **ITALIAN JOURNAL OF AGROMETEOROLOGY.** Text in Italian, English. 1996. 3/yr. free to members (effective 2011). **Document type:** *Journal, Academic/Scholarly.* **Description:** Focuses on the interactions between meteorological, hydrological factors and the agro-forest ecosystem, agriculture and related themes.
Former titles (until 2009): Rivista Italiana di Agrometereologia (1824-8705); (until 2003): A I A M News (2038-5811)
Indexed: AgrForAb, C25, C30, CABA, E12, F08, FCA, H16, MaizeAb, S13, SCOPUS, W10.
Published by: (Associazione Italiana di Agrometereologia), Patron Editore, Via Badini 12, Quarto Inferiore, BO 40050, Italy. TEL 39-051-767003, FAX 39-051-768252, info@patroneditore.com, http://www.patroneditore.com.

551 JPN ISSN 0916-5355
IWATEKEN KISHO GEPPO/IWATE PREFECTURE. MONTHLY REPORT OF METEOROLOGY. Text in Japanese. 1951. m.
Published by: Kishocho, Morioka Chiho Kishodai/Japan Meteorological Agency, Morioka Local Meteorological Observatory, 7-60 Sanno-cho, Morioka-shi, Iwate-ken 020-0821, Japan.

551.5 HRV ISSN 1331-2979
JADRANSKA METEOROLOGIJA/ADRIATIC METEOROLOGY. Text in Croatian. 1955. a.
Former titles (until 1991): Pomorski Meteoroloski Centar Split. Vijesti (0353-264X); (until 1987): Pomorska Meteoroloska Sluzba. Vijesti (0506-9998)
Indexed: ASFA, B21, ESPM, M&GPA.
Published by: Pomorski Meteoroloski Centar Split, Drzavni Hidrometeorolozki Zavod Zagreb, Glagoljaska 11, Split, 21000, Croatia. TEL 385-21-589378, FAX 385-21-591033, hodzic@cirus.dhz.hr, http://www.dalmatianet.com/cmms.

551.5 SAU ISSN 1319-1039
JAME'AT AL-MALIK 'ABDUL 'AZIZ. MAJALA. 'U'LUM AL-ARSAD WA-AL-BI'AT/KING ABDULAZIZ UNIVERSITY. JOURNAL. METEOROLOGY, ENVIRONMENT, AND ARID LAND AGRICULTURE. Text in Arabic, English. 1990. a. **Document type:** *Journal, Academic/Scholarly.*

M

Related titles: Online - full text ed.: ISSN 1658-4287. free (effective 2011).
Indexed: A01, ESPM, M&GPA, PollutAb, SSciA.
Published by: King Abdulaziz University, Scientific Publishing Center/Markaz al-Nashr al-'Ilmi Jami'at al-Malik 'Abd al-'Aziz, PO Box 80200, Jeddah21589, Saudi Arabia. TEL 966-26452017, publisher@kau.edu.sa, http://spc.kau.edu.sa/content.aspx?Site_ID=320&lng=EN&cid=2732&URL=www.kau.edu.sa.

551.65 JPN ISSN 0448-3758
JAPAN METEOROLOGICAL AGENCY. ANNUAL REPORT/KISHOCHO NENPO ZENKOKU KISHOHYO. Text in English, Japanese. 1887. a. (in 2 vols.). JPY 2,163. **Document type:** *Government.*
Indexed: M&GPA.
Published by: Kishocho/Japan Meteorological Agency, 1-3-4 Otemachi, Chiyoda-ku, Tokyo, 100-8122, Japan. Circ: 724.

551.6 JPN ISSN 0075-3467
JAPANESE PROGRESS IN CLIMATOLOGY/NIPPON NO KIKOGAKU NO SHINPO. Text in English. 1964. a., latest 2000, Dec. USD 20 (effective 2001); also available on exchange. **Document type:** *Journal, Academic/Scholarly.*
Indexed: M&GPA, SpeleolAb.
Published by: Japanese Climatological Seminar/Kikogaku Danwakai, Hosei Daigaku Bungakubu Chirigaku Kyoshitsu, 17-1 Fujimi 2-chome, Chiyoda-ku, Tokyo, 102-8160, Japan. TEL 81-3-3264-9457, norihito@i.hosei.ac.jp. Ed. Norihito Satou. Circ: 1,050 (controlled).

551.6 USA ISSN 1942-2466
▼ ➤ JOURNAL OF ADVANCES IN MODELING EARTH SYSTEMS. Abbreviated title: J A M E S. Text in English. 2009. irreg. free (effective 2011). **Document type:** *Journal, Academic/Scholarly.* **Description:** Publishes research related to a wide range of problems in climate science.
Media: Online - full text.
Indexed: M&GPA.
Published by: Colorado State University, Department of Atmospheric Science, 200 W Lake St, Fort Collins, CO 80523. TEL 970-491-8682, FAX 970-491-8449, info@atmos.colostate.edu, http://www.atmos.colostate.edu. Ed. David Randall.

➤ JOURNAL OF AGROMETEOROLOGY. *see* AGRICULTURE

551.5 USA ISSN 1558-8424
QC851 CODEN: JOAMEZ
➤ JOURNAL OF APPLIED METEOROLOGY AND CLIMATOLOGY. Text in English. 1962. m. USD 1,075 combined subscription domestic to non-members (print & online eds.); USD 1,145 combined subscription foreign to non-members (print & online eds.) (effective 2011). adv. abstr.; bibl.; charts; illus.; stat. index. back issues avail.; reprints avail. **Document type:** *Journal, Academic/Scholarly.* **Description:** Focuses on applied research pertinent to physical meteorology, weather modification, cloud physics, satellite meteorology and air pollution.
Formerly (until Jan.2006): Journal of Applied Meteorology (0894-8763); Which supersedes in part (in 1988): Journal of Climate and Applied Meteorology (0733-3021); Which was formerly (1962-1983): Journal of Applied Meteorology (0021-8952)
Related titles: Online - full text ed.: ISSN 1558-8432. USD 540 to non-members (effective 2011).
Indexed: A01, A02, A03, A05, A08, A22, A23, A24, A26, A28, APA, APD, AS&TA, AS&TI, ASCA, ASFA, ApMecR, B04, B13, BRD, BiolDig, BrCerAb, C&ISA, C10, CA, CA/WCA, CIA, CPEI, CerAb, ChemAb, CivEngAb, CorrAb, CurCont, E&CAJ, E01, E04, E05, E08, E11, EEA, EMA, ESPM, EngInd, EnvEAb, FR, G01, G08, GEOBASE, GeoRef, H15, I05, INIS AtomInd, ISR, Inspec, M&GPA, M&TEA, M09, MBF, METADEX, OceAb, P02, P10, P26, P47, P48, P52, P53, P54, P56, PQC, PollutAb, RefZh, S01, S04, S09, S10, SCI, SCOPUS, SPPI, SWRA, SolStAb, SpeleolAb, T02, T04, W03, W05, W07, WAA.
—BLDSC (4943.065000), AskIEEE, CASDDS, IE, Infotrieve, Ingenta, INIST, Linda Hall. **CCC.**
Published by: American Meteorological Society, 45 Beacon St, Boston, MA 02108. TEL 617-227-2425, FAX 617-742-8718, amspubs@ametsoc.org. Ed. Robert M Rauber TEL 217-333-2046. **Subscr. to:** Allen Press Inc., PO Box 1897, Lawrence, KS 66044. TEL 785-843-1235, FAX 785-843-1274, orders@allenpress.com, http://www.allenpress.com.

▼ ➤ JOURNAL OF ARID LAND. *see* EARTH SCIENCES—Geology

551.5 USA ISSN 0739-0572
➤ JOURNAL OF ATMOSPHERIC AND OCEANIC TECHNOLOGY. Text in English. 1984. m. USD 530 combined subscription domestic to non-members (print & online eds.); USD 605 combined subscription foreign to non-members (print & online eds.); USD 398 combined subscription domestic to non-members (print & online eds.); USD 463 combined subscription foreign to non-members (print & online eds.) (effective 2009). adv. abstr.; bibl.; charts; illus.; stat. index. back issues avail.; reprints avail. **Document type:** *Journal, Academic/Scholarly.* **Description:** Presents information related to the state-of-the-art development of technical support to the atmospheric and oceanic science.
Related titles: Online - full text ed.: ISSN 1520-0426. USD 420 to non-members; USD 315 to members (effective 2009).
Indexed: A01, A03, A05, A08, A22, A28, A37, APA, AS&TA, AS&TI, ASCA, ASFA, BRD, BrCerAb, C&ISA, C10, C25, CA, CA/WCA, CABA, CIA, CPEI, CerAb, ChemAb, CivEngAb, CorrAb, CurCont, E&CAJ, E01, E04, E05, E11, E12, EEA, EMA, ESPM, EngInd, EnvEAb, F08, F12, FLUIDEX, G11, GEOBASE, GH, H15, I11, INIS AtomInd, ISR, Inspec, M&GPA, M&TEA, M09, MBF, METADEX, OceAb, P10, P26, P47, P48, P52, P53, P54, P56, PQC, S01, S04, S10, S13, S16, SCI, SCOPUS, SWRA, SolStAb, T02, T04, TAR, W03, W05, W07, WAA.
—BLDSC (4947.900000), AskIEEE, IE, Infotrieve, Ingenta, INIST, Linda Hall. **CCC.**
Published by: American Meteorological Society, 45 Beacon St, Boston, MA 02108. TEL 617-227-2425, FAX 617-742-8718, amspubs@ametsoc.org. Eds. Julie Haggerty, Scott M Glenn, V Chandrasekar. **Subscr. to:** Allen Press Inc., PO Box 1897, Lawrence, KS 66044. TEL 785-843-1235, FAX 785-843-1274.

➤ JOURNAL OF ATMOSPHERIC AND SOLAR - TERRESTRIAL PHYSICS. *see* EARTH SCIENCES—Geophysics

➤ JOURNAL OF ATMOSPHERIC CHEMISTRY. *see* CHEMISTRY

551 537 JPN
QC960.5 CODEN: RLAEEA
JOURNAL OF ATMOSPHERIC ELECTRICITY. Text in English, Japanese; Summaries in English. 1981. s-a. free to members (effective 2008). **Document type:** *Journal, Academic/Scholarly.*
Formerly (until 1993): Research Letters on Atmospheric Electricity (0286-6188)
Indexed: ChemAb, M&GPA.
—BLDSC (4949.070000), CASDDS.
Published by: Nihon Taiki Denki Gakkai/Society of Atmospheric Electricity of Japan, Osaka Daigaku Kogakubu Denkikogakka, 2-1 Yamada-Oka, Suita-shi, Osaka-fu 565-0871, Japan. TEL 81-6-68797690, FAX 81-6-68797774, saej_secretariat@commf5.comm.eng.osaka-u.ac.jp. Ed. Sigeru Nakae.

551.5 USA ISSN 0894-8755
QC851 CODEN: JLCLEL
➤ JOURNAL OF CLIMATE. Text in English. 1962. s-m. USD 950 combined subscription domestic to non-members (print & online eds.); USD 1,080 combined subscription foreign to non-members (print & online eds.); USD 713 combined subscription domestic to members (print & online eds.); USD 843 combined subscription foreign to members (print & online eds.) (effective 2009). adv. abstr.; bibl.; charts; illus.; stat. index. back issues avail.; reprints avail. **Document type:** *Journal, Academic/Scholarly.* **Description:** Provides articles on climate research and impact analysis.
Supersedes in part (in 1988): Journal of Climate and Applied Meteorology (0733-3021); Which was formerly (1962-1983): Journal of Applied Meteorology (0021-8952)
Related titles: Online - full text ed.: ISSN 1520-0442. USD 755 to non-members; USD 566 to members (effective 2009).
Indexed: A01, A02, A03, A08, A22, A33, A37, ASCA, ASFA, Agr, B04, B21, BRD, BiolDig, C25, C30, CA, CABA, CIS, CPEI, CurCont, E01, E04, E05, E12, ESPM, EngInd, F08, F12, FR, G02, G03, G11, GEOBASE, GH, GSA, GSI, GeoRef, I11, INIS AtomInd, ISR, Inspec, M&GPA, OceAb, P10, P11, P26, P30, P32, P47, P48, P52, P53, P54, P56, PGrRegA, PQC, PollutAb, R12, S01, S04, S10, S13, S16, SCI, SCOPUS, SSciA, SWRA, SpeleolAb, T02, T05, TAR, W03, W05, W07, W11.
—BLDSC (4958.369730), AskIEEE, CASDDS, IE, Infotrieve, Ingenta, INIST, Linda Hall. **CCC.**
Published by: American Meteorological Society, 45 Beacon St, Boston, MA 02108. TEL 617-227-2425, FAX 617-742-8718, amspubs@ametsoc.org. Ed. Andrew Weaver TEL 250-472-4005. **Subscr. to:** Allen Press Inc., PO Box 1897, Lawrence, KS 66044. http://www.allenpress.com/.

➤ JOURNAL OF GEOPHYSICAL RESEARCH. *see* EARTH SCIENCES—Geophysics

551.5 USA
JOURNAL OF GEOPHYSICAL RESEARCH: ATMOSPHERES. Text in English. 1896. s-m. USD 682 to institutional members; USD 8,285 to non-members; USD 864 combined subscription to institutional members (print & online eds.); USD 12,670 combined subscription to non-members (print & online eds.) (effective 2010). charts; illus.; bibl. back issues avail.; reprints avail. **Document type:** *Journal, Academic/Scholarly.* **Description:** Covers the physics and chemistry of the atmosphere, as well as the atmospheric, biospheric, lithospheric, and hydrospheric interface.
Related titles: Online - full text ed.: USD 227 to institutional members; USD 4,480 to non-members (effective 2010).
Indexed: CIN, ChemTitl, EnvAb, SPINweb, SpeleolAb.
Published by: American Geophysical Union, 2000 Florida Ave, NW, Washington, DC 20009. TEL 202-462-6900, FAX 202-328-0566. Eds. Joost de Gouw, Sara C Pryor.

JOURNAL OF HYDROMETEOROLOGY. *see* EARTH SCIENCES—Hydrology

551.56 NLD ISSN 1652-8034
➤ JOURNAL OF LIGHTNING RESEARCH. Text in English. 2006. 3/yr. free (effective 2011). **Document type:** *Journal, Academic/Scholarly.* **Description:** Covers all areas of lightning research.
Media: Online - full text.
Published by: (Uppsala Universitet, Aangstroemlaboratoriet SWE), Bentham Open (Subsidiary of: Bentham Science Publishers Ltd.), PO Box 294, Bussum, AG 1400, Netherlands. TEL 31-35-6923800, FAX 31-35-6980150, subscriptions@bentham.org. Ed. Vernan Cooray.

551.1 JPN ISSN 0368-5942
QC851
JOURNAL OF METEOROLOGICAL RESEARCH/KISHOCHO KENKYU JIHO. Text in Japanese; Summaries in English. 1891. bi-m.
Indexed: JPI, M&GPA, RefZh, SpeleolAb.
—Linda Hall.
Published by: Kishocho/Japan Meteorological Agency, 1-3-4 Otemachi, Chiyoda-ku, Tokyo, 100-8122, Japan. Circ: 879.

551.5 FRA ISSN 2115-7251
▼ JOURNAL OF SPACE WEATHER AND SPACE CLIMATE. Text in English. 2011. free (effective 2012). **Document type:** *Journal, Academic/Scholarly.*
Media: Online - full text.
Published by: E D P Sciences, 17 Ave du Hoggar, Parc d'Activites de Courtaboeuf, BP 112, Cedex A, Les Ulis, F-91944, France. TEL 33-1-69187575, FAX 33-1-69860678, subscribers@edpsciences.org, http://www.edpsciences.org.

551.5 USA ISSN 0022-4928
QC851 CODEN: JATSDF
➤ JOURNAL OF THE ATMOSPHERIC SCIENCES. Text in English. 1944. m. USD 1,500 combined subscription domestic to non-members (print & online eds.); USD 1,570 combined subscription foreign to non-members (print & online eds.) (effective 2011). adv. abstr.; bibl.; charts; illus.; stat. index. back issues avail.; reprints avail. **Document type:** *Journal, Academic/Scholarly.* **Description:** Focuses on basic research related to the physics and dynamics of the atmosphere of the Earth and other planets.
Formerly (until 1962): Journal of Meteorology (0095-9634)
Related titles: Online - full text ed.: ISSN 1520-0469. USD 755 to non-members (effective 2011).
Indexed: A01, A02, A03, A05, A08, A22, A23, A24, A26, A28, A33, APA, APD, AS&TA, AS&TI, ASCA, ASFA, ApMecR, B04, B13, BRD, BrCerAb, C&ISA, C10, CA, CA/WCA, CCMJ, CIA, CIS, CPEI, CerAb, ChemAb, CivEngAb, CorrAb, CurCont, E&CAJ, E01, E04, E05, E08, E11, EEA, EMA, ESPM, EngInd, EnvEAb, FLUIDEX, G01, G03, G08, GEOBASE, GSA, GSI, GeoRef, H15, I05, IBR, IBZ, INIS AtomInd, ISR, Inspec, M&GPA, M&TEA, M06, M09, MBF, METADEX, MSN, MathR, OceAb, P02, P10, P26, P47, P48, P52, P53, P54, P56, PQC, PollutAb, RefZh, S01, S04, S09, S10, SCI, SCOPUS, SPPI, SWRA, SolStAb, SpeleolAb, T02, T04, W03, W05, W07, WAA.
—BLDSC (4949.200000), AskIEEE, CASDDS, IE, Infotrieve, Ingenta, INIST, Linda Hall. **CCC.**
Published by: American Meteorological Society, 45 Beacon St, Boston, MA 02108. TEL 617-227-2425, FAX 617-742-8718, amspubs@ametsoc.org. Ed. Dr. Ka-Kit Tung TEL 206-685-3794. **Subscr. to:** Allen Press Inc., PO Box 1897, Lawrence, KS 66044. http://www.allenpress.com.

551.6 CHN ISSN 1006-8775
➤ JOURNAL OF TROPICAL METEOROLOGY. Text in English. 1995. s-a. USD 106 (effective 2004). 112 p./no.; back issues avail. **Document type:** *Journal, Academic/Scholarly.* **Description:** Covers the latest research achievements in tropical atmospheric science.
Related titles: CD-ROM ed.; Online - full content ed.; Online - full text ed.; ◆ Chinese ed.: Redai Qixiang Xuebao. ISSN 1004-4965.
Indexed: A01, ASFA, B21, ESPM, M&GPA, P52, P56, SCI, W07.
Published by: Guangzhou Redai Haiyang Qixiang Yanjiusuo/Guangzhou Institute of Tropical and Oceanic Meteorology, No 6, Fujin Rd, Dongshan District, Guangzhou, Guangdong 510080, China. TEL 86-20-87776918 ext 331, FAX 86-20-87673470. Ed. Shangsen Wu. Adv. contact Chaoxiong Cao. Circ: 200.

551.6 GBR ISSN 2040-2244
GB651
▼ ➤ JOURNAL OF WATER AND CLIMATE CHANGE. Variant title: Water and Climate. Text in English. 2010 (Jun.). q. EUR 527 combined subscription in Europe to institutions (print & online eds.); USD 623 combined subscription in North America to institutions (print & online eds.); GBP 421 combined subscription to institutions in the UK & elsewhere (print & online eds.) (effective 2011). back issues avail. **Document type:** *Journal, Academic/Scholarly.* **Description:** Covers all aspects of water science, technology, management and innovation in response to climate change.
Related titles: Online - full text ed.
Indexed: CABA, E12, GH, I11, R12, S13, S16, W11.
—IE. **CCC.**
Published by: I W A Publishing (Subsidiary of: International Water Association), Alliance House, 12 Caxton St, London, SW1H 0QS, United Kingdom. TEL 44-20-76545500, FAX 44-20-76545555, publications@iwap.co.uk, http://www.iwapublishing.com. **Subscr. to:** Portland Customer Services, Commerce Way, Colchester CO2 8HP, United Kingdom. TEL 44-1206-796351, FAX 44-1206-799331, sales@portland-services.com, http://www.portlandpress.com.

551.63 USA ISSN 0739-1781
QC926.6 CODEN: JWMOEL
JOURNAL OF WEATHER MODIFICATION. Text in English. 1969. a. USD 50 print or CD ed.; USD 60 print & CD eds. (effective 2004). adv. cum.index: 1969-1999. back issues avail. **Document type:** *Magazine, Trade.*
Indexed: GeoRef, Inspec, M&GPA.
—AskIEEE, Ingenta.
Published by: Weather Modification Association, PO Box 26926, Fresno, CA 93729-6926. TEL 559-434-3486, FAX 559-434-3486. Ed. James A Miller. Adv. contact Hilda Duckering. Circ: 500.

551 JPN ISSN 0916-5126
KAGAWAKEN KISHO GEPPO/KAGAWA PREFECTURE. MONTHLY REPORT OF METEOROLOGY. Text in Japanese. 1946. m.
Published by: Kishocho, Takamatsu Chiho Kishodai/Japan Meteorological Agency, Takamatsu Local Meteorological Observatory, 1277-1 Fuseishi-cho, Takamatsu-shi, Kagawa-ken 761-8071, Japan.

551.6 JPN
KAIJO KISHO GAIHO/MARINE METEOROLOGICAL REPORT. Text in Japanese. 1952. m.
Published by: Kishocho, Maizuru Kaiyo Kishodai/Japan Meteorological Agency, Maizuru Marine Observatory, 901 Shimo-Fukui, Maizuru-shi, Kyoto-Fu 624-0946, Japan.

551 JPN ISSN 0449-7392
KANAGAWAKEN KISHO GEPPO/KANAGAWA PREFECTURE. MONTHLY REPORT OF METEOROLOGY. Text in Japanese. 1950. m.
Published by: Kishocho, Yokohama Chiho Kishodai/Japan Meteorological Agency, Yokohama Local Meteorological Observatory, 99 Yamate-Machi, Naka-ku, Yokohama-shi, Kanagawa-ken 231-0862, Japan.

KANSAS. AGRICULTURAL STATISTICS SERVICE. CROP WEATHER. *see* AGRICULTURE—Abstracting, Bibliographies, Statistics

551.5 RUS
KATALOG RADIATSIONNYKH DANNYKH/CATALOGUE OF SOLAR RADIATION DATA. Text in Russian. 1987. a. USD 15 (effective 1994).
Published by: Glavnaya Geofizicheskaya Observatoriya im. A.I. Voeikova, Mirovoi Tsentr Radiatsionnykh Dannykh/Voeikov Main Geophysical Observatory, World Radiation Data Centre, Ul Karbysheva 7, St Petersburg, 194018, Russian Federation. TEL 812-247-01-03, FAX 812-247-86-61. Ed. E P Borisenkov.

551.5 JPN
KAZE NI KANSURU SHINPOJUMU KOEN YOSHISHU/PROCEEDINGS OF THE WIND SYMPOSIUM. Text in Japanese. a.
Published by: Jishin Gakkai/Seismological Society of Japan, Daigaku Jishin Kenkyujo, 1-1 Yayoi 1-chome, Bunkyo-ku, Tokyo, 113-0032, Japan.

551.63 NZL ISSN 1177-651X
KEN RING'S PREDICT WEATHER ALMANAC AND ISOBARIC MAPS. Text in English. 1999. a. NZD 44.99 (effective 2009). **Document type:** *Handbook/Manual/Guide, Consumer.*
Published by: Random House New Zealand Ltd., Private Bag 102950, North Shore Mail Centre, Auckland, New Zealand. TEL 64-9-4447197, FAX 64-9-4447524, cs@randomhouse.co.nz, http://www.randomhouse.co.nz.

551.656 KEN
KENYA METEOROLOGICAL DEPARTMENT. ANNUAL REPORT. Text in English. 1929. a. **Document type:** *Government.*
Supersedes in part: East African Community. East African Meteorological Department. Annual Report
Published by: Meteorological Department, Dagoretti Corner Ngong Rd., PO Box 30259, Nairobi, Kenya. Circ: 1,200.

551.5 KEN ISSN 1995-9834
QC991.A353
KENYA METEOROLOGICAL SOCIETY. JOURNAL. Text in English. 2007. s-a. **Document type:** *Journal, Trade.*
Published by: Kenya Meteorological Society, PO Box 30259, Nairobi, 00100, Kenya. TEL 254-2-3867880, FAX 254-2-3876955, kms@meteo.go.ke, http://www.meteo.go.ke/kms.

551 JPN ISSN 0916-474X
KIKO EIKYO RIYO KENKYUKAI KAIHO/JAPANESE STUDY GROUP FOR THE W C I P AND W C A P NEWSLETTER. Text in Japanese. 1984. a. **Document type:** *Newsletter.*
Published by: Kiko Eikyo Riyo Kenkyukai/Japanese Study Group for the W C I P and W C A P, c/o Yoshino Kenkyushitsu, Tsukuba Daigaku Chikyu Kagakukei, 1-1 Tenno-Dai 1-chome, Tsukuba-shi, Ibaraki-ken 305-0006, Japan.

551.6 JPN ISSN 0916-166X
KIKOGAKU KISHOGAKU KENKYU HOKOKU/RESEARCH REPORT OF METEOROLOGY AND CLIMATOLOGY. Text in Japanese. a.?.
Published by: University of Tsukuba, Institute of Geoscience/Tsukuba Daigaku Chikyu Kagakukei, 1-1 Tenno-Dai 1-chome, Tsukuba-shi, Ibaraki-ken 305-0006, Japan.

551.636 JPN ISSN 0916-927X
QC994.95
KIKOKEI KANSHI HOKOKU/MONTHLY REPORT ON CLIMATE SYSTEM. Text in English, Japanese. 1960. m. JPY 13,390. stat.
Formerly (until 1987): Japan Meteorological Agency. Mean Maps. Long Range Weather Forecasting
Published by: (Yohobu), Kishocho/Japan Meteorological Agency, 1-3-4 Otemachi, Chiyoda-ku, Tokyo, 100-8122, Japan. Circ: 624.

551.6 JPN ISSN 0388-9653
KISHO EISEI SENTA GIJUTSU HOKOKU/METEOROLOGICAL SATELLITE CENTER TECHNICAL NOTE. Text in English, Japanese. 1980. s-a.
Published by: Kishocho, Kisho Eisei Senta/Japan Meteorological Agency, Meteorological Satellite Center, 3-235 Nakakiyo-To, Kiyose-shi, Tokyo-to 204-0012, Japan. TEL 81-3-42493-4990, FAX 81-3-42492-2433.

551 JPN ISSN 0287-9247
KISHO EISEI SENTA NYUSU/METEOROLOGICAL SATELLITE CENTER NEWS. Text in Japanese. 1983. q.
Published by: Kishocho, Kisho Eisei Senta/Japan Meteorological Agency, Meteorological Satellite Center, 3-235 Nakakiyo-To, Kiyose-shi, Tokyo-to 204-0012, Japan.

551 JPN
KISHO GYOMU HOKOKU CHOSA SHUKEISHO/ANNUAL REPORT OF METEOROLOGICAL SERVICE. Text in Japanese. a.
Published by: (Somubu), Kishocho/Japan Meteorological Agency, 1-3-4 Otemachi, Chiyoda-ku, Tokyo, 100-8122, Japan.

551 JPN
KISHO KANSOKUKYO TETTO KANSOKU SHIRYO/REPORT OF OBSERVATION AT THE METEOROLOGICAL OBSERVATION TOWER. Text in English, Japanese. 1982. triennial.
Published by: Kishocho, Kisho Kenkyujo/Japan Meteorological Agency, Meteorological Research Institute, 1-1 Nagamine, Tsukuba-shi, Ibaraki-ken 305-0052, Japan.

551 JPN ISSN 0386-4049
QC801
KISHO KENKYUJO GIJUTSU HOKOKU/METEOROLOGICAL RESEARCH INSTITUTE. TECHNICAL REPORTS. Text in Japanese; Summaries in English, Japanese. 1978. irreg.
Indexed: INIS AtomInd, JPI.
Published by: Kishocho, Kisho Kenkyujo/Japan Meteorological Agency, Meteorological Research Institute, 1-1 Nagamine, Tsukuba-shi, Ibaraki-ken 305-0052, Japan.

551 JPN
KISHO KENKYUJO NYUSU/METEOROLOGICAL RESEARCH INSTITUTE NEWS. Text in Japanese. 1965. m.
Published by: Kishocho, Kisho Kenkyujo/Japan Meteorological Agency, Meteorological Research Institute, 1-1 Nagamine, Tsukuba-shi, Ibaraki-ken 305-0052, Japan.

551 JPN
KISHO NENKAN/YEARBOOK OF METEOROLOGY. Text in Japanese. 1967. a. JPY 3,780 per issue (effective 2008). **Document type:** *Yearbook.*
Published by: Kishocho/Japan Meteorological Agency, 1-3-4 Otemachi, Chiyoda-ku, Tokyo, 100-8122, Japan. http://www.jma.go.jp/. **Subscr. to:** Japan Meteorological Business Support Center, 3-17, Kanda-Nishikicho, Chiyoda-ku, Tokyo 101-0054, Japan. TEL 81-3-52810440, FAX 81-3-52810443, http://www.jmbsc.or.jp/.

551.6 JPN ISSN 0917-494X
➤ **KISHO RIYO KENKYU/APPLIED CLIMATE RESOURCES RESEARCH.** Text in Japanese. 1988. a. free to members. adv. bk.rev. **Document type:** *Journal, Academic/Scholarly.* **Description:** Contains reports, opinions, lectures, interpretations and reviews on applied meteorology and climate resources.
Published by: Kisho Riyo Kenkyukai/Japanese Society of Applied Meteorology, Kyushu University, Applied Meteorology Laboratory, Hakozaki 6-10-1, Higashi-ku, Fukuoka-shi, 812-8581, Japan. TEL 81-92-6423095, FAX 81-92-6423095. Circ: 280.

551.65 JPN ISSN 0448-374X
KISHOCHO GEPPO ZENKOKU KISHOHYO/JAPAN METEOROLOGICAL AGENCY. MONTHLY REPORT. METEOROLOGICAL OBSERVATIONS. Text in Japanese, English. 1892. m. USD 227.
Published by: Kishocho/Japan Meteorological Agency, 1-3-4 Otemachi, Chiyoda-ku, Tokyo, 100-8122, Japan.

551 JPN
KISHOCHO KAIYO JUNPO/TEN-DAY MARINE REPORT. Text in English, Japanese. 1946. 3/m.
Published by: (Kaiyo Kishobu), Kishocho/Japan Meteorological Agency, 1-3-4 Otemachi, Chiyoda-ku, Tokyo, 100-8122, Japan.

551.5 JPN
KISHOCHO KANSOKU GIJUTSU SHIRYO/JAPAN METEOROLOGICAL AGENCY. TECHNICAL DATA SERIES. Text in English, Japanese. 1956. a. JPY 2,000.
Published by: Kishocho/Japan Meteorological Agency, 1-3-4 Otemachi, Chiyoda-ku, Tokyo, 100-8122, Japan. Circ: 461.

551 JPN
KISHOCHO KISHO KENKYUJO KENKYU HOKOKUSHO/METEOROLOGICAL RESEARCH INSTITUTE. ANNUAL RESEARCH REPORT. Text in Japanese. 1966. a.
Published by: Kishocho, Kisho Kenkyujo/Japan Meteorological Agency, Meteorological Research Institute, 1-1 Nagamine, Tsukuba-shi, Ibaraki-ken 305-0052, Japan.

551.5 JPN ISSN 0387-5369
QC851 CODEN: KNOTDR
KISHOU KENKYU NOTO/METEOROLOGICAL STUDY NOTE. Text in Japanese. irreg., latest vol.175. price varies.
—CASDDS, Linda Hall. **CCC.**
Published by: Meteorological Society of Japan/Nihon Kisho Gakkai, c/o Japan Meteorological Agency, 3-4 Ote-Machi 1-chome, Chiyoda-ku, Tokyo, 100-0004, Japan. TEL 03-3212-8341, FAX 03-3216-4401.

551.6 333.79 NOR ISSN 1504-8136
KLIMA; norsk magasin for klimaforskning. Text in Norwegian. 1992. bi-m. free (effective 2005). back issues avail. **Document type:** *Journal, Academic/Scholarly.* **Description:** Reports on new developments in climate and environmental research, the political arena, and CICERO. The journal also carries reports from important international meetings and conferences.
Formerly (until 2007): Cicerone (0804-0508)
Related titles: Online - full text ed.: ISSN 1504-8594.
Indexed: INIS AtomInd.
Published by: C I C E R O Senter for Klimaforskning/Center for International Climate and Environmental Research, PO Box 1129, Blindern, Oslo, 0318, Norway. TEL 47-22-858750, FAX 47-22-858751, admin@cicero.uio.no. Ed. Tove Kolset.

551.6 NLD ISSN 1878-4984
KLIMAAT. Text in Dutch. 2007. q. EUR 8 (effective 2011). **Document type:** *Magazine, Consumer.*
Published by: Vereniging Klimaat, Postbus 427, Kampen, 8260 AK, Netherlands. http://www.verenigingklimaat.nl. Ed. Dr. J G van der Land.

551.5 RUS
KLIMAT I GIDROGRAFIYA ZABAIKAL'YA. Text in Russian. 1972. irreg. illus.
Indexed: RASB.
Published by: Geograficheskoe Obshchestvo S.S.S.R., Zabaikal'skii Filial, Chita, Russian Federation.

551.6 SWE ISSN 1654-2258
▼ **KLIMATOLOGI.** Text in Swedish. 2009. irreg., latest vol.2, 2010. **Document type:** *Monographic series, Academic/Scholarly.*
Published by: Sveriges Meteorologiska och Hydrologiska Institut/ Swedish Meteorological and Hydrological Institute, Folkborgvaegen 1, Norrkoeping, 60176, Sweden. TEL 46-11-4958000, FAX 46-11-4958001, smhi@smhi.se, http://www.smhi.se.

KOBE KAIYO KISHODAI. IHO/KOBE MARINE OBSERVATORY. BULLETIN. *see* EARTH SCIENCES—Oceanography

551 JPN
KOCHIKEN KISHO GEPPO/KOCHI PREFECTURE. MONTHLY REPORT OF METEOROLOGY. Text in Japanese. 1904. m.
Published by: Kishocho, Kochi Chiho Kishodai/Japan Meteorological Agency, Kochi Local Meteorological Observatory, 3-41 Hon-Machi 4-chome, Kochi-shi, 780-0870, Japan.

551 JPN
KOKUSETSU RISETSU GIJUTSU KENKYU/STUDY ON CONQUEST AND UTILIZATION OF SNOW. Text in Japanese. 1986. a. JPY 8,000.
Published by: Nihon Shisutemu Kaihatsu Kenkyujo/Systems Research and Development Institute of Japan, 16-5 Tomihisa-cho, Shinjuku-ku, Tokyo, 162-0067, Japan.

551.6 630 JPN
KONGETSU NO TENKO TO NORIN SAGYO/MONTHLY NEWS OF WEATHER, AGRICULTURE AND FORESTRY. Text in Japanese. 1967. m.
Published by: Kishocho, Matsue Chiho Kishodai/Japan Meteorological Agency, Matsue Local Meteorological Observatory, 1-11 Nishi-Tsuda 7-chome, Matsue-shi, Shimane-ken 690-0017, Japan.

551.5 NLD ISSN 0169-1708
KONINKLIJK NEDERLANDS METEOROLOGISCH INSTITUUT. TECHNISCHE RAPPORTEN/KONINKLIJK NEDERLANDS METEOROLOGISCH INSTITUUT. TECHNICAL REPORTS. Text in Dutch. 1980. irreg. **Document type:** *Monographic series.*
Indexed: ASFA, GeoRef, M&GPA.
—BLDSC (8753.180000).
Published by: Koninklijk Nederlands Meteorologisch Instituut, Wilhelminalaan 10, PO Box 201, De Bilt, 3730 AE, Netherlands. TEL 31-30-2206911, FAX 31-30-2210407, http://www.knmi.nl/.

551.5 NLD ISSN 0169-1651
KONINKLIJK NEDERLANDS METEOROLOGISCH INSTITUUT. WETENSCHAPPELIJKE RAPPORTEN. Text in Dutch. 1962. irreg.
Indexed: ASFA, M&GPA.
—BLDSC (8198.395000).
Published by: Koninklijk Nederlands Meteorologisch Instituut, Wilhelminalaan 10, PO Box 201, De Bilt, 3730 AE, Netherlands. TEL 31-30-2206911, FAX 31-30-2210407, http://www.knmi.nl/.

551 JPN ISSN 0373-5842
QC851
KOSO KISHODAI IHO/AEROLOGICAL OBSERVATORY AT TATENO. JOURNAL. Text in Japanese; Summaries in English, Japanese. 1923. a.
Indexed: JPI, M&GPA.
Published by: Kishocho, Koso Kishodai/Japan Meteorological Agency, Aerological Observatory, 1-2 Nagamine, Tsukuba-shi, Ibaraki-ken 305-0052, Japan.

551.5 JPN
KUMAMOTO PREFECTURE. MONTHLY REPORT. Text in Japanese. 1953. m.
Published by: Kumamoto Prefecture, 12-20, Kyo-machi 2-chome, Kumamoto, 860, Japan. Circ: 100.

551 JPN ISSN 0916-5169
KYOTOFU KISHO GEPPO/KYOTO PREFECTURE. MONTHLY REPORT OF METEOROLOGY. Text in Japanese. 1951. m.
Published by: Kishocho, Kyoto Chiho Kishodai/Japan Meteorological Agency, Kyoto Local Meteorological Observatory, 38 Nishinokyo-Kasadono-cho, Nakagyo-ku, Kyoto-shi, 604-8482, Japan.

551.5 USA ISSN 1948-2582
L E A R N (BOULDER); atmospheric science explorers. (Laboratory Experience in Atmospheric Research) Text and summaries in English. 1991. irreg. **Document type:** *Newsletter, Consumer.* **Description:** Designed for science teacher professional development.
Formerly (until 1998): Project Learn Update (1948-2574)
Published by: National Center for Atmospheric Research, PO Box 3000, Boulder, CO 80307. TEL 303-497-1000, http://www.ncar.ucar.edu.

551.5 USA ISSN 0198-4683
LOCAL CLIMATOLOGICAL DATA. ABERDEEN, SOUTH DAKOTA. ANNUAL SUMMARY WITH COMPARATIVE DATA. Text in English. 19??. a. USD 39 combined subscription per issue includes 12 monthly summaries & one a. summary (effective 2009); free to qualified government agencies. stat. back issues avail. **Document type:** *Government.* **Description:** Presents the monthly and annual average, resultant and fastest mile wind speed for the current year as well as the monthly and annual mean and fastest mile speed for a long period for Aberdeen, South Dakota.
Related titles: Online - full text ed.: USD 29 per issue (effective 2009); ◆ Cumulative ed(s).: Local Climatological Data. Aberdeen, South Dakota. Monthly Summary. ISSN 0198-4691.
Published by: U.S. National Climatic Data Center (Subsidiary of: U.S. Department of Commerce), Federal Bldg, 151 Patton Ave, Asheville, NC 28801. TEL 828-271-4800, FAX 828-271-4876, NODC.Services@noaa.gov, http://www.ncdc.noaa.gov.

551.5 USA ISSN 0198-4691
LOCAL CLIMATOLOGICAL DATA. ABERDEEN, SOUTH DAKOTA. MONTHLY SUMMARY. Text in English. 19??. m. USD 5 per issue (effective 2009); free to qualified government agencies. stat. back issues avail. **Document type:** *Government.* **Description:** Provides a monthly summary of temperature extremes, degree days, precipitation and winds, hourly precipitation and 3-hourly weather observations in Aberdeen, South Dakota.
Related titles: Online - full text ed.: USD 3 per issue (effective 2009); ◆ Cumulative ed. of: Local Climatological Data. Aberdeen, South Dakota. Annual Summary with Comparative Data. ISSN 0198-4683.
—Linda Hall.
Published by: U.S. National Climatic Data Center (Subsidiary of: U.S. Department of Commerce), Federal Bldg, 151 Patton Ave, Asheville, NC 28801. TEL 828-271-4800, FAX 828-271-4876, NODC.Services@noaa.gov, http://www.ncdc.noaa.gov.

551.5 USA ISSN 0198-4888
LOCAL CLIMATOLOGICAL DATA. ABILENE, TEXAS. ANNUAL SUMMARY WITH COMPARATIVE DATA. Text in English. 19??. a. USD 39 combined subscription per issue includes 12 monthly summaries & one a. summary (effective 2009); free to qualified government agencies. stat. back issues avail. **Document type:** *Government.* **Description:** Presents the monthly and annual average, resultant and fastest mile wind speed for the current year as well as the monthly and annual mean and fastest mile speed for a long period for Abilene, Texas.
Related titles: Online - full text ed.: USD 29 per issue (effective 2009); ◆ Cumulative ed(s).: Local Climatological Data. Abilene, Texas. Monthly Summary. ISSN 0198-4896.
Published by: U.S. National Climatic Data Center (Subsidiary of: U.S. Department of Commerce), Federal Bldg, 151 Patton Ave, Asheville, NC 28801. TEL 828-271-4800, FAX 828-271-4876, NODC.Services@noaa.gov, http://www.ncdc.noaa.gov.

551.5 USA ISSN 0198-4896
LOCAL CLIMATOLOGICAL DATA. ABILENE, TEXAS. MONTHLY SUMMARY. Text in English. 19??. m. USD 5 per issue (effective 2009); free to qualified government agencies. stat. back issues avail. **Document type:** *Government.* **Description:** Provides a monthly summary of temperature extremes, degree days, precipitation and winds, hourly precipitation and 3-hourly weather observations in Abilene, Texas.
Related titles: Online - full text ed.: USD 3 per issue (effective 2009); ◆ Cumulative ed. of: Local Climatological Data. Abilene, Texas. Annual Summary with Comparative Data. ISSN 0198-4888.
—Linda Hall.
Published by: U.S. National Climatic Data Center (Subsidiary of: U.S. Department of Commerce), Federal Bldg, 151 Patton Ave, Asheville, NC 28801. TEL 828-271-4800, FAX 828-271-4876, NODC.Services@noaa.gov, http://www.ncdc.noaa.gov.

551.5 USA ISSN 0198-3873
LOCAL CLIMATOLOGICAL DATA. AKRON, OHIO. ANNUAL SUMMARY WITH COMPARATIVE DATA. Text in English. 19??. a. USD 39 combined subscription per issue includes 12 monthly summaries & one a. summary (effective 2009); free to qualified government agencies. stat. back issues avail. **Document type:** *Government.* **Description:** Presents the monthly and annual average, resultant and fastest mile wind speed for the current year as well as the monthly and annual mean and fastest mile speed for a long period for Akron, Ohio.
Related titles: Online - full text ed.: USD 29 per issue (effective 2009); ◆ Cumulative ed(s).: Local Climatological Data. Akron, Ohio. Monthly Summary. ISSN 0198-3881.
Published by: U.S. National Climatic Data Center (Subsidiary of: U.S. Department of Commerce), Federal Bldg, 151 Patton Ave, Asheville, NC 28801. TEL 828-271-4800, FAX 828-271-4876, NODC.Services@noaa.gov, http://www.ncdc.noaa.gov.

551.5 USA ISSN 0198-3881
LOCAL CLIMATOLOGICAL DATA. AKRON, OHIO. MONTHLY SUMMARY. Text in English. 19??. m. USD 5 per issue (effective 2009); free to qualified government agencies. stat. back issues avail. **Document type:** *Government.* **Description:** Provides a monthly summary of temperature extremes, degree days, precipitation and winds, hourly precipitation and 3-hourly weather observations in Akron, Ohio.

Related titles: Online - full text ed.: USD 3 per issue (effective 2009); ◆ Cumulative ed. of: Local Climatological Data. Akron, Ohio. Annual Summary with Comparative Data. ISSN 0198-3873.
—Linda Hall.
Published by: U.S. National Climatic Data Center (Subsidiary of: U.S. Department of Commerce), Federal Bldg, 151 Patton Ave, Asheville, NC 28801. TEL 828-271-4800, FAX 828-271-4876, NODC.Services@noaa.gov, http://www.ncdc.noaa.gov.

551.5 USA ISSN 0198-7720
LOCAL CLIMATOLOGICAL DATA. ALAMOSA, COLORADO. ANNUAL SUMMARY WITH COMPARATIVE DATA. Text in English. 19??. a. USD 39 combined subscription per issue includes 12 monthly summaries & one a. summary (effective 2009); free to qualified government agencies. stat. back issues avail. **Document type:** *Bulletin, Government.* **Description:** Presents the monthly and annual average, resultant and fastest mile wind speed for the current year as well as the monthly and annual mean and fastest mile speed for a long period for Alamosa, Colorado.
Related titles: Online - full text ed.: USD 29 per issue (effective 2009); ◆ Cumulative ed(s).: Local Climatological Data. Alamosa, Colorado. Monthly Summary. ISSN 0198-7739.
Published by: U.S. National Climatic Data Center (Subsidiary of: U.S. Department of Commerce), Federal Bldg, 151 Patton Ave, Asheville, NC 28801. TEL 828-271-4800, FAX 828-271-4876, NODC.Services@noaa.gov, http://www.ncdc.noaa.gov.

551.5 USA ISSN 0198-7739
LOCAL CLIMATOLOGICAL DATA. ALAMOSA, COLORADO. MONTHLY SUMMARY. Text in English. 19??. m. USD 5 per issue (effective 2009); free to qualified government agencies. stat. back issues avail. **Document type:** *Government.* **Description:** Provides a monthly summary of temperature extremes, degree days, precipitation and winds, hourly precipitation and 3-hourly weather observations in Alamosa, Colorado.
Related titles: Online - full text ed.: USD 3 per issue (effective 2009); ◆ Cumulative ed. of: Local Climatological Data. Alamosa, Colorado. Annual Summary with Comparative Data. ISSN 0198-7720.
—Linda Hall.
Published by: U.S. National Climatic Data Center (Subsidiary of: U.S. Department of Commerce), Federal Bldg, 151 Patton Ave, Asheville, NC 28801. TEL 828-271-4800, FAX 828-271-4876, NODC.Services@noaa.gov, http://www.ncdc.noaa.gov.

551.5 USA ISSN 0198-3539
QC984.N72
LOCAL CLIMATOLOGICAL DATA. ALBANY, NEW YORK. ANNUAL SUMMARY WITH COMPARATIVE DATA. Text in English. 19??. a. USD 39 combined subscription per issue includes 12 monthly summaries & one a. summary (effective 2009); free to qualified government agencies. stat. back issues avail. **Document type:** *Bulletin, Government.* **Description:** Presents the monthly and annual average, resultant and fastest mile wind speed for the current year as well as the monthly and annual mean and fastest mile speed for a long period for Albany, New York.
Related titles: Online - full text ed.: USD 29 per issue (effective 2009); ◆ Cumulative ed(s).: Local Climatological Data. Albany, New York. Monthly Summary. ISSN 0198-3547.
Published by: U.S. National Climatic Data Center (Subsidiary of: U.S. Department of Commerce), Federal Bldg, 151 Patton Ave, Asheville, NC 28801. TEL 828-271-4800, FAX 828-271-4876, NODC.Services@noaa.gov, http://www.ncdc.noaa.gov.

551.5 USA ISSN 0198-3547
LOCAL CLIMATOLOGICAL DATA. ALBANY, NEW YORK. MONTHLY SUMMARY. Text in English. 19??. m. USD 5 per issue (effective 2009). back issues avail. **Document type:** *Bulletin, Government.* **Description:** Provides a monthly summary of temperature extremes, degree days, precipitation and winds, hourly precipitation and 3-hourly weather observations in Albany, New York.
Related titles: Online - full text ed.: USD 3 per issue (effective 2009); ◆ Cumulative ed. of: Local Climatological Data. Albany, New York. Annual Summary with Comparative Data. ISSN 0198-3539.
—Linda Hall.
Published by: U.S. National Climatic Data Center (Subsidiary of: U.S. Department of Commerce), Federal Bldg, 151 Patton Ave, Asheville, NC 28801. TEL 828-271-4800, FAX 828-271-4876, NODC.Services@noaa.gov, http://www.ncdc.noaa.gov.

551.5 USA ISSN 0198-3474
LOCAL CLIMATOLOGICAL DATA. ALBUQUERQUE, NEW MEXICO. ANNUAL SUMMARY WITH COMPARATIVE DATA. Text in English. 19??. a. USD 39 combined subscription per issue includes 12 monthly summaries & one a. summary (effective 2009); free to qualified government agencies. stat. back issues avail. **Document type:** *Bulletin, Government.* **Description:** Presents the monthly and annual average, resultant and fastest mile wind speed for the current year as well as the monthly and annual mean and fastest mile speed for a long period for Albuquerque, New Mexico.
Related titles: Online - full text ed.: USD 29 per issue (effective 2009); ◆ Cumulative ed(s).: Local Climatological Data. Albuquerque, New Mexico. Monthly Summary. ISSN 0198-3482.
Published by: U.S. National Climatic Data Center (Subsidiary of: U.S. Department of Commerce), Federal Bldg, 151 Patton Ave, Asheville, NC 28801. TEL 828-271-4800, FAX 828-271-4876, NODC.Services@noaa.gov, http://www.ncdc.noaa.gov.

551.5 USA ISSN 0198-3482
LOCAL CLIMATOLOGICAL DATA. ALBUQUERQUE, NEW MEXICO. MONTHLY SUMMARY. Text in English. 19??. m. USD 5 per issue (effective 2009). stat. back issues avail. **Document type:** *Bulletin, Government.* **Description:** Provides a monthly summary of temperature extremes, degree days, precipitation and winds, hourly precipitation and 3-hourly weather observations in Albuquerque, New Mexico.
Related titles: Online - full text ed.: USD 3 per issue (effective 2009); ◆ Cumulative ed. of: Local Climatological Data. Albuquerque, New Mexico. Annual Summary with Comparative Data. ISSN 0198-3474.
—Linda Hall.
Published by: U.S. National Climatic Data Center (Subsidiary of: U.S. Department of Commerce), Federal Bldg, 151 Patton Ave, Asheville, NC 28801. TEL 828-271-4800, FAX 828-271-4876, NODC.Services@noaa.gov, http://www.ncdc.noaa.gov.

551.5 USA ISSN 0198-4454
LOCAL CLIMATOLOGICAL DATA. ALLENTOWN, PENNSYLVANIA. ANNUAL SUMMARY WITH COMPARATIVE DATA. Text in English. 19??. a. USD 39 combined subscription per issue includes 12 monthly summaries & one a. summary (effective 2009). stat. back issues avail. **Document type:** *Bulletin, Government.* **Description:** Presents the monthly and annual average, resultant and fastest mile wind speed for the current year as well as the monthly and annual mean and fastest mile speed for a long period for Allentown, Pennsylvania.
Related titles: Online - full text ed.: USD 29 per issue (effective 2009); ◆ Cumulative ed(s).: Local Climatological Data. Allentown, Pennsylvania. Monthly Summary. ISSN 0198-4462.
Published by: U.S. National Climatic Data Center (Subsidiary of: U.S. Department of Commerce), Federal Bldg, 151 Patton Ave, Asheville, NC 28801. TEL 828-271-4800, FAX 828-271-4876, NODC.Services@noaa.gov, http://www.ncdc.noaa.gov.

551.5 USA ISSN 0198-4462
LOCAL CLIMATOLOGICAL DATA. ALLENTOWN, PENNSYLVANIA. MONTHLY SUMMARY. Text in English. 19??. m. USD 5 per issue (effective 2009). stat. back issues avail. **Document type:** *Government.* **Description:** Provides a monthly summary of temperature extremes, degree days, precipitation and winds, hourly precipitation and 3-hourly weather observations in Allentown, Pennsylvania.
Related titles: Online - full text ed.: USD 3 per issue (effective 2009); ◆ Cumulative ed. of: Local Climatological Data. Allentown, Pennsylvania. Annual Summary with Comparative Data. ISSN 0198-4454.
—Linda Hall.
Published by: U.S. National Climatic Data Center (Subsidiary of: U.S. Department of Commerce), Federal Bldg, 151 Patton Ave, Asheville, NC 28801. TEL 828-271-4800, FAX 828-271-4876, NODC.Services@noaa.gov, http://www.ncdc.noaa.gov.

551.5 USA ISSN 0198-2494
LOCAL CLIMATOLOGICAL DATA. ALPENA, MICHIGAN. ANNUAL SUMMARY WITH COMPARATIVE DATA. Text in English. 19??. a. USD 39 combined subscription per issue includes 12 monthly summaries & one a. summary (effective 2009). stat. back issues avail. **Document type:** *Bulletin, Government.* **Description:** Presents the monthly and annual average, resultant and fastest mile wind speed for the current year as well as the monthly and annual mean and fastest mile speed for a long period for Alpena, Michigan.
Related titles: Online - full text ed.: USD 29 per issue (effective 2009); ◆ Cumulative ed(s).: Local Climatological Data. Alpena, Michigan. Monthly Summary. ISSN 0198-2508.
Published by: U.S. National Climatic Data Center (Subsidiary of: U.S. Department of Commerce), Federal Bldg, 151 Patton Ave, Asheville, NC 28801. TEL 828-271-4800, FAX 828-271-4876, ncdc.info@noaa.gov, http://www.ncdc.noaa.gov.

551.5 USA ISSN 0198-2508
LOCAL CLIMATOLOGICAL DATA. ALPENA, MICHIGAN. MONTHLY SUMMARY. Text in English. 19??. m. USD 5 per issue (effective 2009). stat. back issues avail. **Document type:** *Government.* **Description:** Provides a monthly summary of temperature extremes, degree days, precipitation and winds, hourly precipitation and 3-hourly weather observations in Alpena, Michigan.
Related titles: Online - full text ed.: USD 3 per issue (effective 2009); ◆ Cumulative ed. of: Local Climatological Data. Alpena, Michigan. Annual Summary with Comparative Data. ISSN 0198-2494.
—Linda Hall.
Published by: U.S. National Climatic Data Center (Subsidiary of: U.S. Department of Commerce), Federal Bldg, 151 Patton Ave, Asheville, NC 28801. TEL 828-271-4800, FAX 828-271-4876, NODC.Services@noaa.gov, http://www.ncdc.noaa.gov.

551.5 USA ISSN 0198-490X
LOCAL CLIMATOLOGICAL DATA. AMARILLO, TEXAS. ANNUAL SUMMARY WITH COMPARATIVE DATA. Text in English. 19??. a. USD 39 combined subscription per issue includes 12 monthly summaries & one a. summary (effective 2009). stat. back issues avail. **Document type:** *Bulletin, Government.* **Description:** Presents the monthly and annual average, resultant and fastest mile wind speed for the current year as well as the monthly and annual mean and fastest mile speed for a long period for Amarillo, Texas.
Related titles: Online - full text ed.: USD 29 per issue (effective 2009); ◆ Cumulative ed(s).: Local Climatological Data. Amarillo, Texas. Monthly Summary. ISSN 0198-4918.
Published by: U.S. National Climatic Data Center (Subsidiary of: U.S. Department of Commerce), Federal Bldg, 151 Patton Ave, Asheville, NC 28801. TEL 828-271-4800, FAX 828-271-4876, NODC.Services@noaa.gov, http://www.ncdc.noaa.gov.

551.5 USA ISSN 0198-4918
LOCAL CLIMATOLOGICAL DATA. AMARILLO, TEXAS. MONTHLY SUMMARY. Text in English. 19??. m. USD 5 per issue (effective 2009). stat. back issues avail. **Document type:** *Government.* **Description:** Provides a monthly summary of temperature extremes, degree days, precipitation and winds, hourly precipitation and 3-hourly weather observations in Amarillo, Texas.
Related titles: Online - full text ed.: USD 3 per issue (effective 2009); ◆ Cumulative ed. of: Local Climatological Data. Amarillo, Texas. Annual Summary with Comparative Data. ISSN 0198-490X.
—Linda Hall.
Published by: U.S. National Climatic Data Center (Subsidiary of: U.S. Department of Commerce), Federal Bldg, 151 Patton Ave, Asheville, NC 28801. TEL 828-271-4800, FAX 828-271-4876, NODC.Services@noaa.gov, http://www.ncdc.noaa.gov.

551.5 USA ISSN 0197-954X
QC984.A42
LOCAL CLIMATOLOGICAL DATA. ANCHORAGE, ALASKA. ANNUAL SUMMARY WITH COMPARATIVE DATA. Text in English. 19??. a. USD 39 combined subscription per issue includes 12 monthly summaries & one a. summary (effective 2009). stat. back issues avail. **Document type:** *Bulletin, Government.* **Description:** Presents the monthly and annual average, resultant and fastest mile wind speed for the current year as well as the monthly and annual mean and fastest mile speed for a long period for Anchorage, Alaska.
Related titles: Online - full text ed.: USD 29 per issue (effective 2009); ◆ Cumulative ed(s).: Local Climatological Data. Anchorage, Alaska. Monthly Summary. ISSN 0197-9558.
Published by: U.S. National Climatic Data Center (Subsidiary of: U.S. Department of Commerce), Federal Bldg, 151 Patton Ave, Asheville, NC 28801. TEL 828-271-4800, FAX 828-271-4876, NODC.Services@noaa.gov, http://www.ncdc.noaa.gov.

551.5 USA ISSN 0197-9558
QC984.A42 A52
LOCAL CLIMATOLOGICAL DATA. ANCHORAGE, ALASKA. MONTHLY SUMMARY. Text in English. 19??. m. USD 5 per issue (effective 2009). stat. back issues avail. **Document type:** *Government.* **Description:** Provides a monthly summary of temperature extremes, degree days, precipitation and winds, hourly precipitation and 3-hourly weather observations in Anchorage, Alaska.
Related titles: Online - full text ed.: USD 3 per issue (effective 2009); ◆ Cumulative ed. of: Local Climatological Data. Anchorage, Alaska. Annual Summary with Comparative Data. ISSN 0197-954X.
—Linda Hall.
Published by: U.S. National Climatic Data Center (Subsidiary of: U.S. Department of Commerce), Federal Bldg, 151 Patton Ave, Asheville, NC 28801. TEL 828-271-4800, FAX 828-271-4876, NODC.Services@noaa.gov, http://www.ncdc.noaa.gov.

551.5 USA ISSN 0197-9566
QC984.A42
LOCAL CLIMATOLOGICAL DATA. ANNETTE, ALASKA. ANNUAL SUMMARY WITH COMPARATIVE DATA. Text in English. 19??. a. USD 39 combined subscription per issue includes 12 monthly summaries & one a. summary (effective 2009). stat. back issues avail. **Document type:** *Bulletin, Government.* **Description:** Presents the monthly and annual average, resultant and fastest mile wind speed for the current year as well as the monthly and annual mean and fastest mile speed for a long period for Annette, Alaska.
Related titles: Online - full content ed.: USD 29 per issue (effective 2009); ◆ Cumulative ed(s).: Local Climatological Data. Annette, Alaska. Monthly Summary. ISSN 0197-9574.
Published by: U.S. National Climatic Data Center (Subsidiary of: U.S. Department of Commerce), Federal Bldg, 151 Patton Ave, Asheville, NC 28801. TEL 828-271-4800, FAX 828-271-4876, NODC.Services@noaa.gov, http://www.ncdc.noaa.gov.

551.5 USA ISSN 0197-9574
QC984.A42
LOCAL CLIMATOLOGICAL DATA. ANNETTE, ALASKA. MONTHLY SUMMARY. Text in English. 19??. m. USD 5 per issue (effective 2009). stat. back issues avail. **Document type:** *Government.* **Description:** Provides a monthly summary of temperature extremes, degree days, precipitation and winds, hourly precipitation and 3-hourly weather observations in Annette, Alaska.
Related titles: Online - full text ed.: USD 3 per issue (effective 2009); ◆ Cumulative ed. of: Local Climatological Data. Annette, Alaska. Annual Summary with Comparative Data. ISSN 0197-9566.
—Linda Hall.
Published by: U.S. National Climatic Data Center (Subsidiary of: U.S. Department of Commerce), Federal Bldg, 151 Patton Ave, Asheville, NC 28801. TEL 828-271-4800, FAX 828-271-4876, NODC.Services@noaa.gov, http://www.ncdc.noaa.gov.

551.5 USA ISSN 0198-1218
LOCAL CLIMATOLOGICAL DATA. APALACHICOLA, FLORIDA. ANNUAL SUMMARY WITH COMPARATIVE DATA. Text in English. a. USD 39 combined subscription per issue includes 12 monthly summaries & one a. summary (effective 2009). stat. back issues avail. **Document type:** *Government.*
Related titles: Online - full text ed.: USD 29 per issue (effective 2009).
Published by: U.S. National Climatic Data Center (Subsidiary of: U.S. Department of Commerce), Federal Bldg, 151 Patton Ave, Asheville, NC 28801. TEL 828-271-4800, FAX 828-271-4876, NODC.Services@noaa.gov, http://www.ncdc.noaa.gov.

551.5 USA ISSN 0198-3695
LOCAL CLIMATOLOGICAL DATA. ASHEVILLE, NORTH CAROLINA. ANNUAL SUMMARY WITH COMPARATIVE DATA. Text in English. 19??. a. USD 39 combined subscription per issue includes 12 monthly summaries & one a. summary (effective 2009). stat. back issues avail. **Document type:** *Bulletin, Government.* **Description:** Presents the monthly and annual average, resultant and fastest mile wind speed for the current year as well as the monthly and annual mean and fastest mile speed for a long period for Asheville, North Carolina.
Related titles: Online - full text ed.: USD 29 per issue (effective 2009); ◆ Cumulative ed(s).: Local Climatological Data. Asheville, North Carolina. Monthly Summary. ISSN 0198-3709.
Published by: U.S. National Climatic Data Center (Subsidiary of: U.S. Department of Commerce), Federal Bldg, 151 Patton Ave, Asheville, NC 28801. TEL 828-271-4800, FAX 828-271-4876, NODC.Services@noaa.gov, http://www.ncdc.noaa.gov.

551.5 USA ISSN 0198-3709
LOCAL CLIMATOLOGICAL DATA. ASHEVILLE, NORTH CAROLINA. MONTHLY SUMMARY. Text in English. 19??. m. USD 5 per issue (effective 2009). stat. back issues avail. **Document type:** *Government.* **Description:** Provides a monthly summary of temperature extremes, degree days, precipitation and winds, hourly precipitation and 3-hourly weather observations in Asheville, North Carolina.
Related titles: Online - full text ed.: USD 3 per issue (effective 2009); ◆ Cumulative ed. of: Local Climatological Data. Asheville, North Carolina. Annual Summary with Comparative Data. ISSN 0198-3695.
—Linda Hall.
Published by: U.S. National Climatic Data Center (Subsidiary of: U.S. Department of Commerce), Federal Bldg, 151 Patton Ave, Asheville, NC 28801. TEL 828-271-4800, FAX 828-271-4876, NODC.Services@noaa.gov, http://www.ncdc.noaa.gov.

551.5 USA ISSN 0198-4098
QC984.O72
LOCAL CLIMATOLOGICAL DATA. ASTORIA, OREGON. ANNUAL SUMMARY WITH COMPARATIVE DATA. Text in English. 19??. a. USD 39 combined subscription per issue includes 12 monthly summaries & one a. summary (effective 2009). back issues avail. **Document type:** *Bulletin, Government.* **Description:** Presents the monthly and annual average, resultant and fastest mile wind speed for the current year as well as the monthly and annual mean and fastest mile speed for a long period for Astoria, Oregon.
Related titles: Online - full text ed.: USD 29 per issue (effective 2009); ◆ Cumulative ed(s).: Local Climatological Data. Astoria, Oregon. Monthly Summary. ISSN 0198-4101.

Published by: U.S. National Climatic Data Center (Subsidiary of: U.S. Department of Commerce), Federal Bldg, 151 Patton Ave, Asheville, NC 28801. TEL 828-271-4800, FAX 828-271-4876, NODC.Services@noaa.gov, http://www.ncdc.noaa.gov.

551.5 USA ISSN 0198-4101
QC984.O72
LOCAL CLIMATOLOGICAL DATA. ASTORIA, OREGON. MONTHLY SUMMARY. Text in English. 19??. m. USD 5 per issue (effective 2009). stat. back issues avail. **Document type:** *Government.* **Description:** Provides a monthly summary of temperature extremes, degree days, precipitation and winds, hourly precipitation and 3-hourly weather observations in Astoria, Oregon.
Related titles: Online - full text ed.: USD 3 per issue (effective 2009); ◆ Cumulative ed. of: Local Climatological Data. Astoria, Oregon. Annual Summary with Comparative Data. ISSN 0198-4098.
—Linda Hall.
Published by: U.S. National Climatic Data Center (Subsidiary of: U.S. Department of Commerce), Federal Bldg, 151 Patton Ave, Asheville, NC 28801. TEL 828-271-4800, FAX 828-271-4876, NODC.Services@noaa.gov, http://www.ncdc.noaa.gov.

551.5 USA ISSN 0198-1544
QC984.G42
LOCAL CLIMATOLOGICAL DATA. ATHENS, GEORGIA. ANNUAL SUMMARY WITH COMPARATIVE DATA. Text in English. 19??. a. USD 39 combined subscription per issue includes 12 monthly summaries & one a. summary (effective 2009). stat. back issues avail. **Document type:** *Bulletin, Government.* **Description:** Presents the monthly and annual average, resultant and fastest mile wind speed for the current year as well as the monthly and annual mean and fastest mile speed for a long period for Athens, Georgia.
Related titles: Online - full text ed.: USD 29 per issue (effective 2009); ◆ Cumulative ed(s).: Local Climatological Data. Athens, Georgia. Monthly Summary. ISSN 0198-1552.
Published by: U.S. National Climatic Data Center (Subsidiary of: U.S. Department of Commerce), Federal Bldg, 151 Patton Ave, Asheville, NC 28801. TEL 828-271-4800, FAX 828-271-4876, NODC.Services@noaa.gov, http://www.ncdc.noaa.gov.

551.5 USA ISSN 0198-1552
LOCAL CLIMATOLOGICAL DATA. ATHENS, GEORGIA. MONTHLY SUMMARY. Text in English. 19??. m. USD 5 per issue (effective 2009). stat. back issues avail. **Document type:** *Government.* **Description:** Provides a monthly summary of temperature extremes, degree days, precipitation and winds, hourly precipitation and 3-hourly weather observations in Athens, Georgia.
Related titles: Online - full text ed.: USD 3 per issue (effective 2009); ◆ Cumulative ed. of: Local Climatological Data. Athens, Georgia. Annual Summary with Comparative Data. ISSN 0198-1544.
—Linda Hall.
Published by: U.S. National Climatic Data Center (Subsidiary of: U.S. Department of Commerce), Federal Bldg, 151 Patton Ave, Asheville, NC 28801. TEL 828-271-4800, FAX 828-271-4876, NODC.Services@noaa.gov, http://www.ncdc.noaa.gov.

551.5 USA ISSN 0198-1560
LOCAL CLIMATOLOGICAL DATA. ATLANTA, GEORGIA. ANNUAL SUMMARY WITH COMPARATIVE DATA. Text in English. 19??. a. USD 39 combined subscription per issue includes 12 monthly summaries & one a. summary (effective 2009). stat. back issues avail. **Document type:** *Bulletin, Government.* **Description:** Presents the monthly and annual average, resultant and fastest mile wind speed for the current year as well as the monthly and annual mean and fastest mile speed for a long period for Atlanta, Georgia.
Related titles: Online - full text ed.: USD 29 per issue (effective 2009); ◆ Cumulative ed(s).: Local Climatological Data. Atlanta, Georgia. Monthly Summary. ISSN 0198-1579.
Published by: U.S. National Climatic Data Center (Subsidiary of: U.S. Department of Commerce), Federal Bldg, 151 Patton Ave, Asheville, NC 28801. TEL 828-271-4800, FAX 828-271-4876, NODC.Services@noaa.gov, http://www.ncdc.noaa.gov.

551.5 USA ISSN 0198-1579
LOCAL CLIMATOLOGICAL DATA. ATLANTA, GEORGIA. MONTHLY SUMMARY. Text in English. 19??. m. USD 5 per issue (effective 2009). stat. back issues avail. **Document type:** *Government.* **Description:** Provides a monthly summary of temperature extremes, degree days, precipitation and winds, hourly precipitation and 3-hourly weather observations in Atlanta, Georgia.
Related titles: Online - full text ed.: USD 3 per issue (effective 2009); ◆ Cumulative ed. of: Local Climatological Data. Atlanta, Georgia. Annual Summary with Comparative Data. ISSN 0198-1560.
—Linda Hall.
Published by: U.S. National Climatic Data Center (Subsidiary of: U.S. Department of Commerce), Federal Bldg, 151 Patton Ave, Asheville, NC 28801. TEL 828-271-4800, FAX 828-271-4876, NODC.Services@noaa.gov, http://www.ncdc.noaa.gov.

551.5 USA ISSN 0275-1763
LOCAL CLIMATOLOGICAL DATA. ATLANTIC CITY, NEW JERSEY. N A F E C ANNUAL SUMMARY WITH COMPARATIVE DATA. Text in English. 19??. a. USD 39 combined subscription per issue includes 12 monthly summaries & one a. summary (effective 2009). back issues avail. **Document type:** *Bulletin, Government.* **Description:** Presents the monthly and annual average, resultant and fastest mile wind speed for the current year as well as the monthly and annual mean and fastest mile speed for a long period for Atlantic City, New Jersey.
Formerly (until 1979): Local Climatological Data. Atlantic City, New Jersey. Annual Summary with Comparative Data (0198-3407)
Related titles: Online - full text ed.: USD 29 per issue (effective 2009).
Published by: U.S. National Climatic Data Center (Subsidiary of: U.S. Department of Commerce), Federal Bldg, 151 Patton Ave, Asheville, NC 28801. TEL 828-271-4800, FAX 828-271-4876, NODC.Services@noaa.gov, http://www.ncdc.noaa.gov.

551.5 USA ISSN 0198-3415
LOCAL CLIMATOLOGICAL DATA. ATLANTIC CITY, NEW JERSEY. NATIONAL WEATHER SERVICE OFFICE. AVIATION FACILITIES EXPERTISE CENTER. MONTHLY SUMMARY. Text in English. 19??. m. USD 5 per issue (effective 2004). stat. back issues avail. **Document type:** *Government.*
Related titles: Online - full text ed.
—Linda Hall.
Published by: U.S. National Climatic Data Center (Subsidiary of: U.S. Department of Commerce), Federal Bldg, 151 Patton Ave, Asheville, NC 28801. TEL 828-271-4800, FAX 828-271-4876, NODC.Services@noaa.gov, http://www.ncdc.noaa.gov.

551.5 USA ISSN 0198-3423
LOCAL CLIMATOLOGICAL DATA. ATLANTIC CITY, NEW JERSEY. NATIONAL WEATHER SERVICE URBAN SITE. ATLANTIC CITY STATE MARINA. MONTHLY SUMMARY. Text in English. m. USD 5 per issue (effective 2004). stat. back issues avail. **Document type:** *Government.*
Related titles: Online - full text ed.
—Linda Hall.
Published by: U.S. National Climatic Data Center (Subsidiary of: U.S. Department of Commerce), Federal Bldg, 151 Patton Ave, Asheville, NC 28801. TEL 828-271-4800, FAX 828-271-4876, NODC.Services@noaa.gov, http://www.ncdc.noaa.gov.

551.5 USA ISSN 0198-1587
QC984.G42
LOCAL CLIMATOLOGICAL DATA. AUGUSTA, GEORGIA. ANNUAL SUMMARY WITH COMPARATIVE DATA. Text in English. 19??. a. USD 39 combined subscription per issue includes 12 monthly summaries & one a. summary (effective 2009). stat. back issues avail. **Document type:** *Government.* **Description:** Presents the monthly and annual average, resultant and fastest mile wind speed for the current year as well as the monthly and annual mean and fastest mile speed for a long period for Augusta, Georgia.
Related titles: Online - full text ed.: USD 29 per issue (effective 2009); ◆ Cumulative ed(s).: Local Climatological Data. Augusta, Georgia. Monthly Summary. ISSN 0198-1595.
Published by: U.S. National Climatic Data Center (Subsidiary of: U.S. Department of Commerce), Federal Bldg, 151 Patton Ave, Asheville, NC 28801. TEL 828-271-4800, FAX 828-271-4876, NODC.Services@noaa.gov, http://www.ncdc.noaa.gov.

551.5 USA ISSN 0198-1595
QC984.G4
LOCAL CLIMATOLOGICAL DATA. AUGUSTA, GEORGIA. MONTHLY SUMMARY. Text in English. 19??. m. USD 5 per issue (effective 2009). stat. back issues avail. **Document type:** *Government.* **Description:** Provides information about hourly precipitation data for Augusta.
Related titles: Online - full text ed.: USD 3 per issue (effective 2009); ◆ Cumulative ed. of: Local Climatological Data. Augusta, Georgia. Annual Summary with Comparative Data. ISSN 0198-1587.
—Linda Hall.
Published by: U.S. National Climatic Data Center (Subsidiary of: U.S. Department of Commerce), Federal Bldg, 151 Patton Ave, Asheville, NC 28801. TEL 828-271-4800, FAX 828-271-4876, NODC.Services@noaa.gov, http://www.ncdc.noaa.gov.

551.5 USA ISSN 1528-7459
LOCAL CLIMATOLOGICAL DATA. AUSTIN-BERGTROM, TEXAS. AUSTIN-BERGSTROM INTERNATIONAL AIRPORT. ANNUAL SUMMARY WITH COMPARATIVE DATA. Text in English. 19??. a. USD 39 combined subscription per issue includes 12 monthly summaries & one a. summary (effective 2009). stat. back issues avail. **Document type:** *Government.* **Description:** Presents the monthly and annual average, resultant and fastest mile wind speed for the current year as well as the monthly and annual mean and fastest mile speed for a long period for Austin-Bergtrom, Texas.
Related titles: Online - full text ed.: USD 29 per issue (effective 2009).
Published by: U.S. National Climatic Data Center (Subsidiary of: U.S. Department of Commerce), Federal Bldg, 151 Patton Ave, Asheville, NC 28801. TEL 828-271-4800, FAX 828-271-4876, NODC.Services@noaa.gov, http://www.ncdc.noaa.gov.

551.5 USA ISSN 1528-7440
LOCAL CLIMATOLOGICAL DATA. AUSTIN CITY, TEXAS. CAMP MABRY ARMY NATIONAL GUARD. ANNUAL SUMMARY WITH COMPARATIVE DATA. Text in English. 19??. a. USD 39 combined subscription per issue includes 12 monthly summaries & one a. summary (effective 2009). stat. back issues avail. **Document type:** *Government.* **Description:** Presents the monthly and annual average, resultant and fastest mile wind speed for the current year as well as the monthly and annual mean and fastest mile speed for a long period for Austin City, Texas.
Related titles: Online - full text ed.: USD 29 per issue (effective 2009).
Published by: U.S. National Climatic Data Center (Subsidiary of: U.S. Department of Commerce), Federal Bldg, 151 Patton Ave, Asheville, NC 28801. TEL 828-271-4800, FAX 828-271-4876, NODC.Services@noaa.gov, http://www.ncdc.noaa.gov.

551.5 USA ISSN 0198-4926
LOCAL CLIMATOLOGICAL DATA. AUSTIN, TEXAS. ANNUAL SUMMARY WITH COMPARATIVE DATA. Text in English. 19??. a. USD 39 combined subscription includes 12 monthly summaries & one a. summary (effective 2009). stat. back issues avail. **Document type:** *Government.* **Description:** Presents the monthly and annual average, resultant and fastest mile wind speed for the current year as well as the monthly and annual mean and fastest mile speed for a long period for Austin, Texas.
Related titles: Online - full text ed.: USD 29 per issue (effective 2009); ◆ Cumulative ed(s).: Local Climatological Data. Austin, Texas. Monthly Summary. ISSN 0198-4934.
Published by: U.S. National Climatic Data Center (Subsidiary of: U.S. Department of Commerce), Federal Bldg, 151 Patton Ave, Asheville, NC 28801. TEL 828-271-4800, FAX 828-271-4876, NODC.Services@noaa.gov, http://www.ncdc.noaa.gov.

551.5 USA ISSN 0198-4934
LOCAL CLIMATOLOGICAL DATA. AUSTIN, TEXAS. MONTHLY SUMMARY. Text in English. 19??. m. USD 5 per issue (effective 2009). stat. back issues avail. **Document type:** *Government.* **Description:** Provides information about hourly precipitation data for Austin.
Related titles: Online - full text ed.: USD 3 per issue (effective 2009); ◆ Cumulative ed. of: Local Climatological Data. Austin, Texas. Annual Summary with Comparative Data. ISSN 0198-4926.
—Linda Hall.
Published by: U.S. National Climatic Data Center (Subsidiary of: U.S. Department of Commerce), Federal Bldg, 151 Patton Ave, Asheville, NC 28801. TEL 828-271-4800, FAX 828-271-4876, NODC.Services@noaa.gov, http://www.ncdc.noaa.gov.

551.5 USA ISSN 0198-4470
LOCAL CLIMATOLOGICAL DATA. AVOCA, PENNSYLVANIA. ANNUAL SUMMARY WITH COMPARATIVE DATA. Text in English. a. USD 39 combined subscription per issue includes 12 monthly summaries & one a. summary (effective 2009). **Document type:** *Bulletin, Government.*
Related titles: Online - full content ed.: USD 29 per issue (effective 2009); ◆ Cumulative ed(s).: Local Climatological Data. Avoca, Pennsylvania. Monthly Summary. ISSN 0198-4489.
Published by: U.S. National Climatic Data Center (Subsidiary of: U.S. Department of Commerce), Federal Bldg, 151 Patton Ave, Asheville, NC 28801. TEL 828-271-4800, FAX 828-271-4876, NODC.Services@noaa.gov, http://www.ncdc.noaa.gov.

551.5 USA ISSN 0198-4489
LOCAL CLIMATOLOGICAL DATA. AVOCA, PENNSYLVANIA. MONTHLY SUMMARY. Text in English. 19??. m. USD 5 per issue (effective 2009). back issues avail. **Document type:** *Bulletin, Government.* **Description:** Provides a monthly summary of temperature extremes, degree days, precipitation and winds, hourly precipitation and 3-hourly weather observations in Wilkes-Barre Scranton Airport, Avoca, Pennsylvania.
Related titles: Online - full text ed.: USD 3 per issue (effective 2009); ◆ Cumulative ed. of: Local Climatological Data. Avoca, Pennsylvania. Annual Summary with Comparative Data. ISSN 0198-4470.
—Linda Hall.
Published by: U.S. National Climatic Data Center (Subsidiary of: U.S. Department of Commerce), Federal Bldg, 151 Patton Ave, Asheville, NC 28801. TEL 828-271-4800, FAX 828-271-4876, NODC.Services@noaa.gov, http://www.ncdc.noaa.gov.

551.5 USA ISSN 0198-0696
LOCAL CLIMATOLOGICAL DATA. BAKERSFIELD, CALIFORNIA. ANNUAL SUMMARY WITH COMPARATIVE DATA. Text in English. 19??. a. USD 39 combined subscription per issue includes 12 monthly summaries & one a. summary (effective 2009). back issues avail. **Document type:** *Bulletin, Government.* **Description:** Presents the monthly and annual average, resultant and fastest mile wind speed for the current year as well as the monthly and annual mean and fastest mile speed for a long period for Bakersfield, California.
Related titles: Online - full text ed.: USD 29 per issue (effective 2009); ◆ Cumulative ed(s).: Local Climatological Data. Bakersfield, California. Monthly Summary. ISSN 0198-0645.
Published by: U.S. National Climatic Data Center (Subsidiary of: U.S. Department of Commerce), Federal Bldg, 151 Patton Ave, Asheville, NC 28801. TEL 828-271-4800, FAX 828-271-4876, NODC.Services@noaa.gov, http://www.ncdc.noaa.gov.

551.5 USA ISSN 0198-0645
LOCAL CLIMATOLOGICAL DATA. BAKERSFIELD, CALIFORNIA. MONTHLY SUMMARY. Text in English. 19??. m. USD 5 per issue (effective 2009). back issues avail. **Document type:** *Bulletin, Government.* **Description:** Provides information about local climatological data for Bakersfield.
Related titles: Online - full text ed.: USD 3 per issue (effective 2009); ◆ Cumulative ed. of: Local Climatological Data. Bakersfield, California. Annual Summary with Comparative Data. ISSN 0198-0696.
—Linda Hall.
Published by: U.S. National Climatic Data Center (Subsidiary of: U.S. Department of Commerce), Federal Bldg, 151 Patton Ave, Asheville, NC 28801. TEL 828-271-4800, FAX 828-271-4876, NODC.Services@noaa.gov, http://www.ncdc.noaa.gov.

551.5 USA ISSN 0198-2397
LOCAL CLIMATOLOGICAL DATA. BALTIMORE, MARYLAND. ANNUAL SUMMARY WITH COMPARATIVE DATA. Text in English. 19??. a. USD 39 combined subscription per issue includes 12 monthly summaries & one a. summary (effective 2009). back issues avail. **Document type:** *Bulletin, Government.* **Description:** Presents the monthly and annual average, resultant and fastest mile wind speed for the current year as well as the monthly and annual mean and fastest mile speed for a long period for Baltimore, Maryland.
Related titles: Online - full text ed.: USD 29 per issue (effective 2009); ◆ Cumulative ed(s).: Local Climatological Data. Baltimore, Maryland. Monthly Summary. ISSN 0198-2400.
Published by: U.S. National Climatic Data Center (Subsidiary of: U.S. Department of Commerce), Federal Bldg, 151 Patton Ave, Asheville, NC 28801. TEL 828-271-4800, FAX 828-271-4876, NODC.Services@noaa.gov, http://www.ncdc.noaa.gov.

551.5 USA ISSN 0198-2400
LOCAL CLIMATOLOGICAL DATA. BALTIMORE, MARYLAND. MONTHLY SUMMARY. Text in English. 19??. m. USD 5 per issue (effective 2009). back issues avail. **Document type:** *Bulletin, Government.* **Description:** Provides information about local climatological data for Baltimore.
Related titles: Online - full text ed.: USD 3 per issue (effective 2009); ◆ Cumulative ed. of: Local Climatological Data. Baltimore, Maryland. Annual Summary with Comparative Data. ISSN 0198-2397.
—Linda Hall.
Published by: U.S. National Climatic Data Center (Subsidiary of: U.S. Department of Commerce), Federal Bldg, 151 Patton Ave, Asheville, NC 28801. TEL 828-271-4800, FAX 828-271-4876, NODC.Services@noaa.gov, http://www.ncdc.noaa.gov.

551.5 USA ISSN 2151-7789
▼ **LOCAL CLIMATOLOGICAL DATA. BANGOR, MAINE.** Text in English. 2009. m. USD 3 per issue (effective 2010). back issues avail. **Document type:** *Bulletin, Government.*
Published by: U.S. National Climatic Data Center (Subsidiary of: U.S. Department of Commerce), Federal Bldg, 151 Patton Ave, Asheville, NC 28801. TEL 828-271-4800, FAX 828-271-4876, ncdc.info@noaa.gov, http://www.ncdc.noaa.gov.

551.5 USA ISSN 0197-9582
QC984.A42
LOCAL CLIMATOLOGICAL DATA. BARROW, ALASKA. ANNUAL SUMMARY WITH COMPARATIVE DATA. Text in English. 19??. a. USD 39 combined subscription per issue includes 12 monthly summaries & one a. summary (effective 2009). back issues avail. **Document type:** *Bulletin, Government.* **Description:** Presents the monthly and annual average, resultant and fastest mile wind speed for the current year as well as the monthly and annual mean and fastest mile speed for a long period for Barrow, Alaska.
Related titles: Online - full text ed.: USD 29 per issue (effective 2009); ◆ Cumulative ed(s).: Local Climatological Data. Barrow, Alaska. Monthly Summary. ISSN 0197-9590.

Published by: U.S. National Climatic Data Center (Subsidiary of: U.S. Department of Commerce), Federal Bldg, 151 Patton Ave, Asheville, NC 28801. TEL 828-271-4800, FAX 828-271-4876, NODC.Services@noaa.gov, http://www.ncdc.noaa.gov.

551.5 USA ISSN 0197-9590
QC984.A42
LOCAL CLIMATOLOGICAL DATA. BARROW, ALASKA. MONTHLY SUMMARY. Text in English. 19??. m. USD 5 per issue (effective 2009). back issues avail. **Document type:** *Bulletin, Government.* **Description:** Provides information about local climatological data for Barrow.
Related titles: Online - full text ed.: USD 3 per issue (effective 2009); ◆ Cumulative ed. of: Local Climatological Data. Barrow, Alaska. Annual Summary with Comparative Data. ISSN 0197-9582.
—Linda Hall.
Published by: U.S. National Climatic Data Center (Subsidiary of: U.S. Department of Commerce), Federal Bldg, 151 Patton Ave, Asheville, NC 28801. TEL 828-271-4800, FAX 828-271-4876, NODC.Services@noaa.gov, http://www.ncdc.noaa.gov.

551.5 USA ISSN 0197-9604
LOCAL CLIMATOLOGICAL DATA. BARTER ISLAND, ALASKA. ANNUAL SUMMARY WITH COMPARATIVE DATA. Text in English. 19??. a. USD 39 combined subscription per issue includes 12 monthly summaries & one a. summary (effective 2009). back issues avail. **Document type:** *Bulletin, Government.* **Description:** Presents the monthly and annual average, resultant and fastest mile wind speed for the current year as well as the monthly and annual mean and fastest mile speed for a long period for Barter Island, Alaska.
Related titles: Online - full text ed.: USD 29 per issue (effective 2009).
Published by: U.S. National Climatic Data Center (Subsidiary of: U.S. Department of Commerce), Federal Bldg, 151 Patton Ave, Asheville, NC 28801. TEL 828-271-4800, FAX 828-271-4876, NODC.Services@noaa.gov, http://www.ncdc.noaa.gov.

551.5 USA ISSN 0198-2273
LOCAL CLIMATOLOGICAL DATA. BATON ROUGE, LOUISIANA. ANNUAL SUMMARY WITH COMPARATIVE DATA. Text in English. 19??. a. USD 39 combined subscription per issue includes 12 monthly summaries & one a. summary (effective 2009). back issues avail. **Document type:** *Bulletin, Government.* **Description:** Presents the monthly and annual average, resultant and fastest mile wind speed for the current year as well as the monthly and annual mean and fastest mile speed for a long period for Baton Rouge, Louisiana.
Related titles: Online - full text ed.: USD 29 per issue (effective 2009); ◆ Cumulative ed(s).: Local Climatological Data. Baton Rouge, Louisiana. Monthly Summary. ISSN 0198-2281.
Published by: U.S. National Climatic Data Center (Subsidiary of: U.S. Department of Commerce), Federal Bldg, 151 Patton Ave, Asheville, NC 28801. TEL 828-271-4800, FAX 828-271-4876, NODC.Services@noaa.gov, http://www.ncdc.noaa.gov.

551.5 USA ISSN 0198-2281
LOCAL CLIMATOLOGICAL DATA. BATON ROUGE, LOUISIANA. MONTHLY SUMMARY. Text in English. 19??. m. USD 5 per issue (effective 2009). back issues avail. **Document type:** *Bulletin, Government.* **Description:** Provides information about local climatological data for Baton Rouge.
Related titles: Online - full text ed.: USD 3 per issue (effective 2009); ◆ Cumulative ed. of: Local Climatological Data. Baton Rouge, Louisiana. Annual Summary with Comparative Data. ISSN 0198-2273.
—Linda Hall.
Published by: U.S. National Climatic Data Center (Subsidiary of: U.S. Department of Commerce), Federal Bldg, 151 Patton Ave, Asheville, NC 28801. TEL 828-271-4800, FAX 828-271-4876, NODC.Services@noaa.gov, http://www.ncdc.noaa.gov.

551.5 USA ISSN 0198-5590
LOCAL CLIMATOLOGICAL DATA. BECKLEY, WEST VIRGINIA. MONTHLY SUMMARY. Text in English. 19??. m. USD 5 per issue (effective 2009). back issues avail. **Document type:** *Bulletin, Government.* **Description:** Provides information about local climatological data for Beckley.
Related titles: Online - full text ed.: USD 3 per issue (effective 2009).
—Linda Hall.
Published by: U.S. National Climatic Data Center (Subsidiary of: U.S. Department of Commerce), Federal Bldg, 151 Patton Ave, Asheville, NC 28801. TEL 828-271-4800, FAX 828-271-4876, NODC.Services@noaa.gov, http://www.ncdc.noaa.gov.

551.5 USA ISSN 0197-9620
QC984.A42
LOCAL CLIMATOLOGICAL DATA. BETHEL, ALASKA. ANNUAL SUMMARY WITH COMPARATIVE DATA. Text in English. 19??. a. USD 39 combined subscription per issue includes 12 monthly summaries & one a. summary (effective 2009). back issues avail. **Document type:** *Bulletin, Government.* **Description:** Presents the monthly and annual average, resultant and fastest mile wind speed for the current year as well as the monthly and annual mean and fastest mile speed for a long period for Bethel, Alaska.
Related titles: Online - full text ed.: USD 29 per issue (effective 2009); ◆ Cumulative ed(s).: Local Climatological Data. Bethel, Alaska. Monthly Summary. ISSN 0197-9639.
Published by: U.S. National Climatic Data Center (Subsidiary of: U.S. Department of Commerce), Federal Bldg, 151 Patton Ave, Asheville, NC 28801. TEL 828-271-4800, FAX 828-271-4876, NODC.Services@noaa.gov, http://www.ncdc.noaa.gov.

551.5 USA ISSN 0197-9639
QC984.A42
LOCAL CLIMATOLOGICAL DATA. BETHEL, ALASKA. MONTHLY SUMMARY. Text in English. 19??. m. USD 5 per issue (effective 2009). back issues avail. **Document type:** *Bulletin, Government.* **Description:** Provides information about local climatological data for Bethel.
Related titles: Online - full text ed.: USD 3 per issue (effective 2009); ◆ Cumulative ed. of: Local Climatological Data. Bethel, Alaska. Annual Summary with Comparative Data. ISSN 0197-9620.
—Linda Hall.
Published by: U.S. National Climatic Data Center (Subsidiary of: U.S. Department of Commerce), Federal Bldg, 151 Patton Ave, Asheville, NC 28801. TEL 828-271-4800, FAX 828-271-4876, NODC.Services@noaa.gov, http://www.ncdc.noaa.gov.

551.5 USA ISSN 0197-9647
QC984.A42
LOCAL CLIMATOLOGICAL DATA. BETTLES, ALASKA. ANNUAL SUMMARY WITH COMPARATIVE DATA. Text in English. 19??. a. USD 39 combined subscription per issue includes 12 monthly summaries & one a. summary (effective 2009). back issues avail. **Document type:** *Bulletin, Government.* **Description:** Presents the monthly and annual average, resultant and fastest mile wind speed for the current year as well as the monthly and annual mean and fastest mile speed for a long period for Bettles, Alaska.
Related titles: Online - full text ed.: USD 29 per issue (effective 2009); ◆ Cumulative ed(s).: Local Climatological Data. Bettles, Alaska. Monthly Summary. ISSN 0197-9655.
Published by: U.S. National Climatic Data Center (Subsidiary of: U.S. Department of Commerce), Federal Bldg, 151 Patton Ave, Asheville, NC 28801. TEL 828-271-4800, FAX 828-271-4876, NODC.Services@noaa.gov, http://www.ncdc.noaa.gov.

551.5 USA ISSN 0197-9655
QC984.A42
LOCAL CLIMATOLOGICAL DATA. BETTLES, ALASKA. MONTHLY SUMMARY. Text in English. 199?. m. USD 5 per issue (effective 2009). back issues avail. **Document type:** *Bulletin, Government.* **Description:** Provides information about local climatological data for Bettles.
Related titles: Online - full text ed.: USD 3 per issue (effective 2009); ◆ Cumulative ed. of: Local Climatological Data. Bettles, Alaska. Annual Summary with Comparative Data. ISSN 0197-9647.
—Linda Hall.
Published by: U.S. National Climatic Data Center (Subsidiary of: U.S. Department of Commerce), Federal Bldg, 151 Patton Ave, Asheville, NC 28801. TEL 828-271-4800, FAX 828-271-4876, NODC.Services@noaa.gov, http://www.ncdc.noaa.gov.

551.5 USA ISSN 0197-9663
QC984.A42
LOCAL CLIMATOLOGICAL DATA. BIG DELTA, ALASKA. ANNUAL SUMMARY WITH COMPARATIVE DATA. Text in English. a. USD 39 combined subscription per issue includes 12 monthly summaries & one a. summary (effective 2009). **Document type:** *Bulletin, Government.*
Related titles: Online - full content ed.: USD 29 per issue (effective 2009); ◆ Cumulative ed(s).: Local Climatological Data. Big Delta, Alaska. Monthly Summary. ISSN 0197-9671.
Published by: U.S. National Climatic Data Center (Subsidiary of: U.S. Department of Commerce), Federal Bldg, 151 Patton Ave, Asheville, NC 28801. TEL 828-271-4800, FAX 828-271-4876, NODC.Services@noaa.gov, http://www.ncdc.noaa.gov.

551.5 USA ISSN 0197-9671
QC984.A42
LOCAL CLIMATOLOGICAL DATA. BIG DELTA, ALASKA. MONTHLY SUMMARY. Text in English. 19??. m. USD 5 per issue (effective 2009). back issues avail. **Document type:** *Bulletin, Government.* **Description:** Provides information about local climatological data for Big Delta.
Related titles: Online - full text ed.: USD 3 per issue (effective 2009); ◆ Cumulative ed. of: Local Climatological Data. Big Delta, Alaska. Annual Summary with Comparative Data. ISSN 0197-9663.
—Linda Hall.
Published by: U.S. National Climatic Data Center (Subsidiary of: U.S. Department of Commerce), Federal Bldg, 151 Patton Ave, Asheville, NC 28801. TEL 828-271-4800, FAX 828-271-4876, NODC.Services@noaa.gov, http://www.ncdc.noaa.gov.

551.5 USA ISSN 0198-294X
QC984.M92
LOCAL CLIMATOLOGICAL DATA. BILLINGS, MONTANA. ANNUAL SUMMARY WITH COMPARATIVE DATA. Text in English. 19??. a. USD 39 combined subscription per issue includes 12 monthly summaries & one a. summary (effective 2009). back issues avail. **Document type:** *Bulletin, Government.* **Description:** Presents the monthly and annual average, resultant and fastest mile wind speed for the current year as well as the monthly and annual mean and fastest mile speed for a long period for Billings, Montana.
Related titles: Online - full text ed.: USD 29 per issue (effective 2009); ◆ Cumulative ed(s).: Local Climatological Data. Billings, Montana. Monthly Summary. ISSN 0198-2958.
Published by: U.S. National Climatic Data Center (Subsidiary of: U.S. Department of Commerce), Federal Bldg, 151 Patton Ave, Asheville, NC 28801. TEL 828-271-4800, FAX 828-271-4876, NODC.Services@noaa.gov, http://www.ncdc.noaa.gov.

551.5 USA ISSN 0198-2958
QC984.M92
LOCAL CLIMATOLOGICAL DATA. BILLINGS, MONTANA. MONTHLY SUMMARY. Text in English. 19??. m. USD 5 per issue (effective 2009). back issues avail. **Document type:** *Bulletin, Government.* **Description:** Provides information about local climatological data for Billings.
Related titles: Online - full text ed.: USD 3 per issue (effective 2009); ◆ Cumulative ed. of: Local Climatological Data. Billings, Montana. Annual Summary with Comparative Data. ISSN 0198-294X.
—Linda Hall.
Published by: U.S. National Climatic Data Center (Subsidiary of: U.S. Department of Commerce), Federal Bldg, 151 Patton Ave, Asheville, NC 28801. TEL 828-271-4800, FAX 828-271-4876, NODC.Services@noaa.gov, http://www.ncdc.noaa.gov.

551.5 USA ISSN 0198-3555
QC851.N65
LOCAL CLIMATOLOGICAL DATA. BINGHAMTON, NEW YORK. ANNUAL SUMMARY WITH COMPARATIVE DATA. Text in English. 19??. a. USD 39 combined subscription per issue includes 12 monthly summaries & one a. summary (effective 2009). back issues avail. **Document type:** *Bulletin, Government.* **Description:** Presents the monthly and annual average, resultant and fastest mile wind speed for the current year as well as the monthly and annual mean and fastest mile speed for a long period for Binghamton, New York.
Related titles: Online - full text ed.: USD 29 per issue (effective 2009); ◆ Cumulative ed(s).: Local Climatological Data. Binghamton, New York. Monthly Summary. ISSN 0198-3563.
Published by: U.S. National Climatic Data Center (Subsidiary of: U.S. Department of Commerce), Federal Bldg, 151 Patton Ave, Asheville, NC 28801. TEL 828-271-4800, FAX 828-271-4876, NODC.Services@noaa.gov, http://www.ncdc.noaa.gov.

551.5 USA ISSN 0198-3563
LOCAL CLIMATOLOGICAL DATA. BINGHAMTON, NEW YORK. MONTHLY SUMMARY. Text in English. 19??. m. USD 5 per issue (effective 2009). **Document type:** *Bulletin, Government.* **Description:** Provides information about local climatological data for Binghamton.
Related titles: Online - full text ed.: USD 3 per issue (effective 2009); ◆ Cumulative ed. of: Local Climatological Data. Binghamton, New York. Annual Summary with Comparative Data. ISSN 0198-3555.
—Linda Hall.
Published by: U.S. National Climatic Data Center (Subsidiary of: U.S. Department of Commerce), Federal Bldg, 151 Patton Ave, Asheville, NC 28801. TEL 828-271-4800, FAX 828-271-4876, NODC.Services@noaa.gov, http://www.ncdc.noaa.gov.

551.5 USA ISSN 0197-9469
LOCAL CLIMATOLOGICAL DATA. BIRMINGHAM, ALABAMA. ANNUAL SUMMARY WITH COMPARATIVE DATA. Text in English. 19??. a. USD 39 combined subscription per issue includes 12 monthly summaries & one a. summary (effective 2009). back issues avail. **Document type:** *Bulletin, Government.* **Description:** Presents the monthly and annual average, resultant and fastest mile wind speed for the current year as well as the monthly and annual mean and fastest mile speed for a long period for Birmingham, Alabama.
Related titles: Online - full text ed.: USD 29 per issue (effective 2009); ◆ Cumulative ed(s).: Local Climatological Data. Birmingham, Alabama. Monthly Summary. ISSN 0197-9868.
Published by: U.S. National Climatic Data Center (Subsidiary of: U.S. Department of Commerce), Federal Bldg, 151 Patton Ave, Asheville, NC 28801. TEL 828-271-4800, FAX 828-271-4876, NODC.Services@noaa.gov, http://www.ncdc.noaa.gov.

551.5 USA ISSN 0275-1798
LOCAL CLIMATOLOGICAL DATA. BIRMINGHAM, ALABAMA. CITY OFFICE. ANNUAL SUMMARY WITH COMPARATIVE DATA. Text in English. a. USD 300 per issue (effective 2008). **Document type:** *Bulletin, Government.*
Related titles: Online - full content ed.
Published by: U.S. National Climatic Data Center (Subsidiary of: U.S. Department of Commerce), Federal Bldg, 151 Patton Ave, Asheville, NC 28801. TEL 828-271-4800, FAX 828-271-4876, NODC.Services@noaa.gov, http://www.ncdc.noaa.gov.

551.5 USA ISSN 0197-9868
LOCAL CLIMATOLOGICAL DATA. BIRMINGHAM, ALABAMA. MONTHLY SUMMARY. Text in English. m. USD 5 per issue (effective 2009). **Document type:** *Bulletin, Government.*
Related titles: Online - full text ed.: USD 3 per issue (effective 2009); ◆ Cumulative ed. of: Local Climatological Data. Birmingham, Alabama. Annual Summary with Comparative Data. ISSN 0197-9469.
—Linda Hall.
Published by: U.S. National Climatic Data Center (Subsidiary of: U.S. Department of Commerce), Federal Bldg, 151 Patton Ave, Asheville, NC 28801. TEL 828-271-4800, FAX 828-271-4876, NODC.Services@noaa.gov, http://www.ncdc.noaa.gov.

551.5 USA ISSN 0198-0866
LOCAL CLIMATOLOGICAL DATA. BISHOP, CALIFORNIA. ANNUAL SUMMARY WITH COMPARATIVE DATA. Text in English. 19??. a. USD 39 combined subscription per issue includes 12 monthly summaries & one a. summary (effective 2009). back issues avail. **Document type:** *Bulletin, Government.* **Description:** Presents the monthly and annual average, resultant and fastest mile wind speed for the current year as well as the monthly and annual mean and fastest mile speed for a long period for Bishop, California.
Related titles: Online - full text ed.: USD 29 per issue (effective 2009); ◆ Cumulative ed(s).: Local Climatological Data. Bishop, California. Monthly Summary. ISSN 0198-070X.
Published by: U.S. National Climatic Data Center (Subsidiary of: U.S. Department of Commerce), Federal Bldg, 151 Patton Ave, Asheville, NC 28801. TEL 828-271-4800, FAX 828-271-4876, NODC.Services@noaa.gov, http://www.ncdc.noaa.gov.

551.5 USA ISSN 0198-070X
QC984.C2
LOCAL CLIMATOLOGICAL DATA. BISHOP, CALIFORNIA. MONTHLY SUMMARY. Text in English. 19??. m. USD 5 per issue (effective 2009). back issues avail. **Document type:** *Bulletin, Government.* **Description:** Provides information about local climatological data for Bishop.
Related titles: Online - full text ed.: USD 3 per issue (effective 2009); ◆ Cumulative ed. of: Local Climatological Data. Bishop, California. Annual Summary with Comparative Data. ISSN 0198-0866.
—Linda Hall.
Published by: U.S. National Climatic Data Center (Subsidiary of: U.S. Department of Commerce), Federal Bldg, 151 Patton Ave, Asheville, NC 28801. TEL 828-271-4800, FAX 828-271-4876, NODC.Services@noaa.gov, http://www.ncdc.noaa.gov.

551.5 USA ISSN 0198-3814
LOCAL CLIMATOLOGICAL DATA. BISMARCK, NORTH DAKOTA. ANNUAL SUMMARY WITH COMPARATIVE DATA. Text in English. 19??. a. USD 39 combined subscription per issue includes 12 monthly summaries & one a. summary (effective 2009). back issues avail. **Document type:** *Bulletin, Government.* **Description:** Presents the monthly and annual average, resultant and fastest mile wind speed for the current year as well as the monthly and annual mean and fastest mile speed for a long period for Bismarck, North Dakota.
Related titles: CD-ROM ed.; Online - full text ed.: USD 29 per issue (effective 2009); ◆ Cumulative ed(s).: Local Climatological Data. Bismarck, North Dakota. Monthly Summary. ISSN 0198-3822.
Published by: U.S. National Climatic Data Center (Subsidiary of: U.S. Department of Commerce), Federal Bldg, 151 Patton Ave, Asheville, NC 28801. TEL 828-271-4800, FAX 828-271-4876, NODC.Services@noaa.gov, http://www.ncdc.noaa.gov.

551.5 USA ISSN 0198-3822
LOCAL CLIMATOLOGICAL DATA. BISMARCK, NORTH DAKOTA. MONTHLY SUMMARY. Text in English. 19??. m. USD 5 per issue (effective 2009). back issues avail. **Document type:** *Bulletin, Government.* **Description:** Provides information about local climatological data for Bismarck.
Related titles: Online - full text ed.: USD 3 per issue (effective 2009); ◆ Cumulative ed. of: Local Climatological Data. Bismarck, North Dakota. Annual Summary with Comparative Data. ISSN 0198-3814.
—Linda Hall.

Published by: U.S. National Climatic Data Center (Subsidiary of: U.S. Department of Commerce), Federal Bldg, 151 Patton Ave, Asheville, NC 28801. TEL 828-271-4800, FAX 828-271-4876, NODC.Services@noaa.gov, http://www.ncdc.noaa.gov.

551.5 USA ISSN 0198-4578
LOCAL CLIMATOLOGICAL DATA. BLOCK ISLAND, RHODE ISLAND. ANNUAL SUMMARY WITH COMPARATIVE DATA. Text in English. 19??. a. USD 39 combined subscription per issue includes 12 monthly summaries & one a. summary (effective 2009). back issues avail. **Document type:** *Bulletin, Government.* **Description:** Presents the monthly and annual average, resultant and fastest mile wind speed for the current year as well as the monthly and annual mean and fastest mile speed for a long period for Block Island, Rhode Island.
Related titles: Online - full text ed.: USD 29 per issue (effective 2009).
Published by: U.S. National Climatic Data Center (Subsidiary of: U.S. Department of Commerce), Federal Bldg, 151 Patton Ave, Asheville, NC 28801. TEL 828-271-4800, FAX 828-271-4876, NODC.Services@noaa.gov, http://www.ncdc.noaa.gov.

551.5 USA ISSN 0198-0874
LOCAL CLIMATOLOGICAL DATA. BLUE CANYON, CALIFORNIA. ANNUAL SUMMARY WITH COMPARATIVE DATA. Text in English. 19??. a. USD 39 combined subscription per issue includes 12 monthly summaries & one a. summary (effective 2009). back issues avail. **Document type:** *Bulletin, Government.* **Description:** Presents the monthly and annual average, resultant and fastest mile wind speed for the current year as well as the monthly and annual mean and fastest mile speed for a long period for Blue Canyon, California.
Related titles: Online - full text ed.: USD 29 per issue (effective 2009).
Published by: U.S. National Climatic Data Center (Subsidiary of: U.S. Department of Commerce), Federal Bldg, 151 Patton Ave, Asheville, NC 28801. TEL 828-271-4800, FAX 828-271-4876, NODC.Services@noaa.gov, http://www.ncdc.noaa.gov.

551.5 USA ISSN 0198-2435
QC984.M42
LOCAL CLIMATOLOGICAL DATA. BLUE HILL OBSERVATORY. MILTON, MASSACHUSETTS. ANNUAL SUMMARY WITH COMPARATIVE DATA. Text in English. 19??. a. USD 39 combined subscription per issue includes 12 monthly summaries & one a. summary (effective 2009). back issues avail. **Document type:** *Bulletin, Government.* **Description:** Presents the monthly and annual average, resultant and fastest mile wind speed for the current year as well as the monthly and annual mean and fastest mile speed for a long period for Blue Hill Observatory in Milton, Massachusetts.
Formerly: Local Climatological Data. Milton, Massachusetts, Blue Hill Observatory, Annual Summary with Comparative Data
Related titles: Online - full text ed.: USD 29 per issue (effective 2009); ◆ Cumulative ed(s).: Local Climatological Data. Blue Hill Observatory, Milton, Massachusetts. Monthly Summary. ISSN 0198-2443.
Published by: U.S. National Climatic Data Center (Subsidiary of: U.S. Department of Commerce), Federal Bldg, 151 Patton Ave, Asheville, NC 28801. TEL 828-271-4800, FAX 828-271-4876, NODC.Services@noaa.gov, http://www.ncdc.noaa.gov.

551.5 USA ISSN 0198-2443
LOCAL CLIMATOLOGICAL DATA. BLUE HILL OBSERVATORY, MILTON, MASSACHUSETTS. MONTHLY SUMMARY. Text in English. 19??. m. USD 5 per issue (effective 2009). back issues avail. **Document type:** *Bulletin, Government.* **Description:** Provides a monthly summary of temperature extremes, degree days, precipitation and winds, hourly precipitation and 3-hourly weather observations in Blue Hill Observatory, Milton, Massachusetts.
Related titles: Online - full text ed.: USD 3 per issue (effective 2009); ◆ Cumulative ed. of: Local Climatological Data. Blue Hill Observatory. Milton, Massachusetts. Annual Summary with Comparative Data. ISSN 0198-2435.
—Linda Hall.
Published by: U.S. National Climatic Data Center (Subsidiary of: U.S. Department of Commerce), Federal Bldg, 151 Patton Ave, Asheville, NC 28801. TEL 828-271-4800, FAX 828-271-4876, NODC.Services@noaa.gov, http://www.ncdc.noaa.gov.

551.5 USA ISSN 0198-1765
QC984.I22
LOCAL CLIMATOLOGICAL DATA. BOISE, IDAHO. ANNUAL SUMMARY WITH COMPARATIVE DATA. Text in English. 19??. a. USD 39 combined subscription per issue includes 12 monthly summaries & one a. summary (effective 2009). back issues avail. **Document type:** *Bulletin, Government.* **Description:** Presents the monthly and annual average, resultant and fastest mile wind speed for the current year as well as the monthly and annual mean and fastest mile speed for a long period for Boise, Idaho.
Related titles: Online - full text ed.: USD 29 per issue (effective 2009); ◆ Cumulative ed(s).: Local Climatological Data. Boise, Idaho. Monthly Summary. ISSN 0198-1773.
Published by: U.S. National Climatic Data Center (Subsidiary of: U.S. Department of Commerce), Federal Bldg, 151 Patton Ave, Asheville, NC 28801. TEL 828-271-4800, FAX 828-271-4876, NODC.Services@noaa.gov, http://www.ncdc.noaa.gov.

551.5 USA ISSN 0198-1773
QC984.I22
LOCAL CLIMATOLOGICAL DATA. BOISE, IDAHO. MONTHLY SUMMARY. Text in English. 19??. m. USD 5 per issue (effective 2009). back issues avail. **Document type:** *Bulletin, Government.* **Description:** Provides information about local climatological data for Boise.
Related titles: Online - full text ed.: USD 3 per issue (effective 2009); ◆ Cumulative ed. of: Local Climatological Data. Boise, Idaho. Annual Summary with Comparative Data. ISSN 0198-1765.
—Linda Hall.
Published by: U.S. National Climatic Data Center (Subsidiary of: U.S. Department of Commerce), Federal Bldg, 151 Patton Ave, Asheville, NC 28801. TEL 828-271-4800, FAX 828-271-4876, NODC.Services@noaa.gov, http://www.ncdc.noaa.gov.

551.5 USA ISSN 0198-2419
LOCAL CLIMATOLOGICAL DATA. BOSTON, MASSACHUSETTS. ANNUAL SUMMARY WITH COMPARATIVE DATA. Text in English. 19??. a. USD 39 combined subscription per issue includes 12 monthly summaries & one a. summary (effective 2009). back issues avail. **Document type:** *Bulletin, Government.* **Description:** Presents the monthly and annual average, resultant and fastest mile wind speed for the current year as well as the monthly and annual mean and fastest mile speed for a long period for Boston, Massachusetts.
Formerly: Local Climatological Data, with Comparitive Data. Boston, Massachusetts
Related titles: Online - full text ed.: USD 29 per issue (effective 2009); ◆ Cumulative ed(s).: Local Climatological Data. Boston, Massachusetts. Monthly Summary. ISSN 0198-2427.
Published by: U.S. National Climatic Data Center (Subsidiary of: U.S. Department of Commerce), Federal Bldg, 151 Patton Ave, Asheville, NC 28801. TEL 828-271-4800, FAX 828-271-4876, NODC.Services@noaa.gov, http://www.ncdc.noaa.gov.

551.5 USA ISSN 0198-2427
LOCAL CLIMATOLOGICAL DATA. BOSTON, MASSACHUSETTS. MONTHLY SUMMARY. Text in English. 19??. m. USD 5 per issue (effective 2009). back issues avail. **Document type:** *Bulletin, Government.* **Description:** Provides a monthly summary of temperature extremes, degree days, precipitation and winds, hourly precipitation and 3-hourly weather observations in Boston, Massachusetts.
Related titles: Online - full text ed.: USD 3 per issue (effective 2009); ◆ Cumulative ed. of: Local Climatological Data. Boston, Massachusetts. Annual Summary with Comparative Data. ISSN 0198-2419.
—Linda Hall.
Published by: U.S. National Climatic Data Center (Subsidiary of: U.S. Department of Commerce), Federal Bldg, 151 Patton Ave, Asheville, NC 28801. TEL 828-271-4800, FAX 828-271-4876, NODC.Services@noaa.gov, http://www.ncdc.noaa.gov.

551.5 USA ISSN 0198-1129
LOCAL CLIMATOLOGICAL DATA. BRIDGEPORT, CONNECTICUT. ANNUAL SUMMARY WITH COMPARATIVE DATA. Text in English. 19??. a. USD 39 combined subscription per issue includes 12 monthly summaries & one a. summary (effective 2009). back issues avail. **Document type:** *Bulletin, Government.* **Description:** Presents the monthly and annual average, resultant and fastest mile wind speed for the current year as well as the monthly and annual mean and fastest mile speed for a long period for Bridgeport, Connecticut.
Related titles: Online - full text ed.: USD 29 per issue (effective 2009); ◆ Cumulative ed(s).: Local Climatological Data. Bridgeport, Connecticut. Monthly Summary. ISSN 0198-1153.
Published by: U.S. National Climatic Data Center (Subsidiary of: U.S. Department of Commerce), Federal Bldg, 151 Patton Ave, Asheville, NC 28801. TEL 828-271-4800, FAX 828-271-4876, NODC.Services@noaa.gov, http://www.ncdc.noaa.gov.

551.5 USA ISSN 0198-1153
LOCAL CLIMATOLOGICAL DATA. BRIDGEPORT, CONNECTICUT. MONTHLY SUMMARY. Text in English. m. USD 5 per issue (effective 2009). back issues avail. **Document type:** *Bulletin, Government.* **Description:** Provides a monthly summary of temperature extremes, degree days, precipitation and winds, hourly precipitation and 3-hourly weather observations in Bridgeport, Connecticut.
Related titles: Online - full text ed.: USD 3 per issue (effective 2009); ◆ Cumulative ed. of: Local Climatological Data. Bridgeport, Connecticut. Annual Summary with Comparative Data. ISSN 0198-1129.
—Linda Hall.
Published by: U.S. National Climatic Data Center (Subsidiary of: U.S. Department of Commerce), Federal Bldg, 151 Patton Ave, Asheville, NC 28801. TEL 828-271-4800, FAX 828-271-4876, NODC.Services@noaa.gov, http://www.ncdc.noaa.gov.

551.5 USA ISSN 0198-4772
QC984.T2
LOCAL CLIMATOLOGICAL DATA. BRISTOL-JOHNSON, CITY-KINGSPORT, TENNESSEE. MONTHLY SUMMARY. Text in English. 19??. m. USD 5 per issue (effective 2004). **Document type:** *Bulletin, Government.*
Related titles: Online - full text ed.
—Linda Hall.
Published by: U.S. National Climatic Data Center (Subsidiary of: U.S. Department of Commerce), Federal Bldg, 151 Patton Ave, Asheville, NC 28801. TEL 828-271-4800, FAX 828-271-4876, NODC.Services@noaa.gov, http://www.ncdc.noaa.gov.

551.5 USA ISSN 0198-4942
QC984.T42
LOCAL CLIMATOLOGICAL DATA. BROWNSVILLE, TEXAS. ANNUAL SUMMARY WITH COMPARATIVE DATA. Text in English. 19??. a. USD 39 combined subscription per issue includes 12 monthly summaries & one a. summary (effective 2009). back issues avail. **Document type:** *Bulletin, Government.* **Description:** Presents the monthly and annual average, resultant and fastest mile wind speed for the current year as well as the monthly and annual mean and fastest mile speed for a long period for Brownsville, Texas.
Related titles: Online - full text ed.: USD 29 per issue (effective 2009); ◆ Cumulative ed(s).: Local Climatological Data. Brownsville, Texas. Monthly Summary. ISSN 0198-4950.
Published by: U.S. National Climatic Data Center (Subsidiary of: U.S. Department of Commerce), Federal Bldg, 151 Patton Ave, Asheville, NC 28801. TEL 828-271-4800, FAX 828-271-4876, NODC.Services@noaa.gov, http://www.ncdc.noaa.gov.

551.5 USA ISSN 0198-4950
LOCAL CLIMATOLOGICAL DATA. BROWNSVILLE, TEXAS. MONTHLY SUMMARY. Text in English. 19??. m. USD 5 per issue (effective 2009). back issues avail. **Document type:** *Bulletin, Government.* **Description:** Provides a monthly summary of temperature extremes, degree days, precipitation and winds, hourly precipitation and 3-hourly weather observations in Brownsville, Texas.
Related titles: Online - full text ed.: USD 3 per issue (effective 2009); ◆ Cumulative ed. of: Local Climatological Data. Brownsville, Texas. Annual Summary with Comparative Data. ISSN 0198-4942.
—Linda Hall.
Published by: U.S. National Climatic Data Center (Subsidiary of: U.S. Department of Commerce), Federal Bldg, 151 Patton Ave, Asheville, NC 28801. TEL 828-271-4800, FAX 828-271-4876, NODC.Services@noaa.gov, http://www.ncdc.noaa.gov.

551.5 USA ISSN 0198-3571
QC851.N65
LOCAL CLIMATOLOGICAL DATA. BUFFALO, NEW YORK. ANNUAL SUMMARY WITH COMPARATIVE DATA. Text in English. 19??. a. USD 39 combined subscription per issue includes 12 monthly summaries & one a. summary (effective 2009). back issues avail. **Document type:** *Bulletin, Government.* **Description:** Presents the monthly and annual average, resultant and fastest mile wind speed for the current year as well as the monthly and annual mean and fastest mile speed for a long period for Buffalo, New York.
Related titles: Online - full text ed.: USD 29 per issue (effective 2009); ◆ Cumulative ed(s).: Local Climatological Data. Buffalo, New York. Monthly Summary. ISSN 0198-358X.
Published by: U.S. National Climatic Data Center (Subsidiary of: U.S. Department of Commerce), Federal Bldg, 151 Patton Ave, Asheville, NC 28801. TEL 828-271-4800, FAX 828-271-4876, NODC.Services@noaa.gov, http://www.ncdc.noaa.gov.

551.5 USA ISSN 0198-358X
QC983
LOCAL CLIMATOLOGICAL DATA. BUFFALO, NEW YORK. MONTHLY SUMMARY. Text in English. 19??. m. USD 5 per issue (effective 2009). back issues avail. **Document type:** *Bulletin, Government.* **Description:** Provides a monthly summary of temperature extremes, degree days, precipitation and winds, hourly precipitation and 3-hourly weather observations in Buffalo, New York.
Formerly: Local Climatological Data. Buffalo, New York
Related titles: Online - full text ed.: USD 3 per issue (effective 2009); ◆ Cumulative ed. of: Local Climatological Data. Buffalo, New York. Annual Summary with Comparative Data. ISSN 0198-3571.
—Linda Hall.
Published by: U.S. National Climatic Data Center (Subsidiary of: U.S. Department of Commerce), Federal Bldg, 151 Patton Ave, Asheville, NC 28801. TEL 828-271-4800, FAX 828-271-4876, NODC.Services@noaa.gov, http://www.ncdc.noaa.gov.

551.5 USA ISSN 0198-2036
LOCAL CLIMATOLOGICAL DATA. BURLINGTON, IOWA. ANNUAL SUMMARY WITH COMPARATIVE DATA. Text in English. 19??. a. USD 39 combined subscription per issue includes 12 monthly summaries & one a. summary (effective 2009). back issues avail. **Document type:** *Bulletin, Government.* **Description:** Presents the monthly and annual average, resultant and fastest mile wind speed for the current year as well as the monthly and annual mean and fastest mile speed for a long period for Burlington, Iowa.
Related titles: Online - full text ed.: USD 29 per issue (effective 2009).
Published by: U.S. National Climatic Data Center (Subsidiary of: U.S. Department of Commerce), Federal Bldg, 151 Patton Ave, Asheville, NC 28801. TEL 828-271-4800, FAX 828-271-4876, NODC.Services@noaa.gov, http://www.ncdc.noaa.gov.

551.5 USA ISSN 0198-5302
LOCAL CLIMATOLOGICAL DATA. BURLINGTON, VERMONT. ANNUAL SUMMARY WITH COMPARATIVE DATA. Text in English. 19??. a. USD 39 combined subscription per issue includes 12 monthly summaries & one a. summary (effective 2009). back issues avail. **Document type:** *Bulletin, Government.* **Description:** Presents the monthly and annual average, resultant and fastest mile wind speed for the current year as well as the monthly and annual mean and fastest mile speed for a long period for Burlington, Vermont.
Related titles: Online - full text ed.: USD 29 per issue (effective 2009); ◆ Cumulative ed(s).: Local Climatological Data. Burlington, Vermont. Monthly Summary. ISSN 0198-5310.
Published by: U.S. National Climatic Data Center (Subsidiary of: U.S. Department of Commerce), Federal Bldg, 151 Patton Ave, Asheville, NC 28801. TEL 828-271-4800, FAX 828-271-4876, NODC.Services@noaa.gov, http://www.ncdc.noaa.gov.

551.5 USA ISSN 0198-5310
QC984.V4
LOCAL CLIMATOLOGICAL DATA. BURLINGTON, VERMONT. MONTHLY SUMMARY. Text in English. 19??. m. USD 5 per issue (effective 2009). back issues avail. **Document type:** *Bulletin, Government.* **Description:** Provides a monthly summary of temperature extremes, degree days, precipitation and winds, hourly precipitation and 3-hourly weather observations in Burlington, Vermont.
Related titles: Online - full text ed.: USD 3 per issue (effective 2009); ◆ Cumulative ed. of: Local Climatological Data. Burlington, Vermont. Annual Summary with Comparative Data. ISSN 0198-5302.
—Linda Hall.
Published by: U.S. National Climatic Data Center (Subsidiary of: U.S. Department of Commerce), Federal Bldg, 151 Patton Ave, Asheville, NC 28801. TEL 828-271-4800, FAX 828-271-4876, NODC.Services@noaa.gov, http://www.ncdc.noaa.gov.

551.5 USA ISSN 0198-411X
LOCAL CLIMATOLOGICAL DATA. BURNS, OREGON. ANNUAL SUMMARY WITH COMPARATIVE DATA. Text in English. 19??. a. USD 39 combined subscription per issue includes 12 monthly summaries & one a. summary (effective 2009). back issues avail. **Document type:** *Bulletin, Government.* **Description:** Presents the monthly and annual average, resultant and fastest mile wind speed for the current year as well as the monthly and annual mean and fastest mile speed for a long period for Burns, Oregon.
Related titles: Online - full text ed.: USD 29 per issue (effective 2009); ◆ Cumulative ed(s).: Local Climatological Data. Burns, Oregon. Monthly Summary. ISSN 0198-4128.
Published by: U.S. National Climatic Data Center (Subsidiary of: U.S. Department of Commerce), Federal Bldg, 151 Patton Ave, Asheville, NC 28801. TEL 828-271-4800, FAX 828-271-4876, NODC.Services@noaa.gov, http://www.ncdc.noaa.gov.

551.5 USA ISSN 0198-4128
LOCAL CLIMATOLOGICAL DATA. BURNS, OREGON. MONTHLY SUMMARY. Text in English. 19??. m. USD 5 per issue (effective 2009). back issues avail. **Document type:** *Bulletin, Government.* **Description:** Provides a monthly summary of temperature extremes, degree days, precipitation and winds, hourly precipitation and 3-hourly weather observations in Burns, Oregon.
Related titles: Online - full text ed.: USD 3 per issue (effective 2009); ◆ Cumulative ed. of: Local Climatological Data. Burns, Oregon. Annual Summary with Comparative Data. ISSN 0198-411X.
—Linda Hall.

Published by: U.S. National Climatic Data Center (Subsidiary of: U.S. Department of Commerce), Federal Bldg, 151 Patton Ave, Asheville, NC 28801. TEL 828-271-4800, FAX 828-271-4876, NODC.Services@noaa.gov, http://www.ncdc.noaa.gov.

551.5 USA ISSN 0198-182X
LOCAL CLIMATOLOGICAL DATA. CAIRO, ILLINOIS. ANNUAL SUMMARY WITH COMPARATIVE DATA. Text in English. 19??. a. USD 39 combined subscription per issue includes 12 monthly summaries & one a. summary (effective 2009). back issues avail. **Document type:** *Bulletin, Government.* **Description:** Presents the monthly and annual average, resultant and fastest mile wind speed for the current year as well as the monthly and annual mean and fastest mile speed for a long period for Cairo, Illinois.
Related titles: Online - full text ed.: USD 29 per issue (effective 2009).
Published by: U.S. National Climatic Data Center (Subsidiary of: U.S. Department of Commerce), Federal Bldg, 151 Patton Ave, Asheville, NC 28801. TEL 828-271-4800, FAX 828-271-4876, NODC.Services@noaa.gov, http://www.ncdc.noaa.gov.

551.5 USA ISSN 0198-3717
LOCAL CLIMATOLOGICAL DATA. CAPE HATTERAS, NORTH CAROLINA. ANNUAL SUMMARY WITH COMPARATIVE DATA. Text in English. 19??. a. USD 39 combined subscription per issue includes 12 monthly summaries & one a. summary (effective 2009). back issues avail. **Document type:** *Bulletin, Government.* **Description:** Presents the monthly and annual average, resultant and fastest mile wind speed for the current year as well as the monthly and annual mean and fastest mile speed for a long period for Cape Hatteras, North Carolina.
Related titles: Online - full text ed.: USD 29 per issue (effective 2009); ◆ Cumulative ed(s).: Local Climatological Data. Cape Hatteras, North Carolina. Monthly Summary. ISSN 0198-3725.
Published by: U.S. National Climatic Data Center (Subsidiary of: U.S. Department of Commerce), Federal Bldg, 151 Patton Ave, Asheville, NC 28801. TEL 828-271-4800, FAX 828-271-4876, NODC.Services@noaa.gov, http://www.ncdc.noaa.gov.

551.5 USA ISSN 0198-3725
LOCAL CLIMATOLOGICAL DATA. CAPE HATTERAS, NORTH CAROLINA. MONTHLY SUMMARY. Text in English. 19??. m. USD 5 per issue (effective 2009). back issues avail. **Document type:** *Bulletin, Government.* **Description:** Provides a monthly summary of temperature extremes, degree days, precipitation and winds, hourly precipitation and 3-hourly weather observations in Cape Hatteras, North Carolina.
Related titles: Online - full text ed.: USD 3 per issue (effective 2009); ◆ Cumulative ed. of: Local Climatological Data. Cape Hatteras, North Carolina. Annual Summary with Comparative Data. ISSN 0198-3717.
—Linda Hall.
Published by: U.S. National Climatic Data Center (Subsidiary of: U.S. Department of Commerce), Federal Bldg, 151 Patton Ave, Asheville, NC 28801. TEL 828-271-4800, FAX 828-271-4876, NODC.Services@noaa.gov, http://www.ncdc.noaa.gov.

551.5 USA ISSN 0198-2354
LOCAL CLIMATOLOGICAL DATA. CARIBOU, MAINE. ANNUAL SUMMARY WITH COMPARATIVE DATA. Text in English. 19??. a. USD 39 combined subscription per issue includes 12 monthly summaries & one a. summary (effective 2009). back issues avail. **Document type:** *Bulletin, Government.* **Description:** Presents the monthly and annual average, resultant and fastest mile wind speed for the current year as well as the monthly and annual mean and fastest mile speed for a long period for Caribou, Maine.
Related titles: Online - full text ed.: USD 29 per issue (effective 2009); ◆ Cumulative ed(s).: Local Climatological Data. Caribou, Maine. Monthly Summary. ISSN 0198-2362.
Published by: U.S. National Climatic Data Center (Subsidiary of: U.S. Department of Commerce), Federal Bldg, 151 Patton Ave, Asheville, NC 28801. TEL 828-271-4800, FAX 828-271-4876, NODC.Services@noaa.gov, http://www.ncdc.noaa.gov.

551.5 USA ISSN 0198-2362
LOCAL CLIMATOLOGICAL DATA. CARIBOU, MAINE. MONTHLY SUMMARY. Text in English. 19??. m. USD 5 per issue (effective 2009). back issues avail. **Document type:** *Bulletin, Government.* **Description:** Provides a monthly summary of temperature extremes, degree days, precipitation and winds, hourly precipitation and 3-hourly weather observations in Caribou, Maine.
Related titles: Online - full text ed.: USD 3 per issue (effective 2009); ◆ Cumulative ed. of: Local Climatological Data. Caribou, Maine. Annual Summary with Comparative Data. ISSN 0198-2354.
—Linda Hall.
Published by: U.S. National Climatic Data Center (Subsidiary of: U.S. Department of Commerce), Federal Bldg, 151 Patton Ave, Asheville, NC 28801. TEL 828-271-4800, FAX 828-271-4876, NODC.Services@noaa.gov, http://www.ncdc.noaa.gov.

551.5 USA ISSN 0198-5779
LOCAL CLIMATOLOGICAL DATA. CASPER, WYOMING. MONTHLY SUMMARY. Text in English. 19??. m. USD 5 per issue (effective 2009). back issues avail. **Document type:** *Bulletin, Government.* **Description:** Provides a monthly summary of temperature extremes, degree days, precipitation and winds, hourly precipitation and 3-hourly weather observations in Casper, Wyoming.
Related titles: Online - full text ed.: USD 3 per issue (effective 2009).
—Linda Hall.
Published by: U.S. National Climatic Data Center (Subsidiary of: U.S. Department of Commerce), Federal Bldg, 151 Patton Ave, Asheville, NC 28801. TEL 828-271-4800, FAX 828-271-4876, NODC.Services@noaa.gov, http://www.ncdc.noaa.gov.

551.5 USA ISSN 0198-4616
LOCAL CLIMATOLOGICAL DATA. CHARLESTON, SOUTH CAROLINA. ANNUAL SUMMARY WITH COMPARATIVE DATA. Text in English. 19??. a. USD 39 combined subscription per issue includes 12 monthly summaries & one a. summary (effective 2009). back issues avail. **Document type:** *Bulletin, Government.* **Description:** Presents the monthly and annual average, resultant and fastest mile wind speed for the current year as well as the monthly and annual mean and fastest mile speed for a long period for Charleston, South Carolina.
Related titles: Online - full text ed.: USD 29 per issue (effective 2009); ◆ Cumulative ed(s).: Local Climatological Data. Charleston, South Carolina International Airport. Monthly Summary. ISSN 0198-4624.
Published by: U.S. National Climatic Data Center (Subsidiary of: U.S. Department of Commerce), Federal Bldg, 151 Patton Ave, Asheville, NC 28801. TEL 828-271-4800, FAX 828-271-4876, NODC.Services@noaa.gov, http://www.ncdc.noaa.gov.

551.5 USA ISSN 0198-4624
LOCAL CLIMATOLOGICAL DATA. CHARLESTON, SOUTH CAROLINA INTERNATIONAL AIRPORT. MONTHLY SUMMARY. Text in English. m. USD 5 per issue (effective 2009). back issues avail. **Document type:** *Bulletin, Government.*
Related titles: Online - full text ed.: USD 3 per issue (effective 2009); ◆ Cumulative ed. of: Local Climatological Data. Charleston, South Carolina. Annual Summary with Comparative Data. ISSN 0198-4616.
—Linda Hall.
Published by: U.S. National Climatic Data Center (Subsidiary of: U.S. Department of Commerce), Federal Bldg, 151 Patton Ave, Asheville, NC 28801. TEL 828-271-4800, FAX 828-271-4876, NODC.Services@noaa.gov, http://www.ncdc.noaa.gov.

551.5 USA ISSN 0198-4632
LOCAL CLIMATOLOGICAL DATA. CHARLESTON, SOUTH CAROLINA, US CUSTOM HOUSE. MONTHLY SUMMARY. Text in English. m. USD 5 per issue (effective 2004). **Document type:** *Bulletin, Government.*
Related titles: Online - full text ed.
—Linda Hall.
Published by: U.S. National Climatic Data Center (Subsidiary of: U.S. Department of Commerce), Federal Bldg, 151 Patton Ave, Asheville, NC 28801. TEL 828-271-4800, FAX 828-271-4876, NODC.Services@noaa.gov, http://www.ncdc.noaa.gov.

551.5 USA ISSN 0198-5612
LOCAL CLIMATOLOGICAL DATA. CHARLESTON, WEST VIRGINIA. MONTHLY SUMMARY. Text in English. 19??. m. USD 5 per issue (effective 2009). back issues avail. **Document type:** *Bulletin, Government.* **Description:** Provides a monthly summary of temperature extremes, degree days, precipitation and winds, hourly precipitation and 3-hourly weather observations in Charleston, West Virginia.
Related titles: Online - full text ed.: USD 3 per issue (effective 2009).
—Linda Hall.
Published by: U.S. National Climatic Data Center (Subsidiary of: U.S. Department of Commerce), Federal Bldg, 151 Patton Ave, Asheville, NC 28801. TEL 828-271-4800, FAX 828-271-4876, NODC.Services@noaa.gov, http://www.ncdc.noaa.gov.

551.5 USA ISSN 0198-3733
LOCAL CLIMATOLOGICAL DATA. CHARLOTTE, NORTH CAROLINA. ANNUAL SUMMARY WITH COMPARATIVE DATA. Text in English. 19??. a. USD 39 combined subscription per issue includes 12 monthly summaries & one a. summary (effective 2009). back issues avail. **Document type:** *Bulletin, Government.* **Description:** Presents the monthly and annual average, resultant and fastest mile wind speed for the current year as well as the monthly and annual mean and fastest mile speed for a long period for Charlotte, North Carolina.
Related titles: Online - full text ed.: USD 29 per issue (effective 2009); ◆ Cumulative ed(s).: Local Climatological Data. Charlotte, North Carolina. Monthly Summary. ISSN 0198-3741.
Published by: U.S. National Climatic Data Center (Subsidiary of: U.S. Department of Commerce), Federal Bldg, 151 Patton Ave, Asheville, NC 28801. TEL 828-271-4800, FAX 828-271-4876, NODC.Services@noaa.gov, http://www.ncdc.noaa.gov.

551.5 USA ISSN 0198-3741
LOCAL CLIMATOLOGICAL DATA. CHARLOTTE, NORTH CAROLINA. MONTHLY SUMMARY. Text in English. 19??. m. USD 5 per issue (effective 2009). back issues avail. **Document type:** *Bulletin, Government.* **Description:** Provides a monthly summary of temperature extremes, degree days, precipitation and winds, hourly precipitation and 3-hourly weather observations in Charlotte, North Carolina.
Related titles: Online - full text ed.: USD 3 per issue (effective 2009); ◆ Cumulative ed. of: Local Climatological Data. Charlotte, North Carolina. Annual Summary with Comparative Data. ISSN 0198-3733.
—Linda Hall.
Published by: U.S. National Climatic Data Center (Subsidiary of: U.S. Department of Commerce), Federal Bldg, 151 Patton Ave, Asheville, NC 28801. TEL 828-271-4800, FAX 828-271-4876, NODC.Services@noaa.gov, http://www.ncdc.noaa.gov.

551.5 USA ISSN 0198-4780
LOCAL CLIMATOLOGICAL DATA. CHATTANOOGA, TENNESSEE. ANNUAL SUMMARY WITH COMPARATIVE DATA. Text in English. 19??. a. USD 39 combined subscription per issue includes 12 monthly summaries & one a. summary (effective 2009). back issues avail. **Document type:** *Bulletin, Government.* **Description:** Presents the monthly and annual average, resultant and fastest mile wind speed for the current year as well as the monthly and annual mean and fastest mile speed for a long period for Chattanooga, Tennessee.
Related titles: Online - full text ed.: USD 29 per issue (effective 2009); ◆ Cumulative ed(s).: Local Climatological Data. Chattanooga, Tennessee. Monthly Summary. ISSN 0198-4799.
Published by: U.S. National Climatic Data Center (Subsidiary of: U.S. Department of Commerce), Federal Bldg, 151 Patton Ave, Asheville, NC 28801. TEL 828-271-4800, FAX 828-271-4876, NODC.Services@noaa.gov, http://www.ncdc.noaa.gov.

551.5 USA ISSN 0198-4799
LOCAL CLIMATOLOGICAL DATA. CHATTANOOGA, TENNESSEE. MONTHLY SUMMARY. Text in English. 19??. m. USD 5 per issue (effective 2009). back issues avail. **Document type:** *Bulletin, Government.* **Description:** Provides a monthly summary of temperature extremes, degree days, precipitation and winds, hourly precipitation and 3-hourly weather observations in Chattanooga, Tennessee.
Related titles: Online - full text ed.: USD 3 per issue (effective 2009); ◆ Cumulative ed. of: Local Climatological Data. Chattanooga, Tennessee. Annual Summary with Comparative Data. ISSN 0198-4780.
—Linda Hall.
Published by: U.S. National Climatic Data Center (Subsidiary of: U.S. Department of Commerce), Federal Bldg, 151 Patton Ave, Asheville, NC 28801. TEL 828-271-4800, FAX 828-271-4876, NODC.Services@noaa.gov, http://www.ncdc.noaa.gov.

551.5 USA ISSN 0198-5795
LOCAL CLIMATOLOGICAL DATA. CHEYENNE, WYOMING. MONTHLY SUMMARY. Text in English. 19??. m. USD 5 per issue (effective 2009). back issues avail. **Document type:** *Bulletin, Government.* **Description:** Provides a monthly summary of temperature extremes, degree days, precipitation and winds, hourly precipitation and 3-hourly weather observations in Cheyenne, Wyoming.
Related titles: Online - full text ed.: USD 3 per issue (effective 2009).
—Linda Hall.
Published by: U.S. National Climatic Data Center (Subsidiary of: U.S. Department of Commerce), Federal Bldg, 151 Patton Ave, Asheville, NC 28801. TEL 828-271-4800, FAX 828-271-4876, NODC.Services@noaa.gov, http://www.ncdc.noaa.gov.

551.5 USA ISSN 0198-1846
LOCAL CLIMATOLOGICAL DATA. CHICAGO, ILLINOIS. O'HARE INTERNATIONAL AIRPORT. ANNUAL SUMMARY WITH COMPARATIVE DATA. Text in English. 19??. a. USD 39 combined subscription per issue includes 12 monthly summaries & one a. summary (effective 2009). back issues avail. **Document type:** *Bulletin, Government.* **Description:** Presents the monthly and annual average, resultant and fastest mile wind speed for the current year as well as the monthly and annual mean and fastest mile speed for a long period for O'Hare International Airport in Chicago, Illinois.
Related titles: Online - full text ed.: USD 29 per issue (effective 2009); ◆ Cumulative ed(s).: Local Climatological Data. Chicago Illinois O'Hare International Airport. Monthly Summary. ISSN 0198-1854.
Published by: U.S. National Climatic Data Center (Subsidiary of: U.S. Department of Commerce), Federal Bldg, 151 Patton Ave, Asheville, NC 28801. TEL 828-271-4800, FAX 828-271-4876, NODC.Services@noaa.gov, http://www.ncdc.noaa.gov.

551.5 USA ISSN 0198-1854
LOCAL CLIMATOLOGICAL DATA. CHICAGO ILLINOIS O'HARE INTERNATIONAL AIRPORT. MONTHLY SUMMARY. Text in English. 19??. m. USD 5 per issue (effective 2009). back issues avail. **Document type:** *Bulletin, Government.* **Description:** Provides a monthly summary of temperature extremes, degree days, precipitation and winds, hourly precipitation and 3-hourly weather observations in Chicago Illinois O'Hare International Airport.
Related titles: Online - full text ed.: USD 3 per issue (effective 2009); ◆ Cumulative ed. of: Local Climatological Data. Chicago, Illinois. O'Hare International Airport. Annual Summary with Comparative Data. ISSN 0198-1846.
—Linda Hall.
Published by: U.S. National Climatic Data Center (Subsidiary of: U.S. Department of Commerce), Federal Bldg, 151 Patton Ave, Asheville, NC 28801. TEL 828-271-4800, FAX 828-271-4876, NODC.Services@noaa.gov, http://www.ncdc.noaa.gov.

551.5 USA ISSN 2151-7762
▼ **LOCAL CLIMATOLOGICAL DATA. CHILDRESS, TEXAS.** Text in English. 2009. m. USD 3 per issue (effective 2010). **Document type:** *Bulletin, Government.*
Published by: U.S. National Climatic Data Center (Subsidiary of: U.S. Department of Commerce), Federal Bldg, 151 Patton Ave, Asheville, NC 28801. TEL 828-271-4800, FAX 828-271-4876, ncdc.info@noaa.gov, http://www.ncdc.noaa.gov.

551.5 USA ISSN 0198-3911
LOCAL CLIMATOLOGICAL DATA. CINCINNATI, OHIO. GREATER CINCINNATI AIRPORT. ANNUAL SUMMARY WITH COMPARATIVE DATA. Text in English. a. USD 39 combined subscription per issue includes 12 monthly summaries & one a. summary (effective 2009). **Document type:** *Bulletin, Government.*
Related titles: Online - full text ed.: USD 29 per issue (effective 2009); ◆ Cumulative ed(s).: Local Climatological Data. Cincinnati, Ohio. Greater Cincinnati Airport, Boone County, Kentucky. Monthly Summary. ISSN 0198-392X.
Published by: U.S. National Climatic Data Center (Subsidiary of: U.S. Department of Commerce), Federal Bldg, 151 Patton Ave, Asheville, NC 28801. TEL 828-271-4800, FAX 828-271-4876, NODC.Services@noaa.gov, http://www.ncdc.noaa.gov.

551.5 USA ISSN 0198-392X
LOCAL CLIMATOLOGICAL DATA. CINCINNATI, OHIO. GREATER CINCINNATI AIRPORT, BOONE COUNTY, KENTUCKY. MONTHLY SUMMARY. Text in English. 19??. m. USD 5 per issue (effective 2004). **Document type:** *Bulletin, Government.*
Related titles: Online - full text ed.; ◆ Cumulative ed. of: Local Climatological Data. Cincinnati, Ohio. Greater Cincinnati Airport. Annual Summary with Comparative Data. ISSN 0198-3911.
—Linda Hall.
Published by: U.S. National Climatic Data Center (Subsidiary of: U.S. Department of Commerce), Federal Bldg, 151 Patton Ave, Asheville, NC 28801. TEL 828-271-4800, FAX 828-271-4876, NODC.Services@noaa.gov, http://www.ncdc.noaa.gov.

551.5 USA ISSN 0198-3490
LOCAL CLIMATOLOGICAL DATA. CLAYTON, NEW MEXICO. ANNUAL SUMMARY WITH COMPARATIVE DATA. Text in English. 19??. a. USD 39 combined subscription per issue includes 12 monthly summaries & one a. summary (effective 2009). back issues avail. **Document type:** *Bulletin, Government.* **Description:** Presents the monthly and annual average, resultant and fastest mile wind speed for the current year as well as the monthly and annual mean and fastest mile speed for a long period for Clayton, New Mexico.
Related titles: Online - full text ed.: USD 29 per issue (effective 2009); ◆ Cumulative ed(s).: Local Climatological Data. Clayton, New Mexico. Monthly Summary. ISSN 0198-2486.
Published by: U.S. National Climatic Data Center (Subsidiary of: U.S. Department of Commerce), Federal Bldg, 151 Patton Ave, Asheville, NC 28801. TEL 828-271-4800, FAX 828-271-4876, NODC.Services@noaa.gov, http://www.ncdc.noaa.gov.

551.5 USA ISSN 0198-2486
LOCAL CLIMATOLOGICAL DATA. CLAYTON, NEW MEXICO. MONTHLY SUMMARY. Text in English. 19??. m. USD 5 per issue (effective 2009). back issues avail. **Document type:** *Bulletin, Government.* **Description:** Provides a monthly summary of temperature extremes, degree days, precipitation and winds, hourly precipitation and 3-hourly weather observations in Clayton, New Mexico.
Related titles: Online - full text ed.: USD 3 per issue (effective 2009); ◆ Cumulative ed. of: Local Climatological Data. Clayton, New Mexico. Annual Summary with Comparative Data. ISSN 0198-3490.
—Linda Hall.

Published by: U.S. National Climatic Data Center (Subsidiary of: U.S. Department of Commerce), Federal Bldg, 151 Patton Ave, Asheville, NC 28801. TEL 828-271-4800, FAX 828-271-4876, NODC.Services@noaa.gov, http://www.ncdc.noaa.gov.

551.5 USA ISSN 0198-3938
LOCAL CLIMATOLOGICAL DATA. CLEVELAND, OHIO. ANNUAL SUMMARY WITH COMPARATIVE DATA. Text in English. 19??. a. USD 39 combined subscription per issue includes 12 monthly summaries & one a. summary (effective 2009). back issues avail. **Document type:** *Bulletin, Government.* **Description:** Presents the monthly and annual average, resultant and fastest mile wind speed for the current year as well as the monthly and annual mean and fastest mile speed for a long period for Cleveland, Ohio.
Related titles: Online - full text ed.: USD 29 per issue (effective 2009); ◆ Cumulative ed(s).: Local Climatological Data. Cleveland, Ohio. Monthly Summary. ISSN 0198-3946.
Published by: U.S. National Climatic Data Center (Subsidiary of: U.S. Department of Commerce), Federal Bldg, 151 Patton Ave, Asheville, NC 28801. TEL 828-271-4800, FAX 828-271-4876, NODC.Services@noaa.gov, http://www.ncdc.noaa.gov.

551.5 USA ISSN 0198-3946
LOCAL CLIMATOLOGICAL DATA. CLEVELAND, OHIO. MONTHLY SUMMARY. Text in English. 19??. m. USD 5 per issue (effective 2009). back issues avail. **Document type:** *Bulletin, Government.* **Description:** Provides a monthly summary of temperature extremes, degree days, precipitation and winds, hourly precipitation and 3-hourly weather observations in Cleveland, Ohio.
Related titles: Online - full text ed.: USD 3 per issue (effective 2009); ◆ Cumulative ed. of: Local Climatological Data. Cleveland, Ohio. Annual Summary with Comparative Data. ISSN 0198-3938.
—Linda Hall.
Published by: U.S. National Climatic Data Center (Subsidiary of: U.S. Department of Commerce), Federal Bldg, 151 Patton Ave, Asheville, NC 28801. TEL 828-271-4800, FAX 828-271-4876, NODC.Services@noaa.gov, http://www.ncdc.noaa.gov.

551.5 USA ISSN 0197-968X
QC984.A42
LOCAL CLIMATOLOGICAL DATA. COLD BAY, ALASKA. ANNUAL SUMMARY WITH COMPARATIVE DATA. Text in English. 19??. a. USD 39 combined subscription per issue includes 12 monthly summaries & one a. summary (effective 2009). back issues avail. **Document type:** *Bulletin, Government.* **Description:** Presents the monthly and annual average, resultant and fastest mile wind speed for the current year as well as the monthly and annual mean and fastest mile speed for a long period for Cold Bay, Alaska.
Related titles: Online - full text ed.: USD 29 per issue (effective 2009); ◆ Cumulative ed(s).: Local Climatological Data. Cold Bay, Alaska. Monthly Summary. ISSN 0197-9698.
Published by: U.S. National Climatic Data Center (Subsidiary of: U.S. Department of Commerce), Federal Bldg, 151 Patton Ave, Asheville, NC 28801. TEL 828-271-4800, FAX 828-271-4876, NODC.Services@noaa.gov, http://www.ncdc.noaa.gov.

551.5 USA ISSN 0197-9698
QC984.A42
LOCAL CLIMATOLOGICAL DATA. COLD BAY, ALASKA. MONTHLY SUMMARY. Text in English. 19??. m. USD 5 per issue (effective 2009). back issues avail. **Document type:** *Bulletin, Government.* **Description:** Provides a monthly summary of temperature extremes, degree days, precipitation and winds, hourly precipitation and 3-hourly weather observations in Cold Bay, Alaska.
Related titles: Online - full text ed.: USD 3 per issue (effective 2009); ◆ Cumulative ed. of: Local Climatological Data. Cold Bay, Alaska. Annual Summary with Comparative Data. ISSN 0197-968X.
—Linda Hall.
Published by: U.S. National Climatic Data Center (Subsidiary of: U.S. Department of Commerce), Federal Bldg, 151 Patton Ave, Asheville, NC 28801. TEL 828-271-4800, FAX 828-271-4876, NODC.Services@noaa.gov, http://www.ncdc.noaa.gov.

551.5 USA ISSN 0198-7704
LOCAL CLIMATOLOGICAL DATA. COLORADO SPRINGS, COLORADO. ANNUAL SUMMARY WITH COMPARATIVE DATA. Text in English. 19??. a. USD 39 combined subscription per issue includes 12 monthly summaries & one a. summary (effective 2009). back issues avail. **Document type:** *Bulletin, Government.* **Description:** Presents the monthly and annual average, resultant and fastest mile wind speed for the current year as well as the monthly and annual mean and fastest mile speed for a long period for Colorado Springs, Colorado.
Related titles: Online - full text ed.: USD 29 per issue (effective 2009); ◆ Cumulative ed(s).: Local Climatological Data. Colorado Springs, Colorado. Monthly Summary. ISSN 0198-7712.
Published by: U.S. National Climatic Data Center (Subsidiary of: U.S. Department of Commerce), Federal Bldg, 151 Patton Ave, Asheville, NC 28801. TEL 828-271-4800, FAX 828-271-4876, NODC.Services@noaa.gov, http://www.ncdc.noaa.gov.

551.5 USA ISSN 0198-7712
LOCAL CLIMATOLOGICAL DATA. COLORADO SPRINGS, COLORADO. MONTHLY SUMMARY. Text in English. 19??. m. USD 5 per issue (effective 2009). back issues avail. **Document type:** *Bulletin, Government.* **Description:** Provides a monthly summary of temperature extremes, degree days, precipitation and winds, hourly precipitation and 3-hourly weather observations in Colorado Springs, Colorado.
Related titles: Online - full text ed.: USD 3 per issue (effective 2009); ◆ Cumulative ed. of: Local Climatological Data. Colorado Springs, Colorado. Annual Summary with Comparative Data. ISSN 0198-7704.
—Linda Hall.
Published by: U.S. National Climatic Data Center (Subsidiary of: U.S. Department of Commerce), Federal Bldg, 151 Patton Ave, Asheville, NC 28801. TEL 828-271-4800, FAX 828-271-4876, NODC.Services@noaa.gov, http://www.ncdc.noaa.gov.

551.5 USA ISSN 0198-2834
QC984.M82
LOCAL CLIMATOLOGICAL DATA. COLUMBIA, MISSOURI. ANNUAL SUMMARY WITH COMPARATIVE DATA. Text in English. 19??. a. USD 39 combined subscription per issue includes 12 monthly summaries & one a. summary (effective 2009). back issues avail. **Document type:** *Bulletin, Government.* **Description:** Presents the monthly and annual average, resultant and fastest mile wind speed for the current year as well as the monthly and annual mean and fastest mile speed for a long period for Columbia, Missouri.
Related titles: Online - full text ed.: USD 29 per issue (effective 2009); ◆ Cumulative ed(s).: Local Climatological Data. Columbia, Missouri. Monthly Summary. ISSN 0198-2842.
Published by: U.S. National Climatic Data Center (Subsidiary of: U.S. Department of Commerce), Federal Bldg, 151 Patton Ave, Asheville, NC 28801. TEL 828-271-4800, FAX 828-271-4876, NODC.Services@noaa.gov, http://www.ncdc.noaa.gov.

551.5 USA ISSN 0198-2842
LOCAL CLIMATOLOGICAL DATA. COLUMBIA, MISSOURI. MONTHLY SUMMARY. Text in English. 19??. m. USD 5 per issue (effective 2009). back issues avail. **Document type:** *Bulletin, Government.* **Description:** Provides a monthly summary of temperature extremes, degree days, precipitation and winds, hourly precipitation and 3-hourly weather observations in Columbia, Missouri.
Related titles: Online - full text ed.: USD 3 per issue (effective 2009); ◆ Cumulative ed. of: Local Climatological Data. Columbia, Missouri. Annual Summary with Comparative Data. ISSN 0198-2834.
—Linda Hall.
Published by: U.S. National Climatic Data Center (Subsidiary of: U.S. Department of Commerce), Federal Bldg, 151 Patton Ave, Asheville, NC 28801. TEL 828-271-4800, FAX 828-271-4876, NODC.Services@noaa.gov, http://www.ncdc.noaa.gov.

551.5 USA ISSN 0198-4640
LOCAL CLIMATOLOGICAL DATA. COLUMBIA, SOUTH CAROLINA. ANNUAL SUMMARY WITH COMPARATIVE DATA. Text in English. 19??. a. USD 39 combined subscription per issue includes 12 monthly summaries & one a. summary (effective 2009). **Document type:** *Bulletin, Government.* **Description:** Presents the monthly and annual average, resultant and fastest mile wind speed for the current year as well as the monthly and annual mean and fastest mile speed for a long period for Columbia, South Carolina.
Related titles: Online - full text ed.: USD 29 per issue (effective 2009); ◆ Cumulative ed(s).: Local Climatological Data. Columbia, South Carolina. Monthly Summary. ISSN 0198-4659.
Published by: U.S. National Climatic Data Center (Subsidiary of: U.S. Department of Commerce), Federal Bldg, 151 Patton Ave, Asheville, NC 28801. TEL 828-271-4800, FAX 828-271-4876, NODC.Services@noaa.gov, http://www.ncdc.noaa.gov.

551.5 USA ISSN 0198-4659
LOCAL CLIMATOLOGICAL DATA. COLUMBIA, SOUTH CAROLINA. MONTHLY SUMMARY. Text in English. 19??. m. USD 5 per issue (effective 2009). back issues avail. **Document type:** *Bulletin, Government.* **Description:** Provides a monthly summary of temperature extremes, degree days, precipitation and winds, hourly precipitation and 3-hourly weather observations in Columbia, South Carolina.
Related titles: Online - full text ed.: USD 3 per issue (effective 2009); ◆ Cumulative ed. of: Local Climatological Data. Columbia, South Carolina. Annual Summary with Comparative Data. ISSN 0198-4640.
—Linda Hall.
Published by: U.S. National Climatic Data Center (Subsidiary of: U.S. Department of Commerce), Federal Bldg, 151 Patton Ave, Asheville, NC 28801. TEL 828-271-4800, FAX 828-271-4876, NODC.Services@noaa.gov, http://www.ncdc.noaa.gov.

551.5 USA ISSN 0198-1609
LOCAL CLIMATOLOGICAL DATA. COLUMBUS, GEORGIA. ANNUAL SUMMARY WITH COMPARATIVE DATA. Text in English. 19??. a. USD 39 combined subscription per issue includes 12 monthly summaries & one a. summary (effective 2009). back issues avail. **Document type:** *Bulletin, Government.* **Description:** Presents the monthly and annual average, resultant and fastest mile wind speed for the current year as well as the monthly and annual mean and fastest mile speed for a long period for Columbus, Georgia.
Related titles: Online - full text ed.: USD 29 per issue (effective 2009); ◆ Cumulative ed(s).: Local Climatological Data. Columbus, Georgia. Monthly Summary. ISSN 0198-1617.
Published by: U.S. National Climatic Data Center (Subsidiary of: U.S. Department of Commerce), Federal Bldg, 151 Patton Ave, Asheville, NC 28801. TEL 828-271-4800, FAX 828-271-4876, NODC.Services@noaa.gov, http://www.ncdc.noaa.gov.

551.5 USA ISSN 0198-1617
CODEN: AQINDQ
LOCAL CLIMATOLOGICAL DATA. COLUMBUS, GEORGIA. MONTHLY SUMMARY. Text in English. 19??. m. USD 5 per issue (effective 2009). back issues avail. **Document type:** *Bulletin, Government.* **Description:** Provides a monthly summary of temperature extremes, degree days, precipitation and winds, hourly precipitation and 3-hourly weather observations in Columbus, Georgia.
Related titles: Online - full text ed.: USD 3 per issue (effective 2009); ◆ Cumulative ed. of: Local Climatological Data. Columbus, Georgia. Annual Summary with Comparative Data. ISSN 0198-1609.
—Linda Hall.
Published by: U.S. National Climatic Data Center (Subsidiary of: U.S. Department of Commerce), Federal Bldg, 151 Patton Ave, Asheville, NC 28801. TEL 828-271-4800, FAX 828-271-4876, NODC.Services@noaa.gov, http://www.ncdc.noaa.gov.

551.5 USA ISSN 0198-3954
LOCAL CLIMATOLOGICAL DATA. COLUMBUS, OHIO. ANNUAL SUMMARY WITH COMPARATIVE DATA. Text in English. 19??. a. USD 39 combined subscription per issue includes 12 monthly summaries & one a. summary (effective 2009). back issues avail. **Document type:** *Bulletin, Government.* **Description:** Presents the monthly and annual average, resultant and fastest mile wind speed for the current year as well as the monthly and annual mean and fastest mile speed for a long period for Columbus, Ohio.
Related titles: Online - full text ed.: USD 29 per issue (effective 2009); ◆ Cumulative ed(s).: Local Climatological Data. Columbus, Ohio. Monthly Summary. ISSN 0198-3962.

Published by: U.S. National Climatic Data Center (Subsidiary of: U.S. Department of Commerce), Federal Bldg, 151 Patton Ave, Asheville, NC 28801. TEL 828-271-4800, FAX 828-271-4876, NODC.Services@noaa.gov, http://www.ncdc.noaa.gov.

551.5 USA ISSN 0198-3962
LOCAL CLIMATOLOGICAL DATA. COLUMBUS, OHIO. MONTHLY SUMMARY. Text in English. 19??. m. USD 5 per issue (effective 2009). back issues avail. **Document type:** *Bulletin, Government.* **Description:** Provides a monthly summary of temperature extremes, degree days, precipitation and winds, hourly precipitation and 3-hourly weather observations in Columbus, Ohio.
Related titles: Online - full text ed.: USD 3 per issue (effective 2009); ◆ Cumulative ed. of: Local Climatological Data. Columbus, Ohio. Annual Summary with Comparative Data. ISSN 0198-3954.
—Linda Hall.
Published by: U.S. National Climatic Data Center (Subsidiary of: U.S. Department of Commerce), Federal Bldg, 151 Patton Ave, Asheville, NC 28801. TEL 828-271-4800, FAX 828-271-4876, NODC.Services@noaa.gov, http://www.ncdc.noaa.gov.

551.5 USA ISSN 0198-3369
LOCAL CLIMATOLOGICAL DATA. CONCORD, NEW HAMPSHIRE. ANNUAL SUMMARY WITH COMPARATIVE DATA. Text in English. 19??. a. USD 39 combined subscription per issue includes 12 monthly summaries & one a. summary (effective 2009). back issues avail. **Document type:** *Bulletin, Government.* **Description:** Presents the monthly and annual average, resultant and fastest mile wind speed for the current year as well as the monthly and annual mean and fastest mile speed for a long period for Concord, New Hampshire.
Related titles: Online - full text ed.: USD 29 per issue (effective 2009); ◆ Cumulative ed(s).: Local Climatological Data. Concord, New Hampshire. Monthly Summary. ISSN 0198-3377.
Published by: U.S. National Climatic Data Center (Subsidiary of: U.S. Department of Commerce), Federal Bldg, 151 Patton Ave, Asheville, NC 28801. TEL 828-271-4800, FAX 828-271-4876, NODC.Services@noaa.gov, http://www.ncdc.noaa.gov.

551.5 USA ISSN 0198-3377
QC984.N4
LOCAL CLIMATOLOGICAL DATA. CONCORD, NEW HAMPSHIRE. MONTHLY SUMMARY. Text in English. 19??. m. USD 5 per issue (effective 2009). back issues avail. **Document type:** *Bulletin, Government.* **Description:** Provides a monthly summary of temperature extremes, degree days, precipitation and winds, hourly precipitation and 3-hourly weather observations in Concord, New Hampshire.
Related titles: Online - full text ed.: USD 3 per issue (effective 2009); ◆ Cumulative ed. of: Local Climatological Data. Concord, New Hampshire. Annual Summary with Comparative Data. ISSN 0198-3369.
—Linda Hall.
Published by: U.S. National Climatic Data Center (Subsidiary of: U.S. Department of Commerce), Federal Bldg, 151 Patton Ave, Asheville, NC 28801. TEL 828-271-4800, FAX 828-271-4876, NODC.Services@noaa.gov, http://www.ncdc.noaa.gov.

551.5 USA ISSN 0198-2133
LOCAL CLIMATOLOGICAL DATA. CONCORDIA, KANSAS. ANNUAL SUMMARY WITH COMPARATIVE DATA. Text in English. a. USD 39 combined subscription per issue includes 12 monthly summaries & one a. summary (effective 2009). **Document type:** *Bulletin, Government.*
Related titles: Online - full text ed.: USD 29 per issue (effective 2009); ◆ Cumulative ed(s).: Local Climatological Data. Concordia, Kansas. Monthly Summary. ISSN 0198-2141.
Published by: U.S. National Climatic Data Center (Subsidiary of: U.S. Department of Commerce), Federal Bldg, 151 Patton Ave, Asheville, NC 28801. TEL 828-271-4800, FAX 828-271-4876, NODC.Services@noaa.gov, http://www.ncdc.noaa.gov.

551.5 USA ISSN 0198-4969
LOCAL CLIMATOLOGICAL DATA. CORPUS CHRISTI, TEXAS. ANNUAL SUMMARY WITH COMPARATIVE DATA. Text in English. 19??. a. USD 39 combined subscription per issue includes 12 monthly summaries & one a. summary (effective 2009). back issues avail. **Document type:** *Bulletin, Government.* **Description:** Presents the monthly and annual average, resultant and fastest mile wind speed for the current year as well as the monthly and annual mean and fastest mile speed for a long period for Corpus Christi, Texas.
Related titles: Online - full text ed.: USD 29 per issue (effective 2009); ◆ Cumulative ed(s).: Local Climatological Data. Corpus Christi, Texas. Monthly Summary. ISSN 0198-4977.
Published by: U.S. National Climatic Data Center (Subsidiary of: U.S. Department of Commerce), Federal Bldg, 151 Patton Ave, Asheville, NC 28801. TEL 828-271-4800, FAX 828-271-4876, NODC.Services@noaa.gov, http://www.ncdc.noaa.gov.

551.5 USA ISSN 0198-4977
LOCAL CLIMATOLOGICAL DATA. CORPUS CHRISTI, TEXAS. MONTHLY SUMMARY. Text in English. 19??. m. USD 5 per issue (effective 2009). back issues avail. **Document type:** *Bulletin, Government.* **Description:** Provides a monthly summary of temperature extremes, degree days, precipitation and winds, hourly precipitation and 3-hourly weather observations in Corpus Christi, Texas.
Related titles: Online - full text ed.: USD 3 per issue (effective 2009); ◆ Cumulative ed. of: Local Climatological Data. Corpus Christi, Texas. Annual Summary with Comparative Data. ISSN 0198-4969.
—Linda Hall.
Published by: U.S. National Climatic Data Center (Subsidiary of: U.S. Department of Commerce), Federal Bldg, 151 Patton Ave, Asheville, NC 28801. TEL 828-271-4800, FAX 828-271-4876, NODC.Services@noaa.gov, http://www.ncdc.noaa.gov.

551.5 USA ISSN 0198-5043
LOCAL CLIMATOLOGICAL DATA. DALLAS-FORT WORTH, TEXAS. ANNUAL SUMMARY WITH COMPARATIVE DATA. Text in English. a. USD 39 combined subscription per issue includes 12 monthly summaries & one a. summary (effective 2009). **Document type:** *Bulletin, Government.*
Related titles: Online - full text ed.: USD 29 per issue (effective 2009); ◆ Cumulative ed(s).: Local Climatological Data. Dallas-Fort Worth, Texas. Monthly Summary. ISSN 0198-5051.

Published by: U.S. National Climatic Data Center (Subsidiary of: U.S. Department of Commerce), Federal Bldg, 151 Patton Ave, Asheville, NC 28801. TEL 828-271-4800, FAX 828-271-4876, NODC.Services@noaa.gov, http://www.ncdc.noaa.gov.

551.5 USA ISSN 1528-7416
LOCAL CLIMATOLOGICAL DATA. DALLAS, TEXAS. DALLAS LOVE FIELD. MONTHLY SUMMARY. Text in English. 19??. m. USD 39 combined subscription per issue includes 12 monthly summaries & one a. summary (effective 2009). back issues avail. **Document type:** *Bulletin, Government.* **Description:** Provides a monthly summary of temperature extremes, degree days, precipitation and winds, hourly precipitation and 3-hourly weather observations in Dallas, Texas.
Related titles: Online - full text ed.: USD 29 per issue (effective 2009).
Published by: U.S. National Climatic Data Center (Subsidiary of: U.S. Department of Commerce), Federal Bldg, 151 Patton Ave, Asheville, NC 28801. TEL 828-271-4800, FAX 828-271-4876, NODC.Services@noaa.gov, http://www.ncdc.noaa.gov.

551.5 USA ISSN 0198-3970
LOCAL CLIMATOLOGICAL DATA. DAYTON, OHIO. ANNUAL SUMMARY WITH COMPARATIVE DATA. Text in English. a. USD 39 combined subscription per issue includes 12 monthly summaries & one a. summary (effective 2009). back issues avail. **Document type:** *Bulletin, Government.* **Description:** Presents the monthly and annual average, resultant and fastest mile wind speed for the current year as well as the monthly and annual mean and fastest mile speed for a long period for Dayton, Ohio.
Formerly: Local Climatological Summary, with Comparative Data. Dayton, Ohio
Related titles: Online - full text ed.: USD 29 per issue (effective 2009); ◆ Cumulative ed(s).: Local Climatological Data. Dayton, Ohio. Monthly Summary. ISSN 0198-3989.
Published by: U.S. National Climatic Data Center (Subsidiary of: U.S. Department of Commerce), Federal Bldg, 151 Patton Ave, Asheville, NC 28801. TEL 828-271-4800, FAX 828-271-4876, NODC.Services@noaa.gov, http://www.ncdc.noaa.gov.

551.5 USA ISSN 0198-3989
LOCAL CLIMATOLOGICAL DATA. DAYTON, OHIO. MONTHLY SUMMARY. Text in English. 19??. m. USD 5 per issue (effective 2009). back issues avail. **Document type:** *Bulletin, Government.* **Description:** Provides a monthly summary of temperature extremes, degree days, precipitation and winds, hourly precipitation and 3-hourly weather observations in Dayton, Ohio.
Formerly: Station Meteorological Summary. Dayton, Ohio
Related titles: Online - full text ed.: USD 3 per issue (effective 2009); ◆ Cumulative ed. of: Local Climatological Data. Dayton, Ohio. Annual Summary with Comparative Data. ISSN 0198-3970.
—Linda Hall.
Published by: U.S. National Climatic Data Center (Subsidiary of: U.S. Department of Commerce), Federal Bldg, 151 Patton Ave, Asheville, NC 28801. TEL 828-271-4800, FAX 828-271-4876, NODC.Services@noaa.gov, http://www.ncdc.noaa.gov.

551.5 USA ISSN 0198-1226
QC984.F62
LOCAL CLIMATOLOGICAL DATA. DAYTONA BEACH, FLORIDA. ANNUAL SUMMARY WITH COMPARATIVE DATA. Text in English. 19??. a. USD 39 combined subscription per issue includes 12 monthly summaries & one a. summary (effective 2009). back issues avail. **Document type:** *Bulletin, Government.* **Description:** Presents the monthly and annual average, resultant and fastest mile wind speed for the current year as well as the monthly and annual mean and fastest mile speed for a long period for Daytona Beach, Florida.
Related titles: Online - full text ed.: USD 29 per issue (effective 2009); ◆ Cumulative ed(s).: Local Climatological Data. Daytona Beach, Florida. Monthly Summary. ISSN 0198-134X.
Published by: U.S. National Climatic Data Center (Subsidiary of: U.S. Department of Commerce), Federal Bldg, 151 Patton Ave, Asheville, NC 28801. TEL 828-271-4800, FAX 828-271-4876, NODC.Services@noaa.gov, http://www.ncdc.noaa.gov.

551.5 USA ISSN 0198-134X
LOCAL CLIMATOLOGICAL DATA. DAYTONA BEACH, FLORIDA. MONTHLY SUMMARY. Text in English. 19??. m. USD 5 per issue (effective 2009). back issues avail. **Document type:** *Bulletin, Government.* **Description:** Provides a monthly summary of temperature extremes, degree days, precipitation and winds, hourly precipitation and 3-hourly weather observations in Daytona Beach, Florida.
Related titles: Online - full text ed.: USD 3 per issue (effective 2009); ◆ Cumulative ed. of: Local Climatological Data. Daytona Beach, Florida. Annual Summary with Comparative Data. ISSN 0198-1226.
—Linda Hall.
Published by: U.S. National Climatic Data Center (Subsidiary of: U.S. Department of Commerce), Federal Bldg, 151 Patton Ave, Asheville, NC 28801. TEL 828-271-4800, FAX 828-271-4876, NODC.Services@noaa.gov, http://www.ncdc.noaa.gov.

551.5 USA ISSN 0198-4985
LOCAL CLIMATOLOGICAL DATA. DEL RIO, TEXAS. ANNUAL SUMMARY WITH COMPARATIVE DATA. Text in English. 19??. a. USD 39 combined subscription per issue includes 12 monthly summaries & one a. summary (effective 2009). **Document type:** *Bulletin, Government.* **Description:** Presents the monthly and annual average, resultant and fastest mile wind speed for the current year as well as the monthly and annual mean and fastest mile speed for a long period for Del Rio, Texas.
Related titles: Online - full text ed.: USD 29 per issue (effective 2009); ◆ Cumulative ed(s).: Local Climatological Data. Del Rio, Texas. Monthly Summary. ISSN 0198-4993.
Published by: U.S. National Climatic Data Center (Subsidiary of: U.S. Department of Commerce), Federal Bldg, 151 Patton Ave, Asheville, NC 28801. TEL 828-271-4800, FAX 828-271-4876, NODC.Services@noaa.gov, http://www.ncdc.noaa.gov.

551.5 USA ISSN 0198-4993
LOCAL CLIMATOLOGICAL DATA. DEL RIO, TEXAS. MONTHLY SUMMARY. Text in English. 19??. m. USD 5 per issue (effective 2009). back issues avail. **Document type:** *Bulletin, Government.* **Description:** Provides a monthly summary of temperature extremes, degree days, precipitation and winds, hourly precipitation and 3-hourly weather observations in Del Rio, Texas.
Related titles: Online - full text ed.: USD 3 per issue (effective 2009); ◆ Cumulative ed. of: Local Climatological Data. Del Rio, Texas. Annual Summary with Comparative Data. ISSN 0198-4985.
—Linda Hall.
Published by: U.S. National Climatic Data Center (Subsidiary of: U.S. Department of Commerce), Federal Bldg, 151 Patton Ave, Asheville, NC 28801. TEL 828-271-4800, FAX 828-271-4876, NODC.Services@noaa.gov, http://www.ncdc.noaa.gov.

551.5 USA ISSN 0198-7682
LOCAL CLIMATOLOGICAL DATA. DENVER, COLORADO. ANNUAL SUMMARY WITH COMPARATIVE DATA. Text in English. 19??. a. USD 39 combined subscription per issue includes 12 monthly summaries & one a. summary (effective 2009). back issues avail. **Document type:** *Bulletin, Government.* **Description:** Presents the monthly and annual average, resultant and fastest mile wind speed for the current year as well as the monthly and annual mean and fastest mile speed for a long period for Denver, Colorado.
Related titles: Online - full text ed.: USD 29 per issue (effective 2009); ◆ Cumulative ed(s).: Local Climatological Data. Denver, Colorado. Monthly Summary. ISSN 0198-7690.
Published by: U.S. National Climatic Data Center (Subsidiary of: U.S. Department of Commerce), Federal Bldg, 151 Patton Ave, Asheville, NC 28801. TEL 828-271-4800, FAX 828-271-4876, NODC.Services@noaa.gov, http://www.ncdc.noaa.gov.

551.5 USA ISSN 0198-7690
LOCAL CLIMATOLOGICAL DATA. DENVER, COLORADO. MONTHLY SUMMARY. Text in English. 19??. m. USD 5 per issue (effective 2009). back issues avail. **Document type:** *Bulletin, Government.* **Description:** Provides a monthly summary of temperature extremes, degree days, precipitation and winds, hourly precipitation and 3-hourly weather observations in Denver, Colorado.
Related titles: Online - full text ed.: USD 3 per issue (effective 2009); ◆ Cumulative ed. of: Local Climatological Data. Denver, Colorado. Annual Summary with Comparative Data. ISSN 0198-7682.
—Linda Hall.
Published by: U.S. National Climatic Data Center (Subsidiary of: U.S. Department of Commerce), Federal Bldg, 151 Patton Ave, Asheville, NC 28801. TEL 828-271-4800, FAX 828-271-4876, NODC.Services@noaa.gov, http://www.ncdc.noaa.gov.

551.5 USA ISSN 0198-2052
LOCAL CLIMATOLOGICAL DATA. DES MOINES, IOWA. ANNUAL SUMMARY WITH COMPARATIVE DATA. Text in English. 19??. a. USD 39 combined subscription per issue includes 12 monthly summaries & one a. summary (effective 2009). back issues avail. **Document type:** *Bulletin, Government.* **Description:** Presents the monthly and annual average, resultant and fastest mile wind speed for the current year as well as the monthly and annual mean and fastest mile speed for a long period for Des Moines, Iowa.
Related titles: Online - full text ed.: USD 29 per issue (effective 2009); ◆ Cumulative ed(s).: Local Climatological Data. Des Moines, Iowa. Monthly Summary. ISSN 0198-2060.
Published by: U.S. National Climatic Data Center (Subsidiary of: U.S. Department of Commerce), Federal Bldg, 151 Patton Ave, Asheville, NC 28801. TEL 828-271-4800, FAX 828-271-4876, NODC.Services@noaa.gov, http://www.ncdc.noaa.gov.

551.5 USA ISSN 0198-2060
LOCAL CLIMATOLOGICAL DATA. DES MOINES, IOWA. MONTHLY SUMMARY. Text in English. 19??. m. USD 5 per issue (effective 2009). back issues avail. **Document type:** *Bulletin, Government.* **Description:** Provides a monthly summary of temperature extremes, degree days, precipitation and winds, hourly precipitation and 3-hourly weather observations in Des Moines, Iowa.
Related titles: Online - full text ed.: USD 3 per issue (effective 2009); ◆ Cumulative ed. of: Local Climatological Data. Des Moines, Iowa. Annual Summary with Comparative Data. ISSN 0198-2052.
—Linda Hall.
Published by: U.S. National Climatic Data Center (Subsidiary of: U.S. Department of Commerce), Federal Bldg, 151 Patton Ave, Asheville, NC 28801. TEL 828-271-4800, FAX 828-271-4876, NODC.Services@noaa.gov, http://www.ncdc.noaa.gov.

551.5 USA ISSN 0198-2516
LOCAL CLIMATOLOGICAL DATA. DETROIT, MICHIGAN. CITY AIRPORT. ANNUAL SUMMARY WITH COMPARATIVE DATA. Text in English. 19??. a. USD 39 combined subscription per issue includes 12 monthly summaries & one a. summary (effective 2009). back issues avail. **Document type:** *Bulletin, Government.* **Description:** Presents the monthly and annual average, resultant and fastest mile wind speed for the current year as well as the monthly and annual mean and fastest mile speed for a long period for Detroit, Michigan.
Related titles: Online - full text ed.: USD 29 per issue (effective 2009).
Published by: U.S. National Climatic Data Center (Subsidiary of: U.S. Department of Commerce), Federal Bldg, 151 Patton Ave, Asheville, NC 28801. TEL 828-271-4800, FAX 828-271-4876, NODC.Services@noaa.gov, http://www.ncdc.noaa.gov.

551.5 USA ISSN 0198-2532
LOCAL CLIMATOLOGICAL DATA. DETROIT, MICHIGAN. METROPOLITAN AIRPORT. ANNUAL SUMMARY WITH COMPARATIVE DATA. Text in English. 19??. a. USD 39 combined subscription per issue includes 12 monthly summaries & one a. summary (effective 2009). back issues avail. **Document type:** *Bulletin, Government.* **Description:** Presents the monthly and annual average, resultant and fastest mile wind speed for the current year as well as the monthly and annual mean and fastest mile speed for a long period for Detroit, Michigan.
Related titles: Online - full text ed.: USD 29 per issue (effective 2009); ◆ Cumulative ed(s).: Local Climatological Data. Detroit, Michigan. Metropolitan Airport. Monthly Summary. ISSN 0198-2540.
Published by: U.S. National Climatic Data Center (Subsidiary of: U.S. Department of Commerce), Federal Bldg, 151 Patton Ave, Asheville, NC 28801. TEL 828-271-4800, FAX 828-271-4876, NODC.Services@noaa.gov, http://www.ncdc.noaa.gov.

551.5 USA ISSN 0198-2540
LOCAL CLIMATOLOGICAL DATA. DETROIT, MICHIGAN. METROPOLITAN AIRPORT. MONTHLY SUMMARY. Text in English. 19??. m. USD 5 per issue (effective 2009). back issues avail. **Document type:** *Bulletin, Government.* **Description:** Provides a monthly summary of temperature extremes, degree days, precipitation and winds, hourly precipitation and 3-hourly weather observations in Detroit, Michigan.
Related titles: Online - full text ed.: USD 3 per issue (effective 2009); ◆ Cumulative ed. of: Local Climatological Data. Detroit, Michigan. Metropolitan Airport. Annual Summary with Comparative Data. ISSN 0198-2532.
—Linda Hall.
Published by: U.S. National Climatic Data Center (Subsidiary of: U.S. Department of Commerce), Federal Bldg, 151 Patton Ave, Asheville, NC 28801. TEL 828-271-4800, FAX 828-271-4876, NODC.Services@noaa.gov, http://www.ncdc.noaa.gov.

551.5 USA ISSN 0198-215X
LOCAL CLIMATOLOGICAL DATA. DODGE CITY, KANSAS. ANNUAL SUMMARY WITH COMPARATIVE DATA. Text in English. 19??. a. USD 39 combined subscription per issue includes 12 monthly summaries & one a. summary (effective 2009). back issues avail. **Document type:** *Bulletin, Government.* **Description:** Presents the monthly and annual average, resultant and fastest mile wind speed for the current year as well as the monthly and annual mean and fastest mile speed for a long period for Dodge City, Kansas.
Related titles: Online - full text ed.: USD 29 per issue (effective 2009); ◆ Cumulative ed(s).: Local Climatological Data. Dodge City, Kansas. Monthly Summary. ISSN 0198-2168.
Published by: U.S. National Climatic Data Center (Subsidiary of: U.S. Department of Commerce), Federal Bldg, 151 Patton Ave, Asheville, NC 28801. TEL 828-271-4800, FAX 828-271-4876, NODC.Services@noaa.gov, http://www.ncdc.noaa.gov.

551.5 USA ISSN 0198-2168
LOCAL CLIMATOLOGICAL DATA. DODGE CITY, KANSAS. MONTHLY SUMMARY. Text in English. 19??. m. USD 5 per issue (effective 2009). back issues avail. **Document type:** *Bulletin, Government.* **Description:** Provides a monthly summary of temperature extremes, degree days, precipitation and winds, hourly precipitation and 3-hourly weather observations in Dodge City, Kansas.
Related titles: Online - full text ed.: USD 3 per issue (effective 2009); ◆ Cumulative ed. of: Local Climatological Data. Dodge City, Kansas. Annual Summary with Comparative Data. ISSN 0198-215X.
—Linda Hall.
Published by: U.S. National Climatic Data Center (Subsidiary of: U.S. Department of Commerce), Federal Bldg, 151 Patton Ave, Asheville, NC 28801. TEL 828-271-4800, FAX 828-271-4876, NODC.Services@noaa.gov, http://www.ncdc.noaa.gov.

551.5 USA ISSN 0198-2079
LOCAL CLIMATOLOGICAL DATA. DUBUQUE, IOWA. ANNUAL SUMMARY WITH COMPARATIVE DATA. Text in English. 19??. a. USD 5 per issue (effective 2004). **Document type:** *Bulletin, Government.*
Related titles: Online - full text ed.; ◆ Cumulative ed(s).: Local Climatological Data. Dubuque, Iowa. Monthly Summary. ISSN 0198-2087.
Published by: U.S. National Climatic Data Center (Subsidiary of: U.S. Department of Commerce), Federal Bldg, 151 Patton Ave, Asheville, NC 28801. TEL 828-271-4800, FAX 828-271-4876, NODC.Services@noaa.gov, http://www.ncdc.noaa.gov.

551.5 USA ISSN 0198-2087
LOCAL CLIMATOLOGICAL DATA. DUBUQUE, IOWA. MONTHLY SUMMARY. Text in English. 19??. m. USD 5 per issue (effective 2009). back issues avail. **Document type:** *Bulletin, Government.* **Description:** Provides a monthly summary of temperature extremes, degree days, precipitation and winds, hourly precipitation and 3-hourly weather observations in Dubuque, Iowa.
Related titles: Online - full text ed.: USD 3 per issue (effective 2009); ◆ Cumulative ed. of: Local Climatological Data. Dubuque, Iowa. Annual Summary with Comparative Data. ISSN 0198-2079.
—Linda Hall.
Published by: U.S. National Climatic Data Center (Subsidiary of: U.S. Department of Commerce), Federal Bldg, 151 Patton Ave, Asheville, NC 28801. TEL 828-271-4800, FAX 828-271-4876, NODC.Services@noaa.gov, http://www.ncdc.noaa.gov.

551.5 USA ISSN 0198-2699
QC984.M6
LOCAL CLIMATOLOGICAL DATA. DULUTH, MINNESOTA. ANNUAL SUMMARY WITH COMPARATIVE DATA. Text in English. 19??. a. USD 39 combined subscription per issue includes 12 monthly summaries & one a. summary (effective 2009). back issues avail. **Document type:** *Bulletin, Government.* **Description:** Presents the monthly and annual average, resultant and fastest mile wind speed for the current year as well as the monthly and annual mean and fastest mile speed for a long period for Duluth, Minnesota.
Related titles: Online - full text ed.: USD 29 per issue (effective 2009); ◆ Cumulative ed(s).: Local Climatological Data. Duluth, Minnesota. Monthly Summary. ISSN 0198-2702.
Published by: U.S. National Climatic Data Center (Subsidiary of: U.S. Department of Commerce), Federal Bldg, 151 Patton Ave, Asheville, NC 28801. TEL 828-271-4800, FAX 828-271-4876, NODC.Services@noaa.gov, http://www.ncdc.noaa.gov.

551.5 USA ISSN 0198-2702
LOCAL CLIMATOLOGICAL DATA. DULUTH, MINNESOTA. MONTHLY SUMMARY. Text in English. 19??. m. USD 5 per issue (effective 2009). back issues avail. **Document type:** *Bulletin, Government.* **Description:** Provides a monthly summary of temperature extremes, degree days, precipitation and winds, hourly precipitation and 3-hourly weather observations in Duluth, Minnesota.
Related titles: Online - full text ed.: USD 3 per issue (effective 2009); ◆ Cumulative ed. of: Local Climatological Data. Duluth, Minnesota. Annual Summary with Comparative Data. ISSN 0198-2699.
—Linda Hall.
Published by: U.S. National Climatic Data Center (Subsidiary of: U.S. Department of Commerce), Federal Bldg, 151 Patton Ave, Asheville, NC 28801. TEL 828-271-4800, FAX 828-271-4876, NODC.Services@noaa.gov, http://www.ncdc.noaa.gov.

551.5 USA ISSN 0198-5027
LOCAL CLIMATOLOGICAL DATA. EL PASO, TEXAS. ANNUAL SUMMARY WITH COMPARATIVE DATA. Text in English. 19??. a. USD 39 combined subscription per issue includes 12 monthly summaries & one a. summary (effective 2009). back issues avail. **Document type:** *Bulletin, Government.* **Description:** Presents the monthly and annual average, resultant and fastest mile wind speed for the current year as well as the monthly and annual mean and fastest mile speed for a long period for El Paso, Texas.
Related titles: Online - full text ed.: USD 29 per issue (effective 2009); ◆ Cumulative ed(s).: Local Climatological Data. El Paso, Texas. Monthly Summary. ISSN 0198-5035.

Published by: U.S. National Climatic Data Center (Subsidiary of: U.S. Department of Commerce), Federal Bldg, 151 Patton Ave, Asheville, NC 28801. TEL 828-271-4800, FAX 828-271-4876, NODC.Services@noaa.gov, http://www.ncdc.noaa.gov.

551.5 USA ISSN 0198-5035

LOCAL CLIMATOLOGICAL DATA. EL PASO, TEXAS. MONTHLY SUMMARY. Text in English. 19??. m. USD 5 per issue (effective 2009). back issues avail. **Document type:** *Bulletin, Government.* **Description:** Provides a monthly summary of temperature extremes, degree days, precipitation and winds, hourly precipitation and 3-hourly weather observations in El Paso, Texas.

Related titles: Online - full text ed.: USD 3 per issue (effective 2009); ◆ Cumulative ed. of: Local Climatological Data. El Paso, Texas. Annual Summary with Comparative Data. ISSN 0198-5027.

—Linda Hall.

Published by: U.S. National Climatic Data Center (Subsidiary of: U.S. Department of Commerce), Federal Bldg, 151 Patton Ave, Asheville, NC 28801. TEL 828-271-4800, FAX 828-271-4876, NODC.Services@noaa.gov, http://www.ncdc.noaa.gov.

551.5 USA ISSN 0198-5620

LOCAL CLIMATOLOGICAL DATA. ELKINS, WEST VIRGINIA. ANNUAL SUMMARY WITH COMPARATIVE DATA. Text in English. 19??. a. USD 39 combined subscription per issue includes 12 monthly summaries & one a. summary (effective 2009). back issues avail. **Document type:** *Bulletin, Government.* **Description:** Presents the monthly and annual average, resultant and fastest mile wind speed for the current year as well as the monthly and annual mean and fastest mile speed for a long period for Elkins, West Virginia.

Related titles: Online - full text ed.: USD 29 per issue (effective 2009); ◆ Cumulative ed(s).: Local Climatological Data. Elkins, West Virginia. Monthly Summary. ISSN 0198-5639.

Published by: U.S. National Climatic Data Center (Subsidiary of: U.S. Department of Commerce), Federal Bldg, 151 Patton Ave, Asheville, NC 28801. TEL 828-271-4800, FAX 828-271-4876, NODC.Services@noaa.gov, http://www.ncdc.noaa.gov.

551.5 USA ISSN 0198-5639

LOCAL CLIMATOLOGICAL DATA. ELKINS, WEST VIRGINIA. MONTHLY SUMMARY. Text in English. 19??. m. USD 5 per issue (effective 2009). back issues avail. **Document type:** *Bulletin, Government.* **Description:** Provides a monthly summary of temperature extremes, degree days, precipitation and winds, hourly precipitation and 3-hourly weather observations in Elkins, West Virginia.

Related titles: Online - full text ed.: USD 3 per issue (effective 2009); ◆ Cumulative ed. of: Local Climatological Data. Elkins, West Virginia. Annual Summary with Comparative Data. ISSN 0198-5620.

—Linda Hall.

Published by: U.S. National Climatic Data Center (Subsidiary of: U.S. Department of Commerce), Federal Bldg, 151 Patton Ave, Asheville, NC 28801. TEL 828-271-4800, FAX 828-271-4876, NODC.Services@noaa.gov, http://www.ncdc.noaa.gov.

551.5 USA ISSN 0198-3261

LOCAL CLIMATOLOGICAL DATA. ELKO, NEVADA. ANNUAL SUMMARY WITH COMPARATIVE DATA. Text in English. 19??. a. USD 39 combined subscription per issue includes 12 monthly summaries & one a. summary (effective 2009). back issues avail. **Document type:** *Bulletin, Government.* **Description:** Presents the monthly and annual average, resultant and fastest mile wind speed for the current year as well as the monthly and annual mean and fastest mile speed for a long period for Elko, Nevada.

Related titles: Online - full text ed.: USD 29 per issue (effective 2009); ◆ Cumulative ed(s).: Local Climatological Data. Elko, Nevada. Monthly Summary. ISSN 0198-327X.

Published by: U.S. National Climatic Data Center (Subsidiary of: U.S. Department of Commerce), Federal Bldg, 151 Patton Ave, Asheville, NC 28801. TEL 828-271-4800, FAX 828-271-4876, NODC.Services@noaa.gov, http://www.ncdc.noaa.gov.

551.5 USA ISSN 0198-327X

LOCAL CLIMATOLOGICAL DATA. ELKO, NEVADA. MONTHLY SUMMARY. Text in English. 19??. m. USD 5 per issue (effective 2009). back issues avail. **Document type:** *Bulletin, Government.* **Description:** Provides a monthly summary of temperature extremes, degree days, precipitation and winds, hourly precipitation and 3-hourly weather observations in Elko, Nevada.

Related titles: Online - full text ed.: USD 3 per issue (effective 2009); ◆ Cumulative ed. of: Local Climatological Data. Elko, Nevada. Annual Summary with Comparative Data. ISSN 0198-3261.

—Linda Hall.

Published by: U.S. National Climatic Data Center (Subsidiary of: U.S. Department of Commerce), Federal Bldg, 151 Patton Ave, Asheville, NC 28801. TEL 828-271-4800, FAX 828-271-4876, NODC.Services@noaa.gov, http://www.ncdc.noaa.gov.

551.5 USA ISSN 0198-3288

LOCAL CLIMATOLOGICAL DATA. ELY, NEVADA. ANNUAL SUMMARY WITH COMPARATIVE DATA. Text in English. 19??. a. USD 39 combined subscription per issue includes 12 monthly summaries & one a. summary (effective 2009). back issues avail. **Document type:** *Bulletin, Government.* **Description:** Presents the monthly and annual average, resultant and fastest mile wind speed for the current year as well as the monthly and annual mean and fastest mile speed for a long period for Ely, Nevada.

Related titles: Online - full text ed.: USD 29 per issue (effective 2009); ◆ Cumulative ed(s).: Local Climatological Data. Ely, Nevada. Monthly Summary. ISSN 0198-3296.

Published by: U.S. National Climatic Data Center (Subsidiary of: U.S. Department of Commerce), Federal Bldg, 151 Patton Ave, Asheville, NC 28801. TEL 828-271-4800, FAX 828-271-4876, NODC.Services@noaa.gov, http://www.ncdc.noaa.gov.

551.5 USA ISSN 0198-3296

LOCAL CLIMATOLOGICAL DATA. ELY, NEVADA. MONTHLY SUMMARY. Text in English. 19??. m. USD 5 per issue (effective 2009). back issues avail. **Document type:** *Bulletin, Government.* **Description:** Provides a monthly summary of temperature extremes, degree days, precipitation and winds, hourly precipitation and 3-hourly weather observations in Ely, Nevada.

Related titles: Online - full text ed.: USD 3 per issue (effective 2009); ◆ Cumulative ed. of: Local Climatological Data. Ely, Nevada. Annual Summary with Comparative Data. ISSN 0198-3288.

—Linda Hall.

Published by: U.S. National Climatic Data Center (Subsidiary of: U.S. Department of Commerce), Federal Bldg, 151 Patton Ave, Asheville, NC 28801. TEL 828-271-4800, FAX 828-271-4876, NODC.Services@noaa.gov, http://www.ncdc.noaa.gov.

551.5 USA ISSN 0198-4497

LOCAL CLIMATOLOGICAL DATA. ERIE, PENNSYLVANIA. ANNUAL SUMMARY WITH COMPARATIVE DATA. Text in English. 19??. a. USD 39 combined subscription per issue includes 12 monthly summaries & one a. summary (effective 2009). back issues avail. **Document type:** *Bulletin, Government.* **Description:** Presents the monthly and annual average, resultant and fastest mile wind speed for the current year as well as the monthly and annual mean and fastest mile speed for a long period for Erie, Pennsylvania.

Related titles: Online - full text ed.: USD 29 per issue (effective 2009); ◆ Cumulative ed(s).: Local Climatological Data. Erie, Pennsylvania. Monthly Summary. ISSN 0198-4500.

Published by: U.S. National Climatic Data Center (Subsidiary of: U.S. Department of Commerce), Federal Bldg, 151 Patton Ave, Asheville, NC 28801. TEL 828-271-4800, FAX 828-271-4876, NODC.Services@noaa.gov, http://www.ncdc.noaa.gov.

551.5 USA ISSN 0198-4500

LOCAL CLIMATOLOGICAL DATA. ERIE, PENNSYLVANIA. MONTHLY SUMMARY. Text in English. 19??. m. USD 5 per issue (effective 2009). back issues avail. **Document type:** *Bulletin, Government.* **Description:** Provides a monthly summary of temperature extremes, degree days, precipitation and winds, hourly precipitation and 3-hourly weather observations in Erie, Pennsylvania.

Related titles: Online - full text ed.: USD 3 per issue (effective 2009); ◆ Cumulative ed. of: Local Climatological Data. Erie, Pennsylvania. Annual Summary with Comparative Data. ISSN 0198-4497.

—Linda Hall.

Published by: U.S. National Climatic Data Center (Subsidiary of: U.S. Department of Commerce), Federal Bldg, 151 Patton Ave, Asheville, NC 28801. TEL 828-271-4800, FAX 828-271-4876, NODC.Services@noaa.gov, http://www.ncdc.noaa.gov.

551.5 USA ISSN 0198-4136
QC984.O72

LOCAL CLIMATOLOGICAL DATA. EUGENE, OREGON. ANNUAL SUMMARY WITH COMPARATIVE DATA. Text in English. 19??. a. USD 39 combined subscription per issue includes 12 monthly summaries & one a. summary (effective 2009). back issues avail. **Document type:** *Bulletin, Government.* **Description:** Presents the monthly and annual average, resultant and fastest mile wind speed for the current year as well as the monthly and annual mean and fastest mile speed for a long period for Eugene, Oregon.

Related titles: Online - full text ed.: USD 29 per issue (effective 2009); ◆ Cumulative ed(s).: Local Climatological Data. Eugene, Oregon. Monthly Summary. ISSN 0198-4144.

Published by: U.S. National Climatic Data Center (Subsidiary of: U.S. Department of Commerce), Federal Bldg, 151 Patton Ave, Asheville, NC 28801. TEL 828-271-4800, FAX 828-271-4876, NODC.Services@noaa.gov, http://www.ncdc.noaa.gov.

551.5 USA ISSN 0198-4144
QC984.O72

LOCAL CLIMATOLOGICAL DATA. EUGENE, OREGON. MONTHLY SUMMARY. Text in English. 19??. m. USD 5 per issue (effective 2009). back issues avail. **Document type:** *Bulletin, Government.* **Description:** Provides a monthly summary of temperature extremes, degree days, precipitation and winds, hourly precipitation and 3-hourly weather observations in Eugene, Oregon.

Related titles: Online - full text ed.: USD 3 per issue (effective 2009); ◆ Cumulative ed. of: Local Climatological Data. Eugene, Oregon. Annual Summary with Comparative Data. ISSN 0198-4136.

—Linda Hall.

Published by: U.S. National Climatic Data Center (Subsidiary of: U.S. Department of Commerce), Federal Bldg, 151 Patton Ave, Asheville, NC 28801. TEL 828-271-4800, FAX 828-271-4876, NODC.Services@noaa.gov, http://www.ncdc.noaa.gov.

551.5 USA ISSN 0198-0882

LOCAL CLIMATOLOGICAL DATA. EUREKA, CALIFORNIA. ANNUAL SUMMARY WITH COMPARATIVE DATA. Text in English. 19??. a. USD 39 combined subscription per issue includes 12 monthly summaries & one a. summary (effective 2009). back issues avail. **Document type:** *Bulletin, Government.* **Description:** Presents the monthly and annual average, resultant and fastest mile wind speed for the current year as well as the monthly and annual mean and fastest mile speed for a long period for Eureka, California.

Related titles: Online - full text ed.: USD 29 per issue (effective 2009); ◆ Cumulative ed(s).: Local Climatological Data. Eureka, California. Monthly Summary. ISSN 0198-0726.

Published by: U.S. National Climatic Data Center (Subsidiary of: U.S. Department of Commerce), Federal Bldg, 151 Patton Ave, Asheville, NC 28801. TEL 828-271-4800, FAX 828-271-4876, NODC.Services@noaa.gov, http://www.ncdc.noaa.gov.

551.5 USA ISSN 0198-0726

LOCAL CLIMATOLOGICAL DATA. EUREKA, CALIFORNIA. MONTHLY SUMMARY. Text in English. 19??. m. USD 5 per issue (effective 2009). back issues avail. **Document type:** *Bulletin, Government.* **Description:** Provides a monthly summary of temperature extremes, degree days, precipitation and winds, hourly precipitation and 3-hourly weather observations in Eureka, California.

Related titles: Online - full text ed.: USD 3 per issue (effective 2009); ◆ Cumulative ed. of: Local Climatological Data. Eureka, California. Annual Summary with Comparative Data. ISSN 0198-0882.

—Linda Hall.

Published by: U.S. National Climatic Data Center (Subsidiary of: U.S. Department of Commerce), Federal Bldg, 151 Patton Ave, Asheville, NC 28801. TEL 828-271-4800, FAX 828-271-4876, NODC.Services@noaa.gov, http://www.ncdc.noaa.gov.

551.5 USA ISSN 0198-1943

LOCAL CLIMATOLOGICAL DATA. EVANSVILLE, INDIANA. ANNUAL SUMMARY WITH COMPARATIVE DATA. Text in English. 19??. a. USD 39 combined subscription per issue includes 12 monthly summaries & one a. summary (effective 2009). back issues avail. **Document type:** *Bulletin, Government.* **Description:** Presents the monthly and annual average, resultant and fastest mile wind speed for the current year as well as the monthly and annual mean and fastest mile speed for a long period for Evansville, Indiana.

Related titles: Online - full text ed.: USD 29 per issue (effective 2009); ◆ Cumulative ed(s).: Local Climatological Data. Evansville, Indiana. Monthly Summary. ISSN 0198-1951.

Published by: U.S. National Climatic Data Center (Subsidiary of: U.S. Department of Commerce), Federal Bldg, 151 Patton Ave, Asheville, NC 28801. TEL 828-271-4800, FAX 828-271-4876, NODC.Services@noaa.gov, http://www.ncdc.noaa.gov.

551.5 USA ISSN 0198-1951

LOCAL CLIMATOLOGICAL DATA. EVANSVILLE, INDIANA. MONTHLY SUMMARY. Text in English. 19??. m. USD 5 per issue (effective 2009). back issues avail. **Document type:** *Bulletin, Government.* **Description:** Provides a monthly summary of temperature extremes, degree days, precipitation and winds, hourly precipitation and 3-hourly weather observations in Evansville, Indiana.

Related titles: Online - full text ed.: USD 3 per issue (effective 2009); ◆ Cumulative ed. of: Local Climatological Data. Evansville, Indiana. Annual Summary with Comparative Data. ISSN 0198-1943.

—Linda Hall.

Published by: U.S. National Climatic Data Center (Subsidiary of: U.S. Department of Commerce), Federal Bldg, 151 Patton Ave, Asheville, NC 28801. TEL 828-271-4800, FAX 828-271-4876, NODC.Services@noaa.gov, http://www.ncdc.noaa.gov.

551.5 USA ISSN 0197-9728
QC984.A42

LOCAL CLIMATOLOGICAL DATA. FAIRBANKS, ALASKA. ANNUAL SUMMARY WITH COMPARATIVE DATA. Text in English. 19??. a. USD 39 combined subscription per issue includes 12 monthly summaries & one a. summary (effective 2009). back issues avail. **Document type:** *Bulletin, Government.* **Description:** Presents the monthly and annual average, resultant and fastest mile wind speed for the current year as well as the monthly and annual mean and fastest mile speed for a long period for Fairbanks, Alaska.

Related titles: Online - full text ed.: USD 29 per issue (effective 2009); ◆ Cumulative ed(s).: Local Climatological Data. Fairbanks, Alaska. Monthly Summary. ISSN 0197-9736.

Published by: U.S. National Climatic Data Center (Subsidiary of: U.S. Department of Commerce), Federal Bldg, 151 Patton Ave, Asheville, NC 28801. TEL 828-271-4800, FAX 828-271-4876, NODC.Services@noaa.gov, http://www.ncdc.noaa.gov.

551.5 USA ISSN 0197-9736
QC984.A42

LOCAL CLIMATOLOGICAL DATA. FAIRBANKS, ALASKA. MONTHLY SUMMARY. Text in English. 19??. m. USD 5 per issue (effective 2009). back issues avail. **Document type:** *Bulletin, Government.* **Description:** Provides a monthly summary of temperature extremes, degree days, precipitation and winds, hourly precipitation and 3-hourly weather observations in Fairbanks, Alaska.

Related titles: Online - full text ed.: USD 3 per issue (effective 2009); ◆ Cumulative ed. of: Local Climatological Data. Fairbanks, Alaska. Annual Summary with Comparative Data. ISSN 0197-9728.

—Linda Hall.

Published by: U.S. National Climatic Data Center (Subsidiary of: U.S. Department of Commerce), Federal Bldg, 151 Patton Ave, Asheville, NC 28801. TEL 828-271-4800, FAX 828-271-4876, NODC.Services@noaa.gov, http://www.ncdc.noaa.gov.

551.5 USA ISSN 0198-3830
QC984.N92

LOCAL CLIMATOLOGICAL DATA. FARGO, NORTH DAKOTA. ANNUAL SUMMARY WITH COMPARATIVE DATA. Text in English. 19??. a. USD 39 combined subscription per issue includes 12 monthly summaries & one a. summary (effective 2009). back issues avail. **Document type:** *Bulletin, Government.* **Description:** Presents the monthly and annual average, resultant and fastest mile wind speed for the current year as well as the monthly and annual mean and fastest mile speed for a long period for Fargo, North Dakota.

Related titles: Online - full text ed.: USD 29 per issue (effective 2009); ◆ Cumulative ed(s).: Local Climatological Data. Fargo, North Dakota. Monthly Summary. ISSN 0198-3849.

Published by: U.S. National Climatic Data Center (Subsidiary of: U.S. Department of Commerce), Federal Bldg, 151 Patton Ave, Asheville, NC 28801. TEL 828-271-4800, FAX 828-271-4876, NODC.Services@noaa.gov, http://www.ncdc.noaa.gov.

551.5 USA ISSN 0198-3849
QC984.N92

LOCAL CLIMATOLOGICAL DATA. FARGO, NORTH DAKOTA. MONTHLY SUMMARY. Text in English. 19??. m. USD 5 per issue (effective 2009). back issues avail. **Document type:** *Bulletin, Government.* **Description:** Provides a monthly summary of temperature extremes, degree days, precipitation and winds, hourly precipitation and 3-hourly weather observations in Fargo, North Dakota.

Related titles: Online - full text ed.: USD 3 per issue (effective 2009); ◆ Cumulative ed. of: Local Climatological Data. Fargo, North Dakota. Annual Summary with Comparative Data. ISSN 0198-3830.

—Linda Hall.

Published by: U.S. National Climatic Data Center (Subsidiary of: U.S. Department of Commerce), Federal Bldg, 151 Patton Ave, Asheville, NC 28801. TEL 828-271-4800, FAX 828-271-4876, NODC.Services@noaa.gov, http://www.ncdc.noaa.gov.

551.5 USA ISSN 0198-0564

LOCAL CLIMATOLOGICAL DATA. FLAGSTAFF, ARIZONA. ANNUAL SUMMARY WITH COMPARATIVE DATA. Text in English. 19??. a. USD 39 combined subscription per issue includes 12 monthly summaries & one a. summary (effective 2009). back issues avail. **Document type:** *Bulletin, Government.* **Description:** Presents the monthly and annual average, resultant and fastest mile wind speed for the current year as well as the monthly and annual mean and fastest mile speed for a long period for Flagstaff, Arizona.

Related titles: Online - full text ed.: USD 29 per issue (effective 2009); ◆ Cumulative ed(s).: Local Climatological Data. Flagstaff, Arizona. Monthly Summary. ISSN 0198-0467.

Published by: U.S. National Climatic Data Center (Subsidiary of: U.S. Department of Commerce), Federal Bldg, 151 Patton Ave, Asheville, NC 28801. TEL 828-271-4800, FAX 828-271-4876, NODC.Services@noaa.gov, http://www.ncdc.noaa.gov.

551.5 USA ISSN 0198-0467
LOCAL CLIMATOLOGICAL DATA. FLAGSTAFF, ARIZONA. MONTHLY SUMMARY. Text in English. 19??. m. USD 5 per issue (effective 2009). back issues avail. **Document type:** *Bulletin, Government.* **Description:** Provides a monthly summary of temperature extremes, degree days, precipitation and winds, hourly precipitation and 3-hourly weather observations in Flagstaff, Arizona.
Related titles: Online - full text ed.: USD 3 per issue (effective 2009); ◆ Cumulative ed. of: Local Climatological Data. Flagstaff, Arizona. Annual Summary with Comparative Data. ISSN 0198-0564.
—Linda Hall.
Published by: U.S. National Climatic Data Center (Subsidiary of: U.S. Department of Commerce), Federal Bldg, 151 Patton Ave, Asheville, NC 28801. TEL 828-271-4800, FAX 828-271-4876, NODC.Services@noaa.gov, http://www.ncdc.noaa.gov.

551.5 USA ISSN 0198-2559
LOCAL CLIMATOLOGICAL DATA. FLINT, MICHIGAN. ANNUAL SUMMARY WITH COMPARATIVE DATA. Text in English. 19??. a. USD 39 combined subscription per issue includes 12 monthly summaries & one a. summary (effective 2009). back issues avail. **Document type:** *Bulletin, Government.* **Description:** Presents the monthly and annual average, resultant and fastest mile wind speed for the current year as well as the monthly and annual mean and fastest mile speed for a long period for Flint, Michigan.
Related titles: Online - full text ed.: USD 29 per issue (effective 2009); ◆ Cumulative ed(s).: Local Climatological Data. Flint, Michigan. Monthly Summary. ISSN 0198-2567.
Published by: U.S. National Climatic Data Center (Subsidiary of: U.S. Department of Commerce), Federal Bldg, 151 Patton Ave, Asheville, NC 28801. TEL 828-271-4800, FAX 828-271-4876, NODC.Services@noaa.gov, http://www.ncdc.noaa.gov.

551.5 USA ISSN 0198-2567
LOCAL CLIMATOLOGICAL DATA. FLINT, MICHIGAN. MONTHLY SUMMARY. Text in English. 19??. m. USD 5 per issue (effective 2009). back issues avail. **Document type:** *Bulletin, Government.* **Description:** Provides a monthly summary of temperature extremes, degree days, precipitation and winds, hourly precipitation and 3-hourly weather observations in Flint, Michigan.
Related titles: Online - full text ed.: USD 3 per issue (effective 2009); ◆ Cumulative ed. of: Local Climatological Data. Flint, Michigan. Annual Summary with Comparative Data. ISSN 0198-2559.
—Linda Hall.
Published by: U.S. National Climatic Data Center (Subsidiary of: U.S. Department of Commerce), Federal Bldg, 151 Patton Ave, Asheville, NC 28801. TEL 828-271-4800, FAX 828-271-4876, NODC.Services@noaa.gov, http://www.ncdc.noaa.gov.

551.5 USA ISSN 0198-1234
LOCAL CLIMATOLOGICAL DATA. FORT MYERS, FLORIDA. ANNUAL SUMMARY WITH COMPARATIVE DATA. Text in English. 19??. a. USD 39 combined subscription per issue includes 12 monthly summaries & one a. summary (effective 2009). back issues avail. **Document type:** *Bulletin, Government.* **Description:** Presents the monthly and annual average, resultant and fastest mile wind speed for the current year as well as the monthly and annual mean and fastest mile speed for a long period for Fort Myers, Florida.
Related titles: Online - full text ed.: USD 29 per issue (effective 2009); ◆ Cumulative ed(s).: Local Climatological Data. Fort Myers, Florida. Monthly Summary. ISSN 0198-1358.
Published by: U.S. National Climatic Data Center (Subsidiary of: U.S. Department of Commerce), Federal Bldg, 151 Patton Ave, Asheville, NC 28801. TEL 828-271-4800, FAX 828-271-4876, NODC.Services@noaa.gov, http://www.ncdc.noaa.gov.

551.5 USA ISSN 0198-1358
LOCAL CLIMATOLOGICAL DATA. FORT MYERS, FLORIDA. MONTHLY SUMMARY. Text in English. 19??. m. USD 5 per issue (effective 2009). back issues avail. **Document type:** *Bulletin, Government.* **Description:** Provides a monthly summary of temperature extremes, degree days, precipitation and winds, hourly precipitation and 3-hourly weather observations in Fort Myers, Florida.
Related titles: Online - full text ed.: USD 3 per issue (effective 2009); ◆ Cumulative ed. of: Local Climatological Data. Fort Myers, Florida. Annual Summary with Comparative Data. ISSN 0198-1234.
—Linda Hall.
Published by: U.S. National Climatic Data Center (Subsidiary of: U.S. Department of Commerce), Federal Bldg, 151 Patton Ave, Asheville, NC 28801. TEL 828-271-4800, FAX 828-271-4876, NODC.Services@noaa.gov, http://www.ncdc.noaa.gov.

551.5 USA ISSN 0198-0661
LOCAL CLIMATOLOGICAL DATA. FORT SMITH, ARKANSAS. ANNUAL SUMMARY WITH COMPARATIVE DATA. Text in English. 19??. a. USD 39 combined subscription per issue includes 12 monthly summaries & one a. summary (effective 2009). back issues avail. **Document type:** *Bulletin, Government.* **Description:** Presents the monthly and annual average, resultant and fastest mile wind speed for the current year as well as the monthly and annual mean and fastest mile speed for a long period for Fort Smith, Arkansas.
Related titles: Online - full text ed.: USD 29 per issue (effective 2009); ◆ Cumulative ed(s).: Local Climatological Data. Fort Smith, Arkansas. Monthly Summary. ISSN 0198-0610.
Published by: U.S. National Climatic Data Center (Subsidiary of: U.S. Department of Commerce), Federal Bldg, 151 Patton Ave, Asheville, NC 28801. TEL 828-271-4800, FAX 828-271-4876, NODC.Services@noaa.gov, http://www.ncdc.noaa.gov.

551.5 USA ISSN 0198-0610
LOCAL CLIMATOLOGICAL DATA. FORT SMITH, ARKANSAS. MONTHLY SUMMARY. Text in English. 19??. m. USD 5 per issue (effective 2009). back issues avail. **Document type:** *Bulletin, Government.* **Description:** Provides a monthly summary of temperature extremes, degree days, precipitation and winds, hourly precipitation and 3-hourly weather observations in Fort Smith, Arkansas.
Related titles: Online - full text ed.: USD 3 per issue (effective 2009); ◆ Cumulative ed. of: Local Climatological Data. Fort Smith, Arkansas. Annual Summary with Comparative Data. ISSN 0198-0661.
—Linda Hall.
Published by: U.S. National Climatic Data Center (Subsidiary of: U.S. Department of Commerce), Federal Bldg, 151 Patton Ave, Asheville, NC 28801. TEL 828-271-4800, FAX 828-271-4876, NODC.Services@noaa.gov, http://www.ncdc.noaa.gov.

551.5 USA ISSN 0198-196X
LOCAL CLIMATOLOGICAL DATA. FORT WAYNE, INDIANA. ANNUAL SUMMARY WITH COMPARATIVE DATA. Text in English. 19??. a. USD 39 combined subscription per issue includes 12 monthly summaries & one a. summary (effective 2009). back issues avail. **Document type:** *Bulletin, Government.* **Description:** Presents the monthly and annual average, resultant and fastest mile wind speed for the current year as well as the monthly and annual mean and fastest mile speed for a long period for Fort Wayne, Indiana.
Related titles: Online - full text ed.: USD 29 per issue (effective 2009); ◆ Cumulative ed(s).: Local Climatological Data. Fort Wayne, Indiana. Monthly Summary. ISSN 0198-1978.
Published by: U.S. National Climatic Data Center (Subsidiary of: U.S. Department of Commerce), Federal Bldg, 151 Patton Ave, Asheville, NC 28801. TEL 828-271-4800, FAX 828-271-4876, NODC.Services@noaa.gov, http://www.ncdc.noaa.gov.

551.5 USA ISSN 0198-1978
LOCAL CLIMATOLOGICAL DATA. FORT WAYNE, INDIANA. MONTHLY SUMMARY. Text in English. 19??. m. USD 5 per issue (effective 2009). back issues avail. **Document type:** *Bulletin, Government.* **Description:** Provides a monthly summary of temperature extremes, degree days, precipitation and winds, hourly precipitation and 3-hourly weather observations in Fort Wayne, Indiana.
Related titles: Online - full text ed.: USD 3 per issue (effective 2009); ◆ Cumulative ed. of: Local Climatological Data. Fort Wayne, Indiana. Annual Summary with Comparative Data. ISSN 0198-196X.
—Linda Hall.
Published by: U.S. National Climatic Data Center (Subsidiary of: U.S. Department of Commerce), Federal Bldg, 151 Patton Ave, Asheville, NC 28801. TEL 828-271-4800, FAX 828-271-4876, NODC.Services@noaa.gov, http://www.ncdc.noaa.gov.

551.5 USA ISSN 0198-0890
LOCAL CLIMATOLOGICAL DATA. FRESNO, CALIFORNIA. ANNUAL SUMMARY WITH COMPARATIVE DATA. Text in English. 19??. a. USD 39 combined subscription per issue includes 12 monthly summaries & one a. summary (effective 2009). back issues avail. **Document type:** *Bulletin, Government.* **Description:** Presents the monthly and annual average, resultant and fastest mile wind speed for the current year as well as the monthly and annual mean and fastest mile speed for a long period for Fresno, California.
Related titles: Online - full text ed.: USD 29 per issue (effective 2009); ◆ Cumulative ed(s).: Local Climatological Data. Fresno, California. Monthly Summary. ISSN 0198-0734.
Published by: U.S. National Climatic Data Center (Subsidiary of: U.S. Department of Commerce), Federal Bldg, 151 Patton Ave, Asheville, NC 28801. TEL 828-271-4800, FAX 828-271-4876, NODC.Services@noaa.gov, http://www.ncdc.noaa.gov.

551.5 USA ISSN 0198-0734
LOCAL CLIMATOLOGICAL DATA. FRESNO, CALIFORNIA. MONTHLY SUMMARY. Text in English. 19??. m. USD 5 per issue (effective 2009). back issues avail. **Document type:** *Bulletin, Government.* **Description:** Provides a monthly summary of temperature extremes, degree days, precipitation and winds, hourly precipitation and 3-hourly weather observations in Fresno, California.
Related titles: Online - full text ed.: USD 3 per issue (effective 2009); ◆ Cumulative ed. of: Local Climatological Data. Fresno, California. Annual Summary with Comparative Data. ISSN 0198-0890.
—Linda Hall.
Published by: U.S. National Climatic Data Center (Subsidiary of: U.S. Department of Commerce), Federal Bldg, 151 Patton Ave, Asheville, NC 28801. TEL 828-271-4800, FAX 828-271-4876, NODC.Services@noaa.gov, http://www.ncdc.noaa.gov.

551.5 USA ISSN 0742-8731
QC984.F6
LOCAL CLIMATOLOGICAL DATA. GAINESVILLE, FLORIDA. ANNUAL SUMMARY WITH COMPARATIVE DATA. Text in English. 1986. a. USD 39 combined subscription per issue includes 12 monthly summaries & one a. summary (effective 2009). back issues avail. **Document type:** *Bulletin, Government.* **Description:** Presents the monthly and annual average, resultant and fastest mile wind speed for the current year as well as the monthly and annual mean and fastest mile speed for a long period for Gainesville, Florida.
Related titles: Online - full text ed.: USD 29 per issue (effective 2009); ◆ Cumulative ed(s).: Local Climatological Data. Gainesville, Florida. Monthly Summary. ISSN 0742-8723.
Published by: U.S. National Climatic Data Center (Subsidiary of: U.S. Department of Commerce), Federal Bldg, 151 Patton Ave, Asheville, NC 28801. TEL 828-271-4800, FAX 828-271-4876, NODC.Services@noaa.gov, http://www.ncdc.noaa.gov.

551.5 USA ISSN 0742-8723
LOCAL CLIMATOLOGICAL DATA. GAINESVILLE, FLORIDA. MONTHLY SUMMARY. Text in English. 1984. m. USD 5 per issue (effective 2009). back issues avail. **Document type:** *Bulletin, Government.* **Description:** Provides a monthly summary of temperature extremes, degree days, precipitation and winds, hourly precipitation and 3-hourly weather observations in Gainesville, Florida.
Related titles: Online - full text ed.: USD 3 per issue (effective 2009); ◆ Cumulative ed. of: Local Climatological Data. Gainesville, Florida. Annual Summary with Comparative Data. ISSN 0742-8731.
—Linda Hall.
Published by: U.S. National Climatic Data Center (Subsidiary of: U.S. Department of Commerce), Federal Bldg, 151 Patton Ave, Asheville, NC 28801. TEL 828-271-4800, FAX 828-271-4876, NODC.Services@noaa.gov, http://www.ncdc.noaa.gov.

551.5 USA ISSN 0198-506X
LOCAL CLIMATOLOGICAL DATA. GALVESTON, TEXAS. ANNUAL SUMMARY WITH COMPARATIVE DATA. Text in English. 19??. a. USD 39 combined subscription per issue includes 12 monthly summaries & one a. summary (effective 2009). back issues avail. **Document type:** *Bulletin, Government.* **Description:** Presents the monthly and annual average, resultant and fastest mile wind speed for the current year as well as the monthly and annual mean and fastest mile speed for a long period for Galveston, Texas.
Related titles: Online - full text ed.: USD 29 per issue (effective 2009).
Published by: U.S. National Climatic Data Center (Subsidiary of: U.S. Department of Commerce), Federal Bldg, 151 Patton Ave, Asheville, NC 28801. TEL 828-271-4800, FAX 828-271-4876, NODC.Services@noaa.gov, http://www.ncdc.noaa.gov.

551.5 USA ISSN 0198-2966
QC984.M92
LOCAL CLIMATOLOGICAL DATA. GLASGOW, MONTANA. ANNUAL SUMMARY WITH COMPARATIVE DATA. Text in English. 19??. a. USD 39 combined subscription per issue includes 12 monthly summaries & one a. summary (effective 2009). back issues avail. **Document type:** *Bulletin, Government.* **Description:** Presents the monthly and annual average, resultant and fastest mile wind speed for the current year as well as the monthly and annual mean and fastest mile speed for a long period for Glasgow, Montana.
Related titles: Online - full text ed.: USD 29 per issue (effective 2009); ◆ Cumulative ed(s).: Local Climatological Data. Glasgow, Montana. Monthly Summary. ISSN 0198-2974.
Published by: U.S. National Climatic Data Center (Subsidiary of: U.S. Department of Commerce), Federal Bldg, 151 Patton Ave, Asheville, NC 28801. TEL 828-271-4800, FAX 828-271-4876, NODC.Services@noaa.gov, http://www.ncdc.noaa.gov.

551.5 USA ISSN 0198-2974
QC984.M92
LOCAL CLIMATOLOGICAL DATA. GLASGOW, MONTANA. MONTHLY SUMMARY. Text in English. 19??. m. USD 5 per issue (effective 2009). back issues avail. **Document type:** *Bulletin, Government.* **Description:** Provides a monthly summary of temperature extremes, degree days, precipitation and winds, hourly precipitation and 3-hourly weather observations in Glasgow, Montana.
Related titles: Online - full text ed.: USD 3 per issue (effective 2009); ◆ Cumulative ed. of: Local Climatological Data. Glasgow, Montana. Annual Summary with Comparative Data. ISSN 0198-2966.
—Linda Hall.
Published by: U.S. National Climatic Data Center (Subsidiary of: U.S. Department of Commerce), Federal Bldg, 151 Patton Ave, Asheville, NC 28801. TEL 828-271-4800, FAX 828-271-4876, NODC.Services@noaa.gov, http://www.ncdc.noaa.gov.

551.5 USA ISSN 0198-2176
LOCAL CLIMATOLOGICAL DATA. GOODLAND, KANSAS. ANNUAL SUMMARY WITH COMPARATIVE DATA. Text in English. 19??. a. USD 39 combined subscription per issue includes 12 monthly summaries & one a. summary (effective 2009). back issues avail. **Document type:** *Bulletin, Government.* **Description:** Presents the monthly and annual average, resultant and fastest mile wind speed for the current year as well as the monthly and annual mean and fastest mile speed for a long period for Goodland, Kansas.
Related titles: Online - full text ed.: USD 29 per issue (effective 2009); ◆ Cumulative ed(s).: Local Climatological Data. Goodland, Kansas. Monthly Summary. ISSN 0198-2184.
Published by: U.S. National Climatic Data Center (Subsidiary of: U.S. Department of Commerce), Federal Bldg, 151 Patton Ave, Asheville, NC 28801. TEL 828-271-4800, FAX 828-271-4876, NODC.Services@noaa.gov, http://www.ncdc.noaa.gov.

551.5 USA ISSN 0198-2184
LOCAL CLIMATOLOGICAL DATA. GOODLAND, KANSAS. MONTHLY SUMMARY. Text in English. 19??. m. USD 5 per issue (effective 2009). back issues avail. **Document type:** *Bulletin, Government.* **Description:** Provides a monthly summary of temperature extremes, degree days, precipitation and winds, hourly precipitation and 3-hourly weather observations in Goodland, Kansas.
Related titles: Online - full text ed.: USD 3 per issue (effective 2009); ◆ Cumulative ed. of: Local Climatological Data. Goodland, Kansas. Annual Summary with Comparative Data. ISSN 0198-2176.
—Linda Hall.
Published by: U.S. National Climatic Data Center (Subsidiary of: U.S. Department of Commerce), Federal Bldg, 151 Patton Ave, Asheville, NC 28801. TEL 828-271-4800, FAX 828-271-4876, NODC.Services@noaa.gov, http://www.ncdc.noaa.gov.

551.5 USA ISSN 1524-5837
QC984.N92
LOCAL CLIMATOLOGICAL DATA. GRAND FORKS, NORTH DAKOTA. ANNUAL SUMMARY WITH COMPARATIVE DATA. Text in English. 19??. a. USD 39 combined subscription per issue includes 12 monthly summaries & one a. summary (effective 2009). back issues avail. **Document type:** *Bulletin, Government.* **Description:** Presents the monthly and annual average, resultant and fastest mile wind speed for the current year as well as the monthly and annual mean and fastest mile speed for a long period for Grand Forks, North Dakota.
Related titles: Online - full text ed.: USD 29 per issue (effective 2009); ◆ Cumulative ed(s).: Local Climatological Data. Grand Forks, North Dakota. Monthly Summary. ISSN 1524-5829.
Published by: U.S. National Climatic Data Center (Subsidiary of: U.S. Department of Commerce), Federal Bldg, 151 Patton Ave, Asheville, NC 28801. TEL 828-271-4800, FAX 828-271-4876, NODC.Services@noaa.gov, http://www.ncdc.noaa.gov.

551.5 USA ISSN 1524-5829
QC984.N92
LOCAL CLIMATOLOGICAL DATA. GRAND FORKS, NORTH DAKOTA. MONTHLY SUMMARY. Text in English. 19??. m. USD 5 per issue (effective 2009). back issues avail. **Document type:** *Bulletin, Government.* **Description:** Contains summaries from major airport weather stations that include a daily account of temperature extremes, degree days, precipitation amounts and winds in Grand Forks, North Dakota.
Related titles: Online - full text ed.: USD 3 per issue (effective 2009); ◆ Cumulative ed. of: Local Climatological Data. Grand Forks, North Dakota. Annual Summary with Comparative Data. ISSN 1524-5837.
Published by: U.S. National Climatic Data Center (Subsidiary of: U.S. Department of Commerce), Federal Bldg, 151 Patton Ave, Asheville, NC 28801. TEL 828-271-4800, FAX 828-271-4876, NODC.Services@noaa.gov, http://www.ncdc.noaa.gov.

551.5 USA ISSN 0198-3105
LOCAL CLIMATOLOGICAL DATA. GRAND ISLAND, NEBRASKA. ANNUAL SUMMARY WITH COMPARATIVE DATA. Text in English. 19??. a. USD 39 combined subscription per issue includes 12 monthly summaries & one a. summary (effective 2009). back issues avail. **Document type:** *Bulletin, Government.* **Description:** Presents the monthly and annual average, resultant and fastest mile wind speed for the current year as well as the monthly and annual mean and fastest mile speed for a long period for Grand Island, Nebraska.
Related titles: Online - full text ed.: USD 29 per issue (effective 2009); ◆ Cumulative ed(s).: Local Climatological Data. Grand Island, Nebraska. Monthly Summary. ISSN 0198-3253.

Published by: U.S. National Climatic Data Center (Subsidiary of: U.S. Department of Commerce), Federal Bldg, 151 Patton Ave, Asheville, NC 28801. TEL 828-271-4800, FAX 828-271-4876, NODC.Services@noaa.gov, http://www.ncdc.noaa.gov.

551.5 USA ISSN 0198-3253
LOCAL CLIMATOLOGICAL DATA. GRAND ISLAND, NEBRASKA. MONTHLY SUMMARY. Text in English. 19??. m. USD 5 per issue (effective 2009). back issues avail. **Document type:** *Bulletin, Government.* **Description:** Provides a monthly summary of temperature extremes, degree days, precipitation and winds, hourly precipitation and 3-hourly weather observations in Grand Island, Nebraska.
Related titles: Online - full text ed.: USD 3 per issue (effective 2009); ◆ Cumulative ed. of: Local Climatological Data. Grand Island, Nebraska. Annual Summary with Comparative Data. ISSN 0198-3105.
—Linda Hall.
Published by: U.S. National Climatic Data Center (Subsidiary of: U.S. Department of Commerce), Federal Bldg, 151 Patton Ave, Asheville, NC 28801. TEL 828-271-4800, FAX 828-271-4876, NODC.Services@noaa.gov, http://www.ncdc.noaa.gov.

551.5 USA ISSN 0198-7666
LOCAL CLIMATOLOGICAL DATA. GRAND JUNCTION, COLORADO. ANNUAL SUMMARY WITH COMPARATIVE DATA. Text in English. 19??. a. USD 39 combined subscription per issue includes 12 monthly summaries & one a. summary (effective 2009). back issues avail. **Document type:** *Bulletin, Government.* **Description:** Presents the monthly and annual average, resultant and fastest mile wind speed for the current year as well as the monthly and annual mean and fastest mile speed for a long period for Grand Junction, Colorado.
Related titles: Online - full text ed.: USD 29 per issue (effective 2009); ◆ Cumulative ed(s).: Local Climatological Data. Grand Junction, Colorado. Monthly Summary. ISSN 0198-7674.
Published by: U.S. National Climatic Data Center (Subsidiary of: U.S. Department of Commerce), Federal Bldg, 151 Patton Ave, Asheville, NC 28801. TEL 828-271-4800, FAX 828-271-4876, NODC.Services@noaa.gov, http://www.ncdc.noaa.gov.

551.5 USA ISSN 0198-7674
LOCAL CLIMATOLOGICAL DATA. GRAND JUNCTION, COLORADO. MONTHLY SUMMARY. Text in English. 19??. m. USD 5 per issue (effective 2009). back issues avail. **Document type:** *Bulletin, Government.* **Description:** Provides a monthly summary of temperature extremes, degree days, precipitation and winds, hourly precipitation and 3-hourly weather observations in Grand Junction, Colorado.
Related titles: Online - full text ed.: USD 3 per issue (effective 2009); ◆ Cumulative ed. of: Local Climatological Data. Grand Junction, Colorado. Annual Summary with Comparative Data. ISSN 0198-7666.
—Linda Hall.
Published by: U.S. National Climatic Data Center (Subsidiary of: U.S. Department of Commerce), Federal Bldg, 151 Patton Ave, Asheville, NC 28801. TEL 828-271-4800, FAX 828-271-4876, NODC.Services@noaa.gov, http://www.ncdc.noaa.gov.

551.5 USA ISSN 0198-2575
LOCAL CLIMATOLOGICAL DATA. GRAND RAPIDS, MICHIGAN. ANNUAL SUMMARY WITH COMPARATIVE DATA. Text in English. 19??. a. USD 39 combined subscription per issue includes 12 monthly summaries & one a. summary (effective 2009). back issues avail. **Document type:** *Bulletin, Government.* **Description:** Presents the monthly and annual average, resultant and fastest mile wind speed for the current year as well as the monthly and annual mean and fastest mile speed for a long period for Grand Rapids, Michigan.
Related titles: Online - full text ed.: USD 29 per issue (effective 2009); ◆ Cumulative ed(s).: Local Climatological Data. Grand Rapids, Michigan. Monthly Summary. ISSN 0198-2583.
Published by: U.S. National Climatic Data Center (Subsidiary of: U.S. Department of Commerce), Federal Bldg, 151 Patton Ave, Asheville, NC 28801. TEL 828-271-4800, FAX 828-271-4876, NODC.Services@noaa.gov, http://www.ncdc.noaa.gov.

551.5 USA ISSN 0198-2583
LOCAL CLIMATOLOGICAL DATA. GRAND RAPIDS, MICHIGAN. MONTHLY SUMMARY. Text in English. 19??. m. USD 5 per issue (effective 2009). back issues avail. **Document type:** *Bulletin, Government.* **Description:** Provides a monthly summary of temperature extremes, degree days, precipitation and winds, hourly precipitation and 3-hourly weather observations in Grand Rapids, Michigan.
Related titles: Online - full text ed.: USD 3 per issue (effective 2009); ◆ Cumulative ed. of: Local Climatological Data. Grand Rapids, Michigan. Annual Summary with Comparative Data. ISSN 0198-2575.
—Linda Hall.
Published by: U.S. National Climatic Data Center (Subsidiary of: U.S. Department of Commerce), Federal Bldg, 151 Patton Ave, Asheville, NC 28801. TEL 828-271-4800, FAX 828-271-4876, NODC.Services@noaa.gov, http://www.ncdc.noaa.gov.

551.5 USA ISSN 0198-2990
QC984.M92
LOCAL CLIMATOLOGICAL DATA. GREAT FALLS, MICHIGAN. MONTHLY SUMMARY. Text in English. m. USD 5 per issue (effective 2004). **Document type:** *Bulletin, Government.*
Related titles: Online - full text ed.: USD 3 per issue (effective 2009); ◆ Cumulative ed. of: Local Climatological Data. Great Falls, Montana. Annual Summary with Comparative Data. ISSN 0198-2982.
—Linda Hall.
Published by: U.S. National Climatic Data Center (Subsidiary of: U.S. Department of Commerce), Federal Bldg, 151 Patton Ave, Asheville, NC 28801. TEL 828-271-4800, FAX 828-271-4876, NODC.Services@noaa.gov, http://www.ncdc.noaa.gov.

551.5 USA ISSN 0198-2982
QC984.M92
LOCAL CLIMATOLOGICAL DATA. GREAT FALLS, MONTANA. ANNUAL SUMMARY WITH COMPARATIVE DATA. Text in English. 19??. a. USD 39 combined subscription per issue includes 12 monthly summaries & one a. summary (effective 2009). back issues avail. **Document type:** *Bulletin, Government.* **Description:** Presents the monthly and annual average, resultant and fastest mile wind speed for the current year as well as the monthly and annual mean and fastest mile speed for a long period for Great Falls, Montana.
Related titles: Online - full text ed.: USD 29 per issue (effective 2009); ◆ Cumulative ed(s).: Local Climatological Data. Great Falls, Michigan. Monthly Summary. ISSN 0198-2990.
Published by: U.S. National Climatic Data Center (Subsidiary of: U.S. Department of Commerce), Federal Bldg, 151 Patton Ave, Asheville, NC 28801. TEL 828-271-4800, FAX 828-271-4876, NODC.Services@noaa.gov, http://www.ncdc.noaa.gov.

551.5 USA ISSN 0198-5698
LOCAL CLIMATOLOGICAL DATA. GREEN BAY, WISCONSIN. MONTHLY SUMMARY. Text in English. 19??. m. USD 5 per issue (effective 2009). back issues avail. **Document type:** *Bulletin, Government.* **Description:** Provides a monthly summary of temperature extremes, degree days, precipitation and winds, hourly precipitation and 3-hourly weather observations in Green Bay, Wisconsin.
Related titles: Online - full text ed.: USD 3 per issue (effective 2009).
—Linda Hall.
Published by: U.S. National Climatic Data Center (Subsidiary of: U.S. Department of Commerce), Federal Bldg, 151 Patton Ave, Asheville, NC 28801. TEL 828-271-4800, FAX 828-271-4876, NODC.Services@noaa.gov, http://www.ncdc.noaa.gov.

551.5 USA ISSN 0198-375X
LOCAL CLIMATOLOGICAL DATA. GREENSBORO, NORTH CAROLINA. ANNUAL SUMMARY WITH COMPARATIVE DATA. Text in English. 19??. a. USD 39 combined subscription per issue includes 12 monthly summaries & one a. summary (effective 2009). back issues avail. **Document type:** *Bulletin, Government.* **Description:** Presents the monthly and annual average, resultant and fastest mile wind speed for the current year as well as the monthly and annual mean and fastest mile speed for a long period for Greensboro, North Carolina.
Related titles: Online - full text ed.: USD 29 per issue (effective 2009); ◆ Cumulative ed(s).: Local Climatological Data. Greensboro, High Point, Winston-Salem AP, North Carolina. Monthly Summary. ISSN 0198-3768.
Published by: U.S. National Climatic Data Center (Subsidiary of: U.S. Department of Commerce), Federal Bldg, 151 Patton Ave, Asheville, NC 28801. TEL 828-271-4800, FAX 828-271-4876, NODC.Services@noaa.gov, http://www.ncdc.noaa.gov.

551.5 USA ISSN 0198-4667
LOCAL CLIMATOLOGICAL DATA. GREENVILLE-SPARTANBURG AIRPORT. GREER, SOUTH CAROLINA. ANNUAL SUMMARY WITH COMPARATIVE DATA. Text in English. 19??. a. USD 39 combined subscription per issue includes 12 monthly summaries & one a. summary (effective 2009). back issues avail. **Document type:** *Bulletin, Government.* **Description:** Presents the monthly and annual average, resultant and fastest mile wind speed for the current year as well as the monthly and annual mean and fastest mile speed for a long period for Greenville-Spartanburg Airport in Greer, South Carolina.
Related titles: Online - full text ed.: USD 29 per issue (effective 2009); ◆ Cumulative ed(s).: Local Climatological Data. Greenville-Spartanburg AP. Greer, South Carolina. Monthly Summary. ISSN 0198-4675.
Published by: U.S. National Climatic Data Center (Subsidiary of: U.S. Department of Commerce), Federal Bldg, 151 Patton Ave, Asheville, NC 28801. TEL 828-271-4800, FAX 828-271-4876, NODC.Services@noaa.gov, http://www.ncdc.noaa.gov.

551.5 USA ISSN 0198-4675
LOCAL CLIMATOLOGICAL DATA. GREENVILLE-SPARTANBURG AP. GREER, SOUTH CAROLINA. MONTHLY SUMMARY. Text in English. 19??. m. USD 5 per issue (effective 2009). back issues avail. **Document type:** *Bulletin, Government.* **Description:** Provides a monthly summary of temperature extremes, degree days, precipitation and winds, hourly precipitation and 3-hourly weather observations in Greenville-Spartanburg Airport, Greer, South Carolina.
Related titles: Online - full text ed.: USD 3 per issue (effective 2009); ◆ Cumulative ed. of: Local Climatological Data. Greenville-Spartanburg Airport. Greer, South Carolina. Annual Summary with Comparative Data. ISSN 0198-4667.
—Linda Hall.
Published by: U.S. National Climatic Data Center (Subsidiary of: U.S. Department of Commerce), Federal Bldg, 151 Patton Ave, Asheville, NC 28801. TEL 828-271-4800, FAX 828-271-4876, NODC.Services@noaa.gov, http://www.ncdc.noaa.gov.

551.5 USA ISSN 0198-425X
LOCAL CLIMATOLOGICAL DATA. GUAM, PACIFIC. ANNUAL SUMMARY WITH COMPARATIVE DATA. Text in English. 19??. a. USD 39 combined subscription per issue includes 12 monthly summaries & one a. summary (effective 2009). back issues avail. **Document type:** *Bulletin, Government.* **Description:** Presents the monthly and annual average, resultant and fastest mile wind speed for the current year as well as the monthly and annual mean and fastest mile speed for a long period for Guam, Pacific.
Related titles: Online - full text ed.: USD 29 per issue (effective 2009); ◆ Cumulative ed(s).: Local Climatological Data. Guam, Pacific. Monthly Summary. ISSN 0198-4268.
Published by: U.S. National Climatic Data Center (Subsidiary of: U.S. Department of Commerce), Federal Bldg, 151 Patton Ave, Asheville, NC 28801. TEL 828-271-4800, FAX 828-271-4876, NODC.Services@noaa.gov, http://www.ncdc.noaa.gov.

551.5 USA ISSN 0198-4268
LOCAL CLIMATOLOGICAL DATA. GUAM, PACIFIC. MONTHLY SUMMARY. Text in English. m. USD 5 per issue (effective 2009). **Document type:** *Bulletin, Government.*
Related titles: Online - full text ed.: USD 3 per issue (effective 2009); ◆ Cumulative ed. of: Local Climatological Data. Guam, Pacific. Annual Summary with Comparative Data. ISSN 0198-425X.
—Linda Hall.
Published by: U.S. National Climatic Data Center (Subsidiary of: U.S. Department of Commerce), Federal Bldg, 151 Patton Ave, Asheville, NC 28801. TEL 828-271-4800, FAX 828-271-4876, NODC.Services@noaa.gov, http://www.ncdc.noaa.gov.

551.5 USA ISSN 0197-9701
QC984.A42
LOCAL CLIMATOLOGICAL DATA. GULKANA, ALASKA. ANNUAL SUMMARY WITH COMPARATIVE DATA. Text in English. 19??. a. USD 39 combined subscription per issue includes 12 monthly summaries & one a. summary (effective 2009). back issues avail. **Document type:** *Bulletin, Government.* **Description:** Presents the monthly and annual average, resultant and fastest mile wind speed for the current year as well as the monthly and annual mean and fastest mile speed for a long period for Gulkana, Alaska.
Related titles: Online - full text ed.: USD 29 per issue (effective 2009); ◆ Cumulative ed(s).: Local Climatological Data. Gulkana, Alaska. Monthly Summary. ISSN 0197-971X.
Published by: U.S. National Climatic Data Center (Subsidiary of: U.S. Department of Commerce), Federal Bldg, 151 Patton Ave, Asheville, NC 28801. TEL 828-271-4800, FAX 828-271-4876, NODC.Services@noaa.gov, http://www.ncdc.noaa.gov.

551.5 USA ISSN 0197-971X
QC984.A42
LOCAL CLIMATOLOGICAL DATA. GULKANA, ALASKA. MONTHLY SUMMARY. Text in English. 19??. m. USD 5 per issue (effective 2009). back issues avail. **Document type:** *Bulletin, Government.* **Description:** Provides a monthly summary of temperature extremes, degree days, precipitation and winds, hourly precipitation and 3-hourly weather observations in Gulkana, Alaska.
Related titles: Online - full text ed.: USD 3 per issue (effective 2009); ◆ Cumulative ed. of: Local Climatological Data. Gulkana, Alaska. Annual Summary with Comparative Data. ISSN 0197-9701.
—Linda Hall.
Published by: U.S. National Climatic Data Center (Subsidiary of: U.S. Department of Commerce), Federal Bldg, 151 Patton Ave, Asheville, NC 28801. TEL 828-271-4800, FAX 828-271-4876, NODC.Services@noaa.gov, http://www.ncdc.noaa.gov.

551.5 USA ISSN 0198-4519
LOCAL CLIMATOLOGICAL DATA. HARRISBURG, PENNSYLVANIA. ANNUAL SUMMARY WITH COMPARATIVE DATA. Text in English. 19??. a. USD 39 combined subscription per issue includes 12 monthly summaries & one a. summary (effective 2009). back issues avail. **Document type:** *Bulletin, Government.* **Description:** Presents the monthly and annual average, resultant and fastest mile wind speed for the current year as well as the monthly and annual mean and fastest mile speed for a long period for Harrisburg, Pennsylvania.
Related titles: Online - full text ed.: USD 29 per issue (effective 2009).
Published by: U.S. National Climatic Data Center (Subsidiary of: U.S. Department of Commerce), Federal Bldg, 151 Patton Ave, Asheville, NC 28801. TEL 828-271-4800, FAX 828-271-4876, NODC.Services@noaa.gov, http://www.ncdc.noaa.gov.

551.5 USA ISSN 0198-1137
QC984.C82
LOCAL CLIMATOLOGICAL DATA. HARTFORD, CONNECTICUT. ANNUAL SUMMARY WITH COMPARATIVE DATA. Text in English. 19??. a. USD 39 combined subscription per issue includes 12 monthly summaries & one a. summary (effective 2009). back issues avail. **Document type:** *Bulletin, Government.* **Description:** Presents the monthly and annual average, resultant and fastest mile wind speed for the current year as well as the monthly and annual mean and fastest mile speed for a long period for Hartford, Connecticut.
Related titles: Online - full text ed.: USD 29 per issue (effective 2009); ◆ Cumulative ed(s).: Local Climatological Data. Hartford, Connecticut. Monthly Summary. ISSN 0198-1161.
Published by: U.S. National Climatic Data Center (Subsidiary of: U.S. Department of Commerce), Federal Bldg, 151 Patton Ave, Asheville, NC 28801. TEL 828-271-4800, FAX 828-271-4876, NODC.Services@noaa.gov, http://www.ncdc.noaa.gov.

551.5 USA ISSN 0198-1161
LOCAL CLIMATOLOGICAL DATA. HARTFORD, CONNECTICUT. MONTHLY SUMMARY. Text in English. 19??. m. USD 5 per issue (effective 2009). back issues avail. **Document type:** *Bulletin, Government.* **Description:** Provides a monthly summary of temperature extremes, degree days, precipitation and winds, hourly precipitation and 3-hourly weather observations in Hartford, Connecticut.
Related titles: Online - full text ed.: USD 3 per issue (effective 2009); ◆ Cumulative ed. of: Local Climatological Data. Hartford, Connecticut. Annual Summary with Comparative Data. ISSN 0198-1137.
—Linda Hall.
Published by: U.S. National Climatic Data Center (Subsidiary of: U.S. Department of Commerce), Federal Bldg, 151 Patton Ave, Asheville, NC 28801. TEL 828-271-4800, FAX 828-271-4876, NODC.Services@noaa.gov, http://www.ncdc.noaa.gov.

551.5 USA ISSN 0198-3008
LOCAL CLIMATOLOGICAL DATA. HAVRE, MONTANA. ANNUAL SUMMARY WITH COMPARATIVE DATA. Text in English. 19??. a. USD 39 combined subscription per issue includes 12 monthly summaries & one a. summary (effective 2009). back issues avail. **Document type:** *Bulletin, Government.* **Description:** Presents the monthly and annual average, resultant and fastest mile wind speed for the current year as well as the monthly and annual mean and fastest mile speed for a long period for Havre, Montana.
Related titles: Online - full text ed.: USD 29 per issue (effective 2009).
Published by: U.S. National Climatic Data Center (Subsidiary of: U.S. Department of Commerce), Federal Bldg, 151 Patton Ave, Asheville, NC 28801. TEL 828-271-4800, FAX 828-271-4876, NODC.Services@noaa.gov, http://www.ncdc.noaa.gov.

551.5 USA ISSN 0198-3024
LOCAL CLIMATOLOGICAL DATA. HELENA, MONTANA. ANNUAL SUMMARY WITH COMPARATIVE DATA. Text in English. 19??. a. USD 39 combined subscription per issue includes 12 monthly summaries & one a. summary (effective 2009). back issues avail. **Document type:** *Bulletin, Government.* **Description:** Presents the monthly and annual average, resultant and fastest mile wind speed for the current year as well as the monthly and annual mean and fastest mile speed for a long period for Helena, Montana.
Related titles: Online - full text ed.: USD 29 per issue (effective 2008); ◆ Cumulative ed(s).: Local Climatological Data. Helena, Montana. Monthly Summary. ISSN 0198-3032.
Published by: U.S. National Climatic Data Center (Subsidiary of: U.S. Department of Commerce), Federal Bldg, 151 Patton Ave, Asheville, NC 28801. TEL 828-271-4800, FAX 828-271-4876, NODC.Services@noaa.gov, http://www.ncdc.noaa.gov.

551.5 USA ISSN 0198-3032
LOCAL CLIMATOLOGICAL DATA. HELENA, MONTANA. MONTHLY SUMMARY. Text in English. 19??. m. USD 5 per issue (effective 2009). back issues avail. **Document type:** *Bulletin, Government.* **Description:** Provides a monthly summary of temperature extremes, degree days, precipitation and winds, hourly precipitation and 3-hourly weather observations in Helena, Montana.
Related titles: Online - full text ed.: USD 3 per issue (effective 2009); ◆ Cumulative ed. of: Local Climatological Data. Helena, Montana. Annual Summary with Comparative Data. ISSN 0198-3024.
—Linda Hall.
Published by: U.S. National Climatic Data Center (Subsidiary of: U.S. Department of Commerce), Federal Bldg, 151 Patton Ave, Asheville, NC 28801. TEL 828-271-4800, FAX 828-271-4876, NODC.Services@noaa.gov, http://www.ncdc.noaa.gov.

551.5 USA ISSN 0198-1684
QC993
LOCAL CLIMATOLOGICAL DATA. HILO, HAWAII. ANNUAL SUMMARY WITH COMPARATIVE DATA. Text in English. 19??. a. USD 39 combined subscription per issue includes 12 monthly summaries & one a. summary (effective 2009). back issues avail. **Document type:** *Bulletin, Government.* **Description:** Presents the monthly and annual average, resultant and fastest mile wind speed for the current year as well as the monthly and annual mean and fastest mile speed for a long period for Hilo, Hawaii.
Related titles: Online - full text ed.: USD 29 per issue (effective 2009); ◆ Cumulative ed(s).: Local Climatological Data. Hilo, Hawaii. Monthly Summary. ISSN 0198-1692.
Published by: U.S. National Climatic Data Center (Subsidiary of: U.S. Department of Commerce), Federal Bldg, 151 Patton Ave, Asheville, NC 28801. TEL 828-271-4800, FAX 828-271-4876, NODC.Services@noaa.gov, http://www.ncdc.noaa.gov.

551.5 USA ISSN 0198-1692
QC993
LOCAL CLIMATOLOGICAL DATA. HILO, HAWAII. MONTHLY SUMMARY. Text in English. 19??. m. USD 5 per issue (effective 2009). back issues avail. **Document type:** *Bulletin, Government.* **Description:** Provides a monthly summary of temperature extremes, degree days, precipitation and winds, hourly precipitation and 3-hourly weather observations in Hilo, Hawaii.
Related titles: Online - full text ed.: USD 3 per issue (effective 2009); ◆ Cumulative ed. of: Local Climatological Data. Hilo, Hawaii. Annual Summary with Comparative Data. ISSN 0198-1684.
—Linda Hall.
Published by: U.S. National Climatic Data Center (Subsidiary of: U.S. Department of Commerce), Federal Bldg, 151 Patton Ave, Asheville, NC 28801. TEL 828-271-4800, FAX 828-271-4876, NODC.Services@noaa.gov, http://www.ncdc.noaa.gov.

551.5 USA ISSN 0197-9744
QC984.A42
LOCAL CLIMATOLOGICAL DATA. HOMER, ALASKA. ANNUAL SUMMARY WITH COMPARATIVE DATA. Text in English. 19??. a. USD 39 combined subscription per issue includes 12 monthly summaries & one a. summary (effective 2009). back issues avail. **Document type:** *Bulletin, Government.* **Description:** Presents the monthly and annual average, resultant and fastest mile wind speed for the current year as well as the monthly and annual mean and fastest mile speed for a long period for Homer, Alaska.
Related titles: Online - full text ed.: USD 29 per issue (effective 2009); ◆ Cumulative ed(s).: Local Climatological Data. Homer, Alaska. Monthly Summary. ISSN 0197-9752.
Published by: U.S. National Climatic Data Center (Subsidiary of: U.S. Department of Commerce), Federal Bldg, 151 Patton Ave, Asheville, NC 28801. TEL 828-271-4800, FAX 828-271-4876, NODC.Services@noaa.gov, http://www.ncdc.noaa.gov.

551.5 USA ISSN 0197-9752
QC984.A42
LOCAL CLIMATOLOGICAL DATA. HOMER, ALASKA. MONTHLY SUMMARY. Text in English. 19??. m. USD 5 per issue (effective 2009). back issues avail. **Document type:** *Bulletin, Government.* **Description:** Provides a monthly summary of temperature extremes, degree days, precipitation and winds, hourly precipitation and 3-hourly weather observations in Homer, Alaska.
Related titles: Online - full text ed.: USD 3 per issue (effective 2009); ◆ Cumulative ed. of: Local Climatological Data. Homer, Alaska. Annual Summary with Comparative Data. ISSN 0197-9744.
—Linda Hall.
Published by: U.S. National Climatic Data Center (Subsidiary of: U.S. Department of Commerce), Federal Bldg, 151 Patton Ave, Asheville, NC 28801. TEL 828-271-4800, FAX 828-271-4876, NODC.Services@noaa.gov, http://www.ncdc.noaa.gov.

551.5 USA ISSN 0198-1706
LOCAL CLIMATOLOGICAL DATA. HONOLULU, HAWAII. ANNUAL SUMMARY WITH COMPARATIVE DATA. Text in English. 19??. a. USD 39 combined subscription per issue includes 12 monthly summaries & one a. summary (effective 2009). back issues avail. **Document type:** *Bulletin, Government.* **Description:** Presents the monthly and annual average, resultant and fastest mile wind speed for the current year as well as the monthly and annual mean and fastest mile speed for a long period for Honolulu, Hawaii.
Related titles: Online - full text ed.: USD 29 per issue (effective 2009); ◆ Cumulative ed(s).: Local Climatological Data. Honolulu, Hawaii. Monthly Summary. ISSN 0198-1714.
Published by: U.S. National Climatic Data Center (Subsidiary of: U.S. Department of Commerce), Federal Bldg, 151 Patton Ave, Asheville, NC 28801. TEL 828-271-4800, FAX 828-271-4876, NODC.Services@noaa.gov, http://www.ncdc.noaa.gov.

231 USA ISSN 0198-1714
LOCAL CLIMATOLOGICAL DATA. HONOLULU, HAWAII. MONTHLY SUMMARY. Text in English. 19??. m. USD 5 per issue (effective 2009). back issues avail. **Document type:** *Bulletin, Government.* **Description:** Provides a monthly summary of temperature extremes, degree days, precipitation and winds, hourly precipitation and 3-hourly weather observations in Honolulu, Hawaii.
Related titles: Online - full text ed.: USD 3 per issue (effective 2009); ◆ Cumulative ed. of: Local Climatological Data. Honolulu, Hawaii. Annual Summary with Comparative Data. ISSN 0198-1706.
—Linda Hall.
Published by: U.S. National Climatic Data Center (Subsidiary of: U.S. Department of Commerce), Federal Bldg, 151 Patton Ave, Asheville, NC 28801. TEL 828-271-4800, FAX 828-271-4876, NODC.Services@noaa.gov, http://www.ncdc.noaa.gov.

551.5 USA ISSN 0198-2591
LOCAL CLIMATOLOGICAL DATA. HOUGHTON, LAKE, MICHIGAN. ANNUAL SUMMARY WITH COMPARATIVE DATA. Text in English. 19??. a. USD 39 combined subscription per issue includes 12 monthly summaries & one a. summary (effective 2009). back issues avail. **Document type:** *Bulletin, Government.* **Description:** Presents the monthly and annual average, resultant and fastest mile wind speed for the current year as well as the monthly and annual mean and fastest mile speed for a long period for Houghton Lake, Michigan.
Related titles: Online - full text ed.: USD 29 per issue (effective 2009); ◆ Cumulative ed(s).: Local Climatological Data. Houghton Lake, Michigan. Monthly Summary. ISSN 0198-2605.
Published by: U.S. National Climatic Data Center (Subsidiary of: U.S. Department of Commerce), Federal Bldg, 151 Patton Ave, Asheville, NC 28801. TEL 828-271-4800, FAX 828-271-4876, NODC.Services@noaa.gov, http://www.ncdc.noaa.gov.

551.5 USA ISSN 0198-2605
LOCAL CLIMATOLOGICAL DATA. HOUGHTON LAKE, MICHIGAN. MONTHLY SUMMARY. Text in English. 19??. m. USD 5 per issue (effective 2009). back issues avail. **Document type:** *Bulletin, Government.* **Description:** Provides a monthly summary of temperature extremes, degree days, precipitation and winds, hourly precipitation and 3-hourly weather observations in Houghton Lake, Michigan.
Related titles: Online - full text ed.; ◆ Cumulative ed. of: Local Climatological Data. Houghton, Lake, Michigan. Annual Summary with Comparative Data. ISSN 0198-2591.
—Linda Hall.
Published by: U.S. National Climatic Data Center (Subsidiary of: U.S. Department of Commerce), Federal Bldg, 151 Patton Ave, Asheville, NC 28801. TEL 828-271-4800, FAX 828-271-4876, NODC.Services@noaa.gov, http://www.ncdc.noaa.gov.

551.5 USA ISSN 0198-5086
LOCAL CLIMATOLOGICAL DATA. HOUSTON, TEXAS. ANNUAL SUMMARY WITH COMPARATIVE DATA. Text in English. 19??. a. USD 39 combined subscription per issue includes 12 monthly summaries & one a. summary (effective 2009). back issues avail. **Document type:** *Bulletin, Government.* **Description:** Presents the monthly and annual average, resultant and fastest mile wind speed for the current year as well as the monthly and annual mean and fastest mile speed for a long period for Houston, Texas.
Related titles: Online - full text ed.: USD 29 per issue (effective 2009); ◆ Cumulative ed(s).: Local Climatological Data. Houston, Texas. Monthly Summary. ISSN 0198-5094.
Published by: U.S. National Climatic Data Center (Subsidiary of: U.S. Department of Commerce), Federal Bldg, 151 Patton Ave, Asheville, NC 28801. TEL 828-271-4800, FAX 828-271-4876, NODC.Services@noaa.gov, http://www.ncdc.noaa.gov.

551.5 USA ISSN 0198-5094
LOCAL CLIMATOLOGICAL DATA. HOUSTON, TEXAS. MONTHLY SUMMARY. Text in English. 19??. m. USD 5 per issue (effective 2009). back issues avail. **Document type:** *Bulletin, Government.* **Description:** Provides a monthly summary of temperature extremes, degree days, precipitation and winds, hourly precipitation and 3-hourly weather observations in Houston, Texas.
Related titles: Online - full text ed.: USD 3 per issue (effective 2009); ◆ Cumulative ed. of: Local Climatological Data. Houston, Texas. Annual Summary with Comparative Data. ISSN 0198-5086.
—Linda Hall.
Published by: U.S. National Climatic Data Center (Subsidiary of: U.S. Department of Commerce), Federal Bldg, 151 Patton Ave, Asheville, NC 28801. TEL 828-271-4800, FAX 828-271-4876, NODC.Services@noaa.gov, http://www.ncdc.noaa.gov.

551.5 USA ISSN 0198-5655
LOCAL CLIMATOLOGICAL DATA. HUNTINGTON, WEST VIRGINIA. MONTHLY SUMMARY. Text in English. 19??. m. USD 5 per issue (effective 2009). back issues avail. **Document type:** *Bulletin, Government.* **Description:** Provides a monthly summary of temperature extremes, degree days, precipitation and winds, hourly precipitation and 3-hourly weather observations in Huntington, West Virginia.
Related titles: Online - full text ed.: USD 3 per issue (effective 2009).
—Linda Hall.
Published by: U.S. National Climatic Data Center (Subsidiary of: U.S. Department of Commerce), Federal Bldg, 151 Patton Ave, Asheville, NC 28801. TEL 828-271-4800, FAX 828-271-4876, ncdc.info@noaa.gov, http://www.ncdc.noaa.gov.

551.5 USA ISSN 0197-9485
LOCAL CLIMATOLOGICAL DATA. HUNTSVILLE, ALABAMA. ANNUAL SUMMARY WITH COMPARATIVE DATA. Text in English. 19??. a. USD 39 combined subscription per issue includes 12 monthly summaries & one a. summary (effective 2009). back issues avail. **Document type:** *Bulletin, Government.* **Description:** Presents the monthly and annual average, resultant and fastest mile wind speed for the current year as well as the monthly and annual mean and fastest mile speed for a long period for Huntsville, Alabama.
Related titles: Online - full text ed.: USD 29 per issue (effective 2009); ◆ Cumulative ed(s).: Local Climatological Data. Huntsville, Alabama. Monthly Summary. ISSN 0197-9493.
Published by: U.S. National Climatic Data Center (Subsidiary of: U.S. Department of Commerce), Federal Bldg, 151 Patton Ave, Asheville, NC 28801. TEL 828-271-4800, FAX 828-271-4876, NODC.Services@noaa.gov, http://www.ncdc.noaa.gov.

551.5 USA ISSN 0197-9493
LOCAL CLIMATOLOGICAL DATA. HUNTSVILLE, ALABAMA. MONTHLY SUMMARY. Text in English. 19??. m. USD 5 per issue (effective 2009). back issues avail. **Document type:** *Bulletin, Government.* **Description:** Provides a monthly summary of temperature extremes, degree days, precipitation and winds, hourly precipitation and 3-hourly weather observations in Huntsville, Alabama.
Related titles: Online - full text ed.: USD 3 per issue (effective 2009); ◆ Cumulative ed. of: Local Climatological Data. Huntsville, Alabama. Annual Summary with Comparative Data. ISSN 0197-9485.
—Linda Hall.
Published by: U.S. National Climatic Data Center (Subsidiary of: U.S. Department of Commerce), Federal Bldg, 151 Patton Ave, Asheville, NC 28801. TEL 828-271-4800, FAX 828-271-4876, NODC.Services@noaa.gov, http://www.ncdc.noaa.gov.

551.5 USA ISSN 0198-4705
LOCAL CLIMATOLOGICAL DATA. HURON, SOUTH DAKOTA. ANNUAL SUMMARY WITH COMPARATIVE DATA. Text in English. 19??. a. USD 39 combined subscription per issue includes 12 monthly summaries & one a. summary (effective 2009). back issues avail. **Document type:** *Bulletin, Government.* **Description:** Presents the monthly and annual average, resultant and fastest mile wind speed for the current year as well as the monthly and annual mean and fastest mile speed for a long period for Huron, South Dakota.
Related titles: Online - full text ed.: USD 29 per issue (effective 2009); ◆ Cumulative ed(s).: Local Climatological Data. Huron, South Dakota. Monthly Summary. ISSN 0198-4713.
Published by: U.S. National Climatic Data Center (Subsidiary of: U.S. Department of Commerce), Federal Bldg, 151 Patton Ave, Asheville, NC 28801. TEL 828-271-4800, FAX 828-271-4876, NODC.Services@noaa.gov, http://www.ncdc.noaa.gov.

551.5 USA ISSN 0198-4713
LOCAL CLIMATOLOGICAL DATA. HURON, SOUTH DAKOTA. MONTHLY SUMMARY. Text in English. 19??. m. USD 5 per issue (effective 2009). back issues avail. **Document type:** *Bulletin, Government.* **Description:** Provides a monthly summary of temperature extremes, degree days, precipitation and winds, hourly precipitation and 3-hourly weather observations in Huron, South Dakota.
Related titles: Online - full text ed.: USD 3 per issue (effective 2009); ◆ Cumulative ed. of: Local Climatological Data. Huron, South Dakota. Annual Summary with Comparative Data. ISSN 0198-4705.
—Linda Hall.
Published by: U.S. National Climatic Data Center (Subsidiary of: U.S. Department of Commerce), Federal Bldg, 151 Patton Ave, Asheville, NC 28801. TEL 828-271-4800, FAX 828-271-4876, NODC.Services@noaa.gov, http://www.ncdc.noaa.gov.

551.5 USA ISSN 0198-1986
QC984.I62
LOCAL CLIMATOLOGICAL DATA. INDIANAPOLIS, INDIANA. ANNUAL SUMMARY WITH COMPARATIVE DATA. Text in English. 19??. a. USD 39 combined subscription per issue includes 12 monthly summaries & one a. summary (effective 2009). back issues avail. **Document type:** *Bulletin, Government.* **Description:** Presents the monthly and annual average, resultant and fastest mile wind speed for the current year as well as the monthly and annual mean and fastest mile speed for a long period for Indianapolis, Indiana.
Related titles: Online - full text ed.: USD 29 per issue (effective 2009); ◆ Cumulative ed(s).: Local Climatological Data. Indianapolis, Indiana. Monthly Summary. ISSN 0198-2001.
Published by: U.S. National Climatic Data Center (Subsidiary of: U.S. Department of Commerce), Federal Bldg, 151 Patton Ave, Asheville, NC 28801. TEL 828-271-4800, FAX 828-271-4876, NODC.Services@noaa.gov, http://www.ncdc.noaa.gov.

551.5 USA ISSN 0198-2001
LOCAL CLIMATOLOGICAL DATA. INDIANAPOLIS, INDIANA. MONTHLY SUMMARY. Text in English. 19??. m. USD 5 per issue (effective 2009). back issues avail. **Document type:** *Bulletin, Government.* **Description:** Provides a monthly summary of temperature extremes, degree days, precipitation and winds, hourly precipitation and 3-hourly weather observations in Indianapolis, Indiana.
Related titles: Online - full text ed.: USD 3 per issue (effective 2009); ◆ Cumulative ed. of: Local Climatological Data. Indianapolis, Indiana. Annual Summary with Comparative Data. ISSN 0198-1986.
—Linda Hall.
Published by: U.S. National Climatic Data Center (Subsidiary of: U.S. Department of Commerce), Federal Bldg, 151 Patton Ave, Asheville, NC 28801. TEL 828-271-4800, FAX 828-271-4876, NODC.Services@noaa.gov, http://www.ncdc.noaa.gov.

551.5 USA ISSN 0198-2710
LOCAL CLIMATOLOGICAL DATA. INTERNATIONAL FALLS, MINNESOTA. ANNUAL SUMMARY WITH COMPARATIVE DATA. Text in English. 19??. a. USD 39 combined subscription per issue includes 12 monthly summaries & one a. summary (effective 2009). back issues avail. **Document type:** *Bulletin, Government.* **Description:** Presents the monthly and annual average, resultant and fastest mile wind speed for the current year as well as the monthly and annual mean and fastest mile speed for a long period for International Falls, Minnesota.
Related titles: Online - full text ed.: USD 29 per issue (effective 2009); ◆ Cumulative ed(s).: Local Climatological Data. International Falls, Minnesota. Monthly Summary. ISSN 0198-2729.
Published by: U.S. National Climatic Data Center (Subsidiary of: U.S. Department of Commerce), Federal Bldg, 151 Patton Ave, Asheville, NC 28801. TEL 828-271-4800, FAX 828-271-4876, NODC.Services@noaa.gov, http://www.ncdc.noaa.gov.

551.5 USA ISSN 0198-2729
LOCAL CLIMATOLOGICAL DATA. INTERNATIONAL FALLS, MINNESOTA. MONTHLY SUMMARY. Text in English. 19??. m. USD 5 per issue (effective 2009). back issues avail. **Document type:** *Bulletin, Government.* **Description:** Provides a monthly summary of temperature extremes, degree days, precipitation and winds, hourly precipitation and 3-hourly weather observations in International Falls, Minnesota.
Related titles: Online - full text ed.: USD 3 per issue (effective 2009); ◆ Cumulative ed. of: Local Climatological Data. International Falls, Minnesota. Annual Summary with Comparative Data. ISSN 0198-2710.
—Linda Hall.
Published by: U.S. National Climatic Data Center (Subsidiary of: U.S. Department of Commerce), Federal Bldg, 151 Patton Ave, Asheville, NC 28801. TEL 828-271-4800, FAX 828-271-4876, NODC.Services@noaa.gov, http://www.ncdc.noaa.gov.

551.5 USA ISSN 0742-8715
QC984.N7
LOCAL CLIMATOLOGICAL DATA. ISLIP, NEW YORK. ANNUAL SUMMARY WITH COMPARATIVE DATA. Text in English. 1986. a. USD 39 combined subscription per issue includes 12 monthly summaries & one a. summary (effective 2009). back issues avail. **Document type:** *Bulletin, Government.* **Description:** Presents the monthly and annual average, resultant and fastest mile wind speed for the current year as well as the monthly and annual mean and fastest mile speed for a long period for Islip, New York.
Related titles: Online - full text ed.: USD 29 per issue (effective 2009).
Published by: U.S. National Climatic Data Center (Subsidiary of: U.S. Department of Commerce), Federal Bldg, 151 Patton Ave, Asheville, NC 28801. TEL 828-271-4800, FAX 828-271-4876, NODC.Services@noaa.gov, http://www.ncdc.noaa.gov.

551.5 USA ISSN 0278-9140
LOCAL CLIMATOLOGICAL DATA. JACKSON, KENTUCKY. ANNUAL SUMMARY WITH COMPARATIVE DATA. Text in English. 1981. a. USD 39 combined subscription per issue includes 12 monthly summaries & one a. summary (effective 2009). back issues avail. **Document type:** *Bulletin, Government.* **Description:** Presents the monthly and annual average, resultant and fastest mile wind speed for the current year as well as the monthly and annual mean and fastest mile speed for a long period for Jackson, Kentucky.
Related titles: Online - full text ed.: USD 29 per issue (effective 2009); ◆ Cumulative ed(s).: Local Climatological Data. Jackson, Kentucky. Monthly Summary. ISSN 0278-9159.
Published by: U.S. National Climatic Data Center (Subsidiary of: U.S. Department of Commerce), Federal Bldg, 151 Patton Ave, Asheville, NC 28801. TEL 828-271-4800, FAX 828-271-4876, NODC.Services@noaa.gov, http://www.ncdc.noaa.gov.

551.5 USA ISSN 0278-9159
LOCAL CLIMATOLOGICAL DATA. JACKSON, KENTUCKY. MONTHLY SUMMARY. Text in English. 19??. m. USD 5 per issue (effective 2009). back issues avail. **Document type:** *Bulletin, Government.* **Description:** Provides a monthly summary of temperature extremes, degree days, precipitation and winds, hourly precipitation and 3-hourly weather observations in Jackson, Kentucky.
Related titles: Online - full text ed.: USD 3 per issue (effective 2009); ◆ Cumulative ed. of: Local Climatological Data. Jackson, Kentucky. Annual Summary with Comparative Data. ISSN 0278-9140.
—Linda Hall.
Published by: U.S. National Climatic Data Center (Subsidiary of: U.S. Department of Commerce), Federal Bldg, 151 Patton Ave, Asheville, NC 28801. TEL 828-271-4800, FAX 828-271-4876, NODC.Services@noaa.gov, http://www.ncdc.noaa.gov.

551.5 USA ISSN 0198-2796
QC984.M72
LOCAL CLIMATOLOGICAL DATA. JACKSON, MISSISSIPPI. ANNUAL SUMMARY WITH COMPARATIVE DATA. Text in English. 19??. a. USD 39 combined subscription per issue includes 12 monthly summaries & one a. summary (effective 2009). back issues avail. **Document type:** *Bulletin, Government.* **Description:** Presents the monthly and annual average, resultant and fastest mile wind speed for the current year as well as the monthly and annual mean and fastest mile speed for a long period for Jackson, Mississippi.
Related titles: Online - full text ed.: USD 29 per issue (effective 2009); ◆ Cumulative ed(s).: Local Climatological Data. Jackson, Mississippi. Monthly Summary. ISSN 0198-280X.
Published by: U.S. National Climatic Data Center (Subsidiary of: U.S. Department of Commerce), Federal Bldg, 151 Patton Ave, Asheville, NC 28801. TEL 828-271-4800, FAX 828-271-4876, NODC.Services@noaa.gov, http://www.ncdc.noaa.gov.

551.5 USA ISSN 0198-280X
LOCAL CLIMATOLOGICAL DATA. JACKSON, MISSISSIPPI. MONTHLY SUMMARY. Text in English. 19??. m. USD 5 per issue (effective 2009). back issues avail. **Document type:** *Bulletin, Government.* **Description:** Provides a monthly summary of temperature extremes, degree days, precipitation and winds, hourly precipitation and 3-hourly weather observations in Jackson, Mississippi.
Related titles: Online - full text ed.: USD 3 per issue (effective 2009); ◆ Cumulative ed. of: Local Climatological Data. Jackson, Mississippi. Annual Summary with Comparative Data. ISSN 0198-2796.
—Linda Hall.
Published by: U.S. National Climatic Data Center (Subsidiary of: U.S. Department of Commerce), Federal Bldg, 151 Patton Ave, Asheville, NC 28801. TEL 828-271-4800, FAX 828-271-4876, NODC.Services@noaa.gov, http://www.ncdc.noaa.gov.

551.5 USA ISSN 0198-1242
QC984.F62
LOCAL CLIMATOLOGICAL DATA. JACKSONVILLE, FLORIDA. ANNUAL SUMMARY WITH COMPARATIVE DATA. Text in English. 19??. a. USD 39 combined subscription per issue includes 12 monthly summaries & one a. summary (effective 2009). back issues avail. **Document type:** *Bulletin, Government.* **Description:** Presents the monthly and annual average, resultant and fastest mile wind speed for the current year as well as the monthly and annual mean and fastest mile speed for a long period for Jacksonville, Florida.
Related titles: Online - full text ed.: USD 29 per issue (effective 2009); ◆ Cumulative ed(s).: Local Climatological Data. Jacksonville, Florida. Monthly Summary. ISSN 0198-1366.
Published by: U.S. National Climatic Data Center (Subsidiary of: U.S. Department of Commerce), Federal Bldg, 151 Patton Ave, Asheville, NC 28801. TEL 828-271-4800, FAX 828-271-4876, NODC.Services@noaa.gov, http://www.ncdc.noaa.gov.

551.5 USA ISSN 0198-1366
LOCAL CLIMATOLOGICAL DATA. JACKSONVILLE, FLORIDA. MONTHLY SUMMARY. Text in English. 19??. m. USD 5 per issue (effective 2009). back issues avail. **Document type:** *Bulletin, Government.* **Description:** Provides a monthly summary of temperature extremes, degree days, precipitation and winds, hourly precipitation and 3-hourly weather observations in Jacksonville, Florida.
Related titles: Online - full text ed.: USD 3 per issue (effective 2009); ◆ Cumulative ed. of: Local Climatological Data. Jacksonville, Florida. Annual Summary with Comparative Data. ISSN 0198-1242.
—Linda Hall.
Published by: U.S. National Climatic Data Center (Subsidiary of: U.S. Department of Commerce), Federal Bldg, 151 Patton Ave, Asheville, NC 28801. TEL 828-271-4800, FAX 828-271-4876, NODC.Services@noaa.gov, http://www.ncdc.noaa.gov.

551.5 USA ISSN 0198-4276
LOCAL CLIMATOLOGICAL DATA. JOHNSTON ISLAND, PACIFIC. ANNUAL SUMMARY WITH COMPARATIVE DATA. Text in English. 19??. a. USD 39 combined subscription per issue includes 12 monthly summaries & one a. summary (effective 2009). back issues avail. **Document type:** *Bulletin, Government.* **Description:** Presents the monthly and annual average, resultant and fastest mile wind speed for the current year as well as the monthly and annual mean and fastest mile speed for a long period for Johnston Island, Pacific.
Related titles: Online - full text ed.: USD 29 per issue (effective 2009).
Published by: U.S. National Climatic Data Center (Subsidiary of: U.S. Department of Commerce), Federal Bldg, 151 Patton Ave, Asheville, NC 28801. TEL 828-271-4800, FAX 828-271-4876, NODC.Services@noaa.gov, http://www.ncdc.noaa.gov.

551.5 USA ISSN 0197-9760
QC984.A42
LOCAL CLIMATOLOGICAL DATA. JUNEAU, ALASKA. ANNUAL SUMMARY WITH COMPARATIVE DATA. Text in English. 19??. a. USD 39 combined subscription per issue (print, includes 12 monthly summaries & one a. summaryonline & CD-ROM eds.) (effective 2009). back issues avail. **Document type:** *Bulletin, Government.* **Description:** Presents the monthly and annual average, resultant and fastest mile wind speed for the current year as well as the monthly and annual mean and fastest mile speed for a long period for Juneau, Alaska.
Related titles: Online - full text ed.: USD 29 per issue (effective 2009); ◆ Cumulative ed(s).: Local Climatological Data. Juneau, Alaska. Monthly Summary. ISSN 0197-9779.
Published by: U.S. National Climatic Data Center (Subsidiary of: U.S. Department of Commerce), Federal Bldg, 151 Patton Ave, Asheville, NC 28801. TEL 828-271-4800, FAX 828-271-4876, NODC.Services@noaa.gov, http://www.ncdc.noaa.gov.

551.5 USA ISSN 0197-9779
QC984.A42
LOCAL CLIMATOLOGICAL DATA. JUNEAU, ALASKA. MONTHLY SUMMARY. Text in English. 19??. m. USD 5 per issue (effective 2009). back issues avail. **Document type:** *Bulletin, Government.* **Description:** Provides a monthly summary of temperature extremes, degree days, precipitation and winds, hourly precipitation and 3-hourly weather observations in Juneau, Alaska.
Related titles: Online - full text ed.: USD 3 per issue (effective 2009); ◆ Cumulative ed. of: Local Climatological Data. Juneau, Alaska. Annual Summary with Comparative Data. ISSN 0197-9760.
—Linda Hall.
Published by: U.S. National Climatic Data Center (Subsidiary of: U.S. Department of Commerce), Federal Bldg, 151 Patton Ave, Asheville, NC 28801. TEL 828-271-4800, FAX 828-271-4876, NODC.Services@noaa.gov, http://www.ncdc.noaa.gov.

551.5 USA ISSN 0198-1722
LOCAL CLIMATOLOGICAL DATA. KAHULUI, HAWAII. ANNUAL SUMMARY WITH COMPARATIVE DATA. Text in English. a. USD 39 combined subscription per issue includes 12 monthly summaries & one a. summary (effective 2009). back issues avail. **Document type:** *Bulletin, Government.* **Description:** Provides information about local climatological data for Kahului.
Related titles: Online - full text ed.: USD 29 per issue (effective 2009); ◆ Cumulative ed(s).: Local Climatological Data. Kahului, Hawaii. Monthly Summary. ISSN 0198-1730.
Published by: U.S. National Climatic Data Center (Subsidiary of: U.S. Department of Commerce), Federal Bldg, 151 Patton Ave, Asheville, NC 28801. TEL 828-271-4800, FAX 828-271-4876, NODC.Services@noaa.gov, http://www.ncdc.noaa.gov.

551.5 USA ISSN 0198-1730
LOCAL CLIMATOLOGICAL DATA. KAHULUI, HAWAII. MONTHLY SUMMARY. Text in English. 19??. m. USD 5 per issue (effective 2009). back issues avail. **Document type:** *Bulletin, Government.* **Description:** Provides a monthly summary of temperature extremes, degree days, precipitation and winds, hourly precipitation and 3-hourly weather observations in Kahului, Hawaii.
Related titles: Online - full text ed.: USD 3 per issue (effective 2009); ◆ Cumulative ed. of: Local Climatological Data. Kahului, Hawaii. Annual Summary with Comparative Data. ISSN 0198-1722.
—Linda Hall.
Published by: U.S. National Climatic Data Center (Subsidiary of: U.S. Department of Commerce), Federal Bldg, 151 Patton Ave, Asheville, NC 28801. TEL 828-271-4800, FAX 828-271-4876, NODC.Services@noaa.gov, http://www.ncdc.noaa.gov.

551.5 USA ISSN 0198-3040
LOCAL CLIMATOLOGICAL DATA. KALISPELL, MONTANA. ANNUAL SUMMARY WITH COMPARATIVE DATA. Text in English. 19??. a. USD 39 combined subscription per issue includes 12 monthly summaries & one a. summary (effective 2009). back issues avail. **Document type:** *Bulletin, Government.*
Related titles: Online - full text ed.: USD 29 per issue (effective 2009); ◆ Cumulative ed(s).: Local Climatological Data. Kalispell, Montana. Monthly Summary. ISSN 0198-3059.
Published by: U.S. National Climatic Data Center (Subsidiary of: U.S. Department of Commerce), Federal Bldg, 151 Patton Ave, Asheville, NC 28801. TEL 828-271-4800, FAX 828-271-4876, NODC.Services@noaa.gov, http://www.ncdc.noaa.gov.

551.5 USA ISSN 0198-3059
LOCAL CLIMATOLOGICAL DATA. KALISPELL, MONTANA. MONTHLY SUMMARY. Text in English. 19??. m. USD 5 per issue (effective 2009). back issues avail. **Document type:** *Bulletin, Government.* **Description:** Provides a monthly summary of temperature extremes, degree days, precipitation and winds, hourly precipitation and 3-hourly weather observations in Kalispell, Montana.
Related titles: Online - full text ed.: USD 3 per issue (effective 2009); ◆ Cumulative ed. of: Local Climatological Data. Kalispell, Montana. Annual Summary with Comparative Data. ISSN 0198-3040.
—Linda Hall.
Published by: U.S. National Climatic Data Center (Subsidiary of: U.S. Department of Commerce), Federal Bldg, 151 Patton Ave, Asheville, NC 28801. TEL 828-271-4800, FAX 828-271-4876, NODC.Services@noaa.gov, http://www.ncdc.noaa.gov.

551.5 USA ISSN 0743-5347
QC984.M82
LOCAL CLIMATOLOGICAL DATA. KANSAS CITY, MISSOURI. DOWNTOWN AIRPORT. ANNUAL SUMMARY WITH COMPARATIVE DATA. Text in English. a. USD 5 per issue (effective 2004). **Document type:** *Bulletin, Government.*
Related titles: Online - full content ed.
Published by: U.S. National Climatic Data Center (Subsidiary of: U.S. Department of Commerce), Federal Bldg, 151 Patton Ave, Asheville, NC 28801. TEL 828-271-4800, FAX 828-271-4876, NODC.Services@noaa.gov, http://www.ncdc.noaa.gov.

551.5 USA ISSN 0198-2850
QC984.M82
LOCAL CLIMATOLOGICAL DATA. KANSAS CITY, MISSOURI. INTERNATIONAL AIRPORT. ANNUAL SUMMARY WITH COMPARATIVE DATA. Text in English. 19??. a. USD 39 combined subscription per issue includes 12 monthly summaries & one a. summary (effective 2009). back issues avail. **Document type:** *Bulletin, Government.*
Related titles: Online - full text ed.: USD 29 per issue (effective 2009); ◆ Cumulative ed(s).: Local Climatological Data. Kansas City Missouri International Airport. Monthly Summary. ISSN 0198-2877.
Published by: U.S. National Climatic Data Center (Subsidiary of: U.S. Department of Commerce), Federal Bldg, 151 Patton Ave, Asheville, NC 28801. TEL 828-271-4800, FAX 828-271-4876, NODC.Services@noaa.gov, http://www.ncdc.noaa.gov.

551.5 USA ISSN 0198-2877
LOCAL CLIMATOLOGICAL DATA. KANSAS CITY MISSOURI INTERNATIONAL AIRPORT. MONTHLY SUMMARY. Text in English. 19??. m. USD 5 per issue (effective 2009). back issues avail. **Document type:** *Bulletin, Government.* **Description:** Provides a monthly summary of temperature extremes, degree days, precipitation and winds, hourly precipitation and 3-hourly weather observations in Kansas City Missouri International Airport.
Related titles: Online - full text ed.: USD 3 per issue (effective 2009); ◆ Cumulative ed. of: Local Climatological Data. Kansas City, Missouri. International Airport. Annual Summary with Comparative Data. ISSN 0198-2850.
—Linda Hall.
Published by: U.S. National Climatic Data Center (Subsidiary of: U.S. Department of Commerce), Federal Bldg, 151 Patton Ave, Asheville, NC 28801. TEL 828-271-4800, FAX 828-271-4876, NODC.Services@noaa.gov, http://www.ncdc.noaa.gov.

551.5 USA ISSN 0198-1250
LOCAL CLIMATOLOGICAL DATA. KEY WEST, FLORIDA. ANNUAL SUMMARY WITH COMPARATIVE DATA. Text in English. 19??. a. USD 39 combined subscription per issue includes 12 monthly summaries & one a. summary (effective 2009). back issues avail. **Document type:** *Bulletin, Government.*
Related titles: Online - full text ed.: USD 29 per issue (effective 2009); ◆ Cumulative ed(s).: Local Climatological Data. Key West, Florida. Monthly Summary. ISSN 0198-1374.
Published by: U.S. National Climatic Data Center (Subsidiary of: U.S. Department of Commerce), Federal Bldg, 151 Patton Ave, Asheville, NC 28801. TEL 828-271-4800, FAX 828-271-4876, NODC.Services@noaa.gov, http://www.ncdc.noaa.gov.

551.5 USA ISSN 0198-1374
LOCAL CLIMATOLOGICAL DATA. KEY WEST, FLORIDA. MONTHLY SUMMARY. Text in English. 19??. m. USD 5 per issue (effective 2009). back issues avail. **Document type:** *Bulletin, Government.* **Description:** Provides a monthly summary of temperature extremes, degree days, precipitation and winds, hourly precipitation and 3-hourly weather observations in Key West, Florida.
Related titles: Online - full text ed.: USD 3 per issue (effective 2009); ◆ Cumulative ed. of: Local Climatological Data. Key West, Florida. Annual Summary with Comparative Data. ISSN 0198-1250.
—Linda Hall.
Published by: U.S. National Climatic Data Center (Subsidiary of: U.S. Department of Commerce), Federal Bldg, 151 Patton Ave, Asheville, NC 28801. TEL 828-271-4800, FAX 828-271-4876, NODC.Services@noaa.gov, http://www.ncdc.noaa.gov.

551.5 USA ISSN 0197-9787
QC984.A42
LOCAL CLIMATOLOGICAL DATA. KING SALMON, ALASKA. ANNUAL SUMMARY WITH COMPARATIVE DATA. Text in English. 19??. a. USD 39 combined subscription per issue includes 12 monthly summaries & one a. summary (effective 2009). back issues avail. **Document type:** *Bulletin, Government.*
Related titles: Online - full text ed.: USD 29 per issue (effective 2009); ◆ Cumulative ed(s).: Local Climatological Data. King Salmon, Alaska. Monthly Summary. ISSN 0197-9795.
Published by: U.S. National Climatic Data Center (Subsidiary of: U.S. Department of Commerce), Federal Bldg, 151 Patton Ave, Asheville, NC 28801. TEL 828-271-4800, FAX 828-271-4876, NODC.Services@noaa.gov, http://www.ncdc.noaa.gov.

551.5 USA ISSN 0197-9795
QC984.A42
LOCAL CLIMATOLOGICAL DATA. KING SALMON, ALASKA. MONTHLY SUMMARY. Text in English. 19??. m. USD 5 per issue (effective 2009). back issues avail. **Document type:** *Bulletin, Government.* **Description:** Provides a monthly summary of temperature extremes, degree days, precipitation and winds, hourly precipitation and 3-hourly weather observations in King Salmon, Alaska.
Related titles: Online - full text ed.: USD 3 per issue (effective 2009); ◆ Cumulative ed. of: Local Climatological Data. King Salmon, Alaska. Annual Summary with Comparative Data. ISSN 0197-9787.
—Linda Hall.
Published by: U.S. National Climatic Data Center (Subsidiary of: U.S. Department of Commerce), Federal Bldg, 151 Patton Ave, Asheville, NC 28801. TEL 828-271-4800, FAX 828-271-4876, NODC.Services@noaa.gov, http://www.ncdc.noaa.gov.

551.5 USA ISSN 0198-4802
LOCAL CLIMATOLOGICAL DATA. KNOXVILLE, TENNESSEE. ANNUAL SUMMARY WITH COMPARATIVE DATA. Text in English. 19??. a. USD 39 combined subscription per issue includes 12 monthly summaries & one a. summary (effective 2009). back issues avail. **Document type:** *Bulletin, Government.*

M

Related titles: Online - full text ed.: USD 29 per issue (effective 2009); ♦ Cumulative ed(s).: Local Climatological Data. Knoxville, Tennessee. Monthly Summary. ISSN 0198-4810.

Published by: U.S. National Climatic Data Center (Subsidiary of: U.S. Department of Commerce), Federal Bldg, 151 Patton Ave, Asheville, NC 28801. TEL 828-271-4800, FAX 828-271-4876, NODC.Services@noaa.gov, http://www.ncdc.noaa.gov.

551.5 USA ISSN 0198-4810
QC984.T2

LOCAL CLIMATOLOGICAL DATA. KNOXVILLE, TENNESSEE. MONTHLY SUMMARY. Text in English. 19??. m. USD 5 per issue (effective 2009). back issues avail. **Document type:** *Bulletin, Government.* **Description:** Provides a monthly summary of temperature extremes, degree days, precipitation and winds, hourly precipitation and 3-hourly weather observations in Knoxville, Tennessee.

Related titles: Online - full text ed.: USD 3 per issue (effective 2009); ♦ Cumulative ed. of: Local Climatological Data. Knoxville, Tennessee. Annual Summary with Comparative Data. ISSN 0198-4802.

—Linda Hall.

Published by: U.S. National Climatic Data Center (Subsidiary of: U.S. Department of Commerce), Federal Bldg, 151 Patton Ave, Asheville, NC 28801. TEL 828-271-4800, FAX 828-271-4876, NODC.Services@noaa.gov, http://www.ncdc.noaa.gov.

551.5 USA ISSN 0197-9809
QC984.A42

LOCAL CLIMATOLOGICAL DATA. KODIAK, ALASKA. ANNUAL SUMMARY WITH COMPARATIVE DATA. Text in English. 19??. a. USD 39 combined subscription per issue includes 12 monthly summaries & one a. summary (effective 2009). back issues avail. **Document type:** *Bulletin, Government.*

Related titles: Online - full text ed.: USD 29 per issue (effective 2009); ♦ Cumulative ed(s).: Local Climatological Data. Kodiak, Alaska. Monthly Summary. ISSN 0197-9817.

Published by: U.S. National Climatic Data Center (Subsidiary of: U.S. Department of Commerce), Federal Bldg, 151 Patton Ave, Asheville, NC 28801. TEL 828-271-4800, FAX 828-271-4876, NODC.Services@noaa.gov, http://www.ncdc.noaa.gov.

551.5 USA ISSN 0197-9817
QC984.A42

LOCAL CLIMATOLOGICAL DATA. KODIAK, ALASKA. MONTHLY SUMMARY. Text in English. 19??. m. USD 5 per issue (effective 2009). back issues avail. **Document type:** *Bulletin, Government.* **Description:** Provides a monthly summary of temperature extremes, degree days, precipitation and winds, hourly precipitation and 3-hourly weather observations in Kodiak, Alaska.

Related titles: Online - full text ed.: USD 3 per issue (effective 2009); ♦ Cumulative ed. of: Local Climatological Data. Kodiak, Alaska. Annual Summary with Comparative Data. ISSN 0197-9809.

—Linda Hall.

Published by: U.S. National Climatic Data Center (Subsidiary of: U.S. Department of Commerce), Federal Bldg, 151 Patton Ave, Asheville, NC 28801. TEL 828-271-4800, FAX 828-271-4876, NODC.Services@noaa.gov, http://www.ncdc.noaa.gov.

551.5 USA ISSN 0198-4292

LOCAL CLIMATOLOGICAL DATA. KOROR ISLAND, PACIFIC. ANNUAL SUMMARY WITH COMPARATIVE DATA. Text in English. 19??. a. USD 39 combined subscription per issue includes 12 monthly summaries & one a. summary (effective 2009). back issues avail. **Document type:** *Bulletin, Government.*

Related titles: Online - full text ed.: USD 29 per issue (effective 2009); ♦ Cumulative ed(s).: Local Climatological Data. Koror Island, Pacific. Monthly Summary. ISSN 0198-4306.

Published by: U.S. National Climatic Data Center (Subsidiary of: U.S. Department of Commerce), Federal Bldg, 151 Patton Ave, Asheville, NC 28801. TEL 828-271-4800, FAX 828-271-4876, NODC.Services@noaa.gov, http://www.ncdc.noaa.gov.

551.5 USA ISSN 0198-4306

LOCAL CLIMATOLOGICAL DATA. KOROR ISLAND, PACIFIC. MONTHLY SUMMARY. Text in English. 19??. m. USD 5 per issue (effective 2009). back issues avail. **Document type:** *Bulletin, Government.* **Description:** Provides a monthly summary of temperature extremes, degree days, precipitation and winds, hourly precipitation and 3-hourly weather observations in Koror Island, Pacific.

Related titles: Online - full text ed.: USD 3 per issue (effective 2009); ♦ Cumulative ed. of: Local Climatological Data. Koror Island, Pacific. Annual Summary with Comparative Data. ISSN 0198-4292.

—Linda Hall.

Published by: U.S. National Climatic Data Center (Subsidiary of: U.S. Department of Commerce), Federal Bldg, 151 Patton Ave, Asheville, NC 28801. TEL 828-271-4800, FAX 828-271-4876, NODC.Services@noaa.gov, http://www.ncdc.noaa.gov.

551.5 USA ISSN 0197-9825
QC984.A42

LOCAL CLIMATOLOGICAL DATA. KOTZEBUE, ALASKA. ANNUAL SUMMARY WITH COMPARATIVE DATA. Text in English. 19??. a. USD 39 combined subscription per issue includes 12 monthly summaries & one a. summary (effective 2009). back issues avail. **Document type:** *Bulletin, Government.*

Related titles: Online - full text ed.: USD 29 per issue (effective 2009); ♦ Cumulative ed(s).: Local Climatological Data. Kotzebue, Alaska. Monthly Summary. ISSN 0197-9833.

Published by: U.S. National Climatic Data Center (Subsidiary of: U.S. Department of Commerce), Federal Bldg, 151 Patton Ave, Asheville, NC 28801. TEL 828-271-4800, FAX 828-271-4876, NODC.Services@noaa.gov, http://www.ncdc.noaa.gov.

551.5 USA ISSN 0197-9833
QC984.A42

LOCAL CLIMATOLOGICAL DATA. KOTZEBUE, ALASKA. MONTHLY SUMMARY. Text in English. 19??. m. USD 5 per issue (effective 2009). back issues avail. **Document type:** *Bulletin, Government.* **Description:** Provides a monthly summary of temperature extremes, degree days, precipitation and winds, hourly precipitation and 3-hourly weather observations in Kotzebue, Alaska.

Related titles: Online - full text ed.: USD 3 per issue (effective 2009); ♦ Cumulative ed. of: Local Climatological Data. Kotzebue, Alaska. Annual Summary with Comparative Data. ISSN 0197-9825.

—Linda Hall.

Published by: U.S. National Climatic Data Center (Subsidiary of: U.S. Department of Commerce), Federal Bldg, 151 Patton Ave, Asheville, NC 28801. TEL 828-271-4800, FAX 828-271-4876, NODC.Services@noaa.gov, http://www.ncdc.noaa.gov.

551.5 USA ISSN 0198-4314

LOCAL CLIMATOLOGICAL DATA. KWAJALEIN, MARSHALL ISLANDS, PACIFIC. ANNUAL SUMMARY WITH COMPARATIVE DATA. Text in English. 19??. a. USD 39 combined subscription per issue includes 12 monthly summaries & one a. summary (effective 2009). back issues avail. **Document type:** *Bulletin, Government.* **Description:** Presents the monthly and annual average, resultant and fastest mile wind speed for the current year as well as the monthly and annual mean and fastest mile speed for a long period for Kwajalein, Marshall Islands, Pacific.

Related titles: Online - full text ed.: USD 29 per issue (effective 2009); ♦ Cumulative ed(s).: Local Climatological Data. Kwajalein, Pacific. Monthly Summary. ISSN 0198-4322.

Published by: U.S. National Climatic Data Center (Subsidiary of: U.S. Department of Commerce), Federal Bldg, 151 Patton Ave, Asheville, NC 28801. TEL 828-271-4800, FAX 828-271-4876, NODC.Services@noaa.gov, http://www.ncdc.noaa.gov.

551.5 USA ISSN 0198-4322

LOCAL CLIMATOLOGICAL DATA. KWAJALEIN, PACIFIC. MONTHLY SUMMARY. Text in English. 19??. m. USD 5 per issue (effective 2009). back issues avail. **Document type:** *Bulletin, Government.* **Description:** Provides a monthly summary of temperature extremes, degree days, precipitation and winds, hourly precipitation and 3-hourly weather observations in Kwajalein, Pacific.

Related titles: Online - full text ed.: USD 3 per issue (effective 2009); ♦ Cumulative ed. of: Local Climatological Data. Kwajalein, Marshall Islands, Pacific. Annual Summary with Comparative Data. ISSN 0198-4314.

—Linda Hall.

Published by: U.S. National Climatic Data Center (Subsidiary of: U.S. Department of Commerce), Federal Bldg, 151 Patton Ave, Asheville, NC 28801. TEL 828-271-4800, FAX 828-271-4876, NODC.Services@noaa.gov, http://www.ncdc.noaa.gov.

551.5 USA ISSN 0198-571X

LOCAL CLIMATOLOGICAL DATA. LA CROSSE, WISCONSIN. MONTHLY SUMMARY. Text in English. 19??. m. USD 5 per issue (effective 2009). back issues avail. **Document type:** *Bulletin, Government.* **Description:** Provides a monthly summary of temperature extremes, degree days, precipitation and winds, hourly precipitation and 3-hourly weather observations in La Crosse, Wisconsin.

Related titles: Online - full text ed.: USD 3 per issue (effective 2009).

—Linda Hall.

Published by: U.S. National Climatic Data Center (Subsidiary of: U.S. Department of Commerce), Federal Bldg, 151 Patton Ave, Asheville, NC 28801. TEL 828-271-4800, FAX 828-271-4876, NODC.Services@noaa.gov, http://www.ncdc.noaa.gov.

551.5 USA ISSN 0198-229X

LOCAL CLIMATOLOGICAL DATA. LAKE CHARLES, LOUISIANA. ANNUAL SUMMARY WITH COMPARATIVE DATA. Text in English. 19??. a. USD 39 combined subscription per issue includes 12 monthly summaries & one a. summary (effective 2009). back issues avail. **Document type:** *Bulletin, Government.* **Description:** Presents the monthly and annual average, resultant and fastest mile wind speed for the current year as well as the monthly and annual mean and fastest mile speed for a long period for Lake Charles, Louisiana.

Related titles: Online - full text ed.: USD 29 per issue (effective 2009); ♦ Cumulative ed(s).: Local Climatological Data. Lake Charles, Louisiana. Monthly Summary. ISSN 0198-2303.

Published by: U.S. National Climatic Data Center (Subsidiary of: U.S. Department of Commerce), Federal Bldg, 151 Patton Ave, Asheville, NC 28801. TEL 828-271-4800, FAX 828-271-4876, NODC.Services@noaa.gov, http://www.ncdc.noaa.gov.

551.5 USA ISSN 0198-2303

LOCAL CLIMATOLOGICAL DATA. LAKE CHARLES, LOUISIANA. MONTHLY SUMMARY. Text in English. 19??. m. USD 5 per issue (effective 2009). back issues avail. **Document type:** *Bulletin, Government.* **Description:** Provides a monthly summary of temperature extremes, degree days, precipitation and winds, hourly precipitation and 3-hourly weather observations in Lake Charles, Louisiana.

Related titles: Online - full text ed.: USD 3 per issue (effective 2009); ♦ Cumulative ed. of: Local Climatological Data. Lake Charles, Louisiana. Annual Summary with Comparative Data. ISSN 0198-229X.

—Linda Hall.

Published by: U.S. National Climatic Data Center (Subsidiary of: U.S. Department of Commerce), Federal Bldg, 151 Patton Ave, Asheville, NC 28801. TEL 828-271-4800, FAX 828-271-4876, NODC.Services@noaa.gov, http://www.ncdc.noaa.gov.

551.5 USA ISSN 0198-5817

LOCAL CLIMATOLOGICAL DATA. LANDER, WYOMING. MONTHLY SUMMARY. Text in English. 19??. m. USD 5 per issue (effective 2009). back issues avail. **Document type:** *Bulletin, Government.* **Description:** Provides a monthly summary of temperature extremes, degree days, precipitation and winds, hourly precipitation and 3-hourly weather observations in Lander, Wyoming.

Related titles: Online - full text ed.: USD 3 per issue (effective 2009).

—Linda Hall.

Published by: U.S. National Climatic Data Center (Subsidiary of: U.S. Department of Commerce), Federal Bldg, 151 Patton Ave, Asheville, NC 28801. TEL 828-271-4800, FAX 828-271-4876, NODC.Services@noaa.gov, http://www.ncdc.noaa.gov.

551.5 USA ISSN 0198-2613

LOCAL CLIMATOLOGICAL DATA. LANSING, MICHIGAN. ANNUAL SUMMARY WITH COMPARATIVE DATA. Text in English. 19??. a. USD 39 combined subscription per issue includes 12 monthly summaries & one a. summary (effective 2009). back issues avail. **Document type:** *Bulletin, Government.* **Description:** Presents the monthly and annual average, resultant and fastest mile wind speed for the current year as well as the monthly and annual mean and fastest mile speed for a long period for Lansing, Michigan.

Related titles: Online - full text ed.: USD 29 per issue (effective 2009); ♦ Cumulative ed(s).: Local Climatological Data. Lansing, Michigan. Monthly Summary. ISSN 0198-2621.

Published by: U.S. National Climatic Data Center (Subsidiary of: U.S. Department of Commerce), Federal Bldg, 151 Patton Ave, Asheville, NC 28801. TEL 828-271-4800, FAX 828-271-4876, NODC.Services@noaa.gov, http://www.ncdc.noaa.gov.

551.5 USA ISSN 0198-2621

LOCAL CLIMATOLOGICAL DATA. LANSING, MICHIGAN. MONTHLY SUMMARY. Text in English. 19??. m. USD 5 per issue (effective 2009). back issues avail. **Document type:** *Bulletin, Government.* **Description:** Provides a monthly summary of temperature extremes, degree days, precipitation and winds, hourly precipitation and 3-hourly weather observations in Lansing, Michigan.

Related titles: Online - full text ed.: USD 3 per issue (effective 2009); ♦ Cumulative ed. of: Local Climatological Data. Lansing, Michigan. Annual Summary with Comparative Data. ISSN 0198-2613.

—Linda Hall.

Published by: U.S. National Climatic Data Center (Subsidiary of: U.S. Department of Commerce), Federal Bldg, 151 Patton Ave, Asheville, NC 28801. TEL 828-271-4800, FAX 828-271-4876, NODC.Services@noaa.gov, http://www.ncdc.noaa.gov.

551.5 USA ISSN 0198-330X

LOCAL CLIMATOLOGICAL DATA. LAS VEGAS, NEVADA. ANNUAL SUMMARY WITH COMPARATIVE DATA. Text in English. 19??. a. USD 39 combined subscription per issue includes 12 monthly summaries & one a. summary (effective 2009). back issues avail. **Document type:** *Bulletin, Government.* **Description:** Presents the monthly and annual average, resultant and fastest mile wind speed for the current year as well as the monthly and annual mean and fastest mile speed for a long period for Las Vegas, Nevada.

Related titles: Online - full text ed.: USD 29 per issue (effective 2009); ♦ Cumulative ed(s).: Local Climatological Data. Las Vegas, Nevada. Monthly Summary. ISSN 0198-3318.

Published by: U.S. National Climatic Data Center (Subsidiary of: U.S. Department of Commerce), Federal Bldg, 151 Patton Ave, Asheville, NC 28801. TEL 828-271-4800, FAX 828-271-4876, NODC.Services@noaa.gov, http://www.ncdc.noaa.gov.

551.5 USA ISSN 0198-3318

LOCAL CLIMATOLOGICAL DATA. LAS VEGAS, NEVADA. MONTHLY SUMMARY. Text in English. 19??. m. USD 5 per issue (effective 2009). back issues avail. **Document type:** *Bulletin, Government.* **Description:** Provides a monthly summary of temperature extremes, degree days, precipitation and winds, hourly precipitation and 3-hourly weather observations in Las Vegas, Nevada.

Related titles: Online - full text ed.: USD 3 per issue (effective 2009); ♦ Cumulative ed. of: Local Climatological Data. Las Vegas, Nevada. Annual Summary with Comparative Data. ISSN 0198-330X.

—Linda Hall.

Published by: U.S. National Climatic Data Center (Subsidiary of: U.S. Department of Commerce), Federal Bldg, 151 Patton Ave, Asheville, NC 28801. TEL 828-271-4800, FAX 828-271-4876, NODC.Services@noaa.gov, http://www.ncdc.noaa.gov.

551.5 USA ISSN 0198-1781
QC984.I22

LOCAL CLIMATOLOGICAL DATA. LEWISTON, IDAHO. ANNUAL SUMMARY WITH COMPARATIVE DATA. Text in English. 19??. a. USD 39 combined subscription per issue includes 12 monthly summaries & one a. summary (effective 2009). back issues avail. **Document type:** *Bulletin, Government.* **Description:** Presents the monthly and annual average, resultant and fastest mile wind speed for the current year as well as the monthly and annual mean and fastest mile speed for a long period for Lewiston, Idaho.

Related titles: Online - full text ed.: USD 29 per issue (effective 2009); ♦ Cumulative ed(s).: Local Climatological Data. Lewiston, Idaho. Monthly Summary. ISSN 0198-179X.

Published by: U.S. National Climatic Data Center (Subsidiary of: U.S. Department of Commerce), Federal Bldg, 151 Patton Ave, Asheville, NC 28801. TEL 828-271-4800, FAX 828-271-4876, NODC.Services@noaa.gov, http://www.ncdc.noaa.gov.

551.5 USA ISSN 0198-179X
QC984.I22

LOCAL CLIMATOLOGICAL DATA. LEWISTON, IDAHO. MONTHLY SUMMARY. Text in English. 19??. m. USD 5 per issue (effective 2009). back issues avail. **Document type:** *Bulletin, Government.* **Description:** Provides a monthly summary of temperature extremes, degree days, precipitation and winds, hourly precipitation and 3-hourly weather observations in Lewiston, Idaho.

Related titles: Online - full text ed.: USD 3 per issue (effective 2009); ♦ Cumulative ed. of: Local Climatological Data. Lewiston, Idaho. Annual Summary with Comparative Data. ISSN 0198-1781.

—Linda Hall.

Published by: U.S. National Climatic Data Center (Subsidiary of: U.S. Department of Commerce), Federal Bldg, 151 Patton Ave, Asheville, NC 28801. TEL 828-271-4800, FAX 828-271-4876, NODC.Services@noaa.gov, http://www.ncdc.noaa.gov.

551.5 USA ISSN 0198-2230

LOCAL CLIMATOLOGICAL DATA. LEXINGTON, KENTUCKY. ANNUAL SUMMARY WITH COMPARATIVE DATA. Text in English. 19??. a. USD 39 combined subscription per issue includes 12 monthly summaries & one a. summary (effective 2009). back issues avail. **Document type:** *Bulletin, Government.* **Description:** Presents the monthly and annual average, resultant and fastest mile wind speed for the current year as well as the monthly and annual mean and fastest mile speed for a long period for Lexington, Kentucky.

Related titles: Online - full text ed.: USD 29 per issue (effective 2009); ♦ Cumulative ed(s).: Local Climatological Data. Lexington, Kentucky. Monthly Summary. ISSN 0198-2249.

Published by: U.S. National Climatic Data Center (Subsidiary of: U.S. Department of Commerce), Federal Bldg, 151 Patton Ave, Asheville, NC 28801. TEL 828-271-4800, FAX 828-271-4876, ncdc.info@noaa.gov, http://www.ncdc.noaa.gov.

551.5 USA ISSN 0198-2249

LOCAL CLIMATOLOGICAL DATA. LEXINGTON, KENTUCKY. MONTHLY SUMMARY. Text in English. 19??. m. USD 5 per issue (effective 2009). back issues avail. **Document type:** *Bulletin, Government.* **Description:** Provides a monthly summary of temperature extremes, degree days, precipitation and winds, hourly precipitation and 3-hourly weather observations in Lexington, Kentucky.

Related titles: Online - full text ed.: USD 3 per issue (effective 2009); ♦ Cumulative ed. of: Local Climatological Data. Lexington, Kentucky. Annual Summary with Comparative Data. ISSN 0198-2230.

—Linda Hall.
Published by: U.S. National Climatic Data Center (Subsidiary of: U.S. Department of Commerce), Federal Bldg, 151 Patton Ave, Asheville, NC 28801. TEL 828-271-4800, FAX 828-271-4876, NODC.Services@noaa.gov, http://www.ncdc.noaa.gov.

551.5 USA ISSN 0198-1749
LOCAL CLIMATOLOGICAL DATA. LIHUE, HAWAII. ANNUAL SUMMARY WITH COMPARATIVE DATA. Text in English. 19??. a. USD 39 combined subscription per issue includes 12 monthly summaries & one a. summary (effective 2009). back issues avail. **Document type:** *Bulletin, Government.* **Description:** Presents the monthly and annual average, resultant and fastest mile wind speed for the current year as well as the monthly and annual mean and fastest mile speed for a long period for Lihue, Hawaii.
Related titles: Online - full text ed.: USD 29 per issue (effective 2009); ◆ Cumulative ed(s).: Local Climatological Data. Lihue, Hawaii. Monthly Summary. ISSN 0198-1757.
Published by: U.S. National Climatic Data Center (Subsidiary of: U.S. Department of Commerce), Federal Bldg, 151 Patton Ave, Asheville, NC 28801. TEL 828-271-4800, FAX 828-271-4876, NODC.Services@noaa.gov, http://www.ncdc.noaa.gov.

551.5 USA ISSN 0198-1757
LOCAL CLIMATOLOGICAL DATA. LIHUE, HAWAII. MONTHLY SUMMARY. Text in English. 19??. m. USD 5 per issue (effective 2009). back issues avail. **Document type:** *Bulletin, Government.* **Description:** Provides a monthly summary of temperature extremes, degree days, precipitation and winds, hourly precipitation and 3-hourly weather observations in Lihue, Hawaii.
Related titles: Online - full text ed.: USD 3 per issue (effective 2009); ◆ Cumulative ed. of: Local Climatological Data. Lihue, Hawaii. Annual Summary with Comparative Data. ISSN 0198-1749.
—Linda Hall.
Published by: U.S. National Climatic Data Center (Subsidiary of: U.S. Department of Commerce), Federal Bldg, 151 Patton Ave, Asheville, NC 28801. TEL 828-271-4800, FAX 828-271-4876, NODC.Services@noaa.gov, http://www.ncdc.noaa.gov.

551.5 USA ISSN 0198-3113
QC984.N22
LOCAL CLIMATOLOGICAL DATA. LINCOLN, NEBRASKA. ANNUAL SUMMARY WITH COMPARATIVE DATA. Text in English. 19??. a. USD 39 combined subscription per issue includes 12 monthly summaries & one a. summary (effective 2009). back issues avail. **Document type:** *Bulletin, Government.* **Description:** Presents the monthly and annual average, resultant and fastest mile wind speed for the current year as well as the monthly and annual mean and fastest mile speed for a long period for Lincoln, Nebraska.
Related titles: Online - full text ed.: USD 29 per issue (effective 2009); ◆ Cumulative ed(s).: Local Climatological Data. Lincoln, Nebraska. Monthly Summary. ISSN 0198-3121.
Published by: U.S. National Climatic Data Center (Subsidiary of: U.S. Department of Commerce), Federal Bldg, 151 Patton Ave, Asheville, NC 28801. TEL 828-271-4800, FAX 828-271-4876, NODC.Services@noaa.gov, http://www.ncdc.noaa.gov.

551.5 USA ISSN 0198-3121
LOCAL CLIMATOLOGICAL DATA. LINCOLN, NEBRASKA. MONTHLY SUMMARY. Text in English. 19??. m. USD 5 per issue (effective 2009). back issues avail. **Document type:** *Bulletin, Government.* **Description:** Provides a monthly summary of temperature extremes, degree days, precipitation and winds, hourly precipitation and 3-hourly weather observations in Lincoln, Nebraska.
Related titles: Online - full text ed.: USD 3 per issue (effective 2009); ◆ Cumulative ed. of: Local Climatological Data. Lincoln, Nebraska. Annual Summary with Comparative Data. ISSN 0198-3113.
—Linda Hall.
Published by: U.S. National Climatic Data Center (Subsidiary of: U.S. Department of Commerce), Federal Bldg, 151 Patton Ave, Asheville, NC 28801. TEL 828-271-4800, FAX 828-271-4876, NODC.Services@noaa.gov, http://www.ncdc.noaa.gov.

551.5 USA ISSN 0198-067X
QC984.A72
LOCAL CLIMATOLOGICAL DATA. LITTLE ROCK, ARKANSAS. ANNUAL SUMMARY WITH COMPARATIVE DATA. Text in English. 19??. a. USD 39 combined subscription per issue includes 12 monthly summaries & one a. summary (effective 2009). back issues avail. **Document type:** *Bulletin, Government.* **Description:** Presents the monthly and annual average, resultant and fastest mile wind speed for the current year as well as the monthly and annual mean and fastest mile speed for a long period for Little Rock, Arkansas.
Related titles: Online - full text ed.: USD 29 per issue (effective 2009); ◆ Cumulative ed(s).: Local Climatological Data. Little Rock, Arkansas. Monthly Summary. ISSN 0198-0629.
Published by: U.S. National Climatic Data Center (Subsidiary of: U.S. Department of Commerce), Federal Bldg, 151 Patton Ave, Asheville, NC 28801. TEL 828-271-4800, FAX 828-271-4876, NODC.Services@noaa.gov, http://www.ncdc.noaa.gov.

551.5 USA ISSN 0198-0629
LOCAL CLIMATOLOGICAL DATA. LITTLE ROCK, ARKANSAS. MONTHLY SUMMARY. Text in English. 19??. m. USD 5 per issue (effective 2009). back issues avail. **Document type:** *Bulletin, Government.* **Description:** Provides a monthly summary of temperature extremes, degree days, precipitation and winds, hourly precipitation and 3-hourly weather observations in Little Rock, Arkansas.
Related titles: Online - full text ed.: USD 3 per issue (effective 2009); ◆ Cumulative ed. of: Local Climatological Data. Little Rock, Arkansas. Annual Summary with Comparative Data. ISSN 0198-067X.
—Linda Hall.
Published by: U.S. National Climatic Data Center (Subsidiary of: U.S. Department of Commerce), Federal Bldg, 151 Patton Ave, Asheville, NC 28801. TEL 828-271-4800, FAX 828-271-4876, NODC.Services@noaa.gov, http://www.ncdc.noaa.gov.

551.5 USA ISSN 0198-0904
LOCAL CLIMATOLOGICAL DATA. LONG BEACH, CALIFORNIA. ANNUAL SUMMARY WITH COMPARATIVE DATA. Text in English. 19??. a. USD 39 combined subscription per issue includes 12 monthly summaries & one a. summary (effective 2009). back issues avail. **Document type:** *Bulletin, Government.* **Description:** Presents the monthly and annual average, resultant and fastest mile wind speed for the current year as well as the monthly and annual mean and fastest mile speed for a long period for Long Beach, California.
Related titles: Online - full text ed.: USD 29 per issue (effective 2009); ◆ Cumulative ed(s).: Local Climatological Data. Long Beach, California. Monthly Summary. ISSN 0198-0742.
Published by: U.S. National Climatic Data Center (Subsidiary of: U.S. Department of Commerce), Federal Bldg, 151 Patton Ave, Asheville, NC 28801. TEL 828-271-4800, FAX 828-271-4876, NODC.Services@noaa.gov, http://www.ncdc.noaa.gov.

551.5 USA ISSN 0198-0742
LOCAL CLIMATOLOGICAL DATA. LONG BEACH, CALIFORNIA. MONTHLY SUMMARY. Text in English. 19??. m. USD 5 per issue (effective 2009). back issues avail. **Document type:** *Bulletin, Government.* **Description:** Provides a monthly summary of temperature extremes, degree days, precipitation and winds, hourly precipitation and 3-hourly weather observations in Long Beach, California.
Related titles: Online - full text ed.: USD 3 per issue (effective 2009); ◆ Cumulative ed. of: Local Climatological Data. Long Beach, California. Annual Summary with Comparative Data. ISSN 0198-0904.
—Linda Hall.
Published by: U.S. National Climatic Data Center (Subsidiary of: U.S. Department of Commerce), Federal Bldg, 151 Patton Ave, Asheville, NC 28801. TEL 828-271-4800, FAX 828-271-4876, NODC.Services@noaa.gov, http://www.ncdc.noaa.gov.

551.5 USA ISSN 0198-0920
QC984.C2
LOCAL CLIMATOLOGICAL DATA. LOS ANGELES, CALIFORNIA. CIVIC CENTER. ANNUAL SUMMARY WITH COMPARATIVE DATA. Text in English. 19??. a. USD 39 combined subscription per issue includes 12 monthly summaries & one a. summary (effective 2009). back issues avail. **Document type:** *Bulletin, Government.* **Description:** Presents the monthly and annual average, resultant and fastest mile wind speed for the current year as well as the monthly and annual mean and fastest mile speed for a long period for Los Angeles, California.
Related titles: Online - full text ed.: USD 29 per issue (effective 2009); ◆ Cumulative ed(s).: Local Climatological Data. Los Angeles California Civic Center. Monthly Summary. ISSN 0198-0769.
Published by: U.S. National Climatic Data Center (Subsidiary of: U.S. Department of Commerce), Federal Bldg, 151 Patton Ave, Asheville, NC 28801. TEL 828-271-4800, FAX 828-271-4876, NODC.Services@noaa.gov, http://www.ncdc.noaa.gov.

551.5 USA ISSN 0198-0769
QC984.N4
LOCAL CLIMATOLOGICAL DATA. LOS ANGELES CALIFORNIA CIVIC CENTER. MONTHLY SUMMARY. Text in English. 19??. m. USD 5 per issue (effective 2009). back issues avail. **Document type:** *Bulletin, Government.* **Description:** Provides information about local climatological data for Los Angeles California civic center.
Related titles: Online - full text ed.: USD 3 per issue (effective 2009); ◆ Cumulative ed. of: Local Climatological Data. Los Angeles, California. Civic Center. Annual Summary with Comparative Data. ISSN 0198-0920.
—Linda Hall.
Published by: U.S. National Climatic Data Center (Subsidiary of: U.S. Department of Commerce), Federal Bldg, 151 Patton Ave, Asheville, NC 28801. TEL 828-271-4800, FAX 828-271-4876, NODC.Services@noaa.gov, http://www.ncdc.noaa.gov.

551.5 USA ISSN 0198-0912
QC984.C2
LOCAL CLIMATOLOGICAL DATA. LOS ANGELES, CALIFORNIA. INTERNATIONAL AIRPORT. ANNUAL SUMMARY WITH COMPARATIVE DATA. Text in English. 19??. a. USD 39 combined subscription per issue includes 12 monthly summaries & one a. summary (effective 2009). back issues avail. **Document type:** *Bulletin, Government.* **Description:** Presents the monthly and annual average, resultant and fastest mile wind speed for the current year as well as the monthly and annual mean and fastest mile speed for a long period for the international airport in Los Angeles, California.
Related titles: Online - full text ed.: USD 29 per issue (effective 2009); ◆ Cumulative ed(s).: Local Climatological Data. Los Angeles California International Airport. Monthly Summary. ISSN 0198-0750.
Published by: U.S. National Climatic Data Center (Subsidiary of: U.S. Department of Commerce), Federal Bldg, 151 Patton Ave, Asheville, NC 28801. TEL 828-271-4800, FAX 828-271-4876, NODC.Services@noaa.gov, http://www.ncdc.noaa.gov.

551.5 USA ISSN 0198-0750
QC984.N4
LOCAL CLIMATOLOGICAL DATA. LOS ANGELES CALIFORNIA INTERNATIONAL AIRPORT. MONTHLY SUMMARY. Text in English. 19??. m. USD 5 per issue (effective 2009). back issues avail. **Document type:** *Bulletin, Government.* **Description:** Provides information about local climatological data for Los Angeles California international airport.
Related titles: Online - full text ed.: USD 3 per issue (effective 2009); ◆ Cumulative ed. of: Local Climatological Data. Los Angeles, California. International Airport. Annual Summary with Comparative Data. ISSN 0198-0912.
—Linda Hall.
Published by: U.S. National Climatic Data Center (Subsidiary of: U.S. Department of Commerce), Federal Bldg, 151 Patton Ave, Asheville, NC 28801. TEL 828-271-4800, FAX 828-271-4876, NODC.Services@noaa.gov, http://www.ncdc.noaa.gov.

551.5 USA ISSN 0198-2257
QC984.K42
LOCAL CLIMATOLOGICAL DATA. LOUISVILLE, KENTUCKY. ANNUAL SUMMARY WITH COMPARATIVE DATA. Text in English. 19??. a. USD 39 combined subscription per issue includes 12 monthly summaries & one a. summary (effective 2009). back issues avail. **Document type:** *Bulletin, Government.* **Description:** Presents the monthly and annual average, resultant and fastest mile wind speed for the current year as well as the monthly and annual mean and fastest mile speed for a long period for Louisville, Kentucky.
Related titles: Online - full text ed.: USD 29 per issue (effective 2009); ◆ Cumulative ed(s).: Local Climatological Data. Louisville, Kentucky. Monthly Summary. ISSN 0198-2265.
Published by: U.S. National Climatic Data Center (Subsidiary of: U.S. Department of Commerce), Federal Bldg, 151 Patton Ave, Asheville, NC 28801. TEL 828-271-4800, FAX 828-271-4876, NODC.Services@noaa.gov, http://www.ncdc.noaa.gov.

551.5 USA ISSN 0198-2265
LOCAL CLIMATOLOGICAL DATA. LOUISVILLE, KENTUCKY. MONTHLY SUMMARY. Text in English. 19??. m. USD 5 per issue (effective 2009). back issues avail. **Document type:** *Bulletin, Government.* **Description:** Provides information about local climatological data for Louisville.
Related titles: Online - full text ed.: USD 3 per issue (effective 2009); ◆ Cumulative ed. of: Local Climatological Data. Louisville, Kentucky. Annual Summary with Comparative Data. ISSN 0198-2257.
—Linda Hall.
Published by: U.S. National Climatic Data Center (Subsidiary of: U.S. Department of Commerce), Federal Bldg, 151 Patton Ave, Asheville, NC 28801. TEL 828-271-4800, FAX 828-271-4876, NODC.Services@noaa.gov, http://www.ncdc.noaa.gov.

551.5 USA ISSN 0198-5108
LOCAL CLIMATOLOGICAL DATA. LUBBOCK, TEXAS. ANNUAL SUMMARY WITH COMPARATIVE DATA. Text in English. 19??. a. USD 39 combined subscription per issue includes 12 monthly summaries & one a. summary (effective 2009). back issues avail. **Document type:** *Bulletin, Government.* **Description:** Presents the monthly and annual average, resultant and fastest mile wind speed for the current year as well as the monthly and annual mean and fastest mile speed for a long period for Lubbock, Texas.
Related titles: Online - full text ed.: USD 29 per issue (effective 2009); ◆ Cumulative ed(s).: Local Climatological Data. Lubbock, Texas. Monthly Summary. ISSN 0198-5116.
Published by: U.S. National Climatic Data Center (Subsidiary of: U.S. Department of Commerce), Federal Bldg, 151 Patton Ave, Asheville, NC 28801. TEL 828-271-4800, FAX 828-271-4876, NODC.Services@noaa.gov, http://www.ncdc.noaa.gov.

551.5 USA ISSN 0198-5116
LOCAL CLIMATOLOGICAL DATA. LUBBOCK, TEXAS. MONTHLY SUMMARY. Text in English. 19??. m. USD 5 per issue (effective 2009). back issues avail. **Document type:** *Bulletin, Government.* **Description:** Provides information about local climatological data for Lubbock.
Related titles: Online - full text ed.: USD 3 per issue (effective 2009); ◆ Cumulative ed. of: Local Climatological Data. Lubbock, Texas. Annual Summary with Comparative Data. ISSN 0198-5108.
—Linda Hall.
Published by: U.S. National Climatic Data Center (Subsidiary of: U.S. Department of Commerce), Federal Bldg, 151 Patton Ave, Asheville, NC 28801. TEL 828-271-4800, FAX 828-271-4876, NODC.Services@noaa.gov, http://www.ncdc.noaa.gov.

551.5 USA ISSN 0198-5329
QC984.V82
LOCAL CLIMATOLOGICAL DATA. LYNCHBURG, VIRGINIA. ANNUAL SUMMARY WITH COMPARATIVE DATA. Text in English. 19??. a. USD 39 combined subscription per issue includes 12 monthly summaries & one a. summary (effective 2009). back issues avail. **Document type:** *Bulletin, Government.* **Description:** Presents the monthly and annual average, resultant and fastest mile wind speed for the current year as well as the monthly and annual mean and fastest mile speed for a long period for Lynchburg, Virginia.
Related titles: Online - full text ed.: USD 29 per issue (effective 2009); ◆ Cumulative ed(s).: Local Climatological Data. Lynchburg, Virginia. Monthly Summary. ISSN 0198-5337.
Published by: U.S. National Climatic Data Center (Subsidiary of: U.S. Department of Commerce), Federal Bldg, 151 Patton Ave, Asheville, NC 28801. TEL 828-271-4800, FAX 828-271-4876, NODC.Services@noaa.gov, http://www.ncdc.noaa.gov.

551.5 USA ISSN 0198-5337
QC984.V8
LOCAL CLIMATOLOGICAL DATA. LYNCHBURG, VIRGINIA. MONTHLY SUMMARY. Text in English. 19??. m. USD 5 per issue (effective 2009). back issues avail. **Document type:** *Bulletin, Government.* **Description:** Provides information about local climatological data for Lynchburg.
Related titles: Online - full text ed.: USD 3 per issue (effective 2009); ◆ Cumulative ed. of: Local Climatological Data. Lynchburg, Virginia. Annual Summary with Comparative Data. ISSN 0198-5329.
—Linda Hall.
Published by: U.S. National Climatic Data Center (Subsidiary of: U.S. Department of Commerce), Federal Bldg, 151 Patton Ave, Asheville, NC 28801. TEL 828-271-4800, FAX 828-271-4876, NODC.Services@noaa.gov, http://www.ncdc.noaa.gov.

551.5 USA ISSN 0198-1625
LOCAL CLIMATOLOGICAL DATA. MACON, GEORGIA. ANNUAL SUMMARY WITH COMPARATIVE DATA. Text in English. 19??. a. USD 39 combined subscription per issue includes 12 monthly summaries & one a. summary (effective 2009). back issues avail. **Document type:** *Bulletin, Government.* **Description:** Presents the monthly and annual average, resultant and fastest mile wind speed for the current year as well as the monthly and annual mean and fastest mile speed for a long period for Macon, Georgia.
Related titles: Online - full text ed.: USD 29 per issue (effective 2009); ◆ Cumulative ed(s).: Local Climatological Data. Macon, Georgia. Monthly Summary. ISSN 0198-1633.
Published by: U.S. National Climatic Data Center (Subsidiary of: U.S. Department of Commerce), Federal Bldg, 151 Patton Ave, Asheville, NC 28801. TEL 828-271-4800, FAX 828-271-4876, NODC.Services@noaa.gov, http://www.ncdc.noaa.gov.

551.5 USA ISSN 0198-1633
LOCAL CLIMATOLOGICAL DATA. MACON, GEORGIA. MONTHLY SUMMARY. Text in English. 19??. m. USD 5 per issue (effective 2009). back issues avail. **Document type:** *Bulletin, Government.* **Description:** Provides a monthly summary of temperature extremes, degree days, precipitation and winds, hourly precipitation and 3-hourly weather observations in Macon, Georgia.
Related titles: Online - full text ed.: USD 3 per issue (effective 2009); ◆ Cumulative ed. of: Local Climatological Data. Macon, Georgia. Annual Summary with Comparative Data. ISSN 0198-1625.
—Linda Hall.
Published by: U.S. National Climatic Data Center (Subsidiary of: U.S. Department of Commerce), Federal Bldg, 151 Patton Ave, Asheville, NC 28801. TEL 828-271-4800, FAX 828-271-4876, NODC.Services@noaa.gov, http://www.ncdc.noaa.gov.

M

551.5 USA ISSN 0198-5736
LOCAL CLIMATOLOGICAL DATA. MADISON, WISCONSIN. MONTHLY SUMMARY. Text in English. 19??. m. USD 5 per issue (effective 2009). back issues avail. **Document type:** *Bulletin, Government.* **Description:** Provides a monthly summary of temperature extremes, degree days, precipitation and winds, hourly precipitation and 3-hourly weather observations in Madison, Wisconsin.
Related titles: Online - full text ed.: USD 3 per issue (effective 2009).
—Linda Hall.
Published by: U.S. National Climatic Data Center (Subsidiary of: U.S. Department of Commerce), Federal Bldg, 151 Patton Ave, Asheville, NC 28801. TEL 828-271-4800, FAX 828-271-4876, NODC.Services@noaa.gov, http://www.ncdc.noaa.gov.

551.5 USA ISSN 0198-4349
LOCAL CLIMATOLOGICAL DATA. MAJURO, MARSHALL ISLAND, PACIFIC. MONTHLY SUMMARY. Text in English. 19??. m. USD 5 per issue (effective 2009). back issues avail. **Document type:** *Bulletin, Government.* **Description:** Provides a monthly summary of temperature extremes, degree days, precipitation and winds, hourly precipitation and 3-hourly weather observations in Majuro, Marshall Island, Pacific.
Related titles: Online - full text ed.: USD 3 per issue (effective 2009); ◆ Cumulative ed. of: Local Climatological Data. Majuro, Marshall Islands, Pacific. Annual Summary with Comparative Data. ISSN 0198-4330.
—Linda Hall.
Published by: U.S. National Climatic Data Center (Subsidiary of: U.S. Department of Commerce), Federal Bldg, 151 Patton Ave, Asheville, NC 28801. TEL 828-271-4800, FAX 828-271-4876, NODC.Services@noaa.gov, http://www.ncdc.noaa.gov.

551.5 USA ISSN 0198-4330
LOCAL CLIMATOLOGICAL DATA. MAJURO, MARSHALL ISLANDS, PACIFIC. ANNUAL SUMMARY WITH COMPARATIVE DATA. Text in English. 19??. a. USD 39 combined subscription per issue includes 12 monthly summaries & one a. summary (effective 2009). back issues avail. **Document type:** *Bulletin, Government.* **Description:** Presents the monthly and annual average, resultant and fastest mile wind speed for the current year as well as the monthly and annual mean and fastest mile speed for a long period for Majuro, Marshall Islands, Pacific.
Related titles: Online - full text ed.: USD 29 per issue (effective 2009); ◆ Cumulative ed(s).: Local Climatological Data. Majuro, Marshall Island, Pacific. Monthly Summary. ISSN 0198-4349.
Published by: U.S. National Climatic Data Center (Subsidiary of: U.S. Department of Commerce), Federal Bldg, 151 Patton Ave, Asheville, NC 28801. TEL 828-271-4800, FAX 828-271-4876, NODC.Services@noaa.gov, http://www.ncdc.noaa.gov.

551.5 USA ISSN 0198-3997
QC984.O32
LOCAL CLIMATOLOGICAL DATA. MANSFIELD, OHIO. ANNUAL SUMMARY WITH COMPARATIVE DATA. Text in English. 19??. a. USD 39 combined subscription per issue includes 12 monthly summaries & one a. summary (effective 2009). back issues avail. **Document type:** *Bulletin, Government.* **Description:** Presents the monthly and annual average, resultant and fastest mile wind speed for the current year as well as the monthly and annual mean and fastest mile speed for a long period for Mansfield, Ohio.
Related titles: Online - full text ed.: USD 29 per issue (effective 2009); ◆ Cumulative ed(s).: Local Climatological Data. Mansfield, Ohio. Monthly Summary. ISSN 0198-4004.
Published by: U.S. National Climatic Data Center (Subsidiary of: U.S. Department of Commerce), Federal Bldg, 151 Patton Ave, Asheville, NC 28801. TEL 828-271-4800, FAX 828-271-4876, NODC.Services@noaa.gov, http://www.ncdc.noaa.gov.

551.5 USA ISSN 0198-4004
LOCAL CLIMATOLOGICAL DATA. MANSFIELD, OHIO. MONTHLY SUMMARY. Text in English. 19??. m. USD 5 per issue ' (effective 2009). back issues avail. **Document type:** *Bulletin, Government.* **Description:** Provides a monthly summary of temperature extremes, degree days, precipitation and winds, hourly precipitation and 3-hourly weather observations in Mansfield, Ohio.
Related titles: Online - full text ed.: USD 3 per issue (effective 2009); ◆ Cumulative ed. of: Local Climatological Data. Mansfield, Ohio. Annual Summary with Comparative Data. ISSN 0198-3997.
—Linda Hall.
Published by: U.S. National Climatic Data Center (Subsidiary of: U.S. Department of Commerce), Federal Bldg, 151 Patton Ave, Asheville, NC 28801. TEL 828-271-4800, FAX 828-271-4876, NODC.Services@noaa.gov, http://www.ncdc.noaa.gov.

551.5 USA
LOCAL CLIMATOLOGICAL DATA. MARQUETTE COUNTY AIRPORT, MICHIGAN. ANNUAL SUMMARY WITH COMPARATIVE DATA. Text in English. 19??. a. USD 39 combined subscription per issue includes 12 monthly summaries & one a. summary (effective 2009). back issues avail. **Document type:** *Bulletin, Government.* **Description:** Presents the monthly and annual average, resultant and fastest mile wind speed for the current year as well as the monthly and annual mean and fastest mile speed for a long period for Marquette County Airport, Michigan.
Formerly (until 19??): Local Climatological Data. Marquette, Michigan. Annual Summary with Comparative Data (0198-263X)
Related titles: Online - full text ed.: USD 29 per issue (effective 2009); ◆ Cumulative ed(s).: Local Climatological Data. Marquette, Michigan. Monthly Summary. ISSN 0198-2648.
Published by: U.S. National Climatic Data Center (Subsidiary of: U.S. Department of Commerce), Federal Bldg, 151 Patton Ave, Asheville, NC 28801. TEL 828-271-4800, FAX 828-271-4876, NODC.Services@noaa.gov, http://www.ncdc.noaa.gov.

551.5 USA ISSN 0198-2648
LOCAL CLIMATOLOGICAL DATA. MARQUETTE, MICHIGAN. MONTHLY SUMMARY. Text in English. 19??. m. USD 5 per issue (effective 2009). back issues avail. **Document type:** *Bulletin, Government.* **Description:** Provides a monthly summary of temperature extremes, degree days, precipitation and winds, hourly precipitation and 3-hourly weather observations in Marquette, Michigan.
Related titles: Online - full text ed.: USD 3 per issue (effective 2009); ◆ Cumulative ed. of: Local Climatological Data. Marquette County Airport, Michigan. Annual Summary with Comparative Data.
—Linda Hall.
Published by: U.S. National Climatic Data Center (Subsidiary of: U.S. Department of Commerce), Federal Bldg, 151 Patton Ave, Asheville, NC 28801. TEL 828-271-4800, FAX 828-271-4876, NODC.Services@noaa.gov, http://www.ncdc.noaa.gov.

551.5 USA ISSN 0197-9841
QC984.A42
LOCAL CLIMATOLOGICAL DATA. MCGRATH, ALASKA. ANNUAL SUMMARY WITH COMPARATIVE DATA. Text in English. 19??. a. USD 39 combined subscription per issue includes 12 monthly summaries & one a. summary (effective 2009). back issues avail. **Document type:** *Bulletin, Government.* **Description:** Presents the monthly and annual average, resultant and fastest mile wind speed for the current year as well as the monthly and annual mean and fastest mile speed for a long period for McGrath, Alaska.
Related titles: Online - full text ed.: USD 29 per issue (effective 2009); ◆ Cumulative ed(s).: Local Climatological Data. McGrath, Alaska. Monthly Summary. ISSN 0197-985X.
Published by: U.S. National Climatic Data Center (Subsidiary of: U.S. Department of Commerce), Federal Bldg, 151 Patton Ave, Asheville, NC 28801. TEL 828-271-4800, FAX 828-271-4876, NODC.Services@noaa.gov, http://www.ncdc.noaa.gov.

551.5 USA ISSN 0197-985X
QC984.A42
LOCAL CLIMATOLOGICAL DATA. MCGRATH, ALASKA. MONTHLY SUMMARY. Text in English. 19??. m. USD 5 per issue (effective 2009). back issues avail. **Document type:** *Bulletin, Government.* **Description:** Provides a monthly summary of temperature extremes, degree days, precipitation and winds, hourly precipitation and 3-hourly weather observations in McGrath, Alaska.
Related titles: Online - full text ed.: USD 3 per issue (effective 2009); ◆ Cumulative ed. of: Local Climatological Data. McGrath, Alaska. Annual Summary with Comparative Data. ISSN 0197-9841.
—Linda Hall.
Published by: U.S. National Climatic Data Center (Subsidiary of: U.S. Department of Commerce), Federal Bldg, 151 Patton Ave, Asheville, NC 28801. TEL 828-271-4800, FAX 828-271-4876, NODC.Services@noaa.gov, http://www.ncdc.noaa.gov.

551.5 USA ISSN 0198-4152
QC984.O72
LOCAL CLIMATOLOGICAL DATA. MEDFORD, OREGON. ANNUAL SUMMARY WITH COMPARATIVE DATA. Text in English. a. USD 39 combined subscription per issue includes 12 monthly summaries & one a. summary (effective 2009). back issues avail. **Document type:** *Bulletin, Government.* **Description:** Presents the monthly and annual average, resultant and fastest mile wind speed for the current year as well as the monthly and annual mean and fastest mile speed for a long period for Medford, Oregon.
Formerly: Local Climatological Data with Comparative Data. Medford, Oregon
Related titles: Online - full text ed.: USD 29 per issue (effective 2009); ◆ Cumulative ed(s).: Local Climatological Data. Medford, Oregon. Monthly Summary. ISSN 0198-4160.
Published by: U.S. National Climatic Data Center (Subsidiary of: U.S. Department of Commerce), Federal Bldg, 151 Patton Ave, Asheville, NC 28801. TEL 828-271-4800, FAX 828-271-4876, NODC.Services@noaa.gov, http://www.ncdc.noaa.gov.

551.5 USA ISSN 0198-4160
QC984.O72
LOCAL CLIMATOLOGICAL DATA. MEDFORD, OREGON. MONTHLY SUMMARY. Text in English. m. USD 5 per issue (effective 2009). back issues avail. **Document type:** *Bulletin, Government.* **Description:** Provides a monthly summary of temperature extremes, degree days, precipitation and winds, hourly precipitation and 3-hourly weather observations in Medford, Oregon.
Formerly: Station Meteorological Summary. Medford, Oregon
Related titles: Online - full text ed.: USD 3 per issue (effective 2009); ◆ Cumulative ed. of: Local Climatological Data. Medford, Oregon. Annual Summary with Comparative Data. ISSN 0198-4152.
—Linda Hall.
Published by: U.S. National Climatic Data Center (Subsidiary of: U.S. Department of Commerce), Federal Bldg, 151 Patton Ave, Asheville, NC 28801. TEL 828-271-4800, FAX 828-271-4876, NODC.Services@noaa.gov, http://www.ncdc.noaa.gov.

551.5 USA ISSN 2156-6879
QC984.F6
LOCAL CLIMATOLOGICAL DATA. MELBOURNE, FLORIDA. Text in English. 19??. m. USD 29; USD 3 per issue (effective 2010). back issues avail. **Document type:** *Bulletin, Government.* **Description:** Provides a monthly summary of temperature extremes, degree days, precipitation and winds, hourly precipitation and 3-hourly weather observations in Melbourne, Florida.
Related titles: Online - full text ed.: ISSN 2156-6887.
Published by: U.S. National Climatic Data Center (Subsidiary of: U.S. Department of Commerce), Federal Bldg, 151 Patton Ave, Asheville, NC 28801. TEL 828-271-4800, FAX 828-271-4876, ncdc.info@noaa.gov, http://www.ncdc.noaa.gov.

551.5 USA ISSN 0198-4829
QC984.T22
LOCAL CLIMATOLOGICAL DATA. MEMPHIS, TENNESSEE. ANNUAL SUMMARY WITH COMPARATIVE DATA. Text in English. 19??. a. USD 39 combined subscription per issue includes 12 monthly summaries & one a. summary (effective 2009). back issues avail. **Document type:** *Bulletin, Government.* **Description:** Presents the monthly and annual average, resultant and fastest mile wind speed for the current year as well as the monthly and annual mean and fastest mile speed for a long period for Memphis, Tennessee.
Related titles: Online - full text ed.: USD 29 per issue (effective 2009); ◆ Cumulative ed(s).: Local Climatological Data. Memphis, Tennessee. Monthly Summary. ISSN 0198-4837.
Published by: U.S. National Climatic Data Center (Subsidiary of: U.S. Department of Commerce), Federal Bldg, 151 Patton Ave, Asheville, NC 28801. TEL 828-271-4800, FAX 828-271-4876, NODC.Services@noaa.gov, http://www.ncdc.noaa.gov.

551.5 USA ISSN 0198-4837
QC984.T2
LOCAL CLIMATOLOGICAL DATA. MEMPHIS, TENNESSEE. MONTHLY SUMMARY. Text in English. 19??. m. USD 5 per issue (effective 2009). back issues avail. **Document type:** *Bulletin, Government.* **Description:** Provides a monthly summary of temperature extremes, degree days, precipitation and winds, hourly precipitation and 3-hourly weather observations in Memphis, Tennessee.
Related titles: Online - full text ed.: USD 3 per issue (effective 2009); ◆ Cumulative ed. of: Local Climatological Data. Memphis, Tennessee. Annual Summary with Comparative Data. ISSN 0198-4829.
—Linda Hall.
Published by: U.S. National Climatic Data Center (Subsidiary of: U.S. Department of Commerce), Federal Bldg, 151 Patton Ave, Asheville, NC 28801. TEL 828-271-4800, FAX 828-271-4876, NODC.Services@noaa.gov, http://www.ncdc.noaa.gov.

551.5 USA ISSN 0198-2818
LOCAL CLIMATOLOGICAL DATA. MERIDIAN, MISSISSIPPI. ANNUAL SUMMARY WITH COMPARATIVE DATA. Text in English. 19??. a. USD 39 combined subscription per issue includes 12 monthly summaries & one a. summary (effective 2009). back issues avail. **Document type:** *Bulletin, Government.* **Description:** Presents the monthly and annual average, resultant and fastest mile wind speed for the current year as well as the monthly and annual mean and fastest mile speed for a long period for Meridian, Mississippi.
Related titles: Online - full text ed.: USD 29 per issue (effective 2009); ◆ Cumulative ed(s).: Local Climatological Data. Meridian, Mississippi. Monthly Summary. ISSN 0198-2826.
Published by: U.S. National Climatic Data Center (Subsidiary of: U.S. Department of Commerce), Federal Bldg, 151 Patton Ave, Asheville, NC 28801. TEL 828-271-4800, FAX 828-271-4876, NODC.Services@noaa.gov, http://www.ncdc.noaa.gov.

551.5 USA ISSN 0198-2826
LOCAL CLIMATOLOGICAL DATA. MERIDIAN, MISSISSIPPI. MONTHLY SUMMARY. Text in English. 19??. m. USD 5 per issue (effective 2009). back issues avail. **Document type:** *Bulletin, Government.* **Description:** Provides a monthly summary of temperature extremes, degree days, precipitation and winds, hourly precipitation and 3-hourly weather observations in Meridian, Mississippi.
Related titles: Online - full text ed.: USD 3 per issue (effective 2009); ◆ Cumulative ed. of: Local Climatological Data. Meridian, Mississippi. Annual Summary with Comparative Data. ISSN 0198-2818.
—Linda Hall.
Published by: U.S. National Climatic Data Center (Subsidiary of: U.S. Department of Commerce), Federal Bldg, 151 Patton Ave, Asheville, NC 28801. TEL 828-271-4800, FAX 828-271-4876, NODC.Services@noaa.gov, http://www.ncdc.noaa.gov.

551.5 USA ISSN 0198-1269
QC984.F62
LOCAL CLIMATOLOGICAL DATA. MIAMI, FLORIDA. ANNUAL SUMMARY WITH COMPARATIVE DATA. Text in English. 19??. a. USD 39 combined subscription per issue includes 12 monthly summaries & one a. summary (effective 2009). back issues avail. **Document type:** *Bulletin, Government.* **Description:** Presents the monthly and annual average, resultant and fastest mile wind speed for the current year as well as the monthly and annual mean and fastest mile speed for a long period for Miami, Florida.
Related titles: Online - full text ed.: USD 29 per issue (effective 2009); ◆ Cumulative ed(s).: Local Climatological Data. Miami, Florida. Monthly Summary. ISSN 0198-1382.
Published by: U.S. National Climatic Data Center (Subsidiary of: U.S. Department of Commerce), Federal Bldg, 151 Patton Ave, Asheville, NC 28801. TEL 828-271-4800, FAX 828-271-4876, NODC.Services@noaa.gov, http://www.ncdc.noaa.gov.

551.5 USA ISSN 0198-1382
LOCAL CLIMATOLOGICAL DATA. MIAMI, FLORIDA. MONTHLY SUMMARY. Text in English. 19??. m. USD 5 per issue (effective 2009). back issues avail. **Document type:** *Bulletin, Government.* **Description:** Provides a monthly summary of temperature extremes, degree days, precipitation and winds, hourly precipitation and 3-hourly weather observations in Miami, Florida.
Related titles: Online - full text ed.: USD 3 per issue (effective 2009); ◆ Cumulative ed. of: Local Climatological Data. Miami, Florida. Annual Summary with Comparative Data. ISSN 0198-1269.
—Linda Hall.
Published by: U.S. National Climatic Data Center (Subsidiary of: U.S. Department of Commerce), Federal Bldg, 151 Patton Ave, Asheville, NC 28801. TEL 828-271-4800, FAX 828-271-4876, NODC.Services@noaa.gov, http://www.ncdc.noaa.gov.

551.5 USA ISSN 1059-7050
LOCAL CLIMATOLOGICAL DATA. MIDDLETOWN HARRISBURG INTERNATIONAL AIRPORT. MONTHLY SUMMARY. Text in English. 1991. m. USD 5 per issue (effective 2009). back issues avail. **Document type:** *Bulletin, Government.* **Description:** Provides a monthly summary of temperature extremes, degree days, precipitation and winds, hourly precipitation and 3-hourly weather observations in Middletown Harrisburg International Airport.
Related titles: Online - full text ed.: USD 3 per issue (effective 2009).
—Linda Hall.
Published by: U.S. National Climatic Data Center (Subsidiary of: U.S. Department of Commerce), Federal Bldg, 151 Patton Ave, Asheville, NC 28801. TEL 828-271-4800, FAX 828-271-4876, NODC.Services@noaa.gov, http://www.ncdc.noaa.gov.

551.5 USA ISSN 0198-5124
LOCAL CLIMATOLOGICAL DATA. MIDLAND-ODESSA, TEXAS. ANNUAL SUMMARY WITH COMPARATIVE DATA. Text in English. 19??. a. USD 5 per issue (effective 2004). **Document type:** *Bulletin, Government.*
Related titles: Online - full content ed.; ◆ Cumulative ed(s).: Local Climatological Data. Midland-Odessa, Texas. Monthly Summary. ISSN 0198-5132.
Published by: U.S. National Climatic Data Center (Subsidiary of: U.S. Department of Commerce), Federal Bldg, 151 Patton Ave, Asheville, NC 28801. TEL 828-271-4800, FAX 828-271-4876, NODC.Services@noaa.gov, http://www.ncdc.noaa.gov.

551.5 USA ISSN 0198-5132
LOCAL CLIMATOLOGICAL DATA. MIDLAND-ODESSA, TEXAS. MONTHLY SUMMARY. Text in English. 19??. m. USD 5 per issue (effective 2009). **Document type:** *Bulletin, Government.* **Description:** Provides a monthly summary of temperature extremes, degree days, precipitation and winds, hourly precipitation and 3-hourly weather observations in Midland-Odessa, Texas.
Related titles: Online - full text ed.: USD 3 per issue (effective 2009); ◆ Cumulative ed. of: Local Climatological Data. Midland-Odessa, Texas. Annual Summary with Comparative Data. ISSN 0198-5124.
—Linda Hall.
Published by: U.S. National Climatic Data Center (Subsidiary of: U.S. Department of Commerce), Federal Bldg, 151 Patton Ave, Asheville, NC 28801. TEL 828-271-4800, FAX 828-271-4876, NODC.Services@noaa.gov, http://www.ncdc.noaa.gov.

551.5 USA ISSN 0198-3067
LOCAL CLIMATOLOGICAL DATA. MILES CITY, MONTANA. ANNUAL SUMMARY WITH COMPARATIVE DATA. Text in English. 19??. a. USD 39 combined subscription per issue includes 12 monthly summaries & one a. summary (effective 2009). back issues avail. **Document type:** *Bulletin, Government.* **Description:** Presents the monthly and annual average, resultant and fastest mile wind speed for the current year as well as the monthly and annual mean and fastest mile speed for a long period for Miles City, Montana.
Related titles: Online - full text ed.: USD 29 per issue (effective 2009).
Published by: U.S. National Climatic Data Center (Subsidiary of: U.S. Department of Commerce), Federal Bldg, 151 Patton Ave, Asheville, NC 28801. TEL 828-271-4800, FAX 828-271-4876, NODC.Services@noaa.gov, http://www.ncdc.noaa.gov.

551.5 USA ISSN 0198-5264
LOCAL CLIMATOLOGICAL DATA. MILFORD, UTAH. ANNUAL SUMMARY WITH COMPARATIVE DATA. Text in English. 19??. a. USD 39 combined subscription per issue includes 12 monthly summaries & one a. summary (effective 2009). back issues avail. **Document type:** *Bulletin, Government.* **Description:** Presents the monthly and annual average, resultant and fastest mile wind speed for the current year as well as the monthly and annual mean and fastest mile speed for a long period for Milford, Utah.
Related titles: Online - full text ed.: USD 29 per issue (effective 2009).
Published by: U.S. National Climatic Data Center (Subsidiary of: U.S. Department of Commerce), Federal Bldg, 151 Patton Ave, Asheville, NC 28801. TEL 828-271-4800, FAX 828-271-4876, NODC.Services@noaa.gov, http://www.ncdc.noaa.gov.

551.5 USA ISSN 0198-5752
LOCAL CLIMATOLOGICAL DATA. MILWAUKEE, WISCONSIN. MONTHLY SUMMARY. Text in English. 19??. m. USD 5 per issue (effective 2009). back issues avail. **Document type:** *Bulletin, Government.* **Description:** Provides a monthly summary of temperature extremes, degree days, precipitation and winds, hourly precipitation and 3-hourly weather observations in Milwaukee, Wisconsin.
Related titles: Online - full text ed.: USD 3 per issue (effective 2009).
—Linda Hall.
Published by: U.S. National Climatic Data Center (Subsidiary of: U.S. Department of Commerce), Federal Bldg, 151 Patton Ave, Asheville, NC 28801. TEL 828-271-4800, FAX 828-271-4876, NODC.Services@noaa.gov, http://www.ncdc.noaa.gov.

551.5 USA ISSN 0198-2745
LOCAL CLIMATOLOGICAL DATA. MINNEAPOLIS-ST. PAUL, MINNESOTA. MONTHLY SUMMARY. Text in English. 19??. m. USD 5 per issue (effective 2009). back issues avail. **Document type:** *Bulletin, Government.* **Description:** Provides a monthly summary of temperature extremes, degree days, precipitation and winds, hourly precipitation and 3-hourly weather observations in Minneapolis-St. Paul, Minnesota.
Related titles: Online - full text ed.; ◆ Cumulative ed. of: Local Climatological Data. Minneapolis-St. Paul, Minnesota. Annual Summary with Comparative Data. ISSN 0198-2737.
—Linda Hall.
Published by: U.S. National Climatic Data Center (Subsidiary of: U.S. Department of Commerce), Federal Bldg, 151 Patton Ave, Asheville, NC 28801. TEL 828-271-4800, FAX 828-271-4876, NODC.Services@noaa.gov, http://www.ncdc.noaa.gov.

551.5 USA ISSN 0198-3083
LOCAL CLIMATOLOGICAL DATA. MISSOULA, MONTANA. ANNUAL SUMMARY WITH COMPARATIVE DATA. Text in English. 19??. a. USD 39 combined subscription per issue includes 12 monthly summaries & one a. summary (effective 2009). back issues avail. **Document type:** *Bulletin, Government.* **Description:** Presents the monthly and annual average, resultant and fastest mile wind speed for the current year as well as the monthly and annual mean and fastest mile speed for a long period for Missoula, Montana.
Related titles: Online - full text ed.: USD 29 per issue (effective 2009); ◆ Cumulative ed(s).: Local Climatological Data. Missoula, Montana. Monthly Summary. ISSN 0198-3091.
Published by: U.S. National Climatic Data Center (Subsidiary of: U.S. Department of Commerce), Federal Bldg, 151 Patton Ave, Asheville, NC 28801. TEL 828-271-4800, FAX 828-271-4876, NODC.Services@noaa.gov, http://www.ncdc.noaa.gov.

551.5 USA ISSN 0198-3091
LOCAL CLIMATOLOGICAL DATA. MISSOULA, MONTANA. MONTHLY SUMMARY. Text in English. m. USD 5 per issue (effective 2009). back issues avail. **Document type:** *Bulletin, Government.* **Description:** Provides a monthly summary of temperature extremes, degree days, precipitation and winds, hourly precipitation and 3-hourly weather observations in Missoula, Montana.
Related titles: Online - full text ed.: USD 3 per issue (effective 2009); ◆ Cumulative ed. of: Local Climatological Data. Missoula, Montana. Annual Summary with Comparative Data. ISSN 0198-3083.
—Linda Hall.
Published by: U.S. National Climatic Data Center (Subsidiary of: U.S. Department of Commerce), Federal Bldg, 151 Patton Ave, Asheville, NC 28801. TEL 828-271-4800, FAX 828-271-4876, NODC.Services@noaa.gov, http://www.ncdc.noaa.gov.

551.5 USA ISSN 0197-9507
LOCAL CLIMATOLOGICAL DATA. MOBILE, ALABAMA. ANNUAL SUMMARY WITH COMPARATIVE DATA. Text in English. 19??. a. USD 39 combined subscription per issue includes 12 monthly summaries & one a. summary (effective 2009). back issues avail. **Document type:** *Bulletin, Government.* **Description:** Presents the monthly and annual average, resultant and fastest mile wind speed for the current year as well as the monthly and annual mean and fastest mile speed for a long period for Mobile, Alabama.
Related titles: Online - full text ed.: USD 29 per issue (effective 2009); ◆ Cumulative ed(s).: Local Climatological Data. Mobile, Alabama. Monthly Summary. ISSN 0197-9515.
Published by: U.S. National Climatic Data Center (Subsidiary of: U.S. Department of Commerce), Federal Bldg, 151 Patton Ave, Asheville, NC 28801. TEL 828-271-4800, FAX 828-271-4876, NODC.Services@noaa.gov, http://www.ncdc.noaa.gov.

551.5 USA ISSN 0197-9515
LOCAL CLIMATOLOGICAL DATA. MOBILE, ALABAMA. MONTHLY SUMMARY. Text in English. 19??. m. USD 5 per issue (effective 2009). back issues avail. **Document type:** *Bulletin, Government.* **Description:** Provides a monthly summary of temperature extremes, degree days, precipitation and winds, hourly precipitation and 3-hourly weather observations in Mobile, Alabama.
Related titles: Online - full text ed.: USD 3 per issue (effective 2009); ◆ Cumulative ed. of: Local Climatological Data. Mobile, Alabama. Annual Summary with Comparative Data. ISSN 0197-9507.
—Linda Hall.
Published by: U.S. National Climatic Data Center (Subsidiary of: U.S. Department of Commerce), Federal Bldg, 151 Patton Ave, Asheville, NC 28801. TEL 828-271-4800, FAX 828-271-4876, NODC.Services@noaa.gov, http://www.ncdc.noaa.gov.

551.5 USA ISSN 0198-1862
QC984.I32
LOCAL CLIMATOLOGICAL DATA. MOLINE, ILLINOIS. ANNUAL SUMMARY WITH COMPARATIVE DATA. Text in English. 19??. a. USD 39 combined subscription per issue includes 12 monthly summaries & one a. summary (effective 2009). back issues avail. **Document type:** *Bulletin, Government.* **Description:** Presents the monthly and annual average, resultant and fastest mile wind speed for the current year as well as the monthly and annual mean and fastest mile speed for a long period for Moline, Illinois.
Related titles: Online - full text ed.: USD 29 per issue (effective 2009); ◆ Cumulative ed(s).: Local Climatological Data. Moline, Illinois. Monthly Summary. ISSN 0198-1870.
Published by: U.S. National Climatic Data Center (Subsidiary of: U.S. Department of Commerce), Federal Bldg, 151 Patton Ave, Asheville, NC 28801. TEL 828-271-4800, FAX 828-271-4876, NODC.Services@noaa.gov, http://www.ncdc.noaa.gov.

551.5 USA ISSN 0198-1870
LOCAL CLIMATOLOGICAL DATA. MOLINE, ILLINOIS. MONTHLY SUMMARY. Text in English. 19??. m. USD 5 per issue (effective 2009). back issues avail. **Document type:** *Bulletin, Government.* **Description:** Provides a monthly summary of temperature extremes, degree days, precipitation and winds, hourly precipitation and 3-hourly weather observations in Moline, Illinois.
Related titles: Online - full text ed.: USD 3 per issue (effective 2009); ◆ Cumulative ed. of: Local Climatological Data. Moline, Illinois. Annual Summary with Comparative Data. ISSN 0198-1862.
—Linda Hall.
Published by: U.S. National Climatic Data Center (Subsidiary of: U.S. Department of Commerce), Federal Bldg, 151 Patton Ave, Asheville, NC 28801. TEL 828-271-4800, FAX 828-271-4876, NODC.Services@noaa.gov, http://www.ncdc.noaa.gov.

551.5 USA ISSN 0197-9523
LOCAL CLIMATOLOGICAL DATA. MONTGOMERY, ALABAMA. ANNUAL SUMMARY WITH COMPARATIVE DATA. Text in English. 19??. a. USD 39 combined subscription per issue includes 12 monthly summaries & one a. summary (effective 2009). back issues avail. **Document type:** *Bulletin, Government.* **Description:** Presents the monthly and annual average, resultant and fastest mile wind speed for the current year as well as the monthly and annual mean and fastest mile speed for a long period for Montgomery, Alabama.
Related titles: Online - full text ed.: USD 29 per issue (effective 2009); ◆ Cumulative ed(s).: Local Climatological Data. Montgomery, Alabama. Monthly Summary. ISSN 0197-9531.
Published by: U.S. National Climatic Data Center (Subsidiary of: U.S. Department of Commerce), Federal Bldg, 151 Patton Ave, Asheville, NC 28801. TEL 828-271-4800, FAX 828-271-4876, NODC.Services@noaa.gov, http://www.ncdc.noaa.gov.

551.5 USA ISSN 0197-9531
LOCAL CLIMATOLOGICAL DATA. MONTGOMERY, ALABAMA. MONTHLY SUMMARY. Text in English. 19??. m. USD 5 per issue (effective 2009). back issues avail. **Document type:** *Bulletin, Government.* **Description:** Provides a monthly summary of temperature extremes, degree days, precipitation and winds, hourly precipitation and 3-hourly weather observations in Montgomery, Alabama.
Related titles: Online - full text ed.: USD 3 per issue (effective 2009); ◆ Cumulative ed. of: Local Climatological Data. Montgomery, Alabama. Annual Summary with Comparative Data. ISSN 0197-9523.
—Linda Hall.
Published by: U.S. National Climatic Data Center (Subsidiary of: U.S. Department of Commerce), Federal Bldg, 151 Patton Ave, Asheville, NC 28801. TEL 828-271-4800, FAX 828-271-4876, NODC.Services@noaa.gov, http://www.ncdc.noaa.gov.

551.5 USA ISSN 0198-0939
LOCAL CLIMATOLOGICAL DATA. MOUNT SHASTA, CALIFORNIA. ANNUAL SUMMARY WITH COMPARATIVE DATA. Text in English. 19??. a. USD 39 combined subscription per issue includes 12 monthly summaries & one a. summary (effective 2009). back issues avail. **Document type:** *Bulletin, Government.* **Description:** Presents the monthly and annual average, resultant and fastest mile wind speed for the current year as well as the monthly and annual mean and fastest mile speed for a long period for Mount Shasta, California.
Related titles: Online - full text ed.: USD 29 per issue (effective 2009).
Published by: U.S. National Climatic Data Center (Subsidiary of: U.S. Department of Commerce), Federal Bldg, 151 Patton Ave, Asheville, NC 28801. TEL 828-271-4800, FAX 828-271-4876, NODC.Services@noaa.gov, http://www.ncdc.noaa.gov.

551.5 USA ISSN 0198-3393
QC984.N4
LOCAL CLIMATOLOGICAL DATA. MOUNT WASHINGTON OBSERVATORY, GORHAM, NEW HAMPSHIRE. MONTHLY SUMMARY. Text in English. 19??. m. USD 5 per issue (effective 2004). **Document type:** *Bulletin, Government.*
Related titles: Online - full text ed.; ◆ Cumulative ed. of: Local Climatological Data. Mount Washington Observatory. Gorham, New Hampshire. Annual Summary with Comparative Data. ISSN 0198-3385.
—Linda Hall.
Published by: U.S. National Climatic Data Center (Subsidiary of: U.S. Department of Commerce), Federal Bldg, 151 Patton Ave, Asheville, NC 28801. TEL 828-271-4800, FAX 828-271-4876, NODC.Services@noaa.gov, http://www.ncdc.noaa.gov.

551.5 USA ISSN 0198-2656
LOCAL CLIMATOLOGICAL DATA. MUSKEGON, MICHIGAN. ANNUAL SUMMARY WITH COMPARATIVE DATA. Text in English. 19??. a. USD 39 combined subscription per issue includes 12 monthly summaries & one a. summary (effective 2009). back issues avail. **Document type:** *Bulletin, Government.* **Description:** Presents the monthly and annual average, resultant and fastest mile wind speed for the current year as well as the monthly and annual mean and fastest mile speed for a long period for Muskegon, Michigan.
Related titles: Online - full text ed.: USD 29 per issue (effective 2009); ◆ Cumulative ed(s).: Local Climatological Data. Muskegon, Michigan. Monthly Summary. ISSN 0198-2664.
Published by: U.S. National Climatic Data Center (Subsidiary of: U.S. Department of Commerce), Federal Bldg, 151 Patton Ave, Asheville, NC 28801. TEL 828-271-4800, FAX 828-271-4876, NODC.Services@noaa.gov, http://www.ncdc.noaa.gov.

551.5 USA ISSN 0198-2664
LOCAL CLIMATOLOGICAL DATA. MUSKEGON, MICHIGAN. MONTHLY SUMMARY. Text in English. 19??. m. USD 5 per issue (effective 2009). back issues avail. **Document type:** *Bulletin, Government.* **Description:** Provides a monthly summary of temperature extremes, degree days, precipitation and winds, hourly precipitation and 3-hourly weather observations in Muskegon, Michigan.
Related titles: Online - full text ed.: USD 3 per issue (effective 2009); ◆ Cumulative ed. of: Local Climatological Data. Muskegon, Michigan. Annual Summary with Comparative Data. ISSN 0198-2656.
—Linda Hall.
Published by: U.S. National Climatic Data Center (Subsidiary of: U.S. Department of Commerce), Federal Bldg, 151 Patton Ave, Asheville, NC 28801. TEL 828-271-4800, FAX 828-271-4876, NODC.Services@noaa.gov, http://www.ncdc.noaa.gov.

551.5 USA ISSN 0198-4845
LOCAL CLIMATOLOGICAL DATA. NASHVILLE, TENNESSEE. ANNUAL SUMMARY WITH COMPARATIVE DATA. Text in English. 19??. a. USD 39 combined subscription per issue includes 12 monthly summaries & one a. summary (effective 2009). back issues avail. **Document type:** *Bulletin, Government.* **Description:** Presents the monthly and annual average, resultant and fastest mile wind speed for the current year as well as the monthly and annual mean and fastest mile speed for a long period for Nashville, Tennessee.
Related titles: Online - full text ed.: USD 29 per issue (effective 2009); ◆ Cumulative ed(s).: Local Climatological Data. Nashville, Tennessee. Monthly Summary. ISSN 0198-4853.
Published by: U.S. National Climatic Data Center (Subsidiary of: U.S. Department of Commerce), Federal Bldg, 151 Patton Ave, Asheville, NC 28801. TEL 828-271-4800, FAX 828-271-4876, NODC.Services@noaa.gov, http://www.ncdc.noaa.gov.

551.5 USA ISSN 0198-4853
QC984.T2
LOCAL CLIMATOLOGICAL DATA. NASHVILLE, TENNESSEE. MONTHLY SUMMARY. Text in English. 19??. m. USD 5 per issue (effective 2009). back issues avail. **Document type:** *Bulletin, Government.* **Description:** Provides a monthly summary of temperature extremes, degree days, precipitation and winds, hourly precipitation and 3-hourly weather observations in Nashville, Tennessee.
Related titles: Online - full text ed.: USD 3 per issue (effective 2009); ◆ Cumulative ed. of: Local Climatological Data. Nashville, Tennessee. Annual Summary with Comparative Data. ISSN 0198-4845.
—Linda Hall.
Published by: U.S. National Climatic Data Center (Subsidiary of: U.S. Department of Commerce), Federal Bldg, 151 Patton Ave, Asheville, NC 28801. TEL 828-271-4800, FAX 828-271-4876, NODC.Services@noaa.gov, http://www.ncdc.noaa.gov.

551.5 USA ISSN 0198-2311
QC984.L82
LOCAL CLIMATOLOGICAL DATA. NEW ORLEANS, LOUISIANA. ANNUAL SUMMARY WITH COMPARATIVE DATA. Text in English. 19??. a. USD 39 combined subscription per issue includes 12 monthly summaries & one a. summary (effective 2009). back issues avail. **Document type:** *Bulletin, Government.* **Description:** Presents the monthly and annual average, resultant and fastest mile wind speed for the current year as well as the monthly and annual mean and fastest mile speed for a long period for New Orleans, Louisiana.
Related titles: Online - full text ed.: USD 29 per issue (effective 2009); ◆ Cumulative ed(s).: Local Climatological Data. New Orleans, Louisiana. Monthly Summary. ISSN 0198-232X.
Published by: U.S. National Climatic Data Center (Subsidiary of: U.S. Department of Commerce), Federal Bldg, 151 Patton Ave, Asheville, NC 28801. TEL 828-271-4800, FAX 828-271-4876, NODC.Services@noaa.gov, http://www.ncdc.noaa.gov.

551.5 USA ISSN 0198-232X
LOCAL CLIMATOLOGICAL DATA. NEW ORLEANS, LOUISIANA. MONTHLY SUMMARY. Text in English. 19??. m. USD 5 per issue (effective 2009). back issues avail. **Document type:** *Bulletin, Government.* **Description:** Provides information about local climatological data for New Orleans.
Related titles: Online - full text ed.: USD 3 per issue (effective 2009); ◆ Cumulative ed. of: Local Climatological Data. New Orleans, Louisiana. Annual Summary with Comparative Data. ISSN 0198-2311.
—Linda Hall.

Published by: U.S. National Climatic Data Center (Subsidiary of: U.S. Department of Commerce), Federal Bldg, 151 Patton Ave, Asheville, NC 28801. TEL 828-271-4800, FAX 828-271-4876, NODC.Services@noaa.gov, http://www.ncdc.noaa.gov.

551.5 USA ISSN 0198-3598
QC851.N65
LOCAL CLIMATOLOGICAL DATA. NEW YORK, NEW YORK CENTRAL PARK. ANNUAL SUMMARY WITH COMPARATIVE DATA. Text in English. 19??. a. USD 39 combined subscription per issue includes 12 monthly summaries & one a. summary (effective 2009). back issues avail. **Document type:** *Bulletin, Government.* **Description:** Presents the monthly and annual average, resultant and fastest mile wind speed for the current year as well as the monthly and annual mean and fastest mile speed for a long period for New York Central Park, New York.
Related titles: Online - full text ed.: USD 29 per issue (effective 2009); ◆ Cumulative ed(s).: Local Climatological Data. New York, New York Central Park Observatory. Monthly Summary. ISSN 0198-3601.
Published by: U.S. National Climatic Data Center (Subsidiary of: U.S. Department of Commerce), Federal Bldg, 151 Patton Ave, Asheville, NC 28801. TEL 828-271-4800, FAX 828-271-4876, NODC.Services@noaa.gov, http://www.ncdc.noaa.gov.

551.5 USA ISSN 0198-3601
QC984.N7
LOCAL CLIMATOLOGICAL DATA. NEW YORK, NEW YORK CENTRAL PARK OBSERVATORY. MONTHLY SUMMARY. Text in English. 19??. m. USD 5 per issue (effective 2009). back issues avail. **Document type:** *Bulletin, Government.* **Description:** Provides information about local climatological data for New York Central park observatory.
Related titles: Online - full text ed.: USD 3 per issue (effective 2009); ◆ Cumulative ed. of: Local Climatological Data. New York, New York Central Park. Annual Summary with Comparative Data. ISSN 0198-3598.
—Linda Hall.
Published by: U.S. National Climatic Data Center (Subsidiary of: U.S. Department of Commerce), Federal Bldg, 151 Patton Ave, Asheville, NC 28801. TEL 828-271-4800, FAX 828-271-4876, NODC.Services@noaa.gov, http://www.ncdc.noaa.gov.

551.5 USA ISSN 0198-3628
QC984.N72
LOCAL CLIMATOLOGICAL DATA. NEW YORK, NEW YORK JOHN F KENNEDY INTERNATIONAL AIRPORT. MONTHLY SUMMARY. Text in English. 19??. m. USD 5 per issue (effective 2009). back issues avail. **Document type:** *Bulletin, Government.* **Description:** Provides information about local climatological data for New York John F Kennedy international airport.
Related titles: Online - full text ed.: USD 3 per issue (effective 2009).
—Linda Hall.
Published by: U.S. National Climatic Data Center (Subsidiary of: U.S. Department of Commerce), Federal Bldg, 151 Patton Ave, Asheville, NC 28801. TEL 828-271-4800, FAX 828-271-4876, NODC.Services@noaa.gov, http://www.ncdc.noaa.gov.

551.5 USA ISSN 0198-3644
QC984.N7
LOCAL CLIMATOLOGICAL DATA. NEW YORK, NEW YORK LA GUARDIA AIRPORT. MONTHLY SUMMARY. Text in English. 19??. m. USD 5 per issue (effective 2009). back issues avail. **Description:** Provides information about local climatological data for New York La Guardia airport.
Related titles: Online - full text ed.: USD 3 per issue (effective 2009).
—Linda Hall.
Published by: U.S. National Climatic Data Center (Subsidiary of: U.S. Department of Commerce), Federal Bldg, 151 Patton Ave, Asheville, NC 28801. TEL 828-271-4800, FAX 828-271-4876, NODC.Services@noaa.gov, http://www.ncdc.noaa.gov.

551.5 USA ISSN 0198-3431
LOCAL CLIMATOLOGICAL DATA. NEWARK, NEW JERSEY. ANNUAL SUMMARY WITH COMPARATIVE DATA. Text in English. 19??. a. USD 39 combined subscription per issue includes 12 monthly summaries & one a. summary (effective 2009). back issues avail. **Document type:** *Bulletin, Government.* **Description:** Presents the monthly and annual average, resultant and fastest mile wind speed for the current year as well as the monthly and annual mean and fastest mile speed for a long period for Newark, New Jersey.
Related titles: Online - full text ed.: USD 29 per issue (effective 2009); ◆ Cumulative ed(s).: Local Climatological Data. Newark, New Jersey. Monthly Summary. ISSN 0198-344X.
Published by: U.S. National Climatic Data Center (Subsidiary of: U.S. Department of Commerce), Federal Bldg, 151 Patton Ave, Asheville, NC 28801. TEL 828-271-4800, FAX 828-271-4876, NODC.Services@noaa.gov, http://www.ncdc.noaa.gov.

551.5 USA ISSN 0198-344X
LOCAL CLIMATOLOGICAL DATA. NEWARK, NEW JERSEY. MONTHLY SUMMARY. Text in English. 19??. m. USD 5 per issue (effective 2009). back issues avail. **Document type:** *Bulletin, Government.* **Description:** Provides information about local climatological data for Newark.
Related titles: Online - full text ed.: USD 3 per issue (effective 2009); ◆ Cumulative ed. of: Local Climatological Data. Newark, New Jersey. Annual Summary with Comparative Data. ISSN 0198-3431.
—Linda Hall.
Published by: U.S. National Climatic Data Center (Subsidiary of: U.S. Department of Commerce), Federal Bldg, 151 Patton Ave, Asheville, NC 28801. TEL 828-271-4800, FAX 828-271-4876, NODC.Services@noaa.gov, http://www.ncdc.noaa.gov.

551.5 USA ISSN 0198-0688
QC984.A72
LOCAL CLIMATOLOGICAL DATA. NO. LITTLE ROCK, ARKANSAS. ANNUAL SUMMARY WITH COMPARATIVE DATA. Text in English. 19??. a. USD 39 combined subscription per issue includes 12 monthly summaries & one a. summary (effective 2009). **Document type:** *Bulletin, Government.* **Description:** Presents the monthly and annual average, resultant and fastest mile wind speed for the current year as well as the monthly and annual mean and fastest mile speed for a long period for Little Rock, Arkansas.
Related titles: Online - full text ed.: USD 29 per issue (effective 2009); ◆ Cumulative ed(s).: Local Climatological Data. No. Little Rock, Arkansas. Monthly Summary. ISSN 0198-0637.
Published by: U.S. National Climatic Data Center (Subsidiary of: U.S. Department of Commerce), Federal Bldg, 151 Patton Ave, Asheville, NC 28801. TEL 828-271-4800, FAX 828-271-4876, NODC.Services@noaa.gov, http://www.ncdc.noaa.gov.

551.5 USA ISSN 0198-0637
LOCAL CLIMATOLOGICAL DATA. NO. LITTLE ROCK, ARKANSAS. MONTHLY SUMMARY. Text in English. 19??. m. USD 5 per issue (effective 2009). back issues avail. **Document type:** *Bulletin, Government.* **Description:** Provides a monthly summary of temperature extremes, degree days, precipitation and winds, hourly precipitation and 3-hourly weather observations in Little Rock, Arkansas.
Related titles: Online - full text ed.: USD 3 per issue (effective 2009); ◆ Cumulative ed. of: Local Climatological Data. No. Little Rock, Arkansas. Annual Summary with Comparative Data. ISSN 0198-0688.
—Linda Hall.
Published by: U.S. National Climatic Data Center (Subsidiary of: U.S. Department of Commerce), Federal Bldg, 151 Patton Ave, Asheville, NC 28801. TEL 828-271-4800, FAX 828-271-4876, NODC.Services@noaa.gov, http://www.ncdc.noaa.gov.

551.5 USA ISSN 0198-0505
QC984.A42
LOCAL CLIMATOLOGICAL DATA. NOME, ALASKA. ANNUAL SUMMARY WITH COMPARATIVE DATA. Text in English. 19??. a. USD 39 combined subscription per issue includes 12 monthly summaries & one a. summary (effective 2009). back issues avail. **Document type:** *Bulletin, Government.* **Description:** Presents the monthly and annual average, resultant and fastest mile wind speed for the current year as well as the monthly and annual mean and fastest mile speed for a long period for Nome, Alaska.
Related titles: Online - full text ed.: USD 29 per issue (effective 2009); ◆ Cumulative ed(s).: Local Climatological Data. Nome, Alaska. Monthly Summary. ISSN 0198-0408.
Published by: U.S. National Climatic Data Center (Subsidiary of: U.S. Department of Commerce), Federal Bldg, 151 Patton Ave, Asheville, NC 28801. TEL 828-271-4800, FAX 828-271-4876, NODC.Services@noaa.gov, http://www.ncdc.noaa.gov.

551.5 USA ISSN 0198-0408
QC984.A42
LOCAL CLIMATOLOGICAL DATA. NOME, ALASKA. MONTHLY SUMMARY. Text in English. 19??. m. USD 5 per issue (effective 2009). back issues avail. **Document type:** *Bulletin, Government.* **Description:** Provides information about local climatological data for Nome.
Related titles: Online - full text ed.: USD 3 per issue (effective 2009); ◆ Cumulative ed. of: Local Climatological Data. Nome, Alaska. Annual Summary with Comparative Data. ISSN 0198-0505.
—Linda Hall.
Published by: U.S. National Climatic Data Center (Subsidiary of: U.S. Department of Commerce), Federal Bldg, 151 Patton Ave, Asheville, NC 28801. TEL 828-271-4800, FAX 828-271-4876, NODC.Services@noaa.gov, http://www.ncdc.noaa.gov.

551.5 USA ISSN 0198-313X
LOCAL CLIMATOLOGICAL DATA. NORFOLK, NEBRASKA. ANNUAL SUMMARY WITH COMPARATIVE DATA. Text in English. 19??. a. USD 39 combined subscription per issue includes 12 monthly summaries & one a. summary (effective 2009). **Document type:** *Bulletin, Government.* **Description:** Presents the monthly and annual average, resultant and fastest mile wind speed for the current year as well as the monthly and annual mean and fastest mile speed for a long period for Norfolk, Nebraska.
Related titles: Online - full text ed.: USD 29 per issue (effective 2009); ◆ Cumulative ed(s).: Local Climatological Data. Norfolk, Nebraska. Monthly Summary. ISSN 0198-3148.
Published by: U.S. National Climatic Data Center (Subsidiary of: U.S. Department of Commerce), Federal Bldg, 151 Patton Ave, Asheville, NC 28801. TEL 828-271-4800, FAX 828-271-4876, NODC.Services@noaa.gov, http://www.ncdc.noaa.gov.

551.5 USA ISSN 0198-3148
LOCAL CLIMATOLOGICAL DATA. NORFOLK, NEBRASKA. MONTHLY SUMMARY. Text in English. 19??. m. USD 5 per issue (effective 2009). back issues avail. **Document type:** *Bulletin, Government.* **Description:** Provides a monthly summary of temperature extremes, degree days, precipitation and winds, hourly precipitation and 3-hourly weather observations in Norfolk, Nebraska.
Related titles: Online - full text ed.: USD 3 per issue (effective 2009); ◆ Cumulative ed. of: Local Climatological Data. Norfolk, Nebraska. Annual Summary with Comparative Data. ISSN 0198-313X.
—Linda Hall.
Published by: U.S. National Climatic Data Center (Subsidiary of: U.S. Department of Commerce), Federal Bldg, 151 Patton Ave, Asheville, NC 28801. TEL 828-271-4800, FAX 828-271-4876, NODC.Services@noaa.gov, http://www.ncdc.noaa.gov.

551.5 USA ISSN 0198-5345
LOCAL CLIMATOLOGICAL DATA. NORFOLK, VIRGINIA. ANNUAL SUMMARY WITH COMPARATIVE DATA. Text in English. 19??. a. USD 39 combined subscription per issue includes 12 monthly summaries & one a. summary (effective 2009). back issues avail. **Document type:** *Bulletin, Government.* **Description:** Presents the monthly and annual average, resultant and fastest mile wind speed for the current year as well as the monthly and annual mean and fastest mile speed for a long period for Norfolk, Virginia.
Related titles: Online - full text ed.: USD 29 per issue (effective 2009); ◆ Cumulative ed(s).: Local Climatological Data. Norfolk, Virginia. Monthly Summary. ISSN 0198-5353.
Published by: U.S. National Climatic Data Center (Subsidiary of: U.S. Department of Commerce), Federal Bldg, 151 Patton Ave, Asheville, NC 28801. TEL 828-271-4800, FAX 828-271-4876, NODC.Services@noaa.gov, http://www.ncdc.noaa.gov.

551.5 USA ISSN 0198-5353
LOCAL CLIMATOLOGICAL DATA. NORFOLK, VIRGINIA. MONTHLY SUMMARY. Text in English. 19??. m. USD 5 per issue (effective 2009). back issues avail. **Document type:** *Bulletin, Government.* **Description:** Provides a monthly summary of temperature extremes, degree days, precipitation and winds, hourly precipitation and 3-hourly weather observations in Norfolk, Virginia.
Related titles: Online - full text ed.: USD 3 per issue (effective 2009); ◆ Cumulative ed. of: Local Climatological Data. Norfolk, Virginia. Annual Summary with Comparative Data. ISSN 0198-5345.
—Linda Hall.
Published by: U.S. National Climatic Data Center (Subsidiary of: U.S. Department of Commerce), Federal Bldg, 151 Patton Ave, Asheville, NC 28801. TEL 828-271-4800, FAX 828-271-4876, NODC.Services@noaa.gov, http://www.ncdc.noaa.gov.

551.5 USA ISSN 0198-3156
QC984.N22
LOCAL CLIMATOLOGICAL DATA. NORTH PLATTE, NEBRASKA. ANNUAL SUMMARY WITH COMPARATIVE DATA. Text in English. 19??. a. USD 39 combined subscription per issue includes 12 monthly summaries & one a. summary (effective 2009). back issues avail. **Document type:** *Bulletin, Government.* **Description:** Presents the monthly and annual average, resultant and fastest mile wind speed for the current year as well as the monthly and annual mean and fastest mile speed for a long period for North Platte, Nebraska.
Related titles: Online - full text ed.: USD 29 per issue (effective 2009); ◆ Cumulative ed(s).: Local Climatological Data. North Platte, Nebraska. Monthly Summary. ISSN 0198-3164.
Published by: U.S. National Climatic Data Center (Subsidiary of: U.S. Department of Commerce), Federal Bldg, 151 Patton Ave, Asheville, NC 28801. TEL 828-271-4800, FAX 828-271-4876, NODC.Services@noaa.gov, http://www.ncdc.noaa.gov.

551.5 USA ISSN 0198-3164
LOCAL CLIMATOLOGICAL DATA. NORTH PLATTE, NEBRASKA. MONTHLY SUMMARY. Text in English. 19??. m. USD 5 per issue (effective 2009). back issues avail. **Document type:** *Bulletin, Government.* **Description:** Provides a monthly summary of temperature extremes, degree days, precipitation and winds, hourly precipitation and 3-hourly weather observations in North Platte, Nebraska.
Related titles: Online - full text ed.: USD 3 per issue (effective 2009); ◆ Cumulative ed. of: Local Climatological Data. North Platte, Nebraska. Annual Summary with Comparative Data. ISSN 0198-3156.
—Linda Hall.
Published by: U.S. National Climatic Data Center (Subsidiary of: U.S. Department of Commerce), Federal Bldg, 151 Patton Ave, Asheville, NC 28801. TEL 828-271-4800, FAX 828-271-4876, NODC.Services@noaa.gov, http://www.ncdc.noaa.gov.

551.5 USA ISSN 0198-4861
LOCAL CLIMATOLOGICAL DATA. OAK RIDGE, TENNESSEE. ANNUAL SUMMARY WITH COMPARATIVE DATA. Text in English. 19??. a. USD 39 combined subscription per issue includes 12 monthly summaries & one a. summary (effective 2009). back issues avail. **Document type:** *Bulletin, Government.* **Description:** Presents the monthly and annual average, resultant and fastest mile wind speed for the current year as well as the monthly and annual mean and fastest mile speed for a long period for Oak Ridge, Tennessee.
Related titles: Online - full text ed.: USD 29 per issue (effective 2009); ◆ Cumulative ed(s).: Local Climatological Data. Oak Ridge, Tennessee. Monthly Summary. ISSN 0198-487X.
Published by: U.S. National Climatic Data Center (Subsidiary of: U.S. Department of Commerce), Federal Bldg, 151 Patton Ave, Asheville, NC 28801. TEL 828-271-4800, FAX 828-271-4876, NODC.Services@noaa.gov, http://www.ncdc.noaa.gov.

551.5 USA ISSN 0198-487X
QC984.T2
LOCAL CLIMATOLOGICAL DATA. OAK RIDGE, TENNESSEE. MONTHLY SUMMARY. Text in English. 19??. m. USD 5 per issue (effective 2009). back issues avail. **Document type:** *Bulletin, Government.* **Description:** Provides a monthly summary of temperature extremes, degree days, precipitation and winds, hourly precipitation and 3-hourly weather observations in Oak Ridge, Tennessee.
Related titles: Online - full text ed.: USD 3 per issue (effective 2009); ◆ Cumulative ed. of: Local Climatological Data. Oak Ridge, Tennessee. Annual Summary with Comparative Data. ISSN 0198-4861.
—Linda Hall.
Published by: U.S. National Climatic Data Center (Subsidiary of: U.S. Department of Commerce), Federal Bldg, 151 Patton Ave, Asheville, NC 28801. TEL 828-271-4800, FAX 828-271-4876, NODC.Services@noaa.gov, http://www.ncdc.noaa.gov.

551.5 USA ISSN 0198-4055
LOCAL CLIMATOLOGICAL DATA. OKLAHOMA CITY, OKLAHOMA. ANNUAL SUMMARY WITH COMPARATIVE DATA. Text in English. 19??. a. USD 39 combined subscription per issue includes 12 monthly summaries & one a. summary (effective 2009). back issues avail. **Document type:** *Bulletin, Government.* **Description:** Presents the monthly and annual average, resultant and fastest mile wind speed for the current year as well as the monthly and annual mean and fastest mile speed for a long period for Oklahoma City, Oklahoma.
Related titles: Online - full text ed.: USD 29 per issue (effective 2008); ◆ Cumulative ed(s).: Local Climatological Data. Oklahoma City, Oklahoma. Monthly Summary. ISSN 0198-4063.
Published by: U.S. National Climatic Data Center (Subsidiary of: U.S. Department of Commerce), Federal Bldg, 151 Patton Ave, Asheville, NC 28801. TEL 828-271-4800, FAX 828-271-4876, NODC.Services@noaa.gov, http://www.ncdc.noaa.gov.

551.5 USA ISSN 0198-4063
LOCAL CLIMATOLOGICAL DATA. OKLAHOMA CITY, OKLAHOMA. MONTHLY SUMMARY. Text in English. 19??. m. USD 5 per issue (effective 2009). back issues avail. **Document type:** *Bulletin, Government.* **Description:** Provides a monthly summary of temperature extremes, degree days, precipitation and winds, hourly precipitation and 3-hourly weather observations in Oklahoma City, Oklahoma.
Related titles: Online - full text ed.: USD 3 per issue (effective 2009); ◆ Cumulative ed. of: Local Climatological Data. Oklahoma City, Oklahoma. Annual Summary with Comparative Data. ISSN 0198-4055.
—Linda Hall.
Published by: U.S. National Climatic Data Center (Subsidiary of: U.S. Department of Commerce), Federal Bldg, 151 Patton Ave, Asheville, NC 28801. TEL 828-271-4800, FAX 828-271-4876, NODC.Services@noaa.gov, http://www.ncdc.noaa.gov.

551.5 USA ISSN 0198-540X
LOCAL CLIMATOLOGICAL DATA. OLYMPIA, WASHINGTON. ANNUAL SUMMARY WITH COMPARATIVE DATA. Text in English. 19??. a. USD 39 combined subscription per issue includes 12 monthly summaries & one a. summary (effective 2009). back issues avail. **Document type:** *Bulletin, Government.* **Description:** Presents the monthly and annual average, resultant and fastest mile wind speed for the current year as well as the monthly and annual mean and fastest mile speed for a long period for Olympia, Washington.
Related titles: Online - full text ed.: USD 29 per issue (effective 2009); ◆ Cumulative ed(s).: Local Climatological Data. Olympia, Washington. Monthly Summary. ISSN 0198-5418.
Published by: U.S. National Climatic Data Center (Subsidiary of: U.S. Department of Commerce), Federal Bldg, 151 Patton Ave, Asheville, NC 28801. TEL 828-271-4800, FAX 828-271-4876, NODC.Services@noaa.gov, http://www.ncdc.noaa.gov.

551.5 USA ISSN 0198-5418
QC984.W2
LOCAL CLIMATOLOGICAL DATA. OLYMPIA, WASHINGTON. MONTHLY SUMMARY. Text in English. 19??. m. USD 5 per issue (effective 2009). back issues avail. **Document type:** *Bulletin, Government.* **Description:** Provides a monthly summary of temperature extremes, degree days, precipitation and winds, hourly precipitation and 3-hourly weather observations in Olympia, Washington.
Related titles: Online - full text ed.: USD 3 per issue (effective 2009); ◆ Cumulative ed. of: Local Climatological Data. Olympia, Washington. Annual Summary with Comparative Data. ISSN 0198-540X.
—Linda Hall.
Published by: U.S. National Climatic Data Center (Subsidiary of: U.S. Department of Commerce), Federal Bldg, 151 Patton Ave, Asheville, NC 28801. TEL 828-271-4800, FAX 828-271-4876, ncdc.info@noaa.gov, http://www.ncdc.noaa.gov.

551.5 USA ISSN 0198-3199
QC984.N22
LOCAL CLIMATOLOGICAL DATA. OMAHA (NORTH), NEBRASKA. ANNUAL SUMMARY WITH COMPARATIVE DATA. Text in English. a. USD 5 per issue (effective 2004). **Document type:** *Bulletin, Government.*
Related titles: Online - full content ed.; ◆ Cumulative ed(s).: Local Climatological Data. Omaha (North), Nebraska. Monthly Summary. ISSN 0198-3202.
Published by: U.S. National Climatic Data Center (Subsidiary of: U.S. Department of Commerce), Federal Bldg, 151 Patton Ave, Asheville, NC 28801. TEL 828-271-4800, FAX 828-271-4876, NODC.Services@noaa.gov, http://www.ncdc.noaa.gov.

551.5 USA ISSN 0198-3202
LOCAL CLIMATOLOGICAL DATA. OMAHA (NORTH), NEBRASKA. MONTHLY SUMMARY. Text in English. 19??. m. USD 5 per issue (effective 2009). back issues avail. **Document type:** *Bulletin, Government.* **Description:** Provides a monthly summary of temperature extremes, degree days, precipitation and winds, hourly precipitation and 3-hourly weather observations in Omaha (North), Nebraska.
Related titles: Online - full text ed.: USD 3 per issue (effective 2009); ◆ Cumulative ed. of: Local Climatological Data. Omaha (North), Nebraska. Annual Summary with Comparative Data. ISSN 0198-3199.
Published by: U.S. National Climatic Data Center (Subsidiary of: U.S. Department of Commerce), Federal Bldg, 151 Patton Ave, Asheville, NC 28801. TEL 828-271-4800, FAX 828-271-4876, NODC.Services@noaa.gov, http://www.ncdc.noaa.gov.

551.5 USA ISSN 0198-3172
LOCAL CLIMATOLOGICAL DATA. OMAHA, NEBRASKA. ANNUAL SUMMARY WITH COMPARATIVE DATA. Text in English. 19??. a. USD 39 combined subscription per issue includes 12 monthly summaries & one a. summary (effective 2009). back issues avail. **Document type:** *Bulletin, Government.* **Description:** Presents the monthly and annual average, resultant and fastest mile wind speed for the current year as well as the monthly and annual mean and fastest mile speed for a long period for Omaha, Nebraska.
Related titles: Online - full text ed.: USD 29 per issue (effective 2009); ◆ Cumulative ed(s).: Local Climatological Data. Omaha, Nebraska. Monthly Summary. ISSN 0198-3180.
Published by: U.S. National Climatic Data Center (Subsidiary of: U.S. Department of Commerce), Federal Bldg, 151 Patton Ave, Asheville, NC 28801. TEL 828-271-4800, FAX 828-271-4876, NODC.Services@noaa.gov, http://www.ncdc.noaa.gov.

551.5 USA ISSN 0198-3180
LOCAL CLIMATOLOGICAL DATA. OMAHA, NEBRASKA. MONTHLY SUMMARY. Text in English. 19??. m. USD 5 per issue (effective 2009). back issues avail. **Document type:** *Bulletin, Government.* **Description:** Provides a monthly summary of temperature extremes, degree days, precipitation and winds, hourly precipitation and 3-hourly weather observations in Omaha, Nebraska.
Related titles: Online - full text ed.: USD 3 per issue (effective 2009); ◆ Cumulative ed. of: Local Climatological Data. Omaha, Nebraska. Annual Summary with Comparative Data. ISSN 0198-3172.
—Linda Hall.
Published by: U.S. National Climatic Data Center (Subsidiary of: U.S. Department of Commerce), Federal Bldg, 151 Patton Ave, Asheville, NC 28801. TEL 828-271-4800, FAX 828-271-4876, NODC.Services@noaa.gov, http://www.ncdc.noaa.gov.

551.5 USA ISSN 0198-1277
QC984.F62
LOCAL CLIMATOLOGICAL DATA. ORLANDO, FLORIDA. ANNUAL SUMMARY WITH COMPARATIVE DATA. Text in English. 19??. a. USD 5 per issue (effective 2004). **Document type:** *Bulletin, Government.*
Related titles: Online - full content ed.; ◆ Cumulative ed(s).: Local Climatological Data. Orlando, Florida. Monthly Summary. ISSN 0198-1390.
Published by: U.S. National Climatic Data Center (Subsidiary of: U.S. Department of Commerce), Federal Bldg, 151 Patton Ave, Asheville, NC 28801. TEL 828-271-4800, FAX 828-271-4876, NODC.Services@noaa.gov, http://www.ncdc.noaa.gov.

551.5 USA ISSN 0888-9988
LOCAL CLIMATOLOGICAL DATA. PADUCAH, KENTUCKY. ANNUAL SUMMARY WITH COMPARATIVE DATA. Text in English. 19??. a. USD 39 combined subscription per issue includes 12 monthly summaries & one a. summary (effective 2009). back issues avail. **Document type:** *Bulletin, Government.* **Description:** Presents the monthly and annual average, resultant and fastest mile wind speed for the current year as well as the monthly and annual mean and fastest mile speed for a long period for Paducah, Kentucky.
Related titles: Online - full text ed.: USD 29 per issue (effective 2009); ◆ Cumulative ed(s).: Local Climatological Data. Paducah, Kentucky. Monthly Summary. ISSN 8755-058X.
Published by: U.S. National Climatic Data Center (Subsidiary of: U.S. Department of Commerce), Federal Bldg, 151 Patton Ave, Asheville, NC 28801. TEL 828-271-4800, FAX 828-271-4876, NODC.Services@noaa.gov, http://www.ncdc.noaa.gov.

551.5 USA ISSN 8755-058X
LOCAL CLIMATOLOGICAL DATA. PADUCAH, KENTUCKY. MONTHLY SUMMARY. Text in English. 1984. m. USD 5 per issue (effective 2009). back issues avail. **Document type:** *Bulletin, Government.* **Description:** Provides a monthly summary of temperature extremes, degree days, precipitation and winds, hourly precipitation and 3-hourly weather observations in Paducah, Kentucky.
Related titles: Online - full text ed.: USD 3 per issue (effective 2009); ◆ Cumulative ed. of: Local Climatological Data. Paducah, Kentucky. Annual Summary with Comparative Data. ISSN 0888-9988.
—Linda Hall.
Published by: U.S. National Climatic Data Center (Subsidiary of: U.S. Department of Commerce), Federal Bldg, 151 Patton Ave, Asheville, NC 28801. TEL 828-271-4800, FAX 828-271-4876, NODC.Services@noaa.gov, http://www.ncdc.noaa.gov.

551.5 USA ISSN 0198-4357
LOCAL CLIMATOLOGICAL DATA. PAGO PAGO, AMERICAN SAMOA. ANNUAL SUMMARY WITH COMPARATIVE DATA. Text in English. 19??. a. USD 5 per issue (effective 2004). **Document type:** *Bulletin, Government.*
Related titles: Online - full content ed.; ◆ Cumulative ed(s).: Local Climatological Data. Pago Pago, American Samoa, Monthly Summary. ISSN 0198-4365.
Published by: U.S. National Climatic Data Center (Subsidiary of: U.S. Department of Commerce), Federal Bldg, 151 Patton Ave, Asheville, NC 28801. TEL 828-271-4800, FAX 828-271-4876, NODC.Services@noaa.gov, http://www.ncdc.noaa.gov.

551.5 USA ISSN 0198-4179
QC984.O72
LOCAL CLIMATOLOGICAL DATA. PENDLETON, OREGON. ANNUAL SUMMARY WITH COMPARATIVE DATA. Text in English. 19??. a. USD 39 combined subscription per issue includes 12 monthly summaries & one a. summary (effective 2009). back issues avail. **Document type:** *Bulletin, Government.* **Description:** Presents the monthly and annual average, resultant and fastest mile wind speed for the current year as well as the monthly and annual mean and fastest mile speed for a long period for Pendleton, Oregon.
Related titles: Online - full text ed.: USD 29 per issue (effective 2009); ◆ Cumulative ed(s).: Local Climatological Data. Pendleton, Oregon. Monthly Summary. ISSN 0198-4187.
Published by: U.S. National Climatic Data Center (Subsidiary of: U.S. Department of Commerce), Federal Bldg, 151 Patton Ave, Asheville, NC 28801. TEL 828-271-4800, FAX 828-271-4876, NODC.Services@noaa.gov, http://www.ncdc.noaa.gov.

551.5 USA ISSN 0198-4187
QC984.O72
LOCAL CLIMATOLOGICAL DATA. PENDLETON, OREGON. MONTHLY SUMMARY. Text in English. 19??. m. USD 5 per issue (effective 2009). back issues avail. **Document type:** *Bulletin, Government.* **Description:** Provides a monthly summary of temperature extremes, degree days, precipitation and winds, hourly precipitation and 3-hourly weather observations in Pendleton, Oregon.
Related titles: Online - full text ed.: USD 3 per issue (effective 2009); ◆ Cumulative ed. of: Local Climatological Data. Pendleton, Oregon. Annual Summary with Comparative Data. ISSN 0198-4179.
—Linda Hall.
Published by: U.S. National Climatic Data Center (Subsidiary of: U.S. Department of Commerce), Federal Bldg, 151 Patton Ave, Asheville, NC 28801. TEL 828-271-4800, FAX 828-271-4876, ncdc.info@noaa.gov, http://www.ncdc.noaa.gov.

551.5 USA ISSN 0198-1285
LOCAL CLIMATOLOGICAL DATA. PENSACOLA, FLORIDA. ANNUAL SUMMARY WITH COMPARATIVE DATA. Text in English. 19??. a. USD 39 combined subscription per issue includes 12 monthly summaries & one a. summary (effective 2009). back issues avail. **Document type:** *Bulletin, Government.* **Description:** Presents the monthly and annual average, resultant and fastest mile wind speed for the current year as well as the monthly and annual mean and fastest mile speed for a long period for Pensacola, Florida.
Related titles: Online - full text ed.: USD 29 per issue (effective 2009); ◆ Cumulative ed(s).: Local Climatological Data. Pensacola, Florida. Monthly Summary. ISSN 0198-1404.
Published by: U.S. National Climatic Data Center (Subsidiary of: U.S. Department of Commerce), Federal Bldg, 151 Patton Ave, Asheville, NC 28801. TEL 828-271-4800, FAX 828-271-4876, NODC.Services@noaa.gov, http://www.ncdc.noaa.gov.

551.5 USA ISSN 0198-1404
LOCAL CLIMATOLOGICAL DATA. PENSACOLA, FLORIDA. MONTHLY SUMMARY. Text in English. 19??. m. USD 5 per issue (effective 2009). back issues avail. **Document type:** *Bulletin, Government.* **Description:** Provides a monthly summary of temperature extremes, degree days, precipitation and winds, hourly precipitation and 3-hourly weather observations in Pensacola, Florida.
Related titles: Online - full text ed.: USD 3 per issue (effective 2009); ◆ Cumulative ed. of: Local Climatological Data. Pensacola, Florida. Annual Summary with Comparative Data. ISSN 0198-1285.
—Linda Hall.
Published by: U.S. National Climatic Data Center (Subsidiary of: U.S. Department of Commerce), Federal Bldg, 151 Patton Ave, Asheville, NC 28801. TEL 828-271-4800, FAX 828-271-4876, ncdc.info@noaa.gov, http://www.ncdc.noaa.gov.

551.5 USA ISSN 0198-1889
QC984.I32
LOCAL CLIMATOLOGICAL DATA. PEORIA, ILLINOIS. ANNUAL SUMMARY WITH COMPARATIVE DATA. Text in English. 19??. a. USD 39 combined subscription per issue includes 12 monthly summaries & one a. summary (effective 2009). back issues avail. **Document type:** *Bulletin, Government.* **Description:** Presents the monthly and annual average, resultant and fastest mile wind speed for the current year as well as the monthly and annual mean and fastest mile speed for a long period for Peoria, Illinois.
Related titles: Online - full text ed.: USD 29 per issue (effective 2009); ◆ Cumulative ed(s).: Local Climatological Data. Peoria, Illinois. Monthly Summary. ISSN 0198-1897.
Published by: U.S. National Climatic Data Center (Subsidiary of: U.S. Department of Commerce), Federal Bldg, 151 Patton Ave, Asheville, NC 28801. TEL 828-271-4800, FAX 828-271-4876, NODC.Services@noaa.gov, http://www.ncdc.noaa.gov.

551.5 USA ISSN 0198-1897
LOCAL CLIMATOLOGICAL DATA. PEORIA, ILLINOIS. MONTHLY SUMMARY. Text in English. 19??. m. USD 5 per issue (effective 2009). back issues avail. **Document type:** *Bulletin, Government.* **Description:** Provides a monthly summary of temperature extremes, degree days, precipitation and winds, hourly precipitation and 3-hourly weather observations in Peoria, Illinois.
Related titles: Online - full text ed.: USD 3 per issue (effective 2009); ◆ Cumulative ed. of: Local Climatological Data. Peoria, Illinois. Annual Summary with Comparative Data. ISSN 0198-1889.
—Linda Hall.
Published by: U.S. National Climatic Data Center (Subsidiary of: U.S. Department of Commerce), Federal Bldg, 151 Patton Ave, Asheville, NC 28801. TEL 828-271-4800, FAX 828-271-4876, NODC.Services@noaa.gov, http://www.ncdc.noaa.gov.

551.5 USA ISSN 0198-4535
LOCAL CLIMATOLOGICAL DATA. PHILADELPHIA, PENNSYLVANIA. ANNUAL SUMMARY WITH COMPARATIVE DATA. Text in English. 19??. a. USD 39 combined subscription per issue includes 12 monthly summaries & one a. summary (effective 2009). **Document type:** *Bulletin, Government.* **Description:** Presents the monthly and annual average, resultant and fastest mile wind speed for the current year as well as the monthly and annual mean and fastest mile speed for a long period for Philadelphia, Pennsylvania.
Related titles: Online - full text ed.: USD 29 per issue (effective 2009); ◆ Cumulative ed(s).: Local Climatological Data. Philadelphia, Pennsylvania. Monthly Summary. ISSN 0198-4543.
Published by: U.S. National Climatic Data Center (Subsidiary of: U.S. Department of Commerce), Federal Bldg, 151 Patton Ave, Asheville, NC 28801. TEL 828-271-4800, FAX 828-271-4876, NODC.Services@noaa.gov, http://www.ncdc.noaa.gov.

551.5 USA ISSN 0198-4543
LOCAL CLIMATOLOGICAL DATA. PHILADELPHIA, PENNSYLVANIA. MONTHLY SUMMARY. Text in English. 19??. m. USD 5 per issue (effective 2009). back issues avail. **Document type:** *Bulletin, Government.* **Description:** Provides a monthly summary of temperature extremes, degree days, precipitation and winds, hourly precipitation and 3-hourly weather observations in Philadelphia, Pennsylvania.
Related titles: Online - full text ed.: USD 3 per issue (effective 2009); ◆ Cumulative ed. of: Local Climatological Data. Philadelphia, Pennsylvania. Annual Summary with Comparative Data. ISSN 0198-4535.
—Linda Hall.
Published by: U.S. National Climatic Data Center (Subsidiary of: U.S. Department of Commerce), Federal Bldg, 151 Patton Ave, Asheville, NC 28801. TEL 828-271-4800, FAX 828-271-4876, NODC.Services@noaa.gov, http://www.ncdc.noaa.gov.

551.5 USA ISSN 0198-0572
LOCAL CLIMATOLOGICAL DATA. PHOENIX, ARIZONA. ANNUAL SUMMARY WITH COMPARATIVE DATA. Text in English. 19??. a. USD 39 combined subscription per issue includes 12 monthly summaries & one a. summary (effective 2009). back issues avail. **Document type:** *Bulletin, Government.* **Description:** Presents the monthly and annual average, resultant and fastest mile wind speed for the current year as well as the monthly and annual mean and fastest mile speed for a long period for Phoenix, Arizona.
Related titles: Online - full text ed.: USD 29 per issue (effective 2009); ◆ Cumulative ed(s).: Local Climatological Data. Phoenix, Arizona. Monthly Summary. ISSN 0198-0475.
Published by: U.S. National Climatic Data Center (Subsidiary of: U.S. Department of Commerce), Federal Bldg, 151 Patton Ave, Asheville, NC 28801. TEL 828-271-4800, FAX 828-271-4876, NODC.Services@noaa.gov, http://www.ncdc.noaa.gov.

551.5 USA ISSN 0198-0475
LOCAL CLIMATOLOGICAL DATA. PHOENIX, ARIZONA. MONTHLY SUMMARY. Text in English. 19??. m. USD 5 per issue (effective 2009). back issues avail. **Document type:** *Bulletin, Government.* **Description:** Provides a monthly summary of temperature extremes, degree days, precipitation and winds, hourly precipitation and 3-hourly weather observations in Phoenix, Arizona.
Related titles: Online - full text ed.: USD 3 per issue (effective 2009); ◆ Cumulative ed. of: Local Climatological Data. Phoenix, Arizona. Annual Summary with Comparative Data. ISSN 0198-0572.
—Linda Hall.
Published by: U.S. National Climatic Data Center (Subsidiary of: U.S. Department of Commerce), Federal Bldg, 151 Patton Ave, Asheville, NC 28801. TEL 828-271-4800, FAX 828-271-4876, NODC.Services@noaa.gov, http://www.ncdc.noaa.gov.

551.5 USA ISSN 0270-0514
LOCAL CLIMATOLOGICAL DATA. PITTSBURGH, PENNSYLVANIA. GREATER PITTSBURGH AIRPORT. ANNUAL SUMMARY WITH COMPARATIVE DATA. Text in English. 19??. a. USD 39 combined subscription per issue includes 12 monthly summaries & one a. summary (effective 2009). back issues avail. **Document type:** *Bulletin, Government.* **Description:** Presents the monthly and annual average, resultant and fastest mile wind speed for the current year as well as the monthly and annual mean and fastest mile speed for a long period for Pittsburgh, Pennsylvania.

Related titles: Online - full text ed.: USD 29 per issue (effective 2009); ◆ Cumulative ed(s).: Local Climatological Data. Pittsburgh, Pennsylvania. Weather Service Contract Meteorology Observatory. Greater Pittsburgh International Airport. Monthly Summary. ISSN 0270-0522.
Published by: U.S. National Climatic Data Center (Subsidiary of: U.S. Department of Commerce), Federal Bldg, 151 Patton Ave, Asheville, NC 28801. TEL 828-271-4800, FAX 828-271-4876, NODC.Services@noaa.gov, http://www.ncdc.noaa.gov.

551.5 USA ISSN 0198-1803
QC984.I22
LOCAL CLIMATOLOGICAL DATA. POCATELLO, IDAHO. ANNUAL SUMMARY WITH COMPARATIVE DATA. Text in English. 19??. a. USD 39 combined subscription per issue includes 12 monthly summaries & one a. summary (effective 2009). **Document type:** *Bulletin, Government.*
Related titles: Online - full text ed.: USD 29 per issue (effective 2009); ◆ Cumulative ed(s).: Local Climatological Data. Pocatello, Idaho. Monthly Summary. ISSN 0198-1811.
Published by: U.S. National Climatic Data Center (Subsidiary of: U.S. Department of Commerce), Federal Bldg, 151 Patton Ave, Asheville, NC 28801. TEL 828-271-4800, FAX 828-271-4876, NODC.Services@noaa.gov, http://www.ncdc.noaa.gov.

551.5 USA ISSN 0198-1811
QC984.I22
LOCAL CLIMATOLOGICAL DATA. POCATELLO, IDAHO. MONTHLY SUMMARY. Text in English. 19??. m. USD 5 per issue (effective 2009). back issues avail. **Document type:** *Bulletin, Government.* **Description:** Provides a monthly summary of temperature extremes, degree days, precipitation and winds, hourly precipitation and 3-hourly weather observations in Pocatello, Idaho.
Related titles: Online - full text ed.: USD 3 per issue (effective 2009); ◆ Cumulative ed. of: Local Climatological Data. Pocatello, Idaho. Annual Summary with Comparative Data. ISSN 0198-1803.
—Linda Hall.
Published by: U.S. National Climatic Data Center (Subsidiary of: U.S. Department of Commerce), Federal Bldg, 151 Patton Ave, Asheville, NC 28801. TEL 828-271-4800, FAX 828-271-4876, NODC.Services@noaa.gov, http://www.ncdc.noaa.gov.

551.5 USA ISSN 0198-4373
QC933.M625
LOCAL CLIMATOLOGICAL DATA. PONAPE ISLAND, PACIFIC. ANNUAL SUMMARY WITH COMPARATIVE DATA. Text in English. a. USD 39 combined subscription per issue includes 12 monthly summaries & one a. summary (effective 2009). **Document type:** *Bulletin, Government.*
Related titles: Online - full text ed.: USD 29 per issue (effective 2009); ◆ Cumulative ed(s).: Local Climatological Data. Ponape Island, Pacific. Monthly Summary. ISSN 0198-4381.
Published by: U.S. National Climatic Data Center (Subsidiary of: U.S. Department of Commerce), Federal Bldg, 151 Patton Ave, Asheville, NC 28801. TEL 828-271-4800, FAX 828-271-4876, NODC.Services@noaa.gov, http://www.ncdc.noaa.gov.

551.5 USA ISSN 0198-4381
LOCAL CLIMATOLOGICAL DATA. PONAPE ISLAND, PACIFIC. MONTHLY SUMMARY. Text in English. 19??. m. USD 5 per issue (effective 2009). back issues avail. **Document type:** *Bulletin, Government.* **Description:** Provides a monthly summary of temperature extremes, degree days, precipitation and winds, hourly precipitation and 3-hourly weather observations in Ponape Island, Pacific.
Related titles: Online - full text ed.: USD 3 per issue (effective 2009); ◆ Cumulative ed. of: Local Climatological Data. Ponape Island, Pacific. Annual Summary with Comparative Data. ISSN 0198-4373.
—Linda Hall.
Published by: U.S. National Climatic Data Center (Subsidiary of: U.S. Department of Commerce), Federal Bldg, 151 Patton Ave, Asheville, NC 28801. TEL 828-271-4800, FAX 828-271-4876, NODC.Services@noaa.gov, http://www.ncdc.noaa.gov.

551.5 USA ISSN 0198-5140
LOCAL CLIMATOLOGICAL DATA. PORT ARTHUR, TEXAS. ANNUAL SUMMARY WITH COMPARATIVE DATA. Text in English. 19??. a. USD 39 combined subscription per issue includes 12 monthly summaries & one a. summary (effective 2009). **Document type:** *Bulletin, Government.* **Description:** Presents the monthly and annual average, resultant and fastest mile wind speed for the current year as well as the monthly and annual mean and fastest mile speed for a long period for Port Arthur, Texas.
Related titles: Online - full text ed.: USD 29 per issue (effective 2009); ◆ Cumulative ed(s).: Local Climatological Data. Port Arthur, Texas. Monthly Summary. ISSN 0198-5159.
Published by: U.S. National Climatic Data Center (Subsidiary of: U.S. Department of Commerce), Federal Bldg, 151 Patton Ave, Asheville, NC 28801. TEL 828-271-4800, FAX 828-271-4876, NODC.Services@noaa.gov, http://www.ncdc.noaa.gov.

551.5 USA ISSN 0198-5159
LOCAL CLIMATOLOGICAL DATA. PORT ARTHUR, TEXAS. MONTHLY SUMMARY. Text in English. 19??. m. USD 5 per issue (effective 2009). back issues avail. **Document type:** *Bulletin, Government.* **Description:** Provides a monthly summary of temperature extremes, degree days, precipitation and winds, hourly precipitation and 3-hourly weather observations in Port Arthur, Texas.
Related titles: Online - full text ed.: USD 3 per issue (effective 2009); ◆ Cumulative ed. of: Local Climatological Data. Port Arthur, Texas. Annual Summary with Comparative Data. ISSN 0198-5140.
—Linda Hall.
Published by: U.S. National Climatic Data Center (Subsidiary of: U.S. Department of Commerce), Federal Bldg, 151 Patton Ave, Asheville, NC 28801. TEL 828-271-4800, FAX 828-271-4876, NODC.Services@noaa.gov, http://www.ncdc.noaa.gov.

551.5 USA ISSN 0198-2370
LOCAL CLIMATOLOGICAL DATA. PORTLAND, MAINE. ANNUAL SUMMARY WITH COMPARATIVE DATA. Text in English. a. USD 39 combined subscription per issue includes 12 monthly summaries & one a. summary (effective 2009). **Document type:** *Bulletin, Government.* **Description:** Presents the monthly and annual average, resultant and fastest mile wind speed for the current year as well as the monthly and annual mean and fastest mile speed for a long period for Portland, Maine.
Related titles: Online - full text ed.: USD 29 per issue (effective 2009); ◆ Cumulative ed(s).: Local Climatological Data. Portland, Maine. Monthly Summary. ISSN 0198-2389.
Published by: U.S. National Climatic Data Center (Subsidiary of: U.S. Department of Commerce), Federal Bldg, 151 Patton Ave, Asheville, NC 28801. TEL 828-271-4800, FAX 828-271-4876, NODC.Services@noaa.gov, http://www.ncdc.noaa.gov.

551.5 USA ISSN 0198-2389
LOCAL CLIMATOLOGICAL DATA. PORTLAND, MAINE. MONTHLY SUMMARY. Text in English. 19??. m. USD 5 per issue (effective 2009). back issues avail. **Document type:** *Bulletin, Government.* **Description:** Provides a monthly summary of temperature extremes, degree days, precipitation and winds, hourly precipitation and 3-hourly weather observations in Portland, Maine.
Related titles: Online - full text ed.: USD 3 per issue (effective 2009); ◆ Cumulative ed. of: Local Climatological Data. Portland, Maine. Annual Summary with Comparative Data. ISSN 0198-2370.
—Linda Hall.
Published by: U.S. National Climatic Data Center (Subsidiary of: U.S. Department of Commerce), Federal Bldg, 151 Patton Ave, Asheville, NC 28801. TEL 828-271-4800, FAX 828-271-4876, NODC.Services@noaa.gov, http://www.ncdc.noaa.gov.

551.5 USA ISSN 0198-4195
QC984.O72
LOCAL CLIMATOLOGICAL DATA. PORTLAND, OREGON. ANNUAL SUMMARY WITH COMPARATIVE DATA. Text in English. 1966. a. USD 39 combined subscription per issue includes 12 monthly summaries & one a. summary (effective 2009). back issues avail. **Document type:** *Bulletin, Government.* **Description:** Presents the monthly and annual average, resultant and fastest mile wind speed for the current year as well as the monthly and annual mean and fastest mile speed for a long period for Portland, Oregon.
Related titles: Online - full text ed.: USD 29 per issue (effective 2009); ◆ Cumulative ed(s).: Local Climatological Data. Portland, Oregon. Monthly Summary. ISSN 0198-4209.
Published by: U.S. National Climatic Data Center (Subsidiary of: U.S. Department of Commerce), Federal Bldg, 151 Patton Ave, Asheville, NC 28801. TEL 828-271-4800, FAX 828-271-4876, NODC.Services@noaa.gov, http://www.ncdc.noaa.gov.

551.5 USA ISSN 0198-4209
QC984.O7
LOCAL CLIMATOLOGICAL DATA. PORTLAND, OREGON. MONTHLY SUMMARY. Text in English. 19??. m. USD 5 per issue (effective 2009). back issues avail. **Document type:** *Bulletin, Government.* **Description:** Provides a monthly summary of temperature extremes, degree days, precipitation and winds, hourly precipitation and 3-hourly weather observations in Portland, Oregon.
Formerly: Station Meteorological Summary. Portland, Oregon
Related titles: Online - full text ed.: USD 3 per issue (effective 2009); ◆ Cumulative ed. of: Local Climatological Data. Portland, Oregon. Annual Summary with Comparative Data. ISSN 0198-4195.
—Linda Hall.
Published by: U.S. National Climatic Data Center (Subsidiary of: U.S. Department of Commerce), Federal Bldg, 151 Patton Ave, Asheville, NC 28801. TEL 828-271-4800, FAX 828-271-4876, NODC.Services@noaa.gov, http://www.ncdc.noaa.gov.

551.5 USA ISSN 0198-4594
QC984.R52
LOCAL CLIMATOLOGICAL DATA. PROVIDENCE, RHODE ISLAND. ANNUAL SUMMARY WITH COMPARATIVE DATA. Text in English. 19??. a. USD 39 combined subscription per issue includes 12 monthly summaries & one a. summary (effective 2009). back issues avail. **Document type:** *Bulletin, Government.* **Description:** Presents the monthly and annual average, resultant and fastest mile wind speed for the current year as well as the monthly and annual mean and fastest mile speed for a long period for Providence, Rhode Island.
Related titles: Online - full text ed.: USD 29 per issue (effective 2009); ◆ Cumulative ed(s).: Local Climatological Data. Providence, Rhode Island. Monthly Summary. ISSN 0198-4608.
Published by: U.S. National Climatic Data Center (Subsidiary of: U.S. Department of Commerce), Federal Bldg, 151 Patton Ave, Asheville, NC 28801. TEL 828-271-4800, FAX 828-271-4876, NODC.Services@noaa.gov, http://www.ncdc.noaa.gov.

551.5 USA ISSN 0198-4608
LOCAL CLIMATOLOGICAL DATA. PROVIDENCE, RHODE ISLAND. MONTHLY SUMMARY. Text in English. 19??. m. USD 5 per issue (effective 2009). back issues avail. **Document type:** *Bulletin, Government.* **Description:** Provides a monthly summary of temperature extremes, degree days, precipitation and winds, hourly precipitation and 3-hourly weather observations in Providence, Rhode Island.
Related titles: Online - full text ed.: USD 3 per issue (effective 2009); ◆ Cumulative ed. of: Local Climatological Data. Providence, Rhode Island. Annual Summary with Comparative Data. ISSN 0198-4594.
—Linda Hall.
Published by: U.S. National Climatic Data Center (Subsidiary of: U.S. Department of Commerce), Federal Bldg, 151 Patton Ave, Asheville, NC 28801. TEL 828-271-4800, FAX 828-271-4876, NODC.Services@noaa.gov, http://www.ncdc.noaa.gov.

551.5 USA ISSN 0198-7631
LOCAL CLIMATOLOGICAL DATA. PUEBLO, COLORADO. ANNUAL SUMMARY WITH COMPARATIVE DATA. Text in English. 19??. a. USD 39 combined subscription per issue includes 12 monthly summaries & one a. summary (effective 2009). back issues avail. **Document type:** *Bulletin, Government.* **Description:** Presents the monthly and annual average, resultant and fastest mile wind speed for the current year as well as the monthly and annual mean and fastest mile speed for a long period for Pueblo, Colorado.
Related titles: Online - full text ed.: USD 29 per issue (effective 2009); ◆ Cumulative ed(s).: Local Climatological Data. Pueblo, Colorado. Monthly Summary. ISSN 0198-764X.
Published by: U.S. National Climatic Data Center (Subsidiary of: U.S. Department of Commerce), Federal Bldg, 151 Patton Ave, Asheville, NC 28801. TEL 828-271-4800, FAX 828-271-4876, NODC.Services@noaa.gov, http://www.ncdc.noaa.gov.

551.5 USA ISSN 0198-764X
LOCAL CLIMATOLOGICAL DATA. PUEBLO, COLORADO. MONTHLY SUMMARY. Text in English. 19??. m. USD 5 per issue (effective 2009). back issues avail. **Document type:** *Bulletin, Government.* **Description:** Provides a monthly summary of temperature extremes, degree days, precipitation and winds, hourly precipitation and 3-hourly weather observations in Pueblo, Colorado.
Related titles: Online - full text ed.: USD 3 per issue (effective 2009); ◆ Cumulative ed. of: Local Climatological Data. Pueblo, Colorado. Annual Summary with Comparative Data. ISSN 0198-7631.
—Linda Hall.
Published by: U.S. National Climatic Data Center (Subsidiary of: U.S. Department of Commerce), Federal Bldg, 151 Patton Ave, Asheville, NC 28801. TEL 828-271-4800, FAX 828-271-4876, NODC.Services@noaa.gov, http://www.ncdc.noaa.gov.

551.5 USA ISSN 0198-5426
LOCAL CLIMATOLOGICAL DATA. QUILLAYUTE AIRPORT, WASHINGTON. ANNUAL SUMMARY WITH COMPARATIVE DATA. Text in English. a. USD 39 combined subscription per issue includes 12 monthly summaries & one a. summary (effective 2009). **Document type:** *Bulletin, Government.*
Related titles: Online - full text ed.: USD 29 per issue (effective 2009); ◆ Cumulative ed(s).: Local Climatological Data. Quillayute, Washington. Monthly Summary. ISSN 0198-5434.
Published by: U.S. National Climatic Data Center (Subsidiary of: U.S. Department of Commerce), Federal Bldg, 151 Patton Ave, Asheville, NC 28801. TEL 828-271-4800, FAX 828-271-4876, NODC.Services@noaa.gov, http://www.ncdc.noaa.gov.

551.5 USA ISSN 0198-5434
QC984.W2
LOCAL CLIMATOLOGICAL DATA. QUILLAYUTE, WASHINGTON. MONTHLY SUMMARY. Text in English. 19??. m. USD 5 per issue (effective 2009). back issues avail. **Document type:** *Bulletin, Government.* **Description:** Provides a monthly summary of temperature extremes, degree days, precipitation and winds, hourly precipitation and 3-hourly weather observations in Quillayute, Washington.
Related titles: Online - full text ed.: USD 3 per issue (effective 2009); ◆ Cumulative ed. of: Local Climatological Data. Quillayute Airport, Washington. Annual Summary with Comparative Data. ISSN 0198-5426.
—Linda Hall.
Published by: U.S. National Climatic Data Center (Subsidiary of: U.S. Department of Commerce), Federal Bldg, 151 Patton Ave, Asheville, NC 28801. TEL 828-271-4800, FAX 828-271-4876, NODC.Services@noaa.gov, http://www.ncdc.noaa.gov.

551.5 USA ISSN 0198-3776
LOCAL CLIMATOLOGICAL DATA. RALEIGH, NORTH CAROLINA. ANNUAL SUMMARY WITH COMPARATIVE DATA. Text in English. 19??. a. USD 39 combined subscription per issue includes 12 monthly summaries & one a. summary (effective 2009). back issues avail. **Document type:** *Bulletin, Government.* **Description:** Presents the monthly and annual average, resultant and fastest mile wind speed for the current year as well as the monthly and annual mean and fastest mile speed for a long period for Raleigh, North Carolina.
Related titles: Online - full text ed.: USD 29 per issue (effective 2009); ◆ Cumulative ed(s).: Local Climatological Data. Raleigh, North Carolina. Monthly Summary. ISSN 0198-3784.
Published by: U.S. National Climatic Data Center (Subsidiary of: U.S. Department of Commerce), Federal Bldg, 151 Patton Ave, Asheville, NC 28801. TEL 828-271-4800, FAX 828-271-4876, NODC.Services@noaa.gov, http://www.ncdc.noaa.gov.

551.5 USA ISSN 0198-3784
LOCAL CLIMATOLOGICAL DATA. RALEIGH, NORTH CAROLINA. MONTHLY SUMMARY. Text in English. 19??. m. USD 5 per issue (effective 2009). back issues avail. **Document type:** *Bulletin, Government.* **Description:** Provides a monthly summary of temperature extremes, degree days, precipitation and winds, hourly precipitation and 3-hourly weather observations in Raleigh, North Carolina.
Related titles: Online - full text ed.: USD 3 per issue (effective 2009); ◆ Cumulative ed. of: Local Climatological Data. Raleigh, North Carolina. Annual Summary with Comparative Data. ISSN 0198-3776.
—Linda Hall.
Published by: U.S. National Climatic Data Center (Subsidiary of: U.S. Department of Commerce), Federal Bldg, 151 Patton Ave, Asheville, NC 28801. TEL 828-271-4800, FAX 828-271-4876, NODC.Services@noaa.gov, http://www.ncdc.noaa.gov.

551.5 USA ISSN 0198-4721
LOCAL CLIMATOLOGICAL DATA. RAPID CITY, SOUTH DAKOTA. ANNUAL SUMMARY WITH COMPARATIVE DATA. Text in English. 19??. a. USD 39 combined subscription per issue includes 12 monthly summaries & one a. summary (effective 2009). back issues avail. **Document type:** *Bulletin, Government.* **Description:** Presents the monthly and annual average, resultant and fastest mile wind speed for the current year as well as the monthly and annual mean and fastest mile speed for a long period for Rapid City, South Dakota.
Related titles: Online - full text ed.: USD 29 per issue (effective 2009); ◆ Cumulative ed(s).: Local Climatological Data. Rapid City, South Dakota. Monthly Summary. ISSN 0198-473X.
Published by: U.S. National Climatic Data Center (Subsidiary of: U.S. Department of Commerce), Federal Bldg, 151 Patton Ave, Asheville, NC 28801. TEL 828-271-4800, FAX 828-271-4876, NODC.Services@noaa.gov, http://www.ncdc.noaa.gov.

551.5 USA ISSN 0198-473X
LOCAL CLIMATOLOGICAL DATA. RAPID CITY, SOUTH DAKOTA. MONTHLY SUMMARY. Text in English. 19??. m. USD 5 per issue (effective 2009). back issues avail. **Document type:** *Bulletin, Government.* **Description:** Provides a monthly summary of temperature extremes, degree days, precipitation and winds, hourly precipitation and 3-hourly weather observations in Rapid City, South Dakota.
Related titles: Online - full text ed.: USD 3 per issue (effective 2009); ◆ Cumulative ed. of: Local Climatological Data. Rapid City, South Dakota. Annual Summary with Comparative Data. ISSN 0198-4721.
—Linda Hall.
Published by: U.S. National Climatic Data Center (Subsidiary of: U.S. Department of Commerce), Federal Bldg, 151 Patton Ave, Asheville, NC 28801. TEL 828-271-4800, FAX 828-271-4876, NODC.Services@noaa.gov, http://www.ncdc.noaa.gov.

551.5 USA ISSN 0198-0955

LOCAL CLIMATOLOGICAL DATA. RED BLUFF, CALIFORNIA. ANNUAL SUMMARY WITH COMPARATIVE DATA. Text in English. 19??. a. USD 39 combined subscription per issue includes 12 monthly summaries & one a. summary (effective 2009). back issues avail. **Document type:** *Bulletin, Government.* **Description:** Presents the monthly and annual average, resultant and fastest mile wind speed for the current year as well as the monthly and annual mean and fastest mile speed for a long period for Red Bluff, California.

Related titles: Online - full text ed.: USD 29 per issue (effective 2009).

Published by: U.S. National Climatic Data Center (Subsidiary of: U.S. Department of Commerce), Federal Bldg, 151 Patton Ave, Asheville, NC 28801. TEL 828-271-4800, FAX 828-271-4876, NODC.Services@noaa.gov, http://www.ncdc.noaa.gov.

551.5 USA ISSN 0898-3585
QC984.C2

LOCAL CLIMATOLOGICAL DATA. REDDING, CALIFORNIA. ANNUAL SUMMARY WITH COMPARATIVE DATA. Text in English. 1987. a. USD 39 combined subscription per issue includes 12 monthly summaries & one a. summary (effective 2009). back issues avail. **Document type:** *Bulletin, Government.* **Description:** Presents the monthly and annual average, resultant and fastest mile wind speed for the current year as well as the monthly and annual mean and fastest mile speed for a long period for Redding, California.

Related titles: Online - full text ed.: USD 29 per issue (effective 2009); ◆ Cumulative ed(s).: Local Climatological Data. Redding, California. Monthly Summary. ISSN 0890-6904.

Published by: U.S. National Climatic Data Center (Subsidiary of: U.S. Department of Commerce), Federal Bldg, 151 Patton Ave, Asheville, NC 28801. TEL 828-271-4800, FAX 828-271-4876, NODC.Services@noaa.gov, http://www.ncdc.noaa.gov.

551.5 USA ISSN 0890-6904

LOCAL CLIMATOLOGICAL DATA. REDDING, CALIFORNIA. MONTHLY SUMMARY. Text in English. 19??. m. USD 5 per issue (effective 2009). back issues avail. **Document type:** *Bulletin, Government.* **Description:** Provides a monthly summary of temperature extremes, degree days, precipitation and winds, hourly precipitation and 3-hourly weather observations in Redding, California.

Related titles: Online - full text ed.: USD 3 per issue (effective 2009); ◆ Cumulative ed. of: Local Climatological Data. Redding, California. Annual Summary with Comparative Data. ISSN 0898-3585.

—Linda Hall.

Published by: U.S. National Climatic Data Center (Subsidiary of: U.S. Department of Commerce), Federal Bldg, 151 Patton Ave, Asheville, NC 28801. TEL 828-271-4800, FAX 828-271-4876, NODC.Services@noaa.gov, http://www.ncdc.noaa.gov.

551.5 USA ISSN 0198-3326

LOCAL CLIMATOLOGICAL DATA. RENO, NEVADA. ANNUAL SUMMARY WITH COMPARATIVE DATA. Text in English. 19??. a. USD 39 combined subscription per issue includes 12 monthly summaries & one a. summary (effective 2009). back issues avail. **Document type:** *Bulletin, Government.* **Description:** Presents the monthly and annual average, resultant and fastest mile wind speed for the current year as well as the monthly and annual mean and fastest mile speed for a long period for Reno, Nevada.

Related titles: Online - full text ed.: USD 29 per issue (effective 2009); ◆ Cumulative ed(s).: Local Climatological Data. Reno, Nevada. Monthly Summary. ISSN 0198-3334.

Published by: U.S. National Climatic Data Center (Subsidiary of: U.S. Department of Commerce), Federal Bldg, 151 Patton Ave, Asheville, NC 28801. TEL 828-271-4800, FAX 828-271-4876, NODC.Services@noaa.gov, http://www.ncdc.noaa.gov.

551.5 USA ISSN 0198-3334

LOCAL CLIMATOLOGICAL DATA. RENO, NEVADA. MONTHLY SUMMARY. Text in English. 19??. m. USD 5 per issue (effective 2009). back issues avail. **Document type:** *Bulletin, Government.* **Description:** Provides a monthly summary of temperature extremes, degree days, precipitation and winds, hourly precipitation and 3-hourly weather observations in Reno, Nevada.

Related titles: Online - full text ed.: USD 3 per issue (effective 2009); ◆ Cumulative ed. of: Local Climatological Data. Reno, Nevada. Annual Summary with Comparative Data. ISSN 0198-3326.

—Linda Hall.

Published by: U.S. National Climatic Data Center (Subsidiary of: U.S. Department of Commerce), Federal Bldg, 151 Patton Ave, Asheville, NC 28801. TEL 828-271-4800, FAX 828-271-4876, NODC.Services@noaa.gov, http://www.ncdc.noaa.gov.

551.5 USA ISSN 0198-5361
QC984.V82

LOCAL CLIMATOLOGICAL DATA. RICHMOND, VIRGINIA. ANNUAL SUMMARY WITH COMPARATIVE DATA. Text in English. 19??. a. USD 39 combined subscription per issue includes 12 monthly summaries & one a. summary (effective 2009). back issues avail. **Document type:** *Bulletin, Government.* **Description:** Presents the monthly and annual average, resultant and fastest mile wind speed for the current year as well as the monthly and annual mean and fastest mile speed for a long period for Richmond, Virginia.

Related titles: Online - full text ed.: USD 29 per issue (effective 2009); ◆ Cumulative ed(s).: Local Climatological Data. Richmond, Virginia. Monthly Summary. ISSN 0198-537X.

Published by: U.S. National Climatic Data Center (Subsidiary of: U.S. Department of Commerce), Federal Bldg, 151 Patton Ave, Asheville, NC 28801. TEL 828-271-4800, FAX 828-271-4876, NODC.Services@noaa.gov, http://www.ncdc.noaa.gov.

551.5 USA ISSN 0198-537X
QC984.V8

LOCAL CLIMATOLOGICAL DATA. RICHMOND, VIRGINIA. MONTHLY SUMMARY. Text in English. 19??. m. USD 5 per issue (effective 2009). back issues avail. **Document type:** *Bulletin, Government.* **Description:** Provides a monthly summary of temperature extremes, degree days, precipitation and winds, hourly precipitation and 3-hourly weather observations in Richmond, Virginia.

Related titles: Online - full text ed.: USD 3 per issue (effective 2009); ◆ Cumulative ed. of: Local Climatological Data. Richmond, Virginia. Annual Summary with Comparative Data. ISSN 0198-5361.

—Linda Hall.

Published by: U.S. National Climatic Data Center (Subsidiary of: U.S. Department of Commerce), Federal Bldg, 151 Patton Ave, Asheville, NC 28801. TEL 828-271-4800, FAX 828-271-4876, NODC.Services@noaa.gov, http://www.ncdc.noaa.gov.

551.5 USA ISSN 0198-5388
QC984.V8

LOCAL CLIMATOLOGICAL DATA. ROANOKE, VIRGINIA. ANNUAL SUMMARY WITH COMPARATIVE DATA. Text in English. 19??. a. USD 39 combined subscription per issue includes 12 monthly summaries & one a. summary (effective 2009). back issues avail. **Document type:** *Bulletin, Government.* **Description:** Presents the monthly and annual average, resultant and fastest mile wind speed for the current year as well as the monthly and annual mean and fastest mile speed for a long period for Roanoke, Virginia.

Related titles: Online - full text ed.: USD 29 per issue (effective 2009); ◆ Cumulative ed(s).: Local Climatological Data. Roanoke, Virginia. Monthly Summary. ISSN 0198-5396.

Published by: U.S. National Climatic Data Center (Subsidiary of: U.S. Department of Commerce), Federal Bldg, 151 Patton Ave, Asheville, NC 28801. TEL 828-271-4800, FAX 828-271-4876, NODC.Services@noaa.gov, http://www.ncdc.noaa.gov.

551.5 USA ISSN 0198-5396
QC984.V8

LOCAL CLIMATOLOGICAL DATA. ROANOKE, VIRGINIA. MONTHLY SUMMARY. Text in English. 19??. m. USD 5 per issue (effective 2009). back issues avail. **Document type:** *Bulletin, Government.* **Description:** Provides a monthly summary of temperature extremes, degree days, precipitation and winds, hourly precipitation and 3-hourly weather observations in Roanoke, Virginia.

Related titles: Online - full text ed.: USD 3 per issue (effective 2009); ◆ Cumulative ed. of: Local Climatological Data. Roanoke, Virginia. Annual Summary with Comparative Data. ISSN 0198-5388.

—Linda Hall.

Published by: U.S. National Climatic Data Center (Subsidiary of: U.S. Department of Commerce), Federal Bldg, 151 Patton Ave, Asheville, NC 28801. TEL 828-271-4800, FAX 828-271-4876, NODC.Services@noaa.gov, http://www.ncdc.noaa.gov.

551.5 USA ISSN 0198-2753
QC984.M62

LOCAL CLIMATOLOGICAL DATA. ROCHESTER, MINNESOTA. ANNUAL SUMMARY WITH COMPARATIVE DATA. Text in English. 19??. a. USD 39 combined subscription per issue includes 12 monthly summaries & one a. summary (effective 2009). back issues avail. **Document type:** *Bulletin, Government.* **Description:** Presents the monthly and annual average, resultant and fastest mile wind speed for the current year as well as the monthly and annual mean and fastest mile speed for a long period for Rochester, Minnesota.

Related titles: Online - full text ed.: USD 29 per issue (effective 2009); ◆ Cumulative ed(s).: Local Climatological Data. Rochester, Minnesota. Monthly Summary. ISSN 0198-2761.

Published by: U.S. National Climatic Data Center (Subsidiary of: U.S. Department of Commerce), Federal Bldg, 151 Patton Ave, Asheville, NC 28801. TEL 828-271-4800, FAX 828-271-4876, NODC.Services@noaa.gov, http://www.ncdc.noaa.gov.

551.5 USA ISSN 0198-2761

LOCAL CLIMATOLOGICAL DATA. ROCHESTER, MINNESOTA. MONTHLY SUMMARY. Text in English. 19??. m. USD 5 per issue (effective 2009). back issues avail. **Document type:** *Bulletin, Government.* **Description:** Provides a monthly summary of temperature extremes, degree days, precipitation and winds, hourly precipitation and 3-hourly weather observations in Rochester, Minnesota.

Related titles: Online - full text ed.: USD 3 per issue (effective 2009); ◆ Cumulative ed. of: Local Climatological Data. Rochester, Minnesota. Annual Summary with Comparative Data. ISSN 0198-2753.

—Linda Hall.

Published by: U.S. National Climatic Data Center (Subsidiary of: U.S. Department of Commerce), Federal Bldg, 151 Patton Ave, Asheville, NC 28801. TEL 828-271-4800, FAX 828-271-4876, NODC.Services@noaa.gov, http://www.ncdc.noaa.gov.

551.5 USA ISSN 0198-3652
QC984.N72

LOCAL CLIMATOLOGICAL DATA. ROCHESTER, NEW YORK. ANNUAL SUMMARY WITH COMPARATIVE DATA. Text in English. 1966. a. USD 39 combined subscription per issue includes 12 monthly summaries & one a. summary (effective 2009). back issues avail. **Document type:** *Bulletin, Government.*

Formerly: Local Climatological Data with Comparative Data. Rochester, New York

Related titles: Online - full text ed.: USD 29 per issue (effective 2009); ◆ Cumulative ed(s).: Local Climatological Data. Rochester, New York. Monthly Summary. ISSN 0198-3660.

Published by: U.S. National Climatic Data Center (Subsidiary of: U.S. Department of Commerce), Federal Bldg, 151 Patton Ave, Asheville, NC 28801. TEL 828-271-4800, FAX 828-271-4876, NODC.Services@noaa.gov, http://www.ncdc.noaa.gov.

551.5 USA ISSN 0198-3660
CODEN: KIDZDN

LOCAL CLIMATOLOGICAL DATA. ROCHESTER, NEW YORK. MONTHLY SUMMARY. Text in English. 19??. m. USD 5 per issue (effective 2009). back issues avail. **Document type:** *Bulletin, Government.* **Description:** Provides a monthly summary of temperature extremes, degree days, precipitation and winds, hourly precipitation and 3-hourly weather observations in Rochester, New York.

Related titles: Online - full text ed.: USD 3 per issue (effective 2009); ◆ Cumulative ed. of: Local Climatological Data. Rochester, New York. Annual Summary with Comparative Data. ISSN 0198-3652.

—Linda Hall.

Published by: U.S. National Climatic Data Center (Subsidiary of: U.S. Department of Commerce), Federal Bldg, 151 Patton Ave, Asheville, NC 28801. TEL 828-271-4800, FAX 828-271-4876, NODC.Services@noaa.gov, http://www.ncdc.noaa.gov.

551.5 USA ISSN 0198-1900

LOCAL CLIMATOLOGICAL DATA. ROCKFORD, ILLINOIS. ANNUAL SUMMARY WITH COMPARATIVE DATA. Text in English. 19??. a. USD 39 combined subscription per issue includes 12 monthly summaries & one a. summary (effective 2009). back issues avail. **Document type:** *Bulletin, Government.* **Description:** Presents the monthly and annual average, resultant and fastest mile wind speed for the current year as well as the monthly and annual mean and fastest mile speed for a long period for Rockford, Illinois.

Related titles: Online - full text ed.: USD 29 per issue (effective 2009); ◆ Cumulative ed(s).: Local Climatological Data. Rockford, Illinois. Monthly Summary. ISSN 0198-1919.

Published by: U.S. National Climatic Data Center (Subsidiary of: U.S. Department of Commerce), Federal Bldg, 151 Patton Ave, Asheville, NC 28801. TEL 828-271-4800, FAX 828-271-4876, NODC.Services@noaa.gov, http://www.ncdc.noaa.gov.

551.5 USA ISSN 0198-1919

LOCAL CLIMATOLOGICAL DATA. ROCKFORD, ILLINOIS. MONTHLY SUMMARY. Text in English. 19??. m. USD 5 per issue (effective 2009). back issues avail. **Document type:** *Bulletin, Government.* **Description:** Provides a monthly summary of temperature extremes, degree days, precipitation and winds, hourly precipitation and 3-hourly weather observations in Rockford, Illinois.

Related titles: Online - full text ed.: USD 3 per issue (effective 2009); ◆ Cumulative ed. of: Local Climatological Data. Rockford, Illinois. Annual Summary with Comparative Data. ISSN 0198-1900.

—Linda Hall.

Published by: U.S. National Climatic Data Center (Subsidiary of: U.S. Department of Commerce), Federal Bldg, 151 Patton Ave, Asheville, NC 28801. TEL 828-271-4800, FAX 828-271-4876, NODC.Services@noaa.gov, http://www.ncdc.noaa.gov.

551.5 USA ISSN 0198-1641

LOCAL CLIMATOLOGICAL DATA. ROME, GEORGIA. ANNUAL SUMMARY WITH COMPARATIVE DATA. Text in English. 19??. a. USD 39 combined subscription per issue includes 12 monthly summaries & one a. summary (effective 2009). back issues avail. **Document type:** *Bulletin, Government.* **Description:** Presents the monthly and annual average, resultant and fastest mile wind speed for the current year as well as the monthly and annual mean and fastest mile speed for a long period for Rome, Georgia.

Related titles: Online - full text ed.: USD 29 per issue (effective 2009).

Published by: U.S. National Climatic Data Center (Subsidiary of: U.S. Department of Commerce), Federal Bldg, 151 Patton Ave, Asheville, NC 28801. TEL 828-271-4800, FAX 828-271-4876, NODC.Services@noaa.gov, http://www.ncdc.noaa.gov.

551.5 USA ISSN 0198-3512

LOCAL CLIMATOLOGICAL DATA. ROSWELL, NEW MEXICO. ANNUAL SUMMARY WITH COMPARATIVE DATA. Text in English. 19??. a. USD 5 per issue (effective 2004). **Document type:** *Bulletin, Government.*

Related titles: Online - full text ed.; ◆ Cumulative ed(s).: Local Climatological Data. Roswell, New Mexico. Monthly Summary. ISSN 0198-3520.

Published by: U.S. National Climatic Data Center (Subsidiary of: U.S. Department of Commerce), Federal Bldg, 151 Patton Ave, Asheville, NC 28801. TEL 828-271-4800, FAX 828-271-4876, NODC.Services@noaa.gov, http://www.ncdc.noaa.gov.

551.5 USA ISSN 0198-0963

LOCAL CLIMATOLOGICAL DATA. SACRAMENTO, CALIFORNIA. ANNUAL SUMMARY WITH COMPARATIVE DATA. Text in English. 19??. a. USD 39 combined subscription per issue includes 12 monthly summaries & one a. summary (effective 2009). back issues avail. **Document type:** *Bulletin, Government.* **Description:** Presents the monthly and annual average, resultant and fastest mile wind speed for the current year as well as the monthly and annual mean and fastest mile speed for a long period for Sacramento, California.

Related titles: Online - full text ed.: USD 29 per issue (effective 2009); ◆ Cumulative ed(s).: Local Climatological Data. Sacramento, California. Monthly Summary. ISSN 0198-0807.

Published by: U.S. National Climatic Data Center (Subsidiary of: U.S. Department of Commerce), Federal Bldg, 151 Patton Ave, Asheville, NC 28801. TEL 828-271-4800, FAX 828-271-4876, NODC.Services@noaa.gov, http://www.ncdc.noaa.gov.

551.5 USA ISSN 0198-0807

LOCAL CLIMATOLOGICAL DATA. SACRAMENTO, CALIFORNIA. MONTHLY SUMMARY. Text in English. 19??. m. USD 5 per issue (effective 2009). back issues avail. **Document type:** *Bulletin, Government.* **Description:** Provides a monthly summary of temperature extremes, degree days, precipitation and winds, hourly precipitation and 3-hourly weather observations in Sacramento, California.

Related titles: Online - full text ed.: USD 3 per issue (effective 2009); ◆ Cumulative ed. of: Local Climatological Data. Sacramento, California. Annual Summary with Comparative Data. ISSN 0198-0963.

—Linda Hall.

Published by: U.S. National Climatic Data Center (Subsidiary of: U.S. Department of Commerce), Federal Bldg, 151 Patton Ave, Asheville, NC 28801. TEL 828-271-4800, FAX 828-271-4876, NODC.Services@noaa.gov, http://www.ncdc.noaa.gov.

551.5 USA ISSN 0198-277X

LOCAL CLIMATOLOGICAL DATA. SAINT CLOUD, MINNESOTA. ANNUAL SUMMARY WITH COMPARATIVE DATA. Text in English. 19??. a. USD 39 combined subscription per issue includes 12 monthly summaries & one a. summary (effective 2009). back issues avail. **Document type:** *Bulletin, Government.* **Description:** Presents the monthly and annual average, resultant and fastest mile wind speed for the current year as well as the monthly and annual mean and fastest mile speed for a long period for Saint Cloud, Minnesota.

Related titles: Online - full text ed.: USD 29 per issue (effective 2009); ◆ Cumulative ed(s).: Local Climatological Data. Saint Cloud, Minnesota. Monthly Summary. ISSN 0198-2788.

Published by: U.S. National Climatic Data Center (Subsidiary of: U.S. Department of Commerce), Federal Bldg, 151 Patton Ave, Asheville, NC 28801. TEL 828-271-4800, FAX 828-271-4876, NODC.Services@noaa.gov, http://www.ncdc.noaa.gov.

551.5 USA ISSN 0198-2788
LOCAL CLIMATOLOGICAL DATA. SAINT CLOUD, MINNESOTA. MONTHLY SUMMARY. Text in English. 19??. m. USD 5 per issue (effective 2009). back issues avail. **Document type:** *Bulletin, Government.* **Description:** Provides a monthly summary of temperature extremes, degree days, precipitation and winds, hourly precipitation and 3-hourly weather observations in Saint Cloud, Minnesota.
Related titles: Online - full text ed.: USD 3 per issue (effective 2009); ◆ Cumulative ed. of: Local Climatological Data. Saint Cloud, Minnesota. Annual Summary with Comparative Data. ISSN 0198-277X.
—Linda Hall.
Published by: U.S. National Climatic Data Center (Subsidiary of: U.S. Department of Commerce), Federal Bldg, 151 Patton Ave, Asheville, NC 28801. TEL 828-271-4800, FAX 828-271-4876, NODC.Services@noaa.gov, http://www.ncdc.noaa.gov.

551.5 USA ISSN 0198-4217
QC984.O72
LOCAL CLIMATOLOGICAL DATA. SALEM, OREGON. ANNUAL SUMMARY WITH COMPARATIVE DATA. Text in English. 19??. a. USD 39 combined subscription per issue includes 12 monthly summaries & one a. summary (effective 2009). back issues avail. **Document type:** *Bulletin, Government.* **Description:** Presents the monthly and annual average, resultant and fastest mile wind speed for the current year as well as the monthly and annual mean and fastest mile speed for a long period for Salem, Oregon.
Related titles: Online - full text ed.: USD 29 per issue (effective 2009); ◆ Cumulative ed(s).: Local Climatological Data. Salem, Oregon. Monthly Summary. ISSN 0198-4225.
Published by: U.S. National Climatic Data Center (Subsidiary of: U.S. Department of Commerce), Federal Bldg, 151 Patton Ave, Asheville, NC 28801. TEL 828-271-4800, FAX 828-271-4876, NODC.Services@noaa.gov, http://www.ncdc.noaa.gov.

551.5 USA ISSN 0198-4225
QC984.O72
LOCAL CLIMATOLOGICAL DATA. SALEM, OREGON. MONTHLY SUMMARY. Text in English. 19??. m. USD 5 per issue (effective 2009). back issues avail. **Document type:** *Bulletin, Government.* **Description:** Provides a monthly summary of temperature extremes, degree days, precipitation and winds, hourly precipitation and 3-hourly weather observations in Salem, Oregon.
Related titles: Online - full text ed.: USD 3 per issue (effective 2009); ◆ Cumulative ed. of: Local Climatological Data. Salem, Oregon. Annual Summary with Comparative Data. ISSN 0198-4217.
—Linda Hall.
Published by: U.S. National Climatic Data Center (Subsidiary of: U.S. Department of Commerce), Federal Bldg, 151 Patton Ave, Asheville, NC 28801. TEL 828-271-4800, FAX 828-271-4876, NODC.Services@noaa.gov, http://www.ncdc.noaa.gov.

551.5 USA ISSN 0198-5280
LOCAL CLIMATOLOGICAL DATA. SALT LAKE CITY, UTAH. ANNUAL SUMMARY WITH COMPARATIVE DATA. Text in English. 19??. a. USD 39 combined subscription per issue includes 12 monthly summaries & one a. summary (effective 2009). back issues avail. **Document type:** *Bulletin, Government.* **Description:** Presents the monthly and annual average, resultant and fastest mile wind speed for the current year as well as the monthly and annual mean and fastest mile speed for a long period for Salt Lake City, Utah.
Related titles: Online - full text ed.: USD 29 per issue (effective 2009); ◆ Cumulative ed(s).: Local Climatological Data. Salt Lake City, Utah. Monthly Summary. ISSN 0198-5299.
Published by: U.S. National Climatic Data Center (Subsidiary of: U.S. Department of Commerce), Federal Bldg, 151 Patton Ave, Asheville, NC 28801. TEL 828-271-4800, FAX 828-271-4876, NODC.Services@noaa.gov, http://www.ncdc.noaa.gov.

551.5 USA ISSN 0198-5299
LOCAL CLIMATOLOGICAL DATA. SALT LAKE CITY, UTAH. MONTHLY SUMMARY. Text in English. 19??. m. USD 5 per issue (effective 2009). back issues avail. **Document type:** *Bulletin, Government.* **Description:** Provides a monthly summary of temperature extremes, degree days, precipitation and winds, hourly precipitation and 3-hourly weather observations in Salt Lake City, Utah.
Related titles: Online - full text ed.: USD 3 per issue (effective 2009); ◆ Cumulative ed. of: Local Climatological Data. Salt Lake City, Utah. Annual Summary with Comparative Data. ISSN 0198-5280.
—Linda Hall.
Published by: U.S. National Climatic Data Center (Subsidiary of: U.S. Department of Commerce), Federal Bldg, 151 Patton Ave, Asheville, NC 28801. TEL 828-271-4800, FAX 828-271-4876, NODC.Services@noaa.gov, http://www.ncdc.noaa.gov.

551.5 USA ISSN 0198-5167
LOCAL CLIMATOLOGICAL DATA. SAN ANGELO, TEXAS. ANNUAL SUMMARY WITH COMPARATIVE DATA. Text in English. 19??. a. USD 39 combined subscription per issue includes 12 monthly summaries & one a. summary (effective 2009). back issues avail. **Document type:** *Bulletin, Government.* **Description:** Presents the monthly and annual average, resultant and fastest mile wind speed for the current year as well as the monthly and annual mean and fastest mile speed for a long period for San Angelo, Texas.
Related titles: Online - full text ed.: USD 29 per issue (effective 2009); ◆ Cumulative ed(s).: Local Climatological Data. San Angelo, Texas. Monthly Summary. ISSN 0198-5175.
Published by: U.S. National Climatic Data Center (Subsidiary of: U.S. Department of Commerce), Federal Bldg, 151 Patton Ave, Asheville, NC 28801. TEL 828-271-4800, FAX 828-271-4876, NODC.Services@noaa.gov, http://www.ncdc.noaa.gov.

551.5 USA ISSN 0198-5175
LOCAL CLIMATOLOGICAL DATA. SAN ANGELO, TEXAS. MONTHLY SUMMARY. Text in English. 19??. m. USD 5 per issue (effective 2009). back issues avail. **Document type:** *Bulletin, Government.* **Description:** Provides a monthly summary of temperature extremes, degree days, precipitation and winds, hourly precipitation and 3-hourly weather observations in San Angelo, Texas.
Related titles: Online - full text ed.: USD 3 per issue (effective 2009); ◆ Cumulative ed. of: Local Climatological Data. San Angelo, Texas. Annual Summary with Comparative Data. ISSN 0198-5167.
—Linda Hall.
Published by: U.S. National Climatic Data Center (Subsidiary of: U.S. Department of Commerce), Federal Bldg, 151 Patton Ave, Asheville, NC 28801. TEL 828-271-4800, FAX 828-271-4876, NODC.Services@noaa.gov, http://www.ncdc.noaa.gov.

551.5 USA ISSN 0198-5183
LOCAL CLIMATOLOGICAL DATA. SAN ANTONIO, TEXAS. ANNUAL SUMMARY WITH COMPARATIVE DATA. Text in English. 19??. a. USD 39 combined subscription per issue includes 12 monthly summaries & one a. summary (effective 2009). back issues avail. **Document type:** *Bulletin, Government.* **Description:** Presents the monthly and annual average, resultant and fastest mile wind speed for the current year as well as the monthly and annual mean and fastest mile speed for a long period for San Antonio, Texas.
Related titles: Online - full text ed.: USD 29 per issue (effective 2009); ◆ Cumulative ed(s).: Local Climatological Data. San Antonio, Texas. Monthly Summary. ISSN 0198-5191.
Published by: U.S. National Climatic Data Center (Subsidiary of: U.S. Department of Commerce), Federal Bldg, 151 Patton Ave, Asheville, NC 28801. TEL 828-271-4800, FAX 828-271-4876, NODC.Services@noaa.gov, http://www.ncdc.noaa.gov.

551.5 USA ISSN 0198-5191
LOCAL CLIMATOLOGICAL DATA. SAN ANTONIO, TEXAS. MONTHLY SUMMARY. Text in English. 19??. m. USD 5 per issue (effective 2009). back issues avail. **Document type:** *Bulletin, Government.* **Description:** Provides a monthly summary of temperature extremes, degree days, precipitation and winds, hourly precipitation and 3-hourly weather observations in San Antonio, Texas.
Related titles: Online - full text ed.: USD 3 per issue (effective 2009); ◆ Cumulative ed. of: Local Climatological Data. San Antonio, Texas. Annual Summary with Comparative Data. ISSN 0198-5183.
—Linda Hall.
Published by: U.S. National Climatic Data Center (Subsidiary of: U.S. Department of Commerce), Federal Bldg, 151 Patton Ave, Asheville, NC 28801. TEL 828-271-4800, FAX 828-271-4876, NODC.Services@noaa.gov, http://www.ncdc.noaa.gov.

551.5 USA ISSN 0198-0971
QC984.C2
LOCAL CLIMATOLOGICAL DATA. SAN DIEGO, CALIFORNIA. ANNUAL SUMMARY WITH COMPARATIVE DATA. Text in English. 19??. a. USD 39 combined subscription per issue includes 12 monthly summaries & one a. summary (effective 2009). back issues avail. **Document type:** *Bulletin, Government.* **Description:** Presents the monthly and annual average, resultant and fastest mile wind speed for the current year as well as the monthly and annual mean and fastest mile speed for a long period for San Diego, California.
Related titles: Online - full text ed.: USD 29 per issue (effective 2009); ◆ Cumulative ed(s).: Local Climatological Data. San Diego, California. Monthly Summary. ISSN 0198-0815.
Published by: U.S. National Climatic Data Center (Subsidiary of: U.S. Department of Commerce), Federal Bldg, 151 Patton Ave, Asheville, NC 28801. TEL 828-271-4800, FAX 828-271-4876, NODC.Services@noaa.gov, http://www.ncdc.noaa.gov.

551.5 USA ISSN 0198-0815
LOCAL CLIMATOLOGICAL DATA. SAN DIEGO, CALIFORNIA. MONTHLY SUMMARY. Text in English. 19??. m. USD 5 per issue (effective 2009). back issues avail. **Document type:** *Bulletin, Government.* **Description:** Provides a monthly summary of temperature extremes, degree days, precipitation and winds, hourly precipitation and 3-hourly weather observations in San Diego, California.
Related titles: Online - full text ed.: USD 3 per issue (effective 2009); ◆ Cumulative ed. of: Local Climatological Data. San Diego, California. Annual Summary with Comparative Data. ISSN 0198-0971.
—Linda Hall.
Published by: U.S. National Climatic Data Center (Subsidiary of: U.S. Department of Commerce), Federal Bldg, 151 Patton Ave, Asheville, NC 28801. TEL 828-271-4800, FAX 828-271-4876, NODC.Services@noaa.gov, http://www.ncdc.noaa.gov.

551.5 USA ISSN 0198-0998
LOCAL CLIMATOLOGICAL DATA. SAN FRANCISCO, CALIFORNIA. FEDERAL OFFICE BUILDING. ANNUAL SUMMARY WITH COMPARATIVE DATA. Text in English. a. USD 5 per issue (effective 2004). **Document type:** *Bulletin, Government.*
Related titles: Online - full content ed.; ◆ Cumulative ed(s).: Local Climatological Data. San Francisco California Federal Office Building. Monthly Summary. ISSN 0198-0831.
Published by: U.S. National Climatic Data Center (Subsidiary of: U.S. Department of Commerce), Federal Bldg, 151 Patton Ave, Asheville, NC 28801. TEL 828-271-4800, FAX 828-271-4876, NODC.Services@noaa.gov, http://www.ncdc.noaa.gov.

551.5 USA ISSN 0198-0831
LOCAL CLIMATOLOGICAL DATA. SAN FRANCISCO CALIFORNIA FEDERAL OFFICE BUILDING. MONTHLY SUMMARY. Text in English. m. USD 5 per issue (effective 2009). **Document type:** *Bulletin, Government.*
Related titles: Online - full text ed.: USD 3 per issue (effective 2009); ◆ Cumulative ed. of: Local Climatological Data. San Francisco, California. Federal Office Building. Annual Summary with Comparative Data. ISSN 0198-0998.
—Linda Hall.
Published by: U.S. National Climatic Data Center (Subsidiary of: U.S. Department of Commerce), Federal Bldg, 151 Patton Ave, Asheville, NC 28801. TEL 828-271-4800, FAX 828-271-4876, NODC.Services@noaa.gov, http://www.ncdc.noaa.gov.

551.5 USA ISSN 0198-098X
QC984.C22
LOCAL CLIMATOLOGICAL DATA. SAN FRANCISCO, CALIFORNIA. INTERNATIONAL AIRPORT. ANNUAL SUMMARY WITH COMPARATIVE DATA. Text in English. 19??. a. USD 39 combined subscription per issue includes 12 monthly summaries & one a. summary (effective 2009). back issues avail. **Document type:** *Bulletin, Government.* **Description:** Presents the monthly and annual average, resultant and fastest mile wind speed for the current year as well as the monthly and annual mean and fastest mile speed for a long period for the international airport in San Francisco, California.
Related titles: Online - full text ed.: USD 29 per issue (effective 2009); ◆ Cumulative ed(s).: Local Climatological Data. San Francisco, California. International Airport. Monthly Summary. ISSN 0198-0823.
Published by: U.S. National Climatic Data Center (Subsidiary of: U.S. Department of Commerce), Federal Bldg, 151 Patton Ave, Asheville, NC 28801. TEL 828-271-4800, FAX 828-271-4876, NODC.Services@noaa.gov, http://www.ncdc.noaa.gov.

551.5 USA ISSN 0198-0823
LOCAL CLIMATOLOGICAL DATA. SAN FRANCISCO, CALIFORNIA. INTERNATIONAL AIRPORT. MONTHLY SUMMARY. Text in English. 19??. m. USD 5 per issue (effective 2009). back issues avail. **Document type:** *Bulletin, Government.* **Description:** Provides a monthly summary of temperature extremes, degree days, precipitation and winds, hourly precipitation and 3-hourly weather observations in San Francisco California International Airport.
Related titles: Online - full text ed.: USD 3 per issue (effective 2009); ◆ Cumulative ed. of: Local Climatological Data. San Francisco, California. International Airport. Annual Summary with Comparative Data. ISSN 0198-098X.
—Linda Hall.
Published by: U.S. National Climatic Data Center (Subsidiary of: U.S. Department of Commerce), Federal Bldg, 151 Patton Ave, Asheville, NC 28801. TEL 828-271-4800, FAX 828-271-4876, NODC.Services@noaa.gov, http://www.ncdc.noaa.gov.

551.5 USA ISSN 0198-5566
LOCAL CLIMATOLOGICAL DATA. SAN JUAN, PUERTO RICO. ANNUAL SUMMARY WITH COMPARATIVE DATA. Text in English. 19??. a. USD 39 combined subscription per issue includes 12 monthly summaries & one a. summary (effective 2009). back issues avail. **Document type:** *Bulletin, Government.* **Description:** Presents the monthly and annual average, resultant and fastest mile wind speed for the current year as well as the monthly and annual mean and fastest mile speed for a long period for San Juan, Puerto Rico.
Related titles: Online - full text ed.: USD 29 per issue (effective 2009); ◆ Cumulative ed(s).: Local Climatological Data. San Juan, Puerto Rico. Monthly Summary. ISSN 0198-5574.
Published by: U.S. National Climatic Data Center (Subsidiary of: U.S. Department of Commerce), Federal Bldg, 151 Patton Ave, Asheville, NC 28801. TEL 828-271-4800, FAX 828-271-4876, NODC.Services@noaa.gov, http://www.ncdc.noaa.gov.

551.5 USA ISSN 0198-5574
LOCAL CLIMATOLOGICAL DATA. SAN JUAN, PUERTO RICO. MONTHLY SUMMARY. Text in English. 19??. m. USD 5 per issue (effective 2009). back issues avail. **Document type:** *Bulletin, Government.* **Description:** Provides a monthly summary of temperature extremes, degree days, precipitation and winds, hourly precipitation and 3-hourly weather observations in San Juan, Puerto Rico.
Related titles: Online - full text ed.: USD 3 per issue (effective 2009); ◆ Cumulative ed. of: Local Climatological Data. San Juan, Puerto Rico. Annual Summary with Comparative Data. ISSN 0198-5566.
—Linda Hall.
Published by: U.S. National Climatic Data Center (Subsidiary of: U.S. Department of Commerce), Federal Bldg, 151 Patton Ave, Asheville, NC 28801. TEL 828-271-4800, FAX 828-271-4876, NODC.Services@noaa.gov, http://www.ncdc.noaa.gov.

551.5 USA ISSN 0742-8774
QC984.C2
LOCAL CLIMATOLOGICAL DATA. SANTA BARBARA, CALIFORNIA. ANNUAL SUMMARY WITH COMPARATIVE DATA. Text in English. 1986. a. USD 39 combined subscription per issue includes 12 monthly summaries & one a. summary (effective 2009). back issues avail. **Document type:** *Bulletin, Government.* **Description:** Presents the monthly and annual average, resultant and fastest mile wind speed for the current year as well as the monthly and annual mean and fastest mile speed for a long period for Santa Barbara, California.
Related titles: Online - full text ed.: USD 29 per issue (effective 2009); ◆ Cumulative ed(s).: Local Climatological Data. Santa Barbara, California. Municipal Airport. Monthly Summary. ISSN 0742-8766.
Published by: U.S. National Climatic Data Center (Subsidiary of: U.S. Department of Commerce), Federal Bldg, 151 Patton Ave, Asheville, NC 28801. TEL 828-271-4800, FAX 828-271-4876, NODC.Services@noaa.gov, http://www.ncdc.noaa.gov.

551.5 USA ISSN 0742-8766
LOCAL CLIMATOLOGICAL DATA. SANTA BARBARA, CALIFORNIA. MUNICIPAL AIRPORT. MONTHLY SUMMARY. Text in English. m. USD 5 per issue (effective 2009). **Document type:** *Bulletin, Government.*
Related titles: Online - full text ed.: USD 3 per issue (effective 2009); ◆ Cumulative ed. of: Local Climatological Data. Santa Barbara, California. Annual Summary with Comparative Data. ISSN 0742-8774.
—Linda Hall.
Published by: U.S. National Climatic Data Center (Subsidiary of: U.S. Department of Commerce), Federal Bldg, 151 Patton Ave, Asheville, NC 28801. TEL 828-271-4800, FAX 828-271-4876, NODC.Services@noaa.gov, http://www.ncdc.noaa.gov.

551.5 USA ISSN 0198-1005
LOCAL CLIMATOLOGICAL DATA. SANTA MARIA, CALIFORNIA. ANNUAL SUMMARY WITH COMPARATIVE DATA. Text in English. 19??. a. USD 39 combined subscription per issue includes 12 monthly summaries & one a. summary (effective 2009). back issues avail. **Document type:** *Bulletin, Government.* **Description:** Presents the monthly and annual average, resultant and fastest mile wind speed for the current year as well as the monthly and annual mean and fastest mile speed for a long period for Santa Maria, California.
Related titles: Online - full text ed.: USD 29 per issue (effective 2009); ◆ Cumulative ed(s).: Local Climatological Data. Santa Maria, California. Monthly Summary. ISSN 0198-084X.
Published by: U.S. National Climatic Data Center (Subsidiary of: U.S. Department of Commerce), Federal Bldg, 151 Patton Ave, Asheville, NC 28801. TEL 828-271-4800, FAX 828-271-4876, NODC.Services@noaa.gov, http://www.ncdc.noaa.gov.

551.5 USA ISSN 0198-084X
LOCAL CLIMATOLOGICAL DATA. SANTA MARIA, CALIFORNIA. MONTHLY SUMMARY. Text in English. 19??. m. USD 5 per issue (effective 2009). back issues avail. **Document type:** *Bulletin, Government.* **Description:** Provides a monthly summary of temperature extremes, degree days, precipitation and winds, hourly precipitation and 3-hourly weather observations in Santa Maria, California.

Related titles: Online - full text ed.: USD 3 per issue (effective 2009); ◆ Cumulative ed. of: Local Climatological Data. Santa Maria, California. Annual Summary with Comparative Data. ISSN 0198-1005.
—Linda Hall.
Published by: U.S. National Climatic Data Center (Subsidiary of: U.S. Department of Commerce), Federal Bldg, 151 Patton Ave, Asheville, NC 28801. TEL 828-271-4800, FAX 828-271-4876, NODC.Services@noaa.gov, http://www.ncdc.noaa.gov.

551.5 USA ISSN 0198-2672
QC984.M52
LOCAL CLIMATOLOGICAL DATA. SAULT STE. MARIE, MICHIGAN. ANNUAL SUMMARY WITH COMPARATIVE DATA. Text in English. 19??. a. USD 39 combined subscription per issue includes 12 monthly summaries & one a. summary (effective 2009). back issues avail. **Document type:** *Bulletin, Government.* **Description:** Presents the monthly and annual average, resultant and fastest mile wind speed for the current year as well as the monthly and annual mean and fastest mile speed for a long period for Sault Ste. Marie, Michigan.
Related titles: Online - full text ed.: USD 29 per issue (effective 2009); ◆ Cumulative ed(s).: Local Climatological Data. Sault Ste. Marie, Michigan. Monthly Summary. ISSN 0198-2680.
Published by: U.S. National Climatic Data Center (Subsidiary of: U.S. Department of Commerce), Federal Bldg, 151 Patton Ave, Asheville, NC 28801. TEL 828-271-4800, FAX 828-271-4876, NODC.Services@noaa.gov, http://www.ncdc.noaa.gov.

551.5 USA ISSN 0198-2680
LOCAL CLIMATOLOGICAL DATA. SAULT STE. MARIE, MICHIGAN. MONTHLY SUMMARY. Text in English. 19??. m. USD 5 per issue (effective 2009). back issues avail. **Document type:** *Bulletin, Government.* **Description:** Provides a monthly summary of temperature extremes, degree days, precipitation and winds, hourly precipitation and 3-hourly weather observations in Sault Ste Marie, Michigan.
Related titles: Online - full text ed.: USD 3 per issue (effective 2009); ◆ Cumulative ed. of: Local Climatological Data. Sault Ste. Marie, Michigan. Annual Summary with Comparative Data. ISSN 0198-2672.
—Linda Hall.
Published by: U.S. National Climatic Data Center (Subsidiary of: U.S. Department of Commerce), Federal Bldg, 151 Patton Ave, Asheville, NC 28801. TEL 828-271-4800, FAX 828-271-4876, NODC.Services@noaa.gov, http://www.ncdc.noaa.gov.

551.5 USA ISSN 0198-1668
QC984.G42
LOCAL CLIMATOLOGICAL DATA. SAVANNAH, GEORGIA. ANNUAL SUMMARY WITH COMPARATIVE DATA. Text in English. 19??. a. USD 39 combined subscription per issue includes 12 monthly summaries & one a. summary (effective 2009). back issues avail. **Document type:** *Bulletin, Government.* **Description:** Presents the monthly and annual average, resultant and fastest mile wind speed for the current year as well as the monthly and annual mean and fastest mile speed for a long period for Savannah, Georgia.
Related titles: Online - full text ed.: USD 29 per issue (effective 2009); ◆ Cumulative ed(s).: Local Climatological Data. Savannah, Georgia. Monthly Summary. ISSN 0198-1676.
Published by: U.S. National Climatic Data Center (Subsidiary of: U.S. Department of Commerce), Federal Bldg, 151 Patton Ave, Asheville, NC 28801. TEL 828-271-4800, FAX 828-271-4876, NODC.Services@noaa.gov, http://www.ncdc.noaa.gov.

551.5 USA ISSN 0198-1676
LOCAL CLIMATOLOGICAL DATA. SAVANNAH, GEORGIA. MONTHLY SUMMARY. Text in English. 19??. m. USD 5 per issue (effective 2009). back issues avail. **Document type:** *Bulletin, Government.* **Description:** Provides a monthly summary of temperature extremes, degree days, precipitation and winds, hourly precipitation and 3-hourly weather observations in Savannah, Georgia.
Related titles: Online - full text ed.: USD 3 per issue (effective 2009); ◆ Cumulative ed. of: Local Climatological Data. Savannah, Georgia. Annual Summary with Comparative Data. ISSN 0198-1668.
—Linda Hall.
Published by: U.S. National Climatic Data Center (Subsidiary of: U.S. Department of Commerce), Federal Bldg, 151 Patton Ave, Asheville, NC 28801. TEL 828-271-4800, FAX 828-271-4876, NODC.Services@noaa.gov, http://www.ncdc.noaa.gov.

551.5 USA ISSN 0198-3210
LOCAL CLIMATOLOGICAL DATA. SCOTTSBLUFF, NEBRASKA. ANNUAL SUMMARY WITH COMPARATIVE DATA. Text in English. 19??. a. USD 39 combined subscription per issue includes 12 monthly summaries & one a. summary (effective 2009). back issues avail. **Document type:** *Bulletin, Government.* **Description:** Presents the monthly and annual average, resultant and fastest mile wind speed for the current year as well as the monthly and annual mean and fastest mile speed for a long period for Scottsbluff, Nebraska.
Related titles: Online - full text ed.: USD 29 per issue (effective 2009); ◆ Cumulative ed(s).: Local Climatological Data. Scottsbluff, Nebraska. Monthly Summary. ISSN 0198-3229.
Published by: U.S. National Climatic Data Center (Subsidiary of: U.S. Department of Commerce), Federal Bldg, 151 Patton Ave, Asheville, NC 28801. TEL 828-271-4800, FAX 828-271-4876, NODC.Services@noaa.gov, http://www.ncdc.noaa.gov.

551.5 USA ISSN 0198-3229
LOCAL CLIMATOLOGICAL DATA. SCOTTSBLUFF, NEBRASKA. MONTHLY SUMMARY. Text in English. 19??. m. USD 5 per issue (effective 2009). back issues avail. **Document type:** *Bulletin, Government.* **Description:** Provides a monthly summary of temperature extremes, degree days, precipitation and winds, hourly precipitation and 3-hourly weather observations in Scottsbluff, Nebraska.
Related titles: Online - full text ed.: USD 3 per issue (effective 2009); ◆ Cumulative ed. of: Local Climatological Data. Scottsbluff, Nebraska. Annual Summary with Comparative Data. ISSN 0198-3210.
—Linda Hall.
Published by: U.S. National Climatic Data Center (Subsidiary of: U.S. Department of Commerce), Federal Bldg, 151 Patton Ave, Asheville, NC 28801. TEL 828-271-4800, FAX 828-271-4876, NODC.Services@noaa.gov, http://www.ncdc.noaa.gov.

551.5 USA
LOCAL CLIMATOLOGICAL DATA. SEATTLE C.O., WASHINGTON. MONTHLY SUMMARY. Text in English. 198?. m. USD 5 per issue (effective 2004). **Document type:** *Bulletin, Government.*
Former titles (until 198?): Local Climatological Data. Seattle, Washington. National Weather Service Urban Site. Monthly Summary (0198-5477); (until 1984): Local Climatological Data. Seattle, Washington. Monthly Summary (0737-9986)
Related titles: Online - full content ed.
—Linda Hall.
Published by: U.S. National Climatic Data Center (Subsidiary of: U.S. Department of Commerce), Federal Bldg, 151 Patton Ave, Asheville, NC 28801. TEL 828-271-4800, FAX 828-271-4876, NODC.Services@noaa.gov, http://www.ncdc.noaa.gov.

551.5 USA ISSN 1528-7424
QC984.W2
LOCAL CLIMATOLOGICAL DATA. SEATTLE SAND POINT, WASHINGTON. W S F O SEATTLE SAND POINT. Text in English. 19??. a. USD 39 combined subscription per issue includes 12 monthly summaries & one a. summary (effective 2009). back issues avail. **Document type:** *Bulletin, Government.* **Description:** Contains summaries from major airport weather stations that include a daily account of temperature extremes, degree days, precipitation amounts and winds in Seattle Sand Point, Washington.
Related titles: Online - full text ed.: USD 29 per issue (effective 2009).
Published by: U.S. National Climatic Data Center (Subsidiary of: U.S. Department of Commerce), Federal Bldg, 151 Patton Ave, Asheville, NC 28801. TEL 828-271-4800, FAX 828-271-4876, NODC.Services@noaa.gov, http://www.ncdc.noaa.gov.

551.5 USA ISSN 0198-5450
QC984.W22
LOCAL CLIMATOLOGICAL DATA. SEATTLE, WASHINGTON. NATIONAL WEATHER SERVICE OFFICE. SEATTLE-TACOMA AIRPORT. MONTHLY SUMMARY. Text in English. 19??. m. USD 5 per issue (effective 2004). **Document type:** *Bulletin, Government.*
Related titles: Online - full content ed.; ◆ Cumulative ed. of: Local Climatological Data. Seattle, Washington. Seattle-Tacoma Airport. Annual Summary with Comparative Data. ISSN 0198-5442.
—Linda Hall.
Published by: U.S. National Climatic Data Center (Subsidiary of: U.S. Department of Commerce), Federal Bldg, 151 Patton Ave, Asheville, NC 28801. TEL 828-271-4800, FAX 828-271-4876, NODC.Services@noaa.gov, http://www.ncdc.noaa.gov.

551.5 USA ISSN 0198-5442
QC984.W22
LOCAL CLIMATOLOGICAL DATA. SEATTLE, WASHINGTON. SEATTLE-TACOMA AIRPORT. ANNUAL SUMMARY WITH COMPARATIVE DATA. Text in English. 19??. a. USD 39 combined subscription per issue includes 12 monthly summaries & one a. summary (effective 2009). back issues avail. **Document type:** *Bulletin, Government.* **Description:** Presents the monthly and annual average, resultant and fastest mile wind speed for the current year as well as the monthly and annual mean and fastest mile speed for a long period for Seattle-Tacoma Airport in Seattle, Washington.
Related titles: Online - full text ed.: USD 29 per issue (effective 2009); ◆ Cumulative ed(s).: Local Climatological Data. Seattle, Washington. National Weather Service Office. Seattle-Tacoma Airport. Monthly Summary. ISSN 0198-5450.
Published by: U.S. National Climatic Data Center (Subsidiary of: U.S. Department of Commerce), Federal Bldg, 151 Patton Ave, Asheville, NC 28801. TEL 828-271-4800, FAX 828-271-4876, NODC.Services@noaa.gov, http://www.ncdc.noaa.gov.

551.5 USA ISSN 0198-5833
LOCAL CLIMATOLOGICAL DATA. SHERIDAN, WYOMING. MONTHLY SUMMARY. Text in English. 19??. m. USD 5 per issue (effective 2009). back issues avail. **Document type:** *Bulletin, Government.* **Description:** Provides a monthly summary of temperature extremes, degree days, precipitation and winds, hourly precipitation and 3-hourly weather observations in Sheridan, Wyoming.
Related titles: Online - full text ed.: USD 3 per issue (effective 2009).
—Linda Hall.
Published by: U.S. National Climatic Data Center (Subsidiary of: U.S. Department of Commerce), Federal Bldg, 151 Patton Ave, Asheville, NC 28801. TEL 828-271-4800, FAX 828-271-4876, NODC.Services@noaa.gov, http://www.ncdc.noaa.gov.

551.5 USA ISSN 0198-2338
LOCAL CLIMATOLOGICAL DATA. SHREVEPORT, LOUISIANA. ANNUAL SUMMARY WITH COMPARATIVE DATA. Text in English. 19??. a. USD 39 combined subscription per issue includes 12 monthly summaries & one a. summary (effective 2009). back issues avail. **Document type:** *Bulletin, Government.* **Description:** Presents the monthly and annual average, resultant and fastest mile wind speed for the current year as well as the monthly and annual mean and fastest mile speed for a long period for Shreveport, Louisiana.
Related titles: Online - full text ed.: USD 29 per issue (effective 2009); ◆ Cumulative ed(s).: Local Climatological Data. Shreveport, Louisiana. Monthly Summary. ISSN 0198-2346.
Published by: U.S. National Climatic Data Center (Subsidiary of: U.S. Department of Commerce), Federal Bldg, 151 Patton Ave, Asheville, NC 28801. TEL 828-271-4800, FAX 828-271-4876, NODC.Services@noaa.gov, http://www.ncdc.noaa.gov.

551.5 USA ISSN 0198-2346
LOCAL CLIMATOLOGICAL DATA. SHREVEPORT, LOUISIANA. MONTHLY SUMMARY. Text in English. 19??. m. USD 5 per issue (effective 2009). back issues avail. **Document type:** *Bulletin, Government.* **Description:** Provides a monthly summary of temperature extremes, degree days, precipitation and winds, hourly precipitation and 3-hourly weather observations in Shreveport, Louisiana.
Related titles: Online - full text ed.: USD 3 per issue (effective 2009); ◆ Cumulative ed. of: Local Climatological Data. Shreveport, Louisiana. Annual Summary with Comparative Data. ISSN 0198-2338.
—Linda Hall.
Published by: U.S. National Climatic Data Center (Subsidiary of: U.S. Department of Commerce), Federal Bldg, 151 Patton Ave, Asheville, NC 28801. TEL 828-271-4800, FAX 828-271-4876, NODC.Services@noaa.gov, http://www.ncdc.noaa.gov.

551.5 USA ISSN 0198-2095
QC984.I82
LOCAL CLIMATOLOGICAL DATA. SIOUX CITY, IOWA. ANNUAL SUMMARY WITH COMPARATIVE DATA. Text in English. 19??. a. USD 39 combined subscription per issue includes 12 monthly summaries & one a. summary (effective 2009). back issues avail. **Document type:** *Bulletin, Government.* **Description:** Presents the monthly and annual average, resultant and fastest mile wind speed for the current year as well as the monthly and annual mean and fastest mile speed for a long period for Sioux City, Iowa.
Related titles: Online - full text ed.: USD 29 per issue (effective 2009); ◆ Cumulative ed(s).: Local Climatological Data. Sioux City, Iowa. Monthly Summary. ISSN 0198-2109.
Published by: U.S. National Climatic Data Center (Subsidiary of: U.S. Department of Commerce), Federal Bldg, 151 Patton Ave, Asheville, NC 28801. TEL 828-271-4800, FAX 828-271-4876, NODC.Services@noaa.gov, http://www.ncdc.noaa.gov.

551.5 USA ISSN 0198-2109
LOCAL CLIMATOLOGICAL DATA. SIOUX CITY, IOWA. MONTHLY SUMMARY. Text in English. 19??. m. USD 5 per issue (effective 2009). back issues avail. **Document type:** *Bulletin, Government.* **Description:** Provides a monthly summary of temperature extremes, degree days, precipitation and winds, hourly precipitation and 3-hourly weather observations in Sioux City, Iowa.
Related titles: Online - full text ed.: USD 3 per issue (effective 2009); ◆ Cumulative ed. of: Local Climatological Data. Sioux City, Iowa. Annual Summary with Comparative Data. ISSN 0198-2095.
—Linda Hall.
Published by: U.S. National Climatic Data Center (Subsidiary of: U.S. Department of Commerce), Federal Bldg, 151 Patton Ave, Asheville, NC 28801. TEL 828-271-4800, FAX 828-271-4876, NODC.Services@noaa.gov, http://www.ncdc.noaa.gov.

551.5 USA ISSN 0198-4748
QC984.S82
LOCAL CLIMATOLOGICAL DATA. SIOUX FALLS, SOUTH DAKOTA. ANNUAL SUMMARY WITH COMPARATIVE DATA. Text in English. 19??. a. USD 3 combined subscription per issue (print, online & CD-ROM eds.) (effective 2008). back issues avail. **Document type:** *Bulletin, Government.* **Description:** Presents the monthly and annual average, resultant and fastest mile wind speed for the current year as well as the monthly and annual mean and fastest mile speed for a long period for Sioux Falls, South Dakota.
Related titles: CD-ROM ed.; Online - full text ed.; ◆ Cumulative ed(s).: Local Climatological Data. Sioux Falls, South Dakota. Monthly Summary. ISSN 0198-4756.
Published by: U.S. National Climatic Data Center (Subsidiary of: U.S. Department of Commerce), Federal Bldg, 151 Patton Ave, Asheville, NC 28801. TEL 828-271-4800, FAX 828-271-4876, NODC.Services@noaa.gov, http://www.ncdc.noaa.gov.

551.5 USA ISSN 0198-4756
LOCAL CLIMATOLOGICAL DATA. SIOUX FALLS, SOUTH DAKOTA. MONTHLY SUMMARY. Text in English. 19??. m. USD 5 per issue (effective 2009). back issues avail. **Document type:** *Bulletin, Government.* **Description:** Provides a monthly summary of temperature extremes, degree days, precipitation and winds, hourly precipitation and 3-hourly weather observations in Sioux Falls, South Dakota.
Related titles: Online - full text ed.: USD 3 per issue (effective 2009); ◆ Cumulative ed. of: Local Climatological Data. Sioux Falls, South Dakota. Annual Summary with Comparative Data. ISSN 0198-4748.
—Linda Hall.
Published by: U.S. National Climatic Data Center (Subsidiary of: U.S. Department of Commerce), Federal Bldg, 151 Patton Ave, Asheville, NC 28801. TEL 828-271-4800, FAX 828-271-4876, NODC.Services@noaa.gov, http://www.ncdc.noaa.gov.

551.5 USA ISSN 0198-201X
LOCAL CLIMATOLOGICAL DATA. SOUTH BEND, INDIANA. ANNUAL SUMMARY WITH COMPARATIVE DATA. Text in English. 19??. a. USD 39 combined subscription per issue includes 12 monthly summaries & one a. summary (effective 2009). back issues avail. **Document type:** *Bulletin, Government.* **Description:** Presents the monthly and annual average, resultant and fastest mile wind speed for the current year as well as the monthly and annual mean and fastest mile speed for a long period for South Bend, Indiana.
Related titles: Online - full text ed.: USD 29 per issue (effective 2009); ◆ Cumulative ed(s).: Local Climatological Data. South Bend, Indiana. Monthly Summary. ISSN 0198-2028.
Published by: U.S. National Climatic Data Center (Subsidiary of: U.S. Department of Commerce), Federal Bldg, 151 Patton Ave, Asheville, NC 28801. TEL 828-271-4800, FAX 828-271-4876, NODC.Services@noaa.gov, http://www.ncdc.noaa.gov.

551.5 USA ISSN 0198-2028
LOCAL CLIMATOLOGICAL DATA. SOUTH BEND, INDIANA. MONTHLY SUMMARY. Text in English. 19??. m. USD 5 per issue (effective 2009). back issues avail. **Document type:** *Bulletin, Government.* **Description:** Provides a monthly summary of temperature extremes, degree days, precipitation and winds, hourly precipitation and 3-hourly weather observations in South Bend, Indiana.
Related titles: Online - full text ed.: USD 3 per issue (effective 2009); ◆ Cumulative ed. of: Local Climatological Data. South Bend, Indiana. Annual Summary with Comparative Data. ISSN 0198-201X.
—Linda Hall.
Published by: U.S. National Climatic Data Center (Subsidiary of: U.S. Department of Commerce), Federal Bldg, 151 Patton Ave, Asheville, NC 28801. TEL 828-271-4800, FAX 828-271-4876, NODC.Services@noaa.gov, http://www.ncdc.noaa.gov.

551.5 USA ISSN 0198-5485
QC984.W2
LOCAL CLIMATOLOGICAL DATA. SPOKANE, WASHINGTON. ANNUAL SUMMARY WITH COMPARATIVE DATA. Text in English. 19??. a. USD 39 combined subscription per issue includes 12 monthly summaries & one a. summary (effective 2009). back issues avail. **Document type:** *Bulletin, Government.* **Description:** Presents the monthly and annual average, resultant and fastest mile wind speed for the current year as well as the monthly and annual mean and fastest mile speed for a long period for Spokane, Washington.
Related titles: Online - full text ed.: USD 29 per issue (effective 2009); ◆ Cumulative ed(s).: Local Climatological Data. Spokane, Washington. Monthly Summary. ISSN 0198-5493.

Published by: U.S. National Climatic Data Center (Subsidiary of: U.S. Department of Commerce), Federal Bldg, 151 Patton Ave, Asheville, NC 28801. TEL 828-271-4800, FAX 828-271-4876, NODC.Services@noaa.gov, http://www.ncdc.noaa.gov.

551.5 USA ISSN 0198-5493
QC984.W2
LOCAL CLIMATOLOGICAL DATA. SPOKANE, WASHINGTON. MONTHLY SUMMARY. Text in English. 19??. m. USD 5 per issue (effective 2009). back issues avail. **Document type:** *Bulletin, Government.* **Description:** Provides a monthly summary of temperature extremes, degree days, precipitation and winds, hourly precipitation and 3-hourly weather observations in Spokane, Washington.
Related titles: Online - full text ed.: USD 3 per issue (effective 2009); ◆ Cumulative ed. of: Local Climatological Data. Spokane, Washington. Annual Summary with Comparative Data. ISSN 0198-5485.
—Linda Hall.
Published by: U.S. National Climatic Data Center (Subsidiary of: U.S. Department of Commerce), Federal Bldg, 151 Patton Ave, Asheville, NC 28801. TEL 828-271-4800, FAX 828-271-4876, NODC.Services@noaa.gov, http://www.ncdc.noaa.gov.

551.5 USA ISSN 0198-1927
QC984.I32
LOCAL CLIMATOLOGICAL DATA. SPRINGFIELD, ILLINOIS. ANNUAL SUMMARY WITH COMPARATIVE DATA. Text in English. 19??. a. USD 39 combined subscription per issue includes 12 monthly summaries & one a. summary (effective 2009). back issues avail. **Document type:** *Bulletin, Government.* **Description:** Presents the monthly and annual average, resultant and fastest mile wind speed for the current year as well as the monthly and annual mean and fastest mile speed for a long period for Springfield, Illinois.
Related titles: Online - full text ed.: USD 29 per issue (effective 2009); ◆ Cumulative ed(s).: Local Climatological Data. Springfield, Illinois. Monthly Summary. ISSN 0198-1935.
Published by: U.S. National Climatic Data Center (Subsidiary of: U.S. Department of Commerce), Federal Bldg, 151 Patton Ave, Asheville, NC 28801. TEL 828-271-4800, FAX 828-271-4876, NODC.Services@noaa.gov, http://www.ncdc.noaa.gov.

551.5 USA ISSN 0198-1935
LOCAL CLIMATOLOGICAL DATA. SPRINGFIELD, ILLINOIS. MONTHLY SUMMARY. Text in English. 19??. m. USD 5 per issue (effective 2009). back issues avail. **Document type:** *Bulletin, Government.* **Description:** Provides a monthly summary of temperature extremes, degree days, precipitation and winds, hourly precipitation and 3-hourly weather observations in Springfield, Illinois.
Related titles: Online - full text ed.: USD 3 per issue (effective 2009); ◆ Cumulative ed. of: Local Climatological Data. Springfield, Illinois. Annual Summary with Comparative Data. ISSN 0198-1927.
—Linda Hall.
Published by: U.S. National Climatic Data Center (Subsidiary of: U.S. Department of Commerce), Federal Bldg, 151 Patton Ave, Asheville, NC 28801. TEL 828-271-4800, FAX 828-271-4876, NODC.Services@noaa.gov, http://www.ncdc.noaa.gov.

551.5 USA ISSN 0198-2923
QC984.M82
LOCAL CLIMATOLOGICAL DATA. SPRINGFIELD, MISSOURI. ANNUAL SUMMARY WITH COMPARATIVE DATA. Text in English. 19??. a. USD 39 combined subscription per issue includes 12 monthly summaries & one a. summary (effective 2009). back issues avail. **Document type:** *Bulletin, Government.* **Description:** Presents the monthly and annual average, resultant and fastest mile wind speed for the current year as well as the monthly and annual mean and fastest mile speed for a long period for Springfield, Missouri.
Related titles: Online - full text ed.: USD 29 per issue (effective 2009); ◆ Cumulative ed(s).: Local Climatological Data. Springfield, Missouri. Monthly Summary. ISSN 0198-2931.
Published by: U.S. National Climatic Data Center (Subsidiary of: U.S. Department of Commerce), Federal Bldg, 151 Patton Ave, Asheville, NC 28801. TEL 828-271-4800, FAX 828-271-4876, NODC.Services@noaa.gov, http://www.ncdc.noaa.gov.

551.5 USA ISSN 0198-2931
LOCAL CLIMATOLOGICAL DATA. SPRINGFIELD, MISSOURI. MONTHLY SUMMARY. Text in English. 19??. m. USD 5 per issue (effective 2009). back issues avail. **Document type:** *Bulletin, Government.* **Description:** Provides a monthly summary of temperature extremes, degree days, precipitation and winds, hourly precipitation and 3-hourly weather observations in Springfield, Missouri.
Related titles: Online - full text ed.: USD 3 per issue (effective 2009); ◆ Cumulative ed. of: Local Climatological Data. Springfield, Missouri. Annual Summary with Comparative Data. ISSN 0198-2923.
—Linda Hall.
Published by: U.S. National Climatic Data Center (Subsidiary of: U.S. Department of Commerce), Federal Bldg, 151 Patton Ave, Asheville, NC 28801. TEL 828-271-4800, FAX 828-271-4876, NODC.Services@noaa.gov, http://www.ncdc.noaa.gov.

551.5 USA ISSN 0198-2907
QC984.M5
LOCAL CLIMATOLOGICAL DATA. ST. LOUIS, MISSOURI. ANNUAL SUMMARY WITH COMPARATIVE DATA. Text in English. 19??. a. USD 39 combined subscription per issue includes 12 monthly summaries & one a. summary (effective 2009). back issues avail. **Document type:** *Bulletin, Government.* **Description:** Presents the monthly and annual average, resultant and fastest mile wind speed for the current year as well as the monthly and annual mean and fastest mile speed for a long period for St. Louis, Missouri.
Related titles: Online - full text ed.: USD 29 per issue (effective 2009); ◆ Cumulative ed(s).: Local Climatological Data. St. Louis, Missouri. Monthly Summary. ISSN 0198-2915.
Published by: U.S. National Climatic Data Center (Subsidiary of: U.S. Department of Commerce), Federal Bldg, 151 Patton Ave, Asheville, NC 28801. TEL 828-271-4800, FAX 828-271-4876, NODC.Services@noaa.gov, http://www.ncdc.noaa.gov.

551.5 USA ISSN 0198-2915
QC984.M5
LOCAL CLIMATOLOGICAL DATA. ST. LOUIS, MISSOURI. MONTHLY SUMMARY. Text in English. 19??. m. USD 5 per issue (effective 2009). back issues avail. **Document type:** *Bulletin, Government.* **Description:** Provides a monthly summary of temperature extremes, degree days, precipitation and winds, hourly precipitation and 3-hourly weather observations in St. Louis, Missouri.
Related titles: Online - full text ed.: USD 3 per issue (effective 2009); ◆ Cumulative ed. of: Local Climatological Data. St. Louis, Missouri. Annual Summary with Comparative Data. ISSN 0198-2907.
—Linda Hall.
Published by: U.S. National Climatic Data Center (Subsidiary of: U.S. Department of Commerce), Federal Bldg, 151 Patton Ave, Asheville, NC 28801. TEL 828-271-4800, FAX 828-271-4876, NODC.Services@noaa.gov, http://www.ncdc.noaa.gov.

551.5 USA ISSN 0198-0513
QC984.A42
LOCAL CLIMATOLOGICAL DATA. ST. PAUL ISLAND, ALASKA. ANNUAL SUMMARY WITH COMPARATIVE DATA. Text in English. 19??. a. USD 39 combined subscription per issue includes 12 monthly summaries & one a. summary (effective 2009). back issues avail. **Document type:** *Bulletin, Government.* **Description:** Presents the monthly and annual average, resultant and fastest mile wind speed for the current year as well as the monthly and annual mean and fastest mile speed for a long period for St. Paul Island, Alaska.
Related titles: Online - full text ed.: USD 29 per issue (effective 2009); ◆ Cumulative ed(s).: Local Climatological Data. St. Paul Island, Alaska. Monthly Summary. ISSN 0198-0416.
Published by: U.S. National Climatic Data Center (Subsidiary of: U.S. Department of Commerce), Federal Bldg, 151 Patton Ave, Asheville, NC 28801. TEL 828-271-4800, FAX 828-271-4876, NODC.Services@noaa.gov, http://www.ncdc.noaa.gov.

551.5 USA ISSN 0198-0416
QC984.A42
LOCAL CLIMATOLOGICAL DATA. ST. PAUL ISLAND, ALASKA. MONTHLY SUMMARY. Text in English. 19??. m. USD 5 per issue (effective 2009). back issues avail. **Document type:** *Bulletin, Government.* **Description:** Provides a monthly summary of temperature extremes, degree days, precipitation and winds, hourly precipitation and 3-hourly weather observations in St. Paul Island, Alaska.
Related titles: Online - full text ed.: USD 3 per issue (effective 2009); ◆ Cumulative ed. of: Local Climatological Data. St. Paul Island, Alaska. Annual Summary with Comparative Data. ISSN 0198-0513.
—Linda Hall.
Published by: U.S. National Climatic Data Center (Subsidiary of: U.S. Department of Commerce), Federal Bldg, 151 Patton Ave, Asheville, NC 28801. TEL 828-271-4800, FAX 828-271-4876, NODC.Services@noaa.gov, http://www.ncdc.noaa.gov.

551.5 USA ISSN 0198-5507
LOCAL CLIMATOLOGICAL DATA. STAMPEDE PASS, WASHINGTON. ANNUAL SUMMARY WITH COMPARATIVE DATA. Text in English. 19??. a. USD 39 combined subscription per issue includes 12 monthly summaries & one a. summary (effective 2009). back issues avail. **Document type:** *Bulletin, Government.* **Description:** Presents the monthly and annual average, resultant and fastest mile wind speed for the current year as well as the monthly and annual mean and fastest mile speed for a long period for Stampede Pass, Washington.
Related titles: Online - full text ed.: USD 29 per issue (effective 2009).
Published by: U.S. National Climatic Data Center (Subsidiary of: U.S. Department of Commerce), Federal Bldg, 151 Patton Ave, Asheville, NC 28801. TEL 828-271-4800, FAX 828-271-4876, NODC.Services@noaa.gov, http://www.ncdc.noaa.gov.

551.5 USA ISSN 0198-1013
LOCAL CLIMATOLOGICAL DATA. STOCKTON, CALIFORNIA. ANNUAL SUMMARY WITH COMPARATIVE DATA. Text in English. 19??. a. USD 39 combined subscription per issue includes 12 monthly summaries & one a. summary (effective 2009). back issues avail. **Document type:** *Bulletin, Government.* **Description:** Presents the monthly and annual average, resultant and fastest mile wind speed for the current year as well as the monthly and annual mean and fastest mile speed for a long period for Stockton, California.
Related titles: Online - full text ed.: USD 29 per issue (effective 2009); ◆ Cumulative ed(s).: Local Climatological Data. Stockton, California. Monthly Summary. ISSN 0198-0858.
Published by: U.S. National Climatic Data Center (Subsidiary of: U.S. Department of Commerce), Federal Bldg, 151 Patton Ave, Asheville, NC 28801. TEL 828-271-4800, FAX 828-271-4876, NODC.Services@noaa.gov, http://www.ncdc.noaa.gov.

551.5 USA ISSN 0198-0858
LOCAL CLIMATOLOGICAL DATA. STOCKTON, CALIFORNIA. MONTHLY SUMMARY. Text in English. 19??. m. USD 5 per issue (effective 2009). back issues avail. **Document type:** *Bulletin, Government.* **Description:** Provides a monthly summary of temperature extremes, degree days, precipitation and winds, hourly precipitation and 3-hourly weather observations in Stockton, California.
Related titles: Online - full text ed.: USD 3 per issue (effective 2009); ◆ Cumulative ed. of: Local Climatological Data. Stockton, California. Annual Summary with Comparative Data. ISSN 0198-1013.
—Linda Hall.
Published by: U.S. National Climatic Data Center (Subsidiary of: U.S. Department of Commerce), Federal Bldg, 151 Patton Ave, Asheville, NC 28801. TEL 828-271-4800, FAX 828-271-4876, NODC.Services@noaa.gov, http://www.ncdc.noaa.gov.

551.5 USA ISSN 0198-3679
LOCAL CLIMATOLOGICAL DATA. SYRACUSE, NEW YORK. ANNUAL SUMMARY WITH COMPARATIVE DATA. Text in English. 19??. a. USD 39 combined subscription per issue includes 12 monthly summaries & one a. summary (effective 2009). back issues avail. **Document type:** *Bulletin, Government.* **Description:** Presents the monthly and annual average, resultant and fastest mile wind speed for the current year as well as the monthly and annual mean and fastest mile speed for a long period for Syracuse, New York.
Related titles: Online - full text ed.: USD 29 per issue (effective 2009); ◆ Cumulative ed(s).: Local Climatological Data. Syracuse, New York. Monthly Summary. ISSN 0198-3687.
Published by: U.S. National Climatic Data Center (Subsidiary of: U.S. Department of Commerce), Federal Bldg, 151 Patton Ave, Asheville, NC 28801. TEL 828-271-4800, FAX 828-271-4876, NODC.Services@noaa.gov, http://www.ncdc.noaa.gov.

551.5 USA ISSN 0198-3687
QC925.1.U8
LOCAL CLIMATOLOGICAL DATA. SYRACUSE, NEW YORK. MONTHLY SUMMARY. Text in English. m. USD 5 per issue (effective 2009). back issues avail. **Document type:** *Bulletin, Government.* **Description:** Provides a monthly summary of temperature extremes, degree days, precipitation and winds, hourly precipitation and 3-hourly weather observations in Syracuse, New York.
Formerly (until 1975): Local Climatological Data. Syracuse, N.Y.
Related titles: Online - full text ed.: USD 3 per issue (effective 2009); ◆ Cumulative ed. of: Local Climatological Data. Syracuse, New York. Annual Summary with Comparative Data. ISSN 0198-3679.
—Linda Hall.
Published by: U.S. National Climatic Data Center (Subsidiary of: U.S. Department of Commerce), Federal Bldg, 151 Patton Ave, Asheville, NC 28801. TEL 828-271-4800, FAX 828-271-4876, NODC.Services@noaa.gov, http://www.ncdc.noaa.gov.

551.5 USA ISSN 0198-0521
QC984.A42
LOCAL CLIMATOLOGICAL DATA. TALKEETNA, ALASKA. ANNUAL SUMMARY WITH COMPARATIVE DATA. Text in English. 19??. a. USD 39 combined subscription per issue includes 12 monthly summaries & one a. summary (effective 2009). back issues avail. **Document type:** *Bulletin, Government.* **Description:** Presents the monthly and annual average, resultant and fastest mile wind speed for the current year as well as the monthly and annual mean and fastest mile speed for a long period for Talkeetna, Alaska.
Related titles: Online - full text ed.: USD 29 per issue (effective 2009); ◆ Cumulative ed(s).: Local Climatological Data. Talkeetna, Alaska. Monthly Summary. ISSN 0198-0424.
Published by: U.S. National Climatic Data Center (Subsidiary of: U.S. Department of Commerce), Federal Bldg, 151 Patton Ave, Asheville, NC 28801. TEL 828-271-4800, FAX 828-271-4876, NODC.Services@noaa.gov, http://www.ncdc.noaa.gov.

551.5 USA ISSN 0198-0424
QC984.A42
LOCAL CLIMATOLOGICAL DATA. TALKEETNA, ALASKA. MONTHLY SUMMARY. Text in English. 19??. m. USD 5 per issue (effective 2009). back issues avail. **Document type:** *Bulletin, Government.* **Description:** Provides a monthly summary of temperature extremes, degree days, precipitation and winds, hourly precipitation and 3-hourly weather observations in Talkeetna, Alaska.
Related titles: Online - full text ed.: USD 3 per issue (effective 2009); ◆ Cumulative ed. of: Local Climatological Data. Talkeetna, Alaska. Annual Summary with Comparative Data. ISSN 0198-0521.
—Linda Hall.
Published by: U.S. National Climatic Data Center (Subsidiary of: U.S. Department of Commerce), Federal Bldg, 151 Patton Ave, Asheville, NC 28801. TEL 828-271-4800, FAX 828-271-4876, NODC.Services@noaa.gov, http://www.ncdc.noaa.gov.

551.5 USA ISSN 0198-1293
LOCAL CLIMATOLOGICAL DATA. TALLAHASSEE, FLORIDA. ANNUAL SUMMARY WITH COMPARATIVE DATA. Text in English. 19??. a. USD 39 combined subscription per issue includes 12 monthly summaries & one a. summary (effective 2009). back issues avail. **Document type:** *Bulletin, Government.* **Description:** Presents the monthly and annual average, resultant and fastest mile wind speed for the current year as well as the monthly and annual mean and fastest mile speed for a long period for Tallahassee, Florida.
Related titles: Online - full text ed.: USD 29 per issue (effective 2009); ◆ Cumulative ed(s).: Local Climatological Data. Tallahassee, Florida. Monthly Summary. ISSN 0198-1412.
Published by: U.S. National Climatic Data Center (Subsidiary of: U.S. Department of Commerce), Federal Bldg, 151 Patton Ave, Asheville, NC 28801. TEL 828-271-4800, FAX 828-271-4876, NODC.Services@noaa.gov, http://www.ncdc.noaa.gov.

551.5 USA ISSN 0198-1412
LOCAL CLIMATOLOGICAL DATA. TALLAHASSEE, FLORIDA. MONTHLY SUMMARY. Text in English. 19??. m. USD 5 per issue (effective 2009). back issues avail. **Document type:** *Bulletin, Government.* **Description:** Provides a monthly summary of temperature extremes, degree days, precipitation and winds, hourly precipitation and 3-hourly weather observations in Tallahassee, Florida.
Related titles: Online - full text ed.: USD 3 per issue (effective 2009); ◆ Cumulative ed. of: Local Climatological Data. Tallahassee, Florida. Annual Summary with Comparative Data. ISSN 0198-1293.
—Linda Hall.
Published by: U.S. National Climatic Data Center (Subsidiary of: U.S. Department of Commerce), Federal Bldg, 151 Patton Ave, Asheville, NC 28801. TEL 828-271-4800, FAX 828-271-4876, NODC.Services@noaa.gov, http://www.ncdc.noaa.gov.

551.5 USA ISSN 0198-1307
LOCAL CLIMATOLOGICAL DATA. TAMPA, FLORIDA. ANNUAL SUMMARY WITH COMPARATIVE DATA. Text in English. 19??. a. USD 39 combined subscription per issue includes 12 monthly summaries & one a. summary (effective 2009). back issues avail. **Document type:** *Bulletin, Government.* **Description:** Presents the monthly and annual average, resultant and fastest mile wind speed for the current year as well as the monthly and annual mean and fastest mile speed for a long period for Tampa, Florida.
Related titles: Online - full text ed.: USD 29 per issue (effective 2009); ◆ Cumulative ed(s).: Local Climatological Data. Tampa, Florida. Monthly Summary. ISSN 0198-1420.
Published by: U.S. National Climatic Data Center (Subsidiary of: U.S. Department of Commerce), Federal Bldg, 151 Patton Ave, Asheville, NC 28801. TEL 828-271-4800, FAX 828-271-4876, NODC.Services@noaa.gov, http://www.ncdc.noaa.gov.

551.5 USA ISSN 0198-1420
LOCAL CLIMATOLOGICAL DATA. TAMPA, FLORIDA. MONTHLY SUMMARY. Text in English. 19??. m. USD 5 per issue (effective 2009). back issues avail. **Document type:** *Bulletin, Government.* **Description:** Provides a monthly summary of temperature extremes, degree days, precipitation and winds, hourly precipitation and 3-hourly weather observations in Tampa, Florida.

M

Related titles: Online - full text ed.: USD 3 per issue (effective 2009); ◆ Cumulative ed. of: Local Climatological Data. Tampa, Florida. Annual Summary with Comparative Data. ISSN 0198-1307.
—Linda Hall.
Published by: U.S. National Climatic Data Center (Subsidiary of: U.S. Department of Commerce), Federal Bldg, 151 Patton Ave, Asheville, NC 28801. TEL 828-271-4800, FAX 828-271-4876, NODC.Services@noaa.gov, http://www.ncdc.noaa.gov.

551.5 USA ISSN 0198-4012
LOCAL CLIMATOLOGICAL DATA. TOLEDO, OHIO. ANNUAL SUMMARY WITH COMPARATIVE DATA. Text in English. 19??. a. USD 39 combined subscription per issue includes 12 monthly summaries & one a. summary (effective 2009). back issues avail. **Document type:** *Bulletin, Government.* **Description:** Presents the monthly and annual average, resultant and fastest mile wind speed for the current year as well as the monthly and annual mean and fastest mile speed for a long period for Toledo, Ohio.
Related titles: Online - full text ed.: USD 29 per issue (effective 2009); ◆ Cumulative ed(s).: Local Climatological Data. Toledo, Ohio. Monthly Summary. ISSN 0198-4020.
Published by: U.S. National Climatic Data Center (Subsidiary of: U.S. Department of Commerce), Federal Bldg, 151 Patton Ave, Asheville, NC 28801. TEL 828-271-4800, FAX 828-271-4876, NODC.Services@noaa.gov, http://www.ncdc.noaa.gov.

551.5 USA ISSN 0198-4020
LOCAL CLIMATOLOGICAL DATA. TOLEDO, OHIO. MONTHLY SUMMARY. Text in English. 19??. m. USD 5 per issue (effective 2009). back issues avail. **Document type:** *Bulletin, Government.* **Description:** Provides a monthly summary of temperature extremes, degree days, precipitation and winds, hourly precipitation and 3-hourly weather observations in Toledo, Ohio.
Related titles: Online - full text ed.: USD 3 per issue (effective 2009); ◆ Cumulative ed. of: Local Climatological Data. Toledo, Ohio. Annual Summary with Comparative Data. ISSN 0198-4012.
—Linda Hall.
Published by: U.S. National Climatic Data Center (Subsidiary of: U.S. Department of Commerce), Federal Bldg, 151 Patton Ave, Asheville, NC 28801. TEL 828-271-4800, FAX 828-271-4876, NODC.Services@noaa.gov, http://www.ncdc.noaa.gov.

551.5 USA ISSN 0198-2192
QC984.K22
LOCAL CLIMATOLOGICAL DATA. TOPEKA, KANSAS. ANNUAL SUMMARY WITH COMPARATIVE DATA. Text in English. 19??. a. USD 39 combined subscription per issue includes 12 monthly summaries & one a. summary (effective 2009). back issues avail. **Document type:** *Bulletin, Government.* **Description:** Presents the monthly and annual average, resultant and fastest mile wind speed for the current year as well as the monthly and annual mean and fastest mile speed for a long period for Topeka, Kansas.
Related titles: Online - full text ed.: USD 29 per issue (effective 2009); ◆ Cumulative ed(s).: Local Climatological Data. Topeka, Kansas. Monthly Summary. ISSN 0198-2206.
Published by: U.S. National Climatic Data Center (Subsidiary of: U.S. Department of Commerce), Federal Bldg, 151 Patton Ave, Asheville, NC 28801. TEL 828-271-4800, FAX 828-271-4876, NODC.Services@noaa.gov, http://www.ncdc.noaa.gov.

551.5 USA ISSN 0198-2206
LOCAL CLIMATOLOGICAL DATA. TOPEKA, KANSAS. MONTHLY SUMMARY. Text in English. 19??. m. USD 5 per issue (effective 2009). back issues avail. **Document type:** *Government.* **Description:** Provides a monthly summary of temperature extremes, degree days, precipitation and winds, hourly precipitation and 3-hourly weather observations in Topeka, Kansas.
Related titles: Online - full text ed.: USD 3 per issue (effective 2009); ◆ Cumulative ed. of: Local Climatological Data. Topeka, Kansas. Annual Summary with Comparative Data. ISSN 0198-2192.
—Linda Hall.
Published by: U.S. National Climatic Data Center (Subsidiary of: U.S. Department of Commerce), Federal Bldg, 151 Patton Ave, Asheville, NC 28801. TEL 828-271-4800, FAX 828-271-4876, NODC.Services@noaa.gov, http://www.ncdc.noaa.gov.

551.5 USA ISSN 0198-4403
LOCAL CLIMATOLOGICAL DATA. TRUK CAROLINE ISLAND PACIFIC. MONTHLY SUMMARY. Text in English. m. USD 5 per issue (effective 2009). **Document type:** *Bulletin, Government.*
Related titles: Online - full text ed.: USD 3 per issue (effective 2009); ◆ Cumulative ed. of: Local Climatological Data. Truk, Eastern Caroline Island, Pacific. Annual Summary with Comparative Data. ISSN 0198-439X.
—Linda Hall.
Published by: U.S. National Climatic Data Center (Subsidiary of: U.S. Department of Commerce), Federal Bldg, 151 Patton Ave, Asheville, NC 28801. TEL 828-271-4800, FAX 828-271-4876, NODC.Services@noaa.gov, http://www.ncdc.noaa.gov.

551.5 USA ISSN 0198-439X
LOCAL CLIMATOLOGICAL DATA. TRUK, EASTERN CAROLINE ISLAND, PACIFIC. ANNUAL SUMMARY WITH COMPARATIVE DATA. Text in English. 19??. a. **Document type:** *Bulletin, Government.*
Related titles: Online - full content ed.; ◆ Cumulative ed(s).: Local Climatological Data. Truk Caroline Island Pacific. Monthly Summary. ISSN 0198-4403.
Published by: U.S. National Climatic Data Center (Subsidiary of: U.S. Department of Commerce), Federal Bldg, 151 Patton Ave, Asheville, NC 28801. TEL 828-271-4800, FAX 828-271-4876, NODC.Services@noaa.gov, http://www.ncdc.noaa.gov.

551.5 USA ISSN 0198-0580
LOCAL CLIMATOLOGICAL DATA. TUCSON, ARIZONA. ANNUAL SUMMARY WITH COMPARATIVE DATA. Text in English. 19??. a. USD 39 combined subscription per issue includes 12 monthly summaries & one a. summary (effective 2009). back issues avail. **Document type:** *Bulletin, Government.* **Description:** Presents the monthly and annual average, resultant and fastest mile wind speed for the current year as well as the monthly and annual mean and fastest mile speed for a long period for Tucson, Arizona.
Related titles: Online - full text ed.: USD 29 per issue (effective 2009); ◆ Cumulative ed(s).: Local Climatological Data. Tucson, Arizona. Monthly Summary. ISSN 0198-0483.
Published by: U.S. National Climatic Data Center (Subsidiary of: U.S. Department of Commerce), Federal Bldg, 151 Patton Ave, Asheville, NC 28801. TEL 828-271-4800, FAX 828-271-4876, NODC.Services@noaa.gov, http://www.ncdc.noaa.gov.

551.5 USA ISSN 0198-0483
LOCAL CLIMATOLOGICAL DATA. TUCSON, ARIZONA. MONTHLY SUMMARY. Text in English. 19??. m. USD 5 per issue (effective 2009). back issues avail. **Document type:** *Bulletin, Government.* **Description:** Provides a monthly summary of temperature extremes, degree days, precipitation and winds, hourly precipitation and 3-hourly weather observations in Tucson, Arizona.
Related titles: Online - full text ed.: USD 3 per issue (effective 2009); ◆ Cumulative ed. of: Local Climatological Data. Tucson, Arizona. Annual Summary with Comparative Data. ISSN 0198-0580.
—Linda Hall.
Published by: U.S. National Climatic Data Center (Subsidiary of: U.S. Department of Commerce), Federal Bldg, 151 Patton Ave, Asheville, NC 28801. TEL 828-271-4800, FAX 828-271-4876, ncdc.info@noaa.gov, http://www.ncdc.noaa.gov.

551.5 USA ISSN 0198-4071
QC984.O52
LOCAL CLIMATOLOGICAL DATA. TULSA, OKLAHOMA. ANNUAL SUMMARY WITH COMPARATIVE DATA. Text in English. 19??. a. USD 39 combined subscription per issue includes 12 monthly summaries & one a. summary (effective 2009). back issues avail. **Document type:** *Bulletin, Government.* **Description:** Presents the monthly and annual average, resultant and fastest mile wind speed for the current year as well as the monthly and annual mean and fastest mile speed for a long period for Tulsa, Oklahoma.
Related titles: Online - full text ed.: USD 29 per issue (effective 2009); ◆ Cumulative ed(s).: Local Climatological Data. Tulsa, Oklahoma. Monthly Summary. ISSN 0198-408X.
Published by: U.S. National Climatic Data Center (Subsidiary of: U.S. Department of Commerce), Federal Bldg, 151 Patton Ave, Asheville, NC 28801. TEL 828-271-4800, FAX 828-271-4876, NODC.Services@noaa.gov, http://www.ncdc.noaa.gov.

551.5 USA ISSN 0198-408X
LOCAL CLIMATOLOGICAL DATA. TULSA, OKLAHOMA. MONTHLY SUMMARY. Text in English. 19??. m. USD 5 per issue (effective 2009). back issues avail. **Document type:** *Bulletin, Government.* **Description:** Provides a monthly summary of temperature extremes, degree days, precipitation and winds, hourly precipitation and 3-hourly weather observations in Tulsa, Oklahoma.
Related titles: Online - full text ed.: USD 3 per issue (effective 2009); ◆ Cumulative ed. of: Local Climatological Data. Tulsa, Oklahoma. Annual Summary with Comparative Data. ISSN 0198-4071.
—Linda Hall.
Published by: U.S. National Climatic Data Center (Subsidiary of: U.S. Department of Commerce), Federal Bldg, 151 Patton Ave, Asheville, NC 28801. TEL 828-271-4800, FAX 828-271-4876, NODC.Services@noaa.gov, http://www.ncdc.noaa.gov.

551.5 USA ISSN 0742-8782
LOCAL CLIMATOLOGICAL DATA. TUPELO, MISSISSIPPI. ANNUAL SUMMARY WITH COMPARATIVE DATA. Text in English. 19??. a. USD 39 combined subscription per issue includes 12 monthly summaries & one a. summary (effective 2009). back issues avail. **Document type:** *Bulletin, Government.* **Description:** Presents the monthly and annual average, resultant and fastest mile wind speed for the current year as well as the monthly and annual mean and fastest mile speed for a long period for Tupelo, Mississippi.
Related titles: Online - full text ed.: USD 29 per issue (effective 2009); ◆ Cumulative ed(s).: Local Climatological Data. Tupelo, Missouri. Monthly Summary. ISSN 0739-7259.
Published by: U.S. National Climatic Data Center (Subsidiary of: U.S. Department of Commerce), Federal Bldg, 151 Patton Ave, Asheville, NC 28801. TEL 828-271-4800, FAX 828-271-4876, NODC.Services@noaa.gov, http://www.ncdc.noaa.gov.

551.5 USA ISSN 0739-7259
LOCAL CLIMATOLOGICAL DATA. TUPELO, MISSOURI. MONTHLY SUMMARY. Text in English. 1983. m. USD 5 per issue (effective 2004). **Document type:** *Bulletin, Government.*
Related titles: Online - full text ed.; ◆ Cumulative ed. of: Local Climatological Data. Tupelo, Mississippi. Annual Summary with Comparative Data. ISSN 0742-8782.
—Linda Hall.
Published by: U.S. National Climatic Data Center (Subsidiary of: U.S. Department of Commerce), Federal Bldg, 151 Patton Ave, Asheville, NC 28801. TEL 828-271-4800, FAX 828-271-4876, NODC.Services@noaa.gov, http://www.ncdc.noaa.gov.

551.5 USA ISSN 0198-053X
LOCAL CLIMATOLOGICAL DATA. UNALAKLEET, ALASKA. ANNUAL SUMMARY WITH COMPARATIVE DATA. Text in English. 19??. a. USD 39 combined subscription per issue includes 12 monthly summaries & one a. summary (effective 2009). back issues avail. **Document type:** *Bulletin, Government.* **Description:** Presents the monthly and annual average, resultant and fastest mile wind speed for the current year as well as the monthly and annual mean and fastest mile speed for a long period for Unalakleet, Alaska.
Related titles: Online - full text ed.: USD 29 per issue (effective 2009); ◆ Cumulative ed(s).: Local Climatological Data. Unalakleet, Alaska. Monthly Summary. ISSN 0198-0432.
Published by: U.S. National Climatic Data Center (Subsidiary of: U.S. Department of Commerce), Federal Bldg, 151 Patton Ave, Asheville, NC 28801. TEL 828-271-4800, FAX 828-271-4876, NODC.Services@noaa.gov, http://www.ncdc.noaa.gov.

551.5 USA ISSN 0198-0432
QC984.A42
LOCAL CLIMATOLOGICAL DATA. UNALAKLEET, ALASKA. MONTHLY SUMMARY. Text in English. 19??. m. USD 5 per issue (effective 2009). back issues avail. **Document type:** *Bulletin, Government.* **Description:** Provides a monthly summary of temperature extremes, degree days, precipitation and winds, hourly precipitation and 3-hourly weather observations in Unalakleet, Alaska.
Related titles: Online - full text ed.: USD 3 per issue (effective 2009); ◆ Cumulative ed. of: Local Climatological Data. Unalakleet, Alaska. Annual Summary with Comparative Data. ISSN 0198-053X.
—Linda Hall.
Published by: U.S. National Climatic Data Center (Subsidiary of: U.S. Department of Commerce), Federal Bldg, 151 Patton Ave, Asheville, NC 28801. TEL 828-271-4800, FAX 828-271-4876, NODC.Services@noaa.gov, http://www.ncdc.noaa.gov.

551.5 USA ISSN 0198-0548
QC984.A42
LOCAL CLIMATOLOGICAL DATA. VALDEZ, ALASKA. ANNUAL SUMMARY WITH COMPARATIVE DATA. Text in English. 19??. a. USD 39 combined subscription per issue includes 12 monthly summaries & one a. summary (effective 2009). back issues avail. **Document type:** *Bulletin, Government.* **Description:** Presents the monthly and annual average, resultant and fastest mile wind speed for the current year as well as the monthly and annual mean and fastest mile speed for a long period for Valdez, Alaska.
Related titles: Online - full text ed.: USD 29 per issue (effective 2009); ◆ Cumulative ed(s).: Local Climatological Data. Valdez, Alaska. Monthly Summary. ISSN 0198-0440.
Published by: U.S. National Climatic Data Center (Subsidiary of: U.S. Department of Commerce), Federal Bldg, 151 Patton Ave, Asheville, NC 28801. TEL 828-271-4800, FAX 828-271-4876, NODC.Services@noaa.gov, http://www.ncdc.noaa.gov.

551.5 USA ISSN 0198-0440
QC984.A42
LOCAL CLIMATOLOGICAL DATA. VALDEZ, ALASKA. MONTHLY SUMMARY. Text in English. 19??. m. USD 5 per issue (effective 2009). back issues avail. **Document type:** *Bulletin, Government.* **Description:** Provides a monthly summary of temperature extremes, degree days, precipitation and winds, hourly precipitation and 3-hourly weather observations in Valdez, Alaska.
Related titles: Online - full text ed.: USD 3 per issue (effective 2009); ◆ Cumulative ed. of: Local Climatological Data. Valdez, Alaska. Annual Summary with Comparative Data. ISSN 0198-0548.
—Linda Hall.
Published by: U.S. National Climatic Data Center (Subsidiary of: U.S. Department of Commerce), Federal Bldg, 151 Patton Ave, Asheville, NC 28801. TEL 828-271-4800, FAX 828-271-4876, NODC.Services@noaa.gov, http://www.ncdc.noaa.gov.

551.5 USA ISSN 0198-3237
LOCAL CLIMATOLOGICAL DATA. VALENTINE, NEBRASKA. ANNUAL SUMMARY WITH COMPARATIVE DATA. Text in English. 19??. a. USD 39 combined subscription per issue includes 12 monthly summaries & one a. summary (effective 2009). back issues avail. **Document type:** *Bulletin, Government.* **Description:** Presents the monthly and annual average, resultant and fastest mile wind speed for the current year as well as the monthly and annual mean and fastest mile speed for a long period for Valentine, Nebraska.
Related titles: Online - full text ed.: USD 29 per issue (effective 2009); ◆ Cumulative ed(s).: Local Climatological Data. Valentine, Nebraska. Monthly Summary. ISSN 0198-3245.
Published by: U.S. National Climatic Data Center (Subsidiary of: U.S. Department of Commerce), Federal Bldg, 151 Patton Ave, Asheville, NC 28801. TEL 828-271-4800, FAX 828-271-4876, NODC.Services@noaa.gov, http://www.ncdc.noaa.gov.

551.5 USA ISSN 0198-3245
LOCAL CLIMATOLOGICAL DATA. VALENTINE, NEBRASKA. MONTHLY SUMMARY. Text in English. 19??. m. USD 5 per issue (effective 2009). back issues avail. **Document type:** *Bulletin, Government.* **Description:** Provides a monthly summary of temperature extremes, degree days, precipitation and winds, hourly precipitation and 3-hourly weather observations in Valentine, Nebraska.
Related titles: Online - full text ed.: USD 3 per issue (effective 2009); ◆ Cumulative ed. of: Local Climatological Data. Valentine, Nebraska. Annual Summary with Comparative Data. ISSN 0198-3237.
—Linda Hall.
Published by: U.S. National Climatic Data Center (Subsidiary of: U.S. Department of Commerce), Federal Bldg, 151 Patton Ave, Asheville, NC 28801. TEL 828-271-4800, FAX 828-271-4876, NODC.Services@noaa.gov, http://www.ncdc.noaa.gov.

551.5 USA ISSN 0742-8758
QC984.F6
LOCAL CLIMATOLOGICAL DATA. VERO BEACH, FLORIDA. ANNUAL SUMMARY WITH COMPARATIVE DATA. Text in English. 1986. a. USD 39 combined subscription per issue includes 12 monthly summaries & one a. summary (effective 2009). back issues avail. **Document type:** *Bulletin, Government.* **Description:** Presents the monthly and annual average, resultant and fastest mile wind speed for the current year as well as the monthly and annual mean and fastest mile speed for a long period for Vero Beach, Florida.
Related titles: Online - full text ed.: USD 29 per issue (effective 2009); ◆ Cumulative ed(s).: Local Climatological Data. Vero Beach, Florida Municipal Airport. Monthly Summary. ISSN 0742-874X.
Published by: U.S. National Climatic Data Center (Subsidiary of: U.S. Department of Commerce), Federal Bldg, 151 Patton Ave, Asheville, NC 28801. TEL 828-271-4800, FAX 828-271-4876, NODC.Services@noaa.gov, http://www.ncdc.noaa.gov.

551.5 USA ISSN 0742-874X
LOCAL CLIMATOLOGICAL DATA. VERO BEACH, FLORIDA MUNICIPAL AIRPORT. MONTHLY SUMMARY. Text in English. 1984. m. USD 3 per issue (effective 2009). **Document type:** *Bulletin, Government.*
Related titles: Online - full text ed.; ◆ Cumulative ed. of: Local Climatological Data. Vero Beach, Florida. Annual Summary with Comparative Data. ISSN 0742-8758.
—Linda Hall.
Published by: U.S. National Climatic Data Center (Subsidiary of: U.S. Department of Commerce), Federal Bldg, 151 Patton Ave, Asheville, NC 28801. TEL 828-271-4800, FAX 828-271-4876, NODC.Services@noaa.gov, http://www.ncdc.noaa.gov.

551.5 USA ISSN 0198-5205
LOCAL CLIMATOLOGICAL DATA. VICTORIA, TEXAS. ANNUAL SUMMARY WITH COMPARATIVE DATA. Text in English. 19??. a. USD 39 combined subscription per issue includes 12 monthly summaries & one a. summary (effective 2009). back issues avail. **Document type:** *Bulletin, Government.* **Description:** Presents the monthly and annual average, resultant and fastest mile wind speed for the current year as well as the monthly and annual mean and fastest mile speed for a long period for Victoria, Texas.

Related titles: Online - full text ed.: USD 29 per issue (effective 2009); ◆ Cumulative ed(s).: Local Climatological Data. Victoria, Texas. Monthly Summary. ISSN 0198-5213.
Published by: U.S. National Climatic Data Center (Subsidiary of: U.S. Department of Commerce), Federal Bldg, 151 Patton Ave, Asheville, NC 28801. TEL 828-271-4800, FAX 828-271-4876, NODC.Services@noaa.gov, http://www.ncdc.noaa.gov.

551.5 USA ISSN 0198-5213
LOCAL CLIMATOLOGICAL DATA. VICTORIA, TEXAS. MONTHLY SUMMARY. Text in English. 19??. m. USD 5 per issue (effective 2009). back issues avail. **Document type:** *Bulletin, Government.* **Description:** Provides a monthly summary of temperature extremes, degree days, precipitation and winds, hourly precipitation and 3-hourly weather observations in Victoria, Texas.
Related titles: Online - full text ed.: USD 3 per issue (effective 2009); ◆ Cumulative ed. of: Local Climatological Data. Victoria, Texas. Annual Summary with Comparative Data. ISSN 0198-5205.
—Linda Hall.
Published by: U.S. National Climatic Data Center (Subsidiary of: U.S. Department of Commerce), Federal Bldg, 151 Patton Ave, Asheville, NC 28801. TEL 828-271-4800, FAX 828-271-4876, NODC.Services@noaa.gov, http://www.ncdc.noaa.gov.

551.5 USA ISSN 0198-5221
LOCAL CLIMATOLOGICAL DATA. WACO, TEXAS. ANNUAL SUMMARY WITH COMPARATIVE DATA. Text in English. 19??. a. USD 39 combined subscription per issue includes 12 monthly summaries & one a. summary (effective 2009). back issues avail. **Document type:** *Bulletin, Government.* **Description:** Presents the monthly and annual average, resultant and fastest mile wind speed for the current year as well as the monthly and annual mean and fastest mile speed for a long period for Waco, Texas.
Related titles: Online - full text ed.: USD 29 per issue (effective 2009); ◆ Cumulative ed(s).: Local Climatological Data. Waco, Texas. Monthly Summary. ISSN 0198-523X.
Published by: U.S. National Climatic Data Center (Subsidiary of: U.S. Department of Commerce), Federal Bldg, 151 Patton Ave, Asheville, NC 28801. TEL 828-271-4800, FAX 828-271-4876, NODC.Services@noaa.gov, http://www.ncdc.noaa.gov.

551.5 USA ISSN 0198-523X
LOCAL CLIMATOLOGICAL DATA. WACO, TEXAS. MONTHLY SUMMARY. Text in English. 19??. m. USD 5 per issue (effective 2009). back issues avail. **Document type:** *Bulletin, Government.* **Description:** Provides a monthly summary of temperature extremes, degree days, precipitation and winds, hourly precipitation and 3-hourly weather observations in Waco, Texas.
Related titles: Online - full text ed.: USD 3 per issue (effective 2009); ◆ Cumulative ed. of: Local Climatological Data. Waco, Texas. Annual Summary with Comparative Data. ISSN 0198-5221.
—Linda Hall.
Published by: U.S. National Climatic Data Center (Subsidiary of: U.S. Department of Commerce), Federal Bldg, 151 Patton Ave, Asheville, NC 28801. TEL 828-271-4800, FAX 828-271-4876, NODC.Services@noaa.gov, http://www.ncdc.noaa.gov.

551.5 USA ISSN 0198-4411
LOCAL CLIMATOLOGICAL DATA. WAKE ISLAND, PACIFIC. ANNUAL SUMMARY WITH COMPARATIVE DATA. Text in English. 19??. a. USD 3 per issue (effective 2008). **Document type:** *Bulletin, Government.*
Related titles: Online - full content ed.; ◆ Cumulative ed(s).: Local Climatological Data. Wake Island, Pacific. Monthly Summary. ISSN 0198-442X.
Published by: U.S. National Climatic Data Center (Subsidiary of: U.S. Department of Commerce), Federal Bldg, 151 Patton Ave, Asheville, NC 28801. TEL 828-271-4800, FAX 828-271-4876, NODC.Services@noaa.gov, http://www.ncdc.noaa.gov.

551.5 USA ISSN 0198-442X
LOCAL CLIMATOLOGICAL DATA. WAKE ISLAND, PACIFIC. MONTHLY SUMMARY. Text in English. 19??. m. USD 5 per issue (effective 2009). back issues avail. **Document type:** *Bulletin, Government.* **Description:** Provides a monthly summary of temperature extremes, degree days, precipitation and winds, hourly precipitation and 3-hourly weather observations in Wake Island, Pacific.
Related titles: Online - full text ed.: USD 3 per issue (effective 2009); ◆ Cumulative ed. of: Local Climatological Data. Wake Island, Pacific. Annual Summary with Comparative Data. ISSN 0198-4411.
—Linda Hall.
Published by: U.S. National Climatic Data Center (Subsidiary of: U.S. Department of Commerce), Federal Bldg, 151 Patton Ave, Asheville, NC 28801. TEL 828-271-4800, FAX 828-271-4876, NODC.Services@noaa.gov, http://www.ncdc.noaa.gov.

551.5 USA ISSN 0198-5523
LOCAL CLIMATOLOGICAL DATA. WALLA WALLA, WASHINGTON. ANNUAL SUMMARY WITH COMPARATIVE DATA. Text in English. 19??. a. USD 39 combined subscription per issue includes 12 monthly summaries & one a. summary (effective 2009). back issues avail. **Document type:** *Bulletin, Government.* **Description:** Presents the monthly and annual average, resultant and fastest mile wind speed for the current year as well as the monthly and annual mean and fastest mile speed for a long period for Walla Walla, Washington.
Related titles: Online - full text ed.: USD 29 per issue (effective 2009).
Published by: U.S. National Climatic Data Center (Subsidiary of: U.S. Department of Commerce), Federal Bldg, 151 Patton Ave, Asheville, NC 28801. TEL 828-271-4800, FAX 828-271-4876, NODC.Services@noaa.gov, http://www.ncdc.noaa.gov.

551.5 USA ISSN 0198-7658
LOCAL CLIMATOLOGICAL DATA. WALLOPS ISLAND, VIRGINIA. MONTHLY SUMMARY. Text in English. 19??. m. USD 5 per issue (effective 2009). back issues avail. **Document type:** *Bulletin, Government.* **Description:** Provides a monthly summary of temperature extremes, degree days, precipitation and winds, hourly precipitation and 3-hourly weather observations in Wallops Island, Virginia.
Related titles: Online - full text ed.: USD 3 per issue (effective 2009).
—Linda Hall.
Published by: U.S. National Climatic Data Center (Subsidiary of: U.S. Department of Commerce), Federal Bldg, 151 Patton Ave, Asheville, NC 28801. TEL 828-271-4800, FAX 828-271-4876, NODC.Services@noaa.gov, http://www.ncdc.noaa.gov.

551.5 USA ISSN 0198-120X
QC984.W3
LOCAL CLIMATOLOGICAL DATA. WASHINGTON, D.C. DULLES INTERNATIONAL AIRPORT. ANNUAL SUMMARY WITH COMPARATIVE DATA. Text in English. 19??. a. USD 39 combined subscription per issue includes 12 monthly summaries & one a. summary (effective 2009). back issues avail. **Document type:** *Bulletin, Government.* **Description:** Presents the monthly and annual average, resultant and fastest mile wind speed for the current year as well as the monthly and annual mean and fastest mile speed for a long period for D.C. Dulles International Airport, Washington.
Related titles: Online - full text ed.: USD 29 per issue (effective 2009); ◆ Cumulative ed(s).: Local Climatological Data. Washington D.C. Dulles International Airport. Monthly Summary. ISSN 0198-1323.
Published by: U.S. National Climatic Data Center (Subsidiary of: U.S. Department of Commerce), Federal Bldg, 151 Patton Ave, Asheville, NC 28801. TEL 828-271-4800, FAX 828-271-4876, NODC.Services@noaa.gov, http://www.ncdc.noaa.gov.

551.5 USA ISSN 0198-1323
LOCAL CLIMATOLOGICAL DATA. WASHINGTON D.C. DULLES INTERNATIONAL AIRPORT. MONTHLY SUMMARY. Text in English. 19??. m. USD 5 per issue (effective 2009). back issues avail. **Document type:** *Bulletin, Government.* **Description:** Provides a monthly summary of temperature extremes, degree days, precipitation and winds, hourly precipitation and 3-hourly weather observations in Washington D.C. Dulles International Airport.
Related titles: Online - full text ed.: USD 3 per issue (effective 2009); ◆ Cumulative ed. of: Local Climatological Data. Washington, D.C. Dulles International Airport. Annual Summary with Comparative Data. ISSN 0198-120X.
—Linda Hall.
Published by: U.S. National Climatic Data Center (Subsidiary of: U.S. Department of Commerce), Federal Bldg, 151 Patton Ave, Asheville, NC 28801. TEL 828-271-4800, FAX 828-271-4876, NODC.Services@noaa.gov, http://www.ncdc.noaa.gov.

551.5 USA ISSN 0198-1196
QC984.D6
LOCAL CLIMATOLOGICAL DATA. WASHINGTON, D.C. NATIONAL AIRPORT. ANNUAL SUMMARY WITH COMPARATIVE DATA. Text in English. 19??. a. USD 39 combined subscription per issue includes 12 monthly summaries & one a. summary (effective 2009). back issues avail. **Document type:** *Bulletin, Government.* **Description:** Presents the monthly and annual average, resultant and fastest mile wind speed for the current year as well as the monthly and annual mean and fastest mile speed for a long period for D.C. National Airport, Washington.
Related titles: Online - full text ed.: USD 29 per issue (effective 2009); ◆ Cumulative ed(s).: Local Climatological Data. Washington D.C. National Airport. Monthly Summary. ISSN 0198-1188.
Published by: U.S. National Climatic Data Center (Subsidiary of: U.S. Department of Commerce), Federal Bldg, 151 Patton Ave, Asheville, NC 28801. TEL 828-271-4800, FAX 828-271-4876, NODC.Services@noaa.gov, http://www.ncdc.noaa.gov.

551.5 USA ISSN 0198-1188
QC984.D6
LOCAL CLIMATOLOGICAL DATA. WASHINGTON D.C. NATIONAL AIRPORT. MONTHLY SUMMARY. Text in English. 19??. m. USD 5 per issue (effective 2009). back issues avail. **Document type:** *Bulletin, Government.* **Description:** Provides a monthly summary of temperature extremes, degree days, precipitation and winds, hourly precipitation and 3-hourly weather observations in Washington D.C. National Airport.
Related titles: Online - full text ed.: USD 3 per issue (effective 2009); ◆ Cumulative ed. of: Local Climatological Data. Washington, D.C. National Airport. Annual Summary with Comparative Data. ISSN 0198-1196.
—Linda Hall.
Published by: U.S. National Climatic Data Center (Subsidiary of: U.S. Department of Commerce), Federal Bldg, 151 Patton Ave, Asheville, NC 28801. TEL 828-271-4800, FAX 828-271-4876, NODC.Services@noaa.gov, http://www.ncdc.noaa.gov.

551.5 USA ISSN 0198-2117
QC984.I82
LOCAL CLIMATOLOGICAL DATA. WATERLOO, IOWA. ANNUAL SUMMARY WITH COMPARATIVE DATA. Text in English. 19??. a. USD 39 combined subscription per issue includes 12 monthly summaries & one a. summary (effective 2009). back issues avail. **Document type:** *Bulletin, Government.* **Description:** Presents the monthly and annual average, resultant and fastest mile wind speed for the current year as well as the monthly and annual mean and fastest mile speed for a long period for Waterloo, Iowa.
Related titles: Online - full text ed.: USD 29 per issue (effective 2009); ◆ Cumulative ed(s).: Local Climatological Data. Waterloo, Iowa. Monthly Summary. ISSN 0198-2125.
Published by: U.S. National Climatic Data Center (Subsidiary of: U.S. Department of Commerce), Federal Bldg, 151 Patton Ave, Asheville, NC 28801. TEL 828-271-4800, FAX 828-271-4876, NODC.Services@noaa.gov, http://www.ncdc.noaa.gov.

551.5 USA ISSN 0198-2125
LOCAL CLIMATOLOGICAL DATA. WATERLOO, IOWA. MONTHLY SUMMARY. Text in English. 19??. m. USD 5 per issue (effective 2009). back issues avail. **Document type:** *Bulletin, Government.* **Description:** Provides a monthly summary of temperature extremes, degree days, precipitation and winds, hourly precipitation and 3-hourly weather observations in Waterloo, Iowa.
Related titles: Online - full text ed.: USD 3 per issue (effective 2009); ◆ Cumulative ed. of: Local Climatological Data. Waterloo, Iowa. Annual Summary with Comparative Data. ISSN 0198-2117.
—Linda Hall.
Published by: U.S. National Climatic Data Center (Subsidiary of: U.S. Department of Commerce), Federal Bldg, 151 Patton Ave, Asheville, NC 28801. TEL 828-271-4800, FAX 828-271-4876, NODC.Services@noaa.gov, http://www.ncdc.noaa.gov.

551.5 USA ISSN 0198-1315
QC984.F62
LOCAL CLIMATOLOGICAL DATA. WEST PALM BEACH, FLORIDA. ANNUAL SUMMARY WITH COMPARATIVE DATA. Text in English. 19??. a. USD 39 combined subscription per issue includes 12 monthly summaries & one a. summary (effective 2009). back issues avail. **Document type:** *Bulletin, Government.* **Description:** Presents the monthly and annual average, resultant and fastest mile wind speed for the current year as well as the monthly and annual mean and fastest mile speed for a long period for West Palm Beach, Florida.
Related titles: Online - full text ed.: USD 29 per issue (effective 2009); ◆ Cumulative ed(s).: Local Climatological Data. West Palm Beach, Florida. Monthly Summary. ISSN 0198-1439.
Published by: U.S. National Climatic Data Center (Subsidiary of: U.S. Department of Commerce), Federal Bldg, 151 Patton Ave, Asheville, NC 28801. TEL 828-271-4800, FAX 828-271-4876, NODC.Services@noaa.gov, http://www.ncdc.noaa.gov.

551.5 USA ISSN 0198-1439
LOCAL CLIMATOLOGICAL DATA. WEST PALM BEACH, FLORIDA. MONTHLY SUMMARY. Text in English. 19??. m. USD 5 per issue (effective 2009). back issues avail. **Document type:** *Bulletin, Government.* **Description:** Provides a monthly summary of temperature extremes, degree days, precipitation and winds, hourly precipitation and 3-hourly weather observations in West Palm Beach, Florida.
Related titles: Online - full text ed.: USD 3 per issue (effective 2009); ◆ Cumulative ed. of: Local Climatological Data. West Palm Beach, Florida. Annual Summary with Comparative Data. ISSN 0198-1315.
—Linda Hall.
Published by: U.S. National Climatic Data Center (Subsidiary of: U.S. Department of Commerce), Federal Bldg, 151 Patton Ave, Asheville, NC 28801. TEL 828-271-4800, FAX 828-271-4876, NODC.Services@noaa.gov, http://www.ncdc.noaa.gov.

551.5 USA ISSN 0198-5248
LOCAL CLIMATOLOGICAL DATA. WICHITA FALLS, TEXAS. ANNUAL SUMMARY WITH COMPARATIVE DATA. Text in English. 19??. a. USD 39 combined subscription per issue includes 12 monthly summaries & one a. summary (effective 2009). back issues avail. **Document type:** *Bulletin, Government.* **Description:** Presents the monthly and annual average, resultant and fastest mile wind speed for the current year as well as the monthly and annual mean and fastest mile speed for a long period for Wichita Falls, Texas.
Related titles: Online - full text ed.: USD 29 per issue (effective 2009); ◆ Cumulative ed(s).: Local Climatological Data. Wichita Falls, Texas. Monthly Summary. ISSN 0198-5256.
Published by: U.S. National Climatic Data Center (Subsidiary of: U.S. Department of Commerce), Federal Bldg, 151 Patton Ave, Asheville, NC 28801. TEL 828-271-4800, FAX 828-271-4876, NODC.Services@noaa.gov, http://www.ncdc.noaa.gov.

551.5 USA ISSN 0198-5256
LOCAL CLIMATOLOGICAL DATA. WICHITA FALLS, TEXAS. MONTHLY SUMMARY. Text in English. 19??. m. USD 5 per issue (effective 2009). back issues avail. **Document type:** *Bulletin, Government.* **Description:** Provides a monthly summary of temperature extremes, degree days, precipitation and winds, hourly precipitation and 3-hourly weather observations in Wichita Falls, Texas.
Related titles: Online - full text ed.: USD 3 per issue (effective 2009); ◆ Cumulative ed. of: Local Climatological Data. Wichita Falls, Texas. Annual Summary with Comparative Data. ISSN 0198-5248.
—Linda Hall.
Published by: U.S. National Climatic Data Center (Subsidiary of: U.S. Department of Commerce), Federal Bldg, 151 Patton Ave, Asheville, NC 28801. TEL 828-271-4800, FAX 828-271-4876, NODC.Services@noaa.gov, http://www.ncdc.noaa.gov.

551.5 USA ISSN 0198-2214
LOCAL CLIMATOLOGICAL DATA. WICHITA, KANSAS. ANNUAL SUMMARY WITH COMPARATIVE DATA. Text in English. 19??. a. USD 39 combined subscription per issue includes 12 monthly summaries & one a. summary (effective 2009). back issues avail. **Document type:** *Bulletin, Government.* **Description:** Presents the monthly and annual average, resultant and fastest mile wind speed for the current year as well as the monthly and annual mean and fastest mile speed for a long period for Wichita, Kansas.
Related titles: Online - full text ed.: USD 29 per issue (effective 2009); ◆ Cumulative ed(s).: Local Climatological Data. Wichita, Kansas. Monthly Summary. ISSN 0198-2222.
Published by: U.S. National Climatic Data Center (Subsidiary of: U.S. Department of Commerce), Federal Bldg, 151 Patton Ave, Asheville, NC 28801. TEL 828-271-4800, FAX 828-271-4876, NODC.Services@noaa.gov, http://www.ncdc.noaa.gov.

551.5 USA ISSN 0198-2222
LOCAL CLIMATOLOGICAL DATA. WICHITA, KANSAS. MONTHLY SUMMARY. Text in English. 19??. m. USD 5 per issue (effective 2009). back issues avail. **Document type:** *Bulletin, Government.* **Description:** Provides a monthly summary of temperature extremes, degree days, precipitation and winds, hourly precipitation and 3-hourly weather observations in Wichita, Kansas.
Related titles: Online - full text ed.: USD 3 per issue (effective 2009); ◆ Cumulative ed. of: Local Climatological Data. Wichita, Kansas. Annual Summary with Comparative Data. ISSN 0198-2214.
—Linda Hall.
Published by: U.S. National Climatic Data Center (Subsidiary of: U.S. Department of Commerce), Federal Bldg, 151 Patton Ave, Asheville, NC 28801. TEL 828-271-4800, FAX 828-271-4876, NODC.Services@noaa.gov, http://www.ncdc.noaa.gov.

551.5 USA ISSN 0198-4551
QC984.P42
LOCAL CLIMATOLOGICAL DATA. WILLIAMSPORT, PENNSYLVANIA. ANNUAL SUMMARY WITH COMPARATIVE DATA. Text in English. 19??. a. USD 39 combined subscription per issue includes 12 monthly summaries & one a. summary (effective 2009). back issues avail. **Document type:** *Bulletin, Government.* **Description:** Presents the monthly and annual average, resultant and fastest mile wind speed for the current year as well as the monthly and annual mean and fastest mile speed for a long period for Williamsport, Pennsylvania.
Related titles: Online - full text ed.: USD 29 per issue (effective 2009); ◆ Cumulative ed(s).: Local Climatological Data. Williamsport, Pennsylvania. Monthly Summary. ISSN 0198-456X.

Published by: U.S. National Climatic Data Center (Subsidiary of: U.S. Department of Commerce), Federal Bldg, 151 Patton Ave, Asheville, NC 28801. TEL 828-271-4800, FAX 828-271-4876, NODC.Services@noaa.gov, http://www.ncdc.noaa.gov.

551.5 USA ISSN 0198-456X
LOCAL CLIMATOLOGICAL DATA. WILLIAMSPORT, PENNSYLVANIA. MONTHLY SUMMARY. Text in English. 19??. m. USD 5 per issue (effective 2009). back issues avail. **Document type:** *Bulletin, Government.* **Description:** Provides a monthly summary of temperature extremes, degree days, precipitation and winds, hourly precipitation and 3-hourly weather observations in Williamsport, Pennsylvania.
Related titles: Online - full text ed.: USD 3 per issue (effective 2009); ◆ Cumulative ed. of: Local Climatological Data. Williamsport, Pennsylvania. Annual Summary with Comparative Data. ISSN 0198-4551.
—Linda Hall.
Published by: U.S. National Climatic Data Center (Subsidiary of: U.S. Department of Commerce), Federal Bldg, 151 Patton Ave, Asheville, NC 28801. TEL 828-271-4800, FAX 828-271-4876, NODC.Services@noaa.gov, http://www.ncdc.noaa.gov.

551.5 USA ISSN 0198-3857
LOCAL CLIMATOLOGICAL DATA. WILLISTON, NORTH DAKOTA. ANNUAL SUMMARY WITH COMPARATIVE DATA. Text in English. 19??. a. USD 39 combined subscription per issue includes 12 monthly summaries & one a. summary (effective 2009). back issues avail. **Document type:** *Bulletin, Government.* **Description:** Presents the monthly and annual average, resultant and fastest mile wind speed for the current year as well as the monthly and annual mean and fastest mile speed for a long period for Williston, North Dakota.
Related titles: Online - full text ed.: USD 29 per issue (effective 2009); ◆ Cumulative ed(s).: Local Climatological Data. Williston, North Dakota. Monthly Summary. ISSN 0198-3865.
Published by: U.S. National Climatic Data Center (Subsidiary of: U.S. Department of Commerce), Federal Bldg, 151 Patton Ave, Asheville, NC 28801. TEL 828-271-4800, FAX 828-271-4876, NODC.Services@noaa.gov, http://www.ncdc.noaa.gov.

551.5 USA ISSN 0198-3865
LOCAL CLIMATOLOGICAL DATA. WILLISTON, NORTH DAKOTA. MONTHLY SUMMARY. Text in English. 19??. m. USD 5 per issue (effective 2009). back issues avail. **Document type:** *Bulletin, Government.* **Description:** Provides a monthly summary of temperature extremes, degree days, precipitation and winds, hourly precipitation and 3-hourly weather observations in Williston, North Dakota.
Related titles: Online - full text ed.: USD 3 per issue (effective 2009); ◆ Cumulative ed. of: Local Climatological Data. Williston, North Dakota. Annual Summary with Comparative Data. ISSN 0198-3857.
—Linda Hall.
Published by: U.S. National Climatic Data Center (Subsidiary of: U.S. Department of Commerce), Federal Bldg, 151 Patton Ave, Asheville, NC 28801. TEL 828-271-4800, FAX 828-271-4876, NODC.Services@noaa.gov, http://www.ncdc.noaa.gov.

551.5 USA ISSN 0198-1145
LOCAL CLIMATOLOGICAL DATA. WILMINGTON, DELAWARE. ANNUAL SUMMARY WITH COMPARATIVE DATA. Text in English. 19??. a. USD 39 combined subscription per issue includes 12 monthly summaries & one a. summary (effective 2009). back issues avail. **Document type:** *Bulletin, Government.* **Description:** Presents the monthly and annual average, resultant and fastest mile wind speed for the current year as well as the monthly and annual mean and fastest mile speed for a long period for Wilmington, Delaware.
Related titles: Online - full text ed.: USD 29 per issue (effective 2009); ◆ Cumulative ed(s).: Local Climatological Data. Wilmington, Delaware. Monthly Summary. ISSN 0198-117X.
Published by: U.S. National Climatic Data Center (Subsidiary of: U.S. Department of Commerce), Federal Bldg, 151 Patton Ave, Asheville, NC 28801. TEL 828-271-4800, FAX 828-271-4876, NODC.Services@noaa.gov, http://www.ncdc.noaa.gov.

551.5 USA ISSN 0198-117X
LOCAL CLIMATOLOGICAL DATA. WILMINGTON, DELAWARE. MONTHLY SUMMARY. Text in English. 19??. m. USD 5 per issue (effective 2009). back issues avail. **Document type:** *Bulletin, Government.* **Description:** Provides a monthly summary of temperature extremes, degree days, precipitation and winds, hourly precipitation and 3-hourly weather observations in Wilmington, Delaware.
Related titles: Online - full text ed.: USD 3 per issue (effective 2009); ◆ Cumulative ed. of: Local Climatological Data. Wilmington, Delaware. Annual Summary with Comparative Data. ISSN 0198-1145.
—Linda Hall.
Published by: U.S. National Climatic Data Center (Subsidiary of: U.S. Department of Commerce), Federal Bldg, 151 Patton Ave, Asheville, NC 28801. TEL 828-271-4800, FAX 828-271-4876, NODC.Services@noaa.gov, http://www.ncdc.noaa.gov.

551.5 USA ISSN 0198-3792
QC984.N82
LOCAL CLIMATOLOGICAL DATA. WILMINGTON, NORTH CAROLINA. ANNUAL SUMMARY WITH COMPARATIVE DATA. Text in English. 19??. a. USD 5 per issue (effective 2004). **Document type:** *Bulletin, Government.*
Related titles: Online - full text ed.; ◆ Cumulative ed(s).: Local Climatological Data. Wilmington, North Carolina. Monthly Summary. ISSN 0198-3806.
Published by: U.S. National Climatic Data Center (Subsidiary of: U.S. Department of Commerce), Federal Bldg, 151 Patton Ave, Asheville, NC 28801. TEL 828-271-4800, FAX 828-271-4876, NODC.Services@noaa.gov, http://www.ncdc.noaa.gov.

551.5 USA ISSN 0198-3806
LOCAL CLIMATOLOGICAL DATA. WILMINGTON, NORTH CAROLINA. MONTHLY SUMMARY. Text in English. 19??. m. USD 5 per issue (effective 2004). **Document type:** *Government.*
Related titles: Online - full text ed.; ◆ Cumulative ed. of: Local Climatological Data. Wilmington, North Carolina. Annual Summary with Comparative Data. ISSN 0198-3792.
—Linda Hall.
Published by: U.S. National Climatic Data Center (Subsidiary of: U.S. Department of Commerce), Federal Bldg, 151 Patton Ave, Asheville, NC 28801. TEL 828-271-4800, FAX 828-271-4876, NODC.Services@noaa.gov, http://www.ncdc.noaa.gov.

551.5 USA ISSN 0198-3342
LOCAL CLIMATOLOGICAL DATA. WINNEMUCCA, NEVADA. ANNUAL SUMMARY WITH COMPARATIVE DATA. Text in English. 19??. a. USD 39 combined subscription per issue includes 12 monthly summaries & one a. summary (effective 2009). back issues avail. **Document type:** *Bulletin, Government.* **Description:** Presents the monthly and annual average, resultant and fastest mile wind speed for the current year as well as the monthly and annual mean and fastest mile speed for a long period for Winnemucca, Nevada.
Related titles: Online - full text ed.: USD 29 per issue (effective 2009); ◆ Cumulative ed(s).: Local Climatological Data. Winnemucca, Nevada. Monthly Summary. ISSN 0198-3350.
Published by: U.S. National Climatic Data Center (Subsidiary of: U.S. Department of Commerce), Federal Bldg, 151 Patton Ave, Asheville, NC 28801. TEL 828-271-4800, FAX 828-271-4876, NODC.Services@noaa.gov, http://www.ncdc.noaa.gov.

551.5 USA ISSN 0198-3350
LOCAL CLIMATOLOGICAL DATA. WINNEMUCCA, NEVADA. MONTHLY SUMMARY. Text in English. 19??. m. USD 5 per issue (effective 2009). back issues avail. **Document type:** *Bulletin, Government.* **Description:** Provides a monthly summary of temperature extremes, degree days, precipitation and winds, hourly precipitation and 3-hourly weather observations in Winnemucca, Nevada.
Related titles: Online - full text ed.: USD 3 per issue (effective 2009); ◆ Cumulative ed. of: Local Climatological Data. Winnemucca, Nevada. Annual Summary with Comparative Data. ISSN 0198-3342.
—Linda Hall.
Published by: U.S. National Climatic Data Center (Subsidiary of: U.S. Department of Commerce), Federal Bldg, 151 Patton Ave, Asheville, NC 28801. TEL 828-271-4800, FAX 828-271-4876, NODC.Services@noaa.gov, http://www.ncdc.noaa.gov.

551.5 USA ISSN 0198-0599
LOCAL CLIMATOLOGICAL DATA. WINSLOW, ARIZONA. ANNUAL SUMMARY WITH COMPARATIVE DATA. Text in English. 19??. a. USD 39 combined subscription per issue includes 12 monthly summaries & one a. summary (effective 2009). back issues avail. **Document type:** *Bulletin, Government.* **Description:** Presents the monthly and annual average, resultant and fastest mile wind speed for the current year as well as the monthly and annual mean and fastest mile speed for a long period for Winslow, Arizona.
Related titles: Online - full text ed.: USD 29 per issue (effective 2009); ◆ Cumulative ed(s).: Local Climatological Data. Winslow, Arizona. Monthly Summary. ISSN 0198-0491.
Published by: U.S. National Climatic Data Center (Subsidiary of: U.S. Department of Commerce), Federal Bldg, 151 Patton Ave, Asheville, NC 28801. TEL 828-271-4800, FAX 828-271-4876, NODC.Services@noaa.gov, http://www.ncdc.noaa.gov.

551.5 USA ISSN 0198-0491
LOCAL CLIMATOLOGICAL DATA. WINSLOW, ARIZONA. MONTHLY SUMMARY. Text in English. 19??. m. USD 5 per issue (effective 2009). back issues avail. **Document type:** *Bulletin, Government.* **Description:** Provides a monthly summary of temperature extremes, degree days, precipitation and winds, hourly precipitation and 3-hourly weather observations in Winslow, Arizona.
Related titles: Online - full text ed.: USD 3 per issue (effective 2009); ◆ Cumulative ed. of: Local Climatological Data. Winslow, Arizona. Annual Summary with Comparative Data. ISSN 0198-0599.
—Linda Hall.
Published by: U.S. National Climatic Data Center (Subsidiary of: U.S. Department of Commerce), Federal Bldg, 151 Patton Ave, Asheville, NC 28801. TEL 828-271-4800, NODC.Services@noaa.gov, http://www.ncdc.noaa.gov.

551.5 USA ISSN 0198-2451
QC984.W6
LOCAL CLIMATOLOGICAL DATA. WORCESTER, MASSACHUSETTS. ANNUAL SUMMARY WITH COMPARATIVE DATA. Text in English. 19??. a. USD 39 combined subscription per issue includes 12 monthly summaries & one a. summary (effective 2009). back issues avail. **Document type:** *Bulletin, Government.* **Description:** Presents the monthly and annual average, resultant and fastest mile wind speed for the current year as well as the monthly and annual mean and fastest mile speed for a long period for Worcester, Massachusetts.
Related titles: Online - full text ed.: USD 29 per issue (effective 2009); ◆ Cumulative ed(s).: Local Climatological Data. Worcester, Massachusetts. Monthly Summary. ISSN 0198-246X.
Published by: U.S. National Climatic Data Center (Subsidiary of: U.S. Department of Commerce), Federal Bldg, 151 Patton Ave, Asheville, NC 28801. TEL 828-271-4800, FAX 828-271-4876, NODC.Services@noaa.gov, http://www.ncdc.noaa.gov.

551.5 USA ISSN 0198-246X
QC984.W6
LOCAL CLIMATOLOGICAL DATA. WORCESTER, MASSACHUSETTS. MONTHLY SUMMARY. Text in English. 19??. m. USD 5 per issue (effective 2009). back issues avail. **Document type:** *Bulletin, Government.* **Description:** Provides a monthly summary of temperature extremes, degree days, precipitation and winds, hourly precipitation and 3-hourly weather observations in Worcester, Massachusetts.
Related titles: Online - full text ed.: USD 3 per issue (effective 2009); ◆ Cumulative ed. of: Local Climatological Data. Worcester, Massachusetts. Annual Summary with Comparative Data. ISSN 0198-2451.
—Linda Hall.
Published by: U.S. National Climatic Data Center (Subsidiary of: U.S. Department of Commerce), Federal Bldg, 151 Patton Ave, Asheville, NC 28801. TEL 828-271-4800, FAX 828-271-4876, NODC.Services@noaa.gov, http://www.ncdc.noaa.gov.

551.5 USA ISSN 0198-5558
QC984.W2
LOCAL CLIMATOLOGICAL DATA. YAKIMA, WASHINGTON. MONTHLY SUMMARY. Text in English. 19??. m. USD 5 per issue (effective 2009). back issues avail. **Document type:** *Bulletin, Government.* **Description:** Provides a monthly summary of temperature extremes, degree days, precipitation and winds, hourly precipitation and 3-hourly weather observations in Yakima, Washington.
Related titles: Online - full text ed.: USD 3 per issue (effective 2009).
—Linda Hall.

Published by: U.S. National Climatic Data Center (Subsidiary of: U.S. Department of Commerce), Federal Bldg, 151 Patton Ave, Asheville, NC 28801. TEL 828-271-4800, FAX 828-271-4876, NODC.Services@noaa.gov, http://www.ncdc.noaa.gov.

551.5 USA ISSN 0198-0556
QC984.A42
LOCAL CLIMATOLOGICAL DATA. YAKUTAT, ALASKA. ANNUAL SUMMARY WITH COMPARATIVE DATA. Text in English. 19??. a. USD 39 combined subscription per issue includes 12 monthly summaries & one a. summary (effective 2009). back issues avail. **Document type:** *Bulletin, Government.* **Description:** Presents the monthly and annual average, resultant and fastest mile wind speed for the current year as well as the monthly and annual mean and fastest mile speed for a long period for Yakutat, Alaska.
Related titles: Online - full text ed.: USD 29 per issue (effective 2009); ◆ Cumulative ed(s).: Local Climatological Data. Yakutat, Alaska. Monthly Summary. ISSN 0198-0459.
Published by: U.S. National Climatic Data Center (Subsidiary of: U.S. Department of Commerce), Federal Bldg, 151 Patton Ave, Asheville, NC 28801. TEL 828-271-4800, FAX 828-271-4876, NODC.Services@noaa.gov, http://www.ncdc.noaa.gov.

551.5 USA ISSN 0198-0459
QC984.A42
LOCAL CLIMATOLOGICAL DATA. YAKUTAT, ALASKA. MONTHLY SUMMARY. Text in English. 19??. m. USD 5 per issue (effective 2009). back issues avail. **Document type:** *Bulletin, Government.* **Description:** Provides a monthly summary of temperature extremes, degree days, precipitation and winds, hourly precipitation and 3-hourly weather observations in Yakutat, Alaska.
Related titles: Online - full text ed.: USD 3 per issue (effective 2009); ◆ Cumulative ed. of: Local Climatological Data. Yakutat, Alaska. Annual Summary with Comparative Data. ISSN 0198-0556.
—Linda Hall.
Published by: U.S. National Climatic Data Center (Subsidiary of: U.S. Department of Commerce), Federal Bldg, 151 Patton Ave, Asheville, NC 28801. TEL 828-271-4800, FAX 828-271-4876, NODC.Services@noaa.gov, http://www.ncdc.noaa.gov.

551.5 USA ISSN 0198-4438
LOCAL CLIMATOLOGICAL DATA. YAP ISLAND, PACIFIC. ANNUAL SUMMARY WITH COMPARATIVE DATA. Text in English. 19??. a. USD 39 combined subscription per issue includes 12 monthly summaries & one a. summary (effective 2009). back issues avail. **Document type:** *Bulletin, Government.* **Description:** Presents the monthly and annual average, resultant and fastest mile wind speed for the current year as well as the monthly and annual mean and fastest mile speed for a long period for Yap Island, Pacific.
Related titles: Online - full text ed.: USD 29 per issue (effective 2009); ◆ Cumulative ed(s).: Local Climatological Data. Yap Island, Pacific. Monthly Summary. ISSN 0198-4446.
Published by: U.S. National Climatic Data Center (Subsidiary of: U.S. Department of Commerce), Federal Bldg, 151 Patton Ave, Asheville, NC 28801. TEL 828-271-4800, FAX 828-271-4876, NODC.Services@noaa.gov, http://www.ncdc.noaa.gov.

551.5 USA ISSN 0198-4446
LOCAL CLIMATOLOGICAL DATA. YAP ISLAND, PACIFIC. MONTHLY SUMMARY. Text in English. 19??. m. USD 5 per issue (effective 2009). back issues avail. **Document type:** *Bulletin, Government.* **Description:** Provides a monthly summary of temperature extremes, degree days, precipitation and winds, hourly precipitation and 3-hourly weather observations in Yap Island, Pacific.
Related titles: Online - full text ed.: USD 3 per issue (effective 2009); ◆ Cumulative ed. of: Local Climatological Data. Yap Island, Pacific. Annual Summary with Comparative Data. ISSN 0198-4438.
—Linda Hall.
Published by: U.S. National Climatic Data Center (Subsidiary of: U.S. Department of Commerce), Federal Bldg, 151 Patton Ave, Asheville, NC 28801. TEL 828-271-4800, FAX 828-271-4876, NODC.Services@noaa.gov, http://www.ncdc.noaa.gov.

551.5 USA ISSN 0198-4039
LOCAL CLIMATOLOGICAL DATA. YOUNGSTOWN, OHIO. ANNUAL SUMMARY WITH COMPARATIVE DATA. Text in English. 19??. a. USD 39 combined subscription per issue includes 12 monthly summaries & one a. summary (effective 2009). back issues avail. **Document type:** *Bulletin, Government.* **Description:** Presents the monthly and annual average, resultant and fastest mile wind speed for the current year as well as the monthly and annual mean and fastest mile speed for a long period for Youngstown, Ohio.
Related titles: Online - full text ed.: USD 29 per issue (effective 2009); ◆ Cumulative ed(s).: Local Climatological Data. Youngstown, Ohio. Monthly Summary. ISSN 0198-4047.
Published by: U.S. National Climatic Data Center (Subsidiary of: U.S. Department of Commerce), Federal Bldg, 151 Patton Ave, Asheville, NC 28801. TEL 828-271-4800, FAX 828-271-4876, NODC.Services@noaa.gov, http://www.ncdc.noaa.gov.

551.5 USA ISSN 0198-4047
LOCAL CLIMATOLOGICAL DATA. YOUNGSTOWN, OHIO. MONTHLY SUMMARY. Text in English. 19??. m. USD 5 per issue (effective 2009). back issues avail. **Document type:** *Bulletin, Government.* **Description:** Provides a monthly summary of temperature extremes, degree days, precipitation and winds, hourly precipitation and 3-hourly weather observations in Youngstown, Ohio.
Related titles: Online - full text ed.: USD 3 per issue (effective 2009); ◆ Cumulative ed. of: Local Climatological Data. Youngstown, Ohio. Annual Summary with Comparative Data. ISSN 0198-4039.
—Linda Hall.
Published by: U.S. National Climatic Data Center (Subsidiary of: U.S. Department of Commerce), Federal Bldg, 151 Patton Ave, Asheville, NC 28801. TEL 828-271-4800, FAX 828-271-4876, NODC.Services@noaa.gov, http://www.ncdc.noaa.gov.

551.5 USA ISSN 0198-0653
LOCAL CLIMATOLOGICAL DATA. YUMA, ARIZONA. ANNUAL SUMMARY WITH COMPARATIVE DATA. Text in English. 19??. a. USD 39 combined subscription per issue includes 12 monthly summaries & one a. summary (effective 2009). back issues avail. **Document type:** *Bulletin, Government.* **Description:** Presents the monthly and annual average, resultant and fastest mile wind speed for the current year as well as the monthly and annual mean and fastest mile speed for a long period for Yuma, Arizona.

Related titles: Online - full text ed.: USD 29 per issue (effective 2009); ◆ Cumulative ed(s).: Local Climatological Data. Yuma, Arizona. Monthly Summary. ISSN 0198-0602.
Published by: U.S. National Climatic Data Center (Subsidiary of: U.S. Department of Commerce), Federal Bldg, 151 Patton Ave, Asheville, NC 28801. TEL 828-271-4800, FAX 828-271-4876, NODC.Services@noaa.gov, http://www.ncdc.noaa.gov.

551.5 USA ISSN 0198-0602
LOCAL CLIMATOLOGICAL DATA. YUMA, ARIZONA. MONTHLY SUMMARY. Text in English. 19??. m. USD 5 per issue (effective 2009). back issues avail. **Document type:** *Bulletin, Government.* **Description:** Provides a monthly summary of temperature extremes, degree days, precipitation and winds, hourly precipitation and 3-hourly weather observations in Yuma, Arizona.
Related titles: Online - full text ed.: USD 3 per issue (effective 2009); ◆ Cumulative ed. of: Local Climatological Data. Yuma, Arizona. Annual Summary with Comparative Data. ISSN 0198-0653.
—Linda Hall.
Published by: U.S. National Climatic Data Center (Subsidiary of: U.S. Department of Commerce), Federal Bldg, 151 Patton Ave, Asheville, NC 28801. TEL 828-271-4800, FAX 828-271-4876, NODC.Services@noaa.gov, http://www.ncdc.noaa.gov.

LOUISIANA. AGRICULTURAL STATISTICS SERVICE. CROP WEATHER SUMMARY. *see* AGRICULTURE—Abstracting, Bibliographies, Statistics

551.63 JPN ISSN 0460-7317
MAIZURU KAIYO KISHODAI YOHO/MAIZURU MARINE OBSERVATORY. BULLETIN. Text in English, Japanese. 1950. irreg.
Published by: Kishocho, Maizuru Kaiyo Kishodai/Japan Meteorological Agency, Maizuru Marine Observatory, 901 Shimo-Fukui, Maizuru-shi, Kyoto-Fu 624-0946, Japan.

551 USA ISSN 0025-3367
QC994
MARINERS WEATHER LOG. Abbreviated title: M W L. Text in English. 1957-1995 (Summer); N.S. 1996. 3/yr. USD 19 domestic; USD 26.60 foreign (effective 2010). charts; illus.; stat. index. back issues avail.; reprints avail. **Document type:** *Magazine, Government.* **Description:** Contains articles, news and information about marine weather events and phenomena, storms at sea, weather forecasting, the NWS Voluntary Observing Ship Program, Port Meteorological Officers, cooperating ships officers, and their vessels.
Related titles: Online - full text ed.: ISSN 1554-950X. free (effective 2010).
Indexed: A22, ASFA, AmStI, IUSGP, M&GPA, OceAb, RefZh, SPPI.
—Ingenta, Linda Hall.
Published by: (U.S. National Oceanographic Data Center), National Oceanic and Atmospheric Administration, National Weather Service (Subsidiary of: U.S. Department of Commerce), 1325 East West Hwy, Silver Spring, MD 20910. http://www.nws.noaa.gov. **Subscr. to:** U.S. Government Printing Office, Superintendent of Documents, PO Box 371954, Pittsburgh, PA 15250. TEL 202-512-1800, FAX 202-512-2250.

551.5 IND ISSN 0252-9416
QC851 CODEN: MAUSDJ
MAUSAM. Text in English, Hindi. 1950. q. bk.rev. abstr.; charts; illus. index. **Document type:** *Journal, Government.*
Former titles (until 1979): Indian Journal of Meteorology, Hydrology and Geophysics (0376-4796); (until 1975): Indian Journal of Meteorology and Geophysics (0019-5383)
Indexed: ASFA, B21, ChemAb, ESPM, GeoRef, Inspec, M&GPA, SCI, SCOPUS, SpeleolAb, W07.
—BLDSC (5413.279550), AskIEEE, IE, Ingenta, INIST, Linda Hall.
Published by: (India. Positional Astronomy Centre, Meteorological Department), Scientific Publishers, 5-A, New Pali Rd, PO Box 91, Jodhpur, Rajasthan 342 001, India. TEL 91-291-2433323, FAX 91-291-2624154, info@scientificpub.com, http://www.scientificpub.com.

551.5 DEU ISSN 0938-5177
MAX-PLANCK-INSTITUT FUER METEOROLOGIE. EXAMENSARBEIT. Text in Multiple languages. 1990. irreg., latest vol.86, 2002. **Document type:** *Monographic series.*
Indexed: GeoRef, SCOPUS.
Published by: Max-Planck-Institut fuer Meteorologie, Bundesstr. 55, Hamburg, 20146, Germany. TEL 49-40-411730, FAX 49-40-41173298, http://www.mpimet.mpg.de/.

551.5 DEU ISSN 0937-1060
QC851
MAX-PLANCK-INSTITUT FUER METEOROLOGIE. REPORT. Text in Multiple languages. 1987. irreg.
Indexed: M&GPA.
Published by: Max-Planck-Institut fuer Meteorologie, Bundesstr. 55, Hamburg, 20146, Germany. TEL 49-40-411730, FAX 49-40-41173298.

551 JPN
MEIKEN KISHO GEPPO/MIE PREFECTURE. MONTHLY REPORT OF METEOROLOGY. Text in Japanese. 1956. m.
Published by: Kishocho, Tsu Chiho Kishodai/Japan Meteorological Agency, Tsu Local Meteorological Observatory, Tsu Dai 2 Chiho Godo chosha, 327-2 Shimazaki-cho, Tsu-shi, Mie-ken 514-0002, Japan.

551.5 COL ISSN 0124-6984
METEOROLOGIA COLOMBIANA. Text in Spanish; Abstracts in English, Spanish. 2000. s-a.
Indexed: ASFA, ESPM, M&GPA, SWRA.
Published by: Universidad Nacional de Colombia, Departamento de Geociencias, Edificio Manuel Ancizar, Oficina 301, Bogota, Colombia. TEL 57-1-3165000, FAX 57-1-3165390, dgeologia@ciencias.unal.edu.co, http://www.geociencias.unal.edu.co/.

551.5 ARG ISSN 0325-187X
METEOROLOGICA. Text in Multiple languages. 1970. 3/yr. ARS 60 to individuals; ARS 100 to institutions (effective 2010). **Document type:** *Journal, Academic/Scholarly.*
Related titles: Online - full text ed.: ISSN 1850-468X. 2006 (from SciELO).
Indexed: M&GPA.
Published by: Centro Argentino de Meteorologos, Departamento de Ciencia de la Atmosfera, Universidad de Buenos Aires, Nunez - Pabellon 2, Buenos Aires, 1428, Argentina. Circ: 500.

METEOROLOGICAL AND GEOASTROPHYSICAL ABSTRACTS. *see* METEOROLOGY—Abstracting, Bibliographies, Statistics

551.5 GBR ISSN 1350-4827
QC875.A2
METEOROLOGICAL APPLICATIONS. Text in English. 1994. q. GBP 298 in United Kingdom to institutions; EUR 377 in Europe to institutions; USD 583 elsewhere to institutions; GBP 344 combined subscription in United Kingdom to institutions (print & online eds.); EUR 434 combined subscription in Europe to institutions (print & online eds.); USD 671 combined subscription elsewhere to institutions (print & online eds.) (effective 2012). adv. bk.rev. back issues avail.; reprint service avail. from PSC. **Document type:** *Journal, Academic/Scholarly.* **Description:** Covers the analysis and prediction of weather events and the tools, models and methods used.
Related titles: Online - full text ed.: ISSN 1469-8080. GBP 298 in United Kingdom to institutions; EUR 377 in Europe to institutions; USD 583 elsewhere to institutions (effective 2012).
Indexed: A22, A37, ASFA, C25, C30, CA, CABA, CurCont, E01, E12, ESPM, F08, F12, FCA, G11, GH, GeoRef, H16, I11, ISR, LT, M&GPA, MaizeAb, N02, O01, P33, PollutAb, R07, R08, R12, R13, RRTA, RefZh, S12, S13, S16, S17, SCI, SCOPUS, SWRA, SoyAb, T02, T05, TAR, W07, W11.
—BLDSC (5705.280000), IE, Infotrieve, Ingenta, Linda Hall. **CCC.**
Published by: (Royal Meteorological Society), John Wiley & Sons Ltd. (Subsidiary of: John Wiley & Sons, Inc.), 1-7 Oldlands Way, PO Box 808, Bognor Regis, West Sussex PO21 9FF, United Kingdom. TEL 44-1865-778315, FAX 44-1243-843232, cs-journals@wiley.com, http://eu.wiley.com/WileyCDA/. Ed. P J A Burt. **Subscr. to:** 1-7 Oldlands Way, PO Box 809, Bognor Regis, West Sussex PO21 9FG, United Kingdom. TEL 44-1865-778054, cs-agency@wiley.com.

551.65 JPN ISSN 0018-3423
METEOROLOGICAL DATA OF HOKKAIDO/HOKKAIDO NO KISHO. Text in Japanese. 1957. m. (plus special issue). JPY 5,500. bk.rev. illus.; stat. index.
Published by: Japan Weather Association, Administration Division, Kita 4-jo Nish 23-1-18, Chuo-ku, Sapporo-shi, Hokkaido 064, Japan. TEL 011-622-2230, FAX 011-640-2383. Ed. Jigyo Bu.

551 JPN ISSN 0387-4028
METEOROLOGICAL SATELLITE CENTER. MONTHLY REPORT. Text in English. 1978. m.
Related titles: CD-ROM ed.
Published by: Kishocho, Kisho Eisei Senta/Japan Meteorological Agency, Meteorological Satellite Center, 3-235 Nakakiyo-To, Kiyose-shi, Tokyo-to 204-0012, Japan.

551.5 JPN ISSN 0026-1165
QC851 CODEN: JMSJAU
➤ **METEOROLOGICAL SOCIETY OF JAPAN. JOURNAL/KISHO SHUSHI.** Text in English. 1882. bi-m. illus. reprints avail. **Document type:** *Journal, Academic/Scholarly.*
Related titles: Online - full text ed.: free (effective 2011).
Indexed: A22, A37, ASCA, ASFA, C25, C30, CABA, ChemAb, CurCont, E12, ESPM, F08, F12, G11, GEOBASE, GeoRef, H16, I11, IBR, IBZ, INIS AtomInd, ISR, JTA, M&GPA, MaizeAb, PollutAb, R11, RefZh, S13, S16, S17, SCI, SCOPUS, TAR, W07.
—BLDSC (4825.000000), CASDDS, IE, Ingenta, INIST, Linda Hall. **CCC.**
Published by: Meteorological Society of Japan/Nihon Kisho Gakkai, c/o Japan Meteorological Agency, 3-4 Ote-Machi 1-chome, Chiyoda-ku, Tokyo, 100-0004, Japan. TEL 81-3-3212-8341, FAX 81-3-3216-4401, http://www-cmpo.mit.edu/met_links/full/imsjap.full.html.

551 JPN
METEOROLOGICAL SOCIETY OF JAPAN. PREPRINTS OF MEETING/NIHON KISHO GAKKAI TAIKAI KOEN YOKOSHU. Text in English, Japanese. s-a.
Published by: Meteorological Society of Japan/Nihon Kisho Gakkai, c/o Japan Meteorological Agency, 3-4 Ote-Machi 1-chome, Chiyoda-ku, Tokyo, 100-0004, Japan.

551.5 NZL ISSN 0111-1736
METEOROLOGICAL SOCIETY OF NEW ZEALAND. NEWSLETTER. Text in English. 1980. q. free membership (effective 2009). **Document type:** *Newsletter.* **Description:** Provides information about recent weather events with climatological summaries together with general information about the Society's business and activities and members' news and views.
Indexed: M&GPA.
Published by: Meteorological Society of New Zealand, Te Aro, PO Box 6523, Wellington, New Zealand. info@metsoc.rsnz.org.

551.5 GBR ISSN 2042-7190
▼ **METEOROLOGICAL TECHNOLOGY INTERNATIONAL.** Text in English. 2010. a. GBP 60, USD 98 per issue; free to qualified personnel (effective 2010). adv. **Document type:** *Magazine, Trade.* **Description:** Covers the latest developments in climate, weather and hydrometeorological forecasting, measurement and analysis technologies and service providers.
Related titles: Online - full text ed.: free (effective 2010).
Published by: UKIP Media & Events Ltd, Abinger House, Church St, Dorking, Surrey RH4 1DF, United Kingdom. TEL 44-1306-743744, FAX 44-1306-887546, info@ukintpress.com. Ed. Christopher Hounsfield. Circ: 10,000.

551.5 CZE ISSN 0026-1173
QC851 CODEN: MEZPAQ
➤ **METEOROLOGICKE ZPRAVY.** Text in Czech; Summaries in English. 1947. bi-m. CZK 180 domestic; EUR 36 foreign (effective 2008). adv. bk.rev. bibl.; charts; illus.; maps; stat. index. 32 p./no. 2 cols./p.; **Document type:** *Journal, Academic/Scholarly.*
Indexed: ChemAb, M&GPA.
—BLDSC (5739.400000), Linda Hall.
Published by: Cesky Hydrometeorologicky Ustav/Czech Hydrometeorological Institute, Na Sabatce 2050/17, Prague 4, 14306, Czech Republic. eva.firmanova@chmi.cz. Ed. Lubos Nemec. Circ: 250 (paid).

551.654 FRA ISSN 2107-0830
LA METEOROLOGIE. Text in French. 200?. q.
Media: Online - full text.
Published by: Societe Meteorologique de France, 1 Quai Branly, Paris Cedex 07, 75430, France. http://www.smf.asso.fr.

551.5 DEU ISSN 0342-4324
METEOROLOGISCHE ABHANDLUNGEN. SERIE A, MONOGRAPHIEN. Text in German. 1975. irreg., latest vol.9, no.4, 1998. price varies. **Document type:** *Monographic series, Academic/Scholarly.*
Supersedes in part (in 1975): Meteorologische Abhandlungen (0026-1203)
Published by: (Freie Universitaet Berlin, Institut fuer Meteorologie), Dietrich Reimer Verlag GmbH, Berliner Str 53, Berlin, 10713, Germany. TEL 49-30-700138850, FAX 49-30-700138855, vertrieb-kunstverlage@reimer-verlag.de, http://www.dietrichreimerverlag.de.

551.5 DEU ISSN 0941-2948
QC851 CODEN: MEZEEV
➤ **METEOROLOGISCHE ZEITSCHRIFT.** Text and summaries in English, German. 1992. 6/yr. USD 622 combined subscription (print & online eds.) (effective 2010). adv. bk.rev. bibl.; charts; illus. index. back issues avail. **Document type:** *Journal, Academic/Scholarly.* **Description:** Publishes observational, theoretical and computational research covering a full range of current topics in meteorology.
Incorporates (1957-2000): Contributions to Atmospheric Physics (0303-4186); Which was formerly (until 1969): Beitraege zur Physik der Atmosphaere (0005-8173); Formed by the merger of (1947-1992): Meteorologische Rundschau (0026-1211); (1884-1992): Zeitschrift fuer Meteorologie (0084-5361); Which was formerly (until 1946): Meteorologische Zeitschrift (0369-1845)
Related titles: Online - full text ed.: ISSN 1610-1227 (from IngentaConnect).
Indexed: A20, A22, ApMecR, BibCart, ChemAb, CurCont, ESPM, FLUIDEX, GEOBASE, IBR, IBZ, INIS AtomInd, ISR, Inspec, L09, M&GPA, PollutAb, SCI, SCOPUS, SpeleolAb, W07.
—BLDSC (5742.180000), AskIEEE, IE, Ingenta, INIST, Linda Hall. **CCC.**
Published by: (Oesterreichische Gesellschaft fuer Meteorologie AUT, Deutsche Meteorologische Gesellschaft), Gebrueder Borntraeger Verlagsbuchhandlung, Johannesstr 3A, Stuttgart, 70176, Germany. TEL 49-711-3514560, FAX 49-711-35145699. **Co-sponsor:** Schweizerische Gesellschaft fuer Meteorologie.

551.6 NOR ISSN 1504-1549
METEOROLOGISK INSTITUTT. MET.NO-REPORT, KLIMA/NORWEGIAN METEOROLOGICAL INSTITUTE. CLIMATE REPORT. Text in English, Norwegian. 1984. irreg., latest vol.15, 2005. back issues avail. **Document type:** *Monographic series, Academic/Scholarly.*
Formerly (until 2005): Det Norske Meteorologiske Institutt. D N M I-Rapport, Klima (0805-9918)
Related titles: Online - full text ed.
Published by: Meteorologisk Institutt/Norwegian Meteorological Institute, PO Box 43, Blindern, Oslo, 0313, Norway. TEL 47-22-963000, FAX 47-22-963050, met.inst@met.no, http://www.met.no.

551.5 NOR ISSN 0373-4463
METEOROLOGISKE ANNALER. Text in English. 1942. irreg., latest 1975. charts. back issues avail. **Document type:** *Monographic series, Academic/Scholarly.*
Indexed: Inspec.
Published by: Meteorologisk Institutt/Norwegian Meteorological Institute, PO Box 43, Blindern, Oslo, 0313, Norway. TEL 47-22-963000, FAX 47-22-963050, met.inst@met.no, http://www.met.no.

551.5 RUS ISSN 0130-2906
QC851 CODEN: MEGIAC
METEOROLOGIYA I GIDROLOGIYA. Text in Russian. 1935. m. USD 252 foreign (effective 2005). bk.rev. charts; illus. **Document type:** *Journal.* **Description:** Presents articles on the main problems of meteorology, climate changes, environmental pollution monitoring.
Related titles: ◆ English Translation: Russian Meteorology and Hydrology. ISSN 1068-3739.
Indexed: ASFA, CIN, ChemAb, ChemTitl, FR, GeoRef, Inspec, M&GPA, RefZh, SCOPUS, SpeleolAb.
—AskIEEE, CASDDS, East View, INIST, Linda Hall. **CCC.**
Published by: Izdatel'skii tsentr Meteorologiya i Gidrologya, Novovagan'kovskii per 12, Moscow, 123242, Russian Federation. TEL 7-095-2523067, FAX 7-095-2539484. Ed. Y A Izrael. Circ: 4,000. **Dist. by:** East View Information Services, 10601 Wayzata Blvd, Minneapolis, MN 55305. TEL 952-252-1201, 800-477-1005, FAX 952-252-1202, info@eastview.com, http://www.eastview.com.

551.5 AUT ISSN 0177-7971
QC851 CODEN: MAPHEU
➤ **METEOROLOGY AND ATMOSPHERIC PHYSICS.** Text in English. 1948. m. EUR 2,915, USD 3,586 combined subscription to institutions (print & online eds.) (effective 2012). adv. bk.rev. abstr.; illus. back issues avail.; reprint service avail. from PSC. **Document type:** *Journal, Academic/Scholarly.* **Description:** Discusses physical and chemical processes in all atmospheric conditions, including radiation, optical and electrical effects, precipitation and cloud microphysics.
Formerly (until 1986): Archives for Meteorology, Geophysics, and Bioclimatology. Series A: Meteorology and Geophysics - Archiv fuer Meteorologie, Geophysik und Bioklimatologie. Series A. (0066-6416)
Related titles: Microform ed.: (from PQC); Online - full text ed.: ISSN 1436-5065 (from IngentaConnect).
Indexed: A22, A26, A28, A37, APA, ASCA, ASFA, Agr, BrCerAb, C&ISA, C25, CA, CA/WCA, CABA, CIA, CerAb, CivEngAb, CorrAb, CurCont, E&CAJ, E01, E04, E05, E08, E11, E12, EEA, EMA, ESPM, EnvEAb, F08, F12, G11, GEOBASE, GeoRef, H15, I05, I11, ISR, Inspec, M&GPA, M&TEA, M09, MBF, METADEX, P02, P10, P26, P48, P52, P53, P54, P56, PQC, R12, RefZh, S09, S10, S13, S16, SCI, SCOPUS, SolStAb, SpeleolAb, T02, T04, TAR, W07, W11, WAA.
—BLDSC (5744.045000), AskIEEE, IE, Infotrieve, Ingenta, INIST, Linda Hall. **CCC.**
Published by: Springer Wien (Subsidiary of: Springer Science+Business Media), Sachsenplatz 4-6, Vienna, W 1201, Austria. TEL 43-1-33024150, FAX 43-1-3302426, journals@springer.at, http://www.springer.at. Ed. C Simmer. Adv. contact Irene Hofmann. B&W page EUR 1,290; 170 x 230. Circ: 500 (paid). **Subscr. in the Americas to:** Springer New York LLC, Journal Fulfillment, PO Box 2485, Secaucus, NJ 07096. TEL 800-777-4643, 201-348-4033, FAX 201-348-4505, journals-ny@springer.com, http://www.springer.com; **Subscr. to:** Springer Distribution Center, Kundenservice Zeitschriften, Haberstr 7, Heidelberg 69126, Germany. TEL 49-6221-3454303, FAX 49-6221-3454229, subscriptions@springer.com.

551.5 CHE ISSN 1818-7137
QC851
METEOWORLD. Text in English. 2004. bi-m. **Document type:** *Newsletter.*
Related titles: Online - full content ed.: ISSN 1818-7153; French ed.: MeteoMonde. ISSN 1818-7145.
Published by: World Meteorological Organization, 7 bis Avenue de la Paix, Case postale 2300, Geneva 2, 1211, Switzerland. TEL 41-22-7308111, FAX 41-22-7308022, http://www.wmo.int.

551.5 GRC
MINIAIO KLIMATOLOGIKO DELTIO/MONTHLY METEOROLOGICAL BULLETIN. Text in Greek. m.
Published by: National Observatory of Athens, Institute for Environmental Research, Lofos Koufou-Penteli, Athens, Greece. TEL 30-210-8109126, FAX 30-210-8103236, lagouvar@galaxy.meteo.noa.gr, http://www.noa.gr.

551.65 USA
MINNESOTA WEATHERGUIDE CALENDAR. Short title: Weatherguide. Text in English. 1975. a. USD 12.95 (effective 1997).
Former titles: Weather Guide Calendar (0270-9031); Weather Guide Calendar Almanac; (until 1977): Minnesota and Environs Weather Almanac (0095-7348)
Published by: Freshwater Foundation, 2500 Shadywood Rd, Navarre, MN 55331. TEL 612-471-9773, FAX 612-471-7685. Ed. Tom Cousins. Circ: 40,000.

551 JPN ISSN 0916-5398
MIYAGIKEN KISHO GEPPO/MIYAGI PREFECTURE. MONTHLY REPORT OF METEOROLOGY. Text in Japanese. 1964. m.
Published by: Kishocho, Sapporo Kanku Kishodai/Japan Meteorological Agency, Sapporo District Meteorological Observatory, 3-15 Gorin 1-chome, Miyagino-ku, Sendai-shi, Miyagi-ken 983-0842, Japan.

551 JPN ISSN 0916-5290
MIYAZAKIKEN KISHO GEPPO/MIYAZAKI PREFECTURE. MONTHLY REPORT OF METEOROLOGY. Text in Japanese. m.
Published by: Kishocho, Miyazaki Chiho Kishodai/Japan Meteorological Agency, Miyazaki Local Meteorological Observatory, 1-14 Wachikawaracho, Miyazaki-shi, 880-0000, Japan.

551.6 USA ISSN 0027-0296
QC982
MONTHLY CLIMATIC DATA FOR THE WORLD. Text in English. 1948. m. free (effective 2008). charts; illus. back issues avail.; reprints avail. **Document type:** *Government.*
Related titles: Online - full content ed.; Online - full text ed.
Indexed: A26, AmStI, G05, G06, G07, G08, GeoRef, I05, S06, SpeleolAb.
Published by: (U.S. Department of Commerce), U.S. National Climatic Data Center (Subsidiary of: U.S. Department of Commerce), Federal Bldg, 151 Patton Ave, Asheville, NC 28801. TEL 828-271-4800, FAX 828-271-4876, NODC.Services@noaa.gov, http://www.ncdc.noaa.gov. Circ: 500. **Co-sponsor:** World Meteorological Organization.

551.5 USA ISSN 0027-0644
QC983 CODEN: MWREAB
➤ **MONTHLY WEATHER REVIEW.** Text in English. 1872. m. USD 1,600, USD 1,670 combined subscription to non-members (print & online eds.); USD 1,200 combined subscription to members (print & online eds.) (effective 2011). adv. abstr.; bibl.; charts; illus.; stat. Index. back issues avail.; reprints avail. **Document type:** *Journal, Academic/Scholarly.* **Description:** Features research related to weather analysis and forecasting, observed and modeled circulations, including techniques development and verification studies.
Related titles: Microform ed.: (from PMC); Online - full text ed.: ISSN 1520-0493. USD 815 to non-members; USD 611 to members (effective 2011).
Indexed: A01, A03, A05, A08, A22, A23, A24, A28, A33, A37, APA, AS&TA, AS&TI, ASCA, ASFA, ApMecR, B04, B10, B13, BRD, BrCerAb, C&ISA, C10, C25, CA, CA/WCA, CABA, CIA, CIS, CMCI, CPEI, CerAb, ChemAb, CivEngAb, CorrAb, CurCont, E&CAJ, E01, E04, E05, E11, E12, EEA, EMA, ESPM, EngInd, EnvEAb, F08, F12, FCA, G09, G11, GEOBASE, GeoRef, H15, I11, INIS AtomInd, ISR, Inspec, M&GPA, M&TEA, M09, MBF, METADEX, P10, P26, P32, P40, P47, P48, P52, P53, P54, P56, PQC, S01, S04, S13, S16, SCI, SCOPUS, SPPI, SWRA, SolStAb, SpeleolAb, T02, T04, TAR, TriticAb, W03, W05, W07, WAA.
—BLDSC (5965.000000), IE, Infotrieve, Ingenta, INIST, Linda Hall. **CCC.**
Published by: American Meteorological Society, 45 Beacon St, Boston, MA 02108. TEL 617-227-2425, FAX 617-742-8718, amspubs@ametsoc.org. Ed. David M Schultz.

551.5 MOZ
MOZAMBIQUE. INSTITUTO NACIONAL DE METEOROLOGIA. BOLETIM METEOROLOGICO PARA AGRICULTURA. Text in Portuguese. 1963. 3/m. MZM 204,000, USD 17 (effective 2000). stat. reprints avail. **Document type:** *Bulletin.*
Formerly: Mozambique. Servico Meteorologico. Boletim Meteorologico para a Agricultura (0006-6044)
Media: Duplicated (not offset).
Published by: Instituto Nacional de Meteorologia, C.P. 256, Maputo, Mozambique. mozmet@zebra.uem.mz, mozmet@inam.gov.mz. Ed. Filipe Freires Domingos Lucio.

551.5 USA ISSN 2153-2397
N C A R TECHNICAL NOTES. Text in English. 1962. irreg. back issues avail. **Document type:** *Monographic series.*
Related titles: Online - full text ed.: ISSN 2153-2400. free (effective 2010).
—Linda Hall.
Published by: (National Center for Atmospheric Research), University Corporation for Atmospheric Research, PO Box 3000, Boulder, CO 80307. TEL 303-497-1000, ncarref@ucar.edu. **Subscr. to:** U.S. Department of Commerce, National Technical Information Service.

551 JPN ISSN 0916-5185
NAGANOKEN KISHO GEPPO/NAGANO PREFECTURE. MONTHLY REPORT METEOROLOGY. Text in Japanese. 1950. m.
Published by: Kishocho, Nagano Chiho Kishodai/Japan Meteorological Agency, Nagano Local Meteorological Observatory, 2417 Hakoshimizu, Nagano-shi, 380-0801, Japan.

551 JPN ISSN 0916-5312
NAGASAKIKEN KISHO GEPPO/NAGASAKI PREFECTURE. MONTHLY REPORT OF METEOROLOGY. Text in Japanese. 1952. m.
Published by: Kishocho, Nagasaki Kaiyo Kishodai/Japan Meteorological Agency, Nagasaki Marine Observatory, 11-51 Minami-Yamate-Machi, Nagasaki-shi, Nagasaki-ken 850-0931, Japan.

551.6 629.1 JPN
NAGOYA KOKU KISHOHYO/NAGOYA DATA OF AERONAUTICAL METEOROLOGY. Text in Japanese. m.
Published by: Kishocho, Nagoya Koku Sokkojo/Japan Meteorological Agency, Nagoya Aeronautical Meteorological Station, Nakashinden, Toyoba, Nishikasugai-gun, Toyoyama-cho, Aichi-ken 480-0202, Japan.

551 JPN
NARAKEN KISHO GEPPO/NARA PREFECTURE. MONTHLY REPORT OF METEOROLOGY. Text in Japanese. 1965. m.
Published by: Kishocho, Nara Chiho Kishodai/Japan Meteorological Agency, Nara Local Meteorological Observatory, 7 Handa-Biraki-cho, Nara-shi, 630-8111, Japan.

551.5 USA
NATIONAL CENTER FOR ATMOSPHERIC RESEARCH. ANNUAL REPORT. Abbreviated title: N A R. Variant title: N C A R Annual Reports. Text in English. 1997. a. free (effective 2010). back issues avail. **Document type:** *Report, Trade.*
Formerly (until 2005): N C A R Annual Scientific Reports
Media: Online - full text.
Published by: National Center for Atmospheric Research, PO Box 3000, Boulder, CO 80307. TEL 303-497-1000, http://www.ncar.ucar.edu.

551.6 USA ISSN 1949-4319
NATIONAL CENTER FOR ATMOSPHERIC RESEARCH. CLIMATE AND GLOBAL DYNAMICS. NEWS. Text in English. 1991. q. **Document type:** *Journal, Academic/Scholarly.*
Published by: National Center for Atmospheric Research, PO Box 3000, Boulder, CO 80307. TEL 303-497-1000, http://www.ncar.ucar.edu.

551.5 CAN ISSN 1926-447X
NATIONAL COMMUNICATION ON CLIMATE CHANGE; actions to meet commitments under the United Nations framework convention on climate change. Text in English, French. 1994. irreg., latest vol.5, 2010. free (effective 2011). back issues avail. **Document type:** *Report, Government.*
Formerly (until 2006): Canada's National Report on Climate Change (1702-2223)
Related titles: Online - full text ed.
Published by: Government of Canada, Service Canada, Ottawa, ON K1A 0J9, Canada. TEL 613-941-5995, 800-635-7943, FAX 613-954-5779, 800-565-7757, canadasite@canada.gc.ca, http://www.canada.gc.ca.

551.552 USA ISSN 0092-2056
QC851
NATIONAL HURRICANE OPERATIONS PLAN. Text in English. 1962. a. illus. **Document type:** *Government.*
Related titles: Online - full content ed.
—Linda Hall.
Published by: Federal Coordinator for Meteorological Services and Supporting Research, 8455 Colesville Rd, Ste 1500, Silver Spring, MD 20910. TEL 301-427-2002, ofcm.mail@noaa.gov, http://www.ofcm.gov/. Circ: 1,000. **Co-sponsors:** U.S. National Oceanic and Atmospheric Administration; U.S. Department of Commerce.

551.5 JPN
➤ **NATIONAL INSTITUTE OF POLAR RESEARCH. MEMOIRS. SERIES A: UPPER ATMOSPHERE PHYSICS.** Text and summaries in English. 1963. irreg., latest vol.19, 1989. per issue exchange basis. **Document type:** *Monographic series, Academic/Scholarly.*
Former titles: National Institute of Polar Research. Memoirs. Series A: Aeronomy (0386-5517); Japanese Antarctic Research Expedition Scientific Reports.: Aeronomy (0075-3351)
—INIST, Linda Hall.
Published by: National Institute of Polar Research/Kokuritsu Kyokuchi Kenkyujo, Publications, 10-3, Midoricho, Tachikawa, Tokyo, 190-8518, Japan. FAX 81-3-39622225, publication402@nipr.ac.jp, http://www.nipr.ac.jp/. Ed. Okitsugu Watanabe. Circ: 1,000.

551.65 JPN ISSN 0386-5525
QC980
➤ **NATIONAL INSTITUTE OF POLAR RESEARCH. MEMOIRS. SERIES B: METEOROLOGY.** Text and summaries in English. 1969. irreg., latest vol.2, 1974. per issue exchange basis. **Document type:** *Monographic series, Academic/Scholarly.*
Supersedes: Japanese Antarctic Research Expedition, 1956-1962. Scientific Reports. Series B: Meteorology (0075-336X)
Indexed: M&GPA.
—INIST.
Published by: National Institute of Polar Research/Kokuritsu Kyokuchi Kenkyujo, Publications, 10-3, Midoricho, Tachikawa, Tokyo, 190-8518, Japan. FAX 81-3-39622225, publication402@nipr.ac.jp, http://www.nipr.ac.jp/. Ed. Okitsugu Watanabe. Circ: 1,000.

551.63 USA ISSN 0271-1044
QC851
NATIONAL WEATHER ASSOCIATION NEWSLETTER. Text in English. 1976. m. USD 18 (effective 2003). **Document type:** *Newsletter, Trade.* **Description:** Details association news and provides meeting and job announcements for members. Also covers new equipment and techniques.
Related titles: ◆ Supplement to: National Weather Digest. ISSN 0271-1052.
Published by: National Weather Association, 228 W Millbrook Rd, Raleigh, NC 27609. TEL 919-845-1546, natweaasoc@aol.com, http://www.nwas.org. Eds. Eli Jacks, Larry Burch. R&P J Kevin Lavin. Circ: 3,000.

551.63 USA ISSN 0271-1052
QC983
➤ **NATIONAL WEATHER DIGEST.** Text in English. 1976. s-a. USD 60 to non-members; USD 30 per issue to non-members; free to members (effective 2010). bk.rev. bibl.; illus. Index. back issues avail.; reprints avail. **Document type:** *Journal, Trade.* **Description:** Features peer-reviewed articles, technical notes, correspondence, and official news of the Association.
Related titles: Online - full text ed.; ◆ Supplement(s): National Weather Association Newsletter. ISSN 0271-1044.
Indexed: CIS, G05, G06, G07, G08, I05, M&GPA, S06.
—BLDSC (6033.330500), IE, Ingenta, Linda Hall.
Published by: National Weather Association, 228 W Millbrook Rd, Raleigh, NC 27609. TEL 919-845-1546, FAX 919-845-2956, natweaasoc@aol.com. Eds. Tony Lupo, Gary Ellrod. Pub. Steve Harned.

➤ **NATIONAL WINTER STORMS OPERATIONS PLAN.** *see* CIVIL DEFENSE

551.6 GBR ISSN 1758-678X
▼ **NATURE CLIMATE CHANGE.** Text in English. 2011 (Apr.). m. EUR 2,410 in Europe to institutions; USD 3,036 in the Americas to institutions; GBP 1,558 to institutions in the UK & elsewhere (effective 2011). adv. **Document type:** *Journal, Academic/Scholarly.* **Description:** Provides in-depth coverage of the impacts and wider implications of the Earth's changing climate.
Related titles: Online - full text ed.: ISSN 1758-6798. 2011.
Indexed: A34, A37, C25, C30, E12, F08, FCA, R07, S13, SSciA, T05, W11.
—CCC.
Published by: Nature Publishing Group (Subsidiary of: Macmillan Publishers Ltd.), The MacMillan Bldg, 4 Crinan St, London, N1 9XW, United Kingdom. TEL 44-20-78334000, FAX 44-20-78334640. Adv. contact Simon Allardice. **Subscr. to:** Brunel Rd, Houndmills, Basingstoke, Hamps RG21 6XS, United Kingdom. TEL 44-1256-329242, FAX 44-1256-812358, subscriptions@nature.com.

551.5 796.552 FRA ISSN 1247-5327
NEIGE ET AVALANCHES. Text in French. 1977. q.
Indexed: A33, GeoRef, SD.
Published by: Association Nationale pour l'Etude de la Neige et des Avalanches, 15 Rue Ernest Calvat, Grenoble, 38000, France. TEL 33-04-76513939, FAX 33-04-76428166, http://www.anena.org.

551.6 NGA ISSN 0545-9923
NIGERIA. METEOROLOGICAL SERVICE. AGROMETEOROLOGICAL BULLETIN. Text in English. 1965. m. stat. **Document type:** *Bulletin, Government.*
Published by: Meteorological Service, Department Headquarters, Strachan St. (near Tafawa Balewa Sq.), Lagos, Nigeria. Ed. L E Akeh.

551.5 JPN ISSN 0389-1313
NIHON SEIKISHO GAKKAI ZASSHI/JAPANESE JOURNAL OF BIOMETEOROLOGY. Text and summaries in English, Japanese. 1966. 4/yr. JPY 5,000, USD 40 (effective 2001). adv. bk.rev. back issues avail. **Document type:** *Journal, Academic/Scholarly.* **Description:** Covers the effects of climate, weather, season and temperature on homes, physiology, pathology of man, animals and plants.
Related titles: Online - full text ed.: ISSN 1347-7617. free (effective 2011).
Indexed: A36, A38, A39, ASFA, B21, C25, C27, C29, C30, CABA, D03, D04, E12, E13, ESPM, F08, F11, F12, GH, H&SSA, H16, I11, LT, M&GPA, N02, N03, O01, PollutAb, R11, R14, RRTA, S13, S14, S15, S16, S18, SSciA.
—CCC.
Published by: Nihon Seikisho Gakkai/Japanese Society of Biometeorology, Nagoya Institute of Technology, Department of Environmental Technology & Urban Planning, Gokisho-cho, Showa-ku, Nagoya-City, Nagoya 466-8555, Japan. biomet@archi.ace.nitech.ac.jp. Circ: 600. **Subscr. to:** Kanazawa University School of Medicine, Department of Physiology - Kanazawa Daigaku Igakubu Seirigaku Kyoshitsu, 13-1 Takara-Machi, Kanazawa-shi, Ishikawa-ken 920-0934, Japan.

NIHON SHASHIN SOKURYO GAKKAI. GAKUJUTSU KOENKAI HAPPYO RONBUNSHU. *see* GEOGRAPHY

551 JPN
NIIGATAKEN KISHO GEPPO/NIIGATA PREFECTURE. MONTHLY REPORT OF METEOROLOGY. Text in Japanese. 1970. m.
Published by: Kishocho, Niigata Chiho Kishodai/Japan Meteorological Agency, Niigata Local Meteorological Observatory, 4-1 Saiwai-Nishi 4-chome, Niigata-shi, 950-0908, Japan.

551.6 551.31 ITA ISSN 1122-4339
NIMBUS; rivista italiana di meteorologia, clima e ghiacciai. Text in French, Italian. 1993. q. EUR 37 domestic; EUR 43 foreign (effective 2009). adv. bk.rev. illus. 100 p./no.; back issues avail. **Document type:** *Magazine, Consumer.* **Description:** Covers alpine meteorology and climatology and related fields. Includes weather reviews based on 82 meteorological stations of western Alps.
Indexed: IBR, IBZ, M&GPA.
—Ingenta.
Published by: Societa Meteorologica Subalpina, V. G. Re 86, Turin, TO 10146, Italy. TEL 39-011-797620, FAX 39-011-7504478, http://www/nimbus.it. Circ: 1,000 (paid); 500 (controlled).

NIMBUS. *see* GEOGRAPHY

551.5 CHE
NINO UPDATE; El Nino Update. Text in English. irreg.
Media: Online - full text.
Published by: World Meteorological Organization, 7 bis Avenue de la Paix, Case postale 2300, Geneva 2, 1211, Switzerland. TEL 41-22-7308111, FAX 41-22-7308022, pubsales@gateway.wmo.ch. **Co-sponsor:** International Research Institute for Climate Prediction.

551 JPN
NISHINHON KAIKYO JUNPO/TEN-DAY MARINE REPORT OF THE EAST CHINA SEA. Text in Japanese. 1948. 3/m.
Published by: Kishocho, Nagasaki Kaiyo Kishodai/Japan Meteorological Agency, Nagasaki Marine Observatory, 11-51 Minami-Yamate-Machi, Nagasaki-shi, Nagasaki-ken 850-0931, Japan.

551 630 JPN ISSN 0287-9824
NOGYO KISHO KENKYU SHUROKU/COLLECTED PAPERS OF AGRICULTURAL METEOROLOGY. Text in English, Japanese. 1953. a.
Published by: (Kankyo Shigenbu Kisho Kanrika), Norin Suisansho, Nogyo Kankyo Gijutsu Kenkyujo/Ministry of Agriculture, Forestry and Fisheries, National Institute of Agro-Environmental Sciences, Department of Natural Resources, Division of Agrometeorology, 1-1 Kannondai 3-chome, Tsukuba-shi, Ibaraki-ken 305-0856, Japan. TEL 81-298-38-8237, FAX 81-298-38-8199. Circ: 230.

551.5 630 JPN
NOGYO KISHO NENPO/ANNUAL REPORT OF AGRICULTURAL METEOROLOGY. Text in Japanese. 1950. a. membership. **Document type:** *Government.*
Published by: Kishocho/Japan Meteorological Agency, 1-3-4 Otemachi, Chiyoda-ku, Tokyo, 100-8122, Japan. Circ: 383.

551.5 USA ISSN 1932-0396
QC879.72
NORTHERN HEMISPHERE WINTER SUMMARY. Text in English. 19??. a. **Document type:** *Bulletin, Trade.*
Media: Online - full text.
Published by: National Oceanic and Atmospheric Administration, National Weather Service, Climate Prediction Center, 5200 Auth Rd, Camp Springs, MD 20746.

551 JPN
NYUZU RETA SEPPYO HOKUSHIN'ETSU/JAPANESE SOCIETY OF SNOW AND ICE. HOKUSHIN'ETSU BRANCH. NEWSLETTER. Text in Japanese. bi-m. **Document type:** *Newsletter.*
Published by: Nihon Seppyo Gakkai, Hokushin'etsu Shibu/Japanese Society of Snow and Ice, Hokushin'etsu Branch, c/o Prof. Norio Hayakawa, Nagaoka Gijutsu Kagaku Daigaku, 1603-1 Kami-Tomioka-Machi, Nagaoka-shi, Niigata-ken 940-2137, Japan.

551.5 AUT
OESTERREICHISCHE BEITRAEGE ZU METEOROLOGIE UND GEOPHYSIK. Text in English, German. 1989. irreg. back issues avail. **Document type:** *Monographic series, Academic/Scholarly.*
Indexed: SpeleolAb.
Published by: Zentralanstalt fuer Meteorologie und Geodynamik, Hohe Warte 38, Vienna, 1190, Austria. TEL 43-1-36026, FAX 43-1-3691233, TELEX 43-1-131837-METW, dion@zamg.ac.at, http://www.zamg.ac.at. Ed. Peter Steinhauser. Circ: 350.

551.5 JPN ISSN 0916-5320
OITAKEN KISHO GEPPO/OITA PREFECTURE. MONTHLY REPORT OF METEOROLOGY. Text in Japanese. 1956. m. **Description:** Circulated only in the domestic government and municipal office.
Published by: Kishocho, Oita Chiho Kishodai/Japan Meteorological Agency, Oita Local Meteorological Observatory, 1-38 Nagahama-Machi 3-chome, Oita, 870-0023, Japan. FAX 0975-36-0091. Circ: 100.

551 JPN ISSN 0916-5045
OKAYAMAKEN KISHO GEPPO/OKAYAMA PREFECTURE. MONTHLY REPORT OF METEOROLOGY. Text in Japanese. 1936. m.
Published by: Kishocho, Okayama Chiho Kishodai/Japan Meteorological Agency, Okayama Local Meteorological Observatory, 1-36 Kuwada-cho, Okayama-shi, 700-0984, Japan.

551 JPN ISSN 0387-8341
QC990.J32
OKINAWA GIJUTSU NOTO/OKINAWA METEOROLOGICAL OBSERVATORY. TECHNICAL NOTE. Text in Japanese. 1972. s-a.
Indexed: JPI.
Published by: Kishocho, Okinawa Kishodai/Japan Meteorological Agency, Okinawa Meteorological Observatory, 15-15 Higawa 1-chome, Naha-shi, Okinawa-ken 900-0022, Japan.

551.6 JPN
OKINAWA KANNAI IJO KISHO HOKOKU/OKINAWA METEOROLOGICAL OBSERVATORY. UNUSUAL METEOROLOGICAL REPORT. Text in Japanese. 1972. a.
Published by: Kishocho, Okinawa Kishodai/Japan Meteorological Agency, Okinawa Meteorological Observatory, 15-15 Higawa 1-chome, Naha-shi, Okinawa-ken 900-0022, Japan.

551 JPN ISSN 0386-2380
QC990.J32
OKINAWA KANNAI KISHO KENKYUKAISHI/OKINAWA METEOROLOGICAL OBSERVATORY. COLLECTED PAPERS. Text in Japanese. 1973. a.
Published by: Kishocho, Okinawa Kishodai/Japan Meteorological Agency, Okinawa Meteorological Observatory, 15-15 Higawa 1-chome, Naha-shi, Okinawa-ken 900-0022, Japan.

551 JPN ISSN 0916-5339
OKINAWAKEN KISHO GEPPO/OKINAWA PREFECTURE. MONTHLY REPORT OF METEOROLOGY. Text in Japanese. 1974. m.
Published by: Kishocho, Okinawa Kishodai/Japan Meteorological Agency, Okinawa Meteorological Observatory, 15-15 Higawa 1-chome, Naha-shi, Okinawa-ken 900-0022, Japan.

551 JPN
OOSAKA KANKU FUKEN KISHO KENKYUKAISHI/OSAKA DISTRICT METEOROLOGICAL SOCIETY. JOURNAL. Text in Japanese. 1975. a.
Published by: Kishocho, Oosaka Kanku Kishodai/Japan Meteorological Agency, Osaka District Meteorological Observatory, 1-67, Otemachi 4-chome, Chuo-ku, Osaka-shi, 540, Japan.

551 JPN
OOSAKA KANKU IJO KISHO HOKOKU/OSAKA DISTRICT METEOROLOGICAL OBSERVATORY. UNUSUAL METEOROLOGICAL REPORT. Text in Japanese. 1953. a.
Published by: Kishocho, Oosaka Kanku Kishodai/Japan Meteorological Agency, Osaka District Meteorological Observatory, 1-67, Otemachi 4-chome, Chuo-ku, Osaka-shi, 540, Japan.

551 JPN
OOSAKA KANKU KISHODAI GIJUTSU JOHO/OSAKA DISTRICT METEOROLOGICAL OBSERVATORY. TECHNICAL REPORT. Text in Japanese. 3/yr.
Published by: Kishocho, Oosaka Kanku Kishodai/Japan Meteorological Agency, Osaka District Meteorological Observatory, 1-67, Otemachi 4-chome, Chuo-ku, Osaka-shi, 540, Japan.

551.65 JPN ISSN 0030-6088
OOSAKAFU KISHO GEPPO/OSAKA PREFECTURE. MONTHLY REPORT OF METEOROLOGY. Text in Japanese. 1965. m. stat.
Published by: Kishocho, Oosaka Kanku Kishodai/Japan Meteorological Agency, Osaka District Meteorological Observatory, 1-67, Otemachi 4-chome, Chuo-ku, Osaka-shi, 540, Japan. Circ: 120.

551.5 NLD ISSN 1874-2823
QC851
➤ **THE OPEN ATMOSPHERIC SCIENCE JOURNAL.** Text in English. 2007. irreg. free (effective 2011). **Document type:** *Journal, Academic/Scholarly.* **Description:** Covers all areas of climate research and atmospheric science.
Media: Online - full text.
Indexed: A01, A28, A37, A39, APA, BrCerAb, C&ISA, C27, C29, CA/WCA, CABA, CIA, CerAb, CivEngAb, CorrAb, D03, D04, E&CAJ, E11, E12, E13, EEA, EMA, ESPM, H15, I11, M&GPA, M&TEA, M09, MBF, METADEX, PollutAb, R14, S13, S14, S15, S16, S18, SolStAb, T04, TAR, WAA.
Published by: Bentham Open (Subsidiary of: Bentham Science Publishers Ltd.), PO Box 294, Bussum, AG 1400, Netherlands. TEL 31-35-6923800, FAX 31-35-6980150, subscriptions@bentham.org, http://www.bentham.org. Ed. Vernon Cooray.

551.5 CHE ISSN 0250-9237
ORGANISATION METEOROLOGIQUE MONDIALE. CONGRES. PROCES - VERBAUX. Text in French. 1951. quadrennial.
Related titles: Ed.: World Meteorological Congress. Proceedings. ISSN 0084-1935. 1952.
Published by: World Meteorological Organization, 7 bis Avenue de la Paix, Case postale 2300, Geneva 2, 1211, Switzerland. TEL 41-22-7308111, FAX 41-22-7308022, pubsales@gateway.wmo.ch, http://www.wmo.int.

551.5 CHE ISSN 1011-3592
ORGANISATION METEOROLOGIQUE MONDIALE. SESSION DU CONSEIL EXECUTIF. RAPPORT ABREGE ET RESOLUTIONS. Text in French. 1983. a.
Related titles: ◆ English ed.: World Meteorological Organization. Executive Council Session. Abridged Final Reports with Resolutions. ISSN 1011-3231; ◆ Russian ed.: Vsemirnaya Meteorologicheskaya Organizatsiya. Sessiya Ispolnitel'nogo Soveta. Sokrashchennyi Otchet s Rezolyutsiyami. ISSN 1011-3673; ◆ Spanish ed.: Organizacion Meteorologica Mundial. Reunion del Consejo Ejecutivo. Informe Abreviado y Resoluciones. ISSN 1011-3576.
Published by: World Meteorological Organization, 7 bis Avenue de la Paix, Case postale 2300, Geneva 2, 1211, Switzerland. TEL 41-22-7308111, FAX 41-22-7308022, pubsales@gateway.wmo.ch, http://www.wmo.int.

551.5 CHE ISSN 1011-3576
ORGANIZACION METEOROLOGICA MUNDIAL. REUNION DEL CONSEJO EJECUTIVO. INFORME ABREVIADO Y RESOLUCIONES. Text in Spanish. 1983. a.
Related titles: ◆ English ed.: World Meteorological Organization. Executive Council Session. Abridged Final Reports with Resolutions. ISSN 1011-3231; ◆ Russian ed.: Vsemirnaya Meteorologicheskaya Organizatsiya. Sessiya Ispolnitel'nogo Soveta. Sokrashchennyi Otchet s Rezolyutsiyami. ISSN 1011-3673; ◆ French ed.: Organisation Meteorologique Mondiale. Session du Conseil Executif. Rapport Abrege et Resolutions. ISSN 1011-3592.
Published by: World Meteorological Organization, 7 bis Avenue de la Paix, Case postale 2300, Geneva 2, 1211, Switzerland. TEL 41-22-7308111, FAX 41-22-7308022, pubsales@gateway.wmo.ch, http://www.wmo.int.

551.5 JPN
OSHIMA-HIYAMA CHIHO NOGYO KISHO SOKUHO/MONTHLY REPORT OF AGRICULTURAL METEOROLOGY. Text in Japanese. 1979. m.
Published by: Kishocho, Hakodate Kaiyo Kishodai/Japan Meteorological Agency, Hakodate Marine Observatory, 3-4-4 Mihara, Hakodate-shi, Hokkaido 041-0806, Japan. Circ: 100.

551.5 ITA ISSN 1825-6864
OSSERVATORIO METEREOLOGICO DI MACERATA. RENDICONTI. Text in Italian. 1957. irreg. **Document type:** *Journal, Academic/Scholarly.*
Former titles (until 1966): Osservatorio Metereologico di Macerata. Rendiconti. Osservazioni Metereologiche (0393-1013); (until 1963): Osservatorio Metereologico. Osservazioni dell'Anno (1825-6856)
Published by: Osservatorio Geofisico Sperimentale, Centro di Ecologia e Climatologia, Viale Indipendenza 180, Macerata, Italy. TEL 39-0733-279111.

551.6 NZL ISSN 1177-9446
OTAGO CLIMATE AND PASTURE UPDATE. Text in English. m. **Description:** Provides a summary of climate, river flow and rainfall information in Otag.
Formerly (until 2006): Southern Climate and Pasture Outlook
Related titles: Online - full text ed.: ISSN 1177-9454.
Published by: (National Institute of Water and Atmospheric Research Ltd.), Otago Regional Council, 70 Stafford St, Private Bag 1954, Dunedin, New Zealand. TEL 64-3-4740827, FAX 64-3-4790015.

551.6 ESP ISSN 0212-9221
OXYMURA; revista sobre las zonas humedas. Text in Spanish; Summaries in English. 1984. a. free. **Document type:** *Monographic series, Academic/Scholarly.* **Description:** Covers waterfowl and wetlands.
Indexed: IECT.
Published by: Asociacion Amigos de la Malvasia, Apartado 3059, Cordoba, 14080, Spain. Ed. Armando Alcala Zamora Barron. Circ: 1,000. **Co-sponsor:** Patronato de las Reservas y Parajes Naturales del Sur de Cordoba.

551.5 CAN ISSN 1915-1489
OZONE DATA FOR THE WORLD (DVD-ROM)/DONNEES MONDIALES SUR L'OZONE. Text in English, French. 1960. a. Supplement avail.; back issues avail.
Former titles (until 2005): Ozone Data for the World (CD-ROM) (1497-5742); (until 1999): Ozone Data for the World (Print) (0030-7777)
Media: Optical Disk - DVD.
Published by: Environment Canada, Meteorological Service of Canada. World Ozone and Ultraviolet Radiation Data Centre (Subsidiary of: Environment Canada, Meteorological Service of Canada), 4905 Dufferin St, Toronto, ON M3H 5T4, Canada. TEL 416-739-4635, FAX 416-739-4281, woudc@ec.gc.ca, http://www.msc-smc.ec.gc.ca/woudc/index_e.html. Circ: 500.

OZONE NEWS. *see* ENVIRONMENTAL STUDIES—Pollution

551.6 DEU
P I K REPORT (ONLINE). (Potsdam Institut fuer Klimafolgenforschung) Text in English. 1994. irreg., latest vol.113, 2009. free. **Document type:** *Monographic series, Academic/Scholarly.*
Formerly (until 2009): P I K Report (Print) (1436-0179)
Indexed: GEOBASE, SCOPUS.
Published by: Potsdam Institute for Climate Impact Research, PO Box 601203, Potsdam, 14412, Germany. TEL 49-331-2882500, FAX 49-331-2882600, press@pik-potsdam.de.

551.5 551 JPN ISSN 0031-126X
QC851 CODEN: PMGTAW
PAPERS IN METEOROLOGY AND GEOPHYSICS. Text in English, Japanese. 1950. q. JPY 6,180; or on exchange basis. charts; illus. **Document type:** *Journal, Academic/Scholarly.*
Related titles: Online - full text ed.
Indexed: A28, APA, ASFA, ApMecR, BrCerAb, C&ISA, CA/WCA, CIA, CerAb, ChemAb, CivEngAb, CorrAb, E&CAJ, E11, EEA, EMA, ESPM, EnvEAb, GEOBASE, GeoRef, H15, INIS AtomInd, JTA, M&GPA, M&TEA, M09, MBF, METADEX, PollutAb, SCOPUS, SolStAb, T04, WAA.
—CASDDS, Ingenta, INIST, Linda Hall.
Published by: Japan Meteorological Agency, Meteorological Research Institute/Kishocho Kisho Kenkyujo, Office of Planning, 1-1 Nagamine, Tsukuba-shi, Ibaraki-ken 305-0052, Japan. Ed. Kenji Okada.

PHYSICAL GEOGRAPHY. *see* EARTH SCIENCES

551.5 550 RUS ISSN 0555-2648
G575 CODEN: PBAAA4
PROBLEMY ARKTIKI I ANTARKTIKI. Text in Russian. 1959. irreg.
Indexed: ASFA, B21, ESPM, GeoRef, RefZh.
—INIST, Linda Hall. **CCC.**
Published by: Gidrometeoizdat, Ul Beringa 38, St Petersburg, 199397, Russian Federation.

036 PRT ISSN 0870-4724
PROJECTO I2 DO P I D D A C. BOLETIM. (Programa de Investimentos e Despesas de Desenvolvimento da Administracao Publica) Text in Portuguese. 1978. q. stat. **Document type:** *Bulletin, Government.*
Published by: Instituto de Meteorologia, Rua C do Aeroporto, Lisbon, 1749-077, Portugal. TEL 351-21-8447000, FAX 351-21-8402370, informacoes@meteo.pt, http://www.meteo.pt/. Circ: 150.

551.6 USA ISSN 0160-9599
QC981 CODEN: PCTLD6
PUBLICATIONS IN CLIMATOLOGY. Text in English. 1948. a. price varies.
Indexed: GeoRef, SpeleolAb.
—BLDSC (7126.990000), Linda Hall.
Published by: (Laboratory of Climatology), C.W. Thornthwaite Associates, 1725 Parvins Mill Rd., Pittsgrove, NJ 08318-4555. TEL 609-358-2350. Ed. John R Mather. Circ: 500.

551.5 CHN ISSN 1000-0526
QC851
QIXIANG. Text in Chinese. 1975. m. CNY 4.80 per issue. charts; stat. Index. 64 p./no.; back issues avail. **Document type:** *Journal, Academic/Scholarly.* **Description:** Middle-level journal for academic exchange. Covers all aspects of atmospheric science, especially synoptic meteorology, climatology, atmospheric physics, and atmospheric sounding.
Formelry (until 1975): Qixiang Tongxun
Related titles: Online - full text ed.: (from WanFang Data Corp.).
Indexed: ESPM, M&GPA, PollutAb.
—East View, Linda Hall.
Published by: (Zhongguo Qixiangju/China Meteorological Administration), Qixiang Chubanshe/China Meteorological Press, 46, Zhongguancun Nan Dajie, Beijing, 100081, China. http://www.cmp.cma.gov.cn/. Circ: 6,000.

551.5 CHN ISSN 1671-6345
➤ **QIXIANG KEJI/METEOROLOGICAL SCIENCE AND TECHNOLOGY.** Text in Chinese; Abstracts in English. 1973. bi-m. abstr.; charts; illus.; bibl.; maps. Index. back issues avail. **Document type:** *Journal, Academic/Scholarly.* **Description:** Focuses on global progress, new methods, new trends and new viewpoints in atmospheric science. Covers Forecasting theory and methodology, weather and climate analysis, weather and climate analysis, climate and global change, atmospheric physics and atmospheric chemistry, applied meteorology (including urban and environmental meteorology, agricultural and ecological meteorology, and weather modification, natural disaster prevention and mitigation), atmospheric sounding technology, etc.
Related titles: CD-ROM ed.; Online - full text ed.: (from WanFang Data Corp.).
Published by: Zhongguo Qixiang Kexue Yanjiuyuan/Chinese Academy of Meteorological Sciences, 46, Zhongguancun Nandajie, Beijing, 100081, China. TEL 86-10-68407256, FAX 86-10-68407256, http://www.cams.cma.gov.cn/. Ed. Xiaomei Zeng. Pub. Fenjie Yuan. Circ: 1,000. **Co-sponsors:** Beijing Shi Qixiangju/Beijing Meteorological Bureau; Guojia Qixiang Xinxi Zhongxin; Guojia Weixing Qixiang Zhongxin; Zhongguo Qixiangju Qixiang Tance Zhongxin/Meteorological Observation Centre of C M A.

551.5 CHN ISSN 0577-6619
QC851 CODEN: CHIHAW
➤ **QIXIANG XUEBAO.** Text in Chinese. 1941. bi-m. CNY 240 (effective 2011). **Document type:** *Journal, Academic/Scholarly.*
Related titles: Online - full text ed.: (from WanFang Data Corp.); ◆ English ed.: Acta Meteorologica Sinica. ISSN 0894-0525.
Indexed: Inspec.
—AskIEEE, East View, Linda Hall.
Published by: Chinese Meteorological Society/Zhongguo Qixiang Xuehui, 46 Zhongguancun Nan Dajie, Haidian District, Beijing, 100081, China. TEL 86-10-68406942, FAX 86-10-68408571, http://www.cms1924.org/CN/index.html. Ed. Zhou Xiuji. R&P Zhou Shijian TEL 86-10-6840-7092. Circ: 2,000 (paid); 100 (controlled).

551.5 CHN ISSN 1673-8411
QIXIANG YANJIU YU YINGYONG/JOURNAL OF METEOROLOGICAL RESEARCH AND APPLICATION. Text in Chinese. 1956. q. CNY 10 per issue (effective 2011). **Document type:** *Journal, Academic/Scholarly.*
Formerly (until 2007): Guangxi Qixiang/Journal of Guangxi Meteorology (1001-5191)
Related titles: Online - full text ed.
Published by: Guangxi Qixiangju/Guangxi Meteorological Bureau, 81, Minzu Dadao, Nanning, 530022, China. TEL 86-771-5848935, FAX 86-771-5865443, http://www.gxqxj.com/.

551.5 CHN ISSN 1000-0321
QIXIANG ZHISHI/METEOROLOGICAL KNOWLEDGE. Text in Chinese. 1981. bi-m. CNY 66 (effective 2011). **Document type:** *Magazine, Government.*
Related titles: Online - full text ed.
Published by: (Zhongguo Qixiangju/China Meteorological Administration), Chinese Meteorological Society/Zhongguo Qixiang Xuehui, 46 Zhongguancun Nan Dajie, Haidian District, Beijing, 100081, China. TEL 86-10-68406721, FAX 86-10-68406841, cmaywwz@cma.gov.cn, http://www.cms1924.org/CN/index.html.

551.63 JPN
R S M C TOKYO - TYPHOON CENTER. ANNUAL ACTIVITY REPORT. Text in English. a.

Published by: Kishocho/Japan Meteorological Agency, 1-3-4 Otemachi, Chiyoda-ku, Tokyo, 100-8122, Japan.

551.527 NOR
THE RADIATION OBSERVATORY RADIATION YEARBOOK. Text in Norwegian. 2003. a.
Media: Online - full content.
Published by: Universitetet i Bergen, Geofysisk Institutt/University of Bergen, Geophysical Institute, Allegaten 70, Bergen, 5007, Norway. TEL 47-55-582602, FAX 47-55-589883, http://www.gfi.uib.no/middle_and_right_e.html.

551.6 CHN ISSN 1004-4965
QC993.5
➤ **REDAI QIXIANG XUEBAO.** Text in Chinese; Abstracts in English. 1984. q. USD 45 (effective 2009). adv. 96 p./no.; back issues avail. **Document type:** *Journal, Academic/Scholarly.* **Description:** Covers the latest research achievements in tropical atmospheric science.
Formerly (until 1993): Redai Qixiang (1000-4068)
Related titles: ◆ CD-ROM ed.: Chinese Academic Journals Full-Text Database. Science & Engineering, Series A. ISSN 1007-8010; Online - full content ed.; Online - full text ed.; ◆ English ed.: Journal of Tropical Meteorology. ISSN 1006-8775.
—East View.
Published by: Guangzhou Redai Haiyang Qixiang Yanjiusuo/Guangzhou Institute of Tropical and Oceanic Meteorology, No 6, Fujin Rd, Dongshan District, Guangzhou, Guangdong 510080, China. TEL 86-20-87776918 ext 333, FAX 86-20-87673470. Ed. Shangsen Wu. R&P, Adv. contact Cao Myles. Circ: 1,200. **Dist. overseas by:** China International Book Trading Corp, 35 Chegongzhuang Xilu, Haidian District, PO Box 399, Beijing 100044, China.

551.5 MAC ISSN 0460-3060
RESULTADOS DAS OBSERVACOES METEOROLOGICAS DE MACAU. Text in Chinese, Portuguese. 1952. m. (plus a. issue). free. charts; stat. **Document type:** *Government.* **Description:** Contains meteorological results.
Published by: Servicos Meteorologicos e Geofisicos de Macau, Caixa Postal 93, Macau. TEL 853-8986223, FAX 853-850557, meteo@smg.gov.mo, http://www.smg.gov.mo. Eds. Fong Soi Kun, Antonio Viseu. Pub. Fong Soi Kun. R&P, Adv. contact Hao I Pan. Circ: 120.

551.5 630 ARG ISSN 1666-017X
REVISTA ARGENTINA DE AGROMETEOROLOGIA. Text in Multiple languages. 2001. a. **Document type:** *Magazine, Trade.*
Published by: Asociacion Argentina de Agrometeorologia, Facultad de Agronomia y Veterinaria, Universidad del Rio Cuarto, Ruta Nacional 36 Km 601, Rio Cuarto, Cordoba X5804BYA, Argentina. TEL 54-358-4676191, FAX 54-358-4680280, http://www.aada.com.ar.

551.5 630 BRA ISSN 0104-1347
REVISTA BRASILEIRA DE AGROMETEOROLOGIA. Text in Portuguese. 1993. a. **Document type:** *Journal, Academic/Scholarly.*
Indexed: A34, A37, A38, AgrForAb, BA, C25, C30, CABA, E12, ESPM, F08, F12, FCA, G11, H16, I11, M&GPA, MaizeAb, N02, O01, OR, P32, P40, PGegResA, PGrRegA, R11, R13, S12, S13, S16, SWRA, SoyAb, TAR, TriticAb, VS, W10, W11.
Published by: Universidade Federal de Santa Maria, Centro de Ciencias Rurais, Predio 42 - Sala 3104, Santa Maria, 97105-900, Brazil. TEL 55-55-220-8698, FAX 55-55-220-8695, http://www.ufsm.br.

551 BRA ISSN 0102-7786
REVISTA BRASILEIRA DE METEOROLOGIA. Text in Portuguese. 1986. s-a. **Document type:** *Journal, Academic/Scholarly.*
Related titles: Online - full text ed.: ISSN 1982-4351. free (effective 2011).
Indexed: A34, A37, AgrForAb, C25, C30, CABA, D01, E12, F08, F12, FCA, G11, GH, H16, I11, M&GPA, N02, P33, PGrRegA, R08, S13, S16, T05, TAR.
Published by: Sociedade Brasileira de Meteorologia, Rua Mexico 41, Sala 1304, Centro, Rio de Janeiro, 20031-144, Brazil. TEL 55-21-25247890, FAX 55-21-97581995, sbmet@sbmet.org.br, http://www.sbmet.org.br/. Ed. Manoel Alonso Gan.

551.5 ESP ISSN 1578-8768
QC851
REVISTA DE CLIMATOLOGIA. Text in Spanish. 2001. irreg. free (effective 2011). **Document type:** *Journal, Academic/Scholarly.*
Media: Online - full text.
Indexed: CA, E04, E05, F04, T02.
Address: Palma de Majorca, Spain. Ed. Jose Antonio Guijarro.

551.5 MYS
RINGKASAN TAHUNAN PEMERHATIAN KAJICUACA/MALAYSIAN METEOROLOGICAL SERVICE. ANNUAL SUMMARY OF METEOROLOGICAL OBSERVATIONS. Text and summaries in English. 1930. a. MYR 100 (effective 2000). **Document type:** *Government.* **Description:** Provides a summary of meteorological parameters recorded for the year from meteorological and climatological stations.
Former titles: Malaysian Meteorological Service. Summary of Observations for Malaysia (0126-8864); Malaysia. Meteorological Service. Summary of Observations for Malaya, Sabah and Sarawak
Published by: Perkhidmatan Kajicuaca Malaysia/Malaysian Meteorological Service, Jalan Sultan, Petaling Jaya, Selangor 46667, Malaysia. TEL 60-3-7563225, FAX 60-3-7563621, TELEX MA 37243, klim@kjc.gov.my, http://www.kjc.gov.my. Circ: 100 (paid).

551.5 ROM ISSN 1223-1118
➤ **ROMANIAN JOURNAL OF METEOROLOGY.** Text in Romanian. 1994. s-a. per issue exchange basis. **Document type:** *Academic/Scholarly.*
Indexed: M&GPA.
—Linda Hall.
Published by: National Institute of Meteorology and Hydrology/Institutul National de Meteorologie si Hidrologie, Sos. Bucuresti Ploiesti 97, Bucharest, 71581, Romania. TEL 40-1-6793240, FAX 40-1-3129843, TELEX 10460 IMH R. Ed., R&P Sergiu Tumanov. Circ: 250 (controlled).

551.5 RUS ISSN 1023-6317
QC851 CODEN: IFAOAV
ROSSIISKAYA AKADEMIYA NAUK. IZVESTIYA. SERIYA FIZIKA ATMOSFERY I OKEANA. Text in Russian; Summaries in English, Russian. 1951. m. RUR 1,300 for 6 mos. domestic (effective 2004). adv. bk.rev. charts; illus. index. **Document type:** *Journal, Academic/Scholarly.* **Description:** Publishes original scientific research and review articles on vital issues in the physics of the earth's atmosphere and hydrosphere, and climate theory.
Formerly (until 1992): Akademiya Nauk S.S.S.R. Izvestiya. Seriya Fizika Atmosfery i Okeana (0002-3515); Which superseded in part (in 1965): Akademiya Nauk S.S.S.R. Izvestiya. Seriya Geofizicheskaya (0568-5311)
Related titles: Online - full text ed.; ◆ English Translation: Russian Academy of Sciences. Izvestiya. Atmospheric and Oceanic Physics. ISSN 0001-4338.
Indexed: A20, ASFA, B21, BibCart, CCMJ, ChemAb, ESPM, GeoRef, Inspec, M&GPA, MSN, MathR, PhysBer, RefZh, SpeleolAb, Z02.
—BLDSC (0082.309550), AskIEEE, CASDDS, East View, INIST, Linda Hall. **CCC.**
Published by: (Rossiiskaya Akademiya Nauk/Russian Academy of Sciences), Izdatel'stvo Nauka, Profsoyuznaya ul 90, Moscow, 117864, Russian Federation. TEL 7-095-3347151, FAX 7-095-4202220, secret@naukaran.ru, http://www.naukaran.ru. Circ: 1,000.

ROYAL ASTRONOMICAL SOCIETY. MONTHLY NOTICES. *see* ASTRONOMY

ROYAL ASTRONOMICAL SOCIETY. MONTHLY NOTICES. LETTERS (ONLINE). *see* ASTRONOMY

551.5 GBR ISSN 0035-9009
QC851 CODEN: QJRMAM
➤ **ROYAL METEOROLOGICAL SOCIETY. QUARTERLY JOURNAL;** a journal of the atmospheric sciences, applied meteorology, and physical oceanography. Text in English. 18??. 8/yr. GBP 565 in United Kingdom to institutions; EUR 714 in Europe to institutions; USD 1,105 elsewhere to institutions; GBP 650 combined subscription in United Kingdom to institutions (print & online eds.); EUR 821 combined subscription in Europe to institutions (print & online eds.); USD 1,271 combined subscription elsewhere to institutions (print & online eds.) (effective 2012). adv. bk.rev. charts; illus. index. back issues avail.; reprints avail. **Document type:** *Journal, Academic/Scholarly.* **Description:** Includes some oceanographic aspects of meteorology.
Formerly (until 1871): Bibliography of Meteorological Literature
Related titles: Online - full text ed.: ISSN 1477-870X. GBP 565 in United Kingdom to institutions; EUR 714 in Europe to institutions; USD 1,105 elsewhere to institutions (effective 2012).
Indexed: A22, A28, A37, APA, ASCA, ASFA, BrCerAb, C&ISA, C25, CA/WCA, CABA, CIA, CPEI, CTO, CerAb, CivEngAb, CorrAb, CurCont, E&CAJ, E11, E12, EEA, EMA, ESPM, EngInd, EnvEAb, F08, F12, FCA, G11, GEOBASE, GeoRef, H15, I11, IBR, IBZ, ISR, Inspec, M&GPA, M&TEA, M09, MBF, METADEX, MaizeAb, OceAb, R07, RefZh, S13, S16, SCI, SCOPUS, SolStAb, SpeleolAb, T02, T04, TAR, W07, WAA.
—BLDSC (7186.000000), AskIEEE, CASDDS, IE, Infotrieve, Ingenta, INIST, Linda Hall. **CCC.**
Published by: (Royal Meteorological Society), John Wiley & Sons Ltd. (Subsidiary of: John Wiley & Sons, Inc.), 1-7 Oldlands Way, PO Box 808, Bognor Regis, West Sussex PO21 9FF, United Kingdom. TEL 44-1865-778315, FAX 44-1243-843232, cs-journals@wiley.com, http://eu.wiley.com/WileyCDA/. Eds. John Thuburn, Mark P Baldwin. **Subscr. to:** 1-7 Oldlands Way, PO Box 809, Bognor Regis, West Sussex PO21 9FG, United Kingdom. TEL 44-1865-778054, cs-agency@wiley.com.

551.5 RUS ISSN 0001-4338
QC851 CODEN: IRAPEK
RUSSIAN ACADEMY OF SCIENCES. IZVESTIYA. ATMOSPHERIC AND OCEANIC PHYSICS. Text in English. 1957. bi-m. EUR 1,883, USD 2,246 combined subscription to institutions (print & online eds.) (effective 2012). **Document type:** *Journal, Academic/Scholarly.* **Description:** Publishes original scientific research and review articles on vital issues in the physics of the earth's atmosphere and hydrosphere, and climate theory.
Formerly: Academy of Sciences of the U S S R. Izvestiya. Atmospheric and Oceanic Physics; Which superseded in part (in 1965): Academy of Sciences of the U S S R. Bulletin. Geophysics Series (0568-5249)
Related titles: Online - full text ed.: ISSN 1555-628X (from IngentaConnect); ◆ Translation of: Rossiiskaya Akademiya Nauk. Izvestiya. Seriya Fizika Atmosfery i Okeana. ISSN 1023-6317.
Indexed: A22, A26, A37, ASFA, C25, C30, CABA, CCMJ, CurCont, E01, E12, F08, F12, G11, GEOBASE, GeoRef, I05, I11, ISR, Inspec, M&GPA, MSN, MathR, P26, P32, P47, P48, P52, P54, P56, PQC, S13, S16, SCI, SCOPUS, TAR, W07, Z02.
—BLDSC (0412.740550), East View, IE, Infotrieve, Ingenta, INIST, Linda Hall. **CCC.**
Published by: M A I K Nauka - Interperiodica (Subsidiary of: Pleiades Publishing, Inc.), Profsoyuznaya ul 90, Moscow, 117997, Russian Federation. TEL 7-095-3347420, FAX 7-095-3360666, compmg@maik.ru. Ed. Greorgii S Golitsyn. **Distr. in the Americas by:** Springer New York LLC, Journal Fulfillment, PO Box 2485, Secaucus, NJ 07096. TEL 212-460-1500, FAX 201-348-4505; **Distr. outside of the Americas by:** Springer, Haber Str 7, Heidelberg 69126, Germany. TEL 49-6221-3454303, FAX 49-6221-3454229.

551.5 551.4 USA ISSN 1068-3739
QC851 CODEN: RMHYEA
➤ **RUSSIAN METEOROLOGY AND HYDROLOGY.** Text in English. 1976. m. EUR 2,854, USD 3,458 combined subscription to institutions (print & online eds.) (effective 2012). bibl.; charts; illus.; stat.; abstr.; maps. index. back issues avail.; reprints avail. **Document type:** *Journal, Academic/Scholarly.* **Description:** Covers weather forecasting, ocean hydrodynamics, atmospheric turbulence, hydrometeorological anomalies, environmental pollution, and agrometeorology.
Formerly (until 1993): Soviet Meteorology and Hydrology (0146-4108)
Related titles: Online - full text ed.: ISSN 1934-8096; ◆ Translation of: Meteorologiya i Gidrologiya. ISSN 0130-2906.
Indexed: A22, A26, A34, A37, C25, C30, CABA, CPEI, E01, E12, ESPM, EngInd, F08, F11, F12, FCA, G11, GEOBASE, GeoRef, H12, I05, I11, Inspec, M&GPA, P26, P47, P48, P52, P54, P56, PQC, PollutAb, S13, S16, SCI, SCOPUS, TAR, TriticAb, W07, W11.
—BLDSC (0420.772200), AskIEEE, East View, IE, Infotrieve, Ingenta, INIST, Linda Hall. **CCC.**

Published by: (Gidrometeoizdat RUS), Allerton Press, Inc. (Subsidiary of: Pleiades Publishing, Inc.), 18 W 27th St, New York, NY 10001. TEL 646-424-9686, FAX 646-424-9695, journals@allertonpress.com. Ed. Yurii A Izrael.

551.6 GBR
S I R W E C. PROCEEDINGS. (Standing International Road Weather Conference) Text in English. a. **Document type:** *Proceedings.*
Published by: University of Birmingham, Birmingham Climate and Atmospheric Research Centre (BCAR), University Of Birmingham, Edgbaston, Birmingham B15 2TT, United Kingdom. **Co-sponsor:** Vaisala TMI.

M

551.5 SWE ISSN 0283-7730
S M H I METEOROLOGI. Text in Swedish. 1982. irreg., latest vol.142, 2010. **Document type:** *Monographic series, Academic/Scholarly.*
Formerly (until 1985): Sveriges Meteorologiska och Hydrologiska Institut. Klimatsektionen. Meteorologiska Avdelningen. Rapport (0282-261X)
Published by: Sveriges Meteorologiska och Hydrologiska Institut/Swedish Meteorological and Hydrological Institute, Folkborgvaegen 1, Norrkoeping, 60176, Sweden. TEL 46-11-4958000, FAX 46-11-4958001, smhi@smhi.se, http://www.smhi.se.

551.5 SWE ISSN 0347-2116
S M H I RAPPORTER. METEOROLOGI OCH KLIMATOLOGI/S M H I REPORTS. METEOROLOGY AND CLIMATOLOGY. Text in English, Swedish. 1953. irreg., latest vol.113, 2008. **Document type:** *Monographic series, Academic/Scholarly.*
Former titles (until 1973): Sveriges Meteorologiska och Hydrologiska Institut. Notiser och Preliminaera Rapporter. Serie Meteorologi (0373-7691); (until 1959): Notiser och Preliminaera Rapporter. Sveriges Meteorologiska och Hydrologiska Institut. Meteorologiska Byraan
Indexed: M&GPA.
Published by: Sveriges Meteorologiska och Hydrologiska Institut/Swedish Meteorological and Hydrological Institute, Folkborgvaegen 1, Norrkoeping, 60176, Sweden. TEL 46-11-4958000, FAX 46-11-4958001, smhi@smhi.se, http://www.smhi.se.

551.5 USA ISSN 1948-2507
S O A R S NEWSLETTER. (Significant Opportunities in Atmospheric Research and Science) Text in English. 1998. s-a. back issues avail. **Document type:** *Newsletter, Trade.* **Description:** Cointains updates on the Significant Opportunities in Atmospheric Research and Science internship program for undergraduate and graduate students.
Related titles: Online - full text ed.: ISSN 1948-2515.
Published by: National Center for Atmospheric Research, S O A R S, PO Box 3000, Boulder, CO 80307. TEL 303-497-8622, FAX 303-497-8629, SOARS@UCAR.edu, http://www.soars.ucar.edu.

551.5 JPN ISSN 1349-6476
QC851
S O L A. (Scientific Online Letters on the Atmosphere) Text in English. 2005. irreg. free (effective 2011). **Document type:** *Journal, Academic/Scholarly.*
Media: Online - full text.
Indexed: A39, C27, C29, D03, D04, E13, R14, S14, S15, S18, SCI, SCOPUS, W07.
Published by: Meteorological Society of Japan/Nihon Kisho Gakkai, c/o Japan Meteorological Agency, 3-4 Ote-Machi 1-chome, Chiyoda-ku, Tokyo, 100-0004, Japan. TEL 81-3-3212-8341 ext 2546, FAX 81-3-3216-4401. Ed. Dr. Hiroshi L Tanaka.

551.656 MDG
SAISON CYCLONIQUE A MADAGASCAR. Text in French. 1973. a. **Document type:** *Government.* **Description:** Presents cyclonic season in Madagascar.
Published by: Service de la Meteorologie Nationale, BP 1254, Antananarivo, Madagascar. TEL 19-261-2-40241, FAX 19-261-2-40581.

551 JPN ISSN 0916-5215
SAITAMA-KEN KISHO GEPPO/SAITAMA PREFECTURE. MONTHLY REPORT OF METEOROLOGY. Text in Japanese. 1897. m.
Related titles: Online - full text ed.
Published by: Kishocho, Kumagaya Chiho Kishodai/Japan Meteorological Agency, Kumagaya Local Meteorological Observatory, 1-6-10 Sakura, Kumagaya, Saitama 360-0814, Japan. TEL 81-48-5215858, http://www.jma-net.go.jp/kumagaya/.

551 JPN
SAITAMA-KEN NO KISHO SAIGAI/METEOROLOGICAL DISASTER IN SAITAMA PREFECTURE. Text in Japanese. triennial.
Published by: (Japan. Kishocho/Japan Meteorological Agency, Saitamaken. Kumagaya Chiho Kishodai/Kumagaya Local Meteorological Observatory), Saitama Prefectural Government, 15-1 Takasago 3-chome, Urawa-shi, Saitama-ken 336-0011, Japan.

551 JPN
SAPPORO KANKU KISHO KENKYUKAISHI/SAPPORO DISTRICT METEOROLOGICAL OBSERVATORY. JOURNAL. Text in Japanese. a.
Published by: Kishocho, Sapporo Kanku Kishodai/Japan Meteorological Agency, Sapporo District Meteorological Observatory, 2, Nishi 18-chome, Kita 2-jo, Chuo-ku, Sapporo-shi, Hokkaido 060, Japan.

551 JPN
SAPPORO KANKU KISHODAI GIJUTSU JIHO/SAPPORO DISTRICT METEOROLOGICAL OBSERVATORY. TECHNICAL REPORT. Text in Japanese. s-a.
Published by: Kishocho, Sapporo Kanku Kishodai/Japan Meteorological Agency, Sapporo District Meteorological Observatory, 2, Nishi 18-chome, Kita 2-jo, Chuo-ku, Sapporo-shi, Hokkaido 060, Japan.

551.6 CAN ISSN 0821-0284
SASKATCHEWAN RESEARCH COUNCIL. CLIMATOLOGICAL REFERENCE STATION. ANNUAL SUMMARY. Text in English. 1975. a. CAD 40 (effective 2000). **Document type:** *Journal, Academic/Scholarly.* **Description:** Includes monthly weather summaries of various weather elements.
Former titles: Saskatoon S.R.C. Climatological Reference Station. Annual Summary (0848-6964); Saskatchewan Research Council. Physics Division. Annual Climatic Summary (0706-9391)
Published by: (Environment Division), Saskatchewan Research Council, 15 Innovation Blvd, Saskatoon, SK S7N 2X8, Canada. TEL 306-933-8182, FAX 306-933-7817. Ed., R&P Carol Beaulieu. Circ: 100.

551.5 USA ISSN 1948-254X
SCIENCE BRIEFS. Text in English. 1995. q. **Document type:** *Newsletter, Trade.*
Published by: National Center for Atmospheric Research, PO Box 3000, Boulder, CO 80307. TEL 303-497-1000, http://www.ncar.ucar.edu.

551.470 NLD ISSN 8755-6839
GC221.2
SCIENCE OF TSUNAMI HAZARDS. Text in English. 1982. q. **Document type:** *Journal, Academic/Scholarly.*
Formerly: Natural Sciences of Hazards (0736-5306)
Related titles: Online - full text ed.: free (effective 2011).
Indexed: ASFA, ESPM, GeoRef, M&GPA, OceAb, SCOPUS, T02.
—Linda Hall. **CCC.**
Published by: (Tsunami Society USA), Springer Netherlands (Subsidiary of: Springer Science+Business Media), Van Godewijckstraat 30, Dordrecht, 3311 GX, Netherlands. TEL 31-78-6576050, FAX 31-78-6576474, http://www.springer.com. Ed. George Pararas-Carayannis.

551.5 630 JPN ISSN 1346-5368
S600
SEIBUTSU TO KISHO. Text in Japanese. 1943. q. JPY 2,060 per issue. adv. bk.rev. abstr.; charts. index.
Formerly (until 2001): Nogyo Kisho/Journal of Agricultural Meteorology (0021-8588)
Related titles: Online - full text ed.
Indexed: A22, ASFA, Agrind, B25, BIOSIS Prev, ChemAb, ESPM, M&GPA, MycolAb, PollutAb, SSciA, SWRA.
—BLDSC (4922.000000), IE, Ingenta, Linda Hall. **CCC.**
Published by: Society of Agricultural Meteorology of Japan/Nihon Nogyo Kisho Gakkai, University of, Department of Agricultural Engineering, Yayoi, Bunkyo-ku, Tokyo, 113-0032, Japan. FAX 81-3-3813-2437. Ed. Taichi Maki. Circ: 1,100.

551 JPN
SENDAI KANKU CHOSA KENKYUKAI SHIRYO/SENDAI DISTRICT METEOROLOGICAL OBSERVATORY. PROCEEDINGS OF THE MEETING. Text in Japanese. a. **Document type:** *Proceedings.*
Published by: Kishocho, Sapporo Kanku Kishodai/Japan Meteorological Agency, Sapporo District Meteorological Observatory, 3-15 Gorin 1-chome, Miyagino-ku, Sendai-shi, Miyagi-ken 983-0842, Japan.

551 JPN
SENDAI KANKU GIJUTSU SHIRYO/SENDAI DISTRICT METEOROLOGICAL OBSERVATORY. TECHNICAL DATA. Text in Japanese. 1969. irreg.
Published by: Kishocho, Sapporo Kanku Kishodai/Japan Meteorological Agency, Sapporo District Meteorological Observatory, 3-15 Gorin 1-chome, Miyagino-ku, Sendai-shi, Miyagi-ken 983-0842, Japan.

551 JPN
SENDAI KANKU IJO KISHO HOKOKU/SENDAI DISTRICT METEOROLOGICAL OBSERVATORY. UNUSUAL METEOROLOGICAL REPORT. Text in Japanese. 1964. a.
Published by: Kishocho, Sapporo Kanku Kishodai/Japan Meteorological Agency, Sapporo District Meteorological Observatory, 3-15 Gorin 1-chome, Miyagino-ku, Sendai-shi, Miyagi-ken 983-0842, Japan.

551.6 JPN ISSN 0918-1474
SEPPYO HOKUSHIN'ETSU/JAPANESE SOCIETY OF SNOW AND ICE. HOKUSHIN'ETSU BRANCH. JOURNAL. Text in Japanese. 1988. s-a. **Document type:** *Academic/Scholarly.*
Published by: Nihon Seppyo Gakkai, Hokushin'etsu Shibu/Japanese Society of Snow and Ice, Hokushin'etsu Branch, c/o Prof. Norio Hayakawa, Nagoaka Gijutsu Kagaku Daigaku, 1603-1 Kami-Tomioka-Machi, Nagaoka-shi, Niigata-ken 940-2137, Japan.

551.6 CHN ISSN 1004-5732
SHANXI QIXIANG/SHANXI METEOROLOGICAL QUARTERLY. Text in Chinese. 1988. q. CNY 3 newsstand/cover (effective 2006). **Document type:** *Journal, Academic/Scholarly.*
Related titles: Online - full text ed.
Published by: Shanxi Sheng Qixiang Ju/Shanxi Provincial Bureau of Meteorology, 145 Xinjian Lu, Taiyuan, 030002, China. TEL 86-351-4077727.

551 JPN
SHIGAKEN KISHO GEPPO/SHIGA PREFECTURE. MONTHLY REPORT OF METEOROLOGY. Text in Japanese. 1900. m.
Published by: Kishocho, Hikone Chiho Kishodai/Japan Meteorological Agency, Hikone Local Meteorological Observatory, 5-25 Shiro-Machi 2-chome, Hikone-shi, Shiga-ken 522-0068, Japan.

551 JPN
SHIKOKU URYO GEPPO/MONTHLY PRECIPITATION REPORT IN SHIKOKU DISTRICT. Text in Japanese. 1957. m.
Published by: Nihon Kisho Kyokai, Shikoku Shiter/Japan Weather Association, Shikoku Branch, Sunshine 60 Building, 3-1-1, Higashi-Ikebukuro, Toshima-ku, Tokyo, 170, Japan. TEL 81-3-5958-8161, FAX 81-3-5958-8162.

551 JPN ISSN 0916-538X
SHIMANEKEN KISHO GEPPO/SHIMANE PREFECTURE. MONTHLY REPORT OF METEOROLOGY. Text in Japanese. 1967. m. **Document type:** *Academic/Scholarly.*
Published by: Kishocho, Matsue Chiho Kishodai/Japan Meteorological Agency, Matsue Local Meteorological Observatory, 1-11 Nishi-Tsuda 7-chome, Matsue-shi, Shimane-ken 690-0017, Japan.

551 JPN ISSN 0916-5002
SHIZUOKAKEN KISHO GEPPO/SHIZUOKA PREFECTURE. MONTHLY REPORT OF METEOROLOGY. Text in Japanese. 1950. m. stat.
Published by: Shizuoka Chiho Kishodai/Shizuoka Local Meteorological Observatory (Subsidiary of: Kishocho/Japan Meteorological Agency), 2-1-5 Magarikane, Shizuoka, 422-8006, Japan. TEL 81-54-286-6919, http://www.tokyo-jma.go.jp/sub_index/soumu/tokyo/sizuoka/.

551.5 USA ISSN 1948-2493
SIGNAL (BOULDER). Text in English. 1993. s-a.
Published by: National Center for Atmospheric Research, PO Box 3000, Boulder, CO 80307. TEL 303-497-1000, http://www.ncar.ucar.edu.

551.5 SVK ISSN 1335-339X
QC989.S56
SLOVENSKY HYDROMETEOROLOGICKY USTAV. METEOROLOGICKY CASOPSIS/SLOVAK HYDROMETEOROLOGICAL INSTITUT. METEOROLOGICAL JOURNAL. Text in Multiple languages. 1998. s-a.
Indexed: A22, M&GPA.
—BLDSC (5739.445000), IE, Ingenta.
Published by: Slovensky Hydrometeorologicky Ustav/Slovak Hydrometeorological Institut, Jeseniova 17, Bratislava, 833 15, Slovakia. TEL 421-2-54771247, FAX 421-2-54774593, SHMU-GR@shmu.sk, http://www.shmu.sk.

551 BRA ISSN 1676-014X
SOCIEDAD BRASILEIRA DE METEOROLOGIA. BOLETIM. Text in Portuguese. 1960. q. back issues avail. **Document type:** *Bulletin, Academic/Scholarly.*
Related titles: Online - full text ed.
Published by: Sociedade Brasileira de Meteorologia, Rua Mexico 41, Sala 1304, Centro, Rio de Janeiro, 20031-144, Brazil. TEL 55-21-25247890, FAX 55-21-97581995, sbmet@sbmet.org.br. Ed. Marley Cavalcante de Lima.

551.5 JPN
SOKKO JIHO/WEATHER SERVICE BULLETIN. Text in Japanese. 1930. bi-m. JPY 7,800. index. **Document type:** *Bulletin.*
Published by: Kishocho/Japan Meteorological Agency, 1-3-4 Otemachi, Chiyoda-ku, Tokyo, 100-8122, Japan. Circ: 914.

551.65 ZAF ISSN 0011-5517
SOUTH AFRICA. WEATHER BUREAU. DAILY WEATHER BULLETIN/ SUID-AFRIKA. WEERBURO. DAAGLIKSE WEERBULLETIN. Text in Afrikaans, English. 1950. m. ZAR 220 (effective 2001). bibl.; charts; maps; stat. **Document type:** *Bulletin, Government.* **Description:** Reports daily weather conditions in South Africa.
Published by: South African Weather Service, Department of Environmental Affairs and Tourism, Private Bag X97, Pretoria, 0001, South Africa. TEL 27-82-233-8686, FAX 27-12-3093989, pubenq@weathersa.co.za, http://www.weathersa.co.za. Circ: 400.

551.5 ZAF
SOUTH AFRICA. WEATHER BUREAU. REGIONAL DESCRIPTION OF THE WEATHER AND CLIMATE OF THE EXTREME SOUTH-WESTERN CAPE. Text in English. 1996. irreg. ZAR 50 per issue (effective 2001). charts; stat. index. **Document type:** *Government.* **Description:** Surveys the microclimates and meteorological conditions in a particular region of South Africa.
Formerly: South Africa. Weather Bureau. Regional Description of the Weather and Climate of South Africa (1026-1729)
Published by: South African Weather Service, Department of Environmental Affairs and Tourism, Private Bag X97, Pretoria, 0001, South Africa. TEL 27-82-233-8686, FAX 27-12-3093989, pubenq@weathersa.co.za, http://www.weathersa.co.za. Circ: 200.

551.6 ZAF ISSN 0379-6736
SOUTH AFRICA. WEATHER BUREAU. TECHNICAL PAPER/SUID-AFRIKA. WEERBURO. TEGNIESE VERHANDELING. Text in English. 1974. irreg., latest vol.32, 1996. ZAR 45 per issue (effective 2001). back issues avail. **Document type:** *Monographic series, Government.* **Description:** Discusses various topics pertaining to meteorological conditions in South Africa.
Published by: South African Weather Service, Department of Environmental Affairs and Tourism, Private Bag X97, Pretoria, 0001, South Africa. TEL 27-82-233-8686, FAX 27-12-3093989, pubenq@weathersa.co.za, http://www.weathersa.co.za.

551.578 ZAF
SOUTH AFRICA. WEATHER BUREAU. TEN DAILY RAINFALL REPORT. Text in English. 3/m. charts; maps; stat. **Document type:** *Government.*
Media: Online - full content.
Published by: South African Weather Service, Department of Environmental Affairs and Tourism, Private Bag X97, Pretoria, 0001, South Africa. TEL 27-82-233-8686, FAX 27-12-3093989, pubenq@weathersa.co.za, http://www.weathersa.co.za.

551.5 ZAF ISSN 0081-2331
SOUTH AFRICA. WEATHER BUREAU. W.B. SERIES. Text in English. 1971. irreg., latest vol.41, 1990. price varies. **Document type:** *Government.* **Description:** Surveys meteorological phenomena in South Africa.
Published by: South African Weather Service, Department of Environmental Affairs and Tourism, Private Bag X97, Pretoria, 0001, South Africa. TEL 27-82-233-8686, FAX 27-12-3093989, pubenq@weathersa.co.za, http://www.weathersa.co.za. Circ: 1,500.

551.65 ZAF
SOUTH AFRICA. WEATHER BUREAU. YEARLY WEATHER REPORT/ SUID-AFRIKA. WEERBURO. JAARLIKSE WEERVERSLAG. Text and summaries in Afrikaans, English. 1936. a., latest covers 1993. ZAR 60 per issue (effective 2001). charts; maps; stat. back issues avail. **Document type:** *Government.* **Description:** Provides data for climate and rainfall throughout southern Africa.
Supersedes (in 1990): South Africa. Weather Bureau. Monthly Weather Report (0038-1942)
Published by: South African Weather Service, Department of Environmental Affairs and Tourism, Private Bag X97, Pretoria, 0001, South Africa. TEL 27-82-233-8686, FAX 27-12-3093989, pubenq@weathersa.co.za, http://www.weathersa.co.za. Circ: 400.

551.5 ZAF ISSN 1992-2566
SOUTH AFRICAN WEATHER SERVICE. CLIMATE SUMMARY OF SOUTH AFRICA/SUID-AFRIKA. WEERBURO. KLIMAATOPSOMMING VAN SUIDELIKE AFRIKA. Text in Afrikaans, English. 1990. m. ZAR 660 (effective 2006). charts; illus.; maps; stat. **Document type:** *Government.* **Description:** Reviews the highlights and effects of the weather in South Africa over the past month.
Formerly (until 2006): South Africa. Weather Bureau. Climate Summary for Southern Africa (Print) (1025-8280)
Media: Online - full text.
Published by: South African Weather Service, Department of Environmental Affairs and Tourism, Private Bag X97, Pretoria, 0001, South Africa. FAX 27-12-3676031, pubenq@weathersa.co.za. Circ: 300.

551.5 USA ISSN 1932-0418
QC879.72
SOUTHERN HEMISPHERE WINTER SUMMARY. Text in English. 19??. a. **Document type:** *Bulletin, Trade.*
Media: Online - full text.
Published by: National Oceanic and Atmospheric Administration, National Weather Service, Climate Prediction Center, 5200 Auth Rd, Camp Springs, MD 20746.

SPACE WEATHER; the international journal of research and applications. *see* ASTRONOMY

551.5 LKA
SRI LANKA. DEPARTMENT OF METEOROLOGY. REPORT. Text in English. 1907. a. LKR 500, USD 20. charts; illus. **Document type:** *Government.* **Description:** Provides climatological data for meteorological stations in Sri Lanka. Presents descriptions of the weather during the year.
Formerly (until 1967): Colombo Observatory. Report
Published by: Department of Meteorology, Bauddhaloka Mawatha, Colombo, 7, Sri Lanka. TEL 94-1-694846, FAX 94-1-691443.

551.5 LKA
SRI LANKA METEOROLOGICAL SOCIETY. JOURNAL. Text in English. 1972. q. adv. bibl.; charts; stat.
Published by: Sri Lanka Meteorological Society, 26 Clifford Place, Colombo, 4, Sri Lanka. Circ: 190.

551.6 POL
STACJA ARCTOWSKIEGO. ROCZNIK METEOROLOGICZNY. Text in Polish, English. 1978. irreg. USD 200. **Description:** Covers meteorology and observation results at the subantarctic meteorological research station.
Published by: Instytut Meteorologii i Gospodarki Wodnej, Oddzial Morski w Gdyni/Institute of Meteorology and Water Management, Maritime Branch in Gdynia, Ul Waszyngtona 42, Gdynia, 81342, Poland. TEL 4858-203532, FAX 4858-201641. Eds. Danuta Wielbinska, Miroslaw Mietus. Circ: 120.

551.6 POL
STACJA HORNSUND. ROCZNIK METEOROLOGICZNY. Text in Polish, English. 1979. irreg. USD 200. **Description:** Covers meteorology and observation results at the polar meteorological research station.
Published by: Instytut Meteorologii i Gospodarki Wodnej, Oddzial Morski w Gdyni/Institute of Meteorology and Water Management, Maritime Branch in Gdynia, Ul Waszyngtona 42, Gdynia, 81342, Poland. TEL 4858-203532, FAX 4858-201641, TELEX 54216 PL. Eds. Danuta Wielbinska, Miroslaw Mietus. Circ: 120.

551.5 SWE ISSN 0349-0068
QC851.I53
STOCKHOLM UNIVERSITY. INTERNATIONAL METEOROLOGICAL INSTITUTE IN STOCKHOLM. ANNUAL REPORT. Text in English. 1973. biennial. free. **Document type:** *Academic/Scholarly.*
Related titles: Online - full text ed.
Published by: Stockholms Universitet, International Meteorological Institute in Stockholm, Arrhenius Laboratory, Stockholm, 10691, Sweden. TEL 46-8-162000, FAX 46-8-157185, 46-8-159295, imi@misu.su.se. Circ: 400.

551.5 USA ISSN 2157-2283
STORM COURIER. Text in English. 199?. a. free (effective 2010). back issues avail. **Document type:** *Newsletter, Trade.* **Description:** Contains information about weather events, hurricane seasons, rainfall summary etc.
Media: Online - full text.
Published by: National Weather Service, Charleston Weather Forecast Office, 5777 S Aviation Ave, North Charleston, SC 29406. TEL 843-744-0303.

551.55 USA ISSN 0039-1972
QC943.5.U6
STORM DATA. Text in English. 1922. m. USD 6 combined subscription per issue (print, online & CD-ROM eds.) (effective 2008). illus. Index. back issues avail.; reprints avail. **Document type:** *Government.* **Description:** Presents information on storm paths, deaths, injuries, and property damages.
Related titles: CD-ROM ed.; Online - full text ed.: USD 6 per issue (effective 2004).
Indexed: A26, AmStI, G05, G06, G07, G08, I05, S06.
Published by: (U.S. Department of Commerce), U.S. National Climatic Data Center (Subsidiary of: U.S. Department of Commerce), Federal Bldg, 151 Patton Ave, Asheville, NC 28801. TEL 828-271-4800, FAX 828-271-4876, NODC.Services@noaa.gov, http://www.ncdc.noaa.gov. Circ: 1,500.

551.5 USA
STORMTRACK. Text in English. 1977. bi-m. USD 15; USD 22 foreign (effective 2000). adv. bk.rev. charts; illus. back issues avail. **Document type:** *Newsletter.* **Description:** Caters to the scientist and amateur alike who share an avid interest in the acquisition and advancement of knowledge concerning severe storms.
Related titles: CD-ROM ed.: USD 65 (effective 2000); Online - full text ed.
Published by: Tim Marshall, Ed. & Pub., 4041 Bordeaux Cir, Flower, Mound, TX 75022-7050. TEL 800-527-0168, FAX 972-484-1821. Adv. contact Tim Marshall. B&W page USD 250; trim 10 x 7.5. Circ: 900 (paid).

551.5 CHE
STRATUS. Text in English, German. 1994. irreg., latest vol.7, 2000. CHF 32 per issue. **Document type:** *Monographic series, Academic/ Scholarly.*
Published by: (Universitaet Basel), Verlag Wepf und Co., Eisengasse 5, Basel, 4001, Switzerland. TEL 41-61-3119576, FAX 41-61-3119585, wepf@dial.eunet.ch, http://www.wepf.ch.

STUDIA GEOPHYSICA ET GEODAETICA; a journal of geophysics, geodesy, meteorology and climatology. *see* EARTH SCIENCES—Geophysics

551.5 HKG
SUMMARY OF METEOROLOGICAL OBSERVATIONS IN HONG KONG (YEAR). Text in Chinese, English. 1987. a., latest 2000. price varies.
Former titles (until 1993): Hong Kong Observatory. A Summary of Radiosonde - Radiowind Ascents Made in (Year); Hong Kong. Royal Observatory. A Summary of Radiosonde - Radiowind Ascents Made in (Year)
Published by: Hong Kong Observatory, 134 A Nathan Rd, Kowloon, Hong Kong. TEL 852-29263113, FAX 852-23119448, hkopmo@hko.gov.hk, http://www.hko.gov.hk/.

551.5 JPN ISSN 0916-1295
SYMPOSIUM ON ATMOSPHERE/TAIKIKEN SHINPOJUMU. Text in English, Japanese. 1986. a.
Indexed: M&GPA.
Published by: Institute of Space and Aeronautical Science/Uchu Kagaku Kenkyujo, 1-1 Yoshinodai 3-chome, Sagamihara-shi, Kanagawa-ken 229-0022, Japan.

551.5 620 JPN
SYMPOSIUM ON WIND ENGINEERING. PROCEEDINGS. Text in Japanese; Summaries in English. 1970. biennial. price varies. adv. **Document type:** *Proceedings.*
Former titles: Symposium on Wind Effects on Structures in Japan. Proceedings; National Symposium on Wind Engineering. Proceedings
Published by: Nihon Gakujutsu Kaigi, Meteorological Society of Japan/Science Council of Japan, c/o Japan Meteorological Agency, 1-3 Ote-Machi, Chiyoda-ku, Tokyo, 100-0004, Japan.

551 537 JPN ISSN 1882-0549
TAIKI DENKI GAKKAISHI/SOCIETY OF ATMOSPHERIC ELECTRICITY OF JAPAN. JOURNAL. Text in Japanese. 1969; N.S. 2007. s-a. back issues avail. **Document type:** *Journal, Academic/Scholarly.*
Formerly (until 2007): Nihon Taiki Denki Gakkai Kaiho/Society of Atmospheric Electricity of Japan. Proceedings
—BLDSC (8598.517500).
Published by: Nihon Taiki Denki Gakkai/Society of Atmospheric Electricity of Japan, Osaka Daigaku Kogakubu Denkikogakka, 2-1 Yamada-Oka, Suita-shi, Osaka-fu 565-0871, Japan. TEL 81-6-68797690, FAX 81-6-68797774, saej_secretariat@commf5.comm.eng.osaka-u.ac.jp.

551 JPN ISSN 0286-3405
TAIKI DENKI KENKYU/SOCIETY OF ATMOSPHERIC ELECTRICITY OF JAPAN. PROCEEDINGS. Text in English, Japanese. 1969. a. **Document type:** *Proceedings, Academic/Scholarly.*
Published by: Nihon Taiki Denki Gakkai/Society of Atmospheric Electricity of Japan, Osaka Daigaku Kogakubu Denkikogakka, 2-1 Yamada-Oka, Suita-shi, Osaka-fu 565-0871, Japan. TEL 81-6-68797690, FAX 81-6-68797774, saej_secretariat@commf5.comm.eng.osaka-u.ac.jp.

551 539.2 JPN ISSN 0447-3884
TAIKI HOSHANO KANSOKU SEISEKI/BULLETIN OF ATMOSPHERIC RADIOACTIVITY. Text in English, Japanese. 1955. a.
Published by: Kishocho/Japan Meteorological Agency, 1-3-4 Otemachi, Chiyoda-ku, Tokyo, 100-8122, Japan.

551 USA ISSN 0280-6495
QC880 CODEN: TSAOD8
➤ **TELLUS. SERIES A: DYNAMIC METEOROLOGY AND OCEANOGRAPHY.** Text in English, French, German; Summaries in English. 1949. bi-m. GBP 214 in United Kingdom to institutions; EUR 271 in Europe to institutions; USD 358 in the Americas to institutions; USD 419 elsewhere to institutions; GBP 247 combined subscription in United Kingdom to institutions (print & online eds.); EUR 312 combined subscription in Europe to institutions (print & online eds.); USD 412 combined subscription in the Americas to institutions (print & online eds.); USD 482 combined subscription elsewhere to institutions (print & online eds.) (effective 2011). adv. abstr.; charts; illus.; stat. index. back issues avail.; reprint service avail. from PSC. **Document type:** *Journal, Academic/Scholarly.*
Supersedes in part (in 1983): Tellus (0040-2826)
Related titles: Online - full text ed.: ISSN 1600-0870. GBP 214 in United Kingdom to institutions; EUR 271 in Europe to institutions; USD 358 in the Americas to institutions; USD 419 elsewhere to institutions (effective 2011) (from IngentaConnect).
Indexed: A01, A03, A08, A22, A26, A28, A33, APA, APD, ASCA, ASFA, ApMecR, BrCerAb, C&ISA, C25, C30, CA, CA/WCA, CABA, CIA, CIS, CerAb, ChemAb, CivEngAb, CorrAb, CurCont, E&CAJ, E01, E04, E05, E11, E12, EEA, EMA, ESPM, EnvAb, EnvEAb, EnvInd, F08, F12, FCA, GEOBASE, GeoRef, H15, I05, I11, IBR, IBZ, ISR, Inspec, M&GPA, M&TEA, M09, MBF, METADEX, MathR, OceAb, R07, RefZh, S01, S13, S16, SCI, SCOPUS, SWRA, SolStAb, SpeleolAb, T02, T04, TAR, TriticAb, W07, W11, WAA.
—BLDSC (8789.000100), AskIEEE, CASDDS, IE, Ingenta, INIST, Linda Hall. **CCC.**
Published by: (Svenska Geofysiska Foerening SWE, Stockholms Universitet, International Meteorological Institute in Stockholm SWE), Wiley-Blackwell Publishing, Inc. (Subsidiary of: Wiley-Blackwell Publishing Ltd.), Commerce Pl, 350 Main St, Malden, MA 02148. TEL 781-388-8200, FAX 781-388-8210, info@wiley.com, http://www.wiley.com/WileyCDA/. Ed. Harald Lejenaes.

551 USA ISSN 0280-6509
QC879.6 CODEN: TSBMD7
➤ **TELLUS. SERIES B: CHEMICAL AND PHYSICAL METEOROLOGY.** Text in English, French, German; Summaries in English. 1949. bi-m. GBP 214 in United Kingdom to institutions; EUR 271 in Europe to institutions; USD 358 in the Americas to institutions; USD 419 elsewhere to institutions; GBP 247 combined subscription in United Kingdom to institutions (print & online eds.); EUR 312 combined subscription in Europe to institutions (print & online eds.); USD 412 combined subscription in the Americas to institutions (print & online eds.); USD 482 combined subscription elsewhere to institutions (print & online eds.) (effective 2011). adv. abstr.; charts; illus.; stat. index. reprint service avail. from PSC. **Document type:** *Journal, Academic/Scholarly.*
Supersedes in part (in 1983): Tellus (0040-2826)
Related titles: Online - full text ed.: ISSN 1600-0889. GBP 214 in United Kingdom to institutions; EUR 271 in Europe to institutions; USD 358 in the Americas to institutions; USD 419 elsewhere to institutions (effective 2011) (from IngentaConnect).
Indexed: A01, A03, A08, A22, A26, A33, A37, APD, ASFA, ApMecR, B21, B25, BA, BIOSIS Prev, C25, C30, CA, CABA, CIN, CIS, ChemAb, ChemTitl, CurCont, E01, E12, ESPM, EnvAb, EnvInd, F08, F11, F12, FCA, G11, GEOBASE, GH, GeoRef, I05, I11, IBR, IBZ, INIS AtomInd, ISR, Inspec, M&GPA, MaizeAb, MycolAb, OceAb, P30, PollutAb, R12, RefZh, S01, S13, S16, SCI, SCOPUS, SWRA, SoyAb, SpeleolAb, T02, T05, TAR, W07, W11.
—BLDSC (8789.000150), AskIEEE, CASDDS, IE, Infotrieve, Ingenta, INIST, Linda Hall. **CCC.**
Published by: (Stockholms Universitet, International Meteorological Institute in Stockholm SWE, Swedish Geophysical Society SWE), Wiley-Blackwell Publishing, Inc. (Subsidiary of: Wiley-Blackwell Publishing Ltd.), Commerce Pl, 350 Main St, Malden, MA 02148. TEL 781-388-8200, FAX 781-388-8210, info@wiley.com, http://www.wiley.com/WileyCDA/. Ed. H Rode.

551.5 JPN ISSN 0546-0921
QC851 CODEN: TENKBT
TENKI/METEOROLOGICAL SOCIETY OF JAPAN. WEATHER. Text in Japanese. 12/yr. JPY 6,900 to individuals; JPY 9,000 to institutions.
Indexed: JPI, M&GPA.
—CASDDS, Linda Hall. **CCC.**
Published by: Nihon Kisho Gakkai/Meteorological Society of Japan, c/o Japan Meteorological Agency, 3-4 Ote-Machi 1-chome, Chiyoda-ku, Tokyo, 100-0004, Japan. TEL 81-3-3212-8341, FAX 81-3-3216-4401.

551.5 JPN
TENKIZU/DAILY WEATHER MAPS. Text in English, Japanese. 1940. m. JPY 180,000.
Incorporates (in 1989): Taifu Keirozu
Published by: Kishocho/Japan Meteorological Agency, 1-3-4 Otemachi, Chiyoda-ku, Tokyo, 100-8122, Japan. Circ: 501.

551.5 ESP ISSN 1697-1523
➤ **TETHYS**; revista del temps i el clima de la Mediterrania occidental. Text in English, Spanish, Catalan. 1997. irreg. **Document type:** *Journal, Academic/Scholarly.*
Related titles: Online - full text ed.: ISSN 1139-3394. free (effective 2011).
Published by: Associacion Catalana de Metereologia (A C A M), Rambla Solanas 25, Cornella, 08940, Spain. http://www.acam.cat.

551.5 AUT ISSN 0177-798X
QC980 CODEN: TACLEK
➤ **THEORETICAL AND APPLIED CLIMATOLOGY.** Text in English. 1948. m. EUR 3,821, USD 4,528 combined subscription to institutions (print & online eds.) (effective 2012). adv. bk.rev. abstr. back issues avail.; reprint service avail. from PSC. **Document type:** *Journal, Academic/Scholarly.* **Description:** Discusses climate and climatic change modeling, applied meteorology, micrometeorology and atmospheric radiation problems, air pollution, and techniques and technologies to measure climatic phenomena.
Formerly (until 1985): Archives for Meteorology, Geophysics, and Bioclimatology. Series B: Climatology, Environmental Meteorology, Radiation Research - Archiv fuer Meteorologie, Geophysik und Bioklimatologie. Series B (0066-6424)
Related titles: Microform ed.: (from PQC); Online - full text ed.: ISSN 1434-4483 (from IngentaConnect).
Indexed: A01, A03, A08, A20, A22, A26, A33, A34, A37, A38, ASCA, ASFA, AgrForAb, B25, BIOSIS Prev, C25, C30, CA, CABA, CurCont, E01, E04, E05, E08, E12, ESPM, F08, F11, F12, FCA, FR, G11, GEOBASE, GH, GeoRef, H16, I05, I11, IBR, IBZ, INIS AtomInd, ISR, Inspec, LT, M&GPA, MaizeAb, MycolAb, O01, P02, P26, P30, P32, P48, P52, P54, P56, PGrRegA, PQC, PollutAb, R12, R13, RRTA, RefZh, S09, S12, S13, S16, SCI, SCOPUS, SoyAb, SpeleolAb, T02, T05, TAR, TriticAb, VS, W07, W11.
—BLDSC (8814.551500), AskIEEE, IE, Infotrieve, Ingenta, INIST, Linda Hall. **CCC.**
Published by: Springer Wien (Subsidiary of: Springer Science+Business Media), Sachsenplatz 4-6, Vienna, W 1201, Austria. TEL 43-1-33024150, FAX 43-1-3302426, journals@springer.at, http://www.springer.at. Adv. contact Irene Hofmann. B&W page EUR 1,290; 170 x 230. Circ: 500 (paid). **Subscr to:** Springer Distribution Center, Kundenservice Zeitschriften, Haberstr 7, Heidelberg 69126, Germany. TEL 49-6221-3454303, FAX 49-6221-3454229, subscriptions@springer.com**; Subscr. in the Americas to:** Springer New York LLC, Journal Fulfillment, PO Box 2485, Secaucus, NJ 07096. TEL 800-777-4643, 201-348-4033, FAX 201-348-4505, journals-ny@springer.com, http://www.springer.com.

551.5 GBR ISSN 2044-5148
TIDE TIMES. CORNISH COAST. Text in English. 198?. a. GBP 2.45 per issue (effective 2010). **Document type:** *Journal, Trade.* **Description:** Contains tidal time differences for various locations around the designated port.
Formerly (until 2009): High & Low Tide Times and Heights. Cornish Coast (1742-3198); Which superseded in part (in 199?): Tide Times and Heights (0961-2408)
Published by: Holidaymaker Publications Ltd., The Mill Barns, Trevarrick Rd, St Austell, PL25 5JN, United Kingdom. TEL 44-1726-70090, FAX 44-1726-69455, sales@holidaymakerpublications.co.uk.

551.5 GBR ISSN 2044-379X
TIDE TIMES. NORTH DEVON COAST. Text in English. 198?. a. GBP 1.30 newsstand/cover (effective 2010). **Document type:** *Journal, Trade.* **Description:** Contains tidal time differences for various locations around the designated port.
Formerly (until 2009): High & Low Tide Times and Heights. North Devon Coast (1742-321X); Which superseded in part (in 199?): Tide Times and Heights (0961-2408)
Published by: Holidaymaker Publications Ltd., The Mill Barns, Trevarrick Rd, St Austell, PL25 5JN, United Kingdom. TEL 44-1726-70090, FAX 44-1726-69455, sales@holidaymakerpublications.co.uk, http://www.holidaymakerpublications.co.uk.

551.5 GBR ISSN 2045-5674
TIDE TIMES. PLYMOUTH & COAST. Text in English. 198?. a. GBP 2.45 per issue (effective 2010). **Document type:** *Report, Trade.* **Description:** Contains tidal time differences for various locations around the designated port.
Formerly (until 2010): High & Low Tide Times and Heights. Plymouth & Coast (1742-3201); Which superseded in part (in 199?): Tide Times and Heights (0961-2408)
Published by: Holidaymaker Publications Ltd., The Mill Barns, Trevarrick Rd, St Austell, PL25 5JN, United Kingdom. TEL 44-1726-70090, FAX 44-1726-69455, sales@holidaymakerpublications.co.uk.

551.5 GBR ISSN 2044-3803
TIDE TIMES. SOUTH DEVON COAST. Variant title: North Devon Coast. Text in English. 198?. a. GBP 1.30 newsstand/cover (effective 2010). **Document type:** *Journal, Trade.* **Description:** Contains tidal time differences for various locations around the designated port.
Formerly (until 2009): High & Low Tide Times and Heights. South Devon Coast (1742-3228); Which superseded in part (in 199?): Tide Times and Heights (0961-2408)
Published by: Holidaymaker Publications Ltd., The Mill Barns, Trevarrick Rd, St Austell, PL25 5JN, United Kingdom. TEL 44-1726-70090, FAX 44-1726-69455, sales@holidaymakerpublications.co.uk, http://www.holidaymakerpublications.co.uk.

551 JPN ISSN 0916-5010
TOCHIGIKEN KISHO GEPPO/TOCHIGI PREFECTURE. MONTHLY REPORT OF METEOROLOGY. Text in Japanese. 1900. m. **Document type:** *Academic/Scholarly.*
Published by: Kishocho, Utsunomiya Chiho Kishodai/Japan Meteorological Agency, Utsunomiya Local Meteorological Observatory, 1-7 Akebono-cho, Utsunomiya-shi, Tochigi-ken 320-0845, Japan.

551.5 TGO
TOGO. DIRECTION DE LA METEOROLOGIE NATIONALE. RESUME ANNUEL DU TEMPS. Text in French. a.
Published by: Direction de la Meteorologie Nationale, BP 1505, Lome, Togo.

551.5 TGO
TOGO. DIRECTION DE LA METEOROLOGIE NATIONALE. RESUME MENSUEL DU TEMPS. Text in French. m.
Published by: Direction de la Meteorologie Nationale, BP 1505, Lome, Togo.

551.63 JPN
TOHOKU CHIHO CHOKI YOHO SOKUHO/BULLETIN OF LONG RANGE WEATHER FORECASTING OF TOHOKU DISTRICT. Text in Japanese. 1942. 3/yr.
Published by: Kishocho, Sapporo Kanku Kishodai/Japan Meteorological Agency, Sapporo District Meteorological Observatory, 3-15 Gorin 1-chome, Miyagino-ku, Sendai-shi, Miyagi-ken 983-0842, Japan.

551 JPN ISSN 0563-6493
TOHOKU CHIHO KISHO KENKYUKAISHI/JOURNAL OF METEOROLOGICAL RESEARCH OF TOHOKU DISTRICT. Text in English, Japanese. triennial.
Published by: Kishocho, Sapporo Kanku Kishodai/Japan Meteorological Agency, Sapporo District Meteorological Observatory, 3-15 Gorin 1-chome, Miyagino-ku, Sendai-shi, Miyagi-ken 983-0842, Japan.

551 JPN ISSN 0289-3126
QC851
TOHOKU GIJUTSU DAYORI/TOHOKU DISTRICT METEOROLOGICAL OBSERVATORY. TECHNICAL NEWS. Text in Japanese. 1962. bi-m.
Published by: Kishocho, Sapporo Kanku Kishodai/Japan Meteorological Agency, Sapporo District Meteorological Observatory, 3-15 Gorin 1-chome, Miyagino-ku, Sendai-shi, Miyagi-ken 983-0842, Japan.

551 630 JPN ISSN 0287-1173
TOHOKU NO NOGYO KISHO/BULLETIN OF THE AGRICULTURAL METEOROLOGY OF TOHOKU DISTRICT. Text in Japanese. 1956. a. JPY 2,500 (effective 2002). adv. **Document type:** *Bulletin, Academic/Scholarly.* **Description:** Covers the agricultural meteorology in northeast Japan.
Published by: Nihon Nogyo Kisho Gakkai, Tohoku Shibu/Society of Agricultural Meteorology of Japan, Tohoku Branch, Norin Suisansho Tohoku Nogyo Shikenjo, 4 Akahira, Shimokuriyagawa, Morioka-shi, Iwate-ken 020-01, Japan. TEL 81-196-43-3461, FAX 81-196-41-7794. Ed., R&P Takashi Ozawa. Adv. contact Kimio Inoue. Circ: 300 (controlled).

551 JPN ISSN 0385-0625
TOKAN GIJUTSU NYUSU/TOKYO DISTRICT METEOROLOGICAL OBSERVATORY. TECHNICAL INFORMATION NEWS. Text in Japanese. 1968. 4/yr.
Published by: Kishocho, Tokyo Kanku Kishodai/Japan Meteorological Agency, Tokyo District Meteorological Observatory, 3-4 Ote-Machi 1-chome, Chiyoda-ku, Tokyo, 100-0004, Japan.

551 JPN ISSN 0916-5231
TOKUSHIMA-KEN KISHO GEPPO/TOKUSHIMA PREFECTURE. MONTHLY REPORT OF METEOROLOGY. Text in Japanese. 1954. m.
Formerly (until 1965): Tokushima no Kisho
Published by: Kishocho, Tokushima Chiho Kishodai/Japan Meteorological Agency, Tokushima Local Meteorological Observatory, 3-36 Yamato-cho 2-chome, Tokushima-shi, 770-0864, Japan.

551 JPN ISSN 0289-310X
TOKYO KANKU CHIHO KISHO KENKYUKAISHI/TOKYO DISTRICT METEOROLOGICAL OBSERVATORY. GEOPHYSICAL NOTES. Text in Japanese. 1968. a.
Published by: Kishocho, Tokyo Kanku Kishodai/Japan Meteorological Agency, Tokyo District Meteorological Observatory, 3-4 Ote-Machi 1-chome, Chiyoda-ku, Tokyo, 100-0004, Japan.

551.6 JPN
TOKYO KANKU IJO KISHO HOKOKU/TOKYO DISTRICT METEOROLOGICAL OBSERVATORY. UNUSUAL METEOROLOGICAL REPORT. Text in Japanese. 1960. a.
Published by: Kishocho, Tokyo Kanku Kishodai/Japan Meteorological Agency, Tokyo District Meteorological Observatory, 3-4 Ote-Machi 1-chome, Chiyoda-ku, Tokyo, 100-0004, Japan.

551 JPN ISSN 0916-524X
TOKYOTO KISHO GEPPO/TOKYO METROPOLIS. MONTHLY REPORT OF METEOROLOGY. Text in Japanese. 1951. m.
Published by: Kishocho, Tokyo Kanku Kishodai/Japan Meteorological Agency, Tokyo District Meteorological Observatory, 3-4 Ote-Machi 1-chome, Chiyoda-ku, Tokyo, 100-0004, Japan.

551 JPN ISSN 0916-5258
TOTTORIKEN KISHO GEPPO/TOTTORI PREFECTURE. MONTHLY REPORT OF METEOROLOGY. Text in Japanese. 1950. m.
Published by: Kishocho, Tottori Chiho Kishodai/Japan Meteorological Agency, Tottori Local Meteorological Observatory, c/o Tottori Dai 3 Chiho Godo chosha, 109 Yoshikata, Tottori-shi, 680-0842, Japan.

551.5 JPN ISSN 0916-5614
TOTTORIKEN KISHO NENPO/TOTTORI PREFECTURE. ANNUAL REPORT OF METEOROLOGY. Text in Japanese. a.
Published by: Kishocho, Tottori Chiho Kishodai/Japan Meteorological Agency, Tottori Local Meteorological Observatory, c/o Tottori Dai 3 Chiho Godo chosha, 109 Yoshikata, Tottori-shi, 680-0842, Japan.

551.5 JPN ISSN 0916-5266
TOYAMAKEN KISHO GEPPO/TOYAMA PREFECTURE. MONTHLY REPORT OF METEOROLOGY. Text in Japanese. 1951. m.
Published by: Kishocho, Toyama Chiho Kishodai/Japan Meteorological Agency, Toyama Local Meteorological Observatory, 2415 Ishi-Saka, Toyama-shi, 930-0892, Japan.

551.5 JPN ISSN 0916-5630
TOYAMAKEN KISHO NENPO/TOYAMA PREFECTURE. ANNUAL REPORT OF METEOROLOGY. Text in Japanese. a.
Published by: Kishocho, Toyama Chiho Kishodai/Japan Meteorological Agency, Toyama Local Meteorological Observatory, 2415 Ishi-Saka, Toyama-shi, 930-0892, Japan.

M

551.5 USA
TRENDS ONLINE. Text in English. irreg. free. charts; maps; stat. **Document type:** *Monographic series, Government.* **Description:** Provides synopses of critical data related to global environmental change: atmospheric carbon dioxide, atmospheric methane, other trace gases and aerosols, carbon dioxide emissions, temperature, methane emissions, and clouds.
Former titles (until 199?): Trends: A Compendium of Data on Global Change; C02 Technical Report
Media: Online - full text.
Published by: (U.S. Department of Energy, Office of Industrial Technologies), Carbon Dioxide Information Analysis Center, Oak Ridge National Laboratory, Box 2008, MS 6335, Oak Ridge, TN 37831-6335. TEL 865-574-0390, FAX 865-574-2232.

551.5 538 NOR ISSN 1504-1174
TROMSOE GEOPHYSICAL OBSERVATORY. REPORTS. Text in English. 2004. irreg., latest vol.3, 2010. back issues avail. **Document type:** *Monographic series, Academic/Scholarly.*
Related titles: Online - full text ed.: ISSN 0809-6228.
Published by: Universitetet i Tromsoe, Tromsoe Geophysical Observatory, c/o Faculty of Science, Universitet i Tromsoe, Tromsoe, 9037, Norway. TEL 47-77-645150, FAX 47-77-645580, http://www.tgo.uit.no. Ed. Truls Hansen.

TYDSKRIF VIR SKOONLUG/CLEAN AIR JOURNAL. *see* ENVIRONMENTAL STUDIES—Pollution

551.5 USA ISSN 2152-5021
U C A R MAGAZINE. Text in English. 1974. 3/yr. free to qualified personnel (effective 2010). index. back issues avail. **Document type:** *Magazine, Academic/Scholarly.* **Description:** Aims to publicize the activities of the University Corporation for Atmospheric Research (including the National Center for Atmospheric Research and the UCAR Office of Programs) and its collaborators.
Former titles (until 2009): U C A R Quarterly (1948-0296); (until 1994): U C A R Newsletter (0273-0707); Which superseded (in 1997): N C A R Newsletter (1948-0318)
Related titles: Online - full text ed.: ISSN 2152-5005. free (effective 2010).
Indexed: RefZh.
—Linda Hall.
Published by: University Corporation for Atmospheric Research, PO Box 3000, Boulder, CO 80307. TEL 303-497-1000, http://www.ucar.edu.

551.6 USA ISSN 1934-8851
QC980
U.S. NATIONAL OCEANIC AND ATMOSPHERIC ADMINISTRATION. ANNUAL CLIMATE DIAGNOSTICS AND PREDICTION WORKSHOP. PROCEEDINGS. Text in English. 1976. a. back issues avail. **Document type:** *Proceedings, Government.* **Description:** Provides the status and prospects for advancing climate monitoring, assessment, and prediction in the context of the NOAH Climate Services Societal Challenges, along with a session on drought with special emphasis.
Former titles (until 1996): U.S. National Oceanic and Atmospheric Administration. Annual Climate Diagnostics Workshop. Proceedings (0192-8759); (until 1977): N O A A Climate Diagnostics Workshop. Proceedings
Related titles: Online - full text ed.
Indexed: GeoRef, SpeleolAb.
—Ingenta.
Published by: U.S. National Oceanic and Atmospheric Administration, 1401 Constitution Ave, NW, Rm 5128, Washington, DC 20230. TEL 301-713-1208, 800-638-8972, outreach@noaa.gov, http://www.noaa.gov/.

551.5 USA
U.S. NAVAL RESEARCH LABORATORY. MARINE METEOROLOGY DIVISION. MEMORANDUM REPORT. Text in English. irreg.
Former titles (until 1993): U.S. Naval Oceanographic Research and Development Activity. Report; (until 1989): U.S. Naval Environmental Prediction Research Facility. Report
Published by: U.S. Naval Research Laboratory, Marine Meteorology Division, 7 Grace Hopper Ave, Stop 2, Monterey, CA 93943-5502. TEL 831-656-4721, http://www.nrlmry.navy.mil/index.html.

551 JPN ISSN 0287-5276
UMI NO KISHO/MARINE METEROLOGY. Text in Japanese. 1955. bi-m. JPY 2,700 (effective 1999). adv. back issues avail. **Document type:** *Academic/Scholarly.* **Description:** Information, fun, etc. for mariners.
Published by: Kaiyo Kisho Gakkai/Marine Meteorological Society, 1-4-3, Wakinohamakaigan-dori, Chuo-ku, Kobe, 653-0073, Japan. http://www.h6.dion.ne.jp/~marmetsc/. Ed. Junichi Nishizawa. Circ: 500.

551 JPN ISSN 0503-1567
➤ **UMI TO SORA/MARINE METEOROLOGICAL SOCIETY. JOURNAL.** Variant title: Sea and Sky. Text in English, Japanese. 1921. q. free to members. **Document type:** *Journal, Academic/Scholarly.* **Description:** Scientific papers mainly on marine meterology.
Indexed: ASFA, B21, ESPM, JPI.
—Linda Hall.
Published by: Kaiyo Kisho Gakkai/Marine Meteorological Society, 1-4-3, Wakinohamakaigan-dori, Chuo-ku, Kobe, 653-0073, Japan. TEL 81-78-222-8955, FAX 81-78-222-8955, umitosora@k2.dion.ne.jp. Circ: 500.

➤ **UNIVERSIDAD DE GUADALAJARA. INSTITUTO DE ASTRONOMIA Y METEOROLOGIA. BOLETIN INFORMATIVO MENSUAL.** *see* ASTRONOMY

➤ **UNIVERSIDAD NACIONAL AUTONOMA DE MEXICO. INSTITUTO DE GEOGRAFIA. SERIE VARIA.** *see* GEOGRAPHY

551.5 DEU ISSN 0179-5619
UNIVERSITAT KARLSRUHE. INSTITUTS FUER METEOROLOGIE UND KLIMAFORSCHUNG, WISSENSCHAFTLICHE BERICHTE. Text in German. 1985. irreg.
Indexed: M&GPA.
Published by: (Universitaet Karlsruhe, Institut fuer Meteorologie und Klimaforschung), Universitaet Karlsruhe, Kaiserstr 12, Karlsruhe, 76131, Germany. TEL 49-721-6080, FAX 49-721-6084290, http://www.uni-karlsruhe.de.

UNIVERSITATIS SCIENTIARUM BUDAPESTINENSIS DE ROLANDO EOTVOS NOMINATAE. ANNALES. SECTIO GEOPHYSICA ET METEOROLOGICA. *see* EARTH SCIENCES—Geophysics

551.5 551 BEL
UNIVERSITEIT TE GENT. STERRENKUNDIG OBSERVATORIUM. MEDEDELINGEN: METEOROLOGIE EN GEOFYSICA. Text and summaries in Dutch, English. 1961. irreg. free. **Document type:** *Academic/Scholarly.*
Formerly: Rijksuniversiteit te Gent. Sterrenkundig Observatorium. Mededelingen: Meteorologie en Geofysica (0072-4440)
Indexed: ApicAb.
Published by: Universiteit Gent, Sterrenkundig Observatorium, Krijgslaan 281, Ghent, 9000, Belgium. TEL 32-9-2464798, FAX 32-9-2644989.

551.5 NOR ISSN 1502-5519
UNIVERSITY OF BERGEN. REPORTS IN METEOROLOGY AND OCEANOGRAPHY. Text in English. 1984. irreg.
Formerly (until 2001): University of Bergen. Geophysical Institute. Meteorological Report Series (0800-6369)
Indexed: ASFA, B21, M&GPA.
Published by: Universitetet i Bergen, Geofysisk Institutt/University of Bergen, Geophysical Institute, Allegaten 70, Bergen, 5007, Norway. TEL 47-55-582602, FAX 47-55-589883, http://www.gfi.uib.no/middle_and_right_e.html.

551.5 551.46 USA
UNIVERSITY OF MIAMI. ROSENSTIEL SCHOOL OF MARINE & ATMOSPHERIC SCIENCE. TECHNICAL REPORT. Text in English. irreg. **Document type:** *Report, Trade.*
Published by: Rosenstiel School of Marine and Atmospheric Science, 4600 Rickenbacker Causeway, Miami, FL 33149. TEL 305-361-4000, FAX 305-361-4711, http://www.rsmas.miami.edu.

551.5 SWE ISSN 0280-4441
UNIVERSITY OF STOCKHOLM. DEPARTMENT OF METEOROLOGY. REPORT A P. (Atmospheric Physics) Variant title: International Meteorological Institute in Stockholm. Report AP. Text in English. 1977. irreg. **Document type:** *Monographic series.*
Indexed: M&GPA.
Published by: Stockholms Universitet, Department of Meteorology, International Meteorological Institute, Arrhenius Laboratory, Stockholm, 106 91, Sweden. TEL 46-8-16-20-00, FAX 46-8-15-71-85, 46-8-15-92-95, imi@misu.su.se, http://www.misu.su.se.

551.5 SWE ISSN 0280-445X
UNIVERSITY OF STOCKHOLM. DEPARTMENT OF METEOROLOGY. REPORT C M. (Chemical Meteorology) Text in English. 1969. irreg., latest vol.99, 2003. free (effective 2003). back issues avail. **Document type:** *Monographic series, Academic/Scholarly.*
Formerly (until 1981): University of Stockholm. Department of Meteorology. Report A C (0349-0130)
Indexed: M&GPA.
Published by: Stockholms Universitet, Meteorologiska Institutionen/Stockholm University, Department of Meteorology, Stockholm Universitet, Stockholm, 10691, Sweden. TEL 46-8-162395, FAX 46-8-157185, http://www.misu.su.se.

551.5 SWE ISSN 0349-0467
UNIVERSITY OF STOCKHOLM. DEPARTMENT OF METEOROLOGY. REPORT D M. (Dynamic Meteorology) Text in English. 1969. irreg., latest vol.95, 2005. free (effective 2003). **Document type:** *Monographic series, Academic/Scholarly.*
Formerly (until 1974): University of Stockholm. Meteorologiska Institutionen. Report D M
Indexed: M&GPA.
—BLDSC (7524.170000).
Published by: Stockholms Universitet, Meteorologiska Institutionen/Stockholm University, Department of Meteorology, Stockholm Universitet, Stockholm, 10691, Sweden. TEL 46-8-162395, FAX 46-8-157185, http://www.misu.su.se.

UNIVERSUM. *see* ASTRONOMY

551.5 363.7 FIN ISSN 1238-2388
VAISALA NEWS. Text in English. 1959. 3/yr. back issues avail. **Document type:** *Magazine, Academic/Scholarly.* **Description:** Contains scientific articles written by external experts and product news as well as other news items. Two issues are dedicated to weather observations and one issue deals with environmental measurements.
Related titles: Online - full text ed.
Indexed: GeoRef, M&GPA.
Published by: Vaisala Oyj, PO Box 26, Helsinki, 00421, Finland. TEL 358-9-894-91, FAX 358-9-8949-2227.

551.5 IND ISSN 0970-1397
VAYU MANDAL; science journal on the human environment. Text in English. 1971. q. bk.rev. charts; illus. **Document type:** *Journal, Academic/Scholarly.*
Published by: Indian Meteorological Society, Mausam Bhavan, Lodi Rd, New Delhi, 110 003, India. sdatti@yahoo.com, http://www.ncmrwf.gov.in/ims/.

551.6 USA
VIRGINIA CLIMATE ADVISORY (ONLINE). Text in English. 1977. irreg.
Formerly (until 2004): Virginia Climate Advisory (Print) (0743-6785)
Media: Online - full content.
Published by: University of Virginia, Department of Environmental Sciences, Clark Hall, 291 McCormick Rd, Charlottesville, VA 22903. TEL 434-924-7761, FAX 434-982-2137, climate@virginia.edu, http://climate.virginia.edu/index.htm.

551.5 CHE ISSN 0250-8893
VSEMIRNAYA METEOROLOGICHESKAYA ORGANIZATSIYA. GODOVOI OTCHET. Text in Russian. 1951. a.
Related titles: Ed.: World Meteorological Organization. Annual Report. ISSN 0084-1994. 1953. price varies.
Published by: World Meteorological Organization, 7 bis Avenue de la Paix, Case postale 2300, Geneva 2, 1211, Switzerland. TEL 41-22-7308111, FAX 41-22-7308022, pubsales@gateway.wmo.ch, http://www.wmo.int.

551.5 CHE ISSN 1011-3673
VSEMIRNAYA METEOROLOGICHESKAYA ORGANIZATSIYA. SESSIYA ISPOLNITEL'NOGO SOVETA. SOKRASHCHENNYI OTCHET S REZOLYUTSIYAMI. Text in Russian. 1983. a.
Related titles: ◆ English ed.: World Meteorological Organization. Executive Council Session. Abridged Final Reports with Resolutions. ISSN 1011-3231; ◆ Spanish ed.: Organizacion Meteorologica Mundial. Reunion del Consejo Ejecutivo. Informe Abreviado y Resoluciones. ISSN 1011-3576; ◆ French ed.: Organisation Meteorologique Mondiale. Session du Conseil Executif. Rapport Abrege et Resolutions. ISSN 1011-3592.
Published by: World Meteorological Organization, 7 bis Avenue de la Paix, Case postale 2300, Geneva 2, 1211, Switzerland. TEL 41-22-7308111, FAX 41-22-7308022, pubsales@gateway.wmo.ch, http://www.wmo.int.

551.6 USA ISSN 1949-4327
W I A S NEWS. (Women in Atmospheric Sciences) Text in English. 1991. m. **Document type:** *Newsletter, Trade.*
Published by: National Center for Atmospheric Research, PO Box 3000, Boulder, CO 80307. TEL 303-497-1000, http://www.ncar.ucar.edu.

551.5 CHE ISSN 0042-9767
QC851 CODEN: WMOBAR
W M O BULLETIN. Text in English. 1952. q. CHF 85 (effective 2004). adv. bk.rev. illus. index. reprints avail. **Document type:** *Bulletin, Academic/Scholarly.* **Description:** Provides a summary of the work and developments in international meteorology and hydrology.
Related titles: Russian ed.: ISSN 0250-6076; French ed.: ISSN 0510-9019; Spanish ed.: ISSN 0250-6025.
Indexed: A22, A37, ASFA, C25, C30, CABA, E12, ESPM, F08, F12, FCA, GH, GeoRef, H16, I11, IIS, LT, M&GPA, N02, OceAb, R07, R12, RRTA, S12, S16, SCOPUS, SWRA, SpeleolAb, TAR, W11.
—IE, Infotrieve, Ingenta, Linda Hall.
Published by: World Meteorological Organization, 7 bis Avenue de la Paix, Case postale 2300, Geneva 2, 1211, Switzerland. TEL 41-22-7308111, FAX 41-22-7308022, pubsales@gateway.wmo.ch, http://www.wmo.int. Ed. Hong Yan. Adv. contact Monique Yabi. page CHF 2,700; trim 150 x 215. Circ: 6,500. **Dist. in U.S. by:** American Meteorological Society, 45 Beacon St, Boston, MA 02108. TEL 617-227-2425.

551.6 JPN
W N O KAIYO KIKO GAIYO/MARINE CLIMATOLOGICAL SUMMARY. Text in English. 1961. a.
Published by: Kishocho/Japan Meteorological Agency, 1-3-4 Otemachi, Chiyoda-ku, Tokyo, 100-8122, Japan.

551.65 JPN ISSN 0910-4542
WAKAYAMA PREFECTURE. ANNUAL REPORT OF METEOROLOGY/ WAKAYAMA-KEN KISHO NENPO. Text in Japanese. a. charts; stat.
Published by: Wakayama Local Meteorological Observatory/Wakayama Chiho Kishodai, 4 Onoshiba-cho, Wakayama-shi, 640-8230, Japan.

551.65 JPN ISSN 0043-0021
WAKAYAMAKEN KISHO GEPPO/WAKAYAMA PREFECTURE. MONTHLY REPORT OF METEOROLOGY. Text in Japanese. 1917. m. charts; illus.
Published by: Kishocho, Wakayama Chiho Kishodai/Japan Meteorological Agency, Wakayama Local Meteorological Observatory, 4-1 Onoshiba-cho, Wakayama-shi, 640-8230, Japan.

551.5 551.46 NZL ISSN 1172-1014
WATER & ATMOSPHERE. Text in English. 1992. q. back issues avail. **Document type:** *Magazine, Trade.*
Related titles: Online - full text ed.: ISSN 1177-7699.
Indexed: A33, GeoRef, INIS AtomInd.
Published by: National Institute of Water and Atmospheric Research Ltd., Private Bag 14901, Wellington, New Zealand. TEL 64-4-3860300, FAX 64-4-3862153, scicomm@niwa.co.nz, http://www.niwascience.co.nz.

551.6 GBR ISSN 0043-1656
QC851 CODEN: WTHRAL
➤ **WEATHER.** Text in English. 1946. m. GBP 60 in United Kingdom to institutions; EUR 75 in Europe to institutions; USD 116 elsewhere to institutions; GBP 69 combined subscription in United Kingdom to institutions (print & online eds.); EUR 86 combined subscription in Europe to institutions (print & online eds.); USD 134 combined subscription elsewhere to institutions (print & online eds.) (effective 2012). adv. bk.rev.; video rev. charts; illus. index. back issues avail.; reprint service avail. from PSC. **Document type:** *Journal, Academic/Scholarly.* **Description:** Contains articles on the science, technology, informational aspects, and broadcasting of meteorology and climatology, with announcements of conferences, seminars and meetings.
Incorporates (1965-2003): Weather Log
Related titles: Online - full text ed.: ISSN 1477-8696. GBP 60 in United Kingdom to institutions; EUR 75 in Europe to institutions; USD 116 elsewhere to institutions (effective 2012).
Indexed: A20, A22, ASFA, CIS, CTO, ChemAb, CurCont, ESPM, GEOBASE, GeoRef, Inspec, M&GPA, MEA&I, SCI, SCOPUS, SPPI, SWRA, SpeleolAb, W07.
—BLDSC (9282.000000), AskIEEE, IE, Infotrieve, Ingenta, INIST, Linda Hall. **CCC.**
Published by: (Royal Meteorological Society), John Wiley & Sons Ltd. (Subsidiary of: John Wiley & Sons, Inc.), 1-7 Oldlands Way, PO Box 808, Bognor Regis, West Sussex PO21 9FF, United Kingdom. TEL 44-1865-778315, FAX 44-1243-843232, cs-journals@wiley.com, http://eu.wiley.com/WileyCDA/. Ed. Bob Prichard. **Subscr. to:** 1-7 Oldlands Way, PO Box 809, Bognor Regis, West Sussex PO21 9FG, United Kingdom. TEL 44-1865-778054, cs-agency@wiley.com.

551.6 NZL ISSN 0111-5499
QC851
➤ **WEATHER AND CLIMATE.** Text in English. 1981. s-a. NZD 30 to individual members; NZD 90 to institutional members (effective 2008). adv. bk.rev. **Document type:** *Journal, Academic/Scholarly.* **Description:** Deals with meteorological or climatological subject with preference given to contributions related to New Zealand and The Southwest Pacific.
Indexed: ESPM, GeoRef, M&GPA, SWRA, SpeleolAb.
—**CCC.**
Published by: Meteorological Society of New Zealand, Te Aro, PO Box 6523, Wellington, New Zealand. info@metsoc.rsnz.org. Ed., Pub., R&P, Adv. contact Anthony Fowler. Circ: 450.

551.5 310 USA ISSN 0882-8156
QC994.95 CODEN: WEFOE3
➤ **WEATHER AND FORECASTING.** Abbreviated title: W A F. Text in English. 1986. bi-m. USD 530 combined subscription domestic to non-members (print & online eds.); USD 575 combined subscription foreign to non-members (print & online eds.) (effective 2011). adv. abstr.; bibl.; charts; illus.; stat. index. back issues avail.; reprints avail. **Document type:** *Journal, Academic/Scholarly.* **Description:** Features operational forecasting techniques, applications of new analysis methods, forecasting verification studies, and meso-scale and synoptic-scale case studies that have direct applicability to forecasting.
Related titles: Online - full text ed.: ISSN 1520-0434. USD 275 to non-members (effective 2011).
Indexed: A01, A03, A08, A22, ASCA, CA, CPEI, CurCont, E01, E04, E05, Englnd, GEOBASE, GeoRef, ISR, M&GPA, P10, P47, P48, P52, P53, P54, P56, PQC, S01, S10, SCI, SCOPUS, T02, W07.
—BLDSC (9282.600000), IE, Infotrieve, Ingenta, INIST, Linda Hall. **CCC.**
Published by: American Meteorological Society, 45 Beacon St, Boston, MA 02108. TEL 617-227-2425, FAX 617-742-8718, amspubs@ametsoc.org. Eds. Dr. Brian A Colle, Da-Lin Zhang, William A Gallus. **Subscr. to:** Allen Press Inc., PO Box 1897, Lawrence, KS 66044. orders@allenpress.com, http://www.allenpress.com, http://www.allenpress.com.

551 USA ISSN 1948-2450
WEATHER AND SOCIETY WATCH. Text in English. 2007. q. free (effective 2009). back issues avail. **Document type:** *Newsletter, Trade.* **Description:** Provides a forum for those interested in the societal impacts of weather and weather forecasting.
Related titles: Online - full text ed.: ISSN 1948-2469.
Published by: National Center for Atmospheric Research, Societal Impacts Program, PO Box 3000, Boulder, CO 80307. TEL 303-497-2857, lazo@ucar.edu.

551.5 USA ISSN 1948-8327
QC851
▼ **WEATHER, CLIMATE, AND SOCIETY.** Abbreviated title: W C A S. Text in English. 2009. q. USD 355 combined subscription domestic to non-members (print & online eds.); USD 395 combined subscription foreign to non-members (print & online eds.) (effective 2011). **Document type:** *Journal, Academic/Scholarly.* **Description:** Features research and analysis on the interactions of weather and climate with society.
Related titles: Online - full text ed.: ISSN 1948-8335. 2009. USD 185 to non-members (effective 2011).
Indexed: A22, E01, E04, E05, T02.
Published by: American Meteorological Society, 45 Beacon St, Boston, MA 02108. TEL 617-227-2425, FAX 617-742-8718, amspubs@ametsoc.org.

551.6 USA
WEATHERVANE. Text in English. 1955. d. **Document type:** *Trade.* **Description:** Contains information to provide the news media global policy initiatives related to climate change.
Formerly (until 1997): The Fiberglas Canada Weathervane (Print) (0833-3092)
Media: Online - full text.
—CCC.
Published by: Resources for the Future, Inc., 1616 P St, N W, Washington, DC 20036. TEL 202-328-5000, FAX 202-939-3460, info@rff.org.

551.6 USA ISSN 0043-1672
QC851 CODEN: WTHWA2
WEATHERWISE. Text in English. 1948. bi-m. GBP 102 in United Kingdom to institutions; EUR 134, USD 168 to institutions (effective 2012). bk.rev. charts; illus. index, cum.index: vols.1-31. back issues avail.; reprint service avail. from PSC. **Document type:** *Magazine, Consumer.* **Description:** Features fascinating articles and spectacular color photographs that showcase the power, beauty, and excitement of weather.
Related titles: CD-ROM ed.; Microform ed.: (from PQC); Online - full text ed.: ISSN 1940-1310.
Indexed: A01, A02, A03, A08, A11, A22, A25, A26, B04, BRD, BiolDig, C05, CA, CPerI, CTO, ChemAb, E01, E04, E05, E08, EnvAb, EnvInd, G01, G03, G05, G06, G07, G08, GSA, GSI, GeoRef, I05, I06, I07, Inspec, M&GPA, M01, M02, M04, MASUSE, MagInd, P02, P10, P13, P26, P47, P48, P52, P53, P54, P56, PMR, PQC, R03, R04, R06, RGAb, RGPR, S01, S04, S06, S08, S09, S10, S23, SpeleolAb, T02, TOM, W03, W05, WBA, WMB.
—BLDSC (9283.900000), AskIEEE, IE, Infotrieve, Ingenta, INIST, Linda Hall. **CCC.**
Published by: (American Meteorological Society, Helen Dwight Reid Educational Foundation), Taylor & Francis Inc. (Subsidiary of: Taylor & Francis Group), 325 Chestnut St, Ste 800, Philadelphia, PA 19106. TEL 215-625-2940, 800-354-1420, FAX 215-625-8914, customerservice@taylorandfrancis.com.

551.5 NLD ISSN 1568-1629
HET WEER! MAGAZINE. Text in Dutch. 2000. bi-m. EUR 22.50; EUR 4.95 newsstand/cover (effective 2010). adv. **Document type:** *Magazine, Trade.*
Published by: Virtumedia, Postbus 595, Zeist, 3700 AN, Netherlands. TEL 31-30-6920677, FAX 31-30-6913312, info@virtumedia.nl, http://www.virtumedia.nl. Ed. Frank van der Laan. Pub. Pepijn Dobbelaer. Adv. contact Klaartje Grol. color page EUR 720; trim 210 x 297. Circ: 5,000.

551.5 DEU ISSN 0943-0504
DER WETTERLOTSE. Text in German. 1949. bi-m. EUR 13; EUR 3.50 per issue (effective 2009). index. back issues avail. **Document type:** *Bulletin, Trade.* **Description:** Contains meteorological values and reports for weather observers on ships.
Indexed: RefZh.
Published by: Deutscher Wetterdienst, Geschaeftsfeld Forschung und Entwicklung, Bernhard-Nocht-Str 76, Hamburg, 20359, Germany. TEL 49-40-66901444, FAX 49-40-66901499, http://www.dwd.de. Circ: 1,100 (paid and controlled).

551.5 USA ISSN 1098-7215
QC875
WINDSWEPT. Text in English. 1937. q. USD 25 to individuals; USD 45 to institutions. adv. bk.rev. charts; illus.; stat. cum.index: 1937-1960. **Document type:** *Bulletin.*
Formerly (until 1998): Mount Washington Observatory News Bulletin (0027-2523)
Published by: Mount Washington Observatory, PO Box 2310, North Conway, NH 03860. TEL 603-356-8345, FAX 603-356-3060. Ed. Guy Gosselin. R&P Linda Gray. Circ: 4,500.

551.65 AUT ISSN 0043-7077
WITTERUNG IN OESTERREICH. MONATSUEBERSICHT. Text in German. 1946. m. price varies. charts; stat. **Document type:** *Journal, Government.*
Published by: Zentralanstalt fuer Meteorologie und Geodynamik, Hohe Warte 38, Vienna, 1190, Austria. TEL 43-1-36026, FAX 43-1-3691233, dion@zamg.ac.at.

551.5 CHE
WORLD CLIMATE NEWS. Text in English. irreg. back issues avail.
Related titles: Online - full text ed.
Published by: World Meteorological Organization, 7 bis Avenue de la Paix, Case postale 2300, Geneva 2, 1211, Switzerland. TEL 41-22-7308111, FAX 41-22-7308022, pubsales@gateway.wmo.ch, http://www.wmo.int.

551 JPN
WORLD DATA CENTER C2 FOR AURORA. DATA CATALOGUE. Text in English. 1985. irreg., latest vol.5, 1995. per issue exchange basis. **Document type:** *Catalog.*
Supersedes in part (in 1993): Data Catalogue in World Data Center C2 for Aurora.
Published by: National Institute of Polar Research/Kokuritsu Kyokuchi Kenkyujo, Publications, 10-3, Midoricho, Tachikawa, Tokyo, 190-8518, Japan. FAX 81-3-39622225, publication402@nipr.ac.jp, http://www.nipr.ac.jp/. Ed. Okitsugu Watanabe. Circ: 800.

551.5 CHE
WORLD METEOROLOGICAL ORGANIZATION. ABRIDGED FINAL REPORTS OF SESSIONS OF TECHNICAL COMMISSIONS. Text in English. irreg. price varies. **Document type:** *Monographic series, Government.*
Formerly: World Meteorological Association. Technical Commissions Abridged Final Reports (0084-1919)
—Linda Hall.
Published by: World Meteorological Organization, 7 bis Avenue de la Paix, Case postale 2300, Geneva 2, 1211, Switzerland. TEL 41-22-7308111, FAX 41-22-7308022, pubsales@gateway.wmo.ch, http://www.wmo.int. **Dist. in U.S. by:** American Meteorological Society, 45 Beacon St, Boston, MA 02108. TEL 617-227-2425.

551.5 CHE
WORLD METEOROLOGICAL ORGANIZATION. BASIC DOCUMENTS. Text in English. irreg. (in 3 vols.). price varies. **Document type:** *Bulletin.* **Description:** Contains regulations of the W.M.O. and agreements with the U.N. and the Swiss governments by which the W.M.O. operates.
Former titles: World Meteorological Organization. Basic Documents and Official Reports; World Meteorological Organization. Basic Documents, Records and Reports (0084-1943)
Published by: World Meteorological Organization, 7 bis Avenue de la Paix, Case postale 2300, Geneva 2, 1211, Switzerland. TEL 41-22-7308111, FAX 41-22-7308022, pubsales@gateway.wmo.ch, http://www.wmo.int. **Dist. in U.S. by:** American Meteorological Society, 45 Beacon St, Boston, MA 02108. TEL 617-227-2425.

551.3 387.7 CHE ISSN 0510-906X
QC851
WORLD METEOROLOGICAL ORGANIZATION. COMMISSION FOR AERONAUTICAL METEOROLOGY. ABRIDGED FINAL REPORT OF THE (NO.) SESSION. Text in English. 1954. irreg., latest 1994. price varies. **Document type:** *Monographic series, Academic/Scholarly.*
Related titles: French ed.: Organisation Meteorologique Mondiale. Commission de Meteorologie Aeronautique. Rapport Final Abrege de la (No) Session. ISSN 0251-8899; Spanish ed.: Organizacion Meteorologica Mundial. Comision de Meteorologia Aeronautica. Informe Final Abrevido de la (No) Reunion. ISSN 0251-8902; Russian ed.: Vsemirnaya Meteorologicheskaya Organizatsiya. Komissiya po Aviatsionnoi Meteorologii. Okonchatel'nyi Sokrashchennyi Otchet (No) Sessii. ISSN 0251-8880.
—Linda Hall.
Published by: (Commission for Aeronautical Meteorology), World Meteorological Organization, 7 bis Avenue de la Paix, Case postale 2300, Geneva 2, 1211, Switzerland. TEL 41-22-7308111, FAX 41-22-7308022, pubsales@gateway.wmo.ch, http://www.wmo.int. **Dist. in U.S. by:** American Meteorological Society, 45 Beacon St, Boston, MA 02108. TEL 617-227-2425.

551.3 630 CHE ISSN 0510-9078
QC851
WORLD METEOROLOGICAL ORGANIZATION. COMMISSION FOR AGRICULTURAL METEOROLOGY. ABRIDGED FINAL REPORT OF THE (NO.) SESSION. Text in English. 1953. irreg., latest 1995. price varies.
Related titles: French ed.: Organisation Meteorologique Mondiale. Commission de Meteorologie Agricole. Rapport Final Abrege de la (No) Session. ISSN 0251-883X; Spanish ed.: Organizacion Meteorologica Mundial. Comision de Meteorologia Agricola. Informe Final Abrevido de la (No) Reunion. ISSN 0251-8821; Russian ed.: Vsemirnaya Meteorologicheskaya Organizatsiya Komissiya po Sel'skokhozyaistvennoi Meteorologii. Okonchatel'nyi Sokrashchennyi Otchet (No) Sessii. ISSN 0251-8848.
—Linda Hall.
Published by: (Commission for Agricultural Meteorology), World Meteorological Organization, 7 bis Avenue de la Paix, Case postale 2300, Geneva 2, 1211, Switzerland. TEL 41-22-7308111, FAX 41-22-7308022, pubsales@gateway.wmo.ch, http://www.wmo.int. **Dist. in U.S. by:** American Meteorological Society, 45 Beacon St, Boston, MA 02108. TEL 617-227-2425.

551.3 CHE ISSN 0250-9172
WORLD METEOROLOGICAL ORGANIZATION. COMMISSION FOR ATMOSPHERIC SCIENCES. ABRIDGED FINAL REPORT OF THE (NO.) SESSION. Text in English. 1953-1965; N.S. 1970. irreg., latest 1994. price varies.
Formerly (until 1965): World Meteorological Organization. Commission of Aerology. Abridged Final Report of the (No.) Session (1011-3223)
Related titles: French ed.: Organisation Meteorologique Mondiale. Commission des Sciences de l'Atmosphere. Rapport Final Abrege de la (No) Session. ISSN 0250-9156; Spanish ed.: Organizacion Meteorologico Mundial. Comision de Ciencias Atmosfericas. Informe Final Abrevido de la (No) Reunion. ISSN 0250-9180; Russian ed.: Vsemirnaya Meteorologicheskaya Organizatsiya. Komissiya po Atmosfernym Naukam. Okonchatel'nyi Sokrashchennyi Otchet (No) Sessii. ISSN 0250-9164.
Published by: (Commission for Atmospheric Sciences), World Meteorological Organization, 7 bis Avenue de la Paix, Case postale 2300, Geneva 2, 1211, Switzerland. TEL 41-22-7308111, FAX 41-22-7308022, pubsales@gateway.wmo.ch, http://www.wmo.int. **Dist. in U.S. by:** American Meteorological Society, 45 Beacon St, Boston, MA 02108. TEL 617-227-2425.

551.3 CHE ISSN 0251-8953
WORLD METEOROLOGICAL ORGANIZATION. COMMISSION FOR BASIC SYSTEMS. ABRIDGED FINAL REPORT OF THE (NO.) SESSION. Text in English. 1953-1970; N.S. 1974. irreg., latest 1994. price varies.
Formerly (until 1970): World Meteorological Organization. Commission of Synoptic Meteorology. Abridged Final Report of the (No.) Session (0510-9116)
Related titles: Abridged ed.: Organisation Meteorologique Mondiale. Commission des Systems de Base. Rapport Final Abrege de la (No) Session. ISSN 0251-8988; Organizacion Meteorologica Mundial. Comision de Sistemas Basicos. Informe Final Abrevido de la (No) Reunion. ISSN 0251-897X; Vsemirnaya Meteologicheskaya Organizatsiya. Komissiya po Osnovnym Sistemam. Okonchatel'nyi Sokrashchennyi Otchet (No) Sessii. ISSN 0251-8961.
—Linda Hall.
Published by: (Commission for Basic Systems), World Meteorological Organization, 7 bis Avenue de la Paix, Case postale 2300, Geneva 2, 1211, Switzerland. TEL 41-22-7308111, FAX 41-22-7308022, pubsales@gateway.wmo.ch, http://www.wmo.int. **Dist. in U.S. by:** American Meteorological Society, 45 Beacon St, Boston, MA 02108. TEL 617-227-2425.

551.3 551.46 CHE ISSN 0251-8775
WORLD METEOROLOGICAL ORGANIZATION. COMMISSION FOR HYDROLOGY. ABRIDGED FINAL REPORT OF THE (NO.) SESSION. Text in English. 1972. irreg., latest 1993. price varies. **Document type:** *Government.*
Related titles: French ed.: Organisation Meteorologique Mondiale. Commission de'Hydrologie. Rapport Final Abege de la (No) Session. ISSN 0251-8740; Spanish ed.: Organizacion Meteorologica Mundial. Comision de Hidrologia. Informe Final Abrevido de la (No) Reunion. ISSN 0251-8759; Russian ed.: Vsemirnaya Meteorologicheskaya Organizatsiya. Komissiya po Gidrologii. Okonchatel'nyi Sokrashchennyi Otchet (No) Sessii. ISSN 0251-8767.
—Linda Hall.
Published by: (Commission for Hydrology), World Meteorological Organization, 7 bis Avenue de la Paix, Case postale 2300, Geneva 2, 1211, Switzerland. TEL 41-22-7308111, FAX 41-22-7308022, pubsales@gateway.wmo.ch, http://www.wmo.int. **Dist. in the U.S. by:** American Meteorological Society, 45 Beacon St, Boston, MA 02108. TEL 617-227-2425.

551.3 CHE ISSN 0251-8783
WORLD METEOROLOGICAL ORGANIZATION. COMMISSION FOR INSTRUMENTS AND METHODS OF OBSERVATION. ABRIDGED FINAL REPORT OF THE (NO.) SESSION. Text in English. 1953. quadrennial. price varies.
Related titles: French ed.: Organisation Meteorologique Mondiale. Commission des Instruments et des Methodes d'Observation. Rapport Final Abrege de la (No) Session. ISSN 0251-8791; Spanish ed.: Organizacion Meteorologica Mundial. Comision de Instrumentos y Metodos de Observacion. Informe Final Abrevido de la (No) Reunion; Russian ed.: Vsemirnaya Meteorologicheskaya Organizatsiya. Komissiya po Priboram i Metodam Nablyudenii. Okonchatel'nyi Sokrashchennyi Otchet (No) Sessii. ISSN 0251-8813.
Published by: (Commission for Instruments and Methods of Observation), World Meteorological Organization, 7 bis Avenue de la Paix, Case postale 2300, Geneva 2, 1211, Switzerland. TEL 41-22-7308111, FAX 41-22-7308022, pubsales@gateway.wmo.ch, http://www.wmo.int. **Dist. in the U.S. by:** American Meteorological Society, 45 Beacon St, Boston, MA 02108. TEL 617-227-2425.

551.3 387 CHE ISSN 1011-3207
WORLD METEOROLOGICAL ORGANIZATION. COMMISSION FOR MARINE METEOROLOGY. ABRIDGED FINAL REPORT OF THE (NO.) SESSION. Text in English. 1952. quadrennial. price varies. **Document type:** *Government.*
Formerly (until 1968): World Meteorological Organization. Commission for Maritime Meteorology. Abridged Final Report of the (No.) Session (0084-1951)
Related titles: French ed.: Organisation Meteorologique Mondiale. Commission de Meteorologie Maritime. Rapport Final Abrege de la (No) Session. ISSN 0251-8872; Spanish ed.: Organizacion Meteorologica Mundial. Comision de Meteorologia Marina. Informe Final Abrevido de la (No) Reunion. ISSN 0251-8864; Russian ed.: Vsemirnaya Meteorologicheskaya Organizatsiya. Komissiya po Morskoi Meteorologii. Okonchatel'nyi Sokrashchennyi Otchet (No) Sessii. ISSN 0251-8856.
Published by: (Commission for Marine Meteorology), World Meteorological Organization, 7 bis Avenue de la Paix, Case postale 2300, Geneva 2, 1211, Switzerland. TEL 41-22-7308111, FAX 41-22-7308022, pubsales@gateway.wmo.ch, http://www.wmo.int. **Dist. in U.S. by:** American Meteorological Society, 45 Beacon St, Boston, MA 02108. TEL 617-227-2425.

551.5 CHE ISSN 0084-1927
WORLD METEOROLOGICAL ORGANIZATION. CONGRESS. ABRIDGED REPORT WITH RESOLUTIONS. Text in English. 1951. quadrennial. price varies. **Document type:** *Government.*
Related titles: French ed.: Organisation Meteorologique Mondiale. Congres. Rapport Abrege et Resolutions. ISSN 0250-9261; Russian ed.: Vsemirnaya Meteorologicheskaya Organizatsiya. Kongress. Sokrashchennyi Otchet s Rezolyutsiyami. ISSN 0250-9245; Spanish ed.: Organizacion Meteorologica Mundial. Congreso. Informe Abrevido y Resoluciones. ISSN 0250-9253.

Published by: World Meteorological Organization, 7 bis Avenue de la Paix, Case postale 2300, Geneva 2, 1211, Switzerland. TEL 41-22-7308111, FAX 41-22-7308022, pubsales@gateway.wmo.ch, http://www.wmo.int. **Dist. in U.S. by:** American Meteorological Society, 45 Beacon St, Boston, MA 02108. TEL 617-227-2425.

551.5 CHE ISSN 1011-3231
WORLD METEOROLOGICAL ORGANIZATION. EXECUTIVE COUNCIL SESSION. ABRIDGED FINAL REPORTS WITH RESOLUTIONS. Text in English. a. price varies. **Document type:** *Government.*
Former titles: World Meteorological Organization. Executive Committee Reports. Abridged Final Reports with Resolutions; World Meteorological Organization. Executive Committee Sess: Abridged Reports with Resolutions (0084-196X)
Related titles: ◆ French ed.: Organisation Meteorologique Mondiale. Session du Conseil Executif. Rapport Abrege et Resolutions. ISSN 1011-3592; ◆ Russian ed.: Vsemirnaya Meteorologicheskaya Organizatsiya. Sessiya Ispolnitel'nogo Soveta. Sokrashchennyi Otchet s Rezolyutsiyami. ISSN 1011-3673; ◆ Spanish ed.: Organizacion Meteorologica Mundial. Reunion del Consejo Ejecutivo. Informe Abreviado y Resoluciones. ISSN 1011-3576.
Published by: World Meteorological Organization, 7 bis Avenue de la Paix, Case postale 2300, Geneva 2, 1211, Switzerland. TEL 41-22-7308111, FAX 41-22-7308022, pubsales@gateway.wmo.ch, http://www.wmo.int. **Dist. in U.S. by:** American Meteorological Society, 45 Beacon St, Boston, MA 02108. TEL 617-227-2425.

551.656 CHE ISSN 0510-9124
QC851
WORLD METEOROLOGICAL ORGANIZATION. REGIONAL ASSOCIATION I (AFRICA). ABRIDGED FINAL REPORT OF THE (NO.) SESSION. Text in English. irreg., latest 1994. price varies. **Document type:** *Government.*
Related titles: French ed.: Organisation Meteorolgique Mondiale. Association Regionale I (Afrique). Rapport Final Abrege de la Session. ISSN 0250-9059.
—Linda Hall.
Published by: World Meteorological Organization, 7 bis Avenue de la Paix, Case postale 2300, Geneva 2, 1211, Switzerland. TEL 41-22-7308111, FAX 41-22-7308022, pubsales@gateway.wmo.ch, http://www.wmo.int. **Dist. in U.S. by:** American Meteorological Society, 45 Beacon St, Boston, MA 02108. TEL 617-227-2425.

551.655 CHE ISSN 0509-3007
QC851
WORLD METEOROLOGICAL ORGANIZATION. REGIONAL ASSOCIATION II (ASIA). ABRIDGED FINAL REPORT OF THE (NO.) SESSION. Text in English. 1955. irreg., latest 1992. price varies.
Related titles: Russian ed.: Vsemirnaya Meteorologicheskaya Organizatsiya. Regional'naya Assotsiatsiya II (Aziya). Okonchatel'nyi Sokrashchennyi Otchet (No.) Sessii. ISSN 0250-9105; French ed.: Organisation Meteorologique Mondiale. Association Regionale II (Asie). Rapport Final Abrege de la (No.) Session. ISSN 0250-9113.
—Linda Hall.
Published by: World Meteorological Organization, 7 bis Avenue de la Paix, Case postale 2300, Geneva 2, 1211, Switzerland. TEL 41-22-7308111, FAX 41-22-7308022, pubsales@gateway.wmo.ch, http://www.wmo.int. **Dist. in U.S. by:** American Meteorological Society, 45 Beacon St, Boston, MA 02108. TEL 617-227-2425.

551.658 CHE ISSN 0510-9132
WORLD METEOROLOGICAL ORGANIZATION. REGIONAL ASSOCIATION III (SOUTH AMERICA). ABRIDGED FINAL REPORT OF THE (NO.) SESSION. Text in English. 1953. irreg., latest 1993. price varies.
Related titles: Spanish ed.: Organizacion Meteorologica Mundial. Asociacion Regional III (America del Sur). Informe Final Abreviado de la (No.) Reunion. ISSN 0250-9148.
Published by: World Meteorological Organization, 7 bis Avenue de la Paix, Case postale 2300, Geneva 2, 1211, Switzerland. TEL 41-22-7308111, FAX 41-22-7308022, pubsales@gateway.wmo.ch, http://www.wmo.int. **Dist. in U.S. by:** American Meteorological Society, 45 Beacon St, Boston, MA 02108. TEL 617-227-2425.

551.657 CHE ISSN 0250-9121
WORLD METEOROLOGICAL ORGANIZATION. REGIONAL ASSOCIATION IV (NORTH AMERICA AND CENTRAL AMERICA). ABRIDGED FINAL REPORT OF THE (NO.) SESSION. Text in English. 1953. irreg., latest 1993. price varies.
Related titles: Spanish ed.: Organizacion Meteorologica Mundial. Asociacion Regional IV (America del Norte y America Central). Informe Final Abreviado de la (No.) Reunion. ISSN 0250-913X.
Published by: World Meteorological Organization, 7 bis Avenue de la Paix, Case postale 2300, Geneva 2, 1211, Switzerland. TEL 41-22-7308111, FAX 41-22-7308022, pubsales@gateway.wmo.ch, http://www.wmo.int. **Dist. in U.S. by:** American Meteorological Society, 45 Beacon St, Boston, MA 02108. TEL 617-227-2425.

551.659 CHE ISSN 0250-9040
QC851
WORLD METEOROLOGICAL ORGANIZATION. REGIONAL ASSOCIATION V (SOUTH WEST PACIFIC). ABRIDGED FINAL REPORT OF THE (NO.) SESSION. Text in French. 1954. quadrennial. price varies.
Related titles: French ed.: Organisation Meteorologique Mondiale. Association Regionale V (Pacifique Sud-Ouest). Rapport Final Abrege de la (No.) Session. ISSN 0250-9032.
—Linda Hall.
Published by: World Meteorological Organization, 7 bis Avenue de la Paix, Case postale 2300, Geneva 2, 1211, Switzerland. TEL 41-22-7308111, FAX 41-22-7308022, pubsales@gateway.wmo.ch, http://www.wmo.int. **Dist. in U.S. by:** American Meteorological Society, 45 Beacon St, Boston, MA 02108. TEL 617-227-2425.

WORLD METEOROLOGICAL ORGANIZATION. SPECIAL ENVIRONMENTAL REPORTS. *see* ENVIRONMENTAL STUDIES

551.5 CHE ISSN 0084-201X
QC851 CODEN: WMOTAD
WORLD METEOROLOGICAL ORGANIZATION. TECHNICAL NOTES. Text in English. 1954. irreg., latest vol.196. price varies.
Indexed: GeoRef, SpeleolAb.
—INIST.
Published by: World Meteorological Organization, 7 bis Avenue de la Paix, Case postale 2300, Geneva 2, 1211, Switzerland. TEL 41-22-7308111, FAX 41-22-7308022, pubsales@gateway.wmo.ch, http://www.wmo.int. **Dist. in U.S. by:** American Meteorological Society, 45 Beacon St, Boston, MA 02108. TEL 617-227-2425.

551.632 CHE ISSN 0250-9393
WORLD METEOROLOGICAL ORGANIZATION. WEATHER REPORTING. VOLUME A: OBSERVING STATIONS. Text in English, French. 1952. base vol. plus s-a. updates. looseleaf. USD 100 base vol(s). per vol.; USD 180 updates (effective 2001). **Document type:** *Government.* **Description:** Contains information on stations providing synoptic meteorological reports.
Published by: World Meteorological Organization, 7 bis Avenue de la Paix, Case postale 2300, Geneva 2, 1211, Switzerland. TEL 41-22-7308111, FAX 41-22-7308022, pubsales@gateway.wmo.ch, http://www.wmo.int. **Dist. in U.S. by:** American Meteorological Society, 45 Beacon St, Boston, MA 02108. TEL 617-227-2425.

551.632 CHE ISSN 0250-9407
WORLD METEOROLOGICAL ORGANIZATION. WEATHER REPORTING. VOLUME B: DATA PROCESSING. Text in English, French, Russian, Spanish. 1974. base vol. plus s-a. updates. looseleaf. USD 84 base vol(s). per vol. includes binder; USD 35 updates (effective 2001). **Document type:** *Government.*
Published by: World Meteorological Organization, 7 bis Avenue de la Paix, Case postale 2300, Geneva 2, 1211, Switzerland. TEL 41-22-7308111, FAX 41-22-7308022, pubsales@gateway.wmo.ch, http://www.wmo.int. **Dist. in U.S. by:** American Meteorological Society, 45 Beacon St, Boston, MA 02108. TEL 617-227-2425.

551.632 CHE
WORLD METEOROLOGICAL ORGANIZATION. WEATHER REPORTING. VOLUME C1: CATALOGUE OF METEOROLOGICAL BULLETINS. Text in English. base vol. plus bi-m. updates. USD 75 base vol(s). per vol. includes binder; USD 135 updates (effective 2001).
Published by: World Meteorological Organization, 7 bis Avenue de la Paix, Case postale 2300, Geneva 2, 1211, Switzerland. TEL 41-22-7308111, FAX 41-22-7308022, pubsales@gateway.wmo.ch, http://www.wmo.int. **Dist. in U.S. by:** American Meteorological Society, 45 Beacon St, Boston, MA 02108. TEL 617-227-2425.

551.632 CHE ISSN 0250-9415
WORLD METEOROLOGICAL ORGANIZATION. WEATHER REPORTING. VOLUME C2: TRANSMISSIONS. Text in English, French. 1952. base vol. plus bi-m. updates. looseleaf. USD 72 base vol(s). per vol. includes binder; USD 55 updates (effective 2000). **Document type:** *Government.* **Description:** Contains schedules of broadcasts and point-to-point transmission of coded meteorological information.
Published by: World Meteorological Organization, 7 bis Avenue de la Paix, Case postale 2300, Geneva 2, 1211, Switzerland. TEL 41-22-7308111, FAX 41-22-7308022, pubsales@gateway.wmo.ch, http://www.wmo.int. **Dist. in U.S. by:** American Meteorological Society, 45 Beacon St, Boston, MA 02108. TEL 617-227-2425.

551.632 CHE ISSN 0250-9423
WORLD METEOROLOGICAL ORGANIZATION. WEATHER REPORTING. VOLUME D: INFORMATION FOR SHIPPING. Text in English, French. 1952. base vol. plus bi-m. updates. looseleaf. USD 183 base vol(s). includes 3 binders; USD 110 updates (effective 2001). **Document type:** *Government.* **Description:** Information about meteorological forecasts and warnings to shipping and on the collection of ships' weather reports.
Published by: World Meteorological Organization, 7 bis Avenue de la Paix, Case postale 2300, Geneva 2, 1211, Switzerland. TEL 41-22-7308111, FAX 41-22-7308022, pubsales@gateway.wmo.ch, http://www.wmo.int.

551.5 RUS
WORLD RADIATION DATA CENTRE. SOLAR RADIATION AND RADIATION BALANCE DATA. Text in English, Russian. 1964. q. USD 120 foreign (effective 2001). stat. Supplement avail. **Description:** Provides the users with data on solar radiation, radiation balance and sunshine duration.
Former titles: World Radiation Data Centre. Quarterly Report; (until 1994): Solnechnaya Radiatsiya i Radiatsionnyi Balans. Mirovaya Set' - Solar Radiation and Radiation Balance Data. The World Network (0235-4519)
Published by: Glavnaya Geofizicheskaya Observatoriya im. A.I. Voeikova, Mirovoi Tsentr Radiatsionnykh Dannykh/Voeikov Main Geophysical Observatory, World Radiation Data Centre, Ul Karbysheva 7, St Petersburg, 194018, Russian Federation. TEL 812-247-01-03, FAX 812-247-86-61. Ed. E P Borisenkov.

551.6 SGP ISSN 2010-2763
WORLD SCIENTIFIC SERIES ON ASIA-PACIFIC WEATHER AND CLIMATE. Text in English. 2002. irreg., latest vol.4, 2010. price varies. back issues avail. **Document type:** *Monographic series, Academic/Scholarly.*
Published by: World Scientific Publishing Co. Pte. Ltd., 5 Toh Tuck Link, Singapore, 596224, Singapore. TEL 65-6466-5775, FAX 65-6467-7667, wspc@wspc.com.sg, http://www.worldscientific.com. Eds. Chih-Pei Chang, Congbin Fu. **Dist. by:** World Scientific Publishing Co., Inc., 27 Warren St, Ste 401-402, Hackensack, NJ 07601. TEL 201-487-9655, 800-227-7562, FAX 201-487-9656, 888-977-2665, wspc@wspc.com; World Scientific Publishing Ltd., 57 Shelton St, London WC2H 9HE, United Kingdom. TEL 44-207-8360888, FAX 44-207-8362020, sales@wspc.co.uk.

551.5 SGP
WORLD SCIENTIFIC SERIES ON EARTH SYSTEM SCIENCE IN ASIA. Text in English. 2002. irreg., latest vol.3, 2004. price varies. back issues avail. **Document type:** *Monographic series, Academic/Scholarly.*
Published by: World Scientific Publishing Co. Pte. Ltd., 5 Toh Tuck Link, Singapore, 596224, Singapore. TEL 65-6466-5775, FAX 65-6467-7667, wspc@wspc.com.sg, http://www.worldscientific.com. Ed. Chih-Pei Chang. **Subscr. to:** Farrer Rd, PO Box 128, Singapore 912805, Singapore. sales@wspc.com.sg. **Dist. by:** World Scientific Publishing Co., Inc., 27 Warren St, Ste 401-402, Hackensack, NJ 07601. TEL 201-487-9655, 800-227-7562, FAX 201-487-9656, 888-977-2665, wspc@wspc.com; World Scientific Publishing Ltd., 57 Shelton St, London WC2H 9HE, United Kingdom. TEL 44-207-8360888, FAX 44-207-8362020, sales@wspc.co.uk.

551.5 SGP
WORLD SCIENTIFIC SERIES ON METEOROLOGY OF EAST ASIA. Text in English. 2002 (Mar.). irreg., latest vol.3. price varies. **Document type:** *Monographic series, Academic/Scholarly.*
Formerly: World Scientific Series on East Asian Meteorology
Published by: World Scientific Publishing Co. Pte. Ltd., 5 Toh Tuck Link, Singapore, 596224, Singapore. TEL 65-6466-5775, FAX 65-6467-7667, series@wspc.com.sg, wspc@wspc.com.sg, http://www.worldscientific.com. **Dist. by:** World Scientific Publishing Co., Inc., 1060 Main St, River Edge, NJ 07661. TEL 201-487-9655, 800-227-7562, FAX 201-487-9656, 888-977-2665; World Scientific Publishing Ltd., 57 Shelton St, London WC2H 9HE, United Kingdom. TEL 44-207-8360888, FAX 44-207-8362020, sales@wspc.co.uk.

551.58 NLD ISSN 0168-6321
WORLD SURVEY OF CLIMATOLOGY. Text in English. 1969. irreg., latest 2001, vol.1C. price varies. back issues avail. **Document type:** *Monographic series, Academic/Scholarly.* **Description:** Publishes research on all aspects of climatology and meteorological phenomena worldwide.
Related titles: Online - full text ed.
Indexed: GeoRef, Inspec.
Published by: Elsevier BV (Subsidiary of: Elsevier Science & Technology), Radarweg 29, PO Box 211, Amsterdam, 1000 AE, Netherlands. TEL 31-20-4853911, FAX 31-20-4852457, JournalsCustomerServiceEMEA@elsevier.com, http://www.elsevier.nl. Ed. H E Landsberg.

551.63 CHE ISSN 0084-2451
WORLD WEATHER WATCH PLANNING REPORTS. Text in English. 1966. irreg., latest 1983. price varies. **Document type:** *Government.*
Indexed: IIS.
—Linda Hall.
Published by: World Meteorological Organization, 7 bis Avenue de la Paix, Case postale 2300, Geneva 2, 1211, Switzerland. TEL 41-22-7308111, FAX 41-22-7308022, pubsales@gateway.wmo.ch, http://www.wmo.int. **Dist. in U.S. by:** American Meteorological Society, 45 Beacon St, Boston, MA 02108. TEL 617-227-2425.

551 JPN ISSN 0916-5274
YAMAGUCHIKEN KISHO GEPPO/YAMAGUCHI PREFECTURE. MONTHLY REPORT OF METEOROLOGY. Text in Japanese. 1947. m.
Published by: Kishocho, Shimonoseki Chiho Kishodai/Japan Meteorological Agency, Shimonoseki Local Meteorological Observatory, 6-1 Takezaki-cho 4-chome, Shimonoseki-shi, Yamaguchi-ken 750-0025, Japan.

551 JPN ISSN 0916-5282
YAMANASHIKEN KISHO GEPPO/YAMANASHI PREFECTURE. MONTHLY REPORT OF METEOROLOGY. Text in Japanese. 1900. m.
Published by: Kishocho, Kofu Chiho Kishodai/Japan Meteorological Agency, Kofu Local Meteorological Observatory, 7-29 Idacho 4-chome, Kofu-shi, Yamanashi-ken 400-0000, Japan.

551.6 CHN ISSN 1001-7313
QC851
➤ **YINGYONG QIXIANG XUEBAO/JOURNAL OF APPLIED METEOROLOGY.** Text in Chinese; Abstracts in English. 1986. bi-m. CNY 180 (effective 2011). bk.rev. abstr.; bibl.; charts; illus. **Document type:** *Journal, Academic/Scholarly.*
Formerly (until 1990): Qixiang Kexue Yanjiuyuan Yuankan
Related titles: Online - full text ed.: (from WanFang Data Corp.).
Indexed: M&GPA.
—East View.
Published by: (Chinese Meteorological Society/Zhongguo Qixiang Xuehui), Chinese Academy of Meteorological Sciences/Zhongguo Qixiang Kexueyuan, 46 Zhongguancun Nan Dajie, Beijing, 100081, China. TEL 86-10-68407086, FAX 86-10-68407256, wlb@cams.cma.gov.cn, http://www.cams.cma.gov.cn/.
Co-sponsors: National Meteorological Center of China; National Climate Center of China; National Satellite Meteorological Center of China.

551 JPN
YUKIGUNI JOHO SHIRYOSHU/INFORMATION MATERIALS FOR HEAVY SNOW AREA. Text in Japanese. 1986. a.
Published by: Nihon Shisutemu Kaihatsu Kenkyujo/Systems Research and Development Institute of Japan, 16-5 Tomihisa-cho, Shinjuku-ku, Tokyo, 162-0067, Japan.

551.5 ZMB ISSN 0302-5047
ZAMBIA. METEOROLOGICAL DEPARTMENT. TOTALS OF MONTHLY AND ANNUAL RAINFALL; for selected stations in Zambia. Text in English. a. **Document type:** *Government.* **Description:** Lists rainfall of the entire Zambian rainfall network catchment by catchment, including an annual map and its percentage to normal rainfall.
Published by: Meteorological Department, PO Box 30200, Lusaka, Zambia. TEL 260-1-228939, TELEX ZA 41450.

551.6 ZMB
ZAMBIAN CLIMATOLOGICAL SUMMARY; SURFACE AND UPPER AIR DATA. Text in English. m. **Document type:** *Government.* **Description:** Lists hourly, daily and monthly values of weather elements.
Published by: Meteorological Department, PO Box 30200, Lusaka, Zambia. TEL 260-1-228939.

551.5 DEU ISSN 0947-7128
ZENTRUM FUER MEERES- UND KLIMAFORSCHUNG. BERICHTE. REIHE A: METEOROLOGIE. Text in German. 1962. irreg. **Document type:** *Monographic series, Academic/Scholarly.*
Supersedes in part (in 1992): Universitaet Hamburg. Zentrum fuer Meeres- und Klimaforschung. Berichte (0936-949X); Which was formerly (until 1988): Universitaet Hamburg. Instituts fuer Meereskunde. Mitteilungen (0017-6907)
Indexed: ASFA, B21, ESPM, FLUIDEX, GEOBASE, M&GPA, SCOPUS.
—BLDSC (3425.929000), IE, Ingenta.
Published by: (Universitaet Hamburg, Meteorologisches Institut/University of Hamburg, Meteorological Institute), Universitaet Hamburg, Zentrum fuer Meeres- und Klimaforschung/University of Hamburg, Center for Marine and Climate Research, Bundesstr. 55, Hamburg, 20146, Germany. TEL 49-40-42838-4523, FAX 49-40-42838-5235, http://www.uni-hamburg.de/Wiss/SE/ZMK.

551.46 551.5 DEU ISSN 0947-7179
GC1
ZENTRUM FUER MEERES- UND KLIMAFORSCHUNG. BERICHTE. REIHE Z: INTERDISZIPLINAERE ZENTRUMSBERICHTE. Text in German. 1962. a. per issue exchange basis. illus. **Document type:** *Monographic series.*
Supersedes in part (in 1992): Universitaet Hamburg. Zentrum fuer Meeres- und Klimaforschung. Berichte (0936-949X); Which was formerly (until 1988): Universitaet Hamburg. Institut fuer Meereskunde. Mitteilungen (0017-6907)
Indexed: ASFA, B21, ESPM, SpeleolAb.
Published by: Universitaet Hamburg, Zentrum fuer Meeres- und Klimaforschung/University of Hamburg, Center for Marine and Climate Research, Bundesstr. 55, Hamburg, 20146, Germany. TEL 49-40-42838-4523, FAX 49-40-42838-5235, TELEX 212586-IFMHHHD, http://www.uni-hamburg.de/Wiss/SE/ZMK. Ed. Walter Nellen. Circ: 200.

551.5 CHN ISSN 1000-6362
ZHONGGUO NONGYE QIXIANG/CHINESE JOURNAL OF AGROMETEOROLOGY. Text in Chinese. 1979. q. CNY 6 newsstand/cover (effective 2006). **Document type:** *Journal, Academic/Scholarly.*
Related titles: Online - full text ed.
Indexed: M&GPA.
Published by: Zhongguo Nongye Kexueyuan/Chinese Academy of Agricultural Sciences, 12, Zhongguancun Nan Dajie, Beijing, 100081, China. TEL 86-10-68919774. Ed. Min Jinru.

551.5 CHN ISSN 1001-7496
ZHONGGUO QIXIANG KEXUE YANJIUYUAN NANBAO/ACADEMY OF METEOROLOGICAL SCIENCE. ANNUAL REPORT. Text in Chinese. 1986. a.
Related titles: Online - full text ed.
Published by: Zhongguo Qixiang Kexue Yanjiuyuan/Chinese Academy of Meteorological Sciences, 46, Zhongguancun Nandajie, Beijing, 100081, China. TEL 86-10-68407256, http://www.cams.cma.gov.cn/.

551.5 ZWE ISSN 0085-5707
QC875.Z55
ZIMBABWE. DEPARTMENT OF METEOROLOGICAL SERVICES. REPORT OF THE DIRECTOR. Text in English. a. back issues avail. **Document type:** *Government.*
Published by: Department of Meteorological Services, Belvedere, PO Box BE 150, Harare, Zimbabwe. TEL 704955. Circ: 80.

METEOROLOGY—Abstracting, Bibliographies, Statistics

551.5 USA
ALASKA BASIN OUTLOOK REPORT. Text in English. irreg. charts. **Document type:** *Government.* **Description:** Provides statistics on the precipitation and other meteorological data for the state of Alaska.
Published by: U.S. Department of Agriculture, Natural Resources Conservation Service (Anchorage), 949 E 36th Ave, Ste 400, Anchorage, AK 99508-4362.

551.65729021 USA ISSN 0500-4780
QC983
CLIMATOLOGICAL DATA. PUERTO RICO AND VIRGIN ISLANDS. Text in English. 1976. m. USD 63; USD 12 per issue (effective 2009). back issues avail. **Document type:** *Government.*
Formerly (until 1975): United States. Environmental Data Service. Climatological Data, Puerto Rico and Virgin Islands
Related titles: Online - full text ed.: USD 42; USD 4 per issue (effective 2009); Supplement(s): Supplemental Climatological Data, Late Reports and Corrections. Puerto Rico & Virgin Islands.
—Linda Hall.
Published by: U.S. National Climatic Data Center (Subsidiary of: U.S. Department of Commerce), Federal Bldg, 151 Patton Ave, Asheville, NC 28801. TEL 828-271-4800, FAX 828-271-4876, NODC.Services@noaa.gov, http://www.ncdc.noaa.gov.

551.5021 PAN
ESTADISTICA PANAMENA. SITUACION FISICA. SECCION 121. METEOROLOGIA. Text in Spanish. 1952. a. PAB 1 domestic (effective 2000). **Document type:** *Bulletin, Government.* **Description:** Offers a complete list of meteorological stations in Panama. Presents data on rainfall, temperature, humidity, atmospheric pressure, wind, solar radiation and other data.
Former titles: Estadistica Panamena. Situacion Fisica. Seccion 121. Clima - Meteorologia (0378-6757); Estadistica Panamena. Serie L. Meteorologia (0078-8953)
Published by: Direccion de Estadistica y Censo, Contraloria General, Apdo. 5213, Panama City, 5, Panama. FAX 507-269-7494. Circ: 600.

551.5021 FIN ISSN 1458-4530
ILMASTOTILASTOJA SUOMESTA/CLIMATOLOGICAL STATISTICS OF FINLAND. Text in English, Finnish. 2002. irreg. stat. **Document type:** *Government.* **Description:** Contains various climatological statistics.
Published by: Ilmatieteen Laitos/Finnish Meteorological Institute, Vuorikatu 24, PO Box 503, Helsinki, 00101, Finland. TEL 358-9-19291, FAX 358-9-179581, http://www.fmi.fi.

551.65 ITA ISSN 1127-509X
QC851
ITALY. ISTITUTO NAZIONALE DI STATISTICA. STATISTICHE METEOROLOGICHE. Text in Italian. 1959. irreg. **Document type:** *Government.*
Formerly (until 1982): Italy. Istituto Centrale di Statistica. Annuario di Statistiche Meteorologiche (0075-1731)
Published by: Istituto Nazionale di Statistica (I S T A T), Via Cesare Balbo 16, Rome, 00184, Italy. TEL 39-06-46731, http://www.istat.it.

016.5516 JPN ISSN 0289-3118
KOKU KISHO NOTO/ABSTRACTS IN AVIATION METEOROLOGY. Text in Japanese. 1970. s-a. **Document type:** *Abstract/Index.*
Published by: Kishocho/Japan Meteorological Agency, 1-3-4 Otemachi, Chiyoda-ku, Tokyo, 100-8122, Japan.

551.5 LUX
LUXEMBOURG. SERVICE CENTRAL DE LA STATISTIQUE ET DES ETUDES ECONOMIQUES. INDICATEURS RAPIDES. SERIE M: METEOROLOGIE. Text in French. m. looseleaf. **Document type:** *Government.* **Description:** Covers temperature, atmospheric pressure, precipitation, and sunshine.
Published by: Service Central de la Statistique et des Etudes Economiques, 13, rue Erasme, Luxembourg, L-1468, Luxembourg. TEL 352-478-4233, FAX 352-464-289, statec.post@statec.etat.lu, http://www.statec.public.lu.

016.5515 USA ISSN 0026-1130
QC851 CODEN: MGEAAQ
METEOROLOGICAL AND GEOASTROPHYSICAL ABSTRACTS. Text in English. 1950. bi-m. (plus a. cum. index on CD). USD 2,335 combined subscription (includes a. index on CD-ROM) (effective 2011). adv. bk.rev. abstr.; illus. Index. back issues avail.; reprints avail. **Document type:** *Abstract/Index.* **Description:** Presents current abstracts of books, reports, research papers, and miscellaneous literature published worldwide in the areas of environmental sciences, meteorology, astrophysics, hydrology, glaciology, and physical oceanography.
Formerly (until 1960): Meteorological Abstracts and Bibliography (0196-1632)
Related titles: Cumulative ed(s).: ISSN 1066-2707. 1993.
—BLDSC (5705.200000), Linda Hall. **CCC.**
Published by: ProQuest LLC (Bethesda) (Subsidiary of: Cambridge Information Group), 7200 Wisconsin Ave, Ste 715, Bethesda, MD 20814. TEL 301-961-6798, 800-843-7751, FAX 301-961-6799, journals@csa.com. Ed. Christopher Readinger. Circ: 334.
Co-sponsor: American Meteorological Society.

016.551 RUS ISSN 0202-9308
REFERATIVNYI ZHURNAL. METEOROLOGIYA I KLIMATOLOGIYA; vypusk svodnogo toma. Text in Russian. m. USD 492 foreign (effective 2011). **Document type:** *Journal, Abstract/Index.*
Related titles: CD-ROM ed.; Online - full text ed.
—East View.
Published by: VINITI RAN, ul Usievicha 20, Moscow, 125190, Russian Federation. TEL 7-499-1526113, FAX 7-499-9430060, dir@viniti.ru, http://www.viniti.ru. **Dist. by:** Informnauka Ltd., Ul Usievicha 20, Moscow 125190, Russian Federation. alfimov@viniti.ru.

551.5 JPN
REKISHO NENPYO. Text in Japanese. 1946. a. free. charts; stat. **Description:** Publishes astronomical data.
Published by: University of Tokyo, National Astronomical Observatory, 21-1 Osawa 2-chome, Mitaka-shi, Tokyo-to 181-0015, Japan. TEL 81-422-34-3621, FAX 81-422-34-3793.

551.5 MYS ISSN 0126-8872
RINGKASAN BULANAN PEMERHATIAN KAJICUACA/MONTHLY ABSTRACT OF METEOROLOGICAL OBSERVATIONS OF MALAYSIA. Text and summaries in English. 1950. m. MYR 360 (effective 2000). **Document type:** *Government.* **Description:** Provides a summary of meteorological parameters recorded for the month from meteorlogical and climatological stations.
Published by: Perkhidmatan Kajicuaca Malaysia/Malaysian Meteorological Service, Jalan Sultan, Petaling Jaya, Selangor 46667, Malaysia. TEL 60-3-7563225, FAX 60-3-7563621, TELEX MA37243. Circ: 80 (paid).

551.5 JPN ISSN 0388-3515
SEIKEI KISHO KANSOKUJO HOKOKU/SEIKEI METEOROLOGICAL OBSERVATORY. YEARLY DATA REPORT. Text in Japanese. 1958. a. free. stat. **Document type:** *Yearbook, Academic/Scholarly.*
Formerly (until 1979): Seikei Kisho Tenmon Kansokujo Hokoku (0388-3507)
Published by: Seikei Kisho Kansokujo/Seikei Meteorological Observatory, 3-10-13 Kichijoji-kitamachi, Musashin, Tokyo, 180-8633, Japan. obs@th.seikei.ac.jp, http://www.seikei.ac.jp/obs/index-j.htm. Circ: (controlled).

SOLAR TERRESTRIAL ACTIVITY CHART. *see* ASTRONOMY—Abstracting, Bibliographies, Statistics

METROLOGY AND STANDARDIZATION

A 2 L A (YEAR) ANNUAL REPORT. *see* BUSINESS AND ECONOMICS—Trade And Industrial Directories

A 2 L A (YEAR) DIRECTORY OF ACCREDITED LABORATORIES (ONLINE). *see* BUSINESS AND ECONOMICS—Trade And Industrial Directories

A 2 L A NEWS. *see* BUSINESS AND ECONOMICS—Trade And Industrial Directories

389.6 USA ISSN 0038-9676
A N S I REPORTER. (American National Standards Institute) Text in English. 1967. q. USD 100 (effective 2005). adv. reprints avail. **Document type:** *Newsletter.* **Description:** Reports on national and international standards issues.
Formerly: Standards Institute Reporter
Related titles: Microform ed.: (from PQC); Online - full text ed.
Published by: American National Standards Institute, Inc., 25 W. 43rd St., Flr. 4, New York, NY 10036-7406. TEL 212-642-4900, FAX 212-302-1286. Ed. Sharon Phillips. adv.: page USD 2,000; bleed 9 x 11.5. Circ: 8,000 (controlled).

530.8 HUN ISSN 0237-028X
ACTA I M E K O. Text in Hungarian. 1958. triennial. **Document type:** *Proceedings.*
Formerly: International Measurement Conference. Proceedings. Acta IMEKO (0074-6916)
Indexed: ChemAb.
Published by: International Measurement Confederation (IMEKO), PO Box 457, Budapest, 1371, Hungary. FAX 361-153-1406, TELEX 225792. Circ: 500.

389.6 USA
Z7914.A22
AMERICAN NATIONAL STANDARDS INSTITUTE. CATALOG OF AMERICAN STANDARDS. Text in English. 1977. a. free. **Document type:** *Catalog.*
Former titles (until 1997): American National Standards Catalog (1075-6809); (until 1992): Catalog of American National Standards (1043-7002)
Media: Online - full text.
Indexed: FS&TA.
Published by: American National Standards Institute, Inc., 25 W. 43rd St., Flr. 4, New York, NY 10036-7406. TEL 212-642-4900, FAX 212-398-0023.

389.6 USA
TP149
AMERICAN SOCIETY FOR QUALITY CONTROL. WORLD CONFERENCE ON QUALITY AND IMPROVEMENT PROCEEDINGS (CD-ROM). Text in English. 1994. a. **Document type:** *Proceedings.*
Former titles: American Society for Quality Control. World Conference on Quality and Improvement Proceedings (Print Edition); (until 1998): American Society for Quality Control. Annual Quality Congress Proceedings (1080-7764)
Media: CD-ROM.
Indexed: Englnd, SCOPUS.
—Linda Hall. **CCC.**
Published by: American Society for Quality, 600 North Plankinton Ave, P O Box 3005, Milwaukee, WI 53203. TEL 414-272-8575, 800-248-1946, FAX 414-272-1734, help@asq.org, http://www.asq.org.

389.6 USA
TP149 CODEN: AQATAZ
AMERICAN SOCIETY FOR QUALITY. PROCEEDINGS. Text in English. 1947. a. index by category, author and title. **Document type:** *Proceedings.*
Former titles (until 200?): A S Q World Conference on Quality and Improvement Proceedings; (until 2005): A S Q Annual Quality Congress Proceedings; (until 1998): A S Q C Annual Quality Congress Proceedings (1080-7764); (until 1994): American Society for Quality Control. Annual Quality Congress; (until 1992): American Society for Quality Control. Annual Quality Congress Transactions (1067-7267); (until 1981): American Society for Quality Control. Annual Technical Conference Transactions (0360-6929); (until 1965): American Society for Quality Control. Annual Convention Transactions; (until 1960): American Society for Quality Control. National Convention Transactions; (until 1955): American Society for Quality Control. Quality Control Convention Papers; (until 1954): American Society for Quality Control. Quality Control Conference Papers; (until 1951): American Society for Quality Control. Conference Papers
Related titles: Online - full text ed.: free to members (effective 2009).
Indexed: CIS.
—Linda Hall. **CCC.**
Published by: American Society for Quality, 600 North Plankinton Ave, P O Box 3005, Milwaukee, WI 53203. TEL 414-272-8575, 800-248-1946, FAX 414-272-1734, help@asq.org, http://www.asq.org. Circ: 5,500.

389.1 AUT
AUSTRIA. BUNDESAMT FUER EICH- UND VERMESSUNGSWESEN. AMTSBLATT FUER DAS EICHWESEN. Text in German. 1952. 8/yr. index. **Document type:** *Government.*
Published by: Bundesamt fuer Eich- und Vermessungswesen, Schiffamtsgasse 1-3, Vienna, 1025, Austria. TEL 43-1-211760, FAX 43-1-2161062, info@bev.gv.at, http://www.bev.gv.at. Circ: 450.

BENCHMARK (GLASGOW). *see* ENGINEERING

389.6 CHN ISSN 1674-5698
BIAOZHUN KEXUE/STANDARD SCIENCE. Text in Chinese. 1964. m.
Former titles (until 2009): Shijie Biaozhunhua yu Zhiliang Guanli/World Standardization & Quality Management (1002-610X); (until 1986): Guowai Biaozhunhua Dongtai; (until 1979): Biaozhunhua Yicong
Related titles: Online - full text ed.
Published by: Zhongguo Biaozhunhua Yanjiuyuan/China National Institute of Standardization, 4, Zhichun Lu, Beijing, 100088, China. TEL 86-10-58811439, FAX 86-10-64408535.

389.6 GBR
BRITISH STANDARDS INSTITUTION. ANNUAL REVIEW & SUMMARY FINANCIAL STATEMENTS (ONLINE). Text in English. 19??. a. free (effective 2010). back issues avail. **Document type:** *Corporate.*
Former titles (until 2006): British Standards Institution. Annual Review & Summary Financial Statements (Print); (until 2001): British Standards Institution. Annual Reports and Accounts; (until 1995): British Standards Institution. Annual Review (1368-0285); (until 1993): British Standards Institution. Annual Report; (until 1992): British Standards Institution. Annual Report and Accounts (0960-4391); (until 1989): British Standards Institution. Annual Report (0524-675X); Which superseded in part (1959-1982): British Standards Yearbook (0068-2578); Which was formerly (until 1959): British Standards Institution. Yearbook; (until 1946): British Standards Institution. Yearbook
Related titles: ◆ Issued with: Business Standards. ISSN 1366-5650.
Published by: British Standards Institution, 389 Chiswick High Rd, London, W4 4AL, United Kingdom. TEL 44-20-89969001, FAX 44-20-89967001, cservices@bsi-global.com, http://www.bsigroup.com/.

BRUEL & KJAER TECHNICAL REVIEW. *see* PHYSICS—Sound

352.83 CHE ISSN 0106-6080
C B BULLETIN/BULLETIN O C. Text in English. 1967. 3/yr. SEK 120, USD 13. **Document type:** *Bulletin, Trade.* **Description:** Titel: CB bulletin, information from The Certification Body (CB) of the International Commission on Rules for the Approval of Electrical Equipment (CEE), Bulletin OC, information de l'organisme de certification (OC) de la commission internationale de reglementation en vue de l'approbation de l'equipement electrique (CEE).
Related titles: Online - full text ed.
Published by: International Electrotechnical Commission, 3 Rue de Varembe, Geneva 20, 1211, Switzerland. TEL 41-22-9190252, FAX 41-22-9190300, info@iec.ch, http://www.iec.ch.

658.562 CAN ISSN 1204-6299
CALIBRE (ENGLISH EDITION). Text in English. 1993. q. free (effective 2004). **Document type:** *Newsletter.*
Related titles: Online - full text ed.: ISSN 1494-4790.
Published by: Canadian General Standards Board, Place du Portage III, 6B1, 11 Laurier St, Gatineau, PQ K1A 1G6, Canada. TEL 819-956-0425, 800-665-2472, FAX 819-956-5644, ncr.cgsb-ongc@pwgsc.gc.ca.

389.6 CAN
CANADIAN STANDARDS ASSOCIATION. ANNUAL REPORT. Text in English. 1919. a. free. **Document type:** *Corporate.*
Related titles: French ed.
Indexed: AESIS.
Published by: Canadian Standards Association, Public Affairs, 178 Rexdale Blvd, Toronto, ON M9W 1R3, Canada. TEL 416-747-4129, FAX 416-747-4149. Ed. Rosemary MacVicar-Elliott. Circ: 10,000.

389.6 CAN ISSN 0829-0873
CANADIAN STANDARDS ASSOCIATION. CATALOGUE. Text in English. 1930. a. free. **Document type:** *Catalog.*
Supersedes: Canadian Standards Association. Standards Catalogue; Canadian Standards Association. List of Publications
Published by: (Standards Sales), Canadian Standards Association, 178 Rexdale Blvd, Toronto, ON M9W 1R3, Canada. TEL 416-747-4044, FAX 416-747-2475, TELEX 06-989344. Circ: 50,000.

389.6 CAN
CANADIAN STANDARDS ASSOCIATION E - CODE, ELECTRICAL SAFETY STANDARDS. Text in English. 1992. 4/yr. CAD 1,900. **Description:** Includes CSA's collection of Electrical Product Safety Standards (wiring, industrial, environmental, consumer and commercial products), outside wiring standards, electrical installation rules and related information.
Related titles: CD-ROM ed.
Published by: Canadian Standards Association, 178 Rexdale Blvd, Toronto, ON M9W 1R3, Canada. TEL 416-747-4044, FAX 416-747-2475.

389.6 CAN ISSN 1182-0187
CANADIAN STANDARDS ASSOCIATION. INFO UPDATE. Text in English. 1981. 8/yr. CAD 59.50, USD 71.
Formerly: C S A Information Update (0702-7583)
Published by: Canadian Standards Association, 178 Rexdale Blvd, Toronto, ON M9W 1R3, Canada. TEL 416-747-4116, FAX 416-747-2473. Circ: 3,500.

389.6 FRA ISSN 0750-7046
TA368
CATALOGUE AFNOR (NORMES FRANCAISES). Text in French. 1976 (vol.32). a. adv.
Formerly: Catalogue des Normes Francaises
Related titles: CD-ROM ed.; Online - full text ed.
Published by: Association Francaise de Normalisation (A F N O R), Tour Europe - Cedex 7, Paris La Defense, 92080, France. TEL 33-1-42915555, FAX 33-1-42915656, TELEX 611974F, http://www.afnor.org. Circ: 11,000.

352.83 MWI
CATALOGUE OF MALAWI STANDARDS. Text in English. a., latest 1996. MWK 20, USD 35 (effective 1997). **Document type:** *Government.*
Published by: Malawi Bureau of Standards, Library, PO Box 946, Blantyre, Malawi. TEL 265-670-488, FAX 265-670-756.

CEHUI BIAOZHUNHUA/STANDARDIZATION FOR SURVEYING AND MAPPING. *see* GEOGRAPHY

389.1 FRA ISSN 0370-2596
CODEN: PVSPA7
COMITE INTERNATIONAL DES POIDS ET MESURES. PROCES-VERBAUX DES SEANCES. Text in French, English. 1875. irreg. (89th meeting), latest 2000. charts; illus.; stat. index. **Document type:** *Proceedings.*
—INIST, Linda Hall.
Published by: Bureau International des Poids et Mesures, Pavillon de Breteuil, Sevres, Cedex 92312, France. TEL 33-1-45077070, FAX 33-1-45342021, info@bipm.org, http://www.bipm.org. Circ: 650.

389.6 FRA
COMITE INTERNATIONAL DES POIDS ET MESURES. SYSTEME INTERNATIONAL D'UNITES/INTERNATIONAL SYSTEM OF UNITS. Text in French. 1970. irreg., latest vol.7, 1998. EUR 23 (effective 2002). **Document type:** *Proceedings.*
Published by: Bureau International des Poids et Mesures, Pavillon de Breteuil, Sevres, Cedex 92312, France. TEL 33-1-45077070, FAX 33-1-45342021, info@bipm.org, http://www.bipm.org. Circ: 5,000.

389.1 FRA ISSN 1016-5983
CONFERENCE GENERALE DES POIDS ET MESURES. COMPTES RENDUS DES SEANCES/GENERAL CONFERENCE OF WEIGHTS AND MEASURES. Text in French. 1889. every 4 yrs. EUR 23 (effective 2002). **Document type:** *Proceedings.*
—INIST.
Published by: Bureau International des Poids et Mesures, Pavillon de Breteuil, Sevres, Cedex 92312, France. TEL 33-1-45077070, FAX 33-1-45342021, info@bipm.org, http://www.bipm.org.

658.568 MEX
CONGRESO MEXICANO DE CONTROL DE CALIDAD. ANNUAL PROCEEDINGS. Text in Spanish. 1973. a. (in 2 vols.). USD 30. adv. bk.rev.
Published by: Instituto Mexicano de Control de Calidad/Mexican Institute for Quality Control, THIERS 251, Col Anzures, Mexico City, DF 11590, Mexico. Ed. Patricia Gonzalez Prado. Circ: 3,000.

389.6 CAN ISSN 0380-1314
CONSENSUS (OTTAWA); Canada's news magazine of standardization. Text in English. 1974. bi-m. free (effective 2004). adv. **Document type:** *Magazine, Trade.* **Description:** News and feature articles on standards and standardization in Canada and around the world. Provides insight into the use of standards as tools for achieving quality, accuracy and efficiency. Studies technology and trade as they relate to manufacturing, information technology, communications and distribution.
Related titles: French ed.
Indexed: C03, CBCABus, P48, PQC.
Published by: Standards Council of Canada, 270 Albert St, Ste 200, Ottawa, ON K1P 6N7, Canada. TEL 613-238-3222, FAX 613-569-7808, http://www.scc.ca. Ed. Lesly Bauer. R&P Jeff Holt. Adv. contact Guy Ethier. Circ: 5,300 (controlled).

CONSTRUCTION METRICATION. *see* BUILDING AND CONSTRUCTION

389.1 DEU ISSN 0722-7337
D I N HANDBOOK. (Deutsches Institut fuer Normung) Text in English. 197?. irreg. price varies. **Document type:** *Catalog, Trade.*
Formerly (until 1982): D I N Pocketbook (0721-4952)
Published by: (Deutsches Institut fuer Normung e.V.), Beuth Verlag GmbH, Burggrafenstr 6, Berlin, 10787, Germany. TEL 49-30-26012260, FAX 49-30-26011260, postmaster@beuth.de, http://www.beuth.de.

389.1 DEU ISSN 0722-2912
D I N MITTEILUNGEN & ELEKTRONORM. (Deutsches Institut fuer Normung) Text in German. 1977. m. EUR 400 (effective 2009). bk.rev. charts; illus. index. **Document type:** *Journal, Trade.*
Formed by the merger of (1950-1977): D I N Mitteilungen (0011-4952); (1947-1977): Elektronorm (0013-5747)
Indexed: A22, CEABA, CISA, IBR, IBZ, TM.
—IE, Infotrieve. **CCC.**
Published by: (Deutsches Institut fuer Normung e.V.), Beuth Verlag GmbH, Burggrafenstr 6, Berlin, 10787, Germany. TEL 49-30-26012260, FAX 49-30-26011260, postmaster@beuth.de, http://www.beuth.de. Adv. contact Reinhardt Schultz. Circ: 4,000.

389.1 DEU ISSN 0342-801X
D I N - TASCHENBUECHER. (Deutsches Institut fuer Normung) Text in German. 1963. irreg. price varies. **Document type:** *Monographic series, Trade.*
Indexed: GeoRef, SpeleolAb.
Published by: (Deutsches Institut fuer Normung e.V.), Beuth Verlag GmbH, Burggrafenstr 6, Berlin, 10787, Germany. TEL 49-30-26012260, FAX 49-30-26011260, postmaster@beuth.de, http://www.beuth.de.

389.6 DEU
D I T R INFO; Informationen fuer Kunden der DITR-Datenbank. Text in German. 1989. 3/yr. free (effective 2011). **Document type:** *Bulletin, Trade.* **Description:** Discusses various aspects of international technical standards and research in the field.
Published by: (Deutsches Institut fuer Normung e.V., Deutsches Informationszentrum fuer Technische Regeln), Beuth Verlag GmbH, Burggrafenstr 6, Berlin, 10787, Germany. TEL 49-30-26012260, FAX 49-30-26011260, postmaster@beuth.de. Ed. Daniela Trescher.

389.6 DNK ISSN 1602-1746
DANSK STANDARD, LISTESTOF; dansk offentliggoerelse af nye standarder, forslag til standarder og nationale tekniske forskrifter. Text in Danish. 1958. bi-m. **Description:** Contains information on new standards and draft standards, relevant information concerning standardization and certification.
Former titles (until 2002): Dansk Standard (0908-0783); (until 1993): Standardnyt (0107-2870)
Published by: Dansk Standard/Danish Standards Association, Kollegievej 6, Charlottenlund, 2920, Denmark. TEL 45-39-966101, FAX 45-39-966102, dansk.standard@ds.dk, http://www.ds.dk.

389.6 CHE ISSN 1424-6074
RS189 CODEN: DBEIAI
➤ **DEVELOPMENTS IN BIOLOGICALS.** Text in English. 1973. irreg., latest vol.133, 2011. price varies. back issues avail. **Document type:** *Monographic series, Academic/Scholarly.* **Description:** Reports on the development and use of standardized biologicals.
Formerly (until 1999): Developments in Biological Standardization (0301-5149); Which was formed by the merger of (1964-1973): Progress in Immunobiological Standardization (0079-6344); (1966-1973): Symposia Series in Immunobiological Standardization (0082-0768)
Related titles: Online - full text ed.: ISSN 1662-2960.
Indexed: A22, ASCA, Agr, C33, CIN, ChemAb, ChemTitl, EMBASE, ExcerpMed, ISR, IndMed, MEDLINE, P30, R10, Reac, SCOPUS.
—BLDSC (3579.067010), CASDDS, GNLM, IE, Infotrieve, Ingenta, INIST. **CCC.**
Published by: (International Association for Biologicals), S. Karger AG, Allschwilerstr 10, Basel, 4055, Switzerland. TEL 41-61-3061111, FAX 41-61-3061234, karger@karger.ch, http://www.karger.ch.

389.1 CHN ISSN 1000-7105
DIANZI CELIANG YU YIQI XUEBAO/JOURNAL OF ELECTRONIC MEASUREMENT AND INSTRUMENT. Text in Chinese. 1987. bi-m. USD 96 (effective 2009). **Document type:** *Journal, Academic/Scholarly.*
Related titles: Online - full text ed.
Indexed: SCOPUS.
—BLDSC (3580.205210), East View.
Address: 172, Beiyuan Rd., No.9 Bldg., Rm. 201, Beijing, 100101, China. TEL 86-10-84853004, FAX 86-10-84851365.

352.83 MWI
DIRECTORY OF CERTIFIED PRODUCTS AND PROCESS IN MALAWI. Text in English. a., latest vol.2, 1995. MWK 15, USD 25. **Document type:** *Directory, Government.*
Published by: Malawi Bureau of Standards, Library, PO Box 946, Blantyre, Malawi. TEL 265-670-488, FAX 265-670-756.

THE DOZENAL JOURNAL. *see* MATHEMATICS

389.1 PRT ISSN 0874-4769
E A N PORTUGAL. (Electronic Article Number) Text in Portuguese. 1997. q. **Document type:** *Magazine, Trade.*
Published by: Associacao Portuguesa de Identificacao e Codificacao de Produtos, Rua Prof Fernando da Fonseca 16, Esc II, Lisbon, 1600-618, Portugal. TEL 351-21-7520740, FAX 351-21-7520741, info@gs1pt.org, http://www.gs1pt.org.

389.6 FRA ISSN 0223-4866
TA368 E55
ENJEUX. Text in French. 1981. m. adv. bk.rev. abstr.; bibl.; charts; illus.; stat.
Supersedes: Bulletin Mensuel de la Normalisation Francaise (0300-1164); Courrier de la Normalisation (0011-0485)
Indexed: A22, A28, APA, BrCerAb, C&ISA, CA/WCA, CIA, CISA, CerAb, ChemAb, CivEngAb, CorrAb, E&CAJ, E11, EEA, ELLIS, EMA, ESPM, EnvEAb, H15, Inspec, M&TEA, M09, MBF, METADEX, SolStAb, T04, WAA.
—BLDSC (3775.480000), IE, Infotrieve, Ingenta, INIST, Linda Hall.
Published by: Association Francaise de Normalisation (A F N O R), 11 av Francis-de-Pressense, La Plaine, Saint Denis, 93571 Cedex, France. TEL 33-1-42915555, FAX 33-1-42915656, http://www.afnor.org. Ed. Jean Claude Tourneur. Adv. contact Catherine Langros. Circ: 10,300.

EUROPEAN CONFERENCE ON SOFTWARE MAINTENANCE AND REENGINEERING. PROCEEDINGS. *see* COMPUTERS—Software

389.6 RUS
EVROPEISKOE KACHESTVO. Text in Russian. 1994. q. free with subscr. to Standarty i Kachestvo. **Document type:** *Journal, Trade.*
Related titles: ◆ Supplement to: Standarty i Kachestvo. ISSN 0038-9692.
Published by: Standarty i Kachestvo, PO Box 21, Moscow, 115114, Russian Federation. TEL 7-095-7716652, FAX 7-095-7716653, stq@mirq.ru, http://www.stq.ru.

F D C CONTROL NEWSLETTER (ONLINE). (Food, Drug, Cosmetics) *see* FOOD AND FOOD INDUSTRIES

FANGZHI BIAOZHUN YU ZHILIANG. *see* TEXTILE INDUSTRIES AND FABRICS

389.6 USA ISSN 0083-1816
JK468.A8 CODEN: FIPPAT
FEDERAL INFORMATION PROCESSING STANDARDS PUBLICATION. Abbreviated title: F I P S Publication. Text in English. 1968. irreg. back issues avail. **Document type:** *Government.* **Description:** Provides standards and guidelines that are developed by the National Institute of Standards and Technology (NIST) for Federal computer systems.
Formerly: U.S. National Bureau of Standards. Federal Information Processing Standards
Related titles: Online - full text ed.: free (effective 2010).
Published by: U.S. Department of Commerce, National Institute of Standards and Technology, 100 Bureau Dr, Gaithersburg, MD 20899. TEL 301-975-6478, inquiries@nist.gov, http://www.nist.gov.

FLOW MEASUREMENT AND INSTRUMENTATION. *see* INSTRUMENTS

389.6 CAN ISSN 0831-4888
T59.2.C2
FOCUS (TORONTO, 1970). Text in English. 1970. q. free. illus. **Document type:** *Newsletter.*
Formerly: Standards - Canada (0038-965X)
Related titles: French ed.
Indexed: C03, CBCABus, CBPI, PQC.
Published by: Canadian Standards Association, Public Affairs, 178 Rexdale Blvd, Toronto, ON M9W 1R3, Canada. TEL 416-747-4129, FAX 416-747-4149. Ed. Rosemary MacVicar-Elliott. Circ: 30,000.

658.4013 NOR ISSN 0809-8700
G S 1 FOKUS. (Global Standard) Text in Norwegian. 1986. q. adv. back issues avail. **Document type:** *Magazine, Trade.*
Formerly (until 2005): E A N-Nytt (0801-4620)
Related titles: Online - full text ed.: ISSN 0809-8719. 1999.
Published by: GS1 Norway, Haslevangen 15, PO Box 454, Oekern, Oslo, 0513, Norway. TEL 47-22-971320, FAX 47-22-971348, firmapost@gs1.no. Ed. Inger Trine Langebo.

658.2 FIN ISSN 1795-8083
G S 1 INFO. (Global Standards) Text in Finnish. q. **Document type:** *Magazine, Trade.*
Formerly (until 2005): E A N Info (0789-1776)
Published by: GS1 Finland Oy, Aleksanterinkatu 17, PL 1000, Helsinki, 00101, Finland. TEL 358-9-696969, FAX 358-9-650303, etunimi.sukunimi@gs1.fi, http://www.gs1.fi.

006.4 SWE ISSN 1653-2775
G S 1 SWEDEN FOKUS. (Global Standards) Text in Swedish. q. **Document type:** *Magazine, Trade.*
Formerly (until 2005): Svenska E A B Varlden
Published by: GS1 Sweden, Vasagatan 46, Stockholm, 11191, Sweden. TEL 46-8-50101000, FAX 46-8-50101001, support@gs1.se.

389.6 KOR
GISUL PYOJUN/MONTHLY TECHNOLOGY AND STANDARD. Text in Korean. m. **Document type:** *Journal, Academic/Scholarly.*
Related titles: Online - full text ed.
Published by: Korean Agency forTechnology and Standards, Technology & Standards Information Service Division, 96, Gyoyukwongil, Gwacheon-Si, Gyonggi-Do 427-723, Korea, S. TEL 82-2-5097234, FAX 82-2-5097415, info@kats.go.kr, http://www.kats.go.kr/.

658.568 ZAF ISSN 1728-8762
GLOBAL STANDARDS. Text in English. 2003. q.
Published by: GS1 South Africa, PO Box 41417, Craighall, South Africa. TEL 27-11-7895777, FAX 27-11-8864966, info@gs1za.org, http://www.gs1za.org.

I E C BULLETIN. *see* ENGINEERING—Electrical Engineering

389.1 USA ISSN 1094-6969
TK7881 CODEN: IIMMF9
I E E E INSTRUMENTATION AND MEASUREMENT MAGAZINE. (Institute of Electrical and Electronics Engineers) Text in English. 1978. bi-m. USD 205; USD 255 combined subscription (print & online eds.) (effective 2012). back issues avail.; reprints avail. **Document type:** *Magazine, Trade.* **Description:** Features applications-oriented and tutorial articles of general interest in areas of instrumentation system design and measurement, subsequent to peer review.
Formerly (until 1998): I E E E Instrumentation and Measurement Society. Newsletter (0161-1038)
Related titles: CD-ROM ed.; Microfiche ed.; Online - full text ed.: ISSN 1941-0123. USD 185 (effective 2012).
Indexed: A22, A28, APA, BrCerAb, C&ISA, CA/WCA, CIA, CPEI, CerAb, CivEngAb, CorrAb, CurCont, E&CAJ, E11, EEA, EMA, ESPM, EngInd, EnvEAb, H15, Inspec, M&TEA, M09, MBF, METADEX, P30, RefZh, SCI, SCOPUS, SolStAb, T04, TM, W07, WAA.
—BLDSC (4362.934800), IE, Infotrieve, Ingenta, INIST, Linda Hall. **CCC.**
Published by: I E E E, 445 Hoes Ln, Piscataway, NJ 08854. TEL 732-981-0060, 800-678-4333, FAX 732-562-6380, contactcenter@ieee.org, http://www.ieee.org. Ed. Shlomo Engelberg. Adv. contact Onkar Sandal.

I E E E INSTRUMENTATION AND MEASUREMENT TECHNOLOGY CONFERENCE. PROCEEDINGS. (Institute of Electrical and Electronics Engineers) *see* INSTRUMENTS

658.658 USA ISSN 1541-7026
I E E E INTERNATIONAL RELIABILITY PHYSICS SYMPOSIUM. PROCEEDINGS. (Institute of Electrical and Electronics Engineers) Text in English. 1962. a. adv. back issues avail. **Document type:** *Proceedings, Academic/Scholarly.*
Former titles (until 1997): I E E E International Reliability Physics. Proceedings (1082-7285); (until 1994): I E E E International Reliability Physics Symposium. Reliability Physics (0735-0791); (until 1970): I E E Reliability Physics Symposium. Proceedings (0080-0821)
Related titles: Online - full text ed.: ISSN 1938-1891.
Indexed: A22.
—IE, Ingenta. **CCC.**
Published by: I E E E, 445 Hoes Ln, Piscataway, NJ 08855. contactcenter@ieee.org, http://www.ieee.org.

389.6 USA
CODEN: ISBEEX
I E E E STANDARDSWIRE. (Institute of Electrical and Electronics Engineers) Text in English. 1986. m. free (effective 2010). **Document type:** *Newsletter, Trade.* **Description:** Covers topics include IEEE standards, information and news, general topics related to standards, and legal issues.
Former titles (until 2000): The I E E E Standards Bearer (0896-1425); (until 1987): Standards Bearer of the I E E E (0895-7614)

Media: Online - full text. **Related titles:** German ed.: I E E E Normen Nachrichten. ISSN 1050-6187; French ed.: I E E E Nouvelle des Normes. ISSN 1050-6195; Italian ed.: Notiziario degli Standard I E E E. ISSN 1050-6179; Regional ed(s).: I E E E Standards Bearer (British Edition). ISSN 1050-6209.
—CASDDS, Linda Hall. **CCC.**
Published by: (I E E E Standards Association), I E E E, 445 Hoes Ln, Piscataway, NJ 08855. contactcenter@ieee.org, http://www.ieee.org.

530.8 USA ISSN 0018-9456
TK7870 CODEN: IEIMAO
➤ **I E E E TRANSACTIONS ON INSTRUMENTATION AND MEASUREMENT.** (Institute of Electrical and Electronics Engineers) Text in English. 1952. m. USD 1,190; USD 1,490 combined subscription (print & online eds.) (effective 2012). adv. bk.rev. abstr.; illus. index. back issues avail.; reprints avail. **Document type:** *Journal, Academic/Scholarly.* **Description:** Covers measurements and instrumentation using electrical and electronic techniques.
Former titles (until 1963): I R E Transactions on Instrumentation (0096-2260); (until 1955): I R E Professional Group on Instrumentation. Transactions
Related titles: CD-ROM ed.; Microfiche ed.; Online - full text ed.: ISSN 1557-9662. USD 1,080 (effective 2012).
Indexed: A01, A02, A03, A05, A08, A22, A26, A28, APA, AS&TA, AS&TI, ASCA, AcoustA, ApMecR, B01, B06, B07, B09, B10, BrCerAb, C&ISA, C10, CA, CA/WCA, CIA, CIN, CMCI, CPEI, CerAb, ChemAb, ChemTitl, CivEngAb, CompC, CompD, CorrAb, CurCont, E&CAJ, E08, E11, EEA, EMA, ESPM, EngInd, EnvEAb, G01, G08, H15, I05, ISMEC, ISR, Inspec, M&GPA, M&TEA, M05, M09, MBF, METADEX, MathR, P30, RefZh, S01, S09, SCI, SCOPUS, SolStAb, T02, T04, TM, W07, WAA.
—BLDSC (4363.199100), AskIEEE, CASDDS, IE, Infotrieve, Ingenta, INIST, Linda Hall. **CCC.**
Published by: I E E E, 445 Hoes Ln, Piscataway, NJ 08854. TEL 732-981-0060, 800-678-4333, FAX 732-562-6380, contactcenter@ieee.org, http://www.ieee.org. Eds. Reza Zoughi TEL 573-341-4656, Dawn Melley. **Subscr. to:** Universal Subscription Agency, Pvt. Ltd.; Maruzen Co., Ltd. **Co-sponsor:** Instrumentation and Measurement Society.

389.1 USA
I O M NEWSLETTER. (Institute for Objective Measurement) Text in English. q.
Published by: Institute for Objective Measurement, 155 N Harbor Dr, 1002, Chicago, IL 60601. TEL 312-616-6705, FAX 312-616-6704, instobjmeas@worldnet.att.net.

352.83 ARG ISSN 1666-5481
I R A M. BOLETIN. (Instituto Argentino de Normalizacion y Certificacion) Key Title: Boletin I R A M. Text in Spanish. 1996. m. back issues avail. **Document type:** *Bulletin, Consumer.*
Related titles: Online - full text ed.: ISSN 1668-740X. 2001.
Published by: Instituto Argentino de Normalizacion y Certificacion, Peru, 552 - 556, Buenos Aires, 1068, Argentina. TEL 54-11-43460600, iram-iso@iram.org.ar. Ed. Jose F Lopez.

389.6 IRN
I S I R I YEARBOOK. Text in English. 1975. a. free.
Published by: Institute of Standards and Industrial Research of Iran, P O Box 15875-4618, Teheran, Iran. FAX 98-26130664. Ed. M Seifi. Circ: 1,000.

389.6 RUS ISSN 1813-8640
I S O 9000 + I S O 14000 + PO MATERIALAM I S O. Text in Russian. 2001. m. free with subscr. to Standarty i Kachestvo. **Document type:** *Journal, Trade.*
Related titles: ◆ Supplement to: Standarty i Kachestvo. ISSN 0038-9692.
Published by: (International Organization for Standardization CHE), Standarty i Kachestvo, PO Box 21, Moscow, 115114, Russian Federation. TEL 7-095-7716652, FAX 7-095-7716653, stq@mirq.ru, http://www.stq.ru.

389.6 CHE ISSN 1023-327X
Z7914.A22 CODEN: ISCADP
I S O CATALOGUE (ENGLISH EDITION). Text in English. a. (plus quarterly updates). **Document type:** *Catalog, Trade.* **Description:** Lists all published ISO standards.
Formerly (until 1994): I S O Catalogue (0303-3309)
Related titles: Online - full text ed.; French ed.: ISSN 1023-3261; ◆ Supplement(s): I S O Catalogue. Supplement. ISSN 1018-5968.
—CASDDS. **CCC.**
Published by: International Organization for Standardization, 1, ch de la Voie-Creuse, Case Postale 56, Geneva 20, 1211, Switzerland. TEL 41-22-7490111, FAX 41-22-7333430, central@iso.ch, http://www.iso.org. **Dist. in US by:** American National Standards Institute, 11 W 43rd St, 4th Fl, New York, NY 10036. TEL 212-642-4900, FAX 212-398-0023.

389.6 CHE ISSN 1018-5968
I S O CATALOGUE. SUPPLEMENT. Text in English. q. **Document type:** *Catalog, Trade.*
Related titles: ◆ Supplement to: I S O Catalogue (English Edition). ISSN 1023-327X.
Published by: International Organization for Standardization, 1, ch de la Voie-Creuse, Case Postale 56, Geneva 20, 1211, Switzerland. TEL 41-22-7490111, FAX 41-22-7333430, central@iso.ch, http://www.iso.org. **Dist. in U.S. by:** American National Standards Institute, 11 W 43rd St, 4th Fl, New York, NY 10036. TEL 212-642-4900, FAX 212-398-0023.

389.6 CHE ISSN 1729-8709
T59.A1
I S O FOCUS (ENGLISH EDITION). Text in English. 1970. m. illus. **Document type:** *Bulletin, Trade.* **Description:** Includes standardization news, calendar of ISO meetings, lists of new draft standards and newly published standards.
Formerly (until 2004): I S O Bulletin (0303-805X)
Indexed: A22, Cadscan, ConcrAb, LeadAb, SCOPUS, Zincscan.
—IE, Infotrieve. **CCC.**
Published by: International Organization for Standardization, 1, ch de la Voie-Creuse, Case Postale 56, Geneva 20, 1211, Switzerland. TEL 41-22-7490111, FAX 41-22-7333430, central@iso.ch, http://www.iso.org. Circ: 8,600. **Dist. in the U.S. by:** American National Standards Institute, 11 W 43rd St, 4th Fl, New York, NY 10036. TEL 212-642-4900, FAX 212-398-0023.

389.6 DEU
I S O MAINTENANCE AGENCY. ANNUAL REPORT. Text in German. a. **Document type:** *Corporate.*
Published by: International Organization for Standardization, Maintenance Agency, Am Karlsbad 4-5, Berlin, 10772, Germany. TEL 49-30-26012860, FAX 49-30-26011231.

389.6 ESP ISSN 1681-6552
I S O MANAGEMENT SYSTEMS (SPANISH EDITION). Text in Spanish. 2001. bi-m.
Related titles: ◆ English ed.: I S O Management Systems (Swiss Edition). ISSN 1680-8096; French ed.: I S O Management Systems (French Edition). ISSN 1680-810X.
Published by: Asociacion Espanola de Normalizacion y Certificacion, Genova 6, Madrid, 28004, Spain. TEL 34-91-4326000, FAX 34-91-3103172, info@aenor.es, http://www.aenor.es.

389.6 CHE ISSN 1680-8096
I S O MANAGEMENT SYSTEMS (SWISS EDITION). Text in English. 1992. 6/yr. CHF 128 (effective 2007). adv. **Document type:** *Magazine, Trade.* **Description:** News and information on ISO quality system standards and environmental management system standards.
Former titles: I S O 9000 and I S O 14000 News (1561-7742); (until 1999): I S O 9000 News (1018-6638)
Related titles: ◆ Spanish ed.: I S O Management Systems (Spanish Edition). ISSN 1681-6552; French ed.: I S O Management Systems (French Edition). ISSN 1680-810X.
—BLDSC (4583.263900). **CCC.**
Published by: International Organization for Standardization, 1, ch de la Voie-Creuse, Case Postale 56, Geneva 20, 1211, Switzerland. TEL 41-22-7490111, FAX 41-22-7333430, central@iso.ch. Ed., R&P Roger Frost. Adv. contact Martin de Halleux. **Dist. in US by:** American National Standards Institute, 11 W 43rd St, 4th Fl, New York, NY 10036. TEL 212-642-4900, FAX 212-398-0023.

389.6 CHE ISSN 0536-2067
I S O MEMENTO. Text in English, French. a. **Document type:** *Directory, Trade.* **Description:** Gives the scope of responsibility, organizational structure and secretariats for each technical committee.
Related titles: Online - full text ed.
Published by: International Organization for Standardization, 1, ch de la Voie-Creuse, Case Postale 56, Geneva 20, 1211, Switzerland. TEL 41-22-7490111, FAX 41-22-7333430, central@iso.ch, http://www.iso.org. **Dist. in the U.S. by:** American National Standards Institute, 11 W 43rd St, 4th Fl, New York, NY 10036. TEL 212-642-4900, FAX 212-398-0023.

389.6 CHE
I S O TECHNICAL PROGRAMME. Text in English. 1985. 2/yr. **Document type:** *Bulletin, Trade.*
Related titles: Online - full text ed.
Published by: International Organization for Standardization, 1, ch de la Voie-Creuse, Case Postale 56, Geneva 20, 1211, Switzerland. TEL 41-22-7490111, FAX 41-22-7333430, central@iso.ch, http://www.iso.org.

389.6 USA ISSN 0198-9138
JK1679
INDEX OF FEDERAL SPECIFICATIONS, STANDARDS AND COMMERCIAL ITEM DESCRIPTIONS. Text in English. 1952. a. USD 27. **Description:** Provides alphabetic, numeric and Federal Supply Classification listings of specifications, lists and descriptions in general use throughout the Federal Government.
Former titles: Index of Federal Specifications, Standards, and Handbooks (0364-1414); Index of Federal Specifications and Standards
Published by: U.S. Federal Supply Service, General Services Administration, 1941 Jefferson Davis Hwy, Washington, DC 20406. TEL 202-655-4000. **Subscr. to:** U.S. Government Printing Office, Superintendent of Documents, PO Box 371954, Pittsburgh, PA 15250. TEL 202-512-1800, FAX 202-512-2250, orders@gpo.gov, http://www.access.gpo.gov.

INSTITUTE OF MEASUREMENT AND CONTROL. TRANSACTIONS. *see* INSTRUMENTS

INSTRUMENT ENGINEER'S YEARBOOK; manufacturers' - users' guide to instrumentation & control. *see* INSTRUMENTS

389.1 MEX ISSN 0187-8549
INSTRUMENTACION Y DESARROLLO. Text in Multiple languages. 1981. s-a. **Document type:** *Magazine, Trade.*
Indexed: C01.
Published by: Sociedad Mexicana de Instrumentacion, Apartado Postal 70-186, Coyoacan, 04511, Mexico.

INTERNATIONAL CONFERENCE ON DUBLIN CORE AND METADATA APPLICATIONS. PROCEEDINGS (ONLINE). *see* COMPUTERS—Data Communications And Data Transmission Systems

INTERNATIONAL CONFERENCE ON SCIENTIFIC AND STATISTICAL DATABASE MANAGEMENT. PROCEEDINGS. *see* COMPUTERS—Software

INTERNATIONAL CONFERENCE ON SOFTWARE MAINTENANCE. PROCEEDINGS. *see* COMPUTERS—Software

THE INTERNATIONAL DIRECTORY OF MEASURING EQUIPMENT AND SCALES IMPORTERS. *see* BUSINESS AND ECONOMICS—Trade And Industrial Directories

389.1 FRA ISSN 2107-6839
INTERNATIONAL JOURNAL OF METROLOGY AND QUALITY ENGINEERING. Text in English. s-a. GBP 376, EUR 451, USD 620 combined subscription to institutions (print & online eds.) (effective 2012).
Related titles: Online - full text ed.: ISSN 2107-6847. GBP 205, EUR 246, USD 338 to institutions (effective 2012).
Published by: E D P Sciences, 17 Ave du Hoggar, Parc d'Activites de Courtaboeuf, BP 112, Cedex A, Les Ulis, F-91944, France. TEL 33-1-69187575, FAX 33-1-69860678, http://www.edpsciences.org.

INTERNATIONAL JOURNAL OF SERVICES AND STANDARDS. *see* BUSINESS AND ECONOMICS

389.6 CHE ISSN 1029-371X
INTERNATIONAL ORGANIZATION FOR STANDARDIZATION, INTERNATIONAL ELECTROTECHNICAL COMMISSION. GUIDE. Text in English. 1993. irreg.
—BLDSC (4583.262500).
Published by: (International Electrotechnical Commission), International Organization for Standardization, 1, ch de la Voie-Creuse, Case Postale 56, Geneva 20, 1211, Switzerland. TEL 41-22-7490111, FAX 41-22-7333430, http://www.iso.org.

389.1 USA
INTERNATIONAL SOCIETY OF WEIGHING AND MEASUREMENT. MEMBERSHIP DIRECTORY & PRODUCT GUIDE. Text in English. a. USD 50 to non-members. adv. **Document type:** *Directory.*
Published by: International Society of Weighing and Measurement, 10 Kimball St W, Winder, GA 30680. TEL 770-868-5300, FAX 770-868-5301. Ed. Mimi Harlan. Circ: 1,400 (controlled).

INTERNATIONAL SYMPOSIUM ON SOFTWARE METRICS. *see* COMPUTERS—Software

INTERNATIONAL SYMPOSIUM ON SYSTEM SYNTHESIS. PROCEEDINGS. *see* COMPUTERS—Software

389.1 USA
INTERNATIONAL WORKSHOP ON STATISTICAL METHODOLOGY. Text in English. 1996. a., latest 2001. adv. back issues avail.; reprints avail. **Document type:** *Proceedings, Trade.*
Formerly (until 2001): International Workshop on Statistical Metrology
Related titles: Online - full text ed.
Published by: I E E E, 445 Hoes Ln, Piscataway, NJ 08854. TEL 732-981-0060, 800-678-4333, FAX 732-562-6380, customer.service@ieee.org, http://www.ieee.org.

389.1 ITA
ISTITUTO NAZIONALE DI RICERCA METROLOGICA. RAPPORTO ANNUALE/ISTITUTO NAZIONALE DI RICERCA METROLOGICA. ANNUAL REPORT. Text in Italian. 1935. a. free. charts; illus.; stat. index, cum.index. back issues avail. **Document type:** *Journal, Academic/Scholarly.* **Description:** Synthesis of the scientific activities performed by IEN every year in meteorology, materials physics and technology, and innovation technologies.
Formery (until 2005): Istituto Elettrotecnico Nazionale Galileo Ferraris (0018-957X)
Published by: Istituto Nazionale di Ricerca Metrologica (I N RI M), Strada delle Cacce 91, Turin, TO 10135, Italy. TEL 39-011-39191, FAX 39-011-346384, inrim@inrim.it, http://www.inrim.it.

389.6 JPN
J I S YEARBOOK (YEAR). (Japanese Industrial Standards) Text in Japanese. a. JPY 7,350 (effective 2006).
Published by: Japanese Standards Association, 4-1-24 Akasaka Minato-ku, Tokyo, 107-8440, Japan. TEL 81-3-35838005, FAX 81-3-35862014, sitemaster@jsa.or.jp, http://www.jsa.or.jp.

JIANCHUAN BIAOZHUNHUA YU HUANJING TIAOJIAN/SHIP STANDARDIZATION ENGINEER. *see* TRANSPORTATION—Ships And Shipping

389.6 CHN ISSN 1000-0771
T50 CODEN: JIJIEQ
JILIANG JISHU/MEASUREMENT TECHNIQUE. Text in Chinese. 1957. m. USD 62.40 (effective 2009). 52 p./no.; **Document type:** *Trade.*
Related titles: Online - full text ed.
—East View, Linda Hall.
Published by: Zhongguo Jishu Jiandu Qingbao Yanjiusuo/China Information Institute of Technical Supervision, 2 West St Hepingli, Beijing, 100013, China. TEL 86-10-6421-8712. Ed. Shaofang He. Circ: 25,000. **Dist. overseas by:** China International Book Trading Corp, 35 Chegongzhuang Xilu, Haidian District, PO Box 399, Beijing 100044, China.

389.1 CHN ISSN 1000-1158
JILIANG XUEBAO/ACTA METROLOGICA SINICA. Text in Chinese. 1980. q. USD 40.20 (effective 2009). **Document type:** *Journal, Academic/Scholarly.*
Related titles: Online - full text ed.
Indexed: EngInd, SCOPUS.
—East View, Linda Hall.
Published by: Zhongguo Jiliang Ceshi Xuehui/China Metrological Measuring Institute, PO Box 1413, Beijing, 100013, China. http://www.chinajlonline.org/0jljc/jlxh/sjlxh.asp. **Dist. by:** China International Book Trading Corp, 35 Chegongzhuang Xilu, Haidian District, PO Box 399, Beijing 100044, China. TEL 86-10-68412045, FAX 86-10-68412023, cibtc@mail.cibtc.com.cn, http://www.cibtc.com.cn.

389.1 CHN ISSN 1671-4598
JISUANJI CELIANG YU KONGZHI/MEASUREMENT AND CONTROL. Text in Chinese. 1993. m. USD 96 (effective 2009). **Document type:** *Journal, Academic/Scholarly.*
Formerly: Jisuanji Zidong Celiang yu Kongzhi (1007-0257)
Related titles: Online - full content ed.; Online - full text ed.
Indexed: A28, APA, BrCerAb, C&ISA, CA/WCA, CIA, CerAb, CivEngAb, CorrAb, E&CAJ, E11, EEA, EMA, ESPM, EnvEAb, H15, Inspec, M&TEA, M09, MBF, METADEX, SolStAb, T04, WAA.
—BLDSC (4669.206235), East View, Linda Hall.
Address: Haidian-qu, Fucheng Lu 8-hao, PO Box 849-26, Beijing, 100830, China. JZCK@chinajournal.net.cn.

530.8 USA ISSN 1529-7713
QA465
➤ **JOURNAL OF APPLIED MEASUREMENT.** Text in English. 2000. q. USD 58 to individuals; USD 150 to institutions (effective 2011). bk.rev.; software rev. 1 cols./p.; back issues avail.; reprints avail. **Document type:** *Journal, Academic/Scholarly.* **Description:** Publishes scholarly work from all academic disciplines that relates to measurement theory and it's application to developing variables.
Incorporates (1997-2002): Journal of Outcome Measurement (1090-655X)
Indexed: AEI, CA, E03, EMBASE, ERI, ExcerpMed, IndMed, MEDLINE, P03, P30, PsycInfo, PsycholAb, R10, Reac, SCOPUS, T02.
—BLDSC (4942.830000), IE, Ingenta.
Published by: J A M Press, PO Box 1283, Maple Grove, MN 55311. info@jampress.org. Ed. Richard M Smith.

➤ **JOURNAL OF DYNAMIC SYSTEMS, MEASUREMENT AND CONTROL.** *see* ENGINEERING—Engineering Mechanics And Materials

530.8 CHN ISSN 1674-8042
▼➤ **JOURNAL OF MEASUREMENT SCIENCE AND INSTRUMENTATION/CESHI KEXUE YU YIQI.** Text in English. 2010 (Mar.). q. CNY 60, USD 60; CNY 15, USD 15 per issue (effective 2011). bk.rev. abstr.; bibl.; charts; illus.; stat. Index. back issues avail.; reprints avail. **Document type:** *Journal, Academic/Scholarly.*
Description: Covers basic principles, technologies and instrumentation of measurement and control relating to such subject areas as mechanics, electric and electronic engineering, magnetics, optics, chemistry, biology, and so on. Specific contents are as follows:; Precision measurement; new measurement principles; advanced technology of measurement; next generation instruments and systems; nanometer test techniques; remote test and calibration; automated test & diagnostics systems; calibration & self-calibration; virtual measurement systems; non-invasive measurement systems; distributed measurement systems; sensor systems and its application; signal processing techniques; measurement theory and development; optical and laser based techniques; imaging techniques; spectroscopy; novel instrument systems and technology.
Related titles: Online - full text ed.
Published by: Zhongbei Daxue Chubanbu/Press of North University of China, Xueyuan Lu, Taiyuan, 030051, China. TEL 86-351-3923306, FAX 86-351-3922085. Eds. Jilong Zhang, Victor Filippovich Kravchenko. Pub., R&P Jilong Zhang. **Dist. by:** China International Book Trading Corp, 35 Chegongzhuang Xilu, Haidian District, PO Box 399, Beijing 100044, China. TEL 86-10-68412045, FAX 86-10-68412023, cibtc@mail.cibtc.com.cn, http://www.cibtc.com.cn.

530.8 JPN ISSN 0453-4662
TK7870 CODEN: TPRYAV
KEISOKU TO SEIGYO/SOCIETY OF INSTRUMENT AND CONTROL ENGINEERS. JOURNAL. Text in Japanese. 1962. m. JPY 11,000 membership (effective 2005). adv. bk.rev. charts; illus.; tr.lit. **Document type:** *Journal, Academic/Scholarly.*
Formed by the merger of (1951-1961): Keisoku/Society of Instrument Technology. Journal (0450-0024); (1954-1961): Jido Seigyo/ Automatic Control (0447-7235)
Indexed: INIS AtomInd, Inspec, JCT, JTA.
—BLDSC (4889.250000), AskIEEE, INIST, Linda Hall. **CCC.**
Published by: Keisoku Jido Seigyo Gakkai/Society of Instrument and Control Engineers, 1-35-28-303 Hongo, Bunkyo-ku, Tokyo, 113-0033, Japan.

KEY ABSTRACTS - MEASUREMENTS IN PHYSICS. *see* METROLOGY AND STANDARDIZATION—Abstracting, Bibliographies, Statistics

389.6 540 CHN ISSN 1001-4012
LIHUA JIANYAN (WULI FENCE)/PHYSICAL TESTING AND CHEMICAL ANALYSIS PART A: PHYSICAL TESTING. Text in Chinese. 1963. m. USD 49.20 (effective 2009).
Related titles: Online - full text ed.
—East View.
Published by: Shanghai Cailiao Yanjiusuo/Shanghai Research Institute of Materials, 99 Handan Rd, Shanghai, 200437, China. TEL 86-21-65556775 ext 265, FAX 86-21-65557441.

352.83 MWI
M B S INFORMER. Text in English. bi-w. **Document type:** *Government.*
Published by: Malawi Bureau of Standards, Library, PO Box 946, Blantyre, Malawi. TEL 265-670-488, FAX 265-670-756.

352.83 MWI
M B S NEWS. Text in English. q. MWK 15, USD 25 (effective 1997). **Document type:** *Government.*
Published by: Malawi Bureau of Standards, Library, PO Box 946, Blantyre, Malawi. TEL 265-670-488, FAX 265-670-756, mbs@Unima.wn.apc.org.

530.8 DEU ISSN 0945-7143
CODEN: MSPNBZ
M P A - MESSEN, PRUEFEN, AUTOMATISIEREN. Index in English, French, German. 1965. 10/yr. EUR 92 domestic; EUR 102 foreign (effective 2009). adv. bk.rev. abstr.; bibl.; pat. index. **Document type:** *Magazine, Trade.* **Description:** Covers measuring and control techniques in the electronics field.
Former titles (until 1993): Messen und Prufen (0937-3446); (until 1990): Messen, Pruefen, Automatisieren (0177-7297); (until 1984): Messen und Pruefen (0026-0339); (until 1973): M P - Messen und Pruefen (0342-2682); Which incorporated (1956-1972): Automatik (0005-1136); Which incorporated (1958-1968): Automatisierung (0572-2292)
Indexed: A22, ChemAb, CybAb, Inspec.
—CASDDS, IE, INIST, Linda Hall. **CCC.**
Published by: b-Quadrat Verlags GmbH & Co. KG, Kolpingstr 46, Kaufering, 86916, Germany. TEL 49-8191-96410, FAX 49-8191-964141, info@b-quadrat.de. Ed. Wolfgang Klinker. Pub. Gisela Mengling. Adv. contact Werner Duda. B&W page EUR 3,400, color page EUR 4,450; trim 178 x 257. Circ: 14,552 (paid and controlled).

389.6 MWI
MALAWI BUREAU OF STANDARDS. ANNUAL REPORT AND STATEMENT OF ACCOUNTS. Text in English. a. free. back issues avail. **Document type:** *Government.*
Published by: Malawi Bureau of Standards, Library, PO Box 946, Blantyre, Malawi. TEL 265-670-488, FAX 265-670-756.

MALAWI BUREAU OF STANDARDS. LIBRARY. ADDITIONS TO THE LIBRARY. *see* METROLOGY AND STANDARDIZATION—Abstracting, Bibliographies, Statistics

658.568 USA
MANAGEMENT BRIEFING. Text in English. 1990. q. USD 75 in North America; USD 110 elsewhere (effective 2001). **Document type:** *Newsletter, Trade.* **Description:** Contains material designed to assist the management team with effective and efficient process updates, and to recommend action programs to quality assurance professionals.
Published by: Quality Assurance Institute, 2101 Park Center Dr., Ste. 200, Orlando, FL 32835-7614. TEL 407-363-1111, FAX 407-363-1112, stevi@qaiusa.com. Ed. William E Perry.

389.6 CHE ISSN 1422-6634
MANAGEMENT UND QUALITAET. Text in French, German. 1965. 10/yr. adv. bk.rev. **Document type:** *Magazine, Trade.*
Former titles (until 1997): Qualitaet (1422-660X); (until 1995): S A Q Bulletin (0256-2545); (until 1984): Schweizerische Arbeitsgemeinschaft fuer Qualitaetsfoerderung. Bulletin (1422-6642)
Indexed: TM.
Published by: Schweizerische Arbeitsgemeinschaft fuer Qualitaetsfoerderung, Industrie Neuhof 21, Kirchberg, 3422, Switzerland. TEL 41-34-4483366, FAX 41-34-4483365, info@saq.ch. adv.: B&W page CHF 2,700, color page CHF 3,700; trim 225 x 297. Circ: 3,000.

389.1 IND ISSN 0970-3950
QC89.I4
MAPAN. Variant title: Metrology Society of India. Journal. Text in English. 1986. q. EUR 150, USD 227 combined subscription to institutions (print & online eds.) (effective 2012). reprint service avail. from PSC. **Document type:** *Journal, Academic/Scholarly.* **Description:** Publishes research communication or technical articles of current interest in measurement science; original work, tutorial or survey papers in any metrology related area; reviews and analytical studies in metrology; case studies on reliability, uncertainty in measurements; and reports and results of intercomparison and proficiency testing.
Related titles: Online - full text ed.: ISSN 0974-9853 (from IngentaConnect).
Indexed: A22, E01, Inspec, SCI, SCOPUS, W07.
—BLDSC (5369.318310), IE, Linda Hall. **CCC.**
Published by: (Metrology Society of India), Springer (India) Private Ltd. (Subsidiary of: Springer Science+Business Media), 212, Deen Dayal Upadhyaya Marg, 3rd Fl, Gandharva Mahavidyalaya, New Delhi, 110 002, India. TEL 91-11-45755888, FAX 91-11-45755889. Ed. A K Bandyopadhyay.

389.1 ROM ISSN 1582-2834
MASURARI SI AUTOMATIZARI. Text in Romanian. 2001. bi-m. **Document type:** *Magazine, Trade.*
—BLDSC (5390.318000).
Published by: Artecno Bucuresti Srl, Sos Mihai Bravu 110, Bucharest, 021332, Romania. automatizari@artecno.ro, http://www.masurari.ro.

530.8 LTU ISSN 1392-1223
T50
MATAVIMAI/MEASUREMENTS. Text in Lithuanian, English. 1995. s-a. **Document type:** *Journal, Academic/Scholarly.*
Indexed: C10, CA, T02.
Published by: (Kauno Technologijos Universitetas, Metrologijos Institutas), Kauno Technologijos Universitetas/Kaunas University of Technology, K Donelaicio g 73, Kaunas, 44029, Lithuania. TEL 370-37-300000, http://www.ktu.lt. Ed. Rimvydas Zilinskas.

352.83 MUS
MAURITIUS STANDARDS BUREAU. ANNUAL REPORT. Text in English. a., latest 1978.
Published by: Government Printing Office, Elizabeth II Ave, Port Louis, Mauritius.

389.1 NLD ISSN 0263-2241
QC81
➤ **MEASUREMENT.** Text in Dutch. 1983. 10/yr. EUR 1,477 in Europe to institutions; JPY 196,400 in Japan to institutions; USD 1,661 elsewhere to institutions (effective 2012). bk.rev. charts; illus.; abstr. back issues avail.; reprints avail. **Document type:** *Academic/ Scholarly.* **Description:** Gives a worldwide report on the state and progress of the science and technology of measurement.
Incorporates (1990-1992): Industrial Metrology (0921-5956)
Related titles: Microform ed.: (from PQC); Online - full text ed.: ISSN 1873-412X (from IngentaConnect, ScienceDirect).
Indexed: A01, A03, A08, A20, A22, A26, A28, APA, BrCerAb, C&ISA, CA, CA/WCA, CIA, CPEI, CerAb, CivEngAb, CorrAb, CurCont, E&CAJ, E11, EEA, EMA, ESPM, EngInd, EnvAb, EnvEAb, H15, I05, Inspec, M&TEA, M09, MBF, METADEX, S01, SCI, SCOPUS, SolStAb, T02, T04, TM, W07, WAA.
—BLDSC (5413.544700), AskIEEE, IE, Infotrieve, Ingenta, INIST, Linda Hall. **CCC.**
Published by: (International Measurement Confederation), Elsevier BV (Subsidiary of: Elsevier Science & Technology), Radarweg 29, PO Box 211, Amsterdam, 1000 AE, Netherlands. TEL 31-20-4853911, FAX 31-20-4852457, JournalsCustomerServiceEMEA@elsevier.com, http://www.elsevier.nl. Ed. K T V Grattan.

➤ **MEASUREMENT + CONTROL.** *see* INSTRUMENTS

389.1 USA
MEASUREMENT METHODS FOR THE SOCIAL SCIENCES. Variant title: Measurement Methods for the Social Sciences Series. Text in English. 1991. irreg., latest 2002. price varies. adv. **Document type:** *Monographic series, Academic/Scholarly.* **Description:** Provides professionals and students in the social sciences with succinct information on methodology.
Published by: Sage Publications, Inc., Books (Subsidiary of: Sage Publications, Inc.), 2455 Teller Rd, Thousand Oaks, CA 91320. TEL 805-499-0721, 800-818-7243, FAX 805-499-0871, journals@sagepub.com. Ed. Richard M Jaeger. Adv. contact Margaret Travers.

389.1 USA ISSN 0543-1972
TJ1313 CODEN: MSTCAL
➤ **MEASUREMENT TECHNIQUES.** Text in English. 1958. m. EUR 4,718, USD 4,895 combined subscription to institutions (print & online eds.) (effective 2012). adv. back issues avail.; reprint service avail. from PSC. **Document type:** *Journal, Academic/Scholarly.* **Description:** Brings out articles for scientists interested in the study and application of fundamental measurements.
Related titles: Microfilm ed.: (from PQC); Online - full text ed.: ISSN 1573-8906 (from IngentaConnect); ◆ Russian ed.: Izmeritel'naya Tekhnika. ISSN 0368-1025; ◆ Translation of: Izmeritel'naya Tekhnika. ISSN 0368-1025.
Indexed: A01, A03, A08, A12, A20, A22, A26, ABIn, ASCA, ApMecR, BibLing, CA, CPEI, CurCont, E01, EnerRA, EngInd, I05, ISR, Inspec, P17, P26, P48, P51, P53, P54, PQC, RefZh, S01, SCI, SCOPUS, T02, TM, W07.
—BLDSC (0415.830000), AskIEEE, East View, IE, Infotrieve, Ingenta, INIST, Linda Hall. **CCC.**
Published by: Springer New York LLC (Subsidiary of: Springer Science+Business Media), 233 Spring St, New York, NY 10013. TEL 212-460-1500, FAX 212-460-1575, service-ny@springer.com, http://www.springer.com. Ed. V N Krutikov.

➤ **MECHATRONIK**; Design - Entwicklung - Integration. *see* ENGINEERING

389.6 RUS
T59 CODEN: STKABA
METODY MENEDZHMENTA KACHESTVA. Text in Russian; Contents page in English, French. 1969. m. USD 467 foreign (effective 2005). adv. bk.rev.; Website rev. abstr.; bibl.; charts; illus. 64 p./no. 2 cols./p.; **Document type:** *Journal, Trade.* **Description:** Covers quality control and analysis methods; outlays for quality, systems of quality and control of processes; benchmarking; reliability problems; safety of technical systems; statistical methods.
Former titles (until 1999): Nadezhnost' i Kontrol' Kachestva (0130-6898)
Related titles: CD-ROM ed.; Online - full text ed.
Indexed: CIS, ChemAb, RefZh.
—CASDDS.
Published by: (Gosstandart Rossii/Committee for Standardization of the Russian Federation), Standarty i Kachestvo, PO Box 21, Moscow, 115114, Russian Federation. TEL 7-095-7716652, FAX 7-095-7716653, stq@mirq.ru, http://www.stq.ru. Ed. M L Rakhmanov. Pub., R&P Natalia Thomson TEL 7-095-236-8461. adv.: color page USD 700. Circ: 5,700 (paid). **Dist. by:** East View Information Services, 10601 Wayzata Blvd, Minneapolis, MN 55305. TEL 952-252-1201, 800-477-1005, FAX 952-252-1202, info@eastview.com, http://www.eastview.com.

389.16 CAN ISSN 0383-9184
METRIC FACT SHEETS. Text in English. 1973. irreg. USD 5 (effective 2000). adv. **Document type:** *Monographic series, Academic/ Scholarly.* **Description:** Presents various aspects of metrication and international standardization.
Published by: Canadian Metric Association, P O Box 35, Fonthill, ON L0S 1E0, Canada. TEL 416-892-3800. Ed., R&P Albert J Mettler. Circ: 1,000.

389.16 USA
METRIC REPORTER. Text in English. 1973. bi-m. USD 100 to members. adv. bk.rev. **Document type:** *Newsletter.* **Description:** Covers metric use in industry and U.S. government.
Published by: American National Metric Council, 4340 East West Hwy, Ste 401, Bethesda, MD 20814. TEL 301-718-6508, FAX 301-656-0989. Ed. Ruth E Thaler Carter. R&P W Frank Morris. Adv. contact W. Frank Morris. Circ: 5,000 (controlled).

389.16 USA ISSN 1050-5628
METRIC TODAY. Text in English. 1966. bi-m. looseleaf. USD 30 domestic to individual members; USD 35 foreign to individual members; USD 150 to institutional members (effective 2005). bk.rev. illus.; tr.lit. cum.index. 8 p./no.; back issues avail. **Document type:** *Newspaper, Government.* **Description:** Provides information on the progress of the U.S. government's congressionally directed changeover to use only metric system measurements in conducting its business (except where inefficiencies can be proven).
Former titles (until Mar. 1990): U S M A Newsletter (0271-2555); U S Metric Association Newsletter; Metric Association Newsletter (0300-7308)
Published by: U S Metric Association, Inc., 10245 Andasol Ave, Northridge, CA 91325-1504. TEL 818-363-5606, FAX 818-363-5606. Ed., R&P Valerie Antoine TEL 818-363-5606. Circ: 1,500.

389.1 GBR ISSN 0026-1394
QC81 CODEN: MTRGAU
➤ **METROLOGIA**; at the cutting edge of measurement science. Text in English. 1965. bi-m. GBP 659 combined subscription to institutions (print & online eds.) (effective 2010). charts; illus. Index. back issues avail.; reprints avail. **Document type:** *Journal, Academic/Scholarly.* **Description:** Disseminates new and fundamental knowledge in all areas of scientific metrology.
Related titles: Microfiche ed.: USD 664 in the Americas; GBP 415 elsewhere (effective 2007) (from PQC); Online - full text ed.: ISSN 1681-7575. GBP 627 to institutions (effective 2010) (from IngentaConnect).
Indexed: A22, ASCA, C&ISA, CCMJ, CPEI, ChemAb, CurCont, E&CAJ, EngInd, GeoRef, IBR, IBZ, INIS AtomInd, ISMEC, ISR, Inspec, M&GPA, MSN, MathR, P02, P10, P48, P53, P54, PQC, PhysBer, RefZh, S10, SCI, SCOPUS, SolStAb, SpeleolAb, TM, W07.
—BLDSC (5748.800000), AskIEEE, CASDDS, IE, Infotrieve, Ingenta, INIST, Linda Hall. **CCC.**
Published by: (Bureau International des Poids et Mesures FRA), Institute of Physics Publishing Ltd., Dirac House, Temple Back, Bristol, BS1 6BE, United Kingdom. TEL 44-117-9297481, FAX 44-117-9301178, custserv@iop.org, http://publishing.iop.org/. Ed. Janet R Miles. Pub. Sharon d'Souza.

389.1 POL ISSN 0860-8229
METROLOGIA I SYSTEMY POMIAROWE/METROLOGY AND MEASURING SYSTEMS. Text in Polish; Summaries in English. 1988. q. EUR 53 foreign (effective 2005). **Document type:** *Journal, Academic/Scholarly.*
Indexed: B22, Inspec, SCI, SCOPUS, W07.
Published by: Polska Akademia Nauk, Komitet Metrologii i Aparatury Naukowej, ul Miodowa 10, Warsaw, 00251, Poland. TEL 48-22-312738, FAX 48-22-267163. Ed. Krzysztof Badzmirowski. **Dist. by:** Ars Polona, Obroncow 25, Warsaw 03933, Poland. TEL 48-22-5098609, FAX 48-22-5098610, arspolona@arspolona.com.pl, http://www.arspolona.com.pl.

389.6 ROM
METROLOGIE. Text in Romanian; Summaries in English, French. 1954. irreg. ROL 210.
Former titles (until 1991): Calitate Fiabilitate Metrologie (1017-1614); (until 1989): Metrologie Aplicata (0377-8134); (until 1975): Calitatea Productiei si Metrologie (0377-8126); (until 1971): Metrologie Aplicata (0539-5232)
Indexed: CIS, Inspec.
—INIST, Linda Hall.
Published by: Institutul National de Metrologie, Sos. Vitan Birzesti 11, Bucharest, 75669, Romania. TEL 343520, FAX 346585, TELEX 11871 INMB R. Ed. Aurel Millea. **Subscr. to:** ILEXIM, Str. 13 Decembrie 3, PO Box 136-137, Bucharest 70116, Romania.

389.1 USA ISSN 1940-2988
T50
METROLOGIST; human resources handbook. Text in English. 2008. q. free (effective 2011). **Document type:** *Handbook/Manual/Guide, Trade.*
Related titles: Online - full text ed.: ISSN 1940-2996.
Published by: National Conference of Standards Laboratories (N C S L), 2995 Wilderness Pl, Ste 107, Boulder, CO 80301. TEL 303-440-3339, FAX 303-440-3384, info@ncsli.org.

389.1 RUS ISSN 0132-4713
METROLOGIYA. Text in Russian. m. USD 365 in United States.
Indexed: RefZh.
—East View, INIST, Linda Hall.
Published by: Komitet po Standartizatsii Metrologii i Sertifikatsii, Ozernaya ul 46, Moscow, 119361, Russian Federation. TEL 7-095-4372855. **Dist. by:** East View Information Services, 10601 Wayzata Blvd, Minneapolis, MN 55305. TEL 952-252-1201, 800-477-1005, FAX 952-252-1202, info@eastview.com, http://www.eastview.com.

389.6 RUS
MIR IZMERENII. Text in Russian. 2001. m. **Document type:** *Journal, Trade.*
Published by: (Gosstandart Rossii/Committee for Standardization of the Russian Federation), Standarty i Kachestvo, PO Box 21, Moscow, 115114, Russian Federation. TEL 7-095-7716652, FAX 7-095-7716653, stq@mirq.ru, http://www.stq.ru. Ed. V I Krutikov.

389.6 USA ISSN 1536-2264
N C S L I NEWSLETTER. (National Conference of Standards Laboratories International) Text in English. 1972 (vol.12). q. **Document type:** *Newsletter, Trade.*
Formerly (until 2001): National Conference of Standards Laboratories. Newsletter (0194-5149)
—Linda Hall.
Published by: National Conference of Standards Laboratories (N C S L), 2995 Wilderness Pl, Ste 107, Boulder, CO 80301. TEL 303-440-3339, FAX 303-440-3384, info@ncsli.org, http://www.ncsli.org/.

389.6 USA
CODEN: NIHAE2
N I S T HANDBOOK. (National Institute of Standards and Technology) Text in English. 1918. irreg. back issues avail. **Document type:** *Monographic series, Government.*
Former titles (until 1989): N B S Handbook; (until 197?): National Bureau of Standards Handbook (0083-1824); (until 1934): Handbook, Bureau of Standards (1939-8743); (until 192?): Bureau of Standards. Handbook Series (1939-8727)
Related titles: Online - full text ed.: free (effective 2010).
Published by: U.S. Department of Commerce, National Institute of Standards and Technology, 100 Bureau Dr, Gaithersburg, MD 20899. TEL 301-975-6478, inquiries@nist.gov, http://www.nist.gov.

389.6 USA ISSN 1054-013X
QC100 CODEN: NTNOEF
N I S T TECHNICAL NOTES. (National Institute of Standards and Technology) Text in English. 1959. irreg. **Document type:** *Monographic series, Government.*
Formerly (until 1988): U.S. National Bureau of Standards. Technical Notes (0083-1913)
Indexed: A28, APA, BrCerAb, C&ISA, CA/WCA, CIA, CerAb, ChemAb, CivEngAb, CorrAb, E&CAJ, E11, EEA, EMA, GeoRef, H15, Inspec, M&TEA, M09, MBF, METADEX, SolStAb, T04, WAA.
—CASDDS, INIST, Linda Hall.
Published by: U.S. Department of Commerce, National Institute of Standards and Technology, 100 Bureau Dr, Gaithersburg, MD 20899. TEL 301-975-6478, inquiries@nist.gov, http://www.nist.gov.

389.1 JPN ISSN 0916-1546
NAGARE NO KEISOKU/ASSOCIATION FOR THE STUDY OF FLOW MEASUREMENTS OF JAPAN. JOURNAL. Text in Japanese. 1983. a.
Published by: Nagare no Keisoku Kondankai/Association for the Study of Flow Measurements of Japan, Nihon Kagaku Kogyo K.K., 2-1 Shimizu, Suita-shi, Osaka-fu 565-0805, Japan.

389.1 JPN
NAGARE NO KEISOKU OOSAKA SHINPOJUMU KOEN YOSHISHU/ PROCEEDINGS OF THE OSAKA SYMPOSIUM ON FLOW MEASURING TECHNIQUES. Text in English, Japanese. 1983. a. **Document type:** *Proceedings.*
Published by: Nagare no Keisoku Kondankai/Association for the Study of Flow Measurements of Japan, Nihon Kagaku Kogyo K.K., 2-1 Shimizu, Suita-shi, Osaka-fu 565-0805, Japan.

NATIONAL CONFERENCE OF STANDARDS LABORATORIES. DIRECTORY OF STANDARDS LABS. *see* BUSINESS AND ECONOMICS—Trade And Industrial Directories

389.6 USA ISSN 0077-3964
QC100
NATIONAL CONFERENCE ON WEIGHTS AND MEASURES. REPORT. Text in English. 1905. a. cum.index: 1905-60. back issues avail. **Document type:** *Report, Government.*
Related titles: Online - full text ed.: free (effective 2010); ◆ Series of: N I S T Special Publication. ISSN 1048-776X.
Published by: U.S. Department of Commerce, National Institute of Standards and Technology, 100 Bureau Dr, Gaithersburg, MD 20899. TEL 301-975-6478, inquiries@nist.gov, http://www.nist.gov. Eds. Carol Hockert, Linda Crown.

389.6 USA ISSN 1044-677X
CODEN: JRITEF
NATIONAL INSTITUTE OF STANDARDS AND TECHNOLOGY. JOURNAL OF RESEARCH. Text in English. 1977. bi-m. USD 47 domestic; USD 65.80 foreign (effective 2009). illus. index. reprints avail. **Document type:** *Journal, Trade.* **Description:** Reports on research conducted in the fields of the physical and engineering sciences including metrology and standardization.
Formerly (until 1988): U.S. National Bureau of Standards. Journal of Research (0160-1741); Which was formed by the merger of (1959-1977): U.S. National Bureau of Standards. Journal of Research. Section A. Physics and Chemistry (0022-4332); (1968-1977): U.S. National Bureau of Standards. Journal of Research. Section B. Mathematical Sciences (0098-8979); Which was formerly (until 1967): U.S. National Bureau of Standards. Journal of Research. Section B. Mathematics and Mathematical Physics (0022-4340); Which superseded in part (in 1959): U.S. National Bureau of Standards. Journal of Research (0091-0635); Which was formerly (1928-1934): Bureau of Standards. Journal of Research (0091-1801); Which was formed by the merger of (1910-1928): Bureau of Standards. Technologic Papers (0096-5200); (1919-1928): Bureau of Standards. Scientific Papers (0096-6231); Which was formerly (1905-1919): Bureau of Standards. Bulletin (0096-8579)
Related titles: Microform ed.: (from PQC); Online - full text ed.: 1982. free (effective 2011).
Indexed: A05, A22, A23, A24, A26, A28, A39, APA, AS&TA, AS&TI, ASCA, ApMecR, B04, B13, BRD, BrCerAb, C&ISA, C10, C13, C27, C29, CA, CA/WCA, CEABA, CIA, CIN, CIS, CPEI, CRIA, CRICC, CerAb, ChemAb, ChemTitl, CivEngAb, CompD, CorrAb, CurCont, D03, D04, E&CAJ, E08, E11, E13, EEA, EMA, ESPM, EngInd, EnvEAb, FS&TA, G08, GeoRef, H15, I05, ISR, IUSGP, Inspec, M&TEA, M09, MBF, METADEX, MathR, P02, P10, P26, P30, P48, P52, P53, P54, P56, PQC, R14, S04, S06, S09, S14, S15, S18, SCI, SCOPUS, SolStAb, SpeleolAb, T02, T04, W03, W05, W07, WAA, WSCA, Z02.
—BLDSC (5050.600000), AskIEEE, CASDDS, IE, Infotrieve, Ingenta, INIST, Linda Hall.
Published by: U.S. Department of Commerce, National Institute of Standards and Technology, 100 Bureau Dr, Gaithersburg, MD 20899. inquiries@nist.gov, http://www.nist.gov. Ed. Robert A Dragoset. Circ: 2,000 (paid and controlled). **Subscr. to:** U.S. Government Printing Office, Superintendent of Documents, PO Box 371954, Pittsburgh, PA 15250. TEL 202-512-1800, FAX 202-512-2250, orders@gpo.gov, http://www.access.gpo.gov.

389.1 JPN ISSN 0451-6109
CODEN: BNLMAP
NATIONAL RESEARCH LABORATORY OF METROLOGY. BULLETIN. Text in English, Japanese. 1955. s-a. per issue exchange basis. **Document type:** *Bulletin, Academic/Scholarly.*
Indexed: Inspec, JCT.
—IE, Ingenta.
Published by: National Research Laboratory of Metrology/Tsusho Sangyosho Kogyo Gijutsu-in Keiryo Kenkyujo, 1-1-4 Ume-Zono, Tsukuba-shi, Ibaraki-ken 305-0045, Japan. FAX 81-298-54-4135, TELEX 3652570-AIST-J. Ed., R&P Akira Ono TEL 81-3-298-54-4111. Circ: 700.

NONGCHANPIN ZHILIANG YU ANQUAN/QUALITY AND SAFETY OF AGRO-PRODUCTS. *see* AGRICULTURE

389.6 CUB ISSN 0138-8118
NORMALIZACION. Text in Spanish; Summaries in English, Spanish. 1971. q. CUP 72 domestic; USD 30 elsewhere (effective 2011). adv. charts; illus.; stat.; abstr. 48 p./no.; back issues avail. **Document type:** *Magazine, Trade.* **Description:** Deals with standardization, metrology and quality assurance subjects in Cuba.
Related titles: CD-ROM ed.: ISSN 2223-179X. 2010.
Published by: Oficina Nacional de Normalizacion, Instituto de Investigaciones en Normalizacion, Reina 412 e. Escobar y Gervasio, 3 Centro, Havana, C.P.10300, Cuba. TEL 537-863-3282, http://www.inin.cubaindustria.cu. Ed. Gisela Pena Montero. Pub. Nuria Davila Fernandez. Circ: 1,100.

NORMALIZACJA. *see* ENGINEERING

NUCLEAR STANDARDS NEWS. *see* ENERGY—Nuclear Energy

389.6 SWE
NYTT OM 9000 & 14000; kunskap om kvalitet, miljoe och verksamhetsutveckling. Variant title: Nytt om Niotusen och Fjortontusen. Text in Swedish. 1989. 9/yr. SEK 1,975 (effective 2004).
Formerly (until 2000): Nytt om Niotusen (1103-0615)
Published by: Swedish Standards Institute (SIS), Sankt Paulsgatan 6, Stockholm, 11880, Sweden. TEL 46-8-55552000, FAX 46-8-55552001, info@sis.se. Eds. Chatarina Dahlberg, Olle Axenborg. Pub. Olle Axenborg.

389.1 FRA ISSN 0473-2812
ORGANISATION INTERNATIONALE DE METROLOGIE LEGALE. BULLETIN. Variant title: O I M L. Bulletin. Text in Multiple languages. 1963. q.
Indexed: IBR, IBZ, RefZh.
—BLDSC (6252.626000), INIST.
Published by: Organisation Internationale de Metrologie Legale, 11 Rue Turgot, Paris, 75009, France. TEL 33-1-48781282, FAX 33-1-42821727, biml@oiml.org.

530.8 629.892 POL ISSN 1427-9126
P A R. POMIARY AUTOMATYKA ROBOTYKA. Text in Polish. 1997. m.
Indexed: B22.
Published by: Redakcja PAR, Al Jerozolimskie 202, Warsaw, 02486, Poland. TEL 48-22-8740351, FAX 48-22-8740202. Ed. Adela Kaczanowska.

530.8 DEU
CODEN: PTBMAZ
P T B - MITTEILUNGEN FORSCHEN UND PRUEFEN. Text in German. 1890. q. EUR 50; EUR 15 newsstand/cover (effective 2008). adv. bk.rev. **Document type:** *Magazine, Trade.*
Former titles: P T B Mitteilungen (0030-834X); (until 1964): Physikalisch-Technischen Bundesanstalt. Amtsblatt (0340-2932)
Indexed: A20, A22, ASCA, CIN, CISA, Cadscan, ChemAb, ChemTitl, INIS AtomInd, Inspec, LeadAb, PhysBer, SCOPUS, TM, Zincscan.
—BLDSC (6946.570000), CASDDS, IE, Ingenta, INIST, Linda Hall. **CCC.**
Published by: (Physikalisch-Technische Bundesanstalt), Wirtschaftsverlag N W - Verlag fuer Neue Wissenschaft GmbH, Buergermeister-Smidt-Str 74-76, Bremerhaven, 27568, Germany. TEL 49-471-945440, FAX 49-471-9454477, info@nw-verlag.de, http://www.nw-verlag.de. adv.: B&W page EUR 620, color page EUR 1,380. Circ: 1,800 (paid and controlled).

389.6 CUB ISSN 0138-7863
PAGINAS SUELTAS. Text in Spanish. m. **Document type:** *Journal, Academic/Scholarly.*
Media: Online - full text.
Published by: Oficina Nacional de Normalizacion, Instituto de Investigaciones en Normalizacion, Reina 412 e. Escobar y Gervasio, 3 Centro, Havana, C.P.10300, Cuba. TEL 537-863-3282. Ed. Gisela Pena Montero.

658.568 RUS ISSN 1813-9469
PARTNERY I KONKURENTY. LABORATORIUM. Text in Russian. 1999. m. **Document type:** *Journal, Trade.*
Formerly (until 2004): Partnery i Konkurenty
Published by: (Gosstandart Rossii/Committee for Standardization of the Russian Federation), Standarty i Kachestvo, PO Box 21, Moscow, 115114, Russian Federation. TEL 7-095-7716652, FAX 7-095-7716653, stq@mirq.ru, http://www.stq.ru.

PLUMBING STANDARDS MAGAZINE. *see* HEATING, PLUMBING AND REFRIGERATION

POMIARY - AUTOMATYKA - KONTROLA. *see* COMPUTERS—Automation

389.1 USA
POPULAR MEASUREMENT. Text in English. a. USD 15 (effective 2002). back issues avail.
Published by: Institute for Objective Measurement, 155 N Harbor Dr, 1002, Chicago, IL 60601. TEL 312-616-6705, FAX 312-616-6704, instobjmeas@worldnet.att.net.

530.8 629.8 RUS
CODEN: PRSUBT
PRIBORY I SISTEMY. UPRALENIE, KONTROL', DIAGNOSTIKA. Text in Russian; Contents page in English. 1956. m. USD 550 foreign (effective 2006). adv. bk.rev. bibl.; charts; illus. index. **Document type:** *Journal, Trade.* **Description:** Covers the state-of-the-art and trends in the development of instrument-making and the scientific-technical policy in this area.
Former titles (until 2000): Pribory i Sistemy Upravleniya (0032-8154); (until 1967): Priborostroenie (0555-1013)
Indexed: CEABA, CIN, ChemAb, ChemTitl, GeoRef, Inspec, SCOPUS, SpeleolAb.
—CASDDS, INIST, Linda Hall.
Published by: (Mezhdunarodnoe N T O Proborostroitelei i Metrologov), NauchTekhLitIzdat, Alymov per, dom 17, str 2, Moscow, 107258, Russian Federation. TEL 7-095-2690004, FAX 7-095-3239010. adv.: page MRK 4,500. Circ: 2,000. **Dist. by:** East View Information Services, 10601 Wayzata Blvd, Minneapolis, MN 55305. TEL 952-252-1201, 800-477-1005, FAX 952-252-1202, info@eastview.com, http://www.eastview.com.

389.1 POL ISSN 0137-8651
PROBLEMY JAKOSCI; dwumiesiecznik naukowo-techniczny. Text in Polish; Summaries in Multiple languages. 1968. m. PLZ 308.70 domestic; EUR 193 foreign (effective 2011). adv. bk.rev. 40 p./no.; **Document type:** *Journal, Trade.*
Related titles: Online - full text ed.
Indexed: AgrLib, B22, RASB.
Published by: (Federacja Stowarzyszen' Naukowo-Technicznych NOT), Wydawnictwo SIGMA - N O T Sp. z o.o., ul Ratuszowa 11, PO Box 1004, Warsaw, 00950, Poland. TEL 48-22-8180918, FAX 48-22-6192187, sekretariat@sigma-not.pl. Ed. Tomasz Strzelecki TEL 48-22-6549689. adv.: B&W page PLZ 1,400, color page PLZ 3,050. Circ: 2,400. **Dist. by:** Ars Polona, Obroncow 25, Warsaw 03933, Poland. TEL 48-22-5098609, FAX 48-22-5098610, arspolona@arspolona.com.pl, http://www.arspolona.com.pl.

389.6 ITA
QUALITA. Text in Italian. 1974 (vol.4). bi-m. free to members (effective 2008). adv. bk.rev. **Document type:** *Magazine, Trade.*
Published by: Associazione Italiana Cultura Qualita (A I C Q), Via Emilio Cornalia 19, Milan, 20124, Italy. Circ: 6,000.

658.568 DEU
QUALITAET UND ZUVERLAESSIGKEIT; Zeitschrift fuer industrielles Qualitaetsmanagement. Text in German. 1956. m. EUR 179; EUR 18.50 newsstand/cover (effective 2011). adv. bk.rev. bibl.; charts; illus. index. **Document type:** *Magazine, Trade.*
Former titles: Q Z Qualitaet und Zuverlaessigkeit (0720-1214); (until 1980): Qualitaet und Zuverlaessigkeit (0033-5126); (until 1969): Qualitaetskontrolle
Related titles: Online - full text ed.
Indexed: A22, A28, APA, BrCerAb, C&ISA, CA/WCA, CIA, CIS, CerAb, CivEngAb, CorrAb, E&CAJ, E11, EEA, EMA, ESPM, EnvEAb, H15, Inspec, M&TEA, M09, MBF, METADEX, ORMS, QC&AS, RASB, SolStAb, T04, TM, WAA.
—BLDSC (7168.124000), AskIEEE, IE, Ingenta, INIST, Linda Hall. **CCC.**
Published by: (Deutsche Gesellschaft fuer Qualitaet), Carl Hanser Verlag GmbH & Co. KG, Kolbergerstr 22, Munich, 81679, Germany. TEL 49-89-998300, FAX 49-89-984809, info@hanser.de, http://www.hanser.de. Ed. Fritz Taucher. Adv. contact Hermann Kleiner. Circ: 19,758 (paid and controlled).

658.568 USA ISSN 1064-3761
TS156.A1 CODEN: JQAIE3
QUALITY ASSURANCE INSTITUTE. JOURNAL. Text in English. 1987. q. USD 43 in North America to members; USD 68 elsewhere to members; USD 50 in North America to non-members; USD 75 elsewhere to non-members (effective 2001). **Document type:** *Journal, Academic/Scholarly.* **Description:** Dedicated to quality management in the information services function covering such topics as testing, standards, successful programs, measurement and management functions.
Formerly (until 1991): Quality Data Processing
Related titles: Online - full text ed.
Indexed: B01, B07, C10, CA, CompLI, T02.
Published by: Quality Assurance Institute, 2101 Park Center Dr., Ste. 200, Orlando, FL 32835-7614. TEL 407-363-1111, FAX 407-363-1112, stevi@quaiusa.com. Ed. William E Perry.

358.568 GBR ISSN 1352-8769
TS156.A1 CODEN: QUWOEW
QUALITY WORLD; for the quality professional. Text in English. 1935; N.S. 1975. m. GBP 69 domestic; GBP 88 in Europe; GBP 106 elsewhere (effective 2009). adv. bk.rev. charts; illus.; stat. reprints avail. **Document type:** *Journal, Trade.* **Description:** Provides information on all the contemporary developments in quality.
Incorporates (in 200?): Quality World. Technical Supplement (1352-8777); Which was formerly (until 1994): Quality Forum (0959-3268); (1975-1990): Quality Assurance (0306-2856); Which incorporated (1960-1975): Quality Engineer (0033-5215); Former titles (until 1994): Quality News (0959-3756); (until 1990): Q A News (0959-3497); (until 1987): Quality Assurance News (0309-0116)
Indexed: A22, ADPA, BMT, Emerald, ErgAb, Inspec, ORMS, QC&AS, RASB, SCOPUS, TM.
—BLDSC (7168.181500), AskIEEE, IE, Infotrieve, Ingenta, INIST, Linda Hall. **CCC.**
Published by: Chartered Quality Institute, 12 Grosvenor Crescent, London, SW1X 7EE, United Kingdom. TEL 44-20-72456722, FAX 44-20-72456788, info@thecqi.org. adv.: B&W page GBP 1,260, color page GBP 1,595; trim 210 x 274. Circ: 12,000 (paid).

389.1 FRA ISSN 1606-3740
RAPPORT DU DIRECTEUR SUR L'ACTIVITE ET LA GESTION DU BUREAU INTERNATIONAL DES POIDS ET MESURES/ DIRECTOR'S REPORT ON THE ACTIVITY AND MANAGEMENT OF THE INTERNATIONAL BUREAU OF WEIGHTS AND MEASURES. Text in French, English. 2000. a. EUR 23 (effective 2002).
—Linda Hall.

Published by: Bureau International des Poids et Mesures, Pavillon de Breteuil, Sevres, Cedex 92312, France. TEL 33-1-45077070, FAX 33-1-45342021, info@bipm.org, http://www.bipm.org. Ed. J H Williams. Circ: 500.

389.1 BRA ISSN 0102-9789
REVISTA A B N T. (Associacao Brasileira de Normas Tecnicas) Text in Portuguese. 1983. bi-m. **Document type:** *Magazine, Trade.*
Formerly (until 1987): A B N T Noticias (0102-5481)
Published by: Associacao Brasileira de Normas Tecnicas (A B N T), Rua Minas Gerais 190, Higienopolis, Sao Paulo, SP, Brazil. TEL 55-11-30173600, atendimento.sp@abnt.org.br, http://www.abnt.org.br.

389.1 FRA ISSN 1772-1792
QC100.F7
➤ **REVUE FRANCAISE DE METROLOGIE.** Text in French. 1970. q. **Document type:** *Journal, Academic/Scholarly.*
Former titles (until 2005): Bureau National de Metrologie. Bulletin (0982-2232); (until 1986): Bureau National de Metrologie. Bulletin d'Information (0373-3815)
Related titles: Online - full text ed.: ISSN 1776-3215.
Indexed: INIS AtomInd, RefZh.
—BLDSC (2431.030000), INIST, Linda Hall.
Published by: Laboratoire National de Metrologie et d'Essais (L N E), 1 Rue Gaston Boissier, Paris, 75015, France. TEL 33-5-45654400, FAX 33-5-45897285, http://www.lne.fr. Ed. Francoise Le Frious.

352.83 ZAF ISSN 1018-4295
TA368
S A B S CATALOGUE. Text in English. 1963. a. price varies. **Document type:** *Catalog.*
Supersedes: S A B S Katalogus (Afrikaans Edition) (0259-3610); S A B S Catalogue (English Edition) (0259-3602); Formerly: S A B S Yearbook (0081-2137)
Published by: South African Bureau of Standards, Private Bag X191, Pretoria, 0001, South Africa. TEL 27-12-428-7911, FAX 27-12-344-1568, TELEX 321308. Ed. J Guilford. R&P L E Labuschagne. Circ: 800 (controlled).

389.6 FIN ISSN 0356-1089
S F S - TIEDOTUS. Text in Finnish. 1969. s-m. EUR 63 domestic; EUR 69 in Scandinavia and Baltic countries; EUR 73 in Europe; EUR 75 elsewhere (effective 2005). adv. bk.rev. illus. 48 p./no.; back issues avail. **Document type:** *Bulletin, Trade.*
Published by: (Suomen Standardisoimisliitto ry/Finnish Standards Association), Stellatum Oy, Tyopajankatu 6 A, Helsinki, 00580, Finland. TEL 358-9-8689700, FAX 358-9-86897070, info@stellatum.fi, http://www.stellatum.fi. Ed. Pekka Jaervinen. adv.: B&W page EUR 700, color page EUR 1,000; 186 x 274. Circ: 4,000 (paid).

389.6 SWE
S I S STANDARD MAGAZINE. (Swedish Standards Institute) Text in Swedish. 2001. q. SEK 200; SEK 60 per issue (effective 2004). back issues avail. **Document type:** *Journal, Trade.*
Related titles: Online - full text ed.
Published by: Swedish Standards Institute (SIS), Sankt Paulsgatan 6, Stockholm, 11880, Sweden. TEL 46-8-55552000, FAX 46-8-55552001, info@sis.se. Eds. Chatarina Dahlberg, Olle Axenborg. Pub. Olle Axenborg.

389.1 USA
S M A WEIGHLOG. Text in English. q. **Document type:** *Newsletter.*
Published by: Scale Manufacturers Association, 6724 Lone Oak Blvd, Naples, FL 34109-6834. Ed., R&P Robert A Reinfried.

389.6 CHE ISSN 0252-0389
S N V BULLETIN. Text in English, French, German. 1952. m. CHF 60 (effective 2000). adv. index. back issues avail. **Document type:** *Bulletin.*
Indexed: BAS.
Published by: Schweizerische Normen-Vereinigung, Muehlebachstr 54, Zuerich, 8008, Switzerland. TEL 41-1-2545454, FAX 41-1-2545474. Ed., Adv. contact Heinz Kull. page CHF 1,000. Circ: 1,200 (controlled).

389.1 JPN ISSN 1347-1473
T50 CODEN: KKYHAH
SANSOUKEN KEIRYOU HYOUJIN HOUKOKU. Variant title: A I S T Bulletin of Metrology. Text in Japanese. 1951. q. **Document type:** *Bulletin, Academic/Scholarly.*
Former titles (until 2002): Keiryo Kenkyusho Hokoku/National Research Laboratory of Metrology. Reports (0368-6051); (until 1961): Chuo Keiryo Kenteijo Hokoku/Central Inspection Institute of Weights and Measures. Reports (0529-682X)
Indexed: A28, APA, BrCerAb, C&ISA, CA/WCA, CIA, CerAb, CivEngAb, CorrAb, E&CAJ, E11, EEA, EMA, ESPM, EnvEAb, H15, Inspec, M&TEA, M09, MBF, METADEX, RefZh, SolStAb, T04, TM, WAA.
—BLDSC (0785.456250), IE, Ingenta, Linda Hall.
Published by: National Institute of Advanced Industrial Science and Technology/Sangyou Gijutsu Sougou Kenkyuujo, 1-1-1 Umezono, Tsukuba Central 2, Tsukuba, Ibaraki 305-8563, Japan. TEL 81-29-8626217, FAX 81-29-8626212, prpub@m.aist.go.jp, http://www.aist.go.jp/.

SCIENCE AND ENGINEERING IN SOFTWARE DEVELOPMENT. *see* COMPUTERS—Software

650.11 CHN
SHIJIAN PINLU XUEBAO/JOURNAL OF TIME AND FREQUENCY. Text in Chinese. 1978. s-a. CNY 10 newsstand/cover (effective 2008).
Formerly: Shaanxi Tianwentai Taikan/Publications of the Shaanxi Astronomical Observatory (1001-1544)
Published by: Zhongguo Kexueyuan Guojia Shoushi Zhongxin/Chinese Academy of Sciences, National Time Service Center, 3, Shuyuan Dong Lu, Xi'an, 710600, China. TEL 86-29-83890417, FAX 86-29-83890196, http://www.ntsc.ac.cn/.

SHUYU BIAOZHUNHUA YU XINXI JISHU/TERMINOLOGY STANDARDIZATION AND INFORMATION TECHNOLOGY. *see* COMPUTERS—Information Science And Information Theory

658.568 MEX
SISTEMAS DE CALIDAD. Text in Spanish. 1973. bi-m. USD 15. adv. bk.rev. index.
Published by: Instituto Mexicano de Control de Calidad/Mexican Institute for Quality Control, THIERS 251, Col Anzures, Mexico City, DF 11590, Mexico. FAX 525-2547390, TELEX 1763190 IMECME. Ed. Patricia Gonzalez Prado. Circ: 5,000.

SOUTH AFRICA. STATISTICS SOUTH AFRICA. STANDARD CODE LIST FOR STATISTICAL REGIONS, MAGISTERIAL DISTRICTS, CITIES, TOWNS AND NON-URBAN AREAS. *see* METROLOGY AND STANDARDIZATION—Abstracting, Bibliographies, Statistics

SOUTH AFRICA. STATISTICS SOUTH AFRICA. STANDARD INDUSTRIAL CLASSIFICATION OF ALL ECONOMIC ACTIVITIES. *see* METROLOGY AND STANDARDIZATION—Abstracting, Bibliographies, Statistics

389.6 ZAF ISSN 0038-2698
SOUTH AFRICAN BUREAU OF STANDARDS. BULLETIN. Text in Afrikaans, English. 1947. bi-m. free. illus. **Document type:** *Bulletin.*
Indexed: ISAP.
Published by: South African Bureau of Standards, Private Bag X191, Pretoria, 0001, South Africa. FAX 27-12-344-1568, TELEX 3-21308 SA. Ed. C M Meyer. Circ: 5,500.

389.6 USA ISSN 0271-4027
QC89.U5
SPECIFICATIONS, TOLERANCES, AND OTHER TECHNICAL REQUIREMENTS FOR WEIGHING AND MEASURING DEVICES. Text in English. 19??. irreg. free (effective 2011). **Document type:** *Government.*
Former titles (until 1979): Specifications, Tolerances, and Other Technical Requirements for Commercial Weighing and Measuring Devices; Specifications, Tolerances, and Regulations for Commercial Weights and Measures and Weighing and Measuring Devices; Specifications and Tolerances for Weights and Measures and Weighing and Measuring Devices
Related titles: Online - full text ed.: ISSN 1937-4755.
—Linda Hall.
Published by: U.S. Government Printing Office, 732 N Capitol St, NW, Washington, DC 20401. TEL 202-512-1800, 866-512-1800, FAX 202-512-2104, ContactCenter@gpo.gov, http://www.gpo.gov.

389.6 NOR
STANDARD.NO. Text in English, Norwegian. 2001. bi-m. free.
Media: Online - full text.
Published by: Norges Standardiseringsforbund/Norwegian Standards Association, PO Box 353, Skoeyen, Oslo, 0213, Norway. TEL 47-22-04-92-00, FAX 47-22-04-92-77. Ed. Torill Staehr. R&P Jakob Berg.

389.6 USA ISSN 0360-6902
TE200
STANDARD SPECIFICATIONS FOR TRANSPORTATION MATERIALS AND METHODS OF SAMPLING AND TESTING. Text in English. 1935. a. USD 714 to non-members; USD 595 to members (effective 2011). **Document type:** *Handbook/Manual/Guide, Trade.*
Formerly (until 1974): Standard Specifications for Highway Materials and Methods of Sampling and Testing
Published by: American Association of State Highway and Transportation Officials, 444 N Capitol St, NW, Ste 249, Washington, DC 20001. TEL 202-624-5800, 800-231-3475, FAX 202-624-5806, http://www.transportation.org.

389.6 ZAF ISSN 1024-1612
STANDARD TIME & FREQUENCY SERVICE BULLETIN. Text in English. 1994. m. looseleaf. free. back issues avail. **Document type:** *Bulletin, Government.* **Description:** Provides information on IRO time standard in South Africa.
Related titles: E-mail ed.; Online - full text ed.
Published by: Council for Scientific and Industrial Research (C S I R), PO Box 395, Pretoria, 0001, South Africa. TEL 27-12-8412911, FAX 27-12-3491153, http://www.csir.co.za. Circ: 30.

389.1 389.6 MNG
STANDARDIZATION AND METROLOGY. Text in Mongol. 1982. m. MNT 800 (effective 2000). adv. bibl.; charts; illus.; stat. **Document type:** *Bulletin, Academic/Scholarly.* **Description:** Covers all activities related to standardization and metrology in the international and national level, research works, survey, report of the participating international training, meeting, conferences, etc.
Related titles: Diskette ed.
Published by: Mongolian National Centre for Standardization and Metrology, PO Box 48, Ulaanbaatar, 211051, Mongolia. TEL 976-1-458349, FAX 976-1-458032, mncsm@magicnet.mn. Ed., Adv. contact TS Sarangerel. Circ: 150.

389.6 USA ISSN 1094-4656
TA368 CODEN: STDNA
STANDARDIZATION NEWS. Text in English. 1940. bi-m. USD 20; free to members (effective 2011). adv. charts; illus. Index. back issues avail.; reprints avail. **Document type:** *Magazine, Trade.* **Description:** Covers new activities, research and testing of ASTM's standards-writing committees, and events influencing the standards-development process.
Former titles (until 1985): A S T M Standardization News (0090-1210); (until 1973): Materials Research and Standards - MIRS (0025-5394); (until 1961): A S T M Bulletin (0365-7205); (until 1939): American Society for Testing Materials. Bulletin
Related titles: Microform ed.: (from MIM, PMC, PQC).
Indexed: A05, A20, A22, A23, A24, A28, ABIPC, AESIS, APA, AS&TA, AS&TI, ApMecR, B04, B13, BMT, BrCerAb, C&ISA, C10, CA, CA/WCA, CEABA, CIA, CIS, CPEI, CRIA, CRICC, Cadscan, CerAb, ChemAb, CivEngAb, ConcrAb, CoppAb, CorrAb, CurCont, E&CAJ, E11, EEA, EMA, EMBASE, ESPM, EngInd, EnvEAb, ErgAb, ExcerpMed, GeoRef, GeotechAb, H15, HRIS, ICEA, ISMEC, Inspec, JOF, L09, LeadAb, M&TEA, M09, MBF, MEDLINE, METADEX, P06, P30, P34, SCOPUS, SoftAbEng, SolStAb, SpeleolAb, T01, T02, T04, TTI, WAA, WSCA, Zincscan.
—BLDSC (1747.091000), IE, Ingenta, INIST, Linda Hall. **CCC.**
Published by: A S T M International, 100 Barr Harbor Dr, PO Box C700, W Conshohocken, PA 19428. TEL 610-832-9500, FAX 610-832-9555, service@astm.org. Ed. Maryann Gorman TEL 610-832-9606. adv.: page USD 3,534; trim 8.125 x 10.875. Circ: 31,818.

389.1 DEU
STANDARDS. Text in German. 1982. q. EUR 16.50; EUR 5.50 newsstand/cover (effective 2010). adv. **Document type:** *Magazine, Trade.*
Former titles (until 2009): G S 1 Magazin; (until 2004): Coorganisation (0722-9305)
Published by: GS1 Germany GmbH, Maarweg 133, Cologne, 50825, Germany. TEL 49-221-947140, FAX 49-221-94714990, info@gs1-germany.de. Circ: 32,000 (paid and controlled).

389.6 USA ISSN 0038-9633
T59.A1
STANDARDS ACTION. Text in English. 1970. fortn. membership. back issues avail. **Document type:** *Bulletin.* **Description:** Alerts members on domestic, regional and national standards developments.
Former titles (until 1970): Magazine of Standards (0097-2959); (until 1954): Standardization (0097-2991); (until 1949): Industrial Standardization (0360-1919); (until 1943): Industrial Standardization and Commercial Standards Monthly (0097-2940)
Related titles: Microform ed.: (from PQC).
Indexed: A23, A24, B13, P06.
—Linda Hall.
Published by: American National Standards Institute, Inc., 25 W. 43rd St., Flr. 4, New York, NY 10036-7406. TEL 212-642-4900, FAX 212-302-1286. Circ: 8,000.

352.83 CAN ISSN 0706-943X
STANDARDS COUNCIL OF CANADA. ANNUAL REPORT. Text in English, French. 1971. a.
Related titles: Online - full text ed.: ISSN 1701-4247.
Published by: Standards Council of Canada, 270 Albert St, Ste 200, Ottawa, ON K1P 6N7, Canada. TEL 613-238-3222, FAX 613-569-7808.

389.6 USA ISSN 0038-9668
T59
STANDARDS ENGINEERING. Text in English. 1948. bi-m. USD 60 in US & Canada to non-members; USD 100 elsewhere to non-members; free to members (effective 2011). bk.rev. bibl.; charts; illus.; stat. back issues avail. **Document type:** *Journal, Academic/Scholarly.*
Indexed: A22.
—Ingenta, Linda Hall.
Published by: Standards Engineering Society, 1950 Lafayette Rd, PO Box 1, Portsmouth, NH 03801. TEL 603-926-0750, FAX 603-610-7101, admin@ses-standards.org. Ed. Diane C Thompson.

658.568 GBR ISSN 1755-9081
STANDARDS IN DEFENCE NEWS (ONLINE). Text in English. 1976. irreg., latest vol.214, 2009. free (effective 2009). back issues avail. **Document type:** *Monographic series, Trade.*
Formerly (until 2007): Standards in Defence News (Print) (0263-8266)
Media: Online - full text.
Indexed: ErgAb.
Published by: Great Britain. Ministry of Defence, Defence Equipment & Support, Kentigern House, Rm 1138, 65 Brown St, Glasgow, G2 8EX, United Kingdom. TEL 44-141-2242531, FAX 44-141-2242503, enquiries@dstan.mod.uk, http://www.dstan.mod.uk.

389.6 IND ISSN 0970-2628
T59.2.I4 CODEN: STNDE3
STANDARDS INDIA. Text in English. 1949. m. INR 700 (effective 2011). adv. bk.rev. charts; illus. index. 32 p./no. 2 cols./p.; **Document type:** *Journal, Academic/Scholarly.* **Description:** Contains write-ups on subjects of standardization, technical and consumer interest as well as in-depth articles papers of technical nature contributed by eminent professionals from industries, research institutes and government departments.
Formerly (until 1987): Indian Standards Institution .Bulletin (0019-0632)
Indexed: CRIA, CRICC, ChemAb, FS&TA, Inspec.
Published by: Bureau of Indian Standards, 9, Bahadur Shah Zafar Marg, New Delhi, 110002, India. lsc@bis.org.in. **Subscr. to:** I N S I O Scientific Books & Periodicals.

389.6 IND ISSN 0038-9684
STANDARDS: MONTHLY ADDITIONS. Text in English. 1960. m. INR 300 (effective 2011). **Document type:** *Journal, Academic/Scholarly.* **Description:** Covers information regarding the latest publications of Indian Standards, amendments to Indian Standards, standards withdrawn, draft standards circulated and abstracts of WTO-TBTnotifications issued every month.
Formerly (until 1987): I S I Standards: Monthly Additions (Indian Standards Institution)
Published by: Bureau of Indian Standards, 9, Bahadur Shah Zafar Marg, New Delhi, 110002, India. lsc@bis.org.in.

389.6 LKA
STANDARDS NEWS. Text in English. 1975. s-a. free. adv.
Indexed: SLSI.
Published by: Bureau of Ceylon Standards, 53 Dharmapala Mawatha, Colombo, 3, Sri Lanka. Ed. S G Weragoda. Circ: 1,000.

389.6 NZL ISSN 1177-5874
STANDARDS UPDATE (ONLINE). Text in English. 1979. m. free. **Description:** Publishes recent standards, drafts available for public comment, standards superseded and/or withdrawn and current projects.
Formerly (until 2006): Standards Update (Print) (1173-9495)
Media: Online - full text.
Published by: Standards New Zealand, Private Bag 2439, Wellington, 6140, New Zealand. TEL 64-4-4985990, FAX 64-4-4985994, snz@standards.co.nz.

389.1 389.6 BGR ISSN 1310-0831
T58.A2
STANDARTIZATSIA, METROLOGIA, SERTIFIKATSIA. Text in Bulgarian. 1992. m. USD 120 foreign (effective 2002). **Document type:** *Bulletin.*
Formerly (until 1993): Standartizatsia, Metrologia (0861-9379)
Published by: State Agency for Standardization and Metrology, 21, 6th September St., Sofia, 1000, Bulgaria. TEL 359-2-9808920, FAX 359-2-9861707. **Dist. by:** Sofia Books, ul Silivria 16, Sofia 1404, Bulgaria. TEL 359-2-9586257, info@sofiabooks-bg.com, http://www.sofiabooks-bg.com.

389.6 RUS ISSN 0038-9692
STANDARTY I KACHESTVO. Text in Russian. 1926. m. USD 399 foreign (effective 2005). **Document type:** *Journal, Trade.* **Description:** Covers standardization, certification, quality and competitiveness management; information about quality contests and prizes; experience of enterprises successfully operating at home and foreign markets.
Former titles (until 1966): Standartizatsiya (0371-3318); (until 1945): Vestnik Standartizatsii (0372-5650)
Related titles: ◆ Supplement(s): I S O 9000 + I S O 14000 + po Materialam I S O. ISSN 1813-8640; ◆ Evropeiskoe Kachestvo.
Indexed: RefZh, SCOPUS.
—East View, INIST. **CCC.**

Published by: (Gosstandart Rossii/Committee for Standardization of the Russian Federation), Standarty i Kachestvo, PO Box 21, Moscow, 115114, Russian Federation. TEL 7-095-7716652, FAX 7-095-7716653, stq@mirq.ru, http://www.stq.ru. **Dist. by:** East View Information Services, 10601 Wayzata Blvd, Minneapolis, MN 55305. TEL 952-252-1201, 800-477-1005, FAX 952-252-1202, info@eastview.com, http://www.eastview.com.

STILISTICA E METRICA ITALIANA. *see* STATISTICS

530.8 FIN ISSN 0780-7961
SUOMEN STANDARDISOIMISLIITTO. S F S - KASIKIRJA. Text in Finnish. 1971. irreg. price varies. **Document type:** *Monographic series.*
Formerly (until 1982): Suomen Standardisoimisliitto. Kasikirja (0357-0304)
Published by: Suomen Standardisoimisliitto ry/Finnish Standards Association, Maistraatinportti 2, PO Box 116, Helsinki, 00241, Finland. TEL 358-9-1499331, FAX 358-9-1464914, sfs@sfs.fi, http://www.sfs.fi/.

389.6 FIN ISSN 1239-1735
SUOMEN STANDARDISOIMISLIITTO. S F S - LUETTELO/FINNISH STANDARDS ASSOCIATION. S F S CATALOGUE; catalogue of Finnish national standards. Text and summaries in English, Finnish. 1996. a. (plus s-a. updates). price varies. **Document type:** *Catalog, Abstract/Index.*
Formed by the merger of (1935-1996): S F S - Luettelo. Osa 1 (1235-7014); (1935-1996): S F S - Luettelo. Osa 2 (1235-2748); Both of which superseded in part (in 1992): S F S - Luettelo (0357-0312)
Related titles: CD-ROM ed.: ISSN 1239-1743; ◆ Supplement(s): Suomen Standardisoimisliitto. S F S - Luettelo. Taydennysluettelo. ISSN 0780-766X.
Published by: Suomen Standardisoimisliitto ry/Finnish Standards Association, Maistraatinportti 2, PO Box 116, Helsinki, 00241, Finland. TEL 358-9-1499331, FAX 358-9-1464914, sfs@sfs.fi, http://www.sfs.fi/. Ed. Kari Kaartuma. Circ: 2,000.

389.6 FIN ISSN 0780-766X
SUOMEN STANDARDISOIMISLIITTO. S F S - LUETTELO. TAYDENNYSLUETTELO/FINNISH STANDARDS ASSOCIATION. S F S CATALOGUE. CUMULATIVE SUPPLEMENT. Text in English, Finnish. 1975. irreg.
Related titles: ◆ Supplement to: Suomen Standardisoimisliitto. S F S - Luettelo. ISSN 1239-1735.
Published by: Suomen Standardisoimisliitto ry/Finnish Standards Association, Maistraatinportti 2, PO Box 116, Helsinki, 00241, Finland. TEL 358-9-1499331, FAX 358-9-1464914, sfs@sfs.fi, http://www.sfs.fi/.

389.6 TZA ISSN 0856-0374
QC100.T34
TANZANIA. BUREAU OF STANDARDS. ANNOUNCER. Text in English. 1979. q. back issues avail. **Document type:** *Bulletin.*
Published by: Bureau of Standards, PO Box 9524, Dar Es Salaam, Tanzania. TEL 255-51-43298, FAX 255-51-43298, TELEX 41667 TBS TZ. Ed. N N Maingu. Circ: 830.

389.6 TZA ISSN 0856-2539
TANZANIA. BUREAU OF STANDARDS. DIRECTOR'S ANNUAL REPORT. Text in English. 1976. a. **Document type:** *Corporate.*
Published by: Bureau of Standards, PO Box 9524, Dar Es Salaam, Tanzania. TEL 255-51-43298, FAX 255-51-43298, TELEX 416677 TBS TZ. Ed. N N Maingu. Circ: (controlled).

658.568 USA
TECH TALK. Text in English. 1981. m. membership only. bk.rev. back issues avail. **Document type:** *Newsletter, Trade.* **Description:** Directed at providing insight on how to improve professional and managerial skills and practices. Includes extracts and comments on the materials presented by experts, academicians and practitioners on the approaches and practices needed to be effective in an organization.
Formerly: Q A Quest
Published by: Quality Assurance Institute, 2101 Park Center Dr., Ste. 200, Orlando, FL 32835-7614. TEL 407-363-1111, FAX 407-363-1112, stevi@qaiusa.com. Ed., R&P William E Perry. Circ: 1,000.

TELECOM STANDARDS NEWSLETTER. *see* COMMUNICATIONS

TEST & MEASUREMENT WORLD BUYER'S GUIDE. *see* ENGINEERING—Electrical Engineering

530.8 JPN ISSN 0040-8689
CODEN: TDKKA6
TOHOKU DAIGAKU KAGAKU KEISOKU KENKYUJO HOKOKU/TOHOKU UNIVERSITY. RESEARCH INSTITUTE FOR SCIENTIFIC MEASUREMENTS. BULLETIN. Text in Japanese; Summaries in English. 1951. 3/yr. per issue exchange basis only. charts; illus.
Related titles: Microfilm ed.
Indexed: ChemAb, INIS AtomInd, Inspec, JPI, JTA.
—AskIEEE.
Published by: Tohoku Daigaku, Kagaku Keisoku Kenkyujo/Tohoku University, Research Institute for Scientific Measurements, 1-1 Katahira 2-chome, Aoba-ku, Sendai-shi, Miyagi-ken 980-0812, Japan. Ed. Mareo Ishigame.

389.1 JPN
TOHOKU DAIGAKU KAGAKU KEISOKU KENKYUJO KENKYU HOKOKU/TOHOKU UNIVERSITY. RESEARCH INSTITUTE FOR SCIENTIFIC MEASUREMENTS. ANNUAL REPORT. Text in English, Japanese. a.
Published by: Tohoku Daigaku, Kagaku Keisoku Kenkyujo/Tohoku University, Research Institute for Scientific Measurements, 1-1 Katahira 2-chome, Aoba-ku, Sendai-shi, Miyagi-ken 980-0812, Japan.

389.6 629.13 POL ISSN 0860-7222
TA357.5.T87
➤ **TURBULENCE.** Text and summaries in English. 1989. irreg. price varies. **Document type:** *Academic/Scholarly.* **Description:** Presentation of the activity of Polish Pilot Centre of European Research Community on Flow Turbulence and Combustion (ERCOFTAC) on theoretical, computational, and experimental approach to the phenomena of turbulence.
Indexed: ApMecR, B22.
Published by: (Politechnika Czestochowska), Wydawnictwo Politechniki Czestochowskiej, ul Dabrowskiego 69, Czestochowa, Poland. TEL 48-34-3250393, wydawnictwo@adm.pcz.czest.pl. Circ: 400 (controlled). **Dist. by:** Ars Polona, Obroncow 25, Warsaw 03933, Poland. TEL 48-22-5098609, FAX 48-22-5098610, arspolona@arspolona.com.pl, http://www.arspolona.com.pl.

➤ **U.S. DEPARTMENT OF DEFENSE. INDEX OF SPECIFICATIONS AND STANDARDS.** *see* METROLOGY AND STANDARDIZATION—Abstracting, Bibliographies, Statistics

355.6 USA
U.S. DEPARTMENT OF DEFENSE. INDEX OF SPECIFICATIONS AND STANDARDS: PART 1, ALPHABETICAL LISTING. Text in English. irreg., latest 2006. **Document type:** *Government.* **Description:** Lists all current standardization documents in order by the document, as well as all standardization documents cancelled since the last basic DODISS.
Related titles: Online - full text ed.
Published by: U.S. Department of Defense, 1400 Defense Pentagon, Washington, DC 20301. TEL 703-571-3343, http://www.defense.gov/.

U.S. DEPARTMENT OF DEFENSE. INDEX OF SPECIFICATIONS AND STANDARDS: PART 2, NUMERIC LISTING. *see* METROLOGY AND STANDARDIZATION—Abstracting, Bibliographies, Statistics

U.S. DEPARTMENT OF DEFENSE. INDEX OF SPECIFICATIONS AND STANDARDS: PART 3, FEDERAL SUPPLY CLASS LISTING. *see* METROLOGY AND STANDARDIZATION—Abstracting, Bibliographies, Statistics

U.S. DEPARTMENT OF DEFENSE. INDEX OF SPECIFICATIONS AND STANDARDS: PART 4, NUMERICAL LISTING OF CANCELLED DOCUMENTS. *see* METROLOGY AND STANDARDIZATION—Abstracting, Bibliographies, Statistics

352.83 ESP ISSN 0213-9510
UNE. Text in Spanish. 1978. m. (11/yr.). EUR 69.34 (effective 2008). adv. bk.rev. illus. back issues avail. **Document type:** *Bulletin, Trade.* **Description:** Informs on all topics related to quality, standardization and certification.
Formerly (until 1980): Boletin de la Normalizacion Espanola (0210-2315); Which was formed by the merger of (1975-1977): Iranor (0211-3813); (1973-1977): Boletin Informativo Iranor (0211-3694); Which was formerly: I y E - Innovacion y Empresa (0211-3783)
Published by: Asociacion Espanola de Normalizacion y Certificacion, Genova 6, Madrid, 28004, Spain. TEL 34-91-4326000, FAX 34-91-3103172, info@aenor.es, http://www.aenor.es. Ed. Victor Reig. Pub. Ana Maria Lopez. Circ: 8,000.

530.8 DEU ISSN 1615-7184
UNIVERSITAET HANNOVER. INSTITUT FUER MESS- UND REGELUNGSTECHNIK. BERICHTE. Text in German. 2000. irreg., latest vol.17, 2009. price varies. **Document type:** *Monographic series, Academic/Scholarly.*
Published by: (Universitaet Hannover, Institut fuer Mess- und Regelungstechnik), Shaker Verlag GmbH, Kaiserstr 100, Herzogenrath, 52134, Germany. TEL 49-2407-95960, FAX 49-2407-95969, info@shaker.de.

389.1 GBR ISSN 1016-2178
V A M A S. BULLETIN. (Versailles Project on Advanced Materials and Standards) Text in English. 1989. irreg., latest vol.26, 2005. back issues avail. **Document type:** *Bulletin.*
Related titles: Online - full text ed.
Indexed: A28, APA, BrCerAb, C&ISA, CA/WCA, CIA, CerAb, CivEngAb, CorrAb, E&CAJ, E11, EEA, EMA, H15, M&TEA, M09, MBF, METADEX, SolStAb, T04, WAA.
—Linda Hall.
Published by: The Versailles Project on Advanced Materials and Standards, VAMAS Secretariat, National Physical Laboratory, Industry and Innovation Division, G10-A7, Hampton Road, Teddington, Middlesex TW11 0LW, United Kingdom. sam.gnaniah@npl.co.uk.

389.6 DEU ISSN 1435-2176
WAEGEN, DOSIEREN UND MISCHEN. Text in German. 1969. bi-m. EUR 10 newsstand/cover (effective 2003). adv. bk.rev. charts; illus. **Document type:** *Magazine, Trade.* **Description:** Devoted to the technology of weights, measures, and testing. Includes new developments and research results, new materials for construction, and current information, both national and international.
Formerly (until 1998): Waegen und Dosieren (0342-5916)
Indexed: TM.
—IE, Infotrieve. **CCC.**
Published by: Verlag Kirchheim und Co. GmbH, Kaiserstr 41, Mainz, 55116, Germany. TEL 49-6131-96070-0, FAX 49-6131-9607070, info@kirchheim-verlag.de, http://www.kirchheim-verlag.de. adv.: B&W page EUR 2,235, color page EUR 3,515; trim 178 x 250. Circ: 7,800 (paid and controlled).

389.6 USA
WEEKLY STANDARDS AND SPECIFICATIONS BULLETIN. Text in English. 1964. w. **Document type:** *Bulletin, Trade.* **Description:** Reports new, updated, revised and cancelled standards and specifications.
Formerly: Standards and Specifications Information Bulletin (0038-9641)
Published by: Global Engineering Documents, 15 Inverness Way E, Englewood, CO 80112-5710. TEL 303-397-7956, 800-854-7179, FAX 303-397-2740, global@ihs.com, http://www.global@ihs.com.

389.6 USA ISSN 0095-537X
TS410
WEIGHING & MEASUREMENT. Text in English. 1914. bi-m. USD 30; free to qualified personnel (effective 2005). adv. bk.rev. charts; illus.; tr.lit. **Document type:** *Magazine, Trade.*
Formerly: Scale Journal
—Linda Hall.
Published by: W A M Publishing, Inc., 1206 Newman's Trail, Hendersonville, TN 37073. TEL 615-824-6920, FAX 615-824-7092. Ed., Pub. David M Mattieu. Adv. contact David Mathieu Jr. Circ: 12,000 (controlled).

389.6 ZMB
Z A B S REVIEW. (Zambia Bureau of Standards) Text in English. 1988. q. USD 15. adv. bk.rev. **Document type:** *Government.* **Description:** Reports on standards activities carried out by the bureau staff.
Formerly: Zambian Standards Reporter
Published by: Bureau of Standards, PO Box RW 50259, Lusaka, Zambia. TEL 260-1-227171. Ed. Davis Mukuka. Circ: 500 (controlled).

389.1 RUS
ZAKONODATEL'NAYA I PRIKLADNAYA METROLOGIYA. Text in Russian. q.
Address: Ozernaya ul 46, Moscow, 119361, Russian Federation. TEL 7-095-4375577, FAX 7-095-4375666. **Dist. by:** East View Information Services, 10601 Wayzata Blvd, Minneapolis, MN 55305. TEL 952-252-1201, 800-477-1005, FAX 952-252-1202, info@eastview.com, http://www.eastview.com.

530.8 CHN ISSN 1674-5124
ZHONGGUO CESHI/CHINA MEASUREMENT TECHNOLOGY. Text in Chinese. 1975. bi-m. CNY 90; CNY 15 newsstand/cover (effective 2010). **Document type:** *Journal, Academic/Scholarly.*
Former titles: Zhongguo Ceshi Jishu (1672-4984); (until 2002): Shiyong Ceshi Jishu/Practical Measurement Technology (1006-317X)
Related titles: Online - full text ed.
Indexed: A28, APA, BrCerAb, C&ISA, CA/WCA, CIA, CerAb, CivEngAb, CorrAb, E&CAJ, E11, EEA, EMA, ESPM, EnvEAb, H15, M&TEA, M09, MBF, METADEX, RefZh, SolStAb, T04, WAA.
Published by: Zhongguo Ceshi Jishu Yanjiuyuan/National Institute of Measurement and Testing Technology, 10, Yushuang Lu, Chengdu, 610021, China. TEL 86-28-84404872, FAX 86-28-84403677.

METROLOGY AND STANDARDIZATION—Abstracting, Bibliographies, Statistics

016.3896 GBR ISSN 0950-4818
QC39
KEY ABSTRACTS - MEASUREMENTS IN PHYSICS. Text in English. 1976. m. USD 625 in the Americas to institutions (print or online ed.); GBP 365 elsewhere to institutions (print or online ed.); USD 11,275 in the Americas to institutions all 22 Key Abstracts; (print or online ed.); GBP 6,424 elsewhere to institutions all 22 Key Abstracts; (print or online ed.) (effective 2010). index. **Document type:** *Abstract/Index.* **Description:** Covers radiation detectors and measurement, mass spectrometry, plasma diagnostics, measurements and instrumentation in mechanics, heat, optics, fluid dynamics, and the environment.
Formerly (until 1987): Key Abstracts - Physical Measurements and Instrumentation (0307-7969)
Related titles: Online - full text ed.
—**CCC.**
Published by: The Institution of Engineering and Technology, Michael Faraday House, Stevenage, Herts SG1 2AY, United Kingdom. TEL 44-1438-313311, FAX 44-1438-765526, journals@theiet.org.

016.3896 MWI
MALAWI BUREAU OF STANDARDS. LIBRARY. ADDITIONS TO THE LIBRARY. Text in English. 1978. m.
Published by: Malawi Bureau of Standards, Library, PO Box 946, Blantyre, Malawi. TEL 265-670-488, FAX 265-670-756.

016.3891 RUS ISSN 0034-2505
REFERATIVNYI ZHURNAL. METROLOGIYA I IZMERITEL'NAYA TEKHNIKA; otdel'nyi vypusk. Text in Russian. 1963. m. USD 1,063.20 foreign (effective 2011). **Document type:** *Journal, Abstract/Index.*
Related titles: CD-ROM ed.; Online - full text ed.
Indexed: ChemAb.
—East View, Linda Hall.
Published by: VINITI RAN, ul Usievicha 20, Moscow, 125190, Russian Federation. TEL 7-499-1526113, FAX 7-499-9430060, dir@viniti.ru, http://www.viniti.ru. Eds. Stanislav Emelyanov, Yurii Arskii. **Dist. by:** Informnauka Ltd., Ul Usievicha 20, Moscow 125190, Russian Federation. alfimov@viniti.ru.

389.6021 ZAF
SOUTH AFRICA. STATISTICS SOUTH AFRICA. STANDARD CODE LIST FOR STATISTICAL REGIONS, MAGISTERIAL DISTRICTS, CITIES, TOWNS AND NON-URBAN AREAS. Text in English. irreg., latest vol.11, 1993. **Document type:** *Government.*
Formerly (until Aug.1998): South Africa. Central Statistical Service. Standard Code List for Statistical Regions, Magisterial Districts, Cities, Towns and Non-urban Areas
Published by: Statistics South Africa/Statistieke Suid-Afrika, Private Bag X44, Pretoria, 0001, South Africa. TEL 27-12-3108911, FAX 27-12-3108500, info@statssa.gov.za, http://www.statssa.gov.za.

389.6021 ZAF
SOUTH AFRICA. STATISTICS SOUTH AFRICA. STANDARD INDUSTRIAL CLASSIFICATION OF ALL ECONOMIC ACTIVITIES. Text in English. irreg., latest vol.5, 1993. **Document type:** *Government.* **Description:** Statistical classifications of type of activity applied to South African industries, businesses and services, with all divisions, groups, and sub-groups.
Formerly (until Aug.1998): South Africa. Central Statistical Service. Standard Industrial Classification of All Economic Activities
Published by: Statistics South Africa/Statistieke Suid-Afrika, Private Bag X44, Pretoria, 0001, South Africa. TEL 27-12-3108911, FAX 27-12-3108500, info@statssa.gov.za, http://www.statssa.gov.za.

016.3896 USA ISSN 0363-8464
UC263
U.S. DEPARTMENT OF DEFENSE. INDEX OF SPECIFICATIONS AND STANDARDS. Text in English. 1952. bi-m. USD 40.
Related titles: Microfiche ed.; Online - full text ed.: ISSN 1935-1976.
Published by: U.S. Naval Publications and Forms Center, 5801 Tabor Ave, Philadelphia, PA 19111. TEL 215-697-2000. Circ: 8,200. **Subscr. to:** U.S. Government Printing Office, Superintendent of Documents, PO Box 371954, Pittsburgh, PA 15250. TEL 202-512-1800, FAX 202-512-2250, orders@gpo.gov, http://www.access.gpo.gov.

016.3891 USA
U.S. DEPARTMENT OF DEFENSE. INDEX OF SPECIFICATIONS AND STANDARDS: PART 2, NUMERIC LISTING. Text in English. 19??. irreg. **Document type:** *Government.* **Description:** Provides a numerical listing of current standardization documents cancelled since the last DODISS.
Published by: (U.S. Department of Defense), U.S. Government Printing Office, 732 N Capitol St, NW, Washington, DC 20401. TEL 202-512-1800, 866-512-1800, FAX 202-512-2104, ContactCenter@gpo.gov, http://www.gpo.gov.

016.3896 USA
U.S. DEPARTMENT OF DEFENSE. INDEX OF SPECIFICATIONS AND STANDARDS: PART 3, FEDERAL SUPPLY CLASS LISTING. Text in English. 19??. base vol. plus irreg. updates. looseleaf. **Document type:** *Government.* **Description:** Lists all current standardization documents in alphabetical order within each FSC, as well as all standardization documents cancelled since the last basic DODISS.
Published by: (U.S. Department of Defense), U.S. Government Printing Office, 732 N Capitol St, NW, Washington, DC 20401. TEL 202-512-1800, 866-512-1800, FAX 202-512-2104, ContactCenter@gpo.gov, http://www.gpo.gov.

016.3891 USA
U.S. DEPARTMENT OF DEFENSE. INDEX OF SPECIFICATIONS AND STANDARDS: PART 4, NUMERICAL LISTING OF CANCELLED DOCUMENTS. Text in English. 19??. triennial. **Document type:** *Government.* **Description:** Provides a cumulative numerical listing of all standardization documents cancelled since 1964.
Published by: (U.S. Department of Defense), U.S. Government Printing Office, 732 N Capitol St, NW, Washington, DC 20401. **Subscr. to:** U.S. Government Printing Office, Superintendent of Documents.

MICROBIOLOGY

see BIOLOGY—Microbiology

MICROCOMPUTERS

see COMPUTERS—Microcomputers

MICROSCOPY

see BIOLOGY—Microscopy

MILITARY

see also CIVIL DEFENSE

A A M U C FOOTLOCKER. *see* HOBBIES

355 USA
A COMMON PERSPECTIVE. Text in English. s-a. back issues avail. **Document type:** *Newsletter.* **Description:** Contains articles, letters, and opinions to inform of the latest news and issues surrounding Joint Doctrine.
Published by: Joint War Fighting Center (Subsidiary of: U.S. Department of Defense), Fenwick Rd, Bldg 96, Fort Monroe, VA 23551-5000. FAX 804-726-6552, http://www.dtic.mil/doctrine/jel/comm_per/comm_per.htm.

A D F HEALTH. (Australian Defense Force) *see* MEDICAL SCIENCES

355 AUS ISSN 1324-6550
HD9743.A8
A D M; serving the business of defence. (Australian Defence Magazine) Text in English. 1993. 11/yr. AUD 148.50 domestic; AUD 175 in New Zealand; AUD 200 in Asia; AUD 270 elsewhere (effective 2008). adv. bk.rev. back issues avail. **Document type:** *Magazine, Trade.* **Description:** Aims to act as a communication bridge between defense industry and its single source customer, the Department of Defense.
Related titles: CD-ROM ed.; Online - full text ed.
Published by: Yaffa Publishing Group Pty Ltd., 17-21 Bellevue St, Surry Hills, NSW 2010, Australia. TEL 61-2-92812333, FAX 61-2-92812750, subscriptions@yaffa.com.au, http://www.yaffa.com.au/defence. Ed. Katherine Ziesing TEL 61-2-92135077. Pub. Tracy Yaffa TEL 61-2-92138266. adv.: B&W page AUD 2,810, color page AUD 3,350; trim 210 x 297. Circ: 4,047. **Subscr. to:** GPO Box 606, Sydney, NSW 2001, Australia.

A F F FAMILIES JOURNAL. (Army Families Federation) *see* LIFESTYLE

A F V MODELLER. (Armored Fighting Vehicles) *see* HOBBIES

355 USA ISSN 0741-076X
UC263
A L A WORLDWIDE DIRECTORY AND FACT BOOK. Text in English. 1982. a. USD 75 per issue. adv. back issues avail. **Document type:** *Directory.* **Description:** Military resale directory.
Related titles: Microfiche ed.: (from CIS).
Indexed: SRI.
Published by: American Logistics Association, 1133 15th St, N W, Ste 640, Washington, DC 20005. TEL 202-466-2520, http://www.ala-national.org. Ed. Herman Marshall. Circ: 10,000.

A M S STUDIES IN THE EMBLEM. (Abrahams Magazine Service) *see* GENEALOGY AND HERALDRY

355 CHE
A O G MITTEILUNGEN. Text in German. 4/yr. CHF 5 to non-members (effective 2008). **Document type:** *Journal, Trade.*
Published by: Allgemeine Offiziersgesellschaft, Jakob Kaiser-Weg 17, Schwerzenbach, 8603, Switzerland. thomfrey@hotmail.com, http://www.aog.ch.

355 USA ISSN 1933-5679
A S V A B. (Armed Services Vocational Aptitude Battery) Text in English. 2002. biennial (20th ed.). USD 13.95 per issue (effective 2009). 672 p./no.; **Document type:** *Guide, Consumer.* **Description:** Includes more practice tests and more updated test advice and an introduction to hundreds of careers open to enlistees in all 5 military branches.
Related titles: CD-ROM ed.
Published by: Thomson Peterson's (Subsidiary of: Thomson Reuters Corp.), Princeton Pike Corporate Center, 2000 Lenox Dr, 3rd Fl, PO Box 67005, Lawrenceville, NJ 08648. TEL 609-896-1800, 800-338-3282 ext 54229, FAX 609-896-4531, custsvc@petersons.com, http://www.petersons.com.

355 CZE ISSN 1802-4823
A T M. Text in Czech. 2007. m. CZK 890 (effective 2010). adv.
Formed by the merger of (2003-2007): Armady, Technika, Militaria (1214-1518); (1969-2007): A T M - Armadni Technicky Magazin (1210-2849); Which was formerly (1969-1990): A T O M - Armadni Technicky Obrazkovy Mesicnik (0322-8401)
Published by: Aeromedia, a. s., Baranova 38, Prague 8, 130 00, Czech Republic. TEL 420-2-22718814, FAX 420-2-22718814, obchod@aeromedia.cz, http://www.aeromedia.cz. Ed. Jan Cadil. Adv. contact Jiri Navratil.

355.31 USA ISSN 1075-458X
A U S A NEWS. Text in English. 1978. m. **Document type:** *Newsletter, Trade.*
Published by: Association of the United States Army, 2425 Wilson Blvd., Arlington, VA 22201. TEL 703-841-4300, 800-336-4570, ausa-info@ausa.org.

A U V S I'S UNMANNED SYSTEMS NORTH AMERICA. PROCEEDINGS. *see* COMPUTERS—Robotics

A U V S I'S UNMANNED SYSTEMS PROGRAM REVIEW PROCEEDINGS. *see* COMPUTERS—Robotics

355.1 USA ISSN 0001-2874
A V C BULLETIN. (American Veterans Committee) Text in English. 1944. irreg. (2-4/yr.). USD 5 (effective 1999). bk.rev. illus. **Document type:** *Newsletter.* **Description:** Provides information on activities of chapters, officers and members.
Published by: American Veterans Committee, Inc., 6309 Bannockburn Dr, Bethesda, MD 20817-5403. TEL 301-320-6490, FAX 301-320-6490. Ed. June A Willenz. R&P June Willenz. Circ: 15,000.

ACTION REPORT. *see* POLITICAL SCIENCE—International Relations

355 CAN ISSN 0705-0992
ADSUM. Text in French. 1972. w. CAD 24 (effective 1999). adv. bk.rev. index, cum.index. back issues avail. **Document type:** *Newspaper.*
Published by: USS Valcartier, CP1000, Succ Forces, Bldg 200, Courcelette, PQ G0A 4Z0, Canada. TEL 418-844-5000, FAX 418-844-6934. Ed. Caroline Charest. Circ: 5,000.

358.4 GBR ISSN 0262-8791
UG630
AEROMILITARIA; Air-Britain military aviation historical quaterly. Text in English. 1975. q. GBP 6.50 newsstand/cover to non-members; free to members (effective 2010). **Document type:** *Magazine, Trade.* **Description:** Provides detailed notes on, mainly, British and Commonwealth military types, providing data on the use and fates of each individual aircraft.
—**CCC.**
Published by: Air-Britain (Historians) Ltd., Victoria House, Stanbridge Park, Staplefield Ln, Staplefield, W Sussex RH17 6AS, United Kingdom. membership@air-britain.co.uk. Eds. James J Halley, Phil Butler. **Subscr. to:** 41 Penshurst Rd, Leigh, Tonbridge, Kent TN11 8HL, United Kingdom. TEL 44-1732-835637, FAX 44-1732-835637, sales@air-britain.co.uk.

AERONAUTICA E DIFESA. *see* AERONAUTICS AND SPACE FLIGHT

AEROPHILE. *see* HOBBIES

AEROTECNICA, MISSILI E SPAZIO. *see* AERONAUTICS AND SPACE FLIGHT

355 AFG
AFGHAN MILITARY REVIEW. Text in Persian, Modern, Pushto. 1976 (vol.56). m. USD 15.
Published by: Military Press, Urdoo Moojella, Kabul, 23208, Afghanistan.

355.31 ZAF
U1
AFRICAN ARMED FORCES; a monthly journal devoted to defence matters. Text in English. 1975. m. ZAR 160 domestic; USD 90 in Sub-Saharan Africa; USD 120 in UK, Europe, USA & Australia (effective 2010). adv. bk.rev. illus. back issues avail. **Document type:** *Journal, Trade.*
Formerly (until July 1994): Armed Forces (0379-6477)
Indexed: AMB, ISAP.
Published by: Military Publications Pty. Ltd., PO Box 23022, Joubert Park, Johannesburg 2044, South Africa. TEL 27-11-725-2701, FAX 27-11-725-2703. Ed. S J McIntosh.

355 GBR ISSN 1024-6029
UA855.6
AFRICAN SECURITY REVIEW; a working paper series. Text in English. 1992. q. GBP 245 combined subscription in United Kingdom to institutions (print & online eds.); EUR 324, USD 405 combined subscription to institutions (print & online eds.) (effective 2012). bk.rev. illus. reprint service avail. from PSC. **Document type:** *Monographic series.* **Description:** Publishes research reports, policy papers and articles on security and related issues in Africa.
Former titles (until 1995): African Defence Review (1022-6745); (until 1994): South African Defence Review (1018-9335)
Related titles: Online - full text ed.: ISSN 2154-0128. GBP 220 in United Kingdom to institutions; EUR 292, USD 365 to institutions (effective 2012).
Indexed: CA, CJA, I02, ISAP, LID&ISL, M10, P34, P52, S02, S03, T02.
—BLDSC (0733.320000), IE, Ingenta. **CCC.**
Published by: (Institute for Security Studies ZAF), Taylor & Francis Ltd. (Subsidiary of: Taylor & Francis Group), 4 Park Sq, Milton Park, Abingdon, Oxfordshire OX14 4RN, United Kingdom. TEL 44-20-70176000, FAX 44-20-70176336, info@tandf.co.uk. Ed. S.E. Meek. R&P S E Meek. Circ: 1,800.

355 GBR ISSN 0306-154X
AFTER THE BATTLE. Text in English. 1973. q. GBP 19.36 in UK & Channel Islands; GBP 24.36 in Europe; USD 40 in United States; CAD 51.36 in Canada; AUD 69.50 in Australia; NZD 66 in New Zealand; GBP 29.52 elsewhere; GBP 4.25 per issue (effective 2009). back issues avail. **Document type:** *Magazine, Consumer.* **Description:** Features articles on World War II battle fields.
—BLDSC (0735.620000).
Published by: Battle of Britain International Ltd., The Mews, Hobbs Cross House, Hobbs Cross, Old Harlow, Essex CM17 0NN, United Kingdom. TEL 44-1279-418833, FAX 44-1279-419386, hq@afterthebattle.com. **Dist. in US by:** R Z M Imports, 880 Canal St, Stamford, CT 06902. TEL 203-324-5100, FAX 203-324-5106, info@rzm.com, http://www.rzm.com/.

355 RUS ISSN 0134-9171
AGITATOR ARMII I FLOTA. Text in Russian. 1977. s-m.
Formerly: Sobesednik Voina
Published by: (Ministerstvo Oborony Rossiiskoi Federatsii/Ministry of Defence of the Russian Federation), Krasnaya Zvezda, Khoroshevskoye shosse 38, Moscow, 123892, Russian Federation.

358.4 FRA ISSN 0002-2152
AIR ACTUALITES; le magazine de l'armee de l'air. Text in French. 1968. 10/yr. EUR 33 domestic; EUR 54.60 DOM-TOM; EUR 63 elsewhere (effective 2009). adv. bk.rev. illus. **Document type:** *Magazine, Government.* **Description:** Provides editorials, news, reviews of aircrafts.
Supersedes: France. Secretariat d'Etat aux Forces Armees "Air". Bulletin d'Information
Published by: (Service d'Information de Recrutement et de Presse de l'Armee de l'Air), Etablissement de Communication et de Production Audiovisuelle de la Defense - E C P A D, 2 - 8 Route du Fort d'Ivry, Ivry-sur-Seine Cedex, 94205, France. TEL 33-1-45770376, FAX 33-1-45735373. Ed. Cl Gosset. Adv. contact Didier Contoux. Circ: 38,000.

358.4 USA ISSN 1555-385X
UG633
➤ **THE AIR & SPACE POWER JOURNAL.** Text in English. 1947. q. USD 32 domestic; USD 44.80 foreign; USD 16 per issue domestic; USD 22.40 per issue foreign (effective 2009). bk.rev. charts; illus.; stat. Index. 128 p./no.; back issues avail.; reprints avail. **Document type:** *Journal, Academic/Scholarly.* **Description:** Provides an open forum for the discussion of operational-level, as well as strategy and policy issues, with an emphasis on the uses of aerospace power.
Former titles (until 2002): The Aerospace Power Journal (1535-4245); (until 1999): Airpower Journal (0897-0823); (until 1987): Air University Review (0002-2594); (until 1963): Air University Quarterly Review
Related titles: Microform ed.: (from PQC); Online - full text ed.: ISSN 1554-2505. free (effective 2011); ◆ Arabic ed.: Air & Space Power Journal bil-'Arabiya. ISSN 1555-3868; ◆ French ed.: Air & Space Power Journal en Francais. ISSN 1931-728X; ◆ Chinese ed.: Air & Space Power Journal in Chinese. ISSN 1937-1373; ◆ Portuguese ed.: Air & Space Power Journal in Portuguese. ISSN 1555-3825; ◆ Spanish ed.: Air & Space Power Journal Espanol. ISSN 1555-3833.
Indexed: A01, A02, A03, A08, A09, A10, A15, A22, A26, A39, ABIn, ABS&EES, AMB, APA, AUNI, AmH&L, BAS, BRI, C&ISA, C12, C27, C29, CA, CorrAb, D03, D04, DM&T, E&CAJ, E08, E13, EEA, ESPM, EnvEAb, G01, G05, G06, G07, G08, HistAb, I02, I05, IBR, IBZ, IUSGP, LID&ISL, M01, M02, M05, M06, M07, MEA&I, MLA-IB, P02, P06, P10, P16, P26, P30, P34, P47, P48, P51, P52, P53, P54, PAIS, PQC, PRA, R14, RASB, S01, S09, S14, S15, S18, SCOPUS, SolStAb, T02, V02, V03, V04, WAA.
—BLDSC (0774.131500), IE, Ingenta, Linda Hall.
Published by: U.S. Air Force, Air University, 155 N Twining St, Maxwell, AL 36112. TEL 334-953-6455. Ed. Capt Lori Katowich. **Subscr. to:** U.S. Government Printing Office, Superintendent of Documents, 732 N Capitol St, NW, Washington, DC 20401. TEL 202-512-1800, 866-512-1800, FAX 202-512-2104, ContactCenter@gpo.gov, http://www.gpo.gov/.

358.4 USA ISSN 1555-3868
UG633
AIR & SPACE POWER JOURNAL BIL-'ARABIYA. Text in Arabic. 2005. q. back issues avail. **Document type:** *Journal, Academic/Scholarly.*
Related titles: Online - full text ed.: ISSN 1931-7476. free (effective 2010); ◆ English ed.: The Air & Space Power Journal. ISSN 1555-385X; ◆ French ed.: Air & Space Power Journal en Francais. ISSN 1931-728X; ◆ Spanish ed.: Air & Space Power Journal Espanol. ISSN 1555-3833; ◆ Chinese ed.: Air & Space Power Journal in Chinese. ISSN 1937-1373; ◆ Portuguese ed.: Air & Space Power Journal in Portuguese. ISSN 1555-3825.
Published by: U.S. Air Force, Air University, 55 LeMay Plz S, Maxwell, AL 36112. TEL 334-953-2014, FAX 334-953-3379, apj@maxwell.af.mil, http://www.au.af.mil. Ed. Abdullatif El-Nekishbendy.

358.4 629.13 USA ISSN 1931-728X
UG633
AIR & SPACE POWER JOURNAL EN FRANCAIS. Text in French. 2005. q. back issues avail. **Document type:** *Journal, Academic/Scholarly.* **Description:** Designed to serve as an open forum for the presentation and stimulation of innovative thinking on military doctrine, strategy, force structure, readiness, and other matters of national defense.
Related titles: Online - full text ed.: ISSN 1931-7298. free (effective 2010); ◆ English ed.: The Air & Space Power Journal. ISSN 1555-385X; ◆ Arabic ed.: Air & Space Power Journal bil-'Arabiya. ISSN 1555-3868; ◆ Spanish ed.: Air & Space Power Journal Espanol. ISSN 1555-3833; ◆ Chinese ed.: Air & Space Power Journal in Chinese. ISSN 1937-1373; ◆ Portuguese ed.: Air & Space Power Journal in Portuguese. ISSN 1555-3825.
Published by: U.S. Air Force, Air University, 55 LeMay Plz S, Maxwell, AL 36112. TEL 334-953-2014, FAX 334-953-3379, apj@maxwell.af.mil. Ed. Remy Mauduit.

358.4 USA ISSN 1555-3833
AIR & SPACE POWER JOURNAL ESPANOL. Text in Spanish. q.
Related titles: Online - full text ed.: ISSN 1555-3841; ◆ English ed.: The Air & Space Power Journal. ISSN 1555-385X; ◆ French ed.: Air & Space Power Journal en Francais. ISSN 1931-728X; ◆ Arabic ed.: Air & Space Power Journal bil-'Arabiya. ISSN 1555-3868; ◆ Chinese ed.: Air & Space Power Journal in Chinese. ISSN 1937-1373; ◆ Portuguese ed.: Air & Space Power Journal in Portuguese. ISSN 1555-3825.
Published by: U.S. Air Force, Air University, Maxwell Air Force Base, 401 Chennault Cir, Montgomery, AL 36112-6428. TEL 334-953-5322, apj@maxwell.af.mil, http://www.airpower.maxwell.af.mil. Ed. Al B Lopes.

358.4 USA ISSN 1937-1373
UG633
AIR & SPACE POWER JOURNAL IN CHINESE. Text in Chinese. 2007. q. back issues avail. **Document type:** *Journal, Academic/Scholarly.*
Related titles: Online - full text ed.: free (effective 2010); ◆ English ed.: The Air & Space Power Journal. ISSN 1555-385X; ◆ Arabic ed.: Air & Space Power Journal bil-'Arabiya. ISSN 1555-3868; ◆ Spanish ed.: Air & Space Power Journal Espanol. ISSN 1555-3833; ◆ French ed.: Air & Space Power Journal en Francais. ISSN 1931-728X; ◆ Portuguese ed.: Air & Space Power Journal in Portuguese. ISSN 1555-3825.
Published by: U.S. Air Force, Air University, 55 LeMay Plz S, Maxwell, AL 36112. TEL 334-953-2014, FAX 334-953-3379, apj@maxwell.af.mil, http://www.au.af.mil. Ed. Guocheng Jiang.

358.4 USA ISSN 1555-3825
AIR & SPACE POWER JOURNAL IN PORTUGUESE. Text in Portuguese. q.
Related titles: Online - full text ed.: ISSN 1555-3817; ◆ English ed.: The Air & Space Power Journal. ISSN 1555-385X; ◆ French ed.: Air & Space Power Journal en Francais. ISSN 1931-728X; ◆ Arabic ed.: Air & Space Power Journal bil-'Arabiya. ISSN 1555-3868; ◆ Chinese ed.: Air & Space Power Journal in Chinese. ISSN 1937-1373; ◆ Spanish ed.: Air & Space Power Journal Espanol. ISSN 1555-3833.
Published by: U.S. Air Force, Air University, Maxwell Air Force Base, 401 Chennault Cir, Montgomery, AL 36112-6428. TEL 334-953-5322, apj@maxwell.af.mil, http://www.airpower.maxwell.af.mil. Ed. Luis Fuentes.

355 USA
AIR DEFENSE ARTILLERY YEARBOOK. Text in English. a.
Published by: (U.S. Army Defense School), Advertising Ink, 114 S Oregon St, El Paso, TX 79987. **Subscr. to:** U.S. Government Printing Office, Superintendent of Documents.

358.4 FRA ISSN 0223-0038
AIR FAN; mensuel de l'aeronautique militaire internationale. Text in French. 1978. m. EUR 5.50 per issue (effective 2005). bk.rev. charts; illus. 52 p./no.; back issues avail. **Document type:** *Magazine, Consumer.*
Published by: Edimat, 48 bd. des Batignolles, Paris, 75017, France. TEL 33-01-42936724, FAX 33-01-42942540. Ed. Olivier Cabiac. Pub., Adv. contact Martine Cabiac. Circ: 23,000.

THE AIR FORCE CIVIL ENGINEER. *see* ENGINEERING—Civil Engineering

358.4 USA ISSN 0002-2365
UG633 CODEN: AFCTB3
AIR FORCE COMPTROLLER. Text in English. 1967. q. USD 15 domestic; USD 21 foreign (effective 2005). bk.rev. charts; illus. back issues avail.; reprints avail. **Document type:** *Government.* **Description:** Provides timely information to Air Force Comptroller personnel relating to accomplishing objectives, solving problems and improving operation efficiency, and communicating developments and new techniques.
Related titles: Microfiche ed.: (from CIS); Online - full text ed.
Indexed: A10, A12, A13, A17, A22, A26, ABIn, AUNI, AmStI, B01, B02, B06, B07, B08, B09, B15, B17, B18, BPIA, BusI, C12, G04, G05, G06, G07, G08, I02, I05, IUSGP, M05, M06, M07, P02, P10, P47, P48, P51, P52, P53, P54, PQC, T&II, T02, V03.
—Ingenta, Linda Hall.
Published by: U.S. Air Force, Financial Management and Comptroller, S A F/F M, 1130 Air Force Pentagon, Washington, DC 20330-1130. http://www.saffm.hq.af.mil. Circ: 4,500. **Subscr. to:** U.S. Government Printing Office, Superintendent of Documents, PO Box 371954, Pittsburgh, PA 15250. TEL 202-512-1800, FAX 202-512-2250.

358.4 USA ISSN 0270-403X
UG1123
➤ **AIR FORCE JOURNAL OF LOGISTICS.** Text in English. 1976. q. USD 33 domestic; USD 46.20 foreign; USD 13 per issue domestic; USD 18.20 per issue foreign (effective 2009). bk.rev. back issues avail. **Document type:** *Journal, Academic/Scholarly.* **Description:** Provides a forum for the presentation of issues, ideas, research, and information of concern to logisticians who plan, acquire, maintain, supply, transport, and provide supporting engineering and services for military aerospace forces.
Former titles (until 1980): Global Autovon Automatic Voice Network, Defense Communications System Directory (0747-7651); The Pipeline (0747-7562)
Related titles: Online - full text ed.: ISSN 1554-9593. free (effective 2009).
Indexed: A01, A03, A08, A26, AUNI, CA, E08, G05, G06, G07, G08, I02, I05, IBR, IBZ, IUSGP, LogistBibl, M05, M06, M07, P02, P10, P47, P48, P52, P53, P54, PQC, S09, T02.
—Ingenta.
Published by: U.S. Air Force, Logistics Management Agency, 501 Ward St, Gunter Annex, Maxwell AFB, AL 36114. TEL 334-416-2335, FAX 334-416-4392, https://www.aflma.hq.af.mil/. Eds. Cindy Young, Lt.Col. James C Rainey. R&P Lt.Col. James C Rainey. **Subscr. to:** U.S. Government Printing Office, Superintendent of Documents, PO Box 371954, Pittsburgh, PA 15250. TEL 202-512-1800, FAX 202-512-2250.

➤ **AIR FORCE LAW REVIEW.** *see* LAW—Military Law

358.4 USA ISSN 0730-6784
AIR FORCE MAGAZINE; the force behind the force. Text in English. 1927. m. USD 36 domestic to non-members; USD 46 in Canada & Mexico to non-members; USD 65 elsewhere to non-members; USD 21 domestic to members; USD 31 in Canada & Mexico to members; USD 50 elsewhere to members (effective 2009). adv. bk.rev. charts; illus.; tr.lit. back issues avail.; reprints avail. **Document type:** *Magazine, Consumer.* **Description:** Contains articles of interest to persons serving in the U.S. Air Force and their families.
Former titles (until 1972): Air Force and Space Digest (0002-2349); (until 1959): Air Force (0097-0190); (until 1942): Air Forces News Letter; (until 1941): Air Corps News Letter
Related titles: Online - full text ed.
Indexed: A22, A26, A28, ABS&EES, AMB, APA, AUNI, AmH&L, BrCerAb, C&ISA, CA/WCA, CIA, CerAb, CivEngAb, CorrAb, DM&T, E&CAJ, E11, EEA, EMA, G05, G06, G07, G08, H15, HistAb, I02, I05, LID&ISL, M&TEA, M05, M06, M07, M09, MBF, METADEX, P02, P06, P10, P13, P47, P48, P53, P54, PQC, PRA, RASB, SCOPUS, SolStAb, T02, T04, WAA.
—BLDSC (0776.073000), IE, Infotrieve, Ingenta, Linda Hall.
Published by: Air Force Association, 1501 Lee Hwy, Arlington, VA 22209. TEL 703-247-5800, 800-727-3337, FAX 703-247-5853, 800-291-8480, service@afa.org, http://www.afa.org. Ed. Suzann Chapman. adv.: B&W page USD 7,210, color page USD 9,050; trim 8.125 x 10.875. Circ: 138,295 (paid).

355 USA ISSN 0273-4370
UG633
AIR FORCE REPORT. Text in English. a.
Published by: U.S. Air Force, The Pentagon, Washington, DC 20330-1000.

358.4 USA ISSN 0002-2403
CODEN: AJTHAB
AIR FORCE TIMES (U.S. EDITION). Text in English. 19??. w. (Mon.). USD 55; USD 3.25 newsstand/cover (effective 2009). adv. bk.rev. charts; illus.; stat. reprints avail. **Document type:** *Newspaper, Trade.* **Description:** Provides articles and editorial content for all air force personnel and their families.
Formerly (until 1940): Army Times (Air Force Edition)
Related titles: Microform ed.: (from PQC); Online - full text ed.: AirForceTimes.com. ISSN 1943-5762. USD 29.95 (effective 2009); International ed.: Air Force Times (Worldwide Edition); ◆ Supplement(s): Handbook for Military Life. ISSN 1541-4434.
Indexed: A22, AUNI, C12, M01, M02, M05, P34, P52, RASB, T02, V02.
—CCC.
Published by: Army Times Publishing Co. (Subsidiary of: Gannett Company, Inc.), 6883 Commercial Dr, Springfield, VA 22159. TEL 703-750-7400, 800-368-5718, cust-svc@atpco.com, http://www.gannett.com/about/map/armytimes.htm, http://www.armytimes.com. Ed. Tobias Naegele. adv.: color page USD 22,190; 10.25 x 11.25. Circ: 54,153 (paid).

AIR POWER; journal of air power and space studies. *see* AERONAUTICS AND SPACE FLIGHT

355 358.4183 623.746 AUS ISSN 1832-2433
➤ **AIR POWER AUSTRALIA ANALYSES.** Text in English. 2004 (Nov.). irreg. free. cum.index:2004-2009. back issues avail. **Document type:** *Journal, Academic/Scholarly.* **Description:** Covers military science with a focus on military strategy, technology, management, governance; intended audience military professionals and scholars of military science.
Media: Online - full text.
Published by: Air Power Australia, Unit 2 / 14A Bloomfield Rd., Noble Park, VIC 3174, Australia. TEL 61395481585. Ed., Pub., R&P Carlo Kopp. Adv. contact Peter Goon.

➤ **AIR POWER HISTORY.** *see* AERONAUTICS AND SPACE FLIGHT

358.4 GBR ISSN 1463-6298
AIR POWER REVIEW. Text in English. 1997. q. bk.rev. back issues avail. **Document type:** *Magazine, Trade.*
Formerly (until 1998): Air Power (1369-9482)
Related titles: Online - full text ed.: ISSN 1756-1248. free (effective 2009).
Indexed: LID&ISL.
—BLDSC (8028.078000). **CCC.**
Published by: (Great Britain. Royal Air Force), R A F Magazines, Deputy Director of Defence Studies, Headquarters Defence Academy, Shrivenham, Swindon, Wiltshire SN6 8LA, United Kingdom. TEL 44-1793-314847, obarnes.dds@da.mod.uk.

358.4 USA
AIR PULSE. Text in English. 1949. w. (Fri.). free to military personnel (effective 2007). **Document type:** *Newspaper, Consumer.*
Contact Owner: Suburban Newspapers, Inc., 1413 S Washington St., Ste 300, Papillion, NE 68045. TEL 402-339-3331, FAX 402-537-2997. Circ: 13,200 (paid and controlled).

AIR UNIVERSITY LIBRARY INDEX TO MILITARY PERIODICALS. *see* MILITARY—Abstracting, Bibliographies, Statistics

358.4 CAN ISSN 0704-6804
TL501
AIRFORCE; the magazine of Canada's air force heritage. Text in English. 1961. q. CAD 35 (effective 2005). adv. bk.rev.; music rev.; film rev.; video rev. charts; illus. 64 p./no.; back issues avail. **Document type:** *Magazine, Consumer.* **Description:** Focuses on military aviation in Canada past, present and future. Contains updates on developments in the aviation and aerospace industry.
Former titles: Wings at Home (0043-5902); Wings in Space
Indexed: M05.
—CCC.
Published by: (Air Force Association of Canada), Airforce Productions Ltd., P O Box 2460, Ottawa, ON K1P 5W6, Canada. TEL 613-992-7482, FAX 613-995-2196, vjohnson@airforce.ca. Ed. Vic Johnson. Pub. Bob Tracy. Adv. contact John Stuart. Circ: 20,000; 16,068 (paid); 3,271 (controlled).

358.4 GBR ISSN 0955-7091
UG622
AIRFORCES MONTHLY; the world's leading military aviation magazine. Text in English. 1988. m. GBP 41 includes domestic & USA; GBP 51 elsewhere; GBP 4.20 per issue (effective 2010). adv. bk.rev. bibl.; illus.; stat.; maps. back issues avail.; reprints avail. **Document type:** *Magazine, Consumer.* **Description:** Covers every facet of military aviation.
—CCC.
Published by: Key Publishing Ltd., PO Box 300, Stamford, Lincs PE9 1NA, United Kingdom. ann.saundry@keypublishing.com, http://www.keypublishing.com. Ed. Alan Warnes. Adv. contact Ian Maxwell.

358.4 USA ISSN 0002-2756
UG633.A1
AIRMAN. Text in English. 1957. bi-m. USD 6.50 per issue; free to qualified personnel (effective 2009). illus. back issues avail.; reprints avail. **Document type:** *Magazine, Government.* **Description:** Covers Air Force news, information, policies, and programmes. Includes information on personnel.
Related titles: Microform ed.: (from MIM, PQC); Online - full text ed.: ISSN 1554-8988.
Indexed: A09, A10, A22, AUNI, G05, G06, G07, G08, I05, IUSGP, M02, M05, M06, M07, MEA&I, P02, P06, P10, P16, P47, P48, P52, P53, P54, PQC, T02, V02, V03, V04.
—Ingenta, Linda Hall.
Published by: (United States Air Force), Air Force News Agency (Subsidiary of: U.S. Air Force), 203 Norton St, San Antonio, TX 78226. TEL 210-925-7757, FAX 210-925-7219, editor@afnews.af.mil, http://www.af.mil/. **Subscr. to:** U.S. Government Printing Office, Superintendent of Documents, PO Box 371954, Pittsburgh, PA 15250. TEL 202-512-1800, 866-512-1800, FAX 202-512-2250, orders@gpo.gov, http://www.gpo.gov/.

AIRPOWER; the story of combat aviation. *see* AERONAUTICS AND SPACE FLIGHT

AIRSHIP. *see* AERONAUTICS AND SPACE FLIGHT

AIRSHOW AND DEFENSE EXPO INTERNATIONAL. *see* AERONAUTICS AND SPACE FLIGHT

358.4 USA
AIRTIDES. Text in English. 1949. w. adv. **Document type:** *Newspaper.* **Description:** News and features pertaining to Air Force members and their families, military retirees and their families, and government civilian employees.
Published by: Burlington County Times, 2901 Falcon Ln, McGuire Air Force Base, Trenton, NJ 08641. TEL 609-724-4091, FAX 609-724-6999. Ed. S Sgt Mary McHale.

355 LBN ISSN 1991-2382
AL DEFAIYA. Text in Arabic. 1993. bi-m. **Document type:** *Magazine, Trade.*
Published by: Al-Iktissad Wal-Aamal, Hamra, PO Box 113-6194, Beirut, 1103 2100, Lebanon. TEL 961-1-780200, FAX 961-1-780206, info@iktissad.com, http://www.iktissad.com.

ALARMING CRY. *see* RELIGIONS AND THEOLOGY—Protestant

355 ARG ISSN 1852-7248
ALERTA MILITANTE. Text in Spanish. 1999. m. back issues avail. **Document type:** *Magazine, Consumer.*
Related titles: Online - full text ed.: ISSN 1852-7167.
Address: Entre Rios, 1654-3, Buenos Aires, Argentina. correo@alertamilitar.com.ar. Eds. Gacriel Santagata, Miguel Butkoniv.

359 USA ISSN 0002-5577
VA52
ALL HANDS; magazine of the United States Navy. Abbreviated title: A H. Text in English. 1922. m. USD 45 domestic; USD 54 foreign; USD 7.50 per issue domestic; USD 9 per issue foreign (effective 2009). bk.rev. illus. back issues avail. **Document type:** *Magazine, Consumer.* **Description:** Features general-interest articles about the U.S. Navy and its operations.
Former titles (until 1945): United States. Bureau of Naval Personnel. Information Bulletin; (until 1942): United States. Navy Department. Bureau of Navigation Bulletin; (until 1928): United States. Navy Department. Bureau of Navigation News Bulletin
Related titles: Online - full text ed.
Indexed: A09, A10, A22, A26, A33, AMB, AUNI, G05, G06, G07, G08, I05, IUSGP, M01, M02, M05, M06, M07, P06, P10, P16, P47, P48, P52, P53, P54, PQC, T02, V02, V03, V04.
—Ingenta, Linda Hall.
Published by: (Times-Union Military Publications), Naval Media Center, Publishing Division, 2713 Mitscher Rd, SW, Bldg 168, Washington, DC 20373-5819. navynewsservice@dma.mil, http://www.dmaana.dma.mil/. Ed. Marie G Johnston. **Subscr. to:** U.S. Government Printing Office, Superintendent of Documents.

359 NLD ISSN 0002-5674
VA530
ALLE HENS. Text in Dutch. 1947. m. adv. bk.rev. charts; illus. **Document type:** *Government.*
Indexed: A22, AMB.
—IE, Infotrieve.
Published by: Ministerie van Defensie, Directie Voorlichting en Communicatie, Postbus 20701, The Hague, 2500 ES, Netherlands. TEL 31-70-3188188, FAX 31-70-3187888.

355 CHE ISSN 0002-5925
U3
ALLGEMEINE SCHWEIZERISCHE MILITAERZEITSCHRIFT. Short title: A S M Z. Text in German. 1855. m. CHF 78 domestic; CHF 98 foreign (effective 2008). adv. bk.rev. abstr.; bibl.; charts; illus.; maps. index. **Document type:** *Journal, Trade.* **Description:** Covers all aspects of the Swiss military, including training, equipment, information, international news, new publications and positions available.
Incorporates (1963-1965): Artillerie, Armee und Technik (0004-3796); Which was formerly (1922-1963): Schweizer Artillerist (1420-7974)
Indexed: A22, DIP, IBR, IBZ, LID&ISL, PRA, RASB.
—IE, Infotrieve.
Published by: Schweizerische Offiziersgesellschaft, Schaffhauserstr 43, Postfach 321, Zurich, 8042, Switzerland. TEL 41-44-3504994, FAX 41-44-3504432, office@sog.ch, http://www.sog.ch. Circ: 33,806 (paid and controlled).

359 USA ISSN 0736-3559
V1
ALMANAC OF SEAPOWER. Text in English. 1983. a. USD 45 to non-members; USD 22.50 per issue to non-members; free to members (effective 2009).
Related titles: ◆ Supplement to: Sea Power. ISSN 0199-1337.
—CCC.
Published by: Navy League of the United States, 2300 Wilson Blvd, Arlington, VA 22201. TEL 703-528-1775, FAX 703-243-8251. Ed. Amy Wittman. Pub. Michael J McGrath.

353.538 ITA
ALPIN JO, MAME!. Text in Italian. 1967. q. free. **Document type:** *Newspaper, Consumer.* **Description:** Newspaper of the Udine section of Associazione Nazionale Alpini.
Published by: Associazione Nazionale Alpini (A N A), Sezione di Udine, Viale Trieste 137, Udine, 33100, Italy. TEL 39-0432-502456, FAX 39-0432-506279, udine@anaudine.it, http://www.anaudine.it. Ed. Claudio Cojutti. Circ: 16,000.

ALTOS ESTUDIOS. *see* POLITICAL SCIENCE

355 USA ISSN 0883-072X
AMERICAN INTELLIGENCE JOURNAL. Text in English. 1977. 2/yr. USD 75 domestic; USD 135 foreign (effective 2005). adv. bk.rev. **Description:** Contains articles of professional government/industry and academic interest in the areas of defense, national security, intelligence, and counter-intelligence.
Indexed: I02, T02.
Published by: (N M I A Publication Fund of the Intelligence Scholarship Foundation), National Military Intelligence Association, PO Box 6712, Falls Church, VA 22040. TEL 301-840-6642, FAX 301-840-8502, zhi@nmia.org. Ed., R&P Roy K Jonkers. Circ: 3,000 (paid).

THE AMERICAN LEGION. *see* CLUBS

353.538 USA
AMERICAN VETERAN. Text in English. 1985. q. USD 10 (effective 2006). adv. **Document type:** *Magazine, Consumer.* **Description:** Features news and information focusing on veterans' issues, including the benefits provided by veterans' service organizations, services available through the Department of Veterans Affairs, pending federal legislation affecting veterans and retirees, and current news from the military community.

Related titles: Online - full text ed.
Published by: AMVETS, 4647 Forbes Blvd, Lanham, MD 20706-7380. TEL 301-459-9600, 877-726-8387, FAX 301-459-7924, http://www.amvets.org/. Ed. Jonathan Agg TEL 301-683-4083. Adv. contact Joe Chenelly TEL 301-683-4035. B&W page USD 2,160; trim 8.125 x 10.875. Circ: 224,729 (paid and controlled).

AMERICA'S CIVIL WAR. *see* HISTORY—History Of North And South America

359.96 USA ISSN 0886-344X
AMPHIBIOUS WARFARE REVIEW. Text in English. 1983. 3/yr. adv. bk.rev.
Published by: Marine Corps League, Capital Marine Detachment, 9351 Birchwood Court, Site 20122314, Manassas, VA 22110. TEL 703-330-0599, FAX 703-335-6181. Ed. Cyril Kammeier. Circ: 25,000 (controlled).

AMUNA KAI DIPLOMATIA. *see* POLITICAL SCIENCE

355 GRC
AMYNA & TEKNOLOGIA. Text in Greek. m. adv. **Document type:** *Trade.*
Published by: Velos Ltd., 9 Alexandras Ave, Athens, 114 73, Greece. TEL 01-6439641, FAX 01-6461361. Ed. Sotiris Poulopoulos. Adv. contact Ute Steuer. B&W page USD 3,500, color page USD 6,500; trim 175 x 255. Circ: 15,526. **Subscr. to:** Moench Verlagsgesellschaft mbH, Heilsbachstr 26, Bonn 53123, Germany. TEL 49-228-6483-0.

ANALYSEN ZUR SICHERHEITSPOLITIK/GERMAN STRATEGIC STUDIES. *see* POLITICAL SCIENCE—International Relations

355.6 USA ISSN 1930-6830
UA23.2
ANALYSIS OF THE F Y DEFENSE BUDGET REQUEST WITH HISTORICAL DEFENSE BUDGET TABLES. (Fiscal Year) Text in English. 199?. a. **Document type:** *Report, Trade.*
Formerly: Analysis of the President's F Y Defense Budget Request
Published by: The Center for Strategic and Budgetary Assessments (C S B A), 1667 K St. NW, Ste 900, Washington, DC 20006. TEL 202-331-7990, FAX 202-331-8019, info@csbaonline.org, http://www.csbaonline.org/2006-1/index.shtml. Ed. Steven Kosiak.

353.538 FRA ISSN 1243-3306
ANCIENS DES FORCES FRANCAISES EN ALLEMAGNE ET EN AUTRICHE. CEUX. Short title: Ceux des A F F A A. Text in French. 1924. q. adv. illus. **Document type:** *Journal, Academic/Scholarly.*
Former titles (until 1992): Forces Francaises en Allemagne et en Autriche. Ceux (1243-3292); (until 1964): Rhenanie Ruhr et Tyrol (1243-3284); (until 1939): Ceux du Rhin (1243-3276); (until 1938): Anciens de la Ruhr et de la Rhenanie (1243-3268)
Published by: Federation Nationale des Anciens des Forces Francaises en Allemagne et en Autriche, 1404 Rte des Nappes, B P 2, Les Avenieres, 38630, France. TEL 33-4-74336603, FAX 33-4-74338207, AFFAA@wanadoo.fr, http://www.affaa.com. Circ: 7,000.

355.4 NLD ISSN 1874-7019
ANCIENT WARFARE. Text in English. 2007. bi-m. EUR 33.50 (effective 2011). adv. **Document type:** *Magazine, Consumer.*
Published by: Karwansaray BV, PO Box 1110, Rotterdam, 3000 BC, Netherlands.

355.3 FRA ISSN 1638-3931
UA10.5
ANNUAIRE STRATEGIQUE ET MILITAIRE. Text in French. 2002. a. **Document type:** *Journal, Trade.*
Indexed: IBSS.
Published by: Fondation pour la Recherche Strategique, 27 rue Damesme, Paris, 75013, France. TEL 33-01-43137777, FAX 33-01-43137778, webmaster@frstrategie.org, http://www.frstrategie.org.

355.8 USA ISSN 1931-8855
HD9744.F55
ANNUAL FIREARMS MANUFACTURING AND EXPORT REPORT. Text in English. 19??. a., latest 2005. **Document type:** *Government.*
Media: Online - full text.
Published by: U.S. Department of Justice, Bureau of Alcohol, Tobacco, Firearms and Explosives (Subsidiary of: U.S. Department of Justice), 650 Massachusetts Ave, NW, Washington, DC 20226. ATFMail@atf.gov.

355 DEU
ANTENNE. Text in German. q. EUR 18 domestic; EUR 28.50 foreign (effective 2008). adv. **Document type:** *Magazine, Trade.*
Published by: A. Bernecker Verlag, Unter dem Schoeneberg 1, Melsungen, 34212, Germany. TEL 49-5661-7310, FAX 49-5661-731111, info@bernecker.de, http://www.bernecke.de. adv.: page EUR 785.

355 PRT ISSN 0011-765X
U4
ANUARIO ESTADISTICO DA DEFESA NACIONAL. Text in Portuguese. 1934. a. bk.rev. illus. index;cum.index. **Document type:** *Report, Government.*
Published by: Ministerio da Defesa Nacional, Av Ilha da Madeira 1, Lisbon, 1400-204, Portugal. TEL 351-213-010001, FAX 351-213-020284, gcrp@defesa.pt, http://www.mdn.gov.pt.

APPROACH. *see* AERONAUTICS AND SPACE FLIGHT

AQUILA LEGIONIS. *see* HISTORY

358.4 DEU
ARAB DEFENCE AND AEROSPACE BUSINESS. Text in Arabic. bi-m. adv. **Document type:** *Magazine, Trade.*
Published by: Moench Verlagsgesellschaft mbH, Heilsbachstr 26, Bonn, 53123, Germany. FAX 49-228-6483109, http://www.monch.com. Ed. Raouf Abou Zaki. Adv. contact Ute Steuer. B&W page USD 3,400, color page USD 5,500; trim 7.31 x 9.44. Circ: 23,296. **Co-publisher:** Al-Iktissad Wal-Aamal.

355 BEL
ARES. Text in Dutch, French. 1935. q. bk.rev.
Formerly: Officier de Reserve (0030-0551)
Indexed: LID&ISL.
Published by: (Union Royale Nationale des Officiers de Reserve (URNOR)/National Association of Reserve Officers (KNVRO)), F Lepeer Ed & Pub, Rue van Rolleghem 25, Brussels, 1090, Belgium. Circ: 9,000.

623.194 FRA ISSN 1776-1107
L'ARFUPEEN. Variant title: Association pour la Restauration du Fort d'Uxegney et de la Place d'Epinal. Text in French. 1990. 3/yr. **Document type:** *Journal, Trade.*
Published by: Association pour la Restauration du Fort d'Uxegney et de la Place d'Epinal, Fort d'Uxegney, Rue des Forts, Uxegney, 88390, France.

338.473 363.35 GBR ISSN 1749-1258
ARGENTINA DEFENCE & SECURITY REPORT. Text in English. 2005. a. EUR 820, USD 1,030 combined subscription per issue (print & email eds.) (effective 2010). **Document type:** *Report, Trade.* **Description:** Provides professionals, consultancies, government departments, regulatory bodies and researchers with independent forecasts and regional competitive intelligence on the Argentinian defence and security industry.
Related titles: E-mail ed.
Indexed: B01.
Published by: Business Monitor International Ltd., Senator House, 85 Queen Victoria St, London, EC4V 4AB, United Kingdom. TEL 44-20-72480468, FAX 44-20-72480467, subs@businessmonitor.com.

ARGENTINA. ESCUELA DE DEFENSA NACIONAL. REVISTA. *see* POLITICAL SCIENCE—International Relations

ARGENTINA. SERVICIO DE INTELIGENCIA NAVAL. BIBLIOTECAS DE LA ARMADA. BOLETIN BIBLIOGRAFICO. *see* MILITARY—Abstracting, Bibliographies, Statistics

355.31 CHE ISSN 1560-4616
ARMADA COMPENDIUM. Text in English. 1998. irreg. **Document type:** *Directory, Trade.*
Published by: Armada International, Thurgauerstr 39, Zurich, 8050, Switzerland. TEL 41-1-3085050, FAX 41-1-3085055, mail@armada.ch, http://www.armada.ch.

ARMADA INTERNATIONAL. *see* AERONAUTICS AND SPACE FLIGHT

355 NLD ISSN 0168-1672
➤ **ARMAMENTARIA.** Text in Dutch. 1966. a., latest vol.43, 2008. EUR 29.90 (effective 2009). **Document type:** *Monographic series, Academic/Scholarly.* **Description:** Covers Dutch military history, along with the history of arms and uniforms.
Published by: Koninklijk Nederlands Leger- en Wapenmuseum "Generaal Hoefer", Korte Geer 1, Delft, 2611 CA, Netherlands. TEL 31-15-2150500, FAX 31-15-2150566.

355.8 799.202 ESP
ARMAS. Text in Spanish. 1983. m. adv. **Document type:** *Magazine, Consumer.*
Published by: M C Ediciones, Paseo de Sant Gervasi 16-20, Barcelona, 08022, Spain. TEL 34-93-2541250, FAX 34-93-2541262, http://www.mcediciones.net. Circ: 35,000.

ARMCHAIR GENERAL. *see* BIOGRAPHY

355.31 USA ISSN 0095-327X
U21.5
➤ **ARMED FORCES AND SOCIETY**; an interdisciplinary journal on military institutions, civil-military relations, arms control and peacekeeping, and conflict management. Abbreviated title: A F S. Text in English. 1972. q. USD 531, GBP 313 to institutions; USD 542, GBP 319 combined subscription to institutions (print & online eds.) (effective 2012). adv. bk.rev. charts; illus. index. back issues avail.; reprint service avail. from PSC. **Document type:** *Journal, Academic/Scholarly.* **Description:** Provides an international forum for a wide range of topics, including war, revolution, recruitment and conscription policies, arms control, peacekeeping, military history, economics of defense, and strategic issues.
Related titles: Microfilm ed.: (from PQC); Online - full text ed.: ISSN 1556-0848. USD 488, GBP 287 to institutions (effective 2012).
Indexed: A01, A02, A03, A08, A09, A10, A20, A22, A25, A26, ABCPolSci, ABS&EES, AMB, ASCA, AUNI, AmH&L, B04, BAS, BRD, CA, CBRI, ChPerI, CurCont, DIP, E01, E08, ESPM, F09, FR, FamI, G08, H09, HistAb, I02, I05, I13, I14, IBR, IBSS, IBZ, L03, LID&ISL, M05, M06, M07, MEA&I, P02, P06, P10, P13, P16, P27, P30, P34, P42, P43, P45, P46, P47, P48, P53, P54, PAIS, PCI, PQC, PRA, PSA, PsycholAb, RASB, RI-1, RI-2, RiskAb, S02, S03, S05, S08, S09, SCOPUS, SOPODA, SSA, SSAI, SSAb, SSCI, SSI, SociolAb, T02, V02, V03, V04, W01, W02, W03, W04, W07.
—BLDSC (1682.970000), IE, Infotrieve, Ingenta, INIST. **CCC.**
Published by: (Inter-University Seminar on Armed Forces & Society), Sage Publications, Inc., 2455 Teller Rd, Thousand Oaks, CA 91320. TEL 800-818-7243, FAX 800-583-2665, info@sagepub.com, http://www.sagepub.com. Ed. Patricia M Shields. **Subscr. outside the Americas to:** Sage Publications Ltd., 1 Oliver's Yard, 55 City Rd, London EC1Y 1SP, United Kingdom. TEL 44-207-3248701, FAX 44-207-3248733, subscription@sagepub.co.uk.

355.31 USA ISSN 0004-2188
UC20
ARMED FORCES COMPTROLLER. Text in English. 1956. q. USD 15 domestic; USD 18 foreign (effective 2005). adv. bk.rev. charts. **Document type:** *Magazine, Trade.*
Related titles: Microform ed.: (from PQC); Online - full text ed.
Indexed: A09, A10, A26, ATI, AUNI, B01, B02, B06, B07, B08, B09, B15, B17, B18, BPIA, BusI, C12, G04, G05, G06, G07, G08, I02, I05, M01, M02, M05, M06, M07, ManagAb, ManagCont, P02, P10, P16, P47, P48, P53, P54, PQC, S22, T&II, T02, V02, V03, V04.
Published by: American Society of Military Comptrollers, 415 N Alfred St, Alexandria, VA 22314. TEL 703-549-0360, http://www.asmconline.org. Ed. Ltg James F McCall. R&P James F McCall. Circ: 20,000.

355 USA ISSN 1559-162X
U1 CODEN: AFJIE8
ARMED FORCES JOURNAL. Abbreviated title: T F J. Text in English. 1863. m. free domestic to qualified personnel (effective 2009). adv. illus. back issues avail.; reprints avail. **Document type:** *Magazine, Trade.* **Description:** Contains defense news commentary and analyses of career military officers, government officials, and industry executives involved in defense.
Former titles (until 2002): Armed Forces Journal International (0196-3597); (until 1973): Armed Forces Journal (0004-220X); (until 1968): The Journal of the Armed Forces; (until 1964): Army, Navy, Air Force Journal & Register; Which was formed by the merger of (1950-1962): Army, Navy, Air Force Journal; (until 1950): Army and Navy Journal (0275-2360); (until 1924): The American Army and Navy Journal and Gazette of the Regular, National Guard, and Reserve Forces; (until 1921): National Service; Which incorporated (1915-1918): International Military Digest; (1961-1962): Army-Navy-Air Force Register; Which was formerly (until 1961): Army-Navy-Air Force Register & Defense Times; (until 1959): The Army-Navy-Air Force Register; (1879-1949): Army and Navy Register; Which incorporated (1949-1956): The R O T C Journal
Related titles: Microform ed.: (from PQC); Online - full text ed.: ISSN 1930-8698.
Indexed: A01, A03, A08, A22, A26, ABS&EES, AMB, AUNI, CA, DM&T, I02, I05, LID&ISL, M05, M06, MEA&I, P34, P52, RASB, T02.
—BLDSC (1683.007000), IE, Infotrieve, Ingenta. **CCC.**
Published by: Defense News Media Group (Subsidiary of: Army Times Publishing Co.), 6883 Commercial Dr, Springfield, VA 22159. TEL 703-642-7330, 800-252-5825, FAX 703-642-7386, custserv@defensenews.com. Eds. Karen Walker, Tobias Naegele. Adv. contact Donna Peterson. Circ: 23,380. **Subscr. to:** Army Times Publishing Co., P O Box 109, Winchester, MA 01890-0109. TEL 781-729-4200.

355 BFA
ARMEE DU PEUPLE. Text in French. 1982. m. **Description:** Presents armed forces and defense information.
Address: Ouagadougou, Burkina Faso. Ed. Seydou Niang.

355.31 FRA ISSN 1621-4544
ARMEE ET DEFENSE; reserve et nation. Text in French. 1928. q. EUR 18 domestic; EUR 20 foreign (effective 2009). adv. bk.rev. illus. **Document type:** *Magazine.*
Formerly: Officier de Reserve
Indexed: RASB.
Published by: Union Nationale des Officiers de Reserve et des Organisations de Reservistes (U N O R), 12 Rue Marie-Laurencin, Paris, 75012, France. TEL 33-1-43474016, FAX 33-1-49280287, info@unor.org. Circ: 18,000.

355 CHE ISSN 1423-7008
ARMEE-LOGISTIK. Text in German, French, Italian. 1928. m. CHF 32 domestic; CHF 49 foreign (effective 2001). adv. bk.rev. **Document type:** *Bulletin, Trade.*
Formerly (until 1999): Fourier (0015-914X)
Published by: Schweizerischer Fourierverband, Postfach 2840, Luzern, 6002, Switzerland. TEL 41-41-2403868, FAX 41-41-2403869, mas-lu@bluewin.ch. Ed. Schuler Meinrad. Circ: 7,600.

355.31 FRA ISSN 0338-3520
U2
ARMEES D'AUJOURD'HUI. Text in French. 1962. 10/yr. EUR 20 domestic to individuals; FRF 30 DOM-TOM to individuals; FRF 35 elsewhere to individuals (effective 2009). adv. bk.rev. index. **Document type:** *Magazine, Government.* **Description:** Provides editorials, news, reviews of defense and French forces.
Supersedes: Forces Armees Francaises (0338-3512); Armee (0004-2234)
Related titles: Online - full text ed.
Indexed: AMB, FR, RASB.
—IE.
Published by: (Service d'Information et de Relations Publiques des Armees), Etablissement de Communication et de Production Audiovisuelle de la Defense - E C P A D, 2 - 8 Route du Fort d'Ivry, Ivry-sur-Seine Cedex, 94205, France. TEL 33-1-45770376, FAX 33-1-45795373. Ed. Capitaine de Fregate Levet. Adv. contact Didier Contoux. Circ: 150,000.

355 RUS
ARMEISKII SBORNIK; zhurnal dlya voennykh professionalov. Text in Russian. m. USD 129.95 in United States.
Related titles: Microfiche ed.: (from EVP).
Published by: Nachal'nik General'nogo Shtaba Vooruzhennykh Sil, K-175, Moscow, 103175, Russian Federation. TEL 7-095-2967919, FAX 7-095-9414066. Ed. V P Vinnik. **Dist. by:** East View Information Services, 10601 Wayzata Blvd, Minneapolis, MN 55305. TEL 952-252-1201, 800-477-1005, FAX 952-252-1202, info@eastview.com, http://www.eastview.com.

ARMEMUSEUM. MEDDELANDE. *see* MUSEUMS AND ART GALLERIES

355 NLD ISSN 0922-2979
ARMEX; defensiemagazine. Text in Dutch. 1919. bi-m. EUR 25 domestic; EUR 35 foreign (effective 2009). adv. bk.rev. illus. **Description:** Discusses peace, security, arms control, military technology and history, defense policies, and current developments affecting the Netherlands Armed Forces, independent from the Ministry of Defense.
Formerly (until Apr. 1988): Ons Leger (0030-2724)
Published by: Koninklijke Nederlandse Vereniging "Ons Leger", Postbus 90701, The Hague, 2509 LS, Netherlands. http://www.knvol.nl. Ed. P K Smit.

355 UKR
ARMIYA UKRAINY. Text in Russian, Ukrainian. 208/yr. USD 470 in United States.
Address: Ternopol'skaya ul 36, Lvov, Ukraine. TEL 380-32-423518, FAX 380-32-421774. **Dist. by:** East View Information Services, 10601 Wayzata Blvd, Minneapolis, MN 55305. TEL 952-252-1201, 800-477-1005, FAX 952-252-1202, info@eastview.com, http://www.eastview.com.

355 USA ISSN 0004-2420
UE1
ARMOR. Text in English. 1888. bi-m. USD 27 domestic; USD 37.80 foreign; free to qualified personnel (effective 2009). bk.rev. illus.; charts. cum.index: 1888-1968. 54 p./no.; back issues avail. **Document type:** *Magazine, Trade.*
Former titles (until 1950): Armored Cavalry Journal (0097-3688); (until 1946): The Cavalry Journal; (until 1920): United States Cavalry Association. Journal
Related titles: Microfilm ed.; Online - full text ed.
Indexed: A22, A26, ABS&EES, AMB, AUNI, CA, DM&T, G05, G06, G07, G08, I05, IUSGP, LID&ISL, M05, M06, M07, MEA&I, P02, P10, P13, P47, P48, P52, P53, P54, PQC, RASB, T02.
—IE, Infotrieve, Ingenta, Linda Hall.

Published by: U.S. Army Armor Center, 201 6th Ave, Ste 373, Bldg 1109 A, Ft. Knox, KY 40121. TEL 502-624-2249, FAX 502-624-5039, knox.armormag@conus.army.mil. **Subscr. to:** U.S. Government Printing Office, 732 N Capitol St, NW, Washington, DC 20401. TEL 202-512-1800, 866-512-1800, FAX 202-512-2104, gpo@custhelp.com, http://www.gpo.gov/.

355 USA ISSN 2151-190X
U1

▼ **ARMOR & MOBILITY.** Text in English. 2009. bi-m. USD 60 domestic; USD 90 foreign (effective 2009). adv. back issues avail. **Document type:** *Magazine, Trade.* **Description:** Provides latest news and information on current and future armor technologies and tactical missions.
Published by: Tactical Defense Media, Leisure World Plz, PO Box 12115, Silver Spring, MD 20908. TEL 301-974-9792, FAX 443-637-3714, contact@tacticaldefensemedia.com. adv.: page USD 4,600; trim 8.375 x 10.875.

355.8 GBR ISSN 1746-9449
ARMOUR AND WEAPONS. Text in English. 2005. irreg., latest vol.3, 2011. price varies. **Document type:** *Monographic series, Academic/Scholarly.*
Published by: Boydell & Brewer Ltd., Whitwell House, St Audrys Park Rd, Melton, Woodbridge, IP12 1SY, United Kingdom. TEL 44-1394-610600, FAX 44-1394-610316, editorial@boydell.co.uk, http://www.boydell.co.uk.

355 GBR ISSN 1363-1004
ARMOURER; the militaria magazine. Text in English. 1994. bi-m. GBP 24 domestic; GBP 30 in Europe & Republic of Ireland; GBP 35 elsewhere; GBP 3.50 per issue elsewhere (effective 2009). bk.rev. 80 p./no.; back issues avail. **Document type:** *Magazine, Consumer.*
Published by: Warners Group Publications Plc., The Maltings, Manor Ln, Bourne, Lincs PE10 9PH, United Kingdom. TEL 44-1778-391000, wgpsubs@warnersgroup.co.uk, http://www.warnersgroup.co.uk. Ed. Irene Moore.

343.821 355.8 GBR ISSN 1741-6124
U799

➤ **ARMS & ARMOUR.** Text in English. 1997. s-a. GBP 156 combined subscription to institutions (print & online eds.); USD 311 combined subscription in United States to institutions (print & online eds.) (effective 2012). adv. back issues avail.; reprint service avail. from PSC. **Document type:** *Journal, Academic/Scholarly.* **Description:** Aims to encourage and publish serious research in the field from scholars, both professional and amateur, around the world. Its areas of study, include, but are not limited to, the history, development, use, decoration and display of arms and armour throughout history.
Formerly (until 2004): Royal Armouries Yearbook (1366-3925)
Related titles: Online - full text ed.: ISSN 1749-6268. GBP 140 to institutions; USD 280 in United States to institutions (effective 2012) (from IngentaConnect).
Indexed: A01, A03, A08, A20, A30, A31, ArtHuCI, CA, T02, W07.
—BLDSC (1683.079500), IE, Ingenta. **CCC.**
Published by: (Royal Armouries), Maney Publishing, Ste 1C, Joseph's Well, Hanover Walk, Leeds, W Yorks LS3 1AB, United Kingdom. TEL 44-113-2432800, FAX 44-113-3868178, maney@maney.co.uk, http://www.maney.co.uk. **Subscr. in N America to:** Maney Publishing, 875 Massachusetts Ave, 7th Fl, Cambridge, MA 02139. TEL 866-297-5154, FAX 617-354-6875, maney@maneyusa.com

355 USA ISSN 1542-9792
ARMS SALES MONITOR. Text in English. 1991. q. (3-4 per yr.). USD 20 (effective 2002).
Published by: Federation of American Scientists, 1717 K St., NW, Ste. 209, Washington, DC 20036. TEL 202-546-3300, FAX 202-675-1010, fas@fas.org.

355.31 USA ISSN 0004-2455
ARMY. Text in English. 1950. m. USD 33 domestic; USD 58 foreign; free to members (effective 2009). adv. bk.rev. illus. 72 p./no.; back issues avail.; reprints avail. **Document type:** *Magazine, Trade.* **Description:** Focusses on the activities and interests of the US army worldwide and serves a readership interested in issues of national security; past and present issues involving landpower; and future trends in the military arts and sciences.
Former titles (until 1956): The Army Combat Forces Journal (0271-7336); Which incorporated (1948-1954): Antiaircraft Journal; Which was formerly (until 1948): The Coast Artillery Journal (0095-8832); (until 1922): Journal of the United States Artillery (0097-3785); The Army Combat Forces Journal was formerly (until 1954): United States Army Combat Forces Journal (0277-9080); Which was formed by the merger of (1910-1950): Infantry Journal (0019-9540); Which was formerly (1904-1910): United States Infantry Association. Journal; (1911-1950): The Field Artillery Journal
Related titles: Online - full text ed.
Indexed: A01, A22, A26, ABS&EES, AUNI, G05, G06, G07, G08, I02, I05, LID&ISL, M05, M06, M07, P02, P10, P34, P47, P48, P52, P53, P54, PQC, PRA, RASB, S23, T02.
—IE, Infotrieve, Ingenta, Linda Hall.
Published by: Association of the U.S. Army, 2425 Wilson Blvd, Arlington, VA 22201. TEL 703-841-4300, 800-336-4570, FAX 703-841-3505, ausa-info@ausa.org. Ed. Mary Blake French. Adv. contact James E Burke.

355.31 AUS ISSN 0729-5685
ARMY; the soldiers newspaper. Text in English. 1959. bi-w. AUD 39 (effective 2009). bk.rev. back issues avail. **Document type:** *Newspaper, Government.* **Description:** Reports on current events in the military, conditions of service, and current army projects.
Formerly (until 1980): Australian Army (0729-5677)
Related titles: Online - full text ed.: free (effective 2009).
Published by: Department of Defence, Army Newspaper Unit, R8-LG-039, Department of Defence, Russell Offices, Canberra, ACT, Australia. TEL 61-2-62667607, FAX 61-2-62656690. Ed. Maj Rod Horan. Adv. contact Geoff Howard.

355.31 USA ISSN 1529-8507
UC263

ARMY A L & T. (Acquisition, Logistics and Technology) Text in English. 2000. bi-m. USD 20 (effective 2001). **Document type:** *Government.* **Description:** Reports on Army research, development and acquisitions.
Related titles: Online - full text ed.: ISSN 1555-1385.
Indexed: A22, M05, P16, P47, P48, P52, P53, P54, PQC.
—Linda Hall.
Published by: Office of the Assistant Secretary of the Army for Acquisition, Logistics and Technology, 9900 Belvoir Rd Ste 101, Fort Belvoir, VA 22060-5567. TEL 703-805-1034, FAX 703-805-4218, bleicheh@aaesa.belvoir.army.mil. **Subscr. to:** U.S. Government Printing Office, Superintendent of Documents, PO Box 371954, Pittsburgh, PA 15250. TEL 202-512-1800, FAX 202-512-2250, orders@gpo.gov, http://www.access.gpo.gov.

358.4 GBR ISSN 0307-0069
THE ARMY AIR CORPS JOURNAL. Text in English. 1959. a. GBP 6. adv. bk.rev. back issues avail. **Description:** Gives both serving and retired members of the Army Air Corps news about the Corps history, operational accounts, honors, awards, promotions, appointments, and other association-related matters. Includes sporting and adventurous expedition accounts.
Indexed: LID&ISL.
Published by: Headquarters Director, Army Aviation, Middle Wallop, Stockbridge, Hants SO20 8DY, United Kingdom. TEL 01980-674426, FAX 01980-674163. Ed. Maj T M Deane. Adv. contact Maj T C Morley. Circ: 4,000.

358.4 USA ISSN 0004-248X
UG633.A1

ARMY AVIATION. Text in English. 1953. 10/yr. USD 30 (effective 2005). adv. **Document type:** *Magazine, Government.*
Indexed: LID&ISL.
Published by: Army Aviation Publications Inc., 755 Main St, Ste 4D, Monroe, CT 06468-2830. TEL 203-268-2450, FAX 203-268-5870, aaaa@quad-a.org, http://www.quad-a.org/. Ed. James R Bullinger. Pub., R&P William R Harris Jr. Adv. contact Robert C Lachowski. Circ: 13,500 (paid).

355.347 USA ISSN 1542-8907
UH23

ARMY CHAPLAINCY. Text in English. 1972. q. free to qualified personnel. bk.rev. **Document type:** *Government.* **Description:** Seeks to support and strengthen Army chaplains and chaplain assistants.
Formerly (until 1992): Military Chaplains' Review (0360-9693)
Related titles: Online - full text ed.: ISSN 1542-8915.
Indexed: A21, IUSGP, RI-1, RI-2.
—Ingenta.
Published by: U.S. Army Chaplain Center and School, ATSC CMT PAO 10100 Lee Rd, Fort, Jackson, SC 29207-7090. TEL 803-751-8070, FAX 803-751-8740. Ed. Chaplain Larry A Walker. R&P Nella Hobson. Circ: 6,000 (controlled).

354.75 USA ISSN 0362-5745
UA943

ARMY COMMUNICATOR; voice of the Signal Regiment. Text in English. 1976. q. free (effective 2005). bk.rev. **Document type:** *Government.* **Description:** Promotes the professional development of United States Army Signal Regiment by disseminating doctrinal and technical information and presenting new ideas or lessons learned concerning communications and electronics.
Related titles: Microform ed.: (from PQC); Online - full text ed.
Indexed: A01, A22, A26, AMB, E08, G05, G06, G07, G08, I05, IUSGP, LID&ISL, M01, M02, M05, M06, S09.
—Ingenta.
Published by: U.S. Army Signal Center, Signal Towers, Bldg 29808A, Room 713, Fort Gordon, GA 30905. FAX 706-791-3917.

358.4 USA
ARMY FLIER. Text in English. w. adv. **Document type:** *Newspaper, Government.*
Address: PO Box 1140, Enterprise, AL 36331. TEL 205-347-9533, FAX 205-347-0825. Pub. Mark J Cullen. Circ: 10,000.

355.31 USA ISSN 1546-5330
UA25

ARMY HISTORY; the professional bulletin of Army history. Text in English. 1983. q. **Document type:** *Bulletin, Government.*
Formerly (until 1989): Army Historian (0748-2299)
—Linda Hall.
Published by: U.S. Army, Center of Military History, 103 3rd Ave, Ft McNair, Washington, DC 20319-5058. TEL 202-685-2733, http://www.army.mil/cmh-pg/.

355.31 GBR ISSN 0965-9544
ARMY LIST. Text in English. 1845. every 3 yrs., latest 2005. price varies. **Document type:** *Government.* **Description:** Includes three parts: 1, Contains details of major army appointments, headquarters and establishments, as well as regimental and corps lists of officers of the British regular and territorial armies. It also contains details of affiliated institutions and of Commonwealth governments and military forces represented in the United Kingdom. 2, Officers in receipt of retired pay. 3, Restricted document that contains the biographical list of serving active officers.
Related titles: ◆ Supplement(s): Army List. Supplement. ISSN 0965-9552.
—BLDSC (1683.157000).
Published by: (Great Britain. Ministry of Defence. British Army), The Stationery Office, St Crispins, Duke St, Norwich, NR3 1PD, United Kingdom. TEL 44-1603-622211, FAX 44-870-6005533, customer.services@tso.co.uk, http://www.tso.co.uk.

355.31 GBR ISSN 0965-9552
ARMY LIST. SUPPLEMENT. Text in English. 1845. a., latest 2007. **Description:** Provides military related information.
Related titles: ◆ Supplement to: Army List. ISSN 0965-9544.
Published by: The Stationery Office, St Crispins, Duke St, Norwich, NR3 1PD, United Kingdom. TEL 44-1603-622211, customer.services@tso.co.uk, http://www.tso.co.uk. **Subscr. to:** PO Box 29, Norwich NR3 1GN, United Kingdom. TEL 44-870-6005522, FAX 44-870-6005533, subscriptions@tso.co.uk.

ARMY MOTORS. *see* HOBBIES

355.31 USA
U393

ARMY R D & A; professional publication of the R D & A community. (Research, Development and Acquisition) Text in English. 1960. bi-m. USD 11; USD 13.75 foreign. back issues avail. **Document type:** *Government.* **Description:** Reports on U.S. Army research, development and acquisition.
Former titles (until 1995): Army R D and A Bulletin (0892-8657); Army R D and A Magazine (0895-111X); Army R D and A (0162-7082); Army Research and Development (0004-2560)
Related titles: Microform ed.: (from PQC).
Indexed: IUSGP, LID&ISL, RASB.
—IE, Ingenta, Linda Hall.
Published by: U.S. Department of the Army, Office of the Deputy Director, Acquisition Career Management, 9900 Belvoir Rd., Ste. 101, Ft. Belvoir, MD 22060-5567. TEL 703-805-4215, FAX 703-805-4218. Ed. Harvey L Bleicher. Circ: 42,000. **Subscr. to:** U.S. Government Printing Office, Superintendent of Documents.

355.4 USA ISSN 2153-5973
U168

ARMY SUSTAINMENT. Text in English. 1969. bi-m. USD 23 domestic; USD 32.20 foreign (effective 2010). bk.rev. bibl.; charts; illus. back issues avail. **Document type:** *Magazine, Government.* **Description:** Brings out information on Army and Department of Defense sustainment plans, programs, policies, operations, procedures, and doctrine for the benefit of all army personnel.
Formerly (until 2009): Army Logistician (0004-2528)
Related titles: Microform ed.: (from MIM, PQC); Online - full text ed.: ISSN 2153-6015.
Indexed: A01, A22, A26, AMB, AUNI, C12, DM&T, E08, G05, G06, G07, G08, I02, I05, IBR, IBZ, IUSGP, LID&ISL, LogistBibl, M02, M05, M06, P02, P10, P34, P47, P48, P53, P54, PQC, S09, T02.
—IE, Ingenta, Linda Hall.
Published by: Army Logistics University, 2401 Quarters Rd, Ft. Lee, VA 23801. TEL 804-765-4761, FAX 804-765-4463, leeealog@conus.army.mil. **Subscr. to:** U.S. Government Printing Office, Superintendent of Documents, U.S. Government Printing Office, Washington, DC 20401. TEL 866-512-1800, FAX 202-512-2104, ContactCenter@gpo.gov, http://www.gpo.gov/.

355.31 USA ISSN 0004-2595
ARMY TIMES. Text in English. 1940. w. (Mon.). USD 55; USD 3.25 newsstand/cover (effective 2009). adv. bk.rev. charts; illus. reprints avail. **Document type:** *Newspaper, Consumer.* **Description:** Serving all Army personnel and their families.
Related titles: Microform ed.: (from PQC); Online - full text ed.: ArmyTimes.com. ISSN 1943-5770. USD 29.95 (effective 2009); International ed.
Indexed: A22, AUNI, M01, M02, M05, P34, P52, RASB, T02, V02.
—**CCC.**
Published by: Army Times Publishing Co. (Subsidiary of: Gannett Company, Inc.), 6883 Commercial Dr, Springfield, VA 22159. TEL 703-750-7400, 800-368-5718, cust-svc@atpco.com, http://www.gannett.com/about/map/armytimes.htm. Ed. Tobias Naegele. adv.: color page USD 22,190; 10.25 x 11.25. Circ: 107,171 (paid).

355.821 SWE ISSN 0004-3788
ARTILLERI-TIDSKRIFT. Text in Swedish. 1872. 4/yr. adv. bk.rev. charts; illus. index, cum.index every 4 yrs. back issues avail. **Document type:** *Magazine.*
Related titles: Online - full text ed.: 2002.
Published by: Foersvarsmakten, Artilleriregementet, Bodens Garnison, PO Box 9113, Boden, 96119, Sweden. TEL 46-921-68000, FAX 46-921-68698, exp-i19@mil.se. Circ: 1,000.

355 USA ISSN 1446-6880
UA870

ASIA - PACIFIC DEFENCE REPORTER. Text in English. 1974. bi-m. free to qualified personnel (effective 2005). adv. **Document type:** *Magazine, Trade.* **Description:** Covers geopolitical, defence and security issues in the Asia-Pacific region.
Former titles (until 2001): Defence Reporter (1446-6872); (until 2000): Asia - Pacific Defence Reporter (Sydney) (1037-1427); (until 1990): Pacific Defence Reporter (0311-385X)
Related titles: Online - full text ed.
Indexed: AMB, AUNI, CA, DM&T, I02, LID&ISL, RASB, T02.
—BLDSC (1742.260150), IE, Ingenta. **CCC.**
Published by: PRO-Media Sales & Consulting, Inc., 30096 Mine Run Rd, Unionville, VA 22567. TEL 540-854-0910. adv.: B&W page USD 255, color page USD 3,650; trim 205 x 275. Circ: 5,520.

355 USA
ASIA - PACIFIC DEFENSE FORUM. Text in English. 1976. q. free to qualified personnel. back issues avail. **Document type:** *Government.* **Description:** International forum for military personnel of the Asian and Pacific areas.
Related titles: Online - full content ed.
Indexed: SPPI.
Published by: U.S. Pacific Command (USCINCPAC), Editor, HQ USPACOM J39 (FORUM), PO Box 64013, Camp H M Smith, HI 96861-4013. TEL 808-477-0760, FAX 808-477-1471. Ed., R&P Paul R Stankiewicz. Circ: 30,200.

355 MYS ISSN 1394-178X
UA830

ASIAN DEFENCE AND DIPLOMACY. Text in English. 1993. m. MYR 120 domestic; USD 70 in Rest of ASEAN countries; USD 150 in US & Europe; USD 100 in Australia & New Zealand; USD 160 elsewhere; MYR 10 newsstand/cover in ASEAN countries; USD 20 newsstand/cover elsewhere (effective 2000). adv. **Document type:** *Journal, Academic/Scholarly.* **Description:** Provides a wide spectrum of substantive reports and analysis on defence and security issues, updates on new products, systems and technology, and articles and interviews on geo-politics in the region.
Published by: A D P R Consult (M) Sdn. Bhd., 19th Fl, SIME Bank Bldg, No.4 Jalan Sultan Sulaiman, Kuala Lumpur, 50000, Malaysia. TEL 603-22731355, 603-22735315, FAX 603-22735318, sachi@pc.jaring.my, http://www.adprconsult.com/. Ed. R Sachi Thananthan. Adv. contact Norezan Sulaiman. color page USD 4,000, B&W page USD 3,000; trim 285 x 210. Circ: 8,423 (paid); 19,000 (paid and controlled).

355 MYS ISSN 0126-6403
UA830

ASIAN DEFENCE JOURNAL. Text in English. 1971. m. MYR 156 domestic; SGD 120 in Singapore; USD 120 in ASEAN & Hong Kong; USD 156 in Asia & the Pacific; USD 216 in the Americas; USD 192 elsewhere (effective 2005). adv. bk.rev. charts; illus. back issues avail. **Document type:** *Magazine, Trade.* **Description:** Covers military, geopolitical affairs and all spheres of defence activities and industries from an Asia-Pacific perspective.
Related titles: Online - full text ed.; ◆ Special ed(s).: Asian Defence Yearbook.
Indexed: A22, AMB, AUNI, BAS, LID&ISL, PerIslam, RASB.
—BLDSC (1742.407700), IE, Infotrieve, Ingenta.

Published by: S H P Media Sdn Bhd., C-17-1, 17th Fl., Block C, Megan Phileo Ave., 12, Jalan Yap Kwan Seng, PO Box 10836, Kuala Lumpur, 50726, Malaysia. TEL 60-3-21660852 ext 5175, FAX 60-3-2161-0541, info@shpmedia.com. Ed. Ghazemy M. Mahmud. Circ: 20,000.

355 MYS
ASIAN DEFENCE YEARBOOK. Text in English. 1998. a. adv. **Document type:** *Yearbook, Academic/Scholarly.* **Description:** Contains 4 sections: Section one contains research articles on geo-strategic and political developments that took place during the year of publication, focusing on the critical areas of political-security concern. Section Two covers policy decisions, developments and significant events as regards Asia-Pacific militaries force structures, order of battle, force modernization, etc. Section Three lists state-owned or privately-owned defense companies operating in various countries of the Asia-Pacific region, including addresses and other contact information. Section four provides reference to the comparative capabilities of the militaries surveyed, including comprehensive and updated tables enumerating the inventories of Asia-Pacific's land, naval and air forces.
Related titles: ◆ Special ed. of: Asian Defence Journal. ISSN 0126-6403.
—BLDSC (1742.407701).
Published by: S H P Media Sdn Bhd., C-17-1, 17th Fl., Block C, Megan Phileo Ave., 12, Jalan Yap Kwan Seng, PO Box 10836, Kuala Lumpur, 50726, Malaysia.

355 GUM
ASSIGNMENT GUAM. Text in English. 1976. a. free.
Published by: Glimpses of Guam, Inc., P O Box 3191, Agana, Guam 96910, Guam. Ed. Jonathan Needham.

355 BRA ISSN 0102-9223
ASSOCIACAO BRASILEIRA DE ENGENHARIA MILITAR. REVISTA. Text in Portuguese. 1937. m. **Document type:** *Magazine, Trade.*
Published by: Associacao Brasileira de Engenharia Militar, Rua Ipiru 2, Jardim Guanabara, Ilha do Governador, Rio de Janeiro, RJ 21931-090, Brazil. info@engmil.org.br, http://www.engmil.org.br.

355.00711 PRT ISSN 0872-8224
ASSOCIACAO DOS ANTIGOS ALUNOS DO COLEGIO MILITAR. REVISTA. Text in Portuguese. 1965. 4/yr. bk.rev. back issues avail. **Document type:** *Bulletin, Academic/Scholarly.*
Published by: Associacao dos Antigos Alunos do Colegio Militar, Calcada do Marques de Abrantes, 40-1o D, Lisbon, 1200, Portugal. TEL 351-1-3962021, FAX 351-1-3950097. Ed. Antonio Pedro de Oliveira Collares Pereira. Circ: 2,000.

ASSOCIATION AMICALE DES ANCIENS COMBATTANTS DU 8E REGIMENT DE CUIRASSIERS. BULLETIN TRIMESTRIEL. *see* CLUBS

359 796.152 ESP ISSN 1699-4310
EL ASTILLERO; revista de modelismo naval. Text in Spanish. 2003. q. back issues avail. **Document type:** *Magazine, Consumer.*
Media: Online - full text.
Published by: El Astillero astillero@ya.com. Ed. Borja Garcia Cabellos.

355 PRT
▼ **ATENA.** Text in Portuguese. 2010. irreg. **Document type:** *Monographic series, Government.*
Published by: Instituto da Defesa Nacional, Calcadas das Necessidades 5, Lisbon, 1399-017, Portugal. TEL 351-213-924600, idn.instituto@defesa.pt, http://www.idn.gov.pt.

338.473 363.35 GBR ISSN 1749-1266
AUSTRALIA DEFENCE & SECURITY REPORT. Text in English. 2005. q. EUR 820, USD 1,030 combined subscription (print & email eds.) (effective 2010). **Document type:** *Report, Trade.* **Description:** Provides professionals, consultancies, government departments, regulatory bodies and researchers with independent forecasts and regional competitive intelligence on the Australian defence and security industry.
Related titles: E-mail ed.
Indexed: B01.
Published by: Business Monitor International Ltd., Senator House, 85 Queen Victoria St, London, EC4V 4AB, United Kingdom. TEL 44-20-72480468, FAX 44-20-72480467, subs@businessmonitor.com.

AUSTRALIAN & NEW ZEALAND DEFENCE BUSINESS DIRECTORY OF SUPPLIERS; the essential guide for defence procurement sourcing. *see* BUSINESS AND ECONOMICS—Trade And Industrial Directories

355.8 AUS ISSN 1039-1738
AUSTRALIAN AND NEW ZEALAND INDUSTRY DEFENCE EQUIPMENT AND CAPABILITY CATALOGUE. Text in English. 1974. a. AUD 360 (effective 2008). adv. illus. **Document type:** *Catalog, Trade.* **Description:** Lists more than 3500 suppliers to the Australian Defense Industry and is endorsed by Department of Defense.
Former titles: Australian and New Zealand Defence Equipment Catalogue; Australian Defence Equipment Catalogue (0314-156X)
Related titles: Online - full text ed.
Published by: (Australia. Australia. Department of Defence), J P M Media Pty Ltd., 15 Mayfield St, Abbotsford, VIC 3067, Australia. TEL 61-3-99450600, FAX 61-3-99450666, info@jpmmedia.com.au. Circ: 2,300.

355 AUS ISSN 1448-2843
AUSTRALIAN ARMY JOURNAL. Text in English. 2003. s-a. **Document type:** *Magazine, Trade.*
Indexed: AusPAIS.
Published by: Land Warfare Studies Centre, Ian Campbell Rd, Duntroon, ACT 2600, Australia. TEL 61-2-6265-9890, FAX 61-2-62659888. Ed. Scott Hopkins. Pub. Malcolm McGregor.

355.31 AUS ISSN 1832-3286
AUSTRALIAN ARMY ROWELL PROFESSION OF ARMS SEMINAR SERIES. Text in English. 2005. a. **Document type:** *Journal, Trade.*
Published by: Land Warfare Studies Centre, Ian Campbell Rd, Duntroon, ACT 2600, Australia. TEL 61-2-62659624, FAX 61-2-62659888, http://www.defence.gov.au/army/lwsc.

355 AUS ISSN 1329-9980
AUSTRALIAN DEFENCE BUSINESS REVIEW; the national defense industry and astrospace reporter. Abbreviated title: A D B R. Text in English. 1982. 20/yr. AUD 495 combined subscription (print & online eds.) (effective 2008); includes ADBR- Entrepreneur e-Newsletter. adv. 24 p./no.; back issues avail. **Document type:** *Magazine, Trade.* **Description:** Monitors the development of Australian defense policy and its impact on the equipment and logistics purchases of the Australian Defence force. Also monitors the corporate structure of Australia's top 50 defense suppliers.
Former titles (until Oct. 1997): Defence Industry & Aerospace Report (1033-2898); (until 1989): Defence Industry (0811-9449)
Related titles: E-mail ed.; Online - full text ed.
Published by: Business Communications Group, PO Box 250, Mawson, ACT 2607, Australia. TEL 61-2-62604855, FAX 61-2-62603977. Ed. Trevor J Thomas TEL 61-4-12631399. adv.: color page AUD 2,000; 210 x 300. Circ: 3,000 (controlled).

355 AUS ISSN 1320-2545
U1
➤ **AUSTRALIAN DEFENCE FORCE JOURNAL**; journal of the Australian profession of arms. Variant title: A D F J. Text in English. 1976. 3/yr. free. bk.rev. charts; illus. Index. back issues avail. **Document type:** *Journal, Academic/Scholarly.*
Former titles (until 1991): Defence Force Journal (0314-1039); Army Journal (0004-251X)
Related titles: Online - full text ed.: ISSN 1444-7150.
Indexed: A11, AMB, AusPAIS, CA, DM&T, IBR, IBZ, LID&ISL, P47, P48, PQC, RILM, T02.
—BLDSC (1798.390000), IE, Ingenta.
Published by: Australia. Department of Defence, R8-LG-001, Russell Offices, Canberra, ACT 2600, Australia. TEL 61-2-62651193, FAX 61-2-62656972. Circ: 2,200 (controlled).

355 AUS ISSN 1032-1063
AUSTRALIAN DEFENCE INTELLIGENCER; a monthly compilation of commercial intelligence on Australia's defence equipment programs and policies. Text in English. 1988. m. bk.rev. Supplement avail. **Document type:** *Newsletter.* **Description:** Covers Australian defence equipment programs and policies.
Published by: Tom Muir & Associates Pty. Ltd., PO Box 430, Erindale, ACT 2903, Australia. tom.muir@dynamite.com.au. **Dist. in US by:** Tom Muir & Associates.

355 AUS
AUSTRALIAN DEFENCE NEWS. Text in English. 1988. 50/yr. AUD 350 domestic; AUD 500 foreign (effective 2008). back issues avail. **Document type:** *Newsletter, Trade.*
Published by: Yaffa Publishing Group Pty Ltd., 17-21 Bellevue St, Surry Hills, NSW 2010, Australia. TEL 61-2-92812333, 800-807-760, FAX 61-2-92812750, yaffa@yaffa.com.au, http://www.yaffa.com.au. Ed. Gregor Ferguson. Adv. contact Mike Kerr TEL 61-7-33486966. Circ: 300. **Subscr. to:** GPO Box 606, Sydney, NSW 2001, Australia.

355 551.46 AUS ISSN 0157-6429
AUSTRALIAN MARINE SCIENCE BULLETIN. Variant title: A M S A Bulletin. Text in English. 1963. 3/yr. free to members (effective 2008). adv. bk.rev. back issues avail. **Document type:** *Bulletin, Academic/Scholarly.* **Description:** Promotes in the study of marine science and coordinating discussion and debate of marine issues in Australia.
Former titles (until 1970): Australian Marine Sciences Association. Bulletin; (until 1968): Australian Marine Science. Newsletter
Indexed: ASFA, B21, CTO, ESPM, GeoRef.
Published by: Australian Marine Sciences Association Inc., PO Box 8, Kilkivan, QLD 4600, Australia. TEL 61-7-54841179, FAX 61-7-54841456, secretary@amsa.asn.au. Ed. Patricia von Baumgarten. adv.: page AUD 297. Circ: 1,200.

359.00994 AUS ISSN 1832-861X
AUSTRALIAN MARITIME ISSUES. Variant title: S P C - A (Sea Power Centre Australia) Annual. Text in English. 2004. a. free (effective 2009). back issues avail. **Document type:** *Monographic series, Government.* **Description:** Contains the summary of the various naval and maritime issues during the financial year.
Related titles: Online - full text ed.
Published by: Sea Power Centre Australia, Department of Defence, Canberra, ACT 2600, Australia. TEL 61-2-61276512, FAX 61-2-61276519, seapower.centre@defence.gov.au, http://www.navy.gov.au/spc/. Ed. Andrew Forbes.

AUSTRALIAN MILITARY MEDICINE. *see* MEDICAL SCIENCES

AVALON HILL GENERAL. *see* SPORTS AND GAMES

358.4 PER ISSN 0005-2078
AVIACION. Text in Spanish. 1936. m. **Description:** Discusses Peruvian Air Force.
Published by: Fuerza Aerea, Edificio Ministerio de Aeronautica, 28 de Julio, Campo de Marte, Lima, Peru.

AVIATION WEEK'S HOMELAND SECURITY & DEFENSE. *see* AERONAUTICS AND SPACE FLIGHT

AVIONS. *see* TRANSPORTATION—Air Transport

355 AZE
AZERBAIJAN ORDUSU. Text in Azerbaijani. w. USD 325 in the Americas (effective 2000).
Published by: Redaktsiya Azerbaijan Ordusu, Khajibeili Kuch., 26, Baku, 370007, Azerbaijan. TEL 994-12-964696. Ed. Isa Ismayilov. **Dist. by:** East View Information Services, 10601 Wayzata Blvd, Minneapolis, MN 55305. TEL 952-252-1201, 800-477-1005, FAX 952-252-1202, info@eastview.com, http://www.eastview.com.

B I C C BRIEF. *see* POLITICAL SCIENCE—International Relations

B I C C BULLETIN. *see* POLITICAL SCIENCE—International Relations

B I C C PAPER. *see* POLITICAL SCIENCE—International Relations

B I C C REPORT. *see* POLITICAL SCIENCE—International Relations

THE B V A BULLETIN. (Blinded Veterans Association) *see* HANDICAPPED—Visually Impaired

355 ISR
BA-MAHANE. Text in Hebrew. 1948. w. adv. **Document type:** *Magazine, Trade.*
Published by: Israel Defense Forces, Military Post, 01025, Israel. TEL 972-3-694903, FAX 972-3-260279. Circ: 70,000.

353.538 USA ISSN 2154-2627
BADGER LEGIONNAIRE & "WISCONSIN". Text in English. 1923. every 5 wks. USD 5 to non-members. adv. **Document type:** *Newspaper.* **Description:** Contains articles of interest to veterans.
Former titles (until 2010): Badger Legionnaire & American Legion Auxiliary "Wisconsin"; (until 1992): Badger Legionnaire & Wisconsin American Legion Auxiliary (0162-2218); (until 197?): Badger Legionnaire (0005-3767)
Published by: Wisconsin American Legion, 812 E State St, Milwaukee, WI 53202. TEL 414-271-1940. Ed. Rick Barnett. Circ: 96,000.

355 USA
THE BARKSDALE WARRIOR. Text in English. w. **Document type:** *Magazine, Consumer.*
Formerly (until Sep. 2007): The Bombardier
Published by: (Barksdale Air Force Base), Gannett River States Publishing Company DBA the Times, 109 Barksdale Blvd. W., Ste. 209, Barksdale AFB, LA 71110-2164.

358.4 FRA ISSN 1253-5354
BATAILLES AERIENNES. Text in French. 199?. q. back issues avail. **Document type:** *Magazine, Consumer.*
Published by: Lela Presse, 29 Rue Paul Bert, Outreau, 62230, France. TEL 33-3-21338896, FAX 33-3-21320039, lela.presse@wanadoo.fr.

355.8 909 632 FRA ISSN 1765-0828
BATAILLES & BLINDES. Text in French. 2003. bi-m. EUR 35 domestic; EUR 40 in the European Union; EUR 40 DOM-TOM; EUR 40 in Switzerland; EUR 45 elsewhere (effective 2009). back issues avail. **Document type:** *Magazine, Consumer.*
Published by: Caraktere SARL, 29 Bd Rabatau, Marseille, 13008, France. http://www.caraktere.com/.

355 SWE ISSN 0284-3765
BATALJONSBLADET. Text in Swedish. 1984. q. (4-5 yr.). adv. **Description:** Association for Swedish veterans of UN sanctioned missions.
Published by: Fredsbaskarna Sverige/Peace Berets of Sweden, Teglbruksgatan 8, Joenkoeping, 55480, Sweden. TEL 46-36-71-90-07, FAX 46-36-71-90-06, kansliet.fredsbaskarna@telia.com, http://www.fredsbaskarna.org.

355 USA
BATTLE CALL. Text in English. 1963. m. USD 20 (effective 2000). adv. bk.rev. **Document type:** *Newsletter.* **Description:** Presents articles on the Civil War, including military uniform and battle information.
Published by: Army of Tennessee, C S A - U S A, PO Box 91, Rosedale, IN 47874. TEL 765-548-2594. Ed. Ruby I Walker. Pub. K A Walker. Adv. contact Kimberly A Walker. Circ: 350.

BATTLEFIELDS REVIEW. *see* HISTORY

355.31 USA
THE BAYONET. Text in English. 1943. w. (Fri.). USD 21.50; free newsstand/cover (effective 2005). **Document type:** *Newspaper.*
Related titles: Online - full content ed.
Published by: The Bayonet, 6751 Constitution Loop, Ste 602, Fort Benning, GA 31905. TEL 706-545-4622. Ed. Lori Egan. Pub. Richard Benjamin Freakley. Adv. contact Scott Kirk. Circ: 25,000 (paid and free).

355 NOR ISSN 0332-9097
BEFALSBLADET. Text in Norwegian. 1895. 8/yr. adv.
Formerly (until 1930): Underofficersbladet (0333-3272)
Published by: Norges Offisersforbund, Moellergatan 10, Oslo, Norway. TEL 47-2-40-15-74. adv.: B&W page NOK 8,000, color page NOK 12,000. Circ: 7,400.

338.473 947.8 363.35 GBR ISSN 1749-1274
BELARUS DEFENCE & SECURITY REPORT. Text in English. 2005. a. EUR 820, USD 1,030 combined subscription per issue (print & email eds.) (effective 2010). **Document type:** *Report, Trade.* **Description:** Provides professionals, consultancies, government departments, regulatory bodies and researchers with independent forecasts and regional competitive intelligence on the Belarusian defence and security industry.
Related titles: E-mail ed.
Indexed: A15, ABIn, B02, B15, B17, B18, G04, I05, P48, P51, P52, PQC.
Published by: Business Monitor International Ltd., Senator House, 85 Queen Victoria St, London, EC4V 4AB, United Kingdom. TEL 44-20-72480468, FAX 44-20-72480467, subs@businessmonitor.com.

341.72 355 CAN ISSN 1716-2645
BEYOND BOUNDARIES: CANADIAN DEFENCE AND STRATEGIC STUDIES. Key Title: Beyond Boundaries Series. Text in English. 2005. irreg., latest vol.2, 2006. price varies. **Document type:** *Monographic series, Academic/Scholarly.* **Description:** Provides readers with narratives and analysis of the Canadian military. Covers defence policy and security issues, international and external relations, diplomacy and peacekeeping.
Published by: (Canadian Defence and Foreign Affairs Institute), University of Calgary Press, 2500 University Dr NW, Calgary, AB T2N 1N4, Canada. TEL 403-220-7578, FAX 403-282-0085, ucpmail@ucalgary.ca.

900 NLD ISSN 0250-4308
BIBLIOGRAPHIE INTERNATIONALE D'HISTOIRE MILITAIRE. Text in Multiple languages. 1978. s-a. EUR 113, USD 160 to institutions; EUR 124, USD 174 combined subscription to institutions (print & online eds.) (effective 2012). **Document type:** *Bibliography.*
Formerly (until 1978): Commission Internationale d'Histoire Militaire Comparee. Comite de Bibliographie. Bulletin de Bibliographie. (0378-7869)
Related titles: Online - full text ed.: ISSN 2211-5757. EUR 103, USD 145 to institutions (effective 2012).
Published by: (Commission Internationale d'Histoire Militaire), Brill, PO Box 9000, Leiden, 2300 PA, Netherlands. TEL 31-71-5353500, FAX 31-71-5317532, cs@brill.nl.

355.8 CHN ISSN 1672-4054
BINGGONG KEJI/ORDNANCE INDUSTRY SCIENCE TECHNOLOGY. Text in Chinese. 2002. s-a. **Document type:** *Journal, Academic/Scholarly.*
Formerly (until 2002): Keji yu Guoli (1006-8651)
Published by: Binggong Keji Zazhishe, 38, Hanguang Nan Lu, Xi'an, 710065, China. TEL 86-29-88233966. **Co-sponsors:** Gong-Qing-Tuan Shaanxi Sheng Guofang Gong-Wei; Shaanxi Sheng Kejishi Xuehui.

355 CHN ISSN 1000-1093
UF10 CODEN: BIXUD9
BINGGONG XUEBAO/ACTA ARMAMENTARII. Text in Chinese. 1979. m. CNY 240 (effective 2009). back issues avail. **Document type:** *Journal, Academic/Scholarly.*
Related titles: Online - full text ed.; English ed.: Journal of China Ordnance. ISSN 1673-002X.
Indexed: A22, A28, APA, BrCerAb, C&ISA, CA/WCA, CIA, CPEI, CerAb, CivEngAb, CorrAb, E&CAJ, E11, EEA, EMA, EngInd, H15, M&TEA, M09, MBF, METADEX, RASB, SCOPUS, SolStAb, T04, WAA.
—BLDSC (0596.630000), East View, IE, Infotrieve, Linda Hall.
Published by: Zhongguo Binggong Xuehui/China Ordnance Society, PO Box 2431, Beijing, 100089, China. TEL 86-1-68962718, FAX 86-1-68963025. Ed. Dong Wang.

355 629.8 CHN ISSN 1006-1576
UF520
➤ **BINGGONG ZIDONGHUA/ORDNANCE INDUSTRY AUTOMATION.** Text in Chinese; Abstracts in Chinese, English. 1982. m. CNY 120, USD 120; CNY 10 newsstand/cover (effective 2009). **Document type:** *Journal, Academic/Scholarly.* **Description:** Covers the latest developments of theoretical and applied researches in the fields of ordnance industry automation.
Related titles: Online - full text ed.
—East View.
Published by: Zhongguo Bingqi Gongye Di-58 Yanjiusuo/Southwest Automation Research Institute, PO Box 207, Mianyang, Sichuan 621000, China. TEL 86-816-2282073, FAX 86-816-2279300, http://www.58suo.com/. Ed. Li Huang. Circ: 6,000.

355.8 CHN ISSN 1009-3567
BINGQI/WEAPON. Text in Chinese. 1999. m. **Document type:** *Journal, Academic/Scholarly.*
Formerly (until 2000): Wuqi (1008-9683)
Published by: Zhongguo Bingqi Gongye Jituan Gongsi/China North Industries Group Corporation, PO Box 100081-67, Beijing, 100081, China. TEL 86-10-62149673, http://www.cngc.com.cn.

623 CHN ISSN 1004-244X
BINGQI CAILIAO KEXUE YU GONGCHENG/ORDNANCE MATERIAL SCIENCE AND ENGINEERING. Text in Chinese. 1978 (Mar). bi-m. USD 31.20 (effective 2009). back issues avail. **Document type:** *Journal, Academic/Scholarly.*
Related titles: Online - full text ed.
Address: 199, Lingyun Lu, Ningbo, 315103, China. TEL 86-574-87902250, FAX 86-574-87902259.

355.82 CHN ISSN 1000-4912
U799
BINGQI ZHISHI/ORDNANCE KNOWLEDGE. Text in Chinese. 1979. m. USD 88.80 (effective 2009). **Document type:** *Journal, Academic/Scholarly.*
Related titles: Online - full text ed.
—East View.
Published by: Zhongguo Binggong Xuehui/China Ordnance Society, PO Box 2431, Beijing, 100089, China. TEL 86-1-68962718, FAX 86-1-68963025, http://www.cos.org.cn/.

355 610 CHN ISSN 1672-4356
BINGTUAN YIXUE. Text in Chinese. 1984. q. **Document type:** *Journal, Academic/Scholarly.*
Published by: Xinjiang Shengchan Jianshe Bingtuan Yixuehui, 15, Wuxin Lu, Urumqi, 830002, China. TEL 86-991-2621783.

BIT'ON HEL HA-AVIR/ISRAEL AIR FORCE MAGAZINE. *see* AERONAUTICS AND SPACE FLIGHT

THE BLUE & GREY CHRONICLE. *see* HISTORY—History Of North And South America

359 USA
THE BLUEJACKET; Naval support activity mid-south. Text in English. w. (Thu.). USD 22 in state; USD 38 for 2 yrs. in state; USD 28 subscr - mailed out of state (effective 2004). adv. **Document type:** *Newspaper.*
Published by: Millington Star, The, 5107 Easley St, Millington, Shelby, TN 38053. TEL 901-872-2286, FAX 901-872-2965. Ed. Julia Wallis. adv.: col. inch USD 8. Circ: 7,500 (free).

355 SWE ISSN 0347-299X
BOCKEN. Text in Swedish. 1938. a. SEK 75 to members (effective 1990).
Published by: Haelsinge Regementes Kamratfoerening, I 14 Fo 21, Fack 614, Gavle, 80126, Sweden.

BOEI DAIGAKKO KYOKAN KENKYU YOROKU/NATIONAL DEFENSE ACADEMY. DIGEST OF RESEARCHES BY FACULTY MEMBERS. *see* MILITARY—Abstracting, Bibliographies, Statistics

BOEI DAIGAKKO RIKOGAKU KENKYU HOKOKU/NATIONAL DEFENSE ACADEMY. SCIENTIFIC AND ENGINEERING REPORTS. *see* ENGINEERING

355 JPN ISSN 0919-8555
UA10
BOEI GIJUTSU JANARU/DEFENSE TECHNOLOGY JOURNAL. Text in Japanese; Summaries in English, Japanese. 1981. m. JPY 7,000 (effective 2002). **Document type:** *Academic/Scholarly.*
Formerly (until 1993): Boei Gijutsu (0285-0893)
Published by: Boei Gijutsu Kyokai/Defense Technology Foundation, AHMS-1 4F 1-18-4, Ebisu-nisi, Shibuya-ku, Tokyo, 150-0021, Japan. TEL 81-3-3463-2308, FAX 81-3-3463-2149, dtf.journal@dream.com.

355 RUS
BOEVAYA VAKHTA. Text in Russian. 104/yr. USD 475 in the Americas (effective 2000).
Published by: Redaktsiya Boevaya Vakhta, Ul. Pos'etskaya, 22, Vladivostok, 690600, Russian Federation. TEL 4232-412148. Ed. Yi M Trakelo. **Dist. by:** East View Information Services, 10601 Wayzata Blvd, Minneapolis, MN 55305. TEL 952-252-1201, 800-477-1005, FAX 952-252-1202, info@eastview.com, http://www.eastview.com.

355 ESP ISSN 1136-7210
BOINA NEGRA. Text in Spanish. 1960. q. back issues avail. **Document type:** *Magazine, Trade.*
Published by: Ministerio de Defensa, Centro de Publicaciones, Calle de Alcala 18, 4o, Madrid, 28014, Spain. TEL 34-91-522524, FAX 34-91-5227553, http://www.mde.es.

BONN INTERNATIONAL CENTER FOR CONVERSION. JAHRESBERICHT. *see* POLITICAL SCIENCE—International Relations

338.473 497 363.35 GBR ISSN 1749-1282
BOSNIA & HERZEGOVINA DEFENCE & SECURITY REPORT. Text in English. 2005. a. EUR 820, USD 1,030 combined subscription per issue (print & email eds.) (effective 2010). **Document type:** *Report, Trade.* **Description:** Provides professionals, consultancies, government departments, regulatory bodies and researchers with independent forecasts and regional competitive intelligence on the Bosnian defence and security industry.
Related titles: E-mail ed.
Indexed: A15, ABIn, P48, P51, P52, PQC.
Published by: Business Monitor International Ltd., Senator House, 85 Queen Victoria St, London, EC4V 4AB, United Kingdom. TEL 44-20-72480468, FAX 44-20-72480467, subs@businessmonitor.com.

355 DEU
DER BOTE AUS DEM WEHRGESCHICHTLICHEN MUSEUM. Text in German. 1977. s-a. EUR 5 per issue (effective 2010). cum.index every 15 nos. back issues avail. **Document type:** *Bulletin.*
Published by: Vereinigung der Freunde des Wehrgeschichtlichen Museums Schloss Rastatt e.V., Museums Schloss Rastatt e.V., Postfach 1633, Rastatt, 76406, Germany. TEL 49-7222-34244, FAX 49-7222-30712, information@wgm-rastatt.de, http://www.wgm-rastatt.de/foerderverein. Circ: 1,000.

355 RUS
BRATISHKA; zhurnal podrazdelenii spetsial'nogo naznacheniya. Text in Russian. 1997. m. USD 75 in the Americas (effective 2000).
Published by: Bratstvo Krapovykh Beretov, Syromyatnicheskii pr., 8, Moscow, 107120, Russian Federation. TEL 7-095-9171589. **Dist. by:** East View Information Services, 10601 Wayzata Blvd, Minneapolis, MN 55305. TEL 952-252-1201, 800-477-1005, FAX 952-252-1202, info@eastview.com, http://www.eastview.com.

338.473 981 363.35 GBR ISSN 1749-1290
BRAZIL DEFENCE & SECURITY REPORT. Text in English. 2005. q. EUR 820, USD 1,030 combined subscription (print & email eds.) (effective 2010). **Document type:** *Report, Trade.* **Description:** Provides professionals, consultancies, government departments, regulatory bodies and researchers with independent forecasts and regional competitive intelligence on the Brazilian defence and security industry.
Related titles: E-mail ed.
Indexed: B01, P34.
Published by: Business Monitor International Ltd., Senator House, 85 Queen Victoria St, London, EC4V 4AB, United Kingdom. TEL 44-20-72480468, FAX 44-20-72480467, subs@businessmonitor.com.

BRIGADIER. *see* COLLEGE AND ALUMNI

355.02 GBR ISSN 1753-3090
BRITAIN AT WAR MAGAZINE. Text in English. 2007. m. GBP 37.50 domestic; GBP 64 in Europe; GBP 81.60 elsewhere; GBP 3.75 per issue (effective 2009). adv. back issues avail. **Document type:** *Magazine, Consumer.* **Description:** Covers the entire spectrum of British involvement in conflicts from the beginning of the twentieth-century until now.
Published by: Green Arbor Publishing Ltd., Cabbell, Unit 7, Woodman Works, 204 Durnsford Rd, London, SW19 8DR, United Kingdom. TEL 44-208-9718452, FAX 44-208-9718480. Ed. Martin Mace. Adv. contact Leah Grayson.

355 RUS
BRONEKOLLEKTSIYA. Text in Russian. bi-m.
Published by: Redaktsiya Zhurnala Modelist - Konstruktor, Novodmitrovskaya ul 5-a, Moscow, 127015, Russian Federation. TEL 7-095-2851704.

355.8 RUS
BRONEKOLLEKTSIYA. PRILOZHENIE K ZHURNALU MODELIST-KONSTRUKTOR. Text in Russian. bi-m.
Address: Novodmitrovskaya ul 5-a, Moscow, 125015, Russian Federation. TEL 7-095-2858046, FAX 7-095-2852757. Ed. A S Raguzin. **Dist. by:** East View Information Services, 10601 Wayzata Blvd, Minneapolis, MN 55305. TEL 952-252-1201, 800-477-1005, FAX 952-252-1202, info@eastview.com, http://www.eastview.com.

355 NOR ISSN 1504-3363
BUDSTIKKEN. Text in Norwegian. 1974. q. NOK 150 membership (effective 2006). **Document type:** *Magazine, Consumer.*
Formerly (until 2004): Budstikken (Haerens Sambands Kameratforening) (1504-338X)
Published by: Sambandssoldatenes Forening, c/o Finn Berntzen, Lensmannsjordet 7, Kolsaas, 1352, Norway. TEL 47-67-172238, sbsf@sbsf.no, http://www.sbsf.no.

DER BUECHSENMACHER - MESSER UND SCHERE. *see* HOBBIES

BUILD THE RED BARON'S FIGHTER PLANE. *see* HOBBIES

338.473 363.35 GBR ISSN 1749-1304
BULGARIA DEFENCE & SECURITY REPORT. Text in English. 2005. q. EUR 820, USD 1,030 combined subscription (print & email eds.) (effective 2010). **Document type:** *Report, Trade.* **Description:** Provides professionals, consultancies, government departments, regulatory bodies and researchers with independent forecasts and regional competitive intelligence on the Bulgarian defence and security industry.
Related titles: E-mail ed.
Indexed: A15, ABIn, B02, B15, B17, B18, G04, I05, P48, P51, P52, PQC.
Published by: Business Monitor International Ltd., Senator House, 85 Queen Victoria St, London, EC4V 4AB, United Kingdom. TEL 44-20-72480468, FAX 44-20-72480467, subs@businessmonitor.com.

355 BGR
BULGARSKI VOENEN KNIGOPIS. Text in Bulgarian. 1955. bi-m. free. bibl.
Indexed: RASB.
Published by: (Institut po Voena Istoriia), Izdatelstvo na M O, Iv Vazov ul 12, Sofia, Bulgaria. Ed. L Ilieva. Circ: 835.

355 BGR
BULGARSKI VOIN. Text in Bulgarian. m. USD 62 foreign (effective 2002). **Document type:** *Journal, Government.*
Published by: Ministerstvo na Otbranata na Republika Bulgaria/Ministry of Defence of the Republic of Bulgaria, 3 Vassil Levski St, Sofia, 1000, Bulgaria. TEL 359-2-9885885, FAX 359-2-9873228, presscntr@md.government.bg, http://www.md.government.bg/.

355 SWE ISSN 1100-0961
BUMERANGEN. Text in Swedish. 1978-1995; resumed 1997. q. adv. **Document type:** *Consumer.*
Related titles: E-mail ed.
Published by: Svenska Vapenstiftelsen (SVEVAP), PO Box 6100, Haegersten, 12907, Sweden. TEL 46-8-194572, kansli@svevap.se.

355.1 DEU ISSN 0932-8904
BUND UND BERUF. Text in German. 1987. q. EUR 16 (effective 2008). adv. **Document type:** *Magazine, Trade.* **Description:** Provides information and details on available jobs and training for German soldiers about to enter the civilian job market.
Published by: A. Bernecker Verlag, Unter dem Schoeneberg 1, Melsungen, 34212, Germany. TEL 49-5661-7310, FAX 49-5661-731111, info@bernecker.de, http://www.bernecke.de. adv.: B&W page EUR 1,700, color page EUR 2,660. Circ: 15,000 (controlled).

BUNDESPOLIZEI. *see* POLITICAL SCIENCE—International Relations

355 DEU ISSN 0007-5949
DIE BUNDESWEHR. Text in German. 1956. m. EUR 30 (effective 2010). adv. bk.rev.; Website rev. illus. index. 80 p./no.; **Document type:** *Journal, Trade.*
Indexed: RASB.
Published by: Deutscher Bundeswehr-Verband e.V, Suedstr 123, Bonn, 53175, Germany. TEL 49-228-38230, FAX 49-228-3823220, info@dbwv.de. Ed. Frank Henning. Adv. contact Wilhelm Koester. B&W page EUR 4,050; trim 222 x 307. Circ: 179,684 (paid and controlled).

BUNDESWEHRVERWALTUNG; Fachzeitschrift fuer Administration. *see* LAW

355 GBR
BUSINESS RATIO REPORT: THE DEFENCE INDUSTRY. Text in English. 1979. a. GBP 365 per issue (effective 2010). charts; stat. back issues avail. **Document type:** *Report, Trade.* **Description:** Covers companies active in the defence industry.
Formerly (until 199?): Business Ratio Report: Defence Equipment Manufacturers (0261-7781)
Published by: Key Note Ltd. (Subsidiary of: Bonnier Business Information), Harlequin House, 5th Fl, 7 High St, Teddington, Richmond upon Thames, TW11 8EE, United Kingdom. TEL 44-845-5040452, FAX 44-845-5040453, sales@keynote.co.uk.

355.343 USA ISSN 1941-1286
UB251.U5
C 4 I S R; the journal of net-centric warfare. Text in English. 2002. 10/yr. free to qualified personnel (effective 2009). adv. **Document type:** *Journal, Trade.* **Description:** Covers the latest developments in the high-tech realm of military intelligence, surveillance, and reconnaissance (ISR) programs.
Formerly (until 2004): The I S R Journal (1540-9880)
Indexed: P52.
—CCC.
Published by: Army Times Publishing Co. (Subsidiary of: Gannett Company, Inc.), 6883 Commercial Dr, Springfield, VA 22159. TEL 703-750-7400, 800-368-5718, FAX 703-658-8412, cust-svc@atpco.com, http://www.armytimes.com. Ed. Tobias Naegele. Adv. contact Judy McCoy TEL 703-642-7330.

C B W MAGAZINE; a journal on chemical and biological weapons. *see* ENGINEERING—Chemical Engineering

355 USA
C C C O ACTION ALERT. Text in English. 1993. m.?. adv.
Published by: Central Committee for Conscientious Objectors, 1515 Cherry St, Philadelphia, PA 19102-1403. TEL 215-545-4626, FAX 215-545-4628. Ed., Adv. contact Chris Lombard.

355 CAN ISSN 0045-8872
C F B COLD LAKE COURIER. (Canadian Forces Base) Text in English. 1967. w. CAD 20. adv. bk.rev. **Document type:** *Newspaper.*
Published by: Canadian Forces Base, Cold Lake, P O Box 3190, Medley, AB T0A 2M0, Canada. TEL 403-594-5206, FAX 403-594-2139. Ed. Debbie Lawrence. Adv. contact Laura Saueracker. Circ: 4,000.

355 CAN
C F B COMOX TOTEM TIMES. (Canadian Forces Base Comox) Text in English, French. 1960. fortn. CAD 15 (effective 2000). adv. bk.rev. **Document type:** *Newspaper.* **Description:** Provides a mix of military news, community, sports, health, history for serving and retired members of the local military community.
Published by: Canadian Forces Base Comox, Box 100 Stn Main, Lazo, BC V0R 2K0, Canada. TEL 250-339-2541, FAX 250-339-5209, totemtimes@comox.dnd.ca. Ed. Major J C Clarkston. Adv. contact J Cooper. page CAD 600. Circ: 2,100 (controlled).

C H I DISPATCH. *see* HISTORY—History Of North And South America

C M L ARMY CHEMICAL REVIEW. *see* CHEMISTRY—Analytical Chemistry

355 USA
C N A CORPORATION ANNUAL REPORT. Text in English. 1972. irreg. **Document type:** *Corporate.*
Formerly (until 1997): Center for Naval Analyses. Biennial Report
Published by: Center for Naval Analyses (C N A), 4825 Mark Center Dr., Ste. 100, Alexandria, VA 22311-1846.

359 USA ISSN 1931-3624
C N A OCCASIONAL PAPER. (Center for Naval Analyses) Text in English. 19??. irreg. **Document type:** *Report, Trade.*
Published by: Center for Naval Analyses (C N A), 4825 Mark Center Dr., Ste. 100, Alexandria, VA 22311-1846. TEL 703-824-2000, http://www.cna.org.

355 004 USA ISSN 1526-4653
HD9744.E43
C O T S JOURNAL. (Commercial Off-the-Shelf) Text in English. w. free domestic to qualified personnel (effective 2002). adv. back issues avail.; reprints avail. **Document type:** *Journal, Trade.*
Published by: R T C Group, 927 Calle Negocio, G, San Clemente, CA 92673. TEL 949-226-2000, FAX 949-226-2050. Ed. Warren Andrews. Pub. Pete Yeatman.

355 CAN ISSN 1912-0974
C R T I ANNUAL REPORT/I R T C. RAPPORT ANNUEL. (Chemical, Biological, Radiological, and Nuclear Research and Technology Initiative) Text in English. 2003. a. **Document type:** *Report, Trade.*
Formerly (until 2005): C B R N Research and Technology Initiative. Annual Report (1912-094X)

Published by: C B R N Research and Technology Initiative (Subsidiary of: Defence Research and Development Canada/Recherche et Developpement pour la Defense Canada), 305 Rideau St, Ottawa, ON K1A 0K2, Canada. TEL 613-996-2350, FAX 613-995-3402, crti-irtc@drdc-rddc.gc.ca, http://www.crti.drdc-rddc.gc.ca/en/default.asp.

355.309489 DNK ISSN 0902-3488
C S BLADET. Text in Danish. 1971. 10/yr. DKK 300 (effective 2008). adv. back issues avail. **Document type:** *Magazine, Trade.*
Former titles (until 1986): Stampersonel (0105-3000); (until 1976): Fagbladet Stampersonel (0105-2993); (until 1973): Fagblad for Seniorsergenter of Stampersonel (0902-1701); Which incorporates (1966-1971): S F O Bladet (0036-1356)
Related titles: Online - full text ed.
Published by: Centralforeningen for Stampersonel, Trommesalen 3, Copenhagen V, 1614, Denmark. TEL 45-36-908990, FAX 45-33-311033, cs@cs.dk. Eds. Finn H Bengtsen, Jesper K Hansen.

353.358 USA
CALIFORNIA LEGIONNAIRE. Text in English. 1930. m. USD 3 (effective 2000). adv. bk.rev. tr.lit. back issues avail. **Document type:** *Newspaper.*
Related titles: Microfilm ed.: (from LIB).
Published by: American Legion, Department of California, 117 War Memorial Bldg, San Francisco, CA 94102. TEL 415-431-2400. Ed. Donald A Drumheller. Circ: 161,200.

353.538 USA ISSN 1069-8477
CALIFORNIA VETERAN. Text in English. 1954. 8/yr. **Description:** Provides news on legislation, benefits, rights, and other veteran-related information.
Published by: Veterans of Foreign Wars of the United States, 406 W 34th St, Kansas City, MO 64111. TEL 816-756-3390, FAX 816-968-1149, info@vfw.org, http://www.vfw.org.

355 CHL ISSN 0717-4535
CAMARADAS. Text in Spanish. 1991. bi-m. **Document type:** *Magazine, Trade.*
Published by: Fuerza Aerea de Chile, Calle Centeno 45, Piso 2, Santiago de Chile, Chile. TEL 56-2-6948001, http://www.fach.cl/.

CAMBRIDGE MILITARY HISTORIES. *see* HISTORY

CAMOUFLAGE. *see* CHILDREN AND YOUTH—For

355 USA ISSN 1055-2790
CAMP CHASE GAZETTE; where the Civil War comes alive. Text in English. 1972. 10/yr. USD 33 domestic; USD 60 foreign; USD 4.50 per issue (effective 2008). adv. bk.rev.; film rev.; music rev.; video rev. 68 p./no.; back issues avail. **Document type:** *Magazine, Consumer.* **Description:** Source of information for those individuals and organizations that participate in Civil War Reenacting. Each issue contains a complete national calendar of events, articles on topics of interest to Civil War Reenactors, event reports, and letters to the editor.
Published by: Camp Chase Publishing Co., Inc., 1609 W. 1st North St., Morristown, TN 37814. TEL 800-624-0281, FAX 423-551-3061. Ed. Ed Hooper. Pub., R&P William Holschuh. Adv. contact Denise Thacker. Circ: 4,200 (paid); 5,000 (controlled).

355.6 CAN ISSN 1495-3722
UA602.C49
CANADA. CHIEF OF THE DEFENCE STAFF. ANNUAL REPORT. Text in English, French. 199?. a.
Related titles: Online - full content ed.: ISSN 1495-3315.
Published by: (Canada. Department of National Defence, Chief of the Defence Staff), Department of National Defence, Major-General George R Pearkes Bldg, 101 Colonel By Dr, Ottawa, ON K1A 0K2, Canada. TEL 613-995-2534, FAX 613-995-2610, information@forces.gc.ca, http://www.forces.gc.ca.

327.12 CAN ISSN 1206-7490
JL86.I58
CANADA. COMMUNICATIONS SECURITY ESTABLISHMENT COMMISSIONER. ANNUAL REPORT/COMMISSAIRE DU CENTRE DE LA SECURITE DES TELECOMMUNICATIONS. RAPPORT ANNUEL. Text in English, French. 1997. a.
—CCC.
Published by: Canada. Office of the Communications Security Establishment Commissioner, PO Box 1984, Sta B, Ottawa, ON K1P 5R5, Canada. TEL 613-992-3044, FAX 613-992-4096.

338.473 363.35 941 GBR ISSN 2042-4221
▼ **CANADA DEFENCE & SECURITY REPORT.** Text in English. 2009. q. EUR 820, USD 1,030 combined subscription (print & email eds.) (effective 2010). back issues avail. **Document type:** *Report, Trade.* **Description:** Covers independent forecasts and competitive intelligence on the defense and security industry in Canada.
Related titles: E-mail ed.
Published by: Business Monitor International Ltd., Senator House, 85 Queen Victoria St, London, EC4V 4AB, United Kingdom. TEL 44-20-72480468, FAX 44-20-72480467, subs@businessmonitor.com, http://www.businessmonitor.com.

355 CAN ISSN 0383-4638
UA600
CANADA. DEPARTMENT OF NATIONAL DEFENCE. DEFENCE (YEAR). Text in English, French. 1970. a. free. illus.
Published by: Government of Canada Publications, Publishing and Depository Services, Public Works and Government Services Canada, Ottawa, ON K1A 0S9, Canada. TEL 613-951-7277. Circ: 25,000.

355 CAN
CANADA. DEPARTMENT OF NATIONAL DEFENCE. DIRECTORATE OF HISTORY. MONOGRAPH SERIES. Text in English. 1976. irreg. price varies. **Document type:** *Monographic series, Trade.*
Supersedes (in 1983): Canada. Department of National Defence. Directorate of History. Occasional Paper
Published by: Government of Canada Publications, Publishing and Depository Services, Public Works and Government Services Canada, Ottawa, ON K1A 0S9, Canada. TEL 613-951-7277.

CANADA. DEPARTMENT OF NATIONAL DEFENCE. PERFORMANCE REPORT. *see* PUBLIC ADMINISTRATION

355 CAN ISSN 1498-3796
CANADA. DEPARTMENT OF NATIONAL DEFENSE. REPORT ON PLANS AND PRIORITIES. Text in English. a.
Published by: Department of National Defence, Major-General George R Pearkes Bldg, 101 Colonel By Dr, Ottawa, ON K1A 0K2, Canada. TEL 613-995-2534, FAX 613-995-2610, information@forces.gc.ca, http://www.forces.gc.ca.

355 351 CAN ISSN 1912-5178
UA600
CANADA. HOUSE OF COMMONS. STANDING COMMITTEE ON NATIONAL DEFENCE. MINUTES OF PROCEEDINGS. Text in English. 1989. irreg. **Document type:** *Government.*
Supersedes in part (in 2006): Standing Committee on National Defence and Veterans Affairs. Minutes of Proceedings (1204-5179); Which was formerly (until 1995): Standing Committee on National Defence and Veterans Affairs. Minutes of Proceedings and Evidence (0846-4928); Which was formed by the merger of (195?-1989): Standing Committee on Veterans Affairs. Minutes of Proceedings and Evidence (0410-8388); (1986-1989): Standing Committee on National Defence. Minutes of Proceedings and Evidence (0846-4936)
Related titles: French ed.: Canada. Chambre des Communes. Comite Permanent de la Defense Nationale. Proces-verbal. ISSN 1912-516X. 1996.
Published by: Canada, House of Commons. Standing Committee on National Defence, Sixth Flr, 180 Wellington St, Ottawa, ON K1A 0A6, Canada. TEL 613-995-9461, FAX 613-995-2106, NDDN@parl.gc.ca, http://cmte.parl.gc.ca/cmte/CommitteeHome.aspx?Lang=1&PARLSES=391&JNT=0&SELID=e17_&COM=10470.

CANADA. NATIONAL BATTLEFIELDS COMMISSION. PERFORMANCE REPORT. *see* PUBLIC ADMINISTRATION

355 CAN ISSN 1924-9209
CANADA REMEMBERS TIMES. VETERANS' WEEK SPECIAL EDITION. Text in English. 2006. a. free (effective 2011). back issues avail. **Document type:** *Newspaper, Government.*
Related titles: Online - full text ed.
Published by: Veterans Affairs Canada/Anciens Combattants Canada, PO Box 7700, Charlottetown, PE C1A 8M9, Canada. TEL 902-566-8567, 866-522-2122, information@vac-acc.gc.ca.

CANADA. VETERANS AFFAIRS CANADA. PERFORMANCE REPORT. *see* PUBLIC ADMINISTRATION

358.4 CAN ISSN 1916-7032
THE CANADIAN AIR FORCE JOURNAL. Text in English. 2008. q. back issues avail. **Document type:** *Journal, Trade.* **Description:** Dedicated to disseminating the ideas and opinions of Air Force personnel, and also those civilians who have an interest in issues of aerospace power.
Related titles: Online - full text ed.: ISSN 1916-7040. free (effective 2011); French ed.: Revue de la Force Aerienne du Canada. ISSN 1916-7059.
Published by: Canadian Forces Aerospace Warfare Centre, Major-General George R. Pearkes Bldg, 101 Colonel By Dr, Ottawa, ON K1A 0K2, Canada. TEL 613-995-2534, FAX 613-992-4739, http://www.airforce.forces.gc.ca/cfawc/Index_e.asp. Ed. William March.

355.4 CAN ISSN 1713-773X
CA1DN12-11
THE CANADIAN ARMY JOURNAL. Text in English, French. 1998. q.
Formerly (until 2004): Army Doctrine and Training Bulletin (1480-9826)
Related titles: Online - full text ed.: ISSN 1712-9745; French ed.: L' Armee du Canada. Journal. ISSN 1712-9753. 1998.
Indexed: A26, CPerI, G05, G06, G07, G08, I05.
Published by: Department of National Defence, Major-General George R Pearkes Bldg, 101 Colonel By Dr, Ottawa, ON K1A 0K2, Canada. TEL 613-995-2534, FAX 613-995-2610, information@forces.gc.ca, http://www.forces.gc.ca.

355 CAN ISSN 1910-7021
CANADIAN DEFENCE AND SECURITY DIRECTORY. Text in English. 1995. a. **Document type:** *Directory, Trade.*
Former titles (until 2006): Canadian Defence & Security Almanac (1910-7013); (until 2005): Canadian Defence Almanac (1484-9674)
Published by: Canadian Association of Defence and Security Industries, 130 Slater St, Ste 1250, Ottawa, ON K1P 6E2, Canada. TEL 613-235-5337, FAX 613-235-0784, cadsi@defenceandsecurity.ca, https://www.defenceandsecurity.ca/public/index.asp.

355 CAN ISSN 1922-7388
CANADIAN FORCES CHAPLAIN BRANCH. DIALOGUE. Text in English. 1982. q. **Document type:** *Government.*
Published by: Canadian Forces Chaplain Branch, c/o Department of National Defence, National Defence Headquarters, 101 Colonel By Dr, Ottawa, ON K1A 0K2, Canada. TEL 613-995-2534, 800-467-9877, FAX 613-992-4739, 800-467-9877, Christopher.Ryan@forces.gc.ca, http://www.forces.gc.ca.

355.1 CAN ISSN 0706-0823
CANADIAN FORCES PERSONNEL NEWSLETTER/FORCES CANADIENNES. BULLETIN DU PERSONNEL. Text in English, French. 1970. m. **Document type:** *Newsletter.*
Former titles (until 1978): Canadian Armed Forces Personnel Newsletter (0706-0572); (until 1975): Canadian Forces Personnel Newsletter (0715-8424)
Published by: Canadian Armed Forces, Office of the Assistant Deputy Minister, Major-General George R Pearkes Bldg, 15NT, 101 Colonel By Dr, Ottawa, ON K1A 0K2, Canada. TEL 613-995-2534, FAX 613-995-2610, information@forces.gc.ca.

355.821 CAN ISSN 0068-8843
UA602.R64
CANADIAN GUNNER. Text in English. 1965. a. CAD 15. back issues avail.
Published by: (Royal Regiment of Canadian Artillery), Leech Printing Ltd., 18th and Park, Brandon, MB R7A 5B8, Canada. TEL 204-728-3037, FAX 204-727-3338.

355.00971 CAN ISSN 1195-8472
F1028
CANADIAN MILITARY HISTORY. Text in English. 1992. q. CAD 80 domestic to institutions; USD 90 foreign to institutions (effective 2012). adv. bk.rev. illus. back issues avail. **Document type:** *Journal, Academic/Scholarly.* **Description:** Explores the Canadian military experience from the earliest days to the present.
Related titles: Online - full text ed.; Supplement(s): Book Review Supplement.
Indexed: AmH&L, C03, CA, CBCARef, CPerI, HistAb, P48, PQC, T02.
Published by: (Wilfrid Laurier University, Laurier Center for Military, Strategic and Disarmament Studies), Wilfrid Laurier University Press, 75 University Ave W, Waterloo, ON N2L 3C5, Canada. TEL 519-884-0710 ext 6124, FAX 519-725-1399, press@wlu.ca, http://www.wlupress.wlu.ca. Ed. Roger Sarty. adv.: page CAD 400.

355 CAN ISSN 1492-465X
CA1DN12-8
CANADIAN MILITARY JOURNAL (OTTAWA)/REVUE MILITAIRE CANADIENNE. Text in Multiple languages. 2000. q. free (effective 2010).
Related titles: Online - full text ed.: ISSN 1492-0786; French ed.: Revue Militaire Canadienne (Ottawa). ISSN 1492-0808.
Indexed: C03, CBCARef, P48, PQC.
Published by: (Canadian Forces, Canada. Department of National Defence), Minister of National Defence, Department of National Defence, Defence Headquarters, 101 Colonel By Dr, Ottawa, ON K1A 0K2, Canada. http://www.forces.gc.ca/. Ed. David Bashow TEL 613-541-6000 ext 6148.

359 CAN ISSN 0008-4972
CANADIAN SAILOR. Text in English, French. 1950. m. CAD 15.
Published by: Seafarers International Union of Canada, 1333 rue St Jacques, Montreal, PQ H3C 4K2, Canada. FAX 514-931-3667. Ed. D McMillian. Circ: 5,000 (controlled).

355 CAN ISSN 0701-0427
CANADIAN SOCIETY OF MILITARY MEDALS AND INSIGNIA. JOURNAL. Text in English. 1965. q. CAD 15. adv. bk.rev. index. **Document type:** *Monographic series, Academic/Scholarly.* **Description:** Aims to advance the study of military orders, decorations, medals and related insignia along educational and historical lines.
Published by: Canadian Society of Military Medals and Insignia, 34 Blue Spruce Cres, Winnipeg, MB R2M 4C2, Canada. TEL 204-255-8537. Ed. Ian C Steingaszner. Adv. contact Geoff Todd. Circ: 700. **Subscr. to:** 1531 Bayview Ave, P O Box 43536, Toronto, ON M4G 4G8, Canada.

355.033 CAN ISSN 0843-6940
THE CANADIAN STRATEGIC FORECAST. Text in English. 1982. a. price varies. **Document type:** *Proceedings.*
Formerly (until 1990): The Canadian Strategic Review (0824-2216)
Published by: Canadian Institute of Strategic Studies, 10 Adelaide St E, Suite 400, Toronto, ON M5C 1J3, Canada. TEL 416-322-8128, FAX 416-322-8129, info@ciss.ca, http://www.ciss.ca.

CANADIAN WARGAMER'S JOURNAL. *see* SPORTS AND GAMES

355 AUS ISSN 0069-0104
➤ **CANBERRA PAPERS ON STRATEGY AND DEFENCE.** Text in English. 1968. irreg., latest no.171. price varies. abstr.,bibl.,charts,illus,maps. back issues avail. **Document type:** *Monographic series, Academic/Scholarly.* **Description:** Contains information on strategic and defense topics.
Related titles: Online - full text ed.: free (effective 2009).
Indexed: AMB, LID&ISL.
—BLDSC (3046.280000), IE, Ingenta.
Published by: Strategic and Defence Studies Centre, Australian National University, Coombs Bldg # 9, Fellows Rd, Canberra, ACT 0200, Australia. TEL 61-2-61259921, FAX 61-2-61259926, sdsc@anu.edu.au, http://sdsc.anu.edu.au. Ed., R&P, Adv. contact Kitty Eggerking.

358.4 USA
CAPITAL FLYER. Text in English. 1972. w. (Fri.). free to military (effective 2008). 32 p./no. 6 cols./p.; **Document type:** *Newspaper.*
Published by: Comprint, 9030 Comprint Ct., Gaithersburg, MD 20877. TEL 240-473-7538. Ed. Alex Saltekoff. Circ: 15,000 (paid and controlled).

CARRIER AVIATION NEWS. *see* AERONAUTICS AND SPACE FLIGHT

355.26029 USA ISSN 1521-1673
UA23.3
CARROLL'S DEFENSE INDUSTRY CHARTS. Text in English. 1997. q. looseleaf. USD 1,950 (effective 2011). **Document type:** *Directory, Government.* **Description:** Organization charts for 175 of the major aerospace, electronics and military contractors retained by the Department of Defense. Contact information for nearly 9,000 personnel associated with more than 1,200 US defense contractors.
Former titles (until 1997): Defense Industry Service; Defense Organization Service - Industry
Related titles: CD-ROM ed.: USD 1,400; Online - full text ed.
Published by: Carroll Publishing, 4701 Sangamore Rd, Ste S 155, Bethesda, MD 20816. TEL 800-336-4240, FAX 301-263-9801, info@carrollpub.com.

355 USA
UA23.A1
CARROLL'S DEFENSE ORGANIZATION CHARTS. Text in English. 199?. 8/yr. looseleaf. USD 2,050 (effective 2011). charts. **Document type:** *Directory, Government.* **Description:** Includes 213 organization charts covering nearly 12,000 key officials in the Defense Department.
Former titles: Defense Organization Service; Federal Organization Service - Military
Related titles: CD-ROM ed.: ISSN 1521-1681.
Published by: Carroll Publishing, 4701 Sangamore Rd, Ste S 155, Bethesda, MD 20816. TEL 800-336-4240, FAX 301-263-9801, info@carrollpub.com.

355 GBR ISSN 1367-5907
UG405
➤ **CASEMATE.** Text in English. 1976. 3/yr. free to members (effective 2009). bk.rev. 150 p./no.; back issues avail.; reprints avail. **Document type:** *Newsletter, Academic/Scholarly.* **Description:** Devoted to the history and development of military architecture, fortification theory and practice, and related military history throughout the ages.
Formerly (until 198?): Fort (0261-586X)
Related titles: Microfiche ed.
Indexed: AIAP, API, AmH&L, B24, BrArAb, CA, HistAb, NumL, T02.
—BLDSC (4014.820000), IE, Ingenta. **CCC.**
Published by: Fortress Study Group, c/o Alan Fyson, Membership Secretary, 4 Acacia Close, Orpington, BR5 1LL, United Kingdom. TEL 44-168-9826884, http://www.fortress-study-group.com. Ed. Charles Blackwood TEL 44-1352-741556.

355.31 357 USA ISSN 2157-8605
UE1
THE CAVALRY & ARMOR JOURNAL. Text in English. 2008. bi-m. **Document type:** *Journal, Trade.*
Formerly (until 2010): The Armor & Cavalry Journal (1942-8790)
Indexed: CA, M05.
—IE.
Published by: U.S. Armor Association, PO Box 607, Fort Knox, KY 40121. TEL 502-942-6170, FAX 502-942-8624, http://www.usarmor-assn.org/.

THE CAVALRY JOURNAL. *see* HISTORY—History Of North And South America

CENTRAL INTELLIGENCE AGENCY. MONOGRAPHS. ALL COMMUNIST COUNTRIES REPORTS. *see* POLITICAL SCIENCE—International Relations

CENTRAL INTELLIGENCE AGENCY. MONOGRAPHS. CHINA REPORTS. *see* POLITICAL SCIENCE—International Relations

CENTRAL INTELLIGENCE AGENCY. MONOGRAPHS. COMMONWEALTH OF INDEPENDENT STATES REPORT. *see* POLITICAL SCIENCE—International Relations

CENTRE DE LA FAMILLE VALCARTIER. RAPPORT ANNUEL. *see* SOCIAL SERVICES AND WELFARE

359 ARG ISSN 0009-0123
CENTRO NAVAL. BOLETIN. Text in Spanish; Abstracts in English, Spanish. 1882. q. USD 60 (effective 2000). adv. bk.rev. bibl. index. **Document type:** *Bulletin, Government.*
Related titles: Microform ed.
Indexed: AMB, INIS AtomInd.
Published by: Centro Naval Argentina, Florida 826, Buenos Aires, 1005, Argentina. TEL 54-114-3110041, FAX 54-114-3110123, webmaster@centro-naval-argentina.org, http://www.centro-naval-argentina.org. Ed. Rodolfo Remotti. Circ: 5,000 (controlled).

355 900 ITA ISSN 2037-9242
CENTRO UNIVERSITARIO DI STUDI E RICERCHE STORICO - MILITARI. COLLANA. Text in Italian. 2006. irreg. **Document type:** *Monographic series, Academic/Scholarly.*
Published by: (Centro Interuniversitario di Studi e Ricerche Storico - Militari), Edizioni Unicopli, Via Festa del Perdono 12, Milan, 20122, Italy. TEL 39-02-42299666, http://www.edizioniunicopli.it.

355 USA
CHAIRMAN OF THE JOINT CHIEFS OF STAFF STRATEGY ESSAY COMPETITION ESSAYS. Abbreviated title: C J C S Strategy Essay Competition Essays. Text in English. 1984. a., latest vol.28. free (effective 2009). **Document type:** *Government.*
Formerly (until 1998): Essays on Strategy (1045-1544)
Related titles: Online - full text ed.
Published by: National Defense University (Subsidiary of: U.S. Department of Defense), Fort Lesley J McNair, 300 Fifth Ave. Bldg 62, Washington, DC 20319. TEL 202-685-4210, FAX 202-685-4806, ndupress@ndu.edu.

355 900 FRA ISSN 1767-8765
CHAMPS DE BATAILLE. Text in French. 2004. bi-m. EUR 54 domestic (effective 2009). **Document type:** *Magazine, Consumer.*
Published by: Conflits et Strategie, 470 Av. Jean Monnet, Saint-Cannat, 13760, France. TEL 33-4-42201525, FAX 33-4-42201963, societe@conflits-strategie.com.

355 900 FRA ISSN 1957-2409
CHAMPS DE BATAILLE. THEMATIQUE. Text in French. 2007. q. EUR 35 domestic; EUR 56 in Europe; EUR 56 DOM-TOM; EUR 60 elsewhere (effective 2007). **Document type:** *Magazine, Consumer.*
Published by: Conflits et Strategie, 470 Av. Jean Monnet, Saint-Cannat, 13760, France. TEL 33-4-42201525, FAX 33-4-42201963, societe@conflits-strategie.com.

LES CHAMPS DE MARS. *see* SOCIAL SCIENCES: COMPREHENSIVE WORKS

355 USA ISSN 1937-5271
THE CHANGING FACE OF WAR. Text in English. 2007 (Dec.). irreg., latest 2010. price varies. back issues avail. **Document type:** *Monographic series, Academic/Scholarly.*
Published by: Praeger Publishers (Subsidiary of: Greenwood Publishing Group Inc.), 88 Post Rd W, Westport, CT 06881. TEL 800-368-6868, tech.support@greenwood.com, http://www.greenwood.com. Ed. James Carafano.

CHELIANG YU DONGLI JISHU/VEHICLE & POWER TECHNOLOGY. *see* TRANSPORTATION—Automobiles

CHEMICAL AND BIOLOGICAL DEFENSE INFORMATION ANALYSIS CENTER. NEWSLETTER. *see* ENGINEERING—Chemical Engineering

CHEMICAL DISARMAMENT. *see* POLITICAL SCIENCE

338.473983 GBR ISSN 1749-1320
CHILE DEFENCE & SECURITY REPORT. Text in English. 2005. a. EUR 820, USD 1,030 combined subscription per issue (print & email eds.) (effective 2010). **Document type:** *Report, Trade.* **Description:** Provides professionals, consultancies, government departments, regulatory bodies and researchers with independent forecasts and regional competitive intelligence on the Chilean defence and security industry.
Related titles: E-mail ed.
Indexed: A15, ABIn, B01, P48, P51, P52, PQC.
Published by: Business Monitor International Ltd., Senator House, 85 Queen Victoria St, London, EC4V 4AB, United Kingdom. TEL 44-20-72480468, FAX 44-20-72480467, subs@businessmonitor.com.

338.473 951 GBR ISSN 1749-1339
CHINA DEFENCE & SECURITY REPORT. Text in English. 2005. q. EUR 820, USD 1,030 combined subscription (print & email eds.) (effective 2010). **Document type:** *Report, Trade.* **Description:** Provides professionals, consultancies, government departments, regulatory bodies and researchers with independent forecasts and regional competitive intelligence on the Chinese defence and security industry.
Related titles: E-mail ed.
Indexed: B01.
Published by: Business Monitor International Ltd., Senator House, 85 Queen Victoria St, London, EC4V 4AB, United Kingdom. TEL 44-20-72480468, FAX 44-20-72480467, subs@businessmonitor.com.

355 951 USA ISSN 1943-0817
CHINA MARITIME STUDIES. Text in English. 2008 (Aug.). irreg. price varies. back issues avail. **Document type:** *Journal, Academic/Scholarly.* **Description:** Contains research projects of particular interest to policy makers, scholars, and analysts.
Related titles: Online - full text ed.: ISSN 1943-0825. free (effective 2010).
Published by: Naval War College Press, 686 Cushing Rd, Newport, RI 02841. TEL 401-841-2236, FAX 401-841-6309, press@nwc.navy.mil.

355.0751 GBR ISSN 1740-9772
CHINESE MILITARY UPDATE. Text in English. 2003. 10/yr. GBP 50; GBP 10 per issue (effective 2006). **Document type:** *Bulletin, Trade.* **Description:** Designed to look at specific military developments and issues in the country. Provides an objective and balanced analysis of the world's largest military force.
Related titles: Online - full text ed.
—CCC.
Published by: Royal United Services Institute, Whitehall, London, SW1A 2ET, United Kingdom. TEL 44-20-77472600, FAX 44-20-73210943, media@rusi.org.

359 004 USA ISSN 1047-9988
CHIPS MAGAZINE. Text in English. 198?. q.
Formerly (until 198?): Chips Ahoy (0887-4263)
Related titles: Online - full text ed.
Indexed: G06, G07, G08, I05.
Published by: Navy Regional Data Automation Center (N A R D A C), Commanding Officer, Norfolk, VA 23511.

355 USA
CITIZEN'S REPORT ON THE MILITARY AND THE ENVIRONMENT. Text in English. m. free. **Document type:** *Newsletter.* **Description:** Covers current trends in environmental restoration and cleanup of military installations, federal facilities, and brownfields sites emphasizing the issues of community and public participation.
Published by: Pacific Studies Center, 222 B View St, Mountain View, CA 94041. TEL 650-969-1545, FAX 650-968-1126. Ed., R&P Lenny Siegel. **Co-sponsor:** Center for Public Environmental Oversight.

CIVIL WAR TIMES; a magazine for persons interested in the American Civil War, its people, and its era. *see* HISTORY—History Of North And South America

CIVIL WARS. *see* POLITICAL SCIENCE—International Relations

355 USA
CIVILIAN-BASED DEFENSE. Text in English. 1982. 4/yr. looseleaf. USD 15 (effective 1998). bk.rev. back issues avail. **Description:** Explores civilian-based defense, a strategy in which well prepared but unarmed civilians resist invasions and coups d'etat through noncooperation, strikes, demonstrations, and sanctions.
Formerly (until 1992): Civilian - Based Defense: News and Opinion (0886-6015)
Published by: Civilian-Based Defense Association, 333 State St, Salem, OR 97301. pbergel@igc.apc.org. Ed. Peter Bergel. Circ: 500.

CIVILIAN CONGRESS; includes a directory of persons holding executive branch-military office in Congress contrary to constitutional prohibition (Art.1, Sec.6, Cl.2) of concurrent office-holding. *see* LAW

CIVILIAN JOB NEWS. *see* OCCUPATIONS AND CAREERS

355 371.42 GBR ISSN 1746-8426
CIVVY STREET. Text in English. 2005. bi-m. free to qualified personnel (effective 2010). adv. back issues avail. **Document type:** *Magazine, Consumer.* **Description:** Aims to help military personnel to successfully make the move into a new civilian life.
Related titles: Online - full text ed.
—CCC.
Published by: Craven Publishing Ltd, 15-39 Durham St, Kinning Park, Glasgow, G41 1BS, United Kingdom. TEL 44-141-4190044, FAX 44-141-4190077, enquiries@cravenpublishing.co.uk, http://www.cravenpublishing.com/. Ed. James Glasgow. Adv. contact Ian Carr. color page GBP 3,495.

388.04355 GBR ISSN 1473-7779
CLASSIC MILITARY VEHICLE. Abbreviated title: C M V. Text in English. 2001. m. GBP 43.92 domestic; GBP 49.44 in Europe; GBP 54.96 elsewhere (effective 2010). adv. illus. back issues avail. **Document type:** *Magazine, Consumer.* **Description:** Contains detailed articles and features on both modern and historic military vehicles.
Related titles: Online - full text ed.
Published by: Kelsey Publishing Ltd., Cudham Tithe Barn, Berry's Hill, Cudham, Kent TN16 3AG, United Kingdom. TEL 44-1959-541444, FAX 44-1959-541400, info@kelsey.co.uk, http://www.kelsey.co.uk. Ed. John Blackman. Adv. contact Julia Johnston TEL 44-1733-353353.

359 PRT ISSN 1647-404X
CLUBE MILITAR NAVAL. ANAIS. Text in Portuguese. 1870. a. adv. bk.rev. bibl.; charts; illus.; stat. index. **Document type:** *Yearbook, Consumer.*
Indexed: AMB, ASFA, B21, ESPM.
Published by: Clube Militar Naval, Ave Defensores de Chaves 26, Lisbon, 11000-177, Portugal. TEL 351-21-3542122, FAX 351-21-3571641, cmnaval@cmnaval.com, http://www.cmnaval.com. Circ: 2,000 (controlled).

355 BRA ISSN 0101-6547
U4
CLUBE MILITAR. REVISTA. Text in Portuguese. 1926. bi-m. free. adv. bk.rev. **Description:** Covers the history, economics, politics, and strategy of soldiering.
Published by: Clube Militar, Av Rio Branco, 251 9, Centro, Rio De Janeiro, RJ 20040-009, Brazil. TEL 55-21-220-9076. Circ: 40,000.

359 BRA ISSN 0102-0382
V5
CLUBE NAVAL. REVISTA. Text in Portuguese. 1888. 4/yr. free to qualified personnel. adv. bk.rev.
Supersedes (in 1975): Mar (0025-2727); Which was formerly (until 1966): Clube Naval. Boletim, Proceedings
Published by: Clube Naval, Departamento Cultural, Av Rio Branco, 180 Andar 5, Centro, Rio De Janeiro, RJ 20040-003, Brazil. TEL 021-282-1273 ext. 225, FAX 021-220-8681. Circ: 9,700.

355 IRQ ISSN 1942-7166
COALITION CHRONICLE. Text in English. 2006. m. **Document type:** *Magazine, Consumer.*
Media: Online - full text.
Published by: Multi-National Corps - Iraq http://purl.access.gpo.gov/GPO/LPS94635.

355 USA ISSN 1559-6591
VG53
COAST GUARD. Text in English. 1964. m. USD 48 to non-members; USD 6 per issue to non-members; free to members (effective 2010). back issues avail. **Document type:** *Magazine, Trade.* **Description:** Designed for members of the U.S. Coast Guard.
Formerly (until 1996): Commandant's Bulletin
Related titles: Online - full text ed.: ISSN 1559-6605. 1996. free (effective 2010).
Indexed: G05, G06, G07, G08, I05.
Published by: U.S. Coast Guard, 2100 Second St, SW, Washington, DC 20593. TEL 202-267-1061, FAX 202-267-4402, gchappell@comdt.uscg.mil, http://www.uscg.mil/default.asp. Ed. Dan Tremper. **Subscr. to:** Superintendent of Documents, PO Box 371954, Pittsburgh, PA 15250. TEL 202-512-1800, FAX 202-512-2250.

355.223 USA ISSN 1079-0853
THE COAST GUARD RESERVIST. Text in English. 19??. m. back issues avail. **Document type:** *Magazine, Trade.*
Former titles (until 198?): Reservist; (until 1982): Coast Guard Reservist (0364-104X)
Related titles: Online - full text ed.: free (effective 2010).
Published by: U.S. Coast Guard, 2100 Second St, SW, Washington, DC 20593. TEL 202-267-1061, FAX 202-267-4402, gchappell@comdt.uscg.mil, http://www.uscg.mil/default.asp. Ed. Isaac D Pacheco.

COLLEGE ALUMNI AND MILITARY PUBLICATIONS. *see* COLLEGE AND ALUMNI

355.4 USA ISSN 1947-0924
THE COLLINS CENTER UPDATE. Text in English. 1999. q. back issues avail. **Document type:** *Newsletter, Trade.*
Related titles: Online - full text ed.: ISSN 1947-0932. free (effective 2009).
Published by: U.S. Army War College, Center for Strategic Leadership, 650 Wright Ave, Carlisle, PA 17013. TEL 717-245-4552, FAX 717-245-4948, CSL_Info@conus.army.mil.

338.4739861 GBR ISSN 1749-1347
COLOMBIA DEFENCE & SECURITY REPORT. Text in English. 2005. q. EUR 820, USD 1,030 combined subscription (print & email eds.) (effective 2010). **Document type:** *Report, Trade.* **Description:** Provides professionals, consultancies, government departments, regulatory bodies and researchers with independent forecasts and regional competitive intelligence on the Colombian defence and security industry.
Related titles: E-mail ed.
Indexed: B01, P34.
Published by: Business Monitor International Ltd., Senator House, 85 Queen Victoria St, London, EC4V 4AB, United Kingdom. TEL 44-20-72480468, FAX 44-20-72480467, subs@businessmonitor.com.

355.31 USA
COLORADO LEGIONNAIRE. Text in English. 1967. m. USD 1 to non-members. adv.
Published by: American Legion, Department of Colorado, 7465 East 1st Ave, Unit D, Denver, CO 80230. TEL 303-366-5201, FAX 303-366-7618. Ed. Charles Smith. Circ: 27,000.

359 FRA ISSN 0010-1834
COLS BLEUS. Text in French. 1945. 42/yr. EUR 63 domestic to individuals; EUR 63 DOM-TOM to individuals; EUR 117 elsewhere to individuals (effective 2009). adv. bk.rev.; play rev.; film rev. charts; illus.; stat. **Document type:** *Magazine, Government.* **Description:** Provides news of the French navy.
—IE, Infotrieve.
Published by: (France. Service d'Information et des Relations Publiques de la Marine), Etablissement de Communication et de Production Audiovisuelle de la Defense - E C P A D, 2 - 8 Route du Fort d'Ivry, Ivry-sur-Seine Cedex, 94205, France. TEL 33-1-45770376, FAX 33-1-45795373. Ed. C A de Drezigue. Adv. contact Didier Contoux. Circ: 24,000.

COMBAT AIRCRAFT. *see* AERONAUTICS AND SPACE FLIGHT

355 GBR ISSN 0955-9841
U225
COMBAT & SURVIVAL MAGAZINE. Abbreviated title: C & S. Text in English. 1987. m. GBP 40.50 domestic; GBP 48 in Europe; GBP 52.95 elsewhere (effective 2010). adv. back issues avail. **Document type:** *Magazine, Consumer.* **Description:** Contains topics, ranging from comprehensive kit advice, weapons and hardware reviews, and trouble-zone news to battle tactics.
Related titles: Online - full text ed.: GBP 27.30 (effective 2010).
Published by: M A I Publications, Revenue Chambers, St. Peter's St, Huddersfield, W Yorkshire HD1 1DL, United Kingdom. TEL 44-1484-435011, FAX 44-1484-422177, martialartsltd@btconnect.com, http://www.martialartsltd.co.uk. Ed. Bob Morrison. Adv. contact Moira E Spencer. **Dist. by:** Seymour Distribution Ltd.

THE COMBAT EDGE. *see* AERONAUTICS AND SPACE FLIGHT

355.11 USA ISSN 0887-235X
COMBAT STUDIES INSTITUTE. U.S. ARMY COMMAND AND GENERAL STAFF COLLEGE. RESEARCH SURVEY. Text in English. 1982. a. **Document type:** *Government.* **Description:** Provides information on General Services Administration, Defense Logistics Agency, US army Material Command, US Transportation Command, US Transcom Component commands and Direct Reporting Unit, US Army Medical Command and US Total Army Personnel Command.
Indexed: LID&ISL.
Published by: Combat Studies Institute, US Army Command & General Staff College, Fort Leavenworth, KS 66027. TEL 913-684-9327, FAX 913-684-9328, http://cgsc.leavenworth.army.mil/index.asp.

355 PER ISSN 1680-0001
EL COMBATIENTE. Text in Spanish. 2000. bi-m.
Media: Online - full text.
Published by: Ejercito de Peru, Ave Boulevard s-n, Sab Borja, Lima, 41, Peru. TEL 51-1-3171700, FAX 51-1-4369112, oie@ejercito.mil.pe, http://www.ejercito.mil.pe/.

M

355 USA ISSN 0010-2474
COMMAND; Christian perspectives on life in the military. Text in English. 1952. 10/yr. USD 20 domestic to non-members; USD 25 foreign to non-members; free to members (effective 2004). bk.rev. 16 p./no.; back issues avail. **Document type:** *Magazine, Consumer.*
Description: Covers subjects pertinent to Christianity and military life.
Formerly (until 1956): Officers' Christian Union. Bulletin (0471-1505)
Related titles: Fax ed.
Published by: Officers' Christian Fellowship of the United States of America, 3784 S. Inca St., Englewood, CO 80110-3405. TEL 800-424-1984, http://www.ocfusa.org. Ed., Pub., R&P Mike Edwards. Circ: 10,000 (controlled).

COMMANDO; for action and adventure. *see* LITERATURE—Adventure And Romance

341.72 USA ISSN 1947-2323
JZ5588
COMMON DEFENSE QUARTERLY. Abbreviated title: C D Q. Text in English. 200?. q. free to qualified personnel (effective 2009). back issues avail. **Document type:** *Magazine, Trade.* **Description:** Provides thought pieces and factual information for the international defense cooperation community.
Formerly (until 2009): Common Defense Forum
Related titles: Online - full text ed.: ISSN 1947-2331.
Published by: (International Defence Corporation), IDEEA, Inc., 6233 Nelway Dr, McLean, VA 22101. TEL 703-760-0762, FAX 703-760-0764, qwhiteree@ideea.com, http://www.ideea.com/.

CONCISE B2B AEROSPACE (ONLINE); aerospace news from the commonwealth of independent states. *see* AERONAUTICS AND SPACE FLIGHT

CONFLICT, SECURITY & DEVELOPMENT. *see* POLITICAL SCIENCE—International Relations

341.72 355 GBR ISSN 1467-8799
THE CONFLICT, SECURITY & DEVELOPMENT GROUP. WORKING PAPERS. Text in English. 1999 (Sept). irreg. back issues avail. **Document type:** *Monographic series.* **Description:** Consists of five studies carried out during 1999-2001 which examine conceptual, policy-relevant and regional-specific issues in the field of security-sector reform.
Related titles: Online - full text ed.
Published by: The Conflict, Security & Development Group (Subsidiary of: University of London King's College, Centre for Defence Studies), King's College London, Strand, London, WC2R 2LS, United Kingdom. TEL 44-207-8481984, FAX 44-207-8482748, csdg@kcl.ac.uk.

355 USA ISSN 1544-1903
CONNECTICUT GUARDIAN. Text in English. 2000. m. back issues avail. **Document type:** *Magazine, Trade.*
Related titles: Online - full text ed.: ISSN 2157-4359.
Published by: Connecticut National Guard, Public Affairs Office, 360 Broad St, Hartford, CT 06105. TEL 860-524-4911, FAX 860-524-4902, http://www.ng.mil/CT/default.aspx.

355 DEU ISSN 1812-1098
JZ5588
CONNECTIONS (GARMISCH-PARTENKIRCHEN). Text in English. 2002. 3/yr. free. **Document type:** *Journal, Academic/Scholarly.*
Description: Provided to defense and security related institutions, mainly governmental and educational, in countries of the Euro-Atlantic Partnership Council.
Related titles: Online - full text ed.: ISSN 1812-2973; Russian ed.: ISSN 1812-1101.
Indexed: P02, P10, P48, P52, P53, P54, PQC.
—CCC.
Published by: Partnership for Peace, Consortium of Defense Academies and Security Studies Institutes, Gernackerstrasse 2, Bldg 102, Rm 310B, Garmisch-Partenkirchen, 82467, Germany. TEL 49-8821-7502712, FAX 49-8821-7502852, pfpcpublications@marshallcenter.org, https://consortium.pims.org. Ed. Sean S Costigan.

355 USA ISSN 1932-295X
CONTEMPORARY MILITARY, STRATEGIC, AND SECURITY ISSUES. Text in English. 2006 (Nov.). irreg., latest 2010. price varies. back issues avail. **Document type:** *Monographic series, Academic/Scholarly.* **Description:** Provides examination and current perspectives on controversial and in-the-news military, strategic, and security issues both at home and around the world.
Published by: Praeger Publishers (Subsidiary of: Greenwood Publishing Group Inc.), 88 Post Rd W, Westport, CT 06881. TEL 800-368-6868, tech.support@greenwood.com, http://www.greenwood.com.

355 USA ISSN 0883-6884
CONTRIBUTIONS IN MILITARY STUDIES. Text in English. 1969. irreg., latest 2007. price varies. back issues avail. **Document type:** *Monographic series, Academic/Scholarly.*
Formerly (19??): Contributions in Military History (0084-9251)
Indexed: A22.
—BLDSC (3460.805000), IE, Ingenta. **CCC.**
Published by: Greenwood Publishing Group Inc. (Subsidiary of: A B C - C L I O), 88 Post Rd W, PO Box 5007, Westport, CT 06881. TEL 203-226-3571, 800-225-5800, FAX 877-231-6980, sales@greenwood.com, http://www.greenwood.com.

355 IRL ISSN 0010-9460
AN COSANTOIR; Irish defence forces magazine. Text in English. 1940. 10/yr. EUR 22.20 in Ireland & UK; EUR 39.30 elsewhere; EUR 2.20 newsstand/cover (effective 2005). adv. bk.rev. illus. index. back issues avail. **Document type:** *Magazine, Trade.* **Description:** For troops; chronicles the Irish Defence Forces involvement with United Nations Peacekeeping Missions.
Related titles: Microform ed.: (from PQC).
Indexed: LID&ISL.
Published by: Defence Forces, Public Relations Section, Defence Forces Headquarters, Parkgate, Dublin, 8, Ireland. armypr@iol.ie. Circ: 6,600 (paid).

THE COURIER (BROCKTON); North America's foremost miniature wargaming magazine. *see* HOBBIES

327.12 USA ISSN 1076-8645
COVERT INTELLIGENCE LETTER. Text in English. 1974. bi-m. USD 18 for 2 yrs. domestic to individuals; USD 20 for 2 yrs. foreign to individuals; USD 20 for 2 yrs. to institutions (effective 2000). bk.rev. **Document type:** *Newsletter.*
Published by: Horizon, PO Box 67, St. Charles, MO 63302. TEL 314-731-0993, FAX 314-731-0993. Ed. W Waltzer. Circ: 300.

338.473972 GBR ISSN 1749-1355
CROATIA DEFENCE & SECURITY REPORT. Text in English. 2005. q. EUR 820, USD 1,030 combined subscription (print & email eds.) (effective 2010). **Document type:** *Report, Trade.* **Description:** Provides professionals, consultancies, government departments, regulatory bodies and researchers with independent forecasts and regional competitive intelligence on the Croatian defence and security industry.
Related titles: E-mail ed.
Indexed: A15, ABIn, B01, B02, B15, B17, B18, G04, I05, P48, P51, P52, PQC.
Published by: Business Monitor International Ltd., Senator House, 85 Queen Victoria St, London, EC4V 4AB, United Kingdom. TEL 44-20-72480468, FAX 44-20-72480467, subs@businessmonitor.com.

358.4 GBR ISSN 1360-9009
CROSS & COCKADE INTERNATIONAL. Abbreviated title: C C I. Text in English. 1970. q. free to members (effective 2009). bk.rev.; video rev. illus.; maps. 68 p./no. 2 cols./p.; **Document type:** *Journal, Academic/Scholarly.* **Description:** Contains articles by aviation historians, as well as well as photographs from private collections and accurate scale three-views and three quarter-view cut away drawings.
Formerly (until 1986): Cross & Cockade Great Britain Journal
Published by: Cross and Cockade International, Cragg Cottage, The Crag, Bramham, Wetherby, W Yorks LS23 6QB, United Kingdom. TEL 44-1937-845320, http://www.crossandcockade.com. Ed. Mick Davis. Adv. contact Marcus Williams. **Subscr. to:** c/o Roger Tisdale, Membership Secretary, 5 Cave Dr, Downend, Bristol BS16 2TL, United Kingdom. TEL 44-117-9395945, rtbr14643@bluemoonyonder.co.uk.

355 CHL ISSN 0718-3771
CUADERNO DE DIFUSION. Text in Spanish. 1998. a. **Document type:** *Monographic series, Academic/Scholarly.*
Formerly (until 2002): Cuadernos de Difusion (Print) (0717-4187)
Media: CD-ROM.
Published by: Academia de Guerra del Ejercito de Chile, Valenzuela Llanos No. 623, Campo Militar La Reina del Gral., Rene Scheider Sh., Santiago, Chile. TEL 56-2-2907458, http://www.acague.cl/.

355 GBR ISSN 0963-0562
CURRENT DECISIONS REPORTS. Text in English. 1991. q. **Document type:** *Monographic series, Academic/Scholarly.*
—IE, Ingenta.
Published by: Oxford Research Group, Wytham, Oxford, Oxfordshire OX2 8QN, United Kingdom. TEL 44-1865-242819, FAX 44-1865-794652, org@oxfordresearchgroup.org.uk, http://www.oxfordresearchgroup.org.uk.

355.347 200 USA ISSN 2150-5853
▼ **CURTANA**; sword of mercy. Text in English. 2009. q. free (effective 2010). **Document type:** *Journal, Academic/Scholarly.* **Description:** An independent journal on chapliancy history.
Media: Online - full content.
Published by: Scriptorium Novum Press, LLC, PO Box 95, Seabeck, WA 98380. TEL 360-779-2862, curana.editor@gmail.comg.

355.8 USA ISSN 1089-5663
UC263
CUSTOMER ASSISTANCE HANDBOOK. Text in English. a.
Published by: U.S. Defense Logistics Agency, 8725 John J Kingman Rd, Ste 2533, Fort Belvoir, VA 22060-6221. TEL 877-352-2255.

355 CZE ISSN 1802-4300
CZECH DEFENCE INDUSTRY & SECURITY REVIEW. Text in Czech, English. 2001. q. CZK 680 (effective 2009). adv. **Document type:** *Magazine, Trade.*
Formerly (until 2007): Czech Defence & Aviation Industry Review (1213-3531)
Published by: Military System Line s.r.o., PO Box 11, Kounice, 289 15, Czech Republic. info@msline.cz. adv.: page CZK 60,000.

338.47394371 GBR ISSN 1749-1363
CZECH REPUBLIC DEFENCE & SECURITY REPORT. Text in English. 2005. a. EUR 820, USD 1,030 combined subscription per issue (print & email eds.) (effective 2010). **Document type:** *Report, Trade.* **Description:** Provides professionals, consultancies, government departments, regulatory bodies and researchers with independent forecasts and regional competitive intelligence on the Czech defence and security industry.
Related titles: E-mail ed.
Indexed: A15, ABIn, B02, B15, B17, B18, G04, I05, P48, P51, P52, PQC.
Published by: Business Monitor International Ltd., Senator House, 85 Queen Victoria St, London, EC4V 4AB, United Kingdom. TEL 44-20-72480468, FAX 44-20-72480467, subs@businessmonitor.com.

362.4 USA ISSN 0885-6400
D A V MAGAZINE. Text in English. 1960. bi-m. USD 15 to non-members; free to members (effective 2009). back issues avail. **Document type:** *Magazine, Consumer.* **Description:** Covers issues affecting disabled veterans and their families.
Former titles (until 1985): D A V (0276-7465); (until 19??): D A V Magazine
Related titles: Audio cassette/tape ed.; Online - full text ed.: free (effective 2009).
Indexed: G06, G07, G08, I05, I07, S23.
Published by: Disabled American Veterans, PO Box 14301, Cincinnati, OH 45250. TEL 859-441-7300, 877-426-2838, FAX 859-442-2088, http://www.dav.org. Pub. Arthur H Wilson.

D C A A CONTRACT AUDIT MANUAL. (Defense Contract Audit Agency) *see* BUSINESS AND ECONOMICS—Public Finance, Taxation

D C A A OFFICES. DIRECTORY. (Defense Contract Audit Agency) *see* BUSINESS AND ECONOMICS—Public Finance, Taxation

358.4 DEU ISSN 1435-831X
D H S; Die Flugzeuge der Nationalen Volksarmee. (Diensthabendes System) Text in German. 1998. irreg., latest vol.9. EUR 14.50 newsstand/cover (effective 2009). **Document type:** *Magazine, Consumer.* **Description:** Contains articles and features on the military aircraft deployed by the former German Democratic Republic.
Published by: Buchholz Medien Verlag Druck, Arensburger Str 10, Buchholz, 31710, Germany. TEL 49-5751-96460, FAX 49-5751-964646, info@bmvd.de.

355 DEU
D I Z SCHRIFTEN. Text in German. 1989. irreg., latest vol.13, 2005. price varies. **Document type:** *Monographic series, Academic/Scholarly.*
Published by: (Dokumentations und Informations Zentrum Emslandlager), Edition Temmen, Hohenlohestr 21, Bremen, 28209, Germany. TEL 49-421-348430, FAX 49-421-348094, info@edition-temmen.de. Ed. Horst Temmen.

320 IND ISSN 0971-4391
D R D O NEWSLETTER. (Defence Research & Development Organization) Text in English. 1981. m. back issues avail. **Document type:** *Newsletter, Government.* **Description:** Highlights the achievements of DRDO,its future plans and other scientific administrative and cultural activities.
Related titles: Online - full content ed.: free (effective 2010).
Published by: (India. Defence Research & Development Organization, Great Britain. Ministry of Defence GBR), Defence Scientific Information & Documentation Centre, Metcalfe House, New Delhi, 110 054, India. TEL 91-11-23902400, FAX 91-11-23819151. Eds. B Nityanand, A L Moorthy. Circ: 2,500; 2,500 (controlled).

355.8 629.13 USA ISSN 1935-6269
UF533
D T I; the best sources for news and in-depth reporting on defense technology. (Defence Technology International) Text in English. 2007 (Jan.). 10/yr. free (effective 2008). adv. back issues avail. **Document type:** *Magazine, Trade.* **Description:** Designed for senior decision and thought leaders who need technology to be put into perspective with operations, policies, programs and funding etc.
Related titles: Online - full text ed.
Indexed: B01.
—CCC.
Published by: Aviation Week Group (Subsidiary of: McGraw-Hill Companies, Inc.), 2 Penn Plz, 25th Fl, New York, NY 10121. TEL 800-525-5003, FAX 888-385-1428, buccustserv@cdsfulfillment.com. Ed. Sharon Weinberger. Pub. Gregory Hamilton. Adv. contact Katie Taplett TEL 212-383-2335. color page USD 11,250, B&W page USD 9,670; trim 7.75 x 10.5. Circ: 37,481 (paid).

355 IRQ ISSN 1943-0442
THE DAILY CHARGE. Text in English. 200?. d. **Document type:** *Newspaper, Consumer.*
Media: Online - full text.
Published by: Multi-National Division - Baghdad http://pao.hood.army.mil/1stcavdiv/daily%20charge/dailycharge.htm.

355 USA
DAILY DEFENSE NEWS CAPSULE. Text in English. d. USD 89.95 (effective 2003). **Document type:** *Newsletter, Trade.*
Media: E-mail.
Published by: Periscope (Subsidiary of: United Communications Group), 11300 Rockville Pike, Ste 1100, Rockville, MD 20852-3030. TEL 301-287-2652, FAX 301-816-8945, periscope@ucg.com.

623.51 CHN ISSN 1004-499X
UF820
DANDAO XUEBAO/JOURNAL OF BALLISTICS. Text in Chinese. 1989. q. USD 20.80 (effective 2009). **Document type:** *Journal, Academic/Scholarly.*
Related titles: Online - full text ed.
Indexed: A28, APA, BrCerAb, C&ISA, CA/WCA, CIA, CPEI, CerAb, CivEngAb, CorrAb, E&CAJ, E11, EEA, EMA, ESPM, EngInd, EnvEAb, H15, M&TEA, M09, MBF, METADEX, SCOPUS, SolStAb, T04, WAA.
—BLDSC (4951.103000), East View.
Published by: (Zhongguo Binggong Xuehui/China Ordnance Society), Dandao Xuebao, Nanjing University of Science & Technology, 200 Xiao Ling Wei, Nanjing, 210094, China. TEL 86-25-84315487, FAX 86-25-84317482. Ed. Hongzhi Li.

359 CHN ISSN 1006-6071
DANGDAI HAIJUN/MODERN NAVY. Text in Chinese. 1987. m. USD 45.60 (effective 2009). **Document type:** *Consumer.* **Description:** Provides comprehensive coverage of international naval interests.
Formerly: Shuibing (1003-0050)
Related titles: Online - full text ed.
—East View.
Published by: Renmin Haijun Baoshe, 19-27, Xisanhuan Zhonglu, Beijing, 100841, China. TEL 86-10-66960372.

DANJIAN YU ZHIDAO XUEBAO/JOURNAL OF PROJECTILES, ROCKETS, MISSILES AND GUIDANCE. *see* AERONAUTICS AND SPACE FLIGHT

355 DNK ISSN 0011-6203
DANSK ARTILLERI-TIDSSKRIFT. Text in Danish. 1914. 6/yr. DKK 150 (effective 2008). adv. bk.rev. abstr.; charts; illus. index. **Document type:** *Newsletter, Consumer.*
Published by: Artilleriofficersforeningen/Artillery Officers Association, c/o Haerens Artilleriskole, PO Box 182, Varde, 6800, Denmark. TEL 45-76-955132, FAX 45-75-211140. adv.: page DKK 2,895. Circ: 450.

DAODAN YU HANGTIAN YUNZAI JISHU/MISSILES AND SPACE VEHICLES. *see* AERONAUTICS AND SPACE FLIGHT

355.27 359 323 USA ISSN 0747-072X
DECKPLATE. Text in English. bi-m.
Published by: U.S. Naval Sea Systems Command, 1333 Isaac Hull Ave S E, Washington Navy Yard, DC 20362. TEL 202-781-0000, http://www.navsea.navy.mil.

355 GBR ISSN 1024-2694
HC79.D4
➤ **DEFENCE AND PEACE ECONOMICS.** Text in English. 1990. bi-m. GBP 699 combined subscription in United Kingdom to institutions (print & online eds.); EUR 927, USD 1,163 combined subscription to institutions (print & online eds.) (effective 2012). adv. reprint service avail. from PSC. **Document type:** *Journal, Academic/Scholarly.* **Description:** Embraces all aspects of the economics of defence, disarmament, conversion and peace.

Formerly (until 1994): Defence Economics (1043-0717)
Related titles: Microform ed.; Online - full text ed.: ISSN 1476-8267. GBP 629 in United Kingdom to institutions; EUR 834, USD 1,046 to institutions (effective 2012) (from IngentaConnect).
Indexed: A01, A03, A08, A12, A17, A20, A22, ABIn, ASCA, B01, B06, B07, B09, BAS, CA, CurCont, E01, EconLit, I02, IBSS, JEL, LID&ISL, M05, P34, P42, P48, P51, P53, P54, PQC, R02, SCOPUS, SSCI, T02, W07.
—BLDSC (3541.488700), IE, Ingenta. **CCC.**
Published by: Routledge (Subsidiary of: Taylor & Francis Group), 4 Park Sq, Milton Park, Abingdon, Oxon OX14 4RN, United Kingdom. TEL 44-20-70176000, FAX 44-20-70176336, subscriptions@tandf.co.uk, http://www.routledge.com. Ed. Daniel Arce. Adv. contact Linda Hann TEL 44-1344-779945. **Subscr. in N. America to:** Taylor & Francis Inc., Customer Services Dept, 325 Chestnut St, 8th Fl, Philadelphia, PA 19106. TEL 215-625-8900, 800-354-1420, FAX 215-625-2940; **Subscr. to:** Taylor & Francis Ltd., Journals Customer Service, Sheepen Pl, Colchester, Essex CO3 3LP, United Kingdom. TEL 44-20-70175544, FAX 44-20-70175198.

355 GBR ISSN 1475-1798
UA11
➤ **DEFENCE AND SECURITY ANALYSIS.** Text in English. 1985. q. GBP 490 combined subscription in United Kingdom to institutions (print & online eds.); EUR 649, USD 814 combined subscription to institutions (print & online eds.) (effective 2012). adv. back issues avail.; reprint service avail. from PSC. **Document type:** *Journal, Academic/Scholarly.* **Description:** Analyzes defense and intelligence policies.
Formerly (until 2002): Defense Analysis (0743-0175)
Related titles: Online - full text ed.: ISSN 1475-1801. 1999. GBP 441 in United Kingdom to institutions; EUR 584, USD 733 to institutions (effective 2012) (from IngentaConnect).
Indexed: A01, A03, A08, A22, ABS&EES, B21, BAS, CA, CJPI, DIP, E01, E17, ESPM, GEOBASE, I02, I13, IBR, IBZ, LID&ISL, M05, M07, P02, P10, P34, P42, P47, P48, P53, P54, PQC, PSA, R02, RASB, S02, S03, SCOPUS, SociolAb, T02.
—IE, Ingenta. **CCC.**
Published by: Routledge (Subsidiary of: Taylor & Francis Group), 4 Park Sq, Milton Park, Abingdon, Oxon OX14 4RN, United Kingdom. TEL 44-20-70176000, FAX 44-20-70176336, subscriptions@tandf.co.uk, http://www.routledge.com. Ed. Martin Edmonds. Adv. contact Linda Hann TEL 44-1344-779945. **Subscr. to:** Taylor & Francis Ltd., Journals Customer Service, Sheepen Pl, Colchester, Essex CO3 3LP, United Kingdom. TEL 44-20-70175544, FAX 44-20-70175198, tf.enquiries@tfinforma.com.

355.8 GBR ISSN 2042-6240
▼ **DEFENCE AND SECURITY SYSTEMS INTERNATIONAL.** Abbreviated title: D S S I. Text in English. 2009. s-a. GBP 5.95, EUR 8, USD 8.95 per issue; free to qualified personnel (effective 2010). adv. back issues avail. **Document type:** *Magazine, Trade.* **Description:** Delivers intelligence and information on the latest projects, technical and product developments.
Related titles: Online - full text ed.: free (effective 2010).
Published by: Global Trade Media Ltd. (Subsidiary of: Progressive Media Group), Progressive House, 2 Maidstone Rd, Footscray, Sidcup, Kent DA14 5HZ, United Kingdom. TEL 44-20-82697700, FAX 44-20-82697880, info@globaltrademedia.com, http://www.globaltrademedia.com/. Eds. Andrew Tunnicliffe, John Lawrence. Pub. William Crocker.

355 USA ISSN 1011-2200
UA830
DEFENCE ASIA - PACIFIC. Key Title: Mao yu Dun. Text in Chinese, English. 1985. m. SGD 100, SGD 50 domestic; USD 80 foreign. adv. bk.rev. charts; illus. index. back issues avail. **Description:** Dedicated to international defense news and issues: military sales and aid, weapon systems, technology.
Published by: Darti Publications, c/o World Journal Bookstore, 141-07 20 Ave., Whitestone, NY 11357. TEL 779-1702, FAX 779-1703. Ed. D Gan. Circ: 22,500. **US addr.:** Gemini Consultants.

355 USA ISSN 1529-4250
UA23
DEFENCE DAILY INTERNATIONAL. Text in English. 2000. w. USD 1,195 combined subscription (email & online eds.) (effective 2011). adv. **Document type:** *Newsletter, Trade.*
Media: E-mail. **Related titles:** Online - full text ed.: ISSN 1529-4269. 2000.
Indexed: A15, ABIn, I02, M07, P10, P47, P48, P51, P52, P53, P54, PQC.
—**CCC.**
Published by: Access Intelligence, LLC (Subsidiary of: Veronis, Suhler & Associates Inc.), 4 Choke Cherry Rd, 2nd Fl, Rockville, MD 20850. TEL 301-354-2000, 800-777-5006, FAX 301-340-3819, info@accessintel.com, http://www.accessintel.com.

355 IRL ISSN 1649-7066
DEFENCE FORCES REVIEW. Text in English. 1994. a. EUR 3 (effective 2006).
Formerly (until 2003): An Cosantoir Review (0791-9395)
Published by: Defence Forces, Public Relations Section, Defence Forces Headquarters, Parkgate, Dublin, 8, Ireland. http://www.military.ie.

DEFENCE HELICOPTER. *see* AERONAUTICS AND SPACE FLIGHT

355.20941 GBR ISSN 1741-7821
DEFENCE INDUSTRY (HAMPTON). Variant title: Key Note Business Ratio: Defence Industry. Text in English. 1991. irreg., latest 2009. GBP 365 per issue (effective 2010). **Document type:** *Monographic series, Trade.* **Description:** Provides an overview of the UK defense industry, including industry structure, market size and trends, developments, prospects, and major company profiles.
Formerly (until 2003): Key Note Market Review: U K Defence Industry (1362-6396)
Related titles: CD-ROM ed.; Online - full text ed.
Published by: Key Note Ltd. (Subsidiary of: Bonnier Business Information), Harlequin House, 5th Fl, 7 High St, Teddington, Richmond upon Thames, TW11 8EE, United Kingdom. TEL 44-845-5040452, FAX 44-845-5040453, sales@keynote.co.uk.

335 PAK ISSN 0257-2141
UA11
DEFENCE JOURNAL. Text in English. 1975. m. USD 30 in Asia; USD 40 in North America; USD 45 in South America (effective 2010). adv. bk.rev. bibl.; illus. **Document type:** *Journal, Trade.*
Indexed: AMB, BAS, RASB.
Address: Defence Housing Society, 16-B 7th Central St., Karachi, 75500, Pakistan. TEL 21-5894074, FAX 21-5834144, TELEX 23625 EMMAY PK. Ed. M Ikram Sehgal. Circ: 10,000.

355 IND
DEFENCE MANAGEMENT. Abbreviated title: D M J. Text in English. 1974. s-a. bk.rev. bibl.; charts. **Document type:** *Journal, Trade.*
Formerly: Defence Manager
Published by: College of Defence Management, Sainikpuri Post, Secunderabad, Andhra Pradesh 500 094, India. TEL 91-40-27115741, cdm@nic.in. Circ: 800.

355 GBR ISSN 1464-2646
DEFENCE MANAGEMENT JOURNAL. Abbreviated title: D M J. Text in English. 1995. q. GBP 295 (effective 2011). adv. back issues avail. **Document type:** *Journal, Trade.* **Description:** Covers the recent parliamentary committee commentary on responsible defence exports and reinforces the need for transparency, robust export control and ethics in defence trading.
Former titles (until 1998): Public Sector Review. Defence (1462-3056); (until 1997): Defence Review (1368-4418); (until 199?): Defence Yearbook (1367-4412)
Related titles: Online - full text ed.: ISSN 2046-6129. free (effective 2011).
—**CCC.**
Published by: P S C A International Ltd., Ebenezer House, Rycroft, Newcastle-under-Lyme, Staffs ST5 2UB, United Kingdom. TEL 44-1782-630200, FAX 44-1782-625533, mailbox@publicservice.co.uk, http://www.publicservice.co.uk. Ed. Anthony Hall TEL 44-1782-740088. Adv. contact Gerrod Mellor TEL 44-1782-630200.

355.07 CAN ISSN 1702-3599
U395.C2
DEFENCE R & D CANADA. ANNUAL REPORT. (Research & Development) Variant title: Scientific Excellence for Canada's Defence. Text in English, French. 1999. a.
Formerly (until 2001): Canada. Defence Research and Development Branch. Annual Report (1493-9509)
Related titles: Online - full text ed.: ISSN 1702-3602.
Published by: Defence R & D Canada, 3701 Carling Ave, Ottawa, ON K1A 0Z4, Canada. TEL 613-995-2971, FAX 613-996-0392, candidinfo@drdc-rddc.gc.ca, http://www.ottawa.drdc-rddc.gc.ca.

355.4 355.03 GBR
DEFENCE RESEARCH & ANALYSIS. BRIEFS. Text in English. irreg. **Description:** Deals with specific issues of interest to the defence community.
Published by: Defence Research & Analysis, 461 Harrow Rd, London, W10 4RG, United Kingdom. TEL 44-20-8960-4488, FAX 44-20-8960-6886, DRandA@compuserve.com.

355 PAK
DEFENCE REVIEW. Text in English. 1989. 2/yr. USD 8.
Published by: Inspector General Training & Evaluation Branch, Training Publications & Information Directorate, General Staff Branch, General Headquarters, Rawalpindi, Pakistan. TELEX 32854 GHQ PK. Ed. Syed Ishfaq Ali. Circ: 3,500.

355 AUS ISSN 1834-6928
DEFENCE REVIEW ASIA. Abbreviated title: D R A. Text in English. 2007. 8/yr. AUD 84 in Asia; AUD 126 elsewhere (effective 2011). adv. back issues avail. **Document type:** *Magazine, Consumer.* **Description:** Aims to meet the requirements of regional defence professionals with unbiased quality coverage of defence issues in the Asia-Pacific region.
Related titles: Online - full text ed.: AUD 32 (effective 2011).
Published by: Asian Press Group Pte Ltd, PO Box 88, Miranda, NSW 1490, Australia. TEL 61-2-95267188, FAX 61-2-95261779. Ed. Kym Bergmann TEL 61-412-539106. Pub. Marilyn Tangye Butler TEL 61-410-529324. Adv. contact Raymond Boey TEL 65-6-4572340.

355 MYS ISSN 1985-6571
DEFENCE S & T TECHNICAL BULLETIN/BULETIN TEKNIKAL SAINS & TEKNOLOGI PERTAHANAN. Variant title: Defence Science & Technology Technical Bulletin. Text in Malay, English. 2008. s-a. abstr. back issues avail. **Document type:** *Journal, Academic/Scholarly.* **Description:** Contains articles on research findings in various fields of defence science & technology by researchers both within and outside the country.
Related titles: Online - full text ed.
Published by: Malaysia, Ministry of Defence. Science & Technology Research Institute for Defence (STRIDE), Taman Bukit Mewah Fasa 9, Kajang, Selangor 43000, Malaysia. TEL 603-87324400, FAX 603-87348695. Ed. Zalini Yunus.

355 AUS ISSN 1837-8404
DEFENCE SCIENCE AUSTRALIA. Text in English. 1985. q. free (effective 2011). back issues avail. **Document type:** *Magazine, Government.* **Description:** Provides scientific advice and support to the Australian Defence Organisation.
Former titles (until 2010): Australian Defence Science (1441-0818); (until 1998): Australian Defence Science News (1320-1077); (until 1993): D S T O Research News (1033-3983); (until 1986): D S T O News (0818-9536); (until 1985): Defence Research News (0816-5076)
Related titles: Online - full text ed.: ISSN 1838-0093. free (effective 2011).
Published by: Australian Government, Defence Science and Technology Organisation, PO Box 1500, Edinburgh, SA 5111, Australia. TEL 61-8-73896923, FAX 61-8-73896191, stephen.butler@dsto.defence.gov.au. Ed. Tony Cox.

355 IND ISSN 0011-748X
U395.I5 CODEN: DSJOAA
➤ **DEFENCE SCIENCE JOURNAL.** Text in English. 1949. bi-m. INR 150 domestic to individuals; USD 55 foreign to individuals; INR 600 domestic to institutions; USD 70 foreign to institutions (effective 2010). charts; illus. index. back issues avail. **Document type:** *Journal, Academic/Scholarly.* **Description:** Covers engineering and technology, including applied physics, chemical technology, biomedical engineering, computer science and electronics.
Related titles: Online - full text ed.: free (effective 2011).
Indexed: A05, A22, A28, APA, AS&TA, AS&TI, ASCA, ASFA, ApMecR, B04, B21, BMT, BRD, BrCerAb, C&ISA, C10, CA, CA/WCA, CIA, CIN, CPEI, CTE, CerAb, ChemAb, ChemTitl, CivEngAb, CorrAb, E&CAJ, E11, EEA, EMA, ESPM, EngInd, EnvEAb, GeoRef, H&SSA, H15, I02, ISMEC, Inspec, LID&ISL, M&TEA, M09, MBF, METADEX, MathR, P30, RASB, SCI, SCOPUS, SolStAb, T02, T04, W03, W05, W07, WAA, Z02.
—BLDSC (3546.200000), AskIEEE, CASDDS, IE, Infotrieve, Ingenta, Linda Hall.
Published by: (India. Defence Research & Development Organization, Great Britain. Ministry of Defence GBR), Defence Scientific Information & Documentation Centre, Metcalfe House, New Delhi, 110 054, India. TEL 91-11-23902400, FAX 91-11-23819151, director@desidoc.drdo.in, http://www.drdo.gov.in. Ed. Alka Bansal. **Subscr. to:** Indianjournals.com, Divan Enterprises, B-9, Local Shopping Complex, A-Block, Naraina Vihar, Ring Rd, New Delhi 110 028, India. TEL 91-11-25770411, FAX 91-11-25778876, info@indianjournals.com, http://www.indianjournals.com.

355 900 GBR ISSN 1470-2436
UA10.7
➤ **DEFENCE STUDIES.** Text in English. 2001 (Spring). 3/yr. GBP 333 combined subscription in United Kingdom to institutions (print & online eds.); EUR 426, USD 537 combined subscription to institutions (print & online eds.) (effective 2012). adv. bk.rev. annual index. back issues avail.; reprint service avail. from PSC. **Document type:** *Journal, Academic/Scholarly.* **Description:** Aimed at staff colleges and military personnel around the world and at academics interested in all aspects of defence.
Related titles: Online - full text ed.: ISSN 1743-9698. GBP 300 in United Kingdom to institutions; EUR 384, USD 483 to institutions (effective 2012) (from IngentaConnect).
Indexed: A01, A03, A08, A22, AmH&L, CA, E01, ESPM, HistAb, I02, LID&ISL, M05, M07, P02, P10, P34, P42, P47, P48, P53, P54, PAIS, PQC, PSA, R02, RiskAb, SCOPUS, SociolAb, T02.
—IE, Ingenta. **CCC.**
Published by: (Joint Services Command and Staff College), Routledge (Subsidiary of: Taylor & Francis Group), 4 Park Sq, Milton Park, Abingdon, Oxon OX14 4RN, United Kingdom. TEL 44-20-70176000, FAX 44-20-70176336, subscriptions@tandf.co.uk, http://www.routledge.com. Ed. Geoffrey Till. Adv. contact Linda Hann TEL 44-1344-779945. B&W page GBP 195, B&W page USD 285; trim 110 x 178. **Subscr. to:** Taylor & Francis Ltd., Journals Customer Service, Sheepen Pl, Colchester, Essex CO3 3LP, United Kingdom. TEL 44-20-70175544, FAX 44-20-70175198.

➤ **DEFENSE A T & L.** (Acquisition, Technology & Logistics) *see* COMPUTERS—Computer Systems

355.6 USA ISSN 2156-8391
UC260
➤ **DEFENSE ACQUISITION RESEARCH JOURNAL.** Text in English. 1994. q. back issues avail. **Document type:** *Journal, Academic/Scholarly.*
Former titles (until 2011): Defense A R Journal (1553-6408); (until 2004): Acquisition Review Quarterly (1087-3112)
Related titles: Online - full text ed.: ISSN 2156-8405.
Indexed: A01, A03, A26, AUNI, B01, E08, G05, G06, G07, G08, I02, I05, M05, M06, M07, P10, P47, P48, P52, P53, P54, PQC, S09, T02.
Published by: Defense Acquisition University, 9820 Belvoir Rd, Fort Belvoir, VA 22060. TEL 703-805-3459, 866-568-6924, dauhelp@dau.mil, http://www.dau.mil.

➤ **DEFENSE AND AEROSPACE AGENCIES BRIEFING.** *see* AERONAUTICS AND SPACE FLIGHT

➤ **DEFENSE AND AEROSPACE COMPANIES BRIEFING.** *see* AERONAUTICS AND SPACE FLIGHT

➤ **DEFENSE & FOREIGN AFFAIRS STRATEGIC POLICY.** *see* POLITICAL SCIENCE—International Relations

355.947 RUS ISSN 1608-3520
DEFENSE & SECURITY. Text in English. 1992 (Sept.). 3/w. USD 115 per month; USD 1,242 (effective 2003). bk.rev.; music rev.; software rev.; dance rev.; tel.rev.; film rev.; rec.rev. abstr. 10 p./no. 3 cols./p.; back issues avail. **Document type:** *Journal, Trade.* **Description:** Monitors the military political situation in Russia and the former Soviet Union and contains complete coverage of national security issues, the role of the armed forces in society and conversion of the defense industry.
Related titles: Ed.; Supplement(s): Armaments and Technology.
Published by: W P S Agentstvo Obzora Sredstv Massovoi Informatsii/WPS, Russian Media Monitoring Agency, a/ya 90, Moscow, 115191, Russian Federation. TEL 7-095-9552708, FAX 7-095-9552927, http://www.wps.ru/e_index.html. Ed. Igor Frolov. Pub., R&P Zoya Kudriavtseva. Circ: 20. **Dist. by:** East View Information Services, 10601 Wayzata Blvd, Minneapolis, MN 55305. TEL 952-252-1201, 800-477-1005, FAX 952-252-1202, info@eastview.com, http://www.eastview.com.

355 USA ISSN 1934-2543
DEFENSE AND SECURITY REPORT. Text in English. 2001. q. **Document type:** *Report, Trade.*
Formerly (until 2004): Defense and Aerospace Report (1544-9688)
Published by: U.S. - Taiwan Business Council, 1700 N Moore St, Ste 1703, Arlington, VA 22209. TEL 703-465-2930, FAX 703-465-2937, Council@us-taiwan.org, http://www.us-taiwan.org/index.html.

355 USA
DEFENSE BUSINESS BRIEFING. Text in English. 1987. w. looseleaf. USD 695 (print or e-mail ed.) (effective 2011). back issues avail. **Document type:** *Newsletter, Trade.* **Description:** Tracks the award of Pentagon dollars to industry. Reports on all U.S. Department of Defense announced prime contract actions of the previous week.
Related titles: CD-ROM ed.: USD 550 (effective 2011); Diskette ed.; E-mail ed.
Published by: Teal Group Corp., 3900 University Dr, Ste 220, Fairfax, VA 22030. TEL 703-385-1992, FAX 703-691-9591, custserv@tealgroup.com, http://www.tealgroup.com.

355 USA ISSN 1088-9000
DEFENSE COMMUNITIES. Text in English. 1973. bi-m. USD 100 to non-members; free to members (effective 2011). **Document type:** *Magazine, Trade.* **Description:** For military and civilian managers of on- and off-base military housing.
Former titles (until 199?): Defense Housing (1047-6504); (until 1987): Pronotes
—**CCC.**

Published by: (Professional Housing Management Association), Stratton Publishing and Marketing Inc., 5285 Shawnee Rd, Ste 510, Alexandria, VA 22312. TEL 703-914-9200, FAX 703-914-6777, pubpros@strattonpublishing.com, http://www.strattonpub.com/.

355 363.1 USA ISSN 1932-3816
UA927
DEFENSE CONCEPTS. Text in English. 2006. q. **Document type:** *Journal, Trade.* **Description:** Presents news and views on defense and security issue based on a dedication to solving security challenges.
Related titles: Online - full text ed.: ISSN 1933-5288.
Published by: Center for Advanced Defense Studies, 10 G Street NE, Ste 610, Washington, DC 20002. TEL 202-289-3332, FAX 202-789-2786, info.c4ads.org, http://www.c4ads.org. Ed. Jerrold Post.

355 USA ISSN 1062-0613
DEFENSE CONTRACT AWARDS. Text in English. 1993. 32/yr. (three times per month, except once per month in January and August). USD 500 domestic (effective 2001). bk.rev. **Document type:** *Newsletter.* **Description:** Monitors and tracks all contracts let by the various agencies of the U.S. Department of Defense. Directed to industrial companies and consultants doing business with the Department of Defense.
Media: E-mail.
Address: 1057 B National Press Bldg, Washington, DC 20045. Ed., Pub., R&P Murray Felsher. **Subscr. to:** Pentagon Sta., PO Box 47036, Washington, DC 20050-7036.

355.8 658.7 GBR
DEFENSE CONTRACTS INTERNATIONAL. Abbreviated title: D C I. Text in English. 19??. d. GBP 960, EUR 1,105, USD 1,499 (effective 2010). back issues avail. **Document type:** *Newsletter, Trade.* **Description:** Contains information on open contract opportunities and awards from defense organizations around the world.
Media: Online - full text.
Published by: B I P Solutions Ltd, Medius, 60 Pacific Quay, Glasgow, G51 1DZ, United Kingdom. TEL 44-141-3328247, FAX 44-141-3312652, bip@bipsolutions.com, http://www.bipsolutions.com.

DEFENSE DAILY. *see* AERONAUTICS AND SPACE FLIGHT

355 FRA ISSN 1772-788X
DEFENSE ET SECURITE INTERNATIONALE. Key Title: D S I. Text in French. 2005. m. EUR 50 domestic to individuals; EUR 45 domestic to students and military personnel; EUR 60 foreign to individuals; EUR 55 foreign to students and military personnel (effective 2008). back issues avail. **Document type:** *Magazine.*
Published by: Areion Publishing, Chateau de Valmousse, Departementale 572, Lambesc, 13410, France. TEL 33-4-42921738, FAX 33-4-42924872. Circ: 50,000.

327 USA ISSN 0160-5836
UA10
DEFENSE FOREIGN AFFAIRS HANDBOOK; political, economic & defense data on every country in the world. Text in English. 1976. a., latest 2006, 16th ed. USD 397 per issue domestic; USD 457 per issue foreign (effective 2009). back issues avail. **Document type:** *Handbook/Manual/Guide, Trade.* **Description:** Contains comprehensive chapters on 245 countries and territories worldwide, with each chapter giving full cabinet and leadership listings, history, recent developments, demographics, economic statistics, political and constitutional data, including political parties and names, voting records, etc.
Related titles: CD-ROM ed.: USD 379 per issue (effective 2009).
Published by: The International Strategic Studies Association, PO Box 320608, Alexandria, VA 22320. TEL 703-548-1070, FAX 703-684-7476, GRCopley@StrategicStudies.org, http://www.strategicstudies.org/. **Subscr. to:** PO Box 20407, Alexandria, VA 22320.

355 USA
DEFENSE INFORMATION SYSTEMS AGENCY. CIRCULARS. Text in English. irreg. **Document type:** *Government.*
Published by: Defense Information Systems Agency (Subsidiary of: Department of Defense), DISA Headquarters Bldg #12, 701 South Courthouse Rd, Arlington, VA 22204-2199 . TEL 703-607-6900, http://www.disa.mil/.

355 USA
DEFENSE INFORMATION SYSTEMS AGENCY. NOTICES. Text in English. irreg. **Document type:** *Government.*
Published by: Defense Information Systems Agency (Subsidiary of: Department of Defense), DISA Headquarters Bldg #12, 701 South Courthouse Rd, Arlington, VA 22204-2199 . TEL 703-607-6900, http://www.disa.mil/.

355 USA ISSN 0893-0619
DEFENSE MEDIA REVIEW; a survey of the National Security Press with analysis and commentary. Text in English. 1987. m. USD 60. **Description:** Tracks media coverage of defense issues and policies.
Published by: Boston University, Center for Defense Journalism, 67 Bay State Rd, Boston, MA 02215. TEL 617-353-6186, FAX 617-353-8707. Ed. H Joachim Maitre. Circ: 600.

355 USA ISSN 0195-6450
JX1901
THE DEFENSE MONITOR. Text in English. 1972. bi-m. free (effective 2010). illus. back issues avail.; reprints avail. **Document type:** *Newsletter, Trade.* **Description:** Provides expert analysis on various components of U.S. national security, international security and defense policy.
Related titles: Online - full text ed.: ISSN 1943-3506. free (effective 2010).
Indexed: A01, AUNI, C12, DM&T, HRIR, I02, M02, M05, P34, PRA, RASB, T02.
—IE, Infotrieve.
Published by: Center for Defense Information, 1779 Massachusetts Ave, NW, Ste 615, Washington, DC 20036. TEL 202-332-0600, FAX 202-462-4559, info@cdi.org.

355 USA ISSN 0884-139X
CODEN: CORRAK
DEFENSE NEWS. Text in English. 1986. w. (Mon.). adv. charts; stat. reprints avail. **Document type:** *Newspaper, Trade.* **Description:** Covers the international politics and business of the defense community.
Related titles: Microform ed.; Online - full text ed.: free (effective 2009).
Indexed: A22, A26, B03, C33, CA, G08, I05, M05, P52, T02.
—BLDSC (3546.227000), IE, Infotrieve, Ingenta. **CCC.**
Published by: Defense News Media Group (Subsidiary of: Army Times Publishing Co.), 6883 Commercial Dr, Springfield, VA 22159. TEL 703-750-7400, 800-368-5718, FAX 703-658-8412, custserv@defensenews.com. Ed. Vago Muradian. Adv. contact Donna Peterson TEL 703-750-8172. B&W page USD 9,590, color page USD 11,990; bleed 11.25 x 13. Circ: 36,521.

355 362.1 333.792 USA
DEFENSE NUCLEAR FACILITIES SAFETY BOARD. REPORT TO CONGRESS ON ACQUISITIONS MADE FROM MANUFACTURER INSIDE AND OUTSIDE THE UNITED STATES, FISCAL YEAR (YEAR). Text in English. 2004. a. **Document type:** *Government.* **Description:** Summarizes activities during the year, assesses improvements in the safety of defense nuclear facilities, and identifies remaining health and safety problems.
Published by: Defense Nuclear Facilities Safety Board, 625 Indiana Ave, NW, Ste 700, Washington, DC 20004-2901. TEL 202-694-7000, mailbox@dnfsb.gov, http://www.dnfsb.gov/.

355 JPN
DEFENSE OF JAPAN (YEAR); the white paper on defense. Text in Japanese. 1989. a. JPY 5,600. **Description:** Gives a full account of Japan's defense policy and the current state of the Japanese "self-defense" forces. Includes reference material and statistical data related to Japan's defense.
Published by: (Japan. Defense Agency), The Japan Times Ltd., 5-4, Shibaura 4-chome, Minato-ku, Tokyo, 108-0023, Japan. TEL 81-3-3453-2013, FAX 81-3-3453-8023.

355.8 USA ISSN 1558-836X
UA23.A1
DEFENSE SYSTEMS; information technology and net-centric warfare. Text in English. 2006 (Jan.). 10/yr. free to qualified personnel (effective 2008). adv. back issues avail. **Document type:** *Magazine, Government.* **Description:** Focuses on strategic intelligence for info-centric operations.
Published by: 1105 Government Information Group (Subsidiary of: 1105 Media Inc.), 3141 Fairview Park Dr, Ste 777, Falls Church, VA 22042. TEL 703-876-5100, http://www.1105govinfo.com. Ed. Sean Gallagher TEL 410-504-6616. Pub. David Smith TEL 703-645-7876. Circ: 38,007.

355.4 USA ISSN 0011-7625
U1
DEFENSE TRANSPORTATION JOURNAL; magazine of international defense transportation and logistics. Text in English. 1946. bi-m. USD 35 includes membership (effective 2004). adv. bk.rev. charts; illus. index. reprints avail. **Document type:** *Journal, Trade.* **Description:** Covers defense transportation and logistics for the government defense and commercial sectors.
Former titles (until 1967): National Defense Transportation Journal (0193-8851); (until 1949): Army Transportation Journal
Related titles: Microform ed.: (from PQC); Online - full text ed.
Indexed: A22, A26, AMB, AUNI, CLT&T, DM&T, E08, G05, G06, G07, G08, HRIS, I05, LogistBibl, M06, M07, P02, P06, P10, P47, P48, P52, P53, P54, PQC, S09.
—IE, Ingenta, Linda Hall.
Published by: National Defense Transportation Association, 50 South Pickett St, 220, Alexandria, VA 22304-7296. TEL 703-751-5011, FAX 703-823-8761. Pub. Kenneth Wykle. Adv. contact Don Perkins TEL 434-817-2000. Circ: 10,000 (paid).

355 NLD ISSN 0167-0808
DEFENSIEKRANT. Text in Dutch. 1975. w. EUR 13.61 domestic; EUR 15.88 foreign (effective 2010). **Document type:** *Newsletter, Trade.*
Formerly (until 1978): Legerkoerant (0920-6558)
Published by: Ministerie van Defensie, Directie Voorlichting en Communicatie, Postbus 20701, The Hague, 2500 ES, Netherlands. TEL 31-70-3188188, FAX 31-70-3187888. Eds. Andre Twigt TEL 31-70-3397805, Ellen Eggink. Circ: 41,000.

355.1 HRV ISSN 1331-002X
DELTA. Text in Croatian. 1994. m. **Document type:** *Magazine, Trade.*
Published by: Trend d.o.o., Trg Petra Svacica 12-II, Zagreb, 10000, Croatia. TEL 385-1-4856895, FAX 385-1-4554536.

355 RUS
DEN' VOINA; spetsial'nyi vypusk gazeta zavtra. Text in Russian. 1997. m. USD 98 in the Americas (effective 2000).
Published by: Redaktsiya Den' Voina, Komsomol'skii pr., 13, Moscow, 119146, Russian Federation. TEL 7-095-2471327, FAX 7-095-2459626, com@zavtra.msk.rug. Ed. A Prokhanov.

DEPARTMENT OF DEFENSE BUYERS GUIDE. *see* BUSINESS AND ECONOMICS—Trade And Industrial Directories

358.4 USA
THE DESERT AIRMAN. Text in English. 1940. w. (Fri.). free to qualified personnel (effective 2006). 24 cols./p.; **Document type:** *Newspaper.*
Published by: Aerotech News & Review, 456 East Ave K4 Ste 8, Lancaster, CA 93535. Adv. contact Diane Hasse. Circ: 30,000 (controlled).

DESPATCHES. *see* MUSEUMS AND ART GALLERIES

355.3 DEU
DEUTSCHER BUNDESWEHR-KALENDER. Text in German. 1956. 4 base vols. plus updates 2/yr. EUR 99 base vol(s).; EUR 48 updates (effective 2010). adv. **Document type:** *Trade.*
Published by: Walhalla Fachverlag, Haus an der Eisernen Bruecke, Regensburg, 93042, Germany. TEL 49-941-56840, FAX 49-941-5684111, walhalla@walhalla.de. Eds. Karl H Schnell, Wolfgang Schmelzer. adv.: B&W page EUR 1,650. Circ: 20,000 (controlled).

355 DEU ISSN 0417-3635
DEUTSCHES SOLDATENJAHRBUCH. Text in German. 1953. a. EUR 35.80 (effective 2005). adv. bk.rev. bibl.; charts; illus.; stat. **Document type:** *Bulletin, Trade.*
Published by: Schild-Verlag GmbH, Kasernenstr 6-10, Zweibruecken, 66482, Germany. TEL 49-6332-72710, FAX 49-6332-72730, info@vdmedien.de, http://www.vdmedien.de/. Circ: 7,000 (controlled).

355 CHN ISSN 1674-2230
DIANZI XINXI DUIKANG JISHU/ELECTRONIC INFORMATION WARFARE TECHNOLOGY. Text in Chinese. 1986. bi-m. **Document type:** *Journal, Academic/Scholarly.*
Formerly (until 2006): Dianzi Duikang Jishu
Published by: (Xinxi Zonghe Kongzhi Guojia Zhongdian Shiyanshi), Zhongguo Dianzi Keji Jituan Gongsi Di-29 Yanjiusuo/China Electronics Technology Group Corp. (CETC) No.29 Research Institute, PO Box 420-011, Chadianzi, Chengdu, 610036, China. TEL 86-28-87551384.

355 LBN
AL-DIFA' AL-ARABI/ARAB DEFENSE JOURNAL. Text in Arabic. 1976. m. LBP 50,000 domestic; USD 150 in US & Canada; USD 125 in Europe (effective 2003). adv. bk.rev. 120 p./no.; **Document type:** *Magazine.*
Published by: Dar As-Sayad S.A.L., C/o Said Freiha, Hazmieh, P O Box 1038, Beirut, Lebanon. TEL 961-5-456373, FAX 961-5-452700, contactpr@csi.com, alanwar@alanwar.com, http://www.alanwar.com. Ed. Maj Gen Wadih Gebrane. Adv. contact Said Freiha. color page USD 5,460; bleed 215 x 285. Circ: 23,845.

355 RUS
DIGEST OF THE RUSSIAN NONPROLIFERATION JOURNAL YADERNY KONTROL; daidzhest zhurnala yadernyi kontrol'. Text in English. 1996. 3/yr. USD 115 in the Americas (effective 2000).
Published by: P I R - Tsentr, A-ya 17, Moscow, 117454, Russian Federation. TEL 7-095-3351955, FAX 7-095-2349558, info@pircenter.org.

623.043029 GBR ISSN 1759-345X
DIGITAL BATTLESPACE. Text in English. 2005. bi-m. GBP 50; USD 100 to institutions; free to qualified personnel (effective 2010). adv. back issues avail. **Document type:** *Magazine, Trade.* **Description:** Provides news, information and analysis for the global C4ISTAR community.
Related titles: Online - full text ed.: ISSN 1759-3468. free (effective 2010).
—**CCC.**
Published by: Shephard Press Ltd., 268 Bath Rd, Slough, Berkshire SL1 4DX, United Kingdom. TEL 44-1753-727001, FAX 44-1753-727002, info@shephard.co.uk. Ed. Peter Donaldson TEL 44-1753-727023. Adv. contact Mike Wild TEL 44-1753-727007. B&W page GBP 5,200, color page GBP 8,600; 205 x 273. **Subscr. to:** CDS Global, Tower House, Sovereign Park, Market Harborough, Leics LE16 9EF, United Kingdom. TEL 44-1858-438879, FAX 44-1858-461739, shephardgroup@subscription.co.uk.

DIPLOMAT; the review of the diplomatic and consular world. *see* POLITICAL SCIENCE—International Relations

355 USA
DIRECTOR OF SELECTIVE SERVICE. ANNUAL REPORT TO CONGRESS. Text in English. 1967. a. free. charts; stat. **Document type:** *Government.*
Published by: U.S. Selective Service System, 1515 Wilson Blvd, Arlington, VA 22209. TEL 703-605-4100. Ed. Lewis C Brodsky. Circ: (controlled). **Orders to:** U.S. Government Printing Office, Superintendent of Documents, PO Box 371954, Pittsburgh, PA 15250. TEL 202-512-1800, FAX 202-512-2250.

355 UAE
DIR'U AL-WATAN. Text in Arabic. 1971. m. **Description:** Covers military issues.
Published by: General Command for the Armed Forces, Public Relations Administration, P O Box 4224, Abu Dhabi, United Arab Emirates. TEL 447999. Circ: 1,000.

THE DISPATCH (MIDLAND); American airpower a proud heritage. *see* AERONAUTICS AND SPACE FLIGHT

355 USA
DISTRIBUTION OF PERSONNEL BY STATE AND BY SELECTED LOCATIONS. Text in English. a. **Document type:** *Government.*
Media: Online - full content.
Published by: U.S. Department of Defense, Washington Headquarters Services, Directorate for Information Operations and Reports http://web1.whs.osd.mil/mmid/MMIDHOME.HTM.

355 CHE
DIVISIONS KURIER. Text in German. 4/yr.
Address: Juchstr 21, Glattfelden, 8192, Switzerland. TEL 01-8368283, FAX 01-8367414. Ed. Christoph Hagedorn. Circ: 25,000.

355 USA
THE DOLPHIN. Text in English. w. (Thu.). free (effective 2007). adv. 10 p./no. 6 cols./p.; **Document type:** *Newspaper.*
Published by: Journal Register Co., 50 W State St, 12th Fl, Trenton, NJ 08608. TEL 609-396-2200. Ed. Sheryl Walsh. Pub. John Slater. adv.: col. inch USD 11.80. Circ: 8,500 (free).

DONGNAN GUOFANG YIYAO/SOUTHEAST CHINA NATIONAL DEFENCE MEDICAL SCIENCE. JOURNAL. *see* MEDICAL SCIENCES

355 USA ISSN 2157-7749
DOWN RANGE. Text in English. 19??. bi-m. back issues avail. **Document type:** *Newsletter, Trade.* **Description:** Provides information about people, policies, operations, technical developments, trends and ideas about the department of defense.
Formerly (until 2010): Up and Down the Hill (2157-7722)
Media: Online - full text.
Published by: Public Affairs Office (Subsidiary of: East-West Center), 18436 4th St, Bldg 112, Fort A P Hill, VA 22427. TEL 804-633-8120, http://www.aphill.army.mil/sites/installation/pao.asp. Ed. David San Miguel.

355 DNK ISSN 1604-9136
DRAGONEN. Text in Danish. 1934. bi-m. **Document type:** *Magazine, Consumer.*
Formerly (until 2005): Dragonavisen (0903-2231); Which incorporated (1937-1970): Ryttervagten (0903-2258); Which was formerly (until 1937): Danske Soldater
Published by: Jydske Dragonregiment, Dragonkassernen, Holstebro, 7500, Denmark. TEL 45-97-423177, FAX 45-97-412439, jdr@mil.dk. Eds. Tommy Bruhn, Major Peter G Muhs.

DRESDNER HISTORISCHE STUDIEN. *see* HISTORY—History Of Europe

DRILL; for men who serve. *see* MEN'S INTERESTS

355 CHE
DRUE-BLATT. Text in German. 3/yr.
Address: Postfach 246, Liebefeld, 3097, Switzerland. Circ: 25,000.

358.4 USA ISSN 2151-8084
E-MILITARY PRODUCT NEWS FOR AVIATION. Text in English. 2008. q. free (effective 2009). back issues avail. **Document type:** *Magazine, Trade.*
Media: Online - full content.
Published by: Cygnus Business Media, Inc., 3 Huntington Quadrangle, Ste 301 N, Melville, NY 11747. TEL 631-845-2700, 800-308-6397, FAX 631-845-7109, http://www.cygnusb2b.com. Pub. Missy Zingsheim TEL 920-563-1665.

E W REFERENCE AND SOURCE GUIDE. (Electronic Warfare) *see* ENGINEERING

355 USA
EAGLE (NEW YORK). Text in English. 1981. bi-m. USD 3.95 per issue. adv. bk.rev.
Formerly: Eagle: For the American Fighting Man
Published by: Command Publications, Inc., 1115 Broadway, New York, NY 10010. Ed. Harry Kane. Circ: 75,000.

355.27 USA
UG485 CODEN: JELDER
EDEFENSE; detect. decide. shoot. survive. Text in English. 1978. m. USD 499 (effective 2005). adv. reprints avail. **Document type:** *Journal, Trade.* **Description:** Planning and procurement, technology and application of EW equipment and subsystems, EW system integration, performance and operations.
Formerly (until 2004): Journal of Electronic Defense (0192-429X)
Media: Online - full content. **Related titles:** Online - full text ed.
Indexed: A01, A03, A08, A22, A26, AMB, AUNI, B03, B11, CA, DM&T, E08, G01, G05, G06, G07, G08, I02, I05, Inspec, LID&ISL, M05, M06, M07, P02, P10, P26, P34, P47, P48, P52, P53, P54, PQC, R02, S01, S09, T02.
—BLDSC (4974.920000), AskIEEE, IE, Infotrieve, Ingenta. **CCC.**
Published by: (Association of Old Crows), Horizon House Publications, 685 Canton St, Norwood, MA 02062. TEL 781-769-9750, FAX 781-762-9230, http://www.horizonhouse.com. Ed. Michael Puttre. Pub. Michael Boyd. Circ: 25,000.

338.473962 GBR ISSN 1749-1371
EGYPT DEFENCE & SECURITY REPORT. Text in English. 2005. q. EUR 820, USD 1,030 combined subscription (print & email eds.) (effective 2010). **Document type:** *Report, Trade.* **Description:** Provides professionals, consultancies, government departments, regulatory bodies and researchers with independent forecasts and regional competitive intelligence on the Egyptian defence and security industry.
Related titles: E-mail ed.
Indexed: B01.
Published by: Business Monitor International Ltd., Senator House, 85 Queen Victoria St, London, EC4V 4AB, United Kingdom. TEL 44-20-72480468, FAX 44-20-72480467, subs@businessmonitor.com.

355.31 ESP ISSN 1696-7178
EJERCITO DE TIERRA ESPANOL. Text in Spanish. 1940. m. EUR 12 domestic; EUR 18 in Europe; EUR 24 elsewhere (effective 2010). adv. bk.rev. bibl.; charts; illus. index. **Document type:** *Magazine, Trade.*
Formerly (until 1998): Ejercito (0013-2918)
Indexed: IBR, IBZ.
Published by: Ministerio de Defensa, Centro de Publicaciones, Calle de Alcala 18, 4o, Madrid, 28014, Spain. TEL 34-91-522524, FAX 34-91-5227553.

355 USA ISSN 0884-4828
ELECTRONIC WARFARE DIGEST. Text in English. 1977. m. looseleaf. USD 345 domestic; USD 355 in Canada; USD 365 elsewhere (effective 2001). 10 p./no. 2 cols./p.; back issues avail. **Document type:** *Newsletter.*
Published by: Washington National News Reports Inc., 1745 Jeff Davis Hwy, Ste 308, Arlington, VA 22202. TEL 703-416-1950, FAX 703-416-1030. Ed. Brian Thomas. Pub., R&P Brian T Sheehan. Circ: 500 (paid).

355 USA ISSN 1939-3636
EMPLOYMENT SITUATION OF VETERANS. Text in English. 19??. biennial. free (effective 2009). **Document type:** *Government.* **Description:** Provides detailed information on the labor force, employment, and unemployment.
Formerly (until 2003): Employment Situation of Vietnam-Era Veterans (1939-3644)
Media: Online - full content.
Published by: U.S. Department of Labor, Bureau of Labor Statistics, 2 Massachusetts Ave, NE, Rm 2860, Washington, DC 20212. TEL 202-691-5200, FAX 202-691-7890, blsdata_staff@bls.gov.

ENGINEER (FORT LEONARD WOOD); the professional bulletin of Army engineers. *see* ENGINEERING

358.22 USA ISSN 0733-8163
ENGINEER UPDATE. Text in English. 197?. m. **Document type:** *Government.* **Description:** Provides news and features on Corps of Engineers people and projects.
Indexed: GeoRef.
Published by: U.S. Army Corp. of Engineers, Public Affairs Office, 441 G. Street, NW, Washington, DC 20314-1000.

355.45 ARG ISSN 1515-7113
ESCUELA DE DEFENSA NACIONAL. COLECCION ACADEMICA. Text in Spanish. 2000. m.
Media: Online - full text.
Published by: Escuela de Defensa Nacional, Maipu, 262, Buenos Aires, 1084, Argentina. TEL 54-114-3261318, FAX 54-114-3253510, escdef@datamar.com.ar, http://www.mindef.gov.ar/edn.htm.

355.45 ARG
ESCUELA DE DEFENSA NACIONAL. CUADERNOS Y BOLETINES ACADEMICOS. Text in Spanish. 1996. bi-m. back issues avail.
Related titles: Online - full text ed.
Published by: Escuela de Defensa Nacional, Maipu, 262, Buenos Aires, 1084, Argentina. TEL 54-114-3261318, FAX 54-114-3253510, escdef@datamar.com.ar, http://www.mindef.gov.ar/edn.htm.

355 ITA ISSN 1591-3031
ESERCITI NELLA STORIA. Text in Italian. 1999. bi-m. **Document type:** *Magazine, Consumer.*
Published by: Delta Editrice, Borgo Regale 21, Parma, PR 43100, Italy. TEL 39-0521-287883, FAX 39-0521-237546, http://www.deltaeditrice.it.

355 TKM
ESGER. Text in Turkmen. w. USD 445 in the Americas (effective 2000).
Published by: Ministry of Defence, Ul. Khudaiberdyeva, 29, Ashgabat, 744004, Turkmenistan. TEL 3632-356809. **Dist. by:** East View Information Services, 10601 Wayzata Blvd, Minneapolis, MN 55305. TEL 952-252-1201, 800-477-1005, FAX 952-252-1202, info@eastview.com, http://www.eastview.com.

355 CAN ISSN 1194-2266
UA600
ESPRIT DE CORPS; Canadian military then & now. Text in English. 1991. m. CAD 29.95, USD 39.95; CAD 3.50 newsstand/cover (effective 2000 & 2001). adv. bk.rev.; video rev. illus. back issues avail. **Document type:** *Magazine, Consumer.* **Description:** Offers historical articles, policy reviews and company profiles to those interested in the military.
Related titles: Online - full text ed.
Indexed: C03, C05, CBCARef, CPerl, G08, I05, P48, PQC.
Published by: S.R. Taylor Publishing, 204 1066 Somerset St W, Ottawa, ON K1Y 4T3, Canada. TEL 613-725-5060, FAX 613-725-1019. Ed., Pub., Adv. contact Scott Taylor. R&P Julie Simoneau. B&W page CAD 1,350, color page CAD 1,500; trim 10.88 x 8.13. Circ: 10,000 (paid).

355 USA ISSN 1043-1667
DS35.69
THE ESTIMATE; political and security intelligence analysis of the Islamic world and its neighbors. Text in English. 1989. bi-w. USD 150 domestic to institutions; USD 180 foreign to institutions; USD 295 domestic to corporations; USD 330 foreign to corporations (effective 2010). bk.rev. index. back issues avail. **Document type:** *Newsletter, Trade.* **Description:** Contains political and security intelligence and risk analysis on the Islamic world.
Published by: International Estimate, Inc., 3300 Redpine St, Falls Church, VA 22041. TEL 703-671-2997, FAX 703-671-2998, mdunn@theestimate.com. Ed., Pub. Michael Collins Dunn.

355 DEU ISSN 0940-4171
EUROPAEISCHE SICHERHEIT; Politik - Streitkraefte - Wirtschaft - Technik. Text in German. 1983. m. EUR 63.50 domestic; EUR 82.50 foreign (effective 2011). adv. bk.rev. illus. **Document type:** *Magazine, Trade.*
Incorporates (in 1994): Europaeische Sicherheit. Ausgabe "A": Kampftruppen; Formerly (until 1991): Europaeische Wehrkunde, Wehrwissenschaftliche Rundschau (0723-9432); Which was formed by the merger of (1975-1983): Wehrwissenschaftliche Rundschau (0342-4847); Which was formerly (1971-1975): Wehrforschung (0342-4863); (1951-1970): Wehrwissenschaftliche Rundschau (0509-9722); (1936-1951): Militaerwissenschaftliche Rundschau (0935-3623); (1976-1983): Europaeische Wehrkunde (0343-6373); Which was formerly (1952-1976): Wehrkunde (0043-213X)
Indexed: A22, BAS, DIP, HistAb, IBR, IBZ, LID&ISL, MLA-IB, PAIS, PRA, RefZh.
—BLDSC (3829.361650), IE, Infotrieve, Ingenta. **CCC.**
Published by: (Clausewitz-Gesellschaft Arbeitskreis fuer Wehrforschung, Gesellschaft fuer Wehr- und Sicherheitspolitik e.V.), Verlag E.S. Mittler und Sohn GmbH, Hochkreuzallee 1, Bonn, 53175, Germany. TEL 49-228-307890, FAX 49-228-3078915, vertrieb@koehler-mittler.de, http://www.koehler-mittler.de. Ed. Juergen Hensel. adv.: B&W page EUR 3,200, color page EUR 4,400; trim 185 x 270. Circ: 18,493 (paid).

355 DEU ISSN 1617-7983
EUROPEAN SECURITY AND DEFENCE. Text in English. 2001. 3/yr. EUR 17.70 (effective 2009). adv. **Document type:** *Magazine, Trade.* **Description:** Keeps track of events and developments in the defense and security arenas.
Published by: Verlag E.S. Mittler und Sohn GmbH, Hochkreuzallee 1, Bonn, 53175, Germany. TEL 49-228-307890, FAX 49-228-3078915, vertrieb@koehler-mittler.de, http://www.koehler-mittler.de. adv.: B&W page EUR 3,400, color page EUR 4,600. Circ: 7,218 (paid).

355.1 USA ISSN 0014-388X
D769.A15
EX - C B I ROUNDUP. (China - Burma - India) Text in English. 1946. m. (except Aug.-Sep.). USD 13. adv. bk.rev.
Published by: Dwight O. King, Ed. & Pub., PO Box 2665, La Habra, CA 90631. TEL 310-947-2007. Circ: 6,185.

355 USA ISSN 0161-7451
D805.A1
EX - P O W BULLETIN. Text in English. 1949. m. USD 20 (effective 2000). adv. bk.rev. back issues avail.
Published by: American Ex-Prisoners of War, c/o Cheryl Cerbone, Ed., 3201 E Pioneer Pkwy, Ste 40, Arlington, TX 76010. TEL 817-649-2979. Ed., Pub., R&P, Adv. contact Cheryl Cerbone. Circ: 23,000.

355 USA ISSN 0014-4452
EXCHANGE & COMMISSARY NEWS. Abbreviated title: E and C News. Text in English. 1962. m. USD 105 domestic; free to qualified personnel (effective 2012). adv. **Document type:** *Magazine, Trade.* **Description:** Features news, interviews and merchandising reports examining every aspect of the military resale market - from Capitol Hill and the Pentagon to military resale activities around the world.
Published by: Executive Business Media, Inc., 825 Old Country Rd, PO Box 1500, Westbury, NY 11590. TEL 516-334-3030, FAX 516-334-3059, ebm-mail@ebmpubs.com. Ed. Phil Grey. Circ: 8,298.

358.4 DEU ISSN 1430-0117
F-40; Die Flugzeuge der Bundeswehr. Text in German. 1987. irreg., latest vol.49. EUR 14.50 newsstand/cover (effective 2009). **Document type:** *Magazine, Consumer.*
Published by: Buchholz Medien Verlag Druck, Arensburger Str 10, Buchholz, 31710, Germany. TEL 49-5751-96460, FAX 49-5751-964646, info@bmvd.de, http://www.bmvd.de.

355 NOR ISSN 1503-4399
F F I - FOKUS. (Forsvarets Forskningsinstitutt) Text in Norwegian. 2002. irreg. (2-3/yr). **Document type:** *Magazine, Government.*
Formerly (until 2003): Fokus (1503-2914)
Related titles: Online - full text ed.: ISSN 1503-4402.
Published by: Forsvarets Forskningsinstitutt/Norwegian Defence Research Establishment, PO Box 25, Kjeller, 2027, Norway. TEL 47-63-807000, FAX 47-63-807115, ffi@ffi.no.

355 NOR ISSN 0802-2437
F F I RAPPORT. (Forsvarets Forskningsinstitutt) Text in English, Norwegian. 1980. irreg. **Document type:** *Monographic series.*
Related titles: Online - full text ed.
Published by: Forsvarets Forskningsinstitutt/Norwegian Defence Research Establishment, PO Box 25, Kjeller, 2027, Norway. TEL 47-63-807000, FAX 47-63-807115, ffi@ffi.no.

355 SWE ISSN 1650-3201
F O I INFORMERAR OM. Variant title: Briefing Book on. Text in Swedish; Text occasionally in English. 1964-1993; resumed 1995-1996; resumed 2001. irreg., latest vol.5, 2005. SEK 175 per issue (effective 2005). charts; illus. back issues avail. **Document type:** *Monographic series, Government.*
Former titles (until 2001): F O A Informerar om (1401-4319); (until 1995): Om (0014-6013)
Published by: Totalfoersvarets Forskningsinstitut/Swedish Defense Research Agency, Gullfossgatan 6, Stockholm, 16490, Sweden. TEL 46-8-55503000, FAX 46-8-55503100, registrar@foi.se.

355 SWE ISSN 1650-1942
F O I - R. (Totalfoersvarets Forskningsinstitut Rapport) Text in Swedish. 1994. irreg. back issues avail. **Document type:** *Monographic series.*
Formerly (until 2001): F O A - R (1104-9154)
Published by: Totalfoersvarets Forskningsinstitut/Swedish Defense Research Agency, Gullfossgatan 6, Stockholm, 16490, Sweden. TEL 46-8-55503000, FAX 46-8-55503100, registrar@foi.se, http://www.foi.se.

F X O REPORT. *see* ENGINEERING—Electrical Engineering

355.338060489 DNK ISSN 0107-7716
FAGLIGT FORSVAR. Text in Danish. 1982. 6/yr. adv. illus. **Document type:** *Magazine, Consumer.*
Published by: Haerens Konstabel- og Korporalforening, Kronprinsensgade 8, Copenhagen K, 1114, Denmark. TEL 45-33-936522, FAX 45-33-936523, hkkf@hkkf.dk, http://www.hkkf.dk. Eds. Tina Noerholtz, Flemming Vinther.

358.4 USA
FALCON FLYER. Text in English. 1960. w. USD 45. adv. bk.rev. **Document type:** *Newspaper.* **Description:** Covers student activities, military news, sports and current events in government for cadets at the U.S. Air Force Academy.
Published by: Gowdy Printcraft Press, Inc., 22 N Sierre Madre, Colorado Springs, CO 80903. TEL 719-634-1593, FAX 719-632-0762. Ed. Doug Roth. Pub. John Bernheim. Adv. contact Michael Murt. Circ: 7,500.

355 FRA ISSN 0956-2400
UB275
FALLING LEAF. Text in English. 1958. q. EUR 15, GBP 10, USD 20 membership (effective 2007). adv. bk.rev. illus. **Document type:** *Magazine, Consumer.* **Description:** Primarily concerns the dissemination and effects of aerial propaganda leaflets in wars and conflicts.
Related titles: Online - full text ed.
Indexed: E-psyche, RASB.
Published by: Psywar Society, c/o Freddy Dehon, Sec., Villa Jonquille, 5 Avenue de la Paix, Hyeres, 83400, France. freddy.dehon@psywarsoc.org, http://www.psywar.org/psywarsoc/. Ed. Lee Richards. Circ: 150.

355 USA
FAMILY (FLORAL PARK); the magazine for military wives. Text in English. 1958. m. free to military families. adv. bk.rev. illus. **Document type:** *Magazine, Consumer.*
Formerly: Stateside Family
Published by: Military Family Communications, 51 Atlantic Ave, Floral Park, NY 11001. TEL 516-616-1930, FAX 516-616-1936. Ed. Donald Hirst. Pub., Adv. contact Joseph Mugnai Jr. page USD 14,000. Circ: 500,000.

355.6 USA ISSN 1084-7898
KF844.599
FEDERAL ACQUISITION REGULATION (CHICAGO). Abbreviated title: F A R. Text in English. 1987. s-a. (Jan. & Jul.; a. until 2004). USD 77 per issue for Jan. vol.; USD 116 per issue for Jan./Jul. combo vol. (effective 2007). **Document type:** *Government.* **Description:** Contains the uniform policies and procedures for acquisitions by executive agencies of the federal government: Department of Defense, the General Services Administration, and the National Aeronautics and Space Administration.
Related titles: CD-ROM ed.: F A R Archives. ISSN 1068-7041; Online - full text ed.
Published by: (U.S. Air Force), C C H Inc. (Subsidiary of: Wolters Kluwer N.V.), 2700 Lake Cook Rd, Riverwoods, IL 60015. TEL 847-267-7000, 800-248-3248, cust_serv@cch.com, http://www.cch.com. **Subscr. also to:** U.S. Government Printing Office, Superintendent of Documents.

353.538 USA ISSN 0883-3370
UB357
FEDERAL BENEFITS FOR VETERANS AND DEPENDENTS. Text in English. 1961. a. free. **Document type:** *Government.* **Description:** Outlines and describes benefits and services available to US veterans and their dependents. Also lists V.A. facilities nationwide.
Formerly: U.S. Veterans Administration. V A Fact Sheets (0083-3576)
Related titles: Online - full text ed.
Published by: (Office of Public Affairs), U.S. Department of Veterans Affairs, 810 Vermont Ave, NW, Washington, DC 20420. TEL 202-273-5121, http://www.va.gov. Ed. Bonner H Day. **Subscr. to:** U.S. Government Printing Office, Superintendent of Documents, PO Box 371954, Pittsburgh, PA 15250. TEL 202-512-1800, FAX 202-512-2250, orders@gpo.gov.

FEIHANG DAODAN/WINGED MISSILES JOURNAL. *see* AERONAUTICS AND SPACE FLIGHT

355 DEU
FELDPOSTBRIEFE. Text in German. 2008. irreg., latest vol.3, 2009. price varies. **Document type:** *Monographic series, Academic/Scholarly.*
Published by: Trafo Verlag, Finkenstr 8, Berlin, 12621, Germany. TEL 49-30-61299418, FAX 49-30-61299421, info@trafoberlin.de.

355.5 CHE ISSN 0014-9780
FELDWEBEL/SERGENT-MAJOR/SERGENTE MAGGIORE. Text in French, German. 1970 (vol.12). m. CHF 48. adv. charts; illus. **Document type:** *Bulletin, Trade.* **Description:** Covers association news and information, training, technical information. Includes reports and calendar of events.
Published by: (Schweizerischer Feldwebelverband), Huber und Co. AG, Promenadenstr 16, Frauenfeld, 8501, Switzerland. TEL 41-54-271111. Ed. P Roethlin.

FIGURINES. see HOBBIES

FINANCIAL AID FOR VETERANS, MILITARY PERSONNEL, AND THEIR DEPENDENTS. see EDUCATION—School Organization And Administration

355 USA ISSN 1935-4096
UF1
FIRES. Text in English. 2007. bi-m. free to members (effective 2009). bk.rev. illus. back issues avail.; reprints avail. **Document type:** *Magazine, Trade.* **Description:** Contains articles related to Army and Marine Corps field artillery or fire support.
Formed by the merger of (1998-2007): A D A Magazine Online; Which was formerly (until 1998): A D A (1084-6700); (until 1990): Air Defense Artillery (0740-803X); (until 1983): Air Defense Magazine (0192-964X); (until 1976): Air Defense Trends (0091-9225); (1987-2007): Field Artillery (0899-2525); Which was formerly (until 1987): Field Artillery Journal (0191-975X); Which superseded in part (in 1973): Army (0004-2455); Which was formerly (until 1956): The Army Combat Forces Journal (0271-7336); (1950-1954): United States Army Combat Forces Journal (0277-9080); Which was formed by the merger of (1911-1950): The Field Artillery Journal; (1910-1950): Infantry Journal (0019-9540); Which was formerly (1904-1910): United States Infantry Association. Journal; The Army Combat Forces Journal incorporated (1948-1954): Antiaircraft Journal; Which was formerly (until 1948): The Coast Artillery Journal (0095-8832); (until 1922): Journal of the United States Artillery (0097-3785)
Related titles: Online - full text ed.: ISSN 1935-410X. free (effective 2009).
Indexed: A22, A26, ABS&EES, AMB, AUNI, CA, DM&T, G05, G06, G07, G08, I05, LID&ISL, M05, M06, M07, MEA&I, P02, P10, P47, P48, P52, P53, P54, PQC, T02.
—Ingenta, Linda Hall.
Published by: U S Army Fires Center of Excellence, PO Box 33311, Fort Sill, OK 73503. TEL 580-442-5121, FAX 580-442-7773, famag@sill.army.mil. Ed. Sharon McBride. **Subscr. to:** U.S. Government Printing Office, Superintendent of Documents, PO Box 371954, Pittsburgh, PA 15250. gpo@custhelp.com, http://www.gpo.gov/.

359 UKR
FLOT UKRAINY. Text in Ukrainian. 1992. w. **Document type:** *Newspaper, Government.*
Published by: Ministerstvo Oborony Ukrainy, vul Komunistychna 3a, Sevastopol, 99011, Ukraine. TEL 380-692-547838, FAX 380-692-547838, http://www.mil.gov.ua.

359 SWE ISSN 0015-4431
FLOTTANS MAEN; kamratskap, oerlogstradition, sjoefoersvar. Text in Swedish. 1935. q. adv. bk.rev. illus. **Document type:** *Magazine, Trade.*
Indexed: AMB.
Published by: Foereningen Flottans Maen, Teatergatan 3, Stockholm, 11148, Sweden. riksforbundet@flottensman.se, http://www.flottensman.se. Ed. Olle Melin.

FLYING M. see AERONAUTICS AND SPACE FLIGHT

355 SWE ISSN 0046-4643
FOERSVAR I NUTID. Text in Swedish. 1965. bi-m. bk.rev. charts; illus.; stat. **Document type:** *Bulletin.*
Published by: Folk och Foersvar/Society and Defense, Lilla Nygatan 14, Stockholm, 10317, Sweden. TEL 46-8-58882490, FAX 46-8-6606355, http://www.folkochforsvar.se. Ed. Jonas Landahl. Circ: 1,600.

355 SWE ISSN 0347-7576
FOERSVARETS FOERFATTNINGSSAMLING. Text in Swedish. 1977. 40/yr. SEK 370 (effective 2001). **Document type:** *Journal, Government.*
Supersedes in part: Tjaenstemeddelanden fraan Foersvarsmakten
Published by: Militaera Servicekontoret, TF-redaktionen, Stockholm, 10786, Sweden. TEL 46-8-788-75-00, FAX 46-8-788-83-08. Ed. Sven Oeberg. Pub. Barbro Yannelos.

355 SWE ISSN 1100-8245
FOERSVARETS FORUM. Text in Swedish. 1989. 6/yr. SEK 100 domestic; SEK 120 foreign (effective 2005). bk.rev. **Document type:** *Magazine, Government.* **Description:** Focuses on relevant topics of interest to the Swedish armed forces and others with an interest in Swedish defense and national security.
Related titles: Online - full text ed.: ISSN 1402-4594.
Published by: Foersvarsmakten, Informationsavdelingen, Lidingoevaegen 24, Stockholm, 10785, Sweden. TEL 46-8-7887500, FAX 46-8-7887778, exp-hkv@mil.se.

355 SWE ISSN 1653-3720
FOERSVARSUTBILDAREN. Text in Swedish. 1918. 5/yr. SEK 150 membership (effective 2006). adv. bk.rev. illus.; maps; stat. back issues avail. **Document type:** *Magazine, Trade.* **Description:** Provides a source of information about the military to members.
Former titles (until 2006): Befael (1400-6030); (until vol.4, 1994): F B U - Befael (0005-7797); (until vol.4, 1971): Befael; (until 1947): Befael, Landstormsmannen; (until 1946): Landstormsmannen
Related titles: E-mail ed.; Fax ed.; Online - full text ed.
Published by: Centralfoerbundet Foer Befaelsutbildning, Karlavaegen 65, PO Box 5034, Stockholm, 10241, Sweden. TEL 46-8-58774200, FAX 46-8-58774290, info@forsvarsutbildarna.se. Ed. Bert Olof Lax. Pub. Anders Hakansson. adv.: B&W page SEK 12,000, color page SEK 17,000; trim 265 x 186. Circ: 37,000.

355.1 FRA ISSN 1630-5078
FONDATION DE LA FRANCE LIBRE. Text in French. 1945. q. EUR 15 (effective 2008). adv. bk.rev. illus. **Document type:** *Journal.*
Formerly (until 2001): Revue de la France Libre (0035-1210)
Published by: Association des Francais Libres, 59 rue Vergniaud, Paris, 75013, France. TEL 33-1-45887252. Ed. Louise De Bea. Circ: 9,500.

355.3 FRA ISSN 1966-5156
FONDATION POUR LA RECHERCHE STRATEGIQUE. RECHERCHES ET DOCUMENTS. Text in French. 1995. irreg. **Document type:** *Monographic series, Academic/Scholarly.*
Formerly (until 1999): Recherches et Documents du C R E S T (1279-0257)
Published by: Fondation pour la Recherche Strategique, 27 rue Damesme, Paris, 75013, France. TEL 33-01-43137777, FAX 33-01-43137778, webmaster@frstrategie.org, http://www.frstrategie.org.

355 GBR
FORCES WEEKLY ECHO. Text in English. 1980. w. GBP 55. adv.
Published by: Combined Service Publications Ltd., PO Box 4, Combined Service Publications, Farnborough, Hants GU14 7LR, United Kingdom. TEL 44-1252-515891, FAX 44-1252-517918. Ed. D D Crossley. Circ: 25,000.

355 DNK ISSN 1603-483X
FORSVARET. Text in Danish. 1983. bi-m. free. illus. **Document type:** *Magazine, Trade.*
Formerly (until 2003): Vaernskontakt (0109-0100)
Related titles: Online - full text ed.: 2007.
Published by: Forsvarskommandoen, Presse- og Informationstjeneste/ Defence Command Denmark, Danneskiold-Samsoes Alle 1, Copenhagen K, 1434, Denmark. TEL 45-45-674567, FAX 45-45-890748, fko-chkomsek@mil.dk, http://www.forsvaret.dk. Ed. Lennie Fredskov Hansen. Circ: 30,000 (controlled and free).

355.3 NOR ISSN 0809-845X
FORSVARETS FORUM. Text in Norwegian. 1945. 10/yr. adv. bk.rev. illus. back issues avail. **Document type:** *Magazine, Government.*
Incorporates (2004-2005): I Marinen (1504-0305); (2003-2005): Haerfra (1503-6308); (1987-2005): Luftled (0807-9021); Former titles (until 2006): Forsvarsforum (1503-8505); (until 2004): Forsvarets Forum (0332-9062); (until 1980): Mannskapsavisa (0025-2352); Militaer Orienterung
Related titles: Online - full text ed.
—CCC.
Published by: Forsvarets Mediasenter, Akershus Festning, Bygning 65, Oslo, 0015, Norway. TEL 47-23-092030, FAX 47-23-092031. Eds. Erling Eikli, Tor Eigil Stordahl TEL 47-23-092031. Adv. contact Gunn-Hilde Kolstad. Circ: 80,000.

FORT CONCHO GUIDON. see MUSEUMS AND ART GALLERIES

355 USA
FORT JACKSON LEADER. Text in English. w. (Thu.). free (effective 2006). **Document type:** *Newspaper.*
Related titles: Online - full content ed.
Published by: U S Army, 4394 Stroin Thurman Blvd, Fort Jackson, SC 29207. TEL 803-751-5487, FAX 803-751-2722. Ed. Lori Bultman. Circ: 15,000 (free).

355.31 USA
FORT LEWIS RANGER/AIRLIFT. Text in English. 1951. w. (Thu.). free newsstand/cover & home delivery; USD 29 subscr - mailed. **Document type:** *Newspaper.*
Formerly: The Fort Lewis Ranger
Published by: Thomas H. Swarner, The Ranger Publishing Co., Inc., PO Box 98801, Tacoma, WA 98498. TEL 253-584-1212, FAX 253-581-5962. Ed. Kenneth Swarner. Pub. Thomas H. Swarner. Adv. contact Bill White. Circ: 29,000 (controlled and free). Wire service: AP.

355.31 USA
FORT RILEY POST. Text in English. 1958. w. (Fri.). USD 20 subscr - mailed; free (effective 2005). adv. 16 p./no.; **Document type:** *Newspaper.*
Published by: Montgomery Communications, Inc., 222 W. Sixth St., Junction City, KS 66441. TEL 785-762-5000, FAX 785-762-4584. Ed. Michael Heronemus. Pub. John G. Montgomery. adv.: col. inch USD 15.10. Circ: 8,800 (free).

355 USA
FORT SAM NEWS LEADER. Text in English. w. **Document type:** *Newspaper, Consumer.*
Published by: Prime Time, Inc, 17400 Judson Rd, San Antonio, TX 78247. TEL 210-453-3300, http://www.primetimenewspapers.com/.

355.009 USA ISSN 0015-8070
E199
FORT TICONDEROGA MUSEUM. BULLETIN. Text in English. 1927. a. USD 10 (effective 2003). bk.rev. illus.; bibl.; maps. index. 120 p./no. 1 cols./p.; back issues avail. **Document type:** *Bulletin, Consumer.* **Description:** Covers military history from 1609 to 1781.
Published by: Fort Ticonderoga Association Inc., Fort Ticonderoga Museum, PO Box 390, Ticonderoga, NY 12883. TEL 518-585-2821, FAX 518-585-2210, mail@fort-ticonderoga.org, http://www.fort-ticonderoga.org. Ed. Virginia M Westbrook. Pub., R&P Nicholas Westbrook. Circ: 750.

355 CHE
FORTERESSE. Text in French. 11/yr.
Address: 7 rue de Geneve, Lausanne, 1002, Switzerland. TEL 021-505901. Circ: 1,400.

359.96 USA ISSN 0362-9910
VE23.A1
FORTITUDINE. Text in English. 1970. q. USD 15 domestic; USD 21 foreign; USD 3.50 per issue domestic; USD 4.90 per issue foreign (effective 2009). bibl.; charts; illus. back issues avail. **Document type:** *Newsletter, Trade.* **Description:** Seeks to educate and train marines on active duty in the uses of military and Marine Corps history.
Formerly (until 19??): Harumfrodite
Indexed: IUSGP.
Published by: U.S. Marine Corps, History and Museums Division, 3079 Moreell Ave, Quantico, VA 22134. TEL 703-432-4874, http://hqinet001.hqmc.usmc.mil/HD/. **Subscr. to:** U.S. Government Printing Office, Superintendent of Documents, PO Box 371954, Pittsburgh, PA 15250. TEL 202-512-1800, FAX 202-512-2250, ContactCenter@gpo.gov, http://bookstore.gpo.gov.

355 CAN ISSN 0843-5995
FORUM (MARKHAM). Text in English. 1985. q. USD 72 domestic; USD 80 foreign. adv. back issues avail. **Description:** Independent publication whose mandate is to write about issues and events concerning Canada's defense community.
Published by: Synergistic Enterprises, 132 Adrian Cres, Markham, ON L3P 7B3, Canada. TEL 416-472-2801, FAX 416-472-3091. Ed. Peter A Kitchen. Circ: 12,000.

355 930 DEU ISSN 1869-5167
▼ **FORUM MODERNE MILITAERGESCHICHTE.** Text in German. 2009. irreg. price varies. **Document type:** *Monographic series, Academic/Scholarly.*
Published by: Verlag Dr. Koester, Rungestr 22-24, Berlin, 10179, Germany. TEL 49-30-76403224, FAX 49-30-76403227, verlag-koester@t-online.de.

355 SWE ISSN 0280-6215
FORUM NAVALE. Text in Swedish. 1940. irreg. SZL 200 membership (effective 2007). back issues avail. **Document type:** *Monographic series, Academic/Scholarly.*
Formerly (until 1946): Sjoehistoriska Samfundet. Skrifter (1102-8084)
Published by: Sjoehistoriska Samfundet, c/o Per Clason, Krigsarkivet, Stockholm, 11599, Sweden. info@sjohistoriskasamfundet.se. Ed. Leos Mueller.

355 SWE ISSN 1650-1837
FORUM NAVALES SKRIFTSERIE. Text in Swedish; Summaries in English. 2000. irreg., latest vol.21, 2007. back issues avail. **Document type:** *Monographic series, Academic/Scholarly.*
Published by: Sjoehistoriska Samfundet, c/o Per Clason, Krigsarkivet, Stockholm, 11599, Sweden. info@sjohistoriskasamfundet.se.

355 SWE ISSN 1650-2671
UA11
FRAMSYN. Text in Swedish. 1963. 6/yr. SEK 212 (effective 2005). **Document type:** *Magazine, Consumer.*
Former titles (until 2001): F O A Tidningen (0429-9531); (until 1964): F O A Tidning foer Foersvarets Forskningsanstalt
Published by: (Foersvarshoegskolan/Swedish National Defence College), Totalfoersvarets Forskningsinstitut/Swedish Defense Research Agency, Gullfossgatan 6, Stockholm, 16490, Sweden. TEL 46-8-55503000, FAX 46-8-55503100, registrar@foi.se. Ed. Jan Ivar Askelin.

338.473944 GBR ISSN 1749-138X
FRANCE DEFENCE & SECURITY REPORT. Text in English. 2005. q. EUR 820, USD 1,030 combined subscription (print & email eds.) (effective 2010). **Document type:** *Report, Trade.* **Description:** Provides professionals, consultancies, government departments, regulatory bodies and researchers with independent forecasts and regional competitive intelligence on the French defence and security industry.
Related titles: E-mail ed.
Indexed: B01.
Published by: Business Monitor International Ltd., Senator House, 85 Queen Victoria St, London, EC4V 4AB, United Kingdom. TEL 44-20-72480468, FAX 44-20-72480467, subs@businessmonitor.com.

355 FRA ISSN 0015-9727
FRANCE. MINISTERE DE LA DEFENSE NATIONALE. BULLETIN OFFICIEL. Variant title: France. Ministere de la Defense Nationale. Bulletin Officiel des Armees. Text in French. 1947. w. **Document type:** *Bulletin, Government.*
Related titles: Online - full text ed.
Published by: France. Ministere de la Defense Nationale, 14 rue Saint Dominique, Paris, 75007, France.

355 FRA ISSN 2105-2468
UA701
FRANCE. MINISTERE DES ARMEES. BULLETIN OFFICIEL DES ARMEES. Text in French. 1973. w. back issues avail. **Document type:** *Government.*
Incorporates (1997-200?): France. Ministere des Armees. Bulletin Officiel des Armees. Edition Methodique. Administration et Gestion des Militaires, Affectations, Tenue des Dossiers (1277-7390); Formed by the merger of (1973-2006): France. Ministere des Armees. Bulletin Officiel des Armees. Edition Chronologique (Print) (0755-2289); Which was formed by the merger of (1965-1973): France. Ministere des Armees. Bulletin Officiel des Armees. Edition Chronologique, Armee de l'air, Partie Annexe (0532-5277); (1965-1973): France. Ministere des Armees. Bulletin Officiel des Armees. Edition Chronologique, Armee de Terre, Partie Annexe (0532-5293); (1965-1973): France. Ministere des Armees. Bulletin Officiel des Armees. Edition Chronologique, Marine Nationale, Partie Annexe (0532-5315); (1965-1973): France. Ministere des Armees. Bulletin Officiel des Armees. Edition Chronologique, Services Communs, Partie Annexe (0532-534X); (1973-2006): France. Ministere des Armees. Bulletin Officiel des Armees. Edition Chronologique, Partie Principale (Print) (0755-2270); Which was formed by the merger of (1965-1973): France. Ministere des Armees. Bulletin Officiel des Armees. Edition Chronologique, Services Communs, Partie Principale (0532-5358); (1965-1973): France. Ministere des Armees. Bulletin Officiel des Armees. Edition Chronologique, Armee de l'air, Partie Principalle (0532-5285); (1965-1973): France. Ministere des Armees. Bulletin Officiel des Armees. Edition Chronologique, Armee de Terre, Partie Principale (0532-5307); (1965-1973): France. Ministere des Armees. Bulletin Officiel des Armees. Edition Chronologique, Marine Nationale, Partie Principale (0532-5323)
Media: Online - full text.
Published by: France. Ministere de la Defense Nationale, 14 rue Saint Dominique, Paris, 75007, France.

355.31 FRA ISSN 0016-1144
FRERES D'ARMES; organe de Liaison des Forces Armees Francaises, Africaines et Malgaches. Text in French. 1963. bi-m. adv. bk.rev. bibl.; illus. **Description:** News of French military cooperation with Africa, the Indian Ocean and the Pacific regions and Cambodia .
Published by: France. Ministere des Affaires Etrangeres, 37 Quai d'Orsay, Paris, 75007, France. http://www.diplomatie.gouv.fr. Circ: 10,000.

355 USA ISSN 0071-9641
FRONTIER MILITARY SERIES. Text in English. 1951. irreg., latest vol.29, 2010. price varies. index. back issues avail. **Document type:** *Monographic series, Academic/Scholarly.*
Published by: Arthur H. Clark Co. (Subsidiary of: University of Oklahoma Press), 2800 Venture Dr, Norman, OK 73069. TEL 405-325-2000, 800-627-7377, FAX 405-364-5798, 800-735-0476, presscs@ou.edu, http://www.oupress.com/ECommerce/Book/Publishers/0/Title/False?query=publisher%3D14. Pub. Robert A Clark TEL 405-325-4548.

355 CAN ISSN 1715-9296
FRONTLINE DEFENCE. Text in English. 2004. bi-m. CAD 28.50 domestic to qualified personnel; CAD 59.50 domestic to institutions; CAD 69.50 domestic to corporations; USD 69.50 in United States; USD 99.50 elsewhere (effective 2006). bk.rev. **Document type:** *Magazine, Trade.* **Description:** Written by the senior officers and commanders of Canada's Uniformed Forces for themselves and others.
Formerly (until 2005): Frontline (1708-9875)
Published by: Beacon Publishing Inc., 2150 Fillmore Cr., Ottawa, ON K1J 6A4, Canada. TEL 613-747-1138, FAX 613-747-7319, info@frontline-canada.com.

355 CAN ISSN 1715-930X
FRONTLINE SECURITY. Text in English. 2006. bi-m. **Document type:** *Magazine, Trade.*
Published by: Beacon Publishing Inc., 2150 Fillmore Cr., Ottawa, ON K1J 6A4, Canada. TEL 613-747-1138, FAX 613-747-7319, info@frontline-canada.com.

355 DEU ISSN 1862-6017
FUEAK REFLEXIONEN. Text in German. 2006. irreg. **Document type:** *Monographic series, Academic/Scholarly.*
Media: Online - full content.
Published by: Fuehrungsakademie der Bundeswehr, Manteuffelstr 20, Hamburg, 22587, Germany. TEL 49-40-86673112, FAX 49-40-86674009, fueakbwwebmaster@bundeswehr.org.

358.4 ESP ISSN 1575-1090
FUERZA AEREA. Text in Spanish. 1998. m. EUR 56 domestic (effective 2009). **Document type:** *Magazine, Consumer.*
Published by: M C Ediciones, Paseo de Sant Gervasi 16-20, Barcelona, 08022, Spain. TEL 34-93-2541250, FAX 34-93-2541262, http://www.mcediciones.net.

358.4 CHL ISSN 0716-4866
UG635.C5
FUERZA AEREA. Text in Spanish. 1941. q. USD 60. adv.
Formerly: Revista de la Fuerza Aerea
Indexed: IBR, IBZ.
Published by: Editorial Fuerza Aerea, Ave. B O Higgins, 1316 Of 63, Santiago, Chile. Circ: 15,000.

359 ESP ISSN 1695-3258
FUERZA NAVAL. Text in Spanish. 2002. m. EUR 56 domestic (effective 2009). **Document type:** *Magazine, Consumer.*
Published by: M C Ediciones, Paseo de Sant Gervasi 16-20, Barcelona, 08022, Spain. TEL 34-93-2541250, FAX 34-93-2541262, http://www.mcediciones.net.

355.31 ESP ISSN 1698-0131
FUERZA TERRESTRE. Text in Spanish. 2004. m. EUR 56 domestic (effective 2009). **Document type:** *Magazine, Consumer.*
Published by: M C Ediciones, Paseo de Sant Gervasi 16-20, Barcelona, 08022, Spain. TEL 34-93-2541250, FAX 34-93-2541262, http://www.mcediciones.net.

355 ESP ISSN 1887-9144
FUERZAS DE DEFENSA Y SEGURIDAD. Text in Spanish. 1978. m. adv. bk.rev. illus.; bibl.; charts; maps; stat. index. 84 p./no.; back issues avail. **Document type:** *Magazine, Consumer.* **Description:** Covers armies, weapons, and industries for the Spanish and Latin market.
Formerly (until 2007): Defensa (0211-3732)
Published by: Grupo Edefa S.A., C Puerto Principe No. 3-B 1o.-A, Madrid, 28043, Spain. TEL 34-91-38219445, edefa@edefa.com, http://www.edefa.es. Ed. Javier Taibo. Pub. Vicente Talon. Adv. contact Eva Cervera. B&W page USD 3,020, color page USD 4,780; trim 210 x 300. Circ: 22,000.

G I JOBS; get hired. *see* OCCUPATIONS AND CAREERS

355.37 USA ISSN 1559-9922
G X. (Guard Experience) Text in English. 2004. m. adv. **Document type:** *Magazine, Trade.*
Published by: G X Magazine, 1625 Broadway, 3rd flr, Nashville, TN 37203. TEL 615-256-6282, 866-596-4558, FAX 615-256-6860, info@gxonline.com, http://www.gxonline.com.

355 GBR ISSN 2044-0863
▼ **G2 DEFENCE**; intelligence and security. Text in English. 2010. bi-m. free to qualified personnel (effective 2010). back issues avail. **Document type:** *Magazine, Trade.* **Description:** Aims to keep service men and women informed about equipment available or being developed for training and operations.
Related titles: Online - full text ed.: ISSN 2044-0871. free to qualified personnel (effective 2010).
Published by: Jon Philips Ltd., 60 Port St, Manchester, M1 2EQ, United Kingdom. TEL 44-161-2364300, http://www.jonphilips.co.uk. Ed. Will Fowler.

355 GBR ISSN 2043-9318
▼ **G3 DEFENCE.** Text in English. 2009. bi-m. free to qualified personnel (effective 2010). back issues avail. **Document type:** *Magazine, Trade.* **Description:** Aims to keep service men and women informed about equipment available or being developed for training and operations.
Related titles: Online - full text ed.: ISSN 2040-8935. free to qualified personnel (effective 2010).
Published by: Jon Philips Ltd., 60 Port St, Manchester, M1 2EQ, United Kingdom. TEL 44-161-2364300, sales@g3defence.co.uk, http://www.jonphilips.co.uk. Ed. Will Fowler.

355 GBR ISSN 2044-088X
▼ **G4 DEFENCE.** Text in English. 2010. bi-m. free to qualified personnel (effective 2010). back issues avail. **Document type:** *Magazine, Trade.*
Related titles: Online - full text ed.: ISSN 2044-0898. free to qualified personnel (effective 2010).
Published by: Jon Philips Ltd., 60 Port St, Manchester, M1 2EQ, United Kingdom. TEL 44-161-2364300, http://www.jonphilips.co.uk. Eds. David Craig, Will Fowler.

355 GBR ISSN 0966-1158
THE GALLIPOLIAN. Text in English. 1969. 3/yr. free (effective 2009). bk.rev. bibl.; illus.; maps. back issues avail. **Document type:** *Newsletter, Academic/Scholarly.* **Description:** Focuses on the Gallipoli campaign of 1915-1916 and all matters associated with it.
Published by: The Gallipoli Association, PO Box 26907, London, SE21 8WB, United Kingdom. chairman@gallipoli-association.org, http://www.gallipoli-association.org. Ed. Foster Summerson.

355 RUS
GANGUT. Text in Russian. s-a. USD 90 in the Americas (effective 2000).
Published by: Izdatel'stvo Gangut, P.O. Box 10, St. Petersburg, 196135, Russian Federation. **Dist. by:** East View Information Services, 10601 Wayzata Blvd, Minneapolis, MN 55305. TEL 952-252-1201, 800-477-1005, FAX 952-252-1202, info@eastview.com, http://www.eastview.com.

356.1 AUS ISSN 1837-8234
THE GARRISON GAZETTE. Text in English. 200?. q. free (effective 2010). back issues avail. **Document type:** *Newsletter, Trade.*
Media: Online - full text.
Published by: 73rd Regiment of Foot gabriellekoens@hotmail.com. Ed. Dave Sanders.

DAS GELTENDE SEEVOELKERRECHT IN EINZELDARSTELLUNGEN. *see* LAW—International Law

358.4 GBR ISSN 1749-1134
GEN SHEET. Text in English. 1948. q. free to members (effective 2010). **Document type:** *Newsletter, Trade.*
Formerly (until 1998): Royal Air Forces Association. Chelmsford Branch. Branch Newsletter
Related titles: Online - full text ed.: free (effective 2009).
Published by: Royal Air Force Association. Chelmsford Branch, Oliver House, Hall St, Chelmsford, Essex CM2 0GH, United Kingdom. TEL 44-1245-225649, secretary@rafachelms.freeserve.co.uk, http://www.rafa.org.uk/. Ed. Norman Bartlett.

355.0353 FRA ISSN 1161-1715
GEND'INFO. Text in French. 1974. 11/yr. illus. **Description:** Offers a look at the lives of police officials.
Former titles (until 1991): Gendarmerie Informations (0767-3957); (until 1979): Echos de la Direction (0767-3949)
Published by: Direction Generale de la Gendarmerie Nationale, 35 Rue Saint-Didier, Paris, 75016, France. TEL 33-1-56288999, http://www.defense.gouv.fr/gendarmerie/. Circ: 106,000.

353.538 USA ISSN 0741-0611
UB357
GEOGRAPHIC DISTRIBUTION OF V A EXPENDITURES. (Veterans Administration) Text in English. a. **Document type:** *Government.*
Published by: U.S. Department of Veterans Affairs, 810 Vermont Ave, NW, Washington, DC 20420. TEL 202-273-5121, http://www.va.gov.

GEORGE C. MARSHALL FOUNDATION. TOPICS. *see* HISTORY—History Of North And South America

355 629.1 USA ISSN 2150-9468
UA993
GEOSPATIAL INTELLIGENCE FORUM. Abbreviated title: G I F. (vol.4, no.1 (Mar. 2006) has the title: Military - DHS Intelligence) Text in English. 2003. bi-m. free to qualified personnel (effective 2009). adv. back issues avail. **Document type:** *Magazine, Trade.* **Description:** Covers geospatial intelligence in terms of war and homeland security, including technological developments.
Formerly (until 2009): Military Geospatial Technology (1552-7905)
Related titles: Online - full text ed.: ISSN 2150-9476.
Published by: (United States Geospatial Intelligence Foundation), Kerrigan Media International, Inc., 15800 Crabbs Branch Way, Ste 300, Rockville, MD 20855. TEL 301-670-5700, 888-299-8292, FAX 301-670-5701, kmi@kmimediagroup.com, http://www.kerriganmedia.com. Ed. Jeff McKaughan. Adv. contact Scott Parker. B&W page USD 6,219, color page USD 7,259; trim 8.375 x 10.875.

338.473 943 363.35 GBR ISSN 1749-1398
GERMANY DEFENCE & SECURITY REPORT. Text in English. 2005. q. EUR 820, USD 1,030 combined subscription (print & email eds.) (effective 2010). **Document type:** *Report, Trade.* **Description:** Provides professionals, consultancies, government departments, regulatory bodies and researchers with independent forecasts and regional competitive intelligence on the German defence & security industry.
Related titles: E-mail ed.
Indexed: B01.
Published by: Business Monitor International Ltd., Senator House, 85 Queen Victoria St, London, EC4V 4AB, United Kingdom. TEL 44-20-72480468, FAX 44-20-72480467, subs@businessmonitor.com.

GLADIUS; etudes sur les armes anciennes, l'armement, l'art militaire et la vie culturelle en Orient et Occident. *see* ANTIQUES

GLOBAL SURVEY. *see* POLITICAL SCIENCE—International Relations

359 GBR ISSN 0017-1204
GLOBE AND LAUREL. Text in English. 1892. bi-m. GBP 12 in United Kingdom & Northern Ireland; GBP 21 in Europe; GBP 30 elsewhere (effective 2009). adv. bk.rev. charts; illus. index. back issues avail. **Document type:** *Magazine, Trade.* **Description:** Contains reports from all major units, ships detachments, reserves, cadets and association branches, as well as reports on reunions, families pages, corps sport etc.
Indexed: LID&ISL.
Published by: Royal Marines, The Secretary, HMS Excellent, Whale Island, Portsmouth, Hants PO2 8ER, United Kingdom. TEL 44-23-92547209. Ed. Capt. J Hillier. Circ: 13,000.

355 USA
GOODFELLOW MONITOR. Text in English. 1958. w. free. adv. charts; illus.; maps; stat. back issues avail. **Document type:** *Newspaper.* **Description:** Provides news and information concerning all aspects of Goodfellow Air Force Base, Texas, along with news from all branches of the Department of Defense for all persons in San Angelo affiliated with the U.S. military.
Published by: (17th Training Wing), San Angelo Standard - Times, 34 W Harris, San Angelo, TX 76903. TEL 325-653-1221, FAX 325-654-5414. Ed. Mike Briggs. R&P, Adv. contact John Nebling. trim. Circ: 5,000.

353.538 USA
GOPHER OVERSEA'R. Text in English. 1929. 6/yr. USD 2 to non-members. adv. bk.rev. back issues avail.
Published by: Veterans of Foreign Wars of the United States, Department of Minnesota, Veterans Service Bldg., St. Paul, MN 55155. TEL 612-291-1757, FAX 612-291-2753. Ed. Jim Hesselgrave. Circ: 85,000 (controlled).

355 USA
GOSPORT. Text in English. 1921. w. (Fri.). free (effective 2004). 24 p./no. 6 cols./p.; back issues avail.; reprints avail. **Document type:** *Newspaper.*
Published by: Gannett Printing and Publishing Pensacola, Commanding Officer, 190 Radford Blvd, NAS, Pensacola, Escambia, FL 32508-5217. TEL 850-452-2313, FAX 850-452-2760. Ed. Scott Hallford. Pub. Capt. John Pruitt. Circ: 25,000 (paid and controlled).

GOVERNMENT VIDEO; for federal, military, state and local government media professionals. *see* COMMUNICATIONS—Video

353.538 FRA ISSN 1162-5031
GRAND INVALIDE. Text in French. 1924. bi-m. adv.
Former titles (until 1944): Federation Nationale des plus Grands Invalides de Guerre. Circulaire Mensuelle (1162-5023); (until 1940): Le Grand Invalide (1162-5015)
Published by: Federation Nationale des Plus Grands Invalides de Guerre, 13 av. de la Motte Picquet, Paris, 75007, France. TEL 33-1-44113270, FAX 33-1-44113272, pgig@wanadoo.fr. Ed. Jean Claude Gouellain. Circ: 3,800.

355 RUS
GRANITSA ROSSII. Text in Russian. 1994. w. USD 152 in North America (effective 2000).
Indexed: RASB.
Published by: Izdatel'stvo Granitsa, Glavpochtampt, A-ya 848, Moscow, 101000, Russian Federation. TEL 7-095-2248169, FAX 7-095-2565159. Ed. A E Lubovinin. **Dist. by:** East View Information Services, 10601 Wayzata Blvd, Minneapolis, MN 55305. TEL 952-252-1201, 800-477-1005, FAX 952-252-1202, info@eastview.com, http://www.eastview.com.

355.8 GBR ISSN 1479-3865
GREAT BRITAIN. MINISTRY OF DEFENCE. DEFENCE CONTRACTS BULLETIN. Abbreviated title: M O D D C B. Text in English. 1992. fortn. GBP 230, EUR 323.40 combined subscription (print & online eds.) (effective 2010). adv. back issues avail. **Document type:** *Bulletin, Trade.* **Description:** Provides information on possible future purchases/contract notices, giving suppliers advance notification of forthcoming MOD tenders or contracts.
Former titles (until 2002): Works Services Opportunities (1352-447X); (until 1993): M O D Contracts Bulletin. Work Services Opportunities (0965-6197)
Related titles: Diskette ed.; Online - full text ed.
—CCC.
Published by: (Great Britain. Ministry of Defence), B I P Solutions Ltd, Medius, 60 Pacific Quay, Glasgow, G51 1DZ, United Kingdom. TEL 44-141-3328247, FAX 44-141-3312652, bip@bipsolutions.com, http://www.bipsolutions.com.

623 GBR
GREAT BRITAIN. MINISTRY OF DEFENCE. DEFENCE ESTATE ORGANISATION. DESIGN AND MAINTENANCE GUIDE. Text in English. 19??. irreg., latest vol.25, 2001. free (effective 2010). back issues avail. **Document type:** *Government.* **Description:** Provides information relating to the design, procurement, content maintenance and quality parameters of specific building types or facilities.
Formerly: Defence Works Functional Standard. Design and Maintenance Guide (1367-6210)
Related titles: Online - full text ed.
Published by: (Great Britain. Ministry of Defence, Defence Estate Organisation), The Stationery Office, St Crispins, Duke St, Norwich, NR3 1PD, United Kingdom. TEL 44-1603-622211, customer.services@tso.co.uk, http://www.tso.co.uk.

623 GBR
GREAT BRITAIN. MINISTRY OF DEFENCE. DEFENCE ESTATE ORGANISATION. SPECIFICATION. Text in English. irreg., latest vol.49, 2006. **Document type:** *Government.*
Formerly: Defence Works Functional Standard. Specification (1367-6237); Which superseded in part (in 199?): Defence Works Functional Standards
Related titles: Online - full text ed.
Published by: Defence Estate Organisation (Subsidiary of: Great Britain. Ministry of Defence), Kingston Rd., Sutton Coldfield, West Midlands, B75 7RL, United Kingdom. TEL 44-121-3112140, secretariat@de.mod.uk, http://www.mod.uk/DefenceInternet/Microsite/DE/.

359 GBR ISSN 0141-6081
GREAT BRITAIN. MINISTRY OF DEFENCE. NAVY LIST. Text in English. a. GBP 26 (effective 2010). **Document type:** *Directory, Government.* **Description:** Lists officers of the U.K. Royal Navy.
Published by: (Great Britain. Ministry of Defence), The Stationery Office, St Crispins, Duke St, Norwich, NR3 1PD, United Kingdom. TEL 44-1603-622211, FAX 44-870-6005533, customer.services@tso.co.uk, http://www.tso.co.uk. Circ: 900 (paid). **Subscr. to:** PO Box 29, Norwich NR3 1GN, United Kingdom. TEL 44-870-6005522.

GREAT BRITAIN. MINISTRY OF DEFENCE. NEWS. *see* BUSINESS AND ECONOMICS

355.31 GBR
GREAT BRITAIN. ROYAL ARMY CHAPLAINS' DEPARTMENT. JOURNAL. Text in English. 1922. a. bk.rev. back issues avail. **Document type:** *Journal, Trade.*
Formerly: Royal Army Chaplains Department. Quarterly Journal (0035-8657)
Published by: R A Ch D Association, MOD Chaplains (Army) Building 183, Trenchard Lines, Upavon, Pewsey, Wilts SN9 6BE, United Kingdom. armychaplains@armymail.mod.uk, http://www.army.mod.uk/chaplains/chaplains.aspx. Ed. Rev. J Whitton. Adv. contact Major M A Easey. Circ: 750 (paid).

355 USA
GREAT LAKES BULLETIN. Text in English. 1918. w. (Fri.). free domestic to qualified personnel (effective 2005). **Document type:** *Newspaper.*
Published by: U.S. Navy/Great Lakes Bulletin & Lakeland Media, 2601-A Paul Jones St, Bldg One, Rm B25, Great Lakes, Lake, IL 60088. TEL 847-688-4808, FAX 847-223-8810, http://www.nsgreatleakes.mil. Ed. Jeffrey Brown. Pub. William H Schroeder. Circ: 22,000 (free).

338.473 363.35 GBR ISSN 1749-1401
GREECE DEFENCE & SECURITY REPORT. Text in English. 2005. q. EUR 820, USD 1,030 combined subscription (print & email eds.) (effective 2010). **Document type:** *Report, Trade.* **Description:** Provides professionals, consultancies, government departments, regulatory bodies and researchers with independent forecasts and regional competitive intelligence on the Greek defence & security industry.
Related titles: E-mail ed.
Indexed: B01.
Published by: Business Monitor International Ltd., Senator House, 85 Queen Victoria St, London, EC4V 4AB, United Kingdom. TEL 44-20-72480468, FAX 44-20-72480467, subs@businessmonitor.com.

M

355 DEU ISSN 1860-403X
GRIEPHAN BRIEFE. Text in German. 1964. 47/yr. EUR 640 (effective 2010). adv. back issues avail. **Document type:** *Newsletter, Trade.* **Description:** Covers the equipment requirements of the German armed forces and analyses of the German and European defense industries.
Former titles (until 2004): Wehrdienst (1611-0900); (until 2002): Griephan Briefe Wehrdienst (1437-4684)
Published by: Griephan Verlag GmbH und Co. KG, Nordkanalstr 36, Hamburg, 20097, Germany. TEL 49-40-2371404, FAX 49-40-23714259, griephan@dvvmedia.com.

355 DEU ISSN 1619-4403
GRIEPHAN EXECUTIVE SUMMARY; the German newsletter for the defence & security industry. Text in English. 2002. 10/yr. EUR 368 (effective 2010). **Document type:** *Newsletter, Trade.*
Published by: Griephan Verlag GmbH und Co. KG, Nordkanalstr 36, Hamburg, 20097, Germany. TEL 49-40-2371404, FAX 49-40-23714259, griephan@dvvmedia.com.

355 USA ISSN 2157-1503
▼ **GROUND COMBAT TECHNOLOGY.** Abbreviated title: G C T. Text in English. 2010. 8/yr. USD 65 domestic; USD 149 foreign; free to qualified personnel (effective 2010). adv. back issues avail. **Document type:** *Magazine, Consumer.*
Related titles: Online - full text ed.: ISSN 2157-1511. free (effective 2010).
Published by: KMI Media Group, 15800 Crabbs Branch Way, Ste 300, Rockville, MD 20855. TEL 301-670-5700, 888-299-8292, FAX 301-670-5701, kmi@kmimediagroup.com. Ed. Phil Kiver TEL 301-670-5700 ext 140. Adv. contact Mike Appleby.

355 USA ISSN 2157-4405
GUARD TIMES. Text in English. 199?. q. free (effective 2010). back issues avail. **Document type:** *Magazine, Trade.*
Media: Online - full text.
Published by: New York State, Division of Military and Naval Affairs, DMNA-MNPA, 330 Old Niskayuna Rd, Latham, NY 12110. TEL 518-786-4581, FAX 518-786-4649, Richard.Goldenberg@ng.army.mil. Ed. Steven Petibone.

355.31 ESP ISSN 0210-5470
GUARDIA CIVIL. Text in Spanish. 1944. m. adv. back issues avail. **Document type:** *Magazine, Trade.*
Related titles: Online - full text ed.
Published by: Ministerio del Interior, Direccion General de la Guardia Civil, C/ Guzman el Bueno 110, Madrid, 28003, Spain. TEL 34-91-5146000, FAX 34-91-5146018, consulta@guardiacivil.org. Ed. Miguel Lopez Corral. Circ: 60,000 (paid).

355.31 ESP ISSN 1136-4645
GUARDIA CIVIL. CUADERNOS. Text in Spanish. 1968. s-a. **Document type:** *Monographic series, Trade.*
Former titles (until 1988): Guardia Civil. Revista de Estudios Historicos (0210-038X)
Indexed: IBR, IBZ.
Published by: Ministerio del Interior, Direccion General de la Guardia Civil, C/ Guzman el Bueno 110, Madrid, 28003, Spain. TEL 34-91-5146000, FAX 34-91-5146018, consulta@guardiacivil.org.

358.4 USA
THE GUARDIAN (MOODY AIR FORCE BASE). Text in English. w. (Fri.). free to qualified personnel (effective 2005). **Document type:** *Newspaper, Government.*
Formerly: Excalibur
Published by: Moody Air Force Base, 347 RQW/PA, 5113 Austin Ellipse, Ste. 6, Moody AFB, GA 31699-1795. TEL 229-257-1110, FAX 229-257-4804. Ed. Jon Grives. Circ: 5,000 (paid and controlled).

355 USA ISSN 2157-4235
GUARDLIFE. Text in English. 19??. bi-m. free (effective 2010). back issues avail. **Document type:** *Magazine, Trade.* **Description:** Designed for all members of the New Jersey Army and Air National Guard.
Media: Online - full text.
Published by: State of New Jersey, Department of Military and Veterans Affairs, PO Box 340, Trenton, NJ 08625. TEL 888-865-8387, pao@njdmava.state.nj.us. Eds. April Kelly, Patrick Daugherty, Yvonne Mays.

355 GBR ISSN 0017-503X
THE GUARDS MAGAZINE; journal of the household division. Text in English. 1862. q. GBP 16 domestic; GBP 20 foreign (effective 2003). adv. bk.rev. maps; illus. 80 p./no. 2 cols./p.; back issues avail. **Document type:** *Magazine, Trade.*
Formerly: Household Brigade Magazine
Published by: Guards Magazine, c/o Col. O.J.M. Lindsay, Ed., Horse Guards, Whitehall, London, SW1A 2AX, United Kingdom. TEL 44-20-74142271, FAX 44-20-74142207. Ed. O J M Lindsay. Adv. contact Digby Thornewill TEL 44-20-74142270. page GBP 300; 152 x 203. Circ: 2,200.

355 ITA ISSN 1126-7836
GUERRE E PACE. Text in English. 1993. bi-m. (5/yr.). EUR 35 (effective 2008). **Document type:** *Magazine, Consumer.*
Published by: Comitato Golfo, Via Festa del Perdono 6, Milan, 20122, Italy. TEL 39-02-58315437, FAX 39-02-28302611. Ed. Walter Peruzzi.

355.9 ESP ISSN 1697-9842
GUERREROS Y BATALLAS. Text in Spanish. 2000. irreg. back issues avail. **Document type:** *Monographic series, Academic/Scholarly.*
Published by: Editorial Sistesis, Vallehermoso, 34, Madrid, 28015, Spain. TEL 34-91-5932098, FAX 34-91-5458696, info@sintesis.com, http://www.sintesis.com/.

355 BRA ISSN 1414-0438
HF1371
GUIA MARITIMO. Text in Portuguese. 1992. bi-w. USD 120. adv. **Document type:** *Trade.*
Related titles: ◆ Supplement to: Global. ISSN 1415-2649.
Published by: Editora Update do Brasil Ltda., Av. Faria Lima 1234 - CJ 53, Sao Paulo SP, SP 01452-000, Brazil. TEL 55-11-815-9900, FAX 55-11-815-8259. Ed. Cassia Schitini. Pub. Tadeusz Polakiewicz. Adv. contact Tadausz Polakiewicz. page USD 2,500. Circ: 7,500.

GULHANE TIP DERGISI/GULHANE MEDICAL JOURNAL. *see* MEDICAL SCIENCES

GUN DIGEST. *see* HOBBIES

GUOFANG JIAOTONG GONGCHENG YU JISHU/TRAFFIC ENGINEERING AND TECHNOLOGY FOR NATIONAL DEFENCE. *see* TRANSPORTATION—Roads And Traffic

355 600 CHN ISSN 1671-4547
U395.C6
GUOFANG KEJI/NATIONAL DEFENSE SCIENCE & TECHNOLOGY. Text in Chinese. 2001. m. CNY 10 newsstand/cover (effective 2008). **Document type:** *Journal, Academic/Scholarly.*
Related titles: Online - full text ed.
Published by: Guofang Keji Jishu Daxue/National University of Defense Technology, Daya Lu, Changsha, Hunan 410073, China. TEL 86-731-4573570.

355 600 CHN ISSN 1001-2486
UG101
GUOFANG KEJI DAXUE XUEBAO/NATIONAL UNIVERSITY OF DEFENSE TECHNOLOGY. JOURNAL. Text in Chinese. 1956. bi-m. USD 31.20 (effective 2009). **Document type:** *Journal, Academic/Scholarly.*
Related titles: Online - full content ed.; Online - full text ed.
Indexed: A22, A28, APA, BrCerAb, C&ISA, CA/WCA, CIA, CPEI, CerAb, CivEngAb, CorrAb, E&CAJ, E11, EEA, EMA, ESPM, EngInd, EnvEAb, H15, INIS AtomInd, Inspec, M&TEA, M09, MBF, METADEX, RefZh, SCOPUS, SolStAb, T04, WAA.
—BLDSC (4831.247000), East View, IE, Ingenta, Linda Hall.
Published by: Guofang Keji Jishu Daxue/National University of Defense Technology, Daya Lu, Changsha, Hunan 410073, China. TEL 86-731-4572637.

GUOJI HANGKONG/INTERNATIONAL AVIATION. *see* AERONAUTICS AND SPACE FLIGHT

H B S A NEWSLETTER. *see* ANTIQUES

355.37 DNK ISSN 1902-3391
H J V MAGASINET. (Hjemmevaernskommandoen) Text in Danish. 1945. 4/yr. free. adv. charts; illus. **Document type:** *Magazine, Consumer.* **Description:** Membership publication for the Danish Home Guard.
Former titles (until 2007): Hjemmevaernsbladet (1600-2768); (until 1999): Hjemmevaernet (0906-8228); (until 1991): Hjemmevaernsbladet (0108-9978); (until 1974): Hjemmevaernet (0018-2834)
Related titles: Online - full text ed.
Published by: (Hjemmevaernet/The Danish Home Guard), Hjemmevaernskommandoen, Presseafdelingen/The Danish Home Guard, Press Department, c/o Hjemmevaernet, Kastellet 82, Copenhagen OE, 2100, Denmark. TEL 45-33-479300, FAX 45-33-479485, hjk@hjv.dk. Ed. Joergen Jensen TEL 45-33-479396. Adv. contact Joan Schack TEL 45-33-479395. Circ: 55,200.

355 USA ISSN 2156-471X
▼ **H P C INSIGHTS.** (High Performance Computing) Text in English. 2009. s-a. free (effective 2010). back issues avail. **Document type:** *Trade.*
Media: Online - full text.
Published by: High Performance Computing Modernization Program, 10501 Furnace Rd, Ste 101, Lorton, VA 22079. TEL 703-812-8205, habu@hpcmo.hpc.mil.

353.538 351 USA ISSN 1932-0876
UB369
H S R & D RESEARCH BRIEFS. (Health Services Research and Development) Text in English. 2001. s-a. **Document type:** *Newsletter.* **Description:** Summary information about recently completed research projects and publications, descriptions of new initiatives, and studies.
Media: Online - full text.
Published by: U.S. Department of Veterans Affairs, Office of Research and Development, 810 Vermont Ave NW, Washington, DC 20420. TEL 202-745-8000.

353.538 ISR ISSN 0334-357X
HA-LOHEM. Text in Hebrew. 1950. q. adv. bk.rev.
Formerly: Ha-Hayyal Ha-Meshuhrar
Indexed: IHP.
Published by: Organization of Disabled Veterans, Beit Halochame, P O Box 39262, Tel Aviv, 61392, Israel. FAX 972-3-421316, http://www.inz.org.il. Ed. Gil Yudelevich. Circ: 35,000.

355 HUN ISSN 0017-6540
DB925.5
HADTORTENELMI KOZLEMENYEK. Text in Hungarian. 1954. q. **Document type:** *Journal, Academic/Scholarly.*
Indexed: HistAb, P30, RASB.
Published by: Hadtorteneti Intezet es Muzeum/Museum of Military History, Kapisztran ter 2/4, Budapest, 1014, Hungary. TEL 36-1-3569522.

HAIJUN GONGCHENG DAXUE XUEBAO/NAVAL UNIVERSITY OF ENGINEERING. JOURNAL. *see* ENGINEERING

HAIJUN GONGCHENG DAXUE XUEBAO (ZONGHE BAN)/NAVAL UNIVERSITY OF ENGINEERING. JOURNAL (COMPREHENSIVE EDITION). *see* SOCIAL SCIENCES: COMPREHENSIVE WORKS

359 CHN
HAIJUN YUANXIAO JIAOYU/EDUCATION OF NAVAL ACADEMIES. Text in Chinese. 2001. bi-m. **Document type:** *Journal, Academic/Scholarly.*
Related titles: Online - full text ed.
Published by: Haijun Gongcheng Daxue/Naval University of Engineering, 717, Jiefang Dadao, Wuhan, 430033, China. TEL 86-27-83443674.

HAIJUN ZONGYIYUAN XUEBAO/PEOPLE'S LIBERATION ARMY. NAVAL GENERAL HOSPITAL. JOURNAL. *see* MEDICAL SCIENCES

355 FIN ISSN 0017-6796
HAKKU; pioneerien lehti. Text in Finnish. 1925. q. EUR 26 (effective 2005). adv. bk.rev. charts; illus. **Document type:** *Magazine.*
Published by: Pioneeriaselajin Liitto r.y., c/o Kari Melleri, Soederkullantori 3 A 5, Soederkulla, 01150, Finland. TEL 358-9-2721539, FAX 358-40-5587851. Ed. Kari Melleri. Circ: 3,500.

358.4 GBR ISSN 2046-1356
THE HALTONIAN. Text in English. 1980. s-a. free to members (effective 2011). **Document type:** *Magazine, Trade.* **Description:** For the graduates of the RAF Apprentice College at Halton as a means to stay in touch with each other.
Published by: R A F Halton Apprentices Association, The Airfield, RAF Halton, Aylesbury, Bucks HP22 5PG, United Kingdom. TEL 44-1296-623535 ext 6300, FAX 44-1296-696896, RAFHAAA@aol.com.

HAMPTON ROADS INTERNATIONAL SECURITY QUARTERLY. *see* POLITICAL SCIENCE—International Relations

355 USA ISSN 1541-4434
U766
HANDBOOK FOR MILITARY LIFE. Text in English. 1977. a. adv. bk.rev. illus. **Document type:** *Handbook/Manual/Guide, Consumer.* **Description:** Provides US military service personnel and their families with a variety of helpful tips and advice.
Former titles (until 2000): Handbook for Military Living (1540-4021); (until 1999): Handbook for Military Families (1056-1927); (until 198?): Times Magazine Handbook for Military Families
Related titles: ◆ Supplement to: Air Force Times (U.S. Edition). ISSN 0002-2403; ◆ Supplement to: Navy Times. ISSN 0028-1697.
Published by: Army Times Publishing Co. (Subsidiary of: Gannett Company, Inc.), 6883 Commercial Dr, Springfield, VA 22159. TEL 703-750-7400, 800-368-5718, cust-svc@atpco.com, http://www.gannett.com/about/map/armytimes.htm. Ed. Tobias Naegele.

HANDBOOK OF DEFENSE ECONOMICS. *see* PUBLIC ADMINISTRATION

HANDGUNS (YEAR). *see* HOBBIES

358.4 629.1 CHN ISSN 1673-2421
HANGTIAN DIANZI DUIKANG/AEROSPACE ELECTRONIC WARFARE. Text in Chinese. 1985. bi-m. CNY 8 newsstand/cover (effective 2006). **Document type:** *Journal, Academic/Scholarly.*
Related titles: Online - full text ed.
—BLDSC (4262.076440).
Address: 35, Houbiaoying, PO Box 1610, Nanjing, 210007, China. TEL 86-25-84638543, FAX 86-25-84498353.

355 USA
HANSCONIAN. Text in English. w. free (effective 2005). **Document type:** *Newspaper.*
Published by: Hanscom Air Force Base, Hanscom Air Force Base, Bedford, Middlesex, MA 01730. TEL 781-377-5027, FAX 781-377-5077. Ed. Lisa Spilinek.

AL-HARAS AL-WATANI/NATIONAL GUARD MAGAZINE. *see* GENERAL INTEREST PERIODICALS—Saudi Arabia

355 USA
HARRISON POST. Text in English. 1965. w.
Address: 7962 Pendleton Park, Lawrence, KS 46226. TEL 317-542-8149. Circ: 10,000.

▼ **HARVARD NATIONAL SECURITY JOURNAL.** *see* POLITICAL SCIENCE—International Relations

355 AUS ISSN 1833-6531
HEADMARK. Text in English. 1975. q. AUD 60 in Australia & New Zealand membership; AUD 75 in Asia & the Pacific membership; AUD 82 elsewhere membership (effective 2008). bk.rev. charts; illus.; stat. cum.index: 1975-1985. back issues avail. **Document type:** *Journal, Academic/Scholarly.* **Description:** Covers various issues of Australian maritime concerns such as shipping, smuggling and policies. Also covers academic papers on naval subjects.
Formerly (until 2005): Australian Naval Institute. Journal (0312-5807)
Indexed: P47, P48, P52, PQC, RASB.
—Ingenta.
Published by: Australian Naval Institute, PO Box 29, Red Hill, ACT 2603, Australia. TEL 61-2-62950056, FAX 61-2-62953367, businessmanager@navalinstitute.com.au. Ed. Tom Lewis. Circ: 1,000.

HEADQUARTERS HELIOGRAM. *see* HISTORY—History Of North And South America

355 JPN
HEIKI TO GIJUTSU/ORDNANCE AND TECHNOLOGY. Text in Japanese. 1952. m.
Published by: Nihon Boei Sobi Kogyokai/Japan Association of Defence Industry, 21-3 Akasaka 2-chome, Minato-ku, Tokyo, 107-0052, Japan.

355.3 NOR ISSN 0017-985X
HEIMEVERNSBLADET. Variant title: HV-Bladet. Text in Norwegian. 1947. 8/yr. NOK 50; free to members of the Home Guard. adv. bk.rev. index. back issues avail. **Document type:** *Magazine, Trade.*
Related titles: Online - full text ed.
—CCC.
Published by: Heimevernet/Norwegian National Guard, Oslo Mil, Akershus Festning, Oslo, 0015, Norway. TEL 47-23-096678, FAX 47-23-096189. Eds. Stian Stoevland TEL 47-23-095032, Geir Olav Kjoesnes. Circ: 65,000.

HELICOPTER INTERNATIONAL MAGAZINE. *see* AERONAUTICS AND SPACE FLIGHT

355 SWE ISSN 0018-0351
HEMVAERNET; tidskrift foer allmaenna hemvaernet och driftvaernet. Text in Swedish. 1941. 6/yr. SEK 150 (effective 2006). adv. bk.rev. **Document type:** *Magazine, Trade.*
Incorporates (in 1978): Hemvaernsbefael
Published by: Rikshemvaernsraadet, Lidingoevaegen 28, Stockholm, 10787, Sweden. TEL 46-8-788-75-00, FAX 46-8-664-57-90. Ed., Pub. Ulf Ivarsson. adv.: B&W page SEK 15,855, color page SEK 19,845; trim 185 x 263. Circ: 93,000 (controlled).

HERRSCHAFT UND SOZIALE SYSTEME IN DER FRUEHEN NEUZEIT. *see* HISTORY—History Of Europe

358.4 USA ISSN 1933-1843
UG1523
HIGH FRONTIER; the journal for space and cyberspace professionals. Text in English. 2004. q. back issues avail. **Document type:** *Journal, Academic/Scholarly.*
Related titles: Online - full text ed.: ISSN 1933-3366. free (effective 2010).
Published by: Air Force Space Command, 150 Vandenberg St Ste 1105, Peterson AFB, CO 80914. TEL 719-554-3731, FAX 719-554-6013.

355 USA ISSN 2157-7730
HIGH GROUND (CENTENNIAL). Text in English. 2005. m. **Document type:** *Journal, Trade.*
Media: Online - full text.

Published by: Colorado National Guard, Joint Forces Headquarters, 6848 S Revere Pky, Centennial, CO 80112. TEL 720-250-1053, ngcopao@ng.army.mil, http://co.ng.mil/arng/units/JFHQ/default.aspx.

355 PAK
HILAL. Text in Urdu; Summaries in English. 1951. w. PKR 200. bk.rev. **Document type:** *Government.*
Published by: (Great Britain. Ministry of Defence GBR), I S P R Dte., Hilal Rd., Rawalpindi, 46000, Pakistan. TEL 92-9271606, FAX 92-9271605. Ed. Mumtaz Iqbal Malik. Circ: 90,000 (paid).

355 USA
HILLTOP TIMES. Text in English. 1941. w. (Thu.). free (effective 2005). adv. **Document type:** *Newspaper.*
Published by: U.S. Air Force, Ogden Air Logistics Center, 7981 Georgia St., Hill AFB, UT 84056-5824. Ed. Bill Orndorff. Pub. Bill Mulvay. Circ: 22,000 (paid and controlled).

HISTORIA MILITAR DEL PARAGUAY. *see* HISTORY—History Of North And South America

355.009 FRA ISSN 1167-9638
HISTORICA. Text in French. 6/yr.
Formerly (until 1990): 39 - 45 Magazine. Guerres Contemporaines (1167-962X)
Related titles: ♦ Supplement to: 39 - 45 Magazine. ISSN 0761-7348.
Published by: Editions Heimdal, Chateau de Damigny, B P 61350, Bayeux, Cedex 14406, France.

355 GBR ISSN 0305-0440
HISTORICAL BREECHLOADING SMALLARMS ASSOCIATION. JOURNAL. Text in English. 1973. a. USD 23. bk.rev. bibl.; charts; illus. **Description:** Gives a history of both military and civilian firearms and ammunition from 1800-1945.
Published by: Historical Breechloading Smallarms Association, PO Box 12778, London, SE1 6XB, United Kingdom. Ed. B Bergman Field. Circ: 2,000.

HISTORICAL MINIATURE. *see* HOBBIES

355.009 CZE ISSN 0018-2583
DB2070
HISTORIE A VOJENSTVI. Text in Czech; Summaries in English. 1953. q. CZK 340; CZK 95 newsstand/cover (effective 2010). **Document type:** *Journal, Academic/Scholarly.*
Indexed: HistAb, LID&ISL, RASB.
Published by: (Vojensky Historicky Ustav Praha), Aeromedia, a. s., Baranova 38, Prague 8, 130 00, Czech Republic. TEL 420-2-22718814, FAX 420-2-22718814, obchod@aeromedia.cz, http://www.aeromedia.cz. Ed. Jan Cadil. Adv. contact Jiri Navratil.

HISTORY OF WARFARE. *see* HISTORY

355 CZE ISSN 1804-2228
▼ **HOBBY HISTORIE.** Text in Czech. 2010. bi-m. CZK 530 (effective 2010). adv. **Document type:** *Magazine, Consumer.*
Published by: Aeromedia, a. s., Baranova 38, Prague 8, 130 00, Czech Republic. TEL 420-2-22718814, FAX 420-2-22718814, obchod@aeromedia.cz, http://www.aeromedia.cz.

HOMELAND DEFENSE & SECURITY MONITOR. *see* ENVIRONMENTAL STUDIES—Waste Management

355 USA ISSN 1546-7368
UA927
HOMELAND DEFENSE JOURNAL. Text in English. m. **Document type:** *Magazine, Trade.*
Related titles: Online - full text ed.: ISSN 1546-7481.
Indexed: CA, I02, T02.
Address: 4301 Wilson Blvd. Ste. 1003, Arlington, VA 22203-1867. TEL 703-807-2755, FAX 703-807-2728. Ed. David Silverberg. Pub. Doug Dickson.

HOMELAND SECURITY BUYERS GUIDE. *see* BUSINESS AND ECONOMICS—Trade And Industrial Directories

355.31 CMR ISSN 0046-7855
HONNEUR ET FIDELITE; bulletin de liaison des forces armees. Text in French. 1953. 6/yr. free. adv. film rev. charts; illus.
Published by: Bureau Information Presse de Forces Armees de la Republique, BP 1191, Yaounde, Cameroon. Ed. Lt Mpeck Marius. Circ: 2,000.

355.821 GBR ISSN 0046-7863
HONOURABLE ARTILLERY COMPANY JOURNAL. Text in English. 1923. s-a. free to members (effective 2009). bk.rev. **Document type:** *Journal, Trade.*
Published by: Honourable Artillery Company, Armoury House, City Rd, London, EC1Y 2BQ, United Kingdom. TEL 44-20-73821537, FAX 44-20-73821538, hac@hac.org.uk, http://www.hac.org.uk.

355 USA ISSN 0736-9220
VG93
➤ **THE HOOK (SAN DIEGO).** Text in English. 1977. q. free to members (effective 2010). adv. bk.rev. back issues avail. **Document type:** *Journal, Academic/Scholarly.* **Description:** Dedicated to describe the story of U.S. Navy carrier aviation, both past and present.
Published by: Tailhook Association, 9696 Businesspark Ave, San Diego, CA 92131. TEL 858-689-9227, 800-322-4665, FAX 858-578-8839, thookassn@aol.com. Ed. Dennis Irelan.

353.538 USA ISSN 0018-4772
HOOSIER LEGIONNAIRE. Text in English. 1926. q. membership. adv. bk.rev. illus. **Document type:** *Newspaper.* **Description:** Contains news, features and issues of interest to Indiana war time veterans and their families.
Published by: American Legion, Department of Indiana, 777 N Meridian St, Indianapolis, IN 46204. TEL 317-630-1391, FAX 317-237-9891. Ed., R&P Maria L Gottlieb. Circ: 140,000.

355 GBR ISSN 1755-439X
➤ **HOPLITE.** Text in English. 2008. a. free (effective 2011). back issues avail. **Document type:** *Journal, Academic/Scholarly.* **Description:** Focuses on a broad specialized area of Greek military history that stretches from the early Neolithic period to the modern times military records.
Media: Online - full text.
Published by: Markoulakis Publications, The Hive, Nottingham Trent University, Burton St, Nottingham, NG1 4BU, United Kingdom. TEL 44-115-8484354, FAX 44-115-8484612, info@markoulakispublications.org.uk, http://www.markoulakispublications.co.uk.

355.1 HRV ISSN 1330-500X
U4
HRVATSKI VOJNIK. Text in Croatian. 1991. s-m. **Document type:** *Magazine, Trade.*
Incorporates (1992-1993): Hrvatski Zrakoplovac (1331-8047); (1992-1993): Hrvatski Mornar (1331-8039)
Published by: Ministarstvo Obrane Republike Hrvatske, Zvonimirova 12, Zagreb, 10000, Croatia. TEL 385-1-4568041, FAX 385-1-4550075. Ed. Ivan Tolj.

HUABEI GUOFANG YIYAO/MEDICAL JOURNAL OF NATIONAL DEFENDING FORCES IN NORTH CHINA. *see* MEDICAL SCIENCES

338.473 363.35 GBR ISSN 1749-141X
HUNGARY DEFENCE & SECURITY REPORT. Text in English. 2005. a. EUR 820, USD 1,030 combined subscription per issue (print & email eds.) (effective 2010). **Document type:** *Report, Trade.* **Description:** Provides professionals, consultancies, government departments, regulatory bodies and researchers with independent forecasts and regional competitive intelligence on the Hungarian defence & security industry.
Related titles: E-mail ed.
Published by: Business Monitor International Ltd., Senator House, 85 Queen Victoria St, London, EC4V 4AB, United Kingdom. TEL 44-20-72480468, FAX 44-20-72480467, subs@businessmonitor.com.

323 CHN ISSN 1003-1480
HUOGONGPIN/INITIATORS & PYROTECHNICS. Text in Chinese. 1979. q. USD 24.60 (effective 2009). **Document type:** *Journal, Academic/Scholarly.*
Related titles: Online - full content ed.; Online - full text ed.
—BLDSC (4514.342500), IE, Ingenta.
Published by: Jixie Dianzi Gongyebu Di-213 Yanjiusuo, PO Box 213, Xi'an, 710061, China. TEL 86-29-5228473, FAX 86-29-5264165. **Dist. by:** China International Book Trading Corp, 35 Chegongzhuang Xilu, Haidian District, PO Box 399, Beijing 100044, China. TEL 86-10-68412045, FAX 86-10-68412023, cibtc@mail.cibtc.com.cn, http://www.cibtc.com.cn.

355 CHN ISSN 1008-8652
UF848
HUOKONG LEIDA JISHU/FIRE CONTROL RADAR TECHNOLOGY. Text in Chinese. 1972. q. USD 20.80 (effective 2009). **Document type:** *Journal, Academic/Scholarly.*
—BLDSC (4337.528000).
Published by: Xi'an Dianzi Gongcheng Yanjiusuo/Xi'an Electronic Engineering Research Institute, PO Box 132-8, Xi'an, 710100, China. TEL 86-29-85617147, FAX 86-29-85617000.

632 CHN ISSN 1002-0640
CODEN: HYZKEW
HUOLI YU ZHIHUI KONGZHI/FIRE CONTROL & COMMAND CONTROL. Text in Chinese. 1976. m. CNY 180, USD 180; USD 15 newsstand/cover (effective 2009).
Related titles: Online - full text ed.
Indexed: A28, APA, BrCerAb, C&ISA, CA/WCA, CIA, CerAb, CivEngAb, CorrAb, E&CAJ, E11, EEA, EMA, ESPM, EnvEAb, H15, M&TEA, M09, MBF, METADEX, SolStAb, T04, WAA.
—East View.
Published by: Zhongguo Bingqi Gongye Jituan, Beifang Zidong Kongzhi Jishu Yanjiusuo, PO Box 193, Taiyuan, 030006, China. TEL 86-351-8725026, FAX 86-351-8725207. Ed. Bang-da Di. Circ: 2,000. **Dist. by:** China International Book Trading Corp, 35 Chegongzhuang Xilu, Haidian District, PO Box 399, Beijing 100044, China. TEL 86-10-68412045, FAX 86-10-68412023, cibtc@mail.cibtc.com.cn, http://www.cibtc.com.cn.

355 PRT
I D N BRIEF. (Instituto da Defesa Nacional) Text in Portuguese. 2005. irreg. **Document type:** *Bulletin, Government.*
Published by: Instituto da Defesa Nacional, Calcadas das Necessidades 5, Lisbon, 1399-017, Portugal. TEL 351-213-924600, idn.instituto@defesa.pt, http://www.idn.gov.pt.

355 PRT ISSN 1646-4397
I D N CADERNOS. (Instituto da Defesa Nacional) Text in Portuguese. 2006. irreg. **Document type:** *Report, Government.*
Published by: Instituto da Defesa Nacional, Calcadas das Necessidades 5, Lisbon, 1399-017, Portugal. TEL 351-213-924600, idn.instituto@defesa.pt, http://www.idn.gov.pt.

355.31 USA ISSN 0270-8906
UB251.U5
I N S C O M JOURNAL; for the military intelligence professional. (Intelligence and Security Command) Text in English. 1977. q. **Document type:** *Government.*
Formerly (until 1980): Journal of the U.S. Army Intelligence & Security Command (0194-9527)
—Ingenta.
Published by: U.S. Army, Intelligence and Security Command, 8825 Beulah St, Fort Belvoir, VA 22060-5246. TEL 703-428-4553, http://www.inscom.army.mil. Ed. Brian Murphy.

355 USA ISSN 2158-5350
▼ **I O JOURNAL.** (Information Operations) Text in English. 2009. q. free (effective 2010). back issues avail. **Document type:** *Journal, Trade.* **Description:** Promotes public understanding in the science and practice of Information Operations and related disciplines.
Media: Online - full text.
Published by: Association of Old Crows, 1000 N Payne St, Ste 200, Alexandria, VA 22314. TEL 703-549-1600, FAX 703-549-2589, richetti@crows.org. Ed. Joel Harding TEL 703-549-1600. Adv. contact Melissa Zawada TEL 352-333-3407.

355 USA ISSN 1939-2370
U163
I O SPHERE; the professional journal of joint informaiton operations. (Information Operations) Text in English. 2005. q. **Document type:** *Journal, Government.*
Published by: U.S. Department of Defense, Joint Information Operations Center, 2 Hall Blvd, Ste 217, San Antonio, TX 78243. TEL 210-977-2240, FAX 210-977-4166. Ed. John Whisenhunt.

▼ **I S S R A PAPERS.** (Institute of Strategic Studies Research and Analysis) *see* POLITICAL SCIENCE—International Relations

355 USA
ILLINOIS GUARD CHRONICLE. Text in English. 1985. 4/yr. membership. **Document type:** *Newspaper, Government.* **Description:** Informs Guard members on training and events.
Published by: Illinois National Guard, Public Affairs Office, 1301 N MacArthur Blvd, Springfield, IL 62702-2399. TEL 217-785-3569, FAX 217-785-3527. Ed. Capt Brian E Deloche. Circ: 18,000.

359 658.3 FIN ISSN 1795-7672
ILMAVOIMALAINEN. Text in Finnish. 2005. q. **Document type:** *Magazine, Trade.*
Published by: Ilmavoimien Esikunta, PO Box 30, Tikkakoski, 41161, Finland. TEL 358-14-1810111, FAX 358-14-1814351, ilmavoimat@mil.fi.

IN UNIFORM - THE MAGAZINE. *see* HOMOSEXUALITY

355 USA ISSN 1556-8504
IN WAR AND IN PEACE: U.S. CIVIL-MILITARY RELATIONS. Text in English. 2006. irreg., latest 2010. price varies. back issues avail. **Document type:** *Monographic series, Academic/Scholarly.*
Published by: Praeger Publishers (Subsidiary of: Greenwood Publishing Group Inc.), 88 Post Rd W, Westport, CT 06881. TEL 800-368-6868, tech.support@greenwood.com, http://www.greenwood.com. Eds. David Heidler, Jeanne Heidler.

338.473 363.35 GBR ISSN 1749-1428
INDIA DEFENCE & SECURITY REPORT. Text in English. 2005. q. EUR 820, USD 1,030 combined subscription (print & email eds.) (effective 2010). **Document type:** *Report, Trade.* **Description:** Provides industry leaders, defense manufacturers and suppliers, intelligence agencies and governments with independent forecasts and competitive intelligence on the defense and security industry in India.
Related titles: E-mail ed.
Indexed: B01.
Published by: Business Monitor International Ltd., Senator House, 85 Queen Victoria St, London, EC4V 4AB, United Kingdom. TEL 44-20-72480468, FAX 44-20-72480467, subs@businessmonitor.com.

355 IND ISSN 0970-2512
UA840
➤ **INDIAN DEFENCE REVIEW.** Text in English. 1986. 4/yr. USD 100 (effective 2009). adv. bk.rev. **Document type:** *Journal, Academic/Scholarly.* **Description:** Offers an incisive analysis of defence and politico-security affairs focused on South Asia and throughout the Pacific Rim.
Indexed: LID&ISL.
Published by: Lancer Publishers & Distributors, 56 Gautam Nagar, New Delhi, 110 049, India. TEL 91-11-6854691, FAX 91-11-6862077. Ed., R&P, Adv. contact Bharat Verma. Circ: 4,000. **Subscr. in Australia & New Zealand to:** Peter Lewis Young, PO Box 473, Warrnambool, VIC 3280, Australia. TEL 61-3-55-611996, FAX 61-3-55-617138; **Subscr. in N. America to:** Spantech & Lancer. TEL 414-673-9064; **Subscr. to:** I N S I O Scientific Books & Periodicals, PO Box 7234, Indraprastha HPO, New Delhi 110 002, India. iihm@ap.nic.in, http://iihm.ap.nic.in/.

355 USA
INDIANA COMBAT VETERAN. Text in English. 1947. m. USD 2. **Document type:** *Newspaper.* **Description:** Publishes articles of interest to veterans.
Published by: Indiana Veterans of Foreign Wars, 1402 N Shadeland Ave, Indianapolis, IN 46219-3637. TEL 317-634-4331. Ed. Patrick Moran. Circ: 63,400.

355.37 USA
INDIANA GUARDSMAN. Text in English. 19??. q. back issues avail. **Document type:** *Magazine, Trade.* **Description:** Provides information about Indiana Army and Air National Guard.
Related titles: Online - full text ed.: ISSN 2157-7102. free (effective 2010).
Published by: Indiana National Guard, Stout Field, 2002 S Holt Rd, Indianapolis, IN 46241. TEL 317-247-3300.

338.473 363.35 GBR ISSN 1749-1436
INDONESIA DEFENCE & SECURITY REPORT. Text in English. 2005. q. EUR 820, USD 1,030 combined subscription (print & email eds.) (effective 2010). **Document type:** *Report, Trade.* **Description:** Provides professionals, consultancies, government departments, regulatory bodies and researchers with independent forecasts and regional competitive intelligence on the Indonesian defence & security industry.
Related titles: E-mail ed.
Indexed: B01.
Published by: Business Monitor International Ltd., Senator House, 85 Queen Victoria St, London, EC4V 4AB, United Kingdom. TEL 44-20-72480468, FAX 44-20-72480467, subs@businessmonitor.com.

355 IDN ISSN 0303-4992
UA853.I5
INDONESIA. LEMBAGA PERTAHANAN NASIONAL. KETAHANAN NASIONAL. Text in Indonesian. 1965. bi-m. IDR 3,500. adv.
Published by: Lembaga Pertahanan Nasional, Jalan Kebon Sirih 26, Jakarta, Indonesia. Circ: 10,000.

355 IDN ISSN 0216-3217
INDONESIA. LEMBAGA PERTAHANAN NASIONAL. NATIONAL RESILIENCE. Text in English. q.
Published by: Lembaga Pertahanan Nasional, Jalan Kebon Sirih 26, Jakarta, Indonesia.

355 NLD ISSN 1872-4515
INFANTERIE. Text in Dutch. 1995. q. EUR 18 (effective 2009).
Published by: Vereniging van Infanterie Officieren, Postbus 475, Houten, 3990 GG, Netherlands. TEL 31-6-51660085, secretaris@vio.nl, http://www.verenigingInfanterieofficieren.nl.

356.1 USA ISSN 0019-9532
UD1
INFANTRY; a professional bulletin for the U.S. Army infantryman. Text in English. 1930. bi-m. bk.rev. reprints avail. **Document type:** *Government.* **Description:** Provides current information on infantry organization, weapons, equipment, tactics, techniques, and relevant historical articles.
Former titles (until 1957): Infantry School Quarterly; (until 1947): The Infantry School Mailing List; (until 1934): Infantry School. Mailing List
Related titles: Microform ed.: (from PQC); Online - full text ed.

Indexed: A22, A26, AMB, AUNI, CA, DM&T, G05, G06, G07, G08, I05, IUSGP, LID&ISL, M02, M05, M06, M07, P02, P10, P13, P47, P48, P52, P53, P54, PQC, RASB, T02.
—BLDSC (4478.280000), Ingenta.
Published by: U.S. Army Infantry School, PO Box 52005, Ft. Benning, GA 31995. TEL 706-545-3643, http://www.infantry.army.mil/infantry/index.asp.

356.1 USA ISSN 1933-6225
UD23
INFANTRY BUGLER. Text in English. 2001. q. USD 20 membership (effective 2007). **Document type:** *Magazine, Trade.*
Published by: (National Infantry Association), Community Communications, PO Box 672121, Marietta, GA 30006-0036.

355.31 FRA ISSN 1772-3760
INFLEXIONS; civils et militaires. Text in French. 2005. 3/yr. EUR 30 (effective 2007). back issues avail. **Document type:** *Journal, Government.*
Related titles: Online - full text ed.
Indexed: IBSS.
Published by: France. Armee de Terre, La Chargee de Mission, 14 Rue Saint-Dominique, Paris, 00453 Armees, France. TEL 33-1-44424320.

355.31 CHE ISSN 1422-5794
INFO S O L O G. Text in French, German. 1947. m. adv. **Document type:** *Journal, Trade.*
Incorporates (1960-1997): Schweizerische Gesellschaft der Offiziere des Munitionsdienstes. Bulletin (0036-7591); Former titles (until 1998): Armee-Motor (0004-2269); (until 1952): Schweizerische Gesellschaft der Offiziere der Motorisierten Truppen. Mitteilungsblatt (1421-296X)
Published by: Schweizerische Offiziersgesellschaft der Logistik, Opfikonerstr 3, Wallisellen, 8304, Switzerland. TEL 41-44-8774717, FAX 41-44-8774748, mut@solog.ch, http://www.solog.ch. Circ: 4,300.

355 DEU
INFOPOST. Text in German. 1977. q. free (effective 2009). **Document type:** *Magazine, Consumer.* **Description:** Discusses life in the Armed Forces; directed at teenagers.
Published by: Bundesministerium der Verteidigung, Presse- und Informationsstab, Stauffenbergstr 18, Berlin, 10785, Germany. TEL 49-30-18248232, FAX 49-30-18248240, http://www.bmvg.de. Circ: 300,000.

355.14 USA ISSN 1554-0561
UA23.A1
INFORMATION AGE WARFARE QUARTERLY. Text in English. 2005. q. **Document type:** *Journal, Academic/Scholarly.* **Description:** Contributes to the solution of real world information age defense problems.
Media: Online - full content.
Published by: Alidade Press, 31 Bridge St, Newport, RI 02840. TEL 401-367-0040, FAX 401-633-6420, press@alidadepress.com, http://www.alidadepress.com. Ed. James Miskel.

355.31 USA ISSN 1937-0067
INFORMATION AS POWER; an anthology of selected United States Army War College student papers. Text in English. 2006. irreg. **Document type:** *Monographic series, Trade.* **Description:** Coverst topics relating to the importance of information in warfare, including commmunications, networks and intelligence.
Published by: U.S. Army, War College, 122 Forbes Ave, Carlisle, PA 17013. TEL 717-245-3131, FAX 717-245-4224, carl_atwc-cpa@conus.army.mil.

359 SWE ISSN 1652-3571
V5
INSATS & FOERSVAR; foersvarsmaktens forum foer insatsorganisationen. Text in Swedish. 2004. 6/yr. SEK 200 domestic; SEK 250 foreign (effective 2005). charts; illus.; stat. **Document type:** *Magazine, Government.*
Formed by the merger of (1950-2004): Marinnytt (0025-3375); (1960-2004): Flygvapennytt (0011-5479); (1949-2004): Armenytt (0004-2404)
Published by: Foersvarsmakten, Informationsavdelingen, Lidingoevaegen 24, Stockholm, 10785, Sweden. TEL 46-8-7887500, FAX 46-8-7887778, exp-hkv@mil.se, http://www.mil.se.

355 USA
INSIDE MISSILE DEFENSE. Text in English. 1995. bi-w. USD 795 in US & Canada; USD 845 elsewhere (effective 2008). back issues avail. **Document type:** *Newsletter, Trade.* **Description:** Follows both national and theater missile defense systems, arms control issues, counter proliferation efforts and space activities.
Related titles: E-mail ed.; Online - full text ed.: USD 300; USD 25 per issue (effective 2008).
Published by: Inside Washington Publishers, 1919 South Eads St, Ste 201, Arlington, VA 22202. TEL 703-416-8500, 800-424-9068, custsvc@iwpnews.com, http://www.iwpnews.com. Ed. Richard Lardner.

358.4 USA
INSIDE THE AIR FORCE. Text in English. 1989. w. USD 1,180 in US & Canada; USD 1,230 elsewhere (effective 2008). back issues avail. **Document type:** *Newsletter, Trade.* **Description:** Covers the latest developments in air and space warfare, including the F-22A, the Joint strike fighter, strategic airlift, military space and other key programs.
Related titles: E-mail ed.; Online - full text ed.: USD 300; USD 25 per issue (effective 2008).
Published by: Inside Washington Publishers, 1919 South Eads St, Ste 201, Arlington, VA 22202. TEL 703-416-8500, 800-424-9068, custsvc@iwpnews.com, http://www.iwpnews.com.

355 USA
INSIDE THE ARMY. Text in English. 1995. w. USD 1,245 in US & Canada (effective 2008); USD 1,295 elsewhere (effective 2005). back issues avail. **Document type:** *Newsletter, Trade.* **Description:** Follows the service's transformation to a more modular and lethal force including the future combat system.
Related titles: E-mail ed.; Online - full text ed.: USD 300; USD 25 per issue (effective 2008).
Published by: Inside Washington Publishers, 1919 South Eads St, Ste 201, Arlington, VA 22202. TEL 703-416-8500, 800-424-9068, custsvc@iwpnews.com, http://www.iwpnews.com.

359 USA
INSIDE THE NAVY. Text in English. 1995. w. USD 1,290 in US & Canada; USD 1,340 elsewhere (effective 2008). back issues avail. **Document type:** *Newsletter, Trade.* **Description:** Covers navy and marine corps modernization efforts, policies and decision-making and also focuses on shipbuilding, the V-22 Osprey, the submarine force and maritime strategy.
Related titles: E-mail ed.; Online - full text ed.: USD 300; USD 25 per issue (effective 2008).
Published by: Inside Washington Publishers, 1919 South Eads St, Ste 201, Arlington, VA 22202. TEL 703-416-8500, 800-424-9068, service@iwpnews.com, http://www.iwpnews.com. Ed. Richard Lardner.

359 USA
INSIDE THE PENTAGON. Text in English. 1984. w. USD 1,295 in US & Canada; USD 1,345 elsewhere (effective 2008). back issues avail. **Document type:** *Newsletter, Trade.* **Description:** Covers acquisition and strategic policy, the war on terror, budget and program developments, campaigns abroad and Pentagon leadership decisions.
Related titles: E-mail ed.; Online - full text ed.: USD 300; USD 25 per issue (effective 2008).
Published by: Inside Washington Publishers, 1919 South Eads St, Ste 201, Arlington, VA 22202. TEL 703-416-8500, 800-424-9068, custsvc@iwpnews.com, http://www.iwpnews.com.

355 USA
INSIDE THE TURRET. Text in English. 1948. w. (Thu.). free (effective 2005). **Document type:** *Newspaper, Consumer.* **Description:** Includes Fot Knox and Army news in particular, military news in general, along with information about high school and professional sports, and local entertainment and travel.
Formerly: Ft. Knox Inside The Turret
Published by: U.S.Army Garrison, 410 West Dixie Ave., Elizabethtown, Hardin, KY 42701-2433. TEL 502-624-1211, FAX 502-624-6074. Ed. Larry Barnes. Circ: 21,000 (free). Wire service: AP.

INSTITUTE FOR DEFENCE STUDIES AND ANALYSES. STRATEGIC DIGEST. *see* CIVIL DEFENSE

INSTITUTE FOR STRATEGIC STUDIES. BULLETIN/INSTITUUT VIR STRATEGIESE STUDIES. BULLETIN. *see* POLITICAL SCIENCE—International Relations

355.47 ARG ISSN 1851-3697
INSTITUTO GEOGRAFICO MILITAR. BOLETIN INFORMATIVO. Text in Spanish. 2006. m.
Media: Online - full text.
Published by: Instituto Geografico Militar, Ave Cabildo 381, Buenos Aires, 1426, Argentina. TEL 54-11-45765576.

355 ARG ISSN 1852-7205
▼ **INSTITUTO UNIVERSITARIO NAVAL. REVISTA DIGITAL.** Text in Spanish. 2009. 3/yr. **Document type:** *Magazine, Trade.*
Media: Online - full text.
Published by: Instituto Universitario Naval, Edif. Libertad, Ave. Comodoro Py, 2055, Piso 10 Ofic. 104, Argentina, C11043EA, Argentina. TEL 54-11-43172000, http://www.inun.edu.ar/.

355 USA ISSN 1932-3492
INTELLIGENCE AND THE QUEST FOR SECURITY. Text in English. 2006. irreg., latest 2008. price varies. back issues avail. **Document type:** *Monographic series, Academic/Scholarly.*
Published by: Praeger Publishers (Subsidiary of: Greenwood Publishing Group Inc.), 88 Post Rd W, Westport, CT 06881. TEL 800-368-6868, tech.support@greenwood.com, http://www.greenwood.com. Ed. Loch Johnson.

355.3 USA ISSN 2158-7639
INTELLIGENCER; journal of U.S. intelligence studies. Text in English. 1991. s-a. USD 15 per issue to non-members; free to members (effective 2011). back issues avail. **Document type:** *Journal, Academic/Scholarly.* **Description:** Features papers, book announcements and reviews by intelligence professionals, and analyses of important intelligence topics.
Media: Online - full text.
Published by: Association of Former Intellgence Officers, 6723 Whittier Ave, Ste 200, McLean, VA 22101. TEL 703-790-0320, FAX 703-991-1278, afio@afio.com.

355 RUS
INTERFAX. RUSSIA & C I S MILITARY DAILY. (Commonwealth of Independent States) Text in English. d. price varies. **Document type:** *Bulletin, Trade.* **Description:** Reports on key Russian national security events.
Related titles: Online - full text ed.
Indexed: P52.
Published by: Interfax Ltd., 1-ya Tverskaya-Yamskaya, dom 2, stroenie 1, Moscow, 127006, Russian Federation. TEL 7-095-2509840, FAX 7-095-2509727, info@interfax.ru, http://www.interfax.ru.

355 RUS
INTERFAX. RUSSIA & C I S MILITARY INFORMATION WEEKLY. (Commonwealth of Independent States) Text in English. w. price varies. **Document type:** *Bulletin, Trade.* **Description:** Reports on key Russian national security events.
Related titles: Online - full text ed.
Indexed: A15, P48, P51, P52.
Published by: Interfax Ltd., 1-ya Tverskaya-Yamskaya, dom 2, stroenie 1, Moscow, 127006, Russian Federation. TEL 7-095-2509840, FAX 7-095-2509727, info@interfax.ru, http://www.interfax.ru. **Dist. by:** Interfax America, Inc., 3025 S Parker Rd, Ste 737, Aurora, CO 80014. TEL 303-368-1421, FAX 303-368-1458, america@interfax-news.com, http://www.interfax.com.

358.4 387.7 USA ISSN 1473-9917
INTERNATIONAL AIR POWER REVIEW. Text in English. 1990. q. GBP 49.95 domestic; USD 64 in United States; CAD 89 in Canada; EUR 88 in Europe; USD 112 elsewhere (effective 2009). **Document type:** *Journal, Trade.* **Description:** Contains informations and pictues about military aviation aircrafts.
Formerly (until 2001): World Air Power Journal (0959-7050)
—IE.
Published by: Airtime Publishing Ltd., PO Box 5074, Westport, CT 06881. TEL 203-454-4773, 00-800-75737573, 0011-800-75737573, FAX 203-226-5967, http://www.airtimepublishing.com/.

355 GBR ISSN 0950-3714
INTERNATIONAL DEFENCE NEWSLETTER. Short title: I D N. Text in English. 1986. m. (except Dec.). GBP 275; GBP 375 foreign. **Document type:** *Newsletter, Trade.* **Description:** Provides concise, independent news reports on developments in the defense industry worldwide.
Published by: I T X Publishing, PO Box 28, Twickenham, Mddx TW1 1EH, United Kingdom. TEL 44-181-8927471, FAX 44-181-7442704. Ed., Pub. John Jayes. Circ: 600 (paid).

INTERNATIONAL GUIDE TO UNMANNED VEHICLES. *see* AERONAUTICS AND SPACE FLIGHT

335 363.35 USA ISSN 2150-4822
HV551.2
▼ **INTERNATIONAL HOMELAND SECURITY.** Text in English. 2009. q. USD 100 domestic; USD 110 foreign (effective 2009). **Document type:** *Journal, Academic/Scholarly.* **Description:** Covers homeland security, homeland defense, emergency management, first response, communications, and intelligence around the world.
Published by: Government Institutes (Subsidiary of: Scarecrow Press, Inc.), 4501 Forbes Blvd, Ste 200, Lanham, MD 20706. TEL 301-459-3366 ext 5616, custserv@rowman.com.

INTERNATIONAL JOURNAL OF INTELLIGENT DEFENCE SUPPORT SYSTEMS. *see* COMPUTERS

INTERNATIONAL JOURNAL OF NAVAL HISTORY. *see* HISTORY

INTERNATIONAL LIBRARY OF WAR STUDIES. *see* POLITICAL SCIENCE—International Relations

355 DEU ISSN 0942-4598
INTERNATIONALES MILITARIA-MAGAZIN; Das aktuelle Magazin fuer Orden, Militaria, Zeitgeschichte. Abbreviated title: I M M. Text in German. 1990. bi-m. EUR 5.90 newsstand/cover (effective 2009). **Document type:** *Magazine, Consumer.*
Published by: V D M Heinz Nickel, Kasernenstr 6-10, Zweibruecken, 66482, Germany. TEL 49-6332-72710, info@vdmedien.de, http://vdmedien.com.

355 USA ISSN 1557-4687
VG50
INTREP. Text in English. 2003. 3/yr. **Document type:** *Newsletter, Trade.*
Media: Online - full text.
Published by: U.S. Coast Guard Auxiliary (Subsidiary of: U.S. Coast Guard) http://nws.cgaux.org/index.html.

355.1 BEL
INVALIDE BELGE. Text in French. 1917. m. adv. bk.rev.
Related titles: Dutch ed.: Belgische Verminkte.
Address: Pl E Flagey 7-4, Brussels, 1050, Belgium. TEL 32-2-647-0778. Circ: 9,000.

338.473 363.35 GBR ISSN 1749-1444
IRAN DEFENCE & SECURITY REPORT. Text in English. 2005. q. EUR 820, USD 1,030 combined subscription (print & email eds.) (effective 2010). **Document type:** *Report, Trade.* **Description:** Provides professionals, consultancies, government departments, regulatory bodies and researchers with independent forecasts and regional competitive intelligence on the Iranian defence & security industry.
Related titles: E-mail ed.
Indexed: B01.
Published by: Business Monitor International Ltd., Senator House, 85 Queen Victoria St, London, EC4V 4AB, United Kingdom. TEL 44-20-72480468, FAX 44-20-72480467, subs@businessmonitor.com.

338.473 363.35 GBR ISSN 1749-1452
IRAQ DEFENCE & SECURITY REPORT. Text in English. 2005. q. EUR 820, USD 1,030 combined subscription (print & email eds.) (effective 2010). **Document type:** *Report, Trade.* **Description:** Provides professionals, consultancies, government departments, regulatory bodies and researchers with independent forecasts and regional competitive intelligence on the Iraqi defence & security industry.
Related titles: E-mail ed.
Indexed: B01.
Published by: Business Monitor International Ltd., Senator House, 85 Queen Victoria St, London, EC4V 4AB, United Kingdom. TEL 44-20-72480468, FAX 44-20-72480467, subs@businessmonitor.com.

355 IRL ISSN 1649-9999
IRELAND. DEPARTMENT OF DEFENCE AND DEFENCE FORCES. ANNUAL REPORT/TUARASCAIL BHLIANTUIL DON AIRE COSANTA DO. Text in English, Gaelic. 2000. a.
Formerly (until 2006): Ireland. Department of Defence. Annual Report (1649-1211)
Published by: (Defence Forces), Department of Defence, Parkgate, Infirmary Rd, Dublin, 7, Ireland. TEL 353-1-8042000, FAX 353-1-8045000, info@defence.irlgov.ie, http://www.defence.ie.

355 IRL ISSN 0021-1389
DA914
➤ **THE IRISH SWORD**; the journal of the military history society of Ireland. Text in English. 1949. s-a. EUR 32; EUR 20 newsstand/cover (effective 2003). bk.rev. charts; illus. index. back issues avail. **Document type:** *Journal, Academic/Scholarly.* **Description:** Study of warfare in Ireland and of Irishmen in war.
Indexed: AmH&L, BrArAb, CA, FR, HistAb, IBR, IBZ, LID&ISL, MLA-IB, P30, T02.
—BLDSC (4574.840000), INIST.
Published by: Military History Society of Ireland, c/o University College Dublin, Newman House, 86 St Stephen's Green, Dublin, 2, Ireland. TEL 353-1-2985617, FAX 353-1-7067211. Ed. Kenneth Ferguson. Circ: 900.

➤ **ISLAMABAD PAPERS.** *see* POLITICAL SCIENCE—International Relations

338.473 363.35 GBR ISSN 1749-1460
ISRAEL DEFENCE & SECURITY REPORT. Text in English. 2005. q. EUR 820, USD 1,030 combined subscription (print & email eds.) (effective 2010). **Document type:** *Report, Trade.* **Description:** Provides professionals, consultancies, government departments, regulatory bodies and researchers with independent forecasts and regional competitive intelligence on the Israeli defence & security industry.
Related titles: E-mail ed.
Indexed: A15, ABIn, B01, P48, P51, PQC.

Published by: Business Monitor International Ltd., Senator House, 85 Queen Victoria St, London, EC4V 4AB, United Kingdom. TEL 44-20-72480468, FAX 44-20-72480467, subs@businessmonitor.com.

355.405694 340 ISR
ISRAEL DEFENSE FORCES LAW REVIEW. Text in English. 2003. a. **Document type:** *Journal, Trade.*
Published by: Israel Defence Forces, School of Military Law, c/o IDF School of Military Law, Military Post, 03608, Israel. idflawreview@lycos.co.uk.

338.473 363.35 GBR ISSN 1749-1479
ITALY DEFENCE & SECURITY REPORT. Text in English. 2005. q. EUR 820, USD 1,030 combined subscription (print & email eds.) (effective 2010). **Document type:** *Report, Trade.* **Description:** Provides professionals, consultancies, government departments, regulatory bodies and researchers with independent forecasts and regional competitive intelligence on the Italian defence & security industry.
Related titles: E-mail ed.
Indexed: B01, P34.
Published by: Business Monitor International Ltd., Senator House, 85 Queen Victoria St, London, EC4V 4AB, United Kingdom. TEL 44-20-72480468, FAX 44-20-72480467, subs@businessmonitor.com.

355.31 USA
THE IVY LEAVES. Text in English. 1916. q. USD 15 (effective 2003). adv. **Document type:** *Magazine, Consumer.* **Description:** Contains news and items of interest to members of the Fourth Infantry Division U.S. Army.
Published by: Finisterre Publishing Inc., 3 Black Skimmer Ct., Beaufort, SC 29907-1823. finisterre@islc.net. Ed., R&P Richard B. Taylor. Adv. contact Edward McEniry. Circ: 10,000 (paid and controlled).

J A M P. (Journal of America's Military Past) *see* HISTORY—History Of North And South America

J M N R. (Journal of Military Nursing & Research) *see* MEDICAL SCIENCES—Nurses And Nursing

J S - DAS MAGAZIN FUER LEUTE BEIM BUND. (Junge Soldaten) *see* RELIGIONS AND THEOLOGY—Protestant

JANE'S AERO-ENGINES. *see* AERONAUTICS AND SPACE FLIGHT

623.45191 GBR ISSN 0954-3848
UG1270
JANE'S AIR-LAUNCHED WEAPONS. Text in English. 1988. s-a. GBP 885 (effective 2010). illus. **Document type:** *Journal, Trade.* **Description:** Provides reference to over 580 individual air-launched weapons around the world, covers how each weapon works, when it entered service, who purchased it and which aircraft are cleared to carry which weapons. Each system entry contains details on type, development, description, operational status, specifications and contractors together with photographs and scaled diagrams to aid recognition. Analysis tables allow quick comparison of similar systems.
Related titles: CD-ROM ed.: GBP 1,555 (effective 2010); Online - full content ed.: GBP 2,125 (effective 2010).
—CCC.
Published by: I H S Jane's (Subsidiary of: I H S), Sentinel House, 163 Brighton Rd, Coulsdon, Surrey CR5 2YH, United Kingdom. TEL 44-20-87003700, FAX 44-20-87003751, info@janes.co.uk, http://www.janes.com. Ed. Robert Hewson. **US dist. addr.:** 1340 Braddock Pl, Ste 300, Alexandria, VA 22314-1651. TEL 703-683-3700, FAX 703-836-0297, info@janes.com.

358.4 GBR ISSN 1369-7277
JANE'S AMMUNITION HANDBOOK. Text in English. 1992. a. GBP 480 per issue (2010-2011 ed.) (effective 2010). adv. charts; illus.; stat. **Document type:** *Yearbook, Trade.*
Related titles: CD-ROM ed.: GBP 1,245 (effective 2010); Online - full text ed.: GBP 1,685 (effective 2010).
—CCC.
Published by: I H S Jane's (Subsidiary of: I H S), Sentinel House, 163 Brighton Rd, Coulsdon, Surrey CR5 2YH, United Kingdom. TEL 44-20-87003700, FAX 44-20-87003751, info@janes.co.uk, http://www.janes.com. Eds. Anthony G Williams, Leland Ness. Pub. Alan Condron. Adv. contact Richard West. **Dist. in Asia by:** Jane's Information Group Asia, 60 Albert St, #15-01 Albert Complex, Singapore 189969, Singapore. TEL 65-331-6280, FAX 65-336-9921, info@janes.com.sg; **Dist. in Australia by:** Jane's Information Group Australia, PO Box 3502, Rozelle, NSW 2039, Australia. TEL 61-2-8587-7900, FAX 61-2-8587-7901, info@janes.thomson.com.au; **Dist. in the Americas by:** 1340 Braddock Pl, Ste 300, Alexandria, VA 22314-1651. TEL 703-683-3700, 800-824-0768, FAX 703-836-0297, 800-836-0297, info@janes.com.

623.825 GBR ISSN 1748-2577
U261
JANE'S AMPHIBIOUS AND SPECIAL FORCES. Text in English. 2002. s-a. GBP 950 (effective 2010). illus. **Document type:** *Magazine, Trade.* **Description:** Provides detailed assessments, by country, of the forces, vessels and equipment capable of mounting an amphibious operation.
Formerly: Jane's Amphibious Warfare Capabilities
Related titles: CD-ROM ed.: GBP 1,555 (effective 2010); Online - full text ed.: GBP 2,125 (effective 2010).
—CCC.
Published by: I H S Jane's (Subsidiary of: I H S), Sentinel House, 163 Brighton Rd, Coulsdon, Surrey CR5 2YH, United Kingdom. TEL 44-20-87003700, FAX 44-20-87003751, info@janes.co.uk, http://www.janes.com. Ed. Ewen Southby-Tailyour. **Dist. Addr. in Australia:** Jane's Information Group Australia, PO Box 3502, Rozelle, NSW 2039, Australia. TEL 61-2-8587-7900, FAX 61-2-8587-7901, info@janes.thomson.com.au; **Dist. addr. in Asia:** Jane's Information Group Asia, 60 Albert St, #15-01 Albert Complex, Singapore 189969, Singapore. TEL 65-331-6280, FAX 65-336-9921, info@janes.com.sg; **Dist. addr. in the Americas:** 1340 Braddock Pl, Ste 300, Alexandria, VA 22314-1651. TEL 703-683-3700, FAX 703-836-0297, info@janes.com.

355.821 GBR ISSN 0143-9952
UG446.5
JANE'S ARMOUR AND ARTILLERY. Text in English. 1979. a. GBP 605 per issue (2010-2011 ed.) (effective 2010). adv. illus. index. **Document type:** *Yearbook, Trade.* **Description:** Covers development histories, detailed descriptions, lists of variants and modifications, full specifications, lists of user countries and manufacturer contact details for armoured fighting vehicles and artillery worldwide.
Related titles: CD-ROM ed.: GBP 1,445 (effective 2010); Microfiche ed.: USD 615 in the Americas for complete set 1979-1993; GBP 395 elsewhere for complete set 1979-1993 (effective 2002); Online - full text ed.: GBP 2,010 (effective 2010).
—BLDSC (4646.600000). **CCC.**
Published by: I H S Jane's (Subsidiary of: I H S), Sentinel House, 163 Brighton Rd, Coulsdon, Surrey CR5 2YH, United Kingdom. TEL 44-20-87003700, FAX 44-20-87003751, info@janes.co.uk, http://www.janes.com. Ed. Christopher F Foss. Adv. contact Janine Boxall TEL 44-20-87003852. **Dist. in Asia by:** Jane's Information Group Asia, 60 Albert St, #15-01 Albert Complex, Singapore 189969, Singapore. TEL 65-331-6280, FAX 65-336-9921, info@janes.com.sg; **Dist. in Australia by:** Jane's Information Group Australia, PO Box 3502, Rozelle, NSW 2039, Australia. TEL 61-2-8587-7900, FAX 61-2-8587-7901, info@janes.thomson.com.au; **Dist. in the Americas by:** 1340 Braddock Pl, Ste 300, Alexandria, VA 22314-1651. TEL 703-683-3700, 800-824-0768, FAX 703-836-0297, 800-836-0297, info@janes.com.

358.4 GBR ISSN 1360-5682
JANE'S ARMOUR AND ARTILLERY UPGRADES. Text in English. 1988. a. GBP 475 per issue (2010-2011 ed.) (effective 2010). adv. illus. **Document type:** *Yearbook, Trade.* **Description:** Covers the key armoured fighting vehicle and artillery sub-systems available for installation in new and rebuilt vehicles, with development histories, descriptions, specifications, photographs, and supplier contact information for manufacturers worldwide.
Former titles (until 1994): Jane's A F V Retrofit Systems (1369-8206); (until 1993): Jane's Armoured Fighting Vehicle Retrofit Systems (1369-8192); (until 1989): Jane's Amoured Fighting Vehicle Systems (0954-383X)
Related titles: CD-ROM ed.: GBP 1,225 (effective 2010); Online - full text ed.: GBP 1,670 (effective 2010).
—BLDSC (4646.600600). **CCC.**
Published by: I H S Jane's (Subsidiary of: I H S), Sentinel House, 163 Brighton Rd, Coulsdon, Surrey CR5 2YH, United Kingdom. TEL 44-20-87003700, FAX 44-20-87003751, info@janes.co.uk, http://www.janes.com. Eds. Christopher F Foss, Richard Stickland. Adv. contact Richard West. **Dist. in Asia by:** Jane's Information Group Asia, 60 Albert St, #15-01 Albert Complex, Singapore 189969, Singapore. TEL 65-331-6280, FAX 65-336-9921, info@janes.com.sg; **Dist. in Australia by:** Jane's Information Group Australia, PO Box 3502, Rozelle, NSW 2039, Australia. TEL 61-2-8587-7900, FAX 61-2-8587-7901, info@janes.thomson.com.au; **Dist. in the Americas by:** 1340 Braddock Pl, Ste 300, Alexandria, VA 22314-1651. TEL 703-683-3700, 800-824-0768, FAX 703-836-0297, 800-836-0297, info@janes.com.

355 GBR ISSN 1357-0226
JANE'S C 4 I SYSTEMS. (Command, Control, Communications, Computers, and Intelligence) Text in English. 1989. a. GBP 500 per issue (2010-2011 ed.) (effective 2010). adv. illus. **Document type:** *Yearbook, Trade.* **Description:** Guide to all "C4I" systems around the world, including command information systems, communications networks, and intelligence gathering systems.
Former titles (until 1994): Jane's C 3 I Systems (0961-0278); Jane's C 3 I; Which supersedes in part: Jane's Weapon Systems (0075-3068)
Related titles: CD-ROM ed.: GBP 1,280 (effective 2010); Online - full text ed.: GBP 1,770 (effective 2010).
—BLDSC (4646.770000). **CCC.**
Published by: I H S Jane's (Subsidiary of: I H S), Sentinel House, 163 Brighton Rd, Coulsdon, Surrey CR5 2YH, United Kingdom. TEL 44-20-87003700, FAX 44-20-87003751, info@janes.co.uk, http://www.janes.com. Ed. Giles Ebbutt. Pub. Alan Condron. Adv. contact Richard West. **Dist. in Asia by:** Jane's Information Group Asia, 60 Albert St, #15-01 Albert Complex, Singapore 189969, Singapore. TEL 65-331-6280, FAX 65-336-9921, info@janes.com.sg; **Dist. in Australia by:** Jane's Information Group Australia, PO Box 3502, Rozelle, NSW 2039, Australia. TEL 61-2-8587-7900, FAX 61-2-8587-7901, info@janes.thomson.com.au; **Dist. in the Americas by:** 1340 Braddock Pl, Ste 300, Alexandria, VA 22314-1651. TEL 703-683-3700, 800-824-0768, FAX 703-836-0297, 800-836-0297, info@janes.com.

355 GBR
JANE'S DEFENCE EQUIPMENT LIBRARY. Text in English. 1996. q. USD 22,470 (effective 2009). **Document type:** *Directory, Trade.* **Description:** Comprehensive portfolio of information bringing together 23 Jane's products that provide defence equipment-related reference, news and analysis covering air, land, sea and industry.
Formerly: Jane's Land and Systems Library
Media: CD-ROM. **Related titles:** Online - full text ed.: USD 30,750 (effective 2009).
Published by: I H S Jane's (Subsidiary of: I H S), Sentinel House, 163 Brighton Rd, Coulsdon, Surrey CR5 2YH, United Kingdom. TEL 44-20-87003700, FAX 44-20-87003751, info@janes.co.uk, http://www.janes.com. **Dist. in Asia by:** Jane's Information Group Asia, 60 Albert St, #15-01 Albert Complex, Singapore 189969, Singapore. TEL 65-331-6280, FAX 65-336-9921, info@janes.com.sg; **Dist. in Australia by:** Jane's Information Group Australia, PO Box 3502, Rozelle, NSW 2039, Australia. TEL 61-2-8587-7900, FAX 61-2-8587-7901, info@janes.thomson.com.au; **Dist. in the Americas by:** 1340 Braddock Pl, Ste 300, Alexandria, VA 22314-1651. TEL 703-683-3700, 800-824-0768, FAX 703-836-0297, 800-836-0297, info@janes.com.

355 GBR
JANE'S DEFENCE INDUSTRY (ONLINE). Text in English. 200?. d. GBP 1,125, USD 1,855, AUD 2,920 (effective 2010). **Document type:** *Newsletter, Trade.*
Media: Online - full text. **Related titles:** CD-ROM ed.: GBP 810, USD 1,335, AUD 2,100 (effective 2010).
Published by: I H S Jane's (Subsidiary of: I H S), Sentinel House, 163 Brighton Rd, Coulsdon, Surrey CR5 2YH, United Kingdom. TEL 44-20-87003700, FAX 44-20-87003751, info@janes.co.uk, http://www.janes.com.

355 GBR ISSN 0265-3818
JANE'S DEFENCE WEEKLY. Text in English. 1980. w. GBP 280 domestic; GBP 300 in Europe; GBP 420 elsewhere (effective 2010). adv. illus. reprints avail. **Document type:** *Journal, Trade.* **Description:** Contains news of the latest developments in military technology and incisive analysis of current geopolitical and industry issues from around the globe.
Formerly (until 1984): Jane's Defence Review (0144-0470)
Related titles: CD-ROM ed.: GBP 780 (effective 2010); Online - full text ed.: GBP 1,085 (effective 2010).
Indexed: A22, A28, AMB, APA, AUNI, B03, BMT, BrCerAb, C&ISA, CA, CA/WCA, CIA, CerAb, CivEngAb, CorrAb, DM&T, E&CAJ, E11, EEA, EMA, ESPM, EngInd, EnvEAb, G05, G06, G07, G08, H15, I02, I05, LID&ISL, M&TEA, M05, M06, M07, M09, MBF, METADEX, P10, P16, P47, P48, P53, P54, PQC, RASB, SCOPUS, SolStAb, T02, T04, WAA.
—BLDSC (4646.840000), IE, Infotrieve, Ingenta, Linda Hall. **CCC.**
Published by: I H S Jane's (Subsidiary of: I H S), Sentinel House, 163 Brighton Rd, Coulsdon, Surrey CR5 2YH, United Kingdom. TEL 44-20-87003700, FAX 44-20-87003751, info@janes.co.uk, http://www.janes.com. Ed. Peter Felstead. Adv. contact Janine Boxall TEL 44-20-87003852. Circ: 27,543 (paid and controlled). **Dist. in Asia by:** Jane's Information Group Asia, 60 Albert St, #15-01 Albert Complex, Singapore 189969, Singapore. TEL 65-331-6280, FAX 65-336-9921, info@janes.com.sg; **Dist. in Australia by:** Jane's Information Group Australia, PO Box 3502, Rozelle, NSW 2039, Australia. TEL 61-2-8587-7900, FAX 61-2-8587-7901, info@janes.thomson.com.au; **Dist. in the Americas by:** 1340 Braddock Pl, Ste 300, Alexandria, VA 22314-1651. TEL 703-683-3700, 800-824-0768, FAX 703-836-0297, 800-836-0297, info@janes.com.

355 GBR ISSN 1367-5044
JANE'S ELECTRO-OPTIC SYSTEMS. Text in English. 1989. a. GBP 480 per issue (2010-2011 ed.) (effective 2010). adv. illus. **Document type:** *Yearbook, Trade.* **Description:** Contains a complete profile of all the military electro-optic systems or systems with electro-optic elements, either in production, under development or in service with armies, navies and air forces throughout the world.
Formerly (until 1995): Jane's Battlefield Surveillance Systems (0960-6211); Which supersedes in part: Jane's Weapon Systems (0075-3068)
Related titles: CD-ROM ed.: GBP 1,245 (effective 2010); Online - full text ed.: GBP 1,685 (effective 2010).
—BLDSC (4646.950000). **CCC.**
Published by: I H S Jane's (Subsidiary of: I H S), Sentinel House, 163 Brighton Rd, Coulsdon, Surrey CR5 2YH, United Kingdom. TEL 44-20-87003700, FAX 44-20-87003751, info@janes.co.uk, http://www.janes.com. Ed. Michael J Gething. Adv. contact Richard West. **Dist. in Asia by:** Jane's Information Group Asia, 60 Albert St, #15-01 Albert Complex, Singapore 189969, Singapore. TEL 65-331-6280, FAX 65-336-9921, info@janes.com.sg; **Dist. in Australia by:** Jane's Information Group Australia, PO Box 3502, Rozelle, NSW 2039, Australia. TEL 61-2-8587-7900, FAX 61-2-8587-7901, info@janes.thomson.com.au; **Dist. in the Americas by:** 1340 Braddock Pl, Ste 300, Alexandria, VA 22314-1651. TEL 703-683-3700, 800-824-0768, FAX 703-836-0297, 800-836-0297, info@janes.com.

JANE'S ELECTRONIC MISSION AIRCRAFT. *see* AERONAUTICS AND SPACE FLIGHT

JANE'S EXPLOSIVE ORDNANCE DISPOSAL. *see* CIVIL DEFENSE

359 GBR ISSN 0075-3025
VA40
JANE'S FIGHTING SHIPS. Text in English. 1898. a. GBP 605 per issue (2010-2011 ed.) (effective 2010). adv. illus. index. **Document type:** *Yearbook, Trade.* **Description:** Analysis of the fleets, equipment, structures, and personnel of the world's navy.
Formerly (until 1916): Fighting Ships
Related titles: CD-ROM ed.: GBP 1,445 (effective 2010); Microfiche ed.: USD 3,075 in the Americas for complete set 1897-1993; GBP 1,975 elsewhere for complete set 1897-1993; USD 525 in the Americas per individual set; GBP 345 elsewhere per individual set (effective 2002); individual microfiche sets are cumulative and available for each of the following years 1897-1909, 1910-1919, 1920-1929, 1930-1939, 1940-1949, 1950-1959, 1960-1969, 1970-1979, and 1980-1993; Online - full text ed.: GBP 2,010 (effective 2010).
—BLDSC (4647.000000). **CCC.**
Published by: I H S Jane's (Subsidiary of: I H S), Sentinel House, 163 Brighton Rd, Coulsdon, Surrey CR5 2YH, United Kingdom. TEL 44-20-87003700, FAX 44-20-87003751, info@janes.co.uk, http://www.janes.com. Ed. Cmdr. Stephen Saunders. Adv. contact Janine Boxall TEL 44-20-87003852. **Dist. in Asia by:** Jane's Information Group Asia, 60 Albert St, #15-01 Albert Complex, Singapore 189969, Singapore. TEL 65-331-6280, FAX 65-336-9921, info@janes.com.sg; **Dist. in Australia by:** Jane's Information Group Australia, PO Box 3502, Rozelle, NSW 2039, Australia. TEL 61-2-8587-7900, FAX 61-2-8587-7901, info@janes.thomson.com.au; **Dist. in the Americas by:** 1340 Braddock Pl, Ste 300, Alexandria, VA 22314-1651. TEL 703-683-3700, 800-824-0768, FAX 703-836-0297, 800-836-0297, info@janes.com.

381.4562 GBR ISSN 1758-521X
HD9743.A1
JANE'S INDUSTRY QUARTERLY. Text in English. 2008. q. GBP 210 (effective 2010). illus. **Document type:** *Journal, Trade.* **Description:** Provides comprehensive analysis on key issues in the defense industry.
Indexed: A28, APA, BrCerAb, C&ISA, CA/WCA, CIA, CerAb, CivEngAb, CorrAb, E&CAJ, E11, EEA, EMA, H15, M&TEA, M09, MBF, METADEX, SolStAb, T04, WAA.
—Linda Hall.
Published by: I H S Jane's (Subsidiary of: I H S), Sentinel House, 163 Brighton Rd, Coulsdon, Surrey CR5 2YH, United Kingdom. TEL 44-20-87003700, FAX 44-20-87003751, info@janes.co.uk, http://www.janes.com.

356.1 GBR ISSN 0306-3410
JANE'S INFANTRY WEAPONS. Text in English. 1975. a. GBP 540 per issue (2010-2011 ed.) (effective 2010). adv. illus. index. **Document type:** *Yearbook, Trade.* **Description:** Describes and analyzes over 1500 weapons from every manufacturing country in the world.
Related titles: CD-ROM ed.: GBP 1,350 (effective 2010); Online - full text ed.: GBP 1,995 (effective 2010).

—BLDSC (4647.070000). **CCC.**
Published by: I H S Jane's (Subsidiary of: I H S), Sentinel House, 163 Brighton Rd, Coulsdon, Surrey CR5 2YH, United Kingdom. TEL 44-20-87003700, FAX 44-20-87003751, info@janes.co.uk, http://www.janes.com. Ed. Richard Jones. Adv. contact Janine Boxall TEL 44-20-87003852. **Dist. in Asia by:** Jane's Information Group Asia, 60 Albert St, #15-01 Albert Complex, Singapore 189969, Singapore. TEL 65-331-6280, FAX 65-336-9921, info@janes.com.sg; **Dist. in Australia by:** Jane's Information Group Australia, PO Box 3502, Rozelle, NSW 2039, Australia. TEL 61-2-8587-7900, FAX 61-2-8587-7901, info@janes.thomson.com.au; **Dist. in the Americas by:** 1340 Braddock Pl, Ste 300, Alexandria, VA 22314-1651. TEL 703-683-3700, 800-824-0768, FAX 703-836-0297, 800-836-0297, info@janes.com.

355 GBR ISSN 1350-6226
UA15 CODEN: JINRE5
JANE'S INTELLIGENCE REVIEW. Text in English. 1989. m. GBP 355 domestic; GBP 360 in Europe; GBP 390 elsewhere (effective 2010). bk.rev. illus. **Document type:** *Magazine, Trade.* **Description:** Provides open-source intelligence on conflicts, crises and security-related issues.
Incorporates: Pointer (1352-8491); Formerly (until 1991): Jane's Soviet Intelligence Review (0955-1247)
Related titles: CD-ROM ed.: GBP 855 (effective 2010); Online - full text ed.: GBP 1,180 (effective 2010); ◆ Supplement(s): Pointer (Coulsdon). ISSN 1352-8491; Jane's Intelligence Review. Special Report. ISSN 1462-4923. 1994.
Indexed: A22, AUNI, C&CSA, CA, FR, G05, G06, G07, G08, I02, I05, LID&ISL, M05, M06, M07, P10, P16, P34, P47, P48, P53, P54, PQC, T02.
—BLDSC (4647.071000), IE, Infotrieve, Ingenta. **CCC.**
Published by: I H S Jane's (Subsidiary of: I H S), Sentinel House, 163 Brighton Rd, Coulsdon, Surrey CR5 2YH, United Kingdom. TEL 44-20-87003700, FAX 44-20-87003751, info@janes.co.uk, http://www.janes.com. Ed. Christian LeMiere. Pub. Janine Boxall TEL 44-20-87003852. Circ: 3,000. **Dist. in Asia by:** Jane's Information Group Asia, 60 Albert St, #15-01 Albert Complex, Singapore 189969, Singapore. TEL 65-331-6280, FAX 65-336-9921, info@janes.com.sg; **Dist. in Australia by:** Jane's Information Group Australia, PO Box 3502, Rozelle, NSW 2039, Australia. TEL 61-2-8587-7900, FAX 61-2-8587-7901, info@janes.thomson.com.au; **Dist. in the Americas by:** 1340 Braddock Pl, Ste 300, Alexandria, VA 22314-1651. TEL 703-683-3700, 800-824-0768, FAX 703-836-0297, 800-836-0297, info@janes.com.

▼ **JANE'S INTELLIGENCE WEEKLY.** *see* POLITICAL SCIENCE—International Relations

355.4 GBR ISSN 1368-8359
UC260
JANE'S INTERNATIONAL DEFENCE DIRECTORY. Text in English. 1984. a. GBP 600 per issue (2010-2011 ed.) (effective 2010). adv. illus. index. back issues avail. **Document type:** *Directory, Trade.* **Description:** Lists defense companies, organizations worldwide. Includes company name, key personnel and product, service description.
Formerly: International Defense Directory (0256-7822)
Related titles: CD-ROM ed.: GBP 1,165 per issue (effective 2010); Online - full text ed.: GBP 1,605 (effective 2010).
—CCC.
Published by: I H S Jane's (Subsidiary of: I H S), Sentinel House, 163 Brighton Rd, Coulsdon, Surrey CR5 2YH, United Kingdom. TEL 44-20-87003700, FAX 44-20-87003751, info@janes.co.uk, http://www.janes.com. Ed. Jacqui Bowell. **Dist. in Asia by:** Jane's Information Group Asia, 60 Albert St, #15-01 Albert Complex, Singapore 189969, Singapore. TEL 65-331-6280, FAX 65-336-9921, info@janes.com.sg; **Dist. in Australia by:** Jane's Information Group Australia, PO Box 3502, Rozelle, NSW 2039, Australia. TEL 61-2-8587-7900, FAX 61-2-8587-7901, info@janes.thomson.com.au; **Dist. in the Americas by:** 1340 Braddock Pl, Ste 300, Alexandria, VA 22314-1651. TEL 703-683-3700, 800-824-0768, FAX 703-836-0297, 800-836-0297, info@janes.com.

355 GBR ISSN 1476-2129
U1 CODEN: IDRVAL
JANE'S INTERNATIONAL DEFENCE REVIEW. Text in English. 1968. m. GBP 255 domestic; GBP 270 in Europe; GBP 310 elsewhere (effective 2010). adv. illus. reprints avail. **Document type:** *Journal, Trade.* **Description:** Provides expert monthly reporting on the latest equipment, future defense technologies, scientific issues, strategic and security issues, and armed forces briefings.
Incorporates (1998-2004): Jane's Defence Upgrades (1365-4179); Which was formerly (until 1997): Jane's Defence Systems Moderinisation (1367-1251); (until 1994): Defence Systems Moderinisation (0953-4970); Formerly (until 1995): International Defense Review (0020-6512); Which incorporated (1968-1988): International Wehrrevue (1016-3565)
Related titles: CD-ROM ed.: GBP 760 (effective 2010); Microform ed.: (from PQC); Online - full text ed.: GBP 1,035 (effective 2010); ◆ Supplement(s): International Defense Review Extra. ISSN 1362-3974; Janes's International Defense Review Quarterly Report. ISSN 1460-3098. 1977.
Indexed: A22, A28, AMB, APA, AUNI, BrCerAb, C&CSA, C&ISA, CA, CA/WCA, CIA, CerAb, CivEngAb, CorrAb, DM&T, E&CAJ, E11, EEA, EMA, ESPM, EngInd, EnvEAb, H15, I02, I05, Inspec, LID&ISL, M&TEA, M05, M06, M09, MBF, METADEX, PRA, RASB, SCOPUS, SolStAb, T02, T04, WAA.
—BLDSC (4647.072000), IE, Infotrieve, Ingenta, Linda Hall. **CCC.**
Published by: I H S Jane's (Subsidiary of: I H S), Sentinel House, 163 Brighton Rd, Coulsdon, Surrey CR5 2YH, United Kingdom. TEL 44-20-87003700, FAX 44-20-87003751, info@janes.co.uk, http://www.janes.com. Ed. Mark Daly. Pub. Janine Boxall TEL 44-20-87003852. adv.: B&W page USD 7,625, color page USD 8,770; trim 8 x 10.75. **Dist. in Asia by:** Jane's Information Group Asia, 60 Albert St, #15-01 Albert Complex, Singapore 189969, Singapore. TEL 65-331-6280, FAX 65-336-9921, info@janes.com.sg; **Dist. in Australia by:** Jane's Information Group Australia, PO Box 3502, Rozelle, NSW 2039, Australia. TEL 61-2-8587-7900, FAX 61-2-8587-7901, info@janes.thomson.com.au; **Dist. in the Americas by:** 1340 Braddock Pl, Ste 300, Alexandria, VA 22314-1651. TEL 703-683-3700, 800-824-0768, FAX 703-836-0297, 800-836-0297, info@janes.com.

355 GBR ISSN 0959-5821
JANE'S LAND-BASED AIR DEFENCE. Text in English. 1988. a. GBP 510 per issue (2010-2011 ed.) (effective 2010). illus. **Document type:** *Yearbook, Trade.* **Description:** Presents data on land-based air defence weapons, covering all types of static and mobile anti-aircraft, anti-helicopter and anti-missile systems in service or under development all over the world.
Formerly (until 1988): Jane's Battlefield Air Defence (0954-3821)
Related titles: CD-ROM ed.: GBP 1,305 (effective 2010); Online - full text ed.: GBP 1,795 (effective 2010).
—BLDSC (4647.073000). **CCC.**
Published by: I H S Jane's (Subsidiary of: I H S), Sentinel House, 163 Brighton Rd, Coulsdon, Surrey CR5 2YH, United Kingdom. TEL 44-20-87003700, FAX 44-20-87003751, info@janes.co.uk, http://www.janes.com. Ed. James C O'Halloran. **Dist. in Asia by:** Jane's Information Group Asia, 60 Albert St, #15-01 Albert Complex, Singapore 189969, Singapore. TEL 65-331-6280, FAX 65-336-9921, info@janes.com.sg; **Dist. in Australia by:** Jane's Information Group Australia, PO Box 3502, Rozelle, NSW 2039, Australia. TEL 61-2-8587-7900, FAX 61-2-8587-7901, info@janes.thomson.com.au; **Dist. in the Americas by:** 1340 Braddock Pl, Ste 300, Alexandria, VA 22314-1651. TEL 703-683-3700, 800-824-0768, FAX 703-836-0297, 800-836-0297, info@janes.com.

355.27 GBR ISSN 0144-0004
JANE'S MILITARY COMMUNICATIONS. Text in English. 1979. a. GBP 515 per issue (2010-2011 ed.) (effective 2010). adv. illus. index. **Document type:** *Yearbook, Trade.* **Description:** Devoted to communication systems, equipment and ancillaries designed for, and used by, the world's armed forces. Includes sections devoted to test and maintenance, security, surveillance and signal analysis, direction finding and jamming.
Related titles: CD-ROM ed.: GBP 1,280 (effective 2010); Online - full text ed.: GBP 1,760 (effective 2010).
—CCC.
Published by: I H S Jane's (Subsidiary of: I H S), Sentinel House, 163 Brighton Rd, Coulsdon, Surrey CR5 2YH, United Kingdom. TEL 44-20-87003700, FAX 44-20-87003751, info@janes.co.uk, http://www.janes.com. Ed. John Williamson. Adv. contact Janine Boxall TEL 44-20-87003852. **Dist. in Asia by:** Jane's Information Group Asia, 60 Albert St, #15-01 Albert Complex, Singapore 189969, Singapore. TEL 65-331-6280, FAX 65-336-9921, info@janes.com.sg; **Dist. in Australia by:** Jane's Information Group Australia, PO Box 3502, Rozelle, NSW 2039, Australia. TEL 61-2-8587-7900, FAX 61-2-8587-7901, info@janes.thomson.com.au; **Dist. in the Americas by:** 1340 Braddock Pl, Ste 300, Alexandria, VA 22314-1651. TEL 703-683-3700, 800-824-0768, FAX 703-836-0297, 800-836-0297, info@janes.com.

355.4 GBR ISSN 1369-5967
JANE'S MILITARY VEHICLES AND LOGISTICS. Text in English. 1978. a. GBP 625 per vol. (2010-2011 ed.) (effective 2010). adv. illus. index. **Document type:** *Yearbook, Trade.* **Description:** Worldwide survey using text, photographs, drawings and diagrams of logistic vehicles and associated equipment including materials handling equipment, personnel transport, bridging, land and mine warfare plus fuel and water supplies.
Former titles (until 1990): Jane's Military Logistics (0954-4941); (until 1987): Jane's Military Vehicles and Ground Support Equipment (0263-2594); (1978): Jane's Combat Support Equipment (0143-1420)
Related titles: CD-ROM ed.: GBP 1,305 (effective 2010); Online - full text ed.: GBP 1,790 (effective 2010).
—BLDSC (4647.087100). **CCC.**
Published by: I H S Jane's (Subsidiary of: I H S), Sentinel House, 163 Brighton Rd, Coulsdon, Surrey CR5 2YH, United Kingdom. TEL 44-20-87003700, FAX 44-20-87003751, info@janes.co.uk, http://www.janes.com. Eds. Christopher F Foss, Shaun C Conners. Pub. Alan Condron. Adv. contact Richard West. **Dist. in Asia by:** Jane's Information Group Asia, 60 Albert St, #15-01 Albert Complex, Singapore 189969, Singapore. TEL 65-331-6280, FAX 65-336-9921, info@janes.com.sg; **Dist. in Australia by:** Jane's Information Group Australia, PO Box 3502, Rozelle, NSW 2039, Australia. TEL 61-2-8587-7900, FAX 61-2-8587-7901, info@janes.thomson.com.au; **Dist. in the Americas by:** 1340 Braddock Pl, Ste 300, Alexandria, VA 22314-1651. TEL 703-683-3700, 800-824-0768, FAX 703-836-0297, 800-836-0297, info@janes.com.

355.845 623.451 GBR ISSN 1366-5103
JANE'S MINES AND MINE CLEARANCE. Text in English. 1996. a. GBP 480 per vol. (2010-2011 ed.) (effective 2010). illus. **Document type:** *Yearbook, Trade.* **Description:** A guide to identifying and disarming mines and booby traps throughout the world.
Related titles: CD-ROM ed.: GBP 1,195 (effective 2010); Online - full text ed.: GBP 1,635 (effective 2010).
—BLDSC (4647.087150). **CCC.**
Published by: I H S Jane's (Subsidiary of: I H S), Sentinel House, 163 Brighton Rd, Coulsdon, Surrey CR5 2YH, United Kingdom. TEL 44-20-87003700, FAX 44-20-87003751, info@janes.co.uk, http://www.janes.com. Ed. Colin King. **Dist. in Asia by:** Jane's Information Group Asia, 60 Albert St, #15-01 Albert Complex, Singapore 189969, Singapore. TEL 65-331-6280, FAX 65-336-9921, info@janes.com.sg; **Dist. in Australia by:** Jane's Information Group Australia, PO Box 3502, Rozelle, NSW 2039, Australia. TEL 61-2-8587-7900, FAX 61-2-8587-7901, info@janes.thomson.com.au; **Dist. in the Americas by:** 1340 Braddock Pl, Ste 300, Alexandria, VA 22314-1651. TEL 703-683-3700, 800-824-0768, FAX 703-836-0297, 800-836-0297, info@janes.com.

623.4519 GBR ISSN 1365-4187
UG1310
JANE'S MISSILES AND ROCKETS. Text in English. 1997. m. GBP 385 domestic; GBP 390 in Europe; GBP 410 elsewhere (effective 2010). illus. **Document type:** *Newsletter, Trade.* **Description:** News of the latest technology and contract information as well as procurement forecasts for missiles, rockets and precision-guided munitions from around the globe.
Related titles: CD-ROM ed.: GBP 880 (effective 2010); Online - full text ed.: GBP 1,195 (effective 2010).
Indexed: A28, APA, BrCerAb, C&ISA, CA/WCA, CIA, CerAb, CivEngAb, CorrAb, E&CAJ, E11, EEA, EMA, ESPM, EngInd, EnvEAb, H15, M&TEA, M09, MBF, METADEX, SCOPUS, SolStAb, T04, WAA.
—Infotrieve. **CCC.**

Published by: I H S Jane's (Subsidiary of: I H S), Sentinel House, 163 Brighton Rd, Coulsdon, Surrey CR5 2YH, United Kingdom. TEL 44-20-87003700, FAX 44-20-87003751, info@janes.co.uk, http://www.janes.com. Ed. Doug Richardson. **Dist. in Asia by:** Jane's Information Group Asia, 60 Albert St, #15-01 Albert Complex, Singapore 189969, Singapore. TEL 65-331-6280, FAX 65-336-9921, info@janes.com.sg; **Dist. in Australia by:** Jane's Information Group Australia, PO Box 3502, Rozelle, NSW 2039, Australia. TEL 61-2-8587-7900, FAX 61-2-8587-7901, info@janes.thomson.com.au; **Dist. in the Americas by:** 1340 Braddock Pl, Ste 300, Alexandria, VA 22314-1651. TEL 703-683-3700, 800-824-0768, FAX 703-836-0297, 800-836-0297, info@janes.com.

JANE'S NAVAL CONSTRUCTION AND RETROFIT MARKETS. *see* BUILDING AND CONSTRUCTION

359 GBR ISSN 0960-4448
VF346
JANE'S NAVAL WEAPON SYSTEMS; in-depth assessment of naval weapon systems worldwide. Text in English. 1988. s-a. GBP 905 (effective 2010). illus. back issues avail. **Document type:** *Magazine, Trade.* **Description:** Examines naval weapon systems and associated equipment.
Related titles: CD-ROM ed.: GBP 1,765 (effective 2010); Online - full content ed.: GBP 2,410 (effective 2010).
—CCC.
Published by: I H S Jane's (Subsidiary of: I H S), Sentinel House, 163 Brighton Rd, Coulsdon, Surrey CR5 2YH, United Kingdom. TEL 44-20-87003700, FAX 44-20-87003751, info@janes.co.uk, http://www.janes.com. Ed. Malcolm Fuller. **Dist. in Asia by:** Jane's Information Group Asia, 60 Albert St, #15-01 Albert Complex, Singapore 189969, Singapore. TEL 65-331-6280, FAX 65-336-9921, info@janes.com.sg; **Dist. in Australia by:** Jane's Information Group Australia, PO Box 3502, Rozelle, NSW 2039, Australia. TEL 61-2-8587-7900, FAX 61-2-8587-7901, info@janes.thomson.com.au; **Dist. in the Americas by:** 1340 Braddock Pl, Ste 300, Alexandria, VA 22314-1651. TEL 703-683-3700, 800-824-0768, FAX 703-836-0297, 800-836-0297, info@janes.com.

359 GBR ISSN 1358-3719
V1
JANE'S NAVY INTERNATIONAL. Text in English. 1895. 10/yr. GBP 170 domestic; GBP 180 in Europe; GBP 205 elsewhere (effective 2010). adv. bk.rev. illus. reprints avail. **Document type:** *Magazine, Trade.* **Description:** Provides in-depth reporting and analysis of significant developments affecting maritime security and the balance of seapower.
Formerly (until 1995): Navy International (0144-3194); Which incorporated (in 1986): Combat Craft (0264-4649); Which was formerly: Navy (0028-1646)
Related titles: CD-ROM ed.: GBP 635 (effective 2010); Online - full text ed.: GBP 855 (effective 2010).
Indexed: A22, AMB, BMT, CA, DM&T, EngInd, I02, I05, IBR, IBZ, M05, M06, M07, P10, P16, P47, P48, P53, P54, PQC, PRA, RASB, RefZh, SCOPUS, T02.
—IE, Ingenta. **CCC.**
Published by: I H S Jane's (Subsidiary of: I H S), Sentinel House, 163 Brighton Rd, Coulsdon, Surrey CR5 2YH, United Kingdom. TEL 44-20-87003700, FAX 44-20-87003751, info@janes.co.uk, http://www.janes.com. Ed. Nick Brown. Pub., Adv. contact Simon Kay. R&P Robert Hutchinson. B&W page USD 3,468, color page USD 8,770; trim 8 x 10.75. Circ: 19,807 (paid and controlled). **Dist. in Asia by:** Jane's Information Group Asia, 60 Albert St, #15-01 Albert Complex, Singapore 189969, Singapore. TEL 65-331-6280, FAX 65-336-9921, info@janes.com.sg; **Dist. in Australia by:** Jane's Information Group Australia, PO Box 3502, Rozelle, NSW 2039, Australia. TEL 61-2-8587-7900, FAX 61-2-8587-7901, info@janes.thomson.com.au; **Dist. in the Americas by:** 1340 Braddock Pl, Ste 300, Alexandria, VA 22314-1651. TEL 703-683-3700, 800-824-0768, FAX 703-836-0297, 800-836-0297, info@janes.com.

355.4 GBR ISSN 1464-8210
JANE'S NUCLEAR, BIOLOGICAL AND CHEMICAL DEFENCE. Variant title: Jane's N B C Defence Systems. Text in English. 1988. a. GBP 465 per vol. (2010-2011 ed.) (effective 2010). illus. **Document type:** *Yearbook, Trade.* **Description:** Features a thousand key defensive products so you can make informed procurement decisions.
Formerly (until 1997): Jane's N B C Protection Equipment (0954-3791)
Related titles: CD-ROM ed.: GBP 1,200 (effective 2010); Online - full text ed.: GBP 1,650 (effective 2010).
—CCC.
Published by: I H S Jane's (Subsidiary of: I H S), Sentinel House, 163 Brighton Rd, Coulsdon, Surrey CR5 2YH, United Kingdom. TEL 44-20-87003700, FAX 44-20-87003751, info@janes.co.uk, http://www.janes.com. Ed. Neil Gibson. **Dist. in Asia by:** Jane's Information Group Asia, 60 Albert St, #15-01 Albert Complex, Singapore 189969, Singapore. TEL 65-331-6280, FAX 65-336-9921, info@janes.com.sg; **Dist. in Australia by:** Jane's Information Group Australia, PO Box 3502, Rozelle, NSW 2039, Australia. TEL 61-2-8587-7900, FAX 61-2-8587-7901, info@janes.thomson.com.au; **Dist. in the Americas by:** 1340 Braddock Pl, Ste 300, Alexandria, VA 22314-1651. TEL 703-683-3700, 800-824-0768, FAX 703-836-0297, 800-836-0297, info@janes.com.

JANE'S POLICE AND HOMELAND SECURITY EQUIPMENT (YEARS). *see* CRIMINOLOGY AND LAW ENFORCEMENT—Security

354.75 GBR ISSN 0959-5759
JANE'S RADAR AND ELECTRONIC WARFARE SYSTEMS. Text in English. 1989. a. GBP 560 per issue (2010-2011 ed.) (effective 2010). adv. illus. **Document type:** *Yearbook, Trade.* **Description:** Reports on more than 2,000 systems, covering land, sea and airborne surveillance and fire control radars.
Formerly: Jane's Radar and E-W Systems
Related titles: CD-ROM ed.: GBP 1,370 (effective 2010); Online - full text ed.: GBP 2,010 (effective 2010).
—BLDSC (4647.094000), IE, Ingenta. **CCC.**
Published by: I H S Jane's (Subsidiary of: I H S), Sentinel House, 163 Brighton Rd, Coulsdon, Surrey CR5 2YH, United Kingdom. TEL 44-20-87003700, FAX 44-20-87003751, info@janes.co.uk, http://www.janes.com. Ed. Martin Streetly. Adv. contact Richard West. **Dist. in Asia by:** Jane's Information Group Asia, 60 Albert St, #15-01 Albert Complex, Singapore 189969, Singapore. TEL 65-331-6280,

FAX 65-336-9921, info@janes.com.sg; **Dist. in Australia by:** Jane's Information Group Australia, PO Box 3502, Rozelle, NSW 2039, Australia. TEL 61-2-8587-7900, FAX 61-2-8587-7901, info@janes.thomson.com.au; **Dist. in the Americas by:** 1340 Braddock Pl, Ste 300, Alexandria, VA 22314-1651. TEL 703-683-3700, 800-824-0768, FAX 703-836-0297, 800-836-0297, info@janes.com.

JANE'S SECURITY LIBRARY. *see* CRIMINOLOGY AND LAW ENFORCEMENT—Security

355 GBR ISSN 1361-9675
JANE'S SIMULATION AND TRAINING SYSTEMS. Text in English. 1988. a. GBP 460 per issue (2010-2011 ed.) (effective 2010). adv. illus. **Document type:** *Directory, Trade.* **Description:** Comprehensive descriptions and reviews of more than 1,000 items of land, sea and air training equipment from small arms trainers to full flight mission simulations.
Former titles (until 1995): Jane's Military Training and Simulation Systems (1361-9667); (until 1994): Jane's Military Training Systems (0954-3805)
Related titles: CD-ROM ed.: GBP 1,190 (effective 2010); Online - full content ed.: GBP 1,635 (effective 2010).
Indexed: LID&ISL.
—CCC.
Published by: I H S Jane's (Subsidiary of: I H S), Sentinel House, 163 Brighton Rd, Coulsdon, Surrey CR5 2YH, United Kingdom. TEL 44-20-87003700, FAX 44-20-87003751, info@janes.co.uk, http://www.janes.com. Eds. Giles Ebbutt, Huw Williams. Adv. contact Richard West. **Dist. in Asia by:** Jane's Information Group Asia, 60 Albert St, #15-01 Albert Complex, Singapore 189969, Singapore. TEL 65-331-6280, FAX 65-336-9921, info@janes.com.sg; **Dist. in Australia by:** Jane's Information Group Australia, PO Box 3502, Rozelle, NSW 2039, Australia. TEL 61-2-8587-7900, FAX 61-2-8587-7901, info@janes.thomson.com.au; **Dist. in the Americas by:** 1340 Braddock Pl, Ste 300, Alexandria, VA 22314-1651. TEL 703-683-3700, 800-824-0768, FAX 703-836-0297, 800-836-0297, info@janes.com.

338.476234 GBR ISSN 0958-6032
UF500
JANE'S STRATEGIC WEAPON SYSTEMS. Text in English. 1989. s-a. GBP 885 (effective 2010). illus. **Document type:** *Journal, Trade.* **Description:** Contains analysis of offensive and defensive systems in use or under development including land-based, ship/submarine-based, air-launched and space-based systems. Weapon entries include details of type, development status and description including major operating modes, operational status, specifications and contractors together with illustrations.
Related titles: CD-ROM ed.: GBP 1,725 (effective 2010); Online - full text ed.: GBP 2,375 (effective 2010).
—CCC.
Published by: I H S Jane's (Subsidiary of: I H S), Sentinel House, 163 Brighton Rd, Coulsdon, Surrey CR5 2YH, United Kingdom. TEL 44-20-87003700, FAX 44-20-87003751, info@janes.co.uk, http://www.janes.com. Ed. Duncan Lennox. **Subscr. addr. in Asia:** Jane's Information Group Asia, 60 Albert St, #15-01 Albert Complex, Singapore 189969, Singapore. TEL 65-331-6280, FAX 65-336-9921, info@janes.com.sg; **Subscr. addr. in Australia:** Jane's Information Group Australia, PO Box 3502, Rozelle, NSW 2039, Australia. TEL 61-2-8587-7900, FAX 61-2-8587-7901, info@janes.thomson.com.au; **Subscr. addr. in the Americas:** 1340 Braddock Pl, Ste 300, Alexandria, VA 22314-1651. TEL 703-683-3700, 800-824-0768, FAX 703-836-0297, 800-836-0297, info@janes.com.

JANE'S TRANSPORT LIBRARY. *see* TRANSPORTATION

355 GBR ISSN 0959-6283
JANE'S UNDERWATER WARFARE SYSTEMS. Text in English. 1989. a. GBP 475 per issue (2010-2011 ed.) (effective 2010). illus. **Document type:** *Yearbook, Trade.* **Description:** Covers all aspects of the underwater warfare scene, including underwater weapons and their fire control systems, sonar, sonobuoys, MAD, underwater communications ranges and targets.
Related titles: CD-ROM ed.: GBP 1,225 (effective 2010); Online - full text ed.: GBP 1,670 (effective 2010).
—BLDSC (4647.115000). **CCC.**
Published by: I H S Jane's (Subsidiary of: I H S), Sentinel House, 163 Brighton Rd, Coulsdon, Surrey CR5 2YH, United Kingdom. TEL 44-20-87003700, FAX 44-20-87003751, info@janes.co.uk, http://www.janes.com. Ed. Clifford Funnell. **Dist. in Asia by:** Jane's Information Group Asia, 60 Albert St, #15-01 Albert Complex, Singapore 189969, Singapore. TEL 65-331-6280, FAX 65-336-9921, info@janes.com.sg; **Dist. in Australia by:** Jane's Information Group Australia, PO Box 3502, Rozelle, NSW 2039, Australia. TEL 61-2-8587-7900, FAX 61-2-8587-7901, info@janes.thomson.com.au; **Dist. in the Americas by:** 1340 Braddock Pl, Ste 300, Alexandria, VA 22314-1651. TEL 703-683-3700, 800-824-0768, FAX 703-836-0297, 800-836-0297, info@janes.com.

355.8 GBR ISSN 1759-7161
JANE'S UNMANNED GROUND VEHICLES AND SYSTEMS. Text in English. 2008. s-a. GBP 1,130 (effective 2010). illus. **Document type:** *Journal, Trade.* **Description:** Provide informations on unmanned ground platforms as well as their communication and control systems, support equipment and attachments in applications such as reconnaissance, explosive ordnance disposal and mine detection roles.
Related titles: CD-ROM ed.: GBP 1,820 (effective 2010); Online - full text ed.: GBP 2,520 (effective 2010).
Published by: I H S Jane's (Subsidiary of: I H S), Sentinel House, 163 Brighton Rd, Coulsdon, Surrey CR5 2YH, United Kingdom. TEL 44-20-87003700, FAX 44-20-87003751, info@janes.co.uk, http://www.janes.com. Ed. Damian Kemp.

355.8 GBR ISSN 1759-717X
▼ **JANE'S UNMANNED MARITIME VEHICLES AND SYSTEMS.** Text in English. 2009. s-a. GBP 1,130 (effective 2010). illus. **Document type:** *Journal, Trade.* **Description:** Contains information on unmanned surface vehicles, semi-submersibles and underwater vehicles.
Related titles: CD-ROM ed.: GBP 1,820 (effective 2010); Online - full text ed.: 2009. GBP 2,520 (effective 2010).
Published by: I H S Jane's (Subsidiary of: I H S), Sentinel House, 163 Brighton Rd, Coulsdon, Surrey CR5 2YH, United Kingdom. TEL 44-20-87003700, FAX 44-20-87003751, http://www.janes.com. Ed. Clifford Funnell.

358.4 GBR ISSN 1748-2526
JANE'S WORLD AIR FORCES. Text in English. 1996. s-a. GBP 980 (effective 2010). illus. **Document type:** *Handbook/Manual/Guide, Trade.* **Description:** Contains a detailed listing of the aircraft operating in the world's air arms as well as the units that operate them, including national identity markings, air order of battle including chains of command and bases, inventories, future procurement plans, and airbase location maps.
Related titles: CD-ROM ed.: GBP 1,590 (effective 2010); Online - full content ed.: GBP 2,185 (effective 2010).
—CCC.
Published by: I H S Jane's (Subsidiary of: I H S), Sentinel House, 163 Brighton Rd, Coulsdon, Surrey CR5 2YH, United Kingdom. TEL 44-20-87003700, FAX 44-20-87003751, info@janes.co.uk, http://www.janes.com. Eds. Eleanor Keymer, Lindsay Peacock. **Dist. addr. in Asia:** Jane's Information Group Asia, 60 Albert St, #15-01 Albert Complex, Singapore 189969, Singapore. TEL 65-331-6280, FAX 65-336-9921, info@janes.com.sg; **Dist. addr. in Australia:** Jane's Information Group Australia, PO Box 3502, Rozelle, NSW 2039, Australia. TEL 61-2-8587-7900, FAX 61-2-8587-7901, info@janes.thomson.com.au; **Dist. addr. in the Americas:** 1340 Braddock Pl, Ste 300, Alexandria, VA 22314-1651. TEL 703-683-3700, 800-824-0768, FAX 703-836-0297, 800-836-0297, info@janes.com.

355.31 GBR ISSN 1748-2607
JANE'S WORLD ARMIES. Text in English. 1996. s-a. GBP 980 (effective 2010). illus. **Document type:** *Handbook/Manual/Guide, Trade.* **Description:** Covers the structure, operation and equipment of the world's armies, including national inventories and procurement data.
Related titles: CD-ROM ed.: GBP 1,590 (effective 2010); Online - full text ed.: GBP 2,185 (effective 2010).
—BLDSC (4647.135300). **CCC.**
Published by: I H S Jane's (Subsidiary of: I H S), Sentinel House, 163 Brighton Rd, Coulsdon, Surrey CR5 2YH, United Kingdom. TEL 44-20-87003700, FAX 44-20-87003751, info@janes.co.uk, http://www.janes.com. Ed. Eleanor Keymer. **Dist. addr. in Asia:** Jane's Information Group Asia, 60 Albert St, #15-01 Albert Complex, Singapore 189969, Singapore. TEL 65-331-6280, FAX 65-336-9921, info@janes.com.sg; **Dist. addr. in Australia:** Jane's Information Group Australia, PO Box 3502, Rozelle, NSW 2039, Australia. TEL 61-2-8587-7900, FAX 61-2-8587-7901, info@janes.thomson.com.au; **Dist. addr. in the Americas:** 1340 Braddock Pl, Ste 300, Alexandria, VA 22314-1651. TEL 703-683-3700, 800-824-0768, FAX 703-836-0297, 800-836-0297, info@janes.com.

JANE'S WORLD DEFENCE INDUSTRY. *see* BUSINESS AND ECONOMICS

359 GBR ISSN 1757-5710
JANE'S WORLD NAVIES. Variant title: World Navies. Text in English. 2008. 2/yr. GBP 980 (effective 2010). illus. **Document type:** *Handbook/Manual/Guide, Trade.* **Description:** Resource for understanding command, operational and deployment data and analysis on the world's navies, including recent operational activity.
Related titles: CD-ROM ed.: 2008. GBP 1,590 (effective 2010); Online - full text ed.: 2008. GBP 2,185 (effective 2010).
Published by: I H S Jane's (Subsidiary of: I H S), Sentinel House, 163 Brighton Rd, Coulsdon, Surrey CR5 2YH, United Kingdom. TEL 44-20-87003700, FAX 44-20-87003751, info@janes.co.uk, http://www.janes.com. Ed. Eleanor Keymer.

338.473 363.35 GBR ISSN 1749-1487
JAPAN DEFENCE & SECURITY REPORT. Text in English. 2005. q. EUR 820, USD 1,030 combined subscription (print & email eds.) (effective 2010). **Document type:** *Report, Trade.* **Description:** Provides professionals, consultancies, government departments, regulatory bodies and researchers with independent forecasts and regional competitive intelligence on the Japanese defence & security industry.
Related titles: E-mail ed.
Indexed: B01, P34.
Published by: Business Monitor International Ltd., Senator House, 85 Queen Victoria St, London, EC4V 4AB, United Kingdom. TEL 44-20-72480468, FAX 44-20-72480467, subs@businessmonitor.com.

JAPANESE MILITARY AIRCRAFT SERIALS. *see* MILITARY—Abstracting, Bibliographies, Statistics

355 USA
JAX AIR NEWS. Text in English. 1944. w. (Thu.). free newsstand/cover; USD 50 subscr - mailed (effective 2005). adv. **Document type:** *Newspaper.*
Published by: Times-Union Military Publications, One Riverside Ave., Jacksonville, FL 32202. TEL 904-359-4336, FAX 904-366-6230. Ed. Miriam S Gallet TEL 904-542-5588. Adv. contact Linda Edenfield. col. inch USD 16.55. Circ: 12,000 (paid and free).

305.8924 USA ISSN 0047-2018
DS101
JEWISH VETERAN; the patriotic voice of American Jewry. Text in English. 1927. 5/yr. USD 7.50 (effective 2001). adv. bk.rev. charts; illus. **Document type:** *Magazine, Consumer.* **Description:** Updates readers on issues of concern to veterans and Jews, including benefits, entitlement, veteran's health care, the Middle East, Israel, anti-Semitism and racism.
Related titles: Microfilm ed.: (from AJP).
Published by: Jewish War Veterans of the USA, Inc., 1811 R St, N W, Washington, DC 20009. TEL 202-265-6280, FAX 202-234-5662, jwv@jew.org, http://www.jwv.org/. Pub., Adv. contact Alan Zimmerman. Circ: 100,000.

JIANCHUAN ZHISHI. *see* TRANSPORTATION—Ships And Shipping

355.31 CHN
JIEFANGJUN BAO/LIBERATION ARMY DAILY. Text in Chinese. d. CNY 249.60, USD 90 (effective 2005). **Document type:** *Newspaper.*
Related titles: Online - full content ed.
Published by: Zhongguo Renmin Jiefangjun/Chinese People's Liberation Army, 34, Fuwei Dajie, Beijing, 100832, China. **Dist. by:** China International Book Trading Corp, 35 Chegongzhuang Xilu, Haidian District, PO Box 399, Beijing 100044, China. TEL 86-10-68412045, FAX 86-10-68412023, cibtc@mail.cibtc.com.cn, http://www.cibtc.com.cn.

355.1 CHN ISSN 0009-3823
UA837
JIEFANGJUN HUABAO/P L A PICTORIAL. Text in Chinese. 1951. m. USD 144 (effective 2010). illus. **Document type:** *Magazine, Government.*
Indexed: RASB.
—East View.
Published by: Jiefangjun Baoshe/Chinese People's Liberation Army Press, 40 Sanlihe Lu, Ganjiakou, Beijing, 100037, China. **Dist. by:** China International Book Trading Corp, 35 Chegongzhuang Xilu, Haidian District, PO Box 399, Beijing 100044, China. TEL 86-10-68412045, FAX 86-10-68412023, cibtc@mail.cibtc.com.cn, http://www.cibtc.com.cn.

M

JIEFANGJUN JIANKANG/P L A HEALTH. *see* PHYSICAL FITNESS AND HYGIENE

355.1 CHN ISSN 1002-4654
UA838.C45
JIEFANGJUN SHENGHUO/P L A LIFE. Text in Chinese. 1985. m. USD 39.60 (effective 2009). **Document type:** *Journal, Academic/Scholarly.*
Related titles: Online - full text ed.
—East View.
Address: 3, Pinganli, Beijing, 100035, China. TEL 86-10-66169234, FAX 86-10-66733787. **Dist. by:** China International Book Trading Corp, 35 Chegongzhuang Xilu, Haidian District, PO Box 399, Beijing 100044, China. TEL 86-10-68412045, FAX 86-10-68412023, cibtc@mail.cibtc.com.cn, http://www.cibtc.com.cn.

JIEFANGJUN WENYI/LITERATURE AND ART OF PEOPLE'S LIBERATION ARMY. *see* LITERATURE

JIEFANGJUN YIXUE ZAZHI/MEDICAL JOURNAL OF CHINESE PEOPLE'S LIBERATION ARMY. *see* MEDICAL SCIENCES

355 USA ISSN 1521-8708
JING BAO JOURNAL. Text in English. 1948. bi-m. membership only. bk.rev.; film rev.; play rev. **Document type:** *Newsletter.* **Description:** Covers association activities and tales of members during World War II in China.
Published by: Flying Tigers of the 14th Air Force Association, Inc., PO Box 934236, Margate, FL 33093-4236. TEL 954-973-0277, FAX 954-973-1561. Ed. Lt Col C L Mcmillen. Circ: 4,070 (paid).

355 USA ISSN 1070-0692
U260
JOINT FORCE QUARTERLY. Text in English. 1993. q. USD 20 domestic; USD 28 foreign; USD 15 per issue domestic; USD 21 per issue foreign (effective 2009). bk.rev. illus. Index. back issues avail.; reprints avail. **Document type:** *Journal, Government.* **Description:** Promotes understanding of the integrated employment of land, sea, air, space, and special operations forces.
Related titles: Online - full text ed.: ISSN 1559-6702. free (effective 2009).
Indexed: A01, A03, A08, A22, A26, ABS&EES, AUNI, CA, E08, G06, G07, G08, I02, I05, LID&ISL, M05, M06, M07, P10, P34, P47, P48, P52, P53, P54, PAIS, PQC, S09, T02.
—BLDSC (4672.266030), IE, Ingenta.
Published by: National Defense University (Subsidiary of: U.S. Department of Defense), Fort Lesley J McNair, 300 Fifth Ave. Bldg 62, Washington, DC 20319. TEL 202-685-4210, FAX 202-685-4806, ndupress@ndu.edu, http://www.ndu.edu. Ed. David H Gurney TEL 202-685-4220. **Subscr. to:** U.S. Government Printing Office, Superintendent of Documents, PO Box 371954, Pittsburgh, PA 15250. TEL 202-512-1800, FAX 202-512-2250, orders@gpo.gov, http://www.access.gpo.gov.

338.473 363.35 GBR ISSN 1749-1495
JORDAN DEFENCE & SECURITY REPORT. Text in English. 2005. a. EUR 820, USD 1,030 combined subscription per issue (print & email eds.) (effective 2010). **Document type:** *Report, Trade.* **Description:** Provides professionals, consultancies, government departments, regulatory bodies and researchers with independent forecasts and regional competitive intelligence on the Jordanian defence & security industry.
Related titles: E-mail ed.
Indexed: B01.
Published by: Business Monitor International Ltd., Senator House, 85 Queen Victoria St, London, EC4V 4AB, United Kingdom. TEL 44-20-72480468, FAX 44-20-72480467, subs@businessmonitor.com.

355 PRT ISSN 0871-8598
JORNAL DO EXERCITO; orgao de informacao, cultura e recreio do exercito portugues. Text in Portuguese. 1960. m. EUR 16.95 (effective 2005). bk.rev. charts; illus. index. **Document type:** *Magazine, Government.*
Published by: Ministerio da Defesa Nacional, Exercito, Largo da Graca 94, Lisbon, 1170-165, Portugal. TEL 351-218-541025, FAX 351-218-541046, info@mail.exercito.pt, http://www.exercito.pt. Ed. Maj Francisco Marques Fernando. Circ: 6,000.

355 FRA ISSN 1282-738X
JOURNAL DES COMBATTANTS. Text in French. 1916. w. adv. bk.rev. bibl.; illus.; stat.
Formerly (until 1919): Jusqu'au Bout (1635-7434)
Address: 80 rue des Prairies, Paris, 75020, France. Ed. Mrs. Daniel. Circ: 30,000.

359 AUS
➤ **JOURNAL OF AUSTRALIAN NAVAL HISTORY.** Text in English. 2004. s-a. AUD 40 (effective 2007). **Document type:** *Journal, Academic/Scholarly.* **Description:** Aims to encourage the study, research, writing and discussion of Australian naval history.
Published by: Naval Historical Society of Australia, The Boatshed, Bldg 25, Garden Island, NSW 2011, Australia. TEL 61-2-93592372, FAX 61-2-93592383, secretary@navyhistory.org.au. Ed., R&P Ian Pfennigwerth. Pub. Paul Martin. Circ: 250 (paid and controlled).

355 AUS ISSN 1440-5113
➤ **JOURNAL OF BATTLEFIELD TECHNOLOGY.** Text in English. 1998. 3/yr. AUD 165, GBP 70, EUR 110, USD 140 (effective 2008). back issues avail. **Document type:** *Journal, Academic/Scholarly.* **Description:** Provides information on research in battlefield technology for military officers, scientists and engineers.
Related titles: Online - full text ed.
Indexed: I02, T02.
—BLDSC (4951.137000), IE, Ingenta.

Published by: (Australian Defence Force Academy, School of Electrical Engineering), Argos Press Pty Ltd., PO Box 85, Red Hill, ACT 2603, Australia. TEL 61-2-62959404, FAX 61-2-62959404, contact@argospress.com. Eds. Paul Hazell TEL 44-1793-785906, Michael Ryan TEL 61-2-62688200.

➤ **JOURNAL OF CONFLICT AND SECURITY LAW.** *see* LAW—International Law

▼➤ **JOURNAL OF DEFENCE AND SECURITY.** *see* POLITICAL SCIENCE

355 ROM ISSN 2068-9403

▼➤ **JOURNAL OF DEFENSE RESOURCES MANAGEMENT.** Text in English. 2010. s-a. free to qualified personnel. Index. back issues avail. **Document type:** *Journal, Academic/Scholarly.*
Related titles: Online - full text ed.: free (effective 2011).
Published by: Regional Department of Defense Resources Management Studies, 160 Mihai Viteazul St., Brasov, 500183, Romania. TEL 40-268-401800, FAX 40-268-401802, contact@crmra.ro, http://www.dresmara.ro. Ed. Cezar Vasilescu. Circ: 100.

▼➤ **JOURNAL OF FAITH AND WAR.** *see* RELIGIONS AND THEOLOGY

➤ **JOURNAL OF INTERNATIONAL PEACEKEEPING.** *see* POLITICAL SCIENCE—International Relations

355 USA ISSN 1532-4060
K10

THE JOURNAL OF INTERNATIONAL SECURITY AFFAIRS. Text in English. 2001. s-a. USD 16; USD 8 per issue (effective 2009). adv. back issues avail. **Document type:** *Journal, Trade.* **Description:** Dedicated to shaping ideas and framing policy relating to the security of the United States and its allies abroad.
Related titles: Online - full text ed.: ISSN 1947-0967.
Published by: Jewish Institute for National Security Affairs, 1779 Massachusetts Ave NW, Ste 515, Washington, DC 20036. TEL 202-667-3900, FAX 202-667-0601, info@jinsa.org, http://www.jinsa.org. Ed. Ilan Berman. Pub. Tom Neumann.

JOURNAL OF MEDIEVAL MILITARY HISTORY. *see* HISTORY—History Of Europe

355 CAN ISSN 1488-559X
U102

➤ **JOURNAL OF MILITARY AND STRATEGIC STUDIES.** Text in English, French. 1998. s-a. free (effective 2011). bk.rev. **Document type:** *Journal, Academic/Scholarly.* **Description:** Seeks to provide and promote a timely and active discussion on issues of security, defence and strategic studies across disciplines and is intended for academics, military professionals and those interested in security issues.
Media: Online - full text.
Indexed: A39, C27, C29, CA, D03, D04, E13, P42, PAIS, PSA, R14, S14, S15, S18, T02.
Published by: University of Calgary, Centre for Military and Strategic Studies, 2500 University Dr N W, Calgary, AB, Canada. TEL 403-220-4038, FAX 403-282-0594. Eds. Jim Keeley, John Ferris.

355 NOR ISSN 1502-7570
U22

➤ **JOURNAL OF MILITARY ETHICS;** normative aspects of the use of military force. Text in English. 2001. q. GBP 198 combined subscription in United Kingdom to institutions (print & online eds.); EUR 260, USD 327 combined subscription to institutions (print & online eds.) (effective 2012). reprint service avail. from PSC. **Document type:** *Journal, Academic/Scholarly.* **Description:** Contains articles discussing justifications for the resort to military force and/or what may justifiably be done in the use of such force.
Related titles: Online - full text ed.: ISSN 1502-7589. GBP 178 in United Kingdom to institutions; EUR 234, USD 294 to institutions (effective 2012) (from IngentaConnect).
Indexed: A01, A03, A08, A22, CA, E01, I02, LID&ISL, M05, P48, P52, PAIS, PQC, PhilInd, T02.
—IE, Ingenta. **CCC.**
Published by: Taylor & Francis A S (Subsidiary of: Taylor & Francis Group), Biskop Gunnerusgate 14A, PO Box 12 Posthuset, Oslo, 0051, Norway. TEL 47-23-103460, FAX 47-23-103461, journals@tandf.no. Eds. Dr. Baard Maeland, James Turner Johnson. **Subscr. addr. in Europe:** Taylor & Francis Ltd., Journals Customer Service, Sheepen Pl, Colchester, Essex CO3 3LP, United Kingdom. TEL 44-20-70175544, FAX 44-20-70175198, tf.enquiries@tfinforma.com; **Subscr. addr. in N America:** Taylor & Francis Inc., Customer Services Dept, 325 Chestnut St, 8th Fl, Philadelphia, PA 19106. TEL 800-354-1420, FAX 215-625-2940.

▼➤ **JOURNAL OF MILITARY GEOGRAPHY.** *see* GEOGRAPHY

355.009 909 USA ISSN 0899-3718
E181

➤ **JOURNAL OF MILITARY HISTORY.** Text in English. 1937. q. free to members (effective 2009). adv. bk.rev.; film rev.; video rev.; Website rev. bibl.; charts; illus.; maps. cum.index: 1937-1994. 320 p./no.; back issues avail.; reprints avail. **Document type:** *Journal, Academic/Scholarly.* **Description:** Publishes scholarly articles and reviews on all aspects of military history.
Former titles (until 1989): Military Affairs (0026-3931); (until 1941): American Military Institute. Journal (1520-8613); (until 1939): American Military History Foundation. Journal (1520-8621)
Related titles: Microfilm ed.: (from PQC); Online - full text ed.: ISSN 1543-7795.
Indexed: A01, A02, A03, A08, A20, A22, A26, ABS&EES, AMB, ASCA, AUNI, AmH&L, AmHI, ArtHuCI, B04, B14, BAS, BRD, BRI, CA, CBRI, CurCont, DIP, E01, E08, G08, H05, H07, H08, HAb, HistAb, HumInd, I02, I05, IBR, IBZ, LID&ISL, M05, M06, M07, MEA&I, MLA-IB, P02, P06, P10, P13, P30, P42, P47, P48, P53, P54, PCI, PQC, RASB, S09, SCOPUS, SPPI, T02, W03, W04, W07.
—BLDSC (5019.945000), IE, Infotrieve, Ingenta, Linda Hall. **CCC.**
Published by: Society for Military History, George C Marshall Library, Virginia Military Institute, Lexington, VA 24450. TEL 540-464-7468, FAX 540-464-7330. Ed. Bruce Vandervort. Adv. contact Wendy Vandervort. page USD 325; bleed 6 x 9. **Co-sponsor:** George C. Marshall Foundation.

623.0937 GBR ISSN 0961-3684
U35

JOURNAL OF ROMAN MILITARY EQUIPMENT STUDIES. Abbreviated title: J R M E S. Text in English. 1990. a., latest vol.13, 2005. price varies. back issues avail. **Document type:** *Journal, Academic/Scholarly.* **Description:** Dedicated to the study of weapons, armour and fighting within the Roman World.
Indexed: BrArAb, NumL.
—CCC.
Published by: Armatura Press, Braemar Kirkgate, Chirnside Duns, Berks TD11 3XL, United Kingdom. FAX 44-870-940048, info@armatura.co.uk, http://www.armatura.co.uk/. Ed. M C Bishop. **Dist in the UK by:** Oxbow Books, 10 Hythe Bridge St, Oxford OX1 2EW, United Kingdom. TEL 44-1865-241249, FAX 44-1865-794449, oxbow@oxbowbooks.com, http://www.oxbowbooks.com; **Dist. in US by:** David Brown Book Co.

355 GBR ISSN 1351-8046
UA770 CODEN: JSMTE8

➤ **THE JOURNAL OF SLAVIC MILITARY STUDIES.** Text in English. 1988. q. GBP 425 combined subscription in United Kingdom to institutions (print & online eds.); EUR 561, USD 704 combined subscription to institutions (print & online eds.) (effective 2012). bk.rev. illus. index. back issues avail.; reprint service avail. from PSC. **Document type:** *Journal, Academic/Scholarly.* **Description:** Investigates all aspects of military affairs in the Slavic nations of Central and Eastern Europe in a historical and geopolitical context.
Formerly (until 1993): Journal of Soviet Military Studies (0954-254X)
Related titles: Online - full text ed.: ISSN 1556-3006. GBP 383 in United Kingdom to institutions; EUR 504, USD 633 to institutions (effective 2012) (from IngentaConnect).
Indexed: A01, A22, ABS&EES, AUNI, B21, CA, DIP, E01, E17, ESPM, HistAb, I02, I13, IBR, IBSS, IBZ, LID&ISL, M05, M07, P02, P10, P42, P47, P48, P53, P54, PAIS, PCI, PQC, PSA, SCOPUS, T02.
—IE, Infotrieve, Ingenta. **CCC.**
Published by: Routledge (Subsidiary of: Taylor & Francis Group), 4 Park Sq, Milton Park, Abingdon, Oxon OX14 4RN, United Kingdom. TEL 44-20-70176000, FAX 44-20-70176336, subscriptions@tandf.co.uk, http://www.routledge.com. Eds. Christopher Donnelly TEL 44-1793-785075, David M Glantz TEL 843-724-5960. Adv. contact Linda Hann TEL 44-1344-779945. **Subscr. to:** Taylor & Francis Ltd., Journals Customer Service, Sheepen Pl, Colchester, Essex CO3 3LP, United Kingdom. TEL 44-20-70175544, FAX 44-20-70175198.

355 610 USA ISSN 1553-9768
UH201

➤ **JOURNAL OF SPECIAL OPERATIONS MEDICINE.** Text in English. 200?. q. USD 30 (effective 2010). **Document type:** *Journal, Academic/Scholarly.* **Description:** Provides information about operations medicine.
Related titles: Online - full text ed.: free (effective 2010).
Indexed: EMBASE, ExcerpMed, MEDLINE, P30, SCOPUS.
Published by: United States Special Operations Command, 7701 Tampa Point Blvd, MacDill AFB, FL 33621. TEL 813-826-4600, FAX 813-826-4035, Public.Affairs@socom.mil, http://www.socom.mil/SOCOMHome/Pages/default.aspx.

355 AUS ISSN 1327-0141
DU112.3

JOURNAL OF THE AUSTRALIAN WAR MEMORIAL. Text in English. 1982. irreg. adv. bk.rev. illus. back issues avail. **Document type:** *Journal, Consumer.* **Description:** An occasional publication, for the purpose of advancing the Memorial's mission of remembering and interpreting the Australian experience of war and to publicize research into Australian military history.
Formerly (until 1995): Journal of the Australian War Memorial (Print) (0729-6274)
Media: Online - full text.
Indexed: A26, AusPAIS, E08, G08, HistAb, I05, S09.
—Ingenta. **CCC.**
Published by: Australian War Memorial, GPO Box 345, Canberra, ACT 2601, Australia. TEL 61-2-62434211, FAX 61-2-62434325, info@awm.gov.au. Eds. Anne-Marie Conde TEL 61-2-62434390, Peter Londey. Adv. contact Anne-Marie Conde TEL 61-2-62434390.

▼ **JOURNAL OF THE MILITARY JEEP IN ACTION.** *see* TRANSPORTATION—Automobiles

355.821 GBR ISSN 0022-5134

JOURNAL OF THE ROYAL ARTILLERY. Text in English. 1858. s-a. adv. bk.rev. illus.; maps. index every 10 yrs. 72 p./no. 3 cols./p.; back issues avail. **Document type:** *Journal, Academic/Scholarly.*
Formerly: Great Britain. Army. Royal Artillery Institution. Proceedings
Indexed: AUNI, DM&T, LID&ISL.
—BLDSC (4853.100000).
Published by: Royal Artillery Institution, Royal Artillery Barracks, Larkhill, Salisbury, Wilts SP4 8QT, United Kingdom. TEL 44-20-8781-3705, FAX 44-20-8781-3706, gunnermag@aol.com. Eds. J W Timbers, M J N Richards TEL 44-20-8781-3031. R&P M J N Richards TEL 44-20-8781-3031. Circ: 2,500.

JOURNAL OF WAR AND CULTURE STUDIES. *see* SOCIOLOGY

355 UAE

AL-JUNDI. Text in Arabic. 1973. m. USD 84 (effective 1999). adv. back issues avail. **Document type:** *Government.* **Description:** Covers military affairs in the U.A.E., the Gulf region and worldwide, including the latest developments in weapons systems, as well as sports and cultural topics.
Published by: Ministry of Defence, Morale & Cultural Affairs Department/Wizarat al-Difa'a, PO Box 2838, Dubai, United Arab Emirates. TEL 971-4-451515, FAX 971-4-455033, TELEX 45554 MOD EM. Ed. Maj Ismail Khamis Mubarak. R&P Khalid M Al Shaibah. Adv. contact Fahed Al Halabieh. B&W page USD 4,300, color page USD 5,000; trim 210 x 285. Circ: 6,000.

355 059.951 CHN ISSN 1674-1528

JUNDUI DANGDE SHENGHUO. Text in Chinese. 2004. m. **Document type:** *Magazine, Government.*
Formerly (until 2007): Dangdai Junshi Wenzhai/Contemporary Military Digest (1672-7886)
Published by: Jiefangjun Chubanshe, 28, Zhongguancun Nan Dajie, Beijing, 100081, China. TEL 86-10-66801179, FAX 86-10-66801021.

355 CHN ISSN 1673-8888

JUNSAO/ARMY WIVES. Text in Chinese. 2005. bi-m. **Document type:** *Magazine, Consumer.*
Published by: Junsao Zazhishe, 19, Yangfangdian Dong Lu, Haitian Zhongxin Bldg.1, Sect. 2, Rm.202, Beijing, 100038, China. TEL 86-10-63988257.

355 CHN ISSN 1002-4883
DS738

JUNSHI LISHI/MILITARY HISTORY. Text in Chinese. 1983. bi-m. USD 22.80 (effective 2009). **Document type:** *Journal, Academic/Scholarly.*
Related titles: Online - full text ed.
—East View.
Published by: Junshi Kexueyuan, Haidian-qu, Beijing, 100091, China. TEL 86-10-66767464. **Dist. by:** China International Book Trading Corp, 35 Chegongzhuang Xilu, Haidian District, PO Box 399, Beijing 100044, China. TEL 86-10-68412045, FAX 86-10-68412023, cibtc@mail.cibtc.com.cn, http://www.cibtc.com.cn.

JUNSHI YIXUE KEXUEYUAN YUANKAN/ACADEMY OF MILITARY MEDICAL SCIENCES. BULLETIN. *see* MEDICAL SCIENCES

355 620 CHN ISSN 1672-8211

JUNSHI YUNCHOU YU XITONG GONGCHENG/MILITARY OPERATIONS RESEARCH AND SYSTEMS ENGINEERING. Text in Chinese. 1987. q. USD 20.80 (effective 2009). **Document type:** *Journal, Academic/Scholarly.*
Related titles: Online - full text ed.
Published by: Zhongguo Renmin Jiefangjun, Junshi Kexueyuan/Academy of Military Science of the C P L A, 998-Xinxiang 11-Fenxiang, Beijing, 100091, China.

JUNYING WENHUA TIANDI. *see* LITERATURE

355 EST

KAITSE KODU. Text in Estonian. bi-m. USD 205 in North America (effective 2000).
Address: Tartu Riya 2, Tallinn, Estonia. TEL 3702-427550, FAX 3702-427551, kaitseko@online.ee. Ed. Ivar Joesaar. **Dist. by:** East View Information Services, 10601 Wayzata Blvd, Minneapolis, MN 55305. TEL 952-252-1201, 800-477-1005, FAX 952-252-1202, info@eastview.com, http://www.eastview.com.

355 DEU ISSN 1434-4394

KAMERADEN. Text in German. 1953. 10/yr. EUR 40 domestic; EUR 49 foreign; EUR 5 newsstand/cover (effective 2008). **Document type:** *Magazine, Trade.*
Formerly (until 1997): Alte Kameraden (0401-5436)
Published by: Arbeitsgemeinschaft fuer Kameradenwerke und Traditionsverbaende, Tuebinger Str 12-16, Stuttgart, 70178, Germany. TEL 49-711-2260620, FAX 49-711-2260794, info@kameradenwerke.de. Circ: 16,000.

355 AUT ISSN 0029-974X

KAMERADSCHAFT DER WIENER PANZER-DIVISION. MITTEILUNGSBLATT. Text in German. 1961. q. adv. bk.rev. illus. **Document type:** *Newsletter.*
Published by: Kameradschaft der Wiener Panzer-Division, Postfach 159, Vienna, W 1061, Austria. TEL 01-5866357. Ed. Franz Steinzer. Circ: 4,000.

KANRIN/JAPAN SOCIETY OF NAVAL ARCHITECTS AND OCEAN ENGINEERS. BULLETIN. *see* TRANSPORTATION—Ships And Shipping

355 CAN ISSN 1913-3677

KANWA ASIAN DEFENCE. Text in English. 2007. m. HKD 940 in Hong Kong; USD 125 in Asia; USD 130 elsewhere (effective 2011). **Document type:** *Journal, Trade.*
Published by: Kanwa Information Center, 420 Hwy 7 East, PO Box 82023, Richmond Hill, ON L4B 3K2, Canada. info@kanwa.com.

355 CAN ISSN 1712-5049

KANWA DEFENSE REVIEW. Text in English. 2004. irreg. **Document type:** *Journal, Trade.* **Description:** Contains news correspondence, original photos, and reference reports on the foreign and national defense policies of different Asian countries.
Published by: Kanwa Information Center, 420 Hwy 7 East, PO Box 82023, Richmond Hill, ON L4B 3K2, Canada. info@kanwa.com, http://www.kanwa.com.

355.1 LTU ISSN 0022-9199
U4

KARYS. Text in Lithuanian. 1950. m. USD 149 (effective 1999). bk.rev.
Address: Pamenkalnio ul 13, Vilnius, 2000, Lithuania. TEL 3702-613410, FAX 3702-613410. Ed. M Barkauskas. Circ: 1,300. **Dist. by:** East View Information Services, 10601 Wayzata Blvd, Minneapolis, MN 55305. TEL 952-252-1201, 800-477-1005, FAX 952-252-1202, info@eastview.com, http://www.eastview.com.

355 RUS

KASPIETS. Text in Russian. w.
Published by: Komanduyushchii Krasnoznamennoi Kaspiiskoi Flotilii (Subsidiary of: Ministry of Defence of the Russian Federation/Ministerstvo Oborony R F), Ul Latysheva 5, Astrakahan, 414056, Russian Federation. Ed. A I Kuznetsov.

338.473 958 363.35 GBR ISSN 2044-5059

KAZAKHSTAN AND CENTRAL ASIA DEFENCE & SECURITY REPORT. Text in English. 2005. q. GBP 695, EUR 820, USD 1,150 combined subscription (print & email eds.) (effective 2010). **Document type:** *Report, Trade.* **Description:** Provides professionals, consultancies, government departments, regulatory bodies and researchers with independent forecasts and regional competitive intelligence on the Kyrgyzstani, Kazakhstani, Tajikistani, Turkmen and Uzbekistani defence & security industries.
Formerly (until 2009): Central Asia Defence & Security Report (1749-1312)
Related titles: E-mail ed.
Indexed: A15, ABIn, B01, B02, B15, B17, B18, G04, I05, P48, P51, P52, PQC.
Published by: Business Monitor International Ltd., Senator House, 85 Queen Victoria St, London, EC4V 4AB, United Kingdom. TEL 44-20-72480468, FAX 44-20-72480467, subs@businessmonitor.com, http://www.businessmonitor.com.

355 KAZ

KAZAKHSTAN SARBAZY. Text in Kazakh. w.
Related titles: Russian ed.: Voin Kazakhstana.
Published by: Ministerstvo Oborony, Ul Zharokova 210, Almaty, 480057, Kazakstan. TEL 7-327-444551, 7-327-443751, 7-327-443766. Ed. S H Zhagiparov. Circ: 5,060.

355.4 NLD ISSN 1877-2331
KEEP THEM ROLLING. Variant title: K T R. Text in Dutch. 1977. q. **Document type:** *Magazine, Consumer.*
Published by: Nederlandse Vereniging Instandhouding Historische Militaire Voertuigen "Keep Them Rolling", c/o Margaret Roos, Oude Oppenhuizerweg 95, Sneek, 8606 JD, Netherlands. TEL 31-515-417258, http://www.ktr.nl.

355 USA
KELLY U S A OBSERVER. Text in English. 1947. w. **Document type:** *Newspaper, Consumer.*
Formerly: Kelly Observer
Published by: Prime Time, Inc, 17400 Judson Rd, San Antonio, TX 78247. TEL 210-453-3300, http://www.primetimenewspapers.com/.

355.31 DNK ISSN 0023-0057
KENTAUR; kamptroppernes tidsskrift. Text in Danish. 1954. 4/yr. DKK 150; DKK 35 per issue (effective 2010). adv. 26 p./no. 2 cols./p.; **Document type:** *Magazine, Consumer.* **Description:** Deals with issues of primary interest to Army and Home Guard personnel; education, arms and tactics.
Address: c/o SSG Rolf Rasmussen, Haerens Kampskole, Oksbol, 6840, Denmark. TEL 45-76-541429, FAX 45-76-541409, hks@mil.dk. Ed. E Schjoenning. adv.: color page DKK 4,100; 248 x 170.

355.009 USA
KENTUCKY. ADJUTANT-GENERAL'S OFFICE. REPORT. Text in English. a.
Published by: Adjutant-General's Office, Frankfort, KY 40601. TEL 502-564-8558.

355 338 GBR ISSN 1365-8131
KEY NOTE MARKET REPORT: DEFENCE EQUIPMENT. Variant title: Defence Equipment Market Report. Text in English. 198?. irreg., latest 2006, Jul. GBP 420 per issue (effective 2010). **Document type:** *Report, Trade.* **Description:** Provides an overview of the UK defence equipment market, including industry structure, market size and trends, developments, prospects, and major company profiles.
Formerly (until 1996): Key Note Report: Defence Equipment (1357-1435)
Related titles: CD-ROM ed.; Online - full text ed.
Published by: Key Note Ltd. (Subsidiary of: Bonnier Business Information), Harlequin House, 5th Fl, 7 High St, Teddington, Richmond upon Thames, TW11 8EE, United Kingdom. TEL 44-845-5040452, FAX 44-845-5040453, info@keynote.co.uk.

359 USA
KINGS BAY PERISCOPE. Text in English. 1979. w. (Fri.). free (effective 2004). **Document type:** *Newspaper.*
Published by: Times-Union Military Publications, One Riverside Ave., Jacksonville, FL 32202. TEL 904-359-4336, FAX 904-366-6230. Ed. Craig Richardson. Adv. contact Julie H Sandifer TEL 904-359-4527. Circ: 10,000 (free).

355 IRN
KITAB-I MUQAVAMAT. Text in Persian, Modern. 1989. q. IRR 720 per issue. illus.
Published by: Hawzah-i Hunari Sazman-i Tablighat-i Islami, 213 Summaiyah St., P O Box 1677-15815, Teheran, Iran.

KOEHLERS FLOTTENKALENDER; internationales Jahrbuch der Seefahrt. *see* TRANSPORTATION—Ships And Shipping

KOKUSAI ANZEN HOSHO/JOURNAL OF INTERNATIONAL SECURITY. *see* POLITICAL SCIENCE

353.538 POL ISSN 0867-8952
KOMBATANT. Text in Polish. 1990. m. PLZ 14.40; PLZ 1.20 newsstand/cover. adv. back issues avail. **Description:** Deals mainly with subject matter pertaining to ex-combatants organizations and veterans welfare.
Published by: Urzad do Spraw Kombatantow i Osob Represionowanych, Ul. Krucza 36, Warsaw, 00-921, Poland. TEL 48-22-6958000, FAX 48-22-6959926. Ed., Adv. contact Franciszka Gryko. Circ: 5,000.

KONGJUN GONGCHENG DAXUE XUEBAO (ZIRAN KEXUE BAN)/AIR FORCE ENGINEERING UNIVERSITY. JOURNAL (NATURAL SCIENCE EDITION). *see* SCIENCES: COMPREHENSIVE WORKS

355 GBR ISSN 1016-3271
UA830
➤ **THE KOREAN JOURNAL OF DEFENSE ANALYSIS.** Text in English. 1989. q. GBP 193, EUR 307, USD 386 combined subscription to institutions (print & online eds.) (effective 2010). back issues avail.; reprint service avail. from PSC. **Document type:** *Journal, Academic/Scholarly.* **Description:** Discusses all Asian security issues with a focus on the political, economic and military aspects of Northeast Asia.
Related titles: Online - full text ed.: ISSN 1941-4641. GBP 183, EUR 292, USD 366 to institutions (effective 2010).
Indexed: A20, ASCA, BAS, CA, CurCont, LID&ISL, P42, PAIS, PSA, SCOPUS, SSCI, SociolAb, T02, W07.
—BLDSC (5113.529000), IE, Ingenta. **CCC.**
Published by: (Korea Institute for Defense Analyses KOR), Routledge (Subsidiary of: Taylor & Francis Group), 4 Park Sq, Milton Park, Abingdon, Oxon OX14 4RN, United Kingdom. TEL 44-20-70176000, FAX 44-20-70176336, info@routledge.co.uk, http://www.routledge.com. Ed. Tae Am Ohm. Pub. Koo Sub Kim. Adv. contact Linda Hann TEL 44-1344-779945.

355.03 NOR ISSN 1502-6361
KORT-INFO FRA DNAK/SHORTINFO FROM DNAK. (Den Norske Atlanterhavskomite) Text in English. 2001. irreg. back issues avail. **Document type:** *Report, Consumer.* **Description:** Short presentations on current topics in foreign and security policy.
Related titles: Online - full text ed.: ISSN 1502-637X.
Published by: Den Norske Atlanterhavskomite/The Norwegian Atlantic Committee, Fridjof Nansens Plass 8, Oslo, 0160, Norway. TEL 47-22-403600, FAX 47-22-403610, post@dnak.org, http://www.dnak.org. Ed. Neving Rudskjaer.

355 RUS ISSN 0023-4559
KRASNAYA ZVEZDA. Text in Russian. 1924. 260/yr. USD 298 foreign (effective 2003). adv. illus. reprints avail. **Document type:** *Newspaper.* **Description:** Covers primarily military news.
Related titles: Microfilm ed.: (from PQC); Online - full content ed.; Supplement(s): Syn Otechestva.
Indexed: LID&ISL.
Published by: Ministerstvo Oborony Rossiiskoi Federatsii/Ministry of Defence of the Russian Federation, Khoroshevskoe shosse 38, Moscow, 123826, Russian Federation. FAX 7-095-9414066, nikolaev@mil.ru. Ed. A I Dokuchaev. **Dist. by:** East View Information Services, 10601 Wayzata Blvd, Minneapolis, MN 55305. TEL 952-252-1201, 800-477-1005, FAX 952-252-1202, info@eastview.com, http://www.eastview.com; M K - Periodica, ul Gilyarovskogo 39, Moscow 129110, Russian Federation. TEL 7-095-2845008, FAX 7-095-2813798, info@periodicals.ru, http://www.mkniga.ru.

355 RUS
KRASNYI VOIN. Text in Russian. 1921. 104/yr. USD 415 in North America.
Published by: Moscow Military District, Khoroshevskoe shosse 38a, Moscow, 123007, Russian Federation. TEL 7-095-9410901. Ed. Yu V Burylin. **Dist. by:** East View Information Services, 10601 Wayzata Blvd, Minneapolis, MN 55305. TEL 952-252-1201, 800-477-1005, FAX 952-252-1202, info@eastview.com, http://www.eastview.com.

355 SWE ISSN 2000-4206
▼ **KRIGENS HISTORIA.** Text in Swedish. 2009. m. **Document type:** *Magazine, Consumer.*
Published by: Krutroek Media, PO Box 27805, Stockholm, 11593, Sweden. TEL 46-8-55342884. Ed. Patrik Nilsson.

948.95 DNK ISSN 0454-5230
D25
KRIGSHISTORISK TIDSSKRIFT. Text in Danish. 1965. 3/yr. DKK 180; DKK 60 per issue (effective 2009). **Document type:** *Journal, Academic/Scholarly.* **Description:** Journal of military history of Denmark.
Indexed: RILM.
Published by: Det Militaere Laeseselskab Rendsborg, Kastellet 60, Copenhagen OE, 2100, Denmark.

355 359 SWE ISSN 0023-5369
U4
➤ **KUNGLIGA KRIGSVETENSKAPSAKADEMIEN. HANDLINGAR OCH TIDSKRIFT/ROYAL SWEDISH ACADEMY OF WAR SCIENCES. PROCEEDINGS AND JOURNAL.** Text in Swedish; Text occasionally in English; Summaries in English. 1797. 6/yr. SEK 400; SEK 105 per issue (effective 2010). adv. bk.rev. bibl.; charts; maps; illus. index. back issues avail. **Document type:** *Proceedings, Academic/Scholarly.* **Description:** Covers defence, security policy, military technique, strategy, warfare, military history. Qualified analyses of the total defence, the current debate on security and defence policy, historical perspectives and future visions.
Former titles (until 1833): Kungliga Krigsvetenskapsakademien. Handlinger; (until 1804): Svenska Krigsmannasaellskapet. Handlinger
Indexed: HistAb, P30, RASB.
Published by: Kungliga Krigsvetenskapsakademien/Royal Swedish Academy of War Sciences, Teatergatan 3, Stockholm, 11148, Sweden. TEL 46-8-6111400, FAX 46-8-6672253, info@kkrva.se. **Subscr. to:** Marie Brunnberg AB, Marie Brunnberg AB, Faagelsta 212, Oestervaala 74046, Sweden.

338.473 953.67 363.35 GBR ISSN 1749-1509
KUWAIT DEFENCE & SECURITY REPORT. Text in English. 2005. q. EUR 820, USD 1,030 combined subscription (print & email eds.) (effective 2010). **Document type:** *Report, Trade.* **Description:** Provides professionals, consultancies, government departments, regulatory bodies and researchers with independent forecasts and regional competitive intelligence on the Kuwaiti defence & security industry.
Related titles: E-mail ed.
Indexed: B01, P34.
Published by: Business Monitor International Ltd., Senator House, 85 Queen Victoria St, London, EC4V 4AB, United Kingdom. TEL 44-20-72480468, FAX 44-20-72480467, subs@businessmonitor.com.

355.1 DEU
KYFFHAEUSER. Text in German. bi-m. adv. **Document type:** *Newspaper, Consumer.*
Published by: Kyffhaeuserbund e.V., Bahnstr 12, Wiesbaden, 65205, Germany. TEL 49-611-523616, FAX 49-611-590638, kyffhaeuserbund@t-online.de, http://www.kyffhaeuserbund.de. adv.: B&W page EUR 1,616. Circ: 40,500 (controlled).

358.4 USA
LACKLAND TALESPINNER. Text in English. 19??. w. **Document type:** *Newspaper, Consumer.*
Published by: Prime Time, Inc, 17400 Judson Rd, San Antonio, TX 78247. TEL 210-453-3300, http://www.primetimenewspapers.com/.

LADIES AUXILIARY V F W. (Veterans of Foreign Wars) *see* CLUBS

355 GBR ISSN 2042-5317
▼ **LAND WARFARE INTERNATIONAL.** Abbreviated title: L W I. Text in English. 2010. bi-m. GBP 65; free to qualified personnel (effective 2010). adv. back issues avail. **Document type:** *Magazine, Trade.* **Description:** Covers all aspects of the land battle.
Related titles: Online - full text ed.: ISSN 2042-5325.
Published by: Shephard Press Ltd., 268 Bath Rd, Slough, Berkshire SL1 4DX, United Kingdom. TEL 44-1753-727001, FAX 44-1753-727002, info@shephard.co.uk. Ed. Ian Kemp TEL 44-7532-426978. Adv. contact Mike Wild TEL 44-1753-727007.

356 NLD ISSN 1572-1248
U4
LANDMACHT. Text in Dutch. 1951. m. adv. bk.rev.; film rev.; rec.rev. **Document type:** *Government.*
Formerly (until 2003): Legerkoerier (0024-0389)
Published by: Koninklijke Landmacht, Postbus 90701, The Hague, 2509 LS, Netherlands. http://www.landmacht.nl. Eds. Corne Dalebout, Gerard Koot. Circ: 53,000.

DER LANDSER. FLIEGERGESCHICHTEN AUS DEM ZWEITEN WELTKRIEG. *see* LITERATURE—Adventure And Romance

355 CAN ISSN 1910-7587
LAURIER CENTRE FOR MILITARY, STRATEGIC AND DISARMAMENT STUDIES. PROGRAM NOTES. Text in English. 2006. s-a. **Document type:** *Newsletter, Trade.*
Published by: Wilfrid Laurier University, Laurier Centre for Military, Strategic and Disarmament Studies, 75 University Ave West, Waterloo, ON N2L 3C5, Canada. TEL 519-884-1970, FAX 519-886-9351, http://info.wlu.ca/~wwwmsds.

LEADING EDGE (OJAI). *see* AERONAUTICS AND SPACE FLIGHT

358.4 USA
LEADING EDGE (WRIGHT-PATTERSON AIR FORCE BASE). Text in English. m. **Document type:** *Magazine, Trade.*
Published by: Air Force Materiel Command, 4375 Chidlaw Rd., RM N152, Wright-Patterson AFB, OH 45433-5006. TEL 937-257- 1203.

359 USA ISSN 0023-981X
D731
LEATHERNECK; magazine of the Marines. Text in English. 1917. m. free to members (effective 2009). adv. bk.rev. illus. Index. 72 p./no. 3 cols./p.; back issues avail.; reprints avail. **Document type:** *Magazine, Trade.* **Description:** Covers U.S. Marine Corps history and the activities of Marines throughout the world.
Formerly (until 19??): Quantico Leatherneck
Related titles: Microfilm ed.: (from PQC); Online - full text ed.
Indexed: A22, M07, P10, P47, P48, P52, P53, P54, PQC.
—Ingenta.
Published by: Marine Corps Association, 715 Broadway St, PO Boox 1775, Quantico, VA 22134. TEL 800-336-0291, FAX 703-640-0823, mca@mca-marines.org. Pub. Walter G Ford. Adv. contact G Scott Dinkel TEL 718-715-1361. B&W page USD 2,900; trim 8 x 10.875. Circ: 86,857 (paid).

355.31 USA ISSN 0195-3451
U27
LEAVENWORTH PAPERS. Text in English. 1979. irreg. **Document type:** *Government.*
Indexed: LID&ISL.
Published by: Combat Studies Institute, US Army Command & General Staff College, Fort Leavenworth, KS 66027. TEL 913-684-9327, FAX 913-684-9328, http://www.leavenworth.army.mil.

LIAISON FOR CIVIL-MILITARY HUMANITARIAN RELIEF COLLABORATIONS. *see* SOCIAL SERVICES AND WELFARE

338.473 961.2 363.35 GBR ISSN 1749-1517
LIBYA DEFENCE & SECURITY REPORT. Text in English. 2005. q. EUR 820, USD 1,030 combined subscription (print & email eds.) (effective 2010). **Document type:** *Report, Trade.* **Description:** Provides professionals, consultancies, government departments, regulatory bodies and researchers with independent forecasts and regional competitive intelligence on the Libyan defence & security industry.
Related titles: E-mail ed.
Indexed: B01.
Published by: Business Monitor International Ltd., Senator House, 85 Queen Victoria St, London, EC4V 4AB, United Kingdom. TEL 44-20-72480468, FAX 44-20-72480467, subs@businessmonitor.com.

327.1 355 LTU ISSN 1648-8016
LIETUVOS METINE STRATEGINE APZVALGA. Text in Lithuanian. 2003. a. **Document type:** *Journal, Academic/Scholarly.* **Description:** Analyses international and internal Lithuanian security processes.
Related titles: ◆ Translation of: Lithuanian Annual Strategic Review. ISSN 1648-8024.
Indexed: IBSS.
Published by: (Vilniaus Universitetas, Tarptautiniu Santykiu ir Politicos Mokslu/University of Vilnius, Institute of International Relations and Political Science), Generalo Jono Zemaicio Lietuvos Karo Akademija/General Jonas Zemaitis Lithuanian Military Academy, Silo g 5a, Vilnius, 10322, Lithuania. TEL 370-5-2126313, FAX 370-5-2127318, pmk@lka.lt, http://www.lka.lt/en.

355 909 FRA ISSN 1953-0544
LIGNE DE FRONT. Text in French. 2006. bi-m. EUR 35 domestic; EUR 40 in the European Union; EUR 40 DOM-TOM; EUR 40 in Switzerland; EUR 45 elsewhere (effective 2009). **Document type:** *Magazine, Consumer.*
Published by: Caraktere SARL, 29 Bd Rabatau, Marseille, 13008, France. http://www.caraktere.com/.

355 610 CHN ISSN 1671-3826
CODEN: LJZIAT
LINCHUANG JUNYI ZAZHI/CLINICAL JOURNAL OF MEDICAL OFFICER. Text in Chinese; Abstracts in Chinese, English. 1973. bi-m. USD 31.20 (effective 2009). **Document type:** *Journal, Academic/Scholarly.* **Description:** Covers the latest developments of theoretical and applied researches in the fields of medicine.
Formerly (until 2000): Jiefangjun Yixue Gaodeng Zhuanke Xuexiao Xuebao/P L A Junior Colleges of Medicine. Journal (1007-1725)
Related titles: Online - full text ed.
—East View.
Address: 665, Jiefang Lu, Dalian, 116017, China. TEL 86-411-85846149, FAX 86-411-82679439. Ed. Peng Xue. Circ: 4,000. **Dist. by:** China International Book Trading Corp, 35 Chegongzhuang Xilu, Haidian District, PO Box 399, Beijing 100044, China. TEL 86-10-68412045, FAX 86-10-68412023, cibtc@mail.cibtc.com.cn, http://www.cibtc.com.cn.

LINCOLN MEMORIAL ASSOCIATION NEWSLETTER. *see* HISTORY—History Of North And South America

LINK (SAN ANTONIO). *see* FOOD AND FOOD INDUSTRIES

355.31 CYP
LION. Text in English. w. **Document type:** *Newspaper.* **Description:** Includes news and information for British Forces community in Cyprus.
Published by: British Sovereign Base, British Forces Post Office 5e, Nicosia, Cyprus. TEL 357-5-262445, FAX 357-5-263181. Ed. R C Thornton. Pub. J Zavallis. Circ: 4,500.

355.31 GBR
LIONESS. Text in English. 1945. s-a. free to members (effective 2009). bk.rev. **Document type:** *Magazine, Consumer.*
Published by: Women's Royal Army Corps Association, Gould House, Worthy Down, Winchester, Hants SO21 2RG, United Kingdom. TEL 44-1962-887478, FAX 44-1962-887478, wracassociation@googlemail.com, http://www.wracassociation.co.uk/.

355.223 CAN ISSN 0381-3401
VK1245
LIST OF LIGHTS, BUOYS AND FOG SIGNALS. INLAND WATERS. Text in English. 1959. a.
Formerly (until 1966): List of Lights and Fog Signals. Inland Waters (0381-341X)

Published by: Department of Fisheries and Oceans, Canadian Coast Guard Marine Navigation Services Directorate, 200 Kent St, Sta 5150, Ottawa, ON K1A 0E6, Canada. TEL 613-990-3016, FAX 613-998-8428, http://www.notmar.gc.ca.

355.223 CAN ISSN 0382-1080
VK1027.P3
LIST OF LIGHTS, BUOYS AND FOG SIGNALS. PACIFIC COAST. Text in English. 1943. a.
Formerly (until 1967): List of Lights and Fog Signals. Pacific Coast (0382-1099)
Published by: Department of Fisheries and Oceans, Canadian Coast Guard Marine Navigation Services Directorate, 200 Kent St, Sta 5150, Ottawa, ON K1A 0E6, Canada. TEL 613-990-3016, FAX 613-998-8428, http://www.notmar.gc.ca.

327.1 355 LTU ISSN 1648-8024
UA10.5
LITHUANIAN ANNUAL STRATEGIC REVIEW/LIETUVOS METINE STRATEGINE APZVALGA. Text in English. 2003. a. free (effective 2006). **Document type:** *Journal, Academic/Scholarly.* **Description:** Analyses international and internal Lithuanian security processes.
Related titles: ◆ Lithuanian Translation: Lietuvos Metine Strategine Apzvalga. ISSN 1648-8016.
Indexed: CA, I02, IBSS, T02.
Published by: (Vilniaus Universitetas, Tarptautiniu Santykiu ir Politicos Mokslu/University of Vilnius, Institute of International Relations and Political Science), Generalo Jono Zemaicio Lietuvos Karo Akademija/ General Jonas Zemaitis Lithuanian Military Academy, Silo g 5a, Vilnius, 10322, Lithuania. TEL 370-5-2126313, FAX 370-5-2127318, pmk@lka.lt, http://www.lka.lt/en.

355 CAN ISSN 1910-8133
LOOKING FORWARD, STAYING AHEAD. Text in English. 2002. a. **Document type:** *Journal, Trade.*
Media: Online - full text. **Related titles:** Print ed.: ISSN 1716-5911; French ed.: Progressiste, Avant-Gardiste. ISSN 1910-8141.
Published by: Defence Research and Development Canada/Recherche et Developpement pour la Defense Canada, Knowledge and Information Management, Ottawa, ON K1A OK2, Canada. TEL 613-995-2971, FAX 613-996-0392, candidinfo@drdc-rddc.gc.ca, http://www.drdc-rddc.gc.ca/home_e.asp.

355 CAN ISSN 0315-6389
LOOKOUT. Text in English. 1945. w. CAD 27.82; CAD 76 foreign (effective 1999). adv. bk.rev. **Document type:** *Newspaper.* **Description:** Military newspaper with a focus on the West Coast Navy.
Former titles: Maritime Command (Pacific) Lookout (0315-6370); Naden Lookout
Published by: C F B Esquimalt, P O Box 17000, Sta Forces, Victoria, BC V9A 7N2, Canada. TEL 250-385-0313, FAX 250-361-3512. Ed., R&P Corina DeGuire. Adv. contact Ivan Groth. Circ: 5,000.

355.3 NOR
LOTTEBLADET. Text in Norwegian. 1928. 6/yr. NOK 200. adv. bk.rev. illus.
Published by: Norges Lotteforbund/Norwegian Women's Voluntary Defense League, Oslo Mil-Akershus, Oslo 1, Norway. Ed. Astrid Thon. Circ: 4,000.

355.37 DEU ISSN 0343-0103
LOYAL; das Deutsche Wehrmagazin. Text in German. 1960. m. (11/yr.). EUR 23; EUR 2.50 newsstand/cover (effective 2006). adv. illus. back issues avail. **Document type:** *Magazine, Trade.*
Formerly (until 1969): Reserve
Published by: (Verband der Reservisten der Deutschen Bundeswehr e.V.), Frankfurter Societaet, Frankenallee 71-81, Frankfurt Am Main, 60327, Germany. TEL 49-69-75010. adv.: B&W page EUR 3,850, color page EUR 7,000; trim 210 x 280. Circ: 141,736.

M H Q; the quarterly journal of military history. (Military History Quarterly) *see* HISTORY—History Of North And South America

M S M R. (Medical Surveillance Monthly Report) *see* MEDICAL SCIENCES

355 ROM ISSN 1843-3391
M.T.A. REVIEW. Text in English. 2006. q. **Document type:** *Journal, Academic/Scholarly.*
Related titles: Online - full text ed.
Published by: Military Technical Academy Publishing House/Editura Academiei Tehnice Militare, 81-83 George Cosbuc Ave., Sector 5, Bucharest, 050141, Romania. TEL 40-21-3354660, FAX 40-21-3355763.

355.4 USA ISSN 1089-7054
UH805
M W R TODAY. (Morale, Welfare, and Recreation) Text in English. 1961. m. USD 25 membership (effective 2003); Subscr. incld. in membership. adv. illus. index. **Document type:** *Magazine, Trade.*
Former titles (until 1995): Military Clubs & Recreation (0192-2718); Club Executive (0009-9554); Clubs and Recreation
Indexed: H&TI, H06, Hospl.
Published by: International Military Community Executives Association, 2100 E Stan Schleuter Loop Ste G, Killeen, TX 76542. TEL 254-554-6619, FAX 254-554-6629, sarischneider@imcea.com, http://www.imcea.com/. Circ: 7,000.

355 FIN ISSN 1455-7495
MAANPUOLUSTUSKORKEAKOULU. JOHTAMISEN LAITOS. JULKAISUSARJA 1: TUTKIMUKSIA/NATIONAL DEFENCE UNIVERSITY. DEPARTMENT OF LEADERSHIP AND MANAGEMENT STUDIES. PUBLICATION SERIES 1. RESEARCH REPORTS. Text mainly in Finnish; Text occasionally in English. 1993. irreg., latest 2005. **Document type:** *Monographic series, Academic/ Scholarly.*
Formerly (until 1998): Maanpuolustuskorkeakoulu. Johtamisen ja Hallinnon Laitos. Tutkimuksia (1237-0037)
Published by: (Maanpuolustuskorkeakoulu, Johtamisen Laitos/National Defence University. Department of Leadership and Management Studies), Maanpuolustuskorkeakoulu/National Defence University, PO Box 7, Helsinki, 00861, Finland. TEL 358-9-18144511, mpkk@mil.fi.

355 FIN ISSN 1456-7377
MAANPUOLUSTUSKORKEAKOULU. JOHTAMISEN LAITOS. JULKAISUSARJA 2: ARTIKKELIKOKOELMAT/NATIONAL DEFENCE UNIVERSITY. DEPARTMENT OF LEADERSHIP AND MANAGEMENT STUDIES. PUBLICATION SERIES 2. ARTICLE COLLECTION. Text mainly in Finnish; Text occasionally in English. 1999. irreg., latest 2006. **Document type:** *Monographic series, Academic/Scholarly.*
Published by: (Maanpuolustuskorkeakoulu, Johtamisen Laitos/National Defence University. Department of Leadership and Management Studies), Maanpuolustuskorkeakoulu/National Defence University, PO Box 7, Helsinki, 00861, Finland. TEL 358-9-18144511, mpkk@mil.fi.

355 FIN ISSN 1456-7385
MAANPUOLUSTUSKORKEAKOULU. JOHTAMISEN LAITOS. JULKAISUSARJA 3: TYOPAPEREITA. Text in Finnish. 1995. irreg., latest 2004. **Document type:** *Monographic series, Academic/ Scholarly.*
Former ttles (until 1999): Maanpuolustuskorkeakoulu. Johtamisen ja Hallinnon Laitos. Julkaisusarja 2, Tyopapereita (1455-7509); (until 1997): Maanpuolustuskorkeakoulu. Johtamisen ja Hallinnon Laitos. Tyopapereita (1238-6367)
Published by: (Maanpuolustuskorkeakoulu, Johtamisen Laitos/National Defence University. Department of Leadership and Management Studies), Maanpuolustuskorkeakoulu/National Defence University, PO Box 7, Helsinki, 00861, Finland. TEL 358-9-18144511, mpkk@mil.fi.

355 FIN ISSN 1236-4959
MAANPUOLUSTUSKORKEAKOULU. STRATEGIAN LAITOS. JULKAISUSARJA 1: STRATEGIAN TUTKIMUKSIA/NATIONAL DEFENCE UNIVERSITY. DEPARTMENT OF STRATEGIC STUDIES. SERIES 1, STRATEGIC RESEARCH. Text mainly in Finnish; Text occasionally in English. 1972. irreg., latest vol.22, 2005. **Document type:** *Monographic series, Academic/Scholarly.*
Former titles (until 1993): Sotakorkeakoulu. Sotatieteen Laitos. Julkaisusarja 1, Strategian Tutkimuksia (0783-7046); (until 1987): Sotatieteen Laitos. Julkaisusarja 1, Strategian Tutkimuksia (0355-8010)
Related titles: Online - full text ed.
Published by: (Maanpuolustuskorkeakoulu, Strategian Laitos/National Defence College. Department of Strategic and Defence Studies), Maanpuolustuskorkeakoulu/National Defence University, PO Box 7, Helsinki, 00861, Finland. TEL 358-9-18144511, mpkk@mil.fi.

355 FIN ISSN 1455-2108
MAANPUOLUSTUSKORKEAKOULU. STRATEGIAN LAITOS. JULKAISUSARJA 2: STRATEGIAN TUTKIMUSSELOSTEITA/ NATIONAL DEFENCE UNIVERSITY. DEPARTMENT OF STRATEGIC STUDIES. SERIES 2, RESEARCH REPORTS. Text mainly in Finnish; Text occasionally in English. 1971. irreg., latest vol.37, 2007. back issues avail. **Document type:** *Monographic series, Academic/Scholarly.*
Formerly (until 1997): Sotatieteen Laitos. Julkaisusarja 2, Strategian ja Turvallisuuspolitiikan Asiakirjoja (0355-8029)
Related titles: Online - full text ed.
Published by: (Maanpuolustuskorkeakoulu, Strategian Laitos/National Defence College. Department of Strategic and Defence Studies), Maanpuolustuskorkeakoulu/National Defence University, PO Box 7, Helsinki, 00861, Finland. TEL 358-9-18144511, mpkk@mil.fi.

355 FIN ISSN 1236-4975
MAANPUOLUSTUSKORKEAKOULU. STRATEGIAN LAITOS. JULKAISUSARJA 3: STRATEGIAN ASIATIETOA. Text in Finnish. irreg., latest vol.4, 2007. back issues avail. **Document type:** *Monographic series, Academic/Scholarly.*
Former titles (until 1994): Sotakorkeakoulu. Sotatieteen Laitos. Julkaisusarja 3, Strategian Asiatietoa (0782-9205); (until 1986): Sotatieteen Laitos. Julkaisusarja 3, Strategian Asiatietoa (0355-8037)
Related titles: Online - full text ed.
Published by: (Maanpuolustuskorkeakoulu, Strategian Laitos/National Defence College. Department of Strategic and Defence Studies), Maanpuolustuskorkeakoulu/National Defence University, PO Box 7, Helsinki, 00861, Finland. TEL 358-9-18144511, mpkk@email.fi.

355 FIN ISSN 1236-4983
MAANPUOLUSTUSKORKEAKOULU. STRATEGIAN LAITOS. JULKAISUSARJA 4: STRATEGIAN TYOPAPEREITA/NATIONAL DEFENCE COLLEGE. DEPARTMENT OF STRATEGIC AND DEFENCE STUDIES. SERIES 4, WORKING PAPERS. Text mainly in Finnish; Text occasionally in English. 1993. irreg., latest vol.19, 2007. back issues avail. **Document type:** *Monographic series, Academic/ Scholarly.*
Related titles: Online - full text ed.
Published by: (Maanpuolustuskorkeakoulu, Strategian Laitos/National Defence College. Department of Strategic and Defence Studies), Maanpuolustuskorkeakoulu/National Defence University, PO Box 7, Helsinki, 00861, Finland. TEL 358-9-18144511, mpkk@mil.fi.

355 ISR ISSN 0464-2147
MA'ARAKHOT. Text and summaries in Hebrew. 1939. bi-m. ILS 60 (effective 2001). bk.rev.; Website rev. 64 p./no.; back issues avail. **Document type:** *Journal.*
Indexed: IHP.
Published by: Ministry of Defense Publishing House, Hakirya, 3 Mendlev, P O Box 7026, Tel Aviv, 61070, Israel. TEL 972-3-5694343, FAX 972-3-5694343. Eds. Efi Meltzer, Haggai Golan.

338.473 363.35 GBR ISSN 1749-1525
MALAYSIA DEFENCE & SECURITY REPORT. Text in English. 2005. q. EUR 820, USD 1,030 combined subscription (print & email eds.) (effective 2010). **Document type:** *Report, Trade.* **Description:** Provides professionals, consultancies, government departments, regulatory bodies and researchers with independent forecasts and regional competitive intelligence on the Malaysian defence & security industry.
Related titles: E-mail ed.
Indexed: A15, ABIn, B01, P48, P51, P52, PQC.
Published by: Business Monitor International Ltd., Senator House, 85 Queen Victoria St, London, EC4V 4AB, United Kingdom. TEL 44-20-72480468, FAX 44-20-72480467, subs@businessmonitor.com.

MANUAL OF AIR FORCE LAW: AMENDMENTS. *see* LAW—Military Law

MANUAL OF MILITARY LAW - AMENDMENTS. *see* LAW—Military Law

355 CAN ISSN 1480-4336
CA1DN12-7
MAPLE LEAF. Text in Multiple languages. 1996. m. **Document type:** *Journal, Trade.*
Formerly (until 1998): Defence Matters (1203-6161)
Related titles: Online - full text ed.: ISSN 1494-9636. 1998.
Published by: Department of National Defence, Major-General George R Pearkes Bldg, 101 Colonel By Dr, Ottawa, ON K1A 0K2, Canada. TEL 613-995-2534, FAX 613-995-2610, information@forces.gc.ca, http://www.forces.gc.ca.

359.96 FRA ISSN 1151-1397
MARINE. Text in French. 1951. q. adv. bk.rev. **Document type:** *Proceedings.*
Published by: Association Centrale des Officiers de Reserve de l'Armee de Mer, 15 rue de LaBorde, BP 12, Armees, 00312, France. TEL 33-1-53428039, FAX 33-1-45225303. Ed. H Nguyen Tan. Circ: 6,000.

359.96 USA ISSN 0025-3170
MARINE CORPS GAZETTE; the professional journal for United States Marines. Text in English. 1916. m. free to members (effective 2009). adv. bk.rev. illus. index. 72 p./no.; back issues avail.; reprints avail. **Document type:** *Journal, Trade.* **Description:** Provides a forum for discussion of ideas pertinent to the U.S. Marine Corps and military capabilities.
Related titles: Microfilm ed.: (from PQC); Online - full text ed.
Indexed: A22, A26, AMB, AUNI, AmH&L, B14, BRI, CBRI, DM&T, G05, G06, G07, G08, HistAb, I02, I05, LID&ISL, M01, M02, M05, M06, M07, P02, P10, P16, P30, P34, P47, P48, P52, P53, P54, PAIS, PQC, PRA, RASB, SPPI, T02, V02.
—BLDSC (5373.765000), IE, Infotrieve, Ingenta.
Published by: Marine Corps Association, 715 Broadway St, PO Boox 1775, Quantico, VA 22134. TEL 703-640-6161, 800-336-0291, FAX 703-630-9147, mca@mca-marines.org. Ed. John A Keenan. Adv. contact G Scott Dinkel TEL 718-715-1361. page USD 3,325; trim 8 x 10.875. Circ: 29,731.

355 USA
MARINE CORPS LEAGUE. Text in English. q. USD 7.50; USD 2.50 newsstand/cover (effective 2001). adv. **Description:** Official publication of the Marine Corp League includes features on Marine history, columns by league officials and a calendar of events.
Address: 8626 Lee Hwy,201, Fairfax, VA 22031. TEL 703-207-9588, FAX 703-207-0047.

355 USA ISSN 1522-0869
MARINE CORPS TIMES. Text in English. 1940. w. USD 55; USD 3.25 newsstand/cover (effective 2009). adv. **Document type:** *Newspaper, Trade.* **Description:** Provides a exclusive, original, in-depth news and analysis about your career, pay and benefits and issues impacting your professional advancement.
Related titles: Online - full text ed.: MarineCorpsTimes.com. USD 29.95 (effective 2009).
Indexed: P52.
—CCC.
Published by: Army Times Publishing Co. (Subsidiary of: Gannett Company, Inc.), 6883 Commercial Dr, Springfield, VA 22159. TEL 703-750-7400, 800-368-5718, cust-svc@atpco.com, http://www.gannett.com/about/map/armytimes.htm. Ed. Tobias Naegele. adv.: col. inch USD 22,190; 10.25 x 11.25. Circ: 30,929 (paid).

359 USA ISSN 1547-9676
VK23
MARINE SAFETY AND SECURITY COUNCIL. PROCEEDINGS. Text in English. 1944. q. free (effective 2010). **Document type:** *Proceedings, Government.* **Description:** Contains audience of large segment of the private maritime industry population, including retired officers, fishing vessel captains, river pilots, ocean scientists, Departments of Homeland Security and Transportation staff, and allied foreign national readers.
Former titles (until 2004): U.S. Coast Guard. Marine Safety Council. Proceedings (0364-0981); (until 1971): U.S. Coast Guard. Merchant Marine Council. Proceedings (0025-9896)
Related titles: Online - full text ed.
Indexed: A22, B21, BMT, CLT&T, ESPM, H&SSA, HRIS, IUSGP, OceAb, PollutAb, RefZh, SSciA, SWRA.
—BLDSC (6755.400000), IE, Infotrieve, Ingenta, Linda Hall.
Published by: (Commandant G-MP-4), U.S. Coast Guard, 2100 Second St, SW, Washington, DC 20593. TEL 202-267-1061, FAX 202-267-4402, gchappell@comdt.uscg.mil, http://www.uscg.mil/default.asp.

343.01 USA ISSN 1941-7284
V203
MARINE TACTICAL. Text in English. 2007. bi-m. USD 35 (effective 2008). **Document type:** *Magazine, Trade.*
Related titles: Online - full text ed.: ISSN 1941-7292.
Published by: Travis Communications Inc., 2111 Wilson Blvd, Ste 700, Arlington, VA 22201. TEL 703-351-5011, FAX 703-243-1648.

359 NLD ISSN 0025-3340
V5
➤ **MARINEBLAD.** Text in Dutch, English. 1887. 8/yr. EUR 49.50 domestic; EUR 69.50 foreign (effective 2009). adv. bk.rev. charts; illus.; maps. 36 p./no.; **Document type:** *Proceedings, Academic/ Scholarly.* **Description:** Furthers the interest and aims of the Dutch Naval Officers Association. Reports on current and historical topics relating to naval and defense matters, and association news.
Indexed: IBR, IBZ.
—IE, Infotrieve.
Published by: Koninklijke Vereniging van Marine-Officieren, Wassenaarseweg 2b, The Hague, 2596 CH, Netherlands. TEL 31-70-3839504, FAX 31-70-3835911, info@kvmo.nl, http://www.kvmo.nl. Ed. M L G Lijmbach.

359 DNK ISSN 0106-5122
MARINEHISTORISK TIDSSKRIFT. Text in Danish. 1967. 4/yr. DKK 200 membership (effective 2010). bk.rev. cum index: 1969-1997, 1998-2002, 2003-2007. **Document type:** *Magazine, Consumer.* **Description:** Covers naval history.
Related titles: Online - full text ed.
Published by: Orlogsmuseets Venner/Marinehistorisk Selskab/The Naval Historical Society and Friends of the Royal Danish Naval Museum, c/o Poul Grooss, Strandvejen 174, Charlottenlund, 2920, Denmark. http://www.marinehist.dk. Ed. Niels M Probst TEL 45-45-866983.

359 DNK ISSN 0909-0029
MARINEHISTORISKE SKRIFTER. Variant title: Marinehistorisk Selskab. Skriftraekke. Text in Danish. 1952. irreg., latest vol.31, 2005. price varies. back issues avail. **Document type:** *Monographic series, Academic/Scholarly.*
Formerly (until 1990): Marinehistorisk Selskab. Skrift (0464-9850)
Published by: Orlogsmuseets Venner/Marinehistorisk Selskab/The Naval Historical Society and Friends of the Royal Danish Naval Museum, c/o Poul Grooss, Strandvejen 174, Charlottenlund, 2920, Denmark. TEL 45-33-116037, FAX 45-33-937152, http://www.marinehist.dk.

MARINMUSEUM. AARSBOK. *see* MUSEUMS AND ART GALLERIES

359 SWE ISSN 1402-8115
MARINMUSEUM. SKRIFTER. Text in Swedish. 1997. irreg. back issues avail. **Document type:** *Monographic series, Academic/Scholarly.*
Published by: Marinmuseum, PO Box 48, Karlskrona, 37121, Sweden. TEL 46-455-359300, FAX 46-455-359349, registrator@maritima.se, http://www.maritima.se.

359 CAN ISSN 0025-3413
MARITIME COMMAND TRIDENT. Text in English, French. 1966. fortn. CAD 25 domestic; USD 30 in United States; USD 50 elsewhere (effective 2000). adv. bk.rev. **Document type:** *Newspaper.* **Description:** Contains news of the Maritime Command, CFB Halifax, and the naval community at large.
Published by: Trident Military Newspaper Ltd., Bldg S 93, CFB Halifax, P O Box 99000, Sta Forces, Halifax, NS B3K 5X5, Canada. TEL 902-427-4237, FAX 902-427-4238, editortrident@psphalifax.ns.ca, trident.@psphalifax.ns.ca, salestrident@psphalifax.ns.ca. Ed., R&P Kim Cameron TEL 902-427-4237. Adv. contact Susan Holman. Circ: 10,500.

359 SWE ISSN 1651-5374
MARITIME SKRIFTER. Text in Swedish. 2002. irreg. **Document type:** *Monographic series, Academic/Scholarly.*
Published by: Statens Maritima Museer, Sjoehistoriska Museet, PO Box 27131, Stockholm, 10252, Sweden. TEL 46-8-51954900, http://www.maritima.se, FAX 46-8-51954994.

355 USA
MARKET INTELLIGENCE REPORTS: "AN" EQUIPMENT FORECAST. Text in English. base vol. plus d. updates. looseleaf. USD 1,795 base vol(s). domestic; USD 1,880 base vol(s). foreign; USD 3,100 combined subscription domestic (print & DVD eds.); USD 3,280 combined subscription foreign (print & DVD eds.); USD 3,320 combined subscription domestic (print & online eds.); USD 3,405 combined subscription foreign (print & online eds.) (effective 2009). abstr.; charts; illus.; mkt.; stat. back issues avail. **Document type:** *Report, Trade.* **Description:** Covers the full range of electronics equipment being used by U.S. armed forces on land, at sea and in the air.
Formerly: D M S Market Intelligence Reports: "AN" Equipment Forecast
Related titles: Online - full text ed.: USD 1,935 (effective 2009); Optical Disk - DVD ed.: USD 1,765 domestic; USD 1,860 foreign (effective 2009).
Published by: Forecast International Inc., 22 Commerce Rd, Newtown, CT 06470. TEL 203-426-0800, 800-451-4975, FAX 203-426-0233, info@forecast1.com, http://www.forecast1.com.

359.8 USA
MARKET INTELLIGENCE REPORTS: ANTI-SUBMARINE WARFARE FORECAST. Variant title: Anti-Submarine Warfare Forecast. Text in English. 1995. base vol. plus d. updates. looseleaf. USD 1,795 base vol(s). domestic; USD 1,880 base vol(s). foreign; USD 3,100 combined subscription domestic (print & DVD eds.); USD 3,280 combined subscription foreign (print & DVD eds.); USD 3,320 combined subscription domestic (print & online eds.); USD 3,405 combined subscription foreign (print & online eds.) (effective 2009). abstr.; charts; illus.; mkt.; stat. back issues avail. **Document type:** *Report, Trade.* **Description:** Presents a series of detailed reports on the technologies available for countering the submarine threat.
Formerly: D M S Market Intelligence Reports: Anti-Submarine Warfare Forecast
Related titles: Online - full text ed.: USD 1,935 (effective 2009); Optical Disk - DVD ed.: USD 1,765 domestic; USD 1,860 foreign (effective 2009).
Published by: Forecast International Inc., 22 Commerce Rd, Newtown, CT 06470. TEL 203-426-0800, 800-451-4975, FAX 203-426-0233, info@forecast1.com, http://www.forecast1.com.

MARKET INTELLIGENCE REPORTS: CIVIL AIRCRAFT FORECAST. *see* AERONAUTICS AND SPACE FLIGHT

355.85 USA
MARKET INTELLIGENCE REPORTS: COMMAND, CONTROL, COMMUNICATIONS & INTELLIGENCE FORECAST. Short title: C 3 I. Text in English. 19??. a. looseleaf. USD 1,935 per issue (effective 2009). abstr.; charts; illus.; mkt.; stat. back issues avail. **Document type:** *Report, Trade.* **Description:** Presents an analysis of C3I projects worldwide, in 8 technology areas: C2 information, battle management, communications, intelligence, surveillance and warning, communication security, navigation and weather, and the C3I technology base.
Formerly: D M S Market Intelligence Reports: Command, Control, Communications & Intelligence Forecast
Related titles: CD-ROM ed.: USD 1,525 (effective 2001); Online - full content ed.: USD 1,695 (effective 2001).
Published by: Forecast International Inc., 22 Commerce Rd, Newtown, CT 06470. TEL 203-426-0800, 800-451-4975, FAX 203-426-0233, info@forecast1.com, http://www.forecast1.com.

355 USA
MARKET INTELLIGENCE REPORTS: DEFENSE & AEROSPACE COMPANIES. Variant title: Defense & Aerospace Companies. Text in English. 1990. 2 base vols. plus d. updates. looseleaf. USD 1,795 base vol(s). domestic; USD 1,880 base vol(s). foreign; USD 3,100 combined subscription domestic (print & DVD eds.); USD 3,280 combined subscription foreign (print & DVD eds.); USD 3,320 combined subscription domestic (print & online eds.); USD 3,405 combined subscription foreign (print & online eds.) (effective 2009). abstr.; charts; illus.; mkt.; stat. back issues avail. **Document type:** *Report, Trade.* **Description:** Contains reports that provide data for individual corporations on recent mergers, restructurings, and joint ventures, along with a strategic outlook that examines the company's strengths, weaknesses and opportunities.
Formerly: D M S Market Intelligence Reports: Defense & Aerospace Companies; Formed by the merger of: D M S Market Intelligence Reports: Defense Market; D M S Market Intelligence Reports: Aerospace Companies
Related titles: Online - full text ed.: USD 1,935 (effective 2009); Optical Disk - DVD ed.: USD 1,765 domestic; USD 1,860 foreign (effective 2009).
Published by: Forecast International Inc., 22 Commerce Rd, Newtown, CT 06470. TEL 203-426-0800, 800-451-4975, FAX 203-426-0233, info@forecast1.com, http://www.forecast1.com.

355 621.381 USA
MARKET INTELLIGENCE REPORTS: ELECTRONIC SYSTEMS FORECAST. Variant title: Electronic Systems Forecast. Text in English. 1991. base vol. plus d. updates. looseleaf. USD 1,795 base vol(s). domestic; USD 1,880 base vol(s). foreign; USD 3,100 combined subscription domestic (print & DVD eds.); USD 3,280 combined subscription foreign (print & DVD eds.); USD 3,320 combined subscription domestic (print & online eds.); USD 3,405 combined subscription foreign (print & online eds.) (effective 2009). abstr.; charts; illus.; mkt.; stat. back issues avail. **Document type:** *Report, Trade.* **Description:** Examines the latest developments in avionics, air traffic management, C4I, electronic warfare and other select market sectors.
Formerly: D M S Market Intelligence Reports: Electronic Systems Forecast
Related titles: Online - full text ed.: USD 1,935 (effective 2009); Optical Disk - DVD ed.: USD 1,765 domestic; USD 1,860 foreign (effective 2009).
Published by: Forecast International Inc., 22 Commerce Rd, Newtown, CT 06470. TEL 203-426-0800, 800-451-4975, FAX 203-426-0233, info@forecast1.com, http://www.forecast1.com.

355 621.381 USA
MARKET INTELLIGENCE REPORTS: ELECTRONIC WARFARE FORECAST. Variant title: Electronic Warfare Forecast. Text in English. 1995. base vol. plus d. updates. looseleaf. USD 1,795 base vol(s). domestic; USD 1,880 base vol(s). foreign; USD 3,100 combined subscription domestic (print & DVD eds.); USD 3,280 combined subscription foreign (print & DVD eds.); USD 3,320 combined subscription domestic (print & online eds.); USD 3,405 combined subscription foreign (print & online eds.) (effective 2009). abstr.; charts; illus.; mkt.; stat. back issues avail. **Document type:** *Report, Trade.* **Description:** Addresses the growing worldwide interest in self-protection and early warning systems for several types of military platform, both in the skies and on the surface.
Formerly: D M S Market Intelligence Reports: Electronic Warfare Forecast
Related titles: Online - full text ed.: USD 1,935 (effective 2009); Optical Disk - DVD ed.: USD 1,765 domestic; USD 1,860 foreign (effective 2009).
Published by: Forecast International Inc., 22 Commerce Rd, Newtown, CT 06470. TEL 203-426-0800, 800-451-4975, FAX 203-426-0233, info@forecast1.com, http://www.forecast1.com.

355 USA
MARKET INTELLIGENCE REPORTS: INTERNATIONAL CONTRACTORS. Variant title: International Contractors. Text in English. 2 base vols. plus d. updates. looseleaf. USD 1,355 base vol(s). domestic; USD 1,440 base vol(s). foreign (effective 2009). back issues avail. **Document type:** *Report, Trade.* **Description:** Provides contractor and subcontractor information from aerospace, power systems and defense markets.
Formerly: D M S Market Intelligence Reports: International Contractors
Related titles: Online - full text ed.
Published by: Forecast International Inc., 22 Commerce Rd, Newtown, CT 06470. TEL 203-426-0800, 800-451-4975, FAX 203-426-0233, info@forecast1.com, http://www.forecastinternational.com.

355 USA
MARKET INTELLIGENCE REPORTS: INTERNATIONAL MILITARY MARKETS - ASIA, AUSTRALIA & PACIFIC RIM. Text in English. base vol. plus m. updates. looseleaf. USD 1,795 base vol(s).; USD 3,100 combined subscription (print & DVD eds.); USD 3,320 combined subscription (print & online eds.) (effective 2009). abstr.; charts; illus.; mkt.; stat. back issues avail. **Document type:** *Report, Trade.* **Description:** Provides a country by country examination of military capabilities, equipment requirements and current inventories.
Formerly: D M S Market Intelligence Reports: International Military Markets - Asia, Australia & Pacific Rim; Supersedes in part: D M S Market Intelligence Reports: International Military Markets - Latin America and Australasia
Related titles: Online - full content ed.: USD 1,935 (effective 2009); Optical Disk - DVD ed.: USD 1,765 (effective 2009).
Published by: Forecast International Inc., 22 Commerce Rd, Newtown, CT 06470. TEL 203-426-0800, 800-451-4975, FAX 203-426-0233, info@forecast1.com, http://www.forecastinternational.com. Ed. Michael Pinto. R&P Ray Peterson.

355 USA
MARKET INTELLIGENCE REPORTS: INTERNATIONAL MILITARY MARKETS - EURASIA. Text in English. 2008. base vol. plus m. updates. looseleaf. USD 1,840 base vol(s). domestic; USD 1,880 base vol(s). foreign (effective 2009).
Related titles: Online - full text ed.: USD 1,935 (effective 2009); Optical Disk - DVD ed.: USD 1,815 domestic; USD 1,860 foreign (effective 2009).
Published by: Forecast International Inc., 22 Commerce Rd, Newtown, CT 06470. TEL 203-426-0800, 800-451-4975, FAX 203-426-0233, info@forecast1.com, http://www.forecastinternational.com.

355 USA
MARKET INTELLIGENCE REPORTS: INTERNATIONAL MILITARY MARKETS - EUROPE. Text in English. base vol. plus m. updates. looseleaf. USD 1,840 base vol(s). domestic; USD 1,880 base vol(s). foreign (effective 2009). abstr.; charts; illus.; mkt.; stat. back issues avail. **Document type:** *Report, Trade.* **Description:** Country-by-country examination of the military capabilities, equipment requirements, and current inventories for NATO and Europe. Discusses manufacturing capabilities, military budgets, recent transactions, future requirements, strategic environments and military postures.
Former titles: Market Intelligence Reports: International Military Markets - N A T O & Europe; D M S Market Intelligence Reports: International Military Markets - N A T O & Europe
Related titles: Online - full content ed.: USD 1,935 (effective 2009); Optical Disk - DVD ed.: USD 1,815 domestic; USD 1,860 foreign (effective 2009).
Published by: Forecast International Inc., 22 Commerce Rd, Newtown, CT 06470. TEL 203-426-0800, 800-451-4975, FAX 203-426-0233, info@forecast1.com, http://www.forecastinternational.com. Ed. Michael Pinto. R&P Ray Peterson.

355 USA
MARKET INTELLIGENCE REPORTS: INTERNATIONAL MILITARY MARKETS - LATIN AMERICA & CARIBBEAN. Text in English. base vol. plus m. updates. looseleaf. USD 1,795 base vol(s). domestic; USD 1,880 base vol(s). foreign; USD 3,100 combined subscription domestic (print & DVD eds.); USD 3,280 combined subscription foreign (print & DVD eds.); USD 3,320 combined subscription domestic (print & online eds.); USD 3,405 combined subscription foreign (print & online eds.) (effective 2009). abstr.; charts; stat. back issues avail. **Document type:** *Report, Trade.* **Description:** Provides a country-by-country examination of the military capabilities, equipment requirements and inventories for Latin America & the Caribbean.
Formerly: D M S Market Intelligence Reports: International Military Markets - Latin America & Caribbean; Supersedes in part: D M S Market Intelligence Reports: International Military Markets - Latin America and Australasia
Related titles: Online - full content ed.: USD 1,935 (effective 2009); Optical Disk - DVD ed.: USD 1,765 domestic; USD 1,860 foreign (effective 2009).
Published by: Forecast International Inc., 22 Commerce Rd, Newtown, CT 06470. TEL 203-426-0800, 800-451-4975, FAX 203-426-0233, info@forecast1.com, http://www.forecastinternational.com.

355 USA
MARKET INTELLIGENCE REPORTS: INTERNATIONAL MILITARY MARKETS - MIDDLE EAST & AFRICA. Text in English. 1989. base vol. plus d. updates. looseleaf. USD 1,795 base vol(s). domestic; USD 1,880 base vol(s). foreign; USD 3,100 combined subscription domestic (print & DVD eds.); USD 3,280 combined subscription foreign (print & DVD eds.); USD 3,320 combined subscription domestic (print & online eds.); USD 3,405 combined subscription foreign (print & online eds.) (effective 2009). abstr.; charts; illus.; mkt.; stat. **Document type:** *Report, Trade.* **Description:** Provides a country-by-country examination of the military capabilitees, equipment requirements and inventories for the Middle East & Africa.
Formerly: D M S Market Intelligence Reports: International Military Markets - Middle East & Africa
Related titles: Online - full content ed.: USD 1,935 (effective 2009); Optical Disk - DVD ed.: USD 1,765 domestic; USD 1,860 foreign (effective 2009).
Published by: Forecast International Inc., 22 Commerce Rd, Newtown, CT 06470. TEL 203-426-0800, 800-451-4975, FAX 203-426-0233, info@forecast1.com, http://www.forecastinternational.com.

355 USA
MARKET INTELLIGENCE REPORTS: INTERNATIONAL MILITARY MARKETS - NORTH AMERICA. Text in English. 200?. base vol. plus m. updates. looseleaf. USD 1,840 base vol(s). domestic; USD 1,880 base vol(s). foreign (effective 2009).
Related titles: Online - full text ed.: USD 1,935 (effective 2009); Optical Disk - DVD ed.: USD 1,815 domestic; USD 1,860 foreign (effective 2009).
Published by: Forecast International Inc., 22 Commerce Rd, Newtown, CT 06470. TEL 203-426-0800, 800-451-4975, FAX 203-426-0233, info@forecast1.com, http://www.forecastinternational.com.

355 USA
MARKET INTELLIGENCE REPORTS: MILITARY AIRCRAFT FORECAST. Variant title: Military Aircraft Forecast. Text in English. 1989. base vol. plus d. updates. looseleaf. USD 1,795 base vol(s). domestic; USD 1,880 base vol(s). foreign; USD 3,100 combined subscription domestic (print & DVD eds.); USD 3,280 combined subscription foreign (print & DVD eds.); USD 3,320 combined subscription domestic (print & online eds.); USD 3,405 combined subscription foreign (print & online eds.) (effective 2009). abstr.; charts; illus.; mkt.; stat. **Document type:** *Report, Trade.* **Description:** Contains more than 50 individual reports on fixed-wing military aircraft of all types, broken out by market segment.
Formerly: D M S Market Intelligence Reports: Military Aircraft Forecast
Related titles: Online - full text ed.: USD 1,935 (effective 2009); Optical Disk - DVD ed.: USD 1,765 domestic; USD 1,860 foreign (effective 2009).
Published by: Forecast International Inc., 22 Commerce Rd, Newtown, CT 06470. TEL 203-426-0800, 800-451-4975, FAX 203-426-0233, info@forecast1.com, http://www.forecast1.com.

355 USA
MARKET INTELLIGENCE REPORTS: MILITARY FORCE STRUCTURES OF THE WORLD. Variant title: Military Force Structures of the World. Text in English. base vol. plus d. updates. looseleaf. USD 2,510 base vol(s). domestic; USD 2,595 base vol(s). foreign; USD 4,405 combined subscription domestic (print & DVD eds.); USD 4,585 combined subscription foreign (print & DVD eds.); USD 4,815 combined subscription domestic (print & online eds.); USD 4,900 combined subscription foreign (print & online eds.) (effective 2009). **Document type:** *Report, Trade.* **Description:** Provides in-depth descriptions of over 110 national force structures spread across six major regions.
Formerly: D M S Market Intelligence Reports: Military Force Structures of the World
Related titles: Online - full text ed.: USD 2,710 (effective 2009); Optical Disk - DVD ed.: USD 2,470 domestic; USD 2,565 foreign (effective 2009).
Published by: Forecast International Inc., 22 Commerce Rd, Newtown, CT 06470. TEL 203-426-0800, 800-451-4975, FAX 203-426-0233, info@forecast1.com, http://www.forecast1.com.

M

355 USA
MARKET INTELLIGENCE REPORTS: MILITARY VEHICLES FORECAST. Variant title: Military Vehicles Forecast. Text in English. 1985. base vol. plus d. updates. looseleaf. USD 1,795 base vol(s). domestic; USD 1,880 base vol(s). foreign; USD 3,100 combined subscription domestic (print & DVD eds.); USD 3,280 combined subscription foreign (print & DVD eds.); USD 3,320 combined subscription domestic (print & online eds.); USD 3,405 combined subscription foreign (print & online eds.) (effective 2009). abstr.; charts; illus.; mkt.; stat. back issues avail. **Document type:** *Report, Trade.* **Description:** Provides guidance on the world's military vehicle market abd includes 77 reports and three market segment analyses, covering well over 100 individual military vehicle programs.
Formerly: D M S Market Intelligence Reports: Military Vehicles Forecast
Related titles: Online - full text ed.: USD 1,935 (effective 2009); Optical Disk - DVD ed.: USD 1,765 domestic; USD 1,860 foreign (effective 2009).
Published by: Forecast International Inc., 22 Commerce Rd, Newtown, CT 06470. TEL 203-426-0800, 800-451-4975, FAX 203-426-0233, info@forecast1.com, http://www.forecast1.com. Ed. Greg Fetter. R&P Ray Peterson.

355 USA
MARKET INTELLIGENCE REPORTS: MISSILE FORECAST. Variant title: Missile Forecast. Text in English. 1990. base vol. plus d. updates. looseleaf. USD 1,795 base vol(s). domestic; USD 1,880 base vol(s). foreign; USD 3,100 combined subscription domestic (print & DVD eds.); USD 3,280 combined subscription foreign (print & DVD eds.); USD 3,320 combined subscription domestic (print & online eds.); USD 3,405 combined subscription foreign (print & online eds.) (effective 2009). abstr.; charts; illus.; mkt.; stat. back issues avail. **Document type:** *Report, Trade.* **Description:** Provides extensive coverage of the $100+ billion market for tactical and strategic missiles.
Formerly: D M S Market Intelligence Reports: Missile Forecast
Related titles: Online - full text ed.: USD 1,935 (effective 2009); Optical Disk - DVD ed.: USD 1,765 domestic; USD 1,860 foreign (effective 2009).
Published by: Forecast International Inc., 22 Commerce Rd, Newtown, CT 06470. TEL 203-426-0800, 800-451-4975, FAX 203-426-0233, info@forecast1.com, http://www.forecast1.com.

355 USA
MARKET INTELLIGENCE REPORTS: ORDNANCE & MUNITIONS FORECAST. Text in English. 1985. base vol. plus d. updates. looseleaf. USD 1,795 base vol(s). domestic; USD 1,880 base vol(s). foreign; USD 3,100 combined subscription domestic (print & DVD eds.); USD 3,280 combined subscription foreign (print & DVD eds.); USD 3,320 combined subscription domestic (print & online eds.); USD 3,405 combined subscription foreign (print & online eds.) (effective 2009). abstr.; charts; illus.; mkt.; stat. back issues avail. **Document type:** *Report, Trade.* **Description:** Examines worldwide ordnance and munitions programs, including 10-year forecasts. Information on project history, funding, and modification programs.
Former titles: D M S Market Intelligence Reports: Ordnance & Munitions Forecast; D M S Market Intelligence Reports: Ordnance
Related titles: Online - full text ed.: USD 1,935 (effective 2009); Optical Disk - DVD ed.: USD 1,765 domestic; USD 1,860 foreign (effective 2009).
Published by: Forecast International Inc., 22 Commerce Rd, Newtown, CT 06470. TEL 203-426-0800, FAX 203-426-0233, info@forecast1.com, http://www.forecastinternational.com. Ed. Greg Fetter. R&P Ray Peterson.

355 621.381 USA
MARKET INTELLIGENCE REPORTS: RADAR FORECAST. Variant title: Radar Forecast. Text in English. 1995. base vol. plus d. updates. looseleaf. USD 1,795 base vol(s). domestic; USD 1,880 base vol(s). foreign; USD 3,100 combined subscription domestic (print & DVD eds.); USD 3,280 combined subscription foreign (print & DVD eds.); USD 3,320 combined subscription domestic (print & online eds.); USD 3,405 combined subscription foreign (print & online eds.) (effective 2009). abstr.; illus.; mkt.; stat.; charts. back issues avail. **Document type:** *Report, Trade.* **Description:** Provides coverage of some 110 U.S. and international radar systems.
Formerly: D M S Market Intelligence Reports: Radar Forecast
Related titles: Online - full text ed.: USD 1,935 (effective 2009); Optical Disk - DVD ed.: USD 1,765 domestic; USD 1,860 foreign (effective 2009).
Published by: Forecast International Inc., 22 Commerce Rd, Newtown, CT 06470. TEL 203-426-0800, 800-451-4975, FAX 203-426-0233, info@forecast1.com, http://www.forecast1.com.

355 USA
MARKET INTELLIGENCE REPORTS: SPACE SYSTEMS FORECAST. Text in English. 1990. base vol. plus m. updates. looseleaf. USD 1,585 (effective 2003). abstr.; charts; illus.; mkt.; stat. back issues avail. **Document type:** *Report, Trade.* **Description:** Reviews worldwide expendable launch vehicles and upper stages; commercial, scientific remote sensing and military satellites; returnable space vehicles; and RDT&E programs.
Formerly: D M S Market Intelligence Reports: Space Systems Forecast
Related titles: CD-ROM ed.: USD 1,525 (effective 2001); Online - full text ed.: USD 1,695 (effective 2001).
Published by: Forecast International Inc., 22 Commerce Rd, Newtown, CT 06470. TEL 203-426-0800, 800-451-4975, FAX 203-426-0233, info@forecast1.com, http://www.forecast1.com.

355 USA
MARKET INTELLIGENCE REPORTS: U S DEFENSE BUDGET FORECAST. Variant title: U S Defense Budget Forecast. Text in English. base vol. plus d. updates. looseleaf. USD 1,845 base vol(s). domestic; USD 1,930 base vol(s). foreign; USD 3,100 combined subscription domestic (print & DVD eds.); USD 3,280 combined subscription foreign (print & DVD eds.); USD 3,540 combined subscription domestic (print & online eds.); USD 3,625 combined subscription foreign (print & online eds.) (effective 2009). abstr.; charts; illus.; mkt.; stat. **Document type:** *Report, Trade.* **Description:** Examines every line item in the procurement and RDT&E portions of the U.S. defense budget - over 1,800 programs in total.
Formerly: D M S Market Intelligence Reports: U S Defense Budget Forecast
Related titles: Online - full text ed.: USD 2,045 (effective 2009); Optical Disk - DVD ed.: USD 1,810 domestic; USD 1,905 foreign (effective 2009).
Published by: Forecast International Inc., 22 Commerce Rd, Newtown, CT 06470. TEL 203-426-0800, 800-451-4975, FAX 203-426-0233, info@forecast1.com, http://www.forecastinternational.com.

355 USA
MARKET INTELLIGENCE REPORTS: UNMANNED VEHICLES FORECAST. Variant title: World Unmanned Vehicles Forecast. Text in English. base vol. plus d. updates. looseleaf. USD 1,795 base vol(s). domestic; USD 1,880 base vol(s). foreign; USD 3,100 combined subscription domestic (print & DVD eds.); USD 3,280 combined subscription foreign (print & DVD eds.); USD 3,320 combined subscription domestic (print & online eds.); USD 3,405 combined subscription foreign (print & online eds.) (effective 2009). abstr.; charts; illus.; mkt.; stat. **Document type:** *Report, Trade.* **Description:** Features nearly 100 reports on the many military and civil unmanned vehicles currently in development or production.
Formerly: D M S Market Intelligence Reports: Unmanned Vehicles Forecast
Related titles: Online - full text ed.: USD 1,935 (effective 2008); Optical Disk - DVD ed.: USD 1,765 domestic; USD 1,860 foreign (effective 2009).
Published by: Forecast International Inc., 22 Commerce Rd, Newtown, CT 06470. TEL 203-426-0800, 800-451-4975, FAX 203-426-0233, info@forecast1.com, http://www.forecastinternational.com.

359.32 USA
MARKET INTELLIGENCE REPORTS: WARSHIPS FORECAST. Variant title: Warships Forecast. Text in English. 1995. base vol. plus d. updates. looseleaf. USD 1,795 base vol(s). domestic; USD 1,880 base vol(s). foreign; USD 3,100 combined subscription domestic (print & DVD eds.); USD 3,280 combined subscription foreign (print & DVD eds.); USD 3,320 combined subscription domestic (print & online eds.); USD 3,405 combined subscription foreign (print & online eds.) (effective 2009). abstr.; charts; illus.; mkt.; stat. back issues avail. **Document type:** *Report, Trade.* **Description:** Contains reports on the world's leading submarine, aircraft carrier, surface combatant, amphibious warfare, and naval auxiliary warships programs.
Formerly: D M S Market Intelligence Reports: Warships Forecast
Related titles: Online - full text ed.: USD 1,935 (effective 2009); Optical Disk - DVD ed.: USD 1,765 domestic; USD 1,860 foreign (effective 2009).
Published by: Forecast International Inc., 22 Commerce Rd, Newtown, CT 06470. TEL 203-426-0800, 800-451-4975, FAX 203-426-0233, info@forecast1.com, http://www.forecast1.com.

355 BEL ISSN 1376-5493
MARS ET MERCURE/MARS EN MERCURIUS. Text in Dutch, English, French. 1926. q. bk.rev. **Document type:** *Bulletin.*
Published by: Cercle Royal Mars et Mercure/Belgische Koninklijke Kring Mars & Mercurius, Quartier Reine Elisabeth Bloc 10, Rue d'Evere, 1B, Bruxelles, 1140, Belgium. TEL 32-2-701-6184, FAX 32-2-512-8708, mm@mars-mercurius.org, http://www.mars-mercurius.be. Circ: 1,500.

355 USA ISSN 2156-3004
MARYLAND MUSKET. Text in English. 19??. s-a. back issues avail. **Document type:** *Magazine, Consumer.* **Description:** Designed for the members of the Maryland Army National Guard.
Media: Online - full text.
Published by: Maryland Army National Guard, Fifth Regiment Armory, 29th Division St, Baltimore, MD 21201. TEL 410-576-6000, paomd@md.ngb.army.mil. Ed. Rob Barker. Circ: 1,000.

▼ **MAX MODELLER.** *see* HOBBIES

355 USA
MAXWELL PAPERS. Text in English. 1996. irreg. **Document type:** *Monographic series, Academic/Scholarly.* **Description:** Focuses on current and future issues of interest to the Air Force and Department of Defense.
Indexed: LID&ISL.
Published by: Air War College, c/o Dr Lawrence Grinter, 325 Chennault Circle, Maxwell, AL 36112. TEL 334-953-7074, FAX 334-953-1988, Lawrence.Grinter@maxwell.af.mil. Ed. Lawrence Grinter.

355.007 USA ISSN 1934-2241
U408.5
MCGRAW-HILL'S A S V A B. (Armed Services Vocational Aptitude Battery) Text in English. 2005. irreg., latest 2006. USD 16.95 per issue (effective 2008). **Document type:** *Guide, Academic/Scholarly.*
Published by: McGraw-Hill Professional (Subsidiary of: McGraw-Hill Companies, Inc.), 1221 Ave of the Americas, New York, NY 10020. TEL 212-904-2000, FAX 212-512-2000, customer.service@mcgraw-hill.com, http://www.mhprofessional.com/index.php. Ed. Dr. Janet E Wall.

355.5 USA ISSN 1933-4397
U408.5
MCGRAW-HILL'S A S V A B BASIC TRAINING FOR THE A F Q T. (Armed Services Vocational Aptitude Battery / Armed Forces Qualifying Test) Text in English. 2005. irreg. USD 12.95 per issue (effective 2008). **Document type:** *Guide, Academic/Scholarly.*
Related titles: Online - full text ed.: USD 12.95 per issue (effective 2008).
Published by: McGraw-Hill Professional (Subsidiary of: McGraw-Hill Companies, Inc.), 1221 Ave of the Americas, New York, NY 10020. TEL 212-904-2000, FAX 212-512-2000, customer.service@mcgraw-hill.com, http://www.mhprofessional.com/index.php. Ed. Dr. Janet E Wall.

355 USA ISSN 1071-7552
MCNAIR PAPERS. Text in English. 1989. irreg. back issues avail. **Document type:** *Monographic series, Government.*
Related titles: Online - full content ed.
Indexed: LID&ISL.
Published by: National Defense University, Institute for National Strategic Studies, c/o NDU-NSS-PD, 300 5th Ave., Fort Lesley J. McNair, Washington, DC 20319-5066. TEL 202-685-4210, http://www.ndu.edu/inss/insshp.html. **Subscr. to:** U.S. Government Printing Office, Superintendent of Documents, PO Box 371954, Pittsburgh, PA 15250. TEL 202-512-1800, FAX 202-512-2250, orders@gpo.gov, http://www.access.gpo.gov.

359.94 USA ISSN 1093-8753
VG93
MECH. Text in English. 1995. q. free to qualified personnel (effective 2011). back issues avail. **Document type:** *Magazine, Government.*
Supersedes in part (in 1997): Approach Mech (1086-928X); Which was formed by the merger of (1955-1995): Approach (0570-4979); Which was formerly (until 1955): United States Naval Aviation Safety Bulletin; (1968-1995): Mech (0025-6471); Which was formerly (until 1968): Aircraft Mishaps Involving Maintenance and Servicing
Related titles: Online - full text ed.: free (effective 2011).
Indexed: A26, G05, G06, G07, G08, I05, M06.
—Ingenta, Linda Hall.
Published by: Naval Safety Center (Subsidiary of: U.S. Department of the Navy), 375 A St, Norfolk, VA 23511. TEL 757-444-3520, safe-pao@navy.mil, http://www.safetycenter.navy.mil/. Eds. David Robb TEL 757-444-3520 ext 7220, Derek Nelson TEL 757-444-3520 ext 7243. **Subscr. to:** U.S. Government Printing Office, Superintendent of Documents.

MEDAL NEWS. *see* HOBBIES

MEDIA, WAR & CONFLICT. *see* JOURNALISM

MEDICINE, CONFLICT AND SURVIVAL. *see* MEDICAL SCIENCES

623 NLD ISSN 1878-6960
MEERTALIG VERKLAREND WOORDENBOEK WAPENS EN MUNITIE. Text in Dutch. 2006. a. EUR 55 (effective 2011).
Published by: Sdu Uitgevers bv, Postbus 20025, The Hague, 2500 EA, Netherlands. TEL 31-70-3789911, FAX 31-70-3854321, sdu@sdu.nl, http://www.sdu.nl/.

355.31 FRA ISSN 1772-8657
MEMENTO DEFENSE. Text in French. a.
Formerly (until 2005): Agenda des Armees, Terre, Air, Mer, Gendarmerie (1154-3264); Which was formed by the merger of (1972-1977): Agenda de la Gendarmerie (1154-3213); (1976-1977): Agenda des Armees (1154-3256); Which was formerly (1972-1975): Agenda des Armees, Terre, Air (0376-6284)
Published by: Editions Charles Lavauzelle, Le Prouet, BP 8, Panazol, 87350, France. TEL 33-5-55584545, FAX 33-5-55584525.

355 359 FIN ISSN 1796-0800
MERISOTAKOULU. JULKAISUSARJA. A, TUTKIMUKSIA. Text in Finnish. 2005. irreg. **Document type:** *Monographic series, Academic/Scholarly.*
Published by: Merisotakoulu/Finnish Naval Academy, PO Box 5, Suomenlinna, 00190, Finland. TEL 358-9-18144811, FAX 358-9-18146118.

355 359 FIN ISSN 1796-1076
MERISOTAKOULU. JULKAISUSARJA. B, ASIATIETOJA. Text in Finnish. 2005. irreg. **Document type:** *Monographic series, Academic/Scholarly.*
Published by: Merisotakoulu/Finnish Naval Academy, PO Box 5, Suomenlinna, 00190, Finland. TEL 358-9-18144811, FAX 358-9-18146118.

MEXICAN WAR JOURNAL. *see* HISTORY—History Of North And South America

338.473 972 363.35 GBR ISSN 1749-1533
MEXICO DEFENCE & SECURITY REPORT. Text in English. 2005. a. EUR 820, USD 1,030 combined subscription per issue (print & email eds.) (effective 2010). **Document type:** *Report, Trade.* **Description:** Provides professionals, consultancies, government departments, regulatory bodies and researchers with independent forecasts and regional competitive intelligence on the Mexican defence & security industry.
Related titles: E-mail ed.
Indexed: A15, ABIn, B01, P48, P51, P52, PQC.
Published by: Business Monitor International Ltd., Senator House, 85 Queen Victoria St, London, EC4V 4AB, United Kingdom. TEL 44-20-72480468, FAX 44-20-72480467, subs@businessmonitor.com.

355 796 ITA ISSN 1128-6806
MEZZI CORAZZATI. Text in Italian. 1998. bi-m. **Document type:** *Magazine, Consumer.*
Published by: Ermanno Albertelli Editore, Casella Postale 395, Parma, PR 43100, Italy. FAX 39-0521-290387, info@tuttostoria.it, http://www.tuttostoria.it.

353.358 USA ISSN 1067-0661
CODEN: VLDBFR
MICHIGAN OVERSEAS VETERAN. Text in English. 1923. m. USD 2. adv. **Document type:** *Newspaper.* **Description:** Covers veteran information and news in Michigan.
Published by: Michigan Veterans of Foreign Wars of the United States, 924 N Washington Ave, Lansing, MI 48906-5136. TEL 313-722-4090. Ed. Elmer Wurster. Circ: 85,000.

355 USA ISSN 1930-045X
U21.5
MICHIGAN WAR STUDIES REVIEW. Text in English. 2005. a. free (effective 2011). **Document type:** *Journal, Academic/Scholarly.*
Media: Online - full text.
Published by: Michigan War Studies Group jmarwil@umich.edu, http://www.michiganwarstudies.com/. Ed. James P Holoka.

358.4 USA
MILE HIGH GUARDIAN: the news of the front range. Text in English. 1994. w. (Fri.). free (effective 2005). **Document type:** *Newspaper.*
Formerly: Lowry Airman
Published by: Buckley Air Force Base, 660 S. Aspen St., Stop 27, Aurora, CO 80011-9544. TEL 720-847-9431, FAX 720-847-6887. Ed. Chris Smith. Circ: 10,000 (paid and free).

355 SWE ISSN 2000-3471
▼ **MILITAER HISTORIA.** Text in Swedish. 2009. m. SEK 449 (effective 2010). adv. **Document type:** *Magazine, Consumer.*
Published by: Historiska Media AB, PO Box 1206, Lund, 22105, Sweden. TEL 46-46-333450, FAX 46-46-189685, info@militarhistoria.se, http://www.historiskamedia.se. Ed. Marco Smedberg. Adv. contact Sara Jansson TEL 46-40-165485. page SEK 15,000; 210 x 280.

MILITAER & GESCHICHTE; Bilder - Tatsachen - Hintergruende. *see* HISTORY

MILITAER UND GESELLSCHAFT IN DER FRUEHEN NEUZEIT. *see* HISTORY—History Of Europe

MILITAERGESCHICHTE. *see* HISTORY—History Of Europe

355 DEU
DD101
➤ **MILITAERGESCHICHTLICHE ZEITSCHRIFT.** Text in German. 1967. s-a. EUR 39.80; EUR 25 to students; EUR 22.80 newsstand/cover (effective 2011). adv. bk.rev. charts; illus.; stat. cum.index: 1967-1971. reprint service avail. from SCH. **Document type:** *Journal, Academic/Scholarly.*
Formerly (until 2000): Militaergeschichtliche Mitteilungen (0026-3826)
Related titles: Online - full text ed.: EUR 39.80; EUR 25 to students (effective 2011).
Indexed: A20, AmH&L, ArtHuCI, CA, CurCont, DIP, HistAb, IBR, IBZ, LID&ISL, RASB, SCOPUS, T02, W07.
—IE. **CCC.**
Published by: (Militaergeschichtliches Forschungsamt), Oldenbourg Wissenschaftsverlag GmbH, Rosenheimer Str 145, Munich, 81671, Germany. TEL 49-89-450510, FAX 49-89-45051204, orders@oldenbourg.de, http://www.oldenbourg.de. Eds. Hans Ehlert, Winfried Heinemann. Circ: 1,400 (paid and controlled).

355 NOR ISSN 1890-5919
MILITAERHISTORIE. Text in Norwegian. 2008. bi-m. (3 issues in 2008). NOK 189 (effective 2008); NOK 359 (effective 2009); NOK 498 (effective 2008 - 2009). **Document type:** *Magazine, Consumer.*
Published by: Ares Forlag AS, PO Box 54, Skallestad, 3139, Norway. post@mht.no, http://www.mht.no. Pubs. Heine Wang, Per Erik Olsen.

355.1 DEU ISSN 1617-027X
MILITAERHISTORISCHE UNTERSUCHUNGEN. Text in German. 2001. irreg., latest vol.10, 2009. price varies. **Document type:** *Monographic series, Academic/Scholarly.*
Published by: Peter Lang GmbH (Subsidiary of: Peter Lang Publishing Group), Eschborner Landstr 42-50, Frankfurt Am Main, 60489, Germany. TEL 49-69-7807050, FAX 49-69-78070550, zentrale.frankfurt@peterlang.com, http://www.peterlang.com. Ed. Merith Niehuss.

MILITAERHISTORISK TIDSKRIFT. *see* HISTORY—History Of Europe

355.02 DEU ISSN 0171-9033
MILITAERPOLITIK DOKUMENTATION. Text in German. 1976. irreg. price varies. **Document type:** *Monographic series, Academic/Scholarly.*
Indexed: PAIS.
Published by: Haag & Herchen GmbH, Fuchshohl 19a, Frankfurt Am Main, 60431, Germany. TEL 49-69-550911, FAX 49-69-552601, verlag@haagundherchen.de, http://www.haagundherchen.de.

MILITAERSEELSORGE. *see* RELIGIONS AND THEOLOGY

355 DNK ISSN 0026-3850
MILITAERT TIDSSKRIFT. Text in Danish. 1871. 4/yr. adv. bk.rev. index. **Document type:** *Magazine, Academic/Scholarly.*
Indexed: LID&ISL, MLA-IB, RASB.
Published by: Det Krigsvidenskabelige Selskab, c/o Werner Iversen, Forsvarsakademiet, Ryvangs Alle 1, Copenhagen OE, 2100, Denmark. TEL 45-39-151515, info@dkvs.dk, http://www.dkvs.dke. Ed. Niels Bo Poulsen.

355 SWE ISSN 0047-7354
MILITAERTEKNISK TIDSKRIFT/SWEDISH JOURNAL OF MILITARY TECHNOLOGY. Text in Swedish. 1931. q. SEK 150 domestic; SEK 220 elsewhere (effective 2002). adv. bk.rev. back issues avail. **Document type:** *Trade.* **Description:** Concerns the development of military equipment in Sweden and surrounding countries.
Formerly (until 1955): Pansar
Indexed: LID&ISL.
Published by: Verkstaedernas Foerlag AB, PO Box 5510, Stockholm, 11485, Sweden. TEL 46-8-7820800, FAX 46-8-7820994, http://www.verkstaderna.se/mtt. Ed., R&P Eric Hedstroem. Adv. contact Mikael Segerman. color page SEK 11,400; trim 200 x 260. Circ: 3,000.

355 NLD ISSN 0026-3869
➤ **MILITAIRE SPECTATOR.** Text in Dutch, English. 1832. m. adv. bk.rev. charts; illus. index, cum.index. 60 p./no.; back issues avail. **Document type:** *Journal, Academic/Scholarly.*
Incorporates (1969-1988): Mars in Cathedra (0025-4029); Which was formerly (until 1969): Orgaan van de Koninklijke Vereniging ter Beoefening van de Krijgswetenschap (1877-9301); (until 1965): Orgaan der Vereeniging ter Beoefening van de Krijgswetenschap (1877-931X); (1865-1902): Vereeniging ter Beoefening van de Krijgsmacht (1877-9298)
Indexed: CA, P42, PAIS, PSA, RASB, T02.
—IE, Infotrieve.
Published by: (Netherlands. Ministerie van Defensie), Koninklijke Vereniging ter Beoefening van de Krijgswetenschap/Royal Society for Military Science, Gebouw 203, kamer 026, PO Box 20701, The Hague, 2509 LS, Netherlands. TEL 31-70-3186930, FAX 31-70-3165199, secretaris@kvbk.nl, http://www.kvbk.nl. Circ: 8,000.

355 FRA ISSN 0026-3877
MILITANT; revue nationaliste pour la defense de l'identite francaise et europeenne. Text in French. 1967. s-m. adv. bk.rev. illus. **Document type:** *Newspaper, Consumer.* **Description:** Covers world news of a political or nationalistic nature.
Address: B.P. 154, Paris, Cedex 10 75463, France. TEL 33-1-46637971.

355 DEU ISSN 0724-3529
UB435.G3
MILITARIA; Wissenschaftliches Organ fur Orden, Uniformen, Militar- und Zeitgeschicht. Text in German. 1971. bi-m. EUR 34 domestic; EUR 40 foreign (effective 2011). adv. **Document type:** *Magazine, Consumer.* **Description:** Contains articles and features on all aspects of military decorations, uniforms, equipment, flags and organizations.
Indexed: IBR, IBZ.
Published by: Verlag Klaus Patzwall, Aetzberg 1B, Melbeck, 21406, Germany. TEL 49-4134-907570, FAX 49-4134-907571, verlag@patzwall.de, http://www.patzwall.de. Ed. K D Patzwall.

355 ESP ISSN 0214-8765
MILITARIA; revista de cultura militar. Text in Spanish. 1988. a., latest vol.15, 2001. back issues avail. **Document type:** *Journal, Academic/Scholarly.* **Description:** Covers history, geography, armament, militia and related fields. Aims to be the bridge between the society and the army.
Related titles: Online - full text ed.: ISSN 1988-3315.
Indexed: RILM.
Published by: (Asociacion de Amigos de los Museos Militares), Universidad Complutense de Madrid, Servicio de Publicaciones, C/ Obispo Trejo 2, Ciudad Universitaria, Madrid, 28040, Spain. TEL 34-91-3941127, FAX 34-91-3941126, servicio.publicaciones@rect.ucm.es, http://www.ucm.es/publicaciones. Ed. Francisco Castrillo Mazerej.

355 BEL ISSN 0776-7412
UC465.B4
MILITARIA BELGICA; revue d'uniformologie et d'histoire militaire Belge. Text in Dutch, French. 1977. q. includes Revue Belge d'Histoire Militaire. back issues avail. **Description:** Highlights arms and armor.
Indexed: IBR, IBZ.
—INIST.
Published by: Societe Royale des Amis du Musee Royal de l'Armee et d'Histoire Militaire, Parc du Cinquantenaire 3, Brussels, 1040, Belgium. Ed. E A Jacobs. Circ: 1,000.

355.8075 FRA ISSN 0753-1877
UC460
MILITARIA MAGAZINE; Uniformes, equipements et insignes militaires de 1914 a 1970. Text in French. 1984. bi-m. EUR 67 domestic; EUR 80 foreign (effective 2009). back issues avail. **Document type:** *Magazine, Consumer.*
Published by: Histoire et Collection, 5 Av. de la Republique, Paris, 75011, France. TEL 33-1-40211820, FAX 33-1-47005111, fredbey@club-internet.fr, http://www.histoireetcollections.com.

355 USA ISSN 1046-2511
E840.4
MILITARY; WWII, Korea, Vietnam, Cold War & Today. Text in English. 1985. m. USD 16 domestic; USD 26 foreign (effective 2003). adv. bk.rev. illus. 64 p./no.; back issues avail.; reprints avail. **Document type:** *Magazine, Consumer.* **Description:** Covers World War II, Korea, Vietnam, and present military actions worldwide.
Formerly: Military History Review
Indexed: RASB.
Published by: M H R Publishing Corp., 2122 28 St, Sacramento, CA 95818. TEL 916-457-8990, 800-366-9192, FAX 916-457-7339, editor@milmag.com. Ed. Rick McCusker. adv.: B&W page USD 337; trim 10 x 7.5. Circ: 24,000.

355 378 USA ISSN 1938-4165
U716
MILITARY ADVANCED EDUCATION. Abbreviated title: M A E. Text in English. 2006. q. free to qualified personnel (effective 2008). adv. back issues avail. **Document type:** *Magazine, Trade.* **Description:** Features information and advice about using military education benefits.
Published by: Kerrigan Media International, Inc., 1300 Piccard Dr, Ste 200, Rockville, MD 20850. TEL 301-926-5090, 888-299-8292, FAX 301-926-5091, kmi@kmimediagroup.com, http://www.kerriganmedia.com. Ed. Marty Kauchak. adv.: B&W page USD 5,980, color page USD 6,980; trim 8.375 x 10.875.

810 USA
MILITARY ADVANTAGE; relationship marketing for the military community. Text in English. 1999. d. charts; illus.; maps. **Document type:** *Journal, Consumer.*
Formerly: Military.com
Media: Online - full content. **Related titles:** E-mail ed.
Published by: Military.com, 1235 Jefferson Davis, Hwy 304, Arlington, VA 22202. TEL 703-414-3035, FAX 703-414-3095, anne.dwane@military-inc.com, http://www.military.com.

MILITARY ADVISOR; the publication for international military hobbyists and historians. *see* HOBBIES

358.4 GBR
MILITARY AIRCRAFT MARKINGS (YEAR). Text in English. 1980. a. GBP 10.99 per issue (effective 2010). back issues avail.; reprints avail. **Document type:** *Yearbook, Trade.* **Description:** Covers all the latest developments that have affected military aviation throughout the world and will appeal to all aviation enthusiasts who need the most up to date information available.
Published by: Ian Allan Publishing Ltd., Riverdene Business Park, Riverdene Industrial Estate, Molesey Rd, Walton-on-Thames, Surrey KT12 4RG, United Kingdom. TEL 44-1932-266622, FAX 44-1932-266633, magazines@ianallanpublishing.co.uk. Ed. Howard J Curtis.

MILITARY & AEROSPACE ELECTRONICS. *see* AERONAUTICS AND SPACE FLIGHT

355 GBR ISSN 0459-7222
UA15
➤ **THE MILITARY BALANCE (YEAR).** Text in English. 1959. a. GBP 287 combined subscription in United Kingdom to institutions (print & online eds.); EUR 422 combined subscription to institutions (print & online eds.); USD 501 combined subscription in North America to institutions (print & online eds.); USD 531 combined subscription elsewhere to institutions (print & online eds.) (effective 2012). bk.rev. charts; stat. 320 p./no.; back issues avail.; reprint service avail. from PSC. **Document type:** *Journal, Academic/Scholarly.* **Description:** Provides a quantitative assessment of military strength and defense spending of every country with armed forces.
Related titles: Online - full text ed.: ISSN 1479-9022. GBP 258 in United Kingdom to institutions; EUR 380 to institutions; USD 452 in North America to institutions; USD 477 elsewhere to institutions (effective 2012) (from IngentaConnect).
Indexed: A22, CA, E01, I02, P42, PSA, RASB, T02.
—BLDSC (5767.990000), IE, Ingenta. **CCC.**
Published by: (International Institute for Strategic Studies), Routledge (Subsidiary of: Taylor & Francis Group), 4 Park Sq, Milton Park, Abingdon, Oxon OX14 4RN, United Kingdom. TEL 44-20-7017-6000, FAX 44-20-7017-6336, info@routledge.co.uk, http://www.routledge.com. Ed. Hackett James TEL 44-20-73959147. Adv. contact Linda Hann TEL 44-1344-779945.

➤ **MILITARY CAMPAIGNS OF THE CIVIL WAR.** *see* HISTORY—History Of North And South America

355.347 USA ISSN 0026-3958
UH23
THE MILITARY CHAPLAIN. Text in English. 1931. bi-m. USD 14 domestic (effective 2005). adv. bk.rev. illus. 16 p./no. 2 cols./p.; back issues avail. **Document type:** *Newsletter, Trade.* **Description:** Covers the religious activities in all branches of the armed forces and all religious faiths.
Indexed: AUNI, RASB.
Published by: Military Chaplains Association of the United States of America, PO Box 7056, Arlington, VA 22207-0056. TEL 703-276-2189, FAX 703-276-2189, http://www.mca-usa.org. Ed., Adv. contact David E White. Circ: 1,900 (controlled).

MILITARY CLUB & HOSPITALITY. *see* FOOD AND FOOD INDUSTRIES

MILITARY COLLECTOR & HISTORIAN. *see* ANTIQUES

355 USA ISSN 2153-134X
▼ **MILITARY COLLEGE OF SOUTH CAROLINA. JOURNAL.** Variant title: Journal of Military Legitimacy and Leadership. Text in English. 2009. a. free (effective 2010). **Document type:** *Journal, Academic/Scholarly.*
Media: Online - full text.
Published by: The Citadel, Department of Political Science and Criminal Justice, 171 Moultrie St, Charleston, SC 29409. TEL 843-225-3294.

355 USA
MILITARY ELECTRONICS BRIEFING. Abbreviated title: M E B. Text in English. 1994. m. USD 1,995; USD 2,895 combined subscription (print & CD-ROM eds.); USD 3,495 combined subscription (print & online eds.) (effective 2011). **Document type:** *Trade.* **Description:** Researches and analyzes more than 300 of the top U.S. military electronics programs.
Related titles: CD-ROM ed.; Online - full text ed.: USD 1,895 (online or CD-ROM ed.); USD 3,395 combined subscription (online & CD-ROM eds.) (effective 2011).
Published by: Teal Group Corp., 3900 University Dr, Ste 220, Fairfax, VA 22030. TEL 703-385-1992, FAX 703-691-9591, custserv@tealgroup.com.

623 USA ISSN 1930-1316
UG485
MILITARY EMBEDDED SYSTEMS. Variant title: Military Embedded Systems Resource Guide. Text in English. 2005 (May). bi-m. USD 28 in US & Canada; USD 50 elsewhere; free to qualified personnel (effective 2009). adv. back issues avail.; reprints avail. **Document type:** *Magazine, Trade.* **Description:** Focuses on the "Whole Life COTS" and the total military program life cycle.
Related titles: Online - full text ed.: ISSN 1557-3222. free (effective 2009).
Published by: OpenSystems Publishing, 30233 Jefferson Ave, St Clair Shores, MI 48082. TEL 586-415-6500, FAX 586-415-4882, sales@opensystemsmedia.com, http://www.opensystems-publishing.com/. Eds. Chris Ciufo TEL 360-834-7009, Sharon Schnakenburg, Terri Thorson. Adv. contact Dennis Doyle TEL 586-415-6500. B&W page USD 1,400; trim 8 x 10.875. Circ: 40,070 (controlled).

MILITARY ENGINEER. *see* ENGINEERING

355 USA ISSN 1524-8666
D25
MILITARY HERITAGE. Text in English. 1999. bi-m. USD 18.95 domestic; USD 23.95 foreign (effective 2009). adv. **Document type:** *Magazine, Consumer.* **Description:** Covers military history, specific wars, battles, and their significance.
Indexed: AmH&L, HistAb.
Published by: Sovereign Media, 453B Carlisle Dr, Herndon, VA 20170. TEL 703-964-0361, FAX 703-964-0366, laura@sovhomestead.com, http://sovmedia.sovhomestead.com/. Ed. Roy Morris. Adv. contact Jeff Kight TEL 570-322-7848 ext 116.

355.009 GBR ISSN 0026-4008
DA49
MILITARY HISTORICAL SOCIETY. BULLETIN. Text in English. 1951. q. GBP 15 in Europe; GBP 20 elsewhere (effective 2010). bk.rev. charts; illus.; maps. cum.index every 5 yrs. back issues avail. **Document type:** *Bulletin, Academic/Scholarly.* **Description:** Contains a wide range of military research, articles and a forum for members' questions.
—BLDSC.
Published by: Military Historical Society, c/o Mr John Chapman, Membership Secretary, 5 Cecil Aldin Dr, Purley on Thames, Tilehurst, RG31 6YP, United Kingdom. john.chapman@purley.eu. Circ: 1,500 (paid).

MILITARY HISTORY. *see* HISTORY—History Of North And South America

355.1 GBR ISSN 1465-8488
MILITARY HISTORY AND POLICY. Text in English. 1999. irreg., latest 2009. price varies. back issues avail. **Document type:** *Monographic series, Academic/Scholarly.* **Description:** Publishes studies on historical and contemporary aspects of land power, spanning the period from the eighteenth century to the present day.
Published by: Routledge (Subsidiary of: Taylor & Francis Group), 2 Park Sq, Milton Park, Abingdon, Oxon OX14 4RN, United Kingdom. subscriptions@tandf.co.uk. Eds. Brian Holden Reid, John Gooch.

355.009 ZAF ISSN 0026-4016
DT769
MILITARY HISTORY JOURNAL/KRYGSHISTORIESE TYDSKRIF. Text and summaries in Afrikaans, English. 1967. 2/yr. ZAR 70 domestic; ZAR 150 foreign (effective 2003). bk.rev. charts; illus.; stat. cum.index. 40 p./no.; back issues avail. **Document type:** *Academic/Scholarly.*
Incorporates (1985-1991): South African National Museum of Military History. Review (1016-2550)
Indexed: IBR, IBZ, ISAP, LID&ISL.
Published by: South African National Museum of Military History/Suid-Afrikaanse Nasionale Museum vir Krygsgestiederis, PO Box 52090, Saxonwold, Johannesburg 2132, South Africa. TEL 27-11-6465513, FAX 27-11-6465256, milmus@acenet.co.za, http://www.militarymuseum.co.za. Ed. Susanne Blendulf. R&P S Blendulf. Circ: 700. **Co-sponsor:** South African Military History Society.

MILITARY HISTORY OF THE WEST. *see* HISTORY—History Of North And South America

355 GBR ISSN 1479-9677
MILITARY ILLUSTRATED. Text in English. 1986. m. GBP 42 domestic; GBP 62 in Europe; GBP 77 elsewhere; GBP 4.10 per issue domestic; GBP 5.10 per issue in Europe; GBP 6.10 per issue elsewhere (effective 2009). **Document type:** *Magazine, Consumer.* **Description:** Contains feature articles on the most popular periods of military history - including WWI and WWII, the Napoleonic Wars, Roman Empire, Colonial Warfare and Medieval battles - all written by leading military historians.
Formerly (until 1994): Military Illustrated Past & Present (0268-8328)

—CCC.
Published by: A D H Publishing Ltd., Doolittle Mill, Doolittle Ln, Totternhoe, Bedfordshire LU6 1QX, United Kingdom. TEL 44-1525-222573, FAX 44-1525-222574, enquiries@adhpublishing.com.

355 USA ISSN 1040-4961
UA23.A1
MILITARY IMAGES. Text in English. 1979. bi-m. USD 24.95 domestic; USD 50.95 foreign (effective 2010). bk.rev. illus. cum.index every 5 yrs. back issues avail.; reprints avail. **Document type:** *Journal, Academic/Scholarly.* **Description:** Covers U.S. military history from 1839 to 1900, with particular emphasis on the Civil war, biographies of the common soldier, and original, unpublished photographs from private collections.
Formerly (until 19??): Military Images Magazine (0193-9866)
Related titles: Microfiche ed.; Microform ed.: (from PQC); Online - full text ed.
Indexed: AmH&L, M02, M05, M07, P10, P47, P48, P52, P53, P54, PQC, T02.
—Ingenta.
Address: PO Box B, Export, PA 15632.

355 621.3822 USA ISSN 1097-1041
UG478
MILITARY INFORMATION TECHNOLOGY; the voice of military communication and computing. Abbreviated title: M I T. Text in English. 1997. 10/yr. free to qualified personnel (effective 2009). adv. **Document type:** *Magazine, Trade.* **Description:** Features all the aspects of IT in defense and national security applications enterprise technology and systems integration, networking and information sharing, security, satcom and telecom, data warehousing, rugged computing, video conferencing, tactical systems and C4ISR.
Related titles: Online - full text ed.
Published by: Kerrigan Media International, Inc., 15800 Crabbs Branch Way, Ste 300, Rockville, MD 20855. TEL 301-670-5700, 888-299-8292, FAX 301-670-5701, kmi@kmimediagroup.com, http://www.kerriganmedia.com. Ed. Marty Kauchak. adv.: B&W page USD 5,980, color page USD 6,980; trim 8.375 x 10.875.

355 USA ISSN 0026-4024
UB250
MILITARY INTELLIGENCE. Text in English. 1974. q. USD 14 (effective 2001). bk.rev. illus. **Document type:** *Government.* **Description:** The objectives of this publication are to provide a forum for the exchange of ideas, to inform and motivate, and to provide the professional development of all members of the intelligence community.
Related titles: Microfiche ed.; Online - full text ed.
Indexed: A01, A22, A26, AMB, AUNI, C12, G05, G06, G07, G08, I02, I05, IUSGP, LID&ISL, M01, M02, M05, M06, P02, P10, P47, P48, P52, P53, P54, PQC, T02.
—Ingenta.
Published by: U.S. Army Intelligence Center & Fort Huachuca, Attn: ATZS-BDB (73), Ft. Huachuca, AZ 85613-6000. http://usaic.hua.army.mil/. Circ: 5,000.

355 USA ISSN 0740-5065
MILITARY LIVING. Text in English. 1969. q. USD 8. **Document type:** *Magazine, Consumer.* **Description:** Military benefits, facilities, and rest and recreation.
—CCC.
Published by: Military Living Publications, PO Box 2347, Falls Church, VA 22042-0347. TEL 703-237-0203. Ed. L Ann Crawford.

355 USA ISSN 0740-5073
MILITARY LIVING'S R & R REPORT; the voice of the military traveler. Text in English. 1971. bi-m. USD 17. adv. back issues avail. **Document type:** *Magazine, Consumer.* **Description:** Military rest and recreation and travel.
—CCC.
Published by: Military Living Publications, PO Box 2347, Falls Church, VA 22042-0347. TEL 703-237-0203. Ed. L Ann Crawford.

355 GBR ISSN 2043-6807
MILITARY LOGISTICS INTERNATIONAL. Text in English. 2005. bi-m. GBP 65 (effective 2010). adv. back issues avail. **Document type:** *Magazine, Trade.* **Description:** Covers ranges from fresh 'after-action' reports of logistics operations in the field, through logistics transformation issues, to analysis and discussion about industrial aspects of logistics and supply chain matters.
Related titles: Online - full text ed.: ISSN 2043-6815.
Published by: Shephard Press Ltd., 268 Bath Rd, Slough, Berkshire SL1 4DX, United Kingdom. TEL 44-1753-727001, FAX 44-1753-727002, info@shephard.co.uk. Ed. Francis Tusa TEL 44-20-72840331. Adv. contact Paul Barrett TEL 44-1753-727005. color page GBP 8,600; 205 x 273.

MILITARY MACHINES INTERNATIONAL. *see* HOBBIES

MILITARY MEDAL SOCIETY OF SOUTH AFRICA. JOURNAL. *see* NUMISMATICS

MILITARY MEDICAL/C B R N TECHNOLOGY. (Chemical, Biological, Radiological, and Nuclear) *see* MEDICAL SCIENCES

MILITARY MINIATURES IN REVIEW. *see* HOBBIES

355 GBR ISSN 0026-4083
MILITARY MODELLING. Text in English. 1971. 15/yr. GBP 59.25 domestic; GBP 62 in Europe; GBP 65 in United States; GBP 69 elsewhere (effective 2010). adv. bk.rev.; film rev. charts; illus. Index. back issues avail.; reprints avail. **Document type:** *Magazine, Consumer.* **Description:** Contains articles of interest to modellers of military figures and armour, wargamers, and general military enthusiasts.
Incorporates (1974-1978): Battle (0309-7668)
Related titles: Online - full text ed.
—BLDSC (5768.160000).
Published by: MyHobbyStore Ltd., Berwick House, 8-10 Knoll Rise, Orpington, Kent BR6 0EL, United Kingdom. TEL 44-844-4122262, info@myhobbystore.com, http://www.myhobbystoregroup.com. Adv. contact Ben Rayment TEL 44-844-8485240.

355.1 USA ISSN 1549-375X
MILITARY MONEY. Text in English. 2003 (Fall). q. free to qualified personnel (effective 2004). **Document type:** *Magazine, Consumer.* **Description:** Contains information on saving, investing and budgeting on a military income.
Published by: InCharge Institute of America, Inc., 2101 Park Center Dr Ste 310, Orlando, FL 32835. TEL 407-532-5745, 888-436-8714, http://www.incharge.org. Ed. Rebecca Stiehl.

070.431 RUS ISSN 1609-5863
MILITARY NEWS AGENCY. Text in English. 199?. d. **Document type:** *Journal, Trade.* **Description:** Provides full coverage of Russian military reform, the military-industrial complex, Russia's military and technical cooperation with other countries, new developments in weapons systems, and the current state of affairs within the country's security agencies.
Media: Online - full content. **Related titles:** Online - full text ed.; Russian ed.: Agentstvo Voennyh Novostej. ISSN 1609-5871. 2001.
Indexed: A26, B02, B15, B17, B18, G04, G06, G07, G08, I02, I05, M06, R01.
Published by: Interfax - Military News Agency, 2 Pervaya Tverskaya-Yamskaya, Moscow, 127006, Russian Federation. TEL 7-095-2509232, FAX 7-095-2501436, sales@militarynews.ru.

355 USA ISSN 1542-3360
UB413
MILITARY OFFICER. Text in English. 1945. m. USD 24 membership; USD 3 newsstand/cover (effective 2005). adv. bk.rev. charts; illus.; maps; stat. **Document type:** *Magazine, Consumer.* **Description:** For men and women who are or have been commissioned or warrant officers in any component of the seven uniformed services of the United States.
Former titles (until 2003): The Retired Officer Magazine (Alexandria) (1061-3102); The Retired Officer (Washington, DC, 1979) (0034-6160); (until 1978): The Retired Officer Magazine (Washington, DC) (0737-724X); (until 1973): The Retired Officer (Washington, DC, 1945) (0737-6995)
Related titles: Audio cassette/tape ed.; Microfilm ed.: (from PQC).
Published by: The Military Officers Association of America, 201 N Washington St, Alexandria, VA 22314-2539. TEL 703-838-8115, FAX 703-838-8179. Ed. Col. Warren S Lacy. R&P Molly Wyman TEL 703-838-8155. Adv. contact Major Dale Robinson. B&W page USD 5,490, color page USD 7,355. Circ: 383,344 (controlled).

355.4 USA ISSN 0275-5823
U104
➤ **MILITARY OPERATIONS RESEARCH (ALEXANDRIA, 1981).** Text in English. 1981. irreg. price varies. **Document type:** *Monographic series, Academic/Scholarly.*
Indexed: CIS, CMCI, SCI, SCOPUS, W07.
—IE, Infotrieve.
Published by: Military Operations Research Society, 1703 N Beauregard St, Ste 450, Alexandria, VA 22311. TEL 703-751-7290, FAX 703-751-8171, morsoffice@mors.org, http://www.mors.org.

355.4 USA ISSN 1082-5983
U163
➤ **MILITARY OPERATIONS RESEARCH (ALEXANDRIA, 1996).** Variant title: Military Operations Research Society. Journal. Text in English. 1996. q. USD 70 domestic to non-members; USD 135 foreign to non-members; free to members (effective 2010). back issues avail. **Document type:** *Journal, Academic/Scholarly.* **Description:** Provides a forum for researchers and practitioners to share research findings and applications with the military operations research community.
Indexed: CA, M05, T02.
—BLDSC (5768.162700), Ingenta.
Published by: Military Operations Research Society, 1703 N Beauregard St, Ste 450, Alexandria, VA 22311. TEL 703-933-9070, FAX 703-933-9066. Ed. Dr. Richard F Deckro.

355 RUS ISSN 1029-466X
MILITARY PARADE. Text in English. bi-m. USD 245 in United States. **Document type:** *Journal, Consumer.* **Description:** Covers the latest news from the Russian defense industry.
Related titles: ◆ Russian ed.: Voennyi Parad. ISSN 1029-4678; ◆ Translation of: Voennyi Parad. ISSN 1029-4678.
Published by: Military Parade Ltd., Ul Mosfil'movskaya 35, str 1, Moscow, 117330, Russian Federation. TEL 7-095-1439650, FAX 7-095-1439651. **Dist. by:** East View Information Services, 10601 Wayzata Blvd, Minneapolis, MN 55305. TEL 952-252-1201, 800-477-1005, FAX 952-252-1202, info@eastview.com, http://www.eastview.com.

355.0335 USA ISSN 0895-4208
UB825.U54
MILITARY POLICE. Text in English. 1951. s-a. USD 12 domestic; USD 15 foreign (effective 2001). bk.rev. illus. index. back issues avail. **Document type:** *Government.* **Description:** Discusses the functions of military police in combat.
Former titles (until 1987): Military Police Journal (0884-0024); Military Police Law Enforcement Journal (0199-7211)
Related titles: Online - full text ed.: ISSN 1554-9690.
Indexed: A22, A26, AUNI, G06, G07, G08, I02, I05, M02, M05, M06, RASB, S02, S03, T02.
Published by: U.S. Army Military Police School, 320 Manscen Loop, Ste 210, Fort Leonard Wood, MO 65473-8929 . TEL 205-848-4326, FAX 205-848-5885. Ed. Lois C Perry. Circ: 11,000. **Subscr. to:** U.S. Government Printing Office, Superintendent of Documents, PO Box 371954, Pittsburgh, PA 15250. TEL 202-512-1800, FAX 202-512-2250, orders@gpo.gov, http://www.access.gpo.gov.

MILITARY PSYCHOLOGY. *see* PSYCHOLOGY

355 USA
CODEN: EMRAFG
MILITARY REALTOR. Text in English. 1993. s-a. USD 15; free to qualified personnel (effective 2005). adv. software rev. charts; illus.; maps; tr.lit. back issues avail. **Document type:** *Magazine, Trade.* **Description:** For employees of military exchange resale services (AAFES, NEXCOM, CGES, MCX). Covers products, merchandising, people, news, legislature, store profiles, and employee relations.
Formerly: Military Exchange Magazine (1070-0765)
Published by: Downey Communications, Inc., 4800 Montgomery Ln, Ste 700, Bethesda, MD 20814-5341. TEL 301-718-7600, FAX 301-718-7652. Eds. Cati O'Keefe, Lisa Palladino. Pubs., Adv. contacts Michael J Jennings, Richard T Carroll. B&W page USD 3,200, color page USD 3,750; trim 8.13 x 10.88. Circ: 4,000 (controlled and free).

355 USA ISSN 0026-4148
Z6723
MILITARY REVIEW (ENGLISH EDITION); the professional journal of the United States Army. Text in English. 1922. bi-m. USD 42 domestic; USD 58.80 foreign (effective 2009). bk.rev. abstr.; charts; illus.; maps. Index. back issues avail.; reprints avail. **Document type:** *Magazine, Government.* **Description:** Focuses on concepts, doctrine and warfighting at the tactical and operational levels of war and supports the education, training, doctrine development and integration missions of the combined arms center.
Former titles (until 1939): The Command and General Staff School Quarterly; (until 1936): Review of Military Literature; (until 1933): Quarterly Review of Military Literature; (until 1932): Review of Current Military Literature; (until 1931): Review of Current Military Writings; (until 1925): Instructor's Summary of Military Articles
Related titles: Microfilm ed.: (from PQC); Online - full text ed.: ISSN 1943-1147. free (effective 2009); Portuguese ed.: Military Review (Portuguese Edition). ISSN 1067-0653. 1945; Ed.: Military Review (Arabic Edition). ISSN 1559-0313; Spanish ed.: Military Review (Spanish Edition). ISSN 0193-2977. 1945.
Indexed: A01, A02, A03, A08, A22, A26, ABS&EES, AMB, AUNI, AmH&L, BAS, BibInd, DIP, DM&T, G05, G06, G07, G08, HistAb, I02, I05, IBR, IBZ, IUSGP, LID&ISL, M01, M02, M05, M06, M07, P02, P06, P10, P30, P34, P43, P45, P47, P48, P53, P54, PAIS, PQC, PRA, RASB, S02, S03, T02.
—BLDSC (5768.170000), IE, Infotrieve, Ingenta, Linda Hall.
Published by: U.S. Army Combined Arms Center, 294 Grant Ave, Bldg 77, Fort Leavenworth, KS 66027. TEL 913-684-9327, FAX 913-684-9328, leav-milrevweb@conus.army.mil. Ed. Col. John J Smith. **Subscr. to:** U.S. Government Printing Office, Superintendent of Documents, PO Box 371954, Pittsburgh, PA 15250. TEL 202-512-1800, FAX 202-512-2250, orders@gpo.gov, http://www.access.gpo.gov.

MILITARY ROBOTICS NEWSLETTER; covering government and defense applications of robotics. *see* COMPUTERS—Robotics

355 USA ISSN 1944-5008
UG1523
MILITARY SPACE & MISSILE FORUM. Text in English. 2008. bi-m. **Document type:** *Journal, Trade.* **Description:** Dedicated to the military space and communities. Covers strategic space launch, space-based radars and vehicles, theater missiles, and support systems invoved in military space defense.
Related titles: Online - full text ed.: ISSN 1944-5717.
Published by: Kerrigan Media International, Inc., 1300 Piccard Dr, Ste 200, Rockville, MD 20850. TEL 301-926-5090, 888-299-8292, FAX 301-926-5091, kmi@kmimediagroup.com, http://www.kerriganmedia.com. Ed. Marty Kauchak.

051 USA
MILITARY SPOUSE. Text in English. 2004 (Sep.). bi-m. USD 12; USD 3.99 newsstand/cover (effective 2005). adv. **Document type:** *Magazine, Consumer.* **Description:** Addresses interests and current events that are relevant to a military spouse's daily life.
Published by: Anchor Media, Inc., PO Box 288, St. Marys, GA 31558. TEL 912-882-7401. Ed. Regina Galvin. Pubs. Babette Maxwell, Elsie Hammond. Adv. contact Jackie Lindstrom. color page USD 4,875; trim 7.875 x 10. Circ: 75,000.

355 DEU ISSN 0722-3226
U1
MILITARY TECHNOLOGY. Variant title: Miltech. Text in English. 1977. m. EUR 130; EUR 13.50 newsstand/cover (effective 2008). adv. bk.rev. back issues avail.; reprints avail. **Document type:** *Magazine, Trade.* **Description:** Journal of defense technology and economics.
Formerly (until 1981): Military Technology and Economics (0344-6352)
Related titles: Online - full text ed.
Indexed: A01, A22, A26, A28, APA, AUNI, BAS, BrCerAb, C&ISA, C23, CA, CA/WCA, CIA, CerAb, CivEngAb, CorrAb, DM&T, E&CAJ, E11, EEA, EMA, ESPM, EnvEAb, G05, G06, G07, G08, H15, I02, I05, LID&ISL, M&TEA, M05, M06, M07, M09, MBF, METADEX, P02, P10, P34, P47, P48, P52, P53, P54, PQC, RASB, SolStAb, T02, T04, WAA.
—BLDSC (5768.361000), IE, Infotrieve, Ingenta, Linda Hall. **CCC.**
Published by: Wehr und Wissen Verlagsgesellschaft mbH, Heilsbachstr 26, Bonn, 53123, Germany. TEL 49-228-64830, FAX 49-228-6483109, info@moench-group.com. Ed. Ezio Bonsignore. Adv. contact Anne Fichtel. B&W page EUR 4,500, color page EUR 7,500; trim 7.3125 x 10.0625. Circ: 24,343 (paid).

355 USA ISSN 0869-5636
MILITARY THOUGHT; a Russian journal of military theory and strategy. Text in English. 1918. q. USD 570 to institutions; USD 812 combined subscription to institutions (print & online eds.) (effective 2009). adv. index. back issues avail. **Document type:** *Journal, Government.* **Description:** Presents articles on Russian military reform, tactics and strategy of modern combat, experience of counterterrorist operations, international security, etc.
Related titles: Microfiche ed.: (from EVP); Online - full text ed.: USD 114 to individuals; USD 738 to institutions (effective 2009); ◆ Translation of: Voennaya Mysl'. ISSN 0236-2058.
Indexed: A01, A03, A08, A26, DIP, E08, G05, G06, G07, G08, I02, I05, IBR, IBZ, LID&ISL, M05, M06, P42, S09.
—East View.
Published by: (Ministerstvo Oborony Rossiiskoi Federatsii/Ministry of Defence of the Russian Federation RUS), East View Information Services, 10601 Wayzata Blvd, Minneapolis, MN 55305. TEL 952-252-1201, 800-477-1005, FAX 952-252-1202, info@eastview.com. Ed. S Rodikov. Circ: 200 (paid and controlled).

355 GBR ISSN 2043-930X
▼ **MILITARY TIMES.** Text in English. 2010. m. GBP 29.95 (effective 2011). adv. **Document type:** *Magazine, Consumer.* **Description:** Features informative articles and in-depth analysis on military history.
Related titles: Online - full text ed.: GBP 24.97 (effective 2011).
Published by: Church Street Publishing, Lamb House, Church St, London, W4 2PD, United Kingdom. TEL 44-20-88195580, FAX 44-20-88195589, http://www.churchstreetpublishing.com/. Ed. Neil Faulkner. Pub. Luke Bilton. Adv. contact Elliot Stead TEL 44-20-73493181.

355 600 USA ISSN 1097-0975
MILITARY TRAINING TECHNOLOGY. Text in English. 1996. 8/yr. free to qualified personnel (effective 2008). adv. back issues avail. **Document type:** *Magazine, Trade.* **Description:** Focuses on all issues related to training and preparation of the armed forces.

Related titles: Online - full text ed.
Published by: Kerrigan Media International, Inc., 15800 Crabbs Branch Way, Ste 300, Rockville, MD 20855. TEL 301-670-5700, 888-299-8292, FAX 301-670-5701, kmi@kmimediagroup.com, http://www.kerriganmedia.com. Ed. Marty Kauchak. adv.: B&W page USD 5,980, color page USD 6,980; trim 8.375 x 10.875.

MILITARY TRAVEL GUIDE. *see* TRAVEL AND TOURISM

355.27 USA ISSN 1092-7824
UG615
MILITARY VEHICLES MAGAZINE. Text in English. 1987. bi-m. USD 34.98; USD 5.99 newsstand/cover (effective 2012). adv. bk.rev. **Document type:** *Magazine, Trade.* **Description:** Contains news, vintage military photos, collecting advice, market information, show listings, and display and classified advertising sections offering to buy and sell hundreds of beeps, tanks, trucks, vehicle parts, and accessories from dealers and enthusiasts all over the world. Other regular features include book and media reviews, letters to the editor, tech topics, weapons & replica, models, and toys.
Formerly (until 19??): Military Vehicles (0893-3863)
Indexed: G08, I05.
—**CCC.**
Published by: F + W Media Inc., 4700 E Galbraith Rd, Cincinnati, OH 45236. TEL 513-531-2690, contact_us@fwmedia.com, http://www.fwmedia.com/. Ed. John Adams-Graf TEL 715-445-2214 ext 13645. Pub. Jamie Wilkinson TEL 715-445-2214 ext 13447. Circ: 18,000 (controlled and free).

355 IND ISSN 0076-8782
U10.I5
MILITARY YEARBOOK. Text in English. 1965. a. INR 4,975 per issue domestic; USD 700, GBP 395 per issue foreign (effective 2011). adv. illus.; stat. **Description:** Covers organizational and technological aspects, global events affecting the security environment, and a complete equipment catalogue of army, navy, air force of India.
Published by: Guide Publications, P O Box 2525, New Delhi, 110 005, India. TEL 91-11-24644693, FAX 91-11-24647093, guidepub@vsnl.com, http://www.spguidepublications.com/. Circ: 9,575. **Dist. in U.S. by:** Taylor & Francis Inc., 7625 Empire Dr, Florence, KY 41042. cserve@routledge-ny.com.

355 UKR
MILITSEIS'KYI KUR'IER. Text in Ukrainian. w. USD 225 in United States.
Published by: Upravlenie M.V.D. L'vovskoi Oblasti, Ul Sichovykh Stril'tsiv 9, Lvov, Ukraine. TEL 380-32-782798. **Dist. by:** East View Information Services, 10601 Wayzata Blvd, Minneapolis, MN 55305. TEL 952-252-1201, 800-477-1005, FAX 952-252-1202, info@eastview.com, http://www.eastview.com.

355.37 RUS ISSN 0869-558X
HV8224 CODEN: SOMIEC
MILITSIYA. Text in Russian. 1922. m.
Formerly: Sovetskaya Militsiya (0320-2259)
Indexed: RASB.
—East View.
Address: c/o A G Gorlov, Ed, Ul Ivanovskaya 24, Moscow, 127434, Russian Federation. TEL 7-095-9766644, FAX 7-095-9770400. Circ: 107,200. **Dist. by:** East View Information Services, 10601 Wayzata Blvd, Minneapolis, MN 55305. TEL 952-252-1201, 800-477-1005, FAX 952-252-1202, info@eastview.com, http://www.eastview.com.

355 UKR
MILITSIYA UKRAINY. Text in Ukrainian. m. USD 190 in United States.
Address: Ul V Zhytomyrs'ka 32, Kiev, Ukraine. TEL 212-31-63, FAX 380-44-291-3691. **Dist. by:** East View Information Services, 10601 Wayzata Blvd, Minneapolis, MN 55305. TEL 952-252-1201, 800-477-1005, FAX 952-252-1202, info@eastview.com, http://www.eastview.com.

355.4 USA ISSN 1937-9315
U168
MILTARY LOGISTICS FORUM (ROCKVILLE). Text in English. 2007. bi-m. USD 65 domestic; USD 149 foreign; free to qualified personnel (effective 2008). adv. **Document type:** *Magazine, Trade.* **Description:** Covers all aspects of the military supply and demand chain, logistics operations and transportation communities.
Published by: Kerrigan Media International, Inc., 1300 Piccard Dr, Ste 200, Rockville, MD 20850. TEL 301-926-5090, 888-299-8292, FAX 301-926-5091, kmi@kmimediagroup.com, http://www.kerriganmedia.com. Ed. Dawn Onley. Pub. Jack Kerrigan.

MILTARYLIFESTYLE.COM COUPONER. *see* FOOD AND FOOD INDUSTRIES

355.4082 USA ISSN 1938-3649
UB418.W65
➤ **MINERVA JOURNAL OF WOMEN AND WAR.** Text in English. 1983-2005; N.S. 2007. s-a. USD 70 combined subscription domestic to individuals (print & online eds.); USD 80 combined subscription foreign to individuals (print & online eds.); USD 150 combined subscription domestic to institutions (print & online eds.); USD 160 combined subscription foreign to institutions (print & online eds.) (effective 2010). bk.rev.; film rev.; play rev. bibl.; charts; illus. cum.index: 1983-1984. back issues avail.; reprints avail. **Document type:** *Journal, Academic/Scholarly.* **Description:** Contains articles relating to service women, military wives, and women veterans (both military and civilian) from all nations and all eras.
Formerly (until 2007): Minerva (0736-718X)
Related titles: Online - full text ed.: ISSN 1744-1463.
Indexed: A25, A26, AmH&L, CA, CWI, DYW, E08, ERA, FemPer, G06, G07, G08, G10, GW, HistAb, I05, LID&ISL, M06, P30, P48, PQC, S08, S09, S19, S21, T02, T03, W09.
—Infotrieve, Ingenta.
Published by: (Minerva Society for the Study of Women and War), McFarland & Company, Inc., PO Box 611, Jefferson, NC 28640. TEL 336-246-4460, FAX 336-246-5018, info@mcfarlandpub.com. Pub. Rhonda Herman.

355 GBR ISSN 0266-3228
MINIATURE WARGAMES. Text in English. 1983. m. GBP 43 domestic; GBP 53 foreign (effective 2010). adv. bk.rev. illus.; maps. index. 56 p./no. 3 cols./p.; back issues avail.; reprints avail. **Document type:** *Magazine, Consumer.* **Description:** Covers war gaming in all periods of history from sumerians to 21st century throughout the world.
Published by: Pireme Publishing Ltd., Strelley Hall, Nottingham, NG8 6PE, United Kingdom. TEL 44-115-9061218, FAX 44-115-9061251, andrew@miniwargames.com. Pub. Andrew Hubback. adv.: color page GBP 300; trim 210 x 297.

355 USA ISSN 0164-4270
MINNESOTA LEGIONNAIRE. Text in English. 1920. m. USD 10 to non-members; free to members (effective 2005). adv. bk.rev. back issues avail. **Document type:** *Newspaper, Consumer.*
Published by: Minnesota American Legion, 20 W 12th St, St Paul, MN 55155-2069. TEL 651-291-1800, FAX 651-291-1057. Ed., Adv. contact Al Zdon. B&W page USD 1,215. Circ: 113,749 (free).

359 USA
THE MIRROR (MAYPORT). Text in English. 1958. w. (Fri.). USD 40 (effective 2005). adv. **Document type:** *Newspaper.*
Published by: Beaches Leader, Inc., 1114 Beach Blvd., Jacksonville Beach, FL 32250. TEL 904-249-9033. Ed. Paige Gnann. Pub. Tom Wood. adv.: col. inch USD 10.70. Circ: 9,700 (free).

MISSISSIPPI LEGION-AIRE. *see* CLUBS

355 DEU ISSN 0936-4013
DER MITTLER-BRIEF. Text in German. 1986. q. EUR 15.60 (effective 2010). **Document type:** *Newsletter, Consumer.*
Published by: Verlag E.S. Mittler und Sohn GmbH, Striepenweg 31, Hamburg, 21147, Germany. TEL 49-40-7971303, FAX 49-40-79713324, vertrieb@koehler-mittler.de, http://www.koehler-mittler.de.

355 USA ISSN 1559-159X
UC333
THE MOBILITY FORUM; journal of the Air Mobility Command. Text in English. 1954. bi-m. free to qualified personnel. bk.rev. stat. reprints avail. **Document type:** *Magazine, Government.* **Description:** Safety publication.
Former titles (until 1992): M A C Forum (1067-8999); (until 1991): M A C Flyer (0024-788X)
Related titles: Microform ed.: (from MIM, PQC); Online - full text ed.
Indexed: A01, A03, A08, AUNI, IUSGP, M05, M07, P02, P10, P47, P48, P52, P53, P54, PQC, T02.
—Ingenta, Linda Hall.
Published by: (U.S. Air Force, Air Mobility Command, Director of Safety), Schatz Publishing Group, 11950 W. Highland Ave., Blackwell, OK 74631-6511. TEL 580-628-2933, 888-474-6397, FAX 580-628-2011. Ed. Maj John Ward. R&P David Rubelcaba. Circ: 12,000. **Subscr. to:** U.S. Government Printing Office, Superintendent of Documents, PO Box 371954, Pittsburgh, PA 15250. TEL 202-512-1800, FAX 202-512-2250, orders@gpo.gov, http://bookstore.gpo.gov.

MODERN MILITARY TRADITION. *see* HISTORY—History Of North And South America

355.5 GBR ISSN 1471-1052
MODERN SIMULATION AND TRAINING. Short title: M S & T. Text in German. 1985. bi-m. GBP 49 domestic; EUR 69 in the European Union; USD 92 elsewhere (effective 2005). adv. **Document type:** *Report, Trade.* **Description:** Provides reports and descriptions of armed forces training throughout the world, with an emphasis on targeting DODs, serving officers and training establishments.
Formerly (until 2000): Military Simulation and Training (0937-6348)
Indexed: LID&ISL.
—BLDSC (5980.840150), IE, Ingenta. **CCC.**
Published by: Halldale Publishing & Media Ltd., 84 Alexandra Rd, Farnborough, Hants GU14 6DD, United Kingdom. TEL 44-1252-532000, FAX 44-1252-512714. Ed. Chris Lehman. Pub. Andrew Smith. adv.: B&W page GBP 2,335, color page GBP 4,040; 178 x 254. Circ: 13,056.

MONTANA LEGIONNAIRE. *see* CLUBS

359 SRB ISSN 0027-1136
MORNARICKI GLASNIK/NAVY JOURNAL. Text in Serbo-Croatian. 1951. bi-m. USD 20.
Published by: Vojnoizdavacki Zavod, Vojska, Novinsko-itdavacka, ustanova, Bircaninova 5, Belgrade, Serbia 11000. Ed. Malin Malivuk.

359.96 UKR
MORS'KA DERZHAVA; hromads'ko-politychnyi, naukovyi, literaturno-khudozhnii zhurnal. Text in Ukrainian. 2003. bi-m. **Document type:** *Journal, Government.*
Published by: Ministerstvo Oborony Ukrainy, vul Komunistychna 3a, Sevastopol, 99011, Ukraine. TEL 380-692-547838, FAX 380-692-547838, http://www.mil.gov.ua.

355 RUS
MORSKOI PEKHOTINETS. Text in Russian. 1995. m. USD 184 in North America (effective 2000).
Published by: Federal'naya Sluzhba Okhrany Al'fa-Egida, Ul Kosmoduanskaya 46-50, Moscow, Russian Federation. TEL 7-095-2996346. **Dist. by:** East View Information Services, 10601 Wayzata Blvd, Minneapolis, MN 55305. TEL 952-252-1201, 800-477-1005, FAX 952-252-1202, info@eastview.com, http://www.eastview.com.

355.2 NLD ISSN 2210-9285
DE MORTIER VAN 5. Text in Dutch. 199?. 3/yr.
Published by: Stichting Veteranen 5-5-RI, de Kievit 21, Vriezenveen, 7671 ZK, Netherlands. TEL 31-546-561746, http://www.5-5-ri.mysites.nl.

355 USA
MOUNTAINEER (COLORADO SPRINGS). Text in English. 1942. w. adv. bk.rev. **Document type:** *Newspaper, Government.*
Published by: Fort Carson, Public Affairs Office, Bldg 1500, Rm 2180, Fort Carson, CO 80913-5119. TEL 719-579-4144, FAX 719-579-1021. Ed. Alicia Stewart. Circ: 12,000.

355 USA ISSN 2157-0701
MOUNTAINEER DEFENDER. Text in English. 19??. q. back issues avail. **Document type:** *Magazine, Consumer.*
Media: Online - full text.
Published by: West Virginia National Guard, 1679 Coonskin Dr, Charleston, WV 25311. TEL 304-341-6625, FAX 304-341-6010, sharon.peters@wvchar.ang.af.mil.

353.538 AUS
MUFTI. Text in English. 1934. q. bk.rev. **Document type:** *Bulletin.* **Description:** Contains information of interest to the veteran community.
Published by: (Returned & Services League of Australia), Newsprinters Pty Ltd. Shepparton, PO Box 204, Shepparton, VIC 3632, Australia. http://www.newsprinters.com.au.

355 RUS ISSN 0868-9652
PG3227.5
MUZHESTVO/BRAVERY; mezhdunarodnyi literaturno-khudozhestvennyi i istoricheskii zhurnal. Text in Russian. 1991. q. USD 89 in North America (effective 2000). **Document type:** *Journal.* **Description:** Publishes articles about fortitude, heroism, military memoirs.
Indexed: RASB.
Address: Khoroshevskoe shosse 50, korpus 3, of. 410, Moscow, 123007, Russian Federation. TEL 7-095-9401530. Ed. I V Chernykh. **Dist. by:** East View Information Services, 10601 Wayzata Blvd, Minneapolis, MN 55305. TEL 952-252-1201, 800-477-1005, FAX 952-252-1202, info@eastview.com, http://www.eastview.com.

355 POL ISSN 0209-3111
MYSL WOJSKOWA. Text in Polish. 1950. m. EUR 37 foreign (effective 2005). **Document type:** *Journal, Government.*
Published by: Ministerstwo Obrony Narodowej, ul Klonowa 1, Warsaw, 00909, Poland. TEL 48-22-6280031, FAX 48-22-8455378, http://www.wp.mil.pl. **Dist. by:** Ars Polona, Obroncow 25, Warsaw 03933, Poland. TEL 48-22-5098609, FAX 48-22-5098610, arspolona@arspolona.com.pl, http://www.arspolona.com.pl.

355.03109182 NOR ISSN 1891-2346
▼ **N A T O 2020.** (North Atlantic Treaty Organization) Text in English. 2009. irreg. **Document type:** *Monographic series, Consumer.*
Related titles: Online - full text ed.
Published by: Den Norske Atlanterhavskomite/The Norwegian Atlantic Committee, Fridjof Nansens Plass 8, Oslo, 0160, Norway. TEL 47-22-403600, FAX 47-22-403610, post@dnak.org, http://www.dnak.org. Ed. Neving Rudskjaer.

355 BEL
N A T O DATA. Text in English, French. 1993. irreg. free. **Document type:** *Directory, Government.* **Description:** Distributes NATO public information, and studies and reports in the field of international security.
Media: Online - full text.
Indexed: IIS.
Published by: (Integrated Data Service), North Atlantic Treaty Organization (N A T O), Office of Information and Press, Blvd Leopold III, Brussels, 1110, Belgium. TEL 32-2-7074599, FAX 32-2-7075457, http://www.nato.int.

N A T O'S NATIONS AND PARTNERS FOR PEACE. (North Atlantic Treaty Organization) *see* POLITICAL SCIENCE—International Relations

353.538 USA ISSN 0747-0150
THE N C O A JOURNAL. Text in English. bi-m. membership. adv. **Document type:** *Newspaper.* **Description:** Covers news, legislation, association updates and other items of interest to active duty, veteran and Guard members of the NCOA in all five branches of the armed forces.
Published by: Non-Commissioned Officers Association, PO Box 33610, San Antonio, TX 78265. TEL 210-653-6161, FAX 210-656-6225. Ed. Cliff "Scoop" Davis. R&P Cliff Scoop Davis. Adv. contact Cathy John. B&W page USD 3,600, color page USD 5,319; trim 10.75 x 8.25. Circ: 175,000.

355 USA ISSN 1058-9058
THE N C O JOURNAL. (Noncommissioned Officers) Text in English. 1991. m. free to qualified personnel (effective 2011). **Document type:** *Journal, Academic/Scholarly.* **Description:** Provide a forum for the open exchange of ideas and information, to support training, education and development of the NCO Corps and to foster a closer bond among its members.
Related titles: Online - full text ed.: free (effective 2011).
—Ingenta.
Published by: U.S. Army Sergeants Major Academy, 11291 SGT E Churchill St, Fort Bliss, TX 79918. TEL 915-744-8307, ATSS-CD@conus.army.mil, http://usasma.bliss.army.mil/.

355.37 SGP ISSN 0218-690X
N S MAN. Text in English. 1973. bi-m. adv. 44 p./no. 3 cols./p.; **Document type:** *Magazine, Consumer.* **Description:** Covers men's life-style topics for members of the Singapore Armed Forces.
Formerly: Reservist (0218-6896)
Published by: (S A F R A), S P H Magazines Pte Ltd. (Subsidiary of: Singapore Press Holdings Ltd.), 82 Genting Ln Level 7, Media Centre, Singapore, 349567, Singapore. TEL 65-6319-6319, FAX 65-6319-6345, sphmag@sph.com.sg, http://www.sphmagazines.com.sg/. adv.: B&W page SGD 1,500, color page SGD 2,300; 205 x 275. Circ: 108,000.

355 NZL ISSN 1170-8859
N Z ARMY NEWS. (New Zealand) Text in English. 1990. m. free. bk.rev. back issues avail. **Document type:** *Newspaper, Government.* **Description:** Provides news and information for service people, civilians, ex-service people, defense reporters, and those interested in the army.
Formerly (until Oct.2008): Army News (1170-4411)
Related titles: Online - full text ed.: ISSN 1177-3359.
Published by: New Zealand Army, New Zealand Army Defence House, 2-12 Aitken St, Private Bag 39997, Wellington, New Zealand. TEL 64-4-4960999. Ed. Judith Martin TEL 64-4-4960227.

355.1 RUS ISSN 0869-6403
UA770
NA BOEVOM POSTU/AT THE BEAT; ezhemesiachnyi voenno-publitsisticheskii i literaturno-khudozhestvennyi zhurnal vnutrennikh voisk. Text in Russian. 1958. m. USD 175 in United States. **Description:** Covers today's problems and the history of internal troops of Ministry of Internal Affairs as well as the traditions, biographies of military leaders.
Related titles: Microfiche ed.: (from EVP); Microfilm ed.: (from EVP, PQC).
Indexed: RASB.
—East View.
Published by: Glavnoe Upravlenie Komanduyushchego Vnutrennimi Voiskami MVD Rossiiskoi Federatsii, Syromyatnicheskii Proezd, 8, Moscow, 107120, Russian Federation. TEL 7-095-3618171, 7-095-3618257. Ed. L. I. Lukienko. **Dist. by:** East View Information Services, 10601 Wayzata Blvd, Minneapolis, MN 55305. TEL 952-252-1201, 800-477-1005, FAX 952-252-1202, info@eastview.com, http://www.eastview.com. **Co-publisher:** Ministerstvo Vnutrennikh Del Rossiiskoi Federatsii.

355 BLR
NA STRAZHE. Text in Russian. 104/yr. USD 275 in North America (effective 2000).
Published by: Ministerstvo Kul'tury Respubliki Belarus/Ministry of Culture, Vul Chicherina 1, Minsk, 220029, Belarus. TEL 0172-2769467. **Dist. by:** East View Information Services, 10601 Wayzata Blvd, Minneapolis, MN 55305. TEL 952-252-1201, 800-477-1005, FAX 952-252-1202, info@eastview.com, http://www.eastview.com.

355 RUS
NA STRAZHE RODINY; yezhednevnaya gazeta Leningradskogo voennogo okruga. Text in Russian. d. **Document type:** *Newspaper.*
Published by: Komanduyushchii Leningradskim Voennym Okrugom (Subsidiary of: Ministry of Defence of the Russian Federation/ Ministerstvo Oborony R F), Dvortsovaya Ploshad' 10, St. Petersburg, 191186, Russian Federation. TEL 7-812-2192328, 7-812-2192328, 7-812-2192185. Ed. V Yu Shtitsberg.

355 RUS
NA STRAZHE ZAPOLYARYA. Text in Russian. 1937. 104/yr. USD 795 in North America (effective 2000).
Published by: Ministry of Defence of the Russian Federation/Ministerstvo Oborony R F, Ul Sgibneva 9, Severomorsk, 184600, Russian Federation. TEL 6-69-40. Ed. N V Sytsevich. **Dist. by:** East View Information Services, 10601 Wayzata Blvd, Minneapolis, MN 55305. TEL 952-252-1201, 800-477-1005, FAX 952-252-1202, info@eastview.com, http://www.eastview.com.

355 PRT ISSN 0870-757X
NACAO E DEFESA. Text in Portuguese. 1976. irreg. **Document type:** *Journal, Government.*
Published by: Instituto da Defesa Nacional, Calcadas das Necessidades 5, Lisbon, 1399-017, Portugal. TEL 351-213-924600, idn.instituto@defesa.pt, http://www.idn.gov.pt.

NAPOLEON; international journal of the French Revolution and age of Napoleon. *see* HISTORY—History Of Europe

355 UKR
NARODNA ARMIYA. Text in Russian. 1943. 260/yr. UAK 163.68 domestic (effective 2011). **Document type:** *Magazine, Government.*
Formerly (until 1991): Leninskoe Znamya
Related titles: Microfilm ed.: (from EVP).
Indexed: RASB.
Published by: Ministerstvo Oborony Ukrainy, vul Mel'nykova 24, Kyiv, 04050, Ukraine. TEL 380-44-4890664, FAX 380-44-4890664, http://www.mil.gov.ua. Ed. Oleg Mahno.

353.538 USA ISSN 0027-853X
NATIONAL AMVET. Text in English. 1947. q. USD 10; USD 11 foreign (effective 1998). adv. bk.rev. charts; illus.; stat. **Document type:** *Bulletin, Trade.* **Description:** Articles and news of interest to veterans.
Published by: American Veterans of World War II, Korea and Vietnam (AMVETS), 4647 Forbes Blvd, Lanham, MD 20706. TEL 301-459-9600, FAX 301-459-7924. Ed. Richard W Flanagan. R&P Richard Flanagan. Adv. contact Cathy John. Circ: 180,000.

355 USA ISSN 0092-1491
CODEN: NTDFA2
NATIONAL DEFENSE. Text in English. 1920. m. USD 40 domestic; USD 45 foreign (effective 2009). adv. bk.rev. charts; illus.; stat. index. back issues avail.; reprints avail. **Document type:** *Magazine, Trade.* **Description:** Covers the issues influencing US defense policy and the defense industrial base.
Former titles (until 1973): Ordnance (0030-4557); (until 1947): Army Ordnance (0097-3696); Which incorporated (1946-1964): Armed Forces Chemical Journal (0097-4293); Which was formerly (until 1948): Chemical Corps Journal (0095-8611)
Related titles: Microform ed.: 1920 (from PQC); Online - full text ed.: ISSN 1943-3115.
Indexed: A01, A22, A26, AMB, AUNI, ChemAb, DM&T, G05, G06, G07, G08, I02, I05, IBR, IBZ, Inspec, LID&ISL, M05, M06, M07, P02, P10, P34, P47, P48, P52, P53, P54, PQC, RASB, T02.
—BLDSC (6021.869000), IE, Infotrieve, Ingenta, Linda Hall.
Published by: National Defense Industrial Association, 2111 Wilson Blvd, Ste 400, Arlington, VA 22201. TEL 703-522-1820, FAX 703-522-1885, tfletcher@ndia.org, http://www.ndia.org. Ed. Sandra Erwin TEL 703-247-2543. Pub. Lawrence P Farrell TEL 703-247-2549. adv.: B&W page USD 5,995, color page USD 7,715; 8.25 x 10.875. Circ: 28,000 (controlled).

NATIONAL DEFENSE ACADEMY. MEMOIRS. MATHEMATICS, PHYSICS, CHEMISTRY AND ENGINEERING/BOEI DAIGAKKO KIYO RIKOGAKU-HEN. *see* SCIENCES: COMPREHENSIVE WORKS

355 USA ISSN 0163-3945
UA42
NATIONAL GUARD. Text in English. 1947. m. USD 25 to non-members; free to members (effective 2010). adv. bk.rev. illus. back issues avail.; reprints avail. **Document type:** *Magazine, Trade.* **Description:** Features articles on Guard-related issues, programs, and activities at home and abroad.
Former titles (until 1978): Guardsman (0163-3953); (until 1975): National Guardsman (0027-9412)
Related titles: Microform ed.: (from PQC); Online - full text ed.
Indexed: A01, A22, AUNI, M05, M07, P02, P10, P16, P47, P48, P52, P53, P54, PQC, T02.
Published by: National Guard Association of the United States, One Massachusetts Ave, NW, Washington, DC 20001. TEL 202-789-0031, FAX 202-682-9358, ngaus@ngaus.org. Ed. Ron Jensen TEL 202-408-5885. Adv. contact Kim Hanson. B&W page USD 4,235, color page USD 5,865; trim 8.25 x 10.75.

355.4 006.3 USA ISSN 1557-0304
UG475
NATIONAL RECONNAISSANCE; journal of the discipline and practice. Text in English. 2001. a. **Document type:** *Journal, Government.*
Formerly (until 2005): Center for the Study of National Reconnaissance. Bulletin (1534-505X)
Published by: U.S. Department of Defense, Center for the Study of National Reconnaissance, 14675 Lee Rd, Chantilly, VA 20151. TEL 703-488-4733, csnr@nro.mil, http://www.nro.gov/index.html.

355 PHL ISSN 0115-5113
➤ **NATIONAL SECURITY REVIEW.** Text in English. 1973. q. free. bibl.; charts. **Document type:** *Journal, Academic/Scholarly.*
Indexed: ABCT, IPP.
Published by: National Defense College of the Philippines, Logcom Area, Camp Aguinaldo, Quezon City Mm, 1110, Philippines. Circ: 500 (controlled).

355 BGR ISSN 0324-0835
NATSIONALEN VOENNOISTORICHESKI MUZEI, SOFIA. IZVESTIYA. Text in Bulgarian. 1973. a. illus.
Published by: (Natsionalen Voennoistoricheski Muzei, Sofia), Izdatelstvo na M O, Iv Vazov ul 12, Sofia, Bulgaria.

355 RUS
NAUCHNYE ZAPISKI TSENTRA POLITICHESKIKH ISSLEDOVANII V ROSSII. Text in Russian. 1995. 3/yr. USD 105 in North America (effective 2000).
Published by: P I R - Tsentr, A-ya 17, Moscow, 117454, Russian Federation. TEL 7-095-3351955. **Dist. by:** East View Information Services, 10601 Wayzata Blvd, Minneapolis, MN 55305. TEL 952-252-1201, 800-477-1005, FAX 952-252-1202, info@eastview.com, http://www.eastview.com.

355 UKR
NAUKA I OBORONA. Text in Russian, Ukrainian. 1994. q. USD 254 in North America (effective 2000). **Document type:** *Journal, Government.*
Related titles: Online - full text ed.
Published by: (Ministerstvo Oborony Ukrainy), Vydavnytstvo Tekhnika, Vul Observatorna 25, Kyiv, Ukraine. TEL 380-44-2721080, FAX 380-44-2721088. Ed. Volodymyr Vahapov.

359 USA ISSN 0028-1409
VA49
NAVAL AFFAIRS; in the interest of the enlisted active duty, reserve and retired personnel of the U.S. Navy, Marine Corps and Coast Guard. Text in English. 1922. m. USD 7 to non-members; free to members (effective 2005). adv. **Document type:** *Magazine, Trade.*
Published by: Fleet Reserve Association, 125 N West St, Alexandria, VA 22314-2754. TEL 703-683-1400, 800-372-1924, FAX 703-549-6610. Ed., R&P, Adv. contact Lauren Armstrong. B&W page USD 2,850, color page USD 3,550; trim 10.5 x 8.25. Circ: 170,000 (controlled and free).

NAVAL & MILITARY PRESS. BOOKLIST. *see* PUBLISHING AND BOOK TRADE

NAVAL AVIATION NEWS. *see* AERONAUTICS AND SPACE FLIGHT

359 ZAF ISSN 1561-9060
VK119.S6
NAVAL DIGEST. Variant title: S A Naval Heritage Society. Journal. Text in English. 1996. s-a. ZAR 75 (effective 2007).
Published by: South African Naval Heritage Society, PO Box 521, Simon's Town, 7995, South Africa. TEL 27-21-6866309, cb@imt.co.za, http://www.simonstown.com/navalmuseum/sanheritage.htm.

NAVAL ENGINEERS JOURNAL. *see* ENGINEERING

359 DEU ISSN 0722-8880
V1
NAVAL FORCES; international forum for maritime power. Text in English. 1980. bi-m. EUR 85, USD 125; EUR 15, USD 22.50 newsstand/cover (effective 2008). adv. bk.rev. back issues avail. **Document type:** *Magazine, Trade.* **Description:** Provides specialist naval reports and features.
Related titles: Online - full text ed.
Indexed: A09, A10, A22, A26, AMB, AUNI, BMT, DM&T, G05, G06, G07, G08, I02, I05, LID&ISL, M05, M06, M07, P02, P10, P16, P47, P48, P52, P53, P54, PQC, T02, V03, V04.
—BLDSC (6064.210000), IE, Infotrieve, Ingenta. **CCC.**
Published by: Moench Verlagsgesellschaft mbH, Heilsbachstr 26, Bonn, 53123, Germany. TEL 49-228-64830, FAX 49-228-6483109, info@moench-group.com. Ed. Wolfgang Legien. Adv. contact Ute Steuer. B&W page EUR 4,500, color page EUR 7,500; trim 7.31 x 10.63. Circ: 15,957 (paid and controlled).

359.009 AUS ISSN 0158-5738
NAVAL HISTORICAL REVIEW. Text in English. 1970. q. AUD 35 (effective 2007). adv. **Document type:** *Journal, Academic/Scholarly.*
Published by: Naval Historical Society of Australia, The Boatshed, Bldg 25, Garden Island, NSW 2011, Australia. TEL 61-2-93592372, FAX 61-2-93592383, secretary@navyhistory.org.au. Ed., R&P, Adv. contact Tony Howland. Pub. Paul Martin. Circ: 1,200 (paid and controlled).

359 USA ISSN 1042-1920
V27
NAVAL HISTORY. Text in English. 1987. bi-m. USD 20 to members; USD 4.99 newsstand/cover in US & Canada (effective 2009). adv. bk.rev. illus. index. back issues avail.; reprints avail. **Document type:** *Journal, Academic/Scholarly.* **Description:** Covers naval history, including various areas, subjects and countries, and services branches.
Related titles: Online - full text ed.
Indexed: A01, A02, A03, A08, ABS&EES, AmH&L, CA, H05, HistAb, LID&ISL, M02, M05, M07, P02, P10, P47, P48, P52, P53, P54, PQC, T02, W04.
—Ingenta.
Published by: U S Naval Institute, 291 Wood Rd, Annapolis, MD 21401. TEL 410-268-6110, 800-233-8764, FAX 410-295-1049, customer@usni.org. Ed. Richard G Latture. Pub. William Miller. Adv. contact Dave Sheehan TEL 410-295-1041. color page USD 3,261; bleed 8.625 x 11.25.

359 USA ISSN 1057-4581
VA40
NAVAL INSTITUTE GUIDE TO COMBAT FLEETS OF THE WORLD. Text in English. 1976. biennial, latest 2007, 15th ed. USD 250 per issue to non-members; USD 200 per issue to members (effective 2011). back issues avail.; reprints avail. **Document type:** *Handbook/Manual/ Guide, Trade.*
Formerly (until 1991): Combat Fleets of the World (0364-3263)
Related titles: CD-ROM ed.: ISSN 1527-4195; French ed.
—BLDSC (3324.650000).
Published by: (U.S. Naval Institute), Naval Institute Press, 291 Wood Rd, Annapolis, MD 21402. TEL 410-268-6110, 800-233-8764, FAX 410-571-1703, customer@usni.org.

358.4 USA ISSN 1530-650X
VA61
THE NAVAL INSTITUTE GUIDE TO THE SHIPS AND AIRCRAFT OF THE U.S. FLEET. Variant title: Naval Institute Guide to Ships and Aircraft of the United States Fleet. Text in English. 1939. irreg., latest 2005, 18th ed. USD 100 per issue to non-members; USD 80 per issue to members (effective 2011). index. back issues avail.; reprints avail. **Document type:** *Handbook/Manual/Guide, Trade.*
Formerly (until 19??): Ships and Aircraft of the United States Fleet (0080-9292)
Published by: (U.S. Naval Institute), Naval Institute Press, 291 Wood Rd, Annapolis, MD 21402, TEL 410-268-6110, 800-233-8764, FAX 410-571-1703, customer@usni.org.

NAVAL POLICY AND HISTORY. *see* HISTORY

359 USA ISSN 0894-069X
V179 CODEN: NRLOEP
➤ **NAVAL RESEARCH LOGISTICS**; an international journal. Abbreviated title: N R L. Text in English. 1954. 8/yr. GBP 1,352 in United Kingdom to institutions; EUR 1,709 in Europe to institutions; USD 2,395 in United States to institutions; USD 2,507 in Canada & Mexico to institutions; USD 2,647 elsewhere to institutions; GBP 1,556 combined subscription in United Kingdom to institutions (print & online eds.); EUR 1,968 combined subscription in Europe to institutions (print & online eds.); USD 2,754 combined subscription in United States to institutions (print & online eds.); USD 2,866 combined subscription in Canada & Mexico to institutions (print & online eds.); USD 3,006 combined subscription elsewhere to institutions (print & online eds.) (effective 2012). adv. bibl.; charts. index, cum.index. back issues avail.; reprint service avail. from PSC. **Document type:** *Journal, Academic/Scholarly.* **Description:** Publishes articles on both theory and applications in key areas, including mathematical statistics, economics, tactics and strategy.
Formerly (until 1987): Naval Research Logistics Quarterly (0028-1441)
Related titles: Microform ed.: (from PQC); Online - full text ed.: ISSN 1520-6750. 1996. GBP 1,223 in United Kingdom to institutions; EUR 1,546 in Europe to institutions; USD 2,395 elsewhere to institutions (effective 2012).
Indexed: A22, A28, APA, ASCA, ApMecR, BrCerAb, C&ISA, CA, CA/WCA, CCMJ, CIA, CIS, CMCI, CPEI, CerAb, CivEngAb, CorrAb, CurCont, CybAb, E&CAJ, E11, EEA, EMA, ESPM, EngInd, EnvEAb, GeoRef, H15, IAOP, ISMEC, ISR, IUSGP, Inspec, JCQM, M&TEA, M05, M09, MBF, METADEX, MSN, MathR, ORMS, QC&AS, RASB, SCI, SCOPUS, ST&MA, SolStAb, SpeleolAb, T02, T04, W07, WAA, Z02.
—BLDSC (6064.995000), AskIEEE, IE, Infotrieve, Ingenta, INIST, Linda Hall. **CCC.**
Published by: John Wiley & Sons, Inc., 111 River St, Hoboken, NJ 07030. TEL 201-748-6000, FAX 201-748-6088, info@wiley.com, http://www.wiley.com/WileyCDA/. Ed. Awi Federgruen. **Subscr. outside the Americas to:** John Wiley & Sons Ltd.

359 USA
NAVAL RESERVIST NEWS; news of the total force Navy for the Naval Reserve community. Text in English. 1976. m. free to qualified personnel. illus. **Document type:** *Government.*
Published by: Commander, Naval Reserve Force, Public Affairs Office Code 004, 4400 Dauphine St, New Orleans, LA 70146-5046. TEL 504-678-6058, FAX 504-678-5049. Ed. Patricia S Antenucci. Circ: 100,000.

359 USA ISSN 0028-1484
V1
NAVAL WAR COLLEGE REVIEW. Text in English. 1948. q. free to qualified personnel (effective 2009). bk.rev. illus. index. back issues avail.; reprints avail. **Document type:** *Journal, Academic/Scholarly.* **Description:** Covers international security, defense and naval matters.
Related titles: Microform ed.: (from BHP, MIM, PQC); Online - full text ed.
Indexed: A01, A03, A08, A22, A26, ABS&EES, AMB, AUNI, AmH&L, B14, BAS, BRI, CA, CBRI, DIP, DM&T, E08, G05, G06, G07, G08, HistAb, I02, I05, I13, IBR, IBZ, IUSGP, LID&ISL, M05, M06, M07, MEA&I, P02, P06, P10, P13, P34, P42, P45, P47, P48, P52, P53, P54, PAIS, PQC, PRA, PSA, S09, SCOPUS, T02.
—Ingenta.
Published by: U.S. Naval War College, 686 Cushing Rd, Newport, RI 02841. TEL 401-841-2200, FAX 401-841-3579, PAO@usnwc.edu.

NAVAL WARGAMING REVIEW. *see* SPORTS AND GAMES

359 387 FRA ISSN 1280-4290
NAVIRES & HISTOIRE. Text in French. 1999. q. back issues avail. **Document type:** *Magazine, Consumer.*
Published by: Lela Presse, 29 Rue Paul Bert, Outreau, 62230, France. TEL 33-3-21338896, FAX 33-3-21320039, lela.presse@wanadoo.fr.

355 AUS ISSN 1035-6088
VA710
NAVY ANNUAL. Text in English. 1990. a. price varies. adv. back issues avail. **Document type:** *Bulletin, Government.* **Description:** Offers insight into a wide range of navy activities since the Gulf War.
Related titles: Online - full text ed.
Published by: Australia. Department of Defence, Chief of Naval Staff, Canberra, ACT 2600, Australia. Adv. contact Geoff Howard TEL 61-2-62667605. page AUD 5,500. Circ: 5,500 (controlled).

355.347 USA
VG23
NAVY CHAPLAIN. Text in English. 1955. q. free to qualified personnel (effective 2005). bk.rev. **Document type:** *Journal, Trade.*
Incorporates (in 1986): Navy Chaplains Bulletin (0028-1654); Porthole
Indexed: CERDIC.
Published by: (Office of the Navy Chief of Chaplains), U.S. Navy, Bureau of Naval Personnel, Washington, DC 20370. TEL 757-444-7665, FAX 757-445-1006. R&P B Bibson. Circ: 4,200 (controlled).

623 USA ISSN 0096-9419
VG593
NAVY CIVIL ENGINEER. Text in English. 1946. 3/yr. USD 7.50 (effective 2001). bk.rev. abstr.; charts; illus.; stat. index, cum.index. **Document type:** *Government.* **Description:** Features articles on the U.S. Navy's shore establishments throughout the world, along with technical articles on planning and designing, public works, construction and maintenance, utilities, transportation, and housing. Covers research and feature articles on the Civil Engineer Corps and the Seabees.
Related titles: Microform ed.: (from PQC).
Indexed: A22, GeotechAb, IUSGP, L09.

—IE, Ingenta, Linda Hall.
Published by: U.S. Naval Facilities Engineering Command, c/o Superintendent of Documents, US Govt Printing Office, Box 371594, Pittsburgh, PA 15250-7954. TEL 202-512-1800, FAX 202-512-2250. Ed. K Fedele. Circ: 12,700. **Subscr. to:** U.S. Government Printing Office, Superintendent of Documents, PO Box 371954, Pittsburgh, PA 15250. TEL 202-512-1800, FAX 202-512-2250, orders@gpo.gov, http://www.access.gpo.gov.

359 USA
NAVY EXPERIMENTAL DIVING UNIT. REPORT. Text in English. irreg.
Published by: U.S. Navy Experimental Diving Unit, 321 Bullfinch Rd, Panama City, FL 32407-7015. TEL 850-230-3100, FAX 850-234-4238, http://www.nedu.navsea.navy.mil/.

355 GBR
NAVY LIST OF RETIRED OFFICERS. Text in English. a. price varies. **Document type:** *Government.*
Published by: The Stationery Office, St Crispins, Duke St, Norwich, NR3 1PD, United Kingdom. TEL 44-1603-622211, FAX 44-870-6005533, customer.services@tso.co.uk, http://www.tso.co.uk.

359 GBR ISSN 0028-1670
NAVY NEWS. Text in English. 19??. m. GBP 20 domestic; GBP 26 foreign; GBP 2 newsstand/cover (effective 2010). adv. Website rev. illus. 6 cols./p.; back issues avail. **Document type:** *Newspaper, Consumer.* **Description:** Contains information directed to the navy and to naval enthusiasts.
Formerly (until 1954): Portsmouth Navy News : The Official Newspaper of the Portsmouth Command
Related titles: Online - full text ed.: free (effective 2009).
Address: Leviathan Block, H M S Nelson, Queen St, Portsmouth, Hants PO1 3HH, United Kingdom. TEL 44-2392-726284, FAX 44-2392-830149, edit@navynews.co.uk. Ed. Mike Gray TEL 44-23-92725136.

359 USA ISSN 0360-716X
VC35
NAVY SUPPLY CORPS NEWSLETTER. Text in English. 1937. bi-m. USD 20 (effective 2001).
Related titles: Online - full content ed.: ISSN 1554-9615; Online - full text ed.
Indexed: A26, G05, G06, G07, G08, I02, I05, M05, M06, M07, P10, P47, P48, P52, P53, P54, PQC, T02.
Published by: U.S. Department of the Navy, Supply Systems Command, Attn.: Newsletter, SUP 09PA, 5450 Carlisle Pike, PO Box 2050, Mechanicsburg, PA 17055-0791. TEL 703-607-1301, FAX 703-607-2221, Liz_Van_Wye@navsup.navy.mil, http://www.navsup.navy.mil. Ed. Linda Hall. Circ: 15,000 (controlled). **Subscr. to:** U.S. Government Printing Office, Superintendent of Documents, PO Box 371954, Pittsburgh, PA 15250. TEL 202-512-1800, FAX 202-512-2250, orders@gpo.gov, http://www.access.gpo.gov.

359 USA ISSN 0028-1697
NAVY TIMES. Text in English. 1951. w. USD 55; USD 3.25 newsstand/cover (effective 2009). adv. bk.rev. charts; illus.; mkt.; stat. reprints avail. **Document type:** *Newspaper, Trade.* **Description:** Serving all sea service personnel and their families.
Incorporates (1947-1952): Armed Force; Which was formerly (1945-1947): Army and Navy Bulletin
Related titles: Microform ed.: (from PQC); Online - full text ed.: NavyTimes.com. ISSN 1943-5797. USD 29.95 (effective 2009); International ed.; ◆ Supplement(s): Handbook for Military Life. ISSN 1541-4434; Handbook for the Guard & Reserve. ISSN 1936-1599.
Indexed: A22, AUNI, M01, M02, M05, P34, P52, RASB, T02, V02.
—CCC.
Published by: Army Times Publishing Co. (Subsidiary of: Gannett Company, Inc.), 6883 Commercial Dr, Springfield, VA 22159. TEL 703-750-7400, 800-368-5718, cust-svc@atpco.com, http://www.gannett.com/about/map/armytimes.htm. Ed. Tobias Naegele. adv.: color page USD 22,190; 10.25 x 11.25. Circ: 52,501 (paid).

NEDERLANDS MILITAIR GENEESKUNDIG TIJDSCHRIFT. *see* MEDICAL SCIENCES

355 USA ISSN 1548-9256
UG478
NETDEFENSE; the global report on netowrk-centric operations for defense and security leaders. Variant title: Aviation Week's NetDefense. Aviation Week's Netdefense. Text in English. 2004 (Jan.). w. **Document type:** *Journal, Trade.* **Description:** Covers current news, policy developments, programs and business opportunities across all defense and security applications of network-centric operations.
Related titles: E-mail ed.; Online - full content ed.
—CCC.
Published by: Aviation Week Group (Subsidiary of: McGraw-Hill Companies, Inc.), 2 Penn Plz, 25th Fl, New York, NY 10121. TEL 800-525-5003, FAX 888-385-1428, buccustserv@cdsfulfillment.com, http://www.aviationweek.com.

355 NLD ISSN 1877-0800
NETHERLANDS DEFENCE ACADEMY. FACULTY OF MILITARY SCIENCES. ANNUAL RESEARCH REPORT. Text in English. 2008. a.
Published by: Nederlandse Defensie Academie, Faculteit Militaire Wetenschappen, Postbus 90002, Breda, 4800 PA, Netherlands. FAX 31-76-5273521, nlda@mindef.nl.

355 USA
NEW BREED. Text in English. 1982. bi-m. USD 17. adv. bk.rev. **Description:** Covers all areas of the military: history, law enforcement, weapons and intelligence.
Published by: New Breed Publications, Inc., PO Box 428, Nanuet, NY 10954. Ed. Harry Belil. Circ: 68,000.

353.538 USA ISSN 0094-7326
UB358.N6
NEW MEXICO. VETERANS' SERVICE COMMISSION. REPORT. Key Title: Report of the New Mexico Veteran's Service Commission. Text in English. a. free (effective 2005). charts; stat. **Document type:** *Corporate.*
Published by: Veterans' Service Commission, Bataan Memorial Building, 408 Galisteo St, Box 2324, Santa Fe, NM 87503. TEL 505-827-6300, 866-433-8387, FAX 505-827-6372, http://www.state.nm.us/veterans/vschome.html. Circ: 100.

353.538 USA
NEW YORK (STATE) ASSEMBLY. STANDING COMMITTEE ON VETERANS' AFFAIRS. ANNUAL REPORT. Text in English. a. free. **Document type:** *Proceedings, Government.*
Published by: State Assembly, Rm 841, Legislative Office Bldg, Albany, NY 12248. TEL 518-455-4897, FAX 518-455-4861.

363.286 USA
NEW YORK HARBOR WATCH. Text in English. 1989. w. (Thu.). USD 15; free domestic to military (effective 2005). **Document type:** *Newspaper.*
Published by: Courier-Life, Inc., 1733 Sheepshead Bay Rd., Brooklyn, NY 11235-3606. TEL 718-615-2500, 718-615-3830. Eds. Norman Fallick, Susan Blake. Circ: 12,000 (controlled and free).

355.357 NZL ISSN 1176-7014
NEW ZEALAND DEFENCE FORCE. STATEMENT OF INTENT. Text in English. 1995. a. **Document type:** *Government.* **Description:** Provides a summary of what the NZDF intends to achieve over the medium term (three to five years) and how it intends to do this. Statements of Intent form part of the supporting information provided by the annual Estimates of Appropriations.
Formerly (until 2005): New Zealand Defence Force. Departmental Forecast Report (1173-4701)
Related titles: Online - full text ed.: ISSN 1179-013X.
Published by: New Zealand Defence Force, 15-21 Stout St, Private Bag, Wellington, New Zealand. TEL 64-4-4960999, FAX 64-4-4960869.

355.6 NZL ISSN 1177-6161
NEW ZEALAND. MINISTRY OF DEFENCE. STATEMENT OF INTENT. Text in English. 2004. a.
Media: Online - full text.
Published by: Ministry of Defence, PO Box 5347, Lambton Quay, Wellington, New Zealand. TEL 64-4-4960999, FAX 64-4-4960859, info@defence.govt.nz.

359 USA
NEWPORT NAVALOG. Text in English. 1901. w. (Fri.). free (effective 2008). adv. 20 p./no. 5 cols./p.; **Document type:** *Newspaper.* **Description:** Civilian enterprise newspaper published for the naval education and training center, Newport, Rhode Island.
Published by: Edward A. Sherman Publishing Co., 101 Malbone Rd, Newport, RI 02840. TEL 401-849-3300, FAX 401-849-3335. Pub. Albert K Sherman Jr. adv.: col. inch USD 17. Circ: 4,000 (free).

359 USA ISSN 1544-6824
V420
THE NEWPORT PAPERS. Text in English. 1991. irreg. price varies. back issues avail. **Document type:** *Monographic series, Academic/Scholarly.*
Related titles: Online - full text ed.: free (effective 2010).
Indexed: LID&ISL.
Published by: (Naval War College), Naval War College Press, 686 Cushing Rd, Newport, RI 02841. TEL 401-841-2236, FAX 401-841-6309, press@nwc.navy.mil.

355.009 USA
NEWSLETTER OF THE S.L.A. MARSHALL MILITARY HISTORY COLLECTION. Text in English. 1980. irreg., latest vol.16, 1991. free. bk.rev. **Document type:** *Newsletter.* **Description:** Presents news of developments in the collection. Distributed to military historians, active-duty and retired military officers, and libraries with an institutional interest in military history.
Published by: University of Texas at El Paso, University Library, 500 W University Ave, El Paso, TX 79968. TEL 915-747-6717, FAX 915-747-5345. Ed., R&P Thomas F Burdett. Circ: 500.

355 RUS ISSN 1810-1674
NEZAVISIMOE VOENNOE OBOZRENIE. Text in Russian. w. USD 629 foreign (effective 2005). **Document type:** *Newspaper, Consumer.* **Description:** Designed for politically active sections of society, it offers articles and commentaries by independent experts and researchers on problems of the Russian military international security.
Related titles: Online - full content ed.: ISSN 1810-1682; ◆ Supplement to: Nezavisimaya Gazeta. ISSN 1560-1005.
Published by: Nezavisimaya Gazeta, Myasnitskaya 13, Moscow, 101000, Russian Federation. TEL 7-095-9255543, info@ng.ru, http://www.ng.ru. **Dist. by:** East View Information Services, 10601 Wayzata Blvd, Minneapolis, MN 55305. TEL 952-252-1201, 800-477-1005, FAX 952-252-1202, info@eastview.com, http://www.eastview.com.

NIHON SEMPAKU KAIYOU KOUGAKKAI ROMBUNSHUU/JAPAN SOCIETY OF NAVAL ARCHITECTS AND OCEAN ENGINEERS. JOURNAL. *see* TRANSPORTATION—Ships And Shipping

NO LIMITS; life after high school in Wisconsin. *see* CHILDREN AND YOUTH—About

THE NONPROLIFERATION REVIEW. *see* POLITICAL SCIENCE—International Relations

355 NOR ISSN 0029-1692
NORGES FORSVAR. Text in Norwegian. 1951. 10/yr. NOK 395 domestic (effective 2007). bk.rev. illus. index. **Document type:** *Magazine, Trade.*
Related titles: ◆ Supplement(s): Norwegian Defence Review. ISSN 0803-3250.
Indexed: CCMJ, RASB.
—CCC.
Published by: Norges Forsvarsforening/Norwegian Defence Association, Postboks 5235, Majorstua, Oslo, 0303, Norway. TEL 47-23-196262, FAX 47-23-196270, foreningspost@forsvarsforening.no.

355 NOR ISSN 0029-1854
NORSK ARTILLERI-TIDSSKRIFT. Text in Norwegian. 1900. 4/yr. NOK 100 (effective 1997). adv. bk.rev. charts; illus. index. **Document type:** *Academic/Scholarly.*
Published by: Artilleriets Offisersforening, Artilleriregimentet, Haslemoen, 2437, Norway. TEL 47-62-42-92-01, FAX 47-62-42-90-14. Ed. K Gillingsrud. Circ: 600.

355 NOR ISSN 0029-2028
U4
NORSK MILITAERT TIDSSKRIFT/NORWEGIAN MILITARY JOURNAL. Text in Norwegian. 1830. q. NOK 200 domestic; NOK 300 domestic to institutions; NOK 400 elsewhere; NOK 42 per issue (effective 2011). adv. bk.rev. illus. index. back issues avail. **Document type:** *Magazine, Consumer.*
Related titles: Online - full text ed.: 2001.
Indexed: HistAb, RASB.
Published by: (Oslo Militaere Samfund), Norsk Militaert Tidsskrift/Norwegian Military Journal, Tollbugt 10, Oslo, 0152, Norway. Ed. Harald Hoeiback TEL 47-23-095783. Adv. contact Geir Karstensen TEL 47-55-540803. Circ: 2,500.

359 NOR ISSN 0029-2222
V5
NORSK TIDSSKRIFT FOR SJOVESEN. Text in Norwegian. 1882. 6/yr. NOK 90. adv. bk.rev. illus. index.
Indexed: RASB.
Published by: Sjomilitaere Samfund, Postboks 150, Hundvaag, 4086, Norway. Ed. Svein C Sivertsen. Circ: 2,300.

NORTH CAROLINA AMERICAN LEGION NEWS. *see* CLUBS

338.473 951.93 363.35 GBR ISSN 1749-1541
NORTH KOREA DEFENCE & SECURITY REPORT. Text in English. 2005. a. EUR 820, USD 1,030 combined subscription per issue (print & email eds.) (effective 2010). **Document type:** *Report, Trade.* **Description:** Provides industry leaders, defense manufacturers and suppliers, intelligence agencies and governments with independent forecasts and competitive intelligence on the defense and security industry in North Korea.
Related titles: E-mail ed.
Indexed: B01.
Published by: Business Monitor International Ltd., Senator House, 85 Queen Victoria St, London, EC4V 4AB, United Kingdom. TEL 44-20-72480468, FAX 44-20-72480467, subs@businessmonitor.com.

NORTHERN IRELAND NEWS SERVICE; NINS NewsBreak. *see* POLITICAL SCIENCE

358.4 USA
NORTHWEST AIRLIFTER. Text in English. 1968. w. free. adv. **Document type:** *Newspaper, Government.* **Description:** Contains news, mission stories and entertainment for military personnel and families of McChord AFB.
Published by: 62nd Airlift Wing Public Affairs, 100 Main St., Ste. 1050, Mcchord Afb, WA 98438. TEL 206-984-5637, FAX 206-984-5025. Ed. Stuart Camp. Pub. Tom Swarner. Circ: 8,200.

355 USA
NORTHWEST GUARDIAN. Text in English. w. (Fri.). free (effective 2008). **Document type:** *Newspaper.*
Published by: Commanding General of Fort Lewis, Public Affairs Office, Attn.: IMNW-LEW, Fort Lewis, Pierce, WA 98433-9500. TEL 253-967-0173, FAX 253-967-0850. Circ: 20,700 (free).

355 NOR ISSN 0803-3250
UA750
NORWEGIAN DEFENCE REVIEW. Text in Norwegian, English. 1977. a. **Document type:** *Journal, Trade.*
Related titles: ◆ Supplement to: Norges Forsvar. ISSN 0029-1692.
Published by: Norges Forsvarsforening/Norwegian Defence Association, Postboks 5235, Majorstua, Oslo, 0303, Norway. TEL 47-23-196262, FAX 47-23-196270, foreningspost@forsvarsforening.no, http://www.forsvarsforening.no.

355 CHE
NOTRE ARMEE DE MILICE. Text in German. 10/yr.
Address: Postfach 501, Yverdon-les-Bains 1, 1400, Switzerland. TEL 024-217424, FAX 024-220939. Ed. J H Schule. Circ: 15,839.

355 RUS ISSN 1028-9674
NOVOSTI RAZVEDKI I KONTRAZVEDKI. Text in Russian; Summaries in English, Russian. s-m. USD 84 foreign (effective 2003). adv. **Document type:** *Newspaper, Consumer.* **Description:** Provides information about special service activities of Russia and the CIS, as well as many other countries around the world.
Related titles: Microfiche ed.: (from EVP).
Indexed: RASB.
Published by: Novosti Spezsluzhb, A-ya 75, Moscow, 123056, Russian Federation. TEL 7-095-9751302, FAX 7-095-9751179, chief@intelligence.ru. Ed. M.G. Zaugaev. Pub. M A Zaugaev. R&P M G Zaugaev TEL 7-095-2551334. Adv. contact Valery D Isaev. page USD 700. Circ: 50,000. **Dist. by:** East View Information Services, 10601 Wayzata Blvd, Minneapolis, MN 55305. TEL 952-252-1201, 800-477-1005, FAX 952-252-1202, info@eastview.com, http://www.eastview.com; M K - Periodica, ul Gilyarovskogo 39, Moscow 129110, Russian Federation. TEL 7-095-2845008, FAX 7-095-2813798, info@periodicals.ru, http://www.mkniga.ru.

355 USA ISSN 1083-2246
NOW HEAR THIS - U S S CALLAWAY NEWSLETTER. Text in English. 1965. s-a. **Document type:** *Newsletter.* **Description:** Contains news of interest to WWII veterans of USS Callaway and the U.S. Coast Guard.
Published by: U S S Callaway Association, 5319 Manning Pl, N W, Washington, DC 20013-5311. TEL 202-363-3663. Ed. Dorothy Shipp. Pubs. Dorothy Shipp, Wallace Shipp. R&P Wallace Shipp. Circ: 369 (controlled).

358.4183 POL ISSN 1230-1655
U4
NOWA TECHNIKA WOJSKOWA. Text in Polish. 1991. m. EUR 71 foreign (effective 2006). **Document type:** *Magazine, Trade.*
Formerly (until 1992): Technika Wojskowa (0867-5635)
Published by: Wydawnictwo Magnum-X, ul Skrajna 1/25, Warsaw, 03209, Poland. TEL 48-22-8103330, magnum@hbz.com.pl. **Dist. by:** Ars Polona, Obroncow 25, Warsaw 03933, Poland. TEL 48-22-5098609, FAX 48-22-5098610, arspolona@arspolona.com.pl, http://www.arspolona.com.pl.

355 ITA
IL NUOVO GIORNALE DEI MILITARI. Text in Italian. 1952. w. EUR 59 to institutions (effective 2009). adv. **Document type:** *Magazine, Trade.*
Formerly: Giornale dei Militari
Related titles: Online - full text ed.
Published by: Il Nuovo Giornale dei Militari, Via Savona 6, Rome, 00182, Italy. TEL 39-06-70304885. Circ: 60,000.

355 USA
O I W COMMUNIQUE. Text in English. 1979. m. USD 20 (effective 1999). **Document type:** *Newsletter.* **Description:** Devoted to the study and historic preservation of Indian Wars sites.
Published by: Order of the Indian Wars, PO Box 7401, Little Rock, AR 72217. TEL 501-225-3996. Ed. Jerry L Russell. Circ: 500 (paid).

O P C W ANNUAL REPORT. *see* POLITICAL SCIENCE

355 RUS
OBORONNYI KOMPLEKS - NAUCHNO-TEKHNICHESKOMU PROGRESSU ROSSII. Text in Russian. irreg.
Published by: V.I.M.I., Volokolamskoe shosse 77, Moscow, 123584, Russian Federation. TEL 7-095-4911306, FAX 7-095-4916820. **Dist. by:** East View Information Services, 10601 Wayzata Blvd, Minneapolis, MN 55305. TEL 952-252-1201, 800-477-1005, FAX 952-252-1202, info@eastview.com, http://www.eastview.com.

355 HRV ISSN 1332-6856
U4
OBRANA. Text in Croatian. 2000. w. **Document type:** *Magazine, Trade.*
Published by: Ministarstvo Obrane Republike Hrvatske, Zvonimirova 12, Zagreb, 10000, Croatia. TEL 385-1-4568041, FAX 385-1-4550075.

OBRANA A STRATEGIE/DEFENCE & STRATEGY. *see* POLITICAL SCIENCE—International Relations

ODBRANA I ZASTITA. *see* CIVIL DEFENSE

355 AUT ISSN 0048-1440
U3
OESTERREICHISCHE MILITAERISCHE ZEITSCHRIFT. Text in German. 1963. bi-m. EUR 24.30; EUR 12.20 to students; EUR 4.70 newsstand/cover (effective 2006). adv. bk.rev. charts; illus.; maps; stat. index. reprints avail. **Document type:** *Journal, Academic/Scholarly.*
Related titles: CD-ROM ed.: EUR 21.80 (effective 2001).
Indexed: A22, AMB, AmH&L, CA, DIP, HistAb, IBR, IBZ, LID&ISL, P30, PRA, RASB, RefZh, T02.
—IE, Infotrieve.
Published by: Bundesministerium fuer Landesverteidigung, Landesverteidigungsakademie, Stiftgasse 2a, Vienna, W 1070, Austria. TEL 43-1-520040901, FAX 43-1-520017108, http://www.bmlv.gv.at/organisation/beitraege/lvak/index.shtml. Circ: 5,000.

359 USA
OFFICE OF NAVAL RESEARCH. TECHNICAL REPORT. Text in English. irreg.
Published by: U.S. Office of Naval Research, 800 N Quincy St, BCT1, Arlington, VA 22217-5660. TEL 703-696-5031, FAX 703-696-6940, onrpao@onr.navy.mil, http://www.onr.navy.mil.

355 USA ISSN 0030-0268
UA23.A1
THE OFFICER. Text in English. 1924. 10/yr. USD 24 domestic to non-members; USD 34 foreign to non-members; free to members (effective 2007). adv. bk.rev. illus. 72 p./no.; reprints avail. **Document type:** *Magazine, Trade.* **Description:** Covers active and reserve force activities of the Army, Navy, Air Force, Coast Guard, Public Health Service and National Oceanic and Atmospheric Administration, as well as congressional and administrative actions affecting the nation's uniformed services.
Related titles: Microform ed.: (from PQC); Online - full text ed.
Indexed: A01, A22, A26, ABS&EES, AUNI, G05, G06, G07, G08, I02, I05, I06, I07, M05, M06, M07, P02, P10, P47, P48, P52, P53, P54, PQC, RASB, S23, T02.
Published by: Reserve Officers Association of the United States, One Constitution Ave, N E, Washington, DC 20002-5655. TEL 202-479-2200, FAX 202-479-0416, info@roa.org, http://www.roa.org. Ed. Eric Minton. Pub. Lt.Col. Dennis McCarthy. Adv. contact Cari Burnett. B&W page USD 3,475, color page USD 5,000. Circ: 65,000 (controlled).

355 USA ISSN 0736-7317
U56
OFFICER REVIEW. Text in English. 1962. 10/yr. USD 15 (effective 2007). adv. bk.rev. charts; illus. 32 p./no. 2 cols./p.; **Document type:** *Magazine, Consumer.*
Formerly (until 1974): World Wars Officer Review (0512-381X)
Related titles: Online - full text ed.
Indexed: A01, A03, A08, A10, P34, T02, V03.
Published by: Military Order of the World Wars, 435 N Lee St, Alexandria, VA 22314. TEL 703-683-4911, 877-320-3774, FAX 703-683-4501, moww@comcast.net. adv.: page USD 725. Circ: 12,000.

355 USA ISSN 1040-029X
OFFICERS CALL. Text in English. 1981. q. looseleaf. membership only. adv. bk.rev. back issues avail. **Document type:** *Newsletter.* **Description:** Focuses on benefits and entitlement programs for military personnel, as well as on issues relating to financial management, second careers, and other military-related issues.
Published by: National Officers Association, PO Box 4999, Reston, VA 20195-1465. TEL 703-438-3060, FAX 703-438-3072. Ed., R&P, Adv. contact Meghan Monaghan. Circ: 9,000 (controlled).

355.3 SWE ISSN 0280-2759
OFFICERSTIDNINGEN; medlemstidning foerr Officersfoerbundet. Text in Swedish. 1982. 10/yr. SEK 185 in Scandinavia; SEK 225 elsewhere. adv. bk.rev. **Description:** Publishes information and debate about Swedish national defense, military leadership, education and working conditions.
Formed by merger of (1932-1982): Officersfoerbundsbladet (0345-8873); (1972-1982): Kompaniofficeren (0345-634X); Which was formerly: Svenske Underofficeren; (1976-1982): Pluntonofficren (0347-4658); Which was formerly (1972-1976): Plutonofficerstidningen (0345-942X)
Published by: Officersfoerbundet, Fack 5338, Stockholm, 10247, Sweden. TEL 08-440-83-49, FAX 08-440-83-50. Ed., R&P Svante Palme. Adv. contact Monica Wistedt.

358.4 NOR ISSN 0332-7159
OFFISERSBLADET. Text in Norwegian. 1945. 8/yr. NOK 250 domestic; NOK 300 elsewhere (effective 2002). adv. bk.rev. index.
Formerly (until 1948): Medlemsblad - Haerens Offisers-Forbund (0802-524X); Superseded in part (in 1983): Norsk Luftmilitaert Tidsskrift (0029-201X)
Indexed: GeoRef, SpeleolAb.
Published by: Befalets Fellesorganisasjon, Karl Johansgaten 12, PO Box 501, Sentrum, Oslo, 0105, Norway. TEL 47-23-10-02-20, FAX 47-23-10-02-25. Ed. Einar Holst Clausen TEL 47-23-10-02-42. Adv. contact Lars-Kristian Berg TEL 47-22-17-35-23. B&W page NOK 9,800, color page NOK 12,700; 185 x 260. Circ: 10,250.

355 CHE
DER OFFIZIER. Text in German. 1932. 3/yr. **Document type:** *Journal, Trade.*
Formerly (until 2001): O G B Mitteilungen
Published by: Offiziersgesellschaft der Stadt Bern, Hargarte 4, Ueberstorf, 3182, Switzerland. info@ogb.ch, http://www.ogb.ch. Circ: 3,300.

OHIO CIVIL WAR GENEALOGY JOURNAL. *see* GENEALOGY AND HERALDRY

355.31 USA
OHIO LEGION NEWS. Text in English. m. adv. **Document type:** *Newspaper.*
Published by: American Legion, Department of Ohio, 60 Big Run Rd, P O Box 8007, Delaware, OH 43015. TEL 740-362-7478, FAX 740-362-1429, ohlegion@iwaynet.net. Ed., R&P Mike Wiswell. Adv. contact Brian Barr. Circ: 148,000.

355 JPN
OKINAWA GUIDE. Text in English. 1998. a. adv. **Description:** Provides information for US servicemen in Okinawa. Includes news and entertainment listings, classifieds, and a calendar of local events.
Published by: M C C S Marketing, MCB Camp SD Butler, Unit 35023, FPO AP OKINAWA, 96373, Japan. TEL 91-611-745-3970, FAX 81-611-745-0975. Adv. contact Alex Kirkland.

355 JPN
OKINAWA LIVING. Text in English. m. adv. **Description:** Includes recreation information for US servicemen living in Okinawa.
Published by: M C C S Marketing, MCB Camp SD Butler, Unit 35023, FPO AP OKINAWA, 96373, Japan. TEL 91-611-745-3970, FAX 81-611-745-0975.

355 JPN
OKINAWA MARINE. Text in English. w. adv. **Description:** Contains news, entertainment listings, and other information for US servicemen living in Okinawa.
Published by: M C C S Marketing, MCB Camp SD Butler, Unit 35023, FPO AP OKINAWA, 96373, Japan. TEL 91-611-745-3970, FAX 81-611-745-0975.

355 USA
OKINAWA TODAY. Text in English. 1982. fortn. adv. **Description:** Military consumer magazine.
Address: 825 Old Country Rd, Westbury, NY 11590. TEL 516-334-3030. Ed. Kari Valtaoja. Circ: 15,000.

OKLAHOMA LEGIONNAIRE. *see* CLUBS

OKRETY WOJENNE; magazyn milosnikow spraw wojennomorskich. *see* TRANSPORTATION—Ships And Shipping

355 USA ISSN 1064-007X
ON GUARD. Text in English. 1986. s-a. looseleaf. USD 10 (effective 1999). bk.rev. back issues avail. **Document type:** *Newspaper.* **Description:** Covers human rights, civil rights, and liberties; issues for active-duty military personnel.
Related titles: Microform ed.: (from PQC).
Indexed: AltPI.
Published by: Citizen Soldier, 175 Fifth Ave, Ste 2135, New York, NY 10010. TEL 212-679-2250. Ed. Thomas Ensign. Circ: 15,000.

355 USA ISSN 1947-4997
U1
▼ **ON PATROL**; until everyone comes home. Text in English. 2009. q. free to individual members (effective 2009). **Document type:** *Magazine, Consumer.* **Description:** Official magazine of the USO, providing inspirational stories, information and resources for troops.
Related titles: Online - full text ed.: ISSN 1947-5004.
Published by: United Services Association, 2111 Wilson Blvd, Ste 1200, Arlington, VA 22201. TEL 703-908-6446, amitchell@uso.org.

355.31 USA
ON POINT: THE JOURNAL OF ARMY HISTORY. Text in English. q.
Published by: Army Historical Foundation, Inc., 2425 Wilson Boulevard, Arlington, VA 22201. TEL 703-522-7901, FAX 703-522-7929.

359 USA ISSN 1047-1731
ON WATCH. Text in English. 1988. bi-m. free. **Document type:** *Newsletter.* **Description:** For enlisted (active duty and reserve) members of the U.S. Navy, Marine Corps and Coast Guard.
Published by: Fleet Reserve Association, 125 N West St, Alexandria, VA 22314-2754. TEL 703-683-1400, 800-372-1924, FAX 703-549-6610, http://www.fra.org. Ed. Lauren Armstrong. Circ: 165,000.

358.4 NLD ISSN 0030-3208
ONZE LUCHTMACHT. Text in Dutch. 1948. bi-m. EUR 28 domestic; EUR 36.50 foreign (effective 2009). adv. bk.rev. illus. index.
Published by: Koninklijke Nederlandse Vereniging "Onze Luchtmacht", Potgieterlaan 1, Hilversum, 1215 AH, Netherlands. TEL 31-33-2773219, admin@onzeluchtmacht.nl, http://www.onzeluchtmacht.nl. Ed. W F Helfferich TEL 31-35-6247335. Adv. contact Johan C Breukelaar TEL 31-43-4501845.

ORDERS AND MEDALS SOCIETY OF AMERICA. JOURNAL. *see* HOBBIES

355 GUM
ORDERS GUAM. Text in English. 1976. a. free to qualified personnel.
Published by: Glimpses of Guam, Inc., P O Box 3191, Agana, Guam 96910, Guam. Circ: 10,000.

355 ITA
ORDINE DI MALTA. NEWSLETTER. Text in Italian, English. 1969. irreg. charts; illus. **Document type:** *Newsletter, Consumer.*
Media: Online - full text. **Related titles:** Italian ed.; English ed.
Published by: Ordine di Malta, Palazzo Malta, Via Condotti 68, Rome, 00187, Italy. TEL 39-06-675811, FAX 39-06-6797202.

ORDINES MILITARES. *see* HISTORY

355 GBR ISSN 0957-1698
UF145 CODEN: JOSOET
ORDNANCE SOCIETY. JOURNAL. Text in English. 1989. a. GBP 19.50, USD 35 to individual members; GBP 29, USD 50 to institutional members (effective 2009). **Document type:** *Journal, Trade.* **Description:** Provides a forum for the exchange and publication of information about the history and development of artillery.
Indexed: BrArAb, NumL.
—BLDSC (4837.440000).
Published by: Ordnance Society, c/o Mr Ian McKenzie, Membership Secretary, 3 Maskell Way, Farnborough, Hamps GU14 0PU, United Kingdom. TEL 44-1252-521201, ordnance.society@virgin.net, http://freespace.virgin.net/ordnance.society/. Ed. R Jenkins. Circ: 240 (paid).

355 RUS
ORUZHEINYI DVOR. Text in Russian. 1994. bi-m. USD 125 in North America (effective 2000).
Published by: Izdatels'tvo/Promo Media, B Gnezdnikovskii per 10 ofis 819, Moscow, 103009, Russian Federation. TEL 7-095-2296614. **Dist. by:** East View Information Services, 10601 Wayzata Blvd, Minneapolis, MN 55305. TEL 952-252-1201, 800-477-1005, FAX 952-252-1202, info@eastview.com, http://www.eastview.com.

355 KAZ
OTAN SAKSHYSY. Text in Kazakh. w.
Related titles: Russian ed.: Chasovoi Rodiny.
Published by: Komitet po Okhrane Gosudarstvennoi Granitsy Respubliki Kazakhstan, Ul Nauryzbai Batyra 77, Almaty, 480091, Kazakstan. TEL 7-327-60038, 7-327-60091. Ed. Sagidolla Sikhymbaev.

OVERSEAS DEVELOPMENT GROUP. HUMANITARIAN PRACTICE NETWORK PAPERS. *see* POLITICAL SCIENCE

355 FRA ISSN 0154-7313
LE P G - C A T M. (Prisonniers de Guerre Combattants d'Algerie de Tunise et Maroc) Text in French. 1971 (vol.26). m. (11/yr.). EUR 15 domestic; EUR 17 foreign (effective 2008). bk.rev. bibl.; charts; illus. **Document type:** *Newspaper, Consumer.*
Former titles: C A T M; P G - Prisonniers de Guerre (0048-2595)
Indexed: RASB.
Published by: Federation Nationale des Prisonniers de Guerre Combattants d'Algerie de Tunise et Maroc, 46 rue Copernic, Paris, Cedex 16 75782, France. TEL 33-1-53642000, FAX 33-1-53642020. Ed. Jean Dodgio. Pub. Joseph Girard. Circ: 120,000.

355 USA ISSN 1949-7059
P K S O I BULLETIN. Text in English. 2008. q. free (effective 2009). back issues avail. **Document type:** *Bulletin, Trade.*
Media: Online - full content.
Published by: Peacekeeping and Stability Operations Institute, Upton Hall, 22 Ashburn Dr, Carlisle, PA 17013. TEL 717-245-3722, CARL_PKSOI_Operations@conus.army.mil, https://pksoi.army.mil.

P T S D RESEARCH QUARTERLY. (Post-Traumatic Stress Disorder) *see* MEDICAL SCIENCES—Psychiatry And Neurology

355 FIN ISSN 0788-8554
U4
PAALLYSTOLEHTI. Text in Finnish; Summaries in Swedish. 1930. m. free. adv. bk.rev. **Document type:** *Magazine, Trade.*
Former titles (until 1989): Toimiupseeri (0355-726X); (until 1974): Aliupseeri (0002-5445); (until 1954): Sauli
Related titles: Online - full text ed.
Published by: Paallystoliitto/Finnish Noncommissioned Officer Association, Ratamestarinkatu 11, Helsinki, 00520, Finland. TEL 358-70-3247500, FAX 358-70-3247410, http://ww.paallystoliitto.fi. Ed. Mika Oramen.

355 JPN
PACIFIC STARS & STRIPES. Text in Japanese. d. **Document type:** *Newspaper.*
Address: 23-17 Roppongi 7-chome, Minato-ku, Tokyo, 106-0032, Japan. TEL 81-3-3408-8936, FAX 81-3-3408-8936. Ed. Robert Trounson. Circ: 27,000.

PAKISTAN ARMED FORCES MEDICAL JOURNAL. *see* MEDICAL SCIENCES

355.31 PAK ISSN 0030-9656
PAKISTAN ARMY JOURNAL. Text in English. 1956. q. PKR 90, USD 8. bk.rev.
Indexed: LID&ISL, RASB.
Published by: Inspector General Training & Evaluation Branch, Training Publications & Information Directorate, General Staff Branch, General Headquarters, Rawalpindi, Pakistan. Ed. Lt.Col. Syed Ishia Ali. Circ: 3,500.

338.473 954.91 363.35 GBR ISSN 1749-155X
PAKISTAN DEFENCE & SECURITY REPORT. Text in English. 2005. q. EUR 820, USD 1,030 combined subscription (print & email eds.) (effective 2010). **Document type:** *Report, Trade.* **Description:** Provides industry leaders, defense manufacturers and suppliers, intelligence agencies and governments with independent forecasts and competitive intelligence on the defense and security industry in Pakistan.
Related titles: E-mail ed.
Indexed: B01.
Published by: Business Monitor International Ltd., Senator House, 85 Queen Victoria St, London, EC4V 4AB, United Kingdom. TEL 44-20-72480468, FAX 44-20-72480467, subs@businessmonitor.com.

355 ITA ISSN 0394-3429
PANORAMA DIFESA. Text in Italian; Summaries in English. 1982. m. (11/yr.). EUR 43 domestic; EUR 70 in Europe; EUR 89 elsewhere (effective 2009). **Document type:** *Magazine, Consumer.* **Description:** Features a broad view of novelties in the following sectors: Air Force, Navy, ground force, space and civil defense.
Published by: Ediservice Casa Editrice Firenze, Via XX Settembre 60, Florence, 50129, Italy. TEL 39-055-4625293, FAX 39-055-4633331, info@ediservice.it, http://www.ediservice.it.

PANZERSCHRECK. *see* SPORTS AND GAMES

PAPER WARS. *see* SPORTS AND GAMES

355 AUS ISSN 0810-0500
PAR ONERI. Variant title: Australian Army Transport Journal. Text in English. 1980. a.
Published by: (Royal Australian Corps of Transport), 900 Degrees, PO Box 947, Broadway, NSW 2007, Australia. TEL 61-2-85968600, FAX 61-2-85968622, admin@900degrees.com.au. Ed. F M King.

355.31 USA ISSN 0031-1723
U1
➤ **PARAMETERS (CARLISLE).** Text in English. 1971. q. USD 26 domestic; USD 36.40 foreign; free to qualified personnel (effective 2009). bk.rev. charts; illus. index. 160 p./no.; back issues avail.; reprints avail. **Document type:** *Journal, Academic/Scholarly.* **Description:** Provides a forum for the expression of mature, professional thought on the art and science of land warfare; national and international security affairs, military strategy, military leadership and management, military history; ethics and other topics of important and current interest to the U.S. Army, and the Department of Defense.
Related titles: Microfiche ed.: (from PQC); Microfilm ed.: (from PQC); Online - full text ed.

Indexed: A01, A03, A08, A22, A26, ABCPolSci, ABS&EES, AMB, AUNI, AmH&L, B04, B05, B14, BRD, BRI, CA, CBRI, E08, G05, G06, G07, G08, HistAb, I02, I05, IBR, IBZ, IUSGP, LID&ISL, M05, M06, M07, MEA&I, P02, P10, P30, P34, P42, P45, P47, P48, P53, P54, PAIS, PQC, PSA, S02, S03, S09, SCOPUS, SSAI, SSAb, SSI, SociolAb, T02, W03, W05.
—BLDSC (6404.837000), IE, Infotrieve, Ingenta.
Published by: U.S. Army, War College, 122 Forbes Ave, Carlisle, PA 17013. TEL 717-245-4943, FAX 717-245-4233, carl_atwc-cpa@conus.army.mil. Ed. Col. Robert H Taylor. **Subscr. to:** U.S. Government Printing Office, Superintendent of Documents, PO Box 371954, Pittsburgh, PA 15250. TEL 202-512-1800, 866-512-1800, FAX 202-512-2250, orders@gpo.gov, http://www.access.gpo.gov/.

623 USA ISSN 1948-4569
PATHFINDER (BETHESDA); the geospatial intelligence magazine. Text in English. 200?. bi-m. free to members (effective 2009). back issues avail. **Document type:** *Magazine, Trade.* **Description:** Aims to enhance and promote public awareness and understanding of the discipline of geospatial intelligence with news stories of interest to a broad audience.
Media: Online - full content.
Published by: National Geospatial-Intelligence Agency, 4600 Sangamore Rd, Mail Stop D-39, Bethesda, MD 20816. TEL 301-227-7388, 800-455-0899, NGAIG@nga.mil. Ed. Jason K Michas.

358.4 USA
THE PATRIOT (ALTUS). Text in English. w. (Fri.). free (effective 2006). adv. **Document type:** *Newspaper, Government.* **Description:** Military news related to Altus Air Force Base.
Formerly: Galaxy
Published by: Altus Air Force Base, Public Affairs Office, Altus Air Force Base, Altus, OK 73521. TEL 580-481-7213, FAX 580-481-5966. Ed. Aldre Burobers. adv.: page USD 31,655.

PATRIOT ORENBURZH'YA. *see* SOCIAL SERVICES AND WELFARE

PEACE MAGAZINE. *see* POLITICAL SCIENCE—International Relations

358.4 GBR ISSN 0031-4080
PEGASUS JOURNAL. Text in English. 1946. s-a. GBP 15 domestic; GBP 21 foreign (effective 2009). adv. bk.rev. **Document type:** *Journal, Trade.* **Description:** Contains important PRA news as well as obituaries and last post.
Published by: Parachute Regiment and Airborne Forces, Merville Barracks, Circular Rd S, Colchester, Colchester CO2 7UT, United Kingdom. TEL 44-1752-312061, FAX 44-1206-817076, http://www.army.mod.uk/infantry/regiments/3471.aspx.

355.1 GBR ISSN 0048-3192
PENNANT. Text in English. 1946. 2/yr. GBP 2 per issue; GBP 17 membership (effective 2000). adv. bk.rev. **Document type:** *Bulletin.* **Description:** Contains comments on the society's activities.
Published by: Officers' Pensions Society, 68s Lambeth Rd, London, SE1 7PP, United Kingdom. TEL 44-20-7582-0469, FAX 44-20-7820-9948. Ed. Maj Gen Peter Bonnet. Adv. contact Mrs. Judith Foster. Circ: 33,000.

355 USA ISSN 1551-6679
PENTAGON BRIEF; independent monthly review of US defense news. Text in English. 2004. m. back issues avail. **Document type:** *Newsletter, Academic/Scholarly.* **Description:** Current news regarding US defense policy, US defense policy, US armed forces structure, US military operations, and US military equipment.
Related titles: Online - full text ed.: ISSN 1536-9153. 2001; German ed.: Pentagon Brief - Deutsche Ausgabe. ISSN 1536-7304. USD 24 worldwide for PDF; USD 37.60 in US & Canada for print; USD 42.60 elsewhere for print (effective 2004).
Published by: Transatlantic Euro-American Multimedia LLC, PO Box 6793, Portsmouth, VA 23703. service@teamultimedia.com.

PERFIDIOUS ALBION. *see* SPORTS AND GAMES

359 USA ISSN 1045-4381
PERSPECTIVE. UNITED STATES. NAVAL MILITARY PERSONNEL COMMAND; the professional bulletin for Navy officers. Text in English. bi-m. **Document type:** *Bulletin.*
Published by: United States. Naval Military Personnel Command, Department of the Navy, Washington, DC 20370-5000.

355 SWE ISSN 1654-7128
AP48
PERSPEKTIV. Text in Swedish. 1940-1952; resumed 1958. 6/yr. SEK 150 (effective 2008). back issues avail. **Document type:** *Magazine, Consumer.*
Former titles (until 2007): Folk och Foersvar (0345-3529); (until vol.14, 1941): Paa Vakt
Published by: Folk och Foersvar/Society and Defense, Lilla Nygatan 14, Stockholm, 10317, Sweden. TEL 46-8-58882490, FAX 46-8-6606355. Ed. Aurora Carlstroem TEL 46-8-58882493.

355.4 USA ISSN 0195-1920
T57.6
PHALANX; bulletin of military operations research. Text in English. 1965. q. USD 40 domestic to non-members; USD 75 foreign to non-members; free to members (effective 2010). adv. bk.rev. back issues avail. **Document type:** *Bulletin, Trade.*
Related titles: Online - full text ed.: free (effective 2010).
Indexed: CA, M05, T02.
Published by: Military Operations Research Society, 1703 N Beauregard St, Ste 450, Alexandria, VA 22311. TEL 703-933-9070, FAX 703-933-9066, morsoffice@mors.org. Ed. John Willis. Pub. Karen Wilson. Circ: 9,100.

355 CAN
PHARE/BEACON. Text in English. m. CAD 15. adv. back issues avail. **Document type:** *Newspaper.*
Related titles: Diskette ed.
Address: BFC Bagotville, B P 369, Alouette, PQ G0V 1A0, Canada. TEL 418-677-8160, FAX 418-677-8480. Ed. Capt Leonard. Adv. contact Michel Aubin. Circ: 3,000 (controlled).

338.473 959.9 363.35 GBR ISSN 1749-1568
PHILIPPINES DEFENCE & SECURITY REPORT. Text in English. 2005. q. EUR 820, USD 1,030 combined subscription (print & email eds.) (effective 2010). **Document type:** *Report, Trade.* **Description:** Provides industry leaders, defense manufacturers and suppliers, intelligence agencies and governments with independent forecasts and competitive intelligence on the defense and security industry in the Philippines.
Related titles: E-mail ed.
Indexed: B01.
Published by: Business Monitor International Ltd., Senator House, 85 Queen Victoria St, London, EC4V 4AB, United Kingdom. TEL 44-20-72480468, FAX 44-20-72480467, subs@businessmonitor.com.

PILOT UND FLUGZEUG. *see* TRANSPORTATION—Air Transport

355.31 SGP ISSN 0048-4199
UA853.S5
PIONEER; Singapore armed forces news. Text in English. 1969. m. SGD 0.50 per issue. adv. bk.rev. charts; illus.
Indexed: AMB.
Published by: Ministry of Defense, Public Affairs Department, Tanglin Rd, Singapore, 1024, Singapore. Ed. Francis Gomes. Circ: 120,000.

355 CHE
PIONIER. Text in English. m. **Document type:** *Bulletin.*
Published by: Hurter & Partner, Dorfstr. 11, Baden-Daettwil, 5405, Switzerland. TEL 41-56-4934363, FAX 41-56-4933551.

355 NLD ISSN 1877-2226
PIT PRO REGE NIEUWS. Text in Dutch. 1971 (vol.82). q. free (effective 2009). adv. bk.rev. charts; illus.
Former titles (until 2009): Pro Rege Nieuws (1874-4893); (until 2006): P M T - Nieuws (1381-8635); (until 1975): De Nederlandse Krijgsman (0047-9241)
Published by: Koninklijke PIT Pro Rege, Frankenlaan 38, Apeldoorn, 7312 TD, Netherlands. TEL 31-55-3575650, FAX 31-55-3575651, info@pitprorege.net, http://www.pitprorege.net.

338.473 943.8 363.35 GBR ISSN 1749-1576
POLAND DEFENCE & SECURITY REPORT. Text in English. 2005. q. EUR 820, USD 1,030 combined subscription (print & email eds.) (effective 2010). **Document type:** *Report, Trade.* **Description:** Provides industry leaders, defense manufacturers and suppliers, intelligence agencies and governments with independent forecasts and competitive intelligence on the defense and security industry in Poland.
Related titles: E-mail ed.
Indexed: A15, ABIn, B01, P48, P51, PQC.
Published by: Business Monitor International Ltd., Senator House, 85 Queen Victoria St, London, EC4V 4AB, United Kingdom. TEL 44-20-72480468, FAX 44-20-72480467, subs@businessmonitor.com.

POLEMOS; casopis za interdisciplinama istrazivanja rata i mira. *see* POLITICAL SCIENCE

355.5 POL ISSN 1895-3344
POLIGON. Text in Polish. 2006. q.
Published by: Wydawnictwo Magnum-X, ul Borowskiego 2, p 307, Warsaw, 03475, Poland. magnum@hbz.com.pl.

POLITICAL AND MILITARY SOCIOLOGY: AN ANNUAL REVIEW. *see* SOCIOLOGY

POLITICAL Y ESTRATEGIA. *see* POLITICAL SCIENCE

355 POL ISSN 0867-4523
POLSKA ZBROJNA. Text in Polish. 1950. 5/w. PLZ 117 for 6 mos. domestic (effective 2006). **Document type:** *Newspaper, Consumer.*
Former titles: Zolnierz Rzeczypospolitej (0867-4515); (until 1990): Zolnierz Wolnosci (0137-9402)
Published by: (Poland. Ministerstwo Obrony Narodowej), Dom Wydawniczy Bellona, ul Grzybowska 77, Warsaw, 00844, Poland. TEL 48-22-6204286, FAX 48-22-6242273, biuro@bellona.pl, http://www.bellona.pl. Circ: 100,000.

355 NLD ISSN 1567-5238
POLSSLAG; Tijdschrift van de Vereniging officieren van de Geneeskundige Diensten. Text in Dutch. 1966. bi-m. free membership (effective 2010). adv. bk.rev. illus.; maps; stat. back issues avail. **Document type:** *Bulletin.*
Former titles (until 2000): Posslag - V O G T Aktueel (1387-2524); (until 1997): Posslag (0167-8698)
Published by: Vereniging van Officieren van de Geneeskundige Diensten (V O G D), Bellefleur 119, Duiven, 6922 AJ, Netherlands. http://www.vogd.net/vereniging/. Ed. Major H Jonker.

355 CAN
POST - GAZETTE. Text in English. 1960. w. CAD 35. adv. **Document type:** *Newspaper.*
Formed by the 1993 merger of: C F B Gagetown Gazette (0713-391X); Oromocto Post
Address: 291 Restigouche Rd, Oromocto, NB E2V 2H5, Canada. TEL 506-357-9813, FAX 506-357-5222. Ed., R&P James Haley. Adv. contact Karen Jensen. Circ: 4,000 (paid).

355 SRB ISSN 0351-3912
UA18.Y8
POZADINA. Text in Serbo-Croatian. 1947. bi-m. bk.rev.
Formerly (until 1980): Vojnoekonomski Pregled (0350-0578)
Published by: Savezni Sekretarijat za Narodnu Odbranu, Vojska, Novinsko-izdavacka ustanova, Bircaninova 5, Belgrade, 11000. Ed. Borisav Nedic.

355 USA ISSN 1547-206X
PRAEGER ILLUSTRATED MILITARY HISTORY. Text in English. 2004. irreg. price varies. **Document type:** *Monographic series.*
Published by: Greenwood Publishing Group Inc. (Subsidiary of: A B C - C L I O), 88 Post Rd W, PO Box 5007, Westport, CT 06881. TEL 203-226-3571, 800-225-5800, FAX 877-231-6980, sales@greenwood.com.

355.6 USA ISSN 1934-1245
UC267
PRIME CONTRACT AWARDS, SIZE DISTRIBUTION. Text in English. 1967. a. **Document type:** *Government.*
Related titles: Online - full text ed.: ISSN 1934-1237.
Published by: U.S. Department of Defense, Washington Headquarters Services, 1155 Defense Pentagon, Washington, DC 20301. TEL 703-697-7351, http://www.whs.mil/.

355 USA ISSN 2157-0663
▼ **PRISM (WASHINGTON).** Text in English. 2009. q. USD 28 domestic; USD 39.20 foreign (effective 2010). back issues avail. **Document type:** *Journal, Academic/Scholarly.* **Description:** Informs members of U.S. Federal Agencies, allies and other partners on national security operations, reconstruction and nationbuilding.
Related titles: Online - full text ed.: ISSN 2157-0671. free (effective 2010).
Published by: National Defense University Press, 260 Fifth Ave, Bldg 64, Fort McNair, Washington, DC 20319. TEL 202-685-4210, FAX 202-685-4806, NDUPress@ndu.edu. Ed. Michael Miklaucic. Pub. Hans Binnendijk.

355 NOR ISSN 1503-7142
PRO PATRIA/VAART VERN. Text in Norwegian. 2003. 5/yr. NOK 400 membership; NOK 250 to students (effective 2011). adv. bk.rev. bibl.; illus. **Document type:** *Magazine, Trade.*
Formed by the merger of (1924-2002): Pro Patria (0032-910X); Which was formerly (until 1931): De Vernepliktige Officerers Forenings Medlemsblad (0332-8163); (1912-2002): Vaart Vern (0042-2037); Which was formerly (until 1963): Vaar Haer (0333-2160)
Published by: Norske Reserveoffiserers Forbund/Norwegian Reserve Officers Federation, PO Box 908, Sentrum, Oslo, 0104, Norway. TEL 47-22-478259, FAX 47-22-332725, post@nrof.no, http://www.nrof.no. Ed. Liv Hegna TEL 47-22-478250. Circ: 8,000.

355.3 NLD ISSN 2210-7304
PRODEF BULLETIN. Text in Dutch. 2004. 8/yr.
Formerly (until 2010): Federatie van Nederlandse Officieren. Bulletin (1871-6083)
Published by: Federatie van Nederlandse Officieren en Middelbaar en Hoger Burgerpersoneel bij Defensie, Wassenaarseweg 2, The Hague, 2596 CH, Netherlands. TEL 31-70-3839504, FAX 31-70-3835911, info@fvno.nl, http://www.fvno.nl. Eds. Dr. M L G Lijmbach, R C Hunnego.

355 RUS
PROFI. Text in Russian. m.
Address: A-ya 15, Moscow, 121614, Russian Federation. TEL 7-095-4178070, 7-095-4174101, 7-095-4179400. Ed. Irina Komarova. Circ: 3,000.

355 USA ISSN 0145-112X
UA23.A1
➤ **PROFILE (NORFOLK).** Text in English. 1957. m. (Nov.-April). free (effective 2010). **Document type:** *Journal, Academic/Scholarly.* **Description:** Covers various career options offered by the branches of the DOD (Army, Navy, Air Force, and Marines) as well as the Coast Guard. The January issue compares these branches and the other 5 issues provide feature stories on specific careers and specific individuals within those careers.
Formerly: High School News Service Report
Related titles: Online - full text ed.
Indexed: A26, G05, G06, G07, G08, I05, IFP, IUSGP.
—Ingenta.
Published by: U.S. Department of Defense, High School News Service, 9420 Third Ave, Suite 110, Norfolk, VA 23511.

355 UKR
PRYKORDONNYK UKRAINY. Text in Ukrainian, Russian. 1943. w. USD 280 in North America (effective 2000).
Address: Ul Narodnaya 54a, Kiev, Ukraine. TEL 212-87-96. **Dist. by:** East View Information Services, 10601 Wayzata Blvd, Minneapolis, MN 55305. TEL 952-252-1201, 800-477-1005, FAX 952-252-1202, info@eastview.com, http://www.eastview.com.

355 POL ISSN 1640-6281
DK4170
PRZEGLAD HISTORYCZNO-WOJSKOWY. Text in Polish. 1929-1938; resumed 1956-1997; resumed 2000. q. bk.rev. bibl. **Description:** Covers military history of Poland.
Former titles (until 2000): Wojskowy Przeglad Historyczny (0043-7182); (until 1956): Przeglad Historyczno-Wojskowy (1640-6273)
Indexed: HistAb, IBR, IBZ, LID&ISL, RASB.
—INIST.
Published by: Ministerstwo Obrony Narodowej, ul Stefana Banacha 2, pok 335, Warsaw, 00909, Poland. TEL 48-22-6826527. Ed. Grzegorz Nowik. Circ: 15,000.

358.4 POL ISSN 0867-2075
PRZEGLAD WOJSK LOTNICZYCH I OBRONY POWIETRZNEJ. Text in Polish; Summaries in English. 1928. m. PLZ 60 domestic; USD 50 foreign; PLZ 5 newsstand/cover domestic (effective 2002). adv. bk.rev. **Document type:** *Magazine, Government.* **Description:** Discusses tactics, training and flying safety, engineering and operation, education; presents views, opinions, experience.
Former titles (until 1990): Przeglad Wojsk Lotniczych i Wojsk Obrony Powietrznej Kraju (0137-8058); (until 1974): Wojskowy Przeglad Lotniczy (0043-7190)
Related titles: CD-ROM ed.; E-mail ed.
Indexed: LID&ISL.
Published by: (Dowodztwo Wojsk Lotniczych i Obrony Powietrznej), Przeglad Wojsk Lotnicznych i Obrony Powietrznej, Ul Kosciuszki 92-98, PO Box 507, Poznan, 60-967, Poland. TEL 48-61-8572922, FAX 48-61-8572657, redakcja@przeglad-wlop.pl. Ed. Jozef Zielinski. Adv. contact Krzysztof Kakolewski. page USD 1,500. Circ: 1,500.

623.66 GRC ISSN 1105-1310
PTISI KAI DIASTIMA/FLIGHT AND SPACE. Key Title: Ptisi. Text in Greek. 1979. m. adv. Website rev. illus. back issues avail. **Document type:** *Magazine, Consumer.* **Description:** Covers aerospace technology and defense matters.
Related titles: Online - full content ed.
Published by: Technical Press SA, 80 Ioannou Metaxa, Karelas, Koropi, 19400, Greece. TEL 30-210-9792500, FAX 30-210-9792528, info@technicalpress.gr, http://www.technicalpress.gr. Ed. Faidon Karaiosifides. Adv. contact Chrisanthi Bitsori. Circ: 5,978 (paid).

355 USA
PUPUKAHI/HARMONIOUSLY UNITED. Text in English. 1950. 4/yr. free.
Formerly (until 1973): Hawaii Guardsman (0017-8578)
Published by: Department of Defense, 3949 Diamond Head Rd., Honolulu, HI 96816-4495. TEL 808-737-8839, FAX 808-734-8527, http://www.dod.hawaii.gov/pao/pupukahi.html. Circ: 7,500.

353.538 USA ISSN 0279-0653
PURPLE HEART MAGAZINE. Text in English. 1932. bi-m. USD 5 to non-members; free to members (effective 2008). bk.rev. **Document type:** *Magazine, Consumer.*
Published by: Military Order of the Purple Heart of the U.S.A., PO Box 49, Annandale, VA 22003. TEL 703-354-2140, FAX 703-642-2054, Info@PurpleHeart.org. Ed. Cy Kammeier. R&P Nick McIntosh TEL 502-582-6926. Circ: 30,000.

PYRAMID (ONLINE). *see* SPORTS AND GAMES

327.12 CHN ISSN 0258-8005
QINGBAO KEXUE JISHU. Text in Chinese. bi-m. **Document type:** *Journal, Academic/Scholarly.*
Indexed: Inspec.
Address: 26, Fucheng Lu, Beijing, 100036, China. TEL 86-10-66757270.

623.455 CHN ISSN 1000-8810
UD380
QINGBINGQI/SMALL ARMS. Text in Chinese. 1978. s-m. back issues avail. **Document type:** *Academic/Scholarly.*
Related titles: Online - full text ed.
—East View.
Published by: (Zhongguo Binggong Xuehui Qingwuqi Xuehui), Qingbingqi Zazhishe, Changping, 1023 Xingxiang, Beijing, 102202, China. TEL 86-10-89790455, FAX 86-10-89790773. Ed. Qianqian Chu. **Co-sponsor:** Bingqi Gongye Qingbingqi Zhuanye Qingbaowang.

355 USA ISSN 1930-4420
UA23.3
THE QUADRENNIAL DEFENSE REVIEW. REPORT. Text in English. 199?. irreg. free (effective 2011). **Document type:** *Report, Government.*
Media: Online - full text.
Published by: U.S. Department of Defense, 1400 Defense Pentagon, Washington, DC 20301. TEL 703-571-3343, http://www.defense.gov/.

355 TWN ISSN 1010-3228
U4
QUANQIU FANGWEI ZAZHI/DEFENSE INTERNATIONAL. Text in Chinese. 1984. m.
Published by: Quanqiu Fangwei Zazhishe, 9F, 182-2 Sec 1 Ho-Ping Rd, E., Taipei, Taiwan. TEL 02-362-7093, FAX 02-362-7016.

355 USA ISSN 0896-9795
UC30
QUARTERMASTER PROFESSIONAL BULLETIN. Text in English. 1988. q. USD 14 (effective 2001). **Document type:** *Government.* **Description:** Presents material designed to keep Quartermasters knowledgeable of current and emerging developments to enhance their professional development.
Published by: U.S. Army Quartermaster Center and School, Fort Lee, VA 23801-1601. **Subscr. to:** U.S. Government Printing Office, Superintendent of Documents, PO Box 371954, Pittsburgh, PA 15250. TEL 202-512-1800, FAX 202-512-2250, orders@gpo.gov, http://www.access.gpo.gov.

355.31 GBR
QUEEN'S REGULATIONS FOR THE ARMY AMENDMENTS. Text in English. irreg., latest 2009, Amendment 29. looseleaf. GBP 35 per issue (effective 2010). 236 p./no.; back issues avail. **Document type:** *Government.*
Published by: (Great Britain. Ministry of Defence), The Stationery Office, St Crispins, Duke St, Norwich, NR3 1PD, United Kingdom. TEL 44-1603-622211, FAX 44-870-6005533, customer.services@tso.co.uk, http://www.tso.co.uk. **Subscr. to:** PO Box 29, Norwich NR3 1GN, United Kingdom. TEL 44-870-6005522.

358.4 GBR
QUEEN'S REGULATIONS FOR THE R.A.F. AMENDMENTS. (Royal Air Force) Text in English. irreg., latest 2009, Amendment list no. 23, 5th ed. looseleaf. GBP 9 per issue (effective 2010). 38 p./no.; **Document type:** *Government.*
Published by: (Great Britain. Ministry of Defence. Air Force Board), The Stationery Office, St Crispins, Duke St, Norwich, NR3 1PD, United Kingdom. TEL 44-1603-622211, FAX 44-870-6005533, customer.services@tso.co.uk, http://www.tso.co.uk. **Subscr. to:** PO Box 29, Norwich NR3 1GN, United Kingdom. TEL 44-870-6005522.

358.4 FRA ISSN 1963-2150
QUESTION' AIR. Text in French. 200?. irreg.
Formerly (until 2008): C E S A. Les Fiches (1957-3294)
Published by: Centre d'Etudes Strategiques Aerospaciales (C E S A), Ecole Militaire, 1 Place Joffre, B P 43, Paris, 00445 Armees, France. TEL 33-1-44428032, st.cesa@air.defense.gouv.fr.

355 BHR
AL-QUWWA. Text in Arabic. 1974. m. free. **Document type:** *Government.*
Published by: Defence Forces, PO Box 245, Manama, Bahrain. TEL 973-665599, FAX 973-663923, TELEX 8429 DEFFA'A. Ed. Maj Ahmad Muhammad As Suwaidi.

358.4 UAE
AL-QUWWAT AL-JAWWIYYAH/U A E AIR FORCE MAGAZINE. Text in Arabic. 1984. bi-m. AED 120 domestic to individuals; AED 540 foreign to individuals; AED 125 domestic to institutions; AED 480 in Europe to institutions; AED 550 in North America to institutions. adv. **Description:** Covers military aviation and air force and air defence matters.
Published by: General Command for the Armed Forces, Air Force and Air Defence Command, PO Box 3231, Abu Dhabi, United Arab Emirates. TEL 971-2-482400, FAX 971-2-482626, TELEX 24345 AIRFORM EM. Ed. Ahmad Khamis Al Hamili. Circ: 22,000.

358.4 GBR ISSN 0035-8614
R A F NEWS. Text in English. 1961. fortn. GBP 16.50 domestic to non-members; GBP 28 in Europe to non-members; GBP 49 in Australia & New Zealand to non-members; GBP 43.50 elsewhere to non-members; GBP 14.50 domestic to members (effective 2009). adv. bk.rev. illus. **Document type:** *Newspaper, Trade.* **Description:** Features latest news, international news, job vacancies as well as articles on sports and entertainment.
—CCC.
Published by: Royal Air Force, 100B, Greenwood, Walters Ash, High Wycombe, Bucks HP14 4XE, United Kingdom. TEL 44-1494-495546. Ed. Simon Williams.

R & R - A F N CABLE & SATELLITE T V. (Rest & Relaxation) *see* COMMUNICATIONS—Television And Cable

355 USA
R & R ENTERTAINMENT DIGEST. (Rest & Relaxation) Text in English. 1982. m. adv. **Description:** Military consumer magazine.
Address: 825 Old Country Rd, Westbury, NY 11590. TEL 516-334-3030. Ed. Tory Billard. Circ: 182,500.

358.4 CAN ISSN 1910-7889
R C A F MEMORIAL MUSEUM. NEWSLETTER. (Royal Canadian Air Force) Text in English. 2002. s-a. **Document type:** *Newsletter, Consumer.*
Published by: Royal Canadian Air Force Memorial Museum, PO Box 1000, Stn Forces, Astra, ON K0K 3W0, Canada. TEL 613-965-7314, FAX 613-965-7352, foundation@rcafmuseum.on.ca, http://www.rcafmuseum.on.ca.

355 ITA ISSN 1122-7605
R I D. RIVISTA ITALIANA DIFESA. Short title: R I D. Text in Italian. 1982. m. EUR 44 domestic; EUR 85 in Europe; EUR 110 elsewhere (effective 2009). adv. bk.rev. index. back issues avail. **Document type:** *Magazine, Trade.*
Address: Via Martiri della Liberazione 79-3, Chiavari, GE 16043, Italy. TEL 39-0185-308606, FAX 39-0185-309063. Ed. Andrea Nativi. Adv. contact Franco Lazzari TEL 39-0185-301598. B&W page USD 3,950, color page USD 6,950; trim 7.31 x 10.63. Circ: 30,000 (paid and controlled).

R S A REVIEW. (Returned Services Association) *see* SOCIAL SERVICES AND WELFARE

355 GBR ISSN 0307-1847
U1
R U S I JOURNAL. (Royal United Services Institute) Text in English. 1857. bi-m. GBP 561, EUR 876, USD 1,099 combined subscription to institutions (print & online eds.) (effective 2009); includes Whitehall Papers. adv. bk.rev. bibl.; illus. index. back issues avail.; reprint service avail. from PSC. **Document type:** *Journal, Academic/Scholarly.* **Description:** Covers leading forum for the exchange of ideas on national and international defence and security issues.
Former titles (until 1972): Royal United Services Institute for Defence Studies. Journal (0953-3559); (until 1971): Royal United Service Institution. Journal (0035-9289); (until 1860): United Service Institution. Journal
Related titles: Microform ed.: (from PQC); Online - full text ed.: ISSN 1744-0378. GBP 533, EUR 832, USD 1,044 to institutions (effective 2009); includes Whitehall Papers (from IngentaConnect).
Indexed: A22, AMB, AUNI, AmH&L, CA, DIP, DM&T, E01, HistAb, IBR, IBZ, LID&ISL, M05, M07, P02, P06, P10, P47, P48, P52, P53, P54, PAIS, PCI, PQC, PRA, RASB, SCOPUS, T02.
—BLDSC (8052.647530), IE, Infotrieve, Ingenta, Linda Hall. **CCC.**
Published by: (Royal United Services Institute), Routledge (Subsidiary of: Taylor & Francis Group), 4 Park Sq, Milton Park, Abingdon, Oxon OX14 4RN, United Kingdom. TEL 44-20-70176000, FAX 44-20-70176336, subscriptions@tandf.co.uk, http://www.routledge.com. Adv. contact Linda Hann TEL 44-1344-779945. **Subscr. to:** Taylor & Francis Ltd., Journals Customer Service, Sheepen Pl, Colchester, Essex CO3 3LP, United Kingdom. TEL 44-20-70175544, FAX 44-20-70175198, tf.enquiries@tfinforma.com.

355 GBR ISSN 1471-3330
UA11
R U S I NEWSBRIEF. (Royal United Services Institute) Text in English. 1980. m. GBP 84 to non-members; GBP 12 per issue to members; free to members (effective 2009). back issues avail. **Document type:** *Newsletter, Trade.* **Description:** Provides bi-monthly briefings on current issues in international defence, security and the military sciences.
Former titles (until 2000): R U S I News Brief (0268-2656); (until 1985): R U S I News Sheet (0950-0391); (until 1982): R U S I News
Related titles: Online - full text ed.
—CCC.
Published by: Royal United Services Institute, Whitehall, London, SW1A 2ET, United Kingdom. FAX 44-20-73210943, media@rusi.org. Ed. Jonathan Eyal TEL 44-20-77472616.

355.4 FRA ISSN 0769-4814
RAIDS. Text in French. 1986. m. EUR 62.50 domestic; EUR 75 foreign (effective 2009). back issues avail. **Document type:** *Magazine, Consumer.* **Description:** Focuses on the special forces and elite troops of the French and foreign armies.
Published by: Histoire et Collection, 5 Av. de la Republique, Paris, 75011, France. TEL 33-1-40211820, FAX 33-1-47005111, fredbey@club-internet.fr, http://www.histoireetcollections.com.

355 FIN ISSN 0483-9080
RAJAMME VARTIJAT. Text in Finnish. 1934. bi-m. **Document type:** *Government.* **Description:** Deals with matters of particular interest to members of the border patrol.
Formerly (until 1962): Rajajaakari (0481-7338)
Published by: Suomen Rajavartiolaitos/Frontier Guard of Finland, PL 3, Helsinki, 00131, Finland. TEL 358-204106513, FAX 358-20416755. Ed. Pekka Korhola.

355 283 GBR ISSN 1358-0507
READY. Text in English. 1912. s-a. bk.rev. 20 p./no.; back issues avail. **Document type:** *Bulletin, Consumer.* **Description:** Presents claims of Jesus Christ to members of Her Majesty's Armed Forces and their families.
Published by: Soldiers' & Airmen's Scripture Readers Association, Havelock House, Barrack Rd, Aldershot, Hants GU11 3NP, United Kingdom. TEL 44-1252-310033, FAX 44-1252-341804, admin@sasra.org.uk, http://www.sasra.org.uk.

RECON. *see* HISTORY

355 USA
RED THRUST STAR. Text in English. q. **Document type:** *Government.* **Description:** Provides timely, authoritative information on OPFOR training to increase the knowledge and understanding of OPFOR training throughout the Armed Forces.
Related titles: Online - full content ed.
Published by: (United States. U.S. forces Command O P F O R Training Program), 11th Armored Cavalry Regiment, c/o AFZJ-AC-RT, Fort Irwin, CA 92310-5031. TEL 619-380-5289, FAX 619-380-5127, http://call.army.mil/call/fmso/RED-STAR/RED-STAR.HTM.

355 USA ISSN 1059-9878
REENACTOR'S JOURNAL; for Civil War military and civilian reenactors. Text in English. 1990. m. USD 24; USD 36 foreign (effective 1996). adv. bk.rev. illus. **Document type:** *Newsletter, Consumer.* **Description:** Covers the reenactment of notable battles, especially those of the Civil War.
Published by: Rick Keating, Ed. & Pub., PO Box 1864, Varna, IL 61375. TEL 309-463-2123, FAX 309-463-2188. Adv. contact Patricia A Keating. Circ: 2,000.

355.3 FRA ISSN 1964-7859
REFLEXIONS STRATEGIQUES. Text in French. 2008. irreg. **Document type:** *Monographic series, Academic/Scholarly.*
Published by: Fondation pour la Recherche Strategique, 27 rue Damesme, Paris, 75013, France. TEL 33-01-43137777, FAX 33-01-43137778, webmaster@frstrategie.org, http://www.frstrategie.org.

355.223 USA
REGISTER OF OFFICERS. Text in English. a. back issues avail. **Document type:** *Government.*
Former titles (until 200?): U.S. Coast Guard. Register of Officers (0364-8753); (until 1976): United States Coast Guard. Register of Officers and Cadets (0095-2818); (until 19??): United States Coast Guard. Register of Officers and Cadets of the United States Coast Guard in the Order of Precedence
Related titles: Online - full text ed.: free (effective 2010).
—Linda Hall.
Published by: U.S. Coast Guard, 2100 Second St, SW, Washington, DC 20593. TEL 202-267-1061, FAX 202-267-4402, gchappell@comdt.uscg.mil, http://www.uscg.mil/default.asp.

355.1 617.06 USA ISSN 0882-7753
REHABILITATION R & D PROGRESS REPORTS. (Research & Development) Text in English. 1983. a.
Related titles: Online - full text ed.
Indexed: C06, C07, C08, CINAHL, SCOPUS.
—Linda Hall.
Published by: Department of Veterans Affairs, Veterans Health Administration, 103 S Gay St, Baltimore, MD 21202-3517. TEL 410-962-1800, FAX 410-962-9670, mail@rehab-balt.med.va.gov, http://www.va.gov.

RENMIN JUNYI/PEOPLE'S MILITARY SURGEON. *see* MEDICAL SCIENCES—Surgery

355.3 FRA ISSN 1297-2592
REPERES STRATEGIQUES. Text in French. 1999. irreg. **Document type:** *Monographic series, Academic/Scholarly.*
Published by: Fondation pour la Recherche Strategique, 27 rue Damesme, Paris, 75013, France. TEL 33-01-43137777, FAX 33-01-43137778, webmaster@frstrategie.org, http://www.frstrategie.org.

355 USA
REPORT OF THE QUADRENNIAL DEFENSE REVIEW. Text in English. quadrennial. **Document type:** *Government.* **Description:** Provides close and thorough examination of the defense structure of United States as a report to the Congress.
Related titles: Online - full content ed.
Published by: Department of Defense, OASD(PA)/DPC, 1400 Defense Pentagon, Rm 1E757, Washington, DC 20301-1400 . TEL 703-697-5737, http://www.defenselink.mil/.

RESCUES; the quarterly publication that supports the Royal New Zealand Coastguard. *see* SPORTS AND GAMES—Boats And Boating

355.8 USA ISSN 0198-0181
CODEN: ARYTDT
RESEARCH & DEVELOPMENT ASSOCIATES FOR MILITARY FOOD AND PACKAGING SYSTEMS. ACTIVITIES REPORT. Key Title: Activities Report of the R & D Associates. Text in English. 1947. s-a. back issues avail. **Document type:** *Proceedings, Trade.*
Former titles (until 1978): Research and Development Associates for Military Food and Packaging Systems (0099-6335); U.S. Army Natick Laboratories. Activities Report (0041-7505)
Indexed: A22, Agr.
—BLDSC (0676.557000), CASDDS, IE, Ingenta, Linda Hall.
Published by: Research and Development Associates for Military Food & Packaging Systems, Inc., 16607 Blanco Rd, Ste 1506, San Antonio, TX 78232. TEL 210-493-8024, FAX 210-493-8036. Ed. Anna May Schenck. Pub., R&P Jim Fagan. Circ: 2,200.

355.37 USA
RESERVE & NATIONAL GUARD MAGAZINE. Variant title: AmeriForce Reserve & National Guard Magazine. Text in English. 1999. a. adv. **Document type:** *Magazine, Consumer.* **Description:** Focuses on issues important to this branch of the military.
Published by: AmeriForce Publishing, LLC, 11 Tidewater, Irvine, CA 92614. Ed. Sara Graves. Pubs. Brian Dunbar TEL 215-773-0414, Dan Charobee TEL 949-733-1035. adv.: color page USD 8,595; bleed 8 x 10.75.

355.4 ZAF ISSN 1995-1973
THE RESERVE FORCE VOLUNTEER. Text in English. 2007. s-a.
Published by: Republic of South Africa, Department Defence, Reserve Force Division, Private Bag X161, Pretoria, 0001, South Africa. TEL 27-12-3556321, FAX 27-12-3556398, info@mil.za. Ed. Jennifer Render.

355 SWE ISSN 0284-625X
RESERVOFFICEREN. Text in Swedish. 1970. q. adv. charts; illus. **Document type:** *Magazine, Trade.*
Former titles (until1986): Reservbefael (0034-5490); Tidskrift foer Reservofficerare
Published by: Sveriges Reservofficersfoerbund, Lilla Nygatan 14, Gamla Stan, PO Box 2148, Stockholm, 10314, Sweden. http://www.sverof.se. Ed. Johan Hamnegaard.

355.31 USA ISSN 0893-1828
UA25
RESOURCE MANAGEMENT. Text in English. 1980. q.
Formerly (until 1987): Resource Management Journal (0274-5968)
Indexed: AMB, INZP.
—Ingenta.
Published by: U.S. Department of the Army, Comptroller Proponency Office, SAFM-PO, 109 Army Pentagon, Washington, DC 2031-0109. TEL 703-692-7413.

355 SWE ISSN 1653-526X
RESURS. Text in Swedish. 1994. q. back issues avail. **Document type:** *Magazine, Trade.*
Former titles (until 2005): Totalfoersvarsfolket (1401-3274); (until 1995): Personligt (1104-7968)
Media: Online - full content.
Published by: Pliktverket/The National Service Administration, Vaaxnaesgatan 10, Karlstad, Sweden. TEL 46-771-244000, FAX 46-54-1146509, pliktverket@pliktverket.se. Ed. Ulrika Haeggroth TEL 46-54-146663.

355.538 AUS ISSN 0034-6306
REVEILLE; the voice of New South Wales serving and ex-service men and women. Text in English. 1927. bi-m. AUD 4.40 newsstand/cover (effective 2009). bk.rev. **Document type:** *Magazine, Consumer.* **Description:** Covers issues on the well-being, care, compensation and commemoration of serving and ex-service Defence Force members and their dependants.
Published by: Returned and Services League of Australia, New South Wales State Branch, Anzac House, 245 Castlereach St, Sydney, NSW 2000, Australia. TEL 61-2-92648188, FAX 61-2-92648466, statsec@rslnsw.com.au. Ed. Graham Barry.

355 ARG ISSN 0326-6427
U4
REVISTA ARGENTINA DE ESTUDIOS ESTRATEGICOS. Text in Portuguese, Spanish; Summaries in Spanish. 1969. s-a. bibl.; charts; illus.; mkt.; maps; stat. back issues avail. **Document type:** *Academic/ Scholarly.*
Formerly (until 1984): Estrategia (0046-2578)
Related titles: Microfilm ed.
Indexed: AMB, C01, H21, P08, PAIS.
Published by: (Centro Argentino de Estudios Estrategicos y de las Relaciones Internacionales), Olcese Editores, Viamonte, 494 Piso 3, Buenos Aires, 1053, Argentina. TEL 54-114-3120607, FAX 54-114-3117996. Ed. Haroldo Olcese. Circ: 1,500.

REVISTA CUBANA DE MEDICINA MILITAR. *see* MEDICAL SCIENCES

355.31 PRT ISSN 0870-9343
REVISTA DA ARMADA. Text in Portuguese. 1971. m. bk.rev. **Document type:** *Magazine, Government.* **Description:** Contains information relating to naval proceedings, news and reports, exercises, and history.
Address: Ministerio da Marinha, Rua do Arsenal, Lisbon, 1100-001, Portugal. Circ: 7,000.

355 ESP ISSN 0482-5748
D25
REVISTA DE HISTORIA MILITAR. Text in Spanish. 1957. s-a. EUR 9.01 domestic; EUR 12.02 foreign (effective 2002). back issues avail. **Document type:** *Magazine, Consumer.*
Indexed: HistAb, I14, P30.
Published by: Instituto de Historia y Cultura Militar, C. Martires de Alcala, 9, Madrid, 28015, Spain. TEL 34-91-2054222, FAX 34-91-2054025, publicaciones@mde.es, http://www.ejercito.mde.es/ihycm/revista/.

355.49 ESP ISSN 0212-467X
REVISTA DE HISTORIA NAVAL. Text in Spanish. 1983. 3/yr. EUR 16 domestic; EUR 25 foreign (effective 2009). **Document type:** *Magazine, Consumer.*
Indexed: CA, HistAb, T02.
Published by: Instituto de Historia y Cultura Naval, Juan de Mena, 1 1a. Planta, Madrid, 28071, Spain. TEL 34-91-3795050, FAX 34-91-3795940.

355.31 COL ISSN 0120-0631
UA625
REVISTA DE LAS FUERZAS ARMADAS. Text in Spanish. 1976. 6/yr. adv. bibl.; charts; illus.
Published by: Escuela Superior de Guerra, Fuerzas Militares de Colombia, Avenida 81 No. 45a-40, Apartado Aereo 4403, Bogota, DE, Colombia. Ed. Miguel Rodriguez Casas. Circ: 6,800.

359 CHL ISSN 0034-8511
➤ **REVISTA DE MARINA.** Text in Spanish. 1885. bi-m. CLP 25,000 domestic; USD 100 foreign (effective 2003). bk.rev. index. 102 p./no.; back issues avail. **Document type:** *Magazine, Academic/Scholarly.*
Related titles: Microfilm ed.
Indexed: GeoRef, P30.
Published by: Armada de Chile, Casilla 220, Valparaiso, Chile. TEL 56-32-281222, FAX 56-32-509783, revismar@vtr.net. Ed., Adv. contact Jaime Sepulveda. Circ: 3,200.

359 PER ISSN 0034-8538
REVISTA DE MARINA DEL PERU. Text in Spanish. 1916. q. USD 20 (effective 1992). adv.
Published by: Marina de Guerra del Peru, Direccion de Informacion, Ave. Salaverry Cdra, 24, Jesus Maria, Lima, 11, Peru. TEL 5114-634141.

REVISTA DE PUBLICACIONES NAVALES. *see* MILITARY—Abstracting, Bibliographies, Statistics

610 335 MEX ISSN 0301-696X
REVISTA DE SANIDAD MILITAR. Text in Spanish. 1954. bi-m. MXN 200 domestic; USD 20 foreign (effective 2004). back issues avail. **Document type:** *Journal, Government.*
Formerly (until 1953): Boletin de Sanidad Militar
Related titles: Online - full text ed.
Indexed: A01, C01, CA, P30, SCOPUS, T02.
Published by: Secretaria de la Defensa Nacional, Direccion General de Sanidad, Av. Miguel Of Cervantes Saavedra No. 596, Col. Irrigacion Edif. No. "2", Planta Baja, C.P., Mexico, D.F., 11500, Mexico. dgsanidad@mail.sedena.gob.mx. Ed. Jose Jesu Akmanza Munoz.

355.31 MEX ISSN 0034-9046
REVISTA DEL EJERCITO. Text in Spanish. 1906. m. MXN 35,000.
Published by: Secretaria de la Defensa Nacional, c/o Estado Mayor del Ejercito, Mexico City, DF, Mexico. Circ: 4,000.

355.3 ARG ISSN 0327-6953
REVISTA DEL SUBOFICIAL. Text in Spanish. 1919. q. USD 40. adv. **Description:** Publishes contributions from officers and non-commissioned officers of the Argentine army.
Published by: Estado Mayor General del Ejercito, Azopardo, 250 Piso 4, Buenos Aires, 1328, Argentina. TEL 54-114-3422121, FAX 54-114-3311865. Adv. contact Victor Raul Lessler. B&W page USD 1,000; 280 x 200. Circ: 24,000.

355 BRA ISSN 0101-7284
U4
REVISTA DO EXERCITO BRASILEIRO. Text in Portuguese. 1882. q. BRL 20 domestic; USD 40 foreign (effective 1999). adv. bk.rev. **Document type:** *Government.* **Description:** Covers military subjects of interest to non-commissioned officers and junior officers. Includes some topics of interest to a general military audience.
Formerly (until vol.119, 1982): Revista Militar Brasileira (0035-0125); (1920-1923): Boletim do Estado Major do Exercito
Published by: Diretoria de Assuntos Culturais, Biblioteca do Exercito Editora, Palacio Duque De Caxias, 25, Ala Marcilio Dias, 3 andar, Rio De Janeiro, RJ 20221-260, Brazil. TEL 55-21-5195707, FAX 55-21-5195569. Ed. Luis P Macedo Carvalho. Adv. contact Luiz Eugenio Daarte Peixoto. Circ: 2,000 (controlled).

355 ESP ISSN 1131-5172
UA780
REVISTA ESPANOLA DE DEFENSA. Text in Spanish. 1988. 11/yr. **Document type:** *Magazine, Trade.*
Related titles: Online - full text ed.: ISSN 1696-7232. 200?; Optical Disk - DVD ed.: ISSN 1696-7224. 2003.
Published by: Ministerio de Defensa, Centro de Publicaciones, Calle de Alcala 18, 4o, Madrid, 28014, Spain. TEL 34-91-522524, FAX 34-91-5227553, http://www.mde.es. Circ: 30,000.

REVISTA ESPANOLA DE DERECHO MILITAR. *see* LAW—Military Law

355 ESP ISSN 1575-9059
DP78.5
REVISTA ESPANOLA DE HISTORIA MILITAR. Text in Spanish. 2000. bi-m. EUR 9 newsstand/cover (effective 2008). **Document type:** *Magazine, Trade.*
Published by: Alcaniz Fresnos, Calle Cromo 18-20, Prol. San Cristobal, Valladolid, 47012, Spain. TEL 34-983-390583, FAX 34-983-395336, quiron@quironediciones.com, http://www.quironediciones.com/.

359 ESP ISSN 0034-9569
REVISTA GENERAL DE MARINA. Text in Spanish. 1877. m. (except Aug.-Sep.). EUR 14.80 domestic; EUR 19.57 in Europe; EUR 20.16 elsewhere (effective 2009). adv. bk.rev. **Document type:** *Proceedings.*
Related titles: Optical Disk - DVD ed.: ISSN 1696-7305. 2003; Supplement(s): Cuadernos de Pensamiento Naval. ISSN 1697-2333. 2001.
Indexed: AMB, HistAb, IECT, RASB, RefZh.
Published by: Estado Mayor de la Armada, Montalban, 2, Madrid, 28014, Spain. TEL 34-1-3795107, FAX 34-1-3795028, http://www.aramada.mde.es/. Eds. Juan Genova, Mariano Juan y Ferragut. Adv. contact Mercedes Briones. Circ: 3,000.

359 BRA ISSN 0034-9860
V5
REVISTA MARITIMA BRASILEIRA. Text in Portuguese. 1851. q. USD 22. adv. bibl.; charts; illus. index.
Related titles: ◆ Supplement(s): Pesquisa Naval. ISSN 1414-8595.
Indexed: C01, IBR, IBZ.
—Linda Hall.
Published by: Ministerio da Marinha, Servico de Documentacao da Marinha, Rua Dom Manuel, 15, Centro, Rio De Janeiro, RJ 20010-090, Brazil. TEL 55-21-2216696, FAX 55-21-2166716. Ed. Jose Geraldo da Costa Cardoso de Melo. Circ: 4,000.

355 PRT ISSN 0377-4686
REVISTA SERVICO DE ADMINISTRACAO MILITAR. Text in Portuguese. bi-m. illus.
Former titles (until 1978): Servico de Administracao Militar. Revista Bimestral (0037-2714); (until 1955): Boletim de Administracao Militar (0871-8687)
Published by: Servico de Administracao Militar, Rua Rodrigo da Fonseca, 180, Lisbon, 1000, Portugal.

355.009 BEL ISSN 0035-0877
DH540
REVUE BELGE D'HISTOIRE MILITAIRE/BELGISCH TIJDSCHRIFT VOOR MILITAIRE GESCHIEDENIS. Text in Dutch, French. 1924. q. includes Militaria Belgica. bk.rev. back issues avail.
Indexed: FR, HistAb, IBR, IBZ, NumL, P30, RASB.
—INIST.
Published by: Societe Royale des Amis du Musee Royal de l'Armee et d'Histoire Militaire, Parc du Cinquantenaire 3, Brussels, 1040, Belgium. Ed. J Lorette. Circ: 1,000.

355 FRA ISSN 2105-7508
D410
REVUE DEFENSE NATIONALE. Text in French. 1939. m. EUR 90 domestic; EUR 90 DOM-TOM; EUR 120 in the European Union; EUR 130 elsewhere (effective 2009). bk.rev. bibl. back issues avail. **Document type:** *Journal, Consumer.* **Description:** Discusses political, strategic, economical, scientific and military studies.
Former titles (until 2010): Defense Nationale et Securite Collective (1950-3253); (until 2005): Defense Nationale (0336-1489); (until 1973): Revue de Defense Nationale (0035-1075)
Related titles: English ed.: ISSN 1779-3874.
Indexed: A22, AMB, AmH&L, BAS, DIP, ELLIS, FR, HistAb, I13, IBR, IBSS, IBZ, INIS AtomInd, LID&ISL, P30, P42, PAIS, PRA, PSA, RASB, SociolAb.
—BLDSC (7898.260000), IE, Infotrieve, Ingenta. **CCC.**
Published by: Comite d'Etudes de Defense Nationale, BP 8607, Paris, 75325 Cedex 07, France. TEL 33-1-44423192, FAX 33-1-44423189, cednrevu@worldnet.fr. Ed. Jean Dufourcq. Circ: 6,000.

355.009 FRA ISSN 0035-3299
UA700
REVUE HISTORIQUE DES ARMEES. Text in French. 1942. 4/yr. **Document type:** *Journal, Academic/Scholarly.* **Description:** Covers the history of the French military forces.
Former titles (until 1945): Traditions et Souvenirs Militaires (1245-8961); (until 1943): Revue d'Histoire Militaire (1245-8953)
Related titles: Online - full text ed.: ISSN 1965-0779. free (effective 2011).
Indexed: AmH&L, CA, FR, HistAb, IBR, IBZ, P30, RASB, SCOPUS, T02.
Published by: Service Historique de la Defense, Chateau de Vincennes, Av. de Paris, Vincennes, Cedex 94306, France. TEL 33-1-41932222. Circ: 4,000.

355.009 NLD ISSN 0254-8186
D25
REVUE INTERNATIONALE D'HISTOIRE MILITAIRE. Text in English, French, German, Italian, Russian, Spanish. 1939. irreg., latest 2007. price varies. **Document type:** *Magazine, Trade.* **Description:** Each volume devoted to the military history of a single country.
Indexed: HistAb, IBR, IBZ, P30, RASB.
Published by: Commission Internationale d'Histoire Militaire, c/o Institute of Military History, Alexander Barracks, Bldg 204, PO Box 90701, The Hague, 2509 LS, Netherlands. TEL 31-70-3165836, FAX 31-70-3165851, nimh@mindef.nl, http://www.nimh.nl.

355 CHE ISSN 0035-368X
U2
REVUE MILITAIRE SUISSE. Text in French. 1856. m. (11/yr.). CHF 55 domestic; CHF 80 foreign (effective 2002). adv. bk.rev. abstr.; bibl.; charts; illus. 48 p./no.; **Document type:** *Newspaper, Trade.*
Related titles: Online - full text ed.
Indexed: AMB, IBR, IBZ, LID&ISL, PRA, RASB.
Published by: Association de la Revue Militaire Suisse, Case Postale 7, Albeuve, 1669, Switzerland. TEL 41-26-9281977, FAX 41-26-9281977. Ed. Herve de Weck. adv.: page CHF 950; trim 207 x 142. Circ: 5,500 (paid).

355 ROM ISSN 1220-5710
RIVISTA DE ISTORIE MILITARA. Text in Romanian; Summaries in English, French, German, Romanian, Russian, Spanish. 1984. bi-m. USD 25 in Europe; USD 30 elsewhere (effective 1999). adv. bk.rev. illus. **Description:** Covers military history studies, archaeology, numismatics, heraldics, philately, and uniforms.
Formerly (until 1990): Lupta Intregului Popor (1220-5729)
Related titles: English ed.: Review of Military History.
Indexed: RASB.
Published by: Ministerul Apararii Nationale/Ministry of National Defense, Bd. Unirii nr.57, Bl. E4, Sector 3, Bucharest, 70764, Romania. TEL 40-1-3157827, FAX 40-1-3159456. Ed. Gheorghe Vartic. **Dist. by:** Rodipet S.A., Piata Presei Libere 1, sector 1, PO Box 33-57, Bucharest 3, Romania. TEL 40-21-2224126, 40-21-2226407, rodipet@rodipet.ro.

355 ITA ISSN 1826-1906
LA RIVISTA DELL'ARMA. Text in Italian. 1998. m. **Document type:** *Magazine, Trade.*
Published by: Unione Nazionale Arma Carabinieri (U N A C) http://www.carabinieri-unione.it/unac/index.asp.

359 ITA ISSN 0035-6964
V4
RIVISTA MARITTIMA. Text in Italian. 1868. m. (11/yr.). EUR 25 domestic (effective 2009). bk.rev. abstr.; charts; illus. index, cum.index. Supplement avail. **Document type:** *Magazine, Consumer.* **Description:** Deals with a variety of sea-related subjects such as: naval war, naval engineering, naval history, navies of the world, science and technology, weapon systems, shipping and yachting, naval aviation.
Related titles: CD-ROM ed.
Indexed: A22, AMB, AmH&L, DIP, GeoRef, P30, RASB, SpeleolAb.
—IE, Infotrieve.
Published by: Ministero della Difesa, Marina, Lungotevere delle Navi, Rome, RM 00196, Italy.

355 ITA ISSN 0035-6980
U4
RIVISTA MILITARE. Text in Italian, English. 1856. bi-m. EUR 11.40 domestic; EUR 15.50 foreign (effective 2009). adv. bk.rev. bibl.; charts; illus. index. **Document type:** *Magazine, Consumer.*
Indexed: AMB, HistAb, I13, IBR, IBZ, LID&ISL, MLA-IB, P30, RASB.
Published by: Ministero della Difesa, Stato Maggiore Esercito, Centro Pubblicistica dell'Esercito, Via di San Marco 8, Rome, RM 00186, Italy. FAX 39-06-47357371. Circ: 30,000.

355 CHE ISSN 0035-6999
RIVISTA MILITARE DELLA SVIZZERA ITALIANA. Text in Italian. 1927. bi-m. adv. charts; illus. **Document type:** *Journal, Trade.*
Address: Palazzo Oxalis B, Ponte Capriasca, 6946, Switzerland. TEL 41-91-9603330. Ed. Giovanni Galli.

355.31 KWT ISSN 1940-672X
ROCK SLATE. Text in English. 2003. w. **Document type:** *Newspaper, Trade.*
Media: Online - full text.
Published by: U.S. Army, 386th Air Expeditionary Wing in Southwest Asia, Ali Al Salem Air Base, Ali Al Salem, Kuwait.

363.35 338.473 GBR ISSN 1749-1584
ROMANIA DEFENCE & SECURITY REPORT. Text in English. 2005. q. EUR 820, USD 1,030 combined subscription (print & email eds.) (effective 2010). **Document type:** *Report, Trade.* **Description:** Provides professionals, consultancies, government departments, regulatory bodies and researchers with independent forecasts and regional competitive intelligence on the Romanian defence & security industry.
Related titles: E-mail ed.
Indexed: A15, ABIn, P48, P51, P52, PQC.
Published by: Business Monitor International Ltd., Senator House, 85 Queen Victoria St, London, EC4V 4AB, United Kingdom. TEL 44-20-72480468, FAX 44-20-72480467, subs@businessmonitor.com.

355 RUS
ROSSIISKOE VOENNOE OBOZRENIE. Text in Russian. 2003. m. USD 358 foreign (effective 2004). **Document type:** *Journal.*
Related titles: ◆ English Translation: Russian Military Review.
Published by: (Ministerstvo Oborony Rossiiskoi Federatsii/Ministry of Defence of the Russian Federation), Rossiiskoe Agentstvo Mezhdunarodnoi Informatsii R I A Novosti, Zubovskii bulv 4, Moscow, 119021, Russian Federation. TEL 7-095-2012746, marketing@rian.ru, http://en.rian.ru. **Dist. by:** East View Information Services, 10601 Wayzata Blvd, Minneapolis, MN 55305. TEL 952-252-1201, 800-477-1005, FAX 952-252-1202, info@eastview.com, http://www.eastview.com.

358.4 GBR ISSN 2040-8625
▼ **ROYAL AIR FORCE SALUTE.** Text in English. 2009. a. GBP 4.99 per issue (effective 2010). adv. **Document type:** *Magazine, Trade.*
Published by: (Great Britain. Royal Air Force), Key Publishing Ltd., PO Box 100, Stamford, PE9 1XQ, United Kingdom. TEL 44-1780-755131, FAX 44-1780-751323, info@keypublishing.com, http://www.keypublishing.com. Ed. Paul Hamblin. Pub. Adrian Cox. Adv. contact Brodie Baxter. **Subscr. to:** PO Box 300, Stamford, Lincs PE9 1NA, United Kingdom. TEL 44-1780-480404, FAX 44-1780-757812.

610.6 GBR
THE ROYAL ARMY MEDICAL CORPS MAGAZINE. Text in English. 1927. 3/yr. adv. bk.rev. **Document type:** *Newsletter, Government.* **Description:** Unit news of organizations within the Army Medical Services.
Formerly (until 2001): Army Medical Services Magazine

Published by: R A M C Historical Museum, Keogh Barracks, Ash Vale, Aldershot, Hants GU12 5RQ, United Kingdom. TEL 44-1252-868612, FAX 44-1252-868832, armymedicalmuseum@btinternet.com, http://www.ams-museum.org.uk/. Ed. P H Starling. R&P P.H. Starling TEL 44-1252-340250. Circ: 2,500.

355 GBR
ROYAL BRITISH LEGION. ANNUAL REPORT AND ACCOUNTS. Text in English. 1921. a. free (effective 2009). **Document type:** *Corporate.* **Description:** Contains review of Royal British Legion activities and financial position for every financial year.
Related titles: Online - full text ed.: free (effective 2009).
Published by: Royal British Legion, 199 Borough High St, London, SE1 1AA, United Kingdom. TEL 44-20-32072100.

355 CAN ISSN 1719-8844
ROYAL CANADIAN MILITARY INSTITUTE. MEMBERS' NEWS. Text in English. 2004. bi-m. **Document type:** *Newsletter, Trade.*
Published by: Royal Canadian Military Institute, 426 University Ave, Toronto, ON M5G 1S9, Canada. TEL 416-597-0286, 800-585-1072, FAX 416-597-6919, info@rcmi.org, http://www.rcmi.org.

623 GBR ISSN 0035-8878
UG1
ROYAL ENGINEERS JOURNAL. Text in English. 18??. 3/yr. free to members (effective 2009). adv. bk.rev. illus. index. **Document type:** *Journal, Academic/Scholarly.*
Formerly (until 1870): Corps of Royal Engineers. Journal
Indexed: A22, ChemAb, GeoRef, LID&ISL, SpeleolAb.
—BLDSC (8030.000000), IE, Ingenta, INIST, Linda Hall.
Published by: Institution of Royal Engineers, Brompton Barracks, Chatham, Kent ME4 4UG, United Kingdom. TEL 44-1634-822035, enquiries@instre.org, http://www.instre.org.

355 GBR ISSN 0035-9025
ROYAL MILITARY POLICE. JOURNAL. Abbreviated title: R M P Journal. Text in English. 1950. 3/yr. GBP 9 (effective 2009). adv. bk.rev. illus. **Document type:** *Journal, Trade.*
Published by: Royal Military Police, Regimental Headquarters, Defence Police College Policing and Guarding, Southwick Park, PO Box 38, Fareham, Hants PO17 6EJ, United Kingdom. TEL 44-23-92284206, regsec_rhqrmp@btconnect.com, http://www.army.mod.uk/home.aspx. adv.: B&W page GBP 450, color page GBP 650; 186 x 266.

363.35 338.473947 GBR ISSN 1749-1592
RUSSIA DEFENCE & SECURITY REPORT. Text in English. 2005. q. EUR 820, USD 1,030 combined subscription (print & email eds.) (effective 2010). **Document type:** *Report, Trade.* **Description:** Provides professionals, consultancies, government departments, regulatory bodies and researchers with independent forecasts and regional competitive intelligence on the Russian defence & security industry.
Related titles: E-mail ed.
Published by: Business Monitor International Ltd., Senator House, 85 Queen Victoria St, London, EC4V 4AB, United Kingdom. TEL 44-20-72480468, FAX 44-20-72480467, subs@businessmonitor.com.

355 RUS
RUSSIAN MILITARY REVIEW. Text in English. 2004. m. USD 385 (effective 2010). **Document type:** *Journal, Academic/Scholarly.*
Related titles: ◆ Translation of: Rossiiskoe Voennoe Obozrenie.
Published by: (Ministerstvo Oborony Rossiiskoi Federatsii/Ministry of Defence of the Russian Federation), Rossiiskoe Agentstvo Mezhdunarodnoi Informatsii R I A Novosti, Zubovskii bulv 4, Moscow, 119021, Russian Federation. TEL 7-095-2012746, marketing@rian.ru, http://en.rian.ru. Ed. Fyodor Kozanchuk. **Dist. by:** East View Information Services, 10601 Wayzata Blvd, Minneapolis, MN 55305. TEL 952-252-1201, 800-477-1005, FAX 952-252-1202, info@eastview.com, http://www.eastview.com.

355 RWA
RWANDA. MINISTERE DE LA DEFENSE NATIONALE. FORCES DE SECURITE AU SERVICE DE LA NATION. Text in French. bi-m. **Document type:** *Government.*
Published by: Ministere de la Defense Nationale, BP 85, Kigali, Rwanda.

355 GBR
S C S I OCCASIONAL PAPERS. Text in English. irreg., latest vol.40, 2001. free. 70 p./no.; **Document type:** *Monographic series, Academic/Scholarly.*
Indexed: LID&ISL.
Published by: Strategic and Combat Studies Institute, Joint Doctrine & Concepts Centre, Shrivenham, Swindon, Wiltshire SN6 8RF, United Kingdom. TEL 44-1793787266, FAX 44-1793787265, defencestudies@gtnet.gov.uk. Ed. Richard P Cousens. R&P Jahe Darby. Circ: 2,000.

355 ARG ISSN 0328-6126
➤ **S E R EN EL 2000.** (Seguridad Estrategia Regional) Text in Spanish. 1992. 3/yr. USD 21; USD 40 foreign. adv. bk.rev. **Document type:** *Academic/Scholarly.*
Related titles: Online - full text ed.
Address: Hipolito Yrigoyen, 1994, Buenos Aires, 1089, Argentina. TEL 54-114-9510712. Ed., R&P Luis Tibiletti. Pub. Eduardo Pedro Vaca. Adv. contact Marcela R Donadio. Circ: 1,000.

➤ **S I B TERM.** (Sprachinstitut des Bundesheeres) *see* LINGUISTICS

➤ **S O W I ARBEITSPAPIERE.** *see* SOCIAL SCIENCES: COMPREHENSIVE WORKS

355 AUS ISSN 0048-8933
SABRETACHE. Text in English. 1957. q. free to members (effective 2009). bk.rev. Index. **Document type:** *Journal, Trade.* **Description:** Includes articles and letters; publishes member's wants and queries; covers military history, customs, traditions, dress, arms, equipment and kindred matters.
Related titles: Online - full text ed.
Indexed: A26, AusPAIS, E08, G08, I05, M06, S09.
—Ingenta.
Published by: Military Historical Society of Australia, PO Box 5030, Garran, ACT 2605, Australia. members@mhsa.org.au. Ed. Anthony Staunton.

355 USA ISSN 2157-5991
SAFE PASSAGE. Text in English. 2003. s-a. free (effective 2010). back issues avail. **Document type:** *Newsletter, Trade.*
Formerly (until 2004): Mine Action Messenger
Media: Online - full text.
Published by: U.S. Department of State, Office of Weapons Removal and Abatement, Bureau of Political-Military Affairs, 2121 Virginia Ave, NW, Rm 6100, Washington, DC 20522. TEL 202-663-0081, FAX 202-663-0090, DavisSB@state.gov, http://www.state.gov/t/pm/wra/.

355 CAN ISSN 1208-9400
SAFETY DIGEST (OTTAWA)/DIGEST DE SECURITE. Text in English. 1973. 4/yr. CAD 11, USD 13.40. illus. **Document type:** *Government.*
Formerly (until 1996): General Safety Digest (0707-0403)
Related titles: French ed.
Published by: Department of National Defence, Directorate of General Safety, National Defence Headquarters, Major General George Pearkes Bldg, 101 Colonel By Dr, Ottawa, ON K1A 0K2, Canada. TEL 613-995-3291, FAX 613-992-5484. Ed., R&P Bob Britton. Circ: 10,000. **Dist. by:** Canada Communication Group, 45 Sacre-Coeur Blvd, Hull, PQ K1A 0S7, Canada.

355.31 IND ISSN 0036-2743
U4
SAINIK SAMACHAR. Text in Hindi. 1909. fortn. INR 100 domestic; INR 450 foreign (effective 2011). adv. bk.rev. charts; illus. back issues avail. **Document type:** *Magazine, Government.* **Description:** Provides news and entertainment as well as education to those enrolled in Indian Armed Forces.
Formerly (until 1954): Fauji Akhbar
Related titles: Multiple languages ed.
Published by: Ministry of Defence, Directorate of Public Relations, Block L-1, Church Rd, New Delhi, 110 011, India. TEL 91-11-23092768, einc-ss@nic.in, http://mod.nic.in/. Eds. V K Joshi, D J Narain. Pub. Sitanshu Kar.

355 ZAF ISSN 1609-5014
U1
SALUT; S A soldier. Text in English. 1949. m. adv. bk.rev. illus.; maps; stat. 48 p./no.; back issues avail. **Document type:** *Magazine, Government.* **Description:** Covers South African National Defence Force and Department of Defence matters with articles and features.
Former titles (until 1994): Paratus (0031-1839); Commando (0010-2504)
Related titles: E-mail ed.; Online - full text ed.
Indexed: AMB, ISAP, LID&ISL.
—IE.
Published by: South African National Defence Force, Private Bag X158, Pretoria, 0001, South Africa. TEL 27-12-3556341, FAX 27-12-3556399, salut@mil.za. Ed., R&P, Adv. contact Nelda Pienaar. Circ: 60,000 (paid).

355 USA ISSN 1933-5318
SALUTE!. Text in English. 2006. m. **Document type:** *Newsletter, Consumer.*
Related titles: Online - full text ed.: ISSN 1933-5326.
Published by: Red Engine Press, Box 107, Ste F, Branson West, MO 65737. Publisher@redenginepress.com. Ed. Pat McGrath Avery.

355.37 USA ISSN 1942-6836
UA42.A6
SALUTE TO FREEDOM. Text in English. 2007. irreg. **Document type:** *Magazine, Consumer.*
Published by: Lafayette Marketing Group, 503 Althea Rd, Belleair, FL 33756. TEL 727-531-5090, FAX 727-524-3073. Ed. Gabrielle D Wood.

SALVO (SAN FRANCISCO). *see* HISTORY—History Of North And South America

THE SANDHURST CONFERENCE SERIES. *see* POLITICAL SCIENCE—International Relations

355 GBR
THE SAPPER. Text in English. 1895. bi-m. GBP 12 domestic; GBP 15 foreign; GBP 2 per issue domestic; GBP 2.50 per issue foreign (effective 2009). adv. bk.rev. back issues avail. **Document type:** *Magazine.* **Description:** Contains information about units on operational tours, such as operation herrick in Afghanistan and operation telic in Iraq and provides a round up of sports articles and adventure training articles.
Related titles: Online - full text ed.
—BLDSC (8075.770500).
Published by: Corps of Royal Engineers, Brompton Barracks, Dock Rd, Chatham, Kent ME4 4UG, United Kingdom. TEL 44-1634-822299, FAX 44-1634-822397.

051 USA
SATELLITE FLYER. Text in English. w. **Document type:** *Newspaper, Consumer.*
Published by: Colorado Springs Military Newspaper Group (Subsidiary of: Dolan Media Co.), 31 E Platte Ave, Colorado Springs, CO 80903. TEL 719-634-5905, FAX 719-867-0265.

363.35 338.473 953.8 GBR ISSN 1749-1606
SAUDI ARABIA DEFENCE & SECURITY REPORT. Text in English. 2005. q. EUR 820, USD 1,030 combined subscription (print & email eds.) (effective 2010). **Document type:** *Report, Trade.* **Description:** Provides professionals, consultancies, government departments, regulatory bodies and researchers with independent forecasts and regional competitive intelligence on the Saudi defence & security industry.
Related titles: E-mail ed.
Indexed: B01, P34.
Published by: Business Monitor International Ltd., Senator House, 85 Queen Victoria St, London, EC4V 4AB, United Kingdom. TEL 44-20-72480468, FAX 44-20-72480467, subs@businessmonitor.com.

SAVAGE AND SOLDIER. *see* SPORTS AND GAMES

355 TUR ISSN 1300-2082
TL527.T9
SAVUNMA VE HAVACILIK; defence and aerospace. Text in Turkish. 1987. bi-m. TRY 50 domestic; EUR 60 in Europe; USD 100 elsewhere (effective 2009). adv. back issues avail. **Document type:** *Magazine, Trade.* **Description:** Covers technical issues in the defense and civilian sectors of the aviation and aerospace industries.
Published by: Monch Turkiye Yayincilik, Hosdere Caddesi, Halit Ziya Sokak, No 26/9, Cankaya / Ankara, 06540, Turkey. TEL 90-312-4419354, FAX 90-312-4395724, info@monch.com.tr. Ed. Ibrahim Sunnetci. Adv. contact Ute Steuer. B&W page USD 3,500, color page USD 6,500; trim 7.31 x 10.63. Circ: 21,030. **Subscr. to:** Moench Publishing Group, Postfach 140261, Bonn 53057, Germany. TEL 49-228-6483-0, FAX 49-228-6483109.

355 USA ISSN 0036-5408
SCABBARD AND BLADE JOURNAL. Text in English. 1913. 3/yr. USD 3. bk.rev. illus.
Published by: National Society of Scabbard and Blade, 205 Thatcher Hall, Oklahoma State University, Stillwater, OK 74078. TEL 405-624-5000. Ed. Max Rodgers. Circ: 2,000.

355 CHE ISSN 1421-6906
UA800
SCHWEIZER SOLDAT UND M F D; Die Monatszeitschrift fuer Armee und Kader mit MFD-Zeitung. Text in German. 1925. m. CHF 54.50 domestic; CHF 64 foreign (effective 2000). adv. bk.rev. **Document type:** *Journal, Trade.* **Description:** Covers current issues, news, information and new developments concerning the national and foreign military. Includes list of events, new publications and positions available.
Former titles (until 1986): Schweizer Soldat und F H D (1421-6914); (until 1982): Schweizer Soldat (0036-7451); Incorporates: M F D-Zeitung (0014-584X)
Indexed: IBR, IBZ.
—IE, Infotrieve.
Published by: Huber und Co. AG, Promenadenstr 16, Frauenfeld, 8501, Switzerland. TEL 41-54-271111. Ed. Edwin Hofstetter. Circ: 12,500.

355 CHE
SCHWEIZER WEHRSPORT. Text in German. 11/yr.
Address: Endlikerstr 79, Winterthur, 8400, Switzerland. TEL 052-296296. Ed. Heinz Koch. Circ: 3,000.

355 ITA
SCIARPA AZZURRA. Text in Italian. 1988. q. free to members. adv. bk.rev. back issues avail. **Document type:** *Magazine, Trade.* **Description:** Contains technical, historical and current events articles.
Published by: Unione Nazionale Ufficiali in Congedo d'Italia (U N U C I), Via Nomentana 313, Rome, 00162, Italy. TEL 39-06-8548795, FAX 39-06-8414555, http://www.unuci.it. Circ: 1,500.

SCIENTIFIC-TECHNICAL REVIEW. *see* ENGINEERING

359 USA
SCIPIO NEWSLETTER. Text in English. 1979. m. membership. bk.rev. **Document type:** *Newsletter.* **Description:** Covers past and upcoming events and meetings.
Formerly (until 1992): Grenade (0891-124X)
Published by: Scipio Society of Naval and Military History, Inc., PO Box 93, Cold Spring, NY 11724. TEL 631-271-7037, FAX 631-271-7137. Ed. Richard N Hadcock. Circ: 25.

358.4 USA
SCOTT FLIER. Text in English. 1987. w. (Thu.). free (effective 2005). **Document type:** *Newspaper.*
Published by: Herald Publications, P O Box C, Mascoutah, IL 62258. TEL 618-566-8282. Pub. Greg Hoskins. Circ: 4,000 (paid and controlled).

355.1 GBR
SCOTTISH LEGION NEWS. Text in English. 1950. 6/yr. bk.rev. illus. **Document type:** *Magazine, Trade.* **Description:** Contains articles looking at the military past, present and future as well as current affairs.
Incorporates (in 1987): Claymore (0009-8590)
Published by: Royal British Legion Scotland, New Haig House, 66 Logie Green Rd, Edinburgh, EH7 4HR, United Kingdom. info@rblsnewdeer.org.uk.

355 USA
SCOUT ONLINE; informating, educating and entertaining since 1942. Text in English. 1980. w. (Thu.). free (effective 2009). **Document type:** *Newspaper, Consumer.*
Formerly (until Apr.2009): The Scout (Print)
Media: Online - full content.
Published by: U.S. Marine Corps Base Camp Pendleton, Attn: Scout newspaper, Box 555019, Camp Pendleton, CA 92055-5019. TEL 760-725-5799, http://www.pendleton.usmc.mil/. Circ: 25,500 (paid and free).

335 USA
SCREAMING EAGLE. Text in English. 1945. bi-m. USD 20 to members. adv. bk.rev. **Document type:** *Newsletter.* **Description:** News and features for all veterans of the 101st Airborne Division.
Published by: 101st Airborne Division Association, 7698 State Rt. 41, PO Box 101, Bentonvilles, OH 45105. TEL 513-549-4326, FAX 513-549-2018. Ed., R&P Billy A Carrington. Adv. contact Debi Rogers. Circ: 6,200.

359 USA ISSN 0199-1337
VA49
SEA POWER. Text in English. 1949. m. USD 58 domestic; USD 145 foreign; USD 5 per issue domestic; USD 14 per issue foreign (effective 2009). adv. bk.rev. charts; illus. index. back issues avail.; reprints avail. **Document type:** *Magazine, Trade.* **Description:** Aims to educate the American people, their elected representatives, and industry on the need for robust naval and maritime forces.
Formerly (until 1971): Navy (0028-1689); (until 1958): Now Hear This
Related titles: Microform ed.: (from PQC); Online - full text ed.: ISSN 1930-3947; ◆ Supplement(s): Almanac of Seapower. ISSN 0736-3559.
Indexed: A01, A22, A26, ABS&EES, AMB, AUNI, DM&T, G05, G06, G07, G08, I02, I05, M02, M05, M06, M07, P02, P10, P34, P47, P48, P52, P53, P54, P56, PAIS, PQC, RASB, S23, T02.
—Ingenta, Linda Hall. **CCC.**
Published by: Navy League of the United States, 2300 Wilson Blvd, Arlington, VA 22201. TEL 703-528-1775, 800-356-5760, FAX 703-243-8251. Ed. Amy Wittman. Pub. Michael J McGrath. adv.: color page USD 7,670; bleed 8.375 x 11.

355 GBR
SEAFORD HOUSE PAPERS. Text in English. 1970. a. back issues avail. **Document type:** *Journal, Academic/Scholarly.* **Description:** Contains the best of dissertations written by the member of the full 11-month course of the defense academy of United Kingdom.
Related titles: Online - full text ed.: free (effective 2009).
Indexed: LID&ISL.
Published by: Royal College of Defence Studies, Seaford House, 37 Belgrave Sq, London, SW1X 8NS, United Kingdom. TEL 44-20-79154804.

355 CAN ISSN 0048-9883
SEALANDAIR. Text in English. 1969. fortn. CAD 10, USD 20. adv. charts; illus.
Published by: Canadian Forces Base Edmonton, 408 Tactical Helicopter Squadron, Canadian Forces Base Edmonton, PO Box 10500 STN Forces, Edmonton, AB T53 4J5, Canada. Circ: 3,000.

359 USA
SEALIFT (ONLINE). Text in English. 1951-1979 (vol.29, no.12); resumed 1986. m. free to qualified personnel. bk.rev. **Document type:** *Magazine, Trade.*
Former titles (until 1979): Sealift (Print) (0191-135X); (until 1968): Sealift Magazine; (until 1961): M S T S
Media: Online - full content.
Indexed: IUSGP.
Published by: U.S. Navy, Military Sealift Command, 914 Charles Morris Court, S.E., Washington Navy Yard, Washington, DC 20398-5540. TEL 202-685-5055, FAX 202-685-5067. Circ: 7,000.

359 AUS ISSN 1322-6479
SEATALK. Text in English. 1998 (Winter). q. back issues avail. **Document type:** *Magazine, Trade.* **Description:** Covers the conditions of naval service, pay and allowances, housing. Also provides articles covering other varied aspects specific to life in the navy.
Published by: Australia. Department of Defence, R8-LG-001, Russell Offices, Canberra, ACT 2600, Australia. TEL 61-2-62651193, FAX 61-2-62656972, http://www.defence.gov.au/index.htm. Ed. Antony Underwood. Adv. contact Geoff Howard TEL 61-2-62667605.

359 900 CAN ISSN 1710-6966
SEAWAVES TODAY IN HISTORY. Text in English. 2004. w. **Document type:** *Newsletter.*
Media: Online - full text.
Published by: Seawaves Publishing Inc info@seawaves.com, http://www.seawaves.com/index.html.

355 USA ISSN 1533-2535
JZ5588
SECURITY AND DEFENSE STUDIES REVIEW. Abbreviated title: S D S R. Text in English. 2001. s-a. free (effective 2011). back issues avail. **Document type:** *Journal, Academic/Scholarly.*
Media: Online - full text.
Indexed: CA, P42, PAIS, SociolAb, T02.
Published by: National Defense University, Center for Hemispheric Defense Studies, National Defense University, Abraham Lincoln Hall, 260 5th Ave Bldg 64, Washington, DC 20319. TEL 202-685-4670, FAX 202-685-4674, http://www.ndu.edu/chds/. Ed. Martin Edwin Andersen.

355 AUS ISSN 1833-1459
➤ **SECURITY CHALLENGES.** Text in English. 2005. q. AUD 100; AUD 27 per issue; free to members (effective 2009). back issues avail. **Document type:** *Journal, Academic/Scholarly.* **Description:** Covers future security issues for military, government, commercial and academic experts.
Related titles: Online - full text ed.
Indexed: AusPAIS.
Published by: Kokoda Foundation, 1st Fl 182-200 City Walk, Canberra, ACT 2600, Australia. TEL 61-2-62041822, FAX 61-2-61693019, manager@kokodafoundation.org, http://www.kokodafoundation.org. Eds. David Connery, Stephan Fruehling. Circ: 700.

355 363.35 GBR ISSN 1993-4270
➤ **SECURITY INDEX.** Text in English. 2007. 4/yr. GBP 329 combined subscription in United Kingdom to institutions (print & online eds.); EUR 434, USD 542 combined subscription to institutions (print & online eds.) (effective 2012). **Document type:** *Journal, Academic/Scholarly.* **Description:** Features research on urgent issues in the sphere of international security that are relevant to Russian interests.
Related titles: Online - full text ed.: ISSN 2151-7495. 2010. GBP 295 in United Kingdom to institutions; EUR 390, USD 488 to institutions (effective 2012); ◆ Russian ed.: Indeks Bezopasnosti. ISSN 1992-9242.
Indexed: I02, T02.
—East View. **CCC.**
Published by: Taylor & Francis Ltd. (Subsidiary of: Taylor & Francis Group), 4 Park Sq, Milton Park, Abingdon, Oxfordshire OX14 4RN, United Kingdom. TEL 44-20-70176000, FAX 44-20-70176336, info@tandf.co.uk.

➤ **SECURITY STUDIES (QUARTERLY).** *see* POLITICAL SCIENCE—International Relations

355 VEN
SEGURIDAD Y DEFENSA; revista plural sobre temas militares y geopolitica. Text in Spanish. q.
Address: Miracielos a Hospital, Edif. Sur 2, piso 8, Of. 812, Caracas, 1010, Venezuela. TEL 4835853. Ed. Manuel Molina Penaloza.

355 JPN
SEKAI NO KANSEN/SHIPS OF THE WORLD. Text in Japanese. 1957. m. JPY 12,600; JPY 16,130 foreign (effective 1999). adv. bk.rev. illus. **Description:** Covers ships from all over the world including: modern and historic warships, merchant ships, cruise ships, and ferries. Also contains world navy news, maritime events and history, and shipping news. Includes 88 pages of black & white and color photos.
Published by: Kaijinsha Co. Ltd., c/o NAO Bldg, 4 Shinogawa-Machi 1-chome, Shinjuku-ku, Tokyo, 162-0814, Japan. TEL 81-3-3268-6351, FAX 81-3-3268-6354. Ed., R&P Tohru Kizu. Pub. Koji Ishiwata. Adv. contact Hitoshi Hasegawa. Circ: 54,000.

SEKAI NO KESSAKUKI/FAMOUS AIRPLANES OF THE WORLD. *see* AERONAUTICS AND SPACE FLIGHT

355 USA ISSN 1933-2327
SEMPER FI. Text in English. 19??. bi-m. adv. **Document type:** *Magazine, Consumer.*
Former titles (until 2006): Marine Corps League (0888-5923); (until 1986): Marine Corps League News (0746-9594); (until 1983): Proud Tradition (0279-2710); (until 1981): Marine Corps League News (0195-7422)
Published by: Marine Corps League, PO Box 3070, Merrifield, VA 22116.

363.35 338.47355 949.71 GBR ISSN 1749-1614
SERBIA & MONTENEGRO DEFENCE & SECURITY REPORT. Text in English. 2005. q. EUR 475, USD 575 combined subscription (print & email eds.) (effective 2005). **Document type:** *Report, Trade.* **Description:** Provides industry leaders, defense manufacturers and suppliers, intelligence agencies and governments with independent forecasts and competitive intelligence on the defense and security industry in Serbia & Montenegro.
Related titles: E-mail ed.
Published by: Business Monitor International Ltd., Senator House, 85 Queen Victoria St, London, EC4V 4AB, United Kingdom. TEL 44-20-72480468, FAX 44-20-72480467, subs@businessmonitor.com, enquiry@businessmonitor.com.

SERIES ON THE IRAQ WAR AND ITS CONSEQUENCES. *see* POLITICAL SCIENCE—International Relations

355 RUS
SERTIFIKATSIYA - KONVERSIYA - RYNOK. Text in Russian. q. USD 89 in United States (effective 2000).
Indexed: RASB.
Published by: V.I.M.I., Volokolamskoe shosse 77, Moscow, 123584, Russian Federation. TEL 7-095-4911306. **Dist. by:** East View Information Services, 10601 Wayzata Blvd, Minneapolis, MN 55305. TEL 952-252-1201, 800-477-1005, FAX 952-252-1202, info@eastview.com, http://www.eastview.com.

355 CAN ISSN 1495-7167
SERVICES AND BENEFITS. Text in English. 198?. a. **Document type:** *Journal, Consumer.*
Related titles: Online - full text ed.: ISSN 1910-8303. 2006; ◆ French ed.: Services et Avantages. ISSN 1495-7213.
Published by: Veterans Affairs Canada/Anciens Combattants Canada, PO Box 7700, Charlottetown, PE C1A 8M9, Canada. TEL 866-522-2022, 866-522-2122, information@vac-acc.gc.ca, http://www.veterans.gc.ca.

355 CAN ISSN 1495-7213
SERVICES ET AVANTAGES. Text in French. 198?. a. **Document type:** *Journal, Trade.*
Related titles: Online - full text ed.: ISSN 1910-8311; ◆ English ed.: Services and Benefits. ISSN 1495-7167.
Published by: Veterans Affairs Canada/Anciens Combattants Canada, PO Box 7700, Charlottetown, PE C1A 8M9, Canada. TEL 866-522-2022, 866-522-2122, information@vac-acc.gc.ca, http://www.veterans.gc.ca.

355 PRT ISSN 1647-1393
SERVICO MILITAR. Text in Portuguese. 2008. bi-m. **Document type:** *Magazine, Government.*
Published by: Ministerio da Defesa Nacional, Av Ilha da Madeira 1, Lisbon, 1400-204, Portugal. TEL 351-213-010001, FAX 351-213-020284, gcrp@defesa.pt, http://www.mdn.gov.pt.

355 CAN
SERVIR. Text in English, French. 1971. m. free. adv. bk.rev. illus. **Document type:** *Bulletin, Corporate.*
Formerly: Parapet (0384-0417)
Indexed: INI.
Published by: Canadian Forces Base Montreal, Montreal, PQ J0J 1R0, Canada. TEL 514-358-7099, FAX 514-358-7423. Ed., R&P, Adv. contact Gaetane Dion. B&W page CAD 621, color page CAD 882. Circ: 4,000.

355 RUS
SERZHANT/SERGEANT. Text in Russian. 1996. q. USD 30 (effective 2004); includes Shevron Series, 9 iss./yr. adv. **Document type:** *Magazine.* **Description:** Covers world military history: all periods, all countries, weapons, order of battles, uniforms, personalities, etc.
Published by: Izdatel'stvo Reitar, Pr-t Vernadskogo 89, ofis 315, Moscow, 119526, Russian Federation. plotkin@msk.net.ru. Ed. Gennadii L Plotkin. adv.: B&W page USD 110, color page USD 200.

SHENJIAN/GOD SWORD. *see* LITERATURE

SHEPHARD'S ELECTRONIC WARFARE HANDBOOK. *see* ENGINEERING—Electrical Engineering

SHEPHARD'S MILITARY HELICOPTER HANDBOOK. *see* TRANSPORTATION—Air Transport

355 USA ISSN 1559-4807
VG53
THE SHIELD OF FREEDOM. Text in English. a. **Document type:** *Magazine, Consumer.* **Description:** About the United States Coast Guard.
Published by: Faircount Media Group, 701 N. Westshore Blvd., Tampa, FL 33609. TEL 813-639-1900, 888-960-1300, FAX 813-639-4344, rjobson@faircount.com, http://www.faircount.com.

355 CHN ISSN 1002-4891
SHIJIE JUNSHI/WORLD MILITARY AFFAIRS. Text in Chinese. 1989. m. USD 28.80 (effective 2009). **Document type:** *Magazine, Trade.* **Description:** Covers military issues, weapons, equipments, stories, and combat.
Address: 57, Xuanwumen Xi Dajie, Beijing, 100803, China. TEL 86-10-63073570. **Dist. by:** China International Book Trading Corp, 35 Chegongzhuang Xilu, Haidian District, PO Box 399, Beijing 100044, China. TEL 86-10-68412045, FAX 86-10-68412023, cibtc@mail.cibtc.com.cn, http://www.cibtc.com.cn.

355 CAN ISSN 0037-3729
SHILO STAG. Text in English. 1970 (vol.9). s-m. CAD 12.50. adv. bibl.; charts; illus.; tr.lit.
Published by: Leech Printing Ltd., 18th and Park, Brandon, MB R7A 5B8, Canada. TEL 204-728-3037, FAX 204-727-3338.

SHIPMATE. *see* COLLEGE AND ALUMNI

359 USA
SHIPYARD & I M F LOG. (Intermediate Maintenance Facility) Cover title: Pearl Harbor Shipyard & I M F Log. Text in English. 1946. s-m. free. adv. illus. **Document type:** *Newspaper, Government.*
Formerly: Shipyard Log (1073-8258)
Published by: Pearl Harbor Naval Shipyard and Intermediate Maintenance Facility, 401 Ave E, Ste 124, Pearl Harbor, HI 96860-5350. TEL 808-474-3214, FAX 808-474-0269. Ed. Marshall Fukuki. R&P Kelley Spellman. Circ: 4,050 (controlled).

SHOW DAILY. *see* POLITICAL SCIENCE—International Relations

358.4 RUS
SHTURMOVIK. Text in Russian. 24/yr. USD 145 in United States.
Indexed: RASB.
Address: A-ya 27, Moscow, 105484, Russian Federation. TEL 7-095-9773387. **Dist. by:** East View Information Services, 10601 Wayzata Blvd, Minneapolis, MN 55305. TEL 952-252-1201, 800-477-1005, FAX 952-252-1202, info@eastview.com, http://www.eastview.com.

355 USA ISSN 0733-0367
DD253.65
SIEGRUNEN; the Waffen-SS in historical perspective. Text in English. 1975. irreg. Price varies. adv. bk.rev. back issues avail. **Document type:** *Monographic series, Consumer.* **Description:** Covers history of Waffen-SS and biographies of personalities, units, and battles.
Published by: Merriam Press, 133 Elm St Apt 3R, Bennington, VT 05201-2250. TEL 802-447-0313, ray@merriam-press.com, http://www.merriam-press.com/siegrunenmonographs.aspx. Ed. Richard Landwehr. Circ: 375.

355 USA
SILVER WINGS. Text in English. 1958. w. free. **Document type:** *Newspaper.*
Published by: Columbus Air Force Base Public Affairs, 555 Seventh St, Ste 203, Columbus, MS 39710-1009. FAX 601-434-7009. Ed. Sgt. Karin Wickwire.

363.35 338.473 959.57 GBR ISSN 1749-1622
SINGAPORE DEFENCE & SECURITY REPORT. Text in English. 2005. q. EUR 820, USD 1,030 combined subscription (print & email eds.) (effective 2010). **Document type:** *Report, Trade.* **Description:** Covers independent forecasts and competitive intelligence on the defense and security industry in Singapore.
Related titles: E-mail ed.
Indexed: A15, ABIn, B01, P48, P51, P52, PQC.
Published by: Business Monitor International Ltd., Senator House, 85 Queen Victoria St, London, EC4V 4AB, United Kingdom. TEL 44-20-72480468, FAX 44-20-72480467, subs@businessmonitor.com.

355 DEU
SIXTH SENSE. Text in German. w. **Document type:** *Bulletin.*
Published by: GOC UK Support Command Germany, Rochdale Kaserne, Oldentruper Str 65, Bielefeld, 33604, Germany. TEL 49-521-924720, FAX 49-521-9247229.

363.35 338.473 943.73 GBR ISSN 1749-1630
SLOVAKIA DEFENCE & SECURITY REPORT. Text in English. 2005. a. EUR 820, USD 1,030 combined subscription per issue (print & email eds.) (effective 2010). **Document type:** *Report, Trade.* **Description:** Covers independent forecasts and competitive intelligence on the defence and security industry in Slovakia.
Related titles: E-mail ed.
Published by: Business Monitor International Ltd., Senator House, 85 Queen Victoria St, London, EC4V 4AB, United Kingdom. TEL 44-20-72480468, FAX 44-20-72480467, subs@businessmonitor.com.

363.35 338.473 949.73 GBR ISSN 1749-1649
SLOVENIA DEFENCE & SECURITY REPORT. Text in English. 2005. a. EUR 820, USD 1,030 combined subscription per issue (print & email eds.) (effective 2010). **Document type:** *Report, Trade.* **Description:** Covers independent forecasts and competitive intelligence on the defense and security industry in Slovenia.
Related titles: E-mail ed.
Published by: Business Monitor International Ltd., Senator House, 85 Queen Victoria St, London, EC4V 4AB, United Kingdom. TEL 44-20-72480468, FAX 44-20-72480467, subs@businessmonitor.com.

355 RUS
SLUZHBA. Text in Russian. irreg.
Published by: Rossiiskoe Ekonomicheskoe Obshchestvo Voennosluzhashchikh Zapasa, Obshchestvennyi Sovet 300 let Rossiiskomy Flotu, Sadovaya-Kudrinskaya 11, k 335, Moscow, 103001, Russian Federation. TEL 7-095-2527625, FAX 7-095-2521283. Ed. A S Pilipchuk. **Dist. by:** East View Information Services, 10601 Wayzata Blvd, Minneapolis, MN 55305. TEL 952-252-1201, 800-477-1005, FAX 952-252-1202, info@eastview.com, http://www.eastview.com.

355 UKR
SLUZHBA BEZOPASNOSTI. Text in Russian. m. USD 205 in United States.
Published by: Ukrainskaya Federatsiya Negosudarstvennykh Sluzhb Bezopasnosti, Ul Pan'kovskaya 8, Kiev, Ukraine. TEL 216-15-62. **Dist. by:** East View Information Services, 10601 Wayzata Blvd, Minneapolis, MN 55305. TEL 952-252-1201, 800-477-1005, FAX 952-252-1202, info@eastview.com, http://www.eastview.com.

355 RUS
SLUZHBA BEZOPASNOSTI. Text in Russian. bi-m. USD 149.95 in United States.
Indexed: RASB.
Published by: Federal'naya Sluzhba Kontrazvedki Rossiiskoi Federatsii, Lubyanka 2, Zoologicheskii per 8, kom 3, etazh 1, Moscow, 101000, Russian Federation. TEL 7-095-2248771, FAX 7-095-2332073. **Dist. by:** East View Information Services, 10601 Wayzata Blvd, Minneapolis, MN 55305. TEL 952-252-1201, 800-477-1005, FAX 952-252-1202, info@eastview.com, http://www.eastview.com.

SMALL WARS AND INSURGENCIES. *see* POLITICAL SCIENCE—International Relations

355 USA
SMALL WARS JOURNAL. Text in English. 2005. 3/yr. **Document type:** *Journal, Academic/Scholarly.*
Formerly (until 2008): S W J Magazine
Media: Online - full content.
Published by: Small Wars Foundation, 4938 Hampden Ln, Bethesda, MD 20814. TEL 202-380-6329. Ed. Dave Dilegge. Pub. Bill Nagle.

355 CHE
SOCIETE MILITAIRE DU CANTON DE GENEVE. BULLETIN. Text in French. 10/yr. **Document type:** *Bulletin.*
Published by: (Societe Militaire du Canton de Geneve), Bercher SA, Rue de l Athenee 34, Geneva, 1206, Switzerland. TEL 022-3473388, FAX 022-3462047. Circ: 1,300.

355.009 GBR ISSN 0037-9700
DA49
➤ **SOCIETY FOR ARMY HISTORICAL RESEARCH. JOURNAL.** Text in English. 1921. q. free to members (effective 2009). bk.rev. illus.; maps. cum.index. **Document type:** *Journal, Academic/Scholarly.*

Indexed: AmH&L, AmHI, BAS, BrArAb, BrHumI, CA, H07, HistAb, IBR, IBZ, NumL, P30, PCI, RASB, T02.
—BLDSC (4880.790000), IE, Infotrieve, Ingenta. **CCC.**
Published by: Society for Army Historical Research, St. John's College, Cambridge, CB2 1TP, United Kingdom. TEL 44-1223-338661. Ed. Andrew Cormack TEL 44-20-83584869.

➤ **SOCIETY OF COLONIAL WARS. BULLETIN.** *see* HISTORY—History Of North And South America

355.3 ARG ISSN 0038-0954
SOLDADO ARGENTINO. Text in Spanish. 1921. q. adv. **Description:** Educational magazine for volunteer soldiers of the Argentine Army.
Published by: Estado Mayor General del Ejercito, Azopardo, 250 Piso 4, Buenos Aires, 1328, Argentina. TEL 54-114-3422121, FAX 54-114-3311865. Adv. contact Victor Raul Lessler. B&W page USD 800; 280 x 200. Circ: 15,000.

355 AUT ISSN 0038-0962
DER SOLDAT; Oesterreichische Soldaten-Zeitung. Text in German. 1956. fortn. EUR 33.40 (effective 2008). adv. charts; illus. **Document type:** *Newspaper, Trade.*
Published by: Der Soldat Zeitungs- und Zeitschriften Verlagsgesellschaft mbH, Parkring 4/1c, Vienna, W 1010, Austria. TEL 43-1-5232324, FAX 43-1-523232455. Ed. Georg Geyer. Circ: 15,000.

356.1 DEU ISSN 0038-0970
SOLDAT IM VOLK. Text in German. 1950. bi-m. EUR 20 (effective 2007). adv. **Document type:** *Magazine, Trade.*
Published by: Verband Deutscher Soldaten e.V., Rheinallee 55, Bonn, 53173, Germany. TEL 49-228-361007, FAX 49-228-361008, info@verband-deutscher-soldaten.de, http://www.verband-deutscher-soldaten.de. adv.: page EUR 1,030. Circ: 4,000 (paid and controlled).

355 RUS
SOLDAT OTECHESTVA. Text in Russian. w. USD 249 in United States.
Address: Ul Pionerskaya 19, Samara, 443099, Russian Federation. TEL 8462-334598. Ed. A I Dergilev. **Dist. by:** East View Information Services, 10601 Wayzata Blvd, Minneapolis, MN 55305. TEL 952-252-1201, 800-477-1005, FAX 952-252-1202, info@eastview.com, http://www.eastview.com.

355 TJK
SOLDAT ROSSII. Text in Russian. w. USD 299 in United States.
Published by: Ministry of Defence of the Russian Federation, Infantry Division 201, Box 01162, Dushanbe, Tajikistan. **Dist. by:** East View Information Services, 10601 Wayzata Blvd, Minneapolis, MN 55305. TEL 952-252-1201, 800-477-1005, FAX 952-252-1202, info@eastview.com, http://www.eastview.com.

355 RUS
SOLDAT UDACHI. Text in Russian. m. RUR 348; RUR 40 newsstand/cover (effective 2000). **Document type:** *Journal.*
Published by: Firma Meiker, Ul Lyusinovskaya 68, Moscow, 113162, Russian Federation. TEL 7-095-2332178, FAX 7-095-9583461. Ed. Andrei A Kuzminov. Circ: 25,000. **Dist. by:** East View Information Services, 10601 Wayzata Blvd, Minneapolis, MN 55305. TEL 952-252-1201, 800-477-1005, FAX 952-252-1202, info@eastview.com, http://www.eastview.com.

355 GBR ISSN 0038-1004
SOLDIER. Text in English. 1945. m. GBP 23 domestic; GBP 47 foreign; GBP 13.80 to qualified personnel; GBP 3.50 newsstand/cover (effective 2009). adv. bk.rev. illus. back issues avail. **Document type:** *Magazine, Government.* **Description:** Features articles relevant to the British Army.
Related titles: Online - full text ed.: free (effective 2009).
Indexed: RASB.
—IE, Infotrieve. **CCC.**
Published by: Great Britain. Ministry of Defence, Ordnance Rd, Aldershot, Hampshire GU11 2DU, United Kingdom. TEL 44-1252-347352, FAX 44-1252-347358, customer.services@tso.co.uk, http://www.mod.uk/. Ed. Stephen Tyler TEL 44-1252-347356. Adv. contact Heather Shekyls TEL 44-1252-347352.

355 USA ISSN 0145-6784
G539
SOLDIER OF FORTUNE; the journal of professional adventurers. Text in English. 1975. m. USD 34.95 domestic; USD 54.95 in Canada (effective 2005); USD 49.95 elsewhere; USD 4.95 per issue (effective 2004). adv. bk.rev. tr.lit.; illus. back issues avail.; reprints avail. **Document type:** *Magazine, Consumer.* **Description:** Reports on combat from front lines around the world.
Related titles: Online - full text ed.: USD 29.99 (effective 2005).
Indexed: A22, PAIS, PMR.
—Ingenta.
Published by: Omega Group Ltd., 5735 Arapahoe Ave, No A 5, Boulder, CO 80303-1340. TEL 303-449-3750, 888-811-8009, FAX 303-444-5617. Ed., Pub. Robert K Brown. R&P Thomas D Reisinger. Adv. contact Tom Chambers. Circ: 104,593. **Subscr. to:** PO Box 348, Mt Morris, IL 61054. TEL 800-877-5207.

355 USA ISSN 0093-8440
U1
SOLDIERS. Text in English. 1946. m. USD 46 domestic; USD 64 foreign; USD 7 per issue domestic; USD 9.80 per issue foreign (effective 2009). illus. Index. back issues avail.; reprints avail. **Document type:** *Magazine, Government.* **Description:** Provides timely and authoritative information on the policies, plans, operations and technical developments of the Department of the Army.
Former titles (until 1971): Army Digest (0004-2498); (until 1966): Army Information Digest (0896-7687); (until 1946): I & E Digest
Related titles: Microform ed.: (from PQC); Online - full text ed.
Indexed: A09, A10, A22, A26, ABS&EES, AUNI, BAS, G05, G06, G07, G08, H05, I05, I07, IUSGP, L09, M02, M05, M06, M07, P02, P06, P10, P16, P34, P47, P48, P52, P53, P54, PQC, S23, T02, V02, V03, V04.
—Ingenta.
Published by: U.S. Department of the Army, Soldiers Media Center, Box 31, 2511, Arlington, VA 22202. TEL 703-602-0870, APDFCMP@conus.army.mil, http://www.army.mil. Ed. Carrie McLeroy. **Subscr. to:** U.S. Government Printing Office, Superintendent of Documents, PO Box 371954, Pittsburgh, PA 15250. TEL 202-512-1800, FAX 202-512-2250, ContactCenter@gpo.gov, http://bookstore.gpo.gov.

355 907 GBR
SOLDIERS OF THE QUEEN. Text in English. 1974. q. free to members (effective 2009). bk.rev.; video rev. illus.; bibl.; maps. back issues avail. **Document type:** *Journal, Academic/Scholarly.* **Description:** Promotes the study of military history of all nations and races in the period 1837-1914.
Published by: The Victorian Military Society, PO Box 58377, Newbury, RG14 7FJ, United Kingdom. info@victorianmilitarysociety.org.uk. Ed. Dr. Roger Stearn.

355 907 GBR
SOLDIERS SMALL BOOK. Text in English. 1974. 3/yr. bk.rev.; video rev. bibl. back issues avail. **Document type:** *Newsletter.* **Description:** Promotes the study of military history of all nations and races in the period 1837-1914.
Published by: The Victorian Military Society, PO Box 58377, Newbury, RG14 7FJ, United Kingdom. info@victorianmilitarysociety.org.uk. Ed. Dan Allen. Adv. contact Beverly Allen.

355 FIN ISSN 0357-816X
DL1037
SOTAHISTORIALLINEN AIKAKAUSKIRJA/JOURNAL OF MILITARY HISTORY. Text in Finnish, Swedish; Summaries in English. 1948. a. EUR 15 (effective 2003). **Document type:** *Yearbook, Academic/Scholarly.*
Former titles (until 1980): Sotahistoriallinen Seura ja Sotamuseo. Vuosikirja (0356-7877); (until 1955): Sotamuseo (1238-2949)
Indexed: CA, HistAb, IBSS, P30, T02.
Published by: Sotahistoriallinen Seura ry/Society for Military History, Maurinkatu 1, Helsinki, 00170, Finland. TEL 358-9-0105322942. Ed. Markku Palokangas. Circ: 1,000. **Dist. by:** Tiedekirja OY - Vetenskapsbokhandeln. **Co-sponsor:** Sotamuseo.

355 FIN ISSN 0038-1675
U4
SOTILASAIKAKAUSLEHTI/FINNISH MILITARY REVIEW. Text in Finnish; Contents page in English, Finnish. 1921. m. EUR 50 (effective 2003). adv. bk.rev. charts; illus.; maps; stat. index, cum.index. **Document type:** *Academic/Scholarly.*
Indexed: RASB.
Published by: Upseeriliitto Ry, Laivastokatu 1 b, Helsinki, 00160, Finland. TEL 358-0-66894016, FAX 358-0-66894020. Ed. Martti Lehto. Adv. contact Juha Halminen TEL 358-9-8736944. Circ: 6,200 (controlled).

SOTILASLAAKETIETEELLINEN AIKAKAUSLEHTI/ANNALES MEDICINAE MILITARIS FENNIAE. *see* MEDICAL SCIENCES

355.31 USA
SOUNDOFF!. Text in English. w. (Thu.). free. **Document type:** *Newspaper, Consumer.*
Published by: U.S.Army Garrison, 4550 Parade Ville Ln. 102, Post Public Affairs Office, Fort Meade, Anne Arundel, MD 20755-5025. TEL 301-677-1388, FAX 410-799-5911. Ed. Florence Peace. Pub. Jim Quimby. Circ: 18,000 (free).

363.35 338.473 968 GBR ISSN 1749-1657
SOUTH AFRICA DEFENCE & SECURITY REPORT. Text in English. 2005. q. EUR 820, USD 1,030 combined subscription (print & email eds.) (effective 2010). **Document type:** *Report, Trade.* **Description:** Covers independent forecasts and competitive intelligence on the defense and security industry in South Africa.
Related titles: E-mail ed.
Indexed: B01, P34.
Published by: Business Monitor International Ltd., Senator House, 85 Queen Victoria St, London, EC4V 4AB, United Kingdom. TEL 44-20-72480468, FAX 44-20-72480467, subs@businessmonitor.com.

355 ZAF
SOUTH AFRICA. DEPARTMENT OF DEFENSE. WHITE PAPER ON DEFENSE AND ARMAMENT PRODUCTION. Text in Afrikaans, English. irreg. **Document type:** *Government.*
Published by: Department of Defense, Cape Town, South Africa.

363.35 338.473 951.95 GBR ISSN 1749-1665
SOUTH KOREA DEFENCE & SECURITY REPORT. Text in English. 2005. q. EUR 820, USD 1,030 combined subscription (print & email eds.) (effective 2010). **Document type:** *Report, Trade.* **Description:** Provides industry leaders, defense manufacturers and suppliers, intelligence agencies and governments with independent forecasts and competitive intelligence on the defense and security industry in South Korea.
Related titles: E-mail ed.
Indexed: A15, ABIn, B01, P34, P48, P51, P52, PQC.
Published by: Business Monitor International Ltd., Senator House, 85 Queen Victoria St, London, EC4V 4AB, United Kingdom. TEL 44-20-72480468, FAX 44-20-72480467, subs@businessmonitor.com.

327 GBR ISSN 1462-0944
SOVIET (RUSSIAN) MILITARY EXPERIENCE. Variant title: Cass Series on Soviet (Russian) Military Experience. Text in English. 1991. irreg., latest 2007. price varies. back issues avail.; reprints avail. **Document type:** *Monographic series, Trade.* **Description:** Focuses on Soviet military experience in specific campaigns or operations.
Formerly (until 1998): Cass Series on Soviet Military Experience (1369-5517)
—BLDSC (3062.692330).
Published by: Routledge (Subsidiary of: Taylor & Francis Group), 4 Park Sq, Milton Park, Abingdon, Oxon OX14 4RN, United Kingdom. TEL 44-20-70176000, FAX 44-20-70176336, subscriptions@tandf.co.uk. Ed. David M Glantz.

355 GBR
SOVIET (RUSSIAN) MILITARY THEORY AND PRACTICE. Text in English. 1990. irreg., latest 2006. price varies. back issues avail. **Document type:** *Monographic series, Academic/Scholarly.* **Description:** Examines the evolution of Soviet military science, studying the Soviet method of converting theory into practice.
Former titles (until 2000): Cass Series on Soviet (Russian) Military Theory and Practice (1462-0936); (until 1998): Cass Series on Soviet Military Theory and Practice (1362-7678)
—BLDSC (3062.692300).
Published by: Routledge (Subsidiary of: Taylor & Francis Group), 4 Park Sq, Milton Park, Abingdon, Oxon OX14 4RN, United Kingdom. TEL 44-20-70176000, FAX 44-20-70176336, subscriptions@tandf.co.uk.

SOZIALRECHT & PRAXIS; Fachzeitschrift des VdK Deutschland fuer Vertrauensleute der Behinderten und fuer Sozialpolitiker. *see* SOCIAL SERVICES AND WELFARE

SOZIALWISSENSCHAFTLICHES INSTITUT DER BUNDESWEHR. VORTRAEGE. *see* SOCIAL SCIENCES: COMPREHENSIVE WORKS

355.821 USA
SPACE & MISSILE DEFENSE REPORT (EMAIL). Text in English. 2000. w. USD 1,397 (effective 2011). **Document type:** *Newsletter, Trade.* **Description:** Source for information and analysis on space-related developments occurring at NASA, the Missile Defense Agency, the Department of Defense, the labs and in the private sector.
Media: E-mail. **Related titles:** Online - full text ed.: USD 1,097 (effective 2007).
Published by: Access Intelligence, LLC (Subsidiary of: Veronis, Suhler & Associates Inc.), 4 Choke Cherry Rd, 2nd Fl, Rockville, MD 20850. TEL 301-354-2000, 800-777-5006, FAX 301-340-3819, info@accessintel.com.

323 USA
SPACE AND NAVAL WARFARE SYSTEMS CENTER SAN DIEGO. TECHNICAL DOCUMENT. Text in English. irreg. **Document type:** *Monographic series.*
Former titles (until 1997): Naval Command, Control and Ocean Surveillance Center. Naval Research and Development Division. Technical Document; (until 1992): U.S. Naval Ocean Systems Center. Technical Document (0277-8246)
Published by: Space and Naval Warfare Systems Center, 53560 Hull St, San Diego, CA 92152-5001. TEL 619-553-2717, http://www.spawar.navy.mil/sandiego/. **Subscr. to:** U.S. Department of Commerce, National Technical Information Service, 5301 Shawnee Rd, Alexandria, VA 22312. orders@ntis.fedworld.gov, http://www.ntis.gov/ordering.htm.

323 USA
SPACE AND NAVAL WARFARE SYSTEMS CENTER SAN DIEGO. TECHNICAL REPORT. Text in English. irreg.
Former titles (until 1997): Naval Command, Control and Ocean Surveillance Center. Naval Research and Development Division. Technical Report; (until 1992): U.S. Naval Ocean Systems Center. Technical Report
Published by: Space and Naval Warfare Systems Center, 53560 Hull St, San Diego, CA 92152-5001. TEL 619-553-2717, http://www.spawar.navy.mil/sandiego/. **Subscr. to:** U.S. Department of Commerce, National Technical Information Service, 5301 Shawnee Rd, Alexandria, VA 22312. orders@ntis.fedworld.gov, http://www.ntis.gov/ordering.htm.

SPACE AND SECURITY NEWS. *see* AERONAUTICS AND SPACE FLIGHT

358.4 USA
SPACE OBSERVER. Text in English. 1956. w. adv. bk.rev. **Document type:** *Newspaper, Government.*
Published by: Colorado Springs Military Newspaper Group (Subsidiary of: Dolan Media Co.), 31 E Platte Ave, Colorado Springs, CO 80903. TEL 719-634-5905, FAX 719-867-0265. Ed. Butch Wehry. Circ: 7,500.

355 ESP ISSN 0213-2753
SPAIN. MINISTERIO DE DEFENSA. BOLETIN OFICIAL. Text in Spanish. 1940. 3/yr. **Document type:** *Bulletin, Government.*
Formed by the merger of (1940-1985): Spain. Ministerio de Defensa. Boletin Oficial. Diario Oficial del Ejercito del Aire (0213-2745); Which was formerly (until 1977): Spain. Ministerio del Aire. Boletin Oficial (0038-6405); (1900-1985): Spain. Ministerio de Defensa. Boletin Oficial. Diario Oficial de Marina (0213-3253); Which was formerly (until 1977): Spain. Ministerio de Marina. Diario Oficial (0213-327X); (until 1906): Spain. Ministerio de Marina. Boletin Oficial (0213-3261); (1888-1985): Spain. Ministerio de Defensa. Boletin Oficial. Diario Oficial del Ejercito (0213-3245); Which was formerly (until 1977): Spain. Ministerio del Ejercito. Diario Oficial (0213-3237); (until 1939): Spain. Ministerio de Defensa Nacional. Diario Oficial (0213-3229); (until 1937): Spain. Ministerio de la Guerra. Diario Oficial (0213-3210); (until 1931): Spain. Ministerio del Ejercito. Diario Oficial (0213-3202); (until 1928): Spain. Ministerio de la Guerra. Diario Oficial (0213-3199)
Published by: Ministerio de Defensa, Centro de Publicaciones, Calle de Alcala 18, 4o, Madrid, 28014, Spain. TEL 34-91-522524, FAX 34-91-5227553, http://www.mde.es.

355 USA
SPEARHEAD (MONETA). Text in English. 1945. q. membership only. bk.rev. **Document type:** *Newsletter.*
Published by: First Special Service Force Association, 262 Pine Knob Circle, Moneta, VA 24121-2609. TEL 540-297-8304, FAX 540-297-1136. Ed. Bill Story. Circ: 1,200.

355.8 USA ISSN 1552-7891
UA34.S64
SPECIAL OPERATIONS TECHNOLOGY. Text in English. 2003. 8/yr. free to qualified personnel (effective 2008). adv. back issues avail. **Document type:** *Magazine, Trade.* **Description:** Covers all the services and aspects of special operations that includes weapons and gear; communications and net-centric operations; training, transport and tactics; night warfare; counter-insurgency and force protection and new SOF technologies.
Related titles: Online - full text ed.
Published by: Kerrigan Media International, Inc., 15800 Crabbs Branch Way, Ste 300, Rockville, MD 20855. TEL 301-670-5700, 888-299-8292, FAX 301-670-5701, kmi@kmimediagroup.com, http://www.kerriganmedia.com. Ed. Marty Kauchak. adv.: B&W page USD 5,980, color page USD 6,980; trim 8.375 x 10.875.

355 USA ISSN 1058-0123
U262
SPECIAL WARFARE. Text in English. 1988. bi-m. bk.rev. back issues avail. **Document type:** *Bulletin, Government.* **Description:** Contains information to promote professional development of special-operations forces by providing a forum for the examination of established doctrine and new ideas.
Related titles: Online - full text ed.: free (effective 2010).
Indexed: A26, ABS&EES, AUNI, CA, G05, G06, G07, G08, I02, I05, M05, M06, M07, P02, P10, P47, P48, P52, P53, P54, PQC, T02.
—Ingenta.

Published by: John F. Kennedy Special Warfare Center and School, AOJK-DTD-MP, USAJFKSWCS, Ft. Bragg, NC 28310. TEL 910-432-5703, steelman@soc.mil, http://www.training.sfahq.com/. Ed. Jerry D Steelman.

SPECIAL WEAPONS FOR MILITARY & POLICE. *see* CIVIL DEFENSE

SPEEDNEWS DEFENSE. *see* AERONAUTICS AND SPACE FLIGHT

358.4 USA
SPOKESMAN (SAN ANTONIO). Variant title: Spokesman Online. Text in English. m. free. **Document type:** *Magazine, Government.*
Media: Online - full content.
Published by: U.S. Air Force, Air Intelligence Agency, AIA/PAI, c/o: Spokesman Editor, 102 Hall Blvd., Ste. 234, San Antonio, TX 78243-7036. http://aia.lackland.af.mil/aia/index.cfm.

STAND TO!. *see* HISTORY—History Of Europe

353.538 USA ISSN 0894-8542
STARS AND STRIPES. Text in English. 1877. d. adv. bk.rev. 24 p./no. 5 cols./p.; **Document type:** *Newspaper, Consumer.* **Description:** Delivers independent news and information to the U.S. military community worldwide.
Formerly (until 1942): National Tribune. Stars and Stripes
Related titles: Online - full text ed.: free.
Published by: Stars & Stripes, 529 14th St, NW, Ste 350, Washington, DC 20045-1301. TEL 202-761-0900, FAX 202-761-0890. Adv. contact Daniel Krause. B&W page USD 8,771, color page USD 10,300; trim 10.25 x 13.75. Circ: 90,000 morning; 90,000 Saturday; 92,000 Sunday.

358.4 USA ISSN 1059-7468
STATIC LINE; your airborne lifeline. Text in English. 1965. m. USD 30 domestic; USD 35 in Canada & Mexico; USD 40 elsewhere (effective 2006). adv. bk.rev. illus. 40 p./no. 5 cols./p.; **Document type:** *Newspaper.* **Description:** Directed to former military paratroopers; perpetuates the camaraderie of military service.
Published by: Spearhead, Inc., PO Box 87518, College Park, GA 30337-0518. TEL 770-478-5301, FAX 770-961-2838, sales@staticlinemagazine.com, http://www.staticlinemagazine.com. Ed., Pub., R&P, Adv. contact Don Lassen. Circ: 20,000 (paid).

355.8 DEU
STEELMASTER; Rad- und Kettenfahrzeuge von gestern und heute im Original und Modell. Text in German. 1995. bi-m. EUR 7.50 newsstand/cover (effective 2009). **Document type:** *Magazine, Consumer.*
Published by: V D M Heinz Nickel, Kasernenstr 6-10, Zweibruecken, 66482, Germany. TEL 49-6332-72710, info@vdmedien.de, http://vdmedien.com.

STEELMASTERS; le magazine des blindes et du modelisme militaire. *see* HOBBIES

355 AUT ISSN 0039-1085
STEIRISCHE KRIEGSOPFER ZEITUNG. Text in German. 1947. q. membership. adv. bk.rev. bibl.; illus.; stat. index. **Document type:** *Bulletin, Consumer.*
Published by: Kriegsopfer- und Behindertenverband Steiermark, Muenzgrabenstrasse 4, Graz, St 8011, Austria. TEL 43-316-829121, FAX 43-316-83285385, kobvst@nextra.at. Ed. Ingeborg Axmann. Circ: 15,000.

355 DEU ISSN 0944-2766
STIMME UND WEG. Text in German. 1983. q. free to members. adv. illus.; stat. index. **Document type:** *Magazine, Consumer.* **Description:** For members of the German War Graves Commission.
Formerly (until 1992): Kriegsgraeberfuersorge, Stimme und Weg (0934-1390); Which was formed by the merger of (1921-1983): Kriegsgraeberfuersorge (0023-4648); (1963-1983): Stimme und Weg (0934-1382)
Published by: Volksbund Deutsche Kriegsgraeberfuersorge e.V./German War Graves Commission, Werner Hilpert Str 2, Kassel, 34112, Germany. TEL 49-561-70090, FAX 49-561-7009221, info@volksbund.de. Ed. Maurice Bonkat. adv.: page EUR 7,200. Circ: 215,000 (controlled).

355 ITA ISSN 1122-5289
STORIA MILITARE. Text in Italian. 1993. m. bk.rev. illus. back issues avail. **Document type:** *Magazine, Consumer.* **Description:** Covers various elements of military history.
Published by: Ermanno Albertelli Editore, Casella Postale 395, Parma, PR 43100, Italy. FAX 39-0521-290387, info@tuttostoria.it, http://www.tuttostoria.it.

355 AUS ISSN 0158-3751
➤ **STRATEGIC AND DEFENCE STUDIES CENTRE. WORKING PAPERS.** Text in English. 1978. irreg., latest no.411. price varies. abstr.; bibl.; charts; illus.; maps. back issues avail. **Document type:** *Monographic series, Academic/Scholarly.* **Description:** Provides information to general readers on strategic and defense topics.
Related titles: Online - full text ed.: free (effective 2009).
Indexed: LID&ISL.
—BLDSC (9348.675300).
Published by: Strategic and Defence Studies Centre, Australian National University, Coombs Bldg # 9, Fellows Rd, Canberra, ACT 0200, Australia. TEL 61-2-61259921, FAX 61-2-61259926, sdsc@anu.edu.au, http://sdsc.anu.edu.au. Ed., R&P, Adv. contact Kitty Eggerking.

355 327.1 USA ISSN 1938-1670
U162
STRATEGIC INSIGHTS. Text in English. 2002. bi-m. **Description:** Offers concise analysis of domestic and international security and military issues.
Media: Online - full content.
Published by: Naval Postgraduate School, Center for Contemporary Conflict, National Security Affairs Department, 1411 Cunningham Rd, Monterey, CA 93943. TEL 831-656-3055, ccc@nps.navy.mil.

355 PAK
STRATEGIC PERSPECTIVES. Text in English. q. PKR 120, USD 20.
Indexed: LID&ISL.
Published by: Institute of Strategic Studies, Sector F-5/2, Islamabad, Pakistan. TEL 92-51-9204423, FAX 92-51-9204658, strategy@isb.paknet.com.pk.

STRATEGIC REVIEW FOR SOUTHERN AFRICA/STRATEGIESE OORSIG VIR SUIDER AFRIKA. *see* POLITICAL SCIENCE—International Relations

STRATEGIC STUDIES. *see* POLITICAL SCIENCE—International Relations

355 USA
UA832
STRATEGIC SURVEY FOR ISRAEL (YEAR). Text in English. 1983. a. back issues avail. **Document type:** *Monographic series, Academic/Scholarly.* **Description:** Focuses on developments in the internal, regional, and international arenas that shape Israel's strategic environment.
Former titles (until 2009): The Middle East Strategic Balance; (until 2003): Middle East Military Balance (1099-5552)
Indexed: IHP.
Published by: (Institute for National Security Studies ISR), M I T Press, 55 Hayward St, Cambridge, MA 02142. TEL 617-253-5646, FAX 617-258-6779, journals-info@mit.edu, http://mitpress.mit.edu. Circ: 2,000.

356.1 DEU ISSN 1860-5311
U3
STRATEGIE UND TECHNIK. Text in German. 1958. m. EUR 73; EUR 54 to military; EUR 7.80 newsstand/cover (effective 2006). adv. bk.rev. charts; illus.; stat. index. 80 p./no.; **Document type:** *Journal, Trade.*
Formerly (until 2005): Soldat und Technik (0038-0989)
Indexed: BibCart, DIP, DM&T, IBR, IBZ, LID&ISL, PRA, RefZh.
—CCC.
Published by: (Germany. Bundesministerium der Verteidigung), Report Verlag GmbH, Paul-Kemp-Str 3, Bonn, 53173, Germany. TEL 49-228-3680400, FAX 49-228-3680402, info@report-verlag.de, http://www.report-verlag.de. Ed. Juergen Erbe. Pub. Gerhard Hubatschek. adv.: B&W page EUR 3,580, color page EUR 4,990; trim 210 x 297. Circ: 9,293 (paid and controlled).

324.72 FRA ISSN 0224-0424
U162
STRATEGIQUE. Text in French. 1979. q. back issues avail. **Document type:** *Journal, Academic/Scholarly.*
Indexed: I13, IBR, IBSS, IBZ, LID&ISL, PAIS, RASB.
Published by: Institut de Strategie Comparee, 45-47 rue des Ecoles, Esc. E, Paris, 75005, France. TEL 33-1-44424358. Ed. Herve Coutau Begarie. Circ: 1,500.

STRATEGIST. *see* SPORTS AND GAMES

355.4 USA ISSN 1040-886X
STRATEGY AND TACTICS; the magazine of conflict simulation. Abbreviated title: S & T. Text in English. 1967. bi-m. USD 25 per issue (effective 2010). adv. bk.rev. charts; illus.; stat. Index. 64 p./no.; back issues avail.; reprints avail. **Document type:** *Magazine, Consumer.* **Description:** Covers military history and analysis, with complete historical game.
Former titles (until 1988): Strategy and Tactics Magazine (0736-6531); (until 1983): Strategy and Tactics (0049-2310)
Related titles: ◆ Special ed. of: Strategy & Tactics Magazine (Special Edition). ISSN 0736-654X.
Indexed: AMB, AmH&L, HistAb, P30.
—IE.
Published by: Decision Games, PO Box 21598, Bakersfield, CA 93390. TEL 661-587-9633, FAX 661-587-5031, dgservice@earthlink.net. Ed. Joseph Miranda. Circ: 10,000.

355.4 USA ISSN 0736-654X
U310
STRATEGY & TACTICS MAGAZINE (SPECIAL EDITION). Text in English. 1983. s-a.
Related titles: ◆ Special ed(s).: Strategy and Tactics. ISSN 1040-886X.
Published by: Decision Games, PO Box 21598, Bakersfield, CA 93390. TEL 661-587-9633, FAX 661-587-5031.

355 GRC
STRATIOTIKI EPITHEORISIS/MILITARY REVUE. Text in Greek. bi-m. USD 25.
Indexed: AMB.
Published by: Hellenic Army General Staff, STG 1020, Athens, Greece. TEL 301-6553781.

355 USA
THE STRIPE. Text in English. w. (Fri.). free to military; USD 28 others. **Document type:** *Newspaper, Trade.*
Published by: Comprint Military Publications, 9030 Comprint Court, Gaithersburg, MD 301-921-2800. TEL 301-921-2800. Circ: 10,000 (paid and controlled).

355.31074 POL ISSN 0137-5733
STUDIA DO DZIEJOW DAWNEGO UZBROJENIA I UBIORU WOJSKOWEGO. Text in Polish; Summaries in English. 1963. irreg., latest 1988, nos. 9-10. price varies. **Document type:** *Monographic series.*
Related titles: Microfilm ed.
Published by: Muzeum Narodowe w Krakowie/National Museum in Cracow, Ul J Pilsudskiego 12, Krakow, 31109, Poland. Ed. Elzbieta Hyzy. Circ: 1,000. **Dist. by:** Ars Polona, Obroncow 25, Warsaw 03933, Poland. **Co-sponsor:** Association of Old Arms and Uniforms Amateurs.

355 POL ISSN 0562-2786
DK417
STUDIA I MATERIALY DO HISTORII WOJSKOWOSCI. Text in Polish. 1954. a. price varies. **Document type:** *Monographic series, Academic/Scholarly.* **Description:** History of Polish military science and arms.
Formerly (until 1956): Studia i Materialy do Historii Sztuki Wojennej
Indexed: IBR, IBZ, RASB.
Published by: Muzeum Wojska w Bialymstoku, ul J Kilinskiego 7, Bialystok, 15089, Poland. TEL 48-85-7416449 ext 16, FAX 48-85-7415448, biuro@muzwojska-bialystok.pl, http://www.muzwojska-bialystok.pl.

STUDIA NAD DAWNYM WOJSKIEM, BRONIA I BARWA. *see* HISTORY—History Of Europe

355 DEU ISSN 1619-778X
STUDIES FOR MILITARY PEDAGOGY, MILITARY SCIENCE & SECURITY POLICY. Text in German. 1989. irreg., latest vol.10, 2007. price varies. **Document type:** *Monographic series, Academic/Scholarly.*
Formerly (until 2002): Studien zur Verteidigungspaedagogik, Militaerwissenschaft und Sicherheitspolitik (0934-3687)
Published by: Peter Lang GmbH (Subsidiary of: Peter Lang Publishing Group), Eschborner Landstr 42-50, Frankfurt Am Main, 60489, Germany. TEL 49-69-7807050, FAX 49-69-78070550, zentrale.frankfurt@peterlang.com.

358.4 GBR ISSN 1368-5597
STUDIES IN AIR POWER. Text in English. 1995. irreg., latest 2006. price varies. back issues avail. **Document type:** *Monographic series, Academic/Scholarly.* **Description:** Examines both historical and contemporary aspects of air power, focusing on human issues as well as the technical developments.
—BLDSC (3062.692410), IE, Ingenta.
Published by: Routledge (Subsidiary of: Taylor & Francis Group), 4 Park Sq, Milton Park, Abingdon, Oxon OX14 4RN, United Kingdom. TEL 44-20-70176000, FAX 44-20-70176336, subscriptions@tandf.co.uk. Ed. Sebastian Cox.

355.009 GBR ISSN 1354-3679
➤ **STUDIES IN MILITARY HISTORY.** Text in English. 1992. irreg., latest 1994. price varies. back issues avail. **Document type:** *Monographic series, Academic/Scholarly.*
Published by: Berg Publishers (Subsidiary of: Oxford International Publishers Ltd.), 1st Fl Angel Ct, 81 St Clements St, Oxford, Berks OX4 1AW, United Kingdom. TEL 44-1865-245104, FAX 44-1865-791165, enquiry@bergpublishers.com.

355.02 GBR ISSN 1743-1174
STUDIES ON THE NATURE OF WAR. Text in English. 1992. irreg., latest vol.5, 2003. price varies. **Document type:** *Monographic series, Academic/Scholarly.*
Published by: (Center for Interdisciplinary Research on Social Stress SMR), Boydell & Brewer Ltd., Whitwell House, St Audrys Park Rd, Melton, Woodbridge, IP12 1SY, United Kingdom. TEL 44-1394-610600, FAX 44-1394-610316, editorial@boydell.co.uk, http://www.boydell.co.uk.

359 USA
SUBMARINE REVIEW. Text in English. 1982. q. free to members (effective 2009). adv. bk.rev. 144 p./no.; back issues avail.; reprints avail. **Document type:** *Journal, Trade.* **Description:** Aims to further the interests of the submarine service and to inform the public about submarine matters.
Published by: Naval Submarine League, PO Box 1146, Annandale, VA 22003. TEL 703-256-0891, FAX 703-642-5815, nslmem@cavtel.net. Ed. Jim Hay.

359 387.2 USA ISSN 0145-1073
V1
SURFACE WARFARE. Text in English. 1976. q. bk.rev. illus. back issues avail. **Document type:** *Magazine, Government.*
Related titles: Online - full content ed.
Indexed: A22, AMB, DM&T.
—BLDSC (8547.951800), IE, Infotrieve, Ingenta.
Published by: U.S. Office of the Chief of Naval Operations, Surface Warfare Division (N76) (Subsidiary of: Times-Union Military Publications), 2000 Navy Pentagon, Washington, DC 20350-2000 . TEL 703-692-4609, FAX 703-692-4640, http://www.navy.mil/navydata/cno/n76/index.html, http://surfacewarfare.navy.mil.

355 GBR ISSN 0491-6204
SURMACH. Text in Ukrainian. 1955. a. GBP 3 (effective 1999). adv. bk.rev. **Document type:** *Newspaper.* **Description:** Covers historical and military events of Ukraine and other nations with news of the activities of the Association of Ukrainian Former Combatants in Great Britain.
Published by: Association of Ukrainian Former Combatants in Great Britain, 49 Linden Gardens, London, W2 4HG, United Kingdom. TEL 44-171-229-8392, FAX 44-171-792-2499. Ed. S M Fostun. Circ: 1,000.

355 RUS
SUVOROVSKII NATISK; gazeta krasnoznamennogo dal'nevostochnogo voennogo okruga. Text in Russian. 1943. s-w. **Document type:** *Newspaper.*
Published by: Komanduyushchii Voiskami D V O (Subsidiary of: Ministry of Defence of the Russian Federation/Ministerstvo Oborony R F), Ul Zaparina 124, Khabarovsk, 680038, Russian Federation. TEL 7-4212-349120, 7-4212-349178, 7-4212-349031. Ed. M D Snigur. Circ: 3,364.

355 SWE ISSN 1651-727X
SVENSKA FINLANDSFRIVILLIGAS MINNESFOERENING. TIDNING. Variant title: Tidning foer Svenska Finlandsfrivilligas Minnesfoerening. Text in Swedish. 1941. 2/yr. SEK 100 domestic membership; SEK 150 foreign membership (effective 2010). adv. bk.rev. **Document type:** *Bulletin, Consumer.*
Former titles (until 2000): Foerbundet Svenska Finlandsfrivilliga. Tidning (0015-5225); (until 1949): Foerbundet Svenska Frivilligkaaren. Tidning
Published by: Svenska Finlandsfrivilliga Minnesfoerening/Association of Swedish Volunteers in the Finnish Wars, c/o L Lundholm, Dannemansv 7, Lidingoe, 18141, Sweden. bengt.nylander@finlandsfrivilliga.se, ttp://www.finlandsfrivilliga.se. Ed. Goeran Andolf.

355 FRA ISSN 1957-4193
T N T. Variant title: Trucks and Tanks Magazine. Text in French. 2007. bi-m. EUR 35 domestic; EUR 40 in the European Union; EUR 40 DOM-TOM; EUR 40 in Switzerland; EUR 45 elsewhere (effective 2009). back issues avail. **Document type:** *Magazine, Consumer.*
Published by: Caraktere SARL, 29 Bd Rabatau, Marseille, 13008, France. http://www.caraktere.com/.

355.2 USA
TACTICAL GEAR DIGITAL. Text in English. 2005. 9/yr. free (effective 2012). adv. back issues avail. **Document type:** *Magazine, Trade.* **Description:** Guide to all things tactical.
Media: Online - full text.
Published by: F + W Media Inc., 4700 E Galbraith Rd, Cincinnati, OH 45236. TEL 513-531-2690, contact_us@fwmedia.com, http://www.fwmedia.com/. Eds. Andy Belmas, Kevin Michalowski TEL 715-445-2214 ext 13764. Pub. Jim Schlender TEL 715-445-2214 ext 13346.

358.1883 GBR ISSN 0039-9418
TANK (BOVINGTON). Text in English. 1919. q. GBP 14 domestic to members; GBP 15 foreign to members (effective 2009). bk.rev. back issues avail. **Document type:** *Bulletin, Trade.* **Description:** Contains history and present-day activities of the Royal Tank Regiment, along articles on armored warfare past and present.
Indexed: LID&ISL.
Published by: Royal Tank Regiment Publications Ltd., RHQ RTR, Stanley Barracks, Bovington, Dorset BH20 6JA, United Kingdom. TEL 44-1929-403444, FAX 44-1929-403488, rhqrtr@btconnect.com. Ed. Lt.Col. George Forty.

358.1883 CHN ISSN 1001-8778
UG446.5
TANKE ZHUANGJIA CHELIANG/TANK & ARMOURED VEHICLE. Text in Chinese. 1979. m. **Document type:** *Journal, Academic/Scholarly.*
Published by: Zhongguo Beifang Cheliang Yanjiusuo/China North Vehicle Research Institute, PO Box 969-57, Beijing, 100072, China. TEL 86-10-83808795, http://www.noveri.com.cn/.

TANKETTE. *see* HOBBIES

623 CHE
TECHNISCHE MITTEILUNGEN FUER GENIETRUPPEN. Abbreviated title: T M. Text in French, German, Italian. 1936. q. CHF 40; CHF 50 foreign (effective 2000). adv. bk.rev. charts; illus.; stat. index. **Document type:** *Bulletin, Trade.*
Formerly: Technische Mitteilungen fuer Sappeure, Pontoniere und Mineure
Indexed: LID&ISL.
Published by: Gesellschaft fuer Militaerische Bautechnik, Auf der Mauer 2, Zuerich, 8001, Switzerland. TEL 41-1-2526260, FAX 41-1-2521667. Ed. Thomas Kielieger. Circ: 1,000.

355 FRA ISSN 1953-5953
TECHNOLOGIE & ARMEMENT. Text in French, English. 2006. bi-m. EUR 42 domestic to individuals; EUR 55 foreign to individuals (effective 2008). back issues avail. **Document type:** *Magazine, Trade.*
Published by: Areion Publishing, Chateau de Valmousse, Departementale 572, Lambesc, 13410, France. TEL 33-4-42921738, FAX 33-4-42924872.

355 IND ISSN 0971-4413
UA840
TECHNOLOGY FOCUS. Text in English. 1993. bi-m. free (effective 2011). charts; illus. back issues avail. **Document type:** *Bulletin, Government.* **Description:** Covers military products, processes and technologies.
Related titles: Online - full text ed.
Published by: (Russia. Ministry of Defense, India. Defence Research & Development Organisation), Defence Scientific Information & Documentation Centre, Metcalfe House, New Delhi, 110 054, India. TEL 91-11-23902400, director@desidoc.drdo.in. Eds. B Nityanand, Manoj Kumar, A L Moorthy.

TECNOLOGIA & DIFESA. *see* TECHNOLOGY: COMPREHENSIVE WORKS

355.27 DEU ISSN 0722-2904
UA10
TECNOLOGIA MILITAR. Text in Spanish. 1979. 4/yr. USD 35, EUR 25; USD 10, EUR 6 newsstand/cover (effective 2008). adv. **Document type:** *Magazine, Trade.*
Related titles: Online - full text ed.
Indexed: A01, AMB, F03, F04, LID&ISL, R15, T02.
Published by: Moench Verlagsgesellschaft mbH, Heilsbachstr 26, Bonn, 53123, Germany. TEL 49-228-64830, FAX 49-228-6483109, info@moench-group.com, http://www.monch.com. Ed. Franz Thiele. Adv. contact Ute Steuer. B&W page EUR 3,950, color page EUR 6,500; trim 7.31 x 10.63. Circ: 13,756 (paid and controlled).

355 ARG
TECNOLOGIA PARA LA DEFENSA - ARMAS Y MATERIALES. Text in Spanish. 1996. q. adv. **Document type:** *Government.* **Description:** Describes arms, materials and defense technologies for officers, non-commissioned officers and volunteer soldiers of the Argentine Army.
Published by: Estado Mayor General del Ejercito, Azopardo, 250 Piso 4, Buenos Aires, 1328, Argentina. TEL 54-114-3422121, FAX 54-114-3311865. Adv. contact Victor Raul Lessler. B&W page USD 1,500; 280 x 200. Circ: 39,000.

355 RUS
TEKHNIKA I VOORUZHENIE. Text in Russian. 1997. m. USD 170 in United States (effective 2000).
Indexed: LID&ISL.
Published by: Tekhinform, A-ya 10, Moscow, 109144, Russian Federation. TEL 7-095-3627112. **Dist. by:** East View Information Services, 10601 Wayzata Blvd, Minneapolis, MN 55305. TEL 952-252-1201, 800-477-1005, FAX 952-252-1202, info@eastview.com, http://www.eastview.com.

355 DOM
TEMAS SOBRE LA PROFESIONALIZACION MILITAR EN LA REPUBLICA DOMINICANA. Text in Spanish. 1983. m.
Published by: Editora Corripio C. Por A., Apdo 20374, Santo Domingo, Dominican Republic.

355 FRA ISSN 0995-6999
UA703.A6
TERRE INFORMATION MAGAZINE. Key Title: Terre Magazine. Text in French. 1959. m. (10/yr.). illus. **Document type:** *Magazine, Government.* **Description:** Covers news of the ground armies throughout the world.
Supersedes (in 1987): T A M. Terre Air Mer (0018-8395); Which was formerly (until 1962): Bled, 5/5 (0768-5912); (until 1961): 5/5 Forces Francaises (1766-859X)
Published by: Service d'Information et de Relations Publiques des Armees, 14 Rue Saint-Dominique, Armees, 00453, France. Circ: 75,000. **Dist. by:** Etablissement de Communication et de Production Audiovisuelle de la Defense - E C P A D, 2 - 8 Route du Fort d'Ivry, Ivry-sur-Seine Cedex 94205, France.

355 USA
THE TESTER. Text in English. w. (Thu.). free (effective 2006). **Document type:** *Newspaper.*
Published by: Washington Post Co., 1150 15th St, N W, Washington, DC 20071. TEL 202-334-7973. Pub. John Rives. Circ: 5,000 (paid).

353.538 USA
TEXAN VETERAN NEWS. Text in English. q.
Address: PO Box 7440, Ft. Worth, TX 76111-0440. TEL 817-834-7573.

353.538 USA
THUNDER FROM HEAVEN. Text in English. 1954. 3/yr. USD 15 to members (effective 2001). bk.rev. illus.; maps; stat. 100 p./no. 2 cols./p.; **Document type:** *Newsletter.* **Description:** For military veterans of WW II who served in the 17th Airborne Division.
Published by: 17th Airborne Division Association, 4 Cain Ct, Montville, NJ 07045-9151. TEL 973-263-2433, FAX 973-263-2343. Ed., Pub., R&P Joe Quade. Circ: 2,500 (paid).

358.4 USA
THE THUNDERBOLT (LUKE). Text in English. 1974. w. (Fri.). USD 15 (effective 2005). adv. **Document type:** *Newspaper.*
Formerly: Tallyho
Published by: Aerotech News & Review, 456 East Ave., K-4, Ste 8, Lancaster, CA 93535. TEL 661-945-5634, FAX 623-842-6017. adv.: col. inch USD 9.25. Circ: 60,000 (controlled and free).

358.4 USA
THE THUNDERBOLT (MACDIL). Text in English. 1960. w. (Fri.). free (effective 2006). **Document type:** *Newspaper.*
Published by: Media General, Inc., 301 E Grace St, Box C 32333, Richmond, VA 23293. Adv. contact TSgt. Chris Miller. Circ: 10,000 (paid and controlled).

355 SWE ISSN 1650-7606
TIDSKRIFT FOER AMFIBIEKAAREN. Text in Swedish. 1943. q. SEK 300 domestic; SEK 400 elsewhere (effective 2004). adv. bk.rev. abstr.; illus. cum.index.
Formerly (until 2000): Tidskrift foer Kustartilleriet (0040-683X)
Indexed: RASB.
Published by: Amfibiekaarsklubben, c/o Amfibiestridsskolan, Vaxholm, 18582, Sweden. TEL 46-8-54172000, FAX 46-8-57012805, exp@amfss.mil.se, http://www.amfss.mil.se. Eds. Anders Bohman, Bengt Delang. Circ: 1,100.

TIDSKRIFT I FORTIFIKATION. *see* ENGINEERING—Civil Engineering

359 323 SWE ISSN 0040-6945
V5
TIDSKRIFT I SJOEVAESENDET. Text in Swedish. 1836. q. SEK 250 domestic; SEK 350 foreign (effective 2010). bk.rev. **Document type:** *Magazine, Academic/Scholarly.* **Description:** Journal from Royal Swedish Society of Naval Sciences.
Indexed: IBR, IBZ, RASB.
Published by: Kungliga Oerlogsmannasaellskapet/Royal Swedish Society of Naval Sciences, Teatergatan 3,5 tr, Stockholm, 11148, Sweden. TEL 46-8-6647018, akademien@koms.se.

359.009489 DNK ISSN 0040-7186
V5
TIDSSKRIFT FOR SOEVAESEN. Text in Danish. 1827. 6/yr. adv. bk.rev. bibl.; charts; illus.; maps; stat. index; cum.index every 25 yrs. **Document type:** *Magazine, Trade.*
Former titles (until 1856): Nyt Archiv for Soevaesenet (0909-248X); (until 1842): Archiv for Soevaesenet (0909-2471)
Published by: Soe-Lieutenant-Selskabet/Society of Navy Lieutenants, Overgaden oven Vandet 62 B, Copenhagen K, 1415, Denmark. TEL 45-32-959954, sls@post9.tele.dk.

355 FIN ISSN 0358-8882
➤ **TIEDE JA ASE.** Text in English, Finnish. 1933. a., latest vol.60, 2002. EUR 17 (effective 2003). **Document type:** *Monographic series, Academic/Scholarly.*
Published by: Suomen Sotatieteellinen Seura r.y./Finnish Society of Military Science, c/o Risto Tyrvainen, Tapiolantie 11 A-2, Kerava, 04230, Finland. TEL 358-9-27359270, risto.tyrvainen@kolumbus.fi, http://pro.tvs.fi/sotathedeseura. Ed. Major Aarno Vehvilainen. Circ: 1,375.

355.27 388.3 GBR ISSN 2042-5899
▼ **TIGER TANK**; build the model and discover the history of tanks. Text in English. 2010. w. GBP 4.99, EUR 7.99 per issue (effective 2010). **Document type:** *Magazine, Consumer.* **Description:** Provides a complete reference to the world of the mighty tank which reveals everything to know about the armoured vehicles and their famous deployments in battle.
Published by: Hachette Partworks Ltd. (Subsidiary of: Hachette Livre), 4th Fl, Jordan House, 47 Brunswick Pl, London, N1 6EB, United Kingdom. http://www.hachettepartworks.co.uk. **Subscr. to:** PO Box 77, Jarrow NE32 3YJ, United Kingdom. TEL 44-871-4724240, FAX 44-871-4724241, hachettepw@jacklinservice.com.

355.37 USA ISSN 2157-4308
EL TIGRE NEWS. Text in English. 19??. q. free to members (effective 2010). back issues avail. **Document type:** *Newsletter, Trade.*
Media: Online - full text.
Published by: Arizona Air National Guard, 162nd Fighter Wing, 1650 E Perimeter Way, Tucson, AZ 85706. TEL 520-295-6192, 162fw.pa.omb@ang.af.mil.

355 RUS
TIKHOOKEANSKAYA VAKHTA. Text in Russian. 156/yr. USD 399 in United States.
Published by: Ministry of Defence of the Russian Federation/Ministerstvo Oborony R F, Petropavlovsk-Kamchatski, 683000, Russian Federation. TEL 41500-47918. Ed. V F Burduli. **Dist. by:** East View Information Services, 10601 Wayzata Blvd, Minneapolis, MN 55305. TEL 952-252-1201, 800-477-1005, FAX 952-252-1202, info@eastview.com, http://www.eastview.com.

051 USA
TINKER TAKE-OFF. Text in English. w. adv. **Document type:** *Newspaper, Consumer.*
Published by: Journal Record Publishing Co. (Subsidiary of: Dolan Media Co.), 222 N Robinson Ave, Box 26370, Oklahoma City, OK 73102. TEL 405-235-3100, news@journalrecord.com, http://www.journalrecord.com.

355 USA ISSN 1541-5252
TODAY'S OFFICER (ALEXANDRIA). Text in English. 2003 (Spr.). q. USD 36; USD 3 newsstand/cover (effective 2003). adv. **Document type:** *Magazine, Consumer.*
Related titles: Online - full content ed.
Published by: Military Officers Association of America, 201 N. Washington St., Alexandria, VA 22314-2539. TEL 703-549-2311, 800-234-6622, FAX 703-838-8179, http://www.moaa.org. Ed. Col. Warren S. Lacy. Adv. contact Maj. Dale Robinson. B&W page USD 2,000, color page USD 2,300; trim 8.125 x 10.875.

TOJHUSMUSEETS SKRIFTER. *see* HISTORY—History Of Europe

355.31 CAN ISSN 1189-007X
THE TORCH (DARTMOUTH). Text in English. 1989. q. CAD 8.56. adv. **Document type:** *Newspaper, Trade.*
Published by: (Nova Scotia Command), Nationwide Promotions Limited, 12 Dawn Dr, Burnside Industrial Park, Dartmouth, NS B3B 1H9, Canada. TEL 902-468-5709, FAX 902-468-5697, cxna@netcom.ca. Ed. Bill Harris. R&P, Adv. contact Dave Boutilier TEL 902-468-6871. B&W page CAD 1,595; trim 14 x 10. Circ: 28,000.

TOY SOLDIER AND MODEL FIGURE. *see* HOBBIES

TRADING POST. *see* HOBBIES

355 USA ISSN 1530-4159
U405
➤ **TRAINING AND SIMULATION JOURNAL.** Abbreviated title: T S J. Text in English. 2000 (Spring). bi-m. free to qualified personnel (effective 2009). adv. illus. back issues avail.; reprints avail. **Document type:** *Journal, Academic/Scholarly.* **Description:** Provides a forum for industry, government and military service professionals to learn and share information about latest technologies and issues impacting the training and simulation business.
Related titles: Online - full content ed.
Indexed: CA, M05, T02.
—CCC.
Published by: Defense News Media Group (Subsidiary of: Army Times Publishing Co.), 6883 Commercial Dr, Springfield, VA 22159. TEL 703-642-7330, 800-252-5825, FAX 703-642-7386, custserv@defensenews.com. Ed. Tobias Naegele. Adv. contact Donna Peterson. Circ: 16,189.

355 GBR ISSN 1362-3834
TRANSMISSION LINES. Text in English. 1995. q. free to members (effective 2009). back issues avail. **Document type:** *Newsletter, Trade.*
Published by: Bournemouth University, Oral History Research Unit, Fern Barrow, Poole, Dorset BH12 5BB, United Kingdom. TEL 44-1202-524111, FAX 44-1202-962736, histru@bmth.ac.uk.

TRANSMIT. *see* AERONAUTICS AND SPACE FLIGHT

TRANSPORTATION RESEARCH. PART E: LOGISTICS AND TRANSPORTATION REVIEW. *see* TRANSPORTATION

355 USA
TRIAD (WEST SALEM). Text in English. bi-w. (Fri.). free. **Document type:** *Newspaper.*
Published by: Lee Enterprises, Inc., 215 N. Main St., Davenport, IA 52801. TEL 563-383-2100. Ed. Lou Ann Mittelstaedt. Circ: 5,000 (free).

355 NLD ISSN 0925-6237
TRIVIZIER. Text in Dutch. 1990. 10/yr. adv. bk.rev. **Document type:** *Journal, Trade.* **Description:** Union publication for civil and military servants in the Dutch armed forces.
Published by: V B M, Postbus 93037, The Hague, 2509 AA, Netherlands. TEL 31-70-3155111, FAX 31-70-3837000, http://www.vbmnov.nl. Circ: 33,500 (controlled).

355 AUT ISSN 0041-3658
TRUPPENDIENST; Zeitschrift fuer Fuehrung und Ausbildung im Bundesheer. Text in German. 1962. bi-m. EUR 20; EUR 4 newsstand/cover (effective 2005). bk.rev. bibl.; charts; illus.; stat. index. **Document type:** *Magazine, Trade.*
Indexed: IBR, IBZ, LID&ISL, RASB.
—IE, Infotrieve.
Published by: Bundesministerium fuer Landesverteidigung, Rossauer Laende 1, Vienna, 1090, Austria. TEL 43-1-5200, FAX 43-1-520017139, beschwerden@bmlv.gv.at, http://www.bmlv.gv.at. Circ: 12,000.

TRUST AND VERIFY. *see* POLITICAL SCIENCE—International Relations

359 600 GBR ISSN 1479-5574
U D T FORUM. Variant title: Undersea Defence Technology Forum. Text in Chinese. irreg. **Document type:** *Magazine, Trade.*
Published by: Nexus Media Communications Ltd., Media House, Azalea Dr, Swanley, Kent BR8 8HU, United Kingdom. TEL 44-1322-611404, FAX 44-1322-616350, http://www.nexusmedia.co.uk.

355.31 ITA ISSN 0041-5375
U N U C I. RIVISTA. (Unione Nazionale Ufficiali in Congedo d'Italia) Text in Italian. 1964. m. free to members. adv. bk.rev. illus. **Document type:** *Magazine, Trade.* **Description:** Covers the different types of Italian army activities that go on outside of Italy. Describes each section of the army and its responsibilities.
Published by: Unione Nazionale Ufficiali in Congedo d'Italia (U N U C I), Via Nomentana 313, Rome, 00162, Italy. TEL 39-06-8548795, FAX 39-06-8414555, http://www.unuci.it.

U S A C H P P M HEALTH INFORMATION OPERATIONS WEEKLY UPDATE. *see* MEDICAL SCIENCES

358.4 USA
U.S. AIR FORCE ACADEMY. INSTITUTE FOR NATIONAL SECURITY STUDIES. OCCASIONAL PAPER. Variant title: I N S S Occasional Paper. Text in English. 1994. irreg., latest vol.66, 2008, Apr. price varies. back issues avail. **Document type:** *Monographic series, Academic/Scholarly.*
Related titles: Online - full text ed.: free (effective 2010).
Indexed: LID&ISL.
Published by: U.S. Air Force Academy, Institute for National Security Studies., 2354 Fairchild Dr, Ste 5L27, USAF Academy, CO 80840. TEL 719-333-2717, FAX 719-333-2716, inss@usafa.edu.

323 600 USA
U.S. AIR FORCE INSTITUTE OF TECHNOLOGY. REPORT. Text in English. irreg.
Published by: U.S. Air Force Institute of Technology, Wright-Patterson Air Force Base, OH 45433-7765. **Subscr. to:** U.S. Department of Commerce, National Technical Information Service, 5301 Shawnee Rd, Alexandria, VA 22312. orders@ntis.fedworld.gov, http://www.ntis.gov/ordering.htm.

U.S. AIR FORCE. OFFICE OF THE JUDGE GENERAL. THE REPORTER. *see* LAW—Military Law

355 USA
U.S. ARMY MATERIEL COMMAND. ANNUAL HISTORICAL REVIEW. Text in English. a. **Document type:** *Government.* **Description:** Serves as a chronicle of the U.S. Army Materiel Command Headquarters, making the past a means for managing the present and projecting the future.
Published by: U.S. Army, Materiel Command (Headquarters), Historical Office AMC HO, 500 Eisenhower Ave, Alexandria, VA 22333-0001. TEL 703-274-3776. **Orders to:** U.S. Government Printing Office, Superintendent of Documents.

U.S. ARMY MEDICAL DEPARTMENT. JOURNAL. *see* MEDICAL SCIENCES

U S C T CIVIL WAR DIGEST. (United States Colored Troops) *see* HISTORY—History Of North And South America

U.S. COAST GUARD ENGINEERING, ELECTRONICS & LOGISTICS QUARTERLY. *see* ENGINEERING

▼ **U S COAST GUARD FORUM**; dedicated to those who are always ready. *see* TRANSPORTATION—Ships And Shipping

363.286 359.97 USA
U.S. COAST GUARD. MARINE SAFETY MANUAL. VOLUME 1: ADMINISTRATION AND MANAGEMENT. Text in English. 2000. base vol. plus irreg. updates. looseleaf. **Document type:** *Handbook/ Manual/Guide, Academic/Scholarly.* **Description:** Presents background and rationale for the various marine safety activities of the Coast Guard and prescribes the functions which is to be performed to attain the overall marine safety objectives of the Coast Guard.
Related titles: Online - full text ed.
Published by: U.S. Coast Guard, 2100 Second St, SW, Washington, DC 20593. TEL 202-267-1061, FAX 202-267-4402, gchappell@comdt.uscg.mil, http://www.uscg.mil/default.asp. **Subscr. to:** U.S. Government Printing Office, Superintendent of Documents.

363.286 359.97 USA
U.S. COAST GUARD. MARINE SAFETY MANUAL. VOLUME 10: INTERAGENCY AGREEMENTS AND ACRONYMS. Text in English. 19??. base vol. plus irreg. updates. looseleaf. **Document type:** *Government.* **Description:** Presents authority, background and rationale for the various marine safety activities of the United States Coast Guard and prescribes the essential functions which needs to be performed to attain the overall marine safety objectives of the United States Coast Guard.
Published by: U.S. Coast Guard, 2100 Second St, SW, Washington, DC 20593. TEL 202-372-4620, gchappell@comdt.uscg.mil, http://www.uscg.mil/default.asp. **Subscr. to:** U.S. Government Printing Office, Superintendent of Documents.

363.286 359.97 USA
U.S. COAST GUARD. MARINE SAFETY MANUAL. VOLUME 2: MATERIEL INSPECTION. Text in English. 2000. base vol. plus irreg. updates. looseleaf. **Document type:** *Handbook/Manual/Guide, Government.* **Description:** Presents background and rationale for the various marine safety activities of the Coast Guard and prescribes the functions which is to be performed to attain the overall marine safety objectives of the Coast Guard.
Related titles: Online - full text ed.
Published by: U.S. Coast Guard, 2100 Second St, SW, Washington, DC 20593. TEL 202-267-1061, FAX 202-267-4402, gchappell@comdt.uscg.mil, http://www.uscg.mil/default.asp. **Subscr. to:** U.S. Government Printing Office, Superintendent of Documents.

363.286 359.97 USA
U.S. COAST GUARD. MARINE SAFETY MANUAL. VOLUME 3: MARINE INDUSTRY PERSONNEL. Text in English. 1999. base vol. plus irreg. updates. looseleaf. **Document type:** *Handbook/Manual/ Guide, Government.* **Description:** Presents background and rationale for the various marine safety activities of the Coast Guard and prescribes the functions which is to be performed to attain the overall marine safety objectives of the Coast Guard.
Related titles: Online - full text ed.
Published by: U.S. Coast Guard, 2100 Second St, SW, Washington, DC 20593. TEL 202-267-1061, FAX 202-267-4402, gchappell@comdt.uscg.mil, http://www.uscg.mil/default.asp. **Subscr. to:** U.S. Government Printing Office, Superintendent of Documents.

363.286 359.97 USA
U.S. COAST GUARD. MARINE SAFETY MANUAL. VOLUME 4: TECHNICAL. Text in English. base vol. plus irreg. updates. looseleaf. **Document type:** *Handbook/Manual/Guide, Government.* **Description:** Presents background and rationale for the various marine safety activities of the Coast Guard and prescribes the functions which is to be performed to attain the overall marine safety objectives of the Coast Guard.
Related titles: Online - full text ed.
Published by: U.S. Coast Guard, 2100 Second St, SW, Washington, DC 20593. TEL 202-267-1061, FAX 202-267-4402, gchappell@comdt.uscg.mil, http://www.uscg.mil/default.asp. **Subscr. to:** U.S. Government Printing Office, Superintendent of Documents.

363.286 359.97 USA
U.S. COAST GUARD. MARINE SAFETY MANUAL. VOLUME 5: INVESTIGATIONS. Text in English. 19??. base vol. plus irreg. updates. looseleaf. **Document type:** *Government.* **Description:** Presents the authority, background and rationale for the various marine safety activities of the Coast Guard and prescribes the essential functions which must be performed to attain the overall marine safety objectives of the Coast Guard.
Published by: U.S. Coast Guard, 2100 Second St, SW, Washington, DC 20593. TEL 202-267-1061, FAX 202-267-4402, gchappell@comdt.uscg.mil, http://www.uscg.mil/default.asp. **Subscr. to:** U.S. Government Printing Office, Superintendent of Documents.

363.286 359.97 USA
U.S. COAST GUARD. MARINE SAFETY MANUAL. VOLUME 6: PORTS AND WATERWAYS ACTIVITIES. Text in English. base vol. plus irreg. updates. looseleaf. **Document type:** *Handbook/Manual/Guide, Government.* **Description:** Presents background and rationale for the various marine safety activities of the Coast Guard and prescribes the functions which is to be performed to attain the overall marine safety objectives of the Coast Guard.
Related titles: Online - full text ed.
Published by: U.S. Coast Guard, 2100 Second St, SW, Washington, DC 20593. TEL 202-267-1061, FAX 202-267-4402, gchappell@comdt.uscg.mil, http://www.uscg.mil/default.asp. **Subscr. to:** U.S. Government Printing Office, Superintendent of Documents.

363.286 359.97 USA
U.S. COAST GUARD. MARINE SAFETY MANUAL. VOLUME 9: ENVIRONMENTAL PROTECTION. Text in English. base vol. plus irreg. updates. looseleaf. **Document type:** *Handbook/Manual/Guide, Government.* **Description:** Presents background and rationale for the various marine safety activities of the Coast Guard and prescribes the functions which is to be performed to attain the overall marine safety objectives of the Coast Guard.
Related titles: Online - full text ed.
Published by: U.S. Coast Guard, 2100 Second St, SW, Washington, DC 20593. TEL 202-267-1061, FAX 202-267-4402, gchappell@comdt.uscg.mil, http://www.uscg.mil/default.asp. **Subscr. to:** U.S. Government Printing Office, Superintendent of Documents.

U.S. COAST GUARD. NAVIGATION AND VESSEL INSPECTION CIRCULARS. *see* TRANSPORTATION—Ships And Shipping

355 USA
U.S. DEPARTMENT OF DEFENSE. DEFENSE SECURITY COOPERATION AGENCY. D S C A FACTS BOOK. FOREIGN MILITARY SALES, FOREIGN MILITARY CONSTRUCTION SALES AND MILITARY ASSISTANCE FACTS (ONLINE EDITION). Text in English. 1974. irreg., latest 2003. **Document type:** *Government.*
Former titles (until 1999): Foreign Military Sales, Foreign Military Construction Sales and Military Assistance Facts (Print) (8756-5536); (until 1980): Foreign Military Sales and Military Assistance Facts (0362-577X)
Media: Online - full content.
Published by: U.S. Department of Defense, Defense Security Cooperation Agency, 2800 Defense, Pentagon, Washington, DC 20301-2800. TEL 703-601-3710, LPA-WEB@dsca.mil, http://www.dsca.osd.mil/.

355 USA ISSN 1048-7557
U24
U.S. DEPARTMENT OF DEFENSE. DICTIONARY OF MILITARY AND ASSOCIATED TERMS. Text in English. 19??. irreg. **Document type:** *Government.* **Description:** Sets forth military terminology to govern the joint activities and performances of the Armed Forces of the United States in joint operations. Provides terms for use in multinational and interagency operations which involve US Armed Forces.
Formerly (until 1972): Dictionary of United States Military Terms for Joint Usage (0193-7839)
Related titles: Online - full text ed.
Published by: (U.S. Department of Defense), U.S. Government Printing Office, 732 N Capitol St, NW, Washington, DC 20401. TEL 202-512-1800, 866-512-1800, FAX 202-512-2104, ContactCenter@gpo.gov, http://www.gpo.gov.

U.S. DEPARTMENT OF DEFENSE. INDEX OF SPECIFICATIONS AND STANDARDS: PART 1, ALPHABETICAL LISTING. *see* METROLOGY AND STANDARDIZATION

355.6 USA
UA23.2
U.S. DEPARTMENT OF DEFENSE. REPORT OF THE SECRETARY OF DEFENSE TO THE PRESIDENT AND THE CONGRESS. Variant title: Annual Report to the President and the Congress. Text in English. a. USD 9.50. **Document type:** *Government.*
Former titles (until 1990): U.S. Department of Defense. Report of Secretary of Defense to the Congress on the Budget, Authorization Request, and Defense Program (0191-6513); (unitl 1980): U.S. Department of Defense. Annual Report (0082-9854); (until 1979): U.S. Department of Defense. Report of Secretary of Defense to the Congress on the Defense Budget and the Defense Program (0098-3888)
Published by: U.S. Department of Defense, Office of the Secretary, 1000 Defense Pentagon, Washington, DC 20301-1000. TEL 703-695-5261.

359 USA ISSN 0502-3378
QC621 CODEN: XNLMAT
U.S. DEPARTMENT OF THE NAVY. NAVAL RESEARCH LABORATORY. MEMORANDUM REPORT. Text in English. irreg.
Indexed: ASFA, B21, ESPM.
Published by: U.S. Department of the Navy, Naval Research Laboratory, 4555 Overlook Ave, Washington, DC 20375. http://www.nrl.navy.mil.

353.538 USA
U.S. DEPARTMENT OF VETERANS AFFAIRS. FISCAL YEAR (YEAR) PERFORMANCE AND ACCOUNTABILITY REPORT. Text in English. 2001. a. **Document type:** *Government.*
Formerly (until 2003): U.S. Department of Veterans Affairs. Annual Performance Report
Media: Online - full content. **Related titles:** Print ed.
Published by: U.S. Department of Veterans Affairs, Office of Management, Performance Analysis Service (041H), Rm 619, 810 Vermont Ave, NW, Washington, DC 20420-1000. TEL 202-461-6630, http://www.va.gov/budget/index.htm.

355 IND ISSN 0041-770X
U1
➤ **U S I JOURNAL.** Text in English. 1872. q. INR 500 domestic; USD 60, GBP 30 foreign; INR 150 per issue (effective 2011). adv. bk.rev. illus. **Document type:** *Journal, Academic/Scholarly.*
Indexed: AMB, CA, HistAb, I02, LID&ISL, P06, PAA&I, T02.
Published by: United Service Institution of India, Rao Tula Ram Marg (Opposite Signal Enclave), Vasant Vihar PO, PO Box 8, New Delhi, 110 057, India. TEL 91-11-26146755, FAX 91-11-26149773, director@usiofindia.org.

353.538 USA
U S J. (Uniformed Services Journal) Text in English. 1968. bi-m. USD 15 to non-members. adv. bk.rev. charts; illus. **Document type:** *Newsletter.*
Supersedes: N A U S Newsletter
Published by: National Association for Uniformed Services, 5535 Hempstead Way, Springfield, VA 22151. TEL 703-750-1342, FAX 703-354-4380. Ed., R&P, Adv. contact Sharon W Barnes TEL 800-842-3451. Pub. Richard D Murray. Circ: 160,000.

359.96 USA ISSN 1056-9073
U.S. MARINE CORPS. DIVISION OF PUBLIC AFFAIRS, MEDIA BRANCH. MARINES. Text in English. 1970. q. USD 29 domestic; USD 40.60 foreign; USD 7 per issue domestic (effective 2009). illus. reprints avail. **Document type:** *Magazine, Government.* **Description:** Provides information about U.S. Marine Corps.
Former titles (until 1983): H Q M C Hotline; (until 1978): Hotline H Q M C
Related titles: Online - full text ed.: ISSN 1554-9542; Supplement(s): U.S. Marine Corps. (Year) Almanac. USD 6 newsstand/cover (effective 2001).
Indexed: A26, E08, G05, G06, G07, G08, I05, I07, M01, M02, M05, M06, S09, T02, V02.
—Ingenta.
Published by: U.S. Marine Corps, Division of Public Affairs, Media Branch, DMA Crystal City, Marine Corps News, Box 31, 2511 Jefferson Davis Hwy, Arlington, VA 22202. http://www.marines.mil/ units/hqmc/divpa/Pages/default.aspx. Eds. Clinton Firstbrook, Greg Reeder. **Subscr. to:** U.S. Government Printing Office, Superintendent of Documents, PO Box 371954, Pittsburgh, PA 15250. TEL 202-512-1800, FAX 202-512-2250, ContactCenter@gpo.gov, http://bookstore.gpo.gov.

323 355.6 USA
U.S. NAVAL FACILITIES ENGINEERING COMMAND. REPORT. Text in English. irreg.
Published by: U.S. Naval Facilities Engineering Command, 1322 Patterson Ave SE, Ste 1000, Washington Navy Yard, DC 20374-5065. TEL 202-685-9126, documents@navfac.navy.mil, http://www.navfac.navy.mil.

359 USA ISSN 0041-798X
U S NAVAL INSTITUTE. PROCEEDINGS. Text in English. 1874. m. free to members (effective 2009). adv. bk.rev. charts; illus. Index. back issues avail.; reprints avail. **Document type:** *Magazine, Trade.* **Description:** Covers all aspects of naval affairs for the U.S. Navy, Marines and Coast Guard.
Incorporates (1963-1969): Naval Review (0077-6238); Formerly (until 1879): United States Naval Institute. Record
Related titles: Microform ed.: (from PQC); Online - full text ed.
Indexed: A01, A03, A08, A22, ABS&EES, AUNI, AmH&L, BAS, BMT, ChemAb, DM&T, GeoRef, HistAb, I02, LID&ISL, M05, M07, MLA-IB, P02, P10, P30, P34, P47, P48, P52, P53, P54, P56, PAIS, PQC, PRA, RASB, RefZh, SPPI, SpeleolAb, T02.
—BLDSC (6829.000000), IE, Infotrieve, Ingenta.
Published by: U S Naval Institute, 291 Wood Rd, Annapolis, MD 21401. TEL 410-268-6110, 800-233-8764, FAX 410-269-7940, customer@usni.org. Pub. William Miller. Adv. contact William Hughes TEL 724-238-2680. color page USD 7,192; bleed 8.375 x 11.25. Circ: 59,378. **Subscr. to:** Circulation Department, 2062 Generals Hwy, Annapolis, MD 21401. TEL 410-224-3378, FAX 410-224-2406.

U.S. NAVAL POSTGRADUATE SCHOOL. TECHNICAL REPORT. *see* TECHNOLOGY: COMPREHENSIVE WORKS

323 USA
U.S. NAVAL SURFACE WARFARE CENTER. CARDEROCK DIVISION. REPORT. Text in English. irreg.
Formerly (until 1992): David Taylor Research Center. Report
Published by: U.S. Naval Surface Warfare Center, Carderock Division, 9500 MacArthur Blvd, West Bethesda, MD 20817-5700. http://www.dt.navy.mil/. **Subscr. to:** U.S. Department of Commerce, National Technical Information Service, 5301 Shawnee Rd, Alexandria, VA 22312. subscriptions@ntis.gov, http://www.ntis.gov/ ordering.htm.

355 USA
U S S HENRICO A P A - 45 REUNION ASSOCIATION. NEWSLETTER. Text in English. 1974. s-a. looseleaf. USD 20 (effective 2002). **Document type:** *Newsletter.* **Description:** Contains history of the ship, crew and officer muster roll 1943-1968, and reunion information.
Published by: U S S Henrico A P A - 45 Reunion Association, 15875 Interurban Rd, Platte City, MO 64079-9185. TEL 816-858-5411, FAX 816-858-5556. Ed., R&P Don Soper. Circ: 760 (paid).

355 610 USA ISSN 1943-040X
U S U NEWSLETTER. Text in English. 2006. bi-w. **Document type:** *Newsletter.*
Media: Online - full content.
Published by: Uniformed Services University of the Health Sciences, 4301 Jones Bridge Rd, Bethesda, MD 20814. TEL 301-295-9702, http://www.usuhs.mil. Ed. Andre Nicholson.

338.473 947.7 363.35 GBR ISSN 1749-172X
UKRAINE DEFENCE & SECURITY REPORT. Text in English. 2005. a. EUR 820, USD 1,030 combined subscription per issue (print & email eds.) (effective 2010). **Document type:** *Report, Trade.* **Description:** Covers independent forecasts and competitive intelligence on the defense and security industry in Ukraine.
Related titles: E-mail ed.
Published by: Business Monitor International Ltd., Senator House, 85 Queen Victoria St, London, EC4V 4AB, United Kingdom. TEL 44-20-72480468, FAX 44-20-72480467, subs@businessmonitor.com.

355 USA
UNCLASSIFIED REPORT TO CONGRESS ON THE ACQUISITION OF TECHNOLOGY RELATING TO WEAPONS OF MASS DESTRUCTION AND ADVANCED CONVENTIONAL MUNITIONS. Text in English. a., latest 2002. **Document type:** *Government.*
Related titles: Online - full content ed.
Published by: U.S. Central Intelligence Agency, Office of Public Affairs, Washington, DC 20505.

359.93 USA ISSN 1554-0146
VA858
UNDERSEA WARFARE. Text in English. 1998. q. USD 18 (effective 2001). **Document type:** *Government.* **Description:** Contains professional information for the undersea warfare community.
Related titles: Online - full text ed.: ISSN 1554-9828.
Published by: U.S. Navy, Submarine Warfare Division, c/o Military Editor, Undersea Warfare CNO (N87C), 2000 Navy Pentagon, Washington, DC 20350-2000. **Subscr. to:** U.S. Government Printing Office, Superintendent of Documents, PO Box 371954, Pittsburgh, PA 15250. TEL 202-512-1800, FAX 202-512-2250, orders@gpo.gov, http://www.access.gpo.gov.

355 USA ISSN 1932-1341
UNIFORMED SERVICES UNIVERSITY OF THE HEALTH SCIENCES JOURNAL. Text in English. 1999. a. **Document type:** *Journal, Trade.*

Media: Online - full text.
Published by: Uniformed Services University of the Health Sciences, 4301 Jones Bridge Rd, Bethesda, MD 20814. http://www.usuhs.mil.

UNIFORMED SERVICES UNIVERSITY OF THE HEALTH SCIENCES. REPORT. *see* MEDICAL SCIENCES

355.8 ITA ISSN 1825-9391
LE UNIFORMI DEI CARABINIERI. Text in Italian. 2005. s-m. **Document type:** *Magazine, Consumer.*
Published by: R C S Libri (Subsidiary of: R C S Mediagroup), Via Mecenate 91, Milan, 20138, Italy. TEL 39-02-5095-2248, FAX 39-02-5095-2975, http://rcslibri.corriere.it/libri/index.htm.

UNITED ARAB EMIRATES. AL-QIYADAH AL-AAMAH LIL-QUWWAT AL-MUSALLIHAH. MAJALLAH AL-TIBBIYYAH/UNITED ARAB EMIRATES. GENERAL COMMAND FOR THE ARMED FORCES. MEDICAL JOURNAL. *see* MEDICAL SCIENCES

338.473 953.57 363.35 GBR ISSN 1749-1738
UNITED ARAB EMIRATES DEFENCE & SECURITY REPORT. Text in English. 2005. q. EUR 820, USD 1,030 combined subscription (print & email eds.) (effective 2010). **Document type:** *Report, Trade.* **Description:** Covers independent forecasts and competitive intelligence on the defense and security industry in the UAE.
Related titles: E-mail ed.; Online - full text ed.
Indexed: A15, ABIn, B01, B02, B15, B17, B18, G04, I05, P48, P51, P52, PQC.
Published by: Business Monitor International Ltd., Senator House, 85 Queen Victoria St, London, EC4V 4AB, United Kingdom. TEL 44-20-72480468, FAX 44-20-72480467, subs@businessmonitor.com.

338.473 941 363.35 GBR ISSN 1749-1746
UNITED KINGDOM DEFENCE & SECURITY REPORT. Text in English. 2005. q. EUR 820, USD 1,030 combined subscription (print & email eds.) (effective 2010). **Document type:** *Report, Trade.* **Description:** Covers independent forecasts and competitive intelligence on the defense and security industry in UK.
Related titles: E-mail ed.; Online - full text ed.
Indexed: B01, P34.
Published by: Business Monitor International Ltd., Senator House, 85 Queen Victoria St, London, EC4V 4AB, United Kingdom. TEL 44-20-72480468, FAX 44-20-72480467, subs@businessmonitor.com.

338.473 363.35 941 GBR ISSN 2042-423X
▼ **UNITED STATES DEFENCE & SECURITY REPORT.** Text in English. 2009. q. EUR 820, USD 1,030 combined subscription (print & email eds.) (effective 2010). back issues avail. **Document type:** *Report, Trade.* **Description:** Covers independent forecasts and competitive intelligence on the defense and security industry in the US.
Related titles: E-mail ed.
Published by: Business Monitor International Ltd., Senator House, 85 Queen Victoria St, London, EC4V 4AB, United Kingdom. TEL 44-20-72480468, FAX 44-20-72480467, subs@businessmonitor.com, http://www.businessmonitor.com.

353.538 351 USA ISSN 1931-9134
UNITED STATES. DEPARTMENT OF VETERANS AFFAIRS. HEALTH SERVICES RESEARCH AND DEVELOPMENT SERVICE. FORUM. Short title: Forum. Text in English. 19??. irreg. **Document type:** *Newsletter, Consumer.*
Related titles: Online - full text ed.: ISSN 1931-9142.
Published by: (U.S. Department of Veterans Affairs), U.S. Department of Veterans Affairs, Office of Research and Development, 810 Vermont Ave NW, Washington, DC 20420. TEL 202-745-8000, http://www.research.va.gov.

355.115 USA ISSN 0364-4200
KF22
UNITED STATES HOUSE OF REPRESENTATIVES. COMMITTEE ON VETERANS' AFFAIRS. LEGISLATIVE CALENDAR. Text in English. 19??. biennial. free (effective 2011). **Document type:** *Government.*
Related titles: Online - full text ed.: free (effective 2011).
Published by: (U.S. House of Representatives, Committee on Veterans' Affairs), U.S. Government Printing Office, 732 N Capitol St, NW, Washington, DC 20401. TEL 202-512-1800, 866-512-1800, FAX 202-512-2104, ContactCenter@gpo.gov, http://www.gpo.gov.

355 USA ISSN 0364-8176
KF21
UNITED STATES SENATE. COMMITTEE ON VETERANS' AFFAIRS. LEGISLATIVE CALENDAR. Text in English. 19??. biennial. free (effective 2011). back issues avail. **Document type:** *Government.*
Related titles: Online - full text ed.: ISSN 2157-0019.
Published by: (U.S. Senate, Committee on Veterans' Affairs), U.S. Government Printing Office, 732 N Capitol St, NW, Washington, DC 20401. TEL 202-512-1800, 866-512-1800, FAX 202-512-2104, ContactCenter@gpo.gov, http://www.gpo.gov.

355.6 USA ISSN 0363-0706
KF30.8
UNITED STATES SENATE. HOUSE ARMED SERVICES COMMITTEE. REPORT ON THE ACTIVITIES. Key Title: Report on the Activities of the Committee on Armed Services, United States Senate. Text in English. 19??. biennial. free (effective 2011). back issues avail. **Document type:** *Report, Government.*
Media: Online - full text.
Published by: U.S. Government Printing Office, 732 N Capitol St, NW, Washington, DC 20401. TEL 202-512-1800, 866-512-1800, FAX 202-512-2104, ContactCenter@gpo.gov, http://www.gpo.gov.

UNITES & GUERRIERS. *see* HISTORY

UNIVERSITY OF PRETORIA. INSTITUTE FOR STRATEGIC STUDIES. AD HOC PUBLICATION/UNIVERSITEIT VAN PRETORIA. INSTITUUT VIR STRATEGIESE STUDIES. AD HOC PUBLIKASIE. *see* POLITICAL SCIENCE—International Relations

355.6 GBR
UNIVERSITY OF YORK. CENTRE FOR DEFENCE ECONOMICS. RESEARCH MONOGRAPH SERIES. Text in English. 19??. irreg., latest 2006. **Document type:** *Monographic series.*
Published by: University of York, Centre for Defence Economics, Heslington, Yorks YO1 5DD, United Kingdom. TEL 44-1904-430000, FAX 44-1904-433433, admissions@york.ac.uk, http://www.york.ac.uk/depts/econ/research/associated/.

UNMANNED SYSTEMS. *see* COMPUTERS—Robotics

355 RUS
URAL'SKIE VOENNYE VESTI. Text in English. s-w.
Published by: Komanduyushchii Voiskami U R V O (Subsidiary of: Ministry of Defence of the Russian Federation/Ministerstvo Oborony R F), A-ya 102, Ekaterinburg, 620026, Russian Federation. TEL 7-3432-241769, 7-3432-593233, 7-3432-241640. Ed. V V Sklyar.

355 RUS
URAL'SKIIE VOENNYE VESTI. Text in Russian. w. USD 299 in United States.
Published by: Commander of Ural Military Region, Ul Narodni Voli 62, Ekaterinburg, 620000, Russian Federation. TEL 3432-24-16-45. **Dist. by:** East View Information Services, 10601 Wayzata Blvd, Minneapolis, MN 55305. TEL 952-252-1201, 800-477-1005, FAX 952-252-1202, info@eastview.com, http://www.eastview.com.

355 USA ISSN 2157-7714
UTAH MINUTEMAN. Text in English. 2002. 3/yr. free (effective 2010). back issues avail. **Document type:** *Journal, Trade.* **Description:** Provides Utah military related informations.
Media: Online - full text.
Published by: Utah National Guard, Public Affairs Office, 12953 S Minuteman Dr, Draper, UT 84020. TEL 801-432-4400, ileen.kennedy@us.army.mil. Ed. Hank McIntire. Pub. Bob Ulin. Adv. contact Chris Kersbergen.

355 DEU ISSN 1437-8094
V B B MAGAZIN. (Verband der Beamten der Bundeswehr) Text in German. 1962. m. EUR 32.90 to non-members; free to members (effective 2010). adv. **Document type:** *Magazine, Trade.*
Formerly (until 1999): Der Bundeswehrbeamte (0521-7814)
Related titles: Online - full text ed.
Published by: Verband der Beamten der Bundeswehr/Association of Officials of the Federal Armed Forces, Baumschulallee 18a, Bonn, 53115, Germany. TEL 49-228-389270, FAX 49-228-639960, mail@vbb-bund.de. Ed. Walter Schmitz. adv.: B&W page EUR 1,720, color page EUR 2,485. Circ: 23,500 (controlled).

V D K ZEITUNG. (Verband der Kriegsbeschaedigten, Kriegshinterbliebenen und Sozialrentner Deutschlands) *see* SOCIAL SERVICES AND WELFARE

V E R T I C BRIEF. *see* POLITICAL SCIENCE—International Relations

V E R T I C MATTERS. *see* POLITICAL SCIENCE—International Relations

353.538 USA ISSN 0161-8598
E181
V F W MAGAZINE; ensuring rights, recognition, and remembrance. Text in English. 1912. 11/yr. (Jun.& Jul. Combined). USD 24.95 (effective 2009). adv. bk.rev. illus. 60 p./no.; back issues avail.; reprints avail. **Document type:** *Magazine, Consumer.*
Formerly (until 19??): Foreign Service
Related titles: Microfilm ed.: (from PQC); Online - full text ed.
Indexed: A22, G05, G06, G07, G08, I05, I07, M05, M06, M07, P02, P10, P13, P34, P47, P48, P52, P53, P54, PQC, T02.
Published by: Veterans of Foreign Wars of the United States, 406 W 34th St, Kansas City, MO 64111. TEL 816-756-3390, FAX 816-968-1149, info@vfw.org, http://www.vfw.org. adv.: color page USD 35,590, B&W page USD 28,115.

052 USA ISSN 1069-0220
THE V V A VETERAN. (Vietnam Veterans of America) Text in English. bi-m. membership. **Document type:** *Magazine, Consumer.*
Former titles: Veteran (0893-8547); V V A Veteran (8750-359X)
Published by: Vietnam Veterans of America, Inc., 8605 Cameron St, Ste 400, Silver Spring, MD 20910. TEL 202-628-2700, 800-882-1316, FAX 202-628-5880. Ed. Mokie Porter.

355 SWE ISSN 0042-2800
VAART FOERSVAR; foer fred, frihet, framtid. Text in Swedish. 1902. q. SEK 200 membership (effective 2008). adv. bk.rev. abstr.; illus. back issues avail. **Document type:** *Journal, Trade.*
Related titles: Online - full text ed.
Published by: Allmaenna Foersvarsfoereningen, Teatergatan 3, Stockholm, 11148, Sweden. TEL 46-8-6781510, FAX 46-8-6672253, mail@aff.a.se. Ed. Col Bo Hugemark TEL 46-8-871578. adv.: B&W page SEK 4,800, color page SEK 9,300. Circ: 4,000.

VAE VICTIS; le magazine du jeu d'histoire. *see* SPORTS AND GAMES

359.96 NLD ISSN 1572-5162
VAST WERKEN. Text in Dutch. 1986. q. EUR 25 (effective 2008).
Published by: Algemene Vereniging van Oud-Personeel van de Koninklijke Marine, c/o G Tigchelaar, Siersteenlaan 468-41, Groningen, 9743 ES, Netherlands. TEL 31-50-5775818, FAX 31-50-5770126, secretaris@avom.nl, http://www.avom.nl. Circ: 4,000.

355 UZB
VATANPARVAR. Text in Uzbek, Russian. d. USD 535 in United States (effective 2000).
Published by: Tsentral'nyi Pechatyi Organ Ministerstva Oborony Respubliki Uzbekistan, Ul D Kunaeva 21, Tashkent, 700031, Uzbekistan. TEL 998-3712-561798, 998-3712-560460. Ed. I K Abdukarimov. **Dist. by:** East View Information Services, 10601 Wayzata Blvd, Minneapolis, MN 55305. TEL 952-252-1201, 800-477-1005, FAX 952-252-1202, info@eastview.com, http://www.eastview.com.

355 HRV ISSN 1330-7517
VELEBIT. Text in Croatian. 1995. w. **Document type:** *Magazine, Trade.*
Published by: Ministarstvo Obrane Republike Hrvatske, Zvonimirova 12, Zagreb, 10000, Croatia. TEL 385-1-4568041, FAX 385-1-4550075. Ed. Ivan Tolj.

338.473 987 363.35 GBR ISSN 1749-1754
VENEZUELA DEFENCE & SECURITY REPORT. Text in English. 2005. a. EUR 820, USD 1,030 combined subscription per issue (print & email eds.) (effective 2010). **Document type:** *Report, Trade.* **Description:** Covers independent forecasts and competitive intelligence on the defense and security industry in Venezuela.
Related titles: E-mail ed.
Indexed: A15, ABIn, B01, P48, P51, P52, PQC.
Published by: Business Monitor International Ltd., Senator House, 85 Queen Victoria St, London, EC4V 4AB, United Kingdom. TEL 44-20-72480468, FAX 44-20-72480467, subs@businessmonitor.com.

VERIFICATION YEARBOOK. *see* POLITICAL SCIENCE—International Relations

355.37 RUS
VERSIYA. Text in Russian. 1990. 52/yr. USD 150.
Indexed: RASB.
Published by: Z A O "MAPT-Media", Smolenskaya Pl., 13/21, Moscow, 121009, Russian Federation. TEL 7-095-2912376. Ed. Artiom Borovik. Circ: 60,000. **Dist. by:** East View Information Services, 10601 Wayzata Blvd, Minneapolis, MN 55305. TEL 952-252-1201, 800-477-1005, FAX 952-252-1202, info@eastview.com, http://www.eastview.com.

353.538 AUS ISSN 0819-8934
VETAFFAIRS; a newspaper for the veteran community. Text in English. 1987. 3/yr. free to members (effective 2008). back issues avail. **Document type:** *Newspaper, Consumer.* **Description:** Provides regular, up-to-date information of interest to the veteran community, including important information about government policies, programs and initiatives.
Related titles: Online - full text ed.: free (effective 2008).
Published by: Department of Veterans' Affairs, GPO Box 3994, Sydney, NSW 2001, Australia. TEL 61-2-92137900, FAX 61-2-92137400, GeneralEnquiries@dva.gov.au. Ed. Matt Gately.

353.538 USA ISSN 0042-4765
VETERAN. Text in Polish. 1921. m. USD 5. adv. bk.rev. bibl.
Published by: Polish Army Veterans Association of America, Inc., 17 Irving Place, New York, NY 10003. TEL 212-475-5585. Ed. Zbigniew A Konikowski. Circ: 4,500.

355 RUS
VETERAN. Text in Russian. 48/yr.
Related titles: Microfiche ed.: (from EVP); Microfilm ed.: (from EVP).
Indexed: RASB.
Published by: Vserossiiskii Sovet Veteranov Voiny, Ul Shchepkina 8, Moscow, 129090, Russian Federation. TEL 7-095-2089119, FAX 7-095-2086004. Ed. A E Danilov. **Dist. by:** East View Information Services, 10601 Wayzata Blvd, Minneapolis, MN 55305. TEL 952-252-1201, 800-477-1005, FAX 952-252-1202, info@eastview.com, http://www.eastview.com.

355 RUS
VETERAN GRANITSY. Text in Russian. q.
Published by: Izdatel'stvo Granitsa, Glavpochtampt, A-ya 848, Moscow, 101000, Russian Federation. TEL 7-095-2248169, FAX 7-095-2565159. Ed. V I Sharandak. **Dist. by:** East View Information Services, 10601 Wayzata Blvd, Minneapolis, MN 55305. TEL 952-252-1201, 800-477-1005, FAX 952-252-1202, info@eastview.com, http://www.eastview.com.

VETERANS' BULLETIN. *see* CLUBS

VETERAN'S BUSINESS JOURNAL. *see* BUSINESS AND ECONOMICS—Small Business

VETERAN'S ENTERPRISE; the military and veteran's business network. *see* OCCUPATIONS AND CAREERS

VETERANS FOR PEACE JOURNAL. *see* POLITICAL SCIENCE—International Relations

VETERANS FOR PEACE NEWSLETTER. *see* POLITICAL SCIENCE—International Relations

353.538 USA
VETERAN'S OBSERVER. Text in English. 1981. m. free. adv. bk.rev. **Document type:** *Newspaper.*
Address: 7314 Deering Ave, Canoga Park, CA 91303. TEL 818-713-9447, FAX 818-713-8086. Ed. Tamarra Cox. Pub. Richard A Bivona Sr. R&P Richard Bivona Sr. Adv. contact Casandra Punsiari. Circ: 150,000.

353.538 USA
VETERANS OF FOREIGN WARS OF THE UNITED STATES. ANNUAL CONVENTION PROCEEDINGS. Text in English. 1925. a. free to members (effective 2009). **Document type:** *Proceedings, Trade.* **Description:** Aims to educate the young Americans about the commitment made in America's wars.
Former titles (until 1999): Veterans of Foreign Wars of the United States. National Convention Proceedings (0160-1474); (until 1958): Veterans of Foreign Wars of the United States. National Encampment Proceedings; (until 192?): Veterans of Foreign Wars of the United States. Annual Encampment Proceedings
Published by: Veterans of Foreign Wars of the United States, 406 W 34th St, Kansas City, MO 64111. TEL 816-756-3390, FAX 816-968-1149, info@vfw.org, http://www.vfw.org.

353.538 USA
VETERANS OF THE VIETNAM WAR; the "Veteran Leader". Text in English. 1980. q. USD 20 (effective 2001). adv. **Document type:** *Newsletter.*
Published by: Veterans of the Vietnam War, Inc., 805 South Township Blvd., Pittston, PA 18640-3327. TEL 570-603-9740, FAX 570-603-9741. Ed., Pub., Adv. contact Michael Milne. Circ: 15,000.

353.538 USA ISSN 1054-0962
UA23.A1
VETERAN'S VIEW. Text in English. m.
Published by: Central Newspapers, Inc. (Subsidiary of: Gannett Company, Inc.), 8 South Michigan Ave, Chicago, IL 60603. TEL 312-263-5388. Ed. Michael Haddad.

VETERAN'S VISION. *see* OCCUPATIONS AND CAREERS

305.906 USA
THE VETERANS' VOICE; the new stars & stripes. Text in English. m. USD 19 (effective 2005). adv. **Document type:** *Magazine, Consumer.* **Description:** Covers issues of concern to veterans with an emphasis on politics and legislation, both oending and new, as well as health concerns of veterans.
Published by: All American Publishing, 112 E McGowan St, Plains, MT 59859. TEL 406-826-5333, 888-826-3215, FAX 406-826-5149. adv.: B&W page USD 1,920; trim 10.5 x 12. Circ: 9,000.

353.538 USA
VETS' NEWS. Text in English. 1945. bi-m. free. **Document type:** *Newsletter, Government.* **Description:** Informs veterans and dependents of available benefits, and discusses veteran-related activities.
Formerly: Vets' Newsletter
Published by: Department of Veterans Affairs, 700 Summer St, N E, Salem, OR 97310-1201. TEL 503-373-2385, FAX 503-373-2362. Ed. Robert Fleming. Circ: 48,000.

355 ROM ISSN 1018-0400
U4
VIATA ARMATEI. Text in Romanian. 1935. m. ROL 9,600; USD 45 in Europe; USD 50 elsewhere (effective 2000). bk.rev. abstr.; charts; illus. **Description:** Covers art, literature, music, museums and art galleries, theater, movies, hobbies, photography, military news and military technology.
Former titles (until Dec. 1989): Viata Militara (0042-5044); Imagini Militare
Indexed: RASB.
Published by: Ministerul Apararii Nationale/Ministry of National Defense, Bd. Unirii nr.57, Bl. E4, Sector 3, Bucharest, 70764, Romania. TEL 40-1-3142012, FAX 40-1-3159456. Ed. Liviu Visan. **Dist. by:** Rodipet S.A., Piata Presei Libere 1, sector 1, PO Box 33-57, Bucharest 3, Romania. TEL 40-21-2224126, 40-21-2226407, rodipet@rodipet.ro.

355 USA ISSN 1046-2902
VIETNAM. Text in English. 1988. bi-m. USD 21.95 (effective 2009). adv. bk.rev.; software rev. illus.; maps. back issues avail.; reprints avail. **Document type:** *Magazine, Consumer.* **Description:** Features the full story behind America's most controversial war, with gripping firsthand accounts and carefully researched articles by veterans of the conflict and top military historians.
Related titles: Online - full text ed.
Indexed: A22, A26, E08, G05, G06, G07, G08, I05, M06, M07, P10, P14, P47, P48, P53, P54, PQC, S09.
—Ingenta. **CCC.**
Published by: Weider History Group, 19300 Promenade Dr, Leesburg, VA 20176-6500. TEL 703-771-9400, FAX 703-779-8345, comments@weiderhistorygroup.com. Pub. Eric Weider. adv.: color page USD 3,875; trim 8.375 x 10.5. Circ: 36,000.

338.473 959.7 363.35 GBR ISSN 1749-1762
VIETNAM DEFENCE & SECURITY REPORT. Text in English. 2005. q. EUR 820, USD 1,030 combined subscription (print & email eds.) (effective 2010). **Document type:** *Report, Trade.* **Description:** Covers independent forecasts and competitive intelligence on the defense and security industry in Vietnam.
Related titles: E-mail ed.
Indexed: B01, P34.
Published by: Business Monitor International Ltd., Senator House, 85 Queen Victoria St, London, EC4V 4AB, United Kingdom. TEL 44-20-72480468, FAX 44-20-72480467, subs@businessmonitor.com.

355 BEL
VIGILO. Text in French. 1960. q. adv. bk.rev.
Published by: (Cercle des Officiers de Reserve de Bruxelles/National Association of Reserve Officers (KNVRO)), F Lepeer Ed & Pub, Rue van Rolleghem 25, Brussels, 1090, Belgium. Circ: 1,500.

355 UKR
VIIS'KO UKRAINY. Text in Ukrainian. 1992. bi-m. **Document type:** *Magazine, Government.*
Published by: Ministerstvo Oborony Ukrainy, vul Mel'nykova 81, Kyiv, 04050, Ukraine. TEL 380-44- 4830839, http://www.mil.gov.ua. Ed. Volodymyr Horishnyak.

355 USA ISSN 0360-5876
VIRGINIA GUARDPOST. Text in English. 19??. bi-m. back issues avail. **Document type:** *Journal, Trade.*
Related titles: Online - full text ed.: ISSN 2158-690X. free (effective 2011).
Published by: Virginia National Guard, Public Affairs Office, Bldg 316 - Fort Picket, Blackstone, VA 23824. http://vko.va.ngb.army.mil/VirginiaGuard/media/index.html.

355 ARG ISSN 1852-8619
▼ **VISION CONJUNTA.** Text in Spanish. 2009. a. **Document type:** *Magazine, Trade.*
Related titles: Online - full text ed.
Published by: Escuela Superior de Guerra Conjunta de las Fuerzas Armadas, Ave Luis Maria Campos, 480 2o. Piso, Buenos Aires, C1226BOP, Argentina. TEL 54-11-43468734, revistaesgc@fuerzas-aramadas.mil.ar. Ed. Jose Maria Felix-Martin.

VITAL SIGNS (CAMBRIDGE). *see* PUBLIC HEALTH AND SAFETY

355 FRA
VIVAT HUSSAR. Text in French. 1966. a. adv. bk.rev. bibl.; illus. back issues avail. **Document type:** *Journal.* **Description:** Complete history on hussars in the world.
Published by: Association des Amis du Musee International des Hussards, Jardin Massey, Tarbes, 65000, France. TEL 33-5-62363149, FAX 33-5-62443800. Ed. Andre Mengelle. Circ: 1,500.

355 NLD ISSN 0042-7705
VLIEGENDE HOLLANDER. Text in Dutch. 1945. m. adv. bk.rev. charts; illus. **Document type:** *Government.*
Published by: Ministerie van Defensie, Directie Voorlichting en Communicatie, Postbus 20701, The Hague, 2500 ES, Netherlands. TEL 31-70-3188188, FAX 31-70-3187888, http://www.defensie.nl. **Co-sponsor:** Koninklijke Luchtmacht/Royal Dutch Air Force.

355 BGR ISSN 0861-7392
U4
VOENEN JOURNAL. Text in Bulgarian. 1888. bi-m. **Description:** Presents history, theory, practice of military arts.
Published by: (Ministerstvo na Otbranata na Republika Bulgaria/Ministry of Defence of the Republic of Bulgaria), Izdatelstvo na M O, Iv Vazov ul 12, Sofia, Bulgaria. Ed. Georgy Rachev.

355 RUS ISSN 0236-2058
U4
VOENNAYA MYSL'. Text in Russian. 1918. bi-m. USD 169 (effective 2009). **Document type:** *Journal, Government.* **Description:** Military theory journal of the RF Ministry of Defense. Presents articles on Russian military reform, tactics and strategy of modern combat, experience of counterterrorist operations, international security and so on.
Formerly (until 1936): Voina i Revolyutsiya
Related titles: Microfiche ed.: (from EVP); Online - full text ed.; ◆ English Translation: Military Thought. ISSN 0869-5636.
Indexed: A01, A03, A08, CA, DIP, I02, IBR, IBZ, LID&ISL, M05, M07, P02, P10, P34, P47, P48, P52, P53, P54, PAIS, PQC, PSA, RASB, T02.
—East View. **CCC.**
Published by: Ministerstvo Oborony Rossiiskoi Federatsii/Ministry of Defence of the Russian Federation, Khoroshevskoe shosse 38, Moscow, 123826, Russian Federation. TEL 7-095-1312199, nikolaev@mil.ru, http://www.mil.ru. Ed. S Rodikov. Circ: 2,299. **Dist. by:** East View Information Services, 10601 Wayzata Blvd, Minneapolis, MN 55305. TEL 952-252-1201, 800-477-1005, FAX 952-252-1202, info@eastview.com, http://www.eastview.com.

355 RUS ISSN 0042-9058
VOENNO-ISTORICHESKII ZHURNAL. Text in Russian. 1959. bi-m. USD 170 foreign (effective 2005). **Document type:** *Journal.* **Description:** Covers Russian military history. Publishes stories about famous battles as well as outstanding military leaders. Includes memoirs, newly-found documents and debates.
Related titles: Microfiche ed.: (from EVP).
Indexed: AmH&L, HistAb, LID&ISL, NumL, RASB.
Published by: Krasnaya Zvezda, Khoroshevskoe shosse 38a, Moscow, 123007, Russian Federation. TEL 7-095-1956118. Ed. V M Minaev. **Dist. by:** East View Information Services, 10601 Wayzata Blvd, Minneapolis, MN 55305. TEL 952-252-1201, 800-477-1005, FAX 952-252-1202, info@eastview.com, http://www.eastview.com.

623 RUS
VOENNO-TEKHNICHESKOE SOTRUDNICHESTVO. Text in Russian. w. USD 499 in United States.
Address: Tverskoi bulv 10-12, Moscow, 103009, Russian Federation. TEL 7-095-2021127, FAX 7-095-2024937. **Dist. by:** East View Information Services, 10601 Wayzata Blvd, Minneapolis, MN 55305. TEL 952-252-1201, 800-477-1005, FAX 952-252-1202, info@eastview.com, http://www.eastview.com.

VOENNOISTORICHESKI SBORNIK. *see* HISTORY—History Of Europe

355 ISSN 0134-8256
VOENNYE ZNANIYA/MILITARY REVIEW. Text in Russian. 1925. m. USD 84 foreign (effective 2004).
Related titles: Microfiche ed.: (from EVP).
Indexed: LID&ISL.
—East View.
Address: Volokolamskoe shosse 88, str 5, Moscow, 123362, Russian Federation. TEL 7-095-4912935, FAX 7-095-4911598. Ed. G Ya Chernyshev. **Dist. by:** M K - Periodica, ul Gilyarovskogo 39, Moscow 129110, Russian Federation. TEL 7-095-2845008, FAX 7-095-2813798, info@periodicals.ru, http://www.mkniga.ru.

355 353.13263 RUS
VOENNYI DIPLOMAT/MILITARY DIPLOMAT. Text in Russian, English. 2003. bi-m. EUR 126, USD 150 (effective 2005). **Description:** Contains open-access information about life, and activities of the military diplomatic corps in Moscow; achievements of the Russian military-industrial complex; international ties of the Russian Federation Armed Forces, peacekeeping activities, struggle against terrorism.
Address: ul Marshala Biruzova 8, Bldg 1, entry 1A, off 10, Moscow, 123298, Russian Federation. TEL 7-095-9562499. Ed. Alexander Shaverdov.

355.1 RUS ISSN 1029-4678
UA770
VOENNYI PARAD; zhurnal voenno-promyshlennogo kompleksa. Text in Russian. 1994. bi-m. USD 413 foreign (effective 2010). **Document type:** *Journal.* **Description:** Offers information on the latest weapons systems and military equipment and their combat uses, state-of-the-art technologies, civilian production of defense enterprises, state of the international arms market, military reform, and the military policies of Russia and other CIS countries. Aims to promote Russian-made armaments on the international market, help Russian defense enterprises attract foreign investment, and enhance military-technical cooperation with both domestic and foreign partners.
Related titles: ◆ English ed.: Military Parade. ISSN 1029-466X; ◆ English Translation: Military Parade. ISSN 1029-466X.
Published by: Izdatel'stvo Voennyi Parad, a/ya 73, Moscow, 121108, Russian Federation. TEL 7-495-9379632, FAX 7-495-6044246, military@milparade.com. Ed. Aleksandr Andrianov. Adv. contact Alexei Nedelin. Circ: 20,000 (paid). **Dist. by:** East View Information Services, 10601 Wayzata Blvd, Minneapolis, MN 55305. TEL 952-252-1201, 800-477-1005, FAX 952-252-1202, info@eastview.com, http://www.eastview.com.

355 RUS ISSN 0042-9066
VOENNYI VESTNIK. Text in Russian. 1921. m. index.
Related titles: Microfiche ed.: (from EVP).
Indexed: CDSP, LID&ISL, RASB.
Published by: Voenizdat, Ul Zorge 1, Moscow, 103160, Russian Federation. TEL 095-195-4595. **Co-sponsor:** Ministerstvo Oborony.

355 RUS
VOENNYI VESTNIK YUGA ROSSII. Text in Russian. w. USD 249 in United States.
Address: Ul Taganrogskaya 92, Rostov-on-Don, 344069, Russian Federation. TEL 8632-39-72-63, FAX 8632-78-03-27. Ed. G T Alekhin. **Dist. by:** East View Information Services, 10601 Wayzata Blvd, Minneapolis, MN 55305. TEL 952-252-1201, 800-477-1005, FAX 952-252-1202, info@eastview.com, http://www.eastview.com.

355 UKR
VOHNI SLAVUTYCHA. Text in Ukrainian. bi-m. USD 115 in United States.
Address: Ul 77 Gvardeiskoi divizii 3, Slavutych, Ukraine. **Dist. by:** East View Information Services, 10601 Wayzata Blvd, Minneapolis, MN 55305. TEL 952-252-1201, 800-477-1005, FAX 952-252-1202, info@eastview.com, http://www.eastview.com.

355 RUS
VOIN ROSSII (MOSCOW). Text in Russian. m. USD 145 in United States.
Indexed: RASB.
Published by: Ministerstvo Oborony Rossiiskoi Federatsii/Ministry of Defence of the Russian Federation, Khoroshevskoe shosse 38, Moscow, 123826, Russian Federation. FAX 7-095-9412064. Ed. V B Romanchuk. **Dist. by:** East View Information Services, 10601 Wayzata Blvd, Minneapolis, MN 55305. TEL 952-252-1201, 800-477-1005, FAX 952-252-1202, info@eastview.com, http://www.eastview.com.

355 RUS
VOIN ROSSII (NOVOSIBIRSK). Text in Russian. w. USD 249 in United States.
Published by: Ministry of Defence of the Russian Federation/Ministerstvo Oborony R F, Novosibirsk, 630017, Russian Federation. TEL 7-3832-667357. Ed. S I Dorokhov. **Dist. by:** East View Information Services, 10601 Wayzata Blvd, Minneapolis, MN 55305. TEL 952-252-1201, 800-477-1005, FAX 952-252-1202, info@eastview.com, http://www.eastview.com.

355 RUS
VOISKOVOI VESTNIK. Text in Russian. bi-m. USD 99.95 in United States.
Address: Syromyatnicheskii pr-t 8, Moscow, 107120, Russian Federation. TEL 7-095-3618171, FAX 7-095-9177266. Ed. L M Lukienko. **Dist. by:** East View Information Services, 10601 Wayzata Blvd, Minneapolis, MN 55305. TEL 952-252-1201, 800-477-1005, FAX 952-252-1202, info@eastview.com, http://www.eastview.com.

LA VOIX DU COMBATTANT. *see* SOCIAL SERVICES AND WELFARE

VOJENSKE ZDRAVOTNICKE LISTY. *see* MEDICAL SCIENCES

355 SRB ISSN 0042-840X
VOJNI GLASNIK; strucni casopis rodova vojske i sluzbi jna. Text in Macedonian, Serbo-Croatian. 1947. bi-m. USD 20.
Published by: Vojnoizdavacki Zavod, Vojska, Novinsko-itdavacka, ustanova, Bircaninova 5, Belgrade, Serbia 11000. Ed. Sava Krstic. **Dist. by:** Jugoslovenska Knjiga, Postanski Fah 36, Belgrade 11001.

355 SRB ISSN 0067-5660
U4.B37
VOJNI MUZEJ BEOGRAD. VESNIK/MILITARY MUSEUM, BELGRADE. BULLETIN. Text in Serbo-Croatian; Summaries in English, French. 1954. irreg. bk.rev.
Indexed: HistAb.
Published by: Vojni Muzej Beograd, Kalemegdan bb, Belgrade, 11000. http://www.vj.yu/vojni%20muzej. Ed. Marijan Mozgon. Circ: 2,000.

355 SRB ISSN 0042-8426
U4
VOJNO DELO; opstevojni teorijski casopis. Text in Serbo-Croatian. 1949. bi-m. YUN 300,000, USD 5 per issue.
Indexed: LID&ISL.
Published by: Savazni Sekretarijat za Narodnu Odbranu, Vojska, Novinsko - izdavacka, ustanova, Bircaninova 5, Belgrade, 11000. TEL 011-681-565. Ed. Jovan Canak.

355 SRB ISSN 0042-8442
U4
VOJNOISTORIJSKI GLASNIK. Text in Serbo-Croatian; Summaries in English, French. 1950. bi-m. bk.rev. bibl.; charts; illus.; stat. index, cum.index. **Document type:** *Journal, Academic/Scholarly.*
Indexed: HistAb, IBR, IBZ, LID&ISL, P30, RASB.
Published by: Republika Srbija Ministarstvo Odbrane, Institut za Strategijska Istrazivanja, Odeljenje za Vojnu Istoriju, Bircaninova br 5, Belgrade. TEL 381-11-2063852, FAX 381-11-3006137, vojniarhiv@mod.gov.yu, http://www.mod.gov.yu. Ed. Milan Terzic. Circ: 1,000.

610 355 615 SRB ISSN 0042-8450
RC970
VOJNOSANITETSKI PREGLED/MILITARY MEDICAL AND PHARMACEUTICAL; casopis lekara i farmaceuta Srbije i Crne Gore. Text in English, Serbian; Summaries in English. 1944. m. EUR 60, USD 75 foreign (effective 2005). adv. bk.rev. abstr.; charts; illus.; stat. index. 110 p./no. 2 cols./p.; back issues avail. **Document type:** *Journal, Government.* **Description:** Contains editorials, original articles (scientific and professional), preliminary or short communications, general reviews, meta-analyses, current topics, from the medical history of the Yugoslav Medical Corps.
Related titles: E-mail ed.; Fax ed.; Online - full text ed.
Indexed: A01, A03, A08, A22, CA, CISA, ChemAb, DentInd, EMBASE, ErgAb, ExcerpMed, INIS AtomInd, IndMed, MEDLINE, P30, PsychoIAb, R10, Reac, SCI, SCOPUS, T02, W07.
—BLDSC (9251.652000), GNLM, IE, Infotrieve, Ingenta.
Published by: (Vojnomedicinska Akademija, Institut za Naucne Informacije), Savezno Ministarstvo Odbrane, Sanitetska Uprava, Crnotravska 17, Postanski Fah 3335, Belgrade, 11040. vmaini1@eunet.yu. Ed. Vladimir Tadic. Adv. contact Slavko Lukic. Circ: 500.

355 SRB ISSN 0042-8469
VOJNOTEHNICKI GLASNIK. Text in Serbo-Croatian. 1953. bi-m. YUN 70, USD 8.50.
Published by: (Yugoslavia. Savezni Sekretarijat za Narodnu Odbranu), Vojnoizdavacki Zavod, Vojska, Novinsko-itdavacka, ustanova, Bircaninova 5, Belgrade, Serbia 11000. Ed. Nikola Zoric.

355 SRB ISSN 0354-2750
U4
VOJSKA. Text in Serbo-Croatian. 1945. w. **Document type:** *Magazine.*
Formerly (until 1992): Narodna Armija (0027-7908)
Published by: Novinsko-Izdavacki Centar Vojska, Kataniceva 16, Postanski Pregradak 06-1015, Belgrade, Serbia 11002. genstaffinfo@vj.yu, http://www.vj.yu. Ed. Slavoljub Randjelovic TEL 381-11-643341.

355.009 NZL ISSN 0113-1184
VOLUNTEERS. Text in English. 1973. 3/yr. free membership (effective 2009). bibl. back issues avail. **Document type:** *Journal, Trade.* **Description:** Contains a wide range of articles of interest from each of the services, including details of research that has been carried out by members and others.
Indexed: INZP.
Published by: New Zealand Military Historical Society, PO Box 5123, Auckland, New Zealand. http://www.nzmhs.org.nz/. Ed. Ken Stead.

355 RUS
VOPROSY ZASHCHITY INFORMATSII. Text in Russian. q.
Indexed: RASB.
Published by: V.I.M.I., Volokolamskoe shosse 77, Moscow, 123584, Russian Federation. TEL 7-095-4911306. **Dist. by:** East View Information Services, 10601 Wayzata Blvd, Minneapolis, MN 55305. TEL 952-252-1201, 800-477-1005, FAX 952-252-1202, info@eastview.com, http://www.eastview.com.

355 BEL
VOX: MENSUEL MILITAIRE. Text in French. 1974. m. adv. bk.rev. illus. index.
Former titles: Vox: Hebdomadaire Militaire; F M (0014-5963)
Related titles: ◆ Dutch ed.: Vox: Militair Maandblad.
Indexed: RASB.

M

Published by: Ministere de la Defense Nationale, SID-Quartier Reine Elisabeth, Rue d'Evere 1, Bloc 5, Brussels, 1140, Belgium. TEL 32-2-7013931, vox@js.mil.be. Ed. Alain Vereecke. R&P Eric Tripnaux. Adv. contact Claudine Zamparutti. Circ: 30,000.

355 BEL
VOX: MILITAIR MAANDBLAD; military review. Text in Dutch. 1974. m. 32 p./no.; **Document type:** *Magazine.*
Related titles: ◆ French ed.: Vox: Mensuel Militaire.
Published by: Ministere de la Defense Nationale, SID-Quartier Reine Elisabeth, Rue d'Evere 1, Bloc 5, Brussels, 1140, Belgium. vox@js.mil.be. Circ: 40,000.

355.31 CAN ISSN 0300-3213
VOXAIR. Text in English. 1952. s-m. CAD 4. adv. play rev. **Document type:** *Newspaper, Government.*
Published by: Canadian Forces Base Winnipeg, c/o Maj. C. Walton-Simm, Ed., Westwin, MB R3J 3Y5, Canada. TEL 204-889-3963, FAX 204-885-4176. Ed. Maj C Walton Simm. Adv. contact Maureen Walls. Circ: 3,600 (controlled).

355 NLD ISSN 1876-0724
VREDES MAGAZINE. Text in Dutch. 1992. 4/yr. EUR 10 (effective 2011). adv. **Description:** Covers topics relating to war resistance, anti-militarism and issues pertaining to persons who refuse military service.
Formerly (until 2007): Vee Dee Amok (0927-3433); Which was formed by the merger of (1984-1991): A M O K Anti-militaristies Tijdschrift (0168-8847); Which incorporated (1983-1988): Vredesaktie Krant (0168-194X); (1973-1991): VeeDee (0165-9898); Which incorporated (1976-1978): Wapenfeiten (0166-0047)
Related titles: Online - full text ed.: ISSN 1876-0716.
Published by: (AMOK - V D), Vereniging VredesMedia, Vlamingstraat 82, Delft, 2611 LA, Netherlands. TEL 31-30-8901341, info@vredesmedia.nl, http://www.vredesmedia.nl. Circ: 1,300.
Co-sponsor: Antimilitaristies Onderzoekskollektief.

W W II HISTORY. *see* HISTORY—History Of North And South America

355 DEU
DAS WAFFEN-ARSENAL. Text in German. 1973. irreg. price varies. adv. back issues avail. **Document type:** *Monographic series, Academic/Scholarly.*
Published by: Podzun-Pallas Verlag GmbH, Juraquelle 26, Eggolsheim-Bammersdorf, 91330, Germany. TEL 49-9191-6155460, FAX 49-9191-6155466, info@podzun-pallas-verlag.de, http://www.podzun-pallas.de. Circ: 12,000.

WAR & SOCIETY. *see* HISTORY

355.009 GBR ISSN 0968-3445
U27
➤ **WAR IN HISTORY.** Text in English. 1994. q. USD 572, GBP 310 combined subscription to institutions (print & online eds.); USD 561, GBP 304 to institutions (effective 2011). adv. bk.rev. illus. back issues avail.; reprint service avail. from PSC. **Document type:** *Journal, Academic/Scholarly.* **Description:** Explores the military as it is integrated into a broader definition of history. Deals with war in all its aspects: economic, social, and political for all periods.
Related titles: Online - full text ed.: ISSN 1477-0385. USD 515, GBP 279 to institutions (effective 2011).
Indexed: A01, A02, A03, A08, A20, A22, ASCA, AmH&L, AmHI, ArtHuCI, CA, CurCont, DIP, E01, H05, H07, H14, HistAb, I02, I14, IBR, IBZ, LID&ISL, M05, M07, P10, P30, P47, P48, P52, P53, P54, PQC, SCOPUS, SSCI, T02, W04, W07.
—BLDSC (9261.810700), IE, Infotrieve, Ingenta. **CCC.**
Published by: Sage Publications Ltd. (Subsidiary of: Sage Publications, Inc.), 1 Oliver's Yard, 55 City Rd, London, EC1Y 1SP, United Kingdom. TEL 44-20-73248701, 44-20-73248500, FAX 44-20-73248600, info@sagepub.co.uk, http://www.uk.sagepub.com/home.nav. Eds. Dennis Showalter, Hew Strachan. adv.: B&W page GBP 400; 130 x 205.

355 USA ISSN 1556-4924
WAR TECHNOLOGY AND HISTORY. Text in English. 2006. irreg., latest 2010. price varies. back issues avail. **Document type:** *Monographic series, Academic/Scholarly.*
Published by: Praeger Publishers (Subsidiary of: Greenwood Publishing Group Inc.), 88 Post Rd W, Westport, CT 06881. TEL 800-368-6868, tech.support@greenwood.com, http://www.greenwood.com. Ed. Robert Citino.

WARBIRDTECH SERIES. *see* AERONAUTICS AND SPACE FLIGHT

355 GBR ISSN 0308-0676
➤ **WARFARE.** Text in English. 1972. s-a. free (effective 2003). bk.rev.; film rev.; software rev.; tel.rev.; video rev.; Website rev. abstr.; bibl.; charts; illus.; maps; stat. **Document type:** *Journal, Academic/Scholarly.*
Related titles: CD-ROM ed.; Diskette ed.; E-mail ed.; Fax ed.; Online - full text ed.
Published by: Delane Press, 157 Vicarage Rd, London, E10 5DU, United Kingdom. Ed., Pub. Ronald King.

➤ **WARGAMES ILLUSTRATED.** *see* SPORTS AND GAMES

▼ ➤ **WARGAMES, SOLDIERS & STRATEGY.** *see* SPORTS AND GAMES

355.31 USA
UA23.A1
WARRIOR-CITIZEN. Text in English. 1954. q. USD 14 domestic; USD 19.60 foreign; USD 5.50 per issue domestic; USD 7.70 per issue foreign (effective 2010). bk.rev. charts; illus. index. back issues avail. **Document type:** *Magazine, Trade.*
Former titles (until 2007): Army Reserve Magazine (0004-2579); (until 1964): Army Reservist
Related titles: Online - full text ed.: ISSN 2152-596X. free (effective 2010).
Indexed: A01, A09, A10, A22, A26, AUNI, G05, G06, G07, G08, I02, I05, IUSGP, M01, M02, M05, M06, P16, P52, T02, V02, V03, V04.
—Ingenta.
Published by: U.S. Army Reserve, 2400 Army Pentagon, Washington, DC 22202. TEL 800-359-8483. Ed. Paul R Adams.

355 USA ISSN 1949-7709
WARRIOR MEDIC MONTHLY. Abbreviated title: W M M. Text in English. 2008. m. free to members (effective 2009). **Document type:** *Magazine, Trade.*
Media: Online - full content.
Published by: Army Reserve Medical Command, Public Affairs Office, 2801 Grand Ave, Pinellas Park, FL 33782. TEL 877-891-3281, FAX 727-563-3625, ARMEDCOM@usar.army.mil, http://www.usar.army.mil/arweb/organization/commandstructure/USARC/OPS/ARMEDCOM/Pages/default.aspx. Ed. William D Ritter.

359 GBR ISSN 0142-6222
V765
WARSHIP. Text in English. 1977. a. GBP 30 per issue (effective 2009). adv. bk.rev. **Document type:** *Magazine, Consumer.* **Description:** Covers design, development and service history of the world's combat ships.
Indexed: IBR, IBZ, RASB.
—BLDSC (9261.868600), IE, Ingenta.
Published by: Conway Maritime Press (Subsidiary of: Anova Books), The Old Magistrates Ct, 10 Southcombe St, London, W14 0RA, United Kingdom. TEL 44-20-76051400, FAX 44-20-76051401, customerservices@anovabooks.com, http://www.anovabooks.com/imprint/conway. Ed. John Jordan. Circ: 2,500.

355.27 USA ISSN 0043-0374
V750
WARSHIP INTERNATIONAL. Text in English. 1964. q. free to members (effective 2005). adv. bk.rev. charts; illus.; stat. reprints avail. **Document type:** *Magazine, Consumer.* **Description:** Concentrates on warships of various types, brief summaries of their careers and related subjects such as the armoring of ships, elements of ballistics needed for a full understanding of the ships' designs.
Related titles: Microfilm ed.: (from PQC).
Indexed: A22, AMB, AmH&L, HistAb.
—BLDSC (9261.869000), IE, Infotrieve, Ingenta.
Published by: I N R O, Inc., 5905 Reinwood Dr, Toledo, OH 43613-5605. TEL 419-472-1331, FAX 419-472-1331, inro@primenet.com, http://www.primenet.com/~inro. Ed. Christopher C Wright. Circ: 4,000.

359 GBR ISSN 1464-0511
WARSHIP WORLD. Text in English. 1984. bi-m. GBP 22 domestic; GBP 26.50 foreign (effective 2009). bk.rev. back issues avail. **Document type:** *Magazine, Consumer.* **Description:** Provides current information on ships and weapons in the Royal Navy.
Published by: Maritime Books, Lodge Hill, Liskeard, Cornwall PL14 4EL, United Kingdom. TEL 44-1579-343663, FAX 44-1579-346747, sales@navybooks.com, http://www.navybooks.com.

355 AUS ISSN 1328-2727
WARTIME. Text in English. 1997. q. AUD 28 domestic; AUD 52 in Asia & the Pacific; AUD 64 elsewhere (effective 2008). bk.rev. maps. back issues avail. **Document type:** *Magazine, Consumer.* **Description:** Provides information on Australian experience of war, military history; and the effects of war on society.
Published by: Australian War Memorial, GPO Box 345, Canberra, ACT 2601, Australia. TEL 61-2-62434211, FAX 61-2-62434325, info@awm.gov.au. Ed. Dr. Robert Nichols TEL 61-2-62434327. Circ: 10,000.

WEHRMEDIZIN UND WEHRPHARMAZIE. *see* MEDICAL SCIENCES

WEHRTECHNIK; Quartalsschrift fuer wirtschaftliche Fragen der Verteidigung, Luftfahrt und Industrie. *see* AERONAUTICS AND SPACE FLIGHT

623 DEU ISSN 0935-3100
WEHRTECHNISCHER REPORT. Text in German. 1988. irreg. EUR 11 per issue (effective 2006). adv. back issues avail. **Document type:** *Magazine, Trade.*
Published by: Report Verlag GmbH, Paul-Kemp-Str 3, Bonn, 53173, Germany. TEL 49-228-3680400, FAX 49-228-3680402, info@report-verlag.de, http://www.report-verlag.de. Ed. Gerhard Hubatschek. Adv. contact Brigitte Benzing. B&W page EUR 3,580, color page EUR 4,990. Circ: 7,000 (controlled).

355 DEU ISSN 0938-2631
WEISSBUCH ZUR LAGE UND ENTWICKLUNG DER BUNDESWEHR. Text in German. 1970. irreg., latest 2006. price varies. **Document type:** *Trade.*
Formerly (until 1985): Weissbuch zur Sicherheit der Bundesrepublik Deutschland und zur Lage der Bundeswehr (0723-3876)
Published by: Bundesministerium der Verteidigung, Presse- und Informationsstab, Stauffenbergstr 18, Berlin, 10785, Germany. TEL 49-30-18248232, FAX 49-30-18248240, http://www.bmvg.de.

WENHUA YUEKAN/CULTURE MONTHLY. *see* LITERATURE

355.4 NLD ISSN 1878-3481
WERELD IN OORLOG. Text in Dutch. 2007. bi-m. EUR 50 domestic; EUR 60 in Europe; EUR 70 elsewhere (effective 2010). adv. **Document type:** *Magazine, Consumer.*
Published by: Just Publishers, Julianalaan 18, Hilversum, 1213 AP, Netherlands. TEL 31-35-6286090, FAX 31-35-6213536, info@justpublishers.nl, http://www.justpublishers.nl. Adv. contact Hans van Maar.

353.538 USA ISSN 0745-2799
WEST VIRGINIA LEGIONNAIRE. Text in English. m. adv.
Published by: American Legion Post 16, 1421 Sixth Ave, PO Box 1697, Huntington, WV 25701. http://www.americanlegion16.org. Circ: 27,000.

WEST'S VETERANS APPEALS REPORTER. *see* LAW—Legal Aid

355 DEU ISSN 0083-9078
WEYERS FLOTTENTASCHENBUCH/WARSHIPS OF THE WORLD. Text in German. 1900. a. EUR 64 (effective 2009). **Document type:** *Directory, Trade.*
Former titles: Taschenbuch der Kriegsflotten; Taschenbuch der Deutschen Kriegsflotten
Published by: Bernard und Graefe Verlag, Heilsbachstr 26, Bonn, 53123, Germany. TEL 49-228-64830, FAX 49-228-6483109, marketing@moench-group.com, http://www.monch.com.

353.538 USA ISSN 0083-9108
WHAT EVERY VETERAN SHOULD KNOW. Text in English. 1937. a. USD 12; USD 35 combined subscription includes Supplements (effective 2000). Supplement avail. **Document type:** *Newsletter.*
Related titles: Supplement(s): USD 25 (effective 2000).
Published by: Veterans Information Service, PO Box 111, East Moline, IL 61244. TEL 309-757-7760, FAX 309-757-7760, vis111@home.com, http://members.xoom.com/vetsinfosvc. Ed. K Murphy P Murphy.

359 NZL ISSN 1177-8008
VA720
WHITE ENSIGN. Text in English. 3/yr. **Document type:** *Magazine, Consumer.*
Formerly (until 2007): Raggie (1173-4310)
Published by: Royal New Zealand Navy Museum, Private Bag 32 901, Devonport, North Shore City, 0744, New Zealand. TEL 64-9-4455186, FAX 64-9-4455046. Ed. Theresa Manson TEL 64-9-4461824.

355 GBR ISSN 0268-1307
WHITEHALL PAPERS. Text in English. 1985. s-a. GBP 561, EUR 876, USD 1,099 combined subscription to institutions (print & online eds.) (effective 2009); includes R U S I Journal. adv. back issues avail.; reprint service avail. from PSC. **Document type:** *Journal, Academic/Scholarly.* **Description:** Provides in-depth studies of specific developments, issues or themes in the field of national and international defence and security.
Related titles: Online - full text ed.: ISSN 1754-5382. GBP 533, EUR 832, USD 1,044 to institutions (effective 2009); includes R U S I Journal.
Indexed: A22, LID&ISL, P42.
—IE. **CCC.**
Published by: (Royal United Services Institute), Routledge (Subsidiary of: Taylor & Francis Group), 4 Park Sq, Milton Park, Abingdon, Oxon OX14 4RN, United Kingdom. TEL 44-20-70176000, FAX 44-20-70176336, subscriptions@tandf.co.uk, http://www.routledge.com. Adv. contact Linda Hann TEL 44-1344-779945. **Subscr. to:** Taylor & Francis Ltd., Journals Customer Service, Sheepen Pl, Colchester, Essex CO3 3LP, United Kingdom. TEL 44-20-70175544, FAX 44-20-70175198, tf.enquiries@tfinforma.com.

WHO'S WHO IN TRAINING AND SIMULATION. *see* AERONAUTICS AND SPACE FLIGHT

WINDSCREEN. *see* HOBBIES

355 USA
THE WINDSOCK. Text in English. 1912. w. (Thu.). free to members (effective 2011). 24 p./no. 6 cols./p.; back issues avail. **Document type:** *Newspaper, Consumer.*
Related titles: Online - full text ed.: free (effective 2011).
Published by: Freedom Communications, Inc., 17666 Fitch, Irvine, CA 92614. TEL 949-253-2300, FAX 949-474-7675. Eds. Santiago G Colon, Stacey R Swann.

358.4 USA ISSN 1938-3932
WINGMAN; The United States Air Force journal of occupational, operational and off-duty safety. Text in English. 1967-1986 (Aug.); resumed 1988. q. free (effective 2009). back issues avail.; reprints avail. **Document type:** *Magazine, Government.* **Description:** Published for the prevention of vehicular and other ground mishaps.
Incorporates (in 2009): Weapons Journal (1946-2948); Which was formerly (until 1998): U S A F Nuclear Surety Journal; Incorporates (in 2009): Flying Safety (0279-9308); Which was formerly (until 1981): Aerospace Safety (0001-9429); (until 1960): Flying Safety (1041-0465); Aerospace Safety incorporated (1963-1970): Aerospace Maintenance Safety (0001-9380); Which was formerly (until 1963): Aerospace Accident and Maintenance Review (1041-0627); Formerly (until 2008): Road and Rec (1055-7725); Which supersedes in part (in 1988): Air Force Driver (0002-2373)
Related titles: Microform ed.: (from PQC); Online - full text ed.: ISSN 1944-4168.
Indexed: A09, A10, B07, C12, I02, IUSGP, M01, M02, M05, T02, V02, V03, V04.
—Linda Hall.
Published by: U.S. Air Force, Inspection and Safety Center, 9700 G Ave SE, Ste 283, Kirtland A F B, NM 87117. TEL 505-846-1403, FOIAManager@kirtland.af.mil. Ed. Gwendolyn F Dooley. **Subscr. to:** U.S. Government Printing Office, Superintendent of Documents, PO Box 371954, Pittsburgh, PA 15250. TEL 202-512-1800, FAX 202-512-2250.

358.4 DEU
WINGMASTER; Aircraft im Detail - Luftfahrt, Modellbau, Historie. Text in German. 1998. bi-m. EUR 8.55 newsstand/cover (effective 2009). **Document type:** *Magazine, Consumer.*
Published by: V D M Heinz Nickel, Kasernenstr 6-10, Zweibruecken, 66482, Germany. TEL 49-6332-72710, info@vdmedien.de, http://vdmedien.com.

WINGS; world review of aviation & defence. *see* AERONAUTICS AND SPACE FLIGHT

WINGS (GRANADA HILLS). *see* AERONAUTICS AND SPACE FLIGHT

358.4 USA
WINGSPREAD RANDOLPH A F B. (Air Force Base) Text in English. 1974. w. back issues avail. **Document type:** *Newspaper, Government.*
Published by: Prime Time, Inc, 17400 Judson Rd, San Antonio, TX 78247. TEL 210-453-3300, http://www.primetimenewspapers.com/.

THE WIRE (BLANDFORD FORUM). *see* COMMUNICATIONS

353.538 USA
WISCONSIN. DEPARTMENT OF VETERANS AFFAIRS. BIENNIAL REPORT. Text in English. 1977. biennial. free. **Document type:** *Government.*
Published by: Department of Veterans Affairs, 30 W Mifflin St, Box 7843, Madison, WI 53707. TEL 608-266-1311. Ed. Steve L Olson. Circ: 700.

353.538 USA
WISCONSIN. DEPARTMENT OF VETERANS AFFAIRS. UPDATE. Text in English. 1983. q. free. **Document type:** *Government.*
Formerly: Veterans Affairs in Wisconsin
Published by: Department of Veterans Affairs, 30 W Mifflin St, Box 7843, Madison, WI 53707. TEL 608-266-1311. Ed. Steve L Olson. Circ: 4,000.

355 POL ISSN 1234-5865
CODEN: BWATFP
WOJSKOWA AKADEMIA TECHNICZNA. BIULETYN. Key Title: Biuletyn Wojskowej Akademii Technicznej. Text in Polish. 1952. m. EUR 292 foreign (effective 2006). **Document type:** *Bulletin.*
Formerly (until 1991): Wojskowa Akademia Techniczna im. Jaroslawa Dabrowskiego. Biuletyn (0366-4988)
Indexed: B22, INIS AtomInd.

Published by: Wojskowa Akademia Techniczna, ul Gen S Kaliskiego, Warsaw, 00908, Poland. TEL 48-22-6839000, FAX 48-22-6839901, http://www.wat.edu.pl. **Dist. by:** Ars Polona, Obroncow 25, Warsaw 03933, Poland. TEL 48-22-5098609, FAX 48-22-5098610, arspolona@arspolona.com.pl, http://www.arspolona.com.pl.

WORLD AEROSPACE & DEFENSE INTELLIGENCE (ONLINE). *see* AERONAUTICS AND SPACE FLIGHT

355 USA ISSN 1943-9806
D731
WORLD AT WAR; the trategy and tactics of World War II. Text in English. 2008. bi-m. USD 109.97 (effective 2009). **Document type:** *Magazine, Consumer.* **Description:** Provides in-depth coverage of battles and campaigns of World War II. Covers all areas, including the Pacific, Eastern and Western fronts, Mediterranean, as well as games and what-if scenarios.
Published by: Decision Games, PO Box 21598, Bakersfield, CA 93390. TEL 661-587-9633, FAX 661-587-5031, http://strategyandtacticspress.com, http://www.decisiongames.com. Ed. Joseph Miranda. Pub. Christopher R Cummins.

355.4 ZAF ISSN 1991-1262
➤ **WORLD JOURNAL OF DEFENCE AND MILITARY SCIENCES.** Text in English. 2006. q. USD 120 in Africa to individuals; USD 180 elsewhere to individuals; USD 350 in Africa to institutions; USD 450 elsewhere to institutions; USD 85 in Africa to students; USD 100 elsewhere to students (effective 2007). **Document type:** *Journal, Academic/Scholarly.* **Description:** Covers the field of defense theory and analysis.
Published by: (World Research Organization), Isis Press, PO Box 1919, Cape Town, 8000, South Africa. TEL 27-21-4471574, FAX 27-86-6219999, orders@unwro.org, http://www.unwro.org/isispress.html.

➤ **WORLD MILITARY AND CIVIL AIRCRAFT BRIEFING.** *see* TRANSPORTATION—Air Transport

355 USA ISSN 0897-4667
JX1974.A1
WORLD MILITARY EXPENDITURES AND ARMS TRANSFERS. Text in English. a. price varies. **Description:** Provides information on military resources by country throughout the world.
Formerly: World Military Expenditures (0363-7204); Which supersedes: World Military Expenditures and Related Data (0082-8793)
Published by: U.S. Department of State, Bureau of Verification and Compliance, 2201 C St, NW, Washington, DC 20520. TEL 202-647-4000. **Subscr. to:** U.S. Government Printing Office, Superintendent of Documents, PO Box 371954, Pittsburgh, PA 15250. TEL 202-512-1800, FAX 202-512-2250, orders@gpo.gov, http://www.access.gpo.gov.

359 USA
WORLD NAVAL WEAPONS SYSTEMS. Cover title: Naval Institute Guide to World Naval Weapons Systems. Text in English. 1989. irreg. USD 250 per issue (effective 2011). illus. **Document type:** *Magazine, Trade.* **Description:** Covers worldwide naval fleets of ships, aircraft, and armament.
Published by: (Naval Institute), Naval Institute Press, 291 Wood Rd, Annapolis, MD 21402. TEL 410-268-6110, FAX 410-269-7940, customer@usni.org. Ed. Norman Friedman.

WORLD WAR II (LEESBURG). *see* HISTORY—History Of North And South America

940.3 GBR ISSN 0964-6833
WORLD WAR II REVIEW. Text in English. 1990. 6/yr. USD 20. **Document type:** *Newsletter.* **Description:** Publishes news, views and reviews of events and personalities connected with World War II.
Address: Broadhead, Castleshaw, Delph, Oldham 0L3 5L2, United Kingdom. Ed. Jim Auld.

355.0025 USA ISSN 1073-5097
UA15
WORLDWIDE DIRECTORY OF DEFENSE AUTHORITIES. Text in English. a. (plus update). USD 616 (effective 2005). **Document type:** *Directory.* **Description:** Contains names and addresses of defense and national security officials in every country in the world.
Related titles: CD-ROM ed.
—CCC.
Published by: Keesing's Worldwide, LLC (Subsidiary of: C Q Press, Inc.), 4905 Del Ray Ave., Ste. 405, Bethesda, MD 20814-2557. TEL 800-332-3535, info@keesings.com, http://www.keesings.com. Ed. Stephen Lewis.

355.0335 IRL
WORLDWIDE MILITARY AND POLICE AWARD. Text in English. 1980. a. USD 350. **Document type:** *Newsletter.* **Description:** Lists distinguished military and police officers.
Published by: Royal University, Ltd., 6 Lower Hatch St., Dublin, 2, Ireland. FAX 353-1-6686632.

WORLDWIDE W A M M. *see* WOMEN'S INTERESTS

355 CHN ISSN 1000-7385
CODEN: XIBIE4
XIANDAI BINGQI/MODERN WEAPONRY. Text in Chinese. 1979. m. USD 52.80 (effective 2009). adv. bk.rev. 54 p./no.; back issues avail. **Document type:** *Magazine, Consumer.* **Description:** Covers the development of modern defense technology, defense industries and manufacturers, military establishments and colleges.
—East View.
Published by: Xiandai Bingqi Zazhishe, PO Box 2413-8, Beijing, 100089, China. TEL 86-10-68961782, FAX 86-10-68963199. adv.: page USD 3,000; 180 x 250. Circ: 110,000 (paid). **Dist. by:** China International Book Trading Corp, 35 Chegongzhuang Xilu, Haidian District, PO Box 399, Beijing 100044, China. TEL 86-10-68412045, FAX 86-10-68412023, cibtc@mail.cibtc.com.cn, http://www.cibtc.com.cn.

355 600 CHN ISSN 1009-086X
XIANDAI FANGYU JISHU/MODERN DEFENCE TECHNOLOGY. Text in Chinese. 1973. bi-m. USD 31.20 (effective 2009). **Document type:** *Journal, Academic/Scholarly.*
Related titles: Online - full text ed.
Indexed: A28, APA, BrCerAb, C&ISA, CA/WCA, CIA, CerAb, CivEngAb, CorrAb, E&CAJ, E11, EEA, EMA, ESPM, EnvEAb, H15, Inspec, M&TEA, M09, MBF, METADEX, SolStAb, T04, WAA.
—BLDSC (9367.037160), East View, Linda Hall.
Published by: Zhongguo Hangtianke Gongjituan Gongsi/China Aerospace Science & Industry Corp., PO Box 142-30, Beijing, 100854, China. TEL 86-10-68388557, FAX 86-10-68212656. Ed. Chu-Zhi Cheng.

XIBEI GUOFANG YIXUE ZAZHI/MEDICAL JOURNAL OF NATIONAL DEFENDING FORCES IN NORTHWEST CHINA. *see* MEDICAL SCIENCES

353.538 DEU ISSN 1617-5212
U769
Y.; Magazin der Bundeswehr. Text in German. 2001. m. EUR 37 (effective 2005). adv. **Document type:** *Magazine, Trade.* **Description:** Contains stories and articles for soldiers and affiliated personnel of the German Army.
Related titles: Online - full text ed.
Published by: (Streitkraefteamt, Informations- und Medienzentrale), Frankfurter Societaet, Frankenallee 71-81, Frankfurt Am Main, 60327, Germany. TEL 49-69-75010, FAX 49-69-75014877, verlag@fsd.de, http://www.fsd.de. Ed. Dieter Buchholtz. Adv. contact Michael Faida. B&W page EUR 2,100, color page EUR 3,780; trim 210 x 280. Circ: 73,500 (paid and controlled).

338.473 953.3 363.35 GBR ISSN 1749-1770
YEMEN DEFENCE & SECURITY REPORT. Text in English. 2005. a. EUR 820, USD 1,030 combined subscription per issue (print & email eds.) (effective 2010). **Document type:** *Report, Trade.* **Description:** Covers independent forecasts and competitive intelligence on the defense and security industry in Yemen.
Related titles: E-mail ed.
Indexed: B01.
Published by: Business Monitor International Ltd., Senator House, 85 Queen Victoria St, London, EC4V 4AB, United Kingdom. TEL 44-20-72480468, FAX 44-20-72480467, subs@businessmonitor.com.

355 AUS ISSN 1838-7519
▼ **YOUR MEMENTO.** Text in English. 2011. q. free (effective 2011). **Document type:** *Magazine, Government.* **Description:** Highlights important records, particularly those on migration and defence service.
Media: Online - full text. **Related titles:** E-mail ed.
Published by: National Archives of Australia, Canberra Business Centre, PO Box 7425, Canberra, ACT 2610, Australia. TEL 61-2-62123900, FAX 61-2-62123999, naasales@naa.gov.au, http://www.naa.gov.au/.

359 CHN ISSN 1673-1948
YULEI JISHU/TORPEDO TECHNOLOGY. Text in Chinese. 1993. bi-m. CNY 48 (effective 2009). **Document type:** *Journal, Academic/Scholarly.*
Related titles: Online - full text ed.
Published by: Zhongguo Chuanbo Zhonggong Jituan Gongsi. Di-705 Yanjiusuo/China Shipbuilding Industry Corp., 705 Research Institute, PO Box 76, Xi'an, 710075, China. TEL 86-29-88327279, FAX 86-29-88223445.

355 GEO
ZAKAVKAZSKIE VOENNYE VEDOMOSTI. Text in Russian. 260/yr. USD 359 in United States.
Published by: Ministry of Defence of the Russian Federation, Ul R Tabukashvili 27, Tbilisi, 380008, Georgia. TEL 995-32-990320, 995-32-931838, FAX 995-32-990027. Ed. V R Ziyatdinov. **Dist. by:** East View Information Services, 10601 Wayzata Blvd, Minneapolis, MN 55305. TEL 952-252-1201, 800-477-1005, FAX 952-252-1202, info@eastview.com, http://www.eastview.com.

343.01 RUS
ZAKON I ARMIYA. Text in Russian. 1996. m. USD 271 in United States (effective 2006). **Document type:** *Newspaper.* **Description:** Covers legislation in the military field, laws and regulatory documents of military administration bodies.
Address: A-ya 15, Moscow, 125057, Russian Federation. TEL 7-095-2388885, FAX 7-095-2462020. Ed. A N Bolonin. **Dist. by:** East View Information Services, 10601 Wayzata Blvd, Minneapolis, MN 55305. TEL 952-252-1201, 800-477-1005, FAX 952-252-1202, info@eastview.com, http://www.eastview.com.

355 RUS ISSN 0134-921X
ZARUBEZHNOE VOENNOE OBOZRENIE. Text in Russian. m. USD 172 foreign (effective 2006). **Document type:** *Government.* **Description:** Covers military-political situation in various areas around the world, the state of the armed forces in other countries, weapons and equipment standards, etc.
Related titles: Microfiche ed.: (from EVP); Online - full text ed.
Indexed: LID&ISL, RASB.
—East View.
Published by: Ministerstvo Oborony Rossiiskoi Federatsii/Ministry of Defence of the Russian Federation, Khoroshevskoe shosse 38, Moscow, 123826, Russian Federation. TEL 7-095-1312199, http://www.mil.ru. Ed. Yu B Krivoruchko. **Dist. by:** East View Information Services, 10601 Wayzata Blvd, Minneapolis, MN 55305. TEL 952-252-1201, 800-477-1005, FAX 952-252-1202, info@eastview.com, http://www.eastview.com.

355.1 DEU ISSN 0044-2852
UA712
ZEITSCHRIFT FUER HEERESKUNDE. Text in German. 1929. q. EUR 50; EUR 13.50 newsstand/cover (effective 2009). adv. bk.rev. bibl.; illus. index. **Document type:** *Journal, Academic/Scholarly.*
Indexed: HistAb, IBR, IBZ, P30.
Published by: Deutsche Gesellschaft fuer Heereskunde e.V., Berthold-Brecht-Allee 5, Dresden, 01309, Germany. TEL 49-351-8232802, info@deutsche-gesellschaft-fuer-heereskunde.de, http://www.deutsche-heereskunde.de. Ed., R&P Juergen Kraus. Circ: 1,000.

355 DEU ISSN 1864-5321
U4
ZEITSCHRIFT FUER INNERE FUEHRUNG. Text in German. 1956. m. free (effective 2009). bk.rev. **Document type:** *Journal, Trade.* **Description:** Contains articles and features of interest to soldiers in the Bundeswehr.
Formerly (until 2007): Information fuer die Truppe (0443-1243)
Indexed: DIP, IBR, IBZ, RASB.
Published by: Bundesministerium der Verteidigung, Presse- und Informationsstab, Stauffenbergstr 18, Berlin, 10785, Germany. TEL 49-30-18248232, FAX 49-30-18248240, http://www.bmvg.de. Ed. Dieter Buchholtz. Circ: (controlled).

623.4519 CHN ISSN 1671-0576
ZHIDAO YU YINXIN/GUIDANCE & FUZE. Variant title: Guidance and Detonator. Text in Chinese. 1979. q. USD 16.40 (effective 2009). **Document type:** *Journal, Academic/Scholarly.*
Related titles: Online - full text ed.
—East View.
Published by: Shanghai Hangtianju Jishu Yanjiuyuan Di-802 Yanjiusuo, 203, Liping Lu, Shanghai, 200090, China. TEL 86-21-65666006 ext 254, FAX 86-21-65669214. **Dist. by:** China International Book Trading Corp, 35 Chegongzhuang Xilu, Haidian District, PO Box 399, Beijing 100044, China. TEL 86-10-68412045, FAX 86-10-68412023, cibtc@mail.cibtc.com.cn, http://www.cibtc.com.cn.

355 CHN ISSN 1002-5081
ZHONGGUO MINBING/CHINESE MILITIA. Text in Chinese. 1984. m. USD 27.60 (effective 2009). **Document type:** *Government.*
Related titles: Online - full text ed.
Indexed: RASB.
Published by: Jiefangjun Baoshe, 34, Fuwei Dajie, Beijing, 100832, China. TEL 86-10-66720726. **Dist. by:** China International Book Trading Corp, 35 Chegongzhuang Xilu, Haidian District, PO Box 399, Beijing 100044, China. TEL 86-10-68412045, FAX 86-10-68412023, cibtc@mail.cibtc.com.cn, http://www.cibtc.com.cn.

355 CHN ISSN 1005-5819
JQ1519.A5
ZHONGGUO TONGYI ZHANXIAN. Text in Chinese. 1992. m. USD 39.60 (effective 2009). **Document type:** *Journal, Academic/Scholarly.*
Related titles: Online - full content ed.; Online - full text ed.
—East View.
Address: 135, Fuyou Jie, Beijing, 100800, China. TEL 86-10-63094445, FAX 86-10-63094471.

ZHONGWAI JUNSHI YINGSHI/CHINESE AND FOREIGN MILITARY FILMS AND T V PROGRAMME. *see* MOTION PICTURES

355 POL ISSN 0044-4979
ZOLNIERZ POLSKI. Text in Polish. 1945. w. illus. **Document type:** *Newspaper, Consumer.*
Indexed: LID&ISL, RASB.
Published by: Dom Wydawniczy Bellona, ul Grzybowska 77, Warsaw, 00844, Poland. TEL 48-22-6204286, FAX 48-22-6242273, biuro@bellona.pl, http://www.bellona.pl.

940.53 FRA ISSN 0761-7348
D731
39 - 45 MAGAZINE. Text in French. m. (11/yr.). back issues avail. **Description:** Covers World War II.
Related titles: ◆ Supplement(s): Historica. ISSN 1167-9638.
Published by: Editions Heimdal, Chateau de Damigny, B P 61350, Bayeux, Cedex 14406, France.

353.538 USA
43RD INFANTRY DIVISION VETERANS ASSOCIATION. BULLETIN. Text in English. 1953. q. membership only (effective 2000). **Document type:** *Bulletin.* **Description:** Contains personal anecdotes and veterans' information mainly of interest to veterans of the 43rd Infantry Division.
Published by: 43rd Infantry Division Veterans Association, 150 Lakedell Dr., E. Greenwich, RI 02818. TEL 401-884-7052. Ed. Howard F Brown. Circ: 1,900.

355.1 610 USA ISSN 2157-5975
332ND WARRIOR CALL. Text in English. 2008. m. free (effective 2010). back issues avail. **Document type:** *Journal, Trade.*
Media: Online - full text.
Published by: U S Army Reserve Medical Command, 332nd Medical Brigade, 2801 Grand Ave, Pinellas Park, FL 33782. TEL 877-891-3281, ARMEDCOM@usar.army.mil, http://www.usar.army.mil/arweb/organization/commandstructure/USARC/OPS/ARMEDCOM/Pages/default.aspx.

359 900 USA
THE 820 NEWSLETTER. Text in English. 1998 (Feb, vol.5, no.1). q. **Document type:** *Newsletter.*
Media: Online - full content. **Related titles:** Print ed.
Published by: USS RICH DD/DDE-820 Reunion Association, PO Box 506, Pinopolis, SC 29469 . http://www.ussrich.org/. Ed. Robert Baldwin.

MILITARY—Abstracting, Bibliographies, Statistics

016.355 USA ISSN 0002-2586
Z6723
AIR UNIVERSITY LIBRARY INDEX TO MILITARY PERIODICALS. Short title: A U L I M P. Text in English. 1949. q. free to qualified personnel (effective 2003). bk.rev. illus. index, cum.index. reprints avail. **Document type:** *Catalog, Bibliography.*
Related titles: CD-ROM ed.; Microform ed.; Online - full content ed.
Indexed: MLA-IB.
—Linda Hall.
Published by: U.S. Air Force, Air University Library, 600 Chennault Circle, Building 1405, Maxwell Afb, AL 36112-6424. TEL 334-953-2504, FAX 334-953-1192, evita.siebert@maxwell.af.mil, http://www.au.af.mil/au/aul/aul.htm. Ed. Evita M Siebert. Circ: 1,100 (controlled).

016.359 ARG ISSN 0066-7331
ARGENTINA. SERVICIO DE INTELIGENCIA NAVAL. BIBLIOTECAS DE LA ARMADA. BOLETIN BIBLIOGRAFICO. Text in Spanish. 1943. a.
Published by: Servicio de Inteligencia Naval, Bibliotecas de la Armada, Edificio Libertad, Comodoro Py y Corbeta Uruguay, Buenos Aires, Argentina. Ed. Juan A Manon.

016.355 USA ISSN 1040-7995
U1
BIBLIOGRAPHIES AND INDEXES IN MILITARY STUDIES. Text in English. 1988. irreg., latest 2004. price varies. back issues avail. **Document type:** *Monographic series, Bibliography.*
—BLDSC (1993.097425).
Published by: Greenwood Publishing Group Inc. (Subsidiary of: A B C - C L I O), 88 Post Rd W, PO Box 5007, Westport, CT 06881. TEL 203-226-3571, 800-225-5800, FAX 877-231-6980, sales@greenwood.com.

016.355 USA ISSN 1056-7410
BIBLIOGRAPHIES OF BATTLES AND LEADERS. Text in English. 1990. irreg., latest 2005. price varies. back issues avail. **Document type:** *Monographic series, Bibliography.*
Published by: Greenwood Publishing Group Inc. (Subsidiary of: A B C - C L I O), 88 Post Rd W, PO Box 5007, Westport, CT 06881. TEL 203-226-3571, 800-225-5800, FAX 877-231-6980, sales@greenwood.com. Ed. Myron Smith.

016.355 JPN ISSN 0523-8080
T4
BOEI DAIGAKKO KYOKAN KENKYU YOROKU/NATIONAL DEFENSE ACADEMY. DIGEST OF RESEARCHES BY FACULTY MEMBERS. Text in English, Japanese. 1956. a.
Published by: Boei Daigakko/National Defense Academy, 10-20 Hashirimizu 1-chome, Yokosuka-shi, Kanagawa-ken 239-0811, Japan.

▼ **INFORMATSIONNYI BYULLETEN'. INOSTRANNAYA PECHAT' OB EKONOMICHESKOM, NAUCHNO-TEKHNICHESKOM I VOENNOM POTENTSIALE GOSUDARSTV-UCHASTNIKOV SNG I TEKHNICHESKIKH SREDSTVAKH EGO VYIAVLENIYA. SERIYA: TEKHNITCHESKOE OSNASHCHENIE SPETSSLUZHB ZARUBEZHNYKH GOSUDARSTV.** *see* BUSINESS AND ECONOMICS—Abstracting, Bibliographies, Statistics

INFORMATSIONNYI BYULLETEN'. INOSTRANNAYA PECHAT' OB EKONOMICHESKOM, NAUCHNO-TEKHNICHESKOM I VOENNOM POTENTSIALE GOSUDARSTV-UCHASTNIKOV SNG I TEKHNICHESKIKH SREDSTVAKH EGO VYIAVLENIYA. SERIYA: VOORUZHENNYE SILY I VOENNO-PROMYSHLENNYI POTENTSIAL. *see* BUSINESS AND ECONOMICS—Abstracting, Bibliographies, Statistics

016.355 RUS
INOSTRANNAYA VOENNAYA LITERATURA/FOREIGN MILITARY LITERATURE INDEX; annotirovannyi bibliograficheskii ukazatel'. Text in Russian. 1933. q. USD 149 foreign (effective 2010).
Document type: *Bibliography.* **Description:** Includes an index of foreign military literature and select articles.
Related titles: CD-ROM ed.
Published by: (Rossiiskaya Gosudarstvennaya Biblioteka/Russian State Library), Idatel'stvo Rossiiskoi Gosudarstvennoi Biblioteki Pashkov Dom/Pashkov Dom, Russian State Library Publishing House, Vozdizhenka 3/5, Moscow, 101000, Russian Federation. TEL 7-495-6955953, FAX 7-495-6955953, http://www.rsl.ru/pub.asp. Ed. V P Semenko. **Dist. by:** East View Information Services, 10601 Wayzata Blvd, Minneapolis, MN 55305. TEL 952-252-1201, 800-477-1005, FAX 952-252-1202, info@eastview.com, http://www.eastview.com.

016.3584 JPN
JAPANESE MILITARY AIRCRAFT SERIALS. Text in Japanese. a.
Published by: Nihon Kokuki Kenkyukai/Japan Aviation Research Group, c/o Mr Masataka Sato, 28-5 Hiyoshi-cho, Tokorozawa-shi, Saitama-ken 359-1123, Japan.

327 355 GBR
LANCASTER INDEX TO DEFENCE & INTERNATIONAL SECURITY LITERATURE. Text in English. 1996. base vol. plus bi-m. updates. price varies based on the number of users. back issues avail.
Document type: *Database, Abstract/Index.* **Description:** Offers an indexed bibliographic database of articles and monographs on a wide variety of military and international security affairs.
Media: Online - full content. **Related titles:** CD-ROM ed.
Published by: (Lancaster University, The Management School, Centre for Defence and International Security Studies), Military Policy Research, 92a Church Way, Iffley, Oxford OX4 4EF, United Kingdom. FAX 44-1865-396050, mail@mpr.co.uk.

016.355 016.36534 016.327 USA
MILITARY & GOVERNMENT COLLECTION. Text in English. base vol. plus w. updates. **Document type:** *Database, Abstract/Index.*
Media: Online - full text.
Published by: EBSCO Publishing (Subsidiary of: EBSCO Industries, Inc.), 10 Estes St, PO Box 682, Ipswich, MA 01938. TEL 978-356-6500, 800-653-2726, FAX 978-356-6565, information@ebscohost.com.

016.355 USA
MILITARY AND INTELLIGENCE. Text in English. base vol. plus d. updates. **Document type:** *Database, Abstract/Index.*
Media: Online - full text.
Published by: Gale (Subsidiary of: Cengage Learning), 27500 Drake Rd, Farmington Hills, MI 48331. TEL 248-699-4253, 800-877-4253, FAX 248-699-8035, 877-363-4253, gale.customerservice@cengage.com, http://gale.cengage.com.

016.355 USA
MILITARY MODULE. Text in English. base vol. plus d. updates.
Document type: *Database, Abstract/Index.*
Media: Online - full text.
Published by: ProQuest (Subsidiary of: Cambridge Information Group), 789 E Eisenhower Pky, PO Box 1346, Ann Arbor, MI 48106. TEL 734-761-4700, 800-521-0600, FAX 734-997-4040, 888-241-5612, info@proquest.com, http://www.proquest.com.

016.355 POL ISSN 0137-8473
POLSKA BIBLIOGRAFIA WOJSKOWA. Text in Polish. 1971. q.
Document type: *Bibliography.*
Published by: Centralna Biblioteka Wojskowa, ul Ostrobramska 109, Warsaw, 04041, Poland. TEL 48-22-6100887, FAX 48-22-6816940, cbw@wp.mil.pl, http://www.cbw.wp.mil.pl. **Dist. by:** Ars Polona, Obroncow 25, Warsaw 03933, Poland. TEL 48-22-5098609, FAX 48-22-5098610, arspolona@arspolona.com.pl, http://www.arspolona.com.pl.

016.355 016.36534 016.327 USA
PROQUEST MILITARY COLLECTION. Text in English. base vol. plus updates. **Document type:** *Database, Abstract/Index.* **Description:** Covers topics across all government and military branches, including international relations, political science, criminology, defense, aeronautics and space flight, communications, civil engineering, and more.
Media: Online - full text.
Published by: ProQuest (Subsidiary of: Cambridge Information Group), 789 E Eisenhower Pky, PO Box 1346, Ann Arbor, MI 48106. TEL 734-761-4700, 800-521-0600, FAX 734-997-4040, 888-241-5612, info@proquest.com.

016.359 ARG ISSN 0034-8775
REVISTA DE PUBLICACIONES NAVALES. Text in Spanish. 1901. 3/yr. free. adv. bk.rev. **Document type:** *Bibliography.*
Published by: Estado Mayor General de la Armada, Servicio de Inteligencia Naval, Buenos Aires, Argentina. Ed. Emilio J Del Real. Circ: 3,400.

MILITARY LAW

see LAW—Military Law

MINES AND MINING INDUSTRY

see also METALLURGY

622 DEU
A V INFORMATION. Text in German. 1975. bi-m. **Document type:** *Newsletter.*
Published by: Gewerkschaft Auguste Victoria, Victoriastr 43, Marl, 45772, Germany. TEL 02365-402851, FAX 02365-402204, TELEX 0829886-AVMA-D. Circ: 6,000.

622 GRL ISSN 1399-204X
AATSITASSARSIORNEQ PILLUGU NALUNAARUSIAQ/ RAASTOFAKTIVITETER I GROENLAND. Text in Danish, Eskimo. 1999. a. free. **Document type:** *Government.* **Description:** Deals with mineral and petroleum resources in Greenland.
Formed by the merger of (1980-1999): Faellesraadet Vedroerende Mineraliske Raastoffer i Groenland. Beretning - Joint Committee on Mineral Resources in Greenland. Annual Report (0107-3117); Which incorporates (1979): Groenlands Geologiske Undersoegelse. Oversigt over Forundersoegelsestilladelser og Konsessioner vedroerende Mineralske Raastoffer i Groenland (0107-4318); (1995-1999): Aatsitassarsiorneq Pillugu Nalunaarrusiaq (1399-2074); Which was formerly (until 1997): Ukiumoortumik Nalunaarrusiaq (1399-2104); (1980-1999): Kalaallit Nunaanni Aatsitassat Ikummatissallu Pillugit Siunnersuisoqatigiit (1398-8670); Which was formerly (until 1998): Kalaallit Nunaanni Aatsitassanik Atortussiassat Pillugit Siunnersuisoqatigiit Nalunaarutaat (1397-8098); (until 1997): Kalaallit Nunaanni Atortussiassat Aatsitassanit Pisut Pillugit Siunnersuisoqatigiit Sinnerlugit Nalunaarut (1396-7703); (until 1995): Piffissaq..Pillugu Kalaallit Nunaanni Atortussiassat Aatsitassanit Pisut Pillugit Siunnersuisoqatigiit Nalunaarutaat (0908-925X); (until 1993): Ukinmut Nalunaerut..Kalatdlit-nunane augtitagssanik Atortugssiagssanut Faellesraadimit (0903-1367); (until 1985): Kalatdlit-nunane Augtitagssanik Atortugssiagssalerinermut Faellesraadimip Nalunaerutaa (0903-1359); (until 1984): Kalatdlit-nunane Atortotugssiagssat Augtitagssanik Pissut Pivdlugit Siunersuisoqatigit.. Nalunaerutat (0109-839X); (until 1981): Kalatdlit-nunane Augtitagssanik Atortugssiagssat Pivdlugit..Faellesraadimit Nalunaerut (0107-3559); Which incorporates (1979): Kalatdlit-nunane Atorssiagssat Augtitagssanit Pissut Pivdlugit Sujumortumik Misigssuinigssamut Akuerssissutit..Groenlands Geologiske Undersoegelser (0107-4326)
Related titles: English ed.: Annual Report on Mineral and Petroleum Activities. ISSN 1399-2058. 1999.
Published by: Bureau of Minerals and Petroleum, Joint Committee on Mineral Resources in Greenland/Raastofdirektoratet. Faellesraadet vedroerende Mineralske Raastoffer i Groenland, PO Box 930, Nuuk, 3900, Greenland. TEL 299-346800, FAX 299-324302.

549 ESP ISSN 2171-7788
▼ **ACOPIOS.** Text in Spanish. 2010. a. back issues avail. **Document type:** *Monographic series, Academic/Scholarly.*
Media: Online - full text.
Published by: Mineralogia Topografica Iberica http://mti-minas.blogspot.com/. Ed. Jesus Alonso.

ACTA MONTANISTICA SLOVACA. *see* EARTH SCIENCES—Geology

ACTA RESEARCH REPORT. *see* EARTH SCIENCES—Geophysics

549 665.5 HUN ISSN 0365-8066
QE351 CODEN: AUSEA6
ACTA UNIVERSITATIS SZEGEDIENSIS. ACTA MINERALOGICA - PETROGRAPHICA. Text in English. 1943. a., latest vol.42, 2002. exchange basis. bk.rev. charts; illus. **Document type:** *Monographic series, Academic/Scholarly.* **Description:** Discusses geochemistry, mineralogy and petrology with studies of Hungarian topics of global interest.
Indexed: GeoRef, SCOPUS, SpeleolAb.
—CASDDS, INIST, Linda Hall.
Published by: (Szegedi Tudomanyegyetem, Termeszettudomanyi Kar/University of Szeged, Faculty of Science), Szegedi Tudomanyegyetem/University of Szeged, c/o E Szabo, Exchange Librarian, Dugonics ter 13, PO Box 393, Szeged, 6701, Hungary. TEL 36-62-544009, FAX 36-62-420895, Eneh.Szabo@bibl.u-szeged.hu, http://www.u-szeged.hu. Ed. Tibor Szederkenyi. Circ: 200.

622 ARG ISSN 0326-6672
ACTIVIDAD MINERA. Text in Spanish. 1983. m. USD 24.
Indexed: IMMAb.
Published by: Minera Piedra Libre S.R.L., Bolivar, 187 4 B, Buenos Aires, 1066, Argentina. TEL 54-114-3436422, FAX 54-114-3436138. Eds. Horacio Piccinini, Mariode Pablos. Circ: 1,200.

622 CMR ISSN 0575-7258
ACTIVITES MINERES AU CAMEROUN. Text in French. 1962. a., latest 1975.
Published by: Direction des Mines et de la Geologie, Ministere des Mines et de l'Energie, Yaounde, Cameroon.

ADMINISTRATION DES DIRECTIONS REGIONALES DE L'INDUSTRIE, DE LA RECHERCHE ET DE L'ENVIRONNEMENT. ANNUAIRE. *see* ENERGY

AFRICA ENERGY INTELLIGENCE (ENGLISH EDITION). *see* PETROLEUM AND GAS

AFRICA ENERGY INTELLIGENCE (FRENCH EDITION). *see* PETROLEUM AND GAS

622 FRA ISSN 1624-0022
HD9506.A35
AFRICA MINING INTELLIGENCE (ENGLISH EDITION). Text in English. 2000. s-m. (23/yr). EUR 545, USD 765 (effective 2009). **Document type:** *Newsletter, Trade.*
Related titles: Online - full text ed.: ISSN 1624-6217; ◆ French ed.: Africa Mining Intelligence (French Edition). ISSN 1624-0014.
—CIS.
Published by: Indigo Publications, 142 rue Montmartre, Paris, 75002, France. info@indigo-net.com, http://www.indigo-net.com.

622 FRA ISSN 1624-0014
AFRICA MINING INTELLIGENCE (FRENCH EDITION). Text in French. 2000. s-m. (23/yr). EUR 545 (effective 2009). **Document type:** *Magazine, Trade.*
Related titles: Online - full text ed.: ISSN 1624-6209; ◆ English ed.: Africa Mining Intelligence (English Edition). ISSN 1624-0022.
—CCC.
Published by: Indigo Publications, 142 rue Montmartre, Paris, 75002, France. info@indigo-net.com, http://www.indigo-net.com.

622 ZAF ISSN 2071-9280
AFRICAN MINING. Text in English. bi-m. ZAR 250 domestic; USD 80 in Africa; USD 180 elsewhere (effective 2011). adv. **Document type:** *Magazine, Trade.* **Description:** Covers exploration, mining projects, mineral processing technology, environmental issues and equipment suppliers' news.
Indexed: ISAP.
Published by: Brooke Pattrick Publications, Bldg 13, Pinewood Office Park, 33 Riley Rd, Woodmead, Johannesburg, Transvaal, South Africa. TEL 27-11-6033960, FAX 27-11-2346290, bestbook@brookepattrick.co.za.

AKADEMIA GORNICZO-HUTNICZA. ROZPRAWY MONOGRAFIE. *see* METALLURGY

ALBERTA OIL & GAS DIRECTORY. *see* BUSINESS AND ECONOMICS—Trade And Industrial Directories

549 ESP ISSN 2171-777X
AMALGAMA. Text in Spanish. 2007. a. **Document type:** *Monographic series, Academic/Scholarly.*
Media: Online - full text.
Published by: Mineralogia Topografica Iberica http://mti-minas.blogspot.com/.

343.077 USA
AMERICAN LAW OF MINING. Text in English. 1960. latest 2nd ed., 6 base vols. plus irreg. updates. looseleaf. USD 1,167 base vol(s). (effective 2011). **Document type:** *Handbook/Manual/Guide, Trade.* **Description:** Explains various aspects of mining law including federal lands and mineral leases, mining claims and environmental regulation.
Related titles: CD-ROM ed.: USD 1,079 (effective 2008).
Published by: (Rocky Mountain Mineral Law Foundation), Matthew Bender & Co., Inc. (Subsidiary of: LexisNexis North America), 1275 Broadway, Albany, NY 12204. TEL 518-487-3000, 800-424-4200, FAX 518-487-3083, international@bender.com, http://bender.lexisnexis.com. Ed. Karen Kaiser.

622 USA ISSN 1945-3027
THE AMERICAN MINERALOGIST (ONLINE). Text in English. bi-m.
Document type: *Journal, Academic/Scholarly.*
Incorporates (1998-2002): Geological Materials Research (1526-3339)
Media: Online - full text. **Related titles:** Microform ed.; ◆ Print ed.: The American Mineralogist (Print). ISSN 0003-004X.
Published by: Mineralogical Society of America, 3635 Concorde Pkwy Ste 500, Chantilly, VA 20151. TEL 703-652-9950, FAX 703-652-9951, http://www.minsocam.org. Eds. Frank S Spear TEL 518-276-6103, John B Brady.

549 551.9 USA ISSN 0003-004X
QE351 CODEN: AMMIAY
➤ **THE AMERICAN MINERALOGIST (PRINT)**; an international journal of earth and planetary materials. (Guide to Nature (1908-1935) superseded in part: The Mineral Collector) Text in English. 188?. 8/yr. USD 875 combined subscription domestic to institutions (print & online eds.); USD 900 combined subscription foreign to institutions (print & online eds.) (effective 2009). bk.rev. bibl.; illus.; abstr. Index. 200 p./no.; back issues avail.; reprint service avail. from PSC.
Document type: *Journal, Academic/Scholarly.* **Description:** Contains the results of original scientific research in the general fields of mineralogy, crystallography, geochemistry, and petrology.
Former titles (until 1916): The Mineral Collector (0885-4866); (until 1894): Minerals; (until 1893): Mineralogists' Monthly; (until 1890): Exchanger's Monthly
Related titles: Microform ed.; ◆ Online - full text ed.: The American Mineralogist (Online). ISSN 1945-3027.
Indexed: A01, A02, A03, A05, A08, A20, A22, A23, A24, A25, A26, A33, AESIS, AS&TA, AS&TI, ASCA, B04, B13, C10, C33, CA, CIN, CIS, CRIA, Cadscan, ChemAb, ChemTitl, CurCont, E08, G01, G08, GEOBASE, GeoRef, I05, IBR, IBZ, INIS AtomInd, ISR, Inspec, LeadAb, M01, M02, MSCI, MinerAb, OceAb, P02, P10, P26, P48, P52, P53, P54, P56, PQC, PetrolAb, PhotoAb, RefZh, S01, S08, S09, S10, SCI, SCOPUS, SpeleolAb, T02, V02, W07, Zincscan.
—BLDSC (0845.000000), AskIEEE, CASDDS, IE, Infotrieve, Ingenta, INIST, Linda Hall. **CCC.**
Published by: Mineralogical Society of America, 3635 Concorde Pkwy Ste 500, Chantilly, VA 20151. TEL 703-652-9950, FAX 703-652-9951, business@minsocam.org. Eds. Dana T Griffen, Jennifer A Thomson.

➤ **ANALYTICA.** *see* CHEMISTRY—Analytical Chemistry

➤ **ANGOLA. DIRECCAO PROVINCIAL DOS SERVICOS DE GEOLOGIA E MINAS. BOLETIM.** *see* EARTH SCIENCES—Geology

➤ **ANNALES UNIVERSITATIS MARIAE CURIE-SKLODOWSKA. SECTIO B. GEOGRAPHIA, GEOLOGIA, MINERALOGIA ET PETROGRAPHIA.** *see* GEOGRAPHY

➤ **ANNUAL BOOK OF A S T M STANDARDS. VOLUME 05.06. GASEOUS FUELS; COAL AND COKE.** (American Society for Testing and Materials) *see* ENGINEERING—Engineering Mechanics And Materials

549 AUS ISSN 1441-0540
ANNUAL ENVIRONMENTAL WORKSHOP. Text in English. 197?. a.
Formerly (until 1994): Australian Mining Industry Council. Environmental Workshop Proceedings (1441-0532)
Published by: Minerals Council of Australia, PO Box 363, Dickson, ACT 2602, Australia. TEL 61-6-62793600, FAX 61-6-62793699.

ANNUAL INSTITUTE ON MINERAL LAW. *see* LAW

622 700 DEU ISSN 0003-5238
GT5960.M5
DER ANSCHNITT; Zeitschrift fuer Kunst und Kultur im Bergbau. Text in German. 1949. 4/yr. bk.rev. illus.; abstr.; bibl. 56 p./no. 3 cols./p.; back issues avail.; reprints avail. **Document type:** *Journal, Consumer.*

Indexed: A&ATA, A28, APA, B24, BrArAb, BrCerAb, C&ISA, CA/WCA, CIA, CerAb, CivEngAb, CorrAb, E&CAJ, E11, EEA, EMA, ESPM, EnvEAb, FR, GeoRef, H15, IBR, IBZ, M&TEA, M09, MBF, METADEX, NumL, RASB, SolStAb, SpeleolAb, T04, WAA.
—Ingenta, INIST, Linda Hall. **CCC.**
Published by: Vereinigung der Freunde von Kunst und Kultur im Bergbau e.V., Am Bergbaumuseum 28, Bochum, 44791, Germany. TEL 49-234-5877134, FAX 49-234-5877111, sabine.birnfeld@bergbaumuseum.de. Ed. Andreas Bingener.

622 558 CHL ISSN 0066-5096
HD9506.C5
ANUARIO DE LA MINERIA DE CHILE. Text in Spanish. 1961. a. USD 35 (effective 1999). bk.rev. charts; illus.; stat. **Document type:** *Government.*
Indexed: GeoRef, SpeleolAb.
Published by: Servicio Nacional de Geologia y Mineria, Ave. Santa Maria, 104, Providencia, Santiago, Chile. TEL 56-2-737-5050, FAX 56-2-735-6960, mcortes@sernageomin.cl, jwilliams@sernageomin.cl. Ed. Juan Williams. Circ: 1,000.

551 ESP ISSN 2013-0910
ANUARIO DE LA PIEDRA NATURAL. Text in Spanish. 2008. a. **Document type:** *Yearbook.*
Published by: Federacion Espanola de la Piedra Natural, Ave de los Madranos, 39, Parque del Conde, Madrid, 28043, Spain. TEL 34-91-3881467, FAX 34-91-3005055, http://www.fdp.es/.

338.2 BRA ISSN 0100-9303
HD9506.B7 CODEN: AMBRD9
ANUARIO MINERAL BRASILEIRO. Text in Portuguese. 1972. a. USD 25 (effective 1997). illus.; stat. **Document type:** *Bulletin, Government.*
Indexed: GeoRef.
Published by: Departamento Nacional da Producao Mineral, Setor Autarquia Norte, Quadra 1, Bloco B, Brasilia, DF 70040, Brazil. TEL 55-61-224-2670. Ed. Frederico L M Barboza.

622 JOR ISSN 0250-9881
HD9506.A62
ARAB MINING JOURNAL. Text in Arabic, English. 1980. s-a. free. adv. bk.rev. bibl.; stat. index. **Document type:** *Bulletin.* **Description:** Covers issues pertaining to mining throughout the Arab world.
Indexed: AESIS, GeoRef, IMMAb, SpeleolAb.
Published by: Arab Mining Company, P O Box 20198, Amman, Jordan. TEL 962-6-5663148, FAX 962-6-5684114, TELEX 21489 ARMICO JO, armico@go.com.jo. Ed. Talal Sa'di. Adv. contact Sa'd Anani. Circ: 700.

ARAB PETROLEUM. *see* PETROLEUM AND GAS

622 POL ISSN 0860-7001
TN4 CODEN: AMNSE5
ARCHIVES OF MINING SCIENCES. Text in Multiple languages. 1954. q. USD 85 foreign (effective 2006). abstr.; bibl. **Document type:** *Journal, Academic/Scholarly.*
Formerly (until 1987): Archiwum Gornictwa (0004-0754)
Indexed: ApMecR, B22, CIN, ChemAb, ChemTitl, GeoRef, GeotechAb, IMMAb, RefZh, SCI, SpeleolAb, W07.
—BLDSC (1637.941300), CASDDS, IE, Ingenta, INIST, Linda Hall.
Published by: (Polska Akademia Nauk, Komitet Gornictwa), Polska Akademia Nauk, Instytut Mechaniki Gorotworu, ul Reymonta 27, Krakow, 30059, Poland. TEL 48-12-6376200, FAX 48-12-6372884. Ed. Jakub Siemek. Circ: 480. **Dist. by:** Ars Polona, Obroncow 25, Warsaw 03933, Poland. TEL 48-22-5098609, FAX 48-22-5098610, arspolona@arspolona.com.pl, http://www.arspolona.com.pl.

ARGUS RUSSIAN COAL. *see* ENERGY

622.3 USA
ASBESTOS INFORMATION ASSOCIATION - NORTH AMERICA. NEWS AND NOTES. Text in English. m. **Document type:** *Newsletter.*
Published by: Asbestos Information Association - North America, 1235 Jefferson Davis Hwy, PMB, Arlington, VA 22202. TEL 703-560-2980, FAX 703-560-2981.

338.2 AUS ISSN 1832-7966
THE ASIA MINER. Text in Chinese, English. 2004. q. AUD 80 (effective 2008). adv. **Document type:** *Magazine, Trade.*
Published by: Asia's Resource Communications, 1 Sevenoaks St, Balwyn, Melbourne, VIC 3103, Australia. Ed. Yolanda Torrisi TEL 61-3-98168048. Adv. contact Kim Cox TEL 61-4-22811261.

622 AUS ISSN 1321-0408
ASIAN JOURNAL OF MINING. Text in English. 1993. q. adv. **Document type:** *Journal, Trade.* **Description:** Covers all aspects of mining in Asia-Pacific region, including exploration, extraction, investment, marketing, trade and politics.
Related titles: CD-ROM ed.
Indexed: AESIS, GeoRef, IMMAb, SpeleolAb.
Published by: A J M Resources Publishing, Lonsdale Ct. Level 2, Ste. 18, 600 Lonsdale St, Melbourne, VIC 3000, Australia. TEL 61-3-9642-3500, FAX 61-3-9642-3900, info@ajm.com.au. Ed., R&P Geoffrey M Gold. Adv. contact Gordana Morak. Circ: 5,000.

ASSOCIATION OF PROFESSIONAL ENGINEERS, SCIENTISTS AND MANAGERS. COLLIERIES' STAFF DIVISION. EMPLOYMENT & REMUNERATION SURVEY REPORT. *see* BUSINESS AND ECONOMICS—Labor And Industrial Relations

549 THA ISSN 1014-5451
ATLAS OF MINERAL RESOURCES OF THE ESCAP REGION. Text in English. 1989. irreg., latest vol.16, 2001. USD 25 (effective 2003). maps. back issues avail. **Document type:** *Monographic series.*
Indexed: GeoRef, SpeleolAb.
Published by: United Nations Economic and Social Commission for Asia and the Pacific, United Nations Bldg., Rajadamnern Ave., Bangkok, 10200, Thailand. unescap@unescap.org, http://www.unescap.org. **Orders to:** Conference Services Unit, Conference Services Unit, ESCAP, Bangkok 10200, Thailand; United Nations Publications, 2 United Nations Plaza, Rm DC2-853, New York, NY 10017; United Nations Publications, Sales Office and Bookshop, Bureau E4, Geneva 10 1211, Switzerland.

664 DEU ISSN 1434-9302
TN500 CODEN: AUFTAK
AUFBEREITUNGS-TECHNIK - MINERAL PROCESSING. Text in English, German; Summaries in French, Spanish. 1960. 10/yr. EUR 207 domestic; EUR 231 foreign; EUR 24.50 newsstand/cover (effective 2011). adv. bk.rev. **Document type:** *Journal, Trade.*
Formerly (until 1990): Aufbereitungs-Technik (0004-783X)
Related titles: ◆ Supplement(s): MarktFocus Brecher.
Indexed: A22, CEA, CEABA, CIN, CPEI, CRIA, CRICC, Cadscan, ChemAb, ChemTitl, EngInd, F&EA, GeoRef, IBR, IBZ, IMMAb, LeadAb, RefZh, SCOPUS, SpeleolAb, TCEA, TM, Zincscan.
—BLDSC (1790.900000), CASDDS, IE, Ingenta, INIST, Linda Hall. **CCC.**
Published by: Bauverlag BV GmbH (Subsidiary of: Springer Science+Business Media), Avenwedderstr 55, Guetersloh, 33311, Germany. TEL 49-5241-802119, FAX 49-5241-809582, ulrike.mattern@springer-sbm.com, http://www.bauverlag.de. Ed. Petra Strunk. Pub. Rolf Koehling. Adv. contact Erdal Top. Circ: 5,000 (paid and controlled).

622 AUS ISSN 1034-6775
TN121 CODEN: AIBUEP
AUS I M M BULLETIN. Variant title: Australasian Institute of Mining and Metallurgy Bulletin. Text in English. 1990. bi-m. AUD 154 domestic; AUD 180 foreign (effective 2008). adv. **Document type:** *Bulletin, Trade.* **Description:** Provides information on developments, important news, personnel movements, current issues, and new products for mineral industry professionals.
Supersedes in part (in 1989): Aus I M M Bulletin and Proceedings (0818-3848); Which was formerly (until 1986): A I M M Bulletin and Proceedings (0817-2668); (until 1984): A I M M Bulletin (0814-4346); Which was formed by the merger of (1978-1983): Aus. I.M.M. Bulletin (0158-6602); (1933-1983): Australasian Institute of Mining and Metallurgy. Proceedings (0004-8364)
Related titles: Online - full text ed.: free membership.
Indexed: A22, A28, AESIS, APA, BrCerAb, C&ISA, CA/WCA, CIA, CerAb, CivEngAb, CorrAb, E&CAJ, E11, EEA, EMA, EngInd, EnvAb, GeoRef, H15, I05, IMMAb, INIS AtomInd, M&TEA, M09, MBF, METADEX, SCOPUS, SolStAb, SpeleolAb, T04, WAA.
—BLDSC (1792.932000), CASDDS, IE, Infotrieve, Ingenta, INIST, Linda Hall. **CCC.**
Published by: (Australasian Institute of Mining and Metallurgy), RESolutions Publishing & Media Pty Ltd, PO Box 24, Innaloo City, W.A., Australia. TEL 61-8-94463039, FAX 61-8-92443714, greg@resolution-group.com.au, http://www.resolution-group.com.au. Eds. Carmel Murphy, Monika Sarder, Stephanie Omizzolo. Adv. contact Stephen Donaldson TEL 61-2-85968650. color page AUD 3,350, B&W page AUD 2,250; trim 297 x 210. Circ: 8,534.

622.05 669 AUS ISSN 0155-3399
CODEN: MSAMDR
➤ **AUSTRALASIAN INSTITUTE OF MINING AND METALLURGY. MONOGRAPH SERIES.** Text in English. 1962. irreg., latest vol.25, 2006. price varies. back issues avail. **Document type:** *Monographic series, Academic/Scholarly.* **Description:** Covers various mining and metallurgy topics with each issue, including minerals, geology, commerce, and natural resources.
Related titles: CD-ROM ed.
Indexed: GeoRef, IMMAb, SCOPUS, SpeleolAb.
—CASDDS. **CCC.**
Published by: Australasian Institute of Mining and Metallurgy, PO Box 660, Carlton South, VIC 3053, Australia. TEL 61-3-96623166, FAX 61-3-96623662, publications@ausimm.com.au, http://www.ausimm.com.

622.05 669 AUS ISSN 1324-6240
CODEN: CSAMDJ
➤ **AUSTRALASIAN INSTITUTE OF MINING AND METALLURGY PUBLICATIONS.** Text in English. 1989. a. price varies. abstr.; bibl. **Document type:** *Proceedings, Academic/Scholarly.*
Formed by the merger of (1972-1988): Australasian Institute of Mining and Metallurgy Conference Series (0728-7178); (1972-1988): Australasian Institute of Mining and Metallurgy Symposia Series (0314-6154)
Related titles: CD-ROM ed.
Indexed: AESIS, C&ISA, E&CAJ, GeoRef, IMMAb, ISMEC, SolStAb, SpeleolAb.
—CASDDS. **CCC.**
Published by: Australasian Institute of Mining and Metallurgy, PO Box 660, Carlton South, VIC 3053, Australia. TEL 61-3-96623166, FAX 61-3-96623662, membership@ausimm.com.au.

622 550 AUS
AUSTRALIA. GEOSCIENCE AUSTRALIA. MINERAL RESOURCE REPORT. Text in English. 1987. irreg. price varies. **Document type:** *Government.*
Former titles: Australia. Bureau of Mineral Resources, Geology and Geophysics. Mineral Resource Report; Australia. Bureau of Mineral Resources, Geology and Geophysics. Resource Report (0818-6278)
Indexed: GeoRef, IMMAb, SpeleolAb.
Published by: Geoscience Australia, GPO Box 378, Canberra, ACT 2601, Australia. TEL 61-2-62499966, FAX 61-2-62499960, sales@ga.gov.au, http://www.ga.gov.au/.

622.33 AUS ISSN 0814-446X
AUSTRALIAN COAL YEAR BOOK. Abbreviated title: A C Y. Text in English. 1984. a. AUD 195; AUD 360 combined subscription includes Australian General Mining Year Book (effective 2008). adv. back issues avail. **Document type:** *Directory, Trade.* **Description:** Aims to act as a guide for coal mine site operations, exploration companies, mining companies, mining industry supply companies and consultants in Australia. Also lists oil and gas producers.
Related titles: CD-ROM ed.
Published by: Australia's Mining Series, PO Box 5289, Daisy Hill, QLD 4127, Australia. TEL 61-7-38082111, FAX 61-7-38082999, info@austmining.com.au. adv.: color page AUD 1,795. Circ: 1,500 (paid).

THE AUSTRALIAN GEMMOLOGIST. *see* JEWELRY, CLOCKS AND WATCHES

622 AUS ISSN 1034-6953
AUSTRALIAN GENERAL MINING YEAR BOOK. Abbreviated title: A G M. Text in English. 1989. a. AUD 195; AUD 360 combined subscription includes Australian Coal Year Book (effective 2008). adv. back issues avail. **Document type:** *Directory, Trade.* **Description:** Aims to act as a guide for mine site operations, exploration for minerals, mining companies and mining industry consultants in Australia and Papua New Guinea.
Related titles: CD-ROM ed.
Published by: Australia's Mining Series, PO Box 5289, Daisy Hill, QLD 4127, Australia. TEL 61-7-38082111, FAX 61-7-38082999, info@austmining.com.au. adv.: color page AUD 1,795. Circ: 1,500 (paid).

622 620.1 AUS ISSN 0818-9110
SH224.Q4
AUSTRALIAN GEOMECHANICS JOURNAL. Text in English. 1971. q. adv. bk.rev. back issues avail. **Document type:** *Journal, Academic/Scholarly.* **Description:** News journal of Australian Geomechanics Society with news and technical papers in the general field of geomechanics.
Former titles (until 1986): Australian Geomechanics News (0725-1009); Australian Geomechanics Journal (0313-4458)
Indexed: AESIS, CPEI, GEOBASE, GeoRef, HRIS, ICEA, Inspec, SCOPUS, SoftAbEng, SpeleolAb.
—BLDSC (1801.060000), INIST, Linda Hall. **CCC.**
Published by: Australian Geomechanics Society, PO Box 955, St Ives, NSW 2075, Australia. TEL 61-2-91447519, http://www.australiangeomechanics.org/. Circ: 650.

622.184 AUS ISSN 0817-654X
AUSTRALIAN GOLD, GEM AND TREASURE MAGAZINE. Text in English. 1973. m.
Former titles (until 1986): Australian Gem and Treasure Hunter (0159-6322); (until 1980): Australian Gem and Craft Magazine (0312-231X)
Indexed: GeoRef.
Published by: The Magazine Works Pty Ltd, PO Box 1034, Eastwood, NSW 2122, Australia. magworks@ozemail.com.au.

549 AUS ISSN 1323-7640
THE AUSTRALIAN JOURNAL OF MINERALOGY. Abbreviated title: A J M. Text in English. 1995. s-a. AUD 28 domestic; AUD 34 foreign (effective 2009). back issues avail. **Document type:** *Journal, Trade.* **Description:** Contains articles on Australian mineral localities and information of interest to mineral collectors.
Indexed: GeoRef, MinerAb.
Published by: Mineralogical Society of Victoria, A'Beckett St, PO Box 12162, Melbourne, VIC 8006, Australia. Ed. Dermot Henry TEL 61-3-92705048.

622 AUS ISSN 1037-0552
AUSTRALIAN JOURNAL OF MINING. Abbreviated title: A J M. Text in English. 1977. bi-m. AUD 165 domestic; AUD 209 in New Zealand; AUD 262 elsewhere (effective 2008). adv. bk.rev. back issues avail. **Document type:** *Magazine, Trade.* **Description:** Contains news, features and columns, covering issues in minerals exploration, development, processing, features on mining techniques, practices, equipment, technologies and business.
Former titles (until 2000): The Miner (1030-0880); (until 1988): Miner Newspaper with Petroleum News (1443-8542); (until 1987): Miner Newspaper; (until 1978): Mining and Construction Methods and Equipment; (until 1977): Mining Construction and Civil Engineering; Mining News in Australia; Incorporates (in 1991): Australian Journal of Mining: Australian, Asian and Pacific Mining (1037-0609); Which was formerly (until 1988): Australian Journal of Mining (0817-9646)
Related titles: Online - full text ed.
Indexed: A26, ABIX, AESIS, G08, GeoRef, I05.
—BLDSC (1810.500000). **CCC.**
Published by: Informa Australia Pty Ltd., Level 2, 120 Sussex St, GPO Box 2728, Sydney, NSW 2001, Australia. TEL 61-2-90804300, FAX 61-2-92902577, enquiries@informa.com.au, http://www.informa.com.au/. Ed. Paula Wallace TEL 61-2-90804454. Pub. Peter Attwater TEL 61-2-90804480. Adv. contact Adrian O'Mara TEL 61-2-90804427. B&W page AUD 1,180, color page AUD 1,870; trim 210 x 297. Circ: 5,875.

622 AUS
AUSTRALIAN LONGWALL. Text in English. 3/yr. AUD 46.20 domestic; AUD 69 foreign (effective 2008). **Document type:** *Magazine, Trade.* **Description:** Consists of in-depth coverage of longwall mines, groundbreaking technical and equipment news, and the latest coverage of research and development in underground coal mining.
Published by: Aspermont Ltd., 613-619 Wellington St, Perth, W.A. 6000, Australia. TEL 61-8-62639100, FAX 61-8-62639148, corporate@aspermont.com, http://www.aspermont.com/. Ed. Angie Bahr. Adv. contact Lisa Fisher. Circ: 4,000.

622 AUS ISSN 0004-976X
TP1 CODEN: AUMNA3
AUSTRALIAN MINING. Text in English. 1908. m. AUD 140; AUD 9.90 per issue; free domestic to qualified personnel (effective 2008). adv. bk.rev. illus.; mkt.; tr.lit. index. **Document type:** *Magazine, Trade.* **Description:** Provides information on mining technology developments such as exploration, extraction and mineral processing in Australia.
Former titles (until 1965): Mining and Chemical Engineering Review (0368-8860); (until 1960): Chemical Engineering and Mining Review (0366-6220); (until 1917): Mining and Engineering Review (0369-1012); (until 1910): Australian Mining and Engineering Review
Related titles: Online - full text ed.; Supplement(s): Australian Mining's Product Register.
Indexed: A09, A10, A11, A15, A28, ABIX, ABIn, AESIS, APA, ARI, B02, B07, B15, B17, B18, B21, BrCerAb, C&ISA, CA/WCA, CIA, CerAb, ChemAb, CivEngAb, CorrAb, E&CAJ, E11, EEA, EMA, ESPM, EngInd, EnvAb, EnvEAb, F&EA, G04, G08, GeoRef, H&SSA, H15, I05, IMMAb, INIS AtomInd, ISMEC, Inspec, M&TEA, M09, MBF, METADEX, P48, P51, P52, P56, PQC, RefZh, RiskAb, SCOPUS, SSciA, SolStAb, SpeleolAb, T02, T04, V03, V04, WAA.
—BLDSC (1814.600000), CASDDS, CIS, IE, Ingenta, Linda Hall.
Published by: Reed Business Information Pty Ltd. (Subsidiary of: Reed Business Information International), Tower 2, 475 Victoria Ave, Locked Bag 2999, Chatswood, NSW 2067, Australia. TEL 61-2-94222999, FAX 61-2-94222922, customerservice@reedbusiness.com.au, http://www.reedbusiness.com.au. Ed. Daniel Hall TEL 61-2-94222478. Pub. Chris Williams TEL 61-2-94222957. Adv. contact Roger Podmore TEL 61-2-94222867. B&W page AUD 2,510, color page AUD 3,630; trim 248 x 345. Circ: 9,441.

622 665.5 340 AUS ISSN 0812-857X
K1
AUSTRALIAN MINING AND PETROLEUM LAW ASSOCIATION YEARBOOK. Abbreviated title: A M P L A Yearbook. Text in English. 1977. a., latest 2000. AUD 181.50 domestic; AUD 175 foreign (effective 2007). bibl. 604 p./no.; back issues avail. **Document type:** *Yearbook, Trade.* **Description:** Aims to act as a reference source on Australian resources industries law.
Formerly (until 1983): Australian Mining and Petroleum Law Journal (0157-2083)

Indexed: A26, AESIS, CLI, G08, GeoRef, IMMAb, LRI.
Published by: Australian Mining and Petroleum Law Association Ltd., Level 4, 360 Little Bourke St., Melbourne, VIC 3000, Australia. TEL 61-3-96702544, FAX 61-3-96702616, federal@ampla.org. Eds. Barry Barton, Michael Crommelin. Circ: 600.

622 665.5 340 AUS ISSN 1447-9710
AUSTRALIAN RESOURCES AND ENERGY LAW JOURNAL. Text in English. 1982. 3/yr. AUD 258.50 domestic; AUD 235 foreign (effective 2008). back issues avail. **Document type:** *Journal, Trade.*
Description: Presents nationwide reports, articles and case notes on mining, oil and gas law.
Former titles (until 2002): Australian Mining and Petroleum Law Journal (1328-6803); (until 1996): A M P L A Bulletin (1034-327X)
Indexed: AESIS, GeoRef, IMMAb.
Published by: Australian Mining and Petroleum Law Association Ltd., Level 4, 360 Little Bourke St., Melbourne, VIC 3000, Australia. TEL 61-3-96702544, FAX 61-3-96702616, federal@ampla.org. Eds. Barry Barton, Michael Crommelin. Circ: 700. **Co-sponsor:** University of Melbourne, Centre for Resource, Energy and Environmental Law.

338 AUS ISSN 0728-2400
AUSTRALIAN URANIUM ASSOCIATION. NEWSLETTER. Text in English. 1979. bi-m. **Document type:** *Newsletter.*
Formerly (until 2007): U I C Newsletter
Related titles: Online - full text ed.: ISSN 1326-4788.
Indexed: AESIS, GeoRef, INIS AtomInd.
Published by: Australian Uranium Association, GPO Box 1649, Melbourne, VIC 3001, Australia. TEL 61-3-86160440, FAX 61-3-86160441, info@aua.org.au.

622 AUS ISSN 1327-6115
AUSTRALIA'S LONGWALLS. Text in English. 1994. s-a. AUD 10; AUD 20 foreign (effective 1999). adv. **Document type:** *Magazine, Trade.*
Related titles: ◆ Supplement to: Australia's Mining Monthly. ISSN 1328-8032.
Indexed: AESIS, GeoRef.
Published by: Australia's Mining Monthly, PO Box 78, Leederville, W.A. 6902, Australia. TEL 61-8-9489-9100, FAX 61-8-9381-1848, contact@miningmonthgly.com.

622 AUS ISSN 1328-8032
AUSTRALIA'S MINING MONTHLY. Variant title: Surpac Screen Dump. Text in English. 1980. m. AUD 132 domestic; AUD 270 foreign (effective 2008). adv. bk.rev. charts. **Document type:** *Magazine, Trade.* **Description:** Contains exclusive industry surveys and studies, and in-depth reports on mines, mining companies, mining regions, issues and key technical trends.
Former titles (until 1984): Mining Monthly (0725-9131); (until 1981): Mining Quarterly (0725-1173); Which incorporated (1982-1983): Lodestone's Australian Oil and Gas Journal (0812-9398)
Related titles: ◆ Supplement(s): Australia's Longwalls. ISSN 1327-6115.
Indexed: AESIS, GeoRef, IMMAb, INIS AtomInd, SpeleolAb.
—BLDSC (1825.019500), Ingenta.
Published by: Aspermont Ltd., 613-619 Wellington St, Perth, W.A. 6000, Australia. TEL 61-8-62639100, FAX 61-8-62639148, corporate@aspermont.com, http://www.aspermont.com/. Ed. Noel Dyson. Adv. contact Chris Le Messurier TEL 61-8-62639130. B&W page AUD 1,863, color page AUD 2,645; trim 210 x 297. Circ: 8,542.

AUSZUEGE AUS DEN EUROPAEISCHEN PATENTANMELDUNGEN. TEIL 1B. GRUND- UND ROHSTOFFINDUSTRIE, BAUWESEN, BERGBAU/EXTRACTS FROM EUROPEAN PATENT APPLICATIONS. PART 1B. PRIMARY INDUSTRY, FIXED CONSTRUCTIONS, MINING. *see* PATENTS, TRADEMARKS AND COPYRIGHTS—Abstracting, Bibliographies, Statistics

622 CAN
B C MINE RESCUE MANUAL. Text in English. base vol. plus irreg. updates. looseleaf. CAD 18. **Document type:** *Government.*
Description: Provides basic training in the rescue procedures to be followed in the event of an accident at a surface or underground mining operation.
Published by: British Columbia, Ministry of Energy, Mines and Petroleum Resources, 5th Fl, 1810 Blanshard St, Victoria, BC V8V 1X4, Canada. Ed. Dorothe Jakobsen. **Subscr. to:** Crown Publications Inc., 521 Fort St, Victoria, BC BC V8W 1E7, Canada. TEL 604-386-4636.

622 669 AUT ISSN 0005-8912
CODEN: BHMMAM
➤ **B H M/JOURNAL OF MINING, METALLURGICAL, MATERIALS, GEOTECHNICAL AND PLANT ENGINEERING**; Zeitschrift fuer Rohstoffe, Geotechnik, Metallurgie, Werkstoffe, Maschinen- und Anlagentechnik. (Berg- und Huettenmaennische Monatshefte) Text in German; Abstracts in English. 1841. m. EUR 404, USD 472 combined subscription to institutions (print & online eds.) (effective 2012). adv. bk.rev. bibl.; charts; illus.; abstr. index. back issues avail.; reprint service avail. from PSC. **Document type:** *Journal, Academic/Scholarly.*
Incorporates: Montan-Berichte (0026-9875); Montan-Rundschau (0026-9883); Former titles (until 1962): Berg- und Huettenmaennische Monatshefte (0170-0278); (until 1961): Berg- und Huettenmaennische Monatshefte der Montanistischen Hochschule in Leoben (0365-9747)
Related titles: Online - full text ed.: ISSN 1613-7531 (from IngentaConnect).
Indexed: A22, A26, A28, APA, BrCerAb, C&ISA, CA/WCA, CIA, CIN, CerAb, ChemAb, ChemTitl, CivEngAb, CorrAb, E&CAJ, E01, E08, E11, EEA, EMA, GeoRef, H15, IMMAb, Inspec, M&TEA, M09, MBF, METADEX, SolStAb, SpeleolAb, T04, TM, WAA.
—BLDSC (1909.000000), CASDDS, IE, Infotrieve, Ingenta, INIST, Linda Hall. **CCC.**
Published by: Springer Wien (Subsidiary of: Springer Science+Business Media), Sachsenplatz 4-6, Vienna, W 1201, Austria. TEL 43-1-33024150, FAX 43-1-3302426, journals@springer.at, http://www.springer.at. Ed. Helmut Clemens. Adv. contact Irene Hofmann. B&W page EUR 1,500, color page EUR 2,700; 180 x 260. Circ: 3,500 (paid). **Subscr. in the Americas to:** Springer New York LLC, Journal Fulfillment, PO Box 2485, Secaucus, NJ 07096. TEL 201-348-4033, 800-777-4643, FAX 201-348-4505, journals-ny@springer.com, http://www.springer.com; **Subscr. to:** Springer Distribution Center, Kundenservice Zeitschriften, Haberstr 7, Heidelberg 69126, Germany. TEL 49-6221-3454303, FAX 49-6221-3454229, subscriptions@springer.com. **Co-sponsors:** Bergmaennischer Verband Oesterreich; Montanuniversitaet Leoben; Eisenhuette Oesterreich.

622 SVK ISSN 0231-6854
BANICKE LISTY/FOLIA MONTANA. Text in Slovak; Summaries in English, French, Russian. 1974. irreg. illus.
Published by: (Slovenska Akademia Vied/Slovak Academy of Sciences, Banicky Ustav Sav), Vydavatel'stvo Slovenskej Akademie Vied Veda/Veda, Publishing House of the Slovak Academy of Sciences, Dubravska cesta 9, PO Box 106, Bratislava 45, 84005, Slovakia. **Dist. by:** Slovart G.T.G. s.r.o., Krupinska 4, PO Box 152, Bratislava 85299, Slovakia. TEL 421-2-63839472, FAX 421-2-63839485, http://www.slovart-gtg.sk.

622 669 HUN ISSN 0522-3512
TN4 CODEN: BKLBB6
➤ **BANYASZATI ES KOHASZATI LAPOK - BANYASZAT.** Text in Hungarian; Contents page in English. 1868. bi-m. USD 50 (effective 2001). bk.rev. abstr.; charts; illus. 88 p./no.; **Document type:** *Journal, Academic/Scholarly.*
Formerly (until 1968): Banyaszati Lapok (0365-9003); Which supersedes in part (in 1951): Banyaszati es Kohaszati Lapok (0365-9011)
Indexed: CIN, ChemAb, ChemTitl, FR, GeoRef, IMMAb, INIS AtomInd, SpeleolAb.
—CASDDS, INIST, Linda Hall.
Published by: Orszagos Magyar Banyaszati es Kohaszati Egyesulet, Fo utca 68, Budapest, 1027, Hungary. ombke@mtesz.hu, http://www.mtesz.hu/tagegy/ombke. Ed., Adv. contact T Podanyi TEL 36-87-514136. Circ: 100 (paid); 1,800 (controlled).

➤ **BANYASZATI SZAKIRODALMI TAJEKOZTATO/MINING ABSTRACTS.** *see* MINES AND MINING INDUSTRY—Abstracting, Bibliographies, Statistics

➤ **BAO PO/BLASTING.** *see* ENGINEERING—Chemical Engineering

622 669 620 CHN ISSN 1001-053X
TS300 CODEN: BKDXEZ
BEIJING KEJI DAXUE XUEBAO. Text in Chinese; Abstracts in English. 1955. m. USD 186 (effective 2009). abstr. 96 p./no.; back issues avail. **Document type:** *Journal, Academic/Scholarly.* **Description:** Covers many academic fields, such as mineral, metallurgy, materials, mechanical engineering, mathematics, physics, chemistry etc. Many important professional achievements and researches on basic theory and applied theory are published.
Former titles (until 1988): Beijing Gangtie Xueyuan Xuebao (1000-5609); (until 1960): Beijing Gangtie Gongye Xueyuan Xuebao (0476-0255)
Related titles: Online - full text ed.; ◆ English ed.: International Journal of Minerals Metallurgy and Materials. ISSN 1674-4799.
Indexed: A28, APA, BrCerAb, C&ISA, CA/WCA, CIA, CIN, CPEI, CerAb, ChemAb, ChemTitl, CivEngAb, CorrAb, E&CAJ, E11, EEA, EMA, ESPM, EngInd, EnvEAb, H15, M&TEA, M09, MBF, METADEX, RefZh, SCOPUS, SolStAb, T04, TM, WAA, Z02.
—BLDSC (4912.120000), CASDDS, East View, Linda Hall.
Published by: Beijing Keji Daxue/Beijing University of Science and Technology, Editorial Board of University of Science & Technology Beijing, 30 Xueyuan Lu, Haidian-qu, Beijing, 100083, China. TEL 86-10-62332875, FAX 86-10-62333436. Ed. Jinwu Xu.

BELGIUM. GEOLOGICAL SURVEY OF BELGIUM. PROFESSIONAL PAPERS. *see* EARTH SCIENCES—Geology

622 333.8 DEU ISSN 0342-5681
TN3
BERGBAU; Zeitschrift fuer Bergbau und Energiewirtschaft. Text in German. 1949. m. EUR 8 newsstand/cover (effective 2007). adv. **Document type:** *Magazine, Trade.* **Description:** Covers all branches of the mining industry.
Indexed: A22, FR, GeoRef, IMMAb, INIS AtomInd, SpeleolAb, TM.
—IE, Ingenta, INIST. **CCC.**
Published by: (Ring Deutscher Bergingenieure e.V.), Makossa Druck und Medien GmbH, Pommernstr 17, Gelsenkirchen, 45889, Germany. TEL 49-209-980850, FAX 49-209-9808585, druck.medien@makossa.de, http://www.makossa.de. Ed. Werner Makossa. adv.: B&W page EUR 1,520, color page EUR 2,500. Circ: 12,000 (paid).

622 DEU
BERGMANNSKALENDER. Text in German. 1873. a. EUR 10 per issue (effective 2009). back issues avail. **Document type:** *Bulletin, Trade.*
Formerly (until 1999): Saarbruecker Bergmannskalender
Published by: R A G - Deutsche Steinkohle AG, Shamrockring 1, Herne, 44623, Germany. TEL 49-2323-150, FAX 49-2323-152020, post@rag.de, http://www.rag-deutsche-steinkohle.de.

622 669.142 SWE ISSN 0284-0448
HD9525.S85 CODEN: JJAND2
BERGSMANNEN MED JERNKONTORETS ANNALER. Text in Swedish; Section in English. 1817. 7/yr. SEK 180 in Scandinavia; SEK 230 elsewhere (effective 2000). adv. bk.rev. illus.; stat.; tr.lit. index. back issues avail. **Document type:** *Magazine, Trade.* **Description:** Concerns metal and minerals engineering for the steel mining industry.
Former titles (until 1987): J K A - Jernkontorets Annaler (0280-4239); (until 1981): Jernkontorets Annaler med Bergsmannen (0348-6559); Which was formed by the merger of (1976-1977): Jernkontorets Annaler (0347-4410); (1972-1977): Bergsmannen med Moderna Material (0345-1372)
Related titles: Online - full text ed.
Indexed: A28, APA, ApMecR, BrCerAb, C&ISA, CA/WCA, CIA, CerAb, ChemAb, CivEngAb, CorrAb, E&CAJ, E11, EEA, EMA, EngInd, H15, IMMAb, M&TEA, M09, MBF, METADEX, PAIS, SCOPUS, SolStAb, T04, WAA.
—CASDDS, INIST, Linda Hall.
Published by: Bergsmannen Foerlags AB, Fack 5, Soedertaelje, 15121, Sweden. TEL 46-8-550-616-90, FAX 46-8-550-616-90. Ed., Pub. Stefan Ljungberg. Adv. contact Lars Eck. B&W page SEK 14,900, color page SEK 20,000; trim 210 x 297. Circ: 4,400.

338.2 POL ISSN 1234-7833
BIULETYN GORNICZY. Text in Polish. 1995. bi-m. EUR 65 foreign (effective 2006). **Document type:** *Bulletin.*
Published by: Gornicza Izba Przemyslowo-Handlowa/Mining Chamber of Industry and Commerce, ul Kosciuszki 30, Katowice, 40048, Poland. TEL 48-32-7573239, FAX 48-32-7573081, giph@coig.katowice.pl. **Dist. by:** Ars Polona, Obroncow 25, Warsaw 03933, Poland. TEL 48-22-5098609, FAX 48-22-5098610, arspolona@arspolona.com.pl, http://www.arspolona.com.pl.

BLASTING AND FRAGMENTATION. *see* ENGINEERING—Chemical Engineering

622 AUT
BOECKSTEINER MONTANA. Text in German. irreg., latest vol.9, 1991. **Document type:** *Monographic series, Academic/Scholarly.*
Published by: Verein Montandenkmal Altboeckstein, Karl-Imhof-Ring 12, Boeckstein, 5645, Austria. TEL 43-6434-2234.

622 PRT ISSN 0006-5935
CODEN: PBMIBL
BOLETIM DE MINAS. Text in Portuguese. 1912. q. BRL 550 per issue (effective 2001). charts; illus. **Document type:** *Bulletin.*
Indexed: GeoRef, IBR, IBZ, IMMAb, PAIS, SpeleolAb.
Published by: Ministerio da Economia, Instituto Nacional de Engenharia Tecnologia e Inovacao (I N E T I), Apartado 7586, Zambujal-Alfragide, Amadora, 2720-866, Portugal. TEL 351-210-924600, FAX 351-214-719018, http://www.ineti.pt. Circ: 750.

BOLETIN GEOLOGICO Y MINERO. *see* EARTH SCIENCES—Geology

BOLETIN GEOLOGICO Y MINERO. PUBLICACIONES ESPECIALES. *see* EARTH SCIENCES—Geology

622 JPN ISSN 0385-0501
BONANZA. Text in Japanese. m. illus.
Published by: Kinzoku Kogyo Jigyodan/Metal Mining Agency of Japan, 24-14 Toranomon 1-chome, Minato-ku, Tokyo, 105-0001, Japan.

662 RUS
BOR'BA S GAZOM V UGOL'NYKH SHAKHTAKH. Text in Russian. irreg. illus.
Published by: (Nauchno-Issledovatelskii Institut po Bezopasnosti Rabot v Gornoi Promyshlennosti, Makeevka), Izdatel'stvo Nedra, Tverskaya Zastava pl 3, Moscow, 125047, Russian Federation. TEL 7-095-2505255, FAX 7-095-2502772.

BOTSWANA. DEPARTMENT OF MINES. AIR POLLUTION CONTROL. ANNUAL REPORT. *see* ENVIRONMENTAL STUDIES—Pollution

549 BRA ISSN 0102-4728
TN4
BRASIL MINERAL. Text in Portuguese. 1983. m. BRL 99 (effective 2006). back issues avail. **Document type:** *Magazine, Trade.*
Related titles: Online - full text ed.
Published by: Signus Editora, Rua Eugenio de Medeiros, 499, Sao Paulo, SP 05425-000, Brazil. TEL 55-11-38146899, FAX 55-11-38135534, signus@signuseditora.com.br, http://www.signuseditora.com.br/.

622 BRA ISSN 0100-3577
CODEN: BPMBAB
BRAZIL. DEPARTAMENTO NACIONAL DA PRODUCAO MINERAL. BOLETIM. Text in Portuguese. 1972. irreg., latest vol.60, 1986. USD 25 (effective 1997). back issues avail. **Document type:** *Bulletin, Government.*
Indexed: GeoRef, IMMAb, SpeleolAb.
—Linda Hall.
Published by: Departamento Nacional da Producao Mineral, Setor Autarquia Norte, Quadra 1, Bloco B, Brasilia, DF 70040, Brazil. TEL 55-61-224-2670. Ed. Frederico L M Barboza.

338.2 BRA
BRAZIL. DEPARTAMENTO NACIONAL DA PRODUCAO MINERAL. BOLETIM DE PRECOS. Text in Portuguese. 1974. 4/yr. free. **Document type:** *Government.*
Indexed: SpeleolAb.
Published by: Departamento Nacional da Producao Mineral, Setor Autarquia Norte, Quadra 1, Bloco B, Brasilia, DF 70040, Brazil. TEL 55-61-2244670.

622 BRA
BRAZIL. DEPARTAMENTO NACIONAL DA PRODUCAO MINERAL. RELATORIO ANUAL DE ATIVIDADES E PROGRAMACAO. Text in Portuguese. 1972. a. (in 2 vols.). free. **Document type:** *Government.*
Description: Reports on all planned activities of the Department: geochemical and geophysical surveys, geological mapping and more.
Published by: Departamento Nacional da Producao Mineral, Setor Autarquia Norte, Quadra 1, Bloco B, Brasilia, DF 70040, Brazil. TEL 55-61-224-2670, FAX 55-61-2258274. Circ: 150 (controlled).

622 BRA ISSN 0101-8159
TN41
BRAZIL. DEPARTAMENTO NACIONAL DA PRODUCAO MINERAL. SERIE TECNOLOGIA MINERAL. Text in Portuguese. 1979. irreg., latest vol.46, 1994. **Document type:** *Monographic series, Academic/Scholarly.*
Indexed: GeoRef.
Published by: Departamento Nacional da Producao Mineral, Setor Autarquia Norte, Quadra 1, Bloco B, Brasilia, DF 70040, Brazil. TEL 55-61-224-2670, FAX 55-61-2258274. Ed. Frederico L M Barboza.

622 CAN ISSN 0846-0051
TN27.B9
BRITISH COLUMBIA MINERAL EXPLORATION REVIEW. Text in English. a. free. illus. **Document type:** *Government.*
Formerly (until 1985): British Columbia Exploration Review (0828-6094)
Indexed: GeoRef, SpeleolAb.
Published by: British Columbia, Ministry of Energy, Mines and Petroleum Resources, 5th Fl, 1810 Blanshard St, Victoria, BC V8V 1X4, Canada. **Subscr. to:** Crown Publications Inc., 521 Fort St, Victoria, BC BC V8W 1E7, Canada. TEL 604-386-4636.

BRITISH COLUMBIA OIL AND GAS HANDBOOK. *see* PETROLEUM AND GAS

622 GBR ISSN 0308-2199
BRITISH MINING; memoirs and monographs. Text in English. 1975. s-a. GBP 18. **Document type:** *Monographic series, Academic/Scholarly.*
Indexed: GeoRef, IMMAb, SpeleolAb.
—BLDSC (2330.540000), IE, Ingenta.
Published by: Northern Mine Research Society, 38 Main St, Sutton-In-Craven, Keighley, Yorks BD20 7HD, United Kingdom. TEL 44-1535-635388. Ed. Hazel Martell. Circ: 700.

622.2 POL ISSN 1234-5342
BUDOWNICTWO GORNICZE I TUNELOWE. Text in Polish. 1995. q. EUR 125 foreign (effective 2006). **Document type:** *Journal, Academic/Scholarly.*

Published by: (Politechnika Slaska, Wydzial Gornictwa i Geologii), Wydawnictwo Gornicze, ul Plebiscytowa 36, Katowice, 40041, Poland. TEL 48-32-7572142, FAX 48-32-7572043, wydawnictwo.wg@w-g.com.pl, http://www.w-g.com.pl. Ed. Andrzej Karbownik. **Dist. by:** Ars Polona, Obroncow 25, Warsaw 03933, Poland. TEL 48-22-5098609, FAX 48-22-5098610, arspolona@arspolona.com.pl, http://www.arspolona.com.pl.

BULETINI I SHKENCAVE GJEOLOGJIKE. *see* EARTH SCIENCES—Geology

338.2 GBR ISSN 1474-3159
BUSINESS RATIO REPORT. MINING & QUARRYING. Text in English. 1986. a. GBP 365 per issue (effective 2010). charts; stat. **Document type:** *Report, Trade.* **Description:** Covers companies active in the mining and quarrying industry.
Former titles (until 2001): Business Ratio. Mining & Quarrying (1467-9183); (until 1999): Business Ratio Plus: Mining & Quarrying (1355-1833); (until 1994): Business Ratio Report: Mining and Quarrying (0269-9117)
Published by: Key Note Ltd. (Subsidiary of: Bonnier Business Information), Harlequin House, 5th Fl, 7 High St, Teddington, Richmond upon Thames, TW11 8EE, United Kingdom. TEL 44-845-5040452, FAX 44-845-5040453, sales@keynote.co.uk.

622 669 CAN ISSN 0068-9009
TN1
C I M DIRECTORY. Text in English. 1967. a. CAD 100 per issue (effective 2004). adv. **Document type:** *Directory.* **Description:** Lists officers and members, as well as feature articles on a subject dealing with mining in Canada.
Indexed: GeoRef, IMMAb, SpeleolAb.
—Linda Hall. **CCC.**
Published by: Canadian Institute of Mining, Metallurgy and Petroleum, Ste 855, 3400 de Maisonneuve Blvd W, Ste 1210, Montreal, PQ H3Z 3B8, Canada. cim@cim.org, http://www.cim.org. Ed. Perla Gantz. Circ: 12,750.

338.2 CAN ISSN 1923-6026
▼ **C I M JOURNAL.** (Canadian Institute of Mining) Text in English, French. 2010. q. free to members (effective 2010). **Document type:** *Journal, Trade.*
—BLDSC (3198.244050), IE.
Published by: Canadian Institute of Mining, Metallurgy and Petroleum, Ste 1250, 3500 de Maisonneuve Blvd W, Westmount, PQ H3Z 3C1, Canada. TEL 514-939-2710, FAX 514-939-2714, cim@cim.org, http://www.cim.org.

622 665.5 CAN ISSN 1718-4177
TN1 C3 CODEN: CIBUBA
C I M MAGAZINE. Text in English, French. 1898. m. CAD 171.20 domestic; USD 180 foreign (effective 2006). bk.rev. bibl.; charts; illus.; tr.lit. index. back issues avail.; reprints avail. **Document type:** *Magazine, Trade.* **Description:** Technical data and information on mineral engineering subjects to promote the technological interests of people involved in the development of the industry in Canada.
Formerly (until 2006): C I M Bulletin (0317-0926)
Related titles: Online - full text ed.
Indexed: A&ATA, A05, A20, A22, A23, A24, A28, AESIS, AIA, APA, AS&TA, AS&TI, ASCA, B04, B13, B21, BrCerAb, C&ISA, C03, CA/WCA, CADCAM, CBCABus, CBPI, CEA, CIA, CIN, Cadscan, CerAb, ChemAb, ChemTitl, CivEngAb, CorrAb, E&CAJ, E11, EEA, EIA, EMA, ESPM, EngInd, EnvAb, EnvEAb, F&EA, FLUIDEX, FR, GEOBASE, GeoRef, H&SSA, H15, IMMAb, ISR, Inspec, LeadAb, M&TEA, M09, MBF, METADEX, P26, P48, P52, P54, P56, PQC, PollutAb, SCOPUS, SSciA, SolStAb, SpeleolAb, T04, TCEA, TM, WAA, Zincscan.
—BLDSC (3198.244110), CASDDS, IE, Infotrieve, Ingenta, INIST, Linda Hall, PADDS. **CCC.**
Published by: Canadian Institute of Mining, Metallurgy and Petroleum, Ste 855, 3400 de Maisonneuve Blvd W, Ste 1210, Montreal, PQ H3Z 3B8, Canada. cim@cim.org, http://www.cim.org. Ed. Perla Gantz. Pub. Yvan Jacques. Adv. contact Lynda Battista. Circ: 11,000.

622 CAN ISSN 0701-0710
C I M REPORTER. Text in English. 2/yr. free. adv. **Document type:** *Newspaper.* **Description:** Composed of current mining and milling information.
Indexed: SpeleolAb.
Published by: Canadian Institute of Mining, Metallurgy and Petroleum, Ste 855, 3400 de Maisonneuve Blvd W, Ste 1210, Montreal, PQ H3Z 3B8, Canada. cim@cim.org, http://www.cim.org. Ed. Perla Gantz. Circ: 10,119.

549 666 USA ISSN 1521-740X
C M S WORKSHOP LECTURES. Text in English. 1989. irreg., latest vol.16, 2009. price varies. back issues avail. **Document type:** *Proceedings, Academic/Scholarly.* **Description:** Features original papers pertinent to research on clays and other fine-grain materials.
Indexed: CIN, ChemAb, ChemTitl, GEOBASE, GeoRef, SCOPUS, SpeleolAb.
—BLDSC (3287.282400), IE, Ingenta. **CCC.**
Published by: The Clay Minerals Society, 3635 Concorde Pky, Ste 500, Chantilly, VA 20151. TEL 703-652-9960, FAX 703-652-9951, cms@clays.org.

669.142 GBR ISSN 1755-5566
C R U STEEL NEWS WEEKLY. Variant title: C R U Steel News. Text in English. 199?. w. GBP 1,250 (effective 2010). **Document type:** *Newsletter, Trade.*
Formerly (until 2007): Steel Week (1741-3265)
Media: Online - full text.
—CCC.
Published by: C R U International Ltd., 31 Mount Pleasant, London, WC1X OAD, United Kingdom. TEL 44-20-79032000, FAX 44-20-78370976, http://crugroup.com.

622 CHN ISSN 1671-2900
CAIKUANG JISHU/MINING TECHNOLOGY. Text in Chinese. 2001. q. **Document type:** *Journal, Academic/Scholarly.*
Published by: Changsha Kuangshan Yanjiuyuan, 343, Lushan Nan Lu, Changsha, 410012, China. TEL 86-731-8670962.

622 CHN ISSN 1673-3363
CAIKUANG YU ANQUAN GONGCHENG XUEBAO/JOURNAL OF MINING AND SAFETY ENGINEERING. Text in Chinese. 1984. q. adv. **Document type:** *Academic/Scholarly.* **Description:** Covers researches on ground pressure theory and strata control, and engineering practices of coal industry.
Former titles (until 2006): Kuangshan Yali yu Dingban Guanli/Ground Pressure and Strata Control (G P S C) (1003-5923); (until 1990): Kuangshan Yali
Related titles: Online - full text ed.
Indexed: CPEI, SCOPUS.
—East View.
Published by: Zhongguo Kuangye Daxue/China University of Mining and Technology, Jiefang Nan Lu, Xuzhou, Jiangsu 221008, China. http://www.cumt.edu.cn/. **Co-sponsor:** Zhongguo Meitan Gongye Laodong Baohu Kexue Jishu Xuehui.

CALIFORNIA. DIVISION OF MINES AND GEOLOGY. SPECIAL REPORT. *see* EARTH SCIENCES—Geology

553 GBR ISSN 0962-2012
CAMBRIDGE TOPICS IN MINERAL PHYSICS AND CHEMISTRY. Text in English. 1990. irreg., latest 2005. price varies. adv. back issues avail.; reprints avail. **Document type:** *Monographic series, Academic/Scholarly.* **Description:** Covers a broad range of topics relating to the atomic structure of minerals, their physical and chemical properties and relationship to structure, phase transformations and kinetics, and spectroscopic and experimental techniques.
Indexed: GeoRef.
—BLDSC (3015.998815).
Published by: Cambridge University Press, The Edinburgh Bldg, Shaftesbury Rd, Cambridge, CB2 8RU, United Kingdom. TEL 44-1223-312393, FAX 44-1223-315052, journals@cambridge.org, http://www.cambridge.org/uk. Eds. Andrew Putnis, Michael F Hochella Jr., Robert C Liebermann.

CANADA A-Z; oil, gas, mining directory. *see* BUSINESS AND ECONOMICS—Trade And Industrial Directories

338.2 CAN ISSN 0226-4617
CANADA. STATISTICS CANADA. QUARRIES AND SAND PITS/ CANADA. STATISTIQUE CANADA. CARRIERES. (Catalog 26-217) Text in English, French. 1925. a. CAD 0.70, USD 0.85. stat.
Supersedes in part (in 1978): Canada. Statistics Canada. Sand and Gravel Pits (0575-965X); Which was formerly: Canada. Statistics Canada. Stone Quarries (0575-9846); (until 1962): Canada. Bureau of Statistics. Stone Quarrying Industry (0318-2800); (until 1960): Canada. Bureau of Statistics. Stone Industry (0381-9248)
Published by: Statistics Canada/Statistique Canada, Communications Division, 3rd Fl, R H Coats Bldg, Ottawa, ON K1A 0A6, Canada.

622 CAN
HG5159.M4
CANADIAN AND AMERICAN MINES HANDBOOK. Text in English. 1931. a. CAD 103 per issue domestic; USD 85 per issue foreign (effective 2008). adv. **Document type:** *Handbook/Manual/Guide, Trade.* **Description:** Lists information on 2,000 active Canadian mining companies plus details on mines, projects, smelters, refineries and key industry contacts. Includes mining area maps and stock range tables.
Formerly: Canadian Mines Handbook (0068-9289); Supersedes in part (in 2003): American Mines Handbook (0840-8610)
Related titles: CD-ROM ed.: Canadian MineSCAN. CAD 239 per issue domestic; USD 199 per issue foreign (effective 2007).
Indexed: SpeleolAb.
Published by: Business Information Group, 12 Concorde Pl, Ste 800, Toronto, ON M3C 4J2, Canada. TEL 416-442-2122, 800-668-2374, FAX 416-442-2191, orders@businessinformationgroup.ca. adv.: B&W page CAD 2,015. Circ: 8,000 (paid).

622 739.27 CAN ISSN 1719-9638
CANADIAN DIAMONDS. Text in English. 2001. q. CAD 49.95 domestic; CAD 57.95 in United States; CAD 61.95 elsewhere (effective 2006). adv. **Document type:** *Magazine, Trade.* **Description:** Explores all facets of the diamond business in Canada.
Former titles (until 2006): Canadian Diamonds and Jewellery (1717-421X); (until 2005): Canadian Diamonds (1499-5700)
Indexed: C03, CBCABus, G09, P10, P48, P53, P54, PQC.
Published by: Up Here Publishing, Ste 800, 4920 52nd St, Yellowknife, NT X1A 3T1, Canada. TEL 867-920-4343, 800-661-0861, FAX 867-873-2844. Ed. Jake Kennedy. Pub. Marion Lavigne. Adv. contact Kathy Gray. page CAD 3,400; 8.5 x 11. Circ: 5,000.

CANADIAN INSTITUTE OF MINING AND METALLURGY. SPECIAL VOLUME. *see* BUSINESS AND ECONOMICS—Production Of Goods And Services

CANADIAN MINERALOGIST. *see* EARTH SCIENCES—Geology

622 CAN ISSN 0068-9270
TN26
CANADIAN MINERALS YEARBOOK/ANNUAIRE DES MINERAUX DU CANADA. Text in English. 1962. a. price varies. **Document type:** *Government.*
Indexed: AESIS, GeoRef, SpeleolAb.
—CCC.
Published by: (Canada. Publishing and Communication Services), Natural Resources Canada, Minerals and Metals Sector (Subsidiary of: Natural Resources Canada/Ressources Naturelles Canada), 580 Booth St, Ottawa, ON K1A 0E4, Canada. TEL 613-947-6580, FAX 613-952-7501, info-mms@nrcan.gc.ca, http://www.nrcan.gc.ca/mms/hm_e.htm. Ed. E Godin. **Orders to:** Geological Survey of Canada Bookstore, 601 Booth St, Ottawa, ON K1A 0E8, Canada.

338.2 662 CAN ISSN 0008-4492
TN26 CODEN: CAMJA9
CANADIAN MINING JOURNAL. Text in English. 1879. 9/yr. CAD 47.95 domestic; USD 60.95 in United States; USD 72.95 elsewhere (effective 2008). adv. illus.; mkt. index. **Document type:** *Journal, Trade.* **Description:** Leading mining and exploration journal in Canada. Covers mineral exploration trends, metal prices and new geological models, underground mine developments and operating performances, new technology and services.
Incorporates: Mining in Canada (0047-7494)
Related titles: Microfiche ed.: (from MML); Microfilm ed.: (from MML, PMC); Microform ed.: (from MML); Online - full text ed.
Indexed: A09, A10, A12, A15, A17, A20, A22, A23, A24, A33, ABIn, AESIS, ASCA, B01, B03, B06, B07, B08, B09, B11, B13, C03, C05, CA, CBCABus, CBPI, CISA, CPEI, CPerI, Cadscan, ChemAb, CurCont, E04, E05, E14, EngInd, F&EA, FR, G08, GeoRef, IMMAb, Inspec, KES, LeadAb, P48, P51, P52, P53, P54, P56, PQC, PetrolAb, RefZh, SCI, SCOPUS, SpeleolAb, T02, V03, V04, W07, Zincscan.
—BLDSC (3042.000000), CASDDS, IE, Infotrieve, Ingenta, INIST, PADDS. **CCC.**
Published by: Business Information Group, 12 Concorde Pl, Ste 800, Toronto, ON M3C 4J2, Canada. TEL 416-442-2122, 800-668-2374, FAX 416-442-2191, http://www.businessinformationgroup.ca. Ed. Jane Werniuk TEL 416-510-6742. Pub. Ray Perks TEL 416-510-6891. adv.: B&W page CAD 2,350. Circ: 8,495.

CANADIAN NATURAL RESOURCES DIRECTORY. *see* BUSINESS AND ECONOMICS—Trade And Industrial Directories

624 621.9 ESP ISSN 0008-5677
CANTERAS Y EXPLOTACIONES; revista tecnica de maquinaria del sector de mineria, cantera y medio ambiente. Text in Spanish. 1967. m. (11/yr.). EUR 121 domestic; EUR 223 in Europe; EUR 319 elsewhere (effective 2009). **Document type:** *Magazine, Trade.* **Description:** Presents technical information on the open air, subterranean, tunnel and quarry sectors of mining.
Indexed: GeoRef, IECT, IMMAb, INIS AtomInd, SpeleolAb.
—CCC.
Published by: TPI Edita, Ave Manoteras, 26 3a Planta, Madrid, 28050, Spain. TEL 34-91-3396807, FAX 34-91-3396096, info@grupotpi.es, http://www.tpiedita.es. Ed. Jose Luis Padro. Circ: 10,273 (controlled).

622.8 ITA
CARBONE INFORMAZIONI. Text in Italian. m. adv. bk.rev.; software rev.; Website rev. mkt.; charts; stat. back issues avail. **Document type:** *Magazine, Trade.* **Description:** Reports market figures and statistics for solid combustible products.
Related titles: Online - full text ed.
Published by: Rivista Italiana Petrolio Srl, Via Aventina 19, Rome, 00153, Italy. TEL 39-06-5741208, FAX 39-06-5754906, http://www.staffettaonline.com.

622 PER
CARTA MINERA Y PANORAMA PETROLERO. Text in Spanish. 1982. w. USD 290; includes annual directory. adv. charts; stat. **Document type:** *Newsletter.* **Description:** Covers mining and petrolum in Peru.
Published by: Andean Air Mail & Peruvian Times S.A., Pasaje Los Pinos, 156 Piso B Of 6, Miraflores, Lima 18, Peru. TEL 51-14-453761, FAX 51-14-467888. Ed. Juan Hoyos. Pub. Eleanor Zuniga. Adv. contact Luisa Perbuli.

622 CHN ISSN 1005-9784
CODEN: JCSTFT
➤ **CENTRAL SOUTH UNIVERSITY OF TECHNOLOGY. JOURNAL;** science & technology of mining and metallurgy. Text in English. 1994. bi-m. EUR 1,250, USD 1,514 combined subscription to institutions (print & online eds.) (effective 2012). bk.rev. 72 p./no.; reprint service avail. from PSC. **Document type:** *Journal, Academic/Scholarly.*
Related titles: Online - full text ed.: ISSN 1993-0666; ◆ Chinese ed.: Zhongnan Daxue Xuebao (Ziran Kexue Ban). ISSN 1672-7207.
Indexed: A22, A26, A28, APA, BrCerAb, C&ISA, CA/WCA, CIA, CIN, CPEI, CerAb, ChemAb, ChemTitl, CivEngAb, CorrAb, E&CAJ, E01, E11, EEA, EMA, ESPM, EngInd, EnvEAb, GeoRef, H15, I05, Inspec, M&TEA, M09, MBF, METADEX, MSCI, RefZh, SCI, SCOPUS, SolStAb, SpeleolAb, T04, TM, W07, WAA.
—BLDSC (4724.360000), CASDDS, East View, IE, Ingenta, Linda Hall. **CCC.**
Published by: Zhongnan Daxue/Central South University, Lushan Nan Lu, Changsha, 410083, China. TEL 86-731-8879765, FAX 86-731-8877197, http://www.csu.edu.cn/chinese/. Circ: 500. **Co-publisher:** Springer.

622 ZWE ISSN 0009-1162
TN119.R6 CODEN: CHMJBP
CHAMBER OF MINES JOURNAL. Text in English. 1959. m. ZWD 216; ZWD 300 foreign (effective 1999). adv. **Document type:** *Journal, Trade.*
Supersedes (in 1963): Rhodesia Mining and Engineering
Indexed: GeoRef, IMMAb, ISAP, SpeleolAb.
Published by: (Chamber of Mines, Zimbabwe), Thomson Publications Zimbabwe (Pvt) Ltd., Thomson House, PO Box 1683, Harare, Zimbabwe. TEL 263-4-736835, FAX 263-4-752390.

622 ZAF
CHAMBER OF MINES' NEWSLETTER; serving South Africa's private sector mining industry. Text in English. bi-m. free to qualified personnel. charts; illus.; stat. **Document type:** *Newsletter, Trade.* **Description:** Presents articles on South Africa's mining industry and related issues.
Indexed: AESIS.
Published by: Chamber of Mines of South Africa, PO Box 809, Johannesburg, 2000, South Africa. TEL 27-11-4987100, FAX 27-11-8384251, TELEX 4-87057. Ed. Al Smit.

622 ZAF ISSN 0379-4520
HD9536.S6
CHAMBER OF MINES OF SOUTH AFRICA. ANNUAL REPORT. Text in English. 1889. a.
—Linda Hall.
Published by: Chamber of Mines of South Africa, 5 Hollard St, Marshalltown, Johannesburg, 2107, South Africa. TEL 27-11-498-7100, FAX 27-11-834-1884, http://www.bullion.org.za.

338.2 CMR ISSN 0069-2530
CHAMBRE DE COMMERCE, D'INDUSTRIE ET DES MINES DU CAMEROUN. RAPPORT ANNUEL. Text in French. a. XAF 1,000. **Document type:** *Corporate.*
Published by: Chambre de Commerce d'Industrie et des Mines du Cameroun, BP 4011, Douala, Cameroon. TEL 237-42-6855, FAX 237-42-5596. Ed. Saidou A Bobboy. Pub. Claude Juimo Monthe. Circ: 350.

CHILE. SERVICIO NACIONAL DE GEOLOGIA Y MINERIA. MISCELANEA. *see* EARTH SCIENCES—Geology

CLASSIC PLANT & MACHINERY. *see* MACHINERY

666.3 622.3 JPN ISSN 0009-8574
TN943.J3 CODEN: CLASAJ
CLAY SCIENCE. Text mainly in English. 1960. s-a. (1-2/yr.). membership. charts. Index. **Document type:** *Journal, Academic/Scholarly.* **Description:** Contains papers on original research or reviews in clay mineralogy and related fields.
Related titles: ◆ Japanese ed.: Nendo Kagaku. ISSN 0470-6455.
Indexed: A37, C25, CABA, CIN, ChemAb, ChemTitl, E12, F08, F12, FCA, GeoRef, H16, I11, MinerAb, R11, RefZh, S13, S16, SpeleolAb, TAR.
—CASDDS, INIST, Linda Hall. **CCC.**

Published by: Nippon Nendo Gakkai/Clay Science Society of Japan, c/o Takabumi Sakamoto, Okayama University of Science, Dept of Applied Science, 1-1, Ridai-cho, Okayama, 700-0005, Japan. nendo@das.ous.ac.jp. Ed. Akio Henmi. Circ: 700.

549 666 USA ISSN 0009-8604
TN941 CODEN: CLCMAB
➤ **CLAYS AND CLAY MINERALS.** Text in English. 1952. bi-m. free to members (effective 2009). bk.rev. bibl.; charts; illus. Index. back issues avail.; reprint service avail. from PSC. **Document type:** *Journal, Academic/Scholarly.* **Description:** Covers research on clays and other fine-grain minerals.
Former titles (until 1965): Clays and Clay Minerals; (until 1953): National Conference on Clays and Clay Technology. Proceedings
Related titles: Microform ed.; Online - full text ed.: ISSN 1552-8367 (from IngentaConnect).
Indexed: A22, A28, A33, A34, A37, AESIS, APA, ASCA, ASFA, B21, BrCerAb, C&ISA, C25, C30, C33, CA/WCA, CABA, CIA, CIN, CPEI, CerAb, ChemAb, ChemTitl, CivEngAb, CorrAb, CurCont, E&CAJ, E&PHSE, E11, E12, EEA, EMA, ESPM, EngInd, EnvEAb, F08, F12, FCA, G11, GEOBASE, GH, GP&P, GSW, GeoRef, GeotechAb, H15, H16, I11, ISR, M&TEA, M09, MBF, METADEX, MSCI, MinerAb, N02, N03, N04, OffTech, P30, PGrRegA, PetrolAb, R07, RefZh, S12, S13, S16, SCI, SCOPUS, SWRA, SolStAb, SpeleolAb, T04, T05, TAR, TriticAb, W07, W10, WAA.
—BLDSC (3278.100000), CASDDS, IE, Infotrieve, Ingenta, INIST, Linda Hall, PADDS. **CCC.**
Published by: The Clay Minerals Society, PO Box 460130, Aurora, CO 80046. cms@clays.org. Ed. Joseph W Stucki TEL 217-333-9636.

622 USA ISSN 1091-0646
CODEN: COALEN
COAL AGE. Text in English. 1988. m. USD 68 in US & Canada; USD 80 elsewhere (effective 2011). adv. tr.lit.; illus. index. back issues avail.; reprints avail. **Document type:** *Magazine, Trade.* **Description:** Covers the exploration, development, underground and surface mining, preparation and distribution of anthracite, bituminous coal, and ignite.
Formerly (until 1996): Coal (1040-7820); Which was formed by the merger of (1911-1988): Coal Age (0009-9910); (1984-1988): Coal Mining (0749-1948); Which was formerly (1964-1984): Coal Mining and Processing (0009-9961)
Indexed: A05, A09, A10, A15, A22, A23, A24, A26, ABIn, AESIS, AS&TA, AS&TI, B01, B02, B03, B04, B06, B07, B09, B13, B15, B17, B18, BPI, BRD, C10, C12, CIN, CISA, ChemAb, ChemTitl, E08, E14, EIA, EngInd, EnvAb, EnvInd, F&EA, FR, G04, G06, G07, G08, GasAb, GeoRef, I05, P26, P34, P48, P51, P52, P54, P56, PQC, PROMT, RefZh, S04, S09, SCOPUS, SRI, SpeleolAb, T&II, T02, V03, V04, W01, W02, W03, W05.
—BLDSC (3288.000000), CASDDS, IE, Ingenta, INIST, Linda Hall. **CCC.**
Published by: Mining Media, Inc., c/o Peter Johnson, 8751 East Hampden Ave, Ste B-1, Denver, CO 80231. TEL 303-283-0640, FAX 303-283-0641, info@mining-media.com. Ed. Steve Fiscor TEL 904-721-2925. Pub. Peter Johnson. adv.: B&W page USD 5,060, color page USD 6,580; 7 x 10.

553 GBR
HD9551.1
THE COAL AUTHORITY. REPORT AND ACCOUNTS. Text in English. a. price varies. reprints avail. **Document type:** *Government.*
Former titles: British Coal Corporation. Report and Accounts; (until 1983): National Coal Board. Report and Accounts (0305-120X)
Related titles: Online - full text ed.: free.
Published by: (The Coal Authority), The Stationery Office, St Crispins, Duke St, Norwich, NR3 1PD, United Kingdom. TEL 44-1603-622211, FAX 44-870-6005533, customer.services@tso.co.uk, http://www.tso.co.uk. **Subscr. to:** PO Box 29, Norwich NR3 1GN, United Kingdom. TEL 44-870-6005522.

622 USA ISSN 0276-2846
COAL DAILY. Text in English. 197?. d. (5/wk.). **Document type:** *Newsletter, Trade.* **Description:** Contains trade and pricing information for the coal industry throughout the world.
—CCC.
Published by: Energy Argus, Inc. (Subsidiary of: Argus Media Inc.), 129 Washington St, Ste 400, Hoboken, NJ 07030. TEL 201-659-4400, FAX 201-659-6006, info@energyargus.com, http://www.energyargus.com.

622 FRA ISSN 1012-9324
COAL INFORMATION. Variant title: I E A Coal Information. Text in English. 1986. a., latest 2008. EUR 165 (effective 2011). **Document type:** *Trade.* **Description:** Provides comprehensive information on current world coal market trends and long-term prospects.
Formerly (until 1986): Coal Information Report
Related titles: CD-ROM ed.: EUR 550 per issue (effective 2011); Diskette ed.: ISSN 1606-6758; Online - full text ed.: ISSN 1683-4275. EUR 1,100, GBP 880, USD 1,430, JPY 160,400 (effective 2010) (from IngentaConnect).
Indexed: GeoRef, IIS.
Published by: Organisation for Economic Cooperation and Development (O E C D), International Energy Agency, 9 rue de la Federation, Paris, 75739 cedex 15, France. TEL 33-1-40576500, FAX 33-1-40576559, info@iea.org, http://www.iea.org.

622 GBR ISSN 1357-6941
TN808.G6 CODEN: CLGUAL
COAL INTERNATIONAL. Text in English, Chinese, Russian. 1858. bi-m. GBP 140 domestic; GBP 160 foreign (effective 2011). **Document type:** *Magazine, Trade.* **Description:** Provides the latest mining industry news, case studies, technical articles on health and safety, new plant and equipment as well as other feature articles.
Incorporates (1998-2000): Mining & Quarry World (1463-6336); Formerly (until 1994): Colliery Guardian (0264-9799); Which superseded in part (in 1982): Colliery Guardian Coal International (0143-778X); Which was formerly (until 1979): Colliery Guardian (0010-1281); Which superseded: Colliery Guardian and Journal of the Coal and Iron Trades (0366-5917); And incorporated in part (in 1963): Steel & Coal (0371-3628); Which was formerly (until 1962): Iron & Coal (0140-5101); (until 1961): Iron & Coal Trades Review (0367-732X); Which incorporated: British Iron Trade Association Engineering Review. Bulletin
Related titles: Online - full text ed.: ISSN 2045-2985.
Indexed: A09, A10, A22, AESIS, B01, B06, B07, B08, B09, BrGeoL, C12, CA, CISA, ChemAb, E14, EngInd, F&EA, FR, G06, G07, G08, GeoRef, IMMAb, P34, RICS, RefZh, SCOPUS, SpeleolAb, T02, TM, V02, V03, V04.
—BLDSC (3290.090000), IE, Infotrieve, Ingenta, INIST, Linda Hall. **CCC.**
Published by: Tradelink Publications Ltd, British Fields, Ollerton Rd, Tuxford, Newark, Notts NG22 0PQ, United Kingdom. TEL 44-1777-871007, FAX 44-1777-872271, info@tradelinkpub.co.uk, http://www.tradelinkpub.co.uk.

622 USA
THE COAL LEADER; dedicated to public awareness and understanding in the mining industry. Text in English. 1960. m. USD 18. adv. bk.rev. **Document type:** *Newspaper.* **Description:** Explores coal mining and resources.
Former titles: National Coal Leader; National Independent Coal Leader (0192-7329)
Published by: National Independent Coal Operators Association, PO Box 858, Richlands, VA 24641-0858. TEL 540-963-2779. Eds. Barbara F Altizer, Emily B Fisher. Circ: 16,000.

COAL MINE DIRECTORY; United States and Canada. *see* BUSINESS AND ECONOMICS—Trade And Industrial Directories

338.2 622.33 USA ISSN 0162-2714
K3
COAL OUTLOOK. Text in English. 1975. w. USD 2,345 (effective 2010). adv. charts; stat. back issues avail. **Document type:** *Newsletter, Trade.* **Description:** Provides analysis and insights into: coal price trends in all major US producing areas, major coal companies in the financial markets, mine openings, closings and production.
Incorporates: Coal Week (0149-578X); Which incorporated (197?-1975): Mine Regulation & Productivity Report (0277-8696)
Related titles: Online - full text ed.: ISSN 1555-3515. USD 1,795 combined subscription (online & E-mail eds.) (effective 2010).
Indexed: A15, A26, ABIn, E08, G08, P48, P51, P52, P56, PQC, S09.
—CCC.
Published by: Platts (Subsidiary of: McGraw-Hill Companies, Inc.), 1200 G St NW, Ste 1000, Washington, DC 20005. TEL 212-904-3070, 800-752-8878, FAX 202-383-2024, support@platts.com, http://www.platts.com.

051 USA ISSN 0748-6073
COAL PEOPLE. Text in English. 1976. m. USD 25 (effective 1998). adv. bk.rev. **Document type:** *Magazine, Trade.*
Published by: Al Skinner Inc., PO Box 6247, Charleston, WV 25302. TEL 304-342-4129, FAX 304-343-3124. Ed., Pub. Al Skinner. R&P Christina Karawan. Adv. contact Alan Terranova. Circ: 11,500.

622.33 USA ISSN 2153-8190
TN816.A1
▼ **COAL PREPARATION DIRECTORY AND HANDBOOK.** Text in English. 2009. a. USD 95 per issue (effective 2010). **Document type:** *Handbook/Manual/Guide, Trade.* **Description:** Focuses on the preparation aspect of the coal industry, including technical specifications and conversion tables and a complete listing of U.S. suppliers and manufacturers of coal preparation equipment and services.
Published by: (Coal Preparation Society of America), Mining Media, Inc., 13544 Eads Rd, Prairieville, LA 70769. TEL 225-673-9400, FAX 225-677-8277, info@mining-media.com.

622.33 681.3 NLD ISSN 0167-9449
CODEN: CSTYEF
➤ **COAL SCIENCE AND TECHNOLOGY.** Text in English. 1981. irreg., latest vol.22, 1995. price varies. **Document type:** *Monographic series, Academic/Scholarly.* **Description:** Discusses research and other topics in the extraction, preparation, and combustion of coal and coal products.
Related titles: Online - full text ed.
Indexed: A22, CIN, ChemAb, ChemTitl, GeoRef, IMMAb, SpeleolAb.
—CASDDS, INIST. **CCC.**
Published by: Elsevier BV (Subsidiary of: Elsevier Science & Technology), Radarweg 29, PO Box 211, Amsterdam, 1000 AE, Netherlands. TEL 31-20-4853911, FAX 31-20-4852457, JournalsCustomerServiceEMEA@elsevier.com, http://www.elsevier.nl.

622.33 AUS
COAL USA. Text in English. 2004. q. AUD 61.60 domestic; AUD 96 foreign (effective 2008). **Document type:** *Magazine, Trade.* **Description:** Provides in-depth news and features on North America's longwall and room and pillar industries.
Formerly (until 2007): American Longwall Magazine
Published by: Aspermont Ltd., 613-619 Wellington St, Perth, W.A. 6000, Australia. TEL 61-8-62639100, FAX 61-8-62639148, corporate@aspermont.com, http://www.aspermont.com/. Ed. Angie Bahr. Adv. contact Lisa Fisher. Circ: 3,000.

622.33 USA ISSN 1944-5180
COALBED METHANE EXTRA. Text in English. 19??. q. free (effective 2009). back issues avail. **Document type:** *Newsletter, Trade.* **Description:** Provides regular program update that highlights U.S. and global efforts to recover and use coal mine methane.
Media: Online - full content.
Published by: (U.S. Environmental Protection Agency, Coalbed Methane Outreach Program), U.S. Environmental Protection Agency, Office of Air and Radiation, 1310 L St, NW, Washington, DC 20005. http://www.epa.gov/oar/.

622.33 AUS
COALFAX. Text in English. 1987. w. AUD 1,200, USD 895 (effective 2001). charts; mkt.; tr.lit. **Document type:** *Newsletter, Trade.* **Description:** Discusses the Australian coal market.
Media: Fax. **Related titles:** Online - full content ed.: AUD 1,600 incl. archive; AUD 1,200 combined subscription for both Australian Coal Report & Coalfax (effective 2001); Print ed.: AUD 2,490 combined subscription for both Australian Coal Report & Coalfax (effective 2001).
Published by: Barlow Jonker Pty. Ltd., Level 13, 50 Pitt St, Sydney, NSW 2000, Australia. TEL 61-2-82248888, info@barlowjonker.com, http://www.barlowjonker.com/. Pub. Barlow Jonker.

COALTRANS INTERNATIONAL. *see* TRANSPORTATION—Ships And Shipping

622 USA ISSN 0276-8445
CODE OF FEDERAL REGULATIONS. TITLE 30, MINERAL RESOURCES. Text in English. 19??. irreg. price varies. **Document type:** *Government.*
Related titles: Online - full text ed.
Published by: National Archives and Records Administration, U.S. Office of the Federal Register, 8601 Adelphi Rd, College Park, MD 20740. TEL 202-741-6000, FAX 202-741-6012, fedreg.info@nara.gov, http://www.federalregister.gov.

662.72 GBR ISSN 0305-5450
COKE OVEN MANAGERS' ASSOCIATION. YEAR BOOK. Variant title: C O M A Year Book. Text in English. 1917. a. adv. **Document type:** *Yearbook, Trade.*
—BLDSC (9383.300000), Linda Hall.
Published by: Coke Oven Manager's Association, Waveney House, Adwick Rd, Mexborough, W Yorks S64 0BS, United Kingdom. tim.savage@corusgroup.com. Ed. J Dartnell. Circ: 750.

622 ZAF
COLIMPEX MINING EXECUPAD. Text in Afrikaans, English. a. free to qualified personnel. adv.
Published by: Colimpex Africa (Pty) Ltd., PO Box 5838, Johannesburg, 2000, South Africa.

COLORED STONE; the international reporter of the gemstone trade. *see* JEWELRY, CLOCKS AND WATCHES

338.9 LUX ISSN 1680-3469
HD9525.E79
COMMISSION OF THE EUROPEAN COMMUNITIES. INVESTMENT IN THE COMMUNITY COAL MINING AND IRON AND STEEL INDUSTRIES. REPORT ON THE SURVEY. Text in English. 1956. a., latest 2001. price varies.
Related titles: Dutch ed.: 1956; Italian ed.: 1956; German ed.: 1956; French ed.: 1956.
Indexed: IIS.
Published by: European Commission, Office for Official Publications of the European Union, 2 Rue Mercier, Luxembourg, L-2985, Luxembourg. **Dist. in U.S. by:** Bernan Associates, Bernan, 4611-F Assembly Dr., Lanham, MD 20706-4391.

COMMITTEE FOR COORDINATION OF JOINT PROSPECTING FOR MINERAL RESOURCES IN ASIAN OFFSHORE AREAS. TECHNICAL BULLETIN. *see* EARTH SCIENCES—Geology

622
COMPACT. Text in English. 1983. q. membership. **Document type:** *Newsletter.* **Description:** Provides information for member states on mining laws, regulations and other related areas.
Published by: Interstate Mining Compact Commission, 445 Carlisle Dr, Ste A, Herndon, VA 20170. TEL 703-709-8654, FAX 703-709-8655, bbotsis@imcc.isa.us, http://www.imcc.isa.us. Ed. Gregory E Conrad. R&P Gregory Conrad. Circ: 700.

622 CHL ISSN 0716-5153
COMPENDIO DE LA MINERIA CHILENA. Text in Spanish. 1985. a. price varies. adv. bk.rev. index. back issues avail.
Published by: Editec Ltda., Avenida del Condor 844, Oficina 205, Ciudad Empresarial, Huechuraba, Santiago, 09, Chile. TEL 56-2-7574210, FAX 56-2-75754201, editec@editec.cl, http://www.editec.cl. Eds. Ricardo Cortes, Roly Solis. adv.: B&W page USD 2,700, color page USD 3,400; trim 8.13 x 10.88. Circ: 10,000.

622 USA ISSN 0010-6577
CONSOL NEWS. Text in English. 1962. bi-m. free (effective 2008). charts; illus. index. **Description:** Reports on coal mining and resources.
Published by: Consol Energy, c/o William G. Rieland, 1800 Washington Rd, Pittsburgh, PA 15241. TEL 412-831-4401, 412-831-4032, FAX 412-831-4594, http://www.consolenergy.com. Circ: 22,500.

CONSTRUCTION EQUIPMENT BUYERS' GUIDE. *see* BUILDING AND CONSTRUCTION

CONTRIBUTIONS TO MINERALOGY AND PETROLOGY. *see* EARTH SCIENCES—Geology

338.2 GBR
COPPER BRIEFING SERVICE. Text in English. 1993. m. price varies. back issues avail. **Document type:** *Newsletter, Trade.* **Description:** Features statistical analysis and research about the copper market.
Published by: Bloomsbury Minerals Economics Ltd., 5 Warren Mews, London, W1T 6AP, United Kingdom. TEL 44-207-5298911, web@bloomsburyminerals.com.

338.2 669.3 GBR ISSN 2043-9822
▼ **COPPER SURVEY.** Text in English. 2010. a. GBP 325, EUR 440, USD 595 per issue (effective 2010). **Document type:** *Report, Trade.* **Description:** Provides unique and independent analysis of supply and demand fundamentals within the market.
Related titles: Online - full text ed.
Published by: G F M S Ltd., Hedges House, 153-155 Regent St, London, W1B 4JE, United Kingdom. TEL 44-20-74781777, FAX 44-20-74781779, info@gfms.co.uk.

549 CAN ISSN 0526-4553
QE185
CURRENT RESEARCH IN THE GEOLOGICAL SCIENCES IN CANADA. Text in English. 1908. a.
Supersedes in part (in 1967): Canadian Mining and Metallurgical Bulletin (0008-4484); Which was formerly (until 1926): Canadian Institute of Mining and Metallurgy. Monthly Bulletin (0317-0918); (until 1920): Canadian Mining Institute. Monthly Bulletin (0319-3632); (until 1914): Canadian Mining Institute. Bulletin (0319-3624); (until 1913): Canadian Mining Institute. Quarterly Bulletin (0319-3616)
Indexed: A23, A24, B13, GeoRef, L09, SCOPUS.
—INIST, Linda Hall. **CCC.**
Published by: Geological Survey of Canada, 601 Booth St, Ottawa, ON K1A 0E8, Canada. TEL 613-995-4342.

338.2 USA ISSN 2159-791X
D G C MAGAZINE. (Digital Gold Currency) Text in English. 2008. m. free (effective 2011). adv. back issues avail. **Document type:** *Magazine, Trade.* **Description:** Describes legal use of digital gold currency around the world.
Media: Online - full text.
Published by: Alan Smithee, Pub. dgcmagazine@mises.com. Ed. Herpel Mark.

DAKOTA COUNSEL. *see* ENERGY

622 CHN ISSN 1002-8897
DANGDAI KUANGGONG/MODERN MINER. Text in Chinese. 1985. m. CNY 93.60 newsstand/cover (effective 2006). **Document type:** *Journal, Academic/Scholarly.*
Related titles: Online - full text ed.
Published by: Meitan Xinxi Yanjiuyuan, Xinwen Zhongxin, 35, Shaoyaoju, Beijing, 100029, China. TEL 86-10-84657853, FAX 86-10-84657900, xwzx@chinacoalnews.com, http://www.zgmt.com.cn/.

DEVELOPMENTS IN CLAY SCIENCE. see EARTH SCIENCES—Geology

622 DEU ISSN 1868-4459
DIAMANT HOCHLEISTUNGSWERKZEUGE. Variant title: Dihw. Text in German. 1967. q. EUR 48 (effective 2011). adv. bk.rev. back issues avail.; reprints avail. **Document type:** *Magazine, Trade.*
Formerly (until 2009): I D R (0935-1469)
Indexed: TM.
—IE, Linda Hall.
Published by: Dr. Harnisch Verlagsgesellschaft GmbH, Blumenstr 15, Nuernberg, 90402, Germany. TEL 49-911-20180, FAX 49-911-2018100, service@harnisch.com. Ed. Dietmar Biermann. Pub. Claus-Joerg Harnisch. Adv. contact Ilona Gross-Biermann. Circ: 8,450 (paid).

622 ISR
DIAMOND INTELLIGENCE BRIEFS. Text in English. 1985. 20/yr. USD 590 combined subscription print & online eds. (effective 2008). bk.rev. **Document type:** *Newsletter, Trade.* **Description:** Provides insider information on everything that affects the diamond industry from the mine to the retail jeweler.
Formerly: Europa Star Diamond Intelligence Briefs
Related titles: Fax ed.: USD 600 (effective 2002); Online - full text ed.
Published by: IDEX Online S A, PO Box 3441, Ramat Gan, 52133, Israel. TEL 972-3-5750196, FAX 972-3-5754829, office@tacy.co.il, http://www.tacyltd.com.

622 338.0029 MYS ISSN 1511-645X
DIRECTORY OF INDUSTRIAL MINERAL BASED INDUSTRIES. Text in English. 1999. a. MYR 30 per issue (effective 2008). **Document type:** *Directory, Trade.*
Published by: Jabatan Mineral dan Geosains Malaysia/Minerals and Geoscience Department Malaysia, 20th Fl, Tabung Haji Bldg, Jalan Tun Razak, Kuala Lumpur, 50658, Malaysia. TEL 60-3-21611033, FAX 60-3-21611036, jmgkll@jmg.gov.my, http://www.jmg.gov.my/english/mainpage.htm.

622 GBR ISSN 0957-266X
DIRECTORY OF MINES AND QUARRIES. Text in English. 1984. irreg., latest 2008. GBP 40 per issue (effective 2009). **Document type:** *Directory, Trade.* **Description:** Contains information relating to over 2200 active mines, quarries and other mineral workings in Britain, including those in Northern Ireland, the Isle of Man and the Channel Islands.
Related titles: CD-ROM ed.: GBP 47 per issue (effective 2009).
—BLDSC (3594.716100). **CCC.**
Published by: British Geological Survey, Kingsley Dunham Centre, Keyworth, Nottingham, NG12 5GG, United Kingdom. TEL 44-115-9363100, FAX 44-115-9363276, enquiries@bgs.ac.uk.

338.1029 GBR ISSN 1477-9919
DIRECTORY OF QUARRIES & QUARRY EQUIPMENT. Text in English. 1926. a., latest 32 ed. GBP 42 per issue (effective 2009). adv. **Document type:** *Directory.* **Description:** Contains updated listings on 4,347 quarries, pits, operating companies, recycling companies/depots/contractors, suppliers of plant, equipment, materials and services and industry organisations.
Former titles (until 2002): Directory of Quarries, Pits and Quarry Equipment (1356-7586); (until 1992): Directory of Quarries and Pits (0070-6175)
Published by: Q M J Publishing Ltd., 7 Regent St, Nottingham, NG1 5BS, United Kingdom. TEL 44-115-9411315, FAX 44-115-9484035, mail@qmj.co.uk, http://www.qmj.co.uk/. Ed. Stephen Adam TEL 44-115-9453893. Pub. Jack Berridge. Adv. contact Pam Reddish TEL 44-115-9454362.

DISCOVERY; Victoria's earth resources journal. see EARTH SCIENCES—Geology

DOW JONES MONTAN AKTUELL. see BUSINESS AND ECONOMICS—Investments

622 DEU ISSN 0012-5857
CODEN: DRAEAU
DRAEGERHEFT/DRAEGER REVIEW; Das Magazin fuer Technik in der Medizin. Text in German. 1912. s-a. free (effective 2009). charts; illus. cum.index. **Document type:** *Magazine, Trade.*
Related titles: English ed.: Drager Review. ISSN 0366-9610.
Indexed: CEABA, CISA, ChemAb.
—CASDDS, GNLM. **CCC.**
Published by: Draegerwerk AG & Co. KGaA, Moislinger Allee 53-55, Luebeck, 23542, Germany. TEL 49-451-8822009, FAX 49-451-8823197, info@draeger.com, http://www.draeger.com. Ed. Bjoern Woelke. Circ: 13,000.

DYNA. see ENGINEERING

EARTH AND MINERAL SCIENCES. see EARTH SCIENCES

622.33 GBR ISSN 0967-4926
ECOAL; the newsletter of the World Coal Institute. Text in English. 1992. q. free (effective 2009). back issues avail. **Document type:** *Newsletter.* **Description:** Provides information about World Coal Institute.
Related titles: Online - full text ed.: ISSN 1756-9230.
Indexed: Inspec.
Published by: World Coal Institute, 5th Fl, Heddon House, 149 - 151 Regent St, London, W1B 4JD, United Kingdom. TEL 44-20-78510052, FAX 44-20-78510061, info@worldcoal.org, http://www.wci-coal.com.

ECUADOR. MINISTERIO DE ENERGIA Y MINAS. INFORME DE LABORES. see ENERGY

ECUADOR. MINISTERIO DE ENERGIA Y MINAS. SECTOR ENERGETICO ECUATORIANO. see ENERGY

549 551 EGY ISSN 1110-1466
EGYPTIAN MINERALOGIST/AL-MAGALLAT AL-MISRIYYAT LI-'LM AL-MA'ADIN. Text in English. 1989. bi-m. free (effective 2009). **Document type:** *Journal, Academic/Scholarly.*
Published by: Mineralogical Society of Egypt, National Research Center, Geological Sciences Department, Ain-Shams University, Faculty of Science, Cairo, Egypt. TEL 20-2-3355192, FAX 20-2-3370931. Ed. Dr. Muhammad Ezz-El-Din Helmi.

549 548 CAN ISSN 1811-5209
QE351
➤ **ELEMENTS (QUEBEC);** an international magazine of mineralogy, geochemistry, and petrology. Text in English. 2005. bi-m. USD 150 to institutions; free to members (effective 2010); Free to institutions with subscr. to American Mineralogist, The Canadian Mineralogist or Clays and Clay Minerals. adv. back issues avail. **Document type:** *Journal, Academic/Scholarly.* **Description:** Explores a theme of broad and current interest in the mineral and geochemical sciences.
Formed by the merger of (1985-2005): The Lattice (1526-3746); (1961-2005): M A C Newsletter (0076-8936); C M S News
Related titles: Online - full text ed.: ISSN 1811-5217.
Indexed: A20, A22, A28, A35, A36, A37, APA, ASFA, AgBio, BA, BrCerAb, C&ISA, CA/WCA, CABA, CCI, CIA, CerAb, CivEngAb, CorrAb, CurCont, E&CAJ, E11, E12, EEA, EMA, ESPM, EnvEAb, F08, F12, GEOBASE, GH, GeoRef, H15, H16, I11, M&TEA, M09, MBF, METADEX, N02, OR, P30, RefZh, S13, S16, SCI, SCOPUS, SWRA, SolStAb, T04, T05, TAR, W07, W11, WAA.
—BLDSC (3729.034900), IE, Ingenta, INIST, Linda Hall. **CCC.**
Published by: (Mineralogical Society of America USA, The Clay Minerals Society USA, The Geochemical Society USA, Mineralogical Society of Great Britain & Ireland GBR), Mineralogical Association of Canada/Association Mineralogique du Canada, 490 Rue de la Couronne, Quebec, PQ G1K 9A9, Canada. TEL 418-653-0333, FAX 418-653-0777, office@mineralogicalassociation.ca, http://www.mineralogicalassociation.ca. Adv. contact Pierrette Tremblay TEL 418-654-2606. B&W page USD 1,575, color page USD 1,890; 7.625 x 10.125.

622 USA ISSN 2150-377X
TJ163.13
ENERGY AND THE EARTH. Text in English. 2008. a. free (effective 2009). back issues avail. **Document type:** *Magazine, Consumer.*
Related titles: Online - full text ed.
Published by: Colorado School of Mines, 1500 Illinois, Golden, CO 80401. TEL 303-273-3000, 800-446-9488, admit@mines.edu. Ed. Karen Gilbert.

ENERGY REPORT; energy policy and technology news bulletin. see ENERGY

622 AUS
ENERGY SOURCE & DISTRIBUTION. Text in English. 1995. bi-m. AUD 55 domestic to non-members; AUD 95 foreign to non-members; free to members (effective 2008). adv. **Document type:** *Magazine, Trade.* **Description:** Covers power generation, transmission, supply and distribution.
Former titles (until Jul.1997): Power; (until 1996): Queensland Power (1325-8192)
Published by: The Magazine Publishing Company Pty. Ltd., 34 Station St, PO Box 406, Nundah, QLD 4012, Australia. TEL 61-7-38660000, FAX 61-7-38660066, info@tmpc.com.au. adv.: color page AUD 3,450; trim 240 x 340. Circ: 3,785.

622.33 CAN
ENGINEERING AND INSPECTION ANNUAL REPORT. Text in English. a. CAD 15. back issues avail. **Document type:** *Government.*
Formerly: Mining in British Columbia (0823-1265); Which supersedes in part: Geology, Exploration and Mining in British Columbia (0085-1027); Which was formerly: Lode Metals in British Columbia
Indexed: GeoRef, SpeleolAb.
—INIST, Linda Hall.
Published by: British Columbia, Ministry of Energy, Mines and Petroleum Resources, 5th Fl, 1810 Blanshard St, Victoria, BC V8V 1X4, Canada. Ed. Dorothe Jakobsen. **Subscr. to:** Crown Publications Inc., 521 Fort St, Victoria, BC BC V8W 1E7, Canada. TEL 604-386-4636.

622 620 USA ISSN 0095-8948
TA1 CODEN: ENMJAK
ENGINEERING & MINING JOURNAL. Short title: E & M J. Text in English. 1922. m. USD 82 in US & Canada; USD 134 elsewhere (effective 2011). adv. bk.rev. tr.lit. index. **Document type:** *Journal, Trade.* **Description:** Covers exploration, development, milling, smelting, refining, and other extractive processing of metals and nonmetallics, including coal.
Incorporates (in 1991): International Mining; Former title (until 1922): Engineering and Mining Journal - Press; Which was formed by the merger of (1860-1922): Mining and Scientific Press (0096-5723); (1869-1922): Engineering and Mining Journal (0361-3941); Which incorporated (in 1917): Mining and Engineering World (0096-4840); which was formerly (until 1911): Mining World (0361-3992); (1895-1903): Western Mining World (0361-4182)
Indexed: A01, A02, A03, A05, A08, A09, A10, A12, A22, A23, A24, A26, A28, ABIn, AESIS, APA, AS&TI, ASCA, ASFA, B01, B02, B04, B06, B07, B08, B09, B10, B13, B15, B17, B18, B21, BRD, BrCerAb, BrGeoL, BusI, C&ISA, C10, C12, CA, CA/WCA, CADCAM, CIA, CISA, Cadscan, CerAb, ChemAb, CivEngAb, CoppAb, CorrAb, CurCont, E&CAJ, E04, E05, E06, E11, E14, EEA, EIA, EMA, ESPM, EngInd, EnvAb, EnvEAb, EnvInd, FR, G04, G06, G07, G08, GeoRef, GeotechAb, H&SSA, H15, I05, ICEA, IMMAb, INIS AtomInd, LeadAb, M&TEA, M01, M02, M09, MBF, METADEX, MSCI, OceAb, P06, P26, P34, P48, P51, P52, P53, P54, P56, PQC, PetrolAb, RefZh, S04, SCI, SCOPUS, SRI, SWRA, SoftAbEng, SolStAb, SpeleolAb, T&II, T02, T04, V02, V03, V04, W03, W05, W07, WAA, Zincscan.
—IE, Infotrieve, Ingenta, INIST, Linda Hall, PADDS. **CCC.**
Published by: Mining Media, Inc., 13544 Eads Rd, Prairieville, LA 70769. TEL 225-673-9400, 800-225-0899, FAX 225-677-8277, info@mining-media.com, http://www.mining-media.com. Ed. Steve Fiscor. Pub. Paul Johnson. adv.: color page USD 6,580, B&W page USD 5,060. Circ: 21,514 (controlled).

622 CAN ISSN 1718-8512
ENONCE DE POLITIQUE. Text in French. 2006. irreg. **Document type:** *Newsletter, Trade.*
Related titles: English ed.: Policy Brief. ISSN 1718-8504.
Published by: Partenariat Afrique Canada, Diamond Development Initiative (Subsidiary of: Partenariat Afrique Canada), 323, rue Chapel, Ottawa, ON K1N 7Z2, Canada. TEL 613-237-6768, FAX 613-237-6530, info@pacweb.org, http://www.pacweb.org/f/index.php?option=content&task=view&id=69&Itemid=93, http://www.pacweb.org/f/index.php?option=com_frontpage&Itemid=1.

ENVIRONMENTAL GEOCHEMISTRY AND HEALTH; official journal of the Society for Environmental Geochemistry and Health. see ENVIRONMENTAL STUDIES

EQUIPMENT ECHOES. see BUILDING AND CONSTRUCTION

622 USA ISSN 1937-9714
TA4
EQUIPO MINERO. Text in Spanish. 200?. q. adv. **Document type:** *Magazine, Trade.*
Published by: Mining Media, Inc., 9550 Regency Sq Blvd, Ste 1108, Jacksonville, FL 32225. TEL 904-721-2925, FAX 904-721-2930, info@mining-media.com, http://www.mining-media.com. Ed. Steve Fiscor.

EROSION CONTROL. see CONSERVATION

DER ERZGRAEBER. see EARTH SCIENCES—Geology

338.2 BOL ISSN 0014-1194
ESTANO. Text in Spanish. 1961. bi-m. free. adv. illus.
Published by: (Bolivia. Departamento de Relaciones Publicas e Informacion), Corporacion Minera de Bolivia, Casilla 349, Ave. Mariscal Santa Cruz, 1092, La Paz, Bolivia. Ed. Felix R Nieto.

622 RUS ISSN 2072-0823
EURASIAN MINING. Text in English. 2003. s-a. **Document type:** *Journal, Trade.* **Description:** Covers mineral processing, theory and practice of production, and physics and mechanics of rocks.
Related titles: ◆ Supplement to: Gornyi Zhurnal. ISSN 0017-2278.
Indexed: RefZh.
Published by: Izdatel'stvo Ruda i Metally/Ore and Metals Publishers, Leninskii prospekt 6, korpus 1, ofis 622, a/ya 71, Moscow, 119049, Russian Federation. rim@rudmet.ru. Ed. Lev A Puchkov. Circ: 1,000.

622 AUS
EUREKA ECHO. Text in English. 19??. q. free to members (effective 2009). **Document type:** *Newsletter.*
Published by: Prospectors and Miners Association, Meets at Miners Den, 464 Whitehorse Rd, Mitcham, Melbourne, VIC 3132, Australia. TEL 61-3-98731244, melbmetbranch@pmav.asn.au, http://www.pmav.asn.au.

549 DEU ISSN 0935-1221
QE351 CODEN: EJMIER
➤ **EUROPEAN JOURNAL OF MINERALOGY;** an international journal of mineralogy, geochemistry and related sciences. Text in English, French, German, Italian. 1988. 6/yr. EUR 64 per issue (effective 2011). adv. bibl.; charts; illus. index. back issues avail.; reprints avail. **Document type:** *Journal, Academic/Scholarly.* **Description:** Contains original papers, review articles and short notes dealing with mineralogical sciences: mineralogy, petrology, geochemistry, crystallography, ore deposits, and related fields, including applied mineralogy.
Formed by the merger of (1950-1988): Fortschritte der Mineralogie (0015-8186); (1968-1988): Rendiconti della Societa Italiana di Mineralogia e Petrologia (0037-8828); (1878-1988): Bulletin de Mineralogia (0180-9210); Which was formerly (until 1978): Societe Francaise de Mineralogie et de Cristallographie. Bulletin (0037-9328); (until 1949): Societe Francaise de Mineralogie. Bulletin (0366-3248); (until 1886): Societe Mineralogique de France. Bulletin (0150-9640)
Related titles: Online - full text ed.: ISSN 1617-4011 (from IngentaConnect); ◆ Supplement(s): Plinius (CD-ROM). ISSN 1972-1366.
Indexed: A20, A22, A28, APA, ASCA, BrCerAb, C&ISA, C33, CA/WCA, CIA, CIN, CerAb, ChemAb, ChemTitl, CivEngAb, CorrAb, CurCont, E&CAJ, E11, EEA, EMA, ESPM, EnvEAb, GEOBASE, GeoRef, H15, IBR, IBZ, IMMAb, ISR, Inspec, M&TEA, M09, MBF, METADEX, MSCI, MinerAb, RefZh, SCI, SCOPUS, SolStAb, SpeleolAb, T04, W07, WAA.
—BLDSC (3829.731630), AskIEEE, CASDDS, IE, Infotrieve, Ingenta, INIST, Linda Hall. **CCC.**
Published by: (Deutsche Mineralogische Gesellschaft), E. Schweizerbart'sche Verlagsbuchhandlung, Johannesstr 3A, Stuttgart, 70176, Germany. TEL 49-711-3514560, FAX 49-711-35145699, order@schweizerbart.de. Ed. Christian Chopin. **Co-sponsors:** Societe Francaise de Mineralogie et de Cristallographie; Societa Italiana di Mineralogia e Petrologia.

622 665.5 AUS ISSN 1838-3084
▼ **EXECUTIVE COMPLIANCE NEWS. INDEPENDENT NEWS FOR MINING & PETROLEUM.** Text in English. 2010. w. AUD 1,200 combined subscription (online & email eds.) (effective 2011). **Document type:** *Newsletter, Trade.* **Description:** Provides news and analysis impacting on the mining and petroleum industry sector.
Media: Online - full text. **Related titles:** E-mail ed.
Published by: Thomson Reuters (Professional) Australia Limited (Subsidiary of: Thomson Reuters Corp.), PO Box 3502, Rozelle, NSW 2039, Australia. TEL 61-2-85877980, FAX 61-2-85877981, LTA.Service@thomsonreuters.com.

EXPLORATION & MINING GEOLOGY; journal of the geological society of CIM. see EARTH SCIENCES—Geology

622 USA
EXPLORATION AND PROCESSING; exploring best practices for petroleum, natural gas and mineral industry leaders. Text in English. 19??. m. free to qualified personnel (effective 2008). adv. back issues avail.; reprints avail. **Document type:** *Magazine, Trade.* **Description:** Details the best practices in the recovery, processing and marketing of petroleum, natural gas and mineral products.
Related titles: Online - full text ed.: free (effective 2008).
Published by: Schofield Media Ltd., 303 E Wacker Dr, 23rd Fl., Ste 2300, Chicago, IL 60601. TEL 312-236-4090, FAX 312-240-0686, http://www.schofieldmediagroup.com/. Ed. John Krukowski. adv.: B&W page USD 7,610, color page USD 8,210; bleed 8.612 x 10.986.

EXPLORATION IN BRITISH COLUMBIA. see EARTH SCIENCES—Geology

622 CAN
EXTRA. Text in English. 1980. w. **Document type:** *Newsletter.* **Description:** Employee newsletter containing information concerning processes, safety, health, environment, world markets, corporate strategies, and human interest.
Published by: INCO Limited Manitoba Division, Public Affairs Dept, Thompson, MB R8N 1P3, Canada. TEL 204-778-2777, FAX 204-778-2975. Ed., R&P Penny Mellish. Circ: 2,500.

622 GBR
EXTRACTION BRIEFING. Text in English. 1976. 10/yr. GBP 355 (effective 1998). bk.rev. reprints avail. **Document type:** *Newsletter.* **Description:** Provides information on business and career opportunities in mining.
Former titles (until 1991): New Quarrying and Mining (0950-110X); (until 1986): Quarry and Mining News (0309-5606)
Related titles: Microform ed.: (from PQC).
Indexed: IMMAb.
Published by: Marketing Support Services, 7 Vallet Ave, Alcester, Warks B49 6AU, United Kingdom. TEL 44-1789-400222, FAX 44-1789-763629. Ed. Paul Erlanger. adv.: B&W page GBP 420; trim 180 x 280. Circ: 7,000.

549 USA
EXTRALAPIS ENGLISH. Text in English. 2001. irreg., latest 2010. price varies. back issues avail. **Document type:** *Monographic series, Academic/Scholarly.*
Related titles: ◆ Translation of: ExtraLapis. ISSN 0945-8492.
Published by: Lithographie, LLC, PO Box 11613, Denver, CO 80211. TEL 303-495-5521, FAX 303-482-1238, info@lithographie.org.

338.2 665.5 CAN ISSN 1486-4266
HD9506.C2
F P SURVEY - MINES & ENERGY. (Financial Post) Text in English. 1980. a. CAD 259 per issue (effective 2008). adv. **Document type:** *Report, Trade.* **Description:** Contains investment and financial information on publicly owned mining and resource companies in Canada.
Former titles (until 1998): Survey of Mines and Energy Resources (0833-9600); (until 1985): Financial Post Survey of Mines and Energy Resources (0227-1656); Which was formed by the merger of (1926-1980): Financial Post Survey of Mines (0071-5085); (19??-1980): Financial Post Survey of Energy Resources (0705-7091); Which was formerly (until 1978): Financial Post Survey of Oils (0071-5093); (until 1950): Financial Post Survey of Canadian Oils
Published by: Financial Post Datagroup, 300-1450 Don Mills Rd, Don Mills, ON M3B 3R5, Canada. TEL 416-383-2300, FAX 416-510-6830, chall@nationalpost.com, http://www.financialpost.com. Ed. Steven Pattison. Circ: 11,000. **Dist. by:** Owen Media Partners, Inc., 2085 Hurontario St, Ste 208, Mississauga, ON L5A 4G1, Canada. http://www.owen-media.com.

338.2 622 USA
FACTS ABOUT COAL AND MINERALS. Variant title: Facts about Coal. Text in English. 2002. a. USD 15 per issue to non-members; USD 4 per issue to members (effective 2011). index. **Document type:** *Trade.*
Formed by the merger of (19??-2002): Facts About Minerals; (1982-2002): Facts About Coal; Which was formerly (until 1982): Coal Facts (0734-8908); (until 1975): Bituminous Coal Facts (0067-8988); (until 1958): Bituminous Coal Trends; (until 1956): Bituminous Coal Annual; (until 1950): Bituminous Coal Annual, Facts and Figures; (until 1949): Bituminous Coal Facts and Figures
Related titles: Online - full text ed.: free to members (effective 2011).
—Linda Hall.
Published by: National Mining Association, 101 Constitution Ave, NW, Ste 500E, Washington, DC 20001. TEL 202-463-2600, FAX 202-463-2666, MPhelleps@nma.org.

622.33 USA ISSN 0192-3862
TN805
FEDERAL COAL MANAGEMENT REPORT. Text in English. 1977. a. **Document type:** *Government.* **Description:** Discusses the status of Federal Coal Program for preceding fiscal year.
—Linda Hall.
Published by: U.S. Department of the Interior, Bureau of Land Management, 1849 C St, Room 406-LS, Washington, DC 20240. TEL 202-452-5125. Circ: 1,000.

FEDERAL MINE SAFETY AND HEALTH REVIEW COMMISSION DECISIONS. *see* OCCUPATIONAL HEALTH AND SAFETY

549 FJI ISSN 0252-2462
J961
FIJI. MINERAL RESOURCES DEPARTMENT. ANNUAL REPORT. Text in English. 1953. a. price varies. **Document type:** *Government.* **Description:** Summary of the year's activities, statistics of mining and exploration.
Former titles (until 1980): Fiji. Mineral Resources Division. Annual Report; (until 1975): Fiji. Department of Lands and Mineral Resources. Annual Report (0252-2470); (until 1972): Fiji. Geological Survey. Annual Report (0252-2489)
Indexed: GeoRef, IMMAb, SpeleolAb.
Published by: Mineral Resources Department, P.M. Bag, Suva, Fiji. TEL 679-381611, FAX 679-370039. Ed. Peter Rodda. Circ: 500.

549 FJI ISSN 0379-296X
FIJI. MINERAL RESOURCES DEPARTMENT. ECONOMIC INVESTIGATION. Text in English. 1962. irreg. price varies. **Document type:** *Monographic series, Government.* **Description:** Results of mineral explorations.
Supersedes (in 1974): Fiji. Geological Survey. Economic Investigation (0428-3279)
Indexed: GeoRef, IMMAb, SpeleolAb.
Published by: Mineral Resources Department, P.M. Bag, Suva, Fiji. TEL 679-381611, FAX 679-370039. Ed. Peter Rodda. Circ: 300.

622 RUS ISSN 0015-3273
TN4 CODEN: FTRIAR
➤ **FIZIKO-TEKHNICHESKIE PROBLEMY RAZRABOTKI POLEZNYKH ISKOPAEMYKH.** Text in Russian. 1965. bi-m. USD 91 foreign (effective 2005). adv. index. 120 p./no. 1 cols./p.; reprints avail. **Document type:** *Journal, Academic/Scholarly.* **Description:** Covers theory and application of geomechanics, and mining technology and science.
Related titles: ◆ English ed.: Journal of Mining Science. ISSN 1062-7391.
Indexed: C&ISA, CIN, ChemAb, ChemTitl, E&CAJ, GeoRef, GeotechAb, IMMAb, RefZh, SCOPUS, SolStAb, SpeleolAb.
—CASDDS, East View, INIST, Linda Hall. **CCC.**
Published by: (Rossiiskaya Akademiya Nauk, Sibirskoe Otdelenie, Institut Gornogo Dela/Russian Academy of Sciences, Siberian Branch, Institute of Mining), Izdatel'stvo Sibirskogo Otdeleniya Rossiiskoi Akademii Nauk/Publishing House of the Russian Academy of Sciences, Siberian Branch, Morskoi pr 2, a/ya 187, Novosibirsk, 630090, Russian Federation. TEL 7-3832-300570, FAX 7-3832-333755, psb@ad-sbras.nsc.ru. Ed. M V Kurlenya. Pub. A N Mart'anov. R&P L A Nazarov TEL 7-3832-170636. Adv. contact V N Valiyeva. Circ: 280. **Dist. by:** Informnauka Ltd., Ul Usievicha 20, Moscow 125190, Russian Federation. alfimov@viniti.ru.

622 628.1 USA
FLORIDA INSTITUTE OF PHOSPHATE RESEARCH. PUBLICATIONS. Text in English. irreg.
Published by: Florida Institute of Phosphate Research, 1855 W Main St, Bartow, FL 33830. TEL 863-534-7160, FAX 863-534-7165, http://www.fipr.state.fl.us/. **Dist. by:** NTIS, 5285 Port Royal Rd, Springfield, VA 22161. TEL 800-553-6847.

FRANCE. BUREAU DE RECHERCHES GEOLOGIQUES ET MINIERES. MANUELS ET METHODES. *see* EARTH SCIENCES—Geology

549 DEU ISSN 0173-1785
FRANKFURTER GEOWISSENSCHAFTEN ARBEITEN. SERIE C. MINERALOGIE. Text in German. 1984. irreg.
Indexed: GeoRef.
Published by: Johann Wolfgang Goethe Universitaet Frankfurt am Main, Fachbereich Geowissenschaften, Bockenheimer Landstr. 133, 6, OG, Frankfurt am Main, 60054, Germany. TEL 49-69-798-28128, FAX 49-69-798-28416, dekanat-geowiss@em.uni-frankfurt.de.

FUNDACION BARILOCHE. INSTITUTO DE ECONOMIA DE LA ENERGIA. PUBLICACIONES. *see* ENERGY

622 CHL ISSN 0718-3577
G. & M. GESTION MINERA. Text in Spanish. 2006. bi-m.
Published by: Comunikart Ltda, Ave Salvador 985, Providencia, Santiago, Chile. TEL 56-2-7235703, FAX 56-2-7927830, concacto@comunikart.cl, http://www.comunikart.cl/.

338.7 COD
G E C A M I N E S RAPPORT ANNUEL/G E C A M I N E S ANNUAL REPORT. (Generale des Carrieres et des Mines) Text in English. a. charts; stat.
Related titles: French ed.
Published by: (Generale des Carrieres et des Mines, Division des Relations Publiques COG), Generale des Carrieres et des Mines, BP 450, Lubumbashi, Congo, Dem. Republic.

622 338.2741 GBR
G F M S PRECIOUS METALS QUARTERLY. (Gold Fields Mineral Services) Text in English. 1999. q. GBP 495, USD 995, EUR 695 (effective 2009). charts; stat. back issues avail. **Document type:** *Journal, Trade.* **Description:** Analyzes developments in the markets for gold, silver, platinum, and palladium.
Media: Online - full content.
Published by: Gold Field Mineral Services Ltd., Hedges House, 153 - 155 Regent St, London, W1B 4JE, United Kingdom. TEL 44-20-74781777, FAX 44-20-74781779, info@gfms.co.uk.

GAS SUPPLY AND DEMAND STUDY. *see* PETROLEUM AND GAS

555.8 USA
THE GEMSTONE FORECASTER. Text in English. 1983. q. back issues avail. **Document type:** *Newsletter.* **Description:** Includes topical interviews with leaders in the gemstone industry.
Related titles: Online - full text ed.: ISSN 1520-4707. 1994.
Published by: Gemstone Forecaster, Box 42468, Tucson, AZ 85733. TEL 520-577-6222, FAX 800-458-6453. Ed. Robert Genis.

622 COD
GENERALE DES CARRIERES ET DES MINES. MONOGRAPHIE. Text in French. irreg. (approx. 4/yr.). **Document type:** *Government.*
Formerly: Generale des Carrieres et Mines du Zaire. Monographie
Published by: (Generale des Carrieres et des Mines, Division des Relations Publiques COG), Generale des Carrieres et des Mines, BP 450, Lubumbashi, Congo, Dem. Republic.

622 ITA ISSN 1121-9041
GEOIGEGNERIA AMBIENTALE E MINERARIA. Abbreviated title: G E A M. Text in Multiple languages. 1964. q. EUR 63 domestic; EUR 73 foreign (effective 2010). **Document type:** *Journal, Trade.*
Formerly (until 1991): Associazione Mineraria Subalpina. Bollettino (0392-355X)
Indexed: RefZh.
—Linda Hall.
Published by: Patron Editore, Via Badini 12, Quarto Inferiore, BO 40050, Italy. TEL 39-051-767003, FAX 39-051-768252, info@patroneditore.com, http://www.patroneditore.com.

GEOLOGICA CARPATHICA; international geological journal. *see* EARTH SCIENCES—Geology

GEOLOGICAL SURVEY OF BELGIUM. MEMOIRS/BELGISHE GEOLOGISCHE DIENST. VERHANDELING. *see* EARTH SCIENCES—Geology

GEOLOGISCHES JAHRBUCH. REIHE D: MINERALOGIE. PETROGRAPHIE, GEOCHEMIE, LAGERSTAETTENKUNDE. *see* EARTH SCIENCES—Geology

553 RUS ISSN 0016-7770
TN263 CODEN: GRMAA9
➤ **GEOLOGIYA RUDNYKH MESTOROZHDENII.** Text in Russian; Summaries in English. 1959. bi-m. RUR 1,500 for 6 mos. domestic; USD 398 foreign (effective 2010). adv. bk.rev. bibl.; charts; illus. index. **Document type:** *Journal, Academic/Scholarly.* **Description:** Devoted to the metallic and nonmetallic mineral resources and the conditions of their formation and distribution.
Related titles: Online - full text ed.; ◆ English Translation: Geology of Ore Deposits. ISSN 1075-7015.
Indexed: CIN, ChemAb, ChemTitl, GeoRef, IMMAb, RefZh, SCOPUS, SpeleolAb.
—CASDDS, East View, INIST, Linda Hall. **CCC.**
Published by: (Rossiiskaya Akademiya Nauk/Russian Academy of Sciences), Izdatel'stvo Nauka, Profsoyuznaya ul 90, Moscow, 117864, Russian Federation. TEL 7-095-3347151, FAX 7-095-4202220, secret@naukaran.ru, http://www.naukaran.ru. Ed. N S Bortnikov. Circ: 2,750. **Dist. by:** East View Information Services, 10601 Wayzata Blvd, Minneapolis, MN 55305. TEL 952-252-1201, 800-477-1005, FAX 952-252-1202, info@eastview.com, http://www.eastview.com.

➤ **GEOLOGY AND ORE**; exploration and mining in Greenland. *see* EARTH SCIENCES—Geology

553 RUS ISSN 1075-7015
QE390 CODEN: GODEER
➤ **GEOLOGY OF ORE DEPOSITS.** Text in English. 1959. 6/yr. EUR 1,996, USD 2,425 combined subscription to institutions (print & online eds.) (effective 2012). **Document type:** *Journal, Academic/Scholarly.* **Description:** Devoted to metallic and nonmetallic mineral resources and the conditions of their formation and distribution.
Related titles: Online - full text ed.: ISSN 1555-6476 (from IngentaConnect); ◆ Translation of: Geologiya Rudnykh Mestorozhdenii. ISSN 0016-7770.
Indexed: A22, A26, ASCA, CPEI, CurCont, E01, EngInd, GEOBASE, GeoRef, I05, SCI, SCOPUS, SpeleolAb, W07.
—BLDSC (0411.797000), East View, IE, Ingenta. **CCC.**
Published by: (Rossiiskaya Akademiya Nauk/Russian Academy of Sciences), M A I K Nauka - Interperiodica (Subsidiary of: Pleiades Publishing, Inc.), Profsoyuznaya ul 90, Moscow, 117997, Russian Federation. TEL 7-095-3347420, FAX 7-095-3360666, compmg@maik.ru, http://www.maik.ru. Ed. Nikolai S Bortnikov. **Distr. in the Americas by:** Springer New York LLC, Journal Fulfillment, PO Box 2485, Secaucus, NJ 07096. TEL 212-473-6272, 201-348-4033, 800-777-4643; **Distr. outside of the Americas by:** Springer, Haber Str 7, Heidelberg 69126, Germany. TEL 49-6221-3454303, FAX 49-6221-3454229.

622 551 MEX ISSN 0185-1314
TN4 CODEN: GEOMDZ
GEOMIMET. Text in Spanish. 1973. bi-m. USD 25 to non-members. adv. bk.rev. charts; illus.; stat. reprints avail. **Description:** Covers the energy resources sector of Mexico.
Indexed: C01, CIN, ChemAb, ChemTitl, GeoRef, IBR, IBZ, IMMAb, SpeleolAb.
—CASDDS, INIST.
Published by: Asociacion de Ingenieros de Minas Metalurgistas y Geologos de Mexico A.C., Ave. DEL PARQUE 54, Col Napoles, Del. Benito Juarez, Mexico City, DF 03810, Mexico. TEL 525-5471094, FAX 525-5412592. Ed. Alicia Rico Mendez. Adv. contact Blanca Laura Deochoa. B&W page USD 680, color page USD 850; 230 x 165. Circ: 10,000.

GEOMINAS. *see* EARTH SCIENCES

GEOPHYSICAL DIRECTORY. *see* EARTH SCIENCES—Geophysics

338.2 USA ISSN 0278-3398
TN24.G4
GEORGIA GEOLOGIC SURVEY. INFORMATION CIRCULAR. Text in English. 1933. irreg., latest vol.108, 2004. back issues avail. **Document type:** *Monographic series, Government.* **Description:** Hydrologic or geologic reports discussing regional hydrology or mineral resources.
Former titles (until 1978): Georgia. Geologic and Water Resources Division. Information Circular; (until 1974): Georgia. Earth and Water Division. Information Circular (0271-5201); (until 1972): Georgia. Department of Mines, Mining and Geology. Information Circular (0433-5473); (until 1942): Georgia. Division of Mines, Mining and Geology. Information Circular (0097-6644); (until 1939): Georgia. Division of Geology. Information Circular
Indexed: GeoRef, SpeleolAb.
—Linda Hall.
Published by: Georgia Department of Natural Resources, Georgia Geologic Survey, 2 Martin Luther King, Jr Dr, SE, Ste 1062, E Tower, Atlanta, GA 30334. TEL 404-656-3214, FAX 404-657-8535, ggs.store@dnr.state.ga.us, http://ggsstore.dnr.state.ga.us.

622 NLD ISSN 0960-3182
TN1.A1 CODEN: GGENE3
➤ **GEOTECHNICAL AND GEOLOGICAL ENGINEERING**; an international journal. Text in English. 1983-1990; resumed 1991. 6/yr. EUR 994, USD 1,135 combined subscription to institutions (print & online eds.) (effective 2012). adv. index. back issues avail.; reprint service avail. from PSC. **Document type:** *Journal, Academic/Scholarly.* **Description:** Publishes papers in the areas of soil and rock mechanics as they relate to civil engineering, mining and offshore industries. The emphasis is on the practical aspects of geotechnical engineering and engineering geology, although papers on theoretical and experimental advances in soil and rock mechanics are welcomed.
Formerly: International Journal of Mining and Geological Engineering (0269-0136)
Related titles: Online - full text ed.: ISSN 1573-1529 (from IngentaConnect).
Indexed: A22, A26, A28, AESIS, APA, ASFA, ApMecR, BibLing, BrCerAb, C&ISA, C10, CA, CA/WCA, CIA, CPEI, CerAb, CivEngAb, CorrAb, E&CAJ, E01, E11, E14, EEA, EMA, ESPM, EngInd, EnvEAb, GEOBASE, GeoRef, H15, ICEA, IMMAb, M&TEA, M09, MBF, METADEX, RefZh, SCOPUS, SWRA, SolStAb, SpeleolAb, T02, T04, WAA.
—BLDSC (4158.921500), IE, Infotrieve, Ingenta, INIST, Linda Hall. **CCC.**
Published by: Springer Netherlands (Subsidiary of: Springer Science+Business Media), Van Godewijckstraat 30, Dordrecht, 3311 GX, Netherlands. TEL 31-78-6576050, FAX 31-78-6576474, http://www.springer.com. Eds. Pedro S Seco e Pinto, Tuncer B Edil.

622 658 FRA ISSN 0295-4397
TN2
GERER ET COMPRENDRE/TO MANAGE AND TO UNDERSTAND. Text in French; Summaries in English, German, Russian, Spanish. 1985. q. EUR 79 (effective 2009). adv. **Document type:** *Journal, Trade.* **Description:** Discusses the management, administration, and organization of companies. Publishes studies and testimony of instructors and executives.
Formerly: Annales des Mines. Gerer et Comprendre; Supersedes in part: Annales des Mines (0003-4282)
Indexed: A12, ABIn, FR, GeoRef, IBSS, P48, P51, P52, P53, P54, P56, PQC, SpeleolAb.
—IE, Infotrieve, INIST.
Published by: Editions ESKA, 12 Rue du Quatre-Septembre, Paris, 75002, France. TEL 33-1-40942222, FAX 33-1-40942232, eska@eska.fr. Ed. Francois Baratin. Pub. Serge Kebabtchieff.

GESELLSCHAFT FUER BERGBAU, METALLURGIE, ROHSTOFF- UND UMWELTTECHNIK. SCHRIFTENREIHE. *see* METALLURGY

622 DEU ISSN 0340-7896
TN3 CODEN: GLUEAJ
GLUECKAUF; Fachzeitschrift fuer Rohstoff, Bergbau und Energie. Text in German. 1865. 8/yr. EUR 249; EUR 25 newsstand/cover (effective 2011). adv. bk.rev. bibl.; illus.; pat.; stat.; abstr.; mkt.; maps. 64 p./no. 3 cols./p.; back issues avail.; reprints avail. **Document type:** *Journal, Trade.* **Description:** Covers technical, economic and safety aspects of underground and open-pit mining, including transportation and processing-related topics.
Incorporates (1952-1997): Kali und Steinsalz (0022-7951); (1950-1969): Schlaegel und Eisen (0487-6245); (1926-1943): Elektrizitaet im Bergbau (0724-7915); (18??-1943): Der Bergbau (0373-2371); Which incorporated (1904-193?): Kohle und Erz (0368-637X)
Related titles: CD-ROM ed.: EUR 50 (effective 2002); Russian ed.: ISSN 0130-1233. 1961; Chinese ed.: 1986.
Indexed: A22, A28, APA, BrCerAb, C&ISA, CA/WCA, CIA, CIN, CISA, CerAb, ChemAb, ChemTitl, CivEngAb, CorrAb, DokArb, E&CAJ, E11, EEA, ELLIS, EMA, Englnd, F&EA, FR, GeoRef, H15, IMMAb, ISMEC, M&TEA, M09, MBF, METADEX, SCOPUS, SolStAb, SpeleolAb, T04, TM, WAA.
—BLDSC (4196.000000), CASDDS, IE, Infotrieve, Ingenta, INIST, Linda Hall. **CCC.**
Published by: V G E Verlag GmbH, Postfach 185620, Essen, 45206, Germany. TEL 49-2054-924121, FAX 49-2054-924129, vertrieb@vge.de, http://www.vge.de. Ed. Karsten Gutberlet. Adv. contact Ute Perkovic TEL 49-2054-924130. Circ: 2,000 (paid and controlled).

622 DEU ISSN 0176-4101
GLUECKAUF MINING REPORTER; German Journal for Mining Equipment and Technology. Text in English. 1959. 2/yr. free (effective 2011). adv. abstr.; bibl.; charts; illus.; maps; stat. 60 p./no. 3 cols./p.; **Document type:** *Journal, Trade.*
Former titles (until 1983): Mining Reporter (0343-0073); Bergbau-Reporter (0172-1585); (until 1971): Progress in Mining (0079-6476)
Indexed: CPEI, Englnd, IMMAb, SCOPUS, SpeleolAb.
Published by: V G E Verlag GmbH, Postfach 185620, Essen, 45206, Germany. TEL 49-2054-924121, FAX 49-2054-924129, vertrieb@vge.de. Ed. Karsten Gutberlet. Adv. contact Ute Perkovic TEL 49-2054-924130. Circ: 3,000 (controlled).

622 553.41 AUS ISSN 0816-455X
GOLD GAZETTE. Text in English. 1985. m. AUD 148 domestic; AUD 200 foreign (effective 2008); includes quarterly Asian edition. adv. charts; illus.; stat.; tr.lit. index. **Document type:** *Magazine, Trade.* **Description:** Contains news stories related to the Australian gold industry, stock market news, latest in equipment and technology and some international coverage.
Related titles: Online - full text ed.; Regional ed(s).: Gold Gazette (Asian Edition). ISSN 1327-4430.
Indexed: ABIX, AESIS.
Published by: Resource Information Unit, PO Box 1533, Subiaco, W.A. 6904, Australia. TEL 61-8-93823955, FAX 61-8-93881025, riu@riu.com.au. Ed. Tania Winter. adv.: B&W page AUD 1,881, color page AUD 2,937.

338.2 669 USA ISSN 1058-6164
HG289
GOLD NEWS/NOUVELLES DE L'OR. Text in English. 1976. bi-m. USD 35; USD 45 foreign (effective 1999). back issues avail.
—Linda Hall.
Published by: Gold Institute, Administrative Office/Institut de l'Or, Bureau Administratif, PO Box 14264, Washington, DC 20044-4264. TEL 202-835-0185, FAX 202-835-0155. Ed. Larry Kahaner. Circ: 2,000.

622 USA ISSN 0745-6344
GOLD PROSPECTOR. Text in English. 1968. bi-m. USD 25.95 (effective 2006). adv. **Document type:** *Magazine, Consumer.*
—Ingenta.
Published by: Gold Prospectors Association of America, Inc., PO Box 891509, Temecula, CA 92589. TEL 951-699-4749, 800-551-9707. Ed. Perry Massie. Pub. Tom Kraak. R&P Amber Baker. Adv. contact Adella Sanchez. Circ: 75,000.

622 338.2741 GBR ISSN 1471-2814
GOLD SURVEY (YEAR). Text in English. 1990. a. (plus s-a updates). GBP 325, USD 595, EUR 440 per issue (effective 2009). charts; stat. back issues avail. **Document type:** *Journal, Trade.* **Description:** Presents current picture of each aspect of the gold supply and demand equation in global terms.
Supersedes (in 1999): Gold (1353-0178)
Related titles: Online - full content ed.: GBP 595, EUR 850, USD 975 (effective 1999 & 2000); Chinese ed.: 1997; Russian ed.; Japanese ed.: 1968.
Indexed: AESIS, IMMAb.
—BLDSC (4201.173500).
Published by: Gold Field Mineral Services Ltd., Hedges House, 153 - 155 Regent St, London, W1B 4JE, United Kingdom. TEL 44-20-74781777, FAX 44-20-74781779, info@gfms.co.uk.

662.334 CHN ISSN 1671-251X
CODEN: GZOIBW
➤ **GONGKUANG ZIDONGHUA/INDUSTRY AND MINE AUTOMATION.** Text in Chinese; Abstracts in Chinese, English. 1978. bi-m. CNY 180, USD 180; CNY 15 newsstand/cover (effective 2012). back issues avail. **Document type:** *Journal, Academic/Scholarly.* **Description:** Mainly report achievements and development trends of scientific research, new technology, new product and new technics in the fields of safety monitoring and control, production process automation, communication, power supply, electric drive and control in coal and other mines.
Formerly (until 2001): Meikuang Zidonghua/Coal Mine Automation (1001-439X)
Related titles: Online - full text ed.
Indexed: B21, ESPM, H&SSA.
Published by: Zhong-Mei Ke-gong Jituan Changzhou Zidonghua Yanjiuyuan/China Coal Technology and Engineering Group Corporation, Changzhou Automation Research Institute, 1, Mushu Rd., Changzhou, Jiangsu 213015, China. TEL 86-519-86998098. Eds. Sui-yan Hu, Ying Su. Circ: 6,500.

622 RUS ISSN 1609-9192
TN4
GORNAYA PROMYSHLENNOST'. Text in Russian; Abstracts in English. 1994. bi-m. RUR 1,320 domestic; USD 120 foreign (effective 2004). adv. abstr. **Document type:** *Magazine, Trade.* **Description:** Covers the world mining industry, surface mining, underground mining, preparation, geology, and mining equipment.
Indexed: RefZh.
Address: Leninskii pr-t 6, MGGU, str.2, k. 752, Moscow, 119991, Russian Federation. TEL 7-095-2369770, FAX 7-095-2369771. Ed. Konstantin Anistratov. Adv. contact Elena Anistratova. color page USD 1,500. Circ: 3,000. **Dist. by:** East View Information Services, 10601 Wayzata Blvd, Minneapolis, MN 55305. TEL 952-252-1201, 800-477-1005, FAX 952-252-1202, info@eastview.com, http://www.eastview.com.

622 POL ISSN 1732-6702
TN4 CODEN: GORNDL
➤ **GORNICTWO I GEOINZYNIERIA.** Text in English, Polish; Summaries in English, Polish. 1977. q. EUR 66 foreign (effective 2011). illus.; abstr.; bibl. 70 p./no. 1 cols./p.; **Document type:** *Journal, Academic/Scholarly.* **Description:** Mine excavations' stability, rockbursts, mining influence on the ground surface, mining aerology and mine ventilation, mineral processing, drilling, economics and management in mining, problems of the opencast mining, underground and special construction.
Formerly (until 2003): Akademia Gorniczo-Hutnicza im. Stanislawa Staszica. Gornictwo. Kwartalnik (0138-0990)
Indexed: AgrLib, B22, GeoRef, SpeleolAb.
—CASDDS.
Published by: (Akademia Gorniczo-Hutnicza im. Stanislawa Staszica/ University of Mining and Metallurgy), Wydawnictwo A G H, al Mickiewicza 30, Krakow, 30059, Poland. TEL 48-12-6173228, FAX 48-12-6364038, wydagh@uci.agh.edu.pl. Ed. Jerzy Klich. Circ: 100. **Dist. by:** Ars Polona, Obroncow 25, Warsaw 03933, Poland. TEL 48-22-5098609, FAX 48-22-5098610, arspolona@arspolona.com.pl, http://www.arspolona.com.pl.

622 POL ISSN 0043-2075
CODEN: GROKAF
GORNICTWO ODKRYWKOWE. Text in Polish; Abstracts and contents page in English, German, Polish, Russian. 1959. bi-m. EUR 139 foreign (effective 2006). bk.rev. abstr.; bibl. index, cum.index: 1959-1968. **Document type:** *Journal, Academic/Scholarly.*
Formerly: Wegiel Brunatny Gornictwo Odkrywkowe
Indexed: B22, ChemAb, GeoRef.
—CASDDS.
Published by: Instytut Gornictwa Odkrywkowego Poltegor, ul Parkowa 25, Wroclaw, 51616, Poland. TEL 48-71-3488215, FAX 48-71-3484320, poltegor@igo.wroc.pl, http://poltegor.igo.wroc.pl. Circ: 1,200. **Dist. by:** Ars Polona, Obroncow 25, Warsaw 03933, Poland. TEL 48-22-5098609, FAX 48-22-5098610, arspolona@arspolona.com.pl, http://www.arspolona.com.pl.

622 RUS
GORNYI MIR. Text in Russian. s-a. **Document type:** *Journal, Trade.* **Description:** Publishes news and reviews about the foreign mining problems.
Related titles: ◆ Supplement to: Gornyi Zhurnal. ISSN 0017-2278.
Published by: Izdatel'stvo Ruda i Metally/Ore and Metals Publishers, Leninskii prospekt 6, korpus 1, ofis 622, a/ya 71, Moscow, 119049, Russian Federation. rim@rudmet.ru. Ed. Leonid Vaisberg.

622 RUS
GORNYI VESTNIK. Text in Russian. bi-m. USD 99 in United States.
Published by: Institut Gornogo Dela Imeni, Kryukovskii tup 4, Moscow, 111020, Russian Federation. TEL 7-095-5588046. Ed. A A Skochihskogo. **Dist. by:** East View Information Services, 10601 Wayzata Blvd, Minneapolis, MN 55305. TEL 952-252-1201, 800-477-1005, FAX 952-252-1202, info@eastview.com, http://www.eastview.com.

622 RUS ISSN 0017-2278
TN4 CODEN: GOZHA6
GORNYI ZHURNAL/MINING JOURNAL. Text in Russian. 1825. m. USD 1,194 foreign (effective 2009). adv. bk.rev. charts; illus. index. **Document type:** *Journal, Trade.* **Description:** Devoted to all aspects of deposit development and mining of mineral resources.
Related titles: ◆ Supplement(s): Gornyi Mir; ◆ Eurasian Mining. ISSN 2072-0823.
Indexed: CIN, CISA, ChemAb, ChemTitl, F&EA, GeoRef, IMMAb, Inspec, RASB, RefZh, SCOPUS, SpeleolAb, TM.
—CASDDS, East View, INIST, Linda Hall. **CCC.**
Published by: Izdatel'stvo Ruda i Metally/Ore and Metals Publishers, Leninskii prospekt 6, korpus 1, ofis 622, a/ya 71, Moscow, 119049, Russian Federation. rim@rudmet.ru. Ed. Lev A Puchkov. Circ: 2,500. **Dist. by:** East View Information Services, 10601 Wayzata Blvd, Minneapolis, MN 55305. TEL 952-252-1201, 800-477-1005, FAX 952-252-1202, info@eastview.com, http://www.eastview.com.

333.79 549 POL ISSN 0860-0953
TN95.P7 CODEN: GSMIFB
GOSPODARKA SUROWCAMI MINERALNYMI. Text in Polish. 1985. q. EUR 49 foreign (effective 2006). **Document type:** *Journal, Academic/Scholarly.*
Indexed: B22, GeoRef, RefZh, SCI, SCOPUS, W07.
—BLDSC (4201.675000).
Published by: Polska Akademia Nauk, Instytut Gospodarki Surowcami Mineralnymi i Energia, ul J Wybickiego 7, Krakow, 31261, Poland. TEL 48-12-6323835, FAX 48-12-6323524, centrum@min-pan.krakow.pl, http://www.min-pan.krakow.pl. Ed. Roman Ney. **Dist. by:** Ars Polona, Obroncow 25, Warsaw 03933, Poland. TEL 48-22-5098609, FAX 48-22-5098610, arspolona@arspolona.com.pl, http://www.arspolona.com.pl.

622 USA
GOWER FEDERAL SERVICE - MINING. Text in English. 1962. 2 base vols. plus updates 8/yr. looseleaf. USD 275 base vol(s). (effective 2010). back issues avail. **Document type:** *Report, Government.* **Description:** Publishes decisions of the Department of the Interior, Interior Board of Land Appeals, and reports natural resource information from the Federal Register pertaining to mining issues.
Related titles: Online - full text ed.: 1962.
Published by: Rocky Mountain Mineral Law Foundation, 9191 Sheridan Blvd, Ste 203, Westminster, CO 80031. TEL 303-321-8100, FAX 303-321-7657, info@rmmlf.org, http://www.rmmlf.org.

622 USA
GOWER FEDERAL SERVICE - MISCELLANEOUS LAND DECISIONS. Text in English. 1970. base vol. plus updates 5/yr. looseleaf. USD 165 base vol(s). (effective 2010). back issues avail. **Document type:** *Report, Government.* **Description:** Publishes decisions of the Department of the Interior, Interior Board of Land Appeals, pertaining to public land use issues.
Related titles: Online - full text ed.: 1972.
Published by: Rocky Mountain Mineral Law Foundation, 9191 Sheridan Blvd, Ste 203, Westminster, CO 80031. TEL 303-321-8100, FAX 303-321-7657, info@rmmlf.org, http://www.rmmlf.org.

GOWER FEDERAL SERVICE - ROYALTY VALUATION AND MANAGEMENT. *see* PETROLEUM AND GAS

622 GRL ISSN 1602-8171
GREENLAND MINERAL RESOURCES. FACT SHEET. Text in English. 2002. irreg., latest vol.13. back issues avail. **Document type:** *Monographic series, Government.*
Related titles: Online - full text ed.
Published by: (Denmark. De Nationale Geologiske Undersoegelser for Danmark og Groenland/Geological Survey of Denmark and Greenland DNK), Bureau of Minerals and Petroleum, PO Box 930, Nuuk, 3900, Greenland. TEL 299-346800, FAX 299-324302, bmp@gh.gl, http://www.bmp.gl. Ed. Karsten Secher. **Co-publisher:** De Nationale Geologiske Undersoegelser for Danmark og Groenland/ Geological Survey of Denmark and Greenland.

622 SWE ISSN 0432-7632
GRUVARBETAREN. Text in Swedish. 1904. m. SEK 125. adv.
Former titles (until 1957): Gruvindustriarbetaren; (until 1926): Gruvarbetaren
Published by: Svenska Gruvindustriarbetarefoerbundet, Fack 83, Grangesberg, 77222, Sweden. FAX 240-20728, TELEX 12742 FOTEX S. Circ: 9,000.

622.363 USA
CODEN: MIGYDN
GYPSUM (ONLINE). Text in English. 19??. m. free (effective 2011). **Document type:** *Government.*
Formerly (until 2002): Gypsum (Print) (0193-0001)
Media: Online - full text.
Published by: U.S. Department of the Interior, 1849 C St., NW, Washington, DC 20240. TEL 202-208-3100, http://www.doi.gov.

HARRIS DIRECTORY. MISSOURI MANUFACTURING. *see* BUSINESS AND ECONOMICS—Trade And Industrial Directories

HIRE SOUTH AFRICA. *see* BUILDING AND CONSTRUCTION

HIROSHIMA UNIVERSITY. JOURNAL OF SCIENCE. SERIES C. EARTH AND PLANETARY SCIENCES. *see* EARTH SCIENCES—Geology

HOLMES SAFETY ASSOCIATION. BULLETIN. *see* OCCUPATIONAL HEALTH AND SAFETY

338 JPN
HONPO KOGYO NO SUSEI/MINING YEARBOOK OF JAPAN. Text in Japanese. 1906. a. stat. **Document type:** *Yearbook, Government.*
Published by: Keizai Sangyoushou. Keizai Sangyou Seisakukyoku. Chousa Toukeibu/Ministry of Economy, Trade and Industry. Economic and Industrial Policy Bureau. Research and Statistics Department, 1-3-1 Kasumigaseki, Chiyoda-ku, Tokyo, 100-8902, Japan. TEL 81-3-35019945.

HUA'NAN DIZHI YU KUANGCHAN/GEOLOGY AND MINERAL RESOURCES OF SOUTH CHINA. *see* EARTH SCIENCES—Geology

622.8 AUS ISSN 1036-7454
HUNTER VALLEY COAL REPORT. Text in English. 1991. w. AUD 600 (effective 2008). **Document type:** *Newsletter, Trade.* **Description:** Provides latest information on the domestic and international coal mining industry.
Related titles: E-mail ed.: AUD 1,200 (effective 2008); Online - full text ed.
Published by: C. Randall & Associates, PO Box 683, Newcastle, NSW 2300, Australia. TEL 61-2-49252644, FAX 61-2-49263871, hvcr@colinrandall.com.au, http://www.colinrandall.com.au.

IDAHO. GEOLOGICAL SURVEY. BULLETIN. *see* EARTH SCIENCES—Geology

338.2 553 USA
TN24.I3 CODEN: ILMNAS
ILLINOIS MINERALS. Text in English. 1972. irreg., latest vol.127, 2003. abstr.; bibl.; charts; illus.; stat. back issues avail. **Document type:** *Monographic series, Government.*
Formerly (until 1990): Illinois Minerals Notes (0094-9442); Which was formed by the merger of (1961-1972): Illinois. State Geological Survey. Mineral Economic Briefs (0073-5116); (1963-1972): Illinois. State Geological Survey. Industrial Mineral Notes (0073-4853); Which was formerly (until 1963): Illinois. State Geological Survey. Illinois Industrial Mineral Notes (0270-9929)
Related titles: Online - full text ed.: free (effective 2011).
Indexed: AESIS, SpeleolAb.
—Linda Hall.
Published by: State Geological Survey, 615 E Peabody Dr, Champaign, IL 61820. TEL 217-333-4747, isgs@isgs.illinois.edu, http://www.isgs.illinois.edu/.

622 USA
ILLINOIS MINING INSTITUTE. PROCEEDINGS. Text in English. 1928. a. USD 15; free to members, mining schools and technical libraries. adv. **Document type:** *Proceedings.*
Published by: Illinois Mining Institute, 615 E Peabody, Champaign, IL 61820. TEL 217-867-2791. Ed., R&P, Adv. contact Heinz H Damberger TEL 217-333-5115. Circ: 1,100.

338.270954105 GBR ISSN 1755-781X
INDIA MINING REPORT. Text in English. 2007. q. EUR 820, USD 1,030 combined subscription (print & email eds.) (effective 2010). **Document type:** *Report, Trade.* **Description:** Features latest-available data and forecasts covering all headline indicators for mining; company rankings and competitive landscapes covering mining exploration and production; and analysis of latest industry developments, trends and regulatory issues.
Related titles: E-mail ed.
Indexed: A15, ABIn, B02, B15, B17, B18, G04, I05, P48, P51, P52, P56, PQC.

Published by: Business Monitor International Ltd., Senator House, 85 Queen Victoria St, London, EC4V 4AB, United Kingdom. TEL 44-20-72480468, FAX 44-20-72480467, subs@businessmonitor.com.

INDIAN JOURNAL OF GEOLOGY. *see* EARTH SCIENCES—Geology

549 IND ISSN 2229-3574
TN4 CODEN: INMIAR
INDIAN JOURNAL OF GEOSCIENCES. Text in English. 1947. q. INR 176, USD 10 per issue (effective 2011). bk.rev. charts; illus. back issues avail. **Document type:** *Journal, Government.*
Formerly (until 2009): Indian Minerals (0019-5936)
Indexed: CIN, CRIA, CRICC, ChemAb, ChemTitl, FLUIDEX, GEOBASE, GeoRef, IMMAb, INIS AtomInd, P06, SCOPUS, SpeleolAb.
—CASDDS, Ingenta, Linda Hall.
Published by: Geological Survey of India, 29 Jawaharlal Nehru Rd, Kolkata, West Bengal 700 016, India. TEL 91-33-22861676, FAX 91-33-22861656, dg-gsi@gsi.gov.in.

622 IND ISSN 0445-7897
HD9506.I4 CODEN: IMYBAP
INDIAN MINERALS YEAR BOOK. Text in English. 1959. a., latest 2008. **Document type:** *Yearbook, Government.*
Related titles: Online - full text ed.
Indexed: GeoRef, SpeleolAb.
Published by: Indian Bureau of Mines, c/o Controller General, 2nd Fl, Indira Bhawan, Civil Lines, Nagpur, Maharashtra 440 102, India. TEL 91-712-2560041, FAX 91-712-2565073, cgibm@ibm.mah.nic.in.

622 IND ISSN 0019-5944
HD9506.I4 CODEN: IJACAN
INDIAN MINING & ENGINEERING JOURNAL. Text in English. 1961. m. USD 550 (effective 2011). bk.rev. charts; illus.; mkt.; stat.; tr.lit. index. **Document type:** *Journal, Academic/Scholarly.*
Incorporates: Mineral Markets
Related titles: Microform ed.
Indexed: AESIS, CRIA, CRICC, F&EA, GeoRef, IMMAb, ISA.
—Ingenta, Linda Hall.
Published by: (Mining Engineers' Association of India), Scientific Publishers, 1457, Fishery Tank Rd, Chintamaniswar, Laxmisagarpatna, Bhubaneswar, 751006, India. FAX 91-674-2570906, info@scientificpub.com, http://www.scientificpub.com.

338.021 PRT ISSN 0870-2608
HC394.5.I52
INDICES DA PRODUCAO INDUSTRIAL. Text in Portuguese. 1976. m. **Description:** Provides statistical data on mining and manufactured industry. Includes a comparative table on production in a variety of industrial sectors.
Published by: Instituto Nacional de Estatistica, Av Antonio Jose de Almeida 2, Lisbon, 1000-043, Portugal. TEL 351-21-8426100, FAX 351-21-8426380, ine@ine.pt, http://www.ine.pt.

338.209598 GBR ISSN 1755-7828
INDONESIA MINING REPORT. Text in English. 2007. q. EUR 820, USD 1,030 combined subscription (print & email eds.) (effective 2010). **Document type:** *Report, Trade.* **Description:** Features latest-available data and forecasts covering all headline indicators for mining; company rankings and competitive landscapes covering mining exploration and production; and analysis of latest industry developments, trends and regulatory issues.
Related titles: E-mail ed.
Indexed: A15, ABIn, B02, B15, B17, B18, G04, I05, P48, P51, P52, P56, PQC.
Published by: Business Monitor International Ltd., Senator House, 85 Queen Victoria St, London, EC4V 4AB, United Kingdom. TEL 44-20-72480468, FAX 44-20-72480467, subs@businessmonitor.com.

622 669 553 ITA ISSN 0391-1586
TN4 CODEN: INMRAK
L'INDUSTRIA MINERARIA; miniere e cave, metallurgia, geologia applicata, fonti di energia. Text in Italian. 1927; N.S. 1950. q. adv. bk.rev. charts; illus.; mkt.; stat. index. **Document type:** *Magazine, Trade.*
Former titles (until 1956): Industria Mineraria d'Italia e d'Oltremare (0367-892X); (until 1936): Industria Mineraria (0019-7696)
Indexed: CIN, Cadscan, ChemAb, ChemTitl, GeoRef, LeadAb, SpeleolAb, Zincscan.
—CASDDS, Ingenta.
Published by: Associazione Mineraria Italiana, Via delle Tre Madonne, Rome, 00197, Italy. TEL 39-06-8073045, FAX 39-06-8073385, info@assomineraria.org, http://www.assomineraria.org.

622 ESP ISSN 1137-8042
HD9506.A6 CODEN: INMIDU
INDUSTRIA Y MINERIA. Text in Spanish. 1958. q. adv. bk.rev. abstr.; bibl.; charts; pat.; stat.; tr.lit. index. back issues avail. **Document type:** *Journal, Trade.* **Description:** Covers mining, energy, water, environment, geology, and metallurgy.
Former titles (until 1997): Industria Minera (0210-2307); (until 1968): Consejo Superior de Colegios de Ingenieros de Minas de Espana. Boletin de Informacion (0210-2293)
Indexed: ChemAb, GeoRef, IECT, SpeleolAb.
—BLDSC (4442.780000). **CCC.**
Published by: Consejo Superior de Colegios de Ingenieros de Minas, Rios Rosas, 19, Madrid, 28003, Spain. TEL 34-91-4414611, FAX 34-91-4426109. Ed. Emilio Llorente Gomez. Circ: 4,000.

338.2 660 GBR ISSN 0019-8544
TN1 CODEN: IMINBG
INDUSTRIAL MINERALS. Abbreviated title: I M. Text in English. 1967. m. GBP 898, EUR 1,241, USD 1,716 combined subscription (effective 2010). adv. bk.rev. charts; illus.; stat. index. **Document type:** *Magazine, Trade.* **Description:** Covers non-metallic mineral producers internationally.
Related titles: Online - full text ed.
Indexed: A09, A10, A15, A22, A28, ABIn, AESIS, APA, BrCerAb, BrGeoL, C&ISA, CA/WCA, CBNB, CIA, CIN, CRIA, CRICC, CerAb, ChemAb, ChemTitl, CivEngAb, CorrAb, E&CAJ, E11, EEA, EMA, ESPM, EnvEAb, GeoRef, H15, IMMAb, KES, M&TEA, M09, MBF, METADEX, P&BA, P48, P52, P56, PQC, PROMT, RefZh, SolStAb, SpeleolAb, T04, TM, V04, WAA, WSCA.
—BLDSC (4458.150000), CASDDS, IE, Infotrieve, Ingenta, INIST, Linda Hall. **CCC.**

Published by: Metal Bulletin Plc. (Subsidiary of: Euromoney Institutional Investor Plc.), Nestor House, Playhouse Yard, London, EC4V 5EX, United Kingdom. TEL 44-20-77797390, FAX 44-20-77797389, help@indmin.com, http://www.metalbulletin.com. Ed. Mike O'Driscoll TEL 44-20-78276444. Adv. contact Ismene Clarke TEL 44-20-78275252.

553.029 GBR ISSN 1363-2779
INDUSTRIAL MINERALS DIRECTORY (CD-ROM). Text in English. 1996. irreg. stat. **Document type:** *Directory.* **Description:** Lists producers and processors of non-metallic minerals worldwide.
Media: CD-ROM. **Related titles:** ◆ Print ed.: Industrial Minerals Directory (Print). ISSN 0141-5263.
—CCC.
Published by: Industrial Minerals Information Ltd. (Subsidiary of: Metal Bulletin Plc.), 1 Park House, Park Terr, Worcester Park, Surrey KT4 7HY, United Kingdom. TEL 44-2078-279977, FAX 44-2083-378943, enquiries@indmin.com, http://www.indmin.com. **US subscr. to:** Metal Bulletin Inc., 1250 Broadway, 26th fl., New York, NY 10001-7708. TEL 212-213-6202.

553.029 GBR ISSN 0141-5263
INDUSTRIAL MINERALS DIRECTORY (PRINT). Text in English. 1977. a., latest 2008. adv. **Document type:** *Directory, Trade.* **Description:** Contains all the information of sourcing suppliers, targeting processors of raw materials and much more.
Related titles: ◆ CD-ROM ed.: Industrial Minerals Directory (CD-ROM). ISSN 1363-2779.
Published by: Industrial Minerals Information Ltd. (Subsidiary of: Metal Bulletin Plc.), Nestor House, Playhouse Yard, London, EC4V 5EX, United Kingdom. TEL 44-20-77798989, FAX 44-20-77798294, conferences@indmin.com, http://www.indmin.com. Ed. Mike O'Driscoll TEL 44-20-78276444. Adv. contact Ismene Clarke TEL 44-20-78275252.

622 CAN ISSN 0835-5134
INDUSTRIAL SPECIALTIES NEWS. Text in English. 1987. s-m. looseleaf. USD 557; USD 637 combined subscription print & online eds. (effective 2005). index. back issues avail. **Document type:** *Newsletter, Trade.* **Description:** Contains business news for senior executives in the industrial minerals sector.
Related titles: Online - full text ed.: 1987.
Indexed: PROMT.
—CCC.
Published by: Blendon Information Services, 115 Cliff Drive, Victoria, BC V9C 4A9, Canada. TEL 250-391-8820, FAX 250-391-1787, info@blendon.com, http://www.blendon.com. Ed. Robert V Orchard.

622 DEU ISSN 0341-3489
INDUSTRIE DER STEINE UND ERDEN; Das Fachmagazin fuer Arbeit Sicherheit und Gesundheit. Text in German. 1950. 6/yr. EUR 73.50 domestic; EUR 89 foreign; EUR 19.50 newsstand/cover (effective 2010). adv. **Document type:** *Journal, Trade.*
Indexed: GeoRef, SpeleolAb.
—CCC.
Published by: (Steinbruch Berufsgenossenschaft), Schluetersche Verlagsgesellschaft mbH und Co. KG, Hans-Boeckler-Allee 7, Hannover, 30173, Germany. TEL 49-511-85500, FAX 49-511-85501100, info@schluetersche.de, http://www.schluetersche.de. Ed. Helmut Ehnes. Adv. contact Susann Buglass. B&W page EUR 2,169, color page EUR 3,493; trim 188 x 272. Circ: 8,197 (paid and controlled).

549 CAN ISSN 0712-3620
INFORMATION FOR COLLECTORS/RENSEIGNEMENTS AUX COLLECTIONNEURS. Text in English, French. 1979. a. free (effective 2004). **Description:** Contains information for rock and mineral collectors, including a suggested reading list, a catalogue of shows, and a list of gem, rock and mineral clubs.
Published by: Geological Survey of Canada, 601 Booth St, Ottawa, ON K1A 0E8, Canada. TEL 613-995-4342. **Subscr. to:** Geological Survey of Canada Bookstore, 601 Booth St, Ottawa, ON K1A 0E8, Canada. TEL 613-995-4342, 888-252-4301, FAX 613-943-0646, gscbookstore@nrcan.gc.ca, http://www.nrcan.gc.ca/gsc/bookstore/.

622 BRA ISSN 0101-5931
HD9554.B8
INFORMATIVO ANUAL DA INDUSTRIA CARBONIFERA. Text in Portuguese. 1979. a. USD 20 (effective 1997).
Published by: Departamento Nacional da Producao Mineral, Setor Autarquia Norte, Quadra 1, Bloco B, Brasilia, DF 70040, Brazil. TEL 55-61-224-2670. Ed. Frederico L M Barboza.

622 ITA ISSN 0020-0700
L'INFORMATORE DEL MARMISTA. Text in Italian. 1962. m. EUR 89 domestic; EUR 99 in Europe; EUR 129 elsewhere (effective 2009). adv. bk.rev. stat. **Document type:** *Magazine, Trade.* **Description:** Covers techniques in the manufacturing of marble, precious stones and granite. Includes articles on various equipment and machinery used in this field.
Related titles: Online - full text ed.: EUR 44 (effective 2009).
Published by: Giorgio Zusi Editore, Via Unita d'Italia 278A, Verona, VR 37132, Italy. TEL 39-045-8922292, FAX 39-045-970002, http://www.zusieditore.it. Circ: 8,000.

622 CHL ISSN 0717-0572
INGENIERO ANDINO. Text in Spanish. 1991. w. (English edition bi-w.). USD 600. bk.rev. index. back issues avail. **Document type:** *Newsletter.* **Description:** Reports on mining and energy activities in Chile, Peru and Bolivia.
Related titles: English ed.
Published by: G & T International, Matilde Salamanca 736, Santiago, 09, Chile. TEL 56-2-2098100, FAX 56-2-2098101. Ed. Raul Ferro. Pub. Ricardo Cortes.

622 USA
CODEN: PIBABP
INSTITUTE FOR BRIQUETTING AND AGGLOMERATION. BIENNIAL CONFERENCE. PROCEEDINGS. Text in English. 1947. biennial. free to members (effective 2011). Index. **Document type:** *Proceedings, Academic/Scholarly.* **Description:** Contains about 20 technical papers and technical discussions from the conference.

Former titles (until 1977): Institute for Briquetting and Agglomeration. Biennial Conference. Proceedings (0145-8701); (until 1967): International Briquetting Association. Biennial Conference. Proceedings (0145-9414); (until 1963): International Briquetting Association. Biennial Conference (0895-7878); (until 1961): University of Wyoming. Natural Resources Research Institute. Briquetting Conference. Proceedings; (until 1953): University of Wyoming. Natural Resources Research Institute. Coal Briquetting Conference. Proceedings
Related titles: Online - full text ed.
Indexed: CIN, ChemAb, ChemTitl, IMMAb.
—BLDSC (2023.670000), CASDDS, IE, Ingenta, Linda Hall.
Published by: Institute for Briquetting and Agglomeration, c/o Tom Balzola, PO Box 802, Marquette, MI 49855. iba@charter.net.

622 669 GBR ISSN 1474-9009
TN1 CODEN: TIMNAQ
➤ **INSTITUTE OF MATERIALS, MINERALS AND MINING. TRANSACTIONS. SECTION A: MINING TECHNOLOGY.** Text in English. 1892. q. GBP 275 combined subscription to institutions (print & online eds.); USD 462 combined subscription in United States to institutions (print & online eds.) (effective 2012). adv. bibl.; charts; illus. back issues avail.; reprint service avail. from PSC. **Document type:** *Journal, Academic/Scholarly.* **Description:** Covers to all aspects of underground, opencast and offshore mining operations, including: mining finance, economics and evaluation, mineral resources management, taxation and mining law; planning, development and construction of mines; organization and management; operational techniques; mining machinery; and education and training.
Incorporates in part (1990-2003): Australasian Institute of Mining and Metallurgy. Proceedings (1034-6783); Which superseded in part (in 1989): Australasian Institute of Mining and Metallurgy . Bulletin and Proceedings (0818-3848); Which was formerly (until 1986): A I M M. Bulletin and Proceedings (0817-2668); (until 1984): A I M M. Bulletin (0814-4346); Formerly (until 2001): Institution of Mining and Metallurgy. Transactions. Section A: Mining Industry (0371-7844); Which superseded in part (in 1965): Institution of Mining and Metallurgy. Transactions (0371-7836)
Related titles: Online - full text ed.: ISSN 1743-2863. GBP 252 to institutions; USD 423 in United States to institutions (effective 2012) (from IngentaConnect).
Indexed: A01, A03, A08, A22, A28, AESIS, APA, ASCA, B21, BrCerAb, BrGeoL, BrTechI, C&ISA, CA, CA/WCA, CIA, CPEI, Cadscan, CerAb, ChemAb, CivEngAb, CoppAb, CorrAb, E&CAJ, E11, EEA, EIA, EMA, ESPM, EngInd, EnvAb, EnvEAb, ErgAb, GeoRef, H&SSA, H15, IBR, IBZ, IMMAb, Inspec, LeadAb, M&TEA, M09, MBF, METADEX, PollutAb, RefZh, RiskAb, SCOPUS, SSciA, SWRA, SolStAb, SpeleolAb, T02, T04, WAA, Zincscan.
—BLDSC (8968.400000), IE, Infotrieve, Ingenta, INIST, Linda Hall. **CCC.**
Published by: (Institute of Materials, Minerals and Mining), Maney Publishing, Ste 1C, Joseph's Well, Hanover Walk, Leeds, W Yorks LS3 1AB, United Kingdom. TEL 44-113-2432800, FAX 44-113-3868178, maney@maney.co.uk, http://www.maney.co.uk. Adv. contact Robin Fox TEL 44-20-73060300 ext 231. **Subscr. in N America to:** Maney Publishing, 875 Massachusetts Ave, 7th Fl, Cambridge, MA 02139. TEL 866-297-5154, FAX 617-354-6875, maney@maneyusa.com.

622 669 550 GBR ISSN 0371-7453
TN260 CODEN: TIAEA7
➤ **INSTITUTE OF MATERIALS, MINERALS AND MINING. TRANSACTIONS. SECTION B: APPLIED EARTH SCIENCE.** Text in English. 1892. q. GBP 275 combined subscription to institutions (print & online eds.); USD 462 combined subscription in United States to institutions (print & online eds.) (effective 2012). adv. bibl.; charts; illus. index. back issues avail.; reprint service avail. from PSC. **Document type:** *Journal, Academic/Scholarly.* **Description:** Covers all aspects of the application of the earth sciences in the discovery, exploration, development and exploitation of all forms of mineral resources - from ore mineralogy through remote sensing, photogeology, geochemical and geophysical techniques to physical exploration methods, especially drilling.
Incorporates in part (1990-2003): Australasian Institute of Mining and Metallurgy. Proceedings (1034-6783); Which superseded in part (in 1989): Australasian Institute of Mining and Metallurgy. Bulletin and Proceedings (0818-3848); Which was formerly (until 1986): A I M M. Bulletin and Proceedings (0817-2668); (until 1984): A I M M. Bulletin (0814-4346); Supersedes in part (in 1966): Institution of Mining and Metallurgy. Transactions (0371-7836)
Related titles: Online - full text ed.: ISSN 1743-2758. GBP 252 to institutions; USD 423 in United States to institutions (effective 2012) (from IngentaConnect).
Indexed: A01, A03, A08, A22, A28, AESIS, APA, ASCA, BrCerAb, BrGeoL, BrTechI, C&ISA, CA, CA/WCA, CIA, CIN, CPEI, Cadscan, CerAb, ChemAb, ChemTitl, CivEngAb, CorrAb, E&CAJ, E11, EEA, EIA, EMA, ESPM, EngInd, EnvAb, EnvEAb, ErgAb, GEOBASE, GeoRef, H15, IBR, IBZ, IMMAb, ISMEC, ISR, LeadAb, M&TEA, M09, MBF, METADEX, MinerAb, PetrolAb, PollutAb, RefZh, SCOPUS, SPPI, SSciA, SWRA, SolStAb, SpeleolAb, T02, T04, WAA, Zincscan.
—BLDSC (8968.500000), CASDDS, IE, Infotrieve, Ingenta, INIST, Linda Hall, PADDS. **CCC.**
Published by: (Institute of Materials, Minerals and Mining), Maney Publishing, Ste 1C, Joseph's Well, Hanover Walk, Leeds, W Yorks LS3 1AB, United Kingdom. TEL 44-113-2432800, FAX 44-113-3868178, maney@maney.co.uk, http://www.maney.co.uk. Ed. Dr. Iain McDonald. Adv. contact Robin Fox TEL 44-20-73060300 ext 231. **Subscr. in N America to:** Maney Publishing, 875 Massachusetts Ave, 7th Fl, Cambridge, MA 02139. TEL 866-297-5154, FAX 617-354-6875, maney@maneyusa.com

622 669 GBR ISSN 0371-9553
TN496 CODEN: TMEMAB

➤ **INSTITUTE OF MATERIALS, MINERALS AND MINING. TRANSACTIONS. SECTION C: MINERAL PROCESSING & EXTRACTIVE METALLURGY.** Text in English. 1892. q. GBP 275 combined subscription to institutions (print & online eds.); USD 462 combined subscription in United States to institutions (print & online eds.) (effective 2012). adv. bibl.; charts; illus. index. back issues avail.; reprint service avail. from PSC. **Document type:** *Journal, Academic/Scholarly.* **Description:** Covers the scientific, engineering and economic aspects of the preparation, separation, extraction and purification of ores, metals and mineral products by physical and chemical methods, embracing both practical plant operations and the laboratory development of new processes.
Incorporates in part (in 2003): Australasian Institute of Mining and Metallurgy. Proceedings (1034-6783); Which superseded in part (in 1989): Australasian Institute of Mining and Metallurgy . Bulletin and Proceedings (0818-3848); Which was formerly (until 1986): A I M M. Bulletin and Proceedings (0817-2668); (until 1984): A I M M. Bulletin (0814-4346); Supersedes in part (in 1966): Institution of Mining and Metallurgy. Transactions (0371-7836)
Related titles: Online - full text ed.: ISSN 1743-2855. GBP 252 to institutions; USD 423 in United States to institutions (effective 2012) (from IngentaConnect).
Indexed: A01, A03, A08, A10, A22, A28, AESIS, APA, ASCA, BrCerAb, BrGeoL, BrTechI, C&ISA, CA, CA/WCA, CEA, CIA, CPEI, Cadscan, CerAb, ChemAb, ChemTitl, CivEngAb, CorrAb, E&CAJ, E11, E14, EEA, EIA, EMA, ESPM, EngInd, EnvAb, EnvEAb, ErgAb, GeoRef, H15, IBR, IBZ, IMMAb, Inspec, LeadAb, M&TEA, M09, MBF, METADEX, SCOPUS, SolStAb, SpeleolAb, T02, T04, TCEA, V03, WAA, Zincscan.
—BLDSC (8968.600000), CASDDS, IE, Infotrieve, Ingenta, INIST, Linda Hall. **CCC.**
Published by: (Australasian Institute of Mining and Metallurgy AUS, Institute of Materials, Minerals and Mining), Maney Publishing, Ste 1C, Joseph's Well, Hanover Walk, Leeds, W Yorks LS3 1AB, United Kingdom. TEL 44-113-2432800, FAX 44-113-3868178, maney@maney.co.uk, http://www.maney.co.uk. Ed. Dr. R Vasant Kumar. Adv. contact Robin Fox TEL 44-20-73060300 ext 231. **Subscr. in N America to:** Maney Publishing, 875 Massachusetts Ave, 7th Fl, Cambridge, MA 02139. TEL 866-297-5154, FAX 617-354-6875, maney@maneyusa.com

622 ZAF ISSN 0020-2983
CODEN: JMSVAW

INSTITUTE OF MINE SURVEYORS OF SOUTH AFRICA. JOURNAL/ INSTITUUT VAN MYNOPMETERS VAN SUID-AFRIKA. JOERNAAL. Text in English. 1923. q. adv. charts; illus. index every vol. covering 8 issues.
Indexed: ISAP.
—Ingenta, Linda Hall.
Published by: Institute of Mine Surveyors of South Africa, 11 Burnham Rd, Mulbarton, Johannesburg, South Africa. TEL 27-11-4987682, FAX 27-11-4987681, http://www.ims.org.za. Circ: 600.

622 669 IND ISSN 0257-442X
TN1 CODEN: JIEDEK

➤ **INSTITUTION OF ENGINEERS (INDIA). MINING ENGINEERING DIVISION. JOURNAL.** Text in English. 1920. s-a. INR 600 (effective 2011). adv. charts; illus. index. **Document type:** *Journal, Academic/ Scholarly.*
Formerly (until 1984): Institution of Engineers (India). Mining and Metallurgy Division. Journal (0020-3394)
Related titles: Online - full text ed.
Indexed: ChemAb, GeoRef, Inspec, SCOPUS, SpeleolAb.
—CASDDS, INIST, Linda Hall.
Published by: (Mining Engineering Division), The Institution of Engineers (India), 8 Gokhale Rd, Kolkata, West Bengal 700 020, India. TEL 91-33-40155400, technical@ieindia.org.

622 669 PER ISSN 1607-5617

INSTITUTO GEOLOGICO MINERO Y METALURGICO. BOLETIN. SERIE D. ESTUDIOS REGIONALES. Text in Spanish. m.
Formerly (until 1997): Instituto Geologico Minero y Metalurgico. Boletin. Serie D. Estudios Especiales (0253-4592)
Related titles: Online - full text ed.: Boletin Informativo Electronico Mensual.
Indexed: C01, GeoRef, Z01.
—Linda Hall.
Published by: Instituto Geologico Minero y Metalurgico, Ave Canada, 1470, San Borja, Lima, 41, Peru. TEL 51-1-2242965, FAX 51-1-2253063, http://www.ingemmet.gob.pe/.

622 330 HKG

INTERFAX. CHINA MINING AND METALS WEEKLY. Text in English. w. price varies. **Document type:** *Bulletin, Trade.* **Description:** Covers China's metals sector, including coal, precious metals, rare earth, alloys, non-ferrous and ferrous metals. Includes daily updates on prices from local metals exchanges, as well as statistics on imports and exports.
Related titles: Online - full text ed.
Indexed: A15, P48, P51, P52, P56.
Published by: Interfax China, Ste 1601, Wilson House 19-27, Wyndham St Central, Hong Kong, Hong Kong. TEL 852-25372262, FAX 852-25372264. **Dist. by:** Interfax America, Inc., 3025 S Parker Rd, Ste 737, Aurora, CO 80014. TEL 303-368-1421, FAX 303-368-1458, america@interfax-news.com, http://www.interfax.com.

622 669 RUS

INTERFAX. RUSSIA METALS & MINING WEEKLY. Text in English. w. price varies. **Document type:** *Bulletin, Trade.* **Description:** Outlines the range of events in the ferrous and non-ferrous industries, gold and gem mining, as well as mining companies.
Formerly: Interfax. Mining & Metals Report (1072-2645)
Related titles: Online - full content ed.
Indexed: P48, P51, P52, P56.
Published by: Interfax Ltd., 1-ya Tverskaya-Yamskaya, dom 2, stroenie 1, Moscow, 127006, Russian Federation. TEL 7-095-2509840, FAX 7-095-2509727, info@interfax.ru, http://www.interfax.ru. **Dist. elsewhere by:** Interfax America, Inc., 3025 S Parker Rd, Ste 737, Aurora, CO 80014. TEL 303-368-1421, FAX 303-368-1458, http://www.interfax.com; **Dist. in Germany Austria and Switzerland by:** Interfax Deutschland GmbH, 54, Taunusstrasse, Frankfurt 61476, Germany. TEL 49-6171-695750, FAX 49-6171-989995; **Dist. in Western Europe by:** Interfax Europe Ltd., 2-3 Philpot Lane, 3rd Fl, London EC3M 8AQ, United Kingdom. TEL 44-20-76210595, FAX 44-20-79294263.

622.342 RUS

INTERFAX. RUSSIA PRECIOUS METALS & GEMS WEEKLY. Text in English. w. price varies. **Document type:** *Bulletin, Trade.* **Description:** Covers precious metals and gemstones markets in Russia and the Commonwealth of Independent States.
Related titles: Online - full text ed.
Indexed: A15, P48, P51, P52.
Published by: Interfax Ltd., 1-ya Tverskaya-Yamskaya, dom 2, stroenie 1, Moscow, 127006, Russian Federation. TEL 7-095-2509840, FAX 7-095-2509727, info@interfax.ru, http://www.interfax.ru. **Dist. by:** Interfax America, Inc., 3025 S Parker Rd, Ste 737, Aurora, CO 80014. TEL 303-368-1421, FAX 303-368-1458, america@interfax-news.com, http://www.interfax.com.

622 USA ISSN 1526-405X

INTERNATIONAL CALIFORNIA MINING JOURNAL; the magazine for the independent miner. Key Title: I C M J's Prospecting and Mining Journal. Text in English. 1931. m. USD 25.95 domestic; USD 39.50 in Canada; USD 43.50 per issue elsewhere (effective 2006). adv. bk.rev. charts; mkt.; stat. 64 p./no. 3 cols./p.; **Document type:** *Magazine, Trade.* **Description:** Contains articles on mining methods, technology and equipment. A financial section on precious metals and mining stocks. Current information on laws and regulations affecting mining.
Formerly (until 1994): California Mining Journal (0008-1299)
Related titles: Online - full text ed.
Indexed: CalPI, GeoRef, MinerAb, SpeleolAb.
—Ingenta.
Published by: International California Mining Journal, Inc., PO Box 2260, Aptos, CA 95001-2260. TEL 831-479-1500, FAX 831-479-4385. Ed., Pub., R&P Scott M Harn. adv.: B&W page USD 452.40, color page USD 652.40. Circ: 10,000 (paid).

622 GBR ISSN 1747-3292

INTERNATIONAL COAL REPORT (ONLINE). Text in English. 200?. d. USD 2,135 combined subscription (Online & E-mail eds.) (effective 2010). adv. **Document type:** *Newsletter, Trade.*
Media: Online - full text. **Related titles:** E-mail ed.; Fax ed.: International Coal Report Fax Weekly. GBP 550 with subscr. to ICR (effective 2001).
Published by: Platts (Subsidiary of: McGraw-Hill Companies, Inc.), 20 Canada Sq, 12th Fl, Canary Wharf, London, E14 5LH, United Kingdom. TEL 44-20-71766111, FAX 44-20-71766144, support@platts.com. Adv. contact Ann Forte.

622 338.2 USA

INTERNATIONAL COAL REVIEW MONTHLY. Text in English. 19??. m. USD 850 to non-members; free to members (effective 2011). **Document type:** *Report, Trade.* **Description:** Contains digest of current U.S. coal trade statistics, including monthly and year to date summaries of coal exports and imports and their value.
Former titles (until 1995): International Coal Review; (until 1979): Coal Export Review
Indexed: SRI.
Published by: National Mining Association, 101 Constitution Ave, NW, Ste 500E, Washington, DC 20001. TEL 202-463-2600, FAX 202-463-2666, MPhelleps@nma.org.

INTERNATIONAL DIRECTORY OF URANIUM PRODUCERS AND PROCESSORS. *see* ENERGY—Nuclear Energy

INTERNATIONAL DREDGING REVIEW. *see* ENGINEERING—Hydraulic Engineering

INTERNATIONAL EROSION CONTROL ASSOCIATION. CONFERENCE PROCEEDINGS (CD-ROM). *see* CONSERVATION

INTERNATIONAL EROSION CONTROL ASSOCIATION. PRODUCTS AND SERVICES DIRECTORY. *see* BUSINESS AND ECONOMICS—Trade And Industrial Directories

553.029 GBR ISSN 1364-7512
TN808.G6

INTERNATIONAL GUIDE TO THE COALFIELDS. Text in English. 1948. a. GBP 150 per issue (effective 2009). **Document type:** *Directory.* **Description:** Provides listings of mine operators and suppliers alike as well as contains details on producing companies, coal mines, coal consumers, and a comprehensive 'buyers guide' with cross referencing to products and services guide.
Formerly (until 1996): Guide to the Coalfields (0072-8713)
Related titles: CD-ROM ed.
—CCC.
Published by: Tradelink Publications Ltd, British Fields, Ollerton Rd, Tuxford, Newark, Notts NG22 0PQ, United Kingdom. TEL 44-1777-871007, FAX 44-1777-872271, info@tradelinkpub.co.uk, http://www.tradelinkpub.co.uk.

INTERNATIONAL JOURNAL OF COAL GEOLOGY. *see* EARTH SCIENCES—Geology

622.33 USA ISSN 1939-2699
CODEN: IJCPGA

➤ **INTERNATIONAL JOURNAL OF COAL PREPARATION AND UTILIZATION.** Text in English. 1984. bi-m. GBP 939 combined subscription in United Kingdom to institutions (print & online eds.); EUR 1,241, USD 1,550 combined subscription to institutions (print & online eds.) (effective 2012). adv. bk.rev. back issues avail.; reprint service avail. from PSC. **Document type:** *Journal, Academic/ Scholarly.* **Description:** Publishes original research papers, short communications, review articles, and symposium announcements covering all aspects of coal preparation.
Formerly (until 2008): Coal Preparation (0734-9343)
Related titles: Microform ed.; Online - full text ed.: ISSN 1545-5831. GBP 846 in United Kingdom to institutions; EUR 1,117, USD 1,395 to institutions (effective 2012) (from IngentaConnect).
Indexed: A01, A03, A08, A22, A28, AESIS, APA, BrCerAb, C&ISA, C33, CA, CA/WCA, CIA, CPEI, CerAb, ChemAb, CivEngAb, CorrAb, CurCont, E&CAJ, E01, E04, E05, E11, E14, EEA, EMA, ESPM, EngInd, EnvAb, EnvEAb, H15, M&TEA, M09, MBF, METADEX, P26, P52, P54, P56, PQC, SCI, SCOPUS, SolStAb, T02, T04, W07, WAA.
—BLDSC (4542.172280), IE, Infotrieve, Ingenta, INIST, Linda Hall. **CCC.**
Published by: Taylor & Francis Inc. (Subsidiary of: Taylor & Francis Group), 325 Chestnut St, Ste 800, Philadelphia, PA 19106. TEL 215-625-2940, 800-354-1420, orders@taylorandfrancis.com, http://www.taylorandfrancis.com. Ed. B K Parekh. Adv. contact Linda Hann TEL 44-1344-779945.

622 669 NLD ISSN 0301-7516
CODEN: IJMPBL

➤ **INTERNATIONAL JOURNAL OF MINERAL PROCESSING.** Text in Dutch. 1974. 16/yr. EUR 2,056 in Europe to institutions; JPY 272,900 in Japan to institutions; USD 2,299 elsewhere to institutions (effective 2012). bk.rev. bibl.; charts; illus. back issues avail. **Document type:** *Journal, Academic/Scholarly.* **Description:** Covers all aspects of the processing of solid-mineral materials, such as metallic and non-metallic ores, coals and other solid sources of secondary materials, etc.
Related titles: Microform ed.: (from PQC); Online - full text ed.: (from IngentaConnect, ScienceDirect).
Indexed: A01, A03, A08, A22, A26, A28, AESIS, APA, ASCA, BrCerAb, C&ISA, C33, CA, CA/WCA, CIA, CIN, CPEI, CRIA, Cadscan, CerAb, ChemAb, ChemTitl, CivEngAb, CorrAb, CurCont, E&CAJ, E11, EEA, EMA, ESPM, EngInd, EnvAb, EnvEAb, F&EA, GeoRef, H15, I05, IMMAb, ISMEC, ISR, Inspec, LeadAb, M&TEA, M09, MBF, METADEX, MSCI, RefZh, S01, SCI, SCOPUS, SolStAb, SpeleolAb, T02, T04, W07, WAA, Zincscan.
—BLDSC (4542.362000), CASDDS, IE, Infotrieve, Ingenta, INIST, Linda Hall. **CCC.**
Published by: Elsevier BV (Subsidiary of: Elsevier Science & Technology), Radarweg 29, PO Box 211, Amsterdam, 1000 AE, Netherlands. TEL 31-20-4853911, FAX 31-20-4852457, JournalsCustomerServiceEMEA@elsevier.com, http://www.elsevier.nl. Eds. D R Nagaraj, K Heiskanen. **Subscr. to:** Elsevier, Subscription Customer Service, 6277 Sea Harbor Dr, Orlando, FL 32887-4800. TEL 407-345-4020, 877-839-7126, FAX 407-363-1354.

629.8 549 600 CHN ISSN 1674-4799
TS300 CODEN: JSTBFO

INTERNATIONAL JOURNAL OF MINERALS METALLURGY AND MATERIALS. Text in English. 1994. bi-m. EUR 743, USD 1,003 combined subscription to institutions (print & online eds.) (effective 2012). 80 p./no.; back issues avail. **Document type:** *Journal, Academic/Scholarly.* **Description:** Publishes theoretical and experimental studies related to the fields of minerals, metallurgy and materials.
Formerly: University of Science and Technology Beijing. Journal (1005-8850)
Related titles: Online - full content ed.: ISSN 1869-103X; ◆ Chinese ed.: Beijing Keji Daxue Xuebao. ISSN 1001-053X.
Indexed: A22, A28, APA, BrCerAb, C&ISA, CA/WCA, CIA, CPEI, CerAb, CivEngAb, CorrAb, E&CAJ, E11, EEA, EMA, ESPM, EngInd, EnvEAb, H15, M&TEA, M09, MBF, METADEX, MSCI, RefZh, SCI, SCOPUS, SolStAb, T04, W07, WAA.
—BLDSC (4912.130000), East View, IE, Linda Hall. **CCC.**
Published by: Beijing Keji Daxue/Beijing University of Science and Technology, Editorial Board of Journal of University of Science & Technology Beijing, 30 Xueyuan Lu, Haidian-qu, Beijing, 100083, China. TEL 86-10-62332875, FAX 86-10-62332875 ext 804, http://www.ustb.edu.cn/. **Co-publisher:** Springer.

622 620 GBR ISSN 1754-890X
TN1

➤ **INTERNATIONAL JOURNAL OF MINING AND MINERAL ENGINEERING.** Text in English. 2008 (Sep.). 4/yr. EUR 494 to institutions (print or online ed.); EUR 672 combined subscription to institutions (print & online eds.) (effective 2012). charts; illus.; abstr.; bibl. back issues avail. **Document type:** *Journal, Academic/Scholarly.* **Description:** Fosters innovative solutions to design efficient mining systems and mineral processing plants.
Related titles: Online - full text ed.: ISSN 1754-8918 (from IngentaConnect).
Indexed: A26, A28, APA, B21, BrCerAb, C&ISA, CA/WCA, CIA, CerAb, CivEngAb, CorrAb, E&CAJ, E08, E11, EEA, EMA, ESPM, EnvEAb, H&SSA, H15, M&TEA, M09, MBF, METADEX, PollutAb, RiskAb, SWRA, SolStAb, T04, WAA.
—BLDSC (4542.363900), IE, Linda Hall. **CCC.**
Published by: Inderscience Publishers, PO Box 735, Olney, Bucks MK46 5WB, United Kingdom. TEL 44-1234-240519, FAX 44-1234-240515, editorial@inderscience.com. Ed. Dr. Vladislav Kecojevic. **Subscr. to:** World Trade Centre Bldg, 29 Rte de Pre-Bois, Case Postale 856, Geneva 15 1215, Switzerland. FAX 41-22-7910885, subs@inderscience.com.

622.31 GBR ISSN 1748-0930
TN291

➤ **INTERNATIONAL JOURNAL OF MINING, RECLAMATION AND ENVIRONMENT.** Cover title: I J S M. Text in English. 1994. q. GBP 427 combined subscription in United Kingdom to institutions (print & online eds.); EUR 566, USD 710 combined subscription to institutions (print & online eds.) (effective 2012). adv. back issues avail.; reprint service avail. from PSC. **Document type:** *Journal, Academic/ Scholarly.* **Description:** Examines all aspects of surface mining technology and waste disposal systems relating to coals, oilsands, industrial minerals and metalliferous deposits. Includes computer applications and automation processes.
Formerly (until 2006): International Journal of Surface Mining, Reclamation and Environment (1389-5265); Which was formed by the merger of (1992-1993): International Journal of Environmental Issues in Minerals and Energy Industry (0928-4206); (1987-1993): International Journal of Surface Mining and Reclamation (0920-8119)
Related titles: Online - full text ed.: ISSN 1748-0949. GBP 385 in United Kingdom to institutions; EUR 510, USD 640 to institutions (effective 2012) (from IngentaConnect).
Indexed: A01, A03, A05, A08, A22, AS&TA, AS&TI, ASFA, C10, CA, CPEI, E01, E04, E05, E14, ESPM, EngInd, G02, GEOBASE, GeoRef, IMMAb, Inspec, PollutAb, RefZh, SCOPUS, SSciA, SWRA, SpeleolAb, T02.
—BLDSC (4542.364300), IE, Infotrieve, Ingenta, Linda Hall. **CCC.**

Published by: (American Society of Mining and Reclamation USA), Taylor & Francis Ltd. (Subsidiary of: Taylor & Francis Group), 4 Park Sq, Milton Park, Abingdon, Oxfordshire OX14 4RN, United Kingdom. TEL 44-20-70176000, FAX 44-20-70176336, subscriptions@tandf.co.uk, http://www.taylorandfrancis.com. Ed. Raj K Singhal. Adv. contact Linda Hann. **Subscr. to:** Journals Customer Service, Sheepen Pl, Colchester, Essex CO3 3LP, United Kingdom. TEL 44-20-70175544, FAX 44-20-70175198, tf.enquiries@tfinforma.com.

622 GBR ISSN 1365-1609
TA706
➤ **INTERNATIONAL JOURNAL OF ROCK MECHANICS AND MINING SCIENCES.** Text in English. 1997. 8/yr. EUR 3,144 in Europe to institutions; JPY 417,700 in Japan to institutions; USD 3,515 elsewhere to institutions (effective 2012). adv. bk.rev. abstr.; charts; illus. index. back issues avail.; reprints avail. **Document type:** *Journal, Academic/Scholarly.* **Description:** Features original research, new developments and case studies in rock mechanics and rock engineering for mining and civil applications.
Supersedes in part (in 1996): International Journal of Rock Mechanics and Mining Sciences and Geomechanics Abstracts (0148-9062); Which was formed by the merger of (1964-1973): International Journal of Rock Mechanics and Mining Sciences (0020-7624); Geomechanics Abstracts; Which was formerly (until 1973): Rock Mechanics Abstracts (0035-7456)
Related titles: Microfilm ed.: (from PQC); Online - full text ed.: ISSN 1873-4545 (from IngentaConnect, ScienceDirect).
Indexed: A01, A03, A08, A22, A26, ApMecR, B21, C&ISA, CA, CISA, CPEI, Cadscan, CurCont, E&CAJ, ESPM, EngInd, F&EA, GEOBASE, GeoRef, GeotechAb, H&SSA, HRIS, I05, ICEA, IMMAb, ISR, Inspec, LeadAb, MSCI, PetrolAb, RefZh, S01, SCI, SCOPUS, SWRA, SoftAbEng, SolStAb, SpeleolAb, T02, TM, W07, Zincscan.
—BLDSC (4542.540000), IE, Infotrieve, Ingenta, INIST, Linda Hall. **CCC.**
Published by: Pergamon (Subsidiary of: Elsevier Science & Technology), The Blvd, Langford Ln, East Park, Kidlington, Oxford OX5 1GB, United Kingdom. TEL 44-1865-843000, FAX 44-1865-843010, JournalsCustomerServiceEMEA@elsevier.com. Ed. R W Zimmerman. **Subscr. to:** Elsevier BV, Radarweg 29, PO Box 211, Amsterdam 1000 AE, Netherlands. TEL 31-20-4853757, FAX 31-20-4853432, http://www.elsevier.nl.

549 DEU ISSN 0074-7017
INTERNATIONAL MINERALOGICAL ASSOCIATION. PROCEEDINGS OF MEETINGS. (Proceedings usually published in host country) Text in German. 1959. irreg. (every 4 yrs.). price varies. adv. **Document type:** *Proceedings.*
Indexed: MinerAb, SpeleolAb.
Published by: International Mineralogical Association, c/o Dr. S.S. Hafner, Institute of Mineralogy, Univ. of Marburg, Meerweinstr, Marburg, 35043, Germany. TELEX 482-372-UMR-D.

INTERNATIONAL PEAT JOURNAL. *see* BIOLOGY—Botany

553 USA ISSN 1075-7961
TP325 CODEN: PICNE4
INTERNATIONAL PITTSBURGH COAL CONFERENCE. PROCEEDINGS. Text in English. 1977. a. USD 50 combined subscription per issue (print & CD-ROM eds.) (effective 2011). back issues avail. **Document type:** *Monographic series, Academic/ Scholarly.*
Formerly (until 1988): Pittsburgh Coal Conference. Proceedings (1075-8313); Which was formed by the merger of (1977-1984): International Conference on Coal Gasification, Liquefaction and Conversion to Electricity. Proceedings (0733-8988); Whch was formerly (1974-1977): Symposium on Coal Gasification and Liquefaction. Proceedings; (19??-1984): Industrial Coal Utilization Symposium. Proceedings
Related titles: CD-ROM ed.
Indexed: GeoRef.
—BLDSC (1086.727000). **CCC.**
Published by: International Pittsburgh Coal Conference, University of Pittsburgh, 3700 O'Hara St, 1249 Benedum Hall, Pittsburgh, PA 15261. TEL 412-624-7440, FAX 412-624-1480, ipcc@pitt.edu, http://www.engr.pitt.edu/~pccwww/.

INTERNATIONAL SOCIETY OF EXPLOSIVES ENGINEERS. ANNUAL MEMBERSHIP DIRECTORY AND DESK REFERENCE. *see* ENGINEERING—Chemical Engineering

INTERNATIONAL SOCIETY OF EXPLOSIVES ENGINEERS. CONFERENCES ON EXPLOSIVES AND BLASTING TECHNIQUE. PROCEEDINGS. *see* ENGINEERING—Chemical Engineering

INTERNATIONAL SOCIETY OF EXPLOSIVES ENGINEERS. SYMPOSIUM ON EXPLOSIVES AND BLASTING RESEARCH. PROCEEDINGS. *see* ENGINEERING—Chemical Engineering

556 338.2 CIV
IVORY COAST. DIRECTION DES MINES ET DE LA GEOLOGIE. RAPPORT PROVISOIRE SUR LES ACTIVITIES DU SECTEUR. Text in French. irreg.
Indexed: SpeleolAb.
Published by: Direction des Mines et de la Geologie, c/o Ministry of Mining, BP V50, Abidjan, Ivory Coast.

IZVESTIYA VYSSHIKH UCHEBNYKH ZAVEDENII. GEOLOGIYA I RAZVEDKA. *see* EARTH SCIENCES—Geology

IZVESTIYA VYSSHIKH UCHEBNYKH ZAVEDENII. GORNYI ZHURNAL. *see* EARTH SCIENCES—Geology

622 JAM ISSN 0254-5241
J B I JOURNAL. Text in English, Spanish. 1980. a. USD 12.50 to individuals; USD 20 to institutions (effective 2000). adv. bk.rev. **Description:** Contains original socio-economic, legal and technical articles, highlighting development issues as they affect the Third World, with special reference to aluminium but not excluding other mineral industries.
Supersedes (1976-1979): J B I Digest
Indexed: A28, APA, BrCerAb, C&ISA, CA/WCA, CIA, CerAb, CivEngAb, CorrAb, E&CAJ, E11, EEA, EMA, H15, IMMAb, M&TEA, M09, MBF, METADEX, SolStAb, T04, WAA.
Published by: Jamaica Bauxite Institute, Hope Gardens, PO Box 355, Kingston, 6, Jamaica. TEL 809-92-72073, FAX 809-92-71159, TELEX 2309 JAMBAUX JA. Circ: 300.

622 JAM ISSN 1018-2160
J B I QUARTERLY; the Jamaica bauxite alumina sector. Text in English. 1991. q. JMD 250 domestic; USD 20 foreign (effective 2000). adv. charts; mkt.; stat. back issues avail. **Document type:** *Government.* **Description:** Provides relevant data on the Jamaican bauxite and alumina sector.
Related titles: E-mail ed.; Fax ed.
Published by: Jamaica Bauxite Institute, Hope Gardens, PO Box 355, Kingston, 6, Jamaica. TEL 876-92-72073, FAX 876-92-71159, genjbc@cwjamaica.com. Adv. contact Dennis E Morris.

622 DEU
JAHRBUCH DER EUROPAEISCHEN ENERGIE- UND ROHSTOFFWIRTSCHAFT; Bergbau, Erdoel und Erdgas, Petrochemie, Elektrizitaet, Umweltschutz. Text in German. 1893. a. EUR 128 per issue; EUR 253 combined subscription (print & CD-ROM eds.) (effective 2011). adv. charts; illus.; mkt.; stat.; maps. 1200 p./no. 2 cols./p.; **Document type:** *Yearbook, Trade.* **Description:** Contains information on more than 4,000 companies, associations, organizations and statutory bodies.
Former titles: Jahrbuch fuer Bergbau, Erdoel und Erdgas, Petrochemie, Elektrizitaet, Umweltschutz (0943-9056); (until 1991): Jahrbuch fuer Bergbau, Oel und Gas, Elektrizitaet, Chemie (0179-3675); (until 1984): Jahrbuch fuer Bergbau, Energie, Mineraloel und Chemie (0075-255X); (until 1966): Jahrbuch des Deutschen Bergbaus (0446-3781)
Related titles: CD-ROM ed.: EUR 151 per issue (effective 2011); English ed.: Yearbook of the European Energy and Raw Materials Industry.
Indexed: GeoRef, RASB, SpeleolAb.
Published by: (Bundesverband der Energie- und Wasserwirtschaft), V G E Verlag GmbH, Postfach 185620, Essen, 45206, Germany. TEL 49-2054-924121, FAX 49-2054-924129, vertrieb@vge.de, http://www.vge.de. Ed. Ines Henning. Adv. contact Ute Perkovic TEL 49-2054-924130. Circ: 3,000 (paid and controlled).

JAPAN METAL BULLETIN (ONLINE EDITION). *see* METALLURGY

338.2095205 GBR ISSN 1755-7984
JAPAN MINING REPORT. Text in English. 2007. a. EUR 820, USD 1,030 combined subscription per issue (print & email eds.) (effective 2010). **Document type:** *Report, Trade.* **Description:** Features latest-available data and forecasts covering all headline indicators for mining, company rankings and competitive landscapes covering mining exploration and production; and analysis of latest industry developments, trends and regulatory issues.
Related titles: E-mail ed.
Indexed: A15, ABIn, B01, B02, B15, B17, B18, G04, I05, P48, P51, P52, P56, PQC.
Published by: Business Monitor International Ltd., Senator House, 85 Queen Victoria St, London, EC4V 4AB, United Kingdom. TEL 44-20-72480468, FAX 44-20-72480467, subs@businessmonitor.com.

622 669.1 SWE ISSN 1101-5284
JERNKONTORETS BERGSHISTORISKA UTSKOTT. H. Text in Swedish. 1971. irreg. **Document type:** *Monographic series, Academic/Scholarly.*
Formerly (until 1988): Jernkontorets Forskning. Serie H (0280-137X)
Published by: Jernkontoret/Swedish Steel Producers' Association, PO Box 1721, Stockholm, 11187, Sweden. TEL 46-8-6791700, FAX 46-8-6112089, office@jernkontoret.se, http://www.jernkontoret.se.

JERNKONTORETS FORSKNING. SERIE D. *see* METALLURGY

622.33 CHN ISSN 1006-6772
JIEJINGMEI JISHU/CLEAN COAL TECHNOLOGY. Text in Chinese. 1995. q. USD 53.40 (effective 2009). back issues avail. **Document type:** *Journal, Academic/Scholarly.*
Related titles: Online - full text ed.
—East View.
Published by: Meitan Kexue Yanjiu Zongyuan, Heping Li Qingniangou Lu, 5, Beijing, 100013, China. TEL 86-10-84262927, FAX 86-10-84262340.

662.34 CHN ISSN 1001-1250
JINSHU KUANGSHAN/METAL MINE. Text in Chinese. 1966. bi-m. USD 80.40 (effective 2009). **Document type:** *Academic/Scholarly.*
Related titles: Online - full text ed.
Indexed: ESPM, PollutAb, SCOPUS.
—East View.
Published by: Maanshan Kuangshan Yanjiuyuan, 9 Shiju Bei Lu, Maanshan, Anhui 243004, China. TEL 86-555-2481894, 86-555-2404668, FAX 86-555-2481894, cmmmic@mail.ahwhptt.net.cn. Ed. Pingxi Lei.

JOURNAL OF APPLIED GEOPHYSICS. *see* EARTH SCIENCES—Geophysics

622 AUS ISSN 1448-4471
JOURNAL OF AUSTRALASIAN MINING HISTORY. Text in English. 2003. a. (Sep.). membership. bk.rev. **Document type:** *Journal, Academic/Scholarly.* **Description:** Covers all aspects of mining history, mining archaeology and heritage.
Indexed: AusPAIS.
Published by: Australian Mining History Association, c/o Mel Davies, Business School, Economics M251, University of Western Australia, Crawley, W.A. 6009, Australia. TEL 61-8-64882939, FAX 61-8-64881016, mel.davies@uwa.edu.au, http://amha.asn.au/index.html.

622.33 CHN ISSN 1006-9097
TN809.C47
JOURNAL OF COAL SCIENCE & ENGINEERING. Text in English. 1995. 4/yr. EUR 518, USD 778 combined subscription to institutions (print & online eds.) (effective 2012). reprint service avail. from PSC. **Document type:** *Journal, Academic/Scholarly.*
Related titles: Online - full text ed.: ISSN 1866-6566.
Indexed: A22, E01, GeoRef, SCOPUS.
—East View, IE. **CCC.**
Published by: Zhongguo Meitan Xuehui/China Coal Society, Hepingli, 5, Qingnian Guodong Lu, Beijing, 100013, China. TEL 86-10-84262930, FAX 86-10-84262340. **Co-publisher:** Springer.

THE JOURNAL OF EXPLOSIVES ENGINEERING. *see* ENGINEERING—Chemical Engineering

▼ **JOURNAL OF GEOGRAPHY AND MINING RESEARCH.** *see* EARTH SCIENCES—Geology

622 338.2 662 IND ISSN 0022-2755
TN1 CODEN: JMMFAM
JOURNAL OF MINES, METALS AND FUELS. Text in English. 1953. m. INR 1,200 (effective 2011). bk.rev. charts; illus.; tr.lit. 2 cols./p.; **Document type:** *Journal, Trade.* **Description:** Covers mineral exploration, coal and metal mining, petroleum and natural gas, mineral beneficiation, coal preparation, mining equipment and research, smelting and refining, fuel technology, education and research.
Formerly (until 1959): Indian Mining Journal (0367-8911)
Indexed: A22, AESIS, CIN, CISA, CPEI, CRIA, CRICC, ChemAb, ChemTitl, EngInd, F&EA, GeoRef, IMMAb, INIS AtomInd, SCOPUS, SpeleolAb.
—CASDDS, Ingenta, INIST, Linda Hall.
Published by: Books & Journals Private Ltd., 6-2 Madan St, 3rd Fl, Kolkata, West Bengal 700 072, India. TEL 91-33-22126526, FAX 91-33-22126348, books@satyam.net.in. **Subscr. to:** I N S I O Scientific Books & Periodicals, PO Box 7234, Indraprastha HPO, New Delhi 110 002, India.

622 550 NGA ISSN 1116-2775
TN275.A1 CODEN: JMIGA5
➤ **JOURNAL OF MINING AND GEOLOGY.** Text mainly in English; Text occasionally in French; Summaries in English. 1963. s-a. NGN 1,000 domestic; USD 60 foreign (effective 2004). adv. bk.rev. abstr.; charts; illus.; stat. biennial index. back issues avail.; reprints avail. **Document type:** *Journal, Academic/Scholarly.* **Description:** Takes a multidisciplinary look at the geosciences, mining, metallurgy, materials science, and environmental studies.
Former titles (until 1988): Nigerian Journal of Mining and Geology (0022-2763); (until 1982): Nigerian Mining and Geosciences Society. Journal; (until 1965): Nigerian Mining, Geological and Metallurgical Society. Journal
Related titles: Online - full text ed.
Indexed: ChemAb, GEOBASE, GeoRef, INIS AtomInd, SCOPUS, SpeleolAb.
—CASDDS.
Published by: Nigerian Mining and Geosciences Society, University of Ibadan, Department of Geology, Ibadan, Oyo, Nigeria. TEL 234-2-8101100, FAX 234-2-8103034, TELEX CAMPUS 31128 NG, IBA LIB 31233 NG, uigislab@skannet.com. Ed. A Azubuike Elueze. Adv. contact A. Azubuike Elueze. page USD 4,000. Circ: 1,000 (paid and controlled).

622 SRB ISSN 1450-5959
JOURNAL OF MINING AND METALLURGY. SECTION A: MINING. Text in English. 1964. irreg. **Document type:** *Journal, Academic/Scholarly.*
Supersedes in part (in 1997): Glasnik Rudarstva i Metalurgije (0354-0545); Which was formerly (until 1990): Tehnicki Fakultet i Institut za Bakar Bor. Zbornik Radova (0351-2150)
Published by: Technical Faculty Bor, Vojske Jugoslavije 12, Bor, 19210. TEL 381-30-424547, office@tf.bor.ac.yu, http://www.tf.bor.ac.yu.

622 CHE ISSN 2075-1656
▼ ➤ **JOURNAL OF MINING ENGINEERING AND MINERAL PROCESSING.** Text in English. forthcoming 2011. q. free (effective 2011). **Document type:** *Journal, Academic/Scholarly.*
Media: Online - full text.
Published by: M D P I AG, Postfach, Basel, 4005, Switzerland. TEL 41-61-6837734, FAX 41-61-3028918, http://www.mdpi.org/.

622 551 USA ISSN 1062-7391
TN4 CODEN: JMCIEJ
➤ **JOURNAL OF MINING SCIENCE.** Text in English. 1965. bi-m. EUR 4,626, USD 5,025 combined subscription to institutions (print & online eds.) (effective 2012). 115 p./no.; back issues avail.; reprint service avail. from PSC. **Document type:** *Journal, Academic/Scholarly.* **Description:** Covers all areas of mining engineering, including papers on the mechanical properties, pressure distribution, brittleness, drillability, and blast behavior of rock in mines.
Formerly (until 1992): Soviet Mining Science (0038-5581)
Related titles: Microfilm ed.: (from PQC); Online - full text ed.: ISSN 1573-8736 (from IngentaConnect); ◆ Russian ed.: Fiziko-Tekhnicheskie Problemy Razrabotki Poleznykh Iskopaemykh. ISSN 0015-3273.
Indexed: A01, A03, A08, A22, A26, A28, APA, ASCA, Agr, BibLing, BrCerAb, C&ISA, CA, CA/WCA, CIA, CPEI, CerAb, CivEngAb, CorrAb, CurCont, E&CAJ, E01, E11, E14, EEA, EIA, EMA, ESPM, EnerInd, EngInd, EnvEAb, GeoRef, H15, M&TEA, M09, MBF, METADEX, MSCI, S01, SCI, SCOPUS, SolStAb, SpeleolAb, T02, T04, W07, WAA.
—BLDSC (0415.210000), East View, IE, Infotrieve, Ingenta, INIST, Linda Hall. **CCC.**
Published by: Springer New York LLC (Subsidiary of: Springer Science+Business Media), 233 Spring St, New York, NY 10013. TEL 212-460-1500, FAX 212-460-1575, service@springer-ny.com, http://www.springer.com. Ed. Victor N Oparin.

622 340 ZAF ISSN 1562-3181
JUTASTAT MINING AND MINERALS LIBRARY. Variant title: Juta's Mining Library. Text in English. 1999. m. ZAR 2,038 single user; ZAR 1,030 per additional user (effective 2006).
Media: Online - full text. **Related titles:** CD-ROM ed.: ISSN 1561-9982.
Published by: Juta & Company Ltd., Juta Law, PO Box 14373, Lansdowne, 7779, South Africa. TEL 27-21-7970121, FAX 27-11-7970121, cserv@juta.co.za, http://www.jutalaw.co.za.

622.33 CHN ISSN 1001-3946
KANCHA KEXUE JISHU/SITE INVESTIGATION - SCIENCE AND TECHNOLOGY. Text in Chinese; Abstracts in Chinese, English. 1983. bi-m. USD 18 (effective 2009). **Document type:** *Bibliography.* **Description:** Covers engineering geology, geotechnical engineering, hydrogeology, engineering surveying, and engineering geophysical prospecting.
Related titles: Online - full text ed.
Published by: Yejin Gongye Bu, Kancha Kexue Jishu Yanjiusuo/Ministry of Metallurgic Industry, Institute of Prospecting Science and Technology, 51 Dongfeng Zhonglu, Baoding, Hebei 071067, China. TEL 0312-336001, FAX 0312-334561. Ed. Chen Tingzhang. Pub. Gao Xianning. adv.: page USD 500. Circ: 3,000.

622 333.7 658 JPN ISSN 1348-6012
KANKYOU SHIGEN KOUGAKU/RESOURCES PROCESSING. Text in Japanese. 1954. q. **Document type:** *Journal, Academic/Scholarly.*
Former titles (until 2003): Shigen Shori Gijutsu (0912-4764); (until 1985): Fusen/Flotation (0427-7775)
Related titles: Online - full text ed.: ISSN 1349-9262. 2004.

Indexed: ESPM, GEOBASE, PollutAb, SSciA.
—CCC.
Published by: Kankyou Shigen Kougakkai/Resources Processing Society of Japan, c/o Nakanishi Printing Co., Ogawa Higashi-iru, Shimodachiuri, Kamigyo-ku, Kyoto, 602-8048, Japan. TEL 81-75-4153661, FAX 81-75-4153662, rpsj@nacos.com, http://www.nacos.com/rpsj/.

662 POL
TP315 CODEN: KSMGAA
KARBO. Text in Polish; Summaries in English, French, German, Russian. 1956. m. EUR 125 foreign (effective 2006). adv. bk.rev. **Document type:** *Magazine, Trade.*
Former titles: Karbo - Energochemia - Ekologia (1230-0446); (until 1992): Koks, Smola, Gaz (0023-2823)
Indexed: B22, CIN, ChemAb, ChemTitl, F&EA.
—CASDDS, INIST, Linda Hall.
Published by: (Instytut Chemicznej Przerobki Wegla), Wydawnictwo Gornicze, ul Plebiscytowa 36, Katowice, 40041, Poland. TEL 48-32-7572152, FAX 48-32-7572043, wydawnictwo.wg@w-g.com.pl. Ed. Andrzej Karbownik. Circ: 500 (paid). **Dist. by:** Ars Polona, Obroncow 25, Warsaw 03933, Poland. TEL 48-22-5098609, FAX 48-22-5098610, arspolona@arspolona.com.pl, http://www.arspolona.com.pl.

338.2095845 GBR ISSN 1755-7836
KAZAKHSTAN MINING REPORT. Text in English. 2007. q. EUR 820, USD 1,030 combined subscription (print & email eds.) (effective 2010). **Document type:** *Report, Trade.* **Description:** Features latest-available data and forecasts covering all headline indicators for mining; company rankings and competitive landscapes covering mining exploration and production; and analysis of latest industry developments, trends and regulatory issues.
Related titles: E-mail ed.
Indexed: A15, ABIn, B02, B15, B17, B18, G04, I05, P48, P51, P52, P56, PQC.
Published by: Business Monitor International Ltd., Senator House, 85 Queen Victoria St, London, EC4V 4AB, United Kingdom. TEL 44-20-72480468, FAX 44-20-72480467, subs@businessmonitor.com.

KOMPASS; Zeitschrift fuer Sozialversicherung im Bergbau. *see* INSURANCE

669 622 KAZ ISSN 0202-1382
TN265 CODEN: KIMSDD
KOMPLEKSNOE ISPOL'ZOVANIE MINERAL'NOGO SYR'YA/COMPLEX USE OF NATIONAL RESOURCES. Text in Russian. 1978. m. USD 362 foreign (effective 2005). **Document type:** *Journal, Academic/Scholarly.* **Description:** Publishes research papers on mining and metallurgy.
Indexed: AICP, CIN, ChemAb, ChemTitl, GeoRef, INIS AtomInd, SpeleolAb.
—BLDSC (0091.793300), CASDDS, East View, INIST, Linda Hall. **CCC.**
Published by: (Kazakhstan Respublikasy Gylym Zane Zogary Bilim Ministrliginn. Kazakhstan Respublikasy Ulttyk Gylym Akademiasynyn/Ministry of Education and Science of the Republic of Kazakhstan, National Academy of Sciences of the Republic of Kazakhstan, Institute of Metallurgy and Ore Benecation), Gylym, Pushkina 111-113, Almaty, 480100, Kazakhstan. **Dist. by:** East View Information Services, 10601 Wayzata Blvd, Minneapolis, MN 55305. TEL 952-252-1201, 800-477-1005, FAX 952-252-1202, info@eastview.com, http://www.eastview.com.

KUANGCHAN BAOHU YU LIYONG/CONSERVATION AND UTILIZATION OF MINERAL RESOURCES. *see* CONSERVATION

622 CHN ISSN 1674-7801
KUANGCHAN KANCHA/MINERAL EXPLORATION. Text in Chinese. 1998. bi-m. **Document type:** *Journal, Academic/Scholarly.*
Formerly: Yantu Gongchengjie/Geotechnical Engineering World (1009-5098)
Published by: Youse Jinshu Kuangchan Dizhi Diaocha Zhongxin/China Non-ferrous Metals Resource Geological Survey, Anwai Beiyuan no.5 yuan, 4-qu, Chaoyang-qu, Beijing, 100012, China.

549 CHN ISSN 0258-7106
TN101 CODEN: KUDIDM
KUANGCHUANG DIZHI/MINERAL DEPOSITS. Text in Chinese. 1982. bi-m. **Document type:** *Journal, Academic/Scholarly.*
Related titles: Online - full text ed.
Indexed: A22, A28, APA, BrCerAb, C&ISA, CA/WCA, CIA, CerAb, CivEngAb, E&CAJ, E11, EEA, EMA, ESPM, EnvEAb, H15, M&TEA, M09, MBF, METADEX, RefZh, SolStAb, T04.
—BLDSC (5776.775000), IE, Linda Hall.
Published by: Zhongguo Dizhi Kexueyuan, Kuangchuang Ziyuan Yanjiusuo/Chinese Academy of Geological Sciences, Institute of Mineral Resources, Baiwanzhuang Rd. 26, Beijing, 100037, China. TEL 86-10-68327284, 86-10-68999546, http://imr.cags.ac.cn/. **Co-sponsor:** Zhongguo Dizhi Xuehui, Kuangchuang Dizhi Zhuanye Weiyuanhui.

622.33 526.3 CHN ISSN 1001-358X
CODEN: KUCEEG
➤ **KUANGSHAN CELIANG/MINE SURVEYING.** Text in Chinese. 1973. q. USD 31.20 (effective 2009). adv. bk.rev. abstr.; bibl.; charts; illus. back issues avail. **Document type:** *Academic/Scholarly.*
Related titles: CD-ROM ed.; E-mail ed.; Fax ed.; Online - full text ed.
Published by: Meitan Kexueyuan, Tangshan Fenyuan/China Coal Research Institute, No 21, Xinhuanxi Rd, Tangshan, Hebei 063012, China. TEL 86-315-2822145, FAX 86-315-2829275. Eds. Cui Jixian, Sun Fuxing. R&P Jen Sun. Adv. contact Fuxing Sun. Circ: 3,000.

622.33 551 CHN ISSN 1001-5892
KUANGSHAN DIZHI. Text in Chinese. q.
Indexed: GeoRef, SpeleolAb.
Published by: Zhongguo Dizhi Xuehui, Kuangshan Dizhi Zhuanye Weiyuanhui, Sanlidian, Guilin, Guangxi 541004, China. TEL 444987.

622 621.9 CHN ISSN 1001-3954
KUANGSHAN JIXIE/MINING & PROCESSING EQUIPMENT. Text in Chinese; Abstracts in English. 1973. m. USD 160.80 (effective 2009). adv. bk.rev. 80 p./no.; **Document type:** *Journal, Trade.* **Description:** Covers mining and tunneling, hoisting and winching, crushing and grinding, and other aspects of mining and processing equipment.
Related titles: CD-ROM ed.; Online - full text ed.
—East View.

Published by: Luoyang Kuangshan Jixie Yanjiusuo, Chongqing Rd, Luoyang, Henan 471039, China. TEL 86-379-4221660 ext 2706, FAX 86-379-4219734, ksjx@public2.lytt.ha.cn. Ed. Xingcai Liu. Adv. contact Huijie Li. B&W page CNY 1,000, color page CNY 6,500. Circ: 8,000. **Dist. overseas by:** China International Book Trading Corp, 35 Chegongzhuang Xilu, Haidian District, PO Box 399, Beijing 100044, China.

549 CHN ISSN 1000-4734
QE351 CODEN: KUXUEN
KUANGWU XUEBAO/ACTA MINERALOGICA SINICA. Text in Chinese. 1981. q. USD 35.60 (effective 2009). **Document type:** *Journal, Academic/Scholarly.*
Related titles: Online - full text ed.
Indexed: GeoRef.
—BLDSC (0638.705000), East View.
Address: Guanshui Lu 46-hao, Guiyang, Guizhou-sheng 550002, China. TEL 86-851-589-1352, kwxb@ms.gyig.ac.cn. Ed. Guang-Chi Tu. **Dist. by:** China International Book Trading Corp, 35 Chegongzhuang Xilu, Haidian District, PO Box 399, Beijing 100044, China. TEL 86-10-68412045, FAX 86-10-68412023, cibtc@mail.cibtc.com.cn, http://www.cibtc.com.cn.

622 669 CHN ISSN 0253-6099
TN4 CODEN: KUGODL
KUANGYE GONGCHENG/MINING AND METALLURGICAL ENGINEERING. Text in Chinese; Abstracts in English. 1963. bi-m. USD 31.20 (effective 2009). 72 p./no.; **Document type:** *Journal, Academic/Scholarly.*
Related titles: Online - full text ed.: ISSN 1671-8550.
Indexed: A28, APA, BrCerAb, C&ISA, CA/WCA, CIA, CIN, CerAb, ChemAb, ChemTitl, CivEngAb, CorrAb, E&CAJ, E11, EEA, EMA, ESPM, EnvEAb, H15, IMMAb, M&TEA, M09, MBF, METADEX, SCOPUS, SolStAb, T04, WAA.
—CASDDS, East View, Linda Hall.
Published by: (Zhongguo Jinshu Xuehui/Chinese Society for Metals), Kuangye Gongcheng, 35, Nanshengli Lu, Ansha, Hunan 114001, China. TEL 86-412-5537630, FAX 86-412-5538649. **Dist. overseas by:** China International Book Trading Corp, 35 Chegongzhuang Xilu, Haidian District, PO Box 399, Beijing 100044, China. **Co-sponsor:** Changsha Kuangye Yanjiuyuan.

622 CHN ISSN 1674-5876
CODEN: XKUXEM
KUANGYE GONGCHENG YANJIU/MINERAL ENGINEEERING RESEACH. Text in Chinese; Abstracts in English. 1983. q. CNY 10 newsstand/cover (effective 2010). adv. **Document type:** *Journal, Academic/Scholarly.* **Description:** Covers mine engineering, drilling, coalfield geology and prospecting, machinery, automation, architecture, management, and the chemical coal industry.
Former titles (until 2009): Hunan Keji Daxue Xuebao (Ziran Kexue Ban)/Hunan University of Science & Technology. Journal (Natural Science Edition) (1672-9102); (until 2003): Xiangtan Kuangye Xueyuan Xuebao/Xiangtan Mining Institute. Journal (1000-9930)
Related titles: Online - full text ed.
Indexed: CIN, ChemAb, GeoRef, SCOPUS, SpeleolAb.
—BLDSC (4336.872250), CASDDS.
Published by: Hunan Keji Daxue Qikanshe, Xiangtan, 411201, China. TEL 86-731-58290354, xuebaoz@hnust.edu.cn, http://www.hnust.edu.cn/.

622 CHN ISSN 1009-5683
KUANGYE KUAIBAO/EXPRESS INFORMATION OF MINING INDUSTRY. Text in Chinese. 1984. m. CNY 10 newsstand/cover (effective 2006). **Document type:** *Journal, Academic/Scholarly.*
Related titles: Online - full text ed.
Published by: Maanshan Kuangye Yanjiuyuan, 9, Hubei Lu, 158 Xinxiang, Maanshan, 243004, China. TEL 86-555-2404809, FAX 86-555-2475796.

338.2 CAN ISSN 1912-1326
KUANGYE TOUZI ZHINAN/MINING INVESTMENT GUIDE. Text in Chinese, English. 2002. a., latest 2007, May. **Document type:** *Directory, Trade.*
Published by: N A I Interactive Ltd., # 510 - 1199 W Pender St, Vancouver, BC V6E 2R1, Canada. TEL 604-488-8878, 866-833-5517, FAX 604-488-0868, gil@na-investor.com, http://www.naiinteractive.com/index.asp.

KYOTO UNIVERSITY. FACULTY OF SCIENCE. MEMOIRS. SERIES OF GEOLOGY AND MINERALOGY. *see* EARTH SCIENCES—Geology

LANDESAMT FUER GEOLOGIE, ROHSTOFFE UND BERGBAU BADEN-WUERTTEMBERG. ABHANDLUNGEN. *see* EARTH SCIENCES

LANDESMUSEUM JOANNEUM. REFERAT FUER GEOLOGIE UND PALAEONTOLOGIE. MITTEILUNGEN. *see* PALEONTOLOGY

LANDLINE; keeping environmental professionals in touch. *see* ENVIRONMENTAL STUDIES

622 USA ISSN 1526-3762
THE LATIN AMERICA MINING RECORD/PERIODICO DE MINERIA LATINO AMERICANA. Text in English, Spanish. 1994. m. USD 70 domestic; USD 75 foreign (effective 2000). adv. back issues avail. **Document type:** *Magazine, Trade.* **Description:** Covers exploration, discovery, development, production, joint ventures, acquisitions, operating results, stock quotations, and Latin American currencies.
Published by: Howell International Enterprises, PO Box 1630, Castle Rock, CO 80104. TEL 303-663-7820, FAX 303-663-7823. Ed., Pub. Don E Howell. adv.: B&W page USD 1,567, color page USD 1,870; trim 9.75 x 12.75. Circ: 10,000.

622 CHL ISSN 0717-0580
HD9506.L29
LATINOMINERIA. Text in Spanish. 1991. m. free domestic to qualified personnel; CLP 13,000 domestic; USD 70 in South America and United States; USD 85 in Central America and Canada; USD 100 elsewhere (effective 2003). adv. bk.rev. charts; illus. index. back issues avail.
Published by: (G & T International), Editec Ltda., Avenida del Condor 844, Oficina 205, Ciudad Empresarial, Huechuraba, Santiago, 09, Chile. TEL 56-2-7574210, FAX 56-2-75754201, editec@editec.cl, http://www.editec.cl. Eds. Ricardo Cortes, Roly Solis. adv.: B&W page USD 2,700, color page USD 3,400; trim 8.13 x 10.88. Circ: 10,000.

622 AUT ISSN 0259-0751
LEOBENER GRUENE HEFTE. NEUE FOLGE. Text in German. irreg., latest vol.10, 1992. price varies. **Document type:** *Monographic series.*
Published by: Montanhistorischer Verein fuer Oesterreich, Postfach 1, Leoben, St 8704, Austria.

LIBERIA. MINISTRY OF LANDS, MINES AND ENERGY. ANNUAL REPORT. *see* ENGINEERING—Civil Engineering

LIGHT RAILWAYS; Australia's magazine of industrial and narrow gauge railways. *see* TRANSPORTATION—Railroads

622 GUY
LINMINE NEWS. Text in English. 1971. q. free. bk.rev. **Document type:** *Corporate.* **Description:** Promotes the bauxite industry. Contains current and major events and developmental issues.
Former titles (until 1992): Guymine News; Guybau News
Published by: (Public Relations Section), Linden Mining Enterprise Ltd., PO Box 27, Mackenzie, Linden, Guyana. FAX 592-4-2795, TELEX GY-2245. Ed. Jenny George Parkinson. Circ: 3,000.

LIST OF MINERAL AND PETROLEUM LICENSES IN GREENLAND. *see* PETROLEUM AND GAS

LITHOLOGY AND MINERAL RESOURCES. *see* EARTH SCIENCES—Geology

LITHOS. *see* EARTH SCIENCES—Geology

552 622 RUS ISSN 0024-497X
QE420 CODEN: LPIKAQ
LITOLOGIYA I POLEZNYE ISKOPAEMYE. Text in Russian. 1963. bi-m. USD 304 foreign (effective 2010). bk.rev. bibl. **Document type:** *Journal, Academic/Scholarly.* **Description:** Reviews a wide range of problems related to the formation of sedimentary rocks and ores.
Related titles: Online - full text ed.; ◆ English Translation: Lithology and Mineral Resources. ISSN 0024-4902.
Indexed: CIN, ChemAb, ChemTitl, GeoRef, IMMAb, RefZh, SpeleolAb.
—BLDSC (0098.250000), CASDDS, East View, INIST, Linda Hall. **CCC.**
Published by: (Rossiiskaya Akademiya Nauk, Geologicheskii Institut), Izdatel'stvo Nauka, Profsoyuznaya ul 90, Moscow, 117864, Russian Federation. TEL 7-095-3347151, FAX 7-095-4202220, secret@naukaran.ru, http://www.naukaran.ru. Ed. V N Holodov. **Dist. by:** East View Information Services, 10601 Wayzata Blvd, Minneapolis, MN 55305. TEL 952-252-1201, 800-477-1005, FAX 952-252-1202, info@eastview.com, http://www.eastview.com.

622.184 USA ISSN 1544-7774
LOCATING GOLD, GEMS, & MINERALS; the prospector's guide. Text in English. 1947. a. membership. adv. **Document type:** *Guide, Consumer.* **Description:** Covers UPI's claims and restrictions to modes of recovery.
Former titles: Locating Gold (0024-5658); Panning Gold
Published by: United Prospectors Inc., c/o Denise Matula, 19131 Vaughn Ave, Castro Valley, CA 94546. http://www.unitedprospectors.com/. Ed. Walter J Price. Circ: 200.

533.61 USA ISSN 0069-4592
TN941 CODEN: LGCRAM
LOUISIANA GEOLOGICAL SURVEY. CLAY RESOURCES BULLETIN. Text in English. 1967. irreg., latest vol.3, 1972. price varies. **Document type:** *Monographic series, Government.*
Indexed: GeoRef, SpeleolAb.
—Linda Hall.
Published by: Louisiana Geological Survey, 208 Howe-Russell, Louisiana State University, Baton Rouge, LA 70803. TEL 225-578-5320, FAX 225-578-3662, pat@lgs.bri.lsu.edu, http://www.lgs.lsu.edu.

LUXEMBOURG. SERVICE CENTRAL DE LA STATISTIQUE ET DES ETUDES ECONOMIQUES. INDICATEURS RAPIDES. SERIE C: EMPLOI ET CHOMAGE - SIDERURGIE - FINANCES- TRANSPORT ET COMMERCE. *see* BUSINESS AND ECONOMICS—Abstracting, Bibliographies, Statistics

622 550 AUS ISSN 1326-3544
TN122.S7 CODEN: SGQGAY
M E S A JOURNAL. (Mines and Energy South Australia) Text in English. 1996. q. free (effective 2009). back issues avail. **Document type:** *Journal, Government.* **Description:** Provides current information and news items on all aspects of the South Australian mining and mineral industry, energy, and the geosciences.
Formed by the merger of (1962-1996): Quarterly Geological Notes (0584-3219); (1990-1992): Mines and Energy Review, South Australia (1034-8794); (1976-1995): Mineral Industry Quarterly (0313-6086); Which was formerly (until 1988): Mineral Resources Review (0026-525X); (until 1967): Mining Review (0365-6985); (until 1917): Review of Mining Operations; (until 1904): Short review of Mining Operations in the State of South Australia
Related titles: Online - full text ed.
Indexed: AESIS, ARI, CBPI, CRIA, GeoRef, IMMAb, SpeleolAb.
—BLDSC (5682.287200), CASDDS, Ingenta, Linda Hall. **CCC.**
Published by: Primary Industries and Resources South Australia, Level 7, 101 Grenfell St, GPO Box 1671, Adelaide, SA 5001, Australia. TEL 61-8-84633067, FAX 61-8-82263177. Ed. Jacque Hibburt.

622 DNK ISSN 1602-2475
M I N E X. (Mineral Exploration Newsletter) Variant title: Greenland M I N E X News. Text in English. 1992. irreg. (1-2/yr), latest vol.34, 2009. free (effective 2003). illus. 8 p./no. 2 cols./p.; back issues avail. **Document type:** *Newsletter, Government.* **Description:** Information on the mining industry in Greenland, including expeditionary news, geoscientific data and assessments, recent literature, and licence and regulatory information.
Formerly (until 2001): Greenland MINEX News (0909-0649)
Related titles: Online - full content ed.: ISSN 1602-2483.
Indexed: GeoRef, SpeleolAb.
Published by: (Greenland. Bureau of Minerals and Petroleum GRL), De Nationale Geologiske Undersoegelser for Danmark og Groenland/Geological Survey of Denmark and Greenland, Oester Voldgade 10, Copenhagen K, 1350, Denmark. TEL 45-38-142000, FAX 45-38-142050, geus@geus.dk.

622 546 USA
TN24.A4 CODEN: AMIRB8
M I R L REPORTS. (Mineral Industry Research Laboratory) Text in English. 1964. irreg. price varies. back issues avail. **Document type:** *Monographic series.* **Description:** Covers topics in coal, gold, and mineral exploration, mining, and processing, along with geological engineering and other topics.

Indexed: IMMAb, SpeleolAb.
Published by: University of Alaska at Fairbanks, Mineral Industry Research Laboratory, 212B O Neill Bldg, Box 757240, Fairbanks, AK 99775-7240. TEL 907-474-7135, FAX 907-474-5400. Circ: 350.

M M I J INTERNATIONAL CONFERENCES. PROCEEDINGS. (Mining and Materials Processing Institute of Japan) *see* METALLURGY

622 ZAF ISSN 1818-2380
M M S MAG. (Mining and Manufacturing Systems) Text in English. 2004. m. adv. **Document type:** *Magazine, Trade.*
Published by: In-Sync Consultants (Pty) Ltd, PO Box 424, Onrus River, 7201, South Africa. TEL 27-83-2551852, FAX 27-28-3163596. Ed., Pub. Pieter de Villiers. Adv. contact Duane Cannon.

549 ESP ISSN 1885-7264
MACLA. Text in Multiple languages. 1978. s-a. **Document type:** *Magazine, Trade.* **Description:** Covers mineralogy, crystallography, petrology, economic geology, and mineral deposits, geochemistry, environmental mineralogy and petrology, stone conservation.
Formerly (until 2001): Sociedad Espanola de Mineralogia. Boletin (0210-6558)
Indexed: GeoRef, IECT, MinerAb, SpeleolAb.
Published by: Sociedad Espanola de Mineralogia, Museo Nacional de Ciencias Naturales, C/ Jose Gutierrez Abascal 2, Madrid, 28006, Spain.

549 TUR ISSN 0369-223X
HD9506.A1 CODEN: BMRXAD
MADEN TETKIK VE ARAMA DERGISI. Text in Turkish. 1938. s-a. **Document type:** *Bulletin, Academic/Scholarly.* **Description:** Contains article related to Balkans and Eastern Mediterranean Region of geology and geophysics, paleontology, mineralogy and petrology, mining, raw materials and oil deposits, geochemistry and isotope geology, engineering and environmental geology, remote sensing and geographic information systems.
Related titles: Turkish ed.: Mineral Research and Exploration Magazine. ISSN 0026-4563.
Indexed: GeoRef, IMMAb, SpeleolAb.
—CASDDS, Ingenta, INIST.
Published by: Maden Tetkik ve Arama Genel Mudurlugu/General Directorate of Mineral and Exploration, Universiteler Mahallesi Dumlupinar Bulvari No.139, Cankaya - Ankara, 06800, Turkey. TEL 90-312-2011000, FAX 90-312-2879188, mta@mta.gov.tr. Ed. Dr. Eugun Gokten. Circ: 1,500.

669 TUR ISSN 0024-9416
CODEN: MDCKAP
➤ **MADENCILIK**; maden muhendisleri odasi dergisi. Text in Turkish; Summaries in English. 1961. q. adv. bk.rev. abstr.; bibl.; charts; illus.; stat. index. 47 p./no.; back issues avail. **Document type:** *Journal, Academic/Scholarly.* **Description:** Addresses technological development, working conditions and safety, mineral processing and more. Evaluates different methods and practices in production.
Related titles: Online - full text ed.: free (effective 2009).
Indexed: A28, APA, BrCerAb, C&ISA, CA/WCA, CIA, CPEI, CerAb, ChemAb, CivEngAb, CorrAb, E&CAJ, E11, EEA, EMA, ESPM, EngInd, EnvEAb, GEOBASE, GeoRef, H15, IMMAb, M&TEA, M09, MBF, METADEX, SCOPUS, SolStAb, T04, WAA.
—CASDDS, Linda Hall.
Published by: Turk Muhendis ve Mimar Odalari Birligi, Maden Muhendisleri Odasi/Union of Chambers of Engineers and Architects of Turkey, Chamber of Mining Engineers, Selanik Caddesi No.19/4, Kizilay, Ankara, 06650, Turkey. TEL 90-312-4251080, FAX 90-312-4175290, maden@maden.org.tr, http://www.mining-eng.org.tr. Ed. Nese Celebi. Adv. contact Engin Erdogan. Circ: 5,000 (controlled).

622 USA
MAINE GEOLOGICAL SURVEY. MINERAL RESOURCES AND MINING REPORT. Text in English. 19??. irreg. back issues avail. **Document type:** *Report, Government.*
Related titles: Online - full text ed.: free (effective 2011).
Published by: Maine Geological Survey, 22 State House Sta, Augusta, ME 04333. TEL 207-287-2801, FAX 207-287-2353, mgs@maine.gov.

622 USA
MAINE GEOLOGICAL SURVEY. MINERALOGY OF MAINE. Text in English. 19??. irreg., latest vol.2, 2000. USD 50 (effective 2011). back issues avail. **Document type:** *Monographic series, Government.*
Published by: Maine Geological Survey, 22 State House Sta, Augusta, ME 04333. TEL 207-287-2801, FAX 207-287-2353, mgs@maine.gov.

338.20959505 GBR ISSN 1755-7992
MALAYSIA MINING REPORT. Text in English. 2007. a. EUR 820, USD 1,030 combined subscription per issue (print & email eds.) (effective 2010). **Document type:** *Report, Trade.* **Description:** Provides industry strategists, service companies, company analysts and consultants, government departments, trade associations and regulatory bodies with Malaysian mining forecasts industry.
Related titles: E-mail ed.
Indexed: A15, ABIn, B02, B15, B17, B18, G04, I05, P48, P51, P52, P56, PQC.
Published by: Business Monitor International Ltd., Senator House, 85 Queen Victoria St, London, EC4V 4AB, United Kingdom. TEL 44-20-72480468, FAX 44-20-72480467, subs@businessmonitor.com.

338.2 MYS
MALAYSIAN CHAMBER OF MINES. COUNCIL REPORT. Text in English. a.
Formerly: States of Malaya Chamber of Mines. Council Report (0302-6620)
Indexed: GeoRef.
Published by: Malaysian Chamber of Mines, 8th Fl West Block, Wisma Selanger Dredging, Jalan Ampang, PO Box 12560, Kuala Lumpur, 50782, Malaysia. TEL 603-2616171, FAX 603-2616179.

338.2 MYS
MALAYSIAN CHAMBER OF MINES. YEARBOOK. Text in English. 1966. a. MYR 10. stat. **Document type:** *Yearbook, Trade.*
Formerly: States of Malaya Chamber of Mines. Yearbook
Published by: Malaysian Chamber of Mines, 8th Fl West Block, Wisma Selanger Dredging, Jalan Ampang, PO Box 12560, Kuala Lumpur, 50782, Malaysia. TEL 603-2616171, FAX 603-2616179.

622 MYS ISSN 1394-5076
MALAYSIAN MINERALS YEARBOOK. Text in English. 1995. a., latest 2005. **Document type:** *Yearbook, Trade.*
Indexed: GeoRef.
Published by: Jabatan Mineral dan Geosains Malaysia/Minerals and Geoscience Department Malaysia, 20th Fl, Tabung Haji Bldg, Jalan Tun Razak, Kuala Lumpur, 50658, Malaysia. TEL 60-3-21611033, FAX 60-3-21611036, jmgkll@jmg.gov.my, http://www.jmg.gov.my/english/mainpage.htm.

622 MYS
MALAYSIAN MINING INDUSTRY. Text in English. a. MYR 30 per issue (effective 2008). **Document type:** *Directory, Trade.*
Formerly (until 2002): Malaysian Mining Industry Report And Statistics
Published by: Jabatan Mineral dan Geosains Malaysia/Minerals and Geoscience Department Malaysia, 20th Fl, Tabung Haji Bldg, Jalan Tun Razak, Kuala Lumpur, 50658, Malaysia. TEL 60-3-21611033, FAX 60-3-21611036, jmgkll@jmg.gov.my, http://www.jmg.gov.my/english/mainpage.htm.

MANITOBA INDUSTRY, TRADE AND MINES. AGGRAGATE REPORT SERIES. *see* EARTH SCIENCES—Geology

622 CAN
MANITOBA INDUSTRY, TRADE AND MINES. ANNUAL REPORT SERIES. Text in English. 1980. a. **Document type:** *Government.* **Description:** Covers activities of the department and the mining industry in Manitoba.
Former titles: Manitoba. Energy and Mines. Annual Report Series; Manitoba. Mineral Resources Division. Annual Report Series
Published by: Manitoba Industry, Trade and Mines, 360 1395 Ellice Ave, Winnipeg, MB R3G 3P2, Canada. TEL 204-945-4154, FAX 204-945-8427, publications@gov.mb.ca, http://www.infomine.com/index/suppliers/Manitoba_Industry,_Trade_and_Mines.html. Circ: 1,000.

622 557 CAN
MANITOBA INDUSTRY, TRADE AND MINES. FEDERAL - PROVINCIAL ANNUAL PROGRESS REPORTS. Text in English. a. **Document type:** *Government.*
Published by: Manitoba Industry, Trade and Mines, 360 1395 Ellice Ave, Winnipeg, MB R3G 3P2, Canada. TEL 204-945-4154, FAX 204-945-8427, publications@gov.mb.ca.

MANITOBA INDUSTRY, TRADE AND MINES. GEOLOGICAL REPORT SERIES. *see* EARTH SCIENCES—Geology

MANITOBA INDUSTRY, TRADE AND MINES. MINERAL DEPOSIT REPORT SERIES. *see* EARTH SCIENCES—Geology

622 557 CAN
MANITOBA INDUSTRY, TRADE AND MINES. MINERAL EDUCATION SERIES. Text in English. irreg. **Document type:** *Monographic series, Government.*
Published by: Manitoba Industry, Trade and Mines, 360 1395 Ellice Ave, Winnipeg, MB R3G 3P2, Canada. TEL 204-945-4154, FAX 204-945-8427, publications@gov.mb.ca.

622 557 CAN
MANITOBA INDUSTRY, TRADE AND MINES. MISCELLANEOUS PUBLICATION SERIES. Text in English. irreg. **Document type:** *Monographic series, Government.*
Published by: Manitoba Industry, Trade and Mines, 360 1395 Ellice Ave, Winnipeg, MB R3G 3P2, Canada. TEL 204-945-4154, FAX 204-945-8427, publications@gov.mb.ca.

MANITOBA INDUSTRY, TRADE AND MINES. PUBLICATIONS SERIES. *see* EARTH SCIENCES—Geology

622 DEU ISSN 0174-1357
TN273
MARKSCHEIDEWESEN; Altbergbau - Bergbauliche Umweltauswirkungen - Bergbauplanung - Bergschaeden - Bergvermessung - Boden- und Gebirgsbewegungen - Erneubare Geogene Energien - Genehmigungsverfahren - Geoinformation - Lagerstaettenmanagement - Raumordnung. Text in German, English. 1879. 3/yr. EUR 82 (effective 2010). bk.rev. bibl.; charts. index. 36 p./no. 2 cols./p.; back issues avail.; reprints avail. **Document type:** *Journal, Trade.*
Formerly (until 1979): Mitteilungen aus dem Markscheidewesen (0026-685X)
Indexed: GeoRef, SpeleolAb, TM.
Published by: (Deutscher Markscheider-Verein e.V./German Mine-Surveying Society), G D M B Geschaeftsstelle, Paul Ernst Str 10, Clausthal-Zellerfeld, 38678, Germany. TEL 49-5323-93720, FAX 49-5323-937937, info@gdmb.de. Circ: 650.

664 DEU
MARKTFOCUS BRECHER. Text in German. a. EUR 15 newsstand/cover (effective 2011). adv. **Document type:** *Journal, Trade.*
Related titles: ◆ Supplement to: Aufbereitungs-Technik - Mineral Processing. ISSN 1434-9302.
Published by: Bauverlag BV GmbH (Subsidiary of: Springer Science+Business Media), Avenwedderstr 55, Guetersloh, 33311, Germany. TEL 49-5241-802119, FAX 49-5241-809582, ulrike.mattern@springer-sbm.com, http://www.bauverlag.de. Circ: 30,000 (controlled).

622 ITA ISSN 0392-6303
MARMOMACCHINE; attrezzature e accessori vari. Text in Italian; Summaries in English. 1972. bi-m. EUR 52 domestic; EUR 135 foreign (effective 2009). adv. **Document type:** *Magazine, Trade.*
Related titles: Online - full text ed.
Published by: Promorama Srl, Via Cenisio 49, Milan, 20154, Italy. TEL 39-02-3450344, FAX 39-02-316836, editor@marmomacchine.it, http://www.marmomacchine.it.

622 ITA
MARMOMACCHINE INTERNATIONAL. Text in English; Summaries in Arabic, Chinese, French, German, Russian, Spanish. 1993. q. EUR 16 domestic; EUR 56 foreign (effective 2009). adv. **Document type:** *Magazine, Trade.* **Description:** Covers the entire production cycle of marble and natural stone. Covers international market trends. Profiles products, companies, and trade fairs.
Related titles: Online - full text ed.
Published by: Promorama Srl, Via Cenisio 49, Milan, 20154, Italy. TEL 39-02-3450344, FAX 39-02-316836, editor@marmomacchine.it, http://www.marmomacchine.it.

622 ITA ISSN 0393-876X
MARMOR. Text in Italian. 1983. q. adv. bk.rev. **Document type:** *Magazine, Trade.*
Indexed: AIAP.
Published by: Giorgio Zusi Editore, Via Unita d'Italia 278A, Verona, VR 37132, Italy. TEL 39-045-8922292, FAX 39-045-970002, http://www.zusieditore.it. Ed. Lorenzo Iseppi. Circ: 5,400.

622 FIN ISSN 1459-9694
TN4
MATERIA/BERGSHANTERINGEN. Text in English, Finnish, Swedish. 1943. q. EUR 45 (effective 2005). adv. charts; illus.; stat. cum.index: 1943-1969. **Document type:** *Journal, Trade.*
Formerly (until 2004): Vuoriteollisuus (0042-9317)
Related titles: CD-ROM ed.; Online - full text ed.
Indexed: GeoRef, IMMAb, SpeleolAb.
—Linda Hall.
Published by: Vuorimiesyhdistys-Bergsmannaforeningen r.y./Finnish Association of Mining and Metallurgical Engineers, c/o Ulla-Riitta Lahtinen, Kaskilaaksontie 3 D 108, Espoo, 02360, Finland. TEL 358-9-8134758. Ed. Jouko Harkki. Circ: 2,300.

MATERIALS AND COMPONENTS IN FOSSIL ENERGY APPLICATIONS. *see* ENERGY

622.33 CHN ISSN 1674-3970
MEIKUANG BAOPO/COAL MINE BLASTING. Text in Chinese. 1983. q.
Formerly (until 1994): Zhayao yu Baopo
Related titles: Online - full text ed.
Published by: Meitan Kexue Yanjiu Zongyuan, Baopo Jishu Yanjiusuo/China Coal Research Institute, Blasting Technology Research Institute, 150, Dongshan Lu, Huaibei, 235039, China. TEL 86-561-3090434, FAX 86-561-3090826.

MEIKUANG HUANJING BAOHU/COAL MINE ENVIRONMENTAL PROTECTION. *see* ENVIRONMENTAL STUDIES

622.33 CHN ISSN 1003-0794
MEIKUANG JIXIE/COAL MINE MACHINERY. Text in Chinese. 1980. m. CNY 180; CNY 15 per issue (effective 2010). **Document type:** *Journal, Academic/Scholarly.*
Related titles: Online - full text ed.
Indexed: A28, APA, BrCerAb, CA/WCA, CIA, CerAb, CivEngAb, E11, EEA, EMA, ESPM, EnvEAb, H15, M&TEA, M09, MBF, METADEX, RefZh, T04.
—Linda Hall.
Published by: (Haerbin Meikuang Jixie Yanjiusuo), Meikuang Jixie Zazhishe, 30, Guxiang Jie, Ha'erbin, 150036, China. TEL 86-451-55646587, FAX 86-451-55646587.

622.33 CHN ISSN 1671-0959
MEITAN GONGCHENG/COAL ENGINEERING. Text in Chinese. 1954. m. CNY 11 newsstand/cover (effective 2006). **Document type:** *Journal, Academic/Scholarly.*
Formerly (until 2000): Meikuang Sheji/Coalmine Design (1002-6568)
Related titles: Online - full text ed.
Address: 67, Dewaiande Lu, Beijing, 100011, China. TEL 86-10-62377007, FAX 86-10-62023375.

MEITAN JINGJI YANJIU/COAL ECONOMICS STUDY. *see* BUSINESS AND ECONOMICS

622.33 CHN
MEITAN XINXI. Text in Chinese. w. CNY 595 (effective 2006). **Document type:** *Journal, Academic/Scholarly.*
Published by: Meitan Xinxi Yanjiuyuan, Xinwen Zhongxin, 35, Shaoyaoju, Beijing, 100029, China. TEL 86-10-84657853, FAX 86-10-84657900, xwzx@chinacoalnews.com, http://www.zgmt.com.cn/.

622.33 CHN ISSN 0253-9993
TN799.9 CODEN: MTHPDA
MEITAN XUEBAO/CHINA COAL SOCIETY. JOURNAL. Text in Chinese; Abstracts in English. 1964. bi-m. USD 138 (effective 2009). back issues avail. **Document type:** *Journal, Academic/Scholarly.* **Description:** Provides comprehensive coverage of coal science and technology; mainly publishes research papers relating to coal field geology and exploration, mine construction, coal mining, coal mine electrical machinery, mine survey, mine safety, coal processing and utilization, coal mine environmental protection, etc. It reflects the latest research achievements and the highest research level in the coal circles in China.
Related titles: Online - full text ed.
Indexed: CPEI, ChemAb, EngInd, GeoRef, SCOPUS, SpeleolAb.
—CASDDS, East View, Linda Hall.
Published by: Zhongguo Meitan Xuehui/China Coal Society, Hepingli, 5, Qingnian Guodong Lu, Beijing, 100013, China. TEL 86-10-84262930, FAX 86-10-84262340. Circ: 1,000.

622.33 CHN ISSN 1004-4248
CODEN: MEZHE6
MEITAN ZHUANHUA/COAL CONVERSION. Text in Chinese. 1978. q. CNY 12 newsstand/cover (effective 2006). back issues avail. **Document type:** *Journal, Academic/Scholarly.*
Related titles: Online - full text ed.
Indexed: ChemAb, ChemTitl.
—BLDSC (3289.535000), CASDDS.
Published by: Taiyuan Ligong Daxue, Yingze Xi Dajie Xinkuangyuan Lu #18, Taiyuan, 030024, China. TEL 86-351-6010162. Circ: 2,000.
Co-sponsors: State Key Laboratory of Coal Conversion; Shanxi Institute of Scientific and Technical Information.

MEITIAN DIZHI YU KANTAN/COAL GEOLOGY AND PROSPECTING. *see* EARTH SCIENCES—Geology

622 USA
METAL INDUSTRY INDICATORS (ONLINE). Abbreviated title: M I I. Text in English. 1991. m. free (effective 2011). back issues avail. **Document type:** *Newsletter, Government.* **Description:** Analyzes and forecasts the economic health of five metal industries: primary metals, steel, copper, primera and secondary aluminum, and aluminum mill products.
Media: Online - full text.
Published by: U.S. Geological Survey, Mineral Resources Program (Subsidiary of: U.S. Department of the Interior), 12201 Sunrise Valley Dr, 913 National Ctr, Reston, VA 20192. TEL 703-648-6110, FAX 703-648-6057, kjohnson@usgs.gov.

METALLEIOLOGIKA-METALLOURGIKA HRONIKA/MINING AND METALLURGICAL ANNALS. *see* METALLURGY

622 CAN ISSN 0828-0835
METALLURGICAL WORKS IN CANADA, PRIMARY IRON AND STEEL (YEAR)/ACTIVITE METALLURGIQUE AU CANADA. FER ET ACIER DE PREMIERE FUSION. Text in English. 1984. a. CAD 25.95 domestic; CAD 33.75 foreign (effective 2004).
Formed by the merger of 1984 part of: Mines et Uines de Traitement des Mineraux au Canada (0826-2640); Which was formed by the merger of (1977-1980): Activite Metallurgique au Canada. Production de Fer et d'Acier de Premiere Fusion (0705-9876); Activite Metallurgique au Canada. Metaux non Ferreux et Precieux; Mines et Usines de Transformation des Metaux et des Mineraux Industriels au Canada; and part of (1980-1984): Mining and Mineral Processing Operations in Canada (0825-219X); Which was formed by 1980 the merger of: Metallurgical Works in Canada, Primary Iron and Steel (0076-6712); Metallurgical Works in Canada. Nonferrous and Precious Metals (0076-6704); Metal and Industrial Mineral Mines and Processing Plants in Canada (0319-5406); Which was formerly (until 1968): Metal and Industrial Mineral Mines in Canada (0410-6997)
Indexed: GeoRef.
—CCC.
Published by: Natural Resources Canada, Minerals and Metals Sector (Subsidiary of: Natural Resources Canada/Ressources Naturelles Canada), 580 Booth St, Ottawa, ON K1A 0E4, Canada. TEL 613-947-6580, FAX 613-952-7501, info-mms@nrcan.gc.ca, http://www.nrcan.gc.ca/mms/hm_e.htm.

622 CAN
METALS ECONOMICS GROUP STRATEGIC REPORT. Text in English. 1988. bi-m. USD 1,700 (effective 2001). **Document type:** *Newsletter.*
Published by: Metals Economics Group, 1718 Argyle St, Ste 300, Halifax, NS B3J 3N6, Canada. TEL 902-429-2880, FAX 902-429-6593. Ed. Marilyn Beamish.

METALS WATCH. *see* METALLURGY

338.2097205 GBR ISSN 1755-8506
MEXICO MINING REPORT. Text in English. 2007. a. EUR 820, USD 1,030 combined subscription per issue (print & email eds.) (effective 2010). **Document type:** *Report, Trade.* **Description:** Features latest-available data and forecasts covering all headline indicators for mining; company rankings and competitive landscapes covering mining exploration and production; and analysis of latest industry developments, trends and regulatory issues.
Related titles: E-mail ed.
Indexed: A15, ABIn, B02, B15, B17, B18, G04, I05, P48, P51, P52, P56, PQC.
Published by: Business Monitor International Ltd., Senator House, 85 Queen Victoria St, London, EC4V 4AB, United Kingdom. TEL 44-20-72480468, FAX 44-20-72480467, subs@businessmonitor.com.

549 FRA ISSN 1957-4290
MICROMINERAL MAGAZINE. Text in French. 2007. bi-m. EUR 48 domestic to individuals; EUR 68 domestic to institutions; EUR 58 in Europe to individuals; EUR 68 elsewhere to individuals (effective 2007). **Document type:** *Magazine, Consumer.*
Published by: I-Concept Geologie, 59 Av. du General de Gaulle, Perpignan, 66000, France. contact@micromineral-magazine.com.

622 USA ISSN 1049-1805
MINE & QUARRY TRADER; merchandising everything for the mining and quarry industries. Text in English. 1976. m. free domestic to qualified personnel; USD 66 foreign (effective 2011). adv. **Document type:** *Magazine, Trade.*
—CCC.
Published by: Penton Media, Inc., 7355 Woodland Dr, Indianapolis, IN 46278-1769. TEL 800-827-7468, FAX 317-299-1356, information@penton.com, http://www.pentonmedia.com. adv.: B&W page USD 1,570, color page USD 2,500; 6.75 x 9.0625. Circ: 27,618.

549 AUS
MINE REHABILITATION HANDBOOK. Text in English. 1989. irreg. free (effective 2008). **Document type:** *Handbook/Manual/Guide, Consumer.* **Description:** Provides practical guidance on how to rehabilitate areas disturbed by mining in a sensible, scientific way.
Related titles: Online - full text ed.: free (effective 2008).
Published by: Minerals Council of Australia, PO Box 4497, Kingston, ACT 2604, Australia. TEL 61-2-62330600, FAX 61-2-62330699, info@minerals.org.au, http://www.minerals.org.au.

622.8 ZAF
MINE SAFETY DIGEST. Text in English. bi-m. ZAR 64 domestic; ZAR 129 elsewhere (effective 2000). charts; illus.; stat. **Document type:** *Magazine, Trade.* **Description:** Discusses all aspects of mine safety.
Published by: T M L Business Publishing (Subsidiary of: Times Media Ltd.), PO Box 182, Pinegowrie, Gauteng 2123, South Africa. TEL 27-11-789-2144, FAX 27-11-789-3196. Ed. Roy Bennetts.

622 ZAF ISSN 0368-3206
➤ **MINE VENTILATION SOCIETY OF SOUTH AFRICA. JOURNAL.** Text in English. 1948. q. ZAR 275 domestic; USD 85 foreign (effective 2003). bk.rev. charts; illus. index, cum.index every 10 yrs. back issues avail.; reprints avail. **Document type:** *Journal, Academic/Scholarly.* **Description:** Presents technical papers and notes.
Related titles: Microform ed.: (from PQC).
Indexed: CISA, CPEI, EngInd, F&EA, IMMAb, INIS AtomInd, ISAP, ISMEC, SCOPUS.
—BLDSC (4826.500000), IE, Ingenta, INIST, Linda Hall.
Published by: Mine Ventilation Society of South Africa, PO Box 93480, Yeoville, Johannesburg 2143, South Africa. TEL 27-11-487-1073. Ed. Marco Biffi. R&P, Adv. contact Sue Moseley. Circ: 1,250.

➤ **MINE WATER AND THE ENVIRONMENT.** *see* ENVIRONMENTAL STUDIES—Pollution

➤ **THE MINER.** *see* LABOR UNIONS

669 BRA ISSN 0100-6908
TN4 CODEN: MINMAJ
MINERACAO METALURGIA. Text in Portuguese. 1936. m. USD 60. adv. bibl.; charts; illus.; stat. **Document type:** *Trade.*
Former titles (until 1968): Engenharia, Mineracao, Metalurgia (0013-7685); (until 1951): Mineracao Metalurgia (0026-4520)
Indexed: C01, CIN, ChemAb, ChemTitl, FR, GeoRef, IBR, IBZ, IMMAb, SpeleolAb.
—CASDDS, INIST, Linda Hall.
Published by: (Mineracao Metalurgia), Editora Scorpio Ltda., Rua do Catete, 202, Grupo 301, Rio De Janeiro, RJ 22220-001, Brazil. FAX 55-21-205-0648. Ed. Wilson Costa. Circ: 15,000.

MINERAL ECONOMICS. *see* BUSINESS AND ECONOMICS—International Development And Assistance

622 CAN ISSN 1911-0138
MINERAL EXPLORATION MAGAZINE. Text in English. 1976. bi-m. membership. adv. **Document type:** *Magazine, Trade.*
Former titles (until 2006): Mining Review (0711-3277); (until 1981): British Columbia and Yukon Chamber of Mines. Chamber Reports (0318-1766); Incorporates (in 1982): Equipment, Supply and Service Members. Directory (0318-482X)
Indexed: C03, CBCABus, GeoRef, P48, PQC, SpeleolAb.
Published by: (Association for Mineral Exploration British Columbia), Canada Wide Media Ltd., 4180 Lougheed Hwy, 4th Fl, Burnaby, BC V5C 6A7, Canada. TEL 604-299-7311, FAX 604-299-9188, cwm@canadawide.com, http://www.canadawide.com. Circ: 2,500.

549 338.2094105 GBR ISSN 1742-1764
MINERAL EXTRACTION IN GREAT BRITAIN (ONLINE). Variant title: Business Monitor (PA1007). Mineral Extraction in Great Britain. Text in English. 1999. a., latest 2008. free (effective 2010). back issues avail. **Document type:** *Government.* **Description:** Contains data on the extracted sales of chalk, clays, crushed rock, dolomite, granite, gypsum, limestone, ore minerals, peat, salt, sandstone, sand and gravel, slate plus a few minor minerals; and employment for each quarry type.
Media: Online - full text.
Published by: Office for National Statistics, Rm 1.101, Government Bldgs, Cardiff Rd, Newport, S Wales NP10 8XG, United Kingdom. TEL 44-1633-653599, FAX 44-1633-652747, info@statistics.gov.uk, http://www.statistics.gov.uk/default.asp.

622 GUY
MINERAL INDUSTRY SURVEY; a quarterly newsletter. Text in English. 1992. q. free. charts. **Document type:** *Newsletter.*
Published by: Geology and Mines Commission, Upper Brickdam, PO Box 1028, Georgetown, Guyana. TEL 592-2-52862, FAX 592-2-53047. Ed. Karen Livan. Circ: 200.

340 622 USA ISSN 0897-6694
KF1802
MINERAL LAW NEWSLETTER. Text in English. 1967. q. USD 80 (effective 2010). back issues avail. **Document type:** *Newsletter, Government.*
Formerly (until 1984): Rocky Mountain Mineral Law Newsletter (0557-8051)
Related titles: Online - full text ed.
Indexed: GeoRef, SpeleolAb.
—CCC.
Published by: Rocky Mountain Mineral Law Foundation, 9191 Sheridan Blvd, Ste 203, Westminster, CO 80031. TEL 303-321-8100, FAX 303-321-7657, info@rmmlf.org.

MINERAL LAW SERIES. *see* LAW

338.2 551 USA ISSN 1088-1018
TN1
MINERAL RESOURCES DATA SYSTEM. Abbreviated title: M R D S. Text in English. 1996. a. back issues avail. **Document type:** *Database, Trade.*
Media: CD-ROM.
Published by: U.S. Department of the Interior, Geological Survey, 12201 Sunrise Valley Dr, Reston, VA 20192. TEL 703-648-5953, 800-228-0975, ask@usgs.gov, http://www.usgs.gov.

MINERAL REVIEW. *see* EARTH SCIENCES—Geology

622 CHL ISSN 0026-458X
TN43 CODEN: MINCAN
➤ **MINERALES.** Text in Spanish; Abstracts in English. 1945. q. USD 69 (effective 1997). adv. bk.rev. illus. **Document type:** *Academic/Scholarly.*
Indexed: C01, CIN, ChemAb, ChemTitl, GeoRef, IBR, IBZ, IMMAb, SpeleolAb.
—CASDDS, INIST.
Published by: Instituto de Ingenieros de Minas de Chile, Casilla 14668, Correo, 21, Santiago, Chile. TEL 56-2-6953849, FAX 56-2-6972351. Ed. Jorge Menacho. Adv. contact Javier Jofre. Circ: 1,000.

549 ITA ISSN 1824-7709
MINERALI DA COLLEZIONE. Text in Italian. 2004. w. **Document type:** *Magazine, Consumer.*
Published by: R C S Libri (Subsidiary of: R C S Mediagroup), Via Mecenate 91, Milan, 20138, Italy. TEL 39-02-5095-2248, FAX 39-02-5095-2975, http://rcslibri.corriere.it/libri/index.htm.

541 ITA ISSN 2037-2450
▼ **MINERALI E GEMME DA TUTTO IL MONDO.** Text in Italian. 2010. w. **Document type:** *Magazine, Consumer.*
Published by: R B A Italia (Subsidiary of: R B A Edipresse), Largo Richini 6, Milan, 20122, Italy. TEL 39-02-58215840, FAX 39-02-58215389, http://rbaitalia.it.

549 SVK ISSN 0369-2086
QE381.C8 CODEN: MSLOBI
MINERALIA SLOVACA. Text in Czech, Slovak; Abstracts in English. 1969. bi-m. USD 92. **Document type:** *Journal, Academic/Scholarly.*
Indexed: ChemAb, ChemTitl, GeoRef, IMMAb, MinerAb, SpeleolAb, Z01.
—CASDDS, Ingenta, INIST, Linda Hall.
Published by: (Statny Geologicky Ustav Dionyza Stura/State Geological Institute of Dionyz Stur), Dionyz Stur Publishers, Mlynska dolina 1, Bratislava, 81704, Slovakia. TEL 421-2-59375119, FAX 421-2-54771940, http://www.gssr.sk. **Dist. by:** Slovart G.T.G. s.r.o., Krupinska 4, PO Box 152, Bratislava 85299, Slovakia. TEL 421-2-63839472, FAX 421-2-63839485, info@slovart-gtg.sk, http://www.slovart-gtg.sk.

MINERALIUM DEPOSITA; international journal of geology, mineralogy, and geochemistry of mineral deposits. *see* EARTH SCIENCES—Geology

549 SVN ISSN 1854-3995
MINERALNE SUROVINE. Text in Slovenian. 2005. a. **Document type:** *Journal, Academic/Scholarly.*
Related titles: Online - full content ed.: ISSN 1854-293X.
Published by: Geoloski Zavod Slovenije/Geological Survey of Slovenia, Dimiceva ul 14, Ljubljana, 1000, Slovenia. TEL 386-1-2809700, FAX 386-1-2809753. Ed. Slavko Solar.

549 POL ISSN 1899-8291
QE381.P6 CODEN: MNLPBK
➤ **MINERALOGIA.** Text in English; Summaries in Polish. 1970. s-a. charts; illus. index. **Document type:** *Journal, Academic/Scholarly.*
Formerly (until 2008): Mineralogia Polonica (0032-6267)
Related titles: Online - full text ed.: ISSN 1899-8526. free (effective 2011).
Indexed: A01, ChemAb, GeoRef, MinerAb, SCOPUS, SpeleolAb.
—CASDDS, INIST, Linda Hall.
Published by: Polskie Towarzystwo Mineralogiczne, Al Mickiewicza 30, Krakow, 30059, Poland. TEL 48-12-6172373, FAX 48-12-6334330, zabinski@geol.agh.edu.pl. Ed. Marek Michalik.

549 GBR ISSN 0026-461X
QE351 CODEN: MNLMBB
➤ **MINERALOGICAL MAGAZINE.** Text in English. 1876. bi-m. GBP 430 combined subscription domestic to institutions (print & online eds.); GBP 463 combined subscription foreign to institutions (print & online eds.) (effective 2011). adv. bk.rev. charts; illus. index. reprints avail. **Document type:** *Journal, Academic/Scholarly.*
Formerly (until 1969): Mineralogical Magazine and Journal of the Mineralogical Society (0369-0148)
Related titles: Microfiche ed.: (from BHP); Online - full text ed.: ISSN 1471-8022. GBP 393 to institutions (effective 2011) (from IngentaConnect).
Indexed: A01, A03, A08, A22, AESIS, ASCA, BrGeoL, C33, CA, CIN, CPEI, Cadscan, ChemAb, ChemTitl, CurCont, E01, EngInd, F&EA, GEOBASE, GSW, GeoRef, IBR, IBZ, IMMAb, ISR, LeadAb, MSCI, MinerAb, P30, RefZh, SCI, SCOPUS, SpeleolAb, T02, W07, Zincscan.
—BLDSC (5788.000000), CASDDS, IE, Infotrieve, Ingenta, INIST, Linda Hall. **CCC.**
Published by: Mineralogical Society, 12 Baylis Mews, Amyand Park Rd, Twickenham, Middlesex TW1 3HQ, United Kingdom. TEL 44-20-88916600, FAX 44-20-88916599. Ed. M D Welch. Circ: 2,000.

➤ **MINERALOGICAL SOCIETY SERIES.** *see* EARTH SCIENCES—Geology

549 UKR ISSN 0204-3548
QE351 CODEN: MINZDR
➤ **MINERALOGICHESKII ZHURNAL/MINERALOGICAL JOURNAL**; nauchno-teoreticheskii zhurnal. Text in English, Russian, Ukrainian. 1979. bi-m. USD 126 foreign (effective 2004). **Document type:** *Journal, Academic/Scholarly.*
Formerly: Regional'naya i Geneticheskaya Mineralogiya i Konstitutsiya i Svoystva Mineralov
Indexed: CIN, ChemAb, ChemTitl, Djerelo, GeoRef, MinerAb, RefZh, SpeleolAb.
—CASDDS, East View, INIST, Linda Hall. **CCC.**
Published by: Natsional'na Akademiya Nauk Ukrainy, Instytut Heokhimii, Mineralohii ta Rudoutvorennya/National Academy of Sciences of Ukraine, Department of Geosciences, Institute of Geochemistry, Mineralogy and Ore Formation, Pr Akad Palladina 34, Kyiv, 03680, Ukraine. TEL 380-44-4440170, FAX 380-44-4441270. Ed., R&P Mykola Shcherbak. **Dist. by:** East View Information Services, 10601 Wayzata Blvd, Minneapolis, MN 55305. TEL 952-252-1201, 800-477-1005, FAX 952-252-1202, info@eastview.com, http://www.eastview.com.

549 552 AUT ISSN 0930-0708
QE351 CODEN: MIPEE9
➤ **MINERALOGY AND PETROLOGY.** Text in English. 1872. m. EUR 1,579, USD 1,901 combined subscription to institutions (print & online eds.) (effective 2012). adv. bk.rev. charts; illus.; abstr. index. back issues avail.; reprint service avail. from PSC. **Document type:** *Journal, Academic/Scholarly.* **Description:** Devoted to the whole field of mineralogy, petrology and geochemistry.
Former titles (until 1986): T M P M - Tschermaks Mineralogische und Petrographische Mitteilungen (0041-3763); (until 1968): Tschermak's Mineralogische und Petrographische Mitteilungen (0369-1497)
Related titles: Microfiche ed.: (from PQC); Online - full text ed.: ISSN 1438-1168 (from IngentaConnect).
Indexed: A01, A03, A08, A22, A26, AESIS, ASCA, C33, CA, ChemAb, ChemTitl, CurCont, E01, E08, E14, GeoRef, IBR, IBZ, ISR, MSCI, MinerAb, P02, P10, P26, P48, P52, P53, P54, P56, PQC, RefZh, S01, S09, S10, SCI, SCOPUS, SpeleolAb, T02, W07.
—BLDSC (5790.340000), CASDDS, IE, Infotrieve, Ingenta, INIST, Linda Hall. **CCC.**
Published by: Springer Wien (Subsidiary of: Springer Science+Business Media), Sachsenplatz 4-6, Vienna, W 1201, Austria. TEL 43-1-33024150, FAX 43-1-3302426, journals@springer.at, http://www.springer.at. Ed. J G Raith. Adv. contact Irene Hofmann. B&W page EUR 1,290; 170 x 230. Circ: 600 (paid). **Subscr. in the Americas to:** Springer New York LLC, Journal Fulfillment, PO Box 2485, Secaucus, NJ 07096. TEL 800-777-4643, 201-348-4033, FAX 201-348-4505, journals-ny@springer.com, http://www.springer.com; **Subscr. to:** Springer Distribution Center, Kundenservice Zeitschriften, Haberstr 7, Heidelberg 69126, Germany. TEL 49-6221-3454303, FAX 49-6221-3454229, subscriptions@springer.com.

549 CHE ISSN 2075-163X
▼ ➤ **MINERALS.** Text in English. 2011. q. free (effective 2011). **Document type:** *Journal, Academic/Scholarly.* **Description:** Publishes research on mineral resources, mining and mineral processing.
Media: Online - full text.
Published by: M D P I AG, Postfach, Basel, 4005, Switzerland. TEL 41-61-6837734, FAX 41-61-3028918, http://www.mdpi.org/. Ed. Robert Larry Grayson.

622 USA ISSN 0747-9182
TN496 CODEN: MMPRE8
MINERALS AND METALLURGICAL PROCESSING. Abbreviated title: M & M P. Text in English. 1984. q. USD 599 combined subscription to institutions (print & online eds.); USD 149 combined subscription domestic to non-members (print & online eds.); USD 159 combined subscription foreign to non-members (print & online eds.); USD 119 combined subscription to members (print & online eds.) (effective 2010). adv. back issues avail. **Document type:** *Magazine, Trade.*
Related titles: Microfilm ed.: (from PQC); Online - full text ed.: USD 129 to non-members; USD 99 to members (effective 2010).

Indexed: A15, A22, A28, ABIn, AESIS, APA, ASCA, BrCerAb, C&ISA, C33, CA/WCA, CIA, CIN, CPEI, CerAb, ChemAb, ChemTitl, CivEngAb, CorrAb, CurCont, E&CAJ, E11, EEA, EMA, ESPM, EngInd, EnvEAb, GeoRef, H15, IMMAb, ISMEC, M&TEA, M09, MBF, METADEX, MSCI, P26, P48, P51, P52, P54, PQC, SCI, SCOPUS, SolStAb, T04, W07, WAA.
—BLDSC (5790.620000), CASDDS, IE, Infotrieve, Ingenta, INIST, Linda Hall. **CCC.**
Published by: Society for Mining, Metallurgy and Exploration, 8307 Shaffer Pkwy, Littleton, CO 80127. TEL 303-948-4200, 800-763-3132, FAX 303-973-3845, cs@smenet.org.

MINERALS & METALS REVIEW. *see* METALLURGY

622 GBR ISSN 0892-6875
TN1 CODEN: MENGEB
➤ **MINERALS ENGINEERING.** Text in English. 1988. 15/yr. EUR 1,703 in Europe to institutions; JPY 226,100 in Japan to institutions; USD 1,905 elsewhere to institutions (effective 2012). back issues avail.
Document type: *Journal, Academic/Scholarly.* **Description:** Devoted to innovation and developments in mineral processing and extractive metallurgy.
Related titles: Microfilm ed.: (from PQC); Online - full text ed.: ISSN 1872-9444 (from IngentaConnect, ScienceDirect).
Indexed: A01, A03, A08, A22, A26, A28, A35, A37, AESIS, APA, ASCA, AgBio, BA, BrCerAb, C&ISA, C25, C33, CA, CA/WCA, CABA, CEABA, CIA, CPEI, CerAb, ChemAb, ChemTitl, CivEngAb, CorrAb, CurCont, E&CAJ, E11, E12, EEA, EMA, ESPM, EngInd, EnvEAb, F08, FCA, GH, GeoRef, H15, H16, I05, I11, IMMAb, ISMEC, ISR, M&TEA, M09, MBF, METADEX, MSCI, O01, P33, R08, R11, RefZh, S01, S13, S16, SCI, SCOPUS, SolStAb, T02, T04, TAR, TM, TriticAb, W07, W11, WAA.
—BLDSC (5790.678000), CASDDS, IE, Infotrieve, Ingenta, INIST, Linda Hall. **CCC.**
Published by: Pergamon (Subsidiary of: Elsevier Science & Technology), The Blvd, Langford Ln, East Park, Kidlington, Oxford OX5 1GB, United Kingdom. TEL 44-1865-843000, FAX 44-1865-843010, JournalsCustomerServiceEMEA@elsevier.com, http://www.elsevier.nl. Ed. B A Wills TEL 44-1326-318352.

549 GBR ISSN 0265-3923
TN151
MINERALS HANDBOOK. Text in English. 1982. biennial.
Published by: Palgrave Macmillan Ltd. (Subsidiary of: Macmillan Publishers Ltd.), Houndmills, Basingstoke, Hants RG21 6XS, United Kingdom. TEL 44-1256-329242, FAX 44-1256-810526, http://www.palgrave.com.

549 AUS
MINERALS INDUSTRY SURVEY REPORT (ONLINE). Abbreviated title: M I S. Text in English. 1978. a. free (effective 2008). back issues avail.
Document type: *Corporate.* **Description:** Provides a statistical description of the industry for the financial year.
Former titles (until 2005): Minerals Industry Survey Report (Print); (until 1995): Minerals Industry Survey (0727-3800)
Media: Online - full text.
Indexed: AESIS, GeoRef, SpeleolAb.
Published by: Minerals Council of Australia, PO Box 4497, Kingston, ACT 2604, Australia. TEL 61-2-62330600, FAX 61-2-62330699, info@minerals.org.au, http://www.minerals.org.au.

622 GBR
MINERALS POLICY STATEMENTS. Abbreviated title: M P S. Text in English. 1988. irreg., latest vol.2, 2006. price varies. **Document type:** *Bulletin, Trade.* **Description:** Provides advice and guidance to local authorities and the minerals industry on policies and the operation of the planning system with regard to minerals.
Formerly: Minerals Planning Guidance (0960-6831)
Related titles: Online - full text ed.: free (effective 2009).
—CCC.
Published by: Great Britain. Department of Communities and Local Government, Eland House, Bressenden Pl, London, SW1E 5DU, United Kingdom. TEL 44-20-79444400, contactus@communities.gov.uk.

549 USA
MINERALS RESEARCH LABORATORY NEWSLETTER. Text in English. 1959. q. looseleaf. free. **Document type:** *Newsletter, Trade.*
Supersedes: Minerals Research Laboratory Bulletin (0026-4652)
Published by: North Carolina State University, Minerals Research Laboratory, 180 Coxe Ave, Asheville, NC 28801. TEL 828-251-6155. Ed. R Bruce Tippin. Circ: 300.

549 USA ISSN 0076-8952
TN23 CODEN: MYEAAG
MINERALS YEARBOOK. Text in English. 1932. a. (in 3 vols.). price varies. stat. back issues avail. **Document type:** *Yearbook, Government.* **Description:** Reports mineral data on a commodity, state, and foreign-country basis.
Supersedes in part (in 1933): Mineral Resources of the United States
Related titles: Microfiche ed.: (from BHP, PMC); Online - full text ed.: free (effective 2011).
Indexed: GeoRef, RASB, SpeleolAb.
—BLDSC (5791.000000), CASDDS, INIST, Linda Hall.
Published by: U.S. Geological Survey, Mineral Resources Program (Subsidiary of: U.S. Department of the Interior), 12201 Sunrise Valley Dr, 913 National Ctr, Reston, VA 20192. TEL 703-648-6110, FAX 703-648-6057, kjohnson@usgs.gov.

MINERAUX ET FOSSILES; le guide du collectionneur. *see* PALEONTOLOGY

622 PER ISSN 0026-4679
MINERIA. Text in Spanish. 1952. bi-m. USD 55. adv. illus.; mkt.
Document type: *Academic/Scholarly.*
Indexed: ChemAb, IBR, IBZ, IMMAb, SpeleolAb.
Published by: Instituto de Ingenieros de Minas del Peru, Las Camelias, 555-2, San Isidro, Lima 27, Peru. TEL 51-14-423190, FAX 51-14-424393. Ed. Jorge Vargas Fernandez. Circ: 10,000.

622 669 665.5 CHL ISSN 0716-1042
HD9506.C5
MINERIA CHILENA. Text in Spanish. 1980. m. free domestic to qualified personnel; CLP 36,000 domestic; USD 142 in South America and United States; USD 170 in Central America and Canada; USD 198 elsewhere (effective 2003). adv. bk.rev. index. back issues avail.
Document type: *Trade.*
Indexed: GeoRef, SpeleolAb.
Published by: Editec Ltda., Avenida del Condor 844, Oficina 205, Ciudad Empresarial, Huechuraba, Santiago, 09, Chile. TEL 56-2-7574210, FAX 56-2-75754201, editec@editec.cl, http://www.editec.cl. Eds. Ricardo Cortes, Roly Solis. adv.: B&W page USD 1,350, color page USD 1,700; trim 8.13 x 10.88. Circ: 10,000.

622 MEX ISSN 0187-490X
LA MINERIA EN MEXICO. Text in Spanish. 1981. a. MXN 45 (effective 1999). stat.
Published by: Instituto Nacional de Estadistica, Geografia e Informatica, Secretaria de Programacion y Presupuesto, Prol. Heroe de Nacozari 2301 Sur, Puerta 11, Acceso, Aguascalientes, 20270, Mexico. TEL 52-4-918-1948, FAX 52-4-918-0739.

622.33 USA ISSN 1040-5860
MINERIA PAN-AMERICANA. Text in Spanish, English. 1987. q. free to qualified personnel (effective 2005). adv. back issues avail.
Document type: *Magazine, Trade.* **Description:** Covers mining equipment and new products, international trade fairs, methods of mining exploration and production, minerals processing and transport.
Published by: Mineria Pan-Americana, Inc., 4913 SW 75th Ave, Miami, FL 33155-4440. TEL 305-668-4999, FAX 305-668-7774. Ed. Guido Castellanos. Pub. Luis Suao. Circ: 7,200.

622.029 USA
MINERIA PAN-AMERICANA MINING BUYER'S GUIDE. Text in Spanish. 1997. a. adv. **Document type:** *Directory, Trade.* **Description:** Lists more than 1,000 manufacturers and suppliers of mining equipment, accessories, and attachments from around the world.
Published by: Mineria Pan-Americana, Inc., 4913 SW 75th Ave, Miami, FL 33155-4440. TEL 305-668-4999, FAX 305-668-7774, info@cpa-mpa.com, http://www.cpa-mpa.com. adv.: B&W page USD 3,035, color page USD 3,980. Circ: 10,000.

MINERIA Y GEOLOGIA (ONLINE). *see* EARTH SCIENCES—Geology

622 BRA
MINERIOS - MINERALES. Text in Portuguese, English. 1978. 10/yr. USD 60. adv. Website rev. stat. **Document type:** *Magazine, Trade.*
Description: Covers new mineral projects, advances in equipment and process technology, and improvements in prospecting and geology techniques of mineral producers.
Related titles: Supplement(s):.
Published by: Editora Univers Ltda., Rua Diogo Moriera 124, Sao Paolo, SP CEP 05423-904, Brazil. TEL 55-11-3039-8982, FAX 55-11-3039-8983, jyoung@editoraunivers.com.br, http://www.minerios.com.br. Ed., Pub. Joseph Young. Adv. contact Irene Carvalho. color page USD 3,305. Circ: 10,000.

622 USA ISSN 0890-6157
HD9506.A1
MINERS NEWS. Text in English. 1985. bi-m. USD 25 domestic; USD 35 in Canada; USD 70 elsewhere (effective 2001). adv. 32 p./no. 5 cols./p.;
Document type: *Newspaper, Trade.* **Description:** Provides the industry with in-depth coverage of events, plus feature stories and regular columns.
Published by: Graphic One, Inc., PO Box 5694, Boise, ID 83705-0694. TEL 208-345-7488, 800-624-7212, FAX 208-345-7905. Ed. Shirley White. Pub., R&P Gary White. Adv. contact Charles Bagley. B&W page USD 1,695, color page USD 2,245; trim 17.63 x 11.38. Circ: 5,399 (paid and controlled).

622 FRA ISSN 0994-2556
TN2 CODEN: INMNCA
MINES ET CARRIERES; revue de l'industrie minerale. Text in French. 1855. m. EUR 125 in Europe; EUR 161 elsewhere (effective 2009). adv. bk.rev. abstr.; bibl.; charts; illus.; tr.lit. index. **Document type:** *Magazine, Trade.* **Description:** Discusses issues concerning mines and quarries.
Former titles (until 1988): Industrie Minerale, Mines et Carrieres (0296-2918); (until 1984): Industrie Minerale (0302-2129); Which was formed by the 1971 merger of: Revue de l'Industrie Minerale (0035-1431); Mines et Chimie (0398-9194)
Indexed: A22, CISA, ChemAb, CoppAb, F&EA, FR, GeoRef, GeotechAb, IMMAb, INIS AtomInd, SCOPUS, SpeleolAb.
—CASDDS, IE, Infotrieve, INIST, Linda Hall. **CCC.**
Published by: Societe de l'Industrie Minerale, 17 rue Saint-Severin, Paris, 75005, France. TEL 33-1-53101470, FAX 33-1-53101471, http://www.lasim.org. Circ: 4,300.

622 USA ISSN 0096-4859
CODEN: MMCOAW
MINES MAGAZINE. Variant title: Mines. Text in English. 1910. 4/yr. adv. bk.rev. charts; illus.; tr.lit. back issues avail. **Document type:** *Magazine, Consumer.* **Description:** Features articles on alumni, faculty and students of the Colorado School of Mines; technical subjects explained to a broad audience in non-technical terms.
Formerly (until 1932): Colorado School of Mines Magazine (0095-8719)
Indexed: ChemAb, GeoRef, IMMAb, SpeleolAb.
—Ingenta, Linda Hall.
Published by: Colorado School of Mines Alumni Association, Inc., PO Box 1410, Golden, CO 80402. TEL 303-273-3295, csmaa@mines.edu, http://www.mines.edu/, http://www.alumnifriends.mines.edu/. Ed. Nick Sutcliffe. Circ: 1,000 (free); 19,000 (paid).

622 AUS ISSN 1832-4762
MINESAFE WESTERN AUSTRALIA. Text in English. 2004. 3/yr. free (effective 2009). **Document type:** *Magazine, Government.*
Description: Highlights safety issues in the Western Australian minerals industry.
Related titles: Online - full text ed.
Published by: Government of Western Australia. Department of Mines and Petroleum, Resource Safety Division, Mineral House, 100 Plain St, East Perth, W.A. 6004, Australia. TEL 61-8-93588154, FAX 61-8-93588000, RSDComms@dmp.wa.gov.au. Ed. Dr. Susan Ho TEL 61-8-93588149.

622 IND ISSN 0970-7204
MINETECH. Text in English. 1975. q. free (effective 2011). **Document type:** *Journal, Trade.*
Published by: Central Mine Planning & Design Institute Ltd. (Subsidiary of: Coal India Limited), Gondwana Pl, Kanke Rd, Ranchi, Bihar 834 031, India. TEL 91-651-2231850, FAX 91-651-2231447, cmd@cmpdi.co.in.

622 AUS ISSN 0812-0293
MINFO; New South Wales mining and exploration quarterly. Text in English. 1983. 3/yr. free (effective 2009). back issues avail.
Document type: *Magazine, Trade.* **Description:** Features information on key topics such as geology and exploration, mineral occurrences, mining and mineral processing projects, safety, environmental issues and commodity overviews.
Related titles: Online - full text ed.
Indexed: AESIS, GeoRef, INIS AtomInd.
Published by: Department of Primary Industries, Mineral Resources Division, PO Box 344, Hunter Region Mail Centre, NSW 2310, Australia. TEL 61-2-49316666, FAX 61-2-49316790, mineralpublication.orders@dpi.nsw.gov.au, http://www.dpi.nsw.gov.au.

343.0770922 GBR ISSN 1467-7334
MINING (LONDON, 1999). Text in English. 1999. biennial. USD 200 per issue (effective 2011). **Document type:** *Directory, Trade.*
Description: Features research focusing of the following specialisations: dirt law; mine financing; native title law; leasing and financing and general representation of mining companies.
Published by: (Who's Who Legal), Law Business Research Ltd., 87 Lancaster Rd, London, W11 1QQ, United Kingdom. TEL 44-20-79081188, FAX 44-20-72296910, http://www.lbresearch.com/. Eds. Tom Barnes TEL 44-20-79081180, Callum Campbell. Pub. Richard Davey.

343.077 GBR ISSN 1748-3085
MINING (LONDON, 2005). Variant title: Getting the Deal Through. Mining. Text in English. 2005. a. USD 400 per issue (effective 2011). adv. reprints avail. **Document type:** *Journal, Trade.* **Description:** Addresses the key issues which are of concern to corporations and their counsel when conducting mining operations in foreign jurisdictions.
Related titles: Online - full text ed.: ISSN 1748-3093.
Published by: (Global Arbitration Review), Law Business Research Ltd., 87 Lancaster Rd, London, W11 1QQ, United Kingdom. TEL 44-20-79081188, FAX 44-20-72296910, http://www.lbresearch.com/. Ed. Callum Campbell. Pub. Richard Davey.

622 690 AUS ISSN 1833-3125
THE MINING ADVOCATE. Text in English. 2005. 11/yr. AUD 2.75 newsstand/cover (effective 2009). adv. back issues avail. **Document type:** *Newspaper, Trade.* **Description:** Covers news, trends and developments in the mining industry.
Formerly (until 2007): N Q Industry Advocate
Published by: N Q Industry Advocate, PO Box 945, Townsville, QLD 4810, Australia. TEL 61-7-47550336, FAX 61-7-47550338, info@industryadvocate.com.au, http://www.industryadvocate.com.au/index.htm. adv.: B&W page AUD 2,629, color page AUD 3,554; 255 x 370. Circ: 8,500.

622 338.2 ZAF ISSN 1028-5733
MINING & BUSINESS IN SOUTHERN AFRICA. Text in English. 199?. bi-m. ZAR 64 domestic; ZAR 129 foreign (effective 2000). illus.
Document type: *Journal, Trade.* **Description:** Covers the mining industry and trends in South Africa, Zimbabwe, and elsewhere in southern Africa.
Formerly (until 1997): Mining in Southern Africa (1027-2593)
Indexed: SpeleolAb.
Published by: T M L Business Publishing (Subsidiary of: Times Media Ltd.), PO Box 182, Pinegowrie, Gauteng 2123, South Africa. TEL 27-11-789-2144, FAX 27-11-789-3196, samining@tmltrade.co.za. Ed. Ian Robinson. Adv. contact Gill Williamson.

MINING AND MATERIALS PROCESSING INSTITUTE OF JAPAN. METALLURGICAL REVIEW. *see* METALLURGY

622 USA ISSN 1944-2467
MINING & MINERALS. Text in English. 2008. w. USD 2,295 in US & Canada; USD 2,495 elsewhere; USD 2,525 combined subscription in US & Canada (print & online eds.); USD 2,755 combined subscription elsewhere (print & online eds.) (effective 2011). adv. back issues avail. **Document type:** *Newsletter, Trade.* **Description:** Provides reports on the important institutional research into exploration for minerals (coal, metals, salt, precious gems), as well as the science of mineralogy.
Related titles: E-mail ed.; Online - full text ed.: ISSN 1944-2475. USD 2,295 combined subscription (online & e-mail eds.) (effective 2011).
Indexed: A15, ABIn, P10, P11, P26, P48, P51, P52, P53, P54, P56, PQC.
Published by: NewsRx, 2727 Paces Ferry Rd SE, Ste 2-440, Atlanta, GA 30339. TEL 770-435-8286, 800-726-4550, FAX 770-435-6800, pressrelease@newsrx.com, http://www.newsrx.com. Pub., Adv. contact Susan Hasty TEL 770-507-7777.

622 338 USA ISSN 1945-8215
MINING & MINERALS BUSINESS. Text in English. 2008. w. USD 2,295 in US & Canada; USD 2,495 elsewhere; USD 2,525 combined subscription in US & Canada (print & online eds.); USD 2,755 combined subscription elsewhere (print & online eds.) (effective 2011). adv. back issues avail. **Document type:** *Newsletter, Trade.*
Description: Covers the latest news and business developments of the companies that make up the mining and mineral industries, including mergers and acquisitions, financials, and management changes.
Related titles: E-mail ed.; Online - full text ed.: ISSN 1945-8223. USD 2,295 combined subscription (online & e-mail eds.) (effective 2011).
Indexed: A15, ABIn, B02, B15, B17, B18, G04, I05, P10, P11, P26, P48, P51, P52, P53, P54, P56, PQC.
Published by: NewsRx, 2727 Paces Ferry Rd SE, Ste 2-440, Atlanta, GA 30339. TEL 770-435-8286, 800-726-4550, FAX 770-435-6800, pressrelease@newsrx.com, http://www.newsrx.com. Pub., Adv. contact Susan Hasty TEL 770-507-7777.

MINING AND PETROLEUM LEGISLATION SERVICE. *see* LAW

328 AUS
MINING AND PETROLEUM LEGISLATION SERVICE (COMMONWEALTH). Text in English. 2 base vols. plus irreg. updates. looseleaf. AUD 7,590 (effective 2008). **Document type:** *Handbook/Manual/Guide, Trade.* **Description:** Covers resource that brings together legislation and regulations relating to all forms of mining, mineral exploration, onshore and offshore petroleum and pipelines in Australia.
Related titles: ◆ Series of: Mining and Petroleum Legislation Service.

Published by: (Australian Mining and Petroleum Law Association Ltd.), Lawbook Co. (Subsidiary of: Thomson Reuters (Professional) Australia Limited), PO Box 3502, Rozelle, NSW 2039, Australia. TEL 61-2-85877980, 300-304-195, FAX 61-2-85877981, 300-304-196, LTA.Service@thomsonreuters.com, http://www.thomson.com.au.

MINING AND PETROLEUM LEGISLATION SERVICE (NEW SOUTH WALES / AUSTRALIAN CAPITAL TERRITORY). *see* PUBLIC ADMINISTRATION

MINING AND PETROLEUM LEGISLATION SERVICE (QUEENSLAND). *see* PUBLIC ADMINISTRATION

MINING AND PETROLEUM LEGISLATION SERVICE (SOUTH AUSTRALIA / NORTHERN TERRITORY). *see* PUBLIC ADMINISTRATION

MINING AND PETROLEUM LEGISLATION SERVICE (VICTORIA / TASMANIA). *see* PUBLIC ADMINISTRATION

MINING AND PETROLEUM LEGISLATION SERVICE (WESTERN AUSTRALIA MINING ONLY). *see* PUBLIC ADMINISTRATION

MINING AND PETROLEUM LEGISLATION SERVICE (WESTERN AUSTRALIA PETROLEUM ONLY). *see* PUBLIC ADMINISTRATION

MINING AND PETROLEUM LEGISLATION SERVICE (WESTERN AUSTRALIA). *see* PUBLIC ADMINISTRATION

338.7662 USA
HD9506.U6

MINING BUSINESS DIGEST. Text in English. 1987. m. USD 99.95 (effective 2000). index. **Document type:** *Magazine, Trade.* **Description:** Contains a monthly summary of mining and exploration news covering gold and base-metal companies active in the US, Latin America and Oceania.
Former titles (until 2000): Mining Business Digest (Print) (1055-9957); (until 1991): Western Minerals Activity Report (0896-8527)
Media: Online - full text.
Published by: Lumac Enterprises, Inc., 1014 Snow Lilly Ct, Castle Rock, CO 80104-8273. TEL 303-814-2522, FAX 303-814-2522, mbd@mining.com. Ed. Frank Ludeman.

622 USA

MINING CAMP CHRONICLES. Text in English. 1998. irreg. price varies.
Published by: Westernlore Press, PO Box 35305, Tucson, AZ 85740. TEL 520-297-5491, FAX 520-297-1722. Ed. Lynn R Bailey.

622 551 669 IND

THE MINING, GEOLOGICAL AND METALLURGICAL INSTITUTE OF INDIA. PROCEEDINGS. Text in English. 19??. a. **Document type:** *Proceedings, Academic/Scholarly.* **Description:** Covers proceedings of all seminars, symposia, workshop organised by head quarters/branches are released before the commencement of events and distributed to authors for effective utilization of short period of the 'Event' for meaningful interaction.
Published by: The Mining Geological & Metallurgical Institute of India, GN-38/4, Salt Lake, Sector V, Kolkata, West Bengal 700 091, India. TEL 91-33-23573987, FAX 91-33-23573482, mgmikolkata@gmail.com.

622 551 669 IND ISSN 0371-9588
TN1 CODEN: TMGMAL

THE MINING, GEOLOGICAL AND METALLURGICAL INSTITUTE OF INDIA. TRANSACTIONS. Text in English. 1906. s-a. bibl.; charts; illus. **Document type:** *Journal, Academic/Scholarly.* **Description:** Contains original contribution by specialists, review papers by eminent scientists, case histories etc.
Formerly (until 1937): Geological Institute of India. Transactions of the Mining (0371-9642)
Indexed: GeoRef, SpeleolAb.
Published by: The Mining Geological & Metallurgical Institute of India, GN-38/4, Salt Lake, Sector V, Kolkata, West Bengal 700 091, India. TEL 91-33-23573987, FAX 91-33-23573482, mgmikolkata@gmail.com.

622 GBR ISSN 1366-2511
TN58.D4

➤ **MINING HISTORY.** Text in English. 1959. s-a. free to members (effective 2009). adv. bk.rev. charts; illus. cum.index. back issues avail. **Document type:** *Journal, Academic/Scholarly.* **Description:** Contents are anything concerning the history of mining.
Formerly (until 1996): Peak District Mines Historical Society. Bulletin (0031-3637)
Indexed: BrArAb, GEOBASE, GeoRef, NumL, SCOPUS, SpeleolAb, T02.
Published by: Peak District Mines Historical Society Ltd, c/o Peak District Mining Museum, Matlock Bath, S Parade, Matlock, Derbys DE4 3NR, United Kingdom. membership@pdmhs.com. Ed. Richard Shaw.

622 USA

MINING HISTORY ASSOCIATION NEWSLETTER. Text in English. 1990. q. free to members (effective 2010). bk.rev. back issues avail. **Document type:** *Newsletter, Trade.* **Description:** Offers Mining History Association members news and organizational information of interest.
Formerly (until 1993): Mining History Association News
Related titles: Online - full text ed.: free (effective 2010).
Published by: Mining History Association, PO. Box 552, Sedalia, CO 80135. Ed. Eric Nystrom.

622 USA

➤ **MINING HISTORY JOURNAL.** Text in English. 199?. a. free to members (effective 2010). illus. **Document type:** *Journal, Academic/Scholarly.* **Description:** Publishes scholarly research on the history of mines and mining.
Formerly (until 1995): Mining History Association. Annual
Published by: Mining History Association, PO Box 150300, Denver, CO 80215.

622 CAN ISSN 0316-2281
HD9506.C2

MINING IN CANADA - FACTS & FIGURES. Text in English. 1964. a. free. adv. charts; stat. **Document type:** *Report, Trade.*
Related titles: French ed.: Mines au Canada - Faits et Chiffres. ISSN 0316-2311.
Indexed: CSI.
Published by: Mining Association of Canada, 350 Sparks St, No. 1105, Ottawa, ON K1R 7S8, Canada. TEL 613-233-9391. Ed. Robert Keyes. Adv. contact Gisele Jacob. Circ: 12,000.

622 ZWE

MINING IN ZIMBABWE. Text in English. 1950. a. ZWD 105; ZWD 121.20 foreign (effective 1999). **Document type:** *Journal, Trade.*
Former titles: Mining in Zimbabwe Rhodesia; Mining in Rhodesia (0076-8987)
Published by: Thomson Publications Zimbabwe (Pvt) Ltd., Thomson House, PO Box 1683, Harare, Zimbabwe. TEL 263-4-736835, FAX 263-4-752390.

622 GBR ISSN 0026-5225
CODEN: MJOLAS

MINING JOURNAL. Text in English. 1835. w. GBP 320 in UK & Europe(non euro zone); EUR 516.20 in Europe euro zone; USD 578.50 elsewhere; GBP 360 combined subscription (print & online eds.); in UK & Europe (non euro zone); EUR 580 combined subscription in Europe (print & online eds.), non euro zone; USD 650 combined subscription elsewhere (pint & online eds.) (effective 2009); subscr. Includes Mining Magazine, Mining Environmental Management, Country and Commodity Reports Online. adv. bk.rev. illus. index. back issues avail.; reprints avail. **Document type:** *Newspaper, Trade.* **Description:** Provides international coverage of political, financial and technical news affecting the mining industry.
Former titles (until 1908): The Mining Journal, Railway and Commercial Gazette; (until 1844): The Mining Journal and Commercial Gazette
Related titles: Microfiche ed.; Online - full text ed.: GBP 263 in UK & Europe(non euro zone); EUR 423.40 in Europe euro zone; USD 474.50 elsewhere (effective 2009).
Indexed: A22, A26, A32, AESIS, BrGeoL, CRIA, CRICC, ChemAb, E08, EIA, EnerInd, F&EA, G08, GeoRef, I05, IMMAb, KES, RefZh, S09, SCOPUS, SpeleolAb.
—CIS, IE, Ingenta, Linda Hall. **CCC.**
Published by: Aspermont UK, Albert House, 1 Singer St, London, EC2A 4BQ, United Kingdom. TEL 44-20-72166060, FAX 44-20-72166050, info@aspermontuk.com, http://www.aspermontuk.com/. Adv. contact Gareth Hector TEL 44-20-72166070. page GBP 2,350; trim 210 x 297.

MINING LEGISLATION: WORLD (BY COUNTRY). *see* LAW—International Law

338.4 622 USA

MINING MACHINERY AND MINERAL PROCESSING EN ESPANOL. Text in Spanish. 1987. 6/yr. USD 80. adv. bibl.; tr.lit. **Document type:** *Magazine, Trade.* **Description:** Contains technical news, new products reviews, job stories and machinery applications stories for readers in 22 Spanish-speaking countries.
Supersedes in part: Construction and Mining Machinery en Espanol
Published by: Mining Machinery Corp., 5600 S W 135th Ave, Ste 107, Miami, FL 33183. TEL 305-388-4890, FAX 305-388-4991. Ed. Adolfo T Ramos. Pub. Jerry Estevez. Adv. contact Pablo Aguila. B&W page USD 2,143, color page USD 3,152; trim 10.88 x 8. Circ: 17,000 (controlled).

622 GBR ISSN 0308-6631
TN1 CODEN: VAMED2

MINING MAGAZINE. Text in English. 1909. m. GBP 95 combined subscription (print & online eds.); in UK & Europe(non euro zone); EUR 160 combined subscription in Europe (print & online eds.), euro zone; USD 170 combined subscription elsewhere (print & online eds.) (effective 2009). adv. bk.rev. abstr.; bibl.; illus.; mkt.; pat.; stat. index. back issues avail.; reprints avail. **Document type:** *Magazine, Trade.* **Description:** Contains articles that examine a variety of products and techniques, covering their applications, advantages, problems and solutions.
Related titles: Microfiche ed.; Online - full text ed.; Spanish ed.: Mining Magazine (Spanish Edition).
Indexed: A&ATA, A22, A26, A28, AESIS, APA, BrCerAb, BrTechI, C&ISA, CA/WCA, CIA, CRIA, CRICC, Cadscan, CerAb, ChemAb, ChemTitl, CivEngAb, CorrAb, E&CAJ, E08, E11, EEA, EMA, ESPM, EngInd, EnvEAb, F&EA, FR, G08, GeoRef, H15, HRIS, I05, IMMAb, KES, LeadAb, M&TEA, M09, MBF, METADEX, RefZh, S09, SCOPUS, SolStAb, SpeleolAb, T04, TM, WAA, Zincscan.
—BLDSC (5805.000000), CASDDS, CIS, IE, Infotrieve, Ingenta, INIST, Linda Hall. **CCC.**
Published by: Aspermont UK, Albert House, 1 Singer St, London, EC2A 4BQ, United Kingdom. TEL 44-20-72166060, FAX 44-20-72166050, info@aspermontuk.com, http://www.aspermontuk.com/. Ed. Paul Moore. Adv. contact Gareth Hector TEL 44-20-72166070. page GBP 3,755, page EUR 5,605, page USD 7,510; trim 200 x 275.

622 ZAF ISSN 1022-5455

MINING MIRROR; mining in perspective. Text in English. 1988. m. (11/yr.). ZAR 500 domestic; USD 140 in Africa; USD 265 elsewhere (effective 2011). adv. **Document type:** *Magazine, Trade.* **Description:** Covers the mining and mining machinery manufacturing industries.
Incorporates: Drilling News
Indexed: ISAP.
Published by: Brooke Pattrick Publications, Bldg 13, Pinewood Office Park, 33 Riley Rd, Woodmead, Johannesburg, Transvaal, South Africa. TEL 27-11-6033960, FAX 27-11-2346290, bestbook@brookepattrick.co.za, http://www.brookepattrick.com.

622 ZAF

MINING NEWS. Text in English; Text occasionally in Afrikaans. m. adv. **Document type:** *Newspaper.* **Description:** For mining industry personnel in South Africa.
Indexed: AESIS.
Published by: Chamber of Mines of South Africa, PO Box 809, Johannesburg, 2000, South Africa. TEL 27-11-4987100, FAX 27-11-8368070. Ed. C Du Toit Thom. Circ: (controlled).

628 GBR ISSN 2047-0207
TN5

MINING, PEOPLE AND THE ENVIRONMENT; driving change and awareness. Abbreviated title: M P E. Text in English. 1993. q. GBP 95 combined subscription domestic (print & online eds.); EUR 160 combined subscription in Europe (print & online eds.); USD 170 combined subscription elsewhere (print & online eds.) (effective 2011). adv. **Document type:** *Magazine, Trade.* **Description:** Aims to encourage communication within the industry and between the mining industry and other elements of society.
Formerly (until 2010): Mining Environmental Management (0969-4218)
Related titles: Online - full text ed.
Indexed: A32, AESIS, CRIA, GeoRef, RefZh, SpeleolAb.
—Ingenta, Linda Hall. **CCC.**
Published by: Aspermont UK, Albert House, 1 Singer St, London, EC2A 4BQ, United Kingdom. TEL 44-20-72166060, FAX 44-20-72166050, info@aspermontuk.com, http://www.aspermontuk.com/. Ed. Katherine Welch. Adv. contact Gareth Hector TEL 44-20-72166070.

622 ZAF

MINING R & D NEWS. Text in English. 1983. q. free. **Document type:** *Newsletter, Trade.* **Description:** Informs the mining industry of current developments, progress made in research, and consultancy services.
Supersedes (in July 1993): Chamber of Mines Research Organization. R and D News
Indexed: ISAP.
Published by: Council for Scientific and Industrial Research (C S I R), PO Box 395, Pretoria, 0001, South Africa. TEL 27-12-8412911, FAX 27-12-3491153, http://www.csir.co.za. Circ: 3,500.

622 USA ISSN 0026-5241
TN1

THE MINING RECORD. Text in English. 1889. w. USD 45 print or online; USD 75 combined subscription domestic print & online; USD 102 combined subscription in Canada & Mexico print & online; USD 120 combined subscription elsewhere print & online (effective 2005). adv. mkt. 20 p./no.; **Document type:** *Magazine, Trade.*
Former titles (until 1968): Mining and Natural Resources Record (0270-5818); (until 1964): Mining Record (0271-7549)
Related titles: Online - full content ed.
—CCC.
Published by: Howell International Enterprises, 2700 Butte Circle, Sedalia, CO 80135. TEL 303-663-7820. Ed., Pub., R&P Don E Howell. Adv. contact Dale Howell. col. inch USD 30. Circ: 5,000 (paid).

622 NLD ISSN 1674-5264

➤ **MINING SCIENCE AND TECHNOLOGY.** Text in English. 1990. bi-m. CNY 120, USD 120; CNY 20 per issue (effective 2009). **Document type:** *Journal, Academic/Scholarly.* **Description:** Publishes original research papers covering all aspects of mining sciences and technologies, including mining engineering; safety technology and engineering; mineral processing; coalfield geology engineering; mine mechanical engineering and automation.
Formerly (until 2008): China University of Mining and Technology. Journal (1006-1266)
Related titles: Online - full text ed.: (from ScienceDirect); ◆ Chinese ed.: Zhongguo Kuangye Daxue Xuebao. ISSN 1000-1964.
Indexed: A28, APA, BrCerAb, CA/WCA, CIA, CPEI, CerAb, CivEngAb, E11, EEA, EMA, ESPM, EnvEAb, H15, M&TEA, M09, MBF, METADEX, RefZh, SCOPUS, T04.
—BLDSC (5806.470000), IE, Linda Hall. **CCC.**
Published by: (Zhongguo Kuangye Daxue/China University of Mining and Technology CHN), Elsevier BV (Subsidiary of: Elsevier Science & Technology), Radarweg 29, PO Box 211, Amsterdam, 1000 AE, Netherlands. JournalsCustomerServiceEMEA@elsevier.com, http://www.elsevier.nl. Ed. Zhenfu Luo. Circ: 1,000.

622 CAN ISSN 0840-6723
TN26

MINING SOURCEBOOK. Variant title: Canadian Mining Sourcebook. Text in English. 1891. a. (in Dec.). CAD 106 per issue domestic; USD 94 per issue foreign (effective 2008). adv. **Document type:** *Directory, Trade.*
Former titles (until 1989): Canadian Mining Journal's Reference Manual and Buyers' Guide (0315-9140); Canadian Mining Manual (0068-9319)
Published by: Business Information Group, 12 Concorde Pl, Ste 800, Toronto, ON M3C 4J2, Canada. TEL 416-442-2122, 800-668-2374, FAX 416-442-2191, orders@businessinformationgroup.ca. Circ: 2,970.

622 USA
HD9541

MINING WEEK (ONLINE). Text in English. 19??. w. free to members (effective 2011). back issues avail. **Document type:** *Newsletter, Trade.*
Former titles (until 2001): Mining Week (Print); (until 1995): Coal News (0530-0037); (until 195?): Daily Digest
Media: Online - full text.
Published by: National Mining Association, 101 Constitution Ave, NW, Ste 500E, Washington, DC 20001. TEL 202-463-2600, FAX 202-463-2666, MPhelleps@nma.org.

622 ZAF ISSN 1562-9619

MINING WEEKLY. Variant title: Martin Creamer's Mining Weekly. Text in English. 1995. w. ZAR 282 domestic; ZAR 1,500 Sub-Saharan countries; ZAR 2,000 elsewhere; ZAR 722 domestic print & online eds.; ZAR 1,940 Sub-Saharan countries; print & online eds.; ZAR 2,440 elsewhere print & online eds. (effective 2007). adv. illus.; maps. **Document type:** *Newspaper, Trade.*
Related titles: Online - full text ed.
—CCC.
Published by: Martin Creamer Media (Pty) Ltd., PO Box 75316, Garden View, 2047, South Africa. TEL 27-11-6223744, FAX 27-11-6229350. Ed., Pub. Martin Creamer. Adv. contact Ema Oosthuizen. page ZAR 13,900; bleed 216 x 281.

622 ZAF ISSN 1029-3590

MINING WORLD. Variant title: South African Mining World. Text in English. 1982. m. ZAR 126 domestic; ZAR 205 foreign (effective 2003). adv. **Document type:** *Magazine, Trade.*
Former titles (until Sep. 1995): South African Mining World; Mining World S A
Indexed: IMMAb, ISAP.
Published by: (South African Coal Processing Society), Primedia Publishing, 366 Pretoria Ave, Ferndale, Randburg, Transvaal 2194, South Africa. TEL 27-11-787-5725, FAX 27-11-787-5776, http://www.primediapublishing.co.za/. Ed. Alastair Currie. **Co-sponsor:** S.A. Flameproof Association.

622 GBR ISSN 2045-2578

MINING WORLD. Text in English. 2004. 4/yr. GBP 40 domestic; GBP 50 foreign (effective 2011). adv. **Document type:** *Journal, Trade.*
Formerly (until 2011): Mining and Quarry World (1757-6660)
Related titles: Online - full text ed.: ISSN 2045-2586.
—CCC.
Published by: Tradelink Publications Ltd, British Fields, Ollerton Rd, Tuxford, Newark, Notts NG22 0PQ, United Kingdom. TEL 44-1777-871007, FAX 44-1777-872271, info@tradelinkpub.co.uk, http://www.tradelinkpub.co.uk.

MINNO DELO I GEOLOGIA. *see* ENGINEERING

M

622.33 ZAF
MINTEK REPORTS. Text in English. 1966. irreg. (approx. 20-30/yr.). USD 400. bibl.; illus. **Description:** Deals with mineral processing research.
Former titles: M I N T E K Reports; N I M Reports
Indexed: ChemAb, IMMAb, Inspec, MinerAb.
Published by: Mintek, 200 Hans Strijdom Dr, Private Bag X3015, Randburg, Gauteng 2125, South Africa. TEL 27-11-709-4111, FAX 27-11-709-4326.

622.33 ZAF ISSN 1010-2582
MINTEK RESEARCH DIGEST. Text in English. 1974. bi-m. free.
Former titles: M I N T E K Research Digest; N I M Research Digest
Indexed: AESIS.
Published by: Mintek, 200 Hans Strijdom Dr, Private Bag X3015, Randburg, Gauteng 2125, South Africa. TEL 27-11-709-4111, FAX 27-11-709-4326.

622.33 ZAF
MINTEK. SPECIAL PUBLICATIONS. Text in English. 1975. irreg., latest vol.13, 1989. price varies. **Description:** Covers various aspects of metallurgy and mineral technology, including research, production, and conferences.
Formerly: Council for Mineral Technology (MINTEK). Special Publication
Indexed: IMMAb, SpeleolAb.
Published by: Mintek, 200 Hans Strijdom Dr, Private Bag X3015, Randburg, Gauteng 2125, South Africa. TEL 27-11-709-4111, FAX 27-11-709-4326, TELEX 4-24867 SA.

549 RUS
➤ **MIR KAMNYA/WORLD OF STONES.** Text in English; Section in Russian. 1993. q. USD 52 (effective 1995 & 1996). adv. bk.rev. bibl.; illus. index. back issues avail. **Document type:** *Journal, Academic/Scholarly.* **Description:** Popular-science mineralogical journal for mineralogists and collectors.
Indexed: MinerAb.
Published by: Plus Ltd. Publishing, A-ya 162, Moscow, 103050, Russian Federation. TEL 7-095-2033574, FAX 7-095-2926511. Ed. Alexander Evseev. Pubs. Audrey Y Belyakov, Michael B Leybov. Circ: 3,000. **Subscr. in US to:** H. Obodda, PO Box 51, Short Hills, NJ 07078.

622 551 USA
MONTANA. BUREAU OF MINES AND GEOLOGY. BIENNIAL REPORT. Text in English. 19??. biennial. back issues avail. **Document type:** *Report, Trade.*
Former titles: Montana. Bureau of Mines and Geology. Annual Report (0277-0652); (until 1980): Montana. Bureau of Mines and Geology. Biennial Report
Related titles: Online - full text ed.: free (effective 2011).
Indexed: GeoRef.
—Linda Hall.
Published by: Montana Bureau of Mines and Geology, Natural Resource Bldg, 1505 W Park St, Butte, MT 59701. TEL 406-496-4180, FAX 406-496-4451, pubsales@mtech.edu, http://www.mbmg.mtech.edu.

MONTANA. BUREAU OF MINES AND GEOLOGY. BULLETIN. *see* EARTH SCIENCES—Geology

MONTANA. BUREAU OF MINES AND GEOLOGY. MEMOIR. *see* EARTH SCIENCES—Geology

622 USA ISSN 0077-1104
MONTANA. BUREAU OF MINES AND GEOLOGY. MONTANA MINING DIRECTORY. Text in English. 19??. irreg., latest 2001. price varies. back issues avail. **Document type:** *Monographic series, Trade.* **Description:** Lists types of ore produced, mining districts, property locations, owners' and operators' names and addresses, mill capacities, numbers of employees and yearly status.
Formerly: Montana. Bureau of Mines and Geology. Directory of Mining Enterprises
Related titles: Series of: Open-Files Reports.
Published by: Montana Bureau of Mines and Geology, Natural Resource Bldg, 1505 W Park St, Butte, MT 59701. TEL 406-496-4180, FAX 406-496-4451, pubsales@mtech.edu, http://www.mbmg.mtech.edu.

MONTANA. BUREAU OF MINES AND GEOLOGY. SPECIAL PUBLICATIONS. *see* EARTH SCIENCES—Geology

MONTHLY STATISTICS OF MINERAL PRODUCTION. *see* MINES AND MINING INDUSTRY—Abstracting, Bibliographies, Statistics

388.2096405 GBR ISSN 1755-7844
MOROCCO MINING REPORT. Text in English. 2007. q. EUR 820, USD 1,030 combined subscription (print & email eds.) (effective 2010). **Document type:** *Report, Trade.* **Description:** Features latest-available data and forecasts covering all headline indicators for mining; company rankings and competitive landscapes covering mining exploration and production; and analysis of latest industry developments, trends and regulatory issues.
Related titles: E-mail ed.
Indexed: A15, ABIn, B02, B15, B17, B18, G04, I05, P48, P51, P52, P56, PQC.
Published by: Business Monitor International Ltd., Senator House, 85 Queen Victoria St, London, EC4V 4AB, United Kingdom. TEL 44-20-72480468, FAX 44-20-72480467, subs@businessmonitor.com.

338.209679 GBR ISSN 1755-8956
MOZAMBIQUE MINING REPORT. Text in English. 2007. q. EUR 820, USD 1,030 combined subscription (print & email eds.) (effective 2010). **Document type:** *Report, Trade.* **Description:** Provides industry strategists, service companies, company analysts and consultants, government departments, trade associations and regulatory bodies.
Related titles: E-mail ed.
Indexed: A15, ABIn, B02, B15, B17, B18, G04, I05, P48, P51, P52, P56, PQC.
Published by: Business Monitor International Ltd., Senator House, 85 Queen Victoria St, London, EC4V 4AB, United Kingdom. TEL 44-20-72480468, FAX 44-20-72480467, subs@businessmonitor.com.

MUENCHNER GEOWISSENSCHAFTLICHE ABHANDLUNGEN. REIHE B: ALLGEMEINE UND ANGEWANDTE GEOLOGIE. *see* EARTH SCIENCES—Geology

622 COD ISSN 0541-4873
MWANA SHABA; journal d'entreprise de la Gecamines. Text in French. 1957. m.
Published by: (Generale des Carrieres et des Mines, Division des Relations Publiques COG), Generale des Carrieres et des Mines, BP 450, Lubumbashi, Congo, Dem. Republic.

622 USA
N A Q N; the rock to road trade magazine. (North American Quarry News) Text in English. 1997. m. free (effective 2011). adv. **Document type:** *Newspaper, Consumer.* **Description:** Contains a mix of feature articles about the producers in the industry and how the equipment and technology is helping the increase production, along with information on new equipment and health and safety issues.
Published by: Lee Publications, Inc., 6113 State Hwy 5, PO Box 121, Palatine Bridge, NY 13428. FAX 518-673-3245, info@leepub.com, http://www.leepub.com. Ed. Jon Casey.

N B M G. OPEN-FILE REPORT. *see* EARTH SCIENCES—Geology

N R R I NOW. (Natural Resources Research Institute) *see* EARTH SCIENCES

NALK REPORT. *see* METALLURGY

NAMIBIA BRIEF. *see* BUSINESS AND ECONOMICS—International Development And Assistance

338.2709688105 GBR ISSN 1755-7852
NAMIBIA MINING REPORT. Text in English. 2007. q. EUR 820, USD 1,030 combined subscription (print & email eds.) (effective 2010). **Document type:** *Report, Trade.* **Description:** Provides industry strategists, service companies, company analysts and consultants, government departments, trade associations and regulatory bodies.
Related titles: E-mail ed.
Indexed: A15, ABIn, B02, B15, B17, B18, G04, I05, P48, P51, P52, P56, PQC.
Published by: Business Monitor International Ltd., Senator House, 85 Queen Victoria St, London, EC4V 4AB, United Kingdom. TEL 44-20-72480468, FAX 44-20-72480467, enquiry@businessmonitor.com.

622.33 AUS ISSN 1839-0145
NAMOI VALLEY ENERGY. Text in English. 200?. irreg. adv. **Document type:** *Magazine, Trade.* **Description:** Covers the coal, coal seam gas and thermal industries.
Published by: Gunnedah Publishing Company Pty. Ltd, 287 Conadilly St, PO Box 483, Gunnedah, NSW 2380, Australia. TEL 61-2-67420455, FAX 61-2-67423603.

622 USA
NATIONAL INSTITUTE FOR OCCUPATIONAL SAFETY AND HEALTH. INFORMATION CIRCULAR. Text in English. 1925. irreg. price varies. **Document type:** *Government.* **Description:** Reports the results of various economic and special studies.
Formerly (until 1997): U.S. Bureau of Mines. Information Circulars (1066-5544)
Related titles: Microfiche ed.: 1925 (from NTI).
Indexed: AESIS, ChemAb, IMMAb, PetrolAb, SpeleolAb.
—INIST.
Published by: U.S. National Institute for Occupational Safety and Health, 1600 Clifton Rd, Atlanta, GA 30333. TEL 888-232-6348, cdcinfo@cdc.gov, http://www.cdc.gov/niosh/.

622 UKR ISSN 2071-2227
➤ **NATSIONAL'NYI HIRNYCHYI UNIVERSYTET. NAUKOVYI VISNYK/ NATIONAL MINING UNIVERSITY. SCIENTIFIC BULLETIN.** Text in Russian, Ukrainian, English, German. 1998. bi-m. UAK 1,100 domestic; USD 140 foreign (effective 2011). abstr.; bibl.; charts; illus.; maps. back issues avail. **Document type:** *Journal, Academic/ Scholarly.* **Description:** Covers actual problems in mineral resource industry and power industry and tries to find a solution to these problems via fundamental investigations and applied research, new scientific approaches to development of technologies, analysis of economic aspects of their operation and issues of higher school performance improvement.
Published by: Natsional'nyi Hirnychyi Universytet/National Mining University, vul Karla Marksa 19, Dnipropetrovs'k, 79027, Ukraine. TEL 380-563-730847, http://www.nmu.org.ua. Ed. Hennadii Pivniak. Pub. Tamara Barna.

622 551 USA ISSN 1520-7439
TN1 CODEN: NRREFQ
➤ **NATURAL RESOURCES RESEARCH.** Text in English. 1992. q. EUR 618, USD 595 combined subscription to institutions (print & online eds.) (effective 2012). adv. bk.rev. back issues avail.; reprint service avail. from PSC. **Document type:** *Journal, Academic/Scholarly.* **Description:** Provides insight into the understanding, development, and use of mineral resources and other natural resources, both renewable and nonrenewable.
Formerly (until 1999): Nonrenewable Resources (0961-1444)
Related titles: Online - full text ed.: ISSN 1573-8981 (from IngentaConnect).
Indexed: A22, A26, A28, A29, APA, ASFA, Agr, B20, B21, BibLing, BrCerAb, C&ISA, CA, CA/WCA, CIA, CIN, CerAb, ChemAb, ChemTitl, CivEngAb, CorrAb, E&CAJ, E01, E04, E05, E11, EEA, EMA, ESPM, EnvEAb, GeoRef, H15, I05, I10, IMMAb, M&TEA, M09, MBF, METADEX, PollutAb, RefZh, SCOPUS, SolStAb, SpeleolAb, T02, T04, ViroIAbstr, WAA.
—BLDSC (6040.775000), CASDDS, IE, Infotrieve, Ingenta, INIST, Linda Hall. **CCC.**
Published by: (International Association for Mathematical Geology CAN), Springer New York LLC (Subsidiary of: Springer Science+Business Media), 233 Spring St, New York, NY 10013. TEL 212-460-1500, FAX 212-460-1575, service-ny@springer.com, http://www.springer.com. Eds. J L Jensen TEL 403-210-6324, Keith R Long TEL 520-670-5512.

338.2 RUS ISSN 0868-4502
NAUCHNO-TEKHNICHESKIE DOSTIZHENIYA I PEREDOVOI OPYT V OBLASTI GEOLOGII I RAZVEDKI NADER. Text in Russian. m. USD 189.95 in United States.
—East View.
Published by: Informatsionno-Izdatel'skii Tsentr po Geologii i Nedropol'zovaniu Geoinformmark, Goncharnaya 38, Moscow, 115172, Russian Federation. info@geoinform.ru. **Dist. by:** East View Information Services, 10601 Wayzata Blvd, Minneapolis, MN 55305. TEL 952-252-1201, 800-477-1005, FAX 952-252-1202, info@eastview.com, http://www.eastview.com.

NETHERLANDS JOURNAL OF GEOSCIENCES/GEOLOGY AND MINING. *see* EARTH SCIENCES—Geology

549 DEU ISSN 0077-7757
QE351 CODEN: NJMIAK
➤ **NEUES JAHRBUCH FUER MINERALOGIE. ABHANDLUNGEN.** Text in English. 1807. 6/yr. (in 2 vols., 3 nos./vol.). USD 790 combined subscription per vol. (print & online eds.) (effective 2011). adv. back issues avail. **Document type:** *Journal, Academic/Scholarly.*
Formerly (until 1950): Neues Jahrbuch fuer Mineralogie, Geologie und Palaeontologie, Abhandlungen, Abteilung A: Mineralogie, Petrographie (0369-4488); Supersedes in part: Neues Jahrbuch fur Mineralogie, Geologie und Palaontologie, Beilageband; Incorporates (1806-2005): Neues Jahrbuch fuer Mineralogie. Monatshefte (0028-3649); Which was formerly (until 1950): Neues Jahrbuch fuer Mineralogie, Geologie und Palaeontologie. Monatshefte. Abteilung 1: Mineralogie, Gesteinskunde (0369-4526); Which superseded in part (in 1943): Neues Jahrbuch fuer Mineralogie, Geologie und Palaeontologie. Referate (0369-4518); Which was formerly (until 1833): Jahrbuch fuer Mineralogie, Geognosie, Geologie und Petrefaktenkunde
Related titles: Microfiche ed.: (from BHP); Online - full text ed.: (from IngentaConnect).
Indexed: A&ATA, A22, AESIS, ASCA, BrGeoL, C33, ChemAb, CurCont, GEOBASE, GeoRef, IBR, IBZ, ISR, MSCI, MinerAb, SCI, SCOPUS, SpeleolAb, W07.
—CASDDS, IE, Infotrieve, Ingenta, INIST, Linda Hall. **CCC.**
Published by: E. Schweizerbart'sche Verlagsbuchhandlung, Johannesstr 3A, Stuttgart, 70176, Germany. TEL 49-711-3514560, FAX 49-711-35145699, order@schweizerbart.de. Eds. Gene C Ulmer, Heinz-Guenter Stosch.

➤ **NEVADA. BUREAU OF MINES AND GEOLOGY. BULLETIN.** *see* EARTH SCIENCES—Geology

➤ **NEVADA. BUREAU OF MINES AND GEOLOGY. EDUCATIONAL SERIES.** *see* EARTH SCIENCES—Geology

➤ **NEVADA. BUREAU OF MINES AND GEOLOGY. LISTS.** *see* EARTH SCIENCES—Geology

➤ **NEVADA. BUREAU OF MINES AND GEOLOGY. PAMPHLET.** *see* EARTH SCIENCES—Geology

➤ **NEVADA. BUREAU OF MINES AND GEOLOGY. REPORT.** *see* EARTH SCIENCES—Geology

➤ **NEVADA. BUREAU OF MINES AND GEOLOGY. SPECIAL PUBLICATIONS.** *see* EARTH SCIENCES—Geology

➤ **NEVADA MINERAL INDUSTRY (YEAR).** *see* EARTH SCIENCES—Geology

622 NCL ISSN 0758-6485
NEW CALEDONIA. SERVICE DES MINES ET DE L'ENERGIE. RAPPORT ANNUEL. Text in French. 1915. a. KMF 760. illus. **Document type:** *Government.*
Published by: Service des Mines et de l'Energie, Noumea, New Caledonia. FAX 687-272345. Circ: 210.

622 USA ISSN 0096-4581
TN24.N6 CODEN: NEXBAJ
NEW MEXICO. BUREAU OF GEOLOGY AND MINERAL RESOURCES. BULLETIN. Text in English. 1915. irreg., latest vol.160, 2004. price varies. abstr.; bibl.; charts; illus.; maps. back issues avail. **Document type:** *Bulletin, Government.*
Formerly (until 1919): New Mexico. Mineral Resources Survey. Bulletin
Related titles: CD-ROM ed.; Online - full text ed.: free (effective 2010).
Indexed: A23, A24, B13, CIN, ChemAb, ChemTitl, GeoRef, IMMAb, MinerAb, SpeleolAb, Z01.
—Linda Hall.
Published by: Bureau of Geology and Mineral Resources, New Mexico Tech, 801 Leroy Pl, Socorro, NM 87801. TEL 575-835-5420, FAX 505-835-6333, pubsofc@geo.nmt.edu.

622 USA
TN24.N6 CODEN: NEXCAM
NEW MEXICO. BUREAU OF GEOLOGY AND MINERAL RESOURCES. CIRCULAR. Text in English. 1930. irreg., latest vol.212, 2006. price varies. back issues avail. **Document type:** *Newsletter, Trade.*
Formerly (until 2001): New Mexico. Bureau of Mines and Mineral Resources. Circular (0096-4948)
Related titles: CD-ROM ed.; Online - full text ed.
Indexed: A23, A24, B13, GeoRef, IMMAb, SpeleolAb.
—CASDDS, Linda Hall.
Published by: Bureau of Geology and Mineral Resources, New Mexico Tech, 801 Leroy Pl, Socorro, NM 87801. TEL 575-835-5420, FAX 505-835-6333, pubsofc@geo.nmt.edu.

622 USA ISSN 0548-5975
TN24.N5 CODEN: NMMMAJ
NEW MEXICO. BUREAU OF GEOLOGY AND MINERAL RESOURCES. MEMOIR. Text in English. 1956. irreg., latest vol.49, 2003. price varies. **Document type:** *Government.*
Related titles: Online - full text ed.
Indexed: GeoRef, IMMAb, MinerAb, SpeleolAb, Z01.
—Linda Hall.
Published by: Bureau of Geology and Mineral Resources, New Mexico Tech, 801 Leroy Pl, Socorro, NM 87801. TEL 575-835-5420, FAX 505-835-6333, pubsofc@geo.nmt.edu.

NEW SOUTH WALES. GEOLOGICAL SURVEY. METALLOGENIC STUDY AND MINERAL DEPOSIT DATA SHEETS. *see* EARTH SCIENCES—Geology

622 559 AUS ISSN 0077-8729
CODEN: NWMGA3
NEW SOUTH WALES. GEOLOGICAL SURVEY. MINERAL INDUSTRY OF NEW SOUTH WALES. Text in English. 1967. irreg. price varies. **Document type:** *Monographic series, Government.*
Indexed: AESIS, IMMAb, SpeleolAb.
Published by: N S W Department of Primary Industries, Geological Survey of New South Wales, PO Box 344, Hunter Region Mail Centre, Hunter Region Mail Centre, NSW 2310, Australia. TEL 61-2-49316666, 300-736-122, FAX 61-2-49316700, http://www.dpi.nsw.gov.au/minerals/geological. Circ: 400.

622 559 AUS ISSN 0077-8737
TN122 CODEN: MRWGDA
NEW SOUTH WALES. GEOLOGICAL SURVEY. MINERAL RESOURCES SERIES. Variant title: Geological Survey of N.S.W. Mineral Resources. Text in English. 1898. irreg., latest vol.46, 1989. price varies. Index. **Document type:** *Monographic series, Government.* **Description:** Comprehensive treatises on the geology, distribution mining history of particular minerals.
Related titles: Online - full text ed.
Indexed: AESIS, GeoRef, IMMAb, SpeleolAb.
—Ingenta, Linda Hall.
Published by: N S W Department of Primary Industries, Geological Survey of New South Wales, PO Box 344, Hunter Region Mail Centre, Hunter Region Mail Centre, NSW 2310, Australia. TEL 61-2-49316666, 300-736-122, FAX 61-2-49316700, geoscience.products@dpi.nsw.gov.au. Circ: 400.

622 553 CAN ISSN 1189-6108
NEWFOUNDLAND. DEPARTMENT OF MINES AND ENERGY. GEOLOGICAL SURVEY BRANCH. ORE HORIZONS. Key Title: Ore Horizons. Text in English. 1991. biennial. price varies. illus. **Document type:** *Government.* **Description:** Collection of descriptive articles dealing with mineral deposits, exploration case histories, and mineral development projects in the province.
Published by: Department of Mines and Energy, P.O. Box 8700, St. John's, NF A1B 4J6, Canada. TEL 709-729-3159, FAX 709-729-3493. Ed. B Kean. Circ: 600 (paid).

622 333.79 CAN
NEWFOUNDLAND. DEPARTMENT OF NATURAL RESOURCES. GEOLOGICAL SURVEY. CURRENT RESEARCH. Text in English. a. adv. illus. **Document type:** *Government.* **Description:** Presents annual results of studies in all aspects of Newfoundland and Labrador earth science.
Former titles (until 1990): Newfoundland. Department of Mines and Energy. Geological Survey. Current Research (0843-4972); (until 1988): Newfoundland. Department of Mines and Energy. Mineral Development Division. Current Research (0711-804X); (until 1980): Newfoundland. Mineral Development Division. Report of Activities (0703-1017); (until 1973): Newfoundland. Mineral Development Division. Annual Report (0844-8027)
Indexed: IMMAb, SpeleolAb.
—Linda Hall. **CCC.**
Published by: Department of Mines and Energy, Geological Survey, P O Box 8700, St. John's, NF A1B 4J6, Canada. TEL 709-729-3159, FAX 709-729-3493. Ed., Adv. contact B. Kean. Circ: 500 (paid).

NEWS TO USE. *see* CONSERVATION

NIIGATA UNIVERSITY. FACULTY OF SCIENCE. SCIENCE REPORTS. SERIES E: GEOLOGY AND MINERALOGY/NIIGATA DAIGAKU RIGAKUBU KENKYU HOKOKU. E-RUI, CHISHITSU KOBUTSUGAKU. *see* EARTH SCIENCES—Geology

NONFERROUS METALS SOCIETY OF CHINA. TRANSACTIONS. *see* METALLURGY

622 CAN ISSN 0029-3164
THE NORTHERN MINER; devoted to the mineral resources industry of Canada. Text in English. 1915. w. CAD 95 domestic; USD 95 in United States; USD 130 foreign (effective 2008). adv. bk.rev. charts; illus.; mkt.; stat.; tr.lit. **Document type:** *Newspaper, Trade.* **Description:** Covers the North-American and international activities of all North-American based mining companies.
Related titles: CD-ROM ed.: CAD 249 per issue domestic; USD 199 per issue foreign (effective 2008); Microfilm ed.: (from CML, PQC, SOC); Online - full text ed.: CAD 95 domestic; USD 95 in United States; USD 130 foreign (effective 2008).
Indexed: B03, C03, CBCABus, CBPI, CPerI, CWI, G08, GeoRef, IMMAb, P48, P52, P53, P56, PQC, PROMT, SpeleolAb.
—Linda Hall. **CCC.**
Published by: Business Information Group, 12 Concorde Pl, Ste 800, Toronto, ON M3C 4J2, Canada. TEL 416-442-2122, 800-668-2374, FAX 416-442-2191, orders@businessinformationgroup.ca, http://www.businessinformationgroup.ca. Ed. John Cumming TEL 416-510-6764. Pub. Douglas Donnelly TEL 416-442-2098. Circ: 27,000.

622 RUS ISSN 0202-3776
TN500 CODEN: OBOGAD
OBOGASHCHENIE RUD/MINERAL PROCESSING. Text in Russian. 1956. bi-m. USD 294 foreign (effective 2009). adv. bk.rev. **Document type:** *Journal, Trade.* **Description:** Covers mineral processing, concentration processes and technological mineralogy.
Indexed: CIN, ChemAb, ChemTitl, IMMAb, RefZh.
—CASDDS, Linda Hall.
Published by: Izdatel'stvo Ruda i Metally/Ore and Metals Publishers, Leninskii prospekt 6, korpus 1, ofis 622, a/ya 71, Moscow, 119049, Russian Federation. rim@rudmet.ru. Ed. Viktor F Baranov. adv.: page USD 200. Circ: 1,000. **Dist. by:** East View Information Services, 10601 Wayzata Blvd, Minneapolis, MN 55305. TEL 952-252-1201, 800-477-1005, FAX 952-252-1202, info@eastview.com, http://www.eastview.com.

622.33 GBR ISSN 2046-2425
OFFSHORE RIG MONTHLY. Text in English. 1974. m. **Document type:** *Newsletter, Trade.* **Description:** Provides market intelligence on the worldwide offshore drilling business by identifying and analysing emerging trends and industry drivers.
Formerly (until 200?): The Offshore Rig Newsletter (0147-1481)
Related titles: E-mail ed.; Online - full text ed.: ISSN 2046-2433.
Published by: O D S - Petrodata Ltd., 2nd Fl, The Exchange No. 1, Market St, Aberdeen, AB11 5PJ, United Kingdom. TEL 44-1224-597800, FAX 44-1224-580320, customerservice@ods-petrodata.com.

338.2 GBR ISSN 2042-6259
▼ **OIL & GAS AGENDA.** Text in English. 2009. q. GBP 5.95, EUR 8, USD 8.95 per issue; free to qualified personnel (effective 2010). adv. back issues avail. **Document type:** *Magazine, Trade.*
Related titles: Online - full text ed.: free (effective 2010).
Published by: Global Trade Media Ltd. (Subsidiary of: Progressive Media Group), Progressive House, 2 Maidstone Rd, Footscray, Sidcup, Kent DA14 5HZ, United Kingdom. TEL 44-20-82697700, FAX 44-20-82697880, info@globaltrademedia.com, http://www.globaltrademedia.com/. Eds. Lucy Schwerdtfeger TEL 44-20-79366660, John Lawrence. Pub. William Crocker.

553 662 665.4 EST ISSN 0208-189X
TN858.A1 CODEN: OSIHA3
➤ **OIL SHALE/GORYUCHIE SLANTSY.** Text in English, German, Russian; Summaries in English. 1984. q. EUR 140; EUR 28 per issue (effective 2010). bk.rev. **Document type:** *Journal, Academic/Scholarly.* **Description:** Covers geology, mining composition, methods of processing and combustion, economic and utilization of oil shale and bituminous sands, as well as problems of environment protection.
Related titles: Online - full text ed.: ISSN 1736-7492.
Indexed: A26, A28, APA, ASCA, ASFA, B01, B07, B09, B21, BrCerAb, C&ISA, CA, CA/WCA, CIA, CerAb, CivEngAb, CorrAb, CurCont, E&CAJ, E08, E11, E14, EEA, EMA, ESPM, EnvEAb, GeoRef, H15, I05, INIS AtomInd, ISR, M&TEA, M09, MBF, METADEX, P52, P56, S09, SCI, SCOPUS, SolStAb, SpeleolAb, T02, T04, W07, WAA.
—BLDSC (6252.231450), IE, Ingenta, INIST, Linda Hall. **CCC.**
Published by: (Tallinna Tehnikaulikool/Tallinn University of Technology), Teaduste Akadeemia Kirjastus/Estonian Academy Publishers, Kohtu 6, Tallinn, 10130, Estonia. TEL 372-6-454106, FAX 372-6-466026, asta@kirj.ee, http://www.kirj.ee. Ed. Anto Raukas. Circ: 500.
Co-sponsor: Estonian Oil Shale Industry.

622 CAN ISSN 0708-2061
QE376.O6
ONTARIO GEOLOGICAL SURVEY. AGGREGATE RESOURCES INVENTORY PAPER. Text in English. 1979. irreg. price varies. back issues avail. **Document type:** *Government.*
Indexed: GeoRef, SpeleolAb.
Published by: Ontario Geological Survey, 933 Ramsey Lake Rd, Sudbury, ON P3E 6B5, Canada. TEL 705-670-5691, FAX 705-670-5770.

ONTARIO GEOLOGICAL SURVEY. GUIDE BOOKS. *see* EARTH SCIENCES—Geology

549 CAN ISSN 0706-4551
TN27.O4
ONTARIO GEOLOGICAL SURVEY. MINERAL DEPOSITS CIRCULAR. Text in English. 1950. irreg. (1-2/yr.). price varies. back issues avail. **Document type:** *Government.*
Former titles (until 1976): Ontario. Division of Mines. Mineral Resource Circulars (0474-1722); (until 195?): Ontario. Department of Mines. Metal Resources Circular (0706-456X)
Indexed: GeoRef, IMMAb, SpeleolAb.
—Ingenta.
Published by: Ontario Geological Survey, 933 Ramsey Lake Rd, Sudbury, ON P3E 6B5, Canada. TEL 705-670-5691, FAX 705-670-5770, pubsales@ndm.gov.on.ca.

622 CAN ISSN 0704-2752
TN27.O59 CODEN: MPOSDQ
ONTARIO GEOLOGICAL SURVEY. MISCELLANEOUS PAPER. Text in English. 1960. irreg. (3-4/yr.). price varies. back issues avail. **Document type:** *Government.*
Formerly: Ontario. Division of Mines. Miscellaneous Papers
Related titles: ◆ Series: Ontario Geological Survey. Report of Activities, Resident Geologists. ISSN 0838-3677; ◆ Ontario Geological Survey. Exploration Technology Development Fund, Summary of Research; ◆ Ontario Geological Survey. Summary of Field Work. ISSN 0829-8203.
Indexed: GeoRef, IMMAb, SpeleolAb.
—CASDDS, Linda Hall.
Published by: Ontario Geological Survey, 933 Ramsey Lake Rd, Sudbury, ON P3E 6B5, Canada. TEL 705-670-5691, FAX 705-670-5770, pubsales@ndm.gov.on.ca.

622 557 CAN ISSN 0704-2582
QE191 CODEN: OGSRD2
ONTARIO GEOLOGICAL SURVEY. REPORT. Text in English. 1960. irreg. (3-10/yr.). price varies. back issues avail. **Document type:** *Government.*
Former titles: Ontario Geological Survey. Geological Report; Ontario Geological Survey. Geological Report, Geoscience Report (0381-1778); Ontario. Division of Mines. Geological Reports; Incorporates: Ontario. Division of Mines. Geochemical Reports
Indexed: ChemAb, GeoRef, IMMAb, SpeleolAb.
—CASDDS, Ingenta, Linda Hall.
Published by: Ontario Geological Survey, 933 Ramsey Lake Rd, Sudbury, ON P3E 6B5, Canada. TEL 705-670-5691, FAX 705-670-5770, pubsales@ndm.gov.on.ca.

622 551 CAN ISSN 0838-3677
TN27.O4
ONTARIO GEOLOGICAL SURVEY. REPORT OF ACTIVITIES, RESIDENT GEOLOGISTS. Text in English. 1967. a. price varies. back issues avail. **Document type:** *Government.*
Formerly: Ontario Geological Survey. Annual Report of the Regional and Resident Geologists
Related titles: ◆ Series of: Ontario Geological Survey. Miscellaneous Paper. ISSN 0704-2752.
Published by: Ontario Geological Survey, 933 Ramsey Lake Rd, Sudbury, ON P3E 6B5, Canada. TEL 705-670-5691, FAX 705-670-5770, pubsales@ndm.gov.on.ca.

622 CAN ISSN 0704-2590
CODEN: OGSSD5
ONTARIO GEOLOGICAL SURVEY. STUDY. Text in English. irreg. price varies. back issues avail. **Document type:** *Government.*
Formerly: Ontario. Division of Mines. Geological Circular, Geoscience Study
Indexed: ChemAb, GeoRef, IMMAb, SpeleolAb.
—CASDDS, Linda Hall.
Published by: Ontario Geological Survey, 933 Ramsey Lake Rd, Sudbury, ON P3E 6B5, Canada. TEL 705-670-5691, FAX 705-670-5770, pubsales@ndm.gov.on.ca.

622 CAN ISSN 0829-8203
QE191
ONTARIO GEOLOGICAL SURVEY. SUMMARY OF FIELD WORK. Text in English. 1968. a. price varies. back issues avail. **Document type:** *Government.*
Related titles: ◆ Series of: Ontario Geological Survey. Miscellaneous Paper. ISSN 0704-2752.
Published by: Ontario Geological Survey, 933 Ramsey Lake Rd, Sudbury, ON P3E 6B5, Canada. TEL 705-670-5691, FAX 705-670-5770, pubsales@ndm.gov.on.ca.

338.2 CAN ISSN 1195-1427
TN27.O5
ONTARIO MINING AND EXPLORATION DIRECTORY. Text in English. a.
Former titles (until 1993): Mining and Exploration Companies in Ontario. Directory (1188-9241); (until 1992): Directory of Mining and Exploration Companies in Ontario (1180-0011); (until 1989): Directory of Mineral Exploration Companies in Ontario (1180-0062)
Indexed: GeoRef.
Published by: Ontario. Ministry of Northern Development and Mines, Publication Sales, 933 Ramsey Lake Rd, Sudbury, ON P3E 6B5, Canada. TEL 705-670-5691, 888-415-9845, FAX 705-670-5770, pubsales@ndm.gov.on.ca, http://www.mndm.gov.on.ca/.

THE OPEN MINERAL PROCESSING JOURNAL. *see* METALLURGY

549 622 NLD ISSN 1874-4567
➤ **THE OPEN MINERALOGY JOURNAL.** Text in English. 2007. irreg. free (effective 2011). **Document type:** *Journal, Academic/Scholarly.* **Description:** Coversall areas of mineralogy; including petrology, crystallography and geochemistry.
Media: Online - full text.
Indexed: A01, A28, APA, BrCerAb, C&ISA, CA/WCA, CIA, CerAb, CivEngAb, CorrAb, E&CAJ, E11, EEA, EMA, H15, M&TEA, M09, MBF, METADEX, SolStAb, T04, WAA.
Published by: Bentham Open (Subsidiary of: Bentham Science Publishers Ltd.), PO Box 294, Bussum, AG 1400, Netherlands. TEL 31-35-6923800, FAX 31-35-6980150, subscriptions@bentham.org. Ed. Larissa F Dobrzhinetskaya.

622 GBR ISSN 0964-6027
OPENCAST MINING (YEAR). Text in English. a. GBP 6; GBP 10 foreign. **Document type:** *Journal, Trade.*
Published by: Strata Publishing Ltd., 65 Tweedy Rd, Bromley, Kent BR1 3NH, United Kingdom. TEL 44-181-663-3331, FAX 44-181-464-5637. Ed. Simon Jarvis. Circ: 2,000 (paid).

622 ZAF ISSN 0030-4050
HC517.S7
OPTIMA. Text in English. 1951. s-a. free to shareholders. charts; illus.; stat. index.
Indexed: A22, AESIS, Cadscan, EIP, GeoRef, IMMAb, ISAP, KES, LeadAb, MEA&I, MLA-IB, RASB, SpeleolAb, Zincscan.
—BLDSC (6275.000000), IE, Ingenta.
Published by: Anglo American & De Beers of South Africa, PO Box 61587, Marshalltown, Johannesburg 2107, South Africa. TEL 27-11-638-5189, FAX 27-11-638-3771. Ed. Mark Irvine. Circ: 17,000.

▼ **P N G REPORT.** (Papua New Guinea) *see* ENERGY

622 ESP ISSN 0325-7207
TN4 CODEN: PMINES
PANORAMA MINERO. Text in Spanish. 1976. a. price varies. **Document type:** *Monographic series, Trade.* **Description:** Covers the national and international industry of mining.
Indexed: SpeleolAb.
Published by: Ministerio de Ciencia e Innovacion, Instituto Geologico y Minero de Espana, Rios Rosas 23, Madrid, 28003, Spain. TEL 34-91-3495819, FAX 34-91-3495830, publicaciones@igme.es, http://www.igme.es/internet/principal.asp.

622 USA
PAY DIRT. Text in English. 1938. m. USD 30 domestic; USD 40 in Canada; USD 80 elsewhere (effective 2005). adv. bk.rev. back issues avail.; reprints avail. **Document type:** *Magazine, Trade.* **Description:** Covers mining industry in the U.S. and abroad.
Formerly: Pay Dirt. Southwestern Edition (0886-0920); Formed by the 1985 merger of: Pay Dirt. Rocky Mountain Edition (0886-0912); Pay Dirt. Arizona Edition; Pay Dirt. New Mexico Edition (0199-5960)
Indexed: AESIS, SpeleolAb.
—Ingenta.
Published by: Copper Queen Publishing Co., Inc., P O Drawer 48, Bisbee, AZ 85603. TEL 520-432-2244, FAX 520-432-2247. Pub. Nancy Sullivan. R&P, Adv. contact Caryl Larkins. B&W page USD 570; trim 11 x 8.5. Circ: 2,500 (paid).

622.331 553.21 FIN ISSN 1455-8491
CODEN: BIPSDV
PEATLANDS INTERNATIONAL. Text in English. 2/yr. USD 30. illus. **Document type:** *Newsletter.*
Formerly (until l998): International Peat Society. Bulletin (0355-1008)
Indexed: GeoRef, SpeleolAb.
Published by: International Peat Society, Vapaudenkatu 12, Jyvaskyla, 40100, Finland. TEL 358-14-674-042, FAX 358-14-677-405. Ed. Raimo Sopo. Circ: 1,500.

PENNSYLVANIA BAR ASSOCIATION. ENVIRONMENTAL, MINERAL & NATURAL RESOURCES LAW SECTION. NEWSLETTER. *see* ENVIRONMENTAL STUDIES

338.2 USA
PENNSYLVANIA. DEPARTMENT OF ENVIRONMENTAL PROTECTION. ANNUAL REPORT ON MINING ACTIVITIES. Text in English. 1870. a. USD 14. stat. **Document type:** *Government.* **Description:** Covers all phases of mining in Pennsylvania (coal and non-coal).
Former titles: Pennsylvania. Department of Environmental Resources. Annual Report on Mining Activities; Pennsylvania. Office of Mines and Land Protection. Annual Report.; (until 1973): Pennsylvania. Anthracite, Bituminous Coal and Oil and Gas Divisions. Annual Report
Indexed: SpeleolAb.
Published by: Department of Environmental Protection, Bureau of Mining and Reclamation, PO Box 8461, Harrisburg, PA 17105-8467. TEL 717-783-7515, FAX 717-773-4675. Ed. Patsie Nichols. Circ: 1,000.
Subscr. to: Pennsylvania State University, Bookstore, Commonwealth Keystone Bldg., 400 North St, Harrisburg, PA 17120-0053.

549 550 ITA ISSN 0369-8963
QE351 CODEN: PEMIA7
PERIODICO DI MINERALOGIA. Text in Italian. 1930. 3/yr. index. back issues avail. **Document type:** *Journal, Academic/Scholarly.* **Description:** Covers mineralogy, mining industry, crystallography, geochemistry, earth sciences, vulcanology and petrology.
Indexed: GeoRef, MinerAb, RefZh, SCI, SCOPUS, SpeleolAb, W07.
—CASDDS.

M

Published by: (Universita degli Studi di Roma "La Sapienza"), Bardi Editore, Via Piave 7, Rome, 00187, Italy. TEL 39-06-4817656, FAX 39-06-48912574, info@bardieditore.com, http://www.bardieditore.com. Circ: 300.

622 DEU
PERSPEKTIVEN (COLOGNE); Zeitschrift fuer Fuehrungskraefte. Cover title: V D F Fuehrungskraft. Text in German. 2003. 6/yr. **Document type:** *Journal, Trade.*
Formed by the merger of (19??-2003): Perspektiven fuer Fuehrungskraefte V A F; Which was formerly (until 1999): V A F - Nachrichten; (19??-2003): V D F - Die Fuehrungskraefte (1433-4763); Which was formerly (until 1990): Fuehrungskraft (0178-501X); (until 1978): V D F Intern (0342-667X); (until 1975): Die Fuehrungskraft (0342-5509); (until 1970): Bergfreiheit (0342-5495)
Published by: Verband der Fuehrungskraefte V A F - V D F, Postfach 100945, Cologne, 50449, Germany. TEL 49-221-9218290, FAX 49-221-9218296, akkus@die-fuehrungskraefte.de. Circ: 8,500.

662 PER
PERU MINERO. Text in Spanish. bi-m. USD 50 in state; USD 65 out of state; USD 85 in Latin America; USD 110 elsewhere (effective 2000).
Published by: Instituto Mario Samame Boggio, Calle Las Castanitas 117, Oficina 201 Distrito de San Isidro, Lima, Peru. TEL 51-1-422-8125, FAX 51-1-421-6456, mineria@amauta.rcp.net.pe. Circ: 7,000.

338.27098505 GBR ISSN 1755-8514
PERU MINING REPORT. Text in English. 2007. a. EUR 820, USD 1,030 combined subscription per issue (print & email eds.) (effective 2010). **Document type:** *Report, Trade.* **Description:** Provides industry strategists, service companies, company analysts and consultants, government departments, trade associations and regulatory bodies.
Related titles: E-mail ed.
Indexed: A15, ABIn, B02, B15, B17, B18, G04, I05, P48, P51, P52, P56, PQC.
Published by: Business Monitor International Ltd., Senator House, 85 Queen Victoria St, London, EC4V 4AB, United Kingdom. TEL 44-20-72480468, FAX 44-20-72480467, subs@businessmonitor.com.

622 PHL ISSN 0048-3842
TN113
PHILIPPINE MINING & ENGINEERING JOURNAL. Text in English. 1970. m. adv. bk.rev. illus.; stat.
Indexed: AESIS, GeoRef, IPP, SpeleolAb.
Published by: Business Masters International, 55 U.E. Tech. Avenue, University Hills, Subdivision Malabon, Rizal, Philippines. Circ: 5,000.

622 PHL ISSN 0085-4875
PHILIPPINE MINING AND ENGINEERING JOURNAL. MINING ANNUAL AND DIRECTORY. Text in English. 1971. a. PHP 3, USD 15. adv.
Published by: Business Masters International, 55 U.E. Tech. Avenue, University Hills, Subdivision Malabon, Rizal, Philippines. Ed. Luciano B Quitlong. Circ: 10,000.

338.20959905 GBR ISSN 1755-8522
PHILIPPINES MINING REPORT. Text in English. 2007. a. EUR 820, USD 1,030 combined subscription per issue (print & email eds.) (effective 2010). **Document type:** *Report, Trade.* **Description:** Provides industry strategists, service companies, company analysts and consultants, government departments, trade associations and regulatory bodies.
Related titles: E-mail ed.
Indexed: A15, ABIn, B02, B15, B17, B18, G04, I05, P48, P51, P52, P56, PQC.
Published by: Business Monitor International Ltd., Senator House, 85 Queen Victoria St, London, EC4V 4AB, United Kingdom. TEL 44-20-72480468, FAX 44-20-72480467, subs@businessmonitor.com.

PHYSICOCHEMICAL PROBLEMS OF MINERAL PROCESSING. *see* CHEMISTRY—Physical Chemistry

549 DEU ISSN 0342-1791
QE351 CODEN: PCMIDU
➤ **PHYSICS AND CHEMISTRY OF MINERALS.** Text in English. 1977. 10/yr. EUR 2,923, USD 3,561 combined subscription to institutions (print & online eds.) (effective 2012). adv. abstr.; bibl.; charts; illus.; stat. index. back issues avail.; reprint service avail. from PSC. **Document type:** *Journal, Academic/Scholarly.* **Description:** Supports interdisciplinary work in mineralogy and physics or chemistry, with particular emphasis on applications of modern techniques and new theories.
Related titles: Microform ed.: (from PQC); Online - full text ed.: ISSN 1432-2021 (from IngentaConnect).
Indexed: A01, A03, A08, A22, A26, ASCA, C33, CA, CIN, CPEI, ChemAb, ChemTitl, CurCont, E01, EngInd, GEOBASE, GeoRef, IBR, IBZ, ISR, Inspec, MSCI, MinerAb, PhysBer, RefZh, SCI, SCOPUS, SpeleolAb, T02, W07.
—BLDSC (6478.217000), AskIEEE, CASDDS, IE, Infotrieve, Ingenta, INIST, Linda Hall. **CCC.**
Published by: (International Mineralogical Association), Springer (Subsidiary of: Springer Science+Business Media), Tiergartenstr 17, Heidelberg, 69121, Germany. TEL 49-6221-4870, FAX 49-6221-345229. Eds. C McCammon, M Matsui, M Rieder, P C Burnley. **Subscr. in the Americas to:** Springer New York LLC, Journal Fulfillment, PO Box 2485, Secaucus, NJ 07096. TEL 800-777-4643, 201-348-4033, FAX 201-348-4505, journals-ny@springer.com, http://www.springer.com; **Subscr. to:** Springer Distribution Center, Kundenservice Zeitschriften, Haberstr 7, Heidelberg 69126, Germany. TEL 49-6221-3454303, FAX 49-6221-3454229, subscriptions@springer.com.

622.3 FRA ISSN 1628-9595
PIERRE ACTUAL; arts et techniques des roches de qualite. Text in French. 1933. m. EUR 99 domestic; EUR 121 foreign (effective 2009). adv. charts; illus. **Document type:** *Magazine, Trade.*
Formerly (until 2000): Mausolee (0025-6072)
Indexed: GeoRef, SpeleolAb.
Published by: Societe Le Mausolee, Zac de Chassagne, Ternay, 69360, France. TEL 33-4-72248933, FAX 33-4-72246193, le_mausolee@wanadoo.fr. Ed. Claude Gargi. Adv. contact Jacqueline Martin. Circ: 4,500.

622 USA ISSN 0032-0293
TN1 CODEN: PIQUAN
PIT & QUARRY; equipment.operations.solutions. Text in English. 1916. m. free to qualified personnel (effective 2008). adv. bk.rev. charts; illus.; tr.lit. back issues avail.; reprints avail. **Document type:** *Magazine, Trade.* **Description:** Provides the readers with informative articles on equipment and technology used by aggregates producers of mining industry.
Incorporates (1918-1929): Cement - Mill and Quarry (0095-9952); Which superseded in part (in 1918): Engineering and Cement World (0096-0101)
Related titles: Online - full text ed.: free to qualified personnel (effective 2008); Supplement(s): Quarry Safety.
Indexed: A15, A22, A23, A24, ABIn, B02, B03, B11, B13, B15, B17, B18, BusI, C&ISA, CISA, CRIA, CRICC, CWI, ChemAb, E&CAJ, G04, G06, G07, G08, GeoRef, I05, IMMAb, P48, P51, P52, P56, PQC, RefZh, SCOPUS, SRI, SolStAb, SpeleolAb, T&II.
—IE, Infotrieve, Ingenta, INIST, Linda Hall. **CCC.**
Published by: Questex Media Group Inc., 275 Grove St, Bldg 2, Ste 130, Newton, MA 02466. TEL 617-219-8300, 888-552-4346, FAX 617-219-8310, questex@sunbeltfs.com, http://www.questex.com. adv.: B&W page USD 6,180, color page USD 7,460; trim 7.75 x 10.5. Circ: 20,582.

622 338.2 USA ISSN 1076-3937
HD9506.A1
PLATT'S METALS WEEK. Text in English. 1930. w. USD 1,895 (effective 2008). mkt.; stat. **Document type:** *Newsletter, Trade.* **Description:** Contains a wrap-up of the previous week's price movement plus in-depth interviews with key market participants, outlooks for global supply and demand and analysis of strikes, mining projects, legislation, joint ventures and other market-critical events.
Former titles (until 1993): Metals Week (0026-0975); E-MJ Metal and Mineral Markets (Engineering and Mining Journal)
Related titles: E-mail ed.; Fax ed.: USD 1,670 (effective 2004); Online - full text ed.: ISSN 1556-4126. USD 1,395 combined subscription (online & E-mail eds.) (effective 2008).
Indexed: A12, A13, A17, A28, ABIn, APA, B03, BrCerAb, C&ISA, CA/WCA, CIA, Cadscan, CerAb, CivEngAb, CorrAb, E&CAJ, E11, EEA, EMA, GeoRef, H15, LeadAb, M&TEA, M09, MBF, METADEX, P48, P51, P53, P54, PQC, SolStAb, T04, WAA, Zincscan.
—CIS, IE, Linda Hall. **CCC.**
Published by: Platts (Subsidiary of: McGraw-Hill Companies, Inc.), 1200 G St NW, Ste 1000, Washington, DC 20005. TEL 212-904-3070, 800-752-8878, FAX 202-383-2024, support@platts.com. Ed. Andy Blamey.

549 DEU ISSN 1972-1366
QE351
PLINIUS (CD-ROM); supplemento Italiano all'European journal of mineralogy. Text in Italian. 1985. a. USD 55 per issue (effective 2010). **Document type:** *Monographic series, Academic/Scholarly.*
Former titles (until 2006): Plinius (Print) (1120-317X); (until 1989): SIMP Notizie (1972-1374)
Media: CD-ROM. **Related titles:** ◆ Supplement to: European Journal of Mineralogy. ISSN 0935-1221.
Indexed: GeoRef, SpeleolAb.
—INIST, Linda Hall. **CCC.**
Published by: (Societa Italiana di Mineralogia e Petrologia ITA), E. Schweizerbart'sche Verlagsbuchhandlung, Johannesstr 3A, Stuttgart, 70176, Germany. TEL 49-711-3514560, FAX 49-711-35145699, order@schweizerbart.de.

338.20943805 GBR ISSN 1755-7860
POLAND MINING REPORT. Text in English. 2007. q. EUR 820, USD 1,030 combined subscription (print & email eds.) (effective 2010). **Document type:** *Report, Trade.* **Description:** Features latest-available data and forecasts covering all headline indicators for mining; company rankings and competitive landscapes covering mining exploration and production and analysis of latest industry developments, trends and regulatory issues.
Related titles: E-mail ed.
Indexed: A15, ABIn, B02, B15, B17, B18, G04, I05, P48, P51, P52, P56, PQC.
Published by: Business Monitor International Ltd., Senator House, 85 Queen Victoria St, London, EC4V 4AB, United Kingdom. TEL 44-20-72480468, FAX 44-20-72480467, subs@businessmonitor.com.

622 POL ISSN 0372-9508
TN4 CODEN: ZNSGAY
POLITECHNIKA SLASKA. ZESZYTY NAUKOWE. GORNICTWO. Text in Polish; Summaries in English, German, Russian. 1959. irreg. price varies.
Indexed: B22, ChemAb.
—BLDSC (9512.327100), CASDDS, Linda Hall.
Published by: Politechnika Slaska, ul Akademicka 5, Gliwice, 44100, Poland. wydawnictwo_mark@polsl.pl, http://wydawnictwo.polsl.pl. Ed. Walwry Szuscik. Circ: 205. **Dist. by:** Ars Polona, Obroncow 25, Warsaw 03933, Poland.

622 ZAF ISSN 1991-6787
PORTFOLIO. MINING AND ENERGY IN SOUTH AFRICA. Text in English. 2005. a. ZAR 106 (effective 2006). adv.
Published by: Portfolio Business Publications (Pty) Ltd, PO Box 71707, Bryanston, 2021, South Africa. TEL 27-11-7913891, FAX 27-11-7917413, infojhb@portfolio.co.za. Pub. Willie Ramoshaba. Adv. contact Charnee Nel. page ZAR 32,620; trim 210 x 275.

622 POL ISSN 0033-216X
TN4 CODEN: PRGOAI
PRZEGLAD GORNICZY. Text in Polish; Summaries in English, French, German, Russian. 1912. m. PLZ 300 (effective 2010). adv. bk.rev. abstr.; bibl.; charts; illus. index.
Related titles: Microform ed.
Indexed: A22, B22, CIN, CISA, ChemAb, ChemTitl, FR, GeoRef, GeotechAb, RefZh, SpeleolAb.
—BLDSC (6942.300000), CASDDS, IE, Ingenta, INIST, Linda Hall.
Published by: Stowarzyszenie Inzynierow i Technikow Gornictwa, ul. Powstancow 25, PO Box 653, Katowice, 40-958, Poland. TEL 48-32-2554648, FAX 48-32-2554132, zgsekretariat@sitg.pl. Ed. Wieslaw Blaschke.

622 AUS
QUARRY. Text in English. 1973. m. (except Jan.). free to members (effective 2008). adv. bk.rev. **Document type:** *Magazine, Trade.* **Description:** Covers news, editorial, and views on the latest developments and technological innovations from around the world, providing information to the Asia-Pacific quarrying and extractive industries.
Published by: (Institute of Quarrying), Gunnamatta Media Pty Ltd., Level 1, 558 City Rd, Locked Bag 26, South Melbourne, VIC 3205, Australia. TEL 61-3-96967200, FAX 61-3-96968313, art@gunnamattamedia.com.au, http://www.gunnamattamedia.com.au. Ed. Ben Hocking. Pub. Coleby Nicholson. Adv. contact Sam Veal. page AUD 2,950; trim 210 x 297. Circ: 5,000.

622.35 GBR ISSN 0950-9526
TN950.A1
QUARRY MANAGEMENT; the monthly journal for the quarry products industry. Text in English. 1918. m. GBP 45 (effective 2009). adv. bk.rev. charts; illus.; tr.lit. index. back issues avail.; reprints avail. **Document type:** *Journal, Trade.* **Description:** Features technical papers written by top industry specialists from around the world covering all aspects of the extraction, processing, marketing and transportation of quarry products.
Formerly (until 1984): Quarry Management and Products (0305-9421); Which was formed by the merger of (1918-1974): Quarry Managers' Journal (0033-5274); (1926-1974): Cement, Lime and Gravel (0008-8862); Which was formerly (until 1926): British Limemaster
Indexed: A22, AESIS, BrGeoL, C&ISA, CISA, CRIA, CRICC, E&CAJ, F&EA, GeoRef, HRIS, ICEA, IMMAb, Inspec, RICS, SCOPUS, SoftAbEng, SolStAb, SpeleolAb.
—BLDSC (7168.950000), IE, Infotrieve, Ingenta, Linda Hall. **CCC.**
Published by: (Institute of Quarrying), Q M J Publishing Ltd., 7 Regent St, Nottingham, NG1 5BS, United Kingdom. TEL 44-115-9411315, FAX 44-115-9484035, mail@qmj.co.uk, http://www.qmj.co.uk/. Ed. Stephen Adam TEL 44-115-9453893. Pub. Jack Berridge. Adv. contact Pam Reddish TEL 44-115-9454362. B&W page GBP 1,000, color page GBP 1,775; trim 210 x 297.

622.35 ZAF ISSN 2071-9272
QUARRY SOUTHERN AFRICA. Text in English. 1997. bi-m. ZAR 250 domestic; USD 80 in Africa; USD 180 elsewhere (effective 2011). **Document type:** *Journal, Trade.* **Description:** Serves the surface mining, quarrying, and construction industries.
Formerly (until 1997): Pit & Quarry S A
Published by: Brooke Pattrick Publications, Bldg 13, Pinewood Office Park, 33 Riley Rd, Woodmead, Johannesburg, Transvaal, South Africa. TEL 27-11-6033960, FAX 27-11-2346290, bestbook@brookepattrick.co.za, http://www.brookepattrick.com.

338.2 GBR
QUARTERLY REPORT ON COPPER. Text in English. 200?. q. price varies. **Document type:** *Report, Trade.* **Description:** Publishes statistical anlaysis and research about the copper market.
Published by: Bloomsbury Minerals Economics Ltd., Ste 345, 3rd Fl, Craven House, 121 Kingsway, London, WC2B 6PA, United Kingdom. web@bloomsburyminerals.com.

622 CAN ISSN 1910-2585
QUE SE PASSE-T-IL A LA MINE GIANT?. Text in French. 2006. irreg. **Document type:** *Monographic series, Trade.*
Media: Online - full text. **Related titles:** English ed.: What's Happening at Giant Mine?. ISSN 1910-2542.
Published by: Indian and Northern Affairs Canada/Affaires Indiennes et du Nord Canada, Terrasses de la Chaudiere, 10 Wellington St, N Tower, Rm 1210, Gatineau, PQ K1A 0H4, Canada. TEL 800-567-9604, FAX 866-817-3977, infopubs@ainc-inac.gc.ca, http://www.ainc-inac.gc.ca.

QUEBEC (PROVINCE). MINISTERE DES RESSOURCES NATURELLES ET DE LA FAUNE. RAPPORT ANNUEL DE GESTION. *see* ENERGY

622 AUS
TN1 CODEN: QGMJAZ
QUEENSLAND GOVERNMENT MINING JOURNAL. Abbreviated title: Q G M J. Text in English. 1900. q. free (effective 2009). bk.rev. abstr.; charts; illus.; mkt.; stat.; tr.lit. back issues avail. **Document type:** *Journal, Government.* **Description:** Provides information on developments in the geological, mining and mineral processing industries in Queensland. Also covers world trends.
Former titles (until 2001): Queensland Government Mining & Energy Journal (1444-4445); (until 2000): Queensland Government Mining Journal (0033-6149); Which incorporated (1995-1996): Queensland Coal (1325-8214)
Related titles: Microform ed.: (from PMC); Online - full text ed.
Indexed: AESIS, ARI, ChemAb, F&EA, IMMAb, INIS AtomInd, P06, SpeleolAb.
—BLDSC (7214.000000), IE, Ingenta, Linda Hall.
Published by: Queensland, Department of Mines and Energy, PO Box 15216, City East, QLD 4002, Australia. TEL 61-7-38980375, 800-657-567, FAX 61-7-32383088, info@dme.qld.gov.au. Circ: 2,500.

622 AUS ISSN 1834-3708
QUEENSLAND MINES AND QUARRIES SAFETY PERFORMANCE AND HEALTH REPORT. Text in English. 199?. a. **Document type:** *Report, Trade.*
Formerly: Lost Time & Fatal Injuries Queensland Mines and Quarries Statistical Report
Related titles: Online - full text ed.: ISSN 1834-3716. 2006.
Published by: Queensland, Department of Natural Resources and Water, GPO Box 2454, Brisbane, QLD 4001, Australia. FAX 61-7-3896-3111, http://www.nrw.qld.gov.au.

622 AUS ISSN 1449-2016
QUEENSLAND RESOURCES COUNCIL. ANNUAL REPORT. Text in English. 2004. a., latest 2007. free (effective 2009). back issues avail. **Document type:** *Report, Trade.* **Description:** Report of a non-government organization representing the interests of companies that have an interest in exploration, mining, minerals processing, and energy production.
Related titles: Online - full text ed.: free (effective 2009).
Published by: Queensland Resources Council, Level 13, 133 Mary St, Brisbane, QLD 4000, Australia. TEL 61-7-32959560, FAX 61-7-32959570, info@qrc.org.au.

622 ESP ISSN 1130-9644
TN87
R D M. REVISTA DE MINAS. Text in Spanish. 1979. a. bk.rev. illus.
Document type: *Journal, Academic/Scholarly.*
Formerly (until 1991): Revista de Minas (0210-8356)
Indexed: GeoRef, IECT, SpeleolAb.
—CASDDS.
Published by: Universidad de Oviedo, Escuela Tecnica Superior de Ingenieros de Minas, Independencia, 13, Oviedo, Asturias 33004, Spain. Ed. Jose Martinez Alvarez. Circ: 500.

R I C INSIGHT. *see* METALLURGY

R I C NEWS. *see* METALLURGY

622 USA
R M C M I REPORTER. Text in English. 1983. q. membership; membership. adv. 8 p./no.; **Document type:** *Newsletter.*
Description: Contains coal data, institute data, etc.
Published by: Rocky Mountain Coal Mining Institute, 8057 S.Yukon Way, Littleton, CO 80128. TEL 303-948-3300, FAX 303-948-1132, mail@rmcmi.org. Eds. Doris Finnie, Karen Inzano.

669 551 SVN
TN4 CODEN: RMZBAR
➤ **R M Z - MATERIALS AND GEOENVIRONMENT/MATERIALS AND GEOENVIRONMENT**; periodical for mining, metallurgy and geology. (Rudarsko Metalurski Zbornik) Text and summaries in English, German, Slovenian. 1953. q. USD 40; USD 15 newsstand/cover. adv. bk.rev. charts; illus. index. 188 p./no.; **Document type:** *Academic/Scholarly.* **Description:** Covers applications and trends in mining, metallurgy, geology and related technologies in the Republic of Slovenia.
Former titles (until 2001): Materiali in Geookolje (1408-7073); Rudarsko-Metalurski Zbornik - Mining and Metallurgy Quarterly (0035-9645)
Related titles: Microform ed.: (from PQC).
Indexed: A28, APA, BrCerAb, C&ISA, CA/WCA, CIA, CerAb, ChemAb, ChemTitl, CivEngAb, CorrAb, E&CAJ, E11, EEA, EMA, GeoRef, H15, IMMAb, M&TEA, M09, MBF, METADEX, SolStAb, SpeleolAb, T04, WAA.
—BLDSC (5393.985000), CASDDS, IE, Ingenta, INIST, Linda Hall.
Published by: Univerza v Ljubljani, Fakulteta za Naravoslovje in Tehnologijo/University of Ljubljana, Faculty of Natural Sciences and Technology, Askerceva 12, PO Box 594, Ljubljana, SI-1001, Slovenia. TEL 386-61-1704521, 386-61-1704500, FAX 386-61-1258114, rmz@ntfgam.uni-lj.si. Ed. Jose Pezdic. Circ: 700.

➤ **RANGE REMINISCING.** *see* HISTORY—History Of North And South America

➤ **THE RANGELAND JOURNAL.** *see* CONSERVATION

622 526.9 RUS ISSN 0034-026X
TN4 CODEN: RZONAV
RAZVEDKA I OKHRANA NEDR/EXPLORATION AND PROTECTION OF MINERAL RESOURCES. Text in Russian. 1935. m. USD 226 foreign (effective 2005). bk.rev. bibl.; charts; illus. **Document type:** *Journal, Academic/Scholarly.* **Description:** Covers geological exploration, evaluation of mineral deposit resources, signs of petroleum fields in Russia and other countries, international cooperation, modern geophysics, etc.
Indexed: CIN, ChemAb, ChemTitl, GeoRef, IMMAb, RASB, RefZh, SpeleolAb.
—BLDSC (0140.000000), CASDDS, East View, INIST, Linda Hall. **CCC.**
Published by: Roskomnedra, B. Polianka, 54, Moscow, 113184, Russian Federation. TEL 7-095-2307144. Ed. V I Kuzmenko. Circ: 8,400. **Dist. by:** East View Information Services, 10601 Wayzata Blvd, Minneapolis, MN 55305. TEL 952-252-1201, 800-477-1005, FAX 952-252-1202, info@eastview.com, http://www.eastview.com.

622 658 FRA ISSN 1148-7941
CODEN: ANMSA3
REALITES INDUSTRIELLES. Text in French; Summaries in English, German, Russian, Spanish. 1794. 4/yr. adv. bk.rev. abstr.; illus.; stat. index, cum.index every 10 yrs. back issues avail. **Document type:** *Journal, Corporate.* **Description:** Aims to find the common threads in the technological, economic, and social aspects of business and industry and in the management of firms.
Spersedes in part (in 1989): Annales des Mines (0003-4282)
Related titles: Online - full text ed.
Indexed: A12, A22, ABIn, CISA, ChemAb, F&EA, FR, GeoRef, IBR, IBSS, IBZ, INIS AtomInd, P48, P51, P52, P53, P54, P56, PAIS, PQC, SpeleolAb.
—IE, INIST, Linda Hall.
Published by: Editions ESKA, 12 Rue du Quatre-Septembre, Paris, 75002, France. TEL 33-1-40942222, FAX 33-1-40942232, eska@eska.fr. Ed. Francois Baratin. Pub. Serge Kebabtchieff. Circ: 3,500.

RECLAMATION NEWSLETTER. *see* ENVIRONMENTAL STUDIES

016.622 016.55 RUS ISSN 0202-9413
REFERATIVNYI ZHURNAL. RUDNYE MESTOROZHDENIYA; vypusk svodnogo toma. Text in Russian. 1954. m. USD 232.80 foreign (effective 2011). **Document type:** *Journal, Abstract/Index.*
Related titles: CD-ROM ed.; Online - full text ed.
—East View.
Published by: VINITI RAN, ul Usievicha 20, Moscow, 125190, Russian Federation. TEL 7-499-1526113, FAX 7-499-9430060, dir@viniti.ru, http://www.viniti.ru. Ed. Yurii Arskii. **Dist. by:** Informnauka Ltd., Ul Usievicha 20, Moscow 125190, Russian Federation. alfimov@viniti.ru.

622 AUS
REGISTER OF AFRICAN MINING. Text in English. 1998. a. AUD 429 domestic; AUD 435 foreign; AUD 770 combined subscription domestic (print & CD-ROM eds.); AUD 755 combined subscription foreign (print & CD-ROM eds.) (effective 2008). adv. back issues avail. **Document type:** *Report, Trade.* **Description:** Provides details on diamonds, gold and platinum in Africa.
Formerly (until 2000): Register of African Gold
Related titles: CD-ROM ed.: AUD 550 domestic; AUD 575 foreign (effective 2001).
Published by: Resource Information Unit, PO Box 1533, Subiaco, W.A. 6904, Australia. TEL 61-8-93823955, FAX 61-8-93881025, riu@riu.com.au. adv.: B&W page AUD 2,280, color page AUD 3,775.

622 AUS ISSN 0725-9158
REGISTER OF AUSTRALIAN MINING. Text in English. 1976. a. AUD 440 domestic; AUD 455 foreign; AUD 792 combined subscription domestic (print & CD-ROM eds.); AUD 775 combined subscription foreign (print & CD-ROM eds.); AUD 1,243 combined subscription domestic (print, online & CD-ROM eds.); AUD 1,230 combined subscription foreign (print, online & CD-ROM eds.) (effective 2008). adv. charts; illus.; stat.; tr.lit. index. back issues avail. **Document type:** *Report, Trade.* **Description:** Detailed list of mines, projects and prospects covering all different commodities in Australia.
Formerly (until 1978): Australian Mines Handbook (0314-3554)
Related titles: CD-ROM ed.: AUD 990 newsstand/cover domestic; AUD 920 newsstand/cover foreign (effective 2001); Online - full text ed.
Indexed: GeoRef, SpeleolAb.
Published by: Resource Information Unit, PO Box 1533, Subiaco, W.A. 6904, Australia. TEL 61-8-93823955, FAX 61-8-93881025, riu@riu.com.au. adv.: B&W page AUD 2,280, color page AUD 3,775.

662 553.41 AUS ISSN 1446-9898
REGISTER OF INDO-PACIFIC MINING. Text in English. 2001. a. AUD 429 domestic; AUD 435 foreign; AUD 770 combined subscription domestic (print & CD-ROM eds.); AUD 755 combined subscription foreign (print & CD-ROM eds.) (effective 2008). adv. charts; illus.; stat.; tr.lit. index. back issues avail. **Document type:** *Report, Trade.* **Description:** Detailed list of participating companies, mines, projects, and prospects relating to the Indonesian mining industry.
Formed by the merger of (2000-2001): Register of Pacific Mining (1443-5403); (1999-2001): Register of Indonesian Mining (1441-5062); Which was formerly (1997-1998): Register of Indonesian Gold (1327-4449)
Related titles: CD-ROM ed.: AUD 495 per issue (effective 2000).
Published by: Resource Information Unit, PO Box 1533, Subiaco, W.A. 6904, Australia. TEL 61-8-93823955, FAX 61-8-93881025, riu@riu.com.au. adv.: B&W page AUD 2,280, color page AUD 3,775.

338.2 USA ISSN 0747-7333
TN24.O3
REPORT ON OHIO MINERAL INDUSTRIES; with directories of reporting coal and industrial mineral operations. Text in English. 1872. a. charts; illus.; maps; stat. index. back issues avail. **Document type:** *Report, Government.*
Former titles (until 1981): Ohio. Division of Mines. Report (0078-401X); (until 1965): Ohio. Division of Mines. Annual Report with Coal and Industrial Mineral Directories of Reporting Firms; (until 1951): Ohio. Division of Labor Statistics. Annual Coal and Non-Metallic Mineral Report with Directories of Reporting Firms for .. (0472-6715); (until 1946): Ohio. Division of Labor Statistics. Annual Coal Report and Non-Metallic Mineral Report with Directories of Reporting Firms; (until 1945): Ohio. Division of Labor Statistics. Annual Ohio Coal Report and Directory of Coal Operators; (until 1943): Coal Operators
Related titles: Online - full text ed.: free (effective 2011).
Indexed: SpeleolAb.
—Linda Hall.
Published by: Ohio Department of Natural Resources, Division of Geological Survey, 2045 Morse Rd., Bldg. C-1, Columbus, OH 43229. TEL 614-265-6576, FAX 614-447-1918, geo.survey@dnr.state.oh.us, http://www.ohiodnr.com.

333.72 PHL ISSN 0116-2896
REPUBLIC OF THE PHILIPPINES. BUREAU OF MINES AND GEO-SCIENCES. ANNUAL REPORT. Text in English. 1973. a. USD 3. adv. **Document type:** *Government.*
Formerly: Department of Natural Resources Bureau of Mines. Annaul Report (0115-1940)
Published by: Republic of the Philippines. Bureau of Mines and Geo-Sciences, MGB Compound, North Ave, Diliman, Quezon City, 1227, Philippines. TEL 63-2-9288642, http://www.mgb.gov.ph/. Circ: 1,000.

RESERVES OF COAL, PROVINCE OF ALBERTA. *see* ENERGY

RESOURCE WEEK. *see* BUSINESS AND ECONOMICS—Production Of Goods And Services

RESOURCES POLICY. *see* ENERGY

RESSOURCE EN SANTE ET EN SECURITE. *see* OCCUPATIONAL HEALTH AND SAFETY

622 DEU ISSN 0724-4495
REVIER UND WERK. Text in German. 1950. bi-m. bk.rev. **Document type:** *Trade.*
Published by: Rheinbraun AG, Stuttgenweg 2, Cologne, 50935, Germany. TEL 0221-48022273, FAX 0221-4801356. Ed. Wolfgang Trees. Circ: 34,000.

338.2 TZA ISSN 0082-1659
REVIEW OF THE MINERAL INDUSTRY IN TANZANIA. Variant title: Tanzania. Mines Division. Review of the Mineral Industry. Text in English. 1965. a. free. **Document type:** *Government.*
Published by: Ministry of Water Energy and Minerals, Mines Division, PO Box 903, Dodoma, Tanzania. Ed. Anthony Muze. Circ: 400.

549 USA ISSN 1529-6466
CODEN: RMGECB
➤ **REVIEWS IN MINERALOGY AND GEOCHEMISTRY.** Text in English. 1974. irreg., latest vol.70, 2009. USD 40 per vol. (effective 2009). back issues avail. **Document type:** *Monographic series, Academic/Scholarly.* **Description:** Features informative articles on Mineralogy and Geochemistry.
Former titles (until 2000): Reviews in Mineralogy (0275-0279); (until 1980): Mineralogical Society of America Short Course Notes (0362-1758)
Related titles: Online - full text ed.: ISSN 1943-2666.
Indexed: A22, AESIS, GSW, GeoRef, IBR, IBZ, IMMAb, ISR, Inspec, SCI, SCOPUS, SpeleolAb, W07.
—BLDSC (7793.125000), IE, Ingenta, INIST, Linda Hall. **CCC.**
Published by: (The Geochemical Society), Mineralogical Society of America, 3635 Concorde Pkwy Ste 500, Chantilly, VA 20151. TEL 703-652-9950, FAX 703-652-9951, business@minsocam.org, http://www.minsocam.org.

➤ **REVISTA DA ESCOLA DE MINAS.** *see* ENGINEERING—Civil Engineering

622 340 CHL ISSN 0717-2125
REVISTA DE DERECHO DE MINAS. Text in Spanish. 1990. a. **Document type:** *Journal, Academic/Scholarly.*
Supersedes in part (in 1993): Revista de Derecho de Minas y Aguas (0716-9620)
Published by: Universidad de Atacama, Instituto de Derecho de Minas y Aguas, casilla 240, Copiapo, Chile. TEL 56-52-212005, FAX 56-52-212662, http://www.uda.cl.

622 CUB
REVISTA DE MINERIA Y GEOLOGIA. Text in Spanish. 3/yr. USD 24 in North America; USD 25 in South America; USD 26 in Europe. bibl.; charts; illus.
Formerly (until 1984): Mineria en Cuba
Indexed: IMMAb, SpeleolAb.
Published by: (Cuba. Ministerio de Mineria y Geologia, Cuba. Centro de Informacion Cientifico-Tecnica), Ediciones Cubanas, Obispo 527, Havana, Cuba.

622 550 ROM ISSN 1220-2053
TN275.A1 CODEN: REVMEM
➤ **REVISTA MINELOR.** Text in English; Summaries in English. 1974. m. ROL 180 domestic; EUR 45 in Europe; USD 60 elsewhere (effective 2009). adv. bk.rev. bibl.; charts; illus.; maps; tr.lit. back issues avail.; reprints avail. **Document type:** *Journal, Academic/Scholarly.* **Description:** Publishes articles related to the location and presentation of useful mineral substances deposits, design and construction of mines and pits, the main mining operations, development of mining equipment, health and safety in the mines.
Formerly (until 1990): Mine, Petrol si Gaze (0250-3115); Which was formed by the merger of (1950-1974): Petrol si Gaze (1220-2037); (1968-1974): Minerul (1220-2045)
Related titles: CD-ROM ed.
Indexed: A01, CISA, ChemAb, E14, GeoRef, Inspec, PetrolAb, SpeleolAb, T02.
—CASDDS, INIST, Linda Hall, PADDS.
Published by: (Ministerul Economiei si Comertului, Departamentul de Resurse Minerale/Ministry of Economy and Commerce, Directorate of Mineral Resources, Rumania. Universitatea din Petrosani/University of Petrosani), Infomin Deva, Bd 22 Decembrie nr 37/A, Deva, Hunedoara, Romania. TEL 40-254-213915, FAX 40-254-214718, office@infomindeva.ro. Pub. Ioan Manea. Circ: 800 (paid and controlled).

622 BOL ISSN 0252-8460
REVISTA MINERA BAMIN. Text in Spanish. 1929. q.
Published by: (Departamento de Relaciones Publicas), Banco Minero de Bolivia, Casilla 1410, La Paz, Bolivia.

622 MEX
REVISTA MUNDO MINERO. Text in Spanish. m. MXN 220 domestic; USD 50 foreign (effective 2001). adv.
Related titles: Online - full text ed.: Mundo Minero en Linea. ISSN 1605-5713. 1998.
Published by: Geo Publicidad, S.A. de C.V., Septima Privada de Perimetral No. 3, Col. Modelo, Hermosillo, Sonora, Mexico. TEL 52-62-101744, mminero@amsac.com.mx. adv.: color page MXN 12,000. Circ: 2,000.

549 FRA ISSN 2107-299X
LA REVUE DES MICROMONTEURS; la passion des micromineraux. Text in French. 2006. 3/yr. **Document type:** *Journal.*
Published by: Association Micromonteurs, 14 Rue des Vignes, Montreuil, 28500, France.

549 ITA ISSN 1970-2930
RIVISTA GEMMOLOGICA ITALIANA. Text in Italian. 2006. q. EUR 50 (effective 2008). **Document type:** *Magazine, Trade.*
Published by: Michele Macri, Via Latina 31, Rome, Italy. TEL 39-06-71054783, FAX 39-06-71356044.

549 ITA ISSN 0391-9641
CODEN: RMITDX
RIVISTA MINERALOGICA ITALIANA. Text in Italian. 1967. q. EUR 35 domestic (effective 2009). **Document type:** *Journal, Academic/Scholarly.*
Formerly (until 1977): Gruppo Mineralogico Italiano. Notizie
Indexed: GeoRef, MinerAb.
Published by: Gruppo Mineralogico Lombardo, c/o Museo Civico di Storia Naturale, Corso Venezia 55, Milan, 20121, Italy.

622 ESP ISSN 0214-0217
ROC MAQUINA (SPANISH EDITION). Text in Spanish. 1984. bi-m. EUR 131.04 domestic; EUR 162.18 foreign (effective 2010). **Document type:** *Magazine, Trade.*
Formerly (until 1987): Marmomacchine (0214-0209)
Related titles: CD-ROM ed.: 800 Natural Stones. EUR 23.30 per issue (effective 2003); 800 Variedades de Piedras en el Mundo. EUR 23.30 per issue (effective 2003); Online - full text ed.; English ed.: Roc Maquina (English Edition). ISSN 1130-8362. 1991. EUR 105.86 in Asia and the Americas (effective 2003); includes the yearly directory Natural Stone in the World; Supplement(s): Natural Stone in the World. Free with subscription to Roc Maquina (English Edition); La Piedra Natural en Espana. EUR 72.50 per issue (effective 2003).
Indexed: GeoRef, IECT, SpeleolAb.
Published by: Reed Business Information SA (Subsidiary of: Reed Business Information International), Zancoeta 9, Bilbao, 48013, Spain. TEL 34-944-285600, FAX 34-944-425116, rbi@rbi.es. Ed. Elena Sarachu.

622.33 ESP ISSN 0378-3316
ROCAS Y MINERALES; tecnicas y procesos de minas y canteras. Text in Spanish. 1972. m. EUR 90 domestic; EUR 145 in Europe; EUR 225 elsewhere (effective 2009). adv. bk.rev. illus. back issues avail. **Document type:** *Magazine, Trade.* **Description:** Covers developments in mining preparation and extraction techniques, mechanical processing of rocks and minerals, washing techniques and more.
Indexed: GeoRef, IECT, IMMAb, SpeleolAb.
—**CCC.**
Published by: Fueyo Editores, Torrelaguna, 127, Madrid, 28043, Spain. TEL 34-91-4151804, FAX 34-91-4151661, http://www.fueyoeditores.com/. Ed. Laureano Fueyo Cuesta. adv.: B&W page USD 1,600, color page USD 1,650; trim 275 x 210. Circ: 6,000 (controlled).

549 BRA ISSN 0102-4531
ROCHAS DE QUALIDADE. Text in Portuguese. 1967. bi-m. adv. back issues avail. **Document type:** *Journal, Trade.*
Indexed: B03.
Published by: E M C Editores Associados Ltda, Ave Washington Luis, 3001, Marajoara, Sao Paulo, 04627-000, Brazil. TEL 54-11-55410500, FAX 54-11-55483001, assinatura@revistarochas.com.br, http://www.revistarochas.com.br/index.asp.

622 340 USA
ROCK & COAL. Text in English. 1991. q. free to members (effective 2007). adv. **Document type:** *Newsletter, Trade.* **Description:** Keeps members informed about mining regulations, laws and other activities.
Formerly (until Sep. 1995): C M A Communicator
Related titles: Online - full text ed.
Published by: Colorado Mining Association, 216 16th St, Ste 1250, Denver, CO 80202-5198. TEL 303-575-9199, FAX 303-575-9194, colomine@coloradomining.org. Ed., R&P Stuart A Samderson. Circ: 1,300.

ROCK MECHANICS AND ROCK ENGINEERING. *see* EARTH SCIENCES—Geology

ROCK PRODUCTS. *see* BUILDING AND CONSTRUCTION

549 551 USA ISSN 0035-7529
QE351 CODEN: ROCMAR
➤ **ROCKS AND MINERALS;** mineralogy, geology, lapidary. Text in English. 1926. bi-m. GBP 115 in United Kingdom to institutions; EUR 154, USD 191 to institutions (effective 2012). adv. bk.rev. charts; tr.lit.; illus. index. back issues avail.; reprint service avail. from PSC. **Document type:** *Journal, Academic/Scholarly.* **Description:** Features articles on mineralogy, geology, and paleontology.
Related titles: CD-ROM ed.; Microform ed.; Online - full text ed.: ISSN 1940-1191.
Indexed: A01, A02, A03, A08, A22, A26, B14, BRD, BRI, CA, CBRI, ChemAb, E01, E04, E05, E08, G01, G03, G08, GEOBASE, GSA, GSI, GeoRef, H20, I05, I06, I07, IBR, IBZ, M01, M02, MASUSE, MinerAb, P10, P26, P48, P52, P53, P54, P56, PQC, PetrolAb, S01, S04, S06, S09, S10, S23, SCOPUS, SpeleolAb, T02, W03, W05.
—BLDSC (8002.500000), CASDDS, IE, Ingenta, INIST, Linda Hall. **CCC.**
Published by: (Helen Dwight Reid Educational Foundation), Taylor & Francis Inc. (Subsidiary of: Taylor & Francis Group), 325 Chestnut St, Ste 800, Philadelphia, PA 19106. TEL 215-625-2940, 800-354-1420, FAX 215-625-8914, customerservice@taylorandfrancis.com, http://www.taylorandfrancis.com. Ed. Marie E Huizing.

622 USA ISSN 1061-5245
TN1
ROCKY MOUNTAIN COAL MINING INSTITUTE. PROCEEDINGS. Text in English. 1913. a. USD 50 (effective 2001). adv. 160 p./no. 2 cols./p.; back issues avail. **Document type:** *Proceedings.* **Description:** Contains technical papers presented at the annual convention.
Indexed: GeoRef.
—Linda Hall.
Published by: Rocky Mountain Coal Mining Institute, 8057 S.Yukon Way, Littleton, CO 80128. TEL 303-948-3300, FAX 303-948-1132, mail@rmcmi.org. Eds. Doris Finnie, Karen Inzano. Pub., R&P Doris Finnie. Adv. contact Karen Inzano. page USD 250; 6 x 9. Circ: 1,000 (controlled).

622 340 USA
KF1819.A2
ROCKY MOUNTAIN MINERAL LAW FOUNDATION. ANNUAL INSTITUTE PROCEEDINGS. Text in English. 1955. a. USD 195 per issue to non-members; USD 160 per issue to members (effective 2010). back issues avail.; reprints avail. **Document type:** *Proceedings, Academic/Scholarly.* **Description:** Covers mining, oil and gas, landmen, environmental, and water law.
Former titles (until 1992): Rocky Mountain Mineral Law Institute. Annual Institute. Proceedings (0886-747X); (until 1970): Rocky Mountain Mineral Law Institute. Annual (0557-1987)
Related titles: Microform ed.: (from WSH); Online - full text ed.
Indexed: A26, CLI, G08, GeoRef, I01, I03, I05, ILP, LRI, SpeleolAb.
—Ingenta. **CCC.**
Published by: Rocky Mountain Mineral Law Foundation, 9191 Sheridan Blvd, Ste 203, Westminster, CO 80031. TEL 303-321-8100, FAX 303-321-7657, info@rmmlf.org.

347.2 622 USA ISSN 1550-7157
K16
ROCKY MOUNTAIN MINERAL LAW FOUNDATION. JOURNAL. Variant title: R M M L F Journal. Text in English. 1962. s-a. USD 52 (effective 2010). index. back issues avail. **Document type:** *Journal, Academic/Scholarly.* **Description:** Covers mining, oil, gas and water law.
Former titles (until 2004): Public Land & Resources Law Digest (0148-6489); (until 1970): Rocky Mountain Mineral Law Review (0035-7618)
Related titles: Online - full text ed.
Indexed: EIA, EnerInd, EnvAb, GeoRef, MAB, P06, SpeleolAb.
—Ingenta. **CCC.**
Published by: Rocky Mountain Mineral Law Foundation, 9191 Sheridan Blvd, Ste 203, Westminster, CO 80031. TEL 303-321-8100, FAX 303-321-7657, info@rmmlf.org. Ed. Jennifer Roulette TEL 303-321-8100 ext 103.

ROSSING MAGAZINE. *see* CONSERVATION

622 GBR ISSN 0080-4495
ROYAL SCHOOL OF MINES, LONDON. JOURNAL. Text in English. 1951. a. GBP 1. adv. bk.rev.
Indexed: Cadscan, LeadAb, Zincscan.
Published by: Royal School of Mines Union, Royal School Of Mines, Prince Consort Rd, London, SW7 2BP, United Kingdom. TEL 01-589 5111. Ed. Frank W A A Lucas. Circ: 2,000.

RUDARSKO-GEOLOSKO-NAFTNI ZBORNIK/MINING-GEOLOGICAL-PETROLEUM ENGINEERING BULLETIN. *see* EARTH SCIENCES—Geology

622 551 BIH ISSN 0353-9172
TN4 CODEN: ARUTA6
➤ **RUDARSTVO.** Text in Serbian, Croatian. 1963. q. EUR 20 to individuals; EUR 40 to institutions (effective 2002). adv. bk.rev. 60 p./no. 2 cols./p.; **Document type:** *Academic/Scholarly.* **Description:** Presents scientific and technical work in the field of exploitation and preparation of mineral raw materials.
Supersedes (in 1991): Arhiv za Rudarstvo i Geologiju (0351-4692); Which was formerly (until 1980): Arhiv za Rudarstvo i Tehnologiju (0518-5327); (until 1968): Arhiv za Tehnologiju (0365-7558)
Indexed: IMMAb.
—CASDDS.
Published by: Rudarski Institut Tuzla, Rudarska Ul 72, Tuzla, 75000, Bosnia Herzegovina. TEL 387-35-281073, rit@bih.net.ba. Ed., R&P Esad Hadzic. Adv. contact Husein Bakalovic. Circ: 200.

➤ **RUDARSTVO - GEOLOGIJA - METALURGIJA.** *see* METALLURGY

➤ **RUDY I METALE NIEZELAZNE.** *see* METALLURGY

549 RUS ISSN 0869-5997
QE390 CODEN: RUMEEV
➤ **RUDY I METALLY/ORES AND METALS.** Text in Russian. 1992. 6/yr. USD 163 foreign (effective 2005). bk.rev. charts; illus. index. **Document type:** *Journal, Academic/Scholarly.* **Description:** Contains articles concerning theoretical and applied aspects of mineral deposits from their genesis to development and exploitation including economics with the emphasis on Russian mineral deposits.
Indexed: CIN, ChemAb, ChemTitl, GeoRef, RefZh, SpeleolAb.
—CASDDS, East View. **CCC.**
Published by: Tsentral'nyi Nauchno-Issledovatel'skii Institut Tsvetnykh i Blagorodnykh Metallov/Central Research Institute of Geological Prospecting for Base and Precious Metals, Varshavskoe shosse 129 b, Moscow, 117545, Russian Federation. tsnigri@tsnigri.ru, http://www.tsnigri.ru. Ed. Igor F Migachev. R&P I F Migachev TEL 7-095-3131818. Circ: 500 (controlled). **Dist. by:** East View Information Services, 10601 Wayzata Blvd, Minneapolis, MN 55305. TEL 952-252-1201, 800-477-1005, FAX 952-252-1202, info@eastview.com, http://www.eastview.com.

549 GBR ISSN 0263-7839
THE RUSSELL SOCIETY. JOURNAL. Text in English. 1982. a., latest vol.11, 2008. free to members (effective 2009). back issues avail. **Document type:** *Journal, Academic/Scholarly.* **Description:** Features papers, topological reports and notes on all aspects of mineralogy.
Related titles: Online - full text ed.
Indexed: GeoRef, MinerAb.
—BLDSC (4868.550000).
Published by: The Russell Society, c/o Chris Finch, Honorary Gen.Secr., 30, Thirlmere Rd, Barrow-upon-Soar, Leicestershire, LE12 8QQ, United Kingdom. TEL 44-1509-414427, membership@russellsoc.org.

549 GBR
THE RUSSELL SOCIETY. NEWSLETTER. Text in English. 19??. s-a. free to members (effective 2009). back issues avail. **Document type:** *Newsletter.* **Description:** Explores the activities of the Russell Society and includes articles on minerals and mineralogical sites, membership information and programs.
Related titles: Online - full text ed.
Published by: The Russell Society, c/o Chris Finch, Honorary Gen.Secr., 30, Thirlmere Rd, Barrow-upon-Soar, Leicestershire, LE12 8QQ, United Kingdom. TEL 44-1509-414427, membership@russellsoc.org. Ed. John Davidson.

622 RUS ISSN 1683-4097
RUSSIAN MINING. Text in English. 2000. bi-m. USD 99 foreign (effective 2004). **Document type:** *Journal, Trade.* **Description:** Designed for senior executives, managers, general superindendents and other qualified supervisory personnel in mining, mining processing and allied commercial fields.
Published by: Gornaya Promyshlennost', Leninskii pr-t 6, MGGU, str.2, k. 752, Moscow, 119991, Russian Federation. TEL 7-095-2369770, FAX 7-095-2369771. Ed. Konstantin Anistratov. Circ: 2,500.

622 620 ZAF
CODEN: CGBMA5
S A MINING. (South African) Text in English. 1985. m. ZAR 232 domestic; ZAR 370 foreign (effective 2007). adv. illus.; mkt.; stat. index. **Document type:** *Magazine, Trade.*
Formerly: South African Mining, Coal, Gold and Base Minerals (0257-7623); Which was formed by the merger of (1919-1985): South African Mining and Engineering Journal (0038-2477); Which was formerly (1891-1919): South African Mining Journal (0370-8349); (1964-1985): Coal, Gold and Base Minerals of Southern Africa (0530-0029); Which was formerly (1953-1964): Coal and Base Minerals of Southern Africa (0366-7103); Incorporated: South African Mining Equipment
Related titles: Microfilm ed.: (from PMC, PQC).
Indexed: AESIS, GeoRef, IMMAb, ISAP, SpeleolAb.
—CASDDS, IE, Ingenta, INIST, Linda Hall.
Published by: Johnnic Communications Ltd., 4 Biermann Ave, Rosebank, Johannesburg, 2196, South Africa. TEL 27-11-2803000, FAX 27-11-8345063, matisonnj@johncom.co.za, http://www.johncom.co.za/. Ed. Julie Walker. adv.: color page ZAR 7,900; trim 210 x 297. Circ: 5,000 (paid).

SALT AND HIGHWAY DEICING NEWSLETTER. *see* TRANSPORTATION—Roads And Traffic

622.33 CAN ISSN 0839-8518
TN26 CODEN: SMRRAC
SASKATCHEWAN ENERGY & MINES. ANNUAL REPORT. Text in English. 1954. a. charts; illus. **Document type:** *Government.*
Former titles: Saskatchewan Mineral Resources. Annual Report; Saskatchewan. Department of Mineral Resources. Annual Report (0581-8109)
Indexed: GeoRef, SpeleolAb.
—CASDDS.
Published by: Saskatchewan Energy & Mines, Petroleum Statistics Branch, 2101 Scarth St, Regina, SK S4P 3V7, Canada. TEL 306-787-2528, FAX 306-787-2527.

338.2 665.5 CAN ISSN 0707-2570
HD9506.C23
SASKATCHEWAN ENERGY & MINES. MINERAL STATISTICS YEARBOOK. Text in English. 1964. a. CAD 60 (effective 1999). **Document type:** *Government.* **Description:** Includes a summary section on mineral production, disposition, value of disposition and provincial revenues from minerals, and a detailed section containing monthly, annual and historical data on each of fuel, industrial and metallic minerals.
Former titles: Saskatchewan Mineral Resources. Mineral Statistical Yearbook (0080-651X); Saskatchewan. Department of Mineral Resources. Statistical Yearbook
Indexed: GeoRef, SpeleolAb.
Published by: Saskatchewan Energy & Mines, Petroleum Statistics Branch, 2101 Scarth St, Regina, SK S4P 3V7, Canada. TEL 306-787-2528, FAX 306-787-2527.

SASKATCHEWAN GEOLOGICAL SURVEY. SUMMARY OF INVESTIGATIONS (CD-ROM). *see* EARTH SCIENCES—Geology

622 CAN ISSN 1713-6822
SASKATCHEWAN MINING JOURNAL. Text in English. a. **Document type:** *Journal, Trade.*
Indexed: C03, CBCABus, P48, P52, P56, PQC.
Published by: Sunrise Publishing Ltd., 2213 B Hanselman Ct, Saskatoon, SK S7L 6A8, Canada. TEL 306-244-5668, 800-247-5743, FAX 306-244-5679, news@sunrisepublish.com.

622 CHE ISSN 0370-9213
CODEN: SCSTBM
➤ **SCHWEIZER STRAHLER.** Text in German. 1967. q. CHF 63. adv. bk.rev. **Document type:** *Journal, Academic/Scholarly.* **Description:** Covers minerals and fossils of China and European countries; includes geological descriptions; and member information.
Indexed: GeoRef, SpeleolAb.
—CASDDS, Linda Hall.
Published by: Schweizer Vereinigung der Strahler Mineralien- und Fossiliensammler, Freiestr. 22, Thun, 3604, Switzerland. TEL 41-33-3369051, FAX 41-33-3369051, sekretariat@svsmf.ch. Ed. Ruth Buergler. Circ: 3,200.

549 552 CHE ISSN 0036-7699
QE351 CODEN: SMPTA8
SCHWEIZERISCHE MINERALOGISCHE UND PETROGRAPHISCHE MITTEILUNGEN/BOLLETTINO SVIZZERO DI MINERALOGIA E PETROGRAFIA/BULLETIN SUISSE DE MINERALOGIE ET PETROGRAPHIE/SWISS BULLETIN OF MINERALOGY AND PETROLOGY; eine europaeische Zeitschrift fuer Mineralogie, Geochemie und Petrographie. Text in English, French, German, Italian. 1921. 3/yr. CHF 264 (effective 1997). adv. bk.rev. charts; illus. index. **Document type:** *Bulletin.*
Related titles: Online - full text ed.: (from IngentaConnect).
Indexed: A22, AESIS, ASCA, ChemAb, ChemTitl, GeoRef, IBR, IBZ, ISR, MinerAb, SCOPUS, SpeleolAb.
—CASDDS, IE, Infotrieve, Ingenta, INIST, Linda Hall.
Published by: Staeubli Verlag AG, Raeffelstr 11, Postfach, Zuerich, 8045, Switzerland. TEL 41-1-4615858, FAX 41-1-4612272.

622 JPN ISSN 0286-7184
SEIMITSU CHOSA HOKOKUSHO/METAL MINING AGENCY OF JAPAN. CLOSE EXAMINATION REPORT. Text in Japanese. 1965. a. illus. **Document type:** *Academic/Scholarly.*
Supersedes in part (in 1968): Chishitsu Kozo Chosa Hokokusho (0286-7176)
Published by: Kinzoku Kogyo Jigyodan/Metal Mining Agency of Japan, 24-14 Toranomon 1-chome, Minato-ku, Tokyo, 105-0001, Japan.

622 CHN ISSN 1672-3767
CODEN: SKXUE7
SHANDONG KEJI DAXUE XUEBAO (ZIRAN KEXUE BAN)/ SHANDONG UNIVERSITY OF SCIENCE AND TECHNOLOGY. JOURNAL (NATURAL SCIENCE EDITION). Text in Chinese. 1979. q. CNY 10 newsstand/cover (effective 2007). **Document type:** *Journal, Academic/Scholarly.*
Formerly: Shandong Kuangye Xueyuan Xuebao (Ziran Kexue)/ Shandong Mining Institute. Journal (Natural Science) (1000-2308)
Related titles: Online - full text ed.
Indexed: A28, A32, APA, ASFA, B21, BrCerAb, C&ISA, CA/WCA, CCMJ, CIA, CerAb, CivEngAb, CorrAb, E&CAJ, E11, EEA, EMA, ESPM, EnvEAb, H&SSA, H15, M&TEA, M09, MBF, METADEX, MSN, MathR, PollutAb, RefZh, RiskAb, SWRA, SolStAb, T04, WAA.
—BLDSC (4874.735000), IE, Ingenta.
Published by: Shandong Keji Daxue/Shandong University of Science and Technology, 223, Daizong Dajie, Taian, 271019, China. TEL 86-538-6226361, FAX 86-538-6227415.

622.33 CHN ISSN 1672-0652
SHANXI JIAOMEI KEJI/SHANXI COOKING COAL SCIENCE & TECHNOLOGY. Text in Chinese. 1977. m. CNY 6 newsstand/cover (effective 2006). **Document type:** *Journal, Academic/Scholarly.*
Formerly (until 2002): Xishan Keji/Xishan Science & Technology (1009-9824)
Related titles: Online - full text ed.
Address: 325, Xikuang Jie, Taiyuan, 030053, China. TEL 86-351-6213842, FAX 86-351-6215093.

SHIGEN CHISHITSU. *see* EARTH SCIENCES—Geology

622 JPN ISSN 0916-1740
TN275.A1 CODEN: SHSOEB
SHIGEN SOZAI/MINING AND MATERIALS PROCESSING INSTITUTE OF JAPAN. JOURNAL. Text in Japanese; Summaries in English. 1885. m. subscr. incld. with membership. adv. bk.rev. **Document type:** *Journal, Academic/Scholarly.*
Formerly (until 1988): Nihon Kogyokaishi - Mining and Metallurgical Institute of Japan. Journal (0369-4194); Which incorporated (1930-1969): Kyushu Kozan Gakkaishi - Mining Institute of Kyushu. Journal (0368-5926); And (1943-1969): Tohoku Kozan - TohokuMining Society. Journal (0372-0411)
Related titles: Online - full content ed.; Online - full text ed.
Indexed: A22, APA, C&ISA, ChemAb, ChemTitl, CorrAb, E&CAJ, EEA, ESPM, GeoRef, IMMAb, INIS AtomInd, M&GPA, PollutAb, SWRA, SolStAb, SpeleolAb, WAA.
—BLDSC (4827.700000), CASDDS, IE, Ingenta, INIST, Linda Hall. **CCC.**
Published by: Shigen Sozai Gakkai/Mining and Materials Processing Institute of Japan, Nogizaka Bldg, 9-6-41 Akasaka, Minato-ku, Tokyo, 107-0052, Japan. TEL 81-3-34020541, FAX 81-3-34031776, info@mmij.or.jp, http://www.mmij.or.jp/. Circ: 4,000.

SHIGEN TO KANKYO/NATIONAL INSTITUTE FOR RESOURCES AND ENVIRONMENT. JOURNAL. *see* ENVIRONMENTAL STUDIES

549 AUS ISSN 1833-8194
SIFT. Text in English. 2005. q. free (effective 2009). back issues avail. **Document type:** *Newsletter, Trade.*
Related titles: Online - full text ed.: ISSN 1833-8208.
Published by: Intellection Pty Ltd, 27 Mayneview St, Milton, QLD 4064, Australia. TEL 61-7-35129100, FAX 61-7-35129199, info@intellection.com.au. Ed. Jolene Alfred TEL 61-7-35129104.

338.2 669 USA ISSN 0730-8132
SILVER INSTITUTE LETTER; information on silver for industry. Text in English. 1971. bi-m. USD 20; USD 25 foreign (effective 1999). back issues avail. **Description:** Covers recent developments on the uses of silver in the areas of art, finance, mining, coins and photography.
Related titles: Microfiche ed.: (from CIS); Spanish ed.
Indexed: SRI.
Published by: Silver Institute, 14264, Washington, DC 20044-4264. TEL 202-835-0185, FAX 3202-835-0155. Ed. Laarry Kahaner. Circ: 4,000.

622 USA ISSN 0037-6329
TN1
SKILLINGS' MINING REVIEW. Text in English. 1912. w. USD 69 in US & Canada; USD 245 elsewhere (effective 2008). adv. bk.rev. charts; illus.; stat. Index. 36 p./no.; back issues avail.; reprints avail.
Document type: *Magazine, Trade.*
Related titles: Online - full text ed.
Indexed: A28, AESIS, APA, B03, B21, BrCerAb, C&ISA, CA/WCA, CIA, CerAb, CivEngAb, CorrAb, E&CAJ, E11, EEA, EMA, ESPM, EnvEAb, GeoRef, H&SSA, H15, M&TEA, M09, MBF, METADEX, PROMT, RefZh, SolStAb, T04, TM, WAA.
—BLDSC (8295.850000), IE, Ingenta, Linda Hall.
Published by: H.R. Publishing, 11 E. Superior St., Ste. 514, Duluth, MN 55802-2083. TEL 218-722-2310, FAX 218-722-0134. Eds. Harold Webster, Ivan Hohnstadt, Gail Rosenquist. Pubs. Harold Webster, Ivan Hohnstadt. adv.: B&W page USD 1,086, color page USD 2,031; trim 8.25 x 11.25. Circ: 3,500 (paid and controlled).

622 CHL ISSN 0378-0961
SOCIEDAD NACIONAL DE MINERIA. BOLETIN MINERO. Text in Spanish. 1883. irreg.
Former titles (until 1983): Sociedad Nacional de Mineria. Boletin (0716-3223); (until 1980): Sociedad Nacional de Mineria. Boletin Informativo (0716-3215); (until 1972): Sociedad Nacional de Mineria. Boletin Minero (0716-3193); (until 1918): Sociedad Nacional de Mineria. Boletin (0716-2200)
Indexed: GeoRef.
Published by: Sociedad Nacional de Mineria, Apoquindo 3000, Piso 5, Santiago, Chile. TEL 56-2-3359300, FAX 56-2-3349700, sonami@sonami.cl, http://www.sonami.cl.

338.2 FRA ISSN 1163-5959
SOCIETE DE L'INDUSTRIE MINERALE. GUIDE DES MINES ET CARRIERES. Text in French. 1855. a. EUR 58 per issue (effective 2009). adv. index.
Former titles: Societe de l'Industrie Minerale. Mines et Carrieres. Annuaire (1154-8878); Societe de l'Industrie Minerale. Annuaire (0081-0797)
Indexed: GeoRef, SpeleolAb.
Published by: Societe de l'Industrie Minerale, 17 rue Saint-Severin, Paris, 75005, France. TEL 33-1-53101470, FAX 33-1-53101471, indmin@club-internet.fr.

338.7 CIV ISSN 0250-3697
SOCIETE POUR LE DEVELOPPEMENT MINIER DE LA COTE D'IVOIRE. RAPPORT ANNUEL. Text in French. 1962. a. free. illus.
Indexed: SpeleolAb.
Published by: Societe pour le Developpement Minier de la Cote d'Ivoire, 01 BP 2816, Abidjan, Ivory Coast. FAX 011-225-440821, TELEX 26162 SODMI.

622 669 665.5 USA ISSN 1075-8623
TN1 CODEN: TMEIE3
➤ **SOCIETY FOR MINING, METALLURGY, AND EXPLORATION. TRANSACTIONS.** Text in English. 195?. a. abstr.; bibl.; charts; illus. index. **Document type:** *Journal, Academic/Scholarly.*
Former titles (until 1989): Society of Mining Engineers, Inc. Transactions (1073-2187); (until 1985): Society of Mining Engineers of A I M E. Transactions (0037-9964); Which superseded in part (in 1962): American Institute of Mining, Metallurgical and Petroleum Engineers Incorporated. Transactions (0096-4778)
Indexed: A22, ChemAb, EIA, EnerInd, F&EA, GeoRef, IMMAb, SpeleolAb.
—BLDSC (9007.470000), IE, Ingenta, INIST, Linda Hall. **CCC.**
Published by: Society for Mining, Metallurgy and Exploration, 8307 Shaffer Pkwy, Littleton, CO 80127. TEL 303-973-9550, 800-763-3132, FAX 303-973-3845, sme@smenet.org.

622 551 ZAF
SOUTH AFRICA. DEPARTMENT OF MINERALS AND ENERGY. ANNUAL REPORT. Text in English. N.S. 1947. a. price varies.
Document type: *Government.* **Description:** Reflects the department's activities with regard to the optimum utilization and safe exploitation of mineral and energy resources and the rehabilitation of the surface.
Formerly: South Africa. Department of Mines. Annual Report; Incorporates: South Africa. Geological Survey. Report of the Chief Director of the Geological Survey; South Africa. Minerals Buro. Report of the Chief Director of the Minerals Buro
Indexed: SpeleolAb.
Published by: Department of Minerals and Energy, Private Bag X59, Pretoria, 0001, South Africa. TEL 27-12-3179000, FAX 27-12-3223416, http://www.dme@gov.za. Ed. Siyabonga Kheswa. Circ: 2,000. **Orders to:** South Africa. Government Printing Works, 149 Bosman St, Private Bag X85, Pretoria 0001, South Africa. FAX 27-12-3230009.

SOUTH AFRICAN INSTITUTE OF MINING AND METALLURGY. JOURNAL. *see* METALLURGY

SOUTH AFRICAN INSTITUTE OF MINING AND METALLURGY. MONOGRAPH SERIES. *see* METALLURGY

SOUTH AFRICAN LAPIDARY MAGAZINE. *see* EARTH SCIENCES

SOUTH CAROLINA GEOLOGICAL SURVEY. MINERAL RESOURCES SERIES. *see* EARTH SCIENCES—Geology

SOUTH CAROLINA GEOLOGICAL SURVEY. SOUTH CAROLINA MINERALS AND ROCKS. *see* EARTH SCIENCES—Geology

SPAIN. INSTITUTO TECNOLOGICO GEOMINERO DE ESPANA. COLECCION MEMORIAS. *see* EARTH SCIENCES—Geology

SPAIN. INSTITUTO TECNOLOGICO GEOMINERO DE ESPANA. COLECCION TEMAS GEOLOGICOS - MINEROS. *see* EARTH SCIENCES

SPAIN. INSTITUTO TECNOLOGICO GEOMINERO DE ESPANA. INFORMES. *see* EARTH SCIENCES—Geology

622 USA
SPEAKERS' PAPERS: SPEECHES FROM THE GOLD AND SILVER INSTITUTES' (YEAR) ANNUAL MEETING. Text in English. a. USD 90; USD 105 foreign (effective 1999). **Description:** Contains current information direct from industry leaders and experts.
Published by: Gold Institute, Administrative Office/Institut de l'Or, Bureau Administratif, PO Box 14264, Washington, DC 20044-4264. TEL 202-835-0185, FAX 202-835-0155. R&P Paul Bateman.

STANDING COMMITTEE ON ENERGY, MINES AND RESOURCES. MINUTES OF PROCEEDINGS AND EVIDENCE. *see* ENERGY

338.2 CAN ISSN 0707-2767
TN806.C2
STATISTICAL REVIEW OF COAL IN CANADA. Text in English. 1971. a. stat. **Document type:** *Government.*
Formerly: Coal in Canada, Supply and Demand (0700-284X)
Indexed: GeoRef, SpeleolAb.
—Linda Hall.
Published by: Natural Resources Canada, Minerals and Metals Sector (Subsidiary of: Natural Resources Canada/Ressources Naturelles Canada), 580 Booth St, Ottawa, ON K1A 0E4, Canada. TEL 613-947-6580, FAX 613-952-7501, info-mms@nrcan.gc.ca, http://www.nrcan.gc.ca/mms/hm_e.htm.

622 DEU ISSN 0039-1018
TN950
STEINBRUCH UND SANDGRUBE; Das Fachmagazin fuer Entscheider in der Roh- und Baustoffindustrie. Text in German. 1901. m. EUR 56 domestic; EUR 77 foreign; EUR 5.15 newsstand/cover (effective 2010). adv. bk.rev. illus. index. **Document type:** *Magazine, Trade.*
Related titles: Online - full text ed.
Indexed: GeoRef, SpeleolAb, TM.
—CCC.
Published by: Schluetersche Verlagsgesellschaft mbH und Co. KG, Hans-Boeckler-Allee 7, Hannover, 30173, Germany. TEL 49-511-85500, FAX 49-511-85501100, info@schluetersche.de, http://www.schluetersche.de. Ed. Gabriela Schulz. Adv. contact Susann Buglass. B&W page EUR 1,986, color page EUR 3,083; trim 188 x 272. Circ: 10,229 (paid and controlled).

622 305.897 CAN ISSN 1911-2793
STEPPING STONE. Text in English. 2006 (Spring). s-a. **Document type:** *Newsletter, Trade.* **Description:** It aims to increase respect and cooperation between First Nations and the mining sector.
Published by: Association for Mineral Exploration British Columbia, 800 - 889 W Pender St, Vancouver, BC V6C 3B2, Canada. TEL 604-689-5271, FAX 604-681-2363, info@amebc.ca, http://www.amebc.ca.

622 USA
STONE, SAND & GRAVEL REVIEW. Text in English. 1985. bi-m. USD 48 to members; USD 65 to non-members (effective 2007). adv. **Document type:** *Magazine, Trade.* **Description:** Designed to provide a communication forum for the aggregates industry by which to facilitate the exchange of information on industry technology, trends, developments and concerns.
Formerly (until 2006): Stone Review (8750-9210); Which was formed by the merger of (1974-1984): Stone News; (1964-1984): Limestone
Indexed: ConcrAb.
Published by: National Stone, Sand & Gravel Association, 1605 King St, Alexandria, VA 22314. TEL 703-525-8788, 800-342-1415, FAX 709-525-7782, info@nssga.org. Adv. contact Christine Ricci. B&W page USD 1,379. Circ: 6,000.

622.3 USA ISSN 1052-6994
HD9621.U4
STONE WORLD. Abbreviated title: S W. Text in English. 1984. m. USD 104 domestic; USD 137 in Canada; USD 154 elsewhere; free to qualified personnel (print or online ed.) (effective 2009). adv. bk.rev. index. back issues avail.; reprints avail. **Document type:** *Magazine, Trade.* **Description:** Covers the subject of granite, marble, limestone, sandstone, onyx, and other natural stone products for producers and users.
Related titles: Online - full text ed.
Indexed: A09, A10, A15, ABIn, B02, B03, B07, B11, B15, B17, B18, C12, G04, G06, G07, G08, H14, I05, M01, M02, P10, P48, P51, P52, P53, P54, PQC, S22, T02, T03, V03, V04.
—CCC.
Published by: B N P Media, 210 Rte 4 E, Ste 311, Paramus, NJ 07652. TEL 201-291-9001, FAX 201-291-9002, portfolio@bnpmedia.com, http://www.bnpmedia.com. Ed. Michael Reis TEL 201-291-9001 ext 8613. Pub. Alex Bachrach TEL 201-291-9001 ext 8615. Adv. contact Steve Smith TEL 630-694-4339. B&W page USD 3,755, color page USD 5,000; bleed 8.25 x 11. Circ: 24,030.

622 BRA ISSN 0101-2053
HD9506.B72
SUMARIO MINERAL. Text in Portuguese. 1981. a. BRL 3, USD 3.
Indexed: GeoRef, SpeleolAb.
Published by: Departamento Nacional da Producao Mineral, Setor Autarquia Norte, Quadra 1, Bloco B, Brasilia, DF 70040, Brazil. TEL 061-224-2670. Circ: 2,500.

622 SWE ISSN 0039-6435
SVENSK BERGS- & BRUKSTIDNING. Text in Swedish. 1922. 6/yr. SEK 120 (effective 1990). **Document type:** *Journal, Trade.*
Published by: B & J Invest AB, Fack 6040, Malmo, 20011, Sweden. FAX 40-79737. Ed. Joergen Dahlkvist. Circ: 3,000.

622 EGY ISSN 1110-2519
TABBIN INSTITUTE FOR METALLURGICAL STUDIES. BULLETIN/AL-NASRAT AL-'LMIYYAT LI-MA'HAD AL-TIBIN LIL-DIRASAT AL-MA'DANIT. Text in English. 1968. s-a. **Document type:** *Bulletin, Academic/Scholarly.*
Published by: Tabbin Institute for Metallurgical Studies, El-Tabbin, Helwan, PO Box 109, Cairo, Egypt. TEL 20-2-5010171. Ed. Dr. M G Khalifa.

622 CHN ISSN 1672-7428
➤ **TANKUANG GONGCHENG (YANTU ZUANJUE GONGCHENG)/ EXPLORATION ENGINEERING (ROCK & SOIL DRILLING AND TUNNELING).** Text and summaries in Chinese, English. 1957. bi-m. CNY 10 per issue (effective 2009). adv. abstr.; charts; illus. back issues avail. **Document type:** *Magazine, Trade.* **Description:** Subjects covered include rock and soil drilling and tunneling, construction exploration, water wells and geothermal wells, demolition, and equipment and tools for drilling and excavating. Purpose is to introduce new developments in engineering construction and exchange experiences.
Former tites (until 1978): Kantan Jishu; (until 1974): Tankuang Gongcheng/Exploration Engineering (1000-3746)
Related titles: CD-ROM ed.; Online - full text ed.
Indexed: GeoRef, SpeleolAb.
Published by: Zhongguo Dizhi Kexueyuan/Chinese Academy of Geological Sciences, 26 Baiwanzhuang Dajie, Beijing, 100037, China. TEL 86-10-68320471, FAX 86-10-68320471, http://www.cags.cn.net/. Circ: 3,000. **Co-sponsor:** Zhongguo Dizhi Kexueyuan, Kantan Jishu Yanjiusuo/Chinese Academy of Geological Sciences, Institute of Exploration Techniques.

➤ **TANTALUM-NIOBIUM INTERNATIONAL STUDY CENTER. QUARTERLY BULLETIN.** *see* METALLURGY

➤ **TAXATION OF MINING OPERATIONS.** *see* BUSINESS AND ECONOMICS—Public Finance, Taxation

➤ **TECHNIKA.** *see* MACHINERY

➤ **TECHNIKA POSZUKIWAN GEOLOGICZNYCH, GEOSYNOPTYKA I GEOTERMIA/EXPLORATION TECHNOLOGY, GEOSYNOPTICS AND GEOTHERMAL ENERGY.** *see* EARTH SCIENCES—Geology

M

622 DEU ISSN 0040-1501
TECHNISCHE UNIVERSITAET CLAUSTHAL. MITTEILUNGSBLATT. Text in German. 1960. s-a.
Formerly: Technische Hochschule der Bergakademie Clausthal. Mitteilungsblatt
Indexed: SpeleolAb.
—CCC.
Published by: Technische Universitaet Clausthal, Agricolastr 2, Clausthal-Zellerfeld, 38678, Germany. Circ: 1,800.

549 BRA ISSN 0103-7374
TECNOLOGIA AMBIENTAL. Text in Portuguese. 1991. irreg.
Indexed: ASFA, B21, ESPM, GeoRef.
Published by: Centro de Tecnologia Mineral (CETEM), Ministerio da Ciencia e Tecnologia, Av Ipe, 900 - Ilha da Cidade Universitaria - CEP, Rio de Janeiro, 21941-590, Brazil. TEL 55-21-3865-7222, FAX 55-21-2260-2837, http://www.cetem.gov.br/.

622 ALB
TEKNIKA/TECHNIQUE. Text in Albanian; Summaries in French. q. **Document type:** *Journal, Trade.*
Published by: Ministere des Resources Minerales et Energetiques/ Ministry of Energy and Mineral Resources, Tirana, Albania.

622 340 NLD ISSN 1574-5023
TEKST EN TOELICHTING ASBESTRECHT. Text in Dutch. 2004. a. EUR 51.89 (effective 2009).
Published by: Sdu Uitgevers bv, Postbus 20025, The Hague, 2500 EA, Netherlands. TEL 31-70-3789911, FAX 31-70-3854321, sdu@sdu.nl, http://www.sdu.nl/.

TI02 WORLDWIDE UPDATE. *see* CHEMISTRY—Inorganic Chemistry

TIANRANQI GONGYE/NATURAL GAS INDUSTRY. *see* PETROLEUM AND GAS

TOHOKU DAIGAKU SOZAI KOGAKU KENKYUJO IHO/TOHOKU UNIVERSITY. INSTITUTE FOR ADVANCED MATERIALS PROCESSING. BULLETIN. *see* METALLURGY

549 551 JPN ISSN 0371-3903
CODEN: STUMAR
TOHOKU UNIVERSITY. SCIENCE REPORTS. SERIES 3: MINERALOGY, PETROLOGY AND ECONOMIC GEOLOGY/ TOHOKU DAIGAKU RIKA HOKOKU. DAI 3-SHU, GANSEKIGAKU KOBUTSUGAKU KOSHOGAKU. Text in English. 1921. a.
Indexed: ChemAb, GeoRef, IMMAb, SpeleolAb.
—CASDDS, Ingenta, Linda Hall.
Published by: Tohoku Daigaku, Rigakubu/Tohoku University, Faculty of Science, Laboratory of Nuclear Science, Aramaki, Aoba-ku, Sendai-shi, Miyagi-ken 981-0945, Japan.

622.33 CHN ISSN 1000-4866
TONGMEI KEJI/DATONG COAL MINING ADMINISTRATION. SCIENCE AND TECHNOLOGY. Text in Chinese. 1979. q. **Document type:** *Journal, Academic/Scholarly.*
Related titles: Online - full text ed.
Published by: Datong Meikuang Jituan Youxian Zeren Gongsi/Datong Coal Mine Group, Xinpingwangxiao Bei Jie, 5/F, Keji Lou, Datong, 037003, China. TEL 86-352-7980113, FAX 86-352-7020129.

622 FRA ISSN 0982-0655
TRIBUNE DE LA REGION MINIERE. Text in French. 1952. w. adv.
Formerly (until 1986): Tribune des Mineurs (0982-0663)
Published by: Confederation Generale du Travail, Syndicat des Mineurs, 32 rue Casimir-Beugnet, Lens, Pas-de-Calais 62300, France. Circ: 78,000.

622 POL ISSN 1231-9996
TRYBUNA GORNICZA. Text in Polish. 1994. w. **Document type:** *Magazine, Trade.*
Published by: Wydawnictwo Gornicze, ul Plebiscytowa 36, Katowice, 40041, Poland. TEL 48-32-7572142, FAX 48-32-7572043, wydawnictwo.wg@w-g.com.pl. Ed. Jan Czypionka.

622 GBR ISSN 0952-2409
U K JOURNAL OF MINES AND MINERALS. Variant title: Rockbottom. Text in English. 1987. every 9 mos. GBP 16 domestic; USD 30 in United States; AUD 40 in Australia; GBP 17 elsewhere; GBP 8 per issue (effective 2009). adv. bk.rev. back issues avail. **Document type:** *Journal, Trade.* **Description:** Provides articles of interest to mineral collectors, mine historians, museum curators and topographic mineralogists.
Indexed: MinerAb.
Address: The University of Manchester, Oxford Rd, Manchester, M13 9PL, United Kingdom. http://www.ukjmm.co.uk/. Ed. David Green. Adv. contact Peter Briscoe. page GBP 200; 170 x 255.

662 USA
U.S. BUREAU OF MINES. MINERAL INDUSTRY SURVEYS (ONLINE EDITION). Text in English. m. stat. back issues avail. **Document type:** *Government.*
Media: Online - full text.
Published by: U.S. Geological Survey, Mineral Resources Program (Subsidiary of: U.S. Department of the Interior), 12201 Sunrise Valley Dr, 913 National Ctr, Reston, VA 20192. http://minerals.usgs.gov/.

622.33 USA
TN805.A3
U.S. DEPARTMENT OF ENERGY. ENERGY INFORMATION ADMINISTRATION. ANNUAL COAL REPORT (YEAR). Text in English. 1976. a. free (effective 2011). charts; stat. back issues avail. **Document type:** *Report, Government.*

Formerly (until 2001): U.S. Department of Energy. Energy Information Administration. Coal Industry Annual (Year); Which superseded (in 1993): U.S. Department of Energy. Energy Information Administration. Coal Production (Year) (0736-4504); Which was formerly (until 19??): Bituminous Coal and Lignite Production and Mine Operations; Coal Production was incorporated (in 1983): Coal-Pennsylvania Anthracite; Which was formerly (until 1978): Distribution of Pennsylvania Anthracite for the Calendar Year .. (0193-4236); (until 1977): Coal-Pennsylvania Anthracite in ..
Related titles: CD-ROM ed.; Online - full text ed.
—Linda Hall.
Published by: U.S. Department of Energy, Energy Information Administration, 1000 Independence Ave, SW, Washington, DC 20585. TEL 202-586-8800, infoctr@eia.gov, http://www.eia.doe.gov. **Subscr. to:** U.S. Government Printing Office, Superintendent of Documents.

622 USA
U.S. DEPARTMENT OF ENERGY. ENERGY INFORMATION ADMINISTRATION. WEEKLY COAL PRODUCTION. Text in English. 19??. w. free (effective 2011). stat. back issues avail. **Document type:** *Report, Government.*
Media: Online - full text. **Related titles:** ◆ Print ed.: U.S. Department of Energy. Energy Information Administration. Weekly U.S. Coal Production Overview.
Published by: U.S. Department of Energy, Energy Information Administration, 1000 Independence Ave, SW, Washington, DC 20585. TEL 202-586-8800, infoctr@eia.gov.

U.S. DEPARTMENT OF ENERGY. ENERGY INFORMATION ADMINISTRATION. WEEKLY U.S. COAL PRODUCTION OVERVIEW. *see* ENERGY

U.S. GEOLOGICAL SURVEY. MINERAL RESOURCES PROGRAM. MINERAL INDUSTRY SURVEYS. CHROMIUM. *see* MINES AND MINING INDUSTRY—Abstracting, Bibliographies, Statistics

622.021 USA
U.S. GEOLOGICAL SURVEY. MINERAL RESOURCES PROGRAM. MINERALS YEARBOOK: THE MINERAL INDUSTRY OF ALABAMA. Text in English. a. stat.; maps. back issues avail. **Document type:** *Yearbook, Government.*
Media: Online - full text.
Published by: U.S. Geological Survey, Mineral Resources Program (Subsidiary of: U.S. Department of the Interior), c/o Arnold Tanner, 984 National Center, Reston, VA 20192 . TEL 703-648-4758, FAX 703-648-4995, http://minerals.usgs.gov/.

622.021 USA
U.S. GEOLOGICAL SURVEY. MINERAL RESOURCES PROGRAM. MINERALS YEARBOOK: THE MINERAL INDUSTRY OF ALASKA. Text in English. a. stat. back issues avail. **Document type:** *Yearbook, Government.*
Media: Online - full text.
Published by: U.S. Geological Survey, Mineral Resources Program (Subsidiary of: U.S. Department of the Interior), 12201 Sunrise Valley Dr, 913 National Ctr, Reston, VA 20192. http://minerals.usgs.gov/.

622 USA
U.S. GEOLOGICAL SURVEY. MINERAL RESOURCES PROGRAM. MINERALS YEARBOOK: THE MINERAL INDUSTRY OF ARIZONA. Text in English. 19??. a., latest 2007. free (effective 2011). stat. back issues avail. **Document type:** *Yearbook, Government.*
Media: Online - full text.
Published by: U.S. Geological Survey, Mineral Resources Program (Subsidiary of: U.S. Department of the Interior), 12201 Sunrise Valley Dr, 913 National Ctr, Reston, VA 20192. TEL 703-648-6110, FAX 703-648-6057, kjohnson@usgs.gov.

622 USA
U.S. GEOLOGICAL SURVEY. MINERAL RESOURCES PROGRAM. MINERALS YEARBOOK: THE MINERAL INDUSTRY OF ARKANSAS. Text in English. a. stat. back issues avail. **Document type:** *Yearbook, Government.*
Media: Online - full text.
Published by: U.S. Geological Survey, Mineral Resources Program (Subsidiary of: U.S. Department of the Interior), c/o Arnold Tanner, 984 National Center, Reston, VA 20192 . TEL 703-648-4758, FAX 703-648-4995, http://minerals.usgs.gov/.

622 USA
U.S. GEOLOGICAL SURVEY. MINERAL RESOURCES PROGRAM. MINERALS YEARBOOK: THE MINERAL INDUSTRY OF CALIFORNIA. Text in English. a. stat. back issues avail. **Document type:** *Yearbook, Government.*
Media: Online - full text.
Published by: U.S. Geological Survey, Mineral Resources Program (Subsidiary of: U.S. Department of the Interior), c/o Arnold Tanner, 984 National Center, Reston, VA 20192 . TEL 703-648-4758, FAX 703-648-4995, http://minerals.usgs.gov/.

622 USA
U.S. GEOLOGICAL SURVEY. MINERAL RESOURCES PROGRAM. MINERALS YEARBOOK: THE MINERAL INDUSTRY OF COLORADO. Text in English. a. stat. back issues avail. **Document type:** *Yearbook, Government.*
Media: Online - full text.
Published by: U.S. Geological Survey, Mineral Resources Program (Subsidiary of: U.S. Department of the Interior), c/o Arnold Tanner, 984 National Center, Reston, VA 20192 . TEL 703-648-4758, FAX 703-648-4995, http://minerals.usgs.gov/.

622 USA
U.S. GEOLOGICAL SURVEY. MINERAL RESOURCES PROGRAM. MINERALS YEARBOOK: THE MINERAL INDUSTRY OF CONNECTICUT. Text in English. a. stat. back issues avail. **Document type:** *Yearbook, Government.*
Media: Online - full text.
Published by: U.S. Geological Survey, Mineral Resources Program (Subsidiary of: U.S. Department of the Interior), c/o Arnold Tanner, 984 National Center, Reston, VA 20192 . TEL 703-648-4758, FAX 703-648-4995, http://minerals.usgs.gov/.

622 USA
U.S. GEOLOGICAL SURVEY. MINERAL RESOURCES PROGRAM. MINERALS YEARBOOK: THE MINERAL INDUSTRY OF DELAWARE. Text in English. a. back issues avail. **Document type:** *Yearbook, Government.*
Media: Online - full text.
Published by: U.S. Geological Survey, Mineral Resources Program (Subsidiary of: U.S. Department of the Interior), c/o Arnold Tanner, 984 National Center, Reston, VA 20192 . TEL 703-648-4758, FAX 703-648-4995, http://minerals.usgs.gov/.

622 USA
U.S. GEOLOGICAL SURVEY. MINERAL RESOURCES PROGRAM. MINERALS YEARBOOK: THE MINERAL INDUSTRY OF FLORIDA. Text in English. irreg. stat. back issues avail. **Document type:** *Yearbook, Government.*
Media: Online - full text.
Published by: U.S. Geological Survey, Mineral Resources Program (Subsidiary of: U.S. Department of the Interior), c/o Arnold Tanner, 984 National Center, Reston, VA 20192 . TEL 703-648-4758, FAX 703-648-4995, http://minerals.usgs.gov/.

622 USA
U.S. GEOLOGICAL SURVEY. MINERAL RESOURCES PROGRAM. MINERALS YEARBOOK: THE MINERAL INDUSTRY OF GEORGIA. Text in English. a. stat. back issues avail. **Document type:** *Yearbook, Government.*
Media: Online - full text.
Published by: U.S. Geological Survey, Mineral Resources Program (Subsidiary of: U.S. Department of the Interior), c/o Arnold Tanner, 984 National Center, Reston, VA 20192 . TEL 703-648-4758, FAX 703-648-4995, http://minerals.usgs.gov/.

622 USA
U.S. GEOLOGICAL SURVEY. MINERAL RESOURCES PROGRAM. MINERALS YEARBOOK: THE MINERAL INDUSTRY OF HAWAII. Text in English. a. stat. back issues avail. **Document type:** *Yearbook, Government.*
Media: Online - full text.
Published by: U.S. Geological Survey, Mineral Resources Program (Subsidiary of: U.S. Department of the Interior), c/o Arnold Tanner, 984 National Center, Reston, VA 20192 . TEL 703-648-4758, FAX 703-648-4995, http://minerals.usgs.gov/.

622 USA
U.S. GEOLOGICAL SURVEY. MINERAL RESOURCES PROGRAM. MINERALS YEARBOOK: THE MINERAL INDUSTRY OF IDAHO. Text in English. 19??. a. free (effective 2011). stat. back issues avail. **Document type:** *Yearbook, Government.*
Media: Online - full text.
Published by: U.S. Geological Survey, Mineral Resources Program (Subsidiary of: U.S. Department of the Interior), 12201 Sunrise Valley Dr, 913 National Ctr, Reston, VA 20192. TEL 703-648-6110, FAX 703-648-6057, kjohnson@usgs.gov.

622 USA
U.S. GEOLOGICAL SURVEY. MINERAL RESOURCES PROGRAM. MINERALS YEARBOOK: THE MINERAL INDUSTRY OF ILLINOIS. Text in English. a. stat. back issues avail. **Document type:** *Yearbook, Government.*
Media: Online - full text.
Published by: U.S. Geological Survey, Mineral Resources Program (Subsidiary of: U.S. Department of the Interior), c/o Arnold Tanner, 984 National Center, Reston, VA 20192 . TEL 703-648-4758, FAX 703-648-4995, http://minerals.usgs.gov/.

622 USA
U.S. GEOLOGICAL SURVEY. MINERAL RESOURCES PROGRAM. MINERALS YEARBOOK: THE MINERAL INDUSTRY OF INDIANA. Text in English. a. stat. back issues avail. **Document type:** *Yearbook, Government.*
Media: Online - full text.
Published by: U.S. Geological Survey, Mineral Resources Program (Subsidiary of: U.S. Department of the Interior), c/o Arnold Tanner, 984 National Center, Reston, VA 20192 . TEL 703-648-4758, FAX 703-648-4995, http://minerals.usgs.gov/.

622 USA
U.S. GEOLOGICAL SURVEY. MINERAL RESOURCES PROGRAM. MINERALS YEARBOOK: THE MINERAL INDUSTRY OF IOWA. Text in English. a. stat. back issues avail. **Document type:** *Yearbook, Government.*
Media: Online - full text.
Published by: U.S. Geological Survey, Mineral Resources Program (Subsidiary of: U.S. Department of the Interior), c/o Arnold Tanner, 984 National Center, Reston, VA 20192 . TEL 703-648-4758, FAX 703-648-4995, http://minerals.usgs.gov/.

622 USA
U.S. GEOLOGICAL SURVEY. MINERAL RESOURCES PROGRAM. MINERALS YEARBOOK: THE MINERAL INDUSTRY OF KANSAS. Text in English. a. stat. back issues avail. **Document type:** *Yearbook, Government.*
Media: Online - full text.
Published by: U.S. Geological Survey, Mineral Resources Program (Subsidiary of: U.S. Department of the Interior), c/o Arnold Tanner, 984 National Center, Reston, VA 20192 . TEL 703-648-4758, FAX 703-648-4995, http://minerals.usgs.gov/.

622 USA
U.S. GEOLOGICAL SURVEY. MINERAL RESOURCES PROGRAM. MINERALS YEARBOOK: THE MINERAL INDUSTRY OF KENTUCKY. Text in English. a. stat. back issues avail. **Document type:** *Yearbook, Government.*
Media: Online - full text.
Published by: U.S. Geological Survey, Mineral Resources Program (Subsidiary of: U.S. Department of the Interior), c/o Arnold Tanner, 984 National Center, Reston, VA 20192 . TEL 703-648-4758, FAX 703-648-4995, http://minerals.usgs.gov/.

622 USA
U.S. GEOLOGICAL SURVEY. MINERAL RESOURCES PROGRAM. MINERALS YEARBOOK: THE MINERAL INDUSTRY OF LOUISIANA. Text in English. a. stat. back issues avail. **Document type:** *Yearbook, Government.*
Media: Online - full text.
Published by: U.S. Geological Survey, Mineral Resources Program (Subsidiary of: U.S. Department of the Interior), c/o Arnold Tanner, 984 National Center, Reston, VA 20192 . TEL 703-648-4758, FAX 703-648-4995, http://minerals.usgs.gov/.

622 USA
U.S. GEOLOGICAL SURVEY. MINERAL RESOURCES PROGRAM. MINERALS YEARBOOK: THE MINERAL INDUSTRY OF MAINE. Text in English. a. stat. back issues avail. **Document type:** *Yearbook, Government.*
Media: Online - full text.
Published by: U.S. Geological Survey, Mineral Resources Program (Subsidiary of: U.S. Department of the Interior), c/o Arnold Tanner, 984 National Center, Reston, VA 20192 . TEL 703-648-4758, FAX 703-648-4995, http://minerals.usgs.gov/.

622 USA
U.S. GEOLOGICAL SURVEY. MINERAL RESOURCES PROGRAM. MINERALS YEARBOOK: THE MINERAL INDUSTRY OF MARYLAND. Text in English. 19??. a. free (effective 2011). stat. back issues avail. **Document type:** *Yearbook, Government.*
Media: Online - full text.
Published by: U.S. Geological Survey, Mineral Resources Program (Subsidiary of: U.S. Department of the Interior), 12201 Sunrise Valley Dr, 913 National Ctr, Reston, VA 20192. TEL 703-648-6110, FAX 703-648-6057, kjohnson@usgs.gov.

622 USA
U.S. GEOLOGICAL SURVEY. MINERAL RESOURCES PROGRAM. MINERALS YEARBOOK: THE MINERAL INDUSTRY OF MASSACHUSETTS. Text in English. a. stat. back issues avail. **Document type:** *Yearbook, Government.*
Media: Online - full text.
Published by: U.S. Geological Survey, Mineral Resources Program (Subsidiary of: U.S. Department of the Interior), c/o Arnold Tanner, 984 National Center, Reston, VA 20192 . TEL 703-648-4758, FAX 703-648-4995, http://minerals.usgs.gov/.

622 USA
U.S. GEOLOGICAL SURVEY. MINERAL RESOURCES PROGRAM. MINERALS YEARBOOK: THE MINERAL INDUSTRY OF MICHIGAN. Text in English. a. stat. back issues avail. **Document type:** *Yearbook, Government.*
Media: Online - full text.
Published by: U.S. Geological Survey, Mineral Resources Program (Subsidiary of: U.S. Department of the Interior), c/o Arnold Tanner, 984 National Center, Reston, VA 20192 . TEL 703-648-4758, FAX 703-648-4995, http://minerals.usgs.gov/.

622 USA
U.S. GEOLOGICAL SURVEY. MINERAL RESOURCES PROGRAM. MINERALS YEARBOOK: THE MINERAL INDUSTRY OF MINNESOTA. Text in English. a. stat. back issues avail. **Document type:** *Government.*
Media: Online - full text.
Published by: U.S. Geological Survey, Mineral Resources Program (Subsidiary of: U.S. Department of the Interior), c/o Arnold Tanner, 984 National Center, Reston, VA 20192 . TEL 703-648-4758, FAX 703-648-4995, http://minerals.usgs.gov/.

622 USA
U.S. GEOLOGICAL SURVEY. MINERAL RESOURCES PROGRAM. MINERALS YEARBOOK: THE MINERAL INDUSTRY OF MISSISSIPPI. Text in English. a. stat. back issues avail. **Document type:** *Yearbook, Government.*
Media: Online - full text.
Published by: U.S. Geological Survey, Mineral Resources Program (Subsidiary of: U.S. Department of the Interior), c/o Arnold Tanner, 984 National Center, Reston, VA 20192 . TEL 703-648-4758, FAX 703-648-4995, http://minerals.usgs.gov/.

622 USA
U.S. GEOLOGICAL SURVEY. MINERAL RESOURCES PROGRAM. MINERALS YEARBOOK: THE MINERAL INDUSTRY OF MISSOURI. Text in English. a. stat. back issues avail. **Document type:** *Yearbook, Government.*
Media: Online - full text.
Published by: U.S. Geological Survey, Mineral Resources Program (Subsidiary of: U.S. Department of the Interior), c/o Arnold Tanner, 984 National Center, Reston, VA 20192 . TEL 703-648-4758, FAX 703-648-4995, http://minerals.usgs.gov/.

622 USA
U.S. GEOLOGICAL SURVEY. MINERAL RESOURCES PROGRAM. MINERALS YEARBOOK: THE MINERAL INDUSTRY OF MONTANA. Text in English. a. stat. back issues avail. **Document type:** *Yearbook, Government.*
Media: Online - full text.
Published by: U.S. Geological Survey, Mineral Resources Program (Subsidiary of: U.S. Department of the Interior), c/o Arnold Tanner, 984 National Center, Reston, VA 20192 . TEL 703-648-4758, FAX 703-648-4995, http://minerals.usgs.gov/.

622 USA
U.S. GEOLOGICAL SURVEY. MINERAL RESOURCES PROGRAM. MINERALS YEARBOOK: THE MINERAL INDUSTRY OF NEBRASKA. Text in English. a.
Media: Online - full text.
Published by: U.S. Geological Survey, Mineral Resources Program (Subsidiary of: U.S. Department of the Interior), c/o Arnold Tanner, 984 National Center, Reston, VA 20192 . TEL 703-648-4758, FAX 703-648-4995, http://minerals.usgs.gov/.

622 USA
U.S. GEOLOGICAL SURVEY. MINERAL RESOURCES PROGRAM. MINERALS YEARBOOK: THE MINERAL INDUSTRY OF NEVADA. Text in English. a. stat. back issues avail. **Document type:** *Yearbook, Government.*
Media: Online - full text.
Published by: U.S. Geological Survey, Mineral Resources Program (Subsidiary of: U.S. Department of the Interior), c/o Arnold Tanner, 984 National Center, Reston, VA 20192 . TEL 703-648-4758, FAX 703-648-4995, http://minerals.usgs.gov/.

622 USA
U.S. GEOLOGICAL SURVEY. MINERAL RESOURCES PROGRAM. MINERALS YEARBOOK: THE MINERAL INDUSTRY OF NEW HAMPSHIRE. Text in English. a. stat. back issues avail. **Document type:** *Yearbook, Government.*
Media: Online - full text.
Published by: U.S. Geological Survey, Mineral Resources Program (Subsidiary of: U.S. Department of the Interior), c/o Arnold Tanner, 984 National Center, Reston, VA 20192 . TEL 703-648-4758, FAX 703-648-4995, http://minerals.usgs.gov/.

622 USA
U.S. GEOLOGICAL SURVEY. MINERAL RESOURCES PROGRAM. MINERALS YEARBOOK: THE MINERAL INDUSTRY OF NEW JERSEY. Text in English. 19??. a. free (effective 2011). stat. back issues avail. **Document type:** *Yearbook, Government.*
Media: Online - full text.
Published by: U.S. Geological Survey, Mineral Resources Program (Subsidiary of: U.S. Department of the Interior), 12201 Sunrise Valley Dr, 913 National Ctr, Reston, VA 20192. TEL 703-648-6110, FAX 703-648-6057, kjohnson@usgs.gov.

622 USA
U.S. GEOLOGICAL SURVEY. MINERAL RESOURCES PROGRAM. MINERALS YEARBOOK: THE MINERAL INDUSTRY OF NEW MEXICO. Text in English. 19??. a., latest 2007. free (effective 2011). stat. back issues avail. **Document type:** *Yearbook, Government.*
Media: Online - full text.
Published by: U.S. Geological Survey, Mineral Resources Program (Subsidiary of: U.S. Department of the Interior), 12201 Sunrise Valley Dr, 913 National Ctr, Reston, VA 20192. TEL 703-648-6110, FAX 703-648-6057, kjohnson@usgs.gov.

622 USA
U.S. GEOLOGICAL SURVEY. MINERAL RESOURCES PROGRAM. MINERALS YEARBOOK: THE MINERAL INDUSTRY OF NEW YORK. Text in English. a. stat. back issues avail. **Document type:** *Government.*
Media: Online - full text.
Published by: U.S. Geological Survey, Mineral Resources Program (Subsidiary of: U.S. Department of the Interior), c/o Arnold Tanner, 984 National Center, Reston, VA 20192 . TEL 703-648-4758, FAX 703-648-4995, http://minerals.usgs.gov/.

622 USA
U.S. GEOLOGICAL SURVEY. MINERAL RESOURCES PROGRAM. MINERALS YEARBOOK: THE MINERAL INDUSTRY OF NORTH CAROLINA. Text in English. a. stat. back issues avail. **Document type:** *Yearbook, Government.*
Media: Online - full text.
Published by: U.S. Geological Survey, Mineral Resources Program (Subsidiary of: U.S. Department of the Interior), c/o Arnold Tanner, 984 National Center, Reston, VA 20192 . TEL 703-648-4758, FAX 703-648-4995, http://minerals.usgs.gov/.

622 USA
U.S. GEOLOGICAL SURVEY. MINERAL RESOURCES PROGRAM. MINERALS YEARBOOK: THE MINERAL INDUSTRY OF NORTH DAKOTA. Text in English. a. stat. back issues avail. **Document type:** *Government.*
Media: Online - full text.
Published by: U.S. Geological Survey, Mineral Resources Program (Subsidiary of: U.S. Department of the Interior), c/o Arnold Tanner, 984 National Center, Reston, VA 20192 . TEL 703-648-4758, FAX 703-648-4995, http://minerals.usgs.gov/.

622 USA
U.S. GEOLOGICAL SURVEY. MINERAL RESOURCES PROGRAM. MINERALS YEARBOOK: THE MINERAL INDUSTRY OF OHIO. Text in English. a. stat. back issues avail. **Document type:** *Government.*
Media: Online - full text.
Published by: U.S. Geological Survey, Mineral Resources Program (Subsidiary of: U.S. Department of the Interior), c/o Arnold Tanner, 984 National Center, Reston, VA 20192 . TEL 703-648-4758, FAX 703-648-4995, http://minerals.usgs.gov/.

622 USA
U.S. GEOLOGICAL SURVEY. MINERAL RESOURCES PROGRAM. MINERALS YEARBOOK: THE MINERAL INDUSTRY OF OKLAHOMA. Text in English. a. stat. back issues avail. **Document type:** *Yearbook, Government.*
Media: Online - full text.
Published by: U.S. Geological Survey, Mineral Resources Program (Subsidiary of: U.S. Department of the Interior), c/o Arnold Tanner, 984 National Center, Reston, VA 20192 . TEL 703-648-4758, FAX 703-648-4995, http://minerals.usgs.gov/.

622 USA
U.S. GEOLOGICAL SURVEY. MINERAL RESOURCES PROGRAM. MINERALS YEARBOOK: THE MINERAL INDUSTRY OF OREGON. Text in English. a. stat. back issues avail. **Document type:** *Yearbook, Government.*
Media: Online - full text.
Published by: U.S. Geological Survey, Mineral Resources Program (Subsidiary of: U.S. Department of the Interior), c/o Arnold Tanner, 984 National Center, Reston, VA 20192 . TEL 703-648-4758, FAX 703-648-4995, http://minerals.usgs.gov/.

622 USA
U.S. GEOLOGICAL SURVEY. MINERAL RESOURCES PROGRAM. MINERALS YEARBOOK: THE MINERAL INDUSTRY OF PENNSYLVANIA. Text in English. a. stat. back issues avail. **Document type:** *Yearbook, Government.*
Media: Online - full text.
Published by: U.S. Geological Survey, Mineral Resources Program (Subsidiary of: U.S. Department of the Interior), c/o Arnold Tanner, 984 National Center, Reston, VA 20192 . TEL 703-648-4758, FAX 703-648-4995, http://minerals.usgs.gov/.

622 USA
U.S. GEOLOGICAL SURVEY. MINERAL RESOURCES PROGRAM. MINERALS YEARBOOK: THE MINERAL INDUSTRY OF PUERTO RICO. Text in English. 19??. a., latest 2007. free (effective 2011). stat. back issues avail. **Document type:** *Yearbook, Government.*
Media: Online - full text.
Published by: U.S. Geological Survey, Mineral Resources Program (Subsidiary of: U.S. Department of the Interior), 12201 Sunrise Valley Dr, 913 National Ctr, Reston, VA 20192. TEL 703-648-6110, FAX 703-648-6057, kjohnson@usgs.gov.

622 USA
U.S. GEOLOGICAL SURVEY. MINERAL RESOURCES PROGRAM. MINERALS YEARBOOK: THE MINERAL INDUSTRY OF RHODE ISLAND. Text in English. a. stat. back issues avail. **Document type:** *Yearbook, Government.*
Media: Online - full text.
Published by: U.S. Geological Survey, Mineral Resources Program (Subsidiary of: U.S. Department of the Interior), c/o Arnold Tanner, 984 National Center, Reston, VA 20192 . TEL 703-648-4758, FAX 703-648-4995, http://minerals.usgs.gov/.

622 USA
U.S. GEOLOGICAL SURVEY. MINERAL RESOURCES PROGRAM. MINERALS YEARBOOK: THE MINERAL INDUSTRY OF SOUTH CAROLINA. Text in English. 19??. a., latest 2007. free (effective 2011). stat. back issues avail. **Document type:** *Yearbook, Government.*
Media: Online - full text.
Published by: U.S. Geological Survey, Mineral Resources Program (Subsidiary of: U.S. Department of the Interior), 12201 Sunrise Valley Dr, 913 National Ctr, Reston, VA 20192. TEL 703-648-6110, FAX 703-648-6057, kjohnson@usgs.gov.

622 USA
U.S. GEOLOGICAL SURVEY. MINERAL RESOURCES PROGRAM. MINERALS YEARBOOK: THE MINERAL INDUSTRY OF SOUTH DAKOTA. Text in English. a. stat. back issues avail. **Document type:** *Yearbook, Government.*
Media: Online - full text.
Published by: U.S. Geological Survey, Mineral Resources Program (Subsidiary of: U.S. Department of the Interior), c/o Arnold Tanner, 984 National Center, Reston, VA 20192 . TEL 703-648-4758, FAX 703-648-4995, http://minerals.usgs.gov/.

622 USA
U.S. GEOLOGICAL SURVEY. MINERAL RESOURCES PROGRAM. MINERALS YEARBOOK: THE MINERAL INDUSTRY OF TENNESSEE. Text in English. a. stat. back issues avail. **Document type:** *Yearbook, Government.*
Media: Online - full text.
Published by: U.S. Geological Survey, Mineral Resources Program (Subsidiary of: U.S. Department of the Interior), c/o Arnold Tanner, 984 National Center, Reston, VA 20192 . TEL 703-648-4758, FAX 703-648-4995, http://minerals.usgs.gov/.

622 USA
U.S. GEOLOGICAL SURVEY. MINERAL RESOURCES PROGRAM. MINERALS YEARBOOK: THE MINERAL INDUSTRY OF TEXAS. Text in English. a. stat. back issues avail. **Document type:** *Yearbook, Government.*
Media: Online - full text.
Published by: U.S. Geological Survey, Mineral Resources Program (Subsidiary of: U.S. Department of the Interior), c/o Arnold Tanner, 984 National Center, Reston, VA 20192 . TEL 703-648-4758, FAX 703-648-4995, http://minerals.usgs.gov/.

622 USA
U.S. GEOLOGICAL SURVEY. MINERAL RESOURCES PROGRAM. MINERALS YEARBOOK: THE MINERAL INDUSTRY OF UTAH. Text in English. a. stat. back issues avail. **Document type:** *Yearbook, Government.*
Media: Online - full text.
Published by: U.S. Geological Survey, Mineral Resources Program (Subsidiary of: U.S. Department of the Interior), c/o Arnold Tanner, 984 National Center, Reston, VA 20192 . TEL 703-648-4758, FAX 703-648-4995, http://minerals.usgs.gov/.

622 USA
U.S. GEOLOGICAL SURVEY. MINERAL RESOURCES PROGRAM. MINERALS YEARBOOK: THE MINERAL INDUSTRY OF VERMONT. Text in English. irreg. back issues avail. **Document type:** *Yearbook, Government.*
Media: Online - full text.
Published by: U.S. Geological Survey, Mineral Resources Program (Subsidiary of: U.S. Department of the Interior), c/o Arnold Tanner, 984 National Center, Reston, VA 20192 . TEL 703-648-4758, FAX 703-648-4995, http://minerals.usgs.gov/.

622 USA
U.S. GEOLOGICAL SURVEY. MINERAL RESOURCES PROGRAM. MINERALS YEARBOOK: THE MINERAL INDUSTRY OF VIRGINIA. Text in English. a. stat. back issues avail. **Document type:** *Yearbook, Government.*
Media: Online - full text.
Published by: U.S. Geological Survey, Mineral Resources Program (Subsidiary of: U.S. Department of the Interior), c/o Arnold Tanner, 984 National Center, Reston, VA 20192 . TEL 703-648-4758, FAX 703-648-4995, http://minerals.usgs.gov/.

622 USA
U.S. GEOLOGICAL SURVEY. MINERAL RESOURCES PROGRAM. MINERALS YEARBOOK: THE MINERAL INDUSTRY OF WEST VIRGINIA. Text in English. a. stat. back issues avail. **Document type:** *Yearbook, Government.*
Media: Online - full text.
Published by: U.S. Geological Survey, Mineral Resources Program (Subsidiary of: U.S. Department of the Interior), c/o Arnold Tanner, 984 National Center, Reston, VA 20192 . TEL 703-648-4758, FAX 703-648-4995, http://minerals.usgs.gov/.

622 USA
U.S. GEOLOGICAL SURVEY. MINERAL RESOURCES PROGRAM. MINERALS YEARBOOK: THE MINERAL INDUSTRY OF WISCONSIN. Text in English. a. stat. back issues avail. **Document type:** *Yearbook, Government.*
Media: Online - full text.
Published by: U.S. Geological Survey, Mineral Resources Program (Subsidiary of: U.S. Department of the Interior), c/o Arnold Tanner, 984 National Center, Reston, VA 20192 . TEL 703-648-4758, FAX 703-648-4995, http://minerals.usgs.gov/.

622 USA
U.S. GEOLOGICAL SURVEY. MINERAL RESOURCES PROGRAM. MINERALS YEARBOOK: THE MINERAL INDUSTRY OF WYOMING. Text in English. a. stat. back issues avail. **Document type:** *Yearbook, Government.*
Media: Online - full text.
Published by: U.S. Geological Survey, Mineral Resources Program (Subsidiary of: U.S. Department of the Interior), c/o Arnold Tanner, 984 National Center, Reston, VA 20192 . TEL 703-648-4758, FAX 703-648-4995, http://minerals.usgs.gov/.

622 USA
U.S. GEOLOGICAL SURVEY. MINERAL RESOURCES PROGRAM. SPECIAL PUBLICATIONS. Text in English. 199?. irreg., latest 1999. stat. back issues avail. **Document type:** *Government.*
Media: Online - full text.
Published by: U.S. Geological Survey, Mineral Resources Program (Subsidiary of: U.S. Department of the Interior), 12201 Sunrise Valley Dr, 913 National Ctr, Reston, VA 20192. TEL 703-648-6110, FAX 703-648-6057, kjohnson@usgs.gov.

622.8 USA
U.S. MINE SAFETY AND HEALTH ADMINISTRATION. INFORMATIONAL REPORT. Text in English. irreg.
Formerly: U.S. Mining Enforcement and Safety Administration. Informational Report (0097-9376)
Indexed: AESIS, IMMAb.
Published by: U.S. Department of Labor, Mine Safety and Health Administration, 1100 Wilson Blvd, 21st Fl, Arlington, VA 22209-2249.

622 662 RUS ISSN 0041-5790
TN4 CODEN: UGOLAR
UGOL'. Text in Russian. 1925. m. USD 129.95. adv. bk.rev. bibl.; charts; illus.; stat. index.
Related titles: Online - full text ed.
Indexed: CIN, CISA, ChemAb, F&EA, FR, GeoRef, RASB, RefZh, SCOPUS, SpeleolAb, TM.
—CASDDS, East View, INIST, Linda Hall. **CCC.**
Published by: Rossiiskaya Ugol'naya Kompaniya Rosugol, Novyi Arbat 15, Moscow, 121019, Russian Federation. TEL 7-095-2021493. Ed. G V Krasnikovskii. Circ: 8,945. **Dist. by:** East View Information Services, 10601 Wayzata Blvd, Minneapolis, MN 55305. TEL 952-252-1201, 800-477-1005, FAX 952-252-1202, info@eastview.com, http://www.eastview.com.

622 662.6 UKR ISSN 0041-5804
CODEN: UGOUAK
UGOL' UKRAINY. Text in Russian. 1957. m. USD 160. adv. charts; illus. index.
Indexed: CISA, ChemAb, ChemTitl, F&EA, RASB, RefZh.
—CASDDS, East View, INIST, Linda Hall. **CCC.**
Published by: Ministerstvo Ugol'noi Promyshlennosti Ukrainy, Ul Krasnoarmeiskaya 65, Kiev, Ukraine. TEL 227-37-52, FAX 227-98-46. Circ: 10,000. **Dist. by:** East View Information Services, 10601 Wayzata Blvd, Minneapolis, MN 55305. TEL 952-252-1201, 800-477-1005, FAX 952-252-1202, info@eastview.com, http://www.eastview.com.

622 CZE ISSN 1210-7697
TN4 CODEN: UGPREK
UHLI - RUDY - GEOLOGICKY PRUZKUM; technickoekonomicky mesicnik. Text in Czech; Summaries in English, German, Russian. 1992. bi-m. CZK 360; CZK 60 newsstand/cover (effective 2010). adv. bk.rev. charts; illus.; pat. **Document type:** *Journal, Academic/Scholarly.*
Formed by the merger of (1957-1994): Geologicky Pruzkum (0016-772X); (1992-1994): Uhli - Rudy (1210-1699); Which was formed by the merger of (1953-1992): Uhli (0041-5812); (1953-1992): Rudy (0483-5093)
Indexed: CIN, CISA, ChemAb, F&EA, GeoRef, IMMAb, INIS AtomInd, RefZh, SpeleolAb.
—CASDDS, INIST, Linda Hall.
Published by: Zamestnavatelsky Svaz Dulniho a Naftoveho Prumyslu/ The Employers' Association of Mining and Oil Industry, Rumunska 12, Prague 2, 12000, Czech Republic. TEL 420-2-24230588, FAX 420-2-24210830, http://www.zsdnp.cz. Ed. Evzen Synek. Circ: 2,800. **Dist. by:** Kubon & Sagner Buchexport - Import GmbH, Hessstr 39-41, Munich 80798, Germany. TEL 49-89-542180, FAX 49-89-54218218, postmaster@kubon-sagner.de, http://www.kubon-sagner.de.

338.2 GBR ISSN 0957-4697
HD9506.G7
UNITED KINGDOM MINERALS YEARBOOK. Text in English. 1973. a. GBP 25 per issue (effective 2009). stat. back issues avail. **Document type:** *Yearbook, Government.* **Description:** Provide comprehensive statistical data on minerals production.
Formerly (until 1989): United Kingdom Mineral Statistics (0308-5090)
Related titles: Online - full text ed.: free (effective 2009).
Indexed: RASB, SpeleolAb.
—BLDSC (9096.455000). **CCC.**
Published by: Natural Environment Research Council, British Geological Survey, Kingsley Dunham Ctr, Keyworth, Nottingham, NG12 5GG, United Kingdom. TEL 44-115-9363100, 44-115-9363241, FAX 44-115-9363488, enquiries@bgs.ac.uk.

UNITED MINE WORKERS JOURNAL. *see* LABOR UNIONS

549 ITA ISSN 0391-5573
QE1 CODEN: FUMPAU
UNIVERSITA DI FERRARA. ANNALI. SEZIONE 17: SCIENZE MINERALOGICHE E PETROGRAFICHE. Text in Italian. 1936. a. price varies. **Document type:** *Journal, Academic/Scholarly.*
Supersedes in part (in 1951): Universita di Ferrara. Annali (0365-7833)
Indexed: GeoRef.
—Linda Hall.
Published by: Universita degli Studi di Ferrara, Via Savonarola 9, Ferrara, 44100, Italy. TEL 39-0532-293111, FAX 39-0532-293031, http://www.unife.it.

622 546 USA ISSN 0568-8760
TN24.A4
UNIVERSITY OF ALASKA. MINERAL INDUSTRY RESEARCH LABORATORY. ANNUAL REPORT OF RESEARCH PROGRESS. Text in English. a. **Document type:** *Catalog.*
Published by: University of Alaska at Fairbanks, Mineral Industry Research Laboratory, 212B O Neill Bldg, Box 757240, Fairbanks, AK 99775-7240. TEL 907-474-7135, FAX 907-474-5400.

622 HUN ISSN 1417-5428
TN275.A1 CODEN: PTUADT
UNIVERSITY OF MISKOLC. PUBLICATIONS. SERIES A, MINING. MINING AND GEOTECHNOLOGY. Alternating issues in English, German, Hungarian. irreg., latest vol.45, 1988, no.1-4. bibl. index.

Supersedes in part (in 1995): University of Miskolc. Publications. Series A, Mining (1219-008X); Which was formerly (until 1994): Technical University for Heavy Industry. Publications. Series A, Mining (0324-4628); Which superseded in part (in 1976): Nehezipari Muszaki Egyetem Idegennyelvu Kozlemenyei (0369-4852); Which was formerly (until 1960): Soproni Muszaki Egyetemi Karok Banyamernoki es Foldmernoki Karok Kozlemenyei (0371-1099); (until 1955): Banya- es Kohomernoki Osztaly Kozlemenyei (0367-6412); (until 1934): Soproni M Kir. Banyamernoki es Erdomernoki Foiskola Banyaszati es Kohaszati Osztalyanak Kozlemenyei (0324-4474)
Indexed: CRIA, CRICC, GeoRef, IMMAb, SpeleolAb.
Published by: Miskolci Egyetem/University of Miskolc, Miskolc, 3515, Hungary. TEL 36-46-565111, http://www.uni-miskolc.hu. Circ: 350.

622 HUN ISSN 1417-541X
UNIVERSITY OF MISKOLC. PUBLICATIONS. SERIES A, MINING. PROCESS ENGINEERING. Alternating issues in English, German, Hungarian. irreg.
Supersedes in part (in 1995): University of Miskolc. Publications. Series A, Mining (1219-008X); Which was formerly (until 1994): Technical University for Heavy Industry. Publications. Series A, Mining (0324-4628); Which superseded in part (in 1976): Nehezipari Muszaki Egyetem Idegennyelvu Kozlemenyei (0369-4852); Which was formerly (until 1960): Soproni Muszaki Egyetemi Karok Banyamernoki es Foldmernoki Karok Kozlemenyei (0371-1099); (until 1955): Banya- es Kohomernoki Osztaly Kozlemenyei (0367-6412); (until 1934): Soproni M Kir. Banyamernoki es Erdomernoki Foiskola Banyaszati es Kohaszati Osztalyanak Kozlemenyei (0324-4474)
Published by: Miskolci Egyetem/University of Miskolc, Miskolc, 3515, Hungary. TEL 36-46-565111, http://www.uni-miskolc.hu.

622 ROM ISSN 1454-9174
TN1.A1
➤ **UNIVERSITY OF PETROSANI. ANNALS. MINING ENGINEERING/ UNIVERSITATEA DIN PETROSANI. ANNALS. MINING ENGINEERING.** Text in English, French, German, Russian. 1991. a. ROL 46 domestic; USD 14 foreign (effective 2009). bk.rev. charts; abstr.; bibl. 260 p./no.; back issues avail.; reprints avail. **Document type:** *Proceedings, Academic/Scholarly.* **Description:** Covers all areas of mining engineering, including papers on the exploration, mine planning and design, geomechanics, strength and stability of mine workings, drilling and blasting, underground and open-pit mining technologies.
Formerly (until 2000): University of Petrosani. Scientific Papers. Mining (1220-8477)
Related titles: CD-ROM ed.; ◆ Series: University of Petrosani. Annals. Electrical Engineering. ISSN 1454-8518; ◆ University of Petrosani. Annals. Physics. ISSN 1454-5071; ◆ University of Petrosani. Annals. Mechanical Engineering. ISSN 1454-9166.
Indexed: A01, CA, E14, T02.
—CCC.
Published by: Universitatea din Petrosani, Str. Universitatii, nr 20, Petrosani, 332006, Romania. TEL 40-254-542994, FAX 40-254-543491, rector@upet.ro, http://www.upet.ro. Ed. Ioan-Lucian Bolundut. Pub. Ilie Rotunjanu. Circ: 40 (paid); 60 (controlled).

➤ **UNIVERSITY OF TEXAS AT AUSTIN. BUREAU OF ECONOMIC GEOLOGY. MINERAL RESOURCE CIRCULARS.** *see* EARTH SCIENCES—Geology

622 ZWE ISSN 0254-2951
UNIVERSITY OF ZIMBABWE. INSTITUTE OF MINING RESEARCH. REPORT. Variant title: I M R Open Report. Text in English. 1990 (no.104). irreg., latest vol.126, 1990. **Document type:** *Monographic series.* **Description:** Discusses specific aspects of the mining and minerals industries in Zimbabwe and neighboring states.
Indexed: GeoRef, IMMAb, SpeleolAb.
Published by: University of Zimbabwe, Institute of Mining Research, Mount Pleasant, PO Box MP 167, Harare, Zimbabwe.

333.8 FRA ISSN 1996-3459
HD9539.U69
URANIUM (YEAR): RESOURCES, PRODUCTION AND DEMAND. Text in English. 1965. biennial, latest 2007. EUR 120, GBP 86, USD 186, JPY 16,600 combined subscription print & online eds. (effective 2009). charts; illus. **Description:** Compares uranium supply data with the nuclear industry's requirements until the year 2015. Reviews exploration, resources and production.
Related titles: Online - full content ed.: ISSN 2072-5310. EUR 84, GBP 60, USD 130, JPY 11,600 (effective 2009); French ed.: Uranium: Ressources, Production et Demande. ISSN 0252-9173.
Published by: (Organisation for Economic Cooperation and Development (O E C D), Nuclear Energy Agency/Organisation de Cooperation et de Developpement Economiques, Agence pour l'Energie Nucleaire), Organisation for Economic Cooperation and Development (O E C D)/Organisation de Cooperation et de Developpement Economiques (O C D E), 2 Rue Andre Pascal, Paris, 75775 Cedex 16, France. TEL 33-1-45248200, FAX 33-1-45248500, http://www.oecd.org. Circ: 2,030. **Dist. in N. America by:** O E C D Turpin North America, PO Box 194, Downingtown, PA 19335-0194. TEL 610-524-5361, 800-456-6323, FAX 610-524-5417, bookscustomer@turpinna.com.

UTAH GEOLOGICAL SURVEY. BULLETIN. *see* EARTH SCIENCES—Geology

UTAH GEOLOGICAL SURVEY. SPECIAL STUDY. *see* EARTH SCIENCES—Geology

UTAH GEOLOGICAL SURVEY. SURVEY NOTES. *see* EARTH SCIENCES—Geology

622 338.2 VEN
VENEZUELA. MINISTERIO DE ENERGIA Y MINAS. INFORMATIONS. Text in French. 1967. bi-m. free. **Document type:** *Government.*
Formerly: Venezuela. Ministerio de Minas e Hidrocarburos. Informations (0042-3408)
Media: Duplicated (not offset).
Published by: Ministerio de Energia y Minas, Torre Oeste Piso 8, Parque Central, Caracas, DF 1010, Venezuela.

622 665 VEN
VENEZUELA. MINISTERIO DE ENERGIA Y MINAS. MEMORIA Y CUENTA. Text in Spanish. 1952. a. free. charts; stat. **Document type:** *Government.*
Formerly: Venezuela. Ministerio de Minas e Hidrocarburos. Memoria y Cuenta (0083-5374)
Indexed: SpeleolAb.
Published by: Ministerio de Energia y Minas, Torre Oeste Piso 8, Parque Central, Caracas, DF 1010, Venezuela.

622 665.5 VEN
VENEZUELA. MINISTERIO DE ENERGIA Y MINAS. QUARTERLY BULLETIN. Text in English. q. charts; stat. **Document type:** *Bulletin, Government.*
Former titles: Venezuela. Ministerio de Energia y Minas. Monthly Bulletin; Venezuela. Ministerio de Minas e Hidrocarburos. Monthly Bulletin (0042-3416)
Indexed: GeoRef, SpeleolAb.
Published by: Ministerio de Energia y Minas, Torre Oeste Piso 8, Parque Central, Caracas, DF 1010, Venezuela.

622 DEU ISSN 0302-4938
HD9540.5
VEREIN DEUTSCHER KOHLENIMPORTEURE. JAHRESBERICHT. Text in German. 1900. a. **Document type:** *Corporate.*
Published by: Verein Deutscher Kohlenimporteure e.V., Glockengiesserwall 19, Hamburg, 20095, Germany. TEL 49-40-327484, FAX 49-40-326772.

553 622 USA ISSN 0160-4643
CODEN: VDMPDM
VIRGINIA. DIVISION OF MINERAL RESOURCES. PUBLICATIONS. Text in English. 1959. irreg. price varies. **Document type:** *Government.*
Former titles: Virginia. Division of Mineral Resources. Bulletin (0097-5303); Virginia. Division of Mineral Resources. Information Circular (0083-632X); Virginia. Division of Mineral Resources. Mineral Resources Report (0083-6338); Virginia. Division of Mineral Resources. Report of Investigations (0083-6346); Virginia. Division of Mineral Resources. Reports
Indexed: GeoRef, IMMAb, SpeleolAb, Z01.
—Linda Hall.
Published by: Virginia Department of Mines, Minerals and Energy, Division of Mineral Resources, PO Box 3667, Charlottesville, VA 22903. TEL 804-293-5121, FAX 804-293-2239.

VIRGINIA INDUSTRIAL DIRECTORY. *see* BUSINESS AND ECONOMICS—Trade And Industrial Directories

549 USA ISSN 0042-6652
TN24.V8 CODEN: VAMIAB
VIRGINIA MINERALS. Text in English. 1954. q. free. bk.rev. charts; illus.; maps; stat. cum.index every 10 yrs. **Document type:** *Government.*
Indexed: ChemAb, GeoRef, IMMAb, SpeleolAb.
—IE, Ingenta, Linda Hall.
Published by: Virginia Department of Mines, Minerals and Energy, Division of Mineral Resources, PO Box 3667, Charlottesville, VA 22903. TEL 804-293-5121, FAX 804-293-2239. Ed. Eugene K Rader.

622 POL ISSN 1505-0440
W U G. Text in Polish. 1968. m. EUR 151 foreign (effective 2006).
Former titles (until 1996): Bezpieczenstwo Pracy i Ochrona Srodowiska w Gornictwie (1230-3631); (until 1990): Bezpieczenstwo Pracy w Gornictwie (0208-6875)
Indexed: B22.
Published by: Wyzszy Urzad Gorniczy, ul. Poniatowskiego 31, Katowice, 40956, Poland. TEL 48-32-2511471, FAX 48-32-2514884, wug@wug.gov.pl, http://www.wug.gov.pl. **Dist. by:** Ars Polona, Obroncow 25, Warsaw 03933, Poland. TEL 48-22-5098609, FAX 48-22-5098610, arspolona@arspolona.com.pl, http://www.arspolona.com.pl.

622 USA
WASHINGTON. DIVISION OF GEOLOGY AND EARTH RESOURCES. MINES AND MINERALS OF WASHINGTON. ANNUAL REPORT. Text in English. a. **Document type:** *Report, Government.*
Published by: Washington State Department of Natural Resources, Division of Geology and Earth Resources, 1111 Washington St, SE, PO Box 47007, Olympia, WA 98504. TEL 360-902-1450, FAX 360-902-1785, geology@dnr.wa.gov, http://www.dnr.wa.gov/researchscience/geologyearthsciences/pages/home.aspx.

WASHINGTON. DIVISION OF MINES AND GEOLOGY. BULLETIN. *see* EARTH SCIENCES—Geology

622 USA
WASHINGTON MINING BUREAU. ANNUAL REPORT. Text in English. 19??. a. **Document type:** *Report, Government.*
Published by: Washington State Department of Natural Resources, Division of Geology and Earth Resources, 1111 Washington St, SE, PO Box 47007, Olympia, WA 98504. TEL 360-902-1450, FAX 360-902-1785, geology@dnr.wa.gov, http://www.dnr.wa.gov/researchscience/geologyearthsciences/pages/home.aspx.

622 USA
WEST VIRGINIA MINERAL INDUSTRIES DIRECTORY. Text in English. 1971. biennial. USD 28.50 per issue (effective 2000). **Document type:** *Directory, Government.* **Description:** Lists by commodity and county all mineral producers in West Virginia, with addresses and phone numbers.
Former titles: West Virginia Mineral Producers and Processors Directory; West Virginia Mineral Producers Directory
Published by: Geological and Economic Survey, PO Box 879, Morgantown, WV 26507-0879. TEL 304-594-2331. Ed., R&P Charles Gover.

338.2 USA
WEST VIRGINIA. OFFICE OF MINER'S HEALTH, SAFETY & TRAINING. REPORT & DIGEST DIRECTORY. Text in English. 1883. a. USD 10 (effective 1999). **Document type:** *Directory, Government.*
Formed by the merger of: West Virginia. Department of Mines. Annual Report; West Virginia. Department of Mines. Directory of Mines (0083-8462)
Published by: Office of Miner's Health, Safety & Training, 1615 Washington St E, Charleston, WV 25311. TEL 304-348-3500. Circ: 2,500.

622 USA ISSN 0162-9026
TN12
WESTERN MINING DIRECTORY. Text in English. 1977. a. USD 49. back issues avail. **Document type:** *Directory.*
Indexed: GeoRef, SpeleolAb.
Published by: Howell International Enterprises, PO Box 1630, Castle Rock, CO 80104. TEL 303-663-7820, FAX 303-663-7823. Ed. Don E Howell. Circ: 10,000.

622 AUS
WHAT MINERALS MEAN TO AUSTRALIANS. Text in English. 1978. irreg. free. **Document type:** *Monographic series, Trade.*
Formerly (until 1996): What Mining Means to Australians (0312-4584)
Published by: Minerals Council of Australia, PO Box 363, Dickson, ACT 2602, Australia. TEL 61-6-62793600, FAX 61-6-62793699.

622 CAN ISSN 1911-5725
WHAT'S HAPPENING AT TUNDRA?. Text in English. 2006. q. free (effective 2010). **Document type:** *Journal, Trade.* **Description:** Provides all information about the city Tundra Mine.
Related titles: Online - full text ed.
Published by: Indian and Northern Affairs Canada/Affaires Indiennes et du Nord Canada, Terrasses de la Chaudiere, 10 Wellington St, N Tower, Rm 1210, Gatineau, PQ K1A 0H4, Canada. TEL 800-567-9604, FAX 819-934-6103, infopubs@ainc-inac.gc.ca.

622 POL ISSN 0043-5120
WIADOMOSCI GORNICZE. Text in Polish. 1950. m. EUR 237 foreign (effective 2006). adv. bk.rev. **Document type:** *Magazine, Trade.*
Indexed: B22, CISA.
Published by: (Stowarzyszenie Inzynierow i Technikow Gornictwa), Wydawnictwo Gornicze, ul Plebiscytowa 36, Katowice, 40041, Poland. TEL 48-32-7572142, FAX 48-32-7572043, wydawnictwo.wg@w-g.com.pl, http://www.w-g.com.pl. Ed. Andrzej Karbownik. Circ: 2,850. **Dist. by:** Ars Polona, Obroncow 25, Warsaw 03933, Poland. TEL 48-22-5098609, FAX 48-22-5098610, arspolona@arspolona.com.pl, http://www.arspolona.com.pl.

622 USA
WOMEN IN MINING NATIONAL QUARTERLY. Text in English. 1981. q. USD 10. **Document type:** *Magazine, Trade.* **Description:** Educates members on all aspects of the minerals industry.
Published by: Women in Mining National, PO Box 260246, Lakewood, CO 80226-0246. TEL 303-298-1535. Ed. Susan Hanel. Circ: 600.

622 USA
WORLD MINE PRODUCTION OF GOLD. Text in English. 1979. a. USD 55; USD 65 foreign (effective 1999). back issues avail. **Description:** Production of each of 58 countries known to produce at least 1,000 troy ounces of gold from underground, surface and alluvial sources.
Indexed: SRI.
Published by: Gold Institute, Administrative Office/Institut de l'Or, Bureau Administratif, PO Box 14264, Washington, DC 20044-4264. TEL 202-835-0185, FAX 202-835-0155. Ed. John H Lutley.

622 MEX
WORLD MINING CONGRESS. REPORT. (Published and avail. only in Host Country) Text mainly in English, Russian. 1958. triennial. **Document type:** *Proceedings.*
Formerly: International Organizing Committee of World Mining Congresses. Report (0074-2775)
Indexed: IMMAb.
Published by: World Mining Congress, International Organizing Committee, c/o Mr. J.J. Gutierrez Nunez, Minas de Bacis, S.A. de C.V., Selenio 168 CD, Industrial, Durango, 34220, Mexico. TEL 52-181-412997. Circ: 2,250.

622 GBR ISSN 0746-729X
TN345 CODEN: WOMIDL
WORLD MINING EQUIPMENT. Text in English. 1982. 10/yr. adv. bk.rev. back issues avail. **Document type:** *Magazine, Trade.* **Description:** Covers mines and mining equipment, decision makers with purchasing power in such companies.
Formed by the merger of (1977-1983): Mining Equipment International (0192-902X); (1975-1983): World Coal (0361-7483); (1974-1983): World Mining (0043-8707); Which was formed by the merger of (1948-1974): World Mining (International Edition) (1060-7579); (1965-1974): World Mining (United States Edition) (1060-7587); Which both superseded in part (1939-1965): Mining World (0096-5731); Which incorporated (1937-1940): Pacific Chemical and Metallurgical Industries (0099-880X)
Related titles: Online - full text ed.
Indexed: A22, A23, AESIS, B02, B04, B13, B15, B17, B18, BPI, BRD, BrGeoL, CISA, EIA, F&EA, G04, G06, G07, G08, GeoRef, I05, IMMAb, SpeleolAb, T&II, W01, W02, W03.
—BLDSC (9356.684000), CASDDS, IE, Infotrieve, Ingenta, Linda Hall. **CCC.**
Published by: Metal Bulletin Plc. (Subsidiary of: Euromoney Institutional Investor Plc.), Nestor House, Playhouse Yard, London, EC4V 5EX, United Kingdom. TEL 44-20-77797390, FAX 44-20-77797389, help@metalbulletin.com, http://www.metalbulletin.com. Ed. Steve Fiscor. Pub. Peter Johnson.

WORLD OF METALLURGY - ERZMETALL; journal for exploration, mining, processing, metallurgy, recycling and environmental technology. *see* METALLURGY

622 DEU ISSN 1613-2408
TN831 CODEN: SMUIAY
WORLD OF MINING - SURFACE & UNDERGROUND. Text in English, German. N.S. 1993. bi-m. EUR 210 domestic; EUR 230 foreign (effective 2009). adv. **Document type:** *Journal, Trade.* **Description:** International technical and economic journal of the mining of lignite and other raw materials by surface techniques.
Former titles (until 2004): Surface Mining - Braunkohle and Other Minerals (0931-3990); (until 2000): Braunkohle - Surface Mining (1431-2719); (until 1996): Braunkohle - Bergbautechnik (1431-3235); (until 1994): Braunkohle - Tagebautechnik (0944-8721); Which was formed by the merger of (1971-1993): Neue Bergbautechnik (0047-9403); Which was formed by the merger of (1949-1970): Bergakademie (0365-9917); (1951-1970): Bergbautechnik (0365-9941); (1972-1993): Braunkohle (Deusseldorf, 1972) (0341-1060); Which was formerly (1949-1972): Braunkohle, Warme und Energie (0006-9299); (1902-1945): Braunkohle (Halle, 1902) (0366-3043)
Indexed: CPEI, EngInd, FR, GeoRef, IBR, IBZ, IMMAb, INIS AtomInd, RefZh, SCOPUS, SpeleolAb, TM.
—BLDSC (9356.681000), CASDDS, IE, Ingenta, INIST, Linda Hall. **CCC.**
Published by: G D M B Geschaeftsstelle, Paul Ernst Str 10, Clausthal-Zellerfeld, 38678, Germany. TEL 49-5323-93720, FAX 49-5323-937937, info@gdmb.de, http://www.gdmb.de. Ed. Juergen Zuchowski. adv.: B&W page EUR 2,240, color page EUR 3,029; 180 x 270. Circ: 1,700 (free); 1,300 (paid).

338.2 USA ISSN 1059-6992
HD9536.A1
WORLD SILVER SURVEY (YEAR). Text in English. 1990. a. USD 70; USD 80 foreign (effective 1999).

—Linda Hall.
Published by: Silver Institute, 14264, Washington, DC 20044-4264. TEL 202-835-0185, FAX 202-835-0155.

622 CHN ISSN 1000-8918
CODEN: WYHUEZ

➤ **WUTAN YU HUATAN/GEOPHYSICAL AND GEOCHEMICAL EXPLORATION.** Text in Chinese; Abstracts in English. 1979. bi-m. USD 66.60 (effective 2009). adv. bk.rev. **Document type:** *Academic/Scholarly.* **Description:** Covers geophysical and geochemical theories, technology and recent developments in state of the art.
Related titles: Online - full text ed.
Indexed: ChemAb, GeoRef, RefZh, SpeleolAb.
—CASDDS, East View.
Published by: (Zhongguo Guotu Ziyuan Huangkong Wutan Yaogan Zhongxin/China Aerogeophysical Survey and Remote Sensing Center for Land & Resources), Dizhi Chubanshe/Geological Publishing House, 31 Xueyuan Lu, Haidian-qu, Beijing, 100083, China. TEL 86-10-82329089, FAX 86-10-82324536. Circ: 1,600.

622.1 CHN ISSN 1004-5716
TN101 CODEN: XTGOFN

XIBU TANKUANG GONGCHENG/WEST-CHINA EXPLORATION ENGINEERING. Text in Chinese. 1989. m. CNY 10 per issue. bk.rev. 80 p./no.; **Document type:** *Journal, Academic/Scholarly.* **Description:** Reports on new theories, technologies, achievements and engineering examples in domestic and foreign drilling-digging engineering.
Related titles: CD-ROM ed.; Online - full text ed.: (from WanFang Data Corp.).
Indexed: A28, APA, BrCerAb, C&ISA, CA/WCA, CIA, CerAb, CivEngAb, CorrAb, E&CAJ, E11, EEA, EMA, ESPM, EnvEAb, H15, M&TEA, M09, MBF, METADEX, SolStAb, T04, WAA.
—BLDSC (9367.041953), CASDDS, East View, Linda Hall.
Published by: Xibu Tankuang Gongcheng Bianjibu, 279, Karamay Dong Jie, Urumqi, Xinjiang 830000, China. TEL 86-991-4818457, FAX 86-991-4818457. Ed., R&P, Adv. contact Defeng Liu. Circ: 7,000. **Dist. overseas by:** China International Book Trading Corp, 35 Chegongzhuang Xilu, Haidian District, PO Box 399, Beijing 100044, China.

622.33 526.9 CHN ISSN 1001-3571

➤ **XUANMEI JISHU/COAL PREPARATION TECHNOLOGY.** Text in Chinese. 1973. bi-m. USD 31.20 (effective 2009). adv. bk.rev. abstr.; bibl.; charts; illus.; mkt. back issues avail. **Document type:** *Journal, Academic/Scholarly.*
Related titles: CD-ROM ed.; E-mail ed.; Fax ed.; Online - full text ed.
Published by: Meitan Kexueyuan, Tangshan Fenyuan/China Coal Research Institute, No 21, Xinhuanxi Rd, Tangshan, Hebei 063012, China. TEL 86-315-2822145, FAX 86-315-2829275, ccritsb@ts-user.he.cninfo.net. R&Ps Hongxin Zhao TEL 86-315-7759357, Lijuan Shen. Adv. contact Hongxin Zhao TEL 86-315-7759357. B&W page CNY 4,500, color page CNY 9,000; trim 210 x 297. Circ: 5,000.

622 331.8 GBR

YORKSHIRE MINER. Text in English. 1959. m. GBP 4 domestic; GBP 11 foreign. adv. bk.rev. **Document type:** *Magazine, Trade.* **Description:** Covers the Yorkshire miners, their union, families and communities. Also includes articles of general interest.
Published by: National Union of Mineworkers - Yorkshire Area, Miners Offices, 2 Huddersfield Rd, Barnsley, S Yorks S70 2LS, United Kingdom. TEL 0226-284006, FAX 0226-285486. Ed. Mark Hebert. Circ: 17,500.

YOUKUANG DIZHI/URANIUM GEOLOGY. *see* EARTH SCIENCES—Geology

622.34932 CHN ISSN 1000-8063
TN799.U7 CODEN: YOUKEM

YOUKUANGYE/URANIUM MINING AND METALLURGY. Text in Chinese. 1982. q. USD 14.40 (effective 2009). **Document type:** *Journal, Academic/Scholarly.*
Related titles: Online - full text ed.
Indexed: A22, INIS AtomInd.
—BLDSC (9123.140700), IE, Ingenta.
Address: PO Box 234-108, Beijing, 101149, China. TEL 86-10-81524491 ext 4348, FAX 86-10-81527553. **Dist. by:** China International Book Trading Corp, 35 Chegongzhuang Xilu, Haidian District, PO Box 399, Beijing 100044, China. TEL 86-10-68412045, FAX 86-10-68412023, cibtc@mail.cibtc.com.cn, http://www.cibtc.com.cn.

622 669.3 ZMB

ZAMBIA CONSOLIDATED COPPER MINES LTD. ANNUAL REPORT AND ACCOUNTS. Text in English. a. **Document type:** *Corporate.*
Published by: Zambia Consolidated Copper Mines Investments Holdings Plc, PO Box 30048, Lusaka, Zambia. nseluke@zccm-ih.com.zm.

622 ZMB

ZAMBIA INDUSTRIAL AND MINING CORPORATION. ANNUAL REPORT. Text in English. s-a. **Document type:** *Directory.*
Published by: Zambia Industrial and Mining Corp. Ltd., Zimco Information and Publicity Unit, PO Box 30090, Lusaka, Zambia.

338.2 ZMB ISSN 0377-8118

ZAMBIA MINING YEARBOOK. Text in English. 1955. a. free. **Document type:** *Yearbook, Trade.*
Formerly: Copperbelt of Zambia Mining Industry Year Book
Published by: Copper Industry Service Bureau, PO Box 22100, Kitwe, Zambia. Circ: 500.

622 CHN ISSN 1001-0335

➤ **ZHONGGUO JINGKUANGYAN/CHINA WELL AND ROCK SALT.** Text in Chinese; Abstracts in Chinese, English. 1970. bi-m. CNY 60; CNY 10 newsstand/cover (effective 2008). **Document type:** *Journal, Academic/Scholarly.*
Former titles (until 1989): Jingkuangyan Jishu/Well and Rock Salt Technology; (until 1973): Jingkuangyan Jishu Tongxun/Well and Rock Salt Technology Communication
Related titles: Online - full text ed.
—East View.
Address: No.11, Dongxingsi St., Zigong, Sichuan Province 643000, China. TEL 86-813-8706630, FAX 86-813-8102757. Ed. Mei-ying Lin. Circ: 1,200.

622.33 CHN ISSN 1004-4051

ZHONGGUO KUANGYE/CHINA MINING MAGAZINE. Text in Chinese. 1992. m. USD 62.40 (effective 2009). **Document type:** *Magazine, Trade.*
Formerly: Kuangshan Jishu/Mining Technology (1001-5809)
Related titles: Online - full text ed.
Indexed: SpeleolAb.
—East View.
Published by: Yejin Bu, Anshan Heise Yejin Kuangshan Sheji Yanjiusuo, Xizhimen Wai, 1, Wenxinjie, Beijing, Liaoning 100044, China. TEL 86-10-88374940, FAX 86-10-88374941. Ed. Qian Zhanxun.

622.33 CHN ISSN 1006-530X
TN799.9

ZHONGGUO MEITAN. Text in Chinese. 1994. m. USD 87.60 (effective 2009). **Document type:** *Journal, Academic/Scholarly.*
Formerly (until 1994): Shijie Meitan Jishu/World Coal Technology (0257-4896)
Related titles: Online - full text ed.
—East View, Linda Hall.
Published by: Meitan Xinxi Yanjiuyuan, Xinwen Zhongxin, 35, Shaoyaoju, Beijing, 100029, China. TEL 86-10-84657853, FAX 86-10-84657900, xwzx@chinacoalnews.com, http://www.zgmt.com.cn/.

622.33 CHN ISSN 1674-1803

ZHONGGUO MEITAN DIZHI/COAL GEOLOGY OF CHINA. Text in Chinese. 1989. m. **Document type:** *Journal, Academic/Scholarly.*
Formerly (until 2008): Zhongguo Meitian Dizhi (1004-9177)
Related titles: Online - full text ed.
Published by: Zhongguo Meitan Dizhi Zongju. Meitan Ziyuan Xinxi Zhongxin/China National Administration of Coal Geology. Information Center of Coal Resources, 50, Fangyan Xi Lu, Zhuozhou, 072750, China. TEL 86-312-3685214, FAX 86-312-85666504, yanqunic@sina.com.

622.33 CHN ISSN 1008-6528
TN809.C47

ZHONGGUO MEITAN GONGYE NIANJIAN. Text in Chinese. 1982. a. CNY 150 per issue (effective 2008).
Related titles: ◆ English ed.: China Coal Industry Yearbook. ISSN 0258-3062.
Published by: Meitan Xinxi Yanjiuyuan, Xinwen Zhongxin, 35, Shaoyaoju, Beijing, 100029, China.

ZHONGGUO MEITAN GONGYE YIXUE ZAZHI/CHINESE JOURNAL OF COAL INDUSTRY MEDICINE. *see* MEDICAL SCIENCES

ZHONGGUO YOUSE JINSHU XUEBAO. *see* METALLURGY

622 CHN ISSN 1672-7207
TN4 CODEN: ZGDXFY

➤ **ZHONGNAN DAXUE XUEBAO (ZIRAN KEXUE BAN)/CENTRAL SOUTH UNIVERSITY. JOURNAL (SCIENCE AND TECHNOLOGY).** Text in Chinese; Summaries in English. 1956. bi-m. USD 53.40 (effective 2009). adv. abstr. 128 p./no.; **Document type:** *Journal, Academic/Scholarly.*
Formerly (until 2004): Zhongnan Gongye Daxue Xuebao (Ziran Kexue Ban) (1673-517X); Which superseded in part: Zhongnan Gongye Daxue Xuebao (1005-9792); Which was formerly (until 1995): Zhongnan Kuangye Xueyuan Xuebao (0253-4347)
Related titles: Online - full text ed.; ◆ English ed.: Central South University of Technology. Journal. ISSN 1005-9784.
Indexed: A28, APA, BrCerAb, C&ISA, CA/WCA, CIA, CIN, CPEI, CerAb, ChemAb, ChemTitl, CivEngAb, CorrAb, E&CAJ, E11, EEA, EMA, ESPM, EngInd, EnvEAb, GeoRef, H15, Inspec, M&TEA, M09, MBF, METADEX, RefZh, SCOPUS, SolStAb, SpeleolAb, T04, WAA.
—BLDSC (9512.844470), AskIEEE, CASDDS, East View, Linda Hall.
Published by: Zhongnan Daxue/Central South University, Lushan Nan Lu, Changsha, 410083, China. TEL 86-731-8879765, FAX 86-731-8877197. Circ: 2,500. **Dist. by:** China International Book Trading Corp, 35 Chegongzhuang Xilu, Haidian District, PO Box 399, Beijing 100044, China. TEL 86-10-68412045, FAX 86-10-68412023, cibtc@mail.cibtc.com.cn, http://www.cibtc.com.cn.

➤ **ZIMBABWE ENGINEER.** *see* ENGINEERING

➤ **ZIMBABWE. MINISTRY OF LANDS AND NATURAL RESOURCES. REPORT OF THE SECRETARY FOR LANDS AND NATURAL RESOURCES.** *see* CONSERVATION

➤ **ZIZHI YU ZIYUAN/GEOLOGY AND RESOURCES.** *see* EARTH SCIENCES—Geology

MINES AND MINING INDUSTRY—Abstracting, Bibliographies, Statistics

338.2 CAN ISSN 0380-4321
HD9554.C3

ALBERTA COAL INDUSTRY, ANNUAL STATISTICS. Text in English. 1973. a. CAD 40. illus.; stat. **Description:** Statistical data on coal and the coal industry in Alberta including production, supply and disposition, plant operations and inventories.
Formerly: Cumulative Annual Statistics, Alberta Coal Industry (0837-2608)
Indexed: GeoRef, SpeleolAb.
Published by: Energy and Utilities Board, 640 5th Ave, S W, Calgary, AB T2P 3G4, Canada. TEL 403-297-8311, FAX 403-297-7040.

ANUARIO ESTADISTICO DE LA SIDERURGIA Y MINERIA DE HIERRO EN AMERICA LATINA. *see* METALLURGY—Abstracting, Bibliographies, Statistics

622.021 AUS

AUSTRALIA. BUREAU OF STATISTICS. DIRECTORY OF MINING STATISTICS (ONLINE). Text in English. 1999. irreg., latest 2002. free (effective 2009). **Document type:** *Government.* **Description:** Contains comprehensive information on sources of mining statistics in the public and private sectors.
Formerly: Australia. Bureau of Statistics. Directory of Mining Statistics (Print)
Media: Online - full text.
Published by: Australian Bureau of Statistics, Locked Bag 10, Belconnen, ACT 2616, Australia. TEL 61-2-92684909, 300-135-070, FAX 61-2-92684654, client.services@abs.gov.au.

622.021 AUS

AUSTRALIA. BUREAU OF STATISTICS. INNOVATION IN MINING, AUSTRALIA (ONLINE). Text in English. 1998. irreg., latest 1997. free (effective 2009). **Document type:** *Government.* **Description:** Contains statistics on the innovative activities of the Australian mining industry.
Formerly (until 199?): Australia. Bureau of Statistics. Innovation in Mining, Australia (Print)
Media: Online - full text.
Indexed: AESIS.
Published by: Australian Bureau of Statistics, Locked Bag 10, Belconnen, ACT 2616, Australia. TEL 61-2-92684909, 61-2-62527037, 300-135-070, FAX 61-2-62528103, client.services@abs.gov.au, http://www.abs.gov.au.

622.021 AUS

AUSTRALIA. BUREAU OF STATISTICS. MINERAL AND PETROLEUM EXPLORATION, AUSTRALIA (ONLINE). Text in English. 1974. q. free (effective 2009). **Document type:** *Government.* **Description:** Covers actual and expected expenditure and meters drilled by private organizations exploring for minerals and petroleum.
Former titles (until 199?): Australia. Bureau of Statistics. Mineral and Petroleum Exploration, Australia (Print) (1442-7508); (until 1999): Australia. Bureau of Statistics. Actual and Expected Private Mineral Exploration, Australia (1033-0542); (until 1989): Australia. Bureau of Statistics. Private Mineral Exploration, Australia (1032-9323); (until 1988): Australia. Bureau of Statistics. Mineral Exploration, Australia (0727-1581); Which was formed by the merger of (1978-1980): Australia. Bureau of Statistics. Petroleum Exploration, Australia (0727-1735); Which was formerly (until 1978): Australia. Bureau of Statistics. Petroleum Exploration (0312-7761); (1978-1980): Australia. Bureau of Statistics. Mineral Exploration by Principal Enterprises, Australia (0727-1743); Which was formerly (until 1978): Australia. Bureau of Statistics. Mineral Exploration by Principal Enterprises (0728-5663)
Media: Online - full text.
Indexed: AESIS.
Published by: Australian Bureau of Statistics, Locked Bag 10, Belconnen, ACT 2616, Australia. TEL 61-2-92684909, 61-2-62527037, 300-135-070, FAX 61-2-62528103, client.services@abs.gov.au. Circ: 258.

338.2021 AUS
HD9506.A7

AUSTRALIA. BUREAU OF STATISTICS. MINING OPERATIONS AUSTRALIA (ONLINE). Text in English. 1993. a. free. **Document type:** *Government.* **Description:** Provides a broad picture of the structure of the mining industry.
Former titles (until 2003): Australia. Bureau of Statistics. Mining Operations Australia (Print) (1441-1067); (until 1999): Australia. Bureau of Statistics. Australian Mining Industry (1322-7459); Which formed by the merger of (1968-1993): Mining Industry, Australia (1321-2028); Which was formerly (until 1991): Mining Operations, Australia (1039-4737); (until 1990): Census of Mining Establishments: Summary of Operations by Industry Class, Australia; (until 1977): Mining Establishments. Details of Operations, Australia, States and Territories; (until 1971): Economic Censuses: Mining Establishments, Details of Operations, Australia States and Territories; (1968-1993): Mining Production, Australia (1321-1633); Which was formerly: Mineral Production, Australia (0311-8975)
Media: Online - full content.
Indexed: AESIS, GeoRef, SpeleolAb.
—Linda Hall.
Published by: Australian Bureau of Statistics, Locked Bag 10, Belconnen, ACT 2616, Australia. TEL 61-2-62525249, FAX 61-2-6252-6778. Circ: 475.

662.021 AUS ISSN 1447-1159

AUSTRALIAN BUREAU OF AGRICULTURAL AND RESOURCE ECONOMICS. AUSTRALIAN MINERAL STATISTICS. Text in English. 2001. q. free to members (effective 2008). **Document type:** *Report, Trade.* **Description:** Provides detailed research reports and analysis on mineral resources in Australia.
Media: Online - full text.
Indexed: A11, B01, B07, E14.
Published by: Australian Bureau of Agricultural and Resource Economics, 7B London Circuit, GPO Box 1563, Canberra, ACT 2601, Australia. TEL 61-2-62722000, FAX 61-2-62722001, sales@abare.gov.au. Ed., Pub., R&P Andrew Wright TEL 61-2-62722290.

622 669 MEX ISSN 0187-5027
HD9506.M6

AVANCE DE INFORMACION ECONOMICA. INDUSTRIA MINEROMETALURGICA. Text in Spanish. 1986. m. MXN 77, USD 26.
Published by: Instituto Nacional de Estadistica, Geografia e Informatica, Secretaria de Programacion y Presupuesto, Prol. Heroe de Nacozari 2301 Sur, Puerta 11, Acceso, Aguascalientes, 20270, Mexico. TEL 52-4-918-1948, FAX 52-4-918-0739. Circ: 800.

622 016 HUN ISSN 0231-0651

BANYASZATI SZAKIRODALMI TAJEKOZTATO/MINING ABSTRACTS. Text in Hungarian. 1949. m. HUF 8,600. index. **Document type:** *Abstract/Index.*
Supersedes (in 1982): Muszaki Lapszemle. Banyaszat - Technical Abstracts. Mining (0027-495X)
Published by: Orszagos Muszaki Informacios Kozpont es Konyvtar/National Technical Information Centre and Library, Muzeum utca 17, PO Box 12, Budapest, 1428, Hungary. Ed. Denes Panto. Circ: 260. **Subscr. to:** Kultura, PO Box 149, Budapest 1389, Hungary.

549 CAN ISSN 0825-6896
TN27.B9

BRITISH COLUMBIA. MINISTRY OF ENERGY, MINES AND PETROLEUM RESOURCES. MINERAL RESOURCES DIVISION. SUMMARY OF OPERATIONS. Text in English. a. CAD 3.15. back issues avail. **Document type:** *Government.*
Former titles (until 1980): British Columbia. Minister of Energy, Mines and Petroleum Resources. Mineral Resources Branch. Summary of Operations (0825-6446); Which superseded in part: British Columbia. Minister of Energy, Mines and Petroleum Resources. Annual Report (0228-0078); Which was formerly (1960-1977): Province of British Columbia. Minister of Mines and Petroleum Resources. Annual Report (0365-9356); Which was fomed by the merger of (1930-1959): Province of British Columbia. Minister of Mines. Annual Report (0383-3313); Which was formerly: Annual Report of the Minister of Mines; (1974-1989): Mining in British Columbia (0823-1265); Which superseded in part (1969-1974): Geology, Exploration, and Mining in British Columbia (0085-1027); Which was formerly: Lode metals in British Columbia
Indexed: GeoRef, SpeleolAb.
—INIST, Linda Hall.

Published by: British Columbia, Ministry of Energy, Mines and Petroleum Resources, 5th Fl, 1810 Blanshard St, Victoria, BC V8V 1X4, Canada. Ed. Dorothe Jakobsen. **Subscr. to:** Crown Publications Inc., 521 Fort St, Victoria, BC BC V8W 1E7, Canada. TEL 604-386-4636.

C A SELECTS. COAL SCIENCE AND PROCESS CHEMISTRY. *see* CHEMISTRY—Abstracting, Bibliographies, Statistics

549 CAN ISSN 0380-7797
CANADA. STATISTICS CANADA. CANADA'S MINERAL PRODUCTION, PRELIMINARY ESTIMATE/PRODUCTION MINERALE DU CANADA, CALCUL PRELIMINAIRE. Text in English, French. 1924. a. CAD 25 domestic; USD 25 foreign (effective 1999). **Document type:** *Government.* **Description:** Early estimates on mineral production by class and province; quantities and values.
Related titles: Microform ed.: (from MML); Online - full text ed.
Indexed: GeoRef, SpeleolAb.
Published by: Statistics Canada, Operations and Integration Division (Subsidiary of: Statistics Canada/Statistique Canada), Circulation Management, 120 Parkdale Ave, Ottawa, ON K1A 0T6, Canada. TEL 613-951-7277, 800-267-6677, FAX 613-951-1584.

622.33 CAN ISSN 0380-6847
CANADA. STATISTICS CANADA. COAL AND COKE STATISTICS/ CANADA. STATISTIQUE CANADA. STATISTIQUE DU CHARBON ET DU COKE. Text in English, French. 1921. m. CAD 114; USD 114 foreign (effective 1999). **Document type:** *Government.* **Description:** Covers production, imports, exports, stocks and disposition of coal by province and supply and disposition of coke in Canada.
Former titles (until 1950): Coal and Coke Statistics for Canada (0829-9781); (until 1949): Monthly Report on Coal and Coke Statistics for Canada (0829-9773)
Related titles: Microform ed.: (from MML).
—CCC.
Published by: Statistics Canada, Operations and Integration Division (Subsidiary of: Statistics Canada/Statistique Canada), Circulation Management, 120 Parkdale Ave, Ottawa, ON K1A 0T6, Canada. TEL 613-951-7277, 800-267-6677, FAX 613-951-1584.

622.33 CAN ISSN 1481-4404
CANADA. STATISTICS CANADA. COAL MINING/CANADA. STATISTIQUE CANADA. MINES DE CHARBON. Text in English, French. 1917. a. CAD 25 domestic; USD 25 foreign (effective 1999). bibl. **Document type:** *Government.* **Description:** Data on the number of mines, employment, payroll, cost of fuel and electricity, production, disposition, exports and imports and supply and demand of coal by province.
Former titles (until 1997): Canada. Statistics Canada. Coal Mines (0705-436X); (until 1969): Coal Mining Industry (0068-709X); (until 1949): Coal Statistics for Canada
Related titles: Microform ed.: (from MML).
Published by: Statistics Canada, Operations and Integration Division (Subsidiary of: Statistics Canada/Statistique Canada), Circulation Management, 120 Parkdale Ave, Ottawa, ON K1A 0T6, Canada. TEL 613-951-7277, 800-267-6677, FAX 613-951-1584.

338.2 CAN ISSN 0575-8645
CA1BS26C201
CANADA. STATISTICS CANADA. GENERAL REVIEW OF THE MINERAL INDUSTRIES, MINES, QUARRIES AND OIL WELLS/ CANADA. STATISTIQUE CANADA. REVUE GENERALE SUR LES INDUSTRIES MINERALES, MINES, CARRIERES ET PUITS DE PETROLE. Text in English, French. 1949. a. CAD 25 domestic; USD 25 foreign (effective 1999). **Document type:** *Government.* **Description:** Final statistics of the mining industry, including production and value of minerals by kind and province, historical tables of values and principal statistics.
Related titles: Microform ed.: (from MML); Online - full text ed.
Published by: Statistics Canada, Operations and Integration Division (Subsidiary of: Statistics Canada/Statistique Canada), Circulation Management, 120 Parkdale Ave, Ottawa, ON K1A 0T6, Canada. TEL 613-951-7277, 800-267-6677, FAX 613-951-1584.

338.2021 CAN ISSN 1708-6299
CANADA. STATISTICS CANADA. METAL ORE MINING/CANADA. STATISTIQUE CANADA. EXTRACTION DE MINERAIS METALLIQUES. Text in English, French. 1978. a. free (effective 2004).
Former titles (until 2001): Canada. Statistics Canada. Metal Mines (Online Edition) (1481-5184); (until 1996): Canada. Statistics Canada. Metal Mines (Print Edition) (0226-4595)
Media: Online - full content.
Published by: (Statistics Canada, Manufacturing, Construction and Energy Division), Statistics Canada/Statistique Canada, Publications Sales and Services, Ottawa, ON K1A 0T6, Canada. TEL 613-951-8116, infostats@statcan.ca, http://www.statcan.gc.ca.

622 CHL
CHILE. INSTITUTO NACIONAL DE ESTADISTICAS. MINERIA. Text in Spanish. a. CLP 1,200; USD 8.20 in United States; USD 9.40 elsewhere.
Published by: Instituto Nacional de Estadisticas, Casilla 498, Correo 3, Ave. Bulnes, 418, Santiago, Chile. TEL 56-2-6991441, FAX 56-2-6712169.

622.021 ESP ISSN 0213-2559
ESTADISTICA MINERA DE ESPANA. Text in Spanish. 1861. a. **Document type:** *Government.*
Formerly (until 1968): Estadisticas Minera y Metalurgica de Espana (0071-156X)
Published by: Ministerio de Industria, Paseo Castellana, 160, Madrid, 28046, Spain. FAX 259-84-80.

622 669.3 CHL ISSN 0716-8462
ESTADISTICAS DEL COBRE Y OTROS MINERALES ANUARIO. Text in Spanish. 1981. a. USD 200; or exchange basis. **Document type:** *Directory, Government.* **Description:** Contains statistical information on metallic and non-metallic mining. Data on copper and its by-products.
Supersedes: Produccion y Exportaciones Chilenas de Cobre
Published by: Comision Chilena del Cobre, Augustinas 1161, 4o Piso, Apdo. 9493, Santiago, Chile. TEL 562-3828222, FAX 562-3828300. Circ: 500.

338.2 GRC ISSN 0072-7415
GREECE. NATIONAL STATISTICAL SERVICE. ANNUAL STATISTICAL SURVEY ON MINES, QUARRIES AND SALTERNS. Text in English, Greek. 1954. a., latest 1994. back issues avail. **Document type:** *Government.*
Formerly (until 1961): Greece. National Statistical Service. Results of the Annual Statistical Surveys on Mines, Quarries and Salterns
Published by: National Statistical Service of Greece, Statistical Information and Publications Division/Ethniki Statistiki Yperesia tes Ellados, 14-16 Lykourgou St, Athens, 101 66, Greece. TEL 30-1-3089-397, FAX 30-1-3241-102.

338.2 315 KOR ISSN 1599-1369
GWANG GONG'EOB TONG'GYE JO'SA BO'GO'SEO. JIYEOG PYEON/KOREA (REPUBLIC). NATIONAL STATISTICAL OFFICE. REPORT ON MINING AND MANUFACTURING SURVEY. WHOLE COUNTRY. Text in English, Korean. 1971. a. USD 50 newsstand/ cover (effective 2009). **Document type:** *Government.* **Description:** Contains statistics on the structure, locations and production activities in all mining and manufacturing establishments with five or more workers, including data on employment, wages, number of workers, value of shipment, production cost, value added, and tangible fixed assets.
Formerly: Kwang Kongop T'onggye Chosa Pogoso/Korea (Republic). National Bureau of Statistics. Report on Mining and Manufacturing Survey (0075-6849)
Published by: Tong'gyecheong/Korea National Statistical Office, Government Complex Daejeon, 139 Seonsaro (920 Dunsan 2-dong), Seo-gu, Daejeon, 302-701, Korea, S. TEL 82-42-4814114. **Subscr. to:** The Korean Statistical Association, Rm. 103, Seoul Statistical Branch Office Bldg. 71, Nonhyun-Dong, Kangnam-Ku, Seoul 135701, Korea, S. TEL 82-2-34437954, FAX 82-2-34437957, kosa@nso.go.kr.

GWANG'EOB. JEJO'EOB TONG'GYE JOSA BOGOSEO. SAN'EOBPYEON-JEON'GUG/KOREA (REPUBLIC). NATIONAL STATISTICAL OFFICE. REPORT ON MINING AND MANUFACTURING SURVEY. INDUSTRY - NATIONAL AREA. *see* BUSINESS AND ECONOMICS—Abstracting, Bibliographies, Statistics

HANDBOOK OF WORLD MINERAL STATISTICS. *see* BUSINESS AND ECONOMICS—Abstracting, Bibliographies, Statistics

553 622 669 016 GBR ISSN 0019-0020
TN7
I M M ABSTRACTS. (Institution of Mining and Metallurgy) Text in English. 1950. q. GBP 350 to non-members; GBP 240 to members (effective 2010). abstr. reprints avail. **Document type:** *Abstract/Index.* **Description:** Provides a useful alternative for those who like to keep up to date with the technical literature in their field by browsing through a printed journal organised by broad subject areas, rather than searching electronically for specific topics.
Related titles: Online - full text ed.; Supplement(s): I M M Abstracts. Index. ISSN 0268-2516. 1985.
Indexed: GeoRef.
—BLDSC (4369.630000), Linda Hall. **CCC.**
Published by: Institute of Materials, Minerals and Mining, 1 Carlton House Terr, London, SW1Y 5DB, United Kingdom. TEL 44-20-74517300, FAX 44-20-78391702.

338.2 IND ISSN 0027-0261
INDIAN BUREAU OF MINES. BULLETIN OF MINERAL INFORMATION. Text in English, Hindi. 1961. s-a. charts; stat. **Document type:** *Bulletin, Government.*
Former titles (until 1983): Indian Bureau of Mines. Bulletin of Mineral Statistics and Information; (until 19??): Indian Bureau of Mines. Monthly Bulletin of Mineral Statistics and Information
Related titles: Online - full text ed.: free (effective 2011).
Indexed: ChemAb, SpeleolAb.
Published by: Indian Bureau of Mines, c/o Controller General, 2nd Fl, Indira Bhawan, Civil Lines, Nagpur, Maharashtra 440 102, India. TEL 91-712-2560041, FAX 91-712-2565073, cgibm@ibm.mah.nic.in.

INDICES DA PRODUCAO INDUSTRIAL. *see* MINES AND MINING INDUSTRY

INJURY EXPERIENCE IN SAND AND GRAVEL MINING. *see* OCCUPATIONAL HEALTH AND SAFETY—Abstracting, Bibliographies, Statistics

622 IRN ISSN 0075-0514
IRANIAN MINERAL STATISTICS. Text in English, Persian, Modern. 1962. a. free. **Document type:** *Government.*
Published by: (Bureau of Statistics), Ministry of Finance and Economic Affairs, Teheran, Iran.

KAGAKU GIJUTSU BUNKEN SOKUHO. KINZOKU KOGAKU, KOZAN KOGAKU, CHIKYU NO KAGAKU-HEN/CURRENT BIBLIOGRAPHY ON SCIENCE AND TECHNOLOGY: EARTH SCIENCE, MINING AND METALLURGY. *see* EARTH SCIENCES—Abstracting, Bibliographies, Statistics

622 310 MYS ISSN 0126-818X
HD9506.M36
MALAYSIA. DEPARTMENT OF MINES. STATISTICS RELATING TO THE MINING INDUSTRY OF MALAYSIA. Text in English, Malay. 1951. q. MYR 100; MYR 1.50 newsstand/cover. **Document type:** *Government.*
Indexed: GeoRef, SpeleolAb.
Published by: Department of Mines/Jabatan Galian Malaysia, Jbu Pejabat, Tingkat 22 Bangunan Tabung Haji, Jalan Tun Razak, Kuala Lumpur, 50656, Malaysia.

622 MYS
MALAYSIA. DEPARTMENT OF STATISTICS. ANNUAL CENSUSES OF MINING AND STONE QUARRYING, MALAYSIA/MALAYSIA. JABATAN PERANGKAAN. BANCI INDUSTRI PERLOMBONGAN DAN PENGGALIAN BATU TAHUNAN, MALAYSIA. Text in English, Malay. a., latest 1996. **Document type:** *Government.*
Published by: Malaysia. Department of Statistics/Jabatan Perangkaan, Jalan Cenderasari, Kuala Lumpur, 50514, Malaysia. TEL 60-3-294-4264, FAX 60-3-291-4535.

622 MYS
MALAYSIA. DEPARTMENT OF STATISTICS. ANNUAL CENSUSES OF MINING AND STONE QUARRYING, MALAYSIA - ADDITIONAL TABLES/MALAYSIA. JABATAN PERANGKAAN. BANCI TAHUNAN PERLOMBONGAN DAN PENGGALIAN BATU, MALAYSIA - JADUAL TAMBAHAN. Text in English, Malay. a. MYR 20. **Document type:** *Government.*
Published by: Malaysia. Department of Statistics/Jabatan Perangkaan, Jalan Cenderasari, Kuala Lumpur, 50514, Malaysia. TEL 60-3-294-4264, FAX 60-3-291-4535.

622 MYS ISSN 0128-9918
MALAYSIA. DEPARTMENT OF STATISTICS. ANNUAL CENSUSES OF MINING AND STONE QUARRYING, MALAYSIA - PRINCIPAL STATISTICS/MALAYSIA. JABATAN PERANGKAAN. BANCI TAHUNAN PERLOMBONGAN DAN PENGGALIAN BATU, MALAYSIA - PERANGKAAN UTAMA. Text in English, Malay. 1994. a. MYR 12. **Document type:** *Government.*
Published by: Malaysia. Department of Statistics/Jabatan Perangkaan, Jalan Cenderasari, Kuala Lumpur, 50514, Malaysia. TEL 60-3-294-4264, FAX 60-3-291-4535.

622 USA ISSN 1072-768X
MINE SAFETY AND HEALTH NEWS. Text in English. 1994. 24/yr. USD 625 (effective 2010). index. **Document type:** *Newsletter, Trade.* **Description:** Covers proposed and final rules, policies of the Mine Safety and Health Administration and court cases of the Federal Mine Safety and Health Review Commission.
Related titles: Diskette ed.: USD 625 (effective 2000).
Published by: Legal Publication Services, 888 Pittsford Mendon Center Rd, Pittsford, NY 14534. TEL 716-582-3211, FAX 716-582-2879, MineSafety@aol.com. Ed. Melanie Aclander. Pub., R&P Ellen Smith.

622 IND
MONTHLY STATISTICS OF MINERAL PRODUCTION. Abbreviated title: M S M P. Text in English. 19??. m. INR 3,000 (effective 2011). stat. **Document type:** *Report, Abstract/Index.*
Formerly (until 1985): Quick Release to the Mineral Statistics of India
Published by: Indian Bureau of Mines, c/o Shri K.Thomas, 5 th Fl, Block 'D', Indira Bhavan, Civil Lines, Nagpur, 440102, India. TEL 91-712-2564934, mms@ibm.mah.nic.in, http://www.ibm.nic.in.

622 338.2 USA
NATIONAL MINING ASSOCIATION. WEEKLY STATISTICAL SUMMARY. Text in English. 19??. w. USD 500 to non-members; free to members (effective 2011). **Document type:** *Newsletter, Trade.* **Description:** Presents statistical data on coal production and consumption, electrical output and steel production. Also includes data on U.S. petroleum production, stocks and imports.
Formerly (until 2001): National Coal Association. Weekly Statistical Summary
Published by: National Mining Association, 101 Constitution Ave, NW, Ste 500E, Washington, DC 20001. TEL 202-463-2600, FAX 202-463-2666, MPhelleps@nma.org.

622 317 CAN ISSN 0709-292X
PRODUCTION OF CANADA'S LEADING MINERALS/PRODUCTION DES PRINCIPAUX MINERAUX DU CANADA. Text in English, French. 1979. m. looseleaf. free. charts; stat. back issues avail. **Document type:** *Government.*
Formed by the merger of (1946-1978): Salt (0318-7918); (193?-1978): Asbestos (0380-5778); (1927-1978): Copper and Nickel Production (0380-6952); (1949-1978): Gold Production (0318-7977); (1952-1978): Iron Ore (0318-7969); (1930-1978): Production of Canada's Leading Minerals (0008-2619); (1931-1978): Silver, Lead and Zinc Production (0318-7926)
Related titles: Online - full content ed.
Indexed: CSI.
—CCC.
Published by: (Canada. Publishing and Communication Services), Natural Resources Canada, Minerals and Metals Sector (Subsidiary of: Natural Resources Canada/Ressources Naturelles Canada), 580 Booth St, Ottawa, ON K1A 0E4, Canada. TEL 613-947-6580, FAX 613-952-7501, info-mms@nrcan.gc.ca, http://www.nrcan.gc.ca/mms/hm_e.htm. Ed. H Martin. Circ: 1,400. **Subscr. to:** Natural Resources Canada, Minerals and Metals Sector, Minerals and Mining Statistics Division, Ottawa, ON K1A 0E4, Canada.

622 LUX ISSN 1015-6275
TP325 CODEN: PCRSEI
PROGRESS IN COAL STEEL AND RELATED SOCIAL RESEARCH; a European journal. Text in English. q. ECS 180 with Euro Abstracts. abstr.; bibl.; pat. **Document type:** *Newsletter, Abstract/Index.*
Related titles: ◆ Supplement to: Euroabstracts. ISSN 1606-6340.
Indexed: ErgAb.
—Linda Hall.
Published by: European Commission, Office for Official Publications of the European Union, 2 Rue Mercier, Luxembourg, L-2985, Luxembourg. info@publications.europa.eu, http://europa.eu.

622 338.2 MYS ISSN 0025-1313
QUARTERLY BULLETIN OF STATISTICS RELATING TO THE MINING INDUSTRY OF MALAYSIA. Text in English. 1947. q. MYR 50; MYR 1.50 newsstand/cover. stat. **Document type:** *Government.*
Published by: Department of Mines/Jabatan Galian Malaysia, Jbu Pejabat, Tingkat 22 Bangunan Tabung Haji, Jalan Tun Razak, Kuala Lumpur, 50656, Malaysia. Circ: 140.

REFERATIVNYI ZHURNAL. GEOKHIMIYA, MINERALOGIYA, PETROGRAFIYA; vypusk svodnogo toma. *see* EARTH SCIENCES—Abstracting, Bibliographies, Statistics

016.622 RUS ISSN 0034-2386
REFERATIVNYI ZHURNAL. GORNOE DELO; svodnyi tom. Text in Russian. 1964. m. USD 2,022 foreign (effective 2011). **Document type:** *Journal, Abstract/Index.*
Related titles: CD-ROM ed.; Online - full text ed.; ◆ Cumulative ed. of: Referativnyi Zhurnal. Razrabotka Mestorozhdenii Tverdykh Poleznykh Iskopaemykh. Osnovnye Protsessy. ISSN 0202-9499; ◆ Cumulative ed. of: Referativnyi Zhurnal. Razrabotka Mestorozhdenii Tverdykh Poleznykh Iskopaemykh; ◆ Cumulative ed. of: Referativnyi Zhurnal. Obshchie Voprosy Gornogo Dela.
Indexed: GeoRef, SpeleolAb.
—East View. **CCC.**
Published by: VINITI RAN, ul Usievicha 20, Moscow, 125190, Russian Federation. TEL 7-499-1526113, FAX 7-499-9430060, dir@viniti.ru, http://www.viniti.ru. **Dist. by:** Informnauka Ltd., Ul Usievicha 20, Moscow 125190, Russian Federation. alfimov@viniti.ru.

016.622 016.6655 RUS ISSN 0373-6415
REFERATIVNYI ZHURNAL. GORNOE I NEFTEPROMYSLOVOE MASHINOSTROENIE; otdel'nyi vypusk. Text in Russian. 1964. m. USD 307.20 foreign (effective 2011). **Document type:** *Journal, Abstract/Index.*
Formerly: Gornye Mashiny (0034-2394)
Related titles: CD-ROM ed.; Online - full text ed.
—East View, Linda Hall. **CCC.**

Published by: VINITI RAN, ul Usievicha 20, Moscow, 125190, Russian Federation. TEL 7-499-1526113, FAX 7-499-9430060, dir@viniti.ru, http://www.viniti.ru. **Dist. by:** Informnauka Ltd., Ul Usievicha 20, Moscow 125190, Russian Federation. alfimov@viniti.ru.

016.549 RUS ISSN 0202-9383
REFERATIVNYI ZHURNAL. MESTOROZHDENIYA GORYUCHIKH POLEZNYKH ISKOPAEMYKH; vypusk svodnogo toma. Text in Russian. 1954. m. USD 450 foreign (effective 2011). **Document type:** *Journal, Abstract/Index.*
Related titles: CD-ROM ed.; Online - full text ed.
—East View.
Published by: VINITI RAN, ul Usievicha 20, Moscow, 125190, Russian Federation. TEL 7-499-1526113, FAX 7-499-9430060, dir@viniti.ru, http://www.viniti.ru. **Dist. by:** Informnauka Ltd., Ul Usievicha 20, Moscow 125190, Russian Federation. alfimov@viniti.ru.

016.549 RUS ISSN 0202-9464
REFERATIVNYI ZHURNAL. OBOGASHCHENIE POLEZNYKH ISKOPAEMYKH; vypusk svodnogo toma. Text in Russian. 1960. m. USD 315.60 foreign (effective 2011). **Document type:** *Journal, Abstract/Index.*
Related titles: CD-ROM ed.; Online - full text ed.
—East View.
Published by: VINITI RAN, ul Usievicha 20, Moscow, 125190, Russian Federation. TEL 7-499-1526113, FAX 7-499-9430060, dir@viniti.ru, http://www.viniti.ru. **Dist. by:** Informnauka Ltd., Ul Usievicha 20, Moscow 125190, Russian Federation. alfimov@viniti.ru.

016.622 RUS
REFERATIVNYI ZHURNAL. OBSHCHIE VOPROSY GORNOGO DELA; vypusk svodnogo toma. Text in Russian. 1960. m. USD 350.40 foreign (effective 2010). **Document type:** *Journal, Abstract/Index.*
Formerly (until 2010): Referativnyi Zhurnal. Razrabotka Mestorozhdenii Tverdykh Poleznykh Iskopaemykh. Obshchie Problemy, Promyshlennost, Ekonomika, Stroitelstvo (0202-9480)
Related titles: CD-ROM ed.; Online - full text ed.; ◆ Cumulative ed(s).: Referativnyi Zhurnal. Gornoe Delo. ISSN 0034-2386.
—East View.
Published by: VINITI RAN, ul Usievicha 20, Moscow, 125190, Russian Federation. TEL 7-499-1526113, FAX 7-499-9430060, dir@viniti.ru, http://www.viniti.ru. **Dist. by:** Informnauka Ltd., Ul Usievicha 20, Moscow 125190, Russian Federation. alfimov@viniti.ru.

016.622 RUS
REFERATIVNYI ZHURNAL. RAZRABOTKA MESTOROZHDENII TVERDYKH POLEZNYKH ISKOPAEMYKH; vypusk svodnogo toma. Text in Russian. 1960. m. USD 1,294.80 foreign (effective 2011). **Document type:** *Journal, Abstract/Index.*
Formed by the merger of (1960-2010): Referativnyi Zhurnal. Razrabotka Mestorozhdenii Tverdykh Poleznykh Iskopaemykh. Vspomogatelnye Protsessy (0202-9472); (1960-2010): Referativnyi Zhurnal. Razrabotka Mestorozhdenii Tverdykh Poleznykh Iskopaemykh. Osnovnye Protsessy (0202-9499)
Related titles: CD-ROM ed.; Online - full text ed.; ◆ Cumulative ed(s).: Referativnyi Zhurnal. Gornoe Delo. ISSN 0034-2386.
—East View.
Published by: VINITI RAN, ul Usievicha 20, Moscow, 125190, Russian Federation. TEL 7-499-1526113, FAX 7-499-9430060, dir@viniti.ru, http://www.viniti.ru. **Dist. by:** Informnauka Ltd., Ul Usievicha 20, Moscow 125190, Russian Federation. alfimov@viniti.ru.

338.2 316.8 ZAF
SOUTH AFRICA. STATISTICS SOUTH AFRICA. CENSUS OF MINING (YEAR). Text in English. triennial. ZAR 60 (effective 2007). **Document type:** *Government.*
Former titles (until Aug. 1998): South Africa. Central Statistical Service. Census of Mining (1013-7297); South Africa. Central Statistical Service. Mining: Financial Statistics; South Africa. Department of Statistics. Mining: Financial Statistics
Published by: Statistics South Africa/Statistieke Suid-Afrika, Private Bag X44, Pretoria, 0001, South Africa. TEL 27-12-3108911, FAX 27-12-3108500, info@statssa.gov.za, http://www.statssa.gov.za.

338.2 316.8 ZAF
SOUTH AFRICA. STATISTICS SOUTH AFRICA. STATISTICAL RELEASE. MINING - FINANCIAL STATISTICS. Text in English. q. **Document type:** *Government.*
Formerly (until Aug. 1998): South Africa. Central Statistical Service. Statistical Release. Mining - Financial Statistics
Published by: Statistics South Africa/Statistieke Suid-Afrika, Private Bag X44, Pretoria, 0001, South Africa. TEL 27-12-3108911, FAX 27-12-3108500, info@statssa.gov.za, http://www.statssa.gov.za.

338.2 316.8 ZAF
SOUTH AFRICA. STATISTICS SOUTH AFRICA. STATISTICAL RELEASE. MINING - PRODUCTION AND SALES. Text in English. m. free. **Document type:** *Government.*
Formerly (until Aug. 1998): South Africa. Central Statistical Service. Statistical Release. Mining - Production and Sales
Published by: Statistics South Africa/Statistieke Suid-Afrika, Private Bag X44, Pretoria, 0001, South Africa. TEL 27-12-3108911, FAX 27-12-3108500, info@statssa.gov.za, http://www.statssa.gov.za.

622 USA
U.S. BUREAU OF THE CENSUS. (YEAR) ECONOMIC CENSUS. MINING (ONLINE). Text in English. 19??. every 5 yrs., latest 2007. free (effective 2011). stat. back issues avail. **Document type:** *Database, Government.*
Media: Online - full text.
Published by: U.S. Census Bureau (Subsidiary of: U.S. Department of Commerce), 4600 Silver Hill Rd, Washington, DC 20233. TEL 301-763-4636, 800-923-8282, econ@census.gov, http://www.census.gov.

622.021 USA ISSN 1936-6531
U.S. DEPARTMENT OF ENERGY. ENERGY INFORMATION ADMINISTRATION. QUARTERLY COAL REPORT (ONLINE). Text in English. 1982. q. free. stat. **Document type:** *Government.*
Media: Online - full text.
Published by: U.S. Department of Energy, Energy Information Administration, 1000 Independence Ave, SW, Washington, DC 20585. infoctr@eia.gov, http://www.eia.doe.gov.

622 USA
U.S. DEPARTMENT OF THE INTERIOR. GEOLOGICAL SURVEY. MINERAL RESOURCES PROGRAM. MINERAL INDUSTRY SURVEYS. CEMENT. Variant title: Mineral Industry Surveys. Cement. Text in English. m. stat.; maps. **Document type:** *Government.*
Media: Online - full text.
Published by: U.S. Geological Survey, Mineral Resources Program (Subsidiary of: U.S. Department of the Interior), 12201 Sunrise Valley Dr, 913 National Ctr, Reston, VA 20192.

622 USA
U.S. GEOLOGICAL SURVEY. MINERAL RESOURCES MINERAL INDUSTRY SURVEYS. FLUORSPAR. Text in English. q. stat. back issues avail. **Document type:** *Government.*
Media: Online - full text.
Published by: U.S. Geological Survey, Mineral Resources Program (Subsidiary of: U.S. Department of the Interior), c/o M. Michael Miller, 989 National Center, Reston, VA 20192. TEL 703-648-7716, FAX 703-648-7757, http://minerals.usgs.gov/.

U.S. GEOLOGICAL SURVEY. MINERAL RESOURCES PROGRAM. MINERAL COMMODITY SUMMARIES. BARITE. *see* BUSINESS AND ECONOMICS—Production Of Goods And Services

U.S. GEOLOGICAL SURVEY. MINERAL RESOURCES PROGRAM. MINERAL COMMODITY SUMMARIES. BORON. *see* BUSINESS AND ECONOMICS—Production Of Goods And Services

U.S. GEOLOGICAL SURVEY. MINERAL RESOURCES PROGRAM. MINERAL COMMODITY SUMMARIES. BROMINE. *see* BUSINESS AND ECONOMICS—Production Of Goods And Services

622.021 USA
U.S. GEOLOGICAL SURVEY. MINERAL RESOURCES PROGRAM. MINERAL COMMODITY SUMMARIES. CADMIUM. Text in English. 19??. a. free (effective 2011). stat. back issues avail. **Document type:** *Report, Government.* **Description:** Contain information on the domestic industry structure, government programs, tariffs, and 5-year salient statistics for cadmium.
Media: Online - full text.
Published by: U.S. Geological Survey, Mineral Resources Program (Subsidiary of: U.S. Department of the Interior), 12201 Sunrise Valley Dr, 913 National Ctr, Reston, VA 20192. TEL 703-648-6110, FAX 703-648-6057, kjohnson@usgs.gov.

U.S. GEOLOGICAL SURVEY. MINERAL RESOURCES PROGRAM. MINERAL COMMODITY SUMMARIES. CHROMIUM. *see* BUSINESS AND ECONOMICS—Production Of Goods And Services

U.S. GEOLOGICAL SURVEY. MINERAL RESOURCES PROGRAM. MINERAL COMMODITY SUMMARIES. CLAYS. *see* BUSINESS AND ECONOMICS—Production Of Goods And Services

U.S. GEOLOGICAL SURVEY. MINERAL RESOURCES PROGRAM. MINERAL COMMODITY SUMMARIES. CONSTRUCTION SAND AND GRAVEL. *see* BUSINESS AND ECONOMICS—Production Of Goods And Services

U.S. GEOLOGICAL SURVEY. MINERAL RESOURCES PROGRAM. MINERAL COMMODITY SUMMARIES. DIMENSION STONE. *see* BUSINESS AND ECONOMICS—Production Of Goods And Services

U.S. GEOLOGICAL SURVEY. MINERAL RESOURCES PROGRAM. MINERAL COMMODITY SUMMARIES. FELDSPAR. *see* BUSINESS AND ECONOMICS—Production Of Goods And Services

U.S. GEOLOGICAL SURVEY. MINERAL RESOURCES PROGRAM. MINERAL COMMODITY SUMMARIES. GEMSTONES. *see* BUSINESS AND ECONOMICS—Production Of Goods And Services

U.S. GEOLOGICAL SURVEY. MINERAL RESOURCES PROGRAM. MINERAL COMMODITY SUMMARIES. GRAPHITE (NATURAL). *see* BUSINESS AND ECONOMICS—Production Of Goods And Services

U.S. GEOLOGICAL SURVEY. MINERAL RESOURCES PROGRAM. MINERAL COMMODITY SUMMARIES. HELIUM. *see* BUSINESS AND ECONOMICS—Production Of Goods And Services

U.S. GEOLOGICAL SURVEY. MINERAL RESOURCES PROGRAM. MINERAL COMMODITY SUMMARIES. IODINE. *see* BUSINESS AND ECONOMICS—Production Of Goods And Services

U.S. GEOLOGICAL SURVEY. MINERAL RESOURCES PROGRAM. MINERAL COMMODITY SUMMARIES. IRON AND STEEL. *see* BUSINESS AND ECONOMICS—Production Of Goods And Services

U.S. GEOLOGICAL SURVEY. MINERAL RESOURCES PROGRAM. MINERAL COMMODITY SUMMARIES. IRON AND STEEL SCRAP. *see* BUSINESS AND ECONOMICS—Production Of Goods And Services

U.S. GEOLOGICAL SURVEY. MINERAL RESOURCES PROGRAM. MINERAL COMMODITY SUMMARIES. IRON AND STEEL SLAG. *see* BUSINESS AND ECONOMICS—Production Of Goods And Services

U.S. GEOLOGICAL SURVEY. MINERAL RESOURCES PROGRAM. MINERAL COMMODITY SUMMARIES. KYANITE AND RELATED MINERALS. *see* BUSINESS AND ECONOMICS—Production Of Goods And Services

U.S. GEOLOGICAL SURVEY. MINERAL RESOURCES PROGRAM. MINERAL COMMODITY SUMMARIES. LEAD. *see* BUSINESS AND ECONOMICS—Production Of Goods And Services

U.S. GEOLOGICAL SURVEY. MINERAL RESOURCES PROGRAM. MINERAL COMMODITY SUMMARIES. LIME. *see* BUSINESS AND ECONOMICS—Production Of Goods And Services

U.S. GEOLOGICAL SURVEY. MINERAL RESOURCES PROGRAM. MINERAL COMMODITY SUMMARIES. LITHIUM. *see* BUSINESS AND ECONOMICS—Production Of Goods And Services

U.S. GEOLOGICAL SURVEY. MINERAL RESOURCES PROGRAM. MINERAL COMMODITY SUMMARIES. MANGANESE. *see* BUSINESS AND ECONOMICS—Production Of Goods And Services

U.S. GEOLOGICAL SURVEY. MINERAL RESOURCES PROGRAM. MINERAL COMMODITY SUMMARIES. MANUFACTURED ABRASIVES. *see* BUSINESS AND ECONOMICS—Production Of Goods And Services

U.S. GEOLOGICAL SURVEY. MINERAL RESOURCES PROGRAM. MINERAL COMMODITY SUMMARIES. MERCURY. *see* BUSINESS AND ECONOMICS—Production Of Goods And Services

U.S. GEOLOGICAL SURVEY. MINERAL RESOURCES PROGRAM. MINERAL COMMODITY SUMMARIES. MICA. *see* BUSINESS AND ECONOMICS—Production Of Goods And Services

U.S. GEOLOGICAL SURVEY. MINERAL RESOURCES PROGRAM. MINERAL COMMODITY SUMMARIES. MOLYBDENUM. *see* BUSINESS AND ECONOMICS—Production Of Goods And Services

U.S. GEOLOGICAL SURVEY. MINERAL RESOURCES PROGRAM. MINERAL COMMODITY SUMMARIES. NICKEL. *see* BUSINESS AND ECONOMICS—Production Of Goods And Services

U.S. GEOLOGICAL SURVEY. MINERAL RESOURCES PROGRAM. MINERAL COMMODITY SUMMARIES. NIOBIUM (COLUMBIUM). *see* BUSINESS AND ECONOMICS—Production Of Goods And Services

U.S. GEOLOGICAL SURVEY. MINERAL RESOURCES PROGRAM. MINERAL COMMODITY SUMMARIES. NITROGEN (FIXED) - AMMONIA. *see* BUSINESS AND ECONOMICS—Production Of Goods And Services

U.S. GEOLOGICAL SURVEY. MINERAL RESOURCES PROGRAM. MINERAL COMMODITY SUMMARIES. PEAT. *see* BUSINESS AND ECONOMICS—Production Of Goods And Services

U.S. GEOLOGICAL SURVEY. MINERAL RESOURCES PROGRAM. MINERAL COMMODITY SUMMARIES. PHOSPHATE ROCK. *see* BUSINESS AND ECONOMICS—Production Of Goods And Services

U.S. GEOLOGICAL SURVEY. MINERAL RESOURCES PROGRAM. MINERAL COMMODITY SUMMARIES. PLATINUM-GROUP METALS. *see* BUSINESS AND ECONOMICS—Production Of Goods And Services

U.S. GEOLOGICAL SURVEY. MINERAL RESOURCES PROGRAM. MINERAL COMMODITY SUMMARIES. POTASH. *see* BUSINESS AND ECONOMICS—Production Of Goods And Services

U.S. GEOLOGICAL SURVEY. MINERAL RESOURCES PROGRAM. MINERAL COMMODITY SUMMARIES. QUARTZ CRYSTAL (INDUSTRIAL). *see* BUSINESS AND ECONOMICS—Production Of Goods And Services

U.S. GEOLOGICAL SURVEY. MINERAL RESOURCES PROGRAM. MINERAL COMMODITY SUMMARIES. RARE EARTHS. *see* BUSINESS AND ECONOMICS—Production Of Goods And Services

U.S. GEOLOGICAL SURVEY. MINERAL RESOURCES PROGRAM. MINERAL COMMODITY SUMMARIES. SALT. *see* BUSINESS AND ECONOMICS—Production Of Goods And Services

U.S. GEOLOGICAL SURVEY. MINERAL RESOURCES PROGRAM. MINERAL COMMODITY SUMMARIES. SAND AND GRAVEL (INDUSTRIAL). *see* BUSINESS AND ECONOMICS—Production Of Goods And Services

U.S. GEOLOGICAL SURVEY. MINERAL RESOURCES PROGRAM. MINERAL COMMODITY SUMMARIES. SILICON. *see* BUSINESS AND ECONOMICS—Production Of Goods And Services

U.S. GEOLOGICAL SURVEY. MINERAL RESOURCES PROGRAM. MINERAL COMMODITY SUMMARIES. SODIUM SULFATE. *see* BUSINESS AND ECONOMICS—Production Of Goods And Services

U.S. GEOLOGICAL SURVEY. MINERAL RESOURCES PROGRAM. MINERAL COMMODITY SUMMARIES. STONE (CRUSHED). *see* BUSINESS AND ECONOMICS—Production Of Goods And Services

U.S. GEOLOGICAL SURVEY. MINERAL RESOURCES PROGRAM. MINERAL COMMODITY SUMMARIES. SULFUR. *see* BUSINESS AND ECONOMICS—Production Of Goods And Services

U.S. GEOLOGICAL SURVEY. MINERAL RESOURCES PROGRAM. MINERAL COMMODITY SUMMARIES. TANTALUM. *see* BUSINESS AND ECONOMICS—Production Of Goods And Services

U.S. GEOLOGICAL SURVEY. MINERAL RESOURCES PROGRAM. MINERAL COMMODITY SUMMARIES. TIN. *see* BUSINESS AND ECONOMICS—Production Of Goods And Services

U.S. GEOLOGICAL SURVEY. MINERAL RESOURCES PROGRAM. MINERAL COMMODITY SUMMARIES. TITANIUM AND TITANIUM DIOXIDE. *see* BUSINESS AND ECONOMICS—Production Of Goods And Services

U.S. GEOLOGICAL SURVEY. MINERAL RESOURCES PROGRAM. MINERAL COMMODITY SUMMARIES. TITANIUM MINERAL CONCENTRATES. *see* BUSINESS AND ECONOMICS—Production Of Goods And Services

U.S. GEOLOGICAL SURVEY. MINERAL RESOURCES PROGRAM. MINERAL COMMODITY SUMMARIES. TUNGSTEN. *see* BUSINESS AND ECONOMICS—Production Of Goods And Services

U.S. GEOLOGICAL SURVEY. MINERAL RESOURCES PROGRAM. MINERAL COMMODITY SUMMARIES. VANADIUM. *see* BUSINESS AND ECONOMICS—Production Of Goods And Services

U.S. GEOLOGICAL SURVEY. MINERAL RESOURCES PROGRAM. MINERAL COMMODITY SUMMARIES. ZINC. *see* BUSINESS AND ECONOMICS—Production Of Goods And Services

U.S. GEOLOGICAL SURVEY. MINERAL RESOURCES PROGRAM. MINERAL COMMODITY SUMMARIES. ZIRCONIUM AND HAFNIUM. *see* BUSINESS AND ECONOMICS—Production Of Goods And Services

622.021 USA
U.S. GEOLOGICAL SURVEY. MINERAL RESOURCES PROGRAM. MINERAL INDUSTRY SURVEYS. ALUMINUM. Text in English. 19??. m. free (effective 2011). stat. back issues avail. **Document type:** *Report, Government.* **Description:** Contain information on the domestic industry structure, government programs, tariffs, and 5-year salient statistics for aluminum.
Supersedes in part (in 1996): U.S. Bureau of Mines. Mineral Industry Surveys - Commodities: Aluminum, Bauxite, and Alumina; Which was formed by the merger of: U.S. Bureau of Mines. Annual Reports - Commodities: Aluminum; U.S. Bureau of Mines. Annual Reports - Commodities: Bauxite; Both of which superseded: U.S. Bureau of Mines. Annual Reports - Commodities: Bauxite and Aluminum (0276-5039); U.S. Bureau of Mines. Annual Reports - Commodities: Alumina
Media: Online - full text.
Published by: U.S. Geological Survey, Mineral Resources Program (Subsidiary of: U.S. Department of the Interior), 12201 Sunrise Valley Dr, 913 National Ctr, Reston, VA 20192. TEL 703-648-6110, FAX 703-648-6057, kjohnson@usgs.gov.

622.021 USA
U.S. GEOLOGICAL SURVEY. MINERAL RESOURCES PROGRAM. MINERAL INDUSTRY SURVEYS. ANTIMONY. Text in English. q. stat. back issues avail. **Document type:** *Government.*
Media: Online - full text.

Published by: U.S. Geological Survey, Mineral Resources Program (Subsidiary of: U.S. Department of the Interior), c/o James F. Carlin, Jr, 989 National Center, Reston, VA 20192. TEL 703-648-4985, FAX 703-648-7757, http://minerals.usgs.gov/.

622.021 USA
U.S. GEOLOGICAL SURVEY. MINERAL RESOURCES PROGRAM. MINERAL INDUSTRY SURVEYS. BAUXITE AND ALUMINA. Text in English. q. stat. **Document type:** *Government.*
Supersedes in part (in 1996): U.S. Bureau of Mines. Mineral Industry Surveys - Commodities: Aluminum, Bauxite, and Alumina; Which was formed by the merger of: U.S. Bureau of Mines. Annual Reports - Commodities: Aluminum; U.S. Bureau of Mines. Annual Reports - Commodities: Bauxite; Both of which superseded: U.S. Bureau of Mines. Annual Reports - Commodities: Bauxite and Aluminum (0276-5039); U.S. Bureau of Mines. Annual Reports - Commodities: Alumina
Media: Online - full text.
Published by: U.S. Geological Survey, Mineral Resources Program (Subsidiary of: U.S. Department of the Interior), c/o E. Lee Bray, 989 National Center, Reston, VA 20192. TEL 703-648-4979, FAX 703-648-7757, http://minerals.usgs.gov/.

622.021 USA
U.S. GEOLOGICAL SURVEY. MINERAL RESOURCES PROGRAM. MINERAL INDUSTRY SURVEYS. BISMUTH. Text in English. quadrennial. stat. back issues avail. **Document type:** *Government.*
Media: Online - full text.
Published by: U.S. Geological Survey, Mineral Resources Program (Subsidiary of: U.S. Department of the Interior), c/o James F. Carlin, Jr, 989 National Center, Reston, VA 20192. TEL 703-648-4985, FAX 703-648-7757, http://minerals.usgs.gov/.

622.021 USA
U.S. GEOLOGICAL SURVEY. MINERAL RESOURCES PROGRAM. MINERAL INDUSTRY SURVEYS. CHROMIUM. Text in English. m. stat. back issues avail. **Document type:** *Government.*
Supersedes in part: U.S. Bureau of Mines. Mineral Industry Surveys - Commodities: Chromium (Online Edition)
Media: Online - full text.
Published by: U.S. Geological Survey, Mineral Resources Program (Subsidiary of: U.S. Department of the Interior), c/o John F. Papp, 989 National Center, Reston, VA 20192. TEL 703-648-4963, FAX 703-648-7757, http://minerals.usgs.gov/.

622.021 USA
U.S. GEOLOGICAL SURVEY. MINERAL RESOURCES PROGRAM. MINERAL INDUSTRY SURVEYS. COBALT. Text in English. m. stat. back issues avail. **Document type:** *Government.*
Media: Online - full text.
Published by: U.S. Geological Survey, Mineral Resources Program (Subsidiary of: U.S. Department of the Interior), c/o Kim B. Shedd, 989 National Center, Reston, VA 20192. TEL 703-648-4974, FAX 703-648-7757, http://minerals.usgs.gov/.

622.021 USA
U.S. GEOLOGICAL SURVEY. MINERAL RESOURCES PROGRAM. MINERAL INDUSTRY SURVEYS. GOLD. Text in English. m. stat. back issues avail. **Document type:** *Government.*
Media: Online - full text.
Published by: U.S. Geological Survey, Mineral Resources Program (Subsidiary of: U.S. Department of the Interior), c/o Micheal W. George, 989 National Center, Reston, VA 20192. TEL 703-648-4962, FAX 703-648-7757, http://minerals.usgs.gov/.

622.021 USA
U.S. GEOLOGICAL SURVEY. MINERAL RESOURCES PROGRAM. MINERAL INDUSTRY SURVEYS. GYPSUM. Text in English. m. stat. back issues avail. **Document type:** *Government.*
Media: Online - full text.
Published by: U.S. Geological Survey, Mineral Resources Program (Subsidiary of: U.S. Department of the Interior), c/o Alan Founie, 983 National Center, Reston, VA 20192. TEL 703-648-7720, FAX 703-648-7975, http://minerals.usgs.gov/.

U.S. GEOLOGICAL SURVEY. MINERAL RESOURCES PROGRAM. MINERAL INDUSTRY SURVEYS. IRON AND STEEL SCRAP. *see* BUSINESS AND ECONOMICS—Production Of Goods And Services

622.021 USA
U.S. GEOLOGICAL SURVEY. MINERAL RESOURCES PROGRAM. MINERAL INDUSTRY SURVEYS. IRON ORE. Text in English. m. stat. back issues avail. **Document type:** *Government.*
Media: Online - full text.
Published by: U.S. Geological Survey, Mineral Resources Program (Subsidiary of: U.S. Department of the Interior), c/o John D. Jorgenson, 989 National Center, Reston, VA 20192. TEL 703-648-4912, FAX 703-648-7757, http://minerals.usgs.gov/.

622.021 USA
U.S. GEOLOGICAL SURVEY. MINERAL RESOURCES PROGRAM. MINERAL INDUSTRY SURVEYS. MANGANESE. Text in English. m. stat. back issues avail. **Document type:** *Government.*
Supersedes in part: U.S. Bureau of Mines. Mineral Industry Surveys - Commodities - Manganese (Online)
Media: Online - full text.
Published by: U.S. Geological Survey, Mineral Resources Program (Subsidiary of: U.S. Department of the Interior), c/o Lisa A. Corathers, 989 National Center, Reston, VA 20192. TEL 703-648-4973, FAX 703-648-7757, http://minerals.usgs.gov/.

U.S. GEOLOGICAL SURVEY. MINERAL RESOURCES PROGRAM. MINERAL INDUSTRY SURVEYS. MARKETABLE PHOSPHATE ROCK, CROP YEAR. *see* BUSINESS AND ECONOMICS—Production Of Goods And Services

622.021 USA
U.S. GEOLOGICAL SURVEY. MINERAL RESOURCES PROGRAM. MINERAL INDUSTRY SURVEYS. MOLYBDENUM. Text in English. m. stat. back issues avail. **Document type:** *Government.*
Supersedes in part: U.S. Bureau of Mines. Mineral Industry Surveys - Commodities: Molybdenum (Online Edition)
Media: Online - full text.
Published by: U.S. Geological Survey, Mineral Resources Program (Subsidiary of: U.S. Department of the Interior), c/o Michael J. Magyar, 989 National Center, Reston, VA 20192. TEL 703-648-4964, FAX 703-648-7757, http://minerals.usgs.gov/.

622.021 USA
U.S. GEOLOGICAL SURVEY. MINERAL RESOURCES PROGRAM. MINERAL INDUSTRY SURVEYS. NICKEL. Text in English. m. stat. back issues avail. **Document type:** *Government.*
Supersedes in part: U.S. Bureau of Mines. Mineral Industry Surveys - Commodities: Nickel (Online)
Media: Online - full text.
Published by: U.S. Geological Survey, Mineral Resources Program (Subsidiary of: U.S. Department of the Interior), c/o Peter H. Kuck, 989 National Center, Reston, VA 20192. TEL 703-648-4965, FAX 703-648-7757, http://minerals.usgs.gov/.

622.021 USA
U.S. GEOLOGICAL SURVEY. MINERAL RESOURCES PROGRAM. MINERAL INDUSTRY SURVEYS. PLATINUM-GROUP METALS. Text in English. m. stat. back issues avail. **Document type:** *Government.*
Supersedes in part: U.S. Bureau of Mines. Mineral Industry Surveys - Commodities: Platinum-Group Metals (Online)
Media: Online - full text.
Published by: U.S. Geological Survey, Mineral Resources Program (Subsidiary of: U.S. Department of the Interior), c/o Micheal W. George, 989 National Center, Reston, VA 20192. TEL 703-648-4962, FAX 703-648-7757, http://minerals.usgs.gov/.

622.021 USA
U.S. GEOLOGICAL SURVEY. MINERAL RESOURCES PROGRAM. MINERAL INDUSTRY SURVEYS. SILICON. Text in English. m. stat. back issues avail. **Document type:** *Government.*
Supersedes in part: U.S. Bureau of Mines. Mineral Industry Surveys - Commodities: Silicon (Online Edition)
Media: Online - full text.
Published by: U.S. Geological Survey, Mineral Resources Program (Subsidiary of: U.S. Department of the Interior), c/o Lisa A. Corathers, 989 National Center, Reston, VA 20192. TEL 703-648-4973, FAX 703-648-7757.

622.021 USA
U.S. GEOLOGICAL SURVEY. MINERAL RESOURCES PROGRAM. MINERAL INDUSTRY SURVEYS. SILVER. Text in English. m. stat. back issues avail. **Document type:** *Government.*
Media: Online - full text.
Published by: U.S. Geological Survey, Mineral Resources Program (Subsidiary of: U.S. Department of the Interior), c/o William E. Brooks, 989 National Center, Reston, VA 20192. TEL 703-648-7791, FAX 703-648-7757, http://minerals.usgs.gov/.

622.021 USA
U.S. GEOLOGICAL SURVEY. MINERAL RESOURCES PROGRAM. MINERAL INDUSTRY SURVEYS. SODA ASH/MINERAL INDUSTRY SURVEYS. SODA ASH. Text in English. 19??. m. free (effective 2011). stat. back issues avail. **Document type:** *Report, Government.* **Description:** Provide timely statistical data on production, distribution, stocks, and consumption of soda ash.
Media: Online - full text.
Published by: U.S. Geological Survey, Mineral Resources Program (Subsidiary of: U.S. Department of the Interior), 12201 Sunrise Valley Dr, 913 National Ctr, Reston, VA 20192. TEL 703-648-6110, FAX 703-648-6057, kjohnson@usgs.gov.

622.021 USA
U.S. GEOLOGICAL SURVEY. MINERAL RESOURCES PROGRAM. MINERAL INDUSTRY SURVEYS. SULFUR. Text in English. m. stat. back issues avail. **Document type:** *Government.*
Supersedes in part: U.S. Bureau of Mines. Mineral Industry Surveys - Commodities: Sulfur (Online Edition)
Media: Online - full text.
Published by: U.S. Geological Survey, Mineral Resources Program (Subsidiary of: U.S. Department of the Interior), c/o Joyce A. Ober, 983 National Center, Reston, VA 20192. TEL 703-648-7717, FAX 703-648-7757, http://minerals.usgs.gov/.

622.021 USA
U.S. GEOLOGICAL SURVEY. MINERAL RESOURCES PROGRAM. MINERAL INDUSTRY SURVEYS. TIN. Text in English. m. stat. back issues avail. **Document type:** *Government.*
Supersedes in part: U.S. Bureau of Mines. Mineral Industry Surveys - Commodities: Tin
Media: Online - full text.
Published by: U.S. Geological Survey, Mineral Resources Program (Subsidiary of: U.S. Department of the Interior), c/o James F. Carlin, Jr, 989 National Center, Reston, VA 20192. TEL 703-648-4985, FAX 703-648-7757, http://minerals.usgs.gov/.

622.021 USA
U.S. GEOLOGICAL SURVEY. MINERAL RESOURCES PROGRAM. MINERAL INDUSTRY SURVEYS. TITANIUM. Text in English. q. stat. back issues avail. **Document type:** *Government.*
Supersedes in part: U.S. Bureau of Mines. Mineral Industry Surveys - Commodities: Titanium (Online Edition)
Media: Online - full text.
Published by: U.S. Geological Survey, Mineral Resources Program (Subsidiary of: U.S. Department of the Interior), c/o Joseph Gambogi, 983 National Center, Reston, VA 20192. TEL 703-648-7718, FAX 703-648-7975, http://minerals.usgs.gov/.

622.021 USA
U.S. GEOLOGICAL SURVEY. MINERAL RESOURCES PROGRAM. MINERAL INDUSTRY SURVEYS. TUNGSTEN. Text in English. m. stat. back issues avail. **Document type:** *Government.*
Supersedes in part: U.S. Bureau of Mines. Mineral Industry Surveys - Commodities: Tungsten (Online Edition)
Media: Online - full text.
Published by: U.S. Geological Survey, Mineral Resources Program (Subsidiary of: U.S. Department of the Interior), c/o Kim B. Shedd, 989 National Center, Reston, VA 20192. TEL 703-648-4974, FAX 703-648-7757, http://minerals.usgs.gov/.

622.021 USA
U.S. GEOLOGICAL SURVEY. MINERAL RESOURCES PROGRAM. MINERAL INDUSTRY SURVEYS. VANADIUM. Text in English. m. stat. back issues avail. **Document type:** *Government.*
Supersedes in part: U.S. Bureau of Mines. Mineral Industry Surveys - Commodities: Vanadium (Online)
Media: Online - full text.
Published by: U.S. Geological Survey, Mineral Resources Program (Subsidiary of: U.S. Department of the Interior), c/o Michael J. Magyar, 989 National Center, Reston, VA 20192. TEL 703-648-4964, FAX 703-648-7757, http://minerals.usgs.gov/.

622.021 USA
U.S. GEOLOGICAL SURVEY. MINERAL RESOURCES PROGRAM. MINERAL INDUSTRY SURVEYS. ZINC. Text in English. m. stat. back issues avail. **Document type:** *Government.*
Supersedes in part: U.S. Bureau of Mines. Mineral Industry Surveys - Commodities: Zinc (Online Edition)
Media: Online - full text.
Published by: U.S. Geological Survey, Mineral Resources Program (Subsidiary of: U.S. Department of the Interior), c/o Amy C. Tolcin, 989 National Center, Reston, VA 20192. TEL 703-648-4940, FAX 703-648-7757, http://minerals.usgs.gov/.

622 USA
U.S. GEOLOGICAL SURVEY. MINERAL RESOURCES PROGRAM. MINERALS AND MATERIALS INFORMATION CD-ROM. Text in English. 1994. a., latest 2003. **Document type:** *Government.* **Description:** Comprises technical and statistical information on U.S. mining activity available in print format in a number of USBM publications.
Formerly (until 19??): U.S. Bureau of Mines Minerals and Materials Information on CD-ROM
Media: CD-ROM.
Indexed: AmStI.
Published by: U.S. Geological Survey, Mineral Resources Program (Subsidiary of: U.S. Department of the Interior), 12201 Sunrise Valley Dr, 913 National Ctr, Reston, VA 20192. TEL 703-648-6110, FAX 703-648-6057, kjohnson@usgs.gov.

338.2 669 USA
U S SILVER SUMMARY. Text in English. 1968. a. looseleaf. free. mkt.; stat. back issues avail. **Document type:** *Newsletter.* **Description:** Reviews the supply and demand of silver as a raw material, providing a statistical overview of price and government legislation affecting users of the metal. Predicts conditions likely to affect the supply and value of the metal, both for consumers and investors.
Related titles: Online - full text ed.
Published by: Silver Users Association, 1730 M St, N W, Ste 911, Washington, DC 20036-4505. TEL 202-785-3050. Ed. Walter L Frankland Jr. Circ: 300.

622 VEN
VENEZUELA. MINISTERIO DE ENERGIA Y MINAS. ANUARIO ESTADISTICO MINERO. Text in Spanish. 1965. a. **Document type:** *Government.*
Former titles (until 1986): Hierro; Venezuela. Ministerio de Minas e Hidrocarburos. Oficina de Economia Minera. Hierro y Otros Datos Estadisticos (0083-5382)
Published by: (Venezuela. Direccion de Planificacion y Economia Minera), Ministerio de Energia y Minas, Torre Oeste Piso 4, Parque Central Piso 4, Caracas, DF 1010, Venezuela. Ed. Jose Fernandez Betancourt.

VENEZUELA. MINISTERIO DE ENERGIA Y MINAS. APENDICE ESTADISTICO. *see* ENERGY—Abstracting, Bibliographies, Statistics

VENEZUELA. MINISTERIO DE ENERGIA Y MINAS. MEMORIA. *see* ENERGY—Abstracting, Bibliographies, Statistics

338.2 622.33 USA ISSN 0091-5513
HD9547.W39
WEST VIRGINIA COAL FACTS. Text in English. 1971. a. USD 10 (effective 1999). stat.; illus. **Description:** Profiles West Virginia's coal industry statistically.
Indexed: GeoRef.
Published by: West Virginia Coal Association, PO Box 3923, Charleston, WV 25339-3923. TEL 304-342-4153, FAX 304-342-7651. Ed. Sandi J Davison. Circ: 5,000.

338.2 310 GBR
WORLD MINERAL PRODUCTION. Text in English. 19??. a. GBP 30 per issue (effective 2009). **Document type:** *Government.* **Description:** Contains world mineral statistics commodity tables for five years.
Former titles (until 2004): World Mineral Statistics (0951-9475); (until 1978): Institute of Geological Sciences, London. Statistical Summary of the Mineral Industry (0073-9367)
Indexed: GeoRef, SpeleolAb.
Published by: Natural Environment Research Council, British Geological Survey, Kingsley Dunham Ctr, Keyworth, Nottingham, NG12 5GG, United Kingdom. TEL 44-115-9363100, 44-115-9363241, FAX 44-115-9363488, enquiries@bgs.ac.uk, http://www.bgs.ac.uk/.

ZHONGGUO DIZHI WENZHAI. *see* EARTH SCIENCES—Abstracting, Bibliographies, Statistics

MINES AND MINING INDUSTRY—Computer Applications

620 CAN
A P C O M (YEAR). (Application of Computers and Operations Research in the Mineral Industry) Text in English. 1998. irreg., latest 2009. **Document type:** *Proceedings, Academic/Scholarly.*
Formerly: Application of Computers and Operations Research in the Mineral Industry. Proceedings
Indexed: IMMAb.
Published by: Canadian Institute of Mining, Metallurgy and Petroleum, Ste 855, 3400 de Maisonneuve Blvd W, Ste 1210, Montreal, PQ H3Z 3B8, Canada. TEL 514-939-2710, FAX 514-939-2714, cim@cim.org.

622.0285 IND ISSN 0975-3265
▼ ➤ **ADVANCES IN INFORMATION MINING.** Text in English. 2009. 4/yr. USD 425 (effective 2011). **Document type:** *Journal, Academic/Scholarly.* **Description:** Aims to provide a complete information on current developments in the field of mining.
Related titles: Online - full text ed.: ISSN 0975-9093. free (effective 2011).
Indexed: C10, T02.
Published by: Bioinfo Publications, 49/F-72, Vighnahar Complex, Front of Overseas Bank, Sector 12, Kharghar, Navi Mumbai, 410 210, India. TEL 91-22-27743967, FAX 91-22-66736413, editor@bioinfo.in. Eds. Dr. Prasun Chakrabarti, Dr. Virendra S Gomase.

➤ **EARTH SCIENCE COMPUTER APPLICATIONS.** *see* EARTH SCIENCES—Computer Applications

622 USA ISSN 1087-4720
TN1
EARTH SCIENCE SOFTWARE DIRECTORY. Text in English. biennial. USD 90 domestic; USD 95 foreign (effective 2000). **Document type:** *Directory.* **Description:** Lists commercial and public-domain computer programs for mining applications.
Formerly (until 1993-1994): Directory of Mining Programs (0884-917X)
Published by: Gibbs Associates, PO Box 706, Boulder, CO 80306. TEL 303-444-6032, FAX 303-444-6032.

MINICOMPUTERS

see COMPUTERS—Minicomputers

MOTION PICTURES

791.43 ESP ISSN 1139-9635
A G R COLECCIONISTAS DE CINE. Text in Spanish. 1999. q. **Document type:** *Magazine, Consumer.*
Published by: Editorial El Gran Caid, Paseo de Guadalajara 100, San Sebastian de los Reyes, Madrid, 28700, Spain. TEL 34-91-6528057, FAX 34-91-6537561, agr@elgrancaid.com, http://www.elgrancaid.com/.

A M I A NEWSLETTER. *see* LIBRARY AND INFORMATION SCIENCES

791.433 CAN
A S I F A MAGAZINE. Text in English, French, Russian. 1967 (no.15). q. USD 10 per issue to non-members (effective 2008). adv. bk.rev. **Description:** Aimed at professionals working in the field of animation cinema.
Former titles: A S I F A News (0775-9746); (until 1988): International Animated Film Association. Bulletin (0538-4281)
Published by: Association Internationale du Film d'Animation/ International Association of Animated Film, c/o Chris Robinson, Editor, 2 Daly Ave, Ste 120, Ottawa, ON K1N 6E2, Canada. FAX 613-232-6315, secretary@asifa.net. Ed. Chris Robinson. adv.: B&W page USD 735.

A V PRESENTATIONS HANDBOOK. (Audio Visual) *see* EDUCATION—Teaching Methods And Curriculum

791.43 CAN ISSN 1719-6167
A V PRESERVATION TRUST OF CANADA. ANNUAL REPORT. (Audio-Visual) Text in English. 2002. a., latest 2005. **Document type:** *Report, Consumer.*
Media: Online - full text. **Related titles:** Print ed.: ISSN 1714-0714; French ed.: Trust pour la Preservation de l'A V.CA. Rapport Annuel. ISSN 1719-6175.
Published by: Audio - Visual Preservation Trust of Canada, Box 4861, Station E, Ottawa, ON K1S 5J1, Canada. info@avtrust.ca, http://www.avtrust.ca.

791.43 USA
ACADEMY PLAYERS DIRECTORY. Text in English. 3/yr. USD 75 per issue (effective 2000). **Document type:** *Directory.*
Published by: Academy of Motion Picture Arts and Sciences, 8949 Wilshire Blvd, Beverly Hills, CA 90211-1972. TEL 310-247-3000, FAX 310-550-5034. Ed. Keith W Gonzales. R&P Scott Miller.

791.43 ESP
ACCION. Cover title: Cine y Video Accion. Text in Spanish. 1992. m. EUR 24.04; EUR 1.60 newsstand/cover. adv. film rev.; video rev. bibl.; illus. back issues avail. **Document type:** *Magazine, Consumer.* **Description:** Reports on actors, current films, new videos, and future film plans.
Published by: Ediciones Jardin S.L., Ferrac, 11 1o izq, Madrid, 28008, Spain. TEL 34-91-5470529, FAX 34-91-5415055, edijardin@arrakis.es. Ed. Hector Alonso Bautista. Pub., R&P Mariano Alonso Sanchez. Adv. contact Mariano Alonso. color page EUR 1,900; 210 x 297. Circ: 45,000.

791.43 FRA ISSN 2108-6508
ACME (PARIS). Text in French. 2008. q. **Document type:** *Magazine, Consumer.*
Media: Online - full text.
Published by: Association Acme http://www.revue-acme.com.

778.53 USA ISSN 1533-5984
ADAM FILM WORLD GUIDE. Abbreviated title: Film World. Text in English. 1968. m. USD 7.99 newsstand/cover (effective 2007). adv. **Document type:** *Directory, Consumer.*
Formerly: Adam Film World Guide. Movie Illustrated
Published by: Knight Publishing Corporation, 8060 Melrose Ave, Los Angeles, CA 90046. TEL 323-653-8060, FAX 323-655-9452, psi@loop.com. Ed. J C Adams. Adv. contact Gregory Sage. B&W page USD 1,138, color page USD 1,694.

791.43029 USA ISSN 0743-6335
ADAM FILM WORLD GUIDE. DIRECTORY OF ADULT FILM & VIDEO. Text in English. 1984. a. adv. illus. reprints avail. **Document type:** *Directory, Consumer.* **Description:** Lists distributors, producers and other companies involved in adult video.
Former titles: Adam Film World Guide. Directory of Adult Film
Published by: Knight Publishing Corporation, 8060 Melrose Ave, Los Angeles, CA 90046. TEL 323-653-8060, FAX 323-655-9452, psi@loop.com. Ed. J C Adams. Adv. contact Gregory Sage.

ADAPTATION; the journal of literature on screen studies. *see* LITERATURE

AFTERIMAGE; the journal of media arts and cultural criticism. *see* PHOTOGRAPHY

791.43 USA ISSN 1069-3890
PN2289
AGENCIES: WHAT THE ACTOR NEEDS TO KNOW (HOLLYWOOD EDITION). Text in English. 1984. m. USD 50 (effective 2000). adv. tr.lit. **Document type:** *Directory.* **Description:** Update of franchised talent agencies in Hollywood, with full descriptions of representation and staffs; also includes appraisals by industry consultants and career guidance editorials.
Published by: Acting World Books, PO Box 3899, Hollywood, CA 90078. TEL 818-905-1345, 800-210-1197. Ed., Pub., Adv. contact Lawrence Parke. Circ: 7,000.

338.0029 658.0029 USA
AGENTS, MANAGERS & CASTING DIRECTORS 411. Text in English. s-a. (Apr. & Oct.). USD 79; USD 49 per issue (effective 2003). adv. **Document type:** *Directory, Trade.* **Description:** Contains thousands of up-to-date listings of agents, managers and casting directors for the film and television industry in Los Angeles, New York, Chicago and other key cities.
Published by: 411 Publishing, 5700 Wilshire Blvd, Ste 120, Los Angeles, CA 90036. TEL 323-965-2020, FAX 323-965-5052, gdow@cahners.com, http://www.411publishing.com. adv.: B&W page USD 2,200, color page USD 2,950; trim 8.5 x 10.75.

791.43 780 384.5532 USA
ALL ACCESS. Text in English. 2002. irreg. USD 22 (effective 2003). **Document type:** *Magazine, Consumer.* **Description:** Provides exclusive footage of interviews with artists and entertainment celebrities, as well as a variety of entertainment concepts.
Media: Optical Disk - DVD.
Published by: Kraze Access Media Inc., PO Box 8, Brightwaters, NY 11718. Eds. Monique Woods, Sean Goulbourne.

ALTERNATIVE CINEMA MAGAZINE; the magazine of independent and underground movie making. *see* COMMUNICATIONS—Video

791.43 ARG
EL AMANTE CINE. Text in Spanish. 1991. m. **Document type:** *Consumer.* **Description:** Includes reviews, essays and interviews on local and international cinema.
Related titles: Online - full text ed.
Indexed: IIFP, IITV.
Published by: Vaccaro, Sanchez y Cia., SA, Moreno 794, 9o piso, Buenos Aires, Argentina. Ed. Flavia de la Fuente.

AMASS. *see* LITERARY AND POLITICAL REVIEWS

778.53 USA ISSN 0002-7928
TR845
AMERICAN CINEMATOGRAPHER; the international journal of film & digital production techniques. Text in English. 1920. m. USD 29.95 domestic; USD 49.95 in Canada & Mexico; USD 69.95 elsewhere (effective 2010). adv. bk.rev.; film rev. charts; illus.; stat.; abstr. cum.index. back issues avail.; reprints avail. **Document type:** *Magazine, Trade.* **Description:** Features in-depth articles on cinematography.
Related titles: Microform ed.: (from PQC); Online - full text ed.: USD 29.95 (effective 2010); Supplement(s): American Videographer.
Indexed: A06, A07, A10, A22, A30, A31, AA, ABS&EES, ArtInd, B04, BRD, ChemAb, F01, F02, IBR, IBT&D, IBZ, IIFP, IIPA, IITV, MRD, RASB, RILM, T02, V03, W03, W05.
—BLDSC (0812.460000), IE, Infotrieve, Ingenta, Linda Hall.
Published by: (American Society of Cinematographers), A S C Holding Corporation, PO Box 2230, Hollywood, CA 90078. TEL 323-969-4333, 800-448-0145, FAX 323-876-4973, office@theasc.com. Adv. contact Diella Nepomuceno TEL 323-969-4333 ext 124.

791.43 USA ISSN 0195-8267
PN1993
AMERICAN CLASSIC SCREEN. Text in English. 1977. bi-m. USD 15. adv. bk.rev. back issues avail.
Published by: (National Film Society, Inc.), American Classic Screen, Inc., PO Box 7150, Shawnee Mission, KS 66207. TEL 913-341-1919. Ed. John C Tibbetts. Circ: 20,000.

791.45 USA
AMERICAN FILM & VIDEO REVIEW. Text in English. 1962. a. free. **Document type:** *Catalog.*
Formerly: American Film Review (0065-8308)
Published by: (American Educational Film and Video Center), Eastern College, 1300 Eagle Rd., St. Davids, PA 19087-3696. TEL 215-341-5935. Ed., R&P John A Baird Jr. Circ: 30,000.

791.43 GBR
AMERICAN INDIES. Text in English. irreg. price varies. back issues avail. **Document type:** *Monographic series, Academic/Scholarly.* **Description:** Contains original research with clearly defined classroom-orientated frameworks of film analysis which covers a contemporary American independent film with each volume.
Published by: Edinburgh University Press, 22 George Sq, Edinburgh, Scotland EH8 9LF, United Kingdom. TEL 44-131-6504218, FAX 44-131-6503286, journals@eup.ed.ac.uk. Eds. Gary Needham, Yannis Tzioumakis.

791.43 USA
AMERICAN MOVIE CLASSICS MAGAZINE. Text in English. 1988. m. USD 12.95 (effective 2000). adv. back issues avail. **Document type:** *Magazine, Consumer.* **Description:** Serves as the magazine of American Movie Classics network. Aims to cover classic Hollywood through stories from movie writers and personal reflections on America's favorite films.
Published by: Working Media, Inc., 255 Elm St., Ste. 201, Somerville, MA 02144-2957. TEL 617-350-8777. Ed. Katharine Whittemore. Pub. Timothy J Haley. Circ: 140,000.

791.43 IND
ANANDALOK. Text in Bengali. 1975. fortn. adv. **Document type:** *Newspaper, Trade.*
Published by: Anand Bazar Patrika Ltd., 6 Prafulla Sarkar St, Kolkata, West Bengal 700 001, India. TEL 91-33-22378000, FAX 91-33-22253240, http://www.anandabazar.com. Circ: 59,618.

791.43 780 USA
ANGLOFILE. Text in English. 1988. m. USD 15 (effective 2000). adv. bk.rev.; film rev.; music rev.; video rev. **Document type:** *Newsletter, Consumer.* **Description:** News coverage of British entertainment and pop culture.
Published by: Goody Press, PO Box 33515, Decatur, GA 30033. TEL 770-492-0444, FAX 404-321-3109, goodypress@freewwweb.com. Ed., Pub., R&P William P King. Adv. contact Leslie King. Circ: 3,000.

791.43 SWE ISSN 1651-694X
ANIMAGI. Text in Swedish. 2003. q. SEK 200 domestic; USD 44 foreign (effective 2004). **Document type:** *Magazine, Trade.* **Description:** Animation in films.
Published by: Konstfack, Institionen foer Animation och Animerad Film/University College of Arts, Crafts and Design. Institute for Animation and Animated Films, Kaserngatan 26, Eksjoe, 57535, Sweden. TEL 46-381-12645, FAX 46-381-12646, info@animationenshus.eksjo.se, http://www.animationenshus.eksjo.se/konstfack. Ed. Midhat Ajanovic. Pub. Witold Nowak.

791.43 GBR ISSN 1746-8477
TR897.5
➤ **ANIMATION**; an interdisciplinary journal. Text in English. 2006 (Jul.). 3/yr. GBP 332, USD 615 to institutions; GBP 339, USD 628 combined subscription to institutions (print & online eds.) (effective 2012). adv. back issues avail.; reprint service avail. from PSC. **Document type:** *Journal, Academic/Scholarly.* **Description:** Addresses all animation made using known and yet to be developed techniques, from sixteenth century optical devices to contemporary digital media, revealing its implications on other forms of time-based media expression.
Related titles: Online - full text ed.: ISSN 1746-8485. GBP 305, USD 565 to institutions (effective 2012).
Indexed: A20, A22, ArtHuCI, E01, SCOPUS, W07.
—IE. **CCC.**
Published by: Sage Publications Ltd. (Subsidiary of: Sage Publications, Inc.), 1 Oliver's Yard, 55 City Rd, London, EC1Y 1SP, United Kingdom. TEL 44-20-73248500, FAX 44-20-73248600, info@sagepub.co.uk, http://www.uk.sagepub.com/home.nav. Ed. Suzanne Buchan. **Subscr. to:** Sage Publications, Inc., 2455 Teller Rd, Thousand Oaks, CA 91320. TEL 805-499-9774, FAX 805-499-0871, journals@sagepub.com.

791.433 USA ISSN 1061-0308
NC1765
ANIMATION JOURNAL. Text in English. 1992. a., latest vol.9, a. USD 20 for 2 yrs. domestic to individuals; USD 25 for 2 yrs. in Canada to individuals; USD 30 for 2 yrs. elsewhere to individuals; USD 40 for 2 yrs. domestic to institutions; USD 45 for 2 yrs. in Canada to institutions; USD 50 for 2 yrs. elsewhere to institutions (effective 2004 - 2005). bk.rev.; video rev. bibl.; illus. 96 p./no.; back issues avail. **Document type:** *Journal, Academic/Scholarly.* **Description:** Devoted to animation history and theory. Reflects the diversity of animation's production methods and national origins.
Related titles: Online - full text ed.
Indexed: CA, F01, F02, IIFP, IITV, MRD, PCI, T02.
Published by: (Chapman University, School of Law, School of Film and T V), A J Press, 20124 Zimmerman Pl, Santa Clarita, CA 91390-3102. TEL 661-263-7545. Ed., R&P Maureen Furniss. Circ: 500 (paid).

ANIMATION MAGAZINE; the news, business, technology & art of animation. *see* ART

791.433 USA ISSN 1069-2088
TR897.5
➤ **ANIMATRIX.** Text in English. 1984. a. bk.rev. **Document type:** *Journal, Academic/Scholarly.*
Indexed: CA, F01, F02, T02.
Published by: University of California, Los Angeles, Department of Film and Television, 102 E Melnitz Hall, PO Box 951622, Los Angeles, CA 90095. TEL 310-825-5761, FAX 310-825-3383, info@tft.ucla.edu, http://www.tft.ucla.edu/.

➤ **ANIME DO.** *see* ART

➤ **ANIME PLAY.** *see* HOBBIES

778.53 USA ISSN 1521-7205
NC1765
ANIMEFANTASTIQUE. Text in English. 1999. q. USD 20 domestic; USD 23 foreign; USD 5.95 newsstand/cover (effective 2006). adv. software rev.; tel.rev.; video rev. illus. back issues avail. **Document type:** *Magazine, Consumer.* **Description:** Features in-depth coverage of the animation field from Japan, Europe, and the US.
Published by: Cinefantastique, Inc., 3740 Overland Ave Ste E, Los Angeles, CA 90034-6378. TEL 708-366-5566, FAX 708-366-1441, mail@cfq.com, http://www.cfq.com. Ed. Dan Persons. Pub., R&P Frederick S Clarke. Adv. contact Elaine Fiedler. B&W page USD 900, color page USD 1,700; trim 11 x 8.5. Circ: 20,000. **Subscr. to:** PO Box 270, Oak Park, IL 60303. **Dist. by:** Eastern News Distributors Inc., 250 W. 55th St., New York, NY 10019. TEL 800-221-3148.

778.53 FRA ISSN 0180-3492
L'ANNEE DU CINEMA. Text in French. 1977. a. price varies. illus.
Published by: Editions Calmann-Levy, 31 Rue de Fleurus, Paris, 75006, France. TEL 33-1-49543600, FAX 33-1-49543640, http://www.editions-calmann-levy.com.

384.555 FRA ISSN 1969-1750
PN1993.3
ANNUAIRE DU CINEMA ET DE L'AUDIOVISUEL. Text in French. 1948. a., latest 2009. EUR 170 per issue (effective 2009). adv. **Document type:** *Directory, Trade.* **Description:** Includes 25000 addresses of individuals and companies that take part in the audiovisual industry.
Former titles (until 2006): Annuaire du Cinema Television Video (0991-7799); (until 1986): Annuaire du Cinema et Television (0066-2968)
Related titles: CD-ROM ed.: FRF 1,600 (effective 1999).
Published by: S.N. Bellefaye, 38 rue Etienne Marcel, Paris, 75002, France. TEL 33-1-42335252, FAX 33-1-42333900.

791.43 USA ISSN 1932-829X
PN1993
ANNUAL EDITIONS: FILM. Text in English. 2006. a. USD 22.25 per issue (effective 2010). **Document type:** *Journal, Academic/Scholarly.*
Related titles: Online - full text ed.
Published by: McGraw-Hill, Contemporary Learning Series (Subsidiary of: McGraw-Hill Companies, Inc.), 1221 Ave of the Americas, New York, NY 10020. TEL 212-904-2000, FAX 212-512-2000, customer.service@mcgraw-hill.com, http://www.mhhe.com/cls/.

791.43 ITA
ANNUARIO DEGLI ATTORI/EUROPEAN PLAYERS' DIRECTORY; European players' directory. Text in Italian. 1970. a. (in 2 vols.). EUR 140 (effective 2009). back issues avail. **Document type:** *Directory, Trade.* **Description:** Contains photos of actors and actresses.
Related titles: CD-ROM ed.; Online - full text ed.
Published by: Star Edizioni Cinematografiche s.r.l., Piazza Vittorio Bottego 51, Rome, 00154, Italy. FAX 39-6-80665119. Ed. Dulcymary de Oliveira. Circ: 3,600.

778.53 ITA
ANNUARIO DEL CINEMA ITALIANO E AUDIOVISIVI. Text in Italian. 1951. a. EUR 50 (effective 2008). **Document type:** *Directory, Consumer.*
Formerly: Annuario del Cinema Italiano (0392-596X)
Published by: Centro di Studi di Cultura, Corso di Francia 211, Rome, 00191, Italy. TEL 39-06-3296519, FAX 39-06-3296339.

APE CULTURE. *see* COMMUNICATIONS—Television And Cable

791.43 LBN ISSN 0003-7397
ARAB FILM AND TELEVISION CENTER NEWS. Text in English. 1965. s-m. free to qualified personnel. film rev. illus.; stat. cum.index.
Related titles: French ed.; Arabic ed.
Published by: Ministry of Information, Arab Film & Television Centre, P O Box 3434, Beirut, Lebanon. Circ: 3,000.

791.43 ESP ISSN 0214-6606
PN1993
ARCHIVOS DE LA FILMOTECA. Text in Spanish. 1989. q. EUR 30.05 domestic; EUR 42.07 foreign. bk.rev. back issues avail. **Document type:** *Magazine, Academic/Scholarly.* **Description:** Presents historical research on films. Serves as a backbone for film studies in universities and research centers.
Related titles: ◆ Supplement(s): Archivos de la Filmoteca. Suplemento. ISSN 1130-2038.
Indexed: F01, F02, H21, IIFP, MLA-IB, P08, RILM.
—CCC.
Published by: Instituto Valenciano de Cinematografia, Filmoteca, Plaza del Ajuntamiento, 17, Valencia, 46002, Spain. TEL 34-96-3539300, FAX 34-96-3539330, ivac-lafilmoteca_inf@gva.es, http://www.ivac.lafilmoteca.es/. Ed. Vicente Sanchez Biosca. **Dist. by:** Asociacion de Revistas Culturales de Espana, C Covarruvias 9 2o. Derecha, Madrid 28010, Spain. TEL 34-91-3086066, FAX 34-91-3199267, info@arce.es, http://www.arce.es/.

791.43 ESP ISSN 1130-2038
ARCHIVOS DE LA FILMOTECA. SUPLEMENTO. Text in Spanish. 1989. irreg. **Document type:** *Magazine, Academic/Scholarly.*
Related titles: ◆ Supplement to: Archivos de la Filmoteca. ISSN 0214-6606.
Published by: Instituto Valenciano de Cinematografia, Filmoteca, Plaza del Ajuntamiento, 17, Valencia, 46002, Spain. TEL 34-96-3539300, FAX 34-96-3539330, ivac-lafilmoteca_inf@gva.es, http://www.ivac.lafilmoteca.es/.

▼ **ARS BILDUMA.** *see* ART

778.53 FRA ISSN 1262-0424
PN1993
➤ **L'ART DU CINEMA.** Text in French. 1993. 5/yr. EUR 23 domestic; EUR 26 foreign; EUR 20 domestic to students; EUR 23 foreign to students (effective 2008). adv. **Document type:** *Journal, Academic/Scholarly.* **Description:** Contains studies on film as art; covers film theory and analysis.
Indexed: A26, CPerI, E08, F01, F02, I05, IIFP.
Published by: Association Cinema Art Nouveau, 35 rue des Trois Bornes, Paris, 75011, France. TEL 33-1-43555269, artcinema@free.fr, http://www.imaginet.fr/~dloss/adc/. Ed., R&P, Adv. contact Denis Levy.

778.53 PRT
ARTE 7; revista tecnica de cinema. Text in Portuguese. q.
Published by: Terramar, APART, 112, Mem Martins Codex, 2725, Portugal. TEL 9202104. Ed. Manuel Costa E Silva. Circ: 2,000.

791.4375 DEU
ARTECHOCK FILM. Text in German. w. **Document type:** *Magazine, Consumer.* **Description:** Provides a forum for discussion involving all aspects of motion pictures.
Media: Online - full text.
Published by: Artechock, c/o Filmmuseum im Muenchner Stadtmuseum, St-Jakobsplatz 1, Munich, 80331, Germany. TEL 49-89-23322348, FAX 49-89-23323931.

ARTIBUS ET HISTORIAE; international journal for visual arts. *see* ART

791.43 384 ITA ISSN 1824-6184
PN1995
ARTS AND ARTIFACTS IN MOVIE TECHNOLOGY, AESTHETICS, COMMUNICATION. Abbreviated title: A A M - T A C. Text in Multiple languages. 2004. a. EUR 295 combined subscription domestic to institutions (print & online eds.); EUR 395 combined subscription foreign to institutions (print & online eds.) (effective 2009). **Document type:** *Journal, Academic/Scholarly.*
Related titles: Online - full text ed.: ISSN 1825-201X.
Indexed: RILM.
Published by: Fabrizio Serra Editore (Subsidiary of: Accademia Editoriale), c/o Accademia Editoriale, Via Santa Bibbiana 28, Pisa, 56127, Italy. TEL 39-050-542332, FAX 39-050-574888, accademiaeditoriale@accademiaeditoriale.it, http://www.libraweb.net.

ARTS NEWS. *see* THEATER

791.43 GBR ISSN 1744-8719
➤ **ASIAN CINEMA.** Text in English. 2006 (Feb.). irreg., latest 2006. price varies. **Document type:** *Monographic series, Academic/Scholarly.* **Description:** Aims to re-position Asian cinema at the center of film studies.
Published by: Berg Publishers (Subsidiary of: Oxford International Publishers Ltd.), 1st Fl Angel Ct, 81 St Clements St, Oxford, Berks OX4 1AW, United Kingdom. TEL 44-1865-245104, FAX 44-1865-791165, enquiry@bergpublishers.com. Eds. Anne Ciecko, Geraldine Billingham.

778.53 USA ISSN 1059-440X
PN1993.5.A75
ASIAN CINEMA JOURNAL. Text in English. 1984. s-a. membership. adv. bk.rev. back issues avail. **Document type:** *Journal, Academic/Scholarly.*
Indexed: BAS, CA, F01, F02, IIFP, IITV, MLA-IB, T02.
—BLDSC (1742.403560).
Published by: Asian Cinema Studies Society, c/o John A. Lent, Ed & Pub, 669 Ferne Blvd, Drexel Hill, PA 19026. TEL 610-622-3938, FAX 610-622-2124. Ed., Pub. John A Lent. Circ: 375.

791.436 USA
ASIAN CULT CINEMA. Abbreviated title: A C C. Text in English. 19??. q. USD 30 domestic; USD 50 foreign (effective 2010). film rev. back issues avail. **Document type:** *Magazine, Consumer.* **Description:** Explores the cinematic world of horror and exploitation films from all over Asia including Hong Kong and Japan.
Address: PO Box 15249, Fort Pierce, FL 34979. TEL 772-460-8263, FAX 772-462-3768, customerservice@asiancult.com. Ed. Thomas Weisser.

791.43 USA
ASPECT (BOSTON); the chronicle of new media art. Text in English. 2003. s-a. USD 25 (effective 2005).
Published by: Aspect Magazine, 322 Summer St., 5th Fl, Boston, MA 02210. TEL 617-695-0500, FAX 617-778-2231, info@aspectmag.com. Ed. Michael Middleman.

ASSOCIATION OF TALENT AGENTS. NEWSLETTER. *see* THEATER

791.43 USA
THE ASTOUNDING B MONSTER. Text in English. irreg. **Description:** Includes articles, essays, news, reviews and interviews about the motion picture world.
Media: Online - full text.
Published by: Astounding B Monster Ed. Marty Baumann.

791.43 USA
AUDIENCE (ONLINE EDITION). Text in English. 1998 (Sep.). irreg. adv. film rev. **Document type:** *Magazine, Consumer.* **Description:** Contains film reviews, ratings, and articles on the motion picture industry.
Media: Online - full content.
Published by: Wilson Associates, PO Box 215, Simi Valley, CA 93062. Pub. Bob Wilson.

778.53 DEU ISSN 0179-2555
AUGEN-BLICK; Marburger Hefte zur Medienwissenschaft. Text in German. 1986. 3/yr. EUR 9.90 newsstand/cover (effective 2011). illus. reprints avail. **Document type:** *Journal, Academic/Scholarly.*
Indexed: DIP, F01, F02, IBR, IBZ, PCI.
—CCC.
Published by: (Philipps-Universitaet Marburg, Institut fuer Neuere Deutsche Literatur), Schueren Verlag GmbH, Universitaetsstr 55, Marburg, 35037, Germany. TEL 49-6421-63084, FAX 49-6421-681190, info@schueren-verlag.de, http://www.schueren-verlag.de. Circ: 1,000.

791.43 AUS
AUSTRALIAN FILM INSTITUTE NEWSLETTER (EMAIL). Text in English. fortn. free to members (effective 2008). **Document type:** *Newsletter, Consumer.* **Description:** Contains news and information on the Institute's activities and membership issues.
Media: E-mail.
Published by: Australian Film Institute, 236 Dorcas St, South Melbourne, VIC 3205, Australia. TEL 61-3-96961844, FAX 61-3-96967972, info@afi.org.au, http://www.afi.org.au.

AUSTRALIAN FILM, TELEVISION AND RADIO SCHOOL. ANNUAL REPORT. *see* COMMUNICATIONS—Radio

AUSTRALIAN FILM, TELEVISION AND RADIO SCHOOL HANDBOOK. *see* COMMUNICATIONS—Radio

791.43 FRA ISSN 0045-1150
PN1993 CODEN: RTSCDD
L'AVANT-SCENE. CINEMA. Text in French. 1961. 10/yr. illus. index, cum.index: 1961-1977. back issues avail. **Document type:** *Magazine, Consumer.*
Indexed: A20, A22, DIP, F01, F02, IBR, IBZ, IIFP, IIPA, IITV, PdeR, RASB.
—BLDSC (1837.118000), IE, Infotrieve, Ingenta. **CCC.**
Published by: Editions de l' Avant Scene, 6 rue Git-le-Coeur, Paris, 75006, France. TEL 33-01-46342820, FAX 33-01-43545014, astheatre@aol.com.

AXE FACTORY. *see* LITERATURE

778.53 GBR ISSN 1465-2242
B F M; film - music - media. (Black Filmmaker) Text in English. 1998. bi-m. adv. back issues avail. **Document type:** *Magazine, Trade.*
Indexed: IIBP.
Published by: B F M Media, Ste 13, 5 Blackhorse Rd, Walthamstow, London, E17 6DS, United Kingdom. TEL 44-20-85319199, media@bfmmedia.com.

BACKSTAGE; la rivista dello show business. *see* MUSIC

BARBARA EDEN'S OFFICIAL FAN CLUB NEWSLETTER. *see* CLUBS

791.43 CHN ISSN 1002-6142
BEIJING DIANYING XUEYUAN XUEBAO/BEIJING FILM ACADEMY. JOURNAL. Text in Chinese. 1984. bi-m. USD 31.20 (effective 2009). **Document type:** *Journal, Academic/Scholarly.*
Related titles: Online - full text ed.
—East View.
Published by: Beijing Dianying Xueyuan, 4, Tucheng Lu, Beijing, 100088, China. TEL 86-10-62018899 ext 412, FAX 86-10-82042616.

791.43 DEU ISSN 0232-718X
BEITRAEGE ZUR FILM- UND FERNSEHWISSENSCHAFT. Text in German. 1960. irreg., latest vol.63, 2009. price varies. **Document type:** *Monographic series, Academic/Scholarly.*
Former titles (until 1981): Filmwissenschaftliche Beitraege (0015-1769); Which incorporated (1970-1977): Hochschule fuer Film und Fernsehen der D D R. Information (0138-3698); (until 1968): Filmwissenschaftliche Mitteilungen (0430-4195)
Indexed: IIFP.
Published by: (Hochschule fuer Film und Fernsehen "Konrad Wolf"), Vistas Verlag GmbH, Goltzstr 11, Berlin, 10781, Germany. TEL 49-30-32707446, FAX 49-30-32707455, medienverlag@vistas.de.

791.43 CHN ISSN 1005-183X
BEIYING HUABAO/BEIJING FILM STUDIO PICTORIAL. Text in Chinese. 1985. m. CNY 10 newsstand/cover (effective 2005). illus. **Document type:** *Magazine, Consumer.*
Published by: Beijing Dianying Zhipian Chang/Beijing Film Studio, 77, Sanhuan Zhonglu, Beijing, 100088, China. TEL 86-10-82047294, FAX 86-10-62382727. Ed. Han Sanping. Circ: 30,000 (paid).

791.43 ITA ISSN 1824-2588
BEST MOVIE. Text in Italian. 2002. m. EUR 20 (effective 2009). **Document type:** *Magazine, Consumer.*
Published by: Editoriale Duesse SpA, Via Donatello 5b, Milan, 20131, Italy. TEL 39-02-277961, FAX 39-02-27796300, e-duesse@e-duesse.it, http://www.e-duesse.it.

621.388 ITA ISSN 0394-008X
PN1993
BIANCO & NERO. Key Title: B N. Text in Italian; Summaries in English, Italian. 1933. irreg. EUR 67 domestic to individuals; EUR 72 domestic to institutions; EUR 87.50 foreign (effective 2008). bk.rev.; film rev. illus. index. **Document type:** *Magazine, Consumer.*
Formerly (until 1969): Bianco e Nero (0006-0577)
Related titles: Online - full text ed.: ISSN 2036-4598.
Indexed: A20, F01, F02, IBR, IBZ, IIFP, IITV, MLA-IB, RASB.
Published by: (Fondazione Scuola Nazionale di Cinema), Carocci Editore, Via Sardegna 50, Rome, 00187, Italy. TEL 39-06-42818417, FAX 39-06-42747931, clienti@carocci.it, http://www.carocci.it.

791.43 ITA ISSN 1828-8413
BIBLIOTECA. CINEMA E STORIA. Text in Italian. 2000. irreg. **Document type:** *Magazine, Consumer.*
Published by: Liguori Editore, Via Posillipo 394, Naples, 80123, Italy. TEL 39-081-7206111, FAX 39-081-7206244, http://www.liguori.it. Ed. Pasquale Iaccio.

BIDOUN; a quarterly forum for middle eastern talent. *see* ART

791.43 GBR ISSN 1759-0922
▼ **THE BIG PICTURE.** Abbreviated title: B P. Text in English. 2009. bi-m. GBP 36, USD 68 to individuals; GBP 96, USD 162 to institutions (effective 2012). adv. back issues avail.; reprints avail. **Document type:** *Magazine, Consumer.* **Description:** Offers an intelligent take on cinema, focusing on how film affects our lives.
Related titles: Online - full text ed.: ISSN 1759-0930. GBP 60, USD 90 (effective 2012).
Indexed: F01, F02.
Published by: Intellect Ltd., The Mill, Parnall Rd, Fishponds, Bristol, BS16 3JG, United Kingdom. TEL 44-117-9589910, FAX 44-117-9589911, info@intellectbooks.com, http://www.intellectbooks.co.uk/. Ed. Scott Jordon Harris. Pub. Masoud Yazdani.

791.43 ZAF ISSN 1023-8247
BIG SCREEN; South Africa's movie entertainment magazine. Text in English. 1994. m. ZAR 59. adv. illus. **Document type:** *Magazine, Consumer.*
Related titles: Supplement(s): Popcorn.
Published by: Penta Publications, PO Box 781723, Sandton, Transvaal 2146, South Africa. Ed. Alice Bell. R&P Nicholas Leonsins.

791.4375 DEU
BIOGRAPH. Text in German. 1978. m. adv. **Document type:** *Magazine, Consumer.*
Published by: Biograph Verlag Peter Liese, Citadellstr 14, Duesseldorf, 40213, Germany. TEL 49-211-8668212, FAX 49-211-8668222. Eds. Jenny Holzapfel, Peter Liese. Pub. Peter Liese. adv.: B&W page EUR 1,900, color page EUR 2,800; trim 210 x 285. Circ: 41,168 (controlled).

791.43 IND ISSN 0974-9276
▼ ➤ **BIOSCOPE: SOUTH ASIAN SCREEN STUDIES.** Text in English. 2010 (Jan.). s-a. USD 298, GBP 161 to institutions; USD 304, GBP 164 combined subscription to institutions (print & online eds.) (effective 2011). **Document type:** *Journal, Academic/Scholarly.* **Description:** Publishes theoretical and empirical research articles on both creen practices and wider networks, linkages, and patterns of circulation. This involves research into the historical, regional, and virtual spaces of screen cultures, including globalized and multi-sited conditions of production and circulation.
Related titles: Online - full text ed.: ISSN 0976-352X. USD 274, GBP 148 to institutions (effective 2011).
Indexed: A22, E01.
Published by: Sage Publications India Pvt. Ltd. (Subsidiary of: Sage Publications, Inc.), M-32 Market, Greater Kailash-I, PO Box 4215, New Delhi, 110 048, India. TEL 91-11-6444958, FAX 91-11-6472426, sage@vsnl.com, http://www.indiasage.com/. Eds. Ravi S Vasudevan, Rosie Thomas.

778.53 USA ISSN 1536-3155
PN1995.9.N4
BLACK CAMERA; an international film journal. Text in English. 1985. s-a. USD 85 to institutions; USD 119 combined subscription to institutions (print & online eds.) (effective 2011). bk.rev. illus. back issues avail.; reprint service avail. from PSC. **Document type:** *Journal, Academic/Scholarly.* **Description:** Devoted to the study and documentation of the black cinematic experience. It features essays and interviews that engage film in social as well as political distribution, and production of film in local, regional, national, and transnational settings and environments.
Related titles: Online - full text ed.: ISSN 1947-4237. USD 76.50 to institutions (effective 2011).
Indexed: A22, CA, E01, F01, F02, IBT&D, IIBP, IIPA, MLA-IB, T02.
—CCC.
Published by: (Black Film Center - Archive), Indiana University Press, 601 N Morton St, Bloomington, IN 47404. TEL 812-855-8817, FAX 812-855-7931, iupress@indiana.edu, http://iupress.indiana.edu. Ed. Michael T Martin. Circ: 1,000.

BLACK TALENT NEWS; the entertainment trade publication. *see* THEATER

791.43 GBR ISSN 1366-4522
BLAG. Text in English. 1994. s-a. GBP 7.95 per vol. domestic; GBP 9.95 per vol. in Europe; GBP 12.95 per vol. elsewhere (effective 2009). back issues avail. **Document type:** *Magazine, Consumer.* **Description:** Features articles focusing on music, film, art, culture and style.
Published by: Blag UK Ltd.

791.43 DEU ISSN 0947-4390
BLICKPUNKT: FILM. Text in German. 1976. w. EUR 24 per month (effective 2011). adv. bk.rev. charts; stat. back issues avail. **Document type:** *Magazine, Trade.* **Description:** News magazine of the German film industry.
Published by: Entertainment Media Verlag GmbH und Co. oHG (Subsidiary of: Gruner + Jahr AG & Co), Weihenstephaner Str 7, Munich, 81673, Germany. TEL 49-89-451140, FAX 49-89-45114444, redaktion@e-media.de, http://www.mediabiz.de. Adv. contact Susanne Huebner. Circ: 3,850 (paid and controlled).

778.53 AUT ISSN 1027-5991
PN1993
BLIMP; film magazine. Text and summaries in English, German. 1985. q. bk.rev. 240 p./no. 2 cols./p.; back issues avail. **Document type:** *Magazine, Consumer.* **Description:** Analyzes film, video and media art as forms of cultural practices for academic and non-academic audiences.
Indexed: F01, F02, IBR, IBZ, MLA-IB.
Published by: Edition Blimp, Muchargasse 12-III-10, Graz, St 8010, Austria. TEL 43-316-679950, FAX 43-316-679960. Eds. Bernhard Grundner, Bogdan Grbic. Pub. Bogdan Grbic. R&P, Adv. contact Brigitte Scheruebl TEL 43-316-679960. Circ: 3,500. **Dist. in US by:** Fine Print Distributors, 500 Pampa Dr, Austin, TX 78752-3028. TEL 512-452-8709.

791.45 USA
PN1998.A1
BLU-BOOK PRODUCTION DIRECTORY (ONLINE). Text in English. 1978. a. free (effective 2009). adv. bk.rev. **Document type:** *Directory, Trade.* **Description:** Acts as a resource book for the entertainment industry, containing over 30,000 entries in 250 categories. Geared to help the user with the production of a film, TV or video project from start to finish.
Former titles (until 200?): Blu-Book Production Directory (Print) (1930-6520); (until 2004): Blu-Book Film, T V & Commercial Production Directory; (until 1999): Blu-Book Film & T V Production Directory; (until 1996): Blu-Book Film, T V & Video Production Directory; (until 1995): Blu-Book Directory; (until 1989): Hollywood Reporter Studio Blu-Book Directory (0278-419X); (until 19??): Studio Blu-Book Directory; (until 1978): Hollywood Studio Blu-Book Motion Picture, Television, Radio Directory
Published by: Nielsen Business Publications (Subsidiary of: Nielsen Business Media, Inc.), 770 Broadway, New York, NY 10003. TEL 646-654-4500, FAX 646-654-4948, bmcomm@nielsen.com, http://www.nielsenbusinessmedia.com. Ed., Pub. Robert Dowling. R&P Debbie Lockhart. Circ: 7,000.

BOLERO; Das Schweizer Magazin fuer Mode, Beauty, Lifestyle. *see* CLOTHING TRADE—Fashions

778.53 ESP ISSN 1136-8144
BOLETIN ACADEMIA; noticias del cine espanol. Text in Spanish. 1995. m. **Document type:** *Bulletin, Trade.*
Related titles: Online - full text ed.
Published by: Academia de las Artes y las Ciencias Cinematograficas de Espana, C Zurbano, Madrid, 28010, Spain. TEL 34-91-5934648, FAX 34-91-5931492, academia@academiadecine.com, http://www.academiadecine.com. Ed. Atocha Aguinada.

791.43 MUS ISSN 1694-0261
BOLLYWOOD NEWS. Text in French. 2005. m. EUR 2.50 newsstand/cover (effective 2006). **Document type:** *Magazine, Consumer.*
Published by: Bartholdi Ltd., 24a, D'Epinay Ave, Quatre Bornes, Mauritius. TEL 230-586-4507, FAX 230-698-5470, info@bartholdi.intnet.mu, http://bartholdi.intnet.mu.

BOMB; interviews with artists, writers, musicians, directors and actors. *see* ART

791.43 USA
THE BOOK L A. Text in English. 1988. s-a. USD 16.80 (effective 2006). 128 p./no. 2 cols./p.; **Document type:** *Magazine, Consumer.*
Published by: Reel Communication, 844 S Robertson, Los Angeles, CA 90035. TEL 310-659-0122, FAX 310-652-7114. Ed., Pub. Patrick Kahn. Circ: 30,000.

791.43 ITA
BOXOFFICE. Text in Italian. 200?. fortn. (16/yr.). EUR 25 (effective 2009). **Document type:** *Magazine, Consumer.*
Published by: Editoriale Duesse SpA, Via Donatello 5b, Milan, 20131, Italy. TEL 39-02-277961, FAX 39-02-27796300, e-duesse@e-duesse.it, http://www.e-duesse.it.

791.43 USA ISSN 0006-8527
PN1993
BOXOFFICE. Text in English. 1920. m. USD 59.95 domestic; USD 74.95 in Canada & Mexico; USD 135 elsewhere (effective 2010). adv. bk.rev.; film rev.; Website rev. charts; illus.; stat. back issues avail.; reprints avail. **Document type:** *Magazine, Trade.* **Description:** Features exclusive interviews, reviews and up coming attractions covering the business of movies.
Related titles: Online - full text ed.
Indexed: A10, A15, ABIn, F01, F02, IBT&D, IIPA, P48, P51, PQC, T02, V03.
—Ingenta.
Published by: (National Association of Theatre Owners), Media Enterprises, 9107 Wilshire Blvd, Ste 450, Beverly Hills, CA 90210. TEL 310-876-9090, 800-877-5207.

BRAVO. *see* CHILDREN AND YOUTH—For

BRAVO. *see* CHILDREN AND YOUTH—For

BRAVO. *see* CHILDREN AND YOUTH—For

BRAVO. *see* CHILDREN AND YOUTH—For

BRAVO. *see* MUSIC

791.542 DEU ISSN 0406-9595
BRAVO. Text in German. 1956. w. EUR 72.80; EUR 1.40 newsstand/cover (effective 2010). adv. film rev. illus. **Document type:** *Magazine, Consumer.* **Description:** Focuses on pop music, films and television.
Indexed: CMPI, RASB.
Published by: Heinrich Bauer Smaragd KG (Subsidiary of: Bauer Media Group), Charles-de-Gaulle-Str 8, Munich, 81737, Germany. TEL 49-89-67860, FAX 49-89-6702033, kommunikation@hbv.de, http://www.hbv.de. Ed. Alexandra Schnarrenberger. Adv. contact Arne Sill. page EUR 40,821; trim 194 x 262. Circ: 555,934 (paid). **Dist. in U.S. by:** G L P International Inc., 153 S Dean St, Englewood, NJ 07631-3513. TEL 201-871-0870, 201-871-1010, subscribe@glpnews.com.

BRAVO GIRL!. *see* CHILDREN AND YOUTH—For

BRAVO GIRL!. *see* CHILDREN AND YOUTH—For

BRAZEN HUSSIES. *see* LEISURE AND RECREATION

791.43 FRA ISSN 0759-6898
BREF; le magazine du court metrage. Text in French. 1983. 5/yr. EUR 35 domestic to individuals; EUR 25 domestic to students; EUR 47 foreign to individuals (effective 2008). adv. illus. reprints avail. **Document type:** *Magazine, Trade.*
Indexed: F01, F02, IIFP.
Published by: Agence du Court Metrage, 2 rue de Tocqueville, Paris, 75017, France. TEL 33-1-43800300, FAX 33-1-42675971. Ed. Jacques Kermalon. Pub. Philippe Pilard.

778.53 USA
PN1993
BRIGHT LIGHTS (ONLINE); film journal. Abbreviated title: B L F J. Text in English. 1974-1980; resumed 1993. q. free (effective 2011). adv. bk.rev.; film rev. illus. back issues avail. **Document type:** *Journal, Consumer.* **Description:** Covers marginal cinema (women's films, ethnic, independent, fringe, exploitation, pornography, etc.), emphasizing queer film including profiles of film stars and directors, documentation from the studio era, studies of film themes and related news.
Formerly (until 1995): Bright Lights (Print) (0147-4049)
Media: Online - full text.
Indexed: CA, F01, F02, IIFP, IITV, MRD, T02.
Published by: Bright Lights, PO Box 420987, San Francisco, CA 94142-0987. TEL 510-601-5530, brightlightswriters@gmail.com. Ed., Pub., Adv. contact Gary Morris.

BRITISH CINEMATOGRAPHER. *see* PHOTOGRAPHY

791.43 GBR
BRITISH POPULAR CINEMA. Text in English. 1999. irreg., latest 2006. USD 35.95 per issue (effective 2009). **Document type:** *Monographic series, Consumer.* **Description:** Explores the history of British cinema.
Published by: Routledge (Subsidiary of: Taylor & Francis Group), 4 Park Square, Milton Park, Abingdon, Oxon OX14 4RN, United Kingdom. http://www.routledge.com/journals/. **Dist. by:** Taylor & Francis Ltd.

BROADCASTAWAY. *see* COMMUNICATIONS—Television And Cable

BULAWAYO THIS MONTH. *see* TRAVEL AND TOURISM

THE BULLET (NASHVILLE). *see* COMMUNICATIONS—Television And Cable

778.53 GBR ISSN 1474-094X
BUSINESS RATIO REPORT. THE FILM AND TELEVISION INDUSTRY. Text in English. 1986. a., latest no.23, 2008, May. GBP 365 per issue (effective 2010). charts; stat. back issues avail. **Document type:** *Report, Trade.* **Description:** Covers companies active in the film and television industry.
Former titles (until 2001): Business Ratio. The Film and Television Industry (1470-7063); (until 2000): Business Ratio Plus: The Film & TV Industry (1357-9010); (until 1994): Business Ratio Report: Film and Television Producers, Distributors (0269-641X)
Published by: Key Note Ltd. (Subsidiary of: Bonnier Business Information), Harlequin House, 5th Fl, 7 High St, Teddington, Richmond upon Thames, TW11 8EE, United Kingdom. TEL 44-845-5040452, FAX 44-845-5040453, sales@keynote.co.uk.

791.43 CAN ISSN 1719-9883
C F E NEWSLETTER. (Canadian Film Editors) Text in English. m. **Document type:** *Newsletter, Trade.*
Published by: Canadian Film Editors Guild, 47-3 Church St, Toronto, ON M5E 1M2, Canada.

791.43 FRA ISSN 0256-1336
C I C A E BULLETIN D'INFORMATION. Text in French. 1965. irreg. **Document type:** *Bulletin, Consumer.*
Published by: Confederation Internationale des Cinemas d'Art et d'Essai (C I C A E)/International Art Cinemas Confederation, 12 Rue de Vauvenargues, Paris, 75018, France. TEL 33-1-56331320, cicae@art-et-essai.org. Ed. Jean Lescure. Circ: 1,000.

791.43 CAN ISSN 1719-9891
C I F E J INFO. (Centre International du Film pour l'Enfance et la Jeunesse) Text in English, French. 10/yr. **Document type:** *Newsletter, Consumer.*
Published by: Centre International du Film pour l'Enfance et la Jeunesse/International Centre of Film for Children and Young People, 3774, Saint-Denis, ste 200, Montreal, PQ H2W 2M1, Canada. TEL 514-284-9388, FAX 514-284-0168, info@cifej.com, http://www.cifej.com.

C I L E C T NEWS. *see* COMMUNICATIONS—Television And Cable

791.43 USA ISSN 2158-8724
▼➤ **C I N E J.** Variant title: Cinema e-Journal. Text in English. 2011. 2/yr. free (effective 2011). bk.rev. abstr.; bibl.; stat. Index. back issues avail. **Document type:** *Journal, Academic/Scholarly.* **Description:** Committed to publishing fresh and original research in the fields of film and media studies.
Media: Online - full text.
Published by: EMAJ Publishing LLC, 2885 Sanford Ave, SW, Ste 15320, Grandville, MI 49418. TEL 202-288-4453, vakman@emaj.org, http://www.emaj.org. Ed. Cevdet Kizil. R&P Vedat Akman.

778.53 FRA ISSN 1952-3866
C N C. DOSSIER. Cover title: Informations C N C. Text in French. 1947. 6/yr. bk.rev. charts; illus.; stat. index. **Document type:** *Bulletin.*
Former titles (until 2005): C N C Info (1151-0358); (until 1989): Centre National de la Cinematographie. Informations (0397-8435); Which incorporated (1954-198?): Centre National de la Cinematographie. Statistiques (0427-1432); Which was formerly (until 1976): Centre National de la Cinematographie. Bulletin d'Information (0008-9834); (until 1953): Centre National de la Cinematographie. Bulletin (0997-4199)
Related titles: ◆ English ed.: C N C Info (English Edition). ISSN 1246-8312; ◆ Special ed(s).: C N C Info (Special Edition); ◆ Supplement(s): Centre National de la Cinematographie. Statistiques. ISSN 0427-1432.
Published by: Centre National de la Cinematographie, 12 rue de Lubeck, Paris, Cedex 16 75784, France. TEL 33-1-44343440, http://www.cnc.fr/. Ed. Marc Tessier. Circ: 10,000.

778.53 FRA ISSN 1246-8312
C N C INFO (ENGLISH EDITION). (Centre National de la Cinematographie) Text in English. 1994. irreg.
Related titles: ◆ French ed.: C N C. Dossier. ISSN 1952-3866.
Published by: Centre National de la Cinematographie, 12 rue de Lubeck, Paris, Cedex 16 75784, France. TEL 33-1-44343440, http://www.cnc.fr/. Ed. Marc Tessier.

791.43 CAN ISSN 1202-5879
C S C NEWS. Text in English. 1979. m. CAD 95 (effective 2005). **Document type:** *Magazine, Trade.*
Former titles (until 1992): Canadian Society of Cinematographers. News (0820-3431); (until 1986): Canadian Society of Cinematographers. Newsletter (0229-5989)
Published by: Canadian Society of Cinematographers, 131-3007 Kingston Rd, Toronto, ON M1M 1P1, Canada. TEL 416-266-0591, FAX 416-266-3996, editor@csc.ca.

791.43 USA
C-VILLE WEEKLY. Text in English. 1989. w. (Tue.). free. **Document type:** *Newspaper.*
Published by: William Chapman, 308 E Main St, Charlottesville, VA 22902. TEL 434-817-2749, FAX 434-817-2758. Ed. Cathryn Harding. Pub. Frank Dubec. Circ: 22,000 (free).

778.53 FRA ISSN 0764-8499
PN1993
LES CAHIERS DE LA CINEMATHEQUE. Text in French. 1970. irreg. (1-2/yr). adv. bk.rev.; film rev. illus. **Document type:** *Magazine, Consumer.*
Related titles: Supplement(s): Cahiers de la Cinematheque. Collection. ISSN 0764-8510. 1985.
Indexed: F01, F02, IIFP, IIPA, IITV, MLA-IB.
—IE.
Published by: Institut Jean Vigo de Perpignan, 1 Rue Jean Vielledent, Perpignan, 66000, France. TEL 33-4-68340939, FAX 33-4-68354120.

791.43 FRA ISSN 0008-011X
PN1993
LES CAHIERS DU CINEMA. Text in French. 1951. m. EUR 44.90 domestic (effective 2009); EUR 53 foreign (effective 2003). adv. bk.rev.; film rev. illus. reprints avail. **Document type:** *Magazine, Consumer.*
Related titles: Microfiche ed.; ◆ Spanish ed.: Cahiers du Cinema Espana. ISSN 1887-7494; Supplement(s): Les Cahiers du Cinema. Essais. 1982.
Indexed: A07, A22, A30, A31, AA, ArtInd, B04, BrHumI, F01, F02, IIFP, IIPA, IITV, MLA-IB, PCI, PdeR, RASB, T02.
—BLDSC (2948.800000), IE, Infotrieve, Ingenta. **CCC.**
Published by: Editions de l' Etoile, 9 passage de la Boule Blanche, Paris, 75012, France. TEL 33-1-53447575, FAX 33-1-43439504. Ed., Pub. Serge Toubiana. Circ: 80,000.

791.43 ESP ISSN 1887-7494
PN1993
CAHIERS DU CINEMA ESPANA. Text in Spanish. 2007. m. EUR 40 (effective 2009). **Document type:** *Magazine, Consumer.*
Related titles: ◆ French ed.: Les Cahiers du Cinema. ISSN 0008-011X.
Published by: Caiman Ediciones, Calle Soria 9, 4o, Madrid, 28005, Spain. TEL 34-91-4685835, FAX 34-91-5273329, cahiersducinema@caimanediciones.es, http://www.caimanediciones.es.

CALIFORNIA POINTS AND AUTHORITIES. *see* LAW

CALLSHEET!. *see* COMMUNICATIONS—Television And Cable

791.43 ESP ISSN 1886-9858
▼ **CAMARA LENTA**; revista de cine y otros audiovisuales. Text in Spanish. 2009. s-a. EUR 12 (effective 2009). **Document type:** *Magazine, Consumer.*
Published by: Revista Camara Lenta, Calle Urbion 20, 1oD, Seville, 41005, Spain.

808.066791 GBR
CAMBRIDGE FILM CLASSICS. Text in English. 1993. irreg., latest 2004. price varies. back issues avail.; reprints avail. **Document type:** *Monographic series, Academic/Scholarly.*
Published by: Cambridge University Press, The Edinburgh Bldg, Shaftesbury Rd, Cambridge, CB2 8RU, United Kingdom. TEL 44-1223-312393, FAX 44-1223-315052, journals@cambridge.org, http://www.cambridge.org/uk.

791.43 GBR
CAMBRIDGE STUDIES IN FILM. Text in English. 1990. irreg. price varies. adv. back issues avail.; reprints avail. **Document type:** *Monographic series, Academic/Scholarly.* **Description:** Provides scholarly studies of high intellectual standard on the history and criticism of film.
Published by: Cambridge University Press, The Edinburgh Bldg, Shaftesbury Rd, Cambridge, CB2 8RU, United Kingdom. TEL 44-1223-312393, FAX 44-1223-315052, journals@cambridge.org, http://www.cambridge.org/uk. Eds. Dudley Andrew, William Rothman. Adv. contact Rebecca Roberts TEL 44-1223-325083.

791.436 USA ISSN 0270-5346
PN1995.9.W6
➤ **CAMERA OBSCURA**; feminism, culture, and media studies. Text in English. 1976. 3/yr. USD 30 to individuals; USD 155 to institutions; USD 164 combined subscription to institutions (print & online eds.); USD 52 per issue to institutions (effective 2012). adv. bk.rev.; film rev. bibl.; charts; illus. back issues avail.; reprint service avail. from PSC. **Document type:** *Journal, Academic/Scholarly.* **Description:** Provides innovative feminist perspectives on film, television, and visual media.
Related titles: Microform ed.; Online - full text ed.: ISSN 1529-1510. 2000. USD 137 to institutions (effective 2012).
Indexed: A01, A03, A07, A08, A20, A22, A26, A30, A31, AA, ABM, ASCA, AltPI, AmHI, ArtHuCI, ArtInd, B04, BAS, BrHumI, CA, CWI, CurCont, DIP, E01, E08, F01, F02, FemPer, G06, G07, G08, G10, GW, H07, H14, I05, IBR, IBT&D, IBZ, IIFP, IIPA, IITV, MLA-IB, MRD, P10, P48, P53, P54, PCI, PQC, RILM, S09, S21, SCOPUS, T02, W07, W09.
—BLDSC (3016.149800), CIS, IE, Infotrieve, Ingenta. **CCC.**
Published by: (Department of Film and Media Studies), Duke University Press, 905 W Main St, Ste 18 B, Durham, NC 27701. TEL 919-688-5134, 888-651-0122, FAX 919-688-2615, 888-651-0124, subscriptions@dukeupress.edu, http://www.dukeupress.edu.

➤ **CAMPUS CIRCLE.** *see* MUSIC

➤ **CANADIAN COUNCIL FOR THE ARTS. ANNUAL REPORT/CONSEIL DES ARTS DU CANADA. RAPPORT ANNUEL.** *see* ART

791.43 CAN ISSN 1713-6083
CANADIAN FILM ENCYCLOPEDIA. Text in English. 2003. irreg. **Document type:** *Guide, Consumer.*
Media: Online - full text.
Published by: Film Reference Library, 2 Carlton St, East Mezzanine, Toronto, ON M5B 1J3, Canada. TEL 416-967-1517, FAX 416-967-0628, libraryservices@torfilmfest.ca, http://www.filmreferencelibrary.ca/index.asp.

791.43 CAN ISSN 0705-548X
CANADIAN FILM SERIES. Text in English. 1976. irreg., latest vol.6, 1981. price varies.
Published by: Canadian Film Institute, 2 Daly, Ottawa, ON K1N 6E2, Canada. TEL 613-232-6727, FAX 613-232-6315.

M

778.53 384.55 384.558 CAN ISSN 0847-5911
PN1993.5.A1
➤ **CANADIAN JOURNAL OF FILM STUDIES/REVUE CANADIENNE D'ETUDES CINEMATOGRAPHIQUES.** Text in English, French. 1990. s-a. CAD 35 domestic to individuals; USD 35 foreign to individuals; CAD 45 domestic to institutions; USD 45 foreign to institutions (effective 2010). bk.rev. illus.; abstr. 120 p./no. 1 cols./p.; back issues avail.; reprints avail. **Document type:** *Journal, Academic/Scholarly.* **Description:** Publishes articles on history, theory and criticism of film and television.
Related titles: Online - full text ed.
Indexed: A07, A20, A27, A30, A31, AA, ArtHuCI, ArtInd, B04, C03, CA, CBCARef, F01, F02, IBT&D, IIFP, IIPA, IITV, MLA-IB, MRD, P10, P48, P53, P54, PQC, T02, W03, W05, W07.
—CCC.
Published by: Film Studies Association of Canada, Department of Art History and Communication Studies, McGill University, Arts Building W225, 853 Sherbrooke St W, Montreal, PQ H3A 2T6, Canada. http://www.film.queensu.ca/FSAC/CJFS.html.

➤ **CANAL +.** *see* COMMUNICATIONS—Television And Cable

778.53 ZAF
THE CAPE OF FILMS; moviemaking in one of the most beautiful locations in the world. Text in English. 1995. a. illus.; maps. **Description:** Covers filmmaking in Cape Town and surrounding areas.
Published by: Cape Film Office, PO Box 16597, Vlaeberg, Cape Town 8018, South Africa. TEL 27-21-480-3158, FAX 27-21-480-3130.

CARLTON COMMUNICATIONS PLC. ANNUAL REPORT AND ACCOUNTS. *see* COMMUNICATIONS—Television And Cable

791.43 USA
CASHIERS DU CINEMART. Text in English. 1994. irreg. USD 5 per issue (effective 2003). **Document type:** *Bulletin.* **Description:** Film zine with reviews and quirky interviews.
Related titles: Online - full text ed.
Address: PO Box 2401, Riverview, MI 48192. FAX 801-881-0137. Ed. Mike White. Circ: 6,000.

791.43 USA
CASTER. Text in English. 1991. 3/yr. USD 19.95 (effective 2000). adv. dance rev.; film rev.; music rev.; play rev.; tel.rev.; video rev. illus.; stat.; tr.lit. 108 p./no.; back issues avail. **Document type:** *Directory, Trade.* **Description:** Comprehensive listing of Hollywood's casting directors, studio breakdowns, show assignments, astrological signs; and informative articles on how to succeed in motion pictures and television.
Former titles: Astro Caster; Taaffe O'Connell's Astro Caster (1065-7533)
Related titles: Series of: The Industry's Edge Series.
Published by: Canoco Publishing, 11611 Chenault St, Ste 118, Los Angeles, CA 90049. TEL 310-471-2287, FAX 310-471-1944. Ed., R&P Taaffe O'Connell. Adv. contact Susan Moore. B&W page USD 900; 4.5 x 7.5. Circ: 100,000.

053.1 CHE ISSN 1661-1799
CELEBRITY. Text in German. 2003. m. CHF 53, EUR 26.50; EUR 2.60 newsstand/cover (effective 2006). adv. **Document type:** *Magazine, Consumer.*
Published by: Marquard Media AG, Baarerstr 22, Zug, 6300, Switzerland. TEL 41-41-7252020, FAX 41-41-7252025, http://www.marquard-media.com. Ed. Klaus Dahm. Pub. Juerg Marquard. Adv. contact Ulrike Geisert. B&W page EUR 14,100, color page EUR 15,600. Circ: 198,864 (paid and controlled).

CERBERUS; het magazine voor science fiction, fantastiek & griezel. *see* LITERATURE—Science Fiction, Fantasy, Horror

791.43 IND
CHANDRIKA DAILY. Text in English, Malayalam. 1935. d. adv. 8 cols./p.; back issues avail. **Document type:** *Newspaper, Consumer.*
Published by: Muslim Printing & Publishing Co. Ltd., Y.M.C.A. Rd. No. 64, Calicut, Kerala 673 001, India. TEL 91-495-765122, FAX 91-495-765950.

778.53 CHN
CHINESE FILM MARKET. Text in Chinese. m. **Description:** Covers film marketing, film production trends, film distribution and more.
Published by: Chinese Film Market Press, 25 Xinwai Dajie, Beijing, 100088, China. TEL 86-10-225-4488, FAX 86-10-225-1044.

791.43 IND
CHITRABHUMI. Text in Malayalam. 1982. w. INR 500 domestic; INR 871 foreign; INR 12 per issue (effective 2011). **Document type:** *Magazine, Consumer.* **Description:** Contains news and feature from the movie world.
Published by: Mathrubhumi Printing & Publishing Co. Ltd., M J Krishnamohan Memorial Bldg, K P Kesavamenon Rd, P O Box 46, Kozhikode, Kerala 673 001, India. TEL 91-495-2366655, FAX 91-495-2368333, mbiclt@mpp.co.in. Ed. K K Sreedharan Nair.

791.4375 DEU
CHOICES; kino kultur koeln. Text in German. m. adv. **Document type:** *Magazine, Consumer.*
Related titles: Online - full text ed.
Published by: Berndt Media, Dr-C-Otto-Str 196, Bochum, 44879, Germany. TEL 49-234-941910, FAX 49-234-9419191, info@berndt-media.de, http://www.berndt-media.de. Eds. Linda Hoemberg, Ulrike Baumbach. Pub. Joachim Berndt. adv.: B&W page EUR 2,200, color page EUR 3,000; trim 210 x 285. Circ: 52,490 (controlled).

791.43 ITA ISSN 1121-1784
CIAK; mensile di attualita cinematografica. Text in Italian. 1985. m. EUR 25.70 (effective 2009). adv. back issues avail. **Document type:** *Magazine, Consumer.* **Description:** Covers current events in the film industry. Includes reviews of new releases and special features on topics such as special effects, costumes and directors.
Formerly (until 1995): Ciak Si Gira (1122-8040)
Published by: Arnoldo Mondadori Editore SpA, Via Mondadori 1, Segrate, 20090, Italy. TEL 39-02-66814363, FAX 39-030-3198412, infolibri@mondadori.it, http://www.mondadori.com. Ed. Piera Detassis. Circ: 70,224 (paid).

793 FRA ISSN 0153-8519
CINE 9,5 REVUE. Text in French. 1971. m. **Document type:** *Magazine, Consumer.*
Formerly (until 1975): Cine Club 9,5 de France. Bulletin Mensuel (0153-856X)
Published by: Cine Club 9,5 de France, 22 rue de la Belle Feuille, Boulogne, 92100, France. cine9.5mm@caramail.com, http://cine95.freeservers.com/fr.htm.

791.43 MEX ISSN 1563-7611
CINE ALTERNATIVO. Text in Spanish. d. adv. **Document type:** *Newsletter.*
Media: Online - full text. **Related titles:** E-mail ed.
Published by: Inter Planeta Editorial, SERAFIN OLARTE 54, Xol Independencia, Mexico City, DF 03630, Mexico. TEL 52-5-5394142, ventas@alternativo.net, editor@alternativo.com. Eds. Carlos Bazan, Jose Manuel Saucedo.

778.53 IND ISSN 0971-9970
CINE BLITZ. Text in English. 1974. m. INR 40 per issue (effective 2011). film rev. **Document type:** *Magazine, Consumer.*
Published by: Rifa Publication Pvt. Ltd., Masjid Moth, New Delhi, 110 049, India. TEL 91-11-26255506.

778.53 CAN ISSN 0820-8921
PN1993.5C38C485
CINE-BULLES. Text in English. 1982. q. CAD 22.95; CAD 40 foreign (effective 1999). adv. bk.rev. **Document type:** *Magazine, Academic/Scholarly.*
Indexed: F01, F02, IIFP, IITV.
Published by: Association des Cinemas Paralleles du Quebec, 4545 Ave Pierre de Coubertin, Case Postale 1000, Succ M, Montreal, PQ H1V 3R2, Canada. TEL 514-252-3021, FAX 514-251-8038. Ed. Jean-Philippe Gravel. Adv. contact Martine Mauroy. Circ: 1,500.

791.43 CUB ISSN 0009-6946
CINE CUBANO. Text in Spanish. 1960. q. CUP 12; USD 10 in North America; USD 12 in South America; USD 17 in Europe.
Related titles: Online - full text ed.: Revista Cine Cubano. ISSN 1607-6370.
Indexed: F01, F02, IIFP, IITV, RASB.
Published by: Instituto Cubano del Arte e Industria Cinematograficos (I C A I C), Dpto. Publicaciones, Calle 23, No.1115, Apdo. 55, Havana, Cuba. Ed. Gloria Villazon Hernandez. Circ: 20,000. **Dist. by:** Ediciones Cubanas, Obispo 527, Havana, Cuba.

791.43 ARG ISSN 1852-4699
▼ **CINE DOCUMENTAL.** Text in Spanish. 2009. s-a. **Document type:** *Magazine, Consumer.*
Media: Online - full text.
Address: Venezuela, 3318, Buenos Aires, C1211AAL, Argentina. revista@cinedocumental.com.ar, http://www.revistacinedocumental.com.ar. Ed. Javier Campo.

791.43 FRA ISSN 1962-2996
CINE FAN. Text in French. 2008. q. EUR 4.90 newsstand/cover. **Document type:** *Magazine, Consumer.*
Published by: Paperbox, 24 Av. Pierre-et-Marie-Curie, Le Blanc-Mesnil, 93150, France.

791.43 BEL ISSN 0773-2279
CINE-FICHES DE GRAND ANGLE. Text in French. 1972. m. EUR 38 domestic; EUR 58 foreign (effective 2002). adv. bk.rev.; film rev.; music rev.; video rev. illus. index. **Document type:** *Magazine.*
Formerly: Grand Angle; Incorporates (in 1983): Cinemaniac (0770-1640)
Indexed: F01, F02.
Published by: (Centre de Documentation Cinematographie), A.S.B.L. Grand Angle-Opvac, Rue d'Arschot 29, Mariembourg, 5660, Belgium. TEL 32-60-312168, FAX 32-60-312937. Ed., Pub., R&P, Adv. contact Jacques Noel. Circ: 4,500.

CINE NEWS. *see* PHOTOGRAPHY

791.43 VEN
PN1993
CINE-OJA. Text in Spanish. 1967. 4/yr. USD 15. adv. bk.rev.; film rev. illus. **Description:** Includes essays on the economic and cultural development of the Venezuelan and Latinamerican cinema.
Formerly (until no.25, 1984): Cine al Dia (0009-692X)
Related titles: Microform ed.: (from PQC).
Indexed: IIFP, IITV.
Published by: Sociedad Civil Cine al Dia, Sabana Grande, Apdo 50446, Caracas, DF 1050, Venezuela. Ed. Alfredo Roffe. Circ: 2,500 (controlled).

791 ESP ISSN 0302-8828
CINE PARA LEER. Text in Spanish. 1972. a. **Document type:** *Magazine, Consumer.*
Published by: Ediciones Mensajero, Sancho de Azpeitia 2, Bajo, Bilbao, 48014, Spain. TEL 34-94-4470358, FAX 34-94-4472630, mensajero@mensajero.com, http://www.mensajero.com. Ed. Angel Antonio Perez-Gomez.

791.43 MEX
CINE PREMIERE. Text in Spanish. m. adv. **Document type:** *Magazine, Consumer.*
Published by: Grupo Editorial Premiere, Horacio no 804, Colonia Polanco, Mexico DF, 11550, Mexico. TEL 52-55-11011300, FAX 52-55-55528051, reginasb@gepremiere.com, http://www.gepremiere.com.

CINE TELE REVUE. *see* COMMUNICATIONS—Television And Cable

791.43 305.86 USA ISSN 1941-2622
CINE Y ...; revista de estudios interdisciplinarios sobre cine en espanol. Text mainly in English; Text occasionally in Spanish. 2008. 2/yr. USD 30 to individuals; USD 60 to institutions (effective 2009). **Document type:** *Journal, Academic/Scholarly.*
Published by: Texas A & M University, Department of Hispanic Studies, 219 Academic Bldg, College Station, TX 77843. Eds. Miguel Angel Zarate, Richard Curry.

778.53 CAN ISSN 0826-9866
PN1993
CINEACTION!. Text in English. 1985. 3/yr. USD 21 in North America to individuals; USD 40 in North America to institutions (effective 2010). bk.rev. illus. Index. back issues avail.; reprints avail. **Document type:** *Journal, Academic/Scholarly.* **Description:** Features essays and reviews by film critics and scholars as well as covers a wide range of filmmaking-classic and contemporary popular film, third world cinema, political documentary and experimental film and video.
Related titles: Online - full text ed.
Indexed: A26, C03, CBCARef, CPerI, E08, F01, F02, G06, G07, G08, I05, I07, IIFP, IIPA, IITV, MLA-IB, MRD, P48, PQC, S07, S09, S23, T02.
—BLDSC (3198.635705), IE, Ingenta. **CCC.**
Address: 40 Alexander St, Ste 705, Toronto, ON M4Y 1B5, Canada. TEL 416-964-3534.

791.43 USA ISSN 0009-7004
PN1993 CODEN: JECIAR
CINEASTE; America's leading magazine on the art and politics of the cinema. Text in English. 1967. q. USD 20 domestic to individuals; USD 27 in Canada & Mexico to individuals; USD 30 elsewhere to individuals; USD 36 domestic to institutions; USD 50 in Canada & Mexico to institutions; USD 55 elsewhere to institutions (effective 2010). adv. bk.rev.; film rev. illus. index. 80 p./no.; back issues avail.; reprints avail. **Document type:** *Magazine, Consumer.* **Description:** Features contributions from many of America's articulate and outspoken writers, critics, and scholars. Focuses on both the art and politics of the cinema.
Related titles: Microform ed.: (from PQC); Online - full text ed.
Indexed: A01, A02, A03, A07, A08, A09, A10, A11, A20, A22, A25, A26, A27, A30, A31, AA, ABS&EES, ASCA, AltPI, ArtHuCI, ArtInd, B04, BRD, C05, C12, CA,.CPerI, Chicano, CurCont, DIP, E08, F01, F02, G06, G07, G08, I05, I07, IBR, IBT&D, IBZ, IIFP, IIPA, IITV, LeftInd, M01, M02, M06, MASUSE, MLA, MLA-IB, MRD, P02, P10, P13, P48, P53, P54, PCI, PQC, RASB, S07, S08, S09, S23, SCOPUS, SociolAb, T02, U01, V02, V03, V04, W03, W05, W07, WBA, WMB.
—BLDSC (3198.635800), IE, Ingenta. **CCC.**
Published by: Cineaste Publishers, Inc., 243 Fifth Ave, Ste 706, New York, NY 10016. TEL 212-366-5720. Eds. Rahul Hamid, Gary Crowdus. Adv. contact Barbara Saltz TEL 413-230-3488. B&W page USD 500, color page USD 750; 7.25 x 9.875. **Subscr. to:** PO Box 2242, New York, NY 10009.

791.43 GBR ISSN 0957-6290
CINEBLITZ INTERNATIONAL; Asian film sensation. Text in English. 1989. m. GBP 24; GBP 36 in Europe; GBP 48 elsewhere; GBP 2 newsstand/cover; USD 4 newsstand/cover in United States. adv. film rev. back issues avail. **Document type:** *Magazine, Consumer.*
Indexed: F01, F02.
Published by: Cine Asia Publications Ltd., Dolphin Media, Gkp House Spring Villa Park, Spring Villa Rd, Edgware, Mddx HA8 7EB, United Kingdom. TEL 44-181-3811166, FAX 44-181-3811177. Ed. Rita Karl Mehta. Pub. Rajesh Mehra. Adv. contact Arvind Sikand. B&W page GBP 1,000, color page GBP 1,400; trim 220 x 285. Circ: 30,800 (paid). **Dist. by:** Comag, Tavistock Rd, W Drayton, Middlesex UB7 7QE, United Kingdom. TEL 44-1895-444055, FAX 44-1895-433602.

778.53 CHE ISSN 1018-2098
CINEBULLETIN; Zeitschrift der schweizerischen Filmbranche. Text in French, German. 1975. m. CHF 55; CHF 70 foreign (effective 1999). adv. **Document type:** *Bulletin.*
Indexed: F01, F02.
Published by: Schweizerisches Filmzentrum, Neugasse 6, Postfach, Zuerich, 8031, Switzerland. TEL 41-1-2725330, FAX 41-1-2725350. Adv. contact Annemarie Schoch Huber. B&W page CHF 900; trim 278 x 186. Circ: 2,800.

791.4375 DEU
CINECHART. Text in German. 1997. q. adv. **Document type:** *Magazine, Consumer.*
Published by: ProSieben Sat 1 Media AG, Medienallee 7, Unterfoehring, 85774, Germany. TEL 49-89-950710, FAX 49-89-95078429, info@prosieben.de, http://www.pro7.com. adv.: color page EUR 1,300. Circ: 10,000 (controlled).

778.53 ITA ISSN 1827-1952
CINECORRIERE. Text in Italian. 1948. m. adv. **Document type:** *Magazine, Consumer.*
Published by: Giroal Srl, Piazza Verdi 8, Rome, 00198, Italy. TEL 39-06-8841611, FAX 39-06-85831141, info@giroal.it, http://www.giroal.it.

778.53 PRT
CINEDOCFILME. Text in Portuguese. 1951. 12/yr. film rev. reprints avail. **Document type:** *Bulletin.* **Description:** Synopses and analyses of all films released in Portugal.
Formerly (until 1998): B C - Boletim Cinematografico
Related titles: Online - full text ed.
Address: Rua Candido des Reis, 114-3o, Oeiras, 2780-211, Portugal. TEL 351-21-4420701, FAX 351-21-4429781, cinedoc@vizzavi.pt, http://www.vizzavi.pt/cin. Ed. Francisco Perestrello. Circ: 1,000 (paid).

CINEFANTASTIQUE (ONLINE); the website with a sense of wonder. *see* LITERATURE—Science Fiction, Fantasy, Horror

791.43 USA ISSN 0198-1056
TR858
CINEFEX. Text in English. 1980. q. USD 36 combined subscription domestic (print & online eds.); USD 48 combined subscription in Canada & Mexico (print & online eds.); USD 52 combined subscription elsewhere (print & online eds.); USD 12.50 per issue domestic (effective 2010). adv. bk.rev. illus. back issues avail.; reprints avail. **Document type:** *Magazine, Consumer.* **Description:** Features articles devoted to motion picture visual effects.
Related titles: Online - full text ed.: USD 30 (effective 2010).
Indexed: F01, F02, IBT&D, IIFP, IIPA, IITV, MRD, T02.
—Ingenta.
Address: PO Box 20027, Riverside, CA 92516. TEL 951-781-1917, 800-434-3339, FAX 951-781-1793. adv.: B&W page USD 4,250, color page USD 5,350; trim 9 x 8.

778.53 ITA ISSN 0009-7039
PN1993
CINEFORUM; rivista di cultura cinematografica. Text in Italian. 1961. m. (10/yr.). EUR 57 domestic; EUR 70 foreign (effective 2009). bk.rev.; film rev. index. **Document type:** *Magazine, Consumer.*
Indexed: A20, ASCA, ArtHuCI, CurCont, F01, F02, IIFP, IIPA, IITV, RASB, SCOPUS, T02, W07.
Published by: Federazione Italiana dei Cineforum, Via G Reich 49, Torre Boldone, BG 24020, Italy. TEL 39-035-361361, FAX 39-035-341255, info@cineforum.it, http://www.alasca.it/cineforum/. Circ: 5,000.

791.43 ESP ISSN 0069-4134
CINEGUIA; anuario espanol del espectaculo y audiovisuales. Text in Spanish. 1960. a. adv. back issues avail. **Document type:** *Directory, Consumer.* **Description:** Provides over 8000 listings in the fields of cinematography, video and television, photography, advertising, production, theatre and the press.
Published by: F.M. Editores S.A., Mauricio Legendre, 16 4o. Ofic. 2429, Madrid, 28046, Spain. TEL 34-91-3235115, FAX 34-91-3231151, info@cineguia.es. Ed. Isabel Barbero. Circ: 5,500.

778.53 BGD
CINEMA. Text in Bengali. 1974. w. BDT 0.50 per issue.

Indexed: IITV.
Address: 81 Motijheel C A, Dhaka, 1000, Bangladesh. Ed. Sheikh Fazlur Rahman Maruf. Circ: 11,000.

778.53 DEU ISSN 1010-3627
PN1993
CINEMA. Text in German. 1951. a. CHF 28 (effective 2010). adv. bk.rev. illus. back issues avail. **Document type:** *Journal, Academic/ Scholarly.* **Description:** Covers the Swiss independent film scene.
Formerly (until 1961): Der Filmklub (1421-0843)
Indexed: DIP, F01, F02, IBR, IBZ, IIFP, IIPA, IITV, T02.
Published by: (Arbeitsgemeinschaft Cinema CHE), Schueren Verlag GmbH, Universitaetsstr 55, Marburg, 35037, Germany. TEL 49-6421-63084, FAX 49-6421-681190, info@schueren-verlag.de, http://www.schueren-verlag.de. Circ: 2,600.

791.43 UAE
CINEMA. Text in Arabic. 1988. q. per issue exchange basis. **Description:** Covers international film news and presents an overview of world film-making activity, and discusses the department's film series.
Published by: Cultural Foundation, Culture and Arts Department, P O Box 2380, Abu Dhabi, United Arab Emirates. TEL 215300, FAX 336059, TELEX 22414 CULCEN EM. Circ: 1,000.

791.43 DEU ISSN 0720-020X
CINEMA; Europas groesste Filmzeitschrift. Text in German. m. EUR 46.80; EUR 3.90 newsstand/cover (effective 2010). adv. **Document type:** *Magazine, Consumer.* **Description:** Covers all aspects of movies and the people making them.
Related titles: Online - full text ed.
Published by: Verlagsgruppe Milchstrasse (Subsidiary of: Hubert Burda Media Holding GmbH & Co. KG), Mittelweg 177, Hamburg, 22786, Germany. TEL 49-40-41311310, FAX 49-40-41312015, abo@milchstrasse.de, http://www.milchstrasse.de. Ed. Artur Jung. Pub. Andreas Mayer. Adv. contact Katherine Kreiner. Circ: 81,757 (paid).

791.43 HUN ISSN 1215-6043
CINEMA. Text in Hungarian. 1991. m. adv. **Document type:** *Magazine, Consumer.*
Related titles: Optical Disk - DVD ed.: ISSN 1589-5297. 2003.
Published by: Motor-Presse Budapest Lapkiado kft, Hajogyari-sziget 307, Budapest, 1033, Hungary. TEL 36-1-4369244, FAX 36-1-4369248, mpb@motorpresse.hu, http://www.motorpresse.hu.

791.43 CZE ISSN 1210-132X
CINEMA. Text in Czech. 1991. m. CZK 850 domestic; CZK 85 newsstand/ cover (effective 2006). adv. **Document type:** *Magazine, Consumer.*
Published by: Burda Praha spol. s.r.o., Premyslovska 2845/43, Prague 2, 13000, Czech Republic. TEL 420-2-21589111, FAX 420-2-21589368, burda@burda.cz, http://www.burda.cz. Adv. contact Gabriela Hudeckova. page CZK 130,000; trim 173 x 246. Circ: 35,000 (paid and controlled).

791.43 SWE ISSN 2000-348X
CINEMA. Text in Swedish. 2007. m. SEK 618 (effective 2010). adv. film rev. **Document type:** *Magazine, Consumer.*
Formerly (until 2009): Allt om Film (1654-4994); Which was formed by the merger of (2003-2006): Ingmar (1652-3024); (2005-2006): Stardust, Allt om Film (1653-3372); Which was formed by the merger of (2004-2005): Stardust (1652-960X); (2002-2005): Allt om DVD (1651-5307)
Published by: It is Media Svenska AB, Birger Jarlsgatan 20, Stockholm, 11434, Sweden. TEL 46-8-6679210, FAX 46-8-6679211, info@itsmedia.se, http://www.itsmedia.se.

778.53 PRT
CINEMA 15. Text in Portuguese. 12/yr.
Address: Rua Correia Teles, 22 2o, Lisbon, 1300, Portugal. TEL 68-78-80. Ed. Vittoriano Rosa.

791.43 ITA ISSN 2035-5270
CINEMA & CIE. Text in Multiple languages. 2001. a. **Document type:** *Magazine, Consumer.*
Related titles: Online - full text ed.: ISSN 2036-461X.
Published by: Carocci Editore, Via Sardegna 50, Rome, 00187, Italy. TEL 39-06-42818417, FAX 39-06-42747931, clienti@carocci.it, http://www.carocci.it.

791.43 GBR ISSN 1742-7878
CINEMA BUSINESS. Text in English. 2004. m. GBP 53 domestic to individuals; GBP 63 foreign to individuals; GBP 43 to students (effective 2009). adv. back issues avail. **Document type:** *Magazine, Trade.* **Description:** Covers both the mainstream and independent exhibition circuits, the operation of festivals, as well as in-flight, concert and outdoor screenings. Features independent news and articles as well as information from the Film Distribution Association, Cinema Exhibitors Association and the UKFC.
—CCC.
Published by: Landor Publishing Ltd, Apollo House, 359 Kennington Ln, London, SE11 5QY, United Kingdom. TEL 44-845-2707950, business@landor.co.uk, http://www.landor.co.uk. Adv. contact Frank Kingaby TEL 44-20-79245885.

791.43 ITA ISSN 0392-9981
CINEMA D'OGGI. Text in Italian. 1967. fortn. adv. **Document type:** *Magazine, Trade.*
Related titles: Online - full text ed.
Indexed: RASB.
Published by: A N I C A, Viale Regina Margherita 286, Rome, RM 00198, Italy. anica@anica.it. Circ: 11,000.

791.43 IND
CINEMA EXPRESS. Text in Tamil. 1980. m. INR 240 (effective 2011). adv. dance rev.; music rev.; tel.rev.; video rev. 64 p./no. 3 cols./p.; back issues avail. **Document type:** *Magazine, Consumer.* **Description:** Contains events connected to cinema, film reviews and interviews with film stars.
Related titles: E-mail ed.; Online - full text ed.: free (effective 2011).
Published by: Express Publications (Madurai) Ltd., Express Gardens, 29, 2nd Main Rd, Ambattur Industrial Estate, Chennai, 600 058, India. TEL 91-44-23457601, FAX 91-44-23457619, http://www.epmltd.com. Ed. R Sivakumar.

791.43 ITA ISSN 1970-0091
CINEMA GRANDI ROMANZI. Text in Italian. 2006. s-m. **Document type:** *Magazine, Consumer.*
Published by: De Agostini Editore, Via G da Verrazzano 15, Novara, 28100, Italy. TEL 39-0321-4241, FAX 39-0321-424305, info@deagostini.it, http://www.deagostini.it.

791.43 USA ISSN 0009-7101
PN1993
➤ **CINEMA JOURNAL.** Text in English. 1961. q. USD 138 domestic to institutions; USD 167 in Canada to institutions; USD 182 elsewhere to institutions (effective 2011). adv. bk.rev. illus. Index. 144 p./no.; back issues avail.; reprints avail. **Document type:** *Journal, Academic/ Scholarly.* **Description:** Provides a forum for the study and discussion of art cinema and selective mainstream film.
Formerly (until 1967): Society of Cinematologists. Journal (1550-0349)
Related titles: Microform ed.; Online - full text ed.: ISSN 1527-2087. 1999.
Indexed: A01, A02, A03, A06, A07, A08, A20, A22, A26, A27, A30, A31, AA, ABS&EES, ASCA, ArtHuCI, ArtInd, B04, BRD, CA, CurCont, E01, F01, F02, I05, IBR, IBT&D, IBZ, IIFP, IIPA, IITV, MEA&I, MLA, MLA-IB, MRD, P10, P13, P48, P53, P54, PCI, PQC, RASB, RILM, SCOPUS, T02, W03, W05, W07.
—BLDSC (3198.639000), IE, Infotrieve, Ingenta. **CCC.**
Published by: (Society for Cinema and Media Studies), University of Texas Press, Journals Division, PO Box 7819, Austin, TX 78713. TEL 512-471-7233 ext 2, FAX 512-232-7178, journals@uts.cc.utexas.edu, http://www.utexas.edu/utpress/journals/journals.html. Ed. Heather Hendershot. Adv. contact Leah Dixon TEL 512-232-7618.

791.43 100 PRT ISSN 1647-8991
▼ **CINEMA: JOURNAL OF PHILOSOPHY AND THE MOVING IMAGE.** Text in English. 2010. irreg. free (effective 2011). **Document type:** *Journal, Academic/Scholarly.*
Media: Online - full text.
Published by: Universidade Nova de Lisboa, Faculdade de Ciencias Sociais e Humanas, Avenida de Berna 26, Lisbon, 1069-061, Portugal. Ed. Patricia Silveirinha Castello Branco.

791.43 ITA
CINEMA LOMBARDIA. Text in Italian. 1975. m. looseleaf. adv. film rev. abstr.; charts; illus. **Document type:** *Magazine, Consumer.* **Description:** Provides news of regional association activities and reprints news articles dealing with the film industry.
Published by: Associazione Generale Italiana Spettacolo (A G I S) Lombarda, Piazza Luigi di Savoia 24, Milan, 20124, Italy. Ed. Viviana Giorgi. Circ: 800.

791.4305 CAN ISSN 1488-7002
PN1993
CINEMA SCOPE; expanding the frame on international cinema. Text in English. 1999. q. USD 40 in US & Canada to institutions; USD 60 elsewhere to institutions; CAD 21.40 domestic; USD 20 in United States (effective 2010). adv. illus. back issues avail. **Document type:** *Magazine, Consumer.* **Description:** Features articles on international cinema.
Related titles: Online - full text ed.: CAD 20.58 (effective 2010).
Indexed: A10, F01, F02, MLA-IB, T02, V03.
—CCC.
Published by: Cinema Scope Publishing, 465 Lytton Blvd, Toronto, ON M5N 1S5, Canada. Ed., Pub. Mark Peranson TEL 416- 889-5430.

791.43 778.59 ITA ISSN 1125-1727
CINEMA STUDIO. Text in Italian. 1990. irreg., latest vol.45, 2002. price varies. **Document type:** *Monographic series, Academic/Scholarly.*
Indexed: MLA-IB.
Published by: Bulzoni Editore, Via dei Liburni 14, Rome, 00185, Italy. TEL 39-06-4455207, FAX 39-06-4450355, bulzoni@bulzoni.it, http://www.bulzoni.it. Ed. Orio Caldiron.

778.53 GBR ISSN 0955-2251
TR845
CINEMA TECHNOLOGY. Text in English. 1987. q. GBP 60 combined subscription to non-members (print & online eds.); free to members (effective 2009). adv. software rev. bibl.; illus.; stat.; tr.lit. back issues avail. **Document type:** *Magazine, Trade.* **Description:** Provides coverage of technological trends and developments in the world of cinema exhibition.
Related titles: Online - full text ed.: GBP 40 to non-members; free to members (effective 2009).
Indexed: A10, BrTechI, E11, F01, F02, Inspec, SCOPUS, T02, T04, V03.
—BLDSC (3198.640800), AskIEEE, Linda Hall.
Published by: B K S T S - The Moving Image Society, Pinewood Studios, Pinewood Rd, Iver Heath, Buckinghamshire SL0 0NH, United Kingdom. TEL 44-1753-656656, FAX 44-1753-657016, Info@bksts.com, http://www.bksts.com/. Adv. contact Brett Smith TEL 61-417-663803. page GBP 1,185.24; 7.48 x 10.51. **Dist. by:** The Lavenham Press Ltd. TEL 44-1787-247436.

791.43 PAK
CINEMA THE WORLD OVER. Text in English. 1975. m. PKR 40.
Published by: National Film Development Corporation, c/o K.S. Hosain, 204-205 Hotel Metropole, Karachi, Pakistan.

791.43 GBR
CINEMA THEATRE ASSOCIATION. BULLETIN. Text in English. bi-m. free to members (effective 2009). **Document type:** *Bulletin, Consumer.* **Description:** Covers cinema subjects, photographs, information on CTA visits and events, casework reports etc.
Published by: Cinema Theatre Association, c o Neville Taylor, 128 Gloucester Terr, London, W2 6HP, United Kingdom. TEL 44-20-88891376, david.trevorjones@btopenworld.com. Ed. Harry Rigby.

791.4375 IND
CINEMA VIKATAN. Text in Tamil. 200?. w. INR 20 in state; INR 22 out of state (effective 2011). adv. **Document type:** *Magazine, Consumer.*
Related titles: Online - full text ed.: free (effective 2011).
Published by: Vasan Publications Pvt. Ltd., 757 Anna Salai, Chennai, Tamil Nadu 600 002, India. TEL 91-44-28524074, pubonline@vikatan.com, http://www.vikatan.com.

791.43 IND ISSN 0250-6998
PN1993.5.I8
CINEMA VISION INDIA. Text in English. 1980. q. adv. bk.rev. back issues avail. **Document type:** *Magazine, Consumer.*
Address: 501, Adarsh Nagar, M.H.B. Colony, New Link Rd, Jogeshwari (W), Mumbai, Maharashtra 400 102, India. TEL 91-22-6320739, FAX 91-22-6366642, cvi@indiasurabhi.com. Ed. Siddharth Kak. Circ: 5,000.

778.53 791.45 FRA ISSN 0243-4504
CINEMACTION. Text in French. 1978. q. EUR 80 in Europe; EUR 95 elsewhere (effective 2009). illus. back issues avail. **Document type:** *Journal, Trade.* **Description:** In-depth critical coverage of topics relating to the cinema and television, including profiles of filmmakers, national cinemas, genre films.
Incorporates (in 1995): Cinemaction TV (1241-8161)
Indexed: CA, F01, F02, IIFP, IIPA, IITV, T02.
—IE. **CCC.**
Published by: Editions Corlet S.A., Z.I. route de Vire, BP 86, Conde-sur-Noireau, 14110, France. TEL 33-2-31595300, FAX 33-2-31694129, corlet@corlet.fr, http://www.cinemaction.com. Ed. Guy Hennebelle. Pub. Charles Corlet.

344 USA
CINEMAD (ONLINE). Text in English. 3/yr. USD 12; USD 3.95 newsstand/ cover (effective 2006). film rev. **Document type:** *Magazine, Consumer.* **Description:** Includes interviews, features, and film commentary, as well as reviews of films and other zines.
Formerly (until 2006): Cinemad (Print)
Media: Online - full text.
Published by: Cinemad Film Magazine, PO Box 43909, Tucson, AZ 85733-3909. Ed. Mike Plante.

791.43 DEU
CINEMAGICA. Text in German. 1985. bi-m. EUR 35 membership (effective 2009). **Document type:** *Magazine, Consumer.*
Former titles (until 1999): Beaulieumagica; (until 1992): Beaulieu Club-Zeitung; (until 1987): Beaulieu Club-Mitteilung
Published by: Beaulieu Cine Filmclub International, Schoenbergweg 8, Aschaffenburg, 63741, Germany. TEL 49-6021-48229, FAX 49-6021-411341. Ed. Juergen Vanscheidt.

791.4375 USA
CINEMAN SYNDICATE. Text in English. w. USD 398 (effective 2005). bk.rev.; music rev. **Document type:** *Magazine, Consumer.* **Description:** Provides a weekly movie review report that is used by many online services and newspapers. Also includes daily trivia quizz, and star interviews.
Media: Online - full content.
Published by: Cineman Syndicate, LLC, 31 Purchase St, Ste 203, Rye, NY 10580. TEL 914-967-5353, FAX 914-967-5588, cineman@frontiernet.net.

791.43 ESP ISSN 1135-5840
CINEMANIA. Text in Spanish. 1995. m. EUR 30.60 (effective 2010). adv. film rev. **Document type:** *Magazine, Consumer.* **Description:** Contains articles and features aimed at classic and contemporary movie lovers.
Published by: Promotora General de Revistas S.A. (P R O G R E S A) (Subsidiary of: Grupo Prisa), C Fuencarral 6, Madrid, 28004, Spain. TEL 34-91-5386104, FAX 34-91-5222291, correo@progresa.es, http://www.progresa.es.

791.43 FRA ISSN 2108-6737
▼ **CINEMARCHIVES.** Text in French. 2009. irreg.
Media: Online - full text.
Published by: Revues.org, 3 Place Victor Hugo, Case no 86, Marseille, 13331, France. TEL 33-4-13550355, FAX 33-4-13550341, http:// www.revues.org. Ed. Marc Vernet.

778.53 CAN ISSN 1181-6945
PN1995
CINEMAS; revue d'etudes cinematographiques. Text and summaries in English, French. 1990. 3/yr. CAD 30 to individuals; CAD 35 to institutions (effective 2004). adv. illus.
Indexed: C03, CA, CBCARef, F01, F02, IIFP, IITV, MLA-IB, MRD, P48, PQC, T02, U01.
—CCC.
Published by: Universite de Montreal, Departement de l'Histoire de l'Art, C P 6128, Montreal, PQ H3C 3J7, Canada. Ed. Andre Gaudreault. Circ: 650.

791.43 FRA ISSN 1267-4397
PN1993.5.L3
➤ **CINEMAS D'AMERIQUE LATINE.** Text in French. 1992. a. EUR 15 (effective 2008). back issues avail. **Document type:** *Journal, Academic/Scholarly.* **Description:** Contains articles that analyze production, distribution and co-production in Latin American cinema.
Indexed: BibInd, MLA-IB.
—CCC.
Published by: (Universite de Toulouse II (Le Mirail)), Presses Universitaires du Mirail, Universite de Toulouse II (Le Mirail), 5, Allee Antonio Machado, Toulouse, 31058, France. TEL 33-5-6150-4250, FAX 33-5-6150-4209, pum@univ-tlse2.fr, http://www.univ-tlse2.fr. Ed. Francis Saint Dizier.

791.43 CAN ISSN 1912-3094
CINEMAS OFF CENTRE SERIES. Text in French. 199?. irreg., latest vol.2, 2008. price varies. **Document type:** *Monographic series, Academic/Scholarly.* **Description:** Presents research that provokes and inspires new explorations of past, present, and emerging cinematic trends by individuals and groups of filmmakers from around the world.
Published by: University of Calgary Press, 2500 University Dr NW, Calgary, AB T2N 1N4, Canada. TEL 403-220-7578, FAX 403-282-0085, ucpmail@ucalgary.ca, http://www.uofcpress.com. Ed. Darrell Varga.

778.53 URY ISSN 0797-2059
CINEMATECA REVISTA. Text in Spanish. 1977. irreg. (approx. 10/yr.). USD 8. adv. bk.rev. back issues avail.
Formerly: Cinemateca
Indexed: IIFP, IITV.
Published by: Cinemateca Uruguaya, Dr. Lorenzo Carnelli, 1311, Casilla de Correos 1170, Montevideo, 11218, Uruguay. TEL 598-2-482460, FAX 598-2-494572, TELEX 22043 CIMTECA UY. Circ: 2,000.

791.43 CAN
CINEMATHEQUE ONTARIO MONOGRAPH SERIES. Text in English. 1997. irreg., latest 2002. price varies. **Document type:** *Monographic series, Academic/Scholarly.*
Published by: Cinematheque Ontario, 2 Carlton St, Suite 1600, Toronto, ON M5B 1J3, Canada. FAX 416-967-1595. **Dist. by:** Indiana University Press, 601 N Morton St, Bloomington, IN 47404.

791.43 USA ISSN 2162-0814
▼ **CINEMATIQ**; the quarterly resource magazine with a distinct perspective on black cinema. Text in English. 2011. q. USD 8.95 per issue; USD 34.53 (effective 2011). adv. **Document type:** *Magazine, Trade.*
Published by: Brown Ross, Ed. & Pub., Long Island University, Long Island, NY 11120.

791.43 ESP ISSN 0213-1773
PN1993.5.S7
CINEMATOGRAF. Text in Spanish. 1986. a. EUR 11 (effective 2009). **Document type:** *Magazine, Consumer.*
Published by: (Societat Catalana de Comunicacio), Institut d'Estudis Catalans, Carrer del Carme 47, Barcelona, 08001, Spain. TEL 34-932-701620, FAX 34-932-701180, informacio@iecat.net, http://www2.iecat.net.

778.53 USA ISSN 0886-6570
PN1995.25
CINEMATOGRAPH. Text in English. 1985. irreg., latest vol.6. USD 15 per issue to individuals; USD 25 per issue to institutions (effective 2011). bk.rev. bibl. back issues avail. **Document type:** *Monographic series, Academic/Scholarly.* **Description:** Contains articles on various aspects of film studies.
Formerly: Cinematograph 6: Big As Life, An American History of 8mm Film,Cinematograph 5: Sentience
Related titles: Microform ed.: (from PQC).
Published by: (Foundation for Art in Cinema), San Francisco Cinematheque, Independent Film Ctr, 145 Ninth St, Ste 240, San Francisco, CA 94103. TEL 415-552-1990, FAX 415-552-2067, sfc@sfcinematheque.org.

791.43 CZE ISSN 1214-0414
PN1993.5.C9
CINEMATOGRAPHICA. Variant title: Masarykova Univerzita. Filozoficka Fakulta. Sbornik Praci. O: Rada Filmologicka. Text in Czech, Slovak, English, German. 1998. a. price varies. **Document type:** *Monographic series, Academic/Scholarly.*
Formerly (until 2002): Masarykova Univerzita. Filozoficka Fakulta. Sbornik Praci. Rada Teatrologicka a Filmologicka (1212-3358)
Published by: Masarykova Univerzita, Filozoficka Fakulta/Masaryk University, Faculty of Arts, Arna Novaka 1, Brno, 60200, Czech Republic. TEL 420-549-491111, FAX 420-549-491520, podatelna@phil.muni.cz, http://www.phil.muni.cz.

778.53 AUS
CINEMEDIA ACCESS COLLECTION. VIDEO CATALOG. Text in English. 1954. irreg. (in 5 vols.). film rev.; video rev. abstr. Index. 2370 p./no.; Supplement avail.; back issues avail. **Document type:** *Catalog, Consumer.*
Former titles: State Film Centre of Victoria. Film and Video Library. Video Catalog (1036-1839); (until 1988): State Film Centre of Victoria. New Films and Videotapes (0810-4476); State Film Centre of Victoria. New Films
Related titles: Online - full text ed.
Published by: Australian Centre for the Moving Image, 222 Park St, South Melbourne, VIC 3205, Australia. TEL 61-3-99297040, FAX 61-3-99297027, info@acmi.net.au, http://www.acmi.net.au/. Ed. Faye Shortal. Circ: 200.

791.43 USA
PN1993
CINEMONKEY (ONLINE); film, literature & insight. Text in English. 1976. irreg. free (effective 2008). adv. bk.rev.; film rev. **Document type:** *Magazine, Consumer.*
Former titles (until 197?): Cinemonkey (Print) (0162-0126); (until 1978): Scintillation (0147-5789)
Media: Online - full text.
Published by: Cinemonkey, Inc., c/o Doug Holm, PO Box 4146, Portland, OR 97208-4146. TEL 503-255-4043, FAX 760-477-1111, dkholm@europa.com. Ed. Douglas Holm.

791.43 CAN ISSN 1924-7370
CINEPLEX MAGAZINE. Text in English. 1999. m. back issues avail. **Document type:** *Magazine, Consumer.*
Formerly (until 2010): Famous (1493-4477)
Published by: Cineplex Entertainment, Guest Services, 1303 Yonge St, Toronto, ON M4T 2Y9, Canada. TEL 800-333-0061.

384.55 USA ISSN 1077-3363
CINESCAPE. Text in English. 1994. m. USD 29.95; USD 4.99 newsstand/cover (effective 2006). adv. film rev.; video rev. illus. **Document type:** *Magazine, Consumer.* **Description:** Discusses action, adventure, and science fiction films and their stars and directors.
Published by: Mania Entertainment LLC, 220 Main St, Ste C, Venice, CA 90291. TEL 310-399-8001, FAX 310-399-2622. Ed. Anthony Ferrante. Adv. contact Dave Young. B&W page USD 4,240, color page USD 5,500. Circ: 250,000 (paid). **Subscr. to:** PO Box 807, Mt Morris, IL 61054-0617. TEL 800-342-3592.

791.43 ARG
CINESET. Text in Spanish. 6/yr. adv.
Address: Giribone 1325, Piso 5, Apto. 4, Buenos Aires, Argentina.

791.43 AUT ISSN 1605-6035
CINETEXT. Text in German. 1996. irreg. **Document type:** *Academic/Scholarly.* **Description:** Provides an academic and scholarly look at films and filmmaking.
Media: Online - full text.
Published by: Universitaet Wien, Institut fuer Philosophie, Universitaetsstr 7, Vienna, W 1010, Austria. philosophie@univie.ac.at, http://st1hobel.phl.univie.ac.at/cinetext/.

CINEVIDEO 20. *see* COMMUNICATIONS—Video

791.43 USA ISSN 0895-805X
CINEVUE. Text in English. 1986. 4/yr. adv. bk.rev.
Published by: Asian CineVision, Inc., 133 W 19th St, Suite 300, New York, NY 10011. TEL 212-989-1422, FAX 212-727-3584. Circ: 16,000.

778.53 MEX
CINEXS; cine sin limites. Text in Spanish. m.
Related titles: Online - full text ed.
Published by: Grupo Alce, Donato Guerra No. 9, Col. Juarez, Mexico, D.F., 06600, Mexico. TEL 52-55-7030172, FAX 52-55-7030180, http://www.grupo-alce.com/. Ed. Isabel Cardenas. Circ: 60,000.

791.43 BEL
CINOPSIS. Text in French. 1996. w. free. adv. bk.rev.; film rev. **Document type:** *Newspaper.* **Description:** Covers international movies.
Media: Online - full text.
Address: Pl Schweitzer 32, Brussels, 1082, Belgium. TEL 32-2-06620321, http://www.cinopsis.be, http://www.cinopsis.com. Ed., Adv. contact Oliver Loncin. Pub., R&P Eric van Cutsem.

778.53 USA
CITADEL FILM SERIES. Text in English. 1959. bi-m. adv.
Published by: Citadel Press (Subsidiary of: Lyle Stuart Inc.), 850 3rd Ave., Flr. 16, New York, NY 10022-6222. TEL 212-736-1141, FAX 212-486-2231. Ed. Allan J Wilson. R&P Gordon Allen. Adv. contact Sharon Martell.

791.43 USA ISSN 0275-8423
CLASSIC IMAGES. Text in English. 1962. m. USD 52 domestic; USD 78 in Canada & Mexico; USD 108 elsewhere; USD 4 per issue elsewhere; USD 5 per issue in Canada (effective 2010). adv. bk.rev.; film rev. bibl.; illus. cum.index. back issues avail.; reprints avail. **Document type:** *Newspaper, Consumer.* **Description:** Contains articles on classic films, film personalities, film history.
Former titles (until 1979): Classic Film - Video Images (0164-5560); (until 1978): Classic Film Collector (0009-8329); (until 1966): Eight MM Collector
Related titles: Microfilm ed.: (from PQC); Online - full text ed.: free (effective 2010).
Indexed: A22, F01, F02, IBT&D, IIFP, IIPA, IITV, MLA-IB, MRD, T02.
Published by: Muscatine Journal (Subsidiary of: Lee Enterprises, Inc.), 301 E Third St, Muscatine, IA 52761. TEL 563-263-2331, 800-383-3198, FAX 563-262-8042, http://www.muscatinejournal.com. Ed. Bob King.

CLOSE-UP. *see* PHOTOGRAPHY

791.43 DEU ISSN 1433-7673
CLOSE UP; Schriften aus dem Haus des Dokumentarfilms. Text in German. 1992. irreg., latest vol.23, 2011. price varies. **Document type:** *Monographic series, Academic/Scholarly.*
Published by: U V K Verlagsgesellschaft mbH, Schuetzenstr 24, Konstanz, 78462, Germany. TEL 49-7531-90530, FAX 49-7531-905398, nadine.ley@uvk.de, http://www.uvk.de.

▼ **COMEDY STUDIES.** *see* LITERARY AND POLITICAL REVIEWS

791.43 FIN ISSN 1459-1693
COMO. Text in Finnish. 2002. 11/yr. adv. **Document type:** *Magazine, Consumer.*
Related titles: Online - full text ed.
Published by: Pop Media oy, Malminkatu 24, Helsinki, 00100, Finland. TEL 358-9-43692407, FAX 358-9-43692409, http://www.popmedia.fi. Adv. contact Oskari Anttonen TEL 358-40-5630642. page EUR 2,800; 190 x 260. Circ: 70,000 (controlled and free).

▼ **COMPANIONS TO CONTEMPORARY GERMAN CULTURE.** *see* LITERATURE

CONCATENATION. *see* LITERATURE—Science Fiction, Fantasy, Horror

CONSCIOUSNESS, LITERATURE AND THE ARTS. *see* LITERATURE

CONTEMPORARY. *see* ART

CONTEMPORARY ART CENTRE OF SOUTH AUSTRALIA. BROADSHEET. *see* ART

791.43 NLD ISSN 1572-3070
CONTEMPORARY CINEMA. Text in English. 2004. irreg., latest vol.4, 2008. price varies. **Document type:** *Monographic series, Academic/Scholarly.* **Description:** Focuses on the latest in film culture, theory, reception and interpretation.
Indexed: F01, F02, T02.
—BLDSC (3425.177340).
Published by: Editions Rodopi B.V., Tijnmuiden 7, Amsterdam, 1046 AK, Netherlands. TEL 31-20-6114821, FAX 31-20-4472979, info@rodopi.nl. Eds. Dr. Ernest Mathijs, Steven Jay Schneider.

791.43 USA ISSN 1933-1878
CONTEMPORARY FILM DIRECTORS. Abbreviated title: C F D. Text in English. 2003. irreg. price varies. back issues avail. **Document type:** *Monographic series, Academic/Scholarly.* **Description:** Presents information on living directors from around the world including interview with the director, an annotated filmography, illustrations, and a bibliography.
Published by: University of Illinois Press, 1325 S Oak St, Champaign, IL 61820. TEL 217-333-0950, FAX 217-244-8082, uipress@uillinois.edu. Ed. James Naremore.

791.43 USA ISSN 1543-0863
CONTEMPORARY FILM, TELEVISION, AND VIDEO. Text in English. 2004. irreg., latest vol.2, 2004. price varies. **Document type:** *Monographic series, Academic/Scholarly.* **Description:** Publishes research about contemporary American and international film, television, and video practices.
Published by: Peter Lang Publishing, Inc. (Subsidiary of: Peter Lang Publishing Group), 29 Broadway, New York, NY 10006. TEL 212-647-7700, 800-770-5264, FAX 212-647-7707, customerservice@plang.com.

791.43 AUS ISSN 1030-4312
PN1993
➤ **CONTINUUM**; journal of media and cultural studies. Text in English. 1987. q. GBP 685 combined subscription in United Kingdom to institutions (print & online eds.); EUR 894, AUD 980, USD 1,123 combined subscription to institutions (print & online eds.) (effective 2012). adv. bk.rev. back issues avail.; reprint service avail. from PSC. **Document type:** *Journal, Academic/Scholarly.* **Description:** Provides a space for important new voices in media and cultural studies, while also featuring the work of internationally renowned scholars.
Related titles: Online - full text ed.: ISSN 1469-3666. GBP 617 in United Kingdom to institutions; EUR 805, AUD 882, USD 1,011 to institutions (effective 2012) (from IngentaConnect).
Indexed: A01, A03, A08, A20, A22, ArtHuCI, AusPAIS, CA, CMM, CommAb, E01, F01, F02, IBSS, IIFP, IIMP, IITV, MLA-IB, P10, P34, P48, P53, P54, PCI, PQC, S02, S03, S21, SSCI, T02, W07.
—IE, Infotrieve, Ingenta. **CCC.**
Published by: (Cultural Studies Association of Australasia USA, University of Queensland, Media and Cultural Studies Centre), Routledge (Subsidiary of: Taylor & Francis Group), Level 2, 11 Queens Rd, Melbourne, VIC 3004, Australia. TEL 61-03-90098134, FAX 61-03-98668822, http://www.informaworld.com. Circ: 300. **Subscr. in N. America to:** Taylor & Francis Inc., Customer Services Dept, 325 Chestnut St, 8th Fl, Philadelphia, PA 19106. TEL 215-625-8900, 800-354-1420, FAX 215-625-2940, customerservice@taylorandfrancis.com; **Subscr. to:** Taylor & Francis Ltd., Journals Customer Service, Sheepen Pl, Colchester, Essex CO3 3LP, United Kingdom. TEL 44-20-70175544, FAX 44-20-70175198.

791.43 USA ISSN 1556-1593
CONVERSATIONS WITH FILMMAKERS. Text in English. 19??. irreg. price varies. back issues avail. **Document type:** *Monographic series, Academic/Scholarly.*
Published by: University Press of Mississippi, 3825 Ridgewood Rd, Jackson, MS 39211. TEL 601-432-6205, 800-737-7788, FAX 601-432-6217, press@ihl.state.ms.us.

778.53 USA
COUNCIL ON INTERNATIONAL NONTHEATRICAL EVENTS. YEARBOOK; Golden Eagle film awards. Text in English. 1962. a. USD 20. illus.; stat. **Document type:** *Catalog.*
Published by: C I N E, Inc., 1112 16th St NW, Washington, DC 20036. TEL 202-785-1136, FAX 202-785-4114. Circ: 2,500.

791.43 FRA ISSN 1951-4751
LES COUTS DE DISTRIBUTION DES FILMS FRANCAIS. Text in French. 200?. irreg. free. **Document type:** *Newsletter.*
Published by: Centre National de la Cinematographie, 12 rue de Lubeck, Paris, Cedex 16 75784, France. TEL 33-1-44343440, http://www.cnc.fr/.

791.43 FRA ISSN 1951-4743
LES COUTS DE PRODUCTION DES FILMS EN (YEAR). Text in French. 200?. a. free. **Document type:** *Bulletin.*
Published by: Centre National de la Cinematographie, 12 rue de Lubeck, Paris, Cedex 16 75784, France. TEL 33-1-44343440, http://www.cnc.fr/.

791.43 GBR ISSN 1743-4459
CRASH CINEMA. Text in English. 2002. a. **Document type:** *Monographic series, Academic/Scholarly.*
Published by: Bradford College, School of Art, Design & Textiles, Great Horton Rd, Bradford, W Yorks BD7 1AY, United Kingdom. TEL 44-1274-433004, FAX 44-1274-741060, schoolartsandmedia@bradfordcollege.ac.uk, http://artdesign.bradfordcollege.ac.uk/.

791.43 USA ISSN 1084-8665
PN1996
CREATIVE SCREENWRITING. Abbreviated title: C S. Text in English. 1994. bi-m. USD 23.95 combined subscription domestic (print & online eds.); USD 29.95 combined subscription in Canada & Mexico (print & online eds.); USD 43.95 combined subscription elsewhere (print & online eds.); USD 6.95 newsstand/cover (effective 2011). adv. bk.rev. illus. back issues avail.; reprints avail. **Document type:** *Magazine, Consumer.* **Description:** Publishes critical, theoretical, historical, and practical essays on all aspects of writing for feature films and TV.
Related titles: E-mail ed.: free to qualified personnel (effective 2011); Online - full text ed.: USD 11.95 (effective 2011).
Indexed: F01, F02, IBT&D, IIFP, IIPA, IITV, MLA-IB, T02.
—BLDSC (3487.246800).
Published by: Inside Information Group, 6404 Hollywood Blvd, Ste 415, Los Angeles, CA 90028. TEL 323-957-1405, 888-556-6274, FAX 323-957-1406, http://www.insideinfo.com. Ed., Adv. contact Jeff Goldsmith. Circ: 22,000.

CREWFINDER CYMRU WALES; the film and television directory for wales. *see* COMMUNICATIONS—Television And Cable

791.43 USA ISSN 0090-9831
PN1993
CRITIC. Text in English. 1972. bi-m.
Indexed: IIFP.
Published by: American Federation of Film Societies, 144 Bleecker St, New York, NY 10012.

778.53 ESP ISSN 0214-462X
CUADERNOS CINEMATOGRAFICOS. Text in Spanish. 1968. irreg., latest vol.10, 1999. price varies. **Document type:** *Monographic series, Academic/Scholarly.*
Indexed: RILM.
Published by: Universidad de Valladolid, Secretariado de Publicaciones, Juan Mambrilla 14, Valladolid, 47003, Spain. TEL 34-983-187810, FAX 34-983-187812, spic@uva.es, http://www.uva.es.

791.43 MEX ISSN 2007-0667
CUADERNOS DE CINE. Text in Spanish. 1962. m. back issues avail. **Document type:** *Journal, Academic/Scholarly.*
Published by: Universidad Nacional Autonoma de Mexico, Coordinacion General de Difusion Cultural, Ave Insurgentes Sur 3000, Mexico, D.F., 01000, Mexico. TEL 52-56227003, FAX 52-56653918, http://www.cultural.unam.mx/.

778.53 ESP ISSN 1138-2562
PN1993.5.S7
CUADERNOS DE LA ACADEMIA. Text in Spanish. 1997. 3/yr. EUR 15.03 newsstand/cover (effective 2004). 500 p./no.; **Document type:** *Magazine, Trade.* **Description:** Analyses all areas related to Spanish cinema, both past and present with particular emphasis on research projects about the golden period.
Published by: Academia de las Artes y las Ciencias Cinematograficas de Espana, C Zurbano, Madrid, 28010, Spain. TEL 34-91-5934648, FAX 34-91-5931492, academia@academiadecine.com, http://www.academiadecine.com. Ed. Jesus Garcia de Duenas. **Dist. by:** Asociacion de Revistas Culturales de Espana, C Covarruvias 9 2o. Derecha, Madrid 28010, Spain. TEL 34-91-3086066, FAX 34-91-3199267, info@arce.es, http://www.arce.es/.

CUE SHEET. *see* MUSIC

791.43 USA
CULT MOVIES. Text in English. q. USD 30 for 18 mos. domestic; USD 4.95 newsstand/cover domestic; CAD 6.95 newsstand/cover in Canada (effective 2002). **Document type:** *Magazine, Consumer.*
Published by: Cameo Distributors LLC, 6201 Sunset Blvd, 152, Hollywood, CA 90028. info@cult-movies.com. Ed. Michael Copner.

791.43 USA
CULTURAL STUDIES IN CINEMA/VIDEO. Text in English. 1997. irreg., latest 2009. price varies. back issues avail. **Document type:** *Monographic series, Academic/Scholarly.*
Published by: State University of New York Press, 22 Corporate Woods Blvd, 3rd Fl, Albany, NY 12211. TEL 518-472-5000, 866-430-7869, FAX 518-472-5038, info@sunypress.edu. **Dist. by:** CUP Services.

CULTURE & THE MOVING IMAGE. *see* SOCIOLOGY

791.4375 792 700 USA
CULTUREVULTURE.NET; choices for the cognoscenti. Text in English. 1998. m. free (effective 2002). **Description:** Publishes reviews on film, theatre and art.
Media: Online - full content.
Address: arthur@culturevulture.net, http://www.culturevulture.net. Ed., Pub. Arthur Lazere.

778.5307 DNK ISSN 1901-1601
CUT. Text in Danish. 1978. 3/yr. membership. bk.rev. illus. **Document type:** *Magazine, Trade.*
Former titles (until 2005): Dolly (0907-0532); (until 1991): Medielaererforeningen for Gymnasiet og H F. Meddelelser (0903-8981); (until 1987): Foreningen af Filmlaerere i Gymnasiet. Meddelelser (0900-6664)
Published by: Medielaererforeningen for for de Gymnasiale Uddannelser, c/o Henning Boettner Hansen, Frederikshavn Gymnasium, Frederikshavn, 2300, Denmark. Ed. Kathrine Aggebo.

791.4375 DEU ISSN 1438-0218
CYBERKINO. Text in German. 1994. w. adv. **Document type:** *Magazine, Consumer.* **Description:** Contains articles and reviews detailing the latest news on movie releases and productions.
Supersedes in part (in 1998): Deutsches Entertainment Magazin (1435-2214)
Media: Online - full content.
Published by: Next Step Mediendienste GmbH, Bahnhofstr 12, Gemuenden, 55460, Germany. TEL 49-6765-960196, FAX 49-6765-960198, http://www.next-step-mediendienste.de. Ed., Pub. Dirk Jasper. Adv. contact Christine Volkert TEL 49-89-38356380.

CYFRWNG. *see* COMMUNICATIONS

791.43 DNK ISSN 1601-6432
D F I BOGEN. (Danske Filminstitut) Text in Danish. 1984. a. DKK 175 (effective 2009). adv. **Document type:** *Directory, Consumer.*
Formerly (until 2000): F I - Bogen (1397-7814)
Related titles: Online - full text ed.
Published by: Det Danske Filminstitut/The Danish Film Institute, Gothergade 55, Copenhagen K, 1123, Denmark. TEL 45-33-743400, FAX 45-33-743401, dfi@dfi.dk. adv.: page DKK 20,000; 70 x 140.

791.4375 GBR
D V D & BLU-RAY REVIEW. (Digital Video Disc) Text in English. 1999. 13/yr. GBP 34.99; GBP 3.99 newsstand/cover (effective 2009). film rev. 164 p./no.; back issues avail. **Document type:** *Magazine, Consumer.* **Description:** Contains DVD reviews on the latest releases, technological information, products and news.
Formerly (until 2008): D V D Review (1466-593X)
Related titles: Online - full content ed.
—CCC.
Published by: Future Publishing Ltd., Beauford Ct, 30 Monmouth St, Bath, Avon BA1 2BW, United Kingdom. TEL 44-1225-442244, FAX 44-1225-446019, customerservice@subscription.co.uk, http://www.futureplc.com.

D V D SPECIAL. (Digital Video Disc) *see* COMMUNICATIONS—Video

D V D WORLD. (Digital Video Disc) *see* COMMUNICATIONS—Video

DAILY VARIETY (LOS ANGELES); news of the entertainment industry. *see* COMMUNICATIONS—Television And Cable

DANCE ON CAMERA JOURNAL. *see* DANCE

791.43 CHN ISSN 1002-4646
PN1993
DANGDAI DIANYING/CONTEMPORARY CINEMA. Text in Chinese. 1984. bi-m. USD 49.20 (effective 2009). film rev. **Description:** Covers the fields of film theory, film review, film history, film techniques, and film markets.
Related titles: Online - full text ed.
Published by: China Film Art Research Centre, 25-B Xinjiekouwai Dajie, Beijing, 100088, China. TEL 2014422, FAX 2014316. Ed. Chen Bo. Circ: 8,000. **Dist. outside China by:** China National Publishing Industry Trading Corporation, PO Box 782, Beijing 100011, China.

791.43 THA
DARATHAI MAGAZINE. Text in Thai. 1954. s-m. THB 360, USD 14.12; THB 15 newsstand/cover. adv. dance rev.; film rev.; music rev.; play rev. **Document type:** *Consumer.*
Formerly: Darathai T.V. Magazine
Published by: Siam Offset Co. Ltd., Tungmahamek Sathorn, 9-9 1 Soi Sri Ak Sorn Chuapleung Rd, Bangkok, 10120, Thailand. TEL 662-249-5419, FAX 662-249-5415. Ed. Mrs. Suthisa Bukkavesa. Adv. contact Ms. Apirai Bukkavesa. color page THB 50,000. Circ: 60,000.

DARK REALMS; exploring the shadows of art, music and culture. *see* LITERATURE—Science Fiction, Fantasy, Horror

THE DATA BOOK; New Zealand film, television, video, photographic stills and theatre. *see* BUSINESS AND ECONOMICS—Trade And Industrial Directories

791.43 CHN ISSN 0492-0929
PN1993
DAZHONG DIANYING/POPULAR CINEMA. Text in Chinese. 1950. s-m. USD 62.40 (effective 2009). 64 p./no.; **Document type:** *Magazine, Consumer.*
Related titles: Online - full text ed.
—East View.
Published by: Zhongguo Dianying Chubanshe/China Film Press, 22 Beisanhuan Donglu, Beijing, 100013, China. TEL 86-10-64217218, FAX 86-10-64223710. Eds. Cai Shiyong, Ma Rui. **Dist. by:** China International Book Trading Corp, 35 Chegongzhuang Xilu, Haidian District, PO Box 399, Beijing 100044, China. TEL 86-10-68412045, FAX 86-10-68412023, cibtc@mail.cibtc.com.cn, http://www.cibtc.com.cn.

791.43 IND
DEEP FOCUS; film quarterly. Text in English. 1987. q. **Document type:** *Magazine, Consumer.*
Indexed: F01, F02.
Published by: (Bangalore Film Society), A.L. Georgekutty Ed. & Pub., Charles Campbell Rd. no.94, Cox Town, Bangalore, Karnataka 560 005, India.

791.43 DNK ISSN 1396-5980
DENMARK. DET DANSKE FILMINSTITUT. AARSBERETNING. Text in Danish. 1973. a. **Document type:** *Consumer.*
Formerly (until 1989): Det Danske Filminstitut. Beretning og Regnskab (0902-8749); Which incorporates (1983-1984): Film Premierer (0109-1174)
Related titles: Online - full text ed.
Published by: Det Danske Filminstitut/The Danish Film Institute, Gothergade 55, Copenhagen K, 1123, Denmark. TEL 45-33-743400, FAX 45-33-743401, dfi@dfi.dk.

791.43 DNK ISSN 1399-3356
DENMARK. DET DANSKE FILMINSTITUT. KATALOG. SUPPLEMENT. Variant title: Det Danske Filminstitut. Supplementskatalog. Text in Danish. 1996. irreg., latest 1999. free. **Document type:** *Catalog, Consumer.*
Formerly (until 1999): Denmark. Statens Filmcentral. Katalog (1397-3207); Which was formed by the 1996 merger of (1990-1993): Denmark. Statens Filmcentral. Video (0905-5266); (1989-1992): Denmark. Statens Filmcentral. Film og Video (0905-0973); Which was formerly (1977-1986): Denmark. Statens Filmcentral. S F C - 16 MM Film (0105-5526)
Published by: Det Danske Filminstitut/The Danish Film Institute, Gothergade 55, Copenhagen K, 1123, Denmark. TEL 45-33-743400, FAX 45-33-743401, dfi@dfi.dk, http://www.dfi.dk.

791.43 DEU ISSN 1612-3751
DAS DEUTSCHE EXPORT-ADRESSBUCH. 2, NOMENKLATUR, FIRMENDOKUMENTATION. Text in German, English, French, Spanish. 1952. a. EUR 175 (includes Das Deutsche Export-Adressbuch. 1, Suchworte, Bezugsquellen, Produkte) (effective 2010).
Former titles (until 2002): Deutschland Liefert. 2, Nomenklatur, Firmendokumentation (1438-2938); (until 1994): Deutschland Liefert. 2, Firmendokumentation, Nomenklatur (0939-7523); Which superseded in part (in 1987): Deutschland Liefert (0932-8831); Which was formerly (until 1987): Deutsches Export-Adressbuch, Export-Telefonbuch und -Telexverzeichnis. Band 1, Deutschland Liefert (0177-9168); Which superseded in part (in 1984): B D I Deutschland Liefert (0415-7508)
Related titles: CD-ROM ed.
Published by: Verlag W. Sachon GmbH & Co., Schloss Mindelburg, Mindelheim, 87714, Germany. TEL 49-8261-999457, FAX 49-8261-999491, info@sachon.de, http://www.sachon.de.

791.4375 DEU ISSN 1435-2214
DEUTSCHES ENTERTAINMENT MAGAZIN. Text in German. 1994. d. adv. bk.rev.; film rev.; music rev.; software rev.; tel.rev.; video rev. **Document type:** *Magazine, Consumer.* **Description:** Covers all the latest entertainment news and gossip.
Media: Online - full content.
Published by: Next Step Mediendienste GmbH, Bahnhofstr 12, Gemuenden, 55460, Germany. TEL 49-6765-960196, FAX 49-6765-960198, webmaster@next-step-mediendienste.de, http://www.next-step-mediendienste.de. Ed., Pub. Dirk Jasper. Adv. contact Christine Volkert TEL 49-89-38356380.

791.43 CHN ISSN 1671-2528
DIANYING/FILM. Text in Chinese. m. USD 80.40 (effective 2009). **Document type:** *Journal, Academic/Scholarly.*
Formerly (until 2000): Dianying Tongxun/Film Monthly (1003-7306)
Related titles: Online - full text ed.
—East View.
Published by: Zhongguo Dianying Yishu Yanjiu Zhongxin, 3, Xiaoxi Tianwen Huiyuan Lu, Beijing, 100088, China. TEL 86-10-62254422 ext 1011, FAX 86-10-62218571.

778.53 CHN ISSN 0257-0173
PN1993
DIANYING CHUANGZUO/CINEMATIC CREATION. Text in Chinese. 1977. m. CNY 35 newsstand/cover (effective 2005). adv. film rev. **Document type:** *Journal, Academic/Scholarly.* **Description:** Covers China's film industry.
Related titles: Online - full text ed.
Published by: (Beijing Dianying Zhipianchang), Dianying Chuangzuo Zazhishe, 77, Beisanhuan Zhonglu, Beijing, 100088, China. TEL 86-10-82043235, FAX 86-10-62012059. **Dist. by:** China International Book Trading Corp, 35 Chegongzhuang Xilu, Haidian District, PO Box 399, Beijing 100044, China.

791.43 CHN ISSN 0493-2374
DIANYING GUSHI/FILM STORIES. Text in Chinese. m. CNY 7.50 newsstand/cover (effective 2005). **Document type:** *Magazine, Consumer.* **Description:** Contains synopses of new Chinese movies. Also covers news and trends of Chinese movie industry.
Published by: (Shanghai Dianying Faxing Fangying Gongsi/Shanghai Film Distribution and Projection Company), Dianying Gushi Zazhishe, 322, Anfu Lu, Shanghai, 200031, China. TEL 86-21-64747487, FAX 86-21-64332839. **Dist. by:** China International Book Trading Corp, 35 Chegongzhuang Xilu, Haidian District, PO Box 399, Beijing 100044, China. TEL 86-10-68412045, FAX 86-10-68412023, cibtc@mail.cibtc.com.cn, http://www.cibtc.com.cn.

791.43 CHN
DIANYING JIESHAO. Text in Chinese. m.
Published by: Shanxi Dianying Faxing Fangying Gongsi/Shanxi Film Distribution & Projection Company, 58 Yingze Dajie, Taiyuan, Shanxi 030001, China. TEL 443862. Ed. Hua Zhongzhuang.

791.43 CHN ISSN 1006-6756
DIANYING SHIJIE/MOVIE SHOW. Text in Chinese. 1981. s-m. USD 124.80 (effective 2009). **Document type:** *Magazine, Consumer.*
—East View.
Published by: Dianying Shijie Huabaoshe, 20, Hongqijie, Changchun, 130021, China. TEL 86-431-5955322, FAX 86-431-5913678.

791.43 CHN ISSN 0495-5692
DIANYING WENXUE/FILM LITERATURE. Text in Chinese. 1958-1966; resumed 1978. m. USD 124.80 (effective 2009).
Published by: Changchun Dianying Zhipianchang/Changchun Film Studio, 16 Hongqi Jie, Changchun, Jilin 130021, China. Ed. Zhu Jing. Circ: 190,000. **Dist. outside China by:** China Publication Foreign Trade Company, PO Box 782, Beijing 100011, China.

778.53 CHN ISSN 1005-6777
PN1993.5.C4
DIANYING XINZUO/NEW FILMS. Text in Chinese. 1979. bi-m. USD 10.80 (effective 2009). adv. **Document type:** *Journal, Academic/Scholarly.*
Indexed: RASB.
—East View.
Published by: Shanghai Dianying Yishu Yanjiusuo, 50, Yongfu Lu, Shanghai, China. TEL 86-21-64335788.

791.43 CHN ISSN 0257-0181
PN1993
DIANYING YISHU/FILM ART. Text in Chinese. 1956. bi-m. USD 40.20 (effective 2009). adv. bk.rev.; film rev. **Document type:** *Journal, Academic/Scholarly.* **Description:** Covers all aspects of filmmaking, including scriptwriting, directing, acting, cinematography, sound recording, and editing. Critiques current Chinese filmmakers and their works, researches film history, and introduces foreign works on film theory.
Formerly (until July 1959): Zhongguo Dianying
Related titles: Online - full text ed.
Indexed: RASB.
—East View, Ingenta.
Published by: Zhongguo Dianyingjia Xiehui/China Film Association, 22, Beisanhuan Donglu, Beijing, 100013, China. TEL 86-10-64219977, FAX 86-10-64272591. Circ: 5,000. **Dist. by:** China International Book Trading Corp, 35 Chegongzhuang Xilu, Haidian District, PO Box 399, Beijing 100044, China. TEL 86-10-68412045, FAX 86-10-68412023, cibtc@mail.cibtc.com.cn, http://www.cibtc.com.cn.

791.43 CHN ISSN 1001-5582
DIANYING ZUOPIN/FILM SCRIPTS. Text in Chinese. bi-m.
Published by: E'mei Dianying Zhipian Chang/E'mei Film Studio, Chengdu, Sichuan 610072, China. TEL 669571. Ed. Liang Husheng.

791.45 USA
DIGEST OF THE U F V A. Text in English. bi-m. membership. **Document type:** *Newsletter.* **Description:** Includes news of current interest: jobs, festivals, member activities, and more.
Published by: University Film & Video Association (Kalamazoo), Western Michigan University, Communication Department, Kalamazoo, MI 49008. TEL 269-381-4023, FAX 269-387-3990. Eds. Denise Hartsough, Steve Lipkin. Circ: 850. **Institutions subscr. to:** c/o Steve Fore, University of North Texas, Box 13108, Denton, TX 76203.

791.43 USA ISSN 1555-6719
DIGITAL CINEMATOGRAPHY. Text in English. 2001. bi-m. USD 52 domestic; USD 88 in Canada; USD 102 elsewhere; USD 7 newsstand/cover domestic; free domestic to qualified personnel (effective 2008). back issues avail.; reprints avail. **Document type:** *Magazine, Trade.*
Formerly (until Mar./Apr. 2005): Digital Cinema (1534-8709)
Related titles: Online - full text ed.
Indexed: B02, B15, B17, B18, G04, G08, I05, P16, P48, P53, P54, PQC.
—CIS. **CCC.**
Published by: NewBay Media, LLC (Subsidiary of: The Wicks Group of Companies, LLC.), 810 Seventh Ave, 27th Fl, New York, NY 10019. TEL 212-378-0400, FAX 212-378-0470, customerservice@nbmedia.com, http://www.nbmedia.com. Ed. Cristina Clapp TEL 310-429-8484. Adv. contact Doug Krainman TEL 212-378-0411.

DIGITAL MOVIE. *see* COMMUNICATIONS—Video

791.43 384.558 384.5532 GBR
DIRECTORY OF BRITISH FILM-MAKERS. Variant title: Directory of British Directors. Text in English. 2000. a. free (effective 2010). 27 p./no.; **Document type:** *Directory, Trade.* **Description:** Lists film and contact details of over 200 British film directors of features films, shorts and TV work.
Related titles: Online - full text ed.
Published by: British Council, 10 Spring Gardens, London, SW1A 2BN, United Kingdom. arts@britishcouncil.org, http://www.britishcouncil.org.

791.43 384.558 384.5532 GBR ISSN 0268-5256
PN1993.4
DIRECTORY OF INTERNATIONAL FILM AND VIDEO FESTIVALS (YEAR). Text in English. 1981. biennial. 200 p./no.; **Document type:** *Directory, Trade.* **Description:** Provides information for film-makers interested in sending their films to festivals.
Formerly (until 1985): International Film Festivals Directory (0265-2676)
Related titles: Online - full text ed.
Published by: British Council, 10 Spring Gardens, London, SW1A 2BN, United Kingdom. arts@britishcouncil.org, http://www.britishcouncil.org.

778.53 ESP ISSN 0212-7245
PN1993
DIRIGIDO; revista de cine. Text in Spanish. 1972. m. EUR 39 domestic; EUR 75 in Europe; USD 165 elsewhere (effective 2009). adv. bk.rev.; film rev. illus. back issues avail.; reprints avail. **Document type:** *Magazine, Consumer.* **Description:** Publishes studies of the works of the great directors, alternating classic with modern film. Includes interviews, dossiers, and reports on film festivals.
Indexed: F01, F02, IIFP, MLA-IB.
—CCC.
Published by: Dirigido por.. S.L., Consell de Cent 304, Barcelona, 08007, Spain. TEL 34-93-4876202, FAX 34-93-4880896. Ed. Angel Fabregat. R&P Enrique Aragones. Adv. contact Jose Maria Latorre. Circ: 15,000 (paid). **Dist. by:** Asociacion de Revistas Culturales de Espana, C Covarruvias 9 2o. Derecha, Madrid 28010, Spain. TEL 34-91-3086066, FAX 34-91-3199267, info@arce.es, http://www.arce.es/.

DISCURSOS FOTOGRAFICOS. *see* COMMUNICATIONS

791.43 DEU ISSN 0931-1416
➤ **DISKURS FILM**; muenchner beitraege zur filmphilologie. Text in German. 1987. irreg., latest vol.10, 2007. price varies. bibl.; illus. 240 p./no.; **Document type:** *Monographic series, Academic/Scholarly.*
Published by: diskurs film Verlag Schaudig & Ledig GbR, Tristanstr 13, Munich, 80804, Germany. TEL 49-89-36192876, FAX 49-89-365229. Eds., Pubs. Dr. Elfriede Ledig, Dr. Michael Schaudig.

791.43 DEU
➤ **DISKURS FILM BIBLIOTHEK.** Text in German. 1989. irreg., latest vol.17, 2008. price varies. bibl.; illus. **Document type:** *Monographic series, Academic/Scholarly.*
Published by: diskurs film Verlag Schaudig & Ledig GbR, Tristanstr 13, Munich, 80804, Germany. TEL 49-89-36192876, FAX 49-89-365229. Ed. Dr. Klaus Kanzog. Pubs. Dr. Elfriede Ledig, Dr. Michael Schaudig.

791.43 PRT ISSN 1646-477X
DOC ON-LINE; revista digital de cinema documentario. Text in English. 2006. free (effective 2011). **Document type:** *Journal, Academic/Scholarly.*
Media: Online - full text.
Indexed: MLA-IB.

Published by: Universidade de Beira Interior, Faculdade de Artes e Letras, Rua Marques d'Avila e Bolama, Covilha, 6200-001, Portugal. Eds. Manuela Penafria, Marcius Freire.

791.433 USA ISSN 1559-1034
PN1995.9.D6
DOCUMENTARY (LOS ANGELES). Text in English. 1986. q. USD 45 domestic to non-members; USD 55 foreign to non-members; free to members (effective 2010). adv. bk.rev. illus. back issues avail.; reprints avail. **Document type:** *Magazine, Trade.* **Description:** Devoted to non-fiction film and video. Provides valuable information for documentary filmmakers and their audience.
Formerly (until 2006): International Documentary (1077-9361)
Indexed: F01, F02, IIFP, IITV, T02.
Published by: International Documentary Association, 1201 W 5th St, Ste M320, Los Angeles, CA 90017. TEL 213-534-3600, FAX 213-534-3610. Ed. Thomas White TEL 213-534-3600 ext 7443. Pub. Michael Lumpkin TEL 213-534-3600 ext 7485. Adv. contact Jodi Pais Montgomery TEL 626-398-2090.

791.43 051 USA
DOLCE VITA. Text in English. 1999. 7/yr. USD 14 domestic; USD 30 foreign (effective 2006). **Document type:** *Magazine, Consumer.* **Description:** Focuses on cinema; also contains articles on fashion, music, cuisine, art, and travel.
Address: 2014 N. Sycamore Ave, Hollywood, CA 90068. Ed., Pub. Andrea Galante.

791.43 GBR ISSN 2041-9678
▼ **DOUBLE-0-SEVEN MAGAZINE ARCHIVE FILES.** Variant title: 007 Magazine Archive Files. Text in English. 2010. irreg. back issues avail. **Document type:** *Magazine, Consumer.* **Description:** All about the James Bond phenomenon.
Related titles: Online - full text ed.: USD 15.99 in United States; EUR 11.99 in Europe; GBP 9.99 elsewhere (effective 2010).
Published by: 007 Magazine & Archive Ltd., 6 New St Lydd, Romney Marsh, Kent, TN29 9DJ, United Kingdom. TEL 44-1797-322007.

778.53 DNK ISSN 0929-7529
PN1995.9.D6
DOX; documentary film magazine. Text in English. 1993. 6/yr. EUR 28, EUR 39 combined subscription in Europe printed and online editions; USD 32, USD 46 combined subscription elsewhere printed and online editions; EUR 5 newsstand/cover (effective 2009). adv. film rev. illus. 28 p./no.; reprints avail. **Document type:** *Magazine, Trade.* **Description:** Examines documentary film. Discusses reviews, aesthetics, production-distribution, funding, festival and event diaries, and festival reports.
Related titles: Online - full text ed.: EUR 16, USD 18 (effective 2001).
Indexed: F01, F02, T02.
Published by: European Documentary Network, Vognmagergade 10, Copenhagen K, 1120, Denmark. TEL 45-33-131122, FAX 45-33-131144, edn@edn.dk, http://www.edn.dk. Ed. Ulla Jacobsen. Adv. contact Ove Rishoej Jensen.

791.43 USA
DREAMSCAPE. Text in English. 1996. m. adv. bk.rev. **Description:** Focuses on entertainment, film and technology.
Related titles: Online - full text ed.: 1996.
Address: 520 Washington Blvd, Ste 339, Marina del Rey, CA 90292. TEL 310-822-1583, FAX 310-822-0163. Ed. Zacharias J Beckman.

791.43 DEU
DREHEN IN DEUTSCHLAND (YEAR)/SHOOTING IN GERMANY (YEAR); Handbuch fuer Produktions- und Aufnahmeleiter. Text in English, German. a. EUR 12.30 (effective 2009). **Document type:** *Directory, Trade.* **Description:** Lists information and contacts necessary for film production locations throughout Germany.
Published by: D P V Deutscher Presse Verband e.V., Stresemannstr 375, Hamburg, 22761, Germany. TEL 49-40-8997799, FAX 49-40-8997779, briefe@dpv.org, http://www.dpv.org.

DUCKBURG TIMES. *see* HOBBIES

791 NLD ISSN 1872-2490
DUTCH SHORTS/FILMS COURTS NEERLANDAIS. Text in Multiple languages. 200?. a. adv.
Published by: (Holland Film), Holland Animation Film Festival, Hoogt 4, Utrecht, 3512 GW, Netherlands. TEL 31-30-2331733, FAX 31-30-2331079, info@haff.nl, http://haff.awn.com.

791.43 DEU ISSN 0176-2044
PN1993
E P D FILM. (Evangelischen Publizistik) Text in German. 1984. m. EUR 4.90 newsstand/cover (effective 2006). adv. bk.rev.; film rev. index. back issues avail. **Document type:** *Journal, Academic/Scholarly.* **Description:** Articles on film theory, criticism, history and economy.
Indexed: DIP, F01, F02, IBR, IBZ, IIFP, IITV, MLA-IB.
Published by: Gemeinschaftswerk der Evangelischen Publizistik e.V., Emil-von-Behring-Str 3, Frankfurt Am Main, 60439, Germany. TEL 49-69-580980, FAX 49-69-58098272, info@gep.de, http://www.gep.de. Eds. Bettina Thienhaus, Wilhelm Roth. Pub. Norbert Janowski. Adv. contact Klaus Mertens. B&W page EUR 810, color page EUR 990. Circ: 8,498 (controlled).

791.43 USA ISSN 1075-0851
ECHOES & MIRRORS; comparative studies of film. Text in English. 1994. s-a. USD 10. **Description:** Provides a forum for the comparative study of motion pictures, particularly studies that demonstrate the influence of one film on another, studies that examine films and their remakes and studies that illuminate different directorial approaches to the same material.
Published by: Mount Wachusett Community College, 444 Green St, Gardner, MA 01440-1000. TEL 508-632-6600. Ed. Edward R Cronin.

791.43 CAN ISSN 0844-1111
ECHOS VEDETTES. Text in French. 1963. w. CAD 126.89. adv. bk.rev. **Document type:** *Newspaper.*
Related titles: Microform ed.
Address: 801 est, rue Sherbrooke, 2e etage, Montreal, PQ H2L 4X9, Canada. TEL 514-521-7111, FAX 514-521-7115. Circ: 170,000.

791.43 FRA ISSN 1279-6395
ECLIPSES. Text in French. 1994. s-a. EUR 10 newsstand/cover (effective 2008). **Document type:** *Magazine, Consumer.*
Indexed: F01, F02, IIFP.
Published by: (Eclipses), Centre National du Livre, Hotel d'Avejan, 53 Rue de Verneuil, Paris, 75343, France. TEL 33-1-49546868, FAX 33-1-45491021, http://www.centrenationaldulivre.fr. Ed. Youri Deschamps.

778.53 FRA ISSN 0769-1920
L'ECRAN FANTASTIQUE; le magazine du cinema fantastique et de science-fiction. Text in French. 1970. m. adv. bk.rev.; film rev. illus. **Document type:** *Magazine, Consumer.*
Indexed: F01, F02, IIFP, IITV.
Published by: L' Ecran Fantastique, 18-24 Quai de la Marne, Paris, Cedex 19 75164, France. schlock@club-internet.fr. Ed. Alain Schlockoff. Pub. Patrick Volaine TEL 33-1-48837232. Circ: 100,000.

ECRAN TOTAL; l'hebdomadaire de tous les professionnels de l'audiovisuel. *see* COMMUNICATIONS

791.43 025.04 FRA ISSN 1951-4670
ECRANS. Text in French. 2006. w. **Document type:** *Magazine, Consumer.*
Related titles: ◆ Supplement to: Liberation. ISSN 0335-1793.
Published by: Liberation, 11 rue Beranger, Paris, Cedex 3 75154, France. TEL 33-1-42761789, FAX 33-1-42729493, espaceslibe@liberation.fr, http://www.liberation.fr. Ed. Astrid Girardeau.

791.43 GBR
EDINBURGH STUDIES IN FILM. Text in English. irreg. price varies. back issues avail. **Document type:** *Monographic series, Academic/Scholarly.*
Published by: Edinburgh University Press, 22 George Sq, Edinburgh, Scotland EH8 9LF, United Kingdom. TEL 44-131-6504218, FAX 44-131-6503286, journals@eup.ed.ac.uk. Eds. John Orr, Martine Beugnet.

791.43 USA
EDITORS GUILD MAGAZINE. Text in English. 19??. bi-m. USD 45 domestic; USD 65 foreign (effective 2010). adv. back issues avail. **Document type:** *Magazine, Trade.*
Published by: Steven Jay Cohen, IATSE Local 700 MPEG, 7715 Sunset Blvd, Ste 200, Hollywood, CA 90046. TEL 323-876-4770, 800-705-8700. Ed., Adv. contact Tomm Carroll. B&W page USD 1,750, color page USD 2,700; bleed 8.625 x 11.125.

EDUCATIONAL TECHNOLOGY RESEARCH & DEVELOPMENT. *see* EDUCATION—Teaching Methods And Curriculum

791.43 SVN ISSN 0013-3302
PN1993
EKRAN; revija za film in televizijo. Text in Slovenian. 1962. m. adv. film rev. illus. **Document type:** *Magazine, Consumer.*
Related titles: Online - full content ed.: ISSN 1581-0321.
Indexed: F01, F02, IIFP, IITV, MLA-IB.
Published by: (Zveza Kulturnih Organizacij Slovenije), Slovenska Kinoteka, Metelkova 6, Ljubljana, 1000, Slovenia. TEL 386-61-1383830, FAX 386-61-1330279. Ed. Nika Bohinc. Circ: 2,000.

791.43 RUS
EKRAN I STSENA. Text in Russian. 1990. w. USD 255 foreign (effective 2010). **Document type:** *Newspaper, Consumer.*
Related titles: Microfiche ed.: (from EVP).
Published by: Redaktsiya Ekran i Stsena, Strastnoi bul'var, 10, Moscow, 107031, Russian Federation. TEL 7-495-6090046, FAX 7-495-6090046. Ed. Aleksandr Avdeenko. **Dist. by:** East View Information Services, 10601 Wayzata Blvd, Minneapolis, MN 55305. TEL 952-252-1201, FAX 952-252-1202, info@eastview.com, http://www.eastview.com.

791.43 AUS
EMPIRE. Text in English. 2001. m. AUD 80; AUD 8.95 newsstand/cover (effective 2008). adv. **Document type:** *Magazine, Consumer.* **Description:** Provides the most comprehensive reviews on - new films, DVDs, games, books and the latest film soundtracks.
Published by: A C P Magazines Ltd. (Subsidiary of: P B L Media Pty Ltd.), 54-58 Park St, Sydney, NSW 2000, Australia. TEL 61-2-92828000, FAX 61-2-91263769, research@acpaction.com.au. Adv. contact Darren O'Gradey TEL 61-2-81149441. page AUD 3,995; trim 220 x 285. Circ: 21,547.

791.43 GBR ISSN 0957-4948
PN1995
EMPIRE. Text in English. 1989. m. GBP 35.09 domestic; GBP 85 in Europe; GBP 15,070 elsewhere (effective 2008). adv. **Document type:** *Magazine, Consumer.* **Description:** Guide to films. Covers new releases, star interviews, and news.
Related titles: Online - full text ed.
Indexed: F01, F02.
—IE. **CCC.**
Published by: H. Bauer Publishing Ltd. (Subsidiary of: Bauer Media Group), Mappin House, 4 Winsley St, London, W1W 8HF, United Kingdom. TEL 44-20-71828000, john.adams@bauermedia.co.uk, http://www.bauermedia.co.uk. Adv. contact Andrew Turner. Circ: 189,619 (paid).

791.43 CAN ISSN 1190-836X
EN PRIMEUR; edition campus. Text in English. 1991. q. CAD 22 domestic; CAD 32.50 in United States; CAD 48 elsewhere (effective 2001). adv. **Document type:** *Journal, Consumer.* **Description:** Provides previews of upcoming films.
Related titles: Online - full text ed.
Indexed: C05, M02, MASUSE, T02.
Published by: Tribute Entertainment Media Group, 71 Barber Greene Rd, Toronto, ON M3C 2A2, Canada. TEL 416-445-0544, FAX 416-445-2894. Ed. Sandra I Stewart. Pub. Brian A Stewart. R&P Kim Greene. Adv. contact Catherine Bridgman. Circ: 8,500 (controlled).

EN PRIMEUR JEUNESSE. *see* CHILDREN AND YOUTH—For

791.43 AUS ISSN 0815-2063
ENCORE. Text in English. 1984. m. AUD 139 domestic; AUD 149 in New Zealand; AUD 159 elsewhere (effective 2008). adv. illus. **Document type:** *Magazine, Trade.* **Description:** Covers film, television and new media industries in Australia, focusing on major players and projects as well as developments in government policy, financing, technology, exhibitions, pay TV and multimedia distribution.
Formed by the merger of (1983-1984): Australia Film Review (0811-384X); (1982-1984): Encore Australia (0813-6688); Which was formerly (1976-1982): Encore (0155-3925)
Indexed: B02, B15, B17, B18, CMPI, F01, F02, G04, G08, I05.
—IE. **CCC.**
Published by: Reed Business Information Pty Ltd. (Subsidiary of: Reed Business Information International), Tower 2, 475 Victoria Ave, Locked Bag 2999, Chatswood, NSW 2067, Australia. TEL 61-2-94222999, FAX 61-2-94222922, customerservice@reedbusiness.com.au, http://www.reedbusiness.com.au. Ed. Miguel Gonzalez TEL 61-2-94222976. Pub. Jeremy Knibbs TEL 61-2-94222930. Adv. contact Ashley O'Loan TEL 61-2-94222060. color page AUD 2,900, B&W page AUD 2,564; trim 240 x 330. Circ: 2,933.

384.55029 AUS ISSN 0817-6469
ENCORE DIRECTORY. Text in English. 1986. a. AUD 139 domestic; AUD 149 in New Zealand; AUD 159 elsewhere (effective 2009). adv. **Document type:** *Directory, Trade.* **Description:** A contact book for the Australian film and television production industries, which contains over 14,000 listings.
Published by: Reed Business Information Pty Ltd. (Subsidiary of: Reed Business Information International), Tower 2, 475 Victoria Ave, Locked Bag 2999, Chatswood, NSW 2067, Australia. TEL 61-2-94222999, FAX 61-2-94222922, customerservice@reedbusiness.com.au, http://www.reedbusiness.com.au. Pub. Barrie Parsons. Circ: 3,200.

ENGEKI EIZO/STUDIES ON THEATRE AND FILM ARTS. *see* THEATER

791.4375 DEU
ENGELS - KINO KULTUR WUPPERTAL. Text in German. 1980. m. adv. **Document type:** *Magazine, Consumer.*
Published by: Engels Verlag Joachim Berndt, Dr.-C.-Otto-Str 196, Bochum, 44879, Germany. TEL 49-234-941910, FAX 49-234-9419191, info@berndt-media.de. adv.: B&W page EUR 800, color page EUR 1,400; trim 210 x 285. Circ: 27,613 (controlled).

791.43 THA
ENTERTAIN. Text in Thai. w. THB 25 newsstand/cover (effective 2010). adv. **Document type:** *Magazine, Consumer.*
Published by: Inspire Entertainment Co., 115-66 Moo 12, Soi Ramintra 40, Ramintra Rd, Klong-kum, Bung-kum, Bangkok, 10230, Thailand. TEL 662-508-8100, FAX 662-693-3287, contact@inspire.co.th, http://www.inspire.co.th. Adv. contact Arunee Phoorahong. Circ: 95,000 (paid).

791.43 USA
ENTERTAINMENT: AN INDUSTRY OVERVIEW. Text in English. 1991. a. **Description:** Covers film production, distribution and exhibition, prerecorded music, cable and network television, radio broadcasting. Examines trends toward vertical integration and globalization and the struggle of smaller firms for survival in the face of industry giants.
Published by: Dun & Bradstreet Information Services (Subsidiary of: Dun & Bradstreet, Inc.), 103 JFK Pkwy, Short Hills, NJ 07078. TEL 973-921-5500, 800-234-3867, SMSinfo@dnb.com, http://www.dnb.com.

ENTERTAINMENT AND SPORTS LAWYER. *see* LAW

ENTERTAINMENT EMPLOYMENT JOURNAL. *see* BUSINESS AND ECONOMICS—Labor And Industrial Relations

ENTERTAINMENT LAW REPORTER (ONLINE); movies, television, music, theater, publishing, multimedia, sports. *see* LAW

ENTERTAINMENT MAGAZINE ON-LINE. *see* MUSIC

ENTERTAINMENT PLUS. *see* MUSIC

791.43 780 USA ISSN 1549-3369
ENTERTAINMENT POWER PLAYERS. Text in English. 2001. triennial. USD 39.95 per issue. **Document type:** *Directory.*
Published by: Key Quest Publishing, 5042 Wilshire Blvd Ste 343, Los Angeles, CA 90036. TEL 323-993-3354.

791.43 USA ISSN 1063-5343
ENTERTAINMENT RESEARCH REPORT; the unbiased content report for current films. Text in English. 1991. s-m. USD 29.95. back issues avail. **Description:** Provides content information about current movies focusing on potentially objectionable material in language, adult situations, violence and relationships.
Published by: Entertainment Research Group, PO Box 810608, Boca Raton, FL 33481. TEL 407-395-1150, 800-322-1296, FAX 407-395-6129. Ed. David Winston.

791.43 USA
ENTERTAINMENT TODAY. Text in English. 1967. w. (Fri.). adv. bk.rev.; music rev.; play rev.; software rev.; video rev. back issues avail. **Document type:** *Newspaper, Consumer.* **Description:** Covers all aspects of the entertainment industry, including film, music, dining, theater multimedia.
Related titles: Online - full text ed.: free (effective 2011).
Published by: Entertainment Today, Inc., 12021 Wilshire Blvd, Ste 398, Los Angeles, CA 90025. TEL 213-387-2060 ext 1, FAX 213-341-2225, editor@entertainmenttoday.net, http://www.entertainmenttoday.net. Ed. Megan Gaynes. Pub. Mardi Rustam. adv.: B&W page USD 1,820, color page USD 2,200; trim 12.5 x 10.5. Circ: 155,000 (free).

791.43 FIN ISSN 1459-7381
EPISODI. Variant title: HohtoEpisodi. Text in Finnish. 2003. m. EUR 53.50 (effective 2007). adv. **Document type:** *Magazine, Consumer.*
Incorporates (2003-2006): D V D Hohto (1459-5826); (2001-2005): Hohto (1458-7556)
Published by: Pop Media oy, Malminkatu 24, Helsinki, 00100, Finland. TEL 358-9-43692407, FAX 358-9-43692409, http://www.popmedia.fi. Ed. Jouni Vikman TEL 358-40-7691248. Adv. contact Oskari Anttonen TEL 358-40-5630642. page EUR 3,100; 220 x 285. Circ: 15,000.

ERICH POMMER INSTITUT ZU MEDIENWIRTSCHAFT UND MEDIENRECHT. SCHRIFTENREIHE. *see* COMMUNICATIONS

792.73 ESP ISSN 2013-438X
▼ **EL ESPECTADOR IMAGINARIO.** Text in Spanish. 2009. m. **Document type:** *Magazine, Consumer.*
Media: Online - full text.
Published by: Aula Critica admin@aulacritica.com, http://www.aulacritica.com/.

791.43 USA ISSN 0363-0900
PN1993
THE ESSENTIAL CINEMA. Text in English. 1975. irreg. USD 50 membership (effective 2005).
Published by: Anthology Film Archives, 32-34 Second Ave, New York, NY 10003. TEL 212-505-5181.

M

791.43 BRA ISSN 1415-5907
PN1993
ESTUDOS DE CINEMA. Text in Portuguese; Summaries in English, Portuguese. 1998. s-a. bk.rev. back issues avail. **Document type:** *Academic/Scholarly.* **Description:** Articles on national and international cinema from a literary, artistic, historic and sociological perspective.
Published by: Pontificia Universidade Catolica de Sao Paulo, Centro de Estudos de Cinema, Rua Monte Alegre, 984, Perdizes, Sao Paulo, SP 05014-001, Brazil. TEL 55-11-36708400, FAX 55-11-38733359. Eds. Maria Do Carmo Guedes, Maria Eliza Mazzilli Pereira. Circ: 500.

ETIN. *see* LIBRARY AND INFORMATION SCIENCES

EUROPAEISCHE HOCHSCHULSCHRIFTEN. REIHE 30: THEATER-, FILM- UND FERNSEHWISSENSCHAFTEN/EUROPEAN UNIVERSITY PAPERS. SERIES 30: THEATRE, FILM AND TELEVISION. *see* THEATER

791.43 DEU
EUROPEAN MEDIA ART FESTIVAL. Text in English, German. 1988. a. EUR 10 per issue (effective 2009). adv. back issues avail.
Address: Lohstr 45A, Osnabrueck, 49074, Germany. TEL 49-541-21658, FAX 49-541-28327, presse@emaf.de, http://www.emaf.de. Circ: 1,000 (controlled).

791.43 USA
EUROPEAN TRASH CINEMA. Text in English. 198?. q. bk.rev. back issues avail. **Document type:** *Magazine, Consumer.*
Published by: E T C Video, PO Box 12161, Spring, TX 77391-2161. Ed., R&P Craig Ledbetter.

791.43 371.42 USA ISSN 1522-306X
"EXTRA" WORK FOR BRAIN SURGEONS. Text in English. 1997. a. USD 27.50 newsstand/cover (effective 2007). adv. tr.lit. back issues avail. **Document type:** *Directory, Trade.* **Description:** Provides a detailed listing of the extras casting agencies in Southern California. Describes how, where, who and all of the monetary aspects of the industry.
Published by: Hollywood Operating System LLC, 400 S Beverly Dr, Ste 307, Beverly Hills, CA 90212-4405. TEL 310-289-9400, http://hollywoodos.com. Ed. Mr. Mike Wood. Pubs. Angela Bertolino, Carla Lewis. Circ: 15,000.

791.43 NLD ISSN 2212-0335
PN1993.3
EYE INTERNATIONAL CATALOGUE. Text in English. 1969. a. EUR 20 (effective 2011). illus. **Document type:** *Catalog, Consumer.* **Description:** Presents an overview of recent Dutch film.
Former titles (until 2011): Holland Film (1385-0504); (until 1996): Dutch Film (1385-0490)
Published by: EYE Film Institute Netherlands, Vondelpark 3, Amsterdam, 1071 AA, Netherlands. TEL 31-20-5891400, info@eyefilm.nl.

791.43 DEU ISSN 1430-9947
CODEN: FNKTAH
F K T; Fachzeitschrift fuer Fernsehen, Film und elektronische Medien. (Fernseh- und Kino-Technik) Text in German. 1919. 10/yr. EUR 161 domestic; EUR 168 foreign; EUR 15 newsstand/cover (effective 2011). adv. bk.rev. index. **Document type:** *Magazine, Trade.*
Incorporates (1957-2001): Rundfunktechnische Mitteilungen (0035-9890); Former titles (until 1996): Fernseh- und Kino-Technik (0015-0142); (until 1969): Kino-Technik (0936-5516); (until 1951): Foto-Kino-Technik (0367-2433); (until 1947): Kinotechnik und Filmtechnik. Ausgabe A (0936-6180); (until 1943): Kino-Technik (0368-5799)
Indexed: ChemAb, EngInd, Inspec, TM.
—AskIEEE, IE, INIST, Linda Hall. **CCC.**
Published by: (F K T G Gesellschaft fuer Fernsehen, Film und elektronische Medien), Fachverlag Schiele und Schoen GmbH, Markgrafenstr 11, Berlin, 10969, Germany. TEL 49-30-2537520, FAX 49-30-2517248, service@schiele-schoen.de, http://www.schiele-schoen.de. Ed. Reinhard Wagner. Adv. contact Stefan Nepita TEL 49-30-25375241. Circ: 3,082 (controlled).

791.43 AUT
F L I M; Zeitschrift fuer Film. Text in German. 2/yr. EUR 17; EUR 10 newsstand/cover (effective 2007). **Document type:** *Journal, Academic/Scholarly.*
Published by: StudienVerlag, Erlerstr 10, Innsbruck, 6020, Austria. TEL 43-512-395045, FAX 43-512-39504515, order@studienverlag.at, http://www.studienverlag.at.

F W WEEKLY. (Fort Worth) *see* MUSIC

FACE TO FACE WITH TALENT. *see* COMMUNICATIONS—Television And Cable

791.43 USA ISSN 0736-3745
PN1993
FACETS FEATURES. Text in English. 1975. bi-m. USD 12 domestic; USD 24 foreign (effective 2006). bk.rev.; film rev. illus. **Document type:** *Magazine, Consumer.* **Description:** Covers the world of international films and video, including new foreign, independent and classic releases. Each issues describes 300 to 500 new video releases.
Formerly (until 1980): Focus Chicago (0362-0905)
Published by: Facets Multimedia, Inc., 1517 W Fullerton Ave, Chicago, IL 60614. TEL 773-281-9075, FAX 773-929-5437. Ed. Milos Stehlik. Pub. David Edelberg. Adv. contact Catherine Foley. Circ: 60,000 (paid).

791.43 USA ISSN 1533-3779
FADE IN. Text in English. 1995. 5/yr. USD 19.95 domestic; USD 40 foreign (effective 2007). adv. illus. **Document type:** *Magazine, Consumer.* **Description:** Covers all aspects of the film industry.
Indexed: IIFP.
Published by: Fade In Magazine, 289 S Robertson Blvd, Ste 467, Beverly Hills, CA 90211. TEL 310-275-0287, 800-646-3896. Ed. Audrey Kelly. Circ: 223,500 (paid and controlled).

791.43 USA ISSN 1056-5760
FAMA; el secreto del exito. Text in Spanish. 1991. fortn. USD 9; USD 2.49 newsstand/cover (effective 2001). adv. **Document type:** *Magazine, Consumer.*
Published by: Osmus Publishing Group Inc., 331 W 57th St, Ste 282, New York, NY 10019. TEL 212-633-9975, FAX 212-633-9976. Circ: 250,000.

791.43 USA ISSN 0278-4203
PN1995.9.H6
FAMOUS MONSTERS. Text in English. 1958-19??; resumed 1994. irreg. USD 9.95 per issue (effective 2008). adv. bk.rev.; film rev. illus.
Formerly: Famous Monsters of Filmland (0014-7443)
Published by: Filmland Classics, 6185 Magnolia Ave, Ste. 265, Riverside, CA 92506. TEL 775-262-5082, http://www.filmlandclassics.com/zencart/index.php?main_page=index. Pub. Ray Ferry. Circ: 200,000.

FANDOM DIRECTORY. *see* HOBBIES

FANTAZIA. *see* LITERATURE—Science Fiction, Fantasy, Horror

791.43 ITA ISSN 1970-5786
PN1995
FATA MORGANA; cinema, forme audiovisive, contemporaneita. Text in Italian. 2006. 3/yr. EUR 35 (effective 2010). **Document type:** *Journal, Academic/Scholarly.*
Published by: Editrice Luigi Pellegrini, Via de Rada 67c, Cosenza, CS 87100, Italy. TEL 39-0984-795065, FAX 39-0984-792672, http://www.pellegrinieditore.it. Ed. Walter Pellegrini.

791.43 USA ISSN 1062-3906
FEMME FATALES; revealing the sexy sirens of film, TV, music & the web. Text in English. 1992; N.S. 2003. bi-m. USD 39.95 domestic; USD 49.95 foreign; USD 7.99 newsstand/cover (effective 2007). adv. back issues avail. **Document type:** *Magazine, Consumer.* **Description:** Devoted to the actresses who perform in science fiction, fantasy, and horror movies.
Published by: C F Q Media, LLC, 3740 Overland Ave, Ste E, Los Angeles, CA 90034. TEL 310-204-2029, FAX 310-204-0825, mail@cfq.com, http://www.cfq.com. adv.: page USD 4,400; trim 11 x 8.5. Circ: 230,000. **Dist. by:** Eastern News Distributors Inc., 250 W. 55th St., New York, NY 10019. TEL 800-221-3148.

778.53 FRA ISSN 0336-9331
PN1995.5
FICHES DU CINEMA. Text in French. 1934. s-m. adv. film rev. **Document type:** *Magazine, Consumer.* **Description:** Short reviews and ratings of current films.
Address: 69 Rue du Faubourg Saint Martin, Paris, 75010, France. http://www.fichesducinema.com/. Ed. Pierre Deschamps. Adv. contact Claude Brabant. Circ: 3,000.

791.43 USA
FILAMENT. Text in English. 1981. a. free. back issues avail.
Published by: Wright State University, Department of Theatre Arts, T148 Creative Arts Center, 3640 Colonel Glenn Hwy, Dayton, OH 45435-0001. Ed. Glenn Lalich. Circ: 1,500.

778.53 DNK ISSN 0906-6896
FILM. Variant title: Arets Nye Film. Text in Danish. 1949. a. price varies. illus. 80 p./no.; back issues avail. **Document type:** *Yearbook, Trade.*
Former titles (until 1983): Aarets Bedste Film (0109-2774); (until 1976): Filmaarbogen (0902-0292)
Published by: Lindhardt og Ringhof, Vognmagergade 11, Copenhagen K, 1148, Denmark. TEL 45-33-695000, info@lindhardtogringhof.dk, http://www.lindhardtogringhof.dk.

791.43 IRN ISSN 1019-6382
PN1993.5.I7
FILM. Text in Persian, Modern. 1982. m. USD 52 (effective 2002). 128 p./no.; Supplement avail. **Document type:** *Magazine, Consumer.* **Description:** Covers the cinema of Iran and the world and promotes knowledge of the art of film.
Address: P O Box 11635 5875, Tehran, 11389, Iran. TEL 98-21-6709373, FAX 98-21-6459971. Ed., Pub. Massoud Mehrabi. Circ: 50,000.

791.43 POL ISSN 0137-463X
FILM. Text in Polish. 1946. w. film rev. illus. index. **Document type:** *Magazine, Consumer.*
Published by: Hachette Filipacchi Polska, Ul. Pruszkowska 17, Warsaw, 02-119, Poland. TEL 48-22-6689083, FAX 48-22-6689183. Circ: 149,400.

791.43 DNK ISSN 1399-2813
PN1993
FILM. Text in English. 1990. 3/yr. free (effective 2004). **Document type:** *Magazine, Consumer.*
Formerly (until 2000): Dansk Film (0905-5762)
Related titles: Online - full text ed.; Danish ed.: Filmupdate.
Indexed: F01, F02.
Published by: Det Danske Filminstitut/The Danish Film Institute, Gothergade 55, Copenhagen K, 1123, Denmark. TEL 45-33-743400, FAX 45-33-743401, dfi@dfi.dk. Ed. Susanna Neimann.

791.43 CZE ISSN 0015-1068
PN1993
FILM A DOBA; ctvrtletnik pro filmovou a televizni kulturu. Text in Czech; Summaries in English, French, Russian. 1954. q. CZK 75; CZK 25 newsstand/cover (effective 2010). adv. bk.rev. abstr.; charts; illus. index. **Document type:** *Magazine, Consumer.*
Indexed: F01, F02, IIFP, IITV, RASB.
Published by: Sdruzeni Pratel Odborneho Filmoveho Tisku, Parizska 9, Prague 1, 110 00, Czech Republic. Ed. Eva Zaoralova. Circ: 7,000.

791.430 FRA ISSN 1770-1856
LE FILM AFRICAIN & LE FILM DU SUD. Text in French. 1991. bi-m. EUR 34.54 domestic; EUR 46 in Europe; EUR 46 in Africa; EUR 60 elsewhere (effective 2009). **Document type:** *Newsletter, Consumer.*
Formerly (until 2000): Le Film Africain (1288-3425)
Published by: Festival International du Film d'Amiens, MCA Pl Leon-Gontier, Amiens, 80000, France. TEL 33-3-22713570, FAX 33-3-22925304, contact@filmfestamiens.org.

302.2343 USA ISSN 1543-6098
FILM AND CULTURE SERIES. Text in English. 1993. irreg., latest 2010. price varies. back issues avail. **Document type:** *Monographic series, Academic/Scholarly.*
Published by: Columbia University Press, 61 W 62nd St, New York, NY 10023. TEL 212-459-0600, orderentry@perseusbooks.com. Eds. John Belton, Jennifer Crewe.

791.43 GBR ISSN 2045-2667
FILM & FESTIVALS (ONLINE); the place where filmmakers and cinema lovers meet. Text in English. 2006. 10/yr. free (effective 2010). adv. back issues avail. **Document type:** *Magazine, Consumer.* **Description:** Covers films and film festivals plus topics such as the state Asia's film industry, documentary makers, etc.
Former titles (until 200?): Film & Festivals (Print) (1755-5485); (until 2007): The Filmfestival Magazine (1754-4963)
Media: Online - full text.
Published by: Film Culture Ltd., The Hatfactory, 65-67 Bute St, Luton, LU1 2EY, United Kingdom. TEL 44-1582-727330. Ed., Pub. Chris Patmore. Adv. contact Rose Chamberlain.

791.43 IRL ISSN 1649-1580
PN1993
FILM AND FILM CULTURE. Text in English. 2002. a. **Document type:** *Journal, Academic/Scholarly.*
Indexed: MLA-IB.
Published by: Waterford Institute of Technology, Centre for Film Studies & Comparative Literature, Cork Rd, Waterford, Ireland. http://www2.wit.ie/Research/ResearchGroupsCentres/Groups/FilmStudiesandComparativeLiterature/.

791.4309 USA ISSN 0360-3695
PN1995.2
➤ **FILM & HISTORY**; an interdisciplinary journal of film and television studies. Text in English. 1970. s-a. USD 55 to individuals; USD 90 to institutions (effective 2010). adv. bk.rev.; film rev.; tel.rev.; video rev. illus. 125 p./no.; back issues avail.; reprints avail. **Document type:** *Journal, Academic/Scholarly.* **Description:** Aims to facilitate the exchange of information among scholars and others concerned with film.
Formerly (until 1971): Historians Film Committee. Newsletter
Related titles: CD-ROM ed.; Online - full text ed.: ISSN 1548-9922.
Indexed: A01, A03, A07, A08, A22, A26, A27, A30, A31, AA, ABS&EES, AmH&L, ArtInd, B04, CA, CMM, E01, F01, F02, HistAb, I05, IBT&D, IIFP, IIPA, IITV, MLA-IB, MRD, P02, P10, P48, P53, P54, PCI, PQC, S02, S03, T02, W03, W05.
—BLDSC (3925.682100), IE, Infotrieve, Ingenta.
Published by: Historians Film Committee, 800 Algoma Blvd., Polk 305, Oshkosh, WI 54901. TEL 920-424-0976. Ed. Loren Baybrook. adv.: page USD 500.

791.43 USA ISSN 1073-0427
PN1995
FILM AND PHILOSOPHY. Text in English. 1994. a. USD 20 to individuals; USD 30 to institutions (effective 2005). back issues avail. **Description:** Includes articles on filmmaking, and philosophy.
Media: Online - full text.
Indexed: MLA-IB, PhilInd.
—BLDSC (3925.682120), IE, Ingenta.
Published by: Society for the Philosophic Study of the Contemporary Visual Arts, c/o Daniel Shaw, Lock Haven University, Raub Hall, Room 412, Lock Haven, PA 17745. TEL 570-893-2052.

621.388 GBR ISSN 1366-9362
FILM AND T V PRODUCTION REVIEW. Text in English. 1994. q. adv. tr.lit. back issues avail. **Document type:** *Journal, Trade.* **Description:** Offers information on locations, services, facilities and expertise for motion picture production worldwide.
Formerly (until 1996): British Film and T V Production Review (1363-5824)
Published by: Response Publishing Group plc, 41-45 Goswell Rd, London, EC1V 7EH, United Kingdom. TEL 44-171-490-0550. adv.: B&W page GBP 1,950, color page GBP 2,750; trim 210 x 297. Circ: 10,000 (paid).

791.43 USA
FILM BILL. Text in English. 1970. m. free (effective 2006). adv. bk.rev. 2 cols./p.; **Document type:** *Magazine, Consumer.* **Description:** Covers individual films, cast, production credits, synopsis notes, biographical notes, general articles about film personalities, filmmakers, film memorabilia and cinemalogical trends.
Published by: (George Fenmore, Inc.), Film Bill, Inc., 250 W 54 St, New York, NY 10019. TEL 212-977-4140, FAX 212-977-4404. Ed., R&P George Fenmore. Adv. contact Toddy Gelfand. page USD 5,800; 6 x 9. Circ: 500,000 (controlled).

791.43029 CAN ISSN 0831-5175
PN1993.5.C2
FILM CANADA YEARBOOK. Text in English. 1986. a. CAD 40 domestic; USD 40 in United States; USD 50 elsewhere (effective 2003). adv. **Document type:** *Directory, Trade.* **Description:** Lists companies and people in the film, television and video businesses in Canada. Information on film and video production companies, including postproduction, labs, editing, casting and support services; distributors; exhibitors; TV and pay TV; government agencies; unions; and guilds and associations.
Published by: Moving Pictures Media, PO Box 720, Port Perry, ON L9L 1A6, Canada. TEL 905-986-0050, FAX 905-986-1113, djt@globalserve.net, http://www.filmcanadayearbook.com. Ed., Pub., R&P Tiffin Deborah. adv.: B&W page CAD 990; trim 7 x 9.5.

778.53 USA
FILM CLIPS; a publication for film & video professionals. Text in English. 1979. bi-m. USD 25. adv. illus.; tr.lit. 16 p./no. 2 cols./p.; **Document type:** *Newsletter, Trade.* **Description:** Covers events of interest to film and video professionals; contains a directory of firms, services, and agencies working in the industry.
Published by: San Jose Convention and Visitors Bureau, Film and Video Commission, 408 Almaden Blvd., San Jose, CA 95110-2709. TEL 408-295-9600, FAX 408-295-3937, jkane@sanjose.org, http://www.sanjose.org/filmvideo. Ed., Adv. contact Dorea Domschke TEL 408-792-4135. Pub. Joe O'Kane. B&W page USD 250; 10 x 7.5. Circ: 3,975 (controlled).

791.43 USA ISSN 0015-119X
PN1993
FILM COMMENT. Text in English. 19??. bi-m. USD 29.95 domestic; USD 40 in Canada & Mexico; USD 60 elsewhere (effective 2010). adv. bk.rev.; film rev. illus. Index. back issues avail.; reprints avail. **Document type:** *Magazine, Consumer.* **Description:** Offers film criticism and history and elegant, personal writing about film as an art, as a medium, and as an element of modern life.
Formerly (until 1962): Vision
Related titles: CD-ROM ed.; Microfiche ed.: (from NBI); Microfilm ed.: (from PQC); Online - full text ed.: USD 225 (effective 1999).

Indexed: A01, A02, A03, A06, A07, A08, A15, A20, A22, A25, A26, A27, A30, A31, AA, ABIn, ABS&EES, ARG, ASCA, AcaI, AmHI, ArtHuCI, ArtInd, B04, BRD, C05, CA, CBRI, CMM, CPerI, ChPerI, CurCont, E08, F01, F02, G05, G06, G07, G08, H07, H08, H09, H10, HAb, HumInd, I05, I07, IBR, IBT&D, IBZ, IIFP, IIPA, IITV, M01, M02, MASUSE, MLA-IB, MRD, MagInd, P02, P10, P13, P48, P51, P53, P54, PCI, PMR, PQC, R03, R04, R06, RASB, RGAb, RGPR, RILM, S08, S09, S23, SCOPUS, T02, W03, W07.
—BLDSC (3925.690000), IE, Infotrieve, Ingenta. **CCC.**
Published by: Film Society of Lincoln Center, 70 Lincoln Center Plz, New York, NY 10023. TEL 212-875-5610, FAX 212-875-5636, filminfo@filmlinc.com. Ed. Gavin Smith. adv.: B&W page USD 2,500, color page USD 3,600; bleed 8.4375 x 11.125. Circ: 40,000.

791.436 USA ISSN 0163-5069
➤ **FILM CRITICISM.** Text in English. 1976. 3/yr. USD 25 domestic to individuals; USD 30 domestic to institutions; USD 40 foreign (effective 2010). adv. bk.rev.; film rev. illus. back issues avail.; reprints avail. **Document type:** *Journal, Academic/Scholarly.* **Description:** Presents the writing from a new generation of film historians, theorists, and critics representing many different disciplines, cultures, and critical perspectives.
Related titles: Online - full text ed.
Indexed: A01, A02, A03, A07, A08, A20, A22, A26, A30, A31, AA, ABS&EES, ASCA, AmHI, ArtHuCI, ArtInd, B04, B14, BRD, BRI, CA, CBRI, CurCont, E08, F01, F02, G08, H07, H08, H14, HAb, HumInd, I05, I07, IBR, IBT&D, IBZ, IIFP, IIPA, IITV, L06, LCR, MLA, MLA-IB, MRD, P10, P48, P53, P54, PCI, PQC, RILM, S09, S23, SCOPUS, T02, W03, W05, W07.
—BLDSC (3925.705000), IE, Infotrieve, Ingenta.
Published by: Allegheny College, 520 N Main St, Meadville, PA 16335. TEL 814-332-3100, campus@alleg.edu, http://www.allegheny.edu. Ed. Lloyd Michaels.

791.43 NLD
FILM CULTURE IN TRANSITION. Text in English. 1994. irreg., latest vol.33, 2008. price varies. illus. back issues avail. **Document type:** *Monographic series, Academic/Scholarly.* **Description:** Publishes studies of film and television culture from a European perspective.
Published by: Amsterdam University Press, Herengracht 221, Amsterdam, 1016 BG, Netherlands. TEL 31-20-4200050, FAX 31-20-4203214, info@aup.nl, http://www.aup.nl. Ed. Thomas Elsaesser. **In Europe:** Plymbridge Distributors Ltd, Estover Rd, Plymouth, Devon PL6 7PY, United Kingdom. TEL 44-1752-202300, FAX 44-1752-202330, enquiries@plymbridge.com, http://www.plymbridge.com; **In N America:** University of Michigan Press, 839 Greene St, Ann Arbor, MI 48104. TEL 734-764-4388, FAX 734-615-1540, um.press@umich.edu, http://www.press.umich.edu.

791.43 CHE ISSN 1663-8972
▼ **FILM CULTURES.** Text in English. 2010. irreg., latest vol.2, 2010. price varies. **Document type:** *Monographic series, Academic/Scholarly.*
Published by: Peter Lang AG (Subsidiary of: Peter Lang Publishing Group), Hochfeldstr 32, Postfach 746, Bern 9, 3000, Switzerland. TEL 41-31-3061717, FAX 41-31-3061727, info@peterlang.com. Eds. Andrew McGregor, Philippe Met.

791.4375 DEU ISSN 0720-0781
PN1993
FILM-DIENST; das Film-Magazin. Text in German. 1948. fortn. EUR 106.70; EUR 77 to students; EUR 4.40 newsstand/cover (effective 2009). adv. **Document type:** *Magazine, Consumer.*
Indexed: DIP, IBR, IBZ, IIFP, MLA-IB.
—BLDSC (3925.714500). **CCC.**
Published by: Deutsche Zeitung GmbH, Heinrich-Bruening-Str 9, Bonn, 53113, Germany. TEL 49-228-8840. Ed. Horst Peter Koll. Adv. contact Ulrich Merkt. B&W page EUR 800, color page EUR 1,030; trim 199 x 244. Circ: 6,350 (paid and controlled).

791.43 GBR ISSN 0141-3538
FILM DIRECTIONS. Text in English. 1977. q. GBP 4. adv. bk.rev. illus. **Document type:** *Magazine, Consumer.*
Indexed: IIFP, IITV.
Published by: Queen's Film Theatre, 25 College Gardens, Belfast, BT9 6BS, United Kingdom. TEL 44-1232-663733. Ed., R&P Michael Open. Adv. contact Bernadette Owens. Circ: 2,500.

791.43 GBR ISSN 0305-1706
PN1998.A2
FILM DOPE. Text in English. 1972. q. GBP 24.20. adv. bk.rev. back issues avail. **Document type:** *Directory, Bibliography.*
Indexed: F01, F02, IIFP, IITV.
—CCC.
Address: 74 Julian Rd, Nottingham, NG2 4AN, United Kingdom. Eds. Bob Baker, Derek Owen. Circ: 2,000.

791.43 DEU
FILM-ECHO FILMWOCHE. VERLEIH-KATALOG (ONLINE). Text in German. 1949. a. EUR 86.50 (effective 2010). adv. bk.rev. **Document type:** *Catalog.*
Formerly (until 200?): Film-Echo Filmwoche. Verleih-Katalog (0071-4879)
Media: Online - full text.
Published by: Verlag Horst Axtmann GmbH und Co., Marktplatz 13, Wiesbaden, 65183, Germany. TEL 49-611-360980, FAX 49-611-301303, info@chmielorz.de, http://www.chmielorz.de. Circ: 1,500.

791.43 USA
THE FILM ENCYCLOPEDIA. Text in English. 19??. irreg., latest 2008, 6th ed. USD 34.95 per issue (effective 2011). **Document type:** *Handbook/Manual/Guide, Trade.*
Published by: HarperCollins Publishers, Inc., 10 E 53rd St, New York, NY 10022. TEL 212-207-7000, orders@harpercollins.com.

791.43 NLD ISSN 1871-7225
FILM FACTS AND FIGURES. Cover title: Film Facts and Figures of The Netherlands. Text in English, Dutch. 2004. a.
Published by: (Professional School of the Arts Utrecht), Netherlands Film Fund/Nederlands Fonds voor de Film, Jan Luykenstraat 2, Amsterdam, 1071 CM, Netherlands. TEL 31-20-5707676, FAX 31-20-5707689, info@filmfonds.nl.

791.43 GBR ISSN 2044-2823
▼ ➤ **FILM, FASHION & CONSUMPTION.** Text in English. forthcoming 2012. 3/yr. GBP 36, USD 68 to individuals; GBP 132, USD 185 combined subscription to institutions (print & online eds.); GBP 14, USD 24 per issue (effective 2012). **Document type:** *Journal, Academic/Scholarly.* **Description:** Provides an arena for the discussion of research, methods and practice within and between the fields of film, fashion, design, history, art history and heritage.
Related titles: Online - full text ed.: ISSN 2044-2831. forthcoming. GBP 99, USD 140 (effective 2012).
Published by: Intellect Ltd., The Mill, Parnall Rd, Fishponds, Bristol, BS16 3JG, United Kingdom. TEL 44-117-9589910, FAX 44-117-9589911, info@intellectbooks.com, http://www.intellect-net.com/.

778.53 FRA ISSN 0759-0385
PN1993.5.F7
LE FILM FRANCAIS. Text in French. 1944. w. EUR 6 newsstand/cover (effective 2008). **Document type:** *Magazine, Consumer.*
Formerly (until 1983): Nouveau Film Francais (0181-3528); Which incorporated (1976-1982): Cinema de France (0396-406X); Former titles (until 1977): Film Francais (0181-3587); (until 1974): Film Francais, la Cinematographie (0015-1262); Which was formed by the merger of (1944-1966): Film Francais (0397-8702); Which incorporated (1945-1950): Courier du Centre du Cinema (1153-6942); (1945-1966): Cinematographie Francaise (0181-3935); Which was formerly: Le Film (1146-9633); (1918-1940): Cinematographie Francaise (1146-9625)
Indexed: RASB.
Published by: Mondadori France, 1 Rue du Colonel Pierre-Avia, Paris, Cedex 15 75754, France. TEL 33-1-41335001, contact@mondadori.fr, http://www.mondadori.fr.

971.43 GBR ISSN 1757-6431
▼ **FILM GENRES.** Text in English. forthcoming 2011. irreg. price varies. **Document type:** *Monographic series, Academic/Scholarly.* **Description:** Each volumes presents a clear summary of the historial development of and the existing approaches to a genre, then presents original research that uses contemporary approaches to film genres in order to provide alternative ways in which we might think about those genres.
Published by: Berg Publishers (Subsidiary of: Oxford International Publishers Ltd.), 1st Fl Angel Ct, 81 St Clements St, Oxford, Berks OX4 1AW, United Kingdom. TEL 44-1865-245104, FAX 44-1865-791165, enquiry@bergpublishers.com. Eds. Charles Acland, Mark Jancovich.

778.5309 USA ISSN 0892-2160
PN1993 CODEN: FIHIE6
➤ **FILM HISTORY**; an international journal. Text in English. 1987. q. USD 273.50 combined subscription to institutions (print & online eds.) (effective 2012). adv. bk.rev. illus. Index. back issues avail.; reprint service avail. from PSC. **Document type:** *Journal, Academic/Scholarly.* **Description:** Focuses on the historical development of the motion picture, and the social, technological, and economic context in which this has occurred.
Related titles: Online - full text ed.: ISSN 1553-3905. USD 179.50 to institutions (effective 2012).
Indexed: A01, A02, A03, A07, A08, A22, A26, A30, A31, AA, AmH&L, ArtInd, B04, BRD, CA, CMM, CommAb, E01, E08, F01, F02, G08, H05, H14, HistAb, I05, IBT&D, IIFP, IIMP, IIPA, IITV, M02, MLA-IB, MRD, P10, P30, P48, P53, P54, PCI, PQC, S09, SCOPUS, T02, W03, W05.
—BLDSC (3925.745000), IE, Ingenta. **CCC.**
Published by: Indiana University Press, 601 N Morton St, Bloomington, IN 47404. TEL 812-855-8817, 800-842-6796, FAX 812-855-7931, journals@indiana.edu, http://iupress.indiana.edu. Ed. Richard Koszarski. Adv. contact Linda Bannister TEL 812-855-9449. Circ: 800.

791.43 DNK ISSN 1602-5008
FILM I SKOLEN. Text in Danish. 1995. s-a. back issues avail. **Document type:** *Newsletter, Trade.* **Description:** News about educational films.
Formerly (until 2001): B I F Nyt (1397-7687)
Related titles: Online - full text ed.; Includes: Nye Film i Skolekataloget. ISSN 1603-6042. 2003.
Published by: Det Danske Filminstitut/The Danish Film Institute, Gothergade 55, Copenhagen K, 1123, Denmark. TEL 45-33-743400, FAX 45-33-743401, dfi@dfi.dk. Eds. Martin Brandt Pedersen, Flemming Kaspersen. Circ: 7,000.

778.53 GBR ISSN 1651-6826
FILM INTERNATIONAL. Abbreviated title: F I. Text in English. 1973. bi-m. GBP 36, USD 68 to individuals; GBP 260, USD 395 to institutions (effective 2012). adv. bk.rev.; film rev.; video rev. 68 p./no.; back issues avail. **Document type:** *Journal, Academic/Scholarly.* **Description:** Covers film culture as part of the broader culture, history and economy of society.
Formerly (until 2003): Filmhaeftet (0345-3057)
Related titles: Online - full text ed.: ISSN 2040-3801. GBP 214, USD 310 (effective 2012).
Indexed: A07, A30, A31, AA, ArtInd, B04, BRD, CA, F01, F02, IIFP, IITV, MLA-IB, T02, W03, W05.
—IE.
Published by: (Film International SWE), Intellect Ltd., The Mill, Parnall Rd, Fishponds, Bristol, BS16 3JG, United Kingdom. TEL 44-117-9589910, FAX 44-117-9589911, info@intellectbooks.com, http://www.intellectbooks.co.uk/. Ed. Daniel Lindvall. **Subscr. to:** Turpin Distribution Services Ltd.

791.43 IRN ISSN 1021-6510
FILM INTERNATIONAL; Iranian film quarterly. Text in English. 1993. q. USD 40 (effective 2001). adv. bk.rev.; film rev. illus. reprints avail. **Description:** Provides an international perspective on current trends in the film industry, including extended interviews with film producers and directors, reports from international film festivals, discussions of Iranian cinema, and profiles of other national and regional film industries.
Indexed: F01, F02, MLA-IB, T02.
Published by: Film, P O Box 11635 5875, Tehran, 11389, Iran. TEL 98-21-6707373, FAX 98-21-6459971. Ed., Pub. Massoud Mehrabi.

791.43 USA ISSN 1542-0868
PN1993
THE FILM JOURNAL. Text in English. 2002. q. bk.rev.; film rev. **Document type:** *Journal, Trade.* **Description:** Seeks to contribute to the community of serious-minded film websites by being a forum for eclectic film criticism, study and discussion.
Media: Online - full content.
Indexed: MLA-IB.
Published by: Film Journal thefilmjournal@yahoo.com, http://www.thefilmjournal.com. Ed. Richard A Curnutte Jr.

791.43 USA ISSN 1526-9884
PN1993
FILM JOURNAL INTERNATIONAL. Variant title: Film Journal. Text in English. 1934. m. USD 65 domestic; USD 120 foreign (effective 2008). adv. film rev. illus. index. reprints avail. **Document type:** *Magazine, Trade.* **Description:** Includes theatrical exhibition, production, distribution, and allied activities associated with the motion picture industry. Reports on international and US news with features on current production, industry trends, theater construction, equipment, concessions, and other industry-related news.
Former titles (until 1996): Film Journal (0199-7300); (until 1979): Independent Film Journal (0019-3712)
Related titles: Online - full text ed.
Indexed: A07, A10, A11, A26, A30, A31, AA, ArtInd, B04, B07, C05, CA, CPerI, E08, F01, F02, G05, G06, G07, G08, I05, IBT&D, IIPA, M01, M02, MLA-IB, S09, T02, U01, V03, W03, W05.
—CCC.
Published by: Nielsen Business Publications (Subsidiary of: Nielsen Business Media, Inc.), 770 Broadway, New York, NY 10003. FAX 646-654-5370, bmcomm@nielsen.com, http://www.nielsenbusinessmedia.com. Ed., Pub. Robert Sunshine. Adv. contacts Robin Klamfoth TEL 770-291-5448, Andrew Sunshine TEL 646-654-7684. B&W page USD 3,240, color page USD 3,840; trim 8.5 x 10.875. Circ: 9,200.

791.43 GBR ISSN 2042-1869
▼ ➤ **FILM MATTERS**; future film scholars. Abbreviated title: F M. Text in English. 2010. q. GBP 36, USD 68 to individuals; GBP 99, USD 117 to institutions (effective 2012). adv. back issues avail. **Document type:** *Magazine, Academic/Scholarly.* **Description:** Contains service-oriented pieces, such as profiles of film studies departments, articles that engage the undergraduate film studies community and prepare students for graduate study in the film field etc.
Related titles: Online - full text ed.: ISSN 2042-1877. GBP 60, USD 60 (effective 2012).
Published by: Intellect Ltd., The Mill, Parnall Rd, Fishponds, Bristol, BS16 3JG, United Kingdom. TEL 44-117-9589910, FAX 44-117-9589911, info@intellectbooks.com, http://www.intellectbooks.co.uk/. Eds. Liza Palmer, Tim Palmer. Pub. Masoud Yazdani. **Dist. by:** Turpin Distribution Services Ltd., Pegasus Dr, Stratton Business Park, Biggleswade, Bedfordshire SG18 8QB, United Kingdom. TEL 44-1767-604951, FAX 44-1767-601640, subscriptions@turpin-distribution.com, http://www.turpin-distribution.com/.

➤ **FILM MUSIC.** *see* MUSIC

781.542 USA
FILM MUSIC BUYER'S GUIDE. Text in English. 1977. a. USD 9.95 (effective 1999). **Description:** Soundtrack titles, composer, record numbers, years of release and current market value of recordings.
Published by: R T S, PO Box 93897, Las Vegas, NV 89193-3897. TEL 702-896-1300.

791.43 SWE ISSN 0345-3316
FILM & T V. Text in Swedish. 1973. q. SEK 150 (effective 2004). back issues avail. **Document type:** *Journal, Consumer.*
Incorporates (1973-1991): Folkets Bio-Bladet (0283-7005); Incorporates (1968-1972): Rapport Fraan Filmcentrum
Indexed: F01, F02.
Published by: Tidskriftsfoereningen Film & TV, Stora Nygatan 21, PO Box 2066, Stockholm, 10312, Sweden. TEL 46-8-54527500, FAX 46-8-54527509, distribution@filmcentrum.se. Ed. Mari Edman. Circ: 2,000.

791.43 NOR ISSN 0015-1351
PN1993
FILM & KINO; Norsk filmblad. Text in Norwegian. 1930. 10/yr. NOK 400 in Scandinavia; NOK 550 elsewhere (effective 2003). bk.rev.; film rev. charts; illus. index. back issues avail. **Document type:** *Magazine, Consumer.*
Formerly (until 1965): Norsk Filmblad (0332-6594); Which incorporated (1950-1962): Kino og Vi (1500-3396)
Related titles: Online - full text ed.
Indexed: F01, F02, IIFP, IITV, RASB.
—CCC.
Published by: Film&Kino, Postboks 446, Sentrum, Oslo, 0104, Norway. TEL 47-22-474500, FAX 47-22-474699, http://www.filmweb.no/filmogkino/tidsskriftet. Ed. Kalle Loechen TEL 46-22-474628. Adv. contact Geir Greni.

791.43 GBR ISSN 1466-4615
TR845
➤ **FILM-PHILOSOPHY.** Text in English, French. 1996 (Nov.). w. free (effective 2011). back issues avail. **Document type:** *Journal, Academic/Scholarly.* **Description:** Contains articles on philosophically reviewing film studies, philosophical aesthetics, and world cinema.
Media: Online - full content.
Indexed: CA, F01, F02, MLA-IB, T02.
—CCC.
Address: Dean Walters Bldg, St James Rd, Liverpool, Merseyside L1 7BR, United Kingdom. TEL 44-151-2315102, FAX 44-151-2315049.

791.43 USA ISSN 0015-1386
PN1993
➤ **FILM QUARTERLY.** Abbreviated title: F Q. Text in English. 1945. q. USD 214 combined subscription to institutions (print & online eds.) (effective 2012). adv. bk.rev.; film rev. illus. Index. 64 p./no.; back issues avail.; reprint service avail. from PSC. **Document type:** *Journal, Academic/Scholarly.* **Description:** Contains articles and interviews focusing on experimental, documentary, and special-interest films.
Former titles (until 1958): The Quarterly of Film, Radio and Television (1549-0068); (until 1951): The Hollywood Quarterly (1549-0076)
Related titles: Microform ed.: (from PQC); Online - full text ed.: ISSN 1533-8630. USD 163 to institutions (effective 2012).

M

Indexed: A01, A02, A03, A06, A07, A08, A20, A22, A25, A26, A27, A30, A31, AA, ABS&EES, ASCA, AcaI, AmHI, ArtHuCI, ArtInd, B04, B05, B14, BRD, BRI, BrHumI, CA, CBRI, CMM, ChPerI, CommAb, CurCont, DIP, E01, E08, F01, F02, G05, G06, G07, G08, H07, H08, H09, H10, HAb, HumInd, I05, IBR, IBT&D, IBZ, IIFP, IIPA, IITV, M01, M02, MEA&I, MLA-IB, MRD, MagInd, P02, P06, P10, P13, P48, P53, P54, PCI, PQC, R03, R04, RASB, RGAb, RGPR, RILM, S05, S08, S09, S23, SCOPUS, T02, W03, W07.
—BLDSC (3925.840000), IE, Infotrieve, Ingenta. **CCC.**
Published by: University of California Press, Journals Division, 2000 Ctr St, Ste 303, Berkeley, CA 94704. TEL 510-643-7154, 877-262-4226, FAX 510-642-9917, customerservice@ucpressjournals.com, http://www.ucpressjournals.com. Ed. Rob White. Adv. contact Jennifer Rogers TEL 510-642-6188. Circ: 3,591. **Subscr. to:** 149 5th Ave, 8th Fl, New York, NY 10010. participation@jstor.org.

791.4375 GBR ISSN 1357-5252
FILM REVIEW (LONDON, 1944). Text in English. 1944. a. **Document type:** *Journal, Consumer.*
Indexed: PCI.
—BLDSC (3926.225000). **CCC.**
Published by: Virgin Books (Subsidiary of: Random House Group Ltd.), Thames Wharf Studios, Rainville Rd, London, W6 9HA, United Kingdom. TEL 44-20-73863300, FAX 44-20-73863360, http://www.virginbooks.com.

791.43 GBR ISSN 0957-1809
PN1993
FILM REVIEW (LONDON, 196?). Text in English. 196?. 13/yr. GBP 65 domestic; USD 143 in United States; GBP 99 elsewhere; USD 8.99 per issue (effective 2009); includes Film Review Special. adv. back issues avail. **Document type:** *Magazine, Consumer.* **Description:** Covers information about film.
Formerly (196?): A B C Film Review
Related titles: Online - full text ed.: USD 2.99 per issue (effective 2009); ◆ Supplement(s): Film Review Special. ISSN 0967-8816.
Indexed: A22, F01, F02, IBT&D, IIPA, T02.
—IE, Infotrieve, Ingenta.
Published by: Visual Imagination Ltd., 9 Blades Ct, Deodar Rd, London, SW15 2NU, United Kingdom. TEL 44-20-88751520, FAX 44-20-88751588, mailorder@visimag.com. adv.: B&W page GBP 1,270, color page GBP 1,940; trim 300 x 230.

791.43 GBR ISSN 0967-8816
PN1993 CODEN: WINEF8
FILM REVIEW SPECIAL. Text in English. 1992. bi-m. GBP 65 domestic; USD 143 in United States; GBP 99 elsewhere; USD 15.99 per issue (effective 2009); includes Film Review. back issues avail. **Document type:** *Journal, Consumer.* **Description:** Covers film related news.
Related titles: Online - full text ed.: USD 7.99 per issue (effective 2009); ◆ Supplement to: Film Review (London, 196?). ISSN 0957-1809.
Indexed: F01, F02, IBT&D, IIPA.
Published by: Visual Imagination Ltd., 9 Blades Ct, Deodar Rd, London, SW15 2NU, United Kingdom. TEL 44-20-88751520, FAX 44-20-88751588, mailorder@visimag.com.

FILM SCORE MONTHLY; your soundtrack source since 1990. *see* MUSIC

791.4375 SVK ISSN 1335-8286
FILM.SK. Text in Slovak. 2000. m. EUR 5.50 (effective 2009). adv. **Document type:** *Journal.*
Related titles: Online - full text ed.: ISSN 1336-2712.
Published by: Slovensky Filmovy Ustav, Grosslingova 32, Bratislava, 81109, Slovakia. TEL 421-2-57101525, FAX 421-2-52733214, filmskprogram@sfu.sk. Ed. Simona Notova-Tuserova.

791.43 USA ISSN 2151-9188
▼ **FILM SOUTH.** Text in English. 2010 (Mar.). bi-m. USD 25 (effective 2011). **Document type:** *Magazine, Trade.* **Description:** For film, video, audio, and gaming professionals in the South.
Published by: Publications & Communications, Inc., 13581 Pond Springs Rd, Ste 450, Austin, TX 78729. TEL 512-250-9023, 800-678-9724, FAX 512-331-3950, uw@pcinews.com, http://www.pcinews.com/.

778.53 USA
FILM-TAPE WORLD. Text in English. 1988. m. USD 35 (effective 2007). adv. bk.rev. back issues avail. **Document type:** *Magazine, Trade.* **Description:** Trade publication for the film, video and desktop video community of Northern California.
Published by: Planet Communications, 650 5th St, Ste 401, San Francisco, CA 94107. TEL 415-543-6100, FAX 415-546-7556. Ed., R&P Arne Johnson. Circ: 5,000.

791.43 USA
FILM TECHNOLOGY NEWS. Text in English. irreg.
Published by: Film Technology Co., 726 N Cole Ave, Los Angeles, CA 90038. Ed. Alane Stark.

791.43 384.55 USA ISSN 0270-5648
PN1993.3
FILM TV DAILY YEARBOOK OF MOTION PICTURES AND TELEVISION. Text in English. 1970. a.
Published by: Ayer Company Publishers, Inc, 300 Bedford St, Ste B-213, Manchester, NH 03101. FAX 603-669-7945, 888-267-7323, http://www.ayerpub.com/.

791.436 DEU
FILM UND FERNSEHEN. Text in German. 2002. irreg. price varies. **Document type:** *Monographic series, Academic/Scholarly.*
Published by: MultiLingua Verlag GmbH, Querenburger Hoehe 281, Bochum, 44801, Germany. TEL 49-234-707088, info@multi-lingua.com, http://www.multi-lingua.com.

791.43 DEU
FILM UND KRITIK. Text in German. 1992. irreg., latest vol.2. back issues avail. **Document type:** *Academic/Scholarly.* **Description:** Provides an in-depth analysis of a topic in the study of films.
Published by: Stroemfeld Verlag GmbH, Holzhausenstr 4, Frankfurt Am Main, 60322, Germany. TEL 41-69-955226-0, FAX 41-69-95522624, info@stroemfeld.de.

791 DEU ISSN 0939-9410
FILM UND MEDIEN IN DER DISKUSSION. Text in German. 1991. irreg., latest vol.16, 2008. price varies. **Document type:** *Monographic series, Academic/Scholarly.*
Published by: Nodus Publikationen - Klaus D Dutz Wissenschaftlicher Verlag, Lingener Str 7, Muenster, 48155, Germany. TEL 49-251-65514, FAX 49-251-661692, dutz.nodus@t-online.de, http://elverdissen.dyndns.org/~nodus/nodus.htm#adr. Ed. Juergen Mueller.

791.43 302.23 DEU ISSN 1866-3397
FILM- UND MEDIENWISSENSCHAFT. Text in German. 2008. irreg., latest vol.14, 2010. price varies. **Document type:** *Monographic series, Academic/Scholarly.*
Published by: Ibidem Verlag, Melchiorstr 15, Stuttgart, 70439, Germany. TEL 49-711-9807954, FAX 49-711-9807952, ibidem@ibidem-verlag.de, http://www.ibidem-verlag.de.

791.43 DEU ISSN 0343-5571
FILM UND T V KAMERAMANN. Text in German. 1950. m. EUR 68.90; EUR 49.90 to students; EUR 7.50 newsstand/cover (effective 2011). adv. bk.rev. charts; illus. index. **Document type:** *Magazine, Trade.*
Formerly (until 1977): Deutsche Kameramann (0012-0340)
Indexed: F01, F02.
Published by: I. Weber Verlag (Subsidiary of: Ebner Verlag GmbH), Ohmstr 15, Munich, 80802, Germany. TEL 49-89-38308680, FAX 49-89-38308683. Ed. Evelyn Voight-Mueller. Adv. contact Carola Frommer. Circ: 8,064 (paid and controlled).

791 200 DEU
FILM UND THEOLOGIE. Text in German. 2000. irreg., latest vol.15, 2010. price varies. **Document type:** *Monographic series, Academic/Scholarly.*
Published by: Schueren Verlag GmbH, Universitaetsstr 55, Marburg, 35037, Germany. TEL 49-6421-63084, FAX 49-6421-681190, info@schueren-verlag.de, http://www.schueren-verlag.de.

778.5 384.55 DEU ISSN 0938-1627
FILM UND VIDEO; Magazin fuer kreative Filmgestaltung. Text in German. 1982. 5/yr. EUR 38.50 for 2 yrs. domestic; EUR 46 for 2 yrs. foreign (effective 2009). **Document type:** *Magazine, Consumer.*
Formerly (until 1989): Film 8-16 und Video (0179-9371)
Published by: Bund Deutscher Film-Autoren e.V., Kehrbrock 9, Dortmund, 44339, Germany. TEL 49-231-7280461, FAX 49-231-7280461, info@bdfa.de, http://www.bdfa.de. Ed. Gert Richter.

791.43 CAN ISSN 1708-7880
FILM, VIDEO AND AUDIO-VISUAL POST-PRODUCTION. DATA TABLES. Text in English. 2002. irreg. **Document type:** *Report, Trade.*
Media: Online - full text. **Related titles:** French ed.: La Postproduction Cinematographique, Video et Audiovisuelle. Tableaux de Donnees. ISSN 1708-7899.
Published by: Statistics Canada/Statistique Canada, Communications Division, 3rd Fl, R H Coats Bldg, Ottawa, ON K1A 0A6, Canada. TEL 800-263-1136, infostats@statcan.ca, http://www.statcan.gc.ca.

791.43 FRA ISSN 1957-2360
FILM(S). Variant title: Films Paris. Text in French. 2007. q. EUR 17.90 domestic; EUR 24.90 DOM-TOM; EUR 24.90 in Europe; EUR 33.50 elsewhere (effective 2009). back issues avail. **Document type:** *Magazine, Consumer.*
Formerly (until 2007): Cine Films (1767-0799)
Published by: Editions Tournon, 45 rue Broca, Paris, 75005, France. http://www.editionstournon.fr.

791.43 SWE ISSN 0348-9558
FILMAARSBOKEN/FILM YEAR BOOK (YEAR). Text in Swedish. 1962. a. price varies. film rev. illus. back issues avail. **Document type:** *Yearbook, Consumer.* **Description:** Reports on the film repertoire in Sweden. Gives full data on producers, directors, scriptwriters, cinematographers, actors and Swedish release dates and a synopsis of each film. Includes TV films.
Former titles (until 1979): Svenska Filminstitutets Filmbok (0348-1182); (until 1978): Filmaarsboken (0071-4925); (until 1969): Saesonens Filmers
Published by: (Svenska Filminstitutet/Swedish Film Institute), Proprius Foerlag AB, Floragatan 20, Stockholm, 11431, Sweden. TEL 46-8-6609602, FAX 46-8-6609749, info@proprius.se, http://www.proprius.se. Ed. Bertil Wredlund. Circ: 1,000.

791.43 NLD ISSN 1574-955X
FILMBEELD. Text in Dutch. 1984. 3/yr.
Former titles (until 2004): Stichting Nederlands Fonds voor de Film. Nieuwsbrief (1382-7766); (until 1993): Fonds voor de Nederlandse Film. Nieuwsbrief (1382-7758)
Published by: Netherlands Film Fund/Nederlands Fonds voor de Film, Jan Luykenstraat 2, Amsterdam, 1071 CM, Netherlands. TEL 31-20-5707676, FAX 31-20-5707689, info@filmfonds.nl, http://www.filmfonds.nl. Ed. Jonathan Mees. Circ: 5,300.

778.53 CHE ISSN 0257-7852
PN1993
FILMBULLETIN. Text in German. 1958. 9/yr. CHF 69, EUR 45 (effective 2011). adv. film rev. back issues avail. **Document type:** *Magazine, Consumer.*
Indexed: F01, F02, IBR, IBZ, IIFP, IITV.
Address: Hard 4, Postfach 68, Winterthur, 8408, Switzerland. TEL 41-52-2260555, FAX 41-52-2260556. Circ: 5,000 (paid and controlled).

791.43 ITA ISSN 0015-1513
FILMCRITICA; rivista mensile di critica cinematografica. Text in Italian. 1950. m. (10/yr.). adv. bk.rev.; film rev. illus. index. reprints avail. **Document type:** *Magazine, Consumer.*
Related titles: Microform ed.: (from PQC); Online - full text ed.; Series: Lo Spettatore Critico.
Indexed: F01, F02, IBR, IBZ, IIFP, IITV, RASB.
Published by: Editrice Le Balze, Via Montecavallo 16, Montepulciano Siena, 53045, Italy. TEL 39-0578-717090, FAX 39-0578-717091, http://www.lebalze.com.

778.53 ITA
FILMCRONACHE; rivista bimestrale di cultura cinematografica. Text in Italian. 1987. q. EUR 26, EUR 48 (effective 2008). **Document type:** *Magazine, Consumer.*
Published by: Associazione Nazionale Circoli Cinematografici Italiani, Via Nomentana, 251, Rome, RM 00161, Italy. TEL 06-86-67-29.

791.43 DEU ISSN 0015-1149
PN1993
FILMECHO - FILMWOCHE; die Fachzeitschrift der Filmwirtschaft in Deutschland. Text in German. 1947. w. EUR 290; EUR 7.50 newsstand/cover (effective 2011). adv. bk.rev.; film rev. illus.; stat. **Document type:** *Magazine, Trade.*
Incorporates (1949-1969): Filmblaetter; Which was formerly (until 1949): Berliner Filmblaetter
Indexed: RASB.

Published by: Verlag Horst Axtmann GmbH und Co., Marktplatz 13, Wiesbaden, 65183, Germany. TEL 49-611-360980, FAX 49-611-301303, info@chmielorz.de, http://www.chmielorz.de. Ed. Ralf Boegner. Pub., Adv. contact Detlef Schaller. Circ: 2,314 (paid).

791.43 IND ISSN 0015-1548
FILMFARE. Text in Hindi, English. 1952. fortn. bk.rev.; film rev. illus. **Document type:** *Magazine, Consumer.*
Related titles: English ed.
Published by: Bennett Coleman & Co. Ltd., The Times of India Bldg, 4th Fl, Dr. Dadabhoy Naoroji Rd, Mumbai, 400 001, India. TEL 91-22-22733358, FAX 91-22-22731585. **U.S. subscr. to:** M-s. Kalpana, 42 75 Main St, Flushing, NY 11355.

791.43 DEU
FILMGESCHICHTE INTERNATIONAL. Text in German. 1993. irreg., latest vol.19, 2010. price varies. **Document type:** *Monographic series, Academic/Scholarly.*
Published by: Wissenschaftlicher Verlag Trier, Bergstr 27, Trier, 54295, Germany. TEL 49-651-41503, FAX 49-651-41504, wvt@wvttrier.de, http://www.wvttrier.de.

791.43 ESP ISSN 1136-7385
➤ **FILMHISTORIA.** Text in Spanish, English; Summaries in English. 1991. 3/yr. bk.rev. bibl. index. **Document type:** *Journal, Academic/Scholarly.* **Description:** Discusses film history and historiography.
Indexed: F01, F02, IIFP, IITV, MLA-IB, MRD.
—**CCC.**
Published by: (Universitat de Barcelona, Departament de Historia Contemporanea, Centro de Investigaciones Film-Historia), Universitat de Barcelona, Servei de Publicacions, Gran Via Corts Catalanes 585, Barcelona, 08007, Spain. TEL 34-93-4021100, http://www.publicacions.ub.es. Circ: 600.

778.53 FIN ISSN 0782-3797
PN1993
FILMIHULLU. Text in Finnish. 1968. 6/yr. EUR 35 (effective 2005). back issues avail. **Document type:** *Magazine, Consumer.*
Indexed: F01, F02, IIFP, IITV.
Published by: Filmihullu ry, Malminkatu 36, Helsinki, 00103, Finland. TEL 358-9-6851414, FAX 358-9-68552242. Eds. Peter von Bagh, Timo Malmi.

791.4375 DEU
FILMJOURNAL. Text in German. 1980. m. EUR 12; free newsstand/cover (effective 2010). adv. **Document type:** *Magazine, Consumer.*
Published by: FilmForum Duisburg, Dellplatz 16, Duisburg, 47049, Germany. TEL 49-203-2854746, FAX 49-203-2854748, mail@filmforum.de. Circ: 20,000 (controlled).

791.43 FIN ISSN 1235-4686
FILMJOURNALEN (KIMITO). Text in Swedish. 1990. q. EUR 16, SEK 160 (effective 2005). adv. **Document type:** *Magazine, Consumer.* **Description:** Concentrates on Nordic movie-making.
Indexed: F01, F02.
Published by: Finlandssvenskt Filmcentrum, Nylandsgatan 1, Aabo, 20500, Finland. TEL 358-2-2500410, FAX 358-2-2500431, filmcent@netti.fi. adv.: page EUR 100. Circ: 750.

791.43 SWE ISSN 1100-7362
FILMKONST. Variant title: Tidskriften Filmkonst. Text in Swedish. 1989. 6/yr. SEK 250 domestic to individuals; SEK 300 domestic to institutions; SEK 300 elsewhere (effective 2003). adv. **Document type:** *Academic/Scholarly.*
Published by: Goeteborg Film Festival, Olaf Palmes Plats, Goeteborg, 41304, Sweden. TEL 46-31-3393002, FAX 46-31-410063. Ed., R&P Magnus Telander. adv.: color page SEK 24,000; 210 x 275. Circ: 6,000.

791.43 SWE
FILMKRETS (ONLINE); tidskriften foer film- och videointresserade. Variant title: Tidskriften Filmkrets. Text in Swedish. 1976. 5/yr. **Document type:** *Magazine, Consumer.*
Formerly (until 2010): Filmkrets (Print) (0347-5425)
Published by: Sveriges Film- och Videofoerbund, Groena Gatan 14 A, Soedertaelje, 15132, Sweden. info@sfvforbund.se, http://www.sfvforbund.se.

791.43 HUN ISSN 0015-1580
PN1993
FILMKULTURA. Text in Hungarian; Summaries in English. 1965. m. USD 42. adv. bk.rev.; film rev. illus. reprints avail. **Description:** Deals with classical and contemporary film art abroad and in Hungary.
Related titles: Microfilm ed.: (from PQC).
Indexed: F01, F02, IIFP, IITV, RILM.
Published by: Magyar Film Intezet/Hungarian Film Institute, Budakeszi utca 51-B, Budapest, 1021, Hungary. TEL 36-1-1767-106. Ed. Ivan Forgacs. Adv. contact Vera Suranyi. B&W page USD 1,000. Circ: 5,000.

791.43 AUT ISSN 0015-1599
FILMKUNST; Zeitschrift fuer Filmkultur und Filmwissenschaft. Text in German. 1949. q. adv. bk.rev.; film rev. illus. reprints avail. **Document type:** *Journal, Trade.* **Description:** Scientific studies and essays on motion pictures and television.
Indexed: DIP, F01, F02, IBR, IBZ.
Published by: Oesterreichische Gesellschaft fuer Filmwissenschaft Kommunikations- und Medienforschung, Rauhensteingasse 5, Vienna, W 1010, Austria. TEL 43-1-5129936, FAX 43-1-5135330. Circ: 600.

791.43 NOR ISSN 0804-8142
FILMMAGASINET. Text in Norwegian. 1994. 10/yr. adv. **Document type:** *Magazine, Consumer.*
Incorporates (1994-1997): Paa Kino (0805-5750); Which was formerly (1987-1994): Filmaktuelt (0806-3958)
Related titles: Online - full text ed.
Published by: Filmmagasinet AS, Dronningensgate 3, Oslo, 0152, Norway. TEL 47-22-003080. Ed. Le ND Nguyen. Adv. contact Patrick Westbye TEL 47-62-941039. page NOK 39,800. Circ: 80,000 (paid and controlled).

791.43 DNK ISSN 1903-4075
FILMMAGASINET EKKO. Variant title: Ekko. Text in Danish. 2008. bi-m. DKK 325 to individuals; DKK 400 to institutions; DKK 275 to students (effective 2009). adv. bk.rev.; film rev.; video rev. back issues avail. **Document type:** *Magazine, Academic/Scholarly.* **Description:** Articles on television, feature films, documentaries, and educational video programs.

Formed by the merger of (2003-2007): Filmmagasinet Mifune (1603-5704); (2000-2007): Ekko (1600-0315); Which was formed by the merger of (1988-1999): Klip (0904-4159); Which was formerly (1971-1988): Film U V (0107-9522); (1967-1971): Filmlaerer-Nyt (0901-4616); (1980-1998): Praasen (0106-7664); Which was formerly (1976-1980): D B Film/Orientering (0105-015X)
Related titles: Online - full text ed.: ISSN 1903-4083. 2000.
Published by: Ekko, Rosenoerns Alle 35, Frederiksberg C, 1970, Denmark. TEL 45-33-214196, sekretariat@ekkofilm.dk. Eds. Thure Munkholm, Claus Christensen. Circ: 13,000.

791.43 BEL ISSN 1782-6756
FILMMAGIE. Text in Dutch. 1956. 10/yr. EUR 40 (effective 2006). adv. bk.rev.; film rev. index. **Document type:** *Magazine, Consumer.* **Description:** Covers film, television and video productions and festivals, with interviews and reviews.
Former titles (until 2005): Film - DVD - Video (1780-9738); (until 2004): Film en Televisie - Video (1373-1459); (until 1985): Film en Televisie (0015-122X)
Indexed: F01, F02, IIFP, IITV.
Address: Tivolistraat 45, Laken, 1020, Belgium. TEL 32-2-5460810, FAX 32-2-5460819, info@filmmagie.be, http://www.filmmagie.be. Circ: 10,000.

778.53 USA ISSN 1063-8954
PN1993
FILMMAKER; the magazine of independent film. Text in English. 1992. q. USD 18 (effective 2010). adv. bk.rev. illus. back issues avail.; reprints avail. **Document type:** *Magazine, Consumer.* **Description:** Presents an insider's look at the business and creative aspects of independent film.
Formed by the 1992 merger of: Off-Hollywood Report (1045-1706); Montage
Related titles: Online - full text ed.: USD 9 (effective 2010).
Indexed: A07, AA, ArtInd, F01, F02, IBT&D, IIPA, MRD, T02, W03, W05.
—**CCC.**
Address: 68 Jay St, Ste 425, Brooklyn, NY 11201. TEL 212-465-8200, FAX 212-465-8525. Ed. Scott Macaulay. Adv. contact Ian Gilmore. B&W page USD 2,350, color page USD 3,000; trim 8.375 x 10.875. Circ: 42,000.

791.43 USA
FILMMAKER'S REVIEW. Text in English. 1976. q. USD 15. adv. bk.rev. illus.
Published by: Columbia Filmmakers, 313 Ferris Booth Hall, Columbia University, New York, NY 10027. Ed. Jim Berger. Circ: 5,000.

791.43 USA ISSN 1040-5100
FILMMAKERS SERIES (LANHAM). Text in English. 1982. irreg., latest vol.126, 2008. price varies. back issues avail. **Document type:** *Monographic series, Academic/Scholarly.*
—BLDSC (3926.664800), IE, Ingenta. **CCC.**
Published by: Scarecrow Press, Inc. (Subsidiary of: Rowman & Littlefield Publishers, Inc.), 4501 Forbes Blvd, Ste 200, Lanham, MD 20706. TEL 301-459-3366, 800-462-6420, FAX 301-429-5748, 800-338-4550, custserv@rowman.com, http://www.scarecrowpress.com. Ed. Anthony Slide. Pub. Mr. Edward Kurdyla TEL 301-459-3366 ext 5604. R&P Clare Cox TEL 212-529-3888 ext 308.

791.43 USA
FILMMAKERS SERIES (WOODBRIDGE). Text in English. 1992. irreg., latest 1998, Mar. USD 46 per issue (effective 2010). back issues avail. **Document type:** *Monographic series, Academic/Scholarly.* **Description:** Provides guidance to the study of film and its trends by studying individual filmmakers and cinematic movements.
Published by: Twayne Publishers (Subsidiary of: Gale), 12 Lunar Dr, Woodbridge, CT 06525. TEL 800-877-4253, FAX 800-414-5043, gale.galeord@cengage.com, http://www.gale.cengage.com/twayne/index.htm. Ed. Frank Beaver.

791.4375 SVK ISSN 1338-3671
▼ **FILMMAX.** Text in Slovak. 2011. m. EUR 1.99 newsstand/cover (effective 2011). adv. **Document type:** *Magazine, Consumer.*
Published by: Bauer Media SK, v.o.s., Panonska cesta 7, Bratislava, 85104, Slovakia. TEL 421-232-153700, FAX 421-232-153733, dnadova@bauermedia.sk.

791.43 CZE ISSN 0015-1645
PN1998
FILMOVY PREHLED; mesicnik pro film a video. Text in Czech; Summaries in Czech. 1939. m. CZK 360 (effective 2009). adv. bk.rev.; video rev.; film rev. abstr.; stat. 48 p./no.; back issues avail. **Document type:** *Journal.* **Description:** Covers detailed information on film events in the Czech Rep., namely on Czech film producations and distribution.
Related titles: Diskette ed.; E-mail ed.
Indexed: RASB.
Published by: Narodni Filmovy Archiv, Bartolomejska 11, Prague 1, 11000, Czech Republic. TEL 420-2-26211863, FAX 420-2-24237233, tomas.bartosek@nfa.cz. Ed. Tomas Bartosek. adv.: B&W page CZK 6,000; trim 148 x 215. Circ: 2,200.

791.43 SWE ISSN 0015-1661
PN1993
FILMRUTAN; tidskrift foer film och filmstudios. Text in Swedish. 1958. q. SEK 200 (effective 2011). adv. bk.rev.; film rev. illus. **Document type:** *Magazine, Consumer.*
Indexed: A20, F01, F02, IIFP, IITV, T02.
Published by: Sveriges Foerenade Filmstudios/Swedish Federation of Film Societies, PO Box 27126, Stockholm, 10252, Sweden. TEL 46-8-6651100, ssf@sff-filmstudios.org. Ed. Marika Junstroem.

▼ **FILMS FOR THE FEMINIST CLASSROOM.** *see* WOMEN'S STUDIES

791.43 USA
FILMS IN REVIEW (ONLINE EDITION). Text in English. 1997. irreg. adv. **Document type:** *Magazine, Consumer.*
Media: Online - full text.
Published by: Then and There Media LLC frumkoid@earthlink.net. Eds. Rocco Simonelli, Roy Frumkes.

791.43 USA ISSN 1083-5369
PN1993
FILMS OF THE GOLDEN AGE. Abbreviated title: F G A. Text in English. 1995. q. USD 19.80 domestic; USD 30 in Canada & Mexico; USD 38 elsewhere (effective 2010). adv. illus. back issues avail.; reprints avail. **Document type:** *Magazine, Consumer.*
Indexed: F01, F02, IIFP, MRD, T02.

Published by: Muscatine Journal (Subsidiary of: Lee Enterprises, Inc.), 301 E Third St, Muscatine, IA 52761. TEL 563-263-2331, 800-383-3198, FAX 563-262-8042, http://www.muscatinejournal.com. Ed. Bob King. adv.: page USD 220.

791.4375 DEU ISSN 1438-0226
FILMSTAR. Text in German. 1994. m. adv. **Document type:** *Magazine, Consumer.* **Description:** Contains information and news on movie stars.
Supersedes in part (in 1998): Deutsches Entertainment Magazin (1435-2214)
Media: Online - full content.
Published by: Next Step Mediendienste GmbH, Bahnhofstr 12, Gemuenden, 55460, Germany. TEL 49-6765-960196, FAX 49-6765-960198, http://www.next-step-mediendienste.de. Ed., Pub. Dirk Jasper. Adv. contact Christine Volkert TEL 49-89-38356380.

791.43 CHE
FILMSTELLEN V S E T H - V S U. DOKUMENTATION. Text in German. 4/yr. **Document type:** *Bulletin.*
Published by: Filmstellen V S E T H - V S U, Leonhardstr 15, Zuerich, 8092, Switzerland. TEL 01-2564294.

791.4375 DEU
FILMTIPS. Text in German. 1984. w. free newsstand/cover (effective 2009). adv. **Document type:** *Magazine, Consumer.*
Published by: Cinecitta, Gewerbemuseumsplatz 3, Nuernberg, 90403, Germany. TEL 49-911-206660, FAX 49-911-2066612, cinecitta@cinecitta.de, http://www.cinecitta.de. Eds. Birgit Winter, Stephanie Linde. adv.: page EUR 900; trim 210 x 297. Circ: 35,000 (controlled).

FILTER MAGAZINE. *see* MUSIC

791.43 FIN ISSN 1795-9977
FINNISH DOCUMENTARY FILMS. Text in English. 2004. a. **Document type:** *Catalog, Consumer.*
Related titles: Online - full text ed.
Published by: Suomen Elokuvasaatio/The Finnish Film Foundation, Kanavakatu 12, Helsinki, 00160, Finland. TEL 358-9-6220330, FAX 358-9-62203050, ses@ses.fi.

791.43 FIN ISSN 1796-0738
FINNISH FILMS. Text in English. 1988. a. **Document type:** *Catalog, Consumer.*
Supersedes in Part (in 2004): Film from Finland (0786-0218)
Related titles: Online - full text ed.
Published by: Suomen Elokuvasaatio/The Finnish Film Foundation, Kanavakatu 12, Helsinki, 00160, Finland. TEL 358-9-6220330, FAX 358-9-62203050, ses@ses.fi.

791.43 FIN ISSN 1796-072X
FINNISH SHORT FILMS. Text in English. 1988. a. **Document type:** *Catalog, Consumer.*
Supersedes in part (in 2004): Films from Finland (0786-0218)
Related titles: Online - full text ed.
Published by: Suomen Elokuvasaatio/The Finnish Film Foundation, Kanavakatu 12, Helsinki, 00160, Finland. TEL 358-9-6220330, FAX 358-9-62203050, ses@ses.fi.

791.43 SGP ISSN 0219-7529
FIRST; Asia's premier movie magazine. Text in English. 2002. m. SGD 42.30 (effective 2008). **Document type:** *Magazine, Consumer.*
Related titles: Online - full content ed.
Published by: S P H Magazines Pte Ltd. (Subsidiary of: Singapore Press Holdings Ltd.), 82 Genting Ln Level 7, Media Centre, Singapore, 349567, Singapore. TEL 65-6319-6319, FAX 65-6319-6345, sphmag@sph.com.sg, http://www.sphmagazines.com.sg/.

791.43 DEU ISSN 0173-542X
FISCHER FILM ALMANACH (YEAR). Text in German. 1980. a. **Document type:** *Bulletin, Consumer.*
Published by: Fischer Taschenbuch Verlag GmbH, Hedderichstr 114, Frankfurt Am Main, 60596, Germany.

791.43 USA
FLICK. Text in English. 2005. 8/yr. adv. **Document type:** *Magazine, Consumer.*
Published by: Decipher, Inc., 253 Granby St., Norfolk, VA 23510-1831. TEL 757-623-3600, FAX 757-623-8368, http://www.decipher.com. Pub. Peter Lobred TEL 757-664-1110. Adv. contact Marc Michals TEL 757-664-1164. color page USD 73,145; trim 5.25 x 7.

778.53 GBR
FLICKERS. Text in English. 3/yr. **Document type:** *Newsletter.* **Description:** Forum for serious collectors of vintage film, projectors, ephemera and related items.
Published by: Vintage Film Circle, 11 Norton Rd, Knowle, Bristol BS4 2EZ, United Kingdom. TEL 44-1179-721973. Ed. Alex Wooliams.

778.53 GBR
FLICKERS 'N' FRAMES. Text in English. 1991 (no.14). 4/yr. GBP 5.50, USD 14. bk.rev.; film rev.; video rev. **Description:** Publishes film criticism and original science fiction stories.
Address: c/o John Peters, 299 Southway Dr, Southway, Plymouth, Devon PL6 6QN, United Kingdom. **Subscr. in U.S. to:** Anne Marsden, 1052 Calle del Cerro, 708, San Clemente, CA 92672. TEL 714-361-3791.

791.433 NLD ISSN 1872-9975
FOCAL PRESS VISUAL EFFECTS AND ANIMATION SERIES. Text in English. 2001. irreg., latest vol.6, 2005. price varies. **Document type:** *Monographic series.*
Published by: Elsevier BV (Subsidiary of: Elsevier Science & Technology), Radarweg 29, PO Box 211, Amsterdam, 1000 AE, Netherlands. TEL 31-20-4853911, FAX 31-20-4852457, JournalsCustomerServiceEMEA@elsevier.com, http://www.elsevier.com.

791.43 FRA ISSN 1962-4530
FOCUS; world film market trends. Text in French, English, German. 1997. a. **Document type:** *Journal, Trade.*
Related titles: Online - full text ed.: free.
Published by: Observatoire Europeen de l'Audiovisuel/European Audiovisual Observatory, 76 Allee de la Robertsau, Strasbourg, 67000, France. TEL 33-3-88144419.

FOTO. *see* PHOTOGRAPHY

778.53 ESP ISSN 1136-4351
FOTOGRAMAS Y VIDEO. Text in Spanish. 1946. m. EUR 3 newsstand/cover (effective 2009). adv. back issues avail. **Document type:** *Magazine, Consumer.*

Former titles: Fotogramas (0212-2340); (until 1980): Nuevo Fotogramas (0212-2332); (until 1968): Fotogramas (0212-2324)
Related titles: Online - full text ed.
Indexed: MLA-IB.
Published by: Hachette Filipacchi SA, Avda Cardenal Herrera Oria 3, Madrid, 28034, Spain. TEL 34-91-7287000, FAX 34-91-3585473, comunicacion@hachette.es, http://www.hachette.es. Ed. Pere Vall. adv.: color page EUR 7,600; 228 x 300. Circ: 93,654.

FOTOMUNDO. *see* PHOTOGRAPHY

FOTOMUNDO. *see* PHOTOGRAPHY

FOTON; fotografia, cine y sonida (photography, amateur movie and sound). *see* PHOTOGRAPHY

791.43 USA
FRAMELINE NEWS. Text in English. 1985. q. USD 35 to members. back issues avail. **Description:** Devoted to lesbian and gay film and video.
Published by: Frameline, 145 9th St., Ste. 300, San Francisco, CA 94103-2640. TEL 415-703-8650, FAX 415-861-1404. Ed. Michael Lumpkin. Circ: 3,000 (paid).

791.43 USA ISSN 0306-7661
PN1993
➤ **FRAMEWORK;** the journal of cinema and media. Text in English. 1975-1994; resumed. s-a. USD 30 to individuals; USD 70 to institutions; USD 10 to students (effective 2009). adv. bk.rev. illus. back issues avail.; reprints avail. **Document type:** *Journal, Academic/Scholarly.* **Description:** Dedicated to theoretical and historical work on the diverse and current trends in media and film scholarship.
Related titles: Online - full text ed.: ISSN 1559-7989.
Indexed: A07, A22, A26, A30, A31, AA, ArtInd, B04, CA, CommAb, E01, F01, F02, I05, IBR, IBZ, IIFP, IIPA, IITV, MLA-IB, MRD, P02, PCI, T02, W03, W05.
—BLDSC (4032.119000), IE, Ingenta. **CCC.**
Published by: Wayne State University Press, The Leonard N Simons Bldg, 4809 Woodward Ave, Detroit, MI 48201. TEL 313-577-6120, 800-978-7323, FAX 313-577-6131. Ed. Drake Stutesman. Circ: 100.

791.43 USA
FRAMEWORK: THE JOURNAL OF CINEMA AND MEDIA. Text in Spanish. 1971-1992; resumed 1999. irreg.
Related titles: Online - full text ed.
Published by: Framework, PO Box 2010, New York, NY 10159. Ed. Paul Willemen.

302.2343 301 792 USA ISSN 1524-7821
FRAMING FILM; the history and art of cinema. Text in English. 2002. irreg., latest vol.9, 2009. price varies. **Document type:** *Monographic series, Academic/Scholarly.* **Description:** Publishes film studies on topics of national and international interest, including topics on film theory, film and society, gender and race, politics.
Published by: Peter Lang Publishing, Inc. (Subsidiary of: Peter Lang Publishing Group), 29 Broadway, New York, NY 10006. TEL 212-647-7700, 800-770-5264, FAX 212-647-7707, customerservice@plang.com, http://www.peterlangusa.com. Ed. Frank Beaver.

FRANCEVISION - HIT PARADE. *see* MUSIC

791.43 DEU ISSN 0343-7736
PN1995.9.W6
FRAUEN UND FILM. Text in German. 1974. a. EUR 15 (effective 2005). adv. bk.rev. back issues avail. **Document type:** *Journal, Academic/Scholarly.* **Description:** Examines the role of women in film, as actresses, producers, directors, and writers.
Indexed: DIP, F01, F02, IBR, IBZ, IIFP, IIPA, IITV, MLA-IB, PCI.
—**CCC.**
Published by: Stroemfeld Verlag GmbH, Holzhausenstr 4, Frankfurt Am Main, 60322, Germany. TEL 49-69-9552260, FAX 49-69-95522624, info@stroemfeld.de, http://www.stroemfeld.de. Eds. Gertrud Koch, Heide Schluepmann. Circ: 3,000.

778.53 CAN ISSN 0704-9536
FREEZE FRAME. Text in English. 1977. q. free.
Formerly: Film Edmonton
Published by: Edmonton Film Society, 6243 112 A St, Edmonton, AB T6H 3K4, Canada.

791.43 USA
FRENCH FILM DIRECTORS. Text in English. 1998. irreg., latest 2009. price varies. back issues avail. **Document type:** *Monographic series.*
Published by: Palgrave Macmillan (Subsidiary of: Macmillan Publishers Ltd.), 175 Fifth Ave, New York, NY 10010. TEL 212-982-3900, 800-221-7945, FAX 212-982-5562, http://us.macmillan.com/palgrave.aspx.

GADNEY'S GUIDES TO INTERNATIONAL CONTESTS, FESTIVALS & GRANTS IN FILM & VIDEO, PHOTOGRAPHY, TV-RADIO BROADCASTING, WRITING & JOURNALISM. *see* COMMUNICATIONS

791.43 GBR ISSN 2042-1222
▼ **GANGSTERS;** the ultimate DVD collection. Text in English. 2009. bi-w. back issues avail. **Document type:** *Magazine, Consumer.*
Published by: G E Fabbri Ltd., The Communications Bldg, 7th Fl, 48 Leicester Sq, London, WC2H 7LT, United Kingdom. TEL 44-20-30317600, FAX 44-20-30317601, mailbox@gefabbri.co.uk, http://www.gefabbri.co.uk/.

GEORGE EASTMAN HOUSE - INTERNATIONAL MUSEUM OF PHOTOGRAPHY AND FILM. ANNUAL REPORT. *see* PHOTOGRAPHY

791.43 DEU ISSN 1614-6387
GERMAN FILMS QUARTERLY. Text in German. 1994. q. free to qualified personnel (effective 2009). **Document type:** *Magazine, Trade.*
Formerly (until 2004): Kino (0948-2547)
Indexed: F01, F02, MLA-IB, T02.
—**CCC.**
Published by: German Films Service and Marketing GmbH, Herzog-Wilhelm-Str 16, Munich, 80331, Germany. TEL 49-89-5997870, FAX 49-89-59978730, info@german-films.de.

GESELLSCHAFT FUER MEDIENWISSENSCHAFT. SCHRIFTENREIHE. *see* SOCIOLOGY

791.43 USA ISSN 2152-8438
▼ **GET AHEAD.** Text in English. 2010. s-a. USD 11 per issue (effective 2011). **Document type:** *Magazine, Consumer.* **Description:** Features information on the Get Ahead Film Festival. Includes DVD of short films.

Published by: Get Ahead Films, 515 Lafayette Ave, Apt 1, Brooklyn, NY 11205. TEL 973-652-7569, brandon@getaheadfilms.com.

778.53 USA
GO SEES & PHOTOGRAPHERS. Text in English. bi-w. USD 69 (effective 2000).
Published by: The John King Network, 244 Madison Ave, Ste 393, New York, NY 10016. TEL 212-969-8715, 212-969-8715.

791.43 HKG
GOLDEN MOVIE NEWS/CHIA HO TIEN YING. Text in Chinese. m. HKD 60. illus.
Published by: (Ssu Hai Chu Pan Shih Yeh Yu Hsien Kung Ssu), Four Seas Publications Ltd., 1st Fl, 122 B Argyle St, Kowloon, Hong Kong.

791.43 POL
GOMOTION; the secrets behind animation. Text in English. 2008. q. EUR 59.99 (effective 2009). adv. **Document type:** *Magazine, Trade.* **Description:** Deals with the latest and most useful software, hardware news, and reviews involving 3D and 2D animation.
Published by: Software - Wydawnictwo Sp. z o.o., ul Bokserska 1, Warsaw, 02-682, Poland. TEL 48-22-4273530, FAX 48-22-2442459, sdj@software.com.pl, http://www.software.com.pl. Adv. contact Ewa Samulska. page USD 1,500; trim 180 x 248.

791.43 PER ISSN 1025-9937
LA GRAN ILUSION. Text in Spanish. 1993. s-a. **Document type:** *Journal, Academic/Scholarly.*
Indexed: MLA-IB.
Published by: Universidad de Lima, Avenida Javier Prado Este s/n, Lima, 33, Peru. TEL 51-1-4376767, FAX 51-1-4378066, http://www.ulima.edu.pe.

791.43 ITA ISSN 1127-0918
LL GRANDE CINEMA DI GUERRA. Text in Italian. 1998. bi-w. **Document type:** *Magazine, Consumer.*
Published by: R C S Libri (Subsidiary of: R C S Mediagroup), Via Mecenate 91, Milan, 20138, Italy. TEL 39-02-5095-2248, FAX 39-02-5095-2975, http://rcslibri.corriere.it/libri/index.htm.

791.43 ITA ISSN 2038-0992
▼ **GRANDI SCHERMI.** Text in Italian. 2010. m. **Document type:** *Magazine, Consumer.*
Published by: CIGRA 2003 Srl, Viale Vittorio Veneto 28, Milan, 20124, Italy. TEL 39-02-43995439, FAX 39-02-29061863, info@cigra.it.

778.53 ITA ISSN 0393-3857
PN1993
➤ **GRIFFITHIANA.** Text in English, Italian. 1978. s-a. EUR 40 to individuals; EUR 80 to institutions (effective 2008). adv. bk.rev. illus. reprints avail. **Document type:** *Journal, Academic/Scholarly.* **Description:** Devoted to silent cinema and classic animation.
Related titles: Online - full text ed.: ISSN 1086-3206.
Indexed: AmHI, CA, F01, F02, H07, IBT&D, IIFP, IIPA, IITV, MLA-IB, MRD, T02.
—Ingenta.
Published by: Cineteca del Friuli, Via G. Bini, Palazzo Gurisatti, Gemona, UD 33013, Italy. TEL 39-0432-980458, FAX 39-0432-970542, griffithiana@cinetecadelfriuli.org, http://cinetecadelfriuli.org. Eds. Davide Turconi, Peter Lehman. Pub. Livio Jacob. Adv. contact Piera Patat. Circ: 2,500. **Dist in N. America by:** The Johns Hopkins University Press. jrnlcirc@press.jhu.edu.

➤ **LE GRIOT**; hebdomadaire des spectacles, du cinema et de la culture. *see* GENERAL INTEREST PERIODICALS—Africa

384.55 USA
GUIA FAMILIAR. Text in Spanish. 1979. w. free. **Description:** Covers movies, Hollywood and TV.
Address: PO Box 9190, Van Nuys, CA 91409. TEL 818-882-9200, FAX 818-882-2625. Ed. Diane Lerner. adv.: B&W page USD 291,650; 9.88 x 7.38. Circ: 229,644 (controlled).

791.43 CAN ISSN 1719-5802
GUIDE DES PROGRAMMES FEDERAUX D'AIDE FINANCIERE A L'INDUSTRIE DU FILM ET DE LA VIDEO. Text in French. 2000. a., latest 2006. **Document type:** *Handbook/Manual/Guide, Trade.*
Media: Online - full text.
Published by: Canadian Heritage/Patrimoine Canadien, 15 Eddy St, Gatineau, PQ K1A 0M5, Canada. TEL 819-997-0055, 866-811-0055, pch-qc@pch.gc.ca.

GUIDE TO FEDERAL PROGRAMS FOR THE FILM AND VIDEO SECTOR. *see* PUBLIC ADMINISTRATION

778.53 ARG
HACIENDO CINE. Text in Spanish. 1995. q.? ARS 5 newsstand/cover.
Published by: Multimedia Lei S.A., Ciudad de la Paz 580 3o 7, Buenos Aires, 1428, Argentina. TEL 54-114-5535042.

778.53 USA
HANDS ON PAGES. Text in English. m. free. **Document type:** *Newsletter, Trade.* **Description:** Contains interviews with the top movie makers and information for those who appreciate cinema.
Media: Online - full text.
Published by: Moviemaker Pub., 2265 Westwood Blvd, Ste 479, Los Angeles, CA 90064. TEL 310-234-9234, 888-625-3668, FAX 310-234-9293, staff@moviemaker.com.

HECHOS DE MASCARA. *see* LABOR UNIONS

791.43 SWE ISSN 1402-7402
HEMMABIO. Text in Swedish. 1995. 10/yr. **Document type:** *Consumer.*
Formerly (until 1997): Multimedia HemmaBio (1400-4038)
Published by: Tidningen HiFi Musik AB, PO Box 23084, Stockholm, 10435, Sweden. TEL 46-8-342970, FAX 46-8-342971.

HENDERSON'S CASTING DIRECTORS GUIDE. *see* THEATER

HEROES FROM HACKLAND. *see* LITERATURE—Adventure And Romance

HILL VALLEY TELEGRAPH. *see* CLUBS

THE HILTONIAN. *see* LITERATURE

HISTORICAL JOURNAL OF FILM, RADIO AND TELEVISION. *see* HISTORY

781.542 USA
HITCH; journal of pop culture absurdity. Text in English. 1994. q. USD 19.80; USD 4 per issue (effective 2005). adv. bk.rev.; film rev.; music rev.; software rev.; video rev.; rec.rev.; tel.rev.; Website rev. illus. 84 p./no.; back issues avail. **Document type:** *Magazine, Consumer.* **Description:** Contains satire, humor, entertainment reviews and commentary, including interviews. Purpose is to amuse and inform. Audience is anyone with a sense of humor.
Published by: Hitch Publishing Company, PO Box 23621, Oklahoma City, OK 73123-2621. TEL 405-728-7232. Ed., Pub., R&P, Adv. contact Rod M Lott. B&W page USD 100; 7.5 x 10. Circ: 2,000.

791.43 AUS
HOBART FILM NEWS. Text in English. 1948. bi-m. free to members (effective 2009). **Document type:** *Newsletter.* **Description:** Presents reviews of forthcoming films.
Published by: Hobart Film Society Inc., GPO Box 678, Hobart, TAS 7001, Australia. TEL 61-3-62345998, paulb@trump.net.au, http://www.hobartfilmsociety.tassie.org/. Circ: 350 (controlled).

778.53 USA
HOLA PAGES; national directory of Hispanic talent. Text in English. 1979. q. adv. **Document type:** *Directory, Trade.* **Description:** Distributed nationally to casting directors and producers.
Formerly: Directory of Hispanic Talent
Published by: Hispanic Organization of Latin Actors, 107 Suffolk St, Ste 302, New York, NY 10002. TEL 212-253-1015, FAX 212-253-9651. Ed., R&P, Adv. contact Manny Alfaro. Circ: 1,600.

791.43 HRV ISSN 1330-9471
HOLLYWOOD. Text in Croatian. 1995. m. adv. **Document type:** *Magazine, Consumer.*
Published by: Vedis, Hreljinska 5, Zagreb, 10000, Croatia. TEL 385-1-338813, FAX 385-1-340868. Ed. Veljko Krulcic.

HOLLYWOOD ACTING COACHES AND TEACHERS DIRECTORY. *see* EDUCATION—Teaching Methods And Curriculum

791.43 USA ISSN 1533-4813
HD9696.A1
HOLLYWOOD AFTERMARKET. Text in English. 1993. m. USD 895 (effective 2008). **Document type:** *Newsletter.* **Description:** Analyzes film performance in the home video, pay-per-view, pay TV and free TV markets.
Published by: Adams Media Research (Subsidiary of: Screen Digest Ltd.), 27865 Berwick Dr, Carmel, CA 93923. TEL 831-624-0303, FAX 831-624-2190, info@adamsmediaresearch.com, http://www.adamsmediaresearch.com. Pub. Tom Adams.

HOLLYWOOD CALL SHEET. *see* LABOR UNIONS

HOLLYWOOD CREATIVE DIRECTORY'S BELOW-THE-LINE TALENT. *see* BUSINESS AND ECONOMICS—Trade And Industrial Directories

HOLLYWOOD CREATIVE DIRECTORY'S FILM DIRECTORS. *see* BUSINESS AND ECONOMICS—Trade And Industrial Directories

791.4375 230 USA ISSN 1942-5554
PN1993
HOLLYWOOD JESUS REVIEWS. Text in English. 200?. a. USD 17.95 per issue (effective 2008). **Document type:** *Journal, Consumer.* **Description:** Provides movie synopsis and reviews from a spiritual and Christian perspective.
Published by: Hollywood Jesus Books, PO Box 48282, Burien, WA 98166. TEL 206-241-6149, editor@hjbooks.com, http://www.hjbooks.com/HJBooks/index.htm. Eds. Greg Wright, Jenn Wright.

791.43 USA ISSN 1557-7228
PN1993
HOLLYWOOD LIFE. Text in English. 1989. bi-m. USD 13.75 domestic; USD 33 foreign; USD 3.99 newsstand/cover (effective 2008). adv. bk.rev. illus. 100 p./no.; back issues avail.; reprints avail. **Document type:** *Magazine, Consumer.* **Description:** Highlights lifestyles of film and movie makers.
Former titles (until 2005): Movieline's Hollywood Life (1544-0583); (until Apr. 2003): Movieline (1055-0917)
Indexed: ASIP, F01, F02, MRD, T02.
—Ingenta.
Published by: Line Publications LLC, 10537 Santa Monica Blvd., Ste. 250, Los Angeles, CA 90025-4952. TEL 310-234-9501, FAX 310-234-0332. adv.: B&W page USD 14,820, color page USD 20,270. Circ: 312,000.

791.43 USA ISSN 0018-3660
PN1993
THE HOLLYWOOD REPORTER. Text in English. 1930. w. USD 99; USD 199 combined subscription domestic (print & online eds.); USD 299 combined subscription in Canada & Mexico (print & online eds.); USD 322 combined subscription elsewhere (print & online eds.) (effective 2011). adv. bk.rev.; film rev.; play rev. back issues avail.; reprints avail. **Document type:** *Magazine, Trade.* **Description:** Designed for entertainment's most powerful, influential people, that enables success in a continually evolving business and creative environment.
Related titles: Microfilm ed.: (from BHP, LIB, PQC); Online - full text ed.: Hollywood Reporter: Premier Edition. USD 199 domestic; USD 99.95 foreign (effective 2009); Alternate Frequency ed(s).: w. USD 175 domestic; USD 225 in Canada & Mexico; USD 285 in Europe; USD 350 elsewhere (effective 2003).
Indexed: A10, B01, B03, B07, B11, CWI, F01, F02, G08, G09, I05, I07, P10, P48, P53, P54, PQC, S23, V03.
—CIS. **CCC.**
Published by: Prometheus Global Media, 5700 Wilshire Blvd, 5th Fl, Los Angeles, CA 90036. TEL 323-525-2270, http://www.prometheusgm.com.

791.43 USA
THE HOLLYWOOD REPORTER. INTERNATIONAL EDITION. Text in English. 19??. w. (Tue.). adv. bk.rev.; film rev.; play rev. illus. back issues avail.; reprints avail. **Document type:** *Magazine, Trade.* **Description:** Covers the international film, music, cable, and home video scene.
Related titles: Microfilm ed.: (from BHP, LIB, PQC); Online - full text ed.
Published by: Prometheus Global Media, 5700 Wilshire Blvd, 5th Fl, Los Angeles, CA 90036. TEL 323-525-2270, http://www.prometheusgm.com.

791.437 USA ISSN 1097-8577
PN1996
HOLLYWOOD SCRIPTWRITER. Text in English. 1986. bi-m. USD 30 domestic; USD 38.70 in Canada; USD 47.50 elsewhere (effective 2003). adv. **Document type:** *Magazine, Trade.* **Description:** Contains articles and features on the entertainment industry, including profiles screenwriters, producers, directors, and book-to-movie writers.
Related titles: Online - full text ed.
Indexed: A10, F01, F02, IBT&D, T02, V03.
Address: 11163, Carson, CA 90749-1163. TEL 866-479-7483. adv.: B&W page USD 850, color page USD 1,000; 8.5 x 11.

401 791.43 USA ISSN 1061-2327
PM8415
➤ **HOLQED.** Text in English. 1992. q. back issues avail. **Document type:** *Journal, Academic/Scholarly.* **Description:** Contains artwork, feature articles, and regular columns discussing Klingon linguistics, language, and culture.
Indexed: MLA-IB.
Published by: Klingon Language Institute, PO Box 634, Flourtown, PA 19031. http://www.kli.org/kli/.

791.43 GBR ISSN 0967-8239
HOME ENTERTAINMENT. Text in English. 1992. m. GBP 28.97 domestic; GBP 44 in Europe; GBP 50 in North America; GBP 57 elsewhere; GBP 3.25 newsstand/cover (effective 2002). adv. **Document type:** *Magazine, Consumer.* **Description:** Guide to buying widescreen and digital TVs, VCRs, DVD players, cinema sound amplifiers and speakers, and satellite systems.
Related titles: Online - full text ed.
—CCC.
Published by: Future Publishing Ltd., Beauford Ct, 30 Monmouth St, Bath, Avon BA1 2BW, United Kingdom. TEL 44-1225-442244, FAX 44-1225-446019, customerservice@subscription.co.uk, http://www.futureplc.com. Ed. Rob Lane. Circ: 18,323 (paid).

HOMU SHIATA/HOME THEATER. *see* SOUND RECORDING AND REPRODUCTION

791.43 USA
HOPPY TALK. Text in English. 1991. q. USD 20 domestic; USD 25 foreign (effective 2001). adv. bk.rev. back issues avail. **Document type:** *Newsletter.* **Description:** News about William Boyd's career in silent films and his role of Hopalong Cassidy. Stresses the collecting of toys endorsed by Boyd.
Published by: Friends of Hopalong Cassidy, 6310 Friendship Dr, New Concord, OH 43762-9708. TEL 740-826-4850. Ed., Pub., R&P, Adv. contact Laura Bates. Circ: 400 (paid).

HORROR CULT. *see* COMMUNICATIONS—Video

791.43 USA
HOT HOLLYWOOD GOSSIP. Text in English. 1995. w. **Document type:** *Bulletin.* **Description:** Gossip about movie stars and funny TV reviews.
Media: Online - full text. Ed. Steve Gordon.

087.5 ITA ISSN 1723-1205
HOTDOG MAGAZINE. Variant title: Hot Dog Film Magazine. Text in Italian. 2003. m. adv. **Document type:** *Magazine, Consumer.*
Published by: Play Media Company, Via di Santa Cornelia 5A, Formello, RM 00060, Italy. TEL 39-06-33221250, FAX 39-06-33221235, abbonamenti@playmediacompany.it, http://www.playmediacompany.it.

791.43 HRV ISSN 1330-7665
PN1993.5.C79 CODEN: HFLJFV
➤ **HRVATSKI FILMSKI LJETOPIS/CROATIAN CINEMA CHRONICLE.** Text in Croatian; Abstracts in English. 1995. q. HRK 150 domestic; EUR 60 foreign; HRK 50 per issue (effective 2011). adv. **Document type:** *Journal, Academic/Scholarly.*
Related titles: Online - full text ed.
Indexed: A20, ArtHuCI, RILM, W07.
Published by: Hrvatski Filmski Savez/Croatian Film Club's Association, Tuskanac 1, Zagreb, 10000, Croatia. TEL 385-1-4848771, FAX 385-1-4848764, ngilic@yahoo.com. Ed. Nikica Gilic. Pub. Vera Robic-Skarica. adv.: page HRK 4,000. **Co-publisher:** Hrvatski Drzavni Arhiv.

791.43 CHN ISSN 1002-9974
HUANQIU YINMU HUAKAN/WORLD SCREEN. Text in Chinese. 1985. m. USD 54; USD 4.50 newsstand/cover (effective 2001).
—East View.
Published by: Zhongguo Dianying Chubanshe/China Film Press, 22 Beisanhuan Donglu, Beijing, 100013, China. TEL 86-1-4219977. Ed. Cui Junyan. **Dist. by:** China International Book Trading Corp, 35 Chegongzhuang Xilu, Haidian District, PO Box 399, Beijing 100044, China. TEL 86-10-68412045, FAX 86-10-68412023, cibtc@mail.cibtc.com.cn, http://www.cibtc.com.cn.

I A M H I S T NEWSLETTER. *see* SOCIOLOGY

778.53 USA
I D A MEMBERSHIP AND SURVIVAL GUIDE. Text in English. biennial. USD 50 to non-members; USD 25 to members (effective 2000). adv. **Document type:** *Directory.* **Description:** Lists members of the IDA, an international listing of film and video makers, broadcasters, documentary funders, distributors, crew and talent; reference tool for documentarians.
Published by: International Documentary Association, 1201 W 5th St, Ste M320, Los Angeles, CA 90017. TEL 213-534-3600, FAX 301-785-9334, membership@documentary.org. Pub. Betsy A McLane. R&P Darren S Hand.

791.43 NLD
I D F A MAGAZINE. Text in Dutch, English. 1997. m. adv. bk.rev. **Document type:** *Magazine, Consumer.* **Description:** Offers festival information, interviews with filmmakers, and background articles.
Related titles: Online - full text ed.
Published by: International Documentary Filmfestival Amsterdam, Kleine-Gartmanplantsoen 10, Amsterdam, 1017 RR, Netherlands. TEL 31-20-6273329, FAX 31-20-6385388, info@idfa.nl, http://www.idfa.nl.

791.43 USA
I F F; the magazine of film, music, fashion, and travel. (International Film Festival) Text in English. 6/yr. USD 24 (effective 2001). adv. back issues avail. **Document type:** *Magazine, Consumer.* **Description:** Includes film festival news as well as features on celebrities, travel, and related lifestyles.

Published by: D & D Publications, PO Box 1063, Agoura Hills, CA 91376. TEL 818-754-4412, FAX 805-494-8566, iffmag@earthlink.net. Ed. Jane Kellard. adv.: color page USD 3,500; trim 8 x 10.875.

I Q. (Intellect Quarterly) *see* LITERATURE

778.53 ESP ISSN 1137-4438
TR845
IKUSGAIAK. Text in Spanish. 1985. irreg. **Document type:** *Monographic series, Academic/Scholarly.*
Formerly (until 1997): Sociedad de Estudios Vascos. Cuadernos de Seccion. Cinematografia (1130-5541)
Published by: Eusko Ikaskuntza/Sociedad de Estudios Vascos, Palacio Miramar, Miraconcha 48, Donostia, San Sebastian 20007, Spain. TEL 34-943-310855, FAX 34-943-213956, ei-sev@sc.ehu.es, http://www.eusko-ikaskuntza.org/.

791.43 NZL ISSN 0112-9341
PN1993.5.N43
ILLUSIONS; a New Zealand magazine of film, television and theatre criticism. Text in English. 1986. 3/yr. NZD 13 domestic to individuals; NZD 26 domestic to institutions (effective 2008). adv. illus. **Document type:** *Magazine, Academic/Scholarly.*
Indexed: F01, F02, IIFP, IITV, INZP, RILM, T02.
—Ingenta.
Published by: Victoria University of Wellington, Drama Studies, Te Aro, PO Box 600, Wellington, New Zealand.

791.43 CZE ISSN 0862-397X
PN1993
ILUMINACE. Text in Czech. 1989. q. CZK 200 (effective 2009). **Document type:** *Journal.*
Indexed: IIFP.
Published by: Narodni Filmovy Archiv, Malesicka 12, Prague 3, 13003, Czech Republic. TEL 420-2-71770509, FAX 420-2-71770501, http://www.nfa.cz.

IMAGE (ROCHESTER, 1952); journal of photography and motion pictures. *see* PHOTOGRAPHY

791.43 ESP ISSN 1137-6546
IMAGENES DE ACTUALIDAD. Text in Spanish. 1985. m. USD 32 domestic; USD 65 in Europe; USD 158 elsewhere (effective 2009). adv. music rev.; video rev.; bk.rev.; film rev. back issues avail. **Document type:** *Magazine, Consumer.* **Description:** Publishes reports about recent and future films, interviews with American stars of the moment, articles, dossiers, reports on the main film festivals.
Published by: Dirigido por.. S.L., Consell de Cent 304, Barcelona, 08007, Spain. TEL 34-93-4876202, FAX 34-93-4880896. Ed., R&P Enrique Aragones. Adv. contact Jose Maria Latorre. Circ: 45,000 (paid).

778.53 FRA ISSN 1255-3468
IMAGES DOCUMENTAIRES. Text in French. 1990. q. video rev.; film rev. **Document type:** *Magazine.* **Description:** Publishes articles written by film makers, and critics, all based on one central theme. Written for the general public with an interest in documentary film.
Formerly (until 1993): Images en Bibliotheques (1146-1756)
Published by: Association Images Documentaires, 26, rue du Cdt Mouchotte (K110), Paris, 75014, France. Ed. Catherine Blangonnet. **Subscr. to:** Dif'Pop', 21 ter rue Voltaire, Paris 75011, France. TEL 33-1-40242131, FAX 33-1-40241588.

778.53 FRA ISSN 1952-8752
IMAGES EN BIBLIOTHEQUES. LA LETTRE. Text in French. 1997. bi-m. adv. **Document type:** *Newsletter.* **Description:** Offers valuable information for the libraries proposing video collections (fiction, documentary) to be seen in the library, or rent at home.
Formerly (until 2005): La Lucarne (1255-2992)
Published by: Association Images en Bibliotheques, 21 Rue Curial, Paris, 75019, France. TEL 33-1-43381992, ib@imagenbib.com, http://www.imagenbib.com. Adv. contact Dominique Margot.

791.433 GBR ISSN 1748-1244
IMAGINE; the magazine for animation professionals. Text in English. 1999. bi-m. GBP 19.95 domestic; GBP 35.94, EUR 52 foreign (effective 2009). back issues avail. **Document type:** *Magazine, Trade.* **Description:** Dedicated to animation trends and culture: new applications, emerging techniques, in-depth features as well as analysis of the latest news and events in the world of animation.
Formerly (until 2001): Animation U K (Quarterly Edition) (1468-1188)
Published by: Wildfire Communications Ltd., Unit 2.4 Paintworks, Arnos Vale, Tottendown, Bristol BS4 3EN, United Kingdom. TEL 44-117-9029977, FAX 44-117-9029978, lee.haines@wildfirecomms.co.uk, http://www.wildfirecomms.co.uk. Adv. contact Ruth Morris. Circ: 7,500 (controlled).

791.433 GBR ISSN 1755-0718
IMAGINE ANIMATION DIRECTORY. Text in English. 1995. a. GBP 45, EUR 46.90 per issue; free to members (effective 2009). **Document type:** *Directory, Trade.* **Description:** Covers the entire UK and contains over 4000 industry contacts for production companies, post production facilities, distributors and suppliers, web designers, animators and games developers.
Former titles (until 2007): Animation Directory (1742-853X); (until 2004): Animation UK (1360-208X)
—BLDSC (4368.996437).
Published by: Wildfire Communications Ltd., Unit 2.4 Paintworks, Arnos Vale, Tottendown, Bristol BS4 3EN, United Kingdom. TEL 44-117-9029977, FAX 44-117-9029978, lee.haines@wildfirecomms.co.uk, http://www.wildfirecomms.co.uk. Adv. contact Ruth Morris.

IMAGINE F X. *see* COMPUTERS—Computer Graphics

791.43 GBR ISSN 0964-6957
IMPACT (HUDDERSFIELD). Text in English. 1992. m. GBP 23.70 domestic; GBP 32.95 in Europe; USD 79.95 in North America; GBP 44.95 elsewhere; GBP 3.95 newsstand/cover (effective 2010). adv. bk.rev.; film rev.; video rev. illus. **Document type:** *Magazine, Consumer.* **Description:** Features articles covering the eastern and western action entertainment since 1992.
Related titles: Online - full text ed.: GBP 23.70 domestic; USD 79.95 in North America (effective 2010).
Published by: M A I Publications, Revenue Chambers, St. Peter's St, Huddersfield, W Yorkshire HD1 1DL, United Kingdom. TEL 44-1484-435011, FAX 44-1484-422177, martialartsltd@btconnect.com, http://www.martialartsltd.co.uk. Ed. John Mosby. Pub. Roy Jessop. Adv. contact Moira E Spencer. **Dist. by:** Seymour Distribution Ltd.

778.53 USA
IN FOCUS (LOS ANGELES). Text in English. 1984. s-a. USD 35 to members. film rev.; video rev. illus. **Document type:** *Newsletter.* **Description:** For supporters of Asian-American work in visual communications.
Published by: Friends of Visual Communications, 120 Judge John Aiso St BAsement, Los Angeles, CA 90012. TEL 213-680-4462, FAX 213-687-4848. Pub., R&P Linda Mabalot. Circ: 3,000.

791.43 USA ISSN 1557-5799
PN1993
THE INDEPENDENT (NEW YORK). Text in English. 1978. q. (10/yr. until 2007). free to members (effective 2006). adv. bk.rev. illus. 64 p./no.; back issues avail.; reprints avail. **Document type:** *Magazine, Consumer.* **Description:** Covers the technical, legislative, marketing, and artistic facets of film and video production (especially independent production), with new-technology articles, conference reports, film-maker profiles, announcements of festivals, classifieds, notices.
Former titles (until 2005): The Independent Film & Video Monthly (1077-8918); (until 1994): Independent (New York) (0731-5198)
Related titles: Online - full text ed.
Indexed: A27, AltPI, F01, F02, IIPA, MLA-IB, MRD, P02, P10, P16, P48, P53, P54, PQC, T02.
Published by: (Center for Independent Documentary), Independent Media Publications, 304 Hudson St, 6th Fl, New York, NY 10013. Ed. Mike Hofman. Pub. Michele Meek. adv.: B&W page USD 875, color page USD 1,750; trim 10.88 x 8.25. Circ: 42,000.

741.5 USA ISSN 1756-7319
INDIANA JONES. Text in English. 2008. irreg. USD 39 newsstand/cover (effective 2009). adv. back issues avail. **Document type:** *Magazine, Consumer.* **Description:** Features interviews with the cast and crew of the latest blockbuster, Indiana Jones and the Kingdom of the Crystal Skull along with photography and features of Indiana Jones's comic book adventures.
Published by: Titan Magazines, PMB #1-296, 8205 Santa Monica Blvd, W Hollywood, CA 90046-5977.

791.43 USA
PN1993
INDIE; the free monthly guide to independent film. Text in English. 1998. m. free. adv. **Document type:** *Magazine, Consumer.* **Description:** Contains articles and features on independent films and the actors, writers, directors and producers who create them.
Published by: Hachette Filipacchi Media U.S., Inc. (Subsidiary of: Hachette Filipacchi Medias S.A.), 1633 Broadway, New York, NY 10019. TEL 212-767-6000, FAX 212-767-5600, saleshfmbooks@hfmus.com, http://www.hfmus.com. Ed., Pub. Joseph Steuer.

791.43 USA
INDIEVISION. Text in English. 2002. q. **Document type:** *Magazine, Consumer.*
Published by: Gothamwood Entertainment Ltd., 156 Bay 14th Street, Brooklyn, NY 11214. TEL 718-621-9797, FAX 718-621-2121. Ed. Bruno Derlin. Pub. Kevin DelGaudio. **Subscr. to:** PO Box 8191, White Plains, NY 10602. TEL 866-830-9797, FAX 914-686-5673, subscribe@indievision.net. **Dist. by:** Prestige Periodical Distributors, 19 Court St, White Plains, NY 10601. TEL 914-684-2317, FAX 914-684-2319.

791.43 USA
INDIEWIRE; filmmakers, biz, fans. Text in English. 1995. d. adv. **Document type:** *Newspaper, Consumer.* **Description:** Covers the independent film industry.
Media: Online - full text. **Related titles:** E-mail ed.: indieWIRE Daily. free; Print ed.: indieWIRE Monthly.
Published by: indieWIRE LLC, 73 Spring St, Ste 403, New York, NY 10012. TEL 212-343-8717, FAX 212-343-8718. Ed. Eugene Hernandez. Adv. contact James Israel.

791.43 USA
INDIEZINE. Text in English. 1996. m. USD 30. **Description:** For the advancement of independent film, videomaking and screenwriting. Ed., Pub. Michael Carr.

+INFO. (Plusinfo) *see* HOBBIES

791.43 DEU
INFOBRIEF: FILM; ein Kulleraugen Informationsdienst. Text in German. 1994. irreg. (approx. w.). looseleaf. EUR 30 (effective 2001). bk.rev.; film rev.; video rev. back issues avail. **Document type:** *Newsletter, Corporate.*
Formerly: InfoFax: Film (0947-840X)
Media: Fax.
Published by: Kulleraugen Verlag, Laaseweg 4, Schellerten, 31174, Germany. TEL 49-5123-4330, FAX 49-5123-2015, redaktion.kulleraugen@epost.de, http://www.kulleraugen-verlag.de. Ed. Hans-Juergen Tast. Circ: 250 (paid).

791.43 NZL ISSN 1179-7711
INFRAME; your quarterly guide to what's on at rialto cinemas. Text in English. 2000. q. adv. **Document type:** *Magazine, Consumer.*
Formerly (until 2007): Rialto Cinemas
Related titles: Online - full text ed.: ISSN 1179-7843. free (effective 2010).
Published by: Rialto Cinemas, Level 4, 48 Greys Ave, Auckland, New Zealand. TEL 64-9-3099137, rialtofeedback@rialtocinemas.co.nz, http://www.rialto.co.nz. Pub. Mitchell Murphy. Adv. contact Kim Ellett TEL 64-274-796355.

791.43 USA ISSN 1546-7457
PN1993.5.U6
INGENUE. Text in English. 2003 (Fall). q. USD 12.95 domestic; USD 19.95 in Canada (effective 2005). adv. **Document type:** *Magazine, Consumer.*
Published by: Ingenue Publications, 8961 Sunset Blvd Ste 2A, Los Angeles, CA 90069. TEL 310-247-8810. Ed. Dane Lee.

791.43 SWE
INGMAR. Text in Swedish. 2003. 6/yr. SEK 169 (effective 2003). adv. film rev. 100 p./no. **Document type:** *Journal.*
Published by: Filmtidningen Ingmar Foerlag AB, Upplandsgatan 85, Stockholm, 11344, Sweden. Ed., Pub. Emil Hellstroem. adv.: page SEK 17,700; 210 x 275. Circ: 15,000.

INSCENA. *see* THEATER

791.436 AUS ISSN 1447-2252
INSIDE FILM; Australia's filmmaker magazine. Variant title: I F. Text in English. 1997. 11/yr. AUD 78 domestic; AUD 101.25 in Asia & the Pacific; AUD 120 elsewhere (effective 2009). adv. back issues avail. **Document type:** *Magazine, Trade.*
Former titles (until 2001): If (1442-5246); (until 1999): Independent Filmmakers (1329-8690); (until 1997): Independent Filmmakers Journal
Related titles: Online - full content ed.: ISSN 1447-2260. 2001.
Indexed: F01, F02, T02.
Published by: The Intermedia Group Pty Ltd., PO Box 55, Glebe, NSW 2037, Australia. TEL 61-2-96602113, FAX 61-2-96604419, info@intermedia.com.au, http://www.intermedia.com.au. Eds. Brendan Swift, Susan Royal. Pub. Mark Kuban. adv.: color page AUD 2,870; trim 218 x 288. Circ: 4,490.

791.43 USA
PN1993.5.U6
INSIDE FILM MAGAZINE; business magazine of the film industry. Text in English. 1979. q. USD 16 (effective 2005). adv. bk.rev.; film rev. **Document type:** *Magazine, Trade.*
Former titles: American Premiere Magazine (0279-0041); (until 1981): Premiere (0274-7766)
Related titles: Online - full text ed.
Published by: American Premiere, Ltd., 8421 Wilshire Blvd, Penthouse Ste, Beverly Hills, CA 90211. TEL 323-852-0434. Ed., Pub. Susan Royal. Adv. contact Alyssa Boyle. Circ: 17,500 (paid).

791.43 USA
INSIDE POPULAR FILM. Text in English. 1995. irreg., latest 2008. price varies. back issues avail. **Document type:** *Monographic series.*
Published by: Palgrave Macmillan (Subsidiary of: Macmillan Publishers Ltd.), 175 Fifth Ave, New York, NY 10010. TEL 212-982-3900, 800-221-7945, FAX 212-982-5562, subscriptions@palgrave.com, http://us.macmillan.com/palgrave.aspx.

791.43 DEU ISSN 0944-3215
INSTITUT FUER DEN WISSENSCHAFTLICHEN FILM. BEITRAEGE ZU ZEITGESCHICHTLICHEN FILMQUELLEN. Text in German; Summaries in English, French, German. 1995. irreg. **Document type:** *Academic/Scholarly.*
Indexed: RASB.
Published by: Institut fuer den Wissenschaftlichen Film, Nonnenstieg 72, Goettingen, 37075, Germany. TEL 49-551-5024-0, FAX 49-551-5024400, iwf-goe@iwf.de, http://www.iwf.de/.

778.53 FRA ISSN 0985-2395
PN1993
INSTITUT JEAN VIGO. ARCHIVES. Text in French. 1986. 5/yr. adv. **Document type:** *Bulletin.*
Indexed: F01, F02, IIFP, IITV.
Published by: Institut Jean Vigo de Perpignan, 1 Rue Jean Vielledent, Perpignan, 66000, France. TEL 33-4-68340939, FAX 33-4-68354120. Circ: 800.

791.423 GBR ISSN 1471-5031
HM1206
INTENSITIES; the journal of cult media. Text in English. 2001. s-a. **Description:** Publishes articles on all aspects of cult media including cult television, cult film, cult radio, literary cults and cult authors, new media cults, cult figures and celebrities, cult icons, musical cults, cult geographies, historical studies of media cults and their fandoms, cult genres (e.g. science fiction, horror, fantasy, pulp fiction, Manga, anime, Hong Kong film etc.), non-generic modes of cultishness, theorizations of cult media, relevant audience and readership studies, and work that addresses the cult media industry.
Related titles: Online - full text ed.
Published by: Cardiff University, School of Journalism, Media and Cultural Studies, Cardiff, United Kingdom. Ed. Sara Gwenllian Jones.

791.43 AUS ISSN 1833-0533
➤ **INTERACTIVE MEDIA.** Abbreviated title: I M(Interactive Media). Text in English. 2005. a. **Document type:** *Journal, Academic/Scholarly.*
Media: Online - full text.
Published by: National Academy of Screen and Sound, School of Media Communications and Culture, Division of Arts, Murdoch University,S St, Murdoch, W.A. 6150, Australia. Eds. Jenny De Reuck, Josko Petkovic, Dr. Mick Broderick.

➤ **INTERNATIONAL ALLIANCE OF THEATRICAL STAGE EMPLOYES, MOVING PICTURE TECHNICIANS, ARTISTS AND ALLIED CRAFTS OF THE U.S., ITS TERRITORIES AND CANADA. OFFICIAL BULLETIN.** *see* LABOR UNIONS

778.53 USA
INTERNATIONAL DICTIONARY OF FILMS AND FILMMAKERS. Text in English. irreg., latest vol.4, 2000, 4th ed. USD 216 4th ed. (effective 2008). bibl.; illus. back issues avail. **Document type:** *Directory, Trade.* **Description:** Provides information on films, actors and actresses, directors, writers and other production artists.
Related titles: Online - full text ed.
Published by: Gale (Subsidiary of: Cengage Learning), 27500 Drake Rd, Farmington Hills, MI 48331. TEL 248-699-4253, 800-877-4253, FAX 877-363-4253, gale.galeord@thomson.com, http://gale.cengage.com.

▼ **THE INTERNATIONAL JOURNAL OF SCREENDANCE.** *see* DANCE

791.43 USA ISSN 0074-7084
PN1993.3
INTERNATIONAL MOTION PICTURE ALMANAC; reference tool of the film industry. Text in English. 1929. a. USD 140 per issue (effective 2004). adv. **Document type:** *Handbook/Manual/Guide, Trade.*
Former titles (until 1955): Motion Picture and Television Almanac (1043-8106); (until 1952): International Motion Picture Almanac (1043-8122); (until 1936): The Motion Picture Almanac (1044-1697)
Related titles: Microfilm ed.: (from BHP).
Indexed: CA&I, PABMI.
Published by: Quigley Publishing Co. (Subsidiary of: Q P Media, Inc.), 64 Wintergreen Ln, Groton, MA 01450. quigleypub@aol.com, http://www.quigleypublishing.com/. Ed. Tracy Stevens. Pub., R&P Martin Quigley.

791.43 RUS ISSN 0130-6405
PN1993
ISKUSSTVO KINO. Text in Russian; Summaries in English. 1931. m. USD 131. bk.rev.; film rev. illus. index.
Related titles: Microfilm ed.: (from PQC); Online - full text ed.
Indexed: F01, F02, IBT&D, IIFP, IIPA, IITV, MLA-IB.

—East View.
Published by: Soyuz Kinematografistov Rossii/Russian Filmmakers' Union, Usievicha ul 9, Moscow, 125319, Russian Federation. TEL 7-095-1515651, FAX 7-095-1510272. Ed. Daniil Dondurei. Circ: 12,000. **Dist. by:** East View Information Services, 10601 Wayzata Blvd, Minneapolis, MN 55305. TEL 952-252-1201, 800-477-1005, FAX 952-252-1202, info@eastview.com, http://www.eastview.com.

791.43 ITA
ITALIAN CINEMA. Text in English. q. EUR 25 (effective 2009). **Document type:** *Magazine, Consumer.*
Published by: Editoriale Duesse SpA, Via Donatello 5b, Milan, 20131, Italy. TEL 39-02-277961, FAX 39-02-27796300, e-duesse@e-duesse.it, http://www.e-duesse.it.

791.43 NLD ISSN 2211-4351
THE IVENS MAGAZINE. Text in English. 1995. a. free (effective 2011). **Document type:** *Magazine, Consumer.*
Formerly (until 2006): Europese Stichting Joris Ivens. Nieuwsbrief (1568-9131)
Published by: European Foundation Joris Ivens, Postbus 606, Nijmegen, 6500 AP, Netherlands. TEL 31-24-3888774, FAX 31-24-3888776, info@ivens.nl, http://www.ivens.nl.

791.43 GBR ISSN 2040-1167
▼ **JADE SCREEN.** Text in English. 2009. q. GBP 17 (effective 2011). adv. back issues avail. **Document type:** *Magazine, Consumer.* **Description:** Contains all the latest Asian cinema news.
Published by: Screen Power Publishing, PO Box 1989, Bath, BA2 2YE, United Kingdom. office@screen-power.com.

791.43 DEU
JAHRBUCH KAMERA (YEAR). Text in German. 1959. a. EUR 21.80 (effective 2011). adv. **Document type:** *Magazine, Consumer.*
Formerly (until 1990): Jahrbuch des Kameramanns (0075-2509)
Published by: I. Weber Verlag (Subsidiary of: Ebner Verlag GmbH), Ohmstr 15, Munich, 80802, Germany. TEL 49-89-38308680, FAX 49-89-38308683. Ed. Evelyn Voight-Mueller. Adv. contact Carola Frommer.

778.53 DEU
JAHRBUCH VIDEOFILMEN. Text in German. 1984. a. index. **Document type:** *Directory, Consumer.*
Former titles (until 2003): Jahrbuch fuer Videofilmer (0931-1920); (until 1986): Olympus Jahrbuch fuer Videofilmer (0176-6767)
Published by: Fachverlag Schiele und Schoen GmbH, Markgrafenstr 11, Berlin, 10969, Germany. TEL 49-30-2537520, FAX 49-30-2517248, service@schiele-schoen.de, http://www.schiele-schoen.de. Circ: 5,000.

791.43 JPN ISSN 0448-8830
PN1993.5.J3
JAPANESE FILMS. Text in English. 1958. a.
Published by: UniJapan Film, Association for the Diffusion of Japanese Films Abroad Inc., 2-11-6, Takeda Bldg, No. 505, Ginza, Chuo-ku, Tokyo, 104-0061, Japan. TEL 81-3-55657511, FAX 81-3-55657531, office@unijapan.org, http://www.unijapan.org.

778.53 FRA ISSN 0758-4202
PN1993
JEUNE CINEMA. Text in French. 1964. bi-m. EUR 45 (effective 2008). bk.rev. index. 76 p./no.; back issues avail. **Document type:** *Newsletter, Consumer.*
Indexed: F01, F02, IIFP, IIPA, IITV, MLA-IB.
Published by: Association des Amis de Jeune Cinema, 71 rue Robespierre, Montreuil, 93100, France. TEL 33-1-41721030, FAX 33-1-48702302. Ed. Lucien Logette. Pub. Andree Tournes.

791.43 DEU ISSN 0724-7508
JOURNAL FILM. Text in German. 1981. s-a. adv. bk.rev. back issues avail. **Document type:** *Academic/Scholarly.*
Indexed: IBR, IBZ.
Published by: Kommunales Kino Freiburg e.V., Urachstr 40, Freiburg Im Breisgau, 79102, Germany. TEL 49-761-709033, kino@freiburger-medienforum.de, http://www.freiburger-medienforum.de/kino/. Circ: 1,600.

JOURNAL OF ADAPTATION IN FILM AND PERFORMANCE. *see* THEATER

791.43 GBR ISSN 1754-9221
▼ **JOURNAL OF AFRICAN CINEMAS.** Abbreviated title: J A C. Text in English. 2009. s-a. GBP 36, USD 68 to individuals; USD 180 to institutions; USD 290 to individuals (effective 2012). adv. back issues avail. **Document type:** *Journal, Academic/Scholarly.* **Description:** Explores the interactions of visual and verbal narratives in African film.
Related titles: Online - full text ed.: ISSN 1754-923X. GBP 147, USD 220 (effective 2012).
Indexed: CA, F01, F02, T02.
Published by: Intellect Ltd., The Mill, Parnall Rd, Fishponds, Bristol, BS16 3JG, United Kingdom. TEL 44-117-9589910, FAX 44-117-9589911, info@intellectbooks.com. Eds. Keyan Tomaselli, Martin Mhando. Pub. Masoud Yazdani. **Dist. by:** Turpin Distribution Services Ltd.

791.43 GBR ISSN 1750-8061
PN1993.C6
➤ **JOURNAL OF CHINESE CINEMAS.** Abbreviated title: J C C. Text in English. 2007. 3/yr. GBP 36, USD 68 to individuals; GBP 235, USD 368 to institutions (effective 2012). adv. back issues avail. **Document type:** *Journal, Academic/Scholarly.* **Description:** Devoted to the study of Chinese film, drawing on the recent world-wide growth of interest in Chinese cinemas.
Related titles: Online - full text ed.: ISSN 1750-807X. GBP 192, USD 290 (effective 2012).
Indexed: A07, A30, A31, AA, ArtInd, B04, BRD, CA, F01, F02, IIFP, MLA-IB, T02, W03, W05.
—IE.
Published by: Intellect Ltd., The Mill, Parnall Rd, Fishponds, Bristol, BS16 3JG, United Kingdom. TEL 44-117-9589910, FAX 44-117-9589911, info@intellectbooks.com. Ed. Song Hwee Lim. Pub. Masoud Yazdani. **Subscr. to:** Turpin Distribution Services Ltd., Pegasus Dr, Stratton Business Park, Biggleswade, Bedfordshire SG18 8QB, United Kingdom. TEL 44-1767-604951, FAX 44-1767-601640, custserv@turpin-distribution.com, http://www.turpin-distribution.com/.

791.43 USA ISSN 0742-4671
PN1993
➤ **JOURNAL OF FILM AND VIDEO.** Text in English. 1949. q. USD 95 combined subscription to institutions (print & online eds.) (effective 2012). adv. bk.rev.; film rev. illus. cum.index. back issues avail.; reprints avail. **Document type:** *Journal, Academic/Scholarly.* **Description:** Features scholarly articles on film and television history, theory and production.
Former titles (until 1984): University Film and Video Association. Journal (0734-919X); (until 1982): University Film Association. Journal (0041-9311); (until 1968): University Film Producers Association. Journal (2155-8159)
Related titles: Microform ed.: (from PQC); Online - full text ed.: ISSN 1934-6018. USD 75 to institutions (effective 2012).
Indexed: A01, A02, A03, A07, A08, A09, A10, A20, A22, A26, A27, A30, A31, AA, ABS&EES, APC, ASCA, ArtHuCI, ArtInd, B04, B14, CA, CMM, CommAb, CurCont, DIP, E01, E03, E07, E08, ERI, F01, F02, G08, I05, IBR, IBT&D, IBZ, IIFP, IIPA, IITV, MLA-IB, MRD, P02, P10, P16, P48, P53, P54, PQC, RASB, S09, SCOPUS, T02, V02, V03, V04, W03, W05, W07.
—BLDSC (4984.190000), IE, Infotrieve, Ingenta. **CCC.**
Published by: (University Film and Video Association), University of Illinois Press, 1325 S Oak St, Champaign, IL 61820. TEL 217-333-0950, 866-244-0626, FAX 217-244-8082, journals@uillinois.edu. Ed. Stephen Tropiano TEL 800-280-7709. Adv. contact Jeff McArdle TEL 217-244-0381.

➤ **THE JOURNAL OF FILM MUSIC.** *see* MUSIC

791.43 BEL ISSN 1609-2694
JOURNAL OF FILM PRESERVATION. Text in English, French, Spanish. 1991. s-a. EUR 30 (effective 2010). adv. bk.rev.; film rev.; Website rev. stat.; tr.lit.; illus. back issues avail.; reprints avail. **Document type:** *Journal, Academic/Scholarly.*
Formerly (until Oct. 1993): F I A F Bulletin (1017-1126)
Related titles: Online - full text ed.
Indexed: A&ATA, A07, AA, ArtInd, CA, F01, F02, IBT&D, IIFP, IIPA, IITV, T02, W03, W05.
—CCC.
Published by: Federation Internationale des Archives du Film (F I A F)/International Federation of Film Archives, Rue Defacqz 1, Brussels, 1000, Belgium. TEL 32-2-5383065, FAX 32-2-5344774, info@fiafnet.org. Ed. Robert Daudelin. Pub. Christian Dimitriu.

791.43 GBR ISSN 1756-4905
PN1993
▼ ➤ **JOURNAL OF JAPANESE & KOREAN CINEMA.** Abbreviated title: J J K C. Text in English. 2009. s-a. GBP 36, USD 68 to individuals; GBP 180, USD 290 to institutions (effective 2012). adv. back issues avail. **Document type:** *Journal, Academic/Scholarly.* **Description:** Provides a forum for the dissemination of scholarly work devoted to the cinemas of Japan and Korea and the interactions and relations between them.
Related titles: Online - full text ed.: ISSN 1756-4913. 2009. GBP 147, USD 220 (effective 2012).
Indexed: CA, F01, F02, MLA-IB, T02.
Published by: Intellect Ltd., The Mill, Parnall Rd, Fishponds, Bristol, BS16 3JG, United Kingdom. TEL 44-117-9589910, FAX 44-117-9589911, info@intellectbooks.com. Eds. David Desser, Frances Gateward. Pub. Masoud Yazdani. **Subscr. to:** Turpin Distribution Services Ltd., Pegasus Dr, Stratton Business Park, Biggleswade, Bedfordshire SG18 8QB, United Kingdom. TEL 44-1767-604951, FAX 44-1767-601640, custserv@turpin-distribution.com, http://www.turpin-distribution.com/.

791.43 USA ISSN 0195-6051
PN1993
➤ **JOURNAL OF POPULAR FILM AND TELEVISION.** Text in English. 1972. q. GBP 119 combined subscription in United Kingdom to institutions (print & online eds.); EUR 157, USD 197 combined subscription to institutions (print & online eds.) (effective 2012). adv. bk.rev. bibl.; illus. index, cum.index. back issues avail.; reprint service avail. from PSC. **Document type:** *Journal, Academic/Scholarly.* **Description:** Features include essays on the social and cultural background of films and television programs, filmographies, bibliographies, and commissioned book and video reviews.
Formerly (until 1978): The Journal of Popular Film (0047-2719)
Related titles: CD-ROM ed.; Microform ed.; Online - full text ed.: ISSN 1930-6458. GBP 107 in United Kingdom to institutions; EUR 141, USD 177 to institutions (effective 2012).
Indexed: A01, A02, A03, A06, A07, A08, A20, A22, A25, A26, A27, A30, A31, AA, ABS&EES, APW, ASCA, Acal, AmH&L, AmHI, ArtHuCI, ArtInd, B04, B14, BRD, BRI, CA, CBRI, CMM, CWI, ChPerI, CommAb, CurCont, DIP, E08, F01, F02, G05, G06, G07, G08, H07, H08, HAb, HistAb, HumInd, I05, I07, IBR, IBT&D, IBZ, IIFP, IIPA, IITV, L05, L06, M01, M02, MLA, MLA-IB, MRD, P02, P10, P13, P48, P53, P54, PCI, PQC, RI-1, RI-2, RILM, RefSour, S02, S03, S08, S09, S23, SCOPUS, T02, W03, W05, W07.
—BLDSC (5041.141000), CIS, IE, Infotrieve, Ingenta. **CCC.**
Published by: (Helen Dwight Reid Educational Foundation), Routledge (Subsidiary of: Taylor & Francis Group), 325 Chestnut St, Ste 800, Philadelphia, PA 19106. TEL 215-625-8900, FAX 215-625-2940, journals@routledge.com, http://www.routledge.com. Eds. Gary R Edgerton, Michael T Marsden.

778.53 USA ISSN 1092-1311
PN1995.9.R4
➤ **JOURNAL OF RELIGION AND FILM.** Text in English. 1997. s-a. free (effective 2011). adv. bk.rev.; film rev. back issues avail. **Document type:** *Journal, Academic/Scholarly.* **Description:** Covers information about religion & film.
Media: Online - full text.
Indexed: A21, A26, A39, C27, C29, CA, D03, D04, E08, E13, F01, F02, I05, MLA-IB, R14, RI-1, S14, S15, S18, T02.
Published by: University of Nebraska at Omaha, Department of Philosophy and Religion, 60th & Dodge Streets, Omaha, NE 68182. TEL 402-554-2628, FAX 402-554-3296, unonews@unomaha.edu, http://www.unomaha.edu/wwwphrel/. Ed. Michele Desmarais TEL 402-554-2679.

791.43 GBR ISSN 2042-7891
▼ **JOURNAL OF SCANDINAVIAN CINEMA.** Text in English. 2011. s-a. GBP 36, USD 68 to individuals; GBP 132, USD 185 to institutions (effective 2012). adv. back issues avail. **Document type:** *Journal, Academic/Scholarly.* **Description:** Aims to become a prime site for research and discussions on cinema in Scandinavia, both within the national context of Denmark, Finland, Iceland, Norway and Sweden, and as a region existing in a globalized world.
Related titles: Online - full text ed.: ISSN 2042-7905. forthcoming. GBP 99, USD 140 (effective 2012).
Published by: Intellect Ltd., The Mill, Parnall Rd, Fishponds, Bristol, BS16 3JG, United Kingdom. TEL 44-117-9589910, FAX 44-117-9589911, info@intellectbooks.com. Eds. Anders Marklund, Casper Tybjerg. Pub. Masoud Yazdani.

791.43 GBR ISSN 1759-7137
▼ **JOURNAL OF SCREENWRITING.** Abbreviated title: J O S C. Text in English. 2010. s-a. GBP 36, USD 68 to individuals; GBP 132, USD 185 to institutions (effective 2012). adv. back issues avail. **Document type:** *Journal, Academic/Scholarly.* **Description:** Aims to explore the nature of writing for the moving image in the broadest sense, highlighting current academic thinking around scriptwriting whilst also reflecting on this with a truly international perspective and outlook.
Related titles: Online - full text ed.: ISSN 1759-7145. GBP 99, USD 140 (effective 2012).
Indexed: F01, F02, MLA-IB, T02.
—IE.
Published by: Intellect Ltd., The Mill, Parnall Rd, Fishponds, Bristol, BS16 3JG, United Kingdom. TEL 44-117-9589910, FAX 44-117-9589911, info@intellectbooks.com. Eds. Barry Langford, Ian Macdonald, Jule Selbo. Pub. Masoud Yazdani. **Dist. by:** Turpin Distribution Services Ltd., Pegasus Dr, Stratton Business Park, Biggleswade, Bedfordshire SG18 8QB, United Kingdom. TEL 44-1767-604951, FAX 44-1767-601640, custserv@turpin-distribution.com, http://www.turpin-distribution.com/.

791.43 USA ISSN 1558-9846
THE JOURNAL OF SHORT FILM. Text in English. 2005. q. USD 36; USD 10 per issue (effective 2006). **Document type:** *Magazine, Consumer.*
Media: Optical Disk - DVD.
Published by: The Journal of Short Film, P O Box 8217, Columbus, OH 43201. contact@theJSF.org. Eds. Paul Hill, Susan B Halpern.

778.53 USA
➤ **JUMP CUT**; a review of contemporary media. Text in English. 1974. a. free (effective 2010). bk.rev.; film rev. illus. back issues avail.; reprints avail. **Document type:** *Journal, Academic/Scholarly.*
Media: Online - full text. **Related titles:** Microfilm ed.: (from PQC).
Indexed: ChPerI, IIPA, IITV, LeftInd, MRD, SOPODA.
Published by: Jump Cut Associates, PO Box 865, Berkeley, CA 94701. Eds. Chuck Kleinhans, John Hess, Julia Lesage.

➤ **JUYING YUEBAO/DRAMA & MOVIES MONTHLY.** *see* THEATER

792 791.43 780 USA ISSN 1942-4132
K C STUDIO. (Kansas City) Text in English. 19??. bi-m. USD 40 (effective 2008). adv. **Document type:** *Magazine, Consumer.* **Description:** Highlights cinematic, visual and performing arts events in the Kansas City metropolitan area.
Former titles (until 2008): K C P T Magazine (1074-1720); (until 1993): K C P T Public Television 19 (1055-5706); (until 19??): K C P T Magazine (1050-9534); (until 19??): K C P T Program Guide
Published by: K C P T, 125 E 31st St, Kansas City, MO 64108. Ed. Kellie Houx. Adv. contact Christin Turley.

791.43 ITA ISSN 1828-2245
KARASCIO. Text in Italian. 2006. irreg. **Document type:** *Magazine, Consumer.*
Published by: Universita degli Studi di Bergamo, Via Salvecchio 19, Bergamo, 24100, Italy. TEL 39-035-2052530, FAX 39-035-2052537, http://www.unibg.it.

791.43 GBR ISSN 1754-8489
PN1998.A1
KEMPS FILM, TELEVISION, COMMERCIALS PRODUCTION SERVICES HANDBOOK (UK & REPUBLIC OF IRELAND EDITION). Text in English. 1996. a. adv. **Description:** Comprehensive handbook for professionals involved in the film, TV and video industry, containing entries covering products and services in the UK.
Former titles (until 2007): Kemps Film, Television, Commercials (UK Edition) (1742-8432); (until 2003): Kemps Film, TV & Video Handbook (UK Edition) (1363-4496)
—CCC.
Published by: Reed Business Information Ltd. (Subsidiary of: Reed Business), Windsor Court, East Grinstead House, East Grinstead, W Sussex RH19 1XA, United Kingdom. TEL 44-1342-326972, FAX 44-1342-335612, rbi.subscriptions@qss-uk.com, http://www.reedbusiness.co.uk/. Adv. contact Harvey Osborn TEL 44-1342-335779. Circ: 13,500.

791.43 GBR
KEMPS INTERNATIONAL. Text in English. 1956. a. adv. **Document type:** *Directory.* **Description:** Comprehensive handbook for professionals involved in the film, TV and video industry, containing entries covering products and services in the Americas and Canada.
Former titltes (until 2000): International Kemps Film, T V and Video (1466-1721); (until 1998): Kemps Film, T V and Video Handbook (1366-7068); (until 1995): Kemps Film, TV & Video Yearbook; (until 1993): Kemps International Film and Television Year Book (0142-0690); (until 1978): Kemps Film and Television Year Book (0075-5427)
Published by: Reed Business Information Ltd. (Subsidiary of: Reed Business), Windsor Court, East Grinstead House, East Grinstead, W Sussex RH19 1XA, United Kingdom. TEL 44-1342-326972, FAX 44-1342-335612, rbi.subscriptions@qss-uk.com, http://www.reedbusiness.co.uk/.

KEY NOTE MARKET REPORT: CINEMAS & THEATRES. *see* BUSINESS AND ECONOMICS—Production Of Goods And Services

791.43 GBR
KEY NOTE MARKET REPORT: THE FILM INDUSTRY. Variant title: The Film Industry Market Report. Text in English. 1995. irreg., latest 2002, Mar. GBP 340 per issue (effective 2010). **Document type:** *Report, Trade.* **Description:** Provides an overview of a specific UK market segment and includes executive summary, market definition, market size, industry background, competitor analysis, current issues, forecasts, company profiles, and more.

Published by: Key Note Ltd. (Subsidiary of: Bonnier Business Information), Harlequin House, 5th Fl, 7 High St, Teddington, Richmond upon Thames, TW11 8EE, United Kingdom. TEL 44-845-5040452, FAX 44-845-5040453, info@keynote.co.uk.

KIDS' ACTING FOR BRAIN SURGEONS; the insiders guide for kids in the industry. *see* CHILDREN AND YOUTH—For

791.43 JPN ISSN 1342-4149
KINDAI. Text in Japanese. 1945. m. JPY 13,000. adv. film rev. **Document type:** *Consumer.*
Formerly (until Sep. 1996): Kindai Eiga (0023-1460)
Media: Duplicated (not offset).
Published by: Kindai-Eiga Corp., Owaricho Bldg, 2F, 6-8-3 Ginza, Chuo-ku, Tokyo, 104-0061, Japan. TEL 81-3-5568-2811, FAX 81-3-5568-2818. Ed. Yasushi Mizukami. Pub. Shuzo Kosugi. R&P Fumitaka Kosugi. Adv. contact Masatoshi Tanaka. Circ: (controlled).

KINDER JUGEND FILM KORRESPONDENZ. *see* CHILDREN AND YOUTH—For

371.33523 CAN ISSN 1192-6252
➤ **KINEMA**; a journal for film and audiovisual media. Text in English, French. 1993. s-a. CAD 22; USD 22 in United States; USD 25 foreign (effective 2002). adv. bk.rev. illus. reprints avail. **Document type:** *Journal, Academic/Scholarly.*
Related titles: Online - full text ed.
Indexed: CA, F01, F02, IIFP, MLA-IB, MRD, T02.
—CCC.
Published by: University of Waterloo, Department of Fine Arts and Film Studies, 200 University Ave, W, Waterloo, ON N2L 3G1, Canada. TEL 519-885-1211, FAX 519-746-4982. Ed. Jan Uhde. adv.: page CAD 95. Circ: 250.

778.53 DEU ISSN 0936-3777
KINEMATOGRAPH. Text in German. 1984. irreg., latest vol.23, 2007. price varies. adv. **Document type:** *Monographic series, Academic/Scholarly.*
Published by: Deutsches Filmmuseum, Schaumainkai 41, Frankfurt Am Main, 60596, Germany. TEL 49-69-9612200, FAX 49-69-961220999, info@deutsches-filmmuseum.de, http://www.deutsches-filmmuseum.de. Ed., Adv. contact Walter Schobert.

778.53 COL ISSN 0121-3776
PN1993
➤ **KINETOSCOPIO.** Text in Spanish. 1990. q. COP 26,000 domestic; USD 40 foreign (effective 2002). adv. bk.rev.; film rev. 120 p./no.; back issues avail. **Document type:** *Academic/Scholarly.* **Description:** Covers international cinema with a special focus on Latin American cinema through in-depth articles and dossiers. Includes information on all films currently being shown in the country, interviews, and coverage of international film festivals.
Indexed: F01, F02, IIFP, MLA-IB.
Published by: Centro Colombo Americano, Carrera 45 No. 53-24, Apartado Aereo 8734, Medellin, ANT, Colombia. TEL 57-4-513-4444, FAX 57-4-513-2666. Ed. Pedro Adrian Zuluaga TEL 57-4-513-4444. Adv. contact Beatriz Garcia TEL 57-4-513-4444. Circ: 2,500 (paid).

791.43 POL ISSN 0023-1673
PN1993
KINO; miesiecznik poswiecony tworczosci i edukacji filmowej. Text in Polish. 1966. m. EUR 55 foreign (effective 2007). bk.rev.; film rev. illus. index. **Document type:** *Magazine, Consumer.*
Indexed: F01, F02, IIFP, IITV, MLA-IB, RASB.
Published by: Fundacja Kino, ul Chelmska 19/21, Warsaw, 00724, Poland. TEL 48-22-8416843, FAX 48-22-8419057. Ed. Andrzej Kolodynski. Circ: 30,000. **Dist. by:** Ars Polona, Obroncow 25, Warsaw 03933, Poland. TEL 48-22-5098609, FAX 48-22-5098610, arspolona@arspolona.com.pl, http://www.arspolona.com.pl.

791.43 BGR ISSN 0861-4393
PN1993
KINO. Text in Bulgarian. 1946. bi-m. USD 60 foreign; BGL 2.50 newsstand/cover (effective 2002). bk.rev.; film rev. illus. index. **Document type:** *Journal.* **Description:** Covers problems and perspectives of the development of Bulgarian cinema and its creators.
Formerly (until 1990): Kinoizkustvo (0323-9993)
Indexed: IIFP, IITV, RASB.
Published by: (Suiuz na Bulgarskite Kinodeitsite/Union of Bulgarian Cinema Workers), Komitet za Izkustvo i Kultura, 7 Levski ul, Sofia, 1000, Bulgaria. Ed. Kalinka Stoynovska. Circ: 7,500. **Dist. by:** Sofia Books, ul Silivria 16, Sofia 1404, Bulgaria. TEL 359-2-9586257, info@sofiabooks-bg.com, http://www.sofiabooks-bg.com.

791.43 CAN ISSN 1923-7561
▼ **KINO**; the Western undergraduate journal of film studies. Text in English. 2010. irreg., latest vol.1, 2010. free (effective 2010). **Document type:** *Journal, Academic/Scholarly.* **Description:** Serves to exhibit the best of film theory and critique as written by undergraduate students at The University of Western Ontario.
Media: Online - full text.
Published by: University of Western Ontario, Western Libraries, 1151 Richmond St, London, ON N6A 3K7, Canada. TEL 519-661-2111, FAX 519-661-3493, wufsfilm@hotmail.com, http://www.lib.uwo.ca. Eds. Joshua Romphf, Patrick Martini.

791.43 RUS ISSN 0869-4370
PN1993.5.R9
KINO - GLAZ. Text in Russian. 1991. bi-m. USD 83 (effective 1998). adv. film rev.; video rev. illus. back issues avail.; reprints avail. **Document type:** *Trade.* **Description:** Provides information on film market, production and distribution in Russia and CIS countries.
Related titles: Online - full text ed.
Published by: Izdatel'stvo Kino - Glaz Ltd., Aizenstainskaya ul 8, 223-A, Moscow, 129226, Russian Federation. TEL 7-095-1812236, FAX 7-095-2050658. Ed. Yevgeniya Tirdatova. Pub. Py R Chernyaev. Adv. contact Yulia Khomyakova. page USD 1,500. Circ: 30,000.

791.43 DEU
KINO JOURNAL FRANKFURT. Text in German. w. free. **Document type:** *Magazine, Consumer.*
Published by: Presse Verlagsgesellschaft fuer Zeitschriften und Neue Medien mbH, Ludwigstr 33-37, Frankfurt Am Main, 60327, Germany. TEL 49-69-974600, FAX 49-69-97460400. Eds. Andreas Dosch, Shirin Khalik. Adv. contact Thomas Knopp TEL 49-69-97460633. Circ: 22,000 (controlled).

791.43 DEU
KINO NEWS. Text in German. 1986. m. adv. bk.rev.; film rev. illus. **Document type:** *Magazine, Consumer.*
Former titles (until 2007): L O S; (until 2003): Kino News
Published by: T und M Verlagsgesellschaft mbH, Bilser Str 11-13, Hamburg, 22297, Germany. TEL 49-40-514010, FAX 49-40-51401100, info@t-m-media.de, http://www.t-m-media.de. Ed. Christoph Meier Siem. adv.: page EUR 24,500; trim 195 x 278. Circ: 838,030 (controlled).

778.53 792 700 UKR ISSN 1562-3238
PN2859.U47
KINO-TEATR. Text in Ukrainian. 1995. 6/yr. UAK 14 domestic; USD 95 foreign (effective 2000). bk.rev.; film rev.; play rev.; tel.rev.; video rev. illus. back issues avail. **Document type:** *Academic/Scholarly.*
—East View.
Published by: (Ministry of Culture and Arts of Ukraine), Kyivo-Mohylianska Akademiya, Ul G Skovorody 2, Kiev, 254070, Ukraine. TEL 380-44-4166096, FAX 380-44-4636783. Ed., Pub. Larysa Brioukhovetska. **Dist. by:** East View Information Services, 10601 Wayzata Blvd, Minneapolis, MN 55305. TEL 952-252-1201, 800-477-1005, FAX 952-252-1202, info@eastview.com, http://www.eastview.com.

791.4375 DEU
KINO&CO.; Dein Ticket nach Hollywood. Text in German. 2003. 10/yr. EUR 16.99 (effective 2011). adv. **Document type:** *Magazine, Consumer.*
Published by: Kino&Co. Media GmbH, Aidenbachstr. 54, Muenchen, 81379, Germany. TEL 49-89-790862700, FAX 49-89-79086279. adv.: page EUR 16,500. Circ: 520,000 (controlled).

KINOHANDBUCH; Das Nachschlagewerk der Entertainmentbranche. *see* BUSINESS AND ECONOMICS—Trade And Industrial Directories

778.53 DEU
KINOMAGAZIN; Kino und Kultur. Text in German. 1985. m. adv. back issues avail.
Published by: Studio Kino GmbH, Mainzer Str 8, Saarbruecken, 66111, Germany. TEL 0681-399297, FAX 0681-374556. Circ: 10,000.

791.43 DEU
KINOWELT.DE. Text in German. 2000. m. adv. **Document type:** *Magazine, Consumer.* **Description:** Provides insight, commentary and reviews on movies and distribution.
Published by: kinowelt.de AG, Karl-Tauchnitz-Str 10, Leipzig, 04107, Germany. TEL 49-341-355960, FAX 49-341-35596999, info@kinowelt.de, http://www.kinowelt.de. Pubs. Bertil le Claire, Claudia Snehotta.

791.43 DEU ISSN 1024-1906
KINTOP. Text in German. 1992. a. back issues avail. **Document type:** *Journal, Academic/Scholarly.* **Description:** Studies early Swiss and German films.
Indexed: F01, F02, IIFP, IITV.
Published by: Stroemfeld Verlag GmbH, Holzhausenstr 4, Frankfurt Am Main, 60322, Germany. TEL 49-69-9552260, FAX 49-69-95522624, info@stroemfeld.de, http://www.stroemfeld.de.

379.8 HRV ISSN 1333-2406
KLIK. Text in Croatian. 2001. m. HRK 250 (effective 2011). adv. **Document type:** *Magazine, Consumer.*
Related titles: Online - full text ed.: ISSN 1333-9338. 1999.
Published by: Adria Media Zagreb d.o.o., Radnicka Cesta 39, Zagreb, 10000, Croatia. TEL 385-1-4444800, FAX 385-1-4444801, info@adriamedia.hr, http://www.adriamedia.hr.

KOMMUNIKATION AUDIOVISUELL; Beitraege aus der Hochschule fuer Fernsehen und Film Muenchen. *see* COMMUNICATIONS—Television And Cable

KOMPUTER SWIAT FILM NA DVD. *see* COMMUNICATIONS—Video

791.43 KOR
KOREA FILM DATABASE BOOK. Text in English, Korean. irreg., latest 1995-2008. free to qualified personnel. **Document type:** *Directory, Abstract/Index.* **Description:** Contains a list of film titles, directors, actors, international sales companies, and contacts.
Related titles: Online - full text ed.
Published by: Korean Film Council/Tonga Such'ul Kongsa, 206-46, Cheongnyangni-dong, Dongdaemun-gu, Seoul, 130-010, Korea, S. TEL 82-2-9587591, FAX 82-2-9587590, http://www.koreanfilm.or.kr. Eds. You-Jeong Yang, Lee Yoo-Ran. Pub. Han-Sup Kang.

791.43 KOR
KOREAN CINEMA. Text in English. a. **Document type:** *Magazine, Trade.* **Description:** Contains information on films, statistics, and updated list of film organizations and companies in Korea.
Related titles: Online - full text ed.
Published by: Korean Film Council/Tonga Such'ul Kongsa, 206-46, Cheongnyangni-dong, Dongdaemun-gu, Seoul, 130-010, Korea, S. TEL 82-2-9587591, FAX 82-2-9587590.

791.43 KOR
KOREAN FILM DIRECTOR SERIES. Text in English. irreg. (3-6/yr.). free to qualified personnel. **Document type:** *Monographic series, Trade.* **Description:** Promotes Korean films and directors with each issue featuring a specific director.
Published by: Korean Film Council/Tonga Such'ul Kongsa, 206-46, Cheongnyangni-dong, Dongdaemun-gu, Seoul, 130-010, Korea, S. TEL 82-2-9587591, FAX 82-2-9587590.

791.43 KOR
KOREAN FILM OBSERVATORY. Text in English. 2001 (Spr.). q. free to qualified personnel. **Document type:** *Magazine, Trade.*
Published by: Korean Film Council/Tonga Such'ul Kongsa, 206-46, Cheongnyangni-dong, Dongdaemun-gu, Seoul, 130-010, Korea, S. TEL 82-2-9587591, FAX 82-2-9587590. Eds. Daniel D. H. Park, Lee Yoo-Ran. Pub. Han-Sup Kang.

791.43 DNK ISSN 0023-4222
PN1993
KOSMORAMA; tidsskrift for filmkunst og filmkultur. Text in Danish. 1954. s-a. DKK 250; DKK 175 per issue (effective 2009). bk.rev. illus. index. **Document type:** *Journal, Academic/Scholarly.* **Description:** Covers national and international cinema with articles, interviews and reviews.
Related titles: Microfilm ed.: (from WMP); Microform ed.: (from MIM).
Indexed: A20, ASCA, ArtHuCI, CurCont, DIP, F01, F02, IBR, IBZ, IIFP, IIPA, IITV, RASB, RILM, SCOPUS, W07.
Published by: (Koebenhavns Universitet, Institut for Film- og Medievidenskab/University of Copenhagen, Department of Film & Media Studies), Det Danske Filminstitut/The Danish Film Institute, Gothergade 55, Copenhagen K, 1123, Denmark. TEL 45-33-743400, FAX 45-33-743401, dfi@dfi.dk. Eds. Lars-Martin Soerensen, Eva Joerholt.

778.53 DEU ISSN 0171-5208
KULLERAUGEN; Visuelle Kommunikation. Text in German. 1977. s-a. EUR 16 (effective 2001). tel.rev.; video rev.; bk.rev.; film rev. illus. back issues avail. **Document type:** *Bulletin, Consumer.*
Published by: Kulleraugen Verlag, Laaseweg 4, Schellerten, 31174, Germany. TEL 49-5123-4330, FAX 49-5123-2015, redaktion.kulleraugen@epost.de, http://www.kulleraugen-verlag.de. Circ: 1,000.

791.43 DEU ISSN 0174-2582
KULLERAUGEN - MATERIALSAMMLUNG. Text in German. 1978. s-a. bibl.; illus. 36 p./no.; back issues avail. **Document type:** *Bulletin, Consumer.*
Published by: Kulleraugen Verlag, Laaseweg 4, Schellerten, 31174, Germany. TEL 49-5123-4330, FAX 49-5123-2015, redaktion.kulleraugen@epost.de, http://www.kulleraugen-verlag.de. Circ: 1,000.

778.53 POL ISSN 0452-9502
PN1993
KWARTALNIK FILMOWY. Text in Polish. 1951-1962; resumed 1965. q. USD 39 foreign (effective 2005). bk.rev. illus. index. **Document type:** *Journal, Academic/Scholarly.* **Description:** Presents film theory and history as well as audiovisuality with the main focus on the Polish production.
Indexed: IBSS, IIFP.
Published by: Polska Akademia Nauk, Instytut Sztuki/Polish Academy of Science, Institute of Art, ul Dluga 28, Warsaw, 00950, Poland. TEL 48-22-5048200, FAX 48-22-8313149, ispan@ispan.pl. Eds. Piotr Paszkiewicz, Teresa Rutkowska. Circ: 1,500 (paid).

053.1 DEU
L.O.S.; Das Entertainment-Magazin. Text in German. m. adv. **Document type:** *Magazine, Consumer.*
Published by: T und M Verlagsgesellschaft mbH, Bilser Str 11-13, Hamburg, 22297, Germany. TEL 49-40-514010, FAX 49-40-51401100, info@t-m-media.de, http://www.t-m-media.de. adv.: page EUR 24,500. Circ: 1,200,000 (controlled).

791.43 FRA ISSN 1951-0705
L'A A R S E. (Association des Auteurs Realisateurs du Sud Est) Text in French. 2006. q. free. back issues avail. **Document type:** *Magazine.*
Published by: Association des Auteurs-Realisateurs du Sud-Est (A A R S E), 28 Rue Thiers, Marseille, 13001, France. TEL 33-6-83595498, aarsecine@free.fr, http://aarse.free.fr/.

LADYSLIPPER CATALOG AND RESOURCE GUIDE OF RECORDS, TAPES, COMPACT DISCS AND VIDEOS BY WOMEN. *see* WOMEN'S INTERESTS

791.43 FIN ISSN 0782-3053
LAHIKUVA. Text in Finnish. 1980. q. EUR 22 domestic; EUR 25 foreign (effective 2006). **Document type:** *Magazine, Consumer.*
Indexed: F01, F02, IIFP.
Address: c/o Varsinais-Suomen elokuvakeskus, Uudenmaankatu 1, Turku, 20500, Finland. TEL 358-2-2511998. Ed. Susanna Paasonen.

791.43 USA ISSN 1938-4505
PN1993
LEONARD MALTIN'S MOVIE CRAZY; a newsletter for people who love movies. Text in English. 200?. q. USD 30 domestic; USD 40 in Canada; USD 50 elsewhere (effective 2010). **Document type:** *Newsletter, Consumer.* **Description:** Contains behind the scenes information, stories, biographies and interviews and about films, production and actors from the early days of film.
Published by: Leonard Maltin, Ed. & Pub, PO Box 2747, Toluca Lake, CA 91610. http://www.leonardmaltin.com/home.htm.

791.43 USA ISSN 1555-7235
PN1992.8.F5
LEONARD MALTIN'S MOVIE GUIDE. Text in English. 1969. a. USD 20 per vol. (effective 2005). adv. **Description:** Contains over 19,000 entries with indexes by title, star and director.
Former titles (until 2005): Leonard Maltin's Movie and Video Guide (1082-9466); (until 1993): Leonard Maltin's Television Movies and Video Guide (1050-9879); (until 1987): Leonard Maltin's T V Movies (1052-3286)
Published by: Putnam Penguin, Pearson plc, 375 Hudson St, New York, NY 10014. Ed. Leonard Maltin. Pub. Elaine Koster. R&P Leigh Butler. Adv. contact Maryann Palum.

808.066791 USA ISSN 0090-4260
PN1995.3
➤ **LITERATURE FILM QUARTERLY.** Abbreviated title: L F Q. Text in English. 1973. q. USD 80 domestic to institutions; USD 90 foreign to institutions; USD 15 per issue to institutions (effective 2010). adv. bk.rev.; film rev. illus. back issues avail. **Document type:** *Journal, Academic/Scholarly.* **Description:** Focuses on the problems of adapting and transferring fiction and drama to film. Covers various film genres, theory and criticism. Features interviews with screenwriters, directors and actors. Circulates from coast-to-coast and in roughly 30 foreign countries.
Related titles: CD-ROM ed.; Microfilm ed.: (from PQC); Online - full text ed.
Indexed: A01, A02, A03, A08, A20, A22, A26, A27, ABS&EES, AES, ASCA, AmHI, ArtHuCI, B04, BEL&L, BRD, CA, CMM, ChLitAb, CurCont, E08, F01, F02, G08, H07, H08, H09, H10, HAb, HumInd, I05, IBT&D, IIFP, IIPA, IITV, L05, L06, LCR, LIFT, M01, M02, MLA, MLA-IB, MRD, P02, P10, P48, P53, P54, PCI, PQC, RILM, S07, S09, SCOPUS, T02, W03, W05, W07.
—BLDSC (5276.721100), IE, Infotrieve, Ingenta. **CCC.**
Published by: Salisbury State University, 1101 Camden Ave, Salisbury, MD 21801. TEL 410-543-6000. Eds. David T Johnson, Elsie M Walker. Adv. contact Brenda Grodzicki.

➤ **LITTERATUR TEATER FILM**; nya serien. *see* LITERATURE

778.53 USA
LOCATIONS. Text in English. 1987. s-a. USD 5 per issue. adv. **Description:** Lists AFCI members and their services. Covers on-location productions, national and international filming, location highlights, laws and regulations, finance and budgets, news and events.

Published by: Association of Film Commissioners International, I 25 and College Dr, Cheyenne, WY 82002. TEL 307-777-7777. Circ: 17,000.

LONG ISLAND PRESS. *see* MUSIC

791.43 USA
LOS ANGELES CINEMATHEQUE. Text in English. 1973. m. USD 10. adv. bk.rev.
Published by: Los Angeles Cinematheque, Inc., PO Box 24548, Los Angeles, CA 90024. Ed. Jared Rutter. Circ: 2,000.

LOYOLA OF LOS ANGELES ENTERTAINMENT LAW REVIEW. *see* LAW

791.43 781.64 NLD ISSN 2210-7274
LUST FOR LIFE. Text in Dutch. 2006. m. EUR 66 (effective 2010). adv. **Document type:** *Magazine, Consumer.*
Formerly (until 2010): Revolver Magazine (1871-8604)
Published by: Music Maker Media Group, Postbus 720, Arnhem, 6800 AS, Netherlands. TEL 31-26-3518242, FAX 31.26-4433761. Eds. Martin Cuppens, Paul Gersen. Pub. Mark Postema.

M (ENGLEWOOD CLIFFS). *see* MUSIC

M.E.L.O.N. (Multimedia & Entertainment Law Online News) *see* LAW

M MAGAZINE. *see* CHILDREN AND YOUTH—For

791.4375 JPN
M TELEPAL. Text in Japanese. m. JPY 314 newsstand/cover (effective 2002). adv. **Document type:** *Magazine, Consumer.*
Published by: Shogakukan Inc., 3-1 Hitotsubashi 2-chome, Chiyoda-ku, Tokyo, 101-8001, Japan. TEL 81-3-3230-5211, FAX 81-3-3264-8471, http://www.shogakukan.co.jp.

M3 HEMMABIO. *see* COMMUNICATIONS—Video

791.43 CAN ISSN 1924-5874
LE MAGAZINE CINEPLEX. Text in French. 2002. 11/yr. adv. **Document type:** *Magazine, Trade.* **Description:** Covers interviews, design and photography of top movie stars and Hollywood's A-list actors.
Formerly (until 2010): Magazine Famous Quebec (1706-0559)
Published by: Cineplex Media, 102 Atlantic Ave, Toronto, ON M6K 1X9, Canada. TEL 416-539-8800, FAX 416-539-8511, sales@cineplex.com. Circ: 165,000.

778.53 USA ISSN 0739-2141
PN1993.3
MAGILL'S CINEMA ANNUAL. Text in English. 1982. a., latest 2009. USD 165 (effective 2009). film rev. **Document type:** *Yearbook, Consumer.* **Description:** Presents an in-depth retrospective of significant domestic and foreign films released in the U.S.
Published by: Gale (Subsidiary of: Cengage Learning), 27500 Drake Rd, Farmington Hills, MI 48331. TEL 248-699-4253, 800-877-4253, FAX 877-363-4253, gale.customerservice@cengage.com, http://gale.cengage.com. Ed. Beth Fhaner.

MANGA FORCE; the ultimate collection. *see* HOBBIES

791.43 USA ISSN 1073-8924
PN1995.9.P7
MARKEE. Text in English. 1986. m. USD 34 (effective 2002). adv. **Document type:** *Magazine, Trade.* **Description:** For the Southeast and Southwest film and video industries.
Published by: H J K Publications, Inc., 366 E Graves Ave., Ste D, Orange City, FL 32763-5266. TEL 386-774-8881, FAX 386-774-8908. Ed. Jon T Hutchinson. Circ: 22,200 (controlled).

MARQUEE. *see* THEATER

MARTIN & OSA JOHNSON SAFARI MUSEUM. WAIT-A-BIT NEWS. *see* MUSEUMS AND ART GALLERIES

791.43 USA ISSN 1543-7582
MAXIM MOVIES. Variant title: Maxim Goes to the Movies. Text in English. 2003 (Sum.). bi-m. USD 9.97 domestic; USD 19.97 in Canada; USD 29.97 elsewhere; USD 4.99 newsstand/cover domestic; USD 6.99 newsstand/cover in Canada (effective 2003).
Published by: Dennis Publishing, Inc., 1040 Ave of the Americas, 22nd Fl, New York, NY 10018. TEL 212-302-2626, FAX 212-302-2635. Eds. Greg Williams, Keith Blanchard. Adv. contact Deborah Rubin.

791.43 IND
MAYAPURI. Text in Hindi. 1974. w. **Document type:** *Magazine, Trade.*
Address: A-5, Mayapuri, New Delhi, 110 064, India.

MEDIA AND ARTS LAW REVIEW. *see* LAW

791.43 AUT ISSN 1605-4598
MEDIA BIZ; film - tv - radio - video - audio. Text in German. 199?. 10/yr. EUR 36 domestic; EUR 46 foreign; EUR 20 to students (effective 2005). adv. **Document type:** *Magazine, Trade.*
Related titles: Online - full text ed.: ISSN 1605-1122.
Published by: Bergmayer und Partner Producer OEG, Kalvarienberggasse 67, Vienna, W 1170, Austria. TEL 43-1-40335830, FAX 43-1-403358330. Ed. Wolfgang Ritzberger. Pub., Adv. contact Sylvia Bergmayer. B&W page EUR 1,400; trim 187 x 244. Circ: 5,000 (controlled).

MEDIA BIZ BRANCHENFUEHRER; film - tv - radio - video - audio. *see* BUSINESS AND ECONOMICS—Trade And Industrial Directories

MEDIA-EXPERT; la revue suisse au service des photographes et cineastes. *see* PHOTOGRAPHY

302.2343 USA ISSN 2159-7553
▼ **MEDIA FIELDS JOURNAL**; critical explorations in media and space. Text in English. 2010. 3/yr. free (effective 2011). **Document type:** *Journal, Trade.* **Description:** Provides a forum focused on the critical study of media and space.
Media: Online - full text.
Published by: University of California, Santa Barbara, Department of Film and Media Studies, 2433 Social Sciences and Media Studies Bldg, UC Santa Barbara, Santa Barbara, CA 93106. TEL 805-893-2347, FAX 805-893-8630, businessofficer@filmandmedia.ucsb.edu, http://www.filmandmedia.ucsb.edu.

MEDIASCAPE. *see* SOCIOLOGY

MEDIENWIRTSCHAFT; Zeitschrift fuer Medienmanagement und Kommunikationsoekonomie. *see* COMMUNICATIONS—Radio

MEDIENWISSENSCHAFT; Rezensionen - Reviews. *see* COMMUNICATIONS—Television And Cable

MESH (ONLINE); film video - digital media - installation - performance - art. *see* ART

THE METAPHYSICAL REVIEW. *see* LITERARY AND POLITICAL REVIEWS

371.33523 AUS ISSN 0312-2654
PN1993
METRO. Text in English. 1964. 4/yr. AUD 72 domestic to individuals; AUD 102 foreign to individuals; AUD 95 domestic to institutions; AUD 125 foreign to institutions (effective 2007). adv. bk.rev.; dance rev.; film rev.; music rev.; rec.rev.; software rev.; tel.rev.; video rev.; Website rev. illus. 185 p./no.; back issues avail.; reprints avail. **Document type:** *Magazine, Consumer.* **Description:** Covers film, television, video, multimedia, photography, the internet and radio. For secondary and tertiary teachers and students.
Related titles: Online - full text ed.
Indexed: A11, A26, AEI, AusPAIS, BEL&L, CMM, E07, E08, F01, F02, G08, I05, IIFP, M02, S09, T02, U01, WBA, WMB.
—CCC.
Published by: Australian Teachers of Media, PO Box 2211, St Kilda West, St Kilda, VIC 3182, Australia. TEL 61-3-95349986, FAX 61-3-95372325, tapp@netspace.net.au, http://www.metromagazine.com.au/metro/default.asp. Ed., R&P, Adv. contact Peter Tapp TEL 61-3-95253907. B&W page AUD 1,000, color page AUD 1,400; 165 x 260. Circ: 18,000.

791.43 USA ISSN 1949-4122
▼ **MICHIGAN MOVIE MAGAZINE.** Text in English. 2009. bi-m. USD 25 (effective 2009). **Document type:** *Magazine, Trade.* **Description:** For professionals in the movie industry in Michigan.
Related titles: Online - full text ed.: ISSN 1949-4114. 2009.
Published by: Chris Aliapoulios, Ed. & Pub., 9040 N Territorial, Dexter, MI 48130. TEL 734-726-5299, mmmkuba@gmail.com.

791.43 NLD ISSN 1877-8267
MIDDLE EAST FILM. Text in English, Dutch. 200?. m. EUR 30 to individuals; EUR 150 to institutions (effective 2010). **Document type:** *Magazine, Consumer.*
Published by: Stichting Middle East Culture, Louis Armstongstraat 24, Zaandijk, 1544 KL, Netherlands. TEL 31-75-646771, info@mecultuur.nl, http://www.mecultuur.nl.

778.53 USA ISSN 0886-8719
PN1995.9.H6
MIDNIGHT MARQUEE. Text in English. 1963. 3/yr. USD 15 (effective 1998). bk.rev. illus. reprints avail. **Document type:** *Magazine, Consumer.* **Description:** Dedicated to the serious study of horror, fantasy, suspense and science fiction films.
Indexed: F01, F02, T02.
Address: 4000 Glenarm Ave, Baltimore, MD 21206. TEL 410-665-1198, FAX 410-665-9207. Ed. Gary J Svehla. Circ: 4,000.

791.43 CHE
MIESER TON UND GRUNDLOS SCHWARZ-WEISS; ein Fanzine fuer Superachtfilm. Text in German. 1998. 3/yr. CHF 10 (effective 2002). **Document type:** *Magazine, Consumer.*
Address: Nordstr 293, Zurich, 8037, Switzerland. TEL 41-1-2723441, FAX 41-1-6321227, filmstelle@vseth.ethz.ch. Ed. Saro Pepe.

791.43 RUS ISSN 0134-9090
MIFY I REAL'NOST'. Text in Russian. irreg. film rev.
Published by: (Goskino, Institut Teorii i Istorii Kino), Izdatel'stvo Iskusstvo, Vorotnikovskii per 11, Moscow, Russian Federation. Circ: 25,000.

MILITARY ILLUSTRATED. *see* MILITARY

778.53 USA ISSN 1064-5586
PN1993
MILLENNIUM FILM JOURNAL. Text in English. 1977. s-a. USD 8 per issue (effective 2010). adv. film rev. illus. index. back issues avail. **Document type:** *Journal, Academic/Scholarly.* **Description:** Dedicated to avant-garde cinema theory and practice, it provides a forum to discuss and debate issues worldwide.
Related titles: Microfilm ed.; Online - full text ed.
Indexed: A07, A20, A27, A30, A31, AA, ASCA, ArtHuCI, ArtInd, B04, BRD, CA, CurCont, F01, F02, IBT&D, IIFP, IIPA, P10, P48, P53, P54, PCI, PQC, RILM, SCOPUS, T02, W03, W05, W07.
Published by: Millennium Film Workshop, Inc., 66 E Fourth St, New York, NY 10003.

MIROMENTE; Zeitschrift fuer Gut und Boes. *see* LITERATURE

MIRROR MAGAZINE. *see* ART

791.43 USA ISSN 1943-183X
▼ **MODERN FILMMAKERS.** Text in English. 2009. irreg., latest 2010. USD 44.95, GBP 31.95 per issue (effective 2010). back issues avail. **Document type:** *Monographic series, Academic/Scholarly.*
Published by: Praeger Publishers (Subsidiary of: Greenwood Publishing Group Inc.), 88 Post Rd W, Westport, CT 06881. TEL 800-368-6868, tech.support@greenwood.com, http://www.greenwood.com. Ed. Vincent LoBrutto.

791.43 HRV ISSN 0026-8895
MOJ PAS. Text in Serbo-Croatian. 1954. m. USD 12.50.
Published by: Kinoloski Savez Hrvatske, Ilica 61, Zagreb, Croatia. Ed. Vesna Sekalec.

778.53 BEL ISSN 0771-4874
LE MONITEUR DU FILM EN BELGIQUE. Text in French. 1980. m. (11/yr.). EUR 33 domestic; EUR 52 foreign; EUR 3.33 per issue (effective 2005).
Former titles (until 1995): Le Moniteur du Film et de l'Audio-Visuel en Belgique; (until 1988): Le Moniteur du Film en Belgique; (until 1981): Press and Film Service (0771-4823)
Related titles: Dutch ed.: Filmvakblad van Belgie. ISSN 0771-7504.
Indexed: F01, F02.
Published by: Moniteur du Film en Belgique, Rue de Framboisier 35, Brussels, 1180, Belgium. Ed., Pub. Jacques Elias.

791.43 USA ISSN 1530-9436
MONSTERZINE. Text in English. 2000. q. adv. film rev. back issues avail. **Description:** Dedicated to the thoughtful discussions of classic horror films.
Media: Online - full text.
Address: Box 7651, Minneapolis, MN 55407. FAX 253-540-5491. Ed. Pam Keesey. adv.: online banner USD 500. Circ: 7,500.

791.43 CAN ISSN 1488-2531
MONTAGE. Text in English. 1998. q. CAD 19.80 domestic; CAD 29 in United States; CAD 59 elsewhere; CAD 4.95 newsstand/cover (effective 2000). **Document type:** *Magazine, Consumer.*
Published by: X Unlimited Corporation for the Directors Guild of Canada, 333 Adelaide St West, Level 3, Toronto, ON M5V 1R5, Canada. TEL 416-591-8958, montage@xcorporation.com, http://www.dgcmontage.com.

791.43 DEU
MONTAGE AV; Zeitschrift fuer Theorie und Geschichte audiovisueller Kommunikation. Text in German. 1991. 2/yr. EUR 22 domestic; EUR 27 foreign; EUR 18.50 to students (effective 2011). adv. bk.rev. bibl. back issues avail. **Document type:** *Journal, Academic/Scholarly.*
Formerly: Montagelar (0942-4954)
Indexed: F01, F02, IIFP, IITV, MLA-IB.
Published by: Schueren Verlag GmbH, Universitaetsstr 55, Marburg, 35037, Germany. TEL 49-6421-63084, FAX 49-6421-681190, info@schueren-verlag.de, http://www.schueren-verlag.de.

791.43 USA ISSN 1541-2679
MOTION PICTURE EDITORS GUILD MAGAZINE. Text in English. bi-m. USD 45 domestic to non-members; USD 65 foreign to non-members (effective 2001). film rev. **Document type:** *Magazine, Trade.*
Related titles: Online - full content ed.: Motion Picture Editors Guild Magazine & Directory Articles.
Published by: Motion Picture Editors Guild, West Coast Office, 7715 Sunset Blvd Ste 200, Hollywood, CA 90046. TEL 323-876-4770, 800-705-8700, FAX 323-876-0861, http://www.editorsguild.com/index.shtml.

791.43 USA
PN1993
MOTION PICTURE INVESTOR (ONLINE). Text in English. 1984. m. USD 845; USD 1,240 combined subscription (print & e-mail eds.) (effective 2005). adv. charts. index. **Document type:** *Newsletter, Trade.* **Description:** Covers investment in public and private movie production and distribution companies. Tracks the movement and value of motion picture stocks.
Formerly (until 2007): Motion Picture Investor (Print) (0742-8839)
Media: Online - full text. **Related titles:** E-mail ed.: USD 775 (effective 2005).
—CCC.
Published by: S N L Financial LC, One SNL Plz, PO Box 2124, Charlottesville, VA 22902. TEL 434-977-1600, FAX 434-293-0407, salesdept@snl.com. Ed. Luke Meade. adv.: B&W page USD 3,670.

MOTION PICTURE, T V & THEATRE DIRECTORY; for services & products. *see* BUSINESS AND ECONOMICS—Trade And Industrial Directories

791.43 HUN ISSN 1215-234X
PN1993.5.E82
➤ **MOVEAST**; international film periodical. Text in English. 1991. q. **Document type:** *Journal, Academic/Scholarly.*
Indexed: IIFP.
Published by: Magyar Nemzeti Filmarchivum/Hungarian National Film Archive, Budakeszi ut 51/b, Budapest, 1021, Hungary. TEL 36-1-3941018, FAX 36-1-2008739, filmintezet@ella.hu, http://www.filmintezet.hu. Ed. Ivan Forgacs.

791.43 GBR ISSN 2047-1661
PN1993
➤ **MOVIE (ONLINE)**; a journal of film criticism. Text in English. 1962. s-a. free (effective 2011). bk.rev.; film rev. illus. 96 p./no.; back issues avail. **Document type:** *Journal, Academic/Scholarly.* **Description:** Aims to create a forum for the range of analysis, debate and discussion.
Formerly (until 2010): Movie (Print) (0027-268X)
Media: Online - full text.
Indexed: A20, IIFP, IITV, MRD.
—CCC.
Published by: Universities of Warwick, Reading and Oxford, Coventry, CV4 7AL, United Kingdom. TEL 44-24-76523523, FAX 44-24-76461606, helpdesk@warwick.ac.uk. Eds. Douglas Pye, Michael Walker.

791 ZAF ISSN 1817-0331
MOVIE & D V D. (Digital Video Disc) Variant title: South Africa's Film & DVD Magazine. Text in English. 2005. bi-m. ZAR 26.95 newsstand/cover (effective 2007). adv. bk.rev.; music rev. **Document type:** *Magazine, Consumer.*
Published by: Jalo Media Solutions, 545 Colenso St, Pretoria North, 0182, South Africa. TEL 27-12-5466498, FAX 27-12-6872575. Adv. contact Jacqueline Bekker. color page ZAR 4,800; trim 210 x 297.

791.45 CAN
MOVIE ENTERTAINMENT. Text in English. 1990. m. CAD 21 (effective 2005). adv. film rev. illus. **Document type:** *Magazine, Consumer.* **Description:** Publishes stories and descriptions of feature films, as well as programming information for subscribers.
Formerly: Feature (1180-4785)
—CCC.
Published by: Feature Publishing Ltd., 2100 rue Ste-Catherine Ouest, 10th Fl., Montreal, PQ H3H 2T3, Canada. TEL 514-939-5024, FAX 514-939-1515. Ed. David Sherman. Pub. Marvin Boisvert. Circ: 880,610.

791.43 GBR ISSN 1367-0670
MOVIE IDOLS. Text in English. 1997. bi-m. GBP 13 per issue domestic; USD 21 per issue in United States; GBP 15 per issue elsewhere (effective 2009). **Document type:** *Magazine, Consumer.* **Description:** Provides movie related information.
Related titles: Online - full text ed.
Published by: Visual Imagination Ltd., 9 Blades Ct, Deodar Rd, London, SW15 2NU, United Kingdom. TEL 44-20-88751520, FAX 44-20-88751588, mailorder@visimag.com.

791.4375 DEU
MOVIE - KINO KULTUR AACHEN. Text in German. m. adv. **Document type:** *Magazine, Consumer.*
Published by: Berndt Media, Dr-C-Otto-Str 196, Bochum, 44879, Germany. TEL 49-234-941910, FAX 49-234-9419191, info@berndt-media.de, http://www.berndt-media.de. adv.: B&W page EUR 800, color page EUR 1,400; trim 210 x 285. Circ: 18,700 (controlled).

791.43 GBR
MOVIE MAG INTERNATIONAL. Text in English. 1983. m. GBP 18 in United Kingdom; GBP 30 in Europe; GBP 36 elsewhere (effective 2000); GBP 1.50 newsstand/cover; USD 3.50 newsstand/cover in United States; CAD 4.50 newsstand/cover in Canada; ANG 6 newsstand/cover in Netherlands. adv. bk.rev. back issues avail. **Document type:** *Magazine, Consumer.*

Formerly (until 1999): Movie International (0951-421X)
Address: 55 The Broadway, Southall, Mddx UB1 1JY, United Kingdom. TEL 44-181-574-2222, FAX 44-181-813-9911, info@movie-mag.com, Suri.moviemag@btinternet.com. Ed. Ms. Bharathi Pradhan. Pub. Mr. Neermal Suri. Adv. contact Mr. Sundeed Suri. Circ: 22,000.

791.43 USA ISSN 0027-271X
MOVIE MIRROR. Text in English. 1957. bi-m. USD 20 domestic; USD 25 foreign (effective 2007). adv. bk.rev.; film rev.; rec.rev. **Document type:** *Magazine, Consumer.*
Supersedes in part (in 19??): Photoplay Combined with Movie Mirror (0733-2734); Which was formed by the merger of (1916-1940): Photoplay (0732-538X); Which was formerly (until 1916): Photoplay Magazine (0731-8006); (1931-1940): Movie Mirror
Published by: Dorchester Media, PO Box 6640, Wayne, PA 19087. TEL 212-725-8811, 800-481-9191, customerservice@dorchpub.com, http://www.dorchesterpub.com.

778.53 USA
MOVIE REVIEW QUERY ENGINE. Text in English. 1996. w.
Media: Online - full content.
Address: http://www.mrqe.com.

384.55 JPN ISSN 0047-8288
MOVIE - T V MARKETING. Text in English. 1953. m. JPY 30,000 (effective 1999). adv. **Document type:** *Journal, Trade.*
Former titles (until 1966): Movie Marketing; (until 1962): Far East Film News (0425-7111)
Published by: Movie - TV Marketing, CPO Box 30, Tokyo, 100-8691, Japan. TEL 81-3-3587-2855, FAX 81-3-3587-2820. Ed. Asia M Ireton. Circ: 100,000.

791.43 JPN ISSN 0085-3577
MOVIE - T V MARKETING GLOBAL MOTION PICTURE YEAR BOOK. Text in English. 1955. a. JPY 10,000. adv. **Document type:** *Yearbook, Trade.*
Published by: Movie - TV Marketing, CPO Box 30, Tokyo, 100-8691, Japan. TEL 81-3-3587-2855, FAX 81-3-3587-2820. Ed. Asia M Ireton. Circ: 100,000.

778.53 USA
MOVIEMAKER; the art and business of making movies. Text in English. 1993. bi-m. USD 18 domestic; USD 28 in Canada; USD 44 elsewhere; USD 5.95 per issue (effective 2010). adv. illus. back issues avail. **Document type:** *Magazine, Trade.* **Description:** Covers the work and careers of directors, columns on the festival circuit, production techniques, advice and reviews.
Formerly (until 200?): Movie Maker Magazine
Indexed: IIPA, MRD.
Published by: Moviemaker Pub., 174 Fifth Ave, Ste 300, New York, NY 10010. TEL 212-766-4100, FAX 212-766-4102. Eds. Jennifer M Wood, Timothy E Rhys. Pub. Timothy E Rhys.

791.4375 IRL
MOVIES PLUS. Text in English. m. adv. **Document type:** *Magazine, Consumer.*
Address: The Picture Works, 97 Upper Georges St., Dun Laoghaire, Co. Dublin, Ireland. TEL 353-1-8338241, FAX 353-1-8333873. adv.: page EUR 2,160. Circ: 20,000 (controlled).

791.4305 GBR ISSN 1751-1356
MOVIESCOPE; movies from the insider's point-of-view. Variant title: Movie Scope. Text in English. 2006. bi-m. GBP 20.79 domestic; GBP 35.77 in Europe; USD 41.79 in US & Canada; USD 3.46 per issue (effective 2009). adv. back issues avail. **Document type:** *Magazine, Consumer.* **Description:** Provides informative articles for movie makers.
Related titles: Online - full text ed.: GBP 12.11 (effective 2009).
Indexed: A10, V03.
Published by: MovieScope Publishing, Third Fl, Lafone House, The Leathermarket, 11-13 Weston St, London, SE1 3HN, United Kingdom. TEL 44-84-50946263, FAX 44-84-50943846. Ed. Eric Lilleor. Pub. Rinaldo Quacquarini.

791.43 DEU
MOVIESTAR. Text in German. bi-m. EUR 4.60 newsstand/cover (effective 2007). adv. **Document type:** *Magazine, Consumer.* **Description:** Covers all areas of movies and videos from production to release.
Published by: Medien Publikations- und Werbegesellschaft, Spittlertorgraben 39, Nuernberg, 90429, Germany. TEL 49-911-262896, FAX 49-911-262893, info@tvhighlights.de. Ed. Manfred Knorr. adv.: page EUR 4,490. Circ: 41,290 (paid and controlled).

791.43 USA ISSN 1532-3978
PN1993
➤ **THE MOVING IMAGE**; the journal of the Association of Moving Image Archivists. Text in English. 2001. s-a. USD 112.50 combined subscription domestic to institutions (print & online eds.); USD 120 combined subscription foreign to institutions (print & online eds.) (effective 2012). adv. bk.rev.; tel.rev.; video rev.; film rev. illus. back issues avail. **Document type:** *Journal, Academic/Scholarly.* **Description:** Explores topics relevant to both the media archivist and the media scholar.
Related titles: Online - full text ed.: ISSN 1542-4235. USD 75 (effective 2012).
Indexed: A07, A22, A26, A30, A31, AA, ArtInd, B04, BRD, CA, E01, I05, IIFP, IIPA, MLA-IB, T02, W03, W05.
—BLDSC (5980.390500), IE. **CCC.**
Published by: (Association of Moving Image Archivists), University of Minnesota Press, Ste 290, 111 Third Ave S, Minneapolis, MN 55401. TEL 612-627-1970, FAX 612-627-1980, ump@umn.edu. Eds. Devin Orgeron, Marsha Orgeron. Adv. contact Anne Klingbeil TEL 612-627-1938. page USD 300; 6 x 9.

791.43 AUS ISSN 1320-4181
PN1993.5.A8
➤ **THE MOVING IMAGE.** Text in English. 1993. a., latest 2004. AUD 39 domestic; AUD 49 foreign (effective 2008). 120 p./no.; back issues avail. **Document type:** *Monographic series, Academic/Scholarly.* **Description:** Contains articles related to film, television, film practice, multimedia, history, criticism, and theory.
Indexed: A01, A03, A08, A11, CA, CMM, F01, F02, T02, WBA.
—CCC.
Published by: Australian Teachers of Media, PO Box 2211, St Kilda West, St Kilda, VIC 3182, Australia. TEL 61-3-95349986, FAX 61-3-95372325, atom@atomvic.org, http://www.atomvic.org/. Ed. Peter Tapp TEL 61-3-95253907. Circ: 4,000. **Co-sponsors:** Australian Film Institute; Deakin University, School of Visual, Performing and Media Arts.

791.43 780 USA ISSN 1940-7610
MUSIC AND THE MOVING IMAGE. Text in English. 2008 (Mar.). 3/yr. USD 70 to institutions (effective 2012). back issues avail. **Document type:** *Journal, Academic/Scholarly.* **Description:** Covers the relationship between music and moving images, including film, television, music videos, computer games, performance art, and web-based media.
Media: Online - full text.
Indexed: A07, A26, A30, A31, AA, ArtInd, B04, E08, I05, S09, W03, W05.
Published by: (Film Music Society), University of Illinois Press, 1325 S Oak St, Champaign, IL 61820. TEL 217-333-0950, 866-244-0626, FAX 217-244-8082, journals@uillinois.edu. Eds. Gillian B Anderson TEL 301-326-6836, Ronald H Sadoff TEL 212-996-5779. Adv. contact Jeff McArdle TEL 217-244-0381.

MUSIC, SOUND AND THE MOVING IMAGE. *see* MUSIC

N A P A M A NEWS. *see* THEATER

N A R M C HIGHLIGHTS. *see* LIBRARY AND INFORMATION SCIENCES

791.43 USA
NAKED! SCREAMING! TERROR!. Text in English. m.?. USD 1 per issue. **Description:** Covers horror movies.
Address: PO Box 67, Oberlin, OH 44074-0067. Ed. David Todarello.

791.43 IND
NANA FILM WEEKLY. Text in Malayalam. 19??. w. INR 585 (effective 2011). back issues avail. **Document type:** *Magazine, Consumer.*
Address: R. Krishnaswamy Memorial Bldg, Lekshminada, Kollam, Kerala 691 013, India. TEL 91-474-2750330, FAX 91-474-2740710.

791.43 GBR
NATIONAL CINEMA SERIES. Text in English. 1993. irreg., latest 2003. **Document type:** *Monographic series.* **Description:** Presents recent developments in cultural studies and film history.
Published by: Routledge (Subsidiary of: Taylor & Francis Group), 2 Park Sq, Milton Park, Abingdon, Oxon OX14 4RN, United Kingdom. TEL 44-20-70176000, FAX 44-20-70176699, http://www.routledge.com/journals/. Ed. Susan Hayward. Pub. Rebecca Barden. **Subscr. to:** Taylor & Francis Ltd., Journals Customer Service, Sheepen Pl, Colchester, Essex CO3 3LP, United Kingdom. TEL 44-20-70175544, FAX 44-20-70175198, tf.enquiries@tfinforma.com.

791.437 CAN ISSN 1483-7455
CA1BT31-4 51
NATIONAL FILM BOARD OF CANADA. PERFORMANCE REPORT. Text in English, French. 1997. a.
Related titles: Online - full text ed.: ISSN 1498-7546.
Published by: (National Film Board of Canada/Office National du Film du Canada), Treasury Board of Canada Secretariat, Corporate Communications/Secretariat du Conseil du Tresor du Canada, West Tower, Rm P-135, 300 Laurier Ave W, Ottawa, ON K1A 0R5, Canada. TEL 613-995-2855, FAX 613-996-0518, services-publications@tbs-sct.gc.ca, http://www.tbs-sct.gc.ca.

791.43 GBR ISSN 1474-2756
PN1995
➤ **NEW CINEMAS**; journal of contemporary film. Abbreviated title: N C. Text in English. 2002. 3/yr. GBP 36, USD 68 to individuals; GBP 235, USD 368 to institutions (effective 2012). adv. back issues avail. **Document type:** *Journal, Academic/Scholarly.* **Description:** Devoted to the study of contemporary film around the world.
Related titles: Online - full text ed.: ISSN 2040-0578. USD 192, USD 290 (effective 2012).
Indexed: A01, A02, A03, A08, A22, CA, CMM, E01, F01, F02, IIFP, MLA-IB, T02.
—IE. **CCC.**
Published by: Intellect Ltd., The Mill, Parnall Rd, Fishponds, Bristol, BS16 3JG, United Kingdom. TEL 44-117-9589910, FAX 44-117-9589911, info@intellectbooks.com. Eds. Stephanie Dennison, Stuart Green. Pub. Masoud Yazdani. **Subscr. to:** Turpin Distribution Services Ltd., Pegasus Dr, Stratton Business Park, Biggleswade, Bedfordshire SG18 8QB, United Kingdom. TEL 44-1767-604951, FAX 44-1767-601640, custserv@turpin-distribution.com, http://www.turpin-distribution.com/.

791.43 GBR ISSN 2042-8855
▼ **THE NEW SOUNDTRACK.** Text in English. 2011 (Mar.). s-a. GBP 120 domestic to institutions; USD 233 in North America to institutions; GBP 126 elsewhere to institutions; GBP 150 combined subscription domestic to institutions (print & online eds.); USD 291 combined subscription in North America to institutions (print & online eds.); GBP 157 combined subscription elsewhere to institutions (print & online eds.) (effective 2012). adv. back issues avail.; reprints avail. **Document type:** *Journal, Academic/Scholarly.* **Description:** Covers current developments in sound and moving images, such as sound installations, computer-based delivery, and the psychology of the interaction of image and sound. Includes academic and professional contributions from recognized practitioners in the field, including composers, sound designers and directors.
Related titles: Online - full text ed.: ISSN 2042-8863. USD 199 in North America to institutions; GBP 108 elsewhere to institutions (effective 2012).
—CCC.
Published by: Edinburgh University Press, 22 George Sq, Edinburgh, Scotland EH8 9LF, United Kingdom. TEL 44-131-6504218, FAX 44-131-6620053, journals@eup.ed.ac.uk. Adv. contact Ruth Allison TEL 44-131-6504220.

791.4 GBR ISSN 1661-0261
NEW STUDIES IN EUROPEAN CINEMA. Text in English. 2005. irreg., latest vol.12, 2010. price varies. **Document type:** *Monographic series, Academic/Scholarly.* **Description:** Provides an international forum for lively and controversial debate embracing all aspects of European cinema from a broad range of theoretical perspectives.
Published by: Peter Lang Ltd. (Subsidiary of: Peter Lang Publishing Group), Evenlode Ct, Main Rd, Long Hanborough, Oxfordshire OX29 8SZ, United Kingdom. TEL 44-1993-880088, FAX 44-1993-882040, info@peterlang.com. Eds. A Goodbody, W Everett.

791.43 USA
NEW YORK SCREENWRITER MONTHLY; the screenwriting guide to making it. Text in English. m. USD 35 domestic; USD 65 in Canada & Mexico; USD 90 in Asia; USD 80 elsewhere (effective 2001).
Address: 655 Fulton St, 276, Brooklyn, NY 11217. TEL 718-797-9829, editorial@nyscreenwriter.com.

791.43 NZL ISSN 0113-8596
NEW ZEALAND FILM. Variant title: N Z Film. Text in English. 1980. 3/yr. free (effective 2008). tr.lit. back issues avail. **Document type:** *Magazine, Trade.* **Description:** Promotes New Zealand feature films and short films.
Related titles: Online - full text ed.: ISSN 1178-2528.
Indexed: INZP.
Published by: New Zealand Film Commission, PO Box 11-546, Wellington, New Zealand. TEL 64-4-3827680, FAX 64-4-3849719, info@nzfilm.co.nz. Ed. Kathleen Drumm. R&P Lindsay Shelton TEL 64-4-3827686. Circ: 4,000.

778.53 VNM
NGHE THUAT DIEN ANH/CINEMATOGRAPHY. Text in Vietnamese. 1984. fortn.
Address: 65 Tran Hung Dao, Hanoi, Viet Nam. TEL 52473. Ed. Dang Nhat Minh.

791.43 ESP ISSN 1135-7681
PN1993.5.S7
NICKEL ODEON. Text in Spanish. 1995. q. adv. bk.rev. bibl. back issues avail. **Document type:** *Magazine, Consumer.* **Description:** Each issue consists of an in-depth interview, essays on a central theme, and a topical survey of 100 experts.
Indexed: IIFP.
Published by: Nickel Odeon Dos S.A., Barbara de Braganza 12, Madrid, 28004, Spain. TEL 34-91-3085238, FAX 34-91-3085885, revista@nickel-odeon.com. **Dist. by:** Asociacion de Revistas Culturales de Espana, C Covarrubias 9 2o. Derecha, Madrid 28010, Spain. TEL 34-91-3086066, FAX 34-91-3199267, info@arce.es, http://www.arce.es/.

791.43 NLD ISSN 1871-6970
NIEUWE BLOTTO. Text in English, Dutch. 1984. s-a. EUR 22 domestic; EUR 28 in Europe; USD 44 in United States; GBP 19 in United Kingdom; EUR 34 elsewhere (effective 2010). **Description:** Dedicated to the lives and works of Stan Laurel and Oliver Hardy.
Formerly (until 2005): Blotto (0927-2933)
Published by: Stichting Laurel & Hardy Fonds, Postbus 870, Hilversum, 1200 AW, Netherlands. Ed. Bram Reijnhoudt.

NIKKEI ENTERTAINMENT!. *see* COMPUTERS—Internet

791.4 USA
NITRATE ONLINE. Text in English. q. film rev.; video rev. **Description:** Includes film and video features and reviews.
Media: Online - full text.
Published by: Nitrate Productions, Inc., 11635 106th Ave NE, Kirkland, WA 98039. TEL 425-814-4689, FAX 425-821-5881. Ed. Eddie Cockrell.

791.43 NOR ISSN 0807-9862
NORSK FILMINSTITUTT. SKRIFTSSERIE. Text in Norwegian. 1993. irreg., latest vol.18, 2006. price varies. back issues avail. **Document type:** *Monographic series, Academic/Scholarly.*
Published by: Norsk Filminstitutt, PO Box 482, Sentrum, Oslo, 0105, Norway. TEL 47-22-474500, FAX 47-22-475099, post@nfi.no.

791.3 792 ITA ISSN 1826-641X
NORTH - WEST PASSAGE. Text in English. 2004. s-a. **Document type:** *Journal, Academic/Scholarly.*
Related titles: Online - full text ed.: ISSN 2036-5632.
Indexed: CA, IBT&D, T02.
Published by: (Universita degli Studi di Torino, Discipline Arti Musica e Spettacolo (DA M S)), Edizioni di Pagina, Via dei Mille 205, Bari, 70126, Italy. info@paginasc.it, http://www.paginasc.it.

791.43 384 GBR ISSN 1601-829X
➤ **NORTHERN LIGHTS**; film and media studies yearbook. Abbreviated title: N L. Text in English. 1973. a. GBP 36, USD 68 per issue to individuals; GBP 215, USD 330 per issue to institutions (effective 2012). adv. back issues avail. **Document type:** *Yearbook, Academic/Scholarly.* **Description:** Contains papers on film and media written by faculty members.
Former titles (until 2002): Sekvens (0106-2484); (until 1978): Skrifter fra Institut for Filmvidenskab (0105-3671); (until 1976): Koebenhavns Universitet. Institut for Filmvidenskab (0105-3663)
Related titles: Online - full text ed.: ISSN 2040-0586. GBP 177, USD 265 per issue (effective 2012).
Indexed: CA, F01, F02, MLA-IB, RILM, T02.
—IE.
Published by: (Koebenhavns Universitet, Institut for Film- og Medievidenskab/University of Copenhagen, Department of Film & Media Studies DNK), Intellect Ltd., The Mill, Parnall Rd, Fishponds, Bristol, BS16 3JG, United Kingdom. TEL 44-117-9589910, FAX 44-117-9589911, info@intellectbooks.com. Ed. Stig Hjarvard. Pub. Masoud Yazdani. **Subscr. to:** Turpin Distribution Services Ltd., Pegasus Dr, Stratton Business Park, Biggleswade, Bedfordshire SG18 8QB, United Kingdom. TEL 44-1767-604951, FAX 44-1767-601640, custserv@turpin-distribution.com, http://www.turpin-distribution.com/.

778.53 ITA
NOTE DI TECNICA CINEMATOGRAFICA; rivista multimediale dell' ATIC. Text in Italian; Summaries in English. 1962. q. free. adv. bk.rev.; software rev.; tel.rev.; video rev. illus. back issues avail. **Document type:** *Magazine, Trade.* **Description:** Provides technical information and advertisements for the cinematography and TV industry.
Published by: Associazione Tecnica Italiana per la Cinematografia e la Televisione, Viale Regina Margherita 286, Rome, RM 00198, Italy. TEL 39-06-44259622, FAX 39-06-4404128, atic.ntc@tiscali.it. Circ: 3,000.

778.53 ROM ISSN 1220-1200
NOUL CINEMA. Text in Romanian. 1963. m. adv. bk.rev. **Document type:** *Magazine, Consumer.*
Formerly (until 1990): Cinema (0578-2910)
Indexed: IIFP, IITV, RASB.
Published by: Casa Editoriala Femeia, Str. Horia Closea si Crisan 5, PO Box 0-20, Otopen, Romania. TEL 40-21-2331381, FAX 40-21-2331382, redactia@femeia.ro, http://www.femeia.ro. Circ: 100,000.

778.53 RUS
NOVYE PROMYSHLENNYE KATALOGI. OBORUDOVANIE DLYA POLIGRAFICHESKOI PROMYSHLENNOSTI. FOTOKINOTEKHNIKA. SREDSTVA ORGTEKHNIKI. Text in Russian. m. USD 345 in United States.

Published by: Rossiiskii N.I.I. Problem Transporta, Lubyanskii pr 5, Moscow, 101820, Russian Federation. TEL 7-095-9254609, FAX 7-095-2002203. **Dist. by:** East View Information Services, 10601 Wayzata Blvd, Minneapolis, MN 55305. TEL 952-252-1201, 800-477-1005, FAX 952-252-1202, info@eastview.com, http://www.eastview.com.

791.43 SWE ISSN 1650-8882
NYA SVENSKA FILMVAAGEN. Text in Swedish. 2002. q. SEK 960 to individuals; SEK 1,495 to institutions (effective 2004). adv. **Description:** Distribution of new short films including documentaries and cartoons.
Media: Optical Disk - DVD.
Published by: Paradiso, PO Box 133, Haernoesand, 87123, Sweden. TEL 46-611-555595f, FAX 46-611-14413.

OBITUARIES IN THE PERFORMING ARTS. *see* THEATER

778.53 VEN ISSN 1317-1070
PN1993.5.V4
OBJETO VISUAL; cuadernos de investigacion de la cinemateca nacional. Text in Spanish. 1993. 2/yr. USD 38 (effective 2001). **Document type:** *Academic/Scholarly.* **Description:** Focuses on the study of moving images with an emphasis on Venezuelan and Latin American subjects.
Indexed: F01, F02, MLA-IB.
Published by: Fundacion Cinemateca National, Parque Central Torre Este piso 3, Caracas, DF 1010, Venezuela. TEL 58-2-5761491, 58-2-5762336, FAX 58-2-5764075, documentacionfcn@cantv.net, cinemateca.org.ve. Ed. Isabel Gonzalez.

778.53 ESP ISSN 2013-3782
OBSERVATORI DE LA PRODUCCION AUDIOVISUAL. Text in Catalan. 2007. irreg. back issues avail. **Document type:** *Journal, Academic/Scholarly.*
Media: Online - full text.
Published by: Universitat Pompeu Fabra, Placa de la Merce 10-12, Barcelona, 08002, Spain. TEL 34-93-5422000, FAX 34-93-5422002.

OCTOBER. *see* ART

791.43 AUT
DER OESTERREICHISCHE FILM; von seinen Anfaengen bis heute. Text in German. biennial. EUR 35 per vol. (effective 2004). **Document type:** *Directory, Academic/Scholarly.* **Description:** Contains history of Austrian film industry and motion pictures since 1900.
Published by: Synema - Gesellschaft fuer Film und Medien, Neubaugasse 36-1-1-1, Vienna, 1070, Austria. TEL 43-1-5233797, FAX 43-1-5233797, synema@chello.at. Eds. Brigitte Mayr, Gottfried Schlemmer.

791.43 AUT
OESTERREICHISCHE GESELLSCHAFT FUER FILMWISSENSCHAFT, KOMMUNIKATIONS- UND MEDIENFORSCHUNG. MITTEILUNGEN. Text in German. 1952. bi-m. index. **Document type:** *Newsletter, Consumer.*
Formerly: Oesterreichische Gesellschaft fuer Filmwissenschaft. Mitteilungen (0029-9146)
Published by: Oesterreichische Gesellschaft fuer Filmwissenschaft Kommunikations- und Medienforschung, Rauhensteingasse 5, Vienna, W 1010, Austria. TEL 43-1-5129936, FAX 43-1-5135330. Circ: 800.

791.43 AUT ISSN 0029-9057
DER OESTERREICHISCHER FILMAMATEUR. Text in German. 1966. bi-m. looseleaf. adv. bk.rev. bibl. **Document type:** *Newsletter, Consumer.* **Description:** For the amateur filmmaker.
Published by: Klub der Kinoamateure Oesterreichs, Mareschplatz 5a, Vienna, W 1150, Austria. TEL 43-664-5594837, FAX 43-1-5230571, kdkoe@utanet.at, http://kdkoe.nwy.at. Ed., Adv. contact Peter Gruber. Circ: 1,500.

THE OFFICIAL MCCALLUM OBSERVER PRINT JOURNAL. *see* BIOGRAPHY

791.43 CAN
OFFSCREEN. Text in English. irreg. **Description:** Dedicated to film and film criticism.
Media: Online - full text.
Address: Canada. Ed. Donato Totato.

791.43 ESP ISSN 1989-9173
▼ **OJO DE BUEY.** Text in Spanish. 2010. s-a. **Document type:** *Magazine, Consumer.*
Media: Online - full text.
Address: ojodebuey@gmail.com. Ed. Ramon Besonias Roman.

OKEJ. *see* CHILDREN AND YOUTH—For

791.43 USA
OLD TIME WESTERN FILM CLUB NEWSLETTER. Text in English. 1970. bi-m. free. **Document type:** *Newsletter.* **Description:** Encourages interest in old time Westerns, and news of the Club's screenings of Westerns.
Published by: Old Time Western Film Club, PO Box 142, Siler City, NC 27344. Ed. Milo Holt. Circ: 400.

ON THE SPOT. *see* COMMUNICATIONS—Television And Cable

778.53 NZL ISSN 0112-2789
PN1993.5.N43
ONFILM; New Zealand's screen production industry magazine. Text in English. 1984. m. NZD 67.47 (effective 2008). adv. **Document type:** *Magazine, Trade.* **Description:** Provides information for producers, financier, marketers and associated service providers.
Related titles: Online - full text ed.
Indexed: A15, ABIn, B02, B15, B17, B18, F01, F02, G04, G06, G07, G08, I05, IIFP, IITV, INZP, P48, P51, PQC, RILM, T02.
—CCC.
Published by: 3 Media Group, Wellesley St, PO Box 5544, Auckland, 1141, New Zealand. TEL 64-9-9098400, FAX 64-9-9098401, http://www.admedia.co.nz. Ed. Nick Grant TEL 64-9-9098419. adv.: page NZD 2,606; 240 x 340. Circ: 2,245.

791.43 USA
ONMOVIES. Text in English. 2005 (Dec.). 18/yr. film rev. back issues avail. **Document type:** *Magazine, Consumer.* **Description:** Contains excerpts from Times film reviews, top 10 films, articles on the film industry, notable DVD releases, upcoming films, and new personalities.
Published by: New York Times Company, 620 8th Ave, New York, NY 10018. TEL 212-556-1234, FAX 212-556-7088, letters@nytimes.com, http://www.nytimes.com. Pub. Arthur Ochs Sulzberger Jr. Adv. contact Denise Warren TEL 212-556-7894.

791.43 DNK ISSN 1602-5334
ORDET. Text in Danish. 1986. 3/yr. free (effective 2005). adv. **Document type:** *Journal, Academic/Scholarly.*
Formerly (until 2002): Inguirer (0907-7960)
Related titles: Online - full text ed.
Published by: Koebenhavns Universitet, Institut for Film- og Medievidenskab/University of Copenhagen, Department of Film & Media Studies, c/o Institut for Medier, Erkendelse og Formidling, Det Humanistiske Fakultet, Njalsgade 80, trappe 17, Copenhagen S, 2300, Denmark. TEL 45-35-328100, FAX 45-35-328850, mef@hum.ku.dk, http://filmogmedie.ku.dk. Ed. Henrike Oestergaard. Circ: 750.

791.4 SVN ISSN 1408-1687
OSKAR. Text in Slovenian. 1997. bi-m. **Document type:** *Magazine, Consumer.*
Published by: Mladina, Resljeva 16, Ljubljana, 1000, Slovenia. TEL 386-1-4328175, FAX 386-1-4331239, desk@mladina.si.

791.43 AUT
▼ **OSTEUROPA MEDIAL.** Text in German. 2010. irreg., latest vol.5, 2011. price varies. **Document type:** *Monographic series, Academic/Scholarly.*
Published by: Boehlau Verlag GmbH & Co.KG., Wiesingerstr 1, Vienna, W 1010, Austria. TEL 43-1-3302427, FAX 43-1-3302432, boehlau@boehlau.at.

791.43 USA
OTHER DIMENSIONS; the journal of multimedia horror. Text in English. 1993. irreg., latest vol.3, no.2. USD 4.25 per issue (effective 2010). back issues avail. **Document type:** *Journal, Consumer.* **Description:** Covers contemporary manifestations of horror in entertainment and art forms. Includes interviews with filmmakers and producers, discussions of science fiction and horror films, and examinations of the cultural significance of the iconography of horror.
Published by: Necronomicon Press, PO Box 1304, West Warwick, RI 02893. np@necropress.com, http://www.necropress.com. Ed. Stefan Dziemianowicz.

OTTAWA X PRESS; the capital's newsweekly. *see* MUSIC

791.43 USA ISSN 0895-0393
OUTRE (EVANSTON); entertainment from the world of ultramedia. Text in English. 1986. q. USD 20; USD 30 in Canada; USD 50 elsewhere. adv. illus. reprints avail.
Formerly (until 1995): Filmfax
Indexed: F01, F02, IIFP, IITV, T02.
Published by: Filmfax, Inc., 1320 Oakton St, Evanston, IL 60202-2719. Eds. Michael Stein, Ted Okuda.

P C R; films and video in the behavioral sciences. (Psychological Cinema Register) *see* PSYCHOLOGY—Abstracting, Bibliographies, Statistics

791.43 DNK ISSN 1396-1160
➤ **P.O.V.**; a danish journal of film studies. (Point-of-View) Variant title: Journal of Film Studies. Point-of-View Filmtidsskrift. Text in Danish, English; Summaries in English. 1996. s-a. film rev. back issues avail. **Document type:** *Journal, Academic/Scholarly.*
Related titles: Online - full text ed.: ISSN 1902-2131. 200?.
Indexed: F01, F02, IIFP, MLA-IB, T02.
Published by: Aarhus Universitet, Institut for Informations- og Medievidenskab/Aarhus University, Institute of Information and Media Science, Helsingforsgade 14, Aarhus N, 8200, Denmark. TEL 45-89-429200, FAX 45-89-425950, http://www.imv.au.dk. Ed. Richard Raskin.

➤ **P W.** (Production Weekly) *see* COMMUNICATIONS—Television And Cable

➤ **PAPER (NEW YORK).** *see* CLOTHING TRADE—Fashions

➤ **PARTICIP@TIONS**; journal of audience & reception studies. *see* SOCIOLOGY

781.542 USA ISSN 1050-5504
PN1577
PAST TIMES: THE NOSTALGIA ENTERTAINMENT NEWSLETTER. Text in English. 1990. q. USD 20 (effective 2005). adv. bk.rev.; film rev.; music rev. **Document type:** *Newsletter.* **Description:** Perpetuates the entertainment of the 1920s through the 1940s, covering movies, music, radio programs, pop culture, actors, musicians and personalities.
Published by: Past Times Publishing Co., 7308 Fillmore Dr, Buena Park, CA 90620. Ed. Randy Skretvedt. Pub. Jordan Young. adv.: page USD 100. Circ: 3,000 (paid and controlled).

791.43 USA
PEARLS MAGAZINE. Text in English. 1989. irreg. USD 5 newsstand/cover (effective 2006). film rev.; video rev. mkt.; stat.; tr.lit. back issues avail. **Document type:** *Catalog, Consumer.* **Description:** Lists and prices out-of-print videos in their original boxes. Includes articles about the state of the video industry. Covers online sales and video auctions.
Published by: Video Oyster, P O Box 1012, New York, NY 10012. TEL 212-979-6802, FAX 212-989-3533, videooyster@rcn.com, http://videoyster.com. Ed., Pub., R&P Norman Scherer. Circ: 10,000.

791.43 USA ISSN 2161-5829
AP2
PEOPLE HOLLYWOOD DAILY. Text in English. 19??. d. **Document type:** *Magazine, Consumer.*
Published by: Time Inc. (Subsidiary of: Time Warner Inc.), 1271 Ave of the Americas, New York, NY 10020. TEL 212-522-1212, information@timeinc.com, http://www.timeinc.com.

PERFORMING ARTS BUYERS GUIDE. *see* DANCE

791.436 GBR
PERIPHERAL VISIONS. Text in English. 1995 (no.2). irreg. GBP 3, USD 7. **Description:** Provides 50 detailed reviews of genre films.
Address: 28 Hillside Ave, Kilmalcolm, Renfrew PA13 4QL, United Kingdom. Ed. Iain McLachlan.

778.53 CAN
PERSISTENCE OF VISION. Text in English. 1982. a. free membership. adv. bk.rev. **Document type:** *Newsletter.*
Formerly: F A V A Newsletter
Published by: Film and Video Arts Society of Alberta, 9722-102 St, Edmonton, AB T5K 0X4, Canada. info@fava.ca, http://home.fava.ca. Circ: 100.

791.43 USA ISSN 1935-4371
PERSPECTIVE (STUDIO CITY). Text in English. 200?. bi-m. **Document type:** *Magazine, Consumer.*
Published by: Art Directors Guild & Scenic, Title and Graphic Artists, 11969 Ventura Blvd, 2nd Flr, Studio City, CA 91604. TEL 818-762-9995, FAX 818-762-9997, http://www.artdirectors.org/incEngine/?content=main.

791.43 ITA ISSN 1828-1761
IL PESCE VOLANTE. Text in Italian. 2002. m. **Document type:** *Magazine, Consumer.*
Published by: Edizioni Lindau, Corso Re Umberto 37, Turin, 10128, Italy. TEL 39-011-5175324, FAX 39-011-6693929, lindau@lindau.it.

THE PHANTOM OF THE MOVIES' VIDEOSCOPE; the ultimate genre video guide. *see* COMMUNICATIONS—Video

791.43 GBR ISSN 0263-7553
PICTURE HOUSE. Text in English. 1982. a. free to members (effective 2009). illus. 64 p./no.; back issues avail. **Document type:** *Magazine, Academic/Scholarly.* **Description:** Contains a articles on cinema subjects and is packed with photographs and illustrations.
Indexed: API, F01, F02, T02.
Published by: Cinema Theatre Association, c o Neville Taylor, 128 Gloucester Terr, London, W2 6HP, United Kingdom. TEL 44-20-88891376, david.trevorjones@btopenworld.com. Eds. Allen Eyles, Giles Woodforde. **Subscr. to:** c o Jeremy Buck, 34 Pelham Rd, London N22 6LN, United Kingdom.

PLAY (WESTLAKE VILLAGE); video games - anime - movies - music - gear - toys. *see* COMPUTERS—Computer Games

PLAY X. *see* ART

PLAYBACK; Canada's broadcast and production journal. *see* COMMUNICATIONS—Television And Cable

791.43 USA
PLAYER'S GUIDE. Text in English. a. free. **Document type:** *Directory, Trade.* **Description:** Presents professional union actor's photos and acting credits, actors headshots and agent representation. Distributed to over 2,000 management and casting directors across the United States.
Address: 123 W 44th St, #2J, New York, NY 10036. TEL 212-302-9474, FAX 212-302-3495, playersguide@breakdownservices.com. Ed. Thomas Boff. Circ: 2,000.

791.43 USA ISSN 2153-1250
PLUGGED IN HOLLYWOOD. Text in English. 2008. m. free (effective 2010). back issues avail. **Document type:** *Magazine, Consumer.*
Media: Online - full text.
Published by: Smart Girls Productions, Inc., 15030 Ventura Blvd #914, Sherman Oaks, CA 91403. TEL 818-907-6511, smartgirls@smartg.com, http://www.smartgirlsproductions.com.

POLITICS, MEDIA, AND POPULAR CULTURE. *see* SOCIOLOGY

791.43 302.2343 FRA ISSN 1778-5510
POLITIQUE DU CINEMA. Text in French. 2005. **Document type:** *Monographic series.*
Published by: Editions Sulliver, B P 20227, Arles Cedex, 13635, France. TEL 33-6-24273509, 33-4-90967224, editionssulliver@yahoo.fr.

POPCORN; das Teen People Magazin. *see* CHILDREN AND YOUTH—For

POPCORN. *see* CHILDREN AND YOUTH—For

POPCORN. *see* CHILDREN AND YOUTH—For

POPCORN. *see* CHILDREN AND YOUTH—For

POPCORN. *see* CHILDREN AND YOUTH—For

POPULAR NARRATIVE MEDIA. *see* SOCIAL SCIENCES: COMPREHENSIVE WORKS

791.43 FRA ISSN 0048-4911
PN1993
POSITIF; revue mensuelle de cinema. Text in French. 1952. m. EUR 62 (effective 2009). adv. bk.rev.; film rev. illus. reprints avail. **Document type:** *Magazine, Consumer.*
Indexed: A20, A22, ASCA, ArtHuCI, CurCont, DIP, F01, F02, IBR, IBZ, IIFP, IIPA, IITV, MLA-IB, PdeR, RASB, SCOPUS, W07.
—BLDSC (6558.810000), IE, Infotrieve, Ingenta. **CCC.**
Published by: Scope Editions, 7 Rue Gassendi, Paris, 75014, France. TEL 33-1-42184024, FAX 33-1-42184025, http://www.scope-editions.com.

POST SCRIPT (COMMERCE); essays in film and the humanities. *see* HUMANITIES: COMPREHENSIVE WORKS

POWER AGENT. *see* ASTROLOGY

791.43 POL
POZNANSKIE TOWARZYSTWO PRZYJACIOL NAUK. KOMISJA FILMOZNAWCZA. PRACE. Text in Polish. 2000. irreg., latest vol.1, 2000. price varies. **Document type:** *Monographic series, Academic/Scholarly.*
Published by: (Poznanskie Towarzystwo Przyjaciol Nauk, Komisja Filmoznawcza), Poznanskie Towarzystwo Przyjaciol Nauk/Poznan Society for the Advancement of the Arts and Sciences, ul Sew Mielzynskiego 27-29, Poznan, 61725, Poland. TEL 48-61-8527441, FAX 48-61-8522205, sekretariat@ptpn.poznan.pl, wydawnictwo@ptpn.poznan.pl, http://www.ptpn.poznan.pl.

791.433 CAN ISSN 1914-7198
PRAIRIE TALES. Text in English. 199?. a.
Published by: Metro Cinema Society, 622, 7 Sir Winston Churchill Square, Edmonton, AB T5J 2V5, Canada. TEL 780-425-9212, FAX 780-428-3509, metro@metrocinema.org, http://www.metrocinema.org/.

791.43 DEU ISSN 1617-951X
PRAXIS FILM. Text in German. 2001. irreg., latest vol.62, 2011. price varies. **Document type:** *Monographic series, Academic/Scholarly.*
Published by: U V K Verlagsgesellschaft mbH, Schuetzenstr 24, Konstanz, 78462, Germany. TEL 49-7531-90530, FAX 49-7531-905398, nadine.ley@uvk.de, http://www.uvk.de.

791.43 USA
PRE-VUE ENTERTAINMENT MAGAZINE. Text in English. 1991. bi-m. free (effective 2005). adv. **Document type:** *Magazine, Consumer.* **Description:** Highlights new music and movies for moviegoers.

Related titles: Online - full content ed.
Published by: National Pre-Vue Network, PO Box 281, La Jolla, CA 92038. TEL 619-436-6494, FAX 619-325-3649. Pub., Adv. contact Frank Lane. B&W page USD 4,000, color page USD 5,000; trim 5.3125 x 8.3125. Circ: 199,350 (controlled).

778.53 RUS
PREMIERE. Text in Russian. m. USD 159 in United States.
Published by: Compagnie Internationale de Presse et de Publicite, Bersenevskaya nab 20-2, kom 401, Moscow, 109072, Russian Federation. TEL 7-095-9590461, FAX 7-095-9590460. Ed. A B Kulish. **Dist. by:** East View Information Services, 10601 Wayzata Blvd, Minneapolis, MN 55305. TEL 952-252-1201, 800-477-1005, FAX 952-252-1202, info@eastview.com, http://www.eastview.com.

791.43 792 PRT
PREMIERE. Variant title: Revista Premiere. Text in Portuguese. 2008. m. EUR 30 (effective 2011). adv.
Published by: Multipublicacoes, Rua Basilio Teles 35, Lisbon, 1070-020, Portugal. TEL 351-21-0123400, FAX 351-21-0123444.

791.43 ZAF
PREMIERE. Text in English. bi-m. **Document type:** *Magazine, Consumer.*
Published by: Hachette Times Media, 4 Bierman Ave., Nedbank Gardens, Rosebank, Johannesburg, 2169, South Africa. TEL 27-11-2805401, FAX 27-11-2805404.

791.43 FRA ISSN 0399-3698
PREMIERE; le magazine du cinema. Text in French. 1976. m. EUR 25; EUR 3.50 newsstand/cover (effective 2008). adv. **Document type:** *Magazine, Consumer.*
Indexed: A22, RASB.
—IE, Infotrieve.
Published by: Hachette Filipacchi Medias S.A. (Subsidiary of: Lagardere Media), 149/151 Rue Anatole France, Levallois-Perret, 925340, France. TEL 33-1-413462, FAX 33-1-413469, lgardere@interdeco.fr, http://www.lagardere.com.

791.4375 JPN
PREMIERE. Text in Japanese. 1998. m. JPY 580 newsstand/cover (effective 2002). adv. **Document type:** *Magazine, Consumer.* **Description:** Contains critiques of new releases, features on movie events, and a selective guide to movie-related home entertainment.
Published by: Hachette Fujingaho Co. Ltd. (Subsidiary of: Hachette Filipacchi Medias S.A.), 2-9-1 Nishi Shinbashi, Minato-ku, Tokyo, 105-0003, Japan. TEL 81-3-3506-6601, FAX 81-3-3506-6606, http://www.hfm.co.jp. Circ: 137,000 (paid).

791.43 KOR ISSN 1228-081X
PREMIERE (KOREAN EDITION)/PEULIMIEO HAN'GUGPAN. Text in Korean. bi-w. KRW 29,000 (effective 2009). **Document type:** *Magazine, Consumer.*
Related titles: Online - full text ed.
Published by: Hachette Ein*s Media Co., Ltd./A Swe Tteu Negseuteu Mi'dieo., 4, 6, 7 Fl. Pax Tower, 231-13 Nonhyun-dong, Gangnam-gu, Seoul, 135-010, Korea, S. TEL 82-2-21048031, FAX 82-2-21048090, http://www.hemkorea.co.kr/.

791.43 USA
PREMIERE (ONLINE). Text in English. m. **Document type:** *Magazine, Consumer.*
Media: Online - full content.
Published by: Hachette Filipacchi Media U.S., Inc. (Subsidiary of: Hachette Filipacchi Medias S.A.), 1633 Broadway, New York, NY 10019. TEL 212-767-6000, http://www.hfmus.com. Pub. Paul Turcotte.

053.1 DEU
PREVIEW; Das interaktive Magazin fuer Entertainment & Style. Text in German. 2005. m. adv. **Document type:** *Magazine, Consumer.*
Published by: Lightspeed Media GmbH, Nymphenburgerstr 70, Munich, 80335, Germany. TEL 49-89-7266960, FAX 49-89-72669655, info@lightspeed-media.de, http://www.lightspeed-media.de. Ed. Kurt Koelsch. Pub. Stefan Masseck. Adv. contact Hendrik Boeing. page EUR 8,900. Circ: 100,000 (controlled).

791.43 USA ISSN 0892-6468
CODEN: CMLREE
PREVIEW (RICHARDSON). Variant title: Preview Family Movie & TV Review. Text in English. 1980. s-m. USD 34; USD 41 in Canada; USD 58 elsewhere. adv. tel.rev.; video rev. index, cum.index: 1980-1998. back issues avail. **Document type:** *Newsletter, Consumer.* **Description:** Reviews of current films, TV shows and occasional videos from a Biblical perspective for families concerned about moral content of filmed entertainment.
Related titles: Online - full text ed.
Published by: Movie Morality Ministries Inc., PO Box 832567, Richardson, TX 75083-2567. TEL 972-231-9910, FAX 972-669-9040. Ed. Richard Warick. Pub., R&P, Adv. contact John H Evans. Circ: 5,500 (paid).

781.542 USA ISSN 0199-9257
PREVUE. Variant title: Mediascene Prevue. Text in English. 1972. bi-m. USD 19.95. adv. bk.rev.; film rev. illus. back issues avail. **Document type:** *Magazine, Consumer.*
Formerly (until Aug. 1980): Media Scene
Address: PO Box 4489, Reading, PA 19606. TEL 215-370-0666, FAX 215-370-0867. Ed. J Steranko. Circ: 240,000.

791.43 CAN ISSN 0714-5551
PRIX GENIE. Text in French, English. 1980. a.
Former titles (until 1981): Genie Awards (0714-5543); (until 1980): Genie Awards Program (0228-6602)
Published by: Academy of Canadian Cinema & Television/Academie Canadienne du Cinema et de la Television, 172 King St East, Toronto, ON M5A 1J3, Canada. TEL 416-366-2227, 800-644-5194, FAX 416-366-8454, info@academy.ca, http://www.academy.ca.

PRO LIGHTS & STAGING NEWS. *see* ENGINEERING—Electrical Engineering

791.43 BRA ISSN 1981-3376
PRODUCAO PROFISSIONAL CINE. Text in Portuguese. 2005. q. **Document type:** *Magazine, Trade.*
Published by: Editorial Bolina Brasil (Subsidiary of: Grupo Editorial Bolina), Alameda Pucurui 51-59 B, Tamporere - Barueri, Sao Paulo, 06460-100, Brazil. Ed. Fernando Gaio.

384.5532 USA ISSN 0732-6653
PN1993.5.U77
PRODUCER'S MASTERGUIDE; the international production manual for broadcast-television, feature films, television, commercials, cable, digital and videotape industries in the United States, Canada, the United Kingdom, Bermuda, the Caribbean Islands, Mexico, South America, Europe, Israel, the Far East, Australia and New Zealand. Text in English. 1979. a. USD 125 domestic; USD 135 in Canada; USD 155 elsewhere (effective 1999). adv. charts; stat. **Document type:** *Directory.*
Formerly (until 1982): New York Production Manual (0163-1276)
Published by: Producer's Masterguide, 60 E 8th St, 34th Fl, New York, NY 10003-6514. TEL 212-777-4002, FAX 212-777-4101. Ed. Shmuel Bension. Circ: 18,000.

778.53 GBR ISSN 0142-632X
PRODUCTION AND CASTING REPORT. Abbreviated title: P C R. Text in English. 1968. w. GBP 252; GBP 269.47 combined subscription (print & online eds.) (effective 2009). adv. **Document type:** *Newsletter, Trade.* **Description:** Covers advance production and casting news in the film, television and theater industries.
Formed by the 1968 merger of: London Theatre; Casting Directory; Casting Guide; T C R. Television Casting Report; Grapevine; Writer's Weekly; Incorporates (1965-198?): Who's Where Weekly and Who's Who of Casting Directors (0142-6311); Which incorporated: Who's Where (London); Who's Who (London); Who's Whose (London); What's Whose (London); Daily London News
Related titles: Online - full text ed.: GBP 249.14 (effective 2009).
Address: PO Box 11, London, N1 7JZ, United Kingdom. TEL 44-20-75668282.

791.43 FRA ISSN 1951-476X
LA PRODUCTION CINEMATOGRAPHIQUE EN (YEAR). Text in French. 200?. a. free. back issues avail. **Document type:** *Bulletin.*
Related titles: Online - full text ed.
Published by: Centre National de la Cinematographie, 12 rue de Lubeck, Paris, Cedex 16 75784, France. TEL 33-1-44343440, http://www.cnc.fr/.

778.53 USA
PRODUCTION UPDATE; pre production. post production. equipment. technology. location. Text in English. 1985. m. USD 12 domestic; USD 27 in Canada; USD 42 foreign; USD 4.95 newsstand/cover (effective 2005). adv. **Document type:** *Magazine, Trade.* **Description:** Covers elements that evolve when filming and video taping on local and distant location, as well as studios and soundstages.
Formerly: Location Update (1058-3238)
Published by: Location Update, Inc., 7021 Hayvenhurst Ave, Ste 205, Van Nuys, CA 91406-3802. TEL 818-785-6362, FAX 818-785-8092, cineweb@ix.netcom.com, http://www.cineweb.com/reelnewsupdate/update.html. Ed., Pub. James Thompson. adv.: B&W page USD 2,550, color page USD 3,550. Circ: 24,000 (controlled).

791.43 332 DEU
PRODUKTIONSPRAXIS. Text in German. 1997. irreg., latest vol.10, 2002. price varies. **Document type:** *Monographic series, Academic/Scholarly.*
Published by: U V K Verlagsgesellschaft mbH, Schuetzenstr 24, Konstanz, 78462, Germany. TEL 49-7531-90530, FAX 49-7531-905398, nadine.ley@uvk.de, http://www.uvk.de.

778.53 DEU ISSN 0932-0393
PROFESSIONAL PRODUCTION. Text in German. 1987. 10/yr. EUR 51 (effective 2008). adv. **Document type:** *Magazine, Trade.*
Indexed: TM.
Published by: EuBuCo Verlag GmbH, Geheimrat-Hummel-Platz 4, Hochheim, 65239, Germany. TEL 49-6146-6050, FAX 49-6146-605200, verlag@eubuco.de, http://www.eubuco.de. Ed. Ruodlieb Neubauer. adv.: B&W page EUR 1,790, color page EUR 2,990. Circ: 5,369 (paid and controlled).

PROFIFOTO; das Magazin fuer professionelle Fotografie und Digital Imaging. *see* PHOTOGRAPHY

791.43 USA ISSN 1934-9688
PN1993
➤ **PROJECTIONS (NEW YORK)**; the journal for movies and mind. Text in English. 2007. s-a. GBP 108 combined subscription in United Kingdom to institutions (print & online eds.); EUR 129 combined subscription in Europe to institutions (print & online eds.); USD 170 combined subscription elsewhere to institutions (print & online eds.) (effective 2011). adv. reprint service avail. from PSC. **Document type:** *Journal, Academic/Scholarly.* **Description:** Contains critical issues and themes related to the historical and contemporary relationships that societies, civilizations, empires, regions, nation-states have with nature.
Related titles: Online - full text ed.: ISSN 1934-9696. GBP 91 in United Kingdom to institutions; EUR 110 in Europe to institutions; USD 144 elsewhere to institutions (effective 2011) (from IngentaConnect).
Indexed: A07, A26, A30, A31, AA, ArtInd, E08, I05, MLA-IB, S09, W03, W05.
—BLDSC (6924.907615). **CCC.**
Published by: (The Forum for Movies and Mind), Berghahn Books Inc., 150 Broadway, Ste 812, New York, NY 10038. TEL 212-222-6007, FAX 212-222-6004, journals@berghahnbooks.com, http://www.berghahnbooks.com. Ed. Ira Konigsberg. **Dist. in Europe by:** Turpin Distribution Services Ltd., Pegasus Dr, Stratton Business Park, Biggleswade, Bedfordshire SG18 8QB, United Kingdom. TEL 44-1767-604951, FAX 44-1767-601640, berghahnjournalsuk@turpin-distribution.com; **Dist. outside of Europe by:** Turpin Distribution Services Ltd., The Bleachery, 143 W St, New Milford, CT 06776. TEL 860-350-0041, FAX 860-350-0039, berghahnjournalsus@turpin-distribution.com, http://www.turpin-distribution.com.

791.43 AUS ISSN 1833-7848
THE PUNDIT. Text in English. 2006. free (effective 2008). back issues avail. **Document type:** *Magazine, Consumer.*
Related titles: Online - full text ed.: ISSN 1833-9549.
Published by: A New Leaf Media, PO Box 1426, Fitzroy North, VIC 3068, Australia. TEL 61-3-84862154, info@anewleaf.com.au. Ed. Tim Norton.

778.53 USA
PYRAMID MEDIA CATALOG. Text in English. 1960. biennial. free. film rev. **Document type:** *Catalog.* **Description:** Lists a variety of films, videos, CD-ROMs, and laserdiscs distributed by Pyramid.
Formerly: Pyramid Film and Video Catalog
Published by: Pyramid Media, PO Box 1048, Santa Monica, CA 90406-1048. TEL 310-828-7577, FAX 310-453-9083. Ed. J Randolph Wright. Circ: 60,000.

791.43 AUS ISSN 1838-4943
▼ **Q U T E.** Text in English. 2010. m. adv. back issues avail. **Document type:** *Magazine, Consumer.*
Related titles: Online - full text ed.: ISSN 1838-4951.
Published by: Q U T Student Guild, PO Box 2019, Kelvin Grove, QLD 4059, Australia. TEL 61-7-31381666, s.services@guildonline.net, http://www.guildonline.net. Ed. Kieran Salsone. Adv. contact Andrew Knox TEL 61-7-31385581.

791.43 ITA ISSN 1824-2820
QUADERNI DELLA CINETECA. Text in Italian. 1952. irreg. **Document type:** *Monographic series, Academic/Scholarly.*
Published by: Fondazione Scuola Nazionale di Cinema, Via Tuscolana 1524, Rome, 00173, Italy. TEL 39-06-722941, FAX 39-06-72294319, http://www.csc-cinematografia.it.

778.53 USA ISSN 1050-9208
PN1994 CODEN: QRFVEF
➤ **QUARTERLY REVIEW OF FILM AND VIDEO.** Text in English. 1976. 5/yr. GBP 669 combined subscription in United Kingdom to institutions (print & online eds.); EUR 703, USD 882 combined subscription to institutions (print & online eds.) (effective 2012). adv. bk.rev. illus. index. reprint service avail. from PSC. **Document type:** *Journal, Academic/Scholarly.* **Description:** Features critical, historical, and theoretical essays, book reviews, and interviews in the area of moving image studies including film, video, and digital imagery studies.
Formerly (until 1989): Quarterly Review of Film Studies (0146-0013)
Related titles: Microform ed.; Online - full text ed.: ISSN 1543-5326. GBP 602 in United Kingdom to institutions; EUR 632, USD 794 to institutions (effective 2012) (from IngentaConnect).
Indexed: A01, A02, A03, A07, A08, A20, A22, A26, A27, A30, A31, AA, ABS&EES, ASCA, AmHI, ArtInd, B04, BRD, CA, CBRI, CMM, CPLI, CommAb, E01, E08, F01, F02, FamI, G08, H07, H08, H09, H10, HAb, HumInd, I05, IIFP, IITV, MLA, MLA-IB, MRD, P02, P10, P48, P53, P54, PCI, PQC, RASB, S09, T02, W03.
—BLDSC (7206.700000), IE, Ingenta. **CCC.**
Published by: Routledge (Subsidiary of: Taylor & Francis Group), 325 Chestnut St, Ste 800, Philadelphia, PA 19106. TEL 215-625-8900, 800-354-1420, FAX 215-625-2940, orders@taylorandfrancis.com. Eds. Gwendolyn Audrey Foster, Wheeler Winston Dixon. **Subsc. outside N. America:** Taylor & Francis Ltd., Journals Customer Service, Sheepen Pl, Colchester, Essex CO3 3LP, United Kingdom. TEL 44-20-70175544, FAX 44-20-70175198, tf.enquiries@tfinforma.com.

791.43 SAU
RAABTA. Text in Urdu. m. **Description:** Entertainment and movie news.
Published by: Transcontinental Corp., P O Box 9935, Jeddah, Saudi Arabia. TEL 651-3857. Circ: 58,000.

791.43 IND
RASHTRA DEEPIKA CINEMA. Text in Malayalam. 1995. w. **Document type:** *Magazine, Consumer.*
Published by: Rashtra Deepika Ltd., PO Box 7, Kottayam, Kerala 686 001, India. TEL 91-481-3012001, FAX 91-481-3012222, editor@deepika.com.

791.4375 AUT ISSN 1993-811X
RAY; Filmmagazin. Text in German. 2005. 10/yr. EUR 29 domestic; EUR 45 in Europe (effective 2010). adv. **Document type:** *Magazine, Consumer.*
Published by: Substance Media Ltd., Mariahilferst 76/3/31, Vienna, 1070, Austria. TEL 43-1-92020080, FAX 43-1-920200813, office@ray-magazin.at. Adv. contact Hans Nussbaumer.

REAL 2 REEL. *see* COMMUNICATIONS—Television And Cable

REALSCREEN. *see* BUSINESS AND ECONOMICS

REALTIME; +onscreen. *see* THEATER

791.43 305.89607305 USA ISSN 1538-9618
REEL NOIR; for the African American moviegoer. Text in English. 2002 (Jun./Jul.). bi-m. USD 12 domestic; USD 30 in Canada; USD 60 elsewhere (effective 2002).
Published by: Downs Enterprises, Inc., 1300 E. 47th St. Ste.109, Chicago, IL 60653. TEL 773-779-3709, reelnoir@aol.com. Ed. Crystal Downs.

778.59 791.43 CAN ISSN 0831-5388
REEL WEST MAGAZINE. Text in English. 1985. bi-m. USD 35 (effective 2006). **Document type:** *Magazine, Trade.*
Indexed: C03, CBCABus, F01, F02, P48, PQC, T02.
Published by: Reel West Productions, 4012 Myrtle St, Burnaby, BC V5C 4G2, Canada. TEL 604-451-7335, 888-291-7335, FAX 604-451-7305, info@reelwest.com. Ed. Ian Caddell.

791.43 USA ISSN 1090-8234
REFERENCE GUIDES TO THE WORLD'S CINEMA. Text in English. 1997. irreg., latest 2003. price varies. back issues avail. **Document type:** *Monographic series, Consumer.*
Related titles: Online - full text ed.
Published by: Greenwood Publishing Group Inc. (Subsidiary of: A B C - C L I O), 88 Post Rd W, PO Box 5007, Westport, CT 06881. TEL 203-226-3571, 800-225-5800, FAX 877-231-6980, sales@greenwood.com. Ed. Pierre Horn.

791.43 CHE ISSN 0937-5279
REGARDS SUR L'IMAGE. SERIE 2: TRANSFORMATIONS. Text in French. 1990. irreg., latest vol.3, 1999. price varies. **Document type:** *Monographic series, Academic/Scholarly.*
Published by: Peter Lang AG (Subsidiary of: Peter Lang Publishing Group), Hochfeldstr 32, Postfach 746, Bern 9, 3000, Switzerland. TEL 41-31-3061717, FAX 41-31-3061727, info@peterlang.com, http://www.peterlang.com.

791.43 CHE ISSN 0937-5295
REGARDS SUR L'IMAGE. SERIE 4: ESTHETIQUE ET THEORIE DE L'IMAGE. Text in French. 1991. irreg., latest vol.2, 1995. price varies. **Document type:** *Monographic series, Academic/Scholarly.*
Published by: Peter Lang AG (Subsidiary of: Peter Lang Publishing Group), Hochfeldstr 32, Postfach 746, Bern 9, 3000, Switzerland. TEL 41-31-3061717, FAX 41-31-3061727, info@peterlang.com, http://www.peterlang.com.

M

778.53 DEU ISSN 0933-1395
REIHE: KULLERAUGEN STUDIUM; die blauen Schnellhefter. Text in German. 1986. s-a. EUR 24 domestic; EUR 28 foreign (effective 2006). bk.rev.; film rev.; video rev.; tel.rev. illus. 100 p./no.; back issues avail. **Document type:** *Monographic series, Academic/Scholarly.*
Published by: Kulleraugen Verlag, Laaseweg 4, Schellerten, 31174, Germany. TEL 49-5123-4330, FAX 49-5123-2015, kulleraugen-verlag@gmx.de, http://www.kulleraugen-verlag.de.

791.43 USA ISSN 0890-5231
PN1993
RELEASE PRINT. Text in English. 1979. 10/yr. USD 45 to members; USD 65 foreign to members. adv. bk.rev.; film rev.; video rev. back issues avail. **Document type:** *Magazine, Trade.* **Description:** Covers public policy and the media arts, interviews with independent filmmakers and criticism. Includes a local calendar and international festival and funding information.
Indexed: F01, F02, T02.
Published by: Film Arts Foundation, 346 Ninth St, 2nd Fl, San Francisco, CA 94103. TEL 415-552-8760, FAX 415-552-0882. Ed., R&P Thomas J Powers. Pub. Gail Silva. Adv. contact Andy Moore. Circ: 10,000 (paid).

791.43 USA
REMINDER LIST OF ELIGIBLE RELEASES; annual Academy awards for distinguished achievements. Text in English. a. USD 5 (effective 2000). **Document type:** *Directory.* **Description:** List of films with cast that are eligible for Academy awards consideration.
Published by: Academy of Motion Picture Arts and Sciences, 8949 Wilshire Blvd, Beverly Hills, CA 90211-1972. TEL 310-247-3000, FAX 310-859-9619, jgiancoli@oscars.org. Ed. Torene Svitil. R&P Scott Miller.

RENTAL AND STAGING SYSTEMS. *see* BUSINESS AND ECONOMICS—Trade And Industrial Directories

778.5 BEL ISSN 1379-8391
REPENSER LE CINEMA. Text in French. 2003. irreg., latest vol.4, 2009. price varies. **Document type:** *Monographic series, Academic/Scholarly.*
Published by: P I E - Peter Lang SA, 1 avenue Maurice, 6e etage, Brussels, 1050, Belgium. TEL 32-2-3477236, FAX 32-2-3477237, pie@peterlang.com, http://www.peterlang.net. Ed. Dominique Nasta.

REPERTORY REPORT. *see* THEATER

778.53 CAN ISSN 0843-6827
REVUE DE LA CINEMATHEQUE. Text in French. 1989. bi-m. CAD 25 (effective 2000). adv. illus. back issues avail. **Document type:** *Bulletin.*
Supersedes: Copie Zero (0709-0471)
Indexed: C03, CBCARef, CBPI, F01, F02, IIFP, IITV, MRD, P48, P49, PQC, PdeR.
—IE.
Published by: Cinematheque Quebecoise, 335 bd de Maisonneuve E, Montreal, PQ H2X 1K1, Canada. TEL 514-842-9763, FAX 514-842-1816. Ed., R&P Pierre Jutras. Adv. contact Diane Audet. Circ: 40,000.

RISEN; it's not what you think. *see* MUSIC

791.43 ITA ISSN 1827-5184
PN1993
RIVISTA DEL CINEMATOGRAFO. Abbreviated title: R d C. Text in Italian. 1928. m. (10/yr.). EUR 10.90 (effective 2009). bk.rev.; film rev. illus.; stat.; tr.lit. index. **Document type:** *Magazine, Consumer.*
Former titles (until 1995): Rivista del Cinematografo e della Comunicazione Sociale (1827-5176); (until 1974): Rivista del Cinematografo (0035-5879)
Related titles: Online - full content ed.
Indexed: F01, F02.
Published by: Ente dello Spettacolo, Via Giuseppe Palombini 6, Rome, 00165, Italy. TEL 39-06-6637455, FAX 39-06-6637321. Ed. Andrea Piersanti. Circ: 10,000.

791.43 JPN
ROADSHOW. Text in Japanese. 1972. m. **Document type:** *Consumer.*
Published by: Shueisha Inc., 2-5-10 Hitotsubashi, Chiyoda-ku, Tokyo, 101-0003, Japan. TEL 81-3-32306111. Ed. Mantaro Hanami. Circ: 350,000.

ROCKERILLA; mensile di musica e cinema. *see* MUSIC

791.43 USA ISSN 1532-8147
PN1995
ROGER EBERT'S MOVIE YEARBOOK. Text in English. a. USD 24.95 (effective 2008). **Document type:** *Magazine, Consumer.* **Description:** Reviews films available on videotape.
Former titles (until 1999): Roger Ebert's Video Companion (1072-561X); (until 1994): Roger Ebert's Movie Home Companion
Published by: Andrews and McMeel (Subsidiary of: Universal Press Syndicate), 4520 Main St, Ste 700, Kansas City, MO 64111-7701. TEL 816-932-6680, 800-943-9839, FAX 816-931-5018, http://www.andrewsmcmeel.com.

ROLLING STONE. *see* MUSIC

778.53 ROM
ROMANIAN FILM. Text in Romanian. 1972. irreg.
Indexed: IIFP, IITV.
Published by: Romaniafilm, Bd. Aviatorilor 106 Sector 1, Bucharest, Romania. TEL 40-021-2300365, FAX 40-021-2307304, marketing@romfilm.ro, http://www.romaniafilm.ro.

S A C D. JOURNAL DES AUTEURS. (Societe des Auteurs et Compositeurs Dramatiques) *see* THEATER

791.43 FIN ISSN 1237-2366
S E T S - JULKAISU. (Suomen Elokuvatutkimuksen Seura) Text in Finnish. 1994. 2/yr. back issues avail. **Document type:** *Monographic series, Academic/Scholarly.*
Published by: Suomen Elokuvatutkimuksen Seura/Finnish Society for Cinema Studies, c/o cIlona Hongisto, Mediatutkimus, Turun University, Turun, 20014, Finland. anilho@utu.fi, http://www.uta.fi/jarjestot/sets/.

791.4375 794.8 DEU
S F T - SPIELE FILME TECHNIK. Text in German. 2004. m. EUR 49 domestic; EUR 56.50 in Austria; EUR 61 elsewhere; EUR 2.50 newsstand/cover (effective 2011). adv. **Document type:** *Magazine, Consumer.* **Description:** Contains articles, reviews and features on movies, video games, and electronic devices and gadgets.
Related titles: Online - full text ed.
Published by: Computec Media AG, Dr-Mack-Str 83, Fuerth, 90762, Germany. TEL 49-911-2872100, FAX 49-911-2872200, info@computec.de, http://www.computec.de. Ed. Kay Beinroth. Circ: 111,621 (paid and controlled).

791.43 USA ISSN 1545-0279
TR845 CODEN: SMPJDF
S M P T E MOTION IMAGING JOURNAL. Text in English. 1916. 8/yr. USD 140 to non-members; free to members (effective 2011). bk.rev. abstr.; bibl.; illus. index, cum.index every 5 yrs. back issues avail.; reprints avail. **Document type:** *Magazine, Trade.*
Former titles (until 2002): S M P T E Journal (0036-1682); (until 1976): S M P T E. Journal (0361-4573); (until 1956): S M P T E Journal (0898-0438); (until 1955): Society of Motion Picture and Television Engineers. Journal (0898-042X); (until 1950): Society of Motion Picture Engineers. Journal (0097-5834); (until 1930): Society of Motion Picture Engineers. Transactions (0096-6460)
Related titles: Microform ed.: (from PMC, PQC); Online - full text ed.: ISSN 2160-2492.
Indexed: A05, A20, A22, A23, A24, AS&TA, AS&TI, ASCA, ApMecR, B04, B10, B13, BRD, C&ISA, C10, CA, ChemAb, CurCont, E&CAJ, EngInd, F01, F02, FR, GALA, ISR, Inspec, MLA-IB, PCI, PhotoAb, S04, SCI, SCOPUS, SSCI, SolStAb, T02, TM, W03, W05, W07.
—BLDSC (8313.081000), AskIEEE, CASDDS, IE, Ingenta, INIST, Linda Hall. **CCC.**
Published by: Society of Motion Picture and Television Engineers, 3 Barker Ave, 5th Fl, White Plains, NY 10601. TEL 914-761-1100, FAX 914-761-3115, smpte@allenpress.com.

791.43 USA
S P S C V A NEWSLETTER. Text in English. 1991. q. bk.rev. **Description:** Presents the society's activities and some news on philosophy and filmmaking.
Media: Online - full text.
Published by: Society for the Philosophic Study of the Contemporary Visual Arts

SALT FOR SLUGS; contemporary literature for the random reader. *see* MUSIC

SAMEDI MAGAZINE. *see* LIFESTYLE

384.558029 USA
SAN JOSE FILM & VIDEO PRODUCTION HANDBOOK - DIRECTORY. Variant title: Film Commission Directory of Local Services. Text in English. 1981. a. USD 10. adv. illus.; maps; tr.lit. 34 p./no.; **Document type:** *Directory, Trade.* **Description:** Covers local crew personnel available for hire, sample of locations available for filming, general services, and permit information.
Former titles: San Jose Film & Video Production Binder; (until 1992): San Jose Film and Video Commission Directory; Best Performance Film and Video Directory
Related titles: Online - full content ed.
Published by: San Jose Convention & Visitors Bureau, Film & Video Commission, 408 Almaden Blvd., San Jose, CA 95110-2709. TEL 408-295-9600, 800-726-5673, FAX 408-295-3937, http://www.sanjose.org/index.cfm. Ed. Dorea Domschke. Pub., R&P Joe O'Kane TEL 408-792-4135. Circ: 7,000 (controlled).

791.43 LKA
SARASAVIYA. Text in Singhalese. 1963. w.
Address: Lake House, D.R. Wijewardene Mawatha, P O Box 1168, Colombo, 10, Sri Lanka. TEL 1-21181. Ed. Granville Silva. Circ: 56,000.

781.542 USA ISSN 1093-6491
SAVAGE UNDERGROUND. Text in English. q. USD 8 domestic; USD 16 foreign; USD 2 newsstand/cover (effective 2000). bk.rev.; film rev.; music rev.; video rev. illus. **Document type:** *Newsletter.* **Description:** Contains reviews of underground, independent and offbeat "adult" films, videos, music, pulps from the 1930's and 40's, and zines.
Published by: Savage Film Group, PO Box 4011, Capitol Heights, MD 20791. Ed., Pub. Jose Luis Behar. Adv. contact R Savage.

791.43 DEU
SCALA (STUTTGART). Text in German. m. free newsstand/cover (effective 2007). adv. **Document type:** *Magazine, Consumer.*
Published by: P V - Projekt Verlag, Falbenhennenstr 17, Stuttgart, 70180, Germany. TEL 49-711-60171717, FAX 49-711-60171729. adv.: B&W page EUR 1,230, color page EUR 2,150. Circ: 20,580 (controlled).

791.433 USA
SCANNERS. Text in English. 1987. m. USD 10 (effective 1992). **Description:** Covers Japanese anime and comic, including English translations of Japanese animation, and news of events.
Published by: Southern California Anime Network, PO Box 261702, San Diego, CA 92126-1702. Ed. Adam Chaney.

808.066791 USA ISSN 1079-6851
PN1997.A1
SCENARIO; the magazine of screenwriting art. Text in English. 1995. q. USD 59.95 domestic; USD 69.95 in Canada; USD 72.95 elsewhere (effective 2001). adv. illus. reprints avail. **Description:** Each issue features complete screenplays.
Indexed: AIAP, F01, F02, IIFP, IIPA, IITV.
Published by: eDesign Communications, 3200 Tower Oaks Blvd, Rockville, MD 20852. TEL 212-463-0600, 800-222-2654, FAX 212-989-9891, info@scenariomag.com, http://www.scenariomag.com/. Ed. Tod Lippy. Pub. Howard Cadel. **Subscr. to:** R C Communications Inc., 3200 Tower Oaks Blvd, Rockville, MD 20852. TEL 301-984-3203, FAX 301-984-3203.

791.43 USA
SCHLOCK, THE JOURNAL OF LOW-BROW CINEMA & CULTURE. Text in English. 1992. m. USD 10 (effective 1998). adv. bk.rev.; film rev.; music rev.; tel.rev.; video rev. illus. **Document type:** *Newspaper.* **Description:** Aims to educate the public about great, unknown, and underground films. Covers junk culture in general.
Media: Online - full text.
Published by: John Chilson, Ed. & Pub., 3841 Fourth Ave, 192, San Diego, CA 92103. TEL 619-299-4702, FAX 619-295-0487. R&P, Adv. contact John Chilson. page USD 250. Circ: 5,000.

791.43 DEU ISSN 0177-3739
SCHMALFILM; die Zeitschrift fuer Filmamateure. Text in German. 1948. 6/yr. EUR 73.20 domestic; EUR 78.90 foreign; EUR 11 newsstand/cover (effective 2011). adv. bk.rev.; film rev. illus.; stat.; mkt.; pat.; tr.mk. index. **Document type:** *Magazine, Consumer.*
Former titles (until 1985): Schmalfilm und Videofilmen (0176-2230); (until 1979): Schmalfilm (0036-620X)
—**CCC.**
Published by: Fachverlag Schiele und Schoen GmbH, Markgrafenstr 11, Berlin, 10969, Germany. TEL 49-30-2537520, FAX 49-30-2517248, service@schiele-schoen.de, http://www.schiele-schoen.de. Ed. Juergen Lossau. Circ: 1,742 (paid and controlled).

791 DEU ISSN 1434-4572
SCHRIFTENREIHE MUENCHNER FILMZENTRUM. Text in German. 1997. irreg., latest 2004. price varies. **Document type:** *Monographic series, Academic/Scholarly.*
Published by: Muenchner Filmzentrum e.V., c/o Filmmuseum im Muenchner Stadtmuseum, St-Jakobsplatz 1, Munich, 80331, Germany. TEL 49-89-23322348, FAX 49-89-23323931, kontakt@muenchner-filmzentrum.de, http://www.muenchner-filmzentrum.de.

791.4375 USA ISSN 1524-4253
PN1998
SCHWANN D V D ADVANCE. Text in English. 1999. bi-m. USD 28.35, USD 51.95, USD 76.95; USD 6.95 newsstand/cover (effective 2001). adv. film rev. **Document type:** *Magazine, Consumer.* **Description:** Features reviews of new DVDs and articles on topics important to DVD viewers.
Published by: Schwann Publications (Subsidiary of: Valley Media), 1280 Santa Anita Ct, Woodland, CA 95776. TEL 530-661-7886, FAX 530-669-5184, schwann@valley-media.com. Circ: 10,000 (paid).

791.436 GBR ISSN 1754-3770
➤ **SCIENCE FICTION FILM AND TELEVISION.** Text in English. 2008. s-a. GBP 54, USD 94 combined subscription to individuals (print & online eds.); GBP 144, USD 233 combined subscription to institutions (print & online eds.) (effective 2012). adv. back issues avail.; reprints avail. **Document type:** *Journal, Academic/Scholarly.* **Description:** Aims to encourage dialogue among the scholarly and intellectual communities of film studies, sf studies and television studies.
Related titles: Online - full text ed.: ISSN 1754-3789. 2008. GBP 44, USD 76 to individuals; GBP 115, USD 187 to institutions (effective 2012).
Indexed: A22, A26, CA, E01, F01, F02, I05, MLA-IB, T02.
—**CCC.**
Published by: Liverpool University Press, 4 Cambridge St, Liverpool, L69 7ZU, United Kingdom. TEL 44-151-7942233, FAX 44-151-7942235, lup@liv.ac.uk. Eds. Mark Bould, Sherryl Vint. Adv. contact Janet Smith. **Subscr. to:** Marston Book Services Ltd., PO Box 269, Abingdon, Oxon OX14 4YN, United Kingdom. TEL 44-1235-465574, FAX 44-1235-465556, subscriptions@marston.co.uk, http://www.marston.co.uk/.

791.423 GBR ISSN 1465-9166
PN1993.5.A1
➤ **SCOPE (NOTTINGHAM);** an on-line journal of film studies. Text in English. 1999. 3/yr. free (effective 2011). film rev. back issues avail. **Document type:** *Journal, Trade.* **Description:** Provide a forum for discussion of all aspects of film history, theory and criticism.
Media: Online - full content.
Indexed: MLA-IB, RILM.
—**CCC.**
Published by: University of Nottingham, Institute of Film and Television Studies, University Park, Nottingham, NG7 2RD, United Kingdom. TEL 44-115-9514261, FAX 44-115-9514270, american-enquiries@nottingham.ac.uk, http://www.nottingham.ac.uk/film/.

791.43 GBR ISSN 2045-2128
▼ **SCREAM.** Text in English. 2010. bi-m. GBP 4.50 per issue (effective 2011). back issues avail. **Document type:** *Magazine, Consumer.*
Published by: Screen Power Publishing, PO Box 1989, Bath, BA2 2YE, United Kingdom. TEL 44-1563-541484, office@screen-power.com, http://www.screen-power.com.

SCREEN; trade magazine for Chicago's film industry. *see* COMMUNICATIONS—Television And Cable

791.43 JPN
SCREEN. Text in Japanese. 1946. m. JPY 14,000. adv. **Document type:** *Consumer.*
Published by: Kindai-Eiga Corp., Owaricho Bldg, 2F, 6-8-3 Ginza, Chuo-ku, Tokyo, 104-0061, Japan. TEL 81-3-5568-2811, FAX 81-3-5568-2818. Ed. Hisayuki Ui. Pub. Shuzo Kosugi. R&P Fumitaka Kosugi. Adv. contact Masatoshi Tanaka.

791.43 IND ISSN 0036-9551
SCREEN (MUMBAI). Text in English. 1951. d. adv. film rev. 8 cols./p.; back issues avail. **Document type:** *Newspaper, Consumer.*
Related titles: Online - full text ed.: free (effective 2011).
Indexed: RASB.
Published by: Indian Express Newspapers (Mumbai) Pvt. Ltd., Express Towers, Nariman Pt, Mumbai, Maharashtra 400 021, India. TEL 91-22-22022627, FAX 91-22-2885827, onlinesales@expressindia.com, http://www.indianexpress.com. Ed. Priyanka Sinha. Adv. contact Anjali Gokral.

SCREEN ACTOR. *see* LABOR UNIONS

791.43 AUS
SCREEN AUSTRALIA NEWS. Variant title: Australian Film Commission News. Text in English. 1981. m. free (effective 2008). back issues avail. **Document type:** *Newsletter, Government.* **Description:** Provides information on major events in the Australian film industry, news on AFC activities and initiatives, production reports, multimedia and more.
Former titles (until 2008): A F C News (0819-4424); (until 1986): A F C Information Update (0813-720X); (until 1982): Information Update (0729-1639)
Related titles: Online - full text ed.
—**CCC.**
Published by: Screen Australia, GPO Box 3984, Sydney, NSW 2001, Australia. TEL 61-2-81135800, FAX 61-2-93573737, info@screenaustralia.gov.au, http://www.screenaustralia.gov.au. Ed., R&P Mick Broderick.

791.43 305.81306 GBR ISSN 1751-7834
➤ **SCREEN DECADES.** Text in English. 2005 (Dec.). irreg., latest 2007. price varies. back issues avail. **Document type:** *Monographic series, Academic/Scholarly.* **Description:** Explores the impact of cultural issues in film as well as how film has influenced American society.

Published by: Berg Publishers (Subsidiary of: Oxford International Publishers Ltd.), 1st Fl Angel Ct, 81 St Clements St, Oxford, Berks OX4 1AW, United Kingdom. TEL 44-1865-245104, FAX 44-1865-791165, enquiry@bergpublishers.com. Eds. Lester D Friedman, Murray Pomerance.

➤ **SCREEN EDUCATION.** *see* EDUCATION—Teaching Methods And Curriculum

791.43 GBR ISSN 0965-9587
SCREEN FINANCE. Text in English. 1988. fortn. GBP 745 (effective 2010). **Document type:** *Newsletter, Trade.* **Description:** Provides global reporting on the film industry: finance, production, exhibition and distribution.
Related titles: Microform ed.: (from PQC); Online - full text ed.: GBP 2,235 (effective 2010).
Indexed: B02, B03, B15, B17, B18, G04, G06, G07, G08, I05, P48, PQC, T03.
—CIS.
Published by: Informa Telecoms & Media (Subsidiary of: T & F Informa plc), 37-41 Mortimer St, London, W1T 3JH, United Kingdom. TEL 44-20-70175000, FAX 44-20-70175953, telecoms.enquiries@informa.com, http://www.informatm.com. Adv. contact Katrina Coyne TEL 44-20-70175295. **Subscr. to:** Sheepen Pl, Colchester, Essex C03 3LP, United Kingdom. TEL 44-20-70175533, FAX 44-20-70174783.

791.43 GBR ISSN 0307-4617
PN1993.5.G7
SCREEN INTERNATIONAL; the voice of the international film business. Text in English. 1912. w. adv. bk.rev.; film rev. illus.; stat. back issues avail. **Document type:** *Newspaper, Consumer.* **Description:** Gives in-depth weekly analysis and opinion on the people and issues driving the global film industry.
Former titles: Screen International and Cinema T V Today; (until 1975): Cinema T V Today
Related titles: Online - full text ed.
Indexed: P52.
—BLDSC (8211.757800). **CCC.**
Published by: Emap Media Ltd. (Subsidiary of: Emap Communications Ltd.), Greater London House, Hampstead Rd, London, NW1 7EJ, United Kingdom. TEL 44-20-77285000, http://www.emap.com. Ed. Mike Goodridge TEL 323-655-6087. Adv. contact Andrew Dixon TEL 44-20-77285622.

791.43 GBR
SCREEN INTERNATIONAL DAILIES. Text in English. d. back issues avail. **Document type:** *Magazine, Trade.*
Published by: Emap Media Ltd. (Subsidiary of: Emap Communications Ltd.), Greater London House, Hampstead Rd, London, NW1 7EJ, United Kingdom. TEL 44-20-77285000, http://www.emap.com.

791.43 IND ISSN 0971-2305
PN1993.5.I8
SCREEN WORLD. Variant title: Screen World Annual. Text in English. 1987. a. INR 1,500 per issue (effective 2011). adv. Supplement avail. **Document type:** *Directory, Trade.* **Description:** Provides information on the movie, TV, audio and video industry.
Published by: Screen World Publication, H/9, 171, Snehankoor Society, New M H B, L T Rd, Borivali (W), Mumbai, Maharashtra 4000 091, India. TEL 91-22-28692244, info@screenworldindia.com. Ed., Pub. Rajendra Ojha.

791.43 USA ISSN 1545-9020
PN1993.3
SCREEN WORLD; film annual. Text in English. 1949. a., latest vol.61. USD 49.99 per issue (effective 2011). bibl. 384 p./no.; back issues avail. **Document type:** *Trade.* **Description:** Provides cast lists and production information for all films released in the US every year. Includes over 1000 pictures.
Former titles (until 1982): John Willis' Screen World; (until 1970): Screen World (0080-8288); (until 1966): Daniel Blum's Screen World
Published by: Applause Theatre & Cinema Books, 118 E 30th St, New York, NY 10016. TEL 212-532-5525, FAX 646-562-5852, info@halleonardbooks.com. Ed. Barry Monush.

791.43 791.45 305.896 USA ISSN 1557-3109
PN1995.9.N4
➤ **SCREENING NOIR**; a journal of Black film, television & new media culture. Text in English. 2005 (Fall-Win.). s-a. USD 30 to individuals; USD 45 to institutions; USD 15 per issue (effective 2010). **Document type:** *Journal, Academic/Scholarly.* **Description:** Focuses attention on these representational media in terms of their relevance to and impact on African and African diasporic culture.
Published by: University of California, Santa Barbara, Center for Black Studies, 4603 S Hall, Santa Barbara, CA 93106. TEL 805-893-3914, FAX 805-893-7243, ctr4blst@cbs.ucsb.edu, http://www.research.ucsb.edu/cbs/.

791.43 GBR ISSN 1476-198X
SCREENTRADE MAGAZINE; the quarterly journal for the UK, European and US exhibitors. Text in English. 2002 (Feb.). q. GBP 29 in Europe; USD 50 in North America; GBP 33 elsewhere (effective 2009). adv. back issues avail. **Document type:** *Magazine, Trade.* **Description:** Covers all aspects of cinema exhibition and film distribution.
Related titles: Online - full text ed.
Published by: Screentrade Media Ltd, PO Box 144, Orpington, Kent BR6 6LZ, United Kingdom. TEL 44-1689-833117, FAX 44-1689-833117, advertising@screentrademagazine.co.uk. Ed. Philip Turner. Adv. contact Leslie Waller.

SCREENWRITERS MONTHLY. *see* LITERATURE

791.423 USA
SCRIPT (BALDWIN). Text in English. m. USD 29.95 domestic; USD 37.95 in Canada; USD 49.95 elsewhere (effective 2001).
Published by: Script Magazine, 5638 Sweet Air Rd, Baldwin, MD 21013-0007. TEL 410-592-3466, 888-245-2229, FAX 410-592-8062. Ed. Shelly Mellott. Pub. James Kellett.

808.066791 USA ISSN 1092-2016
PN1996
SCR(I)PT; where film begins. Text in English. 1995. bi-m. USD 24.95 domestic; USD 32.95 in Canada & Mexico; USD 44.95 elsewhere (effective 2010). adv. bk.rev.; film rev. illus. 68 p./no.; back issues avail.; reprints avail. **Document type:** *Magazine, Consumer.* **Description:** Includes how-to-write tips, screenwriter interviews, news of what's selling to whom for what price, and departments listing film festivals and writing contests.
Indexed: F01, F02, T02.
Published by: Final Draft, Inc., 26707 W Agoura Rd, Ste 205, Calabasas, CA 91302. TEL 800-231-4055 ext.137, FAX 818-995-4422, http://www.finaldraft.com/. Eds. Maureen Green, Shelly Mellott. **Subscr. to:** PO Box 90846, Long Beach, CA 90809. scriptsubs@pfsmag.com.

808.066791 ESP ISSN 1134-6795
PN1993
SECUENCIAS; revista de historia del cine. Text in Spanish; Abstracts in English. 1994. s-a. adv. bk.rev. illus. **Document type:** *Journal, Academic/Scholarly.* **Description:** Presents research articles, notes and briefs on film history.
Indexed: F01, F02, IIFP, IMMAb.
Published by: Universidad Autonoma de Madrid, Instituto Universitario de Ciencias de la Educacion, Carr. Colmenar Viejo, Km. 15, Cantoblanco, Madrid, 28049, Spain. TEL 34-91-4974054, http://www.uam.es.

SEE MAGAZINE. *see* MUSIC

778.534 ITA ISSN 0393-3865
PN1993
SEGNOCINEMA; rivista cinematografica bimestrale. Text in Italian. 1981. 6/yr. EUR 30 domestic; EUR 60 in Europe; EUR 90 elsewhere (effective 2008). film rev. bibl.; illus. index. back issues avail. **Document type:** *Magazine, Consumer.*
Indexed: F01, F02, IBR, IBZ, IIFP, IITV, RASB.
Published by: Cineforum di Vicenza, Via Giovanni Prati, 34, Vicenza, VI 36100, Italy. TEL 39-0444-545744, FAX 39-0444-300947. Circ: 8,000.

791.43 AUS ISSN 1443-4059
PN1993
➤ **SENSES OF CINEMA**; an online journal devoted to the serious and eclectic discussion of cinema. Text in English. 1999. q. free (effective 2009). bk.rev.; tel.rev.; film rev.; video rev. 90 p./no.; back issues avail. **Document type:** *Journal, Academic/Scholarly.* **Description:** Contains serious and eclectic discussion of cinema.
Media: Online - full text.
Indexed: AusPAIS, F01, F02, MLA-IB.
—CCC.
Published by: Senses of Cinema Inc., AFI Research Collection, School of Applied Communication, RMIT University, GPO Box 2476V, Melbourne, VIC 3001, Australia. Eds. Rolando Caputo, Scott Murray. Adv. contact Peter Beilby.

791.43 ITA
SENTIERI SELVAGGI ONLINE; il cinema e un'invenzione del futuro. Text in Italian. 1999. irreg. **Document type:** *Magazine, Consumer.*
Media: Online - full content.
Published by: Sentieri Selvaggi, Via del Velodromo 56, Rome, 00179, Italy.

791.43 DNK ISSN 1398-6562
SENTURA; magasin for litteratur og levende billeder. Text in Danish. 1998. irreg. (2-3 yr). DKK 220; DKK 440 to institutions; DKK 65 per issue (effective 2009). adv. bk.rev.; film rev. back issues avail. **Document type:** *Magazine, Consumer.*
Related titles: Online - full text ed.: ISSN 1902-6439. 200?.
Published by: Foreningen Sentura, Valdemarsgade 19 A, Copenhagen V, 1665, Denmark. TEL 45-20-331756. Ed. Nina Larsen. adv.: B&W page DKK 3,200, color page DKK 4,400; 166 x 255. Circ: 1,000.

791.43 CAN ISSN 0037-2412
PN1993
SEQUENCES; la revue de cinema. Text in French. 1955. 6/yr. CAD 25 domestic to individuals; CAD 52 foreign to individuals; CAD 42 domestic to institutions. adv. bk.rev.; film rev. illus. cum.index. back issues avail. **Document type:** *Journal, Consumer.* **Description:** Provides reviews, interviews with actors and directors.
Related titles: Microform ed.: (from BNQ).
Indexed: A26, CPerI, F01, F02, I05, IIFP, IITV, PdeR.
—CCC.
Address: Succ Haute Ville, C P 26, Quebec, PQ G1R 4M8, Canada. TEL 418-656-5040, FAX 418-656-7282. Ed., R&P Yves Beauregard. Pub., Adv. contact Yves Beaupre. Circ: 3,500.

808.23 USA
SERIAL REPORT. Text in English. q. USD 15 domestic; USD 20 foreign (effective 2000). **Document type:** *Newsletter.*
Published by: Boyd Magers, Ed. & Pub., 1312 Stagecoach Rd S E, Albuquerque, NM 87123. Circ: 270 (paid).

791.43 BRA ISSN 1516-9294
SESSOES DO IMAGINARIO. Text in Portuguese. 1996. a. **Document type:** *Journal, Academic/Scholarly.*
Related titles: Online - full text ed.: ISSN 1980-3710. free (effective 2011).
Indexed: CA, T02.
Published by: (Pontificia Universidade Catolica do Rio Grande do Sul, Faculdade dos Meios de Comunicacao Social), Editora da P U C R S, Avenida Ipiranga 6681, Predio 33, Porto Alegre, RS 90619-900, Brazil.

778.53 BRA
SET; cinema & video. (Monthly Guia de TV por Assinatura avail.) Text in Portuguese. 1987. m. USD 63. adv. film rev.; video rev. illus.; stat. **Document type:** *Consumer.* **Description:** Presents reviews of new film releases. Profiles actors and actresses.
Published by: Editora Azul, S.A., Ave. NACOES UNIDAS, 5777, Sao Paulo, SP 05479-900, Brazil. TEL 55-11-8673300, FAX 55-11-8673311. Ed. Jorge de Souza. R&P Benjamin Goncalvez TEL 55-11-8673304. Adv. contact Enio Vergeiro. color page USD 11,500; trim 266 x 202. Circ: 58,654 (paid).

SEVENTH SKY AND SEVENTH SKY PEOPLE. *see* SPORTS AND GAMES

SHANGHAI YISHUJIA/SHANGHAI ARTISTS. *see* THEATER

791.43 CHN ISSN 0559-7331
SHANGYING HUABAO/SHANGHAI FILM PICTORIAL. Text in Chinese. 1957. m. USD 106.80 (effective 2009). **Document type:** *Magazine, Consumer.*
—East View.
Published by: Shanghai Dianying Zhipianchang, 595 Caoxibei Lu, Shanghai, 200030, China. TEL 86-21-4386433, FAX 86-21-4382300. **Dist. by:** China International Book Trading Corp, 35 Chegongzhuang Xilu, Haidian District, PO Box 399, Beijing 100044, China. TEL 86-10-68412045, FAX 86-10-68412023, cibtc@mail.cibtc.com.cn, http://www.cibtc.com.cn.

363.47 USA
SHE. Text in English. irreg. USD 6 newsstand/cover. **Document type:** *Magazine, Consumer.*
Published by: Draculina Publishing, PO Box 587, Glen Carbon, IL 62034. FAX 618-659-1129, dracdirect@charter.net. Ed. Cameron Scholes.

SHIDAI YINGSHI/MODERN MOVIE & TV BIWEEKLY. *see* LITERATURE

791.43 CHN ISSN 1002-9966
SHIJIE DIANYING/WORLD CINEMA. Text in Chinese. 1981. bi-m. USD 39.60 (effective 2009). **Document type:** *Magazine, Consumer.*
Related titles: Online - full text ed.
—East View.
Published by: Zhongguo Dianyingjia Xiehui/China Film Association, 22, Beisanhuan Donglu, Beijing, 100013, China. TEL 86-10-64219977 ext 6380.

791.43 GBR ISSN 0965-8238
SHIVERS. Text in English. 1992. 8/yr. GBP 29 domestic; USD 59 in United States; GBP 37 elsewhere; GBP 3.99 newsstand/cover domestic; USD 8.99 newsstand/cover in United States (effective 2009). adv. back issues avail. **Document type:** *Magazine, Consumer.* **Description:** Contains the details of recent fantasy/ horror releases including retrospectives on classic horror/cult films for enthusiasts.
Published by: Visual Imagination Ltd., 9 Blades Ct, Deodar Rd, London, SW15 2NU, United Kingdom. TEL 44-20-88751520, FAX 44-20-88751588, mailorder@visimag.com. adv.: B&W page GBP 735, color page GBP 1,110; trim 298 x 210.

791.436 USA
SHOCK CINEMA. Text in English. s-a. USD 18 for 2 yrs. domestic; USD 32 for 2 yrs. foreign; USD 5 newsstand/cover in US & Canada; USD 8 newsstand/cover elsewhere (effective 2002). adv. film rev.; bk.rev. illus.; tr.lit. 48 p./no.; back issues avail. **Document type:** *Magazine, Consumer.* **Description:** Includes interviews devoted to cult cinema figures, as well as film reviews by both editorial staff and readers.
Address: c/o Steve Pulchaski, PO Box 518, Peter Stuyvesant Station, New York, NY 10009. Ed., Pub. Steve Pulchaski. adv.: page USD 250; 7.5 x 9.5.

791.43 DEU ISSN 1430-1229
SHOMINGEKI; Filmzeitschrift. Text in German. 1995. irreg. adv. **Document type:** *Magazine, Consumer.* **Description:** Presents articles, reviews and discussions involving various styles and genres of motion pictures.
Address: Kanzowstr 11, Berlin, 10439, Germany. TEL 49-30-44737918, FAX 49-30-44737918. Ed. Ruediger Tomczak.

791.43 GBR ISSN 2042-7824
▼ ➤ **SHORT FILM STUDIES.** Text in English. 2011. s-a. GBP 36, USD 68 to individuals; GBP 110, USD 154 to institutions (effective 2012). adv. back issues avail. **Document type:** *Journal, Academic/Scholarly.* **Description:** Designed to stimulate ongoing research on individual short films as a basis for a better understanding of the art form as a whole.
Related titles: Online - full text ed.: ISSN 2042-7832. GBP 75, USD 105 (effective 2012).
Published by: Intellect Ltd., The Mill, Parnall Rd, Fishponds, Bristol, BS16 3JG, United Kingdom. TEL 44-117-9589910, FAX 44-117-9589911, info@intellectbooks.com. Ed. Richard Raskin. Pub. Masoud Yazdani.

791.43 USA
SHORTKUTZ. Text in English. 2002 (Sep.). q. USD 39.95 (effective 2003). **Document type:** *Magazine, Consumer.* **Description:** Showcases the works of aspiring filmmakers.
Media: Optical Disk - DVD.
Address: c/o Ken Westermann, 7619 Greenwood Ave N, Seattle, WA 98103.

778.53 GBR ISSN 1353-0887
SHOTS. Text in English. 1990. bi-m. GBP 1,499 combined subscription (print, online & DVD eds.); GBP 919 combined subscription (print & DVD eds.) (effective 2009). adv. back issues avail. **Document type:** *Magazine, Trade.* **Description:** Provides an international selection of the most innovative and effective new work produced, from top TV ads and music videos to special effects and spots by talented new directors.
Related titles: Online - full content ed.; Optical Disk - DVD ed.
—CCC.
Published by: Emap Inform, Greater London House, Hampstead Rd, London, NW1 3EJ, United Kingdom. TEL 44-20-77285000, http://www.emap.com. Ed. Danny Edwards TEL 44-20-77285672. Adv. contact Amelie Lambert TEL 44-20-77285686. page GBP 2,940; trim 235 x 297.

079.5496 NPL
SHOWBIZ MAGAZINE. Text in English. bi-m. **Document type:** *Magazine, Consumer.* **Description:** Covers lifestyle, cinema, music, TV, fashion, beauty.
Related titles: Online - full content ed.
Published by: Show-Biz Network Pvt. Ltd, PO Box 13442, Kathmandu, Nepal. TEL 977-1-242244, showbiz@enet.com.np.

SIEGENER FORSCHUNGEN ZUR ROMANISCHEN LITERATUR- UND MEDIENWISSENSCHAFT. *see* LITERATURE

791.43 GBR ISSN 0037-4806
PN1993
SIGHT AND SOUND; the international film monthly. Text in English. 1932. m. GBP 38 domestic; GBP 61 foreign (effective 2009). adv. bk.rev.; film rev. illus. index. back issues avail.; reprints avail. **Document type:** *Magazine, Consumer.* **Description:** Contains articles on contemporary and classic cinema from Hong Kong to Hollywood.
Incorporates (1934-1991): Monthly Film Bulletin (0027-0407)
Related titles: Microfilm ed.: (from PQC, WMP); Microform ed.: (from MIM); Online - full text ed.; Supplement(s): Chronicle of Cinema. ISSN 1359-3595.
Indexed: A01, A02, A03, A06, A07, A08, A10, A11, A20, A22, A25, A26, A27, A30, A31, AA, ASCA, AcaI, AmHI, ArtHuCI, ArtInd, B04, B05, B14, BRD, BRI, BrHumI, C12, CA, CBRI, CurCont, E08, F01, F02, G08, GdIns, H07, H08, H09, H10, HAb, HumInd, I05, IBR, IBT&D, IBZ, IIFP, IIPA, IITV, L04, LISTA, M01, M02, M11, MEA&I, MLA-IB, MRD, P02, P10, P48, P53, P54, PCI, PQC, RASB, S08, S09, SCOPUS, T02, U01, V03, W03, W05, W07, WBA, WMB.
—BLDSC (8275.270000), IE, Infotrieve, Ingenta. **CCC.**

Published by: British Film Institute, Belvedere Rd, S Bank, Waterloo, London, SE1 8XT, United Kingdom. publishing@bfi.org.uk. Adv. contact Ronnie Hackston TEL 44-20-79578916. **Subscr. to:** CDS Global, Tower House, Sovereign Park, Market Harborough, Leics LE16 9EF, United Kingdom. TEL 44-1858-438848, FAX 44-1858-434958. **Dist. by:** Macmillan Distribution Limited, Brunel Rd., Houndsmills, Basingstoke, Hampshire RG21 6XS, United Kingdom. TEL 44-1256-329242, FAX 44-1256-328339.

791.43 384.55 BEL ISSN 1726-0426
SIGNIS MEDIA; cine video radio internet television. Text and summaries in English, French, Spanish. 2002. bi-m. EUR 25, USD 25 (effective 2005). music rev.; tel.rev.; Website rev.; bk.rev.; film rev.; video rev. abstr.; bibl.; illus. index. 24 p./no.; back issues avail. **Document type:** *Newsletter, Trade.* **Description:** Covers cinematographic, video, and new media productions from all over the world, especially those largely ignored by the more industrialized countries.
Formed by the merger of (1982-2002): Cine y Medios (1726-0418); Which was formerly (until 1988): O C I C Info (Spanish Edition) (0771-0623); (1980-2002): Cine and Media (1726-040X); Which was formerly (until 1988): O C I C Info (English Edition) (0771-0518); (until 1983): O C I C News (English Edition) (0258-0349); (until 1981): O C I C Newsletter (English Edition) (0772-3490); (1980-2002): Cine et Media (1016-9660); Which was formerly (until 1988): O C I C Info (French Edition) (0771-0461); (until 1982): O C I C Informations (French Edition) (0772-2761); (until 1980): O C I C Newsletter (French Edition) (0772-277X)
Related titles: Online - full text ed.
Indexed: F01, F02.
Published by: Signis. The World Catholic Association for Communication, Rue du Saphir 15, Brussels, 1030, Belgium. TEL 32-2-7349708, FAX 32-2-7347018, ocicbru@compuserve.com, http://www.ocic.org. Ed., Pub. Robert Molhant. R&P, Adv. contact Guido Convents. Circ: 7,000.

SILVER SCREEN. *see* COMPUTERS—Computer Graphics

778.53 BIH ISSN 0587-0054
➤ **SINEAST/FILM MAKER**; filmski casopis. Text in Serbo-Croatian. 1967. q. USD 12; USD 25 foreign. adv. bk.rev.; film rev. cum.index: 1967-1983. back issues avail. **Document type:** *Academic/Scholarly.* **Description:** Discusses Bosnian cinematography.
Published by: Kino Savez Bosne i Hercegovine, Strosmajerova 1-II, Sarajevo, 71000, Bosnia Herzegovina. TEL 38-71-212377, FAX 387-71-212377. Ed. Asaf Dzanic. Adv. contact Teufik Busatlic. Circ: 1,000. **Co-sponsor:** SIZ Kinematografije Bosne i Hercegovine.

791.43 TUR ISSN 1300-8161
SINEMA. Text in Turkish. 1994. m. adv. **Document type:** *Magazine, Consumer.*
Published by: Turkuvaz Magazine Broadcasting Enterprises, Inc., Tevfik Bey Mah. 20 Temmuz Cad. No.24, Sefakoy - Istanbul, 34295, Turkey. TEL 90-212-4112323, FAX 90-212-3543792, http://www.calik.com/.

791.43 ITA ISSN 1123-458X
SIPARIO. Text in Italian. 1946. m. (10/yr.). EUR 62 (effective 2008). adv. bk.rev. **Document type:** *Magazine, Consumer.* **Description:** Contains articles about stage arts: theater, dance, opera, music, cinema, fine arts.
Indexed: IBR, IBZ, MLA, MLA-IB.
Published by: C A M A s.a.s., Via Rosales, 3, Milano, 20124, Italy. TEL 39-02-653270, FAX 39-02-29060005, siparios@tiscalinet.it. Ed. Mario Mattia Giorgetti.

791.43 USA
SIRENS OF CINEMA. Text in English. q. **Description:** Covers the female stars of television, video, and cinema. Includes interviews and features.
Published by: Draculina Publishing, PO Box 587, Glen Carbon, IL 62034. FAX 618-659-1129, dracdirect@charter.net, http://www.draculina.com. Eds. Kevin Collins, Hugh Gallagher. Pub. Hugh Gallagher.

791.43 IND
SITARA TELUGU FILM WEEKLY. Text in Telugu. 1976. w. film rev. 5 cols./p.; **Document type:** *Magazine, Trade.* **Description:** Provides interesting film news, star features and good reading for the entire family.
Published by: Vasundhara Publications, Eenadu Complex, Somajiguda, Hyderabad, Andhra Pradesh 500 082, India. TEL 91-44-23318181, FAX 91-44-23392530.

791.4375 AUT
SKIP. Text in German. 11/yr. EUR 11 (effective 2008). adv. **Document type:** *Magazine, Consumer.* **Description:** Contains articles and reviews on all the latest movies in theaters and on video.
Published by: Wienerin Verlags GmbH & Co. KG (Subsidiary of: Styria Medien AG), Geiselbergstr 15, Vienna, N 1110, Austria. TEL 43-1-60117999, FAX 43-1-60117967. Ed. Kurt Zechner. Adv. contact Michael Ginalis. page EUR 8,500; trim 210 x 273. Circ: 420,000 (paid and free).

778.53 NLD ISSN 0166-1787
➤ **SKRIEN**; filmmagazine voor professionals en connaisseurs. Text in Dutch. 1968. 8/yr. EUR 62.65 to individuals; EUR 109.95 to institutions; EUR 53.70 to students (effective 2010). adv. bk.rev.; film rev. illus. 68 p./no.; back issues avail. **Document type:** *Journal, Academic/Scholarly.* **Description:** Publishes articles and essays on film, television, film and television production in the Netherlands, film history and theory.
Indexed: F01, F02, IIFP, IITV.
—IE, Infotrieve.
Published by: FolioDynamica B.V., Postbus 513, Zandvoort, 2040 EA, Netherlands. uitgever@foliodynamica.nl, http://www.foliodynamica.nl. Ed. Wally Cartigny. Pub. Eric Ravestijn. adv.: color page EUR 1,175; trim 220 x 285. Circ: 1,500.

791.43 DEU ISSN 1862-8877
SMALLFORMAT. Text in English. 2006. bi-m. EUR 69; EUR 10 newsstand/cover (effective 2008). adv. **Document type:** *Magazine, Trade.* **Description:** Provides information on new products, tips for better filming, tests, labs, film material, the history of camera brands, and a collector's marketplace for small gauge film fans.
Published by: Fachverlag Schiele und Schoen GmbH, Markgrafenstr 11, Berlin, 10969, Germany. TEL 49-30-2537520, FAX 49-30-2517248, service@schiele-schoen.de. Ed. Juergen Lossau. adv.: page EUR 1,200.

791.43 367 GBR
THE SMILE. Text in English. 1999. q. GBP 12 domestic membership; USD 20 foreign membership (effective 2000). film rev. illus. back issues avail. **Document type:** *Magazine, Consumer.* **Description:** Dedicated to fans of the very pretty Canadian actress and her winsome smile.
Published by: Fans of Michele Scarabelli, 320 Brook St, Erith, Kent DA8 1DY, United Kingdom.

791.43 780 GBR ISSN 1751-4193
THE SOUNDTRACK. Abbreviated title: T S. Text in English. 2008. s-a. GBP 36, USD 68 to individuals; GBP 215, USD 330 to institutions (effective 2012). adv. back issues avail. **Document type:** *Journal, Academic/Scholarly.* **Description:** Focuses its attention on the aural elements, which combine with moving images.
Related titles: Online - full text ed.: ISSN 1751-4207. GBP 177, USD 265 (effective 2012).
Indexed: A01, CA, F01, F02, M11, T02.
—BLDSC (8330.554200).
Published by: Intellect Ltd., The Mill, Parnall Rd, Fishponds, Bristol, BS16 3JG, United Kingdom. TEL 44-117-9589910, FAX 44-117-9589911, info@intellectbooks.com. Eds. Estella Tincknell, Michael Filimowicz. Pub. Masoud Yazdani. **Subscr. to:** Turpin Distribution Services Ltd., Pegasus Dr, Stratton Business Park, Biggleswade, Bedfordshire SG18 8QB, United Kingdom. TEL 44-1767-604951, FAX 44-1767-601640, custserv@turpin-distribution.com, http://www.turpin-distribution.com/.

SPACE VIEW; TV & Kino. *see* LITERATURE—Science Fiction, Fantasy, Horror

SPANK! YOUTH CULTURE ONLINE. *see* MUSIC

791.43 USA ISSN 1051-0230
PN1993
SPECTATOR. Text in English. 19??. s-a. USD 15 in US & Canada to individuals; USD 20 elsewhere to individuals; USD 30 in US & Canada to institutions; USD 40 elsewhere to institutions (effective 2010). bk.rev. **Document type:** *Journal, Academic/Scholarly.* **Description:** Covers film, television, and cultural criticism.
Formerly (until 1987): U S C Spectator
Related titles: Online - full text ed.
Indexed: ABS&EES, CA, F01, F02, IIPA, MLA-IB, T02.
Published by: University of Southern California, School of Cinema - Television, University Park, SCA 319, Los Angeles, CA 90089. TEL 213-740-3334, FAX 213-740-9471.

SPETTACOLO E COMUNICAZIONE. *see* COMMUNICATIONS

SPOTLIGHT ACTORS. *see* THEATER

SPOTLIGHT ACTRESSES. *see* THEATER

SPOTLIGHT CHILDREN & YOUNG PERFORMERS. *see* THEATER

THE SPOTLIGHT. GRADUATES. *see* THEATER

SPOTLIGHT ON PRESENTERS. *see* THEATER

778.53 LKA
SRI LANKA FILM ANNUAL. Text in Singhalese. 1975 (no.28). a. LKR 6.95. film rev.
Published by: National Catholic Film Office, St. Phillip Neri's Church, Katukurunda, Kalutara, Sri Lanka.

STAGE AND SCREEN STUDIES. *see* THEATER

STAGE SCREEN & RADIO. *see* LABOR UNIONS

STAGECAST - IRISH STAGE AND SCREEN DIRECTORY. *see* THEATER

STAR TREK COMMUNICATOR. *see* COMMUNICATIONS—Television And Cable

791.43 DEU ISSN 1434-0003
STAR WARS (RHEINFELDEN). Text in German. 1996. q. EUR 3.90 newsstand/cover (effective 2010). adv. **Document type:** *Magazine, Consumer.*
Published by: OZ Verlag GmbH, Roemerstr 90, Rheinfelden, 79618, Germany. TEL 49-7623-9640, FAX 49-7623-964200, info@oz-verlag.de, http://www.oz-verlag.com.

791.43 USA ISSN 1083-4486
STAR WARS INSIDER. Text in English. 1987. bi-m. USD 27.95 (effective 2004). adv. bk.rev.; film rev. illus. **Document type:** *Magazine, Consumer.* **Description:** Covers all matters connected to the science fiction trilogy, the new Star Wars prequels and Star Wars fandom.
Formerly (until 1994): Lucasfilm Fan Club (1041-5122)
Published by: Paizo Publishing LLC, 2700 Richards Rd., Ste. 201, Bellevue, WA 98005-4200. customer.service@paizo.com, http://paizo.com. Ed. Dave Gross. Circ: 250,000 (paid).

791.43 FRA ISSN 1954-3018
STARDUST MEMORIES.COM. Text in French. 2005. m. back issues avail. **Document type:** *Magazine, Consumer.*
Media: Online - full text. **Related titles:** Print ed.: ISSN 1957-2956.
Published by: Stardust Memories, c/o Daniel Dos Santos, 11 Rue Erard, Paris, 75012, France. stardustmemories.magazine@gmail.com. Ed. Daniel Dos Santos.

STARLOG. *see* COMMUNICATIONS—Television And Cable

STARS. *see* LEISURE AND RECREATION

STOCK FOOTAGE INDEX (YEAR); the index to specialist stock footage libraries & their websites. *see* PHOTOGRAPHY

STOCK INDEX U K / EUROPE (YEAR). *see* PHOTOGRAPHY

791.43 SWE ISSN 1653-4859
STOCKHOLM CINEMA STUDIES. Text in Swedish. 2006. irreg., latest vol.10, 2010. **Document type:** *Monographic series, Academic/Scholarly.*
Related titles: ◆ Series of: Acta Universitatis Stockholmiensis. ISSN 0346-6418.
Published by: (Stockholms Universitet, Filmvetenskapliga Institutionen/ Stockholm University, Department of Cinema Studies), Stockholms Universitet, Acta Universitatis Stockholmiensis, c/o Stockholms Universitetsbiblioteket, Universitetsvaegen 10, Stockholm, 10691, Sweden. TEL 46-8-162800, FAX 46-8-157776, http://www.sub.su.se. Ed. Margaretha Fathli. **Dist. by:** Eddy.se AB, Norra Kyrkogatan 3, Visby 62155, Sweden. TEL 46-498-253900, FAX 46-498-249789, info@eddy.se, order@eddy.se, http://www.eddy.se, http://acta.bokorder.se.

791.4375 DEU
STRANDGUT; Stadtmagazin Frankfurt am Main. Text in German. m. adv. **Document type:** *Magazine, Consumer.*
Related titles: Online - full text ed.
Published by: Strandgut Verlags GmbH, Postfach 900709, Frankfurt Am Main, 60447, Germany. TEL 49-69-979103-0, FAX 49-69-7075125. Ed. Birgit Siegel. Adv. contact Dietmar Luening TEL 49-69-97910312. B&W page EUR 1,760, color page EUR 2,550. Circ: 41,045 (controlled).

791.43 USA
STUDENT FILMMAKERS. Text in English. 2006. m. free to qualified personnel (effective 2006). **Document type:** *Magazine, Consumer.* **Description:** Contains articles, interviews, reviews, and photographs on new techniques, trends, technologies, and how-to's.
Published by: Welch Media, 42 W. 24th St., New York, NY 10010 . Ed., Pub. Kim E. Welch.

STUDIEN ZUM THEATER, FILM UND FERNSEHEN. *see* THEATER

791.43 DEU ISSN 0175-9590
STUDIEN ZUR FILMGESCHICHTE. Text in German. 1983. irreg., latest vol.8, 1992. price varies. **Document type:** *Monographic series, Academic/Scholarly.*
Indexed: IIFP.
Published by: Georg Olms Verlag, Hagentorwall 7, Hildesheim, 31134, Germany. TEL 49-5121-15010, FAX 49-5121-150150, info@olms.de.

791.43 GBR ISSN 1750-3175
PN1995.65.A75
STUDIES IN AUSTRALASIAN CINEMA. Abbreviated title: S A C. Text in English. 2007. 3/yr. GBP 36, USD 68 to individuals; GBP 235, USD 368 to institutions (effective 2012). adv. back issues avail. **Document type:** *Journal, Academic/Scholarly.* **Description:** Engages in critical discussion of cinema from the Australian, New Zealand and Pacific region.
Related titles: Online - full text ed.: ISSN 1750-3183. GBP 192, USD 290 (effective 2012).
Indexed: A07, A30, A31, AA, ArtInd, B04, BRD, CA, F01, F02, IIFP, MLA-IB, T02, W03, W05.
—IE.
Published by: Intellect Ltd., The Mill, Parnall Rd, Fishponds, Bristol, BS16 3JG, United Kingdom. TEL 44-117-9589910, FAX 44-117-9589911, info@intellectbooks.com, http://www.intellect-net.com/. Ed. Anthony Lambert. Pub. Masoud Yazdani. **Subscr. to:** Turpin Distribution Services Ltd., Pegasus Dr, Stratton Business Park, Biggleswade, Bedfordshire SG18 8QB, United Kingdom. TEL 44-1767-604951, FAX 44-1767-601640, custserv@turpin-distribution.com, http://www.turpin-distribution.com/.

791.43 GBR ISSN 1750-3280
PN1995.9.D6
➤ **STUDIES IN DOCUMENTARY FILM.** Abbreviated title: S D F. Text in English. 2007. 3/yr. GBP 36, USD 68 to individuals; GBP 235, USD 368 to institutions (effective 2012). adv. back issues avail. **Document type:** *Journal, Academic/Scholarly.* **Description:** Covers the history, theory, criticism and practice of documentary film.
Related titles: Online - full text ed.: ISSN 1750-3299. GBP 192, USD 290 (effective 2012).
Indexed: A07, A30, A31, AA, ArtInd, B04, BRD, CA, F01, F02, IIFP, MLA-IB, T02, W03, W05.
—IE.
Published by: Intellect Ltd., The Mill, Parnall Rd, Fishponds, Bristol, BS16 3JG, United Kingdom. TEL 44-117-9589910, FAX 44-117-9589911, info@intellectbooks.com. Ed. Deane Williams. Pub. Masoud Yazdani. **Subscr. to:** Turpin Distribution Services Ltd., Pegasus Dr, Stratton Business Park, Biggleswade, Bedfordshire SG18 8QB, United Kingdom. TEL 44-1767-604951, FAX 44-1767-601640, custserv@turpin-distribution.com, http://www.turpin-distribution.com/.

791.43 GBR ISSN 2040-350X
▼ **STUDIES IN EASTERN EUROPEAN CINEMA.** Abbreviated title: S E E C. Text in English. 2010. s-a. GBP 36, USD 68 to individuals; GBP 132, USD 185 to institutions (effective 2012). adv. back issues avail. **Document type:** *Journal, Academic/Scholarly.* **Description:** Designed for the world-wide community of Eastern European film scholars.
Related titles: Online - full text ed.: ISSN 2040-3518. GBP 99, USD 140 (effective 2012).
Indexed: F01, F02, T02.
Published by: Intellect Ltd., The Mill, Parnall Rd, Fishponds, Bristol, BS16 3JG, United Kingdom. TEL 44-117-9589910, FAX 44-117-9589911, info@intellectbooks.com. Pub. Masoud Yazdani. **Dist. by:** Turpin Distribution Services Ltd., Pegasus Dr, Stratton Business Park, Biggleswade, Bedfordshire SG18 8QB, United Kingdom. TEL 44-1767-604951, FAX 44-1767-601640, custserv@turpin-distribution.com, http://www.turpin-distribution.com/.

791.43 GBR ISSN 1741-1548
PN1993.5.E85
STUDIES IN EUROPEAN CINEMA. Abbreviated title: S E C. Text in English. 2004. 3/yr. GBP 36, USD 68 to individuals; GBP 235, USD 368 to institutions (effective 2012). adv. back issues avail. **Document type:** *Journal, Academic/Scholarly.* **Description:** Provides a place for readers interested in European cinema and the film cultures of Europe, bringing together experts from a variety of fields in order to facilitate interdisciplinary exchange.
Related titles: Online - full text ed.: ISSN 2040-0594. GBP 192, USD 290 (effective 2012).
Indexed: A22, CA, CMM, E01, F01, F02, IIFP, MLA-IB, T02.
—BLDSC (8490.532350), IE. **CCC.**
Published by: Intellect Ltd., The Mill, Parnall Rd, Fishponds, Bristol, BS16 3JG, United Kingdom. TEL 44-117-9589910, FAX 44-117-9589911, info@intellectbooks.com. Eds. Graeme Harper TEL 44-23-92842201, Owen Evans TEL 44-1792-513375. Pub. Masoud Yazdani. **Subscr. to:** Turpin Distribution Services Ltd., Pegasus Dr, Stratton Business Park, Biggleswade, Bedfordshire SG18 8QB, United Kingdom. TEL 44-1767-604951, FAX 44-1767-601640, custserv@turpin-distribution.com, http://www.turpin-distribution.com/.

791.4 305.84 GBR ISSN 1471-5880
PN1993.5.F7
➤ **STUDIES IN FRENCH CINEMA.** Abbreviated title: S F C. Text in English. 2001. 3/yr. GBP 36, USD 68 to individuals; GBP 235, USD 368 to institutions (effective 2012). adv. back issues avail. **Document type:** *Journal, Academic/Scholarly.* **Description:** Pays special attention to three areas in the study of French cinema. These are: film history, film genre and trends, and film technique and cinematic theory.
Related titles: Online - full text ed.: ISSN 1758-9517. GBP 192, USD 290 (effective 2012).
Indexed: A01, A02, A03, A08, A22, AmHI, ArtHuCI, CA, CurCont, E01, F01, F02, H07, IIFP, MLA-IB, T02, W07.
—IE. **CCC.**
Published by: Intellect Ltd., The Mill, Parnall Rd, Fishponds, Bristol, BS16 3JG, United Kingdom. TEL 44-117-9589910, FAX 44-117-9589911, info@intellectbooks.com. Eds. Phil Powrie TEL 44-1912-227492, Sarah Leahy, Susan Hayward TEL 44-1392-264342, Will Higbee. Pub. Masoud Yazdani. **Subscr. to:** Turpin Distribution Services Ltd., Pegasus Dr, Stratton Business Park, Biggleswade, Bedfordshire SG18 8QB, United Kingdom. TEL 44-1767-604951, FAX 44-1767-601640, custserv@turpin-distribution.com, http://www.turpin-distribution.com/.

791.43 GBR ISSN 1478-0488
PN1993.5.L3
➤ **STUDIES IN HISPANIC CINEMAS.** Abbreviated title: S H C. Text in English. 2004. s-a. GBP 36, USD 68 to individuals; GBP 215, USD 330 to institutions (effective 2012). adv. back issues avail. **Document type:** *Journal, Academic/Scholarly.* **Description:** Dedicated to the study of Spanish-speaking cinemas.
Related titles: Online - full text ed.: ISSN 2040-0608. GBP 177, USD 265 (effective 2012).
Indexed: A22, CA, CMM, E01, F01, F02, IIFP, MLA-IB, T02.
—IE. **CCC.**
Published by: Intellect Ltd., The Mill, Parnall Rd, Fishponds, Bristol, BS16 3JG, United Kingdom. TEL 44-117-9589910, FAX 44-117-9589911, info@intellectbooks.com. Eds. Barry Jordan, Kathleen Vernon, Laura Podalsky. Pub. Masoud Yazdani. **Subscr. to:** Turpin Distribution Services Ltd., Pegasus Dr, Stratton Business Park, Biggleswade, Bedfordshire SG18 8QB, United Kingdom. TEL 44-1767-604951, FAX 44-1767-601640, custserv@turpin-distribution.com, http://www.turpin-distribution.com/.

791.43 GBR ISSN 1750-3132
PN1993.5.R9
STUDIES IN RUSSIAN AND SOVIET CINEMA. Abbreviated title: S R S C. Text in English. 2007. 3/yr. GBP 36, USD 68 to individuals; GBP 235, USD 368 to institutions (effective 2012). adv. back issues avail. **Document type:** *Journal, Academic/Scholarly.* **Description:** Focuses on pre-revolutionary, Soviet and post- Soviet film, its aesthetic development, and its position between ideology and industry.
Related titles: Online - full text ed.: ISSN 1750-3140. GBP 192, USD 290 (effective 2012).
Indexed: A07, A30, A31, AA, ABS&EES, ArtInd, B04, CA, F01, F02, IIFP, MLA-IB, T02, W03, W05.
—IE.
Published by: (Association for Slavic, East European and Eurasian Studies USA), Intellect Ltd., The Mill, Parnall Rd, Fishponds, Bristol, BS16 3JG, United Kingdom. TEL 44-117-9589910, FAX 44-117-9589911, info@intellectbooks.com. Ed. Birgit Beumers. Pub. Masoud Yazdani. **Subscr. to:** Turpin Distribution Services Ltd., Pegasus Dr, Stratton Business Park, Biggleswade, Bedfordshire SG18 8QB, United Kingdom. TEL 44-1767-604951, FAX 44-1767-601640, custserv@turpin-distribution.com, http://www.turpin-distribution.com/.

791.43 GBR ISSN 1756-4921
PN1993.5
▼ ➤ **STUDIES IN SOUTH ASIAN FILM & MEDIA.** Abbreviated title: S A F M. Text in English. 2009. s-a. GBP 36, USD 68 to individuals; GBP 180, USD 290 to institutions (effective 2012). adv. back issues avail. **Document type:** *Journal, Academic/Scholarly.* **Description:** Looks at the media and cinema of the Indian subcontinent in their social, political, economic, historical, and increasingly globalized and diasporic contexts.
Related titles: Online - full text ed.: ISSN 1756-493X. GBP 147, USD 220 (effective 2012).
Indexed: CA, F01, F02, MLA-IB, T02.
—CCC.
Published by: Intellect Ltd., The Mill, Parnall Rd, Fishponds, Bristol, BS16 3JG, United Kingdom. TEL 44-117-9589910, FAX 44-117-9589911, info@intellectbooks.com. Eds. Aarti Wani, Alka Kurian, Jyotsna Kapur. Pub. Masoud Yazdani. **Subscr. to:** Turpin Distribution Services Ltd., Pegasus Dr, Stratton Business Park, Biggleswade, Bedfordshire SG18 8QB, United Kingdom. TEL 44-1767-604951, FAX 44-1767-601640, custserv@turpin-distribution.com, http://www.turpin-distribution.com/.

➤ **STUDIES IN THEATRE AND PERFORMANCE.** *see* THEATER

➤ **STUDII SI CERCETARI DE ISTORIA ARTEI. SERIA TEATRU, MUZICA, CINEMATOGRAFIE/STUDIES AND RESEARCH IN ART HISTORY. SERIES: THEATRE, MUSIC, CINEMATOGRAPHY.** *see* THEATER

791.43 FRA ISSN 1969-9441
▼ **STUDIO CINE LIVE.** Text in French. 2009. m. (11/yr). EUR 33 (effective 2009). **Document type:** *Magazine, Consumer.*
Formed by the merger of (1987-2008): Studio Magazine (0982-8354); (1997-2009): Cine Live (1253-4250)
Address: 22 Rue Rene Boulanger, Paris, Cedex 10 5472, France. TEL 33-1-70373154, http://www.studiocinelive.com.

STUNT PERFORMERS. *see* THEATER

STYLUS MAGAZINE. *see* MUSIC

791.43 FRA ISSN 2108-7199
SUEURS FROIDES (ONLINE). Text in French. 1994. irreg. **Document type:** *Consumer.*
Formerly (until 2003): Sueurs Froides (Print) (1294-2995)
Media: Online - full text.
Published by: Sin'Art http://www.sueursfroides.fr.

SUN BELT JOURNAL. *see* BUSINESS AND ECONOMICS

791.43 DEU
SUPER 8 SAMMLER; Futter fuer Ihren Projektor. Text in German. 1995. q. EUR 20; EUR 5 newsstand/cover (effective 2002). **Document type:** *Magazine, Consumer.*
Address: Harannistr 6, Herne, 44623, Germany. TEL 49-2323-917677. Ed. Andre Supanz.

791.43 SWE ISSN 1654-0050
SWEDISH FILM. Text in English. 2003. irreg. **Document type:** *Magazine, Consumer.*
Formerly (until vol.8, 2006): Made in Sweden (1652-0025)
Related titles: Online - full text ed.: ISSN 1654-8167. 2003.
Published by: Svenska Filminstitutet/Swedish Film Institute, Filmhuset, Borgvaegen 1-5, PO Box 27126, Stockholm, 10252, Sweden. TEL 46-8-6651100, FAX 46-8-6611820, registrar@sfi.se.

791.43 AUS
SYDNEY FILM FESTIVAL PROGRAMME. Text in English. 1954. a. adv. film rev. back issues avail. **Document type:** *Catalog.*
Published by: Sydney Film Festival, PO Box 950, Glebe, NSW 2037, Australia. TEL 61-2-96603844, FAX 61-2-96928793, info@sydfilm-fest.com.au, http://www.sydfilm-fest.com.au. Circ: 5,000.

794.6 DEU
T N T MAGAZINE. Text in German. bi-m. EUR 4.90 newsstand/cover (effective 2007). adv. **Document type:** *Magazine, Consumer.*
Published by: Raptor Publishing GmbH, Galvanistr 30, Frankfurt am Main, 60486, Germany. TEL 49-69-977880, FAX 49-69-9778822, cu@raptor.de, http://www.raptor.de. adv.: page EUR 4,000. Circ: 50,000 (paid and controlled).

T V & FILM EXTRAS. *see* COMMUNICATIONS—Television And Cable

TAKE ONE; the video entertainment newspaper. *see* COMMUNICATIONS—Video

TALENT IN MOTION. *see* LIFESTYLE

791.43306 GBR ISSN 1744-9901
➤ **TALKING IMAGES.** Text in English. 2005 (Feb.). irreg., latest 2009. price varies. back issues avail. **Document type:** *Monographic series, Academic/Scholarly.* **Description:** Publishes radical (and classic) work on the key art form of modern times, the moving image. Focusing chiefly on film - but also encompassing video, TV and digital imaging - the series brings together philosophers, critics, directors and artists to analyze the central role of the visual in contemporary culture.
Published by: Berg Publishers (Subsidiary of: Oxford International Publishers Ltd.), 1st Fl Angel Ct, 81 St Clements St, Oxford, Berks OX4 1AW, United Kingdom. TEL 44-1865-245104, FAX 44-1865-791165, enquiry@bergpublishers.com. Ed. Yann Perreau.

791.43 USA
TAYLOROLOGY. Text in English. 1993. m. **Document type:** *Newsletter.* **Description:** Focuses on the life and death of Paramount film director William Desmond Taylor.
Media: Online - full text. Ed., R&P Bruce Long.

TEATER. MUUSIKA. KINO. *see* THEATER

TEATRO CONTEMPORANEO E CINEMA. *see* THEATER

791.45 FRA ISSN 1963-2304
LE TECHNICIEN DU FILM. Text in French. 1954. m. (11/yr.). EUR 55 (effective 2008). adv. illus.; tr.lit. **Document type:** *Magazine, Trade.*
Former titles (until 2008): Profession Film (1960-2537); (until 2007): Le Technicien du Film (1628-1101); (until 2001): Le Technicien du Film et de la Video (0247-6010); (until 1980): Technicien du Film (0040-103X); Incorporates (in 1973): Technique, l'Exploitation Cinematographique (1142-6071); Which was formed by the merger of (1969-1973): Exploitation Cinematographique (1142-6063); (1969-1973): Technique Cinematographique (1142-6055); Both of which superseded in part (in 1969): Technique, l'Exploitation Cinematographique (1142-6047); Which was formed by the merger of (1949-1965): Exploitation Cinematographique (1142-6039); (1930-1965): Technique Cinematographique (1142-6020)
Published by: Editions Dujarric, 33 av. des Champs Elysees, Paris, 75008, France. TEL 33-1-43592484, FAX 33-1-42255997. Ed. Henriette Dujarric. R&P Carole Maillard. Adv. contact Caroline Nguyen. **Subscr. to:** IF Diffusion, 31 Champs-Elysees, Paris 75008, France.

TEKHNIKA KINO I TELEVIDENIYA/MOTION PICTURE AND TELEVISION TECHNOLOGY. *see* COMMUNICATIONS—Television And Cable

791.43 SWE ISSN 1404-8922
TEKNIK & MAENNISKA. Text in Swedish. 1976. 6/yr. SEK 310 domestic; SEK 405 in the European Union; SEK 420 in Scandinavia; SEK 485 elsewhere (effective 2003). adv. film rev. back issues avail. **Document type:** *Magazine.*
Former titles (until 1999): Tidskriften Teknik & Maenniska (1404-7551); (until 1998): Tidskriften TM (0282-5848); (until 1980): TM: Teknik & Maenniska (0347-4143)
Indexed: F01, F02.
Published by: Svenska Filminstitutet/Swedish Film Institute, Filmhuset, Borgvaegen 1-5, PO Box 27126, Stockholm, 10252, Sweden. TEL 46-8-6651100, FAX 46-8-6611820, registrar@sfi.se. Ed. Susanne Roger. adv.: B&W page SEK 10,500, color page SEK 14,800.

778.53 CAN ISSN 0837-2446
CA1CHF1
TELEFILM CANADA. ANNUAL REPORT. Text in English. 1968. a. free. **Document type:** *Government.*
Formerly (until 1984): C F D C Annual Report (0382-2273)
Published by: Canadian Film Development Corporation, Telefilm Canada, 360 St Jacques Street Ste 700, Montreal, PQ H2Y 4A9, Canada. TEL 514-283-6363. Circ: 3,000.

TELERAMA. *see* COMMUNICATIONS—Television And Cable

778.53 USA ISSN 1063-9063
TEN THOUSAND WORDS!. Text in English. 1976. 10/yr. USD 75 (effective 2005). bk.rev. index. reprints avail. **Document type:** *Newsletter, Consumer.* **Description:** Strategies, research, terminology, bibliographies, case studies about appraisal of all AV media for any purpose.
Related titles: Talking Book ed.
Published by: Behavioral Images, Inc., 302 Leland St, Ste 101, Bloomington, IL 61701-5646. TEL 309-829-3931, FAX 309-829-9677, http://www.mediavalue.com. Ed. Steve Johnson. Circ: 3,000.

TESTCARD; Beitraege zur Popgeschichte. *see* MUSIC

791.43 USA ISSN 1557-5896
TEXAS FILM AND MEDIA STUDIES SERIES. Text in English. 1999. irreg. price varies. back issues avail. **Document type:** *Monographic series, Academic/Scholarly.* **Description:** Covers early and modern cinema, hypertext, and virtual reality, primarily focusing on industry practice and critical analyses of media and culture.
Published by: University of Texas Press, Books Division, PO Box 7819, Austin, TX 78713. TEL 512-471-4034, 800-252-3206, FAX 512-232-7178, 800-687-6046, cs@utpress.utexas.edu. Ed. Thomas Schatz.

TEZUKA. *see* HOBBIES

THEATRE ET CINEMA. *see* THEATER

791.43 FRA ISSN 1159-7941
THEOREME. Text in French. 1990. irreg., latest vol.13, 2009. price varies. **Document type:** *Monographic series, Academic/Scholarly.*
Indexed: IIFP.
Published by: (Institut de Recherche sur le Cinema et l'Audiovisuel), Presses de la Sorbonne Nouvelle, 8 Rue de la Sorbonne, Paris, 75005, France. TEL 33-1-40464802, FAX 33-1-40464804, psn@univ-paris3.fr, http://www.univ-paris3.fr/recherche/psn.

791.43 305.4 USA
THEORIES OF REPRESENTATION AND DIFFERENCE. Text in English. 1981. irreg., latest 2008. price varies. **Document type:** *Monographic series.*
Published by: Indiana University Press, 601 N Morton St, Bloomington, IN 47404. TEL 812-855-8817, 800-842-6796, FAX 812-855-7931, journals@indiana.edu, http://iupress.indiana.edu.

791.43 USA
THEY WON'T STAY DEAD. Text in English. 1989. s-a. adv. bk.rev.; music rev. **Document type:** *Newsletter.* **Description:** Covers cult films and music.
Address: 11 Werner Rd, Greenville, PA 16125. TEL 412-588-3471, glorystomper@webtv.net. Ed., Adv. contact Brian Johnson. Circ: 500 (paid).

THIRST. *see* LITERATURE

THIS IS THE SPINAL TAP ZINE. *see* MUSIC

THRESHOLDS (CAMBRIDGE). *see* ART

791.43 NLD ISSN 1387-649X
P92.N4
➤ **TIJDSCHRIFT VOOR MEDIAGESCHIEDENIS.** Text in Dutch. 1998. s-a. EUR 41 to individuals; EUR 87 to institutions; EUR 29.50 newsstand/cover (effective 2010). **Document type:** *Journal, Trade.*
Formed by a merger of (1987-1996): G B G - Nieuws (0922-1689); (1989 -1997): Jaarboek Mediageschiedenis (0924-1701)
Indexed: IIFP.
Published by: Boom Lemma Uitgeverij, Postbus 85576, The Hague, 2508 CG, Netherlands. TEL 31-70-3307033, FAX 31-70-3307030, infodesk@lemma.nl, http://www.lemma-tijdschriften.nl.

▼ ➤ **TINKER BELL.** *see* CHILDREN AND YOUTH—For

➤ **TOP DIVKY.** *see* CHILDREN AND YOUTH—For

➤ **TOPP.** *see* CHILDREN AND YOUTH—For

➤ **TOTAL ACCESS.** *see* COMMUNICATIONS—Television And Cable

791.43 GBR ISSN 1366-3135
TOTAL FILM; the best films first. Text in English. 1997. 13/yr. GBP 39 domestic; GBP 58.50 in Europe; GBP 90 in United States; GBP 80 elsewhere; GBP 3.99 newsstand/cover (effective 2010). adv. back issues avail. **Document type:** *Magazine, Consumer.* **Description:** Contains exclusive pictures and news on forthcoming films as well as features on the stars, directors and behind-the-scenes talent from the hottest movies.
Related titles: Online - full text ed.: free (effective 2010).
—CCC.
Published by: Future Publishing Ltd., Beauford Ct, 30 Monmouth St, Bath, Avon BA1 2BW, United Kingdom. TEL 44-1225-442244, FAX 44-1225-446019, customerservice@subscription.co.uk, http://www.futureplc.com. Ed. Aubrey Day TEL 44-20-70424832. **Subscr. to:** Tower House, Sovereign Park, Market Harborough, Leicestershire LE16 9EF, United Kingdom. TEL 44-844-8481602, FAX 44-1858-438795, future@subscription.co.uk.

791.43 GBR ISSN 1750-8002
TOTAL FILM SPECIAL EDITION. Text in English. 2006. bi-m. **Document type:** *Magazine, Consumer.*
Published by: Future Publishing Ltd., Beauford Ct, 30 Monmouth St, Bath, Avon BA1 2BW, United Kingdom. TEL 44-1225-442244, FAX 44-1225-446019, customerservice@subscription.co.uk, http://www.futureplc.com.

791.4375 USA
TOTAL MOVIE & ENTERTAINMENT. Text in English. 2000-2001 (Feb.); resumed 2001 (Oct./Nov.). bi-m. USD 59.95 (effective 2001). adv. **Document type:** *Magazine, Consumer.* **Description:** Contains irreverent and witty features and reviews aimed at today's hip, young movie audiences.
Formerly (until 2001): Total Movie
Related titles: ◆ Online - full content ed.: Totalmoviemag.com.
Published by: Versatile Media One, 2400 N Lincoln Ave, Altadena, CA 91001. TEL 626-296-6360, FAX 626-296-6361, http://www.insidedvd.com/. adv.: page USD 34,000. Circ: 500,000.

TR7; das schweizer TV-Magazin. *see* COMMUNICATIONS—Television And Cable

778.53 FRA ISSN 1167-2846
TRAFIC. Text in French. 1991. q. EUR 48 domestic; EUR 51 foreign (effective 2009). **Document type:** *Journal, Consumer.* **Description:** Offers diverse opinions and thoughts on every aspect of motion pictures.
Indexed: F01, F02, IIFP, MLA-IB.
Published by: Editions P.O.L, 33 rue Saint-Andre-des-Arts, Paris, 75006, France. TEL 33-1-44581400. Ed. Paul Otchakovsky Laurens.

791.43 DEU
TRAILER - KINO KULTUR RUHRGEBIET. Text in German. m. adv. **Document type:** *Magazine, Consumer.* **Description:** Contains the latest news, reviews and trailers for current movies.
Published by: Berndt Media, Dr-C-Otto-Str 196, Bochum, 44879, Germany. TEL 49-234-941910, FAX 49-234-9419191, info@berndt-media.de, http://www.berndt-media.de. Ed. Christian Meyer. Pub. Joachim Berndt. adv.: B&W page EUR 1,900, color page EUR 2,700; trim 210 x 285. Circ: 34,615 (controlled).

791.43 GBR ISSN 2040-3526
▼ **TRANSNATIONAL CINEMAS.** Text in English. 2010. s-a. GBP 36, USD 68 to individuals; GBP 132, USD 185 to institutions (effective 2012). adv. back issues avail. **Document type:** *Journal, Academic/Scholarly.* **Description:** Aims to break down traditional geographical and area divisions and welcomes submissions from around the world that reflect the global nature of film cultures.
Related titles: Online - full text ed.: ISSN 2040-3534. GBP 99, USD 140 (effective 2012).
Indexed: MLA-IB.
Published by: Intellect Ltd., The Mill, Parnall Rd, Fishponds, Bristol, BS16 3JG, United Kingdom. TEL 44-117-9589910, FAX 44-117-9589911, info@intellectbooks.com. Eds. Armida de la Garza, Claudia Magallanes-Blanco. Pub. Masoud Yazdani. **Dist. by:** Turpin Distribution Services Ltd., Pegasus Dr, Stratton Business Park, Biggleswade, Bedfordshire SG18 8QB, United Kingdom. TEL 44-1767-604951, FAX 44-1767-601640, custserv@turpin-distribution.com, http://www.turpin-distribution.com/.

791.43 DEU
TRANVIA KINO. Text in German. 1996. irreg., latest vol.2, 1999. price varies. **Document type:** *Monographic series, Academic/Scholarly.*
Published by: Edition Tranvia, Duesseldorfer Str 49, Berlin, 10707, Germany. Tranvia@t-online.de, http://www.tranvia.de.

778.53 DEU ISSN 0942-430X
TREFFPUNKT KINO. Text in German. 1985. m. free newsstand/cover (effective 2011). adv. film rev. back issues avail. **Document type:** *Magazine, Consumer.* **Description:** Contains all the latest information on cinematic films.
Formerly (until 1992): Treffpunkt Film (0941-1682)
Related titles: Online - full text ed.
Published by: Entertainment Media Verlag GmbH und Co. oHG (Subsidiary of: Gruner + Jahr AG & Co), Weihenstephaner Str 7, Munich, 81673, Germany. TEL 49-89-451140, FAX 49-89-45114444, redaktion@e-media.de, http://www.mediabiz.de. Adv. contact Susanne Huebner. Circ: 677,179 (controlled).

791.4375 ESP ISSN 1699-2717
TREN DE SOMBRAS. Text in Spanish. 2004. q. **Document type:** *Magazine, Consumer.*
Media: Online - full text.
Published by: Tres de Sombras editores@tresdesombras.com. Ed. Jose Manuel Lopez.

384.8 USA ISSN 1930-1464
PN1993.5.U6
TRENDS IN DOMESTIC BOX OFFICE. Text in English. irreg. USD 2,095 combined subscription print & onlines eds. (effective 2006).
Formerly: The Kagan Box Office Report
Related titles: Online - full text ed.
Published by: S N L Financial LC, One SNL Plz, PO Box 2124, Charlottesville, VA 22902. TEL 434-977-1600, FAX 434-293-0407, salesdept@snl.com, http://www.snl.com.

791.43 CAN ISSN 0823-678X
TRIBUTE. Text in English. 1984. bi-m. CAD 17.50 domestic; CAD 24.50 in United States; CAD 31.50 elsewhere (effective 2000). adv. back issues avail. **Document type:** *Magazine, Consumer.* **Description:** Focuses on new movies, actors, and directors in the entertainment business.
Formerly: Tribute Goes to the Movies (0826-1210)
Published by: Tribute Publishing, Inc., 71 Barber Green Rd, Don Mills, ON M3C 282, Canada. TEL 416-445-0544, FAX 416-445-2894. Ed., Pub., R&P Sandra I Stewart. Adv. contact Katherine Bridgman. B&W page USD 15,148, color page USD 15,945. Circ: 500,000 (controlled).

791.43 CHE
TRIGON-FILM MAGAZIN. Text in German. 4/yr. CHF 7 newsstand/cover (effective 2005). **Document type:** *Magazine, Consumer.* **Description:** Covers and analyzes films produced in Asia, Africa and Latin America.
Published by: Trigon-Film, Klosterstr 42, Wettingen, T 5430, Switzerland. TEL 41-56-4301230, FAX 41-56-4301231, info@trigon-film.org, http://www.trigon-film.org.

791.43 AUS
TWIN PEEKS: AUSTRALIAN AND NEW ZEALAND FEATURE FILMS. Text in English. 1999. quinquennial. back issues avail. **Document type:** *Journal, Academic/Scholarly.* **Description:** Presents a comprehensive listing of all Australian and New Zealand feature films. Includes twelve essays by recognized authorities on both cinemas.
Published by: Damned Publishing, St. Kilda West Post Office, PO Box 2211, St Kilda, VIC 3182, Australia. TEL 61-3-95255302, FAX 61-3-95372325, tapp@netspace.net.au. Ed. Deb Verhoeven.

U.S. DIRECTORY OF ENTERTAINMENT EMPLOYERS. *see* BUSINESS AND ECONOMICS—Trade And Industrial Directories

791.43 GBR
ULTIMATE D V D. (Digital Video Disc) Text in English. 19??. m. GBP 3.99 newsstand/cover domestic; USD 8.99 newsstand/cover in United States (effective 2009). film rev. back issues avail. **Document type:** *Magazine, Consumer.* **Description:** Covers growth in the DVD home cinema market. Contains the latest news, interviews and appraisals of latest DVD players.
Related titles: Online - full text ed.
Published by: Visual Imagination Ltd., 9 Blades Ct, Deodar Rd, London, SW15 2NU, United Kingdom. TEL 44-20-88751520, FAX 44-20-88751588, mailorder@visimag.com.

ULTIMO (MUENSTER); Muensters Stadtmagazin. *see* LITERARY AND POLITICAL REVIEWS

UNCUT. *see* MUSIC

791.43 SEN ISSN 0253-195X
PN1993.5.A35
UNIR CINEMA; revue du cinema africain. Text in French. 1973 (no.36). q. XOF 1,000. adv. bk.rev.; film rev. **Document type:** *Bulletin.* **Description:** Provides news from the African cinema.
Published by: Diocese de Saint-Louis, 1 rue Neuville, BP 160, St Louis, Senegal. TEL 61-10-27, FAX 61-24-08. Ed. Pierre Sagna. Circ: 1,000. **Subscr. to:** P.J. Vast, 8 rue Duret, BP 160, St Louis, Senegal.

UNIR: ECHO DE SAINT LOUIS. *see* LITERATURE

UNIVERSIDAD DE ZARAGOZA. DEPARTAMENTO DE FILOLOGIA INGLESA Y ALEMANA. MISCELANEA; a journal of English and American philology. *see* LINGUISTICS

UNIVERSITA DEGLI STUDI DI PARMA. ISTITUTO DI STORIA DELL'ARTE. CATALOGHI. *see* ART

UNSIGNED THE MAGAZINE. *see* MUSIC

URB; Future Music Culture. *see* MUSIC

778.53 AUS ISSN 1328-6226
URBAN CINEFILE. Text in English. 1997. w. free (effective 2009). adv. **Document type:** *Newsletter, Consumer.* **Description:** Features movie reviews, trailers and latest film news.
Media: Online - full text.
Address: PO Box 173, Seaforth, NSW 2092, Australia. TEL 61-2-99496700, FAX 61-2-99491795, mail@urbancinefile.com.au. Ed., Adv. contact Andrew L Urban.

791.43 ITA ISSN 1970-6391
PN1993.5.A1
LA VALLE DELL'EDEN; semestrale di cinema e audiovisivi. Text in Multiple languages. 1989. s-a. EUR 31 domestic to individuals; EUR 36 domestic to institutions; EUR 51.50 foreign (effective 2008). **Document type:** *Magazine, Consumer.*
Published by: (Universita degli Studi di Torino, Discipline Arti Musica e Spettacolo (DA M S)), Carocci Editore, Via Sardegna 50, Rome, 00187, Italy. TEL 39-06-42818417, FAX 39-06-42747931, clienti@carocci.it, http://www.carocci.it.

VANDERBILT JOURNAL OF ENTERTAINMENT AND TECHNOLOGY LAW. *see* LAW

VARIETY; the international entertainment weekly. *see* THEATER

VARIETY.COM. *see* THEATER

791.43 USA
PN1993.3
VARIETY INTERNATIONAL FILM GUIDE (YEAR); the ultimate annual review of world cinema. Text in English. 1964. a. USD 29.95 per issue (effective 2005). adv. bk.rev. 432 p./no.; back issues avail. **Document type:** *Magazine, Consumer.* **Description:** Covers film production, festivals, archives and schools in more than 60 countries.
Formerly (until 1990): International Film Guide (0074-6053)
—**CCC.**
Published by: Silman-James Press, 3624 Shannon Rd, Los Angeles, CA 90027. TEL 323-661-9922, FAX 323-661-9933, silmanjamespress@earthlink.net, http://www.silmanjamespress.com/. Ed. Daniel Rosenthal.

791.43 IND
VELLINAKSHATRAM. Text in Malayalam. w. INR 15 per issue (effective 2011). adv. back issues avail. **Document type:** *Magazine, Consumer.*
Published by: Kala Kaumudi Publications (P) Ltd., Kaumudi Bldgs, Pettah, Thiruvananthapuram, Kerala 695 024, India. TEL 91-471-3078842, http://www.kalakaumudi.com.

791.43 USA ISSN 0149-1830
PN1993 CODEN: VLTREI
➤ **THE VELVET LIGHT TRAP.** Abbreviated title: V L T. Text in English. 1971. s-a. USD 92 domestic to institutions; USD 103 in Canada to institutions; USD 111 elsewhere to institutions (effective 2011). bk.rev. illus. Index. back issues avail.; reprints avail. **Document type:** *Journal, Academic/Scholarly.* **Description:** Features essays which explores alternative methodological approaches to the analysis of American film and television. Covers studies debate about critical theoretical and historical issues.
Related titles: Microform ed.: (from PQC); Online - full text ed.: ISSN 1542-4251.
Indexed: A01, A02, A03, A08, A22, A26, A27, AmH&L, AmHI, BibInd, CA, CMM, CommAb, E01, E08, F01, F02, G06, G07, G08, H07, HistAb, I05, IIFP, IIPA, IITV, L05, L06, MLA-IB, MRD, P02, P10, P48, P53, P54, PCI, PQC, S09, SCOPUS, SOPODA, SociolAb, T02.
—BLDSC (9154.302000), IE, Infotrieve, Ingenta. **CCC.**
Published by: University of Texas Press, Journals Division, PO Box 7819, Austin, TX 78713. TEL 512-471-7233 ext 2, FAX 512-232-7178, journals@uts.cc.utexas.edu, http://www.utexas.edu/utpress/journals/journals.html. Adv. contact Leah Dixon TEL 512-232-7618.

791.43 FRA ISSN 0985-1402
PN1993.5.F8
VERTIGO; revue d'esthetique et d'histoire du cinema. Text in French. 1987. s-a. **Document type:** *Magazine, Consumer.*
Formerly (until 1987): Avances Cinematographiques (0764-2792)
Indexed: F01, F02, IIFP, IIPA, IITV, MLA-IB.
Published by: Capricci, 27 Rue Adolphe Moitie, Nantes, 44000, France. TEL 33-2-40892059, FAX 33-2-40204459, contact@capricci.fr, http://capricci.fr.

791.43 GBR ISSN 0968-7904
PN1993
VERTIGO. Text in English. 1993. q. GBP 20 combined subscription domestic to individuals; GBP 26 combined subscription in Europe to individuals; GBP 32 combined subscription elsewhere to individuals; GBP 50 combined subscription domestic to institutions; GBP 56 combined subscription in Europe to institutions; GBP 62 combined subscription elsewhere to institutions; GBP 6 per issue domestic; GBP 8 per issue in Europe; GBP 9.50 per issue elsewhere (effective 2009). back issues avail. **Document type:** *Magazine, Consumer.* **Description:** Serves as a gateway to worldwide independent film. Dedicated to promoting independence, innovation and diversity in moving image culture.
Indexed: F01, F02, IIFP, T02.
Address: 26 Shacklewell Lane, 4th Floor, London, E8 2EZ, United Kingdom. TEL 44-20-76900124. Ed. Holly Aylett.

791.4375 USA
VEX; maximum movie culture. Text in English. a. USD 3.95 newsstand/cover (effective 2001). adv. film rev. **Document type:** *Magazine, Consumer.* **Description:** Provides a guide to everything cinema-related - with an eye out for the lost, missing, forgotten or neglected movies, opinions and people covering the whole spectrum of screen history.
Published by: Vex Magazine, PO Box 319, Roselle, NJ 07203. TEL 212-465-7476. Ed., Pub. Rob Hauschild. Adv. contact Aimee Eckert. Circ: 5,000 (paid). **Dist. by:** International Publishers Direct, 27500 Riverview Center Blvd, Bonita Springs, FL 34134. TEL 858-320-4563, FAX 858-677-3220.

VIDEO AGE INTERNATIONAL; the business journal of film, TV broadcasting, cable, pay TV, PPV, home video, DBS, production. *see* COMMUNICATIONS—Television And Cable

VIDEO AKTIV DIGITAL. *see* COMMUNICATIONS—Video

791.43 USA
VIDEO CONFIDENTIAL. Text in English. 1991. bi-m. USD 7 (effective 2000); USD 2 newsstand/cover. adv. bk.rev.; film rev.; music rev.; video rev. back issues avail. **Document type:** *Newsletter.* **Description:** Specializes in reviewing obscure films on video tape and laser disc from around the world. Carries celebrity interviews. Announces forthcoming video releases.
Published by: Morano Movies, 8822 Second Ave, North Bergen, NJ 07047. TEL 201-869-9856, FAX 201-869-9856, http://www.digital-nation.com. Ed. Eric Mache. Pubs. Carl Morano, Eric Mache. R&P, Adv. contact Carl Morano.

791 DEU ISSN 1864-5372
VIDEO- UND FILMREIHE. Text in German. 2006. irreg. **Document type:** *Monographic series, Academic/Scholarly.*
Media: Online - full content.
Published by: Universitaet Leipzig, Institut fuer Kunstgeschichte, Wuenschmanns Hof, Dittrichring 18-20, Leipzig, 04109, Germany. TEL 49-341-9735550, FAX 49-341-9735559, arthistory@uni-leipzig.de, http://www.uni-leipzig.de/~kuge/index.htm.

VIDEOHOBBY. *see* COMMUNICATIONS—Video

778.59 USA ISSN 1095-371X
PN1992.95
VIDEOHOUND'S GOLDEN MOVIE RETRIEVER (YEAR). Text in English. 1991. a. USD 24.95 (effective 2009). back issues avail. **Document type:** *Directory, Consumer.* **Description:** Lists more than 23,000 movies available on video and includes a multitude of cross-referencing within its 10 primary indexes.
Related titles: Online - full text ed.
Published by: Gale (Subsidiary of: Cengage Learning), 27500 Drake Rd, Farmington Hills, MI 48331. TEL 248-699-4253, 800-877-4253, FAX 877-363-4253, gale.galeord@thomson.com, http://gale.cengage.com.

791.43 DEU ISSN 1611-6615
VIDEOKAMERA OBJEKTIV; das grosse Magazin fuer alle Filmer. Text in German. 198?. 6/yr. EUR 41.40 domestic; EUR 50.40 foreign; EUR 6.90 newsstand/cover (effective 2010). adv. **Document type:** *Magazine, Consumer.*
Incorporates (1998-2006): Digital Video; **Formerly** (until 2002): Objektiv (0178-1065)
Published by: Verlag B. Kaemmer, Georgenstr 19, Munich, 80799, Germany. TEL 49-89-34018900, FAX 49-89-34018901, bk@verlag-kaemmer.de, http://www.verlag-kaemmer.de. Ed. Uli Loehneysen. adv.: B&W page EUR 2,630, color page EUR 4,000. Circ: 10,500 (paid and controlled).

VIEWFINDER. *see* EDUCATION—Teaching Methods And Curriculum

▼ **VIEWFINDER (AUCKLAND)**; shoot, edit, play, share. *see* COMMUNICATIONS—Video

055.1 ITA ISSN 1828-7204
VIP. Text in Italian. 1999. w. **Document type:** *Magazine, Consumer.* **Description:** Covers the lifestyles of the rich and famous.
Formerly (until 2006): Settimana Vip (1129-1346)
Published by: Piscopo Editore Srl, Via di Villa Sacchetti 11, Rome, 00197, Italy. TEL 39-06-3200105, FAX 39-06-3200143, http://www.piscopoeditore.it. Ed. Paolo Mosca.

791.12 DEU
VIRUS; the dark side of entertainment. Text in German. bi-m. EUR 39; EUR 6.66 newsstand/cover (effective 2007). adv. **Document type:** *Magazine, Consumer.*
Published by: Raptor Publishing GmbH, Galvanistr 30, Frankfurt am Main, 60486, Germany. TEL 49-69-977880, FAX 49-69-9778822, cu@raptor.de, http://www.raptor.de. adv.: page EUR 4,000. Circ: 45,000 (paid and controlled).

VISUAL CULTURE IN BRITAIN. *see* ART

778.53 ITA
VIVILCINEMA. Text in Italian. 1985. bi-m. EUR 15 (effective 2009). bk.rev.; film rev.; play rev. abstr.; bibl.; charts; illus.; stat.; tr.lit. **Document type:** *Magazine, Consumer.* **Description:** Reviews of the first screening in theatres of films of high artistic standard.
Published by: Federazione Italiana Cinema d'Essai (F I C E), Via di Villa Patrizi 10, Rome, 00161, Italy. TEL 39-06-884731, FAX 39-06-4404255, fice@agisweb.it. Circ: 150,000.

VOUS; le mag' des nouveaux talents. *see* ART

VUE WEEKLY. *see* MUSIC

778.53 USA
W W W BACKSTAGE. Text in English. 1996. m.
Media: Online - full content.
Published by: Entertainment Network News, 267 Lester Ave, Ste 104, Oakland, CA 94606. TEL 800-437-6397, scmetro@aol.com, http://www.backstage.com.

WARREN'S MOVIE POSTER PRICE GUIDE. *see* HOBBIES

791.43 USA
WE REMEMBER DEAN INTERNATIONAL. Text in English. 1978. q. USD 20 in North America; USD 25 elsewhere. adv. bk.rev. **Document type:** *Newsletter.* **Description:** Dedicated to preserving the memory of James Dean.
Formerly: We Remember Dean
Published by: (We Remember Dean International), Myla Kent, Ed. & Pub., 8314 Greenwood Ave, 206, Seattle, WA 98103. TEL 206-782-6133. Adv. contact Myla Kent. Circ: 600.

791 DEU ISSN 1430-7987
WELTWUNDER DER KINEMATOGRAPHIE. Text in German. 1994. irreg., latest vol.9, 2008. price varies. **Document type:** *Monographic series, Academic/Scholarly.*
Indexed: F01, F02.
Published by: (Deutsche Gesellschaft zur Foerderung der Kultur Berlin e.V.), Polzer Media Group GmbH, Postfach 601361, Potsdam, 14413, Germany. TEL 49-331-2797026, info@polzer.org, http://www.polzer.org.

791.43 USA
WESTERN CLIPPINGS. Text in English. 1994. bi-m. USD 27.25 domestic; USD 30 in Canada; USD 40 elsewhere (effective 2000). adv. bk.rev.; film rev.; tel.rev. **Document type:** *Newsletter.* **Description:** Covers historic westerns made for the silver screen and T.V.
Published by: Boyd Magers, Ed. & Pub., 1312 Stagecoach Rd S E, Albuquerque, NM 87123. TEL 505-292-0049. Circ: 900 (paid).

791.43 USA
WESTERNS & SERIALS. Text in English. 1974. s-a. USD 12; USD 16 foreign (effective 1999). adv. bk.rev. back issues avail. **Document type:** *Magazine, Consumer.* **Description:** Club magazine for those interested in old westerns and serials.
Former titles: Favorite Westerns; Serial World
Published by: Norman Kietzer, Ed. & Pub., 527 S Front St, Mankato, MN 56001-3718. TEL 507-549-3677, FAX 507-549-3788. Circ: 2,000.

791.43 USA
WHOLPHIN. Text in English. 2006. q. USD 50; USD 19.95 per issue (effective 2010). **Document type:** *Magazine, Trade.* **Description:** Conains various short films.
Media: Optical Disk - DVD.
Published by: McSweeney's, 849 Valencia St, San Francisco, CA 94110. TEL 415-642-5609, custservice@mcsweeneys.net, http://www.mcsweeneys.net. Ed. Brent Hoff.

WHO'S WHO IN CANADIAN FILM AND TELEVISION (YEAR)/QUI EST QUI AU CINEMA ET A LA TELEVISION AU CANADA. *see* BIOGRAPHY

791.43 KOR
WHO'S WHO IN KOREAN FILM INDUSTRY: PRODUCERS AND INVESTORS. Text in English. a. free to qualified personnel. **Document type:** *Directory, Trade.* **Description:** Provides profiles of producers and investors as well as an appendix of Korean film industry investment system.
Related titles: Online - full text ed.
Published by: Korean Film Council/Tonga Such'ul Kongsa, 206-46, Cheongnyangni-dong, Dongdaemun-gu, Seoul, 130-010, Korea, S. TEL 82-2-9587591, FAX 82-2-9587590, http://www.koreanfilm.or.kr. Ed. Daniel D. H. Park. Pub. Han-Sup Kang.

778.53025 USA ISSN 0278-6516
PN1998.A2
WHO'S WHO IN THE MOTION PICTURE INDUSTRY; directors, producers, writers, & studio executives. Text in English. 1981. biennial. USD 24.95 (effective 1999). back issues avail. **Document type:** *Directory.* **Description:** Directory and reference to key individuals active in the motion picture and entertainment business. Complete credits and fully indexed.
Published by: Packard Publishing Co., PO Box 2187, Beverly Hills, CA 90213. TEL 310-722-2948. Ed. Rodman W Gregg. Circ: 12,000 (paid).

WICKED; the ultimate guide to horror entertainment. *see* LITERATURE—Science Fiction, Fantasy, Horror

791.43 GBR ISSN 1757-3920
PN1993
▼ ➤ **WIDE SCREEN.** Text in English. 2009. irreg. free (effective 2011). **Document type:** *Journal, Academic/Scholarly.* **Description:** Devoted to the critical study of cinema from historical, theoretical, political, and aesthetic perspectives.
Media: Online - full text.
Indexed: F01, F02, T02.
Published by: Wide Screen Journal, 17 Holborn Terrace, Woodhouse, Leeds, LS6 2QA, United Kingdom. Ed. Kishore Budha.

791.4375 DEU
WIDESCREEN; das DVD-, Blu-Ray- und Kino-Magazin. Text in German. 2007. m. EUR 73 domestic; EUR 80 in Austria; EUR 85 elsewhere; EUR 6.50 newsstand/cover (effective 2011). adv. **Document type:** *Magazine, Consumer.*
Formerly (until 2010): Widescreen Vision; Which was formed by the merger of (2002-2007): Widescreen; (2001-2007): D V D Vision (1617-2175)
Published by: Computec Media AG, Dr-Mack-Str 83, Fuerth, 90762, Germany. TEL 49-911-2872100, FAX 49-911-2872200, info@computec.de, http://www.computec.de. Ed. Christian Mueller. Circ: 24,000 (paid).

WONDERLAND. *see* ART

WORD (LONDON). *see* MUSIC

WORDLY REMAINS. *see* MUSIC

791.43 USA
WORKS OF ART; a guide to quality films from around the world. Text in English. 1994. q. free. adv. bk.rev.; film rev. **Document type:** *Magazine, Consumer.* **Description:** Contains synopses of foreign and art films, articles, and interviews with directors and celebrities.
Published by: Sight & Sound Distributors, 120 S. Central Ave., Ste. 750, Saint Louis, MO 63105-1799. TEL 314-253-5437, FAX 314-426-1307. Ed., R&P, Adv. contact Lynn Petersen. Circ: 20,000.

WORLD OF FANDOM. *see* LITERATURE—Science Fiction, Fantasy, Horror

778.53 USA
WORLDWIDE DIRECTORY OF FILM AND VIDEO FESTIVALS AND EVENTS. Text in English. 1988. a. USD 28 (effective 1998). **Document type:** *Directory.*
Published by: C I N E, Inc., 1112 16th St NW, Washington, DC 20036. TEL 202-785-1136, FAX 202-785-4114. Ed. Jay Gemski. Circ: 3,000.

791.433 GBR ISSN 0043-9452
WRANGLER'S ROOST; a magazine for the B-Western aficionado. Text in English. 1970. 3/yr. USD 9 (effective 2001). adv. bk.rev.; film rev. **Document type:** *Magazine, Consumer.*
Media: Duplicated (not offset).
Published by: Colin Momber Photography, 23 Sabrina Way, Bristol, BS9 1ST, United Kingdom. Circ: 350.

THE WRITER'S BLOCK MAGAZINE; students' magazine for writing, literature and film. *see* JOURNALISM

WRITERS GUILD OF AMERICA, EAST. NEWSLETTER. *see* LITERATURE

WRITTEN BY. *see* LITERATURE

WUTAI YU YINMU. *see* THEATER

XIJU SHIJIE/COMEDY WORLD. *see* THEATER

XIJU YU DIANYING/THEATRE AND CINEMA. *see* THEATER

791.43 GBR ISSN 1363-8289
XPOSE. Text in English. 1996. 9/yr. GBP 45 domestic; USD 83 in United States; GBP 53 elsewhere; GBP 4.99 newsstand/cover domestic; USD 9.99 newsstand/cover in United States (effective 2009); includes Xpose Special. back issues avail. **Document type:** *Magazine, Consumer.* **Description:** Film and TV magazine focusing on sci-fi, fantasy and action.
Related titles: Online - full text ed.; ◆ Supplement(s): Xpose Special.
Published by: Visual Imagination Ltd., 9 Blades Ct, Deodar Rd, London, SW15 2NU, United Kingdom. TEL 44-20-88751520, FAX 44-20-88751588, mailorder@visimag.com.

791.43 GBR
XPOSE SPECIAL. Text in English. 1997. 3/yr. GBP 45 domestic; USD 83 in United States; GBP 53 elsewhere (effective 2009); includes Xpose. back issues avail. **Document type:** *Magazine, Consumer.* **Description:** Covers information on fantastic movies and television, exploring behind the screens of new and popular Fantasy TV shows.
Related titles: ◆ Supplement to: Xpose. ISSN 1363-8289.
Published by: Visual Imagination Ltd., 9 Blades Ct, Deodar Rd, London, SW15 2NU, United Kingdom. TEL 44-20-88751520, FAX 44-20-88751588, mailorder@visimag.com, http://www.visimag.com.

052 PHL
YES!; your entertainment source. Text in English. m. PHP 870; PHP 75 newsstand/cover (effective 2005). adv. **Document type:** *Magazine, Consumer.* **Description:** Covers all aspects of the entertainment industry.
Published by: Summit Media, Level 1, Robinsons Galleria, Ortigas Ave, Quezon City, 1100, Philippines. TEL 63-2-6317738, FAX 63-2-6372206, luz.bolos@summitmedia.com.ph, http://www.summitmedia.com.ph. Ed. Joann Maglipon. Adv. contact Danio Caw.

791.43 CHN ISSN 1009-7627
YINGSHI YISHU/FILM AND T V ART. Text in Chinese. 1978. bi-m. USD 63.80 (effective 2009). 80 p./no.; **Document type:** *Journal, Academic/Scholarly.*
Formerly (until 199?): Dianying, Dianshi Yishu Yanjiu (1001-2796)
Published by: Zhongguo Renmin Daxue Shubao Ziliao Zhongxin/Renmin University of China, Information Center for Social Sciences, Dongcheng-qu, 3, Zhangzizhong Lu, Beijing, 100007, China. TEL 86-10-64039458, FAX 86-10-64015080, center@zlzx.org, http://www.zlzx.org/. **Dist. in US by:** China Publications Service, PO Box 49614, Chicago, IL 60649. TEL 312-288-3291, FAX 312-288-8570; **Dist. by:** China International Book Trading Corp, 35 Chegongzhuang Xilu, Haidian District, PO Box 399, Beijing 100044, China. TEL 86-10-68412045, FAX 86-10-68412023, cibtc@mail.cibtc.com.cn, http://www.cibtc.com.cn.

791.43 CHN
YINMU NEIWAI D V D/AROUND FILM. Text in Chinese. 1979. m. USD 124.80 (effective 2009). **Document type:** *Magazine, Consumer.*
Former titles: Yinmu Neiwai/Around Film (1006-4796); Dianying Pingjie/Film Review (1002-6916)
Related titles: Online - full text ed.
Published by: Sichuan Wenyi Yinxiang Chubanshe, 37, Dongchenggen Nanjie, Chengdu, Sichuan 610015, China.

791.43 NOR ISSN 0800-1464
PN1993
Z; filmtidsskrift. Text in Norwegian. 1983. 4/yr. NOK 250 domestic to individuals; NOK 275 domestic to institutions; NOK 190 domestic to students; NOK 300 in Europe; NOK 325 elsewhere (effective 2007). adv. bk.rev.; film rev.; video rev. illus. back issues avail. **Document type:** *Magazine, Consumer.* **Description:** Focuses on film theory and film history. Covers Norwegian short and feature films, as well as international films, with emphasis on art films.
Related titles: Online - full text ed.: Z paa Nett. ISSN 0807-271X. 1996.
Indexed: F01, F02, IIFP, IITV, MLA-IB, RILM.
Published by: Norsk Filmklubbforbund/Norwegian Federation of Film Societies, Dronningens Gate 16, Oslo, 0152, Norway. TEL 47-22-474680, FAX 47-22-474692, nfk@filmklubb.no, http://www.filmklubb.no. Pub. Ole Petter Bakken. Adv. contact Jon Iversen TEL 47-22-47-46-81. B&W page NOK 5,000, color page NOK 6,000.

791.43 CHN ISSN 0578-1922
PN1993.5
ZHONGGUO YINMU. Text in Chinese, English. 1958. m. USD 62.40 (effective 2009). **Document type:** *Magazine, Consumer.* **Description:** Covers new Chinese films. Contains feature articles on actors, actresses, directors, and films.
Indexed: F01, F02.
—East View.
Address: 25 Xinwei Dajie, Beijing, 100088, China. TEL 86-10-62210663, FAX 86-10-62259341. **Dist. by:** China International Book Trading Corp, 35 Chegongzhuang Xilu, Haidian District, PO Box 399, Beijing 100044, China. TEL 86-10-68412045, FAX 86-10-68412023, cibtc@mail.cibtc.com.cn, http://www.cibtc.com.cn.

791.43 355 CHN ISSN 1007-5305
ZHONGWAI JUNSHI YINGSHI/CHINESE AND FOREIGN MILITARY FILMS AND T V PROGRAMME. Text in Chinese. 1982. m. **Document type:** *Magazine, Consumer.*
Formerly (until 1994): Bayi Dianying (1002-5286)
Published by: Zhongwai Junshi Yingshi Zazhishe, 1, Liuliqiao Beilijia, Guanganmen Wai, Beijing, 100073, China. TEL 86-10-63461964.

ZHURNAL NAUCHNOI I PRIKLADNOI FOTOGRAFII. *see* PHOTOGRAPHY

ZOO (LONDON,1999). *see* ART

371.33523 SWE ISSN 1400-2485
ZOOM; filmpedagogisk tidskrift. Text in Swedish. 1989. q. SEK 200 (effective 2004). bk.rev. **Document type:** *Newspaper, Academic/Scholarly.*
Formerly (until 1995): Tusen och en Film (1100-357X)
Published by: Svenska Filminstitutet/Swedish Film Institute, Filmhuset, Borgvaegen 1-5, PO Box 27126, Stockholm, 10252, Sweden. TEL 46-8-6651100, FAX 46-8-6611820, registrar@sfi.se. Ed. Andreas Hoffsten. Pub. Britte Eskilson. R&P, Adv. contact Barbro Furhammar. Circ: 2,500.

791.43 GBR ISSN 0957-3860
007. Text in English. 19??. q. EUR 11.99 per issue in Europe; USD 15.99 per issue in United States; GBP 9.99 per issue elsewhere (effective 2009). back issues avail. **Document type:** *Magazine, Consumer.*
Related titles: Online - full text ed.
Published by: James Bond British Fan Club, Weybridge Rd, PO Box 007, Addlestone, Weybridge KT15 2QS, United Kingdom. TEL 44-1483-756007, FAX 44-1483-756009, jbifc@globalnet.co.uk, http://www.thejamesbondfanclub.co.uk. Ed., Pub., R&P Graham Rye. Adv. contact Carly Jones.

791.43 GBR ISSN 1754-6877
24 FRAMES. Text in English. 2003. irreg. GBP 50 per vol. hardback; GBP 18.99 per vol. softback (effective 2009). back issues avail. **Document type:** *Monographic series, Academic/Scholarly.* **Description:** Focuses on 24 key feature films or documentaries that serve as entry-points to the appreciation and study of the history, industry, social and political significance, and key directors and stars of every national cinema around the world.
Published by: Wallflower Press, 97 Sclater St, London, E1 6HR, United Kingdom. TEL 44-20-77299533, info@wallflowerpress.co.uk. Ed. Yoram Allon.

778.53 USA
24 FRAMES PER SECOND; productions on film. Text in English. 1997. irreg. (approx. bi-w.). **Description:** Provides a forum for personal reactions to films and filmmakers.
Media: Online - full text. Ed. Kirk Hostetter.

778.53 CAN ISSN 0707-9389
PN1993
24 IMAGES. Text in French. 1979. 5/yr. CAD 23.75 domestic to individuals; CAD 29.50 domestic to institutions; CAD 38 foreign to institutions. adv. bk.rev. back issues avail. **Description:** Covers the history and future of cinema, its celebrated producers and directors along with those less well known. Offers reviews and interviews.
Indexed: A22, C03, CBCARef, CPerl, F01, F02, I05, IIFP, IITV, PQC, PdeR.
—IE, Infotrieve. **CCC.**
Address: 3962 rue Laval, Montreal, PQ H2W 2J2, Canada. TEL 514-286-1688. Ed. Marie Claude Loiselle. Pub., R&P Claude Racine. Circ: 10,200.

791.43 DNK ISSN 1603-5194
16:9; filmtidsskrift. Variant title: Seksten:Ni. Text in Danish; Text occasionally in English. 2003. 5/yr. free (effective 2011). back issues avail. **Document type:** *Journal, Academic/Scholarly.*
Media: Online - full text.
Published by: 16:9 Filmtidsskrift, Fuglesangs Alle 88, Aarhus V, 8210, Denmark. TEL 45-35-137545, FAX 45-25-524545, info@16-9.dk. Eds. Henrik Hoejer, Jakob Isak Nielsen.

791.43 BRA
1000 VIDEOS. Text in Portuguese. 1989. a. illus. **Document type:** *Directory, Consumer.* **Description:** Critical guide to movies on video available in Brazil. Arranged by genre.
Published by: Editora Azul, S.A., Ave. NACOES UNIDAS, 5777, Sao Paulo, SP 05479-900, Brazil. TEL 11-816-7866, FAX 11-813-9115. Ed. Angelo Rossi. adv.: color page USD 7,000; trim 274 x 208. Circ: 30,000.

791.43 FRA ISSN 0769-0959
PN1993.5.A1
1895; revue d'histoire du cinema. Variant title: Mille Huit Cent Quatre-Vingt-Quinze. Text in French. 1984. 3/yr. **Document type:** *Journal, Consumer.*
Related titles: Online - full text ed.: ISSN 1960-6176.
Indexed: F01, F02, IIFP, MLA-IB.
Published by: Association Francaise de Recherche sur l'Histoire du Cinema, 15 Rue Lakanal, Paris, 75015, France. http://www.afrhc.fr. Ed. Laurent Veray. **Co-sponsor:** Editions de la Maison des Sciences de l'Homme.

MOTION PICTURES—Abstracting, Bibliographies, Statistics

016.79143 USA ISSN 0163-5123
PN1993
ANNUAL INDEX TO MOTION PICTURE CREDITS. Text in English. 1976. a. USD 50 (effective 2000). **Document type:** *Directory.* **Description:** Contains approximately 15,000 individual credits, and credits for feature films opening in LA area. Index by title, craft, individual names and distributors. Based on primary sources from producers-distributors.
Superseded: A M P A S Credits Bulletin; Formerly (until 1979): Screen Achievement Records Bulletin (0147-2313)
Published by: Academy of Motion Picture Arts and Sciences, 8949 Wilshire Blvd, Beverly Hills, CA 90211-1972. TEL 310-247-3000, FAX 310-859-9619. Ed. Torene Svitil. R&P Scott Miller. Circ: 999.

791.43021 AUS
AUSTRALIA. BUREAU OF STATISTICS. MOTION PICTURE EXHIBITION, AUSTRALIA (ONLINE). Text in English. 1987. irreg., latest 2000. free (effective 2009). back issues avail. **Document type:** *Government.* **Description:** Presents results, in respect of the financial year, from an Australian Bureau of Statistics (ABS) census of businesses mainly engaged in screening motion pictures in cinemas and drive-in theatres.
Formerly: Australia. Bureau of Statistics. Motion Picture Exhibition, Australia (Print)
Media: Online - full text.
Published by: Australian Bureau of Statistics, Locked Bag 10, Belconnen, ACT 2616, Australia. TEL 61-2-92684909, 61-2-62527037, 300-135-070, FAX 61-2-62528103, client.services@abs.gov.au.

BIO-BIBLIOGRAPHIES IN THE PERFORMING ARTS. *see* THEATER—Abstracting, Bibliographies, Statistics

016.79143 DEU
CINEGRAPH; Lexikon zum deutschsprachigen Film. Text in German. 1984. 8 base vols. plus updates 3/yr. looseleaf. EUR 179 base vol(s). (effective 2009). **Document type:** *Monographic series, Academic/Scholarly.*
Published by: Edition Text und Kritik in Richard Boorberg Verlag GmbH & Co. KG (Subsidiary of: Richard Boorberg Verlag GmbH und Co. KG), Levelingstr 6A, Munich, 81673, Germany. TEL 49-89-43600012, FAX 49-89-43600019, info@etk-muenchen.de, http://www.etk-muenchen.de. Ed. Hans Michael Bock.

016.79143 USA
▼ **CINEMA IMAGE GALLERY.** Text in English. 2009. d. USD 2,060 (effective 2011). **Document type:** *Abstract/Index.* **Description:** Comprehensive still image archive of movie, television, and entertainment history.
Media: Online - full content.
Published by: H.W. Wilson, 950 University Ave, Bronx, NY 10452. TEL 718-588-8400, 800-367-6770, FAX 718-590-1617, custserv@hwwilson.com, http://www.hwwilson.com.

011.37 BEL ISSN 1355-1671
F I A F INTERNATIONAL FILMARCHIVE CD-ROM. (International Federation of Film Archives) Text in English. 1994. s-a. EUR 446.21; includes International Index to Film Periodicals (1972-present). **Document type:** *Bibliography.* **Description:** Lists film and television periodicals from all over the world. Contains F.I.A.F. membership lists, a bibliography to members' publications, a directory of holdings of 125 institutions worldwide, a glossary of filmographic terms, a bibliography of national filmographies from 60 countries, and a listing of members' silent film holdings.
Media: CD-ROM.
Published by: Federation Internationale des Archives du Film (F I A F)/International Federation of Film Archives, Rue Defacqz 1, Brussels, 1000, Belgium. TEL 322-534-6130, FAX 322-534-4774.

791.43 384.55 BGR ISSN 0861-9719
PN1993
FILM; kino - televiziya - video. Text in Bulgarian. 1993. m. BGL 21.60 domestic; USD 68 foreign (effective 2002). adv. film rev.; tel.rev.; video rev. illus. back issues avail. **Document type:** *Journal, Consumer.* **Description:** Covers movies, actors, actresses, and directors.
Published by: IPK Rodina, Tsarigradsko shose blv 113-a, Sofia, 1184, Bulgaria. TEL 359-2-761502, FAX 359-2-761502. Ed. Dima Dimova. Pub. Teodora Halacheva. Adv. contact Iskra Dimitrova. color page USD 500; trim 290 x 215. Circ: 11,000. **Dist. by:** Sofia Books, ul Silivria 16, Sofia 1404, Bulgaria. TEL 359-2-9586257, info@sofiabooks-bg.com, http://www.sofiabooks-bg.com.

016.79143 USA
FILM & TELEVISION LITERATURE INDEX. Abbreviated title: F T L I. Text in English. 2002. base vol. plus updates 2/m. reprints avail. **Document type:** *Database, Abstract/Index.* **Description:** Indexes international periodical literature on film, television and video, by author and subject.
Formerly (until 2006): Film Literature Index (Online)
Media: Online - full text.
Indexed: RASB.
Published by: EBSCO Publishing (Subsidiary of: EBSCO Industries, Inc.), 10 Estes St, PO Box 682, Ipswich, MA 01938. TEL 978-356-6500, 800-653-2726, FAX 978-356-6565, information@ebscohost.com.

016.79143 USA
FILM & TELEVISION LITERATURE INDEX WITH FULL TEXT. Text in English. base vol. plus updates 2/m. **Document type:** *Database, Abstract/Index.*
Media: Online - full text.
Published by: EBSCO Publishing (Subsidiary of: EBSCO Industries, Inc.), 10 Estes St, PO Box 682, Ipswich, MA 01938. TEL 978-356-6500, 800-653-2726, FAX 978-356-6565, information@ebscohost.com.

016.79143 USA
PN1993
FILM INDEX INTERNATIONAL (ONLINE). Text in English. 1993. base vol. plus irreg. updates. back issues avail. **Document type:** *Database, Abstract/Index.* **Description:** Provides information resource for entertainment films and personalities produced in collaboration with the British Film Institute.
Formerly (until 1998): Film Index International (CD-ROM) (1355-4506)
Media: Online - full text.
Published by: (British Film Institute GBR, Library and Information Services Department), ProQuest (Subsidiary of: Cambridge Information Group), 789 E Eisenhower Pky, PO Box 1346, Ann Arbor, MI 48106. TEL 734-761-4700, 800-521-0600, FAX 734-997-4040, 888-241-5612, info@proquest.com, http://www.proquest.com.

016.79143 GBR
FILMLOG; index of feature film production and casting in Britain. Text in English. 1968. m. GBP 37.50 (effective 2001). **Document type:** *Abstract/Index.* **Description:** Lists jobs in the motion picture industry.
Address: PO Box 11, London, N1 7JZ, United Kingdom. TEL 44-171-566-8282, FAX 44-171-566-8284. Ed. Bobbi Dunn. Circ: 4,000. **Subscr. to:** PO Box 100, Broadstairs, Kent CT10 1UJ, United Kingdom.

016.79143 DEU ISSN 0071-4941
FILMSTATISTISCHES TASCHENBUCH. Text in German. 1957. a. **Document type:** *Trade.*
Published by: Spitzenorganisation der Filmwirtschaft e.V., Kreuzberger Ring 56, Wiesbaden, 65205, Germany. TEL 49-611-7789114, FAX 49-611-7789169. Ed. Markus Roth. Circ: 900.

016.79143 BEL ISSN 0000-0388
Z5784.M9
INTERNATIONAL INDEX TO FILM PERIODICALS. Text in English. 1972. a. EUR 180 (effective 2006). film rev.; tel.rev. bibl.; illus. back issues avail.; reprints avail. **Document type:** *Abstract/Index.* **Description:** Contains indexing of over 300 important film periodicals titles.
Related titles: Online - full text ed.: F I A F International FilmArchive Database. 2000.
—BLDSC (4541.050000).
Published by: Federation Internationale des Archives du Film (F I A F)/International Federation of Film Archives, Rue Defacqz 1, Brussels, 1000, Belgium. TEL 32-2-5383065, FAX 32-2-5344774, info@fiafnet.org. Ed. Rutger Penne.

016.77853 MEX
MEXICO. CENTRO DE INFORMACION TECNICA Y DOCUMENTACION. INDICE DE PELICULAS. Text in Spanish. a.
Published by: Servicio Nacional de Adiestramiento Rapido de la Mano de Obra en la Industria, Centro de Informacion Tecnica y Documentacion, Calzada Atzcapotzalco-la Villa 209, Apdo. 16-099, Mexico City, DF, Mexico.

016.79143 CAN ISSN 1704-6548
NATIONAL FILM BOARD OF CANADA. RESOURCE CATALOGUE. Text in English. 1974. a.
Former titles (until 2002): National Film Board of Canada (1704-653X); (until 2000): National Film Board of Canada. Catalogue (1486-3774); (until 199?): National Film Board of Canada. Video and Film Catalogue (1196-2895); (until 1992): National Film Board of Canada. Film and Video Catalogue (1187-0427); (until 1985): National Film Board of Canada. Catalogue (0225-9141); (until 1978): Film Catalogue (0382-3369)
Published by: National Film Board of Canada/Office National du Film du Canada, PO Box 6100, Sta Centre-Ville, Montreal, PQ H3C 3H5, Canada. TEL 514-283-9000, 800-267-7710, FAX 514-283-7564, http://www.nfb.ca.

791.43021 NZL ISSN 1177-5939
PN1993.5.N43
NEW ZEALAND. STATISTICS NEW ZEALAND. SCREEN INDUSTRY IN NEW ZEALAND. Text in English. 2006. a. NZD 35 (effective 2007). **Description:** Presents a statistical view of the screen industry. The screen industry covers all businesses involved in the screen production, postproduction, broadcasting, distribution, and exhibition sectors.
Related titles: Online - full text ed.: ISSN 1177-5947.
Published by: Statistics New Zealand/Te Tari Tatau, Statistics House, The Blvd, Harbour Quays, PO Box 2922, Wellington, 6140, New Zealand. TEL 64-4-9314600, FAX 64-4-9314610, info@stats.govt.nz.

791.43021 ZAF
SOUTH AFRICA. STATISTICS SOUTH AFRICA. CENSUS OF SOCIAL, RECREATIONAL AND PERSONAL SERVICES - MOTION PICTURE AND VIDEO PRODUCTION. Text in English. irreg., latest 1990. **Document type:** *Government.*
Formerly (until Aug.1998): South Africa. Central Statistical Service. Census of Social, Recreational and Personal Services - Motion Picture and Video Production
Published by: Statistics South Africa/Statistieke Suid-Afrika, Private Bag X44, Pretoria, 0001, South Africa. TEL 27-12-3108911, FAX 27-12-3108500, info@statssa.gov.za, http://www.statssa.gov.za.

791.43021 ZAF
SOUTH AFRICA. STATISTICS SOUTH AFRICA. CENSUS OF SOCIAL, RECREATIONAL AND PERSONAL SERVICES - MOTION PICTURE DISTRIBUTION AND PROJECTION AND VIDEO DISTRIBUTION SERVICES. Text in English. irreg., latest 1990. **Document type:** *Government.*
Formerly (until Aug.1998): South Africa. Central Statistical Service. Census of Social, Recreational and Personal Services - Motion Picture Distribution and Projection and Video Distribution Services
Published by: Statistics South Africa/Statistieke Suid-Afrika, Private Bag X44, Pretoria, 0001, South Africa. TEL 27-12-3108911, FAX 27-12-3108500, info@statssa.gov.za, http://www.statssa.gov.za.

016.79143 CHN ISSN 1005-0280
PN1993.5.C4
ZHONGGUO DIANYING NIANJIAN/CHINA FILM YEARBOOK. Text in Chinese. 1981. a. CNY 138 newsstand/cover (effective 2005). adv. **Document type:** *Yearbook, Academic/Scholarly.*
Address: 22, Beisanhuandong Lu, Beijing, 100013, China. TEL 86-10-64219977 ext 223.

MUNICIPAL GOVERNMENT

see PUBLIC ADMINISTRATION—Municipal Government

MUSEUMS AND ART GALLERIES

069 USA
A M M NEWS BRIEF. Text in English. 1988. bi-m. (6 vols published annually). USD 40 to individuals; USD 20 to students (effective Jan. 2000). bk.rev. bibl.; charts; illus. 16 p./no. 2 cols./p.; **Document type:** *Newsletter.*
Former titles: M M C (1073-0893); Midwest Museums Conference. News Brief (1071-8184); (until vol.48, no.4, 1988): Midwest Museums Conference Quarterly (0026-3443)
Indexed: SpeleolAb.
Published by: Association of Midwest Museums, PO Box 11940, St. Louis, MO 63112-0040. TEL 314-454-3110, FAX 313-454-3112. Ed., Adv. contact David M Tanner. Circ: 800.

069 USA
A S I POSTEN. Text in English. 1969. m. (11/yr.). membership. adv. back issues avail. **Document type:** *Newsletter.*
Supersedes (in 1982): Happenings; Which superseded: American Swedish Institute. Bulletin
Published by: American Swedish Institute, 2600 Park Ave, Minneapolis, MN 55407. TEL 612-871-4907. Ed. Janice M McElfish. Circ: 6,000.

A S T C DIMENSIONS. *see* SCIENCES: COMPREHENSIVE WORKS

ACADEMIE INTERNATIONALE DES ARTS ET COLLECTIONS. LA LETTRE. *see* ART

708.1 USA ISSN 1935-3502
ACCESS (NEWARK). Text in English. 1944. bi-m. USD 6 to non-members. adv. illus. **Document type:** *Newsletter.*
Former titles: Newark Museum. Exhibitions & Events; (until 1983): Newark Museum. News Notes (0028-9256)
Published by: Newark Museum Association, 49 Washington St, Box 540, Newark, NJ 07101. TEL 973-596-6550, FAX 973-642-0459. Ed. Catherine Jellinek. Adv. contact Bridget Daley. Circ: 12,500.

ACHTER HET BOEK. *see* LITERATURE

ACTA RERUM NATURALIUM. *see* SCIENCES: COMPREHENSIVE WORKS

ADLER MUSEUM BULLETIN. *see* MEDICAL SCIENCES

AGENDA. *see* ART

069 ESP ISSN 0213-876X
AIXA; revista de dialectologia y tradiciones populares. Text in Spanish, Catalan. 1944. a. **Document type:** *Journal, Academic/Scholarly.*
Indexed: RILM.
Published by: Museu Etnologic del Montseny, Major 6, Arbucies, Girona, Cataluna 17401, Spain. TEL 34-972-860908, FAX 34-972-860983, memga@ddgi.es, http://www.lasguias.com/memga/.

069 JPN ISSN 0385-1354
AKITA-KENRITSU HAKUBUTSUKAN KENKYU HOKOKU/AKITA PREFECTURAL MUSEUM. ANNUAL REPORT. Text in Japanese; Summaries in English, Japanese. 1976. a.
Published by: Akita Prefectural Museum/Akita-kenritsu Hakubutsukan, Ushiroyama, Kanashiniozaki, Akita-shi, 010-0124, Japan.

508.074 JPN ISSN 0065-5554
QH188
AKIYOSHI-DAI KAGAKU HAKUBUTSUKAN HOKOKU. Text in English, Japanese; Summaries in English. 1961. irreg., latest vol.6, 1969. **Document type:** *Bulletin.*
Indexed: GeoRef, SpeleolAb, Z01.
—BLDSC (2382.740000).
Published by: Akiyoshi-dai Museum of Natural History/Akiyoshi-dai Kagaku Hakubutsukan, Akiyoshi, Mine-gun, Shuho-cho, Yamaguchi-ken 754-0511, Japan. Ed. M Ota. **Co-sponsor:** Akiyoshi-dai Science Museum.

069 HUN ISSN 0324-542X
AM101
ALBA REGIA. Text in English, German. 1960. a. HUF 2,700; or exchange basis. bk.rev. back issues avail. **Description:** Covers archaeology, ethnography, and local history.
Indexed: AICP, FR, IBR, IBZ.
Published by: Musei Stephani Regis, PO Box 78, Szekesfehervar, 8002, Hungary. TEL 22-315-583. Ed. J Fitz.

069 CAN ISSN 1719-377X
ALBERTA MUSEUMS ASSOCIATION. AWARDS PROGRAM. Text in English. a. **Document type:** *Journal, Consumer.*
Formerly (until 2005): Museums Alberta. Awards (1719-3761)
Published by: Alberta Museums Association, 9829 - 103 St, Edmonton, AB T5K 0X9, Canada. TEL 780-424-2626, FAX 780-425-1679, info@museumsalberta.ab.ca, http://www.museumsalberta.ab.ca.

708.11 CAN ISSN 0380-3279
ALBERTA MUSEUMS REVIEW. Text in English. 1974. s-a. free contr. circ. **Document type:** *Magazine, Consumer.*
Published by: Alberta Museums Association, 9829 - 103 St, Edmonton, AB T5K 0X9, Canada. TEL 780-424-2626, FAX 780-425-1679, info@museumsalberta.ab.ca, http://www.museumsalberta.ab.ca.

ALBURY & DISTRICT HISTORICAL SOCIETY. BULLETIN. *see* HISTORY—History Of Australasia And Other Areas

708.1 USA ISSN 0065-6410
ALLIED ARTISTS OF AMERICA. EXHIBITION CATALOG. Text in English. 1914. a. USD 3. adv.
Published by: Allied Artists of America, 15 Gramercy Park S, New York, NY 10003. TEL 212-582-6411. Circ: 3,000.

708.5 ITA ISSN 0569-1346
ALTAMURA. Text in Italian. 1954. a. free to members. bibl.; illus. **Document type:** *Journal, Academic/Scholarly.*
Indexed: B24, P30.
Published by: (Museo Civico di Altamura), Edizioni di Pagina, Via dei Mille 205, Bari, 70126, Italy. info@paginasc.it, http://www.paginasc.it.

069 DEU ISSN 0440-1417
AM101
ALTONAER MUSEUM IN HAMBURG. NORDEUTSCHES LANDESMUSEUM. JAHRBUCH. Text in German. 1963. a. **Document type:** *Journal, Academic/Scholarly.*
Indexed: AIAP.
Published by: Altonaer Museum in Hamburg, Museumstr 23, Hamburg, 22765, Germany. TEL 49-40-4281353582, FAX 49-40-4281352143, info@altonaermuseum.de, http://www.altonaermuseum.de. Ed. Gerhard Kaufmann. Circ: 1,500.

508.74 USA
AMERICAN MUSEUM OF NATURAL HISTORY. ANNUAL REPORT. Text in English. 1870. a., latest 1999. bibl.; charts; illus. back issues avail. **Document type:** *Report, Trade.* **Description:** Covers topics discussed included the recent articles of incorporation, gifts to the expanding collection, purchases made in Europe, and a circular sent via the U.S. state department and the United States navy soliciting acquisitions from all corners of the globe.
Related titles: Online - full text ed.
Published by: American Museum of Natural History Library, Scientific Publications Distribution, Central Park W at 79th St, New York, NY 10024. TEL 212-769-5420, FAX 212-769-5009, scipubs@amnh.org, http://library.amnh.org/scientific-publications.

508.74 USA
AMERICAN MUSEUM OF NATURAL HISTORY. BIENNIAL REPORT. Text in English. biennial.
Published by: American Museum of Natural History, Central Park West at 79th St, New York, NY 10024-5192. TEL 212-769-5656, FAX 212-769-5653, scipubs@amnh.org, http://www.amnh.org.

069 USA
AMERICAN SWEDISH HISTORICAL MUSEUM NEWSLETTER. Text in English. 195?. q. USD 50 membership (effective 2000). bk.rev. illus. 8 p./no.; **Document type:** *Newsletter.*
Formerly (until 1987): Museum Expressen
Published by: American Swedish Historical Museum, 1900 Pattison Ave, Philadelphia, PA 19145. TEL 215-389-1776, FAX 215-389-7701. Ed., R&P, Adv. contact Anne L Egler. Circ: 800.

THE AMERICAS ART DIRECTORY/DIRECTORIO DE ARTE DE LAS AMERICAS. *see* ART

069 ESP ISSN 1887-6498
AMIGOS DE LOS MUSEOS. Text in Spanish. 1993. s-a. EUR 20 (effective 2009). **Document type:** *Magazine, Consumer.*
Formerly (until 2004): Federacion Espanola de Amigos de los Museos. Boletin Informativo (1134-2757)
Published by: Federacion Espanola de Amigos de los Museos (F E A M), Avenida Reyes Catolicos 6, Madrid, 28040, Spain. TEL 34-913-600057, FAX 34-915-436106, http://www.feam.es.

069 ESP ISSN 1697-1019
AMIGOS DE LOS MUSEOS DE OSUNA. CUADERNOS. Text in Spanish. 1998. a. **Document type:** *Journal, Academic/Scholarly.*
Published by: Amigos de los Museos de Osuna, Iglesia Colegiata, Osuna, Sevilla 41640, Spain.

930.1 069 FRA ISSN 0335-5160
ANNALES DU MUSEUM DU HAVRE. Text in French. 1975. irreg., latest 2001. charts; illus.; maps. back issues avail.
Indexed: FR, GeoRef, SpeleolAb, Z01.

—INIST.
Published by: (Ville du Havre), Editions du Museum du Havre, Place du Vieux Marche, Le Havre, 76600, France. TEL 33-2-35413728, FAX 33-2-35421240. Ed. Gerard Breton. Circ: 500.

069.5 GRC ISSN 0302-1033
QH151 CODEN: AMUGAY
ANNALES MUSEI GOULANDRIS; contributiones ad historiam naturalem graeciae et regionis mediterraneae. Text in English, French, German, Italian, Latin; Summaries in English, Greek. 1973. a. USD 20 (effective 2000). bk.rev. **Document type:** *Journal, Academic/ Scholarly.* **Description:** Covers the natural history of Greece and the Mediterranean.
Indexed: ASFA, B21, B25, BIOSIS Prev, ESPM, GeoRef, MycolAb, SpeleolAb, Z01.
—Linda Hall.
Published by: Goulandris Natural History Museum, 13 Levidou St, Kifissia, Athens 145 62, Greece. TEL 301-8015870, FAX 301-8080-674. Ed. John Robert Akeroyd. R&P Niki Goulandris. Circ: 1,000.

ANNALS OF THE EASTERN CAPE MUSEUMS. *see* SCIENCES: COMPREHENSIVE WORKS

069 ITA ISSN 1971-4815
GN36.I8
ANTROPOLOGIA MUSEALE. Text in Italian. 2002. 3/yr. **Document type:** *Magazine, Consumer.*
Published by: Societa Italiana per la Museografia e i Beni Demoetnoantropologici, c/o Museo Nazionale Preistorico Etnografico L. Pigorini, Piazza Marconi 14, Rome, 00144, Italy. info_simbdea@yahoo.it, http://www.antropologiamuseale.it/associazioneSG.htm.

708.9498 ROM
ANUARUL MUZEULUI NATIONAL DE ISTORIE A ROMANIEI. Text in Romanian; Summaries in English, French. 1974. a. bk.rev. illus. **Document type:** *Academic/Scholarly.*
Formerly (until 1983): Muzeul National (1015-0323)
Indexed: NumL.
Published by: Muzeul National de Istorie a Romaniei, Calea Victoriei 12, Bucharest, Romania. TEL 614-90-78.

708.92 NLD ISSN 2210-6987
APM. Variant title: Allard Pierson Mededelingen. Text in Dutch. 1970. irreg. (2-3/yr.).
Formerly (until 2009): Vereniging van Vrienden van het Allard Pierson Museum. Mededelingenblad (0922-159X)
Published by: (Allard Pierson Museum), Vereniging van Vrienden van het Allard Pierson Museum, Postbus 94057, Amsterdam, 1090 GB, Netherlands. TEL 31-20-5252557, vvapm-uba@uva.nl, http://www.allardpiersonmuseum.nl/museum/vereniging.html.

▼ **ARAGON EDUCA.** *see* EDUCATION

069 ESP ISSN 1579-7511
QE701
ARAGONIA. Text in Spanish. 1998. irreg. free (effective 2009). back issues avail. **Document type:** *Bulletin, Trade.*
Indexed: GeoRef.
Published by: Universidad de Zaragoza, Sociedad de Amigos del Museo Paleontologico, C Pedro Cerbuna No 12, Zaragoza, 50009, Spain. TEL 34-976-762122, museopa2@unizar.es, http://museo-palo.unizar.es/sampuz/index.htm.

069 DEU ISSN 0402-7817
GN814.S27
ARBEITS UND FORSCHUNGSBERICHTE ZUR SAECHSISCHEN BODENDENKMALPFLEGE. Text in German. 1953. irreg. price varies. **Document type:** *Monographic series, Academic/Scholarly.*
Indexed: AICP, B24, BibInd, BrArAb, DIP, FR, IBR, IBZ, NAA, NumL, RASB.
—INIST.
Published by: Landesamt fuer Archaeologie mit Landesmuseum fuer Vorgeschichte Dresden, Zur Wetterwarte 7, Dresden, 01109, Germany. TEL 49-351-8926199, FAX 49-351-8926999, info@lfa.sachsen.de, http://www.archaeologie.sachsen.de.

ARGO. *see* HISTORY—History Of Europe

069 SWE ISSN 0284-3242
ARGUS (DALAROE); aarsbok foer Tullmuseum och Tullhistoriska Foereningen. Text in Swedish. 1979. a. **Document type:** *Academic/ Scholarly.*
Formerly (until 1987): Tullhistorisk Tidskrift (0349-9081)
Published by: Tullmuseum/Customs Museum, P O Box 12854, Stockholm, 11298, Sweden. TEL 46-8-6530503, FAX 46-8-208012, tullmuseet@tullverket.se, http://www.tullverket.se/se/om_oss/museum.

069 700 USA
ARIZONA ARTISTS GUILD NEWSLETTER. Text in English. 1928. m. looseleaf. membership. back issues avail. **Document type:** *Newsletter.*
Published by: Arizona Artists Guild, 5420 W. Del Rio St., Chandler, AZ 85226-1926. TEL 602-944-9713. Ed. Lee Caster. Circ: 500.

355.009485 SWE ISSN 0349-1048
ARMEMUSEUM. MEDDELANDE. Text in Swedish; Summaries in English. 1938. a. SEK 200 membership (effective 2007). **Document type:** *Yearbook, Consumer.* **Description:** Features articles on military history, uniforms and weapons, particularly that of Sweden.
Formerly (until vol.11, 1950): Foereningen Armemusei Vaenner Meddelanden (0284-1983)
Published by: (Armemuseum/Royal Army Museum), Foereningen Armemusei Vaenner, c/o Armemuseum, Riddargatan 13, PO Box 14095, Stockholm, 10441, Sweden. info@armemuseum.se. Ed. Svante Folin TEL 46-8-7689507. Circ: 2,000.

▼ **ARS BILDUMA.** *see* ART

069 HUN ISSN 0133-6673
NK9
ARS DECORATIVA/IPARMUVESZET. Text in English, German, Hungarian. 1973. a. per issue exchange basis. **Document type:** *Bulletin.*
Supersedes: Iparmuveszeti Muzeum. Evkonyve
Indexed: AIAP, BAS, NumL.
Published by: Iparmuveszeti Muzeum, Hopp Ferenc Keletazsiai Muveszeti Muzeum/Museum of Applied Arts, Ulloi ut 33-37, Budapest, 1091, Hungary. TEL 36-1-2175222, FAX 36-1-2175838. Ed. Andras Szilagy. Pub., R&P Zsuzsa Lovag. Circ: 1,000 (controlled).

069.5 USA
ART ACCESS. Text in English. 1992. m. USD 24 to individuals; USD 22 to qualified personnel (effective 2003). music rev.; play rev.; dance rev. maps. **Document type:** *Magazine, Consumer.*
Media: Online - full content.
Address: Box 4163, Seattle, WA 98104. TEL 206-855-9668, FAX 206-855-7854, info@artaccess.com, http://www.artaccess.com. Ed., Pub., Adv. contact Debbi Lester.

ART AND ARCHAEOLOGY MAGAZINE. *see* ART

344.093 USA ISSN 1553-3999
KF4288.A7
ART AND MUSEUM LAW JOURNAL. Text in English. 2004 (Fall). s-a. **Document type:** *Journal, Academic/Scholarly.*
Published by: Thomas M. Cooley Law School, 300 S Capitol Ave, PO Box 13038, Lansing, MI 48901. TEL 517-371-5140, 800-874-3511, FAX 517-334-5718, communications@cooley.edu, http://www.cooley.edu.

069 705 SWE ISSN 1401-2987
N3540
ART BULLETIN OF NATIONALMUSEUM STOCKHOLM. Text in Multiple languages. 1977. a. **Document type:** *Consumer.*
Formerly (until 1996): Nationalmuseum. Bulletin (0347-7835); Which incorporated: Kontakt med Nationalmuseum (0428-8084)
Related titles: Online - full text ed.
Indexed: A07, A30, A31, AA, ArtInd, B04, B24, BRD, W03, W05.
Published by: Nationalmuseum, Sodra Blasieholmshamnen, PO Box 16176, Stockholm, 103 24, Sweden. TEL 46-8-51954300, FAX 46-8-51954450, info@nationalmuseum.se, http://www.nationalmuseum.se. Ed. Gorel Cavalli-Bjorkman.

708.994 AUS ISSN 0066-7935
N3948
➤ **ART BULLETIN OF VICTORIA.** Abbreviated title: A B V (Issue Number). Text in English. 1945. a., latest no.45. back issues avail. **Document type:** *Journal, Academic/Scholarly.* **Description:** Publishes research on the Gallery's collection of Australian and international art by scholars and researchers.
Former titles (until 1967): National Gallery of Victoria. Annual Bulletin (0505-4354); (until 1959): National Gallery of Victoria. Quarterly Bulletin
Indexed: ABCT, AusPAIS, B24.
—Ingenta.
Published by: National Gallery of Victoria, PO Box 7259, Melbourne, VIC 8004, Australia. TEL 61-3-86202222, FAX 61-3-86202555, enquiries@ngv.vic.gov.au, http://www.ngv.vic.gov.au. Circ: 1,500 (paid).

708.11 CAN
ART GALLERY OF ALBERTA. CALENDAR OF EVENTS. Text in English. 1990. q.
Former titles: Edmonton Art Gallery. Calendar of Events (1206-6486); (until 1997): Edmonton Art Gallery. Outlook (1184-2288); Which was formed by the merger of (1980-1989): Edmonton Art Gallery. Update (0225-3224); (1988-1990): Edmonton Art Gallery. Exhibitions (0844-577X)
Indexed: AIAP.
Published by: Art Gallery of Alberta, 2 Sir Winston Churchill Sq., Edmonton, AB T5J 2C1, Canada. TEL 780-422-6223, FAX 780-426-3105, http://www.artgalleryalberta.ca.

708.11 CAN ISSN 1711-733X
ART GALLERY OF NOVA SCOTIA. ANNUAL REPORT (CD-ROM EDITION). Text in English. a.
Formerly (until 2003): Art Gallery of Nova Scotia. Annual Report (Print Edition) (0837-7839)
Published by: Art Gallery of Nova Scotia, PO Box 2262, Halifax, NS B3J 3C8, Canada. TEL 902-424-7542, FAX 902-424-7359, http://www.agns.gov.ns.ca.

708.11 CAN ISSN 0082-5018
N910.T6
ART GALLERY OF ONTARIO. ANNUAL REPORT. Text in English. 1967. a. **Document type:** *Corporate.*
Published by: Art Gallery of Ontario, 317 Dundas St W, Toronto, ON M5T 1G4, Canada. TEL 416-977-0414, FAX 416-979-6646. Ed. Beverly Carret. Circ: 2,500.

069 CAN ISSN 1205-9110
ART GALLERY OF ONTARIO. MEMBERS JOURNAL. Text in English. q. CAD 75 to members. charts; illus. **Document type:** *Newsletter.*
Former titles (until 1996): Art Gallery of Ontario. Journal (1191-9868); A G O News (0829-4437); Art Gallery of Ontario. The Gallery (0709-8413); Art Gallery of Ontario. Coming Events (0044-9024)
Published by: Art Gallery of Ontario, 317 Dundas St W, Toronto, ON M5T 1G4, Canada. TEL 416-979-6648, FAX 416-204-2711. Eds. Bruce Maxwell, Catherine Van Baren. Circ: 26,000.

069 PHL ISSN 0119-6871
AM101.M297
ART I FACTS. Text in English. 1999. 3/yr. **Document type:** *Newsletter, Consumer.* **Description:** Presents news on culture and science for the National Museum of the Philippines.
Related titles: Online - full content ed.
Published by: National Museum of the Philippines, P. Burgos Ave., PO Box 2659, Manila, 1000, Philippines. TEL 63-2-5271215, FAX 63-2-5270306, http://philmuseum.tripod.com/index. Ed. Elenita D. V. Alba.

069 USA ISSN 1044-4599
N530
ART INSTITUTE OF CHICAGO. ANNUAL REPORT. Text in English. 1955. a.
Published by: Art Institute of Chicago, 111 S Michigan Ave, Chicago, IL 60603. TEL 312-443-3540, FAX 312-443-1334.

069 USA ISSN 0069-3235
N81
➤ **ART INSTITUTE OF CHICAGO. MUSEUM STUDIES.** Text in English. 1966-1978; resumed 1984. s-a. USD 35 to individuals; USD 60 to institutions; USD 30 to members; USD 16.95 per issue (effective 2010). illus. Index. 104 p./no.; back issues avail.; reprints avail. **Document type:** *Journal, Academic/Scholarly.* **Description:** Contains articles pertaining to the museum's exhibitions permanent collections and history.
Related titles: Microform ed.: (from PQC); Online - full text ed.
Indexed: A06, A07, A20, A22, A30, A31, AA, ABM, AIAP, ASCA, AmH&L, ArtHuCI, ArtInd, B04, B24, CA, CurCont, HistAb, PCI, RILM, SCOPUS, T02, W07.
—BLDSC (5989.740000), IE, Ingenta.
Published by: Art Institute of Chicago, 111 S Michigan Ave, Chicago, IL 60603. TEL 312-443-3786, FAX 312-443-1334, aic.publicaffairs@artic.edu. Ed. Greg Nosan.

➤ **ART MONTHLY.** *see* ART

708.1 USA
ART NOW GALLERY GUIDE: BOSTON / NEW ENGLAND EDITION. Text in English. 1981. 10/yr. USD 40 (effective 2008). adv. **Document type:** *Magazine, Consumer.* **Description:** Features information on galleries in Boston and New England.
Former titles: Art Now: Boston and New England Gallery Guide; Art Now: Boston Gallery Guide
Published by: Louise Blouin Media (Subsidiary of: L T B Media), 601 West 26th St, Ste 410, New York, NY 10001. TEL 212-447-9555, production@artinfo.com. Ed. Brianne Cavallone. Pub. Roger Peskin. Circ: 13,000.

708 USA
ART NOW GALLERY GUIDE: CHICAGO / MIDWEST EDITION. Text in English. 189?. 10/yr. USD 40 in US & Canada; USD 60 elsewhere (effective 2009). adv. **Document type:** *Magazine, Consumer.* **Description:** Features information on galleries in Chicago and Midwest.
Formerly: Art Now: Chicago and Midwest Gallery Guide; Formed by the merger of (1981-1982): Art Now: Midwest Gallery Guide; (1980-1982): Art Now: Chicago Gallery Guide
Published by: Louise Blouin Media (Subsidiary of: L T B Media), 601 West 26th St, Ste 410, New York, NY 10001. TEL 212-447-9555. Ed. Monica Iannarelli TEL 646-753-9153. Circ: 16,000.

069.5 USA
N510
ART NOW GALLERY GUIDE: COLLECTOR'S EDITION. Text in English. 1982. 10/yr. (includes one combined summer issue). USD 45 domestic; USD 52 foreign (effective 2007). adv. illus. reprints avail. **Document type:** *Magazine, Consumer.* **Description:** Contains information about exhibitions at galleries and museums across the US and Europe, plus gallery-area maps.
Former titles: Art Now Gallery Guide: International Edition (1059-7689); Art Now Gallery Guide: National Edition; Art Now: U S A - National Art Museum and Gallery Guide (0745-5720)
Published by: Louise Blouin Media (Subsidiary of: L T B Media), 601 West 26th St, Ste 410, New York, NY 10001. TEL 212-447-9555. Ed. Patricia Yannotta. Circ: 6,000.

708.1 USA
ART NOW GALLERY GUIDE: NEW YORK EDITION. Text in English. 1969. 10/yr. USD 40 (effective 2008). adv. **Document type:** *Magazine, Consumer.* **Description:** Features information on galleries in New York.
Former titles: Art Now: New York Gallery Guide; (until 1980): Art Now Gallery Guide
Published by: Louise Blouin Media (Subsidiary of: L T B Media), 601 West 26th St, Ste 410, New York, NY 10001. TEL 212-447-9555, production@artinfo.com. Ed. Julia Oswald TEL 646-753-9068. Circ: 38,000.

069.5 USA
ART NOW GALLERY GUIDE: SOUTHEAST EDITION. Text in English. 19??. 10/yr. USD 40 in US & Canada; USD 60 elsewhere (effective 2009). adv. **Document type:** *Magazine, Consumer.* **Description:** Contains information about exhibitions at galleries and museums, plus gallery-area maps.
Formerly (until 200?): Art Now: Southeast Gallery Guide
Published by: Louise Blouin Media (Subsidiary of: L T B Media), 601 West 26th St, Ste 410, New York, NY 10001. TEL 212-447-9555. Ed. Julia Oswald TEL 646-753-9068. Circ: 13,000.

708 USA
ART NOW GALLERY GUIDE: SOUTHWEST EDITION. Text in English. 1981. 10/yr. adv. **Document type:** *Magazine, Consumer.* **Description:** Contains information about exhibitions at galleries and museums, plus gallery-area maps.
Former titles: Art Now: Southwest Gallery Guide; Art Now: Texas, Arizona, New Mexico Gallery Guide
Published by: Louise Blouin Media (Subsidiary of: L T B Media), 601 West 26th St, Ste 410, New York, NY 10001. TEL 212-447-9555. Ed. Julie Schnedeker. Pub. Roger Peskin. Circ: 20,000.

708 USA
ART NOW GALLERY GUIDE: WEST COAST EDITION. Text in English. 19??. 10/yr. USD 40 in US & Canada; USD 60 elsewhere (effective 2009). adv. **Document type:** *Magazine, Consumer.* **Description:** Contains information about exhibitions at galleries and museums, plus gallery-area maps.
Former titles: Art Now Gallery Guide: California - Northwest Edition; Art Now: California and Northwest Gallery Guide; Which was formed by the merger of (1980-1983): Art Now: California Gallery Guide; Art Now: Northwest Gallery Guide
Published by: Louise Blouin Media (Subsidiary of: L T B Media), 601 West 26th St, Ste 410, New York, NY 10001. TEL 212-447-9555. Ed. Monica Iannarelli TEL 646-753-9153. Adv. contact Patricia Yannotta TEL 908-581-5843. Circ: 20,000.

371.3 USA ISSN 0882-6838
ART TO ZOO. Text in English. 1976. q. free. illus. reprints avail. **Document type:** *Magazine, Consumer.* **Description:** Provides creative ideas for teaching and learning in connection with current Smithsonian art, history or science exhibits.
Related titles: Online - full text ed.
—CCC.

Published by: Smithsonian Institution, Office of Elementary and Secondary Education, 955 L Enfant Plaza, Rm 1163, MRC 402, Washington, DC 20560. Ed. Douglas Casey. Circ: 84,000 (controlled).

L'ARTE DEL COLLEZIONARE. *see* ART

069 AUS ISSN 1838-627X
▼ **ARTICULATE.** Text in English. 2010. q. free to members (effective 2011). **Document type:** *Magazine, Trade.*
Published by: Art Gallery of South Australia, N Terr, Adelaide, SA 5000, Australia. TEL 61-8-82077000, FAX 61-8-82077070, agsainformation@artgallery.sa.gov.au, http://www.artgallery.sa.gov.au/agsa/home.

ARTIFACTS (COLUMBIA). *see* ART

708.994 AUS ISSN 1325-8842
ARTLINES. Text in English. 1996. q. free to members (effective 2009). back issues avail. **Document type:** *Magazine, Trade.* **Description:** Covers events, exhibitions, society news and activities.
Related titles: Online - full text ed.: AUD 7.95 (effective 2009).
Published by: Queensland Art Gallery Society, PO Box 3686, South Brisbane, QLD 4101, Australia. TEL 61-7-38407278, FAX 61-7-38407275, gallerymembers@qag.qld.gov.au, http://www.qag.qld.gov.au.

708.994 AUS ISSN 1323-4552
N3916
ARTONVIEW. Text in English. 1981. q. free to members (effective 2009). adv. back issues avail. **Document type:** *Magazine, Trade.* **Description:** Provides in-depth focus on the national collection and includes a wealth of information on leading museum practices and current art news.
Former titles (until 1995): National Gallery News (1038-863X); (until 1992): Australian National Gallery Association. News (0811-7578); (until 1982): A N G News (0727-3843)
Indexed: A07, A30, A31, AA, ABM, ArtInd, B04, BRD, SCOPUS, W03, W05.
Published by: National Gallery of Australia, GPO Box 1150, Canberra, ACT 2601, Australia. TEL 61-2-62406411, FAX 61-2-62406628, information@nga.gov.au, http://www.nga.gov.au. Ed. Eric Meredith. adv.: color page AUD 2,000; trim 233 x 297. Circ: 14,500.

069 USA
ARTS (MINNEAPOLIS). Text in English. 1983. m. membership. adv. reprints avail. **Document type:** *Newsletter.*
Indexed: AIAP.
Published by: Minneapolis Institute of Arts, 2400 Third Ave S, Minneapolis, MN 55404. TEL 612-870-3046, FAX 612-870-3004. Pub. Don Leurquin. R&P Deann Dankowski. Adv. contact Joan Olson. Circ: 26,000.

069 CAN ISSN 1497-6560
ARTS COMMUNIQUE FROM THE VANCOUVER ART GALLERY. Text in English. 3/yr. membership. **Document type:** *Bulletin.* **Description:** Provides a schedule of events and exhibitions at the gallery.
Former titles (until 2000): Vancouver Art Gallery. Newsletter (1490-425X); (until 1998): Vancouver Art Gallery. Quarterly (1485-4627); (until 1997): Vancouver Art Gallery (1203-6323); (until 1996): Vancouver Art Gallery. Member's Calendar (0838-3626)
Published by: Vancouver Art Gallery, 750 Hornby St, Vancouver, BC V6Z 2H7, Canada. TEL 604-662-4700, FAX 604-682-1086.

708 USA
ARTSFOCUS. Text in English. 1968. q. free to members (effective 2010). 32 p./no.; back issues avail. **Document type:** *Magazine, Consumer.* **Description:** Covers exhibitions, performing arts series, library, art school, museum shop, and volunteer and staff activities.
Related titles: Online - full text ed.: free (effective 2010).
Published by: Colorado Springs Fine Arts Center, 30 W Dale St, Colorado Springs, CO 80903. TEL 719-634-5581, FAX 719-634-0570, ehannan@csfineartscenter.org. Ed., Pub., R&P Erin Hannan. Circ: 6,200.

708 AUS ISSN 1323-5885
ARTWORKER. Text in English. 1986. s-a. AUD 55 (individual membership); AUD 110 (institutional membership) (effective 2008). adv. back issues avail. **Document type:** *Magazine, Trade.* **Description:** Contains professional information on contemporary practice, artist and art worker profiles, opinions and debates.
Formerly: Queensland Artworkers Alliance Newsletter
Published by: Artworkers Alliance, Level 3, 381 Brunswick St, Fortitude Valley, QLD 4006, Australia. TEL 61-7-32150850, FAX 61-7-32150851, info@artworkers.org. Ed. Sofie Ham. adv.: B&W page AUD 330; trim 297 x 210. Circ: 1,500 (controlled).

069 ESP ISSN 2172-3982
ASOCIACION DE MUSEOLOGOS Y MUSEOGRAFOS DE ANDALUCIA. E-BOLETIN. Text in Spanish. 2008. a. back issues avail. **Document type:** *Journal, Academic/Scholarly.*
Media: Online - full text.
Published by: Asociacion de Museologos y Museografos de Andalucia info@asoc-amma.org.

069 FRA
ASSOCIATION GENERALE DES CONSERVATEURS DE MUSEES ET COLLECTIONS PUBLIQUES DE FRANCE. ANNUAIRE. Text in French. 1960. biennial. adv.
Published by: Association Generale des Conservateurs des Collections Publiques de France, 6 Av du Mahatma Gandhi, Paris, 75116, France. TEL 33-1-44176000, FAX 33-1-44176060.

069 GBR ISSN 0142-887X
ASSOCIATION OF INDEPENDENT MUSEUMS BULLETIN. Variant title: A I M Bulletin. Text in English. 1977. bi-m. free to members (effective 2009). adv. bk.rev. back issues avail. **Document type:** *Magazine, Trade.* **Description:** Details the activities of independent museums throughout the UK.
Related titles: Online - full text ed.
Published by: Association of Independent Museums, 4 Clayhall Rd, Gosport, PO12 2BY, United Kingdom. TEL 44-2392-587751, admin@aim-museums.co.uk. Ed., Adv. contact Diana Zeuner TEL 44-1730-812419. page GBP 355; 190 x 273.

069 CAN ISSN 0849-5858
ASSOCIATION OF MANITOBA MUSEUMS. NEWSLETTER. Text in English. q. membership. adv. bk.rev. **Document type:** *Newsletter.*
Published by: Association of Manitoba Museums, 153 Lombard St, Ste 206, Winnipeg, MB R3B 0T4, Canada. TEL 204-947-1782, FAX 204-942-3749. Adv. contact Doreen Robertson. Circ: 400.

708 CHE ISSN 1661-691X
L'ATELIER; travaux d'histoire de l'art et de museologie. Text in French, German. 2007. irreg., latest vol.2, 2007. price varies. **Document type:** *Monographic series, Academic/Scholarly.*
Published by: Peter Lang AG (Subsidiary of: Peter Lang Publishing Group), Hochfeldstr 32, Postfach 746, Bern 9, 3000, Switzerland. TEL 41-31-3061717, FAX 41-31-3061727, info@peterlang.com, http://www.peterlang.com. Eds. Pascal Griener, Pierre Alain Mariaux.

ATENEUM/FINNISH NATIONAL GALLERY. BULLETIN. *see* ART

069 SAU ISSN 0256-4009
DS211
ATLAL. Text in English. 1977. a. **Document type:** *Journal, Academic/Scholarly.*
Indexed: GeoRef.
Published by: Ministry of Education, Department of Antiquities and Museums, Antiquities & Museums, Riyadh, 11148, Saudi Arabia. TEL 966-1-4046666, mslimi@moe.gov.sa, http://www.moe.gov.sa/openshare/englishcon.

069 CAN ISSN 1915-0229
AU COURANT (ENGLISH EDITION). Variant title: Canadian Federation of Friends of Museums. Newsletter. Text in English. 2000. q. **Document type:** *Newsletter.*
Related titles: ◆ French ed.: Au Courant (French Edition). ISSN 1915-0237.
Published by: Canadian Federation of Friends of Museums/Federation Canadienne des Amis de Musees, c/o The Art Gallery of Ontario, 317 Dundas Street West, Toronto, ON M5T 1G4, Canada. TEL 416-979-6650, FAX 416-979-6674, cffm_fcam@ago.net, http://www.cffm-fcam.ca.

069 CAN ISSN 1915-0237
AU COURANT (FRENCH EDITION). Variant title: Federation Canadienne des Amis de Musees. Newsletter. Text in French. 2000. q. **Document type:** *Newsletter.*
Related titles: ◆ English ed.: Au Courant (English Edition). ISSN 1915-0229.
Published by: Canadian Federation of Friends of Museums/Federation Canadienne des Amis de Musees, c/o The Art Gallery of Ontario, 317 Dundas Street West, Toronto, ON M5T 1G4, Canada. TEL 416-979-6650, FAX 416-979-6674, cffm_fcam@ago.net, http://www.cffm-fcam.ca.

708.993 NZL
Q93 CODEN: RAUIA7
➤ **AUCKLAND MUSEUM. RECORDS.** Text in English. 1930. a., latest 2001, vol.37/38 combined. price varies. abstr.; bibl.; illus.; maps; stat. index. back issues avail. **Document type:** *Journal, Academic/Scholarly.* **Description:** Contains results of original research on the Museum collections, and research by Museum staff in their particular subjects.
Former titles: Auckland War Memorial Museum. Records (1174-9202); Auckland Institute and Museum. Records (0067-0464)
Indexed: AICP, AnthLit, B25, BIOSIS Prev, FR, GeoRef, INIS AtomInd, INZP, MycolAb, SPPI, SpeleolAb, Z01.
—Ingenta, INIST, Linda Hall.
Published by: Auckland Museum, Domain Dr., Private Bag 92018, Auckland, New Zealand. TEL 64-9-3090443, FAX 64-9-3799956, store@aucklandmuseum.com, http://www.akmuseum.org.nz. Eds. Brian Gill, Nigel Prickett. Circ: 300.

708.993 NZL
CODEN: BUKIAN
➤ **AUCKLAND WAR MEMORIAL MUSEUM. BULLETIN.** Text in English. 1941. irreg., latest 2002. price varies. back issues avail. **Document type:** *Monographic series, Academic/Scholarly.* **Description:** Covers natural history or human history subjects.
Formerly (until 2000): Auckland Institute and Museum. Bulletin (0067-0456)
Indexed: AICP, GeoRef, SpeleolAb.
—INIST.
Published by: Auckland Museum, Domain Dr., Private Bag 92018, Auckland, New Zealand. TEL 64-9-3090443, FAX 64-9-3799956, store@aucklandmuseum.com, http://www.akmuseum.org.nz. Circ: 300.

➤ **AUS ARCHIVEN, BIBLIOTHEKEN UND MUSEEN MITTEL- UND OSTEUROPAS.** *see* HISTORY—History Of Europe

➤ **AUSTRALIAN MUSEUM. RECORDS.** *see* BIOLOGY—Zoology

➤ **AUSTRALIAN MUSEUM, SYDNEY. RECORDS SUPPLEMENT.** *see* BIOLOGY—Zoology

➤ **AUSTRALIAN MUSEUM. TECHNICAL REPORTS (ONLINE).** *see* BIOLOGY—Zoology

387.0074 AUS ISSN 0813-0523
AUSTRALIAN SEA HERITAGE. Text in English. 1984. q. AUD 55 to non-members; AUD 25 to members (effective 2009). adv. bk.rev. charts; illus.; stat. back issues avail. **Document type:** *Magazine, Trade.* **Description:** Reflects the on going work of Australia's museums in preserving maritime history, and provides outlet for articles on Australian maritime history.
—Ingenta.
Published by: Sydney Maritime Museum, Wharf 7, Pirrama Rd, Pyrmont, NSW 2009, Australia. TEL 61-2-92983888, FAX 61-2-92983839, bclayton@shf.org.au. Circ: 5,000.

THE AVIATOR. *see* AERONAUTICS AND SPACE FLIGHT

069 USA ISSN 0739-7747
AM1
AVISO. Text in English. 1968. m. USD 40 domestic to non-members; USD 55 foreign to non-members (effective 2007). tr.lit. **Document type:** *Newsletter, Trade.* **Description:** Reports on museums in the news, federal legislation affecting museums, upcoming seminars and workshops, federal grant deadlines, and AAM activities and services.
Supersedes (in 1975): A A M Bulletin (0044-7536)
Related titles: Microform ed.: (from MML).
Indexed: IBR, IBZ.
—CCC.
Published by: American Association of Museums, 1575 Eye St, NW, Ste 400, Washington, DC 20005. TEL 202-289-1818, FAX 202-289-6578, servicecentral@aam-us.org, http://www.aam-us.org. Circ: 17,000.

069 PRT ISSN 0872-170X
AZULEJO. Text in Portuguese. 1991. irreg. **Document type:** *Magazine, Consumer.*
Published by: Institutos dos Museus e da Conservacao, Palacio Nacional da Ajuda, Lisbon, 1349-021, Portugal. TEL 351-213-650800, FAX 351-213-647821, http://www.ipmuseus.pt.

708.1 USA
B A C A ARTS CALENDAR. (Brooklyn Arts and Culture Association) Text in English. 1971. m. (Sep.-May). USD 20 to individual members; USD 75 to institutional members. **Document type:** *Newsletter.* **Description:** Includes announcements of the council and classified ads.
Formerly: B A C A Calendar of Cultural Events (0045-3242)
Published by: (Brooklyn Arts and Culture Association, Inc.), BACA - Brooklyn Arts Council, 195 Cadman Plaza W, Brooklyn, NY 11201. TEL 718-625-0080, FAX 718-625-3294. Ed. Scott Holman. Circ: 1,500.

069 GBR ISSN 1755-2656
B A F M JOURNAL. Text in English. 1999. 3/yr. free to members (effective 2009). bk.rev. back issues avail. **Document type:** *Journal, Trade.* **Description:** Contains information and news items connected to, about, and of interest to member groups.
Formerly (until 2007): B A F M Newsletter & Museum Visitor (1472-2402); Which was formed by the merger of (1992-1999): Museum Visitor (1360-9629); Which was formerly (1984-1991): British Association of Friends of Museums Yearbook; (1994-1999): B A F M Newsletter (1360-9610); Which was formerly (until 1994): B A F M Broadsheet
Related titles: Online - full text ed.: free (effective 2009).
Published by: British Association of Friends of Museums, c/o Jayne Selwood, Orchard Tax Services Ltd, 141a School Rd, Brislington, Bristol, BS4 4LZ, United Kingdom. TEL 44-1179-777435, admin@bafm.org.uk. Ed. Joy Heffernan.

069 GBR ISSN 0965-8297
AM101.B87
B M MAGAZINE. Text in English. 1969. 3/yr. free to members (effective 2009). adv. bk.rev. illus. **Document type:** *Bulletin, Academic/Scholarly.* **Description:** Contains news and information about current and forthcoming museum exhibitions, news, and other events, as well as articles by curators on new discoveries, or excavations, etc.
Formerly (until 1990): British Museum Society. Bulletin
Indexed: ABM, AICP, BrHumI, RASB.
—IE. CCC.
Published by: British Museum Society, Great Russell St, London, WC1B 3DG, United Kingdom. TEL 44-20-73238000, FAX 44-20-73238616, information@britishmuseum.org, http://www.britishmuseum.org/.

708.95492 BGD
BANGLADESH LALIT KALA. Text in English. 1975. s-a. BDT 100, USD 15.
Indexed: BAS.
Published by: Dhaka Museum, G.P.O. Box 355, Dhaka, 2, Bangladesh.

708.89 DNK ISSN 0908-8725
BANGSBO MUSEUM OG ARKIV. AARBOG. Text in Danish. 1984. a. DKK 110 membership; DKK 120 per issue (effective 2008). **Document type:** *Academic/Scholarly.*
Formerly (until 1993): Bangsbomuseet. Aarbog (0109-8489)
Published by: Bangsbo Museum og Arkiv, Dr. Margrethes Vej 6, Frederikshavn, 9900, Denmark. TEL 45-98-423111, bangsbo@bangsbomuseum.dk, http://www.bangsbomuseum.dk.

069 DEU ISSN 0938-5525
BAYERISCHE MUSEEN. Text in German. 1985. irreg., latest vol.30, 2006. price varies. **Document type:** *Monographic series, Academic/Scholarly.*
Published by: Weltkunst Verlag GmbH, Nymphenburger Str 84, Munich, 80636, Germany. TEL 49-89-1269900, FAX 49-89-12699011, info@weltkunstverlag.de, http://www.weltkunstverlag.de.

508.074 AUS ISSN 0811-3653
CODEN: BEAGET
➤ **BEAGLE**; records of the museums and art galleries of the northern territory. Text in English. 1983. a. (a., occasionally bi-a.), latest vol.24, 2008. AUD 66 per issue (effective 2009). bk.rev. illus. back issues avail. **Document type:** *Journal, Academic/Scholarly.* **Description:** Covers systematic and other studies of the terrestrial, marine and freshwater flora and fauna of the Northern Territory, tropical Australia, Southeast Asia and Oceania; Australian Aboriginal, Southeast Asian and Oceanic art, material culture and archaeology; Northern Territory and Indo-Pacific history, maritime history and archeology; museum conservation, display techniques, taxidermy, publication, public relations, communication and education.
Related titles: Supplement(s): ISSN 1833-7511. 2005.
Indexed: ASFA, B21, B25, BIOSIS Prev, ESPM, GeoRef, MycolAb, Z01.
—Ingenta.
Published by: Museum & Art Gallery of the Northern Territory, GPO Box 4646, Darwin, N.T. 0801, Australia. TEL 61-8-89998203, FAX 61-8-89998148, natsiaa@nt.gov.au, http://www.nt.gov.au. Ed., R&P Chris Glasby.

708 CAN
BEAVERBROOK ART GALLERY. ANNUAL REPORT. Text in English. 1987. a. **Document type:** *Corporate.*
Published by: Beaverbrook Art Gallery, P O Box 605, Fredericton, NB E3B 5A6, Canada. TEL 506-458-8545, FAX 506-459-7450. Ed. Caroline Walker. R&P Laurie Glenn. Circ: 1,500.

069 CHN
BEIJING WENBO/BEIJING CULTURAL RELICS AND MUSEUMS. Text in Chinese. 1995. q. USD 26.80 (effective 2008). **Document type:** *Journal, Academic/Scholarly.*
Published by: Beijing shi Wenwuju/Beijing Municipal Administration of Cultural Heritage, 36, Fuxue Hutong, Dongcheng District, Beijing, 100007, China. TEL 86-10-64032023, FAX 86-10-64074377. **Dist. by:** China International Book Trading Corp, 35 Chegongzhuang Xilu, Haidian District, PO Box 399, Beijing 100044, China. TEL 86-10-68412045, FAX 86-10-68412023, cibtc@mail.cibtc.com.cn, http://www.cibtc.com.cn.

069 DEU ISSN 1433-8475
BEITRAEGE ZUR UR- UND FRUEHGESCHICHTE MECKLENBURG-VORPOMMERNS. Text in German. 1967. irreg., latest vol.48, 2008. price varies. **Document type:** *Monographic series, Academic/Scholarly.*
Formerly (until 1991): Beitraege zur Ur- und Fruehgeschichte der Bezirke Rostock, Schwerin und Neubrandenburg (0138-4279)

Published by: Landesamt fuer Kultur und Denkmalpflege, Domhof 4/5, Schwerin, 19055, Germany. TEL 49-385-52140, FAX 49-385-5214198, poststelle@kulturerbe-mv.de, http://www.kulturwerte-mv.de.

069.09483 NOR ISSN 0808-0402
BERGEN MUSEUM. AARBOK. Text in Norwegian. 1995. a. price varies. **Document type:** *Yearbook.*
Published by: Bergen Museum, PO Box 7800, Bergen, 5020, Norway. TEL 47-55-589360, FAX 47-55-589364, post@bm.uib.no, http://www.bergenmuseum.uib.no.

069 DEU
BERLINER SCHRIFTEN ZUR MUSEUMSFORSCHUNG. Text in German. 1981. irreg., latest vol.24, 2008. price varies. **Document type:** *Monographic series, Academic/Scholarly.*
Formerly (until 2007): Berliner Schriften zur Museumskunde
Published by: Staatliche Museen zu Berlin, Preussischer Kulturbesitz. Institut fuer Museumsforschung, In der Halde 1, Berlin, 14195, Germany. TEL 49-30-8301460, FAX 49-30-8301504, ifm@smb.spk-berlin.de, http://www.smb.museum/ifm/.

BIBLIOTHEQUES ET MUSEES. *see* HISTORY—History Of Europe

THE BIOLOGY CURATOR. *see* BIOLOGY

BLACHREPORT MUSEUM. *see* BUSINESS AND ECONOMICS—Marketing And Purchasing

069 DEU ISSN 0947-3998
BODENDENKMALPFLEGE IN MECKLENBURG-VORPOMMERN. Text in German. 1964. irreg., latest vol.56, 2008. price varies. **Document type:** *Yearbook, Academic/Scholarly.*
Formerly (until 1991): Bodendenkmalpflege in Mecklenburg (0067-9461)
Indexed: AnthLit, B24, BrArAb, FR, IBR, IBZ, NAA, NumL, RASB, RILM. —INIST.
Published by: Landesamt fuer Kultur und Denkmalpflege, Domhof 4/5, Schwerin, 19055, Germany. TEL 49-385-52140, FAX 49-385-5214198, poststelle@kulturerbe-mv.de, http://www.kulturwerte-mv.de. Circ: 400 (paid).

069 ESP ISSN 0210-8445
BOLETIN AURIENSE. Text in Spanish. 1943. a. **Document type:** *Journal, Consumer.*
Supersedes (in 1971): Museo Arqueologico Provincial de Orense. Boletin (0212-3681)
Related titles: ◆ Supplement(s): Boletin Auriense. Anexos. ISSN 0212-3185.
Indexed: FR, RILM.
Published by: Museo Arqueologico Provincial de Orense, C. del Obispo Carrascosa, 1, Apdo. de Correseo 145, Orense, 32080, Spain. TEL 34-988-223884, FAX 34-988-223701.

069 ESP ISSN 0212-3185
BOLETIN AURIENSE. ANEXOS. Text in Spanish. 1982. irreg. **Document type:** *Monographic series, Consumer.*
Related titles: ◆ Supplement to: Boletin Auriense. ISSN 0210-8445.
Published by: Museo Arqueologico Provincial de Orense, C. del Obispo Carrascosa, 1, Apdo. de Correseo 145, Orense, 32080, Spain. TEL 34-988-223884, FAX 34-988-223701.

069 ITA ISSN 1828-4779
BOLOGNA DEI MUSEI. Text in Italian. 2001. s-a. **Document type:** *Magazine, Consumer.*
Published by: Comune di Bologna, Piazza Maggiore 6, Bologna, 40121, Italy. TEL 39-051-2193111, http://www.comune.bologna.it/.

069 NLD ISSN 1872-1249
BONNE FANS. Text in Dutch. 1985. s-a. **Document type:** *Bulletin.*
Published by: Vereniging van Vrienden van het Bonnefantenmuseum, Postbus 1735, Maastricht, 6201 BS, Netherlands. TEL 31-43-3561435, vrienden@bonnefanten.nl, http://www.bonnefanten.nl.

708.89 DNK ISSN 1398-9073
BORNHOLMS MUSEUM, BORNHOLMS KUNSTMUSEUM. Text in Danish. 1932. a. DKK 225 to individual members (effective 2008). illus. back issues avail. **Document type:** *Yearbook, Consumer.*
Former titles (until 1996): Fra Bornholms Museum (0107-4849); (until 1980): Nyt fra Bornholms Museum (0107-4784)
Published by: Bornholms Museum, Sct Mortensgade 29, Roenne, 3700, Denmark. TEL 45-56-950735, FAX 45-56-950745, bm@bornholmmusem.dk, http://www.bornholmsmuseum.dk. Ed. Ann Vibeke Knudsen. Circ: 3,000.

069 NGA ISSN 1115-0335
DT515.9.B597
BORNO MUSEUM SOCIETY. NEWSLETTER. Text in English. 1989. q. **Document type:** *Newsletter, Consumer.*
Indexed: AICP, AnthLit.
Published by: Borno Museum Society, c/o University of Maiduguri, PO Box 1069, Maiduguri, Borno State, Nigeria. TEL 234-76-231900, http://www.univie.ac.at/afrikanistik/homepageneu/african.maiduguri.html. Ed. Gisela Seidensticker-Brikay.

069 USA ISSN 0084-7992
BOWDOIN COLLEGE. MUSEUM OF ART. OCCASIONAL PAPERS. Text in English. 1972. irreg., latest vol.3, 1988. price varies.
Formerly: Walker Art Museum. Bulletin
Published by: Bowdoin College, Museum of Art, 9400 College Station, Brunswick, ME 04011-8494. TEL 207-725-3275, FAX 207-725-3762.

069 USA ISSN 1052-4681
F189.S14
A BRIEF RELATION. Text in English. 1979. q. USD 20 (effective 1999). adv. bk.rev. **Document type:** *Newsletter.* **Description:** Brings news on the activities, exhibits, programs, staffing of and visitations to this national historic landmark in Maryland, which is an outdoor museum of history, archaeology, and natural history.
Former titles: Historic St. Mary's City Newsletter; St. Marie's City Newsletter; Our Town We Call St. Maries
Published by: Historic St. Mary's City Foundation, Inc., PO Box 24, St. Mary's City, MD 20686. TEL 301-862-0990, FAX 301-862-0968. Ed. Karin B Stanford. Circ: 900 (paid).

069 ESP ISSN 0211-318X
BRIGANTIUM. Text in Spanish, Catalan. 1980. a. **Document type:** *Journal, Academic/Scholarly.*
Published by: Museo Arqueologico e Historico de Coruna, Castelo de San Anton, Coruna, 15821, Spain.

708.11 CAN ISSN 0045-3005
F1086
BRITISH COLUMBIA MUSEUMS ASSOCIATION. MUSEUM ROUND UP. Text in English. 1961. q. CAD 36; CAD 48 foreign (effective 1999). adv. **Document type:** *Newsletter.*
Media: Microfilm.
Published by: British Columbia Museums Association, Ste 523 409 Granville St, Vancouver, BC V6C 1T2, Canada. TEL 604-669-5342, FAX 604-669-5343. Ed., R&P, Adv. contact Owen Williams TEL 604-660-0840. Circ: 650.

069.5 GBR
➤ **BRITISH MUSEUM. RESEARCH PUBLICATIONS.** Text in English. 1978. irreg. (6 to 8/yr.), latest no.172, 2009. price varies. back issues avail. **Document type:** *Monographic series, Academic/Scholarly.* **Description:** Aims to make available research and information on different aspects of the Museum's collections.
Formerly (until 2004): British Museum. Occasional Paper (0142-4815)
Related titles: Online - full content ed.
Indexed: FR, GeoRef.
—IE, Ingenta. **CCC.**
Published by: (Trustees of the British Museum), The British Museum, Great Russell St, London, WC1B 3DG, United Kingdom. TEL 44-20-73238000, FAX 44-20-73238616, information@britishmuseum.org. Ed. Dr. Josephine Turquet. **Dist. by:** The British Museum Press, 46 Bloomsbury St, London WC1B 3QQ, United Kingdom.

708.95955 BRN ISSN 0068-2918
BRUNEI MUSEUM JOURNAL. Text in English. 1969. a. BND 10, USD 15. illus.
Indexed: AICP, BAS, BibLing, EI.
Published by: Brunei Museum, Kota Batu, Bandar Seri Begawan, Brunei Darussalam. TEL 02-222952, FAX 02-242727. Ed. P M Dato Shariffiddin. Circ: 3,000.

708.95955 BRN
BRUNEI MUSEUM JOURNAL. MONOGRAPH. Text in English. 1970. irreg., latest vol.6, 1986. BND 10 per issue; BND 20 per issue in United States. **Document type:** *Monographic series, Academic/Scholarly.*
Published by: Brunei Museum, Kota Batu, Bandar Seri Begawan, Brunei Darussalam. TEL 02-244545, FAX 02-242727.

708 BRN ISSN 0084-8131
BRUNEI MUSEUM. SPECIAL PUBLICATION/MUZIUM BRUNEI. PENERBITAN KHAS. Text in English, Malay. 1972. irreg., latest vol.25, 1996. price varies. **Document type:** *Monographic series, Academic/Scholarly.*
Published by: Brunei Museum, Kota Batu, Bandar Seri Begawan, Brunei Darussalam. TEL 02-244545, FAX 02-242727. Ed. P M Dato Shariffiddin. Circ: 1,000.

069 069.1 USA ISSN 0882-651X
GR110.M3
BUGEYE TIMES. Text in English. 1976. q. membership. cum.index: 1976-1992. back issues avail. **Document type:** *Newsletter.* **Description:** Provides information of interest to the Calvert Marine Museum; includes past and coming events; short reports on topics related to local maritime history, paleontology, or marine biology.
Published by: Calvert Marine Museum, PO Box 97, Solomons, MD 20688. TEL 410-326-2042, FAX 410-326-6691. Ed. Paul L Berry. Circ: 2,500.

069 DEU
BUNDESVERBAND FREIBERUFLICHER KULTURWISSENSCHAFTLER. SCHRIFTEN. Text in German. 2007. irreg., latest vol.3, 2010. price varies. **Document type:** *Monographic series, Academic/Scholarly.*
Published by: Transcript, Muehlenstr 47, Bielefeld, 33607, Germany. TEL 49-521-63454, FAX 49-521-61040, live@transcript-verlag.de.

069 USA
BURKE NEWS. Text in English. 1985. q. looseleaf. membership. bk.rev. back issues avail. **Document type:** *Newsletter.* **Description:** Designed to build interest in the areas of natural history, Northwest and Native arts, as well as culture by the museum.
Former titles: Pacific Currents; Thomas Burke Memorial Washington State Museum Newsletter
Indexed: SpeleolAb.
Published by: University of Washington, Thomas Burke Memorial Washington State Museum, DB 10, Seattle, WA 98195. TEL 206-543-5592, FAX 206-685-3039. Ed., R&P Ruth Pelz TEL 206-616-1550. Circ: 1,300.

BYHORNET/BALLERUP HISTORICAL SOCIETY. *see* HISTORY—History Of Europe

C; international contemporary art. *see* ART

069.4 CAN ISSN 1180-3223
C C I NEWSLETTER/BULLETIN DE L'I C C. Text in English. 1988. s-a. free. **Document type:** *Newsletter.* **Description:** Covers various aspects of art conservation, preservation, and restoration.
Formerly (until 1992): Canadian Conservation Institute. Newsletter (1193-4808)
Related titles: Online - full text ed.: ISSN 1719-5853. 1998.
Indexed: A&ATA.
—**CCC.**
Published by: Canadian Conservation Institute/Institut Canadien de Conservation, 1030 Innes Rd, Ottawa, ON K1A 0C8, Canada. TEL 613-998-3721, FAX 613-998-4721, cci-icc_publications@pch.gc.ca. Ed. Mary-Lou Simac.

333.72 CAN
C C I NOTES/NOTES DE L'I C C. Text in English. irreg. CAD 2 newsstand/cover.
Published by: Canadian Conservation Institute/Institut Canadien de Conservation, 1030 Innes Rd, Ottawa, ON K1A 0C8, Canada. TEL 613-998-3721, FAX 613-998-4721, http://www.cci-icc.gc.ca.

333.72 CAN ISSN 0706-4152
AM145
C C I TECHNICAL BULLETINS/I C C BULLETINS TECHNIQUES. Text in English, French. 1975. irreg., latest vol.16. CAD 6. bibl.; illus. back issues avail. **Document type:** *Bulletin.* **Description:** Disseminates information on current techniques and principles of conservation of use to curators and conservators of Canada's cultural artifacts.
Indexed: A&ATA.
Published by: Canadian Conservation Institute/Institut Canadien de Conservation, 1030 Innes Rd, Ottawa, ON K1A 0C8, Canada. TEL 613-998-3721, FAX 613-998-4721. Ed. Mary-Lou Simac.

069.094 FRA ISSN 1019-9977
C I M C I M PUBLICATIONS. (Comite International des Musees et Collections d'Instruments de Musique) Text in English. 1993. irreg.
Indexed: RILM.
Published by: International Council of Museums/Conseil International des Musees, c/o Maison de l'UNESCO, 1 rue Miollis, Paris, Cedex 15 75732, France. TEL 33-1-47340500, FAX 33-1-43067862.

069 PRT ISSN 1646-3714
CADERNOS DE SOCIOMUSEOLOGIA. Text in Portuguese. 1993. irreg. free (effective 2006). back issues avail. **Document type:** *Journal, Academic/Scholarly.*
Media: Online - full text.
Published by: (Universidade Lusofona de Humanidades e Tecnologias, Centro de Estudios de Museologia), Universidade Lusofona de Humanidades e Tecnologia, Edicoes Universitarias, Campo Grande 376, Lisbon, 1749-024, Portugal. TEL 351-217-515500, FAX 351-217-577006, http://ulusofona.pt. Ed. Mario Canova Moutinho.

069 BRA
CADERNOS MUSEOLOGICOS. Text in Portuguese. 1982. irreg., latest vol.3, 1990. **Description:** Contains theoretical and technical texts on museum science.
Published by: Instituto do Patrimonio Historico e Artistico Nacional, Departamento de Promocao, Sala 906, Rua da Imprensa, 16, Centro, Rio De Janeiro, RJ 20030-120, Brazil. TEL 55-21-2965115 ext. 254.

069.5 FRA ISSN 2116-6994
CAHIERS DU MUSEE DES BEAUX-ARTS DE CAEN. Text in French. 1991. a. **Document type:** *Consumer.*
Formerly (until 2007): La Gazette
Published by: Musee des Beaux-Arts de Caen, Le Chateau, Caen, 14000, France. TEL 33-2-31304770.

CAHOKIAN. *see* ARCHAEOLOGY

069 CAN ISSN 0701-0281
THE CAIRN. Text in English. 1977. 2/yr. CAD 30 membership (effective 2004). adv. **Document type:** *Newsletter.* **Description:** Describes the current art gallery, heritage exhibitions and upcoming events for members and the public.
Published by: (Peter and Catharine Whyte Foundation), Whyte Museum of the Canadian Rockies, 111 Bear St, P O Box 160, Banff, AB T0L 0C0, Canada. TEL 403-762-2291, FAX 403-762-8919, info@whyte.org, http://www.whyte.org. Ed. Sally Truss. Circ: 2,500 (controlled).

CANADIAN ARTISTS SERIES. *see* ART

070.594 CAN ISSN 0316-1854
CANADIAN MUSEUM OF CIVILIZATION. MERCURY SERIES/MUSEE CANADIEN DES CIVILISATIONS. COLLECTION MERCURE. Text in English, French. 1972. irreg. adv. **Document type:** *Monographic series, Academic/Scholarly.*
Related titles: Microfiche ed.: (from MML); ◆ Series: Canadian Museum of Civilization. Mercury Series. History Division. Paper (No.). ISSN 0316-1900; ◆ Canadian Museum of Civilization. Mercury Series. Canadian Centre for Folk Culture Studies. Paper (No.). ISSN 0316-1897; ◆ Canadian Museum of Civilization. Mercury Series. Archaeological Survey of Canada. Paper (No.). ISSN 0317-2244; ◆ Canadian Museum of Civilization. Mercury Series. Ethnology Paper. ISSN 1709-5875.
Indexed: SpeleolAb.
Published by: Canadian Museum of Civilization, 100 Laurier St, P O Box 3100, Sta B, Hull, PQ J8X 4H2, Canada. Ed. Jean Francois Blanchette. R&P Nicole Chamberland. Adv. contact Pam Coulas.

621.13074 CAN ISSN 0820-8336
CANADIAN MUSEUM OF FLIGHT & TRANSPORTATION. MUSEUM NEWSLETTER. Text in English. 1975. q. membership. adv. bk.rev. illus. **Document type:** *Newsletter.* **Description:** Describes the museum's activities, functions and services. Includes articles on historic aviation.
Published by: Canadian Museum of Flight & Transportation, Unit 200, 5333 216th St Langley Airport, Langley, BC V3A 4R1, Canada. TEL 604-532-0035, FAX 604-532-0056. Ed. Brad Thomas. Adv. contact George Proulx. Circ: 2,000 (controlled).

708.1 USA ISSN 1530-0218
➤ **CANTOR CENTER FOR VISUAL ART AT STANFORD UNIVERSITY. JOURNAL.** Text in English. 1971. biennial. back issues avail. **Document type:** *Journal, Academic/Scholarly.* **Description:** Contains facts on selected works of art in the museum and a list of acquisitions for the two-year period with descriptions of all exhibits in both the museum and nearby gallery.
Former titles (until 1999): Stanford University Museum of Art Journal (1081-4825); (until 1993): Stanford Museum (0085-6665)
Indexed: AIAP, B24.
Published by: Stanford University, Stanford Museum of Art, 328 Lomita Dr, Stanford, CA 94305. TEL 650-725-2775, FAX 650-725-571.

708.89 DNK ISSN 1395-7961
CARLSBERGFONDET. AARSSKRIFT. Text in Danish. 1976. a. back issues avail. **Document type:** *Yearbook, Consumer.*
Former titles (until 1995): Frederiksborgmuseet. Aarskrift (0105-9858); (until 1977): Frederiksborgmuseet. Beretning
Related titles: Online - full text ed.: 1995.
Published by: Carlsbergfondet, H C Andersens Blvd 35, Copenhagen V, 1553, Denmark. TEL 45-33-435363, FAX 45-33-435364, carlsbergfondet@carlsbergfondet.dk.

708 USA ISSN 1084-4341
N5020
CARNEGIE INTERNATIONAL. Text in English. 1982. triennial. free to members (effective 2011). **Document type:** *Magazine, Trade.* **Description:** Exhibition catalogue of international contemporary art.
Published by: Carnegie Museum of Art, 4400 Forbes Ave, Pittsburgh, PA 15213. TEL 412-622-3131.

069 DNK ISSN 0109-047X
DL291.K44
CARTHA. Variant title: Kerteminde Museum. Aarsskrift. Text in Danish. 1982. a. DKK 100 per issue (effective 2009). illus. **Document type:** *Yearbook, Consumer.*

Published by: Oestfyns Museer, c/o Kerteminde Museum, Strandgade 7, Kerteminde, 5300, Denmark. TEL 45-65-323727, kertemindemuseer@kertemindemuseer.dk, http://www.kertemindemuseer.dk.

741.58074 USA ISSN 1085-0333
NC1420
CARTOON TIMES. Text in English. 1986. q. USD 35 membership individuals; USD 50 membership families. adv. **Document type:** *Newsletter.* **Description:** Informs Cartoon Art Museum members of museum's activities (exhibits, events, classes). Includes articles on cartoonists, and associated artwork and graphics.
Formerly: Cartoon Art Museum Newsletter
Published by: Cartoon Art Museum, c/o Lara Pepp, Publicist, 814 Mission St, San Francisco, CA 94103-3018. TEL 415-CAR-TOON, FAX 415-243-8666. Ed., R&P, Adv. contact Lara Pepp. Circ: 800.

CATALOGO DE LAS EXPOSICIONES DE ARTE. *see* ART

069 USA ISSN 2158-2971
CATALYST (DENVER). Text in English. 200?. bi-m. free to members (effective 2010). back issues avail. **Document type:** *Magazine, Trade.* **Description:** Aims to excites minds of all ages through scientific discovery and the presentation and preservation of the world's unique treasures.
Formerly (until 2010): Denver Museum of Nature & Science. Magazine
Related titles: Online - full text ed.: ISSN 2158-298X. free (effective 2010).
Published by: Denver Museum of Nature & Science, 2001 Colorado Blvd, Denver, CO 80205. TEL 303-370-6000, feedback@dmns.org.

069.5 NLD ISSN 2210-6111
CATHARIJNE. Text in Dutch. 1982. q. **Document type:** *Magazine, Consumer.*
Formerly (until 2008): Catharijnebrief (0923-1684)
Published by: Museum Catharijneconvent, Postbus 8518, Utrecht, 3503 RM, Netherlands. TEL 31-30-2313835, FAX 31-30-2317896, secretariaat@catharijneconvent.nl, http://www.catharijneconvent.nl.

069 USA
CHARLES H. MACNIDER MUSEUM NEWSLETTER. Text in English. 1966. bi-m. membership. **Document type:** *Newsletter.* **Description:** Informs museum members, the public and professional colleagues about events, activities, and exhibitions occurring at the museum.
Published by: Charles H. MacNider Museum, 303 Second St, S E, Mason City, IA 50401-3988. TEL 515-421-3666. Ed. Richard E Leet. Circ: 1,000.

069.094 FRA ISSN 1776-1220
CHATEAU ET DES MUSEES DE BLOIS. CAHIERS. Text in French. 1983. a., latest vol.39, 2009. **Document type:** *Journal, Consumer.*
Former titles (until 2003): Societe des Amis du Chateau et des Musees de Blois. Bulletin (1634-3913); (until 2001): Societe des Amis du Chateau et des Musees de Blois (0984-3469)
Published by: Societe des Amis du Chateau et des Musees de Blois, Chateau de Blois, Blois, 41000, France.

CHICAGO ARTISTS' NEWS. *see* ART

CHILDREN'S MUSEUM NEWSLETTER. *see* CHILDREN AND YOUTH—For

069 BRA ISSN 0103-2909
Q105.A1
CIENCIAS EM MUSEUS. Text mainly in Portuguese; Abstracts in English. 1989. a. BRL 15, USD 20 (effective 2000). charts; illus.
Published by: Museu Paraense Emilio Goeldi, Av Magalhaes Barata 376, Sao Braz, Belem, PA 66040-170, Brazil. TEL 55-91-32193317, FAX 55-91-32490466, editora@museu-goeldi.br.

708.1 USA ISSN 1064-2242
CINCINNATI ART MUSEUM. ANNUAL REPORT. Text in English. 1930; N.S. 1950. a. free. reprints avail.
Formerly: Cincinnati Art Museum. Bulletin (0069-4061)
Related titles: Microform ed.: N.S. (from PQC).
Indexed: A06, A07, A30, A31, AA, AIAP, ArtInd, B04.
Published by: Cincinnati Art Museum, 953 Eden Park, Cincinnati, OH 45202. TEL 513-721-2787, FAX 513-639-2888. Ed. Sarah Sedlacek. R&P Jennifer Reis. Circ: 5,000.

CIRCUIT RIDER (FRANKFORT). *see* HISTORY—History Of North And South America

069 ESP ISSN 2172-1688
COLECCION LA EDAD DE ORO. Text in Spanish. 1995. a. **Document type:** *Monographic series, Academic/Scholarly.*
Published by: Museo de Teruel, Plaza de Fray Anselmo Polanco, 3, Teruel, 44001, Spain. TEL 34-978-600150, FAX 34-978-602832, http://www.aragob.es/edycul/museos/muteruel.htm.

069 TWN ISSN 1726-2038
QH193.T35
COLLECTION AND RESEARCH. Variant title: Baozang yu Yanjiu. Text in English. 1989. irreg. **Document type:** *Monographic series, Academic/Scholarly.*
Formerly (until 1989): National Museum of Natural Science. Bulletin (1015-8448)
Indexed: AICP, B25, BIOSIS Prev, MycolAb, Z01.
—BLDSC (3310.466252).
Published by: Guoli Ziran Kexue Bowuguan/National Museum of Natural Sciences, 1 Kuan Chien Rd, Taichung, 402, Taiwan. TEL 886-4-3226940, FAX 886-4-3235367, http://www.nmns.edu.tw/. Ed. Chia-Wei Li.

508.074 USA ISSN 0831-4985
QH61 CODEN: COLFEQ
COLLECTION FORUM. Text in English. 1985. s-a. free membership (effective 2005). bk.rev. **Description:** Serves as official journal of the Society. Disseminates substantive information concerning the development and preservation of natural history collections.
Indexed: A&ATA, Z01.
Published by: Society for the Preservation of Natural History Collections (SPNHC), PO Box 797, Washington, DC 20044-0797. http://www.spnhc.org/. Circ: 800.

708 USA ISSN 1046-2252
COLLECTIONS (COLUMBIA). Text in English. 1988. bi-m. USD 3 to members. adv. bk.rev. cum.index: 1988-1989. **Document type:** *Newsletter.* **Description:** Presents articles on European and American art.
Indexed: B24.
Published by: Columbia Museum of Art, PO Box 2068, Columbia, SC 29202-2068. TEL 803-799-2810, FAX 803-343-2150. Ed., Adv. contact Genia Weinberg. R&P Kevin Tucker. B&W page USD 500, color page USD 1,075; trim 11 x 8.5. Circ: 3,500.

069 026 USA ISSN 1550-1906
AM133
COLLECTIONS (WALNUT CREEK); a journal for museum and archives professionals. Text in English. 2004. q. USD 43 to individuals; USD 149 to institutions (effective 2010). back issues avail. **Document type:** *Journal, Academic/Scholarly.*
Indexed: B24.
—BLDSC (3310.407174). **CCC.**
Published by: AltaMira Press, 4501 Forbes Blvd, Ste 200, Lanham, MD 20706. TEL 301-459-3366, FAX 301-429-5748, journals@altamirapress.com. Ed. Juilee Decker. Pub. Marcus Boggs TEL 212-529-3888 ext.304.

069.4 CHE ISSN 0010-0781
COLLECTIONS BAUR. BULLETIN. Text in French, English. 1965. s-a. CHF 5 per issue. **Document type:** *Bulletin, Academic/Scholarly.* **Description:** Features descriptions and history of objects in the collection of Japanese and Chinese artifacts. Includes museum events and activities.
Published by: Fondation Alfred et Eugenie Baur-Duret, 8 rue Munier Romilly, Geneva, 1206, Switzerland. TEL 41-22-3461729, FAX 41-22-7891845, email@collections-baur.ch, http://www.collections-baur.ch. Ed. Frank Dunand. Circ: 1,000.

069 USA
COLUMN (ELMIRA). Text in English. bi-m. membership. **Document type:** *Newsletter.* **Description:** Includes articles on current exhibitions, artists, events of interest to members and general public.
Published by: Arnot Art Museum, 235 Lake St, Elmira, NY 14901. TEL 607-734-3697, FAX 607-734-5687. Ed. Carolyn J Warner. Circ: 1,500.

708.1 USA
THE COLUMN (MEMPHIS). Text in English. 1955. bi-m. USD 16 to members (effective 2006). **Document type:** *Newsletter, Consumer.*
Former titles (until 1998): Brooks; (until 1993): Memphis Brooks Museum of Art. Inside Brooks; (until Feb. 1992): Memphis Brooks Museum of Art. Newsletter; Brooks Memorial Art Gallery. Newsletter
Published by: Memphis Brooks Museum of Art, Inc., Board of Directors, 1934 Poplar Ave, Memphis, TN 38104. TEL 901-544-6200, FAX 901-725-4071, brooks@brooksmuseum.org, http://www.brooksmuseum.org. Ed. Claudia Towell. R&P Diane Jalfon. Circ: 3,700 (controlled).

069 ARG ISSN 1852-8600
COMISION NACIONAL DE MUSEOS Y DE MONUMENTOS Y LUGARES HISTORICOS. BOLETIN INFORMATIVO. Text in Spanish. 2006. q. **Document type:** *Bulletin, Consumer.*
Published by: Comision Nacional de Museos y de Monumentos y Lugares Historicos, Ave. de Mayo, 556, Buenos Aires, C1084AAN, Argentina. TEL 54-11-43435835, FAX 54-11-43436960, comisiondemuseos@cultura.gov.ar, http://www.monumentosysitios.gov.ar/.

069.1 USA
CONFLUENCE (WENATCHEE). Text in English. 1984. q. USD 25 to members. adv. bk.rev. back issues avail. **Description:** Covers regional history.
Published by: North Central Washington Museum Association, 127 S Mission St, Wenatchee, WA 98801. TEL 509-664-5989, FAX 509-664-5997. Ed. Mary L Thomsen. Circ: 1,000 (paid).

CONSERVATION SCIENCE IN CULTURAL HERITAGE; historical - technical journal. *see* ART

508.074 USA
CONSERVE O GRAM. Text in English. 1993. base vol. plus s-a. updates. looseleaf. back issues avail. **Document type:** *Government.* **Description:** Contains technical advice on the care and preservation of museum artifacts and guides N.P.S. staff in carrying out projects identified in collection management planning documents.
Related titles: Online - full text ed.: free (effective 2011).
Published by: U.S. Department of the Interior, National Parks Service, 1849 C St NW, Washington, DC 20240. TEL 202-208-6843.

069 USA
CONSTITUTION CHRONICLE. Text in English. 1976. q. membership. **Document type:** *Newsletter.* **Description:** Keeps members of the U.S.S. Constitution Museum informed of museum activities and exhibits.
Formerly (until 1981): U S S Constitution Museum. News and Notes
Published by: U S S Constitution Museum Foundation, PO Box 1812, Boston, MA 02129. TEL 617-426-1812, FAX 617-242-0496. Ed., R&P Stephanie M Nichols. Circ: 14,000.

069 DEU
COOLIBRI; Kultur Freizeit Programm im Ruhrgebiet. Text in German. 1983. m. EUR 20; free newsstand/cover (effective 2006). adv. **Document type:** *Magazine, Consumer.*
Published by: Roland Scherer Verlag und Werbeservice GmbH, Ehrenfeldstr 34, Bochum, 44789, Germany. TEL 49-234-937370, FAX 49-234-9373799. Ed. Werner Dickob. Adv. contact Christa Sielhorst. B&W page EUR 5,150, color page EUR 7,750; trim 190 x 260. Circ: 134,156 (controlled).

069 NLD
CORPUS VASORUM ANTIQUORUM (LEIDEN). Text in Dutch. 1972. irreg., latest vol.15, 2003. price varies. **Document type:** *Monographic series.*
Published by: Allard Pierson Museum, Oude Turfmarkt 127, Amsterdam, 1012 GC, Netherlands. TEL 31-20-5252552, FAX 31-20-5252561, allard.pierson.museum@uva.nl, http://www.allardpiersonmuseum.nl.

CORRAL DUST. *see* HISTORY

069.5 BEL ISSN 1783-8509
LE COURRIER DU MUSEE ET DE SES AMIS. Text in French. 1988. q. EUR 1.50 per issue (effective 2007). illus. 20 p./no.; back issues avail. **Document type:** *Bulletin, Academic/Scholarly.* **Description:** Reviews and documents temporary exhibits at the museum at the Catholic University of Louvain.
Formerly (until 2006): Le Courrier du Passant (0775-8073)
Published by: (Universite Catholique de Louvain), Universite Catholique de Louvain, Musee de Louvain-la-Neuve, Musee, College Erasme, Pl Blaise Pascal 1, Louvain-la-Neuve, 1348, Belgium. TEL 32-10-474841, FAX 32-40-472413, acc@muse.ucl.ac.be. Ed. B Van den Driessche.

069 700 GBR
COURTAULD INSTITUTE OF ART. COURTAULD RESEARCH PAPERS. Text in English. 2000. irreg., latest 2002, Nov. price varies. 152 p./no.; back issues avail. **Document type:** *Monographic series, Academic/Scholarly.* **Description:** Contains original recently researched material on western art history from classicism to the 20th century.
Published by: (Courtauld Institute of Art), Ashgate Publishing Ltd (Subsidiary of: Gower Publishing Co. Ltd.), Wey Ct E, Union Rd, Farnham, Surrey GU9 7PT, United Kingdom. TEL 44-1252-736600, FAX 44-1252-736736, ashgate.online@ashgate.com.

069 GBR ISSN 2046-8814
▼ **THE COWPER AND NEWTON JOURNAL.** Text in English. 2011. a. GBP 6 domestic to non-members; GBP 12 foreign to non-members; free to members (effective 2011). **Document type:** *Journal, Trade.* **Description:** Focuses on scholarly research and criticism in the fields listed above, but it will also take in subjects of more general interest such as local topography, family connections, and reminiscences of people and places.
Published by: The Cowper and Newton Museum, Orchard Side, Market Place, Olney, Buckinghamshire MK46 4AJ, United Kingdom. TEL 44-1234-711516, FAX 44-1234-711516, cowpernewtonmuseum@btconnect.com.

CRYSTAL PALACE FOUNDATION. NEWS BULLETIN. *see* HISTORY—History Of Europe

CRYSTAL PALACE MATTERS. *see* HISTORY—History Of Europe

069 ESP ISSN 1133-0783
CUADERNOS DEL SUROESTE. Text in Spanish. 1989. a. **Document type:** *Journal, Academic/Scholarly.*
Published by: Museo de Huelva, Alameda Sundheim, 13, Huelv, Andalucia 21003, Spain. TEL 34-959-259300, FAX 34-959-285547.

069 ESP ISSN 1988-7426
CULTURA MUSEUS. Text in Catalan. 199?. irreg. **Document type:** *Monographic series, Academic/Scholarly.*
Published by: Generalitat de Catalunya, Departament de Cultura/Museu d'Arqueologia de Catalunya, Parque de Montjuich, Ps De Santa Madrona, 39-41, Barcelona, 08038, Spain. TEL 34-972-770208, FAX 34-972-774260, macempuries.cultura@gencat.net, http://www.mac.es/.

708.1 792 780 USA ISSN 1542-5347
CULTURAL EVENTS OF NEW JERSEY. Text in English. 10/yr. (monthly Mar. through Oct., bimonthly Jan./Feb., Nov./Dec.). USD 12 (effective 2002).
Published by: Cultural Events of NJ, 325 Morristown Rd., Gillette, NJ 07933-1817. culturaleventsnj@aol.com. Pub. Elissa Merkl.

069.4 USA ISSN 0011-3069
QH70 CODEN: CRTRAH
➤ **CURATOR**; the Museum journal. Text in English. 1958. q. GBP 173 in United Kingdom to institutions; EUR 202 in Europe to institutions; USD 281 elsewhere to institutions; GBP 191 combined subscription in United Kingdom to institutions (print & online eds.); EUR 222 combined subscription in Europe to institutions (print & online eds.); USD 310 combined subscription elsewhere to institutions (print & online eds.) (effective 2012). adv. bk.rev. charts; illus. cum.index. 120 p./no.; back issues avail.; reprint service avail. from PSC. **Document type:** *Magazine, Academic/Scholarly.*
Related titles: Microform ed.: (from PQC); Online - full text ed.: ISSN 2151-6952. GBP 173 in United Kingdom to institutions; EUR 202 in Europe to institutions; USD 281 elsewhere to institutions (effective 2012).
Indexed: A&ATA, A07, A22, A30, A31, AA, ABM, AbAn, AmH&L, ArtInd, B04, BRD, BrArAb, CA, E01, E03, ERI, GeoRef, IBR, IBZ, NumL, RASB, SpeleolAb, T02, W03, W05.
—BLDSC (3493.500000), IE, Infotrieve, Ingenta. **CCC.**
Published by: (California Academy of Sciences), Wiley-Blackwell Publishing, Inc. (Subsidiary of: Wiley-Blackwell Publishing Ltd.), 111 River St, Hoboken, NJ 07030. TEL 201-748-6000, FAX 201-748-6088, info@wiley.com, http://www.wiley.com/. Ed. Zahava D Doering.

069 CAN ISSN 0384-9627
AM21
CURRENTLY: ONTARIO MUSEUM NEWS. Text in English. 1972. bi-m. CAD 25 (effective 2000). adv. bk.rev. back issues avail. **Document type:** *Newsletter.* **Description:** Issues of interest to workers in Ontario museums.
Formerly: Ontario Museum News
Published by: Ontario Museum Association, George Brown House, 50 Baldwin St, Toronto, ON M5T 1L4, Canada. TEL 416-348-8672, FAX 416-348-0438, http://www.museumsontario.com. Ed., Adv. contact Sarah Palmer. B&W page CAD 500; trim 10 x 7. Circ: 2,000.

708.2 GBR ISSN 1750-9394
DACORUM HERITAGE TRUST. ANNUAL REVIEW. Text in English. 2000. a. **Document type:** *Journal, Trade.*
Published by: Dacorum Heritage Trust, The Museum Store, Clarence Rd, Berkhamsted, Herts HP4 3YL, United Kingdom. http://www.dacorumheritage.org.uk/.

069 SWE ISSN 0070-2528
➤ **DAEDALUS (STOCKHOLM)**; tekniska museets aarsbok. Text in Swedish; Text occasionally in English. 1931. a. price varies. adv. cum.index; 1931-1981, 1982-1993. **Document type:** *Journal, Academic/Scholarly.* **Description:** Contains articles on science and technology, their interdependence with society both today and yesterday.
Related titles: Online - full text ed.
Indexed: ABS&EES, AcaI, CLOSS, FR, GSS&RPL, HECAB, MLA, MagInd, SWR&A.
—INIST.
Published by: Tekniska Museet/Swedish National Museum of Science and Technology, Museivaegen 7, Norre Djurgaarden, PO Box 27842, Stockholm, 11593, Sweden. TEL 46-8-4505600, FAX 46-8-4505601, info@tekniskamuseet.se, http://www.tekniskamuseet.se. Ed. Mats Hojeberg. R&P Peter Larsson TEL 46-8-4505663. Circ: 4,000.

➤ **DANGAN TIANDI/ARCHIVES WORLD.** *see* LIBRARY AND INFORMATION SCIENCES

069 DNK ISSN 0905-1600
AM5
DANSK TIDSSKRIFT FOR MUSEUMSFORMIDLING. Variant title: Tidsskrift for Museumsformidling. Text in Danish. 1976. irreg., latest vol.28, 2008. price varies. back issues avail. **Document type:** *Monographic series, Academic/Scholarly.*
Former titles (until 1990): D T M (0901-9138); (until 1984): Dansk Tidsskrift for Museumsformidling (0105-130X)
Published by: Forlaget Hikuin, Moesgaard, Moesgaard Alle 20, Hoejbjerg, 8270, Denmark. TEL 45-86-272443, henvendelser@hikuin.dk. Ed., Pub. Jens Vellev TEL 45-89-424603.

069.5 USA ISSN 1067-8808
N531.D38
DAVID & ALFRED SMART MUSEUM OF ART. BULLETIN. Text in English. 1988. a. membership; USD 5 to non-members (effective 2001). illus. **Document type:** *Bulletin.* **Description:** Contains articles concerning art objects in the Smart collection; reports on exhibitions, accessions, loans, events, and gifts to the Museum, and programs for Museum audiences.
Formerly (until 1989): David and Alfred Smart Gallery Bulletin (1041-6005)
Indexed: B24.
Published by: David & Alfred Smart Museum of Art, University of Chicago, 5550 S Greenwood Ave, Chicago, IL 60637. TEL 773-702-0180, FAX 773-702-3121. Ed. Stephanie Smith. R&P Jennifer Widman. Circ: 1,000.

DAYTON ART INSTITUTE. MEMBER QUARTERLY. *see* ART

070.594 USA
DELAWARE ART MUSEUM NEWSLETTER. Text in English. 1984. bi-m. membership. **Document type:** *Newsletter.*
Former titles: Delaware Art Museum Quarterly; Delaware Art Museum Bulletin
Published by: Delaware Art Museum, 2301 Kentmere Pkwy, Wilmington, DE 19806. TEL 302-571-9590, FAX 302-571-0220. Ed. Lise Monty. R&P Eliz Appleby. Circ: 5,000.

069 355 NZL ISSN 1179-7789
DESPATCHES. Text in English. 200?. m. free to qualified personnel (effective 2010). back issues avail. **Document type:** *Newsletter, Trade.*
Related titles: Online - full text ed.: ISSN 1179-7797. free (effective 2010).
Published by: New Zealand National Army Museum, State Hwy One, PO Box 45, Waiouru, New Zealand. TEL 64-6-3876911, FAX 64-6-3876319. Ed. Carlene Sykes.

069.5 DEU
DEUTSCHE GUGGENHEIM MAGAZINE. Text in English. 2007. irreg., latest vol.15, 2011. **Document type:** *Magazine, Consumer.* **Description:** Provides an overview of the latest exhibitions and art activities of the Deutsche Guggenheim museum.
Published by: Deutsche Guggenheim, Unter den Linden 13/15, Berlin, 10117, Germany. TEL 49-30-2020930, FAX 49-30-20209320, berlin.guggenheim@db.com.

069 DEU ISSN 1438-0595
AM49
DEUTSCHER MUSEUMSBUND. BULLETIN. Text in German. 1996. q. **Document type:** *Journal, Academic/Scholarly.* **Description:** Reports on internal discussions, announces news, and publishes information and resolutions of the Deutscher Museumsbund.
Indexed: ABM.
Published by: Deutscher Museumsbund e.V., In der Halde 1, Berlin, 14195, Germany. TEL 49-30-84109517, FAX 49-30-84109519, office@museumsbund.de, http://www.museumsbund.de. Ed. Vera Neukirchen.

069 DEU ISSN 0012-1339
AM101
➤ **DEUTSCHES MUSEUM. ABHANDLUNGEN UND BERICHTE.** Text in German. 1929. irreg., latest vol.17, 2002. price varies. bibl.; charts; illus. **Document type:** *Monographic series, Academic/Scholarly.*
Indexed: ChemAb, MLA-IB, P30.
—Linda Hall. **CCC.**
Published by: Deutsches Museum, Museumsinsel 1, Munich, 80538, Germany. TEL 49-89-21791, FAX 49-89-2179324, information@deutsches-museum.de, http://www.deutsches-museum.de. Circ: 7,000.

708.1 USA ISSN 2160-5262
DEVELOPMENTS (PHILADELPHIA). Text in English. 199?. q. **Document type:** *Magazine, Consumer.*
Published by: Philadelphia Museum of Art, PO Box 7646, Philadelphia, PA 19101. TEL 215-763-8100, FAX 215-236-4465, library@philamuseum.org, http://www.philamuseum.org.

069 GBR ISSN 1743-8608
DIRECTORY OF MUSEUMS, GALLERIES AND BUILDINGS OF HISTORIC INTEREST IN THE UNITED KINGDOM. Text in English. 1993. a., latest 2008. GBP 350 per issue (effective 2009). **Document type:** *Directory.*
Formerly (until 2003): Directory of Museums and Special Collections in the United Kingdom
—**CCC.**
Published by: (Museums Association, Publications Centre), Routledge (Subsidiary of: Taylor & Francis Group), 2 Park Sq, Milton Park, Abingdon, Oxon OX14 4RN, United Kingdom. TEL 44-20-70176000, FAX 44-20-70176699, info@routledge.co.uk, http://www.routledge.com.

069.5 730 NLD ISSN 1879-4580
DRENTS MUSEUM OVER HEDENDAAGSE FIGURATIEVE KUNSTENAARS. MONOGRAFIEEN. Text in Dutch. 1999. irreg., latest vol.15, 2009. price varies.
Published by: (Drents Museum), Waanders Uitgevers, Postbus 1129, Zwolle, 8001 BC, Netherlands. TEL 31-38-4673400, FAX 31-38-4673401, info@waanders.nl, http://www.waanders.nl.

708 DEU ISSN 0418-0615
DRESDENER KUNSTBLAETTER. Text in German. 1956. bi-m. EUR 18; EUR 4 newsstand/cover (effective 2006). adv. bk.rev. abstr.; illus. index. back issues avail. **Document type:** *Magazine, Consumer.*
Indexed: B24, DIP, IBR, IBZ, NumL.
—BLDSC (3623.400000).
Published by: Staatliche Kunstsammlungen Dresden, Residenzschloss, Taschenberg 2, Dresden, 01067, Germany. TEL 49-351-4914701, FAX 49-351-4914777, info@skd.smwk.sachsen.de, http://www.skd-dresden.de. Ed. Karin Perssen. adv.: B&W page EUR 103, color page EUR 255. Circ: 800 (controlled).

708.11 CAN ISSN 1920-8308
▼ **THE EAR.** Text in English. 2009. 3/yr. **Document type:** *Journal, Consumer.* **Description:** Devoted to perspectives of mental health, philosophy and ideologies communicated through words and visual art.
Published by: Gallery Gachet, Publications Group, 88 E Cordova St, Vancouver, BC V6A 1K2, Canada. TEL 604-687-2468, FAX 604-687-1196.

THE EARLY BIRD. *see* HISTORY—History Of North And South America

069 USA ISSN 1070-8618
EARTHSONG. Text in English. 1960. 6/yr. USD 50 to members (effective 2006). bk.rev. **Document type:** *Newsletter, Consumer.* **Description:** Covers museum events, art exhibits, artist profiles, member trips, other institutions of interest, collecting.
Former titles (until 1993): Heard Museum Newsletter (1052-6544); (until 1990): Heard Museum (1049-8729); (until vol.10, no.1, 1968): Museum Notes (Phoenix)
Published by: Heard Museum, 2301 N Central Ave, Phoenix, AZ 85004-1323. TEL 602-252-8840, FAX 602-252-9757, andrear@heard.org, http://www.heard.org. Ed. Rebecca Stenholm. Pub. Wendy Johnston. Circ: 5,000 (paid and controlled).

069 DEU
▼ **EDITION MUSEUMSAKADEMIE JOANNEUM.** Text in German. 2010. irreg. price varies. **Document type:** *Monographic series, Academic/Scholarly.*
Published by: Transcript, Muehlenstr 47, Bielefeld, 33607, Germany. TEL 49-521-63454, FAX 49-521-61040, live@transcript-verlag.de.

070 ZAF ISSN 1011-193X
ELEPHANT'S CHILD; newsletter of the Albany Museum. Text in English. 1978. 3/yr. free. 10 p./no.; **Document type:** *Newsletter.*
Published by: Albany Museum, Somerset St, Grahamstown, East Cape 6139, South Africa. TEL 27-46-622312, FAX 27-46-622398. Ed. P Black.

708 790.1 USA
ENCYCLOPEDIA OF EXHIBITIONS. Text in English. 1990. a. USD 90 (effective 1999). adv. **Document type:** *Monographic series, Trade.*
Published by: National Association of Theatre Owners, 46051 Lankershim Blvd., Ste. 340, N. Hollywood, CA 91602-1891. TEL 818-406-1778, FAX 818-506-0269. Ed. Jim Kozak. R&P, Adv. contact Mary Delacruz. Circ: 3,000.

069 DEU
ERLEBNIS: MUSEUM. Text in German. 1980. 4/yr. free. 8 p./no.; back issues avail. **Document type:** *Newspaper, Consumer.* **Description:** Contains current and comprehensive information on exhibitions and museums in Schleswig-Holstein.
Former titles (until 1999): Museum Spezial; (until 1996): Museen in Schleswig-Holstein (0720-7883)
Published by: Museumsamt Schleswig-Holstein, Haddebyer Chausee 14, Busdorf, 24866, Germany. TEL 49-4621-9365-0, FAX 49-4621-936555, museumsamts-h@t-online.de, http://www.museumsamt-sh.de. Circ: 220,000.

708 CAN
EUROPEAN AND AMERICAN PAINTING, SCULPTURE AND DECORATIVE ARTS, VOLUME 1: 1300-1800. Text in English. 1987. biennial. USD 97.50. illus. **Document type:** *Catalog.* **Description:** Catalogs the permanent collection at the National Gallery of Canada.
Related titles: French ed.: Peinture, Sculpture et Arts Decoratifs Europeens et Americains, Volume 1: 1300-1800.
Published by: National Gallery of Canada, Publications Division, c/o Irene Lillico, 380 Sussex Dr, Ottawa, ON K1N 9N4, Canada. TEL 613-990-0537, FAX 613-990-7460.

069 USA ISSN 1068-2317
N800
EVERSON MUSEUM OF ART BULLETIN. Text in English. 1959. q. USD 35 to non-members (effective 2001). adv. bibl.; illus. 20 p./no.; **Document type:** *Bulletin.*
Indexed: AIAP.
Published by: Everson Museum of Art, 401 Harrison St, Syracuse, NY 13202. TEL 315-474-6064, FAX 315-474-6943. Ed. Katherine E Blodgett. R&P Michael Flanagan. Circ: 3,500.

070.594 GBR ISSN 2044-7582
▼ **EVOLVE.** Text in English. 2009. q. GBP 13 to non-members; GBP 3.50 per issue to non-members; free to members (effective 2010). **Document type:** *Magazine, Consumer.* **Description:** Features interviews, exhibition news and research information of Natural History Museum.
Published by: Natural History Museum, Cromwell Rd, London, SW7 5BD, United Kingdom. TEL 44-20-79425000, publishing@nhm.ac.uk.

069 GBR
EXETER CITY MUSEUMS & ART GALLERY. Text in English. q. GBP 5 to members. **Document type:** *Newsletter.* **Description:** Contains retrospective news and information about Exeter's four museums, including exhibition reviews and news of recent acquisitions.
Former titles: Museums of Exeter; Exeter Museum News; Exeter Museums Bulletin and View; Exeter Museums News Event and Exhibitors
Published by: Exeter Museums Service, Royal Albert Memorial Museum, Queen St, Exeter, Devon EX4 3RX, United Kingdom. TEL 44-1932-265858, FAX 44-1392-421252. Ed. Ruth Randall. Circ: 3,000.

EXHIBITION FOOTNOTES. *see* ART

069 USA
EXHIBITIONIST (WASHINGTON). Text in English. 1996 (Spring, vol.15, no.1). s-a. free to members (effective 2011). back issues avail. **Document type:** *Journal, Academic/Scholarly.* **Description:** Features exhibit reviews and commentary, project and practical reports, book reviews, exhibit reviews, technical articles, and other essays of interest to the museum exhibition profession.
Published by: National Association for Museum Exhibition, 1220 L St NW, Ste 100-270, Washington, DC 20005.

708.38 POL ISSN 0867-0625
N7255.P6
EXIT; nowa sztuka w Polsce. Text in English, Polish. 1990. q. PLZ 36 domestic; USD 24 foreign (effective 2002 - 2003). **Document type:** *Magazine, Consumer.* **Description:** Aims to promote new art in Poland.
Published by: Staromiejski Dom Kultury, Galeria Promocyjna, Rynek Starego Miasta 2, Warsaw, 00272, Poland. Ed. Jacek Werbanowski. Circ: 3,000. **Co-sponsor:** Ministerstwo Kultury i Sztuki/Ministry of Culture and National Heritage.

EXPLORE. *see* SCIENCES: COMPREHENSIVE WORKS

069 385 CAN ISSN 1912-0494
EXPORAIL NEWS. Text in English. 2001. s-a. **Document type:** *Newsletter, Consumer.*
Published by: Exporail, 110, rue Saint-Pierre, Saint-Constant, PQ J5A 1G7, Canada. TEL 450-632-2410, 450-638-1522, FAX 450-638-1563, http://www.exporail.org/public/index.asp.

F W WEEKLY. (Fort Worth) *see* MUSIC

707.4 USA ISSN 1043-3740
FAIR NEWS. Text in English. 1968. bi-m. looseleaf. USD 20 domestic; USD 20 in Canada; USD 30 elsewhere (effective 2001). adv. bk.rev. back issues avail. **Document type:** *Newsletter.*
Published by: World's Fair Collectors Society, Inc., PO Box 20806, Sarasota, FL 34276-3806. TEL 941-923-2590. Ed., Pub., R&P Michael R Pender. Adv. contact Fran Pender. page USD 50; 11 x 8.5. Circ: 450 (paid).

FINSKT MUSEUM. *see* ARCHAEOLOGY

▼ **FLATLAND JOURNAL.** *see* ART

FOCUS ON SECURITY; the magazine of library, archive and museum security. *see* CRIMINOLOGY AND LAW ENFORCEMENT—Security

FOLIA HISTORICO-NATURALIA MUSEI MATRAENSIS. *see* SCIENCES: COMPREHENSIVE WORKS

069 ITA ISSN 2037-3570
▼ **FONDAZIONE DINO ED ERNESTA SANTARELLI.** Text in Italian. 2009. irreg. price varies. **Document type:** *Monographic series, Academic/Scholarly.*
Published by: L' Erma di Bretschneider, Via Cassiodoro 19, Rome, 00193, Italy. TEL 39-06-6874127, FAX 39-06-6874129, lerma@lerma.it, http://www.lerma.it.

069 ITA ISSN 2036-1998
FONDAZIONE MUSEI SENESI. Text in Italian. 2005. irreg. **Document type:** *Monographic series, Academic/Scholarly.*
Published by: Silvana Editoriale, Via Margherita de Vizzi 86, Cinisello Balsamo, MI 20092, Italy. TEL 39-02-61836337, FAX 39-02-6172464, silvanaeditoriale@silvanaeditoriale.it, http://www.silvanaeditoriale.it.

355.31074 USA ISSN 1071-7110
F394 .F62
FORT CONCHO GUIDON. Text in English. 1982. q. free to members (effective 2010). 16 p./no. 2 cols./p.; back issues avail. **Document type:** *Newsletter, Trade.*
Formerly: Fort Concho Members Dispatch
Related titles: Online - full text ed.: free (effective 2010).
Published by: (Fort Concho Museum), Fort Concho Museum Press, 630 S Oakes St, San Angelo, TX 76903. TEL 325-481-2646, FAX 325-657-4540, admin@fortconcho.com, http://www.fortconcho.com.

FORT TICONDEROGA MUSEUM. BULLETIN. *see* MILITARY

708.1 USA ISSN 1534-2948
FORUM NEWS (WASHINGTON, D C). Text in English. 1994. bi-m. free to members (effective 2010). back issues avail. **Document type:** *Newsletter, Trade.*
Formerly (until 1999): Historic Preservation Forum News (1079-4441)
Published by: National Trust for Historic Preservation, 1785 Massachusetts Ave, NW, Washington, DC 20036. TEL 202-588-6000, 800-944-6847, FAX 202-588-6038, members@nthp.org, http://www.preservationnation.org.

069 GBR ISSN 2045-1113
FRIENDS OF YORK ART GALLERY. NEWSLETTER. Text in English. 2003. s-a. **Document type:** *Newsletter, Trade.*
Formerly (until 2008): News from the Friends of York Art Gallery (1742-0237)
Published by: York Art Gallery, Exhibition Sq, York, YO1 7EW, United Kingdom. TEL 44-1904-687687.

069 USA
FRIENDS' QUARTERLY (ENFIELD). Text in English. 1988. q. USD 36 to members. illus. **Document type:** *Newsletter.* **Description:** Covers news and activities of the local museum.
Published by: Museum at Lower Shaker Village, Rt 4A, Enfield, NH 03748. TEL 603-632-4346. Ed. Deborah L Coffin. Circ: 600.

069.7 NLD ISSN 1872-1273
FRIES MUSEUM MAGAZINE. Text in Dutch. 2006. s-a.
Published by: (Fries Museum), Uitgeverij Intermed, Postbus 2306, Groningen, 9704 CH, Netherlands. TEL 31-50-3120042, FAX 31-50-3139373, info@intermed.nu, http://www.intermed.nu. Circ: 35,000.

069.5 387.2 NLD ISSN 1877-878X
FRIES SCHEEPVAART MUSEUM EN OUDHEIDKAMER. JAARBOEK. Text in Dutch. 1965. a. EUR 12.50 (effective 2011).
Published by: Fries Scheepvaart Museum, Postbus 186, Sneek, 8600 AD, Netherlands. TEL 31-515-414057, info@friesscheepvaartmuseum.nl.

709.05 FRA ISSN 1769-7433
FROG. Text in French. 2005. s-a. **Document type:** *Magazine, Consumer.*
Address: 17 Rue du Palais, Dijon, 21000, France.

FUJIAN WENBO/FUJIAN RELICS AND MUSEUM. *see* ARCHAEOLOGY

708.6 ESP ISSN 1130-9849
FUNDACION LA CAIXA. PANORAMA. Text in Spanish. 1991. m. free. illus. **Document type:** *Magazine, Trade.* **Description:** Covers art exhibits and musical performances supported by the foundation.
Formerly (until 1991): Fundacio Caixa de Pensiones. Informatiu (1130-7870)
Related titles: English ed.: ISSN 1130-9865; Catalan ed.: ISSN 1130-9857.
Published by: Fundacion la Caixa, Via Laietana 56, Barcelona, 08003, Spain. TEL 34-93-4046076. Ed. Jesus Val Jarrin. Circ: 130,000.

069 SWE ISSN 0282-7301
DL621
FYND. Text in Swedish. 1985. s-a. SEK 150 membership (effective 2007). **Document type:** *Magazine, Consumer.*
Formed by the merger of (1968-1985): Fyndmeddelanden (0345-3804); (1982-1984): Goeteborg Arkeologiska Museum. Aarsbok (0280-3429); Which was formerly (1958-1980): Goeteborg Arkeologiska Museum. Aarstryck (0348-3657)
Indexed: NAA.
Published by: (Goeteborgs Stadsmuseum), Fornminnesfoereningen i Goeteborg/The Archaeological Association in Gothenburg, Postgatan 8, Goeteborg, 41113, Sweden. TEL 46-31-7018474, info@fornminnesforeningen-gbg.se, http://www.fornminnesforeningen-gbg.se.

069 ITA ISSN 0072-0070
NC27.I8
GABINETTO DISEGNI E STAMPE DEGLI UFFIZI. CATALOGHI. Text in Italian. 1951. irreg., latest vol.87, 2001. price varies. **Document type:** *Catalog, Academic/Scholarly.*
Published by: Casa Editrice Leo S. Olschki, Viuzzo del Pozzetto 8, Florence, 50126, Italy. TEL 39-055-6530684, FAX 39-055-6530214, celso@olschki.it, http://www.olschki.it. Circ: 2,000.

069 ITA ISSN 1122-0848
GABINETTO DISEGNI E STAMPE DEGLI UFFIZI. INVENTARIO. Text in Italian. 1986. irreg., latest vol.3, 1992. price varies. **Document type:** *Monographic series, Academic/Scholarly.*
Published by: Casa Editrice Leo S. Olschki, Viuzzo del Pozzetto 8, Florence, 50126, Italy. TEL 39-055-6530684, FAX 39-055-6530214, celso@olschki.it, http://www.olschki.it.

708.9892 PRY ISSN 1017-2823
GALERIA MICHELE MALINGUE. CATALOGO. Text in English, Spanish. 1988. q. USD 50.
Published by: (Galeria Michele Malingue), Distribuidor Internacional Publicaciones Paraguayas, Ayoreos e-4a y 5a, PO Box 2507, Asuncion, Paraguay. TEL 595-21-495367, FAX 595-21-447460. Ed. Adriana Almada. Circ: 1,000.

708.3 DEU ISSN 0072-0089
GALERIE NIERENDORF. KUNSTBLAETTER. Text in German. 1963. irreg., latest vol.87, 2010. price varies. **Document type:** *Catalog, Trade.*
Published by: Galerie Nierendorf, Hardenbergstr 19, Berlin, 10623, Germany. TEL 49-30-8325013, FAX 49-30-3129327, galerie@nierendorf.com, http://www.nierendorf.com. Ed., Pub. Florian Karsch. Circ: 2,000.

708.36 AUT
GALERIE SANCT LUCAS. GEMAELDE ALTER MEISTER. Text in German. 1930. a. illus. **Document type:** *Catalog, Trade.*
Published by: Galerie Sanct Lucas, Palais Pallavicini, Josefsplatz 5, Vienna, W 1010, Austria. TEL 43-1-5128237, FAX 43-1-513320316, roman.herzig@eunet.at.

708.5 ITA
GALLERIA DEL CAVALLINO. ARTE. Text in Italian. 1956. irreg. price varies. illus. **Document type:** *Monographic series, Academic/Scholarly.*
Published by: Cavallino Edizioni d'Arte, Calle delle Bande, Castello 5269A, Venice, VE 30122, Italy. TEL 39-041-5210488, FAX 39-041-5210642, cavallino@edcavallino.it, http://www.edcavallino.it.

GALLERIES. *see* ART

708 USA
GALLERY GUIDE. Text in English. 2008. m. adv. **Document type:** *Magazine, Consumer.*
Formed by the merger of (200?-2007): Art Now Gallery Guide: Philadelphia / Mid-Atlantic Edition; Which was formerly (until 200?): Art Now / Philadelphia Gallery Guide; (Nov.2007-Dec.2007): Gallery Guide. New York / New England; Which was formed by the merger of (2005-2007): Gallery Guide. New York; (200?-2007): Gallery Guide. Boston / New England; (until 200?): Art Now Boston/New England Gallery Guide
Related titles: Online - full text ed.
Published by: Louise Blouin Media (Subsidiary of: L T B Media), 601 West 26th St, Ste 410, New York, NY 10001. TEL 212-447-9555.

069.094895 DNK ISSN 0909-945X
AM101
DEN GAMLE BY. Text in Danish. 1928. a. DKK 300 membership; DKK 150 to students (effective 2009). cum.index: 1927-1996. back issues avail. **Document type:** *Consumer.* **Description:** Publishes studies of Danish and European cultural history.
Formerly (until 1994): Koebstadmuseet den Gamle By. Aarbog (0105-9254)
Indexed: RASB.
Published by: Den Gamle By - Danmarks Koebstadsmuseum, Viborgvej 2, Aarhus C, 8000, Denmark. TEL 45-86-123188, FAX 45-86-760687, mail@dengamleby.dk, http://www.dengamleby.dk.

069 GBR ISSN 2044-1576
GARDEN MUSEUM. JOURNAL. Text in English. 2001. s-a. free to members (effective 2010). **Document type:** *Journal, Trade.*
Formerly (until 2009): Museum of Garden History. Journal (1475-8431)
Published by: Garden Museum, Lambeth Palace Rd, London, SE1 7LB, United Kingdom. TEL 44-20-74018865, FAX 44-20-74018869, info@gardenmuseum.org.uk.

069 USA
GAZETTE (CLAYTON). Text in English. 1969. 3/yr. membership. adv. bk.rev. **Document type:** *Newsletter.*
Published by: Antique Boat Museum, 750 Mary St, Clayton, NY 13624. TEL 315-686-4104, FAX 315-686-2775. Ed. Judy Foster. R&P Rebecca Hopfinger. Circ: 2,500.

GELDERS ERFGOED. *see* HISTORY—History Of Europe

069 JPN ISSN 0435-219X
GENDAI NO ME. Text in Japanese. 1954. bi-m. JPY 3,300 (effective 2000). **Document type:** *Newsletter.* **Description:** Contains articles on exhibitions and events of the three institutions, for the purpose of supplying fundamental information.
Published by: National Museum of Modern Art Tokyo, 3 Kitano-Marukoen, Chiyoda-ku, Tokyo, 102-8322, Japan. TEL 81-3-3561-1400, FAX 81-3-3561-8100.

069 IRL ISSN 0144-5294
QE50
GEOLOGICAL CURATOR. Text in English. 1974. s-a. free (effective 2003). adv. bk.rev. 2 cols./p.; Supplement avail.; back issues avail. **Document type:** *Bulletin, Trade.* **Description:** Provides information and advice on all matters relating to geology in museums, including professional codes, and fosters the advancement of the documentation and conservation of geological sites.
Formerly (until 1980): Geological Curators' Group. Newsletter (0308-681X)
Indexed: GeoRef, SpeleolAb, Z01.
—Ingenta, INIST, Linda Hall.
Published by: Geological Curators' Group, c/o Patrick N. Wyse Jackson, Ed., Dept. of Geology, Trinity College, Dublin, 2, Ireland. TEL 353-1-6081477, FAX 353-1-6711199, wysjcknp@tcd.ie. Ed. Patrick Wyse Jackson. R&P Patrick N Wyse Jackson. Adv. contact Patrick N. Wyse Jackson.

069 IRL ISSN 0265-0126
GEOLOGICAL CURATOR. SUPPLEMENT. Text in English. 1974. irreg. price varies. **Document type:** *Bulletin.*
Formerly (until 1978): Geological Curators' Group. Newsletter. Supplement
Indexed: GeoRef, SpeleolAb.
Published by: Geological Curators' Group, c/o Patrick N. Wyse Jackson, Ed., Dept. of Geology, Trinity College, Dublin, 2, Ireland. TEL 353-1-6081477, FAX 353-1-6711199, wysjcknp@tcd.ie.

069 USA
GEORGIA MUSEUM OF ART NEWSLETTER. Text in English. 1983. bi-m. back issues avail. **Document type:** *Newsletter.*
Former titles: Doings; Georgia Museum of Art. News
Published by: Georgia Museum of Art, University of Georgia, Athens, GA 30602. TEL 706-542-4662, FAX 706-542-1051, buramsey@arches.uga.edu, http://www.uga.edu/gamuseum/. Ed. Bonnie Ramsey. R&P Annelies Mondi TEL 706-542-0439. Circ: 4,000.

069 AUT ISSN 1013-6800
GESELLSCHAFT FUER VERGLEICHENDE KUNSTFORSCHUNG IN WIEN. MITTEILUNGEN. Text in German. 1930. q. adv. bk.rev. **Document type:** *Bulletin, Academic/Scholarly.*
Indexed: B24, FR.
Published by: Gesellschaft fuer Vergleichende Kunstforschung in Wien, Universitaetsstr 7, Vienna, W 1010, Austria. Ed. Eckart Vancsa. **Subscr. to:** Institut fuer Kunstgeschichte der Universitatscampus Altes AKH, Spitalgasse 2-4, Vienna, W 1090, Austria.

GIFU-KEN HAKUBUTSUKAN CHOSA KENKYU HOKOKU/GIFU PREFECTURAL MUSEUM. BULLETIN. *see* SCIENCES: COMPREHENSIVE WORKS

069.5 305.897 USA
GILCREASE. Text in English. 19??. s-a. free to members (effective 2010). illus. **Document type:** *Newsletter, Trade.* **Description:** Provides members of noteworthy exhibits and offers perspectives on issues related to the museum's collections.
Published by: Thomas Gilcrease Museum Association, 1400 N Gilcrease Museum Rd, Tulsa, OK 74127. TEL 918-596-2788, FAX 918-596-2700, membership@gilcrease.org, http://www.gilcrease.org.

069.1 NLD ISSN 1878-4720
GLANS. Variant title: Nieuwsbrief Westfries Museum. Westfries Museum Nieuwsbrief. Text in Dutch. a. **Document type:** *Newsletter, Consumer.*
Published by: (Stichting Vrienden van het Westfries Museum), Westfries Museum, Achterom 2-4, Hoorn, 1621 KV, Netherlands. TEL 31-229-280028, http://www.westfriesmuseum.nl.

708.11 CAN ISSN 1926-4593
GLENBOW MUSEUM. CALENDAR. Text in English. 200?. 3/yr. free to members (effective 2011). **Document type:** *Consumer.* **Description:** Includes all exhibitions and programs happening at Glenbow plus information about upcoming events.
Related titles: Online - full text ed.: free (effective 2011).
Published by: Glenbow Museum, 130 Ninth Ave SE, Calgary, AB T2G 0P3, Canada. TEL 403-268-4100, FAX 403-265-9769, glenbow@glenbow.org.

708.92 NLD ISSN 1872-4590
GOEDE PAPIEREN. Text in Dutch. 1992. s-a.
Formerly (until 2006): De Weduwe Ida (0928-270X); Which superseded in part (in 1992): Juffrouw Ida (0927-4847); Which was formerly (until 1982): Juffrouw Idastraat 11 (0927-4839)
Published by: Letterkundig Museum, Postbus 90515, The Hague, 2509 LM, Netherlands. TEL 31-70-3339666, FAX 31-70-3477941, info@nlmd.nl, http://www.letterkundigmuseum.nl.

069 500 SWE ISSN 0374-7921
GOETEBORGS NATURHISTORISKA MUSEUM. AARSTRYCK. Text in Swedish. 1906. a. back issues avail. **Document type:** *Yearbook.*
Supersedes in part (in 1953): Goeteborgs Museum. Aarsstryck (0282-7980)
Related titles: Online - full text ed.
Indexed: Z01.
Published by: Goeteborgs Naturhistoriska Museum/Goeteborg Natural History Museum, Slottskrogen, PO Box 7283, Stockholm, 40235, Sweden. TEL 46-31-7752400, FAX 46-31-129807, info@gnm.se.

GOOD EARTH ASSOCIATION. NEWSLETTER. *see* AGRICULTURE

069 HRV ISSN 1332-9308
GRADSKI MUZEJ SISAK. GODISNJAK. Text in Croatian. 2000. a. **Document type:** *Yearbook.*
Indexed: RILM.
Published by: Gradski Muzej Sisak, Ul Kralja Tomislava 10, Sisak, 44000, Croatia. TEL 385-44-811811, FAX 385-44-543225, gradski-muzej-sisak@sk.htnet.hr, http://www.muzej-sisak.hr.

708 FRA ISSN 1959-1764
GRANDE GALERIE. Text in French. 2007. q. EUR 14.90 (effective 2007 - 2008). **Document type:** *Magazine, Consumer.*
Published by: Musee du Louvre, 34-36 Quai du Louvre, Paris, Cedex 01 75058, France. TEL 33-1-44848039, http://www.louvre.fr.

069 760 NLD ISSN 1877-816X
▼ **GRAPHIC DESIGN MUSEUM. MUSEUM MAGAZINE.** Variant title: G D M Magazine. Museum Magazine. Text in Dutch. 2009. irreg., latest vol.3, 2009. **Document type:** *Magazine, Consumer.*
Published by: Graphic Design Museum, Boschstraat 22, Breda, 4811 GH, Netherlands. TEL 31-76-5299900, FAX 31-76-5299929, info@graphicdesignmuseum.com, http://www.graphicdesignmuseum.nl.

069 GBR ISSN 0958-9864
GUERNSEY MUSEUM & ART GALLERY. MONOGRAPHS. Text in English. 198?. irreg., latest 2007. back issues avail. **Document type:** *Monographic series, Consumer.*
Related titles: Online - full text ed.
—BLDSC (4224.070000).
Published by: Guernsey Museum & Art Gallery, Candie Gardens, St Peter Port, Guernsey, GY1 1UG, United Kingdom. TEL 44-1481-726518, FAX 44-1481-715177.

708.51 TWN ISSN 1011-9078
N8.C5
GUGONG WENWU YUEKAN/NATIONAL PALACE MUSEUM. MONTHLY OF CHINESE ART. Text in Chinese. 1983. m. USD 150 (effective 2001). bk.rev. illus. index. **Description:** Presents articles, analysis, and photographs of Chinese art and antiques from the museum's collection.
Published by: National Palace Museum/Kuo Li Ku Kung Po Wu Yuan, Wai Shuang Hsi, Shih Lin, Taipei, Taiwan. TEL 886-2-2882-1230, FAX 886-2-2882-1440, webmaster@npm.gov.tw, http://www.npm.gov.tw. Ed. Chang Yueh Yun. Circ: 10,000. **US subscr. to:** World Journal Bookstore, 141-07 20th Ave., Whitestone, NY 11357. TEL 718-748-8889.

708.951249 TWN ISSN 1011-9094
N7340
GUGONG XUESHU JIKAN/NATIONAL PALACE MUSEUM RESEARCH QUARTERLY. Text in Chinese. 1966. q. USD 250. charts; illus. index. **Document type:** *Bulletin.* **Description:** Journal to further an atmosphere of scholarly and professional exchange.
Formerly (until 1983): National Palace Museum Quarterly (0454-675X)
Indexed: BAS, CA, T02.
Published by: National Palace Museum/Kuo Li Ku Kung Po Wu Yuan, Wai Shuang Hsi, Shih Lin, Taipei, Taiwan. FAX 886-2-2882-1440, http://www.npm.gov.tw. Eds. Ming-Chu Fung, Tieng-Jen Lin. R&P Sai-Lan Hu. Circ: 1,000.

069 JPN ISSN 0911-9892
AM77.A1
HAKUBUTSUKAN KENKYU/MUSEUM STUDIES. Text in Japanese. 1928. m. JPY 12,600 (effective 2001). **Document type:** *Bulletin.*
Incorporates (in 1986): Hakubutsukan Nyusu
Published by: Japanese Association of Museums/Nihon Hakubutsukan Kyokai, Shoyu-Kaikan 3-3-1, Kasumigaseki, Chiyoda-ku, Tokyo, 100-0013, Japan. TEL 81-3-3591-7190. Ed. Koichi Igarashi.

613.075 AUS ISSN 1447-445X
HAMMER. Text in English. 1991. s-a. **Document type:** *Newsletter.* **Description:** Each issue contains: a main article on some aspect of acquiring, managing or utilizing collections, news of health and medicine museums and exhibitions around Australia, notices of new publications and journal articles.
Former titles (until 2002): Health and Medicine Museums. Newsletter (1442-1283); (until 1993): Museums Association of Australia. Health and Medicine Museums Section. Newsletter (1036-3041)
Related titles: Online - full text ed.
Published by: Health and Medicine Museums, 57 Queen Victoria St, Bexley, NSW 2207, Australia. TEL 61-2-95872834, FAX 61-3-95872834, cornell@netspace.net.au, http://amol.org.au/hmm/.

HANGAR HAPPENIN'S; what's happening in and about the Yankee Air Museum. *see* AERONAUTICS AND SPACE FLIGHT

069 USA ISSN 0093-1047
Z999
HARRIS AUCTION GALLERIES. COLLECTORS' AUCTION. Key Title: Collectors' Auction (Baltimore). Text in English. 1962. 6/yr. USD 25.
Published by: Harris Auction Galleries, Inc., 873 875 N Howard St, Baltimore, MD 21201. TEL 301-728-7040. Eds. Barr Harris, Christopher Bready. Circ: 1,000.

069 USA ISSN 1523-4401
E98.A7
HEARD MUSEUM JOURNAL. Text in English. 1999. 2/yr. USD 50 membership (effective 2006). **Document type:** *Journal, Consumer.*
Published by: Heard Museum, 2301 N Central Ave, Phoenix, AZ 85004-1323. TEL 602-252-8840, FAX 602-252-9757, andrear@heard.org, http://www.heard.org. Ed. Elizabeth Reynolds. Pub. Wendy Johnston.

069 NLD ISSN 1875-6034
HEIMVIZIER. Variant title: Periodieke Uitgave van het Twents Techniekmuseum H E I M. Text in Dutch. 1991. 3/yr. **Document type:** *Bulletin.*
Formerly (until 2007): H E I M - Hengelo's Educatief Industrie-Museum (1876-052X)
Published by: Twents Techniekmuseum HEIM, Industriestr 9, Hengelo (OV), 7553 CK, Netherlands. TEL 31-74-2430054, FAX 31-74-2435645, info@techniekmuseumheim.nl, http://www.techniekmuseumheim.nl.

708.89 DNK ISSN 1902-6447
HELSINGOER KOMMUNES MUSEER. AARBOG. Text in Danish. 1977. a. illus. **Document type:** *Consumer.*
Former titles (until 2005): Helsingoer Kommunes Museer (0900-1611); (until 1984): Helsingoer Kommunes Museer. Aarbog (0108-0393); (until 1982): Helsingoer Bymuseum. Aarbog (0106-0317)
Indexed: NAA.
Published by: Helsingoer Kommunes Museer, Sct. Anna Gade 36, Helsingoer, 3000, Denmark. TEL 45-49-281800, FAX 45-49-281801, museerne@helsingor.dk, http://www.museerne.helsingor.dk.

HERITAGE AND HISTORY. *see* HISTORY—History Of North And South America

069 GBR
HIGHLIGHT (EDINBURGH). Text in English. 1988. m. free. bk.rev. **Document type:** *Newsletter.* **Description:** Events and activities of the National Museums of Scotland.
Formerly (until 1994): Museum Reporter (0954-0423)
Indexed: NumL.
Published by: National Museums of Scotland, Chambers St, Edinburgh, Midlothian EH1 1JF, United Kingdom. TEL 44-131-225-7534, FAX 44-131-220-4819. R&P Barbara Buchan. Circ: 10,000.

HILL COUNTRY SUN. *see* TRAVEL AND TOURISM

M

HISTORIC FARM BUILDINGS GROUP. REVIEW. *see* ARCHITECTURE

HISTORIC HOUSE NEWS. *see* ARCHITECTURE

069 USA
HISTORICAL DEERFIELD NEWSLETTER. Text in English. 1952. q. free. **Document type:** *Newsletter.*
Formerly: Historic Deerfield Quarterly
Published by: Historic Deerfield, Inc., PO Box 321, Deerfield, MA 01342. TEL 413-774-5581, FAX 413-775-7220, jcameron@historic-deerfield.org. Ed. Grace Friary. Circ: 5,500.

708.89 948.95 DNK ISSN 1399-199X
DL291.B63
HISTORISK AARBOG FOR BOV OG HOLBOEL SOGNE. Text in Danish. 1978. a. DKK 100 membership (effective 2009). back issues avail. **Document type:** *Yearbook, Consumer.*
Former titles (until 1998): Historisk Forening for Visherred, Bov Museum (0905-4723); (until 1989): Fra Bov Museum (0106-8229)
Published by: Historisk Forening for Bov og Holboel Sogne, c/o Asmus J. Brylle, Oestergade 1, Padborg, 6330, Denmark. TEL 45-74-775717, jobry@post.tele.dk, http://www.bovhistorisk.dk.

HISTORY NEWS. *see* HISTORY—History Of North And South America

HIWA KAGAKU HAKUBUTSUKAN KENKYU HOKOKU/HIWA MUSEUM FOR NATURAL HISTORY. MISCELLANEOUS REPORTS. *see* SCIENCES: COMPREHENSIVE WORKS

069 JPN ISSN 0912-778X
HOBETSU CHORITSU HAKUBUTSUKANPO. Text in Japanese. 1982. a. **Document type:** *Academic/Scholarly.*
Published by: Hobetsu Choritsu Hakubutsukan/Hobetsu Museum, 80-6, Hobetsu, Yufutsu, Hobetsu, Hokkaido 054-0211, Japan. http://www.bekkoame.ne.jp/~hobemus/.

069 JPN ISSN 0915-5511
HOKKAIDO KAITAKU KINENKAN CHOSA HOKOKU. Cover title: Historical Museum of Hokkaido. Memoirs. Text in Japanese. 1972. a. 112 p./no.; **Document type:** *Corporate.*
Published by: Hokkaido Kaitaku Kinenkan/Historical Museum of Hokkaido, Konopporo, Atsubetsu-cho, Atsubetsu-ku, Sapporo-shi, Hokkaido 004-0006, Japan. TEL 81-11-8980456, FAX 81-11-8982657, http://www.hmh.pref.hokkaido.jp/. Circ: 1,000.

069 JPN ISSN 1341-2795
DS894.215
HOKKAIDO KAITAKU KINENKAN KENKYU KIYO/HISTORICAL MUSEUM OF HOKKAIDO. BULLETIN. Text in Japanese; Summaries in English. 1972. a. Not for sale. 136 p./no.; **Document type:** *Bulletin, Academic/Scholarly.*
Formerly (until 1995): Hokkaido Kaitaku Kinenkan Kenkyu Nenpo/Historical Museum of Hokkaido. Annual Report (0287-9433)
Published by: Hokkaido Kaitaku Kinenkan/Historical Museum of Hokkaido, Konopporo, Atsubetsu-cho, Atsubetsu-ku, Sapporo-shi, Hokkaido 004-0006, Japan. TEL 81-11-8980456, FAX 81-11-8982657, http://www.hmh.pref.hokkaido.jp/. Circ: 1,000.

069 JPN ISSN 0918-3159
GN301
HOKKAIDORITSU HOPPO MINZOKU HAKUBUTSUKAN KENKYU KIYO/HOKKAIDO MUSEUM OF NORTHERN PEOPLES. BULLETIN. Text and summaries in Japanese, English. 1992. a. **Document type:** *Bulletin.*
Indexed: AICP.
Published by: Hokkaidoritsu Hoppo Minzoku Hakubutsukan/Hokkaido Museum of Northern Peoples, 309-1 Shiomi, Abashiri-shi, Hokkaido 093-0042, Japan. TEL 81-152-45-3888, FAX 81-152-45-3889.

069 JPN ISSN 1348-169X
HOKKAIDOU DAIGAKU SOUGOU HAKUBUTSUKAN KENKYUU HOUKOKU/HOKKAIDO UNIVERSITY MUSEUM. BULLETIN. Text in Japanese. 2003. irreg. **Document type:** *Journal, Academic/Scholarly.*
Indexed: C25, CABA, E12, F08, F12, FCA, G11, H16, O01, P32, P40, PGegResA, R07, S13, S16, Z01.
Published by: Hokkaidou Daigaku Sougou Hakubutsukan/Hokkaido University Museum, N10 W8, Sapporo, 060-0810, Japan. TEL 81-11-7062658, FAX 81-11-7064029, museum-jimu@museum.hokudai.ac.jp, http://www.museum.hokudai.ac.jp/.

069.7 NLD ISSN 1872-4086
HORIZON. Text in Dutch. 1997. q. EUR 10 (effective 2010).
Published by: Stichting Streekmuseum / Volkssterrenwacht Burgum, Menno van Coehoornweg 9, Burgum, 9251 LV, Netherlands. TEL 31-511-465544, info@streekmuseum-volkssterrenwachtburgum.nl. Ed. Jantinus Kleinhuis TEL 31-511-482187. Circ: 625.

HORIZONT; veszprem megyei kozmuvelodesi tajekoztato. *see* CLUBS

707.4 USA
HUNTINGTON LIBRARY, ART COLLECTIONS, AND BOTANICAL GARDENS. CALENDAR. Text in English. 1936. bi-m. free to members (effective 2011). **Document type:** *Newsletter, Consumer.*
Former titles: Huntington Library, Art Gallery and Botanical Gardens. Collections; Huntington Library, Art Gallery and Botanical Gardens. Calendar; Henry E. Huntington Library and Art Gallery. Calendar of Exhibitions (0018-0408)
Published by: Huntington Library, Art Collections and Botanical Gardens, 1151 Oxford Rd, San Marino, CA 91108. TEL 626-405-2100, publicinformation@huntington.org, http://www.huntington.org.

069 USA
I A S M H F NEWSLETTER. Text in English. 1971. bi-m. USD 20. adv. bk.rev. **Document type:** *Newsletter.* **Description:** Covers association and member news.
Formerly: Association of Sports Museums and Halls of Fame. Newsletter
Published by: International Association of Sports Museums and Halls of Fame, 101 W Sutton Pl, Wilmington, DE 19810-4115. TEL 302-475-7068, FAX 302-475-7038. Ed. Al Cartwright. Circ: 200.

708 700 NLD ISSN 1566-760X
I C N-INFORMATIE. Text in Dutch. 2000. irreg., latest vol.15, 2007. free (effective 2009).
Related titles: ◆ English ed.: I C N-Information. ISSN 1873-0396.
Published by: Instituut Collectie Nederland, Postbus 76709, Amsterdam, 1070 KA, Netherlands. TEL 31-20-3054545, FAX 31-20-3054600, info@icn.nl, http://www.icn.nl.

708 700 NLD ISSN 1873-0396
I C N-INFORMATION. Text in English. 2000. irreg. free (effective 2009).
Related titles: ◆ Dutch ed.: I C N-Informatie. ISSN 1566-760X.
Published by: Instituut Collectie Nederland, Postbus 76709, Amsterdam, 1070 KA, Netherlands. TEL 31-20-3054545, FAX 31-20-3054600, info@icn.nl, http://www.icn.nl.

069.094 FRA ISSN 1020-6418
AM1
I C O M NEWS (ENGLISH EDITION). Text in English. 1948. q. free to individual members. bk.rev. abstr.; bibl. **Document type:** *Newsletter, Trade.* **Description:** Provides news of ICOM activities, related international committees, and topics of interest to museum workers. Reports on stolen art, illicit traffic, conferences and events.
Formerly (until 19??): I C O M News (Bilingual Edition) (0018-8999)
Related titles: Spanish ed.: I C O M. Noticias. ISSN 1020-6434; French ed.: I C O M. Nouvelles. ISSN 1020-6426.
Indexed: BrArAb, ChemAb, NumL, RASB, RILM, SCOPUS.
—CCC.
Published by: International Council of Museums/Conseil International des Musees, c/o Maison de l'UNESCO, 1 rue Miollis, Paris, Cedex 15 75732, France. TEL 33-1-47340500, FAX 33-1-43067862, http://www.icom.org. Ed. Laura Gutman. Circ: 18,000.

069 FRA ISSN 1020-5543
AM1
I C O M STUDY SERIES/I C O M CAHIERS D'ETUDE. Text and summaries in English, French, Spanish. 1995. irreg. **Document type:** *Academic/Scholarly.* **Description:** Gives an account of the state of affairs in the museum field for museum professionals.
Related titles: Online - full text ed.: free.
Published by: International Council of Museums/Conseil International des Musees, c/o Maison de l'UNESCO, 1 rue Miollis, Paris, Cedex 15 75732, France. TEL 33-1-4340500, FAX 33-1-43067862, http://www.icom.org. Ed. Laura Gutman.

069 ITA
I LOVE MUSEUMS. Text in Italian. 200?. s-a. **Document type:** *Newspaper, Consumer.*
Published by: (Associazione Musei d'Arte Contemporanea Italiani (A M A C I)), Silvana Editoriale, Via Margherita de Vizzi 86, Cinisello Balsamo, MI 20092, Italy. TEL 39-02-61836337, FAX 39-02-6172464, silvanaeditoriale@silvanaeditoriale.it, http://www.silvanaeditoriale.it.

069 JPN ISSN 1343-8921
IBARAKI-KEN SHIZEN HAKUBUTSUKAN KENKYU HOKOKU/IBARAKI NATURE MUSEUM. BULLETIN. Text in Japanese. 1998. a. **Document type:** *Academic/Scholarly.*
Indexed: Z01.
Published by: Ibaraki-ken Shizen Hakubutsukan/Ibaraki Nature Museum, 700 Osaki, Iwai-city, Ibaraki 306-0622, Japan. TEL 81-297-382000, http://www.nat.pref.ibaraki.jp/index.html.

508.74 USA
E78.I18
IDAHO MUSEUM OF NATURAL HISTORY. OCCASIONAL PAPERS. Text in English. 1958. irreg., latest 2006. price varies. back issues avail. **Document type:** *Monographic series, Trade.*
Former titles (until 1991): Idaho Museum of Natural History. Occasional Papers (0196-7703); (until 1979): Idaho State University Museum. Occasional Papers (0073-4551); (untl 1963): Idaho State College Museum. Occasional Papers (1931-6526)
Indexed: AbAn.
Published by: Idaho Museum of Natural History, Idaho State University, PO Box 8096, Pocatello, ID 83209. TEL 208-236-3168, murddena@isu.edu, http://imnh.isu.edu/.

069 USA ISSN 0737-5093
QH1
IDAHO MUSEUM OF NATURAL HISTORY. SPECIAL PUBLICATIONS. Text in English. 1970 (no.2). irreg., latest 1999. price varies. **Document type:** *Monographic series.* **Description:** Represents unique contributions to the professional literature.
Indexed: GeoRef.
Published by: Idaho Museum of Natural History, Idaho State University, PO Box 8096, Pocatello, ID 83209. TEL 208-236-3168, murddena@isu.edu, http://imnh.isu.edu/.

629.130174 JPN
IKOMAYAMA UCHU KAGAKUKAN NYUSU. Text in Japanese. 1969. irreg. **Description:** News of the museum.
Published by: Ikomayama Uchu Kagakukan/Mount Ikoma Space Science Museum, 2312-1 Nabata-cho, Ikoma-shi, Nara-ken 630-0231, Japan.

069 USA ISSN 0095-2893
➤ **ILLINOIS. STATE MUSEUM. INVENTORY OF THE COLLECTIONS.** Text in English. 1969. irreg. price varies. back issues avail. **Document type:** *Monographic series, Academic/Scholarly.*
Indexed: GeoRef, SpeleolAb, WildRev.
Published by: Illinois State Museum, 502 S Spring St, Springfield, IL 62706. TEL 217-782-7386, FAX 217-782-1254, info@museum.state.il.us.

069 FRA ISSN 1268-1210
IMPRESSIONS (PARIS, 1995). Text in French. 1995. q. **Document type:** *Magazine, Trade.*
Published by: Editions de la Reunion des Musees Nationaux, 49 Rue Etienne Marcel, Paris, Cedex 1 75039, France. TEL 33-1-40134800, FAX 33-1-40134400, http://www.rmn.fr.

069 GBR
IN FOCUS (WARRINGTON). Text in English. 2004 (Sept.). s-a. free (effective 2005). back issues avail. **Document type:** *Magazine, Trade.*
Related titles: Online - full content ed.
Published by: Museums Libraries and Archives North West, Ground Floor, The Malt Building, Wilderspool Park, Greenall's Ave, Warrington, WA4 6HL, United Kingdom. TEL 44-1925-625050, FAX 44-1925-243453, info@mlanorthwest.org.uk, http://www.mlanorthwest.org.uk.

IN TOUCH (MOORESTOWN). *see* ETHNIC INTERESTS

708.954 IND ISSN 0019-5987
AM101
INDIAN MUSEUM BULLETIN. Text in English. 1966. a. bk.rev. bibl.; charts; illus. index, cum.index: 1966-1969. **Document type:** *Bulletin, Trade.* **Description:** Provides a forum for research activities on museum collection, acquisition, preservation, display, exhibition and other cultural activities.
Related titles: Fax ed.
Indexed: BAS, NumL.
Published by: Indian Museum Kolkata, 27 Jawaharlal Nehru Rd, Kolkata, West Bengal 700 016, India. TEL 91-33-2495699, FAX 91-33-2495696, imbot@cal2.vsnl.net.in, http://www.indianmuseumkolkata.org.

708 USA ISSN 1949-9795
INDIANAPOLIS MUSEUM OF ART. PREVIEWS MAGAZINE. Text in English. 1911. bi-m. free to members (effective 2009). illus. **Document type:** *Magazine, Trade.*
Former titles (until 1988): Indianapolis Museum of Art. Quarterly Magazine (0894-8828); Indianapolis Museum of Art. Newsletter; Indianapolis Museum of Art. Bulletin (0004-3060); Art Association of Indianapolis. Bulletin
Published by: Indianapolis Museum of Art, 4000 Michigan Rd, Indianapolis, IN 46208. TEL 317-920-2660, FAX 317-931-1978, ima@imamuseum.org, http://www.imamuseum.org.

069 HRV ISSN 0350-2325
AM1
INFORMATICA MUSEOLOGICA. Text in Croatian; Summaries in English. 1970. q. USD 28 (effective 2001). bk.rev.; Website rev. bibl.; illus. 150 p./no.; **Document type:** *Journal, Academic/Scholarly.*
Formerly (until 1973): Bilten-Informatica Museologica
Published by: Muzejski Dokumentacijski Centar, Mesnicka 5, Zagreb, 10000, Croatia. TEL 385-1-4847897, FAX 385-1-4847913, info@mdc.hr. Ed. Drazin Trbugak Lada. Pub. Zgaga Visnja. Circ: 1,000.

069 ESP ISSN 2013-2468
INFORMATIU MUSEUS. Text in Catalan. 1988. q. back issues avail. **Document type:** *Bulletin, Consumer.*
Media: Online - full text.
Published by: Generalitat de Catalunya, Departament de Cultura/Museu d'Arqueologia de Catalunya, Parque de Montjuich, Ps De Santa Madrona, 39-41, Barcelona, 08038, Spain. TEL 34-972-770208, FAX 34-972-774260, http://www.mac.es/.

069 CAN ISSN 1718-9144
INSIDER'S GUIDE TO ONTARIO MUSEUMS. Text in English. 2007. a. **Document type:** *Handbook/Manual/Guide, Consumer.*
Published by: Ontario Museum Association, George Brown House, 50 Baldwin St, Toronto, ON M5T 1L4, Canada. TEL 416-348-8672, FAX 416-348-0438, omachin@planeteer.com.

INSITES (CHICAGO). *see* ARCHITECTURE

INTERNATIONAL DIRECTORY OF ARTS & MUSEUMS OF THE WORLD CD-ROM. *see* ART

THE INTERNATIONAL JOURNAL OF KOREAN ART AND ARCHAEOLOGY. *see* ARCHAEOLOGY

069 AUS ISSN 1835-2014
➤ **THE INTERNATIONAL JOURNAL OF THE INCLUSIVE MUSEUM.** Text in English. 2008. irreg. USD 50 to individuals; USD 300 to institutions (effective 2009). back issues avail. **Document type:** *Journal, Academic/Scholarly.* **Description:** Contains discussions by academics, curators, museum and public administrators, cultural policy makers and research students on the role of museums in society.
Published by: Common Ground Publishing, PO Box 463, Altona, VIC 3018, Australia. TEL 61-3-93988000, FAX 61-3-93988088, mail@commongroundpublishing.com, http://commongroundpublishing.com. Eds. Amareswar Galla, Dr. Bill Cope. Pub., R&P Kathryn Otte. Circ: 100.

➤ **INTERNATIONAL MUSEUM OF WOMEN;** newsletter. *see* WOMEN'S STUDIES

➤ **INTERNATIONAL SWIMMING HALL OF FAME HEADLINES.** *see* SPORTS AND GAMES

➤ **INVENTAIRE GENERAL DES MONUMENTS ET DES RICHESSES ARTISTIQUES DE LA FRANCE.** *see* ARCHITECTURE

➤ **IRISH ARTS REVIEW.** *see* ART

069 USA
IROQUOIS INDIAN MUSEUM. MUSEUM NOTES. Text in English. 1981. irreg. free to members (effective 2011). film rev. back issues avail. **Document type:** *Newsletter, Trade.* **Description:** Reviews museum events, programs and activities.
Formerly: Schoharie Museum of the Iroquois Indian. Museum Notes
Published by: Iroquois Indian Museum, 324 Caverns Rd, PO Box 7, Howes Cave, NY 12092. info@iroquoismuseum.org, http://www.iroquoismuseum.org. Circ: 800.

069 ISR ISSN 0333-7499
N3750.J5
ISRAEL MUSEUM JOURNAL. Text in English. 1965. a., latest vol.26, 2008. USD 7.50 (effective 2003). adv. charts; illus. 90 p./no.; **Document type:** *Journal, Academic/Scholarly.*
Formerly: Israel Museum News (0021-227X)
Indexed: AIAP, AICP, B24, NumL.
Published by: Israel Museum, P O Box 71117, Jerusalem, Israel. FAX 972-2-631833, shop@imj.org.il. Circ: 3,000.

333.72 ITA ISSN 0021-2822
DG420.5
ITALIA NOSTRA. Text in Italian. 1956. m. adv. charts; illus. index. Supplement avail.
Published by: (Associazione Nazionale per la Tutela del Patrimonio Storico Artistico e Naturale della Nazione), Gangemi Editore, Piazza San Pantaleo 4, Rome, Italy. TEL 39-06-6872774, FAX 39-06-68806189, info@gangemieditore.it, http://www.gangemi.com. Ed. Nicola Caracciolo. Circ: 20,000.

708.92 949.2 NLD ISSN 2210-6448
J H M MAGAZINE. Text in Dutch. 1985. 3/yr. adv.
Former titles (until 2009): Joods Historisch Museum. Museumkrant (0928-2963); (until 1992): Joods Historisch Museum. Nieuwsbrief (0920-9190)
Published by: (Joods Historisch Museum/Jewish Historical Museum), Uitgeverij Intermed, Postbus 2306, Groningen, 9704 CH, Netherlands. TEL 31-50-3120042, FAX 31-50-3139373, info@intermed.nu, http://www.intermed.nu. Circ: 15,000.

JAHRBUCH DER AUKTIONSPREISE FUER BUECHER, HANDSCHRIFTEN UND AUTOGRAPHEN; Ergebnisse der Auktionen in Deutschland, den Niederlanden, Oesterreich und der Schweiz. *see* PUBLISHING AND BOOK TRADE

069 DEU ISSN 0075-2207
N3
JAHRBUCH DER BERLINER MUSEEN. Text in German. 1959. a., latest vol.52, 2010. price varies. reprints avail. **Document type:** *Journal, Academic/Scholarly.*
Indexed: A06, A07, A20, A30, A31, AA, AIAP, ASCA, ArtHuCI, ArtInd, B04, B24, CA, CurCont, DIP, IBR, IBZ, PCI, SCOPUS, T02, W07.
—CCC.
Published by: (Staatliche Museen zu Berlin, Preussischer Kulturbesitz. Institut fuer Museumsforschung), Gebr. Mann Verlag, Berliner Str 53, Berlin, 10713, Germany. TEL 49-30-70013880, FAX 49-30-700138811, vertrieb-kunstverlage@reimer-verlag.de, http://www.reimer-mann-verlag.de.

069 DEU ISSN 1863-026X
JAHRBUCH FUER DIE OBERBAYERISCHEN FREILICHTMUSEEN GLENTLEITEN UND AMERANG. Text in German. 1976. a. EUR 19.90 (effective 2011). **Document type:** *Journal, Academic/Scholarly.*
Formerly (until 2006): Freundeskreis Blaetter (0177-011X)
Published by: (Freundeskreis Freilichtmuseum Suedbayern e.V.), Waxmann Verlag GmbH, Steinfurter Str 555, Muenster, 48159, Germany. TEL 49-251-265040, FAX 49-251-2650426, info@waxmann.com. Ed. Helmut Keim.

069 DEU ISSN 0938-6998
JAHRBUCH FUER GLOCKENKUNDE. Text in German. 1989. biennial. EUR 43 per issue (effective 2009). **Document type:** *Bulletin, Consumer.*
Indexed: DIP, IBR, IBZ, RILM.
Published by: Deutsches Glockenmuseum auf Burg Greifenstein e.V., Talstr 19, Greifenstein, 35753, Germany. TEL 49-6449-6460, FAX 49-6449-6073, dgm.greifenstein@t-online.de, http://www.glockenmuseum.de. Circ: 600 (controlled).

069 HUN ISSN 0553-4429
JANUS PANNONIUS MUZEUM. EVKONYVE. Variant title: Janus Pannonius Museum. Yearbook. Musei de Iano Pannonio Nominati. Annales. Muzeja im. Janusa Pannoniusa. Ezegodnik. Text in Multiple languages. 1956. a.
Indexed: FR.
—INIST.
Published by: Janus Pannonius Muzeum, Kaptalan utca 4, Pecs, 7621, Hungary. TEL 36-72-324822, jpm@jpm.hu, http://www.jpm.hu.

069 JPN ISSN 0040-8948
JAPAN. NATIONAL MUSEUM NEWS. Text in Japanese. 1947. bi-m. JPY 2,500 (effective 2001). **Document type:** *Newsletter.*
Published by: Tokyo National Museum/Tokyo Kokuritsu Hakubutsukan, 13-9 Ueno Park, Taito-ku, Tokyo, 110-8712, Japan. TEL 81-3-3822-1111, FAX 81-3-3822-9130. Circ: 10,000.

069 GRC
JEWISH MUSEUM OF GREECE. NEWSLETTER. Text in English; Alternating issues in Greek. 1981. q. membership. bk.rev. illus. **Document type:** *Newsletter.* **Description:** Covers the heritage of the Sephardic and Romaniot communities in the Hellenic world. Includes acquisition news.
Published by: Jewish Museum of Greece, 39 Nikis St, Athens, 105 58, Greece. TEL 30-1-322-5582, FAX 30-1-323-1577. Circ: 1,500. **Dist. in U.S. by:** American Friends of the Jewish Museum of Greece, PO Box 2010, New York, NY 10185-0017. TEL 212-661-9843.

708.1 USA
N742.S5
THE JOHN & MABLE RINGLING MUSEUM OF ART. Text in English. 1964. q. membership. illus. **Document type:** *Newsletter.*
Former titles: Ringling Museums (0731-7956); Ringling Museums Newsletter (0035-5461)
Published by: John and Mable Ringling Museum of Art Foundation, 5401 Bay Shore Rd, Sarasota, FL 34243-2161. TEL 941-359-5700, FAX 941-359-5745. Ed. Barbara Kate Linick. Circ: 6,000 (controlled).

708.1 USA
JOSLYN NEWS; a publication for members. Text in English. 1974. bi-m. USD 35 to individuals membership; USD 25 to senior citizens membership; USD 25 to students membership (effective 2000). illus. **Document type:** *Newsletter.* **Description:** Provides information on Joslyn's permanent collection, special exhibitions, and events.
Former titles: Joslyn Art Museum Members' Calendar; Joslyn Art Museum Calendar of Events
Published by: Joslyn Art Museum, 2200 Dodge St, Omaha, NE 68102. TEL 402-342-3300, FAX 402-342-2376, http://www.joslyn.org. Ed. Amy Krobot. Circ: 8,000 (controlled).

069 GBR ISSN 0260-9126
JOURNAL OF EDUCATION IN MUSEUMS. Text in English. 1980. a. free to members (effective 2009). bk.rev. illus. back issues avail. **Document type:** *Journal, Academic/Scholarly.* **Description:** Covers all aspects of museum education both in Britain and abroad.
Indexed: BrArAb, CPE, NumL, RASB.
—BLDSC (4973.150500). **CCC.**
Published by: Group for Education in Museums, Primrose House, 193 Gillingham Rd, Gillingham, Kent, United Kingdom. TEL 44-1634-853424, FAX 44-1634-853424, office@gem.org.uk.

069 IND ISSN 0970-9894
AM1
JOURNAL OF INDIAN MUSEUMS. Text in English. 1945. a. free to members (effective 2011). **Document type:** *Journal, Academic/Scholarly.*
Indexed: A&ATA, AIAP, BAS.
Published by: Museums Association of India, c/o National Museum of Natural History, F I C C I Museum Bldg, Barakhamba Rd, New Delhi, 110 002, India. pradumman@hotmail.com, http://www.museumsai.com.

069 JPN ISSN 0288-2051
AS552.T696
JOURNAL OF KOKUGAKUIN UNIVERSITY/KOKUGAKUIN ZASSHI. Text in Japanese. 1894. m. **Document type:** *Academic/Scholarly.*
Indexed: RILM.
—Ingenta.
Published by: Kokugakuin University, 4-10-28 Higashi, Shibuya-ku, Tokyo, 150, Japan. Ed. Futaki Keiichi.

069.07 USA ISSN 1059-8650
AM7
JOURNAL OF MUSEUM EDUCATION. Text in English. 1973. 3/yr. USD 159 to institutions; USD 259 combined subscription to institutions (print & online eds.); free to members (effective 2010). adv. back issues avail. **Document type:** *Journal, Academic/Scholarly.* **Description:** Focuses on a specific theme of interest to museum educators, informal educators, museum administrators, researchers, and other education and museum practitioners.
Formerly (until 1985): Museum Education Roundtable. Roundtable Reports (0739-4365)
Related titles: Online - full text ed.
Indexed: ERIC.
—BLDSC (5021.127000), IE, Ingenta.
Published by: (Museum Education Roundtable), Left Coast Press, Inc., 1630 N Main St, Ste 400, Walnut Creek, CA 94596. TEL 925-935-3380, FAX 925 935-2916, Explore@LCoastPress.com. Eds. Cynthia Robinson, Tina Nolan.

JOURNAL OF MUSEUM ETHNOGRAPHY. *see* ANTHROPOLOGY

JOURNAL OF THE AUSTRALIAN WAR MEMORIAL. *see* MILITARY

708.048921 DNK ISSN 1603-5313
N6264.D4
JOURNAL OF THE DAVID COLLECTION. Text in English. 2003. irreg. DKK 200 per issue (effective 2008). **Document type:** *Journal, Academic/Scholarly.* **Description:** The journal features brief presentations of new acquisitions and more in-depth discussions of individual works of art or groups of objects.
Indexed: I14.
Published by: Davids Samling/David Collection, Kronprinsessegade 30-32, Copenhagen K, 1306, Denmark. TEL 45-33-734949, FAX 45-33-734948, museum@davidmus.dk, http://www.davismus.dk.

069 GBR ISSN 0954-6650
AM221 CODEN: JHCOE2
➤ **JOURNAL OF THE HISTORY OF COLLECTIONS.** Text in English. 1989. s-a. GBP 194 in United Kingdom to institutions; EUR 288 in Europe to institutions; USD 385 in US & Canada to institutions; GBP 194 elsewhere to institutions; GBP 211 combined subscription in United Kingdom to institutions (print & online eds.); EUR 314 combined subscription in Europe to institutions (print & online eds.); USD 420 combined subscription in US & Canada to institutions (print & online eds.); GBP 211 combined subscription elsewhere to institutions (print & online eds.) (effective 2012). adv. bk.rev. back issues avail.; reprint service avail. from PSC. **Document type:** *Journal, Academic/Scholarly.* **Description:** Dedicated to the study of collections, ranging from the contents of palaces and accumulations in more modest households, to the most systematic collection of academic institutions.
Related titles: Online - full text ed.: ISSN 1477-8564. GBP 176 in United Kingdom to institutions; EUR 262 in Europe to institutions; USD 350 in US & Canada to institutions; GBP 176 elsewhere to institutions (effective 2012) (from IngentaConnect).
Indexed: A07, A22, A30, A31, AA, ABM, AICP, AmH&L, ArtInd, B04, B24, BRD, BrArAb, CA, E01, HistAb, IBR, IBZ, NumL, PCI, RILM, SCOPUS, T02, W03, W05.
—BLDSC (5000.740000), IE, Infotrieve, Ingenta. **CCC.**
Published by: Oxford University Press, Great Clarendon St, Oxford, OX2 6DP, United Kingdom. TEL 44-1865-556767, FAX 44-1865-556646, enquiry@oup.co.uk, http://www.oxfordjournals.org. Eds. Arthur MacGregor TEL 44-1865-278000, Dr. Kate Heard. Adv. contact Linda Hann TEL 44-1344-779945. **Subscr. in the Americas to:** Oxford University Press, 2001 Evans Rd, Cary, NC 27513. TEL 919-677-0977 ext 5777, 800-852-7323, FAX 919-677-1714, jnlorders@oup-usa.org, http://www.us.oup.com.

➤ **THE JOURNAL OF VENTURA COUNTY HISTORY.** *see* HISTORY—History Of North And South America

069 FIN ISSN 1459-9678
K A S - TAIDETTA. Text in Finnish. 1991. 2/yr. **Document type:** *Newsletter.*
Formerly (until 2002): Concordia (0789-9335)
Related titles: Online - full text ed.: ISSN 1459-9724; Swedish ed.: Concordia. ISSN 1236-1100.
Indexed: ABM.
Published by: Valtion Taidemuseo/Finnish National Gallery, Kaivokato 2, Helsinki, 00100, Finland. TEL 358-9-173361, FAX 358-9-17336259, info@fng.fi. Ed. Anne Nikula.

639.2074 USA
K W M NEWSLETTER; the quarterly journal of the kendall whaling museum. Text in English. 1983. q. USD 25 to members (effective 2000). bk.rev. back issues avail. **Document type:** *Newsletter.* **Description:** Desseminates news of collections and programs of the Kendall Whaling Museum which is concerned with the history of whaling, marine art, maritime history, ethnology, natural history and cetology.
Published by: Kendall Whaling Museum, 27 Everett St, Box 297, Sharon, MA 02067. TEL 781-784-5642, FAX 781-784-0451. Ed. Elizabeth McGregor. R&P Jane Bowers. Circ: 1,000.

069 DEU ISSN 0022-7587
KAERNTNER MUSEUMSSCHRIFTEN. Text in German. 1954. irreg., latest vol.76, 2001. price varies. adv. **Document type:** *Monographic series, Academic/Scholarly.*
Published by: (Landesmuseum Kaernten AUT), Dr. Rudolf Habelt GmbH, Am Buchenhang 1, Bonn, 53115, Germany. TEL 49-228-923830, FAX 49-228-923836, info@habelt.de, http://www.habelt.de. Circ: 200.

069 JPN
KAGOSHIMA DAIGAKU SOUGOU KENKYUU HAKUBUTSUKAN KENKYUU HOUKOKU. Text in Japanese. irreg., latest no.2. **Document type:** *Monographic series, Academic/Scholarly.*
Published by: Kagoshima University Museum, 1-21-30, Korimoto, Kagoshima, 890-0065, Japan. TEL 81-99-2858141, FAX 81-99-2857267, museum@kaum.kagoshima-u.ac.jp, http://www.museum.kagoshima-u.ac.jp/.

069 JPN ISSN 1348-3471
KAGOSHIMA DAIGAKU SOUGOU KENKYUU HAKUBUTSUKAN NEMPOU/KAGOSHIMA UNIVERSITY MUSEUM. ANNUAL REPORT. Text in Japanese. 2003. a. **Document type:** *Journal, Academic/Scholarly.*
Published by: Kagoshima University Museum, 1-21-30, Korimoto, Kagoshima, 890-0065, Japan. TEL 81-99-2858141, FAX 81-99-2857267, museum@kaum.kagoshima-u.ac.jp, http://www.museum.kagoshima-u.ac.jp/.

069 JPN ISSN 1347-2747
KAGOSHIMA UNIVERSITY MUSEUM MONOGRAPHS. Text in English. 2002. a. **Document type:** *Monographic series, Academic/Scholarly.*
Indexed: GeoRef, Z01.
—BLDSC (5081.138110).
Published by: Kagoshima University Museum, 1-21-30, Korimoto, Kagoshima, 890-0065, Japan. TEL 81-99-2858141, FAX 81-99-2857267, museum@kaum.kagoshima-u.ac.jp, http://www.museum.kagoshima-u.ac.jp/.

069 JPN ISSN 1346-7220
KAGOSHIMA UNIVERSITY MUSEUM. NEWSLETTER. Variant title: Kagoshima Daigaku Sougou Kenkyuu Hakubutsukan Newsletter. Text in Japanese. 2001. irreg. (1-3/yr.). **Document type:** *Newsletter, Academic/Scholarly.*
Related titles: Online - full content ed.
Published by: Kagoshima University Museum, 1-21-30, Korimoto, Kagoshima, 890-0065, Japan.

KAMISHIHORO-CHO HIGASHI TAISETSU HAKUBUTSUKAN KENKYU HOKOKU/HIGASHI TAISETSU MUSEUM OF NATURAL HISTORY. BULLETIN. *see* SCIENCES: COMPREHENSIVE WORKS

069 JPN
KANAGAWA-KEN HAKUBUTSUKAN KYOKAI KAIHO/KANAGAWA-KEN MUSEUM GAZETTE. Text in Japanese. 1958. irreg. JPY 500. **Document type:** *Bulletin.* **Description:** A bulletin of natural and cultural sciences.
Published by: Kanagawa-ken Hakubutsukan Kyokai/Museums Association of Kanagawa Prefecture, 5-60 Minami-Nakadori, Naka-ku, Yokohama-shi, Kanagawa-ken 231-0000, Japan. TEL 045-201-0926, FAX 045-201-7364. Circ: (controlled).

KANAGAWA-KENRITSU HAKUBUTSUKAN KENKYU HOKOKU. SHIZEN KAGAKU/KANAGAWA PREFECTURAL MUSEUM OF NATURAL HISTORY. BULLETIN. NATURAL SCIENCE. *see* SCIENCES: COMPREHENSIVE WORKS

KANAGAWA-KENRITSU HAKUBUTSUKAN SHIRYO MOKUROKU. SHIZEN KAGAKU/KANAGAWA PREFECTURAL MUSEUM OF NATURAL HISTORY. CATALOGUE OF THE COLLECTION. *see* SCIENCES: COMPREHENSIVE WORKS

069.1 USA
KEEPING PLACE, KEEPING PACE. Text in English. 1976. q. looseleaf. free to qualified personnel (effective 2006). bk.rev. back issues avail. **Document type:** *Newsletter, Consumer.* **Description:** Covers activities of the museum including fundraising and new research.
Formerly: New Gleanings
Published by: Historic Cherry Hill, 523 1/2 S Pearl St, Albany, NY 12202. TEL 518-434-4806. Ed. Liselle Lafrance. Circ: 700.

069 FIN ISSN 1455-173X
KIASMA. Text in Finnish. 1997. q.
Related titles: English ed.: ISSN 1456-9124.
Published by: Nykytaiteen Museo Kiasma/Museum of Contemporary Art, Mannerheiminaukio 2, Helsinki, 00100, Finland. TEL 358-9-17336501, FAX 358-9-17336503, info@kiasma.fi.

069 DEU ISSN 0173-4695
KIRCHLICHE SCHATZKAMMERN UND MUSEEN. Text in German. 1976. irreg. **Document type:** *Monographic series, Academic/Scholarly.*
Published by: Verlag Schnell und Steiner GmbH, Leibnizstr 13, Regensburg, 93055, Germany. TEL 49-941-787850, FAX 49-941-7878516, post@schnell-und-steiner.de, http://www.schnell-und-steiner.de.

KITAKAMI-SHIRITSU HAKUBUTSUKAN KENKYU HOKOKU/KITAKAMI CITY MUSEUM. BULLETIN. *see* SCIENCES: COMPREHENSIVE WORKS

KITAKYUUSHUU SHIRITSU SHIZENSHI, REKISHI HAKUBUTSUKAN KENKYUU HOUKOU. ARUI, SHIZENSHI/KITAKYUSHU MUSEUM OF NATURAL HISTORY AND HUMAN HISTORY. BULLETIN. SERIES A, NATURAL HISTORY. *see* SCIENCES: COMPREHENSIVE WORKS

069.4 DEU ISSN 0933-257X
AM51.C64
KOELNER MUSEUMS BULLETIN. Text in German. 1961. q. EUR 23 (effective 2003). adv. bk.rev. illus. cum.index in prep. (1961-1975). **Document type:** *Bulletin, Academic/Scholarly.* **Description:** Reports on new acquisitions, exhibitions, and research.
Former titles: Museen der Stadt Koeln. Bulletin (0178-4218); Museen in Koeln. Bulletin (0027-3813)
Indexed: AIAP, RASB.
Published by: Museumsdienst Koeln, Richartzstr 2-4, Cologne, 50667, Germany. TEL 49-221-22124764, FAX 49-221-22124544, museumsdienst@stadtkoeln.de, http://www.museenkoeln.de. Ed., R&P Peter Noelke. Circ: 2,000.

507.4 JPN
KOKURITSU KAGAKU HAKUBUTSUKAN NENPO. Text in Japanese. 1972. a. **Description:** Annual report of the museum.
Published by: Kokuritsu Kagaku Hakubutsukan/National Science Museum, Tokyo, 7-20 Ueno-Koen, Taito-ku, Tokyo, 110-0007, Japan.

KOMATSU-SHIRITSU HAKUBUTSUKAN KENKYU KIYO/KOMATSU CITY MUSEUM. MEMOIRS. *see* SCIENCES: COMPREHENSIVE WORKS

069 AUT
KONSERVIERUNGSWISSENSCHAFT, RESTAURIERUNG, TECHNOLOGIE. Text in German. 2001. irreg., latest vol.7, 2010. price varies. **Document type:** *Monographic series, Academic/Scholarly.*
Published by: Boehlau Verlag GmbH & Co.KG., Wiesingerstr 1, Vienna, W 1010, Austria. TEL 43-1-3302427, FAX 43-1-3302432, boehlau@boehlau.at, http://www.boehlau.at.

707.4 SWE
KONSTKALENDERN. Text in Swedish. 1993. irreg. (3-4/yr.). SEK 70. adv. **Document type:** *Consumer.* **Description:** Publishes information on all art exhibits in Stockholm and surrounding area.
Related titles: Online - full text ed.

Published by: Foerlag ARB - Anders Blume, Fack 17176, Stockholm, 10462, Sweden. TEL 46-8-669-6409, FAX 46-8-669-6409. Ed., Pub., Adv. contact Anders Blume.

507.4 JPN
KOTONOURA. Text in Japanese. 1986. q. **Description:** Publishes news of Wakayama Prefecture's natural science museum.
Published by: Wakayama-kenritsu Shizen Hakubutsukan Tomo no Kai, Wakayama-kenritsu Shizen Hakubutsukan, 370-1 Funo, Kainan-shi, Wakayama-ken 642-0001, Japan.

069 USA
KRESGE FOUNDATION. ANNUAL REPORT. Text in English. a.
Published by: Kresge Foundation, 2701 Troy Center Dr., Ste. 150, Troy, MI 48084-4755. TEL 313-643-9630, FAX 313-643-0588.

707.4 DEU
KULTUR LIFE; Veranstaltungsvorschau. Text in German. 1950. m. free. **Document type:** *Bulletin, Consumer.* **Description:** Provides a calendar of performances and events within the city of Darmstadt.
Formerly (until 1998): Lebendiges Darmstadt
Published by: ProRegio Darmstadt, Luisenplatz 5a, Darmstadt, 64283, Germany. TEL 49-6151-132781.

069 DEU
▼ **KULTUR- UND MUSEUMSSTANDORT HEILIGENGRABE.** Text in German. 2009. irreg., latest vol.2, 2009. price varies. **Document type:** *Monographic series, Academic/Scholarly.*
Published by: Lukas Verlag fuer Kunst- und Geistesgeschichte, Kollwitzstr 57, Berlin, 10405, Germany. TEL 49-30-44049220, FAX 49-30-4428177, lukas.verlag@t-online.de, http://www.lukasverlag.com.

069 DEU ISSN 0344-5690
T14.7 CODEN: KUTEEN
KULTUR UND TECHNIK; Das Magazin aus dem Deutschen Museum. Text in German. 1977. q. EUR 24; EUR 7 newsstand/cover (effective 2011). adv. bk.rev. **Document type:** *Journal, Academic/Scholarly.* **Description:** Examines the inter-relationships of culture and technology.
Indexed: A22, DIP, HistAb, IBR, IBZ, P30, PCI, RASB.
—IE, Infotrieve, Linda Hall. **CCC.**
Published by: (Deutsches Museum), Verlag C.H. Beck oHG, Wilhelmstr 9, Munich, 80801, Germany. TEL 49-89-381890, FAX 49-89-38189398, abo.service@beck.de, http://www.beck.de. Circ: 16,380 (controlled).

069.09489521 DNK ISSN 1601-6254
KULTURHISTORISK MUSEUMS SKRIFTER. Text in Danish. 2000. irreg., latest vol.3, 2006. price varies. back issues avail. **Document type:** *Monographic series, Academic/Scholarly.*
Published by: (Jysk Arkaeologisk Selskab/Jutland Archeological Society), Aarhus Universitetsforlag/Aarhus University Press, Langelandsgade 177, Aarhus N, 8200, Denmark. TEL 45-89-425370, FAX 45-89-425380, unipress@au.dk, http://www.unipress.dk.

069 DEU ISSN 0937-9541
KUNST IN KOELN. Variant title: K I K: Kunst in Koeln. Text in German. 1965. m. free. **Document type:** *Newsletter.* **Description:** Press release by the museums of the city of Cologne.
Published by: Museumsreferat der Museen Koeln, Richartzstr 2-4, Cologne, 50667, Germany. TEL 49-221-2212334. Ed. Karin Bolenius. Circ: 900.

069 DEU ISSN 0023-5474
N3
KUNSTCHRONIK; Monatsschrift fuer Kunstwissenschaft, Museumswesen und Denkmalpflege. Text in German. 1948. 11/yr. EUR 65.90 domestic; EUR 77.90 in Europe; EUR 108.90 elsewhere; EUR 7.90 newsstand/cover (effective 2010). adv. bk.rev. bibl.; charts; illus. index. **Document type:** *Journal, Academic/Scholarly.* **Description:** Covers art, museums, and the care and preservation of works of art.
Indexed: A22, AIAP, B24, DIP, FR, IBR, IBZ, MLA-IB, PCI, RASB, RILM. —IE, Infotrieve. **CCC.**
Published by: (Zentralinstitut fuer Kunstgeschichte in Muenchen), Fachverlag Hans Carl, Andernacher Str 33A, Nuernberg, 90411, Germany. TEL 49-911-952850, FAX 49-911-9528548, info@hanscarl.com. Ed. Peter Diemer. Adv. contact Sabine Raab. Circ: 2,069 (paid).

708 DEU ISSN 1860-0530
KUNSTQUARTAL. Text in German. 1965. q. EUR 32 domestic; EUR 33 foreign; EUR 9 newsstand/cover (effective 2010). adv. **Document type:** *Magazine, Trade.* **Description:** Basic information for anyone with an interest in art.
Formerly (until 2005): Belser Kunst Quartal (0947-8701)
Published by: Hatje Cantz Verlag, Zeppelinstr 32, Ostfildern, 73760, Germany. TEL 49-711-44050, FAX 49-711-4405220, contact@hatjecantz.de, http://www.hatjecantz.de. Ed. Renate Palmer. Circ: 25,000 (controlled).

KUNTSI. *see* ART

KURASHIKI-SHIRITSU SHIZENSHI HAKUBUTSUKAN KENKYU HOKOKU/KURASHIKI MUSEUM OF NATURAL HISTORY. BULLETIN. *see* SCIENCES: COMPREHENSIVE WORKS

069 JPN ISSN 0913-1558
KURASHIKI-SHIRITSU SHIZENSHI HAKUBUTSUKANPO. Text in Japanese. 1986. a. free. **Description:** Annual report of the museum.
Published by: Kurashiki-shiritsu Shizenshi Hakubutsukan/Kurashiki Museum of Natural History, 6-1 Chuo 2-chome, Kurashiki-shi, Okayama-ken 710-0046, Japan. TEL 0864-25-6037, FAX 0864-25-6038. Circ: 1,000.

KUSHIRO-SHIRITSU HAKUBUTSUKAN KIYO/KUSHIRO CITY MUSEUM. MEMOIRS. *see* SCIENCES: COMPREHENSIVE WORKS

069 JPN ISSN 0288-9102
KYODO TO HAKUBUTSUKAN. Text in Japanese. 1953. s-a.
Published by: Tottori-kenritsu Hakubutsukan/Tottori Prefectural Museum, 2-124 Higashi-Machi, Tottori-shi, 680-0011, Japan. FAX 0857-26-8041. Circ: 1,000.

069 SWE ISSN 1651-5706
LAENSMUSEET HALMSTAD. SKRIFTSERIE. Text in Swedish. 2003. irreg., latest vol.3, 2004. price varies. back issues avail. **Document type:** *Monographic series.*
Published by: Laensmuseet Halmstad, Tollsgatan, Halmstad, 30231, Sweden. TEL 46-35-162300, FAX 46-35-162318, kansli@hallmus.se, http://www.hallmus.se.

069 DNK ISSN 1903-8372
LAESOE MUSEUM. MUSEUMSFORENINGEN FOR LAESOE. Text in Danish. 1983. a. DKK 60 membership (effective 2010). cum index: 1983-2008. **Document type:** *Monographic series, Consumer.*
Former titles (until 2009): Museumsforeningen for Laesoe. Laesoe Museum (0902-3690); (until 1987): Museumsforeningen for Laesoe (0109-5854)
Published by: Museumsforeningen for Laesoe, c/o Kay Johannsen, Plantagevej 1, Laesoe, 9940, Denmark. TEL 45-98-499605, mail@laesoe-museumsforening.dk, http://www.laesoe-museumsforening.dk.

069 AUT ISSN 0007-280X
LANDESMUSEUM FUER KAERNTEN. BUCHREIHE. Text in German. 1954. irreg., latest vol.41, 1996. price varies. adv. **Document type:** *Monographic series, Academic/Scholarly.*
Indexed: SpeleolAb.
Published by: Landesmuseum Kaernten, Museumgasse 2, Klagenfurt, K 9021, Austria. TEL 43-50-53630599, FAX 43-50-53630540, info@landesmuseum-ktn.at, http://www.landesmuseum-ktn.at. Circ: 400.

708.3 DEU ISSN 0070-7201
LANDESMUSEUM FUER VORGESCHICHTE DRESDEN. VEROEFFENTLICHUNGEN. Text in German. 1952. irreg., latest vol.44, 2005. price varies. **Document type:** *Monographic series, Academic/Scholarly.*
Published by: Landesmuseum fuer Vorgeschichte Dresden, Zur Wetterwarte 7, Dresden, 01109, Germany. TEL 49-351-8926603, FAX 49-351-8926604, info@archsax.smwk.sachsen.de, http://www.archsax.sachsen.de/lmv/index.html.

708 DEU ISSN 0072-940X
LANDESMUSEUM FUER VORGESCHICHTE, HALLE. VEROEFFENTLICHUNGEN. Text in German. 1964. irreg. price varies. **Document type:** *Monographic series, Academic/Scholarly.*
Published by: Landesmuseum fuer Vorgeschichte Halle, Richard-Wagner-Str 9, Halle, 06114, Germany. TEL 49-345-5247363, FAX 49-345-5247351, poststelle@lda.mk.sachsen-anhalt.de1, http://www.lda-lsa.de/landesmuseum_fuer_vorgeschichte/.

069 DEU
LANDESMUSEUM WUERTTEMBERG. SAMMLUNGEN. Text in German. 1993. irreg., latest vol.3, 2007. price varies. **Document type:** *Monographic series, Academic/Scholarly.*
Formerly (until 2007): Wuerttembergisches Landesmuseum. Sammlungen
Published by: (Wuerttembergisches Landesmuseum), Konrad Theiss Verlag GmbH, Moenchhaldenstr 28, Stuttgart, 70191, Germany. TEL 49-711-255270, FAX 49-711-2552717, service@theiss.de, http://www.theiss.de.

069 ESP ISSN 1133-0600
DP302.V334
LAURO; revista del Museu de Granollers. Text in Spanish, Catalan. 1990. a. **Document type:** *Journal, Academic/Scholarly.*
Related titles: Online - full content ed.
Published by: Museu de Granollers, Carrer Anselm Clave 40, Granollers, Barcelona 08400, Spain. TEL 34-93-8426840, FAX 34-93-8793919, http://www.museugranollers.org.

387.0074 NZL ISSN 1170-4918
LEADING LIGHT. Text in English. 1990. q. free. back issues avail. **Document type:** *Newsletter.* **Description:** Update on museum's activities-exhibitions, friends' news, staff, and special projects.
Published by: Museum of Wellington, City and Sea, Queens Wharf, PO Box 893, Wellington, 6011, New Zealand. TEL 64-4-4728904, FAX 64-4-4961949, museumofwellington@wmt.org.nz. Ed., R&P Wendy Adlam TEL 64-4-4728904. Circ: 900 (controlled).

069.7 373 NLD ISSN 1872-3659
LESSEN. Text in Dutch. 1983. q. EUR 20 (effective 2009).
Formerly (until 2006): De School Anno (0167-8035)
Published by: (Vereniging Vrienden van het Nationaal Onderwijsmuseum), Het Nationaal Onderwijsmuseum, Postbus 21536, Rotterdam, 3001 AM, Netherlands. TEL 31-10-2170370, info@onderwijsmuseum.nl.

069 FRA ISSN 0994-1908
LA LETTRE DE L'O C I M. (Office de Cooperation et d'Information Museographiques) Text in French. 1985. bi-m. EUR 60 domestic; EUR 70 foreign; EUR 30 to students (effective 2010). **Document type:** *Newsletter, Trade.*
Formerly (until 1988): Office de Cooperation et d'Information Museographiques. Note Technique (0298-6760)
Related titles: Online - full text ed.: ISSN 2108-646X. 200?.
Published by: Office de Cooperation et d'Information Museographiques, 36 Rue Chabot Charny, Dijon, 21000, France. TEL 33-3-80589850.

LIBRARY COMPANY OF PHILADELPHIA. OCCASIONAL MISCELLANY. *see* HISTORY—History Of North And South America

708.47 LTU ISSN 1648-7109
LIETUVOS MUZIEJAI/LITHUANIAN MUSEUMS. Text in Lithuanian. 2003. q.
Related titles: ◆ Supplement(s): Muziejininkystes Biuletenis. ISSN 1392-5326.
Published by: Lietuvos Muzieju Asociacija, Saltoniskiu g 58, Vilnius, 08105, Lithuania. TEL 370-5-2790371, FAX 370-5-2790213, muzbiuleten@takas.lt, http://www.museums.lt.

069 ISL ISSN 1021-6626
➤ **LISTASAFN SIGURJONS OLAFSSONAR. ARBOK.** Text in Icelandic; Summaries in English. 1986. a., latest 2002. price varies. back issues avail. **Document type:** *Journal, Academic/Scholarly.*
Published by: Sigurjon Olafsson Museum/Listasafn Sigurjons Olafssonar, Laugarnestanga 70, Reykjavik, 105, Iceland. TEL 354-553-2906, FAX 354-581-4553, lso@lso.is, http://www.lso.is. Ed. Birgitta Spur.

➤ **LITHUANIAN MUSEUM REVIEW.** *see* ETHNIC INTERESTS

506 USA ISSN 1944-4346
Q1
LIVE (SAN FRANCISCO). Text in English. 1940. q. free to members (effective 2009). **Document type:** *Magazine, Consumer.*
Former titles (until 2008): California Academy of Sciences. Member Publication (1935-8121); (until 2006): Academy (1098-0164); (until 1996): California Academy of Sciences. Academy Newsletter (0897-5523); (until 1986): California Academy of Sciences. Newsletter (0271-020X); (until 1974): California Academy of Sciences. Academy Newsletter (0008-0829)
Related titles: Online - full text ed.
—CCC.
Published by: California Academy of Sciences, 55 Music Concourse Dr, Golden Gate Park, San Francisco, CA 94118. TEL 415-379-8000, 800-794-7576, info@calacademy.org. Ed. Stephanie Stone.

630.74 USA ISSN 0047-4851
LIVING HISTORICAL FARMS BULLETIN. Text in English. 1970. bi-m. membership. adv. bk.rev. bibl. **Document type:** *Bulletin.*
Published by: Association for Living Historical Farms and Agricultural Museums, Conner Prairie, Fishers, IN 46038. TEL 317-776-6000, FAX 317-776-6014. Ed. Stephen L Cox. Circ: 1,200.

LIVINGSTONE MUSEUM. RESEARCH NOTES. *see* HISTORY—History Of Africa

069 SWE ISSN 0024-5372
U800.A1
LIVRUSTKAMMAREN. Variant title: Journal of the Royal Armoury. Text in English, Swedish; Summaries in English, French, German. 1915. s-a. bk.rev. Index. back issues avail. **Document type:** *Journal, Academic/Scholarly.*
Formerly (until 1937): Maerkligare Nytt
Indexed: P30, RILM.
Published by: Kungliga Livrustkammaren/Royal Armoury, Slottsbacken 3, Kungliga Slottet, Stockholm, 11130, Sweden. TEL 46-8-51955500, FAX 46-8-51955511, livrustkammaren@lsh.se, http://www.lsh.se. Ed. Ingemar Karlsson.

LOGBOEK. *see* AERONAUTICS AND SPACE FLIGHT

708.29 AUS ISSN 0817-8445
LOOK MAGAZINE. Text in English. m. free to members (effective 2008). bk.rev. **Document type:** *Magazine, Consumer.* **Description:** Covers coming exhibitions, acquisitions, gallery events, educational and social events for members of the society.
Former titles (until 1985): Art Gallery Society of New South Wales. Bulletin (0818-3767); (until 1980): A G S Bulletin; (until 1979): Art Gallery Society News; A G S News
Related titles: Online - full text ed.
Published by: (Art Gallery of New South Wales), Hardie Grant Magazines, 85 High St, Prahran, VIC 3181, Australia. TEL 61-3-85206444, FAX 61-3-85206422, colinritchie@hardiegrant.com.au, http://www.hardiegrant.com.au. Ed. Jill Sykes. Pub. Paul Becker. Adv. contact Lyn Morey Edwards.

THE LOOKDOWN. *see* EARTH SCIENCES—Oceanography

708.891 DNK ISSN 1601-1724
LOUISIANA MAGASIN. Text in Danish. 1976. q. **Document type:** *Magazine, Consumer.*
Formerly (until 2001): Louisiana Klubben (0105-1695)
Published by: Louisiana Museum of Modern Art, Gl Strandvej 13, Humlebaek, 3050, Denmark. TEL 45-49-190719, FAX 45-49-193505, post@louisiana.dk, curator@louisiana.dk, http://www.louisiana.dk.

069 CAN ISSN 1923-1113
LYTTON MUSEUM AND ARCHIVES. Text in English. 1999. s-a. free to members (effective 2010). back issues avail. **Document type:** *Newsletter, Trade.*
Related titles: Online - full text ed.
Published by: The Lytton Museum and Archives, 420 Fraser St, Lytton, BC, Canada. TEL 250-455-2394.

069 USA
M A M NEWS. Text in English. 1982. q. free to members. back issues avail. **Document type:** *Newsletter, Consumer.* **Description:** Features fine art, design, photography, and sculpture at the museum of current exhibitions and the permanent collection, which focuses on works of the western hemisphere from the 1940's to the present.
Formerly: C F A News (Miami)
Published by: Miami Art Museum, 101 W Flagler St, Miami, FL 33130. TEL 305-375-3000, FAX 305-375-1725. Ed. Troy Moss.

069.5 NLD ISSN 1877-0983
▼ **M B.** Text in Dutch. 2009. q. EUR 5 newsstand/cover (effective 2011). **Document type:** *Magazine, Consumer.*
Published by: Museum Belvedere, Oranje Nassaulaan 12, Heerenveen, 8448 MT, Netherlands. TEL 31-513-644999, FAX 31-513-644998, http://www.museumbelvedere.nl.

069 MEX
M MUSEOS DE MEXICO Y DEL MUNDO. Text in Spanish, English. 2004. s-a. USD 38 in North America; USD 38 in Central America; USD 45 in South America; USD 45 in Europe; USD 52 elsewhere (effective 2004). **Document type:** *Magazine, Consumer.*
Published by: Instituto Nacional de Antropologia e Historia (I N A H), Cordoba 45, Mexico City 7, DF 06700, Mexico. TEL 52-50-619100, administracion.dg@inah.gob.mx, http://www.inah.gob.mx.

069 DEU
M P Z INFO; Sonderausstellungen Muenchner Museen. Text in German. 1983. 2/yr. free. **Document type:** *Bulletin, Consumer.*
Media: Online - full text.
Published by: Museums-Paedagogisches Zentrum, Barer Str 29, Munich, 80799, Germany. TEL 49-89-23805120, FAX 49-89-23805197, mpz@mpz.bayern.de, http://www.mpz.bayern.de.

069 DEU
M P Z MUSEUMSDIENST. Text in German. 2000. a. **Document type:** *Magazine, Consumer.* **Description:** Contains listings of museum programs for children and adults in the greater Munich area.
Media: Online - full text.
Published by: Museums-Paedagogisches Zentrum, Barer Str 29, Munich, 80799, Germany. TEL 49-89-23805120, FAX 49-89-23805197, mpz@mpz.bayern.de, http://www.mpz.bayern.de.

069 DEU
M P Z PROGRAMM; Schule und Museum. Text in German. 1973. a. free. 100 p./no.; back issues avail. **Document type:** *Magazine, Consumer.* **Description:** Contains news about programs for children and youth groups in museums in Bavaria and the greater Munich area.
Former titles: M P Z Angebot; Angebote fuer Schulen, Kinder- und Jugendgruppen Fortbildungsangebote fuer Paedagogen; M P Z - Kooperationsprojekt; Schueler im Museum

Media: Online - full text.
Published by: Museums-Paedagogisches Zentrum, Barer Str 29, Munich, 80799, Germany. TEL 49-89-23805120, FAX 49-89-23805197, mpz@mpz.bayern.de, http://www.mpz.bayern.de.

069 DEU ISSN 1866-122X
MAECENATA-SCHRIFTEN. Text in German. 2007. irreg., latest vol.8, 2010. price varies. **Document type:** *Monographic series, Academic/Scholarly.*
Published by: Lucius und Lucius Verlagsgesellschaft mbH, Gerokstr 51, Stuttgart, 70184, Germany. TEL 49-711-242060, FAX 49-711-242088, lucius@luciusverlag.com, http://www.luciusverlag.com.

MAGASINET KUNST. *see* ART

069 USA
MAGNES NEWS. Text in English. 1968. s-a. USD 40 membership (effective 2000). illus. **Document type:** *Newsletter.* **Description:** Covers activities of the museum. Includes a calendar of exhibitions.
Published by: Judah L. Magnes Museum, 2911 Russell St, Berkeley, CA 94705. TEL 510-549-6950, FAX 510-849-3673, http://jfed.org/magnes/magnes.htm. Ed., R&P Paula Friedman. Circ: 3,000 (paid).

069 SWE ISSN 1651-9795
MALMOE MUSEER. E-SKRIFTER. Text in Swedish. 2003. irreg. back issues avail. **Document type:** *Monographic series, Academic/Scholarly.*
Media: Online - full content.
Published by: Malmoe Museer, Malmohusvaegen, PO Box 460, Malmoe, 20124, Sweden. TEL 46-40-341000, FAX 46-40-124097, malmomuseer@malmo.se, http://www.malmo.se/museer.

069 SWE ISSN 1650-9811
MALMOE MUSEER. SKRIFTSERIE. Text in Swedish. irreg., latest vol.1, 2002. SEK 125 per issue (effective 2006). **Document type:** *Monographic series.*
Published by: Malmoe Museer, Malmohusvaegen, PO Box 460, Malmoe, 20124, Sweden. TEL 46-40-341000, FAX 46-40-124097, malmomuseer@malmo.se, http://www.malmo.se/museer.

708.11 CAN ISSN 0715-0105
MANITOBA MUSEUM OF MAN AND NATURE. ANNUAL REPORT. Text in English. 1966. a. membership. **Document type:** *Corporate.*
Formerly (until 1984): Manitoba Museum of Man and Nature. Biennial Report (0076-3888)
Published by: Manitoba Museum of Man and Nature, 190 Rupert Ave, Winnipeg, MB R3B 0N2, Canada. TEL 204-956-2830, FAX 204-942-3679, TELEX 94236-79. Ed. Sue Caughlin. Circ: 2,000 (controlled).

508.074 CAN ISSN 0843-9133
MANITOBA MUSEUM OF MAN AND NATURE. HAPPENINGS. Text in English. bi-m. membership. **Document type:** *Newsletter.*
Published by: Manitoba Museum of Man and Nature, 190 Rupert Ave, Winnipeg, MB R3B 0N2, Canada. TEL 204-956-2830, FAX 204-942-3679. Ed. Sue Caughlin. Circ: 2,800.

069 POL ISSN 1429-1290
NX430.B28
MARE ARTICUM; the Baltic art magazine. Text in English, Polish. 1998. s-a. 128 p./no. 2 cols./p.; back issues avail.
Published by: Muzeum Narodowe Szczecin/National Muzeum in Szczecin, ul Staromlynska 27, Szczecin, 70561, Poland. TEL 48-91-4315200, FAX 48-91-4315204, biuro@muzeum.szczecin.pl, http://www.muzeum.szczecin.pl. Ed. Tadeusz Galinski. Circ: 800. **Dist. by:** Ars Polona, Obroncow 25, Warsaw 03933, Poland. TEL 48-22-5098609, FAX 48-22-5098610, arspolona@arspolona.com.pl, http://www.arspolona.com.pl.

069 BEL ISSN 0776-1317
MARIEMONT. CAHIERS; bulletin du Musee Royal de Mariemont. Text in French. 1970. a. back issues avail. **Document type:** *Bulletin, Academic/Scholarly.*
Published by: Musee Royal de Mariemont, 100 chaussee de Mariemont, Morlanwelz - Mariemont, 7140, Belgium. TEL 32-64-212193, FAX 32-64-262924, info@musee-mariemont.be, http://www.musee-mariemont.be. Ed. P Dartevelle. Circ: 1,500.

069 359 SWE ISSN 1404-0581
VM6.V3
MARINMUSEUM. AARSBOK. Text in Swedish. 1964. a. SEK 250 membership (effective 2007). back issues avail. **Document type:** *Consumer.*
Former titles (until 1999): Aktuellt-Marinmuseum (1103-5595); (until 1978): Aktuellt fraan Foereningen Marinmusei Vaenner i Karlskrona (0430-8441)
Published by: Marinmuseum, PO Box 48, Karlskrona, 37121, Sweden. TEL 46-455-359300, FAX 46-455-359349, registrator@maritima.se, http://www.maritima.se.

MARISIA: STUDII SI MATERIALE (ARHEOLOGIE). *see* ARCHAEOLOGY

MARITIEM MUSEUM MAGAZINE. *see* TRANSPORTATION—Ships And Shipping

069 USA
MARTIN & OSA JOHNSON SAFARI MUSEUM. WAIT-A-BIT NEWS. Text in English. 1980. q. USD 20 to individual members; USD 40 families (effective 2001). bk.rev. back issues avail. **Document type:** *Newsletter.* **Description:** Provides museum members and supporters with information on museum exhibits, collections, programs, research and activities.
Formerly: Johnson Safari Wait-a-Bit Newsletter
Published by: Martin and Osa Johnson Safari Museum, Inc., 111 N Lincoln Ave, Chanute, KS 66720. TEL 316-431-2730. Eds. Barbara E Henshall, Conrad G Froehlich. Circ: 500.

MASTERPIECES IN THE NATIONAL GALLERY OF CANADA/CHEFS-D'OEUVRE DE LA GALERIE NATIONALE DU CANADA. *see* ART

708.11 USA
MASTERWORKS FOR LEARNING: A COLLEGE CATALOGUE. Text in English. 1998. irreg. USD 29.95 (effective 2000). **Document type:** *Catalog.* **Description:** Consists of 171 full scholarly entries on the most important works of art in the collection.
Media: CD-ROM.
Published by: Oberlin College, Allen Memorial Art Museum, 87 N Main St, Oberlin, OH 44074. TEL 440-775-8665, FAX 440-775-8799. Ed. Sharon F Patton. R&P Lucille Stiger TEL 440-775-8668.

623 USA
THE MASTHEAD (PHILADELPHIA). Text in English. 1963. 3/yr. USD 35 to members (effective 2000). **Document type:** *Newsletter.* **Description:** Carries articles on museum exhibits and programs and Delaware Valley maritime history.
Formerly: Spindrift (0896-7466)
Published by: Independence Seaport Museum, 211 S Columbus Blvd, Philadelphia, PA 19106-3100. TEL 215-925-5439, FAX 215-925-6713, http://www.libertynet.org/seaport. Ed. Amber Alexander. Circ: 2,000.

069 POL ISSN 0076-5236
➤ **MATERIALY ZACHODNIOPOMORSKIE.** Text in Polish; Summaries in English, French, German. 1957. a. PLZ 30 per vol. (effective 2006). bk.rev. 250 p./no.; back issues avail. **Document type:** *Journal, Academic/Scholarly.* **Description:** Publishes papers on various fields: archaeology, ethnology, numismatics, history, history of art, sociology, museum management.
Indexed: NumL, RASB.
Published by: Muzeum Narodowe Szczecin/National Muzeum in Szczecin, ul Staromlynska 27, Szczecin, 70561, Poland. TEL 48-91-4315200, FAX 48-91-4315204, biuro@muzeum.szczecin.pl, http://www.muzeum.szczecin.pl. Eds. Lech Karkowski, Tadeusz Galinski. Circ: 700. **Dist. by:** Ars Polona, Obroncow 25, Warsaw 03933, Poland. TEL 48-22-5098609, FAX 48-22-5098610, arspolona@arspolona.com.pl, http://www.arspolona.com.pl.

069 USA
MATURANGO MUSEUM NEWSLETTER. Text in English. 1964. m. free membership (effective 2008). bk.rev. **Description:** Covers current events, lectures, field trips as well as new exhibits of local natural and cultural history.
Published by: Maturango Museum, 100 E Las Flores Ave, Ridgecrest, CA 93555. TEL 760-375-6900, FAX 760-375-0479, matmus@maturango.org, http://www.maturango.org. Ed. Penny Loper.

MAURITIANA (ALTENBURG). *see* SCIENCES: COMPREHENSIVE WORKS

708 CAN ISSN 1208-0721
MCMICHAEL CANADIAN ART COLLECTION. ANNUAL REPORT. Text in English. 1974. a.
Formerly (until 1988): McMichael Canadian Collection. Annual Report (0705-9787)
Published by: McMichael Canadian Art Collection, 10365 Islington Ave, Kleinburg, ON L0J 1C0, Canada. TEL 905-893-1121, 888-213-1121, FAX 905-893-0692, info@mcmichael.com, http://www.mcmichael.com.

069 USA ISSN 2161-2358
NA7615. M43
▼ **MEADOW BROOK.** Text in English. 2010. s-a. **Document type:** *Magazine, Trade.*
Published by: Meadow Brook Hall, 480 South Adams Rd, Rochester, MI 48309. TEL 248-364-6200, FAX 248-364-6201, upward@oakland.eduThis e-mail address is being protected from spambots. You need JavaScript enabled to view it, http://www.meadowbrookhall.org/.

▼ **MEDDELELSER OM GROENLAND/MONOGRAPHS ON GREENLAND.** *see* HISTORY—History Of Europe

MEDELHAVSMUSEET/FOCUS ON THE MEDITERRANEAN; focus on the Mediterranean. *see* ARCHAEOLOGY

069.1 USA
MESSENGER LINE. Text in English. bi-m. USD 15 membership (effective 2006). **Document type:** *Newsletter, Consumer.* **Description:** Keeps members, visitors and others informed of museum activities, the history of organized life saving, and the maritime heritage of Boston Harbor and the region.
Published by: Hull Lifesaving Museum, 1117 Nantasket Ave, Hull, MA 02045. TEL 781-925-5433, FAX 781-925-0992, lifesavingmuseum@comcast.net, http://www.lifesavingmuseum.org. Ed. Lory Newmyer. Circ: 1,200 (controlled).

708.1 BEL ISSN 0077-8958
N610
➤ **METROPOLITAN MUSEUM JOURNAL.** Text in English. 1968. a., latest vol.35, 2000. EUR 105.20 combined subscription (print & online eds.) (effective 2009). bk.rev. illus. back issues avail.; reprints avail. **Document type:** *Monographic series, Academic/Scholarly.* **Description:** Contains first-time investigations and critical reassessments of individual works; monographic surveys relating objects to their cultural contexts; new information drawing on archival research and technical analyses, and other scholarly articles.
Related titles: Online - full text ed.
Indexed: A06, A07, A20, A22, A30, A31, AA, AIAP, ASCA, ArtHuCI, ArtInd, B04, B24, BAS, CA, CurCont, I14, MLA-IB, RASB, RILM, T02, W07.
Published by: (Metropolitan Museum of Art USA), Brepols Publishers, Begijnhof 67, Turnhout, 2300, Belgium. TEL 32-14-448030, FAX 32-14-428919, periodicals@brepols.net, http://www.brepols.net. Ed. Barbara Burn.

708.1 USA ISSN 0026-1521
N610
METROPOLITAN MUSEUM OF ART BULLETIN. Text in English. 1905; N.S. 1942. q. USD 30 to non-members; USD 12.95 per issue to non-members; free to members (effective 2009). illus. index. reprints avail. **Document type:** *Bulletin.* **Description:** General information on art in the museum's collections; each issue organized around a category or an artist.
Incorporates (1986-1988): Metropolitan Museum of Art. Recent Acquisitions (0889-6585); Which was formerly (1979-1985): Metropolitan Museum of Art. Notable Acquisitions (0192-6950)
Related titles: Online - full text ed.
Indexed: A&ATA, A01, A02, A03, A06, A07, A08, A20, A30, A31, AA, ABM, AIAP, ASCA, AmHI, ArtHuCI, ArtInd, B04, B24, BAS, CA, CurCont, FR, H07, M01, M02, MEA&I, MLA-IB, NumL, RASB, RILM, SCOPUS, T02, W07.
—Ingenta, INIST.
Published by: Metropolitan Museum of Art, 1000 Fifth Ave, New York, NY 10028. TEL 212-535-7710, communications@metmuseum.org, http://www.metmuseum.org. Eds. Sue Potter, John P O'Neill.

069 DNK ISSN 1901-2144
MIDTJYSKE FORTAELLINGER. Text in Danish. 2005. a. DKK 125; DKK 160 per issue (effective 2009). back issues avail. **Document type:** *Yearbook, Consumer.*
Published by: Herning Museum, Museumsgade 32, Herning, 7400, Denmark. TEL 45-96-261900, FAX 45-96-261901, herningmuseum@herningmuseum.dk, http://www.herningmuseum.dk.

MIDWEST MUSEUM BULLETIN. *see* ART

508.074 JPN ISSN 0911-2111
MIKUMANO GENERAL MUSEUM. RESEARCH REPORTS. Text in Japanese. 1985. a.
Published by: Mikumano Sogo Shiryokan Kenkyu Iinkai/Mikumano General Museum, Research Committee, Shingushi Kyoiku Iinkai, 6760-1 Shingu, Shingu-shi, Wakayama-ken 647-0081, Japan.

MILLER NOTES. *see* MUSIC

069 USA
MINERVA (SAN FRANCISCO); a journal of museum studies and conservation. Text in English. 1998. q. **Description:** Presents articles written by professionals and students in the museum and conservation fields.
Media: Online - full text.
Published by: San Francisco State University, Museum Studies Program, 1600 Holloway Ave, San Francisco, CA 94132. TEL 415-338-2664. Ed. Andrew Fox.

069 USA ISSN 0076-9096
MINNEAPOLIS INSTITUTE OF ARTS. ANNUAL REPORT. Text in English. 1961. a. **Document type:** *Corporate.*
Published by: Minneapolis Institute of Arts, 2400 Third Ave S, Minneapolis, MN 55404. TEL 612-870-3046, FAX 612-870-3004. Ed. Jodie Ahern. R&P Deann Dankowski. Circ: 15,000.

708 USA ISSN 2152-6176
MINNETRISTA COLUMNS. Text in English. 19??. q. free to members (effective 2010). **Document type:** *Magazine, Trade.*
Published by: Minnetrista Cultural Foundation, Inc, 1200 N Minnetrista Pky, Muncie, IN 47303. TEL 765-282-4848, 800-428-5887, FAX 765-741-5110, minnetristainfo@minnetrista.net, http://www.minnetrista.net.

069 USA
MINT NEWS OF THE MINT MUSEUMS. Text in English. 1986. bi-m. looseleaf. USD 40 to members (effective 1999). 10 p./no.; back issues avail. **Document type:** *Newsletter.* **Description:** Coverage of current art exhibitions, art issues affecting the museum, additions and spotlights to the collections, educational programs, and affiliate organization news.
Former titles (until 1998): Mint Museum MemberNews; (until 1986): Mint Museum Newsletter
Related titles: CD-ROM ed.
Published by: Mint Museum of Art, 2730 Randolph Rd, Charlotte, NC 28207. TEL 704-337-2000, FAX 704-337-2101. Ed., R&P Phil Busher TEL 704-337-2009. Circ: 5,500 (paid); 8,500 (controlled).
Co-sponsor: Mint Museum of Craft & Design.

069 RUS ISSN 0869-8171
AM1
MIR MUZEYA. Text in Russian. 1938. m. USD 199 in United States (effective 2007). **Document type:** *Journal.*
Formerly (until 1993): Sovetskii Muzei (0256-1417)
Indexed: RASB, RILM.
Published by: Redaktsiya Zhurnala Mir Muzeya, ul Nizhnyaya Syromyatnicheskaya, dom 5, str. 3a, ofis 148, Moscow, 121019, Russian Federation. Ed. Yurii Pishchurin. **Dist. by:** East View Information Services, 10601 Wayzata Blvd, Minneapolis, MN 55305. TEL 952-252-1201, 800-477-1005, FAX 952-252-1202, info@eastview.com, http://www.eastview.com.

MISULJARYO/NATIONAL MUSEUM JOURNAL OF ARTS. *see* ART

708.1 USA
MONTCLAIR ART MUSEUM. BULLETIN. Text in English. 1929. bi-m. free to members. adv. illus. **Document type:** *Bulletin, Consumer.*
Formerly: Montclair Art Museum. Bulletin - Newsletter; Which was formed by the merger of: Montclair Art Museum. Bulletin (0027-0059); Montclair Art Museum. Newsletter
Published by: Montclair Art Museum, 3 S Mountain Ave, Montclair, NJ 07042-1747. TEL 973-746-5555, FAX 973-746-9118, aboulier@montclair-art.com, http://www.montclair-art.com/. Circ: 5,000.

069 ROM
MONUMENTE ISTORICE SI DE ARTA. Summaries in English, French, Russian; Text in Romanian. s-a. ROL 100, USD 73. illus.
Former titles: Revista Muzeelor si Monumentelor. Monumente Istorice si de Arta; Revista Muzeelor si Monumentelor. Monumente
Indexed: NumL.
Published by: Ministerul Culturii, Piata Presi Libere 1, Sector 1, Bucharest, Romania.

708.5 ITA
MONUMENTI MUSEI E GALLERIE PONTIFICIE MUSEO GREGORIANO ETRUSCO. CATALOGHI. Text in Italian. 1985. irreg., latest vol.3, 1994. price varies. **Document type:** *Catalog, Academic/Scholarly.*
Published by: (Monumenti Musei e Gallerie Pontificie Museo Gregoriano Etrusco), L'Erma di Bretschneider, Via Cassiodoro 19, Rome, 00193, Italy. TEL 39-06-6874127, FAX 39-06-6874129, lerma@lerma.it, http://www.lerma.it.

708.1 USA
MORRIS MUSEUM. NEWSLETTER. Text in English. 3/yr. free membership. **Document type:** *Newsletter.* **Description:** Informs members and the general public about the museum's collections of fine art and artifacts reflecting the cultural (both European and Native American) and natural histories of the Morris County, NJ, region. Announces forthcoming theatrical productions, workshops, lectures, and temporary exhibits for adults and children.
Published by: Morris Museum, 6 Normandy Heights Rd, Morristown, NJ 07960. TEL 973-971-3700, FAX 973-538-0154, http://www.MorrisMuseum.org. Ed. Paula Hunchar TEL 973-971-3700 ext 3705.

069.4 USA
MOSAIC (SAINT PETERSBURG). Text in English. 19??. q. free to members (effective 2011). illus. back issues avail. **Document type:** *Magazine, Consumer.* **Description:** Publishes news and announcements of art acquisitions, events, exhibitions and educational programs of the Museum of Fine Arts, St. Petersburg, Florida.
Indexed: AES.
Published by: Museum of Fine Arts, St. Petersburg, 225 Beach Dr NE, St. Petersburg, FL 33701. TEL 727-896-2667, FAX 727-894-4638, judy@fine-arts.org, http://www.fine-arts.org.

069 JPN ISSN 2185-1824
▼ **MUKAWA CHOURITSU HOBETSU HAKUBUTSUKAN KAMPOU/ HOBETSU MUSEUM. ANNUAL REPORT.** Text in Japanese. 2010. a. exchange basis. **Document type:** *Report, Corporate.*
Media: CD-ROM.
Published by: Hobetsu Museum/Hobetsu-choritsu Hakubutsukan, 80-6 Hobetsu, Hobetsu-cho, Yufutsu-gun, Hokkaido, 054-0211, Japan. TEL 86-145-453141, FAX 86-145-453141.

069 USA ISSN 0027-3627
N11.M83
MUNSON-WILLIAMS-PROCTOR INSTITUTE. BULLETIN. Text in English. 1941. m. free to members. illus. **Document type:** *Bulletin.* **Description:** Presents upcoming events and information on programming.
Published by: Munson-Williams-Proctor Institute, 310 Genesee St, Utica, NY 13417-4799. TEL 315-797-0000, FAX 315-797-5608. Ed. Joe Schmidt. Circ: 5,000.

069 CAN ISSN 0820-0165
➤ **MUSE (OTTAWA);** the voice of Canada's museum community. Text in English, French. 1966. 6/yr. CAD 35 domestic; USD 42 in United States; USD 50 elsewhere; CAD 7 per issue (effective 2005). adv. bk.rev.; software rev.; video rev.; Website rev. illus. back issues avail. **Document type:** *Magazine, Consumer.* **Description:** Provides a forum for the expression of ideas, opinions and research in museology.
Formerly (until 1983): C M A Gazette - A M C Gazette (0317-6045)
Indexed: A&ATA, BrArAb, C03, CBCARef, CBPI, CMPI, CPerI, NumL, P48, PQC, RASB, SCOPUS.
—IE. **CCC.**
Published by: Canadian Museums Association, 280 Metcalfe St, Ste 400, Ottawa, ON K2P 1R7, Canada. TEL 613-567-0099, FAX 613-233-5438, info@museums.ca, http://www.museums.ca. Ed., R&P Natasha Gauthier. Circ: 2,500.

069 BEL ISSN 0778-1350
MUSEA NOSTRA. Variant title: Reeks Musea Nostra. Text in Dutch. 1987. irreg., latest vol.38. illus. back issues avail. **Document type:** *Monographic series.* **Description:** Presents an overview of the origins and collections of specific museums in Belgium, with a discussion of the most significant works in the collection.
Related titles: French ed.
Published by: (Services Ventes), Credit Communal de Belgique/ Gemeentekrediet van Belgie, Bd Pacheco 44, Brussels, 1000, Belgium. TEL 32-2-222-1111, FAX 32-2-214-4038. **Dist. by:** Exhibitions International, Kolonel Begaultlaan 17, Leuven 3012, Belgium. TEL 32-16-202900, FAX 32-16-296129.

069 PRT ISSN 1646-4206
MUSEAL. Text in Portuguese. 2006. a. **Document type:** *Magazine, Consumer.*
Published by: Camara Municipal de Faro, Largo Dr Francisco Sa Carneiro, Mercado Municipal, Faro, 8000, Portugal. TEL 351-289-801678, http://www.cm-faro.pt.

708.4 FRA ISSN 1765-2480
N2080
MUSEE DES BEAUX-ARTS DE LYON. CAHIERS. Text in French. 1952. q. illus. index. back issues avail. **Document type:** *Bulletin.*
Formerly (until 2003): Musees et Monuments Lyonnais. Bulletin (0521-7032)
Indexed: B24, FR, RASB.
—INIST.
Published by: Musee des Beaux Arts, Association des Amis du Musee, Palais St. Pierre, 20 Place des Terreaux, Lyon, 69001, France. TEL 33-4-72101740, FAX 33-4-78281245. Ed. Vincent Pomarede. R&P Phippe Durey.

069 FRA ISSN 0181-1525
N6490
MUSEE NATIONAL D'ART MODERNE. CAHIERS. Text in French. 1979. q. EUR 88.50 domestic; EUR 95 foreign (effective 2008). adv. bk.rev. **Document type:** *Journal, Academic/Scholarly.* **Description:** Specializes in contemporary art history and aesthetics.
Indexed: A07, A20, A22, A30, A31, AA, ABM, AIAP, ArtInd, B04, B24, CA, FR, RASB, RILM, SCOPUS, T02.
—IE, Infotrieve, INIST. **CCC.**
Published by: (Editions du Centre Georges Pompidou, Musee National d'Art Moderne), Centre Georges Pompidou, Paris, Cedex 4 75191, France. TEL 33-1-44784288, FAX 33-1-44781205. Ed. Jean Pierre Criqui. Adv. contact Mathilde Tournier. Circ: 3,300.

069 POL ISSN 0027-3791
N3160
➤ **MUSEE NATIONAL DE VARSOVIE. BULLETIN.** Text in English, French, German, Italian. 1960. q. USD 34 (effective 2003). illus. 160 p./no. 1 cols./p.; back issues avail. **Document type:** *Journal, Academic/Scholarly.*
Indexed: B24.
Published by: Muzeum Narodowe w Warszawie/National Museum in Warsaw, Al Jerozolimskie 3, Warsaw, 00495, Poland. TEL 48-22-6211031, FAX 48-22-6228559, bulletin@mnw.art.pl, http://www.mnw.art.pl. Ed. Antoni Ziemba. Circ: 500.

708.36 AUT
MUSEEN DES MOBILIENDEPOTS. PUBLIKATIONSREIHE. Variant title: Eine Publikationsreihe der Museen des Mobiliendepots. Text in German. 1996. irreg., latest vol.29, 2010. price varies. **Document type:** *Monographic series, Academic/Scholarly.*
Published by: Boehlau Verlag GmbH & Co.KG., Wiesingerstr 1, Vienna, W 1010, Austria. TEL 43-1-3302427, FAX 43-1-3302432, boehlau@boehlau.at, http://www.boehlau.at.

069 CAN ISSN 0706-098X
AM21.A1
MUSEES. Text in French. 1978. a., latest vol.24, 2003. CAD 16.60 per issue (effective 2004). adv. back issues avail. **Document type:** *Magazine.* **Description:** Looks at museum-related subjects from around the world.
Indexed: PdeR.
Published by: Societe des Musees Quebecois, Succ Centre Ville, UQAM, C P 8888, Montreal, PQ H3C 3P8, Canada. TEL 514-987-3264, FAX 514-987-3379, museesadecouvrir@smq.uqam.ca, http://www.smq.qc.ca. Ed. Helene Panaioti. Circ: 1,500.

708.4 FRA ISSN 0027-383X
AM46.A1
MUSEES ET COLLECTIONS PUBLIQUES DE FRANCE. Text in French. 1932. 3/yr. EUR 22 to individual members; EUR 37 to individuals; EUR 52 in the European Union to institutions; EUR 59 elsewhere to institutions (effective 2008). adv. bk.rev. charts; illus. index. **Document type:** *Journal, Trade.*
Published by: Association Generale des Conservateurs des Collections Publiques de France, 6 Av du Mahatma Gandhi, Paris, 75116, France. TEL 33-1-44176000, FAX 33-1-44176060.

069 BEL ISSN 0776-1414
N1835
MUSEES ROYAUX D'ART ET D'HISTOIRE. BULLETIN/KONINKLIJKE MUSEA VOOR KUNST EN GESCHIEDENIS. BULLETIN. Text in Dutch, French. 1901. s-a. price varies. back issues avail. **Document type:** *Bulletin, Consumer.*
Former titles (until 1928): Musees Royaux du Cinquantenaire. Bulletin (0776-1406); (until 1911): Musees Royaux des Arts Decoratifs et Industriels. Bulletin (0776-1392)
Indexed: AIAP, B24, BrArAb, FR, IBR, IBZ, NumL, RASB.
—INIST.
Published by: Musees Royaux d'Art et d'Histoire/Koninklijke Musea voor Kunst en Geschiedenis, Jubelpark 10, Brussels, 1000, Belgium. TEL 32-2-2417213, http://www.kmkg-mrah.be.

708.97282 BEL ISSN 0027-3856
N1830
MUSEES ROYAUX DES BEAUX-ARTS DE BELGIQUE. BULLETIN/ KONINKLIJKE MUSEA VOOR SCHONE KUNSTEN VAN BELGIE. BULLETIN. Text in Dutch, French. 1928-1929; resumed 1938-1944; resumed 1952. irreg. price varies. illus. index. **Document type:** *Journal, Academic/Scholarly.* **Description:** Publishes scholarly articles reflecting the life of the museum, including discussions of exhibitions, acquisitions and technical matters.
Former titles (until 1944): Musees Royaux des Beaux-Arts de Belgique. Annuaire (0776-3026); (until 1929): Musees Royaux des Beaux-Arts de Belgique. Bulletin (0776-3085)
Indexed: A06, A07, A30, A31, AA, ArtInd, B04, CA, P30, RASB, T02.
—IE. **CCC.**
Published by: Musees Royaux des Beaux-Arts de Belgique/Koninklijke Musea voor Schone Kunsten van Belgie, Museumstraat 9, Brussels, 1000, Belgium. TEL 32-2-5083211, FAX 31-2-5083232, vanderauwera@fine-arts-museum.be.

069 700 ITA
MUSEI CIVICI D'ARTE ANTICA. BOLLETTINO. Text in Italian. 2008. irreg. **Document type:** *Bulletin, Consumer.*
Published by: Silvana Editoriale, Via Margherita de Vizzi 86, Cinisello Balsamo, MI 20092, Italy. TEL 39-02-61836337, FAX 39-02-6172464, silvanaeditoriale@silvanaeditoriale.it, http://www.silvanaeditoriale.it.

069 700 ITA
MUSEI CIVICI GENOVESI. BOLLETTINO. Text in Italian. 1979. a. **Document type:** *Bulletin, Consumer.*
Published by: Silvana Editoriale, Via Margherita de Vizzi 86, Cinisello Balsamo, MI 20092, Italy. TEL 39-02-61836337, FAX 39-02-6172464, silvanaeditoriale@silvanaeditoriale.it, http://www.silvanaeditoriale.it.

069 ITA
MUSEI CIVICI VENEZIANI. BOLLETTINO. Text in Italian. 1956. a. price varies. adv. back issues avail. **Document type:** *Bulletin, Consumer.* **Description:** Covers art and history of Venice.
Former titles (until 1991): Civici Musei Veneziani d'Arte e di Storia. Bollettino (0394-1027); (until 1979): Musei Civici Veneziani. Bollettino (0027-3864)
Related titles: Microform ed.
Indexed: AIAP.
Published by: Musei Civici Veneziani, Venice, VE, Italy. http://www.museiciviciveneziani.it. Circ: 1,650.

069 ITA ISSN 0523-9346
AM55.R6
MUSEI COMUNALI DI ROMA. BOLLETTINO. Text in Italian. 1954; N.S. 1987. irreg., latest vol.12, 1998. price varies. back issues avail. **Document type:** *Monographic series, Academic/Scholarly.*
Indexed: B24.
Published by: (Musei Comunali di Roma, Associazione Amici dei Musei di Roma), Gangemi Editore, Piazza San Pantaleo 4, Rome, Italy. TEL 39-06-6872774, FAX 39-06-6806189, info@gangemieditore.it, http://www.gangemi.com. Ed. Lucia Stefanelli Pirzio Biroli.

MUSEI D'ITALIA. *see* TRAVEL AND TOURISM

069 ITA ISSN 1824-0593
MUSEI E COLLEZIONI D'ETRURIA. Text in Italian. 1974. irreg. **Document type:** *Magazine, Consumer.*
Published by: (Consiglio Nazionale delle Ricerche, Istituto di Studi sulle Civilta Italiche e del Mediterraneo Antico), Consiglio Nazionale delle Ricerche (C N R)/Italian National Research Council, Piazzale Aldo Moro 7, Rome, 00185, Italy. TEL 39-06-49931, FAX 39-06-4461954, http://www.cnr.it.

069 ESP ISSN 1136-601X
AM121
MUSEO. Text in Spanish. 1996. s-a. back issues avail. **Document type:** *Magazine, Trade.*
Published by: Asociacion Profesional de Museologos de Espana (A P M E), Avenida Alfonso XII 68, Madrid, 28014, Spain. TEL 34-91-5306418.

069 ITA ISSN 2037-9226
MUSEO ARCHEOLOGICO DELLA FONDAZIONE DE PALO UNGARO. CATALOGO. Text in Italian. 2003. irreg. **Document type:** *Catalog, Consumer.*
Published by: (Fondazione De Palo Ungaro), Edipuglia Srl, Via Dalmazia 22-B, Santo Spirito, BA 70050, Italy. TEL 39-080-5333056, FAX 39-080-5333057, http://www.edipuglia.it.

069 ITA ISSN 0392-1859
MUSEO ARCHEOLOGICO DI TARQUINIA. MATERIALI. Text in Italian. 1980. irreg., latest vol.13, 1995. price varies. back issues avail. **Document type:** *Monographic series, Academic/Scholarly.*
Published by: Giorgio Bretschneider, Via Crescenzio 43, Rome, 00193, Italy. TEL 39-06-6879361, FAX 39-06-6864543, info@bretschneider.it, http://www.bretschneider.it.

069 ARG
MUSEO ARGENTINO DE CIENCIAS NATURALES "BERNARDINO RIVADAVIA". EXTRA. Text in Spanish. 1949. irreg. **Document type:** *Monographic series, Academic/Scholarly.*
Formerly: Museo Argentino de Ciencias Naturales "Bernardino Rivadavia". Instituto Nacional de Investigacion de las Ciencias Naturales. Extra (0325-1845)
Indexed: ASFA, B21, ESPM.
Published by: Museo Argentino de Ciencias Naturales Bernardino Rivadavia, Instituto Nacional de Investigacion de las Ciencias Naturales, Avda. Angel Gallardo 470, Casilla de Correo 220-Sucursal 5, Buenos Aires, Argentina. TEL 54-11-49820306, FAX 54-11-49824494, macn@musbr.org.secyt.gov.ar, http://www.macn.secyt.gov.ar/.

069 ARG ISSN 1515-7652
MUSEO ARGENTINO DE CIENCIAS NATURALES BERNARDINO RIVADAVIA. MONOGRAFIAS. Text in Spanish. 2001. irreg. back issues avail. **Document type:** *Monographic series, Academic/Scholarly.*
Indexed: B25, BIOSIS Prev, C01, GeoRef, MycolAb, Z01.
Published by: Museo Argentino de Ciencias Naturales Bernardino Rivadavia, Instituto Nacional de Investigacion de las Ciencias Naturales, Avda. Angel Gallardo 470, Casilla de Correo 220-Sucursal 5, Buenos Aires, Argentina. TEL 54-11-49820306, FAX 54-11-49824494, info@macn.gov.ar, http://www.macn.secyt.gov.ar/.

069 ARG ISSN 1853-0400
MUSEO ARGENTINO DE CIENCIAS NATURALES. REVISTA. Text in Spanish. 2005. s-a. **Document type:** *Magazine, Consumer.*
Published by: Museo Argentino de Ciencias Naturales Bernardino Rivadavia, Instituto Nacional de Investigacion de las Ciencias Naturales, Avda. Angel Gallardo 470, Casilla de Correo 220-Sucursal 5, Buenos Aires, Argentina. TEL 54-11-49820306, FAX 54-11-49824494, info@macn.gov.ar, http://www.macn.secyt.gov.ar/.

708.5 ITA ISSN 0392-2413
N2740.6
MUSEO BODONIANO DI PARMA. BOLLETTINO. Text in Italian. 1972. a. bk.rev. **Document type:** *Bulletin, Consumer.* **Description:** Covers the history of printing art.
Published by: Museo Bodoniano, Biblioteca Palatina, Palazzo della Pilotta, Parma, PR 43100, Italy. TEL 39-0521-220411, FAX 39-0521-235662.

069 ESP ISSN 1133-8741
MUSEO DE AMERICA. ANALES. Text in Spanish. 1993. a. back issues avail. **Document type:** *Monographic series, Academic/Scholarly.*
Indexed: AICP.
Published by: (Museo de America), Ministerio de Educacion, Cultura y Deporte, Centro de Publicaciones, c/o Ciudad Universitaria, S/N, Madrid, 28040, Spain. TEL 34-91-453-9800, FAX 34-91-4539884.

069 COL
MUSEO DE ARTE COLONIAL DE BOGOTA. BOLETIN INFORMATIVO. Text in Spanish. 1975. m. free.
Published by: Museo Colonial de Bogota, Carrera 6, 9-77, Bogota, CUND, Colombia. Circ: 500.

069 ARG ISSN 0326-7202
MUSEO DE LA PLATA. NOTAS. Text in Spanish. 1931. irreg. **Document type:** *Monographic series, Academic/Scholarly.*
Formerly (until 1934): Museo de la Plata. Notas Preliminares (0327-3393)
Related titles: ◆ Series: Museo de la Plata. Notas. Antropologia. ISSN 0375-4634; ◆ Museo de la Plata. Notas. Zoologia. ISSN 0372-4549.
Published by: Universidad Nacional de La Plata, Facultad de Ciencias Naturales y Museo, Paseo el Bosque s-n, La Plata, 1900, Argentina. TEL 54-221-4257744, FAX 54-221-4259161, museo@museo.fcnym.unlp.edu.ar, http://www.fcnym.unlp.edu.ar/ museo/.

069 ESP ISSN 0210-7791
EL MUSEO DE PONTEVEDRA. Text in Spanish, Catalan. 1942. a. **Document type:** *Magazine, Consumer.*
Indexed: RILM.
Published by: Museo de Pontevedra, Pasanteria, 10, Pontevedra, 36002, Spain. TEL 34-986-851455, FAX 34-986-843238.

069 ESP ISSN 0212-548X
MUSEO DE ZARAGOZA. BOLETIN. Text in Spanish. 1917. a. **Document type:** *Bulletin, Consumer.*
Supersedes (in 1982): Boletin del Museo Provincial de Bellas Artes de Zaragoza y de la Real Academia de Nobles y Bellas Artes de San Luis (0212-5455); Which was superseded (in 1950): Boletin de la Academia Aragonesa de Nobles y Bellas Artes de San Luis y del Museo Provincial de Bellas Artes de Zaragoza (0212-5463); Which was formerly (until 1934): Museo Provincial de Bellas Artes. Boletin (0212-5471)
Indexed: FR.
—INIST.
Published by: Museo de Zaragoza, Plaza de los Sitios, 6, Zaragoza, 50001, Spain. TEL 34-976-222181, FAX 34-976-225682, http://www.aragonesasi.com/museopz2.htm/.

069 DOM
MUSEO DEL HOMBRE DOMINICANO. SERIE CATALOGOS Y MEMORIAS. Text in Spanish. 1976. irreg., latest vol.41. illus.
Published by: Museo del Hombre Dominicano, Plaza de la Cultura, Calle Pedro Henriquez Urena, Santo Domingo, Dominican Republic.

069 DOM
MUSEO DEL HOMBRE DOMINICANO. SERIE MESA REDONDA CONFERENCIAS. Text in Spanish. 1974. irreg., latest vol.12, 1981. price varies. illus.
Published by: Museo del Hombre Dominicano, Plaza de la Cultura, Calle Pedro Henriquez Urena, Santo Domingo, Dominican Republic.

069 ESP ISSN 0210-8143
AM101.M238
MUSEO DEL PRADO. BOLETIN. Text in Spanish. 1980. a., latest vol.23, no.41, 2005. **Document type:** *Bulletin, Consumer.* **Description:** Provides information on the activities of the Prado Museum.
Indexed: A20, B24, FR.
Published by: Ministerio de Educacion y Cultura, Museo del Prado, C. Ruiz de Alarcon 23, Madrid, 28014, Spain. TEL 34-91-3302800, FAX 34-91-3302856, museo.nacional@prado.mcu.es, http://museoprado.mcu.es.

069 ESP ISSN 0211-3171
N7
MUSEO E INSTITUTO CAMON AZNAR. BOLETIN. Text in Spanish. 1980. q. USD 65 foreign (effective 2002).
Indexed: B24, P09, PCI, RILM.
Published by: Museo e Instituto Camon Aznar, Espoz y Mina, 23, Zaragoza, Aragon 50003, Spain. TEL 34-976-397328. Ed. Pilar Camon Alvarez.

508.74 CHL ISSN 0716-0224
QH119
MUSEO NACIONAL DE HISTORIA NATURAL. PUBLICACIONES OCASIONALES. Text in Spanish. 1963. irreg., latest vol.51, 1997. price varies. adv. **Document type:** *Monographic series.*
Formerly: Museo Nacional de Historia Natural. Publicacion Ocasional (0581-6424)
Indexed: ASFA, B21, C01, ESPM, Z01.
Published by: Museo Nacional de Historia Natural, Casilla 787, Santiago, Chile. TEL 56-2-6814095, FAX 56-2-6817182. Ed. Daniel Frassinetti C. Adv. contact Luis Hidalgo.

508.74 URY ISSN 1510-7353
➤ **MUSEO NACIONAL DE HISTORIA NATURAL Y ANTROPOLOGIA. PUBLICACION EXTRA.** Text in Spanish; Summaries in English. 1970. irreg. per issue exchange basis. back issues avail. **Document type:** *Monographic series, Academic/Scholarly.* **Description:** Deals with biology, anthropology, earth sciences, paleontology and history of science.
Formerly (until 1999): Museo Nacional de Historia Natural. Publicacion Extra (0797-0420)
Indexed: C01, GeoRef, SpeleolAb, WildRev, Z01.
Published by: Museo Nacional de Historia Natural, Casilla de Correos 399, Montevideo, 11000, Uruguay. TEL 598-2-916-0908, FAX 598-2-917-0213. Ed. Alvaro Mones.

069 ESP ISSN 0212-8438
MUSEO PROVINCIAL DE LUGO. BOLETIN. Text in Spanish. 1941. a. back issues avail.
Supersedes (in 1983): Comision Provincial de Monumentos Historicos y Artisticos de Lugo (0210-8569)
Published by: Museo Provincial de Lugo, Plaza de la Soledad, s-n, Lugo, 27001, Spain. TEL 34-982-242112, FAX 34-982-240240, http://www.museolugo.org/.

MUSEO SEFARDI. NOTICIAS. *see* RELIGIONS AND THEOLOGY—Judaic

069 ITA ISSN 1723-9400
MUSEO STIBBERT FIRENZE. Text in Multiple languages. 1999. s-a. EUR 25 (effective 2008). **Document type:** *Bulletin, Consumer.*
Related titles: Online - full text ed.: ISSN 1974-4005. 2003.
Published by: Edizioni Polistampa, Via Livorno 8-32, Florence, FI 50142, Italy. TEL 39-055-737871, FAX 39-055-229430, info@polistampa.com.

069 CAN ISSN 0380-4623
MUSEOGRAMME. Text in English, French. 1973. 6/yr. CAD 26.75; CAD 34.25 in United States; CAD 42.80 elsewhere. adv. **Document type:** *Newsletter.* **Description:** Membership newsletter of the association.
Indexed: RASB.
Published by: Canadian Museums Association, 280 Metcalfe St, Ste 400, Ottawa, ON K2P 1R7, Canada. TEL 613-567-0099, FAX 613-233-5438. Ed. Natalie Blais.

069 BRA ISSN 1984-3917
➤ **MUSEOLOGIA E PATRIMONIO.** Text in English, French, Portuguese, Spanish. 2008. s-a. free. abstr. back issues avail. **Document type:** *Journal, Academic/Scholarly.* **Description:** Covers museum and heritage studies, including scientific articles, reviews, reports, abstracts of dissertations, and reprint of rare classic text.
Media: Online - full content.
Published by: Universidade Federal do Estado do Rio de Janeiro. Programa de Pos-Graduacao em Museologia e Patrimonio tacnet.cultural@uol.com.br, http://www.unirio.br/cch/ppg-pmus/. Eds. Luiz Carlos Borges, Nilson Alves de Moraes, Tereza Scheiner.

069 PRT ISSN 1646-6705
MUSEOLOGIA.PT. Text in Portuguese. 2007. a. **Document type:** *Magazine, Consumer.*
Published by: Institutos dos Museus e da Conservacao, Palacio Nacional da Ajuda, Lisbon, 1349-021, Portugal. TEL 351-213-650800, FAX 351-213-647821, http://www.ipmuseus.pt.

069 ITA ISSN 1123-265X
➤ **MUSEOLOGIA SCIENTIFICA.** Text in English, French, Italian; Summaries in English, French. 1973. s-a. illus.; maps. index. back issues avail. **Document type:** *Proceedings, Academic/Scholarly.* **Description:** Covers scientific museology, history of museums, and related activities.
Formerly (until 1983): A N M S (1721-1514)
Related titles: Supplement(s): Museologia Scientifica. Memorie. ISSN 1972-6848.
Indexed: Z01.
—BLDSC (5986.845000).
Published by: Associazione Nazionale Musei Scientifici Orti Botanici Giardini Zoologici Acquari, c/o Museo Botanico, Via Giorgio La Pira 4, Florence, FI 50121, Italy. musbot@unifi.it, http://www.anms.it. Ed. Guido Moggi. Pub. Michele Lanzinger. Circ: 500.

069 GBR ISSN 1354-5825
MUSEOLOGICAL REVIEW. Text in English. 1994. a. bk.rev. back issues avail. **Document type:** *Journal, Academic/Scholarly.* **Description:** Features experimental research in museum studies.
Related titles: Online - full text ed.: free (effective 2009).
Published by: University of Leicester, Department of Museum Studies, 103/105 Princess Road E, Leicester, Leics LE1 7LG, United Kingdom. TEL 44-116-2523963, FAX 44-116-2523960, http://www2.le.ac.uk/Members/mjs76/structure/arts/museum.

069 FRA ISSN 1951-3283
MUSEOLOGIES. Text in French. 2006. irreg. back issues avail. **Document type:** *Monographic series, Consumer.*
Published by: L' Harmattan, 5 Rue de l'Ecole Polytechnique, Paris, 75005, France. TEL 33-1-43257651, FAX 33-1-43258203.

069 CAN ISSN 1718-5181
AM111
MUSEOLOGIES; les cahiers d'etudes superieures. Text in French. 2006 (Oct.). s-a. CAD 48; CAD 37 to students (effective 2007). **Document type:** *Journal, Academic/Scholarly.*
Published by: Universite du Quebec a Montreal, Institut du Patrimoine, CP 8888, Succursale Centre-ville, Montreal, PQ H3C 3P8, Canada. TEL 514-987-3000, institutdupatrimoine@uqam.ca.

069 ITA ISSN 0541-377X
MUSEOSCIENZA. Text in Italian. 1962-1976 (no.6); N.S. 1991. bi-m. adv. bk.rev. bibl.; charts; illus. **Document type:** *Journal, Academic/Scholarly.*
Indexed: RASB.
Published by: Museo Nazionale della Scienza e della Tecnica Leonardo da Vinci/National Museum of Science and Technology Leonardo da Vinci, Via San Vittore 21, Milan, MI 20123, Italy. TEL 39-02-485551, FAX 39-02-48010016, museo@museoscienza.org, http://www.museoscienza.org. Circ: 2,000.

069 ESP ISSN 1695-470X
MUSEU ARQUEOLOGIC D'ELVISSA I FORMENTERA. TREBALLS/ MUSEO ARQUEOLOGICO DE IBIZA Y FORMENTERA. TRABAJOS. Text in Multiple languages. 1979. s-a. **Document type:** *Monographic series, Academic/Scholarly.*
Formerly (until 1994): Museo Arqueologico de Ibiza. Trabajos (1130-8095)
Published by: Museo Arqueologico de Ibiza, Plaza de la Catedral, 3, Ibiza, Baleares 07800, Spain. Ed. Jorge Humberto Fernandez Gomez.

069 PRT ISSN 1646-5008
MUSEU DA POLVORA NEGRA. CADERNOS. Text in Portuguese. 2006. a. **Document type:** *Magazine, Consumer.*
Published by: Camara Municipal de Oeiras, Largo Marques de Pombal, Oeiras, 2784-501, Portugal. TEL 351-21-4408300, FAX 351-21-4408712, geral@cm-oeiras.pt, http://www.cm-oeiras.pt.

069 ESP ISSN 2013-0384
MUSEU EPISCOPAL DE VIC. QUADERNS. Key Title: Quaderns del Museu Episcopal de Vic. Text in Spanish, Catalan. 2005. a. EUR 20 (effective 2010). **Document type:** *Monographic series, Academic/Scholarly.*
Related titles: Online - full text ed.: ISSN 2013-7400. 2005.
Published by: Museu Episcola de Vic, Placa Bisbe Oliba, 7, Vic, Barcelona, 08500, Spain. TEL 34-938-869360, FAX 34-938-869361, informacio@museuepiscopalvic.com, http://www.museuepiscopalvic.com/.

069 ESP ISSN 2172-1378
MUSEU I BIBLIOTECA EPISCOPALS DE VIC. SERIE CATALEGS. Text in Catalan. 1989. a. **Document type:** *Catalog.*
Published by: Musei i Biblioteca Episcopals de Vic, Placa Bisbe Oliba, 3, Vic, Barcelona, 08500, Spain. TEL 34-938-869360, FAX 34-938-869361, informacio@museuepiscopalvic.com, http://www.museuepiscopalvic.com/.

MUSEU NACIONAL D'ART DE CATALUYNA. BUTLLETI. *see* ART

069.1 USA ISSN 1938-3940
AM1 CODEN: MUNSAJ
MUSEUM. Text in English. 1924. bi-m. USD 38 domestic to non-members (effective 2010). adv. bk.rev. illus. Index. back issues avail. **Document type:** *Magazine, Consumer.* **Description:** Magazine for museum professionals and others interested in all types of museums.
Formerly (until 2008): Museum News (0027-4089)
Related titles: Online - full text ed.
Indexed: A&ATA, A06, A07, A20, A22, A30, A31, AA, ABM, ABS&EES, AIAP, ASCA, AbAn, ArtInd, B04, B24, BAS, BRI, BrArAb, CBRI, E06, I14, NumL, P48, PQC, RASB, RILM, SCOPUS.
—BLDSC (5987.090000), IE, Infotrieve, Ingenta. **CCC.**
Published by: American Association of Museums, 1575 Eye St, NW, Ste 400, Washington, DC 20005. TEL 202-289-1818, FAX 202-289-6578, servicecentral@aam-us.org. Pub. John Strand. Adv. contact Anne Curran Conrad. Circ: 17,000.

069 GBR ISSN 1479-8360
➤ **MUSEUM & SOCIETY.** Text in English. 1990; N.S. 2003. 3/yr. free (effective 2011). bk.rev.; film rev. abstr.; bibl.; illus.; stat. index. back issues avail. **Document type:** *Journal, Academic/Scholarly.* **Description:** Covers all issues associated with museums and other places of public culture concerned with collecting, exhibiting and display.
Formerly (until 2003): New Research in Museum Studies (Print) (1362-6329)
Media: Online - full text.
Indexed: A07, A30, A31, A39, AA, ArtInd, B04, BRD, BrArAb, C27, C29, CA, D03, D04, E13, R14, S14, S15, S18, T02, W03, W05.
—BLDSC (6087.760300). **CCC.**
Published by: University of Leicester, Department of Museum Studies, 105 Princess Rd E, Leicester, LE1 7LG, United Kingdom. TEL 44-116-2523963, FAX 44-116-2523960, museum.studies@leicester.ac.uk, http://www.le.ac.uk/museumstudies/.

➤ **MUSEUM ANTHROPOLOGY.** *see* ANTHROPOLOGY

➤ **THE MUSEUM ARCHAEOLOGIST.** *see* ARCHAEOLOGY

708.92 NLD ISSN 0077-2275
MUSEUM BOIJMANS-VAN BEUNINGEN. AGENDA/MUSEUM BOYMANS-VAN BEUNINGEN. DIARY. Text in Dutch, English. 1949. a. EUR 19 (effective 2009). adv.
Published by: Museum Boijmans van Beuningen, Postbus 2277, Rotterdam, 3000 CG, Netherlands. TEL 31-10-4419400, FAX 31-10-4360500, info@boijmans.nl, http://www.boijmans.nl.

069 USA
MUSEUM CURRENTS. Text in English. 1968. bi-m. membership. 4 p./no.; back issues avail. **Document type:** *Newsletter.*
Formerly: Triton Museum of Art. Members' Bulletin
Published by: Triton Museum of Art, 1505 Warburton Ave, Santa Clara, CA 95050. TEL 408-247-3754, FAX 408-247-3796, triton246@aol.com, tritonpublicity@aol.com. Ed., Adv. contact Cindy Millan TEL 408-247-3754 ext 21. R&P Jill Meyers TEL 408-247-3754 ext 23. Circ: 1,500 (controlled).

708.92 NLD ISSN 1871-9015
MUSEUM DE FUNDATIE. BULLETIN. Text in Dutch. 1991. 3/yr.
Formerly (until 2005): Hannema-de Stuers Fundatie. Bulletin (1380-1716)
Published by: Museum de Fundatie, Blijmarkt 20, Zwolle, 8011 NE, Netherlands. http://www.museumhsf.nl.

MUSEUM ETHNOGRAPHERS GROUP. OCCASIONAL PAPER. *see* ANTHROPOLOGY

708 DEU ISSN 1865-4355
MUSEUM FUER VOELKERKUNDE DRESDEN. STAATLICHE ETHNOGRAPHISCHE SAMMLUNGEN. ABHANDLUNGEN UND BERICHTE. Text in English, German; Abstracts in English, German, Russian. 1881-1989; resumed 19??. irreg., latest vol.53, 2008. price varies. bk.rev. back issues avail. **Document type:** *Journal, Academic/Scholarly.* **Description:** Volume of separate treatises concerning different regional fields of ethnology research.
Former titles (until 2005): Staatliches Museum fuer Voelkerkunde Dresden. Abhandlungen und Berichte (0070-7295); (until 1962): Staatliches Museum fuer Voelkerkunde und Tierkunde. Abhandlungen und Berichte
Indexed: AICP, AnthLit, BAS, DIP, IBR, IBZ, MLA-IB, P30.
Published by: (Museum fuer Voelkerkunde Dresden, Staatliche Ethnographische Sammlungen), V W B - Verlag fuer Wissenschaft und Bildung, Postfach 110368, Berlin, 10833, Germany. TEL 49-30-2510415, FAX 49-30-2511136, info@vwb-verlag.com, http://www.vwb-verlag.com. Ed. Dr. Claus Deimel. Circ: 1,000.

069 DEU ISSN 1865-4347
MUSEUM FUER VOELKERKUNDE DRESDEN. STAATLICHE ETHNOGRAPHISCHE SAMMLUNGEN. JAHRBUCH. Text in German. 1907. irreg., latest 2007. **Document type:** *Monographic series, Academic/Scholarly.*
Former titles: Museum fuer Voelkerkunde, Leipzig. Jahrbuch (0075-8663); (until 1952): Staedtisches Museum fuer Voelkerkunde zu Leipzig. Jahrbuch (0138-3450)
Indexed: AICP, AnthLit, FR, IBR, IBZ, RASB.
Published by: (Museum fuer Voelkerkunde Dresden, Staatliche Ethnographische Sammlungen), V W B - Verlag fuer Wissenschaft und Bildung, Postfach 110368, Berlin, 10833, Germany. TEL 49-30-2510415, FAX 49-30-2511136, info@vwb-verlag.com.

069 USA
MUSEUM HIGHLIGHTS. Text in English. 1982. q. USD 25. **Document type:** *Newsletter.* **Description:** Covers donating exhibitions, programs, educational activities and collections management of South-Western art and history.
Published by: (Maricopa County Historical Society), Desert Caballeros Western Museum, 21 N Frontier St, Wickenburg, AZ 85390-1417. TEL 602-684-2272. Ed., R&P Michael Ettema. Circ: 600.

069 USA ISSN 1936-9816
➤ **MUSEUM HISTORY JOURNAL.** Text in English. 2008 (Jan.). s-a. USD 40 to individuals; USD 159 to institutions; USD 259 combined subscription to institutions (print & online eds.) (effective 2009). **Document type:** *Journal, Academic/Scholarly.* **Description:** Covers traditional museums on natural history and fine art, as well as related cultural institutions such as aquaria, zoos, architectural sites, archives and planetariums.
Related titles: Online - full text ed.: ISSN 1936-9824. 2008 (Jan.).
—BLDSC (5987.706000). **CCC.**
Published by: Left Coast Press, Inc., 1630 N Main St, Ste 400, Walnut Creek, CA 94596. TEL 925-935-3380, FAX 925 935-2916, journals@lcoastpress.com, http://www.lcoastpress.com.

069 GBR ISSN 1350-0775
AM1
➤ **MUSEUM INTERNATIONAL (ENGLISH EDITION).** Text in English. 1927. q. GBP 231 in United Kingdom to institutions; EUR 292 in Europe to institutions; USD 384 in the Americas to institutions; USD 449 elsewhere to institutions; GBP 265 combined subscription in United Kingdom to institutions (print & online eds.); EUR 337 combined subscription in Europe to institutions (print & online eds.); USD 443 combined subscription in the Americas to institutions (print & online eds.); USD 517 combined subscription elsewhere to institutions (print & online eds.) (effective 2012). adv. bk.rev. charts; illus. index, cum.index: 1948-1973. back issues avail.; reprint service avail. from PSC. **Document type:** *Journal, Academic/Scholarly.* **Description:** Aims to foster dialogue between research in the social sciences and political decision-making in a changing cultural environment.
Formerly (until 1993): Museum (English Edition) (0027-3996); Which was Superseded (in 1972): Museum (Bilingual Edition) (1012-4225); Which was formerly (1927 -1946): Mouseion (0369-1349)
Related titles: CD-ROM ed.; Online - full text ed.: ISSN 1468-0033. GBP 231 in United Kingdom to institutions; EUR 292 in Europe to institutions; USD 384 in the Americas to institutions; USD 449 elsewhere to institutions (effective 2012) (from IngentaConnect); ♦ French ed.: Museum International (French Edition). ISSN 1020-2226.
Indexed: A01, A03, A06, A07, A08, A20, A22, A26, A30, A31, AA, ABM, AIAP, AICP, API, ASCA, AmHI, ArtHuCI, ArtInd, B04, BNNA, BrArAb, CA, ChemAb, CurCont, E01, H07, IBR, IBZ, IIFP, IITV, MEA&I, NumL, PCI, PerIslam, RASB, RILM, SCOPUS, T02.
—BLDSC (5987.708000), IE, Ingenta. **CCC.**
Published by: (UNESCO FRA), Wiley-Blackwell Publishing Ltd. (Subsidiary of: John Wiley & Sons, Inc.), 9600 Garsington Rd, Oxford, OX4 2DQ, United Kingdom. TEL 44-1865-776868, FAX 44-1865-714591, customerservices@blackwellpublishing.com. Ed. Isabelle Vinson TEL 33-1-45684353. Adv. contact Craig Pickett TEL 44-1865-476267.

069 GBR ISSN 1020-2226
➤ **MUSEUM INTERNATIONAL (FRENCH EDITION).** Text in French. 1927. bi-m. GBP 231 in United Kingdom to institutions; EUR 292 in Europe to institutions; USD 384 in the Americas to institutions; USD 449 elsewhere to institutions; GBP 265 combined subscription in United Kingdom to institutions (print & online eds.); EUR 337 combined subscription in Europe to institutions (print & online eds.); USD 443 combined subscription in the Americas to institutions (print & online eds.); USD 517 combined subscription elsewhere to institutions (print & online eds.) (effective 2012). charts; illus. **Document type:** *Journal, Academic/Scholarly.*
Formerly (until 1993): Museum (French Edition) (0304-3002); Which superseded in part (in 1972): Museum (1012-4225); Which was formerly (until 1948): Museion (0369-1349)
Related titles: Online - full text ed.: ISSN 1755-5825. GBP 231 in United Kingdom to institutions; EUR 292 in Europe to institutions; USD 384 in the Americas to institutions; USD 449 elsewhere to institutions (effective 2012) (from IngentaConnect); ◆ English ed.: Museum International (English Edition). ISSN 1350-0775.
Indexed: A22, A30, A31, ArtHuCI, CA, CurCont, E01, FR, T02, W07.
—IE. **CCC.**
Published by: (UNESCO Publishing FRA), Wiley-Blackwell Publishing Ltd. (Subsidiary of: John Wiley & Sons, Inc.), 9600 Garsington Rd, Oxford, OX4 2DQ, United Kingdom. TEL 44-1865-776868, FAX 44-1865-714591, customerservices@blackwellpublishing.com, http://www.wiley.com/WileyCDA/. Eds. Isabelle Vinson, Monique Couratier.

069 GBR ISSN 0964-7775
AM121
➤ **MUSEUM MANAGEMENT AND CURATORSHIP.** Abbreviated title: M M C. Text in English. 1982. q. GBP 478 combined subscription in United Kingdom to institutions (print & online eds.); EUR 746, USD 937 combined subscription to institutions (print & online eds.) (effective 2012). adv. bk.rev. illus.; abstr. Index. back issues avail.; reprint service avail. from PSC. **Document type:** *Journal, Academic/Scholarly.* **Description:** Encourages a continuous reassessment of the disciplines governing the establishment, care, presentation and understanding of museum collections.
Formerly (until 1990): International Journal of Museum Management and Curatorship (0260-4779)
Related titles: Microform ed.: (from PQC); Online - full text ed.: ISSN 1872-9185. GBP 431 in United Kingdom to institutions; EUR 671, USD 843 to institutions (effective 2012) (from IngentaConnect).
Indexed: A&ATA, A07, A22, A26, A30, A31, AA, AIAP, API, ArtInd, B04, B24, BrArAb, CA, E01, I05, NumL, P10, P48, P53, P54, PQC, RASB, SCOPUS, T02.
—BLDSC (5987.763000), IE, Infotrieve, Ingenta. **CCC.**
Published by: Routledge (Subsidiary of: Taylor & Francis Group), 4 Park Sq, Milton Park, Abingdon, Oxon OX14 4RN, United Kingdom. TEL 44-20-70176000, FAX 44-20-70176336, subscriptions@tandf.co.uk, http://www.routledge.com. Ed. Robert R Janes. Adv. contact Linda Hann TEL 44-1344-779945. **Subscr. to:** Taylor & Francis Ltd., Journals Customer Service, Sheepen Pl, Colchester, Essex CO3 3LP, United Kingdom. TEL 44-20-70175544, FAX 44-20-70175198.

069 AUS ISSN 1320-2677
MUSEUM MATTERS. Text in English. 1975. q. bk.rev. charts; illus.; tr.lit. back issues avail. **Document type:** *Newsletter.* **Description:** Contains technical information on museological and conservation issues as well as museum news.
Former titles (until 1993): Museums Association of Australia. N.S.W. Branch. Quarterly News (0815-4082); (until 1983): Museums Association of Australia. N.S.W. Branch. Quarterly Newsletter (0728-5817); (until 1981): Quarterly Newsletter of the Museums Association of Australia. New South Wales Branch (0313-0827); (until 1975): Museum Profile (0310-3528); (until 1973): Museums Association of Australia. N.S.W. Branch. News sheet
Indexed: BrArAb, NumL.
Published by: Museums Australia (N.S.W.) Inc., c/o Paul Bentley, PO Box 250, Sydney, NSW 2006, Australia. TEL 61-2-92110113, FAX 61-2-93864259, mansw@museumsaustralia.org.au, http://www.museumsaustralia.org.au.

069 USA
MUSEUM NOTES (SPOKANE). Text in English. 196?. q. USD 25. back issues avail. **Document type:** *Newsletter.* **Description:** Aimed at informing members of events, programs, exhibits, acquisitions, and future plans of the museum.
Published by: Eastern Washington State Historical Society, Cheney Cowles Museum, W 2316 First Ave, Spokane, WA 99204. TEL 509-456-3931, FAX 509-456-7690. Ed. Glenn Mason. R&P Yvonne Lopez Morton. Circ: 1,500.

069.5 SWE ISSN 0081-5691
DS714
➤ **MUSEUM OF FAR EASTERN ANTIQUITIES. BULLETIN.** Text mainly in English. 1929. a. SEK 425 per issue (effective 2010). back issues avail. **Document type:** *Yearbook, Academic/Scholarly.* **Description:** Covers archeology and art history of Asia, ancient and classical.
Indexed: AICP, BAS, FR, MLA, MLA-IB, RASB, SCOPUS.
—BLDSC (2624.500000), INIST.
Published by: Oestasiatiska Museet/Museum of Far Eastern Antiquities, P O Box 16301, Stockholm, 10327, Sweden. TEL 46-8-51955750, FAX 46-8-51955755, info@ostasiatiska.se. Ed. Dr. Martin Svensson Ekstroem TEL 46-8-51955752.

069.1 USA
MUSEUM OF MODERN ART FILM AT THE GRAMERCY THEATRE : FILM AND MEDIA EXHIBITIONS. Text in English. 1950. m. (11/yr.). illus. **Description:** Publishes schedule of events at the museum with description of exhibitions and film programs.
Former titles (until Nov.2002): M o M A Film at the Gramercy Theatre; (until 2002): Calendar; (until 1998): Members Calendar (0195-105X); (until 1980): Calendar; (until 1968): Members Calendar; (until 1965): Members Calendar of Events
Published by: Museum of Modern Art, 11 W 53rd St, New York, NY 10019. TEL 212-708-9400, http://www.moma.org.

069 948.5 SWE ISSN 1101-9301
MUSEUM OF NATIONAL ANTIGUITIES. MONOGRAPHS. Text in Multiple languages. 1991. irreg., latest vol.6, 2003. price varies. back issues avail. **Document type:** *Monographic series, Academic/Scholarly.*
Published by: Statens Historiska Museum/Museum of National Antiguities in Sweden, Narvavaegen 13-17, Stockholm, 11484, Sweden. TEL 46-8-51955600, info@historiska.se.

MUSEUM OF NATIONAL ANTIGUITIES. STUDIES. *see* HISTORY—History Of Europe

069 USA
MUSEUM OF THE AMERICAN PIANO. NEWSLETTER. Text in English. 1988. q. looseleaf. membership. adv. charts; illus. **Document type:** *Newsletter.*
Published by: Museum of the American Piano, 291 Broadway, New York, NY 10007. TEL 212-246-4646. Ed. Kalman Detrich. Circ: 2,000.

069.4 GBR ISSN 1359-771X
AM111
MUSEUM PRACTICE. Abbreviated title: M P. Text in English. 1996. q. GBP 56 domestic to non-members; GBP 110 foreign to non-members; free to members (effective 2009). adv. bk.rev. bibl.; tr.lit. back issues avail. **Document type:** *Magazine, Academic/Scholarly.* **Description:** Contains information and guidance on practical and technical aspects of work in museums and galleries.
Related titles: Online - full text ed.
—IE. **CCC.**
Published by: Museums Association, 24 Calvin St, London, E1 6NW, United Kingdom. TEL 44-20-74266920, FAX 44-20-74266962, info@museumsassociation.org. Ed. Javier Pes. Adv. contact Dennis Jarrett TEL 44-20-74266941. page GBP 110; trim 210 x 278. Circ: 7,500.

708.1 USA
MUSEUM RECORD. Text in English. 1982. bi-m. USD 15; USD 22 foreign (effective 1999). back issues avail. **Document type:** *Newsletter.* **Description:** Focuses on activities sponsored by the society.
Formerly: Bay County Crier
Published by: Bay County Historical Society, 321 Washington Ave, Bay City, MI 48708. TEL 517-893-5733, FAX 517-893-5741. Ed. Claire O'Laughlin. Circ: 500. **Co-sponsor:** Historical Museum of Bay County.

MUSEUM STORE. *see* BUSINESS AND ECONOMICS—Marketing And Purchasing

069 USA
MUSEUM TRUSTEESHIP. Text in English. 1986. 4/yr. membership. adv. back issues avail. **Document type:** *Newsletter.* **Description:** Publishes articles and newsworthy pieces on the subject of museum governance, the roles and responsibilities of museum trustees, trustee education, and legislative updates.
Published by: Museum Trustee Association, 2025 M St, 800, Washington, DC 20036-3409. TEL 202-367-1180, FAX 202-367-2180, http://www.mta-hq.org. Ed. Ellen Hirzy. R&P Amanda Ohlke. Adv. contact James Collins TEL 202-293-7728. page USD 10,000; 8.5 x 11. Circ: 8,500.

069 USA ISSN 0740-0403
N520
MUSEUM YEAR. Text in English. 1962. a. USD 3. **Description:** Annual report of the Boston Museum of Fine Arts, focusing on annual projects and exhibits, staff activities, publications, programs, and curatorial acquisitions.
Formerly: Boston Museum of Fine Arts. Museum Year. Annual Report
Published by: Museum of Fine Arts, 465 Huntington Ave, Boston, MA 02115. TEL 617-267-9300, FAX 617-267-0280. Ed. Cynthia Purvis. Circ: 27,000.

069 NLD ISSN 2211-9280
▼ **MUSEUMGIDS.** Text in Dutch. 2010. a.
Published by: Huis voor de Kunsten Limburg, Postbus 203, Roermond, 6040 AE, Netherlands. TEL 31-475-399299, FAX 31-475-399298, info@hklimburg.nl, http://www.hklimburg.nl.

708.92 NLD ISSN 1566-3418
MUSEUMKRANT (GRONINGEN). Text in Dutch. 1999. s-a. adv.
Published by: (Museum voor Moderne Kunst), Uitgeverij Intermed, Postbus 2306, Groningen, 9704 CH, Netherlands. TEL 31-50-3120042, FAX 31-50-3139373, info@intermed.nu, http://www.intermed.nu. Circ: 15,000.

708.11 CAN ISSN 1191-0925
MUSEUMNEWS; from the Nova Scotia Museum, 25 sites throughout Nova Scotia. Text in English. 1985. bi-m. free. **Description:** Covers events and offers information about provincial museums, historic houses, and restored mills.
Former titles (until 1992): Museum News and Views from the Nova Scotia Museum Complex (0828-2773); (until 1985): News and Views from the Nova Scotia Museum Complex (0842-7666); Which was formed by the merger of: Latest Word from the Nova Scotia Museum (0703-2277); Nova Scotia Museum Program of Events (0225-5006)
Published by: Nova Scotia Museum, 1747 Summer St, Halifax, NS B3H 3A6, Canada. TEL 902-424-7344. Ed. John Henniear Shuh. Circ: 10,000.

069 GBR ISSN 1477-8572
MUSEUMS & GALLERIES YEARBOOK; (Year) guide to museums & galleries. Text in English. 1955. a. GBP 160 to non-members; GBP 60 to members (effective 2009). adv. **Document type:** *Directory, Trade.* **Description:** Contains addresses, staff, admission fees, attendance and facilities.
Former titles (until 2002): Museums Yearbook (0307-7675); (until 1976): Museums Calendar (0580-2652)
Published by: Museums Association, 24 Calvin St, London, E1 6NW, United Kingdom. TEL 44-20-74266920, FAX 44-20-74266962, info@museumsassociation.org. Adv. contact Dennis Jarrett TEL 44-20-74266941. Circ: 2,500.

069 FRA ISSN 0077-233X
MUSEUMS AND MONUMENTS SERIES. Text in French. 1950. irreg., latest 2009. price varies. **Document type:** *Monographic series.*
Related titles: French ed.: Musees et Monuments. ISSN 0251-5040.
Indexed: GeoRef, SpeleolAb.
Published by: UNESCO Publishing, 7 place de Fontenoy, Paris, 75352, France. TEL 33-1-45684300, FAX 33-1-45685737, http://publishing.unesco.org/default.aspx. **Dist. in U.S. by:** Bernan Associates, Bernan, 4611-F Assembly Dr., Lanham, MD 20706-4391. TEL 800-274-4447, FAX 800-865-3450.

MUSEUMS & MORE; specialty shop product news. *see* BUSINESS AND ECONOMICS—Small Business

MUSEUMS & SOCIAL ISSUES. *see* SOCIAL SCIENCES: COMPREHENSIVE WORKS

069 USA
AM2
MUSEUMS AND THE WEB. Text in English. 1997. a. USD 50 per vol. (effective 2006).
Related titles: Online - full text ed.: ISSN 1558-9609.
Published by: Archives and Museum Informatics, 5600 Northumberland St, Pittsburgh, PA 15217. info@archimuse.com, http://www.archimuse.com/index.html.

069 NZL ISSN 1178-2439
MUSEUMS AOTEAROA. DIRECTORY. Text in English. 2002. a. NZD 15 to non-members (effective 2009). **Document type:** *Directory.* **Description:** Lists contact details, staff, opening hours and admission charges for museums/public art galleries throughout New Zealand.
Published by: Museums Aotearoa, PO Box 10 928, Wellington, 6143, New Zealand. TEL 64-4-4991313, FAX 64-4-4996313, mail@museums-aotearoa.org.nz, http://www.museums-aotearoa.org.nz.

069 NZL ISSN 1177-7362
MUSEUMS AOTEAROA QUARTERLY. Text in English. 2006. q. free membership (effective 2009). adv. **Document type:** *Newsletter, Consumer.* **Description:** Contains information, opinion, discussion, ideas, and opportunities.
Published by: Museums Aotearoa, PO Box 10 928, Wellington, 6143, New Zealand. TEL 64-4-4991313, FAX 64-4-4996313, mail@museums-aotearoa.org.nz, http://www.museums-aotearoa.org.nz.

069 AUS ISSN 1449-4043
MUSEUMS AUSTRALIA MAGAZINE. Abbreviated title: M A M. Text in English. 1992. q. AUD 143 domestic; AUD 132 foreign; free to members (effective 2009). adv. bk.rev. back issues avail. **Document type:** *Magazine, Government.* **Description:** Presents news, opinions and debates on issues of museum practice within art, history, and science museums. Represents interests of individuals, institutions within Australia's museum community.
Formerly (until 2003): Museum National (1038-1694); Which was formed by the merger of (1986-1990): A M A A News (0810-1027); (1982-1990): Muse News (0728-8948); Which was formerly (until 1982): Kalori Quarterly Newsletter (0314-3333)
Related titles: Online - full text ed.
Indexed: BrArAb, NumL.
Published by: Museums Australia Inc., PO Box 266, Civic Square, ACT 2608, Australia. TEL 61-2-62732437, FAX 61-2-62732451, ma@museumsaustralia.org.au. Ed., Adv. contact Roslyn Russell TEL 61-2-62816805. B&W page AUD 1,089, color page AUD 1,529; bleed 210 x 297. Circ: 2,300.

069 USA
MUSEUMS CHICAGO. Text in English. 2000. 4/yr. adv. **Document type:** *Magazine, Consumer.* **Description:** Contains museum coverage and commentary on special exhibitions, permanent collections, major events, and the state of the arts in the Chicago area.
Published by: Louise Blouin Media (Subsidiary of: L T B Media), 601 West 26th St, Ste 410, New York, NY 10001. TEL 212-447-9555, production@artinfo.com, http://www.artinfo.com. Circ: 150,000 (paid and controlled).

069 USA
MUSEUMS FLORIDA. Text in English. 19??. q. **Document type:** *Magazine, Consumer.* **Description:** Written for the active museum goer covering exhibitions, collections, news and events with color photography.
Published by: Louise Blouin Media (Subsidiary of: L T B Media), 601 West 26th St, Ste 410, New York, NY 10001. TEL 212-447-9555.

708.11 CAN ISSN 0709-955X
AM21.M3
MUSEUMS IN MANITOBA (YEAR)/MUSEES DU MANITOBA (YEAR); preserving Manitoba's heritage. Text in English, French. a. free. **Document type:** *Directory.* **Description:** Lists and describes the many museums throughout the province of Manitoba.
Published by: (Manitoba. Culture, Heritage and Citizenship), Association of Manitoba Museums, 153 Lombard St, Ste 206, Winnipeg, MB R3B 0T4, Canada. TEL 204-947-1782, FAX 204-942-3749.

069 DEU ISSN 0933-0593
N3
MUSEUMS JOURNAL; Berichte aus den Museen, Schloessern und Sammlungen in Berlin und Potsdam. Text in German. 1981. q. EUR 27.60; EUR 7.20 newsstand/cover (effective 2006). bk.rev. illus. back issues avail. **Document type:** *Journal, Academic/Scholarly.* **Description:** Reports on exhibits and events in musuems in Berlin and Potsdam.
Incorporates (1919-1988): Berliner Museen (0934-3911); Which was formerly (until 1984): B M (0341-4612); (until 1974): Berliner Museen (0005-9315); (until 1919): Amtliche Berichte aus den Preuszischen Kunstsammlungen (0934-5795)
Indexed: B24, DIP, IBR, IBZ, RILM.
—**CCC.**
Published by: Museumspaedagogischer Dienst Berlin, Klosterstr 68-70, Berlin, 10179, Germany. TEL 49-30-9026993, FAX 49-30-2826183, info@mdberlin.de, http://www.mdberlin.de. Circ: 7,000 (paid).

070.594 GBR ISSN 0027-416X
AM1
MUSEUMS JOURNAL. Abbreviated title: M J. Text in English. 1890. m. (plus supplement). GBP 108 domestic to non-members; GBP 165 foreign to non-members; free to members (effective 2009). adv. bk.rev. bibl.; tr.lit. back issues avail. **Document type:** *Journal, Academic/Scholarly.* **Description:** Contains up-to-date news and information on the museum and gallery sector.
Formerly (until 1901): Museums Association. Report of Proceedings; Incorporates (1974-1989): Museums Bulletin (0307-2525); Which was formerly (1961-1974): Museums Association. Monthly Bulletin (0027-4151)
Related titles: Microfiche ed.: (from BHP); Microfilm ed.: (from BHP); Microform ed.: (from BHP).
Indexed: A06, A07, A22, A30, A31, AA, ABM, AICP, API, AmHI, ArtInd, B04, B24, BrArAb, BrGeoL, BrHumI, E06, H07, I14, L04, LISTA, MLA-IB, NumL, PCI, RASB, SCOPUS, T02.
—BLDSC (5990.000000), IE, Infotrieve, Ingenta. **CCC.**

Published by: Museums Association, 24 Calvin St, London, E1 6NW, United Kingdom. TEL 44-20-74266920, FAX 44-20-74266962, info@museumsassociation.org. Ed. Sharon Heal. Adv. contact Richard Eckles TEL 44-20-74266930. page GBP 1,400; bleed 236 x 303. Circ: 7,799.

708 069 GBR ISSN 1746-4951
MUSEUMS LIBRARIES AND ARCHIVES NORTH WEST. ANNUAL REPORT AND ACCOUNTS. Variant title: M L A Northwest. Annual Reports and Accounts. Text in English. 2003. a. **Document type:** *Report, Trade.*
Published by: Museums Libraries and Archives North West, Ground Floor, The Malt Building, Wilderspool Park, Greenall's Ave, Warrington, WA4 6HL, United Kingdom. TEL 44-1925-625050, FAX 44-1925-243453, info@mlanorthwest.org.uk, http://www.mlanorthwest.org.uk.

069 USA
MUSEUMS LOS ANGELES. Text in English. 2000. 4/yr. adv. **Document type:** *Magazine, Consumer.* **Description:** Contains museum coverage and commentary on special exhibitions, permanent collections, major events, and the state of the arts in the Los Angeles area.
Published by: Louise Blouin Media (Subsidiary of: L T B Media), 601 West 26th St, Ste 410, New York, NY 10001. TEL 212-447-9555, production@artinfo.com, http://www.artinfo.com. Circ: 150,000 (paid and controlled).

069 USA ISSN 0190-406X
AM1
MUSEUMS NEW YORK. Text in English. 1979. 4/yr. **Document type:** *Magazine, Consumer.* **Description:** Contains museum coverage and commentary on special exhibitions, permanent collections, major events, and the state of the arts.
Related titles: Supplement(s): Museums Philadelphia.
—CCC.
Published by: Louise Blouin Media (Subsidiary of: L T B Media), 601 West 26th St, Ste 410, New York, NY 10001. TEL 212-447-9555, production@artinfo.com. Circ: 150,000 (paid and controlled).

069.0993 NZL ISSN 1177-7176
MUSEUMS NEWS (ONLINE). Text in English. 2000. m. free to members. **Document type:** *Newsletter.* **Description:** Compilation of museum and art gallery press clippings.
Former titles (until 2006): Museums News (Print) (1175-3323); Museums Aotearoa. News; Museums News (Print) incorporated: Museums Aotearoa. Annual General Meeting
Media: Online - full text.
Published by: Museums Aotearoa, PO Box 10 928, Wellington, 6143, New Zealand. TEL 64-4-4991313, FAX 64-4-4996313, mail@museums-aotearoa.org.nz, http://www.museums-aotearoa.org.nz.

069 DEU
MUSEUMS OF THE WORLD. Text in English. 1973. irreg. (in 2 vols.), latest vol.15, 2008. EUR 458 base vol(s). (effective 2009). adv. **Document type:** *Directory, Trade.* **Description:** Lists museums in over 180 countries, providing a broad outline of historical, geographical and ethnological information. Subject index describes museum holdings.
Related titles: ◆ Series: International Directory of Arts & Museums of the World CD-ROM; ◆ International Directory of Arts. ISSN 0074-4565.
Published by: De Gruyter Saur (Subsidiary of: Walter de Gruyter GmbH & Co. KG), Mies-van-der-Rohe-Str 1, Munich, 80807, Germany. TEL 49-89-769020, FAX 49-89-76902150, info@degruyter.com.

069 USA
MUSEUMS SOUTH FLORIDA. Text in English. 19??. 3/yr. **Document type:** *Magazine, Consumer.*
Published by: Louise Blouin Media (Subsidiary of: L T B Media), 601 West 26th St, Ste 410, New York, NY 10001. TEL 212-447-9555, http://www.artinfo.com.

069 USA ISSN 1529-2789
AM13.W3
MUSEUMS WASHINGTON. Text in English. 1999. 4/yr. adv. **Document type:** *Magazine, Consumer.* **Description:** Contains museum coverage and commentary on special exhibitions, permanent collections, major events, and the state of the arts in the Washington DC area.
—CCC.
Published by: Louise Blouin Media (Subsidiary of: L T B Media), 601 West 26th St, Ste 410, New York, NY 10001. TEL 212-447-9555, production@artinfo.com, http://www.artinfo.com. Circ: 150,000 (paid and controlled).

708.89 DNK ISSN 0108-8858
MUSEUMSAVISEN. Text in Danish. 1980. s-a. DKK 125 membership (effective 2009). illus. **Document type:** *Magazine, Consumer.*
Related titles: Online - full text ed.
Published by: Museumsforeningen Soenderskov, Soenderskovsvej 2, Broerup, 6650, Denmark. TEL 45-75-383866, FAX 45-75-383865, post@sonderskov.dk.

069 DEU ISSN 0027-4178
N1
MUSEUMSKUNDE. Text in German. 1905. 2/yr. adv. bk.rev. index. **Document type:** *Journal, Academic/Scholarly.* **Description:** Contains information about activities and developments in museums.
Indexed: ABM, DIP, IBR, IBZ, MLA-IB, PCI, RASB, RILM, SCOPUS.
—IE.
Published by: Deutscher Museumsbund e.V., In der Halde 1, Berlin, 14195, Germany. TEL 49-30-84109517, FAX 49-30-84109519, office@museumsbund.de, http://www.museumsbund.de. Circ: 2,000 (controlled).

069 DEU ISSN 0941-9802
MUSEUMSMAGAZIN. Text in German. 1983. irreg., latest vol.8, 2001. price varies. **Document type:** *Monographic series, Academic/Scholarly.*
Formed by the merger of (1962-1983): Der Museumsfreund (0580-2695); (1952-1983): Museen in Baden-Wuerttemberg (0941-9861); Which was formerly (until 1962): Das Wuerttembergische Museum (0509-4216)
Published by: (Landesstelle fuer Museumsbetreuung Baden-Wuerttemberg), Konrad Theiss Verlag GmbH, Moenchhaldenstr 28, Stuttgart, 70191, Germany. TEL 49-711-255270, FAX 49-711-2552717, service@theiss.de, http://www.theiss.de.

069 NOR ISSN 1504-520X
MUSEUMSNYTT. Text in Norwegian. 2003. 5/yr. NOK 200 (effective 2011). adv. bk.rev. bibl.; illus. **Document type:** *Magazine, Consumer.*
Supersedes in part (in 2004): Memento (1503-8572); Which was formed by the merger of (1975-2003): Fortidsvern (0332-7205); (1951-2003): Museumsnytt (0027-4186); Which incorporated (1978-1997): Norsk I C O M Nytt (0800-8493); Which was formerly (until 1983): I C O M Nytt (0800-9449)
Related titles: Online - full text ed.
Indexed: A&ATA, NAA.
Published by: (Norges Museumsforbund/Association of Norwegian Museums), A B M - Media AS, PO Box 4, St Olavs Plass, Oslo, 0130, Norway. TEL 47-22-452878, post@abm-media.no, http://www.abm-media.no. Ed. Signy Norendal. Adv. contact John Larsson TEL 47-22-096919.

069 DEU ISSN 0931-4857
AM50.S3
MUSEUMSVERBAND FUER NIEDERSACHSEN UND BREMEN. MITTEILUNGSBLATT. Text in German. 1966. s-a. EUR 35 (effective 2005). back issues avail. **Document type:** *Bulletin, Academic/Scholarly.* **Description:** For staff members of museums in Lower Saxony and Bremen.
Published by: Museumsverband fuer Niedersachsen und Bremen e.V., Foessestr 99, Hannover, 30453, Germany. TEL 49-511-214498, FAX 49-511-21449844, kontakt@mvnb.de, http://www.mvnb.de. Ed. Elke Meyer.

069 NLD ISSN 1874-9798
MUSEUMTIJDSCHRIFT. Variant title: Onafhankelijk Museumtijdschrift. Text in Dutch. 1988. 8/yr. EUR 55.70; EUR 6.75 newsstand/cover (effective 2010); includes Tentoonstellingsboekje. adv. illus. **Document type:** *Magazine, Consumer.*
Formerly (until 2007): Vitrine (0922-226X)
Related titles: ◆ Supplement(s): De Tentoonstellingsagenda.
—IE, Infotrieve.
Published by: Waanders Uitgevers, Postbus 1129, Zwolle, 8001 BC, Netherlands. TEL 31-38-4673400, FAX 31-38-4673401, info@waanders.nl, http://www.waanders.nl. Eds. Lidewijn Reckman TEL 31-20-5512950, Din Pieters TEL 31-20-5512951. Adv. contact Thora Johansen TEL 31-20-4228799. color page EUR 1,390; trim 230 x 290. Circ: 15,000 (paid).

069 NLD ISSN 0166-2074
MUSEUMVISIE. Text in Dutch. 1977. 4/yr. EUR 45 to non-members; EUR 37.50 to members (effective 2009). adv. bk.rev. **Document type:** *Magazine, Trade.*
—BLDSC (5990.135000), IE, Infotrieve.
Published by: Nederlandse Museumvereniging, Postbus 2975, Amsterdam, 1000 CZ, Netherlands. TEL 31-20-5512900, FAX 31-20-5512901, info@museumvereniging.nl, http://www.museumvereniging.nl.

069.4 HUN ISSN 1216-1195
MUTARGYVEDELEM. Text in Hungarian. 1970. a.
Formerly (until 1991): Muzeumi Mutargyvedelem (0139-4398)
Indexed: A&ATA, RILM.
Published by: Magyar Nemzeti Muzeum/Hungarian National Museum, Muzeum krt 14-16, Budapest, 1088, Hungary. TEL 36-1-3382122, FAX 36-1-3177806, hnm@hnm.hu, http://www.hnm.hu.

708.38 POL ISSN 0464-1086
MUZEALNICTWO. Text in Polish. 1952. a. price varies. **Document type:** *Journal, Academic/Scholarly.*
Indexed: RASB.
Published by: Narodowy Instytut Dziedzictwa, ul. Szwolezerow 9, Warsaw, 00464, Poland. TEL 48-22-6293791, FAX 48-22-6226595, zamowienia@nid.pl, http://www.kobidz.pl.

MUZEJSKI VJESNIK/MUSEUM NEWS MAGAZINE. *see* ARCHAEOLOGY

069 SVK ISSN 0027-5263
MUZEUM; metodicky, studijny a informacny bulletin. Text in Slovak; Abstracts and contents page in English. 1953. q. per issue exchange basis. bk.rev. charts; illus. 48 p./no.; **Document type:** *Bulletin.* **Description:** Guidance, information and study material for museum and art gallery workers.
Indexed: B24, IBR, IBZ.
Published by: Slovenske Narodne Muzeum, Narodne Muzejne Centrum, Vajanskeho nabr 2, Bratislava, 81436, Slovakia. TEL 421-2-52961973, FAX 421-2-52966653, nmc@snm.sk. Ed. Beata Egyhazy Jurovska. Circ: 320.

708.371 CZE ISSN 1803-0386
DB2001
MUZEUM. Text in Czech; Contents page in English, French, German, Russian. 1961. s-a. EUR 65, USD 98 (effective 2009). bk.rev. **Document type:** *Journal, Academic/Scholarly.*
Formerly (until 2008): Muzejni a Vlastivedna Prace (0027-5255)
Indexed: B24, CA, NumL, RASB, RILM, T02.
Published by: Narodni Muzeum, Vaclavske nam 68, Prague 1, 11579, Czech Republic. TEL 420-22-4497111, nm@nm.cz. Ed. Pavel Dousa. Circ: 1,600. **Subscr. to:** Myris Trade Ltd., V Stihlach 1311, PO Box 2, Prague 4 14201, Czech Republic. TEL 420-2-34035200, FAX 420-2-34035207, myris@myris.cz, http://www.myris.cz.

MUZEUM LITERATURY IM. ADAMA MICKIEWICZA. BLOK-NOTES. *see* LITERATURE

069 POL ISSN 0208-8193
MUZEUM NARODOWE W KRAKOWIE. KATALOGI ZBIOROW/NATIONAL MUSEUM IN CRACOW. CATALOGUES OF THE COLLECTIONS. Text in English, Polish. 1973. irreg., latest 1994. price varies. adv. **Document type:** *Monographic series, Consumer.*
Published by: Muzeum Narodowe w Krakowie/National Museum in Cracow, Ul J Pilsudskiego 12, Krakow, 31109, Poland. Ed. Ewa Harenczyk. R&P Anna Studnicka. Adv. contact Katarzyna Rzehak. **Subscr. to:** Ars Polona, Obroncow 25, Warsaw 03933, Poland.

MUZEUM ROMSKE KULTURY. BULLETIN. *see* HISTORY—History Of Europe

069 SVK ISSN 1336-4693
MUZEUM.SK. Text in Slovak, English. 2000. s-w.
Media: Online - full text.
Published by: Decus, s.r.o., PO Box 6, Zilina, 01015, Slovakia. TEL 421-903-452471, kontakt@decus.sk, http://www.decus.sk.

943.7 708.371 CZE ISSN 0507-1992
MUZEUM VYSOCINY. ODDELENI VED SPOLECENSKYCH. VLASTIVEDNY SBORNIK VYSOCINY. Text in Czech. 1956. biennial. price varies. **Document type:** *Monographic series, Academic/Scholarly.*
Indexed: RILM.
Published by: Muzeum Vysociny, Oddeleni Ved Spolecenskych, Masarykovo nam 55, Jihlava, 58601, Czech Republic. TEL 420-56-7573896, muzeum@muzeum.ji.cz. Ed. Rudolf Schebesta.

708.47 LTU ISSN 1392-5326
MUZIEJININKYSTES BIULETENIS. Text in Lithuanian. 1992. q.
Related titles: ◆ Supplement to: Lietuvos Muziejai. ISSN 1648-7109.
Published by: Lietuvos Muzieju Asociacija, Saltoniskiu g 58, Vilnius, 08105, Lithuania. TEL 370-5-2790371, FAX 370-5-2790213, http://www.museums.lt.

910.2 USA
MY SMITHSONIAN. Text in English. 2002. s-a. adv. **Document type:** *Magazine, Consumer.* **Description:** Contains information and floor plans for each of the nine Smithsonian Institution's museums, as well as the National Zoo, located on or near the National Mall.
Published by: Smithsonian Institution, 750 9th St NW, Ste 7100, Washington, DC 20001. TEL 202-275-2000. Pub. Amy P. Wilkins. Adv. contact Don Cataldi. Circ: 2,500,000.

069 ZAF
N A L N NUUSBRIEF. Text in Afrikaans. 1994. q. free. illus. **Document type:** *Newsletter.* **Description:** Articles about Afrikaans literature and authors, extracts from items in the collection of the museum, short items about newsworthy subjects, list of new books published in Afrikaans.
Published by: Nasionale Afrikaanse Letterkundige-museum en Navorsingsentrum, c/o Afdeling Museumdiens, Privaatsak X20543, Bloemfontein, 9300, South Africa. TEL 27-51-4054147, FAX 27-51-4054259. Ed. L Lategan. R&P E Terblanche. Circ: 1,200.

069 GBR
N E M S ANNUAL REPORT. Text in English. a. GBP 2. bk.rev. **Document type:** *Corporate.*
Published by: North of England Museums Service, House Of Recovery, Bath Ln, Newcastle upon Tyne, Northd NE4 5SQ, United Kingdom. TEL 44-191-222-1661, FAX 44-191-261-4725. Ed. Sue Underwood.

507.4 JPN
N K H NAGAOKA-SHIRITSU KAGAKU HAKUBUTSUKANPO. Text in Japanese. irreg. adv.
Published by: Nagaoka-shiritsu Kagaku Hakubutsukan/Nagaoka Municipal Science Museum, 2-1 Yanagihara-Machi, Nagaoka-shi, Niigata-ken 940-0072, Japan. TEL 81-258-35-0184. Ed. Hisashi Watanabe.

069 JPN
NAGOYA DAIGAKU HAKUBUSUKAN HOKOKU/NAGOYA UNIVERSITY MUSEUM. BULLETIN. Text and summaries in English, Japanese. 1985. a., latest no.16, 2002. free. bk.rev.; software rev. charts; maps. 10 p./no.; **Document type:** *Journal, Academic/Scholarly.*
Former titles (until 1999): Nagoya Daigaku Furukawa Sogo Kenkyu Shiryokan Hokoku/Nagoya University Furukawa Museum. Bulletin (0916-6319); (until 1989): Nagoya Daigaku Sogo Kenkyu Shiryoukan Houkoku - Nagoya University Museum. Bulletin. (0912-5604)
Indexed: Z01.
Published by: Nagoya Daigaku, Hakubutsukan/Nagoya University Museum, 1 Furo-cho, Chikusa-ku, Nagoya-shi, Aichi-ken 464-0814, Japan. TEL 81-52-7895767, FAX 81-52-7895896, dora@num.nagoya-u.ac.jp, http://www.num.nagoya-u.ac.jp. Ed., Adv. contact H Yoshida TEL 81-52-7895763. Circ: 1,000.

NARINKKA. *see* HISTORY—History Of Europe

708.371 943.7 CZE ISSN 1214-0627
H8
NARODNI MUZEUM. RADA HISTORICKA. CASOPIS. Text in Czech, English, German. 1827. q. EUR 60, USD 90 foreign (effective 2009). bk.rev. charts; illus. **Document type:** *Journal, Academic/Scholarly.*
Former titles (until 1991): Narodni Muzeum v Praze. Rada Historicka. Casopis (0139-9543); (until 1977): Narodni Muzeum v Praze. Oddil Ved Spolecenskych. Casopis (0008-7343)
Indexed: CA, HistAb, RASB, RILM, T02.
—BLDSC (3060.550000).
Published by: Narodni Muzeum, Vaclavske nam 68, Prague 1, 11579, Czech Republic. TEL 420-22-4497111, nm@nm.cz. Ed. Jaroslav Cechura. Circ: 1,000. **Subscr. to:** Myris Trade Ltd., V Stihlach 1311, PO Box 2, Prague 4 14201, Czech Republic. TEL 420-2-34035200, FAX 420-2-34035207, myris@myris.cz, http://www.myris.cz.

708.371 943.7 CZE ISSN 1214-0635
QH7 CODEN: CMOPAJ
NARODNI MUZEUM. RADA PRIRODOVEDNA. CASOPIS. Text in Czech, English. 1827. q. EUR 58, USD 87 foreign (effective 2009). bk.rev. abstr.; illus. index. **Document type:** *Journal, Academic/Scholarly.*
Former titles (until 1990): Narodni Muzeum v Praze. Rada Prirodovedna. Casopis (0139-9497); (until 1977): Narodni Muzeum. Oddil Prirodovedny. Casopis (0008-7351)
Indexed: ChemAb, GeoRef, MycolAb, SpeleolAb.
—CASDDS, INIST.
Published by: Narodni Muzeum, Vaclavske nam 68, Prague 1, 11579, Czech Republic. TEL 420-22-4497111, nm@nm.cz. Ed. Jiri Moravec. **Subscr. to:** Myris Trade Ltd., V Stihlach 1311, PO Box 2, Prague 4 14201, Czech Republic. TEL 420-2-34035200, FAX 420-2-34035207, myris@myris.cz, http://www.myris.cz.

943.7 708.371 CZE ISSN 0036-5335
AM101
➤ **NARODNI MUZEUM V PRAZE. SBORNIK. RADA A: HISTORIE/ACTA MUSEI NATIONALIS PRAGAE. SERIES A: HISTORIA.** Text mainly in Czech; Summaries in English, French, German, Russian. 1937. q. EUR 60, USD 90 foreign (effective 2009). adv. illus. index, cum.index. **Document type:** *Journal, Academic/Scholarly.*
Formerly: Narodni Muzeum v Praze. Sbornik: Historie
Indexed: CA, FR, HistAb, NumL, P30, RefZh, T02.
—BLDSC (8082.990000), Infotrieve, INIST.

Published by: (Historicke Muzeum), Narodni Muzeum, Vaclavske nam 68, Prague 1, 11579, Czech Republic. TEL 420-22-4497111, nm@nm.cz. Ed. Lubomir Srsen. **Subscr. to:** Myris Trade Ltd., V Stihlach 1311, PO Box 2, Prague 4 14201, Czech Republic. TEL 420-2-34035200, FAX 420-2-34035207, myris@myris.cz, http://www.myris.cz.

500 708.371 CZE ISSN 0036-5343
QH7 CODEN: SNMPAM

➤ **NARODNI MUZEUM V PRAZE. SBORNIK. RADA B: PRIRODNI VEDY/ACTA MUSEI NATIONALIS PRAGAE. SERIES B: HISTORIA NATURALIS.** Text in English. 1937. q. EUR 60, USD 90 foreign (effective 2009). charts; illus. index. **Document type:** *Journal, Academic/Scholarly.*
Formerly: Narodni Muzeum v Praze. Sbornik: Prirodni Vedy
Indexed: A01, B25, BIOSIS Prev, C30, CA, CABA, ChemAb, E12, F08, F12, GeoRef, MycolAb, P30, P32, P33, P39, P40, PGegResA, RASB, S13, S16, SpeleolAb, T02, Z01.
—CASDDS.
Published by: (Prirodovedecke Muzeum), Narodni Muzeum, Vaclavske nam 68, Prague 1, 11579, Czech Republic. TEL 420-22-4497111, nm@nm.cz. Ed. Jiri Kvacek. **Subscr. to:** Myris Trade Ltd., V Stihlach 1311, PO Box 2, Prague 4 14201, Czech Republic. TEL 420-2-34035200, FAX 420-2-34035207, myris@myris.cz, http://www.myris.cz.

708.371 491.86 CZE ISSN 0036-5351
PG5000

➤ **NARODNI MUZEUM V PRAZE. SBORNIK. RADA C: LITERARNI HISTORIE/ACTA MUSEI NATIONALIS PRAGAE. SERIES C: HISTORIA LITTERARUM.** Text in Czech; Summaries in English, German. 1955. q. EUR 58, USD 87 foreign (effective 2009). bibl.; illus. **Document type:** *Journal, Academic/Scholarly.*
Formerly: Narodni Muzeum v Praze. Sbornik: Literarni Historie
Indexed: CA, HistAb, P30, RASB, RILM, T02.
—BLDSC (8083.100000).
Published by: Narodni Muzeum, Vaclavske nam 68, Prague 1, 11579, Czech Republic. TEL 420-22-4497111, nm@nm.cz. Ed. Helga Turkova. **Subscr. to:** Myris Trade Ltd., V Stihlach 1311, PO Box 2, Prague 4 14201, Czech Republic. TEL 420-2-34035200, FAX 420-2-34035207, myris@myris.cz, http://www.myris.cz.

069 CZE

NARODNI TECHNICKE MUZEUM. KATALOG. Text in English. 1956. irreg., latest vol.17, 2008. CZK 880 per vol. (effective 2009). **Document type:** *Catalog.*
Published by: Narodni Technicke Muzeum, Kostelni 42, Prague 7, 17078, Czech Republic. TEL 420-2-20399101, FAX 420-2-20399200, info@ntm.cz.

069 ESP ISSN 0210-9441
GR229

NARRIA. Text in Spanish. 1975. a. **Document type:** *Journal, Academic/Scholarly.*
Indexed: P09, PCI, RILM.
Published by: Universidad Autonoma de Madrid, Museo de Artes y Tradiciones Populares, Carr. Colmenar Viejo, Km. 15, Madrid, 28693, Spain. museo.arte@uam.es, http://www.uam.es/.

069 ZAF ISSN 1993-3770
DT1752

➤ **NATIONAL CULTURAL HISTORY MUSEUM. RESEARCH JOURNAL/NATIONAL CULTURAL HISTORY MUSEUM. RESEARCH.** Text in Afrikaans, English. 1986. a., latest vol.9, 2000. price varies. illus.; maps. back issues avail. **Document type:** *Journal, Academic/Scholarly.* **Description:** Publishes archaeological, historical, sociological and natural history studies relating to South Africa.
Former titles (until 2006): Nasionale Kultuurhistoriese Museum. Navorsing (1024-350X); (until 1994): Nasionale Kultuurhistoriese en Opelugmuseum. Navorsing (0259-5567)
Indexed: AICP, ISAP.
Published by: Nasionale Kultuurhistoriese Museum/National Cultural History Museum, Posbus 28088, Sunnyside, Pretoria 0132, South Africa. TEL 27-12-3246082, FAX 27-12-3285173, nchm@nfi.co.za, http://www.nfi.org.za/NCHM/nchmindex.htm. Circ: 300.

➤ **NATIONAL DIRECTORY OF NONPROFIT ORGANIZATIONS**; a comprehensive guide providing profiles and procedures for nonprofit organizations. *see* SOCIAL SERVICES AND WELFARE

708.29 GBR

NATIONAL GALLERIES OF SCOTLAND. ANNUAL REVIEW. Text in English. 19??. a. free (effective 2009). **Document type:** *Journal, Trade.*
Former titles (until 2005): National Galleries of Scotland. Review, Report and Accounts (1362-7457); (until 1993): National Galleries of Scotland. Annual Review (0269-0969); (until 1984): National Galleries of Scotland. Review (0263-4589); (until 1981): National Galleries of Scotland. Annual Report (0260-9207); (until 1978): National Galleries of Scotland. Report of the Board of Trustees (0954-3015)
Related titles: Online - full text ed.
—CCC.
Published by: National Galleries of Scotland, The Mound, Edinburgh, EH2 2EL, United Kingdom. TEL 44-131-6246200, publications@nationalgalleries.org.

708.29 GBR ISSN 0953-024X

NATIONAL GALLERIES OF SCOTLAND. BULLETIN. Text in English. 1981. 6/yr. free. illus. **Document type:** *Bulletin, Trade.* **Description:** Photographic and informational brochure on temporary exhibits, permanent displays, new acquisitions, and current activities at the Gallery.
Formerly (until 1987): National Galleries of Scotland. News (0261-3220)
—CCC.
Published by: National Galleries of Scotland, The Mound, Edinburgh, EH2 2EL, United Kingdom. TEL 44-131-6246200, FAX 44-131-3433250, publications@nationalgalleries.org, http://www.nationalgalleries.org. Ed. Anne Marie Wagener. Circ: 60,000.

NATIONAL GALLERY, LONDON. TECHNICAL BULLETIN. *see* ART

708.994 AUS ISSN 1323-5192

NATIONAL GALLERY OF AUSTRALIA. ANNUAL REPORT. Text in English. 1977. a. free (effective 2009). back issues avail. **Document type:** *Report, Trade.* **Description:** Provides achievements of National Gallery of Australia for each financial year.
Formerly (until 1993): Australian National Gallery. Annual Report (0314-9919)
Related titles: Online - full text ed.: ISSN 1833-9859.
Published by: National Gallery of Australia, GPO Box 1150, Canberra, ACT 2601, Australia. TEL 61-2-62406411, FAX 61-2-62406628, information@nga.gov.au, http://www.nga.gov.au.

NATIONAL GALLERY OF CANADA. ANNUAL REPORT. *see* ART

708.11 CAN ISSN 0826-9726

NATIONAL GALLERY OF CANADA CATALOGUE. CANADIAN ART. Text in English. 1988. irreg. (in 2 vols.). USD 74.95. illus. **Document type:** *Catalog.* **Description:** Information on the gallery's holdings.
Related titles: French ed.: Musee des Beaux-Arts du Canada. Catalogue. Art Canadien. ISSN 0826-9734.
Published by: National Gallery of Canada, Publications Division, c/o Irene Lillico, 380 Sussex Dr, Ottawa, ON K1N 9N4, Canada. TEL 613-990-0537, FAX 613-990-7460.

708.96891 ZWE

NATIONAL GALLERY OF ZIMBABWE. ANNUAL REPORT AND BALANCE SHEET AND INCOME AND EXPENDITURE ACCOUNT. Text in English. 1953. a. free. illus. **Document type:** *Corporate.*
Former titles: National Gallery of Zimbabwe - Rhodesia. Annual Report and Balance Sheet and Income and Expenditure Account; National Gallery of Rhodesia. Annual Report and Balance Sheet and Income and Expenditure Account
Published by: National Gallery of Zimbabwe, Causeway, PO Box CY 848, Harare, Zimbabwe. Circ: 400.

708.2 GBR ISSN 2042-9452

THE NATIONAL GALLERY REVIEW. Text in English. 19??. a. back issues avail. **Document type:** *Journal, Trade.* **Description:** Aims to study and care for the collection, while encouraging the widest possible access to the pictures.
Formerly (until 1999): National Gallery Report (0143-9065)
Related titles: Online - full text ed.: free (effective 2010).
Published by: National Gallery Company Ltd., Trafalgar Sq, London, WC2N 5DN, United Kingdom. TEL 44-20-77472885, FAX 44-20-77472423, information@ng-london.org.uk. Ed. Kate Bell.

069 ZAF

NATIONAL MUSEUM, BLOEMFONTEIN. ANNUAL REPORT. Text in Afrikaans, English. 1877. a. free. **Document type:** *Corporate.*
Published by: Nasionale Museum Bloemfontein/National Museum, Bloemfontein, PO Box 266, Bloemfontein, 9300, South Africa. TEL 27-51-4479609, FAX 27-51-4476273, htttp://www.nasmus.co.za. Ed. C D Lynch. Circ: 120.

069 JPN

NATIONAL MUSEUM OF MODERN ART, TOKYO. ANNUAL REPORT. Text in English, Japanese. 1957. a. **Document type:** *Government.* **Description:** Listing of all exhibitions, events, and collected works of the three institutions.
Published by: National Museum of Modern Art Tokyo, 3 Kitano-Marukoen, Chiyoda-ku, Tokyo, 102-8322, Japan. TEL 81-3-3561-1400, FAX 81-3-3561-8100. Circ: 1,000.

708.1 USA ISSN 1931-8782

NATIONAL MUSEUM OF NATURAL HISTORY. ARCTIC STUDIES CENTER. NEWSLETTER. Text in English. 1992. a. free (effective 2010). back issues avail. **Document type:** *Newsletter, Academic/Scholarly.*
Related titles: Online - full text ed.
Published by: Smithsonian Institution, National Museum of Natural History. Arctic Studies Center, Department of Anthropology MRC 112, PO Box 37012, Washington, DC 20013. TEL 202-633-1887, FAX 202-357-2684, arctics@si.edu. Ed. William Fitzhugh.

708.11 CAN ISSN 1187-3728

NATIONAL MUSEUM OF SCIENCE AND TECHNOLOGY. ANNUAL REPORT. Text in English. 1969. a.
Supersedes in part (in 1991): National Museums of Canada. Annual Report (0704-1616)
Related titles: French ed.: Musee National des Sciences et de la Technologie. Rapport Annuel. ISSN 1187-3736.
Published by: Canada Science and Technology Museum Corp/Musee National des Sciences et de la Technologie, P O Box 9724, Sta T, Ottawa, ON K1G 5A3, Canada. TEL 613 991-3044, FAX 613 991-9207.

708.9678 TZA ISSN 0082-1675

NATIONAL MUSEUM OF TANZANIA. ANNUAL REPORT. Text in English. 1966. a. USD 3. adv. bk.rev. **Document type:** *Corporate.*
Indexed: AICP.
Published by: National Museum of Tanzania, PO Box 511, Dar Es Salaam, Tanzania. TEL 255-51-31365, FAX 255-51-20843. Circ: 5,000.

708.9599 PHL ISSN 0076-3756

NATIONAL MUSEUM OF THE PHILIPPINES. ANNUAL REPORT. Text in English. 1967. a. free. **Document type:** *Report, Corporate.* **Description:** Contains the accomplishments of the National Museum in the fields of science, culture and education during the year under review. Includes brief scientific papers on anthropology, archeology, botany, geology, zoology and conservation.
Published by: National Museum of the Philippines, P. Burgos Ave., PO Box 2659, Manila, 1000, Philippines. TEL 63-2-5271215, FAX 63-2-5270306, nmuseum@i-next.net, http://philmuseum.tripod.com/index. Ed. Elenita D. V. Alba. Circ: 500 (controlled).

069 GBR

NATIONAL MUSEUMS OF WALES. ANNUAL REVIEW/AMGUEDDFEYDD AC ORIELAU CENEDLAETHOL CYMRU. ADRODDIAD BLYNYDDOL. Text in English, Welsh. 1907. a. free (effective 2009). illus. 80 p./no. 2 cols./p.; back issues avail. **Document type:** *Corporate.*
Former titles (until 2005): National Museums & Galleries of Wales. Annual Report (1368-1583); (until 1995): National Museum of Wales. Annual Report (0083-7032)
Related titles: Online - full text ed.
—BLDSC (1366.200000). **CCC.**
Published by: National Museum Wales/Amgueddfa Genedlaethol Cymru, Cathays Park, Cardiff, CF10 3NP, United Kingdom. TEL 44-29-20397951, FAX 44-29-20573321, post@nmgw.ac.uk, http://www.nmgw.ac.uk. Ed. Robin Gwyn.

708.951 TWN ISSN 1011-906X
N3750.T32

NATIONAL PALACE MUSEUM BULLETIN/GUGONG TONGXUN YINGWEN SHUANGYUEKAN. Text in English. 1966. s-a. TWD 1,200 per issue (effective 2004). bibl.; illus. Index. **Document type:** *Bulletin, Academic/Scholarly.* **Description:** Articles of scholarly research on artistic and cultural subjects.
Formerly: National Palace Museum Bulletin (Bi-Monthly Edition) (0027-9846)
Indexed: A&ATA, BAS.
Published by: National Palace Museum/Kuo Li Ku Kung Po Wu Yuan, Wai Shuang Hsi, Shih Lin, Taipei, Taiwan. TEL 886-2-2882-1230, FAX 886-2-2882-1440, http://www.npm.gov.tw. Ed. Yao-Ting Wang. R&P Sai-Lan Hu. Circ: 1,000.

708.951 TWN ISSN 1011-9086
N3750.T32

NATIONAL PALACE MUSEUM. NEWSLETTER. Key Title: Gugong Zhanlan Tongxun. Variant title: National Palace Museum. Newsletter & Gallery Guide. Text in Chinese, English. 1968. q. free. charts; illus. **Document type:** *Newsletter.* **Description:** Highlights of the National Palace Museum's newest publications, exhibitions and activities.
Published by: National Palace Museum/Kuo Li Ku Kung Po Wu Yuan, Wai Shuang Hsi, Shih Lin, Taipei, Taiwan. FAX 886-2-2882-1440, webmaster@npm.gov.tw, http://www.npm.gov.tw. Ed. Shou-Chien Shih. Circ: 25,000.

NATIONAL SCIENCE MUSEUM. BULLETIN. SERIES E: PHYSICAL SCIENCES AND ENGINEERING/KOKURITSU KAGAKU HAKUBUTSUKAN KENKYU HOKOKU. E RUI, RIKOGAKU. *see* ENGINEERING

708.89 DNK ISSN 0084-9308
AS281.A2

NATIONALMUSEETS ARBEJDSMARK. Text in Danish; Summaries in English. 1928. a. price varies. back issues avail. **Document type:** *Yearbook, Consumer.*
Formerly (until 1958): Fra Nationalmuseets Arbejdsmark
Indexed: AIAP, AnthLit, B24, NAA, NumL, PCI, RILM.
Published by: Nationalmuseet, Frederiksholms Kanal 12, Copenhagen K, 1220, Denmark. TEL 45-33-134411, FAX 45-33-473333, doga@natmus.dk, http://www.natmus.dk.

NATURA CROATICA; periodicum musei historiae naturalis Croatici - casopis Hrvatskoga prirodslovnog muzeja. *see* SCIENCES: COMPREHENSIVE WORKS

NATURA SOMOGYIENSIS. *see* BIOLOGY

070.594 JPN ISSN 0917-8902

NATURAL HISTORY MUSEUM AND INSTITUTE, CHIBA. ANNUAL REPORT. Text in Japanese. 1990. a. **Document type:** *Corporate.*
Published by: Natural History Museum and Institute Chiba, 955-2 Aoba-cho, Chuo-ku, Chiba-shi, 260-0852, Japan. TEL 81-43-265-3111, FAX 81-43-266-2481. Circ: 1,000 (controlled).

NATURAL HISTORY MUSEUM. ANNUAL REVIEW. *see* SCIENCES: COMPREHENSIVE WORKS

NATURALEZA ARAGONESA. *see* PALEONTOLOGY

NATURHISTORISCHES MUSEUM IN WIEN. KATALOGE DER WISSENSCHAFTLICHEN SAMMLUNGEN. *see* SCIENCES: COMPREHENSIVE WORKS

500.907 AUT ISSN 0028-095X

NATURHISTORISCHES MUSEUM IN WIEN. MONATSPROGRAMM. Text in German. 1949. m. looseleaf. **Document type:** *Newsletter, Academic/Scholarly.*
Published by: Naturhistorisches Museum in Wien, Burgring 7, Postfach 417, Vienna, W 1014, Austria. TEL 43-1-52177-497, FAX 43-1-52177-229, http://www.nhm-wien.ac.at. Circ: 4,400.

570 DEU ISSN 1438-440X

NATURKUNDEMUSEUM LEIPZIG. VEROEFFENTLICHUNGEN. Text in German. 1970. a. **Document type:** *Monographic series, Academic/Scholarly.*
Indexed: Z01.
Published by: Naturkundemuseum Leipzig, Lortzingstr 3, Leipzig, 04105, Germany. TEL 49-341-982210, FAX 49-341-9822122, www.naturkundemuseum-leipzig.de.

069 NLD ISSN 1875-2489

NEDERLAND MUSEUMLAND. Text in Dutch. 2006. irreg. EUR 12.95 newsstand/cover (effective 2009).
Published by: Inmerc, Postbus 13288, Utrecht, 3507 LG, Netherlands. TEL 31-30-2528500, FAX 31-30-2528598, publish@inmerc.nl, http://www.inmerc.nl.

069 820 741.5 NLD ISSN 1875-3779

NEDERLANDS STRIPMUSEUM GRONINGEN. VRIENDENBLAD. Text in Dutch. 2006. q. EUR 27 membership (effective 2010).
Published by: Stichting Het Nederlands Stripmuseum Groningen, Shoppingcentre de Westerhaven, Westerhaven 71, Groningen, 9718 AC, Netherlands. http://www.stripmuseumgroningen.nl.

708.1 USA

NELSON-ATKINS MUSEUM OF ART. CALENDAR OF EVENTS. Text in English. 1934. 10/yr. membership. illus. **Document type:** *Newsletter.* **Description:** Provides news for museum members.
Formerly: Nelson Gallery and Atkins Museum. Gallery Events (0047-9322)
Published by: Nelson-Atkins Museum of Art, 4525 Oak St, Kansas City, MO 64111-1873. TEL 816-561-4000, FAX 816-561-7154. Ed. Gina L Kelley. R&P Stacey Sherman TEL 816-751-1293. Circ: 16,000; 16,000 (controlled).

708.1 USA ISSN 0077-7919

NEVADA. STATE MUSEUM, CARSON CITY. OCCASIONAL PAPERS. Text in English. 1968. irreg., latest vol.6, 2004. price varies. back issues avail. **Document type:** *Monographic series, Trade.*
Published by: (Department of Anthropology), Nevada State Museum, 600 N Carson St, Carson City, NV 89701. TEL 775-687-4810, FAX 775-687-4168, http://museums.nevadaculture.org/index.php?option=com_content&view=article&id=486&Itemid=439.

708.1 USA ISSN 0077-7927
AM101

NEVADA. STATE MUSEUM, CARSON CITY. POPULAR SERIES. Text in English. 1965. irreg., latest vol.10, 1990. price varies. back issues avail. **Document type:** *Monographic series, Trade.*

Published by: Nevada State Museum, 600 N Carson St, Carson City, NV 89701. TEL 775-687-4810, FAX 775-687-4168, http://museums.nevadaculture.org/index.php?option=com_content&view=article&id=486&Itemid=439.

069 USA
NEVADA STATE MUSEUM NEWSLETTER. Text in English. 1972. q. (Aug., Nov., Feb. & May). free to members. back issues avail. **Document type:** *Newsletter, Consumer.*
Related titles: Online - full text ed.
Published by: Nevada Department of Cultural Affairs, Division of Museums and History, 716 N. Carson St., Ste. B, Carson City, NV 89701. TEL 775-687-4340, FAX 775-687-4333, http://dmla.clan.lib.nv.us/docs/museums/. Ed. Jack Gibson. Circ: 1,165 (controlled).

069 USA
NEW MUSEUM MEMBERS' BULLETIN. Text in English. 1977. q. USD 35. **Document type:** *Newsletter.*
Former titles: New Museum Newsletter; New Museum News
Published by: New Museum of Contemporary Art, Public Relations, 583 Broadway, New York, NY 10012. TEL 212-219-1222, FAX 212-431-5328. Ed. Katie Clifford. Circ: 15,000.

069.1 USA
NEW MUSEUM PAPER. Text in English. 1977. irreg. (2-3/yr). USD 75 membership (effective 2007). 32 p./no.; **Document type:** *Newsletter.*
Former titles: New Museum News; New Museum Newsletter
Published by: New Museum of Contemporary Art, 210 Eleventh Ave., 2nd Fl, New York, NY 10001. TEL 212-219-1222, FAX 212-431-5328, newmu@newmuseum.org. Ed. Chelsea Scott. Circ: 5,000 (paid and controlled).

069 USA
NEW YORK (CITY). MUSEUM OF THE CITY OF NEW YORK. ANNUAL REPORT. Text in English. 1923. a. free. charts; illus. **Document type:** *Corporate.*
Supersedes (1970?-1982): New York (City). Museum of the City of New York. Bulletin
Published by: Museum of the City of New York, 1220 Fifth Ave at 103rd St, New York, NY 10029. TEL 212-534-1672, FAX 212-423-0758. Ed. Billie Heller. R&P Marguerite Levine. Adv. contact Lia M Gravier. Circ: 5,000.

069 USA
Q224.3.U62
NEW YORK STATE MUSEUM. BIENNIAL REPORT. Text in English. 19??. biennial. free (effective 2011). back issues avail. **Document type:** *Report, Government.*
Formerly: New York State Science Service. Biennial Report (0883-1548)
Related titles: Online - full text ed.
Published by: New York State Museum, Cultural Education Center, Rm 3023, Albany, NY 12230. TEL 518-474-5877, nysmpub@mail.nysed.gov.

NEWS FROM THE BAKKEN. *see* LIBRARY AND INFORMATION SCIENCES

NEWS FROM THE FORD. *see* LIBRARY AND INFORMATION SCIENCES

069 USA ISSN 2158-5261
NEXT (CAMBRIDGE). Text in English. 2008. 3/yr. **Document type:** *Newsletter, Trade.*
Published by: Harvard Art Museum, 32 Quincy St, Cambridge, MA 02138 . http://www.harvardartmuseums.org/.

069 SWE ISSN 1652-9855
NOBEL MUSEUM. OCCASIONAL PAPERS. Text in English. 2005. irreg. **Document type:** *Monographic series, Academic/Scholarly.*
Published by: Nobel Museum, PO Box 2245, Stockholm, 10316, Sweden. TEL 46-8-53481800, nobelmuseum@nobel.se, http://www.nobelmuseum.se. Ed. Eva Aahren.

069 SWE ISSN 1103-8152
➤ **NORDISK MUSEOLOGI.** Text in Danish, Norwegian, Swedish; Text occasionally in English; Summaries in English. 1993. s-a. DKK 285; DKK 195 to students (effective 2009). back issues avail. **Document type:** *Journal, Academic/Scholarly.* **Description:** Forum for theoretical and scholarly discussions in museology.
Related titles: Online - full text ed.
Published by: Umeaa Universitet, Institutionen foer Kultur och Medier, Umeaa Universitet, Humanisthuset, Umeaa, 90187, Sweden. TEL 46-90-7865785, FAX 46-90-7867845, http://www.kulturmed.umu.se. Ed. Ane Hejlskov Larsen. **Co-publishers:** Jyvaskylan Yliopisto/University of Jyvaskyla; Aarhus Universitet, Institut for Aestetiske Fag. Center for Museologi; A B M - Utvikling/Norwegian Archive, Library and Museum Authority.

069 USA ISSN 1070-468X
NORTH CAROLINA NATURALIST. Text in English. 1993. s-a. free membership (effective 2006). bk.rev. **Document type:** *Magazine, Consumer.* **Description:** Promotes the museum across the state. Educates and informs the membership of the friends about the museum and the natural history of North Carolina.
Published by: Friends of the North Carolina State Museum of Natural Sciences, 11 W Jones St, Raleigh, NC 27601-1029. TEL 919-733-7450, FAX 919-733-1573, friends@nando.net, http://www.naturalsciences.org. Ed., R&P Margaret Martin. Circ: 2,000.

069.1 ZAF ISSN 1995-5995
NORTHERN FLAGSHIP INSTITUTION. ANNUAL REPORT. Text in English. 2000. a.
Published by: Northern Flagship Institution, PO Box 413, Pretoria, 0001, South Africa. TEL 27-12-3227632, FAX 27-12-3227668, http://www.nfi.org.za.

NYE FAMILY NEWSLETTER. *see* GENEALOGY AND HERALDRY

O K V TENTO. (Openbaar Kunstbezit in Vlaanderen) *see* ART

708.9494 CHE
OEFFENTLICHE KUNSTSAMMLUNG BASEL. KUNSTMUSEUM. MUSEUM FUER GEGENWARTSKUNST. JAHRESBERICHT. Text in German. 1904. irreg., latest 1994. price varies. **Document type:** *Bulletin, Corporate.*
Former titles: Oeffentliche Kunstsammlung Basel. Museum fuer Gegenwartskunst. Jahresbericht; Oeffentliche Kunstsammlung. Museum fuer Gegenwart. Jahresbericht; Oeffentliche Kunstsammlung. Jahresbericht (0067-4311)
Published by: Oeffentliche Kunstsammlung Basel, Museum fuer Gegenwartskunst, St Alban Graben 16, Basel, 4010, Switzerland. TEL 41-61-2066262, FAX 41-61-2066252, pressoffice@linstmuse.umbasel.ch, http://www.kunstmuseumbasel.ch.

OESTERREICHISCHES MUSEUM FUER VOLKSKUNDE. KATALOGE. *see* MUSEUMS AND ART GALLERIES—Abstracting, Bibliographies, Statistics

OESTERREICHISCHES THEATERMUSEUM. SCHRIFTENREIHE. *see* THEATER

069 CAN ISSN 0829-0474
AM21.A1
OFFICIAL DIRECTORY OF CANADIAN MUSEUMS AND RELATED INSTITUTIONS/REPERTOIRE OFFICIEL DES MUSEES CANADIENS ET INSTITUTIONS CONNEXES. Text in English, French. 1978. irreg.
Formerly (until 1985): Directory of Canadian Museums and Related Institutions (0714-2188)
Published by: Canadian Museums Association, 280 Metcalfe St, Ste 400, Ottawa, ON K2P 1R7, Canada. TEL 613-567-0099, FAX 613-233-5438, info@museums.ca.

069 USA ISSN 0090-6700
AM10.A2
OFFICIAL MUSEUM DIRECTORY. Abbreviated title: O M D. Text in English. 1961. a. USD 307 per issue to non-members; USD 207 per issue to members (effective 2011). adv. index. **Document type:** *Directory, Trade.* **Description:** Lists more than 7,800 institutions in 85 categories, including museums, art associations, nature centers, aquariums, botanical gardens, planetariums, zoos, and others. Lists where they are, what they exhibit, and who manages them.
Incorporates (1981-1992): The Official Museum Products and Services Directory (0276-637X); Formerly (until 1971): Museums Directory of the United States and Canada (0090-6697)
Related titles: Online - full text ed.
—CCC.
Published by: (American Association of Museums), National Register Publishing (Subsidiary of: Marquis Who's Who LLC.), 300 Connell Dr, Ste 2000, Berkeley Heights, NJ 07922. TEL 800-473-7020, FAX 908-673-1189, NRPsales@marquiswhoswho.com, http://www.nationalregisterpub.com. Adv. contact Anne Collins TEL 212-689-2500 ext 2503.

708.4 FRA ISSN 1957-0392
L'OFFICIEL GALERIES & MUSEES (ED. DE PARIS ET REGIONS). Text in French. 200?. bi-m. **Document type:** *Magazine, Consumer.*
Supersedes in part (in 2005): L' Officiel Galeries et Musees (1955-9011); Which was formerly (until 2004): L' Officiel des Galeries (1957-0384)
Published by: Editions Theles, 11 Rue Martel, Paris, 75010, France. TEL 33-1-40209842, FAX 33-1-40200512.

708.4 FRA ISSN 1955-902X
L'OFFICIEL GALERIES & MUSEES (PARIS EDITION). Text in French. 200?. bi-m. **Document type:** *Magazine, Consumer.*
Supersedes in part (2004-2005): L' Officiel Galeries et Musees (1955-9011); which was formerly (until 2004): L' Officiel des Galeries (Paris) (1957-0384)
Published by: Editions Theles, 11 Rue Martel, Paris, 75010, France. TEL 33-1-40209842, FAX 33-1-40200512.

507.4 JPN ISSN 0385-0285
OKINAWA KENRITSU HAKUBUTSUKAN KIYO/OKINAWA PREFECTURAL MUSEUM. BULLETIN. Text in Japanese. 1975. a. **Document type:** *Bulletin.*
Published by: Okinawa Kenritsu Hakubutsukan/Okinawa Prefectural Museum, 1-1 Shiyurionaka-cho, Naha-shi, Okinawa-ken 903-0823, Japan. TEL 098-884-2243, FAX 098-886-4353. Ed. Katumori Kugai.

069 JPN ISSN 0385-0293
OKINAWA KENRITSU HAKUBUTSUKAN NENPO/OKINAWA PREFECTURAL MUSEUM. ANNUAL REPORT. Text in Japanese. 1975. a.
Published by: Okinawa Kenritsu Hakubutsukan/Okinawa Prefectural Museum, 1-1 Shiyurionaka-cho, Naha-shi, Okinawa-ken 903-0823, Japan. TEL 098-884-2243, FAX 098-886-4353.

OKLAHOMA MUSEUM OF NATURAL HISTORY. NEWSLETTER. *see* SCIENCES: COMPREHENSIVE WORKS

OKLAHOMA MUSEUM OF NATURAL HISTORY. SCIENTIFIC PUBLICATION. *see* SCIENCES: COMPREHENSIVE WORKS

708.993 NZL ISSN 1177-4614
ON SHOW. Text in English. q. free (effective 2008). **Document type:** *Bulletin, Consumer.* **Description:** Covers events and exhibitions.
Former titles (until 2006): Gallery News (1174-8729); (until 1999): Auckland Art Gallery. News
Published by: Auckland Art Gallery, PO Box 5449, Auckland, New Zealand. TEL 64-9-3077700, FAX 64-9-3021096, gallery@aucklandartgallery.govt.nz.

069 JPN ISSN 0389-8105
QH70.J32
OOSAKA-SHIRITSU SHIZENSHI HAKUBUTSUKAN KANPO/OSAKA MUSEUM OF NATURAL HISTORY. ANNUAL REPORT. Text in Japanese. 1964. a. **Document type:** *Yearbook.*
Indexed: JPI.
Published by: Oosaka-shiritsu Shizenshi Hakubutsukan/Osaka Museum of Natural History, 1-23 Nagaikoen, Higashisumiyoshi-ku, Osaka-shi, 546-0034, Japan. TEL 81-6-6697-6221, FAX 81-6-6697-6225. Ed. Takayoshi Nasu. Circ: 1,200.

069 DNK ISSN 1903-9581
▼ **OPDATERING.** Text in Danish. 2009. a. illus. index: 1965-1995. **Document type:** *Yearbook, Consumer.*
Formed by the merger of (1965-2007): Mark og Montre (0105-0826); Which was formerly (1963-1964): Fra Esbjerg Museums Virke; (1971-2007): Oelgod Museum (0902-9613); Which was formerly (1965-1970): Oelgod Egnsmuseum (0903-6407)
Indexed: B24, NAA.
Published by: Museet for Varde By og Omegn, Lundvej 4, Varde, 6800, Denmark. TEL 45-75-220877, http://www.vardemuseum.dk.

069 CUB ISSN 1025-3084
F1799.H3
OPUS HABANA. Text in Spanish. 1995. q.
Related titles: Online - full text ed.: ISSN 1605-9085. 1997.
Published by: Museo de la Ciudad de la Habana, Oficios No. 6, 1er. Piso, Esq. Obispo, Havana, Cuba. TEL 537-639343, FAX 537-669281, opus@cultural.ohch.cu. Ed. Angel Calcines Pedreira.

069 USA
ORANGE EMPIRE RAILWAY MUSEUM GAZETTE. Text in English. 1956. m. USD 25 to members. **Document type:** *Newsletter.* **Description:** Covers the documents, technology, history, and impact of rail transportation industry in the West.
Published by: Orange Empire Railway Museum, Inc., PO Box 548, Perris, CA 92572-0548. TEL 909-943-3020, FAX 909-943-2676. Ed., R&P Paul Hammond TEL 916-445-1705. Circ: 1,400.

708.92 NLD ISSN 0922-775X
ORANJE-NASSAU MUSEUM. JAARBOEK. Text in Dutch. 1975. a. price varies.
Formerly (until 1985): Vereniging Oranje-Nassau Museum. Jaarboek (0923-3296)
Indexed: B24.
Published by: Geschiedkundige Vereniging Oranje-Nassau, Postbus 11509, 's-Gravenhage, 2502 AM, Netherlands. http://www.oranje-nassau.org.

708 USA ISSN 2154-8366
ORIENTAL INSTITUTE MUSEUM PUBLICATIONS. Text in English. 1951. irreg., latest 2002. price varies. illus. back issues avail. **Document type:** *Monographic series.* **Description:** Describes materials in the Near Eastern collections of the museums.
Published by: University of Chicago, Oriental Institute, 1155 E 58th St, Chicago, IL 60637. TEL 773-702-9508, FAX 773-702-9853. R&P Thomas G Urban.

069 NOR ISSN 0030-6703
DL401 CODEN: OTTADD
OTTAR. Text in Norwegian. 1954. 5/yr. NOK 220 (effective 2011). adv. charts; illus. cum.index: nos.1-190 (1954-1990). back issues avail. **Document type:** *Journal, Academic/Scholarly.* **Description:** Popular-scientific descriptions of old nordic and arctic nature and culture.
Indexed: AICP, E-psyche, GeoRef, NAA, SpeleolAb.
Published by: Tromsoe Museum - Universitesmuseet, Lars Thoeringsvei 10, Tromsoe, 9037, Norway. TEL 47-77-645000, FAX 47-77-645520, museumspost@uit.no, http://www2.uit.no/ikbViewer/page/tmu?p_lang=2. Circ: 5,500.

069 USA
LAS PALABRAS (TAOS). Text in English. 1979. a. membership. **Document type:** *Newsletter.* **Description:** Covers the collection and interpretation of the art, history, and culture of the Native American, Hispanic, and Anglo peoples of the Southwest, focusing on Taos and northern New Mexico.
Published by: Millicent Rogers Museum, PO Box A, Taos, NM 87571. TEL 505-758-2462, FAX 505-758-5751. Ed. David R McFadden. Circ: 1,500.

PAM'YATKY UKRAINY: ISTORIYA TA KUL'TURA/UKRAINIAN HERITAGE: HISTORY & CULTURE. *see* HISTORY—History Of Europe

069 ESP ISSN 1137-6864
CODEN: sp
PAPERS DEL MONTGRI. Text in Catalan. 1982. a. **Document type:** *Monographic series, Academic/Scholarly.*
Published by: Museu de la Mediterrania, C Ulla 27-31, Torroella de Montgri, Girona 17257, Spain. TEL 34-97-2755180, FAX 34-97-2755182, info@museudelamediterrania.org, http://www.museudelamediterrania.org/ca/museu-de-la-mediterrania.html.

069 SWE ISSN 1103-0100
PAPERS IN MUSEOLOGY. Text in English, Swedish. 1992. irreg., latest vol.5, 2000. **Document type:** *Monographic series, Academic/Scholarly.*
Published by: Umeaa Universitet, Institutionen foer Kultur och Medier, Umeaa Universitet, Humanisthuset, Umeaa, 90187, Sweden. TEL 46-90-7865785, FAX 46-90-7867845, http://www.kulturmed.umu.se.

069 USA
PEABODY ESSEX MUSEUM CALENDAR. Text in English. 1987. q. USD 40 membership (effective 2000). illus. **Description:** Covers new exhibitions and items of interest to museum members.
Formerly: Peabody Essex Museum Magazine; Which superseded: Peabody Museum of Salem. Register
Published by: Peabody Essex Museum of Salem, East India Sq, Salem, MA 01970-3783. TEL 978-745-9500 ext. 32042, FAX 978-741-9012. Ed. Martha Rush Mueller. Circ: 3,200.

069 USA ISSN 1074-0457
F72.E7
PEABODY ESSEX MUSEUM COLLECTIONS. Text in English. 1859. a. USD 45 (effective 2000). cum.index through 1969. back issues avail.; reprints avail. **Document type:** *Monographic series.* **Description:** Highlights and promotes all facets of the Museum's international holdings in arts and culture.
Formerly (until vol.129, no.4, Oct. 1993): Essex Institute Historical Collections (0014-0953)
Related titles: Microform ed.: (from PQC).
Indexed: A20, AIAP, ASCA, IBR, IBZ, MLA-IB, P30, PCI.
—BLDSC (6413.749000), Ingenta.
Published by: Peabody Essex Museum of Salem, East India Sq, Salem, MA 01970-3783. TEL 978-745-9500 ext. 32042, FAX 978-741-9012. Ed. William T La Moy TEL 978-745-9500 ext 3042. Circ: 1,100.

069 USA ISSN 0079-0354
AM101 CODEN: PSSEAL
PEARCE-SELLARDS SERIES. Text in English. 1963. irreg., latest vol.48, 1991. price varies. back issues avail. **Document type:** *Monographic series, Academic/Scholarly.*
Indexed: GeoRef, SpeleolAb.
Published by: Texas Memorial Museum, 2400 Trinity St, Austin, TX 78705. TEL 512-471-1604, FAX 512-471-4794, etheriot@austin.utexas.edu.

PENNSYLVANIA HERITAGE. *see* HISTORY—History Of North And South America

069 CAN ISSN 1719-5071
PETERBOROUGH CENTENNIAL MUSEUM AND ARCHIVES. ANNUAL REPORT. Text in English. a. **Document type:** *Report, Consumer.*
Published by: Peterborough Centennial Museum and Archives, PO Box 143, Peterborough, ON K9J 6Y5, Canada. TEL 705-743-5180, FAX 705-743-2614, http://www.pcma.ca/index.htm.

708.1 USA ISSN 0031-7314
N685
PHILADELPHIA MUSEUM OF ART. BULLETIN. Text in English. 1903. irreg. illus. back issues avail.; reprints avail. **Document type:** *Bulletin, Academic/Scholarly.*
Former titles (until 1956): The Philadelphia Museum Bulletin (0899-059X); (until 1938): Pennsylvania Museum. Bulletin (0891-3609)
Indexed: A&ATA, A06, A07, A20, A30, A31, AA, ABM, AIAP, ASCA, ArtInd, B04, B24, CA, IBR, IBZ, RILM.
—Ingenta.
Published by: Philadelphia Museum of Art, PO Box 7646, Philadelphia, PA 19101. TEL 215-763-8100, FAX 215-236-4465, library@philamuseum.org.

570.74 DEU ISSN 0343-7620
CODEN: PABKDZ
PHILIPPIA. Text in German; Summaries in English. 1970. s-a. EUR 7.62 (effective 2003). back issues avail. **Document type:** *Journal, Academic/Scholarly.*
Indexed: B25, BIOSIS Prev, GeoRef, IBR, IBZ, MycolAb, RefZh, SpeleolAb, Z01.
Published by: Naturkundemuseum der Stadt Kassel, Steinweg 2, Kassel, 34117, Germany. TEL 49-561-7874014, FAX 49-567-787-4058. Circ: 800.

069 PHL ISSN 0117-0686
AM79.P6
PHILIPPINES. NATIONAL MUSEUM PAPERS. Text in English. 1990. s-a. USD 20 (effective 1999). **Document type:** *Journal, Academic/Scholarly.* **Description:** Contain brief scientific papers on anthropology, archaeology, botany, geology, zoology and conservation.
Indexed: IPP.
Published by: National Museum of the Philippines, P. Burgos Ave., PO Box 2659, Manila, 1000, Philippines. TEL 63-2-5271215, FAX 63-2-5270306, nmuseum@i-next.net, http://philmuseum.tripod.com/index. Ed. Elenita D. V. Alba. Circ: 500 (controlled).

PIA KANSAI EDITION. *see* LEISURE AND RECREATION

708.11 971 CAN ISSN 1912-0109
PICKERING JUNCTION NEWS. Text in English. 1999. s-a. **Document type:** *Newsletter, Consumer.*
Published by: Pickering Museum Village Foundation, PO Box 66035, Pickering, ON L1V 6P7, Canada. TEL 905-839-4672, http://www.pineridgearts.org/pmvf.html. Ed. Laura Drake.

PLATEAU JOURNAL; land and people of the Colorado Plateau. *see* ANTHROPOLOGY

069 USA
PONY EXPRESS MAIL. Text in English. 1972. m. looseleaf. USD 10 domestic; USD 15 foreign (effective 2000). adv. **Document type:** *Newsletter.* **Description:** Chronicles news and activities of the Patee House Museum, headquarters of the Pony Express, and the Jesse James Home, and events pertaining to the Pony Express and Jesse James.
Indexed: SpeleolAb.
Published by: Pony Express Historical Association, Inc., 12th and Penn, PO Box 1022, St. Joseph, MO 64502. TEL 816-232-8206, FAX 816-232-8206. Ed., R&P, Adv. contact Gary Chilcote. Pub. Jondenna Johnston. Circ: 428 (paid). **Co-sponsors:** Jesse James Home; Patee House Museum.

069 USA
PORTLAND ART MUSEUM NEWSLETTER. Text in English. 1949. q. free to members (effective 2005). adv. 36 p./no.; **Document type:** *Newsletter.*
Former titles (until 1991): Oregon Art Institute Newsletter; Portland Art Association Newsletter; Portland Art Association Calendar; Portland Art Museum Calendar
Published by: Portland Art Museum, 1219 S W Park Ave, Portland, OR 97205. TEL 503-226-2811, FAX 503-226-4842. Ed. Ellen Lewis. Circ: 24,000 (controlled).

069.4 USA ISSN 1523-4967
PRESERVATION TIPS. Text in English. 1993. q. back issues avail. **Document type:** *Newsletter, Trade.* **Description:** Contains information on preserving archives, historic sites, museums and libraries.
Related titles: Online - full text ed.
Published by: Chicora Foundation, Inc., PO Box 8664, Columbia, SC 29202. TEL 803-787-6910, FAX 803-787-6910, info@chicora.org.

PREVIEW. *see* ART

708.1 CAN ISSN 1481-2258
N400
PREVIEW; the gallery guide. Text in English. 198?. 5/yr. free. adv. **Description:** Covers exhibitions in museums and art galleries in Alberta, British Columbia, Washington and Oregon.
Former titles (until 1997): Preview of the Visual Arts in Vancouver, Victoria, Seattle, Portland (1197-8740); (until 1989): Art (Vancouver) (1197-8732)
Address: PO Box 549, Sta A, Vancouver, BC V6C 2N3, Canada. TEL 604-254-1405, FAX 604-254-1314, preview@portal.ca, http://www.preview-art.com/.

708.1 USA ISSN 0032-843X
N1
PRINCETON UNIVERSITY ART MUSEUM. RECORD. Text in English. 1942. a. USD 18 per issue to non-members; free to members (effective 2011). bibl.; illus. cum.index every 10 yrs. back issues avail.; reprints avail. **Document type:** *Journal, Academic/Scholarly.* **Description:** Publishes research on the museum's collection.
Formerly (until 1948): Princeton University Museum of Historic Art. Record (0899-0603)
Related titles: Microform ed.: (from PQC); Online - full text ed.
Indexed: A06, A07, A22, A30, A31, AA, ABM, AIAP, AmHI, ArtInd, B04, B24, BRD, CA, FR, H07, I14, PCI, SCOPUS, T02, W03, W05.
—Ingenta, INIST. **CCC.**
Published by: Princeton University Art Museum, Princeton, NJ 08544. TEL 609-258-3788, mcason@princeton.edu.

PTAH. *see* ARCHITECTURE

069 ESP ISSN 0214-1000
PUIG CASTELLAR; boletin de la Seccion de Estudios del Centro Excursionista. Text in Spanish. 1961. s-a. **Document type:** *Bulletin, Consumer.*
Indexed: GeoRef.
Published by: Museu Torre Balldovina, Placa de Pau Casals, s-n, Santa Coloma de Gramanet, Barcelona, 08922, Spain. TEL 34-93-3857142, FAX 34-93-4660974, mtbsc@minorisa.es, http://www.minorisa.es/mtbsc.

069 CHN ISSN 1004-4973
QIMENG/ENLIGHTENMENT. Text in Chinese. 1986. m. USD 25.20 (effective 2009). **Document type:** *Journal, Academic/Scholarly.*
—East View.
Published by: Tianjin Jiaoyu Zazhishe, 9, Ya'an Dao, Nankai-qu, Tianjin, 300113, China. TEL 86-22-27362429. **Dist. by:** China International Book Trading Corp, 35 Chegongzhuang Xilu, Haidian District, PO Box 399, Beijing 100044, China. TEL 86-10-68412045, FAX 86-10-68412023, cibtc@mail.cibtc.com.cn, http://www.cibtc.com.cn.

QUADERNI DEL MUSEO ANTONIANO. *see* MUSIC

387 USA ISSN 0891-2661
QUARTERDECK. Text in English. 1973. q. USD 25 (effective 2000). adv. illus. 16 p./no.; back issues avail. **Document type:** *Newsletter, Corporate.* **Description:** News, historical vignettes, and announcements pertaining to the activities of the Columbia River Maritime Museum in Oregon.
Formerly (until Fall 1989): Quarterdeck Review
Published by: Columbia River Maritime Museum, Inc., 1792 Marine Dr, Astoria, OR 97103. TEL 503-325-2323, FAX 503-325-2331. Ed., Adv. contact Mary Davis. Circ: 1,900.

708.994 AUS ISSN 1039-8090
QUEEN VICTORIA MUSEUM AND ART GALLERY. ANNUAL REPORT. Text in English. 1902. a., latest 2006. back issues avail. **Document type:** *Corporate.* **Description:** Discusses the museum's accomplishments over the past year and its plans.
Published by: Queen Victoria Museum and Art Gallery, PO Box 403, Launceston, TAS 7250, Australia. TEL 61-3-63233777, FAX 61-3-63233776, enquiries@qvmag.tas.gov.au, http://www.qvmag.tas.gov.au.

708.994 AUS ISSN 1441-6506
AM101 CODEN: RQVMAY
THE QUEEN VICTORIA MUSEUM AND ART GALLERY, LAUNCESTON. RECORDS. Text in English. 1942. irreg., latest vol.114, 2008. price varies. illus. back issues avail. **Document type:** *Report, Academic/Scholarly.*
Formerly (until 1997): Queen Victoria Museum and Art Gallery. Launceston, Tasmania. Records (0085-5278)
Indexed: AESIS, ASFA, B21, ESPM, GeoRef, SpeleolAb, Z01.
—BLDSC (7323.975000), INIST.
Published by: Queen Victoria Museum and Art Gallery, PO Box 403, Launceston, TAS 7250, Australia. TEL 61-3-63233777, FAX 61-3-63233776, enquiries@qvmag.tas.gov.au.

708.994 AUS ISSN 1038-2224
QUEEN VICTORIA MUSEUM AND ART GALLERY. OCCASIONAL PAPERS. Text in English. 1989. irreg., latest vol.8, 2006. price varies. back issues avail. **Document type:** *Monographic series, Academic/Scholarly.*
Published by: Queen Victoria Museum and Art Gallery, PO Box 403, Launceston, TAS 7250, Australia. TEL 61-3-63233777, FAX 61-3-63233776, enquiries@qvmag.tas.gov.au.

QUEENSLAND MUSEUM. MEMOIRS. *see* SCIENCES: COMPREHENSIVE WORKS

QUEENSLAND MUSEUM. MEMOIRS. CULTURAL HERITAGE SERIES. *see* HUMANITIES: COMPREHENSIVE WORKS

R.E. OLDS TRANSPORTATION MUSEUM NEWSLETTER. *see* TRANSPORTATION

069 CAN ISSN 1910-8591
R Q A B M INFO. (Regroupement Quebecois des Amis et Benevoles de Musees) Text in French. 2001. 3/yr. **Document type:** *Newsletter, Trade.*
Media: Online - full text.
Published by: Regroupement Quebecois des Amis et Benevoles de Musees (R Q A B M), C P 1222, Succursale Saint-Laurent, Montreal, PQ H4L 4X1, Canada. TEL 514-744-9182, FAX 514-744-9758, rqabm@qc.aira.com.

READING ROOM; a journal of art and culture. *see* ART

RECERQUES DEL MUSEU D'ALCOI. *see* ARCHAEOLOGY

069.0994 AUS ISSN 1833-1335
➤ **RECOLLECTIONS (CANBERRA).** Text in English. 2006. s-a. AUD 49.95 per issue (effective 2009). back issues avail. **Document type:** *Journal, Academic/Scholarly.* **Description:** Focuses on museology and museum practice.
Related titles: Online - full text ed.: ISSN 1833-4946. free (effective 2009).
Published by: National Museum of Australia, GPO Box 1901, Canberra, ACT 2601, Australia. TEL 61-2-62085040, FAX 61-2-62085014, information@nma.gov.au, http://www.nma.gov.au. Eds. Dr. Mike Smith TEL 61-2-62085335, Dr. Peter Stanley, Dr. Stephen Foster TEL 61-2-61255885, Dr. Therese Weber TEL 61-2-62085059.

061 ESP ISSN 2172-0983
RECORRIDOS CRUZADOS. Text in Spanish. 2001. irreg. **Document type:** *Monographic series, Academic/Scholarly.*
Published by: Universidad de Salamanca, Ediciones, Apartado 325, Salamanca, 37080, Spain. TEL 34-923-294598, FAX 34-923-262579, pedidos@universitas.usal.es, http://www.eusal.es/.

THE RECRUIT. *see* HISTORY—History Of North And South America

069 ESP ISSN 1134-0576
REVISTA DE MUSEOLOGIA. Text in Spanish. 1994. q. EUR 33 domestic (effective 2002). adv. back issues avail. **Document type:** *Journal, Academic/Scholarly.*
Related titles: Online - full text ed.
Published by: Asociacion Espanola de Museologos, Ave. Reyes Catolicos, 6 5a. planta, Madrid, 28040, Spain. TEL 34-91-5430917, FAX 34-91-5440225, aem@museologia.net. Ed. Margarita Ruyra de Andrade. adv.: color page EUR 690, B&W page EUR 600; 220 x 270. Circ: 2,000.

069 ARG
REVISTA DEL MUSEO AMERICANISTA. Text in Spanish. 1969. a.
Published by: Museo Americanista de Antropologia Historia Numismatica y Ciencias Naturales, Manuel Castro, 254, Lomas De Zamora, Buenos Aires 1832, Argentina.

069 ROM ISSN 1220-1723
REVISTA MUZEELOR. Text in Romanian; Summaries in English, French, Russian. 1964. 10/yr. ROL 360, USD 91. bk.rev. bibl.; charts; illus.
Formerly (until 1990): Revista Muzeelor si Monumentelor. Seria Muzee (1220-1731); Which was formed by the 1974 merger of: Revista Muzeelor (0035-0206); Revista Monumentelor Istorice (0253-1569); Which was previously (1908-1970): Buletinul Comisi Unii Monumentelor Istorice (1220-1715)
Indexed: FR, MLA-IB, NumL, RASB.
Published by: Ministerul Culturii, Piata Presi Libere 1, Sector 1, Bucharest, Romania. Ed. Gavril Sarafoleanu. **Subscr. to:** Calea Grivitei, Calea Grivitei 66-68, PO Box 12201, Bucharest, Romania.

708.4 FRA ISSN 1962-4271
➤ **LA REVUE DES MUSEES DE FRANCE.** Text in French; Summaries in English, German. 1951. bi-m. EUR 69 (effective 2008). adv. bk.rev. illus. index. **Document type:** *Journal, Academic/Scholarly.*
Former titles (until 2008): La Revue du Louvre et des Musees de France (0035-2608); (until 1961): La Revue des Arts (0482-7872); (until 1951): Musees de France (1144-1216); (until 1948): Bulletin des Musees de France (1144-1208); (until 1915): Les Musees de France (1144-1194); (until 1911): Bulletin des Musees de France (1144-1186); (until 1908): Musees et Monuments de France (1144-1178)
Related titles: Online - full text ed.
Indexed: A&ATA, A06, A07, A20, A30, A31, AA, AIAP, ASCA, ArtHuCI, ArtInd, B04, B24, BAS, BRD, CurCont, DIP, FR, IBR, IBZ, P30, PCI, RASB, RILM, SCOPUS, W03, W05, W07.
—IE, Infotrieve, INIST. **CCC.**
Published by: Editions de la Reunion des Musees Nationaux, 49 Rue Etienne Marcel, Paris, Cedex 1 75039, France. TEL 33-1-40134800, FAX 33-1-40134400, http://www.rmn.fr. Eds. Danielle Gaborit Chopin, Jean Pierre Cuzin. Adv. contact Francoise Gachin.

069 NLD ISSN 1574-4787
RIJKSMUSEUM AMSTERDAM. JAARVERSLAG. Text in Dutch. 1998. a.
Published by: Rijksmuseum Amsterdam, Postbus 74888, Amsterdam, 1070 DN, Netherlands. TEL 31-20-6747000, FAX 31-20-6747001, info@rijksmuseum.nl.

069 700 NLD ISSN 1875-3604
RIJKSMUSEUM-DOSSIERS. Text in Dutch. 2000. irreg. price varies.
Published by: (Rijksmuseum Amsterdam), Waanders Uitgevers, Postbus 1129, Zwolle, 8001 BC, Netherlands. TEL 31-38-4673400, FAX 31-38-4673401, info@waanders.nl, http://www.waanders.nl.

069 ITA ISSN 2038-4068
▼ **RIVISTA MUSEO TORINO.** Text in Italian. 2010. 3/yr. **Document type:** *Handbook/Manual/Guide, Consumer.*
Related titles: Online - full text ed.: ISSN 2038-4076.
Published by: Comune di Torino, Piazza Palazzo di Citta 1, Turin, 10122, Italy. TEL 39-011-4421111, FAX 39-011-4422723, http://www.comune.torino.it.

708.1 CAN ISSN 1911-1231
ROYAL B C MUSEUM. ANNUAL REPORT. (British Columbia) Text in English. 1992. a. **Document type:** *Report, Trade.*
Formerly (until 2004): Royal British Columbia Museum. Annual Report (1194-5907)
Published by: Royal British Columbia Museum, 675 Belleville St, Victoria, BC V8V 1X4, Canada. TEL 250-356-7226, 888-447-7977, FAX 250-387-5674, reception@royalbcmuseum.bc.ca, http://www.royalbcmuseum.bc.ca/MainSite/default.aspx.

708.11 CAN ISSN 0082-5115
AM101
ROYAL ONTARIO MUSEUM. ANNUAL REPORT. Text in English. 1949. a. free. **Document type:** *Corporate.*
—CCC.
Published by: Royal Ontario Museum, Publications Dept, 100 Queen's Park, Toronto, ON M5S 2C6, Canada. TEL 416-586-5581, FAX 416-586-5887. Ed. Sandra Shaul.

069.5 AUT
RUDOLFINUM. Text in German. 2000. a. **Document type:** *Journal, Academic/Scholarly.*
Published by: Landesmuseum Kaernten, Museumgasse 2, Klagenfurt, K 9021, Austria. TEL 43-50-53630599, FAX 43-50-53630540, info@landesmuseum-ktn.at, http://www.landesmuseum-ktn.at.

▼ **S C I R E S - I T.** (Scientific Research and Information Technology) *see* COMPUTERS

SADO HAKUBUTSUKAN KENKYU HOKOKU/PUBLICATIONS FROM THE SADO MUSEUM. *see* SCIENCES: COMPREHENSIVE WORKS

708.1 USA ISSN 0009-7691
N729
ST. LOUIS ART MUSEUM. BULLETIN. Text in English. 1914; N.S. 1965. s-a. USD 10 (effective 1999). illus. reprints avail. **Document type:** *Bulletin.*
Formerly (until 1972): City Art Museum of Saint Louis. Bulletin (0364-8141)
Indexed: A06, A07, A30, A31, AA, ABM, AIAP, ArtInd, B04, B24.
Published by: St. Louis Art Museum, Publications Department, No. 1 Fine Arts Dr., Forest Park, St. Louis, MO 63110. TEL 314-721-0072, FAX 314-721-6172. Ed. Mary Ann Steiner. R&P Pat Woods. Circ: 17,000 (paid).

SAITAMA-KENRITSU SHIZENSHI HAKUBUTSUKAN KENKYU HOKOKU/SAITAMA MUSEUM OF NATURAL HISTORY. BULLETIN. *see* SCIENCES: COMPREHENSIVE WORKS

SAITAMA-KENRITSU SHIZENSHI HAKUBUTSUKAN SHUZO SHIRYO MOKUROKU/SAITAMA MUSEUM OF NATURAL HISTORY. CATALOGUE OF THE MATERIALS. *see* SCIENCES: COMPREHENSIVE WORKS

SAITO HO-ON KAI MUSEUM OF NATURAL HISTORY. RESEARCH BULLETIN. *see* SCIENCES: COMPREHENSIVE WORKS

SAM NOBLE OKLAHOMA MUSEUM OF NATURAL HISTORY. OCCASIONAL PAPER. *see* SCIENCES: COMPREHENSIVE WORKS

708 792.8 780 USA
SAN FRANCISCO ARTS MONTHLY. Text in English. m. adv. **Description:** Provides information about cultural events in the San Francisco area.
Related titles: Online - full text ed.
Address: 20 Sycamore St, San Francisco, CA 94110. TEL 415-934-9300, http://www.sfarts.org. Ed., Pub. Elizabeth B. Crabtree.

069.5 AUT
SCHAETZE DES ARCHIVS. Text in German. 2008. irreg., latest vol.2, 2010. price varies. **Document type:** *Monographic series, Academic/Scholarly.*
Published by: Boehlau Verlag GmbH & Co.KG., Wiesingerstr 1, Vienna, W 1010, Austria. TEL 43-1-3302427, FAX 43-1-3302432, boehlau@boehlau.at, http://www.boehlau.at.

069 DEU
SCHLESWIG-HOLSTEINISCHEN LANDESMUSEUM. JAHRBUCH. Text in German. 1986. biennial. EUR 25 per issue (effective 2010). **Document type:** *Journal, Academic/Scholarly.*
Published by: (Schleswig-Holsteinischen Landesmuseum), Wachholtz Verlag GmbH, Rungestr 4, Neumuenster, 24537, Germany. TEL 49-4321-250930, FAX 49-4321-2509315, info@wachholtz.de, http://www.wachholtz.de.

069 DEU
SCHRIFTENREIHE MUSEUM EUROPAEISCHER KULTUREN. Text in German. 1999. irreg., latest vol.9, 2010. price varies. **Document type:** *Monographic series, Academic/Scholarly.*
Published by: Lukas Verlag fuer Kunst- und Geistesgeschichte, Kollwitzstr 57, Berlin, 10405, Germany. TEL 49-30-44049220, FAX 49-30-4428177, lukas.verlag@t-online.de, http://www.lukasverlag.com.

SCOPOLIA. *see* BIOLOGY

385 USA
SEASHORE TROLLEY MUSEUM DISPATCH. Text in English. 1958. bi-m. USD 30 to members (effective 2000). bk.rev.; video rev. charts; illus.; maps. back issues avail. **Document type:** *Newsletter.* **Description:** Contains news of the museum and historical information on transit systems worldwide.
Published by: New England Electric Railway Historical Society, Inc., 195 Log Cabin Rd, PO Box A, Kennebunkport, ME 04046-1690. TEL 207-967-2712, FAX 207-967-0867. Ed. Dann E Chamberlin TEL 207-871-9432. R&P Phil Morse. Circ: 1,300.

069 ESP ISSN 2172-1998
SERIE CURSOS Y CONFERENCIAS. Text in Spanish. 2001. a. **Document type:** *Monographic series, Academic/Scholarly.*
Published by: Museo de San Isidro, Plaza San Andres, 2, Madrid, 28005, Spain. TEL 34-913-667415, FAX 34-913-541719, museodelosorigenes@madrid.es.

069 USA
SHILOH SCRAPBOOK. Text in English. 1978. q. looseleaf. USD 10 to members. back issues avail. **Document type:** *Newsletter.* **Description:** Discusses history of Ozark Mountain region and museum programs for people of all ages.
Formerly (until 1995): Shiloh Museum. Newsletter
Published by: Shiloh Museum of Ozark History, 118 W Johnson Ave, Springdale, AR 72764. TEL 501-750-8165, FAX 501-750-8171. Ed. Susan Young. Circ: 2,500.

SHIRETOKO HAKUBUTSUKAN KENKYU HOKOKU/SHIRETOKO MUSEUM. BULLETIN. *see* SCIENCES: COMPREHENSIVE WORKS

SHIZEN KYOIKUEN HOKOKU/JAPAN. MINISTRY OF EDUCATION. NATIONAL SCIENCE MUSEUM. INSTITUTE FOR NATURE STUDY. MISCELLANEOUS REPORTS. *see* SCIENCES: COMPREHENSIVE WORKS

508.074 JPN ISSN 1340-2285
SHIZENSHI DAYORI. Text in Japanese. 1985. 3/yr. **Description:** Reports news of the museum.
Published by: Saitama-kenritsu Shizenshi Hakubutsukan/Saitama Museum of Natural History, 1417-1 Nagatoro, Chichibu-gun, Nagatoro-machi, Saitama-ken 369-1305, Japan. TEL 81-494-660404, FAX 81-494-691002, sizensi@po.kumagaya.or.jp, http://www.kumagaya.or.jp/~sizensi.

069.5 CHN ISSN 1005-0655
N8395.C6
SHOUCANGJIA/COLLECTOR AND CONNOISSEUR. Text in Chinese. 1993. bi-m. USD 148.80 (effective 2009). **Document type:** *Magazine, Consumer.*
—East View.
Address: 5, Chongwenmen Xi Dajie, Beijing, 100005, China. TEL 86-10-65593940, FAX 86-10-65127493. **Dist. by:** China International Book Trading Corp, 35 Chegongzhuang Xilu, Haidian District, PO Box 399, Beijing 100044, China. TEL 86-10-68412045, FAX 86-10-68412023, cibtc@mail.cibtc.com.cn, http://www.cibtc.com.cn.

069 AUS ISSN 1033-4688
SIGNALS. Text in English. 1986. q. free to members; AUD 4.95 per issue (effective 2008). adv. bk.rev. back issues avail. **Document type:** *Magazine, Consumer.* **Description:** Publishes articles on Australian maritime heritage and museum news.
Formerly (until 1988): Australian National Maritime Museum. Newsletter (0818-5662)
Indexed: Inspec.
—Ingenta.
Published by: Australian National Maritime Museum, GPO Box 5131, Sydney, NSW 2001, Australia. TEL 61-2-92983777, FAX 61-2-92983780, info@anmm.gov.au. Ed. Jeffrey Mellefont TEL 61-2-92983647. adv.: color page AUD 1,200; 178 x 262. Circ: 6,000 (controlled).

069 900 SWE ISSN 0280-8439
SIGTUNA MUSEERS SKRIFTSERIE. Text mainly in Swedish; Text occasionally in English. 1982. irreg., latest vol.12, 2005. price varies. back issues avail. **Document type:** *Academic/Scholarly.*
Published by: Sigtuna Museum, Stora Gatan 55, Sigtuna, 19330, Sweden. TEL 46-8-59783870, FAX 46-8-59783883, sigtunamuseum@sigtuna.se, http://195.190.203.17/museer/index.htm.

SLATE. *see* ART

SMITHSONIAN. *see* SOCIAL SCIENCES: COMPREHENSIVE WORKS

069 USA ISSN 1949-2359
▼ **SMITHSONIAN CONTRIBUTIONS TO MUSEUM CONSERVATION.** Text in English. 2010 (Jan.). irreg., latest vol.1, 2010. price varies. **Document type:** *Monographic series, Academic/Scholarly.* **Description:** A book series focusing on museum conservation issues, such as pest control, mold, water damage and preservation techniques.
Related titles: Online - full text ed.: ISSN 1949-2367. 2010 (Jan.).
Published by: (Smithsonian Museum Conservation Institute), Smithsonian Institution Scholarly Press, MRC 957, PO Box 37012, Washington, DC 20013. TEL 202-633-3016, straderg@si.edu, http://www.scholarlypress.si.edu/.

SOCIETE HISTORIQUE DE SAINT-BONIFACE. BULLETIN. *see* HISTORY—History Of North And South America

069 SLB
SOLOMON ISLANDS MUSEUM ASSOCIATION. JOURNAL. Text in English. 1975. a. **Document type:** *Journal, Academic/Scholarly.*
Indexed: AICP.
Published by: (Solomon Islands Museum Association), Solomon Islands Government Printing, PO Box 313, Honiara, Solomon Isl.

707.4 USA ISSN 2152-2545
SOTHEBY'S AT AUCTION. Text in English. 1986. 8/yr. USD 150 domestic; USD 200 foreign (effective 2010). back issues avail. **Document type:** *Magazine, Trade.*
Formerly (until 2009): Sotheby's Preview
Published by: Sotheby's Inc., 1334 York Ave, 72nd St, New York, NY 10021. TEL 212-606-7000, FAX 212-606-7107.

069 ZAF ISSN 0370-8314
AM89.A1 CODEN: SAMAAM
SOUTH AFRICAN MUSEUMS ASSOCIATION. BULLETIN. Text in English. 1936. s-a. ZAR 75, USD 60; free to members. adv. bk.rev. charts; illus. index every 2 yrs. **Document type:** *Bulletin, Consumer.*
Formerly: Southern African Museums Association. Publication (0036-0791)
Indexed: ISAP.
Published by: South African Museums Association, PO Box 699, Grahamstown, East Cape 6140, South Africa. TEL 27-46-6361340. Ed. W Holleman. adv.: B&W page ZAR 342, color page ZAR 684. Circ: 800.

SOUTHWESTERN & MEXICAN PHOTOGRAPHY. *see* PHOTOGRAPHY

SPORVEJSMUSEET SKJOLDENAESHOLM. AARSBERETNING. *see* TRANSPORTATION—Railroads

708.3 DEU ISSN 0075-5133
STAATLICHE KUNSTHALLE KARLSRUHE. BILDHEFTE. Text in German. 1958. irreg. price varies. **Document type:** *Catalog.*
Published by: Staatliche Kunsthalle Karlsruhe, Hans-Thoma-Str 2, Karlsruhe, 76133, Germany. TEL 49-721-9263355, FAX 49-721-9266788.

069 DEU ISSN 0419-733X
STAATLICHE KUNSTSAMMLUNGEN DRESDEN. JAHRBUCH. Text in German. 1960. a. EUR 25 (effective 2005). **Document type:** *Yearbook, Academic/Scholarly.*
Indexed: B24, DIP, IBR, IBZ, RILM.
Published by: Staatliche Kunstsammlungen Dresden, Residenzschloss, Taschenberg 2, Dresden, 01067, Germany. TEL 49-351-4914701, FAX 49-351-4914777, info@skd.smwk.sachsen.de.

069 DEU ISSN 0067-284X
N6886.B27
STAATLICHE KUNSTSAMMLUNGEN IN BADEN-WUERTTEMBERG. JAHRBUCH. Text in German. 1964. a. EUR 30.80 (effective 2009). **Document type:** *Journal, Academic/Scholarly.*
Indexed: AIAP, B24, DIP, IBR, IBZ, RILM.
Published by: (Staatliche Kunstsammlungen in Baden-Wuerttemberg), Deutscher Kunstverlag GmbH, Nymphenburger Str 90e, Munich, 80636, Germany. TEL 49-89-961608610, FAX 49-89-961608644, info@deutscherkunstverlag.de, http://www.deutscherkunstverlag.de. Circ: 600.

069 BEL ISSN 0773-9559
NX555.A57
STAD ANTWERPEN. CULTUREEL JAARBOEK. Text in Dutch; Summaries in English. 1983. a. bk.rev. back issues avail. **Document type:** *Government.* **Description:** Presents various cultural and social events in and around Antwerp.
Indexed: RILM.
Published by: Stad Antwerpen, Stadhuis, Antwerp, 2000, Belgium. TEL 32-3-2060355, FAX 32-3-2060360, TELEX 31807 HAVANT. Ed. Luc Gorsele. Circ: 1,500.

069 DEU ISSN 0078-2777
STADTBIBLIOTHEK NUERNBERG. AUSSTELLUNGSKATALOG. Text in German. 1955. irreg., latest vol.102, 2000. price varies. **Document type:** *Catalog, Academic/Scholarly.*
Published by: Stadtbibliothek Nuernberg, Egidienplatz 23, Nuernberg, 90317, Germany. TEL 49-911-2312790, FAX 49-911-2315476, stb@stadt.nuernberg.de, http://www.stadtbibliothek.nuernberg.de.

069 DEU ISSN 0936-6644
STANDBEIN SPIELBEIN. Text in German. 1984. 3/yr. EUR 21 domestic; EUR 23.50 foreign; EUR 8 newsstand/cover (effective 2009). bk.rev. back issues avail. **Document type:** *Magazine, Consumer.*
Published by: Bundesverband Museumspaedagogik e.V., c/o Stefan Bresky, Deutsches Historisches Museum, Unter den Linden 2, Berlin, 10117, Germany. TEL 49-30-20304753, FAX 49-30-20304759, bresky@dhm.de. Ed. Romy Steinmeier. Circ: 1,000 (controlled).

708.994 AUS ISSN 1443-721X
STATE OF THE ARTS. Text in English. 1996. 4/yr. adv. bk.rev.; dance rev.; film rev.; music rev.; play rev.; software rev. back issues avail. **Document type:** *Magazine, Consumer.* **Description:** Event guide to arts and entertainment in Australia. Includes art galleries, museums, theatre, opera, dance, classical music and related resources.
Former titles (until 2001): State of the Arts South Australia; (until 1998): State of the Arts (1326-4796); Which was formed by the merger of (1992-1996): State of the Art (1324-6658); (1995-1996): State of the Art in Music (1324-6666)
Related titles: Online - full text ed.
Published by: State of the Art Publications (Subsidiary of: Arts Diary D/L), Level 3, 85 William St., East Sydney, NSW 2011, Australia. http://www.staeart.com.au. adv.: B&W page AUD 2,195, color page AUD 3,990; trim 260 x 360. Circ: 32,000. **Subscr. to:** PO Box 243, Kings Cross, NSW 1340, Australia.

069.5 SWE ISSN 1404-4870
STATENS HISTORISKA MUSEUMS UTSTAELLNINGSKATALOG. Text in Swedish. 1991. irreg. price varies. **Document type:** *Catalog, Consumer.*
Formerly (until 1998): Statens Historiska Museum. Utstaellningskatalog (1101-8224)
Published by: Statens Historiska Museum/Museum of National Antiguities in Sweden, Narvavaegen 13-17, Stockholm, 11484, Sweden. TEL 46-8-51955600, info@historiska.se.

069 USA
THE STATESMAN (SPIEGEL GROVE). Text in English. 1981. q. free. back issues avail. **Document type:** *Newsletter.* **Description:** News about the Hayes Presidential Center, its collections, exhibits, and programs that are available to the public.
Related titles: Online - full text ed.
Published by: Rutherford B. Hayes Presidential Center, Spiegel Grove, Fremont, OH 43420-2796. TEL 419-332-2081, FAX 419-332-4952. Ed., R&P Nancy Kleinhenz. Circ: 7,000.

069.1 USA
STATION LOG. Text in English. 1981. 2/yr. USD 15 to members (effective 2006). film rev. illus. back issues avail. **Document type:** *Newsletter, Consumer.* **Description:** Keeps members, visitors and others informed of museum activities, the history of organized life saving, and the maritime heritage of Boston Harbor.
Published by: Hull Lifesaving Museum, 1117 Nantasket Ave, Hull, MA 02045. TEL 781-925-5433, FAX 781-925-0992, lifesavingmuseum@comcast.net, http://www.lifesavingmuseum.org. Ed. Lory Newmyer. Circ: 2,500.

708.81 NOR ISSN 0333-0664
STAVANGER MUSEUM. SKRIFTER. Text in Norwegian; Summaries in English. 1920. irreg., latest vol.11, 1985. price varies. illus. back issues avail. **Document type:** *Monographic series, Academic/Scholarly.*
Published by: Stavanger Museum, Musegate 16, Stavanger, 4010, Norway. TEL 47-51-842700, FAX 47-51-842701, firmapost@stavanger.museum.no, http://www.stavanger.museum.no.

STEARNS NEWSLETTER; the Stearns collection of musical instruments at the University of Michigan. *see* MUSIC

069.5 NLD ISSN 1877-8143
STICHTING VRIENDEN VAN HET GELDMUSEUM. NIEUWSBRIEF. Text in Dutch. 1998. irreg. EUR 25 membership (effective 2011). **Document type:** *Newsletter, Consumer.*
Former titles (until 2007): Stichting Vrienden van het Geld- en Bankmuseum. Nieuwsbrief (1877-8135); (until 2005): Stichting Vrienden van het Nederlands Muntmuseum. Nieuwsbrief (1389-8590)
Published by: Stichting Vrienden van het Geldmuseum, Postbus 2407, Utrecht, 3500 GK, Netherlands. TEL 31-30-2910492, FAX 31-30-2910467, info@geldmuseum.nl, http://www.geldmuseum.nl.

STOCKMAN'S NEWS. *see* HISTORY—History Of Australasia And Other Areas

069 NLD ISSN 0923-9286
STRAATGRAS. Text in Dutch. 1981. 5/yr. EUR 30 membership (effective 2010). **Document type:** *Newsletter, Consumer.*
Incorporates (2000-2009): Natuurlijk Rotterdam (1572-2317); Formerly (until 1989): Brug (0924-2724)
Published by: Natuurmuseum Rotterdam/Natural History Museum, Rotterdam, Westzeedijk 345, Postbus 23452, Rotterdam, 3001 KL, Netherlands. TEL 31-10-4364222, FAX 31-10-4364399, info@nmr.nl, http://www.nmr.nl.

069 USA
STRECKER MUSEUM NEWS. Text in English. 1971. irreg. (approx. 4/yr.). looseleaf. free. back issues avail. **Document type:** *Newsletter.* **Description:** Covers the museum and its research, other programs, museum studies, Strecker associates, volunteers, donors, and interested friends.
Published by: Baylor University, John. K. Strecker Museum, PO Box 97154, Waco, TX 76798. TEL 254-710-1110, FAX 254-710-1173. Ed. David Lintz. Circ: 2,000.

069 HUN ISSN 0133-3046
STUDIA COMITATENSIA. Text in Hungarian; Summaries in English, German, Russian. 1972. irreg., latest vol.27, 1994. price varies or on exchange basis. illus. **Document type:** *Academic/Scholarly.* **Description:** Interdisciplinary studies on Pest County. Includes art, history, sociology, culture, anthropology, ethnology, archeology, literature and history.
Indexed: AICP, FR.
—INIST.
Published by: Pest Megyei Muzeumok Igazgatosaga/Direction of Pest County Museums, Fo ter 6, Szentendre, 2000, Hungary. TEL 26-310-244, FAX 26-310-790. Ed., Pub. Soos Sandor. Circ: 800.

STUDIA DO DZIEJOW DAWNEGO UZBROJENIA I UBIORU WOJSKOWEGO. *see* MILITARY

STUDIA NATURALIA. *see* SCIENCES: COMPREHENSIVE WORKS

069 FIN ISSN 1235-9122
V13.F52
SUOMEN MERIMUSEO. NAUTICA FENNICA. Text in English. 1992. s-a. price varies. back issues avail. **Document type:** *Monographic series, Academic/Scholarly.* **Description:** Articles relating to Finnish maritime history.
Formed by the merger of (1976-1990): Nautica Fennica (0355-8711); (1969-1991): Maritime Museum of Finland. Annual Report (0359-873X); Which was formerly (until 1981): Maritime Museum Helsinki. Annual Report (0355-8975)
Published by: Suomen Merimuseo/Maritime Museum of Finland, Nervanderinkatu 13, PO Box 913, Helsinki, 00101, Finland. TEL 358-9-40501, FAX 358-9-40509300, suomenmerimuseo@nba.fi. **Co-publisher:** Suomen Merihistoriallinen Yhdistys.

708.85 700 SWE
SWEDEN. NATIONALMUSEUM. SKRIFTSERIE. Text in Multiple languages. 1954. irreg. price varies. adv. back issues avail. **Document type:** *Monographic series, Academic/Scholarly.*
Formerly (until 1984): Sweden. Nationalmusei. Skriftserie (0081-5683)
Published by: Nationalmuseum, Sodra Blasieholmshamnen, PO Box 16176, Stockholm, 103 24, Sweden. TEL 46-8-51954300, FAX 46-8-51954450, info@nationalmuseum.se, http://www.nationalmuseum.se. Circ: 2,500.

708.1 CAN ISSN 0845-8081
TABLEAU (FREDERICTON). Text in English. 1970. 3/yr. free. **Document type:** *Newsletter.* **Description:** Provides information on exhibitions held, programs available, recent acquisitions etc.
Formerly (until 1988): Beaverbrook Art Gallery (0045-1592)
Indexed: RILM.

Published by: Beaverbrook Art Gallery, P O Box 605, Fredericton, NB E3B 5A6, Canada. TEL 506-458-8545, FAX 506-459-7450. Ed., R&P Laurie Glenn. Circ: 1,800.

708.11 CAN
TABLEAU (WINNIPEG); involving people in the visual arts. Text in English. bi-m. free. **Document type:** *Newsletter.* **Description:** Discusses exhibits and events at the Winnipeg Art Gallery.
Published by: Winnipeg Art Gallery, 300 Memorial Blvd, Winnipeg, MB R3C 1V1, Canada. TEL 204-786-6641, FAX 204-788-4998. Ed. Heather Mousseau.

TAIDE. *see* ART

069.5 TWN
TAIWAN MUSEUM OF ART NEWSLETTER/GUANXUN ZAZHI. Text in Chinese. 1988. m. free. illus. **Document type:** *Academic/Scholarly.* **Description:** Provides information on shows, special presentations, and displays, with the latest museum news and art reviews.
Published by: Taiwan Museum of Art, 2 Wu-Chuan W. Rd, Taichung, Taiwan. TEL 886-4-3623552, FAX 886-4-3721195. Ed. Kun Fu Liu.

069 CAN ISSN 0713-3901
TALES OF THE TWELVE. Text in English. 1973. q. free to members. **Document type:** *Newsletter.*
Formerly (until 1982): St. Catharines Historical Museum. Newsletter (0706-7461)
Published by: St. Catharines Museum, Box 3012, St. Catharines, ON L2R 7C2, Canada. TEL 905-984-8880, 800-305-5134, FAX 905-984-6910, museuminfo@stcatharines.ca, http://www.stcatharineslock3museum.ca/index.html.

708.9691 MDG ISSN 0496-7801
TALOHA. Text in French, Malagasy. 1965. irreg., latest vol.10, 1987. MGF 5,400. **Description:** Articles on the archeology, anthropology, history and art of ancient Madagascar.
Related titles: Online - full text ed.: ISSN 1816-9082. 2005.
Indexed: AICP.
Published by: Universite de Madagascar, Musee d'Art et d'Archeologie, Isoraka, BP 564, Antananarivo, Madagascar.

069 GBR
TATE GALLERY LIVERPOOL. CRITICAL FORUM SERIES. Variant title: Tate Liverpool Critical Forum. Text in English. 1993. irreg. price varies. back issues avail. **Document type:** *Monographic series, Academic/Scholarly.* **Description:** Focuses attention on the dynamic construction of art histories as stimulated by the fact of exposition.
Published by: (University of Liverpool, Tate Liverpool), Liverpool University Press, 4 Cambridge St, Liverpool, L69 7ZU, United Kingdom. TEL 44-151-7942233, FAX 44-151-7942235, lup@liv.ac.uk. Ed. Jonathan Harris.

069 FRA ISSN 1254-7867
N8560
TECHNE. Text in French. 1956-1968; resumed 19??-1982; resumed 1984-1985; resumed 1994. a. EUR 23 (effective 2010). **Document type:** *Magazine, Consumer.*
Former titles (until 1994): Laboratoire de Recherche des Musees de France. Annales (0373-8027); (until 1968): Laboratoire du Musee du Louvre. Bulletin (0553-2566)
Indexed: A&ATA, B24.
Published by: Laboratoire de Recherche des Musees de France, Palais du Louvre, 6 Rue des Pyramides, Paris, 75041, France. **Subscr. to:** Editions de la Reunion des Musees Nationaux, 49 Rue Etienne Marcel, Paris Cedex 1 75039, France. TEL 33-1-40134800, FAX 33-1-40134400, http://www.rmn.fr.

TEKNISKA MUSEET. RAPPORTSERIE. *see* ENGINEERING

069 NLD
N2450
DE TENTOONSTELLINGSAGENDA. Text in Dutch. 1959. 8/yr. adv. **Document type:** *Journal, Consumer.* **Description:** Covers complete listing of exhibitions in Dutch museums, galleries and other cultural institutions, as well as a number of exhibitions in museums and galleries in nearby foreign countries.
Former titles (until 2002): Tentoonstellingsboekje (0920-7430); (until 1987): Tentoonstellingsagenda (0040-3520)
Related titles: ◆ Supplement to: Museumtijdschrift. ISSN 1874-9798.
Published by: (Netherlands. Openbaar Kunstbezit), Waanders Uitgevers, Postbus 1129, Zwolle, 8001 BC, Netherlands. TEL 31-38-4673400, FAX 31-38-4673401, info@waanders.nl, http://www.waanders.nl. Circ: 16,000.

069 USA ISSN 0082-3074
QH105.T4 CODEN: TXMBAR
TEXAS MEMORIAL MUSEUM. BULLETIN. Text in English. 1960. irreg., latest vol.36, 1994. price varies. back issues avail.; reprints avail. **Document type:** *Monographic series, Academic/Scholarly.*
Indexed: GeoRef, SpeleolAb.
Published by: Texas Memorial Museum, 2400 Trinity St, Austin, TX 78705. TEL 512-471-1604, FAX 512-471-4794, etheriot@austin.utexas.edu.

069 USA ISSN 0082-3082
CODEN: TMMMBI
TEXAS MEMORIAL MUSEUM. MISCELLANEOUS PAPERS. Text in English. 1968. irreg., latest vol.8, 1990. price varies. back issues avail.; reprints avail. **Document type:** *Monographic series, Academic/Scholarly.*
Indexed: GeoRef, SpeleolAb.
Published by: Texas Memorial Museum, 2400 Trinity St, Austin, TX 78705. TEL 512-471-1604, FAX 512-471-4794, etheriot@austin.utexas.edu.

708.1 USA
TEXAS MEMORIAL MUSEUM. MUSEUM NOTES. Text in English. 1938. irreg., latest vol.12, 1974. price varies. back issues avail.; reprints avail. **Document type:** *Monographic series, Academic/Scholarly.*
Published by: Texas Memorial Museum, 2400 Trinity St, Austin, TX 78705. TEL 512-471-1604, FAX 512-471-4794, etheriot@austin.utexas.edu.

TEXAS MEMORIAL MUSEUM. SPELEOLOGICAL MONOGRAPHS. *see* EARTH SCIENCES—Geology

677.0074 USA
THE TEXTILE MUSEUM MEMBERS' MAGAZINE. Text in English. 1971. q. free to members (effective 2010). 16 p./no.; **Document type:** *Magazine, Trade.* **Description:** Includes exhibition information, calendar of events, development, travel, education, special events, and Museum Shop news.
Former titles (until 2009): Textile Museum Bulletin; (until 1987): Textile Museum Newsletter; (until 197?): Textile Museum Newsletter for Associates; (until 1973): Textile Museum Associate's Newsletter; (until 1972): Textile Museum Member's Newsletter
Published by: The Textile Museum, 2320 S St, NW, Washington, DC 20008. TEL 202-667-0441, FAX 202-483-0994, info@textilemuseum.org, http://www.textilemuseum.org.

069 677 NLD ISSN 1874-2297
TEXTUUR. Text in Dutch. 1984. s-a.
Former titles (until 2006): Nederlands Textielmuseum. Museumkrant (1389-0700); (until 1999): Textuur (0169-2097)
Published by: (Stichting Vrienden van het Textielmuseum), Audax Textielmuseum Tilburg, Goirkestraat 96, Tilburg, 5046 GN, Netherlands. TEL 31-13-5367475, FAX 31-13-5363240, vrienden@textielmuseum.nl, http://www.textielmuseum.nl.

708.9593 THA ISSN 1686-770X
THE THAILAND NATURAL HISTORY MUSEUM JOURNAL. Text in English. s-a. **Document type:** *Journal, Academic/Scholarly.*
Indexed: Z01.
—BLDSC (8814.130050), IE.
Published by: National Science Museum, Technopolis, Khlong 5, Khlong Luang, Pathum Thani, 12120, Thailand. http://www.nsm.or.th. Ed. Jarujin Nabhitabhata.

560 USA ISSN 1046-4891
THOMAS BURKE MEMORIAL WASHINGTON STATE MUSEUM. RESEARCH REPORT. Text in English. 1968. a. **Document type:** *Report, Consumer.*
Indexed: GeoRef, Z01.
Published by: Burke Museum of Natural History and Culture, P O Box 353010, Seattle, WA 98195-3010. TEL 206-543-5590, http://www.washington.edu/burkemuseum.

735.22 DNK ISSN 0085-7262
N1925
THORVALDSENS MUSEUM. MEDDELELSER/THORVALDSEN MUSEUM. BULLETIN. Text in Multiple languages; Summaries in English. 1929. irreg. price varies. illus. index. back issues avail. **Document type:** *Academic/Scholarly.* **Description:** Contains studies about Danish art during the first half of the 19th century - the Golden Age of Danish Art.
Indexed: RILM.
Published by: Thorvaldsens Museum, Bertel Thorvaldsens Plads 2, Copenhagen K, 1213, Denmark. TEL 45-33-321532, FAX 45-33-321771, thm@thorvaldsensmuseum.dk, http:/www.thorvaldsensmuseum.dk.

069 CHE
THURGAUISCHES MUSEUM. MITTEILUNGEN. Text in German. 1946. irreg., latest 1999. **Document type:** *Academic/Scholarly.*
Published by: (Thurgauischen Museum), Thurgauische Museumsgesellschaft, Frauenfeld, 8500, Switzerland. heinz.reinhart@kttg.ch. Ed. H Guhl Widmer.

069 AUT ISSN 0379-0231
DB761
➤ **TIROLER LANDESMUSEUM FERDINANDEUM, INNSBRUCK. VEROEFFENTLICHUNGEN.** Text in German; Text occasionally in English, Italian. 1825. a. 350 p./no. 1 cols./p.; back issues avail. **Document type:** *Journal, Academic/Scholarly.*
Indexed: B24, DIP, GeoRef, IBR, IBZ, SpeleolAb, Z01.
Published by: Tiroler Landesmuseum Ferdinandeum, Museumstrasse 15, Innsbruck, T 6020, Austria. TEL 43-512-59489, FAX 43-512-5948988, http://www.tiroler-landesmuseum.at. Ed. Josef Riedmann. Pubs. Ellen Hastaba, Georg Gaertner. Circ: 600.

➤ **TOCHIGI-KENRITSU HAKUBUTSUKAN KENKYU HOKOKUSHO/ TOCHIGI PREFECTURAL MUSEUM. MEMOIRS.** *see* SCIENCES: COMPREHENSIVE WORKS

069 JPN ISSN 1346-2040
TOHOKU UNIVERSITY MUSEUM. BULLETIN. Text in English. 2001. a. **Document type:** *Journal, Academic/Scholarly.*
Indexed: Z01.
Published by: Tohoku University Museum, 6-3 Aoba, Aramaki, Aoba-ku, Sendai, 980-8578, Japan. http://www.museum.tohoku.ac.jp/.

069 JPN ISSN 0916-8001
AM101.T5523
TOKUSHIMA KENRITSU HAKUBUTSUKAN KENKYU HOKOKU/ TOKUSHIMA PREFECTURAL MUSEUM. BULLETIN. Text in English, Japanese; Summaries in English. 1991. a. **Document type:** *Bulletin.* **Description:** Covers geology, zoology, botany, archaeology (including conservation science), history, folklore and pre-modern art.
Formerly (until 1988): Tokushima-ken Hakubutsukan Kiyo (0387-6268)
Indexed: ASFA, B21, ESPM, EntAb, Z01.
—BLDSC (2780.042000).
Published by: Tokushima Prefectural Museum, Bunka-no-mori Park, Hachiman-cho, Tokushima-shi, 770-8070, Japan. TEL 81-88-668-3636, FAX 81-88-668-7197. Circ: 1,000 (controlled).

TOKYO-TO TAKAO SHIZEN KAGAKU HAKUBUTSUKAN KENKYU HOKOKU/TAKAO MUSEUM OF NATURAL HISTORY. SCIENCE REPORT. *see* SCIENCES: COMPREHENSIVE WORKS

708.6 USA
N820
TOLEDO MUSEUM OF ART MEMBERS NEWSLETTER. Text in English. 1907. q. USD 50 to individual members; USD 35 to senior citizens; USD 75 family members (effective 2004). illus. **Document type:** *Newsletter.*
Formerly: Toledo Museum News; Supesedes in part (in 1983): Toledo Museum of Art. Annual Report (0888-9643); (until 1982): Museum News (0049-4062)
Indexed: A06, AIAP, RILM.
Published by: Toledo Museum of Art, PO Box 1013, Toledo, OH 43697. TEL 419-254-5770, 800-644-6862, information@toledomuseum.org, http://www.toledomuseum.org. Circ: (controlled).

TOTTORI-KENRITSU HAKUBUTSUKAN KENKYU HOKOKU/TOTTORI PREFECTURAL MUSEUM. BULLETIN. *see* SCIENCES: COMPREHENSIVE WORKS

507.4 JPN
TOYAMA TO SHIZEN. Text in Japanese. q. **Document type:** *Newsletter.* **Description:** Contains news of the center.
Published by: Toyama-shi Kagaku Bunka Senta/Toyama Science Museum, 1-8-31 Nishi-Nakano-Machi, Toyama-shi, 939-0000, Japan. TEL 0764-92-2123, FAX 0764-21-5950. Ed. Michiharu Goto.

TOYOHASHI MUSEUM OF NATURAL HISTORY. MISCELLANEOUS REPORT/TOYOHASHI-SHI SHIZENSHI HAKUBUTSUKAN SHIRYOSHU. *see* SCIENCES: COMPREHENSIVE WORKS

TOYOHASHI MUSEUM OF NATURAL HISTORY. SCIENCE REPORT/ TOYOHASHI-SHI SHIZENSHI HAKUBUTSUKAN KENKYU HOKOKU. *see* SCIENCES: COMPREHENSIVE WORKS

069 CAN ISSN 1188-2964
TRANSFORMATION SERIES. Variant title: Collection Transformation. Text in English. 1992. irreg.
Published by: Canada Science and Technology Museum Corp/Musee National des Sciences et de la Technologie, P O Box 9724, Sta T, Ottawa, ON K1G 5A3, Canada. TEL 613 991-3044, FAX 613 991-9207, http://www.sciencetech.technomuses.ca.

TRANSVAAL MUSEUM. MONOGRAPHS. *see* BIOLOGY—Zoology

069.1 USA ISSN 1072-0073
N4390
TRAVELER'S GUIDE TO ART MUSEUM EXHIBITIONS; for art lovers who travel and travelers who love art. Text in English. 1989. a.
Formerly (until 1992): Traveler's Guide to Museum Exhibitions (1041-0724)
Published by: Museum Guide Publications, Inc., 1619 31st St NW, Washington, DC 20007-2998. TEL 202-338-1500, FAX 202-338-1500.

707.4 USA ISSN 0733-463X
TRAVELING EXHIBITION INFORMATION SERVICE. NEWSLETTER. Text in English. 1980. bi-m. USD 45 (effective 1998). adv. **Document type:** *Newsletter.* **Description:** Provides descriptions of traveling exhibits in arts, humanities and sciences available for loan.
Published by: Humanities Exchange, Inc., PO Box 1608, Largo, FL 33779. TEL 813-581-7328, FAX 813-585-6398. Ed. Shirley R Howarth. Pub. S R Howarth. Circ: 1,000.

707.4 USA
N5310.7
➤ **TRIBAL ART/MONDE DE L'ART TRIBAL.** Text in English. 1994. q. adv. bk.rev. illus. 120 p./no. 4 cols./p.; back issues avail. **Document type:** *Magazine, Academic/Scholarly.* **Description:** For anthropologists, artists, museum curators, historians, art enthusiasts, and collectors. Contains articles on themes ranging from tribal sculpture to Pre-Columbian ceramics and textiles.
Former titles (until 2006): Tribal (1549-4691); (until 2002): The World of Tribal Arts (1354-2990)
Related titles: Online - full text ed.; French ed.
Indexed: A07, A30, A31, AA, ABM, AICP, ArtInd, B04, BRD, CA, MLA-IB, T02, W03, W05.
—Ingenta.
Published by: Primedia Inc., 2261 Market St, Ste 644, San Francisco, CA 94114. TEL 415-970-0220, 866-882-0220, FAX 415-431-8321, jmfogel@pacbell.net. Ed. Jonathan Fogel. Pub. Alex Arthur.

069 USA ISSN 1041-9632
TROLLEY FARE. Text in English. 1953. bi-m. USD 35 to members. back issues avail. **Document type:** *Newsletter.* **Description:** Covers streetcar preservation and restoration, plus operations of existing street railways and light rail systems, and reports on the planning and progress of new systems worldwide.
Published by: Pennsylvania Railway Museum Association, 1 Museum Rd, Washington, PA 15301. TEL 412-228-9256, FAX 412-228-9675. Ed. Harold M Englund. Circ: 800.

708.81 NOR ISSN 0085-7394
TROMSOE MUSEUM. SKRIFTER. Text in English, Norwegian. 1925. irreg., latest vol.30, 2003. price varies. back issues avail. **Document type:** *Monographic series, Academic/Scholarly.*
Indexed: GeoRef, NAA.
Published by: Tromsoe Museum - Universitesmuseet, Lars Thoeringsvei 10, Tromsoe, 9037, Norway. TEL 47-77-645000, FAX 47-77-645520, museumspost@uit.no, http://www2.uit.no/ikbViewer/page/tmu?p_lang=2.

THE TRUMPETER (WESTBROOK). *see* THEATER

069 NZL ISSN 1173-4337
AM101.W4715
➤ **TUHINGA: RECORDS OF THE MUSEUM OF NEW ZEALAND TE PAPA TONGAREWA.** Text in English. 1975. a., latest vol.13. price varies. bk.rev. bibl.; charts; illus. 150 p./no.; **Document type:** *Journal, Academic/Scholarly.* **Description:** Collects together papers by Te Papa's curators, collection managers, and research associates on a range of topics, from archaeology to zoology.
Supersedes (in June 1995): Museum of New Zealand Records (1171-6908); (in 1992): National Museum of New Zealand Records (0110-943X); Dominion Museum Records; Dominion Museum Records in Ethnology
Indexed: B25, BIOSIS Prev, GeoRef, INIS AtomInd, MycolAb, RefZh, SpeleolAb, WildRev, Z01.
—BLDSC (9068.745000), INIST, Linda Hall. **CCC.**
Published by: (Museum of New Zealand), Te Papa Press, PO Box 467, Wellington, New Zealand. TEL 64-4-3817000, FAX 64-4-3817070, mail@tepapa.govt.nz, http://www.tepapa.govt.nz/TePapa/English/TePapaPress/. Ed. Janet Davidson. Pub. Geoff Norman. Circ: 550.

708.993 NZL ISSN 1177-4975
TUI TUI TUITUIA. Text in English. 1996. q. free membership. **Document type:** *Newsletter, Academic/Scholarly.*
Related titles: Online - full text ed.: ISSN 1177-5890. 2006.
Published by: Tairawhiti Museum, PO Box 716, Gisborne, New Zealand. TEL 64-6-8673832, FAX 64-6-8672728, info@tairawhitimuseum.org.nz, http://www.tairawhitimuseum.org.nz.

TULUFANXUE YANJIU/TURFANOLOGICAL RESEARCH. *see* HISTORY

708.77 CAN ISSN 0824-5991
UKRAINIAN CULTURAL AND EDUCATIONAL CENTRE. VISTI - NEWS. Text in English, Ukrainian. 1976. s-a. membership. **Document type:** *Newsletter.* **Description:** Informs members of activities, events, and recent archival, museum, library and art collections.

Published by: Ukrainian Cultural and Educational Centre, 184 Alexander Ave E, Winnipeg, MB R3B 0L6, Canada. TEL 204-942-0218, FAX 204-943-2857. Ed., R&P Rick Horocholyn. Circ: 2,000.

069.3 BRA
UNIVERSIDADE DE SAO PAULO. MUSEU PAULISTA. COLECAO. SERIE DE MOBILIARIO. Text in Portuguese. irreg.
Supersedes in part (in 1975): Museu Paulista. Colecao (0080-6382)
Published by: Universidade de Sao Paulo, Museu Paulista, Ipiranga, Caixa Postal 42503, Sao Paulo, SP 04299-970, Brazil. Ed. Setembrino Petri.

069 ITA ISSN 1824-2707
UNIVERSITA DI FERRARA. ANNALI. SEZIONE: MUSEOLOGIA SCIENTIFICA E NATURALISTICA. Text in Italian. 2004. a. **Document type:** *Journal, Academic/Scholarly.*
Related titles: Online - full text ed.: free (effective 2011).
Indexed: Z01.
—PADDS.
Published by: (Universita degli Studi di Ferrara), Editografica Srl, Via Verdi 15, Rastignano, BO 40067, Italy. http://www.editografica.com.

069 USA ISSN 0093-7436
AM101.F3
UNIVERSITY OF ALASKA MUSEUM. ANNUAL REPORT. Text in English. a.
Published by: University of Alaska Museum, 907 Yukon Dr, Fairbanks, AK 99775-1200. TEL 907-474-7505, FAX 907-474-5469. Circ: (controlled).

069 USA
UNIVERSITY OF CALIFORNIA AT LOS ANGELES. FOWLER MUSEUM OF CULTURAL HISTORY. MONOGRAPH SERIES. Text in English. irreg., latest vol.28. price varies. back issues avail. **Document type:** *Monographic series.*
Published by: University of California, Los Angeles, Fowler Museum of Cultural History, Box 951549, Los Angeles, CA 90095-1549. TEL 310-825-4361, FAX 310-206-7007.

708.1 USA
UNIVERSITY OF CALIFORNIA AT LOS ANGELES. FOWLER MUSEUM OF CULTURAL HISTORY. OCCASIONAL PAPERS. Text in English. 1969. irreg., latest vol.5, 1985. price varies. back issues avail. **Document type:** *Monographic series.*
Formerly: University of California at Los Angeles. Museum of Cultural History. Occasional Papers (0068-628X)
Published by: University of California, Los Angeles, Fowler Museum of Cultural History, Box 951549, Los Angeles, CA 90095-1549. TEL 310-825-4361, FAX 310-206-7007.

708.1 USA
UNIVERSITY OF KENTUCKY ART MUSEUM NEWSLETTER. Text in English. 1986. 6/yr. free (effective 2007). **Document type:** *Newsletter, Consumer.* **Description:** Provides information on acquisitions, exhibitions and programs of the museum.
Published by: University of Kentucky Art Museum, Rose and Euclid Sts, Lexington, KY 40506-0241. TEL 859-257-5716, FAX 859-323-1994. Ed. Kathy Walsh-Piper. Circ: 3,000 (paid and controlled).

708.1 USA ISSN 0270-1642
N513
➤ **UNIVERSITY OF MICHIGAN. MUSEUMS OF ART AND ARCHAEOLOGY. BULLETIN.** Text in English. 1978. s-a. USD 12 per issue (effective 2010). illus. reprints avail. **Document type:** *Bulletin, Trade.* **Description:** Presents scholarly articles focusing on University of Michigan collections.
Supersedes (in 1977): University of Michigan. Museum of Art. Bulletin (0076-8391)
Indexed: AIAP.
Published by: (University of Michigan Museum of Art), University of Michigan, Kelsey Museum of Archaeology, 434 S State St, Ann Arbor, MI 48109. TEL 734-764-9304, http://www.lsa.umich.edu/kelsey.

069.1 USA ISSN 0041-9885
UNIVERSITY OF NEBRASKA STATE MUSEUM. MUSEUM NOTES. Text in English. 1956. 3/yr. bibl.; charts; illus. reprints avail.
Related titles: Microform ed.: (from PQC).
Published by: University of Nebraska State Museum, W436 Nebraska Hall, University of Nebraska, Lincoln, NE 68588-0514. TEL 402-472-7211. Ed., Pub., R&P Brett C Ratcliffe. Circ: (controlled).

708.1 USA ISSN 0077-8583
N512.A5
UNIVERSITY OF NEW MEXICO ART MUSEUM. BULLETIN. Text in English. 1965. irreg., latest 1981-83, no.14. USD 7. **Document type:** *Bulletin.* **Description:** Provides information and illustrations on recent acquisitions.
Published by: University of New Mexico, Art Museum, FAC 1017, Albuquerque, NM 87131. TEL 505-277-4001. Ed. Peter Walch. Circ: 1,000.

069 JPN ISSN 0910-2566
UNIVERSITY OF TOKYO. UNIVERSITY MUSEUM. MATERIAL REPORTS. Text in English, Japanese. 1979. irreg., latest no.45, 2001. **Document type:** *Report, Academic/Scholarly.*
Indexed: GeoRef, Z01.
Published by: University of Tokyo, University Museum, 3-1 Hongo 7-chome, Bunkyo-ku, Tokyo, 1130033, Japan. FAX 86-3-5841-8451, shomu@um.u-tokyo.ac.jp, http://www.um.u-tokyo.ac.jp.

069 JPN ISSN 1346-6356
UNIVERSITY OF TOKYO. UNIVERSITY MUSEUM. MONOGRAPH. Text in English. 2001. irreg., latest no.1, 2001. **Document type:** *Monographic series, Academic/Scholarly.*
Published by: University of Tokyo, University Museum, 3-1 Hongo 7-chome, Bunkyo-ku, Tokyo, 1130033, Japan. FAX 86-3-5841-8451, shomu@um.u-tokyo.ac.jp, http://www.um.u-tokyo.ac.jp.

069 POL ISSN 0239-9989
QE327.N5 CODEN: RGSNAK
UNIWERSYTET JAGIELLONSKI. ZESZYTY NAUKOWE. OPUSCULA MUSEALIA; czasopismo muzeologiczne. Text in Polish. 1986. irreg., latest vol.18, 2010. price varies. **Document type:** *Monographic series, Academic/Scholarly.*
Published by: (Uniwersytet Jagiellonski, Muzeum), Wydawnictwo Uniwersytetu Jagiellonskiego/Jagiellonian University Press, ul Grodzka 26, Krakow, 31044, Poland. TEL 48-12-4312364, FAX 48-12-4301995, wydaw@if.uj.edu.pl. Ed. S Waltos.

069.5 USA ISSN 0272-0345
Q11
UPDATE (SMITHSONIAN INSTITUTION. TRAVELING EXHIBITION SERVICE). Text in English. a.
Formerly: Smithsonian Institution. Traveling Exhibition Service. Catalogue
Published by: Smithsonian Institution Traveling Exhibition Service, 1100 Jefferso Dr SW, Ste 3146, Washington, DC 20013-7012. TEL 202-633-3168, http://www.sites.si.edu/.

069 POL ISSN 1508-9851
UPPER SILESIAN MUSEUM. MONOGRAPHS/MUZEUM GORNOSLASKIE W BYTOMIU. MONOGRAPHS. Text in Multiple languages. irreg.
Indexed: B21, B25, BIOSIS Prev, EntAb, MycolAb, Z01.
Published by: Muzeum Gornoslaskie w Bytomiu/The Museum of Upper Silesia, Pl Jana III Sobieskiego 2, Bytom, 41902, Poland. TEL 48-32-28182941, mgbytom@us.edu.pl, http://www.um.bytom.pl.

069 USA
UPSTATE HISTORY ALLIANCE NEWSLETTER. Text in English. 1971. q. USD 25 to individuals; USD 35 to institutions (effective 2000). adv. bk.rev. bibl. back issues avail. **Document type:** *Newsletter.*
Formerly: R C H A Newsletter
Published by: Upstate History Alliance, 11 Ford Ave, Oneonta, NY 13820. TEL 800-895-1648, FAX 607-431-9524. Ed. Linda Norris. Adv. contact Shelley McFee.

708.2 GBR ISSN 1465-8291
V & A MAGAZINE. (Victoria & Albert) Text in English. 1998. 3/yr. GBP 11 to non-members; free to members (effective 2009). back issues avail. **Document type:** *Magazine, Consumer.* **Description:** Covers all aspects of the visual arts -architecture, design, craft, photography, fashion and fine art.
Incorporates (199?-1997): In-view; Friends News
Indexed: ABM, D05, I14, SCOPUS.
Published by: Friends of the Victoria and Albert Museum, Cromwell Rd, South Kensington, London, SW7 2RL, United Kingdom. TEL 44-20-79422000, vanda@vam.ac.uk.

069 GBR ISSN 2043-667X
V & A ONLINE JOURNAL. (Victoria and Albert) Text in English. 2008. a. free (effective 2010). back issues avail. **Document type:** *Journal, Trade.* **Description:** Features research undertaken in connection with the V and A - its collections, public programme and history.
Media: Online - full text.
Published by: Victoria and Albert Museum, Cromwell Rd, London, SW7 2RL, United Kingdom. TEL 44-20-79422000, vanda@vam.ac.uk.

069 USA
THE VALENTINE MUSEUM - RICHMOND HISTORY CENTER. NEWSLETTER. Text in English. 1898. q. USD 45 to members (effective 2001). back issues avail. **Document type:** *Newsletter.*
Former titles (until Oct. 2000): Valentine Museum News; (until 1985): Visitor
Published by: The Valentine Museum - Richmond History Center, 1015 E Clay St, Richmond, VA 23219. TEL 804-649-0711, FAX 804-643-3510, valmus@mindspring.com, http://www.valentinemuseum.com. Circ: 3,000.

708.11 CAN ISSN 0083-5161
N910.V3
VANCOUVER ART GALLERY. ANNUAL REPORT. Text in English. 1932. a. free. **Document type:** *Corporate.*
Published by: Vancouver Art Gallery, 750 Hornby St, Vancouver, BC V6Z 2H7, Canada. TEL 604-662-4700, FAX 604-682-1086. Circ: 9,000.

069 SWE ISSN 0083-5536
AM101
VARBERGS MUSEUM. AARSBOK. Text in Swedish. 1950. a. SEK 120 (effective 1998). **Document type:** *Proceedings.*
Indexed: MLA-IB, NAA.
Published by: Ideella Foereningen Laensmuseet Halmstad, c/o Laensmuseet Halmsted, Tollsgatan, Halmsted, 30231, Sweden. FAX 0340-14722. Ed. Thomas Thieme.

708.95492 BGD
VARENDRA RESEARCH MUSEUM. JOURNAL. Text in English. 1972. a. BDT 15, USD 3.
Published by: Varendra Research Museum, University of Rajshahi, Rajshahi, Bangladesh.

069 ESP ISSN 1130-9776
VERDOLAY; revista del Museo de Murcia. Text in Spanish. 1989. a. **Document type:** *Magazine, Consumer.*
Published by: Museo de Murcia, Alfonso X el Sabio 5, Murcia, 30003, Spain. TEL 34-968-239346, museo.ciudad@ayto_murcia.es, http://www.murcia_museociudad.org.

069 NLD ISSN 1872-6585
VERENIGING VAN VRIENDEN VAN MUSEUM HET VALKHOF. NIEUWSBRIEF. Text in Dutch. 2004. 4/yr.
Published by: Vereniging van Vrienden van Museum Het Valkhof, Kelfkensbos 59, Nijmegen, 6511 TB, Netherlands. TEL 31-24-3608805, FAX 31-24-3608656, info@museumhetvalkhof.nl, http://www.museumhetvalkhof.nl.

708 CAN ISSN 1481-4943
CA1NG10-X1
VERNISSAGE. Text in English, French. 1999. q. CAD 25 domestic to individuals; USD 25 foreign to individuals; CAD 35 domestic to institutions; USD 35 foreign to institutions (effective 2004).
Published by: National Gallery of Canada, Publications Division, PO Box 427, Stn A, Ottawa, ON K1N 9N4, Canada. subscriptions@gallery.ca.

VEROEFFENTLICHUNGEN ZUR BRANDENBURGISCHEN LANDESARCHAEOLOGIE. *see* HISTORY

VESTERHEIM NEWS. *see* ETHNIC INTERESTS

069 HRV ISSN 0042-6083
VIJESTI MUZEALACA I KONZERVATORA HRVATSKE. Text in Croatian; Summaries in German. 1960. bi-m. USD 12. bk.rev. bibl.; illus.
Supersedes: Drusto Muzejsko-Konzervatorskih Radnika N.R. Hrvatske. Vijesti
Published by: Muzejsko Drustvo Hrvatske, Mesnicka 5, Zagreb, 41000, Croatia. Ed. Zdenko Kuzmic. **Co-sponsor:** Drustvo Konzervatora Hrvatske.

708.1 USA ISSN 1084-676X
N716.V45
VIRGINIA MUSEUM OF FINE ARTS CALENDAR. Text in English. 1940. bi-m. USD 8; USD 9 foreign (effective 2001). bk.rev.; video rev. illus. back issues avail. **Document type:** *Newsletter.* **Description:** Covers art exhibitions and related events held at the Virginia Museum and at affiliated arts organizations throughout Virginia.
Former titles (until 1995): Virginia Museum of Fine Arts Bulletin (0363-3519); Virginia Museum Bulletin (0042-6687)
Published by: Virginia Museum of Fine Arts, 200 N. Boulevard., Richmond, VA 23220-4007. TEL 804-204-2724, FAX 804-204-2710, mwilson@vmfa.state.va.us. Ed., R&P Monica S Rumsey TEL 804-204-2711. Circ: 17,500.

708.11 CAN ISSN 0828-7023
VISTA (REGINA). Text in English. 1965. 4/yr. free. adv. bk.rev. illus. **Document type:** *Newsletter.* **Description:** Information on exhibitions, permanent collection, events, education classes and volunteer news.
Former titles (until 1984): Mackenzie M A G (0828-7015); Mag (0824-5312); (until 1983): N - M A G (0712-9238); (until 1974): N M A G Review (0384-1022); (until 1973): Norman Mackenzie Art Gallery (0712-922X); (until 1970): Norman Mackenzie Art Gallery. Newsletter (0384-1014)
Published by: Mackenzie Art Gallery, 3475 Albert St, Regina, SK S4S 6X6, Canada. TEL 306-522-4242, FAX 306-569-8191. Ed. Kathryn Weisshaar. Adv. contact Kathy Weisshaar. Circ: 4,500.

VISUAL RESOURCES; an international journal of documentation. *see* ART

069 RUS
VSEROSSIISKII VYSTAVOCHNYI TSENTR. Text in Russian. q.
Address: A-ya 18, Moscow, 129223, Russian Federation. TEL 7-095-2161581, FAX 7-095-2161587. Ed. A V Glushenko. **Dist. by:** East View Information Services, 10601 Wayzata Blvd, Minneapolis, MN 55305. TEL 952-252-1201, 800-477-1005, FAX 952-252-1202, info@eastview.com, http://www.eastview.com.

069 SVK
VYROCNE SPRAVY O CINNOSTI MUZEI NA SLOVENSKU. Text in Slovak. 1966. a. free.
Former titles: Vyrocne Spravy o Cinnosti Slovenskych Muzei; Vyrocne Spravy o Cinnosti Slovenskych Muzei a Galerii; Ustredna Sprava Muzei a Galerii. Vyrocne Spravy o Cinnosti Slovenskych Muzei; Slovenske Narodne Muzeum. Muzeologicky Kabinet. Vyrocne Spravy o Cinnosti Slovenskych Muzei
Published by: Slovenske Narodne Muzeum, Narodne Muzejne Centrum, Vajanskeho nabr 2, Bratislava, 81436, Slovakia. TEL 421-2-52961973, FAX 421-2-52966653, nmc@snm.sk. Ed. Milan Rybecky.

508.074 JPN
WAKAYAMA KENRITSU SHIZEN HAKUBUTSUKAN KANPO/ WAKAYAMA PREFECTURAL MUSEUM OF NATURAL HISTORY. ANNUAL REPORT. Text in Japanese. 1983. a.
Published by: Wakayama-kenritsu Shizen Hakubutsukan Tomo no Kai, Wakayama-kenritsu Shizen Hakubutsukan, 370-1 Funo, Kainan-shi, Wakayama-ken 642-0001, Japan.

708.2 GBR ISSN 0306-0888
N1410
WALKER ART GALLERY. ANNUAL REPORT AND BULLETIN. Text in English. 1971. a. **Document type:** *Journal, Trade.*
Formed by the merger of (1938-1971): Walker Art Gallery. Annual Report (1356-1669); (19??-1971): Walker Art Gallery. Liverpool Bulletin
—CCC.
Published by: Walker Art Gallery, William Brown St, Liverpool, L3 8EL, United Kingdom. TEL 44-151-4784199, http://www.liverpoolmuseums.org.uk/walker/.

THE WALTERS MAGAZINE. *see* ART

WARTIME. *see* MILITARY

WEEKLY PIA. *see* LEISURE AND RECREATION

069 CAN
WELLAND HISTORICAL MUSEUM NEWSLETTER. Text in English. 1988. q. looseleaf. CAD 12 to members. **Document type:** *Newsletter.*
Published by: Welland Historical Museum, 65 Hooker St, Welland, ON L3C 5G9, Canada. TEL 416-732-2215. Ed. Bill Sanderson. Circ: 450.

069 USA
WELLESLEY COLLEGE FRIENDS OF ART NEWSLETTER. Text in English. 1965. a. membership. **Document type:** *Newsletter.* **Description:** Provides current information on acquisitions, benefits, exhibitions, publications, educational programs, and editorial viewpoints.
Published by: Davies Museum and Cultural Center, Wellesley College, Wellesley, MA 02181. TEL 617-283-2081, FAX 617-235-2064. Ed. Nancy Gunn. Circ: 5,000.

069 CHN ISSN 1000-7954
WEN BO/JOURNAL OF MUSEUMS & ARCHAEOLOGY. Variant title: Relics and Museology. Text in Chinese. 1984. bi-m. USD 42.60 (effective 2009). adv. bk.rev. **Document type:** *Journal, Academic/Scholarly.* **Description:** Covers research achievements and academic discussions on archaeology and museology.
Related titles: Online - full text ed.
Indexed: RASB.
—East View.
Published by: Shaanxi Sheng Wenwu Shiye Guanliju/Shaanxi Provincial Administration of Archaeological Data, Xi'an Wenwu Baohu Xiufu Zhongxin, 12, Xingshansi Donglu, Xi'an, Shaanxi 710001, China. Ed. Chen Quanfang. Adv. contact Wuang Chunhui. Circ: 3,000; 4,000 (paid). **Dist. by:** China International Book Trading Corp, 35 Chegongzhuang Xilu, Haidian District, PO Box 399, Beijing 100044, China. TEL 86-10-68412045, FAX 86-10-68412023, cibtc@mail.cibtc.com.cn, http://www.cibtc.com.cn.

WENHUA ZICHAN BAOCUN XUEKAN/JOURNAL OF CULTURAL PROPERTY CONSERVATION. *see* HISTORY—History Of Asia

WEST COAST PEDDLER; oldest journal of antiques, art & collectibles in the Pacific states. *see* ANTIQUES

708.994 AUS
WESTERN AUSTRALIAN MUSEUM. ANNUAL REPORT (ONLINE). Text in English. 1960. a. free (effective 2009). **Document type:** *Corporate.* **Description:** Reports on issues affecting the Western Australian Museum, Perth.

Former titles (until 2000): Western Australian Museum. Annual Report (Print) (0083-8721); Western Australia Museum, Perth. Report of the Museum Board
Media: Online - full content.
Indexed: ApicAb, GeoRef, SpeleolAb.
Published by: Western Australian Museum, Locked Bag 49, Welshpool DC, W.A. 6986, Australia. TEL 61-8-94272766, FAX 61-8-94272827.

708.994 AUS ISSN 0312-3162
QH1 CODEN: REMUDY
➤ **WESTERN AUSTRALIAN MUSEUM. RECORDS.** Text in English. 1974. irreg. AUD 11 per issue (effective 2009). 120 p./no.; back issues avail.; reprints avail. **Document type:** *Journal, Academic/Scholarly.* **Description:** Contains new research in the natural sciences.
Formerly: Western Australia. Public Library, Museum and Art Gallery. Record
Related titles: ◆ Supplement(s): Western Australian Museum. Records. Supplement. ISSN 0313-122X.
Indexed: AESIS, ASFA, ASI, B21, B25, BIOSIS Prev, ESPM, GeoRef, MycolAb, SPPI, SpeleolAb, Z01.
—BLDSC (7325.306000), IE, Ingenta.
Published by: Western Australian Museum, Locked Bag 49, Welshpool DC, W.A. 6986, Australia. TEL 61-8-94272766, FAX 61-8-94272827, perth.shop@museum.wa.gov.au, http://www.museum.wa.gov.au. Ed. Fred Wells. R&P Ann Ousey TEL 64-8-9427-2779. Circ: 263.

069 AUS ISSN 0313-122X
➤ **WESTERN AUSTRALIAN MUSEUM. RECORDS. SUPPLEMENT.** Text in English. 1975. irreg. price varies. abstr. back issues avail. **Document type:** *Magazine, Academic/Scholarly.*
Related titles: ◆ Supplement to: Western Australian Museum. Records. ISSN 0312-3162.
Indexed: AESIS, ASI, GeoRef.
—BLDSC (7325.308000).
Published by: Western Australian Museum, Locked Bag 49, Welshpool DC, W.A. 6986, Australia. TEL 61-8-94272766, FAX 61-8-94272827, reception@museum.wa.gov.au, perth.shop@museum.wa.gov.au, http://www.museum.wa.gov.au. Ed. Fred Wells. R&P Ann Ousey TEL 64-8-9427-2779.

069 USA
WHISPERS NEAR THE INGLENOOK. Text in English. 1978. q.
Published by: 1890 House Museum and Center for Victorian Arts, 37 Tompkins St, Cortland, NY 13045. Ed. John H Nozynski. Circ: 1,300.

WHO'S WHO IN AMERICAN ART. *see* BIOGRAPHY

069 USA
WILLIAM HAMMOND MATHERS MUSEUM. OCCASIONAL PAPERS AND MONOGRAPHS. Text in English. 1974. irreg. free. **Document type:** *Monographic series.*
Formerly: Indiana University Museum. Occasional Papers and Monographs
Published by: Indiana University, William Hammond Mathers Museum, 601 E Eighth St, Bloomington, IN 47405. TEL 812-855-6873, FAX 812-855-0205.

069 USA ISSN 1542-5800
THE WINDMILL CLIPPER. Text in English. 1994. q. free to members. **Document type:** *Newsletter.*
Published by: Kendallville Windmill Museum and Historical Society, 732 S Allen Chapel Rd, Kendallville, IN 46755. TEL 260-347-2334.

069 USA ISSN 1937-271X
WINGS (MILWAUKEE). Text in English. 2005. q. free (effective 2010). **Document type:** *Newsletter, Trade.* **Description:** Chronicles activities taking place at the museum, important acquisitions, displays and exhibits.
Published by: Milwaukee Public Museum, 800 W Wells St, Milwaukee, WI 53233. TEL 414-278-2702, 888-700-9069, MuseumNews@mpm.edu, http://www.mpm.edu.

069 USA
WOODROW WILSON BIRTHPLACE NEWSLETTER. Text in English. 1973. q. membership. bk.rev. back issues avail. **Document type:** *Newsletter.* **Description:** Provides coverage of presidential museum activities, including exhibits, seminars, lectures, collections, and school programs.
Published by: Woodrow Wilson Birthplace Foundation, Inc., PO Box 24, Staunton, VA 24401. TEL 703-885-0897, FAX 703-886-9874. Ed. Patrick Clarke. Circ: 1,000.

708.1 USA ISSN 0084-3539
N10
YALE UNIVERSITY ART GALLERY BULLETIN. Key Title: Bulletin - Yale University Art Gallery. Text in English. 1926. a. USD 12 per issue (effective 2005). bk.rev. illus. reprints avail. **Document type:** *Bulletin.* **Description:** Articles and notes relating to works in the gallery's collection. Includes annual director's report and a complete acquisitions list for the previous year.
Former titles (until 1965): Yale Art Gallery Bulletin (0360-3180); (until 1958): Associates in Fine Arts at Yale University. Bulletin (0898-1922)
Related titles: Microform ed.: (from PQC).
Indexed: A06, A07, A30, A31, AA, ABCT, AIAP, ArtInd, B04, B24, IBR, IBZ, PCI.
—Ingenta.
Published by: Yale University Art Gallery, PO Box 208271, New Haven, CT 06520-8271. TEL 203-432-0660, FAX 203-432-7159. Ed. Leslie Baier. Circ: 2,100.

069 JPN
YAMA TO HAKUBUTSUKAN/MOUNTAIN AND MUSEUM. Text in Japanese. 1956. m. JPY 1,500 (effective 2000). **Description:** Contains reviews and news of the museum.
Published by: Omachi-shiritsu Omachi Sangaku Hakubutsukan/Omachi Alpine Museum, 8056-1 Kamisakae-cho, Omachi-shi, Nagano-ken 398-0002, Japan. TEL 81-261-22-0211, FAX 81-261-21-2133, sanpaku@rose.ocn.ne.jp, http://www.ntcs.ne.jp/sanpaku/alpine.htm. Circ: 1,000.

YAMAGUCHI KENRITSU YAMAGUCHI HAKUBUTSUKAN KENKYU HOKOKU/YAMAGUCHI MUSEUM. BULLETIN. *see* SCIENCES: COMPREHENSIVE WORKS

YOKOSUKA-SHI HAKUBUTSUKAN KENKYU HOKOKU. SHIZEN KAGAKU/YOKOSUKA CITY MUSEUM. SCIENCE REPORT. *see* SCIENCES: COMPREHENSIVE WORKS

YOKOSUKA-SHI HAKUBUTSUKAN SHIRYOSHU/YOKOSUKA CITY MUSEUM. MISCELLANEOUS REPORT. *see* SCIENCES: COMPREHENSIVE WORKS

069 JPN ISSN 0385-8472
QH188
YOKOSUKA-SHI HAKUBUTSUKANPO/YOKOSUKA CITY MUSEUM. ANNUAL REPORT. Text in Japanese. a.
Published by: Yokosuka-shi Shizen Hakubutsukan/Yokosuka City Museum, 95 Fukadadai, Yokosuka-shi, Kanagawa-ken 238-0000, Japan.

069 GBR ISSN 2047-0479
▼ **YOUR DAY AT THE MUSEUM.** Text in English. 2011. 3/yr. free (effective 2011). adv. **Document type:** *Magazine, Consumer.*
Related titles: Online - full text ed.
Published by: (Chiltern Open Air Museum), Rosewood Publishing Ltd., PO Box 1217, Tring, HP23 5XY, United Kingdom. Pub. Sandra Smith. Adv. contact Dawn Lucas.

708.96894 ZMB ISSN 0084-4977
ZAMBIA. NATIONAL MUSEUMS BOARD. REPORT. Text in English. a. ZMK 1. **Document type:** *Government.*
Published by: National Museums Board, Livingstone Museum, PO Box 60498, Livingstone, Zambia.

502 708.371 CZE ISSN 0232-0738
QH178.C8
ZAPADOCESKE MUZEUM V PLZNI. SBORNIK. PRIRODA. Text in Czech. 1967. irreg. (1-2/yr.). price varies. **Document type:** *Monographic series, Academic/Scholarly.*
Indexed: CABA, E12, F08, F12, G11, S13, S16, W10, Z01.
Published by: Zapadoceske Muzeum v Plzni, Kopeckeho sady 2, Plzen, 30135, Czech Republic. TEL 420-377-324105, FAX 420-378-370113, reditelstvi@zcm.cz, http://www.zcm.cz. Eds. Jaromir Sofron, Jaroslav Kraft, Roman Vacik.

069 BWA
THE ZEBRA'S VOICE; lentswe la pitse ya naga. Text in English. 1980. q. USD 15 foreign in overseas & African countries (effective 2001); Not available in SADC countries. 24 p./no. 3 cols./p.; back issues avail. **Document type:** *Magazine, Government.*
Published by: National Museum, Monuments and Art Gallery, Independence Ave 331, Private Bag 00114, Gaborone, Botswana. TEL 267-374616, FAX 267-302797, natiionalmuseum@gov.bw. Ed. Rudolph Mojalemotho. R&P Tickey Pyle. Circ: 5,000.

070.594 DEU
ZEITSCHRIFT FUER MUSEUM UND BILDUNG. Text in German. 1977. 2/yr. EUR 15.90 (effective 2010). **Document type:** *Journal, Academic/Scholarly.*
Formerly (until 2003): Mitteilungen und Materialen (0934-9650)
Published by: Lit Verlag, Grevener Str/Fresnostr 2, Muenster, 48159, Germany. TEL 49-251-235091, FAX 49-251-231972, lit@lit-verlag.de.

069 CHN
ZHONGGUO BOWUGUAN/CHINESE MUSEUMS. Text in Chinese, English. q. USD 3 per issue. **Document type:** *Academic/Scholarly.*
Published by: Zhongguo Bowuguan Xuehui/China Museum Society, 29 Wusi Dajie, Beijing, 100009, China. TEL 4015577, FAX 5123119. Ed. Su Donghai. Circ: 4,000.

708.371 CZE ISSN 1210-5538
N6
➤ **ZPRAVY PAMATKOVE PECE.** Text in Czech; Summaries in German. 1937. bi-m. EUR 77 foreign (effective 2009). adv. illus. **Document type:** *Journal, Academic/Scholarly.* **Description:** Contains articles and studies on research, conservation, and preservation of the historic buildings, monuments and conservation areas in the Czech Republic.
Formerly (until 1992): Pamatky a Priroda (0139-9853); Formed by the merger of (1962-1976): Pamatkova Pece (0231-7966); (1946-1976): Ochrana Prirody (0029-8204)
Related titles: CD-ROM ed.
Indexed: A&ATA, GeoRef, SpeleolAb.
Published by: Narodni Pamatkovy Ustav, Valdstejnske nam 3, Prague, 11801, Czech Republic. TEL 420-2-34653111, FAX 420-2-34653119, praha@praha.npu.cz. Ed. Kristyna Kolajova. R&P Lucie Ernstova. adv.: page CZK 10,000. Circ: 1,100. **Dist. by:** Kubon & Sagner Buchexport - Import GmbH, Hessstr 39-41, Munich 80798, Germany. TEL 49-89-542180, FAX 49-89-54218218, postmaster@kubon-sagner.de, http://www.kubon-sagner.de. **Co-sponsor:** Ministerstvo Kultury Ceske Respubliky.

069 RUS ISSN 0207-9739
Z6935
ZRELISHCHNYE ISKUSSTVA. Text in Russian. 1983. bi-m. USD 143 foreign (effective 2010). **Document type:** *Bibliography.*
Indexed: RASB.
—East View.
Published by: (Rossiiskaya Gosudarstvennaya Biblioteka/Russian State Library), Idatel'stvo Rossiiskoi Gosudarstvennoi Biblioteki Pashkov Dom/Pashkov Dom, Russian State Library Publishing House, Vozdizhenka 3/5, Moscow, 101000, Russian Federation. TEL 7-495-6955953, FAX 7-495-6955953, pashkov_dom@rsl.ru, http://www.rsl.ru/pub.asp. **Dist. by:** East View Information Services, 10601 Wayzata Blvd, Minneapolis, MN 55305. TEL 952-252-1201, 800-477-1005, FAX 952-252-1202, info@eastview.com, http://www.eastview.com.

069 USA ISSN 1944-589X
AM101.N534
1220 FIFTH. Text in English. 2008. q.
Published by: Museum of the City of New York, 1220 Fifth Ave at 103rd St, New York, NY 10029. TEL 212-534-1672, FAX 212-423-0758, info@mcny.org, http://www.mcny.org.

069 DEU
20_21; Das Magazin der Kunstsammlung Nordrhein-Westfalen. Variant title: Zwanzig Unterstrich Einundzwanzig. Text in German. 2004. 2/yr. EUR 2.50 newsstand/cover (effective 2009). adv. **Document type:** *Magazine, Consumer.*
Published by: corps - Corporate Publishing Services GmbH, Kasernenstr 69, Duesseldorf, 40213, Germany. TEL 49-211-54227700, FAX 49-211-54227722, info@corps-verlag.de. Ed. Dorothee Vogt-Christiansen. Adv. contact Ebru Aksan-Loebe. color page EUR 3,950; trim 210 x 280. Circ: 65,000 (controlled).

MUSEUMS AND ART GALLERIES—Abstracting, Bibliographies, Statistics

069.021 AUS
AUSTRALIA. BUREAU OF STATISTICS. COMMERCIAL ART GALLERIES, AUSTRALIA (ONLINE). Text in English. 1996. irreg., latest 2001. free (effective 2009). back issues avail. **Description:** Contains detailed information on the commercial art gallery industry in Australia. Includes sources of income and expenditure, characteristics of employment and persons working, state and territory data, details of artworks sold, as well as a range of performance ratios for the industry.
Formerly: Australia. Bureau of Statistics. Commercial Art Galleries, Australia (Print)
Media: Online - full text.
Published by: Australian Bureau of Statistics, Locked Bag 10, Belconnen, ACT 2616, Australia. TEL 61-2-92684909, 300-135-070, FAX 61-2-92684654, client.services@abs.gov.au.

069.021 AUS
AUSTRALIA. BUREAU OF STATISTICS. MUSEUMS, AUSTRALIA (ONLINE). Text in English. 2001 (Jun). quadrennial, latest 2008. free (effective 2009). back issues avail. **Document type:** *Government.* **Description:** Contains information about museums. Data includes: number and type of museums, employment, volunteers, income and expenses, with breakdowns of key characteristics by size and by State. Also includes: information on admissions, acquisitions, artefacts, art works, special exhibitions, web presence and other museum/gallery activity.
Formerly: Australia. Bureau of Statistics. Museums, Australia (Print)
Media: Online - full text.
Published by: Australian Bureau of Statistics, Locked Bag 10, Belconnen, ACT 2616, Australia. TEL 61-2-92684909, 300-135-070, FAX 61-2-92684654, client.services@abs.gov.au.

069.021 020.021 AUS
AUSTRALIA. BUREAU OF STATISTICS. PUBLIC LIBRARIES, AUSTRALIA (ONLINE). Text in English. 1997. irreg., latest 2004. free (effective 2009). back issues avail. **Document type:** *Government.* **Description:** Presents results from an Australian Bureau of Statistics (ABS) survey of public library operations.
Former titles: Australia. Bureau of Statistics. Public Libraries, Australia (Print); (until 2000): Australia. Bureau of Statistics. Libraries and Museums, Australia
Media: Online - full text.
Published by: Australian Bureau of Statistics, Locked Bag 10, Belconnen, ACT 2616, Australia. TEL 61-2-92684909, 61-2-62527037, 300-135-070, FAX 61-2-62528103, client.services@abs.gov.au.

069.021 AUS
AUSTRALIA. BUREAU OF STATISTICS. SELECTED MUSEUMS, AUSTRALIA (ONLINE). Text in English. 1996. irreg., latest 1997. free (effective 2009). **Description:** Features information on employment, volunteers, admissions, Internet web-sites, artefacts on display, exhibitions developed, income and expenditure, conservation and preservation measures, documentation of collections and data by state and territory.
Formerly: Australia. Bureau of Statistics. Selected Museums, Australia (Print)
Media: Online - full text.
Published by: Australian Bureau of Statistics, Locked Bag 10, Belconnen, ACT 2616, Australia. TEL 61-2-92684909, 300-135-070, FAX 61-2-92684654, client.services@abs.gov.au.

069.021 CAN ISSN 0847-0146
CANADA. STATISTICS CANADA. HERITAGE INSTITUTIONS/ CANADA. STATISTIQUE CANADA. ETABLISSEMENTS DU PATRIMOINE; data tables. Cover title: Culture Statistics, Heritage Institutions, Preliminary Statistics. Text in English, French. 1985. a.
Formerly (until 1986): Canada. Statistics Canada. Culture Statistics. Heritage Institutions, Museums, Parks, Historic Sites, Archives, Other Related Institutions, e.g. Zoos, Botanical Gardens, Exhibition Centres (0833-0344)
Related titles: ◆ Online - full text ed.: Canada. Statistics Canada. Heritage Institutions. ISSN 1708-8151.
Published by: (Statistics Canada, Education, Culture and Tourism Division), Statistics Canada/Statistique Canada, Publications Sales and Services, Ottawa, ON K1A 0T6, Canada. TEL 613-951-8116, infostats@statcan.ca, http://www.statcan.gc.ca.

069.021 CAN ISSN 1708-8151
CANADA. STATISTICS CANADA. HERITAGE INSTITUTIONS; data tables. Text in English. irreg.
Media: Online - full text. **Related titles:** ◆ Print ed.: Canada. Statistics Canada. Heritage Institutions. ISSN 0847-0146; French ed.: Canada. Statistiques Canada. Etablissements du Patrimoine, Tableaux de Donnees. ISSN 1708-816X.
Published by: Statistics Canada/Statistique Canada, Communications Division, 3rd Fl, R H Coats Bldg, Ottawa, ON K1A 0A6, Canada. TEL 800-263-1136, infostats@statcan.ca, http://www.statcan.gc.ca.

016.069 AUT ISSN 1018-6077
AM101
KATALOGE DES OBEROESTERREICHISCHE LANDESMUSEUMS. Text in German. 1985. irreg. **Document type:** *Catalog, Trade.*
Indexed: Z01.
Published by: Oberoesterreichisches Landesmuseum, Museumstr 14, Linz, 4010, Austria. TEL 43-732-7744820, bio.buch@landesmuseum.at, http://www.landesmuseum.at.

069 DEU
M P Z PUBLIK. Text in German. 1994. a. free. **Document type:** *Catalog, Bibliography.*
Formerly (until 2001): M P Z Verlagsprogramm
Media: Online - full text.
Published by: Museums-Paedagogisches Zentrum, Barer Str 29, Munich, 80799, Germany. TEL 49-89-23805120, FAX 49-89-23805197, mpz@mpz.bayern.de, http://www.mpz.bayern.de.

016.069 RUS ISSN 0208-2012
Z5052
MUZEINOE DELO I OKHRANA PAMYATNIKOV; referativno-bibliograficheskaya informatsiya. Text in Russian. 1974. bi-m. USD 143 foreign (effective 2010). **Document type:** *Bibliography.*
Description: Consists of abstracts from museum and heritage protection publications. Covers museum management, theory, history, heritage interpretation and conservation policy.
Related titles: CD-ROM ed.
Indexed: RASB.
—East View.
Published by: (Rossiiskaya Gosudarstvennaya Biblioteka/Russian State Library), Idatel'stvo Rossiiskoi Gosudarstvennoi Biblioteki Pashkov Dom/Pashkov Dom, Russian State Library Publishing House, Vozdizhenka 3/5, Moscow, 101000, Russian Federation. TEL 7-495-6955953, FAX 7-495-6955953, pashkov_dom@rsl.ru, http://www.rsl.ru/pub.asp. Ed. Tamara Lapteva. Circ: 300. **Dist. by:** East View Information Services, 10601 Wayzata Blvd, Minneapolis, MN 55305. TEL 952-252-1201, 800-477-1005, FAX 952-252-1202, info@eastview.com, http://www.eastview.com.

016.069 AUT
OESTERREICHISCHES MUSEUM FUER VOLKSKUNDE. KATALOGE. Text in German. 1946. irreg., latest vol.79, 2001. price varies. **Document type:** *Catalog, Academic/Scholarly.*
Published by: (Oesterreichisches Museum fuer Volkskunde), Verlag Ferdinand Berger und Soehne GmbH, Wienerstr 21-23, Horn, N 3580, Austria. TEL 43-2982-4161332, FAX 43-2982-4161382, office@berger.at, http://www.berger.at.

MUSIC

see also DANCE ; SOUND RECORDING AND REPRODUCTION

780 USA ISSN 1075-816X
ML3790
A & R JOURNAL. (Artist & Repertoire) Text in English. a. USD 15; USD 16 in Canada; USD 25 elsewhere. **Description:** Used by vocalists, songwriters, music students and musicians for career advancement opportunities and talent discovery resources.
Published by: A & R Journal, 244 W 54th St, Ste 800, New York, NY 10019. TEL 212-330-9183, FAX 212-489-1302. Ed. K Morgan. Pub. Richard Davis.

780 BRA ISSN 1518-2630
MT3.B7
A B E M. REVISTA. (Associacao Brasileira de Educacao Musical) Text in Portuguese. 1992. s-a. **Document type:** *Magazine, Trade.*
Indexed: M11.
Published by: Associacao Brasileira de Educacao Musical, Rua Coronel Dulcidio 638 Batel, Curitiba, 80420-170, Brazil. http://www.abem.pop.com.br.

780 USA
➤ **A C M R NEWSLETTER.** Text in English. 1988. s-a. free to members (effective 2010). back issues avail. **Document type:** *Newsletter, Trade.*
Former titles (until 2008): A C M R Reports; (until 1994): A C M R Newsletter (1071-0639)
Related titles: Online - full text ed.: free (effective 2010).
Indexed: RILM.
Published by: Association for Chinese Music Research, c/o Alan L. Kagan, 1376 Christensen Ave, West St. Paul, MN 55118. kagan001@umn.edu. Ed. Valerie Samson.

780 FRA ISSN 1962-4646
A CONTRETEMPS. Text in French. 1990. s-a. **Document type:** *Magazine.*
Formerly (until 2007): Papier Musique (1293-6707)
Published by: Conservatoire Maurice Ravel, 29 Cours du Comte de Cabarrus, Bayonne, 64100, France. TEL 33-5-59312170, contact@cmdt-ravel.fr, http://www.orbcb.fr/conservatoire.

780.23 USA ISSN 0002-0990
A G M A ZINE. Text in English. 1936. 5/yr. free. bk.rev. illus. **Document type:** *Newsletter.* **Description:** For artists, stage directors, and stage management in the fields of opera, dance and concert.
Published by: American Guild of Musical Artists, 1430 Broadway., New York, NY 10018-3308. Ed. Dianne James. Circ: 6,000 (controlled).

A H A! HISPANIC ARTS NEWS. *see* ART

A I C F NEWSLETTER. *see* ART

782.3 USA ISSN 1079-459X
BV169
A I M: LITURGY RESOURCES. Text in English. 1973. q. USD 15 per issue domestic; USD 25 per issue foreign (effective 2011). adv. back issues avail. **Document type:** *Magazine, Trade.* **Description:** Abounds in liturgy and music resources. Contains articles, comments, workshops and new music.
Formerly (until 1993): A I M
Related titles: Online - full text ed.: USD 12 (effective 2011).
Published by: World Library Publications, Inc. (Subsidiary of: J.S. Paluch Co., Inc.), 3708 River Rd, Ste 400, Franklin Park, IL 60131. TEL 847-233-2752, 800-621-5197, FAX 847-233-2762, 888-957-3291, wlpcs@jspaluch.com. Ed. Mr. Alan Hommerding.

A K M INFORMATIONEN. (Autoren, Komponisten und Musikverleger) *see* PATENTS, TRADEMARKS AND COPYRIGHTS

789 USA ISSN 1043-5379
ML1050
THE A M I C A NEWS BULLETIN. Text in English. 1963. bi-m. membership. adv. bk.rev. index. **Document type:** *Newsletter.* **Description:** Contains news and articles of interest to owners, collectors, and sellers of antique automatic musical instruments that run on perforated paper rolls.
Former titles: Automatic Musical Instrument Collectors' Association. News Bulletin (0884-0644); (until 1973): A M I C A Bulletin (0884-0652); (until 1972): Automatic Musical Instrument Collectors' Association. News Bulletin (0884-0660)
Media: Duplicated (not offset).
Published by: Automatic Musical Instrument Collectors' Association, c/o John Fisher, 73 Navada, Rochester, MI 48309. Circ: 950.

780 USA
A M P MAGAZINE. Text in English. 2002. bi-m. USD 1.99 newsstand/cover (effective 2007). adv. **Document type:** *Magazine, Consumer.*
Published by: American Music Press, PO Box 1070, Martinez, CA 94553.

780 USA ISSN 1941-7861
A M S STUDIES IN MUSIC. Text in English. 2008 (Sep.). a., latest 2008. USD 92.50 per issue (effective 2010). **Document type:** *Monographic series, Academic/Scholarly.* **Description:** Provides musicologists and performers, as well as students of literature, with important information and fresh insights into a diverse and compelling musical tradition and the cultural and religious conditions that helped shape it.
Published by: A M S Press, Inc., Brooklyn Navy Yard, 63 Flushing Ave, Bldg 292, Unit #221, Brooklyn, NY 11205. TEL 718-875-8100, FAX 718-875-3800.

789.91 USA
A P M MONOGRAPH SERIES. (Antique Phonograph Monthly) Text in English. 1973. irreg. USD 15. adv. bk.rev. **Document type:** *Monographic series.* **Description:** Devoted to the history of the phonograph and popular music.
Published by: A P M Press, 502 E 17th St, Brooklyn, NY 11226. TEL 718-941-6835. Ed. Allen Koenigsberg. Circ: 2,000.

780 USA
➤ **A-R SPECIAL PUBLICATIONS.** Text in English. 1990. irreg., latest vol.13, 2009. price varies. back issues avail. **Document type:** *Monographic series, Academic/Scholarly.* **Description:** Designed for use in a variety of settings, including churches, early music ensembles, and other venues.
Formerly (until 200?): A-R Performer's Library
Published by: A-R Editions, Inc., 8551 Research Way, Ste 180, Middleton, WI 53562. TEL 608-836-9000, 800-736-0070, FAX 608-831-8200, orders@areditions.com. Ed. James L Zychowicz TEL 608-836-9000 ext 14.

780 800 070.5 920 USA
A S C A P BIOGRAPHICAL DICTIONARY. Text in English. irreg. (4th ed. 1980). USD 41.95.
Indexed: CA&I, PABMI.
Published by: American Society of Composers, Authors and Publishers, One Lincoln Plaza, New York, NY 10023. TEL 212-621-6222, FAX 212-721-0955.

780.23 USA ISSN 0145-5265
ML128.O5
A S C A P SYMPHONIC CATALOG. Text in English. irreg. **Document type:** *Catalog.*
Published by: American Society of Composers, Authors and Publishers, One Lincoln Plaza, New York, NY 10023. TEL 212-595-3050, FAX 212-721-0955.

780 GBR
A T M. Text in English. 1992. q. GBP 12 in British Isles; GBP 16 in Europe; GBP 20 in United States (effective 2000); GBP 2.40 newsstand/cover. **Document type:** *Magazine, Consumer.* **Description:** Covers all aspects of the constantly evolving world of dance music and culture.
Formerly (until June 1998): Atmosphere
Published by: Progressive Advocates Ltd., Southend, PO Box 5307, Southend-on-Sea, Essex SS1 1TW, United Kingdom. TEL 44-1702-512189, FAX 44-1702-529800. Ed. Jason O'Connor. **Dist. by:** Portman Distribution, Gadoline House, 2 Godstone Rd, Whyteleafe, Surrey CR3 0EA, United Kingdom. TEL 44-20-8645-8200, FAX 44-20-8645-8239.

780 ITA ISSN 1973-0241
A TRE VOCI. Text in Italian. 1999. irreg. **Document type:** *Monographic series, Academic/Scholarly.*
Published by: (Universita degli Studi di Parma), Edizioni Unicopli, Via Festa del Perdono 12, Milan, 20122, Italy. TEL 39-02-42299666, http://www.edizioniunicopli.it.

789.49 IND
A V MAX. (Audio Video) Text in English. 19??. m. INR 599 domestic; INR 3,750 foreign; INR 100 per issue (effective 2011). **Document type:** *Magazine, Consumer.* **Description:** Contains indepth and incisive reviews of audio-video equipment.
Published by: Infomedia 18 Ltd., A Wing, Ruby House, J K Sawant Marg, Dadar (West), Mumbai, 400 028, India. TEL 91-22-30245000, FAX 91-22-30034499, ho@infomedia18.in. Adv. contact Ruby Roy TEL 91-22-30034582.

A V STATE OF THE ART. *see* ELECTRONICS

781.66 DEU
A5; Musik - Kultur - Christsein. Text in German. 2007. 6/yr. EUR 15; EUR 2.50 newsstand/cover (effective 2008). **Document type:** *Magazine, Consumer.*
Published by: Edition Nachtigall, Kirchstr 10, Lindenfels, 64678, Germany. TEL 49-6255-9680292, nachtigall@fishpost.de. Ed., Pub. Volker Gruch.

781.62 NOR ISSN 0803-5954
AARBOK FOR NORSK FOLKEMUSIKK. Text in Norwegian. 1991. a. NOK 200 membership (effective 2006). **Document type:** *Yearbook, Consumer.*
Indexed: RILM.
Published by: Norsk Folkemusikk- og Danselag/Norwegian Traditional Music and Dance Association, Kirkegaten 20, PO Box 440, Blindern, Oslo, 0103, Norway. TEL 47-22-005690, FAX 47-22-423208, nfd@folkogdans.no. Ed. Tore Skaug.

780 DEU
ABHANDLUNGEN ZUR MUSIKGESCHICHTE. Text in German. 1997. irreg., latest vol.20, 2009. price varies. **Document type:** *Monographic series, Academic/Scholarly.*
Published by: V & R Unipress GmbH (Subsidiary of: Vandenhoeck und Ruprecht), Robert-Bosch-Breite 6, Goettingen, 37079, Germany. TEL 49-551-5084303, FAX 49-551-5084333, info@vr-unipress.de, http://www.v-r.de/en/publisher/unipress.

792 GBR ISSN 1471-9010
ML1699
ABOUT THE HOUSE; the magazine of The Royal Ballet, The Royal Opera and Birmingham Royal Ballet. Text in English. 1962. 5/yr. free to members (effective 2009). adv. illus. **Document type:** *Magazine, Consumer.* **Description:** Aims at keeping its members up to date on news and performance information.
Former titles (until 2000): Opera House (London) (1351-3443); (until 1993): About the House (0001-3242)
Related titles: Microfilm ed.: (from PQC).
Indexed: A20, IBT&D, IDP, M11, MusicInd, T02.
—Ingenta.
Published by: (Royal Opera House), B B C Magazines Ltd. (Subsidiary of: B B C Worldwide Ltd.), Tower House, Fairfax St, Bristol, BS1 3BN, United Kingdom. TEL 44-117-9279009, FAX 44-117-9349008, enquiries@bbccustomerpublishing.com. Circ: 30,000. **Co-sponsor:** Friends of Covent Garden.

781.65 USA ISSN 1559-7636
ABYSS JAZZ MAGAZINE. Text in English. m. USD 24.95 (effective 2007). **Document type:** *Magazine, Consumer.*
Formerly (until 200?): Abyss Voice
Address: 8947 Washington Ave, Jacksonville, FL 32208. TEL 904-264-4642, FAX 904-264-4667, mailbox@abyssjazz.com.

780 ITA
ACCADEMIA DEI CONCORDI ROVIGO. COLLANA DI MUSICHE. Text in Italian. 1977 (no.12). irreg. price varies. **Document type:** *Monographic series, Academic/Scholarly.*
Published by: Fabrizio Serra Editore (Subsidiary of: Accademia Editoriale), c/o Accademia Editoriale, Via Santa Bibbiana 28, Pisa, 56127, Italy. TEL 39-050-542332, FAX 39-050-574888, accademiaeditoriale@accademiaeditoriale.it, http://www.libraweb.net.

780.43 ITA
ACCADEMIA FILARMONICA ROMANA. NEWSLETTER. Text in Italian. 1992. m. free. **Document type:** *Newsletter, Consumer.*
Formerly (until 199?): Giornale della Filarmonica
Published by: Accademia Filarmonica Romana, Via Flaminia, 118, Rome, RM 00196, Italy. TEL 06-32-01-752, FAX 06-32-10-410.

780 USA
ACCESS TO THE MUSIC ZONE. Abbreviated title: A M Z. Text in English. 1996. m. free. back issues avail. **Description:** Dedicated to covering music of all shapes and sizes, from all around the world.
Media: Online - full text. Ed. Mary Ellen Gustafson.

786.97 USA
ACCORDIONISTS AND TEACHERS GUILD, INTERNATIONAL. BULLETIN. Text in English. 1941. q. free to members (effective 2007); $30 for membership. adv. bk.rev.; rec.rev. back issues avail. **Document type:** *Bulletin, Trade.* **Description:** Includes biographies, events calendar, human-interest articles, accordion news, member news, and information about performances.
Formerly: A T G Bulletin (0001-2734)
Media: Duplicated (not offset).
Published by: Accordionists and Teachers Guild, International, 2312 West 71 Terrace, Prairie Village, KS 66208-3322. TEL 913-722-5625, Sommersj@umkc.edu. Ed., R&P, Adv. contact Amy Jo Sawyer. Circ: 200.

ACHE. *see* ART

787.6 ESP ISSN 1885-5563
ACORDES. Text in Spanish. 2001. m. EUR 40 domestic (effective 2010). adv. **Document type:** *Magazine, Consumer.*
Published by: R D M Editorial, Poligono Industrial Norte, c/ Gomera, 10-2 B, San Sebastian de los Reyes, 28700, Spain. TEL 34-91-6518227, FAX 34-91-6518227, rdm@rdmeditorial.com.

398.8 ESP ISSN 1886-2896
ACORDES DE FLAMENCO. Text in Spanish. 2006. bi-m. EUR 45 domestic; EUR 63 in Europe; EUR 68 elsewhere (effective 2010). adv. **Document type:** *Magazine, Consumer.*
Published by: R D M Editorial, Poligono Industrial Norte, c/ Gomera, 10-2 B, San Sebastian de los Reyes, 28700, Spain. TEL 34-91-6518227, FAX 34-91-6518227, rdm@rdmeditorial.com.

787.87 GBR ISSN 1745-4468
ACOUSTIC. Text in English. 2004. m. GBP 29.95 domestic; GBP 39.95 in Europe; GBP 33.75 in United States; GBP 45 elsewhere (effective 2009). adv. back issues avail. **Document type:** *Magazine, Consumer.* **Description:** Features include: interviews with high profile players; reviews and tests of existing and new acoustic guitar and related products; instructional columns by some of the world's most successful and gifted acoustic guitar players.
Published by: Oyster House Media Ltd., Oyster House, Hunter's Lodge, Kentisbeare, Devon EX15 2DY, United Kingdom. TEL 44-1884-266100, FAX 44-1884-266101, info@oysterhousemedia.co.uk, http://www.oysterhousemedia.co.uk. Ed. Ben Cooper.

787 USA ISSN 1049-9261
ML1015.G9
ACOUSTIC GUITAR. Text in English. 1990. m. USD 29.95 (effective 2010). adv. bk.rev.; rec.rev. back issues avail. **Document type:** *Magazine, Consumer.* **Description:** Features articles written by and for musicians that covers a variety of musical styles, including transcriptions from recordings and solo pieces for guitars.
Related titles: Online - full text ed.: USD 19.95 (effective 2010).
Indexed: A27, IIMP, M11, MusicInd, P10, P48, P53, P54, PQC, RILM, T02.
Published by: String Letter Publishing, PO Box 767, San Anselmo, CA 94979. TEL 415-485-6946, FAX 415-485-0831, http://www.stringletter.com. Ed. Scott Pepper Nygaard. Pub. David A Lusterman.

787.87 USA ISSN 1079-0845
ML3469
ACOUSTIC MUSICIAN MAGAZINE. Text in English. 1994. m. **Document type:** *Magazine, Consumer.*
Indexed: IIMP, MusicInd.
Published by: Border Crossing Publications, Inc., PO Box 1349, New Market, VA 22844-1349. TEL 703-740-4005, FAX 703-740-4006. Ed. Steve Spence.

780 792 DEU ISSN 2191-253X
▼ **ACT**; zeitschrift fuer musik & performance. Text in Multiple languages. 2010. s-a. free (effective 2011). **Document type:** *Journal, Academic/Scholarly.*
Media: Online - full text.
Published by: Universitaet Bayreuth, Forschungsinstitut fuer Musiktheater

780 920 DEU ISSN 0001-6233
ML5
ACTA MOZARTIANA. Text in German. 1954. 2/yr. EUR 36 (effective 2009). adv. bk.rev. charts; illus. **Document type:** *Journal, Academic/Scholarly.*
Formerly (until 1992): Deutsches Mozartfest

Indexed: A20, ASCA, ArtHuCI, CurCont, IIMP, M11, MusicInd, P54, PCI, RASB, RILM, SCOPUS, W07.
—IE. **CCC.**
Published by: Deutsche Mozart-Gesellschaft e.V., Frauentorstr 30, Augsburg, 86152, Germany. TEL 49-821-518588, FAX 49-821-157228, info@deutsche-mozart-gesellschaft.de, http://www.deutsche-mozart-gesellschaft.de. Ed. Laurenz Luetteken. Circ: 2,900 (controlled).

780.01 DEU ISSN 0001-6241
ML5
➤ **ACTA MUSICOLOGICA.** Text in English, French, German. 1928. 2/yr. EUR 94 (effective 2011). bibl.; illus. index, cum.index: vols.1-25 (1928-1953). reprints avail. **Document type:** *Journal, Academic/Scholarly.*
Formerly (until 1931): Internationale Gesellschaft fuer Musikwissenschaft. Mitteilungen (0378-8903)
Related titles: Online - full text ed.
Indexed: A20, A22, ASCA, ArtHuCI, CA, CurCont, DIP, FR, IBR, IBZ, IIMP, M11, MLA-IB, MusicInd, PCI, RASB, RILM, SCOPUS, T02, W07.
—IE, Infotrieve, Ingenta, INIST. **CCC.**
Published by: (International Musicological Society CHE), Baerenreiter Verlag, Heinrich-Schuetz-Allee 35, Kassel, 34131, Germany. TEL 49-561-3105154, FAX 49-561-3105195, order@baerenreiter.com, http://www.baerenreiter.com. Ed. Philippe Vendrix. Circ: 1,900 (paid and controlled).

780.42 CZE ISSN 1214-5955
➤ **ACTA MUSICOLOGICA**; revue pro hudebni vedu. Text in Czech. 2004. q. free. **Document type:** *Journal, Academic/Scholarly.*
Media: Online - full text.
Published by: Masarykova Univerzita, Filozoficka Fakulta, Ustav Hudebni Vedy/Masaryk University, Faculty of Arts, Institute of Musicology, Arna Novaka 1, Brno, 60200, Czech Republic. TEL 420-549-497478, FAX 420-549-497478, music@phil.muni.cz, http://www.phil.muni.cz/music. Ed. Lubomir Spurny.

780 FIN ISSN 0587-2448
ACTA MUSICOLOGICA FENNICA. Text in English, Finnish. 1968. irreg., latest vol.22, 2003. back issues avail. **Document type:** *Monographic series, Academic/Scholarly.*
Published by: Suomen Musiikkitieteellinen Seura/Finnish Musicological Society, c/o Musiikkitieteen Laitos, University of Jyvaskyla, Jyvaskyla, 40014, Finland. http://www.jyu.fi/musica/mts.

786.5 DEU ISSN 0567-7874
ML5
ACTA ORGANOLOGICA. Text in German. 1967. irreg., latest vol.31, 2009. price varies. illus. **Document type:** *Monographic series, Academic/Scholarly.*
Indexed: RILM.
Published by: (Gesellschaft der Orgelfreunde e.V.), Verlag Merseburger Berlin GmbH, Naumburger Strasse 40, Kassel, 34127, Germany. TEL 49-561-78980911, FAX 49-561-78980916, vertrieb@merseburger.de, http://www.merseburger.de.

780 DEU ISSN 0001-6942
ACTA SAGITTARIANA. Text in English, French, German. 1963. a. EUR 30 (effective 2009). adv. bk.rev. illus. back issues avail. **Document type:** *Journal, Academic/Scholarly.*
Indexed: MusicInd, RILM.
—**CCC.**
Published by: Internationale Heinrich Schuetz-Gesellschaft e.V., Heinrich-Schuetz-Allee 35, Kassel, 34131, Germany. TEL 49-561-31050, FAX 49-561-3105240, info@schuetzgesellschaft.de, http://www.schuetzgesellschaft.de. Ed. Sieglinde Froehlich. Circ: 1,000.

780 USA ISSN 1545-4517
➤ **ACTION, CRITICISM & THEORY FOR MUSIC EDUCATION.** Text in English. 2002. irreg. free (effective 2011). **Document type:** *Journal, Academic/Scholarly.* **Description:** Proposes areas and strategies for broadly needed change in music education, and embraces a wide range of related topics, content, questions and issues.
Media: Online - full text.
Indexed: A39, C27, C29, CA, D03, D04, E03, E13, ERI, M11, R14, S14, S15, S18, T02.
Published by: Southern Illinois University at Edwardsville, SIUE Campus, Edwardsville, IL 62026. TEL 888-328-5168, http://www.siue.edu.

780 USA ISSN 1931-4736
ACTIVATE!; movement, music & more. Text in English. 2006. 5/yr. USD 64.95 (effective 2007). **Document type:** *Magazine, Consumer.* **Description:** For children in kindergarten through grade 6.
Published by: Lorenz Corporation, 501 E Third St, Dayton, OH 45402. TEL 937-228-6118, FAX 937-223-2042, info@lorenz.com, http://www.lorenz.com. Ed. Kris Kropff.

780 ROM ISSN 1220-742X
ACTUALITATEA MUZICALA. Text in Romanian. 1990. w. **Document type:** *Magazine, Consumer.*
Published by: Uniunea Compozitorilor si Muzicologilor din Romania, Calea Victoriei 141, Bucharest, Romania. ucmr@clicknet.ro, http://www.ucmr.org.ro.

781.7 DEU ISSN 0001-7965
ML3630
AD MARGINEM; Randbemerkungen zur Musikalischen Volkskunde. Text in German. 1964. a. looseleaf. free. bk.rev. abstr. back issues avail. **Document type:** *Journal, Academic/Scholarly.*
Indexed: RILM.
Published by: Universitaet zu Koeln, Institut fuer Musikalische Volkskunde, Gronewaldstr 2, Cologne, 50931, Germany. TEL 49-221-470-5269. Eds. Gisela Probst-Effah, Reinhard Schneider. Circ: (controlled).

785 ITA ISSN 1722-3954
ML195
➤ **AD PARNASSUM**; a journal of eighteenth- and nineteenth-century instrumental music. Text in English. 2003. s-a. EUR 100 to institutions (effective 2009). **Document type:** *Journal, Academic/Scholarly.* **Description:** Deals exclusively with instrumental music of the 18th and 19th centuries.
Indexed: IBR, IBZ, M11, MusicInd, RILM.
Published by: Ut Orpheus Edizioni S.r.l., Piazza di Porta Ravegnana 1, Bologna, 40126, Italy. TEL 39-051-226468, FAX 39-051-263720, website@utorpheus.com, http://www.utorpheus.com. Ed. Roberto De Caro.

782.4 NZL ISSN 1176-872X
ADD-A-LINE. Variant title: Adeline. Text in English. 200?. 3/yr. **Document type:** *Newsletter.*
Incorporates: Harmony Hi!
Published by: Sweet Adelines International, New Zealand Region 35, c/o Pam Hewett, 143 Moore St, RD 4, Invercargill, New Zealand. communications@sweetadelines.co.nz.

780 BEL ISSN 0001-8171
ADEM; driemaandelijks tijdschrift voor muziekkultuur. Text in Dutch. 1965. q. adv. bk.rev. reprints avail. **Document type:** *Academic/Scholarly.*
Indexed: A22, IIMP, M11, MusicInd, RILM.
—BLDSC (0680.420000), IE, Infotrieve, Ingenta.
Published by: Madrigaal V.Z.W., Herestraat 53, Leuven, 3000, Belgium. FAX 32-16-22-2477. Ed. P Schollaert. Circ: 1,800.

780 681 374 USA
ADVANCE BAND MAGAZINE; the international voice of adult bands. Text in English. 1977. q. USD 30 domestic; USD 45 foreign (effective 2008). adv. bk.rev. bibl.; illus. back issues avail. **Document type:** *Newsletter.* **Description:** For band directors and band music enthusiasts and music educators. Focuses on community concert and band advancement in America and abroad.
Former titles (until 1991): A B C Newsmagazine; (until 1987): A B C Newsletter
Published by: Association of Concert Bands, Inc., c/o Nada Venci, Sec., 6613 Cheryl Ann Dr, Independence, OH 44131-3718. TEL 800-726-8720, secretary@acbands.org, http://www.acbands.org. Circ: 2,000.

780 USA ISSN 1062-404X
AESTHETICS IN MUSIC SERIES. Text in English. 1983. irreg., latest 2010. price varies. back issues avail. **Document type:** *Monographic series, Trade.*
—BLDSC (0730.421000). **CCC.**
Published by: Pendragon Press, PO Box 190, Hillsdale, NY 12529. TEL 518-325-6100, FAX 518-325-6102, orders@pendragonpress.com.

AFRICALIA THE NEWSLETTER. *see* ART

780 ZAF ISSN 0065-4019
ML5
➤ **AFRICAN MUSIC.** Text in English, French. 1948. irreg. (approx. a), latest vol.7, no.4, 1999. ZAR 80, USD 40 per vol. (effective 2001). adv. bk.rev.; music rev. charts; illus.; maps. index. back issues avail.; reprints avail. **Document type:** *Journal, Academic/Scholarly.* **Description:** Publishes articles on all aspects of African music, both traditional and modern, with an emphasis on original reports for a readership of academics and musicians.
Supersedes (in 1954): African Music Society. Newsletter
Indexed: A22, AICP, AbAn, CCA, FR, ISAP, M11, MLA-IB, MusicInd, PCI, RILM.
—BLDSC (0732.900000), IE, Ingenta.
Published by: International Library of African Music, Institute of Social and Economic Research, Rhodes University, Grahamstown, East Cape 6140, South Africa. TEL 27-46-603-8557, FAX 27-46-622-4411, http://ilam.ru.ac.za. Ed., R&P Andrew Tracey. Circ: 300.

781.64 USA
AIDING & ABETTING. Text in English. bi-w. **Document type:** *Magazine, Consumer.* **Description:** Covers the independent music world and features reviews, tour dates, label info, and charts.
Media: Online - full text.
Address: 1308 Shawnee, Durham, NC 27701. TEL 919-682-0045, FAX 919-682-0045, jworley@cent.com. Ed., Pub. Jon Worley.

780 POL ISSN 0239-7080
AKADEMIA MUZYCZNA. PRACE SPECJALNE. Text in Polish. 1984. irreg. per issue exchange basis.
Formerly: Panstwowa Wyzsza Szkola Muzyczna. Prace Specjalne
Published by: Akademia Muzyczna, Ul Zacisze 3, Katowice, 40025, Poland. TEL 48 32 155-4017. **Dist. by:** Ars Polona, Obroncow 25, Warsaw 03933, Poland.

780 POL
AKADEMIA MUZYCZNA. SKRYPTY. Text in Polish. 1984. irreg. per issue exchange basis.
Formerly: Panstwowa Wyzsza Szkola Muzyczna. Skrypty
Published by: Akademia Muzyczna, Ul Zacisze 3, Katowice, 40025, Poland. TEL 48-32-155-4017. **Dist. by:** Ars Polona, Obroncow 25, Warsaw 03933, Poland.

780 POL
AKADEMIA MUZYCZNA. SPRAWOZDANIA. Text in Polish. a. per issue exchange basis.
Formerly: Panstwowa Wyzsza Szkola Muzyczna. Sprawozdania
Published by: Akademia Muzyczna, Ul Zacisze 3, Katowice, 40025, Poland. TEL 48 32 155-4017. **Dist. by:** Ars Polona, Obroncow 25, Warsaw 03933, Poland.

780 POL
AKADEMIA MUZYCZNA. WYDAWNICTWA OKOLICZNOSCIOWE. Text in Polish. irreg. per issue exchange basis.
Formerly: Panstwowa Wyzsza Szkola Muzyczna. Wydawnictwa Okolicznosciowe
Published by: Akademia Muzyczna, Ul Zacisze 3, Katowice, 40025, Poland. TEL 48 32 155-4017. **Dist. by:** Ars Polona, Obroncow 25, Warsaw 03933, Poland.

780 DEU ISSN 1861-9053
ML410.M9
AKADEMIE FUER MOZART-FORSCHUNG DER INTERNATIONALEN STIFTUNG MOZARTEUM SALZBURG. MOZART-JAHRBUCH. Text in English, German. 1950. a. adv. index. **Document type:** *Journal, Academic/Scholarly.*
Former titles (until 2005): Mozart-Jahrbuch (0342-0256); (until 1955): Internationalen Stiftung Mozarteum Salzburg. Mozart-Jahrbuch (0077-1805)
Indexed: DIP, IBR, IBZ, PCI, RILM.
—IE.
Published by: (Internationale Stiftung Mozarteum AUT), Baerenreiter Verlag, Heinrich-Schuetz-Allee 35, Kassel, 34131, Germany. TEL 49-561-3105154, FAX 49-561-3105195, order@baerenreiter.com, http://www.baerenreiter.com. Circ: 1,000.

780 NLD ISSN 0929-3787
AKKOORD. Text in Dutch. 1951. 6/yr. EUR 32.50 domestic; EUR 42.50 in Europe; EUR 52.50 elsewhere (effective 2009). adv. bk.rev. illus. **Document type:** *Magazine, Consumer.* **Description:** Covers music history, building of musical instruments, music interpretation, music making, musicians, association news, and reports of music events. Includes list of courses and activities, classified adds.
Formerly (until 1993): Huismuziek (0018-7097)
Indexed: RILM.
Published by: Uitgeverij de Inzet, Postbus 11497, Amsterdam, 1001 GL, Netherlands. TEL 31-20-6755308, FAX 31-20-5312019. Eds. Diet Scholten, Tettje Halbertsma. **Co-publisher:** Keijser 18 Mediaproducties.

787.87 DEU ISSN 0946-9397
AKUSTIK GITARRE. Text in German. 1994. bi-m. EUR 22.80 domestic; EUR 33 in Europe; EUR 44 elsewhere; EUR 4.20 newsstand/cover (effective 2008). adv. bk.rev.; music rev.; play rev.; video rev. 116 p./no.; back issues avail. **Document type:** *Magazine, Consumer.*
Related titles: Online - full text ed.
Indexed: IBR, IBZ.
Published by: Acoustic Music GmbH & Co. KG, Jahnstr 1a, Osnabrueck, 49080, Germany. TEL 49-541-710020, FAX 49-541-708667, office@acoustic-music.de, http://www.acoustic-music.de. Ed. Andreas Schulz. Pub. Peter Finger. Adv. contact Mecthild Moreno TEL 49-541-63613. B&W page EUR 1,680, color page EUR 2,650; trim 185 x 254. Circ: 20,000 (paid).

780 BEL ISSN 2032-5371
ML265
▼ **ALAMIRE FOUNDATION. JOURNAL.** Text in English. 2009. s-a. EUR 65 combined subscription (print & online eds.) (effective 2012). **Document type:** *Journal, Academic/Scholarly.* **Description:** Covers musicological research, including analysis, music theory, palaeography and notation, source studies, archival research, music and institutions, and aesthetics.
Related titles: Online - full text ed.
Published by: Brepols Publishers, Begijnhof 67, Turnhout, 2300, Belgium. TEL 32-14-448020, FAX 32-14-428919, periodicals@brepols.net, http://www.brepols.net.

780 USA ISSN 1555-8819
ALARM. Text in English. 1995. bi-m. USD 25 domestic; USD 35 in Canada; USD 45 elsewhere (effective 2009). adv. **Document type:** *Magazine, Consumer.* **Description:** Features unique, inspiring, and astonishing stories from the independent music and art community.
Formerly (until 200?): Straight Force
Published by: Alarm Press LLC, 53 W Jackson, Ste 1005, Chicago, IL 60604. TEL 312-341-1290, FAX 312-341-1301, music@alarmpress.com. Pub. Chris Forle. Adv. contact Andrew Myers. page USD 2,500; trim 8.375 x 10.813. Circ: 4,000 (paid).

780 USA
ALARM CLOCK; women in alternative music and female vocalists. Text in English. 1990. 4/yr. USD 6 for 3 issues (effective 2000). bk.rev.; rec.rev.
Address: PO Box 1551, Royal Oak, MI 48068. TEL 313-593-9677, FAX 313-593-9306. Ed., Pub. Allen Salyer. Circ: 250.

780 GBR ISSN 0969-3548
ALDEBURGH STUDIES IN MUSIC. Text in English. 1993. irreg., latest vol.8, 2009. USD 90, GBP 45 per vol. (effective 2010). back issues avail. **Document type:** *Monographic series, Trade.*
—BLDSC (0786.808440).
Published by: (Britten-Pears Library), Boydell Press (Subsidiary of: Boydell & Brewer Ltd.), Whitwell House, St Audry's Park Rd, Melton, Woodbridge, Suffolk IP12 1SY, United Kingdom. TEL 44-1394-610600, FAX 44-1394-610316, trading@boydell.co.uk. Ed. Dr. Jenny Doctor.

780 USA
ALL ABOUT JAZZ. Text in English. 1995. d. adv. **Document type:** *Magazine, Consumer.* **Description:** Covers the past, present, and future of jazz from an international perspective. It is for jazz fans by jazz fans. It offers fans the opportunity to express their opinion on a variety of jazz and jazz-related subjects.
Media: Online - full text.
Address: 761 Sproul Road, #211, Springfield, PA 19064 . TEL 215-362-2852. Pub. Michael Ricci TEL 610-690-0326.

ALL ACCESS. *see* MOTION PICTURES

780 CAN ISSN 0838-7796
ALL ACCESS PASS. Text in English. 1987. m.
Address: 3 Manorcrest St, Bramlea, ON L6S 2W6, Canada. TEL 416-791-5574.

ALLEGRO. *see* LABOR UNIONS

782.3 DEU ISSN 0569-0609
ALLGEMEINER CAECILIEN-VERBAND. SCHRIFTENREIHE. Text in German. 1956. irreg., latest vol.15. price varies. **Document type:** *Monographic series, Academic/Scholarly.*
Published by: Allgemeiner Caecilien-Verband fuer Deutschland, Andreasstr 9, Regensburg, 93059, Germany. TEL 49-941-84339, FAX 49-941-8703432, info@acv-deutschland.de, http://www.acv-deutschland.de.

781.64 USA
ALLMUSIC. Text in English. 1991. m. adv. **Document type:** *Guide, Trade.* **Description:** A comprehensive database of 21th century popular music and musicians, including discographies and a glossary.
Formerly (until 2005): All-Music Guide
Media: Online - full text.
Published by: All Media Guide, 1168 Oak Valley Dr, Ann Arbor, MI 48108. http://www.allmusicguide.com. Adv. contact Chris Smith TEL 310-210-9344.

780 DEU ISSN 0942-9034
ML5
ALTE MUSIK AKTUELL; aktuelle Information fuer alte Musik. Text in German. 1985. m. (11/yr.). EUR 30.50 domestic; EUR 33 in Europe; EUR 35 elsewhere (effective 2002). index. back issues avail. **Document type:** *Bulletin, Academic/Scholarly.*
Published by: Pro Musica Antiqua, Postfach 100830, Regensburg, 93008, Germany. TEL 49-941-52687, FAX 49-941-53094, pro.musica.antiqua@t-online.de, http://www.promusicaantiqua.de. Ed. Stephan Schmid. Circ: 2,000.

781.6 USA ISSN 1937-2701
ALTERCATION. Text in English. 2001. q. USD 15 (effective 2007).
Document type: *Magazine, Consumer.* **Description:** Reports the latest in the punk, alternative, rockabilly and independent music scene including album releases and reviews, concerts, and artist interviews.
Published by: Altercation Press, PO Box 1509, Austin, TX 78767. altercation@altercation.net. Ed. Justin Habersaat.

781.66 USA ISSN 1524-6272
ML1
ALTERNATE MUSIC PRESS; an online music archive. Abbreviated title: A M P. Text in English. 1997. irreg. free (effective 2007). adv. bk.rev. back issues avail. **Document type:** *Newsletter, Consumer.* **Description:** Features interviews, music news, articles and links of music Web sites.
Media: Online - full text.
Address: PO Box 2643, Los Angeles, CA 90078-2643. TEL 323-934-4602. Ed., Pub., R&P, Adv. contact Ben Kettlewell. Circ: 3,000,000.

ALTERNATE ROOTS NEWSLETTER. *see* THEATER

781.64 USA ISSN 1065-1667
ML3533.8
ALTERNATIVE PRESS. Variant title: A P. Text in English. 1969. m. USD 12 (effective 2009). adv. illus. reprints avail. **Document type:** *Magazine, Consumer.*
Related titles: Online - full text ed.
Indexed: IIMP.
Published by: Alternative Press Magazine, Inc., 1305 W 80th St, Ste 2 F, Cleveland, OH 44102-1996. TEL 216-631-1510, 800-339-2675, FAX 216-631-1016. Ed. Jason Pettigrew. Pub. Norman Wonderly.

780.43 ITA ISSN 1120-4540
ML5
AMADEUS. Text in Italian. 1989. m. EUR 78.40 (effective 2009). adv. music rev. illus. **Document type:** *Magazine, Consumer.* **Description:** Explores the world of classical music, from its rich history to today's performances; includes critical analyses by leading authorities.
Related titles: Online - full text ed.; Optical Disk - DVD ed.: ISSN 1828-2504. 2006; French ed.; Supplement(s): Amadeus Plus. ISSN 1828-2512. 2006.
Indexed: RILM.
Published by: De Agostini Editore, Via G da Verrazzano 15, Novara, 28100, Italy. TEL 39-0321-4241, FAX 39-0321-424305, info@deagostini.it, http://www.deagostini.it. Circ: 27,644 (paid).

780 USA ISSN 0065-6704
AMATEUR CHAMBER MUSIC PLAYERS. DIRECTORY. Text in English. 1949. a. membership. **Document type:** *Directory.*
Published by: Amateur Chamber Music Players, Inc., 1123 Broadway, Ste 304, New York, NY 10010-2007. TEL 212-645-7424, FAX 212-741-2678. Circ: 4,800.

780 USA
AMATEUR CHAMBER MUSIC PLAYERS. NEWSLETTER. Text in English. 1947. 3/yr. membership. **Document type:** *Newsletter.*
Formerly: Amateur Chamber Music Players. Annual Newsletter
Published by: Amateur Chamber Music Players, Inc., 1123 Broadway, Ste 304, New York, NY 10010-2007. TEL 212-645-7424, FAX 212-741-2678. Eds. Sally R Bagg, Susan M Lloyd. Circ: 1,800.

781 ESP ISSN 2013-3553
AMAZING SOUNDS. Text in Spanish. 1996. m. back issues avail. **Document type:** *Magazine, Consumer.*
Media: Online - full text.
Address: Apdo de Correso 727, Tarrasa, Barcelona, Spain. amazingsounds@amazings.com, http://www.amazings.com/.

781.64 USA
AMAZING SOUNDS; the alternative music e-magazine. Text in English. 1996. irreg.
Media: Online - full content.

784.18 NOR ISSN 1890-3932
AMBIS. Text in Norwegian. 1980. q. adv. **Document type:** *Magazine, Consumer.*
Formerly (until 2007): Musikkorpsavisa (0808-1840); Which superseded in part (in 1995): Bedre Korps (0802-6343); Which was formerly (until 1989): Janitsjar'n (0332-9437)
Related titles: Online - full text ed.: 2004.
Published by: Norges Musikkorps Forbund/Norwegian Band Federation, PO Box 674, Sentrum, Bergen, 5807, Norway. TEL 47-81-556777, FAX 47-40-001707, post@musikkorps.no, http://www.musikkorps.no. Ed. Haakon Magstad. Adv. contact Birgit Berg-Olsen. Circ: 50,000.

AMERICAN BELL ASSOCIATION. DIRECTORY. *see* HOBBIES

780.6 USA ISSN 8756-8357
ML410.B81
AMERICAN BRAHMS SOCIETY. NEWSLETTER. Text in English. 1983. s-a. USD 25; USD 20 to senior citizens; USD 15 to students (effective 2003). bk.rev. 2 cols./p.; back issues avail. **Document type:** *Newsletter, Trade.* **Description:** Publishes essays on Johannes Brahms and his music; reports on new publications and research on Brahms and his circle.
Indexed: MAG, RILM.
Published by: American Brahms Society, University of Washington, School of Music, Box 353450, Seattle, WA 98195. TEL 206-543-0400, http://pubpages.unh.edu/~dbmk/webpage.html. Ed. William Horne. R&P George Bozarth. Circ: 1,500.

784 USA ISSN 0002-788X
ML27.U5
AMERICAN CHORAL FOUNDATION. RESEARCH MEMORANDUM SERIES. Abbreviated title: R M S. Text in English. 1959. s-a. free to members (effective 2010). adv. bibl. back issues avail. **Document type:** *Journal, Academic/Scholarly.*
Media: Duplicated (not offset).
Indexed: IBT&D, MAG.
Published by: (American Choral Directors Association), Chorus America, PO Box 2646, Arlington, VA 22202. TEL 202-331-7577, FAX 202-331-7599, service@chorusamerica.org. Ed. L Brett Scott.

784 USA ISSN 0002-7898
ML1
AMERICAN CHORAL REVIEW. Text in English. 1958. s-a. free to members (effective 2010). adv. bk.rev. bibl.; charts; illus. back issues avail. **Document type:** *Journal, Academic/Scholarly.*
Formerly (until 1961): American Choral Foundation. Bulletin
Related titles: Online - full text ed.
Indexed: A01, A20, A22, IIMP, M11, MAG, MLA-IB, MusicInd, PCI, RILM, T02.
—Ingenta.
Published by: Chorus America, 1156 15th St, NW, Ste 310, Washington, DC 20005. TEL 202-331-7577, FAX 202-331-7599, service@chorusamerica.org. Ed. William Weinert.

780 USA
AMERICAN COMPOSERS ALLIANCE BULLETIN. Text in English. 1938. irreg. back issues avail.; reprints avail. **Document type:** *Bulletin.* **Description:** Contains articles and a list of works by and about American composers.
Published by: American Composers Alliance, 170 W 74th St, New York, NY 10023. TEL 212-362-8900, FAX 212-362-8902. Circ: (controlled).

781.62 USA
AMERICAN FOLK MUSIC AND MUSICIANS SERIES. Text in English. 1995. irreg., latest vol.11, 2008. price varies. **Document type:** *Monographic series, Trade.* **Description:** Provides information about folk music, which includes the blues, traditional country, ethnic, bluegrass, singer-songwriters, record companies, various venues and styles, and much more.
Published by: Scarecrow Press, Inc. (Subsidiary of: Rowman & Littlefield Publishers, Inc.), 4501 Forbes Blvd, Ste 200, Lanham, MD 20706. TEL 301-459-3366, 800-462-6420, FAX 301-429-5748, 800-338-4550, custserv@rowman.com, http://www.scarecrowpress.com. Eds. Ron Pen, Ronald D Cohen TEL 219-980-6661. Pub. Mr. Edward Kurdyla TEL 301-459-3366 ext 5604.

780 USA ISSN 0888-8701
ML410.H13
AMERICAN HANDEL SOCIETY. NEWSLETTER. Text in English. 1986. 3/yr. USD 20 (effective 1998). bk.rev. **Document type:** *Newsletter.* **Description:** Conducts research in the life and work of the composer.
Indexed: RILM.
Published by: American Handel Society, Inc., c/o University of Maryland, School of Music, 2114 Tawes Fine Arts Bldg, College Park, MD 20742. TEL 301-405-5523, FAX 301-314-9504. Ed., R&P Richard King. Circ: 170.

787.5 USA ISSN 0002-869X
ML1
➤ **AMERICAN HARP JOURNAL.** Text in English. 19??. s-a. free to members (effective 2010). adv. bk.rev. bibl.; illus. **Document type:** *Journal, Academic/Scholarly.* **Description:** Contains biographies of major figures of the past and present, bibliographies, historical studies, listings of publications and recordings, articles of educational content for students and teachers, and articles concerning construction and maintenance of the harp.
Incorporates (1997-2004): A H S Teachers Forum; Former titles (until 1967): Harp News (0440-3215); (until 1950): Harp News of the West
Indexed: A01, A26, E08, I05, IIMP, M11, MAG, MusicInd, RILM, S09, T02.
—Ingenta.
Published by: American Harp Society, Inc., c/o Kathleen Moon, PO Box 38334, Los Angeles, CA 90038. TEL 323-469-3050, FAX 323-469-3050, execsecretary@harpsociety.org. Ed. Elizabeth Huntley TEL 518-893-7495. Adv. contact Stacie Johnston TEL 212-243-8511.

780 791.45 USA
AMERICAN IDOL. Text in English. 2005 (Feb.). a. price varies. **Document type:** *Magazine, Consumer.* **Description:** Provides information on the TV show, contest results, and the contestants, etc.
Published by: (19 TV Ltd. GBR, FremantleMedia North America, Inc.), C S M Group, 481 Old Post Rd., Ste. C, North Attleboro, MA 02760. TEL 508-643-4010, FAX 508-643-4025, http://www.csmgroupinc.com/.

780 USA ISSN 0065-8855
AMERICAN INSTITUTE OF MUSICOLOGY. MISCELLANEA. Text in German. 1951. irreg., latest vol.7, 2008. price varies. back issues avail. **Document type:** *Monographic series, Academic/Scholarly.*
Published by: American Institute of Musicology, 8551 Research Way, Ste 180, Middleton, WI 53562. TEL 608-836-9000, 800-736-0070, FAX 608-831-8200, info@corpusmusicae.com. Ed. Paul L Ranzini.

780 USA ISSN 0147-4413
ML410.L7
➤ **AMERICAN LISZT SOCIETY. JOURNAL.** Text in English. 1977. s-a. free to members (effective 2010). adv. bk.rev. abstr.; bibl. reprints avail. **Document type:** *Journal, Academic/Scholarly.* **Description:** Contains articles written by scholars who research topics related to Liszt, his work or his interests and ideals.
Related titles: Microform ed.: (from PQC).
Indexed: A22, ABS&EES, CA, IIMP, M11, MAG, MLA-IB, MusicInd, PCI, RILM, T02.
—Ingenta.
Published by: American Liszt Society, Inc., c/o Justin Kolb, 1136 Hog Mountain Rd, Fleischmanns, NY 12430. TEL 845-586-4457, mellon@catskill.net. Ed. Rena Charnin Muller.

780.6 USA ISSN 0749-341X
ML410.L7
AMERICAN LISZT SOCIETY. NEWSLETTER. Text in English. 1984. s-a. free to members (effective 2010). back issues avail. **Document type:** *Newsletter, Trade.* **Description:** Covers regional activities and worldwide society events, member activities and information on the annual festival.
Related titles: Online - full text ed.: free (effective 2010).
Published by: American Liszt Society, Inc., c/o Justin Kolb, 1136 Hog Mountain Rd, Fleischmanns, NY 12430. TEL 845-586-4457, mellon@catskill.net. Ed. Edward Rath TEL 217-244-2670. Circ: 600.

787 USA ISSN 1041-7176
ML755
AMERICAN LUTHERIE. Text in English. 1973. q. USD 45 domestic membership; USD 49 in Canada & Mexico membership; USD 55 elsewhere membership (effective 2005). adv. bk.rev. illus. 2 cols./p.; back issues avail. **Document type:** *Journal, Trade.* **Description:** Information sharing system for string instrument makers and repairers of all interests and skill levels.
Former titles (until 1985): Guild of American Luthiers. Quarterly; (until vol.4): G.A.L. Newsletter
Indexed: IIMP, M11, MusicInd, RILM, T02.
Published by: Guild of American Luthiers, 8222 S Park Ave, Tacoma, WA 98408-5226. tim@luth.org, http://www.luth.org. Ed., R&P Tim Olsen. Adv. contact Debra Olsen. Circ: 3,000 (controlled).

780 USA ISSN 0734-4392
ML1
➤ **AMERICAN MUSIC.** Text in English. 1983. q. USD 116 combined subscription to institutions (print & online eds.) (effective 2012). adv. bk.rev.; rec.rev.; film rev.; video rev. illus. 128 p./no.; back issues avail. **Document type:** *Journal, Academic/Scholarly.* **Description:** Presents articles on composers, performers, publishers, institutions, events, and the music industry.
Related titles: Microform ed.: (from PQC); Online - full text ed.: ISSN 1945-2349. USD 106 to institutions (effective 2012).
Indexed: A01, A02, A03, A08, A20, A22, A25, A26, A27, ABS&EES, ASCA, AmHI, ArtHuCI, B04, B14, BRD, BRI, CA, CBRI, CurCont, DIP, E01, E08, G08, H07, H08, HAb, HumInd, I05, IBR, IBT&D, IBZ, IIMP, M01, M02, M11, MAG, MLA-IB, MusicInd, P02, P10, P13, P48, P53, P54, PCI, PQC, RASB, RILM, S08, S09, SCOPUS, T02, W03, W07.
—BLDSC (0845.800000), IE, Infotrieve, Ingenta. **CCC.**
Published by: University of Illinois Press, 1325 S Oak St, Champaign, IL 61820. TEL 217-244-0626, 866-244-0626, FAX 217-244-8082, journals@uillinois.edu. Ed. Neil Lerner. Adv. contact Jeff McArdle TEL 217-244-0381.

780 USA ISSN 1943-9385
ML28.B81
AMERICAN MUSIC REVIEW. Text in English. 1971. s-a. free (effective 2011). adv. bk.rev. bibl.; illus. reprints avail. **Document type:** *Newsletter, Academic/Scholarly.*
Formerly (until 2008): Institute for Studies in American Music. Newsletter (0145-8396)
Related titles: Online - full text ed.: ISSN 1943-9393.
Indexed: A01, CA, IIMP, M11, MAG, MusicInd, RILM, T02.
—BLDSC (0845.840000).
Published by: H. Wiley Hitchcock Institute for Studies in American Music, Brooklyn College, City University of New York, 2900 Bedford Ave, Brooklyn, NY 11210. TEL 718-951-5655, FAX 718-951-4858, isam@brooklyn.cuny.edu, http://depthome.brooklyn.cuny.edu/isam. Eds. Jeffrey Taylor, Ray Allen. R&P, Adv. contact Ray Allen.

780.7 USA ISSN 0003-0112
➤ **AMERICAN MUSIC TEACHER.** Abbreviated title: A M T. Text in English. 19??. bi-m. USD 30 domestic to non-members; USD 40 foreign to non-members; USD 24 domestic to libraries; USD 6 per issue domestic; USD 7 per issue foreign (effective 2010). adv. bk.rev.; dance rev.; music rev.; software rev.; video rev. illus.; mkt. back issues avail.; reprints avail. **Document type:** *Magazine, Trade.* **Description:** Presents feature articles on aesthetics, composition, criticism, interpretation, musicology, pedagogy and performances.
Former titles (until 1951): Music Teachers National Association. Bulletin; (until 1938): Advisory Council Bulletin
Related titles: Online - full text ed.
Indexed: A01, A02, A03, A08, A22, A25, A26, A27, B04, B14, BRD, BRI, CA, CBRI, DIP, E02, E03, E06, E07, E08, E09, ERI, EdA, EdI, G08, I05, I06, I07, IBR, IBZ, IIMP, L09, M11, MAG, MusicInd, P02, P04, P07, P10, P13, P18, P48, P53, P54, P55, PCI, PQC, RILM, S08, S09, S23, T02, W03, W05.
—BLDSC (0845.850000), IE, Ingenta.
Published by: Music Teachers National Association, 441 Vine St, Ste 3100, Cincinnati, OH 45202. TEL 513-421-1420, 888-512-5278, FAX 513-421-2503, mtnanet@mtna.org. Adv. contact Chad Schwalbach TEL 513-421-1420 ext 232. page USD 1,630; trim 8.125 x 10.875.

781.9 USA ISSN 0362-3300
ML1
➤ **AMERICAN MUSICAL INSTRUMENT SOCIETY. JOURNAL.** Text in English. 1974. a. free to members (effective 2010). adv. bk.rev. bibl.; charts; illus. back issues avail. **Document type:** *Journal, Academic/Scholarly.* **Description:** Promotes understanding of all aspects of the history, design, construction, restoration, and usage of musical instruments in all cultures and from all periods.
Related titles: Online - full text ed.
Indexed: A20, A22, ASCA, ArtHuCI, B24, CA, CurCont, IIMP, M11, MAG, MusicInd, PCI, RILM, SCOPUS, T02, W07.
—IE, Infotrieve, Ingenta.
Published by: American Musical Instrument Society, c/o The Guild Associates, Inc, 389 Main St, Ste 202, Malden, MA 02148. TEL 781-397-8870, FAX 781-397-8887, amis@guildassoc.com. Ed. Janet K Page TEL 901-678-1400. Adv. contact Susan Dearborn TEL 617-876-0934.

781.9 USA ISSN 0160-2365
ML1
AMERICAN MUSICAL INSTRUMENT SOCIETY. NEWSLETTER. Text in English. 1971. s-a. free to members (effective 2010). adv. **Document type:** *Newsletter, Trade.* **Description:** Contains news of members, recent acquisition lists from member institutions, articles and communications, and official notices and news of the Society's activities.
Related titles: Online - full text ed.: free (effective 2010).
Indexed: IIMP, M11, MusicInd, RILM, T02.
Published by: American Musical Instrument Society, c/o The Guild Associates, Inc, 389 Main St, Ste 202, Malden, MA 02148. TEL 781-397-8870, FAX 781-397-8887, amis@guildassoc.com. Ed. Kelly J White TEL 505-507-6992.

780 USA ISSN 1099-6796
ML27.U5
AMERICAN MUSICOLOGICAL SOCIETY. DIRECTORY. Abbreviated title: A M S Directory. Text in English. a. free to members (effective 2004). **Document type:** *Directory, Trade.*
Former titles (until 1987): American Musicological Society. Directory of Members and Subscribers (0192-8368); (until 1978): American Musicological Society. List of Members and Subscribers
Published by: American Musicological Society, 201 S 34th St, Philadelphia, PA 19104-6316. TEL 215-898-8698, 888-611-4267, FAX 215-573-3673, ams@sas.upenn.edu, http://www.ams-net.org.

780 USA ISSN 0003-0139
ML27.U5
➤ **AMERICAN MUSICOLOGICAL SOCIETY. JOURNAL.** Abbreviated title: J A M S. Text in English. 1931. 3/yr. USD 156 combined subscription to institutions (print & online eds.) (effective 2012). adv. bk.rev. charts; illus. Index. back issues avail.; reprint service avail. from PSC. **Document type:** *Journal, Academic/Scholarly.*
Description: Publishes scholarship from all fields of musical inquiry: from historical musicology, critical theory, music analysis, iconography and organology, to performance practice, aesthetics and hermeneutics, ethnomusicology, gender and sexuality, popular music and cultural studies.
Former titles (until 1948): American Musicological Society. Bulletin (1544-4708); (until 1936): New York Musicological Society. Bulletin
Related titles: Online - full text ed.: ISSN 1547-3848. USD 130 to institutions (effective 2012).
Indexed: A01, A02, A03, A08, A20, A21, A22, A25, A26, A27, ABS&EES, ASCA, AmHI, ArtHuCI, B04, B24, BAS, BRD, CA, CurCont, DIP, E01, E08, G08, H07, H08, H09, H10, HAb, HumInd, I05, IBR, IBRH, IBZ, IIMP, M11, MAG, MLA-IB, MusicInd, P02, P10, P48, P53, P54, PCI, PQC, RASB, RI-1, RI-2, RILM, S08, S09, SCOPUS, T02, W03, W07. —IE, Infotrieve, Ingenta. **CCC.**
Published by: (American Musicological Society), University of California Press, Journals Division, 2000 Ctr St, Ste 303, Berkeley, CA 94704. TEL 510-643-7154, 877-262-4226, FAX 510-642-9917, customerservice@ucpressjournals.com. Ed. Kate van Orden. Adv. contact Jennifer Rogers TEL 510-642-6188. Circ: 4,259. **Subscr. to:** 149 5th Ave, 8th Fl, New York, NY 10010. participation@jstor.org.

➤ **AMERICAN MUSICOLOGICAL SOCIETY. L G B T Q STUDY GROUP. NEWSLETTER.** (Lesbian, Gay, Bisexual, Transgender, Queer) *see* HOMOSEXUALITY

786.6 USA ISSN 0164-3150
ML1
THE AMERICAN ORGANIST MAGAZINE. Text in English. 1967. m. USD 52 domestic to non-members; USD 70 foreign to non-members (effective 2007). adv. bk.rev.; music rev.; software rev.; video rev. tr.lit. cum.index. back issues avail. **Document type:** *Magazine, Trade.*
Incorporates (in 1979): A G O Times (0362-5907); Formerly (until 1978): Music (0027-4208)
Related titles: Microfilm ed.: (from PQC).
Indexed: A01, A22, IIMP, M11, MAG, MusicInd, P34, PCI, RILM, T02. —Ingenta.
Published by: American Guild of Organists, 475 Riverside Dr, Ste 1260, New York, NY 10115. TEL 212-870-2310, FAX 212-870-2163, abaglivi@agohq.org. Ed., R&P, Adv. contact Anthony Baglivi. B&W page USD 890; trim 7 x 10. Circ: 25,000. **Co-sponsor:** Royal Canadian College of Organists.

789.91 USA ISSN 0003-0716
ML1
AMERICAN RECORD GUIDE. Text in English. 1932-1972; resumed 1976. bi-m. USD 43 domestic; USD 55 in Canada; USD 65 in Western Europe; USD 70 elsewhere (effective 2010). adv. bk.rev.; rec.rev. illus. index. 300 p./no. 2 cols./p.; back issues avail.; reprints avail. **Document type:** *Magazine, Consumer.* **Description:** Contains feature articles and reviews of music concert as well as 500 classical recordings.
Former titles (until 1944): Listener's Record Guide; (until Sep.1944): The American Music Lover; (until 1935): Music Lover's Guide
Related titles: Microform ed.; Online - full text ed.
Indexed: A01, A02, A03, A08, A09, A10, A22, A26, A27, C05, C12, CBRI, CPerI, G05, G06, G07, G08, G09, H20, I05, I07, IIMP, M01, M02, M06, M11, MAG, MASUSE, MagInd, MusicInd, P02, P10, P48, P53, P54, PMR, PQC, R04, S23, T02, V02, V03, V04.
Published by: Record Guide Productions, 4412 Braddock St, Cincinnati, OH 45204. TEL 513-941-1116, 888-658-1907, subs@americanrecordguide.com. Ed. Donald R Vroon. Adv. contact Elaine Fine TEL 217-345-4310.

788.53 USA ISSN 0003-0724
AMERICAN RECORDER. Text in English. 1960. 2/yr. USD 20 to members; USD 32 to non-members (effective 2005). adv. bk.rev.; music rev.; rec.rev.; software rev. illus. cum.index every 5 yrs. back issues avail.; reprints avail. **Document type:** *Magazine, Consumer.*
Related titles: Microform ed.: (from PQC); Online - full content ed.: ISSN 1930-3831. 199?; Online - full text ed.; ◆ Supplement(s): American Recorder Society Members' Library.
Indexed: A01, A22, CA, IIMP, M11, MAG, MusicInd, PCI, RILM, T02. —BLDSC (0853.530000), IE, Ingenta.
Published by: American Recorder Society, Inc., 1129 Ruth Dr, Saint Louis, MO 63122-1019. TEL 314-966-4082, 800-491-9588, http://www.recorderonline.org. Ed. Benjamin Dunham. Pub., R&P Gail Nickless. adv.: page USD 500. Circ: 4,000.

780 USA
AMERICAN RECORDER SOCIETY MEMBERS' LIBRARY. Text in English. 1986. irreg. looseleaf. membership. 4 p./no.; back issues avail. **Document type:** *Bulletin, Consumer.* **Description:** Covers sheet music for recorder consort.
Related titles: Online - full content ed.; ◆ Supplement to: American Recorder. ISSN 0003-0724.
Published by: American Recorder Society, Inc., 1129 Ruth Dr, Saint Louis, MO 63122-1019. TEL 303-347-1120, 508-748-1750, FAX 508-748-1928, 303-347-1181. Ed. Benjamin Dunham. Circ: 4,000.

780 USA
AMERICAN RECORDER SOCIETY NEWSLETTER. Text in English. 1980. 5/yr. looseleaf. free membership (effective 2005). **Document type:** *Newsletter, Consumer.* **Description:** Covers calendar of recorder and early music events worldwide and news of society's activities.
Published by: American Recorder Society, Inc., 1129 Ruth Dr, Saint Louis, MO 63122-1019. TEL 314-966-4082, 800-491-9588, FAX 314-966-4649, http://www.americanrecorder.org. Ed. Gail Nickless. Circ: 4,000.

AMERICAN REVIEW. *see* ART

780 USA ISSN 0896-8993
AMERICAN SONGWRITER. Text in English. 1984. bi-m. USD 19.95 domestic; USD 26.95 in Canada & Mexico; USD 39.95 elsewhere (effective 2008). adv. bk.rev. illus. **Document type:** *Magazine, Trade.*
Address: 1303 16th Ave S, 2nd Fl, Nashville, TN 37212. TEL 615-321-6096, FAX 615-321-6097.

780.7 USA ISSN 0003-1313
ML27.U5
AMERICAN STRING TEACHER. Text in English. 1950. q. free to members (effective 2007). adv. bk.rev.; music rev. reprints avail. **Document type:** *Journal, Trade.* **Description:** Keeps members informed of developments and news within the string profession.
Related titles: Microform ed.: (from PQC); Online - full text ed.
Indexed: A22, CA, E03, ERI, IIMP, M11, MAG, MusicInd, RILM, T02. —Ingenta.
Published by: American String Teachers Association, 4153 Chain Bridge Rd, Fairfax, VA 22030. TEL 703-279-2113, FAX 703-279-2114, asta@astaweb.com. Ed. Mary Jane Dye TEL 703-279-2113 ext 12. R&P Laura J Racin. Adv. contact Steve Dilauro. page USD 1,262; trim 7.5 x 10. Circ: 11,500. **Subscr. to:** ASTA National Office, 1806 Robert Fulton Dr, Ste 300, Reston, VA 22091. TEL 703-476-1316.

780 USA ISSN 0193-5372
MT1
AMERICAN SUZUKI JOURNAL. Text in English. 1972. q. free to members. adv. bk.rev. **Document type:** *Journal, Trade.* **Description:** Publication of interest to teachers, parents, and educators dedicated to the advancement of the Suzuki method of music education in the western world.
Indexed: IIMP, M11, MAG, MusicInd, RILM, T02. —Ingenta. **CCC.**
Published by: Suzuki Association of the Americas, PO Box 17310, Boulder, CO 80308-7310. TEL 303-444-0948, 888-378-9854, FAX 303-444-0984, info@suzukiassociation.org. Ed. Pamela Brasch. Circ: 6,700.

787 USA ISSN 0898-5987
ML900
➤ **AMERICAN VIOLA SOCIETY. JOURNAL.** Text in English. 1973. 2/yr. (Spring & Fall). USD 50 domestic; USD 60 foreign (effective 2010). adv. bk.rev. back issues avail. **Document type:** *Journal, Academic/Scholarly.*
Supersedes (after no.28, 1985): American Viola Society. Newsletter
Related titles: Online - full text ed.
Indexed: CA, IIMP, M11, MAG, MusicInd, RILM, T02. —Ingenta.
Published by: American Viola Society, 13140 Colt Rd, Ste 320, LB 120, Dallas, TX 75240-5737. TEL 972-233-9107, info@avsnationaloffice.org, http://www.americanviolasociety.org. Ed., Adv. contact David M. Bynog. B&W page USD 325. Circ: 1,500.

780 FRA ISSN 0154-7283
AMIS DE L'OEUVRE ET LA PENSEE DE GEORGES MIGOT. BULLETIN D'INFORMATION. Text in French. 1976. 2/yr.
Published by: (Amis de l'Oeuvre et la Pensee de Georges Migot), Institut de Musicologie, 22 rue Rene Descartes, Strasbourg, Cedex 67084, France. Ed. Dr. Marc Honegger. Circ: 200.

781.64 USA
AMPLIFIER; indie rock and artists that matter. Text in English. 1997. bi-m. adv. music rev. **Document type:** *Magazine, Consumer.* **Description:** Covers the spectrum of music and sounds loosely termed indie rock.
Media: Online - full content. **Related titles:** Online - full text ed.
Address: 5 Calista Terrace, Westford, MA 01886.

780 IND ISSN 0972-2335
➤ **AMRIT KIRTAN.** Text in English, Hindi, Panjabi. 1989. m. INR 15 newsstand/cover (effective 2011). bk.rev.; music rev. Index. back issues avail. **Document type:** *Magazine, Consumer.* **Description:** Preaches and teaches sikh music. Scholarly and research coverage of sikh scriptures and music.
Related titles: Online - full text ed.
Published by: Amrit Kirtan Trust, c/o Dr Jagir Singh, 422 Sector 15 A, Chandigarh, Uttranjal 160 015, India. TEL 91-172-2772660. Ed. Jagir Singh.

780 USA ISSN 0402-012X
ML27.U5
AMS NEWSLETTER. Text in English. 1971. s-a. free to members; free with subscr. to journal. **Document type:** *Newsletter.* **Description:** Presents current events, awards, conference and regional chapter announcements, and calls for papers.
Indexed: RILM. —**CCC.**
Published by: American Musicological Society, 201 S 34th St, Philadelphia, PA 19104-6316. TEL 215-898-8698, 888-611-4267, FAX 215-573-3673. Ed. Susan Jackson. R&P Robert Judd. Circ: 4,800.

780 DEU ISSN 0569-9827
ML5
ANALECTA MUSICOLOGICA. Text in German. 1963. irreg., latest vol.30, 1998. price varies. illus. **Document type:** *Monographic series, Academic/Scholarly.*
Indexed: RILM. —**CCC.**
Published by: (Deutsches Historisches Institut in Rom, Musikgeschichtliche Abteilung ITA), Laaber-Verlag, Regensburger Str 19, Laaber, 93164, Germany. info@laaber-verlag.de, http://www.laaber-verlag.de.

785 USA ISSN 0091-7176
ML1
THE ANCIENT TIMES. Text in English. 1973. q. USD 15 membership (effective 1999). adv. bk.rev. illus. **Document type:** *Newsletter.*
Published by: Company of Fifers & Drummers, Inc., PO Box 525, Ivoryton, CT 06442. TEL 914-565-8416. Ed., R&P, Adv. contact Vincent J Czepiel. Circ: 2,000.

780 USA
ANDY'S FRONT HALL. Text in English. 1977. s-a. USD 2. bk.rev.; rec.rev. **Document type:** *Catalog.* **Description:** Covers books, recordings and instruments of folk, celtic and world music.
Related titles: Special ed(s).: Andy's Front Hall. Buyer's Guide.
Published by: Front Hall Enterprises, Inc., Wormer Rd, Box 307, Voorheesville, NY 12186. TEL 518-765-4193, FAX 518-765-4344. Ed. Kay L Spence. Circ: 8,000.

ANGLOFILE. *see* MOTION PICTURES

780 CHE
ANNALES PADEREWSKI. Text in French. 1979. a., latest vol.26, 2003. bk.rev. **Document type:** *Bulletin, Academic/Scholarly.* **Description:** Publication containing reminiscences about the life of the Polish pianist. Includes society's news.
Published by: Societe Paderewski a Morges, Centre Culturel, Place du Casino 1, Morges, 1110, Switzerland. info@paderewski.ch, http://www.paderewski.ch. Eds. Rita Rosenstiel, Xavier Salina. Circ: 1,000.

780 USA ISSN 1051-287X
ML156.2
ANNOUNCED..; this month in classical recordings. Text in English. 1988. m. USD 28; USD 44 foreign. adv. **Document type:** *Catalog.* **Description:** Provides a current source of information about new recordings of classical music on compact disc in the United States.
Published by: Bushnell Corporation, 880 W Williams Rd, Bloomington, IN 47404. TEL 812-339-2258, TELEX 966420. Ed., R&P Vinson Bushnell. Circ: 200.

384.554 FRA ISSN 1296-705X
ANNUAIRE DE LA MUSIQUE, DE L'IMAGE ET DU SON. (Partie 1: Radio, Television, HiFi, Electronique, Electroacoustique; Partie 2: Musique) Text in French. a. EUR 22 newsstand/cover (effective 2009). adv. **Document type:** *Directory, Trade.*
Formed by the merger of (1993-1997): Annuaire de la Musique (1257-4066); (1993-1997): HiFi, Radio, TV, Sono, Video (1257-4074); Which superseded in part (in 1993): Annuaire O.G.M. (0066-3565)
Published by: (Office General de la Musique), Alphamedian & Johanet, 38 Bd Henri Sellier, Suresnes, 92156, France. TEL 33-1-47287070, FAX 33-1-47287383, secretariat@alphamedian.fr, http://www.alphamedian.fr.

780 ITA
ANNUARIO MUSICALE ITALIANO. Text in Italian. 1981. biennial. price varies. adv. **Document type:** *Directory, Trade.*
Published by: Comitato Nazionale Italiano Musica, Largo di Torre Argentina 11, Rome, 00186, Italy. TEL 39-06-6819061, FAX 39-06-68190651, info@cidim.it, http://www.cidim.it.

780 POL ISSN 1509-4308
ML3469
ANTENA KRZYKU; magazyn kultury kultowej. Text in Polish. 1987. bi-m. 80 p./no.; **Document type:** *Magazine, Consumer.*
Address: ul Na Polance 10d/6, Wroclaw, 51109, Poland. Ed. Arkadiusz Marczynski. Circ: 3,000.

780 746.9 USA
ANTHEM. Text in English. 6/yr. USD 19 domestic; USD 40 in Canada; USD 55 elsewhere (effective 2006). **Document type:** *Magazine, Consumer.*
Published by: Anthem Magazine, 110 West Ocean Blvd., 10th Fl, Long Beach, CA 90802. info@anthem-magazine.com. Ed. Dustin A Beatty.

780 306 USA
ANTHEM (NASHVILLE). Text in English. irreg. USD 1 per issue. **Description:** Covers music and other areas of popular culture, including comparative reviews of men's magazines.
Address: PO Box 158324, Nashville, TN 37215. Ed. Keith A Gordon.

ANTHEM (ST. PETERSBURG); the American experience in words, music and art. *see* LITERATURE

ANTIMOVSKI HAN. *see* ART

780 ESP ISSN 1136-2642
ANUARIO DE GAITA. Text in Spanish. 1986. a. **Document type:** *Yearbook, Consumer.*
Indexed: RILM.
Published by: Escola Provincial de Gaitas, Deputacion de Ourense, Ourense, E-32080, Spain. TEL 34-988-227314, FAX 34-988-244350.

780 ESP ISSN 0211-3538
ANUARIO MUSICAL; revista de musicologia del CSIC. Text in Spanish. 1946. a. abstr. back issues avail. **Document type:** *Journal, Academic/Scholarly.* **Description:** Contains articles of musicographers, musicians and related fields.
Related titles: Online - full text ed.: ISSN 1988-4125. free (effective 2011).
Indexed: IBR, IBZ, IIMP, M11, MLA-IB, MusicInd, P09, PCI, RILM. —**CCC.**
Published by: (Consejo Superior de Investigaciones Cientificas (C S I C), Institucion "Mila I. Fontanals"), Consejo Superior de Investigaciones Cientificas (C S I C), Departamento de Publicaciones, Vitruvio 8, Madrid, 28006, Spain. publ@csic.es, http://www.publicaciones.csic.es.

781.654 USA ISSN 1524-6728
ANY SWING GOES; swing music magazine. Text in English. 1997. w. free (effective 2006). adv. bk.rev.; dance rev.; music rev.; video rev. illus. back issues avail. **Document type:** *Newsletter, Consumer.* **Description:** Focuses on swing music, dancing and information related to music. Includes current news, show reviews, interviews with revival artists.
Media: Online - full text.
Published by: Douglas Leclair, Ed. & Pub., PO Box 721675, San Diego, CA 92172-7716. TEL 858-484-7716, FAX 801-382-6409, dleclair@anyswinggoes.com. Ed., R&P, Adv. contact Douglas LeClair. Circ: 64,000 (controlled).

APPLAUS; Kultur-Magazin. *see* THEATER

051 USA ISSN 1067-5108
THE AQUARIAN WEEKLY. Text in English. 1969. w. USD 99 (effective 1998). adv. bk.rev.; film rev. illus.; tr.lit. **Document type:** *Newspaper, Consumer.* **Description:** Covers the New Jersey tri-state area alternative music world.
Former titles (until Oct. 1992): East Coast Rocker; (until 1986): Aquarian (0739-1919)
Related titles: Microfilm ed.
Published by: Arts Weekly, Inc., 52 Sindle Ave, PO Box 1140, Little Falls, NJ 07424. TEL 973-812-6766, FAX 973-812-5420, editor@theaquarian.com, http://www.theaquarian.com. Ed. Chris Uhl. Pubs. Chris Farinas, Diane Casazza. adv.: B&W page USD 1,352; trim 14.75 x 11. Circ: 40,000.

780 USA
AQUI MILWAUKEE. Text in English. bi-m. USD 11.95 domestic (effective 2008). adv. **Document type:** *Magazine, Consumer.* **Description:** Presents local Latino performers spanning various artistic disciplines and genres.
Published by: Milwaukee Journal Sentinel, Specialty Media Division, 4101 W Burnham St, Milwaukee, WI 53215. TEL 414-647-4721, FAX 414-647-4723. Ed. Raul Vasquez. Pub. Cristy Garcia-Thomas. Adv. contact Javier Lopez. color page USD 2,480; trim 8.125 x 10.75. Circ: 10,000.

780 DEU ISSN 0948-1222
ARBEITSGEMEINSCHAFT FUER RHEINISCHE MUSIKGESCHICHTE. MITTEILUNGEN. Text in German. 1955. irreg. membership. bk.rev. cum.index. **Document type:** *Journal, Academic/Scholarly.*
Indexed: RILM.
Published by: Arbeitsgemeinschaft fuer Rheinische Musikgeschichte e.V., c/o Musikwissenschaftliches Institut der Universitaet zu Koeln, Albertus-Magnus-Platz, Cologne, 50931, Germany. TEL 49-221-4702249, FAX 49-221-4705151, Robert.v.Zahn@t-online.de, http://www.ag-musikgeschichte.uni-koeln.de. Circ: 400.

787 ITA ISSN 1971-2022
ARCHI MAGAZINE. Text in Italian. 2006. bi-m. **Document type:** *Journal, Trade.*
Published by: Accademia Italiana drgli Archi, Via Eschilo 231, Rome, 00124, Italy. TEL 39-06-5098155, FAX 39-06-96708622, info@accademia-archi.it, http://www.accademia-archi.it.

780 DEU ISSN 0003-9292
ML5
➤ **ARCHIV FUER MUSIKWISSENSCHAFT.** Text in English, German. 1918. q. EUR 174.80; EUR 53 newsstand/cover (effective 2012). adv. charts; illus. index. back issues avail.; reprint service avail. from SCH. **Document type:** *Journal, Academic/Scholarly.*
Related titles: Online - full text ed.; ◆ Supplement(s): Archiv fuer Musikwissenschaft. Beihefte. ISSN 0570-6769.
Indexed: A20, A22, ASCA, ArtHuCI, CA, CurCont, DIP, H14, IBR, IBZ, IIMP, M11, MLA-IB, MusicInd, P10, P48, P53, P54, PCI, PQC, RASB, RILM, SCOPUS, T02, W07.
—IE, Infotrieve. **CCC.**
Published by: Franz Steiner Verlag GmbH, Birkenwaldstr 44, Stuttgart, 70191, Germany. TEL 49-711-25820, FAX 49-711-2582290, service@steiner-verlag.de. Ed. Albrecht Riethmueller. R&P Thomas Schaber. Adv. contact Susanne Szoradi. Circ: 750 (paid and controlled).

780 DEU ISSN 0570-6769
ML5
ARCHIV FUER MUSIKWISSENSCHAFT. BEIHEFTE. Text in English, German. 1966. irreg., latest vol.68, 2011. price varies. **Document type:** *Monographic series, Academic/Scholarly.*
Related titles: ◆ Supplement to: Archiv fuer Musikwissenschaft. ISSN 0003-9292.
Published by: Franz Steiner Verlag GmbH, Birkenwaldstr 44, Stuttgart, 70191, Germany. TEL 49-711-25820, FAX 49-711-2582290, franz.steiner.verlag@t-online.de, http://www.steiner-verlag.de.

ARCHIVI DI LECCO E DELLA PROVINCIA. *see* ART

780.903 ITA
ARCHIVUM MUSICUM; collana di testi rari. Text in Italian. 1978. irreg. price varies. **Document type:** *Monographic series, Academic/Scholarly.*
Published by: Studio per Edizioni Scelte (S P E S), Lungarno Guicciardini 9, Florence, FI 50125, Italy. TEL 39-055-218690, FAX 39-055-280592, http://www.spes-editore.com.

786.2 GBR ISSN 1465-9387
ARIETTA. Text in English. 1999. a. free to members (effective 2010). back issues avail. **Document type:** *Journal, Trade.* **Description:** Provides articles, reviews and society news and views.
Published by: Beethoven Piano Society of Europe, c/o The Membership Secretary, 12 Heybridge Dr, Barkingside, Essex IG6 1PE, United Kingdom. TEL 44-208-5519290. Ed. Malcolm Miller.

781.65 USA
ARIZONA JAZZ. Text in English. q. adv.
Related titles: Online - full text ed.
Published by: Targeted Media Communications, 1241 E. Washington St., # 206, Phoenix, AZ 85034-1172. TEL 602-230-8161, FAX 602-230-8162. Pub. Tony Brown. adv.: color page USD 2,450, B&W page USD 2,205; trim 7.125 x 9.4375.

780 USA ISSN 0518-6129
ARIZONA MUSIC NEWS. Text in English. 1956. 3/yr. USD 15 to non-members; USD 5 per issue to non-members; free to members (effective 2010). adv. tr.lit. **Document type:** *Journal, Academic/Scholarly.* **Description:** Covers issues in music education at all levels.
Published by: Arizona Music Educators Association, Inc., 1806 Robert Fulton Dr, Reston, VA 20191. TEL 703-860-4000, 800-336-3768, FAX 703-860-1531, william.patterson@dvusd.org.

ARKANSAS COUNTRY DANCER. *see* DANCE

781.64 ITA
ARLEQUINS. Text in English, Italian. 1990. 4/yr. **Document type:** *Magazine, Consumer.* **Description:** Aimed at promoting and spreading all aspects of progressive rock music.
Former titles (until 2000): Arlequins Newsletter (Print Edition); (until 1997): Arlequins
Media: Online - full text.
Address: c/o Alberto Nucci, Via Paparoni 6, Siena, 53100, Italy. Ed., Pub. Alberto Nucci.

780 MEX ISSN 0188-8854
ARMONIA. Text in Spanish. q. MXN 12.50 per issue (effective 1999). **Description:** Includes original papers, interviews, essays and news on music and related issues.
Indexed: C01.
Published by: Universidad Nacional Autonoma de Mexico, Escuela Nacional de Musica, XICOTENCATL 126, Del Carmen, Mexico City, DF 04100, Mexico. TEL 52-5-6054570, FAX 52-5-6041127. Ed. Graciela Agudelo Murgia.

783 028.5 ITA ISSN 0391-5425
M1
ARMONIA DI VOCI. Text in Italian. 1946. 4/yr. EUR 55 domestic; EUR 64 foreign (effective 2009). adv. **Document type:** *Magazine, Consumer.*
Published by: (C E C Don Bosco), Editrice Elledici, Corso Francia 214, Cascine Vica - Rivoli, TO 10098, Italy. TEL 39-011-9552111, FAX 39-011-9574048, mail@elledici.org, http://www.elledici.org.

780 AUT ISSN 2072-182X
ARNOLD SCHOENBERG CENTER. NEWSLETTER. Text in German. 1998. a. **Document type:** *Newsletter, Trade.*
Published by: Wissenschaftszentrum Arnold Schoenberg, Palais Fanto, Schwarzenbergplatz 6, Vienna, 1030, Austria. TEL 43-1-7121888, FAX 43-1-712188888, office@schoenberg.at.

781.65 USA
ARNOLD SHAW RESEARCH CENTER FOR POPULAR MUSIC. NEWSLETTER. Text in English. m. **Document type:** *Newsletter.* **Description:** Discusses the lives and works of jazz legends.
Published by: University of Nevada, Las Vegas, Arnold Shaw Research Center for Popular Music, 4505 S Maryland Pkwy, Box 455053, Las Vegas, NV 89154-5053. Ed. Bill Willard.

780 HUN ISSN 0571-1304
AM100.G9
ARRABONA. Text in Hungarian. 1959. 3/w.
Indexed: AICP, FR, RILM.
Published by: Xantus Janos Muzeum, Szechenyi Platz 5, Gyor, Hungary.

781.64 DEU
ARS!; Das Magazin fuer Musik, HighEnd, HiFi und Zubehoer. Text in German. 1989. 5/yr. EUR 15; EUR 3 newsstand/cover (effective 2008). adv. **Document type:** *Magazine, Consumer.*
Published by: Ars! Joerg Kessler, Osdorfer Landstr 251 A, Hamburg, 22549, Germany. TEL 49-40-8502345, FAX 49-40-8505656, arskessler@t-online.de. Ed. Joerg Kessler. adv.: B&W page EUR 890, color page EUR 1,250. Circ: 6,000 (paid and controlled).

▼ **ARS BILDUMA.** *see* ART

782 USA ISSN 1043-3848
ML1
➤ **ARS LYRICA.** Text in English. 1981. irreg. (approx 1/yr.). USD 65.30 combined subscription (print & online eds.) (effective 2010). bk.rev. **Document type:** *Journal, Academic/Scholarly.* **Description:** Articles and other works dealing with relations of words and music in any aspect.
Related titles: Online - full text ed.
Indexed: A01, CA, IIMP, M11, MLA-IB, MusicInd, PCI, T02.
Published by: Lyrica Society for Word - Music Relations http://www.lyricasociety.org.

786.6 DEU ISSN 0004-2919
ML5
ARS ORGANI; Zeitschrift fuer das Orgelwesen. Text in German. 1951. q. adv. bk.rev.; music rev. illus. **Document type:** *Journal, Academic/Scholarly.*
Indexed: IBR, IBZ, IIMP, M11, MusicInd, RILM.
—**CCC.**
Published by: (Gesellschaft der Orgelfreunde e.V.), Verlag Merseburger Berlin GmbH, Naumburger Strasse 40, Kassel, 34127, Germany. TEL 49-561-78980911, FAX 49-561-78980916, vertrieb@merseburger.de, http://www.merseburger.de. Ed. Martin Balz.

ART & ACADEME. *see* ART

ART MATTERS. *see* THEATER

780 USA
ARTHUR MAGAZINE (GLENDALE); a review of life, arts and thought. Text in English. 2002. bi-m. USD 6 per issue domestic; USD 8 per issue in Canada; USD 11 per issue elsewhere (effective 2008). adv. **Document type:** *Magazine, Consumer.* **Description:** Presents a mixture of travel writing, investigative journalism and creative nonfiction alongside ahead-of-the-curve music coverage, film commentary and profiles of international icons.
Published by: Arthur Publishing Corp., 1146 N Central Ave, #441, Glendale, CA 91202. TEL 323-633-1424, FAX 323-395-0734. Ed., Pub. Jay Babcock. Adv. contact Jesse Locks TEL 916-548-7716. color page USD 2,430; trim 10 x 12. Circ: 50,000 (paid and controlled).

780 HRV ISSN 0587-5455
ML5
ARTI MUSICES/CROATIAN MUSICOLOGICAL REVIEW. Text in Croatian; Summaries in English. 1969. s-a. USD 46. adv. bk.rev. bibl.; illus. back issues avail. **Document type:** *Journal, Academic/Scholarly.*
Indexed: A20, ArtHuCI, IIMP, M11, MusicInd, PCI, RILM, T02, W07.
Published by: Hrvatsko Muzikolosko Drustvo/Croatian Musicological Society, Ilica 16/III, Zagreb, 10000, Croatia. info@hmd-music.hr, http://www.hmd-music.hr. Ed. Vjera Katalinic.

ARTISTEN. *see* LABOR UNIONS

▼ **ARTS.** *see* ART

ARTS MANAGEMENT. *see* THEATER

ARTSFOCUS. *see* MUSEUMS AND ART GALLERIES

780 950 USA ISSN 0044-9202
ML1
➤ **ASIAN MUSIC.** Text in English. 1968. s-a. USD 68 domestic to institutions; USD 78 in Canada to institutions; USD 85 elsewhere to institutions (effective 2011). adv. bk.rev.; music rev.; video rev. bibl.; charts; illus.; maps. back issues avail.; reprints avail. **Document type:** *Journal, Academic/Scholarly.* **Description:** Brings out all aspects of the performing arts of Asia and their cultural context.
Related titles: Online - full text ed.: ISSN 1553-5630.
Indexed: A20, A22, A27, AICP, ASCA, ArtHuCI, BAS, CurCont, E01, FR, IBR, IBZ, IIMP, M11, MAG, MLA, MLA-IB, MusicInd, P10, P48, P53, P54, PCI, PQC, RASB, RILM, SCOPUS, T02, W07.
—BLDSC (1742.701000), IE, Infotrieve, Ingenta, INIST. **CCC.**
Published by: (Society for Asian Music), University of Texas Press, Journals Division, PO Box 7819, Austin, TX 78713. TEL 512-471-7233 ext 2, FAX 512-232-7178, journals@uts.cc.utexas.edu, http://www.utexas.edu/utpress/journals/journals.html. Eds. Ricardo Trimillos, Stephen Slawek. Adv. contact Leah Dixon TEL 512-232-7618.

780 PRT
ASSOCIACAO PORTUGUESA DE EDUCACAO MUSICAL. BOLETIM. Text in Portuguese. bi-m.
Published by: Associacao Portuguesa de Educacao Musical, Rua Rosa Araujo 6-3, Lisboa, P-1200, Portugal. TEL 351-1-3557118, FAX 351-1-3557118.

780 USA ISSN 1098-8009
ML3919
ASSOCIATION FOR MUSIC AND IMAGERY. JOURNAL. Variant title: Journal of the Association for Music and Imagery. Text in English. 1992. a. USD 24 per issue (effective 2011). back issues avail. **Document type:** *Journal, Academic/Scholarly.*
Related titles: Online - full text ed.
Indexed: A04, C11, CA, M11, P03, PsycholAb, RILM, T02.
Published by: Association for Music & Imagery, 6003 Dawn Vista Oval, Parma, OH 44129. TEL 440-886-4299, FAX 440-888-4134, office@ami-bonnymethod.org.

780 FRA ISSN 1266-7870
ASSOCIATION GEORGE ONSLOW. BULLETIN. Text in French. 1994. irreg. **Document type:** *Journal, Consumer.*
Indexed: RILM.
Published by: Association George Onslow, 5 Rue Armand Guery, Reims, 51100, France. contact@georgeonslow.com.

780 FRA ISSN 0243-3559
ML410.B51
ASSOCIATION NATIONALE HECTOR BERLIOZ. BULLETIN DE LIAISON. Text in French. 1964. a. **Document type:** *Bulletin, Trade.*
Indexed: RILM.
Published by: Association Nationale Hector Berlioz, 69 Rue de la Republique, La Cote St Andre, 38260, France. http://www.berlioz-anhb.com.

M

781.643 USA ISSN 1531-7676
ML3520.8
ATLANTA BLUES SOCIETY NEWS. Text in English. 1996. q.
Published by: Atlanta Blues Society, 931 Monroe Dr. Ste. 102, Atlanta, GA 30308. TEL 404-237-9595, absmail@mindspring.com, http://www.atlantablues.org. Ed. Pat Kreeft. Adv. contact Ronda Wenger.

AUDIO MEDIA; the world's leading professional audio technology magazine. *see* SOUND RECORDING AND REPRODUCTION

781.546 CAN ISSN 1481-8515
AUDIO PROGRAMMERS' DATABASE. Text in English. 1996. a. USD 249 (effective 1999). charts. back issues avail. **Description:** Aimed primarily at radio programmers to assist in music programming and at music lovers interested in music chart performance from l955 to present.
Formed by the merger of (1989-1996): Maple Music (1189-0150); Country Canada (Calgary) (1189-0061)
Related titles: CD-ROM ed.; Online - full text ed.
Published by: Canadian Chart Research, 630 3rd Ave S W, 7th Fl, Calgary, AB T2P 4L4, Canada. TEL 403-269-2969, FAX 403-269-2969. Ed. Ted Kennedy.

AUFGANG; Jahrbuch fuer Denken, Dichten, Musik. *see* PHILOSOPHY

781.642 AUS ISSN 1832-2557
AUSTRALIAN COUNTRY MUSIC. Variant title: A C M. Text in English. 2003. a., latest no.3. AUD 27.50 per issue (effective 2008). **Document type:** *Magazine, Consumer.* **Description:** Designed for Australian country music fans having interest in its history from a researched perspective.
Published by: aicmPress, PO Box 994, Gympie, QLD 4570, Australia. TEL 61-7-54828644. Eds. Geoff Walden, Mark Evans, Philip Hayward.

781.7 AUS
AUSTRALIAN COUNTRY MUSIC NEWSLETTER. Text in English. 1979 (May, no.36). 3/yr. illus. **Document type:** *Newsletter.*
Published by: Don & Noela Gresham, PO Box 186, Murwillumbah, NSW 2484, Australia.

787 AUS ISSN 1329-7686
AUSTRALIAN GUITAR MAGAZINE. Text in English. 1997. bi-m. AUD 49 domestic; AUD 60 in New Zealand; AUD 80 elsewhere (effective 2008). adv. **Document type:** *Magazine, Consumer.* **Description:** Provides in-depth coverage of all elements of guitar playing in this country to a loyal readership made up of serious musicians, novices and recording professionals.
Published by: Next Media, 78 Renwick St, Redfern, NSW 2016, Australia. TEL 61-2-96990333, FAX 61-2-93101315, subs@next.com.au. Ed. Lachlan Marks TEL 61-2-96990314. Pub. Phillip Keir. Adv. contact Chris M Peridis TEL 61-2-96990328. page AUD 2,265; trim 220 x 300. Circ: 20,000.

780 AUS ISSN 1838-3335
▼ **AUSTRALIAN HYSTERIA.** Text in English. 2010. q. AUD 39; AUD 12 per issue (effective 2011). adv. **Document type:** *Magazine, Trade.* **Description:** Bridges the gap between independent artists, bands and businesses with international artists. Exposes Aussie talent and international artists.
Published by: Australian Hysteria Pty Ltd., PO Box 3872, Burleigh Town, QLD 4220, Australia. TEL 61-7-55749113, FAX 61-7-55748110. Circ: 5,000.

780 370 AUS ISSN 0004-9484
ML5
AUSTRALIAN JOURNAL OF MUSIC EDUCATION. (First issue in print; the second issue e-journal) Text in English. 1967. s-a. AUD 75 to non-members; free to members (effective 2011). adv. bk.rev.; rec.rev. abstr.; bibl. **Document type:** *Journal, Academic/Scholarly.* **Description:** Publishes articles that enhance knowledge regarding the teaching and learning of music with a special interest toward the Australian music education community. This may include articles that report results of quantitative or qualitative research studies, summarize bodies of research, present theories, models, or philosophical positions, etc. Articles should include a discussion of implications and applications to music teaching and learning, defined broadly.
Related titles: E-mail ed.; ◆ Supplement to: International Journal of Music Education. ISSN 0255-7614.
Indexed: A26, CA, E03, E07, E08, I05, M11, S09, T02.
Published by: Australian Society for Music Education, PO Box 5, Parkville, VIC 3052, Australia. TEL 61-3-99257807, publications@asme.edu.au, http://www.asme.edu.au/. Ed., Pub., R&P, Adv. contact David Forrest. Circ: 1,000.

615.851540994 AUS ISSN 1036-9457
➤ **AUSTRALIAN JOURNAL OF MUSIC THERAPY.** Abbreviated title: A J M T. Text in English. 1990. a. AUD 46 per issue; free to members (effective 2008). back issues avail. **Document type:** *Journal, Academic/Scholarly.* **Description:** Covers the current research and debate in music therapy.
Related titles: Online - full text ed.
Indexed: A11, A26, C06, C07, CA, I05, IIMP, M11, P03, P24, P25, P48, PQC, PsycInfo, PsycholAb, RILM, T02.
—BLDSC (1810.650000), Ingenta. **CCC.**
Published by: Australian Music Therapy Association Inc., PO Box 79, Turramurra, NSW 2074, Australia. TEL 61-2-94495279, FAX 61-2-99883856, info@austmta.org.au. Ed. Dr. Felicity Baker.

780 AUS ISSN 1323-7292
ML5
AUSTRALIAN MUSIC CALENDAR. Text in English. 1995. m. free (effective 2008). adv. 2 p./no.; back issues avail. **Document type:** *Bulletin, Consumer.* **Description:** Lists concerts and events featuring music by Australian composers and sound artists.
Related titles: Online - full text ed.
Published by: Australian Music Centre Ltd., PO Box N690, Grosvenor Place, NSW 1220, Australia. TEL 61-2-92474677, FAX 61-2-92412873, info@amcoz.com.au, http://www.amcoz.com.au/. Ed. Caitlin Rowley. R&P Harriet Cunningham. Adv. contact Victoria White. B&W page AUD 60; trim 70 x 84. Circ: 200 (controlled); 1,400 (paid).

780 AUS ISSN 1325-5266
ML5
AUSTRALIAN MUSIC RESEARCH. Abbreviated title: A M R. Text in English. 1996. irreg. price varies. back issues avail. **Document type:** *Monographic series, Trade.* **Description:** Aims to promote the study of various areas of research relevant to Australian music and musicians as well as institutions and organizations, in all styles and genres.
Related titles: Online - full text ed.
Indexed: AusPAIS, IIMP, M11, MusicInd, RILM.
—Ingenta.
Published by: Lyrebird Press, University of Melbourne, Faculty of Music, Melbourne, VIC 3010, Australia. TEL 61-3-83443023, FAX 61-3-83445346, lyrebirdpress-info@unimelb.edu.au. Ed. Suzanne Robinson.

615.83706294 AUS ISSN 0156-5184
AUSTRALIAN MUSIC THERAPY ASSOCIATION. BULLETIN. Text in English. 1977. q. free to members. **Document type:** *Bulletin, Academic/Scholarly.* **Description:** Contains articles on pertinent Music Therapy topics, reports on activities of the Association and gives notice of events.
Published by: Australian Music Therapy Association Inc., PO Box 79, Turramurra, NSW 2074, Australia. TEL 61-2-94495279, FAX 61-2-99883856, info@austmta.org.au, http://www.austmta.org.au/.

615.851540994 AUS
AUSTRALIAN MUSIC THERAPY ASSOCIATION. NETWORK. Text in English. irreg. free to members. **Document type:** *Newsletter, Trade.* **Description:** Provides a forum for discussion of professional issues, and includes regular features such as reports on the activities of the various interest groups.
Published by: Australian Music Therapy Association Inc., PO Box 79, Turramurra, NSW 2074, Australia. TEL 61-2-94495279, FAX 61-2-99883856, info@austmta.org.au, http://www.austmta.org.au/.

782 AUS
AUSTRALIAN VOICE (ONLINE). Text in English. irreg. AUD 150 domestic; AUD 165 foreign (effective 2011). back issues avail. **Document type:** *Journal, Academic/Scholarly.* **Description:** Publishes original articles and research articles in fields as voice science and physiology, vocal pedagogy, music literature, voice therapy and performance practice and style.
Media: Online - full text.
Published by: (Australian National Association of Teachers of Singing Inc.), Australian Academic Press Pty. Ltd., 32 Jeays St, Bowen Hills, QLD 4006, Australia. TEL 61-7-32571176, FAX 61-7-32525908, info@australianacademicpress.com.au, http://www.australianacademicpress.com.au. Eds. Helen Mitchell, Scott Harrison.

781.64 USA ISSN 1154-5720
AUTOFACE INK; the manual for the everyday independent. Text in English. 2003. m. USD 2.50 newsstand/cover (effective 2003). adv. **Document type:** *Magazine, Consumer.* **Description:** Dedicated to arts and media.
Published by: AutoFace Records, 5532 Oak Center Dr., Oak Lawn, IL 60453-3864. carol@autofacerecords.com. Ed. Rebecca Mis. R&P John Terrell. Adv. contact April Banks. B&W page USD 325.

780 FRA ISSN 0295-1371
ML5
L'AVANT-SCENE. OPERA. Text in French. 1976. 7/yr. **Document type:** *Magazine, Consumer.*
Formerly (until 1986): L' Avant-Scene. Opera, Operette (0764-2873); Which superseded in part (in 1983): L' Avant-Scene. Opera, Operette, Musique (0764-2881); Which was formerly (until 1982): L' Avant-Scene. Opera (0395-0670)
Indexed: A20, ASCA, ArtHuCI, CurCont, IBT&D, IIPA, RASB, RILM, SCOPUS, W07.
—IE, Infotrieve.
Published by: Editions Premieres Loges, 15 rue Tiquetonne, Paris, 75002, France. TEL 33-1-42335151, FAX 33-1-42338091. Ed., Pub. Michel Pazdro.

781.64 USA ISSN 1072-5032
AP2
AXCESS. Text in English. 1993. 10/yr. USD 25. adv. bk.rev. illus. reprints avail. **Document type:** *Magazine, Consumer.*
Published by: Axcess Ventures, 1214 Stonegate Dr., Eagle Point, OR 97524-9010. Ed., Pub., R&P Matt Drewien. Adv. contact Staci Worthington. Circ: 85,000.

780 746.9 POL ISSN 2081-0938
▼ **B 2 B.** Variant title: Back to Black. Czarne jest Czarne. Text in Polish. 2010. m. PLZ 5.99 newsstand/cover (effective 2011). adv. **Document type:** *Magazine, Consumer.*
Published by: Egmont Polska, ul Dzielna 60, Warsaw, 01029, Poland. TEL 48-22-8384100, FAX 48-22-8384200, poczta@egmont.pl, http://www.egmont.pl. Ed. Agnieszka Wieladek.

780 USA
B A MAGAZINE. Text in English. 1977 (vol.6). irreg. illus.
Published by: Brooklyn Academy of Music, 30 Lafayette Ave, Brooklyn, NY 11217. TEL 718-636-4100.

781.68 GBR ISSN 0966-7180
ML5
B B C MUSIC MAGAZINE; the complete monthly guide to classical music. (British Broadcasting Corporation) Text in English. 1992. m. GBP 58.50; GBP 4.50 newsstand/cover (effective 2009). adv. music rev. illus. Index. reprints avail. **Document type:** *Magazine, Consumer.* **Description:** Contains reviews of new classical music releases, broadcasts and performances. Includes features on instrumentalists, composers, and individual works, as well as listings, interviews, and a music course section.
Related titles: Online - full text ed.; ◆ Supplement(s): B B C Music Magazine. Opera a Celebration. ISSN 1361-9039; ◆ B B C Music Magazine. Symphony Special. ISSN 1359-7744.
Indexed: IBT&D, IIMP, IIPA, M11, MusicInd, PCI, RILM, T02, U01, WBA, WMB.
—CIS.
Published by: (British Broadcasting Corporation (B B C)), B B C Worldwide Ltd., Tower House, 14 Fl, Fairfax St, Bristol, BS1 3BN, United Kingdom. TEL 44-117-9279009, FAX 44-117-9349008, info@bbcmagazinesbristol.com, http://www.bbcworldwide.com, http://www.bbcmagazinesbristol.com/. Ed. Rebecca Franks. Adv. contact Tom Drew TEL 44-117-9338043. page GBP 4,060. Circ: 45,144. **Subscr. to:** Dovetail Services UK Ltd, 800 Guillat Ave, Kent Science Park, Sittingbourne, Kent ME9 8GU, United Kingdom. TEL 44-844-8150855, contact@dovetailservices.com, http://www.dovetailservices.com/. **Dist. by:** Frontline Ltd.

784.2 GBR ISSN 1359-7744
B B C MUSIC MAGAZINE. SYMPHONY SPECIAL. (British Broadcasting Corporation) Text in English. 1994. a. includes with subscr. to B B C Music Magazine.
Related titles: ◆ Supplement to: B B C Music Magazine. ISSN 0966-7180; ◆ Supplement to: B B C Music Magazine (North American Edition).
Published by: (British Broadcasting Corporation (B B C)), B B C Worldwide Ltd., 80 Wood Ln, London, W12 0TT, United Kingdom. TEL 44-181-576-2000, FAX 44-181-576-3824, bbcworldwide@bbc.co.uk, http://www.bbcworldwide.com. **U.S. subscr. to:** Connell Communications, Inc., P O Box 538, Peterborough, NH 03458.

780 USA
B B GUN. Text in English. q. USD 6 newsstand/cover (effective 2004). **Document type:** *Journal, Consumer.*
Published by: B B Gun Magazine, P O Box 5074, Hoboken, NJ 07030. linda@bbgun.org. Ed. Bob Bert.

780.7 CAN ISSN 0705-9019
B C MUSIC EDUCATOR. (British Columbia) Text in English. 1959. q. CAD 82.42 to non-members; CAD 60 to members (effective 2008). adv. bk.rev. illus.; stat. index. **Document type:** *Newsletter, Trade.* **Description:** Covers the study and teaching of music.
Formed by the 1977 merger of: British Columbia Music Educator (0007-0564); B.C. Music Educators' Association. Newsletter (0382-8182)
Indexed: C03, CEI, CMPI, PQC.
Published by: (B.C. Music Educators' Association), British Columbia Teachers' Federation, 100-550 W 6th Ave, Vancouver, BC V5Z 4P2, Canada. TEL 604-871-2283, 800-663-9163, FAX 604-871-2286, http://www.bctf.ca. Eds. Chris Trinidad, Karen V Lee.

780 DEU ISSN 1610-1529
B D M V INFO. Text in German. 1997. q. adv. **Document type:** *Magazine, Trade.*
Formerly (until 2001): B D B V Info (1434-6753)
Published by: (Bundesvereinigung Deutscher Musikverbaende), ConBrio Verlagsgesellschaft mbH, Brunnstr 23, Regensburg, 93053, Germany. TEL 49-941-945930, FAX 49-941-9459350, info@conbrio.de, http://www.conbrio.de. adv.: B&W page EUR 1,250, color page EUR 1,500. Circ: 11,000 (controlled).

786.5 GBR ISSN 0141-4992
B I O S JOURNAL. Cover title: Journal of the British Institute of Organ Studies. Text in English. 1977. a. free to members (effective 2009). bk.rev. **Document type:** *Journal, Academic/Scholarly.* **Description:** Contains about nine essays on organ related subjects from contributors, detailed reviews of restored and new instruments in the UK and music for organ.
Indexed: PCI, RILM.
Published by: (British Institute of Organ Studies), Positif Press, 130 Southfirled Rd, Oxford, OX4 1PA, United Kingdom. TEL 44-1865-243220, FAX 44-1865-243272, http://www.positifpress.com/.

780 CHE
B K G V INFORMATION. Text in German. q.
Address: Birbach 9, Krauchthal, 3326, Switzerland. TEL 034-511930. Ed. Alfred Iseli. Circ: 1,500.

780 USA ISSN 1042-6736
ML3469
B M I: MUSIC WORLD. Text in English. 1962. 4/yr. free to qualified personnel. abstr.
Formerly (until 1987): B M I: The Many Worlds of Music (0045-317X)
Media: Duplicated (not offset). **Related titles:** Microfilm ed.: (from PQC).
Indexed: IIMP, M11, MAG, MusicInd, T02.
Published by: Broadcast Music Inc., 320 W 57th St, New York, NY 10019. TEL 212-586-2000. Ed. Robin Ahrold. Circ: 100,000.

780 USA
B# NEWSLETTER. Text in English. 2000. m. **Description:** Provides articles and columns about music industry and independent musicians.
Media: E-mail.
Published by: National Music Agency, Box 1404, Crockett, TX 75835-1404. bsharpnews@yahoo.com. Ed. Kenny Love.

B P I STATISTICAL HANDBOOK. *see* MUSIC—Abstracting, Bibliographies, Statistics

B P M; music, tech, nightlife, style. (Beats Per Minute) *see* LIFESTYLE

780 JPN
B-PASS. (Backstage Pass) Text in Japanese. m. back issues avail. **Document type:** *Magazine, Consumer.*
Published by: Shinko Music Publishing Co. Ltd., 2-1 Kanda-Ogawa-Machi, Chiyoda-ku, Tokyo, 101-0052, Japan. TEL 81-3-32922865, FAX 81-3-32915135, http://www.shinko-music.co.jp.

780 USA
B-SIDE. Text in English. bi-m. USD 18. adv.
Address: PO Box 1860, Birlington, NJ 08016. TEL 609-387-9424. Ed. Carol Schutzbank. Pub. Sandra A Garcia.

784.4 USA
B X FACTOR; an online hiphop magazine. Text in English. q. **Document type:** *Magazine, Consumer.* **Description:** Dedicated to people who appreciate the original lyrics and innovative music in hip-hop culture.
Address: PO Box 1007, Bronx, NY 10472. TEL 212-726-3990. Ed. Russel Carringtion.

780 USA ISSN 0005-3600
ML410.B1
➤ **BACH.** Text in English. 1970. s-a. free to members (effective 2010). bk.rev.; rec.rev. charts; illus. index. back issues avail. **Document type:** *Journal, Academic/Scholarly.* **Description:** Provides articles concerned with Bach and baroque styles, forms, and performance practices, with a historical background.
Related titles: Online - full text ed.
Indexed: A20, A22, ASCA, ArtHuCI, CA, CurCont, IIMP, M11, MAG, MusicInd, PCI, RILM, SCOPUS, T02, W07.
—IE, Infotrieve, Ingenta.
Published by: Riemenschneider Bach Institute, Baldwin-Wallace College, 275 Eastland Rd, Berea, OH 44017. TEL 440-826-2900, bachinst@bw.edu. Ed. Melvin Unger.

780 DEU ISSN 0084-7682
ML410.B1
BACH-JAHRBUCH. Text in German. 1904. a. price varies. bk.rev. bibl.; charts; illus. **Document type:** *Yearbook, Academic/Scholarly.* **Description:** Contains scientific findings, bibliographies and facsimiles.
Indexed: DIP, IBR, IBZ, IIMP, M11, MusicInd, RILM.
Published by: (Bach-Archiv Leipzig), Evangelische Verlagsanstalt GmbH, Blumenstr 76, Leipzig, 04155, Germany. TEL 49-341-7114115, FAX 49-341-7114150, info@eva-leipzig.de, http://www.eva-leipzig.de. Circ: 3,700.

780 USA ISSN 1072-1924
ML410.B1
➤ **BACH PERSPECTIVES.** Text in English. 1995. irreg., latest vol.4, 1999. price varies. back issues avail. **Document type:** *Monographic series, Academic/Scholarly.* **Description:** Contains contributions by nine scholars on two broad themes: the analysis of Johann Sebastian Bach's orchestral works, especially his concertos, and the interpretation and performance of his music in general.
Related titles: Online - full text ed.
Indexed: A01, A02, A03, A08, M01, M02, M11, RILM, T02.
Published by: University of Nebraska Press, 1111 Lincoln Mall, Lincoln, NE 68588. TEL 402-472-3581, FAX 402-472-6214, pressmail@unl.edu.

786.2 786.5 HUN ISSN 1216-9005
BACH TANULMANYOK. Text in Hungarian. 1993. a. **Document type:** *Journal, Academic/Scholarly.*
Indexed: RILM.
Published by: Magyar Bach Tarsasag/Bach Society of Hungary, Deak Ferenc ter 4, Budapest, 1052, Hungary. TEL 36-1-4832150, info@bachsociety.hu, http://www.bachsociety.hu.

781.64 DEU
BACKSPIN; Hip Hop Magazin. Text in German. 10/yr. EUR 39.90, EUR 79.90; EUR 4.80 newsstand/cover (effective 2008). adv. **Document type:** *Magazine, Consumer.*
Related titles: Online - full text ed.
Published by: Backspin Falk & Petering OHG, Hongkongstr 5, Hamburg, 20457, Germany. TEL 49-40-2292980, FAX 49-40-22929850. adv.: page EUR 3,600; trim 210 x 280. Circ: 50,000 (paid and controlled).

780 BRA ISSN 1414-6398
BACKSTAGE; audio musica e instrumentos. Text in Portuguese. 1984. m. BRL 60, USD 52; BRL 5 newsstand/cover (effective 1998). adv. music rev. mkt. back issues avail. **Document type:** *Newsletter, Consumer.* **Description:** Features articles, news on musical instruments, audio equipment and music in general.
Published by: H. Sheldon Servicos de Marketing Ltda., Rua dos Invalidos, 212 Sala 102, Centro, Rio De Janeiro, RJ 20231-020, Brazil. TEL 55-21-509-3572, FAX 55-21-509-3572. Ed. Carlos Eduardo. Pub. Nelson Cardoso. Adv. contact Marco Antonio Walker. Circ: 17,000.

791.43 780 792 ITA ISSN 2035-9306
BACKSTAGE; la rivista dello show business. Text in Italian. 2008. bi-m. EUR 35 domestic; EUR 70 in Europe; EUR 90 elsewhere (effective 2011). **Document type:** *Magazine, Consumer.*
Published by: Tecniche Nuove SpA, Via Eritrea 21, Milan, MI 201, Italy. TEL 39-02-390901, FAX 39-02-7570364, info@tecnichenuove.com, http://www.tecnichenuove.com. Ed. Lorenzo Ortolani.

780.42 USA ISSN 0746-990X
ML420.S77
BACKSTREETS. Text in English. 1980. q. USD 18; USD 25 foreign (effective 1999). adv. bk.rev. back issues avail. **Document type:** *Magazine, Consumer.* **Description:** Deals with the music and performances of Bruce Springsteen and other Jersey shore acts.
—CCC.
Published by: Backstreets Publishing Empire, LLC, PO Box 51225, Seattle, WA 98115. FAX 206-728-8827. Ed., Pub., R&P, Adv. contact Christopher Phillips. Circ: 20,000.

784 DEU ISSN 1612-0345
BADISCHE SAENGERZEITUNG; Organ des Badischen Saengerbundes. Text in German. 1972. 11/yr. EUR 15.80 (effective 2009). adv. **Document type:** *Magazine, Consumer.*
Published by: Badischer Saengerbund e.V., Gartenstr 56a, Karlsruhe, 76133, Germany. TEL 49-721-849669, FAX 49-721-853886, info@badischersaengerbund.de. Ed. Ingrid Vollmer. Circ: 9,000.

780.71 DEU
BAERENREITER STUDIENBUECHER MUSIK. Text in German. 1993. irreg., latest vol.17, 2009. price varies. **Document type:** *Monographic series, Academic/Scholarly.*
Published by: Baerenreiter Verlag, Heinrich-Schuetz-Allee 35, Kassel, 34131, Germany. TEL 49-561-3105154, FAX 49-561-3105195, order@baerenreiter.com, http://www.baerenreiter.com. Eds. Jutta Schmoll Barthel, Silke Leopold.

BALL MAGAZINE. *see* LITERARY AND POLITICAL REVIEWS

780 800 DEU
BALLADS AND SONGS, INTERNATIONAL STUDIES. Text in English. 2004. irreg., latest vol.6, 2010. price varies. **Document type:** *Monographic series, Academic/Scholarly.*
Published by: Wissenschaftlicher Verlag Trier, Bergstr 27, Trier, 54295, Germany. TEL 49-651-41503, FAX 49-651-41504, wvt@wvttrier.de, http://www.wvttrier.de.

782.81 USA
BALTIMORE OPERA MAGAZINE. Text in English. 2002. 5/yr. adv. **Document type:** *Magazine, Consumer.* **Description:** Contains articles about operas guest artists, behind-the-scene topics, program news and events, and current concert program notes.
Published by: MediaTwo Publications, 22 W. Pennsylvania Ave, Ste 305, Towson, MD 21204. TEL 770-723-9707, FAX 770-723-9761. adv.: B&W page USD 1,265, color page USD 1,670; trim 8.125 x 10.875. Circ: 70,000 (free).

780.6 USA ISSN 0885-7113
ML1
➤ **BALUNGAN.** Text in English. 1984. a. USD 25 combined subscription to individuals (print & online eds.); USD 100 combined subscription to institutions (print & online eds.) (effective 2011). bk.rev. back issues avail.; reprints avail. **Document type:** *Journal, Academic/Scholarly.* **Description:** Focuses on all forms of gamelan, Indonesian performing arts, and their international counterparts.
Related titles: Online - full text ed.
Indexed: A01, CA, IIMP, M11, MusicInd, PCI, RILM, T02.
—Ingenta.
Published by: American Gamelan Institute, PO Box 1052, Lebanon, NH 03766. TEL 603-643-9037, FAX 603-643-9037, agi@gamelan.org. Ed. Jody Diamond.

785.067 JPN ISSN 0005-4933
BAND JOURNAL. Text in Japanese. 1959. m. JPY 950. adv. bk.rev. illus. **Document type:** *Consumer.* **Description:** Contains commentaries, lectures, analysis of compositions and reports on items of interest. Also includes scores for parts in the supplement of each issue to make the publication practical.
Published by: Ongaku No Tomo Sha Corp., c/o KakuyukiNabeshima, 6-30 Kagura-Zaka, Shinjuku-ku, Tokyo, 162-0825, Japan. FAX 81-3-3235-2129. Ed. Kenji Kawamoto. Pub. Jun Meguro. R&P Tetsuo Morita TEL 81-3-3235-2111. Adv. contact Takao Oya. B&W page JPY 240,000, color page JPY 480,000; trim 210 x 275. Circ: 100,000.

785 USA ISSN 0084-7704
BAND MUSIC GUIDE. Text in English. 1959. irreg. **Document type:** *Guide, Trade.*
Published by: The Instrumentalist Co., 200 Northfield Rd, Northfield, IL 60093. TEL 847-446-5000, 888-446-6888, FAX 847-446-6263, advertising@instrumentalistmagazine.com, http://www.theinstrumentalist.com.

784.18 NLD ISSN 1876-1356
▼ **BANDCOACH.** Text in Dutch. 2009. bi-m. EUR 39.95 domestic; EUR 57.20 in Europe; EUR 73.20 elsewhere (effective 2011). adv. **Document type:** *Magazine, Trade.*
Published by: Septime bv, Postbus 125, 's-Heerenberg, 7040 AC, Netherlands. TEL 31-314-626436, info@bandcoach.eu. Ed. Reinout Burgers. Pub. Ben van Uhm. Adv. contact Gerrit Hiddink. Circ: 9,000.

780 USA ISSN 0887-9036
MT733
BANDWORLD. Text in English. 1985. 5/yr. index. back issues avail. **Document type:** *Journal, Academic/Scholarly.* **Description:** Details tips and information for music students and band directors.
Related titles: Diskette ed.; Online - full text ed.: USD 4.99 (effective 2011).
Published by: W I B C, Inc., 407 Terrace St, Ashland, OR 97520. TEL 541-840-4888, FAX 541-482-5030, maxmekee@jeffnet.org.

780 051 CAN ISSN 1718-3529
BANGBANG. Text in French. 2006. bi-w. **Document type:** *Magazine, Consumer.*
Published by: Editions BangBang, 355, rue Ste-Catherine west 7th flr, Montreal, PQ H3B 1A5, Canada. info@bangbangtemort.com. Ed. Nelson Roberge.

780 USA ISSN 0190-1559
ML1
BANJO NEWSLETTER; the 5-string banjo magazine. Text in English. 1973. m. USD 25 domestic; USD 32 foreign (effective 2005). adv. bk.rev.; rec.rev.; music rev. illus. index. 40 p./no. 3 cols./p.; back issues avail.; reprints avail. **Document type:** *Newsletter, Consumer.* **Description:** Contains information on the 5-string banjo, a musical instrument used in folk, bluegrass, jazz, and classical music. Includes tablature for the instrument.
Indexed: IIMP, M11, MusicInd, T02.
Published by: Banjo Newsletter, Inc., PO Box 3418, Annapolis, MD 21403-0418. bnl@tiac.net. Ed., R&P Donald Nitchie TEL 508-645-3648. Pub., Adv. contact Spencer Nitchie. B&W page USD 500; trim 8.5 x 11. Circ: 6,900.

780 051 GBR ISSN 2040-428X
▼ **BANTER.** Text in English. 2009. m. **Document type:** *Magazine, Consumer.* **Description:** Features the latest music news, reviews and gigs, movies and interviews with some of the top stars of the music world.
Related titles: Online - full text ed.: free (effective 2010).
Published by: The Banter Magazine, Arcadia Business Ctr, Miller Ln, Clydebank, W Dunbartonshire G81 1UJ, United Kingdom. TEL 44-141-2800115. Ed. Ritchie Marshall.

790.43 USA
THE BARD MUSIC FESTIVAL. Text in English. 1990. irreg., latest 2009. price varies. illus. back issues avail. **Document type:** *Monographic series, Academic/Scholarly.* **Description:** Discusses the lives and works of important classical composers.
Published by: Princeton University Press, 41 William St, Princeton, NJ 08540. TEL 609-258-4900, 800-777-4726, FAX 609-258-6305, cpriday@pupress.co.uk. **Subscr. addr. in US:** California - Princeton Fulfillment Services, Inc., 1445 Lower Ferry Rd, Ewing, NJ 08618. TEL 609-883-1759, 800-777-4726, FAX 609-883-7413, 800-999-1958, orders@cpfsinc.com. **Dist. in Canada, Australia & New Zealand, and Latin America:** University Press Group.; **Dist. in Europe & Africa:** John Wiley & Sons Ltd.

BARFOUT!/TO EXHALE. *see* ART

781.62 HRV ISSN 1330-1128
BASCINSKI GLASI. Text in Croatian. 1991. q. **Document type:** *Magazine, Consumer.*
Indexed: RILM.
Published by: (Festival Dalmatinskih Klapa), Centar za Kulturu Omis, Ul Punta 1, PP 28, Omis, 21310, Croatia. czk-omis@st.htnet.hr.

780 810 USA ISSN 1085-1984
THE BASEMENT MAGAZINE. Text in English. 1994. w. free. adv. music rev.; software rev. back issues avail. **Document type:** *Magazine, Consumer.*
Related titles: Online - full text ed.
Published by: Basement Enterprises, 39 Setalcott Pl., Setauket, NY 11733. TEL 516-689-5106, FAX 516-689-2403, tin@basementmag.com. Ed., Pub., Adv. contact Tin Dizdarevic. page USD 495. Circ: 2,000.

A BASIC MUSIC LIBRARY. *see* MUSIC—Abstracting, Bibliographies, Statistics

780 CHE ISSN 1424-7666
BASLER STUDIEN ZUR MUSIK IN THEORIE UND PRAXIS. Text in German. 1998. irreg., latest vol.2, 2000. price varies. **Document type:** *Monographic series, Academic/Scholarly.*
Published by: Peter Lang AG (Subsidiary of: Peter Lang Publishing Group), Hochfeldstr 32, Postfach 746, Bern 9, 3000, Switzerland. TEL 41-31-3061717, FAX 41-31-3061727, info@peterlang.com. Eds. Eduard Desax, Hans Linnartz.

787.65 USA ISSN 1050-785X
ML1015.B35
BASS PLAYER; for bassists of all styles and every level of ability. Text in English. 1989. m. USD 18.99 domestic; USD 33.99 in Canada; USD 43.99 elsewhere (effective 2008). adv. reprints avail. **Document type:** *Magazine, Consumer.* **Description:** For professional, semi-pro and amateur bass players in all styles.
Supersedes in part (in 1989): G P I Collector's Edition (1044-6656)
Related titles: Microfilm ed.: (from PQC); Online - full text ed.
Indexed: A22, G05, G06, G07, G08, G09, I05, I07, IIMP, M01, M02, M11, MASUSE, MusicInd, P10, P48, P53, P54, PQC, RILM.
—CIS, Ingenta. **CCC.**
Published by: NewBay Media, LLC (Subsidiary of: The Wicks Group of Companies, LLC.), 810 Seventh Ave, 27th Fl, New York, NY 10019. TEL 212-378-0400, FAX 212-378-0470, customerservice@nbmedia.com, http://www.nbmedia.com. Eds. Jonathan Herrera TEL 650-238-0281, Bill Leigh TEL 650-238-0280. Pub. Joe Perry TEL 770-343-9978. adv.: page USD 7,035; trim 8 x 10.5. Circ: 46,581.

DE BASSIST. *see* INSTRUMENTS

780 FIN ISSN 1796-3753
BASSO; urbaani musiikki & kultuuri. Text in Finnish. 2001. q. EUR 25 (effective 2006). **Document type:** *Magazine, Consumer.*
Formerly (until 2005): Posse (1458-3461)
Published by: Oy Basso Media Ltd., Pursimiehenkatu 26 C 6, Helsinki, 00150, Finland. TEL 358-9-677889, asiakaspalvelu@basso.fi, http://www.basso.fi.

BATON. *see* PHILATELY

781.66 786 FRA ISSN 1768-0700
BATTERIE MAGAZINE. Text in French. 2004. m. EUR 71; EUR 6.50 per issue (effective 2009). back issues avail. **Document type:** *Magazine, Consumer.* **Description:** Contains information on drums as well as the latest on drummers and their techniques.
Published by: Societe B G O, 15 Rue de l'Eglise, Paris, 75015, France. redaction@batteriemagazine.com.

780 FRA ISSN 1146-0512
BATTERIES - FANFARES. Text in French. 1980. q. EUR 20 domestic; EUR 22 foreign (effective 2009). **Document type:** *Magazine, Consumer.*
Formerly (until 1989): Confederation Francaise des Batteries - Fanfares. Bulletin Officiel (0980-2843)
Indexed: RILM.
Published by: Confederation Francaise des Batteries - Fanfares (C F B F), BP 20, Vaucresson, 92420, France. TEL 33-1-47419482, FAX 33-1-47014691.

786.9193 FRA ISSN 0981-8936
BATTEUR MAGAZINE. Text in French. 1986. bi-m. EUR 59.90 (effective 2009). adv. **Document type:** *Magazine, Consumer.*
Incorporates (2001-2002): Drummer (1630-5159)
Published by: M V M Editions, 168 Rue Ordener, Paris, 75018, France.

784.18 DEU ISSN 0178-4161
ML5
BAYERISCHE BLASMUSIK. Text in German. 1950. m. EUR 36.90 (effective 2009). adv. **Document type:** *Magazine, Consumer.*
Formerly (until 1985): Die Bayerische Volksmusik (0408-7178)
Published by: (Bayersicher Blasmusikverband e.V.), Druck und Verlag Obermayer GmbH, Bahnhofstr 33, Buchloe, 86807, Germany. TEL 49-8241-500816, FAX 49-8241-500846, info@dvo-verlag.de, http://www.dvo-verlag.de. Ed. Klaus Haertel. adv.: B&W page EUR 1,119, color page EUR 1,977; 185 x 262. Circ: 6,000 (paid and controlled).

BAYREUTH AFRICAN STUDIES SERIES. *see* ETHNIC INTERESTS

780 DEU ISSN 1866-3737
BEAT. Text in German. 2005. 11/yr. EUR 54.90; EUR 5.90 newsstand/cover (effective 2011). adv. **Document type:** *Magazine, Consumer.*
Published by: Falkemedia, An der Halle 400, Kiel, 24149, Germany. TEL 49-431-2007660, FAX 49-431-20076650, info@falkemedia.de, http://www.falkemedia.de. Ed. Alexander Weber. Pub., Adv. contact Kassian Alexander Goukassian. Circ: 17,145 (paid and controlled).

784.5 NOR ISSN 0801-5279
BEAT. Text in Norwegian. 1985. 4/yr. NOK 150.
Published by: Beat Bulldog, c/o Aller Familiejournalen, Postboks 250, Oekern, Oslo, 0103, Norway.

780 USA ISSN 1063-5319
ML3469
THE BEAT (LOS ANGELES); reggae, African, Caribbean, world music. Text in English. 1982. 5/yr. USD 20 domestic; USD 25 in Canada & Mexico; USD 40 elsewhere; USD 3.95 newsstand/cover (effective 2009). adv. music rev.; video rev.; bk.rev. illus. back issues avail.; reprints avail. **Document type:** *Magazine, Consumer.* **Description:** Devoted to popular and traditional music of the Caribbean, Africa and Brazil, and the new world beat movement.
Formerly: Reggae and African Beat
Indexed: ENW, RILM.
Published by: Bongo Productions, PO Box 65856, Los Angeles, CA 90065. TEL 818-500-9299, FAX 818-500-9454. Ed., Pub., R&P C C Smith. Circ: 10,000 (paid).

784.505 AUS ISSN 1445-4610
BEAT MAGAZINE. Text in English. 1986. w. AUD 153 (effective 2008). adv. bk.rev.; film rev.; music rev.; play rev.; video rev. **Document type:** *Magazine, Consumer.* **Description:** Covers art, music and club life.
Formerly (until 1989): Beat (1030-9993)
Related titles: Online - full text ed.
Published by: Furst Media Pty Ltd., 3 Newton St, Richmond, VIC 3121, Australia. TEL 61-3-94283600, FAX 61-3-94283611, info@furstmedia.com.au, http://www.furstmedia.com.au. Ed. Harley Augustine. adv.: B&W page AUD 690, color page AUD 1,165; trim 275 x 390. Circ: 28,000.

780.42 USA ISSN 0274-6905
ML421.B4
BEATLEFAN. Text in English. 1978. bi-m. USD 17 (effective 2000). adv. bk.rev. **Document type:** *Magazine, Consumer.* **Description:** News and features for fans and collectors of the Beatles and the group's individual members: John Lennon, Paul McCartney, George Harrison, Ringo Starr.
Published by: Goody Press, PO Box 33515, Decatur, GA 30033. TEL 770-492-0444, FAX 404-321-3109, goodypress@freewwweb.com. Ed., R&P William P King. Adv. contact Leslie King. B&W page USD 210; trim 9.75 x 7. Circ: 16,000.

784 PER ISSN 1609-9869
THE BEATLES CONNECTION. Text in Spanish. 1996. irreg.
Media: Online - full text.
Published by: Beatles Connection, Ave. Brasil 1275 Stand 34-A, Primer Nivel, Jesus Maria, Lima, Peru. connectab@yahoo.com, http://www.geocities.com/sunsetstrip/show/1970/. Ed. Alfonso Barrera.

780.42 USA
BEATLES FAN CLUB: LIVERPOOL PRODUCTIONS. Text in English. 1980. bi-m. USD 15 domestic; USD 25 foreign (effective 2007). adv. bk.rev.; film rev.; play rev. illus.; tr.lit. back issues avail. **Document type:** *Newsletter, Consumer.* **Description:** For Beatles fans, collectors and appreciators of music from the '60s; includes news, reviews, convention reports, and photos.
Formerly (until 2007): Good Day Sunshine (1041-4118); Which incorporated: Dark Horse; Here There and Everywhere
Published by: Liverpool Productions, 315 Derby Ave, Orange, CT 06477. TEL 203-891-8131, FAX 213-891-8433, http://www.liverpooltours.com. Ed. Charles F Rosenay. Adv. contact Mike Streeto. Circ: 5,200 (paid and controlled).

780 NLD ISSN 1384-296X
BEATLES UNLIMITED MAGAZINE. Variant title: B U Magazine. Text in English; Summaries in Dutch, German. 1963. bi-m. EUR 27 domestic; EUR 28 in Europe; USD 48 in United States; EUR 34 elsewhere (effective 2009). adv. bk.rev.; music rev.; software rev.; video rev. bibl.; charts; illus.; stat. 60 p./no. 2 cols./p.; back issues avail. **Document type:** *Magazine, Consumer.* **Description:** Covers everything pertaining to the Beatles and the subsequent lives and careers of the musicians as solo artists.
Formerly (until 1992): Beatles Unlimited (1385-3155); Which incorporated (1980-1985): Beatles Visie (1385-3163); Which was formerly: Nota Beatles
Related titles: Online - full text ed.
Published by: Beatles Unlimited, PO Box 602, Nieuwegein, 3430 AP, Netherlands. TEL 31-30-6063678, FAX 31-30-2445292, http://www.beatles-unlimited.com. Ed. Patrick Tersteeg. Pub., R&P, Adv. contact Rene van Haarlem. Circ: 3,800.

BEATLOLOGY; the magazine for collectors of beatles memorabilia. *see* HOBBIES

780 USA
BEATTHIEF. Text in English. 1995. q. back issues avail. **Description:** Focuses on contemporary American music, mainly rap and jazz. Also covers poetry and the arts.
Media: Online - full text.
Address: 1708 Mcallister St, San Francisco, CA 94115. scooter@beatthief.com, wayneb@beatthief.com. Ed. Wayne Bremser.

780 USA ISSN 1087-8262
BEETHOVEN JOURNAL. Text in English. 1986. s-a. USD 25 domestic to institutions; USD 35 foreign to institutions; free to members (effective 2010). bk.rev. back issues avail. **Document type:** *Journal, Academic/Scholarly.* **Description:** Devoted to to Beethoven and includes substantial essays, reviews of books and recordings, bibliographies of the latest books and dissertations, reports on the auction market, and much more.
Formerly (until 1995): Beethoven Newsletter (0898-6185)
Related titles: Online - full text ed.
Indexed: IIMP, M11, MAG, MLA-IB, MusicInd, PCI, RILM, T02.
Published by: (Center for Beethoven Studies), San Jose State University, One Washington Sq, San Jose, CA 95192. TEL 408-924-1000, Rose.Lee@sjsu.edu. **Co-sponsor:** American Beethoven Society.

780 DEU
ML410.B4
BEETHOVEN-STUDIEN. Text in German. 1954. irreg., latest vol.8, 2009. EUR 30 per vol. (effective 2010). bk.rev. bibl. **Document type:** *Monographic series, Academic/Scholarly.*
Formerly (until 1999): Beethoven-Jahrbuch (0522-5949)
Indexed: MusicInd, PCI.
Published by: (Der Verein Beethoven-Haus), Verlag Beethoven-Haus, Bonngasse 18, Bonn, 53111, Germany. TEL 49-228-9817521, FAX 49-228-9817572, info@beethoven-haus-bonn.de, http://www.beethoven-haus-bonn.de. Circ: 1,000.

781.621079496 USA
BEHIND THE ORANGE CURTAIN. Text in English. d. **Description:** Features reviews, news and interviews about music and entertainment from Orange County, California.
Media: Online - full text. Ed. Marie Loggia.

780 CHN ISSN 1002-767X
BEIFANG YINYUE/NORTHERN MUSIC. Text in Chinese. 1980. bi-m. USD 54 (effective 2009).
Related titles: Online - full text ed.

M

Published by: (Heilongjiang Sheng Wenlian), Beifang Yinyue Zazhishe, 16, Yaojingjie, Nangang-qu, Harbin, Heilongjiang 150006, China. TEL 30847. Ed. Shu Feng.

780 DEU ISSN 0946-7769
BEITRAEGE ZUR EUROPAEISCHEN MUSIKGESCHICHTE. Text in German. 1995. irreg., latest vol.14, 2009. price varies. **Document type:** *Monographic series, Academic/Scholarly.*
Published by: Peter Lang GmbH (Subsidiary of: Peter Lang Publishing Group), Eschborner Landstr 42-50, Frankfurt Am Main, 60489, Germany. TEL 49-69-7807050, FAX 49-69-78070550, zentrale.frankfurt@peterlang.com. Ed. Ekkehard Kreft.

780 DEU ISSN 0940-4236
BEITRAEGE ZUR GESCHICHTE DER MUSIKPAEDAGOGIK. Text in German. 1995. irreg., latest vol.18, 2009. price varies. **Document type:** *Monographic series, Academic/Scholarly.*
Published by: Peter Lang GmbH (Subsidiary of: Peter Lang Publishing Group), Eschborner Landstr 42-50, Frankfurt Am Main, 60489, Germany. TEL 49-69-7807050, FAX 49-69-78070550, zentrale.frankfurt@peterlang.com. Ed. Eckhard Nolte.

782.3222 DEU ISSN 0935-9044
ML169.8
BEITRAEGE ZUR GREGORIANIK. Text in Multiple languages. 1985. s-a. EUR 40; EUR 23 newsstand/cover (effective 2009). **Document type:** *Journal, Academic/Scholarly.*
Indexed: DIP, IBR, IBZ, RILM.
Published by: Internationale Gesellschaft fuer Studien des Gregorianischen Chorals, c/o Christian Dostal, Rotdornweg 28, Regensburg, 93055, Germany. consiglio@aiscgre.de, http://www.aiscgre.org. Ed. Christian Dostal.

780 AUT ISSN 0067-5067
BEITRAEGE ZUR HARMONIKALEN GRUNDLAGENFORSCHUNG. Text in German. 1968. irreg., latest vol.12, 1980. price varies. **Document type:** *Monographic series, Academic/Scholarly.*
Published by: Lafite Verlag, Hegelgasse 13-22, Vienna, 1010, Austria. TEL 43-1-5126869, FAX 43-1-51268699, edition@musikzeit.at. Ed. Marion Diederichs-Lafite. Adv. contact Christine Goldenberg.

780 AUT
BEITRAEGE ZUR JAZZFORSCHUNG/STUDIES IN JAZZ RESEARCH. Text in German. 1969. irreg., latest vol.10, 1996. price varies. back issues avail. **Document type:** *Monographic series, Academic/Scholarly.*
Published by: (International Society for Jazz Research), Akademische Druck- und Verlagsanstalt Dr. Paul Struzl GmbH, Auersperggasse 12, Graz, St 8010, Austria. TEL 43-316-364432, FAX 43-316-364424, info@adeva.com, http://www.adeva.com. R&P Doris Kellnhofer.

780 DEU ISSN 1616-2927
BEITRAEGE ZUR KULTUR- UND SOZIALGESCHICHTE DER MUSIK. Text in German. 2000. irreg., latest vol.8, 2010. price varies. **Document type:** *Monographic series, Academic/Scholarly.*
Published by: Centaurus Verlag & Media KG, Kaiser-Joseph-Str 267, Freiburg, 79098, Germany. TEL 49-761-1525861, FAX 49-761-1525868, info@centaurus-verlag.de, http://www.centaurus-verlag.de.

789.9 DEU ISSN 0943-9242
BEITRAEGE ZUR POPULARMUSIKFORSCHUNG. Text in German. 1986. irreg., latest vol.37, 2011. price varies. **Document type:** *Monographic series, Academic/Scholarly.*
Indexed: DIP, IBR, IBZ.
Published by: (Arbeitskreis Studium Populaere Musik e.V.), Transcript, Muehlenstr 47, Bielefeld, 33607, Germany. TEL 49-521-63454, FAX 49-521-61040, live@transcript-verlag.de.

780 DEU ISSN 1617-8424
BEITRAEGE ZUR WESTSLAWISCHEN MUSIKFORSCHUNG. Text in German. 2001. irreg., latest vol.3, 2004. price varies. **Document type:** *Monographic series, Academic/Scholarly.*
Published by: Peter Lang GmbH (Subsidiary of: Peter Lang Publishing Group), Eschborner Landstr 42-50, Frankfurt Am Main, 60489, Germany. TEL 49-69-7807050, FAX 49-69-78070550, zentrale.frankfurt@peterlang.com. Eds. Bert Greiner, Kathinka Rebling.

BELL TOWER. *see* HOBBIES

780.378 USA ISSN 1052-3839
MT4.B7
BERKLEE TODAY; a forum for contemporary music and musicians. Abbreviated title: B T. Text in English. 1989. 3/yr. free to members (effective 2011). adv. back issues avail. **Document type:** *Journal, Academic/Scholarly.* **Description:** Provides a forum for contemporary music and musicians; features college news, musical instruction pieces; contains editorials dealing with current issues in the music industry, and a survey of new publications, recordings, and professional achievements of Berklee alumni.
Published by: Berklee College of Music, 1140 Boylston St, Boston, MA 02215. TEL 617 266-1400, 800 237-5533, msmall@berklee.edu. Ed. Mark Small TEL 617-747-2325. Adv. contact Joseph Burke TEL 617-747-2432. Circ: 49,000.

780.6 DEU
BERLINER PHILHARMONIKER. Text in German. 1960. 6/yr. EUR 15 domestic; EUR 30 in Europe; EUR 62 elsewhere (effective 2009). adv. music rev.; rec.rev. illus. back issues avail. **Document type:** *Magazine, Consumer.*
Formerly: Philharmonische Blaetter (Berlin)
Address: Herbert-von-Karajan-Str 1, Berlin, 10785, Germany. TEL 49-30-25488359, FAX 49-30-25488390, presseinfo@berlin-philharmonic.com. Ed., Adv. contact Helge Gruenewald. Circ: 27,500.

780 CHE ISSN 1661-4283
BERNER VEROEFFENTLICHUNGEN ZUR MUSIKFORSCHUNG. Text in German. 2006. irreg. price varies. **Document type:** *Monographic series, Academic/Scholarly.*
Published by: Peter Lang AG (Subsidiary of: Peter Lang Publishing Group), Hochfeldstr 32, Postfach 746, Bern 9, 3000, Switzerland. TEL 41-31-3061717, FAX 41-31-3061727, info@peterlang.com, http://www.peterlang.ch.

780.42 JPN
BEST HIT. Text in Japanese. 1983. m. JPY 5,880.
Published by: Gakken Co. Ltd., 1-17-15, Nakaikegami, Otaku, Tokyo, 145-0064, Japan. Ed. Kin'ichi Iina.

781.64 CAN ISSN 1201-4826
BETWEEN THE LINES. Text in English. 1989. m. CAD 4.25; USD 4.25 in United States; USD 6 elsewhere. **Description:** Contains the latest information, transcriptions of other sources, reviews and opinions about Debbie Gibson and her music.
Formerly: Electric Youth (1200-5215)
Related titles: Online - full text ed.: ISSN 1201-4834.
Address: 2137 Qualicum Dr, Vancouver, BC V5P 2M3, Canada. TEL 604-322-1588, fng@btl.org, btl@btl.org, mkwong@ucsd.edu. Eds. Felix Ng, Myra Wong.

BIDOUN; a quarterly forum for middle eastern talent. *see* ART

780 SWE ISSN 1404-1863
BIDRAG TILL KUNGLIGA MUSIKALISKA AKADEMIENS HISTORIA. Text in Swedish. 2000. irreg. price varies. **Document type:** *Monographic series, Academic/Scholarly.*
Published by: Kungliga Musikaliska Akademien/Royal Swedish Academy of Music, Blasieholmstorg 8, Stockholm, 11148, Sweden. TEL 46-8-4071800, FAX 46-8-6118718, adm@musakad.se, http://www.musakad.se.

789.91 DEU ISSN 0721-7153
ML156.2
BIELEFELDER KATALOG - KLASSIK. Text in German. 1952. a. EUR 39.50 (effective 2010). adv. **Document type:** *Catalog, Consumer.*
Formerly: Bielefelder Katalog (0006-2103)
Published by: New Media Verlag GmbH, Auf der Wies 3, Muehldorf, 84453, Germany. TEL 49-8631-162785, FAX 49-8631-162786, shop@plattensammeln.de, http://www.funwithmusic.de.

780 USA
BIG APPLE BLUES. Text in English. 1981. irreg. USD 10 (effective 1997). adv. bk.rev.; music rev. **Document type:** *Newsletter.* **Description:** Covers blues performances in New York metro area.
Published by: Eric Lesselbaum, Ed. & Pub., c/o Dr Boogie, Box 655, Bronxville, NY 10708. Circ: 250.

780.904 AUS
BIG BEAT OF THE 50'S. Text in English. 1974. q. AUD 35 domestic; AUD 40 in New Zealand; AUD 50 elsewhere (effective 2008).
Published by: Australian Rock 'n' Roll Appreciation Society, PO Box 21, World Trade Centre, VIC 3005, Australia. http://www.myspace.com/australianrocknroll.

780.700 GBR ISSN 1469-316X
BIG DADDY. Text and summaries in English. 1999. q. **Description:** Covers mainly hip-hop, funk, soul and jazz; also covers graffiti.
Address: editor@thebigdaddy.com, http://www.thebigdaddy.com. Ed. George Mahood.

780 USA
BIG SHOT. Text in English. 2003. bi-m. USD 15; USD 3.99 newsstand/cover (effective 2005). **Document type:** *Magazine, Consumer.*
Published by: Big Media Group, 138 Court St., #410, Brooklyn, NY 11201. info@bigshotmag.com. Ed., Pub. Darren Ressler.

780 USA
THE BIG TAKEOVER; music with heart. Text in English. 1980. 2/yr. USD 20 for 2 yrs. domestic; USD 32 for 2 yrs. foreign (effective 2008). adv. **Document type:** *Magazine, Consumer.* **Description:** Covers concerts, recordings of new alternative music, and interviews.
Related titles: Online - full text ed.
Published by: Big Takeover, 1713 8th Ave, Rm 5-2, Brooklyn, NY 11215. jrabid@bigtakeover.com. Ed., Pub., R&P, Adv. contact Jack Rabid. B&W page USD 360, color page USD 900. Circ: 11,500 (paid).

781.64 USA
BIGSHOT. Text in English. 2003. bi-m. USD 15 (effective 2003). adv. **Document type:** *Magazine, Consumer.* **Description:** Covers the latest DJ/dance music trends and personalities.
Published by: BigShot Magazine, 138 Court St., # 410, Brooklyn, NY 11201-6209.

781.64 USA
BIGTIME; the magazine of urban art and expression. Text in English. q. USD 19; USD 4.95 newsstand/cover (effective 2001). adv. **Document type:** *Magazine, Consumer.* **Description:** Contains articles and features on urban music, fashion and lifestyles.
Published by: BigTime Magazine, PO Box 11262, Glendale, CA 91266. TEL 323-960-7923. **Dist. by:** Rider Circulation Services, 3700 Eagle Rock Blvd, Los Angeles, CA 90065. TEL 323-344-1200.

791 USA ISSN 0006-2510
PN2000
BILLBOARD (NEW YORK); the international newsweekly of music, video, and home entertainment. Text in English. 1894. w. USD 299 combined subscription in US & Canada (print & online eds.); USD 450 combined subscription in Europe (print & online eds.); USD 925 combined subscription in Japan (print & online eds.); USD 609 combined subscription elsewhere (print & online eds.) (effective 2011). adv. bk.rev.; film rev.; music rev. illus. back issues avail.; reprints avail. **Document type:** *Magazine, Trade.* **Description:** Entertains and informs, drives markets, influences decisions, platforms debate, builds community and captures the emotional power of music for professionals and fans.
Formerly: Billboard Music Week
Related titles: Online - full text ed.: Billboard.com.
Indexed: A01, A02, A03, A08, A09, A10, A11, A15, A22, A25, A26, ABIn, B01, B02, B03, B04, B06, B07, B08, B09, B11, B15, B17, B18, BPI, BRD, BusI, C05, CBRI, CPerI, CWI, Chicano, E08, F01, F02, G04, G05, G06, G07, G08, G09, I05, I06, I07, IBRH, IBT&D, IIMP, IIPA, M01, M02, M04, M06, M11, MASUSE, MusicInd, P02, P06, P10, P34, P48, P51, P53, P54, PMR, PQC, R06, RASB, RILM, S08, S09, S23, T&II, T02, U01, V03, V04, W01, W02, W03, W05, WBA, WMB.
—BLDSC (2060.700000), CIS. **CCC.**
Published by: Prometheus Global Media, 770 Broadway, 7th Fl, New York, NY 10003. TEL 212-493-4100, http://www.prometheusgm.com.

780.65 USA
BILLBOARD BULLETIN; daily news for the international music industry. Text in English. 1997. d. (52/wk). charts. **Document type:** *Bulletin, Trade.*
Media: Fax. **Related titles:** E-mail ed.: includes subcr. with Billboard.
Published by: Prometheus Global Media, 770 Broadway, 7th Fl, New York, NY 10003. TEL 212-493-4100, http://www.prometheusgm.com.

780 USA ISSN 1098-3732
ML18
BILLBOARD'S INTERNATIONAL BUYER'S GUIDE (YEAR). Text in English. 1958. a. (Dec.). USD 189 per issue (effective 2011). reprints avail. **Document type:** *Directory.* **Description:** Worldwide music and video business to business directory.
Former titles (until 1971): Billboard's International Buyer's Guide of the Music - Record - Tape Industry (0067-8600); (until 1960): Billboard. International Buyer's Guide of the Music - Record Industry
Related titles: Microfilm ed.: (from PQC).
—**CCC.**
Published by: Billboard Directories (Subsidiary of: Nielsen Business Publications), PO Box 15158, North Hollywood, CA 91606. TEL 818-487-4582, 800-562-2706, info@billboard.com, http://www.billboard.com.

792 USA
BILLBOARD'S YEAR-END AWARDS ISSUE. Text in English. 1970. a.
Former titles: Billboard's Year-End Issue Talent in Action; Billboard's Year-End Awards - Talent in Action; Billboard's Talent in Action
Related titles: Microfilm ed.: (from PQC).
Published by: Prometheus Global Media, 770 Broadway, 7th Fl, New York, NY 10003. TEL 212-493-4100, http://www.prometheusgm.com. Circ: 45,000.

781.7 367 USA
BILLIE JO WILLIAMS INTERNATIONAL FAN CLUB. Text in English. 1982. q. USD 10 to individuals; USD 7 to senior citizens. back issues avail. **Description:** Provides news of the artist, including his show dates, merchandise price list and photos.
Address: PO Box 1408, N Wilkesboro, NC 28659. Ed. Billie Jo Williams.

782.42 SWE ISSN 0523-6908
BIRGER SJOEBERG-SAELLSKAPET. SKRIFTSERIE. Text in Swedish. 1962. a. price varies. back issues avail. **Document type:** *Monographic series, Academic/Scholarly.* **Description:** Annual dedicated to the Swedish songwriter Birger Sjoeberg.
Indexed: MLA-IB.
Published by: Birger Sjoeberg-Saellskapet, PO Box 115, Vaenersborg, 46222, Sweden. TEL 46-46-152334, FAX 46-46-387074, bengt.kaage@telia.com. Ed. Lars Helge Tunving.

780 USA
BLACK HOLE; urban music magazine. Text in English. 1999. fortn. free. adv. back issues avail. **Document type:** *Newsletter, Consumer.*
Media: Online - full text. **Related titles:** E-mail ed.
Published by: Tag It, 1837 26th Ave., # 2F, Astoria, NY 11102-3541. TEL 718-726-1938, FAX 718-504-3512, info@eyeofthehole.com. Eds. Sabrina Eller, Sounni de Fontenay. Pub., R&P Sounni de Fontenay. Circ: 800.

780 910.03 USA ISSN 0276-3605
ML3556
➤ **BLACK MUSIC RESEARCH JOURNAL.** Abbreviated title: B M R J. Text in English. 1980. s-a. USD 69 combined subscription to institutions (print & online eds.) (effective 2012). adv. illus. Index. 100 p./no. 1 cols./p.; back issues avail.; reprints avail. **Document type:** *Journal, Academic/Scholarly.* **Description:** Features articles about the philosophy, aesthetics, history, and criticism of black music.
Related titles: Online - full text ed.: ISSN 1946-1615. USD 58 to institutions (effective 2012).
Indexed: A20, A22, A25, A26, A27, ASCA, AmHI, ArtHuCI, B04, BRD, CA, CurCont, DIP, E08, G05, G06, G07, G08, H07, H08, HAb, HumInd, I05, I07, IBR, IBZ, IIBP, IIMP, M08, M11, MAG, MusicInd, P10, P48, P53, P54, PCI, PQC, RILM, S08, S09, S23, SCOPUS, T02, W03, W05, W07.
—BLDSC (2105.965600), IE, Ingenta. **CCC.**
Published by: (Center for Black Music Research), University of Illinois Press, 1325 S Oak St, Champaign, IL 61820. TEL 217-333-0950, 866-244-0626, FAX 217-244-8082, journals@uillinois.edu. Ed. Christopher Wilkinson. Adv. contact Jeff McArdle TEL 217-244-0381.

➤ **BLACK TALENT NEWS**; the entertainment trade publication. *see* THEATER

780 GBR
BLACK VELVET. Abbreviated title: B V. Text in English. 1995. q. GBP 8 domestic; CAD 30 in Canada; AUD 25 in Australia; EUR 18 in Europe; USD 25 elsewhere; GBP 2.70 per issue domestic; EUR 5 per issue in Europe; USD 8 per issue elsewhere (effective 2009). adv. **Document type:** *Magazine, Consumer.* **Description:** Contains band interviews and mega-reviews of CDs, band demos, concert DVDs and live performances.
Address: 336 Birch Field Rd, Webheath, Redditch, Worcs B97 4NG, United Kingdom. Ed. Shari Black Velvet. adv.: page GBP 80; 216 x 303.

780 DEU ISSN 0344-8231
ML5
DIE BLASMUSIK. Text in German. 1950. m. EUR 19.90; EUR 2 newsstand/cover (effective 2010). adv. bk.rev.; music rev.; software rev. bibl.; illus.; stat. back issues avail. **Document type:** *Magazine, Consumer.*
Formerly (until 1970): Allgemeine Volksmusikzeitung (0174-8742)
Indexed: IBR, IBZ.
Published by: (Bund Deutscher Blasmusikverbaende e.V.), HeBu Musikverlag GmbH, Gottlieb-Daimler Str 22, Kraichtal, 76703, Germany. TEL 49-7250-92280, FAX 49-7250-921231, noten@hebu-music.de.

780 JPN
BLAST. Text in Japanese. m. back issues avail. **Document type:** *Magazine, Consumer.*
Published by: Shinko Music Publishing Co. Ltd., 2-1 Kanda-Ogawa-Machi, Chiyoda-ku, Tokyo, 101-0052, Japan. TEL 81-3-32922865, FAX 81-3-32915135, http://www.shinko-music.co.jp.

781.57 NLD ISSN 0921-2558
ML5
BLOCK; magazine for blues. Text in Dutch. 1975. q. EUR 16 domestic; EUR 17 in Europe; EUR 20 elsewhere (effective 2008). adv. bk.rev.; play rev.; rec.rev.; tel.rev.; video rev.; music rev. illus. 72 p./no. 3 cols./p.; back issues avail. **Document type:** *Magazine, Consumer.*
Address: Postbus 244, Almelo, 7600 AE, Netherlands. TEL 31-546-819976, FAX 31-546-820106. Ed., R&P, Adv. contact Rien Wisse. Pubs. Marion Wisse, Rien Wisse. Circ: 4,500.

781.64 USA
BLOODY STUMP. Text in English. 1999. bi-m. **Document type:** *Magazine, Consumer.* **Description:** Contains creative graphic art and literature for the purposes of entertainment, news and announcements regarding Stump Records and it's roster of musical artists, as well as a forum for the release of new music works in digital form.
Media: Online - full text.
Published by: Stump Records, 4009 W. Lupine Ave., Phoenix, AZ 85029-3037. Ed. Matt Murman.

780 USA ISSN 1542-0655
ML1015.G9
BLUE BOOK OF GUITAR AMPLIFIERS. Text in English. 2002 (Oct.). a. USD 24.95 newsstand/cover (effective 2003).
Published by: Blue Book Publications, 8009 34th Ave S, Ste 175, Minneapolis, MN 55425. TEL 952-854-5229, FAX 952-853-1486, bluebook@bluebookinc.com, http://www.bluebookinc.com.

780 TUR ISSN 1300-5855
BLUE JEAN. Text in Turkish. 1986. m. adv. **Document type:** *Magazine, Consumer.* **Description:** Features news, stories, articles and interviews with world's top artists and stars form every scene possible. It is about youth & music.
Related titles: Online - full text ed.: free (effective 2009).
Published by: D B R - Dogan Burda Rizzoli Dergi Yayyncylyk ve Pazarlama A.S., Hurriyet Medya Towers, Gunesli - Istanbul, 34212, Turkey. TEL 90-212-4780300, FAX 90-212-4103200, abone@dbr.com.tr, http://www.dbr.com.tr.

781.643 781.65 ITA ISSN 1124-5263
BLUE NOTE MAGAZINE. Text in Italian. 1996. m. **Document type:** *Magazine, Consumer.* **Description:** Provides information on selected jazz artists. Each issue is accompanied by a CD with highlights from each chosen artist.
Published by: E M I Music Italy SpA, Piazza San Babila, 3, Milano, MI 20122, Italy. http://www.emimusic.it. **Dist. by:** Messaggerie Periodici SpA, Via Giulio Carcano 32, Milano 20141, Italy.

781.6 USA ISSN 1075-6647
ML1
BLUE SUEDE NEWS; the house organ of the church of rock and roll. Text in English. 1986. q. USD 18 domestic; USD 23 in Canada; USD 30 in Europe & S. America; USD 31 in Australia & Japan; USD 5.50 newsstand/cover (effective 2006). adv. 52 p./no.; **Document type:** *Magazine, Consumer.* **Description:** About American roots music: rockabilly, blues, R&B, country, western swing, bluegrass, folk, cajun, zydeco, jazz, doo-wop, etc. Contains articles, interviews, photos, and a review section with well over 150 CD titles plus videos, cassettes, books, etc.
Indexed: IIMP, M11, MusicInd, RILM, T02.
Address: PO Box 25, Duvall, WA 98019-0025. TEL 425-788-2776. Ed., Adv. contact Marc Bristol. Pub. Gaby Maag Bristol. Circ: 3,000.

781.7 DEU ISSN 0936-2479
ML3519
BLUEGRASS - BUEHNE; old time and bluegrass magazine. Text in German. 1981. bi-m. EUR 25 (effective 2009). adv. bk.rev.; music rev.; rec.rev. Index. 16 p./no. 3 cols./p.; **Document type:** *Magazine, Consumer.*
Address: Schuelinstr 3/3, Ulm, 89073, Germany. TEL 49-731-761771, FAX 49-731-761771, eb.finke@t-online.de. Ed. Eberhard Finke. adv.: page EUR 153.39; trim 190 x 260. Circ: 600.

781.62 CAN ISSN 1180-761X
ML3519
BLUEGRASS CANADA MAGAZINE; uniting bluegrassers. Text in English. 1989. bi-m. CAD 21 domestic to individuals; USD 28 in United States to individuals; CAD 36 elsewhere to individuals; CAD 3.50 newsstand/cover domestic (effective 2000). music rev. illus. **Document type:** *Magazine, Consumer.*
Indexed: CMPI, IIMP.
Published by: Jim Jesson, Ed & Pub, 11-1925 Bowen Rd, Nanaimo, BC V9S 1H1, Canada. TEL 250-518-0549, campainfo@campa.ca, http://www.cmpa.ca/pa1.html. R&P Jim Jesson.

780.71 USA ISSN 0006-5129
BLUEGRASS MUSIC NEWS. Text in English. 1950. 4/yr. adv. bk.rev. charts; illus. **Document type:** *Magazine, Consumer.* **Description:** Articles on music education.
Indexed: M11.
Published by: Kentucky Music Educators Association, PO Box 1058, Richmond, KY 40476. Ed. Ben Hawkins. adv.: B&W page USD 260; 10 x 7.5. Circ: 2,000.

781.7 USA ISSN 0006-5137
ML1
BLUEGRASS UNLIMITED. Text in English. 1966. m. USD 25 domestic; USD 39 in Canada; USD 44 elsewhere (effective 2010). adv. bk.rev.; music rev.; video rev.; rec.rev. illus. 92 p./no. 3 cols./p.; back issues avail.; reprints avail. **Document type:** *Magazine, Consumer.* **Description:** Covers old-time, traditional country music and bluegrass.
Related titles: Online - full text ed.
Indexed: IIMP, M11, MLA-IB, MusicInd, PMPI, RILM, T02.
Published by: Bluegrass Unlimited Inc., PO Box 771, Warrenton, VA 20188. TEL 540-349-8181, 800-258-4727, FAX 540-341-0011, info@bluegrassmusic.com. Ed. Peter Kuykendall. adv.: B&W page USD 825, color page USD 1,145; 7.25 x 10.

780 USA
BLUEMONT MUSE. Text in English. 1979. bi-m. **Document type:** *Newsletter.*
Published by: Bluemont Concert Series, PO Box 208, Leesburg, VA 20178. TEL 703-777-6306. Ed. Peter H Dunning. Circ: 5,000.

781.57 GBR
BLUES & RHYTHM; the gospel truth. Abbreviated title: B & R. Text in English. 1984. 10/yr. GBP 48 domestic; GBP 58 in Europe; GBP 56 elsewhere; GBP 4.75 per issue domestic; GBP 5.25 per issue foreign (effective 2009). adv. bk.rev.; rec.rev. back issues avail. **Document type:** *Magazine, Academic/Scholarly.* **Description:** Contains in-depth articles, ground breaking interviews, discographies, regular feature columns and all the latest blues news, CD and DVD reviews.
Address: c/o Tony Burke, 82 Quenby Way, Bromham, Beds MK43 8QP, United Kingdom. TEL 44-123-4826158, tonyburke@bluesandrhythm.co.uk. Ed. Tony Burke. Adv. contact Mike Stephenson TEL 44-130-4825102. **Subscr. to:** c/o Byron Foulger, 2 South Edge, Shipley, W Yorks BD18 4RA, United Kingdom. TEL 44-127-4598531, FAX 44-127-4590072.

781 GBR ISSN 0959-6550
BLUES & SOUL. Text in English. 1966. fortn. bk.rev. illus. back issues avail. **Document type:** *Magazine, Consumer.* **Description:** Dedicated for music writing, comment, integrity, opinion and listings.
Formerly (until 1990): Blues and Soul Music Review (0045-2297); Incorporates (1978-1984): Black Music and Jazz Review (0141-7738); Which was formerly (until 1978): Black Music (0307-2169)
Related titles: Online - full text ed.
Indexed: IIMP, M11, RASB, T02.
Published by: Blues & Soul Ltd., 153 Praed St, London, W2 1RL, United Kingdom. TEL 44-208-6565651. Circ: 65,000. **Dist. by:** Seymour Distribution Ltd, 86 Newman St, London W1T 3EX, United Kingdom. FAX 44-207-396-8002, enquiries@seymour.co.uk.

781.57 USA
BLUES AT THE FOUNDATION. Text in English. q. free to members. adv. **Document type:** *Newsletter.*
Published by: Blues Foundation, 49 Union Ave, Memphis, TN 38103-2420. TEL 901-527-2583, FAX 901-529-4030. Ed. Doug Bacon. R&P, Adv. contact Pat Mitchell. Circ: 5,000 (controlled).

780 USA
THE BLUES AUDIENCE. Text in English. m. USD 25 (effective 2000). **Document type:** *Magazine, Consumer.* **Description:** Performance listings for New England blues bands and clubs.
Published by: Across The Board Graphic Design, 104 Old Nelson Rd, Marlborough, NH 03455-4004. TEL 603-827-3952. Ed., Pub. Diana Shonk. Adv. contact Joe Anderson.

781.643 GBR ISSN 1475-9721
BLUES IN BRITAIN; the magazine of the british blues connection. Text in English. 1989. m. GBP 45 domestic; GBP 55 in Europe; GBP 66 in United States; GBP 77 elsewhere (effective 2009). adv. bk.rev. back issues avail. **Document type:** *Magazine, Consumer.* **Description:** Contains news, reviews and interviews about the blues and has a four page guide to blues events and gigs in the UK.
Formerly (until 2002): Blueprint (1369-1392)
Related titles: CD-ROM ed.: free (effective 2009); Online - full text ed.
Published by: Abacabe Publishing, 10 Messaline Ave, London, W3 6JX, United Kingdom. TEL 44-20-87237376, FAX 44-20-87237380. Adv. contact Don Cleary TEL 44-1580-712323.

781.57 FIN ISSN 0784-7726
BLUES NEWS. Variant title: B N. Text in Finnish. 1968. bi-m. EUR 33 domestic; EUR 35 in Estonia, Norway and Sweden; EUR 42 elsewhere (effective 2005). adv. bk.rev.; rec.rev. **Document type:** *Magazine, Consumer.* **Description:** Covers all forms of Afro-American music.
Published by: Suomen Afroamerikkalaisen Musiikin Yhdistys ry/Finnish Blues Society, P O Box 257, Helsinki, 00531, Finland. TEL 358-9-760755. Ed. Sami Ruokangas TEL 358-40-5892321. Circ: 1,300.

781.643 DEU ISSN 0948-5643
BLUES NEWS; das deutsche Bluesmagazin. Text in German. 1995. q. EUR 22.50 (effective 2011). adv. music rev.; play rev.; rec.rev.; video rev.; Website rev.; bk.rev. cum. index: 1995-2001. 84 p./no. 8 cols./p.; back issues avail. **Document type:** *Magazine, Consumer.* **Description:** Examines developments in the blues music scene.
Published by: Verlag Dirk Foehrs, Freiherr von Stein Str 28, Altena, 58762, Germany. TEL 49-2352-21680, FAX 49-2352-2847. Ed., Pub. Dirk Foehrs. adv.: B&W page EUR 550, color page EUR 725; trim 210 x 297. Circ: 11,000.

780 USA ISSN 1091-7543
ML3520.8
BLUES REVUE. Text in English. 1991. bi-m. USD 27.95 domestic; USD 33.95 in Canada & Mexico; USD 5.99 newsstand/cover (effective 2007). adv. bk.rev. 100 p./no.; **Document type:** *Magazine, Consumer.*
Formerly (until 1994): Blues Revue Quarterly (1076-6162)
Related titles: Online - full text ed.
Indexed: IIMP, M11, MusicInd, T02.
Address: Rte 1, Box 75, Salem, WV 26426-9604. TEL 304-782-1971, 800-258-7388, FAX 304-782-1993. Ed., Pub. Chip Eagle. R&P Christine Kreiser. Adv. contact Dan Ramage. color page USD 2,090, B&W page USD 1,640; trim 8.125 x 10.875. Circ: 31,515 (paid). **Dist. in UK by:** Comag, Tavistock Rd, W Drayton, Middlesex UB7 7QE, United Kingdom. TEL 44-1895-444055, FAX 44-1895-433602.

781.643 USA
BLUES TO-DO'S MONTHLY. Text in English. 1992. m. free newsstand/cover (effective 1997). adv. bk.rev.; dance rev.; film rev.; music rev.; play rev.; tel.rev.; video rev. 16 p./no. 3 cols./p.; back issues avail. **Document type:** *Newspaper.* **Description:** Calendar of blues events for adults 21-54 in the Northwest.
Formerly: All Blues To-Do's Monthly
Related titles: Online - full text ed.
Published by: Blues Media, PO Box 22950, Seattle, WA 98122-0950. TEL 206-328-0662, FAX 206-328-0439. Ed., Adv. contact Marlee Walker. page USD 900; trim 13 x 10.25. Circ: 15,000.

780 AUS
BLUNT. Text in English. 200?. 10/yr. AUD 49 domestic; AUD 70 in New Zealand; AUD 90 elsewhere (effective 2008). adv. **Document type:** *Magazine, Consumer.* **Description:** Delivers irreverent coverage of the very best alternative music from Australia and the world. It has established a distinct, independent voice that continues to turn heads in the rock & roll world.
Published by: Next Media, 78 Renwick St, Redfern, NSW 2016, Australia. TEL 61-2-96990333, FAX 61-2-93101315, subs@next.com.au. Ed. Matt Reekie TEL 61-2-96990353. Pub. Phillip Keir. adv.: page AUD 2,890; trim 210 x 297. Circ: 20,000.

780 USA
▼ **BLURT MAGAZINE (EAST LANSING).** Text in English. 2009. s-a. USD 12; USD 4.95 newsstand/cover (effective 2010). illus. **Document type:** *Magazine, Consumer.*
Related titles: Online - full text ed.: free (effective 2010).
Published by: Second Motion Entertainment, Inc., c/o Stephen H Judge, Pub., P O Box 862, East Lansing, MI 48826. TEL 517-668-6011, stephen@secondmotionrecords.com. Ed. Scott Crawford. Pub. Stephen H Judge.

780 USA
THE BOB. Text in English. 1980. q. USD 12.95 domestic 4 issues; USD 30 foreign 6 issues; USD 3.50 newsstand/cover (effective 2006). adv. bk.rev.; music rev.; video rev. back issues avail. **Document type:** *Magazine, Consumer.* **Description:** Provides indie rock and roll.
Published by: David Janssen Publishing, 112 Warwick Dr, Wilmington, DE 19803-2625. TEL 302-477-1248, FAX 302-655-3357, DJpublishing@aol.com, http://www.djpublishing.com. Ed., R&P Gregory C Beaudoin. Pub. David Janssen. Adv. contact Greg Greenstein. page USD 700; trim 10 x 14. Circ: 10,000 (paid).

780 DEU
BOCHUMER ARBEITEN ZUR MUSIKWISSENSCHAFT. Text in German. 1993. irreg., latest vol.5, 2006. price varies. **Document type:** *Monographic series, Academic/Scholarly.*
Published by: Baerenreiter Verlag, Heinrich-Schuetz-Allee 35, Kassel, 34131, Germany. TEL 49-561-3105154, FAX 49-561-3105195, order@baerenreiter.com, http://www.baerenreiter.com.

BOLETIN DM. (Documentacion Musical) *see* LIBRARY AND INFORMATION SCIENCES

BOMBIN' MAGAZINE. *see* ART

780 USA
BOMP. Text in English. 1966. 6/yr. USD 12. adv. bk.rev.
Formerly: Who Put the Bomp (0039-7873)
Published by: Bomp Magazine, PO Box 7112, Burbank, CA 91510. Ed. Gregory Shaw. Circ: 40,000.

BON. *see* CLOTHING TRADE—Fashions

780 GBR ISSN 2046-1399
BONAFIDE. Text in English. 2008. q. GBP 14 domestic; GBP 19 in Europe; GBP 23 elsewhere; GBP 4.75 per issue domestic; GBP 6.50 per issue in Europe; GBP 7 per issue elsewhere (effective 2011). back issues avail. **Document type:** *Magazine, Trade.* **Description:** Aims to highlight the originators of hip hop and those that strive to keep it original. Celebration of design and music originality.
Published by: Bonafide Magazine, 52a St Jude St, London, N16 8JT, United Kingdom. advertising@bonafidezine.com. Ed. James Griffin.

780 DEU ISSN 0949-1139
BONNER SCHRIFTEN ZUR MUSIKWISSENSCHAFT. Text in German. 1996. irreg., latest vol.9, 2010. price varies. **Document type:** *Monographic series, Academic/Scholarly.*
Published by: Peter Lang GmbH (Subsidiary of: Peter Lang Publishing Group), Eschborner Landstr 42-50, Frankfurt Am Main, 60489, Germany. TEL 49-69-7807050, FAX 49-69-78070550, zentrale.frankfurt@peterlang.com. Eds. Renate Groth, Wolfram Steinbeck.

781.973 USA ISSN 0006-7598
ML1
BOOSEY AND HAWKES NEWSLETTER. Text in English. 1965. 3/yr. free. bk.rev.; music rev. illus. **Document type:** *Newsletter.* **Description:** Provides articles and information about the work of composers published by Boosey and Hawkes and its affiliates.
Published by: Boosey and Hawkes, Inc., 35 E 21st St, New York, NY 10010-6212. TEL 212-228-3300, FAX 212-473-5730, TELEX 650-284-8790 MCI. Ed. Steven Swartz. Circ: 12,000 (controlled).

BOP. *see* CHILDREN AND YOUTH—For

780 USA
BORDER X-INGS. Text in English. q. USD 2.50 per issue. **Description:** Features Irish rock music and Celtic life.
Address: PO Box 5173, North Bergen, NJ 07047. Ed. Mary Ann O'Brien.

781.643 USA
BOSTON BLUES NEWS. Text in English. 1988. bi-m. USD 20. adv. dance rev.; music rev. tr.lit. back issues avail. **Description:** Contains local, national, and international news, reviews and interviews of blues performers.
Published by: Boston Blues Society, PO Box 1438, Boston, MA 02205-1438. Ed., R&P Brian M Owens. Adv. contact Bill McGowan TEL 781-545-3633. B&W page USD 220. Circ: 3,000 (controlled).

780.15 USA
BOSTON SYMPHONY ORCHESTRA PROGRAM. Text in English. 1882. w. (during season). USD 75 (effective 2000). adv. bk.rev. index. reprints avail.
Formerly: Boston Symphony Orchestra Program Book-Notes (0006-8020)
Related titles: Microfilm ed.: (from PQC); Microform ed.: (from BHP, PQC).
Published by: Boston Symphony Orchestra, Program Office, Symphony Hall, Boston, MA 02115. TEL 617-266-1492, FAX 617-638-9440. Ed., R&P Marc Mandel TEL 617-638-9331. Adv. contact Steve Ganak. Circ: 234,000.

780 NLD ISSN 1380-4545
DE BOUWBRIEF. Text in Dutch. 1975. q. adv. bk.rev. illus. **Description:** Devoted to the building and designing of musical instruments. Covers materials, tools, and measurements. Includes announcements of events, exhibitions, and courses.
Indexed: RILM.
Published by: Vereniging voor Muziek en Instrumentenbouw, Huismuziek, Postbus 9, Arnhem, 6800 AA, Netherlands. TEL 31-26-3612922, FAX 31-26-3612925, info@huismuziek.nl, http://www.huismuziek.nl. Ed. Jan Bouterse TEL 31-172-445957.

BOX. *see* SPORTS AND GAMES

781 AUS
BRAG MAGAZINE. Text in English. m. AUD 153 (effective 2008). **Document type:** *Magazine, Consumer.*
Published by: Furst Media Pty Ltd., 3 Newton St, Richmond, VIC 3121, Australia. TEL 61-3-94283600, FAX 61-3-94283611, info@furstmedia.com.au, http://www.furstmedia.com.au.

780 920 DEU ISSN 0341-941X
ML410.B8
BRAHMS STUDIEN. Text in German. 1974. biennial. EUR 20 per vol. (effective 2003). bk.rev. illus. 180 p./no.; back issues avail. **Document type:** *Monographic series, Academic/Scholarly.*
Formerly: Brahms-Gesellschaft Hamburg. Jahresgabe
Indexed: IIMP, M11, MusicInd, PCI, RILM.
Published by: Johannes Brahms Gesellschaft, Internationale Vereinigung e.V., Peterstr 39, Hamburg, 20355, Germany. TEL 49-40-488327, FAX 49-40-4808026, info@brahms-hamburg.de, http://www.brahms-hamburg.de. Ed. Martin Meyer. Circ: 500.

BRAILLE MUSIC MAGAZINE. *see* HANDICAPPED—Visually Impaired

781.64 USA
THE BRAIN. Text in English. w. **Description:** Focuses on bringing independent music fans comprehensive information on websites and bands.
Media: Online - full text.
Published by: Brainwashed, PO Box 7, Arlington, MA 02476-0001. Ed. Jon Whitney.

780.42 USA
BRAIN DAMAGE; the international Pink Floyd magazine. Text in English. 1986. q. USD 28 in North America; USD 40 elsewhere; USD 4.95 newsstand/cover. adv. bk.rev.; music rev.; video rev. illus. back issues avail. **Document type:** *Newsletter.* **Description:** Devoted to reporting current news and reviews of Pink Floyd. Also provides in-depth coverage of the history of the group through retrospective articles. Includes discographies and reviews for collectors.
Published by: Brain Damage Magazine, Inc., PO Box 923, Montgomery, IL 60538-0923. TEL 630-968-4900, FAX 630-968-4944, http://www.brain-damage.com. Ed., R&P, Adv. contact Jeff Jensen. B&W page USD 350, color page USD 420; trim 11.63 x 8.25. Circ: 6,000 (paid).

780 BRA ISSN 1516-2427
ML5
BRASILIANA. Text in Portuguese. 1999. 3/yr.
Indexed: RILM.
Published by: Academia Brasileira de Musica, Rua da Lapa 120, 12 Andar, Rio de Janeiro, 20021-180, Brazil. TEL 55-21-2221-0277, FAX 55-21-2292-5845.

780 CHE
BRASS BAND. Text in English. 1993. m. CHF 72 domestic; CHF 88 foreign (effective 2010). adv. **Document type:** *Magazine, Consumer.*
Published by: Obrasso Verlag AG, Baselstr 23 C, Wiedlisbach, 4537, Switzerland. TEL 41-32-6363727, FAX 41-32-6362644. Ed. Werner Obrecht. Circ: 4,000 (paid and controlled).

780 USA
BRASS BAND NOTES. Text in English. 1970. bi-m. USD 7 membership.
Published by: Chatfield Brass Band, Inc., 81 Liberty Ln, Box 578, Chatfield, MN 55923. TEL 507-867-3275. Ed. Rita Kramer. Circ: 200.

784.18 GBR ISSN 0961-6373
BRASS BAND WORLD; an independent magazine for bands. Text in English. 1991. m. GBP 32.50 domestic; GBP 39.50 in Europe; GBP 42 elsewhere; GBP 3.50 newsstand/cover (effective 2001). adv. music rev. back issues avail. **Document type:** *Magazine, Trade.* **Description:** Aimed at brass-band players and enthusiasts. Contains profiles of bands and individual players, reviews, and interviews.
—CCC.
Published by: Caron Publications, Peak Press Bldg, Eccles Rd, Chapel-En-Le-Frith, High Peak, SK23 9RQ, United Kingdom. TEL 44-1298-812738, FAX 44-1298-815220. Ed. Robert G Mulholland. R&P Robert Mulholland. Adv. contact Liz Winter. B&W page GBP 451, color page GBP 616; trim 297 x 210. Circ: 4,000 (paid).

781.57 USA ISSN 1041-3308
ML1
THE BRASS PLAYER. Text in English. q.
Indexed: MusicInd, RILM.
Published by: New York Brass Conference for Scholarships, 315 W 53rd St, New York, NY 10019. TEL 212-581-1480, FAX 212-489-5186.

780 USA ISSN 0197-8845
BRASS PLAYERS GUIDE (YEAR). Text in English. 1975. a. USD 8 (effective 1999). adv. **Document type:** *Catalog.*
Published by: Robert King Music Sales, Inc., 140 Main St, Bldg 15, N, Easton, MA 02356. FAX 508-238-2571. Ed. Dennis Hugh Avey. Circ: 20,000.

780 USA ISSN 0363-454X
BRASS RESEARCH SERIES. Text in English. irreg. **Description:** Music history and research.
Published by: Brass Press, c/o RKMS, 140 Main St, N, Easton, MA 02356. FAX 508-238-2571. Ed. Stephen L Glover.

780 CAN
BRAVE WORDS & BLOODY KNUCKLES. Abbreviated title: B W + B K. Text in English. 1965. 10/yr. CAD 75 domestic; USD 70 in United States; USD 7.95 newsstand/cover (effective 2003).
Published by: B W & B K, 368 Yonge St, Toronto, ON M5B 1S5, Canada. TEL 416-229-2966, FAX 416-586-0819, bwbk@inforamp.net. Eds. Martin Popoff, Tim Henderson.

BRAVO. *see* CHILDREN AND YOUTH—For

BRAVO. *see* CHILDREN AND YOUTH—For

BRAVO. *see* CHILDREN AND YOUTH—For

BRAVO. *see* CHILDREN AND YOUTH—For

BRAVO. *see* ART

781.64 ROM ISSN 1453-5181
BRAVO. Text in Romanian. 1997. 2/m. adv. film rev.; music rev.; video rev. illus. 32 p./no.; back issues avail. **Document type:** *Magazine, Consumer.* **Description:** Presents the latest news in Romanian and international music and motion pictures, VIPS, etc.
Published by: Ringier Romania S.R.L., Novo Parc, Bulevardul Dimitrie Pompeiu nr 6, Sector 2, Bucharest, Romania. TEL 40-21-2030800, FAX 40-21-2030801, office@ringier.ro, http://www.ringier.ro. Ed. Cristian Constantin. Adv. contact Gabriel Geru. Circ: 66,850 (paid and controlled).

781.64 BGR ISSN 1312-4250
BRAVO. Text in Bulgarian. 2004. fortn. BGL 1.70 newsstand/cover (effective 2011). adv. **Document type:** *Magazine, Consumer.*
Published by: Egmont Bulgaria Ltd., 21 Hristo Belchev St, Sofia, 1000, Bulgaria. TEL 359-2-9880120, FAX 359-2-9880223, http://www.egmontbulgaria.com.

BRAVO. *see* MOTION PICTURES

BRAVO GIRL!. *see* CHILDREN AND YOUTH—For

BRAVO GIRL!. *see* CHILDREN AND YOUTH—For

781.64 GBR ISSN 1368-2938
BREAKTHRU; the magazine about people making it in music. Text in English. 1998. bi-m. GBP 13.50 domestic; GBP 14.10 in Europe; GBP 19.90 elsewhere. adv. back issues avail. **Document type:** *Magazine, Consumer.* **Description:** Covers all aspects of the music entertainment industry. Contains featured on unsigned and newly signed musicians/bands and information on how to get a foothold into the music industry.
Published by: Sequel Publications, PO Box 723, Windsor, Berks SL4 1GP, United Kingdom. TEL 44-20-79003101, FAX 44-20-79003103, all@breakthru-magazine.com, http://www.breakthru-magazine.com. Circ: 20,000.

780 DEU ISSN 0948-0285
BREMER JAHRBUCH FUER MUSIKKULTUR. Text in German. 1995. a. **Document type:** *Journal, Academic/Scholarly.*
Indexed: RILM.
Published by: Verein Bremer Rockmusiker e.V., Vahrer Str 176a, Bremen, 28309, Germany. TEL 49-421-411155, FAX 49-421-411160, info@musikpol.de.

BRIO. *see* LIBRARY AND INFORMATION SCIENCES

780 GBR
BRITISH & INTERNATIONAL FEDERATION OF FESTIVALS. YEARBOOK. Text in English. 1921. a. GBP 8.50 per issue to non-members; free to members (effective 2009). adv. **Document type:** *Directory.* **Description:** Contains detailed information about 300 plus affiliated festivals in the U.K., Hong Kong, and Bermuda. Includes music, dance, speech, and drama festivals for amateur performers.
Former titles (until 19??): British Federation of Festivals. Yearbook; (until 1991): British Federation of Music Festivals. Yearbook (0309-8044)
Published by: British & International Federation of Festivals, 198 Park Ln, Macclesfield, Ches SK11 6UD, United Kingdom. TEL 44-1625-428297, FAX 44-1625-503229, info@federationoffestivals.org.uk, http://www.federationoffestivals.org.uk. Circ: 2,500.

780 GBR ISSN 1742-7762
ML21
BRITISH AND INTERNATIONAL MUSIC YEARBOOK. Text in English. 1972. a. GBP 39, EUR 57.80, USD 57.80, AUD 105, JPY 6,800, DKK 3,884 per issue (effective 2009). adv. stat. index. **Document type:** *Directory, Consumer.* **Description:** Provides a comprehensive directory of British classical music industry.
Former titles (until 1999): British Music Yearbook (0306-5928); (until 1975): Music Yearbook
Published by: Rhinegold Publishing Ltd., 239-241 Shaftesbury Ave, London, WC2H 8TF, United Kingdom. TEL 44-20-73331720, FAX 44-20-73331765, enquiries@rhinegold.co.uk. Adv. contact Neil Cording TEL 44-20-73331733.

785 GBR ISSN 0007-0319
BRITISH BANDSMAN; the leading international brass magazine. Abbreviated title: B B. Text in English. 1887. w. GBP 56 domestic; GBP 75 in Europe; GBP 115 elsewhere (effective 2009). adv. bk.rev. illus. back issues avail. **Document type:** *Newspaper, Consumer.* **Description:** Keeps brass band enthusiasts informed and entertained with the latest news and features about their interest.
Incorporates: Brass Band News; International Bandsman
Related titles: Online - full text ed.
Published by: Kapitol Media and Events, 66-78 Denington Rd, Wellingborough, Northants NN8 2QH, United Kingdom. TEL 44-1933-445442, FAX 44-1933-445435. Ed. Kenneth Crookston TEL 44-1506-882985. Adv. contact John Ward TEL 44-1132-707214.

788.305 GBR ISSN 2045-4074
BRITISH FLUTE SOCIETY. FLUTE. Text in English. 1983. q. free to members (effective 2010). adv. back issues avail. **Document type:** *Journal, Trade.* **Description:** Covers all aspects of the flute and flute playing including the latest flute news, listings of concerts, course and reviews of new music, books and recordings.
Formerly (until 2010): Pan The Flute Magazine (1360-1563)
Indexed: A01, M11, MusicInd, RILM, T02.
—IE.
Published by: British Flute Society, c/o Anna Munks, 27 Eskdale Gardens, Purley, Surrey CR8 1ET, United Kingdom. TEL 44-20-86683360, FAX 44-20-86683360, secretary@bfs.org.uk. Ed. Robert Bigio TEL 44-20-88822627. Adv. contact Anna Munks.

780.89 GBR
BRITISH FORUM FOR ETHNOMUSICOLOGY. NEWSLETTER (ONLINE). Text in English. 1991. 3/yr. free (effective 2009). bk.rev.; music rev. back issues avail. **Document type:** *Newsletter, Trade.* **Description:** Publishes less formal articles on traditional and ethnic music.
Former titles (until Aug. 2008): British Forum for Ethnomusicology. Newsletter (Print); (until 1995): International Council for Traditional Music. Newsletter
Media: Online - full text.
Published by: British Forum for Ethnomusicology, c/o Caroline Bithell,, Martin Haris Center for Music and Drama,, The University of manchester, Coupland St,, Manchester, M13 9P, United Kingdom. TEL 44-161-2753346, Caroline.Bithell@manchester.ac.uk, http://www.bfe.org.uk. Ed. Ruth Hellier-Tinoco.

650 GBR ISSN 0265-0517
ML5
➤ **BRITISH JOURNAL OF MUSIC EDUCATION.** Variant title: B J M E. Text in English. 1984. 3/yr. GBP 166, USD 285 to institutions; GBP 171, USD 294 combined subscription to institutions (print & online eds.) (effective 2012). adv. bk.rev. back issues avail.; reprint service avail. from PSC. **Document type:** *Journal, Academic/Scholarly.* **Description:** Covers classroom music teaching, individual instrumental teaching and group teaching, and music in higher education.
Related titles: Microform ed.: (from PQC); Online - full text ed.: ISSN 1469-2104. GBP 155, USD 264 to institutions (effective 2012).
Indexed: A01, A03, A08, A20, A22, ArtHuCI, B29, CA, CPE, CurCont, DIP, E01, E03, ERA, ERI, IBR, IBZ, IIMP, M11, M12, MusicInd, P03, P18, P25, P48, P53, P54, PCI, PQC, PsycInfo, PsycholAb, RILM, S21, SSCI, T02, V05, W07.
—BLDSC (2311.890000), IE, Infotrieve, Ingenta. **CCC.**
Published by: Cambridge University Press, The Edinburgh Bldg, Shaftesbury Rd, Cambridge, CB2 8RU, United Kingdom. TEL 44-1223-312393, FAX 44-1223-315052, journals@cambridge.org, http://www.cambridge.org/uk. Eds. Gary Spruce, Pamela Burnard. R&P Linda Nicol TEL 44-1223-325702. Adv. contact Rebecca Roberts TEL 44-1223-325083. page GBP 470, page USD 895. Circ: 750. **Subscr. to:** Cambridge University Press, 32 Ave of the Americas, New York, NY 10013. TEL 212-337-5000, FAX 212-691-3239, journals_subscriptions@cup.org.

➤ **BRITISH JOURNAL OF MUSIC THERAPY.** *see* MEDICAL SCIENCES—Physical Medicine And Rehabilitation

780.6 GBR ISSN 0958-5664
ML5
BRITISH MUSIC. Text in English. 1979. a. GBP 5 per issue to non-members; free to members (effective 2009). 72 p./no. 1 cols./p.; back issues avail. **Document type:** *Journal, Academic/Scholarly.* **Description:** Covers British opera, chamber music, orchestral music; reviews of works, interviews and information about lesser known British composers, especially from the period 1850-1975.
Formerly (until 1989): British Music Society. Journal (0143-7402)
Indexed: CA, M11, MusicInd, PCI, RILM, T02.
—BLDSC (2330.620000).
Published by: British Music Society, 7 Tudor Gardens, Upminster, Essex RM14 3DE, United Kingdom. TEL 44-1708-224795, sct.bms1943@amserve.com. Ed. Jonathan Woolf.

780.7 GBR ISSN 1758-3667
ML21.G7
BRITISH MUSIC EDUCATION YEARBOOK (YEAR); the essential guide for students, teachers, parents and musicians. Text in English. 1984. a. GBP 35, EUR 57.80, USD 57.80, AUD 105, JPY 6,800, DKK 38,840 per issue (effective 2010). **Document type:** *Yearbook, Academic/Scholarly.* **Description:** Provides information for music students, parents and teachers from primary school to adult and continuing education level.
Former titles (until 2009): Rhinegold Guide to Music Education (1744-277X); (until 2004): Music Education Yearbook (1353-8896); (until 1994): Music Teachers' Yearbook (1353-548X); (until 1993): British Music Education Yearbook (0266-2329)
—BLDSC (2330.641000). **CCC.**
Published by: Rhinegold Publishing Ltd., 239-241 Shaftesbury Ave, London, WC2H 8TF, United Kingdom. TEL 44-20-73331720, FAX 44-20-73331765, subs@rhinegold.co.uk, enquiries@rhinegold.co.uk. Adv. contact Neil Cording TEL 44-20-73331733.

780 GBR ISSN 1462-9860
BRITISH MUSIC SOCIETY NEWS. Variant title: B M S News. Text in English. 1978. q. free to members (effective 2009). bk.rev.; music rev.; rec.rev. 32 p./no.; reprints avail. **Document type:** *Newsletter, Academic/Scholarly.* **Description:** Contains news, reviews, and short articles relating to lesser-known British composers.
Indexed: M11, MusicInd, RILM, T02.
Published by: British Music Society, 7 Tudor Gardens, Upminster, Essex RM14 3DE, United Kingdom. TEL 44-1708-224795, sct.bms1943@amserve.com, http://www.musicweb-international.com/BMS/. Ed. Rob Barnett TEL 44-151-4233783.

BRITISH PERFORMING ARTS YEARBOOK. *see* THEATER

780 GBR
➤ **BRITISH POSTGRADUATE MUSICOLOGY (ONLINE).** Abbreviated title: B P M. Text in English. 1997. a. free (effective 2011). back issues avail. **Document type:** *Journal, Academic/Scholarly.* **Description:** Aims to display the quality and diversity of scholarly studies.
Formerly (until 1999): British Postgraduate Musicology (Print) (1460-9231)
Media: Online - full text.
Indexed: A01, A39, C27, C29, CA, D03, D04, E13, IIMP, M11, R14, RILM, S14, S15, S18, T02.
Published by: British Postgraduate Musicology, Wolfson College, University of Cambridge, Cambridge, CB3 9BB, United Kingdom. Ed. Rachel Foulds.

780 DEU
BROT & SPIELE; das Kulturmagazin fuer die Region Aschaffenburg. Text in German. 1999. m. adv. **Document type:** *Magazine, Consumer.*
Published by: MorgenWelt Kommunikation & Verlag GmbH, Herstallstr 31, Aschaffenburg, 63739, Germany. TEL 49-6021-444880, FAX 49-6021-373010, info@morgen-welt.de, http://www.morgen-welt.de. Ed. Bettina Bogner. Adv. contact Rainer Koehl. Circ: 15,000 (controlled).

780 GBR
BRUM BEAT (ONLINE). Text in English. 1980. m. free (effective 2009). bk.rev. **Document type:** *Magazine, Consumer.* **Description:** Covers music informatiion.
Former titles: Brum Beat (Print); Midlands Beat
Media: Online - full text.
Published by: Brum Beat Ltd., Premier House, 43-48 New St, Birmingham, Warks B2 4LJ, United Kingdom. john@brumbeat.net.

780.1 USA ISSN 1089-375X
BUCINA; the Historic Brass Society series. Text in English. 1996. irreg., latest vol.7, 2008. price varies. back issues avail. **Document type:** *Monographic series, Trade.* **Description:** Examines the history of brass instruments, their music, and their social function from antiquity through the 19th century.
Published by: Pendragon Press, PO Box 190, Hillsdale, NY 12529. TEL 518-325-6100, FAX 518-325-6102, orders@pendragonpress.com.

BUEHNE. *see* THEATER

780 BGR ISSN 0204-823X
ML5
BULGARSKO MUZIKOZNANIE/BULGARIAN MUSICOLOGY. Text in Bulgarian; Summaries in English, French, German. 1977. q. BGL 6 (effective 2002). **Document type:** *Magazine, Academic/Scholarly.* **Description:** Presents works on a variety of historical and theoretical issues, interpreting predominantly Bulgarian music culture from the Middle Ages, National Revival and modern times. Issues of national music specificity, music culture of the world, traditional music cultures and music of the Balkan region are largely analyzed.
Related titles: Online - full text ed.
Indexed: M11, MusicInd, RILM.

Published by: (Institut za Izkustvoznanie), Sofiiski Universitet Sv. Kliment Ohridski, Universitetsko Izdatelstvo/Sofia University St. Kliment Ohridski University Press, Akad G Bonchev 6, Sofia, 1113, Bulgaria. Ed. Dimiter Khristoff.

780 JPN
BURRN. Text in Japanese. m. back issues avail. **Document type:** *Magazine, Consumer.*
Published by: Shinko Music Publishing Co. Ltd., 2-1 Kanda-Ogawa-Machi, Chiyoda-ku, Tokyo, 101-0052, Japan. TEL 81-3-32922865, FAX 81-3-32915135, http://www.shinko-music.co.jp.

780.42 ITA
BUSCADERO; mensile d'informazione rock. Text in Italian. 1980. m. (11/yr.). EUR 40 domestic; EUR 65 in Europe; EUR 85 in United States (effective 2008). adv. bk.rev. back issues avail. **Document type:** *Magazine, Consumer.*
Published by: Buscadero Srl, Casella Postale 239, Gallarate, VA 21013, Italy. http://www.buscadero.com/. Circ: 25,000.

780 746.9 USA ISSN 1947-6159
▼ **BUTTON MAGAZINE.** Text in English. 2009. bi-m. USD 20; USD 4.99 per issue (effective 2009). **Document type:** *Magazine, Consumer.* **Description:** Covers the music and fashion scene in Portland, Oregon.
Published by: Brittany McGrath, Ed. & Pub., 18722 SW Frank Ct, Aloha, OR 97007. TEL 503-819-8172, brittany@buttonmag.com.

780 USA
BUZZINE. Text in English. 2002. 9/m. USD 29.99; USD 5.99 newsstand/cover (effective 2003). adv. **Document type:** *Magazine, Consumer.* **Description:** Covers the music and entertainment world and behind the scenes experience.
Related titles: Online - full content ed.
Published by: Buzzine Magazine, LLC, PO Box 18857, Encino, CA 91416-8857. TEL 818-995-6161, FAX 818-995-6136, advertising@buzzine.com. Pub. Aaron Stipkovivh. adv.: color page USD 11,000; trim 10 x 12.

780 026 CAN ISSN 1496-9963
ML27.C3
C A M L REVIEW/REVUE DE L'A C B M. (Canadian Association of Music Libraries) Text in English, French. 1957. 3/yr. CAD 45 domestic to individuals; USD 45 foreign to individuals; CAD 35 domestic to students; USD 35 foreign to students; CAD 20 domestic to members CUMS; USD 20 foreign to members CUMS; CAD 80 combined subscription domestic to individuals includes Fontes Artis Musicae; USD 80 combined subscription foreign to individuals includes Fontes Artis Musicae; CAD 110 combined subscription domestic to institutions includes Fontes Artis Musicae; USD 110 combined subscription foreign to institutions includes Fontes Artis Musicae; CAD 70 combined subscription domestic to students includes Fontes Artis Musicae; USD 70 combined subscription foreign to students includes Fontes Artis Musicae (effective 2005). adv. bk.rev. back issues avail. **Document type:** *Newsletter, Trade.* **Description:** Publishes official Association business, conference reports, news and articles of interest to the music library community and reviews of musical Canadiana.
Former titles (until 2001): Canadian Association of Music Libraries, Archives and Documentation Centres. Newsletter (1709-3228); (until 1996): Canadian Association of Music Libraries. Newsletter (0383-1299); (until 1978): C A M L Newsletter (0825-3730); (until 1972): Canadian Music Library Association. Newsletter (0068-9343)
Related titles: Online - full text ed.: ISSN 1708-6701.
Indexed: BibInd, CMPI, M11, MusicInd.
Published by: Canadian Association of Music Libraries, Archives and Documentation Centres, Music Section, Library and Archives Canada, 395 Wellington St, Ottawa, ON K1A 0N4, Canada. TEL 613-996-7519. Ed. Mr. Desmond Maley TEL 705-673-4126 ext 220. adv.: B&W page CAD 100. Circ: 105.

780 CAN
C A M M A C TORONTO REGION NEWSLETTER. (Canadian Amateur Musicians - Musiciens Amateurs du Canada) Text in English. 1970. m. CAD 25 (effective 1999). adv. **Document type:** *Newsletter.* **Description:** Provides news and information about upcoming musical events, activities and workshops of interest to amateur musicians of all ages and abilities.
Formerly: C A M M A C Southern Ontario Region Newsletter
Indexed: CMPI.
Published by: Canadian Amateur Musicians, Toronto Region/Musiciens Amateurs du Canada, 83 Bellefair Ave, Toronto, ON M4L 3T7, Canada. TEL 416-694-9266. Ed., Pub., Adv. contact Jenny Ono. Circ: 400 (controlled).

785.06 CAN ISSN 1487-9123
C B A FANFARE. (Canadian Band Association) Text in English. 1971. q. free to members. adv. bk.rev. **Document type:** *Newsletter, Trade.* **Description:** Promotes and develops the musical, educational and cultural values of bands in Ontario.
Former titles (until 1996): Canadian Band Association. Ontario Chapter. Newsletter (0833-9503); (until 1985): Canadian Band Directors Association. Newsletter (0381-9159)
Indexed: CMPI.
Published by: Canadian Band Association, 34 Sunset Dr North, Yorkton, SK S3N 3K9, Canada. TEL 306-783-2263, FAX 306-783-2060, sask.band@sasktel.net, http://www.canadianband.ca. Circ: 170.

780 CAN ISSN 0711-9828
C B C CLASSICAL RECORD REFERENCE BOOK. (Canadian Broadcasting Corporation) Text in English, French. 1980. a.
Published by: C B C / Radio-Canada, 1400 E Rene Levesque, Montreal, PQ H3C 3A8, Canada. TEL 514-285-3211.

780 910.03 USA ISSN 1043-1241
ML3556
C B M R DIGEST. Text in English. 1988. s-a. free to members (effective 2010). 12 p./no. 2 cols./p.; **Document type:** *Newsletter, Trade.* **Description:** Contains items of interest in black music research.
Formerly (until 1988): Inside C B M R; Supersedes in part (in 1988): Black Music Research Newsletter (0271-3799)
Indexed: A01, IIBP, IIMP, M11, MusicInd, RILM, T02.
—CCC.
Published by: Center for Black Music Research, Columbia College Chicago, 600 S Michigan Ave, Chicago, IL 60605. TEL 312-663-1600, FAX 312-344-8076, cbmr.contact@colum.edu.

780 910.03 USA ISSN 1042-8836
C B M R MONOGRAPHS. Text in English. 1989. irreg., latest vol.5. USD 10 per vol. domestic; USD 13 per vol. foreign (effective 2010). back issues avail.; reprints avail. **Document type:** *Monographic series, Academic/Scholarly.* **Description:** Contains reference material in Black music.
Published by: Center for Black Music Research, Columbia College Chicago, 600 S Michigan Ave, Chicago, IL 60605. TEL 312-663-1600, FAX 312-344-8076, cbmr.contact@colum.edu.

783 USA
C C M UPDATE. (Contemporary Christian Music) Text in English. 1983. 50/yr. USD 120 (effective 1999). adv. **Document type:** *Magazine, Consumer.* **Description:** Contains news and information about the contemporary gospel music industry, including airplay and sales reports.
Formerly (until 1986): MusicLine (0746-7656)
Published by: C C M Communications, 104 Woodmont Blvd, Ste 300, Nashville, TN 37205. TEL 615-386-3011, FAX 615-386-3380. Ed. Lindy Warren. Pub. John W Styll. R&P Sarah Aldridge. Adv. contact David Berndt. Circ: 5,000.

C C T NEWSLETTER. (Choreographers Theatre) *see* DANCE

780 USA ISSN 1062-6883
ML156.9
C D GUIDE. (Compact Disc) Text in English. 19??. s-a.
Published by: Connell Communications, Inc. (Subsidiary of: International Data Group), 86 Elm St, Peterborough, NH 03458. TEL 603-924-7271, 800-216-2225, FAX 603-924-7013.

780.7 USA ISSN 0007-845X
C I M NOTES. (Cleveland Institute of Music) Text in English. 1973. bi-m. (Sep.-May). free. illus. **Document type:** *Newsletter.* **Description:** Provides information on events at the Cleveland Institute of Music and on faculty, student, and trustee activities. Scholarly articles are also included as well as profiles on alumni and donors.
Published by: Cleveland Institute of Music, 11021 E Boulevard, Cleveland, OH 44106. TEL 216-791-5000, FAX 216-791-3063. Ed. Rory Sanders. Circ: 12,000 (controlled).

780.71 AUS ISSN 1321-196X
C I R C M E LECTURE SERIES. (Callaway International Resource Centre) Key Title: C I R C M E Series. Text in English. 1991. irreg., latest vol.13, 1998. AUD 5 newsstand/cover (effective 2003). **Document type:** *Journal, Academic/Scholarly.* **Description:** Contains a series of articles related to music education.
Published by: University of Western Australia, Callaway International Resource Centre (C I R C M E), University of Western, School of Music, 35 Stirling Hwy, Crawley, W.A. 6009, Australia. TEL 61-8-64882051, FAX 61-8-64881076, music@uwa.edu.au.

780 USA ISSN 1050-9887
ML1100
C M A MATTERS; the technical bulletin of Chamber Music America. Text in English. q. free to members. **Document type:** *Newsletter, Trade.* **Description:** Provides practical advice on topics of professional concern.
Related titles: Online - full text ed.
Published by: Chamber Music America, 305 Seventh Ave, New York, NY 10001. TEL 212-242-2022, FAX 212-242-7955, info@chamber-music.org, http://www.chamber-music.org.

372.87 USA
C M E A MAGAZINE. Text in English. 1947. q. free to members (effective 2005). adv. 40 p./no.; **Document type:** *Newsletter, Trade.*
Formerly: C M E A News (0007-8638)
Indexed: IIMP, MAG.
Published by: California Music Educators Association, 2565 Beverly Glen Blvd, Los Angeles, CA 90077. TEL 310-500-3617, FAX 253-295-5717, cmea@calmusiced.com. Ed., Adv. contact Margaret Stevens. R&P John Larrieau. B&W page USD 329, color page USD 675; trim 8.5 x 11. Circ: 3,650.

780.42 USA ISSN 1074-6978
ML156.9
C M J NEW MUSIC MONTHLY. (College Media Journal) Text in English. 1993. m. USD 39.95 domestic; USD 69.95 in Canada; USD 74.95 elsewhere; USD 4.99 newsstand/cover (effective 2006). adv. bk.rev.; film rev.; music rev. charts. back issues avail. **Document type:** *Magazine, Consumer.* **Description:** Contains in-depth interviews, charts, genre focus, unbiased reviews, and the "Localzine" guide to music scenes across the country. Every issue comes with an exclusive compact disc featuring 16 to 22 tracks by as many artists.
Indexed: IIMP, M11, T02.
Published by: C M J Network, 151 W 25th St, 12th Fl, New York, NY 10001. TEL 516-466-6000, FAX 516-466-7159. Ed. Steve Ciabattoni. Pub. Robert K Haber. adv.: page USD 7,000; trim 10.88 x 8.38. Circ: 45,000 (paid). **Subscr. to:** PO Box 57414, Boulder, CO 80322-7414.

780.42 USA ISSN 0890-0795
C M J NEW MUSIC REPORT. (College Media Journal) Text in English. 1978. w. USD 345 domestic; USD 450 in Canada; USD 625 elsewhere (effective 2005). adv. bk.rev.; film rev. back issues avail. **Document type:** *Magazine, Trade.*
Former titles: Progressive Media (0731-5708); C M J Progressive Media (0195-7430)
Published by: C M J Network, 151 W 25th St, 12th Fl, New York, NY 10001. TEL 917-606-1908, FAX 917-606-1914. Ed. Steve Ciabattoni. Pub. Robert Haber. Circ: 3,000.

780 USA
C M S MONOGRAPHS AND BIBLIOGRAPHIES IN AMERICAN MUSIC. Text in English. 19??. irreg., latest vol.22, 2010. price varies. bibl. back issues avail. **Document type:** *Monographic series, Trade.*
Published by: Pendragon Press, PO Box 190, Hillsdale, NY 12529. TEL 518-325-6100, FAX 518-325-6102, orders@pendragonpress.com.

784 DEU
C S - JOURNAL. Text in German. 1879. q. EUR 12 (effective 2011). adv. bk.rev. **Document type:** *Magazine, Consumer.*
Formerly: Gemeindechor
Published by: (Christlicher Saengerbund e.V.), Verlag Singende Gemeinde, Westfalenweg 207, Wuppertal, 42111, Germany. TEL 49-202-750633, FAX 49-202-755304, cs-vsg@cs-vsg.de.

C V C REPORT. *see* COMMUNICATIONS—Video

781.64 DEU
CAB NIGHTFLIGHT; Das Musikmagazin. Text in German. bi-m. adv. **Document type:** *Magazine, Consumer.*
Published by: Hopf & Schmitz Agentur fuer Kommunikation GmbH, Schlesische Str 28, Berlin, 10997, Germany. TEL 49-30-6100920, FAX 49-30-61009297. adv.: B&W page EUR 2,732, color page EUR 4,554; trim 210 x 297. Circ: 80,000 (controlled).

CABINET. *see* ART

780 USA ISSN 0162-6973
ML3505.8
CADENCE (REDWOOD); the review of jazz & blues: creative improvised music. Text in English. 1976. q. (as of October 2007). USD 60 (effective 2007). adv. bk.rev.; music rev. index. 256 p./no. 2 cols./p.; back issues avail. **Document type:** *Magazine, Consumer.* **Description:** Features interviews, oral histories, news and coverage of record scenes.
Indexed: APC, IIMP, M11, MusicInd, PMPI, T02.
—Ingenta.
Published by: Cadence Jazz & Blues Magazine Ltd., Cadence Bldg, Redwood, NY 13679-9612. TEL 315-287-2852, FAX 315-287-2860. Ed. Robert Rusch. R&P Larry Raye. Adv. contact Carl Ericson. Circ: 7,500.

780.7 USA ISSN 0007-9405
ML1
CADENZA. Text in English. 1942. 3/yr. USD 12 to non-members; free to members (effective 2011). adv. bk.rev. illus. **Document type:** *Journal, Academic/Scholarly.* **Description:** Offers a forum covering the study and teaching of music.
Published by: Montana Music Educators Association, 500 32nd Ave, NE, Great Falls, MT 59404. TEL 406-761-0420. Ed., Adv. contact Dennis Granlie. Circ: 1,000.

780.71 CAN ISSN 0703-8380
CADENZA. Text in English. s-a. CAD 50 (effective 2000). bk.rev. **Document type:** *Newsletter.*
Former titles: S M E A. Journal (0317-5073); S M E A. Newsletter (0381-9051)
Indexed: C03, CEI, CMPI, PQC.
Published by: (Saskatchewan Music Educators' Association), Saskatchewan Teachers' Federation, 2317 Arlington Ave., Saskatoon, SK S7J 2H8, Canada. stf@stf.sk.ca. Ed. Ian Cochrane. Circ: 500.

780.42 810 USA ISSN 1089-5728
CAFE EIGHTIES MAGAZINE; the perfect blend of yesterday's grinds and what's brewing in your mind today. Text in English. 1993. q. USD 18; USD 4.95 newsstand/cover (effective 2006). adv. bk.rev.; music rev.; play rev.; tel.rev.; video rev. illus. back issues avail. **Document type:** *Magazine, Consumer.* **Description:** Caters to a readership that grew out of the early 80s. Includes feature articles, literature, celebrity and personality profiles, columns, and product reviews.
Address: 1562 First Ave, Ste 180, New York, NY 10028. TEL 212-570-5599, 800-627-6247, FAX 212-861-0588. Ed., Pub., R&P Kimberly Brittingham. Adv. contact Ingrid Ogden. B&W page USD 600; trim 10.5 x 8. Circ: 2,500. **Dist. by:** Ingram Periodicals, 1240 Heil Quaker Blvd, La Vergne, TN 37086. TEL 615-793-5522.

780 FRA ISSN 1969-881X
LES CAHIERS DE FRANCIS POULENC. Text in French. 2008. s-a. **Document type:** *Consumer.*
Published by: (Association des Amis de Francis Poulenc), Editions Michel de Maule, 41 Rue de Richelieu, Paris, 75001, France. TEL 33-1-42979356, FAX 33-1-42979490, studio@micheldemaule.com, http://www.micheldemaule.com.

LES CAHIERS DE L'EVEIL. *see* PSYCHOLOGY

780.92 FRA ISSN 0395-1200
ML410.D28
CAHIERS DEBUSSY. Text in French; Text occasionally in English. 1974. a., latest vol.28, 2004. EUR 20 to members (effective 2009). adv. illus. 100 p./no.; **Document type:** *Academic/Scholarly.*
Indexed: PCI, RILM.
Published by: Centre de Documentation Claude Debussy, 2 rue de Louvois, Paris, 75002, France. contact@debussy.fr. Ed. Pierre Boulez.

780.89 CHE
CAHIERS D'ETHNOMUSICOLOGIE. Text in French. 1988. a. price varies. **Document type:** *Monographic series, Academic/Scholarly.*
Formerly (until 2006): Cahiers de Musiques Traditionnelles (1015-5775)
Indexed: AICP, MLA-IB.
Published by: (Ateliers d'Ethnomusicologie), Georg Editeur, Case Postale 46, Geneva, 1211, Switzerland. TEL 41-11-7029311, FAX 41-11-7029355. Ed. Laurent Aubert.

782.42 FRA ISSN 1292-7198
CAHIERS D'ETUDES LEO FERRE. Text in French. 1998. s-a. **Document type:** *Journal, Consumer.*
Published by: Editions du Petit Vehicule, 20 rue du Coudray, Nantes, 44300, France. TEL 33-2-40521494, FAX 33-2-40521508.

781.62 CHN
CAIFENG BAO/FOLK SONG WEEKLY. Text in Chinese. w. CNY 52.20 (effective 2004). **Document type:** *Consumer.*
Published by: Tianjin Ribao Baoye Jituan, 873, Dagu Nanlu, Tianjin, 300211, China. TEL 86-22-28201211.

780 USA ISSN 0886-4594
CALENDAR FOR NEW MUSIC. Text in English. 1979. 9/yr. USD 15 domestic; USD 18 foreign; USD 11 to students; USD 3 newsstand/cover (effective 2005). adv. **Document type:** *Newsletter.*
Former titles (until 1982): New Music News; (until 1981): New Music Calendar
Published by: SoundArt Foundation, Inc., PO Box 900, Philmont, NY 12565-0900. Ed. William Hellermann. Circ: 8,500 (paid and controlled).

782.42 USA ISSN 1537-2286
ML3477.7.C15
CALIFORNIA SONG. Text in English. 2002 (Jan.). every 6 wks. USD 30.95 (effective 2002).
Published by: McCarley Entertainment Media, 465 Stony Point Rd. Ste. 240, Santa Rosa, CA 95401. TEL 310-281-1934. Ed., Pub. Kevin McCarley.

780.7 USA
➤ **CALIFORNIA STUDIES IN 19TH CENTURY MUSIC.** Text in English. 1980. irreg., latest vol.13, 2005. price varies. back issues avail. **Document type:** *Monographic series, Academic/Scholarly.* **Description:** Discusses theory in music of the 19th century.

Related titles: Online - full text ed.
Published by: University of California Press, Book Series, 2120 Berkeley Way, Berkeley, CA 94704. TEL 510-642-4247, FAX 510-643-7127, foundation@ucpress.edu. **Subscr. to:** California - Princeton Fulfillment Services, Inc., 1445 Lower Ferry Rd, Ewing, NJ 08618. TEL 609-883-1759, 800-777-4726, FAX 800-999-1958, orders@cpfsinc.com.

➤ **CALL TO WORSHIP**; liturgy, music, preeching and the arts. *see* RELIGIONS AND THEOLOGY—Protestant

782.81 GBR
CAMBRIDGE OPERA HANDBOOKS. Text in English. 1981. irreg., latest 2006. price varies. back issues avail. **Document type:** *Monographic series, Academic/Scholarly.* **Description:** Covers the history of work and a detailed musical analysis.
Published by: Cambridge University Press, The Edinburgh Bldg, Shaftesbury Rd, Cambridge, CB2 8RU, United Kingdom. TEL 44-1223-312393, FAX 44-1223-315052, information@cambridge.org, http://www.cambridge.org/uk. Ed. Richard Wagner.

782.1 GBR ISSN 0954-5867
ML1699
➤ **CAMBRIDGE OPERA JOURNAL.** Text in English. 1989. 3/yr. GBP 131, USD 222 to institutions; GBP 138, USD 238 combined subscription to institutions (print & online eds.) (effective 2012). adv. bk.rev. illus. back issues avail.; reprint service avail. from PSC. **Document type:** *Journal, Academic/Scholarly.* **Description:** Addresses audiences from a variety of disciplines, ranging from musicology to literature, theater, and history.
Related titles: Online - full text ed.: ISSN 1474-0621. GBP 124, USD 216 to institutions (effective 2012).
Indexed: A20, A22, AmHI, ArtHuCI, BrHumI, CA, CurCont, E01, H07, IBT&D, IIMP, IIPA, M11, MLA-IB, MusicInd, P10, P48, P53, P54, PCI, PQC, RASB, RILM, SCOPUS, T02, W07.
—BLDSC (3015.966900), IE, Infotrieve, Ingenta. **CCC.**
Published by: Cambridge University Press, The Edinburgh Bldg, Shaftesbury Rd, Cambridge, CB2 8RU, United Kingdom. TEL 44-1223-312393, FAX 44-1223-315052, journals@cambridge.org, http://www.cambridge.org/uk. Eds. Steven Huebner, Suzanne Aspden. R&P Linda Nicol TEL 44-1223-325702. Adv. contact Rebecca Roberts TEL 44-1223-325083. page GBP 405, page USD 770. Circ: 750. **Subscr. to:** Cambridge University Press, 32 Ave of the Americas, New York, NY 10013. TEL 212-337-5000, FAX 212-691-3239, journals_subscriptions@cup.org.

780 GBR
CAMBRIDGE STUDIES IN MUSIC THEORY AND ANALYSIS. Text in English. 1992. irreg., latest 2007. price varies. adv. back issues avail.; reprints avail. **Document type:** *Monographic series, Academic/Scholarly.* **Description:** Designed for those interested in the theoretical and intellectual issues of music, whether as historians of ideas, as practical analysts, or as theoreticians.
Published by: Cambridge University Press, The Edinburgh Bldg, Shaftesbury Rd, Cambridge, CB2 8RU, United Kingdom. TEL 44-1223-312393, FAX 44-1223-315052, journals@cambridge.org, http://www.cambridge.org/uk. Ed. Ian Bent. R&P Linda Nicol TEL 44-1223-325702. Adv. contact Rebecca Roberts TEL 44-1223-325083.

781.542 USA
CAMPUS CIRCLE. Text in English. 1990. bi-w. free. film rev.; music rev. illus. **Document type:** *Newspaper, Consumer.* **Description:** Covers entertainment, focusing on college students.
Published by: Campus Circle, Inc, 5042 Wilshire Blvd, Ste 600, Los Angeles, CA 90036. TEL 323-939-8477, FAX 323-939-8656. Eds. Joy Calisoff, Mike Dutra. Circ: 40,000.

780 CAN ISSN 1910-6963
CANADA COUNCIL FOR THE ARTS. CANADIAN MUSICAL DIVERSITY PROGRAM. ANNUAL REPORT. Text in English. 2004. a. **Document type:** *Report, Trade.*
Published by: Canada Council for the Arts, 350 Albert St, P O Box 1047, Ottawa, ON K1P 5V8, Canada. TEL 613-566-4414, 800-263-5588, FAX 613-566-4390, http://www.canadacouncil.ca.

780 CAN ISSN 1719-9808
CANADA MUSIC FUND. ANNUAL REPORT. Text in English, French. 2004. a., latest 2004. **Document type:** *Report, Trade.*
Media: Online - full text. **Related titles:** Print ed.: ISSN 1910-9466. 2001; French ed.: Fonds de la Musique du Canada. Rapport Annuel. ISSN 1719-9816.
Published by: Canadian Heritage/Patrimoine Canadien, 15 Eddy St, Gatineau, PQ K1A 0M5, Canada. TEL 819-997-0055, 866-811-0055, pch-qc@pch.gc.ca.

780 CAN ISSN 1910-8613
CANADA MUSIC FUND. POLICY MONITORING PROGRAM. ANNUAL REPORT/FONDS DE LA MUSIQUE DU CANADA. PROGRAMME DE SUIVI DE LA POLITIQUE. RAPPORT ANNUEL. Text in English, French. 2001. a. **Document type:** *Government.*
Published by: (Heritage Canada, Cultural Affairs, Canada Music Fund), Heritage Canada/Patrimoine Canadien, P O Box 1358, Sta B, Ottawa, ON K1P 5R4, Canada. service@rcip.gc.ca.

CANADA MUSIC FUND. SUPPORT TO SECTOR ASSOCIATIONS PROGRAM. ANNUAL REPORT/FONDS DE LA MUSIQUE DU CANADA. PROGRAMME D'AIDE AUX ASSOCIATIONS SECTORIELLES. RAPPORT ANNUEL. *see* BUSINESS AND ECONOMICS

CANADA'S ATLANTIC FOLKLORE AND FOLKLIFE SERIES. *see* FOLKLORE

781.62 CAN ISSN 1925-3265
ML3563
CANADIAN FOLK MUSIC. Text in English, French. 1981. q. free to members (effective 2011). bk.rev. back issues avail. **Document type:** *Magazine, Trade.*
Former titles (until 2003): Canadian Folk Music Bulletin (0829-5344); (until 1982): Canadian Folk Music Society. Bulletin (0820-0742); Which was formed by the merger of (1965-1981): Canadian Folk Music Society Newsletter (0576-5234); (1978-1981): Canada Folk Bulletin (0703-2234); Which was formerly (1972-1978): Come All Ye (0316-0378); Canadian Folk Music Society. Bulletin incorporated (198?-1984): Canadian Folk Festival Directory (0827-2492)
Media: Online - full text.
Indexed: A01, CA, CMPI, IIMP, M11, MLA, MLA-IB, MusicInd, RILM, T02.
—Ingenta.
Published by: Canadian Society for Traditional Music, 4907 54th St, Athabasca, AB T9S 1L2, Canada. Eds. David Gregory, Rosaleen Gregory.

780 158 CAN ISSN 1199-1054
ML3919
➤ **CANADIAN JOURNAL OF MUSIC THERAPY/REVUE CANADIENNE DE MUSICOTHERAPIE.** Text in English, French. 1993. a. looseleaf. bk.rev. bibl.; charts; illus.; stat. back issues avail. **Document type:** *Journal, Academic/Scholarly.* **Description:** Covers the therapeutic application of music for clients and patients. Serves children with disabilities, including emotional behavior delays, individuals with psychiatric diagnoses, and the elderly.
Indexed: A01, C03, CBCARef, CMPI, E-psyche, P03, P24, P25, P48, PQC, PsycInfo, PsycholAb, RILM, T02.
—CCC.
Published by: Canadian Association for Music Therapy/Association de Musicotherapie du Canada, Wilfrid Laurier University, Waterloo, ON N2L 3C5, Canada. TEL 519-884-1970 ext 6828, 800-996-CAMT, FAX 519-886-9351, camt@musictherapy.ca, http://www.musictherapy.ca. Ed. Carolyn Bereznak Kenny. Circ: 430 (paid).

➤ **CANADIAN MUSIC DIRECTORY.** *see* BUSINESS AND ECONOMICS—Trade And Industrial Directories

780.7 CAN ISSN 0008-4549
ML5
➤ **CANADIAN MUSIC EDUCATOR.** Variant title: Canadian Journal of Research in Music Education. Text in English. 1959. q. CAD 60 domestic; USD 75 in United States; USD 80 elsewhere (effective 2005). adv. bk.rev. charts; illus.; stat. index. back issues avail. **Document type:** *Journal, Academic/Scholarly.* **Description:** Presents selected articles and research on music education aimed at improving curriculum and instruction in Canadian schools.
Incorporates: Canadian Music Educators Association. Newsletter (0045-5172)
Related titles: Microform ed.: (from MML); Online - full text ed.
Indexed: A01, C03, CEI, CMPI, E03, IIMP, M11, MusicInd, P48, PQC, RILM, T02.
—Ingenta. **CCC.**
Published by: Canadian Music Educators Association, Faculty of Music, University of Toronto, Toronto, ON M5S 1A1, Canada. TEL 416-978-0535, FAX 416-978-5771, lbartel@chass.utoronto.ca, http://www.musiceducationonline.org/cmea. Ed. Lee Bartel. Circ: 2,800.

➤ **THE CANADIAN MUSIC INDUSTRY. ECONOMIC PROFILE/ INDUSTRIE CANADIENNE DE LA MUSIQUE. PROFIL ECONOMIQUE.** *see* BUSINESS AND ECONOMICS—Production Of Goods And Services

780.7 CAN ISSN 1193-9567
ML27.C2
CANADIAN MUSIC TEACHER. Text in English. 1935. 3/yr. membership. adv. bk.rev.
Former titles (until 1991): Music News (1187-676X); (until 1990): Canadian Federation of Music Teachers' Association. Newsletter (0381-6494); (until 1975): Canadian Music Teacher (0319-6356); (until 1971): Canadian Federation of Music Teachers' Association. News Bulletin (0008-3534)
Indexed: CMPI.
Published by: Canadian Federation of Music Teachers' Associations, 616 Andrew St, Thunder Bay, ON P7B 2C9, Canada. Ed. Laura Gresch. Circ: 4,000.

780 CAN ISSN 0225-9435
CANADIAN MUSIC TRADE. Text in English. 1979. bi-m. adv. **Document type:** *Journal, Trade.*
Related titles: Microfiche ed.: (from MML); Microform ed.: (from MML).
Indexed: C03, CBCABus, CMPI, PQC.
Published by: Norris - Whitney Communications Inc., 23 Hannover Dr, 7, St Catharines, ON L2W 1A3, Canada. TEL 905-641-3471, FAX 905-641-1648. Ed. Jeff MacKay. Pub. Jim Norris. R&P Maureen Jack. Circ: 3,000 (controlled).

780 CAN ISSN 0708-9635
ML3848
CANADIAN MUSICIAN. Text in English. 1979. bi-m. CAD 19 domestic; USD 24 foreign (effective 2005). adv. back issues avail. **Document type:** *Magazine, Consumer.*
Related titles: Microfiche ed.: (from MML); Microform ed.: (from MML); Online - full text ed.
Indexed: A01, A03, A08, A11, A26, C03, C05, CA, CBCARef, CBPI, CMPI, CPerI, G05, G06, G07, G08, H20, I05, I06, I07, IIMP, M02, M11, MusicInd, P48, PQC, S23, T02.
—CIS, Ingenta. **CCC.**
Published by: Norris - Whitney Communications Inc., 23 Hannover Dr, 7, St Catharines, ON L2W 1A3, Canada. TEL 905-641-3471, FAX 905-641-1648. Ed. Jeff MacKay. Pub. Jim Norris. R&P Maureen Jack. Circ: 28,000.

784.18 CAN ISSN 1703-5295
CANADIAN WINDS. Text in English. 2002. s-a. CAD 50 to individuals; CAD 200 to institutions (effective 2007). adv. **Document type:** *Journal, Academic/Scholarly.*
Indexed: A01, CMPI, M11, MusicInd, PQC, RILM, T02.
Published by: Canadian Band Association, 34 Sunset Dr North, Yorkton, SK S3N 3K9, Canada. TEL 306-783-2263, FAX 306-783-2060, sask.band@sasktel.net. Ed., Pub. Tim Linsley. adv.: B&W page CAD 645; trim 8.375 x 10.875. Circ: 1,700.

781.65 AUS ISSN 1832-4649
CANBERRA JAZZ CLUB NEWSLETTER. Text in English. 1982. m. **Document type:** *Newsletter, Consumer.*
Former titles (until 1995): Canberra Jazz Club Letter; (until 1993): Canberra Jazz Club News; (until 1991): Canberra Jazz Club Newsletter; (until 1986): Jazz in Canberra
Published by: Canberra Jazz Club, GPO Box 1304, Canberra, ACT 2601, Australia. TEL 61-2-62486339, FAX 61-2-62956752, cjcact@bigpond.com, http://canberrajazzclub.org.

CANCIONES PARA EL AULA. *see* EDUCATION

CANCIONES PARA MI ESCUELA. *see* EDUCATION

780 POL ISSN 1230-1515
CANOR; pismo poswiecone interpretacjom muzyki dawnej. Text in Polish. 1991. q. 76 p./no.
Indexed: RILM.
Published by: Agencja Promocji Artystycznej Canor, Konopnickiej 31/6, Torun, 87100, Poland. Ed. Cezary Zych. Circ: 1,000.

784 ZAF
CANTANDO GAUDEAMUS. Text in Afrikaans, English. 1994 (no.24). q. membership. adv. bk.rev. **Document type:** *Bulletin.*
Formerly (until 1994): Suid-Afrikaanse Koorvereniging. Nuusbrief
Published by: Suid-Afrikaanse Koorvereniging/South African Choral Society, Fichardt Park, PO Box 31950, Bloemfontein, 9137, South Africa. TEL 27-51-4214284, FAX 27-51-4482003. Ed. Marius Pretorius.

782.5 DEU
CANTATE. Text in German. bi-m. EUR 30 domestic; EUR 36 in Europe; EUR 45 elsewhere; EUR 4.60 newsstand/cover (effective 2003). adv. **Document type:** *Magazine, Consumer.* **Description:** Covers all aspects of choral music and choirs.
Published by: Kontrapunkt Verlags GmbH, Im Sand 56, Rheinbreitbach, 53619, Germany. TEL 49-2224-76482, FAX 49-2224-900292. Ed., Pub. Erwin Bidder. adv.: page EUR 500. Circ: 4,800 (paid and controlled).

780 ITA ISSN 1972-3865
IL CANTIERE MUSICALE. Text in Italian. 2001. m. **Document type:** *Magazine, Consumer.*
Published by: Conservatorio Niccolo Paganini, Via Albaro 38, Genoa, 16145, Italy. TEL 39-010-3620747, FAX 39-010-3620819, http://www.conservatoriopaganini.org.

780 HRV ISSN 1330-4747
ML5
CANTUS. Text in Croatian. 1971. 3/yr. **Document type:** *Journal, Academic/Scholarly.*
Former titles (until 1993): H D S (Hrvatsko Drustvo Skladatelja) (1330-4720); (until 1990): D S H (Drustvo Skladatelja Hrvatske) (1330-4712); (until 1983): Bilten D S H (1330-4704); (until 1979): Bilten Drustva Hrvatskih Skladatelja (1333-7718)
Indexed: RILM.
Published by: Hrvatsko Drustvo Skladatelja/Croatian Composers' Society, Berislaviceva 9, Zagreb, 10000, Croatia. TEL 385-1-4872370, FAX 385-1-4872372, info@hds.hr, http://www.hds.hr.

781.7 398 GBR ISSN 0967-0599
ML3653
CANU GWERIN/FOLK SONG. Text in English. 1909. a. GBP 6 domestic; GBP 8 foreign (effective 2000). bk.rev. back issues avail. **Document type:** *Bulletin.*
Formerly (until 1978): Welsh Folk-Song Society. Journal
Indexed: IIMP, RILM.
Published by: Welsh Folk-Song Society/Cymdeithas Alawon Gwerin Cymru, c/o Mrs. B.L. Roberts, Hafan, Cricieth, Gwynedd, United Kingdom. Eds. Rhiannon Ifans, Rhidian Griffiths. Circ: 250.

780 NZL ISSN 0110-7771
CANZONA. Text in English. 1974. a. free membership (effective 2009). 70 p./no.; back issues avail. **Document type:** *Yearbook, Trade.* **Description:** Contains numerous articles of interest covering events within the preceding year.
Formerly (until 1979): Composers' Association of New Zealand. Newsletter (0110-6600)
Related titles: Online - full text ed.
Indexed: A11, CA, M11, RILM, T02.
—CCC.
Published by: Composers Association of New Zealand Inc., PO Box 4065, Wellington, New Zealand.

780 NZL ISSN 1172-0492
CANZONETTA. Text in English. 19??. bi-m. free to members (effective 2010). **Document type:** *Newsletter, Trade.* **Description:** Contains news, events, features and opportunities that relate to New Zealand composers.
Formerly (until 1979): Composers' Association of New Zealand. Newsletter Supplement
Related titles: Online - full text ed.: ISSN 1179-9951.
Published by: Composers Association of New Zealand Inc., PO Box 4065, Wellington, New Zealand. info@canz.net.nz.

780 ITA ISSN 1970-5166
I CAPOLAVORI DELLA MUSICA CLASSICA. Text in Italian. 2006. w. **Document type:** *Magazine, Consumer.*
Published by: Poligrafici Editoriale (Subsidiary of: Monrif Group), Via Enrico Mattei 106, Bologna, BO 40138, Italy. TEL 39-051-6006111, FAX 39-051-6006266, http://www.monrifgroup.net.

CARBON 14. *see* ART

789.5 USA ISSN 0730-5001
ML1039
CARILLON NEWS. Text in English. 1969. s-a. USD 10 (effective 2001). bk.rev. **Document type:** *Newsletter.*
Formerly: Randschriften; a Newsletter for the Guild of Carillonneurs (0085-5383)
Published by: Guild of Carillonneurs in North America, 5339 S. Ellis #3D, Chicago, IL 60615. fackent1@midway.uchicago.edu. Eds. Donna Fackenthal, Jim Fackenthal TEL 773-288-0725. R&P Jim Fackenthal TEL 773-288-0725. Circ: 525.

780.9221 DNK ISSN 1603-3663
ML410.N625
CARL NIELSEN STUDIES. Text in English. 2003. irreg., latest vol.3, 2008. price varies. back issues avail. **Document type:** *Monographic series, Academic/Scholarly.*
Published by: Det Kongelige Bibliotek/The Royal Library, Christians Brygge, PO Box 2149, Copenhagen K, 1016, Denmark. TEL 45-33-474747, FAX 45-33-932218, kb@kb.dk. Ed. Niels Krabbe.

CARNEGIE; dedicated to art, and science. *see* ART

784 ITA ISSN 1120-4621
ML5
LA CARTELLINA; rivista della coralita italiana. Text in Italian. 1977. bi-m. EUR 45.90 (effective 2008). adv. bk.rev. bibl. cum.index. back issues avail.
Indexed: MusicInd, RILM.
Published by: Edizioni Musicali Europee, Via Forze Armate 13, Milan, 20147, Italy. TEL 39-02-48713103. Circ: 3,000.

781.64 USA
CATALOGUE OF CONTEMPORARY MUSIC. Text in English. irreg. (2-4/yr.). free. back issues avail. **Document type:** *Catalog.* **Description:** Sales and rental performance materials (scores and parts) for 20th century music written by members of ACA.

Published by: (American Composers Alliance), American Composers Edition, 170 W 74th St, New York, NY 10023. TEL 212-362-8900, FAX 212-874-8605.

780 DEU ISSN 0069-116X
ML113
CATALOGUS MUSICUS. Text in German. 1963. irreg., latest vol.18, 2004. price varies. **Document type:** *Monographic series, Academic/Scholarly.*
Published by: (International Association of Music Libraries), Baerenreiter Verlag, Heinrich-Schuetz-Allee 35, Kassel, 34131, Germany. TEL 49-561-3105154, FAX 49-561-3105195, order@baerenreiter.com, http://www.baerenreiter.com. **Co-sponsor:** International Musicological Society.

780 ESP ISSN 1136-7458
CATALUNYA MUSICA. Text in Spanish, Catalan. 1983. m. **Document type:** *Magazine, Consumer.*
Formerly (until 1990): Revista Musical Catalana (1136-744X)
Published by: Palau de la Musica Catalana, Sant Francesc de Paula, 2, Barcelona, 08003, Spain. TEL 34-93-2957200, FAX 34-93-2957210, palau@palaumusica.org, http://www.palaumusica.org/.

780 CAN
CAUSTIC TRUTHS!. Text in English. 2001. bi-m. USD 17.50 in US & Canada; USD 25 elsewhere (effective 2002). **Document type:** *Magazine, Consumer.*
Published by: Caustic Truths Communications, PO Box 92548, Toronto, ON M5A 2K0, Canada. TEL 416-935-0651, FAX 416-935-0609, editor@wehatedancemusic.tv. Ed. Richard Tanana.

783 ITA
CELEBRARE CANTANDO. Text in Italian. a. **Document type:** *Magazine, Consumer.*
Published by: Istituto Diocesano di Musica e Liturgia Don Luigi Guglielmi (I D M L), Viale Timavo 93, Reggio Emilia, 42100, Italy. TEL 39-0522-437959, http://www.idml.altervista.org.

782.3 ITA ISSN 0008-8706
CELEBRIAMO; rivista bimestrale di musica vocale per la liturgia. Text in Italian. 1915. bi-m. EUR 45 (effective 2008). adv. **Document type:** *Journal, Academic/Scholarly.*
Supersedes: Organista; Musica Sacra; Scholare Assemblea; Lodiamo Il Signore; Fiori dell'Organo; Maestri dell'Organo
Published by: Casa Musicale Edizioni Carrara, Via Ambrogio Calepio 4, Bergamo, BG 24125, Italy. TEL 39-035-243618, FAX 39-035-270298, http://www.edizionicarrara.it. Circ: 5,000.

CELEBRITY. *see* MOTION PICTURES

CENTRE CULTUREL FRANCAIS DE YAOUNDE. PROGRAMME SAISON. *see* ART

780.903 FRA ISSN 1762-7907
CENTRE DE MUSIQUE BAROQUE DE VERSAILLES. ANTHOLOGIES. Text in French. 19??. irreg. **Document type:** *Monographic series, Academic/Scholarly.*
Published by: Centre de Musique Baroque de Versailles, Hotel des Menus-Plaisirs, 22, avenue de Paris, Versailles Cedex, 78003, France. TEL 33-1-39207810, FAX 33-1-39207801, accueil@cmbv.com, http://www.cmbv.com.

780.92 FRA ISSN 1285-2880
CENTRE DE MUSIQUE BAROQUE DE VERSAILLES. PUBLICATIONS A. Text in French. 1995. irreg. **Document type:** *Monographic series, Academic/Scholarly.*
Published by: Centre de Musique Baroque de Versailles, Hotel des Menus-Plaisirs, 22, avenue de Paris, Versailles Cedex, 78003, France. TEL 33-1-39207810, FAX 33-1-39207801, accueil@cmbv.com, http://www.cmbv.com.

780.902 FRA ISSN 1285-5979
CENTRE DE MUSIQUE BAROQUE DE VERSAILLES. PUBLICATIONS B. Text in French. 1997. irreg. **Document type:** *Monographic series, Academic/Scholarly.*
Published by: Centre de Musique Baroque de Versailles, Hotel des Menus-Plaisirs, 22, avenue de Paris, Versailles Cedex, 78003, France. TEL 33-1-39207810, FAX 33-1-39207801, accueil@cmbv.com, http://www.cmbv.com.

780 AUS ISSN 1443-9018
ML5
CENTRE FOR STUDIES IN AUSTRALIAN MUSIC. REVIEW. Text in English. 1995. irreg., latest vol.23, 2008. back issues avail. **Document type:** *Journal, Academic/Scholarly.* **Description:** Features in-depth feature articles and reviews on Australian music.
Formerly (until 2000): Centre for Studies in Australian Music. Newsletter (1324-0897)
Related titles: Online - full text ed.: free (effective 2009).
Indexed: RILM.
Published by: University of Melbourne, Centre for Studies in Australian Music, Ground Fl, Conservatorium Bldg, Melbourne, VIC 3010, Australia. TEL 61-3-83445256, FAX 61-3-83445346, ozcentre@music.unimelb.edu.au. Ed. Johanna Selleck.

780 020 ITA
CENTRO INTERNAZIONALE DI RICERCA SUI PERIODICI MUSICALI. NEWSLETTER. Text in Italian. 1992. irreg. free. bk.rev. **Document type:** *Bulletin.* **Description:** Provides information about activities of the center and research on music journals. Promotes research on 18th, 19th and 20th century musical life.
Media: Online - full text.
Published by: Centro Internazionale di Ricerca sui Periodici Musicali, Piazzale San Francesco 1, Parma, PR 43100, Italy. TEL 39-0521-031130, FAX 39-0521-031134, cirpem@lacasadellamusica.it.

780 ITA ISSN 0411-5384
ML5
CENTRO ROSSINIANO DI STUDI. BOLLETTINO. Text in Italian. 1955. a. **Document type:** *Journal, Academic/Scholarly.*
Indexed: RILM.
Published by: Fondazione G. Rossini, Palazzo Olivieri Machirelli, Pesaro, Italy. rossini@abanet.it, www.fondazionerossini.org. Ed. Bruno Cagli.

783 SVN ISSN 0351-496X
CERKVENI GLASBENIK. Text in Slovenian; Summaries in English. 1878. q. EUR 23.40 (effective 2007). **Document type:** *Magazine, Consumer.*
Indexed: RILM.
Published by: Druzina, Krekov trg 1, p.p. 95, Ljubljana, 1001, Slovenia. TEL 386-1-3602845, FAX 386-1-3602800. Ed. Tomas Faganel. Circ: 1,500.

780 USA ISSN 1071-1791
ML1
CHAMBER MUSIC. Text in English. 1978. bi-m. free to members (effective 2010). adv. bk.rev. back issues avail. **Document type:** *Magazine, Trade.* **Description:** Contains news, features, profiles, events, and lists pertaining to chamber, instrumental ensembles, vocal ensembles, jazz ensembles, concert presenters, and audiences.
Former titles (until 1986): Chamber Music Magazine (8755-0725); (until 1984): American Ensemble (0197-3134)
Related titles: Online - full text ed.
Indexed: IIMP, M11, MAG, MusicInd, RILM, T02.
—Ingenta.
Published by: Chamber Music America, 305 Seventh Ave, New York, NY 10001. TEL 212-242-2022, FAX 212-242-7955, membership@chamber-music.org. Ed. Ellen Goldenshn TEL 212-242-2022 ext 26. Adv. contact Brenden O'Hanlon TEL 718-812-8826. B&W page USD 2,350, color page USD 3,200; trim 8.25 x 10.875.

780 USA
CHAMBER MUSIC DIRECTORY. Text in English. 1978. a. USD 65. **Document type:** *Directory, Trade.*
Formerly: Chamber Music America. Membership Directory (0277-4054)
Published by: Chamber Music America, 305 Seventh Ave, New York, NY 10001. TEL 212-242-2022, FAX 212-242-7955. Circ: 15,000.

780 FRA ISSN 2107-0539
LA CHANSON DE LA RENAISSANCE 1480-1600. CATALOGUE. Text in French. 1997. **Document type:** *Catalog, Academic/Scholarly.*
Media: Online - full text.
Published by: Universite de Tours (Francois-Rabelais), Centre d'Etudes Superieures de la Renaissance de Tours. Programme Ricercar, 59, Rue Nericault-Destouches, BP 11328, Tours Cedex, 37013, France. TEL 33-2-47367784, FAX 33-2-47367762, ricercar@univ-tours.fr, http://ricercar.cesr.univ-tours.fr/index.htm.

784 CAN ISSN 1192-1900
ML1499 C53
CHANTER. Text in English. 1976. q. CAD 10. adv. bk.rev.; rec.rev. illus. index. back issues avail. **Description:** Covers choral music and singers.
Formerly (until 1992): A l'Ecoute (0700-3900)
Indexed: CMPI, IIMP, M11, MusicInd.
Published by: Alliance des Chorales du Quebec, 4545 av Pierre De Coubertin, C P 1000, Succursale M, Montreal, PQ H1V 3R2, Canada. TEL 514-252-3020, FAX 514-251-8038, TELEX 05-829647 SECADMIBEC. Ed. Daniel Gauvreau. Adv. contact Chantal Paquette. Circ: 6,000.

780 USA
CHAOS CONTROL DIGIZINE. Text in English. 1992. d. **Description:** Focuses on various styles of electronic and experimental music, including techno, industrial, ambient and gothic.
Media: Online - full text.
Address: PO Box 1065, Hoboken, NJ 07030. Ed. Bob Gourley.

780 DNK ISSN 1904-2078
▼ **CHARA**; tidsskrift for kreativitet, spontaneitet og laering. Text in Danish. 2010. q. **Document type:** *Magazine, Academic/Scholarly.*
Related titles: Online - full text ed.: ISSN 1904-2094.
Published by: Rytmisk Musikkonservatorium/Rhythmic Music Conservatory, Leo Mathiesens Vej 1, Holmen, Copenhagen K, 1437, Denmark. TEL 45-32-686700, FAX 45-32-686766, rmc@rmc.dk, http://www.rmc.dk. Ed. Jens Skov Olsen.

781.546 CAN
CHART (ONLINE); Canada's music magazine. Text in English. 1990. d. adv. bk.rev.; music rev.; software rev.; tel.rev.; video rev. charts; illus. back issues avail. **Document type:** *Magazine, Consumer.* **Description:** Coverage of the Canadian and international music scenes with an emphasis on the cutting-edge tastes of today's youth. Explores the lifestyle and culture of today's youth.
Former titles (until 2009): Chart (Print) (1198-7235); (until 1993): National Chart (1193-4069)
Media: Online - full content.
Indexed: C03, CBCARef, CMPI, CPerI, G08, P48, PQC.
Published by: Chart Communications Inc., 41 Britain St, Ste 200, Toronto, ON M5A 1R7, Canada. TEL 416-363-3101, FAX 416-363-3109. Ed., R&P Nada Laskovski. Pubs. Edward Skira, Nada Laskovski. Adv. contact Edward Skira. Circ: 40,000 (paid).

780.65 DEU ISSN 1438-4779
CHART REPORT GERMANY; Der Informationsdienst fuer die Musikbranche. Text in English, German. 1999. m. EUR 260 (effective 2009). **Document type:** *Magazine, Trade.* **Description:** Provides insider information on the German music market.
Published by: Josef Keller Verlag GmbH & Co. KG, Seebreite 9, Berg, 82335, Germany. TEL 49-8151-7710, FAX 49-8151-771190, info@keller-verlag.de. Ed. Thomas Berger.

780 GBR ISSN 0262-9577
CHART WATCH. Text in English. 1981. q. USD 22.60. adv. bk.rev. charts.
Published by: ChartWatch, 8 Worcester House, Bumpstead Rd, Haverhill, Suffolk CB9 8QB, United Kingdom. Eds. John Hancock, Neil Rawlings. Circ: 300.

380.1 ITA
CHI E DOVE (YEAR). Text in Italian. 1971. a. EUR 100 (effective 2009). **Document type:** *Directory, Trade.* **Description:** Lists over 4000 addresses of people and companies operating in the Italian music and home video business.
Related titles: ◆ Supplement to: Musica e Dischi. ISSN 0027-4526.
Published by: Editoriale Musica e Dischi, Via Edmondo De Amicis, 47, Milan, MI 20123, Italy. info@musicaedischi.it, http://www.musicaedischi.it.

CHICAGO MAGAZINE. *see* TRAVEL AND TOURISM

787 USA
CHICAGO SYMPHONY ORCHESTRA. Text in English. q. adv. **Document type:** *Magazine, Trade.*
Published by: Orchestral Association, 220 South Michigan Ave, Chicago, IL 60604-2559. TEL 312-294-3087, FAX 312-294-3107. Ed., R&P Denise Wagner. Adv. contact Gail McGrath.

780 ITA ISSN 0069-3391
ML5
CHIGIANA; rassegna annuale di studi musicologici. Text in Italian. 1964. a. price varies. bk.rev. **Document type:** *Journal, Academic/Scholarly.*
Formerly: Accademia Musicale Chigiana. Quaderni (0065-0714)
Indexed: IIMP, MLA-IB, MusicInd, PCI, RILM.
Published by: (Accademia Musicale Chigiana, Siena), Casa Editrice Leo S. Olschki, Viuzzo del Pozzetto 8, Florence, 50126, Italy. TEL 39-055-6530684, FAX 39-055-6530214, celso@olschki.it, http://www.olschki.it. Circ: 500.

781.62 USA
CHILDREN'S MUSIC GAZETTE. Text in English. m. free (effective 2006). music rev. **Document type:** *Newsletter, Consumer.* **Description:** Announces news of great music for children.
Media: E-mail.
Published by: Children's Music Web, 305 Dickens Way, Santa Cruz, CA 95064.

781.7 NLD ISSN 0926-7263
ML336
CHIME. Text in English. 1990. a. EUR 23 in the European Union; EUR 25 elsewhere (effective 2009). film rev.; music rev. illus. **Document type:** *Journal, Academic/Scholarly.*
Indexed: CA, M11, MusicInd, RILM, T02.
Published by: European Foundation for Chinese Music Research, PO Box 11092, Leiden, 2301 EB, Netherlands. TEL 31-71-5133974, FAX 31-71-5123183, chime@wxs.nl, http://home.wxs.nl/~chime/. Eds. Dr. Antoinet Schimmelpenninck, Frank Kouwenhoven.

781.7 NLD ISSN 1574-2490
CHIME STUDIES IN EAST ASIAN MUSIC. Text in English. 1997. irreg., latest vol.2, 2004. price varies. **Document type:** *Monographic series.*
Published by: European Foundation for Chinese Music Research, PO Box 11092, Leiden, 2301 EB, Netherlands. TEL 31-71-5133974, FAX 31-71-5123183, chime@wxs.nl. Ed. Frank Kouwenhoven.

CHINMUSIC!. *see* SPORTS AND GAMES—Ball Games

780 USA ISSN 1937-7223
CHITTLIN' CIRCUIT. Text in English. 2004. bi-m. USD 15; USD 3 per issue (effective 2008). **Document type:** *Magazine, Consumer.*
Published by: Blackground Entertainment Group, 2405 N L St, Pensacola, FL 32502. TEL 850-433-9617. Ed. Jerome Knight.

780 GBR ISSN 0968-7262
ML5
CHOIR & ORGAN. Text in English. 1993. bi-m. GBP 22.99 domestic; GBP 44.90 in Europe; GBP 47.50 elsewhere (effective 2009). adv. illus. back issues avail. **Document type:** *Magazine, Consumer.* **Description:** For organists, singers, organ-builders, directors of sacred and secular choirs and those who enjoy choral and organ music.
Related titles: Online - full text ed.
Indexed: A01, A02, A03, A08, AmHI, BrHumI, C05, DIP, H07, IBR, IBZ, IIMP, M01, M02, M11, MASUSE, MusicInd, PCI, RILM, SCOPUS, T02, U01.
—Ingenta. **CCC.**
Published by: Rhinegold Publishing Ltd., 239-241 Shaftesbury Ave, London, WC2H 8TF, United Kingdom. TEL 44-845-1948944, FAX 44-845-1948945, rhinegoldcs@optimabiz.co.uk, http://www.rhinegold.co.uk. Ed. Maggie Hamilton.

780 UKR
CHOMUSIK. Text in Ukrainian. 1995. m. USD 125 in the Americas (effective 2000).
Published by: Litopis Publishing Center, Pr-t Pobedy, 50, Kiev, Ukraine. TEL 229-23-18. **Dist. by:** East View Information Services, 10601 Wayzata Blvd, Minneapolis, MN 55305. TEL 952-252-1201, 800-477-1005, FAX 952-252-1202, info@eastview.com, http://www.eastview.com.

786 POL ISSN 0239-8567
ML410.C54
➤ **CHOPIN STUDIES.** Text in English. 1985. a. PLZ 40 per issue domestic; USD 50 per issue foreign (effective 2003). bk.rev. **Document type:** *Journal, Academic/Scholarly.*
Related titles: ◆ Polish ed.: Rocznik Chopinowski. ISSN 0208-5992.
Indexed: RILM.
Published by: Towarzystwo im. F. Chopina/Frederick Chopin Society, Ul Okolnik 1, Warsaw, 00368, Poland. TEL 48-22-8265935, FAX 48-22-8279599, muzeum@chopin.pl, http://www.chopin.pl. Adv. contact Grazyna Michniewicz. Circ: 150 (controlled).

782.5 AUT
CHOR AKTUELL; oesterreichische Saengerzeitung. Text in German. q. EUR 9.08 domestic; EUR 19.08 in Europe; EUR 27.08 elsewhere (effective 2005). adv. bk.rev. **Document type:** *Newsletter, Consumer.*
Published by: Chorverband Oesterreich, Opernring 11-10, Vienna, W 1010, Austria. TEL 43-1-5869494, FAX 43-1-58694944, office@chorverband.at.

782.5 DEU ISSN 1613-6063
CHOR LIVE. Text in German. 2004. 5/yr. **Document type:** *Magazine, Consumer.*
Published by: ChorVerband Nordrhein-Westfalen e.V., Gallenkampstr 20, Duisburg, 47051, Germany. TEL 49-203-2988401, FAX 49-203-2988411, geschaeftsstelle@cvnrw.de.

782.5 USA
CHORAL DIRECTOR. Text in English. 19??. bi-m. free to qualified personnel (effective 2009). adv. back issues avail. **Document type:** *Magazine, Trade.* **Description:** Gives practical articles and profiles focusing on producing creative educational performances, recruitment, retention, travel, and fundraising for choral directors.
Indexed: P16.
Published by: Symphony Publishing LLC, 21 Highland Cir, Ste One, Needham, MA 02494. TEL 781-453-9310, 800-964-5150, FAX 781-453-9389, http://www.symphonypublishing.com. Ed. Christian Wissmuller TEL 781-453-9310 ext 16. Pub. Richard E Kessel TEL 781-453-9310 ext 14. Adv. contact Sidney L Davis TEL 781-453-9310 ext 13.

784 USA ISSN 0009-5028
ML1
➤ **CHORAL JOURNAL.** Text in English. 1959. m. (Aug.-July). USD 45 domestic to libraries; USD 50 in Canada to libraries; USD 85 elsewhere to libraries; USD 3 per issue to libraries; free to members (effective 2010). adv. bk.rev.; rec.rev. illus. index, cum.index: vols.1-32. back issues avail.; reprints avail. **Document type:** *Journal, Academic/Scholarly.* **Description:** Provides members with practical and scholarly information about choral music and its performance.
Incorporates (1959-1964): Texas Choirmaster
Related titles: Microfiche ed.: (from PQC); Microfilm ed.: (from PQC); Online - full text ed.
Indexed: A01, A22, ABS&EES, CA, IIMP, M11, MAG, MusicInd, RILM, T02.
—IE, Infotrieve, Ingenta.
Published by: American Choral Directors Association, 545 Couch Dr, Oklahoma City, OK 73102. TEL 405-232-8161, FAX 405-232-8162. Ed. Carroll Gonzo. Adv. contact Heidi Harmon TEL 405-232-8161. B&W page USD 1,647, color page USD 2,718; 7 x 9.75.

782.5 USA ISSN 1948-3058
ML1499
▼ ➤ **THE CHORAL SCHOLAR.** Abbreviated title: T C S. Text in English. 2009. s-a. free (effective 2009). **Document type:** *Journal, Academic/Scholarly.* **Description:** Contains articles on the study and performance of choral music.
Media: Online - full content.
Published by: National Collegiate Choral Organization, c/o Bonnie Borshay Sneed, 100 Campus Dr, Southwestern Oklahoma State University, Weatherford, OK 73096-3098. contact@ncco-usa.org. Ed. David Schildkret.

782.5 GBR ISSN 2042-4728
▼ **CHORAL SPECIAL REPORT.** Text in English. 2009. a. GBP 7 per issue (effective 2010). **Document type:** *Report, Consumer.*
Published by: Rhinegold Publishing Ltd., 239-241 Shaftesbury Ave, London, WC2H 8TF, United Kingdom. TEL 44-20-73331720, FAX 44-20-73331765, enquiries@rhinegold.co.uk.

782.5 FRA ISSN 2108-2952
CHORALIES, LE MAG. Text in French. 2002. 3/yr. back issues avail. **Document type:** *Magazine, Consumer.*
Formerly (until 2010): Polyphonies (Lyon) (1962-4182)
Related titles: Online - full text ed.: free.
Published by: A Coeur Joie, Les Passerelles, 24 Av. Joannes Masset, B P 9151, Lyon, Cedex 9 69263, France. TEL 33-4-72198330, edacj.france@wanadoo.fr, http://acj.musicanet.org.

781.64 USA
CHORD MAGAZINE. Text in English. bi-m. USD 12 domestic; USD 21 in Canada; USD 35 elsewhere; free newsstand/cover (effective 2006). adv. **Document type:** *Magazine, Consumer.* **Description:** Presents articles and features on new and upcoming bands as well as veteran groups.
Published by: Insomniac Media, PO Box 56821, Sherman Oaks, CA 91413. TEL 818-905-9347, gus@insomniacmedia.com, http://www.insomniacmedia.com. Ed., Pub., Adv. contact Gus Pena. page USD 1,200; trim 8.375 x 10.875. Circ: 55,000 (paid and controlled).

784 028.5 USA ISSN 1948-4976
ML1
THE CHORISTER. Text in English. 1949. bi-m. free to members (effective 2009). bk.rev.; music rev. bibl.; charts; illus. index. back issues avail. **Document type:** *Newsletter, Trade.* **Description:** Focuses on music with young people. Includes articles, news releases, reviews, and study plans pertaining to choral compositions, with announcements and news on the members and activities of the guild.
Formerly (until 1996): Choristers Guild Letters (0412-2801)
Indexed: MAG.
Published by: Choristers Guild, 12404 Park Central Dr, Ste 100, Dallas, TX 75251. TEL 469-398-3606, 800-246-7478, FAX 469-398-3611, membership@mailcg.org. Ed. Lois Trego TEL 713-622-3600.

784 658.048 AUT
CHORMAGAZIN. Text in German. 1974. 2/yr. free to members. adv. charts; illus. 22 p./no. 2 cols./p.; **Document type:** *Magazine, Consumer.*
Formerly: Oesterreichische Arbeitersaenger
Published by: Oesterreichischer Arbeiter-Saengerbund, Arndtstrasse 27, Vienna, W 1120, Austria. TEL 43-1-8150220, FAX 43-1-8150220, oeasb.bund-linz-her@netway.at. Ed., Pub., Adv. contact Fritz Hinterdorfer.

784 DEU ISSN 1614-2861
CHORPFALZ. Text in German. 1949. bi-m. EUR 9.60 (effective 2009). adv. **Document type:** *Magazine, Consumer.*
Formerly (until 2004): Pfaelzer Saenger (0031-6687)
Published by: (Pfaelzischer Saengerbund), Edition Omega Wolfgang Layer, Eschweg 12, Kirchlinteln-Otersen, 27308, Germany. TEL 49-4238-943642, FAX 49-4238-943613, info@edition-omega.de. adv.: page EUR 620; trim 188 x 257. Circ: 4,200 (paid).

780 DEU ISSN 0172-2255
DER CHORSAENGER. Text in German. 1951. q. membership. adv. bk.rev. **Document type:** *Newsletter.*
Published by: Mitteldeutscher Saengerbund e.V., Ulmenstr 16, Kassel, 34117, Germany. TEL 0561-15888, FAX 0561-107567. Ed. Helmuth Breiter. Circ: 3,800.

781.62 FRA ISSN 1241-7076
CHORUS; les cahiers de la chanson. Text in French. 1992. q. EUR 47 domestic; EUR 56 in Europe; EUR 62 elsewhere (effective 2009). bk.rev.; music rev. index. **Document type:** *Magazine, Consumer.* **Description:** Studies the news and history of French songs and music.
Indexed: RILM.
Published by: Editions du Verbe, 11 Rue des Olivettes, Nantes, 44000, France. TEL 33-2-37436660, FAX 33-2-37436271. Ed., Adv. contact Fred Hidalgo. Circ: 20,000.

784 CAN ISSN 0821-1108
CHORUS. Text in English. 1976. q. CAD 35 membership (effective 2004). adv. **Document type:** *Newsletter.* **Description:** Publishes articles of interest to members and choral music enthusiasts. Information on federation programs and services.
Indexed: CMPI.
Published by: Nova Scotia Choral Federation, 1113 Marginal Rd, Halifax, NS B3H 4P7, Canada. TEL 902-423-4688, FAX 902-422-0881, office@nscf.ns.ca, http://www.chebucto.ns.ca/Culture/NSCF/nscf-home.html. Ed., R&P Tim Cross. adv.: B&W page CAD 100. Circ: 400.

780 USA ISSN 1092-5252
ML156.4
THE CHRISTIAN MUSIC FINDER. Abbreviated title: C M F. Text in English. 2002. q. USD 142.50 (effective 2009). **Document type:** *Handbook/Manual/Guide, Consumer.* **Description:** Contains more than 700,000 searchable entries of printed and recorded Christian music.
Formed by the merger of (1976-2002): The Christian Music Directories. Printed Music (Print) (1095-2640); Which was formerly (until 1990): The Music Locator (0899-0115); (1974-2002): The Christian Music Directories. Recorded Music (Print) (1048-6844); Which was formerly (until 1990): Recording Locator (0899-0123); (until 1981): Misicatalog
Media: CD-ROM.
Published by: Resource Publications, Inc., 160 E Virginia St, Ste 290, San Jose, CA 95112. TEL 408-286-8505, FAX 408-287-8748, info@rpinet.com. Adv. contact Josh Burns.

791.546 USA
THE CHRISTIANNET. Text in English. 1996. m. USD 15 for 6 issues. adv. bk.rev. illus.
Published by: ChristianNet, PO Box 314, Anniston, AL 36202. TEL 800-287-2638. Ed. Darryal W Ray. Pub. H Brandt Ayers. R&P Kristy Farmer. Circ: 100,000.

781.66 CAN
CHRONICLES OF CHAOS. Text in English. 1995. m. free (effective 2004). rec.rev. **Document type:** *Magazine, Consumer.* **Description:** Covers extreme music including death-black metal, industrial, heavy techo-electronica, ambient, hardcore and various other subgenres.
Media: Online - full text.
Address: 57 Lexfield Ave, Downsview, ON M3M 1M6, Canada. Ed. Gino Filicetti.

782.42166 USA
CHUNKLET. Text in English. irreg., latest vol.15, 2000. USD 6.95 per issue (effective 2006). music rev. back issues avail. **Document type:** *Magazine, Consumer.* **Description:** Presents reviews and surveys of the indie rock and underground music scenes.
Address: PO Box 2814, Athens, GA 30612-0814. TEL 404-627-8883, advertising@chunklet.com, http://www.chunklet.com. Ed., Pub. Henry Owings. Circ: 70,000.

783 GBR ISSN 0307-6334
ML5
CHURCH MUSIC QUARTERLY. Text in English. 1963. q. free to members (effective 2009). adv. bk.rev.; rec.rev. bibl.; charts; illus. 52 p./no. 4 cols./p.; back issues avail.; reprints avail. **Document type:** *Magazine, Academic/Scholarly.* **Description:** Provides the members and friends of the RSCM with latest church music news and helps them to learn from leading practioners and theologians.
Formerly (until 1977): Promoting Church Music (0033-1112)
Indexed: RILM.
—IE.
Published by: The Royal School of Church Music, 19 The Close, Salisbury, Wiltshire SP1 2EB, United Kingdom. TEL 44-1722-424848, FAX 44-1722-424849, enquiries@rscm.com. Adv. contact Stephen Dutton TEL 44-20-7 7761011. color page GBP 1,125, B&W page GBP 795; 262 x 185. Circ: 13,500.

781.71 USA
THE CHURCH MUSIC REPORT. Text in English. 1984. m. USD 39.95 (effective 2006). adv. bk.rev.; rec.rev.; software rev.; video rev. 40 p./no. 2 cols./p.; **Document type:** *Newsletter.* **Description:** For ministers of music or anyone who has an interest in church music. Contains a chart of the best selling choral products as well as special offers and new product announcements from publishers and other church music-oriented vendors. Lists items for sale or wanted by members. Includes a listing for churches seeking music leadership or music leadership looking for churches.
Former titles (until 1999): Sacred Music News & Reviews; (until 1992): Church Music Report (1071-9903)
Related titles: Online - full text ed.
Published by: T C M R Enterprises, Inc., PO Box 1179, Grapevine, TX 76099-1179. TEL 817-488-0141, FAX 817-481-4191, tcmrtalk@airmail.net, http://www.tcmr.com. Ed. William H Rayborn. Circ: 5,500.

786 USA ISSN 0890-9032
M21
THE CHURCH PIANIST. Abbreviated title: C P. Text in English. 1984. bi-m. USD 39.95 domestic; USD 44.95 in Canada; USD 75.95 elsewhere (effective 2008). adv. **Document type:** *Magazine, Consumer.* **Description:** Contains appealing preludes, offertories and postludes based on hymns or the classics, as well as new, original compositions all at an intermediate level and in a variety of musical styles.
Published by: Lorenz Publishing Co., 501 E 3rd St, Box 802, Dayton, OH 45402. TEL 937-228-6118, 800-444-1144, FAX 937-223-2042, info@lorenz.com, http://www.lorenz.com.

780 CHN ISSN 1003-174X
PL2543
CIKAN/VERSES. Text in Chinese. 1990. bi-m. USD 46.80 (effective 2009). **Document type:** *Journal, Academic/Scholarly.*
Related titles: Online - full text ed.
—East View.
Published by: Zhongguo Yinyuejia Xiehui/Chinese Musicians Association, c/o China Federation of Literary and Art Circles, Zhaoyang-qu, 22, Anyuan Bei Li, Beijing, 100029, China. TEL 86-10-64920154. **Dist. by:** China International Book Trading Corp, 35 Chegongzhuang Xilu, Haidian District, PO Box 399, Beijing 100044, China. TEL 86-10-68412045, FAX 86-10-68412023, cibtc@mail.cibtc.com.cn, http://www.cibtc.com.cn.

780.904 CAN ISSN 1183-1693
ML5
CIRCUIT; revue nord-americaine de musique du XXe siecle. Text in English. 1991. 2/yr. CAD 45 in US & Canada to individuals; CAD 60 elsewhere to individuals; CAD 87 in US & Canada to institutions; CAD 114 elsewhere to institutions; CAD 33 in US & Canada to students; CAD 50 elsewhere to students (effective 2005). **Document type:** *Journal, Academic/Scholarly.*
Indexed: CMPI, DIP, IBR, IBZ, M11, MusicInd, RILM.
Published by: (Nouvel Ensemble Moderne), Presses de l'Universite de Montreal, 3535, chemin Queen-Mary, Bureau 206, Montreal, PQ H3V 1H8, Canada. TEL 514-343-6933, FAX 514-343-2232, pum@umontreal.ca, http://www.pum.umontreal.ca. Ed. Jean Boivin. Circ: 500. **Subscr. to:** Periodica, C P 444, Outremont, PQ H2V 4R6, Canada. TEL 514-274-5468.

CIRCUS FANFARE. *see* THEATER

780 GBR
CITY OF BIRMINGHAM SYMPHONY ORCHESTRA. MAIN SEASON BROCHURE. Variant title: City of Birmingham Symphony Orchestra. Season Brochure. Text in English. a. free (effective 2010). **Document type:** *Bulletin, Trade.*
Formerly (until 19??): City of Birmingham Symphony Orchestra. Broadsheet
Related titles: Online - full text ed.: free (effective 2010).
Published by: City of Birmingham Symphony Orchestra, CBSO Centre, Berkley St, Birmingham, W Mids B1 2LF, United Kingdom. TEL 44-121-6166500, FAX 44-121-6166518, information@cbso.co.uk, http://www.cbso.co.uk.

051 USA ISSN 1544-3736
CITYSLICKER ENTERTAINMENT MAGAZINE. Text in English. 1989. m. free newsstand/cover (effective 2007). **Document type:** *Magazine, Consumer.* **Description:** Covers food, drink, movies, music, arts, events and more in the Greater Louisville area.
Published by: Synergy Publishing, LLC., PO Box 4441, Louisville, KY 40204. TEL 502-295-6308, FAX 502-277-0973. Pub. Bob Glaser. Circ: 10,000 (controlled).

780 ITA ISSN 1593-1277
CIVILTA MUSICALE. Text in Italian. 1987. 3/yr. **Document type:** *Magazine, Consumer.*
Related titles: Online - full text ed.: ISSN 1974-4080. 2000.
Published by: (Centro Francescano Culturale Artistico Rosetum), LoGisma Editore, Via Zufolana 4, Vicchio Firenze, 50039, Italy. TEL 39-055-8497054, FAX 39-055-8497663, http://www.logisma.it.

786 USA ISSN 1054-5824
ML1039
CLAPPER. Text in English. 1973. q. USD 15 domestic; CAD 20 in Canada; USD 23 elsewhere. adv. bk.rev. **Document type:** *Newsletter.* **Description:** Provides information regarding educational materials, activities and issues concerning the practice of change ringing for guild members.
Published by: North American Guild of Change Ringers, c/o Mary Platt, Ed., Kennesaw State Univ., 1000 Chastain Rd, Kennesaw, GA 30144. TEL 770-423-6197, mplatt@kennesaw.edu. Ed. Mary Platt. Circ: 450 (paid).

780 USA ISSN 0361-5553
ML1
➤ **THE CLARINET.** Text in English. 1973. q. free to members (effective 2011). adv. bk.rev.; music rev.; rec.rev. charts; illus.; stat. Index. back issues avail. **Document type:** *Journal, Academic/Scholarly.* **Description:** Contains articles and a wide range of subjects written by the world's leading performers, teachers and scholars.
Indexed: IIMP, M11, MAG, MusicInd, RILM, T02.
—Ingenta.
Published by: International Clarinet Association, PO Box 1310, Lyons, CO 80540. TEL 405-651-6064, FAX 212-457-6124, membership@clarinet.org. Ed. James Gillespie TEL 940-565-4096. Adv. contact So Rhee. Circ: 4,000.

788 GBR ISSN 0260-390X
CLARINET AND SAXOPHONE. Text in English. 1976 (vol.5). q. free to members (effective 2009). adv. illus. back issues avail. **Document type:** *Magazine, Trade.*
Formerly (until 1980): C A S S News (0308-9053)
Indexed: RILM.
Published by: Clarinet and Saxophone Society of Great Britain, The Membership Secretary, Hanbury Close, Ingleby Barwick, Stockton-on-Tees, Cleveland, TS17 0UQ, United Kingdom. Ed., Adv. contact Richard Edwards.

784.18 DEU ISSN 0937-5864
ML929
CLARINO; Blaesermusik International. Text in German. 1989. 11/yr. EUR 50 domestic; EUR 57 foreign; EUR 5 newsstand/cover (effective 2009). adv. **Document type:** *Magazine, Consumer.*
Published by: Druck und Verlag Obermayer GmbH, Bahnhofstr 33, Buchloe, 86807, Germany. TEL 49-8241-500816, FAX 49-8241-500846, info@dvo-verlag.de, http://www.dvo-verlag.de. Ed. Uschi Mohr-Busduga. adv.: B&W page EUR 1,449, color page EUR 2,307; trim 185 x 262. Circ: 16,900 (paid and controlled).

781.66 GBR ISSN 1743-0801
CLASH MAGAZINE. Text in English. 2004. 10/yr. GBP 35 domestic; GBP 63 in US & Canada includes europe; GBP 89 elsewhere (effective 2009). adv. **Document type:** *Magazine, Consumer.* **Description:** Covers underground and mainstream music as well as fashion, film and entertainment.
Related titles: Online - full text ed.: free to members (effective 2009).
—CCC.
Published by: Clash Music, 29 D Arblay St, London, W1F 8EP, United Kingdom. TEL 44-20-77349351. adv.: page GBP 2,200.

780 ESP
CLASICA AUDIO. Text in Spanish. m. EUR 5 newsstand/cover (effective 2009). adv. **Document type:** *Magazine, Consumer.*
Published by: Grupo V, C Valportillo Primera, 11, Alcobendas, Madrid, 28108, Spain. TEL 34-91-6622137, FAX 34-91-6622654, secretaria@grupov.es, http://www.grupov.es/. Ed. Angel d'Anton. Adv. contact Amador Moreno. page EUR 3,620; trim 22 x 28.5. Circ: 30,000.

781.68 GBR ISSN 1356-2592
CLASSIC F M MAGAZINE. Text in English. 1995. m. GBP 43 (effective 2009). adv. music rev. back issues avail. **Document type:** *Magazine, Consumer.* **Description:** Brings classical music alive, enhancing its readers' musical knowledge and enjoyment. Includes profiles of the stars and reviews of CDs.
—CCC.

Published by: Haymarket Publishing Ltd. (Subsidiary of: Haymarket Media Group), 174 Hammersmith Rd, London, W6 7JP, United Kingdom. TEL 44-20-82674210, info@haymarket.com, http://www.haymarket.com. Ed. John Evans TEL 44-20-82675149. Adv. contact Sandra Spencer TEL 44-20-82675959. Circ: 35,751. **Subscr. to:** PO Box 568, Haywards Heath RH16 3XQ, United Kingdom. TEL 44-8456-777800, Haymarket.subs@qss-uk.com, http://www.themagazineshop.com.

780.42 GBR ISSN 1464-7834
CLASSIC ROCK. Text in English. 1998. m. GBP 43.80 domestic; GBP 61.90 in Europe; GBP 63.58 elsewhere; GBP 6.50 per issue domestic; GBP 7.50 per issue in Europe; GBP 8.50 per issue elsewhere; GBP 4.99 newsstand/cover (effective 2010). adv. back issues avail. **Document type:** *Magazine, Consumer.* **Description:** Presents stories and features on bands and stars of classic guitar based rock.
Related titles: Online - full text ed.: GBP 79.30; GBP 6.10 per issue (effective 2010).
—CCC.
Published by: Future Publishing Ltd., Beauford Ct, 30 Monmouth St, Bath, Avon BA1 2BW, United Kingdom. TEL 44-1225-442244, FAX 44-1225-446019, customerservice@subscription.co.uk, http://www.futureplc.com. Ed. Scott Rowley. **Subscr. to:** Tower House, Sovereign Park, Market Harborough, Leicestershire LE16 9EF, United Kingdom. TEL 44-844-8481602, FAX 44-1858-438795.

781.66 GBR ISSN 2045-2268
▼ **CLASSIC ROCK PRESENTS PROG.** Text in English. 2010. q. **Document type:** *Magazine, Trade.*
Published by: Future Publishing Ltd., 2 Balcombe St, London, NW1 6NW, United Kingdom. TEL 44-20-70424000, FAX 44-20-70424329, http://www.futureplc.com.

782.8 FRA ISSN 1287-4329
CLASSICA; repertoire. Text in French. 1998. m. EUR 46 domestic (effective 2009). adv. music rev. **Document type:** *Magazine, Consumer.*
Published by: Groupe Express-Roularta, 29 Rue de Chateaudun, Paris Cede, 75308, France. TEL 33-1-75551000. Ed. Stephane Chabenat TEL 33-1-75554330. adv.: page EUR 4,300;. Circ: 21,000.

787 GBR ISSN 0950-429X
ML5
CLASSICAL GUITAR. Text in English. 1982. m. GBP 54 domestic; GBP 64.50 in Europe; GBP 72.60 elsewhere; GBP 3.95 newsstand/cover (effective 2009). adv. back issues avail. **Document type:** *Magazine, Consumer.* **Description:** Features classical guitar news, events, festivals and competitions, concert diary, gruppetto, music supplement, book review, private CD releases, music reviews, CD reviews as well as concert reviews.
Indexed: IIMP, M11, MusicInd, PCI, RILM, T02.
—Ingenta.
Published by: Ashley Mark Publishing Co., 1 & 2 Vance Ct, Unit 10 Hill Court, Transbritannia Enterprise Park, Blaydon-on-tyne, NE21 5NH, United Kingdom. TEL 44-191-4149000, FAX 44-191-4149001, david@ashleymark.co.uk, http://www.ashleymark.co.uk/. Adv. contact David English TEL 44-191-4149006.

781.68 GBR
CLASSICAL LONDON. Text in English. m. free. music rev. **Document type:** *Journal, Academic/Scholarly.* **Description:** Includes CD reviews, information about competitions and jobs for performers and composers, classical music news, information about classical music on the internet, and information about concerts in London.
Media: E-mail.
Address: sub@classical-london.com.

780.43 GBR ISSN 0961-2696
CLASSICAL MUSIC. Text in English. 1978. fortn. GBP 84.50 domestic; GBP 102 in Europe; GBP 108 elsewhere; GBP 3.45 per issue (effective 2009). adv. bk.rev.; music rev. illus. back issues avail. **Document type:** *Magazine, Trade.* **Description:** Provides news, previews and features to inform anyone who works in the classical music business in any capacity.
Former titles (until 1979): Classical Music and Album Reviews; (until 1978): Classical Music Weekly (0308-9762)
Related titles: ◆ Supplement(s): Guide to Summer Schools (Year); ◆ Classical Music Guide to Festivals; Music Scholarships. ISSN 1757-2673; Classical Music. Music Competitions. ISSN 1757-2355.
Indexed: IIMP, M11, MusicInd, T02.
—BLDSC (3274.556900). **CCC.**
Published by: Rhinegold Publishing Ltd., 239-241 Shaftesbury Ave, London, WC2H 8TF, United Kingdom. TEL 44-20-73331720, FAX 44-20-73331765, enquiries@rhinegold.co.uk. Ed. Keith Clarke. Adv. contact Neil Cording TEL 44-20-73331733.

781.68 GBR ISSN 2045-6247
ML156.9
CLASSICAL RECORDINGS QUARTERLY. Abbreviated title: C R Q. Text in English. 1995. q. GBP 20 domestic; GBP 24 in Europe; GBP 28 elsewhere (effective 2011). adv. back issues avail. **Document type:** *Magazine, Consumer.* **Description:** Covers articles on great artists of the past, histories of record companies and labels, tales of rare recordings, interviews with famous producers and engineers etc.
Former titles (until 2010): Classic Record Collector (1472-5797); (until 2000): International Classical Record Collector (1357-8189)
Related titles: Online - full text ed.: GBP 18 (effective 2011).
Indexed: A01, IBR, IBZ, M11, MusicInd, RILM, T02.
—CCC.
Address: 8 Locksmeade Rd, Richmond, Surrey TW10 7YT, United Kingdom. TEL 44-20-89401988. Adv. contact Jiri Musil TEL 44-20-83950158.

782.1 USA ISSN 1534-276X
ML3795
CLASSICAL SINGER. Text in English. 1987. m. (10/yr.). USD 58 domestic; USD 78 in Canada; USD 88 elsewhere (effective 2011). adv. play rev.; bk.rev.; music rev. 52 p./no.; back issues avail. **Document type:** *Magazine, Trade.* **Description:** Provides specific information for classical vocal artists at all levels, with interviews, articles, and coverage of auditions, competitions, training programs.
Formerly (until Sep. 1998): New York Opera Newsletter (1043-2361)
Related titles: Online - full content ed.
Indexed: M11, MusicInd.
Published by: Classical Singer Corporation, PO Box 1710, Draper, UT 84020. TEL 801-254-1025, subscriptions@classicalsinger.com. Circ: 3,500 (paid and controlled).

781.68 USA
CLASSICS TODAY; your online guide to classical music. Variant title: Classicstoday.com. Text in English. 1999. d. free (effective 2010). music rev. back issues avail. **Document type:** *Journal, Academic/Scholarly.* **Description:** Provides audience for classical music with comprehensive review coverage of new recordings that are both accurate and completely up-to-date.
Media: Online - full text. Ed. David Vernier. Adv. contact David Hurwitz.

780 ESP ISSN 1138-2554
CLAVE PROFESIONAL. Text in Spanish. 1996. m. USD 80 (effective 1999). adv. **Document type:** *Magazine, Trade.*
Address: Ave Gaudi, 10 Piso 2, Barcelona, 08025, Spain. TEL 34-93-3475199, FAX 34-93-4561729, clave@revistaclave.com. Ed. Carlos Bosch. Pub. Jordi Rueda. R&P Laura Oviedo. Adv. contact Josep Valles.

780 ITA ISSN 2036-9352
IL CLAVICEMBALO. Text in Italian. 2001. irreg. **Document type:** *Monographic series, Academic/Scholarly.*
Published by: Silvana Editoriale, Via Margherita de Vizzi 86, Cinisello Balsamo, MI 20092, Italy. TEL 39-02-61836337, FAX 39-02-6172464, silvanaeditoriale@silvanaeditoriale.it, http://www.silvanaeditoriale.it.

786 USA ISSN 2152-4491
ML1
CLAVIER COMPANION; a practical magazine on piano teaching. Text in English. 1962. bi-m. USD 29.95 domestic; USD 39.95 in Canada; USD 41.95 elsewhere; USD 9.95 per issue (effective 2010). adv. bk.rev.; rec.rev. illus. index. back issues avail.; reprints avail. **Document type:** *Magazine, Trade.* **Description:** Addresses the needs of piano teachers, professionals, parents and students of all ages.
Formed by ther merger of (1990-2009): Keyboard Companion (1086-0819); (1962-2009): Clavier (0009-854X); Which was formerly (until 1966): Piano Teacher
Indexed: A01, A20, A22, ABS&EES, ASCA, B04, BRD, E02, E03, E06, ERI, EdA, EdI, IIMP, M11, MAG, MusicInd, RILM, SCOPUS, T02, W03.
—IE, Infotrieve, Ingenta.
Published by: Frances Clark Center for Keyboard Pedagogy, PO Box 651, Kingston, NJ 08528. TEL 888-881-5861, FAX 609-392-6822, exdir@francesclarkcenter.org, http://www.francesclarkcenter.org. Ed. Peter Jutras. Adv. contact Tiffany Ogden TEL 214-341-6755. color page USD 1,655; trim 8.375 x 10.675.

786 USA ISSN 0279-0858
ML3930.A2
CLAVIER'S PIANO EXPLORER. Text in English. 1981. 10/yr. USD 10 domestic; USD 16 foreign; USD 5 domestic to qualified personnel; USD 11 foreign to qualified personnel (effective 2009). **Document type:** *Magazine, Consumer.* **Description:** Contains articles on composers, music history, interesting facts, theory, practice tips, and more.
Published by: The Instrumentalist Co., 200 Northfield Rd, Northfield, IL 60093. TEL 847-446-5000, 888-446-6888, FAX 847-446-6263, advertising@instrumentalistmagazine.com, http://www.theinstrumentalist.com.

780 CHE ISSN 1422-0466
CLINGKLONG. Text in German, French. 1991. q.
Indexed: RILM.
Published by: FrauenMusik Forum Schweiz, FMF Secretariat and European Archive, Konsumstrasse 6, Bern, 3007, Switzerland. TEL 41-31-3727215, FAX 41-31-3727258, fmf@dplanet.ch, http://www.fmf.ch.

781.6 SWE ISSN 1103-3568
CLOSE-UP MAGAZINE. Text in Swedish. 1991. bi-m. SEK 245; SEK 445 foreign; SEK 45 newsstand/cover (effective 2002). adv. bk.rev.; music rev.; video rev. charts. back issues avail. **Document type:** *Magazine, Consumer.* **Description:** Specializes in metal and hardcore punk music.
Published by: C U Tidnings AB, PO Box 4411, Stockholm, 102 69, Sweden. TEL 46-8-462-0214, FAX 46-8-462-0215. Ed., R&P, Adv. contact Robert Becirovic. B&W page SEK 4,995, color page SEK 7,995; trim 297 x 210. Circ: 20,000 (paid).

781.7 USA ISSN 0896-372X
ML1
CLOSE UP MAGAZINE. Variant title: C M A Close Up. Text in English. 1959. bi-m. USD 50 membership (effective 2005). bk.rev. illus. **Document type:** *Magazine, Trade.*
Formerly: Close-Up (0009-9449)
Indexed: A01, A10, M11, V03.
Published by: Country Music Association, Inc., One Music Circle S, Nashville, TN 37203. TEL 615-244-2840, FAX 615-242-4783. Ed., R&P Angie Crabtree. Circ: 6,500. **Dist. by:** Southern Post, 1500 Elm Hill Pike., Nashville, TN 37210-3602. TEL 615-256-7615.

782.421 USA
COAST 2 COAST MAGAZINE; the magazine dedicated to hip hop and the art and culture of mixtapes. Text in English. 2007. q. USD 14.99; USD 3.99 newsstand/cover (effective 2007). adv. **Document type:** *Magazine, Consumer.*
Related titles: Online - full text ed.
Published by: Lil Fats, Inc., Coast 2 Coast Mixed Tapes and Magazine, 1233 S E 122nd Ave, Portland, OR 97233. TEL 503-367-8773, FAX 503-762-6025, coast2coastmagazine@hirollerz.com, http://www.hirollerz.com. Ed. Lil Fats. Adv. contact Nick Hiersche. color page USD 1,000; trim 8.5 x 11. Circ: 20,000.

780 USA ISSN 1535-1726
ML1
THE COBBETT ASSOCIATION'S CHAMBER MUSIC JOURNAL. Text in English. q.
Published by: Cobbett Association, 601 Timber Trail, Riverwoods, IL 60015.

781.64 FRA ISSN 1249-2345
CODA; nouvelles cultures magazine. Text in French. m. **Description:** Provides information on artists and concerts of house and techno music.
Published by: Coda Presse, 9 passage de Crimee, Paris, 75019, France. TEL 33-1-42095854, FAX 33-1-42095928, http://www.france-techno.fr. Ed. Eric Napora Chassang. Pub. Paulo Fernandes.

781.57 CAN ISSN 0820-926X
CODA MAGAZINE; the journal of jazz and improvised music. Text in English. 1958. 6/yr. CAD 28 domestic; USD 24 in United States; CAD 36 elsewhere; CAD 5 newsstand/cover Canada & elsewhere; USD 4.50 newsstand/cover in United States (effective 2000). adv. bk.rev.; rec.rev. back issues avail.; reprints avail. **Document type:** *Magazine, Consumer.* **Description:** Contains articles and interviews covering the entire spectrum of the music.
Formerly: Coda (0010-017X)
Related titles: Microfiche ed.: (from MML); Microfilm ed.: (from MML, PQC).
Indexed: A22, A26, C03, CBCARef, CBPI, CMPI, CPerI, G08, IIMP, M11, MusicInd, NPI, P48, PMPI, PQC, RASB, T02.
—Ingenta.
Published by: Coda Publications, 161 Frederick St, Toronto, ON M5A 4P3, Canada. TEL 416-593-7230, FAX 416-593-7230, broomer@sprynet.com, http://mars.ark.com/~codawest. Pub., R&P John Norris. Circ: 3,000 (paid).

780 700 ESP
COLECCION ETHOS. Text in Spanish. 1980. irreg., latest vol.17, 1992. price varies. **Document type:** *Monographic series, Academic/Scholarly.*
Published by: (Universidad de Oviedo, Area de Musicologia), Universidad de Oviedo, Servicio de Publicaciones, Campus de Humanidades, Edificio de Servicios, Oviedo, Asturias 33011, Spain. TEL 34-985-109504, FAX 34-985-109507, servipub@uniovi.es, http://www.uniovi.es/publicaciones/.

780.903 FRA ISSN 1775-1527
COLLECTION ENSEMBLE BAROQUE DE LIMOGES. Text in French. 2005. irreg. **Document type:** *Monographic series, Academic/Scholarly.*
Published by: Ensemble Baroque de Limoges, Administration Siege Social - Solignac/Limoges, Solignac, 87110, France. TEL 33-5-55318484, FAX 33-5-55318485, http://www.ebl-laborie.com.

780.902 FRA ISSN 1954-3344
COLLECTION OEUVRE LYRIQUE. Text in French. 1997. irreg. **Document type:** *Monographic series, Academic/Scholarly.*
Formerly (until 2007): Cahiers de Musique (1636-9408)
Published by: Centre de Musique Baroque de Versailles, Hotel des Menus-Plaisirs, 22, avenue de Paris, Versailles Cedex, 78003, France. TEL 33-1-39207810, FAX 33-1-39207801, accueil@cmbv.com, http://www.cmbv.com.

780.922 FRA ISSN 1766-0181
COLLECTION PAROLES DE MUSICIEN. Text in French. 2004. irreg. **Document type:** *Monographic series, Consumer.*
Published by: Institut National de l'Audiovisuel, 4 av de l'Europe, Bry-sur-Marne, 94366, France.

780 FRA ISSN 2105-908X
▼ **COLLECTION PENSEE MUSICALE.** Text in French. 2010. irreg., latest 2010. **Document type:** *Monographic series.*
Published by: Editions Delatour, Le Vallier, Sampzon, 07120, France. infos@editions-delatour.com, http://www.editions-delatour.com.

COLLECTOR (GRAINVILLE). *see* BIOGRAPHY

780 GBR ISSN 0261-2550
ML156.4.J3
COLLECTORS ITEMS. Text in English. 1980. bi-m. GBP 17 domestic; GBP 19.50 in Europe; GBP 25 in North America; GBP 26 elsewhere. bk.rev. bibl. back issues avail. **Document type:** *Magazine, Consumer.* **Description:** Contains material of interest to jazz and blues collectors.
Published by: J & M Records, J & M Records, Fivehead, PO Box 276, Taunton, TA3 6YZ, United Kingdom. TEL 44-1823-481234, FAX 44-1823-480167. Ed. John Holley. Circ: 1,000.

780.711 USA
COLLEGE MUSIC SOCIETY. NEWSLETTER. Text in English. 19??. 5/yr. free to members (effective 2010). adv. bk.rev. back issues avail. **Document type:** *Newsletter, Consumer.*
Related titles: Online - full text ed.
Published by: College Music Society, 312 E Pine St, Missoula, MT 59802. TEL 406-721-9616, FAX 406-721-9419, cms@music.org, http:/www.music.org. Ed. Ann Sears TEL 508-286-3592. Adv. contact Peter Park. Circ: 9,500.

780 USA ISSN 0069-5696
ML1
➤ **COLLEGE MUSIC SYMPOSIUM.** Text in English. 1961. a. USD 25 per issue (effective 2010). adv. bk.rev. illus. back issues avail.; reprints avail. **Document type:** *Journal, Academic/Scholarly.*
Related titles: Online - full text ed.
Indexed: A20, A22, ASCA, ArtHuCI, CA, CurCont, IIMP, M11, MAG, MusicInd, PCI, RILM, SCOPUS, T02, W07.
—BLDSC (3311.175000), Ingenta.
Published by: College Music Society, 312 E Pine St, Missoula, MT 59802. TEL 406-721-9616, FAX 406-721-9419, cms@music.org, http:/www.music.org. Ed. Glenn Stanley. Adv. contact Peter Park.

780 USA ISSN 0147-0108
M2
➤ **COLLEGIUM MUSICUM: YALE UNIVERSITY.** Text in English. 1955. irreg., latest vol.16, 2007. price varies. back issues avail. **Document type:** *Monographic series, Academic/Scholarly.* **Description:** Presents a selection of works that draws from a particular repertory or historical context or that reflects a particular thematic focus.
Published by: (Yale University, Yale University, Department of Music), A-R Editions, Inc., 8551 Research Way, Ste 180, Middleton, WI 53562. TEL 608-836-9000, 800-736-0070, FAX 608-831-8200, orders@areditions.com. Eds. Gerald R Hoekstra, James L Zychowicz TEL 608-836-9000 ext 14.

264 USA ISSN 1938-419X
BV169
COLLOQUIUM, MUSIC, WORSHIP, ARTS. Text in English. 2004. a., latest 2008. **Document type:** *Journal, Academic/Scholarly.*
Related titles: Online - full text ed.: ISSN 1938-4203.
Published by: Yale Institute of Sacred Music, PO Box 208273, New Haven, CT 06520. TEL 203-432-5180, FAX 203-432-5296.

780 GBR
COMES WITH A SMILE. Text in English. q. USD 9.99 (effective 2005). **Document type:** *Magazine, Consumer.*
Address: 69 St. Mary's Grove, London, Chiswick W4 3LW, United Kingdom. TEL 44-0794-1010250. Ed. Matt Dornan.

COMITATUS; a journal of Medieval and Renaissance studies. *see* LITERATURE

COMPANY NORTH AMERICA. *see* LITERARY AND POLITICAL REVIEWS

780 POL
COMPENDIUM MUSICUM. Text in Polish; Summaries in English. 1983. irreg. price varies. adv. **Document type:** *Academic/Scholarly.* **Description:** Series of elementary textbooks covering all fields of music.
Published by: Polskie Wydawnictwo Muzyczne, Al Krasinskiego 11 a, Krakow, 31111, Poland. TEL 48-12-4227044, FAX 48-12-4220174. R&P Janina Warzecha. Adv. contact Elzbieta Widlak.

780 USA ISSN 1089-3733
THE COMPLETE ORGAN. Text in English. 1997. irreg., latest vol.8, 2005. price varies. back issues avail. **Document type:** *Monographic series, Trade.*
Published by: Pendragon Press, PO Box 190, Hillsdale, NY 12529. TEL 518-325-6100, FAX 518-325-6102, orders@pendragonpress.com. Ed. Rollin Smith.

780 USA
COMPLETE WORKS OF G.B. PERGOLESI. Text in English. 19??. irreg. price varies. back issues avail. **Document type:** *Monographic series, Trade.*
Published by: Pendragon Press, PO Box 190, Hillsdale, NY 12529. TEL 518-325-6100, FAX 518-325-6102, orders@pendragonpress.com, http://www.pendragonpress.com.

COMPLEX MAGAZINE. *see* LIFESTYLE

781.66 MEX
COMPLOT INTERNACIONAL. Text in Spanish. 1996. m. MXN 200 (effective 1999). back issues avail. **Description:** Includes interviews, reports and news on rock in Spanish.
Related titles: Online - full text ed.
Published by: Gunna S.A. de C.V., Ave. UNIVERSIDAD 1377-202, Col Axotla, Mexico City, DF 01030, Mexico. TEL 525-5-662-3820, FAX 52-5-662-3818.

780 USA ISSN 1086-1998
ML1
COMPOSER - U S A. Text in English. 1932. 3/yr. USD 20 (effective 2001). adv. bk.rev.; music rev. back issues avail. **Document type:** *Newsletter.* **Description:** Contains news and articles of interest to musicians and art enthusiasts. Profiles composers, lists competitions, performances, publications, recordings, commissions and awards.
Indexed: MAG, MusicInd.
Published by: National Association of Composers - U S A, PO Box 49256, Barrington Sta, Los Angeles, CA 90049. TEL 310-541-8213, FAX 310-541-8213. Ed., Adv. contact Albert Benner TEL 318-357-0924. Circ: 1,000.

780 GBR ISSN 1758-9541
▼ **COMPOSERS.** Text in English. 2009. a. **Document type:** *Consumer.* **Description:** Provides key insights for incredibly varied and vibrant industry.
Published by: Rhinegold Publishing Ltd., 239-241 Shaftesbury Ave, London, WC2H 8TF, United Kingdom. TEL 44-20-73331720, FAX 44-20-73331765, enquiries@rhinegold.co.uk, http://www.rhinegold.co.uk. Ed. Kimon Daltas. Pub. Derek B Smith.

780 USA
COMPOSERS OF NORTH AMERICA SERIES. Text in English. 1985. irreg., latest vol.25, 2006. price varies. back issues avail. **Document type:** *Monographic series.*
Published by: Scarecrow Press, Inc. (Subsidiary of: Rowman & Littlefield Publishers, Inc.), 4501 Forbes Blvd, Ste 200, Lanham, MD 20706. TEL 301-459-3366, 800-462-6420, FAX 301-429-5748, 800-338-4550, custserv@rowman.com, http://www.scarecrowpress.com. Eds. M Lowens, Sam Dennison, W C Loring Jr.

780 FRA ISSN 1285-6177
COMPOSITEURS D'AUJOURD'HUI. Text in French. 1992. irreg. **Document type:** *Monographic series, Academic/Scholarly.*
Formerly (until 1998): Les Cahiers de l'I R C A M. Compositeurs d'Aujourd'hui (1242-8493)
Indexed: RILM.
Published by: (Institut de Recherche et Coordination Acoustique Musique (I R C A M)), L' Harmattan, 5 Rue de l'Ecole Polytechnique, Paris, 75005, France. TEL 33-1-43257651, FAX 33-1-43258203, http://www.editions-harmattan.fr.

785.06 USA
CON BRIO; the newsletter of the Las Vegas Philharmonic. Text in English. q.
Published by: The Las Vegas Philharmonic, 1289 S Torrey Pines Dr, Las Vegas, NV 89146.

780 DEU
CONCENTUS MUSICUS. Text in German. 1973. irreg., latest vol.10, 1997. price varies. illus. **Document type:** *Monographic series, Academic/Scholarly.*
Published by: (Deutsches Historisches Institut in Rom, Musikgeschichtliche Abteilung ITA), Laaber-Verlag, Regensburger Str 19, Laaber, 93164, Germany. info@laaber-verlag.de, http://www.laaber-verlag.de.

780.6 USA ISSN 1551-2266
ML12
CONCERT ARTISTS GUILD. GUIDE TO COMPETITIONS. Text in English. 1978. a. adv. **Document type:** *Directory.*
Supersedes: Concert Artists Guild. Bulletin
Published by: Concert Artists Guild, Inc., 850 Seventh Ave, New York, NY 10019. TEL 212-333-5200. Ed. Mary Madigan. Adv. contact Mary G Madigan. Circ: 1,500.

780 DEU ISSN 1611-4698
ML5
CONCERTINO; Das Magazin fuer Gitarre, Mandoline und Laute. Text in German. 1961. q. EUR 24 domestic; EUR 28 foreign; EUR 5 newsstand/cover (effective 2009). adv. illus. **Document type:** *Magazine, Consumer.*
Former titles (until 2003): Zupfmusik Magazin (0176-0971); (until 1984): Zupfmusik - Gitarre (0722-0545); (until 1974): Zupfmusik (0722-2963); Incorporates: Gitarre
Indexed: RILM.
Published by: Bund Deutscher Zupfmusiker e.V., Huulkamp 26, Hamburg, 22397, Germany. TEL 49-40-60889013, FAX 49-40-60889014, webmaster@bdz-online.de. Ed. Eckhard Richter.

780 DEU ISSN 0177-5944
ML169.8
CONCERTO; magazin fuer alte musik. Text in German. 1983. bi-m. EUR 39 domestic; EUR 45 foreign (effective 2009). adv. **Document type:** *Magazine, Consumer.*
Indexed: CMPI, IIMP, M11, MusicInd, RILM.
Published by: Concerto Verlag, Montanusstr 87, Cologne, 51065, Germany. TEL 49-221-9624207, FAX 49-221-9624208, info@concerto-verlag.de, http://www.concerto-verlag.de. Pub. Johannes Jansen. adv.: page EUR 635; trim 214 x 288.

780 ITA ISSN 1971-0011
CONCERTO GROSSO. Text in Italian. 2006. m. **Document type:** *Magazine, Consumer.*
Published by: F M A Edizioni Musicali e Discografiche Srl, Via Boccaccio 47, Milan, 20123, Italy. TEL 39-02-435093, FAX 39-02-48194098, reception@fma.it, http://www.fma.it.

745 GBR
THE CONDUCTOR. Text in English. 1947. q. free to members (effective 2009). bk.rev.; music rev.; rec.rev.; video rev. tr.lit.; illus. 36 p./no.; back issues avail. **Document type:** *Journal, Trade.* **Description:** Designed for the members of the National Association of Brass Band Conductors.
Published by: National Association of Brass Band Conductors, Marrey, 7 Carr View Rd, Hepworth, Holmfirth, W Yorks HD9 1HX, United Kingdom. TEL 44-1484-683793, FAX 44-1484-686209. Ed. Chris Helme.

780 USA ISSN 0734-1032
ML457
CONDUCTORS GUILD. JOURNAL. Text in English. 1980. s-a. free to members (effective 2009). adv. bk.rev. illus. reprints avail. **Document type:** *Journal, Academic/Scholarly.*
Indexed: MAG, RILM.
—Ingenta.
Published by: Conductors Guild, Inc., 5300 Glenside Dr, Ste 2207, Richmond, VA 23228. TEL 804-553-1378, FAX 804-553-1876, guild@conductorsguild.net, http://www.conductorsguild.net. Ed. Jonathan D Green. Circ: 1,800.

784.2 USA ISSN 1051-8649
ML17
CONDUCTORS' GUILD MEMBERSHIP DIRECTORY. Text in English. a.
Published by: Conductors Guild, Inc., 5300 Glenside Dr, Ste 2207, Richmond, VA 23228. TEL 804-553-1378, FAX 804-553-1876, guild@conductorsguild.net, http://www.conductorsguild.net.

780 ITA
CONGRESSO INTERNAZIONALE DI STUDI VERDIANI. ATTI/ INTERNATIONAL CONGRESS OF VERDI STUDIES. PROCEEDINGS. Text in English, French, German, Italian, Spanish. irreg. price varies. **Document type:** *Proceedings, Academic/ Scholarly.*
Published by: Istituto Nazionale di Studi Verdiani, Strada della Repubblica 56, Parma, PR 43100, Italy. TEL 39-0521-385275, FAX 39-0521-287949, amministrazione@studiverdiani.it, http://www.studiverdiani.it.

781 USA ISSN 1076-2485
CONNECTIONS (LITCHFIELD). Text in English. 1986. s-a. USD 50 domestic membership; USD 55 foreign membership (effective 2008). adv. bk.rev. illus. back issues avail. **Document type:** *Newsletter.* **Description:** Offers educational programs, performances, products and a network designed to introduce people of all ages to music-making.
Published by: Music for People, PO Box 397, Goshen, CT 06756. TEL 860-491-3763, FAX 860-491-4513, mfp@musicforpeople.org, http://www.musicforpeople.org. Eds. Katrin Hall, Mary Knysh. Adv. contact Peter Hawes. B&W page USD 180; 9 x 7. Circ: 1,000.

780.7 CHE ISSN 0010-6550
CONSERVATOIRE DE MUSIQUE DE GENEVE. BULLETIN. Text in French. 1933. 10/yr. CHF 30 (effective 2001). adv. **Document type:** *Bulletin.*
Indexed: RASB.
Published by: Conservatoire de Musique de Geneve, Case Postale 5155, Geneva 11, 1211, Switzerland. TEL 41-22-3196060, FAX 41-22-3196062. Ed. Philippe Dinkel. Circ: 3,500.

780.6 ITA
CONSERVATORIO GIUSEPPE VERDI DI MILANO. QUADERNI DEL CORSO DI MUSICOLOGIA. Text in Italian. 1993. a., latest vol.6. EUR 25 (effective 2009). **Document type:** *Journal, Academic/Scholarly.*
Published by: (Conservatorio di Musica "Giuseppe Verdi" (Conservatorio di Milano)), LIM Editrice Srl, Via di Arsina 296/f, Lucca, LU 55100, Italy. TEL 39-0583-394464, FAX 39-0583-394469, lim@lim.it, http://www.lim.it.

780 ITA
CONSERVATORIO STATALE DI MUSICA GIOACCHINO ROSSINI. ANNUARIO. Text in Italian. a. **Document type:** *Yearbook, Trade.*
Published by: Conservatorio Statale di Musica "Gioacchino Rossini", Piazza Olivieri 5, Pesaro, 61100, Italy. TEL 39-072-133670, FAX 39-072-135295, info@conservatoriorossini.it, http://www.conservatoriorossini.it.

780 GBR ISSN 0268-9111
ML5 CODEN: MENED4
➤ **THE CONSORT.** Text in English. 1929. a. (plus s-a. Bulletin). free to members (effective 2009). bk.rev.; music rev.; rec.rev. charts; illus. cum.index: 1929-1987. 96 p./no.; back issues avail.; reprints avail. **Document type:** *Journal, Academic/Scholarly.* **Description:** Contains scholarly articles relating to music composed before 1800, with non-exclusive emphasis on instrumental music, performance issues, and the nature of 'authentic' performance.
Related titles: Microfilm ed.
Indexed: AmHI, BrHumI, H07, IIMP, M11, MusicInd, PCI, RILM, SCOPUS, T02.
—Ingenta.
Published by: Dolmetsch Foundation Inc., Jesses, Graywood Road, Haslemeve, Surrey GU27 2BS, United Kingdom. http://www.dolmetsch.com/dolmetschfoundation.htm. Ed. Elizabeth Rees TEL 44-1458-851561.

780 USA
CONSUMABLE ONLINE. Text in English. 1993. 3/m. free. music rev. back issues avail. **Document type:** *Newsletter.* **Description:** Consists of collaborative music reviews, interviews, tour information and other music related information. Reviews are primarily of the alternative genre, but also hit pop, rock and other musical formats.
Related titles: Online - full text ed.
Address: 409 Washington St, PMB 294, Hoboken, NJ 07030. editor@consumableonline.com, reproduction@consumableonline.com. Ed. Bob Gajarsky. Circ: 120,000.

782 USA
CONTEMPORARY A CAPPELLA NEWS. Text in English. 1990. bi-m. USD 20 membership; USD 25 foreign membership. adv. bk.rev.; music rev.; rec.rev. back issues avail. **Document type:** *Newsletter.* **Description:** Contains news, articles, reviews and interviews for a cappella groups and fans of vocal music.
Formerly: Contemporary A Cappella Newsletter
Published by: Contemporary A Cappella Society, PMB 1449, 1850 Union, No.4, San Francisco, CA 94123. TEL 415-563-5224, FAX 415-563-5523. Ed., Adv. contact Beth Olliges. Pub., R&P Deke Sharon. Circ: 8,000.

781 USA ISSN 1065-4712
ML197
CONTEMPORARY MUSIC FORUM. Text in English. 1989. a. **Document type:** *Proceedings.*
Indexed: RILM.
Published by: Bowling Green State University, MidAmerican Center for Contemporary Music, Moore Musical Arts Cntr, Bowling Green, OH 43403. TEL 419-372-2685, http://www.bgsu.edu/colleges/music/MACCM/index.html.

780 GBR ISSN 0749-4467
ML197
➤ **CONTEMPORARY MUSIC REVIEW.** Text in English. 1984. bi-m. GBP 769 combined subscription in United Kingdom to institutions (print & online eds.); EUR 877, USD 1,102 combined subscription to institutions (print & online eds.) (effective 2012). adv. back issues avail.; reprint service avail. from PSC. **Document type:** *Journal, Academic/Scholarly.* **Description:** Covers composition today - its techniques, aesthetics, technology and its relationship to other disciplines as well as current thought.
Related titles: Microform ed.; Online - full text ed.: ISSN 1477-2256. GBP 692 in United Kingdom to institutions; EUR 789, USD 992 to institutions (effective 2012) (from IngentaConnect).
Indexed: A01, A02, A03, A08, A20, A22, A26, AmHI, ArtHuCI, B04, BRD, BrHumI, CA, CurCont, E01, E08, G08, H07, H08, HAb, HumInd, I05, IIMP, M02, M11, MusicInd, P10, P48, P53, P54, PCI, PQC, RILM, S09, SCOPUS, T02, W03, W07.
—BLDSC (3425.192200), IE, Infotrieve, Ingenta. **CCC.**
Published by: Routledge (Subsidiary of: Taylor & Francis Group), 4 Park Sq, Milton Park, Abingdon, Oxon OX14 4RN, United Kingdom. TEL 44-20-70176000, FAX 44-20-70176336, subscriptions@tandf.co.uk, http://www.routledge.com/journals/. Eds. Joshua Fineberg, Peter Nelson. Adv. contact Linda Hann TEL 44-1344-779945. **Subscr. in N America to:** Taylor & Francis Inc., Customer Services Dept, 325 Chestnut St, 8th Fl, Philadelphia, PA 19106. TEL 215-625-8900, 800-354-1420, FAX 215-625-2940, customerservice@taylorandfrancis.com; **Subscr. to:** Taylor & Francis Ltd., Journals Customer Service, Sheepen Pl, Colchester, Essex CO3 3LP, United Kingdom. TEL 44-20-70175544, FAX 44-20-70175198, tf.enquiries@tfinforma.com.

920 USA ISSN 1044-2197
ML385
CONTEMPORARY MUSICIANS; profiles of the people in music. Text in English. 1989. q. USD 135 per issue (effective 2009). **Document type:** *Monographic series, Consumer.* **Description:** Provides comprehensive information on more than 4,000 musicians and groups from around the world.
Related titles: Diskette ed.; Magnetic Tape ed.; Online - full text ed.
Published by: Gale (Subsidiary of: Cengage Learning), 27500 Drake Rd, Farmington Hills, MI 48331. TEL 248-699-4253, 800-877-4253, FAX 877-363-4253, gale.galeord@cengage.com.

780 USA
CONTEMPORARY RECORD SOCIETY. SOCIETY NEWS MAGAZINE. Text in English. 1983. s-a. USD 45 domestic membership; USD 65 foreign membership (effective 2000). adv. bk.rev.; music rev.; rec.rev.; video rev. index. back issues avail. **Document type:** *Magazine, Trade.* **Description:** Includes members' progress notes, award and performance possibilities, concert listings, employment opportunities and feature articles on renowned composers and performers.
Related titles: Online - full text ed.
Published by: Contemporary Record Society, 724 Winchester Rd, Broomall, PA 19008. TEL 610-544-5920, FAX 610-544-5921. Ed. John Perotti. R&P Caroline Hunt. Adv. contact Jack Shusterman. page USD 1,900; 7.3333 x 10. Circ: 90,000 (controlled).

784 USA
ML1
CONTEMPORARY SONGWRITER MAGAZINE. Text in English. m. USD 12. illus.
Former titles (until 1998): Songwriter (0274-5917); (until 1978): Songwriter Magazine (0362-7373)
Indexed: M11, MusicInd.
Address: Box 25879, Colorado Springs, CO 80936-5879. TEL 719-232-4489, contemporarysong@yahoo.com, http://www.contemporary.bigstep.com. Ed. Roberta Redford. Circ: 5,000.

780 USA ISSN 0705-6656
CONTINUO; an early music magazine. Text in English. 1977. 5/yr. USD 30 domestic; USD 35 in Canada; USD 63 elsewhere; USD 6 newsstand/cover. adv. bk.rev. **Document type:** *Newsletter.*
Supersedes: Early Music Directory (0705-6648); Which was formerly: Toronto Early Music Directory (0229-9690)
Indexed: CMPI, RILM.

Published by: Matthew James Redsell, Ed.& Pub., PO Box 327, Hammondsport, NY 14840. TEL 607-569-2489, 800-231-2489, FAX 607-569-2776. adv.: B&W page USD 150; trim 9.75 x 7.25. Circ: 1,200.

780 AUS ISSN 0310-6802
ML26
CONTINUO. Text in English. 1970. a. free to members (effective 2009). adv. bk.rev. back issues avail. **Document type:** *Journal, Trade.*
Indexed: AEI, L04, LISTA, M11, MusicInd, RILM, T02.
Published by: International Association of Music Libraries, Archives & Documentation Centres (Australian Branch), Performing Arts Library, University of Adelaide, Adelaide, SA 5001, Australia. Ed., Adv. contact Peter Campbell TEL 61-3-93487528. Circ: 90.

781.7 NLD ISSN 0921-2280
CONTINUO. Text in Dutch. 1986. q. EUR 52.50 domestic; EUR 55 in Belgium (effective 2010).
Published by: Gooi en Sticht, Postbus 5018, Kampen, 8260 GA, Netherlands. TEL 31-38-3392556, FAX 31-38-3311776, gens@kok.nl, http://www.kok.nl.

780.902 BEL ISSN 1377-0330
➤ **CONTRA**; stemmen over muziek. Text in Dutch. 1984. bi-m. EUR 30 domestic; EUR 38 foreign; EUR 24 domestic to students; EUR 32 foreign to students (effective 2003). adv. bk.rev.; music rev. 48 p./no.; **Document type:** *Journal, Academic/Scholarly.* **Description:** The emphasis lies on discussion and polemic on music topics.
Formerly (until 2001): Musica Antiqua (0771-7016)
Indexed: M11, MusicInd, RILM.
Published by: Alamire vzw, PO Box 45, Peer, 3990, Belgium. TEL 32-11-610510, FAX 32-11-610511, info@alamire.com, http://www.alamire.com. Ed. Peter Berge. Pub. Herman Baeten. R&P Karolien Selhorst. Adv. contact Annelies Van Boxel. B&W page EUR 600, color page EUR 1,250; trim 210 x 297. Circ: 2,000.

780 BEL ISSN 0779-1569
CONTREPOINTS. Text in French. 1992. 4/yr.
Formerly: Prologue
Indexed: RILM.
Published by: Opera Royal de Wallonie, Rue des Dominicains 1, Liege, 4000, Belgium. TEL 32-4-221-4720, FAX 32-4-221-0201, http://www.orw.be/intro.php. Ed. Paul Danblon. Circ: 2,000.

780 USA ISSN 0190-4922
ML1
➤ **CONTRIBUTIONS TO MUSIC EDUCATION.** Abbreviated title: C M E. Text in English. 1972. s-a. USD 18 in US & Canada to individuals; USD 30 elsewhere to individuals; USD 28 in US & Canada to institutions; USD 36 elsewhere to institutions; free to members (effective 2010). bk.rev. **Document type:** *Journal, Academic/Scholarly.* **Description:** Covers experimental, theoretical, and historical research in music education.
Related titles: Online - full text ed.
Indexed: A22, CA, E02, E03, ERI, EdA, EdI, IIMP, M11, MusicInd, RILM, T02, W03, W05.
—BLDSC (3461.026000), IE, Ingenta.
Published by: Ohio Music Education Association, 1806 Robert Fulton Dr, Reston, VA 20191. FAX 888-275-6362, mbrserv@menc2.org, https://www.omea-ohio2.org. Ed. Birch Browning TEL 216-687-3768.

➤ **CONVERGENCIAS**; revista de invesitigacao e ensino das artes. *see* ART

➤ **COOL.** *see* CHILDREN AND YOUTH—For

555 USA
COOL AND STRANGE MUSIC!; dedicated to unusual sounds. Text in English. q. USD 15 domestic; USD 20 in Canada; USD 30 elsewhere (effective 2002). rec.rev. **Description:** Includes features on more unusual recordings and culture, interviews, CD reviews,. and more.
Published by: Dana Countryman for Labor of Love Productions, 1101 Colby Ave, Everett, WA 98201. FAX 425-303-3404, editor@coolandstrange.com. Eds. Dana Countryman, Leonard Cutler. Pub. Dana Countryman.

781.64 USA
COOL BEANS!. Text in English. 1993. 3/yr. USD 20 domestic; USD 24 in Canada; USD 28 Europe & Asia; USD 32 elsewhere; USD 5.95 newsstand/cover (effective 2006). adv. music rev. back issues avail. **Document type:** *Magazine, Consumer.* **Description:** Offers interviews with great indie, punk and alternative bands as well as articles about different themes including sex, cooking, travel, bootlegs, MP3s, sports and other zines.
Address: 3020 El Cerrito Plaza, Ste 253, El Cerrito, CA 94530. Ed. Matt Kelly. adv.: page USD 175; 7.5 x 10. Circ: 3,000 (paid).

780 USA
COOL'EH; magazine. Text in English. m. **Document type:** *Magazine, Consumer.*
Published by: Cool'eh Magazine, 1325, 6th Ave, 23rd Fl, New York, NY 10019. Ed. Reuben Grigory.

CORE; a magazine for the future generation. *see* LIFESTYLE

780 FRA ISSN 2107-0504
LE CORPUS DES LUTHISTES. Text in French. 2007. irreg. **Document type:** *Academic/Scholarly.*
Media: Online - full text.
Published by: Universite de Tours (Francois-Rabelais), Centre d'Etudes Superieures de la Renaissance de Tours. Programme Ricercar, 59, Rue Nericault-Destouches, BP 11328, Tours Cedex, 37013, France. TEL 33-2-47367784, FAX 33-2-47367762, ricercar@univ-tours.fr, http://ricercar.cesr.univ-tours.fr/index.htm.

780 USA ISSN 0070-0363
M2
CORPUS MENSURABILIS MUSICAE. Abbreviated title: C M M. Text in German. 1948. irreg., latest vol.111, no.1, 2010. price varies. back issues avail. **Document type:** *Monographic series, Academic/Scholarly.* **Description:** Presents a complete collection of polyphonic music from the 14th to the 16th centuries.
Published by: American Institute of Musicology, 8551 Research Way, Ste 180, Middleton, WI 53562. TEL 608-836-9000, 800-736-0070, FAX 608-831-8200, info@corpusmusicae.com. Ed. Paul L Ranzini.

781.62 AUT
CORPUS MUSICAE POPULARIS AUSTRIACAE. Text in German. 1993. irreg., latest vol.20, 2010. price varies. **Document type:** *Monographic series, Academic/Scholarly.*
Published by: Boehlau Verlag GmbH & Co.KG., Wiesingerstr 1, Vienna, W 1010, Austria. TEL 43-1-3302427, FAX 43-1-3302432, boehlau@boehlau.at, http://www.boehlau.at.

781.7 ITA
CORPUS MUSICUM FRANCISCANUM. Text in Italian. irreg. price varies. **Document type:** *Monographic series, Academic/Scholarly.* **Description:** Covers various works by Franciscan musicians. Contains musical transcriptions.
Published by: Centro Studi Antoniani, Piazza del Santo 11, Padua, PD 35123, Italy. TEL 39-049-8762177, FAX 39-049-8762187, asscsa@tin.it, http://www.centrostudiantoniani.it.

780 USA
CORPUS OF EARLY KEYBOARD MUSIC; transcription of all known sources of keyboard music of the 14th and 15th centuries. Abbreviated title: C E K M. Text in German. 1963. irreg., latest vol.48, 1999. price varies. back issues avail. **Document type:** *Monographic series, Academic/Scholarly.* **Description:** Devoted to the keyboard music of the fourteenth and fifteenth centuries.
Published by: American Institute of Musicology, 8551 Research Way, Ste 180, Middleton, WI 53562. TEL 608-836-9000, 800-736-0070, FAX 608-831-8200, info@corpusmusicae.com. Ed. John Caldwell.

780 USA
COSMIK DEBRIS. Text in English. w. free. **Description:** Features music of all genres for people who refuse to limit their musical diets. Includes articles, columnns, CD giveaways, and sound clips in real audio format.
Media: Online - full text. Ed. D J Johnson.

780.7 USA ISSN 0010-9894
ML1
➤ **COUNCIL FOR RESEARCH IN MUSIC EDUCATION. BULLETIN.** Text in English. 1963. q. USD 112 combined subscription to institutions (print & online eds.) (effective 2012). bk.rev. charts; illus. index. back issues avail.; reprints avail. **Document type:** *Journal, Academic/Scholarly.* **Description:** Presents articles, doctoral dissertation reviews, and conference papers for the international music profession.
Related titles: Microform ed.: (from PQC); Online - full text ed.: USD 73 to institutions (effective 2012).
Indexed: A20, A22, ASCA, ArtHuCI, B04, BRD, CA, CDA, CPE, CurCont, DIP, E02, E03, E06, ERI, EdA, EdI, IBR, IBZ, IIMP, M11, MAG, MEA&I, MLA-IB, MusicInd, PCI, PsycholAb, RASB, RILM, S21, SCOPUS, T02, W03, W07.
—BLDSC (2462.570000), IE, Ingenta.
Published by: (Council for Research in Music Education), University of Illinois at Urbana-Champaign, School of Music, 1114 W Nevada St, Urbana, IL 61801. TEL 217-333-1027, FAX 217-244-8136, musicadmissions@illinois.edu, http://www.music.uiuc.edu/. Ed. Gregory Denardo.

781.642 CAN ISSN 1180-8047
COUNTRY; Canada's country music magazine. Text in English. 1989. 6/yr. CAD 12.84 domestic; USD 24 in United States; USD 48 elsewhere; CAD 4 newsstand/cover; USD 5 newsstand/cover in United States. adv. bk.rev.; film rev. **Document type:** *Magazine, Consumer.* **Description:** Covers country music from a Canadian perspective.
Indexed: CMPI.
Published by: Jim Baine, Ed., 9120 Leslie St, Unit 104, Richmond, ON L4B 3J9, Canada. TEL 905-886-4225, FAX 905-886-0037. Pub. George Leslie. Adv. contact Doug Hammond. Circ: 22,000.

781.7 USA
COUNTRY CRAZY. Text in English. 1976. 3/yr. USD 6.
Published by: Jammie Ann Club - Rebel International Fan Club, PO Box 3525, York, PA 17402. FAX 717-792-3060. Circ: 3,500.

781.7 AUS ISSN 1440-995X
COUNTRY MUSIC CAPITAL NEWS. Text in English. 1975. m. AUD 51 (effective 2007). adv. bk.rev. **Document type:** *Magazine, Consumer.* **Description:** Specializing in country music in Australia with stories, artist bios and products available.
Former titles (until 1998): Australian Country Music Capital News; Capital News (0812-1494)
Published by: Rural Press Ltd. (Subsidiary of: Fairfax Media), 2-6 Lockheed St., PO Box W520, Tamworth, NSW 2340, Australia. TEL 61-2-67622399, http://www.ruralpress.com. Ed. Mike Smith. Adv. contact Cheryl Byrnes TEL 61-2-67622399. Circ: 8,000 (paid).

781.7 USA
COUNTRY MUSIC LIVE. Text in English. 2000. bi-m. USD 18 domestic; USD 33 in Canada; USD 48 in Europe; USD 58 Australia, New Zealand & Japan; USD 3.99 newsstand/cover; USD 4.99 newsstand/cover in Canada (effective 2001). adv. music rev. **Document type:** *Magazine, Consumer.* **Description:** Covers the current country music scene.
Address: 909 18th Ave S., Ste. B, Nashville, TN 37212-2186. TEL 215-925-9333, FAX 215-925-9201.

780 CAN ISSN 0714-8356
COUNTRY MUSIC NEWS; the voice of country music in Canada. Text in English. 1980. m. CAD 26.75, USD 40 domestic; CAD 42 foreign (effective 1997). adv. bk.rev. back issues avail. **Document type:** *Newspaper.* **Description:** Covers the country music scene in Canada; aimed at both fans and the industry.
Indexed: CMPI.
Published by: 97594 Canada Ltd., P O Box 7323, Vanier Terminal, Ottawa, ON K1L 8E4, Canada. TEL 613-745-6006, FAX 613-745-0576. Ed., Pub., R&P Larry Delaney. Adv. contact Joanne Delaney. Circ: 12,500.

781.7 GBR ISSN 0591-2237
ML5
COUNTRY MUSIC PEOPLE. Abbreviated title: C M P. Text in English. 1970. m. GBP 35 domestic; GBP 49 in Europe; GBP 47 elsewhere (effective 2009). adv. bk.rev.; music rev.; rec.rev. back issues avail. **Document type:** *Magazine, Consumer.* **Description:** Reports on American country music, including artist features and record reviews.
Published by: Kickin' Cuts Ltd., PO Box 75, Attleborough, Norfolk NR17 1WL, United Kingdom. TEL 44-1953-853068, info@countrymusicpeople.co.uk.

781.7 GBR ISSN 0140-5721
COUNTRY MUSIC ROUND UP. Text in English. 1976. m. GBP 20.40 in British Isles; GBP 30.72 in Europe & the Rep. of Ireland; GBP 36.24 in US & Canada; GBP 36.48 in Australia & New Zealand (effective 2001). adv. bk.rev.; music rev. **Document type:** *Newspaper, Consumer.* **Description:** Country music magazine for Britain and abroad. Includes artist profiles, record reviews, tour schedules, and regional reports.
Published by: Country Music Round-up Publishing Co., PO Box 111, Waltham, Grimsby, N E Lincs DN37 0YN, United Kingdom. TEL 44-1472-821707, FAX 44-1472-821808, countrymusic@lineone.net. Ed., Pub., R&P John Emptage. Adv. contact Doreen Holder TEL 44-1522-750150. Circ: 18,500.

M

781.642 USA ISSN 1081-4221
COUNTRY MUSIC SCENE. Text in English. 1974. 12/yr. USD 24 (effective 2000). adv. music rev. 52 p./no.; back issues avail. **Document type:** *Newsletter, Trade.* **Description:** Contains a calendar of events listing local and Nashville acts, jamborees, local and national country music articles and local clubs and venues. For country music, line dancing, etc. Dedicated to promoting an interest in country music.
Published by: Country Music Scene, Inc., c/o New Jersey Country Music Association, 804 Main St, Hackensack, NJ 07601. TEL 973-904-0470. Ed., Pub., R&P, Adv. contact Jackie Hinczynski TEL 201-488-3423. B&W page USD 60. Circ: 5,000.

781.642 USA ISSN 1550-9176
ML3523
COUNTRY MUSIC TODAY; the country music magazine with an attitude. Text in English. 2000. bi-m. USD 19.95; USD 3.95 newsstand/cover (effective 2001). adv. **Document type:** *Magazine, Consumer.*
Published by: Country Media Publications, LLC, 3113 S. University Dr., Ste. 202, Fort Worth, TX 76109-5618. http://www.countrymusictoday.com. Ed. Stephen L Betts. Pub. Daniel Collins.

781 AUS ISSN 1327-0664
COUNTRY UPDATE. Text in English. 1994. q. AUD 26.95 domestic; AUD 46.95 foreign; AUD 6.95 newsstand/cover (effective 2009). adv. back issues avail. **Document type:** *Magazine, Consumer.* **Description:** Covers the country music of Australia with news, reviews and interviews.
Address: PO Box 16, Noosa Heads, QLD 4567, Australia. TEL 61-7-54553055, FAX 61-7-54553033. Ed. Bob Anthony. Adv. contact Denise Torenbeek.

781.642 USA ISSN 1074-3235
ML3523
COUNTRY WEEKLY. Text in English. 1994. w. USD 2.49 newsstand/cover (effective 2009). adv. illus. back issues avail. **Document type:** *Magazine, Consumer.* **Description:** Designed for country loving Middle Americans, covering everything from red carpet style extras to star-powered food features.
Incorporates (in 2003): Country Music
Related titles: Online - full content ed.
Published by: American Media, Inc., PO Box 37098, Boone, IA 50037. TEL 561-998-7479, FAX 518-283-9101, http://www.americanmediainc.com. Ed. Larry Holden. Adv. contact Melanie Kolbasowski TEL 212-743-6635. color page USD 35,155, B&W page USD 24,625; trim 7.75 x 10.5. Circ: 435,000 (paid).

781.642 USA ISSN 1096-1488
COUNTRY WESTERN CORNER. Text in English. 1986. m. USD 35; USD 2.50 newsstand/cover (effective 2006). adv. **Document type:** *Magazine, Consumer.* **Description:** Dedicated to the artists and writers of country and gospel music.
Published by: Entertainment News, PO Box 40, Santa Fe, TX 77517. TEL 409-925-4539. Ed., Pub. Edward King. adv.: page USD 65.

052 AUS ISSN 1329-4016
CREAM MAGAZINE. Text in English. 1998. q. AUD 49 domestic; AUD 125 foreign (effective 2009). adv. back issues avail. **Document type:** *Magazine, Consumer.* **Description:** Features the latest in fashion, music, the arts, lifestyle, travel, cuisine and more.
Address: PO Box A 2389, Sydney, NSW 2000, Australia. Adv. contact Antonino Tati TEL 61-2-92679559.

780 200 USA ISSN 1045-0815
ML2999
CREATOR; the bimonthly magazine of balanced music ministries. Text in English. 1978. bi-m. USD 32.95 domestic; USD 44 in Canada; USD 54 elsewhere (effective 2000). adv. music rev.; rec.rev.; bk.rev. index. back issues avail. **Document type:** *Magazine, Consumer.* **Description:** Focuses on music program for all denominations, emphasizing balance of music and worship styles.
Indexed: ChrPI, IIMP, RILM.
Published by: Creator Magazine, 480, Healdsburg, CA 95448-0480. TEL 707-473-9836, creatormag@aol.com. Ed. Rod E Ellis. Pub., Adv. contact Vernon Sanders. Circ: 6,000.

781.66 USA
CREEM (ONLINE EDITION). Text in English. 2003. m. **Document type:** *Magazine, Consumer.*
Media: Online - full content.
Published by: Creem Media, Inc., 28 W 25th St, New York, NY 10010. TEL 212-647-0222, BrianJBowe@CreemMagazine.com, http://www.creemmedia.com. Ed. Brian Bowe. Pub. Robert Matheu.

780 NZL ISSN 0111-8994
ML26
CRESCENDO. Text in English. 1980. 3/yr. **Document type:** *Bulletin, Trade.*
Formerly (until 1982): New Zealand Music Libraries Newsletter (0111-4557)
Indexed: A11, L04, LISTA, M11, RILM.
Published by: International Association of Music Libraries, Archives and Documentation Centres (New Zealand Branch), C/o Marilyn Portman, PO Box 4138, Auckland, New Zealand. TEL 64-9-307-7761, FAX 64-9-307-7741, http://www.iaml.info/en/organization/national_branches/new_zealand.

780 CAN
CRESCENDO. Text in English. 1958. q. adv.
Indexed: CMPI, INZP.
Published by: Toronto Musicians' Association, 101 Thorncliffe Park Dr, Toronto, ON M4H 1M2, Canada. TEL 416-421-1020, FAX 416-421-7011. Ed. Joe Macerollo. R&P, Adv. contact Richard Mendonca. Circ: 4,000 (controlled).

781.62 DEU
CRESCENDO (EUSKIRCHEN). Text in German. 1991. bi-m. EUR 2.90 newsstand/cover (effective 2006). adv. **Document type:** *Magazine, Consumer.*
Published by: (Volksmusikerbund Nordrhein-Westfalen), Loos Marketing und Verlagsgesellschaft mbH, von-Laue-Str 12, Euskirchen, 53881, Germany. TEL 49-2255-94110, FAX 49-2255-941111, info@loos-merketing.de, http://www.loos-marketing.de. adv.: B&W page EUR 768, color page EUR 1,084.60. Circ: 5,000 (paid and controlled).

780 DEU ISSN 1436-5529
CRESCENDO (MUNICH). Text in German. 1963. 6/yr. EUR 15 (effective 2006). adv. bk.rev.; music rev.; play rev.; rec.rev. charts; illus. **Document type:** *Magazine, Consumer.*
Formerly (until 1998): Oper und Konzert (0030-3518)
Indexed: IIMP, M11, MusicInd, RILM.
Published by: Port Media GmbH, Senefelderstr 14, Munich, 80336, Germany. TEL 49-89-7415090, FAX 49-89-74150911, info@portmedia.de, http://www.portmedia.de. Ed. Klemens Hippel. Pub., R&P Winfried Hanuschik. Adv. contact Natalie Lenz. color page EUR 6,090. Circ: 103,841 (paid and controlled).

781.65 GBR ISSN 0962-7472
ML3505.8
CRESCENDO AND JAZZ MUSIC. Text in English. 1962. bi-m. **Document type:** *Magazine, Consumer.* **Description:** Covers jazz and the big band scene as well as technical features about instruments and production.
Former titles (until 1991): Crescendo International (0011-118X); (until 1967): Crescendo (0574-4156)
Indexed: IIMP, M11, MusicInd, RILM, T02.
—BLDSC (3487.309800).
Published by: Crescendo & Jazz Music, 40 Lambs Conduit St, London, WC1N 3HQ, United Kingdom. TEL 44-20-74056556, FAX 44-20-74056505. Ed. Denis Matthews.

780.01 GBR ISSN 1468-6066
➤ **CRITICAL MUSICOLOGY.** Text in English. 1997. irreg., latest 1998. free (effective 2009). **Document type:** *Journal, Academic/Scholarly.* **Description:** Designed to encompass a plurality of topics, discourses, and methodologies.
Media: Online - full text.
Published by: University of Leeds, School of Music, Leeds, LS2 9JT, United Kingdom. TEL 44-113-3432583, FAX 44-113-3432586, music@leeds.ac.uk.

781.57 CAN ISSN 1712-0624
MT68
➤ **CRITICAL STUDIES IN IMPROVISATION - ETUDES CRITIQUES EN IMPROVISATION.** Text in English, French. 2004. s-a. free (effective 2011). back issues avail. **Document type:** *Journal, Academic/ Scholarly.* **Description:** Covers improvisational music, community and social practice.
Media: Online - full text.
Indexed: A39, C27, C29, D03, D04, E13, R14, S14, S15, S18.
—CCC.
Published by: University of Guelph, School of English and Theatre Studies, c/o Dr. Ajay Heble, Guelph, ON N1G 2W1, Canada. TEL 519-824-4120, csi-eci@uoguelph.ca.

780 JPN
CROSSBEAT. Text in Japanese. m. back issues avail. **Document type:** *Magazine, Consumer.*
Published by: Shinko Music Publishing Co. Ltd., 2-1 Kanda-Ogawa-Machi, Chiyoda-ku, Tokyo, 101-0052, Japan. TEL 81-3-32922865, FAX 81-3-32915135, http://www.shinko-music.co.jp.

780 700 CAN ISSN 0704-6588
CROSSCURRENTS. Text in English. 1973. q. USD 15 (effective 2003). bk.rev. **Document type:** *Newsletter, Consumer.* **Description:** A newsletter on music and art and the environment.
Related titles: Online - full text ed.
Indexed: A01, A03, A08, CA, H05, M11, T02.
—CCC.
Published by: Greenwich, 516 Ave K South, Saskatoon, SK S7M 2E2, Canada. TEL 306-244-0679, FAX 306-244-0795, green@link.ca. Ed. Robert Fink. Circ: 500.

781.65 ESP ISSN 1134-7457
CUADERNOS DE JAZZ. Text in Spanish. 1990. bi-m. EUR 27 domestic; EUR 44 in Europe; EUR 60 in the Americas (effective 2008). adv. bk.rev.; music rev. bibl.; illus. 68 p./no.; back issues avail. **Document type:** *Magazine, Consumer.* **Description:** Devoted to reflecting the diverse facets of this music, publishing essays about the links between jazz and other artistic disciplines.
Related titles: Online - full text ed.
Published by: Cuadernos de Jazz Editores S.L., Hortaleza 75, Madrid, 28004, Spain. TEL 34-91-3080302, FAX 34-91-3080599, cuadernos@cuadernorsdejazz.com. Ed. Raul A Mao. R&P Raul Mao. Adv. contact Maria Garcia. Circ: 10,000. **Dist. by:** Asociacion de Revistas Culturales de Espana, C Covarruvias 9 2o. Derecha, Madrid 28010, Spain. TEL 34-91-3086066, FAX 34-91-3199267, info@arce.es, http://www.arce.es/.

780 MEX ISSN 0185-1896
CUADERNOS DE MUSICA. Text in Spanish. 1981. irreg., latest 1985. price varies.
Indexed: C01, RILM.
Published by: Universidad Nacional Autonoma de Mexico, Instituto de Investigaciones Esteticas, Circuito Mario de la Cueva, Ciudad Universitaria, Coyoacan, Mexico, DF 04510, Mexico. TEL 52-55-56652465, FAX 52-55-56654740.

780 700 COL ISSN 1794-6670
ML5
CUADERNOS DE MUSICA, ARTES VISUALES Y ARTES ESCENICAS/ JOURNAL OF MUSIC, VISUAL ARTS, AND PERFORMING ARTS. Text in Spanish. 2004. s-a. COP 30,000 domestic; USD 27 in the Americas; USD 30 rest of world (effective 2009). back issues avail. **Document type:** *Journal, Academic/Scholarly.*
Related titles: Online - full text ed.: free (effective 2011).
Indexed: F04, H08, HAb, HumInd, I04, I05, MLA-IB, T02, W03, W05.
Published by: Pontificia Universidad Javeriana, Faculta de Artes, Carrera 7 No. 40-62, Edif. Pablo VI Piso 2, Bogota, Colombia. TEL 57-1-3208320 ext. 2449, http://www.javeriana.edu.co/Facultades/ Artes/index.php. Ed. Carolina Santamaria Delgado.

780 ESP ISSN 1136-5536
ML199
CUADERNOS DE MUSICA IBEROAMERICANA. Text in Spanish. 1996. s-a. **Document type:** *Journal, Academic/Scholarly.*
Indexed: RILM.
Published by: (Universidad Complutense de Madrid, Instituto Complutense de Ciencias Musicales), Universidad Complutense de Madrid, Servicio de Publicaciones, C/ Obispo Trejo 2, Ciudad Universitaria, Madrid, 28040, Spain. TEL 34-91-3941127, FAX 34-91-3941126, servicio.publicaciones@rect.ucm.es, http:// www.ucm.es/publicaciones. Ed. Olivia Garcia Balboa.

781.542 USA ISSN 0888-9015
ML2074
CUE SHEET. Text in English. 1984. q. USD 35 to individuals; USD 50 to institutions. adv. bk.rev. illus. back issues avail.; reprints avail. **Description:** Provides news and studies on the art of composing for film. Features interviews with film composers.
Indexed: F01, F02, IBT&D, IIFP, IIMP, IIPA, IITV, M11, MusicInd, RILM, T02.
Published by: Film Music Society, PO Box 93536, Los Angeles, CA 90093-0536. TEL 213-469-8307, FAX 818-248-8681. Ed. Jon Burlingame. Adv. contact Jeannie Pool. Circ: 800 (paid).

CULTURAL EVENTS OF NEW JERSEY. *see* MUSEUMS AND ART GALLERIES

CULTURE ET COGNITION MUSICALES. *see* ANTHROPOLOGY

780.01 USA ISSN 0011-3735
ML1
➤ **CURRENT MUSICOLOGY.** Abbreviated title: C M. Text in English. 1965. s-a. USD 25 in North America to individuals; USD 36 in North America to institutions; USD 18 in North America to students (effective 2010). adv. bk.rev. abstr.; bibl.; charts; illus.; stat. cum.index every 5 yrs. back issues avail.; reprints avail. **Document type:** *Journal, Academic/Scholarly.* **Description:** Covers to reflect the forefront of thought in historical musicology, ethnomusicology, and music theory, as well as music cognition, philosophy of music, and interdisciplinary studies.
Related titles: Microfilm ed.: (from PQC); Online - full text ed.
Indexed: A01, A02, A03, A08, A20, A22, A25, A26, A27, ABS&EES, AmHI, B04, BRD, CA, DIP, E08, G08, H07, H08, H09, H10, HAb, HumInd, I05, IBR, IBRH, IBZ, IIMP, M11, MAG, MEA&I, MusicInd, P02, P10, P48, P53, P54, PCI, PQC, PhilInd, RILM, S08, S09, T02, W03.
—IE, Ingenta.
Published by: Columbia University, Department of Music, 614 Dodge Hall, Mail Code 1812, New York, NY 10027. TEL 212-854-1632, FAX 212-854-8191. Ed. Louise Chernosky. Adv. contact Kristy Riggs. page USD 225; trim 6 x 9.

780 USA ISSN 1944-4877
▼ **CURRENT RESEARCH IN JAZZ.** Text in English. 2009. irreg. free (effective 2011). **Document type:** *Journal, Academic/Scholarly.*
Media: Online - full text.
Published by: Michael Fitzgerald, Ed. & Pub.

CYBER-PSYCHOS A O D; the magazine of mental aberrations. *see* LITERATURE—Science Fiction, Fantasy, Horror

780 AUS ISSN 1832-4835
CYCLIC DEFROST. Text in English. 2002. q. free (effective 2009). back issues avail. **Document type:** *Magazine, Consumer.* **Description:** Covers independent electronic music, avant-rock, experimental sound art and leftfield hip hop.
Media: Online - full text. **Related titles:** Print ed.: ISSN 1835-1190. free (effective 2009).
Address: PO Box A2073, Sydney South, NSW 1235, Australia. Eds. Matthew Levinson, Chan Sebastian. Adv. contact Chan Sebastian. Circ: 5,000.

780 USA ISSN 0895-6936
CYMBIOSIS; the marriage of music and magazine. Text in English. 1986. q. USD 39.98. adv. bk.rev. **Description:** Articles feature six new age, jazz and progressive artists included in a one-hour music sampler.
Media: Audio cassette/tape. **Related titles:** CD-ROM ed.
Published by: Cymbiosis, Inc., 6201 W. Sunset Blvd., Ste. 80, Hollywood, CA 90028-8704. TEL 213-463-3808, FAX 213-463-5426. Ed. Ric Levine. Circ: 15,000.

780 CZE ISSN 1211-0264
CZECH MUSIC. Text in English. 1964. bi-m. EUR 25 in Europe; USD 36 elsewhere (effective 2009). adv. bk.rev.; music rev. illus. index. back issues avail. **Document type:** *Magazine, Consumer.*
Formerly (until 1995): Music News from Prague (0027-4410)
Related titles: Online - full text ed.
Indexed: A01, A26, E08, G08, I05, IBR, IBZ, IIMP, M11, MusicInd, RILM, S09, T02.
—Ingenta.
Published by: Hudebni Informacni Stredisko/Czech Music Information Centre, Besedni 3, Prague 1, 118 00, Czech Republic. TEL 420-2-57312422, FAX 420-2-57317424, his@vol.cz, http:// www.musica.cz. Ed. Petr Bakla. adv.: page USD 320. Circ: 1,000. **Co-sponsors:** Bohuslav Martinu Foundation; Nadace Cesky Hudebni Fond/Czech Music Fund; Leos Janacek Foundation.

780 USA
D I W MAGAZINE; independent thought on independent music. (Devil in the Woods) Text in English. 2000. 5/yr. USD 15 domestic; USD 25 in Canada; USD 45 elsewhere (effective 2006). adv. **Document type:** *Magazine, Consumer.*
Published by: Insomniac Media, PO Box 56821, Sherman Oaks, CA 91413. TEL 818-905-9347, gus@insomniacmedia.com, http:// www.insomniacmedia.com. Ed., Adv. contact Andrew Parks. Pub. Gus Pena. color page USD 1,185; trim 7.5 x 10. Circ: 42,500 (paid and controlled).

780 GBR ISSN 0965-4364
D J MAGAZINE. (Disc Jockey) Text in English. 1986. 25/yr. GBP 38.20 combined subscription domestic (print & online eds.); GBP 62.50 combined subscription in Europe (print & online eds.); GBP 76.80 combined subscription elsewhere (print & online eds.) (effective 2010). adv. back issues avail. **Document type:** *Magazine, Trade.* **Description:** Provides the inside scoop on the dance music and club scene.
Formerly (until 1991): Jocks (0951-5143)
Related titles: Online - full text ed.
—CCC.
Published by: Future Publishing Ltd., Beauford Ct, 30 Monmouth St, Bath, Avon BA1 2BW, United Kingdom. TEL 44-1225-442244, FAX 44-1225-446019, customerservice@subscription.co.uk, http:// www.futureplc.com. Ed. David Eserin TEL 44-20-72478855 ext 262. Adv. contact Heath Holmes TEL 44-7977-203843. **Subscr. to:** Tower House, Sovereign Park, Market Harborough, Leicestershire LE16 9EF, United Kingdom. TEL 44-844-8481602, FAX 44-1858-438795, future@subscription.co.uk.

780.42 USA ISSN 1045-9693
D J TIMES; the international magazine for the professional mobile & club DJ. (Disc Jockey) Text in English. 1988. m. USD 19.40 domestic; USD 39.99 in Canada; USD 59.99 elsewhere (effective 2010). adv. illus. back issues avail.; reprints avail. **Document type:** *Magazine, Consumer.* **Description:** Provides a primary source for products, technologies, news and information involving club and mobile DJing.
Related titles: Online - full text ed.
Indexed: IIMP, M11, T02.
Published by: Testa Communications, Inc., 25 Willowdale Ave, Port Washington, NY 11050. TEL 516-767-2500, FAX 516-767-9335. Ed. Jim Tremayne. Adv. contact John Grecco TEL 516-767-2500 ext 507.

780 DNK ISSN 0106-5629
ML5
➤ **D M T.** (Dansk Musik Tidsskrift) Text in Danish. 1925. 6/yr. DKK 280 in Scandinavia; DKK 195 to students; DKK 280 elsewhere; DKK 50 per issue (effective 2007). music rev.; rec.rev.; bk.rev. charts; illus. cum index:1925-1935, 1936-1945. back issues avail. **Document type:** *Magazine, Academic/Scholarly.* **Description:** About modern music and composers with emphasis on Danish subjects.
Formerly (until 1966): Dansk Musiktidsskrift (0011-6386)
Related titles: Online - full text ed.: ISSN 1901-3523. 200?.
Indexed: IIMP, M11, MusicInd, RASB.
Published by: Foreningen Dansk Musik Tidsskrift, Strandvejen 100 D, Snekkersten, 3070, Denmark. TEL 45-33-244248, FAX 45-33-244246, http://www.danskmusiktidsskrift.dk. Ed. Anders Beyer.

782.421 USA ISSN 1543-0960
D V 8. Variant title: Deviate. Text in English. 2005 (Nov.). bi-m. adv. **Document type:** *Magazine, Consumer.* **Description:** Covers urban music, fashion, entertainment, and lifestyle.
Address: 1744 Alvarado Terrace, Atlanta, GA 30310. TEL 404-756-9868, FAX 404-756-0494. Pub. Desmick Perkins. Circ: 5,000.

DA-CAPO. *see* EDUCATION—Higher Education

DAILY VARIETY (LOS ANGELES); news of the entertainment industry. *see* COMMUNICATIONS—Television And Cable

781.62 SWE ISSN 0280-6584
DALARNAS SPELMANSBLAD; tidning foer Dalarnas Spelmansfoerbund. Text in Swedish. 1981. q. SEK 70; SEK 100 foreign (effective 1998). **Document type:** *Newspaper.*
Published by: Dalarnas Spelmansfoerbund/Association of Folk Musicians in Dalarna, Kung Magnigatan, Falun, 79162, Sweden. TEL 46-23-21240. Ed. Tomas Fahlander. R&P Thomas Fahlander.

DANCE ANNUAL DIRECTORY. *see* DANCE

781.554 793.3 USA ISSN 1083-7574
ML3469
DANCE MUSIC AUTHORITY. Short title: D M A. Text in English. 1993. m. USD 35 domestic; USD 40 in Canada; USD 70 elsewhere; USD 2.95 newsstand/cover. adv. **Document type:** *Magazine, Consumer.* **Description:** Features dance music news and reviews along with interviews with clubland's hottest groups and artists.
Address: 7943 Paxton Ave, Tinley Park, IL 60477. TEL 708-614-8417, FAX 708-429-7830. Ed., R&P Gary Hayslett. Pub. Gary Haylett. Adv. contact Kim Kulchawik. Circ: 38,000.

▼ **DANCECULT**; journal of electronic dance music culture. *see* DANCE

DANCESPORT AMERICA. *see* DANCE

DANCING U S A. *see* DANCE

780 CHN ISSN 1005-7099
DANGDAI GETAN/MODERN SONG CIRCLES. Text in Chinese. 1994. m. **Document type:** *Magazine, Consumer.*
Published by: Dangdai Getan Zazhishe, 188, Bei Dong Jie, Ha'erbin, 150001, China. TEL 86-451-82639387, FAX 86-451-82639387.

780 DNK ISSN 1904-237X
ML5
DANISH MUSICOLOGY ONLINE. Text in Danish, English, German. 1975. irreg., latest vol.31, 2007. price varies. back issues avail. **Document type:** *Monographic series, Academic/Scholarly.*
Former titles (until 2010): Musik og Forskning (Online) (1903-3060); (until 2007): Musik og Forskning (Print) (0903-188X)
Media: Online - full text.
Indexed: MLA-IB, RILM.
Published by: Koebenhavns Universitet, Musikvidenskab, c/o Institut for Kunst- og Kulturvidenskab, Klerkegade 2, Copenhagen K, 1308, Denmark. TEL 45-35-323739, FAX 45-35-323738, musik@hum.ku.dk, http://www.musikvidenskab.ku.dke.

780 DNK ISSN 1604-9896
ML5
➤ **DANISH YEARBOOK OF MUSICOLOGY.** Text in Multiple languages. 1961. a. back issues avail. **Document type:** *Yearbook, Academic/ Scholarly.*
Formerly (until 2004): Dansk Aarbog for Musikforskning (0416-6884)
Indexed: RILM.
Published by: Dansk Selskab for Musikforskning/Danish Musicological Society, c/o Musikvidenskabeligt Institut, Klerkegade 2, Copenhagen K, 1308, Denmark. TEL 45-35-323756, ttlind@hum.ku.dk, http:// www.musikforskning.dk. Eds. Michael Fjeldsoe TEL 45-35-323761, Thomas Holme Hansen TEL 45-89-425154.

780.9489 DNK ISSN 0905-6300
ML21.D29
DANSK MUSIK AARBOG/DANISH MUSIC YEARBOOK. Text in Danish. 1990. a. DKK 338 domestic (effective 2008). adv. back issues avail. **Document type:** *Directory, Consumer.* **Description:** Contains articles and statistics on the Danish popular music industry. Directories of the Danish record industry, sheet music publishing, composers and performers. Lists of releases, first performances, charts, and manufacturers listed by product.
Published by: Dansk Musik Aarbog ApS, Sankt Hans Torv 26, Copenhagen N, 2200, Denmark. TEL 45-35-240262, FAX 45-35-240266, musikinfo@musikinfo.dk, http://www.musikinfo.dk. Ed. Nils Harbo. Adv. contact Torben Kruse TEL 45-35-240265.

781 USA
DUSTED. Text in English. d. **Document type:** *Magazine, Consumer.*
Media: Online - full content.
Address: 150 Devoe St, Brooklyn, NY 11211. Eds. Otis Hart, Sam Hunt.

784 CAN
DYNAMIC. Text in English. 1970. 4/yr. membership. adv. **Document type:** *Newsletter.* **Description:** Information and articles of interest to Ontario Choirs and other choral enthusiasts.
Formerly: Choirs Ontario (0822-4749)
Indexed: CMPI.
Published by: Choirs Ontario, 112 St Claire Ave W, Ste 403, Toronto, ON M4V 2Y3, Canada. TEL 416-363-7488, FAX 416-363-8236, info@choirsontario.org. Ed. Julia Armstrong.

781.64 DEU ISSN 1865-4274
DYNAMITE!. Text in German. 1994. bi-m. EUR 34; EUR 6.50 newsstand/cover (effective 2010). adv. **Document type:** *Magazine, Consumer.*
Published by: Huber Verlag GmbH & Co. KG, Markircher Str 9 a, Mannheim, 68229, Germany. TEL 49-621-483610, FAX 49-621-4836111, szeneshop@huber-verlag.de, http://www.huber-verlag.de. Ed. Jessica Hierschbiel. Adv. contact Christin Nagy.

780 NLD ISSN 0012-7418
DYNAMITE INTERNATIONAL. Text in English. 1961. bi-m. EUR 12 domestic; JPY 1,560 in Japan; USD 18 in United States; GBP 11 in United Kingdom; EUR 12 elsewhere (effective 2009). adv. illus. 4 p./no. 5 cols./p.; **Document type:** *Newsletter, Consumer.* **Description:** Provides international news of interest to fans of Cliff Richard, a British singer.
Formerly: Dynamite
Published by: International Cliff Richard Movement, PO Box 94164, Amsterdam, 1090 GD, Netherlands. icrm@cliffrichard.info, http://www.cliffrichard.info.

▼ **DYOU.** *see* CHILDREN AND YOUTH—For

780 POL ISSN 2082-6303
▼ **DYOU.** Text in Polish. 2011. m. PLZ 7.99 newsstand/cover (effective 2011). adv. **Document type:** *Magazine, Consumer.*
Published by: Egmont Polska, ul Dzielna 60, Warsaw, 01029, Poland. TEL 48-22-8384100, FAX 48-22-8384200, poczta@egmont.pl, http://www.egmont.pl. Ed. Magdalena Jaworska.

780 POL ISSN 1429-2629
DYSONANSE; pismo poswiecone muzyce XX wieku oraz innym sztukom. Text in Polish. 1998. q. 56 p./no.; **Document type:** *Magazine, Consumer.*
Published by: Stowarzyszenie Polskich Artystow Muzykow, Ul Kolibrow 4/6, Katowice, 40534, Poland. TEL 48-32-2519807, promarcos@promarcos.com.pl. Circ: 1,000.

780 792 NLD ISSN 1876-9217
E B LIVE. (Entertainment Business) Text in Dutch. 2008. bi-m. EUR 75 (effective 2009). adv. **Document type:** *Magazine, Consumer.*
Published by: iMediate, Postbus 2227, Hilversum, 1200 CE, Netherlands. TEL 31-35-6465800, FAX 31-35-6465899, sales@imediate.nl, http://www.imediate.nl. Eds. Mieke Krammer, Thijs Jaski. Pub. Joost Driessen. adv.: color page EUR 2,250; trim 240 x 297. Circ: 3,500.

780 004.678 GBR
E-JAY. Text in English. 2000. m. USD 7.49 newsstand/cover (effective 2001). adv. **Document type:** *Magazine, Consumer.*
Published by: Future Publishing Ltd., Beauford Ct, 30 Monmouth St, Bath, Avon BA1 2BW, United Kingdom. TEL 44-1225-442244, FAX 44-1225-446019, customerservice@subscription.co.uk, http://www.futureplc.com. Ed. Helen Burge.

780 370 NZL ISSN 1179-7851
➤ **E-JOURNAL OF STUDIES IN MUSIC EDUCATION.** Variant title: Canterbury Studies in Music Education. Text in English. 1997. 3/yr. free (effective 2010). back issues avail. **Document type:** *Journal, Academic/Scholarly.*
Former titles (until 2010): Sound Ideas (Online) (1176-3795); (until 2009): Sound Ideas (Print) (1174-2267)
Media: Online - full text.
Indexed: RILM.
Published by: Te Puna Puoru National Centre for Research in Music Education and Sound Arts, c/o University of Canterbury, Private Bag 4800, Christchurch, 8020, New Zealand. TEL 64-3-3642987, FAX 64-3-3642728, merc@canterbury.ac.nz, http://www.merc.canterbury.ac.nz.

780 USA
E M A BULLETIN. Text in English. 1989. s-a. free to members (effective 2010). adv. **Document type:** *Newsletter, Trade.*
Related titles: Online - full text ed.
Published by: Early Music America, 2366 Eastlake Ave E #429, Seattle, WA 98102. TEL 206-720-6270, 888-722-5288, FAX 206-720-6290, info@earlymusic.org. Adv. contact Patrick Nugent.

791.546 GBR
E.P. MAGAZINE; Music, Video, Games..and Other Crimes. (Extended Play) Text in English. 1991. m. free. adv. music rev.; play rev.; rec.rev.; software rev.; video rev.; Website rev.; bk.rev. 16 p./no.; back issues avail. **Document type:** *Magazine, Consumer.* **Description:** News and information on music, films, television and other activities for young people in eastern England.
Related titles: Online - full text ed.
Published by: Vigilante Publications, Huntingdon House, 35 Field Rd, Reading, Berks RG1 6AP, United Kingdom. TEL 44-118-958-1878, FAX 44-870-734-5174. Ed. Jon Ewing. Adv. contact Emma Coop.

EARLY DRAMA, ART, AND MUSIC MONOGRAPH SERIES. *see* THEATER

784 USA ISSN 0899-8132
ML549.8
➤ **EARLY KEYBOARD JOURNAL.** Text in English. 1982. a., latest vol.24, 2008. free (effective 2010). bk.rev. 100 p./no.; back issues avail. **Document type:** *Journal, Academic/Scholarly.* **Description:** Promotes the study of early keyboard instruments, principally harpsichord, clavichord, fortepiano and the organ prior to 1860, and the music intended for these instruments.
Indexed: A01, CA, IIMP, M11, MusicInd, RILM, T02.
—Ingenta.
Published by: Southeastern Historical Keyboard Society, c/o Elaine Dykstra, PO Box 50092, Dallas, TX 78763. khjacob@gmail.com, http://www.sehks.org. **Co-sponsor:** Midwestern Historical Keyboard Society.

780.43 GBR ISSN 0306-1078
➤ **EARLY MUSIC.** Text in English. 1973. q. GBP 162 in United Kingdom to institutions; EUR 242 in Europe to institutions; USD 324 in US & Canada to institutions; GBP 162 elsewhere to institutions; GBP 177 combined subscription in United Kingdom to institutions (print & online eds.); EUR 265 combined subscription in Europe to institutions (print & online eds.); USD 353 combined subscription in US & Canada to institutions (print & online eds.); GBP 177 combined subscription elsewhere to institutions (print & online eds.) (effective 2012). adv. bk.rev.; music rev. illus. 25 year index available. back issues avail.; reprint service avail. from PSC. **Document type:** *Journal, Academic/Scholarly.* **Description:** Covers the field of Medieval, Renaissance, Baroque and Classical music history, critical surveys and performance practice.
Related titles: Microform ed.: (from PQC); Online - full text ed.: ISSN 1741-7260. GBP 147 in United Kingdom to institutions; EUR 220 in Europe to institutions; USD 295 in US & Canada to institutions; GBP 147 elsewhere to institutions (effective 2012) (from IngentaConnect).
Indexed: A01, A02, A03, A08, A20, A22, A26, A27, ASCA, AmHI, ArtHuCI, B04, B24, BRD, BrHumI, CA, CurCont, DIP, E01, E07, E08, G08, H07, H08, HAb, HistAb, HumInd, I05, IBR, IBZ, IIMP, M11, MLA-IB, MusicInd, P02, P07, P10, P48, P53, P54, PCI, PQC, RILM, S09, SCOPUS, T02, W03, W05, W07.
—BLDSC (3642.993000), IE, Infotrieve, Ingenta. **CCC.**
Published by: Oxford University Press, Great Clarendon St, Oxford, OX2 6DP, United Kingdom. TEL 44-1865-556767, FAX 44-1865-556646, enquiry@oup.co.uk, http://www.oxfordjournals.org. Ed. Tess Knighton. Pub. Nina Curtis. Adv. contact Jane Beeson. B&W page GBP 400, B&W page USD 840; trim 186 x 240. Circ: 3,500.

780 USA ISSN 1083-3633
ML1
EARLY MUSIC AMERICA. Abbreviated title: E M A. Text in English. 1988. q. USD 24 in US & Canada to non-members; USD 34 elsewhere to non-members; free to members (effective 2010). adv. bk.rev. charts; illus. back issues avail. **Document type:** *Magazine, Consumer.* **Description:** Covers news, scholarship, and events in the field of historical performance in North America. Explores the passions, insights and realities behind today's exciting world of early music.
Formerly (until 1995): Historical Performance (0898-8587)
Related titles: Online - full text ed.
Indexed: IIMP, M11, MAG, MusicInd, RILM, T02.
—Ingenta.
Address: 2366 Eastlake Ave E #429, Seattle, WA 98102. TEL 206-720-6270, 888-722-5288, FAX 206-720-6290, info@earlymusic.org. Ed. Benjamin Dunham. Adv. contact Patrick Nugent.

780.43 GBR ISSN 0261-1279
ML169.8
➤ **EARLY MUSIC HISTORY**; studies in medieval and early modern music. Text in English. 1982. a. GBP 126, USD 205 to institutions; GBP 133, USD 225 combined subscription to institutions (print & online eds.) (effective 2012). adv. bk.rev. illus. back issues avail.; reprint service avail. from PSC. **Document type:** *Journal, Academic/Scholarly.* **Description:** Encourages British, American and European work in manuscript studies, analytical work, iconography, textual criticism, and the relationship between music and society before 1700.
Related titles: Microform ed.: (from PQC); Online - full text ed.: ISSN 1474-0559. GBP 117, USD 197 to institutions (effective 2012).
Indexed: A20, A22, A27, ASCA, AmHI, ArtHuCI, CA, CurCont, E01, H07, IBR, IBZ, IIMP, M11, MusicInd, P10, P48, P53, P54, PCI, PQC, RILM, SCOPUS, T02, W07.
—BLDSC (3642.998100), IE, Infotrieve, Ingenta. **CCC.**
Published by: Cambridge University Press, The Edinburgh Bldg, Shaftesbury Rd, Cambridge, CB2 8RU, United Kingdom. TEL 44-1223-312393, FAX 44-1223-315052, journals@cambridge.org, http://www.cambridge.org/uk. Ed. Iain Fenlon. R&P Linda Nicol TEL 44-1223-325702. Adv. contact Rebecca Roberts TEL 44-1223-325083. **Subscr. to:** Cambridge University Press, 32 Ave of the Americas, New York, NY 10013. TEL 212-337-5000, FAX 212-691-3239, journals_subscriptions@cup.org.

788 USA
EARLY MUSIC NEWSLETTER. Text in English. 1976 (vol.16). m. (Sep.-June). USD 20 (effective 1999). adv. bk.rev. **Document type:** *Newsletter.*
Published by: New York Recorder Guild, c/o Eleanor Brodkin, 197 New York Ave, Dumont, NJ 07628. Ed., R&P, Adv. contact Miriam Poser. Circ: 185.

780.43 GBR ISSN 1477-478X
ML5
EARLY MUSIC PERFORMER. Text in English. 1984. s-a. GBP 14 to non-members; free to members (effective 2009). adv. bk.rev. **Document type:** *Journal, Academic/Scholarly.* **Description:** Contains features and articles of special interest to practical musicians, both amateur and professional.
Former titles (until 1998): Leading Notes (0960-6297); (until 1991): N E M A Journal (0951-6573)
Indexed: A01, CA, IIMP, M11, MusicInd, RILM, T02.
—CCC.
Published by: National Early Music Association, 126 Shanklin Dr, Leicester, LE2 3QB, United Kingdom. TEL 44-116-2709984, http://www.nema-uk.org. Ed. Andrew Woolley TEL 44-1636-525705. Pub. Jeremy Burbidge. Adv. contact Jane Beeson.

780.5 GBR ISSN 1355-3437
ML5
EARLY MUSIC REVIEW. Text in English. 1994. 6/yr. GBP 22.50 domestic; GBP 27.50 foreign (effective 2009). adv. bk.rev. **Document type:** *Magazine, Trade.* **Description:** Contains articles, letters and reviews of editions and CD's of early music.
Indexed: RILM.
Published by: The Early Music Company Ltd., The New House, The Fen, Fenstanton, Huntingdon, Cambs PE28 9JT, United Kingdom. Adv. contact Helen Shabetai TEL 44-1707-889893. page GBP 100.

780.43 GBR ISSN 1352-0059
EARLY MUSIC TODAY. Text in English. 1993. bi-m. GBP 21.50 domestic; GBP 25.50 in Europe; GBP 30 elsewhere; GBP 3.75 per issue (effective 2009). adv. bk.rev.; music rev.; rec.rev. illus. **Document type:** *Magazine, Consumer.* **Description:** Provides people involved in the promotion, performance, study or sheer enjoyment of early music with essential news and information.
Indexed: IIMP, M11, MusicInd, T02.
—CCC.
Published by: Rhinegold Publishing Ltd., 239-241 Shaftesbury Ave, London, WC2H 8TF, United Kingdom. TEL 44-20-73331720, FAX 44-20-73331765, enquiries@rhinegold.co.uk. Ed. Jonathan Wikeley. Adv. contact Neil Cording TEL 44-20-73331733.

780.1 GBR ISSN 2046-7168
ML12
THE EARLY MUSIC YEARBOOK & PERFORMERS DIRECTORY. Text in English. 1971. a. **Document type:** *Directory, Trade.* **Description:** Provides information on societies, music publishers, providers of performing material, concert promoters and artists' agents, record companies, early music fairs and courses, including summer schools.
Former titles (until 2009): The Early Music Yearbook (0967-6619); (until 1992): Register of Early Music (0307-0816)
Indexed: MusicInd.
Published by: National Early Music Association, 126 Shanklin Dr, Leicester, LE2 3QB, United Kingdom. TEL 44-116-2709984, http://www.nema-uk.org.

781.57 USA ISSN 1077-0984
ML3508.7.W3
EARSHOT JAZZ; a mirror and focus for the jazz community. Text in English. 1984. m. USD 35 (effective 2001). bk.rev. **Document type:** *Newsletter.*
Address: 3429 Fremont Pl, Ste 309, Seattle, WA 98103. TEL 206-547-6763. Ed. Peter Monaghan. R&P John R Gilbreath. Circ: 4,500.

780.42 USA
EAST END LIGHTS; the Elton John magazine. Text in English. 1990. q. USD 26 domestic; USD 35 foreign (effective 2000). **Document type:** *Newsletter, Consumer.* **Description:** Focuses on the rock star for devoted fans and collectors.
Published by: Anchor Bay Publishing, PO Box 636, New Baltimore, MI 48047-0636. TEL 810-725-3200, FAX 810-725-7077. Ed., Pub. Tom Stanton. Circ: 1,700 (paid).

EASTERN RAINBOW. *see* LITERATURE

780 USA ISSN 0147-345X
MT4.R6
EASTMAN NOTES. Text in English. 1966. a. free to qualified personnel. illus. **Document type:** *Newsletter.* **Description:** Alumni newsletter.
Former titles: Notes from Eastman; (until 1979): Eastman Notes; (until 1976): Notes from Eastman (0550-0958)
Indexed: MAG.
Published by: University of Rochester, Eastman School of Music, 26 Gibbs St, Rochester, NY 14604. TEL 716-274-1040, FAX 716-274-1089. Ed., R&P Allison Duffey. Circ: 11,000.

780.01 USA ISSN 1071-9989
EASTMAN STUDIES IN MUSIC. Text in English. 19??. irreg., latest 2009. price varies. back issues avail. **Document type:** *Monographic series, Academic/Scholarly.*
Former titles (until 1994): Studies in Music (1054-0911); Studies in Musicology
Published by: University of Rochester Press, 668 Mt Hope Ave, Rochester, NY 14620. TEL 585-275-0419, FAX 585-271-8778, boydell@boydellusa.net.

780 USA
EASY REEDING. Text in English. 1985. s-a. adv. **Document type:** *Magazine, Consumer.* **Description:** For those interested in the harmonica and the accordion, its music and artists, related events and activities.
Published by: Hohner Inc., 1000 Technology Park Dr, Glen Allen, VA 23059-4500. TEL 804-591-3741, 800-446-6010, FAX 804-515-0189, webinfo@hohnerusa.com, http://www.hohnerUSA.com. Ed. Andy Garrigue. Circ: 3,000 (controlled).

780 USA ISSN 1535-1807
ML1
➤ **ECHO (LOS ANGELES)**; a music-centered journal. Text in English. 1999. irreg., latest 2005. free (effective 2011). illus. **Document type:** *Journal, Academic/Scholarly.* **Description:** Creates a forum for discussion about music and culture which includes voices from diverse backgrounds.
Media: Online - full text.
Indexed: A39, C27, C29, D03, D04, E13, R14, S14, S15, S18.
Published by: University of California, Los Angeles, Department of Musicology, PO Box 951623, Los Angeles, CA 90095. http://www.musicology.ucla.edu/index.php?option=com_content&view=article&id=789&Itemid=175. Eds. Jonathan Greenberg, Olivia Carter Mather, Philip Gentry.

780 808 USA
ECHO ROOM. Text in English. 1988. 4/yr. USD 4. adv.
Address: 211 Morris St, Phillipsburg, NJ 08865. TEL 908-213-0994. Eds. Rab Sharpe, Steve Gilbert.

781.57 GBR ISSN 0959-4981
ECHOES (LONDON); the U K's essential Black music monthly. Text in English. 1983. m. GBP 36 domestic; GBP 46 in Europe; USD 110 in United States; GBP 62 elsewhere (effective 2010). adv. **Document type:** *Magazine, Consumer.*
Formerly (until 1983): Black Echoes
Related titles: Online - full text ed.
—BLDSC (3647.574300).
Published by: N B M Publishing Ltd., 3 Elsinore Rd, London, SE23 2SH, United Kingdom. Ed. Chris Wells. Adv. contact Paul Phillips TEL 44-1763-244366.

780 CAN ISSN 1910-4650
ECONTACT. Text in English, French. 1998. q. **Document type:** *Journal, Consumer.*
Media: Online - full text.
Published by: Canadian Electroacoustic Community

781.64 GBR
THE EDGE (SOUTHAMPTON). Text in English. 1994. 11/yr. free. adv. **Document type:** *Newspaper, Consumer.* **Description:** Music news, interviews, articles, album and concert reviews.
Published by: University of Southampton, Students Union, University Rd, Southampton, Hants SO17 1BJ, United Kingdom. TEL 44-23-80595200, susu@soton.ac.uk, http://www.susu.org/. Circ: 3,000 (controlled).

780.7 FRA ISSN 0013-1415
ML5
L'EDUCATION MUSICALE; revue culturelle et pedagogique de tout l'enseignement de la musique. Text in French. 1945. 10/yr. EUR 12 newsstand/cover domestic; EUR 15 newsstand/cover foreign (effective 2010). adv. bk.rev.; rec.rev. charts. Supplement avail. **Document type:** *Journal, Academic/Scholarly.* **Description:** Presents study and teaching methods.
Indexed: DIP, IBR, IBZ, RILM.
—CCC.
Published by: Editions Beauchesne, 7 cite Cardinal Lemoine, Paris, 75005, France. TEL 33-1-53100818, FAX 33-1-53108519, contact@editions-beauchesne.com. Circ: 7,000.

780 USA ISSN 0363-4558
EDWARD H. TARR SERIES. Text in English. irreg. **Description:** Music for trumpet.
Published by: Brass Press, c/o RKMS, 140 Main St, N, Easton, MA 02356. FAX 508-238-2571.

781.64 USA
EGG (BAR HARBOR). Text in English. irreg. **Document type:** *Magazine, Consumer.* **Description:** All about music.
Address: PO Box 336, Bar Harbor, ME 04609. TEL 207-288-8344, FAX 207-288-9069.

780 GBR ISSN 1478-5706
ML195
➤ **EIGHTEENTH-CENTURY MUSIC.** Variant title: 18th Century Music. Text in English. 2004. s-a. GBP 98, USD 160 to institutions; GBP 101, USD 175 combined subscription to institutions (print & online eds.) (effective 2012). adv. bk.rev.; music rev. back issues avail.; reprint service avail. from PSC. **Document type:** *Journal, Academic/Scholarly.* **Description:** Addresses a conspicuous gap in its field and serves as a prestigious forum for all eighteenth-century music research.
Related titles: Online - full text ed.: ISSN 1478-5714. GBP 92, USD 160 to institutions (effective 2012).
Indexed: A20, A22, ArtHuCI, CurCont, E01, IIMP, M11, MLA-IB, MusicInd, W07.
—BLDSC (3665.232000), IE. **CCC.**
Published by: Cambridge University Press, The Edinburgh Bldg, Shaftesbury Rd, Cambridge, CB2 8RU, United Kingdom. TEL 44-1223-312393, FAX 44-1223-315052, journals@cambridge.org, http://www.cambridge.org/uk. Eds. David R M Irving, Keith Chapin, W Dean Sutcliffe. Adv. contact Rebecca Roberts TEL 44-1223-325083. **Subscr. to:** Cambridge University Press, 32 Ave of the Americas, New York, NY 10013. TEL 212-337-5000, FAX 212-691-3239, journals_subscriptions@cup.org.

➤ **EIGHTEENTH-CENTURY STUDIES.** *see* HISTORY

➤ **ELECTROMUSICATIONS**; everything except the programmes. *see* COMMUNICATIONS—Television And Cable

789 USA ISSN 0884-4720
ML1380
ELECTRONIC MUSICIAN. Abbreviated title: E M. Text in English. 1976. m. USD 23.97 domestic; USD 30 in Canada; USD 50 elsewhere; USD 29.97 combined subscription domestic (print & online eds.); USD 36 combined subscription in Canada (print & online eds.); USD 56 combined subscription elsewhere (print & online eds.); USD 1.84 per issue (effective 2011). adv. bk.rev.; rec.rev.; software rev. back issues avail. **Document type:** *Magazine, Consumer.* **Description:** Provides a high-tech music equipment and applications news.
Formerly (until 1985): Polyphony (0163-4534)
Related titles: Online - full text ed.: ISSN 2161-9867. USD 23.96 (effective 2011).
Indexed: A01, A03, A08, A09, A10, A22, A26, B07, BPI, BRD, C05, C10, C12, C23, CA, CPerI, CompD, E08, G06, G07, G08, H20, I05, I06, I07, IIMP, M01, M02, M11, MusicInd, S09, S23, T02, V03, V04, W01, W02, W03, W05.
—CIS, Ingenta. **CCC.**
Published by: Penton Media, Inc., 249 W 17th St, New York, NY 10011. TEL 212-204-4200, FAX 212-206-3622, information@penton.com, http://www.penton.com.

781.01 BRA ISSN 1415-9538
➤ **ELECTRONIC MUSICOLOGICAL REVIEW.** Text in Portuguese, English. 1996. irreg., latest 2005, July. free (effective 2011). bk.rev.; music rev. abstr.; illus. **Document type:** *Journal, Academic/Scholarly.*
Media: Online - full content.
Published by: Universidade Federal do Parana, Editora, Rua Joao Negrao 280, Curitiba, Parana 80060-200, Brazil. TEL 55-41-33605000. Ed. Rogerio Budasz.

780.01 DEU
ELEMENTA MUSICAE. Text in German. 1998. irreg., latest vol.5, 2006. price varies. **Document type:** *Monographic series, Academic/Scholarly.*
Published by: Dr. Ludwig Reichert Verlag, Tauernstr 11, Wiesbaden, 65199, Germany. TEL 49-611-461851, FAX 49-611-468613, info@reichert-verlag.de, http://www.reichert-verlag.de.

782.421649 USA ISSN 1557-5438
ML3531
ELEMENTAL; underground culture. Variant title: Elemental Magazine. Text in English. m. USD 20; USD 3.99 per issue domestic; USD 5.50 per issue in Canada (effective 2006). adv. **Document type:** *Magazine, Consumer.* **Description:** Deals with "underground" hip-pop and rap music scene, covering new music, artists, and graffiti art.
Published by: Elemental Publishing, Inc., 184 Kent Ave., #314, Brooklyn, NY 11211. info@elementalmag.com. Ed. Mike Piroli. Circ: 38,000.

780.92 GBR ISSN 0143-1269
ML410.E41
ELGAR SOCIETY. JOURNAL. Text in English. 1973. 3/yr. free to members (effective 2009). adv. bk.rev.; music rev.; rec.rev. back issues avail.; reprints avail. **Document type:** *Journal, Academic/Scholarly.* **Description:** Contains articles on Elgar's life and music and society news and events, book and record reviews, and details of performances by Elgar.
Formerly (until 1979): Elgar Society. Newsletter (0309-4405)
Indexed: M11, RILM.
Published by: Elgar Society, c/o Michael Butterfield, 2, Leigh Rd, Bristol, BS8 2DA, United Kingdom. TEL 44-117-9092503, butterfieldm1@googlemail.com.

780.92 GBR ISSN 1368-5163
ELGAR SOCIETY. NEWS. Text in English. 1997. 3/yr. free to members (effective 2009). **Document type:** *Newsletter, Trade.*
Indexed: M11.
Published by: Elgar Society, c/o Michael Butterfield, 2, Leigh Rd, Bristol, BS8 2DA, United Kingdom. TEL 44-117-9092503, butterfieldm1@googlemail.com, http://www.elgar.org.

780.42 NLD
ELVIS COSTELLO INFORMATION SERVICE. Text in English. 1979. bi-m. USD 20 (effective 2009). adv. bk.rev.; film rev.; music rev.; tel.rev.; video rev. bibl.; charts; illus.; stat. index. back issues avail. **Document type:** *Newsletter, Consumer.* **Description:** Serves Elvis Costello music collectors and fans.
Address: Primulastraat 46, Purmerend, 1441 HC, Netherlands. Ed., Adv. contact Richard Groothuizen. page USD 40. Circ: 700. **Subscr. in the U.K. and Ireland to:** Ian R Cheetham, 91 Durban Rd, Watford, Herts WD18 7DS, United Kingdom. ros-ian@ntlworld.com.

051 USA
ELVIS INTERNATIONAL. Text in English. 1988. 2/yr. USD 16.95 (effective 2005). adv. bk.rev. illus. **Document type:** *Magazine, Consumer.* **Description:** Contains informative and entertaining articles, with rare full color pictures, on Elvis Presley.
Formerly: Elvis International Forum (1070-2164)
Indexed: RILM.
Published by: Darwin Lamm, Ed. & Pub., PO Box 7749, Thousand Oaks, CA 91359. TEL 818-991-3892, FAX 818-991-3894. Ed., Pub. Darwin Lamm. adv.: color page USD 3,500. Circ: 84,000 (controlled).

ELVIS NOW FAN CLUB. *see* CLUBS

ELVIS - THE OFFICIAL COLLECTOR'S EDITION. *see* HOBBIES

780 USA
ELVIS WORLD. Text in English. 1986. q. USD 18 domestic; USD 23 foreign (effective 2007). adv. bk.rev.; music rev.; tel.rev.; video rev.; film rev.; rec.rev. illus. 16 p./no. 3 cols./p.; back issues avail. **Document type:** *Magazine, Consumer.* **Description:** Features rare photos and stories (factual) relating to Elvis Presley.
Published by: Burk Enterprises, PO Box 225, Memphis, TN 38111-0225. TEL 901-327-1128, FAX 901-323-1528. Ed. Connie Lauridsen Burk. Pub., R&P, Adv. contact Bill E Burk. page USD 325; trim 10 x 8. Circ: 5,800 (paid).

780 USA
EMBELLISHMENTS; a newsletter about recent researches. Text in English. 1997. 3/yr. free (effective 2010). back issues avail. **Document type:** *Newsletter, Academic/Scholarly.* **Description:** Features about new or recent publications, a spotlight on music already published in the Recent Researches catalog, and a complete list of new and forthcoming titles.
Related titles: Online - full text ed.: free (effective 2010).
Published by: A-R Editions, Inc., 8551 Research Way, Ste 180, Middleton, WI 53562. TEL 608-836-9000, 800-736-0070, FAX 608-831-8200, orders@areditions.com. Eds. Albrecht Gaub TEL 608-836-9000 ext 18, James L Zychowicz TEL 608-836-9000 ext 14.

780.1 USA ISSN 1559-5749
ML3797
➤ **EMPIRICAL MUSICOLOGY REVIEW.** Abbreviated title: E M R. Text in English. 2006 (Jan.). q. free (effective 2011). back issues avail. **Document type:** *Journal, Academic/Scholarly.* **Description:** Provides an international forum promoting the understanding of music in all of its facets.
Media: Online - full text.
Indexed: A01, A39, C27, C29, D03, D04, E13, M11, P30, R14, RILM, S14, S15, S18, T02.
Published by: Ohio State University, School of Music, 1866 College Rd, 110 Weigel Hall, Columbus, OH 43210. TEL 614-292-6571, FAX 614-292-1102, blatti.1@osu.edu, http://www.music.osu.edu. Ed. Peter E Keller.

780 ESP ISSN 2171-4762
EN CONCIERTO; revista profesional de instrumentos musicales, sonido e iluminacion. Text in Spanish. 1989. q. free (effective 2010). **Document type:** *Magazine, Consumer.*
Published by: Comusica, C Marques de Urquijo, 17 1o., Madrid, 28008, Spain. TEL 34-91-5421082, FAX 34-91-5421086, comusica@comusica.com, http://www.comusica.com/.

780 ESP ISSN 2171-4304
▼ **EN CONCIERTO CLASICO.** Text in Spanish. 2009. s-a. **Document type:** *Magazine, Consumer.*
Published by: Comusica, C Marques de Urquijo, 17 1o., Madrid, 28008, Spain. TEL 34-91-5421082, FAX 34-91-5421086, comusica@comusica.com, http://www.comusica.com/.

787.87 SWE ISSN 1102-5964
ENCORDADO; revista de guitarra. Text in Spanish. 1992. q. SEK 152; USD 30 foreign.
Address: Cervins vaeg 19 D, 5 tr, Spanga, 16358, Sweden. TEL 46-8-7957318. Ed. Luciano Carbone.

781.64 IRL
ENERGY MAGAZINE. Text in English. bi-m. adv. **Document type:** *Magazine, Consumer.* **Description:** Contains the latest news and listings for the Dublin entertainment scene.
Address: 43-44 Lower Dorset St., Dublin, 1, Ireland. TEL 353-1-8170066, FAX 353-1-8170455. adv.: page EUR 1,524; trim 210 x 297. Circ: 20,000 (controlled).

793.31 781.62 GBR ISSN 0013-8231
ML5
ENGLISH DANCE AND SONG. Text in English. 1936. q. GBP 2.50 per issue to non-members; free to members (effective 2009). adv. bk.rev.; rec.rev. illus. back issues avail.; reprints avail. **Document type:** *Magazine, Trade.* **Description:** Devoted to folk music, dance and song in the country.
Incorporates: E F D S S News (0012-7647)
Related titles: Microform ed.: (from PQC); Online - full text ed.
Indexed: AICP, AmHI, BrHumI, H07, IBT&D, IDP, IIMP, IIPA, M11, MLA, MLA-IB, MusicInd, RILM, T02.
—BLDSC (3773.400000), Ingenta.
Published by: English Folk Dance and Song Society, Cecil Sharp House, 2 Regents Park Rd, London, NW1 7AY, United Kingdom. TEL 44-20-74852206, FAX 44-20-72840534, info@efdss.org, http://www.efdss.org/. Ed., Adv. contact Derek Schofield. B&W page GBP 250, color page GBP 300; 185 x 273.

ENGLISH FOLK DANCE AND SONG SOCIETY. ANNUAL REPORT AND ACCOUNTS. *see* DANCE

ENSUITE; Kulturmagazin. *see* LITERATURE

ENTERTAINMENT AND SPORTS LAWYER. *see* LAW

658.8 781.91 789.91 NLD ISSN 1875-2888
ENTERTAINMENT BUSINESS. Text in Dutch. 1951. m. EUR 125 for 6 mos. domestic; EUR 125 for 6 mos. in Benelux, Netherlands Antilles & Suriname; EUR 180 for 6 mos. elsewhere (effective 2009). adv. bk.rev. charts; illus.; mkt.; pat.; tr.lit.; tr.mk. **Document type:** *Magazine, Trade.*
Former titles (until 2008): Muziek en Beeld (0929-6050); (until 1993): Muziek en Beeld Info (0165-599X); Which incorporated (1987-1989): Videovak (0929-6069); (until 1978): Muziek Mercuur (0027-5298); (until 1951): Radio-TV Wereld (0033-8109)
Published by: iMediate, Postbus 2227, Hilversum, 1200 CE, Netherlands. TEL 31-35-6465800, FAX 31-35-6465899, sales@imediate.nl, http://www.imediate.nl. adv.: color page EUR 1,900; trim 240 x 320. Circ: 2,600.

780.42 USA
ENTERTAINMENT EYES. Text in English. 1979. m. USD 12.60. adv. bk.rev. bibl.; charts. back issues avail.
Published by: Alsaman Rec. and Comm. Group, Inc., PO Box 8263, Haledon, NJ 07508. TEL 201-942-6810. Eds. Maureen Ellis, Samuel Cummings. Circ: 10,000.

780 792 USA ISSN 1087-8971
ENTERTAINMENT MAGAZINE ON-LINE. Text in English. 1995. irreg. free. **Document type:** *Magazine, Consumer.*
Media: Online - full content.
Published by: B Z B Publishing, Inc., PO Box 3355, Tucson, AZ 85722. TEL 520-623-3733. Circ: 15,000.

781.542 USA
ENTERTAINMENT PLUS. Text in English. w.
Address: PO Box 11707, Rock Hill, SC 29731. TEL 803-329-4000.

ENTERTAINMENT POWER PLAYERS. *see* MOTION PICTURES

EQUILIBRIUM MAGAZINE. *see* LITERATURE

780 150 700 ITA ISSN 1122-9462
L'ERBAMUSICA; pensare altrimenti la musica e l'educazione. Text in Italian. 1991. 2/yr. adv. 120 p./no.; **Document type:** *Monographic series, Academic/Scholarly.*
Published by: Esagramma, Via Bartolini 48, Milan, 20155, Italy. esagramma.onlus@tin.it. Circ: 1,500 (paid); 500 (controlled).

780 NLD ISSN 1384-6329
EREDIENST. Text in Dutch. 1973. bi-m. EUR 35 (effective 2010). adv. bk.rev. **Description:** Covers topics relating to liturgy and church music.
Formerly (until 1996): Orgeldienst (1382-1377)
Published by: Vereniging van Gereformeerde Kerkmusici, H Van Steenwijckstraat 10, Steenwijk, 8331 KK, Netherlands. TEL 31-521-521276, secretariaat@eredienst.com, http://www.eredienst.com. Ed. Jan Smelik. Circ: 220.

781.7 NLD ISSN 0169-4677
EREDIENSTVAARDIG; tijdschrift voor liturgie en kerkmuziek. Text in Dutch. 5/yr. EUR 25; EUR 20.40 to students; EUR 5.50 newsstand/cover (effective 2008). adv.
Formed by the 1985 merger of: Musica Pro Deo (0167-1677); Eredienst (0167-2711); Which was formerly (until 1968): Liturgische Vereniging in de Nederlandse Hervormde Kerk. Mededelingen (0926-6909)
Published by: (Stichting Eredienstvaardig), Boekencentrum Uitgevers, Goudstraat 50, Postbus 29, Zoetermeer, 2700 AA, Netherlands. TEL 31-79-3615481, FAX 31-79-3615489, info@boekencentrum.nl, http://www.boekencentrum.nl. Ed. Jan van Laar. adv.: page EUR 310; trim 200 x 260. Circ: 1,800.

780.711 USA ISSN 0071-1187
ERNEST BLOCH LECTURES. Text in English. 1966. irreg., latest vol.13, 2006. price varies. back issues avail. **Document type:** *Monographic series, Academic/Scholarly.* **Description:** Discusses Western and Eastern musical traditions.
Published by: University of California Press, Book Series, 2120 Berkeley Way, Berkeley, CA 94704. TEL 510-642-4247, FAX 510-643-7127, foundation@ucpress.edu. **Subscr. to:** California - Princeton Fulfillment Services, Inc., 1445 Lower Ferry Rd, Ewing, NJ 08618. TEL 609-883-1759, 800-777-4726, FAX 800-999-1958, orders@cpfsinc.com.

780 USA
ERNEST BLOCH SOCIETY. BULLETIN. Text in English. 1967. a. USD 3.50. bk.rev. **Document type:** *Bulletin.* **Description:** Devoted entirely to correspondence between the composer and his friends and colleagues.
Former titles: Ernest Bloch Society. Newsletter; (until 1983): Ernest Bloch Society. Bulletin (0071-1195)
Published by: Ernest Bloch Society, c/o Susan Bloch, Ed, 448 Riverside Dr, New York, NY 10027. Circ: 2,000.

790.92 USA ISSN 1053-9948
ML410.K7365
ERNST KRENEK ARCHIVE. NEWSLETTER. Text in English. 1990. 2/yr. USD 10. **Document type:** *Newsletter.*
Indexed: RILM.
Published by: Ernst Krenek Archive, University of California, San Diego, La Jolla, CA 92093-0175. TEL 619-534-1267, FAX 619-534-0189. Ed. Garrett H Bowles.

780 CHN ISSN 0421-3653
ERTONG YINYUE/CHILDREN'S MUSIC. Text in Chinese. 1957. m. USD 62.40 (effective 2009). **Document type:** *Journal, Academic/Scholarly.*
—East View.
Published by: Zhongguo Yinyuejia Xiehui/Chinese Musicians Association, 10, Nongzhanguan Nanli, Beijing, 100026, China. TEL 86-10-65389293. **Dist. by:** China International Book Trading Corp, 35 Chegongzhuang Xilu, Haidian District, PO Box 399, Beijing 100044, China. TEL 86-10-68412045, FAX 86-10-68412023, cibtc@mail.cibtc.com.cn, http://www.cibtc.com.cn.

780.42 ARG
ESCENARIOS; de musica popular argentina. Text in Spanish. 1990. m.
Published by: Editorial Escenarios, Juncal, 971 4o A, Buenos Aires, 1062, Argentina. TEL 54-114-3936298.

780 920 DNK ISSN 0909-9050
ESPANSIVA. Text in Danish; Abstracts in English. 1994. s-a. DKK 175 membership (effective 2008). **Document type:** *Journal, Academic/Scholarly.* **Description:** Journal devoted to Carl Nielsen and his music.
Indexed: RILM.
Published by: Carl Nielsen Selskabet/Carl Nielsen Society, c/o Knud Ketting, Nr. Farimagsgade 11, Copenhagen K, 1364, Denmark. TEL 45-33-119626, info@carlnielsenl.dk, hjttp://www.carlnielsen.dk.

780.89 USA ISSN 0014-1836
➤ **ETHNOMUSICOLOGY.** Text in English. 1953. 3/yr. USD 160 combined subscription to institutions (print & online eds.) (effective 2012). adv. bk.rev.; film rev.; rec.rev.; video rev. bibl.; charts; illus. cum.index: vols.1-10, 11-20, 21-30. 192 p./no.; back issues avail.; reprints avail. **Document type:** *Journal, Academic/Scholarly.* **Description:** Explores the music of people throughout the world.
Related titles: Microform ed.: (from PQC); Online - full text ed.: USD 145 to institutions (effective 2012).
Indexed: A01, A02, A03, A08, A20, A21, A22, A25, A26, A27, ABS&EES, AICP, ASCA, AbAn, AmHI, AnthLit, ArtHuCI, B04, BAS, BNNA, BRD, CA, CCA, ChPerI, CurCont, DIP, E08, FR, G08, H07, H08, H09, H10, H14, HAb, HumInd, I05, IBR, IBRH, IBSS, IBZ, IIBP, IIMP, M01, M02, M08, M11, MEA&I, MLA, MLA-IB, MusicInd, P02, P10, P48, P53, P54, PCI, PQC, RI-1, RILM, RefSour, S02, S03, S08, S09, SCOPUS, SPPI, T02, W03, W07.
—BLDSC (3815.150000), IE, Infotrieve, Ingenta, INIST.
Published by: (Society for Ethnomusicology), University of Illinois Press, 1325 S Oak St, Champaign, IL 61820. TEL 217-333-0950, 866-244-0626, FAX 217-244-8082, journals@uillinois.edu. Ed. J Lawrence Witzleben TEL 301-405-5502. Adv. contact Jeff McArdle TEL 217-244-0381.

780.89 GBR ISSN 1741-1912
ML3797.6
➤ **ETHNOMUSICOLOGY FORUM.** Text in English. 1992. s-a. GBP 232 combined subscription in United Kingdom to institutions (print & online eds.); EUR 308, USD 387 combined subscription to institutions (print & online eds.) (effective 2012). adv. rec.rev.; software rev.; video rev.; bk.rev.; music rev. 1 cols./p.; back issues avail.; reprint service avail. from PSC. **Document type:** *Journal, Academic/Scholarly.* **Description:** Publishes scholarly essays on all kinds of music from an ethnomusicological perspective.
Formerly (until 2004): British Journal of Ethnomusicology (0968-1221); Which superseded in part (in 1992): International Council for Traditional Music (U K Chapter). Bulletin
Related titles: Online - full text ed.: ISSN 1741-1920. GBP 209 in United Kingdom to institutions; EUR 277, USD 348 to institutions (effective 2012) (from IngentaConnect).
Indexed: A01, A02, A03, A08, A22, AICP, CA, E01, IBR, IBSS, IBZ, IIMP, M11, MLA-IB, MusicInd, PCI, RILM, T02.
—IE, Ingenta. **CCC.**
Published by: (British Forum for Ethnomusicology), Routledge (Subsidiary of: Taylor & Francis Group), 4 Park Square, Milton Park, Abingdon, Oxon OX14 4RN, United Kingdom. subscriptions@tandf.co.uk, http://www.routledge.com. Ed. Andrew Killick. Adv. contact Linda Hann TEL 44-1344-779945. Circ: 300 (paid). **Subscr. to:** Taylor & Francis Ltd., Journals Customer Service, Sheepen Pl, Colchester, Essex CO3 3LP, United Kingdom. TEL 44-20-70175544, FAX 44-20-70175198.

780 FRA ISSN 1952-9864
L'ETINCELLE. Text in French. 2006. irreg. **Document type:** *Magazine.*
Published by: Institut de Recherche et Coordination Acoustique Musique (I R C A M), 1 Place Igor Stravinsky, Paris, 75004, France. TEL 33-1-44784843, FAX 33-1-44781540, http://www.ircam.fr/institut.html.

ETNOMUSIKOLOGIAN VUOSIKIRJA. *see* FOLKLORE

780 BEL ISSN 2031-2431
ETUDES DE MUSICOLOGIE/MUSICOLOGICAL STUDIES. Text in French, English. 2008. irreg., latest vol.2, 2008. price varies. **Document type:** *Monographic series, Academic/Scholarly.*
Published by: P I E - Peter Lang SA, 1 avenue Maurice, 6e etage, Brussels, 1050, Belgium. TEL 32-2-3477236, FAX 32-2-3477237, pie@peterlang.com, http://www.peterlang.net. Ed. Henri Vanhulst.

783 FRA ISSN 0071-2086
ETUDES GREGORIENNES; revue de musicologie religieuse. Text in English, French, Italian. 1954. a., latest vol.27, 1999. bk.rev. **Document type:** *Journal, Academic/Scholarly.* **Description:** Contains information on Gregorian chants, Medieval musicology, liturgy, and sacred music.
Indexed: IBR, IBZ, PCI, RILM.
Published by: Editions Abbaye Saint-Pierre de Solesmes, c/o SAS La Froidfontaine, 1 Pl. Dom Gueranger, Solesmes, 72300, France. TEL 33-2-43950308, FAX 33-2-43953893, http://www.abbayedesolesmes.fr. Ed. Patrick Hala. Circ: 500.

780.7 ESP ISSN 1135-6308
EUFONIA; didactica de la musica. Text in Spanish. 1995. q. EUR 58.50 domestic; EUR 61.50 foreign (effective 2009). adv. bk.rev.; music rev. bibl. back issues avail. **Document type:** *Monographic series, Academic/Scholarly.* **Description:** Presents an investigation of music pedagogy.
Indexed: RILM.
Published by: Editorial Grao, C Hurtado, 29, Barcelona, 08022, Spain. TEL 34-93-4080464, FAX 34-93-3524337, web@grao.com, http://www.grao.com. Circ: 1,900 (paid).

780 KOR
EUMAK DONG-A. Text in Korean. 1984. m.
Published by: Dong-A Ilbo, 139, Chungjongno 3-Ga Seodaemun-Gu, Seoul, 120-715, Korea, S. TEL 02-721-7114. Ed. Kwon O Kie. Circ: 85,000.

780 ITA
EUNOMIOS. Text in Multiple languages. 2000. s-a. back issues avail. **Document type:** *Journal, Academic/Scholarly.* **Description:** Contains various contributed papers on topics concerning theory, analysis, and semiotics of music.
Media: Online - full text.
Address: staff@eunomios.org, http://www.eunomios.org/.

780.7 DEU ISSN 0721-3611
EUROPAEISCHE HOCHSCHULSCHRIFTEN. REIHE 36: MUSIKWISSENSCHAFTEN. Text in German. 1978. irreg., latest vol.259, 2010. price varies. **Document type:** *Monographic series, Academic/Scholarly.*
Published by: Peter Lang GmbH (Subsidiary of: Peter Lang Publishing Group), Eschborner Landstr 42-50, Frankfurt Am Main, 60489, Germany. TEL 49-69-7807050, FAX 49-69-78070550, zentrale.frankfurt@peterlang.com, http://www.peterlang.com.

780.01 USA
EUROPEA: ETHNOMUSICOLOGIES AND MODERNITIES. Text in English. 2003. irreg., latest vol.10, 2010. price varies. back issues avail. **Document type:** *Monographic series, Academic/Scholarly.* **Description:** Provides a critical framework for the study of the dynamics of music performance, and the forces behind the senses of identity, selfhood, and belonging that shape "European" musical experience.
—BLDSC (3829.482817).
Published by: Scarecrow Press, Inc. (Subsidiary of: Rowman & Littlefield Publishers, Inc.), 4501 Forbes Blvd, Ste 200, Lanham, MD 20706. TEL 301-459-3366, 800-462-6420, FAX 301-429-5748, 800-338-4550, custserv@rowman.com. Eds. Martin Stokes, Philip V Bohlman.

781.62 780.89 ROM ISSN 1582-5841
ML3797.6
➤ **EUROPEAN MEETINGS IN ETHNOMUSICOLOGY.** Text in English. 1994. a., latest vol.8, 2001. ROL 300,000 domestic; USD 20 foreign (effective 2001). bk.rev.; dance rev.; music rev.; rec.rev. abstr.; bibl.; charts; illus.; stat. back issues avail. **Document type:** *Journal, Academic/Scholarly.* **Description:** Contains scholarly/academic papers, essays, reports, and book reviews on traditional, folk, ethnic and popular music from all over the world.
Formerly (until 2000): Eastern European Meetings in Ethnomusicology (1221-9711)
Indexed: AICP, CA, M11, MLA-IB, MusicInd, RILM, T02.
—INIST.
Published by: Romanian Society for Ethnomusicology, str. Take Ionescu 25, Bucharest, 70166, Romania. marinBmarian@hotmail.com. Ed., Pub., R&P Marin Marian Balasa. Circ: 450.

786 CHE
EUROPIANO. Text in German. q. **Document type:** *Bulletin.*
Published by: Schweizerischer Verband der Klavierbauer und -stimmer, c/o Madlen Bloesch, Vetlingerstr 151, Basel, 4057, Switzerland. TEL 41-61-6934939.

786.23 DEU ISSN 0014-2387
EUROPIANO. Text in English, French, German, Italian. 1960. q. EUR 48; EUR 13.50 per issue (effective 2009). adv. charts; illus.; stat. **Document type:** *Magazine, Trade.* **Description:** Information and workshop service for piano manufacturers. Features latest technology, computerization, association news and events, readers' comments.
Indexed: IBR, IBZ.
—CCC.
Published by: (Union Europaeischer Pianomacher-Fachverbaende), P P V Medien GmbH, Postfach 57, Bergkirchen, 85230, Germany. TEL 49-8131-56550, FAX 49-8131-565510, http://www.ppvmedien.de. Ed. Jan Grossbach TEL 49-69-314513. adv.: B&W page EUR 875, color page EUR 1,315; trim 210 x 280. Circ: 3,100 (paid and controlled).

784 NLD ISSN 1879-9779
EUROVISION ARTISTS MAGAZINE. Text in Dutch. q. EUR 23 domestic; EUR 25 foreign (effective 2011). **Document type:** *Magazine, Consumer.*
Former titles (until 2010): E A-Nieuws (1389-8310); (until 1996): Eurovision Artists (1382-7855)
Published by: Stichting Eurovision Artists, Grote Spie 297, Breda, 4819 CV, Netherlands. TEL 31-345-618887, info@eurovisionartists.nl, http://www.eurovisionartists.nl.

780.65 DEU
EVENT. Text in German. m. adv. **Document type:** *Magazine, Consumer.*
Published by: K P S Magazin Verlags GmbH, Dingolfinger Str 6, Munich, 81673, Germany. TEL 49-89-41600453, FAX 49-89-41600445. adv.: B&W page EUR 6,696, color page EUR 8,240. Circ: 200,528 (controlled).

780.65 DEU ISSN 0949-9504
EVENT PARTNER; Fachmagazin fuer Event-Marketing. Text in German. 1995. bi-m. EUR 52.15 domestic; EUR 61.35 foreign; EUR 10.20 newsstand/cover (effective 2011). adv. **Document type:** *Magazine, Trade.*
Published by: Musik - Media Verlag GmbH (Subsidiary of: Ebner Verlag GmbH), Emil-Hoffmann-Str 13, Cologne, 50996, Germany. TEL 49-2236-962170, FAX 49-2236-962175, info@musikmedia.de, http://www.musikmedia.de. Ed. Walter Wehrhan. Adv. contact Angelika Mueller. Circ: 14,061 (paid and controlled).

781.64 CAN ISSN 1207-6600
EXCLAIM!. Text in English. 1992. m. CAD 25. **Document type:** *Magazine, Consumer.* **Description:** Features emerging music and popular culture.
Related titles: Online - full text ed.
Indexed: CMPI.
Address: 7B Pleasant Blvd, 966, Toronto, ON, Canada. TEL 416-535-9735, FAX 416-535-0566. Ed. James Keast. Pub. Ian Danzig. Circ: 102,000.

EXETER STUDIES IN AMERICAN & COMMONWEALTH ARTS. *see* LITERATURE

780 USA ISSN 1936-220X
ML3533.8
EXPLICITLY INTENSE. Text in English. irreg., latest no.8, 2002. USD 14 domestic; CAD 3.95 newsstand/cover in Canada; GBP 2.50 newsstand/cover in United Kingdom; ANG 9.90 newsstand/cover in Netherlands (effective 2007). music rev. back issues avail. **Document type:** *Magazine, Consumer.* **Description:** Covers both hard rock and heavy metal music. Includes CD reviews, live reviews, and interviews.
Published by: Explicitly Intense Magazine, PO Box 10683, Glendale, CA 91209-0683. Ed., Pub. Sarjoo Devani.

783 NLD
EXPRESSIE. Text in Dutch. 1975. a. adv. bk.rev.
Formerly: Gospel Informatie-Handboek
Published by: Continental Sound, Postbus 81065, Rotterdam, 3009 GB, Netherlands. TEL 31-10-4568688, FAX 31-10-4559022, http://www.cnvkunstenbond.nl.

780 USA
F.E.D.S.; finally every dimension of the streets. Text in English. 2000. q. USD 3.95 newsstand/cover (effective 2001). adv. **Document type:** *Magazine, Consumer.*
Published by: Clark, Inc., 1369 Madison Ave, Ste 406, New York, NY 10128. Ed. Monique Clark. Pub. A Clark.

787 USA ISSN 0196-187X
ML1
F I G A MAGAZINE. Text in English. 1960. bi-m. USD 20 domestic; USD 26.50 in Canada; USD 37 elsewhere (effective 2001). adv. bibl. **Document type:** *Newsletter.*
Former titles: F I G A Review (0196-1861); (until 1980): F I G A News (0014-5890)
Published by: Fretted Instrument Guild of America, 3101 Shadow Pond Terrace, Winter Garden, FL 34787. TEL 407-654-8057, allfrets@aol.com. Ed., Pub. John Baier. Circ: 2,000.

780.01 GBR
F O M R H I QUARTERLY. Text in English. 1975. q. GBP 34 (effective 2009). bk.rev. cum.index. back issues avail. **Document type:** *Journal, Academic/Scholarly.* **Description:** Promotes authenticity in the reproduction, preservation and use of historical musical instruments.
Formerly (until 1985): Fellowship of Makers and Restorers of Historical Instruments Quarterly
Published by: Fellowship of Makers and Researchers of Historical Instruments, Southside Cottage, Brook Hill, Albury, Guildford GU5 9DJ, United Kingdom. TEL 44-1483-202159, FAX 44-1483-203088, Lutesoc@aol.com, http://www.nrinstruments.demon.co.uk/fomrhi.html. Ed. Chris Goodwin.

F W D HOME ENTERTAINMENT MAGAZINE. (Forward) *see* COMMUNICATIONS—Television And Cable

780 791.4375 069 USA
F W WEEKLY. (Fort Worth) Text and summaries in English. w. free. adv. **Description:** Covers the entertainment scene in the Ft. Worth area.
Related titles: Online - full content ed.
Address: 1204 B-West 7th St, Fort Worth, TX 76102. TEL 817-335-9559, feedback@fwweekly.com, http://www.fwweekly.com. Ed. Gayle Reaves.

780.42 USA ISSN 0882-2921
ML3533.8
FACES ROCKS. Text in English. 1983. irreg., latest 1993, June. USD 24.95; USD 4.95 newsstand/cover (effective 2004). adv. illus. **Document type:** *Magazine, Consumer.* **Description:** Features hard rock and heavy metal music.
Formerly (until 1983): Faces (0883-8658)
Published by: Faces Magazines, Inc., 210 E State Rt 4, Ste 401, Paramus, NJ 07652-5103. TEL 201-843-4004, FAX 201-843-8636. Ed. Renee Daigle. Pub. Scott Figman. Adv. contacts Victor Sierkowski, Mitch Hershowitz. Circ: 150,000 (paid).

051 USA ISSN 1533-5194
ML3531
THE FADER. Text in English. 1999. 8/yr. USD 19.95 domestic; USD 50 in Canada; USD 75 elsewhere; USD 5.99 newsstand/cover (effective 2006). adv. **Document type:** *Magazine, Consumer.* **Description:** Focuses on global music, art, fashion, technology and film, with an emphasis on insightful journalism, beautiful photography, and cutting-edge design.
Indexed: A01, F01, F02, G05, G06, G07, I05, M11.
Published by: The Fader, 71 W 23rd St, 13th Fl, New York, NY 10010. TEL 212-741-7100, FAX 212-741-4747, advertising@thefader.com, info@thefader.com, editorial@thefader.com. Pub. Peter Ferraro TEL 212-652-9247. Adv. contact Eric Shorter TEL 212-652-9261. B&W page USD 8,752, color page USD 11,989; trim 9 x 10.875. **Dist. by:** International Publishers Direct, 27500 Riverview Center Blvd, Bonita Springs, FL 34134. TEL 858-320-4563, FAX 858-677-3220.

FANCY. *see* CHILDREN AND YOUTH—For

789.91 USA ISSN 0148-9364
ML156.9
FANFARE (TENAFLY); the magazine for serious record collectors. Text in English. 1977. bi-m. USD 50 domestic; USD 75 foreign (effective 2010). adv. bk.rev. illus. back issues avail.; reprints avail. **Document type:** *Magazine, Consumer.*
Related titles: Online - full text ed.
Indexed: A01, A20, A22, BRI, CA, CBRI, IIMP, M11, MAG, MusicInd, T02.
—IE, Ingenta.
Published by: Fanfare, Inc., 17 Lancaster Rd, PO Box 17, Tenafly, NJ 07670. TEL 201-567-3908, FAX 201-816-0125. Ed., Pub., Adv. contact Joel Flegler.

780 GBR ISSN 1759-9423
▼ **FANTASTIC EXPEDITION.** Text in English. 2010. s-a. GBP 4 per issue domestic; GBP 4.50 per issue in Europe; GBP 5 per issue elsewhere (effective 2010). back issues avail. **Document type:** *Magazine, Consumer.* **Description:** Covers all aspects of late 60s and early 70s US West coast music.
Published by: J. Smith, Ed. & Pub., 57 Hempstead Rd, Kings Langley, Hertfordshire WD4 8BS, United Kingdom.

780 USA ISSN 1087-4879
FARANDULA INTERNACIONAL. Text in Spanish. 1993. m. adv. **Document type:** *Magazine, Consumer.*
Indexed: G08.
Published by: Ibarra Brothers, 1009 Valencia St, San Francisco, CA 94110. TEL 415-826-6700, FAX 415-826-6701. Ed. Arturo Ibarra. R&P Armando Ibarra. Adv. contact Jose M Ibarra.

FASHION ROCKS. *see* CLOTHING TRADE—Fashions

781.7 USA ISSN 8755-9137
ML3551
FAST FOLK MUSICAL MAGAZINE. Text in English. 1984. 10/yr. USD 100; USD 125 foreign (effective 1992). adv. bk.rev. **Description:** Focuses on the contemporary folk singer-songwriter scene. Each CD contains a dozen or more songs, while the print publication contains articles, news and commentaries, interviews, lyrics, and biographies of performers-authors.
Related titles: CD-ROM ed.
Published by: Fast Folk Musical Magazine, Inc., PO Box 938, Village Sta, New York, NY 10014. TEL 212-274-1636, FAX 212-927-1831. Ed. Jack Hardy. Circ: 1,500.

781.64 GBR ISSN 1465-9174
FATLACE; the magazine for ageing b-boys. Text in English. 1997. irreg. **Document type:** *Magazine, Consumer.* **Description:** Provides insight into the history and future of hip hop music.
Published by: Fatlace Productions, PO Box 12809, London, NW3 4WT, United Kingdom. Eds. Dan Huge, Drew Huge.

780 621.389 ITA ISSN 1121-5313
FEDELTA DEL SUONO. Text in Italian. 1991. m. (9/yr.). adv. **Document type:** *Magazine, Consumer.*
Published by: Societa Fedelta del Suono, Via Cavour 63 A, Terni, TR 05100, Italy. TEL 39-0744-441339, FAX 39-0744-435352. Ed. Andrea Bassanelli.

781.57 USA ISSN 1081-5988
ML3505.8
FEDERATION JAZZ. Text in English. 1985. q. free to members; USD 25 to non-members (effective 2003). adv. bk.rev. illus. 8 p./no.; **Document type:** *Newsletter, Trade.* **Description:** Covers the activities of the federation and its members. Includes items of interest to jazz enthusiasts.
Published by: The American Federation of Jazz Societies, Inc., 20137 Skyline Ranch Dr., Apple Valley, CA 92308-5035. TEL 760-247-5165, FAX 760-247-5145, info@jazzfederation.com. Pub. J. Donald Jones. Circ: 1,800 (controlled).

780 AUS ISSN 1039-4354
FELLOWSHIP OF AUSTRALIAN COMPOSERS. JOURNAL. Text in English. 19??. irreg., latest 2006. free to members (effective 2009). adv. **Document type:** *Newsletter.* **Description:** Features updates on FAC projects, composers' opportunities, members' news and upcoming events of interest to the composing community.
Published by: Fellowship of Australian Composers, PO Box 520, Epping, NSW 1710, Australia. enquiries@fellowshipofaustraliancomposers.com.

780 JPN ISSN 1341-0601
FERISU JOGAKUIN DAIGAKU ONGAKU GAKUBU KIYO/FERRIS UNIVERSITY. COLLEGE OF MUSIC. FERRIS STUDIES. Text in Japanese. 1995. a. **Document type:** *Journal, Academic/Scholarly.*
Indexed: RILM.
Published by: Ferisu Jogakuin Daigaku, Ongaku Gakubu/Ferris University, College of Music, 4-5-3 Ryokuen, Izumi-ku, Yokohama, 245-8650, Japan. http://www.ferrismusic.com/.

780 DEU ISSN 0939-4664
FERMATE; rheinisches Musikmagazin. Text in German. 1982. q. EUR 16; EUR 4.80 newsstand/cover (effective 2010). adv. bk.rev. 48 p./no. 3 cols./p.; back issues avail. **Document type:** *Magazine, Consumer.*
Published by: Verlag Christoph Dohr, Kasselberger Weg 120, Cologne, 50769, Germany. TEL 49-221-707002, FAX 49-221-704395, info@dohr.de. Ed. Christoph Dohr. adv.: page EUR 390.

780.1 USA ISSN 1062-4074
FESTSCHRIFT SERIES. Text in English. 1977. irreg. price varies. back issues avail. **Document type:** *Monographic series, Academic/Scholarly.*
Published by: Pendragon Press, PO Box 190, Hillsdale, NY 12529. TEL 518-325-6100, FAX 518-325-6102, orders@pendragonpress.com. Ed. Robert J Kessler.

788 ITA ISSN 1724-2487
FIATI; cultura e informazione sugli strumenti a fiato. Text in Italian. 1993. q. free to qualified personnel (effective 2008). **Document type:** *Magazine, Trade.*
Published by: Accademia Italiana del Flauto, Via Ferruccio 32/b, Rome, 00187, Italy. http://www.accademiaitalianadelflauto.it. Ed. Gian Luca Morseletto.

781.7 ARG
FICTA-DIFUSORA DE MUSICA ANTIQUA. Text in Spanish. 1977. s-a. adv. bk.rev.
Published by: Centro de Musica Antiqua, Mexico 1208, Buenos Aires, 1097, Argentina. Ed. Jorge V Gonzalez. Circ: 1,500.

781.62 CAN ISSN 1079-9974
ML1
FIDDLER MAGAZINE. Text in English. 1994. q. USD 25 domestic; USD 30 in Canada & Mexico; USD 40 elsewhere (effective 2005); USD 7 newsstand/cover (effective 2004). adv. bk.rev.; music rev.; video rev. back issues avail. **Document type:** *Magazine, Consumer.* **Description:** Presents over sixty pages of columns, features and tunes for fiddlers of all levels and styles (Irish, Scottish, Cape Breton, old-time, bluegrass, Texas, swing, Cajun and others.).
Related titles: Online - full text ed.
Indexed: CMPI, RILM.
—CCC.
Address: PO Box 101, North Sydney, NS B2A 3M1, Canada. TEL 902-794-2558, info@fiddle.com. Ed., Pub., R&P, Adv. contact Mary E Larsen. B&W page USD 300; trim 8.5 x 11. Circ: 3,000. **Dist. by:** IPD, 674 Via de la Valle, Ste 200, Solana Beach, CA 92075. TEL 619-793-9486, FAX 619-481-5848.

781 USA
FIDDLIN' AROUND; the journal of American roots music. Text in English. m. free newsstand/cover (effective 2002). **Document type:** *Journal, Trade.*
Published by: R A M, PO Box 174, Grantville, GA 30220. Pub. Steve Robertson.

780.65 AUS ISSN 1448-9295
FIEND. Text in English. 2002. q. AUD 35 domestic; AUD 40 in Asia & the Pacific; AUD 50 elsewhere (effective 2009). adv. back issues avail. **Document type:** *Magazine, Consumer.* **Description:** Provides the dark alternative community in Australasia with articles on fashion, music, nightlife and dark alternative culture.
Formerly (until 2003): Goth Nation (1447-4476)
Published by: Ground Under Productions, PO Box 246, Northcote, VIC 3070, Australia. TEL 61-3-94437265, FAX 61-3-94437520, info@gup.net.au, http://www.gup.net.au. Ed. Amaya Booker. Pub. Joseph Chillari. Adv. contact Gerry Meehan. color page AUD 450; 210 x 297.

780 USA ISSN 1520-3891
ML2074
FILM MUSIC. Text in English. 1998. m. USD 35 domestic; USD 45 in Canada & Mexico; USD 65 elsewhere (effective 2003). **Document type:** *Magazine, Trade.* **Description:** Covers the music for film, television and multimedia, including industry news, technology, personalities and business information.
Indexed: F01, F02, M11, MusicInd, T02.
Published by: Film Music Network, 11601 Wilshire Blvd, Ste 500, Los Angeles, CA 90025. TEL 310-575-1820, 888-456-5020, http://www.filmmusic.net/.

FILM MUSIC BUYER'S GUIDE. *see* MOTION PICTURES

781.542 USA ISSN 1077-4289
ML2074
FILM SCORE MONTHLY; your soundtrack source since 1990. Text in English. 1990. bi-m. USD 36.95 domestic; USD 42.95 in Canada & Mexico; USD 50 elsewhere; USD 4.95 newsstand/cover (effective 2010). bk.rev.; music rev.; video rev. illus.; tr.lit. 48 p./no. 3 cols./p.; back issues avail.; reprints avail. **Document type:** *Magazine, Trade.* **Description:** Covers music in the movies, news, CD reviews, interviews, and commentary.
Related titles: Online - full content ed.; Online - full text ed.: ISSN 1939-974X.
Indexed: F01, F02, IIMP, IIPA, M11, MusicInd, RILM, T02.
Address: 6311 Romaine St, Ste 7109, Hollywood, CA 90038. TEL 323-461-2240, FAX 323-461-2241, lukas@filmscoremonthly.com.

780 ESP ISSN 1576-0464
ML5
FILOMUSICA; revista de musica culta. Text in Spanish. 2000. bi-m. back issues avail. **Document type:** *Magazine, Consumer.*
Media: Online - full text. Ed. Daniel Mateos Moreno.

780 USA
FILTER. Text in English. 5/yr. USD 24.95 (effective 2006). music rev. **Document type:** *Magazine, Consumer.* **Description:** Covers music, musicians, new artists and interviews.
Address: 5908 Barton Ave., Los Angeles, CA 90038. TEL 323-464-4775.

781.542 USA ISSN 1544-2861
ML3469
FILTER MAGAZINE. Text in English. 1997. 5/yr. USD 24.95 (effective 2008); CAD 36; USD 3.95, CAD 5.75 newsstand/cover. adv. **Document type:** *Magazine, Consumer.* **Description:** Features stories on personal heroes, musicians and the emerging hip-hop counter culture. Includes profiles, story on the science fiction novels.
Formerly (until 2002): Mean (1529-3440)
Related titles: Online - full text ed.
Published by: Filter Magazine, LLC, 5908 Barton Ave, Los Angeles, CA 90038. TEL 323-464-4217, http://www.filter-mag.com. Ed. Andy Hunter. Pub. Kashy Khalen. Adv. contact Jamie Fraser. **Dist. by:** Rider Distribution Services, 3700 Eagle Rock Blvd, Los Angeles, CA 90065. TEL 323-344-1200.

780 USA
FILTER MINI. Text in English. 2004. bi-m. **Document type:** *Magazine, Consumer.*
Address: 5908 Barton Ave, Los Angeles, CA 90038. TEL 323-464-4170, info@filtermmm.com. Ed. Chris Martins. Pub. Alan Miller.

780 FIN ISSN 1456-7946
FINAALI. Text in Finnish; Abstracts in English. 1994. q. **Document type:** *Journal, Academic/Scholarly.*
Related titles: Online - full text ed.
Indexed: RILM.
Published by: Sibelius-Akatemia/The Sibelius Academy, PO Box 86, Helsinki, 00251, Finland. TEL 358-20-75390, FAX 358-20-7539600, info@siba.fi, http://www.siba.fi.

FINE F A C T A. *see* EDUCATION

781.57 AUS
FINE MUSIC. Text in English. 1975. m. AUD 90 (effective 2009). adv. bk.rev.; dance rev.; play rev.; Website rev.; film rev.; rec.rev.; music rev. illus.; tr.lit. 80 p./no.; back issues avail. **Document type:** *Magazine, Consumer.* **Description:** Features articles, CD and book reviews on classical, jazz, blues, and some contemporary-experimental music.
Former titles (until 2001): 2 M B S F M Stereo F M Radio (1324-1990); (until 1979): Stereo F M Radio (0313-0797)
Published by: Music Broadcasting Society of N.S.W., 76 Chandos St, St Leonards, NSW 2065, Australia. TEL 61-2-94394777, FAX 61-2-94394064, info@2mbs.com, http://www.2mbs.com. Adv. contact Mike Smith TEL 61-2-94394901.

780 CHE ISSN 1661-9978
FINGER; our favorites' favorites. Text in English. 2005. 2/yr. CHF 15 domestic; EUR 10 in Europe; GBP 5 in United Kingdom; USD 11 elsewhere (effective 2007). adv. **Document type:** *Magazine, Consumer.*
Address: Bertastr 10, Zurich, 8003, Switzerland. Ed. Adrian Hoenicke.

787.87 USA ISSN 1521-3579
FINGERSTYLE GUITAR. Text in English. 1993. bi-m. USD 39.95 domestic; USD 49.95 in Canada & Mexico; USD 82.95 elsewhere; USD 44.95 combined subscription domestic (print & online eds.); USD 54.95 combined subscription in Canada & Mexico (print & online eds.); USD 87.95 combined subscription elsewhere (print & online eds.); USD 8.95 per issue (effective 2010). adv. back issues avail. **Document type:** *Magazine, Consumer.* **Description:** Covers all types of musical genres.
Related titles: Online - full text ed.
Published by: M I Media Llc., 442 US Hwy 202/206 N, 504, Bedminster, NJ 07921. TEL 888-223-3340, FAX 888-316-9624. Ed. Bill Piburn. Pub., Adv. contact Alfred Foss.

THE FINNISH AMERICAN REPORTER; an English language journal for Finnish Americans and their friends. *see* ETHNIC INTERESTS

780.94897 FIN ISSN 0782-1069
ML3619
FINNISH MUSIC QUARTERLY. Variant title: F M Q: Music Magazine. Text in English. 1985. q. EUR 24 in Finland and Scandinavia; EUR 30 elsewhere (effective 2008). adv. rec.rev. back issues avail.; reprints avail. **Document type:** *Magazine, Consumer.* **Description:** Publishes information on Finnish music and music life in Finland.
Indexed: IIMP, M11, MusicInd, T02.
—Ingenta. **CCC.**
Published by: Esittavan Saveltaiteen Edistamiskeskus/Finnish Performing Music Promotion Centre, Pieni Roobertinkatu 16, Helsinki, 00120, Finland. TEL 358-9-68034040, FAX 358-9-68034033, http://www.gramex.fi/index.php?mid=327. Eds. Anu Ahola, Juha Torvinen. Adv. contact Timo Jaakola. page EUR 500; 140 x 210.
Co-sponsors: Foundation for the Promotion of Finnish Music (LUSES); Finnish Composers' International Copyright Bureau (TEOSTO); Sibelius-Akatemia/The Sibelius Academy.

781.66 GBR ISSN 1754-9582
FIREWORKS (STOCKPORT). Text in English. 2000. bi-m. GBP 27 domestic; GBP 40 in Europe; GBP 54, USD 80 elsewhere (effective 2009). adv. back issues avail. **Document type:** *Magazine, Consumer.*
Published by: Fireworks Magazine, 10 Dunnock Close, Offerton, Stockport, SK2 5XD, United Kingdom.

787 USA
FIRST BASS. Text in English. 1987. q. USD 14.95; USD 24.95 foreign. bk.rev. **Description:** Directed to the electric and acoustic bass player of all ages, levels and backgrounds with emphasis on the intelligent creative reader, thinker and music lover. Educational tool for students and guide for consumers.
Published by: (Bass Players Hall of Fame Museum), First Bass International, 33 Essex St, Hackensack, NJ 07601. TEL 201-489-5057, FAX 201-489-2508. Ed. Joe Campagna.

FLAMENCOTIDNINGEN DUENDE. *see* DANCE

788.32 AUS ISSN 0311-0559
FLAUTIST. Text in English. 1971. q. free to members (effective 2009). bk.rev.; music rev.; Website rev. 20 p./no. 3 cols./p.; **Document type:** *Journal, Academic/Scholarly.* **Description:** Publishes articles relevant to flute players.
Published by: Victorian Flute Guild Inc., PO Box 95, Malvern, VIC 3144, Australia. TEL 61-3-98222241, azsloan@bigpond.com.au, http://www.victorianfluteguild.org. Ed. Margaret Rogers.

780 USA
FLIPSIDE. Text in English. 1977. bi-m. USD 24; USD 30 in Canada; USD 36 in Mexico and South America; USD 42 in Europe and New Zealand. adv. bk.rev. **Description:** Features punk music and interviews with new bands.
Address: 24 N. Roosevelt Ave., Pasadena, CA 91107-3621. TEL 626-585-0395, FAX 626-585-0395. Ed. Hal Flipside.

788.32 DEU ISSN 0930-8563
ML935
FLOETE AKTUELL. Text in German. 1985. q. EUR 8 per academic year to members; EUR 12 per academic year to non-members (effective 2009). adv. **Document type:** *Magazine, Consumer.*
Indexed: RILM.
Published by: Deutsche Gesellschaft fuer Floete e.V., Strubbergstr 80, Frankfurt am Main, 60489, Germany. TEL 49-69-5962443, FAX 49-69-590277, floete@floete.net. adv.: B&W page EUR 640; trim 210 x 297. Circ: 2,200 (controlled).

784 USA ISSN 0160-5119
ML1
FLORIDA FRIENDS OF BLUEGRASS SOCIETY. NEWSLETTER. Text in English. bi-m. illus. **Document type:** *Newsletter.*
Published by: Florida Friends of Bluegrass Society, 7318 Sequaia Dr, Tampa, FL 33617.

780.7 USA ISSN 0046-4155
ML1
➤ **FLORIDA MUSIC DIRECTOR.** Text in English. 1959. 8/yr. free to members (effective 2011). bk.rev. illus. 56 p./no. 2 cols./p.; back issues avail.; reprints avail. **Document type:** *Journal, Academic/Scholarly.*
Formerly (until 1969): Music Director (0027-4313); Incorporates: Florida Music Teacher
Related titles: Online - full text ed.: free (effective 2011); ◆ Supplement(s): Research Perspectives in Music Education. ISSN 1947-7457; Florida Music Teacher.
Indexed: MAG.
Published by: Florida Music Educators Association, The Hinckley Ctr for Fine Arts Education, 402 Office Plz, Tallahassee, FL 32301. TEL 850-878-6844, 800-301-3632, FAX 850-942-1793, sales@flmusiced.org, http://www.flmusiced.org/dnn/FMEA.aspx. Adv. contact Val Anderson. Circ: 4,500. **Co-sponsor:** Florida State Music Teachers Association.

780.01 GBR ISSN 1463-4244
FLOURISH (LONDON). Text in English. 1966. 2/yr. bk.rev.; rec.rev. **Document type:** *Magazine, Consumer.*
Formerly (until 1994): Trinity Magazine
Related titles: E-mail ed.: free (effective 2009).
Published by: Trinity College London, 89 Albert Embankment, London, SE1 7TP, United Kingdom. TEL 44-20-78206100, FAX 44-20-78206161, info@trinitycollege.co.uk, http://www.trinitycollege.co.uk.

788 NZL ISSN 1177-0686
FLUTE FOCUS. Text in English. 2005. q. NZD 35 domestic; NZD 50 foreign (effective 2008). adv. back issues avail. **Document type:** *Magazine, Trade.* **Description:** Covers all types of flute from classical to wooden flutes and all types of music from classical to jazz to Irish music.
Published by: Mary O'Brien, Ed. & Pub., 112 Postman Rd, RD 4, Albany, 0794, New Zealand. mary.obrien@xtra.co.nz.

780 FRA ISSN 0398-9038
LA FLUTE HARMONIQUE. Text in French. 1976. q. **Document type:** *Magazine, Consumer.*
Indexed: RILM.
Published by: Association Aristide Cavaille-Coll, 5 Rue Roquepine, Paris, 75008, France.

780 USA ISSN 0744-6918
ML929
FLUTE TALK. Text in English. 1980. m. (except Jun. & Aug.). USD 13 domestic; USD 28 foreign (effective 2009). bk.rev.; rec.rev. **Document type:** *Magazine, Trade.* **Description:** Features interviews with performers and teachers, performance guides, practice ideas, teaching suggestions, a piccolo column and music reviews.
Indexed: IIMP, M11, MAG, MusicInd, RILM.
—Ingenta.
Published by: The Instrumentalist Co., 200 Northfield Rd, Northfield, IL 60093. TEL 847-446-5000, 888-446-6888, FAX 847-446-6263, advertising@instrumentalistmagazine.com, http://www.theinstrumentalist.com.

780 USA ISSN 8756-8667
ML27.U5
➤ **THE FLUTIST QUARTERLY.** Text in English. 1974. q. free to members (effective 2011). adv. bk.rev. back issues avail. **Document type:** *Magazine, Consumer.*
Formerly (until 1984): National Flute Association. Newsletter
Related titles: Microfilm ed.: 1974 (from BHP); Online - full text ed.
Indexed: A01, A26, CA, I05, IIMP, M11, MAG, MusicInd, RILM, T02.
Published by: National Flute Association, Inc., 26951 Ruether Ave, Ste H, Santa Clarita, CA 91351. TEL 661-713-2072, FAX 661-299-6681, memberservices@nfaonline.org. Adv. contact Steve Wafalosky TEL 440-247-1068.

781.64 GBR
FLY MUSIC MAGAZINE. Text in English. 1995. m. free (effective 2009). back issues avail. **Document type:** *Magazine, Consumer.*
Description: Focuses on popular and urban music.
Media: Online - full content.
Address: 59-65 Worship St, London, EC2A 2DU, United Kingdom. TEL 44-20-76889000, FAX 44-20-76888999. Ed. Niall Doherty. Adv. contact Phil Haslehurst TEL 44-20-78747463.

780 371.3 USA ISSN 1077-498X
ML1
FLYING TOGETHER. Text in English. 1989. 3/yr. free to members (effective 2006). **Document type:** *Newsletter, Trade.* **Description:** Offers educators, performers and administrators a forum to exchange ideas and information related to chamber music education.
Related titles: Online - full text ed.
Published by: Chamber Music America, 305 Seventh Ave, New York, NY 10001. TEL 212-242-2022, FAX 212-242-7955, info@chamber-music.org, http://www.chamber-music.org.

FOERBUNDET FOER MUSIKTERAPI I SVERIGE. *see* MEDICAL SCIENCES—Physical Medicine And Rehabilitation

FOLIO (NORTH HOLLYWOOD). *see* COMMUNICATIONS—Radio

781.62 CZE ISSN 0862-9900
FOLK & COUNTRY. Text in Czech. 1991. m. CZK 330; CZK 30 newsstand/cover (effective 2010). adv. **Document type:** *Magazine, Consumer.*
Published by: F M Production, s.r.o, Husinecka 21, Prague 3, 130 00, Czech Republic. TEL 420-2-22541889, FAX 420-2-22541887.

781.7 USA ISSN 1076-4119
ML3476.8
FOLK ERA TODAY!. Text in English. 1981. q. USD 8. adv. bk.rev. back issues avail. **Description:** Covers popular acoustic folk music.
Former titles: Folk Era Newsletter; Kingston Korner Newsletter
Published by: Folk Era Productions, Inc., 17 Middle Dunstable Rd, Nashua, NH 03062. TEL 603-888-3457. Ed. Bob Grand. Circ: 15,000.

780 USA ISSN 0094-8934
ML1
FOLK HARP JOURNAL. Text in English. 1973. q. USD 16 to institutions. adv. bk.rev. bibl.; charts; illus. **Document type:** *Magazine, Consumer.*
Description: Covers folk (nonpedal) harp playing, construction, and history. Aims to provide communication among harpers and builders.
Indexed: IIMP, M11, MusicInd, RILM, T02.
—IE.
Published by: International Society of Folk Harpers and Craftsmen, Inc., 1034 Santa Barbara St, Santa Barbara, CA 93101. TEL 714-998-5717, FAX 714-998-5717. Ed. Nadine Bunn. Circ: 1,400.

781.62 793.31 GBR ISSN 0531-9684
ML5
➤ **FOLK MUSIC JOURNAL.** Abbreviated title: F M J. Text in English. 1932. a. GBP 7.50 per issue to non-members; free to members (effective 2009). adv. bk.rev. illus. cum.index. back issues avail.; reprint service avail. from PSC. **Document type:** *Journal, Academic/Scholarly.*
Formerly (until 1965): English Folk Dance and Song Society. Journal (0071-0563); Which was formed by the merger of (1927-1932): English Folk Dance Society. Journal (1756-0985); Which was formerly (1914-1915): English Folk Dance Society. Journal (0376-8899); (1899-1932): Folk-Song Society. Journal (0377-0567)
Related titles: Microform ed.: (from PQC); Online - full text ed.
Indexed: A01, A02, A03, A08, A20, A22, A26, A27, ASCA, AmHI, ArtHuCI, B04, BRD, BrHumI, CA, CurCont, DIP, E08, G06, G07, G08, H07, H08, HAb, HumInd, I05, IBR, IBZ, IDP, IIMP, IIPA, M11, MLA, MLA-IB, MusicInd, P02, P10, P48, P53, P54, PCI, PQC, RILM, S09, SCOPUS, T02, W03, W05, W07.
—BLDSC (3974.572000), IE, Ingenta.
Published by: English Folk Dance and Song Society, Cecil Sharp House, 2 Regents Park Rd, London, NW1 7AY, United Kingdom. TEL 44-20-74852206, FAX 44-20-72840534, info@efdss.org, http://www.efdss.org/. Ed., Adv. contact David Atkinson. page GBP 225; 130 x 200. Circ: 4,000.

781.7 793.31 GBR ISSN 1350-8083
FOLK NORTH-WEST. Text in English. 1977. q. GBP 10.50 domestic; GBP 14.50 foreign; GBP 2 per issue (effective 2009). adv. bk.rev.; play rev. back issues avail. **Document type:** *Magazine, Consumer.*
Description: Contains News and articles on folk music in Northwest England.
Formerly: North-West Federation of Folk Clubs. Newsletter
Published by: North-West Federation of Folk Clubs, 118 Bolton Rd, Aspull, Wigan, Lancs WN2 1XF, United Kingdom. Ed. John Webb. Adv. contact Paul Holden TEL 44-1942-258459. **Subscr. to:** 7 Sunleigh Rd, Hindley, Wigan, Lancs WN2 2RE, United Kingdom.

FOLK OCH MUSIK. *see* FOLKLORE

781.62 793.31 NOR ISSN 1891-6473
ML3704
FOLKEMUSIKK. Text in Norwegian. 1941. 5/yr. NOK 360 domestic; NOK 500 elsewhere (effective 2011). adv. back issues avail. **Document type:** *Magazine, Consumer.* **Description:** Covers folk music and dancing with an emphasis on Nordic traditions.
Formerly (until 2010): Spelemannsbladet for Folkemusikk og Bygdedans (0333-0370)
Published by: Folkemusikk- og Folkedansorganisasjonen i Norge/ Norwegian Traditional Music and Dance Association, P O Box 4613, Sofienberg, Oslo, 0506, Norway. TEL 47-22-005690, FAX 47-48-105075, post@folkemusikk.no. Ed. Knut Aastad Braaten TEL 47-90-768797.

781.7 DEU
ML3544
FOLKER!; das Musikmagazin. Text in German. 1998. bi-m. EUR 23 domestic; EUR 28 foreign; EUR 5 newsstand/cover (effective 2005). adv. bk.rev. cum.index. **Document type:** *Magazine, Consumer.*
Description: Provides information on international and national folk music, both traditional and contemporary.
Formed by the merger of: Folksblatt; (1977-1998): Folk-Michel (0934-6449); Which was formerly (until 1987): Michel - Zeitschrift fuer Volksmusik
Address: Rommersdorferstr 65 a, Bad Honnef, 53604, Germany. TEL 49-2224-76510, FAX 49-2224-71464. Ed. Mike Kamp. Adv. contact Juergen Brehme. B&W page EUR 770, color page EUR 1,150; trim 190 x 267. Circ: 3,500. **Subscr. to:** Anna-Vandenhoeck-Ring 36, Goettingen 37081, Germany.

780 792.8 USA
THE FOLKFIRE; St. Louis dance & music. Text in English. bi-m. USD 10 (effective 2011). adv. illus. **Document type:** *Newsletter, Consumer.*
Published by: The FolkFire, PO Box 511067, St Louis, MO 63151-1067. TEL 314-846-7964. adv.: page USD 400.

781.62 DEU
FOLKMAGAZIN. Text in German. 1979. bi-m. adv. **Document type:** *Magazine, Consumer.*
Address: Dorfstr 45, Luettenmark, 19258, Germany. TEL 49-38842-20623, FAX 49-38842-21888. Ed. Hedo Holland.

780 DEU ISSN 1861-3047
FOLKWANG STUDIEN. Text in German. 2005. irreg., latest vol.9, 2009. price varies. **Document type:** *Monographic series, Academic/ Scholarly.*
Published by: Georg Olms Verlag, Hagentorwall 7, Hildesheim, 31134, Germany. TEL 49-5121-15010, FAX 49-5121-150150, info@olms.de.

781.62 USA ISSN 2154-6398
▼ **FOLKWAYSMAGAZINE.** Variant title: Smithsonian Folkways Magazine. Text in English. 2009. q. free (effective 2010). **Document type:** *Magazine, Consumer.* **Description:** Features articles on folk music and the Folkways program at the Smithsonian Institute.
Media: Online - full text.
Published by: Smithsonian Institution, Center for Folklife and Cultural Heritage, 600 Maryland Ave, SW, Ste 2001, Washington, DC 20024. TEL 202-633-6450, FAX 202-633-6477, folklife-info@si.edu, http://www.folklife.si.edu.

789.91 621.389 DEU ISSN 0015-6140
FONOFORUM; Klassik, Jazz und HiFi. Text in German. 1957. m. EUR 69.60 domestic; EUR 70.80 foreign (effective 2011). adv. bk.rev.; rec.rev. illus.; tr.lit. index. **Document type:** *Magazine, Consumer.*
Indexed: IBR, IBZ, RASB, RILM.
Published by: Reiner H. Nitschke Verlags GmbH, Eifelring 28, Euskirchen, 53879, Germany. TEL 49-2251-650460, FAX 49-2251-6504699, service@nitschke-verlag.de, http://www.nitschke-verlag.de. **Subscr. to:** P M S GmbH & Co. KG, Postfach 104139, Duesseldorf 40032, Germany. TEL 49-211-6907890, FAX 49-211-69078950.

780 POL ISSN 0867-0501
FONORAMA; pismo kolekcjonerow plyt. Text in English, Polish. 1990. bi-m. PLZ 72 (effective 2003). adv. bk.rev.; music rev. back issues avail. **Document type:** *Newspaper, Consumer.* **Description:** For record collectors, music lovers, archivists.
Media: Online - full content.
Published by: Fonopress, Ul Jozefitow 3-12, Krakow, 30-039, Poland. TEL 48-12-4234116, 48-12-4234116, FAX 48-12-4234116. Ed., Adv. contact Wojciech Zajac. page USD 40; trim 160 x 240. Circ: 500 (paid).

FORCED EXPOSURE. *see* LITERARY AND POLITICAL REVIEWS

784.18 DEU ISSN 1434-6338
FORTE. Text in German. 1997. 10/yr. EUR 25.90 domestic; EUR 34 foreign (effective 2009). adv. **Document type:** *Magazine, Consumer.*
Published by: Druck und Verlag Obermayer GmbH, Bahnhofstr 33, Buchloe, 86807, Germany. TEL 49-8241-500816, FAX 49-8241-500846, info@dvo-verlag.de, http://www.dvo-verlag.de. Ed. Uschi Mohr-Busduga. adv.: B&W page EUR 1,119, color page EUR 1,977; trim 185 x 262. Circ: 6,000 (paid and controlled).

783 DEU ISSN 1434-2340
FORUM KIRCHENMUSIK. Text in German. 1950. bi-m. EUR 21; EUR 5.50 newsstand/cover (effective 2006). adv. bk.rev.; rec.rev. illus. index. **Document type:** *Journal, Academic/Scholarly.*
Formerly (until 1996): Kirchenmusiker (0023-1819)
Indexed: IIMP, M11, MusicInd, RILM.
—CCC.
Published by: (Verband Evangelischer Kirchenmusiker Deutschlands), Strube Verlag GmbH, Pettenkoferstr 24, Munich, 80336, Germany. TEL 49-89-54426611, FAX 49-89-54426630, strube.verlag@strube.de, http://www.strube.de. adv.: page EUR 520; trim 123 x 174. Circ: 6,500 (paid and controlled).

780.71 DEU ISSN 0946-543X
FORUM MUSIKPAEDAGOGIK. Text in German. 1992. irreg., latest vol.97, 2011. price varies. **Document type:** *Monographic series, Academic/Scholarly.*
Indexed: DIP, IBR, IBZ.
Published by: Wissner Verlag, Im Tal 12, Augsburg, 86179, Germany. TEL 49-821-259890, FAX 49-821-594932, info@wissner.com. Ed. Rudolf Dieter Kraemer.

FOTNOTEN; tidningen foer dig som arbetar pedagogiskt med musik, dans eller drama. *see* EDUCATION

781.7 USA ISSN 0887-1892
ML3168.8
FOUNDER'S SOUNDER. Text in English. 1979. s-a. free. **Document type:** *Newsletter.* **Description:** Covers African American gospel music and current events of MARGMF.
Published by: (Middle Atlantic Regional Gospel Music Festival), Middle Atlantic Regional Press, PO Box 6021, Washington, DC 20005. TEL 202-265-7609. Ed. E Myron Noble.

780 DEU ISSN 0949-5282
FRAGMEN; Beitraege, Meinungen und Analysen zur neuen Musik. Text in German. 1993. irreg., latest vol.51, 2008. price varies. **Document type:** *Monographic series, Academic/Scholarly.*
Published by: Pfau Verlag, Hafenstr 33, Saarbruecken, 66111, Germany. TEL 49-681-4163394, FAX 49-681-4163395, info@pfau-verlag.de. Ed. Stefan Fricke.

781.542 USA
ML3489
FRANCEVISION - HIT PARADE. Text in English, French. 1988. bi-m. USD 12. back issues avail. **Document type:** *Newsletter.*
Description: Dedicated to French language popular arts. Major emphasis on music, but includes film.
Formerly: Le Hit Parade (1044-5056)
Published by: Version Francaise, 4930 Saint Elmo Ave., Bethesda, MD 20814-6008. TEL 301-654-2224, 800-835-7537, FAX 301-656-1658. Ed. John Snoody. R&P Donna Sayada. Circ: 12,000.

780 CHE ISSN 1438-857X
ML3797
FRANKFURTER ZEITSCHRIFT FUER MUSIKWISSENSCHAFT. Text in German. 1998. irreg. free (effective 2011). **Document type:** *Journal, Academic/Scholarly.*
Media: Online - full content.
Address: c/o Arne Stollberg, Hallerstr 5, Bern, 3012, Switzerland. arne.stollberg@muwi.unibe.ch.

780 USA
FRANZ LISZT STUDIES SERIES. Text in English. 1991. irreg., latest vol.11, 2010. price varies. back issues avail. **Document type:** *Monographic series, Trade.*
Formerly (until 1992): American Liszt Society Studies Series (1062-4031)
Published by: Pendragon Press, PO Box 190, Hillsdale, NY 12529. TEL 518-325-6100, FAX 518-325-6102, orders@pendragonpress.com. Ed. Michael Saffle.

780 DNK ISSN 1601-2127
FREEMUSE REPORT; freedom of musical expression. Text in English. 2001. irreg. **Document type:** *Monographic series, Academic/ Scholarly.* **Description:** Reports from independent international organisation which advocates freedom of expression for musicians and composers worldwide.
Related titles: Online - full text ed.: ISSN 1601-2135.
—CCC.
Published by: Freemuse, Nytorv 17, 3rd Fl, Copenhagen, 1450, Denmark. TEL 45-33-321027, freemuse@freemuse.org.

FREIBURGER BEITRAEGE ZUR MUSIKERMEDIZIN. *see* MEDICAL SCIENCES

780 USA ISSN 1062-4082
FRENCH OPERA IN THE 17TH AND 18TH CENTURIES. Text in English. 1984. irreg., latest vol.12, 2006. price varies. back issues avail. **Document type:** *Monographic series, Trade.*
Published by: Pendragon Press, PO Box 190, Hillsdale, NY 12529. TEL 518-325-6100, FAX 518-325-6102, orders@pendragonpress.com. Ed. Claire Brook.

787 USA ISSN 1558-0326
ML999
FRETBOARD JOURNAL. Text in English. 2005. q. USD 34 domestic; USD 48 in Canada; USD 80 elsewhere; USD 12.95 newsstand/cover domestic; USD 18.95 per issue foreign (effective 2006). adv. **Document type:** *Magazine, Consumer.* **Description:** Covers all forms of music and instruments for collectors and players of guitars, banjos, mandolins and ukuleles.
Address: PO Box 60032, Palo Alto, CA 94306-0032. TEL 206-854-4357, 800-614-9632. Ed. Michael J Simmons. Pub. Jason Verlinde.

780 230 DEU ISSN 1434-873X
FRIEDENSAUER SCHRIFTENREIHE. REIHE C: MUSIK - KIRCHE - KULTUR. Text in German. 1998. irreg., latest vol.12, 2009. price varies. **Document type:** *Monographic series, Academic/Scholarly.*
Published by: Peter Lang GmbH (Subsidiary of: Peter Lang Publishing Group), Eschborner Landstr 42-50, Frankfurt Am Main, 60489, Germany. TEL 49-69-7807050, FAX 49-69-78070550, zentrale.frankfurt@peterlang.com. Eds. Horst Rolly, Johann Gerhardt, Wolfgang Kabus.

780 USA
FRIENDS OF JULIO INTERNATIONAL NEWSLETTER. Abbreviated title: F O J I Newsletter. Text in English. 1986. q. looseleaf. USD 18 domestic membership; USD 20 in Canada membership; USD 25 in Europe membership (effective 2001). adv. **Document type:** *Newsletter.* **Description:** Reports on Julio's concerts, albums, tour schedules, benefits; includes photos of Julio.
Published by: Friends of Julio International, 28 Farmington Ave, Longmeadow, MA 01106. TEL 413-567-0845, FAX 413-567-9530. Ed., Pub., Adv. contact Isabel Butterfield. Circ: 100.

781.64 USA ISSN 1520-0175
THE FRITZ; the new college music magazine. Text in English. 1995. m. USD 7. adv. bk.rev.; film rev.; music rev.; play rev.; video rev. illus. back issues avail. **Document type:** *Newspaper, Consumer.*
Description: Serves college students across Florida with reviews of over 100 album releases each month, reviews of alternative cinema, and interviews with directors, musicians, and writers.
Formerly (until 1996): Fritz Cesspool
Related titles: Online - full text ed.: ISSN 1520-2747.
Published by: Fritz Media Group, Inc., 2352 Springs Landing Blvd, Longwood, FL 32779. TEL 941-351-9192, FAX 407-862-2115, http://www.thefritz.com. Ed. Aaron Gustafson. Adv. contact Alicia Smith. page USD 1,750; trim 16 x 10. Circ: 20,000 (paid).

787 ITA ISSN 1125-811X
ML5
IL FRONIMO; rivista trimestrale di chitarra e liuto. Text in Italian. 1972. q. EUR 40 domestic; EUR 60 foreign (effective 2009). adv. bk.rev. bibl.; charts; illus. index. **Document type:** *Magazine, Consumer.*
Published by: Edizioni Il Dialogo, Via Orti 14, Milan, 20122, Italy.

781.7 GBR ISSN 1748-6882
FROOTS; local music from out there. Text in English. 1980. m. GBP 46 domestic; GBP 63 foreign; GBP 4.20 per issue (effective 2009). adv. music rev.; rec.rev.; bk.rev. back issues avail. **Document type:** *Magazine, Consumer.* **Description:** Features news, reviews and information about modern and traditional music with roots from around the world.
Former titles (until 2002): Folk Roots (0951-1326); (until 1985): Southern Rag
Related titles: Online - full text ed.: GBP 36 (effective 2009).
Indexed: IIMP, M11, MusicInd, RILM.
Published by: Southern Rag Ltd., PO Box 337, London, N4 1TW, United Kingdom. TEL 44-20-83409651, FAX 44-20-83485626. Ed. Ian Anderson. Adv. contact Gina Jennings. B&W page GBP 725, color page GBP 930; trim 210 x 297. **Dist. by:** Seymour Distribution Ltd, 86 Newman St, London W1T 3EX, United Kingdom. TEL 44-20-73968000, FAX 44-20-73968002.

780 CAN
FULL CONTACT. Abbreviated title: F C. Text in English. bi-m. USD 4.95 newsstand/cover domestic; USD 5.95 newsstand/cover in Canada (effective 2003). illus. **Document type:** *Magazine, Consumer.*
Published by: Full Contact Magazine, 401-485 Huron St, Toronto, ON M5R 2R5, Canada.

780 ESP ISSN 1132-0621
FUNDACION ARCHIVO MANUEL DE FALLA. BOLETIN. Text in Spanish. 1991. irreg. **Document type:** *Bulletin, Consumer.*
Published by: Fundacion Archivo Manuel de Falla, Calle de Darro, 22 Portal B-8, Madrid, 2008002, Spain. TEL 958-228318, FAX 958-215955, archivo@manueldefalla.com, http://www.manueldefalla.com/.

781.7 398 VEN
FUNDACION DE ETNOMUSICOLOGIA Y FOLKLORE. ANUARIO. Text in Spanish. 1975. a. USD 15. bk.rev. illus.
Formerly (until 1989): Centro para las Culturas Populares y Tradicionales. Boletin; Supersedes (in 1987): Instituto Interamericano de Etnomusicologia y Folklore. Revista
Published by: Fundacion de Etnomusicologia y Folklore, Prados del Este, Apdo 81015, Caracas, DF 1080, Venezuela. TEL 612118, FAX 627296.

FUNDACION LA CAIXA. PANORAMA. *see* MUSEUMS AND ART GALLERIES

780 ESP
FUTURE MUSIC. Text in Spanish. m. EUR 5.95 newsstand/cover (effective 2009). adv. **Document type:** *Magazine, Consumer.*
Published by: Grupo V, C Valportillo Primera, 11, Alcobendas, Madrid, 28108, Spain. TEL 34-91-6622137, FAX 34-91-6622654, secretaria@grupov.es, http://www.grupov.es/. Adv. contact Amador Moreno. page EUR 2,350; trim 18.7 x 27.6. Circ: 40,000.

789.5 USA ISSN 0827-5955
ML1
G C N A BULLETIN. Text in English. 1940. a. adv. bk.rev. back issues avail. **Document type:** *Bulletin, Consumer.* **Description:** Covers the carillon, the players and their music.
Published by: (Guild of Carillonneurs in North America (San Antonio)), G C N A Bulletin, c/o George Gregory, Ed, 132 Linda Dr, San Antonio, TX 78216. TEL 210-822-0416. Ed. George Gregory. R&P Arla Jo Anderton TEL 806-795-4040. Adv. contact Laurel Buckwalter TEL 607-587-8090. Circ: 500. **Subscr. to:** William DeTurk, Bok Tower Gardens. Box 3810, Lake Wales, FL 33853. bokbells@cs.com.

780 DEU ISSN 0945-8867
G E M A JAHRBUCH. Text in German. 1991. a. **Document type:** *Journal, Academic/Scholarly.*
Published by: Gesellschaft fuer Musikalische Auffuehrungs- und Mechanische Vervielfaeltigungsrechte, Postfach 301240, Berlin, 10722, Germany. TEL 49-30-2124500, FAX 49-30-21245950, gema@gema.de.

780 DEU ISSN 0946-0055
K1450.A15
G E M A NACHRICHTEN. Text in German. 1948. s-a. **Document type:** *Journal, Academic/Scholarly.*
Indexed: RILM.
Published by: Gesellschaft fuer Musikalische Auffuehrungs- und Mechanische Vervielfaeltigungsrechte, Postfach 301240, Berlin, 10722, Germany. TEL 49-30-2124500, FAX 49-30-21245950, gema@gema.de, http://www.gema.de. Eds. Elfriede Rossori, Hans-Herwig Geyer.

782.2 USA ISSN 1070-7794
ML2999
G I A QUARTERLY. Text in English. 1990. q. USD 18 domestic; USD 28 foreign (effective 2006). **Document type:** *Journal, Trade.* **Description:** Contains articles for pastoral musicians with a clear emphasis on imparting information and building skills.
Indexed: RILM.
—CCC.
Published by: Gregorian Institute of America, 7404 S Mason Ave, Chicago, IL 60638. TEL 708-496-3800, FAX 708-496-3828, custserv@giamusic.com. Ed. Fred Moleck.

G I AKTUELL. (Goethe-Institut) *see* ART

781.64 DEU
G K E; das Tontraegerverzeichnis auf CD-ROM. Text in German. a. (plus 12 updates). EUR 459.36 (effective 2006). **Document type:** *Catalog.*
Media: CD-ROM.
Published by: Josef Keller Verlag GmbH & Co. KG, Seebreite 9, Berg, 82335, Germany. TEL 49-8151-7710, FAX 49-8151-771190, info@keller-verlag.de, http://www.keller-verlag.de.

780.7309489 DNK ISSN 0109-0097
GAFFA. Text in Danish. 1983. m. DKK 399 membership (effective 2009). adv. bk.rev. illus. **Document type:** *Magazine, Consumer.* **Description:** Concerned primarily with rock, techno, hip-hop and jazz.
Related titles: Online - full content ed.: ISSN 1901-354X. 200?.
Published by: Gaffa A/S, Moellegade 9-13, Aarhus C, 8000, Denmark. TEL 45-70-270600, FAX 45-86-189222, gaffa@gaffa.dk. adv.: page DKK 36,500. Circ: 76,500 (controlled and free); 3,500 (paid).

784.19 GBR ISSN 0072-0127
➤ **THE GALPIN SOCIETY JOURNAL**; for the study of musical instruments. Abbreviated title: G S J. Text in English. 1948. a. free to members (effective 2009). adv. bk.rev. charts; illus. cum.index: vols.1-20. 2 cols./p.; back issues avail.; reprints avail. **Document type:** *Journal, Academic/Scholarly.* **Description:** Contains articles, reviews, notes and queries on all aspects of musical instruments.
Related titles: Microfiche ed.: (from PQC); Online - full text ed.
Indexed: A22, B24, CA, FR, IIMP, M11, MusicInd, PCI, RASB, RILM, T02.
—BLDSC (4067.550000), IE, Ingenta, INIST. **CCC.**
Published by: Galpin Society, c/o Maggie Kilbey, Admin, 37 Townsend Dr, St Albans, Herts AL3 5RF, United Kingdom. administrator@galpinsociety.org. Ed. Michael Fleming. Adv. contact Charles Mould TEL 44-1451-860876.

780 USA ISSN 1938-6990
➤ **GAMUT.** Text in English. 2008. s-a. free (effective 2010). **Document type:** *Journal, Academic/Scholarly.* **Description:** Covers all aspects of music theory and related disciplines, including criticism, commentary, research, and scholarship.
Media: Online - full text.
Indexed: M11, T02.
Published by: (Music Theory Society of the Mid-Atlantic), University of Tennessee Libraries, Newfound Press, 1015 Volunteer Blvd, Knoxville, TN 37996. TEL 865-974-6600, FAX 865-974-4259, http://www.newfoundpress.utk.edu/.

780.65 USA
THE GAVIN REPORT. Text in English. w.
Published by: Gavin Report, 140 Second St, 2nd Fl, San Francisco, CA 94105-3727. TEL 415-495-1990, FAX 415-495-2580. Ed. Ron Fell.

780 DEU ISSN 1430-9971
LA GAZZETTA. Text in German. 1991. a. EUR 5 per issue (effective 2011). **Document type:** *Journal, Academic/Scholarly.*
Indexed: RILM.
Published by: (Deutsche Rossini-Gesellschaft e.V. CHE), Leipziger Universitaetsverlag GmbH, Oststr 41, Leipzig, 04317, Germany. TEL 49-341-9900440, FAX 49-341-9900440, info@univerlag-leipzig.de. Ed. Reto Mueller.

784.19 AUS
GEARHEAD EZINE. Text in English. 1998. m. free (effective 2009). bk.rev. back issues avail. **Document type:** *Magazine, Consumer.* **Description:** Features reviews of guitars, amplifiers, effects and general musical instruments.
Media: Online - full text. **Related titles:** E-mail ed.
Address: 47 John Ln, Salisbury, SA 5108, Australia. chris@1800instruments.com, http://www.1800instruments.com/gearhead.htm. Ed. Christopher Carr.

GEARHEAD MAGAZINE. *see* LIFESTYLE

782 CHN
GECHANG YISHU/ART OF SINGING. Text in Chinese. 1988. m. **Document type:** *Magazine, Consumer.*
Formerly (until 2009): Yinxiang Shijie/Audio & Video World (1004-2628)
—East View.
Published by: (Shanghai Changpian Zonggongsi/Shanghai Record Corporation), Yinxiang Shijie Zazhishe, 55, Chaoyangmen Nei Dajie Jia, Dongcheng-qu, Beijing, 100010, China.

▼ **GEGENSTROPHE**; Blaetter zur Lyrik. *see* LITERATURE

780 DNK ISSN 1600-8871
GEIGER. Variant title: Musiktidsskriftet Geiger. Text in Danish. 2000. q. DKK 120 domestic to individuals; DKK 160 domestic to institutions; DKK 160 in Europe; DKK 220 elsewhere; DKK 40 per issue (effective 2009). adv. music rev.; rec.rev. back issues avail. **Document type:** *Magazine, Consumer.*
Related titles: Online - full text ed.: ISSN 1901-3558. 2000.
Published by: (Dansk Rock Samraad (ROSA)), Musiktidsskriftet Geiger, Saltholmsgade 82, Aarhus C, 8000, Denmark. TEL 45-86-196548, info@geiger.dk. Eds. Peter Tapdrup Andersen, Rasmus Steffensen. Circ: 5,000 (controlled and free).

780 USA ISSN 1931-3756
➤ **GENERAL MUSIC TODAY (ONLINE).** Text in English. 2002. 3/yr. USD 58, GBP 34 to institutions (effective 2011). **Document type:** *Journal, Academic/Scholarly.*
Media: Online - full content.
Indexed: BRD, E02, EdA, EdI, IIMP, W03, W05.
—CCC.
Published by: (M E N C: National Association for Music Education), Sage Publications, Inc., 2455 Teller Rd, Thousand Oaks, CA 91320. TEL 805-499-9774, FAX 805-499-0871, info@sagepub.com, http://www.sagepub.com. Ed. Diane Persellin.

780 USA ISSN 1939-8158
ML1
GEORGIA MUSIC MAGAZINE. Text in English. 2005. q. USD 15 (effective 2007). adv. **Document type:** *Magazine, Consumer.* **Description:** Covers Georgia's music industry, including artist profiles, event calendar, reviews and news about all genres of music found in Georgia.
Published by: Georgia Music Hall of Fame Foundation, Inc, PO Box 1073, Macon, GA 31202. TEL 478-741-2020, FAX 478-751-3100, info@georgiamusicmag.com. Ed. Lisa Love. adv.: page USD 1,650; 7.25 x 9.875. Circ: 15,000.

780 USA ISSN 0046-5798
ML1
GEORGIA MUSIC NEWS. Text in English. 1938. q. adv. charts; illus. **Document type:** *Journal, Academic/Scholarly.* **Description:** Aims at K-12, college, university music educators. Deals with music education.Constitutes the official publication of the Georgia Music Educators Association.
Indexed: MAG.
Published by: Georgia Music Educators Association, 218 Willis Dr, Hudson 75 Business Park, Stockbridge, GA 30281. TEL 678-289-9299, FAX 678-289-9250, Ryan@gmea.org. Ed. Mary A Leglar. Adv. contact Aleta Womack.

784 CHN ISSN 0454-0816
GEQU/SONGS MONTHLY. Text in Chinese. 1952. m. USD 48 (effective 2009). **Document type:** *Journal, Academic/Scholarly.*
—East View.
Published by: Zhongguo Yinyuejia Xiehui/Chinese Musicians Association, c/o China Federation of Literary and Art Circles, Zhaoyang-qu, 22, Anyuan Bei Li, Beijing, 100029, China. TEL 86-10-65389290, http://www.cflac.org.cn/xh/yinyue/. **Dist. by:** China International Book Trading Corp, 35 Chegongzhuang Xilu, Haidian District, PO Box 399, Beijing 100044, China. TEL 86-10-68412045, FAX 86-10-68412023, cibtc@mail.cibtc.com.cn, http://www.cibtc.com.cn.

780 CAN ISSN 0537-9423
M2
GESAMTAUSGABEN; collected works. Text in English. 1960. irreg. **Document type:** *Monographic series, Academic/Scholarly.*
Published by: Institute of Mediaeval Music, 1270 Lampman Crescent, Lions Bay, BC V0N 2E0, Canada. TEL 604-912-0258, medievalmusic@shaw.ca.

782.81 AUT
DIE GESELLSCHAFT DER OPER; Musikkultur europaeischer Metropolen im 19. und 20. Jahrhundert. Text in German. 2006. irreg., latest vol.8, 2011. price varies. **Document type:** *Monographic series, Academic/Scholarly.*
Published by: Boehlau Verlag GmbH & Co.KG., Wiesingerstr 1, Vienna, W 1010, Austria. TEL 43-1-3302427, FAX 43-1-3302432, boehlau@boehlau.at.

780.784 GBR ISSN 1744-0904
GIG. Text in English. 2004. fortn. GBP 70.80 domestic; EUR 131 in Europe; USD 182 in United States; GBP 95 elsewhere (effective 2009). adv. **Document type:** *Magazine, Trade.* **Description:** Contains industry information for classical music and performing arts executives.
Incorporates (1987-2006): International Arts Manager (1355-6169)
Indexed: IIMP.
—CCC.
Published by: Impromptu Publishing Ltd., Century House, 2nd Fl, St Peter's Sq, Manchester, M2 3DN, United Kingdom. TEL 44-161-2369526, FAX 44-161-2477978, info@impromptupublishing.com, http://www.impromptupublishing.com. Ed. Christian Lloyd TEL 44-161-2369526 ext 29. Adv. contact Zaynab Benabdelhafid TEL 44-161-2369526 ext 22. page GBP 2,495; trim 240 x 340.

780 JPN
GIGS. Text in Japanese. m. back issues avail. **Document type:** *Magazine, Consumer.*
Published by: Shinko Music Publishing Co. Ltd., 2-1 Kanda-Ogawa-Machi, Chiyoda-ku, Tokyo, 101-0052, Japan. TEL 81-3-32922865, FAX 81-3-32915135, http://www.shinko-music.co.jp.

780 ITA ISSN 1120-6195
ML5
IL GIORNALE DELLA MUSICA. Text in Italian. 1985. m. EUR 14 combined subscription (print & online eds.) (effective 2011). adv. bk.rev.; dance rev.; music rev.; play rev.; rec.rev.; software rev.; Website rev. bibl. 40 p./no.; back issues avail. **Document type:** *Magazine, Consumer.* **Description:** Contains information about musical events, new recordings and music publications, Italian university musicological activities.
Related titles: Online - full text ed.
Published by: E D T Srl, Via Pianezza 17, Torino, 10149, Italy. TEL 39-011-5591811, FAX 39-011-2307034, http://www.edt.it. Circ: 18,000.

GIORNALE DELLO SPETTACOLO. *see* DANCE

780.43 ITA ISSN 1824-8055
IL GIORNALE DI MUSICALIA. Text in Italian. 1992. m. **Document type:** *Magazine, Consumer.*
Published by: Editoriale Pantheon, Via Alatri 30, Rome, 00171, Italy. http://www.editorialepantheon.it.

GIORNO POETRY SYSTEMS L P'S, C D'S, CASSETTES & GIORNO VIDEO PAK SERIES. *see* LITERATURE—Poetry

787.87 POL ISSN 1428-0027
GITARA; czasopismo muzyczne. Text in Polish. 1997. q. PLZ 30 (effective 2002 - 2003). 40 p./no.; **Document type:** *Magazine, Consumer.*
Published by: Rosetti Sp. z o.o., ul Paulinska 14, Wroclaw, 50247, Poland. nieborak@kki.net.pl. Ed. Krzysztof Nieborak. Circ: 1,000.

787.87 POL ISSN 1230-1809
GITARA I BAS. Text in Polish. 1992. bi-m. PLZ 48 (effective 2003). 100 p./no.; **Document type:** *Magazine, Consumer.*
Related titles: Online - full content ed.: Gitara i Bas + Bebny Online. ISSN 1689-3581.
Published by: Professional Music Press, ul. Krasickiego 2A/82, Gdynia, 81385, Poland. TEL 48-58-6200139, FAX 48-58-6200584. Ed. Krzysztof Kuczkowski. Circ: 9,000.

GITARIST. *see* SOUND RECORDING AND REPRODUCTION

787.8 SWE ISSN 0283-474X
GITARR OCH LUTA. Text in Swedish; Summaries in English. 1968. q. SEK 260 domestic membership; SEK 310 elsewhere membership (effective 2011). bk.rev. back issues avail. **Document type:** *Newsletter, Trade.* **Description:** Contains articles on guitar and lute music; musicians, instrument makers, composers, sheet music and discs. Essays on music history.
Formerly (until 1985): S G L S. Svenska Gitarr och Luta Saellskapet (0346-0991)
Indexed: RILM.
Published by: Svenska Gitarr och Luta Saellskapet/Swedish Guitar and Lute Society, c/o Roland Hogman, Riastigen 6, Aelvsjoe, 12533, Sweden. http://www.sgls.nu.

787.61 DEU ISSN 0934-4241
GITARRE AKTUELL. Text in German. 1979. q. EUR 25; EUR 4 newsstand/cover (effective 2006). **Document type:** *Magazine, Consumer.*
Indexed: RILM.
Address: Postfach 130707, Hamburg, Germany. TEL 49-40-452347, FAX 49-40-4500534.

780 DEU ISSN 0172-9683
GITARRE & LAUTE; das Magazin fuer alle Gitarristen und Lautenisten. Text in German. 1979. bi-m. adv. 64 p./no.; back issues avail. **Document type:** *Magazine, Consumer.*
Indexed: DIP, IBR, IBZ, IIMP, M11, MusicInd, PCI, RILM.
—CCC.
Published by: Gitarre & Laute Verlags GmbH, Sielsdorfer Str 1a, Cologne, 50935, Germany. TEL 49-221-3461623, FAX 49-221-9439864. Ed. Peter Paeffgen. Circ: 6,500.

780 DEU ISSN 0937-4213
GITARRE UND BASS; Das Musiker-Fachmagazin. Text in German. 1988. m. EUR 50; EUR 4.90 newsstand/cover (effective 2011). adv. **Document type:** *Magazine, Consumer.*
Formerly (until 1989): Musiker, Gitarre und Bass (0934-7674)
Published by: Musik - Media Verlag GmbH (Subsidiary of: Ebner Verlag GmbH), Emil-Hoffmann-Str 13, Cologne, 50996, Germany. TEL 49-2236-962170, FAX 49-2236-962175, info@musikmedia.de, http://www.musikmedia.de. Ed. Dieter Roesberg. Adv. contact Christiane Weyres. Circ: 28,335 (paid and controlled).

780 CHE
GLAREANA. Text in French. 1951. s-a. CHF 30 to individuals; CHF 50 to institutions. adv. bk.rev. bibl. **Document type:** *Bulletin.* **Description:** Contains news and information concerning old and ancient musical instruments. Features reports of events, exhibitions, museums, history.
Published by: Gesellschaft der Freunde alter Musikinstrumente, Zaehringerstr 17, Bern, 3012, Switzerland. Ed. Rebekka Reichlin. R&P Georg Senn.

GLENDORA REVIEW; an African quarterly on the arts. *see* LITERATURE

338.47791 NOR ISSN 1356-8280
THE GLOBAL GIG GUIDE. Text in Norwegian. 1994. a. **Document type:** *Trade.*
Published by: Jonathan Ellison Sumpton, Postboks 82, Skei I Jolster, 6850, Norway. TEL 47-909-26-456, FAX 47-90-48-91-52.

781.6 USA ISSN 1553-9814
ML3469
GLOBAL RHYTHM; the music, the culture, the movement. Text in English. 1992. m. (11/yr.). USD 29.95; USD 49.95 with CDs; USD 3.95 newsstand/cover (effective 2001). adv. bk.rev.; film rev.; music rev. illus. back issues avail. **Document type:** *Magazine, Consumer.* **Description:** Covers the spectrum of world music and culture. Provides a forum for musicians, indigenous peoples, and urban minds to express ideas, thoughts, and insights into global music and culture.
Former titles (until June 2002): Rhythm (1538-5671); (until 1998): Rhythm Music Magazine (1074-8660)
Related titles: Online - full text ed.
Indexed: A01, ChPerI, M11, MusicInd.
Published by: Rhythm Music Magazine, 928 Broadway., Ste. 204, New York, NY 10010-8162. TEL 212-253-8869, 800-464-2767, FAX 212-253-8892. Ed. Larry Birnbaum. Pub., Adv. contact Alecia J Cohen. B&W page USD 4,100. Circ: 78,000 (paid). **Dist. by:** International Publishers Direct, 27500 Riverview Center Blvd, Bonita Springs, FL 34134. TEL 858-320-4563, FAX 858-677-3220.

781.71 USA ISSN 0731-0781
M2062
GLORY SONGS. Text in English. 198?. q. price varies. back issues avail. **Document type:** *Magazine, Consumer.* **Description:** Contains 3-and 4-part arrangements with easy accompaniments that would be useful for medium-sized choir.
Related titles: Audio cassette/tape ed.: Glory Songs Cassette. ISSN 1553-3530; CD-ROM ed.: ISSN 1523-7729.
Published by: LifeWay Christian Resources, 1 Lifeway Plz, Nashville, TN 37234. TEL 615-251-2000, 800-458-2772, FAX 615-251-5933, customerservice@lifeway.com, http://www.lifeway.com.

782.81 GBR ISSN 0434-1066
GLYNDEBOURNE FESTIVAL PROGRAMME BOOK. Text in English. 1952. a. adv. **Document type:** *Handbook/Manual/Guide, Consumer.*
Published by: (Glyndebourne Festival Opera), Glyndebourne Productions Ltd., Glyndebourne, Lewes, E Sussex BN8 5UU, United Kingdom. TEL 44-1273-812321, FAX 44-1273-812783, info@glyndebourne.com.

781.64 DEU
GO NIGHTLIFE. Text in German. 1996. m. adv. **Document type:** *Magazine, Consumer.*
Published by: Muenchner Stadtmedien GmbH, Arcisstr 68, Munich, 80801, Germany. TEL 49-89-5505660, FAX 49-89-55056612, go@gomuenchen.com, http://www.gomuenchen.com. adv.: B&W page EUR 2,065, color page EUR 2,950. Circ: 50,000 (controlled).

780 DEU ISSN 0177-7319
ML410.H13
➤ **GOETTINGER HAENDEL-BEITRAEGE.** Text in German. 1984. irreg., latest vol.13, 2010. price varies. **Document type:** *Monographic series, Academic/Scholarly.*
Indexed: RILM.
Published by: (Goettinger Haendel-Gesellschaft), Vandenhoeck und Ruprecht, Theaterstr 13, Goettingen, 37073, Germany. TEL 49-551-508440, FAX 49-551-5084422, info@v-r.de. Ed. Hans Joachim Marx.

780 DEU
GOETTINGER MUSIKWISSENSCHAFTLICHE ARBEITEN. Text in German. 1941. irreg., latest vol.12, 1990. price varies. **Document type:** *Monographic series, Academic/Scholarly.*
Published by: Baerenreiter Verlag, Heinrich-Schuetz-Allee 35, Kassel, 34131, Germany. TEL 49-561-3105154, FAX 49-561-3105195, order@baerenreiter.com, http://www.baerenreiter.com.

781.64 367 USA
GOIL TALK. Text in English. 1971. bi-m. USD 25 domestic; USD 30 foreign (effective 2007). 6 p./no.; **Document type:** *Newsletter, Consumer.* **Description:** Reports information on Engelbert Humperdinck's concert tours and album releases. Discusses other information regarding the pop singer's career, with the aim of supporting him in a dignified manner. Announces memorabilia for sale.
Published by: Engelbert's Goils, 22249 Berry Dr., Cleveland, OH 44116. TEL 440-331-5601. Eds. Dot Gillberg, Jeanne Friedl. Circ: 200 (paid).

780 USA ISSN 1078-3806
ML27.U5
GOLD BOOK (NEW YORK). Text in English. a. **Document type:** *Magazine, Trade.* **Description:** A compendium of successful volunteer projects in the areas of ticket sales, fundraising, and educational programs.
Formerly: Symphony Gold Book (0275-9381)
Related titles: Online - full text ed.
Published by: League of American Orchestras, 33 W 60th St, New York, NY 10023. TEL 212-262-5161, FAX 212-262-5198, http://www.americanorchestras.org.

780 ESP ISSN 1699-9606
ML5
GOLDBERG (ENGLISH EDITION); early music magazine. Text in English. 1997. bi-m. 112 p./no.; **Document type:** *Magazine, Consumer.* **Description:** Dedicated to the entire history of music until 1750.
Supersedes in part (in 2003): Goldberg (Spanish and English Edition) (1138-1531)
Indexed: MusicInd.
—BLDSC (4201.190220).
Published by: Goldberg Ediciones, Ave de Bayona 40-E, Pamplona, Navarra 31011, Spain. TEL 34-948-250372, FAX 34-948-196276, goldberg@teleline.es. **Dist. by:** Asociacion de Revistas Culturales de Espana, C Covarrubias 9 2o. Derecha, Madrid 28010, Spain. TEL 34-91-3086066, FAX 34-91-3199267, info@arce.es, http://www.arce.es/.

780 USA ISSN 1055-2685
ML156.2
GOLDMINE; the collector's record and compact disc marketplace. Text in English. 1974. 14/yr. USD 49.95; USD 4.95 newsstand/cover (effective 2012). adv. bk.rev.; music rev. illus. back issues avail.; reprints avail. **Document type:** *Magazine, Trade.* **Description:** Provides a marketplace for collectors and dealers in collectible records, ads, and music memorabilia covering rock 'n' roll, blues, country, folk, and jazz. Includes articles on recording stars of the past and present with discographies listing all known releases, a listing of upcoming record-and-ad-collector conventions, album reviews, hobby and music news, a collecting column, a letters section, a "best of discoveries" section, and "collector mania," which focuses mainly on hobby trends and questions on collecting.
Incorporates (1988- 2006): DISCoveries (0896-8322); Former titles (until 1985): The Record Collector's Goldmine (8750-2577); (until 198?): Goldmine (0271-2520)
Related titles: Online - full text ed.: USD 49.95 foreign (effective 2003).
Indexed: G08, I05, IIMP, M11, MusicInd, T02.
—CCC.
Published by: F + W Media Inc., 4700 E Galbraith Rd, Cincinnati, OH 45236. TEL 513-531-2690, contact_us@fwmedia.com, http://www.fwmedia.com/. Ed. Patrick Prince TEL 212-447-1400 ext 12266. Pub. David Blansfield TEL 212-447-1400 ext 12261.

GOLDMINE RECORDS & PRICES. see HOBBIES

781.64 CHE
GOOD NEWS. Text in German. 10/yr. CHF 21.50 (effective 2000). adv. **Document type:** *Magazine, Consumer.* **Description:** Covers all aspects of local and international music performers and performances.
Published by: Good News Productions AG, Talackerstr 5, Glattbrugg, 8152, Switzerland. TEL 41-1-8096666, FAX 41-1-8096600. Ed. Manuel Leuenberger. Pub. Andre Bechir. adv.: B&W page CHF 7,100, color page CHF 10,200; trim 210 x 280. Circ: 106,644 (paid and controlled).

780 DEU
GOOD TIMES; musik from the 60s to the 80s. Text in German. 1992. bi-m. EUR 33; EUR 5.90 newsstand/cover (effective 2010). adv. **Document type:** *Magazine, Consumer.*
Published by: NikMa - Musikbuch Verlag, Eberdinger Str 37, Vaihingen/Enz, 71665, Germany. TEL 49-7042-102861, FAX 49-7042-102862, info@nikma.de. Pub. Fabian Leibfried. Adv. contact Petra Czerny.

GOOD VIBRATIONS. see HANDICAPPED—Visually Impaired

▼ **THE GOPHER ILLUSTRATED.** see ART

780.7 USA ISSN 0017-2235
GOPHER MUSIC NOTES; the Minnesota music educators journal. Text in English. 1930. q. USD 15 to non-members; free to members (effective 2007). adv. bk.rev. tr.lit. **Document type:** *Newsletter.*
Indexed: MAG, RILM.
Published by: Minnesota Music Educators Association, 6860 Shingle Creek Pkwy, Ste 103, Brooklyn Center, MN 55430. TEL 763-566-1460, 888-678-6632, FAX 763-566-1578, info@mmea.org. Circ: 4,600.

783.7 USA
GOSPEL AND CONTEMPORARY CHRISTIAN MUSIC NETWORKING GUIDE. Text in English. 1971. a. USD 37.95 (effective 2002); free to qualified personnel. adv. illus. **Document type:** *Directory.* **Description:** Contains over 4500 listings of those involved in the Gospel music industry: artists, managers, booking agents, licensing organizations, professional organizations, publishers, radio stations, retailers, record companies, etc.
Former titles (until 2001): Christian Music Networking Guide (1522-113X); Gospel Music Association. Resource Guide; Gospel Music Official Directory (0739-604X); (until 1983): Complete Guide to Gospel Music (0733-4133); (until 1981): Gospel Music (0197-2715); Gospel Music Association. Annual Directory; Gospel Music Association. Annual Directory and Yearbook (0362-7330); Gospel Music Directory and Yearbook
Published by: Gospel Music Association, Inc., 1205 Division St, Nashville, TN 37203-4011. TEL 615-242-0303, FAX 615-254-9755. Ed., Adv. contact Tim Marshall. Circ: 10,000.

782.25 USA ISSN 1536-7096
ML3186.8
GOSPEL ENTERTAINMENT MAGAZINE. Text in English. 1999. s-a. USD 12.95 (effective 2008). **Document type:** *Magazine, Consumer.*
Published by: K D C Publishing, PO Box 3161, Portsmouth, VA 23701. Pub. Thelma Bryant-Brown.

782 USA
GOSPEL FLAVA MAGAZINE. Text in English. 2000. bi-m. USD 14.97; USD 2.99 newsstand/cover (effective 2001). adv. **Document type:** *Magazine, Consumer.*
Published by: Worship Publishing, Inc., 2501 S 15th Ave, Broadview, IL 60155. TEL 708-216-0091, http://www.gospelflavamagazine.com. Ed., Pub. Andre L Brown.

782.254 USA ISSN 1081-8162
ML3186.8
GOSPEL TODAY MAGAZINE; America's leading christian lifestyle magazine. Text in English. 1989. bi-m. USD 19.97 (effective 2009). adv. bk.rev.; music rev.; video rev. illus. back issues avail. **Document type:** *Magazine, Consumer.* **Description:** Covers African American gospel news and events. Includes convention calendars, health and beauty tips and family-oriented subjects.
Formerly (until 1995): Score (1074-5769)
Related titles: Online - full text ed.: free (effective 2009).
Published by: Horizon Concepts, 4660 Main St, Ste A170, Springfield, OR 97478. TEL 541-284-8600, 800-448-1967, FAX 541-284-8700, sales@horizonconcepts.net, http://www.horizonconcepts.com/. **Subscr. to:** MicahTek, Inc., 8215 S Elm Pl, Broken Arrow, OK 74011. TEL 918-449-3300, FAX 918-449-3301, micahtek@micahtek.com, http://www.micahtek.com.

783.7 USA ISSN 1087-9153
THE GOSPEL VOICE. Text in English. m. USD 20; USD 25 in Canada; USD 35 elsewhere. **Document type:** *Magazine, Consumer.*
Published by: Gottem Entertainment Publications Inc., PO Box 682427, Franklin, TN 37068. TEL 615-859-7239.

782.25 USA ISSN 1545-763X
GOSPEL VOICE (SUGARLAND). Text in English. 2003. 2/yr. USD 19.95 domestic; USD 49.95, USD 62.95 in Canada (effective 2003).
Published by: Solomon Media, LLC, 11569 Hwy. 6, S., P. O. Box 124, Sugarland, TX 77478. TEL 214-663-8928. Ed. Sallie B. Middlebrook. Pub. Avery Shepherd.

780 USA ISSN 1533-841X
GOTHIC BEAUTY. Text in English. 2000. q. USD 19; USD 4.95 newsstand/cover domestic; USD 6.17 newsstand/cover in Canada (effective 2005). **Document type:** *Magazine, Consumer.*
Published by: Gothic Beauty Magazine, 4110 SE Hawthorne Blvd., #501, Portland, OR 97214. Ed., Pub. Steven Holiday.

783 DEU ISSN 0017-2499
ML5
GOTTESDIENST UND KIRCHENMUSIK. Text in German. 1951. bi-m. EUR 9.30; EUR 1.60 newsstand/cover (effective 2006). adv. bk.rev. abstr. index. **Document type:** *Journal, Academic/Scholarly.*
Indexed: IIMP, M11, MusicInd.
Published by: Strube Verlag GmbH, Pettenkoferstr 24, Munich, 80336, Germany. TEL 49-89-54426611, FAX 49-89-54426630, strube.verlag@strube.de, http://www.strube.de. Ed. Stefan Uhlenbrock. Adv. contact Isabella Weit. B&W page EUR 310; trim 118 x 177. Circ: 2,500 (paid and controlled).

780 SWE ISSN 1401-6540
GRAENSLOEST; magasin foer samtida musik. Text in Swedish. 1995. q. SEK 160 (effective 1999). adv.
Published by: Ord & Saant Roesnes AB, Fack 19, Haverdal, 31042, Sweden. TEL 46-3-5-512-10, FAX 46-35-481-32. Ed. Thore Roesnes. Adv. contact Birgitta Olsson.

780 USA ISSN 0141-5085
ML410.G75
GRAINGER SOCIETY JOURNAL. Text in English. 1978. s-a. USD 28 to members. adv. bk.rev. **Document type:** *Bulletin.* **Description:** To promote the life and works of Percy Grainger.
Formerly: Grainger Journal
Indexed: IIMP, MusicInd.
Published by: Percy Grainger Society, 7 Cromwell Pl, White Plains, NY 10601. Ed. Matthew McGarrell. Circ: 500. **Subscr. to:** Matthew McGarrell, Brown University, Department of Music, Providence, RI 02912.

784 GBR ISSN 0017-310X
ML5
GRAMOPHONE; your guide to the best in recorded classical music. Text in English. 1923 (Apr.). 13/yr. GBP 47.39 (effective 2009). adv. bk.rev.; rec.rev. illus.; bibl. index. back issues avail.; reprints avail. **Document type:** *Magazine, Consumer.* **Description:** Contains all major classical recordings released in the U.K. and reports audio-equipment news and reviews.
Incorporates (1929-1930): Vox; Radio Critic; Broadcast Review; Cassettes and Cartridges
Indexed: A22, IIMP, M11, MusicInd, RASB.
—BLDSC (4209.000000), IE, Infotrieve, Ingenta.
Published by: Haymarket Publishing Ltd. (Subsidiary of: Haymarket Media Group), Teddington Studios, Broom Rd, Teddington, Middlesex, TW11 9BE, United Kingdom. TEL 44-20-82675050, FAX 44-20-82675844, info@haymarket.com, http://www.haymarket.com. Eds. James Inverne, James Jolly. Pub. Simon Temlett TEL 44-20-82675057. Circ: 34,628. **Subscr. to:** PO Box 568, Haywards Heath RH16 3XQ, United Kingdom. TEL 44-8456-777800, Haymarket.subs@qss-uk.com, http://www.themagazineshop.com.

784 GBR
THE GRAMOPHONE CLASSICAL MUSIC GUIDE. Text in English. 1987. a. GBP 26.95 per issue (effective 2010). back issues avail. **Document type:** *Handbook/Manual/Guide, Consumer.* **Description:** Reviews high-quality classical music recordings available on compact disc.
Former titles (until 2008): The Classical Good C D & D V D Guide; (until 2005): The Gramophone Classical Good C D Guide; (until 1996): The Gramophone Good C D Guide; (until 1994): The Good C D Guide
Indexed: IIPA.
Published by: Gramophone Publications Ltd., Teddington Studios, Broom Rd, Middlesex, Teddington, TW11 9BE, United Kingdom. TEL 44-2082-675000, info@haymarket.com, www.haymarket.com. Ed. James Jolly.

780 USA ISSN 0434-3336
LE GRAND BATON. Text in English. 1964. irreg. USD 20; USD 20 foreign. bk.rev.; music rev. charts; illus. **Description:** For music lovers and collectors, focusing on life and times of Sir Thomas Beecham.
Indexed: MAG.
Published by: Sir Thomas Beecham Society, Inc., 121 Morningside Dr, Falling Waters, WV 25419-9694. Ed., R&P Joseph G Ayers. Pub. Charles Niss. Circ: 500 (paid).

782.81 JPN
GRAND OPERA. Text in Japanese. s-a. JPY 1,800; USD 13 foreign. adv. music rev. back issues avail. **Description:** Features articles on operas staged at the world's famous opera houses, interviews with great artists and producers, and much more.
Related titles: Fax ed.
Published by: Ongaku No Tomo Sha Corp., c/o KakuyukiNabeshima, 6-30 Kagura-Zaka, Shinjuku-ku, Tokyo, 162-0825, Japan. FAX 81-3-5227-2129. Ed. Mitsuomi Fukuzawa. Pub. Jun Meguro. R&P Tetsuo Morita TEL 81-3-3235-2111. Adv. contact Takao Oya. B&W page JPY 480,000, color page JPY 840,000; trim 210 x 277. Circ: 100,000.

781.65 ITA ISSN 1824-1530
IL GRANDE JAZZ. Text in Italian. 2004. s-m. **Document type:** *Magazine, Consumer.*
Published by: De Agostini Editore, Via G da Verrazzano 15, Novara, 28100, Italy. TEL 39-0321-4241, FAX 39-0321-424305, info@deagostini.it, http://www.deagostini.it.

781.64 USA
GREEN MOUNTAIN MUSIC REVIEW. Text in English. 1998. bi-m. **Document type:** *Magazine, Consumer.* **Description:** Dedicated to music aficionados resisting the blanding of America.
Media: Online - full text.
Address: PO Box 391386, Mountain View, CA 94039-1386. Ed., Pub. J Laramie.

781.7 USA ISSN 0272-0264
GREENWOOD ENCYCLOPEDIA OF BLACK MUSIC. Text in English. 1981. irreg., latest 1993. price varies. back issues avail. **Document type:** *Monographic series, Academic/Scholarly.*

M

Published by: Greenwood Publishing Group Inc. (Subsidiary of: A B C - C L I O), 88 Post Rd W, PO Box 5007, Westport, CT 06881. TEL 203-226-3571, 800-225-5800, FAX 877-231-6980, sales@greenwood.com, http://www.greenwood.com.

780 USA ISSN 1551-0271
GREENWOOD GUIDES TO AMERICAN ROOTS MUSIC. Text in English. 2005. irreg., latest 2007. price varies. back issues avail. **Document type:** *Monographic series, Consumer.*
Related titles: Online - full text ed.
Published by: Greenwood Publishing Group Inc. (Subsidiary of: A B C - C L I O), 88 Post Rd W, PO Box 5007, Westport, CT 06881. TEL 203-226-3571, 800-225-5800, FAX 877-231-6980, sales@greenwood.com. Ed. Norm Cohen.

783 NLD ISSN 0017-4122
ML5
GREGORIUSBLAD; tijdschrift tot bevordering van liturgische muziek. Text in Dutch. 1876. q. EUR 33.50 domestic; EUR 40 in Belgium; EUR 10 newsstand/cover (effective 2009). bk.rev.; music rev. charts; illus. cum.index.
Formerly (until 1959): Sint Gregoriusblad (1382-2322)
Indexed: CERDIC, IIMP, M11, MusicInd, RILM.
—IE, Infotrieve.
Published by: (Landelijke Commissie voor Liturgische Muziek), Gooi en Sticht, Postbus 5018, Kampen, 8260 GA, Netherlands. TEL 31-38-3392556, FAX 31-38-3311776, gens@kok.nl, http://www.kok.nl.

780 DEU ISSN 0946-0942
GREIFSWALDER BEITRAEGE ZUR MUSIKWISSENSCHAFT. Text in German. 1995. irreg., latest vol.17, 2009. price varies. **Document type:** *Monographic series, Academic/Scholarly.*
Published by: Frank und Timme GmbH, Wittelsbacherstr 27a, Berlin, 10707, Germany. TEL 49-30-88667911, FAX 49-30-86398731, info@frank-timme.de.

780.42 CHL
GRINDER; extreme metal underground magazine. Text in Spanish. m. CLP 3,000; USD 10 foreign. **Document type:** *Consumer.*
Description: Covers heavy metal music.
Related titles: Online - full text ed.
Address: Correo Central, PO Box 50091, Santiago, 1, Chile. TEL 56-2-5313192, FAX 56-2-5313192.

780 USA ISSN 2159-7510
▼ **GROOVE.** Text in English. 2010. q. USD 10.20 combined subscription (print & online eds.) (effective 2011). **Document type:** *Magazine, Trade.*
Related titles: Online - full text ed.: ISSN 2159-7537. free (effective 2011).
Published by: Void Media Group, 86 Irving St, Midland Park, NJ 07432. http://voidmedia.net. Eds. Brittany Mahady, Mike Lagomarsino, A J May.

780 SWE ISSN 1401-7091
GROOVE. Text in Swedish. 1995. 9/yr. SEK 249; SEK 199 to students (effective 2004). adv. **Document type:** *Magazine, Consumer.*
Description: Mostly contemporary music.
Related titles: Online - full text ed.: ISSN 1402-4772.
Published by: Musikfoereningen Groove, PO Box 11291, Goeteborg, 40426, Sweden. info@groove.se.

781.64 DEU
GROOVE. Text in German. 1989. bi-m. EUR 26 domestic; EUR 46 in Europe (effective 2007). adv. **Document type:** *Magazine, Consumer.*
Published by: Pop Media People Over Profit GmbH, Koepenicker Str 178-179, Berlin, 10997, Germany. TEL 49-30-44312020, FAX 49-30-44312070. Ed. Heiko Hoffmann. Adv. contact Susanne Battke. color page EUR 4,000; trim 210 x 297. Circ: 47,067 (paid and controlled).

781.64 ITA ISSN 1592-7814
GROOVE; urban music & lifestyle. Variant title: Magazine Groove. Text in Italian. 2001. bi-m. adv. music rev. **Document type:** *Magazine, Consumer.*
Published by: Acacia Edizioni, Via Copernico 3, Binasco, MI 20082, Italy. http://www.acaciaedizioni.com.

780.01 DEU ISSN 0177-4190
GROSSE KOMPONISTEN UND IHRE ZEIT. Text in German. 1981. irreg., latest vol.20, 2005. price varies. **Document type:** *Monographic series, Academic/Scholarly.*
Published by: Laaber-Verlag, Regensburger Str 19, Laaber, 93164, Germany. TEL 49-9498-2307, FAX 49-9498-2543, info@laaber-verlag.de, http://www.laaber-verlag.de.

780.42 DEU ISSN 1614-1482
DER GROSSE ROCK & POP L P - PREISKATALOG. Variant title: Der Grosse Rock & Pop L P - C D Preiskatalog. Text in German. 1983. a. EUR 29.80 (effective 2007). adv. bk.rev. bibl.; charts; illus. **Document type:** *Catalog, Consumer.*
Former titles (until 1994): Der Grosse Rock & Pop Preiskatalog (0943-3686); (until 1991): Rock & Pop L P - Preiskatalog (0930-6994)
Published by: NikMa - Musikbuch Verlag, Eberdinger Str 37, Vaihingen/Enz, 71665, Germany. TEL 49-7042-102861, FAX 49-7042-102862, info@nikma.de, http://www.nikma.de. Circ: 6,000.

780.42 DEU ISSN 1868-1972
DER GROSSE ROCK & POP PREISKATALOG - SINGLE. Text in German. 1994. a. EUR 29.80 newsstand/cover (effective 2010). adv. **Document type:** *Catalog, Consumer.*
Formerly (until 2008): Rock & Pop Single - Preiskatalog (1431-374X)
Published by: NikMa - Musikbuch Verlag, Eberdinger Str 37, Vaihingen/Enz, 71665, Germany. TEL 49-7042-102861, FAX 49-7042-102862, info@nikma.de, http://www.nikma.de. Pub. Fabian Leibfried. Adv. contact Petra Czerny.

780.7 DEU ISSN 1436-8447
GRUNDSCHULE MUSIK. Text in German. 1997. q. EUR 78; EUR 12 newsstand/cover (effective 2011). adv. bk.rev.; music rev. illus. back issues avail. **Document type:** *Journal, Academic/Scholarly.*
Description: Offers elementary school music teachers concepts and material for their lessons.
Indexed: DIP, IBR, IBZ.
Published by: Erhard Friedrich Verlag GmbH, Im Brande 17, Seelze, 30926, Germany. TEL 49-511-400040, FAX 49-511-40004170, info@friedrich-verlag.de. Adv. contact Bianca Kraft. Circ: 8,000 (paid).

780 ESP ISSN 1988-754X
GUIAS PARA ENSENANZAS MEDIAS. MUSICA. Text in Spanish. 2007. m. **Document type:** *Monographic series, Academic/Scholarly.*
Media: Online - full text.
Published by: Wolters Kluwer Espana - Educacion (Subsidiary of: Wolters Kluwer N.V.), C Collado Mediano 9, Las Rozas, Madrid, 28230, Spain. TEL 34-902-250510, FAX 34-902-250515, cleintes@wkeducacion.es, http://www.wkeducacion.es/index.asp. Ed. Joaquin Gairin.

780 FRA ISSN 1958-802X
LE GUIDE DES METHODES DE MUSIQUE & RECUEILS PEDAGOGIQUES. Text in French. 2007. biennial. EUR 23 domestic; EUR 27 foreign (effective 2010).
Related titles: ◆ Supplement to: La Lettre du Musicien. ISSN 0766-916X.
Published by: La Lettre du Musicien, 14 Rue Violet, Paris, 75015, France. TEL 33-1-56770400, FAX 33-1-56770409, http://www.la-lettre-du-musicien.com.

GUILDNOTES. *see* ART

787.87 DEU ISSN 1430-9769
GUITAR; alles, was Guitarristen Spass macht. Text in German. 1996. bi-m. EUR 29.40 domestic; EUR 37.20 foreign; EUR 5.40 newsstand/cover (effective 2002). adv. **Document type:** *Magazine, Consumer.*
Related titles: Online - full text ed.
Published by: P P V Medien GmbH, Postfach 57, Bergkirchen, 85230, Germany. TEL 49-8131-56550, FAX 49-8131-87288, ppv@ppvmedien.de, http://www.ppvmedien.de. Ed. Chris Hauke. Adv. contact Sabine Frischmuth.

787.87 USA ISSN 1949-0690
▼ **GUITAR AFICIONADO.** Text in English. 2009. q. USD 24.95 domestic; USD 34.95 in Canada; USD 39.95 elsewhere (effective 2010). adv. illus. back issues avail. **Document type:** *Magazine, Consumer.*
Published by: Future U S, Inc. (Subsidiary of: Future Publishing Ltd.), 4000 Shoreline Ct, Ste 400, South San Francisco, CA 94080. TEL 650-872-1642, FAX 650-872-1643, http://www.futureus.com. Eds. Brad Tolinski, Jon Phillips TEL 650-238-2490. Pub. Greg Di Benedetto TEL 646-723-5413. adv.: color page USD 12,000; trim 9 x 10.875. Circ: 100,000 (paid and controlled).

787.87 GBR ISSN 1755-3385
GUITAR & BASS. Text in English. 1991. m. GBP 34.99 domestic; USD 99.90 in US & Canada; EUR 67.20 in Europe; GBP 62.40 elsewhere; GBP 3.99 newsstand/cover (effective 2009). adv. music rev. illus. back issues avail. **Document type:** *Magazine, Consumer.*
Description: Provides any serious guitarist with dozens of guitar tests, playing techniques, an exclusive bass section and in-depth features on guitar heroes past, present and future.
Formerly (until 2004): Guitar Magazine (0962-2640)
Published by: I P C Country & Leisure Media Ltd. (Subsidiary of: I P C Media Ltd.), The Blue Fin Bldg, 110 Southwark St, London, SE1 0SU, United Kingdom. TEL 44-20-31485000, http://www.ipcmedia.com. Ed. John Callaghan TEL 44-20-87268305. Pub. Richard Marcroft TEL 44-20-87268343. Adv. contact Susan Bann TEL 44-20-87268412. page GBP 895; trim 210 x 297. Circ: 11,994. **Subscr. to:** Rockwood House, Perrymount Rd, Haywards Heath RH16 3DH, United Kingdom. TEL 44-845-1231231, IPCsubs@quadrantsubs.com, http://www.magazinesdirect.co.uk. **Dist. by:** MarketForce UK Ltd. salesinnovation@marketforce.co.uk, http://www.marketforce.co.uk/.

787.87 USA ISSN 2151-0482
M125
GUITAR EDGE. Text in English. 200?. bi-m. USD 17.99 domestic; USD 23.99 in Canada (effective 2009). adv. back issues avail. **Document type:** *Magazine, Consumer.* **Description:** Features authentic tab, gear reviews, artist interviews and more for guitarists of all styles and skill levels.
Related titles: Online - full text ed.: ISSN 2151-0539. free (effective 2009).
Published by: Music Dispatch, 306 Hwy 1 S, PO Box 170, Mount Vernon, IA 52314. TEL 319-895-0050, 877-704-4327, FAX 319-895-8573, info@musicdispatch.com, http://www.musicdispatch.com. Eds. Michael Mueller, Jeff Schroedl.

787.87 USA ISSN 2153-8581
▼ **GUITAR GODDESS.** Text in English. 2009. m. USD 24.95 (effective 2010). **Document type:** *Magazine, Consumer.* **Description:** Reviews new works by female guitarists and shares guitar tips and tricks for women.
Related titles: Online - full text ed.: ISSN 2153-8158. USD 14.95 (effective 2010).
Published by: Guitar Goddess Inc., 269 S Beverly Dr, Beverly Hills, CA 90212. TEL 213-283-6951, info@guitargoddess.com.

787.87 USA
ML1015.G9
GUITAR LEGENDS. Text in English. 19??. 4/yr. USD 7.99 newsstand/cover (effective 2009). adv. **Document type:** *Magazine, Consumer.*
Published by: Future U S, Inc. (Subsidiary of: Future Publishing Ltd.), 4000 Shoreline Ct, Ste 400, South San Francisco, CA 94080. TEL 650-872-1642, FAX 650-872-1643, http://www.futureus.com. Pub. Steve Aaron. Adv. contact Robert Dye TEL 646-723-5431. color page USD 5,925.

787.87 FRA ISSN 1256-737X
GUITAR PART. Text in French. 1994. m. EUR 54 (effective 2009). **Document type:** *Magazine, Consumer.*
Published by: Groupe Express-Roularta, 29 Rue de Chateaudun, Paris Cede, 75308, France. TEL 33-1-75551000, http://www.groupe-exp.com.

787.61 USA ISSN 0017-5463
GUITAR PLAYER; for professional and amateur guitarists. Text in English. 1967. m. USD 14.99 domestic; USD 29.99 in Canada; USD 39.99 elsewhere (effective 2008). adv. bk.rev. charts; illus. cum.index. back issues avail.; reprints avail. **Document type:** *Magazine, Consumer.*
Description: For professional, semi-pro and amateur guitar players in all styles.
Indexed: A11, A22, C05, CPerl, Chicano, G05, G06, G07, G08, G09, I05, I06, I07, IIMP, M01, M02, M11, MAG, MASUSE, MagInd, MusicInd, P02, P10, P48, P53, P54, PMR, PQC, RASB, RILM, S23, TOM, U01.
—CIS, Ingenta. **CCC.**
Published by: NewBay Media, LLC (Subsidiary of: The Wicks Group of Companies, LLC.), 810 Seventh Ave, 27th Fl, New York, NY 10019. TEL 212-378-0400, FAX 212-378-0470, customerservice@nbmedia.com, http://www.nbmedia.com. Ed. Michael Molenda TEL 650-238-0300. Pub. Joe Perry TEL 770-343-9978. adv.: page USD 9,965; trim 8 x 10.5. Circ: 145,393.

787.61 USA ISSN 0017-5471
ML1
GUITAR REVIEW. Text in English. 1946. q. USD 28 domestic; USD 32 foreign (effective 2010). adv. bk.rev.; rec.rev. illus. index. back issues avail. **Document type:** *Journal, Academic/Scholarly.* **Description:** Aimed at the entire musical world.
Indexed: A20, A22, CA, IIMP, M11, MAG, MusicInd, RILM, T02.
—BLDSC (4230.231000), IE, Ingenta.
Published by: Albert Augustine, Ltd., 151 W 26th St Fl 4, New York, NY 10001-6810. TEL 917-661-0220, FAX 917-661-0223. Ed. Stephen L Griesgraber.

787.87193 GBR ISSN 1476-6736
GUITAR TUTOR. Text in English. 1995. 3/yr. free to members (effective 2009). adv. back issues avail. **Document type:** *Magazine, Trade.*
Description: Designed for the registered guitar tutors.
Formerly (until 2000): Guitar Teacher (1361-2190)
Related titles: Online - full text ed.
—**CCC.**
Published by: Registry of Guitar Tutors, Registry Mews, 11-13 Wilton Rd, Bexhill-on-Sea, E Sussex TN40 1HY, United Kingdom. TEL 44-1424-222222, FAX 44-1424-213221, office@RGT.org, http://www.registryofguitartutors.com.

787.87 028.5 USA ISSN 2150-1238
▼ **GUITAR VIBRATIONS.** Text in English. 2009. q. USD 20 (effective 2009). **Document type:** *Magazine, Consumer.* **Description:** An interactive magazine for young classical guitar students with games and exercises.
Published by: Wave Dancer Publications, 3309 Katherine Ave, Fayetteville, AR 72703. TEL 479-443-9064, quiltedmaple@sbcglobal.net.

787 USA ISSN 1045-6295
ML1015.G9
GUITAR WORLD. Text in English. 1980. m. USD 12 domestic; USD 27 in Canada; USD 47 elsewhere; USD 24.95 combined subscription domestic (print & CD-ROM eds.); USD 39.95 combined subscription in Canada (print & CD-ROM eds.); USD 59.95 combined subscription elsewhere (print & CD-ROM eds.) (effective 2008). adv. rec.rev. illus. reprints avail. **Document type:** *Magazine, Consumer.* **Description:** Features broad-ranging interviews that cover techniques, instruments and lifestyles as well as famously thorough transcriptions.
Related titles: CD-ROM ed.; Online - full text ed.; Supplement(s): Guitar Buyer's Guide. ISSN 1063-4231.
Indexed: M11, MusicInd, RASB, T02.
—**CCC.**
Published by: Future U S, Inc. (Subsidiary of: Future Publishing Ltd.), 4000 Shoreline Ct, Ste 400, South San Francisco, CA 94080. TEL 650-872-1642, FAX 650-872-1643, http://www.futureus.com. Ed. Brad Tolinski. Pub. Greg Di Benedetto TEL 646-723-5413. Adv. contact Robert Dye TEL 646-723-5431. B&W page USD 8,614, color page USD 11,485; trim 8 x 10.5. Circ: 200,000 (paid).

787.87 FRA ISSN 1294-8055
GUITARE CLASSIQUE. Text in French. 1999. q. EUR 24 (effective 2009). adv. **Document type:** *Magazine, Consumer.*
Published by: Groupe Express-Roularta, 29 Rue de Chateaudun, Paris Cede, 75308, France. TEL 33-1-75551000, http://www.groupe-exp.com.

787.87 FRA ISSN 1776-0879
GUITARE LIVE. Text in French. 2004. m. EUR 49 (effective 2008). back issues avail. **Document type:** *Magazine, Consumer.*
Media: Online - full text.
Published by: Audio Print, 76-78 Rue Beaubourg, Paris, 75003, France.

780 GBR ISSN 0953-7023
ML1015.G9
GUITARIST; the best in daily guitar news and views. Text in English. 1984. 13/yr. GBP 54.95 domestic; GBP 76 in Europe; GBP 90 in United States; GBP 85 elsewhere; GBP 5.50 newsstand/cover (effective 2010). adv. illus. back issues avail. **Document type:** *Magazine, Consumer.*
Related titles: ◆ Spanish ed.: Guitarrista. ISSN 1885-5571.
—**CCC.**
Published by: Future Publishing Ltd., Beauford Ct, 30 Monmouth St, Bath, Avon BA1 2BW, United Kingdom. TEL 44-1225-442244, FAX 44-1225-446019, customerservice@subscription.co.uk, http://www.futureplc.com. Ed. Mick Taylor. **Subscr. to:** Tower House, Sovereign Park, Market Harborough, Leicestershire LE16 9EF, United Kingdom. TEL 44-844-8481602, FAX 44-1858-438795, future@subscription.co.uk.

787.61 AUS
GUITARIST AUSTRALIA. Text in English. bi-m. AUD 44.98; AUD 9.95 newsstand/cover (effective 2007). adv. **Document type:** *Magazine, Consumer.*
Published by: Derwent Howard Media Pty Ltd., PO Box 1037, Bondi Junction, NSW 1355, Australia. TEL 61-2-83056900, FAX 61-2-83056999, enquiries@derwenthoward.com.au. Adv. contact Daniel Ferguson.

787.87 FRA ISSN 0997-3443
GUITARIST MAGAZINE. Text in French. 1989. m. s-a. index. **Document type:** *Magazine, Consumer.*
Published by: Master Press International, 10 rue de la Paix, Boulogne-Billancourt, 92100, France. TEL 33-1-46031551, FAX 33-1-46038969. Circ: 50,000.

787 USA ISSN 0434-9350
ML1
GUITARRA MAGAZINE. Text in English. 1979. bi-m. USD 15.50. adv. bk.rev. back issues avail. **Description:** Classic and flamenco guitar and music.
Indexed: MAG, MusicInd.
Published by: Sherry - Brener, Inc., 3145 W 63rd St, Chicago, IL 60629. Ed. James Sherry. Circ: 4,500.

785.161 ESP ISSN 1885-5571
GUITARRISTA. Text in Spanish. 1998. m. EUR 27.50 domestic (effective 2010). adv. **Document type:** *Magazine, Consumer.*

Related titles: ◆ English ed.: Guitarist. ISSN 0953-7023.
Published by: R D M Editorial, Poligono Industrial Norte, c/ Gomera, 10-2 B, San Sebastian de los Reyes, 28700, Spain. TEL 34-91-6518227, FAX 34-91-6518227, rdm@rdmeditorial.com.

H.A.S. MAGAZINE. (Hip Artistic Stylish) *see* CLOTHING TRADE—Fashions

H D K MAGAZIN. (Hochschule der Kuenste Berlin) *see* ART

782.421 USA ISSN 1949-3568
▼ **H H H MAGAZINE.** (Hunks & Hotties of HipHop) Text in English. 2010 (Jan.). q. USD 3.99 newsstand/cover (effective 2010). **Document type:** *Magazine, Consumer.* **Description:** Features hip-hop music and artists.
Related titles: Online - full text ed.: ISSN 1949-3576. 2010 (Jan.).
Published by: H H H Entertainment, 477 Triton Ct, Salt Lake City, UT 84107. TEL 704-236-2806, hhhmagazine@gmail.com.

780 CZE ISSN 1213-2438
H I S VOICE. Text in Czech. 1996. bi-m. CZK 330 domestic (effective 2009). **Document type:** *Magazine, Consumer.*
Formerly (until 2001): Hudebni Informacni Stredisko. Bulletin (1212-4516)
Published by: Hudebni Informacni Stredisko/Czech Music Information Centre, Besedni 3, Prague 1, 118 00, Czech Republic. TEL 420-2-57312422, FAX 420-2-57317424, his@vol.cz, http://www.musica.cz. Ed. Matej Kratochvi.

780 230 USA
H M MAGAZINE; the hard music magazine. (Hard Music) (Includes CD with each issue to subscribers) Text in English. 1985. bi-m. USD 15; USD 3.50 newsstand/cover; USD 4.95 newsstand/cover in Canada (effective 2007). adv. bk.rev.; music rev.; software rev.; video rev. back issues avail. **Document type:** *Magazine, Consumer.* **Description:** Contains interviews, news, record and concert reviews, with Christian rock, metal, alternative and industrial bands.
Formerly: Heaven's Metal (1066-6923)
Published by: H M, 6307 Cele Rd, Ste 573, Pflugerville, TX 78660. TEL 512-989-7309, 877-897-0368, FAX 512-670-2764. Ed., Pub. Doug Van Pelt. R&P Andrew Hazen. Adv. contact Lee Haley TEL 512-482-8590. color page USD 1,067, B&W page USD 553; trim 8.38 x 10.75. Circ: 15,000 (paid).

781.64 GBR ISSN 1467-6923
H M V CHOICE. Text in English. 1999. 5/yr. GBP 9.99 domestic; GBP 12.99 in Europe; GBP 17.50 elsewhere (effective 2009). adv. **Document type:** *Magazine, Consumer.* **Description:** Designed to help the readers to discover new music and new artists.
Published by: Origin Publishing Ltd. (Subsidiary of: B B C Worldwide Ltd.), Tower House, Fairfax St, Bristol, BS1 3BN, United Kingdom. TEL 44-117-9279009, FAX 44-117-9349008, http://www.originpublishing.co.uk. Ed. Claire White. Adv. contact Geoff Pullin.

780 DEU ISSN 0440-0615
HAENDEL-JAHRBUCH; im Auftrage der Georg-Friedrich-Haendel-Gesellschaft. Text in German. 1928. a. EUR 69 (effective 2009). **Document type:** *Journal, Academic/Scholarly.*
Indexed: DIP, IBR, IBZ, PCI, RILM.
Published by: (Georg-Friedrich-Haendel-Gesellschaft), Baerenreiter Verlag, Heinrich-Schuetz-Allee 35, Kassel, 34131, Germany. TEL 49-561-3105154, FAX 49-561-3105195, order@baerenreiter.com, http://www.baerenreiter.com.

780 HRV ISSN 1332-1129
HAGEZE; glasilo Hrvatskog Glazbenog Zavoda. Text in Croatian. 1997. m.
Related titles: Online - full content ed.: ISSN 1332-1137.
Indexed: RILM.
Published by: Hrvatski Glazbeni Zavod, Gunduliceva 6, Zagreb, 10000, Croatia. hgz@zg.tel.hr.

780 USA ISSN 1939-6171
HALFTIME MAGAZINE; sights, sounds & spirit of the marching arts. Text in English. 2007 (Jul.). bi-m. USD 19.95 to individuals; USD 4.95 newsstand/cover (effective 2008). adv. **Document type:** *Magazine, Consumer.* **Description:** Connects high school and college musician-athletes through shared experiences about competitions, school spirit, and band traditions with profiles, first-person accounts and thought-provoking feature stories.
Related titles: Online - full text ed.: ISSN 1939-618X.
Published by: Muse Media, PO Box 661355, Los Angeles, CA 90066. TEL 310-594-0050, FAX 310-390-5351. Adv. contact Erich Steinert TEL 310-577-6104. B&W page USD 1,495; trim 8.375 x 10.875. Circ: 9,000 (controlled); 1,000 (paid).

780.6 GBR ISSN 0262-7272
HALLE YEAR BOOK. Text in English. 1858. a. GBP 3. adv. **Document type:** *Bulletin.* **Description:** Lists activities of the Halle Orchestra. Includes a preview of the season's concerts, news of the sponsoring society and sponsorship, lists of members and patrons, and articles on music.
Formed by the merger of: Halle; And: Halle Prospectus
Published by: Halle Concerts Society, Bridgewater Hall, Lower Mosley St, Manchester, M2 3WJ, United Kingdom. TEL 44-161-237-7000, FAX 44-161-237-7029. Ed. Helen Dunnett. Circ: 6,000.

780.6 GBR
HALLMARK. Text in English. 1946. q. membership. adv. **Document type:** *Newsletter.* **Description:** Features current activities of the Halle Concerts Society.
Former titles (until 1992): Halle News; Halle Magazine
Published by: Halle Concerts Society, Bridgewater Hall, Lower Mosley St, Manchester, M2 3WJ, United Kingdom. TEL 44-161-237-7000, FAX 44-161-237-7029, TELEX 666140. Ed. Patsy Lawler. Circ: 6,500.

780 USA
HALLMARKS. Text in English. q. membership. **Description:** Includes a calendar of events, previews upcoming DSO events, reviews recent concerts and projects, and contains human interest stories related to DSO staff and musicians.
Published by: Detroit Symphony Orchestra, 3663 Woodward Ave, Ste 100, Detroit, MI 48201-2444. TEL 313-576-5100, FAX 313-576-5101, http://www.detroitsymphony.com. Ed. Tiffany Stozicki.

780 DEU ISSN 0342-8303
ML5
HAMBURGER JAHRBUCH FUER MUSIKWISSENSCHAFT. Text in German. 1974. irreg., latest vol.26, 2009. price varies. **Document type:** *Journal, Academic/Scholarly.*
Indexed: DIP, IBR, IBZ, PCI, RILM.
Published by: (Universitaet Hamburg, Musikwissenschaftliches Institut), Peter Lang GmbH (Subsidiary of: Peter Lang Publishing Group), Eschborner Landstr 42-50, Frankfurt Am Main, 60489, Germany. TEL 49-69-7807050, FAX 49-69-78070550, zentrale.frankfurt@peterlang.com, http://www.peterlang.com.

781.71 USA ISSN 8756-7407
M147
HANDBELLS; for directors and ringers. Text in English. 1985. q. price varies. back issues avail. **Document type:** *Magazine, Consumer.* **Description:** Contains seven to nine selections of music for ringers in a variety of octave combinations.
Published by: LifeWay Christian Resources, 1 Lifeway Plz, Nashville, TN 37234. TEL 615-251-2000, 800-458-2772, FAX 615-251-5933, customerservice@lifeway.com, http://www.lifeway.com. Ed. Sharron Lyon. Circ: 15,000.

HANDBUCH FUER MUSIKER. *see* SOUND RECORDING AND REPRODUCTION

780 DEU ISSN 0440-2863
HANS - PFITZNER - GESELLSCHAFT. MITTEILUNGEN. Text in German. 1954. a. free to members. bk.rev.; play rev. bibl.; illus. **Document type:** *Newsletter, Academic/Scholarly.*
Indexed: DIP, IBR, IBZ, IIMP, M11, MusicInd.
Published by: (Hans-Pfitzner-Gesellschaft e.V.), Verlag Dr. Hans Schneider GmbH, Mozartstr 6, Tutzing, 82323, Germany. TEL 49-815-83050, FAX 49-815-87636, Musikbuch@aol.com, http://www.schneider-musikbuch.de. Ed. Hans Schneider. Circ: 250.

780 USA
HARD 'N' FAST. Text in English. 1988. m. USD 15. back issues avail. **Document type:** *Newsletter.* **Description:** News, interviews and reviews relating to rock music.
Published by: Qmax Press Services Inc., 1651 Dublin Rd, Dresher, PA 19025-1243. TEL 215-654-9200, FAX 215-654-1895. Ed. Alex Richter. adv.: B&W page USD 200. Circ: 5,000.

781.64 FRA ISSN 1252-2279
HARD 'N' HEAVY. Text in French. 1994. m. (11/yr). EUR 47.50 (effective 2009). **Document type:** *Magazine, Consumer.*
Address: 2 bis rue Tarbe, Paris, 75017, France. TEL 33-1-47667765, FAX 33-1-47661070. Ed. James Petit.

781.64 FRA ISSN 0764-1346
HARD ROCK MAGAZINE. Text in French. 1984. m. EUR 33 domestic; EUR 42 in Europe; EUR 48 elsewhere (effective 2009). illus. **Document type:** *Consumer.*
Published by: Divarius, 4 Rue Galvani, Paris, 75017, France. http://www.eshop.divarius.fr. Circ: 100,000.

780 702 USA
HARDCORE INK. Text in English. 2000. q. USD 5.95 newsstand/cover (effective 2001). **Document type:** *Magazine, Consumer.*
Address: 5 Marine View Plaza, No207, Hoboken, NJ 07030. TEL 201-653-2700, FAX 201-653-7892, tattoo1@ix.netcom.com. Ed. Megan Rogers. Pub. Jean Chris Miller.

780 JPN ISSN 0914-2541
ML5
HARMONIA. Text in Japanese. 1954. a. **Document type:** *Journal, Academic/Scholarly.*
Former titles (until 1967): Kenkyu Kiyo; (until 1954): Kyoto Shiritsu Ongaku Tanki Daigaku Kenkyu Kiyo
Indexed: RILM.
Published by: Kyoto Shiritsu Geijutsu Daigaku, Ongaku Gakubu./Kyoto City University of Arts, Deparment of Music, 13-6 Ohe-Kutsukake-cho, Nishikyo-ku, Kyoto, 610-1197, Japan. http://www.kcua.ac.jp/music/.

780 USA
HARMONICA. Text in English. 6/yr. USD 30. bk.rev.; rec.rev.; video rev. **Document type:** *Magazine, Consumer.* **Description:** For beginners to advanced; contains interviews; covers history, styles, theory, instruments, diatonic, chromatic, extended techniques.
Published by: Harmonica Information Press, 203 14th Ave, San Francisco, CA 94118-1007.

788.82 FRA ISSN 1775-0121
HARMONICAS DE FRANCE FEDERATION MAGAZINE. Text in French. 2005. q. **Document type:** *Magazine, Consumer.*
Published by: Harmonicas de France Federation, 5 Rue Alexandre Fleming, Perpignan, 66000, France.

780 CHE
HARMONIENACHRICHTEN. Text in German. 6/yr.
Address: Poststr 8, Russikon, 8332, Switzerland. TEL 01-2162855. Circ: 1,200.

786.9 DEU ISSN 0938-6629
HARMONIKA INTERNATIONAL; Zeitschrift fuer Musik, Unterhaltung und alle Freunde der Harmonika. Text in German. 1931. 6/yr. EUR 26; EUR 4.90 newsstand/cover (effective 2009). adv. bk.rev. illus. **Document type:** *Magazine, Consumer.*
Formerly (until 1989): Harmonika-Revue (0938-6610)
Published by: Deutscher Harmonika-Verband e.V., Rudolf Maschke Platz 6, Trossingen, 78647, Germany. TEL 49-7425-326646, FAX 49-7425-326648, info@dhv-ev.de. adv.: page EUR 1,150; trim 185 x 267. Circ: 10,000 (controlled).

781 AUT ISSN 1727-5792
HARMONIKALES DENKEN. Text in German. 1999. irreg., latest 2003. price varies. **Document type:** *Monographic series, Academic/Scholarly.*
Published by: Wilhelm Braumueller Universitaets-Verlagsbuchhandlung GmbH, Servitengasse 5, Vienna, 1090, Austria. TEL 43-1-3191159, FAX 43-1-3102805, office@braumueller.at.

780 USA
MT170 CODEN: HAH01
HARMONIOUS HARMONICA/HARMONIJNA HARMONIJKA. Text and summaries in English, Polish. 1997. base vol. plus bi-m. updates. looseleaf. USD 30 base vol(s).; USD 40 updates (effective 2010). adv. bk.rev.; music rev. bibl. back issues avail. **Document type:** *Magazine, Consumer.* **Description:** Contains advice and assistance on learning and mastering the harmonica.
Media: Large Type (14 pt.). **Related titles:** Online - full text ed.
Published by: Whitney Publications, Inc., 147 Lake Valley Rd, Morristown, NJ 07960. TEL 908-219-0284, FAX 908-219-0182, gniking@excite.com. Ed. Chris King. Circ: 10,000 (paid and controlled).

784.96 USA ISSN 0017-7849
HARMONIZER. Text in English. 1942. bi-m. USD 21 domestic to non-members; USD 31 foreign to non-members (effective 2005). adv. music rev. illus. index. back issues avail. **Document type:** *Magazine, Trade.*
Indexed: IIMP, M11, RILM, T02.
Published by: SPEBSQSA, Inc., 7930 Sheridan Road, Kenosha, WI 53143-5199. TEL 262-653-8440, 800-876-7464, FAX 262-654-5552. Ed. Brian Lynch. Circ: 33,000 (controlled).

780 USA ISSN 1062-4090
HARMONOLOGIA: STUDIES IN MUSIC THEORY. Text in English. 1978. irreg., latest vol.15, 2009. price varies. back issues avail. **Document type:** *Monographic series, Trade.*
Published by: Pendragon Press, PO Box 190, Hillsdale, NY 12529. TEL 518-325-6100, FAX 518-325-6102, orders@pendragonpress.com. Ed. David Damschroder.

780 USA ISSN 1536-1438
HARP; it's about the music. Text in English. m. USD 19.95 domestic; USD 29.95 in Canada & Mexico; USD 39.95 elsewhere; USD 4.95 newsstand/cover domestic; USD 5.95 newsstand/cover in Canada (effective 2007). adv. music rev. illus. back issues avail. **Document type:** *Magazine, Consumer.* **Description:** Devoted to covering the alternative music scene and artists.
Published by: Harp Magazine, 8737 Colesville Rd, 9th Fl, Silver Spring, MD 20910-3921. TEL 301-588-4114, 866-427-7624, FAX 301-588-5531. Ed. Scott Crawford.

786.221 GBR ISSN 1463-0036
ML5
HARPSICHORD AND FORTEPIANO. Text in English. 1973. s-a. adv. bk.rev. illus. back issues avail. **Document type:** *Journal, Academic/Scholarly.*
Former titles (until 1989): Harpsichord and Forte Piano Magazine (0953-0797); (until 1987): English Harpsichord Magazine and Early Keyboard Instrument Review (0306-4395); (until 1974): Harpsichord Magazine (0301-7206)
Indexed: A01, CA, M11, PCI, RILM, T02.
—Ingenta.
Published by: Recorder Music Mail, Scout Bottom Farm, Mytholmroyd, Hebden Bridge, West Yorkshire, HX7 5JS, United Kingdom. TEL 44-1422-882751, FAX 44-1422-886157, jerry@recordermail.demon.co.uk. Ed. Micaela Schmitz TEL 44-1386-859648. Circ: 800.

780 USA ISSN 0073-0629
M5
➤ **HARVARD PUBLICATIONS IN MUSIC.** Text in English. 1967. irreg., latest vol.20, 2000. price varies. back issues avail. **Document type:** *Monographic series, Academic/Scholarly.*
Published by: Harvard University, Department of Music, Music Bldg, Cambridge, MA 02138. TEL 617-495-2791, FAX 617-496-8081, musicdpt@fas.harvard.edu.

782.81 DEU
HASSE-STUDIEN. Text in German. 1990. irreg., latest vol.5, 2002. price varies. **Document type:** *Monographic series, Academic/Scholarly.*
Published by: Carus-Verlag GmbH, Sielminger Str 51, Leinfelden-Echterdingen, 70771, Germany. TEL 49-711-7973300, FAX 49-711-79733029, info@carus-verlag.com, http://www.carus-verlag.com.

780 GBR ISSN 1350-1267
➤ **HAYDN SOCIETY. JOURNAL.** Text in English. 1980. a., latest no.21. adv. rec.rev.; bk.rev.; music rev. 50 p./no.; back issues avail. **Document type:** *Journal, Academic/Scholarly.* **Description:** Disseminates scholarly studies and reviews of research into the work of Franz Joseph Haydn.
Formerly (until 1992): Haydn Society Newsletter
Indexed: T02.
Published by: Haydn Society, c/o Secretary, 2, Hindley Hall, Stocksfield, Northumberland NE43 7RY, United Kingdom. TEL 44-1661-842167, D.McCaldin@lancaster.ac.uk.

780 920 DEU ISSN 0440-5323
ML410.H4
HAYDN - STUDIEN. Text in English, German. 1965. irreg., latest vol.9, 2006. price varies. adv. bk.rev. illus. index. **Document type:** *Monographic series, Academic/Scholarly.*
Indexed: A20, A22, IBR, IBZ, M11, MusicInd, PCI.
—IE.
Published by: Joseph Haydn-Institut e.V., Blumenthalstrasse 23, Cologne, 50670, Germany. TEL 49-221-733796, FAX 49-221-1208695, info@haydn-institut.de. Circ: 750.

781.64 DEU ISSN 1863-2130
HEAVY. Text in German. 1991. bi-m. EUR 33; EUR 2.50 newsstand/cover (effective 2010). adv. **Document type:** *Magazine, Consumer.*
Formerly (until 2005): Heavy, Oder Was!? (1860-000X)
Published by: Heavy, Oder Was!?, Im Hirschgarten 9, Rottenburg-Ergenzingen, 72108, Germany. TEL 49-7457-94460, FAX 49-7457-944699.

780.42 ESP
HEAVYROCK; metal magazine. Text in Spanish. 1982. m. EUR 28 domestic (effective 2009). **Document type:** *Magazine, Consumer.*
Related titles: ◆ Special ed(s).: Heavyrock Especial.
Published by: M C Ediciones, Paseo de Sant Gervasi 16-20, Barcelona, 08022, Spain. TEL 34-93-2541250, FAX 34-93-2541262, http://www.mcediciones.net.

781.66 ESP
HEAVYROCK ESPECIAL. Text in Spanish. 1982. bi-m. EUR 28 domestic (effective 2009). adv. **Document type:** *Magazine, Consumer.* **Description:** Covers heavy metal music for Latin American young people.
Related titles: ◆ Special ed. of: Heavyrock.
Published by: M C Ediciones, Paseo de Sant Gervasi 16-20, Barcelona, 08022, Spain. TEL 34-93-2541250, FAX 34-93-2541262, http://www.mcediciones.net. Circ: 241,000.

HECKLER. *see* SPORTS AND GAMES

DER HEIMATPFLEGER; Zeitschrift fuer Volkstanz, Volksmusik, Brauchtum und Heimatpflege. *see* FOLKLORE

780 370 GRC ISSN 1792-2518
▼ ➤ **HELLENIC JOURNAL OF MUSIC, EDUCATION AND CULTURE.** Text in Greek, English. 2010. a. free (effective 2011). **Document type:** *Journal, Academic/Scholarly.*
Media: Online - full text.
Published by: Greek Association of Primary Music Education Teachers, 2-4 Zoodochou Pigis Str, Athens, 106 79, Greece. Eds. Anastasia Siopsi, Graham Welch.

780 UKR
HELLRAISER. Text in Russian. irreg.
Address: Vladimir Kazakov a-ya 5, Kiev 232, 02232, Ukraine.

HEMBYGDEN. *see* DANCE

780 MEX ISSN 0018-1137
ML5
➤ **HETEROFONIA**; revista musical semestral. Text in Spanish. 1968. s-a. MXN 70 domestic; USD 30 foreign; effective 1995. adv. bk.rev.; music rev. abstr.; illus. index. **Document type:** *Academic/Scholarly.*
Indexed: A20, C01, IBR, IBZ, M11, MusicInd, P09, PCI, RILM.
Published by: Centro Nacional de las Artes, Centro Nacional de Investigacion, Documentacion e Informacion Musical, Torre de Investigacion, 7o. Piso, Col. Country Club, Mexico, D.F., 04220, Mexico. TEL 52-55-12539415, FAX 52-55-54204454, http://www.cenart.gob.mx/centros/cenidim/. Ed. Eugenio Delgado Parra. Circ: 1,000.

➤ **HI-FI +**; reproducing the recorded arts. *see* SOUND RECORDING AND REPRODUCTION

781.6 RUS ISSN 1680-581X
HI-FI & MUSIC. Text in Russian. 2001. m. **Document type:** *Magazine, Consumer.*
Published by: Izdatel'skii Dom L K Press, Bol'shoi Savvinskii per, dom 9, Moscow, 119435, Russian Federation. info@lkpress.ru, http://www.lkpress.ru. Circ: 50,000.

780 GBR ISSN 2042-0374
HI-FI NEWS & RECORD REVIEW. Text in English. 1971. m. GBP 34.99 domestic; USD 99.90 in US & Canada; EUR 76.20 in Europe; GBP 64.10 elsewhere; GBP 4 newsstand/cover domestic (effective 2009). adv. bk.rev.; rec.rev. charts; illus.; tr.lit. index. back issues avail.; reprints avail. **Document type:** *Magazine, Consumer.* **Description:** Explores classical, pop and jazz music including hi-fi equipment reviews and ratings, articles, and news of product developments.
Former titles (until 2009): Hi-Fi News (1472-2569); (until 2000): Hi-Fi News and Record Review (0142-6230); Which was formed by the merger of (1956-1971): Hi-Fi News (0018-1226); (1970-1971): Record Review
Related titles: Microform ed.: (from PQC).
Indexed: A28, APA, BrCerAb, BrTechI, C&ISA, CA/WCA, CIA, CerAb, CivEngAb, CorrAb, E&CAJ, E11, EEA, EMA, H15, M&TEA, M09, MBF, METADEX, SolStAb, T04, WAA.
—BLDSC (4307.180000), Linda Hall.
Published by: I P C Country & Leisure Media Ltd. (Subsidiary of: I P C Media Ltd.), Leon House, 233 High St, Croydon, CR9 1HZ, United Kingdom. TEL 44-20-87268311, FAX 44-20-87268397, http://www.ipcmedia.com. Ed. Paul Miller TEL 44-20-87268311. Pub. Richard Marcroft TEL 44-20-87268343. Adv. contact Susan Bann TEL 44-20-87268412. page GBP 1,500; trim 210 x 297. Circ: 10,013.
Subscr. to: Rockwood House, Perrymount Rd, Haywards Heath RH16 3DH, United Kingdom. TEL 44-845-1231231, IPCsubs@quadrantsubs.com, http://www.magazinesdirect.co.uk.
Dist. by: MarketForce UK Ltd. salesinnovation@marketforce.co.uk, http://www.marketforce.co.uk/.

789.91 621.389 BEL
HIFI MUSIQUE. REVUE DES DISQUES ET DE LA HAUTE FIDELITE. Text in French. 1950. bi-m. adv. bk.rev. charts; illus.
Formerly: Revue des Disques et de la Haute Fidelite (0035-1970)
Published by: Editions Dereume, Rue Golden Hope 1, Drogenbos, 1620, Belgium. Ed. Serge Martin. Circ: 5,000.

HIFI & MUSIK. *see* SOUND RECORDING AND REPRODUCTION

780.904 DEU ISSN 0172-956X
ML410.H685
HINDEMITH-JAHRBUCH/ANNALES HINDEMITH. Text in German. 1971. a. EUR 22.95 (effective 2011). bk.rev. **Document type:** *Journal, Academic/Scholarly.*
Indexed: DIP, IBR, IBZ, RILM.
Published by: (Paul-Hindemith-Institut), Schott Musik International GmbH, Weihergarten 5, Mainz, 55116, Germany. TEL 49-6131-2460, FAX 49-6131-246211, info@schott-musik.de, http://www.schott-musik.de. Circ: 1,200.

781.64 USA
HIP HOP BUSINESS JOURNAL. Text in English. 2008. bi-m. **Document type:** *Magazine, Consumer.* **Description:** Focuses on the business aspect of the hip hop culture and the impact it has worldwide by highlighting topics related to the value of education, wealth management and entrepreneurship.
Published by: Vegas Style Publishing, 468 North Camden Dr, Ste 200, Beverly Hills, CA 90210. TEL 310-862-4967, FAX 973-821-5005, vcarroll@vegasstyle.net, http://www.vegasstyleent.nstemp.com. Pub. Vincent Carroll. Circ: 100,000.

780.42 GBR ISSN 1465-4407
HIP-HOP CONNECTION. Text in English. 1988. m. GBP 26.64 domestic; GBP 48.80 in Europe; GBP 58.80 elsewhere; GBP 2.99 newsstand/cover. adv. music rev. illus. back issues avail. **Document type:** *Magazine, Consumer.*
Former titles (until 1998): H H C (0967-7089); (until 1992): Hip-Hop Connection (0957-6363)
—CCC.
Published by: Future Publishing Ltd., Beauford Ct, 30 Monmouth St, Bath, Avon BA1 2BW, United Kingdom. TEL 44-1225-442244, FAX 44-1225-446019, customerservice@subscription.co.uk, http://www.futureplc.com. Ed. Andy Cowan. Pub., R&P Peter Stothard. Adv. contact Gary Povey. Circ: 9,057.

782 USA ISSN 1932-5177
HIP HOP WEEKLY; covering the entire hip hop culture. Text in English. 2007. w. USD 3.99 newsstand/cover (effective 2010). adv. **Document type:** *Magazine, Consumer.* **Description:** Celebrity magazine for 18-39 year old men and women who identify with the hip hop culture.
Published by: Z & M Media, LLC, 1835 N E Miami Gardens Dr, Miami, FL 33179. TEL 305-919-9478, FAX 305-919-9477. Ed. Cynthia Horner. adv.: color page USD 4,400; trim 8 x 10.5. Circ: 100,000 (paid).

780 ITA ISSN 0073-2516
HISTORIAE MUSICAE CULTORES BIBLIOTECA. Text in Italian. 1952. irreg., latest vol.89, 2001. price varies. **Document type:** *Monographic series, Academic/Scholarly.*
Published by: Casa Editrice Leo S. Olschki, Viuzzo del Pozzetto 8, Florence, 50126, Italy. TEL 39-055-6530684, FAX 39-055-6530214, celso@olschki.it, http://www.olschki.it. Circ: 1,000.

780 USA ISSN 1045-4616
ML933
➤ **HISTORIC BRASS SOCIETY JOURNAL.** Text in English. 1989. a. free to members (effective 2010). adv. Website rev.; bk.rev.; music rev.; rec.rev. bibl.; charts; illus. 400 p./no. 1 cols./p.; back issues avail. **Document type:** *Journal, Academic/Scholarly.* **Description:** Provides scholarly articles on the entire range of historic brass music subjects.
Related titles: Online - full text ed.: ISSN 1943-5215.
Indexed: IIMP, M11, MusicInd, PCI, RILM, T02.
—Ingenta.
Published by: Historic Brass Society, Inc., 148 W 23rd St #5F, New York, NY 10011. TEL 212-627-3820, FAX 212-627-3820, president@historicbrass.org. Ed. Howard Weiner. Adv. contact John Benoit TEL 515-961-2845.

780 USA
ML929.5
HISTORIC BRASS SOCIETY NEWSLETTER (ONLINE). Text in English. 1989. a. free to members (effective 2010). adv. bk.rev.; rec.rev. bibl.; charts; illus. 100 p./no.; back issues avail. **Document type:** *Newsletter, Trade.* **Description:** Presents articles concerning the early brass music field.
Formerly (until 2005): Historic Brass Society Newsletter (Print) (1045-4594)
Media: Online - full text.
Indexed: IIMP, M11, MusicInd, RILM, T02.
—Ingenta.
Published by: Historic Brass Society, Inc., 148 W 23rd St #5F, New York, NY 10011. TEL 212-627-3820, FAX 212-627-3820, president@historicbrass.org. Ed. Bryan Proksch TEL 337-475-5023. Adv. contact John Benoit TEL 515-961-2845.

787.9 USA ISSN 1543-8317
ML1005
THE HISTORICAL HARP SOCIETY JOURNAL. Text in English. 1991. q. USD 25 (effective 2003).
Published by: Historical Harp Society, c/o Jean Humphrey, 631 N. 3rd Ave., St. Charles, IL 60174. http://www.historicalharps.org. Ed. Paula Fagerberg.

780 USA ISSN 1043-2523
ML651
HISTORICAL HARPSICHORD SERIES. Text in English. 1984. irreg., latest vol.5, 2010. price varies. back issues avail. **Document type:** *Monographic series, Trade.*
Published by: Pendragon Press, PO Box 190, Hillsdale, NY 12529. TEL 518-325-6100, FAX 518-325-6102, orders@pendragonpress.com. Ed. John Koster.

780 USA ISSN 0162-0266
HIT PARADER. Text in English. 1942. m. USD 29.50; USD 2.46 newsstand/cover (effective 2005). adv. bk.rev. charts; illus.; tr.lit. **Document type:** *Magazine, Consumer.* **Description:** Features music reviews and interviews for fans of hard rock and heavy metal music.
Indexed: PMR.
Published by: Hit Parader Publications, Inc., 40 Violet Ave, Poughkeepsie, NY 12601. TEL 845-454-7420. Ed. Andy Secher. Adv. contacts Vic Sierkowski, Mitch Herskowitz. Circ: 150,000. **Subscr. to:** PO Box 611, Mt Morris, IL 61054-1793. **Dist. by:** Curtis Circulation Co., 730 River Rd, New Milford, NJ 07646. TEL 201-634-7400.; **Dist. in the UK by:** Comag, Tavistock Rd, W Drayton, Middlesex UB7 7QE, United Kingdom. TEL 44-1895-444055, FAX 44-1895-433602.

781.64 USA
HIT SENSATIONS PRESENTS: POP HITS. Text in English. 2000. m. **Document type:** *Magazine, Consumer.*
Published by: Fanzine International, Inc., 230 W 41st St, New York, NY 10036.

HITCH; journal of pop culture absurdity. *see* MOTION PICTURES

781.546 USA
HITMAKERS - WEEKLY TOP 40 RADIO & MUSIC INDUSTRY MAGAZINE. Text in English. w. **Description:** Contains breaking news, weekly features, and major happenings in the radio and music industry.
Media: Online - full text.

780 AUT
HOCHSCHULE FUER MUSIK FRANZ LISZT. SCHRIFTENREIHE. Text in German. 1995. irreg., latest vol.8, 2011. price varies. **Document type:** *Monographic series, Academic/Scholarly.*
Published by: Boehlau Verlag GmbH & Co.KG., Wiesingerstr 1, Vienna, W 1010, Austria. TEL 43-1-3302427, FAX 43-1-3302432, boehlau@boehlau.at, http://www.boehlau.at.

780.7 DEU ISSN 0936-2940
HOCHSCHULE FUER MUSIK KOELN. JOURNAL. Text in German. 1982. s-a. free. adv. **Document type:** *Academic/Scholarly.* **Description:** Music and reports on the school and the world of musicology and teaching methods.
Published by: Hochschule fuer Musik Koeln, Dagobertstr 38, Cologne, 50668, Germany. TEL 49-221-912818105, FAX 49-221-131204.

780 792 DEU ISSN 1868-8896
▼ **HOCHSCHULE FUER MUSIK UND THEATER FELIX MENDELSSOHN BARTHOLDY LEIPZIG. SCHRIFTEN.** Text in German. 2009. irreg., latest vol.3, 2010. price varies. **Document type:** *Monographic series, Academic/Scholarly.*
Published by: (Hochschule fuer Musik und Theater Felix Mendelssohn Bartholdy Leipzig), Georg Olms Verlag, Hagentorwall 7, Hildesheim, 31134, Germany. TEL 49-5121-15010, FAX 49-5121-150150, info@olms.de.

780 792 DEU
HOCHSCHULE FUER MUSIK UND THEATER HANNOVER. PUBLIKATIONEN. Text in German. 1988. irreg., latest vol.14, 2003. price varies. **Document type:** *Monographic series, Academic/Scholarly.*
Published by: Wissner Verlag, Im Tal 12, Augsburg, 86179, Germany. TEL 49-821-259890, FAX 49-821-594932, info@wissner.com.

780.65 DEU
HOER_BAR. Text in German. bi-m. adv. **Document type:** *Magazine, Consumer.*
Published by: M W K Zimmermann & Haehnel GmbH, Elisenstr 24, Cologne, 50667, Germany. TEL 49-221-123435, FAX 49-221-138560, info@mwk-koeln.de, http://www.mwk-koeln.de. adv.: B&W page EUR 2,075, color page EUR 2,350. Circ: 25,000 (controlled).

HOLIDAYS AT THE KINDERGARTEN. *see* CHILDREN AND YOUTH—For

HOLLOW EAR. *see* LITERATURE—Poetry

621.389 780 USA ISSN 1559-5471
ML18
HOLLYWOOD MUSIC INDUSTRY DIRECTORY. Text in English. 2004. a., latest 2007. USD 64.95 per issue (effective 2007). 350 p./no.; **Document type:** *Directory, Trade.*
Published by: Hollywood Creative Directory, 5055 Wilshire Blvd, Los Angeles, CA 90036. TEL 323-525-2369, 800-815-0503, FAX 323-525-2398, hcdcustomerservice@hcdonline.com, http://www.hcdonline.com/index.aspx.

HOOK (IRVINGTON); art, ideas & evolution. *see* ART

780.7 USA ISSN 0046-7928
ML1
THE HORN CALL. Text in English. 1971. 3/yr. adv. bk.rev. index. back issues avail. **Document type:** *Journal, Trade.* **Description:** Includes membership news, workshop reports, feature articles, a variety of clinics, biographical sketches, music and recording reviews, and advertisements for horn-related products and services.
Incorporates: I H S Newsletter
Related titles: Online - full text ed.
Indexed: A01, A26, G08, I05, IIMP, M11, MAG, MusicInd, RILM, T02.
—Ingenta.
Published by: International Horn Society, c/o Heidi Vogel, PO Box 630158, Laniai City, HI 96763. TEL 808-565-7273, FAX 808-565-7273, exec-secretary@hornsociety.org. Ed. William Scharnberg. Adv. contact Paul Austin TEL 616-475-5919.

780 GBR
THE HORN PLAYER. Text in English. 1993. 3/yr. GBP 28 domestic membership; GBP 30 foreign membership (effective 2009). adv. bk.rev.; music rev. **Document type:** *Magazine, Consumer.*
Formerly (until 2004): The Horn Magazine (1475-9632)
Published by: British Horn Society, CAF Administration Service, Kings Hill, West Malling, Kent ME19 4TA, United Kingdom. bhs.membership@ntlworld.com. Ed. Paul Kampen. adv.: page GBP 150; trim 210 x 297.

781.64 BLR
HOT 7. Text in Russian. 2003. bi-m. illus. 64 p./no.; **Document type:** *Magazine, Consumer.*
Published by: Izdatel'stvo Nestor, A/ya 563, Minsk, 220113, Belarus. nestorpb@nestor.minsk.by, http://www.nestor.minsk.by.

780 USA
HOT HOUSE; jazz nightlife guide. Text in English. m. USD 14; USD 27 foreign.
Published by: On Target Features - Hot House, 13 Mekeel Dr., Dover, NJ 07801-2243. TEL 201-627-5349. Ed. Gene Kalbacher.

780.43 USA
MT125
HOUSTON SYMPHONY MAGAZINE. Text in English. 1914. m. distributed to attendees. adv. **Document type:** *Magazine, Trade.* **Description:** Contains program notes for the month's concerts, biographies, interviews, history, social events, corporate sponsor articles, symphony and city news.
Published by: (Houston Symphony Orchestra), New Leaf Publishing, Inc., 2006 Huldy St., Houston, TX 77019. TEL 713-523-5323, FAX 713-523-5995, newleaf@houston.rr.com. Ed. Elaine Reeder Mayo. Pub., R&P, Adv. contact Janet Meyer. B&W page USD 1,910, color page USD 2,660. Circ: 28,000 (free).

780.7 USA ISSN 1936-167X
HOW TO PLAY DRUMS. Text in English. 2006. a. USD 12 newsstand/cover domestic; USD 14 newsstand/cover in Canada; USD 20 newsstand/cover elsewhere (effective 2008). adv. **Document type:** *Magazine, Consumer.* **Description:** Provides instruction and advice for beginning and intermediate drum players on all aspects of drumming, including reading drum notation, setting up and tuning drums, stick grip and practice tips.
Related titles: Online - full text ed.: ISSN 1936-1688; Optical Disk - DVD ed.: ISSN 1936-1696.
Published by: Enter Music Publishing, Inc., 95 South Market St. #200, San Jose, CA 95113. TEL 408-971-9794, 888-378-6624, FAX 408-971-0382, http://drummagazine.americommerce.com. Ed. Andy Doerschuk.

780 HRV ISSN 1330-0490
ML262
HRVATSKA AKADEMIJA ZNANOSTI I UMJETNOSTI. RAZRED ZA GLAZBENU UMJETNOST I MUZIKOLOGIJU. RAD. MUZIKOLOGIJA. Text in Croatian; Summaries in English. 1965. a. **Document type:** *Journal, Academic/Scholarly.*
Former titles (until 1992): Jugoslavenska Akademija Znanosti i Umjetnosti. Razred za Glazbenu Umjetnost i Muzikologiju. Rad. Muzikologija (0353-4545); (until 1980): Jugoslavenska Akademija Znanosti i Umjetnosti. Razred za Muzicku Umjetnost. Rad (0351-3335); (until 1970): Jugoslavenska Akademija Znanosti i Umjetnosti. Odjel za Muzicku Umjetnost. Rad (1330-6421)

Indexed: RILM.
—INIST.
Published by: Hrvatska Akademija Znanosti i Umjetnosti, Razred za Glazbenu Umjetnost i Muzikologiju, Andrije Hebranga 1, Zagreb, 10000, Croatia. TEL 385-1-4895171, http://www.hazu.hr/Raz8.html.

780 CHN ISSN 1003-7721
➤ **HUANG ZHONG.** Text in Chinese. 1986. q. USD 28.40 (effective 2009). adv. bk.rev. **Document type:** *Academic/Scholarly.*
Related titles: Online - full text ed.
Indexed: RILM.
—East View.
Published by: Wuhan Yiyue Xueyuan, No 255, Jiefang Lu, Wuchang, Wuhan, Hubei 430060, China. TEL 86-27-8066354. Ed. Zhou Zhenxi. Adv. contact Cai Jizhou.

780 SVK ISSN 1336-8044
HUDBA. Text in Slovak. 2006. q. **Document type:** *Magazine, Consumer.*
Published by: Hevhetia s.r.o., Pri Hati 1, Kosice, 040 01, Slovakia. TEL 421-55-6367552, FAX 421-55-7994001, hevhetia.ke@stonline.sk.

780 CZE ISSN 0018-6996
ML5
HUDEBNI ROZHLEDY. Text in Czech. 1948. m. CZK 360; CZK 40 per issue (effective 2009). adv. bk.rev. bibl.; illus. index. **Document type:** *Journal, Academic/Scholarly.*
Indexed: IBR, IBZ, IIMP, M11, MusicInd, RASB, RILM.
Published by: Spolecnost Hudebni Rozhledy, Radlicka 99, Prague 5, 150 00, Czech Republic. TEL 420-2-251550208, FAX 420-2-251554088. Ed. Hana Jarolimkova. Circ: 4,200.

780 CZE ISSN 0018-7003
ML5
➤ **HUDEBNI VEDA/MUSICOLOGY.** Text in Czech, German, English, French; Summaries in English, German. 1964. q. CZK 200 (effective 2010). bk.rev.; music rev. bibl.; illus. index. **Document type:** *Journal, Academic/Scholarly.* **Description:** Focuses on the history of Czech music. Also includes bibliographies, a colloquy, and other communications.
Indexed: A20, ASCA, ArtHuCI, CERDIC, CurCont, FR, IIMP, M11, MusicInd, RASB, RILM, SCOPUS, W07.
Published by: Akademie Ved Ceske Republiky, Etnologicky Ustav, Oddeleni Hudebni Historie/Academy of Sciences of the Czech Republic, Institute of Ethnology, Department of Music History, Puskinovo nam 9, Prague 6, 160 00, Czech Republic. TEL 420-22-4311212, FAX 420-22-4323728, http://www.eu.cas.cz. Ed. Ondrej Manour. Circ: 550. **Subscr. to:** Mediaservis s.r.o., Pacericka 2773/1, Prague 9 193 00, Czech Republic. TEL 420-2-71199100, FAX 420-2-72700025, info@mediaservis.cz, http://www.mediaservis.cz.

➤ **HUDEBNI VYCHOVA.** see EDUCATION

780 SVK ISSN 0862-416X
HUDOBNY ARCHIV. Text in Slovak; Summaries in English, German. 1974. irreg. price varies. **Document type:** *Proceedings.*
Indexed: RASB, RILM.
Published by: Matica Slovenska, Archiv Literatury a Umenia, Nam J C Hronskeho 1, Martin, 03652, Slovakia. TEL 421-842-31371, FAX 421-842-33160. Ed. Viera Sedlakova. Circ: 300.

781.57 780.42 SVK ISSN 1335-4140
HUDOBNY ZIVOT/MUSICAL LIFE. Text in Slovak. 1968. s-m. USD 25 foreign (effective 2008). **Document type:** *Magazine, Consumer.* **Description:** Contains information about festivals, concerts; reviews CDs and books; analyses current issues; looks back into the history of Slovak music.
Indexed: RASB.
Published by: Hudobne Centrum, Michalska 10, Bratislava, 81536, Slovakia. TEL 421-2-59204845, FAX 421-2-54430366, suba@hc.sk. Ed. Andrea Serecinova.

780 NLD ISSN 1878-9889
HUISMUZIEK NIEUWSBRIEF. Text in Dutch. 1993. 5/yr. adv.
Formerly (until 2008): Huismuziek (1380-829X); Which superseded in part (in 1993): Akkord (0929-3787)
Published by: Vereniging voor Muziek en Instrumentenbouw, Huismuziek, Postbus 9, Arnhem, 6800 AA, Netherlands. TEL 31-26-8450788, FAX 31-26-8450787, info@huismuziek.nl, http://www.huismuziek.nl. Eds. Chris Eken, Sonja van Dijk. Circ: 2,500.

783.9 USA ISSN 0018-8271
ML1
➤ **THE HYMN;** a journal of congregational song. Text in English. 1949. q. free to members (effective 2009). bk.rev.; rec.rev. index. back issues avail. **Document type:** *Journal, Academic/Scholarly.* **Description:** Provides exemplary hymn texts and tunes in various styles and reflects diverse cultural, ethnic, and theological identities.
Indexed: A21, A22, CA, ChrPI, IIMP, M11, MAG, MLA-IB, MusicInd, R&TA, RI-1, RI-2, RILM, T02.
—BLDSC (4352.607000), IE, Ingenta.
Published by: Hymn Society in the United States and Canada, 745 Commonwealth Ave, Boston, MA 02215. TEL 800-843-4966, FAX 617-353-7322, hymnsoc@bu.edu, http://www.thehymnsociety.org.

780 GBR ISSN 0018-828X
ML5
HYMN SOCIETY OF GREAT BRITAIN AND IRELAND. BULLETIN. Text in English. 1937. q. free to members (effective 2009). bk.rev.; rec.rev. cum.index every 3 yrs. back issues avail. **Document type:** *Bulletin, Trade.*
Indexed: IIMP, M11, MLA-IB, MusicInd, RILM, T02.
Published by: Hymn Society of Great Britain and Ireland, c/o Robert Canham, 99 Barton Rd, Lancaster, LA1 4EN, United Kingdom. TEL 44-1524-66740, robcanham@haystacks.fsnet.co.uk. Ed. Andrew Pratt.

HYMNOLOGI; nordisk tidsskrift. see RELIGIONS AND THEOLOGY—Protestant

783.9 USA ISSN 1054-7495
ML3270
THE HYMNOLOGY ANNUAL. Text in English. 1991. a.
Indexed: R&TA, RILM.
Published by: Hymn Society in the United States and Canada, 745 Commonwealth Ave, Boston, MA 02215. TEL 800-843-4966, FAX 617-353-7322, hymnsoc@bu.edu, http://www.thehymnsociety.org.

780.42 USA ISSN 1065-6200
HYPE; monitoring the black image in the media. Text in English. 1991. m. USD 25; USD 45 foreign (effective 1999). adv. bk.rev.; rec.rev. back issues avail. **Document type:** *Magazine, Consumer.* **Description:** Features interviews, fiction and alternative music reviews.
Related titles: Online - full text ed.
Published by: Center for Media and the Black Experience, 305 E Pine St, Seattle, WA 98122. TEL 206-623-1275, FAX 206-343-5173. Circ: 15,000.

781 ZAF ISSN 1811-086X
HYPE; South Africa's only hip hop magazine. Text in English. 2004. bi-m. ZAR 18.95 newsstand/cover (effective 2007). adv. **Document type:** *Magazine, Consumer.*
Published by: Intelligence Publishing, PostNet Ste 254, Private Bag X30500, Houghton, Johannesburg 2041, South Africa. TEL 27-11-4840877, FAX 27-11-6431881, editor@intelligence.co.za, http://www.intelligence.co.za. Ed. Simone Harris. Adv. contact Nicky Lloyd. Circ: 27,888 (paid).

781.57 CAN ISSN 0098-9487
ML156.9
I A J R C JOURNAL. Text in English. 1967. q. USD 35 to individuals; USD 45 to institutions (effective 2003). adv. bk.rev.; rec.rev. back issues avail. **Document type:** *Journal, Academic/Scholarly.* **Description:** Contains news, reviews and research articles on the subject of jazz music and musicians and related fields of interest to the collector and interested public.
Related titles: Online - full text ed.
Indexed: A01, CA, H20, IIMP, M11, MusicInd, RILM, T02.
—Ingenta.
Published by: International Association of Jazz Record Collectors, c/o Janet Daly, 41 Brentwood Dr, Dundas, ON L9H 3N4, Canada. TEL 905-628-6813, phuntoon@comcast.net. Ed. Art Garcia. Adv. contact Scott MacKenzie. B&W page USD 100. Circ: 1,500 (paid).

780 USA ISSN 1082-1872
ML82
I A W M JOURNAL. Text in English. 1995. 2/yr. free to members; USD 15 per issue to non-members (effective 2008). adv. bk.rev. back issues avail. **Document type:** *Newsletter, Trade.* **Description:** Provides articles on women in the field of music.
Formed by the merger of (1989-1995): International League of Women Composers Journal (1048-5031); Which was formerly (1981-1989): International League of Women Composers Newsletter (0748-5735); (1982-1995): American Women Composers News Forum; Which was formerly (1977-1982): A W C News (0193-0850)
Indexed: IIMP, M11, MAG, MusicInd, RILM, T02.
—Ingenta.
Published by: International Alliance for Women in Music, c o Susan Lackman, Rollins College, 1000 Holt Ave, PO Box 2731, Winter Park, FL 32789. Ed., R&P Eve R Meyer. Adv. contact Jennifer M Barker. Circ: 1,000.

782.1 DEU
I B S AKTUELL. Text in German. 1981. 5/yr. EUR 15 (effective 2006). adv. bk.rev. **Document type:** *Bulletin.*
Published by: Interessenvereins des Bayerischen Staatsopernpublikums e.V., Postfach 100829, Munich, 80082, Germany. ibs.koehle@t-online.de. Circ: 850.

791.44 GBR ISSN 1471-0641
I D J. (International Disc Jockey) Text in English. 1999. m. GBP 39 domestic; GBP 59 in Europe; GBP 79 elsewhere; GBP 3.60 per issue domestic (effective 2009). adv. back issues avail. **Document type:** *Magazine, Consumer.*
Formerly (until 2000): X Fade (1466-6154)
—CCC.
Published by: I D J Magazine, 2nd Fl, 15-16 Lower Park Row, Bristol, BS1 5BN, United Kingdom. TEL 44-117-9297462, FAX 44-117-9276535. Adv. contact Adam Portingale.

780 GBR ISSN 2047-2226
▼ **I E B S NEWSLETTER.** Text in English. 2009. s-a. free to members (effective 2011). back issues avail. **Document type:** *Newsletter, Trade.*
Related titles: Online - full text ed.: ISSN 2047-2234. free (effective 2011).
Published by: International Ernest Bloch Society, 135 Stevenage Rd, Fulham, London, SW6 6PB, United Kingdom. TEL 44-20-73819751, FAX 44-20-73812406, jaellison@btinternet.com. Ed. Robert Sargant.

781.7 367 USA
I F C O CLUB HOUSE. (International Fan Club Organization) Text in English. 1993. q. USD 25 domestic membership; USD 35 foreign membership (effective 2007). **Document type:** *Directory, Consumer.* **Description:** Profiles country music artists, their fans, and their fan club officers.
Published by: Tri-Son, Inc., PO Box 40328, Nashville, TN 37204-0328. TEL 615-371-9596, FAX 615-371-9597. Ed. Loudilla Johnson. Circ: 2,500 (paid).

781.7 367 USA
I F C O JOURNAL. Text in English. 1965. q. USD 30; USD 45 foreign (effective 1999). **Document type:** *Directory, Consumer.*
Published by: (International Fan Club Organization), Tri-Son, Inc., PO Box 40328, Nashville, TN 37204-0328. TEL 615-371-9596, FAX 615-371-9597. Ed. Loudilla Johnson. Circ: 1,100.

I F O STUDIEN ZU KULTUR UND WIRTSCHAFT. (Information und Forschung) see BUSINESS AND ECONOMICS

781.62 IRL
I M R O NEWS. Text in English. q. adv. **Document type:** *Magazine, Consumer.*
Published by: (Irish Music Rights Organisation), Lacethorn Ltd., 11 Clare St, Dublin, 2, Ireland. TEL 353-1-6624887, FAX 353-1-6624886. adv.: color page EUR 1,143; trim 210 x 279. Circ: 3,500 (controlled).

780 DEU ISSN 1022-8667
Z286.I56
I S M N NEWSLETTER. (International Standard Music Number) Text in English. 1994. a. free. **Document type:** *Newsletter.* **Description:** Contains the minutes of its annual meetings and offers up-to-date information about the development of ISMN.
Related titles: Online - full text ed.
Published by: International I S M N Agency, Schlossstr 50, Berlin, 12165, Germany. TEL 49-30-79745002, FAX 49-30-79745254, ismn@ismn-international.org, http://ismn-international.org.

780 SWE ISSN 1607-0348
ML549.8
I S O JOURNAL. (International Society of Organbuilders) Text in English, French, German. 1969. q. adv. bk.rev. **Document type:** *Journal, Trade.*
Former titles (until 1998): I S O News (1017-7515); I S O Information (0579-5613)
Related titles: Supplement(s): I S O Yearbook. ISSN 1028-8023. 1991.
Indexed: IIMP, M11, MusicInd, RILM, T02.
Published by: International Society of Organbuilders, c/o Goeran Grahn, Jupitervaegen 14B, Lidingoe, Sweden. http://www.internationalorganbuilders.com.

780.6 USA ISSN 1549-5426
ML1
I T E A JOURNAL. (International Tuba - Euphonium Association) Text in English, Japanese. 1973. 4/yr. USD 43 domestic to libraries; USD 55 foreign to libraries (effective 2004). adv. bk.rev.; music rev. bibl.; charts; illus.; tr.lit. index. back issues avail. **Document type:** *Journal, Consumer.*
Former titles (until 2001): T.U.B.A. Journal (0363-4787); (until 1976): T.U.B.A. Newsletter (0363-4779)
Indexed: IIMP, M11, MusicInd, PCI, T02.
—Ingenta.
Published by: Tubists Universal Brotherhood Association, c/o Kathy Aylsworth Brantigan, 2253 Downing St, Denver, CO 80205. TEL 303-832-4676, FAX 303-832-0839, http://www.tubaonline.org/. Ed., R&P Jerry Young. Adv. contact Kathy Brantigan. Circ: 1,800.

780 USA
➤ **I T G JOURNAL.** Text in English. 1976. q. free to members (effective 2011). adv. bk.rev. **Document type:** *Journal, Academic/Scholarly.*
Formerly: International Trumpet Guild. Journal (0363-2849); Incorporates (1976-1988): International Trumpet Guild. Newsletter (0363-2857)
Indexed: A22, IIMP, M11, MAG, MusicInd, PCI, T02.
Published by: International Trumpet Guild, 109 McCain Auditorium, Kansas State University, Manhattan, KS 66506. president@trumpetguild.org. Ed. Gary Mortenson. Adv. contact Joseph Walters TEL 505-821-3751. **Subscr. to:** David Jones.

789.91 621.38 GRC
ICHOS & EIKONA/SOUND & HI FI. Text in Greek. 1973. m. adv. Website rev. illus.; mkt. back issues avail. **Document type:** *Magazine, Consumer.* **Description:** Discusses music and high-quality high-fidelity equipment.
Formerly: Echos kai Hi Fi (1105-1302)
Related titles: Online - full text ed.
Published by: Technical Press SA, 80 Ioannou Metaxa, Karelas, Koropi, 19400, Greece. TEL 30-210-9792500, FAX 30-210-9792528, info@technicalpress.gr, http://www.technicalpress.gr. Ed. Fotis Fotiades. Adv. contact Chrisanthi Bitsori. Circ: 5,848 (paid).

IDAHO ARTS QUARTERLY. see ART

780 MEX ISSN 2007-1345
▼ **IDENTIDAD GRUPERA;** la guia de musica grupera y mucho mas. Text in Spanish. 2009. m. **Document type:** *Magazine, Consumer.*
Address: Lago Michigan No. 44, Col. Tacuba, Del. Miguel Hidalgo, Mexico, D.F., 11410, Mexico. TEL 52-55-273969, http://www.identidadgrupera.com.mx/inicio/.

IDOL OF MY HEART ELVIS PRESLEY FAN CLUB NEWSLETTER. see CLUBS

IDOLS. WEST AFRICA. see LEISURE AND RECREATION

781.64 USA ISSN 1078-1986
ML3469
ILLINOIS ENTERTAINER; Chicagoland's music monthly. Text in English. 1974. m. USD 35 (effective 2007). adv. bk.rev.; rec.rev. illus. **Document type:** *Magazine, Trade.* **Description:** Covers the music, film, arts and entertainment industries nationally and in the Chicago area.
Related titles: Online - full content ed.; Supplement(s): Studio Directory.
Published by: Roberts Publishing, Inc., 657-A West Lake St, Chicago, IL 60660. TEL 312-930-9363, FAX 312-930-9341. Ed. Steve Forstneger. Pub. John Vernon. Circ: 50,000 (paid and free).

780.7 371.3 USA ISSN 0019-2147
ML1
➤ **ILLINOIS MUSIC EDUCATOR.** Text in English. 1970 (vol.30). 3/yr. free to members (effective 2011). adv. bk.rev. illus. 100 p./no. 3 cols./p.; back issues avail. **Document type:** *Journal, Academic/Scholarly.* **Description:** Presents teaching methods and current association activities.
Related titles: Online - full text ed.
Indexed: A01, A02, A03, A08, CA, E03, ERI, M11, T02.
Published by: Illinois Music Educators Association, 18700 Wolf Rd, Ste 208, Mokena, IL 60448. TEL 708-479-4000, FAX 708-479-5638, info@ilmea.org. Adv. contact Bill Froom TEL 309-224-4628.

780 DEU ISSN 1615-908X
IMAGINATIO BOREALIS; Bilder des Nordens. Text in German. 2001. irreg., latest vol.21, 2010. price varies. **Document type:** *Monographic series, Academic/Scholarly.*
Published by: Peter Lang GmbH (Subsidiary of: Peter Lang Publishing Group), Eschborner Landstr 42-50, Frankfurt Am Main, 60489, Germany. TEL 49-69-7807050, FAX 49-69-78070550, zentrale.frankfurt@peterlang.com. Ed. Olaf Moerke.

IMAGINE (SILVER SPRING). see PSYCHOLOGY

780 975 ITA ISSN 0255-8831
ML85
IMAGO MUSICAE; international yearbook of musical iconography. Text in English, French, German, Italian. 1984-1990; resumed 1991. a., latest vol.19, 2002. EUR 80 domestic; EUR 85 foreign (effective 2009). back issues avail. **Document type:** *Journal, Academic/Scholarly.*
Indexed: B24, DIP, IBR, IBZ, RILM.
Published by: LIM Editrice Srl, Via di Arsina 296/f, Lucca, LU 55100, Italy. TEL 39-0583-394464, FAX 39-0583-394469, lim@lim.it, http://www.lim.it. **Co-publisher:** Barenreiter-Verlag Basel.

781.65 USA
IMASSJAZZ EZINE. Text in English. 2001. w. adv. **Description:** Includes updates and weekly info on jazz performers in the New England area.
Media: Online - full content. **Related titles:** E-mail ed.
Published by: iMassJazz, 459 High St, No.202, Medford, MA 02155. http://www.imassradio.com/. Ed. Marc Lemay.

780 USA
IMPROVIJAZZATION NATION. Text in English. 1989. q. USD 8; USD 2.25 newsstand/cover. **Description:** Covers self-produced music, all genres.
Address: 5308 65th Ave., S.E., Lacey, WA 98513. Ed. Dick Metcalf.

780 BEL ISSN 2031-3098
IN MONTE ARTIUM. Text in French. 2008. a. EUR 66 combined subscription (print & online eds.) (effective 2012). **Document type:** *Journal, Academic/Scholarly.*
Related titles: Online - full text ed.
Published by: Brepols Publishers, Begijnhof 67, Turnhout, 2300, Belgium. TEL 32-14-448020, FAX 32-14-428919, periodicals@brepols.net, http://www.brepols.net.

781.64 USA
IN MUSIC WE TRUST. Text in English. 1997. m. music rev.; rec.rev. **Document type:** *Magazine, Consumer.* **Description:** Covers everything from indie, punk, rock, ska, jazz and bluegrass to the blues.
Media: Online - full text.
Published by: In Music We Trust, Inc., 15213 SE Bevington Ave, Portland, OR 97267. TEL 503-557-9661, FAX 503-231-0420. Ed. Alex Steininger.

IN THE GROOVE. *see* ANTIQUES

780 USA ISSN 0360-4365
ML1
➤ **IN THEORY ONLY.** Abbreviated title: I T O. Text in English. 1975. irreg., latest vol.13, 2008. USD 40 per vol. domestic to institutions; USD 50 per vol. foreign to institutions (effective 2011). adv. bk.rev. bibl.; charts; illus. index. back issues avail. **Document type:** *Journal, Academic/Scholarly.*
Related titles: Online - full text ed.
Indexed: A20, A22, IBR, IBZ, IIMP, M11, MAG, MusicInd, RILM.
—IE, Ingenta.
Published by: Bowling Green State University, College of Musical Arts, Bowling Green State University, Bowling Green, OH 43403. TEL 419-372-0522. Ed. William E Lake. Circ: 450 (paid).

780 USA
IN-TUNE (ENFIELD). Text in English. 1999. m. free. adv. **Document type:** *Newsletter.* **Description:** Dedicated to piano lovers. Each issue contains interesting facts, tips and information about pianos.
Media: Online - full text.
Published by: Piano World, 38 Park Dr, Enfield, CT 06082. TEL 860-741-2625, FAX 860-741-2625. Ed. Frank Baxter.

780 370 USA ISSN 1554-4370
ML3469
IN TUNE MONTHLY. Text in English. 2003. 8/yr. (Oct.-May). price varies. **Document type:** *Magazine, Consumer.* **Description:** Covers traditional music curriculum for music making students in middle & high schools and their teachers.
Published by: In Tune Partners, LLC., 55 Larry's Ln., Pleasantville, NY 10570. TEL 866-361-4904, 866-361-4904, FAX 914-741-1136.

780 GBR ISSN 2044-9380
ML27.G7
INCORPORATED SOCIETY OF MUSICIANS. HANDBOOK. Text in English. 1898. a. free to members (effective 2010). back issues avail. **Document type:** *Handbook/Manual/Guide, Trade.* **Description:** Reports activities of the society with membership lists in the United Kingdom and elsewhere.
Former titles (until 2010): Incorporated Society of Musicians. Yearbook (0951-6220); (until 1984): Incorporated Society of Musicians. Handbook and Register of members
Published by: Incorporated Society of Musicians, 10 Stratford Pl, London, W1C 1AA, United Kingdom. TEL 44-20-76294413, FAX 44-20-74081538, membership@ism.org.

690 GBR ISSN 0073-5744
INCORPORATED SOCIETY OF ORGAN BUILDERS. JOURNAL. Text in English. 1949. irreg. GBP 3.50.
Published by: Incorporated Society of Organ Builders, Petersfield, Hants GU32 3AT, United Kingdom. Ed. C J Gordon Wells. Circ: 400.

THE INDEPENDENT MIND. *see* LITERATURE

780 IND ISSN 0251-012X
ML5
INDIAN MUSICOLOGICAL SOCIETY. JOURNAL. Abbreviated title: J I M S. Text in English. 1970. s-a. INR 250 domestic to individuals; USD 30 foreign to individuals; INR 500 domestic to institutions; USD 40 foreign to institutions; free to members (effective 2011). bk.rev. 150 p./no. 1 cols./p.; back issues avail.; reprints avail. **Document type:** *Journal, Academic/Scholarly.*
Formerly: Sangeet Kala Vihar (0036-4320)
Related titles: Microform ed.: (from PQC).
Indexed: A20, ASCA, CA, IIMP, M11, MusicInd, PCI, RILM, T02.
—Ingenta.
Published by: Indian Musicological Society, c/o Lee & Muirhead Pvt. Ltd, Oricon House, 2nd Fl, 12 K Dubash Marg, Mumbai, 400 023, India. info@musicology.in, http://web.me.com/wvdm/JIMS/Home/Home.html. Eds. Suvarnalata Rao, Wim van der Meer.

780.71025 USA ISSN 0742-2474
INDIANA DIRECTORY OF MUSIC TEACHERS. Text in English. 1941. a. USD 20 per issue (effective 2010). index. **Document type:** *Directory, Trade.* **Description:** Lists faculties-teachers of music at Indiana public and parochial schools, colleges and universities, and state schools and hospitals.
Formerly (until 1968): Indiana School Music Teachers' Directory (0742-2490)
Published by: Indiana University, School of Music, 1201 E Third St, Bloomington, IN 47405. gta@indiana.edu, http://www.music.indiana.edu.

780.71 USA ISSN 0273-9933
ML1
➤ **INDIANA MUSICATOR.** Text in English. 1945. q. back issues avail. **Document type:** *Journal, Academic/Scholarly.*
Indexed: MAG.
Published by: Indiana Music Educators Association, Ball State University, School of Music, Muncie, IN 47306. TEL 765-285-5496, FAX 765-285-1139, manager@imeamusic.org.

780.7 USA ISSN 0271-8022
MT6
INDIANA THEORY REVIEW. Text in English. 1977. s-a. USD 22 to individuals; USD 30 to institutions (effective 2010). adv. bk.rev. abstr.; charts. back issues avail.; reprint service avail. from PSC. **Document type:** *Journal, Academic/Scholarly.* **Description:** Articles on music theory.
Indexed: IIMP, M11, MusicInd, PCI, RILM, T02.
—Ingenta.
Published by: (Graduate Theory Association), Indiana University, School of Music, 1201 E Third St, Bloomington, IN 47405. gta@indiana.edu. Ed. John Reef. Adv. contact Timothy K Chenette.

782.42166 USA
INDIECENT. Text in English. 4/yr. USD 10; USD 2.95 newsstand/cover (effective 2000). **Document type:** *Magazine, Consumer.* **Description:** Contains reviews, interviews, articles and features on the independent music scene.
Address: 506 Grand St., Apt. 4, Brooklyn, NY 11211-3522. indiecente@aol.com.

781 USA ISSN 1939-3091
INDIELABEL. Text in English. 2007. m. USD 14 (effective 2007). adv. **Document type:** *Magazine, Consumer.*
Related titles: Online - full text ed.: ISSN 1939-3105.
Published by: Kamitri Eworld Resource, PO Box 924113, Houston, TX 77292. TEL 877-404-6343, info@indielabelmagazine.com. Ed. Gerardo Rodriguez. Pub. Kyla Statin.

L'INDUSTRIE CANADIENNE DE LA MUSIQUE. PROFIL ECONOMIQUE (YEAR). *see* BUSINESS AND ECONOMICS—Economic Situation And Conditions

781.66 FIN ISSN 1796-7600
INFERNO MAGAZINE. Text in Finnish. 2001. 10/yr. adv. **Document type:** *Magazine, Consumer.*
Published by: Pop Media oy, Malminkatu 24, Helsinki, 00100, Finland. TEL 358-9-43692407, FAX 358-9-43692409, http://www.popmedia.fi. Ed. Matti Riekki. Adv. contact Oskari Anttonen TEL 358-40-5630642. page EUR 1,400; 210 x 285. Circ: 10,000.

780 DEU
INFO R I S M (ONLINE). Text in English, French, German. 1989. irreg. free. **Document type:** *Newsletter, Academic/Scholarly.*
Formerly: Info R I S M (Print) (0940-7820)
Indexed: RILM.
Published by: Repertoire International des Sources Musicales/International Inventory of Musical Sources, Sophienstr 26, Frankfurt am Main, 60487, Germany. TEL 49-69-706231, FAX 49-69-706026.

051 USA ISSN 1075-8933
INK 19. Text in English. 1991. m. adv. **Document type:** *Magazine, Consumer.* **Description:** Promotes awareness of the best new music, media and thought available today.
Media: Online - full content.
Address: 624 Georgia Ave, Melbourne, FL 32901-7710. Pub. Ian Koss. Adv. contact Mark Harris. Circ: 55,000.

781.64 USA
INK BLOT MAGAZINE. Text in English. fortn. **Document type:** *Magazine, Consumer.* **Description:** Aims to keep one abreast of quality rock, dance, jazz and more through insightful features on bands and musicians.
Published by: Ink Blot, 385 8th St, Ste 203, San Francisco, CA 94103. Ed. Patrick Bennison. Adv. contact Dave Rosenheim.

780 USA
INK DISEASE. Text in English. irreg. USD 2.50 per issue. music rev. **Description:** Features rock music, interviews and band photos.
Address: 4563 Marmion Way, Los Angeles, CA 90065.

780 USA
INNERCITY MAGAZINE. Text in English. 2001-suspended; N.S. 2004. 6/yr. USD 9.95 (effective 2005). **Document type:** *Magazine, Consumer.* **Description:** Urban youth entertainment magazine targeting the 14-24 year old market. Contains news, interviews, profiles, and releases.
Related titles: Online - full content ed.
Published by: Inner City Broadcasting Corp., 67 Wall St, Ste 2212, New York, NY 10005. TEL 212-859-5028, FAX 212-943-2300. Ed., Pub. Farrah Gray. Circ: 300,000.

780 AUT ISSN 1993-1565
INNSBRUCKER BEITRAEGE ZUR MUSIKWISSENSCHAFT. Text in German. 1977. irreg. price varies. adv. charts; illus. index. **Document type:** *Monographic series, Academic/Scholarly.*
Published by: Helbling Verlagsgesellschaft mbH, Kaplanstr 9, Rum, T 6063, Austria. TEL 43-512-2623330, FAX 43-512-262333111, office@helbling.co.at, http://www.helbling.com.

LES INROCKUPTIBLES; l'hebdo musique, cinema, livres, etc. *see* GENERAL INTEREST PERIODICALS—France

INSCENA. *see* THEATER

INSIDE ARTS. *see* THEATER

781.7 USA ISSN 0891-0537
ML3519
INSIDE BLUEGRASS. Text in English. 1974. m. USD 20 domestic to individuals; USD 32 foreign to individuals (effective 2000). adv. bk.rev. back issues avail. **Document type:** *Newsletter.* **Description:** Offers a variety of feature stories, a comprehensive monthly Calendar of events, a number of regular columns etc.
Published by: Minnesota Bluegrass and Old Time Music Association, PO Box 16408, Minneapolis, MN 55416-0408. TEL 612-688-7757, http://www.minnesotabluegrass.org/. Ed., Adv. contact Bob Waltz. Circ: 1,000.

780 CAN
INSIDE TRACKS. Text in English. bi-m.
Address: 93 Goulding Ave, North York, ON M2M 1L3, Canada. TEL 416-229-9213. Ed. Stephen Hubbard. Circ: 5,000 (controlled).

781.64 USA ISSN 1096-4320
ML3540.5
INSIDER (ROSEMEAD); club culture & urban lifestyles magazine. Text in English. 1984. w. (Fri.). USD 20; USD 4.50 newsstand/cover; CAD 6.50 newsstand/cover in Canada (effective 1999). adv. back issues avail. **Document type:** *Newsletter, Consumer.* **Description:** Club culture magazine dedicated to urban lifestyles regardless of the music that drives it.
Related titles: Online - full text ed.
Published by: Industry Insider, Inc., 954 N. Amelia Ave., Ste. B, San Dimas, CA 91773-1407. TEL 626-285-5095, FAX 626-614-0727. Ed. Chang Weisberg. Adv. contact Myles Kovac. Circ: 1,706 (paid and free).

780 USA
INSTANT MAGAZINE; your guide to good rock. Text in English. 1995. bi-m. adv. bk.rev.; film rev.; music rev.; tel.rev.; video rev. illus. back issues avail. **Document type:** *Magazine, Consumer.* **Description:** Delivers exciting coverage on the best local and national acts while staying focused on the indie aspect that makes new artists so relevant and refreshing.
Related titles: Online - full text ed.
Published by: Instant Entertainment, PO Box 2224, Woburn, MA 01888-0324. TEL 617-246-0334, FAX 617-246-0587. Ed., Adv. contact Chris Hinckley. page USD 350; trim 10.75 x 8.13. Circ: 10,000 (controlled).

780 CHE ISSN 0945-6260
INSTITUT FUER MUSIKANALYTIK WIEN. PUBLIKATIONEN. Variant title: Publikationen des Instituts fuer Musikanalytik Wien. Text in German. 1994. irreg., latest vol.6, 2001. price varies. **Document type:** *Monographic series, Academic/Scholarly.*
Published by: Peter Lang AG (Subsidiary of: Peter Lang Publishing Group), Hochfeldstr 32, Postfach 746, Bern 9, 3000, Switzerland. TEL 41-31-3061717, FAX 41-31-3061727, info@peterlang.com, http://www.peterlang.com.

780 DEU ISSN 1862-6173
INSTITUT FUER WESTSLAWISCHE MUSIKFORSCHUNG. SCHRIFTEN. Text in German. 2005. irreg., latest vol.2, 2006. price varies. **Document type:** *Monographic series, Academic/Scholarly.*
Published by: Frank und Timme GmbH, Wittelsbacherstr 27a, Berlin, 10707, Germany. TEL 49-30-88667911, FAX 49-30-86398731, info@frank-timme.de.

780.71171 CAN ISSN 1705-1452
INSTITUTE FOR CANADIAN MUSIC. NEWSLETTER. Text in English. 2003. 3/yr. **Document type:** *Newsletter, Academic/Scholarly.*
Related titles: Online - full text ed.: ISSN 1705-1460.
Indexed: A01, M11, RILM, T02.
—CCC.
Published by: Institute for Canadian Music, Faculty of Music, University of Toronto, Edward Johnson Bldg, 80 Queen's Park, Toronto, ON M5S 2C5, Canada. TEL 416-946-8622, FAX 416-946-3353, ChalmersChair@yahoo.ca.

781.5 USA
INSTITUTE FOR STUDIES IN AMERICAN MUSIC. MONOGRAPHS. Text in English. 1973. irreg., latest 2005. price varies. back issues avail. **Document type:** *Monographic series, Academic/Scholarly.*
Published by: H. Wiley Hitchcock Institute for Studies in American Music, Brooklyn College, City University of New York, 2900 Bedford Ave, Brooklyn, NY 11210. TEL 718-951-5655, FAX 718-951-4858, isam@brooklyn.cuny.edu.

INSTITUTO BRASIL - ESTADOS UNIDOS. BOLETIM. *see* EDUCATION

780 ARG ISSN 1515-050X
ML5
INSTITUTO DE INVESTIGACION MUSICOLOGICA CARLOS VEGA. REVISTA. Text in Spanish. 1977. s-a. USD 18 per issue (effective 2005). **Document type:** *Journal, Academic/Scholarly.*
Published by: (Pontificia Universidad Catolica Argentina, Facultad de Artes y Ciencias Musicales), Pontificia Universidad Catolica Argentina, E D U C A, Av Alicia M de Justo 1400, Buenos Aires, C1107AFD, Argentina. educa@uca.edu.ar, http://www.uca.edu.ar/educa.htm. Ed. Ana Maria Locatelli de Pergamo.

780 ESP ISSN 2172-4997
▼ **INSTITUTO TRISTAN ESPANA. BOLETIN.** Text in Spanish. 2010. m. **Document type:** *Bulletin, Consumer.*
Published by: Instituto Tristan Espana, Ave Pablo Iglesias 134-137, Almeria, 04003, Spain. TEL 34-950-240334, indo@tristan-instituto.es, http://www.tristan-instituto.es/.

780.71 USA ISSN 0020-4331
ML1
THE INSTRUMENTALIST. Text in English. 1946. m. USD 21 domestic; USD 40 foreign (effective 2009). adv. bk.rev.; rec.rev. illus. index, cum.index. back issues avail.; reprints avail. **Document type:** *Magazine, Trade.* **Description:** Contains articles written by music educators, interviews with directors, composers, and performers, instrument clinics, teaching ideas, new music reviews, marching band articles, and middle school tips.
Indexed: A22, A27, B04, BRD, E02, E03, ERI, EdA, EdI, IIMP, JHMA, M11, MAG, MusicInd, P02, P10, P18, P48, P53, P54, PCI, PQC, RILM, T02, W03.
—BLDSC (4528.900000), IE, Ingenta.
Published by: The Instrumentalist Co., 200 Northfield Rd, Northfield, IL 60093. TEL 847-446-5000, 888-446-6888, FAX 847-446-6263, advertising@instrumentalistmagazine.com.

781.91 DEU ISSN 0934-3962
ML5
INSTRUMENTBAU-ZEITSCHRIFT - MUSIK INTERNATIONAL. Text in German. 1880. bi-m. EUR 36; EUR 6.50 newsstand/cover (effective 2006). adv. charts; illus. index. **Document type:** *Magazine, Trade.*
Former titles (until 1988): Musik International (0720-0439); (until 1980): Instrumentbau (0342-1775); (until 1975): Instrumentbau-Zeitschrift (0020-4390)
Indexed: IBR, IBZ, M11, MusicInd, RILM, T02.
—Linda Hall.
Published by: (Musik International Instrumentenbau), Verlag Franz Schmitt, Kaiserstr 99-101, Siegburg, 53721, Germany. TEL 49-2241-62925, FAX 49-2241-53891, verlagschmitt@aol.com, http://www.verlagfranzschmitt.de. Ed. M Moeckel. adv.: B&W page EUR 1,392, color page EUR 2,018. Circ: 2,520 (paid and controlled).

780 DEU ISSN 0936-014X
INSTRUMENTENBAU REPORT; aktuelle Informationen fuer Musikfreunde und Instrumentenbauer. Text in German. 1984. s-a. EUR 10 (effective 2006). bk.rev.; music rev.; rec.rev. 30 p./no. 2 cols./p.; back issues avail. **Document type:** *Consumer.*
Address: Laerchenstr 23, Zorneding, 85604, Germany. TEL 49-8106-22476, http://www.wilhelmerlewein.homepage.t-online.de/. Ed., Adv. contact Wilhelm Erlewein. Circ: 1,200.

M

780 POL
INSTRUMENTY OD A DO Z. Text in Polish. 1966. irreg. price varies. adv. **Document type:** *Monographic series.* **Description:** Series about musical instruments: their history, description, sound properties, orchestral use.
Published by: Polskie Wydawnictwo Muzyczne, Al Krasinskiego 11 a, Krakow, 31111, Poland. TEL 48-12-4227044, FAX 48-12-4220174. R&P Janina Warzecha. Adv. contact Elzbieta Widlak.

780 100 USA ISSN 1073-6913
ML1
➤ **INTEGRAL.** Text in English. 1987. a. USD 25 per issue to individuals; USD 55 per issue to institutions; USD 15 per issue to students (effective 2011). bk.rev. back issues avail. **Document type:** *Journal, Academic/Scholarly.* **Description:** Publishes articles and reviews on music theory, analysis, criticism and their relationship to composition and performance.
Indexed: A01, CA, IIMP, M11, MAG, MusicInd, PCI, RILM, T02.
Address: Eastman School of Music, 26 Gibbs St, Rochester, NY 14604. Eds. Justin Lundberg, Michael Callahan.

➤ **L'INTEGRALE (GRAINVILLE).** *see* BIOGRAPHY

780 USA
INTENSITY. Text in English. 1990. 6/yr. USD 14. adv. back issues avail. **Description:** Covers new music bands from Washington.
Address: 2502 W Opal St, Pasco, WA 99301-3352. TEL 509-545-6747. Ed. John Book.

780 USA ISSN 0195-6655
ML1
INTER-AMERICAN MUSIC REVIEW. Text in English. 1978. irreg. price varies. bk.rev.; music rev. bibl.; illus. **Document type:** *Journal, Academic/Scholarly.*
Related titles: Online - full text ed.
Indexed: H21, IBR, IBZ, IIMP, M11, MusicInd, P08, PCI, RILM.
—Ingenta.
Published by: Theodore Front Musical Literature, Inc., 16122 Cohasset St, Van Nuys, CA 91406. TEL 818-994-1902, FAX 818-994-0419, music@tfront.com. Ed. Robert Stevenson.

780 DEU ISSN 1435-5590
INTERCULTURAL MUSIC STUDIES. Text in German. 1990. irreg., latest vol.14, 2009. price varies. **Document type:** *Monographic series, Academic/Scholarly.*
Indexed: AnthLit.
Published by: (International Institute for Traditional Music), V W B - Verlag fuer Wissenschaft und Bildung, Postfach 110368, Berlin, 10833, Germany. TEL 49-30-2510415, FAX 49-30-2511136, info@vwb-verlag.com.

INTERFACE (AMSTERDAM, 1995). *see* SOUND RECORDING AND REPRODUCTION

781.57 USA
INTERMISSION (LONG BEACH). Text in English. 1968. m. USD 15 (effective 2000). adv. bk.rev. back issues avail. **Document type:** *Newsletter.* **Description:** Preservation and education of Dixieland jazz. Information on scheduled jazz shows and places to perform jazz music.
Published by: New Orleans Jazz Club of Southern California, PO Box 15212, Long Beach, CA 90815. TEL 562-867-7501. Ed., Pub., Adv. contact Bill McCormack. R&P Joy McCormack TEL 714-532-5039. Circ: 300.

781.62 USA ISSN 1933-4974
ML3551.7.U89
INTERMOUNTAIN ACOUSTIC MUSICIAN. Text in English. m. adv. **Document type:** *Magazine, Consumer.* **Description:** Dedicated to the preservation, furtherance and spread of acoustic music, including bluegrass, British Isles, folk, old-time and related musical forms.
Published by: Intermountain Acoustic Music Association, PO Box 520521, Salt Lake City, UT 84152. TEL 801-339-7664, iamaprez@iamaweb.org. Ed. Barb Cantonwine. Adv. contact Bangs Tapscott.

791.547 USA ISSN 1095-0605
ML3519
INTERNATIONAL BLUEGRASS. Text in English. 1985. bi-m. USD 40 (effective 2001). bk.rev.; film rev.; music rev.; rec.rev.; video rev. 20 p./no.; back issues avail. **Document type:** *Newsletter, Trade.* **Description:** Contains news and articles aimed at bluegrass music professionals and fans.
Related titles: Audio cassette/tape ed.
Published by: International Bluegrass Music Association, 2 Music Cir S., Ste. 100, Nashville, TN 37203-4381. TEL 270-684-9025, FAX 270-686-7863, ibma1@occ-uky.campus.mci.net. Ed., R&P Nancy Cardwell TEL 888-438-4262. Circ: 4,600.

784 USA ISSN 0896-0968
ML1499
INTERNATIONAL CHORAL BULLETIN. Text in English, French, German, Spanish. 1981. q. USD 46 to individuals; USD 25 to libraries (effective 2000). adv. back issues avail. **Document type:** *Bulletin.* **Description:** Contains articles dealing with choral music and choral activities throughout the world. Lists festivals, workshops and competitions.
Indexed: MAG.
—Ingenta.
Published by: International Federation for Choral Music, c/o Michael J Anderson, University of Illinois at Chicago, Dept of Performing Arts (M/C 255), 1040 West Harrison St, L042, Chicago, IL 60607-7130. TEL 312-996-8744, FAX 312-996-0954. Ed. Jutta Tagger. Circ: 2,500.

788.8419 GBR ISSN 1744-7356
➤ **INTERNATIONAL CONCERTINA ASSOCIATION. PAPERS.** Abbreviated title: P I C A. Text in English. 2004. a. GBP 5 per issue to non-members; free to members (effective 2009). bk.rev. back issues avail. **Document type:** *Journal, Academic/Scholarly.* **Description:** Covers all aspects of the concertina including the development and history of the instrument, its sociology, iconography, repertories, and performance practices, biographies of concertinists, etc.
Related titles: Online - full text ed.: ISSN 1744-7364.
Indexed: RILM.
—CCC.
Published by: International Concertina Association, 17 Nursery Rd, Bishops Stortford, Herts CM23 3HJ, United Kingdom. TEL 44-1279-656664, FAX 44-1279-863353, secretary@comcertina.org. Ed. Allan W Atlas TEL 212-817-8590. **Co-publisher:** City University of New York, Centre for the Study of Free-Reed Instruments.

781.7 AUS ISSN 0739-1390
ML26
INTERNATIONAL COUNCIL FOR TRADITIONAL MUSIC. BULLETIN. Short title: Bulletin of the I C T M. Text in English, French, German. 1948. s-a. includes subscr. with Yearbook for Traditional Music. back issues avail. **Document type:** *Bulletin, Trade.* **Description:** Features ICTM news, calendar of future events and reports from study groups, national committees and liaison officers.
Formerly (until 1981): International Folk Music Council. Bulletin (0020-6768)
Related titles: Online - full text ed.: free (effective 2009).
Indexed: AICP, IIMP, M11, RILM, T02.
—INIST. CCC.
Published by: International Council for Traditional Music, ICTM Secretariat, Australian National University, School of Music, Bldg 100, Canberra, ACT 0200, Australia. TEL 61-2-61255700, FAX 61-2-61259775, secretariat@ictmusic.org. Ed. Lee Anne Proberts.

780.71 AUS
INTERNATIONAL DIRECTORY OF MUSIC EDUCATION AND MUSIC EDUCATION INSTITUTIONS. Text in English. 1996. quadrennial. AUD 180 (effective 2000). **Document type:** *Directory.* **Description:** Provides information on over 4000 music institutions in 160 countries.
Formerly: International Directory of Music Education
Related titles: CD-ROM ed.
Published by: The Callaway Centre, University of Western Australia, School of Music, 35 Stirling Hwy, Crawley, W.A. 6009, Australia. TEL 61-8-64882051, FAX 61-8-64881076, callaway@uwa.edu.au, http://www.callaway.uwa.edu.au/.

786 USA
INTERNATIONAL HORN SOCIETY. DIRECTORY (ONLINE). Text in English. 19??. a. free to members (effective 2010). **Document type:** *Directory, Trade.*
Formerly: International Horn Society. Directory (Print)
Media: Online - full text.
Published by: International Horn Society, c/o Heidi Vogel, PO Box 630158, Laniai City, HI 96763. TEL 808-565-7273, FAX 808-565-7273, exec-secretary@hornsociety.org, http://www.hornsociety.org.

781.65 USA ISSN 1077-9892
ML3505.8
INTERNATIONAL JAZZ ARCHIVES JOURNAL. Text in English. 1993. a. **Document type:** *Journal, Academic/Scholarly.* **Description:** Presents research on jazz scholarship and publishes manuscripts and transcriptions of the music of internationally acclaimed musicians.
Indexed: RILM.
Published by: University of Pittsburgh, Sonny Rollins International Jazz Archives, Jazz Studies, Pittsburgh, PA 15260. TEL 412-624-4187, FAX 412 624-8805, ndavis@pitt.edu, http://www.pitt.edu/~pittjazz/sonny.html. Ed. Nathan Davis.

780 GBR ISSN 1548-145X
ML1087
INTERNATIONAL JEW'S HARP SOCIETY. JOURNAL. Text in Multiple languages. 1982. a. free to members (effective 2011). bk.rev.; Website rev.; rec.rev. bibl.; illus. 90 p./no.; back issues avail. **Document type:** *Journal, Academic/Scholarly.* **Description:** Publishes articles, reviews, checklists, discographies, bibliographies relating to the Jew's-harp.
Formerly (until 2004): Vierundzwanzigsteljahrsschrift der Internationalen Maultrommelvirtuosengenossenschaft (1090-1302)
Indexed: RILM.
Address: c/o Michael Wright, 77 Beech Rd, Wheatley, Oxon OX33 1UD, United Kingdom. TEL 44-1865-872161, jewsharper@btinternet.com.

780 DEU ISSN 0723-9769
INTERNATIONAL JOSEPH MARTIN KRAUS-GESELLSCHAFT. MITTEILUNGEN. Text in German. 1983. irreg. EUR 4 per vol. (effective 2003). adv. music rev.; bk.rev. **Document type:** *Bulletin, Academic/Scholarly.*
Indexed: RILM.
Published by: Internationale Joseph Martin Kraus-Gesellschaft e.V., Kellereistr 25-29, Buchen, 74722, Germany. TEL 49-6281-8898, FAX 49-6281-556898, info@kraus-gesellschaft.de, http://www.kraus-gesellschaft.de.

780 USA ISSN 1550-7327
MT87
➤ **INTERNATIONAL JOURNAL OF COMMUNITY MUSIC.** Text in English. 2004. s-a. **Document type:** *Journal, Academic/Scholarly.* **Description:** Publishes research articles, practical discussions, timely reviews, readers' notes and special issues concerning all aspects of Community Music.
Media: Online - full text.
Indexed: A39, C27, C29, D03, D04, E13, R14, S14, S15, S18.
Published by: New York University, The Steinhardt School, Office of the Dean, 82 Washington Sq E, 4th Fl, New York, NY 10003. TEL 212-998-5000, http://steinhardt.nyu.edu/. Eds. David J Elliott, Lee Higgens.

780 GBR ISSN 1752-6299
➤ **INTERNATIONAL JOURNAL OF COMMUNITY MUSIC.** Abbreviated title: I J C M. Text in English. 200?. 3/yr. GBP 36, USD 68 to individuals; GBP 235, USD 195 to institutions (effective 2012). adv. back issues avail. **Document type:** *Journal, Academic/Scholarly.* **Description:** Publishes research articles, practical discussions, timely reviews, readers' notes and special issues concerning all aspects of community music.
Related titles: Online - full text ed.: ISSN 1752-6302. GBP 192, USD 145 (effective 2012).
Indexed: A01, CA, M11, T02.
—BLDSC (4542.172603). CCC.
Published by: Intellect Ltd., The Mill, Parnall Rd, Fishponds, Bristol, BS16 3JG, United Kingdom. TEL 44-117-9589910, FAX 44-117-9589911, info@intellectbooks.com, http://www.intellectbooks.co.uk/. Ed. Lee Higgins. Pub. Masoud Yazdani. **Subscr. to:** Turpin Distribution Services Ltd., Pegasus Dr, Stratton Business Park, Biggleswade, Bedfordshire SG18 8QB, United Kingdom. TEL 44-1767-604951, FAX 44-1767-601640, custserv@turpin-distribution.com, http://www.turpin-distribution.com/.

780.7 GBR ISSN 0255-7614
ML5
➤ **INTERNATIONAL JOURNAL OF MUSIC EDUCATION.** Text in English; Summaries in French, German, Spanish. 1967. q. USD 685, GBP 370 combined subscription to institutions (print & online eds.); USD 671, GBP 363 to institutions (effective 2011). adv. bk.rev. illus. back issues avail.; reprint service avail. from PSC. **Document type:** *Journal, Academic/Scholarly.* **Description:** Provides academic papers on various aspects of music education throughout the world.
Incorporates (2002-2003): Music Education International (1448-3238)
Related titles: Microfiche ed.: (from PQC); Microform ed.: (from PQC); Online - full text ed.: ISSN 1744-795X. USD 617, GBP 333 to institutions (effective 2011); ◆ Supplement(s): Australian Journal of Music Education. ISSN 0004-9484.
Indexed: A20, A22, AEI, ASSIA, ArtHuCI, B29, CA, CPE, CurCont, DIP, E01, E03, ERI, ERO, I14, IBR, IBZ, IIMP, M11, MusicInd, P03, PCI, PsycInfo, PsychoIAb, RILM, SCOPUS, T02, W07.
—BLDSC (4542.368500), IE, Ingenta. CCC.
Published by: (International Society for Music Education AUS), Sage Publications Ltd. (Subsidiary of: Sage Publications, Inc.), 1 Oliver's Yard, 55 City Rd, London, EC1Y 1SP, United Kingdom. TEL 44-20-73248500, FAX 44-20-73248600, info@sagepub.co.uk, http://www.uk.sagepub.com/home.nav. Eds. Beatriz Ilari, Christopher Johnson. adv.: B&W page GBP 450; 140 x 210. **Subscr. in the Americas to:** Sage Publications, Inc., 2455 Teller Rd, Thousand Oaks, CA 91320. TEL 805-499-9774, FAX 805-499-0871, journals@sagepub.com.

780 DEU ISSN 0941-9535
ML5
INTERNATIONAL JOURNAL OF MUSICOLOGY. Text in English, French, German, Italian, Spanish. 1992. a. EUR 75 domestic; CHF 98 in Switzerland; EUR 70 in Europe; GBP 61, USD 98 (effective 2011). **Document type:** *Journal, Academic/Scholarly.* **Description:** Disseminates research and study into the theory of music throughout the ages.
Indexed: DIP, E16, ERA, IBR, IBZ, M12, MusicInd, RILM, S19, S21, V05.
Published by: Peter Lang GmbH (Subsidiary of: Peter Lang Publishing Group), Eschborner Landstr 42-50, Frankfurt Am Main, 60489, Germany. TEL 49-69-7807050, FAX 49-69-78070550, zentrale.frankfurt@peterlang.com. Eds. Elliott Antokoletz, Michael von Albrecht. Circ: 400.

790 HUN ISSN 0133-8749
INTERNATIONAL KODALY SOCIETY. BULLETIN. Text mainly in English; Text occasionally in German, French. 1976. s-a. USD 15 (effective 2004). **Document type:** *Journal, Academic/Scholarly.* **Description:** Contains articles about Kodaly's compositions, about the application of his principles of music education, and about other topics of interest to its members.
Indexed: RILM.
Published by: International Kodaly Society, PO Box 67, Budapest, H-1364, Hungary. kodaly@axelero.hu, http://www.iks.hu/.

780 ZAF
INTERNATIONAL LIBRARY OF AFRICAN MUSIC. SYMPOSIA ON ETHNOMUSICOLOGY. Text in English. 1980. a. USD 22 (effective 2000). **Document type:** *Proceedings, Academic/Scholarly.*
Indexed: AbAn.
Published by: International Library of African Music, Institute of Social and Economic Research, Rhodes University, Grahamstown, East Cape 6140, South Africa. TEL 27-46-603-8557, FAX 27-46-622-4411, c.webbstock@ru.ac.za, http://ilam.ru.ac.za. Ed. Andrew Tracey.

780 CAN ISSN 1922-3293
INTERNATIONAL MILITARY MUSIC SOCIETY. CANADIAN BRANCH. NEWSLETTER. Text in English. 1978. q. free to members (effective 2010). back issues avail. **Document type:** *Newsletter, Trade.*
Published by: International Military Music Society, Canadian Branch, c/o Roger McGuire, 132 Wellington Ave, Victoria, BC V8V 4H7, Canada. xcv@telus.net, http://www.imms-online.org/canada.html.

780 GBR ISSN 2047-3516
INTERNATIONAL MILITARY MUSIC SOCIETY. UNITED KINGDOM (FOUNDER) BRANCH. NEWSLETTER. Text in English. 1988. q. free to members (effective 2011). **Document type:** *Newsletter, Trade.*
Published by: International Military Music Society, United Kingdom (Founder) Branch, c/o Nigel P Ellis, 3 Rydal Close, Stowmarket, Suffolk, IP14 1QX, United Kingdom. http://www.imms-uk.org.uk/. Ed. Andy Smith.

780 DEU ISSN 1613-866X
INTERNATIONAL MUSIC DIRECTORY. VOL. 1: PERFORMED MUSIC, CONCERT MANAGEMENT AND PROMOTION AGENCIES, TEACHING AND INSTRUCTION. Text in English. 1999. biennial. EUR 368 (effective 2008). **Document type:** *Directory, Trade.* **Description:** Documents all genres and sectors of the European music industry, including music publishers, orchestras, concert managers, and promotion agencies.
Formerly (until 2004): European Music Directory. Vol. 1: Orchestras, Competitions and Prizes, Festivals, Agencies, Radio and Television, Associations and Foundations, Teaching and Instruction, Documentation and Research (1438-5392)
Published by: De Gruyter Saur (Subsidiary of: Walter de Gruyter GmbH & Co. KG), Mies-van-der-Rohe-Str 1, Munich, 80807, Germany. TEL 49-89-769020, FAX 49-89-76902150, wdg-info@degruyter.com.

780 DEU ISSN 1613-8678
INTERNATIONAL MUSIC DIRECTORY. VOLUME 2: RADIO AND TELEVISION, MUSIC PUBLISHERS, DOCUMENTATION AND RESEARCH, NATIONAL MUSIC COUNCILS, ASSOCIATIONS AND FOUNDATIONS, INDEXES. Text in English. 1999. biennial. EUR 368 per vol. (effective 2008). **Document type:** *Directory, Trade.*
Formerly (until 2004): European Music Directory. Volume 2: Music Industry, Trade, Studios and Record Companies, Music Publishers, Indexes (1438-5406)
Published by: De Gruyter Saur (Subsidiary of: Walter de Gruyter GmbH & Co. KG), Mies-van-der-Rohe-Str 1, Munich, 80807, Germany. TEL 49-89-769020, FAX 49-89-76902150, wdg-info@degruyter.com.

331.8 780 USA ISSN 0020-8051
ML1
INTERNATIONAL MUSICIAN. Text in English. 1901. m. USD 39 domestic to non-members; USD 54 foreign to non-members; free to members (effective 2010). adv. bk.rev. illus. reprints avail. **Document type:** *Magazine, Trade.* **Description:** Provides professional musicians with book and website reviews, new product spotlights, health topics, instrument sales, audition notices, and an extensive classified advertising section.
Related titles: Microform ed.: (from PQC); Online - full text ed.
Indexed: A22, IIMP, M11, MAG, MusicInd, PMR, T02.
Published by: American Federation of Musicians of the United States and Canada, 120 Walton St., Ste 300, Syracuse, NY 13202. TEL 315-422-4488, FAX 315-422-3837, http://www.afm.org. Pub. Sam Folio. Adv. contact Honore Stockley. color page USD 5,145. Circ: 94,886 (paid).

786.2 GBR ISSN 2042-0773
INTERNATIONAL PIANO. Text in English. 1997. bi-m. GBP 33 domestic; GBP 51 in Europe; GBP 83 elsewhere (effective 2011). adv. back issues avail. **Document type:** *Magazine, Consumer.* **Description:** Covers interviews with the world's leading pianists and rising talent, and retrospectives on the piano greats of the past.
Formerly (until 2001): International Piano Quarterly (1368-9770)
Indexed: A01, IBR, IBZ, M11, RILM, T02.
—IE. **CCC.**
Published by: Rhinegold Publishing Ltd., 239-241 Shaftesbury Ave, London, WC2H 8TF, United Kingdom. TEL 44-845-1948944, FAX 44-845-1948945, rhinegoldcs@optimabiz.co.uk, http://www.rhinegold.co.uk.

780 HRV ISSN 0351-5796
ML5
INTERNATIONAL REVIEW OF THE AESTHETICS AND SOCIOLOGY OF MUSIC. Text in English, French, German; Summaries in English, Croatian. 1970. s-a. USD 42 (effective 2005). adv. bk.rev. bibl. back issues avail.; reprints avail. **Document type:** *Journal, Academic/Scholarly.* **Description:** Features original scholarly articles on music aesthetics, the sociology of music, the social history of music, and the history of ideas in music.
Formerly: International Review of Music Aesthetics and Sociology (0047-1208)
Related titles: Online - full text ed.
Indexed: A01, A20, A22, ASCA, ArtHuCI, CA, CurCont, DIP, IBR, IBZ, IIMP, M11, MusicInd, PCI, RILM, S02, S03, SCOPUS, T02, W07.
—IE, Infotrieve, Ingenta.
Published by: Hrvatsko Muzikolosko Drustvo/Croatian Musicological Society, Ilica 16/III, Zagreb, 10000, Croatia. TEL 385-1-4851370, FAX 385-1-4684701, info@hmd-music.hr, http://www.hmd-music.hr. Ed. Stanislav Tuksar. Circ: 800.

781.91 USA
INTERNATIONAL SHAKUHACHI SOCIETY. ANNALS. Text in English. a.
Published by: International Shakuhachi Society, Box 294, Willits, CA 95490. TEL 707-459-3402, FAX 707-459-3434, monty@shakuhachi.com, http://www.shakuhachi.com/.

INTERNATIONAL SINATRA SOCIETY NEWSLETTER. *see* CLUBS

780 281.9 FIN ISSN 1796-9581
INTERNATIONAL SOCIETY FOR ORTHODOX CHURCH MUSIC. PUBLICATIONS. Text in Multiple languages. 2007. irreg. EUR 25 per issue (effective 2007). **Document type:** *Monographic series, Academic/Scholarly.*
Published by: International Society for Orthodox Church Music, c/o Faculty of Music, University of Joensuu, PO Box 111, Joensuu, 80101, Finland. mtakala@joensuu.fi. Ed. Ivan Moody.

370 780 729.8 792 USA ISSN 2153-3776
▼ **INTERNATIONAL STUDIES FOR NON-TRADITIONAL STUDENTS: PEDAGOGY OF PERFORMING ARTS AND MUSIC.** Text in English. forthcoming 2010 (Aug.). a. USD 25 per issue (effective 2010). **Document type:** *Academic/Scholarly.* **Description:** Guide for music, theater and dance teachers working with non-traditional students.
Published by: International Consultation for Educators, LLC, 1015 Essex St, SE, Minneapolis, MN 55414. TEL 612-245-4471, publication@eduice.com, http://www.eduice.com/.

780 USA
INTERNATIONAL TALENT & TOURING GUIDE. Text in English. 1978. a. (Oct.). USD 179 per issue (effective 2011). adv. **Document type:** *Directory, Trade.* **Description:** Source for US and international talent, booking agencies, facilities, services and products.
Former titles (until 1986): Billboard International Talent and Touring Directory (Year) (0732-0124); (until 1982): Billboard's International Talent Directory (0190-9649); Incorporates: Billboard's on Tour (0361-5383); Campus Attractions (0067-8597); Which was formerly (1964-1968): Billboard. Music on Campus
Related titles: Microfilm ed.: (from PQC); Online - full text ed.
—**CCC.**
Published by: Billboard Directories (Subsidiary of: Nielsen Business Publications), PO Box 15158, North Hollywood, CA 91606. TEL 818-487-4582, 800-562-2706, info@billboard.com, http://www.billboard.com.

780 USA ISSN 0145-3513
ML1
INTERNATIONAL TROMBONE ASSOCIATION. JOURNAL. Text in English. 1971. 3/yr. USD 20. adv. bk.rev.
Formerly (until 1981): International Trombone Association. Newsletter
Indexed: A01, H20, IIMP, M11, MusicInd, RILM, T02.
—Ingenta.
Published by: International Trombone Association, Music Department, North Texas State University, Denton, TX 76203. Ed. Vern Kagarice. Circ: 3,500.

780 USA ISSN 0363-5708
INTERNATIONAL TROMBONE ASSOCIATION SERIES. Text in English. irreg.
Published by: Brass Press, c/o RKMS, 140 Main St, N, Easton, MA 02356. FAX 508-238-2571. Ed. Stephen L Glover.

780 USA ISSN 8755-5964
ML17
INTERNATIONAL TRUMPET GUILD. MEMBERSHIP DIRECTORY. Text in English. 19??. a. free to members (effective 2010). **Document type:** *Directory, Academic/Scholarly.*
Published by: International Trumpet Guild, 109 McCain Auditorium, Kansas State University, Manhattan, KS 66506. president@trumpetguild.org.

780 GBR ISSN 1740-0155
ML105
INTERNATIONAL WHO'S WHO IN CLASSICAL MUSIC (YEAR). Text in English. 1935. a. USD 460 per issue (effective 2009). 1104 p./no.; **Document type:** *Directory, Trade.* **Description:** Contains details of approximately 8,000 composers, singers, conductors, arrangers, writers, soloists, orchestral players, managers, impressarios, and others connected with the world of classical and light classical music.
Formerly (until 2002): International Who's Who in Music and Musicians' Directory. Vol. 1: Classical and Light Classical; Which superseded in part: International Who's Who in Music and Musicians' Directory (0307-2894); Which was formerly: Who's Who in Music and Musicians' International Directory (0083-9647)
Indexed: CA&I, PABMI.
—BLDSC (4552.107000). **CCC.**
Published by: Routledge (Subsidiary of: Taylor & Francis Group), 2 Park Sq, Milton Park, Abingdon, Oxon OX14 4RN, United Kingdom. TEL 44-20-70176000, FAX 44-20-70176699, orders@taylorandfrancis.com.

781.64 GBR ISSN 1740-0163
ML105
INTERNATIONAL WHO'S WHO IN POPULAR MUSIC (YEAR). Text in English. 1996. a. USD 420 per issue (effective 2009). reprints avail. **Document type:** *Directory, Trade.* **Description:** Provides biographical information for approximately 5,000 of the world's leading and up-and-coming singers, musicians, managers and other individuals involved in all fields of popular music.
Formerly (until 2002): International Who's Who in Music and Musicians' Directory. Vol. 2: Popular Music; Which superseded in part: International Who's Who in Music and Musicians' Directory (0307-2894); Which was formerly: Who's Who in Music and Musicians' International Directory (0083-9647)
—BLDSC (4552.114250). **CCC.**
Published by: Routledge (Subsidiary of: Taylor & Francis Group), 2 Park Sq, Milton Park, Abingdon, Oxon OX14 4RN, United Kingdom. TEL 44-20-70176000, FAX 44-20-70176699, orders@taylorandfrancis.com.

780 DEU ISSN 1012-8034
INTERNATIONALE BACHAKADEMIE STUTTGART. SCHRIFTENREIHE. Text in German. 1988. irreg., latest vol.14, 2004. **Document type:** *Monographic series, Academic/Scholarly.*
Published by: Internationale Bachakademie Stuttgart, Johann-Sebastian-Bach-Platz, Stuttgart, 70178, Germany. TEL 49-711-619210, FAX 49-711-6192123, office@bachakademie.de, http://www.bachakademie.de.

781 DEU ISSN 1616-8380
INTERNATIONALE MAX REGER GESELLSCHAFT. MITTEILUNGEN. Text in German. 2000. 2/yr. **Document type:** *Journal, Academic/Scholarly.*
Indexed: RILM.
Published by: Internationale Max Reger Gesellschaft e.V., Pfinztalstr 7, Karlsruhe, 76227, Germany. TEL 49-721-854501, FAX 49-721-854502, mri@uni-karlsruhe.de. Ed. Wolfgang Rihm.

780 AUT
INTERNATIONALE SCHOENBERG-GESELLSCHAFT. PUBLIKATIONEN. Text in German. 1978. irreg., latest vol.4, 2001. **Document type:** *Monographic series, Academic/Scholarly.*
Published by: Internationale Schoenberg-Gesellschaft, Hegelgasse 13-22, Vienna, 1010, Austria. TEL 43-1-5126869, FAX 43-1-51268699.

780 DEU
INTERNATIONALE SIEGFRIED WAGNER GESELLSCHAFT. NEUE SCHRIFTENREIHE. Text in German. 1972. irreg. price varies. **Document type:** *Monographic series, Academic/Scholarly.*
Formerly (until 2003): Internationale Siegfried Wagner Gesellschaft. Schriftenreihe (1612-4049)
Published by: (Internationale Siegfried Wagner Gesellschaft e.V.), Centaurus Verlag & Media KG, Kaiser-Joseph-Str 267, Freiburg, 79098, Germany. TEL 49-761-1525861, FAX 49-761-1525868, info@centaurus-verlag.de, http://www.centaurus-verlag.de.

780 AUT ISSN 0541-2331
➤ **INTERNATIONALE STIFTUNG MOZARTEUM. MITTEILUNGEN.** Text in German. 1952. s-a. adv. bk.rev. illus. index. **Document type:** *Journal, Academic/Scholarly.* **Description:** Features historical and musical information, reviews and analysis of his works, Mozart's contemporaries, foundation news, and news of Mozart societies. Includes announcement of events and exhibitions.
Indexed: DIP, IBR, IBZ, IIMP, M11, MusicInd, RILM.
Published by: Internationale Stiftung Mozarteum, Schwarzstrasse 26, Salzburg, Sa 5020, Austria. TEL 43-662-88940, FAX 43-662-8894036, schmutzler@mozarteum.at. Ed., R&P, Adv. contact Rudolph Angermueller. Circ: 2,000.

780 AUT ISSN 0580-1184
INTERNATIONALE STIFTUNG MOZARTEUM SALZBURG. SCHRIFTENREIHE. Text in German. 1966. irreg., latest vol.10, 1993. price varies. **Document type:** *Monographic series, Academic/Scholarly.*
Published by: Internationale Stiftung Mozarteum Salzburg, Schwarzstr 26, Salzburg, 5020, Austria. TEL 43-662-8894030, FAX 43-662-8894036, office@mozarteum.at, http://www.mozarteum.at.

780 USA
INTERPLAY (HILLSDALE); music in interdisciplinary dialogue. Text in English. 2000. irreg., latest vol.7, 2009. price varies. back issues avail. **Document type:** *Monographic series, Trade.*
Published by: Pendragon Press, PO Box 190, Hillsdale, NY 12529. TEL 518-325-6100, FAX 518-325-6102, orders@pendragonpress.com. Ed. Sigland Bruhn.

780.71 CAN ISSN 1911-0146
ML5
➤ **INTERSECTIONS/REVUE DE MUSIQUE DES UNIVERSITES CANADIENNES.** Text in English, French. 1971; N.S. 1980. s-a. CAD 40 in North America; USD 45 foreign (effective 2005). bk.rev. back issues avail.; reprints avail. **Document type:** *Journal, Academic/Scholarly.* **Description:** Publishes articles on all aspects of music research or criticism as well as reports on musical conferences held in Canada.
Former titles (until 2005): Canadian University Music Review (0710-0353); (until 1980): Canadian Association of University Schools of Music. Journal. (0315-3541)
Related titles: Microfilm ed.: N.S. (from PQC).
Indexed: A01, A22, A26, C03, CA, CBCARef, CMPI, CPerl, E08, I05, IIMP, M11, MusicInd, P48, PQC, RILM, S09, T02.
—IE, Ingenta.
Published by: Canadian University Music Society, PO Box 507, Sta Q, Toronto, ON M4T 2M5, Canada. TEL 416-483-7282, FAX 416-489-1713, intersections@cums-smuc.ca. Ed. James Deaville. Circ: 400 (paid). **Subscr. to:** Becker Associates, Station Q, PO Box 507, Toronto, ON M4T 2M5, Canada. TEL 416-483-7282, FAX 416-489-1713, journals@interlog.com, http://www.interlog.com/~jbecker.

780.01 CHE ISSN 1661-5883
INTERUNIVERSITAERE SCHRIFTEN ZUR MUSIKPAEDAGOGIK UND MUSIKWISSENSCHAFT. Text in German. 2007. irreg. price varies. **Document type:** *Monographic series, Academic/Scholarly.*
Published by: Peter Lang AG (Subsidiary of: Peter Lang Publishing Group), Hochfeldstr 32, Postfach 746, Bern 9, 3000, Switzerland. TEL 41-31-3061717, FAX 41-31-3061727, info@peterlang.com. Eds. Christoph Khittl, Peter Maria Krakauer.

780.6 DEU ISSN 0579-8353
INTERVALLE; A M J Informationen. Text in German. s-a. adv. bk.rev. back issues avail. **Document type:** *Journal, Trade.* **Description:** Reports on the activities of the Arbeitskreis.
Published by: Arbeitskreis Musik in der Jugend, Adersheimer Str 60, Wolfenbuettel, 38304, Germany. TEL 49-5331-46016, FAX 49-5331-43723, AMJMusikinderJugend@t-online.de. Ed. Wolfram Koessler.

780 020 FIN ISSN 1796-7392
INTERVALLI (ONLINE). Text in Finnish. 1988. q. Index. back issues avail. **Document type:** *Magazine, Trade.*
Formerly (until 2007): Intervalli (Print) (0785-2843)
Media: Online - full content.
Published by: Suomen Musiikkikirjastoyhdistys ry/Finnish Music Library Association, PO Box 148, Vantaa, 01301, Finland. TEL 358-9-83923473, FAX 358-9-8736471, musakir@kaapeli.fi. Ed. Heikki Poroila.

781.64 DEU
INTRO. Text in German. 1991. 11/yr. EUR 25 domestic; EUR 30 foreign (effective 2006). adv. **Document type:** *Magazine, Consumer.* **Description:** Contains a wide variety of information and reviews for music fans and professionals.
Published by: Intro GmbH & Co. KG, Herwarthstr 12, Cologne, 50672, Germany. TEL 49-221-5890903, FAX 49-221-5626509, redaktion@intro.de. Ed. Thomas Venker. Adv. contact Oliver Bresch. B&W page EUR 4,600, color page EUR 5,350. Circ: 122,796 (paid and controlled).

780.7 USA ISSN 0021-0609
THE IOWA MUSIC EDUCATOR. Text in English. 1946. 3/yr. adv. bk.rev. tr.lit. **Document type:** *Magazine, Trade.* **Description:** Deals with music activities in the state of Iowa as well as music education in general.
Published by: Iowa Music Educators Association, c/o Lance Lehmberg, Ed, Department of Music, Morningside College, Sioux City, IA 51106. TEL 712-274-5218, FAX 712-274-5101, hllool@calpha.morningside.edu. Ed., Pub., R&P, Adv. contact Lance Lehmberg. Circ: 1,400.

781.64 USA
IPROPAGANDA. Text in English. 2000. bi-m. USD 14; USD 4.50 newsstand/cover (effective 2001). adv. **Document type:** *Magazine, Consumer.* **Description:** Contains diverse articles and features on music, fashion, cinema, art and politics.
Address: PO Box 1479, FDR Sta, New York, NY 10150-1479. TEL 212-868-0046.

780 IRL ISSN 0332-298X
ML3654
IRISH FOLK MUSIC STUDIES/EIGSE CHEOL TIRE. Text in English. 1972. irreg., latest vol.6, 2001. price varies. adv. bk.rev. bibl.
Indexed: MLA-IB, MusicInd, PCI, RILM.
Published by: Folk Music Society of Ireland, c/o Irish Traditional Music Archive, 63 Merrion Square, Dublin, 2, Ireland. http://homepage.eircom.net/~shields/fmsi/. Ed. Hugh Shields. Circ: 1,000.

781.7415 IRL ISSN 1393-211X
ML3654
IRISH MUSIC. Text in English. 1995. m. EUR 35 domestic; EUR 60 in Europe; USD 65 in United States; CAD 102 in Canada; EUR 55 elsewhere (effective 2005). adv. back issues avail. **Document type:** *Magazine, Consumer.*
Published by: Lacethorn Ltd., 11 Clare St, Dublin, 2, Ireland. TEL 353-1-6622266, FAX 353-1-6624981. adv.: color page EUR 1,073; trim 182 x 270. Circ: 18,500 (paid and controlled).

781.7 793.31 USA
IRISH MUSIC AND DANCE ASSOCIATION NEWSLETTER. Text in English, Gaelic. 1983. m. looseleaf. USD 18 domestic; USD 20 foreign (effective 2000). adv. music rev. **Document type:** *Newsletter.* **Description:** Covers items of interest to the Irish community in Minnesota.
Published by: Irish Music and Dance Association, 7563 Humboldt Cir N., Minneapolis, MN 55444-2461. TEL 612-227-5090, mnimda@hotmail.com. Ed. Joe Dowling. Adv. contact John Winston. Circ: 275 (paid).

781.7415 IRL
IRISH MUSIC NEWSLETTER. Text in English. 1999. w. **Document type:** *Newsletter.* **Description:** Provides a comprehensive round up of Irish music news.
Media: E-mail.
Published by: Irish Supplies, 52 Meadow Grove, Dundalk, Co Louth, Ireland. TEL 353-42-932-9086, FAX 353-42-932-9086, news@irishsupplies.com. Ed. Gerry Callan.

780 IRL ISSN 1393-4171
IRISH MUSICAL STUDIES. Text in English. 1990. irreg. **Document type:** *Monographic series, Academic/Scholarly.*
—BLDSC (4573.400000).
Published by: Four Courts Press, 7 Malpas St, Dublin, 8, Ireland. TEL 353-1-4534668, FAX 353-1-4534672, info@four-courts-press.ie, http://www.four-courts-press.ie.

781.64 DEU
IRON PAGES (ONLINE). Text in German. 1987. q. adv. **Document type:** *Magazine, Consumer.*
Formerly (until 2000): Iron Pages (Print)
Media: Online - full text.
Published by: I P Verlag Jeske - Mader GbR, Haydnstr 2, Berlin, 12203, Germany. TEL 49-30-86200981, FAX 49-30-86200982.

ISLENSK HLJODRITASKRA/BIBLIOGRAPHY OF ICELANDIC SOUND RECORDINGS. *see* SOUND RECORDING AND REPRODUCTION—Abstracting, Bibliographies, Statistics

780 USA
ISOLATION (KALAMAZOO). Text in English. irreg. **Description:** Features underground music, focusing on death and black metal, and industrial.
Published by: Isolation Magazine, 720-F Garland Cir, Kalamazoo, MI 49008.

780 ITA
ISTITUTO NAZIONALE DI STUDI VERDIANI. BOLLETTINO. Text in Italian. a. **Document type:** *Journal, Academic/Scholarly.*
Published by: Istituto Nazionale di Studi Verdiani, Strada della Repubblica 56, Parma, PR 43100, Italy. TEL 39-0521-385275, FAX 39-0521-287949, amministrazione@studiverdiani.it, http://www.studiverdiani.it.

ITALIANA. PER LA STORIA DELLA LINGUA SCRITTA IN ITALIA. *see* LINGUISTICS

780 IRL ISSN 1649-0215
ML287
THE J M I. (Journal of Music in Ireland) Text in English. 2000. bi-m. EUR 24.75 in Ireland & U.K.; EUR 31.75 in Europe; USD 40 elsewhere (effective 2002). adv. **Document type:** *Magazine, Consumer.* **Description:** Contains new writing on contemporary, jazz and traditional music in Ireland.
Related titles: Online - full text ed.
Indexed: IIMP, M11.
Published by: The J M I, Edenvale, Esplanade, Bray, Co. Wicklow, Ireland. TEL 353-1-2867292, FAX 353-1-2867292.

780 GBR ISSN 1749-1975
JACQUES OFFENBACK SOCIETY. NEWSLETTER. Text in English. 1997. q. free to members (effective 2009). **Document type:** *Newsletter.* **Description:** Contains articles, reviews, research and other matters surrounding the music of Jacques Offenbach.
Published by: The Jacques Offenbach Society, c/o Richard Duployen, First Fl Flat, 92 Abingdon Rd, Grandpont, Oxford, OX1 4PX, United Kingdom. duployenrichard@hotmail.com. Ed. Robert L Folstein.

780 DEU ISSN 0937-1095
JAHRBUCH ALTE MUSIK. Text in German. 1989. a. **Document type:** *Bulletin.*
Indexed: RILM.
Published by: (Akademie fuer Alte Musik), Florian Noetzel Verlag, Heinrichshofen Buecher, Holtermannstr 32, Wilhelmshaven, 26384, Germany. Eds. Gisela Jaacks, Thomas Albert. **Dist. in N. America by:** C. F. Peters Corporation, 373 Park Ave S, New York, NY 10016.

JAHRBUCH FUER LITURGIK UND HYMNOLOGIE. *see* RELIGIONS AND THEOLOGY—Protestant

780 DEU ISSN 1867-3600
JAHRBUCH MUSIK UND GENDER. Text in German. 2008. irreg., latest vol.3, 2010. price varies. **Document type:** *Monographic series, Academic/Scholarly.*
Published by: Georg Olms Verlag, Hagentorwall 7, Hildesheim, 31134, Germany. TEL 49-5121-15010, FAX 49-5121-150150, info@olms.de.

JAHRBUCH MUSIKTHERAPIE. *see* PSYCHOLOGY

780 USA ISSN 1094-9488
JAM RAG. Text in English. 1985. m. USD 27 (effective 2005). adv. rec.rev.; bk.rev.; music rev. 48 p./no. 4 cols./p.; back issues avail. **Document type:** *Magazine, Consumer.* **Description:** For ages 15-40, covers underground music scene, rock bands, politics, environmental issues, and local news.
Published by: Jam Rag Press, PO Box 20076, Ferndale, MI 48220. TEL 248-545-4215, jamrag@glis.net. Ed. Stephanie Loveless. Pub. Tom Ness. R&P Susan Ness. Adv. contact Michele Beck. Circ: 12,000.

781.64 USA
JANE'S XINE. Text in English. 1995. bi-m. **Description:** Focuses on the history of the alternative music band Jane's Addiction and the resulting bands spawned from its self destruction.
Media: Online - full text.
Address: 72 N Merkle, Columbus, OH 43209. Ed. Phil Hayes.

780 USA ISSN 1948-5921
▼ **JAQUETTA'S RECORDS NATIONWIDE ENTERTAINMENT.** Text in English. 2009. m. USD 12.99 (effective 2009). **Document type:** *Magazine, Consumer.* **Description:** Gives exposure to the artists who record at Jaquetta's Records.
Published by: Jaquetta's Records, 4045 Fairfield Ave, South Saint Petersburg, FL 33711. TEL 866-586-1118, jaquettasrecords@yahoo.com.

JAUNA GAITA. *see* ART

781.57 NLD ISSN 1568-2714
JAZZ. Text in Dutch. 1976. bi-m. EUR 36.50; EUR 7.95 newsstand/cover (effective 2009). adv. bk.rev. illus. index. back issues avail. **Document type:** *Magazine, Consumer.* **Description:** Provides information for jazz musicians and aficionados.
Former titles (until 2001): Jazz Nu (0166-7025); (until 1978): Jazz-Press (0921-6855)
Published by: Argo Media Groep bv, Postbus 9308, Amsterdam, 1006 AH, Netherlands. TEL 31-20-4107800, FAX 31-20-4107805, http://www.argomediagroep.nl. adv.: B&W page EUR 2,140, color page EUR 2,890; trim 230 x 300. Circ: 18,000.

781.57 USA ISSN 1085-8415
ML3505.8
JAZZ ARCHIVIST. Text in English. 1986. a. USD 25 to members (effective 2001). bk.rev. back issues avail. **Document type:** *Newsletter.* **Description:** Presents short, scholarly articles based on research conducted at the Archive, news of exhibits, recent donations and related features.
Published by: Hogan Jazz Archive, 304 Jones Hall, 6801 Freret St, Tulane University, New Orleans, LA 70118. TEL 504-865-5688, FAX 504-865-5761. Ed. Dr. John J Joyce. Circ: 1,500.

780 NLD ISSN 1871-9201
JAZZ BULLETIN. Text in Dutch. q. EUR 17.50; EUR 4.95 newsstand/cover (effective 2010). adv. bk.rev.; music rev. illus. back issues avail. **Document type:** *Bulletin, Academic/Scholarly.* **Description:** Covers the history of jazz and jazz musicians in the Netherlands from 1920 to the present.
Former titles (until 2005): Nederlands Jazz Archief Bulletin (0928-8120); (until 1991): National Jazz Archief Bulletin
Related titles: E-mail ed.
Published by: Stichting Nederlands Jazz Archief, Rokin 111, Amsterdam, 1012 KN, Netherlands. TEL 31-20-3446020, FAX 31-20-6733588, mic@mcn.nl, http://www.jazzarchief.nl.

781.57 AUS ISSN 0155-9680
JAZZ DOWN UNDER. Text in English. 1974. bi-m. adv. illus.
Address: PO Box 202, Camden, NSW 2570, Australia.

781.65 SWE ISSN 1654-0654
JAZZ FACTS. Text in English. 2007. 3/yr. back issues avail. **Document type:** *Newsletter, Consumer.*
Related titles: Online - full text ed.
Published by: S T I M/ Svensk Music/Swedish Performing Rights Society. Swedish Music Information Centre, Sandhamnsgatan 79, PO Box 27327, Stockholm, 10254, Sweden. TEL 46-8-7838800, FAX 46-8-7839510, swedmic@stim.se. Eds. Folke Mueller, Odd Sneeggen.

781.57 POL ISSN 0324-8801
ML3505.8
JAZZ FORUM. Text in Polish. 1965. 8/yr. USD 50 foreign (effective 2000). adv. bk.rev.; rec.rev. illus. Supplement avail.; back issues avail.; reprints avail. **Document type:** *Trade.*
Related titles: Microform ed.: (from PQC).
Published by: For Jazz Inc., Nowogrodzka 49, PO Box 102, Warsaw 81, 00-963, Poland. TEL 48-22-219451, FAX 48-22-6217758, jazzfor@jazzforumcom.pl. Ed., R&P Pawel Brodowski. Circ: 12,000.

781.65 USA
JAZZ GUITAR ONLINE. Text in English. 1995. bi-w.
Media: Online - full content.
Address: 719-B Rugby St, Orlando, FL 32804. TEL 407-481-8575, bob@jazzguitar.com. Ed. Bob Patterson.

781.57 FRA ISSN 0021-5643
ML3505.8
JAZZ HOT; la revue internationale du jazz. Text in French. 1935. 11/yr. adv. rec.rev. illus. **Document type:** *Magazine, Consumer.*
Indexed: IIMP, M11, MusicInd, T02.
Published by: Jazz Hot Publications, BP 405, Paris, Cedex 20 75969, France. TEL 33-1-43667488, FAX 33-1-43667260. Ed. Yves Sportis.

781.65 USA ISSN 1080-3572
ML3505.8
JAZZ IMPROV. Text in English. 1997. q. USD 39.95; USD 9.95 newsstand/cover (effective 2001). adv. **Document type:** *Magazine, Consumer.*
Indexed: M11, MusicInd, T02.
Published by: E.S. Proteus, Inc., P O Box 26770, Elkins Park, PA 19027. TEL 215-887-8808, FAX 215-887-8803, jazz@jazzimprov.com, http://www.jazzimprov.com. Ed. Jennifer Karpin Nemeyer. Pub. Eric Nemeyer.

781.65 USA ISSN 1556-0600
JAZZ IMPROV MAGAZINE'S NEW YORK JAZZ GUIDE. Text in English. 2005. m. USD 36 (effective 2005). **Document type:** *Magazine, Consumer.*
Related titles: Online - full text ed.
Published by: E.S. Proteus, Inc., P O Box 26770, Elkins Park, PA 19027. TEL 215-887-8808, FAX 215-887-8803, jazz@jazzimprov.com, http://www.jazzimprov.com. Eds. Graeme Dean, Winthrop Bedford. Pub. Eric Nemeyer.

781.65 USA ISSN 2150-3397
ML3505.8
▼ **JAZZ INSIDE.** Text in English. 2009. q. USD 44.95 (effective 2009). **Document type:** *Magazine, Consumer.* **Description:** Covers jazz improvization for fans and performers.
Related titles: Online - full text ed.: ISSN 2150-3400.
Indexed: T02.
Published by: Eric Nemeyer Corp., PO Box 30284, Elkins Park, PA 19027. TEL 215-885-0670, bizegzll@verizon.net.

781.65 USA ISSN 2150-3419
ML1
▼ **JAZZ INSIDE NY.** (New York) Text in English. 2009. m. USD 49.95 (effective 2009). **Document type:** *Magazine, Consumer.* **Description:** News and listings for jazz in the New York area.
Related titles: Online - full text ed.: ISSN 2150-3427.
Published by: Eric Nemeyer Corp., PO Box 30284, Elkins Park, PA 19027. TEL 215-885-0670, bizegzll@verizon.net.

781.57 658.048 USA
JAZZ INTERACTIONS. Text in English. 1965. s-m. USD 25. adv. back issues avail. **Description:** Comprehensive listing of jazz clubs and artists in NYC and its vicinity. Includes information on free summer jazz park concerts.
Published by: Jazz Interactions, Inc., PO Box 268, Glen Oaks, NY 11004. TEL 718-465-7500. Ed. R Neufeld. Circ: 300.

781.57 GBR ISSN 2041-8833
ML5
JAZZ JOURNAL. Text in English. 1974. m. GBP 45 domestic; USD 125 in United States; GBP 58 elsewhere (effective 2009). bk.rev.; rec.rev.; film rev.; video rev. illus. index. back issues avail. **Document type:** *Journal, Consumer.* **Description:** Contains articles on all aspects of Jazz music.
Incorporates (1999-2008): Jazz Review (1468-3865); Former titles (until vol.62, no.3, May 2009): Jazz Journal International (0140-2285); (until 1977): Jazz Journal; Which was formerly (until 1977): Jazz Journal and Jazz & Blues (0307-4439); Which was formed by the merger of (1948-1974): Jazz Journal (0021-5651); (1971-1974): Jazz and Blues; Which was formerly (until 1971): Jazz Monthly
Related titles: Microform ed.: (from PQC).
Indexed: A22, IIMP, M11, MusicInd, RASB, RILM, T02.
—IE, Ingenta.
Published by: Jazz Journal Ltd., 3 & 3A Forest Rd, Loughton, Essex IG10 1DR, United Kingdom. TEL 44-20-85160994. **Subscr. to:** Unit H, Ashford Business Park, Foster Rd, Ashford TN24 0SH, United Kingdom. TEL 44-1233-503614.

781.65 BLR
JAZZ-KVADRAT/JAZZ-QUAD. Text in Russian. 1997. bi-m. **Document type:** *Magazine, Consumer.*
Related titles: Online - full content ed.
Published by: Izdatel'stvo Nestor, A/ya 563, Minsk, 220113, Belarus. nestorpb@nestor.minsk.by.

781.65 JPN
JAZZ LIFE. Text in Japanese. m. **Document type:** *Consumer.*
Published by: Rittor-Sha Co. Ltd., Shioseven Bldg, 7-4 Honshio-cho, Shinjuku-ku, Tokyo, 160-0003, Japan. TEL 03-3358-6321, FAX 03-3355-2295. Ed. Kazuya Henry Masuda.

781.57 FRA ISSN 0021-566X
ML3505.8
JAZZ MAGAZINE. Text in French. 1954. m. EUR 45 domestic; EUR 60 foreign (effective 2008). adv. bk.rev.; rec.rev. illus. reprints avail. **Document type:** *Magazine, Consumer.*
Related titles: Microform ed.: (from PQC).
Indexed: IIMP, M11, MusicInd, RASB, RILM.
Published by: N E M M et Cie, 63 av. des Champs Elysees, Paris, 75008, France. Circ: 25,000.

781.65 USA
JAZZ NOTES. Text in English. 1978. m. USD 25 (effective 1999). adv. rec.rev. **Document type:** *Newsletter.* **Description:** Reviews and previews of local events of interest to jazz musicians and people who love jazz.
Published by: Twin Cities Jazz Society, PO Box 4487, St. Paul, MN 55104-0487. TEL 612-633-0329. Ed., Pub., Adv. contact Starla Barker.

781.57 USA
JAZZ NOW; the jazz world magazine. Text in English. 1991. m. (except Jan.). USD 21.65 domestic; USD 68 foreign; USD 3.50 newsstand/cover (effective 1999). adv. bk.rev.; music rev. illus. index, cum.index: 1991-1998. back issues avail. **Document type:** *Magazine, Consumer.* **Description:** Devoted to all types of jazz music, blues, and improvised music, with special emphasis on players overlooked by the media.
Formerly: California Jazz Now (1067-5213)
Related titles: Online - full text ed.
Published by: Jazz Now Magazine, PO Box 19266, Oakland, CA 94619-0266. TEL 510-531-2839, FAX 510-531-8875. Ed., Pub., Adv. contact Haybert K Houston. B&W page USD 1,088, color page USD 1,713; trim 11 x 8.5. Circ: 12,000.

781.57 CHE
JAZZ PASSION. Text in French. m. adv. bk.rev. illus. **Description:** Provides festival coverage, interviews and information to jazz fans of Switzerland.
Address: Rue a Ornette, Lussy-sur-Morges, 1133, Switzerland. TEL 021-701-1071.

781.65 GBR ISSN 1749-4060
ML3505.8
➤ **JAZZ PERSPECTIVES.** Text in English. 2007 (Apr.). 3/yr. GBP 204 combined subscription in United Kingdom to institutions (print & online eds.); EUR 293, USD 367 combined subscription to institutions (print & online eds.) (effective 2012). adv. back issues avail.; reprint service avail. from PSC. **Document type:** *Journal, Academic/Scholarly.* **Description:** Aims to bridge the jazz-as-music and jazz-as-culture divide of contemporary jazz studies, as well as to promote broader international perspectives on the jazz tradition and its legacy.
Related titles: Online - full text ed.: ISSN 1749-4079. GBP 183 in United Kingdom to institutions; EUR 264, USD 331 to institutions (effective 2012).
Indexed: A01, A22, BrHumI, CA, E01, M11, P10, PQC, RILM, T02.
—IE. **CCC.**
Published by: (Rutgers University, Institute of Jazz Studies USA), Routledge (Subsidiary of: Taylor & Francis Group), 4 Park Sq, Milton Park, Abingdon, Oxon OX14 4RN, United Kingdom. TEL 44-20-70176000, FAX 44-20-70176336, subscriptions@tandf.co.uk, http://www.routledge.com. Ed. John Howland. Adv. contact Linda Hann TEL 44-1344-779945. **Subscr. to:** Taylor & Francis Ltd., Journals Customer Service, Sheepen Pl, Colchester, Essex CO3 3LP, United Kingdom. TEL 44-20-70175544, FAX 44-20-70175198.

781.65 USA
JAZZ PLAYER. Text in English. 1993. bi-m. USD 35; USD 45 foreign; includes instructional compact disc. music rev.; video rev. **Document type:** *Magazine, Trade.* **Description:** Helps jazz musicians improve their technique. Also contains articles and columns to enthusiasts of all forms of jazz.
Indexed: IIMP.
Published by: Dorn Publications, Inc., PO Box 206, Medfield, MA 02052.

781.57 DEU ISSN 0021-5686
ML5
JAZZ PODIUM. Text in German. 1952. m. EUR 36 domestic; EUR 48 foreign (effective 2007). adv. bk.rev.; film rev.; music rev.; rec.rev.; video rev. **Document type:** *Magazine, Consumer.*
Indexed: DIP, IBR, IBZ, IIMP, M11, MusicInd, RASB, RILM.
Published by: Jazz Podium Verlags GmbH, Vogelsangstr 32, Stuttgart, 70197, Germany. TEL 49-711-99337780, FAX 49-711-993377899, vertrieb@jazzpodium.de. Ed. Gudrun Endress. Adv. contact Frank Zimmerle TEL 49-711-631530. B&W page EUR 750, color page EUR 1,749; trim 185 x 261. Circ: 10,100 (paid).

JAZZ PULSIONS; le magazine des danses jazz. *see* DANCE

781.57 GBR ISSN 1365-7410
THE JAZZ RAG. Text in English. 1986. bi-m. GBP 15.50 domestic; GBP 18.50 in Europe; GBP 22.50 elsewhere; GBP 2.75 newsstand/cover (effective 2009). adv. bk.rev.; film rev.; rec.rev.; music rev.; video rev. illus. back issues avail. **Document type:** *Magazine, Consumer.* **Description:** Contains the latest news on Jazz music and upcoming events from the UK and abroad. It includes reviews of jazz releases, CDs, videos, books, and live concerts, interviews and news.
Published by: Big Bear Music Group, PO Box 944, Edgbaston, Birmingham B16 8UT, United Kingdom. TEL 44-121-4547020, FAX 44-121-4549996, agency@bigbearmusic.com. Ed., Pub. Jim Simpson. Adv. contact Steve Kelly. B&W page GBP 485, color page GBP 970; trim 210 x 297.

781.65 CAN ISSN 0843-3151
THE JAZZ REPORT; voice of the artist. Text in English. 1987. q. CAD 18 domestic; USD 20 elsewhere (effective 2004). adv. bk.rev. illus. reprints avail. **Description:** Provides coverage of the jazz and blues genres. For academics, collectors, and musicians in terms that the lay reader can understand.
Indexed: CMPI.
Published by: King Sutherland Productions, 592 Markham St, Ste 7, Toronto, ON M6G 2L8, Canada. TEL 416-533-2813, FAX 416-588-3501. Ed. Greg Sutherland.

781.6505 GBR ISSN 1753-8637
JAZZ RESEARCH JOURNAL. Text in English. 2004. s-a. USD 220 combined subscription in North America to institutions (print & online eds.); GBP 135 combined subscription elsewhere to institutions (print & online eds.) (effective 2012). adv. rec.rev.; film rev.; bk.rev. back issues avail.; reprints avail. **Document type:** *Journal, Academic/Scholarly.* **Description:** Presents innovative research that either extends the boundaries of jazz scholarship or explores themes which are central to a critical understanding of the music.
Formerly (until 2007): The Source (1740-5777)
Related titles: Online - full text ed.: ISSN 1753-8645. USD 176 in North America; GBP 108 elsewhere (effective 2012).
Indexed: M11.
—IE. **CCC.**
Published by: Equinox Publishing Ltd., Unit S3, Kelham House, 3 Lancaster St, Sheffield, S6 3AF, United Kingdom. TEL 44-114-2725957, FAX 44-560-3459046, journals@equinoxpub.com, http://www.equinoxpub.com/. Eds. Catherine Tackley, Tony Whyton. Adv. contact Val Hall.

781.65 DEU
JAZZ THING & BLUE RHYTHM. Text in German. 1993. 5/yr. EUR 27 (effective 2010). adv. **Document type:** *Magazine, Consumer.*
Formerly (until 2010): Jazz Thing
Published by: Verlag Axel Stinshoff, Suelzburgstr 74, Cologne, 50937, Germany. TEL 49-221-9414888, FAX 49-221-413166. Ed. Martin Laurentius. adv.: B&W page EUR 1,600, color page EUR 2,605; trim 180 x 268. Circ: 25,500 (paid and controlled).

781.65 GBR ISSN 1472-0728
JAZZ U K. Text in English. 1995. bi-m. GBP 15; free to qualified personnel (effective 2009). adv. back issues avail. **Document type:** *Magazine, Consumer.* **Description:** Designed to help players, promoters and the general public share the beauty of Jazz.
Published by: Jazz Newspapers Ltd., 26 The Balcony, Castle Arcade, Cardiff, CF10 2BY, United Kingdom. TEL 44-29-20665161, FAX 44-29-20665160. Adv. contact Nick Brown TEL 44-2920-665161. page GBP 500; 148 x 210.

781.57 USA ISSN 0749-4564
ML3505.8
JAZZ WORLD. Text in English. 1972. bi-m. USD 35. adv. bk.rev. back issues avail.
Former titles (until 1984): Jazz World Index (0886-1927); (until 1981): Jazz Echo (0277-5980); (until 1979): Swinging Newsletter
Indexed: MusicInd.
Published by: World Jazz Society, PO Box 777, Times Square Sta, New York, NY 10108-0777. TEL 201-939-0836. Ed. Jan A Byrczek. Circ: 6,000.

781.57 DEU ISSN 1618-9140
JAZZ ZEITUNG. Text in German. 1976. 5/yr. EUR 18 domestic; EUR 22.50 foreign; EUR 3.80 newsstand/cover (effective 2009). adv. bk.rev. **Document type:** *Magazine, Consumer.* **Description:** Jazz portraits, record reviews, information about concerts and musicians in and around Munich.
Published by: ConBrio Verlagsgesellschaft mbH, Brunnstr 23, Regensburg, 93053, Germany. TEL 49-941-945930, FAX 49-941-9459350, info@conbrio.de, http://www.conbrio.de. Ed. Andreas Kolb. Pub. Theo Geissler. Adv. contact Martina Wagner. B&W page EUR 1,080, color page EUR 1,960. Circ: 15,000 (paid and controlled).

785.4 ARG
JAZZBAND. Text in Spanish. 1972. bi-m. USD 7. adv. bk.rev. illus.
Address: c/o Alberto Miguel Consiglio, Yerbal, 2291, Buenos Aires, 1406, Argentina. Circ: 10,000.

781.65 DEU
DER JAZZBRIEF. Text in German. 1992. irreg. **Document type:** *Newsletter, Consumer.*
Published by: Jazzinstitut Darmstadt, Bessunger Str 88d, Darmstadt, 64285, Germany. TEL 49-6151-963700, FAX 49-6151-963744, jazz@jazzinstitut.de, http://www.jazzinstitut.de.

781.65 370 USA
JAZZED; practical ideas & techniques for jazz educators. Text in English. 2006. bi-m. free to qualified personnel (effective 2009). adv. back issues avail. **Document type:** *Magazine, Trade.* **Description:** Designed for jazz educators. Provides hands-on information to help school and independent music educators teach jazz to high-school and college students.
Published by: Symphony Publishing LLC, 21 Highland Cir, Ste One, Needham, MA 02494. TEL 781-453-9310, 800-964-5150, FAX 781-453-9389, http://www.symphonypublishing.com. Ed. Christian Wissmuller TEL 781-453-9310 ext 16. Pub. Richard E Kessel TEL 781-453-9310 ext 14. Adv. contact Iris Fox TEL 954-973-3555. Circ: 13,000.

780 AUT ISSN 0075-3572
ML5
JAZZFORSCHUNG/JAZZ RESEARCH. Text and summaries in English, German. 1969. a. free to members. **Document type:** *Academic/Scholarly.*
Indexed: IBR, IBZ, IIBP, IIMP, M11, MusicInd, PCI, RILM.
—CCC.
Published by: (International Society for Jazz Research), Akademische Druck- und Verlagsanstalt Dr. Paul Struzl GmbH, Auersperggasse 12, Graz, St 8010, Austria. TEL 43-316-3644, FAX 43-316-364424, info@adeva.com, http://www.adeva.com. R&P Doris Kellnhofer. **Co-sponsor:** Hochschule fuer Musik und Institut fuer Jazz Darstellende Kunst.

781.65 POL ISSN 1232-681X
ML3505.8
JAZZI MAGAZINE; the music business magazine. Text in Polish. 1994. bi-m. PLZ 76; USD 90 in United States. adv. bk.rev.; music rev. illus. back issues avail. **Document type:** *Consumer.*
Published by: Polonia Records Sp. z o.o., Ul Jana Pawla 18-13, Warsaw, 00116, Poland. TEL 48-22-243213, FAX 48-22-243213. Ed. Stanislaw Sobola. Adv. contact Joanna Kowalska. page USD 1,000. Circ: 12,000.

781.65 NLD ISSN 1873-0698
JAZZISM. Text in Dutch. 2006. bi-m. EUR 36; EUR 7.50 newsstand/cover (effective 2009). adv. **Document type:** *Magazine, Consumer.*
Published by: BCM Publishing, Postbus 1392, Eindhoven, 5602 BJ, Netherlands. TEL 31-40-8447644, FAX 31-40-8447655, bcm@bcm.nl, http://www.bcm.nl. Pub. Eric Bruger. Adv. contact Eddy van den Berg. B&W page EUR 1,995, color page EUR 2,695; 230 x 300. Circ: 21,200.

781.57 USA ISSN 0741-5885
ML3505.8
JAZZIZ. Text in English. 1983. m. USD 69.95 domestic; USD 79.95 in Canada & Mexico; USD 99.95 elsewhere; USD 3.95 newsstand/cover (effective 2005). adv. bk.rev. illus. Supplement avail.; reprints avail. **Document type:** *Magazine, Consumer.* **Description:** Music lifestyle publication devoted to jazz and music for adults.
Related titles: Online - full text ed.
Indexed: A22, IIMP, M11, MAG, MusicInd, P10, P48, P53, P54, PQC.
—Ingenta.
Published by: Jazziz Magazine, Inc., 3620 N W 43rd St Ste D, Gainesville, FL 32606. TEL 904-375-3705, FAX 904-375-7268, jazziz@sprintmail.com. Eds. Fernando Gonzales, Mike Koretzky. Pub. Michael Fagien. Adv. contact Lori B Fagien. B&W page USD 2,375, color page USD 3,325; trim 11.13 x 8.38. Circ: 110,000 (paid). **Dist. in UK by:** Comag, Tavistock Rd, W Drayton, Middlesex UB7 7QE, United Kingdom. TEL 44-1895-444055, FAX 44-1895-433602.

781.57 973 USA ISSN 0890-6440
ML3505.8
JAZZLETTER. Text in English. 1981. 12/yr. USD 60; USD 70 foreign. adv. bk.rev. cum.index. back issues avail. **Document type:** *Newsletter, Consumer.* **Description:** Biographical portraits of major artists, and articles on the evolution and contemporary state of American jazz.
Indexed: CMPI.
Address: PO Box 240, Ojai, CA 93024-0240. TEL 805-640-8307, FAX 805-640-0253. Ed. Gene Lees. Circ: 2,000.

781.57 AUS
JAZZLINE. Text in English. 1975. q. AUD 30 to non-members; free to members (effective 2009); subscr. includes Jazzbeat. bk.rev. **Document type:** *Magazine, Consumer.* **Description:** Contains articles and news on local and overseas jazz, audio and video reviews, and photographs.
Published by: Victorian Jazz Club, GPO Box 2421V, Melbourne, VIC 3001, Australia. TEL 61-3-95173009. Ed. Mike McKeon TEL 61-3-95517363.

781.57 USA ISSN 8756-6540
JAZZLINE. Text in English. 1965. s-m. USD 25. **Description:** Provides information on jazz and jazz events in the New York metropolitan area.
Published by: Jazz Interactions, Inc., PO Box 268, Glen Oaks, NY 11004. TEL 718-465-7500. Ed. R Neufeld. Circ: 250.

781.65 FRA ISSN 1240-2044
JAZZMAN; le journal de tous les jazz. Text in French. m. (11/yr). EUR 39.80 (effective 2010). **Document type:** *Magazine, Consumer.* **Description:** Includes interviews, concert guide, CD selection.
Related titles: Online - full text ed.
Published by: Iena Presse, 12 bis Place Henri Bergson, BP 443, Paris, Cedex 8 75366, France. TEL 33-1-40085050, FAX 33-1-40085075. Eds. Alex Dutilh, Franck Bergerot. Pub. Mario Calaiacovo. **Subscr. to:** Dipresse. abo@dipinfo.fr.

781.57 USA
JAZZMEN'S REFERENCE BOOK; Jazz World Direct. Text in English. 1973. a. USD 95 to non-members. adv.
Published by: Jazz World Society, PO Box 777, Times Sq Sta, New York, NY 10108-0777. Ed. Jan A Byrczek. Circ: 8,000.

781.65 DEU ISSN 0933-8926
ML3505.8
JAZZTHETIK; Magazin fuer Jazz und Anderes. Text in German. 1987. 10/yr. EUR 48 domestic; EUR 60 foreign; EUR 5 newsstand/cover (effective 2005). adv. **Document type:** *Magazine, Consumer.*
Indexed: RILM.
Address: Frie-Vendt-Str 16, Muenster, 48153, Germany. TEL 49-251-533420, FAX 49-251-533428. Ed. Joachim Weis. Pub. Christine Stephan. adv.: B&W page EUR 1,150; trim 177 x 258.

781.57 CHE
JAZZTIME; Schweizer Jazz Magazin. Text in German. 1981. m. CHF 42 domestic; CHF 65 foreign (effective 2001). **Document type:** *Magazine, Consumer.* **Description:** Publishes information about jazz concerts, festivals and CD-news.
Published by: Jazztime Verlag AG, Taefernstr 37, Baden, 5405, Switzerland. TEL 41-56-4833737, FAX 41-56-4833739, verlag@jazztime.com, http://www.jazzcd.ch. Ed. Eduard Keller. Circ: 8,000; 6,000 (paid).

781.57 USA ISSN 0272-572X
ML1
JAZZTIMES; America's jazz magazine. Text in English. 1972. 10/yr. USD 23.95 domestic; USD 35.95 in Canada; USD 59.95 elsewhere (effective 2010). adv. bk.rev. illus. reprints avail. **Document type:** *Magazine, Consumer.* **Description:** Comprehensive consumer jazz publication covering swing and big band to Brazilian, blues and contemporary jazz.
Supersedes: Radio Free Jazz (0145-5125)
Related titles: Microfiche ed.: (from PQC); Supplement(s): Jazztimes Jazz Education Guide. ISSN 1526-4661. 1999.
Indexed: A22, IIMP, M11, MAG, MusicInd, RILM, T02.
—Ingenta.
Published by: Jazz Times Inc., Madavor Media, 85 Quincy Ave, Ste B, Quincy, MA 02169. TEL 617-706-9110, FAX 617-536-0102, editor@jazztimes.com, subscriptions@jazztimes.com, jtimes@aol.com. Ed. Lee Mergner. Adv. contact Joe Wensell. Circ: 100,000 (paid). **Dist. in UK by:** Seymour Distribution Ltd, 86 Newman St, London W1T 3EX, United Kingdom. TEL 44-20-73968000, FAX 44-20-73968002, http://www.seymour.co.uk.

781.65 USA
JAZZUSA 'ZINE. Text in English. m. **Description:** Features music reviews, new releases, links to home pages, women in jazz, events listing, puzzle contests and jazz news.
Media: Online - full text.

781.65 USA ISSN 1554-4338
JAZZWEEK. Text in English. 2001. w. USD 249; USD 7.95 per issue (effective 2005). adv.
Formerly (until 2004): Yellow Dog Jazz Reporter
Media: Online - full content.
Published by: Yellow Dog Communications, 2117 Buffalo Rd Ste 317, Rochester, NY 14624. TEL 585-235-4685, FAX 775-878-7482. Ed. Ed Trefzger. Pub., Adv. contact Tony Gasparre.

781.650 GBR ISSN 1368-0021
JAZZWISE. Text in English. 1997. m. (except Dec./Jan. combined). GBP 41 domestic; GBP 55 in Europe; GBP 62 elsewhere (effective 2009). adv. back issues avail. **Document type:** *Magazine, Consumer.* **Description:** Covers various styles and all areas of jazz music.
Related titles: Online - full text ed.: GBP 27.50 (effective 2009).
—CCC.
Published by: Jazzwise Publications, Gleneagle Mews, Ambleside Ave2b, London, SW16 6AE, United Kingdom. TEL 44-20-86770012, FAX 44-20-86777128, http://www.jazzwise.com. Ed., Pub. Jon Newey. Adv. contact Ros McRae TEL 44-141-3341735.

780 FRA ISSN 1155-3464
JE CHANTE!; la revue de la chanson francaise. Text in French. 1990. q. EUR 28 (effective 2008). **Document type:** *Magazine, Consumer.*
Published by: Association Je Chante!, 7 Rue du Panorama, Chelles, 7750, France. TEL 33-1-64266503, FAX 33-1-64216352, je.chante@wanadoo.fr. Ed. Raoul Bellaiche.

782.81 BEL
JEAN DE CASTRO OPERA OMNIA. Text in Dutch. 1993. irreg., latest vol.4, 1997. price varies. **Document type:** *Monographic series, Academic/Scholarly.*
Related titles: CD-ROM ed.
Published by: Leuven University Press, Blijde Inkomststraat 5, Leuven, 3000, Belgium. TEL 32-16-325345, FAX 32-16-325352, university.press@upers.kuleuven.ac.be, http://www.kuleuven.ac.be/upers.

781.6 SWE ISSN 0345-5653
ML5
JEFFERSON; Scandinavian magazine for blues and related music. Text in Swedish. 1968. q. SEK 265 domestic; SEK 350 in Europe; SEK 500 elsewhere (effective 2011). adv. bk.rev. bibl. **Document type:** *Magazine, Consumer.* **Description:** Contains related music styles like zydeco, rock 'n roll, gospel, and reggae.
Formerly (until vol.7, 1969): Jefferson Blues Magazine
Related titles: Online - full text ed.: ISSN 1402-4691.
Indexed: RILM.
Published by: Scandinavian Blues Association, P O Box 4119, Stockholm, 10262, Sweden. http://www.jeffersonbluemag.com. Ed., Adv. contact Anders Lillsunde.

780 USA
JERSEY BEAT. Text in English. 1982. q. USD 12; USD 3 newsstand/cover (effective 2001). adv. bk.rev. 132 p./no.; back issues avail. **Document type:** *Magazine, Consumer.* **Description:** Covers alternative music and media with a focus on the Greater NY area.
Published by: Jim Testa, Ed. & Pub., 418 Gregory Ave., Weehawken, NJ 07086. TEL 201-864-9054. R&P, Adv. contact Jim Testa. Circ: 5,000.

781.57 USA ISSN 0740-5928
ML3505.8
JERSEY JAZZ. Text in English. 1973. 11/yr. USD 35 (effective 2000). adv. bk.rev. illus. **Document type:** *Newsletter.* **Description:** Covers traditional and mainstream jazz.
Published by: New Jersey Jazz Society, 834 Country Club rd, Brookside, NJ 08807-1127. TEL 908-707-9824, FAX 973-543-2829. Ed. Paul White. Circ: 1,500 (controlled).

780 CHN
JIANGSU YINYUE/JIANGSU MUSIC. Text in Chinese. m.
Published by: Jiangsu Wenxue Yishu Jie Lianhehui/Jiangsu Literary and Art Circle Association, 126 Ninghai Lu, Nanjing, Jiangsu 210024, China. TEL 306362. Ed. Xie Hua.

780 CHN ISSN 1003-1499
JIAOXIANG - XI'AN YINYUE XUEYUAN XUEBAO/JIAOXIANG - JOURNAL OF XI-AN CONSERVATORY OF MUSIC. Text in Chinese. 1982. q. USD 20.80 (effective 2009). **Document type:** *Journal, Academic/Scholarly.*
Related titles: Online - full text ed.
Indexed: RILM.
—East View.
Published by: Xi'an Yinyue Xueyuan, 108, Chang'an Zhong Lu, Xi'an, 710061, China. TEL 86-29-85217708.

016.78164 USA ISSN 0195-4040
ML156.4.P6
JOEL WHITBURN'S TOP POP SINGLES. Text in English. 1978. irreg. USD 44.95 per issue (effective 2006).
Published by: Record Research, Inc., PO Box 200, Menomonee Falls, WI 53052-0200. TEL 262-251-5408, books@recordresearch.com.

780 USA
JOHNNY WINTER. Text in English. q. USD 5; USD 10 foreign. **Document type:** *Newsletter, Consumer.*
Published by: Johnny Winter International Fan Club, 2442 N W Market, Ste 208, Seattle, WA 98107.

781.6 USA
JOLSON JOURNAL. Text in English. 1950. s-a. free to members (effective 2010). bk.rev. illus. **Document type:** *Journal, Academic/Scholarly.*
Published by: International Al Jolson Society, c/o Tom Nestor, 1709 Billingshurst Ct, Orlando, FL 32825. http://www.jolson.org/.

781.6 USA
JOLSON JOURNALETTE. Text in English. 19??. q. free to members (effective 2010). **Document type:** *Newsletter, Consumer.*
Former titles (until 1995): Jolsonews; (until 1992): Jolie Journalette; (until 1991): The International Al Jolson Society. Newsletter
Published by: International Al Jolson Society, c/o Tom Nestor, 1709 Billingshurst Ct, Orlando, FL 32825. http://www.jolson.org/.

780 DEU ISSN 0446-9577
JOSEPH HAAS GESELLSCHAFT. MITTEILUNGSBLATT. Text in German. 1950. a. membership. bk.rev.; music rev. bibl. index. **Document type:** *Bulletin, Consumer.*
Published by: Joseph Haas Gesellschaft e.V., c/o Wolfgang Haas, Kreuzeckstr 18, Pullach, 82049, Germany. TEL 49-89-794345, FAX 49-89-794345, info@joseph-haas.de, http://www.joseph-haas.de. Ed. Klaus Zoephel. Circ: 300.

780 USA ISSN 1937-6804
ML1
THE JOURNAL OF A MUSICIAN. Text in English. 2007. q. USD 35; USD 25 to students (effective 2008). **Document type:** *Journal, Consumer.* **Description:** Presents biography, interviews and musical theory of musicians, composers and conductors in a wide variey of musical genres.
Published by: Journal of a Musician, PO Box 14149, Chicago, IL 60614. TEL 847-404-7089, journalofamusicin@gmail.com, http://www.georgelepauw.com/journal/home. Ed. George Lepauw.

JOURNAL OF AESTHETICS AND ART CRITICISM. *see* ART

780 694 USA ISSN 1048-2482
ML549.8
JOURNAL OF AMERICAN ORGANBUILDING. Text in English. 1986. q. USD 12 domestic; USD 16 foreign (effective 2007). adv. bk.rev. back issues avail. **Document type:** *Magazine, Trade.* **Description:** Includes technical articles and product reviews for pipe organ builders and tuning and maintenance technicians.
Indexed: A09, A10, CA, T02, V03, V04.
Published by: American Institute of Organbuilders, PO Box 130982, Houston, TX 77219-0982. TEL 713-529-2212, FAX 713-529-2212, pipes@pipeorgan.org, http://www.pipeorgan.org. Ed. Jeff Weiler. R&P, Adv. contact Howard Maple. Circ: 600 (paid).

786.067 USA ISSN 0021-9207
JOURNAL OF BAND RESEARCH. Text in English. 1964. s-a. USD 15 domestic; USD 20 foreign (effective 2011). bk.rev. abstr.; bibl.; charts; illus.; stat. cum.index: vols.1-8. reprints avail. **Document type:** *Journal, Academic/Scholarly.* **Description:** Provides a wide range of band and wind ensemble research including historical, analytical, descriptive, and experimental studies.
Related titles: Microform ed.: (from PQC).
Indexed: A01, A20, A22, ASCA, ArtHuCI, CA, CurCont, IIMP, M11, MAG, MusicInd, PCI, RILM, SCOPUS, T02, W07.
—Ingenta.
Published by: (American Bandmasters Association), Journal of Band Research, c/o Dr. John R. Locke, Editor, UNCG School of Music, P O Box 26170, Greensboro, NC 27402-6170. TEL 334-670-3252, lockej@uncg.edu, dernsberger@troy.edu. Circ: 1,000 (paid). **Co-sponsors:** American School Band Directors Association; National Band Association.

780.01 USA
ML1
JOURNAL OF COUNTRY MUSIC (ONLINE). Text in English. 1971. 3/yr. free (effective 2010). adv. bk.rev.; rec.rev. bibl.; illus. back issues avail.; reprints avail. **Document type:** *Journal, Consumer.* **Description:** Presents biographical reviews of performers and their musical development, question-and-answer interviews with performers and music business people, and overview essays on historical development of specific styles of music.
Former titles (until 200?): Journal of Country Music (Print) (0092-0517); (until 1971): Country Music Foundation Newsletter
Media: Online - full text.
Indexed: A20, A22, ASCA, ArtHuCI, CurCont, IIMP, M11, MLA, MLA-IB, MusicInd, RILM, T02.
—Ingenta.
Published by: Country Music Foundation, Inc., 222 5th Ave., S, Nashville, TN 37203. TEL 615-416-2001, info@countrymusichalloffame.com.

781.542 GBR ISSN 1087-7142
ML2074
➤ **THE JOURNAL OF FILM MUSIC.** Abbreviated title: J F M. Text in English. 2002. s-a. USD 300 combined subscription in North America to institutions (print & online eds.); GBP 185 combined subscription elsewhere to institutions (print & online eds.) (effective 2012). adv. back issues avail.; reprints avail. **Document type:** *Journal, Academic/Scholarly.* **Description:** Provides a forum for the musicological study of film from the standpoint of dramatic musical art.
Related titles: Online - full text ed.: ISSN 1758-860X. USD 240 in North America to institutions; GBP 148 elsewhere to institutions (effective 2012).
Indexed: CA, F01, F02, IBT&D, IIFP, IIMP, IIPA, M11, MusicInd, RILM, T02.
—CCC.
Published by: (Film Music Society USA), Equinox Publishing Ltd., Unit S3, Kelham House, 3 Lancaster St, Sheffield, S6 3AF, United Kingdom. TEL 44-114-2725957, FAX 44-560-3459046, journals@equinoxpub.com, http://www.equinoxpub.com/. Ed. William H Rosar. Adv. contact Val Hall.

780.1 USA ISSN 1536-6006
ML1
➤ **JOURNAL OF HISTORICAL RESEARCH IN MUSIC EDUCATION.** Text in English. 1980. s-a. USD 25 to individuals; USD 50 to institutions (effective 2011). bk.rev. bibl. back issues avail. **Document type:** *Journal, Academic/Scholarly.* **Description:** Publishes scholarly articles and reviews pertinent in any way to the history of music education.
Formerly (until Oct.1999): The Bulletin of Historical Research in Musical Education (0739-5639)
Indexed: A26, CA, E03, E07, E08, ERI, I05, IIMP, M11, MusicInd, PCI, RILM, S09, T02.
—Ingenta.
Published by: Ithaca College, School of Music, 953 Danby Rd, Ithaca, NY 14850. TEL 607-274-1563, FAX 607-274-1727. Ed. Mark Fonder. Circ: 227.

780 TUR ISSN 1307-0401
➤ **JOURNAL OF INTERDISCIPLINARY MUSIC STUDIES/ DISIPLINLERARASI MUZIK ARATIRMALARI DERGISI.** Text in English. 2007. s-a. EUR 80 to institutions (effective 2009). **Document type:** *Journal, Academic/Scholarly.* **Description:** Aims to establish a broad interdisciplinary platform for music researchers.
Related titles: Online - full text ed.: ISSN 1306-9055. free (effective 2011).
Indexed: A01, CA, M11, T02.
Address: c/o Yonetim Yeri, Executive Office, 235 sok. No: 106/7, Izmir, 35360, Turkey. TEL 90-232-2323423, editor@musicstudies.org. Eds. Ali C Gedick, Richard Parncutt.

781.65 USA ISSN 2158-1401
▼ **JOURNAL OF JAZZ STUDIES.** Text in English. 2011. s-a. free (effective 2011). **Document type:** *Journal, Academic/Scholarly.*
Media: Online - full text.
Published by: Rutgers University, Institute of Jazz Studies, John Cotton Dana Library, 185 University Ave, Newark, NJ 07102. TEL 973-353-5595, FAX 973-353-5944, http://newarkwww.rutgers.edu/IJS.

782.29 USA ISSN 0197-0100
ML3195
JOURNAL OF JEWISH MUSIC AND LITURGY. Text in English, Hebrew. 1976. a., latest vol.23, 2001. bk.rev. **Document type:** *Journal, Academic/Scholarly.* **Description:** Informs the professional and layman of aspects of Jewish music and liturgy from the Biblical period to present. Scholarly articles in the field of Jewish music and Liturgy.
Related titles: Online - full text ed.
Indexed: IIMP, M11, MusicInd, RILM.
Published by: (Yeshiva University), Cantorial Council of America, c/o Yeshiva University, 500 W 185th St, New York, NY 10033. TEL 212-960-5400, http://www.yu.edu/belz.

JOURNAL OF MATHEMATICS AND MUSIC; mathematical and computational approaches to music theory, analysis, composition and performance. *see* MATHEMATICS

780 792.8 NGA
➤ **JOURNAL OF MUSIC AND DANCE.** Text in English. m. free (effective 2010). adv. **Document type:** *Journal, Academic/Scholarly.*
Media: Online - full text.
Published by: Academic Journals, PO Box 73023, Victoria Island, Lagos, Nigeria. service@academicjournals.org.

780 DNK ISSN 1603-7170
ML3800
➤ **THE JOURNAL OF MUSIC AND MEANING.** Abbreviated title: J M M. Text in English. 2003. irreg. free (effective 2011). **Document type:** *Journal, Academic/Scholarly.* **Description:** Aims to bridge the gap between various studies in meaning and signification and areas of research in music.
Media: Online - full text.
Indexed: A01, A39, C27, C29, D03, D04, E13, M11, R14, S14, S15, S18, T02.
Published by: Syddansk Universitet, Institut for Filosofi, Paedagogik og Religionsstudier/University of Southern Denmark, Institute of Philosophy, Education and the Study of Religions, Campusvej 55, Odense M, 5230, Denmark. TEL 45-65-503334, FAX 45-65-432375, ifpr@ifpr.sdu.dk, http://www.sdu.dk/Om_SDU/Institutter_centre/Ifpr.aspx. Ed. Cynthia M Grund.

780 USA ISSN 2155-109X
▼ **JOURNAL OF MUSIC HISTORY PEDAGOGY.** Text in English. 2010 (Sep.). s-a. free (effective 2011). **Document type:** *Journal, Academic/Scholarly.* **Description:** Publishes original articles and reviews related to teaching music history of all levels (undergraduate, graduate, or general studies) and disciplines (western, non-western, concert and popular musics).
Media: Online - full text.
Published by: American Musicological Society, 201 S 34th St, Philadelphia, PA 19104-6316. TEL 215-898-8698, FAX 215-573-3673, ams@sas.upenn.edu.

780 USA ISSN 1092-1710
ML336
JOURNAL OF MUSIC IN CHINA. Text in English. 1999. s-a. USD 40 to individuals; USD 70 to institutions; USD 30 to students (effective 2004).
Related titles: CD-ROM ed.: E-Journal of Music in China. ISSN 1558-8815.
Indexed: RILM.
Published by: Music in China, Inc, Box 25177, Los Angeles, CA 90025-0177. TEL 310-312-1675. Ed. Zhou Qinru.

780.7 USA ISSN 1945-0079
➤ **JOURNAL OF MUSIC TEACHER EDUCATION (ONLINE).** Text in English. 2002. 2/yr. USD 58, GBP 34 to institutions (effective 2011). **Document type:** *Journal, Academic/Scholarly.* **Description:** Offers philosophical, historical, descriptive, or methodological articles related to music teacher education. Some issues offer media reviews and "perspectives," essays that discuss opinions and viewpoints.
Media: Online - full content.
Indexed: BRD, E02, EdA, EdI.
—CCC.
Published by: (M E N C: National Association for Music Education), Sage Publications, Inc., 2455 Teller Rd, Thousand Oaks, CA 91320. TEL 805-499-9774, 800-818-7243, FAX 805-499-0871, 800-583-2665, info@sagepub.com, http://www.sagepub.com. Ed. William E Fredrickson.

780 GBR ISSN 1752-7066
➤ **JOURNAL OF MUSIC, TECHNOLOGY AND EDUCATION.** Abbreviated title: J M T E. Text in English. 2008. 3/yr. GBP 36, USD 68 to individuals; GBP 235, USD 368 to institutions (effective 2012). adv. back issues avail. **Document type:** *Journal, Academic/Scholarly.* **Description:** Covers the educational aspects of music technology and the technological aspects of music.
Related titles: Online - full text ed.: ISSN 1752-7074. GBP 235, USD 368 (effective 2012).
Indexed: A01, B29, CA, M11, T02.
Published by: Intellect Ltd., The Mill, Parnall Rd, Fishponds, Bristol, BS16 3JG, United Kingdom. TEL 44-117-9589910, FAX 44-117-9589911, info@intellectbooks.com. Ed. Andrew King. Pub. Masoud Yazdani. **Subscr. to:** Turpin Distribution Services Ltd., Pegasus Dr, Stratton Business Park, Biggleswade, Bedfordshire SG18 8QB, United Kingdom. TEL 44-1767-604951, FAX 44-1767-601640, custserv@turpin-distribution.com, http://www.turpin-distribution.com/.

781 USA ISSN 0022-2909
ML1
➤ **JOURNAL OF MUSIC THEORY.** Abbreviated title: J M T. Text in English. 1957. s-a. USD 30 to individuals; USD 70 to institutions; USD 72 combined subscription to institutions (print & online eds.); USD 35 per issue to institutions (effective 2012). adv. bk.rev. bibl.; charts; illus. index. back issues avail.; reprint service avail. from PSC. **Document type:** *Journal, Academic/Scholarly.* **Description:** Brings out research and applications in the analysis of music and the history of music theory as well as theoretical or metatheoretical work that engages and stimulates ongoing discourse in the field.
Related titles: Microform ed.: (from MIM, PQC); Online - full text ed.: ISSN 1941-7497. USD 62 to institutions (effective 2012).
Indexed: A01, A20, A22, ASCA, ArtHuCI, CA, CurCont, DIP, FR, IBR, IBRH, IBZ, IIMP, M11, MAG, MusicInd, PCI, RASB, RILM, SCOPUS, T02, W07.
—IE, Ingenta.
Published by: (Yale University, School of Music), Duke University Press, 905 W Main St, Ste 18 B, Durham, NC 27701. TEL 919-688-5134, 888-651-0122, FAX 919-688-2615, 888-651-0124, subscriptions@dukeupress.edu, http://www.dukeupress.edu. Ed. Ian Quinn.

780.71 USA ISSN 0891-7639
MT10
➤ **JOURNAL OF MUSIC THEORY PEDAGOGY.** Text in English. 1987. a., latest 1996. USD 40 per issue domestic to institutions; USD 50 per issue foreign to institutions (effective 2011). bk.rev. back issues avail. **Document type:** *Journal, Academic/Scholarly.* **Description:** International publication for music theorists and music theory teachers that combines scholarly research with practical applications of pedagogical issues. Devoted exclusively to matters directly related to the problems and solutions of teaching and learning music theory.
Indexed: CA, IIMP, M11, MAG, MusicInd, RILM, T02.
—Ingenta.
Published by: University of Oklahoma, School of Music, c/o Alice Lanning, Wagner 175/1005 Asp, Norman, OK 73019. TEL 405-325-3967, FAX 405-325-7383, music@ou.edu, http://music.ou.edu/. Ed. Steven G Laitz.

➤ **JOURNAL OF MUSIC THERAPY.** *see* MEDICAL SCIENCES—Physical Medicine And Rehabilitation

788.2 USA
THE JOURNAL OF MUSICAL INSTRUMENT TECHNOLOGY. Text in English. 1993. 2/yr. USD 30 domestic; USD 36 foreign (effective 2006). **Document type:** *Journal, Trade.* **Description:** Contains articles on repairing, building and designing musical instruments.
Formerly (until 2002): The Woodwind Quarterly (1070-2512)
Indexed: RILM.
Published by: The JournalofMusicalInstrumentTechnology, 23916 SE Kent-Kangley Rd, Maple Valley, WA 98038. TEL 425-413-4343, FAX 425-413-4338, musictrader@musictrader.com, http://www.musictrader.com/mitindex.html.

780.7 USA ISSN 0141-1896
ML5
➤ **JOURNAL OF MUSICOLOGICAL RESEARCH.** Text in English. 1974. q. GBP 198 combined subscription in United Kingdom to institutions (print & online eds.); EUR 263, USD 331 combined subscription to institutions (print & online eds.) (effective 2012). adv. bk.rev. illus. back issues avail.; reprint service avail. from PSC. **Document type:** *Journal, Academic/Scholarly.* **Description:** Focuses on study and teaching.
Formerly (until 1979): Music and Man (0306-2082)
Related titles: Microform ed.; Online - full text ed.: ISSN 1547-7304. GBP 178 in United Kingdom to institutions; EUR 237, USD 297 to institutions (effective 2012) (from IngentaConnect).
Indexed: A01, A02, A03, A08, A20, A22, A26, ASCA, AmHI, ArtHuCI, B04, BRD, BrHumI, CA, CurCont, E01, E08, G08, H07, H08, HAb, HumInd, I05, IBR, IBRH, IBZ, IIMP, M11, MAG, MLA-IB, MusicInd, PCI, PhilInd, RILM, S09, SCOPUS, T02, W03, W07.
—IE, Infotrieve, Ingenta. **CCC.**
Published by: Routledge (Subsidiary of: Taylor & Francis Group), 325 Chestnut St, Ste 800, Philadelphia, PA 19106. TEL 800-354-1420, FAX 215-625-2940, journals@routledge.com, http://www.routledge.com. Ed. Deborah Kauffman. Adv. contact Linda Hann TEL 44-1344-779945.

780.01 USA ISSN 0277-9269
ML1
➤ **THE JOURNAL OF MUSICOLOGY;** a quarterly review of music history, criticism, analysis, and performance practice. Abbreviated title: J M. Text in English. 1982. q. USD 214 combined subscription to institutions (print & online eds.) (effective 2012). adv. bk.rev. illus. 128 p./no.; back issues avail.; reprint service avail. from PSC. **Document type:** *Journal, Academic/Scholarly.* **Description:** Covers articles in every period, field and methodology of musicological scholarship.
Related titles: Microform ed.: (from PQC); Online - full text ed.: ISSN 1533-8347. USD 178 to institutions (effective 2012).
Indexed: A01, A02, A03, A08, A20, A22, A25, A26, A27, ABS&EES, ASCA, AmHI, ArtHuCI, B04, BRD, CA, CurCont, DIP, E01, E08, G08, H07, H08, HAb, HistAb, HumInd, I05, IBR, IBT&D, IBZ, IIMP, M11, MAG, MLA-IB, MusicInd, P02, P10, P48, P53, P54, PCI, PQC, RASB, RILM, S08, S09, SCOPUS, T02, W03, W07.
—BLDSC (5021.163700), IE, Infotrieve, Ingenta. **CCC.**
Published by: University of California Press, Journals Division, 2000 Ctr St, Ste 303, Berkeley, CA 94704. TEL 510-643-7154, 877-262-4226, FAX 510-642-9917, customerservice@ucpressjournals.com, http://www.ucpressjournals.com. Eds. Daniel R Melamed, Floyd Grave, Klara Moricz. Circ: 878. **Subscr. to:** 149 5th Ave, 8th Fl, New York, NY 10010. participation@jstor.org.

➤ **JOURNAL OF NEW MUSIC RESEARCH.** *see* COMPUTERS—Computer Music

➤ **JOURNAL OF PERFORMING ARTS.** *see* THEATER

780 USA ISSN 1524-2226
ML3469
➤ **JOURNAL OF POPULAR MUSIC STUDIES.** Text in English. 1988. q. GBP 255 in United Kingdom to institutions; EUR 325 in Europe to institutions; USD 306 in the Americas to institutions; USD 499 elsewhere to institutions; GBP 293 combined subscription in United Kingdom to institutions (print & online eds.); EUR 374 combined subscription in Europe to institutions (print & online eds.); USD 352 combined subscription in the Americas to institutions (print & online eds.); USD 574 combined subscription elsewhere to institutions (print & online eds.) (effective 2012). adv. music rev. back issues avail.; reprint service avail. from PSC. **Document type:** *Journal, Academic/Scholarly.* **Description:** Covers mutli-disciplinary studies on popular music.
Formerly (until 1993): Tracking
Related titles: Online - full text ed.: ISSN 1533-1598. GBP 255 in United Kingdom to institutions; EUR 325 in Europe to institutions; USD 306 in the Americas to institutions; USD 499 elsewhere to institutions (effective 2012) (from IngentaConnect).
Indexed: A01, A20, A22, A26, ArtHuCI, CA, CurCont, E01, M11, MLA-IB, MusicInd, RILM, SCOPUS, T02, W07.
—BLDSC (5041.142600), IE, Infotrieve, Ingenta. **CCC.**
Published by: (International Association for the Study of Popular Music, USA Branch), Wiley-Blackwell Publishing, Inc. (Subsidiary of: Wiley-Blackwell Publishing Ltd.), 111 River St, Hoboken, NJ 07030. TEL 201-748-6000, FAX 201-748-6088, info@wiley.com. Ed. Kevin J H Dettmar. Adv. contact Kristin McCarthy TEL 201-748-7683.

780.71 USA ISSN 0022-4294
CODEN: ENMJAK
➤ **JOURNAL OF RESEARCH IN MUSIC EDUCATION.** Text in English. 1953. q. USD 151, GBP 89 combined subscription to institutions (print & online eds.); USD 148, GBP 87 to institutions (effective 2011). illus. reprint service avail. from PSC. **Document type:** *Journal, Academic/Scholarly.* **Description:** Covers research on music education, its history and possible future directions.
Related titles: Microform ed.: (from PQC); Online - full text ed.: ISSN 1945-0095. USD 136, GBP 80 to institutions (effective 2011).
Indexed: A01, A02, A03, A08, A20, A22, A26, ASCA, ArtHuCI, B04, B07, BRD, CA, CPE, CurCont, E01, E02, E03, E06, E07, E08, E09, ERA, ERI, ERIC, EdA, EdI, FamI, G08, I05, I07, IBR, IBZ, IIMP, Inspec, M11, MAG, MLA-IB, MusicInd, P03, P04, P07, P10, P18, P25, P43, P48, P53, P54, PCI, PQC, PsycInfo, PsycholAb, RILM, S09, S21, S23, SCOPUS, T02, V05, W03, W05, W07.
—BLDSC (5052.020000), IE, Infotrieve, Ingenta. **CCC.**
Published by: (Society for Research in Music Education), Sage Publications, Inc., 2455 Teller Rd, Thousand Oaks, CA 91320. TEL 805-499-9774, FAX 805-499-0871, info@sagepub.com, http://www.sagepub.com. Ed. Wendy L Sims. Circ: 3,300.

780.1 USA ISSN 1558-268X
MT6
➤ **JOURNAL OF SCHENKERIAN STUDIES.** Text in English. 2005. a. back issues avail. **Document type:** *Journal, Academic/Scholarly.* **Description:** Devoted to the Schenkerian philosophy of music theory and its application to individual works of music.
Published by: Center for Schenkerian Studies, College of Music, University of North Texas, PO Box 311367, Denton, TX 76203. Eileen.Hayes@unt.edu. Ed. Colin Davis.

780.6 920 USA ISSN 1089-747X
ML194
➤ **JOURNAL OF SEVENTEENTH CENTURY MUSIC.** Text mainly in English; Text occasionally in French, German, Spanish, Italian. 1995. irreg. free (effective 2011). bk.rev.; music rev.; rec.rev. illus. back issues avail.; reprints avail. **Document type:** *Journal, Academic/Scholarly.* **Description:** Provides a refereed forum for scholarly studies of the musical cultures of the seventeenth century including historical and archival studies, performance practice, music theory, aesthetics, dance, and theater.
Media: Online - full text.
Indexed: A07, A30, A31, A39, AA, ArtInd, B04, C27, C29, D03, D04, E13, H08, HAb, HumInd, R14, RILM, S14, S15, S18, W03, W05.
Published by: Society for Seventeenth - Century Music, 337 W James St, Lancaster, PA 17603. kimberlyn.montford@trinity.edu, http://www.arts.uci.edu/sscm/. Ed. Bruce Gustafson.

782.0071 USA ISSN 1086-7732
ML27.U5
➤ **JOURNAL OF SINGING.** Abbreviated title: J O S. Text in English. 1944. 5/yr. USD 55 domestic to individuals; USD 85 foreign to individuals; USD 60 domestic to institutions; USD 10 per issue domestic to non-members; USD 15 per issue foreign to non-members; free to members (effective 2010). adv. bk.rev.; music rev.; rec.rev. charts; illus. index. back issues avail.; reprints avail. **Document type:** *Journal, Academic/Scholarly.* **Description:** Features articles devoted to the art of singing, vocal function, vocal literature, care of the professional voice, and the teaching of singing.
Former titles (until Sep.1995): N A T S Journal (0884-8106); (until May1985): N A T S Bulletin (0027-6073); (until 1962): National Association of Teachers of Singing. Bulletin
Related titles: Microfilm ed.: (from PQC); Online - full text ed.
Indexed: A22, A26, ABS&EES, B04, BRD, C06, C07, C08, CA, CINAHL, E02, E03, E07, ERI, EdA, EdI, H12, I05, IIMP, M11, MAG, MusicInd, P70, RILM, T02, W03, W05.
—BLDSC (5064.620000), Ingenta.
Published by: National Association of Teachers of Singing (N A T S), 9957 Moorings Dr, Ste 401, Jacksonville, FL 32257. TEL 904-992-9101, 888-262-2065, FAX 904-262-2587, info@nats.org. Ed. Richard Dale Sjoerdsma. Adv. contact Joan Adams. page USD 1,295; trim 8.5 x 11.

780 USA ISSN 1542-0221
ML1
JOURNAL OF TECHNOLOGY IN MUSIC LEARNING. Text in English. 2001. s-a. USD 27 domestic; USD 33 foreign (effective 2002).
Indexed: M11, MusicInd.
Published by: Florida State University, Center for Music Research, 214 KMU, Tallahassee, FL 32306-1180. Ed. Kimberly C. Walls.

781 USA ISSN 1535-7104
ML200.7.T35
THE JOURNAL OF TEXAS MUSIC HISTORY. Abbreviated title: J T M H. Text in English. 2001. a. free (effective 2010). back issues avail. **Document type:** *Journal, Academic/Scholarly.* **Description:** Focuses on the entire spectrum of Southwestern music history.
Related titles: Online - full text ed.
Indexed: RILM.
Published by: Texas State University - San Marcos, Center for Texas Music History, Brazos Hall, 601 University Dr, San Marcos, TX 78666. TEL 512-245-6465, gh08@txstate.edu, http://www.txstate.edu/ctmh/. Eds. Gary Hartman, Gregg Andrews, Jimmy McWilliams.

780 ZAF ISSN 1812-1004
ML350
JOURNAL OF THE MUSICAL ARTS IN AFRICA. Text in English. 2004. a. GBP 59 combined subscription in United Kingdom to institutions (print & online eds.); EUR 83, USD 106 combined subscription to institutions (print & online eds.) (effective 2012). bk.rev.; software rev. reprint service avail. from PSC. **Document type:** *Journal, Academic/Scholarly.*
Related titles: Online - full text ed.: ISSN 2070-626X. GBP 53 in United Kingdom to institutions; EUR 76, USD 96 to institutions (effective 2012) (from IngentaConnect).
Indexed: A01, A20, ArtHuCI, CA, M11, RILM, SCOPUS, T02, W07.
—CCC.
Published by: South African College of Music, Private Bag, Rondebosch, 7701, South Africa.

780 296 DEU ISSN 1613-7493
JUEDISCHE MUSIK; Studien und Quellen zur juedischen Musikkultur. Text in German. 2004. irreg., latest vol.10, 2010. price varies. **Document type:** *Monographic series, Academic/Scholarly.*
Published by: Harrassowitz Verlag, Kreuzberger Ring 7b-d, Wiesbaden, 65205, Germany. TEL 49-611-5300, FAX 49-611-530560, verlag@harrassowitz.de, http://www.harrassowitz.de.

JUGEND MUSIZIERT. *see* CHILDREN AND YOUTH—About

781.64 DEU ISSN 1614-9033
JUICE. Text in German. 1997. 11/yr. EUR 45 domestic; EUR 60 foreign; EUR 4.90 newsstand/cover (effective 2006). adv. **Document type:** *Magazine, Consumer.*
Published by: Piranha Media GmbH, Rolandstr 69, Cologne, 50677, Germany. TEL 49-221-5797800, FAX 49-221-5797879. adv.: page EUR 3,950. Circ: 27,561 (paid and controlled).

780.7 USA ISSN 1064-1580
JUILLIARD JOURNAL; monthly newspaper. Text in English. 1962. 8/yr. USD 15; free to alumni. adv. bk.rev. illus. reprints avail. **Document type:** *Newspaper.*
Formerly (until 1985): Juilliard News Bulletin (0022-6173)
Related titles: Microform ed.: (from PQC).
Indexed: MAG.
Published by: Juilliard School, Lincoln Center, New York, NY 10023. TEL 212-799-5000, FAX 212-769-6422. Ed., R&P Jane Rubinsky. Adv. contact Stacey Bernstein. Circ: 16,000.

781.57 GBR ISSN 1351-5551
JUKE BLUES; blues, soul, zydeco, gospel & jazz. Text in English. 1985. q. GBP 22 domestic; GBP 25, EUR 38 in Europe; GBP 28 in Canada and South America; GBP 29 in Australia, New Zealand and Japan; USD 40 in United States; GBP 6 per issue domestic; GBP 8 per issue in Europe (effective 2009). adv. music rev.; rec.rev.; video rev.; bk.rev. 86 p./no.; back issues avail. **Document type:** *Magazine, Consumer.* **Description:** Contains articles, photographs, news, and reviews about African-American blues, soul, zydeco, and gospel music.
Address: PO Box 4083, Bath, BA1 0FA, United Kingdom. FAX 44-1225-758375, info@jukeblues.com. Ed. Cilla Huggins. **US subscr. to:** c/o Dick Shurman, 3 S 321 Winfield Rd, Warrenville, IL 60555.

JUKEBOX COLLECTOR. *see* HOBBIES

780 FRA ISSN 0296-6395
JUKEBOX MAGAZINE. Text in French. 1984. m. EUR 65 (effective 2008). bk.rev.; film rev.; music rev.; video rev. back issues avail. **Document type:** *Magazine, Consumer.* **Description:** Covers rock and roll, pop music and record collecting.
Published by: Jacques Leblanc Editions S.A.R.L., 54 Rue St Lazare, Paris, 75009, France. TEL 33-1-55078107, FAX 33-1-43219700. Ed., Pub. Jacques Leblanc. Adv. contact Annie Vincent. Circ: 21,000.

780 USA ISSN 0022-6629
ML1
JUNIOR KEYNOTES. Text in English. 1927. 4/yr. (during school year). USD 5 (effective 1998 & 1999). adv. bk.rev. illus. **Description:** Contains organization news.
Published by: National Federation of Music Clubs, 1336 N Delaware St, Indianapolis, IN 46202. TEL 317-638-4003, FAX 317-638-0503. Ed., R&P Mary Alice Cox TEL 265-282-9405. Pub. C S Kern. Adv. contact Marjorie Neville. Circ: 6,000.

JUNKANOO. *see* THEATER

JUSTCIRCUIT.MAG. *see* HOMOSEXUALITY

780 FIN ISSN 0359-629X
JYVASKYLAN YLIOPISTO. MUSIIKIN LAITOS. JULKAISUSARJA. A, TUTKIELMIA JA RAPORTTEJA/UNIVERSITY OF JYVASKYLA. DEPARTMENT OF MUSIC. RESEARCH REPORTS. Text in Multiple languages. 1982. irreg. price varies. **Document type:** *Monographic series, Academic/Scholarly.*
Indexed: RILM.
Published by: Jyvaskylan Yliopisto, Musiikin Laitos/University of Jyvaskyla. Department of Music, PO Box 35, Jyvaskyla, 40014, Finland. TEL 358-14-2601330, FAX 358-14-2601331.

K C STUDIO. (Kansas City) *see* MOTION PICTURES

781.64 LTU
K N K. (Koks Nors Kelias) Text in Lithuanian. 1988. irreg. **Document type:** *Newsletter.* **Description:** Reviews and information on alternative and underground bands.
Related titles: Online - full text ed.
Address: c/o Karalius, PO Box 114, Kaunas, 30005, Lithuania. jo@socl.klp.osf.lt, jurena@soften.ktu.lt. Ed. Jonas Oskinis.

K48. *see* LITERARY AND POLITICAL REVIEWS

KAGAN'S MEDIA TRENDS. *see* COMMUNICATIONS—Television And Cable

780 891.85 POL ISSN 1233-8249
KAMERTON; pismo muzyczno-literackie. Text in Polish. 1990. q. free. music rev.; play rev. back issues avail. **Document type:** *Magazine, Consumer.*
Published by: Rzeszowskie Towarzystwo Muzyczne, ul Okrzei 7, Rzeszow, 35959, Poland. TEL 48-17-8532535, FAX 48-17-8624640, wdk@kki.net.pl. Ed. Andrzej Szypula.

780.71 USA ISSN 0022-8702
ML1
KANSAS MUSIC REVIEW. Text in English. 1938. 4/yr. free to members. adv. bk.rev.; music rev.; software rev. tr.lit. back issues avail. **Document type:** *Journal, Trade.* **Description:** Presents study and teaching methods.
Indexed: MAG.
Published by: Kansas Music Educators Association, c/o Harold Popp, Editor, 11302 Bekemeyer, Wichita, KS 67212. TEL 316-978-3103, FAX 316-729-6785, editor@ksmea.org, http://www.ksmea.org. Ed. Harold Popp. Adv. contact Robert E Lee. B&W page USD 210; trim 10 x 7. Circ: 3,000.

781 DEU ISSN 0179-9894
KARG-ELERT-GESELLSCHAFT. MITTEILUNGEN. Text in German. 1986. a. **Document type:** *Journal, Academic/Scholarly.*
Indexed: RILM.
Published by: Karg-Elert-Gesellschaft e.V., Knaackstr 35, Berlin, 10405, Germany. mail@karg-elert.de, http://www.karg-elert.de.

780 DEU ISSN 1434-4270
KARLSRUHER BEITRAEGE ZUR MUSIKWISSENSCHAFT. Text in German. 1999. irreg., latest vol.10, 2009. price varies. **Document type:** *Monographic series, Academic/Scholarly.*
Published by: Peter Lang GmbH (Subsidiary of: Peter Lang Publishing Group), Eschborner Landstr 42-50, Frankfurt Am Main, 60489, Germany. TEL 49-69-7807050, FAX 49-69-78070550, zentrale.frankfurt@peterlang.com. Ed. Siegfrid Schmalzriedt.

780 DEU
KASSELER SCHRIFTEN ZUR MUSIK. Text in German. 1988. irreg., latest vol.3, 1993. price varies. **Document type:** *Monographic series, Academic/Scholarly.*
Published by: Baerenreiter Verlag, Heinrich-Schuetz-Allee 35, Kassel, 34131, Germany. TEL 49-561-3105154, FAX 49-561-3105195, order@baerenreiter.com, http://www.baerenreiter.com.

780 RUS
KAZANSKII GOSUDARSTVENNYI PEDAGOGICHESKII INSTITUT. VOPROSY ISTORII, TEORII MUZYKI I MUZYKAL'NOGO VOSPITANIYA. SBORNIK. Text in Russian. 1970. irreg. price varies. **Description:** Contains the research of theoretical and historical materials about professional training of the school musical teachers.
Published by: Kazanskii Gosudarstvennyi Pedagogicheskii Institut, Ul Mezhlauk 1, Kazan, 420021, Russian Federation. Circ: 600.

781.64 GBR ISSN 0262-6624
ML3533.8
KERRANG!; life is loud. Text in English. 1981. w. adv. back issues avail. **Document type:** *Magazine, Consumer.* **Description:** Covers heavy metal music for young men.
—CCC.
Published by: H. Bauer Publishing Ltd. (Subsidiary of: Bauer Media Group), Media House, Lynchwood, Peterborough, Cambridgeshire PE2 6EA, United Kingdom. http://www.bauer.co.uk. Ed. Nichola Browne. Adv. contact Marco Soares TEL 44-20-72958511. page GBP 4,785.

781.66 ESP
KERRANG! (SPANISH EDITION). Text in Spanish. m. EUR 28 domestic (effective 2009). adv. **Document type:** *Magazine, Consumer.*
Published by: M C Ediciones, Paseo de Sant Gervasi 16-20, Barcelona, 08022, Spain. TEL 34-93-2541250, FAX 34-93-2541262, http://www.mcediciones.net. Circ: 241,000.

780 330 GBR ISSN 1751-9314
KEY NOTE MARKET REVIEW: MUSIC INDUSTRY. Variant title: Music Industry Market Review. Text in English. 2006. irreg., latest 2010, Feb. GBP 750 per issue (effective 2010). **Document type:** *Report, Trade.* **Description:** Provides an overview of a music industry and includes executive summary, market research survey, consumer lifestyles, forecasts, music production and distribution information of entertainment and more.
Incorporates (1997-200?): Key Note Market Report: C D & Tapes (1460-7492)
Published by: Key Note Ltd. (Subsidiary of: Bonnier Business Information), Harlequin House, 5th Fl, 7 High St, Teddington, Richmond upon Thames, TW11 8EE, United Kingdom. TEL 44-845-5040452, FAX 44-845-5040453, info@keynote.co.uk.

786 USA ISSN 0730-0158
KEYBOARD; the world's leading music technology magazine. Text in English. 1975. m. USD 12 domestic; USD 27 in Canada & Mexico; USD 37 elsewhere (effective 2008). adv. bk.rev. charts; illus. cum.index. back issues avail.; reprints avail. **Document type:** *Magazine, Consumer.* **Description:** For keyboard musicians of all styles and levels of ability. Teaches how to put more music in your technology.
Formerly (until 1981): Contemporary Keyboard (0361-5820)
Related titles: Microfilm ed.: (from PQC); Online - full text ed.
Indexed: A22, A27, C12, G05, G06, G07, G08, I05, I07, IIMP, M01, M02, M11, MAG, MusicInd, P10, P16, P48, P53, P54, PQC, RASB, RILM, V02.
—BLDSC (5091.840500), IE, Infotrieve, Ingenta. **CCC.**
Published by: NewBay Media, LLC (Subsidiary of: The Wicks Group of Companies, LLC.), 810 Seventh Ave, 27th Fl, New York, NY 10019. TEL 212-378-0400, FAX 212-378-0470, customerservice@nbmedia.com, http://www.nbmedia.com. Ed. Ernie Rideout TEL 650-238-0289. Pub. Joe Perry TEL 770-343-9978. adv.: page USD 6,690; trim 8 x 10.5. Circ: 36,317.

786 GBR ISSN 0269-3836
KEYBOARD PLAYER; keyboards, organs, pianos, synthesizers. Text in English. 1979. m. GBP 35 domestic; GBP 48 in Europe; GBP 60 elsewhere; GBP 2.75 per issue (effective 2009). adv. bk.rev. back issues avail. **Document type:** *Magazine, Consumer.* **Description:** Features articles that cover all types of keyboard instruments including portables, workstations, synthesizers, pianos and organs, plus amplification/speaker systems, computer music software and ancillary equipment.
Incorporates (1979-1985): Organ Player and Keyboard Review (0144-8331)
Related titles: Online - full text ed.: GBP 3.50 per issue (effective 2009).
Address: 48 Mereway Rd, Twickenham, Middlesex TW2 6RG, United Kingdom. TEL 44-20-82413695. Adv. contact Paul Cohen.

786.6 USA ISSN 1083-835X
ML1
KEYBOARD TEACHER. Text in English. 1964. bi-m. (except Jul. and Aug.). USD 25 to members (effective 1998). bk.rev. **Document type:** *Newsletter.*
Former titles: Organ Teacher; N A O T Notes (0027-5948)
Published by: Keyboard Teachers Association International, Inc., 361 Pin Oak Ln, Westbury, NY 11590-1941. Ed. Albert Devito. Circ: 2,000.

780 DEU ISSN 0178-4641
KEYBOARDS. Text in German. 1984. bi-m. EUR 29 domestic; EUR 33 foreign; EUR 5.50 newsstand/cover (effective 2011). adv. bk.rev. **Document type:** *Magazine, Consumer.*
Indexed: IBR, IBZ.
Published by: Musik - Media Verlag GmbH (Subsidiary of: Ebner Verlag GmbH), Emil-Hoffmann-Str 13, Cologne, 50996, Germany. TEL 49-2236-962170, FAX 49-2236-962175, info@musikmedia.de, http://www.musikmedia.de. Ed. Gerald Dellmann. Adv. contact Christiane Weyres. Circ: 8,126 (paid and controlled).

789.49 621.389 FRA ISSN 1773-1526
KEYBOARDS RECORDING. Text in French. 2005. m. (11/yr). EUR 45 (effective 2009). **Document type:** *Magazine, Consumer.*
Formed by the merger of (2001-2005): Recording Musicien (1628-3392); (2004-2005): Keyboards Home Studio (1638-7155); Which was formerly (1987-2004): Keyboards Magazine (0981-2008)
Published by: Groupe Express-Roularta, 29 Rue de Chateaudun, Paris Cede, 75308, France. TEL 33-1-75551000, http://www.groupe-exp.com.

780 DEU ISSN 0938-3573
KEYS; Magazin fur Musik und Computer. Text in German. 1989. m. EUR 51.60; EUR 5 newsstand/cover (effective 2007). adv. bk.rev.; music rev.; software rev. back issues avail. **Document type:** *Magazine, Consumer.* **Description:** Contains information about music and the use of computers.
Related titles: Online - full text ed.
Published by: P P V Medien GmbH, Postfach 57, Bergkirchen, 85230, Germany. TEL 49-8131-56550, FAX 49-8131-565510, ppv@ppvmedien.de, http://www.ppvmedien.de. Ed. Anselm Roessler. Adv. contact Marion Heinemann. B&W page EUR 3,000, color page EUR 5,000; trim 185 x 254. Circ: 15,574 (paid). **Subscr. to:** Verlag Erwin Bochinsky GmbH, Muenchener Str 45, Frankfurt Am Main 60329, Germany. **Dist. by:** IPV, Postfach 103246, Hamburg 20022, Germany.

780 USA ISSN 0199-6657
KICKS. Text in English. 1979. a. USD 5 per issue (effective 2007). adv. bk.rev.; film rev.; rec.rev. **Document type:** *Magazine, Consumer.* **Description:** Covers rock & roll and popular culture.
Published by: Norton Records, PO Box 646, Cooper Sta, New York, NY 10276-0646. TEL 718-789-4438, FAX 718-398-9215. Ed., Adv. contact Billy Miller. Pubs. Billy Miller, Miriam Linna. R&P Miriam Linna. Circ: 10,000.

KIDSHOP; was Kinder wuenschen und Eltern wissen muessen. *see* CHILDREN AND YOUTH—About

780 DEU
KIELER SCHRIFTEN ZUR MUSIKWISSENSCHAFT. Text in German. 1967. irreg., latest vol.51, 2006. price varies. **Document type:** *Monographic series, Academic/Scholarly.*
Published by: Baerenreiter Verlag, Heinrich-Schuetz-Allee 35, Kassel, 34131, Germany. TEL 49-561-3105154, FAX 49-561-3105195, order@baerenreiter.com, http://www.baerenreiter.com. Eds. Friedhelm Krummacher, Heinrich Schwab.

780.82 SWE ISSN 1653-3348
KIM. Text in Swedish. 1992. q. SEK 200 domestic to individuals; SEK 300 foreign to individuals; SEK 400 domestic to institutions; SEK 500 foreign to institutions (effective 2006). adv. back issues avail. **Document type:** *Journal, Trade.* **Description:** Devoted to women in the field of music in the past as well as in the present.
Former titles (until 2005): Musikmagasin Evterpe (1650-4747); (until 2000): Evterpe (1403-8838)
Published by: Foereningen Evterpe - Kvinnor i Musik, c/o Suzanne Persson, Nejlikevaegen 14, Tullinge, 650, Sweden. info@evterpe.se, http://www.evterpe.se.

782.5 DEU ISSN 1863-2440
KINDER- UND JUGENDSTIMME. Text in German. 2007. irreg., latest vol.5, 2010. price varies. **Document type:** *Monographic series, Academic/Scholarly.*
Published by: Logos Verlag Berlin, Comeniushof, Gubener Str 47, Berlin, 10243, Germany. TEL 49-30-42851090, FAX 49-30-42851092, redaktion@logos-verlag.de. Ed. Michael Fuchs.

781.64 DEU
KING. Text in German. 1999. m. adv. **Document type:** *Magazine, Consumer.*
Published by: Piranha Media GmbH, Rolandstr 69, Cologne, 50677, Germany. TEL 49-221-5797800, FAX 49-221-5797879. adv.: page EUR 7,500. Circ: 399,600 (paid and controlled).

781.64 SWE ISSN 1502-7783
KINGSIZE (NORWEGIAN ED.). Text in Norwegian. 2001. 6/yr. SEK 219 (effective 2010). adv. **Document type:** *Magazine, Consumer.* **Description:** Covers Scandinavian and international hiphop culture and lifestyle.
Related titles: Online - full text ed.; ◆ Swedish ed.: Kingsize (Swedish Ed.). ISSN 1652-8190.
Published by: Kingsize Publishing AB, Erik Dahlbergsgatan 30, Stockholm, 115 32, Sweden. TEL 46-8-52800055, FAX 46-8-52800051. Ed. Martin Brandt. Adv. contact Matthias Sjodin.

781.64 SWE ISSN 1652-8190
KINGSIZE (SWEDISH ED.). Text in Swedish. 2004. 6/yr. SEK 189 (effective 2007). adv. **Document type:** *Magazine, Consumer.* **Description:** Covers Scandinavian and international hiphop culture and lifestyle.
Related titles: Online - full text ed.; ◆ Norwegian ed.: Kingsize (Norwegian Ed.). ISSN 1502-7783.
Published by: Kingsize Publishing AB, Erik Dahlbergsgatan 30, Stockholm, 115 32, Sweden. TEL 46-8-52800055, FAX 46-8-52800051. Ed. Martin Brandt. Pub. Camilla Berg.

782.3 DEU ISSN 1436-0276
KIRCHENMUSIKALISCHE MITTEILUNGEN DER DIOEZESE ROTTENBURG-STUTTGART. Text in German. 1967. 2/yr. bk.rev. **Document type:** *Magazine, Consumer.* **Description:** Contains information about church music in the diocese of Rottenburg-Stuttgart.
Formerly (until 1997): Kirchenmusikalische Mitteilungen (0174-2116)
Published by: Amt fuer Kirchenmusik, St Meinrad Weg 6, Rottenburg Am Neckar, 72108, Germany. TEL 49-7472-93840, FAX 49-7472-938420, kontakt@amt-fuer-kirchenmusik.de. Ed. Ursula Kluike. Circ: 3,850 (controlled).

780 200 DEU ISSN 0939-4761
ML5
KIRCHENMUSIKALISCHE NACHRICHTEN. Text in German. 1950. s-a. EUR 5 to members (effective 2010). bk.rev. **Document type:** *Newsletter, Consumer.*
Published by: Evangelische Kirche in Hessen und Nassau in Frankfurt, Amt fuer Kirchenmusik, Markgrafenstr 14, Frankfurt Am Main, 60487, Germany. TEL 49-69-713790, FAX 49-69-71379131, info@kirchenmusik-ekhn.de, http://www.kirchenmusik-ekhn.de. Circ: 1,800.

782.3 DEU ISSN 0075-6199
ML5
KIRCHENMUSIKALISCHES JAHRBUCH. Text in German. 1876. a. bk.rev. **Document type:** *Journal, Academic/Scholarly.*
Formerly (until 1886): Caecilienkalender
Indexed: A21, DIP, IBR, IBZ, IIMP, M11, MusicInd, RI-1, RI-2, RILM.
Published by: Allgemeiner Caecilien-Verband fuer Deutschland, Andreasstr 9, Regensburg, 93059, Germany. TEL 49-941-84339, FAX 49-941-8703432, info@acv-deutschland.de. Ed. Guenther Massenkeil.

780.01 DEU
KLANG UND BEGRIFF. Text in German. 2004. irreg., latest vol.2, 2005. price varies. **Document type:** *Monographic series, Academic/Scholarly.*
Published by: Stiftung Preussischer Kulturbesitz, Staatliches Institut fuer Musikforschung, Tiergartenstr 1, Berlin, 10785, Germany. TEL 49-30-254810, FAX 49-30-25481172, http://www.sim.spk-berlin.de.

780 DEU
KLANGZEITEN; Musik, Politik und Gesellschaft. Text in German. 2004. irreg., latest vol.9, 2011. price varies. **Document type:** *Monographic series, Academic/Scholarly.*
Published by: Boehlau Verlag GmbH & Cie, Ursulaplatz 1, Cologne, 50668, Germany. TEL 49-221-913900, FAX 49-221-9139011, vertrieb@boehlau.de, http://www.boehlau.de.

780 NLD ISSN 1569-9420
DE KLANK. Text in Dutch. 1970. 8/yr. EUR 45 (effective 2010). adv. bk.rev. illus.
Formerly (until 2001): Klank en Weerklank (0030-3836); Supersedes: Opmaat
Indexed: MusicInd.
Published by: Stichting Vrienden van het Brabants Orkest/Friends of the Brabant Orchestra Foundation, Postbus 230, Eindhoven, 5600 AE, Netherlands. TEL 31-40-2655699, FAX 31-40-2463459, info@brabantsorkest.nl, http://www.brabantsorkest.nl/.

780 NLD ISSN 2211-5250
KLANKWIJZER. Text in Dutch. 2003. m. EUR 25 domestic to individuals; EUR 30 foreign to individuals (effective 2011). adv. bk.rev.; rec.rev. illus. **Document type:** *Bulletin, Trade.* **Description:** Publishes news and information relating to music, performance and related matters.
Formerly (until 2011): Music and Show (1571-6791); Which was formed by the merger of (1953-2003): St. Caecilia (0036-2786); (1993-2003): Klank en Show (0929-161X); Which was formed by the 1993 merger of: Muziek en Show (0929-1601); Which was formerly (1980-1987): Muziek (0929-1598); (1978-1993): A N U M Klanken (0929-158X); Which superseded (1921-1978): Musica (0027-450X)
Published by: Verenigde Nederlandse Muziekbonden, Postbus 3535, Thorn, 6017 ZG, Netherlands. TEL 31-475-563054, office@fkm-nederland.nl, http://www.fkm-nederland.nl.

782 NLD ISSN 1388-4581
KLASSIEKE ZAKEN. Text in Dutch. 1993. bi-m. EUR 12.50 (effective 2009). adv. **Document type:** *Magazine, Trade.*
Formerly (until 1998): Klassiek (1388-4573)
Published by: (Vereniging Klassieke Zaken), iMediate, Postbus 2227, Hilversum, 1200 CE, Netherlands. TEL 31-35-6465800, FAX 31-35-6465899, sales@imediate.nl, http://www.imediate.nl.

787 DEU ISSN 1619-5663
KLASSIK HEUTE (ONLINE). Text in German. 1998. w. **Document type:** *Magazine, Consumer.*
Formerly (until 2002): Klassik Heute (Print) (1435-2419)
Media: Online - full content.
Indexed: RILM.
Published by: Klassik-Treff.GmbH, Jaegerstr 17, Hoergertshausen, 85413, Germany. TEL 49-8764-920942, FAX 49-8764-920943.

780.78 DNK ISSN 1901-595X
KLASSISK; magasinet for musikelskere. Text in Danish. 2005. q. DKK 229; DKK 69 per issue (effective 2009). music rev.; rec.rev. **Document type:** *Magazine, Consumer.* **Description:** Devoted to news about classical music worldwide.
Published by: Klassisk ApS, PO Box 2517, Copenhagen OE, 2100, Denmark. TEL 45-29-909571, info@klassisk.org, http://www.klassisk.org. Ed. Per Rask Madsen.

781.68 NOR ISSN 1502-0274
KLASSISK MUSIKKMAGASIN; gallerirunden, aktuelt musikk, programsider. Text in Norwegian. 1999. q. NOK 229 (effective 2007). adv. **Document type:** *Magazine, Consumer.*
Published by: Mezzo Media AS, PO Box 11, Sandefjord, 3201, Norway. TEL 47-33-421575, FAX 47-33-421571, http://www.mezzomedia.no. Ed. Mona Levin. Adv. contact Morten Olsen. page NOK 33,000; 208 x 278.

786.2 SWE ISSN 1654-3734
KLAVERNYTT. Text in Swedish. 2007. q. **Document type:** *Magazine, Consumer.*
Published by: Klaverens Hus, Centrum foer Svensk Klaverkultur/ Swedish Research Center for Keyboard Instruments, Oxtorget 4, Soederhamn, 82632, Sweden. TEL 46-76-2951472, info@klaverenshus.com, http://www.klaverenshus.com.

KLIK. *see* MOTION PICTURES

789.5 NLD ISSN 0023-2181
KLOK EN KLEPEL. Text in Dutch. 1959. q. EUR 17.50 domestic; EUR 20 foreign (effective 2009). adv. bk.rev.; music rev.; rec.rev.; Website rev. illus. 36 p./no. 2 cols./p.; back issues avail. **Document type:** *Magazine, Academic/Scholarly.* **Description:** Covers carillons, carillon music and the history of bells.
Published by: Nederlandse Klokkenspel-Vereniging, Oranjestraat 27, Utrecht, 3511 RA, Netherlands. TEL 31-30-2935114, http://www.klokkenspel.org. Ed. Hylke Banning. adv.: page EUR 140. Circ: 550.

781.64 LVA ISSN 1407-1649
KLUBS. Text in Latvian. 1994. m. **Document type:** *Magazine, Consumer.*
Indexed: MLA-IB.
Published by: Zurnals Santa, Balasta Dambis 3, PO Box 32, Riga, LV-1081, Latvia. TEL 371-762-8275, FAX 371-746-5450, santa@santa.lv.

781.64 LVA ISSN 1691-0257
KLUBS EXCLUSIVE. Text in Latvian. 2002. q. **Document type:** *Magazine, Consumer.*
Published by: Zurnals Santa, Balasta Dambis 3, PO Box 32, Riga, LV-1081, Latvia. TEL 371-762-8275, FAX 371-746-5450, santa@santa.lv.

780 CHE
KNABENMUSIK DER STADT ZUERICH. MITTEILUNGSBLATT. Text in German. 6/yr.
Address: Postfach 6817, Zuerich, 8023, Switzerland. TEL 01-9802903. Circ: 1,200.

781.64 GBR ISSN 1464-1453
KNOWLEDGE; the drum and bass magazine. Text in English. 1994. bi-m. GBP 12.50 domestic; GBP 17.50 in Europe; GBP 26 in North & South America; GBP 27.50 elsewhere; GBP 2.95 newsstand/cover (effective 2000). **Document type:** *Magazine, Consumer.* **Description:** Covers all aspects of the underground dance music scene and includes record reviews, interviews, competitions, and scene commentary.
Published by: Vision Publishing, 14 King Sq, 2nd Fl, Bristol, Avon BS2 8JJ, United Kingdom. TEL 44-117-914-3306, FAX 44-117-914-3305. Eds. Colin Steven, Rachel Patey. **Dist. by:** Lakeside Newsagents, Unit 10, Tideway Industrial Estate, 87 Kirtling St, London SW8 5BP, United Kingdom. TEL 44-20-7720-6680.

780 USA ISSN 1084-1776
ML1
KODALY ENVOY. Text in English. 1975. q. adv. bk.rev. illus. index. **Document type:** *Journal, Trade.*
Indexed: A01, CA, E03, ERI, IIMP, M11, MusicInd, RILM, T02.
Published by: Organization of American Kodaly Educators, 1612 29th Ave S., Moorhead, MN 56560. TEL 218-227-6253, FAX 218-227-6254, http://www.oake.org. Ed. Beth Pontiff. Circ: 1,600 (paid).

780.7 CAN ISSN 1180-1344
KODALY SOCIETY OF CANADA. ALLA BREVE. Text in English, French. 1976. 2/yr. CAD 20 to institutions. adv. bk.rev. back issues avail. **Document type:** *Journal, Academic/Scholarly.*
Former titles: Kodaly Society of Canada. Notes; Kodaly Institute of Canada. Notes (0700-3269)
Indexed: CMPI.
Published by: Kodaly Society of Canada, Velvet Neufeld, 314-25 Valhalla Dr., Winnipeg, MB R2G 0X7, Canada. Ed. Malcolm Bradley. Pub. Sylvia Chodas. Adv. contact Maureen MacDougall. Circ: 550.

780 DEU
KOELNER BEITRAEGE ZUR MUSIKFORSCHUNG. Text in German. 1980. irreg., latest vol.211, 2002. price varies. **Document type:** *Monographic series, Academic/Scholarly.*
Published by: Gustav Bosse Verlag, Heinrich-Schuetz-Allee 35, Kassel, 34131, Germany. TEL 49-561-3105140, FAX 49-561-3105240, info@bosse-verlag.de, http://www.bosse-verlag.de. Ed. Wendelin Goebel.

780.65 DEU
KOELNER PHILHARMONIEPERSOENLICH. Text in German. 2000. bi-m. adv. **Document type:** *Journal, Consumer.*
Published by: M W K Zimmermann & Haehnel GmbH, Elisenstr 24, Cologne, 50667, Germany. TEL 49-221-123435, FAX 49-221-138560, info@mwk-koeln.de, http://www.mwk-koeln.de. adv.: B&W page EUR 2,390, color page EUR 3,175. Circ: 54,000 (controlled).

782.5 SWE ISSN 1401-498X
KOERSAANG. Text in Swedish. 1928. q. SEK 80 to members (effective 1999). adv. bk.rev. bibl.; charts; illus. 32 p./no.; **Document type:** *Bulletin.*
Former titles (until 1996): Koerlivet (1400-2450); (until 1994): Musiklivet - Vaar Saang (0027-4836)
Indexed: RILM.
Published by: Riksfoerbundet Svensk Koersaang/Swedish Choral Association, Nybrokajen 11, Stockholm, 11148, Sweden. TEL 46-8-643 53 33, FAX 46-8-643 53 33. Ed. Stellan Sagvik. Adv. contact Marie Olausson. color page SEK 10,000; 190 x 255. Circ: 18,000.

780.01 DEU
KOMPONISTEN DER GEGENWART. Text in German. 1992. 7 base vols. plus s-a. updates. looseleaf. EUR 112.50 base vol(s). (effective 2009). **Document type:** *Directory, Academic/Scholarly.*
Published by: Edition Text und Kritik in Richard Boorberg Verlag GmbH & Co. KG (Subsidiary of: Richard Boorberg Verlag GmbH und Co. KG), Levelingstr 6A, Munich, 81673, Germany. TEL 49-89-43600012, FAX 49-89-43600019, info@etk-muenchen.de. Eds. Hanns Werner Heister, Walter Wolfgang Sparrer.

780 920 AUT
KOMPONISTEN UNSERER ZEIT. Text in German. 1964. irreg., latest vol.28, 2000. **Document type:** *Monographic series, Academic/Scholarly.*
Formerly: Oesterreichische Komponisten des 20. Jahrhunderts (0078-3501)
Published by: Lafite Verlag, Hegelgasse 13-22, Vienna, 1010, Austria. TEL 43-1-5126869, FAX 43-1-51268699, edition@musikzeit.at. Ed. Marion Diederichs-Lafite. Adv. contact Christine Goldenberg.

780.7 DEU
KONGRESSBERICHT BUNDESSCHULMUSIKWOCHE. Text in German. 1955. biennial, latest vol.28, 2010. price varies. back issues avail. **Document type:** *Monographic series.*
Formerly: Vortraege der Bundesschulmusikwoche (0172-9624)

Published by: (Verband Deutscher Schulmusiker), Schott Musik International GmbH, Weihergarten 5, Mainz, 55116, Germany. TEL 49-6131-2460, FAX 49-6131-246211, info@schott-musik.de, http://www.schott-musik.de. Ed. Dieter Zimmerschied. Circ: 800.

780.9 NLD ISSN 1383-7079
ML27.N4

➤ **KONINKLIJKE VERENIGING VOOR NEDERLANDSE MUZIEKGESCHIEDENIS. TIJDSCHRIFT/ROYAL SOCIETY FOR MUSIC HISTORY OF THE NETHERLANDS. REVIEW.** Text in Dutch, English; Summaries in English. 1869. s-a. price varies. bk.rev. cum.index: vols. 1-30. back issues avail.; reprints avail. **Document type:** *Monographic series, Academic/Scholarly.* **Description:** Covers the musical historiography of the Low Countries, including research on the life and work of major and minor composers.
Former titles (until 1996): Vereniging voor Nederlandse Muziekgeschiedenis. Tijdschrift (0042-3874); (until 1960): Vereeniging voor Noord-Nederland's Muziekgeschiedenis. Tijdschrift (0921-3260); (until 1882): Bouwsteenen (Amsterdam) (1571-9529)
Related titles: Microfiche ed.; Online - full text ed.: ISSN 1875-6409.
Indexed: A20, A22, ArtHuCI, CurCont, IIMP, M11, MusicInd, PCI, RILM, SCOPUS, T02, W07.
—IE, Ingenta.
Published by: Koninklijke Vereniging voor Nederlandse Muziekgeschiedenis/Royal Society for Music History of The Netherlands, PO Box 1514, Utrecht, 3500 BM, Netherlands. secretaris@kvnm.nl, http://www.kvnm.nl. Ed. Eric Jas.

781.64 ITA ISSN 1722-0270
KONSEQUENZ; rivista semestrale di musiche contemporanee. Text in Italian. 1994. s-a. EUR 54 domestic; EUR 60.50 in the European Union; EUR 87.50 elsewhere (effective 2008). **Document type:** *Magazine, Consumer.*
Published by: (Associazione Musicale Ferenc Liszt), Liguori Editore, Via Posillipo 394, Naples, 80123, Italy. TEL 39-081-7206111, FAX 39-081-7206244, liguori@liguori.it, http://www.liguori.it. Ed. Girolamo de Simone.

782.5 NLD ISSN 1381-9097
KOORINFORMATIE. Text in Dutch. 1967. 8/yr. EUR 34.50 domestic; EUR 40.50 in Belgium (effective 2010). **Document type:** *Magazine, Trade.*
Published by: Gooi en Sticht, Postbus 5018, Kampen, 8260 GA, Netherlands. TEL 31-38-3392556, FAX 31-38-3311776, gens@kok.nl, http://www.kok.nl.

781.642 SWE ISSN 0349-7208
KOUNTRY KORRAL MAGAZINE. Text in Swedish. 1968. 4/yr. SEK 160, DKK 150, NOK 170 (effective 2002); to members. adv. bk.rev.; music rev.; rec.rev. bibl.; charts; illus. back issues avail.
Formerly (until 1979): Kountry Korral (0023-429X)
Published by: Kountry Korral Foereningen, PO Box 6031, Falun, 79106, Sweden. TEL 46-243-853-85, FAX 46-243-139-44. Ed., Pub. Lars Kjellberg.

KUENSTE - WELTEN - UEBERGAENGE. *see* LITERATURE

KUERSCHNERS MUSIKER-HANDBUCH. *see* BIOGRAPHY

KULTUR NEWS; Mitteilungen des Kulturrings in Berlin. *see* ART

KULTURA-EXTRA; das online-magazin. *see* ART

KULTURSMOCKAN. *see* EDUCATION

780 SWE ISSN 1100-2751
KUNGLIGA MUSIKALISKA AKADEMIEN. AARSSKRIFT. Text in Swedish. 1943. a. back issues avail. **Document type:** *Yearbook.*
Formerly (until 1987): Kungliga Musikaliska Akademiens Aarsskrift (0349-3466)
Related titles: Online - full text ed.
Published by: Kungliga Musikaliska Akademien/Royal Swedish Academy of Music, Blasieholmstorg 8, Stockholm, 11148, Sweden. TEL 46-8-4071800, FAX 46-8-6118718, adm@musakad.se.

780 SWE ISSN 0347-5158
KUNGLIGA MUSIKALISKA AKADEMIEN. SKRIFTSERIE. Text in Multiple languages. 1957. irreg., latest vol.119, 2009. price varies. back issues avail. **Document type:** *Monographic series, Academic/ Scholarly.*
Former titles (until 1977): Kungliga Musikaliska Akademien. Publikationer; (until 1971): Kungliga Musikaliska Akademien med Musikhoegskolan. Publikationer (0464-0578)
Published by: Kungliga Musikaliska Akademien/Royal Swedish Academy of Music, Blasieholmstorg 8, Stockholm, 11148, Sweden. TEL 46-8-4071800, FAX 46-8-6118718, adm@musakad.se.

KUNST-, MUSIK- UND THEATERWISSENSCHAFT. *see* ART

780.7 NLD ISSN 1570-7989
KUNSTZONE; tijdschrift voor kunst en cultuur in het onderwijs. Text in Dutch. 10/yr. EUR 49.75 domestic; EUR 72.50 foreign; EUR 30 to students (effective 2010). adv. bk.rev. bibl.; illus. index. **Document type:** *Magazine, Trade.*
Formerly (until 2002): All'Art (1568-2986); Incorporates (1963-2004): Muziek en Onderwijs (0378-0651)
Published by: Stichting Kunstzone, Lisztstraat 2, Berkel en Rodenrijs, 2651 VL, Netherlands. TEL 31-10-5114397. Ed. Jos Herfs. adv.: B&W page EUR 1,000, color page EUR 1,400; trim 210 x 297. Circ: 2,800.

780 DEU ISSN 1613-7787
KURT-WEILL-GESELLSCHAFT DESSAU. VEROEFFENTLICHUNGEN. Text in German. 1996. irreg., latest vol.6, 2006. price varies. **Document type:** *Monographic series, Academic/Scholarly.*
Published by: Waxmann Verlag GmbH, Steinfurter Str 555, Muenster, 48159, Germany. TEL 49-251-265040, FAX 49-251-2650426, info@waxmann.com.

780.6 USA ISSN 0899-6407
ML410.W395
KURT WEILL NEWSLETTER. Text in English. 1983. 2/yr. free. bk.rev. **Document type:** *Newsletter, Consumer.* **Description:** Devoted to the life and works of Kurt Weill and Lotte Lenya. Includes feature articles, news about current productions and publications, bibliographies, and critical reviews of performances, books and recordings.
Indexed: IBT&D, IIMP, M11, MLA-IB, MusicInd, PCI, RILM, T02.
—Ingenta.
Published by: Kurt Weill Foundation for Music, 7 E 20th St, New York, NY 10003-1106. TEL 212-505-5240, FAX 212-353-9663. Ed. Elmar Juchem. Circ: 6,000 (paid and controlled).

780 DNK ISSN 0907-7626
KVINDER I MUSIK. Text in Danish. 1984. a. DKK 259 membership (effective 2009). bk.rev.; music rev. **Document type:** *Yearbook, Consumer.* **Description:** Contains articles and features on women in classical and modern music.
Formerly (until 1992): K I M -Nyt (0903-6598)
Address: c/o Det Kongelige Danske Musikkonservatorium, Niels Brocks Gade 1, Copenhagen V, 1574, Denmark. TEL 45-33-692246, info@kvinderimusik.dk, http://www.kvinderimusik.dk.

780.71 JPN ISSN 0388-7502
KYOIKU ONGAKU, CHUGAKU KOKO-BAN/EDUCATIONAL MUSIC, JUNIOR HIGH AND HIGH SCHOOL. Text in Japanese. m. JPY 1,000. adv. **Description:** Presents study and teaching methods.
Formerly: Educational Music, Secondary School
Published by: Ongaku No Tomo Sha Corp., c/o KakuyukiNabeshima, 6-30 Kagura-Zaka, Shinjuku-ku, Tokyo, 162-0825, Japan. FAX 81-3-3235-5731. Ed. Hisatsugu Shimizu. Pub. Jua Meguro. R&P Tetsuo Morita TEL 81-3-3235-2111. Adv. contact Takao Oya. B&W page JPY 120,000, color page JPY 300,000; trim 182 x 257. Circ: 35,000.

780.71 JPN ISSN 0388-7480
KYOIKU ONGAKU, SHOGAKU-BAN/EDUCATIONAL MUSIC, ELEMENTARY SCHOOL. Text in Japanese. 1946. m. JPY 1,000. adv. **Document type:** *Consumer.* **Description:** Presents study and teaching methods.
Published by: Ongaku No Tomo Sha Corp., c/o KakuyukiNabeshima, 6-30 Kagura-Zaka, Shinjuku-ku, Tokyo, 162-0825, Japan. FAX 81-3-3235-5731. Ed. Hisatsugu Shimizu. Pub. Jun Meguro. R&P Testsuo Morita TEL 81-3-3235-2144. Adv. contact Takao Oya. B&W page JPY 120,000, color page JPY 300,000; trim 182 x 257. Circ: 35,000.

781.71 781.5 SWE ISSN 1101-9670
KYRKOKOERJOURNALEN; tidning foer svenska kyrkans koerer. Text in Swedish. 1990. bi-m. SEK 132 (effective 2011). adv. **Document type:** *Magazine, Consumer.*
Related titles: Online - full text ed.: 2010.
Published by: Sveriges Kyrkosaangsfoerbund, c/o Drew Baldwin, Ploglandsvaegen 2, Ekeroe, 17837, Sweden. TEL 46-70-8870244, http://www.sjungkyrkan.nu. Ed. Marita Skoeldberg. Adv. contact MariAnne Widner. Circ: 5,000.

783 SWE ISSN 0281-286X
ML5
KYRKOMUSIKERNAS TIDNING. Short title: K M T. Text in Swedish. 1935-1982; resumed 1984. 12/yr. SEK 280 (effective 1999). adv. bk.rev. illus.
Former titles (until 1984): Svensk Kyrkomusik. Uppl. A - B. och Uppl.B; (until 1970): K M T - K S F; Which was formed by the 1967 merger of: Kyrkosaangsfoerbundet; (until 1967): Kyrkomusikernas Tidning (0347-416X)
Indexed: RILM.
Published by: Kyrkomusikernas Riksfoerbund (KMR), Fack 12229, Stockholm, 10226, Sweden. TEL 46-8-7376615, FAX 46-8-7376611. Ed. Carl Johan Wilson. Circ: 4,000. **Subscr. to:** Fack 2100, Ytterby 44202, Sweden.

789.6 305.896 USA ISSN 1525-853X
L A RITMO.COM; Latin American Rhythm & Sound Magazine. (Latin American) Text in English, Spanish. 1998. bi-w. free (effective 2010). adv. music rev. back issues avail. **Document type:** *Magazine, Consumer.* **Description:** Provides in-depth coverage of Latin music, including soft rock.
Media: Online - full text.
Published by: Tag It, 18-14 Astoria Bd., LIC, NY 11102. TEL 718-278-0662, stratagem@taggin.com, http://taggin.com/home/tagit.about.php3.

780 371.3 ESP ISSN 1575-9563
MT1
L E E M E. REVISTA ELECTRONICA. (Lista Electronica Europea de Musica en la Educacion) Text in Multiple languages. 1998. s-a. free (effective 2011). **Document type:** *Journal, Academic/Scholarly.*
Media: Online - full text.
Indexed: CA, F04, T02.
—CCC.
Published by: Universidad de la Rioja, Departamento de Expresion Artistica, Av de la Paz 93, Logrono, 26006, Spain. TEL 34-941-299100. Ed. Jesus Tejada.

L.O.S.; Das Entertainment-Magazin. *see* MOTION PICTURES

780.42 DEU
L P MAGAZIN; Magazin fuer analoges HIFI & Vinyl-Kultur. (Langspielplatten) Text in German. 2005. bi-m. EUR 24.90; EUR 4.80 newsstand/cover (effective 2011). adv. **Document type:** *Magazine, Consumer.*
Published by: Michael E. Brieden Verlag GmbH, Gartroper Str 42, Duisburg, 47138, Germany. TEL 49-203-42920, FAX 49-203-4292149, info@brieden.de, http://www.brieden.de. Ed. Holger Barske. Adv. contact Udo Schulz. Circ: 25,000 (paid and controlled).

781.624 USA ISSN 1947-265X
▼ **LADIES OF COUNTRY MUSIC MAGAZINE**; the new ladies of country music. Abbreviated title: L O C M Magazine. Text in English. 2009. m. USD 39.97; USD 6.99 per issue (effective 2009). **Document type:** *Magazine, Consumer.* **Description:** Contains news, photos and features of the new women in country music.
Published by: L O C M Publications, 2000 Carsley Rd, Jackson, MS 39209. TEL 601-925-5271, thomas@locpublications.com, http://www.locmpublications.com.

LADYSLIPPER CATALOG AND RESOURCE GUIDE OF RECORDS, TAPES, COMPACT DISCS AND VIDEOS BY WOMEN. *see* WOMEN'S INTERESTS

781.64 POL
LAIF; magazyn kultury klubowej. Text in Polish. 2002. bi-m. 80 p./no.; **Document type:** *Magazine, Consumer.*
Related titles: Online - full content ed.
Published by: Vindobona Development Polska Sp. z. o.o., ul Dzielna 7/89, Warsaw, 00154, Poland. Ed. Kamila Kicinska. Circ: 35,000.

780 FRA ISSN 1145-2048
LARIGOT. Text in French. 1988. irreg. **Document type:** *Magazine, Consumer.*
Indexed: RILM.
Published by: Association des Collectionneurs d'Instruments de Musique a Vent, 136 Bd Magenta, Paris, 75010, France.

781.7 USA ISSN 0163-0350
ML199
➤ **LATIN AMERICAN MUSIC REVIEW/REVISTA DE MUSICA LATINO AMERICANA.** Abbreviated title: L A M R. Text in English, Spanish, Portuguese. 1965. s-a. USD 97 domestic to institutions; USD 106 in Canada to institutions; USD 112 elsewhere to institutions (effective 2011). adv. bk.rev. illus. Index. back issues avail.; reprints avail. **Document type:** *Journal, Academic/Scholarly.* **Description:** Explores the historical, ethnographic, and socio-cultural dimensions of Latin American music in Latin American social groups.
Former titles (until 1980): Anuario Interamericano de Investigacion Musical (0886-2192); (until 1970): Anuario - Tulane University. Inter-American Institute for Musical Research (0564-4429)
Related titles: Microform ed.: (from PQC); Online - full text ed.: ISSN 1536-0199.
Indexed: A01, A02, A03, A08, A20, A22, A26, A27, ASCA, ArtHuCI, BibInd, C32, CA, ChPerI, CurCont, E01, E08, FR, G08, H21, I04, I05, IBR, IBZ, IIMP, M11, MLA, MLA-IB, MusicInd, P08, P10, P48, P53, P54, PCI, PQC, RILM, S09, SCOPUS, T02, W07.
—IE, Infotrieve, Ingenta, INIST. **CCC.**
Published by: University of Texas Press, Journals Division, PO Box 7819, Austin, TX 78713. TEL 512-471-7233 ext 2, FAX 512-232-7178, journals@uts.cc.utexas.edu, http://www.utexas.edu/utpress/journals/journals.html. Ed. Robin Moore. Adv. contact Leah Dixon TEL 512-232-7618.

780 USA ISSN 1553-5460
ML199
LATIN BEAT MAGAZINE; salsa, latin jazz, latin pop, afro-world and more. Text in English. 1991. m. (10/yr). adv. back issues avail. **Document type:** *Magazine, Consumer.*
Related titles: Online - full text ed.
Indexed: I04, I05, I07, IIMP, M11, MusicInd, S23.
Address: 15900 Crenshaw Blvd, Ste 223, Gardena, CA 90249. TEL 310-516-6767, FAX 310-516-9916. Ed., Pub. Rudolph Mangual.

781.62 USA
LATIN VIBES. Text in English. 2000. m. USD 21; USD 3.50 newsstand/cover (effective 2001). adv. **Document type:** *Magazine, Consumer.*
Published by: D'Vinci International, 3013 Fountainview, #100, Houston, TX 77057. TEL 713-706-4486, FAX 713-334-9454, http://www.latinvibesmagazine.com. Ed. J R Ramos. Pub. Dvorah Hasheeve.

781.7 JPN ISSN 0288-8661
LATINA. Text in Japanese. 1952. m. JPY 6,360. adv. illus.
Formerly: Musica Iberoamericana (0027-4534)
Related titles: Online - full text ed.
Indexed: WSI.
Published by: Musica Iberoamericana Co., 1-13-6 Ebisu, Shibuya-ku, Tokyo, 150-0013, Japan. FAX 03-443-7123. Ed. Kenji Honda. Circ: 30,000.

781.7 USA
LATVJU MUZIKA. Text in Latvian. 1968. a. USD 10 (effective 2005). bk.rev. back issues avail.
Published by: Latvian Choir Association in the United States, Inc., 7886 Anita Dr, Philadelphia, PA 19111. Ed. Roberts Zuika. Circ: 1,200.

781.7 CAN ISSN 1914-4199
LAUDEM. Text in French. 1990. s-a. **Document type:** *Journal.*
Formerly (until 2005): Laudem. Bulletin (1181-9189)
Indexed: CMPI.
Published by: (Association des Musiciens Liturgiques du Canada), Editions Laudem, 1085 Rue de la Cathedrale, Montreal, PQ H3B 2V3, Canada. TEL 514-866-1661, info@laudem.org.

781.64 USA
LAUNCH. Text in English. m. USD 19.95; USD 59 foreign (effective 1999). adv. **Document type:** *Magazine, Consumer.* **Description:** Presents exclusive video concert performances by top bands, interviews with today's hottest musicians and movie stars, and video game demos.
Related titles: CD-ROM ed.; Online - full text ed. **Subscr. to:** PO Box 54041, Boulder, CO 80322-4041.

787 USA ISSN 1056-5329
ML420.L277
LEAD BELLY LETTER; to appreciate and celebrate Lead Belly music. Text in English. 1990. 4/yr. USD 17 domestic; USD 21 in Canada; USD 24 elsewhere (effective 2001). bk.rev. bibl. 8 p./no.; back issues avail. **Document type:** *Newsletter, Consumer.* **Description:** Devoted to furthering appreciation of Lead Belly music. Contains critical articles and rare photographs.
Indexed: RILM.
Published by: Lead Belly Society, PO Box 6679, Ithaca, NY 14851. TEL 607-273-6615, FAX 607-273-4816, SK86@cornell.edu. Ed., R&P Sean Killeen. Circ: 3,000.

780.42 USA ISSN 0892-1830
LEFSETZ LETTER; first in music analysis. Text in English. 1986. bi-w. USD 110 (effective 2001). **Document type:** *Newsletter.*
Address: 2128 Oak St, Ste B, Santa Monica, CA 90405. TEL 310-450-3798. Ed. Robert Scott Lefsetz.

781.66 USA
LEFT OFF THE DIAL; music for you, not them.. Text in English. w. adv. **Document type:** *Magazine, Consumer.* **Description:** Covers music spanning from classic punk of the late 70's, to 80's indie and college rock, along with artists of the 90's and today keeping the spirit alive.
Media: Online - full content.
Address: 917 N. Wayne St., Apt. 305, Arlington, VA 22201-5926. Ed. Catherine Nicholas.

780 DEU ISSN 0947-8655
ML410.B1
LEIPZIGER BEITRAEGE ZUR BACH-FORSCHUNG. Text in German. 1995. irreg., latest vol.8, 2006. price varies. **Document type:** *Monographic series, Academic/Scholarly.*
Published by: (Bach-Archiv Leipzig), Georg Olms Verlag, Hagentorwall 7, Hildesheim, 31134, Germany. TEL 49-5121-15010, FAX 49-5121-150150, info@olms.de. Ed. H J Schulze. R&P Christiane Busch.

LEISURE INDUSTRY REPORT. *see* LEISURE AND RECREATION

LEONARDO & LEONARDO MUSIC JOURNAL. *see* ART

780 500 USA ISSN 0961-1215
ML197 CODEN: LMJOEQ
➤ **LEONARDO MUSIC JOURNAL.** Abbreviated title: L M J. Text in English. 1991. a. USD 73 combined subscription per issue in US & Canada to institutions (print & online eds.) (effective 2012). adv. back issues avail.; reprints avail. **Document type:** *Journal, Academic/ Scholarly.* **Description:** Features the latest in music, multimedia art, sound science & technology.
Related titles: CD-ROM ed.: USD 50 per issue in US & Canada to institutions (effective 2012); Online - full text ed.: ISSN 1531-4812. USD 66 in US & Canada to institutions (effective 2012); ◆ Supplement to: Leonardo & Leonardo Music Journal. ISSN 0024-094X.
Indexed: A01, A02, A03, A08, A20, A22, A26, A27, ABM, ASCA, AmHI, ArtHuCI, B04, BRD, BrHumI, CA, CurCont, DIP, E01, E08, G08, H07, H08, HAb, HumInd, IBR, IBZ, IIMP, M11, MAG, MusicInd, P02, P10, P48, P53, P54, PCI, PQC, RILM, S09, SCOPUS, T02, W03, W07. —BLDSC (5182.620000), IE, Infotrieve. **CCC.**
Published by: (International Society for the Arts, Sciences and Technology), M I T Press, 55 Hayward St, Cambridge, MA 02142. TEL 617-253-2889, FAX 617-577-1545, journals-cs@mit.edu, http://mitpress.mit.edu. Ed. Nicolas Collins.

780.42 BRA ISSN 0104-2289
LETRAS TRADUZIDAS. Text in Portuguese. 1987. m.
Related titles: ◆ Supplement to: Showbizz. ISSN 0104-1649.
Published by: Editora Azul, S.A., Ave. NACOES UNIDAS, 5777, Sao Paulo, SP 05479-900, Brazil. TEL 55-11-816-7866, FAX 55-11-8673311, benjamin.goncalvez@email.abril.br.com.

780 FRA ISSN 0766-916X
LA LETTRE DU MUSICIEN. Text in French. 1984. 15/yr. EUR 43 domestic; EUR 60 foreign (effective 2010). adv. Supplement avail. **Document type:** *Newsletter.*
Related titles: ◆ Supplement(s): Le Guide des Methodes de Musique & Recueils Pedagogiques. ISSN 1958-802X; ◆ La Lettre du Musicien. Hors Serie. Piano. ISSN 0999-5404.
Published by: La Lettre du Musicien, 14 Rue Violet, Paris, 75015, France. TEL 33-1-56770400, FAX 33-1-56770409. Ed., Pub. Michele Worms. Adv. contact Denise Marinier. Circ: 5,000.

786 FRA ISSN 0999-5404
LA LETTRE DU MUSICIEN. HORS SERIE. PIANO. Text in French. 1987. a., latest 2010. adv. bk.rev. **Document type:** *Magazine.*
Related titles: ◆ Supplement to: La Lettre du Musicien. ISSN 0766-916X.
Indexed: RILM.
Published by: La Lettre du Musicien, 14 Rue Violet, Paris, 75015, France. TEL 33-1-40612030, FAX 33-1-42731847. Ed. Michele Worms. Adv. contact Denise Marinier.

781.49 USA ISSN 1096-7079
ML3533.8
LEXICON; new wave and beyond. Text in English. 1996. q. USD 15 domestic; USD 17 in Canada & Mexico; USD 27 out of North America; USD 3.95, CAD 4.95 newsstand/cover (effective 2000). adv. bk.rev.; music rev.; rec.rev.; software rev.; tel.rev.; video rev. illus. back issues avail. **Document type:** *Magazine, Consumer.* **Description:** Covers music and artists from the 1980's plus current synthpop and other new music.
Published by: Ninthwave Records and Publishing, 9826 Hollow Glen Pl., Silver Springs, MD 20910. TEL 301-588-2369. Ed., Pub., Adv. contact David Richards. B&W page USD 200, color page USD 550; trim 11 x 8. **Subscr. to:** Lexicon, PO Box 1734, Wheaton, MD 20915. **Dist. by:** Desert Moon Periodicals, 1226 A Calle de Comercio, Santa Fe, NM 87505. TEL 505-474-6311.

LIAISON (VANIER); la revue des arts en Ontario Francais. *see* ART

780.6 DEU ISSN 0460-0932
DAS LIEBHABERORCHESTE. Text in German. 1956. 2/yr. EUR 7.50; EUR 4 newsstand/cover (effective 2009). adv. bk.rev.; music rev. bibl. back issues avail. **Document type:** *Magazine, Consumer.*
Indexed: RILM.
Published by: Bundesverband Deutscher Liebhaberorchester e.V., Schlegelstr 14, Nuernberg, 90491, Germany. TEL 49-911-591309, FAX 49-911-594836, bdlo@bdlo.de. Ed., R&P Michael Goldbach. Circ: 4,700 (controlled).

784.4 398 DEU ISSN 1619-0548
ML3630
LIED UND POPULAERE KULTUR/SONG AND POPULAR CULTURE. Text in German. 1928. a. EUR 39.90 per vol. (effective 2011). adv. bk.rev. index. back issues avail. **Document type:** *Journal, Academic/ Scholarly.*
Formerly (until 2001): Jahrbuch fuer Volksliedforschung (0075-2789)
Related titles: Online - full text ed.
Indexed: A20, ASCA, ArtHuCI, CurCont, DIP, IBR, IBZ, IIMP, M11, MLA, MLA-IB, RASB, RILM, SCOPUS, W07.
Published by: (Deutsches Volksliedarchiv), Waxmann Verlag GmbH, Steinfurter Str 555, Muenster, 48159, Germany. TEL 49-251-265040, FAX 49-251-2650426, info@waxmann.com. Eds. Max Matter, Nils Grosch.

780.01 LTU ISSN 1392-9313
ML305
LIETUVOS MUZIKOLOGIJA/LITHUANIAN MUSICOLOGY. Text in Lithuanian, English. 2000. a.
Indexed: AmHI, CA, H07, M11, MLA-IB, RILM, T02.
Published by: Lietuvos Muzikos ir Teatro Akademija, Gedimino prospektas 42, Vilnius, 01110, Lithuania. TEL 370-52-612691, FAX 370-52-126982, rektoratas@lmta.lt, http://lmta.lt.

782.421 USA
LIFE SUCKS DIE. Text in English. 2000. q. USD 20; USD 5 newsstand/ cover (effective 2001). adv. **Document type:** *Magazine, Consumer.*
Published by: Life Sucks Die, Inc., Box 14801, Minneapolis, MN 55414. TEL 612-379-4151, lifesucks@winternet.com, http://www.lifesucksdie.com. Ed. Khaki Bikini.

780 USA ISSN 1068-8404
LIGHTNING STRIKES. Text in English. 1977. 2/yr. USD 11 (effective 2000). adv. bk.rev. back issues avail. **Description:** Covers all aspects of the career and music of Lou Christie.
Published by: (Lou Christie International Fan Club), Universal Mind Press, c/o Harry Young, Ed, Box 748, Chicago, IL 60690-0748. TEL 773-241-5412. Circ: 650.

781.7 COD
LIKEMBE. Text in French. bi-m. illus.
Published by: Maison d'Editions "Jeunes pour Jeunes", BP 9624, Kinshasa, 1, Congo, Dem. Republic. Ed. Mulongo Mulunda Mukena.

780 CHN ISSN 1671-413X
LINGNAN YINYUE/MUSIC OF SOUTH MOUNTAIN. Text in Chinese. 1957. q. CNY 10 newsstand/cover (effective 2005). **Document type:** *Magazine, Consumer.*
Address: 550, Tianhebeikou Xilu, 13/F, Guangzhou, 510635, China. TEL 86-10-68319671, 86-755-2200069. **Dist. by:** China International Book Trading Corp, 35 Chegongzhuang Xilu, Haidian District, PO Box 399, Beijing 100044, China. TEL 86-10-68412045, FAX 86-10-68412023, cibtc@mail.cibtc.com.cn, http://www.cibtc.com.cn.

780.7094105 GBR ISSN 1741-6140
LINK (MANCHESTER); connecting the music education community. Text in English. 2004. q. GBP 15.80 domestic; GBP 20.80 in Europe; GBP 24.40 elsewhere (effective 2010). **Document type:** *Magazine, Trade.* **—CCC.**
Published by: Impromptu Publishing Ltd., Century House, 2nd Fl, St Peter's Sq, Manchester, M2 3DN, United Kingdom. TEL 44-161-2369526, FAX 44-161-2477978, info@impromptupublishing.com.

780 FRA ISSN 1772-2470
L'INOUI. Text in French. 2005. a. EUR 25 newsstand/cover (effective 2009). **Document type:** *Journal, Consumer.*
Published by: Institut de Recherche et Coordination Acoustique Musique (I R C A M), 1 Place Igor Stravinsky, Paris, 75004, France. TEL 33-1-44784843, FAX 33-1-44781540, http://www.ircam.fr/institut.html.

780 BIH ISSN 0024-4244
LIRA. Text in Serbo-Croatian. 1974. m.
Published by: Opstinska Konferencija Muzicke Omladine, AVNOJ-a 5, Bihac, Bosnia Herzegovina. Ed. Safet Curtovic.

780 SWE ISSN 1401-1026
LIRA; magasinet foer jazz, klubb-, folk- och vaerldsmusik. Text in Swedish. 1994. 5/yr. SEK 395 (effective 2011). adv. back issues avail. **Document type:** *Magazine, Consumer.*
Related titles: Online - full text ed.
Published by: Lira Ekonomisk Foerening, PO Box 31036, Goeteborg, 40032, Sweden. TEL 46-31-134410. Ed. Jonas Bergroth. Adv. contact Elisabeth Tingdal. Circ: 3,700.

780 USA ISSN 1947-4431
ML1
▼ **LISTEN (BRYN MAWR);** life with classical music. Text in English. 2009. bi-m. USD 9.95 (effective 2010). **Document type:** *Magazine, Consumer.* **Description:** Explores classical music in our daily lives.
Published by: ArkivMusic, PO Box 654, Bryn Mawr, PA 19010. TEL 215-493-1126, service@arkivmusic.com, http://www.arkivmusic.com.

780 GBR ISSN 0141-0792
M1410.L7
THE LISZT SOCIETY. JOURNAL. Text in English. 1965. a. free (effective 2009). bk.rev. bibl. **Document type:** *Journal, Academic/Scholarly.* **Description:** Contains original articles and reviews on Liszt's music.
Formerly (until 1976): Liszt Society. Newsletter (0459-5084)
Indexed: RILM.
Published by: The Liszt Society, 14 Mardley Dell, Welwyn, Herts AL6 0UR, United Kingdom. TEL 44-1438-717724, FAX 44-1438-717724, enquiries@LisztSoc.org.uk.

LITERARNO - MUZEJNY LETOPIS. *see* LITERATURE

786.5 NLD ISSN 1879-4149
LITERATA. Text in Dutch. 2006. a. EUR 22.90 (effective 2010).
Related titles: Optical Disk - DVD ed.: Improvisata. ISSN 1879-4130. EUR 16.90 (effective 2010).
Published by: Stichting Promotie Orgel Projecten, Pastorielaan 131, Amersfoort, 3828 EZ, Netherlands. TEL 31-33-4553256, twillert_organist@hetnet.nl, http://www.stichting-pop.nl.

780 LTU ISSN 1648-3219
LITHUANIAN MUSIC REVIEW. Text in Lithuanian. 2001. a. **Document type:** *Journal, Academic/Scholarly.*
Indexed: RILM.
Published by: Lithuanian Musicians Union, Gedimino pr 32-2, Vilnius, 01104, Lithuania. TEL 370-5-2623043, FAX 370-5-2120302, ltmkm@takas.lt, http://teatras.mch.mii.lt/Muzika/Musicians_Union.en.htm.

781.64 USA
THE LITTLE CRACKED EGG (ONLINE). Text in English. 1998. irreg. music rev. **Document type:** *Magazine, Consumer.*
Formerly (until 1999): The Little Cracked Egg (Print)
Media: Online - full text.
Published by: Little Cracked Egg, c/o Spencer Lloyd, PO Box 1648, New York, NY 10009. Eds., Pubs. Johnny Pontiac, Spencer Lloyd.

LITURGIA SACRA; przeglad liturgiczno-muzyczny. *see* RELIGIONS AND THEOLOGY

781.64 DEU
LIVE MAGAZIN. Text in German. 1992. m. adv. **Document type:** *Magazine, Consumer.*
Published by: K I Mediengesellschaft mbH, Im Mediapark 2, Cologne, 50670, Germany. TEL 49-221-9347270, FAX 49-221-93472742, vertrieb@koelner.de. adv.: B&W page EUR 3,440, color page EUR 4,825. Circ: 65,204 (controlled).

780 USA
LIVES IN MUSIC. Text in English. 2000. irreg., latest vol.8, 2005. price varies. back issues avail. **Document type:** *Monographic series, Trade.*
Published by: Pendragon Press, PO Box 190, Hillsdale, NY 12529. TEL 518-325-6100, FAX 518-325-6102, orders@pendragonpress.com. Ed. Claire Brook.

781.573 USA ISSN 0024-5232
ML1
LIVING BLUES; the magazine of the African American blues tradition. Text in English. 1970. bi-m. USD 25.95 domestic; USD 31.95 in Canada; USD 41.95 elsewhere (effective 2010). adv. bk.rev.; rec.rev.; video rev. illus. back issues avail.; reprints avail. **Document type:** *Magazine, Consumer.* **Description:** Features interviews with blues musicians and spotlights performers on the blues scene.
Incorporates: Living Bluesletter
Related titles: Microfilm ed.: (from PQC).
Indexed: A22, AFS, IIBP, IIMP, M11, MLA, MLA-IB, MusicInd, PMPI, RILM, T02. —Ingenta.
Published by: University of Mississippi, Center for the Study of Southern Culture, Barnard Observatory, Sorority Row and Grove Loop, PO Box 1848, University, MS 38677. TEL 662-915-5993, FAX 662-915-5814, cssc@olemiss.edu, http://www.olemiss.edu/depts/south/. Ed. Brett Bonner. adv.: B&W page USD 1,331, color page USD 1,815; trim 8.125 x 10.875.

781.573 USA ISSN 1044-1026
ML12
LIVING BLUES BLUES DIRECTORY. Variant title: Blues Directory. Text in English. 1989. a. USD 25. adv. **Document type:** *Directory.* **Description:** Includes listings of blues artists and agents, festival dates, radio shows, record labels, night clubs, blues societies, and other resources pertinent to the blues.
Published by: University of Mississippi, Center for the Study of Southern Culture, Barnard Observatory, Sorority Row and Grove Loop, PO Box 1848, University, MS 38677. TEL 601-232-5742, FAX 601-232-7842. Ed. David Nelson. Adv. contact Brett Bonner.

780 USA
LIVING MUSIC. Text in English. 1983. s-a. free to members (effective 2011). adv. bk.rev.; music rev.; rec.rev. back issues avail. **Document type:** *Journal, Trade.* **Description:** Publishes original articles, information on competitions and opportunities for composers and performers of new music.
Published by: Living Music Foundation, Inc., c/o Dr. Charles Norman Mason, 900 Arkadelphia Rd, Birmingham-Southern College, PO Box 549033, Birmingham, AL 35254. dwight@dwightwinenger.net.

781.62 GBR ISSN 1351-4105
ML3650
THE LIVING TRADITION. Text in English. 1993. bi-m. GBP 3.25 per issue (effective 2009). adv. music rev. back issues avail. **Document type:** *Magazine, Consumer.* **Description:** Covers folk, traditional, and Celtic music throughout Scotland, England, Ireland, and Wales.
Related titles: Online - full text ed.
Published by: The Living Tradition Ltd, PO Box 1026, Kilmarnock, Ayrshire KA2 0LG, United Kingdom. TEL 44-1563-571220, FAX 44-1563-544855. Adv. contact Janetta Fairbairn TEL 44-1563-571220. B&W page GBP 345, color page GBP 575; trim 210 x 297.

782.3 CAN ISSN 0703-6752
LIVING WITH CHRIST - COMPLETE EDITION. Text in English. 1976. m. CAD 18.95; USD 18.95 in United States; USD 40 elsewhere (effective 2000). **Description:** Liturgical texts of the Mass for Sundays and weekdays.
Related titles: ◆ French ed.: Prions en Eglise - Edition Complete. ISSN 0383-8285.
Published by: Novalis, St Paul University, 223 Main St, Ottawa, ON K1S 1C4, Canada. TEL 613-236-1393, FAX 613-782-3004. Ed. Louise Pambrun. **Subscr. to:** 49 Front St E, 2nd Fl, Toronto, ON M5E 1B3, Canada. TEL 800-387-7164.

782.3 CAN ISSN 0703-6760
LIVING WITH CHRIST - SUNDAY EDITION. Text in English. 1936. bi-m. (plus 2 special issues). CAD 8.40 domestic; USD 8.40 in United States; USD 25 elsewhere (effective 2000). **Description:** Liturgical texts for Sunday Mass.
Related titles: ◆ French ed.: Prions en Eglise - Edition Dominicale. ISSN 0383-8277.
Published by: Novalis, St Paul University, 223 Main St, Ottawa, ON K1S 1C4, Canada. TEL 613-236-1393, 800-387-7164, FAX 613-782-3004. Ed. Louise Pambrun.

LOGIQUES SOCIALES. SERIE MUSIQUES ET CHAMP SOCIAL. *see* SOCIOLOGY

781.64 USA
LOLLIPOP MAGAZINE. Text in English. 1993. 6/yr. USD 20; USD 5 newsstand/cover (effective 2007). adv. bk.rev.; film rev.; music rev.; tel.rev.; video rev. illus. back issues avail. **Document type:** *Magazine, Consumer.* **Description:** Contains alternative music and underground culture for media-addicted youth and hipsters of all ages.
Published by: Scott Hefflon, Ed. & Pub., PO Box 441493, Boston, MA 02144. TEL 617-623-5319, FAX 617-623-5103. Adv. contact Scott Hefflon. B&W page USD 775, color page USD 1,000; trim 8.5 x 11.

780 GBR
LONDON COLLEGE OF MUSIC MAGAZINE. Text in English. 1960. s-a. GBP 8.50. adv. bk.rev. **Document type:** *Newsletter.* **Description:** For students, staff and LCM Society members.
Media: Duplicated (not offset).
Published by: London College of Music, Thames Valley University, London, St Marys Rd, London, W5 5RF, United Kingdom. TEL 44-181-231-2364, FAX 44-181-231-2433. Circ: (controlled).

780 GBR
LONDON PHILHARMONIC ORCHESTRA YEARBOOK. Text in English. a. donations. **Document type:** *Yearbook, Trade.* **Description:** Covers the events of the season as well as interviews and articles relating to the London Philharmonic Orchestra and its private and corporate sponsors.
Published by: London Philharmonic Orchestra, 89 Albert Embankment, London, SE1 7TP, United Kingdom. TEL 44-20-78404200, FAX 44-20-78404201, boxoffice@lpo.org.uk.

781.542 USA
LONG ISLAND PRESS. Text in English. 1978. w. (Thu.). free newsstand/ cover (effective 2008). **Document type:** *Newspaper, Consumer.*
Formerly: The Island Ear (1041-3812)
Published by: Morey Publishing, Inc., 575 Underhill Blvd #210, Syosset, NY 11791. TEL 516-284-3300, FAX 516-284-3311. Ed. Robbie Woliver. Pub. Jed Morey. Circ: 100,001 (free).

781.64 USA
LOUD FAST RULES!. Text in English. 2005. 3/yr. USD 3.99 newsstand/ cover (effective 2007). adv. **Document type:** *Magazine, Consumer.*
Published by: American Music Press, PO Box 1070, Martinez, CA 94553.

781.6 USA ISSN 1072-4427
ML14.L8
LOUISIANA MUSIC DIRECTORY. Text in English. 1990. a., latest 2001. USD 35 (effective 2001). adv. back issues avail. **Document type:** *Directory, Trade.* **Description:** Contains listings and categories of musicians and music-related businesses throughout the state of Louisiana.
Related titles: Online - full content ed.: 1990.

Published by: Offbeat, Inc., 421 Frenchmen St, Ste 200, New Orleans, LA 70116. TEL 504-944-4300, FAX 504-944-4306. Ed., Pub., R&P, Adv. contact Jan V Ramsey. Circ: 15,000.

780 ROM ISSN 1222-894X
LUCRARI DE MUZICOLOGIE. Text in Romanian; Summaries in English, French, German. 1965. a. price varies.
Published by: Academia de Muzica "Gheorge Dima", Str. I.C. Bratianu 25, Cluj-napoca, 3400, Romania. Ed. Dan Voiculescu. Circ: 300.

781.6 NLD ISSN 0024-7286
LUISTER. Text in Dutch. 1952. 8/yr. EUR 48 combined subscription (print & online eds.); EUR 4.95 newsstand/cover (effective 2009). adv. bk.rev.; rec.rev. **Document type:** *Magazine, Consumer.* **Description:** Covers classical music.
Related titles: Online - full text ed.: EUR 25.75 (effective 2009).
—IE, Infotrieve.
Published by: Uitgeverij Scala bv, Postbus 38, Amersfoort, 3800 AA, Netherlands. TEL 31-33-4892900, FAX 31-33-4802281, info@scalapublishing.nl, http://www.uitgeverijscala.nl. Ed. Bert Huisjes. Pubs. Ashja Bosboom, Eric Bruger.

LUST FOR LIFE. *see* MOTION PICTURES

780 GBR ISSN 0952-0759
ML5
➤ **THE LUTE.** Text in English. 1959. a. GBP 35 per issue (effective 2009); subscr. includes quarterly magazine, Lute news. bk.rev. back issues avail. **Document type:** *Journal, Academic/Scholarly.* **Description:** Contains musicology studies.
Formerly (until 1982): Lute Society Journal (0460-007X)
Indexed: RILM.
Published by: Lute Society, Southside Cottage, Brook Hill, Albury, Guildford, Surrey GU5 9DJ, United Kingdom. TEL 44-1483-202159, FAX 44-1483-203088, lutesoc@aol.com, http://www.lutesoc.co.uk.

780 USA ISSN 0076-1524
ML1
LUTE SOCIETY OF AMERICA. JOURNAL. Text in English. 1968. a. membership. adv. bk.rev. index.
Indexed: CA, M11, RILM, T02.
—Ingenta.
Published by: Lute Society of America, c/o Beedle Hinely, Box 1328, Lexington, VA 24450. TEL 703-463-5812. Ed. Victor Coelho. Circ: 600.

780 USA ISSN 1547-982X
ML1
LUTE SOCIETY OF AMERICA. QUARTERLY. Text in English. q. membership.
Formerly: Lute Society of America. Newsletter
Indexed: M11, MAG, MusicInd, T02.
Published by: Lute Society of America, c/o Beedle Hinely, Box 1328, Lexington, VA 24450. TEL 703-463-5812. Ed. Phillip Rukavina.

780 CHE
LUZERNER SAENGERBLATT. Text in German. 8/yr. **Document type:** *Consumer.*
Address: Stauffacherweg 2 a, Luzern, 6006, Switzerland. Ed. Edwin Wartenweiler. Circ: 1,850.

780 NOR ISSN 1502-8860
LYDSKRIFT. Text in Norwegian. 1997. a.
Formerly: Arbok for Norsk Samtidsmusikk (0809-1471)
Indexed: RILM.
Published by: Blamann Musikkforlag Norge, Universitetsg 20, Oslo, 0162, Norway. TEL 2240-3434g, FAX 2242-6422. Ed. Viktor Mjoen.

786 USA ISSN 1538-8700
ML424.S76
LYRA (LONG ISLAND CITY); the music magazine. Text in English. 1935. q. free to libraries, colleges and conservatories. bk.rev. illus. **Document type:** *Newsletter.* **Description:** Provides information on piano competitions. Profiles Steinway artists.
Formerly (until 1994): Steinway News
Published by: Steinway & Sons, Steinway Pl, Long Island City, NY 11105. TEL 718-721-2600, http://www.steinway.com. Ed. Leo Spellman. Circ: 50,000.

782.1 USA ISSN 0024-7839
ML28.C4
LYRIC OPERA NEWS. Text in English. 1956. s-a. membership (effective 2000). adv. bk.rev.; music rev. illus. **Document type:** *Newsletter.*
Indexed: MAG.
Published by: Lyric Opera of Chicago, 20 N Wacker Dr, Chicago, IL 60606. TEL 312-332-2244, FAX 312-332-2633. Ed., R&P Roger Pines. Adv. contact Judie Kate. Circ: 23,000.

781.64 791.437 USA
M (ENGLEWOOD CLIFFS). Text in English. 2000. m. USD 9.97; USD 1 newsstand/cover (effective 2001). **Document type:** *Magazine, Consumer.*
Published by: Bauer Creative Services, Inc., 270 Sylvan Ave., Englewood Cliffs, NJ 07632. TEL 800-846-1597. Ed. Richard Spencer. Pub. Lynette Parillo.

M A R GOSPEL MINISTRIES NEWSLETTER. (Middle Atlantic Regional) *see* RELIGIONS AND THEOLOGY

780 FRA ISSN 2108-3142
▼ **M B O A MAGAZINE.** Text in French. 2010. bi-m. EUR 22 (effective 2011). **Document type:** *Magazine, Consumer.*
Published by: M B O A - T V, 95 Rue des Grands Champs, Paris, 75020, France. http://www.mboatv.com.

▼ **M D W GENDER WISSEN.** *see* WOMEN'S STUDIES

M E I E A JOURNAL. *see* LEISURE AND RECREATION

781.64 DEU
M E M I. (Magazin fuer Elektronische Musik im Internet) Text in German. 1994. irreg. **Document type:** *Consumer.* **Description:** Contains news, reviews, concert dates, and other relevant information for fans of electronic and synthesizer music in Germany and the Netherlands.
Media: Online - full text.
Address: Friedrich-Syrup-Str 3, Koblenz Am Rhein, 56073, Germany. TEL 49-2642-41870. Eds. Frank Korf, Martin Rothhaar.

M E P. ANNUAL REPORT. (Music Entrepreneur Program) *see* SOCIAL SERVICES AND WELFARE

338.476213893 GBR ISSN 1750-4198
M I PRO. (Musical Instrument) Text in English. 1999. m. GBP 50 domestic; GBP 60 in Europe; GBP 90 elsewhere (effective 2009). adv. back issues avail. **Document type:** *Magazine, Trade.*
Incorporates (2003-2005): Audio Pro (1740-648X)
Related titles: Online - full text ed.: free (effective 2009).
—CCC.
Published by: Intent Media Ltd., Saxon House, 6a St Andrew St, Hertford, Hertfordshire SG14 1JA, United Kingdom. TEL 44-1992-535646, FAX 44-1992-535648, http://www.intentmedia.co.uk. Pub. Dave Roberts. Adv. contact Darrell Carter. **Subscr. to:** PO Box 35, Robertsbridge TN32 5WN, United Kingdom. TEL 44-1580-883848, FAX 44-1580-883849, mipro.subscriptions@c-cms.com.

781.64 DEU
M K - Z W O; Magazin fuer HipHop und Dancehall Music. Text in German. 10/yr. EUR 16.35 (effective 2003). adv. **Document type:** *Magazine, Consumer.*
Related titles: Online - full text ed.
Address: Skalitzer Str. 97, Berlin, 10997, Germany. TEL 49-30-61627414, FAX 49-30-61627415. adv.: page EUR 1,250. Circ: 50,000 (paid and controlled).

780 DEU ISSN 0722-9119
M M BRANCHEN HANDBUCH. Text in German. 1980. a. EUR 62.50 (effective 2006). index. **Document type:** *Bulletin.*
Published by: (Musik Markt), Josef Keller Verlag GmbH & Co. KG, Seebreite 9, Berg, 82335, Germany. TEL 49-8151-7710, FAX 49-8151-771190, info@keller-verlag.de, http://www.keller-verlag.de.

M MAGAZINE. *see* CHILDREN AND YOUTH—For

780 USA ISSN 2156-2377
ML3533.8
▼ **M MUSIC & MUSICIANS.** Text in English. 2010. 8/yr. USD 12 domestic; USD 24 in Canada; USD 40 elsewhere (effective 2010). **Document type:** *Magazine, Consumer.* **Description:** Provides information about music and musicians.
Published by: Merlin P. David, Ed. & Pub., PO Box 919, Redondo Beach, CA 90277. katie@mmusicmag.com. Ed. Rick Taylor TEL 615-837-4070. Pub. Merlin David TEL 310-265-1153.

780 792 DEU
M T - JOURNAL. (Musik Theater) Text in German. 1995. 2/yr. **Document type:** *Journal, Trade.*
Published by: Hochschule fuer Musik und Theater Felix Mendelssohn Bartholdy Leipzig, Grassistr 8, Leipzig, 04107, Germany. TEL 49-341-214455, FAX 49-341-2144503, rektor@hmt-leipzig.de.

780 USA ISSN 2152-7210
▼ ➤ **M T N A E-JOURNAL.** Text in English. 2009. q. free to members (effective 2010). back issues avail. **Document type:** *Journal, Academic/Scholarly.* **Description:** Features in-depth, scholarly, research-oriented articles enhanced through the use of sound, image, and video links.
Media: Online - full text.
Published by: Music Teachers National Association, 441 Vine St, Ste 3100, Cincinnati, OH 45202. TEL 513-421-1420, 888-512-5278, FAX 513-421-2503, mtnanet@mtna.org. Pub. Gary L Ingle. Adv. contact Chad Schwalbach TEL 513-421-1420 ext 232.

780 USA
M T V MAGAZINE. (Music Television) Text in English. 2003 (Oct.). bi-m. USD 599 newsstand/cover (effective 2003). **Document type:** *Magazine, Consumer.*
Published by: Nickelodeon Magazine, Inc. (Subsidiary of: Viacom International Inc.), 1515 Broadway, New York, NY 10036.

780 791.45 USA
M T V S S N. (Music Television's Spankin New) Text in English. q. USD 7 newsstand/cover domestic; USD 7.95 newsstand/cover in Canada (effective 2003).
Published by: M T V Networks, 1515 Broadways, New York, NY 10036. http://www.mtv.com.

780 USA ISSN 0740-5812
MADAMINA!. Text in English. 1980. a. USD 20 (effective 1999). adv. bk.rev. back issues avail. **Document type:** *Bulletin.*
Indexed: RILM.
Published by: Music Associates of America, 224 King St, Englewood, NJ 07631. TEL 201-569-2898, FAX 201-569-7023. Ed., R&P, Adv. contact George Sturm. Circ: 5,000 (controlled).

780.6 FRA ISSN 2108-8802
MAG SACEM; le magazine des societaires Sacem. Text in French. 2004. q. **Document type:** *Magazine, Trade.*
Former titles (until 2010): La Lettre des Societaires (1766-6120); (until 2004): La Lettre Bimestrielle des Societaires S A C E M (1277-1392)
Published by: Societe des Auteurs, Compositeurs et Editeurs de Musique, 225, Av Charles-de-Gaulle, Neuilly-sur-Seine Cedex, 92528, France. TEL 33-1-47154715. Ed. Fabienne Herenberg.

780 POL
MAGAZYN C C M. (Centrum Czystej Muzyki) Text in Polish. 1995. q. **Document type:** *Magazine, Consumer.*
Published by: Studio DR Sp. z o.o., Malinka 65D/2, Wisla, 43460, Poland. TEL 48-33-8553621, FAX 48-33-8553664, bkrol@drstudio.com.pl. Ed. Boguslawa Krol. Circ: 3,500.

780.902 DEU ISSN 0541-8968
MAGDEBURGER TELEMANN STUDIEN. Text in German. 1966. irreg., latest vol.20, 2009. price varies. **Document type:** *Monographic series, Academic/Scholarly.*
Related titles: Supplement(s): Telemann Beitraege. ISSN 1437-4293. 1987.
Indexed: RILM.
Published by: Georg Olms Verlag, Hagentorwall 7, Hildesheim, 31134, Germany. TEL 49-5121-15010, FAX 49-5121-150150, info@olms.de.

781.64 FRA ISSN 1262-0378
MAGIC; revue pop moderne. Text in French. 1995. m. (10/yr). EUR 49 (effective 2009). music rev. back issues avail. **Document type:** *Magazine, Consumer.*
Formerly (until 1995): Magic Mushrooms (1156-8585)
Published by: Bonne Nouvelle Editions, 15-17 Rue Vivienne, Paris, 75002, France. TEL 33-1-73038900, FAX 33-1-73038984. Ed. Franck Vergeade TEL 33-1-73034237. Adv. contact Miriem Chibikh. Circ: 32,000. **Subscr. to:** Logodata, 50 Rue Notre-Dame de Lorette, Paris 75009, France. TEL 33-1-55310315.

781.64 USA
MAGNET (ONLINE); real music alternatives. Text in English. w. adv. **Document type:** *Magazine, Consumer.*
Media: Online - full content. **Related titles:** ◆ Print ed.: Magnet (Print). ISSN 1088-7806.
Published by: Magnet Magazine Inc., 1218 Chestnut St., Ste. 508, Philadelphia, PA 19107-4813. TEL 215-413-8570, FAX 215-413-8569.

MAILOUT; arts work with people. *see* ART

783.9 DEU ISSN 1862-2658
MAINZER HYMNOLOGISCHE STUDIEN. Text in German. 2000. irreg., latest vol.24, 2010. price varies. **Document type:** *Monographic series, Academic/Scholarly.* **Description:** Contains interdisciplinary research on hymns and other forms of spiritual music.
Published by: A. Francke Verlag GmbH, Dischinger Weg 5, Tuebingen, 72070, Germany. TEL 49-7071-97970, FAX 49-7071-979711, info@francke.de, http://www.francke.de.

780 792 AUS
MAJOR ATTRACTIONS. ANNUAL DIARY. Text in English. 1978. a.
Published by: Sydney Opera House Trust, Royal Exchange, GPO Box R239, Sydney, NSW 1225, Australia. TEL 61-2-92507111, FAX 61-2-92513843, infodesk@sydneyoperahouse.com, http://www.sydneyoperahouse.nsw.gov.au.

780 USA ISSN 1552-2946
ML1
MAKING MUSIC; better living through recreational music making. Text in English. 2004. bi-m. USD 16.95 domestic; USD 34.95 in Canada; USD 59.95 elsewhere (effective 2009). adv. **Document type:** *Magazine, Consumer.* **Description:** Offers inspiration, instruction and information for the amateur musician.
Published by: Bentley-Hall, Inc., 120 Walton St, Ste 201, Syracuse, NY 13202. TEL 315-422-4488, FAX 315-422-3837, sales@bentley-hall.com, http://www.bentley-hall.com. Ed. Antoinette Follett. Adv. contact Krista Ward TEL 312-422-4488 ext 101. color page USD 3,000; trim 8.125 x 10.875. Circ: 9,396 (paid).

780 POL
MALE MONOGRAFIE MUZYCZNE; monografie popularne. Text in Polish. 1952. irreg. price varies. adv. **Document type:** *Monographic series.* **Description:** Presents life and work of great composers.
Published by: Polskie Wydawnictwo Muzyczne, Al Krasinskiego 11 a, Krakow, 31111, Poland. TEL 48-12-4227044, FAX 48-12-4220174. Ed. Stanislaw Haraschin. R&P Janina Warzecha. Adv. contact Elzbieta Widlak.

787.8 USA ISSN 1081-3918
MANDOLIN QUARTERLY. Text in English. 1995. q. **Document type:** *Magazine, Consumer.* **Description:** Covers all styles of mandolin playing and techniques.
Indexed: RILM.
Published by: Plucked String, Inc., PO Box 2770, Kensington, MD 20891. TEL 301-530-1749, FAX 301-530-2165.

781.5 USA
MANDOZINE. Text in English. 1996. bi-m.
Media: Online - full content.
Address: http://www.mandozine.com. Ed. John Baxter.

780 DEU ISSN 1611-129X
MANNHEIMER HOCHSCHULSCHRIFTEN. Text in German. 1995. irreg., latest vol.7, 2009. price varies. **Document type:** *Monographic series, Academic/Scholarly.*
Published by: Peter Lang GmbH (Subsidiary of: Peter Lang Publishing Group), Eschborner Landstr 42-50, Frankfurt Am Main, 60489, Germany. TEL 49-69-7807050, FAX 49-69-78070550, zentrale.frankfurt@peterlang.com. Ed. Hermann Jung.

MANNHEIMER LIEDERTAFEL. MITTEILUNGEN. *see* CLUBS

780 700 USA
MAP. Variant title: Music. Art. People. Text in English. 2007. q. USD 25 (effective 2007). adv. **Document type:** *Magazine, Consumer.* **Description:** Covers art, music, personalities, issues, trends, and events shaping the art & music world.
Published by: Map Media Group, 2400 NE 2nd Ave, Studio D, Miami, FL 33137. TEL 305-438-0001, FAX 305-576-3799, info@mapmediagroup.com, http://www.mapmediagroup.com/. Ed. Francesca Mora. adv.: page USD 3,200; trim 9 x 11.

780 DEU
MARBURGER BEITRAEGE ZUR MUSIKWISSENSCHAFT. Text in German. 1967. irreg., latest vol.10, 2003. price varies. **Document type:** *Monographic series, Academic/Scholarly.*
Published by: Baerenreiter Verlag, Heinrich-Schuetz-Allee 35, Kassel, 34131, Germany. TEL 49-561-3105154, FAX 49-561-3105195, order@baerenreiter.com, http://www.baerenreiter.com.

MARCATO. *see* LIBRARY AND INFORMATION SCIENCES

781.62 MEX
EL MARIACHI SUENA. Text in Spanish. 1997. irreg. USD 30 (effective 1999 & 2000). adv. **Document type:** *Consumer.* **Description:** Includes articles, songs and news about mariachi, Mexican folk music.
Media: Online - full text.
Published by: Mariachi Suena, San CAMILITO 9-104,, Col Centro, Mexico City, DF 06010, Mexico. TEL 52-5-5265793. Ed. Antonio Covarrubias. Adv. contact Rafael Covarrubias.

780 CHE ISSN 1662-5366
MARTINU-STUDIEN. Text in German. 1996. irreg., latest vol.2, 2009. price varies. **Document type:** *Monographic series, Academic/Scholarly.*
Formerly (until 2009): Bohuslav-Martinu-Stiftung. Jahrbuch (1424-2788)
Published by: Peter Lang AG (Subsidiary of: Peter Lang Publishing Group), Hochfeldstr 32, Postfach 746, Bern 9, 3000, Switzerland. TEL 41-31-3061717, FAX 41-31-3061727, info@peterlang.com.

780.7 USA ISSN 0025-4312
MARYLAND MUSIC EDUCATOR. Text in English. 1954. q. free to members (effective 2006). bk.rev. illus. **Document type:** *Journal, Trade.* **Description:** Covers all areas of music education: choral, band, orchestra, general music, research, music teachers and supervisors.
Indexed: MAG.
Published by: Maryland Music Educators Association, 27 Meadow Ln, Thurmont, MD 21788-1737. TEL 301-271-7269, FAX 301-271-7032, raybach@aol.com. Ed., R&P, Adv. contact Thomas W Fugate.

781.64 USA ISSN 1532-1649
MASS APPEAL. Text in English. 1996. bi-m. USD 20 domestic; USD 30 in Canada; USD 50 elsewhere; USD 4.99 newsstand/cover (effective 2006). adv. illus. **Document type:** *Magazine, Consumer.*
Description: Covers all aspects of hip-hop culture including fashion, art, and music.
Address: 976 Grand St, Brooklyn, NY 11211-2707. TEL 718-625-9033, FAX 718-625-0541, adrian@massappealmag.com. Eds. Sacha Jenkins, Noah Callahan-Bever. Pub. Adrian Moeller. Adv. contact Joanne Carolino. color page USD 13,442, B&W page USD 11,398; trim 8.375 x 10.875. Circ: 75,000 (paid).

781.65 ESP ISSN 1138-5405
MASS JAZZ. Text in Spanish. 1998. s-a. 66 p./no.; **Document type:** *Magazine, Consumer.*
Published by: Orfeo Ediciones, Avda Espana 133, Bloque 3, Of 2, Las Rozas, Madrid 28231, Spain. TEL 34-91-3510253, FAX 34-91-3510587, info@orfeoed.com, http://www.orfeoed.com. **Dist. by:** Asociacion de Revistas Culturales de Espana.

780.7 USA ISSN 0147-2550
ML1
MASSACHUSETTS MUSIC NEWS. Text in English. 1953. q. free to members (effective 2005). adv. bk.rev.; film rev.; music rev. illus.; stat. 68 p./no.; **Document type:** *Newsletter.* **Description:** Documents the progress of music education in Massachusetts.
Formerly: M.M.E.A. Music News (0024-8258)
Indexed: MAG.
Published by: Massachusetts Music Educators Association, Inc. (Subsidiary of: M E N C: National Association for Music Education), c/o Anne Connolly Potter, Executive Secretary-Treasurer, PO Box 2278, Hamilton, MA 01982. TEL 978-468-0211, http://www.mmeaonline.org/index.htm. Ed. Christine K Borning. adv.: B&W page USD 175; trim 10 x 7.5. Circ: 1,500.

870 RUS
MASTER PERFORMERS. Text in Russian. 1977. 2/yr.
Published by: Izdatel'stvo Muzyka, Petrovka 26, Moscow, 127051, Russian Federation. TEL 7-095-9215170, FAX 7-095-9283304, muz-sekretar@yandex.ru, jvolk@mail.ru.

786.2 USA ISSN 0360-8484
ML423.M42
THE MATTHAY NEWS. Text in English. 1927. s-a. free to members (effective 2010). bk.rev.; music rev. illus. **Document type:** *Journal, Academic/Scholarly.*
Published by: American Matthay Association, c/o Elizabeth Vandevander, 100 Minty Dr, Dayton, OH 45415. evanhands@aol.com. Circ: 200.

780 GBR ISSN 2047-2706
MAVERICK (ONLINE); the country, folk, bluegrass & roots digital music magazine. Text in English. 2002. m. GBP 20; GBP 2 per issue (effective 2011). adv. back issues avail. **Document type:** *Magazine, Consumer.*
Formerly: Maverick (Print) (1477-8173)
Media: Online - full text.
Published by: A A G Publishing Ltd., 24 Bray Gardens, Loose, Maidstone, Kent ME15 9TR, United Kingdom. Ed. Alan Cackett TEL 44-1622-744481. Adv. contact Jim Soars TEL 44-1604 456561.

780 USA ISSN 1559-6508
MAVRIK MAGAZINE. Text in English. 2005. bi-m. **Document type:** *Magazine, Consumer.*
Published by: Gruene Music Publishing, LLC, 1243 Gruene Rd, New Braunfels, TX 78130. http://mavrik.lonestarmusic.com/index.asp. Ed. Summer Worn.

781.64 USA ISSN 0743-3530
MAXIMUM ROCK 'N' ROLL. Abbreviated title: M R R. Text in English. 1982. m. USD 42 domestic; USD 57 in Canada & Mexico; USD 112 elsewhere; USD 4.20 per issue (effective 2011). adv. film rev.; rec.rev.; video rev.; Website rev.; bk.rev.; music rev. illus. 160 p./no.; back issues avail.; reprints avail. **Document type:** *Magazine, Consumer.* **Description:** Provides information on the "punk-garage" underground. Contains scene reports, fanzine reviews, interviews, concert coverage and ads for do-it-yourself punk labels. Also includes political articles.
Published by: Maximum Rock'n'Roll, PO Box 460760, San Francisco, CA 94146-0760. TEL 415-923-9814, FAX 415-923-9617.

781.64 DEU
MBEAT. Text in German. m. adv. **Document type:** *Magazine, Consumer.*
Formerly (until 2006): Musicprint
Published by: Mueller Ltd. & Co. KG, Albstr 92, Ulm - Jungingen, 89081, Germany. TEL 49-731-1740, FAX 49-731-174174, info@mueller.de, http://www.mueller.de. adv.: color page EUR 2,690. Circ: 200,000 (controlled).

780 DEU ISSN 0721-6092
ML1049.8
DAS MECHANISCHE MUSIKINSTRUMENT. Text in German. 1975. 3/yr. EUR 60; EUR 22.50 newsstand/cover (effective 2011). music rev. bibl.; pat. back issues avail. **Document type:** *Magazine, Consumer.*
Indexed: IBR, IBZ, RILM.
Published by: Gesellschaft fuer Selbstspielende Musikinstrumente, Emmastr 56, Essen, 45130, Germany. TEL 49-201-784927, FAX 49-201-7266240, vorsitzender@musica-mechanica.de.

780 AUT
MECHANISCHE MUSIKINSTRUMENTE. Text in German. 1999. irreg., latest vol.7, 2009. price varies. **Document type:** *Monographic series, Academic/Scholarly.*
Published by: Verlag der Oesterreichischen Akademie der Wissenschaften, Postgasse 7/4, Vienna, W 1011, Austria. TEL 43-1-515813402, FAX 43-1-515813400, verlag@oeaw.ac.at.

781.7 280.4 USA
MEDIA UPDATE (ONLINE). Text in English. 1982. bi-m. free. back issues avail. **Document type:** *Newsletter, Consumer.* **Description:** Evaluates today's secular and Christian entertainment, especially music. Provides information for teachers, church leaders, and parents to make decisions consistent with Biblical values.
Formerly: Media Update (Print) (1043-4216)
Media: E-mail.
Published by: Al Menconi Ministries, PO Box 131147, Carlsbad, CA 92013-1147. TEL 760-591-4696, Al@AlMenconi.com, http://www.almenconi.com. Ed. Al Menconi. Circ: 10,000.

MEDICAL PROBLEMS OF PERFORMING ARTISTS. *see* MEDICAL SCIENCES

MEIER. *see* LIFESTYLE

MEIER - UNI EXTRA. *see* LIFESTYLE

781.62 DEU
MEINE MELODIE; das Magazin fuer Schlager und Volksmusik. Text in German. 1992. m. EUR 25.20; EUR 1.95 newsstand/cover (effective 2010). adv. **Document type:** *Magazine, Consumer.* **Description:** Contains articles and features on folk music and stars from Germany.
Published by: Pabel-Moewig Verlag KG (Subsidiary of: Bauer Media Group), Karlsruherstr 31, Rastatt, 76437, Germany. TEL 49-7222-130, FAX 49-7222-13218, empfang@vpm.de, http://www.vpm-online.de. adv.: B&W page EUR 3,630, color page EUR 5,100; trim 210 x 280. Circ: 52,319 (paid). **Subscr. to:** G L P International. TEL 201-871-1010, FAX 201-871-0870, info@glpnews.com, http://www.glpnews.com.

781.62 DEU
MEINE STARS HAUTNAH!. Text in German. bi-m. EUR 17.40; EUR 2.90 newsstand/cover (effective 2010). adv. **Document type:** *Magazine, Consumer.*
Published by: Bauer Media Group, Burchardstr 11, Hamburg, 20077, Germany. TEL 49-40-30190, FAX 49-40-30191043, kommunikation@bauermedia.com, http://www.bauermedia.com. Ed. Joerg Schumacher. Adv. contact Karsten Voelker. page EUR 8,500.

780 RUS ISSN 0206-8052
MELODIYA. Text in Russian. 1979. bi-m. USD 110 in North America (effective 2000).
—East View.
Published by: Redaktsiya Melodiya, A-ya 90, Moscow, 103104, Russian Federation. TEL 7-095-2926511. Ed. N Bril'. **Dist. by:** East View Information Services, 10601 Wayzata Blvd, Minneapolis, MN 55305. TEL 952-252-1201, 800-477-1005, FAX 952-252-1202, info@eastview.com, http://www.eastview.com.

780 ESP ISSN 1136-4939
MELOMANO. Text in Spanish. 1996. m. (11/yr.). EUR 69.30 domestic; EUR 150 in Europe; EUR 220 elsewhere (effective 2010). **Document type:** *Magazine, Consumer.* **Description:** Aims to reach an ample public within the musical spectrum in Spain.
Published by: Orfeo Ediciones, Avda Espana 133, Bloque 3, Of 2, Las Rozas, Madrid 28231, Spain. TEL 34-91-3510253, FAX 34-91-3510587, info@orfeoed.com, http://www.orfeoed.com. **Dist. by:** Asociacion de Revistas Culturales de Espana.

781 SWE ISSN 1103-0968
MELOS; en musiktidskrift. Text in English, Swedish. 1992. q. SEK 240. adv. bk.rev. **Document type:** *Newsletter, Academic/Scholarly.*
Indexed: RASB, RILM.
Published by: Kantat HB, Fack 27278, Stockholm, 10253, Sweden. TEL 46-8-664-16-20, FAX 46-8-664-16-20. Ed. Vahid Salehieh. R&P Anna Komar. Adv. contact Bjoern Westberg. Circ: 500.

781.64 DEU
MEMORY; Das Magazin fuer Freunde deutscher Oldies. Text in German. 1978. irreg. **Document type:** *Magazine, Consumer.*
Address: Am Stutenanger 5a, Oberschleissheim, 85764, Germany. TEL 49-89-3151913, FAX 49-89-3154014. Eds., Pubs. Manfred Guenther, Marlene Guenther.

780 NLD ISSN 0025-9462
ML5
MENS EN MELODIE. Text in Dutch. 1946. 6/yr. EUR 55 (effective 2010). adv. bk.rev. bibl.; illus. index. **Description:** Covers classical music for enthusiasts and players.
Incorporates (1999-2007): Vrienden Nederlandse Muziek. Nieuwsbrief (2211-5919); Which was formerly (until 2005): Nieuwsbrief Nederlandse Nuziek (1574-7662); (until 2004): OORsprong (1569-7037); Which incorporated (2000-2002): MuziekGroep Nederland Info (1567-777X)
Indexed: A22, IIMP, M11, MLA-IB, MusicInd, RILM.
—BLDSC (5678.461000), IE, Infotrieve, Ingenta.
Published by: Stichting Mens en Melodie, Burg vd Heijdenlaan 6, Kaatsheuvel, 5171 JD, Netherlands.

780.42 USA
METAL CURSE. Text in English. 1989. s-a. USD 18; USD 5 newsstand/cover (effective 2006). adv. bk.rev.; music rev.; video rev. illus. back issues avail. **Document type:** *Magazine, Consumer.* **Description:** Music magazine that is dedicated to underground extreme metal in all its various forms.
Related titles: Online - full content ed.
Published by: Cursed Productions, Inc., PO Box 302, Elkhart, IN 46515-0302. TEL 574-294-6610, FAX 574-295-1501. Ed., Pub., R&P, Adv. contact Ray Miller. page USD 150; trim 10.75 x 8.25. Circ: 5,000 (controlled).

780 USA ISSN 1068-2872
ML3533.8
METAL EDGE; rock's hardest magazine. Text in English. 1957. 10/yr. USD 5.99 newsstand/cover (effective 2009). adv. bk.rev.; film rev.; music rev.; rec.rev. illus. back issues avail.; reprints avail. **Document type:** *Magazine, Consumer.* **Description:** Covers hard rock, heavy metal music and musicians. Includes interviews and information on contests.
Former titles (until 199?): T V Picture Life, Metal Edge (1059-8006); (until 1984): T V Picture Life (0039-856X)
Related titles: Online - full text ed.: free (effective 2009).
Published by: Zenbu Media, Llc., 104 W 29th St, 11th Fl, New York, NY 10001. TEL 646-230-0100, FAX 646-230-0200, info@zenbumedia.com, http://www.zenbumedia.com. Ed. Phil Freeman. Pub. Steve Bernstein. Adv. contact John McDonald TEL 646-674-3307. color page USD 6,400; trim 8.25 x 10.75. Circ: 98,000.

780.904 DEU
METAL HAMMER. Text in German. 1984. m. EUR 4.90 newsstand/cover; EUR 5.90 newsstand/cover with DVD (effective 2011). adv. bk.rev.; film rev.; music rev.; video rev. bibl.; charts. back issues avail. **Document type:** *Magazine, Consumer.* **Description:** Aimed at people between the ages of 14 and 35 who are interested in hard rock and heavy metal music. Includes tour dates, instruments, album reviews, concert reviews and music news as well as lists of media such as music books, videos and cinema.
Former titles (until 2004): Hammer; Hard Rock and Metal Hammer (1422-9048); (until 1999): New Rock and Metal Hammer (1422-884X); (until 1997): Metal Hammer (1421-2404)
Published by: Axel Springer Mediahouse Berlin GmbH (Subsidiary of: Axel Springer Verlag AG), Mehringdamm 33, Berlin, 10961, Germany. TEL 49-30-30881880, FAX 49-30-3088188223, info@axel-springer-mediahouse-berlin.de, http://www.asmm.de. Ed. Christof Leim. Adv. contact Gernot Krebs. Circ: 42,383 (paid).

781.66 GBR ISSN 0955-1190
METAL HAMMER. Text in English. 1994. m. GBP 39 domestic; GBP 60 in Europe; GBP 75 in United States; GBP 72 elsewhere; GBP 3.99 newsstand/cover (effective 2010). adv. back issues avail. **Document type:** *Magazine, Consumer.* **Description:** Takes an in-depth look at all forms of guitar based rock and the lifestyles of its followers.
Related titles: Online - full text ed.: GBP 79.30; GBP 6.10 per issue (effective 2010).
—CCC.
Published by: Future Publishing Ltd., Beauford Ct, 30 Monmouth St, Bath, Avon BA1 2BW, United Kingdom. TEL 44-1225-442244, FAX 44-1225-446019, customerservice@subscription.co.uk, http://www.futureplc.com. Ed. Alexander Milas. Pub. Chris Ingham. Adv. contact Ian Williamson TEL 44-20-70424104.

781.66 GRC ISSN 1108-5045
METAL HAMMER & HEAVY METAL. Text in Greek. 1988. m. **Document type:** *Magazine, Consumer.*
Related titles: Online - full content ed.
Address: Agamemnonos 51-53, Kallithea, Athens 17675, Greece. TEL 30-210-9421500, FAX 30-210-9425568.

780 BRA ISSN 1413-6163
METAL HEAD. Text in Portuguese. 1995. m. BRL 6.90 newsstand/cover (effective 2006). **Document type:** *Magazine, Consumer.*
Published by: Editora Escala Ltda., Av Prof Ida Kolb, 551, Casa Verde, Sao Paulo, 02518-000, Brazil. TEL 55-11-38552100, FAX 55-11-38579643, escala@escala.com.br, http://www.escala.com.br.

780 BLR
METAL MUSIC MAGAZINE. Variant title: M. Muzykal'nyi Zhurnal. Text in Russian. 1999. bi-m. RUR 24.63 domestic; USD 73.80 foreign to individuals; USD 82 foreign to institutions (effective 2002). illus. **Document type:** *Magazine, Consumer.*
Formerly (until 1999): Legion (Minsk)
Related titles: Online - full content ed.: ISSN 1606-7037.
Published by: Izdatel'stvo Nestor, A/ya 563, Minsk, 220113, Belarus. nestorpb@nestor.minsk.by. Ed. Andrei Grishel TEL 375-172-346790.

780 USA ISSN 1056-2826
ML3533.8
METAL REVOLUTION. Text in English. q.
Published by: Flip Magazines, Inc., 801 Second Ave, New York, NY 10017. TEL 212-661-7878.

783 GBR
METHODIST CHURCH MUSIC SOCIETY. NOTES. Text in English. 1970. s-a. GBP 2.50 per issue domestic to non-members; GBP 3 per issue foreign to non-members; free to members (effective 2009). bk.rev. **Document type:** *Bulletin, Trade.* **Description:** Includes an introduction to the Methodist Church collection of modern art.
Formerly (until 1994): Methodist Church Music Society. Bulletin (0047-6919)
Related titles: Microform ed.: (from WMP).
Published by: Methodist Church Music Society, c/o John Bailey, 23A,The Quadrant, Totley, Sheffield, S17 4DB, United Kingdom. TEL 44-114-2367196, FAX 44-114-2367196, john.baileymcms@btinternet.com.

780.01 DEU ISSN 1618-842X
METHODOLOGY OF MUSIC RESEARCH. Text in English. 2002. irreg., latest vol.4, 2005. price varies. **Document type:** *Monographic series, Academic/Scholarly.*
Published by: Peter Lang GmbH (Subsidiary of: Peter Lang Publishing Group), Eschborner Landstr 42-50, Frankfurt Am Main, 60489, Germany. TEL 49-69-7807050, FAX 49-69-78070550, zentrale.frankfurt@peterlang.com, http://www.peterlang.com. Ed. Nico Schueler.

780 USA
METRONOME MAGAZINE. Text in English. 1986. m. USD 20 (effective 2001). adv. rec.rev. back issues avail. **Description:** Focuses on music and entertainment. Contains interviews with local, national and international musicians.
Published by: Brian M. Owens, Ed. and Pub., PO Box 921, Billerica, MA 01821. TEL 978-957-0925. Adv. contact Brian M Owens. Circ: 30,000.

MI MLADI. *see* CHILDREN AND YOUTH—For

780 USA ISSN 1526-2324
MI2N; music industry news network. Text in English. 1998. d. free. adv. back issues avail. **Document type:** *Newsletter, Trade.*
Media: Online - full text. **Related titles:** E-mail ed.
Published by: Tag It, 1837 26th Ave., # 2F, Astoria, NY 11102-3541. TEL 718-726-1938, FAX 718-504-3512, info@mi2n.com. Ed. Eric de Fontenay. Circ: 6,500.

780 DEU
MICHAELSTEINER KONFERENZBERICHTE. Text in German. 1975. irreg., latest vol.75, 2010. price varies. **Document type:** *Monographic series, Academic/Scholarly.*
Former titles (until 1995): Studien zur Auffuehrungspraxis und Interpretation der Musik des 18. Jahrhunderts; (until 1985): Studien zur Auffuehrungspraxis und Interpretation von Instrumentalmusik des 18. Jahrhunderts
Published by: Wissner Verlag, Im Tal 12, Augsburg, 86179, Germany. TEL 49-821-259890, FAX 49-821-594932, info@wissner.com.

780 USA
MIDWEST BEAT MAGAZINE. Text in English. 1977. m. USD 25 (effective 2005). adv. bk.rev.; music rev.; tel.rev.; video rev.; rec.rev. illus.; stat.; tr.lit. back issues avail. **Document type:** *Newspaper.* **Description:** Covers regional entertainment focus on midwest talents in music and other arts, targeting audiences between 18 to 35.
Former titles (until 1999): Beat (Highland); (until 1984): Illiana Beat; (until 1983): Night Rock News
Published by: Lounge Lizard - Lounges Publications, 2613 41st St., Highland, IN 46322. TEL 219-972-9131, FAX 219-972-9131, beatboss@aol.com, http://www.midwestbeat.com. Ed., Pub., R&P Thomas E Lounges. Adv. contact Julie Lounges. B&W page USD 575, color page USD 800; trim 10.5 x 13. Circ: 30,000.

M

780 USA
MIDWEST MUSICIANS HOTLINE. Text in English. m. USD 14.95 (effective 1999).
Published by: Heartland Construction Group, Inc., 1003 Central Ave, Fort Dodge, IA 50501. TEL 515-955-1600, 888-247-2009, FAX 515-574-2217. Adv. contact Trent Salter. Circ: 6,000 (paid).

780 DEU
MIK'X NEWS; Das deutschsprachige Magazin fuer Vibrationen. Text in German. 1994. 4/yr. EUR 2 newsstand/cover (effective 2009). **Document type:** *Magazine, Consumer.*
Published by: Eisclub Mik Kostevc, Jonasstr 47, Berlin, 12053, Germany. TEL 49-30-61626749, info@eisclub.de. Ed., Pub. Mik Kostevc. Circ: 500 (paid and controlled).

780 USA ISSN 1940-8994
E185.86
MILK. Text in English. 2008 (Mar.). q. USD 11.99 (effective 2008). **Document type:** *Magazine, Consumer.*
Published by: Purple Vine, LLC, 2214 Frederick Douglass Blvd, Ste 142, New York, NY 10026. info@milkmusicmag.com, http://www.milkmusicmag.com.

781.6 USA
MILK MAGAZINE. Text in English. 1993. bi-m. USD 10 (effective 1998). adv. music rev.; software rev.; video rev. back issues avail. **Document type:** *Magazine, Consumer.*
Address: TEL 414-961-7304, FAX 414-332-8095. Ed., Adv. contact Josh Modell. B&W page USD 300, color page USD 550; trim 10 x 8. Circ: 7,500.

785 USA
MILLER NOTES. Text in English. 1980. 4/yr. looseleaf. USD 20 domestic membership; USD 25 foreign membership (effective 2000). adv. bk.rev. **Document type:** *Newsletter, Consumer.* **Description:** Presents news of personnel associated with big band leader Glenn Miller, his records, and the Society's festival.
Published by: Glenn Miller Birthplace Society, PO Box 61, Clarinda, IA 51632. TEL 712-542-2461. Ed., Adv. contact Elaine Armstrong. R&P Marvin Negley. Circ: 1,400.

784.2 780.15 USA ISSN 1046-5413
ML42.M45
MILWAUKEE SYMPHONY ORCHESTRA. Variant title: Milwaukee Symphony Program. Text in English. 1980. s-m. free. adv. **Document type:** *Magazine, Consumer.*
Formerly: Milwaukee Symphony Orchestra. Stagebill
Published by: Encore, Inc., 4532 N Oakland Ave, Milwaukee, WI 53211. TEL 414-964-5669. Ed., Pub. John Stone. R&P Andy Bvehlow TEL 414-291-6020. Adv. contact Cynthia Collyer.

781.7 ISR ISSN 1565-0618
ML5
➤ **MIN-AD: ISRAEL STUDIES IN MUSICOLOGY ONLINE.** Text in English. -1996; N.S. 1999. irreg. free (effective 2011). **Document type:** *Journal, Academic/Scholarly.* **Description:** Aimed at a diverse community of music scholars.
Media: Online - full text.
Indexed: A01, CA, IIMP, J01, M11, T02.
Published by: Israel Musicology Society, POB 39105, Jerusalem, 91390, Israel. TEL 972-2-6585059, FAX 972-2-5611156, http://www.biu.ac.il/hu/mu/ims/Min-ad/. Ed. Adena Portowitz.

781.7 CHN
MINZU MINJIAN YINYUE/NATIONAL AND FOLK MUSIC. Text in Chinese. q. CNY 4.80. **Description:** Introduces folk music popular among nationalities in Guangdong Province.
Published by: (Guangdongsheng Minjian Yinyue Yanjiushi/Guangdong Folk Music Research Office), Minzu Minjian Yinyue Bianjibu, 79 Wende Lu, 7th Fl, Guangzhou, Guangdong 510030, China. TEL 340465. Eds. Lin Yun, Ma Ming.

MINZU YILIN/WORLD OF NATIONAL ART. *see* ART

780 CHN
MINZU YINYUE/ETHNIC MUSIC. Text in Chinese. bi-m. USD 53.40 (effective 2009). **Document type:** *Magazine, Consumer.*
Formerly (until 2006): Yunling Gesheng (1671-2196)
Indexed: RILM.
Published by: Minzu Yinyue Zazhishe, 356, Renmin Xi Lu, Kunming, 650118, China. **Dist. by:** China International Book Trading Corp, 35 Chegongzhuang Xilu, Haidian District, PO Box 399, Beijing 100044, China. TEL 86-10-68412045, FAX 86-10-68412023, cibtc@mail.cibtc.com.cn, http://www.cibtc.com.cn.

MIROMENTE; Zeitschrift fuer Gut und Boes. *see* LITERATURE

MIRROR MAGAZINE. *see* ART

780 CZE ISSN 0544-4136
ML3797
➤ **MISCELLANEA MUSICOLOGICA.** Text in English, German. 1956. irreg., latest vol.38, 2006. price varies. illus. **Document type:** *Journal, Academic/Scholarly.*
Indexed: AICP, CERDIC, MusicInd, PCI, RASB, RILM.
Published by: Univerzita Karlova v Praze, Filozoficka Fakulta, Ustav Hudebni Vedy, nam Jana Palacha 2, Prague, 11638, Czech Republic. TEL 420-2-21619224, FAX 420-2-21619386, musicology@ff.cuni.cz, http://musicology.ff.cuni.cz. Circ: 300.

780.71 USA
MISSISSIPPI MUSIC EDUCATOR. Text in English. 1941. 3/yr. free to members (effective 2007). adv. bk.rev.; film rev. illus.; stat.; tr.lit. **Document type:** *Magazine, Consumer.*
Formerly: Mississippi Notes (0026-6353)
Published by: Mississippi Music Educators Association, c/o Andrea Coleman, Ed, 5025 Hwy 80 E, Pearl, MS 39208. TEL 601-936-6791, msmea@msmea.org, http://www.msmea.org. Ed. Andrea Coleman. adv.: page USD 138. Circ: 500 (controlled).

781.57 USA ISSN 0742-4612
ML3508
THE MISSISSIPPI RAG; the voice of traditional jazz and ragtime. Text in English. 1973 (Nov.). m. USD 24 domestic; USD 28 foreign; USD 3 newsstand/cover (effective 2004). adv. bk.rev.; music rev. 40 p./no. 4 cols./p.; back issues avail. **Document type:** *Newspaper.* **Description:** Contains historical articles, current jazz and ragtime news, photos and articles on performers and festivals, and listings of gigs and festivals.
Indexed: IIMP, M11, MusicInd, PMPI, RILM, T02.
Published by: Mississippi Rag, Inc., 9448 Lyndale Ave S Ste 120, Bloomington, MN 55420-4245. TEL 952-885-9918, FAX 952-885-9943. Ed., Pub., R&P Ms. Leslie Carole Johnson. Adv. contacts Ms. Jody Hughes, Ms. Leslie Carole Johnson. B&W page USD 300; trim 11.38 x 16.25. Circ: 4,200 (paid). **Subscr. to:** PO Box 19068, Minneapolis, MN 55419.

780.1 USA ISSN 0085-350X
ML1
➤ **MISSOURI JOURNAL OF RESEARCH IN MUSIC EDUCATION.** Text in English. 1962. a. abstr. back issues avail. **Document type:** *Journal, Academic/Scholarly.* **Description:** Reports of original research related to music teaching and learning.
Indexed: CA, IIMP, M11, MAG, MusicInd, RILM, T02.
—Ingenta.
Published by: Missouri Music Educators Association, Conservatory of Music, 4949 Cherry St, University of Missouri, Kansas City, MO 64110. TEL 816-235-2900, FAX 816-235-5264, president@mmea.net, http://www.mmea.net.

780 FIN ISSN 1458-3763
MIX. Text in Finnish. 1998. m. adv. **Document type:** *Magazine, Consumer.* **Description:** Contains articles and features on popular music.
Published by: Aller Julkaisut Oy, PO Box 124, Helsinki, 00151, Finland. TEL 358-9-7777777, FAX 358-9-77777225, ilmot@aller.fi, http://www.aller.fi. Ed. Antti Aro. adv.: page EUR 3,400; 207 x 280. Circ: 40,393 (paid).

780 USA
MIXER; the future sound of america. Text in English. 1996. m. USD 3.50 newsstand/cover (effective 2001). adv. **Document type:** *Magazine, Consumer.* **Description:** Contains articles and reviews of the music and lifestyle trends involving club and DJ culture.
Published by: DMC America, 213 W 35th St, Ste 402, New York, NY 10001. TEL 212-777-6676, FAX 212-777-7167, usa@dmcworld.com, http://www.dmcworld.com. **Dist. by:** International Publishers Direct, 27500 Riverview Center Blvd, Bonita Springs, FL 34134. TEL 858-320-4563, FAX 858-677-3220.

780 GBR ISSN 0957-6622
MIXMAG. Text in English. 1982. m. GBP 36 domestic; GBP 52.50 in Europe; GBP 60 elsewhere (effective 2009). adv. film rev. back issues avail. **Document type:** *Magazine, Consumer.* **Description:** Contains information about dance music and the club culture scene.
Related titles: Online - full text ed.
—**CCC.**
Published by: Development Hell Ltd., 90-92, Pentonville Rd, London, N1 9HS, United Kingdom. TEL 44-20-70788400, FAX 44-20-78339900, info@developmenthell.co.uk, http://www.developmenthell.co.uk/. adv.: page GBP 4,005; trim 230 x 300. Circ: 37,139.

782.421 621.389 USA
MIXTAPE. Text in English. 2005. q. USD 3.95 newsstand/cover (effective 2005). adv. music rev. **Document type:** *Magazine, Consumer.* **Description:** Covers mixtap DJ's, including urban culture, artists interviews, profiles of music producers, fashion, reviews, and industry products.
Published by: Entertainment Group Publishing, 244 5th Ave., Ste. 2371, New York, NY 10001-7604. TEL 212-340-1999. adv.: page USD 1,500; trim 6 x 4. Circ: 10,000.

786.5 CAN ISSN 1201-5741
ML549.8
MIXTURES. Text in French. 1995. s-a. **Document type:** *Bulletin.*
Indexed: RILM.
Published by: Federation Quebecoise des Amis de l'Orgue, 1203 Ave d'Argenteuil, Sainte-Foy, PQ G1W 3S1, Canada.

780 USA ISSN 1058-0212
MOBILE BEAT; the DJ magazine. Text in English. 1991. bi-m. USD 23; USD 3.95 newsstand/cover (effective 2001). bk.rev.; music rev.; rec.rev.; software rev. illus.; charts. back issues avail.; reprints avail. **Document type:** *Magazine, Consumer.* **Description:** Of particular interest to disc jockeys, musicians, and audiophiles, with articles on new music and new technology in the field, profiles, advice on buying strategies, product reviews, and marketing tips.
Published by: L A Communications, Inc., PO Box 309, East Rochester, NY 14445. TEL 716-385-9920, FAX 716-385-3637. Eds. Dan Walsh, Robert A Lindquist. Pub. Michael Buonaccorso. R&P Robert A Lindquist. Adv. contact Art Bradley TEL 716-385-9920 ext 103. Circ: 18,000.

780 USA ISSN 0194-4533
MODERN DRUMMER. Text in English. 1977. m. USD 29.97 domestic; USD 4.99 newsstand/cover (effective 2005). adv. bk.rev. illus. **Document type:** *Magazine, Consumer.* **Description:** Dedicated entirely to the art of drumming. Caters to the needs of amateur, semi-pro and professional drummers. Features include new product reviews, industry news as well as full-length feature columns, authored by some of the most respected performers. Offers practical advice on a range of topics that encompasses all phases of the art and the instrument.
Incorporates (in 1988): Modern Percussionist (8750-7838)
Related titles: Online - full text ed.
Indexed: A22, IIMP, M11, MusicInd, T02.
—Ingenta.
Published by: Modern Drummer Publications, Inc., 12 Old Bridge Rd, Cedar Grove, NJ 07009-1288. TEL 973-239-4140, FAX 973-239-7139, rons@moderndrummer.com. Ed. Isabel Spagnardi. Pub. Ronald L Spagnardi. Adv. contact Bob Berenson. Circ: 101,000 (paid). **Subscr. to:** PO Box 480, Mt Morris, IL 61054.

MODEST PROPOSALS. *see* COMMUNICATIONS—Television And Cable

780 PRT
MODUS; revista do Instituto Gregoriano de Lisboa. Text in Multiple languages. 1987. a.
Published by: Instituto Gregoriano de Lisboa, Av. 5 de Outubro 258, Lisbon, 1100, Portugal. TEL 351-21-7930004, FAX 351-21-7950451.

780.729489 DNK ISSN 0902-6711
MODUS. Text in Danish. 1987. 11/yr. DKK 675 (effective 2009). adv. **Document type:** *Magazine, Trade.*
Published by: Dansk Musikpaedagogisk Forening, Noerrebrogade 45 A, Copenhagen N, 2200, Denmark. TEL 45-35-356333, FAX 45-35-350698, dmpf@dmpf.dk, http://www.dmpf.dk. Ed. Dan Johnsen. adv.: color page DKK 4,600; 178 x 255. Circ: 1,400.

MOFA; magazine of performing arts. *see* THEATER

781.46 GBR ISSN 1351-0193
MOJO; the music magazine. Text in English. 1993. m. GBP 40 domestic; GBP 58.50 in Europe & USA; GBP 84.50 elsewhere (effective 2009). adv. illus. back issues avail. **Document type:** *Magazine, Consumer.* **Description:** Designed for people who buy music - vinyl, and CDs, new and old - and want to read about music.
Related titles: Online - full text ed.
Indexed: M11, MusicInd.
—IE. **CCC.**
Published by: H. Bauer Publishing Ltd. (Subsidiary of: Bauer Media Group), Mappin House, 4 Winsley St, London, W1W 8HF, United Kingdom. TEL 44-20-74361515, FAX 44-20-71828596, http://www.bauer.co.uk. Adv. contact Marco Soares TEL 44-20-72958511. page GBP 4,890.

MOLODEZHNAYA ESTRADA. *see* CHILDREN AND YOUTH—For

780 ITA ISSN 0544-7763
IL MONDO DELLA MUSICA; rassegna internazionale di vita musicale, concerti, opera, balletto. Text in Italian. 1963. q. EUR 16 domestic; EUR 20 foreign (effective 2009). adv. bk.rev. **Document type:** *Magazine, Consumer.*
Published by: Mondo della Musica, Via Flaminia Nuova 241, Rome, 00191, Italy.

781.62 FRA ISSN 1772-8916
MONDOMIX; la musique en couleurs. Text in French. 2003. bi-m. free domestic (effective 2010). **Document type:** *Magazine, Consumer.*
Formerly (until 2005): Mondomix Papier (1639-8726)
Published by: Mondomix Media, 9 Cite Paradis, Paris, 75010, France. TEL 33-1-56039089, FAX 33-1-56039084, info@mondomix.com.

780 POL ISSN 1234-172X
MONOCHORD. Text in Polish. 1993. q. PLZ 12.08 per issue (effective 2011). **Document type:** *Journal, Academic/Scholarly.* **Description:** Publishes articles about music theory and links between music studies and other fields of knowledge.
Indexed: RILM.
Published by: Wydawnictwo Adam Marszalek, ul Lubicka 44, Torun, 87100, Poland. TEL 48-56-6485070, FAX 48-56-6608160, info@marszalek.com.pl, http://www.marszalek.com.pl.

780.01 USA ISSN 1062-4112
MONOGRAPHS IN MUSICOLOGY SERIES. Text in English. 1983. irreg. price varies. back issues avail. **Document type:** *Monographic series, Trade.*
Published by: Pendragon Press, PO Box 190, Hillsdale, NY 12529. TEL 518-325-6100, FAX 518-325-6102, orders@pendragonpress.com. Ed. Robert J Kessler.

780 DEU
MONOLITHOGRAPHIEN. Text in German. 2000. irreg., latest vol.4, 2007. price varies. **Document type:** *Monographic series, Academic/Scholarly.*
Published by: Franz Steiner Verlag GmbH, Birkenwaldstr 44, Stuttgart, 70191, Germany. TEL 49-711-25820, FAX 49-711-2582290, service@steiner-verlag.de, http://www.steiner-verlag.de.

780 USA
MONSTA; the ulimate hip hop experience. Text in English. 2008 (Feb.). m. USD 4.99 newsstand/cover (effective 2008). adv. **Document type:** *Magazine, Consumer.* **Description:** Designs for men and women 18-39 years who identify with the hip-hop culture.
Published by: Monsta Publishing, LLC, 1835 N E Miami Dardens Dr, Miami, FL 33179. TEL 305-919-9478, FAX 305-919-9477, hhw.monstasales@gmail.com. Adv. contact Denada Jackson TEL 704-957-1447. color page USD 5,885; trim 10 x 12. Circ: 75,000 (controlled).

780 USA ISSN 2153-6104
▼ **MONTAGUE STREET**; the art of bob dylan. Text in English. 2009. s-a. adv. **Document type:** *Journal, Trade.*
Published by: Charles Haeussler, Ed. & Pub., 1804 76th St, PH C, Brooklyn, NY 11214. Eds. Lucas Stensland, Nina Goss.

780 DEU ISSN 0544-9987
MONUMENTA MONODICA MEDII AEVI. Text in German. 1956. irreg. price varies. **Document type:** *Monographic series, Academic/Scholarly.*
Published by: (Universitaet Erlangen-Nuernberg, Institut fuer Musikwissenschaft), Baerenreiter Verlag, Heinrich-Schuetz-Allee 35, Kassel, 34131, Germany. TEL 49-561-3105154, FAX 49-561-3105195, order@baerenreiter.com, http://www.baerenreiter.com.

783.026 DNK ISSN 0105-3566
MONUMENTA MUSICAE BYZANTINAE. Text in Latin, Greek, Classical. 1935. irreg., latest vol.12, 2000. price varies. **Document type:** *Monographic series, Academic/Scholarly.*
Published by: Museum Tusculanum Press, c/o University of Copenhagen, Njalsgade 126, Copenhagen S, 2300, Denmark. TEL 45-35-329109, FAX 45-35-329113, info@mtp.dk, http://www.mtp.dk.

780 AUT
MONUMENTA MUSICAE BYZANTINAE. CORPUS SCRIPTORUM DE RE MUSICA. Text in German. 1985. irreg., latest vol.5, 1998. price varies. **Document type:** *Monographic series, Academic/Scholarly.*
Published by: Verlag der Oesterreichischen Akademie der Wissenschaften, Postgasse 7/4, Vienna, W 1011, Austria. TEL 43-1-515813402, FAX 43-1-515813400, verlag@oeaw.ac.at.

780 DNK ISSN 0105-3418
MONUMENTA MUSICAE BYZANTINAE. SUBSIDIA. Text in Greek, Classical, Latin. 1935. irreg., latest vol.8, 1966. price varies. **Document type:** *Monographic series, Academic/Scholarly.*
Published by: Museum Tusculanum Press, c/o University of Copenhagen, Njalsgade 126, Copenhagen S, 2300, Denmark. TEL 45-35-329109, FAX 45-35-329113, info@mtp.dk, http://www.mtp.dk.

780 SWE ISSN 0077-1473
M2
MONUMENTA MUSICAE SUECICAE. Text in English, German, Swedish. 1958. irreg., latest vol.9, 1979. Price varies. **Document type:** *Monographic series, Academic/Scholarly.*
Published by: (Svenska Samfundet foer Musikforskning/Swedish Society for Musicology), Edition Reimers AB, Maardvaegen 44, PO Box 17051, Bromma, 16117, Sweden. TEL 46-8-7040280, FAX 46-8-804228, info@editionreimers.se, http://www.editionreimers.se. Pub. Marianne Reimers.

780.902 FRA ISSN 1762-7915
MONUMENTALES. Text in French. 19??. irreg. **Document type:** *Monographic series, Academic/Scholarly.*
Published by: Centre de Musique Baroque de Versailles, Hotel des Menus-Plaisirs, 22, avenue de Paris, Versailles Cedex, 78003, France. TEL 33-1-39207810, FAX 33-1-39207801, accueil@cmbv.com, http://www.cmbv.com.

780 USA ISSN 0077-1503
M2
MONUMENTS OF RENAISSANCE MUSIC. Text in English. 1967. irreg., latest vol.9, 1996. price varies. reprints avail.
Published by: University of Chicago, 5801 S Ellis Ave, Chicago, IL 60637. TEL 773-702-7899. Ed. Bonnie J Blackburn.

781.642 NZL ISSN 1177-0163
MOORE COUNTRY. Text in English. 2003. m. NZD 75 (effective 2008). illus. **Document type:** *Magazine, Consumer.*
Published by: Country Music Promotions New Zealand, PO Box 5550, Papanui, Christchurch, New Zealand. Ed. Ron Moore.

787 USA ISSN 1948-500X
MORAVIAN MUSIC FOUNDATION NEWSLETTER. Text in English. 1985. q. back issues avail. **Document type:** *Newsletter, Trade.* **Description:** Features informative articles on Moravian music.
Formerly (until 1996): Moravian Music Foundation. Newsletter (1948-6898)
Related titles: Online - full text ed.: free (effective 2009).
—CCC.
Published by: Moravian Music Foundation, 457 S Church St, Winston-Salem, NC 27101. TEL 336-725-0651, FAX 336-725-4514, info@moravianmusic.org.

780 051 USA ISSN 1948-9242
▼ **MOTOR DETROIT MAGAZINE.** Short title: Motor Detroit. Text in English. 2009. q. USD 4.95 per issue (effective 2009). **Document type:** *Magazine, Consumer.* **Description:** Promotes and illustrates the essence of Detroit, through its elements, events and the circumstances and situations that drive it. Spotlights the careers of both, the up-and-coming, as well as the established artist and talent, in all mediums and forms.
Related titles: Online - full text ed.: ISSN 1948-9250. 2009.
Published by: Pfalcon Media Group, 190 Mclean St, Detroit, MI 48203. TEL 248-416-9989, paul.a.motley@gmail.com.

780 USA ISSN 1089-8522
MOTORBOOTY; the better magazine. Text in English. 1987. s-a. USD 16. adv. bk.rev.; music rev. charts; illus.; maps; stat. back issues avail. **Document type:** *Magazine, Consumer.* **Description:** Contains comics and satirical essays to mock those who need mocking, proving the point that the truth really does hurt.
Related titles: Online - full text ed.
Published by: Clownskull Graphics, PO Box 02007, Detroit, MI 48202. TEL 313-871-8419, FAX 313-871-4840. Ed., Pub. Mark Dancey. Adv. contact Scott Hamilton. B&W page USD 1,500, color page USD 2,500; trim 11 x 8.5. Circ: 20,000 (paid).

780 AUS ISSN 1836-6856
▼ **MOUNTAIN FOLD MUSIC JOURNAL.** Text in English. 2009. q. free (effective 2011). back issues avail. **Document type:** *Journal, Academic/Scholarly.* **Description:** Focuses primarily on music and also provides a forum to discuss art, film, literature and culture.
Related titles: Online - full text ed.
Address: 46-758 Bourke St, Redfern, NSW 2016, Australia. Ed. Douglas Lance Gibson.

MOVEMENTS IN THE ARTS. *see* ART

MOVIES PLUS. *see* MOTION PICTURES

780 USA ISSN 1527-3733
ML410.M9
MOZART SOCIETY OF AMERICA. NEWSLETTER. Text in English. 1997. s-a. free to members (effective 2011). back issues avail. **Document type:** *Newsletter, Consumer.* **Description:** Contains research about the life, works, historical context, and reception of Wolfgang Amade Mozart.
Related titles: Online - full text ed.: free (effective 2011).
Indexed: RILM.
Published by: Mozart Society of America, 389 Main St, Ste 202, Malden, MA 02148. TEL 781-397-8870, FAX 781-397-8887, Mozart@guildassoc.com. Ed. Stephen C Fisher.

781.7 780.42 ITA ISSN 1121-354X
IL MUCCHIO SELVAGGIO; mensile di musica e cultura rock. Text in Italian. 1977. m. (11/yr. plus two specials). EUR 50 (effective 2009). illus. **Document type:** *Magazine, Consumer.*
Published by: Stemax Coop, Via Lorenzo il Magnifico 148, Rome, 00162, Italy. FAX 39-06-44231301, http://www.ilmucchio.it.

780 DEU
MUENCHNER PHILHARMONIKER. Text in German. 1985. s-m. **Document type:** *Bulletin.*
Address: Kellerstr 4, Munich, 81667, Germany. TEL 49-89-480985500, FAX 49-89-480985400, http://www.mphil.de.

781.7 USA
ML1
MUGWUMPS ONLINE; the magazine of folk instruments. Text in English. 1972. irreg. USD 9. adv. bk.rev. illus. **Document type:** *Magazine, Consumer.*
Former titles (until 1997): Mugwumps (0149-8517); Mugwumps' Instrument Herald
Media: Online - full content.
Indexed: MusicInd.
Published by: Mugwumps, PO Box 1755, Orleans, MA 02653. Ed., Pub. Mike Holmes. Circ: 3,000.

784.4 AUS ISSN 0157-3381
ML3544
MULGA WIRE. Text in English. 1955. bi-m. AUD 2 to non-members; free to members (effective 2008). adv. bk.rev. illus. **Document type:** *Magazine, Consumer.* **Description:** Covers social aspects of the present-day organizations, reviews and events.
Formerly (until 1967): Singabout (0037-5632)
Published by: Bush Music Club Inc., PO Box 433, Sydney, NSW 2001, Australia. TEL 61-2-96427950, info@bushmusic.org.au. Eds. Bob Bolton TEL 61-2-95697244, Colin Fong. Circ: 300.

782.421 USA ISSN 1542-4405
MURDER DOG. Text in English. bi-m. USD 26 domestic; USD 55 foreign; USD 3.95 newsstand/cover domestic (effective 2006). adv. music rev. back issues avail. **Document type:** *Magazine, Consumer.* **Description:** Covers underground rap and hip hop music, musicians, and the current scene with interviews and more.
Related titles: Online - full content ed.
Published by: Automatic Alligator Publishing, 164 Robles Dr, Ste 257, Vallejo, CA 9459. TEL 707-553-8191. Ed. Black Dog Bone.

780 ITA ISSN 0394-4808
N15
MUSEO DEGLI STRUMENTI MUSICALI. RASSEGNA DI STUDI E NOTIZIE; raccolta delle stampe A. Bertarelli, raccolta di arte applicata. Text in Italian. 1973. a. **Document type:** *Journal, Academic/Scholarly.*
Indexed: B24, RILM.
Published by: Comune di Milano, Palazzo Marino, Piazza della Scala 2, Milan, 20121, Italy. TEL 39-02-88451, http://www.comune.milano.it.

780 USA
MUSE'S NEWS. Text in English. 1998. m. free. back issues avail. **Document type:** *Newsletter, Consumer.* **Description:** Provides information to song writers, including song writing tools, articles, song writing contest, market information, copyright issues, publishing advice, and web site reviews.
Media: Online - full text. **Related titles:** E-mail ed.
Published by: Jodi Krangle Ed.& Pub. Circ: 8,500.

780.89 DEU
MUSEUM FUER VOELKERKUNDE, BERLIN. VEROEFFENTLICHUNGEN. NEUE FOLGE. ABTEILUNG: MUSIKETHNOLOGIE. Text in German. 1961. irreg., latest vol.8, 1991. price varies. **Document type:** *Monographic series.*
Published by: Staatliche Museen zu Berlin - Preussischer Kulturbesitz, Generalverwaltung, Stauffenbergstr 41, Berlin, 10785, Germany. TEL 030-266-6, FAX 030-2662612.

MUSEUM OF THE AMERICAN PIANO. NEWSLETTER. *see* MUSEUMS AND ART GALLERIES

780 USA ISSN 0895-1543
ML128.P63
MUSI - KEY; the reference guide of note. Text in English. 1987. bi-m. USD 312. **Document type:** *Catalog.* **Description:** Lists popular and standard music currently in print, both sheets and collections.
Related titles: Diskette ed.
Address: PO Box 2009, Idaho Falls, ID 83403-2009. TEL 520-742-0880, FAX 520-742-1881. Eds. Linda Rucker, Randy Rucker. Circ: 1,400.

780 USA ISSN 1089-6643
ML120.U5
MUSI - KEY INSTRUMENTAL. Text in English. 1985. s-a. USD 132 (effective 2000). **Document type:** *Catalog.*
Related titles: Diskette ed.
Published by: Musi - Key, PO Box 2009, Idaho Falls, ID 83403-2009. TEL 520-742-0880, FAX 520-742-1881. Eds. Linda Rucker, Randy Rucker.

780 USA ISSN 1542-4634
ML128.K5
MUSI - KEY KEYBOARD. Text in English. 1998. a. USD 115 (effective 2000). **Document type:** *Catalog.* **Description:** Lists classical and popular solo and ensemble music in print for piano and organ.
Published by: Musi - Key, PO Box 2009, Idaho Falls, ID 83403-2009. TEL 520-742-0880, FAX 520-742-1881. Eds. Linda Rucker, Randy Rucker.

780 IND
MUSIC ACADEMY. CONFERENCE SOUVENIR. Text in English, Sanskrit, Tamil. 1940. a. INR 50 per issue (effective 2011). **Document type:** *Academic/Scholarly.* **Description:** Contains articles on music contributed by international writers, and documented programmes of music and dance recitals.
Published by: Music Academy, New No. 168 (Old No. 306), T.T.K. Rd, Royapettah, Chennai, Tamil Nadu 600 014, India. TEL 91-44-28112231, FAX 91-44-42359362, music@musicacademymadras.com, http://www.musicacademymadras.in.

780 IND ISSN 0970-3101
ML5
MUSIC ACADEMY. JOURNAL. Text in English, Sanskrit, Tamil. 1929. a. INR 150 per issue (effective 2011). **Document type:** *Journal, Academic/Scholarly.* **Description:** Devoted to the advancement of the science and art of music.
Indexed: RILM.
—Ingenta.
Published by: Music Academy, New No. 168 (Old No. 306), T.T.K. Rd, Royapettah, Chennai, Tamil Nadu 600 014, India. TEL 91-44-28112231, FAX 91-44-42359362, music@musicacademymadras.com. Ed. Pappu Venugopala Rao. **Subscr. to:** I N S I O Scientific Books & Periodicals. **Dist. by:** H P C Publishers Distributors Pvt. Ltd.

780.7 USA ISSN 1051-8975
MUSIC ALIVE!. Text in English. 19??. 8/yr. USD 300 domestic for 30 student copies, 1 teacher's guide & CD; USD 410 foreign for 30 student copies, 1 teacher's guide & CD (effective 2011). back issues avail. **Document type:** *Magazine, Trade.* **Description:** Contains informative articles on the music kids love along with a comprehensive teacher's guide and lesson plan.
Published by: Cherry Lane Magazines, Inc., 149 Fifth Ave, 9th Fl, New York, NY 10010.

780 GBR ISSN 0262-5245
ML1
➤ **MUSIC ANALYSIS.** Text in English. 1982. 3/yr. GBP 458 in United Kingdom to institutions; EUR 582 in Europe to institutions; USD 946 in the Americas to institutions; USD 1,098 elsewhere to institutions; GBP 527 combined subscription in United Kingdom to institutions (print & online eds.); EUR 670 combined subscription in Europe to institutions (print & online eds.); USD 1,088 combined subscription in the Americas to institutions (print & online eds.); USD 1,263 combined subscription elsewhere to institutions (print & online eds.) (effective 2012). adv. bk.rev. back issues avail.; reprint service avail. from PSC. **Document type:** *Journal, Academic/Scholarly.* **Description:** International forum for the presentation of new writing focused on musical works and repertoires.
Related titles: Online - full text ed.: ISSN 1468-2249. GBP 458 in United Kingdom to institutions; EUR 582 in Europe to institutions; USD 946 in the Americas to institutions; USD 1,098 elsewhere to institutions (effective 2012) (from IngentaConnect).
Indexed: A01, A03, A08, A20, A22, A26, ArtHuCI, CA, CurCont, DIP, E01, IBR, IBZ, IIMP, M11, MusicInd, PCI, RASB, RILM, SCOPUS, T02, W07.
—BLDSC (5990.185300), IE, Infotrieve, Ingenta. **CCC.**
Published by: (The Society for Music Analysis USA), Wiley-Blackwell Publishing Ltd. (Subsidiary of: John Wiley & Sons, Inc.), 9600 Garsington Rd, Oxford, OX4 2DQ, United Kingdom. TEL 44-1865-776868, FAX 44-1865-714591, customerservices@blackwellpublishing.com. Ed. Alan Street. Adv. contact Craig Pickett TEL 44-1865-476267. B&W page GBP 445, B&W page USD 823; 110 x 185. Circ: 550.

➤ **MUSIC & ANTHROPOLOGY;** journal of Mediterranean musical anthropology. *see* ANTHROPOLOGY

780 700 GBR ISSN 1754-7105
ML3849
➤ **MUSIC AND ARTS IN ACTION.** Text in English. 2008. irreg. free (effective 2011). **Document type:** *Journal, Academic/Scholarly.*
Media: Online - full text.
Indexed: SociolAb.
Published by: University of Exeter, Department of Sociology & Philosophy, Amory Bldg, Rennes Dr, Exeter, EX4 4RJ, United Kingdom. Ed. Arild Bergh.

780 341.758 GBR ISSN 0968-0322
K1450.A13
MUSIC & COPYRIGHT. Text in English. 1992. fortn. GBP 920, USD 1,610, EUR 1,150 (effective 2010). **Document type:** *Newsletter, Trade.* **Description:** Provides global reporting on the commercial aspects of the music industry.
Related titles: Online - full text ed.: GBP 2,760, USD 4,830, EUR 3,450 (effective 2010).
Indexed: B03, P48, PQC, T03.
—CIS. **CCC.**
Published by: Informa Telecoms & Media (Subsidiary of: T & F Informa plc), 37-41 Mortimer St, London, W1T 3JH, United Kingdom. TEL 44-20-70175000, FAX 44-20-70175953, telecoms.enquiries@informa.com. Ed. Simon Dyson TEL 44-20-70174249. **Subscr. to:** Sheepen Pl, Colchester, Essex C03 3LP, United Kingdom. TEL 44-20-70175533, FAX 44-20-70174783.

MUSIC & DANCE NEWS. *see* DANCE

780.7 USA
MUSIC AND ENTERTAINMENT INDUSTRY EDUCATORS' NOTES. Short title: M I E A Notes. Text in English. 1978. q. looseleaf. USD 6. **Document type:** *Newsletter.*
Formerly: Music Industry Educators' Notes
Published by: Music Industry Educators Association, c/o Music Department, New York State University, Oneonta, NY 13820. TEL 703-568-6863. Ed. Janet Nepkie. Circ: 500.

780.07 GBR ISSN 0027-4224
ML5
➤ **MUSIC AND LETTERS.** Text in English. 1920. q. GBP 160 in United Kingdom to institutions; EUR 240 in Europe to institutions; USD 309 in US & Canada to institutions; GBP 160 elsewhere to institutions; GBP 174 combined subscription in United Kingdom to institutions (print & online eds.); EUR 262 combined subscription in Europe to institutions (print & online eds.); USD 337 combined subscription in US & Canada to institutions (print & online eds.); GBP 174 combined subscription elsewhere to institutions (print & online eds.) (effective 2012). adv. bk.rev.; music rev. illus. index, cum.index: vols.1-40, 1920-1959. 180 p./no.; back issues avail.; reprint service avail. from PSC. **Document type:** *Journal, Academic/Scholarly.* **Description:** Covers all fields of musical enquiry, from earliest times to present day. Includes wide range of reviews: scholarly editions of music of the past; new music.
Related titles: Microform ed.: (from PQC); Online - full text ed.: ISSN 1477-4631. GBP 145 in United Kingdom to institutions; EUR 218 in Europe to institutions; USD 281 in US & Canada to institutions; GBP 145 elsewhere to institutions (effective 2012) (from IngentaConnect).
Indexed: A01, A02, A03, A06, A08, A20, A22, A27, AES, ASCA, AmHI, ArtHuCI, B04, BRD, BrHumI, CA, CRCL, CurCont, E01, FR, H07, H08, H09, H10, HAb, HistAb, HumInd, IBRH, IBT&D, IIMP, M11, MLA, MLA-IB, MusicInd, P02, P10, P30, P48, P53, P54, PCI, PQC, RASB, RILM, S05, SCOPUS, T02, W03, W05, W07.
—BLDSC (5990.190000), IE, Infotrieve, Ingenta, INIST. **CCC.**
Published by: Oxford University Press, Great Clarendon St, Oxford, OX2 6DP, United Kingdom. TEL 44-1865-556767, FAX 44-1865-556646, enquiry@oup.co.uk, http://www.oxfordjournals.org. Eds. Daniel K L Chua, Daniel Grimley, Rebecca Herrisone, Sam Barrett.

780 USA ISSN 1053-9255
MUSIC AND LITERATURE IN SOCIETY. Text in German. 1991. irreg. price varies. **Document type:** *Monographic series, Academic/Scholarly.*
Published by: Peter Lang Publishing, Inc. (Subsidiary of: Peter Lang Publishing Group), 29 Broadway, New York, NY 10006. TEL 212-647-7700, 800-770-5264, FAX 212-647-7707, customerservice@plang.com.

203.8 GBR ISSN 0305-4438
ML5
➤ **MUSIC AND LITURGY.** Text in English. 1974. q. free to members (effective 2009). adv. bk.rev. back issues avail. **Document type:** *Journal, Academic/Scholarly.* **Description:** Covers the study of liturgy and church music.
Formed by the merger of (1959-1974): Church Music (0009-644X); (1970-1974): Life and Worship (0024-5119); Which was formerly (until 1970): Liturgy; (until 194?): Music and Liturgy
Related titles: Microform ed.: (from PQC).
Indexed: A22, CERDIC, CPL, RI-1.
Published by: Society of St. Gregory, c/o Paul Moynihan, 33 Brockenhurst Rd, Addiscombe, Croydon, CR0 7DR, United Kingdom.

▼ ➤ **MUSIC AND MEDICINE.** *see* MEDICAL SCIENCES

780 320 USA ISSN 1938-7687
ML3916
MUSIC AND POLITICS. Text in English. 2007. s-a. free (effective 2011). **Document type:** *Journal, Academic/Scholarly.* **Description:** Explores the connection between music and politics, including music as a form of political discourse and the impact of politics on musicians.

Media: Online - full text.
Indexed: A39, C27, C29, D03, D04, E13, R14, S14, S15, S18.
Published by: University of California, Santa Barbara, Music Department, 1315 Music Bldg, Santa Barbara, CA 93106. TEL 805-893-3261, FAX 805-893-7194, music@music.ucsb.edu. Ed. Patricia Hall.

780 621.389 658 USA ISSN 0894-1238
ML1092
MUSIC AND SOUND RETAILER; the newsmagazine for musical instrument and sound product merchandisers. Text in English. 1978. m. USD 18; free to qualified personnel. adv. charts; illus.; stat.; tr.lit. back issues avail. **Document type:** *Magazine, Trade.* **Description:** For professional musicians and retailers.
Former titles: Music and Sound Electronics Retailer; Sound Arts Merchandising Journal
Published by: Testa Communications, Inc., 25 Willowdale Ave, Port Washington, NY 11050. TEL 516-767-2500, FAX 516-767-9335. Ed. Jon Mayer. Circ: 10,000.

MUSIC AND THE MOVING IMAGE. *see* MOTION PICTURES

MUSIC AND THE TEACHER. *see* EDUCATION—Teaching Methods And Curriculum

781.7 GBR ISSN 1744-0963
MUSIC ARCHIVE PUBLICATIONS. SERIES A, CHANT (EASTERN AND WESTERN). Variant title: Chant (Eastern and Western). Text in English. 1999. irreg., latest 2001. **Document type:** *Monographic series, Academic/Scholarly.*
Published by: Routledge (Subsidiary of: Taylor & Francis Group), 2 Park Sq, Milton Park, Abingdon, Oxon OX14 4RN, United Kingdom. TEL 44-20-70176000, FAX 44-20-70176699, info@routledge.co.uk, http://www.tandf.co.uk.

787 782 GBR ISSN 1744-0971
MUSIC ARCHIVE PUBLICATIONS. SERIES C, RENAISSANCE VOCAL AND INSTRUMENTAL MUSIC. Variant title: Renaissance Vocal and Instrumental Music. Text in English. 1998. irreg., latest 1998. **Document type:** *Monographic series, Academic/Scholarly.*
Published by: Routledge (Subsidiary of: Taylor & Francis Group), 2 Park Sq, Milton Park, Abingdon, Oxon OX14 4RN, United Kingdom. TEL 44-20-70176000, FAX 44-20-70176699, info@routledge.co.uk, http://www.tandf.co.uk.

780 IRL
MUSIC ASSOCIATION OF IRELAND. ANNUAL REPORT. Text in English. 1975. a. stat. **Document type:** *Newsletter.*
Published by: Music Association of Ireland Ltd., 69 S. Great Georges St., Dublin, 2, Ireland. TEL 01-4785368, FAX 01-4754426. Ed. Rodney Senior.

780 028.5 RUS
MUSIC AT THE KINDERGARTEN. Text in Russian. a.
Published by: Izdatel'stvo Muzyka, Petrovka 26, Moscow, 127051, Russian Federation. TEL 7-095-9215170, FAX 7-095-9283304, muz-sekretar@yandex.ru, jvolk@mail.ru.

780 AUS ISSN 1832-8911
MUSIC AUSTRALIA GUIDE; where music lives. Abbreviated title: M A G. Text in English. 2003. m. free (effective 2009). adv. **Document type:** *Magazine, Consumer.* **Description:** Features music reviews and news articles on famous personalities from the world of music.
Published by: The Slattery Media Group, AFL House, Ground Fl, 140 Harbour Esplanade, Docklands, VIC 3008, Australia. TEL 61-3-96272600, FAX 61-3-96272650, http://www.slatterymedia.com. Ed. Jonathan Alley TEL 61-3-96272665. Adv. contact Andrew Slattery TEL 61-3-96272620. page AUD 3,850; bleed 148 x 210. Circ: 80,000.

780 CAN
MUSIC BOOKS PLUS. Text in French. 1990. s-a. (with quarterly updates). free. **Document type:** *Catalog.* **Description:** Features best sellers and new titles including books, instructional videos, CD-ROMs and software. Areas covered include; the music business, songwriting, instrument technique, voice instruction, audio, video, recording, broadcast production, biographies, and songbooks.
Published by: Norris - Whitney Communications Inc., 23 Hannover Dr, 7, St Catharines, ON L2W 1A3, Canada. TEL 905-641-3471, 800-265-8481, FAX 905-641-1648. Ed. Maureen Jack. Circ: 30,000.

745.1 780 GBR ISSN 0027-4275
THE MUSIC BOX; an international journal of mechanical music. Text in English. 1962. q. GBP 24 in Europe; GBP 26 elsewhere (effective 2003). adv. bk.rev. bibl.; charts; illus. index. cum.index every 8 nos. 32 p./no. 3 cols./p.; back issues avail. **Document type:** *Journal, Consumer.* **Description:** Covers all aspects of mechanical music, musical boxes, disc boxes, organs, player pianos, etc.
Indexed: IBR, IBZ.
Published by: Musical Box Society of Great Britain, PO Box 299, Waterbeach, Cambridge, CB4 4PJ, United Kingdom. mbsgb@kreedman.globalnet.co.uk, http://www.mbsgb.org.uk. Ed., Pub., R&P Alan Pratt TEL 44-1564-775000. Adv. contact Ted Brown TEL 44-1403-823533. color page GBP 560. Circ: 1,500 (paid).

780 USA ISSN 1941-2231
THE MUSIC BOX. Text in English. 1994. m. **Document type:** *Newsletter, Consumer.* **Description:** Features concert, album and DVD reviews in a wide array of musical genres, as well as articles, interviews and concert listings.
Related titles: Online - full text ed.: ISSN 1941-224X.
Published by: The Music Box, PO Box 3911, Oak Park, IL 60303. Ed. John Metzger.

780 USA ISSN 1071-0191
MUSIC BOX SOCIETY INTERNATIONAL. NEWS BULLETIN. Text in English. 198?. bi-m.
Former titles (until 199?): M B S I News Bulletin (1058-7241); M B S News Bulletin (0732-7897)
Indexed: IIMP, M11.
Published by: Musical Box Society International, PO Box 10196, Springfield, MO 65808-0196. FAX 417-886-8839, http://www.mbsi.org.

MUSIC CATALOGING BULLETIN (ONLINE). *see* LIBRARY AND INFORMATION SCIENCES

780 USA ISSN 0161-2654
ML1
MUSIC CLUBS MAGAZINE. Text in English. 1922. 4/yr. USD 6. adv. bk.rev.; film rev.; music rev. **Description:** Promotes American music and musicians.
Related titles: Microform ed.: (from PQC); Online - full text ed.
Indexed: A22, IIMP, M11, MAG, MusicInd, T02.
Published by: National Federation of Music Clubs, 1336 N Delaware St, Indianapolis, IN 46202. TEL 317-638-4003, FAX 317-638-0503. Ed. Isabella Laude. Adv. contact Burke Neville. Circ: 4,000.

781.64 USA
MUSIC.COM MAGAZINE. Text in English. 2001. q. USD 12.79; USD 4.99 newsstand/cover; USD 5.99 newsstand/cover in Canada (effective 2001). adv. **Document type:** *Magazine, Consumer.* **Description:** Covers all aspects of the music world and puts them in the context of today's modern technologies and media.
Published by: Music.com, Inc., 580 Howard Ave., Ste. F, Somerset, NJ 08873-1136. TEL 212-997-6879, FAX 212-997-6876, comments@staff.music.com.

780.65 USA ISSN 1091-9791
MUSIC CONNECTION. Text in English. 1977. bi-w. USD 45 domestic; USD 70 foreign; USD 2.95 newsstand/cover; USD 75 for 2 yrs. domestic (effective 2005). adv. bk.rev.; music rev.; software rev.; video rev.; rec.rev.; Website rev. tr.lit. back issues avail. **Document type:** *Magazine, Trade.* **Description:** Trade magazine for musicians.
Indexed: IIMP, M11, T02.
Published by: Music Connection Inc., 16130 Ventura Blvd., Ste. 540, Encino, CA 91436-2579. contactmc@musicconnection.com. Ed. Mark Nardone. Pubs. Eric Bettelli, Michael Dolan TEL 818-995-0101 ext 102. R&P Michael Dolan TEL 818-995-0101 ext 102. Adv. contact Eric Bettelli. B&W page USD 1,740, color page USD 2,460; trim 8.5 x 11. Circ: 75,000.

780 USA
MUSIC CRITICS ASSOCIATION. NEWSLETTER. Text in English. 1963. q. bk.rev. back issues avail. **Document type:** *Newsletter.*
Published by: Music Critics Association, 51 Primrose Cir., Princeton, NJ 08540-9418. TEL 908-233-8468, FAX 908-233-8468, brdh97a@prodigy.com. Eds. A H Cohen, Doris La Mar. Circ: 1,000 (controlled).

780 CAN ISSN 0820-0416
ML21.C3
MUSIC DIRECTORY CANADA. Text in English. 1983. biennial. CAD 39.95 (effective 2001). **Document type:** *Directory.*
Published by: Norris - Whitney Communications Inc., 23 Hannover Dr, 7, St Catharines, ON L2W 1A3, Canada. TEL 905-641-3471, FAX 905-641-1648, info@nor.com, http://www.musicbooksplus.com. Ed. Jim Norris. Circ: 6,000.

781.642 DEU
MUSIC-EAGLE; Zeitschrift fuer die Freunde der Country & Western Music. Text in German. 1995. q. EUR 14 (effective 2005). adv. **Document type:** *Magazine, Consumer.*
Address: Pinneberger Weg 13, Hamburg, 20257, Germany. TEL 49-40-857414, FAX 49-40-3603114173. Ed., Pub. Rolf Baerenwald.

780 371.3 GBR ISSN 1461-3808
MT1
➤ **MUSIC EDUCATION RESEARCH.** Text in English. 1999. q. GBP 391 combined subscription in United Kingdom to institutions (print & online eds.); EUR 519, USD 652 combined subscription to institutions (print & online eds.) (effective 2012). adv. back issues avail.; reprint service avail. from PSC. **Document type:** *Journal, Academic/Scholarly.* **Description:** Aims to provide a forum for debate arising from research findings as well as methods and methodologies.
Related titles: Online - full text ed.: ISSN 1469-9893. GBP 352 in United Kingdom to institutions; EUR 467, USD 587 to institutions (effective 2012) (from IngentaConnect).
Indexed: A01, A02, A03, A08, A20, A22, ArtHuCI, B29, CA, CPE, DIP, E01, E03, ERI, ERIC, IBR, IBZ, M11, MusicInd, P04, P10, P48, P53, P54, PQC, RILM, SCOPUS, SSCI, T02, W07.
—IE, Infotrieve, Ingenta. **CCC.**
Published by: (Research in Music Education Conference), Routledge (Subsidiary of: Taylor & Francis Group), 4 Park Sq, Milton Park, Abingdon, Oxon OX14 4RN, United Kingdom. TEL 44-20-70176000, FAX 44-20-70176336, subscriptions@tandf.co.uk, http://www.routledge.com. Ed. Sarah Hennessy. Adv. contact Linda Hann TEL 44-1344-779945. **Subscr. to:** Taylor & Francis Ltd., Journals Customer Service, Sheepen Pl, Colchester, Essex CO3 3LP, United Kingdom. TEL 44-20-70175544, FAX 44-20-70175198.

780 USA ISSN 1938-6435
➤ **MUSIC EDUCATION RESEARCH INTERNATIONAL.** Text in English. 2007 (Oct.). a. free (effective 2010). **Document type:** *Journal, Academic/Scholarly.* **Description:** Contributes to global views of music education, which contains two different meanings.
Media: Online - full text.
Published by: University of South Florida, School of Music, 4202 E Fowler Ave FAH 110, Tampa, FL 33620. TEL 813-974-2311, FAX 813-974-8721, info@arts.usf.edu, http://music.arts.usf.edu/.

780.71 USA ISSN 0027-4321
➤ **MUSIC EDUCATORS JOURNAL.** Text in English. 1914. 4/yr. USD 165, GBP 98 combined subscription to institutions (print & online eds.); USD 162, GBP 96 to institutions (effective 2011). bk.rev. illus. Index. 3 cols./p.; reprint service avail. from PSC. **Document type:** *Journal, Academic/Scholarly.* **Description:** Offers timely articles on teaching approaches and philosophies, current trends and issues in music education and the latest in products and services.
Former titles (until 1934): Music Supervisors' Journal (1559-2472); (until 1915): Music Supervisors' Bulletin (1559-2464)
Related titles: Microform ed.: (from PQC); Online - full text ed.: ISSN 1945-0087. USD 149, GBP 88 to institutions (effective 2011).
Indexed: A01, A02, A03, A08, A20, A22, A26, B04, B14, BAS, BRD, BRI, CA, CBRI, CPE, DIP, E01, E02, E03, E06, E07, E09, ECER, ERI, ERIC, EdA, EdI, G05, G06, G07, G08, I05, IBR, IBZ, IIMP, M01, M02, M11, MAG, MLA-IB, MusicInd, P04, P07, P10, P18, P48, P53, P54, P55, PCI, PMR, PQC, RILM, SPPI, T02, W03, W05.
—BLDSC (5990.270000), IE, Ingenta. **CCC.**
Published by: (M E N C: National Association for Music Education), Sage Publications, Inc., 2455 Teller Rd, Thousand Oaks, CA 91320. TEL 805-499-9774, 800-818-7243, FAX 805-499-0871, 800-583-2665, info@sagepub.com, http://www.sagepub.com. Ed. Mitchell Robinson. Circ: 80,000. **Subscr. outside the Americas to:** Sage Publications Ltd., 1 Oliver's Yard, 55 City Rd, London EC1Y 1SP, United Kingdom. TEL 44-20-73248701, FAX 44-20-73248733, subscription@sagepub.co.uk.

780 CAN
MUSIC FOR ONE MUSIC FOR ALL. Text in English. 1988. a. CAD 10 (effective 2003). **Document type:** *Monographic series, Academic/Scholarly.* **Description:** The written history of the Association.
Published by: Saskatchewan Music Festival Association, 207 2314 11th Ave, Regina, SK S4P 0K1, Canada. TEL 306-757-1722, FAX 306-347-7789. Ed. Doris Covey Lazecki. Circ: 2,500.

780 USA ISSN 0898-8757
ML395
MUSIC FOR THE LOVE OF IT. Text in English. 1988. bi-m. looseleaf. USD 30 domestic; USD 40 foreign (effective 2006). adv. bk.rev.; music rev. illus. 8 p./no.; back issues avail. **Document type:** *Newsletter, Consumer.* **Description:** Aims to help amateur musicians share their love of making music. Contains news items on amateur music-making, lists of music resources, original music and drawings, interviews, essays and opinions.
Related titles: Special ed(s).: Adult Amateur Summer Music Workshop Directory.
Indexed: H20, M11.
Address: 67 Parkside Dr, Berkeley, CA 94705. TEL 510-654-9134, FAX 510-654-4656, http://www.music.Holloww.com. Ed., Pub., R&P, Adv. contact Ted Rust. 1/2 page USD 200. Circ: 1,100 (paid).

780 USA ISSN 1071-2801
MUSIC FROM CHINA. NEWS/CHANG FENG YUE XUN. Text in Chinese, English. 1991. a. USD 10 (effective 2001). bk.rev.; music rev. back issues avail. **Document type:** *Newsletter.* **Description:** Aims to foster interest in Chinese music. Introduces musicians, works, and events.
Indexed: RILM.
Published by: Music from China/Chang Feng Zhongyuetuan, 170 Park Row, Ste 12 D, New York, NY 10038. TEL 212-962-5698, 212-941-8733, FAX 212-625-8586, muschina@echonyc.com, http://www.musicfromchina.org/. Eds. Chen Yi, Paul Shackman, Wang Guowei. Circ: 1,200 (controlled).

781.64 USA
MUSIC GIGS. Text in English. bi-w. USD 69 (effective 2000).
Published by: The John King Network, 244 Madison Ave, Ste 393, New York, NY 10016. TEL 212-969-8715, 212-969-8715.

780 GBR ISSN 2046-3057
MUSIC HALL STUDIES. Text in English. 2008. s-a. GBP 7 per issue domestic; GBP 9.50 per issue in Europe; GBP 11 per issue in United States (effective 2011). **Document type:** *Journal, Academic/Scholarly.* **Description:** Devoted to the furtherance of research into music hall and the variety theatre.
Address: 11 Grand Parade, Leigh-on-Sea, Essex SS9 1DX, United Kingdom.

780 USA
➤ **MUSIC IN AMERICAN LIFE.** Text in English. 1972. irreg. price varies. back issues avail.; reprints avail. **Document type:** *Monographic series, Academic/Scholarly.*
Published by: University of Illinois Press, 1325 S Oak St, Champaign, IL 61820. TEL 217-333-0950, 866-244-0626, FAX 217-244-8082, uipress@uillinois.edu.

780 USA ISSN 1522-7464
ML26
➤ **MUSIC IN ART**; international journal for music iconography. Text in English, French, German, Italian, Spanish; Summaries in English. 1975. s-a. USD 40 to individuals; USD 125 to institutions (effective 2010). adv. bk.rev.; dance rev.; music rev. charts; illus.; abstr. 250 p./no.; back issues avail. **Document type:** *Journal, Academic/Scholarly.* **Description:** Covers all aspects of representation of music, music making, and musical life found in visual arts.
Formerly (until 1998): R I D I M - R C M I Newsletter (0360-8727)
Related titles: Chinese ed.: Yishu Zhongde Yinyue. 2006.
Indexed: A07, A30, A31, AA, ArtInd, B04, B24, M11, MLA-IB, MusicInd, RILM, T02, W03, W05.
—BLDSC (5990.227850).
Published by: (Research Center for Music Iconography/Repertoire Internationale d'Iconographie Musicale), City University of New York, Research Center for Music Iconography, 365 Fifth Ave, New York, NY 10016. TEL 212-817-1992, FAX 212-817-1569. Ed. Zdravko Blazekovic.

780 GBR ISSN 1752-1904
MUSIC IN BRITAIN, 1600-1900. Text in English. 2006. irreg., latest 2010. price varies. **Document type:** *Monographic series, Academic/Scholarly.*
Published by: Boydell & Brewer Ltd., Whitwell House, St Audrys Park Rd, Melton, Woodbridge, IP12 1SY, United Kingdom. TEL 44-1394-610600, FAX 44-1394-610316, editorial@boydell.co.uk, http://www.boydell.co.uk.

780 EST ISSN 1406-9490
ML303
MUSIC IN ESTONIA. Text in English, Estonian. 1993. irreg. **Document type:** *Monographic series, Academic/Scholarly.*
Indexed: RILM.
Published by: Eesti Muusikanoukogu, Suur-Karja 23, Tallinn, 10148, Estonia. emn@kul.ee, http://www.emc.ee.

780 057.85 POL ISSN 0860-911X
ML5
MUSIC IN POLAND. Text in English. 1966. s-a. free. bk.rev. bibl. **Description:** Contains articles especially on Polish music and musical life in Poland.
—Ingenta.
Published by: Polish Music Council, Fredry 8, Warsaw, 00097, Poland. Circ: 900. **Co-sponsor:** Ministry of Culture and Arts.

780 ISR
MUSIC IN TIME. Text in English. 1984. a., latest 2007. free (effective 2008). **Document type:** *Journal, Academic/Scholarly.* **Description:** Covers musical activities in Israel and subjects of interest to the music and dance world. Presents contributions from internationally-known musicians and music educators.
Published by: Jerusalem Academy of Music and Dance, Campus Givat Ram, Jerusalem, 91904, Israel. TEL 972-2-675-9911, FAX 972-2-652-7713, http://www.jamd.ac.il/english. Ed. Mrs. Michal Smoira-Cohn. Circ: 1,000.

780.65 381 USA ISSN 1050-1681
MUSIC INC. Text in English. 19??. 11/yr. adv.

Former titles (until 1990): Up Beat Monthly (0892-113X); (until 198?): Up Beat (0164-7121)
Published by: Maher Publications, 102 North Haven Rd, Elmhurst, IL 60126. TEL 630-941-2030, FAX 630-941-3210.

780 GBR ISSN 0951-5135
ML5
MUSIC JOURNAL. Text in English. 1929. m. GBP 32 to non-members; free to members (effective 2010). adv. back issues avail. **Document type:** *Magazine, Trade.* **Description:** Carries general musical news and reports of members' activities.
Formed by the 1929 merger of: Incorporated Society of Musicians. Report; British Music Society Bulletin
Indexed: CMPI.
—CCC.
Published by: Incorporated Society of Musicians, 10 Stratford Pl, London, W1C 1AA, United Kingdom. TEL 44-20-76294413, FAX 44-20-74081538, membership@ism.org. Ed. Deborah Annetts. Circ: 5,100.

782 USA ISSN 1086-6671
ML1
MUSIC K-8. Text in English. 1990 (Sept/Oct). 5/yr. USD 44.95; USD 64.90 includes Parts; USD 99.75 includes audio CD; USD 119.70 includes audio CD and Parts (effective 2007); Parts contain every recorded tune with the singers' part extracted for fast, less expensive photocopying. 72 p./no.; **Document type:** *Magazine, Consumer.* **Description:** A resource magazine for elementary and middle school music teachers.
Related titles: Audio CD ed.
Published by: Plank Road Publishing, Inc., PO Box 26627, Wauwatosa, WI 53226. TEL 262-790-5210, 800-437-0832, FAX 262-781-8818, 888-272-0212. Ed. Teresa M Jennings. R&P Julie Gaulke. Circ: 16,000 (paid).

780 027.6 USA ISSN 1074-1259
ML27.U5
MUSIC LIBRARY ASSOCIATION. MEMBERSHIP HANDBOOK. Text in English. 19??. a. USD 25 per issue to non-members; USD 5 per issue to members (effective 2009).
Former titles (until 1993): Music Library Association. Membership Directory (0884-982X); Music Library Association. Music Library Association Membership List
—BLDSC (5547.670000).
Published by: Music Library Association, 8551 Research Way, Ste 180, Middleton, WI 53562. TEL 608-836-5825, FAX 608-831-8200, mla@areditions.com.

780 USA
ML27.U5
MUSIC LIBRARY ASSOCIATION. NEWSLETTER. Variant title: M L A Newsletter. Text in English. 1969. q. free (effective 2009). back issues avail. **Document type:** *Newsletter, Academic/Scholarly.* **Description:** Aims to keep the membership of the association abreast of events, ideas, and trends related to music librarianship.
Media: Online - full content.
Published by: Music Library Association, 8551 Research Way, Ste 180, Middleton, WI 53562. TEL 608-836-5825, FAX 608-831-8200, mla@areditions.com. Ed. Steven Mantz.

MUSIC LIBRARY ASSOCIATION. NOTES. *see* LIBRARY AND INFORMATION SCIENCES

MUSIC LIBRARY ASSOCIATION - SOUTHERN CALIFORNIA CHAPTER. NEWSLETTER. *see* LIBRARY AND INFORMATION SCIENCES

MUSIC LIBRARY ASSOCIATION. TECHNICAL REPORTS. *see* LIBRARY AND INFORMATION SCIENCES

780 JPN
MUSIC LIFE. Text in Japanese. 1952. m. JPY 33,000.
Published by: Shinko Music Publishing Co. Ltd., 2-1 Kanda-Ogawa-Machi, Chiyoda-ku, Tokyo, 101-0052, Japan. Ed. Yo Masuda.

780 GBR ISSN 1755-8123
MUSIC MAKER. Text in English. 1997. m. GBP 30; GBP 2.95 newsstand/cover (effective 2007). adv. **Document type:** *Magazine, Consumer.* **Description:** Contains features about instruments and playing techniques as well as profiles of performers, gig and gear reports.
Formerly (until 200?): Traditional Music Maker (1464-4606)
Published by: (Music Maker Association), Magnet Publishing Ltd., 28 Grafton Ter, London, NW5 4JJ, United Kingdom. TEL 44-20-74240027.

781.64 AUT
MUSIC MANUAL; the best of everything. Text in German. q. EUR 26; EUR 5 newsstand/cover in Germany; EUR 4.40 newsstand/cover in Austria (effective 2005). adv. **Document type:** *Magazine, Consumer.*
Related titles: Online - full text ed.: ISSN 1605-816X.
Published by: VIVO Zeitschriftenverlag GesmbH, Hauptstr 36, Klosterneuburg-Weidling, 3400, Austria. TEL 43-2243-349400, FAX 43-2243-3494012, office@vivo.co.at. Adv. contact Sandra Stadler. B&W page EUR 3,543, color page EUR 4,960; trim 230 x 300. Circ: 80,000 (paid and controlled).

780 CAN ISSN 0702-9012
MUSIC MCGILL. Text in English. 1976. s-a. free.
Indexed: CMPI.
Published by: McGill University, Faculty of Music, 555 Sherbrooke St W, Montreal, PQ H3A 1E3, Canada. TEL 514-398-4535. Circ: 4,500.

780 USA ISSN 1531-6726
MUSIC - MEANINGS. Text in English. 2003. irreg., latest vol.6, 2007. price varies. **Document type:** *Monographic series, Academic/Scholarly.*
Published by: Peter Lang Publishing, Inc. (Subsidiary of: Peter Lang Publishing Group), 29 Broadway, New York, NY 10006. TEL 212-647-7700, 800-770-5264, FAX 212-647-7707, customerservice@plang.com.

780 USA
MUSIC MONITOR. Text in English. 1999. m. **Description:** Covers a broad range of musical styles.
Media: Online - full text.
Address: 107 E Aycock St, Raleigh, NC 27608. TEL 919-460-1941. Ed. Charlie Johnson.

780 USA
MUSIC MONTHLY. Text in English. m. USD 25 (effective 2001). adv.
Published by: Maryland Musician Magazine, 2807 Goodwood Rd., Baltimore, MD 21214-2205. TEL 410-494-0566, FAX 410-494-0565. Ed. Kelly Connelly. adv.: page USD 690; 10.25 x 12.5.

780 AUS ISSN 1837-607X
THE MUSIC NETWORK. Text in English. 1994. w. AUD 335 (effective 2010). adv. **Document type:** *Magazine, Trade.* **Description:** Contains music industry news and information.
Related titles: Online - full text ed.: AUD 300 (effective 2010).
Published by: The Music Network, St James Hall, 153 Bridge Rd, Glebe, NSW 2037, Australia. TEL 61-2-93581600, FAX 61-2-95526866. Ed. Nicole Fossati. Pub. Adam Zammit. Adv. contact Luke Death.

780.42 USA
MUSIC NEWS NETWORK. Text in English. 1993. m. USD 10 (effective 2008). adv. bk.rev.; music rev.; video rev. **Description:** Includes news, international tour dates, album release info, and interviews regarding progressive music (bands like Yes, Genesis, and King Crimson).
Address: 3663 Commercial Way, Spring Hill, FL 34606. musicnewsnetwork@aol.com, http://www.musicnewsnetwork.net. Ed. Christine Holz.

780 USA ISSN 0027-4437
MUSIC NOW. Text in English. 1951. q. membership. bk.rev. **Document type:** *Newsletter.*
Media: Duplicated (not offset).
Indexed: MAG.
Published by: Southeastern Composers' League, 715 Morehead Ave, Greensboro, NC 27401. TEL 601-329-7203, FAX 601-329-7348. Ed. Jonathan D Green. R&P Richard Montalto. Circ: 600 (paid).

MUSIC O C L C USERS GROUP. NEWSLETTER. (Online Computer Library Center) *see* LIBRARY AND INFORMATION SCIENCES

MUSIC OF THE SPHERES; a quarterly magazine of art and music for the New Age. *see* NEW AGE PUBLICATIONS

780 USA ISSN 1066-8217
➤ **MUSIC OF THE UNITED STATES OF AMERICA.** Abbreviated title: M U S A. Text in English. 1993. irreg., latest vol.20, 2009. price varies. back issues avail. **Document type:** *Monographic series, Academic/Scholarly.* **Description:** Features to reflect the character and diversity of American music making.
Related titles: ◆ Issued with: Recent Researches in American Music. ISSN 0147-0078; ◆ Supplement to: Recent Researches in American Music. ISSN 0147-0078.
Published by: (American Musicological Society), A-R Editions, Inc., 8551 Research Way, Ste 180, Middleton, WI 53562. TEL 608-836-9000, 800-736-0070, FAX 608-831-8200, orders@areditions.com. Eds. James L Zychowicz TEL 608-836-9000 ext 14, Richard Crawford.

780.01 USA ISSN 0730-7829
ML1
➤ **MUSIC PERCEPTION.** Abbreviated title: M P. Text in English. 1983. 5/yr. USD 431 combined subscription to institutions (print & online eds.) (effective 2012). adv. bk.rev. illus. Index. 128 p./no.; back issues avail.; reprint service avail. from PSC. **Document type:** *Journal, Academic/Scholarly.* **Description:** Focuses on scientific and musical approaches to the study of musical phenomena.
Related titles: Microform ed.: USD 180 to institutions (effective 2002 - 2003) (from PQC); Online - full text ed.: ISSN 1533-8312. USD 334 to institutions (effective 2012).
Indexed: A01, A02, A03, A08, A20, A22, A26, A27, ASCA, ArtHuCI, BrHumI, CA, CurCont, DIP, E-psyche, E01, E08, G08, I05, IBR, IBZ, IIMP, M11, MusicInd, P03, P10, P25, P30, P48, P53, P54, PCI, PQC, PsycInfo, PsycholAb, RASB, RILM, S09, SCOPUS, SOPODA, SSCI, T02, W07.
—BLDSC (5990.381000), IE, Infotrieve, Ingenta. **CCC.**
Published by: University of California Press, Journals Division, 2000 Ctr St, Ste 303, Berkeley, CA 94704. TEL 510-643-7154, 877-262-4226, FAX 510-642-9917, customerservice@ucpressjournals.com. Ed. Lola L Cuddy. Adv. contact Jennifer Rogers TEL 510-642-6188. Circ: 640. **Subscr. to:** 149 5th Ave, 8th Fl, New York, NY 10010. participation@jstor.org.

780 GBR ISSN 1755-9219
➤ **MUSIC PERFORMANCE RESEARCH.** Text in English. 2007. a. free (effective 2011). back issues avail. **Document type:** *Journal, Academic/Scholarly.* **Description:** Disseminates theoretical and empirical research on the performance of music.
Media: Online - full text.
Indexed: A01, M11, T02.
Published by: Royal Northern College of Music, 124 Oxford Rd, Manchester, M13 9RD, United Kingdom. TEL 44-161-9075200, info@rncm.ac.uk, http://www.rncm.ac.uk/.

➤ **MUSIC REFERENCE SERVICES QUARTERLY.** *see* LIBRARY AND INFORMATION SCIENCES

780 JPN ISSN 0289-2278
➤ **MUSIC RESEARCH/ONGAKU KENKYU.** Text in Japanese. 1972. a., latest vol.17. free. bk.rev. illus. 100 p./no.; back issues avail. **Document type:** *Academic/Scholarly.* **Description:** Contains papers on music culture, modern music, folk music, acoustics, music physiology, and music education.
Former titles (until 1982): Music Culture; (until 1978): Data of Music in Western Japan; (until 1975): Data of Music in Kansai District
Published by: Music Research Institute, Osaka College of Music/Osaka Ongaku Daigaku Ongaku Kenkyujo, 1-1-4 Meishin-Guchi, Toyonaka-shi, Osaka-fu 561-0841, Japan. TEL 81-6-6868-1503, FAX 81-6-6865-1221, http://www.daion.ac.jp. Ed. Hiroko Takahashi. Circ: 1,000.

780 USA ISSN 1042-1262
ML1
MUSIC RESEARCH FORUM. Text in English. 1986. biennial.
Indexed: IIMP, M11, MusicInd, RILM, T02.
—BLDSC (5990.401560).
Published by: University of Cincinnati, College - Conservatory of Music, Mary Emery Hall, P O Box 210003, Cincinnati, OH 45221-0003. TEL 513-556-6638, http://www.ccm.uc.edu/default.htm.

781.642 USA ISSN 0745-5054
CODEN: LBBBD5
MUSIC ROW; Nashville's music industry publication. Text in English. 1981. 23/yr. USD 80; USD 3.50 newsstand/cover (effective 1998). adv. music rev.; video rev. charts; stat. back issues avail. **Document type:** *Newsletter, Trade.*
Indexed: IIMP.
Published by: Music Row Publications, Inc., 1231 17th Ave South, Nashville, TN 37212. TEL 615-321-3617, FAX 615-329-0852. Ed. David M Ross. Adv. contact Dave Ross. B&W page USD 760, color page USD 1,290; trim 11 x 8.5. Circ: 4,000.

778.5344 GBR ISSN 1753-0768
ML2074
➤ **MUSIC, SOUND AND THE MOVING IMAGE.** Text in English. 2007. s-a. GBP 69, USD 118 combined subscription to individuals (print & online eds.); GBP 89, USD 159 combined subscription to institutions (print & online eds.) (effective 2012). adv. back issues avail.; reprints avail. **Document type:** *Journal, Academic/Scholarly.* **Description:** Features articles devoted to the study of the interaction between music and sound with the entirety of moving image media - film, television, music video, advertising, computer games, mixed-media installation, digital art, live cinema, etc.
Related titles: Online - full text ed.: ISSN 1753-0776. 2007. GBP 56, USD 93 to individuals; GBP 71, USD 127 to institutions (effective 2012).
Indexed: A07, A22, A26, A30, A31, AA, AmHI, ArtInd, B04, CA, E01, F01, F02, H07, H08, HAb, HumInd, I05, M11, MLA-IB, T02, W03, W05.
—IE. **CCC.**
Published by: Liverpool University Press, 4 Cambridge St, Liverpool, L69 7ZU, United Kingdom. TEL 44-151-7942233, FAX 44-151-7942235, lup@liv.ac.uk. Ed. Anahid Kassabian. Adv. contact Janet Smith. **Subscr. to:** Marston Book Services Ltd., PO Box 269, Abingdon, Oxon OX14 4YN, United Kingdom. TEL 44-1235-465574, FAX 44-1235-465556, subscriptions@marston.co.uk, http://www.marston.co.uk/.

➤ **MUSIC TEACHER.** *see* EDUCATION—Teaching Methods And Curriculum

780.7 AUS
MUSIC TEACHER INTERNATIONAL. Text in English. 1981. bi-m. AUD 59 domestic; NZD 79.89 in New Zealand; GBP 33.94 in United Kingdom; USD 47.98 in United States; CAD 74.97 in Canada; AUD 86.80 elsewhere (effective 2004). bk.rev.; music rev.; software rev.; video rev. illus. **Document type:** *Journal, Academic/Scholarly.* **Description:** National music education journal covering news and events; also includes interviews and feature articles.
Former titles (until 2006): Music Teacher (1445-5072); (until 2001): Australian Music Teacher (1035-1752); (until 1998): Australian Music Teacher Magazine (1441-1695); (until 1990): Australian Guitar Journal (1033-5161)
Indexed: RILM.
Published by: Boss Publishing Pty. Ltd., PO Box 2231, Templestowe Heights, NSW 3107, Australia. TEL 61-3-09521111, FAX 61-3-98521847. Ed., Adv. contact Ronald Payne. R&P Glenda Walsh. Circ: 4,000.

781.64 USA
MUSIC TECHNOLOGY BUYER'S GUIDE. Text in English. a. **Document type:** *Magazine, Trade.* **Description:** Covers the latest information on musical equipment for home recording and live performance.
Published by: NewBay Media, LLC (Subsidiary of: The Wicks Group of Companies, LLC.), 810 Seventh Ave, 27th Fl, New York, NY 10019. TEL 212-378-0400, FAX 212-378-0470, customerservice@nbmedia.com, http://www.nbmedia.com.

780.01 USA ISSN 1067-3040
MT6
➤ **MUSIC THEORY ONLINE.** Abbreviated title: M T O. Text in English. 1993. bi-m. free (effective 2011). bk.rev.; software rev. illus. back issues avail.; reprints avail. **Document type:** *Journal, Academic/Scholarly.* **Description:** Contains articles, commentaries on articles from previous issues, reviews, and essays all related to the field of professional music theory.
Media: Online - full text.
Indexed: A39, C27, C29, D03, D04, E13, R14, S14, S15, S18.
Published by: Society for Music Theory, University of Chicago, Department of Music, 1010 E 59th St, Chicago, IL 60637. TEL 773-834-3821, vlong@uchicago.edu. Ed. Matthew Shaftel.

780 USA ISSN 0195-6167
MT6
➤ **MUSIC THEORY SPECTRUM.** Abbreviated title: M T S. Text in English. 1979. s-a. USD 175 combined subscription to institutions (print & online eds.) (effective 2012). adv. bk.rev. back issues avail.; reprint service avail. from PSC. **Document type:** *Journal, Academic/Scholarly.* **Description:** Features the best work in music theory and analysis, including aesthetics, history of theory, post-tonal theory, critical theory, linear analysis, rhythm, and music cognition.
Related titles: Online - full text ed.: ISSN 1533-8339. USD 141 to institutions (effective 2012).
Indexed: A01, A02, A03, A08, A20, A22, A27, ASCA, ArtHuCI, BrHumI, CA, CurCont, DIP, E01, IBR, IBZ, IIMP, M11, MAG, MusicInd, P10, P48, P53, P54, PCI, PQC, RILM, SCOPUS, T02, W07.
—BLDSC (5990.425000), IE, Infotrieve, Ingenta. **CCC.**
Published by: (Society for Music Theory), University of California Press, Journals Division, 2000 Ctr St, Ste 303, Berkeley, CA 94704. TEL 510-643-7154, 877-262-4226, FAX 510-642-9917, customerservice@ucpressjournals.com. Ed. Severine Neff. Adv. contact Jennifer Rogers TEL 510-642-6188. Circ: 1,257. **Subscr. to:** 149 5th Ave, 8th Fl, New York, NY 10010. participation@jstor.org.

780 616.89 GBR
ML3919
MUSIC THERAPY NOW. Text in English. 1987. 3/yr. free to members (effective 2009). **Document type:** *Newsletter, Trade.* **Description:** Contains news items, reports of meetings and conferences, new publications, and forthcoming events.
Formerly (until 2007): British Society for Music Therapy. Bulletin (0953-7511); Which superseded in part (in 1987): British Journal of Music Therapy (0308-244X)
Indexed: E-psyche.
—BLDSC (5990.432000), GNLM.
Published by: (Association of Professional Music Therapists), British Society for Music Therapy, 24-27 White Lion St, London, N1 9PD, United Kingdom. TEL 44-20-78376100, FAX 44-20-78376142, info@bsmt.org.

780 150 USA ISSN 0734-6875
ML3920
➤ **MUSIC THERAPY PERSPECTIVES.** Text in English. 1983. s-a. USD 20 per issue; free to members (effective 2009). adv. back issues avail.; reprints avail. **Document type:** *Journal, Academic/Scholarly.* **Description:** Focuses on the theory, practice and administration of music therapy.
Related titles: Online - full text ed.
Indexed: A22, A27, C06, DIP, E-psyche, IBR, IBZ, IIMP, M11, MusicInd, P03, P10, P12, P25, P48, P53, P54, PQC, PsycInfo, PsycholAb, RILM, T02.
—BLDSC (5990.435100), IE, Ingenta.
Published by: American Music Therapy Association, 8455 Colesville Rd, Ste 1000, Silver Spring, MD 20910. TEL 301-589-3300, FAX 301-589-5175, info@musictherapy.org. Ed. Brian Wilson. adv.: B&W page USD 575; 7 x 10. **Subscr. to:** Allen Press Inc., PO Box 1897, Lawrence, KS 66044. http://www.allenpress.com.

780 615.85154 DEU ISSN 1610-191X
ML3919
➤ **MUSIC THERAPY TODAY.** Text in Multiple languages. 2001. q. **Document type:** *Journal, Academic/Scholarly.*
Media: Online - full text.
Indexed: IIMP.
Published by: Universitaet Witten - Herdecke, Alfred Herrhausen Str 50, Witten, 58448, Germany. TEL 49-2302-9260, FAX 49-2302-926407, public@uni-wh.de, http://www.uni-wh.de. Ed., Pub. David Aldridge.

781.71 USA ISSN 0164-7180
MUSIC TIME. Text in English. 19??. w. **Document type:** *Magazine, Consumer.* **Description:** For preschool choir members and their parents.
Published by: LifeWay Christian Resources, 1 Lifeway Plz, Nashville, TN 37234. TEL 615-251-2000, 800-458-2772, FAX 615-251-5933, customerservice@lifeway.com, http://www.lifeway.com.

780 USA ISSN 0027-4488
ML1
THE MUSIC TRADES. Text in English. 1890. m. USD 16; USD 3 per issue (effective 2005); includes Purchaser's Guide to the Music Industries. charts; illus. reprints avail. **Document type:** *Magazine, Trade.*
Related titles: Microform ed.: (from PQC); Online - full text ed.
Indexed: A01, A22, A26, E07, G06, G07, G08, I05, IIMP, M11, MusicInd, P07, S23, T02.
—Ingenta.
Published by: Music Trades Corporation, 80 West St, PO Box 432, Englewood, NJ 07631. TEL 201-871-1965, FAX 201-871-0455. Ed. Brian T Majeski. Pub. Paul A Majeski. Adv. contact Juanita Hampton. Circ: 12,000 (paid).

780 310 USA ISSN 0197-4173
ML3795
MUSIC U S A; annual statistical review of the musical instrument industry. Text in English. 195?. a. **Document type:** *Report, Trade.*
Indexed: SRI.
Published by: N A M M - International Music Products Association, 5790 Armada Dr, Carlsbad, CA 92008. TEL 760-438-8001, FAX 760-438-7327. Ed. John Maher. Circ: 1,750.

780.65 789.91 GBR ISSN 0265-1548
MUSIC WEEK. Text in English. 1959. w. GBP 225 domestic; GBP 265 in Europe; GBP 340 elsewhere (effective 2009). adv. bk.rev.; rec.rev. charts. **Document type:** *Magazine, Consumer.* **Description:** News for the music industry and music retailer.
Incorporates: R M; Supersedes in part (in 1983): Music and Video Week (0261-0817); Which was formerly (until 1981): Music Week (0144-5782); (until 1972): Record Retailer (0034-1606)
Related titles: Online - full text ed.
Indexed: A09, A10, A15, A26, ABIn, B01, B03, B06, B07, B09, B11, C12, E08, G08, I05, I06, I07, M02, M11, MASUSE, P10, P34, P48, P51, P53, P54, PQC, S09, S23, T02, V03, V04.
—CIS. **CCC.**
Published by: C M P Information Ltd. (Subsidiary of: United Business Media Limited), Ludgate House, 245 Blackfriars Rd., London, SE1 9UR, United Kingdom. TEL 44-20-73781188, FAX 44-20-73781199, info@cmpinformation.com, http://www.cmpi.biz/. Ed. Paul Williams. Adv. contact Bill Fahey. Circ: 13,468.

780 GBR ISSN 0267-3290
ML3790
MUSIC WEEK DIRECTORY. Text in English. 1976. a. GBP 32 per issue (effective 2009). **Document type:** *Directory.* **Description:** Directory of UK record and music industry institutions, companies and individuals.
Former titles (until 1984): Music and Video Week Directory (0264-3383); Music and Video Week Yearbook; Music Week Industry Year Book
—CCC.
Published by: C M P Information Ltd. (Subsidiary of: United Business Media Limited), Ludgate House, 245 Blackfriars Rd., London, SE1 9UR, United Kingdom. TEL 44-20-73781188, FAX 44-20-73781199, info@cmpinformation.com, http://www.cmpi.biz/. Ed. Paul Williams.

MUSIC WEEK INTERNATIONAL DIRECTORY. *see* BUSINESS AND ECONOMICS—International Commerce

780 ITA ISSN 0392-5544
ML5
MUSICA; rivista di cultura musicale e discografica. Text in Italian. 1977. 10/yr. EUR 59 domestic; EUR 90 foreign (effective 2009). adv. bk.rev.; music rev.; rec.rev.; video rev.; Website rev. index. 112 p./no. 2 cols./p.; back issues avail. **Document type:** *Magazine, Consumer.* **Description:** Classical music magazine featuring reviews of live and recorded performances plus in-depth articles and news.
Indexed: IIMP, RILM.
Published by: Zecchini Editore, Via Tonale 60, Varese, VA 21100, Italy. TEL 39-0332-331041, FAX 39-0332-331013, editoriale@zecchini.com, http://www.zecchini.com. Eds. Roberto Zecchini, Stephen Hastings. Adv. contact Germano Ruscitto TEL 39-02-2829158. Circ: 35,000.

780.902 DEU ISSN 1863-6667
MUSICA ANTIQUO-MODERNA. Text in German. 2006. irreg. price varies. **Document type:** *Monographic series, Academic/Scholarly.*
Published by: Georg Olms Verlag, Hagentorwall 7, Hildesheim, 31134, Germany. TEL 49-5121-15010, FAX 49-5121-150150, info@olms.de.

780 GBR ISSN 0580-2954
M2
MUSICA BRITANNICA; a national collection of music. Text in English. 1951. a. price varies. back issues avail. **Document type:** *Journal, Academic/Scholarly.* **Description:** Explores the vast heritage of material detailing the British contribution to music in Europe.
—CCC.
Published by: (Musica Britannica Trust), Stainer and Bell Ltd., Victoria House, 23 Gruneisen Rd, Finchley, PO Box 110, London, N3 1DZ, United Kingdom. TEL 44-20-83433303, FAX 44-20-83433024, post@stainer.co.uk, http://www.stainer.co.uk. Ed. H Diack Johnstone.

780 700 792 ITA
MUSICA CINEMA IMMAGINE TEATRO. Text in Italian, English, French. 1984. irreg., latest vol.28. price varies. **Document type:** *Monographic series, Academic/Scholarly.* **Description:** Studies on photography, music, cinema and theatre.
Former titles: Musica, Cinema, Teatro; Musica, Immagine, Teatro
Published by: Angelo Longo Editore, Via Paolo Costa 33, Ravenna, 48121, Italy. TEL 39-0544-217026, FAX 39-0544-217554, longo@longo-editore.it, http://www.longo-editore.it.

780 ESP ISSN 1138-6002
MUSICA D'ARA. Text in Spanish, Catalan. 1998. a. back issues avail. **Document type:** *Journal, Bibliography.*
Related titles: Online - full text ed.
Published by: Associacio Catalana de Compositors, Passeig de Colom, 6 Espai IV, Barcelona, 08002, Spain. TEL 34-93-2683719, FAX 34-93-2681259, acc@compositors.com, http://www.accompositors.com/. Circ: 1,000.

780.9 USA ISSN 0077-2461
ML5
➤ **MUSICA DISCIPLINA**; a yearbook of the history of music. Abbreviated title: M D. Text in English; Text occasionally in French, German, Italian. 1946. a. price varies. **Document type:** *Monographic series, Academic/Scholarly.* **Description:** Covers scholarly exploration of early music. Brings out traditional area of focus studies on Medieval and Renaissance music, and music of the seventeenth century.
Formerly (until 1948): Journal of Renaissance and Baroque Music (1059-8529)
Related titles: Online - full text ed.
Indexed: A20, DIP, IBR, IBZ, IIMP, M11, MLA-IB, MusicInd, PCI, RILM, T02.
—BLDSC (5990.610000), Ingenta. **CCC.**
Published by: American Institute of Musicology, 8551 Research Way, Ste 180, Middleton, WI 53562. TEL 608-836-9000, 800-736-0070, FAX 608-831-8200, info@corpusmusicae.com. Ed. Stanley Boorman.

780.904 780.7 ITA ISSN 0391-4380
MT3.I8
MUSICA DOMANI; trimestrale di cultura e pedagogia musicale. Text in Italian. 1971. q. EUR 18 domestic; EUR 22 foreign (effective 2009). adv. bk.rev. 50 p./no.; back issues avail. **Document type:** *Journal, Academic/Scholarly.*
Indexed: RILM.
Published by: (Societa Italiana per l'Educazione Musicale), E D T Srl, Via Pianezza 17, Torino, 10149, Italy. TEL 39-011-5591811, FAX 39-011-2307034. Circ: 4,500.

781.7 ITA ISSN 0392-6508
MUSICA E ASSEMBLEA. Text in Italian. 1975. q. EUR 30 domestic; EUR 37.80 in the European Union; EUR 40.20 elsewhere (effective 2008). **Document type:** *Magazine, Consumer.*
Published by: Centro Editoriale Dehoniano, Via Scipione dal Ferro 4, Bologna, BO 40138, Italy. TEL 39-051-4290451, FAX 39-051-4290491, ced-amm@dehoniane.it, http://www.dehoniane.it.

789.91 ITA ISSN 0027-4526
MUSICA E DISCHI. Text in Italian. 1945. m. EUR 100 (effective 2009). adv. rec.rev. illus.; bibl. Supplement avail. **Document type:** *Magazine, Consumer.* **Description:** Information on music industry, audio (professional) and home video.
Related titles: ◆ Supplement(s): Chi E Dove (Year).
Published by: Editoriale Musica e Dischi, Via Edmondo De Amicis, 47, Milan, MI 20123, Italy. info@musicaedischi.it, http://www.musicaedischi.it. adv.: B&W page EUR 1,512, color page EUR 2,563.

780 ARG ISSN 0329-224X
ML5
MUSICA E INVESTIGACION. Text in Spanish. 1997. irreg. **Document type:** *Monographic series, Academic/Scholarly.*
Indexed: RILM.
Published by: Instituto Nacional de Musicologia Carlos Vega, Mexico, 564, Buenos Aires, 1097, Argentina. TEL 54-11-43616520, FAX 54-11-43616013, inmuvega@ciudad.com.ar, http://www.inmuega.gov.ar.

780 800 ITA ISSN 1828-177X
MUSICA E LETTERATURA. Text and summaries in Italian. 1996. irreg. price varies. **Document type:** *Monographic series, Academic/Scholarly.*
Published by: Edizioni dell' Orso, Via Urbano Rattazzi 47, Alessandria, 15100, Italy. TEL 39-0131-252349, FAX 39-0131-257567, direzione.editoriale@ediorso.it, http://www.ediorso.it.

780 ITA ISSN 1127-0063
ML5
MUSICA E STORIA. Text in Italian. 1993. 3/yr. EUR 85.50 combined subscription domestic to institutions (print & online eds.); EUR 135 combined subscription foreign to institutions (print & online eds.) (effective 2009). adv. **Document type:** *Journal, Academic/Scholarly.* **Description:** Covers the history of music from the ancient world to the contemporary age.
Related titles: Online - full text ed.
Published by: (Fondazione Ugo e Olga Levi), Societa Editrice Il Mulino, Strada Maggiore 37, Bologna, 40125, Italy. TEL 39-051-256011, FAX 39-051-256034, riviste@mulino.it. Ed. L Bianconi.

780 FRA ISSN 1284-4578
MUSICA FALSA. Text in French. 1997. s-a. EUR 35 for 2 yrs. (effective 2009). **Document type:** *Magazine, Consumer.*
Indexed: RILM.
Published by: Editions M F (Musica Falsa), Les Douches, 5 Rue Legouve, Paris, 75010, France.

780 ARG
MUSICA HOY; opera danza teatro conciertos. Text in Spanish. 1993 (vol.12). m. ARS 5 per issue.
Published by: Musica Hoy Producciones, Donato Alvarez 419, Buenos Aires, 1406, Argentina. TEL 54-114-6324591. Ed. Juan Gelaf.

780 POL ISSN 1233-9679
ML297
MUSICA IAGELLONICA. Text in Polish. 1995. a. **Document type:** *Magazine, Consumer.*
Indexed: RILM.
Published by: Musica Iagellonica sp. z o.o., ul Westerplatte 10, Krakow, 31033, Poland. TEL 48-12-4228211, FAX 48-12-6631671.

781.57 ITA ISSN 0027-4542
ML5
MUSICA JAZZ. Text in Italian. 1945. 11/yr. EUR 63.60 (effective 2009). adv. bk.rev.; film rev.; music rev.; play rev.; rec.rev. bibl.; illus. index. back issues avail. **Document type:** *Magazine, Consumer.*
Published by: (Messaggerie Musicali), Hachette Rusconi SpA (Subsidiary of: Hachette Filipacchi Medias S.A.), Viale Sarca 235, Milan, 20126, Italy. TEL 39-02-66192629, FAX 39-02-66192469, dirgen@rusconi.it, http://portale.hachettepubblicita.it. Ed. Pino Candini. Adv. contact Eduardo Giliberti. Circ: 40,000.

296.462 USA ISSN 0147-7536
ML1
MUSICA JUDAICA. Text in English, Hebrew. 1976. a. USD 25. adv. bk.rev. **Document type:** *Magazine, Consumer.*
Related titles: Online - full text ed.
Indexed: IJP, MusicInd, PCI, RILM.
—BLDSC (5990.665000).
Published by: American Society for Jewish Music, Center for Jewish History, 15 West 16th St, New York, NY 10011. TEL 917-606-8200, boxoffice@cjh.org, http://www.jewishmusic-asjm.org. Ed., R&P, Adv. contact Neil W Levin. Circ: 1,500.

780 ITA ISSN 1125-7261
MUSICA LATINO - AMERICANA. Text in Italian. 1997. bi-w. **Document type:** *Magazine, Consumer.*
Published by: Hobby & Work, Via XXV Aprile 39, Bresso, MI 20091, Italy. TEL 39-02-66527, FAX 39-02-66503, info@hobbyework.it, http://www.hobbyeworkpublishing.com.

780.902 DEU ISSN 1860-7136
MUSICA MENSURABILIS. Text in German. 2005. irreg., latest vol.4, 2008. price varies. **Document type:** *Monographic series, Academic/Scholarly.*
Published by: Georg Olms Verlag, Hagentorwall 7, Hildesheim, 31134, Germany. TEL 49-5121-15010, FAX 49-5121-150150, info@olms.de.

786 JPN ISSN 0289-3630
MUSICA NOVA. Text in Japanese. m. JPY 880. adv. **Description:** Provides information directed at pianists and piano instructors.
Published by: Ongaku No Tomo Sha Corp., c/o KakuyukiNabeshima, 6-30 Kagura-Zaka, Shinjuku-ku, Tokyo, 162-0825, Japan. TEL 81-3-3235-2675, FAX 81-3-3260-6415. Ed. Eiko Soda. Pub. Jun Meguro. R&P Tetsuo Morita TEL 81-3-3235-2111. Adv. contact Takao Oya. B&W page JPY 174,000, color page JPY 360,000; trim 187 x 257. Circ: 65,000.

780 ESP ISSN 1138-8579
ML3544
MUSICA ORAL DEL SUR. Text in Multiple languages. 1995. a., latest 2002. back issues avail. **Document type:** *Monographic series, Academic/Scholarly.*
Indexed: RILM.
Published by: Junta de Andalucia, Centro de Documentacion Musical de Andalucia, C/ Carrera del Darro 29, Granada, 18010, Spain. TEL 34-958-575691, FAX 34-958-228464, informacion.cdma.ccul@juntadeandalucia.es, http://www.juntadeandalucia.es/cultura/centrodocumentacionmusical/.

780.7 ITA
MUSICA - REALTA. Text in Italian, English, German, French. 1980. 3/yr. EUR 31 domestic; EUR 47 foreign (effective 2009). **Document type:** *Journal, Academic/Scholarly.* **Description:** Covers music, culture and society, past and present.
Indexed: IIMP.
Published by: (Fondazione Italiana per la Musica Antica), LIM Editrice Srl, Via di Arsina 296/f, Lucca, LU 55100, Italy. TEL 39-0583-394464, FAX 39-0583-394469, lim@lim.it, http://www.lim.it. Ed. Luigi Pestalozza. Circ: 1,000.

780 DEU ISSN 0943-5093
MUSICA REANIMATA MITTEILUNGEN. Text in German. 1992. q. EUR 13 (effective 2006). **Document type:** *Journal, Academic/Scholarly.*
Indexed: RILM.
Published by: Musica Reanimata - Foerderverein zur Wiederentdeckung NS-Verfolgter Komponisten und Ihrer Werke e.V., c/o Peter Sarkar, Steubenstr 35, Weimar, 99423, Germany. TEL 49-3643-400156. Ed., Pub. Albrecht Duemling.

782.3 DEU ISSN 0179-356X
ML5
MUSICA SACRA. Text in German. 1950. bi-m. EUR 31; EUR 15.50 to students (effective 2008). adv. **Document type:** *Journal, Academic/Scholarly.*
Formerly (until 1956): Zeitschrift fuer Kirchenmusik (0179-3578)
Related titles: Microfiche ed.: (from IDC).
Indexed: DIP, IBR, IBZ, RILM.
—CCC.
Published by: Allgemeiner Caecilien-Verband fuer Deutschland, Andreasstr 9, Regensburg, 93059, Germany. TEL 49-941-84339, FAX 49-941-8703432, info@acv-deutschland.de, http://www.acv-deutschland.de. Ed. Martin Dippon. Adv. contact Kerstin Lehmann. page EUR 580; trim 160 x 240.

780 600 ITA ISSN 1974-0042
ML73
MUSICA TECNOLOGIA. Text in Multiple languages. 2007. a. EUR 70 combined subscription domestic to institutions (print & online eds.); EUR 80 combined subscription foreign to institutions (print & online eds.) (effective 2011). **Document type:** *Journal, Academic/Scholarly.*
Related titles: Online - full text ed.: ISSN 1974-0050. free (effective 2011).

Published by: Firenze University Press, Borgo Albizi 28, Florence, 50122, Italy. TEL 39-055-2743051, FAX 39-055-2743058, info@fupress.com, www.fupress.com/index.asp. Ed. Claudio Leonardi.

MUSICA, TERAPIA Y COMUNICACION. *see* MEDICAL SCIENCES—Physical Medicine And Rehabilitation

780 ESP ISSN 0214-4786
MUSICA Y EDUCACION; revista trimestral de pedagogia musical. Text in Spanish. 1988. q. **Document type:** *Journal, Academic/Scholarly.*
Indexed: RILM.
Published by: Musicalis, S.A., Escosura 27, 5a. Derecha, Madrid, 28015, Spain. TEL 34-91-4470694, FAX 34-91-5942506, http://www.musicalis.es/.

780 GBR ISSN 1029-8649
ML5
➤ **MUSICAE SCIENTIAE**; the journal of the European Society for the Cognitive Sciences of Music. Text in English, French, German; Abstracts in English, French, German, Italian, Spanish. 1992. 3/yr. USD 363 to institutions; USD 370 combined subscription to institutions (print & online eds.) (effective 2011). adv. bk.rev. abstr. 130 p./no.; reprint service avail. from PSC. **Document type:** *Journal, Academic/Scholarly.* **Description:** Focuses on all sciences of music.
Formerly (until 1997): European Society for the Cognitive Sciences of Music. Bulletin d'Information (1022-9299)
Related titles: Online - full text ed.: USD 333 (effective 2011).
Indexed: A20, A22, ArtHuCI, CA, CurCont, IBR, IBZ, M11, MusicInd, P03, P30, PsycInfo, PsycholAb, RILM, SCOPUS, SSCI, T02, W07.
—BLDSC (5990.736000), IE, Ingenta. **CCC.**
Published by: (European Society for the Cognitive Sciences of Music BEL), Sage Publications Ltd. (Subsidiary of: Sage Publications, Inc.), 1 Oliver's Yard, 55 City Rd, London, EC1Y 1SP, United Kingdom. TEL 44-20-73248500, FAX 44-20-73248600, info@sagepub.co.uk, http://www.uk.sagepub.com/home.nav. adv.: B&W page EUR 250; trim 165 x 240.

780 BRA ISSN 0104-5423
ML3797
MUSICAHOJE. Text in Portuguese. 1993. s-a. back issues avail. **Document type:** *Journal, Academic/Scholarly.*
Published by: Universidade Federal de Minas Gerais, Escola de Musica, Ave Antonio Carlos, 6627, Campus Pampulha, Belo Horizonte, MG 31270-901, Brazil. TEL 55-31-34994707, FAX 55-31-34994720, mestrado@musica.ufmg.br, http://www.ufmg.br/. Ed. Rosangela Pereira de Tugny.

790 USA ISSN 1933-3250
ML12
MUSICAL AMERICA WORLDWIDE. Text in English. 1960. a. USD 125 (effective 2008). adv. illus. Index. reprints avail. **Document type:** *Directory, Trade.* **Description:** Contains over 14,000 detailed listings of businesses and organizations worldwide, contacts for over 10,000 artists, and more than 16,000 updated e-mail and web site addresses.
Former titles (until 2006): Musical America International Directory of the Performing Arts (0735-7788); (until 1973): Musical America. Directory of the Performing Arts (1041-4614); (until 1968): Musical America Annual Directory Issue (0580-308X); (until 196?): High Fidelity/Musical America. Special Directory Issue
Related titles: Online - full text ed.: USD 135 (effective 2008).
—**CCC.**
Published by: Commonwealth Business Media, Inc. (Subsidiary of: United Business Media Limited), 400 Windsor Corporate Park, 50 Millstone Rd, Ste 200, East Windsor, NJ 08520. TEL 888-215-6084, 800-221-5488, FAX 609-371-7883, cbizservices@sunbeltfs.com, http://www.cbizmedia.com. Pub. Stephanie Challener. Adv. contact Nicole Pace TEL 609-371-7877. B&W page USD 2,730, color page USD 3,295; 7 x 10. Circ: 15,000 (paid and controlled).

780 USA ISSN 0160-3876
ML1
MUSICAL HERITAGE REVIEW MAGAZINE. Text in English. 1977. 18/yr. membership only. adv. bk.rev.
Published by: Musical Heritage Society, 1710 Highway 35, Ocean, NJ 07712. TEL 201-531-7000. Circ: (controlled).

780 001.3 SWE ISSN 0349-988X
MUSICAL INTERPRETATION RESEARCH. Short title: M I R. Text in Swedish. 1982. irreg. price varies. bk.rev. back issues avail. **Description:** Concerns the artistic aspects of musical performance, particularly the aesthetics of conductors.
Published by: Mirage, Radmansgatan 3, 4 tr, Stockholm, 11425, Sweden. TEL 08-108052. Ed. Nils Goran Sundin.

780 USA ISSN 0364-7501
ML1
MUSICAL MAINSTREAM (LARGE PRINT EDITION). Text in English. 1942. q. free to blind and physically handicapped (effective 2010). bk.rev. reprints avail. **Document type:** *Magazine, Government.* **Description:** Contains selected articles from national magazines about classical music, music criticism, and music teaching; lists new NLS music acquisitions.
Former titles (until Dec.1976): New Braille Musician (0093-2817); Braille Musician
Media: Large Type (16 pt.). **Related titles:** Audio cassette/tape ed.; Braille ed.; Online - full text ed.
—Ingenta.
Published by: (U.S. Library of Congress, National Library Service for the Blind and Physically Handicapped, Music Section), U.S. Library of Congress, National Library Service for the Blind and Physically Handicapped, 1291 Taylor St, NW, Washington, DC 20011. TEL 202-707-5100, 888-657-7323, FAX 202-707-0712, nls@loc.gov, http://www.loc.gov/nls. Circ: 1,900.

658.8 781.91 USA ISSN 0027-4615
ML1
MUSICAL MERCHANDISE REVIEW; pianos, musical instruments, organs, accessories. Abbreviated title: M M R. Text in English. 1879. m. free to qualified personnel (effective 2009). adv. bk.rev.; film rev.; rec.rev. illus.; mkt.; pat.; tr.lit.; tr.mk. Index. **Document type:** *Magazine, Trade.* **Description:** Covers all types of musical instruments, accessories, and related services, and also for wholesalers, importers/exporters and manufacturers of musical products.
Formed by the merger of (1925-1957): Musical Merchandise Magazine; (1956-195?): Piano & Organ Review; Which was formerly (until 1956): Music Trade Review; (until 188?): The Musical Critic and Trade Review; (until 1880): The Music Trade Journal
Related titles: Online - full text ed.
Indexed: B02, B15, B17, G04, G06, G07, G08, I05, M11, P48, PQC.
Published by: Symphony Publishing LLC, 21 Highland Cir, Ste One, Needham, MA 02494. TEL 781-453-9310, 800-964-5150, FAX 781-453-9389, http://www.symphonypublishing.com. Ed. Christian Wissmuller TEL 781-453-9310 ext 16. Pub. Sidney L Davis TEL 781-453-9310 ext 13. Adv. contact Iris Fox TEL 954-973-3555. B&W page USD 2,110; trim 8.125 x 10.875. Circ: 9,311.

780.7 GBR ISSN 0027-4623
MUSICAL OPINION. Text in English. 1877. bi-m. GBP 28 domestic; USD 75 in United States; GBP 40 elsewhere (effective 2009). adv. bk.rev.; music rev.; rec.rev.; dance rev.; video rev. illus. 80 p./no. 3 cols./p.; back issues avail. **Document type:** *Magazine, Consumer.* **Description:** Contains articles of worth and interest to people involved with and interested in classical music.
Formerly (until 1927): Musical Opinion and Music Trade Review
Related titles: Microfilm ed.: (from WMP); Microform ed.: (from PQC); Online - full text ed.; Supplement(s): Musical Opinion Supplement.
Indexed: A01, A22, IIMP, M11, MusicInd, P10, P48, P53, P54, PQC, RILM.
—BLDSC (5990.770000), IE, Ingenta.
Published by: Musical Opinion Ltd., 1 Exford Rd, London, SE12 9HD, United Kingdom. TEL 44-20-88571582. Ed. Robert Matthew-Walker. Adv. contact Gordon Roland-Adams TEL 44-20-89718451.

780 GBR ISSN 1354-8182
MUSICAL PRAXIS. Text in English. 1994. 3/yr. GBP 12 to individuals; GBP 25 to institutions; GBP 7 to students. **Document type:** *Journal, Academic/Scholarly.*
Published by: University of Edinburgh, Faculty of Music, Alison House, 12 Nicolson Sq, Edinburgh, EH8 9DH, United Kingdom. Eds. Emilios Cambouropoulos, Lawrence Shuster.

780 USA ISSN 0027-4631
ML1
➤ **THE MUSICAL QUARTERLY.** Abbreviated title: M Q. Text in English. 1915. q. GBP 124 in United Kingdom to institutions; EUR 178 in Europe to institutions; USD 187 in US & Canada to institutions; GBP 124 elsewhere to institutions; GBP 136 combined subscription in United Kingdom to institutions (print & online eds.); EUR 194 combined subscription in Europe to institutions (print & online eds.); USD 204 combined subscription in US & Canada to institutions (print & online eds.); GBP 136 combined subscription elsewhere to institutions (print & online eds.) (effective 2012). bk.rev. bibl.; illus. index, cum.index: 1915-1959, vols.1-45. back issues avail.; reprint service avail. from PSC. **Document type:** *Journal, Academic/Scholarly.* **Description:** Contains original articles covering the entire range of musical composition and performance, from early music to the Classical-Romantic tradition to twentieth-century jazz and pop to the latest developments in theory and practice.
Related titles: Microform ed.: (from PMC, PQC); Online - full text ed.: ISSN 1741-8399. GBP 113 in United Kingdom to institutions; EUR 162 in Europe to institutions; USD 170 in US & Canada to institutions; GBP 113 elsewhere to institutions (effective 2012) (from IngentaConnect).
Indexed: A01, A02, A03, A08, A20, A22, A25, A26, A27, ABS&EES, ASCA, AcaI, AmHI, ArtHuCI, B04, BRD, BrHumI, CA, CBRI, CRCL, CurCont, DIP, E01, E08, G05, G06, G07, G08, H07, H08, H09, H10, HAb, HumInd, I05, IBR, IBRH, IBT&D, IBZ, IIMP, M11, MAG, MLA-IB, MagInd, MusicInd, P02, P10, P48, P53, P54, PCI, PQC, R04, RASB, RILM, S05, S08, S09, SCOPUS, T02, W03, W05, W07.
—BLDSC (5990.790000), IE, Infotrieve, Ingenta. **CCC.**
Published by: Oxford University Press (Subsidiary of: Oxford University Press), 2001 Evans Rd, Cary, NC 27513. TEL 919-677-0977, 800-445-9714, FAX 919-677-1303, http://www.us.oup.com. Ed. Leon Botstein. Adv. contact Linda Hann.

➤ **MUSICAL SHOW**; devoted to the amateur presentation of Broadway musical shows on the stage. *see* THEATER

780 GBR ISSN 0027-4666
ML5
MUSICAL TIMES. Abbreviated title: M T. Text in English. 1844. q. GBP 75 domestic to institutions; GBP 105 in Europe to institutions; GBP 92 in US & Canada to institutions; GBP 141 elsewhere to institutions (effective 2011). bk.rev.; music rev.; rec.rev. index. back issues avail.; reprints avail. **Document type:** *Magazine, Consumer.* **Description:** Features informative articles on UK's classical music.
Formerly (until 1903): Musical Times and Singing Class Circular (0958-8434)
Related titles: Microfilm ed.: (from WMP); Microform ed.: (from PQC); Online - full text ed.
Indexed: A01, A03, A08, A20, A22, A26, ASCA, AmHI, ArtHuCI, B04, B14, BRD, BRI, BrHumI, CA, CurCont, DIP, E08, G08, H07, H08, H14, HAb, HumInd, IBR, IBRH, IBZ, IIMP, M02, M11, MLA-IB, MusicInd, P10, P48, P53, P54, PCI, PQC, RASB, RILM, S09, SCOPUS, T02, W03, W05, W07.
—BLDSC (5990.810000), IE, Infotrieve, Ingenta. **CCC.**
Published by: Musical Times Publications Ltd., 7 Brunswick Mews, Hove, E Sussex BN3 1HD, United Kingdom. **Subscr. to:** Musical Times, PO Box 464, Berkhamsted, Herts HP4 2UR, United Kingdom. TEL 44-1442-879097, FAX 44-1442-872279, subs@webscribe.co.uk, http://www.webscribe.co.uk/.

780 ITA ISSN 1824-6206
ML3797
MUSICALIA; annuario internazionale di studi musicologici. Text in Multiple languages. 2004. a. EUR 295 combined subscription domestic to institutions (print & online eds.); EUR 395 combined subscription foreign to institutions (print & online eds.) (effective 2009). **Document type:** *Journal, Academic/Scholarly.*
Related titles: Online - full text ed.: ISSN 1826-7858.
Published by: Fabrizio Serra Editore (Subsidiary of: Accademia Editoriale), c/o Accademia Editoriale, Via Santa Bibbiana 28, Pisa, 56127, Italy. TEL 39-050-542332, FAX 39-050-574888, accademiaeditoriale@accademiaeditoriale.it, http://www.libraweb.net.

780.43 ITA ISSN 1723-9451
MUSICALIA (ROME); il fascino della musica. Text in Italian. 1992. bi-m. **Document type:** *Magazine, Consumer.*
Published by: Editoriale Pantheon, Via Alatri 30, Rome, 00171, Italy. http://www.editorialepantheon.it.

450 HUN ISSN 0230-8223
M2
MUSICALIA DANUBIANA. Text in Hungarian. 1982. irreg.
Published by: Magyar Tudomanyos Akademia, Zenetudomanyi Intezet/Hungarian Academy of Sciences, Institute of Musicology, Tancsics M u 7, Budapest, 1014, Hungary. TEL 36-1-2146770, FAX 36-1-3759282, info@zti.hu.

MUSICALS; das Musicalmagazin. *see* THEATER

780 USA ISSN 1526-1107
MUSICDISH; music industry magazine. Text in English. 1997. w. free. back issues avail. **Document type:** *Newsletter, Trade.* **Description:** Showcases the hottest indie artists and labels with interviews and reviews. Provides insightful analysis from industry experts, tips to help careers, as well as news on the companies and events affecting the evolving online music market.
Formerly (until 1999): Beats E-Zine (1520-8109)
Media: Online - full text. **Related titles:** E-mail ed.
Published by: Tag It, 1837 26th Ave., # 2F, Astoria, NY 11102-3541. Eds. Eric de Fontenay, Sounni de Fontenay. Pub., R&P Sounni de Fontenay. Circ: 4,750.

780 FRA ISSN 0982-3476
MUSICHAMP L'ESSENTIEL. Text in French. 1986. irreg. **Document type:** *Monographic series, Academic/Scholarly.*
Published by: Honore Champion, 3 Rue Corneille, Paris, 75006, France. TEL 33-1-46340729, FAX 33-1-46346406, champion@honorechampion.com, http://www.honorechampion.com.

780.903 ITA ISSN 1122-0783
MUSICHE DEL RINASCIMENTO ITALIANO. Text in Italian. 1990. irreg., latest vol.2, 1990. price varies. **Document type:** *Monographic series, Academic/Scholarly.*
Published by: Casa Editrice Leo S. Olschki, Viuzzo del Pozzetto 8, Florence, 50126, Italy. TEL 39-055-6530684, FAX 39-055-6530214, celso@olschki.it, http://www.olschki.it.

780.01 ITA ISSN 1122-4282
M2
MUSICHE RINASCIMENTALI SICILIANE. Text in Italian. 1970. irreg., latest vol.21, 2000. price varies. **Document type:** *Monographic series, Academic/Scholarly.*
Published by: Casa Editrice Leo S. Olschki, Viuzzo del Pozzetto 8, Florence, 50126, Italy. TEL 39-055-6530684, FAX 39-055-6530214, celso@olschki.it, http://www.olschki.it. Circ: 1,000.

780 GBR
MUSICIAN. Text in English. 19??. q. free to members (effective 2009). bk.rev.; music rev.; rec.rev. illus. **Document type:** *Magazine, Consumer.* **Description:** Includes interviews, articles, news for members, campaigns and reviews.
Published by: Musicians' Union, 33 Palfrey Pl, London, SW8 1PE, United Kingdom. TEL 44-20-78405504, FAX 44-20-78405599, london@musiciansunion.org.uk, http://www.musiciansunion.org.uk. Ed. Keith Ames.

338.4 USA ISSN 1062-4759
ML18
THE MUSICIAN'S GUIDE TO TOURING AND PROMOTION. Variant title: Billboard Musician's Guide to Touring and Promotion. Guide to Touring & Promotion. Musician's Guide. Text in English. 1993. s-a. USD 15.95 per issue in US & Canada; USD 18.95 per issue elsewhere (effective 2011). adv. **Document type:** *Directory, Trade.* **Description:** Features an updated A and R directory to major and independent labels, showcase contacts at music conferences, directory of agents, attorneys and managers and a directory of nationwide music publications.
—**CCC.**
Published by: Prometheus Global Media, 770 Broadway, 7th Fl, New York, NY 10003. TEL 212-493-4100, http://www.prometheusgm.com.

780 CHE
MUSICIEN NEUCHATELOIS. Text in French. 6/yr.
Address: Plage 12, St Blaise, 2072, Switzerland. TEL 038-335433. Ed. Donald Bacuzzi. Circ: 2,000.

780 CAN ISSN 0226-8620
ML5
MUSICK. Text in English. 1979. q. free. adv. bk.rev. **Document type:** *Newsletter, Consumer.* **Description:** Covers medieval, Renaissance, baroque and classical music.
Indexed: CMPI, RILM.
—Ingenta.
Published by: Vancouver Society for Early Music, 1254 W Seventh Ave, Vancouver, BC V6H 1B6, Canada. TEL 604-732-1610, FAX 604-732-1602, staff@earlymusic.bc.ca, http://www.earlymusic.bc.ca. Adv. contact Jose Verstappen. Circ: 4,000.

780 USA
MUSICK OF THE FIFES & DRUMS SERIES. Text in English. 1976. irreg. price varies. back issues avail. **Document type:** *Monographic series, Consumer.*
Published by: Colonial Williamsburg Foundation, PO Box 1776, Williamsburg, VA 23187. TEL 757-229-1000.

780 NLD ISSN 0165-5884
MUSICMAKER; maandblad voor de muziekbeoefenaar. Text in Dutch. 1977. m. EUR 65 (effective 2009). adv. **Document type:** *Magazine, Trade.* **Description:** Offers amateur and professional musicians in the Netherlands and Belgium news and information on their vocations.
Published by: Music Maker Media Group, Postbus 720, Arnhem, 6800 AS, Netherlands. FAX 31.26-4433761.

780 USA
MUSICO PRO; la revista para el musico. Text in Spanish. 1996. m. USD 19.95; USD 3.50 newsstand/cover (effective 2005). adv. 80 p./no.; **Document type:** *Magazine, Consumer.*
Published by: Music Maker Publications Inc., 5412 Idylwild Trail, Ste 100, Boulder, CO 80301-3523. TEL 303-516-9118, FAX 303-516-9119, info@musicopro.com, http://www.musicopro.com. Ed. Rodrigo Sanchez. Pub. Tom Hawley. Adv. contacts Gerardo Porraz, Brent Heintz. B&W page USD 2,069. Circ: 36,523 (paid and controlled).

789 AUT ISSN 1016-1066
ML5
MUSICOLOGICA AUSTRIACA. Text in German. 1977. irreg., latest vol.28, 2009. price varies. **Document type:** *Monographic series, Academic/Scholarly.*
Indexed: PCI.
Published by: (Oesterreichische Gesellschaft fuer Musikwissenschaft), Praesens VerlagsgesmbH, Wehlistr 154/12, Vienna, W 1020, Austria. FAX 43-1-25330334660, m.ritter@praesens.at, http://www.praesens.at.

780.42 CZE ISSN 1212-0391
ML5.B75
➤ **MUSICOLOGICA BRUNENSIA.** Variant title: Studia Musicologica. Text in Multiple languages. 1966. s-a. CZK 250 domestic; USD 15 foreign (effective 2011). bk.rev. **Document type:** *Journal, Academic/Scholarly.* **Description:** Provides articles in the various fields of the theory and history of music: Czech, German, Russian, Italian, modern, folk and more.
Former titles (until 1998): Masarykova Univerzita. Filozoficka Fakulta. Sbornik Praci. H: Rada Hudebnevedna (0231-522X); Univerzita J.E. Purkyne. Filozoficka Fakulta. Sbornik Praci.: Rada Hudebnevedna
Indexed: RILM.
Published by: Masarykova Univerzita, Filozoficka Fakulta/Masaryk University, Faculty of Arts, Arna Novaka 1, Brno, 60200, Czech Republic. TEL 420-549-491111, FAX 420-549-491520, podatelna@phil.muni.cz.

780.01 BEL
MUSICOLOGICA NEOLOVANIENSIA STUDIA. Text in French. 1980. irreg., latest vol.8, 1995. price varies. **Document type:** *Monographic series, Academic/Scholarly.*
Published by: (Universite Catholique de Louvain, Departement d'Etudes Greques, Latines et Orientales, Publications d'Archeologie et d'Histoire de l'Art), Universite Catholique de Louvain, College Erasme, Pl Blaise Pascal 1, Louvain-la-Neuve, 1348, Belgium. TEL 32-10-474882, FAX 32-10-474870, moucharte@fltr.ucl.ac.be. R&P Ghislaine Moucharte.

780 SVK ISSN 0581-0558
ML5
MUSICOLOGICA SLOVACA. Text in Slovak. 1969. irreg. price varies.
Indexed: MusicInd, RASB, RILM.
Published by: (Slovenska Akademia Vied/Slovak Academy of Sciences, Umenovedny Ustav), Vydavatel'stvo Slovenskej Akademie Vied Veda/Veda, Publishing House of the Slovak Academy of Sciences, Dubravska cesta 9, PO Box 106, Bratislava 45, 84005, Slovakia. **Dist. by:** Slovart G.T.G. s.r.o., Krupinska 4, PO Box 152, Bratislava 85299, Slovakia. TEL 421-2-63839472, FAX 421-2-63839485, http://www.slovart-gtg.sk.

780 CAN ISSN 1711-9235
ML5
➤ **MUSICOLOGICAL EXPLORATIONS.** Text in English. 1995. s-a. CAD 15 in Canada to individuals; CAD 10 in Canada to students (effective 2004). bk.rev. bibl. 70 p./no. 1 cols./p.; back issues avail. **Document type:** *Journal, Academic/Scholarly.* **Description:** Features articles and reviews by music graduate students across North America.
Formerly (until 2004): Fermata (1201-6624)
Indexed: A01, CA, CMPI, M11, MusicInd, RILM, T02.
Published by: University of Victoria, School of Music, PO Box 1700, Sta CSC, Victoria, BC V8W 2Y2, Canada. TEL 250-721-7903, FAX 250-721-6597, musi@finearts.uvic.ca, http://finearts.uvic.ca/music/. Circ: 100.

780 AUS ISSN 0155-0543
ML5
MUSICOLOGICAL SOCIETY OF AUSTRALIA. NEWSLETTER. Text in English. 1977. s-a. free (effective 2008). adv. back issues avail. **Document type:** *Newsletter.* **Description:** Carries news of Australian musicology and musicologists, as well as international matters of interest to members.
Related titles: Online - full text ed.: free (effective 2008).
Indexed: RILM.
Published by: Musicological Society of Australia Inc., GPO Box 2404, Canberra, ACT 2601, Australia. membership@msa.org.au, http://www.msa.org.au. Ed. John A Phillips. Circ: 300.

780 USA ISSN 0077-2496
MUSICOLOGICAL STUDIES AND DOCUMENTS. Abbreviated title: M S D. Text in English; Text occasionally in French. 1948. irreg., latest vol.55, 2009. price varies. back issues avail. **Document type:** *Monographic series, Academic/Scholarly.* **Description:** Contains commentaries on translated treatises, source facsimiles, music editions, commentary and expanded documentation for editions, and analyses of selected historic or music theory subjects.
Formerly (until 1957): American Institute of Musicology. Studies and Documents
Published by: American Institute of Musicology, 8551 Research Way, Ste 180, Middleton, WI 53562. TEL 608-836-9000, 800-736-0070, FAX 608-831-8200, info@corpusmusicae.com. Ed. Paul L Ranzini.

450 781.62 AUS ISSN 0814-5857
ML5
➤ **MUSICOLOGY AUSTRALIA.** Text in English. 1964. s-a. GBP 108 combined subscription in United Kingdom to institutions (print & online eds.); EUR 142, AUD 225, USD 179 combined subscription to institutions (print & online eds.) (effective 2012). adv. bk.rev. illus. back issues avail.; reprint service avail. from PSC. **Document type:** *Journal, Academic/Scholarly.* **Description:** Features articles on the music of Europe, America, Asia, Indian Ocean, Pacific Ocean, Australian Aborigines and Australian musical composition.
Formerly (until 1985): Musicology (0077-250X)
Related titles: Online - full text ed.: ISSN 1949-453X. GBP 98 in United Kingdom to institutions; EUR 128, AUD 202, USD 161 to institutions (effective 2012).
Indexed: A01, AusPAIS, CA, IIMP, M11, MLA-IB, MusicInd, PCI, RILM, T02.
—BLDSC (5990.890100), IE, Ingenta. **CCC.**
Published by: (Musicological Society of Australia Inc.), Routledge (Subsidiary of: Taylor & Francis Group), Level 2, 11 Queens Rd, Melbourne, VIC 3004, Australia. TEL 61-03-90098134, FAX 61-03-98668822, http://www.informaworld.com. Ed. Paul Watt. adv.: page AUD 500. Circ: 450.

780 CAN ISSN 1497-5122
MUSICOLOGY, ETHNOMUSICOLOGY & COMPOSITION AT YORK UNIVERSITY. Text in English. 1985. a. **Document type:** *Newsletter.*
Formerly (until 1998): Musicology and Ethnomusicology at York (0846-426X)
Indexed: CMPI, RILM.
Published by: York University, Graduate Programme in Music, Accolade East, Suite 371, 4700 Keele St, Toronto, ON M3J 1P3, Canada. TEL 416-736-2100, FAX 416-736-5321, http://www.yorku.ca/grdmusic/. Eds. Marie-Eve Sarrazin, Rob Bowman, Tere Tilban-Rios.

MUSICOPYRIGHT INTELLIGENCE; a newsletter of financial success through copyright ownership. *see* PATENTS, TRADEMARKS AND COPYRIGHTS

780.65 DEU ISSN 1616-0282
MUSICOUTLOOK; Das online Magazin fuer Musik, Markt, Technik und Pop-Politik. Text in German. 2000. m. **Document type:** *Magazine, Trade.*
Media: Online - full content.
Published by: Musicoutlook oHG, Regenburger Str 19, Nittendorf, 93152, Germany. TEL 49-9404-954325, FAX 49-9404-954328. Eds., Pubs. Ralf Weller, Sven Ferchow.

780 GBR
MUSICSTAND. Text in English. 19??. q. free to members (effective 2009). **Document type:** *Magazine, Trade.* **Description:** Contains articles about the Symphony Chorus and Orchestra, youth chorus, and area music education work, along with profiles, interviews, and news of the society's activities.
Published by: City of Birmingham Symphony Orchestra, CBSO Centre, Berkley St, Birmingham, W Mids B1 2LF, United Kingdom. TEL 44-121-6166500, FAX 44-121-6166518, information@cbso.co.uk, http://www.cbso.co.uk. Ed. Ruth Green. Circ: 5,000.

781.62 CAN ISSN 1920-4213
➤ **MUSICULTURES.** Text in English, French. 1973. a. CAD 30, USD 45 (effective 2010). bk.rev.; rec.rev.; video rev. abstr.; bibl.; charts; illus. **Document type:** *Journal, Academic/Scholarly.* **Description:** Contains scholarly articles and reviews on ethnomusicology topics in Canada and abroad. The Journal is intended for universities, and other academic and scholarly institutions and communities. .
Former titles (until 2009): Canadian Journal for Traditional Music (1485-4422); (until 1997): Canadian Folk Music Journal/Revue de Musique Folklorique Canadienne (0318-2568)
Related titles: Online - full text ed.
Indexed: C03, CMPI, IIMP, MLA, MLA-IB, MusicInd, PCI, PQC, RILM.
—Ingenta. **CCC.**
Published by: Canadian Society for Traditional Music, c/o c/o folkwaysAlive!, 3-47 Arts Bldg., University of Alberta, Edmonton, AB T6G 2E6, Canada. Ed. Gordon E. Smith. Circ: 500.

780.7 ZAF ISSN 0256-8837
ML5
➤ **MUSICUS.** Text in Afrikaans, English. 1973. s-a. ZAR 80 domestic to individuals; USD 35 foreign to individuals; ZAR 100 domestic to institutions; USD 100 foreign to institutions (effective 2006). adv. bk.rev.; music rev. illus. back issues avail.; reprints avail. **Document type:** *Journal, Academic/Scholarly.* **Description:** Presents articles written on different aspects of music, music teaching and music examinations.
Indexed: AbAn, ISAP, RILM.
Published by: (University of South Africa), UniSA Press, PO Box 392, Pretoria, 0003, South Africa. TEL 27-12-4292953, FAX 27-12-4293449, unisa-press@unisa.ac.za, http://www.unisa.ac.za/press. Ed. Hubert H van der Spuy. R&P H H van der Spuy TEL 27-12-429-2913. Adv. contact H.H. van der Spuy. Circ: 1,000.

780 700 CAN ISSN 0225-686X
MUSICWORKS; journal of sound exploration. Text in English, French. 1978. 3/yr. CAD 33 domestic to individuals magazine and cd; CAD 39 in United States to individuals magazine and cd; CAD 42 elsewhere to individuals magazine and cd; CAD 55 domestic to institutions magazine and cd (effective 2005). adv. bk.rev. bibl.; charts; illus. back issues avail. **Document type:** *Journal, Consumer.* **Description:** Explores, contemporary (including ethnic and indigenous) thought about music and sound.
Related titles: Microfiche ed.: (from MML); Microfilm ed.: (from MML); Microform ed.: (from MML).
Indexed: C03, CBCARef, CBPI, CMPI, P48, PQC, RILM.
—IE. **CCC.**
Published by: Music Gallery, 401 Richmond St W, No.358, Toronto, ON M5V 3A8, Canada. TEL 416-977-3546, FAX 416-977-4181, sound@musicworks.ca. Circ: 3,000 (paid).

780 FIN ISSN 0780-0703
ML269.1
MUSIIKIN SUUNTA/DIRECTION OF MUSIC. Text in Finnish. 1979. q. EUR 23 (effective 2004). **Document type:** *Journal, Academic/Scholarly.*
Formerly (until 1982): Suomen Etnomusikologisen Seuran Aanenkannattaja (0359-3401)
Indexed: RILM.
Published by: Suomen Etnomusikologinen Seura ry/Finnish Society for Ethnomusicology, Vironkatu 1, PO Box 35, Helsinki, 00014, Finland. **Subscr. to:** Academic Bookstore, PO Box 128, Helsinki FIN-00101, Finland. TEL 358-9-1214322, FAX 358-9-1214252.

780.5 FIN ISSN 0355-1059
➤ **MUSIIKKI.** Text in Finnish, Swedish; Summaries in English. 1954. q. EUR 35 membership (effective 2007). bk.rev. back issues avail. **Document type:** *Journal, Academic/Scholarly.*
Former titles (until 1971): Suomen Musiikin Vuosikirja (0491-5542); (until 1959): Uusi Musiikkilehti (0500-8468)
Indexed: RILM.
Published by: Suomen Musiikkitieteellinen Seura/Finnish Musicological Society, c/o Musiikkitieteen Laitos, University of Jyvaskyla, Jyvaskyla, 40014, Finland. TEL 358-14-2601330, FAX 358-14-2601331. Ed. Susanna Vaelimaeki TEL 358-9-19124674. Circ: 400.

780 SWE ISSN 1652-4659
MUSIK. Text in Swedish. 2004. irreg., latest vol.1, 2004. SEK 180 per issue (effective 2006). **Document type:** *Monographic series, Academic/Scholarly.*
Published by: Oerebro Universitet, Universitetsbiblioteket/University of Oerebro. University Library, Fakultetsgatan 1, Oerebro, 70182, Sweden. TEL 46-19-303240, FAX 46-19-331217, biblioteket@ub.oru.se. Ed. Joanna Jansdotter.

780 DEU ISSN 0930-8954
ML21.G3
MUSIK - ALMANACH; Daten und Fakten zum Musikleben in Deutschland. Text in German. 1986. triennial. EUR 49.90 per vol. (effective 2010). adv. **Document type:** *Directory, Trade.*
Related titles: CD-ROM ed.
Published by: (Deutscher Musikrat), ConBrio Verlagsgesellschaft mbH, Brunnstr 23, Regensburg, 93053, Germany. TEL 49-941-945930, FAX 49-941-9459350, info@conbrio.de, http://www.conbrio.de.

780.7 DEU ISSN 1436-6037
MUSIK ALS MEDIUM. Text in German. 1998. irreg., latest vol.5, 2010. price varies. **Document type:** *Monographic series, Academic/Scholarly.*
Published by: Waxmann Verlag GmbH, Steinfurter Str 555, Muenster, 48159, Germany. TEL 49-251-265040, FAX 49-251-2650426, info@waxmann.com. Ed. Hans Hermann Wickel.

780 792 CHE ISSN 0931-8194
ML5
MUSIK & THEATER; die aktuelle Kulturzeitschrift. Text in German. 1979. 10/yr. CHF 120 domestic; CHF 150 foreign; CHF 12 newsstand/cover (effective 2007). adv. rec.rev. illus. **Document type:** *Magazine, Consumer.* **Description:** News and information from the music and theater world. Includes lists of new records and performances, announcements of events, and classified ads.
Indexed: IDP, M11, MusicInd, RILM.
Published by: Meuli & Masueger Media GmbH, Albisriederstr 80A, Zurich, 8003, Switzerland. TEL 41-1-4917188, FAX 41-1-4931176. Ed. Andrea Meuli. adv.: B&W page CHF 3,900, color page CHF 5,300. Circ: 15,000 (paid and controlled).

780 DEU
MUSIK AUS DER STEIERMARK. Text in German. 1959. irreg. (4-6/yr.). price varies. adv. **Document type:** *Newsletter.* **Description:** Publication of contemporary music by young composers. Features musical arrangements for all instruments. Each issue includes a single piece of music.
Published by: (Styrian Composers Society), Musikverlag Schulz GmbH, Am Maerzengraben 6, Freiburg Im Breisgau, 79112, Germany. FAX 49-7664-5123. Ed. Wolfgang Suppan. Adv. contact Klaus Schulz. Circ: 200.

DER MUSIK D V D MARKT. (Digital Video Disc) *see* COMMUNICATIONS—Video

780.3 DEU ISSN 0580-3225
MUSIK DES OSTENS. Text in German. 1962. irreg. price varies. **Document type:** *Monographic series, Academic/Scholarly.*
Indexed: IBR, IBZ, PCI, RILM.
Published by: Baerenreiter Verlag, Heinrich-Schuetz-Allee 35, Kassel, 34131, Germany. TEL 49-561-3105154, FAX 49-561-3105195, order@baerenreiter.com, http://www.baerenreiter.com.

780 SWE ISSN 0077-2518
➤ **MUSIK I SVERIGE**; dokument och foerteckning. Text in English, German, Swedish. 1969. irreg., latest vol.12, 2001. price varies. back issues avail. **Document type:** *Monographic series, Academic/Scholarly.*
Published by: Statens Musiksamlingar, Musikbibliotek/Swedish National Collections of Music. The Music Library of Sweden, PO Box 16326, Stockholm, 10326, Sweden. TEL 46-8-51955412, FAX 46-8-51955445. Eds. Anders Lonn, Veslemoy Heintz. R&P Veslemoey Heintz.

780 DEU ISSN 0947-8302
MUSIK IN BADEN-WUERTTEMBERG. Text in German. 1994. a. EUR 19 (effective 2006). **Document type:** *Journal, Academic/Scholarly.*
Indexed: DIP, IBR, IBZ, RILM.
Published by: (Gesellschaft fuer Musikgeschichte in Baden-Wuerttemberg), Strube Verlag GmbH, Pettenkoferstr 24, Munich, 80336, Germany. TEL 49-89-54426611, FAX 49-89-54426630, strube.verlag@strube.de, http://www.strube.de.

780 DEU ISSN 0937-583X
MUSIK IN BAYERN. Text in German. 1975. s-a. **Document type:** *Journal, Academic/Scholarly.*
Indexed: A20, ASCA, ArtHuCI, CurCont, DIP, IBR, IBZ, RILM, SCOPUS, W07.
Published by: (Gesellschaft fuer Bayerische Musikgeschichte e.V.), Verlag Dr. Hans Schneider GmbH, Mozartstr 6, Tutzing, 82323, Germany. TEL 49-815-83050, FAX 49-815-87636, Musikbuch@aol.com, http://www.schneider-musikbuch.de.

780.7 DEU ISSN 1433-1489
MUSIK IN DER GRUNDSCHULE; Das Praxismagazin fuer fantasievollen Musikunterricht in den Klassen 1-6. Text in German. 1997. q. EUR 32; EUR 28 to students; EUR 8.90 newsstand/cover (effective 2011). adv. bk.rev. bibl.; charts; illus. index. **Document type:** *Magazine, Trade.*
Published by: Schott Musik International GmbH, Weihergarten 5, Mainz, 55116, Germany. TEL 49-6131-2460, FAX 49-6131-246211, info@schott-musik.de. Ed. Friedrich Neumann. Adv. contact Dieter Schwarz. Circ: 8,500 (paid).

780.7 DEU ISSN 0027-4704
ML5
MUSIK IN DER SCHULE; Zeitschrift fuer Theorie und Praxis des Musikunterrichts. Text in German. 1949. q. EUR 37.50; EUR 23 to students; EUR 11.20 newsstand/cover (effective 2003). adv. bk.rev. abstr.; illus. index. **Document type:** *Journal, Academic/Scholarly.* **Description:** Presents study and teaching methods.
Indexed: A22, DIP, IBR, IBZ, IIMP, M11, MusicInd, RILM.
—IE, Infotrieve.
Published by: Paedagogischer Zeitschriftenverlag GmbH & Co. KG, Axel-Springer-Str. 54b, Berlin, 10117, Germany. TEL 49-30-20183592, FAX 49-30-20183593, info@pzv-berlin.de, http://www.pzv-berlin.de. adv.: B&W page EUR 400, color page EUR 640. Circ: 1,400 (paid and controlled). **Subscr. to:** CVK Cornelsen Verlagskontor, Postfach 100271, Bielefeld 33502, Germany. TEL 49-521-9719-0.

780 DEU ISSN 0931-3311
MUSIK - KONZEPTE; die Reihe ueber Komponisten. Text in German. 1977. 4/yr. EUR 45; EUR 16 newsstand/cover (effective 2009). adv. **Document type:** *Journal, Academic/Scholarly.*
Indexed: DIP, IBR, IBZ, MLA-IB, RILM.

Published by: Edition Text und Kritik in Richard Boorberg Verlag GmbH & Co. KG (Subsidiary of: Richard Boorberg Verlag GmbH und Co. KG), Levelingstr 6A, Munich, 81673, Germany. TEL 49-89-43600012, FAX 49-89-43600019, info@etk-muenchen.de. Ed. Ulrich Tadday. adv.: page EUR 650. Circ: 2,500 (paid).

780 DEU
MUSIK - KULTUR - GENDER. Text in German. 2006. irreg., latest vol.10, 2011. price varies. **Document type:** *Monographic series, Academic/Scholarly.*
Published by: Boehlau Verlag GmbH & Cie, Ursulaplatz 1, Cologne, 50668, Germany. TEL 49-221-913900, FAX 49-221-9139011, vertrieb@boehlau.de.

780 SWE ISSN 0027-4720
MUSIK & LJUDTEKNIK. Variant title: M o L T. Text in Swedish. 1960. q. SEK 300 to members (effective 2011). adv. bk.rev. bibl.; charts; illus.; mkt. index. **Document type:** *Magazine, Trade.*
Formed by the merger of (1959): L P - Bladet; (1959): Ljudteknik (0458-1091)
Published by: Ljudtekniska Saellskapet/Sound Technological Society, PO Box 8096, Stockholm, 10420, Sweden. Ed. Pekka Johanson.

780 DEU
MUSIK UND; eine Schriftenreihe der Hochschule fuer Musik und Theater Hamburg. Text in German. 2001. irreg., latest vol.10, 2010. price varies. **Document type:** *Monographic series, Academic/Scholarly.*
Published by: (Hochschule fuer Musik und Theater Hamburg), Weidler Buchverlag Berlin, Luebecker Str 8, Berlin, 10559, Germany. TEL 49-30-3948668, FAX 49-30-3948698, weidler_verlag@yahoo.de, http://www.weidler-verlag.de.

780 DEU ISSN 1432-9425
ML5
MUSIK UND AESTHETIK. Text in German. 1997. q. EUR 68; EUR 56 to students; EUR 21 newsstand/cover (effective 2011). adv. **Document type:** *Journal, Academic/Scholarly.*
Indexed: DIP, IBR, IBZ, M11, MusicInd, RILM, SCOPUS.
Published by: (Gesellschaft fuer Musik und Aesthetik), Verlag Klett-Cotta, Rotebuehlstr 77, Stuttgart, 70178, Germany. TEL 49-711-66720, FAX 49-711-66722030, info@klett-cotta.de, http://www.klett-cotta.de. Ed. Richard Klein. Adv. contact Friederike Kamann. Circ: 900 (paid).

780.7 DEU ISSN 0027-4747
ML5
MUSIK UND BILDUNG; Zeitschrift fuer Musik in den Klassen 5-13. Text in German. 1969. q. EUR 32; EUR 28 to students; EUR 8.90 newsstand/cover (effective 2011). adv. bk.rev.; music rev.; rec.rev. bibl.; charts; illus. index. **Document type:** *Magazine, Trade.*
Formed by the merger of (1956-1969): Musik im Unterricht. Allgemeine Ausgabe (0179-6798); (1956-1969): Musik im Unterricht. Ausgabe B (0179-6801); (1958-1969): Kontakte (0452-4977); Which was formerly (19??-1958): Junge Musik (0179-6836)
Related titles: CD-ROM ed.: USD 176.50 domestic; USD 183.50 foreign (effective 1999).
Indexed: DIP, IBR, IBZ, IIMP, M11, MusicInd, RASB, RILM.
Published by: (Verband Deutscher Schulmusikerzieher), Schott Musik International GmbH, Weihergarten 5, Mainz, 55116, Germany. TEL 49-6131-2460, FAX 49-6131-246211, info@schott-musik.de, http://www.schott-musik.de. Ed. Caren Benischek. Adv. contact Dieter Schwarz. Circ: 8,000 (paid and controlled).

780 DEU ISSN 0259-076X
MUSIK UND GESELLSCHAFT. Text in German. 1967. irreg., latest vol.28, 2010. price varies. **Document type:** *Monographic series, Academic/Scholarly.* **Description:** Devoted to changes in musical praxis with special emphasis on legal, economical, technical, aesthetical, historical and methodological aspects.
Published by: (Hochschule fuer Musik und Darstellende Kunst AUT, Institut fuer Musiksoziologie AUT), Peter Lang GmbH (Subsidiary of: Peter Lang Publishing Group), Eschborner Landstr 42-50, Frankfurt Am Main, 60489, Germany. TEL 49-69-7807050, FAX 49-69-78070550, zentrale.frankfurt@peterlang.com. Ed. Alfred Smudits.

783 CHE ISSN 1015-6798
ML5
MUSIK & GOTTESDIENST. Text in German. 1923. bi-m. CHF 70 newsstand/cover (effective 2008). adv. bk.rev. reprints avail. **Document type:** *Magazine, Consumer.*
Incorporates (1895-1974): Evangelische Kirchenchor (0014-3448); Formerly (until 1947): Der Organist (1023-3180)
Related titles: Microform ed.: (from PQC).
Indexed: IIMP, M11, MusicInd.
Published by: Friedrich Reinhardt Verlag, Missionsstr 36, Basel, 4012, Switzerland. TEL 41-61-2646450, FAX 41-61-2646488, verlag@reinhardt.ch, http://www.reinhardt.ch. Eds. Andreas Marti, Heinz Roland Schneeberger. Circ: 3,700.

781.7 DEU ISSN 0027-4771
ML5
MUSIK UND KIRCHE. Text in German. 1930. bi-m. EUR 34; EUR 19.95 to students (effective 2008). adv. bk.rev. bibl.; illus. **Document type:** *Journal, Academic/Scholarly.*
Indexed: A20, A22, ASCA, ArtHuCI, CurCont, DIP, IBR, IBZ, IIMP, M11, MusicInd, RILM, SCOPUS, W07.
—IE, Infotrieve. **CCC.**
Published by: Baerenreiter Verlag, Heinrich-Schuetz-Allee 35, Kassel, 34131, Germany. TEL 49-561-3105154, FAX 49-561-3105195, order@baerenreiter.com, http://www.baerenreiter.com. Ed. Klaus Roehring. Adv. contact Kerstin Lehmann. B&W page EUR 500; trim 141 x 208. Circ: 2,500 (paid).

780 808 DEU ISSN 1869-019X
▼ **MUSIK UND LITERATUR.** Text in German. 2009. irreg. price varies. **Document type:** *Monographic series, Academic/Scholarly.*
Published by: Peter Lang GmbH (Subsidiary of: Peter Lang Publishing Group), Eschborner Landstr 42-50, Frankfurt Am Main, 60489, Germany. TEL 49-69-7807050, FAX 49-69-78070550, zentrale.frankfurt@peterlang.com. Ed. Edwin Vanacek.

780 CHE ISSN 1660-8135
MUSIK UND LITURGIE. Text in German. 1876. bi-m. CHF 53 domestic; EUR 42 foreign; CHF 9 newsstand/cover (effective 2006). adv. **Document type:** *Magazine, Consumer.*
Former titles (until 2004): Singen und Musizieren im Gottesdienst (1420-5904); (until 1991): Katholische Kirchenmusik (1420-5912); (until 1960): Der Chorwaechter (1420-6145)
Indexed: RILM.
Published by: Schweizerischer Katholischer Kirchenmusikverband, Hiltiweg 3, Niederrohrdorf, 5443, Switzerland. TEL 41-56-4701047, FAX 41-56-4701048, http://www.kirchenmusik.ch/skmv/. adv.: B&W page CHF 495; trim 166 x 251. Circ: 1,800.

781.64 DEU
MUSIK UND MESSAGE. Text in German. q. EUR 14; EUR 5 newsstand/cover (effective 2006). adv. **Document type:** *Magazine, Consumer.*
Published by: Strube Verlag GmbH, Pettenkoferstr 24, Munich, 80336, Germany. TEL 49-89-54426611, FAX 49-89-54426630, strube.verlag@strube.de, http://www.strube.de. adv.: page EUR 300; trim 185 x 270. Circ: 1,000 (paid and controlled).

780.71 DEU ISSN 0937-9568
➤ **MUSIK UND UNTERRICHT.** Text in German. 1976. q. EUR 23.60; EUR 9.70 newsstand/cover (effective 2008). adv. bk.rev.; music rev. illus. index. back issues avail. **Document type:** *Journal, Academic/Scholarly.* **Description:** Offers music teachers concepts and material for their lessons.
Formerly (until 1990): Zeitschrift fuer Musikpaedagogik (0341-2830)
Indexed: DIP, IBR, IBZ, RILM.
—IE, Infotrieve. **CCC.**
Published by: Lugert Verlag GmbH, Oldershausener Hauptstr 34, Marschacht, 21436, Germany. TEL 49-4133-214911, FAX 49-4133-214918, info@lugert-verlag.de. Adv. contact Bernd Schrader. B&W page EUR 726, color page EUR 1,089. Circ: 6,000 (paid and controlled).

780.65 DEU ISSN 1618-114X
MUSIK.WOCHE; das Fachmagazin fuer die Musikbranche. Text in German. 1993. w. EUR 24 per month (effective 2011). adv. **Document type:** *Magazine, Trade.* **Description:** Contains up-to-date information on the music trade and business.
Formerly (until 2001): MusikWoche (0947-4404)
Published by: Entertainment Media Verlag GmbH und Co. oHG (Subsidiary of: Gruner + Jahr AG & Co), Weihenstephaner Str 7, Munich, 81673, Germany. TEL 49-89-451140, FAX 49-89-45114444, redaktion@e-media.de, http://www.mediabiz.de. Adv. contact Susanne Huebner. Circ: 4,050 (paid).

780.92 SWE ISSN 1653-2945
MUSIKANT OCH KAMMARMUSIK-NYTT. Text in Swedish. 2005. q. SEK 150 (effective 2011). adv. **Document type:** *Magazine, Trade.*
Formed by the merger of (1983-2005): Kammarmusik-Nytt (0283-4146); (1949-2005): Musikant (0345-8210); Which was formerly (until 1967): R S A O; (until 1965): Fanfaren
Indexed: RILM.
Published by: (Kammarmusikfoerbundet R S K), Sveriges Orkesterfoerbund/Association of Swedish Orchestras, PO Box1148, Stockholm, 17123, Sweden. TEL 46-8-4702442, FAX 46-8-4702424, info@orkester.nu. Eds. Claes Bjoernberg, Sverker Ahlenius TEL 46-33-239518. Circ: 13,000. **Co-publisher:** Kammarmusikfoerbundet R S K.

MUSIKBIBLIOTEKSNYTT. *see* LIBRARY AND INFORMATION SCIENCES

780.7 DNK ISSN 1604-049X
MUSIKBLADET. Text in Danish. 19??. 10/yr. membership. **Document type:** *Magazine, Trade.*
Former titles (until 2003): Gymnasiemusik (0108-321X); (until 1982): Gymnasieskolernes Musiklaererforening - Medlemsorientering (0108-4054); (until 1975): Gymnasieskolernes Musiklaererforening. Meddelelser (0901-4640)
Related titles: Online - full text ed.
Published by: Gymnasieskolernes Musiklaererforening, c/o Peter Drenck, Frugthaven 24, Morud, 5462, Denmark. TEL 45-64-801425, drenck@post1.tele.dk, http://www.emu.dk/gym/fag/mu/foreningen/forening.html. Ed. Joergen Aagaard. Adv. contact Jakob M Jensen TEL 45-33-249935.

780.01 NLD ISSN 1824-7199
➤ **MUSIKE**; international journal of ethnomusicological studies. Text in English; Abstracts in English. 2004. 3/yr. EUR 25, GBP 18, USD 32 newsstand/cover (effective 2010). **Document type:** *Journal, Academic/Scholarly.* **Description:** Covers technical, scientific, artistic, ethic, philosophic and symbolic aspects of preservation, conservation, spread of ethnomusicological and choreutical heritage.
Related titles: Online - full content ed.: ISSN 1824-7180.
Indexed: A01, CA, M11, T02.
Published by: Semar Publishers S.r.l., PO Box 18543, The Hague, 2502 EM, Netherlands. TEL 31-70-3560403, FAX 31-70-3629848, info@semar.org, http://www.semarweb.com/.

780 ESP ISSN 1137-4470
ML315.7.B37
MUSIKER. Text in Spanish. 1983. irreg. **Document type:** *Monographic series, Academic/Scholarly.*
Formerly (until 1997): Sociedad de Estudios Vascos. Cuadernos de Seccion. Musica (0213-0815)
Indexed: RILM.
Published by: Eusko Ikaskuntza/Sociedad de Estudios Vascos, Palacio Miramar, Miraconcha 48, Donostia, San Sebastian 20007, Spain. TEL 34-943-310855, FAX 34-943-213956, ei-sev@sc.ehu.es, http://www.eusko-ikaskuntza.org/.

781.64 DEU ISSN 1618-386X
MUSIKER MAGAZIN; Kulturzeitschrift fuer Rock & Pop Musiker. Text in German. 1983. q. EUR 20 (effective 2009). adv. **Document type:** *Magazine, Consumer.*
Former titles (until 2001): Rock- und Pop-Musiker (1436-6088); (until 1997): Rockmusiker (0936-1413)
Published by: Deutsche Rock- und Pop Musikerverband, Kulturelles Jugendbildungswerk, Kolberger Str 30, Lueneburg, 21339, Germany. TEL 49-4131-233030, FAX 49-4131-2330315, info@drmv.de, http://www.drmv.de. Ed., Adv. contact Ole Seelenmeyer. B&W page EUR 1,960, color page EUR 2,890; trim 210 x 280.

331.881178094 DNK ISSN 0905-9962
MUSIKEREN; fagblad for professionelle musikere. Text in Danish. 1911. 11/yr. DKK 399 (effective 2009). adv. music rev. back issues avail. **Document type:** *Magazine, Trade.* **Description:** News, debates, and information for professional and amateur musicians.
Formerly (until 1990): Dansk Musiker Tidende (0902-9141)
Related titles: Online - full text ed.
Published by: Dansk Musiker Forbund/Danish Union of Musicians, Sankt Hans Torv 26, Copenhagen N, 2200, Denmark. TEL 45-35-240265, FAX 45-35-240266, dmf@dmf.dk, http://www.dmf.dk. Ed. Henrik Strube TEL 45-35-240264. Adv. contact Torben Kruse. B&W page DKK 7,550, color page DKK 10,150; 220 x 293. Circ: 7,800.

780 SWE ISSN 0027-478X
ML5
MUSIKERN. Text in Swedish. 1907. 10/yr. SEK 370 membership (effective 2004). adv. bk.rev. charts; illus.; mkt. **Document type:** *Magazine, Trade.*
Former titles (until 1920): Svenska Musikerfoerbundets Tidning; (until 1910): Musikern
Related titles: Audio cassette/tape ed.
Indexed: M11, MusicInd, RASB, RILM.
Published by: Svenska Musikerfoerbundet/Swedish Musicians Union, Allstroemgatan 25B, PO Box 49144, Stockholm, 10029, Sweden. TEL 46-8-58706000, FAX 46-8-168020, info@musikerforbundet.se. Ed. Benny Soederberg. Adv. contact Rune Liedstroem. B&W page SEK 7,900, color page SEK 9,900; trim 270 x 184.

780 AUT ISSN 0027-4798
MUSIKERZIEHUNG; Zeitschrift der Musikerzieher Oesterreichs. Text in German. 1947. 5/yr. EUR 44 (effective 2003). adv. bk.rev.; rec.rev. bibl.; charts; illus. index. **Document type:** *Magazine, Academic/Scholarly.*
Indexed: DIP, IBR, IBZ, IIMP, M11, MLA-IB, MusicInd, RILM.
Published by: Oe B V & H P T Verlagsgesellschaft mbH & Co. KG, Frankgasse 4, Vienna, W 1090, Austria. TEL 43-1-40136-0, FAX 43-1-40136185, office@oebvhpt.at, http://www.oebvhpt.at. Circ: 1,800.

780 DEU ISSN 1618-5129
ML5
MUSIKEXPRESS. Text in German. 1983. m. EUR 5.90 newsstand/cover (effective 2011). adv. music rev.; video rev. charts. **Document type:** *Magazine, Consumer.*
Formerly (until 2000): Musikexpress - Sounds (0254-5187); Which was formed by merger of (19??-1983): Musik-Express (0723-4651); (1967-1983): Sounds (0724-6501)
Indexed: RILM.
Published by: Axel Springer Mediahouse Berlin GmbH (Subsidiary of: Axel Springer Verlag AG), Mehringdamm 33, Berlin, 10961, Germany. TEL 49-30-30881880, FAX 49-30-3088188223, info@axel-springer-mediahouse-berlin.de, http://www.asmm.de. Ed. Rainer Schmidt. Adv. contact Oliver Horn. Circ: 52,631 (paid).

780.01 DEU ISSN 0027-4801
ML5
DIE MUSIKFORSCHUNG. Text in German. 1947. q. EUR 24.80 newsstand/cover (effective 2008). adv. bk.rev. abstr.; bibl.; charts; illus. index. **Document type:** *Journal, Academic/Scholarly.*
Indexed: A20, A22, ASCA, ArtHuCI, CurCont, DIP, IBR, IBZ, IIMP, M11, MLA-IB, MusicInd, PCI, RASB, RILM, SCOPUS, W07.
—IE, Infotrieve. **CCC.**
Published by: (Gesellschaft fuer Musikforschung), Baerenreiter Verlag, Heinrich-Schuetz-Allee 35, Kassel, 34131, Germany. TEL 49-561-3105154, FAX 49-561-3105195, order@baerenreiter.com, http://www.baerenreiter.com. Eds. Bettina Berlinghoff-Eichler, Doerte Schmidt. Adv. contact Kerstin Lehmann. B&W page EUR 500; trim 153 x 208. Circ: 2,500.

780 DEU ISSN 0935-2562
ML5.I579
MUSIKFORUM. Text in German. 1965. 2/yr. EUR 31 domestic; EUR 37 foreign (effective 2011). **Document type:** *Journal, Academic/Scholarly.* **Description:** Contains articles, reports, documents, and other information on musical life and cultural politics in Germany.
Formerly (until 1988): International Music Council. German Committee. Referate Informationen (0538-8791)
Indexed: DIP, IBR, IBZ.
Published by: Deutscher Musikrat, Schumannstr 17, Berlin, 10117, Germany. TEL 49-30-30881010, FAX 49-30-30881011, generalsekretariat@musikrat.de, http://www.deutscher-musikrat.de. Circ: 3,000 (controlled).

780 DEU ISSN 0027-481X
ML5
MUSIKHANDEL. Text in German. 1949. 8/yr. EUR 37 domestic; EUR 41 foreign (effective 2008). adv. bk.rev.; rec.rev. charts; illus. **Document type:** *Journal, Trade.* **Description:** Trade publication fo retailers of sheet music, musical instruments and records. Features news, record reviews, new publications, and available positions.
Incorporates (1950-1990): Der Jung-Musikhandel (0447-1342)
Indexed: IBR, IBZ, IIMP, M11, MusicInd.
Published by: (Gesamtverband Deutscher Musikfachgeschaefte e.V.), Musikhandel Verlagsgesellschaft mbH, Friedrich-Wilhelm-Str 31, Bonn, 53113, Germany. TEL 49-228-539700, FAX 49-228-5397070. adv.: B&W page EUR 1,106, color page EUR 1,565. Circ: 2,810 (paid and controlled). **Co-sponsor:** Deutsches Musikverleger-Verband e.V.

780 SWE ISSN 2000-5555
MUSIKHOEGSKOLAN LIVE. Text in Swedish. 199?. 5/yr. **Document type:** *Magazine, Consumer.*
Formerly (until 2009): Lunds Universitet. Musikhoegskolan i Malmoe. Info (1104-2109)
Related titles: Online - full text ed.
Published by: Lunds Universitet, Musikhoegskolan, Ystadvaegen 25, Malmoe, 20041, Sweden. TEL 46-40-325450. Ed. Ove Torstensson TEL 46-40-325456. Circ: 4,000.

781.64 621.389 DEU
MUSIKINDUSTRIE IN ZAHLEN. Text in German. 1994. a. EUR 29.90 (effective 2009). **Document type:** *Directory, Trade.*
Former titles (until 2007): Die Phonographische Wirtschaft; (until 2006): Jahrbuch der Phonographischen Wirtschaft; (until 2005): Phonographische Wirtschaft Jahrbuch (0949-4391)
Published by: Bundesverband Musikindustrie e.V., Oranienburger Str 67-68, Berlin, 10117, Germany. TEL 49-30-5900380, FAX 49-30-59003838, info@musikindustrie.de.

681.8 DEU ISSN 0027-4828
ML5
DAS MUSIKINSTRUMENT; Business Magazin fuer Handel, Hersteller und Vertrieb. Text in German. 1952. m. EUR 60.50; EUR 5 newsstand/cover (effective 2007). adv. bk.rev. charts; illus.; pat. index. **Document type:** *Magazine, Trade.* **Description:** International trade magazine devoted to the manufacturing, trade, handicraft and research of musical instruments and musical electronics.
Indexed: IBR, IBZ, RASB, RILM.
—CCC.
Published by: P P V Medien GmbH, Postfach 57, Bergkirchen, 85230, Germany. TEL 49-8131-56550, FAX 49-8131-565510, ppv@ppvmedien.de, http://www.ppvmedien.de. adv.: B&W page EUR 1,680, color page EUR 2,220. Circ: 4,800 (paid and controlled).

780 372.87 NOR ISSN 1890-7792
MUSIKK I SKOLEN. Text in Norwegian. 1956. q. (4-6/yr). NOK 300 (effective 2011). adv. bk.rev. **Document type:** *Magazine, Trade.*
Former titles (until 2008): Arabesk (0809-0807); (until 1997): Musikk og Skole (0332-6926)
Indexed: RILM.
Address: PO Box 4703, Sofienberg, Oslo, 0506, Norway. TEL 47-22-005680, FAX 47-22-005601, musikkiskolen@musikk.no, http://www.musikkiskolen.no. Ed. Tori Skrede TEL 47-22-005686. Circ: 2,200.

780.7 NOR ISSN 0808-5005
MUSIKK - KULTUR. Text in Norwegian. 1997. m. NOK 448 domestic; NOK 485 in the Nordic countries; NOK 520 elsewhere; NOK 54 per issue (effective 2002). adv. bk.rev.; music rev. back issues avail. **Document type:** *Consumer.*
Former titles (until 1997): Musikk - Fokus (0802-8176); (until 1990): N M P F - Nytt (0800-1782); (until 1982): Norsk Musikkpedagogisk Forening Nytt (0333-4317)
Related titles: Diskette ed.; E-mail ed.; Fax ed.; Online - full text ed.
Published by: Musikk - Kultur AS, Sentrum, PO Box 871, Oslo, 0104, Norway. TEL 47-23-35-61-00, FAX 47-23-35-61-01. Ed. Geir Storli TEL 47-23-35-61-02. Adv. contact Rune Eriksen TEL 47-23-35-61-03. B&W page NOK 6,900, color page NOK 8,600; trim 185 x 260. Circ: 7,977 (controlled).

781.62 NOR ISSN 1892-0772
ML3704
➤ **MUSIKK OG TRADISJON.** Text in Multiple languages. 1984. a. back issues avail. **Document type:** *Monographic series, Academic/Scholarly.*
Formerly (until 2010): Norsk Folkemusikklag. Skrifter (0800-3734)
Indexed: RILM.
Published by: (Norsk Folkemusikklag/Norwegian Folk Music Research Association), Novus Forlag AS, Herman Foss Gate 19, Oslo, 0171, Norway. TEL 47-22-717450, FAX 47-22-718107, novus@novus.no, http://www.novus.no. Eds. Hans-Hinrich Thedens, Gjermund Kolltveit.

780 DEU ISSN 1616-5209
MUSIKKONTEXT. Text in German. 2001. irreg., latest vol.4, 2008. price varies. **Document type:** *Monographic series, Academic/Scholarly.*
Published by: Peter Lang GmbH (Subsidiary of: Peter Lang Publishing Group), Eschborner Landstr 42-50, Frankfurt Am Main, 60489, Germany. TEL 49-69-7807050, FAX 49-69-78070550, zentrale.frankfurt@peterlang.com, http://www.peterlang.com.

780 DEU ISSN 0946-5642
MUSIKLEBEN; Studien zur Musikgeschichte Oesterreichs. Text in German. 1992. irreg., latest vol.12, 2005. price varies. **Document type:** *Monographic series, Academic/Scholarly.*
Published by: Peter Lang GmbH (Subsidiary of: Peter Lang Publishing Group), Eschborner Landstr 42-50, Frankfurt Am Main, 60489, Germany. TEL 49-69-7807050, FAX 49-69-78070550, zentrale.frankfurt@peterlang.com, http://www.peterlang.com. Ed. Claudia Szabo-Knotik.

785 DNK ISSN 1902-5742
MUSIKMAGASINET. Variant title: D A M. Text in Danish. 2006. q. DKK 100 (effective 2008). **Document type:** *Magazine, Consumer.*
Formerly (until 2006): Dansk Amatoer Musik (1901-6468); Which was formed by the merger of (1983-2006): D A O Bladet (0903-7659); (1995-2006): Boernekorenes Blad (1396-092X)
Published by: Dansk Amatoer Musik/Danish Amateur Music, c/o Poul Svanberg, Ryvangs Alle 77, Hellerup, 2900, Denmark. TEL 45-39-611726, FAX 45-39-611719, damu@amatormusik.dk, http://www.danskamatormusik.dk. Ed. Poul Svanborg.

780 658.8 DEU ISSN 0047-8474
DER MUSIKMARKT. Text in German. 1959. w. EUR 197.60 domestic; EUR 260 foreign; EUR 132.60 to students; EUR 5.50 newsstand/cover (effective 2008). adv. bk.rev. **Document type:** *Magazine, Trade.*
—CCC.
Published by: Josef Keller Verlag GmbH & Co. KG, Seebreite 9, Berg, 82335, Germany. TEL 49-8151-7710, FAX 49-8151-771190, info@keller-verlag.de, http://www.keller-verlag.de. Ed. Stefan Zarge. adv.: B&W page EUR 1,700, color page EUR 2,600; 210 x 297. Circ: 4,950 (paid and controlled).

780 DNK ISSN 1902-9411
MUSIKMUSEET, MUSIKHISTORISK MUSEUM & CARL CLAUDIUS' SAMLING. MEDDELELSER. Text in Danish. 1982. biennial. price varies. adv. illus. back issues avail. **Document type:** *Monographic series, Academic/Scholarly.* **Description:** Articles on musical instruments and the history of Danish musical life.
Former titles (until 2007): Musikhistorisk Museum og Carl Claudius' Samling. Meddelelser (0900-2111); (until 1984): Musikhistorisk Museum og Carl Claudius' Samling (0109-2618)
Indexed: RILM.
Published by: Musikmuseet, Musikhistorisk Museum og Carl Claudius' Samling, Aabenraa 30, Copenhagen K, 1124, Denmark. TEL 45-33-112726, FAX 45-33-116044, fogf@natmus.dk, http://www.natmus.dk/sw25193.asp.

780 DEU ISSN 1867-4097
MUSIKORTE NIEDERSACHSEN. Text in German. 2008. irreg., latest vol.2, 2008. price varies. **Document type:** *Monographic series, Academic/Scholarly.*
Published by: Wehrhahn Verlag, Am Mittelfelde 1, Hannover, 30519, Germany. TEL 49-511-8988906, FAX 49-511-8988245, info@wehrhahn-verlag.de.

780 DEU
MUSIKPAEDAGOGIK IM FOKUS. Text in German. 2008. irreg. price varies. **Document type:** *Monographic series, Academic/Scholarly.*
Published by: Wissner Verlag, Im Tal 12, Augsburg, 86179, Germany. TEL 49-821-259890, FAX 49-821-594932, info@wissner.com.

780 DEU
MUSIKPAEDAGOGISCHE BIBLIOTHEK. Text in German. 1962. irreg., latest vol.37, 1993. price varies. **Document type:** *Monographic series.*
Published by: Florian Noetzel Verlag, Heinrichshofen Buecher, Holtermannstr 32, Wilhelmshaven, 26384, Germany. Ed. Walter Kolneder. **Dist. in U.S. by:** C.F. Peters Corp., 373 Park Ave. S., New York, NY 10016.

780 DEU
▼ **MUSIKPHILOSOPHIE.** Text in German. 2011. irreg., latest vol.3, 2011. price varies. **Document type:** *Monographic series, Academic/Scholarly.*
Published by: Verlag Karl Alber, Hermann-Herder-Str 4, Freiburg, 79104, Germany. TEL 49-761-2717436, FAX 49-761-2717212, info@verlag-alber.de.

780 DEU ISSN 0177-350X
ML3830
MUSIKPSYCHOLOGIE. Text in German. 1984. a. EUR 39.95 (effective 2010). back issues avail. **Document type:** *Journal, Academic/Scholarly.*
Indexed: DIP, E-psyche, IBR, IBZ, M11, MusicInd, RILM.
Published by: (Deutsche Gesellschaft fuer Musikpsychologie), Hogrefe Verlag GmbH & Co. KG, Rohnsweg 25, Goettingen, 37085, Germany. TEL 49-551-496090, FAX 49-551-4960988, verlag@hogrefe.de, http://www.hogrefe.de. Circ: 1,000.

306.484 DEU
MUSIKSOZIOLOGIE. Text in German. 1997. irreg., latest vol.16, 2006. price varies. **Document type:** *Monographic series, Academic/Scholarly.*
Published by: Baerenreiter Verlag, Heinrich-Schuetz-Allee 35, Kassel, 34131, Germany. TEL 49-561-3105154, FAX 49-561-3105195, order@baerenreiter.com, http://www.baerenreiter.com.

780 DEU ISSN 0178-8884
ML197
MUSIKTEXTE; Zeitschrift fuer neue Musik. Text in German. 1983. q. EUR 22 (effective 2011). adv. bk.rev. **Document type:** *Magazine, Consumer.*
Indexed: RILM.
Published by: Verlag MusikTexte, Postfach 190155, Cologne, 50498, Germany. TEL 49-221-9520215, FAX 49-221-9520216. Ed., Pub. Reinhard Oehlschlaegel. adv.: B&W page EUR 300; trim 170 x 260. Circ: 1,300 (paid and controlled).

780 DEU
MUSIKTHEATER; Beitraege zur Didaktik und Methodik. Text in German. 2003. irreg., latest vol.3, 2005. price varies. **Document type:** *Monographic series, Academic/Scholarly.*
Published by: Wissner Verlag, Im Tal 12, Augsburg, 86179, Germany. TEL 49-821-259890, FAX 49-821-594932, info@wissner.com.

780 DEU ISSN 0177-4182
ML5
MUSIKTHEORIE. Text in German. 1986. 4/yr. EUR 64 domestic; EUR 70 foreign; EUR 22 newsstand/cover (effective 2005). index. back issues avail. **Document type:** *Journal, Academic/Scholarly.*
Formerly (until 1986): Z F M T H - Zeitschrift fuer Musiktheorie (0342-3395)
Indexed: A20, ASCA, ArtHuCI, CurCont, DIP, IBR, IBZ, IIMP, M11, MLA-IB, MusicInd, PCI, RILM, SCOPUS, W07.
Published by: Laaber-Verlag, Regensburger Str 19, Laaber, 93164, Germany. TEL 49-9498-2307, FAX 49-9498-2543, info@laaber-verlag.de, http://www.laaber-verlag.de.

MUSIKTHERAPEUTISCHE UMSCHAU; Forschung und Praxis der Musiktherapie. *see* PSYCHOLOGY

780 370 DEU
MUSIKUNTERRICHT; Materialien, Methoden, Modelle. Text in German. 1993. irreg., latest vol.4, 2005. price varies. **Document type:** *Monographic series, Academic/Scholarly.*
Published by: Wissner Verlag, Im Tal 12, Augsburg, 86179, Germany. TEL 49-821-259890, FAX 49-821-594932, info@wissner.com.

780 DEU ISSN 0944-8608
MUSIKWISSENSCHAFTLICHE PUBLIKATIONEN. Text in German. 1994. irreg., latest vol.33, 2009. price varies. **Document type:** *Monographic series, Academic/Scholarly.*
Published by: Georg Olms Verlag, Hagentorwall 7, Hildesheim, 31134, Germany. TEL 49-5121-15010, FAX 49-5121-150150, info@olms.de. Ed. Herbert Schneider. R&P Christiane Busch.

780 CAN
MUSIMAGAZINE. Text in English. 6/yr. adv. **Document type:** *Magazine, Trade.*
Published by: Publiart, Inc., 1741 Leprohon, Montreal, PQ H4E 1P3, Canada. TEL 514-769-7032, FAX 514-769-5884. Ed. Andre Boulet. Adv. contact Napolean Major. Circ: 12,000.

780 FRA ISSN 1771-3641
MUSIQUE & TECHNIQUE; revue professionnelle de la facture instrumentale. Text in French. 2004. a. **Document type:** *Journal, Academic/Scholarly.* **Description:** Explores the conception, manufacturing, practice, and history of various musical instruments. For the instrument maker and musicien alike.
Published by: Institut Technologique Europeen des Metiers de la Musique, 71 Av. Olivier Messiaen, Le Mans, 72000, France. TEL 33-2-43393900, FAX 33-2-43393939, contact@itemm.fr.

780 FRA ISSN 1264-7020
MUSIQUE, IMAGES, INSTRUMENTS. Text in French, English. 1995. irreg. price varies. back issues avail. **Document type:** *Monographic series, Academic/Scholarly.*
Indexed: B24, M11, MusicInd, RILM.
Published by: Centre National de la Recherche Scientifique, 15 Rue Malebranche, Paris, 75005, France. TEL 33-1-53102700, FAX 33-1-53102727.

785.16 FRA ISSN 1283-3584
MUSIQUE INFO; le mensuel de la filiere musicale. Text in French. 1997. m. EUR 195 (effective 2009); subscr. includes weekly Newsletter. adv. **Document type:** *Magazine, Consumer.*
Published by: Editions Lariviere, 6 Rue Olof Palme, Clichy, 92587, France. TEL 33-1-47565400, http://www.editions-lariviere.fr.

781.7 FRA ISSN 1141-5177
LA MUSIQUE SACREE. Variant title: Musique Sacree. L'Organiste. Text in French. 1874. q. **Document type:** *Journal, Academic/Scholarly.*
Former titles (until 1947): Les Cahiers de la Musique Sacree (1153-558X); (until 1945): La Musique Sacree (1153-5571)
Indexed: RILM.
Published by: Association Jeanne d'Arc, 2 Chemin des Meix Lemaire, Fontenay, 88600, France. TEL 33-3-29346005, FAX 33-3-29347325.

780 SVN ISSN 1408-2403
MUSKA. Text in Slovenian. 1970. a. **Document type:** *Magazine, Consumer.*
Formerly (until 1996): Glasbena Mladina (0351-8841)
Indexed: RILM.
Published by: Zveza Glasbene Mladine Slovenije., Kersnikova 4, p.p. 1578, Ljubljana, 1000, Slovenia. http://www.gms-drustvo.si.

780.7805 GBR ISSN 1476-9212
MUSO; the music magazine that rewrites the score. Text in English. 2002. bi-m. GBP 15.75 domestic; GBP 21 in Europe; GBP 30 elsewhere; GBP 3.50 per issue domestic (effective 2010). adv. back issues avail. **Document type:** *Magazine, Consumer.* **Description:** Provides essential advice on courses and careers as well as celebrity interviews, great competitions and practical resources.
Indexed: RILM.
—CCC.
Published by: Rhinegold Publishing Ltd., 239-241 Shaftesbury Ave, London, WC2H 8TF, United Kingdom. TEL 44-20-73331720, FAX 44-20-73331765, enquiries@rhinegold.co.uk, http://www.rhinegold.co.uk. Ed. Claire Jackson. adv.: page GBP 1,495; trim 232 x 290.

780.01 FRA ISSN 1257-7537
ML5
MUSURGIA; analyse et pratique musicales. Text in French. 1994. q. EUR 90 (effective 2009). **Document type:** *Journal, Academic/Scholarly.* **Description:** Analyses classical and contemporary pieces.
Indexed: RILM.
Published by: Editions ESKA, 12 Rue du Quatre-Septembre, Paris, 75002, France. TEL 33-1-40942222, FAX 33-1-40942232, eska@eska.fr. Ed. Andre Riotte. Pub. Serge Kebabtchieff.

780 EST ISSN 1406-9466
ML5
MUUSIKA. Text in Estonian. 2002. m. EUR 19.49 (effective 2011). **Document type:** *Journal, Academic/Scholarly.*
Published by: (Eesti Muusikanoukogu), SA Kultuurileht, Voorimehe St 9, Tallinn, 10146, Estonia. TEL 372-6833110, FAX 372-6833111, info@kl.ee, http://www.kl.ee. Ed. Ia Remmel.

780 FIN ISSN 0356-7923
MUUSIKKO/MUSICIAN. Text in Finnish. 1922. 11/yr. EUR 35 (effective 2005). adv. bk.rev.; rec.rev. **Document type:** *Magazine, Trade.*
Formerly (until 1945): Muusikerilehti
Published by: Suomen Muusikkojen Liitto r.y./Finnish Musicians' Union, Pieni Roobertinkatu 16, Helsinki, 00120, Finland. TEL 358-9-68034072, FAX 358-9-68034087, sml@musicfinland.com. Ed. Jouri Nieminen. Circ: 4,300.

780 ROM ISSN 0580-3713
ML5
MUZICA/MUZICA MAGAZINE. Text in Romanian; Summaries in French. 1950. m. bk.rev. **Document type:** *Magazine, Consumer.*
Related titles: Online - full text ed.: ISSN 2247-0727.
Indexed: MLA-IB, RASB, RILM.
Published by: Uniunea Compozitorilor si Muzicologilor din Romania, Calea Victoriei 141, Bucharest, Romania. ucmr@clicknet.ro, http://www.ucmr.org.ro.

780 SRB ISSN 0354-9313
MUZICKI TALAS. Text in Serbian. 1995. s-a.
Indexed: RILM.
Published by: Clio, Zmaja od Noceja 12/I, Belgrade, 11000. TEL 381-11-2622754, FAX 381-11-2626257, info@clio.co.yu, http://www.clio.co.yu.

781.71 230 NLD ISSN 1569-416X
ML5
MUZIEK EN LITURGIE. Text in Dutch. 1932. bi-m. EUR 50 (effective 2009). adv. **Document type:** *Bulletin.*
Formerly (until 2002): Organist en Eredienst (0167-0840)
Related titles: Braille ed.
Published by: Koninklijke Vereniging van Organisten en Kerkmusici, c/o Harco Clevering, Jabbingelaan 21, Onstwedde, 9591 AL, Netherlands. TEL 31-599-331890, ledenadministratieknov@hetorgel.nl, http://www.kvok.nl. Ed. Peter Ouwerkerk.

783 200 NLD ISSN 0167-2274
MUZIEKBODE. Text in Dutch. 1932. m. (11/yr.). EUR 21.25 (effective 2009). adv. bk.rev.; play rev. abstr.; bibl.; illus.; stat.; tr.lit. **Document type:** *Newsletter, Consumer.*
Formerly: Christelijke Muziekbode (0009-5176)
Published by: Nederlandse Federatie van Christelijke Muziekbonden, Hulsmaatstraat 88, Enschede, 7523 WG, Netherlands. TEL 31-53-4330890, FAX 31-53-4342162, http://www.nfcm.nl. Circ: 5,300.

780 ITA ISSN 1970-1594
MUZIKA. Text in Italian. 2006. m. **Document type:** *Magazine, Consumer.*
Media: Online - full text.
Published by: Edizioni Donegani, Via Turati 9, Milan, 20121, Italy.

780 BGR ISSN 1310-2443
ML252
MUZIKA VCERA, DNES I UTRE/MUSIC YESTERDAY, TODAY AND TOMORROW. Text in Bulgarian. 1994. bi-m. BGL 2.50; USD 54 foreign (effective 2002). adv. bk.rev.; music rev.; rec.rev.; tel.rev.; video rev. 88 p./no.; back issues avail.; reprints avail. **Document type:** *Magazine.* **Description:** Covers great composer-created world of music that some call classical: its past and present, its genial creators, its great performers (singers and players) and its listeners, covering Bach to Stravinsky and the latest creations of Bulgarian composers.
Indexed: RILM.

Published by: Music Society "Vassil Stefanov", c/o Dimiter Christoff, Pub., Mavrovets 7, Sofia - Dragalevtsi, 1415, Bulgaria. TEL 359-2-9672351, FAX 359-2-874378. Ed. Konstantin Karapetrov. Pub., Adv. contact Dimiter Christoff. page USD 320. **Co-sponsor:** Suyuz na Bulgarskite Kompozitory - Union of Bulgarian Composers.

780 BGR ISSN 1311-1515
MUZIKA VIVA. Text in Bulgarian. 1998. bi-w. BGL 1 newsstand/cover (effective 2002). **Document type:** *Newspaper, Consumer.* **Description:** Presents an open forum for the free exchange of opinions, impressions, criticism, and ideas. Gives an overview of musical life in the country and abroad: new talents, musical events, festivals, concerts, competitions, jobs, etc.
Published by: Musica Viva Ltd., 17 Krakra St., Sofia, 1504, Bulgaria. TEL 359-2-449277, andypa@hotmail.com. Ed. Anda Palieva.

780 BGR ISSN 1310-0076
MUZIKALNI HORIZONTI. Text in Bulgarian. 1966. 10/yr. BGL 1 newsstand/cover (effective 2002). **Description:** Publishes materials on the art of performance and music pedagogic. Examines problems in music history, music theory and aesthetics and publishes information about the most significant music events and competitions.
Published by: Union of Bulgarian Musicians and Dance Performers, 12 Vitosha Blv., 5th Fl., Sofia, 1000, Bulgaria. TEL 359-2-9877332, FAX 359-2-9871410. Ed. Julian Kujomdiev.

780 ZAF ISSN 1812-5980
ML350
➤ **MUZIKI;** journal of music research in Africa. Text in Afrikaans, English. 1969. s-a. GBP 124 combined subscription in United Kingdom to institutions (print & online eds.); EUR 193, USD 242 combined subscription to institutions (print & online eds.) (effective 2012). adv. bk.rev. back issues avail.; reprint service avail. from PSC. **Document type:** *Journal, Academic/Scholarly.* **Description:** Publishes articles by lecturers and postgraduate students of the musicology department.
Formerly (until 2004): Ars Nova (0379-6485)
Related titles: Online - full text ed.: ISSN 1753-593X. GBP 111 in United Kingdom to institutions; EUR 174, USD 218 to institutions (effective 2012).
Indexed: A01, AmHI, CA, H07, ISAP, M11, P10, P48, P53, P54, PQC, RILM, T02.
—IE. **CCC.**
Published by: (University of South Africa), UniSA Press, PO Box 392, Pretoria, 0003, South Africa. TEL 27-12-4292953, FAX 27-12-4293449, unisa-press@unisa.ac.za, http://www.unisa.ac.za/press. Eds. Chris Walton, George T King. Circ: 470. **Subscr. outside Africa to:** Routledge, Customer Services Dept, Rankine Rd, Basingstoke, Hants RG24 8PR, United Kingdom. TEL 44-1256-813000, FAX 44-1256-330245, tf.enquiries@tfinforma.com.

780 SRB ISSN 1450-9814
MUZIKOLOGIJA. Text in Serbian, German, English. 2001. a. **Document type:** *Journal, Academic/Scholarly.*
Related titles: Online - full text ed.: free (effective 2011).
Published by: Srpska Akademija Nauka i Umetnosti, Muzikoloskog Institut, Knez Mikhailova 35, Beograd, 11000. Ed. Katarina Tomasevic.

780 SVN ISSN 0580-373X
ML5
MUZIKOLOSKI ZBORNIK/MUSICOLOGICAL ANNUAL. Text in Multiple languages; Summaries in English, Slovenian. 1965. a., latest vol.38, 2002. illus.; bibl. index. 200 p./no. 1 cols./p.; back issues avail. **Document type:** *Yearbook.*
Indexed: A20, ArtHuCI, IIMP, MusicInd, RILM, W07.
Published by: (Univerza v Ljubljani, Filozofska Fakulteta, Oddelek za Muzikologijo), Univerza v Ljubljani, Filozofska Fakulteta/University of Ljubljana, Faculty of Philosophy, Askerceva 2, Ljubljana, 1000, Slovenia. TEL 386-1-2411000, http://www.ff.uni-lj.si. Ed. Matjaz Barbo. Circ: 500.

781.7 USA
MUZIKOS ZINIOS/MUSIC NEWS. Text in Lithuanian. 1911. s-a. USD 5 to members. bk.rev. **Document type:** *Bulletin, Consumer.* **Description:** Contains news of composers, musicians and singers of Lithuanian descent. Provides information on programs and concerts worldwide.
Published by: (Siaures Amerikos Lietuviu Muzikos Sajunga/North American Lithuanian Music Organization), Morkunas Press, c/o Antanas Giedraitis, 7310 S California Ave, Chicago, IL 60629. TEL 773-737-2421. Ed. Kazys Skaisgirys. Circ: 300 (paid).

780 RUS
MUZOBOZ. Text in Russian. 1996. m. USD 139 in North America (effective 2000).
Published by: Izdatel'stvo MuzOboz, Izmailovskoe shosse 71 korp D k 1260, Moscow, 105613, Russian Federation. TEL 7-095-1665114. Ed. S Panfilov. **Dist. by:** East View Information Services, 10601 Wayzata Blvd, Minneapolis, MN 55305. TEL 952-252-1201, 800-477-1005, FAX 952-252-1202, info@eastview.com, http://www.eastview.com.

780 HUN ISSN 0027-5336
ML5
MUZSIKA. Text in Hungarian. 1958. m. adv. bk.rev. illus. **Document type:** *Journal.*
Related titles: Online - full text ed.: ISSN 1588-1415.
Indexed: IIMP, M11, MusicInd, RASB, RILM.
Published by: Pro Musica Alapitvany, Kiraly u 49, Budapest, 1077, Hungary. Circ: 7,500.

780 POL
MUZYCZNE CRACOVIANA. Text in Polish. 1983. irreg. price varies. adv. **Description:** Series presenting Krakow as artistic center of events, facts, and phenomena connected with music.
Published by: Polskie Wydawnictwo Muzyczne, Al Krasinskiego 11 a, Krakow, 31111, Poland. TEL 48-12-4227044, FAX 48-12-4220174. Ed. Leszek Polony. R&P Janina Warzecha. Adv. contact Elzbieta Widlak.

781 POL ISSN 0027-5344
ML5
MUZYKA; kwartalnik poswiecony historii i teorii muzyki. Text in Polish; Summaries in English. 1956. q. EUR 26 foreign (effective 2005). bk.rev.; music rev.; rec.rev. bibl.; illus. 150 p./no.; back issues avail.; reprints avail. **Document type:** *Journal, Academic/Scholarly.* **Description:** Covers articles on history, theory of music and ethnomusicology. Contains information on the activity of music departments in universities and music academies in Poland.
Indexed: DIP, IBR, IBZ, IIMP, M11, MusicInd, RASB, RILM.
Published by: Polska Akademia Nauk, Instytut Sztuki/Polish Academy of Science, Institute of Art, ul Dluga 28, Warsaw, 00950, Poland. TEL 48-22-5048200, FAX 48-22-8313149, ispan@ispan.pl. Ed. Elzbieta Witkowska-Zaremba. Circ: 500. **Dist. by:** Ars Polona, Obroncow 25, Warsaw 03933, Poland. TEL 48-22-5098609, FAX 48-22-5098610, arspolona@arspolona.com.pl, http://www.arspolona.com.pl.

781.62 782.81 781.64 USA ISSN 1556-9276
➤ **MUZYKA;** Russian music past and present. Text in English, French, German, Russian. 2000. a. bk.rev.; film rev.; music rev.; tel.rev.; video rev.; rec.rev. bibl. 150 p./no.; reprints avail. **Document type:** *Journal, Academic/Scholarly.* **Description:** Contains articles, scores and notations.
Indexed: CA, M11, T02.
Published by: Charles Schlacks, Jr., PO Box 1256, Idyllwild, CA 92512. TEL 951-659-4641, info@schlacks.com.

780 RUS
MUZYKA I VREMYA. Text in Russian. 1999. m. USD 168 foreign (effective 2006). **Document type:** *Journal.*
Published by: NauchTekhLitIzdat, Alymov per, dom 17, str 2, Moscow, 107258, Russian Federation. TEL 7-095-2690004, FAX 7-095-3239010, pribor@tgizdat.ru. **Dist. by:** East View Information Services, 10601 Wayzata Blvd, Minneapolis, MN 55305. TEL 952-252-1201, 800-477-1005, FAX 952-252-1202, info@eastview.com, http://www.eastview.com.

780 POL
MUZYKA MOJA MILOSC. Text in Polish. 1970. irreg. price varies. adv. **Description:** Series containing essays devoted to the most prominent persons of the world of music.
Published by: Polskie Wydawnictwo Muzyczne, Al Krasinskiego 11 a, Krakow, 31111, Poland. TEL 48-12-4227044, FAX 48-12-4220174. Ed. Leszek Polony. R&P Janina Warzecha. Adv. contact Elzbieta Widlak.

781.71 POL
MUZYKA POLSKA W DOKUMENTACJACH I INTERPRETACJACH. Text in Polish. 1980. irreg. price varies. adv. **Document type:** *Academic/Scholarly.* **Description:** Papers on Polish music, devoted to composers, material and folklore papers.
Published by: Polskie Wydawnictwo Muzyczne, Al Krasinskiego 11 a, Krakow, 31111, Poland. TEL 48-12-4227044, FAX 48-12-4220174. Ed. Leszek Polony. R&P Janina Warzecha. Adv. contact Elzbieta Widlak.

780 RUS ISSN 0869-4516
ML5
MUZYKAL'NAYA AKADEMIYA. Text in Russian. 1933. q. USD 100 foreign (effective 2003). bk.rev.; music rev. bibl.; illus. index. **Document type:** *Magazine, Academic/Scholarly.*
Formerly: Sovetskaya Muzyka (0038-5085)
Indexed: CDSP, IIMP, M11, MusicInd, RASB, RILM.
—East View.
Published by: Izdatel'stvo Kompozitor, Sadovaya-Triumfal'naya 12/14, Moscow, 127006, Russian Federation. TEL 7-095-2094105, FAX 7-095-2095498, music@sumail.ru. Ed. Yurii Korev. Circ: 1,500. **Dist. by:** M K - Periodica, ul Gilyarovskogo 39, Moscow 129110, Russian Federation. TEL 7-095-2845008, FAX 7-095-2813798, info@periodicals.ru, http://www.mkniga.ru; **Dist. in U.S. by:** Victor Kamkin Inc., 220 Girard St, Ste 1, Gaithersburg, MD 20877. http://www.kamkin.com.

781.64 BLR ISSN 1606-7010
MUZYKAL'NAYA GAZETA. Text in Russian. 2000. w. **Document type:** *Newspaper, Consumer.*
Media: Online - full content.
Published by: Izdatel'stvo Nestor, A/ya 563, Minsk, 220113, Belarus. nestorpb@nestor.minsk.by.

780 RUS ISSN 0027-5352
MUZYKAL'NAYA ZHIZN'. Text in Russian. 1957. m. USD 120 foreign (effective 2003). adv. illus. index. reprints avail. **Document type:** *Magazine, Consumer.*
Indexed: RASB, RILM.
Published by: (Soyuz Kompozitorov Rossiiskoi Federatsii), Izdatel'stvo Kompozitor, Sadovaya-Triumfal'naya 12/14, Moscow, 127006, Russian Federation. TEL 7-095-2094105, FAX 7-095-2095498, music@sumail.ru. Ed. Ya M Platek. Circ: 3,500. **Dist. by:** M K - Periodica, ul Gilyarovskogo 39, Moscow 129110, Russian Federation. TEL 7-095-2845008, FAX 7-095-2813798, info@periodicals.ru, http://www.mkniga.ru; **Dist. in U.S. by:** Victor Kamkin Inc., 220 Girard St, Ste 1, Gaithersburg, MD 20877. TEL 301-881-1637, kamkin@kamkin.com.

780 RUS
MUZYKAL'NOE OBOZRENIE. Text in Russian. m. USD 99.95 in United States.
Published by: Izdatel'skoe Ob'edinenie Kompozitor, Sadovaya-Triumfal'naya 12-14, Moscow, 103006, Russian Federation. TEL 7-095-2092188, FAX 7-095-2006306. Ed. A A Ustinov. **Dist. by:** East View Information Services, 10601 Wayzata Blvd, Minneapolis, MN 55305. TEL 952-252-1201, 800-477-1005, FAX 952-252-1202, info@eastview.com, http://www.eastview.com.

780 RUS
MUZYKAL'NOE OBRAZOVANIE. Text in Russian. m. USD 120 in United States.
Indexed: RASB.
Published by: Izdatel'stvo Kifara, Novoostapovskaya ul 10, Moscow, 109088, Russian Federation. TEL 7-095-2744410, FAX 7-095-2744771. Ed. I Yu Bel'skaya. **Dist. by:** East View Information Services, 10601 Wayzata Blvd, Minneapolis, MN 55305. TEL 952-252-1201, 800-477-1005, FAX 952-252-1202, info@eastview.com, http://www.eastview.com.

780.7 USA ISSN 0027-576X
ML27.U5
➤ **N A C W P I JOURNAL.** Text in English. 1952. q. free to members (effective 2010). bk.rev.; music rev.; rec.rev.; video rev. charts; illus. back issues avail.; reprints avail. **Document type:** *Journal, Academic/Scholarly.* **Description:** Contains articles in which the national officers, project chairpersons, and division chairpersons reports on their activities.
Former titles (until 1970): N A C W P I Bulletin; (until 1958): "Nack-Wappy" Bulletin; (until 1954): National Association of College Wind and Percussion Instrument Instructors. Bulletin
Related titles: Microform ed.: (from PQC).
Indexed: A22, IIMP, M11, MAG, MusicInd, RILM, T02.
—Ingenta.
Published by: National Association of College Wind & Percussion Instructors, c/o Ken Broadway, Department of Music, University of Florida, 125 MUB, PO Box 117900, Gainesville, FL 32611. kbroadway@arts.ufl.edu.

789.91 USA
N A R M SOUNDING BOARD. Text in English. s-m.
Published by: National Association of Recording Merchandisers, 3 Eves Dr, Ste 307, Marlton, NJ 08053.

N D. *see* ART

780 GBR ISSN 0028-6362
ML5
N M E. (New Musical Express) Text in English. 1952. w. GBP 77.40 domestic; USD 165.75 in United States; USD 217.60 in Canada; EUR 119 in Europe; GBP 147.90 elsewhere (effective 2010). adv. rec.rev. illus. back issues avail.; reprints avail. **Document type:** *Magazine, Consumer.* **Description:** Features a unique blend of irreverent journalism and musical expertise, plus exclusive coverage of the latest music scene.
Incorporates (1926-2001): Melody Maker (0025-9012); Which was formerly (until 1926): Rhythm; Former titles (until 1952): Musical Express; (until 1948): Accordion Times and Musical Express
Related titles: Microfilm ed.: (from RPI); Online - full text ed.
Indexed: IIMP, RASB.
—CIS. **CCC.**
Published by: I P C ignite! Ltd. (Subsidiary of: I P C Media Ltd.), Blue Fin Bldg, Southwark St, 4th Fl, London, SE1 0SU, United Kingdom. TEL 44-20-31486985, http://www.ipcmedia.com/about/ignite/. Ed. Krissi Murison TEL 44-20-31486864. Pub. Faith Hill TEL 44-20-31486833. Adv. contact Chris Dicker TEL 44-20-31486709. page GBP 6,920. Circ: 38,486. **Subscr. to:** Rockwood House, Perrymount Rd, Haywards Heath RH16 3DH, United Kingdom. TEL 44-845-1231231, IPCsubs@quadrantsubs.com, http://www.magazinesdirect.co.uk. **Dist. by:** MarketForce UK Ltd.

780 NLD ISSN 0926-0692
N N O MAGAZINE. Text in Dutch. 1990. 3/yr. EUR 25 membership (effective 2010). adv. bk.rev.; music rev. illus. **Document type:** *Magazine, Consumer.* **Description:** Announces appearances of Noord-Nederlands Orkest concerts.
Formed by the merger of: N F O Magazine (0924-6967); (1948-1990): Paukenslag (Leeuwarden) (0926-7654); Which was formerly (until 1962): Orkestniews (0924-6959)
Related titles: Microfilm ed.
Published by: Noord - Nederlands Orkest, Trompsingel 19, Groningen, 9724 CZ, Netherlands. TEL 31-50-3695800, FAX 31-50-3695815, info@nno.nu, http://www.noordnederlandsorkest.nl.

N Y C - ON STAGE. (New York City) *see* THEATER

780 USA
N Y ROCK. (New York) Text in English. 1996. m. free. adv. bk.rev. **Document type:** *Magazine, Consumer.* **Description:** Features music reviews and articles on local and international artists.
Media: Online - full text.
Published by: Scott Communications Inc., PO Box 563, New York, NY 10028-0005. TEL 212-426-4657. Ed. Sandra Boerum. R&P, Adv. contact Stuart Newman. Circ: 500,000.

780 AUT ISSN 1608-8956
ML410.M23
NACHRICHTEN ZUR MAHLER FORSCHUNG. Text in English, German. 1976. s-a. back issues avail. **Document type:** *Newsletter, Academic/Scholarly.*
Related titles: Online - full text ed.; English ed.: News About Mahler Research. ISSN 1609-0349. 1976.
Published by: Internationale Gustav Mahler Gesellschaft, Wiedner Guertel 6, Vienna, W 1040, Austria. TEL 43-1-5057330, FAX 43-1-5057330, info@gustav-mahler.org. Ed. Erich Partsch. Circ: 1,000.

NACHTFLUG. *see* HOTELS AND RESTAURANTS

NACHTLICHTER. *see* HOTELS AND RESTAURANTS

780 792 USA
NASHVILLE SCENE. Text in English. w. USD 39 (effective 2000). adv. bk.rev. **Document type:** *Newspaper, Consumer.* **Description:** Covers entertainment, arts and leisure.
Address: 2120 8th Ave S, Nashville, TN 37204-2204. TEL 615-244-7989, FAX 615-244-8578, editor@nashvillescene.com, http://www.nashvillescene.com. Ed. Bruce Dobie. Pub. Albie Del Favero. R&P Albie Delfavero. Adv. contact Jackson Vahaly. Circ: 50,000 (controlled).

780 SVN ISSN 0027-8270
➤ **NASI ZBORI;** revija za pevce, zborovodje in ljubitelje petja. Text in Slovenian; Summaries in English. 1945. 3/yr. USD 30 foreign (effective 2007). music rev. abstr.; bibl. 60 p./no.; **Document type:** *Journal, Academic/Scholarly.*
Indexed: RILM.
Published by: Javni Sklad Republike Slovenije za Kulturne Dejavnosti/Slovenia. Public Fund for Cultural Activities, Stefanova 5, Ljubljana, 1000, Slovenia. TEL 386-1-2410500, FAX 386-1-2410510, info@jskd.si. Eds. Mihela Jagodic, Stojan Kuret.

780 ESP ISSN 0213-7305
ML315.7.A7
➤ **NASSARRE;** revista aragonesa de musicologia. Text in Spanish. 1985. s-a. EUR 28 per issue (effective 2009). adv. **Document type:** *Monographic series, Academic/Scholarly.*
Indexed: IIMP, M11, MusicInd, P09, PCI, RILM.
Published by: Institucion Fernando el Catolico, Plaza de Espana 2, Zaragoza, 50071, Spain. TEL 34-976-288878, FAX 34-976-288869, ifc@dpz.es. Ed. Alvaro Zaldivar. R&P Felix Sanchez TEL 34-976-288858. Adv. contact Maria Luz Cortes TEL 34-976-288879. Circ: 750.

780.71 USA ISSN 0547-4175
ML27.U5
NATIONAL ASSOCIATION OF SCHOOLS OF MUSIC. DIRECTORY. Text in English. 1950. a., latest 2003. USD 20 per vol. (effective 2007). **Document type:** *Directory, Trade.* **Description:** Lists accredited institutions and degree programs, with addresses, telephone numbers, and music executives of all member institutions.

Published by: National Association of Schools of Music, 11250 Roger Bacon Dr, Ste 21, Reston, VA 20190-5148. TEL 703-437-0700, FAX 703-437-6312, info@arts-accredit.org, http://nasm.arts-accredit.org.

780.71 USA ISSN 0164-2847
ML27.U5
NATIONAL ASSOCIATION OF SCHOOLS OF MUSIC. HANDBOOK. Text in English. 1930. biennial. USD 20 per issue (effective 2007).
Description: Contains the organizations constitution, bylaws, code of ethics, procedures, and standards for accredited institutional membership.
Published by: National Association of Schools of Music, 11250 Roger Bacon Dr, Ste 21, Reston, VA 20190-5148. TEL 703-437-0700, FAX 703-437-6312, info@arts-accredit.org, http://nasm.arts-accredit.org. Circ: 2,200.

780.7 USA ISSN 0190-6615
ML27.U5
NATIONAL ASSOCIATION OF SCHOOLS OF MUSIC. PROCEEDINGS OF THE ANNUAL MEETING. Key Title: Proceedings of the Annual Meeting - National Association of Schools of Music. Text in English. 1934. a., latest vol.79, 2003. USD 20 per vol. (effective 2004). **Document type:** *Proceedings.*
Supersedes: National Association of Schools of Music. Proceeding of the Annual Meeting (0077-3409)
Indexed: IIMP, M11, MusicInd, RILM.
Published by: National Association of Schools of Music, 11250 Roger Bacon Dr, Ste 21, Reston, VA 20190-5148. TEL 703-437-0700, FAX 703-437-6312, info@arts-accredit.org, http://nasm.arts-accredit.org.

786.3 USA ISSN 0077-4642
NATIONAL GUILD OF PIANO TEACHERS. GUILD SYLLABUS. Text in English. 1951. a. USD 15.
Published by: National Guild of Piano Teachers, PO Box 1807, Austin, TX 78767. TEL 512-478-5775. Ed. Pat McCabe-Leche. Circ: 12,000.

780.65 USA
NATIONAL MUSIC PUBLISHERS' ASSOCIATION. NEWS & VIEWS. Text in English. 1965. q. free to qualified personnel. illus. **Document type:** *Newsletter.*
Formerly (until 1991): National Music Publishers' Association. Bulletin
Published by: National Music Publishers' Association, 711 3rd Ave, 8th Fl, New York, NY 10017-4014. TEL 212-370-5330, FAX 212-953-2471. Ed., R&P Margaret Drum. Circ: 6,000.

NEDERLANDSE ORGELMONOGRAFIEEN. *see* INSTRUMENTS

782.25 305.896 USA ISSN 1546-6078
ML3556
THE NEGRO SPIRITUAL; keeping the bond with our enslaved ancestors and their song. Text in English. 1999 (Win.). s-a. USD 16 to non-members; free to members (effective 2003).
Published by: Friends of Negro Spirituals, PO Box 71956, Oakland, CA 94612. fns3@juno.com, http://www.dogonvillage.com/negrospirituals/index.htm.

780 USA
NETWORK AUDIO BITS. Text in English. 1987. m. music rev.
Media: Online - full text.
Address: PO Box 328, Orono, ME 04473-0328. n-audio@maine.maine.edu, murph@maine.maine.edu. Ed. Michael A Murphy.

784 DEU
ML5
NEUE CHORZEIT. Text in German. 1908. m. EUR 19.20; EUR 2.10 newsstand/cover (effective 2009). adv. bk.rev. illus. **Document type:** *Magazine, Trade.*
Formed by the merger of (1947-2005): Chor (0940-600X); (1908-2005): Lied und Chor (1616-3001); Which was formerly (until 1994): Lied und Chor. Ausgabe A (0720-9509); (until 1979): Lied und Chor (0024-290X)
Published by: Deutscher Chorverband - Verlags- und Projektgesellschaft mbH, Eichendorffstr 18, Berlin, 10115, Germany. TEL 49-30-84710896, FAX 49-30-84710898, verlag@dcvg.de, http://www.dcvg.de. Ed. Eva Krautter. Adv. contact Renata Plis. page EUR 1,687.40; trim 193 x 275. Circ: 40,000 (paid).

781 DEU ISSN 0550-6212
NEUE HEIDELBERGER STUDIEN ZUR MUSIKWISSENSCHAFT. Text in German. 1969. irreg., latest vol.23. price varies. **Document type:** *Monographic series, Academic/Scholarly.*
Published by: Laaber-Verlag, Regensburger Str 19, Laaber, 93164, Germany. TEL 49-9498-2307, FAX 49-9498-2543, info@laaber-verlag.de, http://www.laaber-verlag.de.

780 DEU
▼ **NEUE INNSBRUCKER BEITRAEGE ZUR MUSIKWISSENSCHAFT.** Text in German. 2011. irreg. price varies. **Document type:** *Monographic series, Academic/Scholarly.*
Published by: Lit Verlag, Grevener Str/Fresnostr 2, Muenster, 48159, Germany. TEL 49-251-235091, FAX 49-251-231972, lit@lit-verlag.de, http://www.lit-verlag.de.

780 DEU ISSN 0171-0133
NEUE MUSIKZEITUNG. Text in German. 1978. 10/yr. EUR 38 domestic; EUR 45 foreign; EUR 21.50 to students; EUR 4.50 newsstand/cover (effective 2009). adv. bk.rev.; play rev. illus. **Document type:** *Newspaper, Consumer.*
Formed by the merger of (1952-1978): Neue Musikzeitung. Landesverband Niedersachsen (0344-9904); (1952-1978): Neue Musikzeitung. Ausgabe Baden-Wuerttemberg (0344-9920); (1952-1978): Neue Musikzeitung. Ausgabe Landesverband Bayern (0344-9912); (1952-1978): Neue Musikzeitung. Landesverband Nordrhein-Westfalen (0344-9890); Which all superseded in part (in 197?): N M Z - Neue Musikzeitung (0028-3290); Which incorporated (19??-1973): Landesverband der Tonkuenstler und Musiklehrer. Mitteilungsblatt (0047-3979); Which was formerly (until 1969): Musikalische Jugend (0464-0535)
Related titles: Special ed(s).: Neue Musikzeitung. Allgemeine Ausgabe J M D. ISSN 0944-8136. 1952.
Indexed: IIMP, RASB.
Published by: (Verband Deutscher Musikschulen), ConBrio Verlagsgesellschaft mbH, Brunnstr 23, Regensburg, 93053, Germany. TEL 49-941-945930, FAX 49-941-9459350, info@conbrio.de, http://www.conbrio.de. Ed. Theo Geissler. Adv. contact Petra Pfaffenheuser. B&W page EUR 2,922, color page EUR 4,294. Circ: 18,224 (paid).

780 DEU ISSN 0945-6945
NEUE ZEITSCHRIFT FUER MUSIK. Text in German. 1975. 6/yr. EUR 48; EUR 38 to students; EUR 9.50 newsstand/cover (effective 2011). adv. bk.rev.; music rev.; rec.rev. charts; illus. index. **Document type:** *Magazine, Consumer.*
Formerly (until 1991): N Z - Neue Zeitschrift fuer Musik (0170-8791); Which superseded in part (in 1979): Melos, N Z (0343-0138); Which was formed by the merger of (1920-1975): Melos (0025-9020); (1955-1975): Neue Zeitschrift fuer Musik (0343-0332); Which was formerly (until 1972): Neue Zeitschrift fuer Musik (0028-3509)
Related titles: Microfilm ed.: (from BHP).
Indexed: A20, A22, ASCA, ArtHuCI, CurCont, DIP, IBR, IBZ, IDP, IIMP, M11, MLA-IB, MusicInd, PCI, RASB, RILM, SCOPUS, W07.
—BLDSC (6077.827500), IE, Infotrieve. **CCC.**
Published by: Schott Musik International GmbH, Weihergarten 5, Mainz, 55116, Germany. TEL 49-6131-2460, FAX 49-6131-246211, info@schott-musik.de, http://www.schott-musik.de. Adv. contact Dieter Schwarz. B&W page EUR 975, color page EUR 1,725; trim 185 x 260. Circ: 8,000 (paid and controlled).

780 DEU
NEUES MUSIKWISSENSCHAFTLICHES JAHRBUCH. Text in German. 1984. a. EUR 35 (effective 2011). **Document type:** *Journal, Academic/Scholarly.*
Formerly (until 1992): Augsburger Jahrbuch fuer Musikwissenschaft (0178-1758)
Indexed: RILM.
Published by: Wissner Verlag, Im Tal 12, Augsburg, 86179, Germany. TEL 49-821-259890, FAX 49-821-594932, info@wissner.com.

NEUES RHEINLAND; Zeitschrift fuer Landschaft und Kultur. *see* LITERATURE

NEW CULTURE; a review of contemporary African arts. *see* ART

781 USA ISSN 1949-0801
NEW DIMENSION NOTES. Text in English. 1998. m. free (effective 2009). back issues avail. **Document type:** *Newsletter, Trade.* **Description:** Aims to develop public appreciation of barbershop harmony and to teach a cappella vocal music in our schools and communities.
Formerly (until 2008): New Dimension Chorus
Media: Online - full content.
Published by: (Barbershop Harmony Society), New Dimension Chorus, 2530 Silsby Ave, Union City, CA 94587. Ed. Jeff Harris TEL 510-280-6948.

780.42 GBR ISSN 0260-3330
NEW GANDY DANCER; the magazine for instrumental rock music. Text in English. 1976. irreg. (3-4/yr.). USD 24. adv. bk.rev.; rec.rev. charts. **Document type:** *Newsletter.* **Description:** Devoted to instrumental rock music. Includes features and artist profiles.
Published by: Dama Publishing, 87 Napier Rd, Swalwell, Newcastle upon Tyne, NE16 3BT, United Kingdom. TEL 0191-488-8349. Ed., Pub., R&P, Adv. contact Davy Peckett. Circ: 1,000.

780.7 USA ISSN 0028-6265
NEW MEXICO MUSICIAN. Text in English. 1954. 3/yr. USD 9 (effective 2001). adv. bk.rev. charts; illus. 48 p./no.; **Document type:** *Newsletter.* **Description:** Contains information of interest to association members.
Published by: New Mexico Music Educators Association, 93 Mimbres Dr, Los Alamos, NM 87544. FAX 505-672-9840, gerheart@thuntek.net. Ed., Pub., R&P, Adv. contact Donald E Gerheart. Circ: 1,600.

781.12 USA
NEW MUSIC CONNOISSEUR; the magazine devoted to the contemporary music scene. Text in English. q. USD 18; USD 4.95 newsstand/cover (effective 2006). adv. **Document type:** *Magazine, Trade.* **Description:** Focuses on the work of current modern composers, with additional coverage of rare and neglected classical music from all national and ethnic sources.
Former titles (until 1997): Music Connoisseur (1081-2709); (until 19??): Connoisseur's Rack
Indexed: RILM.
Address: PO Box 476, Peck Slip Sta, New York, NY 10272-0476. Ed., Pub. Barry Cohen. adv.: page USD 195.

781.64 IRL ISSN 0791-5268
ML5
NEW MUSIC NEWS. Text in English. 1990. 3/yr. free. **Document type:** *Bulletin.* **Description:** Features news and articles about contemporary music in Ireland. Includes score and CD acquisition information, a CD sales page and a calendar of forthcoming music events.
Indexed: RILM.
Published by: Contemporary Music Centre, 19 Fishamble St, Temple Bar, Dublin, 8, Ireland. TEL 353-1-6612105, FAX 353-1-6489100. Ed. Eve O'Kelly. Circ: 3,500; 3,500 (controlled).

780 USA ISSN 0276-7031
ML18
NEW ON THE CHARTS. Text in English. 1976. m. USD 225 (effective 1999). adv. **Document type:** *Journal, Trade.*
Published by: Music Business Reference, Inc., 70 Laurel Pl, New Rochelle, NY 10801. TEL 914-632-3349, FAX 914-633-7690. Ed., Pub. Leonard Kalikow. Circ: 2,500 (controlled).

780.7 GBR
NEW OXFORD HISTORY OF MUSIC. Text in English. 1954. irreg., latest 2001. price varies. **Document type:** *Monographic series, Academic/Scholarly.*
Published by: Oxford University Press, Great Clarendon St, Oxford, OX2 6DP, United Kingdom. TEL 44-1865-556767, FAX 44-1865-556646, enquiry@oup.co.uk, http://www.oup-usa.org/catalogs/general/series/. Eds. Bonnie J Blackburn, Reinhard Strohm.

780 USA ISSN 2156-5627
THE NEW POWER MAGAZINE. Text in English. 2003. bi-m. USD 9 (effective 2010). adv. back issues avail. **Document type:** *Magazine, Trade.* **Description:** Provides independent artists, labels, DJs, models, recording studios, night clubs, photographers, graphics artists, and small businesses an avenue for exposure, while catering to major recording artist, labels, and corporations looking for added exposure in the Southern urban-market place.
Related titles: Online - full text ed.: free (effective 2010).
Published by: Colom Media Group, Llc., PO Box 8465, Columbus, MS 39705. TEL 662-251-0075. Ed., Pub. Anthony Colom.

780 BGR ISSN 1310-9626
NEW RHYTHM. Text in Bulgarian. 1997. m. BGL 2.99 newsstand/cover (effective 2002). 84 p./no.; **Document type:** *Magazine, Consumer.* **Description:** Covers all of the basic styles in modern rock, pop, techno and dance. Publishes music news from all over the world, interviews with different artists and reviews of all the albums officially released in Bulgaria.
Published by: Public Art Ltd., 2 Biser St., Sofia, 1000, Bulgaria. TEL 359-2-665529, rhythm@rhythm.biscom.net. Ed. Juliana Tancheva.

780 SRB ISSN 0354-818X
NEW SOUND. Text in English. s-a. EUR 10 (effective 2005).
Related titles: ◆ Serbian ed.: Novi Zvuk. ISSN 0354-4362.
Indexed: A01, CA, IIMP, M11, MusicInd, RILM, T02.
Published by: Savez Organizacija Kompozitora Jugoslavije (SOKOJ), Music Information Centre/Union of Yugoslav Composers' Organizations, Misarska 12-14, Belgrade, 11000. TEL 381-11-3245192, FAX 381-11-3224056.

▼ **THE NEW SOUNDTRACK.** *see* MOTION PICTURES

780 USA
NEW YORK MUSIC. Text in English. 1993. m. USD 9. **Document type:** *Magazine, Consumer.*
Published by: Music Marketing Enterprises, 19 W 44th St, Ste 1217, New York, NY 10036. TEL 212-221-7065. Ed. Peter Comas. adv.: B&W page USD 4,594. Circ: 75,000.

781.7 398 USA ISSN 1041-4150
ML3544
NEW YORK PINEWOODS FOLK MUSIC CLUB NEWSLETTER. Text in English. 1965. m. (except Aug.). USD 38 membership (effective 2008). adv. bk.rev. **Document type:** *Newsletter.*
Published by: Folk Music Society of New York, 444 W 54th St #7, New York, NY 10019. TEL 718-651-1115, NYpinewood@aol.com, http://www.folkmusicny.org. Ed. Eileen Pentel. Circ: 1,200.

780 158 NZL ISSN 1176-3264
➤ **THE NEW ZEALAND JOURNAL OF MUSIC THERAPY.** Text in English. 1982. a. **Document type:** *Journal, Academic/Scholarly.*
Former titles (until 2003): New Zealand Society for Music Therapy. Annual Journal (0113-9479); (until 1986): New Zealand Society for Music Therapy. Journal (0111-9664); New Zealand Society for Music Therapy. Newsletter
Indexed: A11, CA, M11, RILM, T02.
Published by: New Zealand Society for Music Therapy, The Terrace, PO Box 10352, Wellington, 6006, New Zealand. lgestro@xtra.co.nz.

781.660993 NZL ISSN 0114-9032
NEW ZEALAND MUSICIAN. Text in English. 1988. bi-m. NZD 25 domestic; AUD 30 in Australia; USD 25 in United States; GBP 15 in United Kingdom; NZD 50 elsewhere (effective 2009). adv. back issues avail. **Document type:** *Magazine, Consumer.*
Indexed: RILM.
Address: Newmarket, PO Box 99-315, Auckland, New Zealand. TEL 64-9-3732572, FAX 64-9-3033349. Ed., Pub. Richard Thorne. Adv. contact Lydia Jenkin.

780 ZAF ISSN 1684-0399
NEWMUSICSA. Variant title: International Society for Contemporary Music. South African Section. Bulletin. Text in English. 2002. a. **Document type:** *Bulletin.*
Indexed: RILM.
Published by: International Society for Contemporary Music, South African Section, PO Box 685, Wits, 2050, South Africa. info@newmusicsa.org.za, http://www.newmusicsa.org.za.

780 782.81 FRA ISSN 1993-310X
NEWS INTEGRAL. Variant title: Integral News. Text in French. 19??. q. back issues avail. **Document type:** *Magazine, Consumer.*
Published by: Integral Distribution, 15 Passage des Abbesses, Paris, 75018, France. TEL 33-1-42543108, FAX 33-1-42540509, integralclassic@wanadoo.fr.

780 JPN ISSN 1342-2308
ML3797
NIHON ONGAKUSHI KENKYU/UENO GAKUEN UNIVERSITY. RESEARCH ARCHIVES FOR JAPANESE MUSIC. BULLETIN. Variant title: Studies in the Historiography of Japanese Music. Text in Japanese. 1996. a. **Document type:** *Journal, Academic/Scholarly.*
Indexed: RILM.
Published by: Ueno Gakuen Nihon Ongaku Shiryoshitsu/Ueno Gakuen University, Research Archives for Japanese Music, 4-24-12 Higashiueno, Taito-ku, Tokyo, 110-8642, Japan.

NIKKEI ENTERTAINMENT!. *see* COMPUTERS—Internet

780 IND ISSN 0973-3787
MT3.I48
NINAD. Variant title: I T C Sangeet Research Academy. Journal. Text in English. 1980. a. free (effective 2011). **Document type:** *Journal, Academic/Scholarly.* **Description:** Covers music acoustics, music cognition, music synthesis, music analysis and composition, music signal processing, psychoacoustics, musicology, music aesthetics, philosophy of music, and music and society.
Formerly (until 2005): Sangeet Research Academy. Journal
Published by: ITC Sangeet Research Academy, 1, Netaji Subash Chandra Bose Rd, Tollygunge, Kolkata, 700 040, India. TEL 91-33-24713395, FAX 91-33-24714371, 000ITCSangeet. Eds. Asoke Kumar Datta, Ranjan Sengupta.

780 USA ISSN 0148-2076
ML1
➤ **NINETEENTH CENTURY MUSIC.** Text in English. 1977. 3/yr. USD 223 combined subscription to institutions (print & online eds.) (effective 2012). adv. bk.rev. illus. cum.index. back issues avail.; reprint service avail. from PSC. **Document type:** *Journal, Academic/Scholarly.* **Description:** Covers all aspects of Western art music between the mid-eighteenth and mid-twentieth centuries.
Related titles: Microfiche ed.; Online - full text ed.: ISSN 1533-8606. USD 178 to institutions (effective 2012).
Indexed: A01, A02, A03, A08, A20, A22, A26, A27, ABS&EES, ASCA, AmH&L, AmHI, ArtHuCI, B04, BRD, BrHumI, CA, CurCont, DIP, E01, E08, G08, H07, H08, H09, H10, HAb, HistAb, HumInd, I05, IBR, IBRH, IBT&D, IBZ, IIMP, M11, MAG, MLA-IB, MusicInd, P02, P10, P30, P48, P53, P54, PCI, PQC, RASB, RILM, S09, SCOPUS, T02, W03, W07.
—BLDSC (9725.475000), IE, Infotrieve, Ingenta.

Published by: University of California Press, Journals Division, 2000 Ctr St, Ste 303, Berkeley, CA 94704. TEL 510-643-7154, FAX 510-642-9917, customerservice@ucpressjournals.com. Ed. Lawrence Kramer. Adv. contact Jennifer Rogers TEL 510-642-6188. **Subscr. to:** 149 5th Ave, 8th Fl, New York, NY 10010. participation@jstor.org.

780 GBR ISSN 1479-4098
ML5
➤ **NINETEENTH CENTURY MUSIC REVIEW.** Text in English. 1940. s-a. GBP 120, USD 192 combined subscription to institutions (print & online eds.) (effective 2012). back issues avail. **Document type:** *Journal, Academic/Scholarly.* **Description:** Aims to locate music within the widest possible framework of intellectual activity pertaining to the long century (c.1780-1914).
Formerly (until 2004): Music Review (0027-4445)
Related titles: Online - full text ed.: ISSN 2044-8414. GBP 109, USD 175 to institutions (effective 2012).
Indexed: A01, A02, A03, A08, A11, A20, A22, A26, A27, AmHI, B04, BRD, E08, G08, H07, H08, H09, H10, HAb, HumInd, I05, IIMP, M11, MLA-IB, MusicInd, P02, P10, P48, P53, P54, PCI, PQC, RILM, S05, S09, U01, W03.
—BLDSC (6113.230600), Ingenta.
Published by: (University of Durham, Centre for Nineteenth-Century Music), Cambridge University Press, The Edinburgh Bldg, Shaftesbury Rd, Cambridge, CB2 8RU, United Kingdom. TEL 44-1223-326070, FAX 44-1223-325150. Ed. Dr. Bennett Zon.

781.642 DEU
NO FENCES; Country & Western Magazine. Text in German. 1995. 3/yr. EUR 14; EUR 2.75 newsstand/cover (effective 2005). **Document type:** *Magazine, Consumer.*
Address: Friedrichsstr 16, Kassel, 34117, Germany. TEL 49-561-773106, FAX 49-561-7397287. Ed., Pub. Harald Harland. Circ: 1,000 (paid and controlled).

780 ROM ISSN 2067-6972
➤ **NO14 PLUS MINUS**; contemporary music journal. Text in Romanian; Abstracts in English. bi-m. free. **Document type:** *Journal, Academic/Scholarly.*
Media: Online - full text.
Published by: S.C. Sieben ER Publishing SRL, CP 13, OP 56, sector 6, Bucharest, Romania. TEL 40-745-550073. Ed. Veronica Anghelescu.

781.6 HRV ISSN 1331-534X
NOMAD. Text in Croatian. 1998. m. HRK 220 domestic; EUR 55, USD 65 foreign; HRK 20 newsstand/cover (effective 2001). adv. **Document type:** *Magazine, Consumer.* **Description:** Contains news, articles and reviews of popular music and artists.
Related titles: Online - full text ed.
Published by: Faust Vrancic d.o.o., Kersovanijev trg 1, Zagreb, 10000, Croatia. TEL 385-1-2313646, FAX 385-1-2313646. Ed. Tonci Kozul. Pub. Valerij Juresic.

NORDIC JOURNAL OF MUSIC THERAPY/NORDISK TIDSSKRIFT FOR MUSIKKETERAPI. *see* MEDICAL SCIENCES—Physical Medicine And Rehabilitation

780.948 SWE ISSN 0108-2914
ML5
NORDIC SOUNDS. Text in English. 1968. 4/yr. DKK 150 in Scandinavia; free elsewhere (effective 2003). bk.rev.; rec.rev. **Document type:** *Magazine, Academic/Scholarly.*
Formerly (until 1980): NOMUS Nytt-Music i Norden (0345-8504)
Indexed: IIMP, M11, MusicInd, RASB, RILM, T02.
Published by: (Nordisk Ministerraad/Nordic Council of Ministers DNK), N O M U S, Nybrokajen 11, Stockholm, 11148, Sweden. TEL 46-8-4071720, FAX 46-8-4071645. Ed. Anders Beyer. Circ: 6,500.

780 371.3 NOR ISSN 1504-5021
NORDISK MUSIKKPEDAGOGISK FORSKNING/NORDIC RESEARCH IN MUSIC EDUCATION. Text in English, Norwegian. 1997. a., latest vol.7, 2004. price varies. back issues avail. **Document type:** *Journal, Academic/Scholarly.*
Related titles: ◆ Series of: Norges Musikhoegskole. N M H Publikasjoner. ISSN 0333-3760.
Published by: Norges Musikhoegskole/Norwegian Academy of Music, PO Box 5190, Majorstua, Oslo, 0303, Norway. TEL 47-23-367000, FAX 47-23-367001, mh@nmh.no, http://www.nmh.no.

780 NOR ISSN 0333-3760
NORGES MUSIKHOEGSKOLE. N M H PUBLIKASJONER. Text in English, Norwegian. 1982. irreg. back issues avail. **Document type:** *Monographic series, Academic/Scholarly.*
Related titles: ◆ Series: Nordisk Musikkpedagogisk Forskning. ISSN 1504-5021.
Published by: Norges Musikhoegskole/Norwegian Academy of Music, PO Box 5190, Majorstua, Oslo, 0303, Norway. TEL 47-23-367000, FAX 47-23-367001, mh@nmh.no.

781.7 NOR ISSN 0333-0176
NORSK KIRKEMUSIKK. Text in Norwegian. 1947. 10/yr. NOK 300 domestic; NOK 350 foreign (effective 2006). adv. back issues avail. **Document type:** *Magazine, Trade.*
Formerly (until 1959): Norges Organistforbund. Medlemsblad (0802-8141)
Indexed: RILM.
Published by: Musikernes Fellesorganisasjon/Norwegian Musicians' Union, Youngstorget, PO Box 8806, Oslo, 0028, Norway. TEL 47-23-062150, FAX 47-23-062151, mfo@musikerorg.no, http://www.musikerorg.no. Ed. Gunnar Jess. Adv. contact Bente J Gundersen. page NOK 1,450.

781.7 NOR ISSN 0807-6685
NORSK KIRKESANG. Text in Norwegian. 1965. q. adv. **Document type:** *Newsletter, Consumer.*
Related titles: Online - full text ed.
Published by: Norges Kirkesangforbund, PO Box 216, Sola, 4097, Norway. TEL 47-51-690477, FAX 47-51-619589, halvor@kirkesang.no.

780.7 USA ISSN 0029-2753
NORTH DAKOTA MUSIC EDUCATOR. Text in English. 1961. 3/yr. USD 10; USD 4 per issue (effective 2007). adv. bk.rev. **Document type:** *Journal, Trade.* **Description:** Publishes articles of interest to music educators and music industry professionals at the state and national level.
Published by: North Dakota Music Educator's Association, c/o Erin Odegaard, 3033 38 1/2 Ave S, Fargo, ND 58104, ND 58104. TEL 701-293-1564, erinodegaard@hotmail.com, http://www.ndmea.org. Ed. Erin Odegaard TEL 701-729-8289. R&P Shawn Brekke TEL 701-446-3637. adv.: page USD 115. Circ: 834.

780 GBR ISSN 2045-9378
NORTHUMBRIAN PIPERS' SOCIETY. JOURNAL. Text in English. 1980. a. free to members (effective 2011). bk.rev.; rec.rev. **Document type:** *Magazine, Trade.* **Description:** Contains news items, articles, and reviews relating to Northumbrian bagpipes and Northumbrian music.
Formerly (until 2010): Northumbrian Pipers' Society Magazine (0261-5096)
Published by: Northumbrian Pipers' Society, c/o Julia Say, Park House, Lynemouth, Morpeth, Northumberland NE61 5XQ, United Kingdom. TEL 44-1670-860215, secretary@northumbrianpipers.org.uk, http://www.northumbrianpipers.org.uk. Ed. Barry Say TEL 44-1670-860215.

781.66 NOR ISSN 1890-5838
NORWAY ROCK MAGAZINE. Text in Norwegian. 2001. 6/yr. NOK 235; NOK 40 per issue (effective 2008). back issues avail. **Document type:** *Magazine, Consumer.* **Description:** Covers Rock, Metal & Retro music.
Formerly (until 2008): Monster (1502-8658)
Related titles: Online - full text ed.
Published by: Kuloert Kultur, P O Box 1070, Trondheim, 7446, Norway. TEL 47-72-880505, FAX 47-72-880504, post@monstermagazine.no. Ed. Geir Larzen. Adv. contact Martin Kvan.

NOSTALGIA. *see* SOUND RECORDING AND REPRODUCTION

781.71 NLD ISSN 1876-2921
NOTABENE. Text in Dutch. 1996. m. EUR 60 domestic includes Het Orgel; EUR 70 in Europe includes Het Orgel; EUR 75 elsewhere includes Het Orgel; EUR 30 domestic; EUR 40 in Europe; EUR 45 elsewhere (effective 2009). adv. bk.rev.; music rev. illus. back issues avail. **Document type:** *Newspaper.*
Formerly (until 2008): De Orgelkrant (1387-1358)
Related titles: Online - full text ed.; ◆ Supplement to: Het Orgel. ISSN 0166-0101.
Published by: Koninklijke Vereniging van Organisten en Kerkmusici, Klipper 49, Zuidhorn, 9801 MT, Netherlands. ledenadministratieknov@hetorgel.nl, http://www.kvok.nl. Eds. Jan Smelik, Peter Ouwerkerk. adv.: B&W page EUR 417; 199 x 232. Circ: 2,700.

780 ARG ISSN 1852-2343
▼ **NOTAS NEGRAS.** Text in Spanish. 2009. q. **Document type:** *Journal, Academic/Scholarly.*
Related titles: Online - full text ed.: ISSN 1852-2351. 2008.
Published by: Escuela de Blues, Republica Dominicana, 3492, Buenos Aires, C1425GKD, Argentina. TEL 54-11-48212722, info@escueladeblues.com.ar/.

780.01 USA
NOTES (ANN ARBOR); a publication for friends and supporters of the University Musical Society. Text in English. 1989. q. free. adv. bk.rev. back issues avail. **Description:** Concerned with artists, programming, and composers as they relate to upcoming presentations of the University Musical Society.
Published by: University Musical Society, c/o University of Michigan, Burton Memorial Tower, Ann Arbor, MI 48109-1270. TEL 313-747-1177, FAX 313-747-1171. Ed. Catherine S Arcure. Circ: 12,000.

781 USA ISSN 0029-3946
NOTES A TEMPO. Text in English. 1951. q. membership. adv. stat. back issues avail. **Document type:** *Newsletter, Trade.* **Description:** Covers all aspects of music education within the state of West Virginia.
Published by: West Virginia Music Educators Association, Inc., c/o David Bess, Division of Music, CAC WVU, Morgantown, WV 26506-6111. TEL 304-293-4841 ext 3174, dasayre@access.k12.wv.us, http://members.tripod.com/~wvmea/. Eds. Becky Taylor, David Bess. Circ: 950.

780 ESP ISSN 2171-5688
▼ **NOTES ALTERADAS.** Text in Multiple languages. 2010. 3/yr. **Document type:** *Bulletin, Consumer.*
Published by: Ayuntament de Riba-Roja del Turia, Conservatori Professional Municipal de Musica i Dansa, Calle Bodeguetes, 68, Valencia, 46190, Spain. notesalterades@ayto-ribarroja.es, http://www.ayto-ribarroja.es/. Ed. Juan Jose Campos Sanchis.

780 CAN ISSN 1910-1422
NOTES NOUVELLES. Text in French. 197?. q. **Document type:** *Journal, Consumer.*
Published by: Chanson Nouvelle, CP 2391, Terminus Postal, Quebec, PQ G1K 7P5, Canada. TEL 418-666-3867, FAX 418-666-8139, chansonnouvelle@qc.aira.com, http://www.chansonnouvelle.qc.ca/index.htm.

780 RUS
NOTNYI AL'BOM. Text in Russian. m. **Document type:** *Magazine.*
Published by: NauchTekhLitIzdat, Alymov per, dom 17, str 2, Moscow, 107258, Russian Federation. TEL 7-095-2690004, FAX 7-095-3239010, pribor@tgizdat.ru.

780 SRB ISSN 0354-4362
ML5
NOVI ZVUK; internationalni casopis za musiku. Text in Serbian. 1955. s-a. EUR 10; EUR 18 combined subscription print & CD-ROM (effective 2005). adv. bk.rev.; rec.rev. **Document type:** *Consumer.* **Description:** Provides reviews on the most significant music events, musicological studies, interviews.
Former titles: Novi; (until 1993): Zvuk (0044-555X)
Related titles: CD-ROM ed.: EUR 10; ◆ English ed.: New Sound. ISSN 0354-818X.
Indexed: M11, MusicInd, RILM.
Published by: Savez Organizacija Kompozitora Jugoslavije (SOKOJ), Music Information Centre/Union of Yugoslav Composers' Organizations, Misarska 12-14, Belgrade, 11000. TEL 381-11-3245192, FAX 381-11-3224056. Ed. Mirjana Veselinovic Hofman. Circ: 1,500.

780 GBR ISSN 1741-685X
NUDE; beyond the counter-culture. Text in English. 2003 (Aug.). q. GBP 15.95 domestic; GBP 24 in Europe; GBP 35 elsewhere; GBP 3.95 per issue domestic; GBP 5.50 per issue in Europe; GBP 7 per issue elsewhere (effective 2009). back issues avail. **Document type:** *Magazine, Consumer.* **Description:** Aims to celebrate the spirit of wayward creativity in all its forms, serving up an eclectic mix of contemporary graphics, deviant design, outsider and alternative musics, eccentric architecture, cult writing, indie film, cutting-edge fashion and profiles of maverick genius the world over.
Published by: Poke-in-the-Eye Publishing, Ltd., P O Box 587, London, WC1H 9WB, United Kingdom. TEL 44-79-10034505.

780 ITA ISSN 0029-6228
ML5
NUOVA RIVISTA MUSICALE ITALIANA; trimestrale di cultura e informazione musicale. Text in Italian. 1894. q. EUR 52 (effective 2008). bk.rev.; rec.rev. bibl. **Document type:** *Magazine, Consumer.*
Formerly (until 1955): Rivista Musicale Italiana (1125-3657)
Indexed: A20, A22, ASCA, ArtHuCI, CurCont, IBR, IBZ, IIMP, M11, MLA-IB, MusicInd, RASB, RILM, SCOPUS, W07.
—IE, Infotrieve.
Published by: E R I Edizioni R A I (Subsidiary of: R A I - Radiotelevisione Italiana), Via Verdi 16, Turin, TO 10121, Italy. http://www.eri.rai.it. Circ: 3,500.

780.904 SWE ISSN 1652-6082
ML5
NUTIDA MUSIK/CONTEMPORARY MUSIC. Text in Swedish. 2002. q. SEK 240 domestic; SEK 260 in Nordic countries; SEK 320 elsewhere; SEK 65 per issue (effective 2005). adv. bk.rev. illus. cum.index. **Document type:** *Magazine, Consumer.*
Supersedes in part (in 2004): N M - T. Nutida Musik - Tritonus (Print) (1652-005X); Which was formed by the merger of (1957-2002): Nutida Musik (0029-6597); (2001-2002): Tritonus (Online)
Related titles: ◆ Online - full text ed.: Tritonus.
Indexed: IIMP, MusicInd.
Published by: International Society for Contemporary Music (ISCM), Swedish Section, c/o Engstroem, Sankt Eriksgatan 114, Stockholm, 11331, Sweden. TEL 46-739-842489, http://www.iscm.a.se/iscm. Ed. Andreas Engstroem. Adv. contact Johanna Paulsson TEL 46-702-097845.

▼ **[NXTLVL] MAGAZINE**; Christ. life. music. *see* RELIGIONS AND THEOLOGY—Protestant

780.6 CAN
O C NEWS. Text in English, French. 1974. bi-m. CAD 27; CAD 37 foreign (effective 1999). adv. **Description:** Contains reviews of government legislation, cultural issues, news, people, and orchestras.
Formerly: Orchestra Canada (0380-1799)
Indexed: CMPI.
Published by: Orchestras Canada/Orchestres Canada, 56 The Esplanade, Ste 311, Toronto, ON M5E 1A7, Canada. TEL 416-366-8834. Ed. Ulla Colgrass. R&P, Adv. contact Madeline Fiala. Circ: 3,000.

786.5 AUS ISSN 0314-4623
O H T A NEWS. (Organ Historical Trust of Australia) Text in English. 1977. q. **Document type:** *Journal, Trade.*
Indexed: RILM.
Published by: Organ Historical Trust of Australia, PO Box 200, Camberwell, VIC 3124, Australia. http://www.ohta.org.au.

781.57 SWE ISSN 1102-7428
ML5
O J. (Om Jazz) Variant title: Orkesterjournalen. Text in Swedish. 1933. 11/yr. SEK 380; SEK 450 in Scandinavia; SEK 500 elsewhere (effective 1999). adv. bk.rev.; rec.rev. back issues avail. **Document type:** *Newspaper.* **Description:** Focuses on jazz music from a Swedish perspective.
Formerly (until 1991): Orkester Journalen (0030-5642); Incorporated (in 1991): Jazznytt fraan S.J.R. (0047-195X); Which was formerly (until Nov. 1967): Jazznyt
Indexed: IIMP, M11, MusicInd, RILM.
Published by: Orkester Journalen, Nybrokajen 11, Stockholm, 11148, Sweden. TEL 46-8-407-17-45, FAX 46-407-17-49. Ed. Lars Westin. Adv. contact Ewert Duell. B&W page SEK 4,400, color page SEK 7,050; trim 290 x 215. Circ: 3,500.

780.65 DEU
O.TON. Text in German. 2004. 5/yr. EUR 10 newsstand/cover (effective 2007). adv. **Document type:** *Magazine, Consumer.*
Published by: M W K Zimmermann & Haehnel GmbH, Elisenstr 24, Cologne, 50667, Germany. TEL 49-221-123435, FAX 49-221-138560, info@mwk-koeln.de, http://www.mwk-koeln.de. adv.: B&W page EUR 1,350, color page EUR 1,650. Circ: 17,500 (paid and controlled).

OBITUARIES IN THE PERFORMING ARTS. *see* THEATER

780 JPN ISSN 1344-672X
OCHANOMIZU ONGAKU RONSHU. Text in Japanese. 1999. a. **Document type:** *Journal, Academic/Scholarly.*
Indexed: RILM.
Published by: Ochanomizu Ongaku Kenkyukai/Ochanomizu University, Musicological Society, 2-1-1 Ohtsuka, Bunkyo-ku, Tokyo, 112-8610, Japan.

780 NLD ISSN 0926-0684
ODEON. Text in Dutch. 1990. 4/yr. EUR 14; EUR 3.50 newsstand/cover (effective 2009). adv. back issues avail. **Document type:** *Magazine, Consumer.* **Description:** Contains interviews, background information on staged operas performed by De Nederlande Opera. Includes cast lists and synopses of operas.
Published by: Nederlandse Opera, Waterlooplein 22, Amsterdam, 1011 PG, Netherlands. TEL 31-20-5518922, FAX 31-20-5518311, info@dno.nl, http://www.dno.nl. Eds. Frits Vliegenthart, Marc N Chahin. Circ: 25,000.

780.71 SWE ISSN 1653-056X
OEREBRO STUDIES IN MUSIC EDUCATION. Text in Swedish. 2005. irreg., latest vol.2, 2005. SEK 180 per issue (effective 2006). back issues avail. **Document type:** *Monographic series, Academic/Scholarly.*
Published by: Oerebro Universitet, Universitetsbiblioteket/University of Oerebro. University Library, Fakultetsgatan 1, Oerebro, 70182, Sweden. TEL 46-19-303240, FAX 46-19-331217, biblioteket@ub.oru.se. Ed. Joanna Jansdotter.

780 DEU ISSN 0078-3471
OESTERREICHISCHE GESELLSCHAFT FUER MUSIK. BEITRAEGE. Text in German. 1967. irreg., latest vol.12, 2006. price varies. **Document type:** *Monographic series, Academic/Scholarly.*
Published by: (Oesterreichische Gesellschaft fuer Musik), Baerenreiter Verlag, Heinrich-Schuetz-Allee 35, Kassel, 34131, Germany. TEL 49-561-3105154, FAX 49-561-3105195, order@baerenreiter.com, http://www.baerenreiter.com.

780 AUT
OESTERREICHISCHE GESELLSCHAFT FUER MUSIKWISSENSCHAFT. MITTEILUNGEN. Text in German. 1973. s-a. **Document type:** *Newsletter, Trade.*
Published by: Oesterreichische Gesellschaft fuer Musikwissenschaft, c/o Institut fuer Musikwissenschaft der Universitaet Wien, Campus Altes AKH, Spitalgasse 2-4, Vienna, W 1090, Austria. office@oegmw.at, http://www.oegmw.at. Ed. Theophil Antonicek.

780 AUT
ML5
➤ **OESTERREICHISCHE MUSIKZEIT**; journal for music and culture in central europe. Text in German. 1946. bi-m. EUR 44; EUR 9.50 newsstand/cover (effective 2011). adv. bk.rev.; music rev.; rec.rev. illus. cum.index: 1970, 2000. 96 p./no.; back issues avail. **Document type:** *Journal, Academic/Scholarly.* **Description:** Contains scientific and cultural articles on old and new music.
Formerly: Oesterreichische Musikzeitschrift (0029-9316); Which incorporated (in 1979): Komponist
Indexed: A01, A20, ArtHuCI, CurCont, DIP, IBR, IBZ, IIMP, M11, MusicInd, RASB, RILM, SCOPUS, W07.
Published by: Boehlau Verlag GmbH & Co.KG., Wiesingerstr 1, Vienna, W 1010, Austria. TEL 43-1-3302427, FAX 43-1-3302432, boehlau@boehlau.at, http://www.boehlau.at. Eds. Daniel Ender, Doris Weberberger.

784 AUT ISSN 0473-8624
OESTERREICHISCHES VOLKSLIEDWERK. JAHRBUCH. Text in German. 1952. a. EUR 30 (effective 2003). bk.rev.; dance rev.; music rev. bibl. index. back issues avail. **Document type:** *Yearbook, Academic/Scholarly.* **Description:** Articles on the subjects of Austrian folkmusic, folksongs and folkdance.
Formerly: Volkslied, Volkstanz, Volksmusik
Indexed: RASB, RILM.
Published by: Oesterreichisches Volksliedwerk, Operngasse 6, Vienna, W 1010, Austria. TEL 43-1-5126335, FAX 43-1-512633513, office@volksliedwerk.at, http://www.volksliedwerk.at. Ed. Michaela Brodl. Circ: 500.

781.6 USA ISSN 1090-0810
ML1
OFF BEAT; Louisiana music and culture. Text in English. 1988. m. USD 39 domestic; USD 45 in Canada; USD 90 elsewhere; USD 6 per issue (effective 2011). adv. bk.rev.; music rev.; rec.rev.; video rev.; Website rev. illus.; charts; maps; bibl. back issues avail. **Document type:** *Magazine, Consumer.* **Description:** Focuses on American roots music indigenous to New Orleans and Louisiana. Features interviews, reviews, club listings, festival information, and schedules.
Related titles: E-mail ed.; Online - full text ed.: ISSN 2162-2744. 1988.
Indexed: A01, M11, MusicInd, T02.
Published by: Offbeat, Inc., 421 Frenchmen St, Ste 200, New Orleans, LA 70116. TEL 504-944-4300, 877-944-4300, FAX 504-944-4306.

780 NLD ISSN 1876-1275
OFF THE RECORD. Text in Dutch. 2008. bi-m. EUR 19.95 (effective 2009). **Document type:** *Magazine, Consumer.*
Published by: BCM Publishing, Postbus 1392, Eindhoven, 5602 BJ, Netherlands. TEL 31-40-8447644, FAX 31-40-8447655, bcm@bcm.nl, http://www.bcm.nl. Ed. Jean-Paul Heck. Adv. contact Alexander den Braber.

780 USA
ML1
THE OHIO STATE ONLINE MUSIC JOURNAL. Abbreviated title: O S O M. Text in English. 1969. irreg., latest vol.2, 2009. free (effective 2010). back issues avail. **Document type:** *Journal, Academic/Scholarly.* **Description:** Features articles, book reviews and comments pertaining to articles and reviews.
Formerly (until 198?): Journal of the Graduate Music Students at the Ohio State University (Print) (0364-2216)
Media: Online - full text.
Indexed: MusicInd.
Published by: Ohio State University, School of Music, 1866 College Rd, 110 Weigel Hall, Columbus, OH 43210. TEL 614-292-6571, FAX 614-292-1102, blatti.1@osu.edu, http://www.music.osu.edu. Eds. Benjamin Williams, Blake R Henson.

786.2 DEU ISSN 1023-7054
OKEY!; Magazin fuer Orgel und Keyboard. Text in German. 1994. bi-m. EUR 24 (effective 2005). adv. **Document type:** *Magazine, Consumer.*
Published by: Mautner Medien GmbH, Schwalbenweg 2, Ense, 59469, Germany. TEL 49-2938-805510, FAX 49-2938-805501. adv.: B&W page EUR 1,900, color page EUR 2,660; trim 210 x 280.

781.7 USA ISSN 1044-3649
OKLAHOMA BLUEGRASS GAZETTE. Text in English. 1975. m. USD 10 to members (effective 2000). adv. bk.rev. illus.; tr.lit. **Document type:** *Newsletter.* **Description:** Keeps members informed of events and bands.
Published by: Oklahoma Bluegrass Club Inc., 8700 Hillview, Midwest City, OK 73150. TEL 405-737-9944. Ed. Charles Doris Lamb. R&P, Adv. contact Pat Pogue TEL 405-677-1509. Circ: 600.

780 USA ISSN 1543-0197
ML3477.7.O4
OKLAHOMA MUSIC MAGAZINE. Text in English. 2003 (Spr.). q. USD 11.80; USD 3.95 newsstand/cover (effective 2003).
Published by: Oklahoma Music, 7134 S. Yale St. Ste. 720, Tulsa, OK 74136. TEL 918-491-9088, FAX 918-491-9946, http://www.oklahomamusic.biz. Ed. Chris Greer. Pub. Bill Bowman.

780 USA ISSN 1040-3582
ML3551
OLD-TIME HERALD; a magazine dedicated to old-time music. Text in English. 1987. q. USD 20 to individuals; USD 25 to institutions. adv. illus. **Document type:** *Magazine, Trade.*
Indexed: A01, IIMP, M11, MLA-IB, MusicInd, RILM, T02.
Published by: Old-Time Music Group, Inc., 1812 House Ave, Durham, NC 27707. TEL 919-416-9433, FAX 919-416-9433. Ed. Alice Gerrard. R&P Alice Gerard TEL 919-402-8495. Adv. contact Molly Nagel. Circ: 4,000.

780.01 DEU
OLDIE - MARKT. Text in German. 1977. m. EUR 85.20 domestic; EUR 94.60 foreign; EUR 8.54 newsstand/cover (effective 2010). adv. bk.rev. **Document type:** *Magazine, Consumer.*
Published by: New Media Verlag GmbH, Auf der Wies 3, Muehldorf, 84453, Germany. TEL 49-8631-162785, FAX 49-8631-162786, shop@plattensammeln.de.

780 DEU ISSN 1612-4162
OLMS FORUM. Text in German. 1998. irreg., latest vol.6, 2005. price varies. **Document type:** *Monographic series, Academic/Scholarly.*
Published by: Georg Olms Verlag, Hagentorwall 7, Hildesheim, 31134, Germany. TEL 49-5121-15010, FAX 49-5121-150150, info@olms.de.

780 800 USA
ON.. Text in English. m. **Description:** Provides running cultural commentary.
Media: Online - full text. Ed. A H Badiner.

782.4 USA ISSN 1933-2351
ON WAX; the no-page music magazine. Text in English. 2006. m. USD 15 (effective 2007). **Document type:** *Magazine, Consumer.* **Description:** Features information on individual artists and genres of popular music in a condensed format.
Published by: K Kreations, PO Box 84373, Baton Rouge, LA 70884. kkreationsonline@gmail.com. Ed. Janene Tate. Pub. Kivoli Thomas.

781.64 USA ISSN 1542-3018
ML156.4.P6
ONE WAY; a showcase for new music. Text in English. 2002. q. USD 25 domestic; USD 55 foreign (effective 2008). adv. **Document type:** *Magazine, Consumer.* **Description:** Showcases established and up-and-coming performers and their music in a wide variety of genres that appeal to an adult audience.
Published by: Pat Mavromatis, Ed. & Pub., 311 N Robertson Blvd, Ste 208, Beverly Hills, CA 90211. TEL 310-275-5141, FAX 310-765-4765.

780 JPN ISSN 0289-3606
ONGAKU NO TOMO/FRIENDS OF MUSIC. Text in Japanese. 1941. m. JPY 970. adv. illus. **Document type:** *Consumer.* **Description:** Contains commentary and explanations of outstanding works and performances, stories of great composers and musicians, movements of music circles in the world as well as in Japan.
Published by: Ongaku No Tomo Sha Corp., c/o KakuyukiNabeshima, 6-30 Kagura-Zaka, Shinjuku-ku, Tokyo, 162-0825, Japan. FAX 81-3-3235-2129. Ed. Natsuo Tsukatani. Pub. Jun Meguro. R&P Tetsuo Marita TEL 81-3-3235-2144. Adv. contact Takao Oya. B&W page JPY 324,000; trim 210 x 277. Circ: 150,000.

ONGAKU ONKYO KENKYUKAI SHIRYO/ACOUSTICAL SOCIETY OF JAPAN. TECHNICAL COMMITTEES. TRANSACTIONS. *see* PHYSICS—Sound

780.01 JPN ISSN 0030-2597
ML5
➤ **ONGAKUGAKU/MUSICOLOGY.** Variant title: Musicological Society of Japan. Journal. Text in Japanese; Summaries in English, German, French. 1954. 3/yr. JPY 9,000, USD 60. adv. bk.rev. abstr.; bibl.; charts; illus. **Document type:** *Academic/Scholarly.* **Description:** Aims to present original articles in the field of musicology.
Related titles: CD-ROM ed.; Microform ed.
Indexed: RILM.
Published by: Nippon Ongaku Gakkai/Musicological Society of Japan, c/o National University of Fine Arts and Music, Department of Musicology, Ueno-Koen, Taito-ku, Tokyo, 110-0007, Japan. TEL 81-3-5685-7500, FAX 81-3-5685-7797. Circ: 1,600. **Subscr. to:** Academia Music Ltd., 3-16-5 Hongo, Bunkyo-ku, Tokyo 113-0033, Japan.

787.5 USA ISSN 1552-9657
ML920
➤ **THE ONLINE JOURNAL OF BASS RESEARCH.** Abbreviated title: O J B R. Text in English. 2003 (Jul). irreg., latest 2004. free (effective 2011). **Document type:** *Journal, Academic/Scholarly.*
Media: Online - full text.
Indexed: CA, M11, T02.
Published by: International Society of Bassists, 13140 Coit Rd Ste 320 LB 120, Dallas, TX 75244. TEL 972-233-9107, FAX 972-490-4219, info@isbworldoffice.com, http://www.isbworldoffice.com. Ed. Jeremy Baguyos.

780 USA
➤ **ONLINE TROMBONE JOURNAL.** Abbreviated title: O T J. Text in English. 1996. irreg. free (effective 2011). bk.rev.; music rev. illus. back issues avail. **Document type:** *Journal, Academic/Scholarly.* **Description:** Covers the advancement of trombone performance and pedagogy though education, communication, and creativity.
Media: Online - full text.
Published by: Richard Human, Jr., Ed. & Pub.

780 NLD ISSN 0921-1616
ML5
OOR. Text in Dutch. 1971. bi-w. EUR 66.95 domestic; EUR 73.95 in Belgium (effective 2010). adv. **Document type:** *Magazine, Consumer.*
Formerly (until 1984): Muziekkrant Oor (0301-6501)
Related titles: Online - full text ed.
Address: Postbus 9308, Amsterdam, 1006 AH, Netherlands. TEL 31-20-5849020. Eds. Erik van den Berg, Koen Poolman.

780 FRA ISSN 1289-0294
OPEN MAG; le magazine des labels musicaux. Text in French. 1998. m. EUR 20 domestic (effective 2007). **Document type:** *Magazine, Consumer.*
Related titles: Online - full text ed.: free.
Address: 22 Rue Richer, Paris, 75009, France. Ed. Joss Danjean.

780 USA ISSN 1525-4267
ML197
THE OPEN SPACE MAGAZINE. Text in English. 1999. irreg. USD 15 per issue to individuals; USD 10 per issue to students (effective 2004).
Indexed: M11, RILM.
Published by: Open Space Magazine, 29 Sycamore Dr, Red Hook, NY 12571. TEL 845-758-5785, FAX 845-758-6740, postmaster@the-open-space.org, http://www.the-open-space.org. Eds. Benjamin Boretz, Mary Lee Roberts.

782.1 DEU ISSN 1431-8318
OPER AKTUELL. Text in German. 1959. a. EUR 22 (effective 2006). back issues avail. **Document type:** *Journal, Consumer.*
Formerly (until 1996): Jahrbuch der Bayerischen Staatsoper (0938-4952)
Indexed: RILM.
Published by: (Gesellschaft zur Foerderung der Muenchner Opernfestspiele), S M G - Stiebner Medien GmbH, Nymphenburger Str 86, Munich, 80636, Germany. TEL 49-89-1257414, FAX 49-89-12162282, info@stiebner.com, http://www.stiebner.com. Circ: 5,000.

782.1 GBR ISSN 0030-3526
OPERA. Text in English. 1950. m. GBP 58.40 domestic; GBP 75 in United States; GBP 97 per issue elsewhere (effective 2009). adv. bk.rev.; music rev.; rec.rev. illus. index. back issues avail.; reprints avail. **Document type:** *Magazine, Consumer.* **Description:** Features comprehensive listings of forthcoming productions and thorough analysis of the latest operatic events and recordings.
Related titles: Microform ed.: (from PQC).
Indexed: A20, A22, A26, AmHI, ArtHuCI, B04, BRD, BrHumI, CurCont, E08, G08, H07, H08, H09, H10, HAb, HumInd, I05, IBT&D, IIMP, IIPA, M11, MLA-IB, MusicInd, PCI, RASB, RILM, S09, SCOPUS, T02, W03, W07.
—BLDSC (6266.400000), IE, Infotrieve, Ingenta.
Published by: Opera Magazine, 36 Black Lion Ln, London, W6 9BE, United Kingdom. TEL 44-20-85638893, FAX 44-20-85638635. Ed. John Allison. Adv. contact Jane Stoggles.

782.81 ESP ISSN 1133-4134
OPERA ACTUAL. Text in Spanish. 1991. 10/yr. USD 45.08 (effective 2010). adv. back issues avail. **Document type:** *Magazine, Consumer.* **Description:** Covers the increasing amount of opera being performed in Spain.
Related titles: Online - full text ed.
Published by: Opera Actual S.L., C Bruc 6, Pral 2a, Barcelona, 08010, Spain. TEL 34-93-3191300, FAX 34-93-3107338, director@operaactual.es, http://www.operaactual.es. **Dist. by:** Asociacion de Revistas Culturales de Espana. info@arce.es, http://www.arce.es/.

782.1 USA
ML27.U5
OPERA AMERICA. Text in English. 1972. q. USD 5.99 per issue (effective 2011). adv. bk.rev. abstr.; stat. back issues avail. **Document type:** *Magazine, Trade.* **Description:** Covers opera company news from around the world, issues affecting the field, professional opportunities, repertoire, and dates on Opera America's programs and activities.
Former titles (until 2007): Opera America Newsline (1062-7243); (until 1991): Intercompany Announcements
Related titles: Online - full text ed.: free (effective 2011).
Indexed: RILM.
Address: 330 Seventh Ave, New York, NY 10001. TEL 212-796-8620, FAX 212-796-8631, Info@operaamerica.org. Ed. Kelley Rourke.

780 792 USA
OPERA AMERICA. ANNUAL FIELD REPORT. Abbreviated title: A F R. Text in English. 19??. a. back issues avail. **Document type:** *Report, Trade.* **Description:** Provides statistics on opera company attendance, operating budgets, earned and unearned income, and the number of performances produced; notes trends in public and private giving, and lists world premiers and the 20 most-produced operas of the season.
Formerly (until 1998): Profile
Indexed: SRI.
Published by: Opera America, 330 Seventh Ave, New York, NY 10001. TEL 212-796-8620, FAX 212-796-8631, Info@operaamerica.org, http://www.operaamerica.org/.

780 792 USA
OPERA AMERICA. SEASON SCHEDULE OF PERFORMANCES. Text in English. 19??. a. **Document type:** *Database, Trade.* **Description:** Lists mainstage repertoire, performance dates, production teams, performance halls and seating capacities for all Opera America professional and intenational company members.
Formerly (until 1998): Opera America. Repertoire Survey
Indexed: MAG.
Published by: Opera America, 330 Seventh Ave, New York, NY 10001. TEL 212-796-8620, FAX 212-796-8631, Info@operaamerica.org.

782.1 CAN ISSN 0030-3577
ML5
OPERA - CANADA. Text in English. 1960. 4/yr. CAD 20 domestic to individuals; USD 20 foreign to individuals; CAD 30 domestic to institutions; USD 30 foreign to institutions; CAD 5.95 newsstand/cover (effective 2000). adv. bk.rev.; rec.rev. illus. back issues avail.; reprints avail. **Document type:** *Journal, Consumer.*
Related titles: Online - full text ed.
Indexed: A26, C03, CBCARef, CBPI, CMPI, CPerI, G05, G06, G07, G08, I05, IBT&D, IIMP, IIPA, M11, MusicInd, P48, PQC, RILM, T02.
—Ingenta.
Published by: Opera Canada Publications, 366 Adelaide St, Ste 434, Toronto, ON M5A 3X9, Canada. TEL 416-363-0395, FAX 416-363-0396. Ed. Wayne Gooding. R&P Robert Devrij. Adv. contact Robert de Vrij. Circ: 5,500.

782.81 USA
OPERA CUES. Text in English. q. **Description:** Covers the events of the Grand Houston Opera and other general opera news.
Published by: Walker Communications, 1014 Montrose Blvd., # D, Houston, TX 77019-4214. TEL 713-524-3560, FAX 713-524-3560.

782.1 USA ISSN 0891-3757
OPERA FANATIC; the magazine for lovers of expressive singing. Text in English. 1986. q. USD 20 domestic; USD 25 foreign.
Published by: Bel Canto Society, Inc., Department A, 85 Furniture Dr, Milford, CT 06460. TEL 212-877-5813, 800-347-5056, FAX 212-877-2792, http://www.belcantosociety.org/index.html.

782.1 USA ISSN 0030-3607
OPERA NEWS. Text in English. 1936. m. USD 31.95 domestic; USD 71.95 foreign (effective 2009). bk.rev.; music rev.; rec.rev.; tel.rev.; video rev. bibl.; illus. index. back issues avail. **Document type:** *Magazine, Consumer.* **Description:** Contains interviews with prominent singers and conductors, historical background articles, performance reviews worldwide, along with cast lists, photographs, and plot summaries for weekly Metropolitan Opera radio broadcasts.
Related titles: Microform ed.: (from PQC); Online - full text ed.: ISSN 1938-1506.

Indexed: A01, A02, A03, A08, A20, A22, A25, A26, A27, ABS&EES, ASCA, AmHI, ArtHuCI, B04, B05, B14, BRD, BRI, C05, CA, CBRI, CPerI, CurCont, E08, G05, G06, G07, G08, H07, H08, H09, H10, HAb, HumInd, I05, I07, IBT&D, IIMP, IIPA, M01, M02, M11, MAG, MASUSE, MLA-IB, MagInd, MusicInd, P02, P10, P13, P48, P53, P54, PMR, PQC, R03, R04, RASB, RGAb, RGPR, RILM, S08, S09, S23, SCOPUS, T02, W03, W05, W07.
—BLDSC (6267.500000), IE, Ingenta.
Published by: Metropolitan Opera Guild, Inc., 70 Lincoln Center Plaza, New York, NY 10023. TEL 212-769-7080, http://www.metguild.org/. Ed. F. Paul Driscoll. Adv. contact Sandra Ourusoff. Circ: 100,000 (paid).

782.1 GBR ISSN 0958-501X
ML1800
OPERA NOW; the most influential opera magazine in the world. Text in English. 1989. bi-m. GBP 34 domestic; GBP 44 in Europe; GBP 57 elsewhere; GBP 5.25 per issue (effective 2009). adv. bk.rev.; music rev.; rec.rev. back issues avail. **Document type:** *Magazine, Consumer.* **Description:** Provides an international perspective on the world of opera.
Indexed: IBT&D, IIMP, IIPA, M11, MLA-IB, MusicInd, RILM, T02.
—CCC.
Published by: Rhinegold Publishing Ltd., 239-241 Shaftesbury Ave, London, WC2H 8TF, United Kingdom. TEL 44-20-73331720, FAX 44-20-73331765, enquiries@rhinegold.co.uk. Ed. Ashutosh Khandekar. Adv. contact Neil Cording TEL 44-20-73331733.

780 USA ISSN 0736-0053
ML1699
➤ **THE OPERA QUARTERLY.** Text in English. 1983. q. GBP 144 in United Kingdom to institutions; EUR 207 in Europe to institutions; USD 215 in US & Canada to institutions; GBP 144 elsewhere to institutions; GBP 156 combined subscription in United Kingdom to institutions (print & online eds.); EUR 226 combined subscription in Europe to institutions (print & online eds.); USD 235 combined subscription in US & Canada to institutions (print & online eds.); GBP 156 combined subscription elsewhere to institutions (print & online eds.) (effective 2012). bk.rev.; rec.rev. illus. back issues avail.; reprint service avail. from PSC. **Document type:** *Journal, Academic/ Scholarly.* **Description:** Contains articles on all aspects of opera and operatic production.
Related titles: Online - full text ed.: ISSN 1476-2870. GBP 130 in United Kingdom to institutions; EUR 188 in Europe to institutions; USD 196 in US & Canada to institutions; GBP 130 elsewhere to institutions (effective 2012) (from IngentaConnect).
Indexed: A01, A02, A03, A08, A20, A22, A25, A26, A27, ABS&EES, ASCA, AmH&L, AmHI, ArtHuCI, B04, BRD, CA, CurCont, DIP, E01, E08, G08, H07, H08, HAb, HistAb, HumInd, I05, IBR, IBT&D, IBZ, IIMP, IIPA, M11, MAG, MLA-IB, MusicInd, P02, P10, P48, P53, P54, PCI, PQC, RASB, RILM, S08, S09, SCOPUS, T02, W03, W05, W07.
—BLDSC (6267.512000), IE, Infotrieve, Ingenta. **CCC.**
Published by: Oxford University Press (Subsidiary of: Oxford University Press), 2001 Evans Rd, Cary, NC 27513. TEL 919-677-0977, 800-445-9714, FAX 919-677-1303, http://www.us.oup.com. Ed. David J Levin. Adv. contact Linda Hann.

782.81 USA
OPERA TODAY. Text in English. 1986. 2/yr. looseleaf. adv. bk.rev.; music rev. 8 p./no.; **Document type:** *Newsletter.* **Description:** Presents information about American opera and tangential subjects.
Published by: Center for Contemporary Opera, Inc., PO Box 258, Island Station, New York, NY 10044-0205. TEL 212-308-6728, FAX 212-308-6744. Ed. Leonard Lehrman. Adv. contact Lorna Opatow TEL 212-421-4837. Circ: 20,000.

782.1 DNK ISSN 0900-6354
OPERABLADET ASCOLTA. Text in Danish. 1982. 8/yr. DKK 200 in Scandinavia membership; DKK 255 elsewhere (effective 2009). adv. music rev.; bk.rev. illus. back issues avail. **Document type:** *Magazine, Consumer.* **Description:** Information on opera events in Denmark and abroad.
Formerly (until 1983): Ascolta (0108-2124)
Published by: Operaens Venner, c/o Joergen Krisand, Toldbodgade 36 B, Copenhagen K, 1253, Denmark. TEL 45-44-987166, FAX 45-44-987188, http://www.ascolta.dk. Ed. J Krisand.

782.1 HUN ISSN 1215-6590
OPERAELET/OPERALIFE. Text in Hungarian. 1991. bi-m. HUF 1,600 domestic (effective 2008). adv. bk.rev. back issues avail. **Document type:** *Journal, Academic/Scholarly.* **Description:** Includes interviews with Hungarian and international opera singers, directors, conductors, essays about Hungarian opera life and opera lovers.
Indexed: IBT&D.
Published by: (Budapesti Operabarat Alapitvany), Kulkey Laszlo, c/o Szomory Gyorgy, Hajos u 19, Budapest, 1065, Hungary. TEL 36-1-3329544. Ed. Szomory Gyorgy. adv.: page HUF 100,000. Circ: 2,000.

782.1 USA
OPERANET. Text in English, French. irreg. adv. bk.rev. **Description:** Offers news, features, opera reviews, interviews of leading opera stars and directors.
Media: Online - full text.
Published by: Culture Kiosque Publications, Ltd., 164 Madison Ave, 5th Fl, New York, NY 10016-5411. Ed. Joel Kasow.

782.1 DEU ISSN 0935-6398
DAS OPERNGLAS. Text in German. 1980. m. EUR 6.50 newsstand/cover (effective 2007). adv. bk.rev.; rec.rev. **Document type:** *Magazine, Consumer.* **Description:** Features opera reviews, interviews, opera information, artist information and a calendar.
Published by: Opernglas Verlagsgesellschaft mbH, Grelckstr 36, Hamburg, 22529, Germany. TEL 49-40-585501, FAX 49-40-585505, opernglas@compuserve.com. Ed. Ralf Tiedemann. Pubs. Juergen Bartels, Michael Lehnert. Adv. contact Christine Muth. B&W page EUR 3,000, color page EUR 4,000. Circ: 9,000 (paid).

782.1 DEU ISSN 0030-3690
ML5
OPERNWELT; das internationale Opernmagazin. Text in German. 1959. m. EUR 137.60 domestic; EUR 155 foreign; EUR 95 to students; EUR 9.80 newsstand/cover (effective 2008). adv. illus. **Document type:** *Magazine, Consumer.*
Indexed: A22, DIP, IBR, IBZ, IIMP, IIPA, M11, MLA-IB, MusicInd, PCI, RASB, RILM.
—IE, Infotrieve. **CCC.**
Published by: Friedrich Berlin Verlagsgesellschaft mbH, Knesebeckstr 59-61, Berlin, 10719, Germany. TEL 49-30-25449520, FAX 49-30-25449512, verlag@friedrichberlin.de, http://www.friedrich-berlin.de. Eds. Bernd Feuchtner, Stefan Moesch. Adv. contact Marion Schamuthe TEL 49-30-25449510. B&W page EUR 3,000, color page EUR 3,810; trim 215 x 276. Circ: 10,000 (controlled).

782.81 POL ISSN 1642-8463
OPEROMANIA. Text in Polish. 2000. m.
Indexed: RILM.
Published by: Teatr Wielki im. Stanislawa Moniuszki w Poznaniu, ul Fredry 9, Poznan, Poland. TEL 48-61-8528291, FAX 48-61-8527464, opera@info.com.pl, http://www.opera.poznan.pl.

780 GBR
OPPROBRIUM. Text in English. irreg.
Address: c/o Nick Cain, 15a West Bank, London, N16 5DG, United Kingdom.

780 BRA ISSN 1517-7017
OPUS. Text in Portuguese. 1999. a. **Document type:** *Monographic series, Academic/Scholarly.*
Published by: Associacao Nacional de Pesquisa e Pos-Graduacao em Musica, Ave Papa Pio XII 199, Apto 72, Campinas, SP 13070-091, Brazil. anppom@iar.unicamp.br. Ed. Maria Lucia Senna Pascoal.

787 CAN ISSN 1494-9393
ML5
OPUS (MISSISSAUGA); Canada's essential jazz and classical music source. Text in English. 1978. 4/yr. CAD 20 domestic; USD 30 foreign (effective 2006). **Document type:** *Magazine, Consumer.* **Description:** Presents news on composers, musicians and their recorded works in Canada and on the international stage.
Former titles (until 1999): Classical Music Magazine (1185-9717); (until 1991): Music Magazine (0705-4009); Which incorporated (in 1987): R C M Bulletin (0820-4578); Which was formerly (until 1986): ConNotes (0227-8693); (until 1974): Royal Conservatory of Music. Bulletin (0495-8977); (1950-1965): Royal Conservatory of Music of Toronto. Monthly Bulletin (0319-2326)
Indexed: C03, CBCARef, CMPI, IIMP, M11, MusicInd, P48, PQC, RILM, T02.
—BLDSC (6276.708000), Ingenta.
Published by: Warwick Publishing, 161 Frederick St, Toronto, ON M5A 4P3, Canada. TEL 416-596-1555, FAX 416-596-1520, http://www.warwickgp.com.

780.7 CAN ISSN 0846-3085
OPUS (REGINA). Text in English. 1953. q. free. adv. **Document type:** *Newsletter.* **Description:** Includes reports from various branches of the provincial association on activities and competitions, and reports and information from associated agencies.
Indexed: CMPI, RILM.
Published by: Saskatchewan Registered Music Teachers' Association, 94 Green Meadow Rd, Regina, SK S4V 0A8, Canada. TEL 306-376-2054. Ed., R&P, Adv. contact Lore Ruschiensky. Circ: 350.

780 CZE ISSN 0862-8505
OPUS MUSICUM. Text in Czech. 1969. 6/yr. CZK 45 newsstand/cover (effective 2006). adv. bk.rev.; music rev. illus. back issues avail. **Document type:** *Journal.* **Description:** Contains musicological studies, interviews and reviews of books and CDs.
Indexed: M11, MusicInd, RILM.
Published by: Opus Musicum Foundation, Krkoskova 45a, Brno, 61300, Czech Republic. TEL 420-725-593460, FAX 42-5-542218272, opus.musicum@post.cz, http://www.czechia.com/opusmusicum. Ed. Martin Flasar. Circ: 1,500.

780 DEU
ORBIS MUSICARUM. Text in German. 1987. irreg., latest vol.123, 2010. price varies. **Document type:** *Monographic series, Academic/ Scholarly.*
Published by: Cuvillier Verlag, Nonnenstieg 8, Goettingen, 37075, Germany. TEL 49-551-547240, FAX 49-551-5472421, info@cuvillier.de.

ORBIT MAGAZINE. *see* LEISURE AND RECREATION

785 DEU ISSN 0030-4468
ML5
DAS ORCHESTER; Zeitschrift fuer deutsche Orchesterkultur und Rundfunk-Chorwesen. Text in German. 1953. 11/yr. EUR 78; EUR 9.50 newsstand/cover (effective 2011). adv. bk.rev. bibl.; charts; illus. index. **Document type:** *Magazine, Consumer.*
Indexed: A22, DIP, IBR, IBZ, IIMP, M11, MusicInd, P30, RASB, RILM.
—BLDSC (6277.925000), IE, Infotrieve, Ingenta.
Published by: (Deutsche Orchestervereinigung), Schott Musik International GmbH, Weihergarten 5, Mainz, 55116, Germany. TEL 49-6131-2460, FAX 49-6131-246211, info@schott-musik.de, http://www.schott-musik.de. Eds. Gerald Mertens, Ulrich Ruhnke. Adv. contact Dieter Schwarz. Circ: 19,700 (paid and controlled).

780 AUS ISSN 1832-4533
ORCHESTRAL OUTLOOK. Text in English. 1993. 3/yr. free to members (effective 2009). adv. **Document type:** *Magazine, Trade.* **Description:** Presents industry news, updates, and articles for and about Australian Orchestras.
Formerly (until 2003): Toan Newsletter
Published by: Orchestras of Australian Network, PO Box 20223, World Square, NSW 2002, Australia. TEL 61-2-83333719, FAX 61-2-83331678, services@orchestrasaustralia.org.au.

785 CAN ISSN 1705-2807
ORCHESTRAS CANADA. MEMBERSHIP DIRECTORY/ANNUAIRE CANADIEN DES ORCHESTRES ET ENSEMBLES MUSICAUX. Text in English, French. 1976. a. CAD 26; CAD 35 foreign (effective 1999). **Document type:** *Directory, Trade.* **Description:** Current list of orchestra personnel.
Former titles (until 2002): Canadian Orchestras, Ensembles, Music Organizations Directory (1701-9818); (until 2001): Canadian Orchestras, Small Ensembles, Music Organizations Directory (1486-4150); (until 1998): Directory of Canadian Orchestras and Small Ensembles (1483-7110); (until 1996): Directory of Canadian Orchestras and Youth Orchestras (0705-6249)
Published by: Orchestras Canada/Orchestres Canada, 56 The Esplanade, Ste 311, Toronto, ON M5E 1A7, Canada. TEL 416-366-8834, FAX 416-366-1780. R&P Madeline Fiala.

780 USA ISSN 0095-2613
ML1
➤ **THE ORFF ECHO.** Text in English. 1968. 4/yr. USD 90 membership (effective 2005). adv. bk.rev. **Document type:** *Journal, Academic/ Scholarly.*
Indexed: IIMP, M11, MAG, MusicInd, RILM, T02.
—Ingenta.
Published by: American Orff-Schulwerk Association, 3105 Lincoln Blvd, Cleveland, OH 44118-2035. TEL 216-321-7573, FAX 216-321-1946, bxfn94b@prodigy.com. Ed. Carlos Abril. Circ: 5,100.

786.6 GBR ISSN 0030-4883
THE ORGAN; review for its makers, its players and its lovers. Text in English. 1921. q. GBP 24 domestic to individuals; GBP 34 foreign to individuals; GBP 12 to students (effective 2009). adv. rec.rev.; bk.rev.; music rev. charts; illus.; stat. 60 p./no. 3 cols./p.; back issues avail. **Document type:** *Magazine, Consumer.* **Description:** Contains articles on new and historic instruments worldwide, organists, composers, festivals and competitions, along with reviews of concerts, recordings, books and new music.
Related titles: Microfilm ed.: (from WMP); Online - full text ed.
Indexed: A01, A20, A22, IIMP, M11, MusicInd, P30, PCI, RILM, T02.
—IE, Infotrieve, Ingenta.
Published by: Musical Opinion Ltd., 453 Battle Rd, St.Leonards-on-sea, E Sussex TN37 7BB, United Kingdom. Adv. contact Gordon Roland-Adams TEL 44-20-89718451.

786.6 DEU ISSN 1435-7941
ORGAN; Journal fuer die Orgel. Text in German. 1998. q. EUR 42; EUR 33 to students; EUR 9.90 newsstand/cover (effective 2011). adv. **Document type:** *Journal, Academic/Scholarly.*
Indexed: RILM.
Published by: Schott Musik International GmbH, Weihergarten 5, Mainz, 55116, Germany. TEL 49-6131-2460, FAX 49-6131-246211, info@schott-musik.de, http://www.schott-musik.de. Ed. Wolfram Adolph. Adv. contact Dieter Schwarz. Circ: 5,500 (paid and controlled).

786 USA ISSN 1943-6912
ML549.8
ORGAN ATLAS. Text in English. 1956. a. free to members (effective 2010); includes subscr. to: Tracker. adv. illus. back issues avail. **Document type:** *Proceedings, Trade.*
Former titles (until 2006): Annual Organ Handbook (0882-2085); (until 1983): Organ Historical Society. Annual National Convention (0148-3099)
Related titles: Online - full text ed.
Indexed: A01, IIMP, M11, MusicInd, P18, T02.
Published by: Organ Historical Society, Inc., PO Box 26811, Richmond, VA 23261. TEL 804-353-9226, FAX 804-353-9266, mail@organsociety.org, http://www.organsociety.org. Adv. contact Rollin Smith TEL 516-334-2789.

786.5 AUS ISSN 1832-8725
ORGAN AUSTRALIA. Text in English. 2005. q. AUD 44 domestic to non-members; AUD 60 foreign to non-members; free to members (effective 2009). back issues avail. **Document type:** *Journal, Trade.* **Description:** Provides information about pipe organ, its history, its music and its players, all those who are separated geographically by the vastness of Australia.
Formed by the merger of (1991-2005): Organ Voice (1037-6984); Which was formerly (until 1991): Organ Society of Queensland. Newsletter (1031-3273); (1999-2005): Organo Pleno (1442-1186); Which was formerly (until 1998): Victorian Organ Journal (0310-4834)
Published by: The Society of Organists, PO Box 315, Camberwell, VIC 3124, Australia. TEL 61-3-95292043, FAX 61-3-95290564, president@sov.org.au, http://www.sov.org.au. Ed. Bruce Steele TEL 61-3-98172151.

786.5 CAN ISSN 1486-2492
ORGAN CANADA. Text in English. 1978. q. CAD 30 domestic; CAD 40 foreign (effective 2005). adv. **Document type:** *Journal, Academic/ Scholarly.*
Former titles (until 1997): R C C O Newsletter (1204-122X); (until 1995): Royal Canadian College of Organists. Newsletter (0829-4291); (until 1985): Royal Canadian College of Organists. College Newsletter (0826-2950); (until 1983): Stretto (0710-6440)
Indexed: CMPI.
Published by: Royal Canadian College of Organists, 204 St. George St, Ste 202, Toronto, ON M5R 2N5, Canada. TEL 416-929-6400, FAX 416-929-2265, http://www.rcco.ca. adv.: B&W page CAD 400; 7.5 x 9.875.

786 GBR ISSN 0306-0357
ORGAN CLUB JOURNAL. Text in English. 1964. 3/yr. free to members (effective 2009). bk.rev. **Document type:** *Journal, Trade.*
Indexed: RILM.
Published by: Organ Club, c/o Mark D. Jameson, 92 The Hawthorns, Charvil, Reading, RG10 9TS, United Kingdom. http://www.organclub.org. Ed. Richard Blanch. **Subscr. to:** James Treloar.

786 USA ISSN 0193-6670
M6
THE ORGAN PORTFOLIO. Text in English. 1937. bi-m. USD 39.95 domestic; USD 44.95 in Canada; USD 75.95 elsewhere (effective 2008). 32 p./no.; **Document type:** *Magazine, Consumer.* **Description:** Features a balanced variety of music ranging from moderately easy to moderately difficult, meeting the needs of the trained organist.
Published by: Lorenz Publishing Co., 501 E 3rd St, Box 802, Dayton, OH 45402. TEL 937-228-6118, 800-444-1144, FAX 937-223-2042, info@lorenz.com, http://www.lorenz.com. Ed. Dorothy Wells.

780 GBR ISSN 1355-7718
ML1379
➤ **ORGANISED SOUND**; an international journal of music and technology. Text in English. 1996. 3/yr. (Plus an annual CD). GBP 166, USD 292 to institutions; GBP 171, USD 306 combined subscription to institutions (print & online eds.) (effective 2012). adv. bk.rev. back issues avail.; reprint service avail. from PSC. **Document type:** *Journal, Academic/Scholarly.* **Description:** Covers methods and issues arising from the use of contemporary technology in fields such as multimedia, performance art, sound sculpture and electroacoustic composition.
Related titles: CD-ROM ed.; Online - full text ed.: ISSN 1469-8153. GBP 153, USD 274 to institutions (effective 2012).

Indexed: A20, A22, ArtHuCI, CA, E01, IIMP, M11, MusicInd, P17, P48, P53, P54, PQC, RILM, T02, W07.
—BLDSC (6289.793000), IE, Infotrieve, Ingenta. **CCC.**
Published by: Cambridge University Press, The Edinburgh Bldg, Shaftesbury Rd, Cambridge, CB2 8RU, United Kingdom. TEL 44-1223-312393, FAX 44-1223-315052, journals@cambridge.org, http://www.cambridge.org/uk. Ed. Leigh Landy. R&P Linda Nicol TEL 44-1223-325702. Adv. contact Rebecca Roberts TEL 44-1223-325083. page GBP 365, page USD 695. Circ: 400. **Subscr. to:** Cambridge University Press, 32 Ave of the Americas, New York, NY 10013. TEL 212-337-5000, FAX 212-691-3239, journals_subscriptions@cup.org.

786 USA ISSN 1931-6178
M6
THE ORGANIST; the service music companion for the church organist. Text in English. 1897. bi-m. USD 39.95 domestic; USD 44.95 in Canada; USD 75.95 elsewhere (effective 2008). 32 p./no.; **Document type:** *Magazine, Consumer.* **Description:** Provides arrangements of classics, hymns, gospel songs and original works by today's leading composers, along with helpful editorial comments on performance hints and historical information.
Published by: Lorenz Publishing Co., 501 E 3rd St, Box 802, Dayton, OH 45402. TEL 937-228-6118, 800-444-1144, FAX 937-223-2042, info@lorenz.com, http://www.lorenz.com. Ed. Gilbert M Martin. R&P Joe Sengl.

786.5 ITA
ORGANISTICA. Text in Italian. 1992. bi-m. EUR 45 (effective 2008). adv. **Document type:** *Magazine, Consumer.*
Published by: Casa Musicale Edizioni Carrara, Via Ambrogio Calepio 4, Bergamo, BG 24125, Italy. TEL 39-035-243618, FAX 39-035-270298, http://www.edizionicarrara.it.

786.5 GBR ISSN 0048-2161
ML549.8
➤ **ORGANISTS' REVIEW.** Text in English. 1913. q. GBP 24.10 domestic to non-members; GBP 29 in Europe; GBP 35 elsewhere; GBP 22.10 domestic to members (effective 2009). adv. bk.rev.; rec.rev.; music rev. reprints avail. **Document type:** *Journal, Academic/Scholarly.* **Description:** Contents include articles. commentary and educational items on: pipe organs; organ music, composer and builders. Reviews of organ and choral CDs and published music.
Related titles: Microform ed.: (from PQC); Online - full text ed.: GBP 24.10 (effective 2009).
Indexed: A01, A22, CA, IIMP, M11, MusicInd, RILM, T02.
—Ingenta.
Published by: Incorporated Association of Organists (IAO), c/o Jane Beeson, Rose Cottage, Brigg Rd, South Kelsey, Market Rasen, Lincolnshire LN7 6PQ, United Kingdom. TEL 44-1652-678230, FAX 44-1652-678230. Ed. Sarah Beedle. Adv. contact Jane Beeson. page GBP 395; 210 x 297.

786 ITA ISSN 0474-6376
ML5
L'ORGANO; rivista di cultura organaria e organistica. Text in Italian. 1960. a. EUR 50 domestic; EUR 68 foreign (effective 2009). bibl. back issues avail. **Document type:** *Magazine, Trade.* **Description:** Reviews research into the field of organ technique and history, and organ music history and interpretation.
Indexed: DIP, IBR, IBZ, M11, MusicInd, RILM.
Published by: Patron Editore, Via Badini 12, Quarto Inferiore, BO 40050, Italy. TEL 39-051-767003, FAX 39-051-768252, info@patroneditore.com, http://www.patroneditore.com. Ed. Luigi Tagliavini.

786.5 ITA
L'ORGANO NELLA LITURGIA. Text in English. 1919. bi-m. EUR 45 (effective 2008). adv. **Document type:** *Magazine, Consumer.*
Published by: Casa Musicale Edizioni Carrara, Via Ambrogio Calepio 4, Bergamo, BG 24125, Italy. TEL 39-035-243618, FAX 39-035-270298, http://www.edizionicarrara.it.

781.71 NLD ISSN 0166-0101
➤ **HET ORGEL.** Text in Dutch. 1886. bi-m. EUR 60 domestic; EUR 70 in Europe; EUR 75 elsewhere (effective 2009); includes NotaBene. adv. music rev. bibl.; illus. back issues avail. **Document type:** *Journal, Academic/Scholarly.* **Description:** Publishes scholarly articles on pipe organ music improvisation and the building and restoration of pipe organs.
Related titles: Online - full text ed.; ◆ Supplement(s): NotaBene. ISSN 1876-2921.
Indexed: RILM.
Published by: Koninklijke Vereniging van Organisten en Kerkmusici, Klipper 49, Zuidhorn, 9801 MT, Netherlands. ledenadministratieknov@hetorgel.nl, http://www.kvok.nl. Ed. Jan Smelik. adv.: B&W page EUR 481; 180 x 245. Circ: 1,800.

786.5 SWE ISSN 0280-0047
ORGELFORUM. Text in Swedish. 1979. q. SEK 250 domestic membership; SEK 350 foreign membership; SEK 150 to students (effective 2007). adv. back issues avail. **Document type:** *Magazine, Trade.*
Indexed: RILM.
Published by: Svenska Orgelsaellskapet, c/o Jan Cedmark, Praestgaardsaengen 2, Goeteborg, 41271, Sweden. jan.cedmark@swipnet.se. Ed. Dag Edholm. adv.: page SEK 2,670.

786.5 NLD ISSN 1386-1417
ML549.8
DE ORGELVRIEND. Text in Dutch. 1959. m. (11/yr.). EUR 49 (effective 2008). adv. **Document type:** *Magazine, Consumer.*
Published by: Boekencentrum Uitgevers, Goudstraat 50, Postbus 29, Zoetermeer, 2700 AA, Netherlands. TEL 31-79-3615481, FAX 31-79-3615489, info@boekencentrum.nl, http://www.boekencentrum.nl. Ed. Gerco Schaap. adv.: B&W page EUR 400, color page EUR 500; trim 210 x 297. Circ: 3,500.

786.6 DNK ISSN 0106-1011
ORGLET. Text in Danish. 1971. s-a. adv. bk.rev. bibl.; illus. cum.index every 5 yrs. back issues avail. **Document type:** *Magazine, Trade.*
Indexed: RILM.
Published by: Det Danske Orgelselskab, c/o Hans Joergen Oestergaard, PO Box 78, Maribo, 4930, Denmark. TEL 45-54-786378, FAX 45-54-786379, domorganist.maribo@mail.dk, http://www.orgelselskabet.dk. Ed. Bent C Van TEL 45-36-300388.

786.6 FRA ISSN 0030-5170
ML5
L'ORGUE; histoire-technique-esthetique-musique. Text in French. 1929. q. EUR 65 domestic to individuals; EUR 72 in Europe to individuals; EUR 80 elsewhere to individuals; EUR 36 domestic to students; EUR 43 in Europe to students; EUR 51 elsewhere to students (effective 2009). adv. bk.rev. bibl.; charts; illus. **Document type:** *Journal.*
Formerly (until 1939): Amis de l'Orgue. Bulletin Trimestriel (0398-8082)
Related titles: ◆ Supplement(s): L' Orgue Dossier. ISSN 1149-6851.
Indexed: RILM.
Published by: (Association des Amis de l'Orgue), Symetrie, 30 Rue Jean-Baptiste Say, Lyon, 69001, France. TEL 33-4-78295214, FAX 33-4-78300111, contact@symetrie.com.

786.6 FRA ISSN 1149-6851
L'ORGUE DOSSIER. Text in French. 1981. irreg.
Related titles: ◆ Supplement to: L' Orgue. ISSN 0030-5170.
Published by: Symetrie, 30 Rue Jean-Baptiste Say, Lyon, 69001, France.

780 FRA ISSN 0985-3642
ML574
L'ORGUE FRANCOPHONE. Text in French. 1986. s-m. **Document type:** *Magazine, Consumer.*
Indexed: RILM.
Published by: Federation Francophone des Amis de l'Orgue, 21 Rue de la Liberte, Saint Jean de Losne, 21170, France. http://www.ffao.com.

781.64 DEU ISSN 1863-5350
ORKUS. Text in German. 10/yr. EUR 49.90 domestic; EUR 77.90 in Europe; EUR 119 elsewhere (effective 2010). adv. **Document type:** *Magazine, Consumer.*
Related titles: Online - full text ed.
Published by: Zoomia Medien Gruppe Claus Mueller, Im Buhles 4, Glashuetten/Taunus, 61479, Germany. TEL 49-6174-961368, FAX 49-6174-2577743. Pub., Adv. contact Claus Mueller. B&W page EUR 3,790. Circ: 40,000 (paid).

780 DEU ISSN 0932-6111
ORPHEUS. Text in German. 1972. 13/yr. adv. play rev.; bk.rev. index. back issues avail. **Document type:** *Magazine, Consumer.*
Indexed: RASB.
Published by: Neue Gesellschaft fuer Musikinformation mbH, Ritterstr 11, Berlin, 10969, Germany. TEL 49-30-6146840, FAX 49-30-6146865. Ed. Geerd Heinsen. Circ: 12,000.

780 FRA ISSN 1251-3369
OSTINATO RIGORE. Text in French. 1994. s-a. **Document type:** *Magazine, Consumer.*
Indexed: RILM.
Published by: Editions Jean-Michel Place, 3 rue Lhomond, Paris, 75005, France. TEL 33-1-44320590, FAX 33-1-44320591, place@jmplace.com, http://www.jeanmichelplace.com. Ed. Jean Claude Teboul.

781.542 CAN
OTTAWA X PRESS; the capital's newsweekly. Text in English. 1993. w. CAD 115 (effective 1997); free in Ottawa. adv. bk.rev.; dance rev.; film rev.; play rev.; tel.rev. 36 p./no. 5 cols./p.; back issues avail. **Document type:** *Newspaper, Consumer.* **Description:** Arts and entertainment listings with alternative news, reviews and interviews for a primarily urban readership from 18 to 55 years of age.
Related titles: Online - full text ed.
Published by: Ottawa X Press Publishing Inc., 69 Sparks St, Ottawa, ON K1P 5A5, Canada. TEL 613-237-8226, FAX 613-232-9055. Ed. Dereck Raymaker. Pubs. Jim Creskey, Ross Dickson. Adv. contact Bill Scott. Circ: 38,500.

780.42 USA ISSN 1542-1309
ML3533.8
OUTBURN; subversive and post alternative. Text in English. 1996. 5/yr. USD 9.95 domestic; USD 22.95 in Canada; USD 3.95 newsstand/cover (effective 2008). adv. music rev. back issues avail. **Document type:** *Magazine, Consumer.* **Description:** Dedicated to the underground music culture within the realms of industrial, gothic, ethereal, and electronic.
Address: PO Box 3187, Thousand Oaks, CA 91359-0187. Eds. Octavia Laird, Rodney Kusano. Pub. Rodney Kusano. Adv. contact Octavia Laird. page USD 825; trim 8.75 x 11.75. Circ: 8,000.

780 CAN
OVERTURE. Text in English. 9/yr. free. adv. back issues avail. **Description:** Provides information on the activities, repertoire, artists and composers featured in the orchestra's annual season.
Published by: Winnipeg Symphony Orchestra, 101 555 Main St, Winnipeg, MB R3B 1C3, Canada. TEL 204-949-3950, FAX 204-956-4271. Ed. Geoffrey Hayes. Adv. contact Carol Cassels. Circ: 14,000 (controlled).

780 USA ISSN 0885-3347
MT125
OVERTURE (BALTIMORE). Text in English. 1977. 5/yr. free. adv. **Description:** Covers news, upcoming events and interviews with guest artists and members of the Baltimore Symphony Orchestra.
Published by: Baltimore Symphony Orchestra, Inc., 1212 Cathedral St, Baltimore, MD 21201-5545. TEL 410-783-8100, FAX 410-783-8077, TELEX 87770 BAL. Ed. Jan Bedell. Circ: 40,000.

780 331.8 USA ISSN 0030-7556
ML1
OVERTURE (LOS ANGELES). Text in English. 1919. m. free membership (effective 2005). adv. charts; illus. **Document type:** *Newspaper, Trade.*
Indexed: M11, P34, T02.
Published by: Professional Musicians, Local 47 of A.F.M., 817 N Vine St, Los Angeles, CA 90038. TEL 213-462-2161, FAX 213-461-3090. Ed., R&P Serena Kay Williams. Pub. John McManan. Adv. contact Terri Markham. Circ: 10,000 (paid).

OVERZICHT VAN DE GEZANGEN. *see* RELIGIONS AND THEOLOGY

780.43 NLD ISSN 1879-5668
OVHO. Variant title: Orkest van het Oosten. Text in Dutch. 1983. 4/yr. EUR 35 (effective 2010). illus. back issues avail. **Document type:** *Magazine, Consumer.* **Description:** Includes information on the concert programmes and repertoire of the Netherlands Symphony Orchestra.
Formerly (until 2009): Podium (1386-0402)
Indexed: MLA-IB.
Published by: Orkest van het Oosten, Van Essengaarde 10, Enschede, 7511 PN, Netherlands. TEL 31-53-4878700, FAX 31-53-4342339, info@orkestvanhetoosten.nl, http://www.orkestvanhetoosten.nl.

781.64 DEU
OX FANZINE. Text in German. 1989. q. EUR 25 domestic; EUR 30 foreign (effective 2006). adv. bk.rev.; film rev.; music rev.; video rev. 160 p./no.; back issues avail. **Document type:** *Magazine, Consumer.* **Description:** Covers the local and international punk rock scenes.
Published by: Ox-Fanzine, Postfach 102225, Haan, 42766, Germany. TEL 49-2104-810828, FAX 49-2104-810830. Pub. Joachim Hiller. Circ: 13,500.

780 GBR
OXFORD MONOGRAPHS ON MUSIC. Text in English. 19??. irreg., latest 2006. price varies. back issues avail. **Document type:** *Monographic series, Academic/Scholarly.*
Published by: Oxford University Press, Great Clarendon St, Oxford, OX2 6DP, United Kingdom. TEL 44-1865-556767, FAX 44-1865-556646, enquiry@oup.co.uk, http://www.oup-usa.org/catalogs/general/series/. **Orders in N. America to:** Oxford University Press, 2001 Evans Rd, Cary, NC 27513. TEL 919-677-0977 ext 5777, 800-852-7323, FAX 919-677-1714, jnlorders@oup-usa.org, http://www.us.oup.com.

780 GBR ISSN 0078-7264
OXFORD STUDIES OF COMPOSERS. Text in English. 19??. irreg., latest 1997. price varies. back issues avail. **Document type:** *Monographic series, Academic/Scholarly.*
Published by: Oxford University Press, Great Clarendon St, Oxford, OX2 6DP, United Kingdom. TEL 44-1865-556767, FAX 44-1865-556646, enquiry@oup.co.uk, http://www.oup-usa.org/catalogs/general/series/.

781.64 USA
OZONE MAGAZINE. Text in English. 2002. 11/yr. USD 11; USD 3.99 newsstand/cover (effective 2006). adv. **Document type:** *Magazine, Consumer.* **Description:** Covers all aspects of southern hip-hop music and culture.
Published by: Ozone Magazine, Inc., 1516 E Colonial Dr, Ste 205, Orlando, FL 32803. TEL 407-447-6063, FAX 407-447-6064. adv.: page USD 3,480; trim 8.375 x 10.875. Circ: 50,000 (paid and controlled).

P A J; a journal of performance and art. (Performing Arts Journal) *see* THEATER

780.7 USA ISSN 0030-8102
ML27.U5
P M E A NEWS; the official journal of the Pennsylvania Music Educators Association. Text in English. 1952. 4/yr. USD 16 (effective 2005). adv. bk.rev. charts; illus. index. 80 p./no.; back issues avail. **Document type:** *Magazine, Trade.* **Description:** Contains information pertinent to music educators and music education.
Indexed: MAG.
—Ingenta.
Published by: Pennsylvania Music Educators Association, Inc., 101 S Fourth St, Hamburg, PA 19526. TEL 610-436-9281, http://www.pmea.net. Ed. David Weiss. adv.: B&W page USD 315, color page USD 685. Circ: 58,000.

780 USA ISSN 0030-8153
P M O NOTES. Text in English. 1943. q. free. illus. **Document type:** *Newsletter.* **Description:** Features articles and pictures on recent events, including musical shows, concerts, tours and student organization activities.
Media: Duplicated (not offset).
Published by: Purdue University Musical Organizations, Edward C Elliott Hall of Music, W, Lafayette, IN 47907-1093. TEL 317-494-3941. Ed. Kitty Campbell Laird. Pub. Brian Breed. Circ: 8,500.

780 GBR ISSN 0964-9875
P R S MEMBERS HANDBOOK. Text in English. 1991. irreg. free to members (effective 2010). **Document type:** *Bulletin, Trade.*
Published by: Performing Right Society Ltd., Copyright House, 29-33 Berners St, London, W1T 3AB, United Kingdom. TEL 44-20-75805544, FAX 44-20-73064455, http://www.prsformusic.com.

780 USA ISSN 2151-7045
ML1
➤ **PACIFIC REVIEW OF ETHNOMUSICOLOGY (ONLINE).** Text in English; Text occasionally in Portuguese, Spanish. 1984. a. free (effective 2011). bk.rev.; music rev.; rec.rev.; video rev.; Website rev. back issues avail. **Document type:** *Journal, Academic/Scholarly.* **Description:** Contains articles on substantive ethnographic research, and reviews of recently released books, audiovisual recordings, websites, theses and dissertations on ethnomusicology.
Formerly (until 2006): Pacific Review of Ethnomusicology (Print) (1096-1291)
Indexed: MLA-IB.
Published by: University of California, Los Angeles, Department of Ethnomusicology, 2539 Schoenberg Music Bldg, Los Angeles, CA 90095. trice@arts.ucla.edu.

➤ **PALACE PEEPER.** *see* THEATER

780 POL
PAMIETNIKI MUZYCZNE. Text in Polish. 1983. irreg. price varies. adv. illus. **Description:** Contains memoirs of great artists.
Published by: Polskie Wydawnictwo Muzyczne, Al Krasinskiego 11 a, Krakow, 31111, Poland. TEL 48-12-4227044, FAX 48-12-4220174. Ed. Leszek Polony. R&P Janina Warzecha. Adv. contact Elzbieta Widlak.

780 USA ISSN 0889-7581
ML1
PAN PIPES. Text in English. 1909. q. USD 30 domestic to non-members; USD 35 foreign to non-members; USD 5 per issue to non-members; free to members (effective 2010). bk.rev.; music rev.; rec.rev. illus. back issues avail. **Document type:** *Journal, Academic/Scholarly.*
Formerly (until 1980): Pan Pipes of Sigma Alpha Iota (0031-0611)
Indexed: M11, MAG, MusicInd, T02.
—Ingenta.
Published by: Sigma Alpha Iota Philanthropies, Inc., 1 Tunnel Rd, Asheville, NC 28805. TEL 828-251-0606, FAX 828-251-0644, nh@sai-national.org. Ed. Heather Davis.

781.62 AUT
PANNONISCHE FORSCHUNGSSTELLE OBERSCHUETZEN. ARBEITSBERICHTE - MITTEILUNGEN. Text in German. 1990. a. bk.rev. **Document type:** *Proceedings, Academic/Scholarly.*
Description: Working papers on all aspects of the life and music of Johann Joseph Fux (1660-1741) as well as research in band music, wind instruments, and music publishing houses.
Published by: Pannonische Forschungsstelle Oberschuetzen, Hauptplatz 8, Oberschuetzen, B 7432, Austria. TEL 43-316-3893120, FAX 43-316-3893121, barbara.fueloep@kug.ac.at, http://www.kug.ac.at/studium/institut_12.shtml. Eds. Bernhard Habla, Thomas Hochradner. Circ: 500 (controlled).

PAPER (NEW YORK). *see* CLOTHING TRADE—Fashions

781.64 GBR
PAPER BOAT; forum for Alisha's fanattics. Text in English. q. GBP 1 per issue domestic; GBP 1.50 per issue in Europe; GBP 2 per issue elsewhere. **Document type:** *Newsletter.* **Description:** News, pictures, exclusives and articles for and by fans of the band Alisha's Attic.
Address: 3 Willow Rd, Blaydon, Tyne & Wea NE21 5BB, United Kingdom. Ed. Alan Sawyers.

PARTYSAN. *see* LIFESTYLE

781.62 USA
PASS IT ON! (EVANSTON). Text in English. 1987. 2/yr. free to members (effective 2006). music rev. illus. 44 p./no. 2 cols./p.; **Document type:** *Newsletter, Consumer.* **Description:** Profiles notable writers and performers of songs for children; contains scores for children and adults who love to be with them to sing.
Published by: Children's Music Network, PO Box 1341, Evanston, IL 60204-1341. TEL 847-733-8003, office@cmnonline.org. Ed. Susan Keniston.

PAST TIMES: THE NOSTALGIA ENTERTAINMENT NEWSLETTER. *see* MOTION PICTURES

781.62 FRA ISSN 0996-4878
PASTEL. Text in French. 1989. q. EUR 11.80 (effective 2009). **Document type:** *Magazine, Consumer.*
Indexed: RILM.
Published by: Conservatoire Occitan, CMDT Toulouse Midi-Pyrenees, 5 Rue du Pont de Tounis, Toulouse, 31000, France. TEL 33-5-34512838, FAX 33-5-61421259, contact@conservatoire-occitan.org.

782.3 USA ISSN 1946-9586
PASTORAL LITURGY. Text in English. 1970. bi-m. USD 24 domestic; USD 32 foreign (effective 2009). adv. Index. back issues avail. **Document type:** *Magazine, Consumer.* **Description:** Provides guidance for liturgy preparation, faith formation, liturgical art and architecture, and the many areas of parish ministry that flow from the liturgy to witness the Gospel and build the kingdom of God.
Former titles (until 2008): Rite (1931-8634); (until 2000): Liturgy 90 (1046-9990); (until 1990): Liturgy 80 (1040-6603); (until 1980): Liturgy 70
Indexed: CPL.
Published by: (Archdiocese of Chicago), Liturgy Training Publications, 1800 N Hermitage Ave, Chicago, IL 60622. TEL 773-579-4900, 800-933-1800, FAX 773-486-7094, 800-933-7094, orders@ltp.org, http://www.ltp.org. Ed. Mary Fox TEL 773-579-4900 ext 3579.

783 USA ISSN 0363-6569
ML1
PASTORAL MUSIC. Text in English. 1976. bi-m. USD 52 domestic to individual members; USD 62 in Canada to individual members; USD 66 elsewhere to individual members; USD 7 per issue (effective 2005). adv. bk.rev. illus. 64 p./no.; back issues avail.; reprints avail. **Document type:** *Journal, Trade.* **Description:** Covers church music and liturgy, especially congregational singing.
Supersedes: Musart (0027-3724)
Related titles: Microfilm ed.: (from PQC); Online - full text ed.
Indexed: A22, CERDIC, CPL, IIMP, M11, MAG, MusicInd, RILM.
—Ingenta.
Published by: National Association of Pastoral Musicians, 962 Wayne Ave, Ste 210, Silver Spring, MD 20910-4461. TEL 202-723-5800, FAX 202-723-2262, NPMSING@npm.org. Pub. Dr. J Michael McMahon. R&P Gordon E Truitt. Adv. contact Ms. Nancy Bannister TEL 503-297-1212. Circ: 9,500. **Subscr. to:** PO Box 4207, Silver Spring, MD 20914-4207.

783 USA ISSN 0145-6636
ML2999
PASTORAL MUSIC NOTEBOOK. Text in English. 1977. bi-m. membership. 8 p./no.
Published by: National Association of Pastoral Musicians, 962 Wayne Ave, Ste 210, Silver Spring, MD 20910-4461. TEL 202-723-5800, FAX 202-723-2262, NPMSING@npm.org, http://www.npm.org. Ed. Gordon E Truitt. Circ: 8,500.

PEABODY MAGAZINE. *see* COLLEGE AND ALUMNI

787 USA ISSN 1088-7954
PEDAL STEEL NEWSLETTER. Text in English. 1973. 10/yr. USD 25 domestic; USD 30 foreign (effective 2001). adv. music rev.; rec.rev.; software rev.; video rev.; bk.rev. back issues avail. **Document type:** *Newsletter, Trade.* **Description:** Concerns the pedal steel guitar, how it is played, and those who play it.
Published by: Pedal Steel Guitar Association, Inc., PO Box 20248, Floral Park, NY 11002-0248. TEL 516-616-9214, FAX 516-616-9214. Ed. Doug Mack. R&P Bob Maickel. Adv. contact Darlene De Maille. Circ: 1,500 (paid).

781.71 USA ISSN 0272-9199
ML2999
PEDALPOINT. Text in English. 190?. q. price varies. back issues avail. **Document type:** *Magazine, Consumer.* **Description:** Provides keyboardists with eight fresh, new arrangements in varying degrees of difficulty each quarter for piano, organ and an occasional duet or multiple keyboard arrangement for some combination of piano, organ and synthesizer.
Published by: LifeWay Christian Resources, 1 Lifeway Plz, Nashville, TN 37234. TEL 615-251-2000, 800-458-2772, FAX 615-251-5933, customerservice@lifeway.com, http://www.lifeway.com.

780 USA
PEEL; stickers, stencils, street art. Text in English. q. USD 19.99 domestic; USD 49.99 foreign; USD 6.99 newsstand/cover domestic; USD 8.99 newsstand/cover foreign (effective 2007). **Document type:** *Magazine, Consumer.*
Related titles: Online - full text ed.
Published by: Wicked Style Productions, 1727 N. Collidge Ave, Indianapolis, IN 46219.

780 USA ISSN 1046-0292
ML200.7.P3
PENN SOUNDS. Text in English. 1989. q. looseleaf. USD 10 domestic; USD 15 foreign (effective 2002). adv. bk.rev. illus. index, cum.index: 1989-1996. back issues avail. **Document type:** *Journal, Trade.*
Description: Serves the needs and interests of Pennsylvania composers. Features articles on aesthetics, technical articles related to composition; lists Pennsylvania composer activities, and lists and reviews classical concerts featuring Pennsylvania composers. Comments on recent technical or social developments that affect the lines of composers.
Indexed: MAG, MusicInd.
Published by: Composer Services Inc., 345 S 19th St, Philadelphia, PA 19103. TEL 215-985-0963, FAX 215-985-0736, eh1958@voicenet.com. Eds. Elizabeth R Hewitt, Harry D. R&P Elizabeth R Hewitt. adv.: B&W page USD 50. Circ: 250.

780.6 USA
PEOPLE'S SONGLETTER. Text in English. 4/yr. membership.
Published by: Newsong Network, 61 Wurts St, Kingston, NY 12401. TEL 914-338-8587.

780 BRA ISSN 1517-7599
ML457
PER MUSI; revista de performance musical. Text in Portuguese, English. 2000. s-a. back issues avail. **Document type:** *Journal, Academic/Scholarly.*
Related titles: Online - full text ed.
Indexed: M11, RILM, T02.
Published by: Universidade Federal de Minas Gerais, Escola de Musica, Ave Antonio Carlos, 6627, Campus Pampulha, Belo Horizonte, MG 31270-901, Brazil. TEL 55-31-34994703, FAX 55-31-34994720, mestrado@musica.ufmg.br, http://www.ufmg.br/. Ed. Fausto Borem.

781.62 DEU
PERCUSSION CREATIV. Text in German. 1996. bi-m. EUR 50 membership (effective 2005). **Document type:** *Magazine, Consumer.*
Published by: Percussion Creativ e.V., Berliner Platz 10a, Nuernberg, 90489, Germany. TEL 49-911-2875781, FAX 49-911-2875725, office@percussion-creativ.de.

780 USA ISSN 1534-9764
ML1
PERCUSSION NEWS. Text in English. bi-m. USD 85; USD 55 to students (effective 2003); includes Percussive Notes. **Document type:** *Newsletter.*
Related titles: Online - full content ed.: USD 40; USD 25 to students (effective 2003).
Indexed: IIMP.
Published by: Percussive Arts Society, Inc., 701 NW Ferris Ave, Lawton, OK 73507-5442. TEL 580-353-1455, FAX 580-353-1456. Ed. Rick Mattingly. R&P, Adv. contact Teresa Peterson.

789 USA ISSN 0553-6502
ML1
PERCUSSIVE NOTES. Text in English. 1961. 6/yr. includes Percussion News. adv. bk.rev. illus. index, cum.index. 88 p./no.; reprints avail. **Document type:** *Magazine, Trade.*
Incorporates (in 1983): Percussive Notes. Research Edition (0749-1344); Which was formerly (until 1982): Percussive Notes. Research Edition, Percussionist (0749-1336); Which superseded in part (in 1980): Percussionist (0553-6499); Which incorporated: Percussionist and Percussive Notes (0031-5168)
Related titles: Microform ed.: (from PQC); Online - full content ed.: USD 40; USD 25 to students (effective 2003).
Indexed: A22, IIMP, M11, MAG, MusicInd, RILM, T02.
—BLDSC (6423.560000), IE, Ingenta.
Published by: Percussive Arts Society, Inc., 701 NW Ferris Ave, Lawton, OK 73507-5442. TEL 580-353-1455, FAX 580-353-1456, percarts@pas.org, http://www.pas.org. Circ: 7,000.

791.43 GBR ISSN 1038-2909
ML5
➤ **PERFECT BEAT.** Abbreviated title: P B. Text in English. 1992. s-a. USD 220 combined subscription in North America to institutions (print & online eds.); GBP 135 combined subscription elsewhere to institutions (print & online eds.) (effective 2012). adv. illus. back issues avail.; reprints avail. **Document type:** *Journal, Academic/Scholarly.*
Description: Focuses on the popular music of the 'Pacific rim' and includes historical and contemporary studies with contributions invited from popular music studies, musicology, cultural studies and ethnomusicological perspectives.
Related titles: Online - full text ed.: ISSN 1836-0343. USD 176 in North America to institutions; GBP 108 elsewhere to institutions (effective 2012).
Indexed: A01, CA, M11, MusicInd, RILM, T02.
—Ingenta. **CCC.**
Published by: Equinox Publishing Ltd., Unit S3, Kelham House, 3 Lancaster St, Sheffield, S6 3AF, United Kingdom. TEL 44-114-2725957, FAX 44-560-3459046, journals@equinoxpub.com, http://www.equinoxpub.com/. Eds. Denis Crowdy, Mark Evans. Adv. contact Val Hall.

780 USA
PERFECT SOUND FOREVER; online music magazine. Text in English. 1993. bi-m. free (effective 2006). **Document type:** *Magazine, Consumer.* **Description:** Contains information on unconventional music and unjustly overlooked artists. Also includes interviews, articles, tributes, book excerpts, and essays by writers and musicians.
Media: Online - full text.
Published by: Mentally Unsound Underground Alternatives, 105 E 24th St, Ste 4F, New York, NY 10010. Ed., Pub., R&P Jason Gross.

782.1 CAN
PERFORMANCE (CANADIAN OPERA COMPANY EDITION). Text in English. 1978. 3/yr. adv.
Formerly: Canadian Opera Company Magazine (0844-384X)
Indexed: CMPI.
Published by: St. Clair Group, 30 St Clair Ave W 805, Toronto, ON M4V 3A1, Canada. TEL 416-926-7595, FAX 416-926-0407.

▼ **PERFORMANCE AND SPIRITUALITY.** *see* THEATER

792 USA
PN2289
PERFORMANCE MAGAZINE. Text in English. 1971. a. USD 75 (effective 2004). adv. back issues avail. **Document type:** *Directory, Trade.*
Formerly: Performance Guide (0896-9973)
Indexed: IBT&D.
Published by: Performance Magazine, Inc., 1203 Lake St., Ste. 200, Fort Worth, TX 76102-4504. TEL 817-338-9444, FAX 817-877-4273, sales@performancemagazine.com. Ed. James Leasing. Pub. Rufus G Clay Jr.

780 USA
ML1
➤ **PERFORMANCE PRACTICE REVIEW (ONLINE).** Text in English. 1988. s-a. free (effective 2010). bk.rev. bibl. **Document type:** *Journal, Academic/Scholarly.* **Description:** Addresses the concerns of historically authentic performance.
Formerly (until 1997): Performance Practice Review (Print) (1044-1638)
Media: Online - full text.
Indexed: IIMP, MAG, MusicInd, PCI, RILM.
—Ingenta.
Published by: Claremont Graduate University, 150 E 10th St, Claremont, CA 91711. TEL 909-621-8000, http://www.cgu.edu. Ed. Robert Zappulla.

➤ **PERFORMANCE RESEARCH**; a journal of the performing arts. *see* THEATER

➤ **PERFORMANCES**; theatre program and lifestyle. *see* THEATER

➤ **PERFORMING ARTS AND ENTERTAINMENT IN CANADA.** *see* THEATER

▼ ➤ **PERFORMING ARTS YEARBOOK.** *see* THEATER

780 GBR ISSN 1755-5744
PERFORMING MUSICIAN PLUS LIVE SOUND WORLD. Text in English. 1987. m. GBP 24 combined subscription domestic (print & online eds.); GBP 35 combined subscription in Europe (print & online eds.); USD 60 combined subscription in North America (print & online eds.); GBP 45 combined subscription elsewhere (print & online eds.); GBP 3.50 per issue (effective 2009). adv. bk.rev. back issues avail. **Document type:** *Magazine, Consumer.* **Description:** Features product reviews of guitars, basses and keyboards.
Formerly (until 2007): Music Mart (0956-6619)
Related titles: Online - full text ed.: GBP 15, USD 22.50 (effective 2009).
—**CCC.**
Published by: S O S Publications Ltd., Media House, Trafalgar Way, Bar Hill, Cambridge, CB23 8SQ, United Kingdom. TEL 44-1954-789888, FAX 44-1954-789895, subscribe@soundonsound.com, http://www.soundonsound.com. Ed., Pub. Dave Lockwood.

782 USA ISSN 2162-2868
ML3469
PERFORMING SONGWRITER (ONLINE). Text in English. 1993. 8/yr. free (effective 2011). adv. **Document type:** *Magazine, Trade.*
Description: Provides songwriters of any musical genre with indepth interviews, regular columns and festival information.
Formerly (until 2009): Performing Songwriter (Print) (1068-9664)
Media: Online - full text.
Indexed: A01, IIMP, M11, MusicInd, T02.
Published by: Desktop Communications, PO Box 40931, Nashville, TN 37204.

780 USA ISSN 0898-8722
ML410.P29
PERGOLESI STUDIES/STUDI PERGOLESIANI. Text in English. 1986. irreg. price varies. **Document type:** *Monographic series, Trade.*
Related titles: ◆ Italian ed.: Studi Pergolesiani. ISSN 1826-8021.
Indexed: RILM.
Published by: Pendragon Press, PO Box 190, Hillsdale, NY 12529. TEL 518-325-6100, FAX 518-325-6102, orders@pendragonpress.com.

780 USA ISSN 0822-7594
PERIODICA MUSICA. Variant title: Repertoire International de la Presse Musicale du XIXe Siecle. Newsletter. Text in Multiple languages. 1983. a. **Document type:** *Journal.*
Indexed: CMPI, RILM.
—Ingenta.
Published by: University of Maryland, Center for Studies in Nineteenth Century Music, 2123 Lee Bldg, College Park, MD 20742-5121. TEL 301-405-7780. Ed. H Robert Cohen.

780.904 USA ISSN 0031-6016
➤ **PERSPECTIVES OF NEW MUSIC.** Text in English. 1962. s-a. USD 46 domestic to individuals; USD 62 foreign to individuals; USD 126 domestic to institutions; USD 142 foreign to institutions (effective 2009). adv. bk.rev.; rec.rev. charts; illus.; bibl. index, cum.index. 250 p./no.; back issues avail.; reprints avail. **Document type:** *Journal, Academic/Scholarly.* **Description:** Publishes interviews, analyses, technical reports, position papers by composers, sociological and philosophical articles relating to contemporary music.
Related titles: CD-ROM ed.; Microform ed.: (from PQC); Online - full text ed.
Indexed: A01, A02, A03, A08, A20, A22, A25, A26, A27, ABS&EES, ASCA, AmHI, B04, BRD, CA, DIP, E08, G06, G07, G08, H07, H08, HAb, HumInd, I05, IBR, IBRH, IBZ, IIMP, M01, M02, M11, MAG, MLA-IB, MusicInd, P02, P10, P48, P53, P54, PCI, PQC, RASB, RILM, S08, S09, S23, T02, W03, W05.
—BLDSC (6428.145900), IE, Ingenta.
Published by: Perspectives of New Music, Inc., University of Washington, Music, Box 353450, Seattle, WA 98195-3450. TEL 206-543-0196, FAX 206-543-9285, http://www.perspectiveofnewmusic.org/. Eds. Benjamin Boretz, John Rahn, Robert Morris. R&P, Adv. contact Brandon Derfler TEL 206-543-0196. Circ: 1,350 (paid).

780 GBR ISSN 1947-4091
▼ ➤ **PERSPECTIVES ON WORLD MUSIC.** Text in English. forthcoming 2013. s-a. **Document type:** *Journal, Academic/Scholarly.*
Description: Features new research on world music and enthomusicology.
Related titles: Online - full text ed.: ISSN 1947-4105. forthcoming.

Published by: Routledge (Subsidiary of: Taylor & Francis Group), 4 Park Square, Milton Park, Abingdon, Oxon OX14 4RN, United Kingdom. TEL 44-1235-828600, FAX 44-1235-829000, info@routledge.co.uk, http://www.routledge.com/journals/.

782.81 DEU ISSN 0178-6121
PERSPEKTIVEN DER OPERNFORSCHUNG. Text in German. 1994. irreg., latest vol.17, 2009. price varies. **Document type:** *Monographic series, Academic/Scholarly.*
Published by: Peter Lang GmbH (Subsidiary of: Peter Lang Publishing Group), Eschborner Landstr 42-50, Frankfurt Am Main, 60489, Germany. TEL 49-69-7807050, FAX 49-69-78070550, zentrale.frankfurt@peterlang.com. Eds. Juergen Maehder, Thomas Betzwieser.

780 DEU
PERSPEKTIVEN ZUR MUSIKPAEDAGOGIK UND MUSIKWISSENSCHAFT. Text in German. 1984. irreg., latest vol.29, 2003. price varies. **Document type:** *Monographic series, Academic/Scholarly.*
Published by: Gustav Bosse Verlag, Heinrich-Schuetz-Allee 35, Kassel, 34131, Germany. TEL 49-561-3105140, FAX 49-561-3105240, info@bosse-verlag.de, http://www.bosse-verlag.de.

780 GBR ISSN 0266-366X
PETER WARLOCK SOCIETY NEWSLETTER. Text in English. 1965. 6/m. GBP 8 to members. bk.rev. **Document type:** *Newsletter.*
Media: Duplicated (not offset).
Published by: Peter Warlock Society, Persiz Ct, Flat 10, 2a Oliver Grove, London, SE25 6EJ, United Kingdom. Ed. Brian Collins. Circ: 150.

780.01 BEL
PHILIPPE DE MONTE OPERA. SERIES A, MOTETS. Text mainly in English. 1975. irreg., latest vol.7, 1986. price varies. back issues avail. **Document type:** *Academic/Scholarly.* **Description:** Presents a musicological analysis of the motet.
Published by: Leuven University Press, Blijde Inkomststraat 5, Leuven, 3000, Belgium. TEL 32-16-325345, FAX 32-16-325352, university.press@upers.kuleuven.ac.be, http://www.kuleuven.ac.be/upers.

782.5 BEL
PHILIPPE DE MONTE OPERA. SERIES B, MASSES. Text mainly in English. 1976. irreg., latest vol.2, 1979. price varies. back issues avail. **Document type:** *Academic/Scholarly.* **Description:** Presents a musicological analysis of choral masses.
Published by: Leuven University Press, Blijde Inkomststraat 5, Leuven, 3000, Belgium. TEL 32-16-325345, FAX 32-16-325352, university.press@upers.kuleuven.ac.be, http://www.kuleuven.ac.be/upers.

782.5 BEL
PHILIPPE DE MONTE OPERA. SERIES D, MADRIGALS. Text mainly in English. 1977. irreg., latest vol.4, 1988. price varies. back issues avail. **Document type:** *Academic/Scholarly.* **Description:** Presents a musicological study and analysis of the madrigal.
Published by: Leuven University Press, Blijde Inkomststraat 5, Leuven, 3000, Belgium. TEL 32-16-325345, FAX 32-16-325352, university.press@upers.kuleuven.ac.be, http://www.kuleuven.ac.be/upers.

780 ITA ISSN 1826-9001
ML290
PHILOMUSICA ON-LINE; rivista del Dipartimento di Scienze Musicologihe e Paleografico-Filologiche. Text in Italian, English. 2001. a. free (effective 2011). **Document type:** *Journal, Academic/Scholarly.*
Media: Online - full text.
Published by: (Universita degli Studi di Pavia), Pavia University Press, Via Ferrata 1, Pavia, 27100, Italy. TEL 39-0382-987743, FAX 39-0382-987262, unipress@unipv.it, http://www.paviauniversitypress.it. Ed. Maria Caraci Vela.

780.71 USA ISSN 1063-5734
ML1
➤ **PHILOSOPHY OF MUSIC EDUCATION REVIEW.** Text in English. 1988. s-a. USD 89.50 combined subscription to institutions (print & online eds.) (effective 2012). bk.rev. back issues avail.; reprint service avail. from PSC. **Document type:** *Journal, Academic/Scholarly.* **Description:** Disseminates philosophical research in music education to an international community of scholars, artists, and teachers.
Formerly (until 1992): Philosophy of Music Education Newsletter (2156-5902)
Related titles: Online - full text ed.: ISSN 1543-3412. USD 59 to institutions (effective 2012).
Indexed: A22, A26, B04, BRD, CA, CPE, E01, E02, E03, E07, E08, ERA, ERI, ERIC, EdA, Edl, G08, I05, IIMP, M11, M12, MAG, MusicInd, P18, P48, P53, P54, PCI, PQC, PhilInd, RILM, S09, T02, W03, W05.
—BLDSC (6464.955200), IE. **CCC.**
Published by: (Indiana University, School of Music), Indiana University Press, 601 N Morton St, Bloomington, IN 47404. TEL 812-855-9449, 800-842-6796, FAX 812-855-8507, journals@indiana.edu, http://iupjournals.org. Ed. Estelle R. Jorgensen.

➤ **PHONOLOG REPORTER**; all-in-one-reporter. *see* MUSIC—Abstracting, Bibliographies, Statistics

➤ **PIA KANSAI EDITION.** *see* LEISURE AND RECREATION

786.2 FRA ISSN 1627-0452
PIANISTE. Text in French. 2000. s-m. EUR 41 (effective 2009). adv. **Document type:** *Magazine, Consumer.*
Published by: Groupe Express-Roularta, 29 Rue de Chateaudun, Paris Cede, 75308, France. TEL 33-1-75551000, http://www.groupe-exp.com.

786.2 GBR ISSN 1369-9547
PIANO. Text in English. 1993. bi-m. GBP 21.50 domestic; GBP 25.50 in Europe; GBP 30 elsewhere; GBP 3.75 per issue (effective 2009). adv. illus. back issues avail. **Document type:** *Magazine, Consumer.* **Description:** Provides pianists with opinions, tips and insights on the works of the great composers. Also features advise on improvisation, playing jazz and practicing, with regular tips on fingering, sight-reading, pedalling, memorization etc.
Formerly (until 1998): Classical Piano (0969-5818)
Indexed: IIMP, M11, MusicInd, RILM, T02.
—**CCC.**
Published by: Rhinegold Publishing Ltd., 239-241 Shaftesbury Ave, London, WC2H 8TF, United Kingdom. TEL 44-20-73331720, FAX 44-20-73331765, enquiries@rhinegold.co.uk. Ed. Jeremy Siepmann. Adv. contact Neil Cording TEL 44-20-73331733.

780 NLD ISSN 0920-0983
PIANO BULLETIN. Text in Dutch. 1983. 3/yr. EUR 28.80 to non-members (effective 2009). adv. bk.rev. illus. back issues avail. **Document type:** *Bulletin, Trade.* **Description:** Provides information for professional pianists and piano teachers about repertoire, technique, history of music, interpretation, and new recordings.
Published by: E P T A Netherlands, Postbus 130, Voorburg, 2270 AC, Netherlands. TEL 31-70-3019693, FAX 31-70-3274029, http://www.eptanetherlands.nl. Ed. Christo Lelie. Circ: 1,200.

786.2 USA
PIANO EXPLORER. Text in English. bi-m. USD 8 (effective 2005). **Document type:** *Magazine, Trade.*
Published by: Instrumentalist Co., 200 Northfield Rd., Northfield, IL 60093. TEL 847-446-5000, FAX 847-446-6263. Ed. Anna Ravestein. Pub. James Rohner.

786.3 USA ISSN 0031-9546
PIANO GUILD NOTES. Text in English. 1951. bi-m. USD 15. adv. bk.rev. illus. reprints avail.
Related titles: Microfilm ed.: (from PQC).
Indexed: A22, RILM.
—Ingenta.
Published by: National Guild of Piano Teachers, PO Box 1807, Austin, TX 78767. TEL 512-478-5775. Ed. Pat McCabe-Leche. Circ: 12,000.

780.71 GBR ISSN 0267-7253
ML5
PIANO JOURNAL. Text in English. 1980. 3/yr. free membership. adv. bk.rev.; music rev. tr.lit. back issues avail. **Document type:** *Journal, Academic/Scholarly.* **Description:** Includes articles on pianists and piano teaching, reviews, and association news.
Published by: E P T A Europe, 28 Emperor's Gate, London, SW7 4HS, United Kingdom. TEL 44-20-73737307, FAX 44-20-73735440, carogrindea@yahoo.com, http://www.epta-europe.org. adv.: B&W page GBP 150, color page GBP 290. Circ: 2,800.

786.23 USA ISSN 0031-9562
ML1
PIANO TECHNICIANS JOURNAL. Text in English. 1958. m. USD 104.50 (effective 2005). adv. bk.rev. charts; illus. index. **Document type:** *Magazine, Trade.*
Indexed: IIMP, M11, MusicInd, T02.
—Ingenta.
Published by: Piano Technicians Guild, Inc., 4444 Forest Ave, Kansas City, KS 66106-3750. TEL 913-432-9975, FAX 913-432-9986, ptg@ptg.org, http://www.ptg.org. Ed. Steve Brady. Pub. Dan Hall. R&P Joe Zeman TEL 816-753-7747. Adv. contact Midge Sheldon. Circ: 4,300 (paid).

786 USA ISSN 1082-8753
PIANO TODAY; the magazine you can play. Text in English. 1993. q. USD 18.97 (effective 2000). adv. bk.rev. illus. **Document type:** *Magazine, Consumer.*
Formerly (until 1995): Keyboard Classics & Piano Stylist (1069-4285); Which was formed by the 1993 merger of: Piano Stylist & Jazz Workshop (1041-2492); Which was formerly (198?-1988): Jazz & Keyboard Workshop (0893-4797); (1983-1993): Keyboard Classics (1044-3266); Which was formerly: Keyboard Classics & Virtuoso (0744-3218); (in 1981): Sheet Music Magazine's Keyboard Classics (0273-9526)
Related titles: Online - full text ed.
Indexed: IIMP, M11, MAG, MusicInd, T02.
—Ingenta.
Published by: Keyboard Classics, Inc., 333 Adams St, Bedford, NY 10507-2001. TEL 914-244-8500, FAX 914-244-8560. Ed., R&P, Adv. contact Stuart Isacoff. Pub. Edward Shanaphy. Circ: 25,000 (paid).

PIANO-TUNERS QUARTERLY. *see* HANDICAPPED—Visually Impaired

PIESN SKRZYDLATA. *see* HISTORY—History Of Europe

781 AUS ISSN 1329-0460
PIG MEAT ZINE. Text in English. 1990. irreg.
Media: Online - full text. **Related titles:** Print ed.
Published by: Pig Meat, PO Box 2064, Fitzroy MDC, VIC 3065, Australia. TEL 61-3-86215535, pig_meat@yahoo.com, http://www.pigmeat.cjb.net. Ed. Nick Potter.

781.62 IRL ISSN 1649-9220
AN PIOBAIRE. Text in English. 1968. 5/yr. EUR 45 to individuals; EUR 19 to students (effective 2006). **Document type:** *Newsletter.*
Published by: Na Piobairi Uilleann, 15 Henrietta St, Dublin, 1, Ireland. TEL 353-1-8730093, FAX 353-1-8735094, info@pipers.ie.

781.64 DEU
PIRANHA. Text in German. 1995. 11/yr. adv. **Document type:** *Magazine, Consumer.*
Published by: Piranha Media GmbH, Rolandstr 69, Cologne, 50677, Germany. TEL 49-221-5797800, FAX 49-221-5797879. adv.: page EUR 5,000. Circ: 110,600 (paid and controlled).

787 USA
PITCH (NEW YORK); for the international microtonalist. Text in English. 1986. q. USD 62 domestic; USD 66 in Canada; USD 70 elsewhere. bk.rev. **Document type:** *Bibliography.*
Media: Audio cassette/tape.
Published by: American Festival of Microtonal Music, Inc., 318 E 70th St, Ste 5FW, New York, NY 10021. TEL 212-517-3550, FAX 212-517-5495. Ed. Johnny Reinhard. Circ: 1,000.

784 USA ISSN 0882-214X
ML1
THE PITCH PIPE. Text in English. 1949. q. USD 12 domestic to non-members; USD 24 foreign to non-members (effective 2007). adv. 44 p./no.; **Document type:** *Magazine, Consumer.*
Indexed: IIMP, M11, T02.
Published by: Sweet Adelines International, Inc., PO Box 470168, Tulsa, OK 74147-0168. TEL 918-622-1444, 800-992-7464, FAX 918-665-0894, admindept@sweetadelineintl.org. Ed. Joey Mechelle Stenner. adv.: B&W page USD 1,160, color page USD 1,760. Circ: 30,000 (controlled).

781.64 USA
PITCHFORK. Text in English. d. adv. **Document type:** *Journal, Consumer.* **Description:** Provides daily indie-focused record reviews and music news.
Media: Online - full content.
Published by: Pitchfork Media, 1834 W North Ave, Ste 2, Chicago, IL 60622. TEL 773-395-5937, FAX 773-395-5992. Ed., Pub. Ryan Schreiber.

780 331.8 USA ISSN 0032-034X
PITTSBURGH MUSICIAN. Text in English. 1949. m. membership only. adv. charts; illus. **Document type:** *Newspaper.* **Description:** News and items of interest to local union musicians.
Published by: Pittsburgh Musicians Union, Local 60 471, A F M, 709 Forbes Ave, Pittsburgh, PA 15219. TEL 412-281-1822. Ed. Vincent Ventresca. Circ: 1,200 (controlled).

785.06 USA ISSN 0032-0358
PITTSBURGH SYMPHONY ORCHESTRA PROGRAM. Text in English. 1926. w. (Sep.-May). adv. index.
Published by: Pittsburgh Symphony Society, Heinz Hall, 600 Penn Ave, Pittsburgh, PA 15222. TEL 412-392-4878, FAX 412-392-4909. Ed. Melissa Farris. Circ: 8,550.

PLACE DES ARTS. MAGAZINE. *see* THEATER

783 GBR ISSN 0961-1371
ML169.8
➤ **PLAINSONG & MEDIEVAL MUSIC.** Text in English. 1978. s-a. GBP 107, USD 185 to institutions; GBP 112, USD 197 combined subscription to institutions (print & online eds.) (effective 2012). adv. music rev. back issues avail.; reprint service avail. from PSC. **Document type:** *Journal, Academic/Scholarly.* **Description:** Covers the entire field of plainchant and medieval music, including monophonic, polyphonic, and liturgical music from the East and West.
Formerly (until 1992): Plainsong and Mediaeval Music Society. Journal (0143-4918)
Related titles: Online - full text ed.: ISSN 1474-0087. GBP 102, USD 178 to institutions (effective 2012).
Indexed: A20, A22, A27, ArtHuCI, CA, CurCont, E01, IIMP, M11, MLA-IB, MusicInd, P10, P48, P53, P54, PCI, PQC, RILM, SCOPUS, T02, W07.
—BLDSC (6507.109000), IE, Infotrieve, Ingenta. **CCC.**
Published by: Cambridge University Press, The Edinburgh Bldg, Shaftesbury Rd, Cambridge, CB2 8RU, United Kingdom. TEL 44-1223-312393, FAX 44-1223-315052, journals@cambridge.org, http://www.cambridge.org/uk. Eds. Helen Deeming, James Borders. R&P Linda Nicol TEL 44-1223-325702. adv.: page GBP 415, page USD 785. Circ: 400. **Subscr. to:** Cambridge University Press, 32 Ave of the Americas, New York, NY 10013. TEL 212-337-5000, FAX 212-691-3239, journals_subscriptions@cup.org

780 USA ISSN 1534-3820
PLAINSONGS. Text in English. 1980. 3/yr. **Document type:** *Magazine, Consumer.*
Indexed: AmHI, H07, T02.
Published by: Peru State College, 600 Hoyt St, P O Box 10, Peru, NE 68421. TEL 800-742-4412, http://www.hpcnet.org/cgi-bin/global/a_bus_card.cgi?SiteID=75.

781.6505 CAN ISSN 1206-4696
PLANET JAZZ. Text in English. 1993. s-a. USD 3.95 (effective 2002). **Document type:** *Magazine, Consumer.*
Former titles (until 1997): Jazz Vine (1196-9431); (until 1993): Montreal Jazz Grapevine (1196-9423)
Indexed: CMPI, M11, MusicInd.
Published by: Haarlem River Publications, 1 Westmount Sq, 1001, Montreal, PQ H3Z 2P9, Canada. TEL 514-931-5821, FAX 514-931-3602. Ed. Carol Robertson. Pub. David Watson.

DAS PLATEAU. *see* ART

780 700 USA ISSN 1942-6976
PLATEAU (RICHMOND HILL). Text in English. 2007. q. USD 13.50 (effective 2008). adv. **Document type:** *Magazine, Consumer.* **Description:** Focuses on independent artists in all genres of music, film and art.
Published by: Plateau Magazine, 95-12 131st St, Ste 1B, Richmond Hill, NY 11419. TEL 718-614-7419. Ed. Alex Clermont. Adv. contact June Medrano. page USD 450.

781.66 305.89607305 746.9 USA ISSN 2150-9387
▼ **PLATINUM PLUS ONLINE MAGAZINE.** Text in English. 2009. q. USD 4.99 (effective 2009). **Document type:** *Magazine, Consumer.* **Description:** Features music, fashion, style and hip-hop.
Related titles: Online - full text ed.: ISSN 2150-9395.
Published by: Thandiwe Clinton, Ed. & Pub., 67 Thorn Creek Way, Dallas, GA 30157. TEL 404-246-5181, teeplatinum@gmail.com.

PLAY (WESTLAKE VILLAGE); video games - anime - movies - music - gear - toys. *see* COMPUTERS—Computer Games

PLAY METER. *see* SPORTS AND GAMES

658.8 780 USA
ML3790
PLAYBACK (CARLSBAD). Text in English. 1947. 10/yr. membership. tr.lit. **Document type:** *Newsletter.*
Former titles: N A M M News; N A M M Music Retailer News (0027-5913); N A M M Members Monthly Bulletin
Published by: N A M M - International Music Products Association, 5790 Armada Dr, Carlsbad, CA 92008. TEL 760-438-8001. Ed. Jerry Derloshon. Circ: 10,500 (controlled).

780.3 USA ISSN 1520-9334
ML27.U5
PLAYBACK (NEW YORK). Text in English. 1990. irreg. back issues avail. **Document type:** *Monographic series, Trade.* **Description:** Covers the music industry. For songwriters, composers, and publishers.
Former titles (until 1998): A S C A P Play Back (1080-1391); (until 1994): Play Back (1059-6925)
Related titles: Online - full text ed.
Indexed: RILM.
Published by: American Society of Composers, Authors and Publishers, One Lincoln Plaza, New York, NY 10023. TEL 212-621-6000, FAX 212-362-7328. Ed. Erik Philbrook. Circ: 90,000.

PLAYBOARD; skateboard - snowboard - music. *see* SPORTS AND GAMES—Outdoor Life

786 GBR ISSN 0140-7589
PLAYER PIANO GROUP BULLETIN. Abbreviated title: P P G Bulletin. Text in English. 1959. q. free to members (effective 2009). bk.rev. back issues avail. **Document type:** *Bulletin, Trade.* **Description:** Provides information and opportunities for people interested in player and reproducing pianos.
Published by: Player Piano Group, c/o George Fleming, 2 St Giles Barton, Hillesley, Gloucestershire GL12 8RG, United Kingdom. membership@pianolasociety.com. Ed. Julian Dyer TEL 44-118-9771057.

781.64 DEU ISSN 1862-2488
PLAYMUSIC; Ihr spielt die Musik. Text in German. 2004. q. adv. **Document type:** *Magazine, Consumer.*
Formerly (until 2006): Spass mit Musik (1613-1274)
Published by: P P V Medien GmbH, Postfach 57, Bergkirchen, 85230, Germany. TEL 49-8131-56550, FAX 49-8131-565510, ppv@ppvmedien.de, http://www.ppvmedien.de. Adv. contact Frank Wunderlich.

PLAZM. *see* ART

780 USA
PODIUM NOTES. Text in English. 1978. q. USD 85 domestic; USD 115 foreign (effective 2000). **Document type:** *Newsletter.*
Formerly: Conductors Guild Newsletter
Published by: Conductors Guild, Inc., 5300 Glenside Dr, Ste 2207, Richmond, VA 23228. TEL 804-553-1378, FAX 804-553-1876, guild@conductorsguild.net, http://www.conductorsguild.net. Ed. Otis French. Circ: 1,800.

780 CAN ISSN 1910-1147
POLICY MONITORING PROGRAM; keeping track. Text in English. 2004. a. **Document type:** *Handbook/Manual/Guide, Trade.*
Media: Online - full text. **Related titles:** French ed.: Programme de Suivi de la Politique, au Rythme de l'Industrie. ISSN 1910-1155.
Published by: (Canadian Heritage, Canada Music Fund/Fonds de la Musique du Canada), Canadian Heritage/Patrimoine Canadien, 15 Eddy St, Gatineau, PQ K1A 0M5, Canada. TEL 819-997-0055, 866-811-0055, pch-qc@pch.gc.ca.

784 ITA ISSN 1593-8735
POLIFONIE; storia e teoria della coralita. Text in Italian. 2001. 3/yr. **Document type:** *Journal, Academic/Scholarly.* **Description:** Dedicated to all aspects of choral music.
Published by: Fondazione Guido d'Arezzo, Corso Italia 102, Arezzo, 52100, Italy. TEL 39-0575-356203, FAX 39-0575-324735, fondguid@polifonico.org. Ed. Francesco Luisi.

781.7 POL ISSN 0032-2946
ML5
POLISH MUSIC/POLNISCHE MUSIK. Text in English, German. 1966. q. USD 14. adv. bk.rev.
Indexed: IBR, IBZ, M11, MusicInd, RILM.
—Ingenta.
Published by: Agencja Autorska/Authors' Agency, Ul Hipoteczna 2, Warszawa, 00950, Poland. TEL 48-22-341859, TELEX ZAIKS PL 812470. Ed. Jan Grzybowski. Circ: 1,200.

781.7 USA ISSN 0741-9945
➤ **POLISH MUSIC HISTORY SERIES.** Text in English. 1982. irreg., latest vol.10, 2007. price varies. bibl.; illus. back issues avail. **Document type:** *Monographic series, Academic/Scholarly.* **Description:** Designed to fill the lack of information in America on music of Polish origin.
Published by: Polish Music Center, University of Southern California, Thornton School of Music, 840 W 34th St, Los Angeles, CA 90089. TEL 213-740-9369, FAX 213-821-4040, polmusic@thornton.usc.edu. Ed. Linda Schubert.

781.7 USA ISSN 1521-6039
ML27.P7
➤ **POLISH MUSIC JOURNAL.** Text in English. 1998. s-a. bk.rev. bibl.; illus.; abstr. back issues avail. **Document type:** *Journal, Academic/Scholarly.* **Description:** Covers the study of Polish music.
Media: Online - full text.
Indexed: RILM.
Published by: Polish Music Center, University of Southern California, Thornton School of Music, 840 W 34th St, Los Angeles, CA 90089. TEL 213-740-9369, FAX 213-821-4040, polmusic@thornton.usc.edu. Ed. Linda Schubert.

781.7 USA
POLISH MUSIC NEWSLETTER. Text in English. 1994. m. free (effective 2010). bk.rev.; music rev. 20 p./no.; back issues avail. **Document type:** *Newsletter, Trade.*
Formerly (until 2000): P M R C Newsletter (1098-9188)
Media: Online - full text.
Published by: Polish Music Center, University of Southern California, Thornton School of Music, 840 W 34th St, Los Angeles, CA 90089. TEL 213-740-9369, FAX 213-821-4040, polmusic@thornton.usc.edu. Ed. Krysta Close.

780.65 USA ISSN 1067-6945
ML13
POLLSTAR. Text in English. 1981. 50/yr. USD 315; GBP 199 in Europe (effective 2000). adv. **Document type:** *Directory, Trade.* **Description:** Covers the international concert business. Includes artist itineraries, box office results, news, ratings charts, contacts.
Published by: Promoters On-Line Listings, 4697 W Jacquelyn Ave, Fresno, CA 93722-6413. TEL 559-271-7900, FAX 559-271-7979. Ed. Gary Bongiovanni. R&P, Adv. contact Gary Smith. **Subscr. in Europe to:** Pollstar U.K., Ste. 8, 24 Highbury Grove, London N5 2EA, United Kingdom.

POLYAESTHETIK UND BILDUNG. *see* EDUCATION—Teaching Methods And Curriculum

783 ITA
POLYPHONIA; musica sacra corale - sacred choral music - geistliche Vokal-musik. Text in English, German, Italian. 1991. q. EUR 45 (effective 2008). **Document type:** *Journal, Academic/Scholarly.*
Published by: Casa Musicale Edizioni Carrara, Via Ambrogio Calepio 4, Bergamo, BG 24125, Italy. TEL 39-035-243618, FAX 39-035-270298, http://www.edizionicarrara.it.

780 GRC
POP & ROCK. Text in Greek. 2002. m. EUR 5.98 newsstand/cover (effective 2006). adv. **Document type:** *Magazine, Consumer.*
Published by: Motorpress Hellas (Subsidiary of: Gruner + Jahr AG & Co), 132 Lefkis Str, Krioneri, 14568, Greece. TEL 30-210-6262000, FAX 30-210-6262401, info@motorpress.gr, http://www.motorpress.gr. Circ: 20,000 (paid and controlled).

781.64 GBR
POP GIRL. Text in English. 2003. m. GBP 1.50 newsstand/cover (effective 2009). adv. **Document type:** *Magazine, Consumer.* **Description:** Contains articles on pop music, fashion, puzzles, gossip as well as interviews with the hottest pop stars.
Published by: B B C Worldwide Ltd., Media Centre, 201 Wood Ln, London, W12 7TQ, United Kingdom. TEL 44-20-84332000, 44-20-84333847, bbcworldwide@bbc.co.uk.

POP POLITICS.COM. *see* POLITICAL SCIENCE

POPCORN; das Teen People Magazin. *see* CHILDREN AND YOUTH—For

POPCORN. *see* CHILDREN AND YOUTH—For

POPCORN. *see* CHILDREN AND YOUTH—For

POPCORN. *see* CHILDREN AND YOUTH—For

POPCORN. *see* CHILDREN AND YOUTH—For

POPCORN. *see* CHILDREN AND YOUTH—For

781.64 028.5 USA ISSN 1539-9508
POPSTAR!. Text in English. 1998. m. USD 19.99 domestic; USD 35 foreign (effective 2007). adv. **Document type:** *Magazine, Consumer.* **Description:** Includes interviews and features on celebrities popular with teenage girls.
Address: 1000 W Washington, Ste 442, Chicago, IL 60607. TEL 312-942-0824, FAX 312-942-0834. Adv. contact Michelle Balaz.

▼ **POPULAERE KULTUR UND MUSIK.** *see* SOCIOLOGY

780 150 700 AUS ISSN 1837-9303
▼ ➤ **POPULAR ENTERTAINMENT STUDIES.** Text in English. 2010. s-a. free (effective 2010). **Document type:** *Journal, Academic/Scholarly.* **Description:** Dedicated to the exploration of all aspects of popular entertainment.
Media: Online - full text.
Published by: University of Newcastle, University Dr, Callaghan, NSW 2308, Australia. TEL 61-2-49215000, FAX 61-2-49854200, EnquiryCentre@newcastle.edu.au. Ed. Victor Emeljanow.

780.42 GBR ISSN 0261-1430
ML3469
➤ **POPULAR MUSIC.** Text in English. 1982. 3/yr. GBP 185, USD 305 to institutions; GBP 195, USD 335 combined subscription to institutions (print & online eds.) (effective 2012). adv. bk.rev.; music rev. illus. back issues avail.; reprint service avail. from PSC. **Document type:** *Journal, Academic/Scholarly.* **Description:** Provides multidisciplinary coverage of all aspects of popular music: musicology, literary studies, sociology, and economic and social history.
Related titles: Microform ed.: (from PQC); Online - full text ed.: ISSN 1474-0095. GBP 175, USD 295 to institutions (effective 2012).
Indexed: A01, A02, A03, A08, A20, A22, A25, A26, A27, AmHI, ArtHuCI, B04, BRD, BrHumI, CA, CurCont, E01, E08, G08, G09, H07, H08, HAb, HumInd, I05, I14, IIBP, IIMP, M11, MLA-IB, MusicInd, P02, P10, P48, P53, P54, PCI, PQC, RASB, RILM, S08, S09, SCOPUS, T02, W03, W07.
—BLDSC (6550.760800), IE, Infotrieve, Ingenta. **CCC.**
Published by: Cambridge University Press, The Edinburgh Bldg, Shaftesbury Rd, Cambridge, CB2 8RU, United Kingdom. TEL 44-1223-312393, FAX 44-1223-315052, journals@cambridge.org, http://www.cambridge.org/uk. Eds. Keith Negus, Nicola Dibben. R&P Linda Nicol TEL 44-1223-325702. adv.: page GBP 470, page USD 895. Circ: 800. **Subscr. to:** Cambridge University Press, 32 Ave of the Americas, New York, NY 10013. TEL 212-337-5000, FAX 212-691-3239, journals_subscriptions@cup.org.

306.484 GBR ISSN 0300-7766
➤ **POPULAR MUSIC & SOCIETY.** Text in English. 1972. 5/yr. GBP 181 combined subscription in United Kingdom to institutions (print & online eds.); EUR 242, USD 304 combined subscription to institutions (print & online eds.) (effective 2012). adv. bk.rev. stat.; charts; illus. index. 120 p./no.; back issues avail.; reprint service avail. from PSC. **Document type:** *Journal, Academic/Scholarly.* **Description:** Contains articles on all aspects of popular, mainly rock, music and society, authors, and performers.
Related titles: Microform ed.: (from PQC); Online - full text ed.: ISSN 1740-1712. GBP 163 in United Kingdom to institutions; EUR 218, USD 274 to institutions (effective 2012) (from IngentaConnect).
Indexed: A01, A02, A03, A08, A20, A22, A25, A26, A27, ASCA, AmH&L, AmHI, ArtHuCI, B04, B14, BRD, BRI, BrHumI, CA, CBRI, CMM, CommAb, CurCont, DIP, E01, E08, G08, H07, H08, HAb, HumInd, I05, I06, IBR, IBRH, IBSS, IBZ, IIMP, M11, MLA-IB, MRD, MusicInd, P02, P10, P48, P53, P54, PQC, RILM, S02, S03, S08, S09, S11, S23, SCOPUS, T02, W03, W05, W07.
—BLDSC (6550.761000), IE, Ingenta. **CCC.**
Published by: (Bowling Green State University USA), Routledge (Subsidiary of: Taylor & Francis Group), 4 Park Square, Milton Park, Abingdon, Oxon OX14 4RN, United Kingdom. TEL 44-1235-828600, FAX 44-1235-829000, subscriptions@tandf.co.uk, http://www.routledge.com. Eds. Gary Burns, Thomas M Kitts. Adv. contact Linda Hann TEL 44-1344-779945. **Subscr. to:** Taylor & Francis Ltd., Journals Customer Service, Sheepen Pl, Colchester, Essex CO3 3LP, United Kingdom.

781.6309 GBR ISSN 1740-7133
ML3469
POPULAR MUSIC HISTORY. Abbreviated title: P M H. Text in English. 2004. 3/yr. USD 300 combined subscription in North America to institutions (print & online eds.); GBP 185 combined subscription elsewhere to institutions (print & online eds.) (effective 2012). adv. back issues avail.; reprints avail. **Document type:** *Journal, Academic/Scholarly.* **Description:** Features original historical and historiographical research that draws on the wide range of disciplines and intellectual trajectories that have contributed to the establishment of popular music studies as a recognized academic enterprise.
Related titles: Online - full text ed.: ISSN 1743-1646. USD 240 in North America to institutions; GBP 148 elsewhere to institutions (effective 2012).
Indexed: A01, A03, A08, AmH&L, CA, HistAb, M11, MLA-IB, RILM, T02.
—BLDSC (6550.763500), IE. **CCC.**
Published by: Equinox Publishing Ltd., Unit S3, Kelham House, 3 Lancaster St, Sheffield, S6 3AF, United Kingdom. TEL 44-114-2725957, FAX 44-560-3459046, journals@equinoxpub.com, http://www.equinoxpub.com/. Ed. Robert Strachan. Adv. contact Val Hall.

781.64 GBR ISSN 1357-0951
➤ **POPULAR MUSICOLOGY ONLINE.** Text in English. 1994. q. free (effective 2011). **Document type:** *Journal, Academic/Scholarly.* **Description:** Addresses the problematic of examining popular music, offering a platform to academics seeking new methodological venue for musicological inquiry.
Formerly (until 2000): Popular Musicology Quarterly (Print)
Media: Online - full text.
Indexed: A39, C27, C29, D03, D04, E13, R14, S14, S15, S18.
Published by: (Cyberstudia), University of Salford, Popular Music Research Unit, Salford, Greater Manchester, M5 4WT, United Kingdom. TEL 44-161-295-5000, FAX 44-161-295-5999, press-office@salford.ac.uk, http://www.salford.ac.uk.

782.5 DEU
POSAUNENCHOR. Text in German. q. EUR 8; EUR 2.50 newsstand/cover (effective 2006). adv. **Document type:** *Magazine, Consumer.*
Published by: Strube Verlag GmbH, Pettenkoferstr 24, Munich, 80336, Germany. TEL 49-89-54426611, FAX 49-89-54426630, strube.verlag@strube.de, http://www.strube.de. adv.: page EUR 660; trim 153 x 235. Circ: 9,000 (paid and controlled).

780.7 DEU ISSN 1867-4593
▼ **POTSDAMER FORSCHUNGEN ZUR MUSIK- UND KULTURGESCHICHTE.** Text in German. 2009. irreg. price varies. **Document type:** *Monographic series, Academic/Scholarly.*
Published by: Frank und Timme GmbH, Wittelsbacherstr 27a, Berlin, 10707, Germany. TEL 49-30-88667911, FAX 49-30-86398731, info@frank-timme.de.

780 DEU ISSN 1861-8529
POTSDAMER SCHRIFTENREIHE ZUR MUSIKPAEDAGOGIK. Text in German. 2006. irreg. price varies. **Document type:** *Monographic series, Academic/Scholarly.*
Published by: Universitaetsverlag Potsdam, Am Neuen Palais 10, Potsdam, 14469, Germany. TEL 49-331-9774458, FAX 49-331-9774625, ubpub@uni-potsdam.de, http://info.ub.uni-potsdam.de/verlag.htm.

780 USA
POWER HOUSE MAGAZINE. Text in English. 2006. s-a. USD 20 (effective 2007). adv. illus. **Document type:** *Magazine, Consumer.*
Published by: The Power House Magazine, 37 Main St, Brooklyn, NY 11201. TEL 212-604-9074, FAX 212-366-5247, subscriptions@powerhousebooks.com, magazine@powerhousebooks.com. Ed. Sara Rosen. Pub. Daniel Power.

780 POL ISSN 1230-0187
POZNANSKIE TOWARZYSTWO PRZYJACIOL NAUK. KOMISJA MUZYKOLOGICZNA. PRACE. Text in Polish. 1991. irreg., latest vol.14, 2003. price varies. **Document type:** *Monographic series, Academic/Scholarly.*
Published by: (Poznanskie Towarzystwo Przyjaciol Nauk, Komisja Muzykologiczna), Poznanskie Towarzystwo Przyjaciol Nauk/Poznan Society for the Advancement of the Arts and Sciences, ul Sew Mielzynskiego 27-29, Poznan, 61725, Poland. TEL 48-61-8527441, FAX 48-61-8522205, sekretariat@ptpn.poznan.pl, wydawnictwo@ptpn.poznan.pl, http://www.ptpn.poznan.pl.

780 POL
PRACE ARCHIWUM SLASKIEJ KULTURY MUZYCZNEJ. Text in Polish. 1972. irreg., latest vol.8, 1980. per issue exchange basis.
Published by: (Biblioteka Glowna), Akademia Muzyczna, Ul Zacisze 3, Katowice, 40025, Poland. TEL 32-155-4017. **Dist. by:** Ars Polona, Obroncow 25, Warsaw 03933, Poland.

780 USA ISSN 1553-3484
THE PRAEGER SINGER-SONGWRITER COLLECTION. Text in English. 2006. irreg., latest 2010. price varies. back issues avail. **Document type:** *Monographic series, Academic/Scholarly.* **Description:** Provides analysis and commentary on the lyrics of singer-songwriters. Each volume features a profile of the life and works of a particular artist, including Bruce Springsteen, Bob Marley, John Lennon, Carole King and Stevie Wonder.
Published by: Praeger Publishers (Subsidiary of: Greenwood Publishing Group Inc.), 88 Post Rd W, Westport, CT 06881. TEL 800-368-6868, tech.support@greenwood.com, http://www.greenwood.com. Ed. James Perone.

780 CAN ISSN 0822-7500
PRAIRIE SOUNDS. Text in English. 1980. 2/yr. free. adv. back issues avail. **Document type:** *Newsletter.* **Description:** News and events concerning Canadian composers of the 3 prairie provinces.
Related titles: Online - full text ed.
Indexed: CMPI.
Published by: Canadian Music Centre, Prairie Region, 911 Library Tower, 2500 University Dr, N W, Calgary, AB T2N 1N4, Canada. TEL 403-220-7403, FAX 403-289-4877, http://www.culturenet.ca/cmc/. Ed. John C Reid. Circ: 2,200.

780.7 DEU ISSN 1436-1949
PRAXIS DES MUSIKUNTERRICHTS; die Gruenen Hefte. Text in German. 1981. q. EUR 18; EUR 6.30 newsstand/cover (effective 2008). adv. bk.rev.; music rev. illus. back issues avail. **Document type:** *Journal, Academic/Scholarly.* **Description:** Offers music teachers concepts and materials for their lessons.
Former titles (until 1997): Zeitschrift fuer die Praxis des Musikunterrichts (1431-973X); (until 1996): Die Gruenen Hefte (0937-9584); (until 1989): Populaere Musik im Unterricht (0722-0030)
Indexed: DIP, IBR, IBZ.
Published by: Lugert Verlag GmbH, Oldershausener Hauptstr 34, Marschacht, 21436, Germany. TEL 49-4133-214911, FAX 49-4133-214918, info@lugert-verlag.de. Adv. contact Bernd Schrader. color page EUR 1,365, B&W page EUR 910. Circ: 8,000 (paid and controlled).

785.06 CAN ISSN 0381-890X
PRELUDE (CALGARY). Text in English. 1975. q. adv. illus. back issues avail. **Document type:** *Magazine, Consumer.*
Formerly: Bravura (0381-8918)
Indexed: CMPI.

Published by: Calgary Philharmonic Orchestra, 205 8th Ave, S E, 2nd Fl, Calgary, AB T2P 0K9, Canada. TEL 403-571-0294, FAX 403-294-7424, info@cpo-live.com, http://www.cpo-live.com. Ed. Laurel S Davis. Circ: 4,500.

782.1 CAN
PRELUDE (TORONTO). Text in English. 1982. 3/yr. CAD 50 (effective 2000). **Document type:** *Newsletter.* **Description:** Information on forthcoming productions, as well as other activities and events.
Former titles: Canadian Opera Company News (0820-4896); (until 1986): C O C News (0822-8922)
Indexed: CMPI.
Published by: Canadian Opera Company, 227 Front St E, Toronto, ON M5A 1E8, Canada. TEL 416-363-6671, FAX 416-363-5584. Ed., Adv. contact Helmut Reichenbacher. Circ: 14,000.

787 USA ISSN 1945-077X
ML1015.G9
PREMIER GUITAR. Text in English. 2007. m. USD 14.95 (effective 2008). adv. **Document type:** *Magazine, Consumer.* **Description:** Provides comprehensive coverage for serious guitar enthusiasts, including product reviews, industry profiles, artist interviews and educational articles.
Related titles: Online - full text ed.: ISSN 1945-0788.
Published by: Gearhead Communications, 301 Hwy 1 S, PO Box 127, Mount Vernon, IA 52314. TEL 877-704-4327, FAX 319-895-0058. Ed. Adam Moore.

PREVIEW; Das interaktive Magazin fuer Entertainment & Style. *see* MOTION PICTURES

PREVUE. *see* MOTION PICTURES

372.87 GBR ISSN 1356-5745
PRIMARY MUSIC TODAY. Text in English. 1995. 3/yr. GBP 24 (effective 2009). back issues avail. **Document type:** *Magazine, Trade.* **Description:** Covers significant articles on primary music education.
Indexed: B29.
—CCC.
Published by: Peacock Press, Scout Bottom Farm, Mytholmroyd, Hebden Bridge, HX7 5JS, United Kingdom. TEL 44-1422 882751, FAX 44-1422-886157, liz@recordermail.demon.co.uk. Eds. Ian Shirley TEL 44-1695-650998, Vanessa Young TEL 44-1227-782427.

781.9 AUT ISSN 1560-8921
PRIMO OTTOCENTO; Studien zum italienischen Musiktheater des (fruehen) 19. Jahrhunderts. Text in German. 1998. irreg., latest vol.3, 2004. price varies. **Document type:** *Monographic series, Academic/Scholarly.*
Published by: Praesens VerlagsgesmbH, Wehlistr 154/12, Vienna, W 1020, Austria. TEL 43-1-720703506, FAX 43-1-25330334660, m.ritter@praesens.at, http://www.praesens.at.

782.1 USA
➤ **PRINCETON STUDIES IN OPERA.** Text in English. 1991. irreg., latest 2005. price varies. charts; illus. back issues avail. **Document type:** *Monographic series, Academic/Scholarly.*
Formerly (until 1998): Princeton Series in Opera
Published by: Princeton University Press, 41 William St, Princeton, NJ 08540. TEL 609-258-4900, 800-777-4726, FAX 609-258-6305, cpriday@pupress.co.uk. Eds. Carolyn Abbate, Roger Parker. **Subscr. addr. in US:** California - Princeton Fulfillment Services, Inc., 1445 Lower Ferry Rd, Ewing, NJ 08618. TEL 609-883-1759, 800-777-4726, FAX 609-883-7413, 800-999-1958, orders@cpfsinc.com. **Dist. addr. in Canada:** University Press Group.; **Dist. addr. in UK:** John Wiley & Sons Ltd.

➤ **PRODUCTIV'S SOLO.** *see* SOUND RECORDING AND REPRODUCTION

780 USA
PROFANE EXISTENCE. Text in English. 1989. q. USD 8 in North America; USD 12 elsewhere (effective 2003). adv. **Description:** Features political coverage of music.
Formerly: M.A.S.
Related titles: Online - full text ed.
Published by: Profane Existence Magazine, PO Box 8722, Minneapolis, MN 55408. Ed. Claire Troll. Circ: 2,000.

780 CAN ISSN 1186-1797
PROFESSIONAL SOUND. Text in English. 1990. bi-m. CAD 19.95 domestic; CAD 22.95 foreign (effective 2002). adv. **Document type:** *Journal, Trade.*
Related titles: Online - full text ed.
Indexed: C03, CBCABus, CMPI, P48, PQC.
—CIS.
Published by: Norris - Whitney Communications Inc., 23 Hannover Dr, 7, St Catharines, ON L2W 1A3, Canada. TEL 905-641-3471, FAX 905-641-1648. Ed. Jeff MacKay. Circ: 13,500.

780 CAN ISSN 1910-2291
PROGRAMME D'AIDE AUX ASSOCIATIONS SECTORIELLES, UN PROGRAMME A L'ECOUTE. Text in French. 2004. a. **Document type:** *Journal, Trade.*
Media: Online - full text. **Related titles:** English ed.: Support to Sector Associations Program, a 'Sound' Program. ISSN 1910-2283.
Published by: Heritage Canada, Cultural Affairs, Canada Music Fund (Subsidiary of: Heritage Canada/Patrimoine Canadien), 15 Eddy St, Gatineau, PQ K1A 0M5, Canada. TEL 819-997-0055, 866-811-0055, http://www.canadianheritage.gc.ca, http://www.pch.gc.ca/progs/ac-ca/progs/fmusc-cmusf/index_e.cfm.

780.65 CAN ISSN 1910-9520
PROGRAMME DES ENTREPRENEURS DE LA MUSIQUE. RAPPORT ANNUEL. Text in French. 2004. a. **Document type:** *Report, Trade.*
Published by: Canadian Heritage, Canada Music Fund/Fonds de la Musique du Canada (Subsidiary of: Canadian Heritage/Patrimoine Canadien), 15, rue Eddy, 15-4-E, Gatineau, PQ K1A 0M5, Canada. TEL 819-934-3208, 866-686-1102, FAX 819-934-9244, cmf-music@pch.gc.ca, http://www.pch.gc.ca/progs/ac-ca/progs/fmusc-cmusf/music_fund_f.cfm#entrepreneur.

781.64 USA ISSN 1087-2744
PROGRESSION; the quarterly journal of progressive music. Text in English. 1992. q. USD 20 domestic; USD 23 in Canada; USD 36 Europe & S. America; USD 46 Pacific Rim (effective 2000). adv. **Document type:** *Magazine, Consumer.* **Description:** Devoted to news, reviews, interviews and features covering a wide range of progressive, electronic, and avant-garde music artists from around the globe.
Address: PO Box 7164, Lowell, MA 01852. TEL 800-545-7371, FAX 978-970-2728, progzine@aol.com, http://progressionmagazine.com. Ed., Pub., Adv. contact John Collinge.

PROPAGANDA; counterculture chronicle. *see* LIFESTYLE

780 CAN
PROVINCIAL NEWSLETTER. Text in English. 3/yr. looseleaf. free. adv. bk.rev. back issues avail. **Document type:** *Newsletter.* **Description:** Presents articles on the teaching of music and reports of the branches of the Association.
Published by: British Columbia Registered Music Teachers' Association, 197 Vancouver Ave, Penticton, BC V2A 1A1, Canada. TEL 250-492-8944, FAX 250-493-9130, ernst_schneider@telus.net. Ed. Ernst Schneider. Circ: 1,000 (controlled).

780 POL ISSN 1643-3319
PRZEGLAD MUZYKOLOGICZNY. Text in Polish. 2001. a., latest vol.2, 2002. price varies. **Document type:** *Monographic series, Academic/Scholarly.*
Indexed: RILM.
Published by: (Uniwersytet Warszawski, Instytut Muzykologii), Wydawnictwa Uniwersytetu Warszawskiego, ul Nowy Swiat 4, Warsaw, 00497, Poland. TEL 48-22-5531319, FAX 48-22-5531318, wuw@uw.edu.pl. Ed. Zbigniew Skowton. Circ: 300. **Dist. by:** Ars Polona, Obroncow 25, Warsaw 03933, Poland. TEL 48-22-5098609, FAX 48-22-5098610, arspolona@arspolona.com.pl, http://www.arspolona.com.pl.

PSALTICNOTES. *see* ART

780.01 USA ISSN 1946-7540
PSALTIKI. Text in English. 2008. s-a. free. reprints avail. **Document type:** *Journal, Academic/Scholarly.* **Description:** Contains articles of scholarship and readings in Byzantine Chant, Musicology, Hymnology and Typikon, as well as any subject relating to the Psaltic Art. Topics address any historical period or related liturgical tradition.
Media: Online - full text. **Related titles:** Print ed.: ISSN 1946-7532.
Published by: Psaltiki Inc., PO Box 149161, Orlando, FL 32814. TEL 404-433-1716. Ed. Dr. Konstantinos Terzopoulos.

781.15 GBR ISSN 0305-7356
ML5
➤ **PSYCHOLOGY OF MUSIC.** Abbreviated title: P O M. Text in English. 1973. q. GBP 319, USD 590 combined subscription to institutions (print & online eds.); GBP 313, USD 578 to institutions (effective 2010); subscr. includes: Research Studies in Music Education. adv. bk.rev. illus. cum.index every 5 vols. back issues avail.; reprint service avail. from PSC. **Document type:** *Journal, Academic/Scholarly.* **Description:** Provides an international forum for researchers working in the fields of psychology of music and music education, to encourage the exchange of ideas and to disseminate research findings.
Related titles: Online - full text ed.: ISSN 1741-3087. GBP 287, USD 531 to institutions (effective 2010).
Indexed: A20, A22, ASD, ArtHuCI, B29, CPE, CommAb, CurCont, DIP, E-psyche, E01, IBR, IBZ, IIMP, IPsyAb, M11, MusicInd, P03, PCI, PsycInfo, PsycholAb, RILM, SCOPUS, SSCI, W07.
—BLDSC (6946.536000), IE, Infotrieve, Ingenta. **CCC.**
Published by: (Society for Education, Music and Psychology Research), Sage Publications Ltd. (Subsidiary of: Sage Publications, Inc.), 1 Oliver's Yard, 55 City Rd, London, EC1Y 1SP, United Kingdom. TEL 44-20-73248500, FAX 44-20-73248600, info@sagepub.co.uk, http://www.uk.sagepub.com/home.nav. Ed. Raymond A R Macdonald. adv.: B&W page GBP 450; 130 x 205. **Subscr. in the Americas to:** Sage Publications, Inc., 2455 Teller Rd, Thousand Oaks, CA 91320. TEL 805-499-9774, FAX 805-499-0871, journals@sagepub.com.

780.01 CAN ISSN 0275-3987
ML3830
➤ **PSYCHOMUSICOLOGY**; a journal of music cognition. Text in English. 1981. s-a. USD 30 in United States; USD 36 elsewhere (effective 2011). bk.rev. bibl.; charts; stat. back issues avail. **Document type:** *Monographic series, Academic/Scholarly.* **Description:** Serves as a journal of research in music cognition, providing a forum for reports of experimental research, reviews of research and theoretical papers that are based on experimental research.
Related titles: Online - full text ed.: ISSN 2162-1535.
Indexed: A01, A22, CA, E-psyche, IIMP, M11, MusicInd, P03, P25, P48, PCI, PQC, PsycInfo, PsycholAb, RILM, T02.
—BLDSC (6946.540070), IE, Ingenta.
Published by: University of Prince Edward Island, Department of Psychology, Charlottetown, PE C1A 4P3, Canada. TEL 902-628-4325, FAX 902-628-4359. Ed. Annabel Cohen. Circ: 300.

780 USA
PURCHASER'S GUIDE TO THE MUSIC INDUSTRIES. Text in English. 1897. a. free with subscription to Music Trades. adv. reprints avail. **Document type:** *Handbook/Manual/Guide, Trade.*
Published by: Music Trades Corporation, 80 West St, PO Box 432, Englewood, NJ 07631. TEL 201-871-1965. Ed. Brian T Majeski. Adv. contact Juanita Hampton. Circ: 8,000.

780 USA ISSN 1940-2112
ML3534.6.J3
PURPLE SKY; a Japanese rock magazine. Text in English. 200?. q. USD 26 in US & Canada (effective 2007). **Document type:** *Magazine, Consumer.* **Description:** Dedicated to promoting Japanese rock music and alternative culture.
Published by: Clear Phoenix Media, PO Box 1271, West Caldwell, NJ 07007. info@purpleskymagazine.com.

781.64 GBR ISSN 0955-4955
ML3533.8
Q; the modern guide to music and more. Text in English. 1986. m. GBP 30 domestic; GBP 44 in Europe; GBP 90 elsewhere (effective 2009). adv. music rev. illus. back issues avail. **Document type:** *Magazine, Consumer.* **Description:** Covers the music scene in the UK and throughout the world, with extensive reviews of recent releases and reissues, profiles of bands, and interviews with musicians and rock 'n' roll personalities.
Related titles: Online - full text ed.
Indexed: M11, MusicInd, RILM.
—IE. **CCC.**
Published by: Bauer Consumer Media Ltd., Mappin House, 4 Winsley St, London, W1W 8HF, United Kingdom. TEL 44-20-71828000, http://www.bauermedia.co.uk. Eds. Nasarene Asghar TEL 44-20-71828482, Paul Rees. Adv. contact Chris Shepperson TEL 44-20-72956715. **Subscr. to:** CDS Global. **Dist. by:** Frontline.

780 GBR
Q MAGAZINE. Text in English. 1986. m. GBP 36 domestic; GBP 44 in Europe & USA; GBP 80 elsewhere; GBP 4.90 per issue domestic; GBP 5.99 per issue foreign (effective 2010). adv. back issues avail. **Document type:** *Magazine, Consumer.* **Description:** Compares to Rolling Stone on which it was originally modeled, though it focuses more on bands of longevity and retrospective import.
Related titles: Online - full text ed.
Published by: Bauer London Lifestyle Ltd. (Subsidiary of: H. Bauer Publishing Ltd.), Mappin House, 4 Winsley St, London, W1W 8HF, United Kingdom. TEL 44-20-71828000, john.adams@bauermedia.co.uk, http://www.bauermedia.co.uk. Adv. contact Chris Shepperson TEL 44-20-72956715. **Subscr. to:** Tower House, Sovereign Park, Market Harborough, Leicestershire LE16 9EF, United Kingdom. TEL 44-845-1204600, subs@greatmagazines.co.uk, http://www.greatmagazines.co.uk.

780.6 CHN
QING YINYUE/LIGHT MUSIC. Text in Chinese. bi-m.
Published by: Jilin Sheng Yinyuejia Xiehui/Jilin Musicians' Association, Fu 111 Stalin St Bldg. No 14, Changchun, Jilin 130021, China. TEL 884953. Ed. Wang Guanqun.

QINTONG/LITTLE MUSICIAN. *see* CHILDREN AND YOUTH—For

708.1 ITA
QUADERNI DEL MUSEO ANTONIANO. Abbreviated title: Q M A. Text in Italian. 1996. irreg., latest vol.2, 1998. price varies. **Document type:** *Monographic series, Academic/Scholarly.*
Published by: Centro Studi Antoniani, Piazza del Santo 11, Padua, PD 35123, Italy. TEL 39-049-8762177, FAX 39-049-8762187, asscsa@tin.it, http://www.centrostudiantoniani.it.

780 ITA
QUADERNI ROSSINIANI. Text in Italian. 1954. irreg., latest vol.19, 1976. price varies. **Document type:** *Monographic series, Academic/Scholarly.*
Published by: (Fondazione G. Rossini), Casa Editrice Leo S. Olschki, Viuzzo del Pozzetto 8, Florence, 50126, Italy. TEL 39-055-6530684, FAX 39-055-6530214, celso@olschki.it, http://www.olschki.it.

780 ESP ISSN 1989-8851
▼ **QUADRIVIUM.** Text in Spanish, Gallegan. 2010. a. **Document type:** *Monographic series, Academic/Scholarly.*
Media: Online - full text.
Published by: Asociacio Valenciana de Musicologia, Academia de la Llengua, 86, Nules - Castello, 12520, Spain. TEL 34-652-282869.

615.85 780 USA
QUALITATIVE INQUIRIES IN MUSIC THERAPY (ONLINE). Text in English. 2004. irreg. free (effective 2010). **Document type:** *Monographic series, Academic/Scholarly.*
Formerly (until 2008): Qualitative Inquiries in Music Therapy (Print) (1559-7326)
Media: Online - full text.
Indexed: A01, CA, M11, T02.
Published by: Barcelona Publishers, 4 White Brook Rd - Lower Village, PO Box 89, Gilsum, NH 03448. TEL 603-357-0236, 800-345-6665, FAX 603-357-2073, barcelonapublishers@comcast.net.

780 331.8 USA
QUARTERNOTE. Text in English. 1976. q. USD 5 (effective 1998). adv. bk.rev. illus. **Document type:** *Newsletter.* **Description:** Provides information of interest to members of the union.
Published by: American Musicians Union, Inc., 8 Tobin Ct, Dumont, NJ 07628. TEL 201-384-5378. Ed. Ben Intorre. Circ: 250 (controlled).

780 GBR
QUARTERNOTE. Text in English. 1979. q. free to members. bk.rev. illus. **Document type:** *Newsletter.* **Description:** Contains news and features surrounding the activities of the orchestra.
Formerly (until 1988): W O S News
Published by: Bournemouth Symphony Orchestra, c/o Naomi Lake, Membership Officer, BSO Membership, 2 Seldown Ln, Poole, Dorset BH15 1UF, United Kingdom. TEL 44-1202-644734, nlake@bsorchestra.co.uk, http://www.bsolive.com/. Circ: 3,000.

781.7 DEU ISSN 0939-9747
QUELLEN UND STUDIEN ZUR GESCHICHTE DER MANNHEIMER HOFKAPELLE. Text in German. 1993. irreg., latest vol.9, 2002. price varies. **Document type:** *Monographic series, Academic/Scholarly.*
Published by: Peter Lang GmbH (Subsidiary of: Peter Lang Publishing Group), Eschborner Landstr 42-50, Frankfurt Am Main, 60489, Germany. TEL 49-69-7807050, FAX 49-69-78070550, zentrale.frankfurt@peterlang.com.

780 DEU ISSN 0175-6257
QUELLEN UND STUDIEN ZUR MUSIKGESCHICHTE VON DER ANTIKE BIS IN DIE GEGENWART. Text in German. 1984. irreg., latest vol.42, 2005. price varies. **Document type:** *Monographic series, Academic/Scholarly.*
Published by: Peter Lang GmbH (Subsidiary of: Peter Lang Publishing Group), Eschborner Landstr 42-50, Frankfurt Am Main, 60489, Germany. Ed. Michael von Albrecht.

780 DEU ISSN 0079-905X
QUELLENKATALOGE ZUR MUSIKGESCHICHTE. Text in German. 1966. irreg., latest vol.25, 1993. **Document type:** *Monographic series.*
Published by: Florian Noetzel Verlag, Heinrichshofen Buecher, Holtermannstr 32, Wilhelmshaven, 26384, Germany. Ed. Richard Schaal. **Dist. in U.S. by:** C. F. Peters Corporation, 373 Park Ave S, New York, NY 10016.

780 DEU ISSN 1436-3631
QUELLENTEXTE ZUR MUSIK DES 20. JAHRHUNDERTS. Text in German. 1991. irreg., latest vol.11, 2004. price varies. **Document type:** *Monographic series, Academic/Scholarly.*
Published by: Pfau Verlag, Hafenstr 33, Saarbruecken, 66111, Germany. TEL 49-681-4163394, FAX 49-681-4163395, info@pfau-verlag.de.

780 AUT
QUERSTAND; Beitraege zu Kunst und Kultur. Text in German. 2005. irreg., latest vol.3, 2007. price varies. **Document type:** *Monographic series, Academic/Scholarly.*
Published by: (Anton Bruckner Privatuniversitaet), Trauner Verlag und Buchservice GmbH, Koeglstr 14, Linz, 4020, Austria. TEL 43-732-778241212, FAX 43-732-778241400, office@trauner.at, http://www.trauner.at.

782.5 CAN ISSN 1922-7442
QUIRES. Text in English. 2003. 3/yr. free to members (effective 2010). adv. **Document type:** *Magazine, Trade.*
Published by: Alberta Choral Federation, 103, 10612-124 St, Edmonton, AB T5N 1S4, Canada. TEL 780-488-7464, FAX 780-488-6403, info@albertachoralfederation.ca. adv.: page USD 180; 7.5 x 9.25.

780 ESP ISSN 1134-8615
ML5
QUODLIBET. Text in Spanish. 1985. 3/yr. EUR 39 domestic; EUR 55 in the Americas; EUR 75 elsewhere (effective 2009). **Document type:** *Journal, Academic/Scholarly.*
Indexed: IIMP, RILM.
Published by: (Universidad de Alcala de Henares, Aula de Musica), Universidad de Alcala de Henares, Fundacion Caja Madrid, Ca Colegios, 10, Alcala de Henares, Madrid, 28801, Spain. TEL 34-91-8788128, FAX 34-91-8802911, auladeмusica@musicalcala.com, http://www.fundacioncajamadrid.org. Ed. Jacobo Duran Loriga.

784 USA ISSN 0885-9442
QUODLIBET. Text in English. 1967. 2/yr. looseleaf. membership. bk.rev. back issues avail.
Published by: Intercollegiate Men's Choruses, Inc., c/o KSU, Dept of Music, McCain Auditorium, Manhattan, KS 66506-4706. TEL 913-532-5740. Ed. Gerald Polish. Circ: 75.

QUYI/VARIETY SHOW. see THEATER

R & R DIRECTORY. (Radio and Records) see COMMUNICATIONS—Radio

R & R HEADLINE NEWS AND RATINGS. (Radio and Records) see COMMUNICATIONS—Radio

R & R TODAY. (Radio and Records) see COMMUNICATIONS—Radio

780 USA ISSN 0889-6607
ML140
R I D I M - R C M I INVENTORY OF MUSIC ICONOGRAPHY. (Repertoire Internationale d'Iconographie Musicale - Research Center for Music Iconography) Text in English. 1987. irreg., latest vol.8. price varies.
Description: Features catalogues of the music iconography in individual museums in the U.S.A.
Published by: (Research Center for Music Iconography/Repertoire Internationale d'Iconographie Musicale), City University of New York, Research Center for Music Iconography, 365 Fifth Ave, New York, NY 10016. TEL 212-817-1992, FAX 212-817-1569.

780 370 USA ISSN 1532-8090
MT1
➤ **R I M E.** (Research and Issues in Music Education) Text in English. 2003. a. free (effective 2011). back issues avail. **Document type:** *Journal, Academic/Scholarly.*
Media: Online - full text.
Indexed: A26, CA, E03, ERI, ERIC, I05, M11, T02.
Published by: Research and Issues in Music Education, 2115 Summit Ave, LOR 103, St. Paul, MN 55105. Ed. Dr. Bruce Gleason.

784.5 NOR ISSN 0800-0549
R-O-C-K. Text in Norwegian, Swedish. 1978. 5/yr. NOK 150, USD 25 (effective 1999). adv. bk.rev. illus. **Document type:** *Consumer.*
Supersedes (1972-1977): Rock and Roll International Magazine; Whole Lotta Rockin
—CCC.
Published by: Rock and Roll Society of Scandinavia, Postboks 59, Furuset, Oslo, 1001, Norway. TEL 47-22-21-41-30. Ed. Tor Arne Petzold. Circ: 1,000.

780.42 780.7 GBR ISSN 1028-9968
R P M: REVIEW OF POPULAR MUSIC. Text in English. 1981. s-a. bk.rev. **Document type:** *Magazine, Consumer.*
Published by: International Association for the Study of Popular Music, c/o Institute of Popular Music, University of Liverpool, Chatham St, Liverpool, L69 7ZT, United Kingdom. FAX 44-151-7942566, webmaster@iaspm.net. Ed. Geoff Stahl. Circ: 400.

780 ITA ISSN 1824-632X
I RACCONTI DELLA MUSICA. Text in Italian. 2001. irreg. **Document type:** *Magazine, Consumer.*
Published by: Zecchini Editore, Via Tonale 60, Varese, VA 21100, Italy. TEL 39-0332-331041, FAX 39-0332-331013, editoriale@zecchini.com, http://www.zecchini.com.

780 USA
RADIO FREE ROCK. Text in English. 1978 (vol.2). m. free. adv. illus. **Document type:** *Newsletter.*
Incorporates: Gulcher
Published by: Cyco Publishing, 633 Crestmoore Pl, Venice, CA 90291-4814. Ed., R&P David F Myers. Circ: 10,000.

780 USA ISSN 1061-9879
ML3469
RAG MAGAZINE; Florida's music magazine. Text in English. 1977. m. USD 25 (effective 2005). adv. **Document type:** *Magazine, Consumer.*
Published by: Rag Magazine, Inc., 8930 State Rd 84, Ste 322, Ft. Lauderdale, FL 33324. TEL 954-234-2888, FAX 954-473-4551. Ed. Crystal Clark. Pub. Sean McCloskey. adv.: B&W page USD 400, color page USD 550; trim 7.25 x 9.5.

785.4 USA ISSN 0090-4570
ML1
RAG TIMES. Text in English. 1967. bi-m. USD 12 in US & Canada; USD 19 elsewhere. adv. bk.rev. illus. back issues avail. **Document type:** *Newsletter.* **Description:** News, articles, announcements, and reviews pertaining to rag-time music and musicians across the nation.
Published by: Maple Leaf Club, 15522 Ricky Ct, Grass Valley, CA 95949. Ed. Richard Zimmerman. Circ: 550.

780 USA
RAGING SMOLDER MUSIC REVIEW. Text in English. 1996. m.
Description: Features reviews of music recordings by new and independent musicians, bands, singers and songwriters.
Media: Online - full text.
Address: 1012 Forest Hills Ave, Annapolis, MD 21403. TEL 410-263-7264. Ed. Riff Gibson.

780 EST ISSN 1406-7099
RAHVUSVAHELISE EDUARD TUBINA UHINGU AASTARAAMAT. Text in Estonian, English. 2001. irreg., latest vol.3, 2003. price varies. **Document type:** *Monographic series, Academic/Scholarly.*
Indexed: RILM.
Published by: Rahvusvaheline Eduard Tubina Uhing, Estonian Academy of Music, Ravala 16, Rm B224, Tallinn, 10143, Estonia. TEL 372-6675736, tubin.society@mail.ee, http://www.kul.ee/emc/ets.

RALPH; coffee, jazz and poetry. see LITERATURE—Poetry

RAMPIKE MAGAZINE. see ART

780 BRA ISSN 1517-1833
ML3531
RAP BRASIL. Text in Portuguese. 1999. bi-m. BRL 4.90 newsstand/cover (effective 2006). **Document type:** *Magazine, Consumer.*
Published by: Editora Escala Ltda., Av Prof Ida Kolb, 551, Casa Verde, Sao Paulo, 02518-000, Brazil. TEL 55-11-38552100, FAX 55-11-38579643, escala@escala.com.br, http://www.escala.com.br.

785.16 FRA ISSN 1966-6748
RAP & GROOVE. Text in French. 1997. m. adv. **Document type:** *Magazine, Consumer.*
Formerly (until 2008): Groove (1279-8991)
Related titles: Supplement(s): Rap U S. ISSN 1628-3384. 2000.
Published by: Euro Services Internet, 60 rue Vitruve, Paris, 75020, France. FAX 33-1-55253101.

782.421 IRL
RAP IRELAND. Text in English. 2004. bi-m. EUR 30 (effective 2006). adv. **Document type:** *Magazine, Consumer.*
Formerly: Hip-Hop Ireland (1649-6094)
Address: 17 Stockton Dr, Castleknock, Dublin, 15, Ireland. TEL 353-879-892011, info@rapireland.com, http://rapireland.com. Pub. Kev Storrs. Adv. contact Timi Martins.

782.421 FRA ISSN 1773-5858
RAP MAG. Text in French. 2004. m. EUR 45 domestic; EUR 48.50 in Europe; EUR 50 elsewhere (effective 2008). **Document type:** *Magazine, Consumer.*
Published by: B & B Media, 40 Rue de Paradis, Paris, 75010, France. TEL 33-1-53249970, FAX 33-1-53249979, info@bandbmedia.com. **Subscr. to:** Viapresse, 7 Impasse Marie Blanche, Paris 75018, France. serviceclients@viapresse.com.

781.57 305.896 USA ISSN 1063-1283
ML3531
RAP PAGES; the survival guide for hip-hop culture, lifestyles & music. Text in English. 1991. 9/yr. USD 12; USD 24 foreign; USD 3.99 newsstand/cover; GBP 1.95 newsstand/cover in United Kingdom; CAD 4.50 newsstand/cover in Canada (effective 1999). adv. bk.rev.; music rev.; rec.rev. illus. **Document type:** *Magazine, Consumer.* **Description:** Covers rap music releases and performers, along with related hip-hop and African American culture.
Related titles: Online - full text ed.
Published by: L F P, Inc., 8484 Wilshire Blvd., Ste. 900, Beverly Hills, CA 90211. TEL 310-858-7100, 800-304-1849, FAX 310-274-7985. Ed. Dorothy Stefanski. Pub. Larry Flynt. Adv. contact Manny Gonzalez. **Dist. by:** Seymour Distribution Ltd, 86 Newman St, London W1T 3EX, United Kingdom. FAX 44-207-396-8002, enquiries@seymour.co.uk.

782.421 USA
RAP SHEET. Text in English. m. adv.
Related titles: Online - full text ed.
Published by: J C I Publishing, 2270 Centinela Ave, B4, Los Angeles, CA 90064. TEL 310-670-7200, FAX 310-670-6236. Ed., Pub. Daryl James.

781.57 USA ISSN 1943-4006
RAP-UP. Text in English. 2005. 6/yr. USD 11.99 (effective 2009). adv. music rev. **Document type:** *Magazine, Consumer.* **Description:** Covers various aspects of hip-hop and R&B music and culture.
Published by: Rap-Up LLC, 23679 Calabasas Rd #368, Calabasas, CA 91302. Pub. Devin Lazerine.

RAPPORT; the modern guide to books, music & more. see PUBLISHING AND BOOK TRADE

780 790.13 ITA
RARO!; mensile di collezionismo e cultura musicale. Text in Italian. 1987. 11/yr. EUR 80 in Europe; EUR 100 elsewhere (effective 2009). adv. bk.rev.; music rev.; video rev. charts; illus.; mkt. back issues avail.
Description: For collectors of record albums.
Related titles: Online - full text ed.
Published by: Edizioni/R A Srl, Via G B Tiepolo 7, Rome, 00196, Italy. TEL 39-06-36086481, FAX 39-06-36086482. Pub. Andrea Tinari. Circ: 20,000.

780 USA ISSN 1084-6379
THE RASTAMON TIMES. Text in English. 1994. m.
Published by: RastaMon Times, PO Box 12882, Milwaukee, WI 53212. Pub. Ras Loosus.

780 USA
RATIONAL ALTERNATIVE DIGITAL CYBERZINE. Text in English. 1993. bi-m. **Description:** Covers alternative, college, or underground music.
Media: Online - full text.
Address: PO Box 171144, Salt Lake City, UT 84117-1144. Ed. Jeff Jolley.

781.64 DEU
RAVELINE; visions of electronic music. Text in German. 1995. m. EUR 38.50 domestic; EUR 52 foreign; EUR 3.50 newsstand/cover (effective 2008). adv. **Document type:** *Magazine, Consumer.* **Description:** Contains information on all aspects of electronic dance music, nightlife, clubbing, technical equipment and fashion.
Published by: A.E.C. Geronimo Verlag GmbH, Provinzialstr 65, Datteln, 45711, Germany. TEL 49-2363-567612, FAX 49-2363-567694. Ed. Sven Schaefer. R&P Frank van Lieshaut. Adv. contact Sebastian Spohr. B&W page EUR 5,000, color page EUR 7,550. Circ: 64,257 (paid).

RBXPRESS. see LIFESTYLE

781.24 USA ISSN 2151-7851
ML1
RE-NOTATION OF MUSIC NEWSLETTER. Text in English. 1986. q. bk.rev. back issues avail. **Document type:** *Newsletter, Academic/Scholarly.* **Description:** Research on new methods of music notation.
Formerly (until 2010): Music Notation News (0258-963X)
Indexed: RILM.
Published by: R I L M International Center, City University of New York, 365 Fifth Ave, Ste 3108, New York, NY 10016. TEL 212-817-1990, FAX 212-817-1569, questions@rilm.org, http://www.rilm.org.

RE-SOUNDINGS. see ART

780 USA
READ MAGAZINE (ASTORIA). Text in English. 1996. q. USD 10; USD 6.99 newsstand/cover domestic; USD 8.99 newsstand/cover in Canada (effective 2005). **Document type:** *Magazine, Consumer.*
Published by: Read Magazine, P O Box 3437, Astoria, NY 11103. Ed. Adam Liebling.

781.605 NZL ISSN 1172-2096
THE REAL GROOVE. Variant title: Groove. Text in English. 1992 (Oct.). 10/yr. NZD 49.95 (effective 2009). **Document type:** *Magazine, Consumer.*
Published by: Real Groovy Promotions, 438 Queen St, Auckland Central, PO Box 91285, Auckland, New Zealand. TEL 64-9-3023940, FAX 64-9-3023955, help@realgroovy.co.nz, http://www.realgroovy.co.nz/.

780 USA ISSN 0147-0078
M2.3.U6
➤ **RECENT RESEARCHES IN AMERICAN MUSIC.** Text in English. 1977. irreg., latest vol.68, 2009. price varies. back issues avail. **Document type:** *Monographic series, Academic/Scholarly.* **Description:** Provides information about music of the eighteenth and early nineteenth centuries. Designed to fill some of the gaps that have persisted in the music of the United States.
Related titles: ◆ Includes: Music of the United States of America. ISSN 1066-8217; ◆ Supplement(s): Music of the United States of America. ISSN 1066-8217.
Published by: A-R Editions, Inc., 8551 Research Way, Ste 180, Middleton, WI 53562. TEL 608-836-9000, 800-736-0070, FAX 608-831-8200, orders@areditions.com. Eds. James L Zychowicz TEL 608-836-9000 ext 14, John M Graziano.

780 USA ISSN 0484-0828
M2
➤ **RECENT RESEARCHES IN THE MUSIC OF THE BAROQUE ERA.** Text in English. 1964. irreg., latest vol.164, 2010. price varies. back issues avail. **Document type:** *Monographic series, Academic/Scholarly.* **Description:** Features as a source for new editions of early music.
Published by: A-R Editions, Inc., 8551 Research Way, Ste 180, Middleton, WI 53562. TEL 608-836-9000, 800-736-0070, FAX 608-831-8200, orders@areditions.com. Eds. Christoph Wolff, James L Zychowicz TEL 608-836-9000 ext 14.

780 USA ISSN 0147-0086
M2
➤ **RECENT RESEARCHES IN THE MUSIC OF THE CLASSICAL ERA.** Text in English. 1975. irreg., latest vol.80, 2010. price varies. back issues avail. **Document type:** *Monographic series, Academic/Scholarly.* **Description:** Aims to provide a balanced presentation of the period as a whole for both performers and scholars.
Formerly: Recent Researches in the Music of the Classical and Early Romantic Era
Published by: A-R Editions, Inc., 8551 Research Way, Ste 180, Middleton, WI 53562. TEL 608-836-9000, 800-736-0070, FAX 608-831-8200, orders@areditions.com. Eds. James L Zychowicz TEL 608-836-9000 ext 14, Neal Zaslaw.

780 USA ISSN 0362-3572
M2
➤ **RECENT RESEARCHES IN THE MUSIC OF THE MIDDLE AGES AND EARLY RENAISSANCE.** Text in English. 1975. irreg., latest vol.40, 2009. price varies. back issues avail. **Document type:** *Monographic series, Academic/Scholarly.* **Description:** Presents modern editions of both monophonic and polyphonic music that result from research into specific composers, repertories, manuscripts, and genres of music dating from approximately 500-1500 C.E.
Published by: A-R Editions, Inc., 8551 Research Way, Ste 180, Middleton, WI 53562. TEL 608-836-9000, 800-736-0070, FAX 608-831-8200, orders@areditions.com. Eds. Charles M Atkinson, James L Zychowicz TEL 608-836-9000 ext 14.

780.904 USA ISSN 0193-5364
M2
➤ **RECENT RESEARCHES IN THE MUSIC OF THE NINETEENTH AND EARLY TWENTIETH CENTURIES.** Text in English. 1979. irreg., latest vol.54, 2010. price varies. back issues avail. **Document type:** *Monographic series, Academic/Scholarly.* **Description:** Contains several anthologies of lieder by various neglected composers on texts by Eichendorff, Goethe, Heine, Morike, and other poets. Features include collections devoted to a single genre.
Published by: A-R Editions, Inc., 8551 Research Way, Ste 180, Middleton, WI 53562. TEL 608-836-9000, 800-736-0070, FAX 608-831-8200, orders@areditions.com. Eds. James L Zychowicz TEL 608-836-9000 ext 14, Rufus Hallmark.

780 USA ISSN 0486-123X
M2
➤ **RECENT RESEARCHES IN THE MUSIC OF THE RENAISSANCE.** Text in English. 1964. irreg., latest vol.151, 2008. price varies. back issues avail. **Document type:** *Monographic series, Academic/Scholarly.* **Description:** Features collected works of a composer within a chosen genre.
Published by: A-R Editions, Inc., 8551 Research Way, Ste 180, Middleton, WI 53562. TEL 608-836-9000, 800-736-0070, FAX 608-831-8200, orders@areditions.com. Eds. James L Zychowicz TEL 608-836-9000 ext 14, James Haar.

780 USA ISSN 1066-8209
M1495
➤ **RECENT RESEARCHES IN THE ORAL TRADITIONS OF MUSIC.** Text in English. 1993. irreg., latest 2010. price varies. back issues avail. **Document type:** *Monographic series, Academic/Scholarly.* **Description:** Designed for scholars to rethink the critical edition as a component in the current rapprochement between ethnomusicology, historical musicology, and cultural studies.
Published by: A-R Editions, Inc., 8551 Research Way, Ste 180, Middleton, WI 53562. TEL 608-836-9000, 800-736-0070, FAX 608-831-8200, orders@areditions.com. Eds. James L Zychowicz TEL 608-836-9000 ext 14, Philip V Bohlman.

780 ESP ISSN 0211-6391
ML315.7.C18
RECERCA MUSICOLOGICA. Text in Spanish, Catalan, English. 1981. a., latest 2006. back issues avail. **Document type:** *Monographic series, Academic/Scholarly.*
Indexed: IIMP, P09, PCI, RILM.

M

Published by: Universitat Autonoma de Barcelona, Servei de Publicacions, Edifici A, Bellaterra, Cardanyola del Valles, Barcelona, 08193, Spain. TEL 34-93-5811022, FAX 34-93-5813239, sp@uab.es, http://www.uab.es/publicacions/.

780 ITA ISSN 1120-5741
ML5
RECERCARE; rivista per lo studio e la pratica della musica antica - journal for the study and practice of early music. Text in English, French, German, Italian. 1971. a., latest vol.13, 2001. EUR 24 domestic; EUR 29 foreign (effective 2009). adv. bk.rev. abstr. **Document type:** *Journal, Academic/Scholarly.*
Formerly (until 1988): Flauto Dolce (1825-8212)
Indexed: DIP, IBR, IBZ, IIMP, M11, MusicInd, RILM.
Published by: (Fondazione Italiana per la Musica Antica), LIM Editrice Srl, Via di Arsina 296/f, Lucca, LU 55100, Italy. TEL 39-0583-394464, FAX 39-0583-394469, lim@lim.it, http://www.lim.it. Ed. Arnaldo Morelli.

780.7 CAN ISSN 1491-4166
RECHERCHE EN EDUCATION MUSICALE. Text in French. 1982. a. **Document type:** *Journal, Academic/Scholarly.*
Former titles (until 1998): Recherche en Education Musicale au Quebec (0844-5923); (until 1989): Cahiers d'Information sur la Recherche en Education Musicale (0821-5456)
Indexed: CMPI, RILM.
Published by: Universite Laval, Faculte de Musique, Pavillon Louis-Jacques-Casault, Sainte-Foy, PQ G1K 7P4, Canada.

780 FRA ISSN 1284-7119
RECHERCHES ET EDITIONS MUSICALES. Text in French. 1999. irreg. **Document type:** *Monographic series, Academic/Scholarly.*
Related titles: ◆ Series of: Arts du Spectacle. ISSN 0296-2292.
Published by: Centre National de la Recherche Scientifique, Campus Gerard-Megie, 3 Rue Michel-Ange, Paris, 75794, France. TEL 33-1-44964000, FAX 33-1-44965390, http://www.cnrseditions.fr.

789.91 GBR ISSN 0034-1568
THE RECORD COLLECTOR (CHELMSFORD). Text in English. 1946. q. GBP 24 domestic; EUR 27 in Europe; GBP 34 elsewhere (effective 2009). bk.rev.; rec.rev. charts; illus. index. back issues avail. **Document type:** *Journal, Academic/Scholarly.* **Description:** Contains full biographies and discographies of two or more singers and articles of interest to the enthusiast, both novice and advanced.
Formerly (until 1947): Record Collector's Bulletin
Published by: Record Collector (Chelmsford), 111 Longshots Close, Broomfield, Chelmsford, CM1 7DU, United Kingdom. TEL 44-1245-441661, FAX 44-1245-443642, larrylusti@aol.com, http://www.members.aol.com/reccoll/collector. Ed. Larry Lustig.

789.9 GBR ISSN 0261-250X
RECORD COLLECTOR (LONDON); serious about music. Text in English. 1980. m. GBP 45 domestic; GBP 72 includes Europe, USA & Canada; GBP 98 elsewhere (effective 2010). adv. bk.rev. illus. back issues avail. **Document type:** *Magazine, Consumer.* **Description:** Spans 50 years of music history, covering every genre - pop, rock, psychedelia, soul, rock & roll, reggae, soundtracks. Uses expert writers from around the world to present news, reviews, interviews, valuations and advice.
Supersedes in part (in 1980): Beatles Book & Record Collector
Related titles: Online - full text ed.
Published by: Metropolis International Ltd, 140 Wales Farm Rd, London, W3 6UG, United Kingdom. TEL 44-20-87528181, FAX 44-20-87528185, metropolis@metropolis.co.uk, http://www.metropolis.co.uk/. Ed. Alan Lewis. Adv. contact Bill Edwards.

780 621.389 USA ISSN 0557-9147
RECORD EXCHANGER. Text in English. 1969. q. USD 11.95. adv. bk.rev. charts; illus. index.
Published by: Vintage Records, PO Box 6144, Orange, CA 92667. TEL 714-639-3383. Ed. Art Turco. Circ: 22,000.

789.91 JPN ISSN 0289-3614
RECORD GEIJUTSU/ART OF RECORDS, DISCOGRAPHY REVIEW. Text in Japanese. 1952. m. JPY 1,250. adv. **Document type:** *Academic/Scholarly.* **Description:** Carries critical commentaries by authorities in the field that serve as guidelines for new record selections as well as enhances the knowledge of music.
Published by: Ongaku No Tomo Sha Corp., c/o KakuyukiNabeshima, 6-30 Kagura-Zaka, Shinjuku-ku, Tokyo, 162-0825, Japan. FAX 81-3-3235-2129. Ed. Ryusuke Nozawa. Pub. Jun Meguro. R&P Tetsuo Morita TEL 81-3-3235-2111. Adv. contact Takao Oya. B&W page JPY 312,000, color page JPY 624,000; trim 182 x 257. Circ: 150,000.

780.7 CAN ISSN 0704-7231
THE RECORDER. Text in English. 1958. q. **Document type:** *Journal, Trade.*
Indexed: C03, CEI, CMPI, P48, PQC.
Published by: Ontario Music Educators' Association, c/o Carolyn Otto, 255 Boland Ave, Sudbury, ON P3E 1Y1, Canada. TEL 705-674-1109. Eds. Dr. Rodger Beatty, Sharon Fitzsimmins.

789.91 GBR ISSN 0961-3544
ML5
THE RECORDER MAGAZINE. Text in English. 1963. q. GBP 25 domestic; USD 26 in United States (effective 2009). adv. bk.rev.; music rev. illus. **Document type:** *Journal, Trade.* **Description:** Features articles on the history of the recorder and its present-day use.
Former titles (until 1900): Recorder and Music Magazine (0961-3242); (until 1983): Recorder and Music (0306-4409); (until 1973): Recorder and Music Magazine (0034-1665)
Indexed: A01, CMPI, H20, IIMP, M11, MusicInd, RILM, T02.
—Ingenta. **CCC.**
Published by: Peacock Press, Scout Bottom Farm, Mytholmroyd, Hebden Bridge, HX7 5JS, United Kingdom. TEL 44-1422 882751, FAX 44-1422-886157, liz@recordermail.demon.co.uk. adv.: page GBP 250; trim 180 x 264. Circ: 3,000.

781.642 GBR
RED HOT COUNTRY MAGAZINE. Text in English. 1996. w.
Published by: Red Hot, 20 College Rd, Wembley, Middlesex, HA9 8RL, United Kingdom.

781.64 USA
RED MAGAZINE. Text in English. 1998. m. **Document type:** *Magazine, Consumer.* **Description:** Covers the local art, music and cultural scenes in Chicago.
Media: Online - full content.
Address: http://www.redmagazine.com. Adv. contacts Mike Ferguson, Scott Johnson.

786 USA ISSN 0736-9549
ML549.8
REED ORGAN SOCIETY BULLETIN. Short title: R O S Bulletin. Text in English. 1982. q. USD 17.50; USD 25 foreign. adv. bk.rev. bibl. back issues avail. **Document type:** *Bulletin.* **Description:** For musicians, historians, collectors and restorers of all types of free-reed instruments, including melodeons, "pump" organs, harmoniums and more.
Formerly: Reed Organ Society Newsletter
Published by: (Reed Organ Society, Inc.), Reed Organ Society Publications, 6907 Rix St, S E, Ada, MI 49301. TEL 616-676-1188. Ed., R&P Edward A Peterson. Pub. Gordon Deyoung. Adv. contact Carl Shannon. Circ: 700. **Subscr. to:** Reed Organ Society Inc., c/o James Quashnock, Membership Sec, 258 Hwy 258E, Wichita Falls, TX 76308-7037. TEL 817-691-7809.

780 DEU ISSN 0342-4936
REGER-STUDIEN. Text in German. 1978. irreg., latest vol.7. price varies. **Document type:** *Monographic series, Academic/Scholarly.*
Indexed: RILM.
Published by: (Max-Reger-Institut, Bonn), Carus-Verlag GmbH, Sielminger Str 51, Leinfelden-Echterdingen, 70771, Germany. TEL 49-711-7973300, FAX 49-711-79733029, info@carus-verlag.com, http://www.carus-verlag.com.

780 USA ISSN 1065-3023
ML3532
REGGAE REPORT. Text in English. 1983. 10/yr. USD 24; USD 40 in Canada; USD 45 elsewhere. adv. bk.rev.; music rev.; video rev. **Document type:** *Magazine, Consumer.* **Description:** Covers all aspects of reggae music and news from Jamaica, America and the world.
Indexed: IIMP, M11, MusicInd.
Published by: R R International Magazine Inc., 21300 N E 24 Ct, Miami, FL 33180. TEL 305-933-1178, FAX 305-933-1077. Ed. M Peggy Quattro. Pub., R&P, Adv. contact M. Peggy Quattro. B&W page USD 1,600, color page USD 2,380.

780 JAM
REGGAE TIMES. Text in English. 1994. bi-m. USD 12 domestic; USD 15 Eastern Caribbean; USD 20 in US & Canada; USD 24 in Europe; USD 26 elsewhere (effective 2000). adv. **Document type:** *Magazine, Consumer.* **Description:** Contains current and topical information on reggae music, people and lifestyles.
Address: The Beverley Hills Ctr, Ste 1, 94N Old Hope Rd, Kingston, 6, Jamaica.

780 FRA ISSN 1773-6498
REGGAE VIBES. Text in French. 199?. bi-m. EUR 6.95 newsstand/cover (effective 2011). adv. **Document type:** *Magazine, Consumer.*
Formerly (until 2008): Ragga (1626-4142)
Published by: Detroit Media, 6, Rue Desargues, Paris, 75011, France. TEL 33-1-42471825.

780 GBR ISSN 0959-7603
REGISTER OF PERFORMERS & COMPOSERS. Text in English. 1976. a. free to members (effective 2010). **Document type:** *Directory, Trade.* **Description:** Features lists members working professionally as performers, conductors, and composers.
Former titles (until 1990): Register of Professional Artists (0951-6247); (until 1987): Professional Register of Artists
Published by: Incorporated Society of Musicians, 10 Stratford Pl, London, W1C 1AA, United Kingdom. TEL 44-20-76294413, FAX 44-20-74081538, membership@ism.org. Circ: 4,000.

780.7 GBR ISSN 0951-6239
ML21.G7
REGISTER OF PROFESSIONAL PRIVATE MUSIC TEACHERS. Text in English. 19??. a. free to members (effective 2010). **Document type:** *Directory, Trade.* **Description:** Feature lists professional teachers of music to private pupils.
Formerly (until 1987): Professional Register of Private Teachers of Music
Published by: Incorporated Society of Musicians, 10 Stratford Pl, London, W1C 1AA, United Kingdom. TEL 44-20-76294413, FAX 44-20-74081538, membership@ism.org.

781.64 808.8 USA
REGULARLY SCHEDULED DEPROGRAMMING. Text in English. irreg., latest 1994. music rev. **Description:** Covers punk rock, the punk lifestyle, the do-it-yourself ethic, and anarchist politics.
Formerly (until 1993): Disinformation
Published by: Tim Nevaker, Ed. & Pub., 8248 Rupert Rd S, Millersville, MD 21108. TEL 410-987-4738. Circ: 100 (paid).

780 DEU ISSN 0931-3087
REIHE MUSIKWISSENSCHAFT. Text in German. 1987. irreg., latest vol.8, 2010. price varies. **Document type:** *Monographic series, Academic/Scholarly.*
Published by: Centaurus Verlag & Media KG, Kaiser-Joseph-Str 267, Freiburg, 79098, Germany. TEL 49-761-1525861, FAX 49-761-1525868, info@centaurus-verlag.de, http://www.centaurus-verlag.de.

780 USA
RELEASE MAGAZINE; christian music covered in style. Text in English. 1991. bi-m.
Published by: Vox Publishing, 3670 Central Pike, Ste J, Hermitage, TN 37076. TEL 615-872-8080, FAX 615-872-9786, editorial@voxcorp.com, http://www.releasemagazine.com. Ed. Chris Well. Circ: 110,000.

780.42 USA ISSN 0146-3489
RELIX; music for the mind. Variant title: Dead Relix. Text in English. 1974. 8/yr. USD 19.95 domestic; USD 29.95 foreign (effective 2005). adv. bk.rev.; film rev. charts; illus.; stat. back issues avail. **Document type:** *Magazine, Consumer.* **Description:** Specializes in classic rock, currently focusing on the next generation of classic rock: Rusted Root, Widespread Panic, MDE, Blues Traveler, etc.
Indexed: IIMP, M11, MusicInd, RILM, T02.
Published by: Relix Magazine, Inc, 180 Varick St, 4th Fl., Ste 410, New York, NY 10014 . TEL 646-230-0100, FAX 646-230-0200. Ed. Aeve Baldwin. Pub. Steve Bernstein. Circ: 70,000 (paid).

780 USA ISSN 0889-8790
ML3469
REMEMBER THAT SONG; newsletter for sheet music collectors. Text in English. 1981. m. USD 20 (effective 1999). bk.rev. illus. **Document type:** *Newsletter.* **Description:** Covers the historical aspects and implications of collecting American popular music, and the evolution of song, from before the Civil War to the present.
Address: 5623 N 64th Ave, Glendale, AZ 85301. TEL 602-931-2835. Ed. Lois A Cordrey. Pub., R&P Lois Cordrey. Circ: 425 (paid).

780 USA ISSN 1532-1347
ML1379
REMIX; underground music production - D J performance. Text in English. 1999. m. (13/yr.). USD 14.97; USD 19.95 combined subscription (print & online eds.) (effective 2008). adv. illus. back issues avail. **Document type:** *Magazine, Consumer.* **Description:** Contains in-depth interviews with major personalities in the DJ/remix scene with a major focus on studio production and performance styles, technology as it effects the creative process, and the gear that is used.
Formerly (until 2000): Electronic Musician Presents Remix (1540-4676)
Related titles: Online - full text ed.
Indexed: A09, A10, B07, M01, M02, M11, T02, V02, V03, V04.
—**CCC.**
Published by: Penton Media, Inc., 6400 Hollis St, Ste 12, Emeryville, CA 94608. TEL 510-653-3307, FAX 510-653-5142, information@penton.com, http://www.pentonmedia.com. Eds. Kylee Swenson, Tom Kenny. adv.: color page USD 5,775; trim 7.4375 x 10.875.

780 USA ISSN 0196-7037
ML169.8
RENAISSANCE MANUSCRIPT STUDIES. Text in English. 1979. irreg., latest vol.6, 1994. price varies. **Document type:** *Monographic series, Academic/Scholarly.* **Description:** Brings out reference works that support the study of early music.
Published by: American Institute of Musicology, 8551 Research Way, Ste 180, Middleton, WI 53562. TEL 608-836-9000, 800-736-0070, FAX 608-831-8200, info@corpusmusicae.com. Ed. Charles Hamm.

780 USA ISSN 0034-4451
RENFRO VALLEY BUGLE. Text in English. 1943. m. USD 9. adv. illus. **Document type:** *Newspaper.* **Description:** Covers news of the local and national country music scene, with listings of upcoming events, and articles on past and present country music entertainers.
Published by: Renfro Valley Entertainment Center, Inc., US 25 S, Renfro Valley, KY 40473. TEL 606-256-2638, FAX 606-256-2679. Ed. Anne Brosnan. Circ: 4,000.

780 CHN ISSN 0447-6573
ML5
➤ **RENMIN YINYUE/PEOPLE'S MUSIC.** Text in Chinese; Contents page in English. 1950. m. USD 159.60 (effective 2009). adv. **Document type:** *Magazine, Academic/Scholarly.* **Description:** Provides information for professional musicians and music lovers.
Related titles: Online - full text ed.
Indexed: RILM.
—Ingenta.
Published by: Zhongguo Yinyuejia Xiehui/Chinese Musicians Association, c/o China Federation of Literary and Art Circles, Zhaoyang-qu, 22, Anyuan Bei Li, Beijing, 100029, China. TEL 86-10-64920154. **Dist. by:** China International Book Trading Corp, 35 Chegongzhuang Xilu, Haidian District, PO Box 399, Beijing 100044, China. TEL 86-10-68412045, FAX 86-10-68412023, cibtc@mail.cibtc.com.cn, http://www.cibtc.com.cn.

➤ **REPLAY MAGAZINE**; a monthly publication for the coin-operated amusement machine industry. *see* BUSINESS AND ECONOMICS—Production Of Goods And Services

780.7 USA ISSN 1947-7457
➤ **RESEARCH PERSPECTIVES IN MUSIC EDUCATION.** Abbreviated title: R P M E. Text in English. 1990. a. USD 60 per issue to non-members; USD 30 per issue to members (effective 2009). back issues avail. **Document type:** *Journal, Academic/Scholarly.* **Description:** Publishes music education research using qualitative and/or quantitative methodologies and manuscripts of a philosophical, historical, or theoretical nature.
Related titles: Online - full text ed.; ◆ Supplement to: Florida Music Director. ISSN 0046-4155.
Published by: Florida Music Educators Association, The Hinckley Ctr for Fine Arts Education, 402 Office Plz, Tallahassee, FL 32301. TEL 850-878-6844, FAX 850-942-1793, http://www.flmusiced.org/dnn/FMEA.aspx. Ed. C Victor Fung.

780.71 GBR ISSN 1321-103X
ML5
➤ **RESEARCH STUDIES IN MUSIC EDUCATION.** Abbreviated title: R S M E. Text in English. 1993. s-a. GBP 319, USD 590 combined subscription to institutions (print & online eds.); GBP 313, USD 578 to institutions (effective 2010); subscr. includes: Psychology of Music. adv. back issues avail.; reprint service avail. from PSC. **Document type:** *Journal, Academic/Scholarly.* **Description:** Reports the outcomes of quality research in music education.
Related titles: Online - full text ed.: ISSN 1834-5530. GBP 287, USD 531 to institutions (effective 2010); subscr. includes: Psychology of Music.
Indexed: A22, AEI, B29, CPE, E01, M11, P03, PsycInfo, RILM, S21, SCOPUS.
—BLDSC (7773.234000), IE. **CCC.**
Published by: (Society for Education, Music and Psychology Research), Sage Publications Ltd. (Subsidiary of: Sage Publications, Inc.), 1 Oliver's Yard, 55 City Rd, London, EC1Y 1SP, United Kingdom. TEL 44-20-73248500, 44-20-73248701, FAX 44-20-73248600, info@sagepub.co.uk, http://www.uk.sagepub.com/home.nav. Ed. Margaret S Barrett. adv.: B&W page GBP 450; 170 x 242.

780 USA
RESISTANCE. Text in English. 1994. q. USD 20 in US & Canada; USD 30 elsewhere (effective 2004). back issues avail. **Document type:** *Magazine, Consumer.* **Description:** Source for music of the White Resistance.
Published by: (National Alliance), Resistance LLC, PO Box 67, Hillsboro, WV 24946. TEL 304-653-4691, FAX 304-653-4690, resist@resistance.com, http://www.resistance.com.

781.64 USA
RESONANCE; mildly subversive music, art & style. Text in English. 1994. bi-m. USD 14.95; USD 3.50 newsstand/cover (effective 2002). adv. film rev.; music rev.; play rev. back issues avail. **Document type:** *Magazine, Consumer.* **Description:** Contains articles and reviews on artists from all over the music spectrum, including electronic, jazz, hip-hop underground, pop, indie rock, and avante garde.
Published by: Resonance Magazine, 95620, Seattle, WA 98145-2620. Ed. Raymond Hovey. Pub. Andrew Monko. **Dist. by:** Rider Circulation Services, 3700 Eagle Rock Blvd, Los Angeles, CA 90065. TEL 323-344-1200.

780 PRI ISSN 1537-8292
RESONANCIAS; la revista puertorriquena de musica. Text in Spanish. 2001. a. **Document type:** *Monographic series, Academic/Scholarly.*
Published by: Instituto de Cultura Puertorriquena, Apdo 9024184, San Juan, 00905, Puerto Rico. TEL 787-724-0700, FAX 787-724-8393, www@icp.gobierno.pr, http://www.icp.gobierno.pr/.

780 AUS
➤ **RESONATE**; engage with Australia's new music scene. Text in English. 1978. s-a. free to members (effective 2008). adv. music rev.; software rev.; bk.rev. bibl.; illus. 48 p./no.; back issues avail. **Document type:** *Magazine, Consumer.* **Description:** Features in-depth articles and discussions, concert reviews, news and commentary, interviews with composers, sound artists and performers, calendar listings of forthcoming events in the new music community.
Former titles (until 2006): Sounds Australian (1030-4908); (until 1987): A M C News (0815-371X); (until 1984): Australia Music Centre. Quarterly Newsletter (0811-3149); (until 1981): Music Co-ordination (0158-3956)
Media: Online - full text.
Indexed: PCI, RILM.
Published by: Australian Music Centre Ltd., PO Box N690, Grosvenor Place, NSW 1220, Australia. TEL 61-2-92474677, 1300-651-834, FAX 61-2-92412873, info@amcoz.com.au, http://www.amcoz.com.au/. Ed. Danielle Carey. Adv. contact Philippa Horn. B&W page AUD 600, color page AUD 1,200. Circ: 1,400 (paid); 200 (controlled).

780 USA
ML459 .D6
RESONATOR GUITARIST. Text in English. 1982. m. USD 29 domestic; USD 37 in Canada; USD 39 elsewhere (effective 2004). adv. bk.rev. illus. **Document type:** *Magazine, Consumer.* **Description:** Centers around Dobro and other resonator guitars. Also covers traditional country music in general.
Formerly (until 2004): Country Heritage (0733-8759); Which incorporated (1974-1982): Resophonic Echoes (0273-3242); Which was formerly (until 1976): Dobro Nut
Published by: Resonator Guitarist Publications, 4660 S Hwy 360, Ste 220, Fort Worth, TX 75052. TEL 972-522-1711, FAX 972-522-1730, support@resonatorguitarist.com. Circ: 300 (paid and controlled).

781 USA ISSN 0749-2472
ML3544
RESOUND. Text in English. 1982. q. USD 25 (effective 2000). adv. illus.; tr.lit. index. back issues avail. **Document type:** *Newsletter.* **Description:** Reports on the Archives' collections of traditional music from all regions of the world.
Indexed: MLA-IB, RILM.
Published by: Indiana University, Archives of Traditional Music, Morrison Hall 117, Bloomington, IN 47405-2501. TEL 812-855-4679, FAX 812-855-6673. Ed., Pub., R&P, Adv. contact Jonathan Cargill. Circ: 500.

▼ **RESPECT.** *see* PHOTOGRAPHY

781.64 USA
RETILA. Text in Spanish. bi-m. **Document type:** *Magazine, Consumer.* **Description:** Information on all aspects of the Rock en Espanol alternative music scene.
Related titles: Online - full text ed.
Published by: Barbano Publishing, 6363 Wilshire Blvd, Ste 117, Los Angeles, CA 90048. TEL 323-653-7714, FAX 323-653-7347. Ed. Octavio Hernandez Diaz. Pub. Frank Barbano.

781.63 USA ISSN 1099-6206
REVIEW ADDICT. Text in English. 1998. w. bk.rev.; music rev. **Description:** Covers mostly pop and indie music.
Media: Online - full text.
Address: PO Box 542, Berea, OH 44017-0542. Ed., Pub. Michael Stutz.

780 ARG ISSN 1666-1060
REVISTA ARGENTINA DE MUSICOLOGIA. Text in Spanish. 1996. a. ARS 65 domestic to individuals; USD 23 in the Americas to individuals; USD 33 elsewhere to individuals; ARS 110 domestic to institutions; USD 33 in the Americas to institutions; USD 70 elsewhere to institutions (effective 2010). back issues avail. **Document type:** *Monographic series, Academic/Scholarly.*
Published by: Asociacion Argentina de Musicologia, Mexico, 564, Buenos Aires, C1097AAL, Argentina. info@aamusicologia.org.ar, http://www.aamusicologia.org.ar/. Ed. Susana Anton Priasco. Circ: 500.

781.7 BRA ISSN 0103-7595
ML5
REVISTA BRASILEIRA DE MUSICA. Text in Portuguese. 1934-1947; resumed 1981. irreg., latest 1986. adv. **Document type:** *Journal, Academic/Scholarly.* **Description:** Covers folk music of Brazil.
Indexed: H21, IIMP, M11, MusicInd, P08, RILM.
Published by: Universidade Federal do Rio de Janeiro, Escola de Musica, Rua de Passeio 98-Lapa, Rio De Janeiro, RJ 20021, Brazil. Circ: 1,000.

780 ESP ISSN 1578-5297
ML3793.2.S7
REVISTA CATALANA DE MUSICOLOGIA. Text in Multiple languages. 1979. a. EUR 12.50 (effective 2009). **Document type:** *Journal, Academic/Scholarly.*
Formerly (until 2000): Societat Catalana de Musicologia. Butlleti (0210-8208)
Related titles: Online - full text ed.: ISSN 2013-3960. 1979.
Published by: (Societat Catalana de Musicologia), Institut d'Estudis Catalans, Carrer del Carme 47, Barcelona, 08001, Spain. TEL 34-932-701620, FAX 34-932-701180, informacio@iecat.net, http://www2.iecat.net.

780.01 COL
REVISTA COLOMBIANA DE INVESTIGACION MUSICAL. Text in Spanish. 1985. 2/yr. per issue exchange basis. bk.rev.
Published by: (Seccion de Musicologia), Universidad Nacional de Colombia, Instituto de Investigaciones Esteticas, Bogota, CUND, Colombia. Eds. Egberto Bermudez, Ellie Duque. Circ: 1,000.

780.01 ESP ISSN 0210-1459
ML5
REVISTA DE MUSICOLOGIA. Abbreviated title: R d M. Text in Spanish. 1978. s-a. music rev. bibl.; illus. back issues avail. **Document type:** *Journal, Academic/Scholarly.*
Indexed: IIMP, M11, MusicInd, P09, PCI, RILM.
—CCC.
Published by: Sociedad Espanola de Musicologia, Carretas 14, 7o. Desp. B-3, Madrid, 28012, Spain. TEL 34-915-231712, sedem@sedem.es, http://www.sedem.es/.

780 ESP ISSN 1698-7454
MT1
➤ **REVISTA ELECTRONICA COMPLUTENSE DE INVESTIGACION EN EDUCACION MUSICAL.** Text in English, Spanish. 2004. a. free (effective 2011). **Document type:** *Journal, Academic/Scholarly.*
Media: Online - full text.
Indexed: H21, P08, P18, P48, P53, P54, PQC, SCOPUS.
—CCC.
Published by: (Universidad Complutense de Madrid, Departamento de Expresion Musical y Corporal), Universidad Complutense de Madrid, Servicio de Publicaciones, C/ Obispo Trejo 2, Ciudad Universitaria, Madrid, 28040, Spain. TEL 34-91-3941127, FAX 34-91-3941126, servicio.publicaciones@rect.ucm.es, http://www.ucm.es/publicaciones.

➤ **REVISTA GOIANA DE ARTES.** *see* ART

780 BRA ISSN 0103-5525
ML5
REVISTA MUSICA. Text in Portuguese. 1990. s-a. per issue exchange basis.
Indexed: RILM.
Published by: Universidade de Sao Paulo, Departamento de Musica, Av. Prof. Lucio Martins Rodrigues 443, Butanta, SP 05508, Brazil. TEL 813-3222, FAX 815-4272, TELEX 80629 UVSI BR.

780.7 CHL ISSN 0716-2790
ML5
➤ **REVISTA MUSICAL CHILENA.** Text in Spanish. 1945. s-a. USD 55 (effective 2011). adv. bk.rev.; rec.rev.; video rev. bibl.; charts; illus. index, cum.index. back issues avail. **Document type:** *Journal, Academic/Scholarly.* **Description:** Review of Chilean and Latin American art and indigenous and folk music from the colonial epoch to present.
Related titles: Microfiche ed.; Online - full text ed.: ISSN 0717-6252. 1996. free (effective 2011) (from SciELO).
Indexed: A20, ArtHuCI, C01, FR, H21, IBR, IBZ, IIMP, M11, MusicInd, P08, RILM, SCOPUS, W07.
—INIST.
Published by: Universidad de Chile, Facultad de Artes, Casilla 2100, Compania, 1264, Santiago, Chile. TEL 56-2-6781337, FAX 56-2-6781327, lmerino@abello.dic.uchile.cl, http://www.uchile.cl/facultades/artes/. Ed. Luis Merino Montero. Pub. Nancy Sattler. Adv. contact Fernando Garcia. Circ: 400.

780.5 VEN ISSN 0254-7376
ML238
REVISTA MUSICAL DE VENEZUELA. Text in Spanish. 1980. 3/yr. **Document type:** *Academic/Scholarly.*
Indexed: DIP, H21, IBR, IBZ, P08, RILM.
Published by: Instituto Latinoamericano de Investigaciones y Estudios Musicales Vicente Emilio Sojo, Apartado Postal 70537, Caracas, DF 1071-A, Venezuela. Ed. Jose Penin.

780 FRA ISSN 1957-9241
REVOLUTIC. Text in French. 2007. irreg. **Document type:** *Monographic series, Consumer.*
Published by: Centre d'Information et de Ressources pour les Musiques Actuelles (I R M A), 22 Rue Soleillet, Paris, Cedex 20 75980, France. TEL 33-1-43151111, FAX 33-1-43151110.

781.66 USA ISSN 1527-408X
ML3533.8
REVOLVER; the world's loudest rock magazine. Text in English. 2000. m. USD 12 domestic; USD 15.60 in Canada; USD 24 elsewhere (effective 2008). adv. 125 p./no.; back issues avail. **Document type:** *Magazine, Consumer.* **Description:** Features the best and brightest coverage of heavy metal and hard rock music.
Published by: Future U S, Inc. (Subsidiary of: Future Publishing Ltd.), 4000 Shoreline Ct, Ste 400, South San Francisco, CA 94080. TEL 650-872-1642, FAX 650-872-1643, http://www.futureus.com. Ed. Tom Beaujour TEL 646-723-5467. Adv. contacts Alana Zinn TEL 646-723-5473, Jon Rayvid TEL 646-723-5489. color page USD 12,180; trim 8 x 10.5. Circ: 150,000 (paid).

781.66 AUS
REVOLVER MAGAZINE; one week to live. Text in English. 1997. w. free. film rev.; rec.rev.; Website rev.; bk.rev.; dance rev.; music rev.; play rev.; software rev.; tel.rev.; video rev. abstr. back issues avail. **Document type:** *Magazine, Consumer.* **Description:** Consists of music, music news, CD reviews, and band and artist interviews for the sixteen to thirty-five year old market. Also includes articles about fashion, arts, gis and clubs.
Published by: Six Shooter Publications, 5-13 Aarness Ave, Marrickville, NSW 2204, Australia.

780.01 BEL ISSN 0771-6788
ML5
REVUE BELGE DE MUSICOLOGIE/BELGISCH TIJDSCHRIFT VOOR MUZIEKWETENSCHAP. Text in Dutch, English, French, German. 1946. a. USD 14. adv. bk.rev. illus. **Document type:** *Journal, Academic/Scholarly.*
Indexed: A22, DIP, IBR, IBZ, IIMP, M11, MusicInd, PCI, RILM, T02.
—IE.
Published by: Societe Belge de Musicologie, Rue de la Regence 30, Brussels, 1000, Belgium. Eds. H Vanhulst, R Wangermee. Circ: 600.

780.01 FRA ISSN 0035-1601
ML5
REVUE DE MUSICOLOGIE. Text in French. 1917. s-a. EUR 35 (effective 2008). adv. bk.rev. illus. cum.index. reprint service avail. from PSC. **Document type:** *Journal, Academic/Scholarly.*
Formerly (until 1921): Societe Francaise de Musicologie. Bulletin (0991-9228)
Related titles: Microform ed.: (from PQC); Online - full text ed.: ISSN 1958-5632.
Indexed: A20, A22, ASCA, ArtHuCI, CA, CurCont, DIP, FR, IBR, IBRH, IBZ, IIMP, M11, MLA-IB, MusicInd, PCI, RASB, RILM, SCOPUS, T02, W07.
—IE, Infotrieve, INIST. **CCC.**
Published by: Societe Francaise de Musicologie, 2 rue de Louvois, Paris, 75002, France. TEL 33-1-47037549. Ed. Christian Meyer. Adv. contact Patrick Taieb. Circ: 1,250.

LA REVUE DES INITIATIVES. *see* PSYCHOLOGY

780 CHE ISSN 0035-3744
ML5
REVUE MUSICALE DE SUISSE ROMANDE. Text in French. 1948. q. CHF 42 domestic; CHF 60 in Europe; CHF 70 elsewhere (effective 2002). adv. bk.rev.; music rev.; rec.rev. charts; illus. **Document type:** *Bulletin, Consumer.*
Indexed: IIMP, M11, MusicInd, RILM.
Address: Rue Laurent 19, Case postale 35, Lausanne 24, 1000, Switzerland. TEL 41-21-6523086, FAX 41-21-6523086. Ed. Vincent Arlettaz. R&P Olga Tercier. Adv. contact Tordjinan Rina. Circ: 3,000.

780.7 GBR ISSN 2040-2449
▼ **RHINEGOLD WORLD CONSERVATOIRES.** Text in English. 2009. a. GBP 12.95, EUR 21.40 per issue (effective 2010). **Document type:** *Directory, Trade.*
Published by: Rhinegold Publishing Ltd., 239-241 Shaftesbury Ave, London, WC2H 8TF, United Kingdom. TEL 44-20-73331720, FAX 44-20-73331765, sales@rhinegold.co.uk. Ed. Toby Deller.

780 GBR ISSN 0957-6592
RHYTHM; every drummer needs it. Text in English. 1987. 13/yr. GBP 46.80 domestic; GBP 58 in Europe; GBP 70 in United States; GBP 66 elsewhere; GBP 4.75 newsstand/cover (effective 2010). adv. back issues avail. **Document type:** *Magazine, Consumer.* **Description:** Includes new electronic drum technology, interviews with rhythm professionals and drumming news.
—CCC.
Published by: Future Publishing Ltd., Beauford Ct, 30 Monmouth St, Bath, Avon BA1 2BW, United Kingdom. TEL 44-1225-442244, FAX 44-1225-446019, customerservice@subscription.co.uk, http://www.futureplc.com. Ed. Phil Ascott. Adv. contact Steve Grigg TEL 44-1225-732392. **Subscr. to:** Tower House, Sovereign Park, Market Harborough, Leicestershire LE16 9EF, United Kingdom. TEL 44-844-8481602, FAX 44-1858-438795, future@subscription.co.uk.

786 USA ISSN 1545-1380
ML1049
RHYTHM BONES PLAYER. Variant title: Rhythm Bones Society. Newsletter. Text in English. 199?. q. USD 25 membership (effective 2007). **Document type:** *Newsletter, Consumer.*
Published by: Rhythm Bones Society, 1060 Lower Brow Rd., Signal Mountain, TN 37377-2910. http://www.rhythmbones.com. Ed. Steve Wixson.

780 FRA ISSN 2107-0601
RICERCAR. Text in French. 1992. **Document type:** *Academic/Scholarly.*
Media: Online - full text.
Published by: Universite de Tours (Francois-Rabelais), Centre d'Etudes Superieures de la Renaissance de Tours. Programme Ricercar, 59, Rue Nericault-Destouches, BP 11328, Tours Cedex, 37013, France. TEL 33-2-47367784, FAX 33-2-47367762, ricercar@univ-tours.fr, http://ricercar.cesr.univ-tours.fr/index.htm.

780 DEU
ML410.S93
RICHARD STRAUSS ANNUAL. Text in English, German. 1979. s-a. EUR 45 per vol. (effective 2010). **Document type:** *Journal, Academic/Scholarly.*
Formerly (until 2009): Richard Strauss Blaetter (0720-9827)
Indexed: RILM.
Published by: (Internationale Richard Strauss Gesellschaft AUT), Verlag Dr. Hans Schneider GmbH, Mozartstr 6, Tutzing, 82323, Germany. TEL 49-815-83050, FAX 49-815-87636, Musikbuch@aol.com, http://www.schneider-musikbuch.de.

782.10924 AUT
RICHARD WAGNER NACHRICHTEN. Text in German. 1989. 5/yr. looseleaf. EUR 15 (effective 2003). **Document type:** *Newsletter, Consumer.* **Description:** Contains essays on Richard Wagner's work.
Published by: Oesterreichische Richard Wagner Gesellschaft, Vorbeckgasse 5, Graz, St 8020, Austria. TEL 43-316-713423, FAX 43-316-677305. Ed., Pub. Franz Ehgartner. Circ: 460 (paid and controlled).

781.64 DEU ISSN 1614-9068
RIDDIM. Text in German. 2001 (Aug.). 6/yr. EUR 25 domestic; EUR 35 foreign; EUR 4.90 newsstand/cover (effective 2007). adv. **Document type:** *Magazine, Consumer.* **Description:** Contains articles and reviews on dancehall and reggae albums and artists.
Published by: Piranha Media GmbH, Rolandstr 69, Cologne, 50677, Germany. TEL 49-221-5797800, FAX 49-221-5797879. Ed. Pete Lilly. adv.: page EUR 3,000. Circ: 40,000 (paid and controlled).

780 NOR ISSN 1891-7119
RIDE RANKE: MUSIKK FRA LIVETS BEGYNNELSE. Text in Norwegian. 1991. q. NOK 290 (effective 2011). **Document type:** *Newsletter, Consumer.*
Former titles (until 2010): Musikk fra Livets Begynnelse (1890-095X); (until 2006): Foreningen Musikk fra Livets Begynnelse. Medlemsblad (1501-6021)
Published by: Foreningen Musikk fra Livets Begynnelse/Early Childhood Music Association of Norway, Sandvigaa 27, Stavanger, 4007, Norway. TEL 47-51-846655, FAX 47-51-846650, musikk.fra.livets.begynnelse@musikk.no, http://www.musikk.no/musikkfralivetsbegynnelse.

780.42 BEL
RIFRAF. Text in Dutch, French. 1989. 10/yr. EUR 13 (effective 2005).

Published by: B Z & T b.v.b.a., Kerkstraat 110, Antwerp, 2060, Belgium. TEL 32-3-236-4501, FAX 32-3-237-7100. Ed. Ina De Ridder. Circ: 30,000.

RIME MAGAZINE. *see* LIFESTYLE

780 USA ISSN 1931-4779
RING AND REJOICE!. Text in English. q. USD 24.95 (effective 2009); minimum 5 copies. **Document type:** *Magazine, Consumer.* **Description:** Provides information about music and rejoice in seasons.
Published by: Lorenz Publishing Co., 501 E 3rd St, Box 802, Dayton, OH 45402. TEL 937-228-6118, 800-444-1144, FAX 937-223-2042, info@lorenz.com, http://www.lorenz.com. Ed. Douglas E Wagner.

789.5 GBR ISSN 0035-5453
RINGING WORLD. Text in English. 1911. w. GBP 55 domestic; GBP 70 in Western Europe; GBP 73.50 elsewhere; GBP 1.70 newsstand/cover (effective 2009). adv. bk.rev. back issues avail. **Document type:** *Magazine, Trade.* **Description:** Contains articles, advice, reports, training material, notices of ringing events and many other items of interest.
Related titles: Online - full text ed.: free (effective 2009).
Published by: (Central Council of Church Bell Ringers), Ringing World Ltd., 35 A High St, Andover, SP10 1LJ, United Kingdom. TEL 44-1264-366620, FAX 44-1264-360594, letters@ringingworld.co.uk. Ed. Robert A Lewis. **Co-sponsors:** Whitechapel Bell Foundry Ltd.; Taylors Eayre and Smith Ltd.

784.54005 NZL ISSN 0114-0876
RIP IT UP. Text in English. 1977. bi-m. NZD 45 domestic; NZD 75 foreign; NZD 39 to students (effective 2008). adv. **Document type:** *Magazine, Consumer.*
Indexed: RILM.
Published by: Satellite Media Group, Mt. Eden, PO Box 10218, Auckland, New Zealand. TEL 64-9-623-8251, FAX 64-9-623-8261. Ed. Scott Kara. Adv. contact Mark Hobday.

306 028.5 USA
RISEN; it's not what you think. Text in English. 2004. bi-m. USD 14.99; USD 4.95 newsstand/cover (effective 2005). adv. **Document type:** *Magazine, Consumer.*
Published by: Risen Media LLC, 11772 Sorrento Valley Rd, Ste 257, San Diego, CA 92121. TEL 858-481-5650, FAX 858-481-5660. Pub. Michael Sherman. Adv. contact Amber Jacobson. B&W page USD 4,660, color page USD 5,178; trim 9 x 10.875. Circ: 65,353.

780.43 ESP ISSN 0035-5658
RITMO; revista de musica clasica. Text in Spanish. 1929. m. (11/yr.). adv. music rev.; rec.rev. 116 p./no.; **Document type:** *Magazine, Consumer.* **Description:** Devoted to classical music and records published in Europe.
Indexed: IBR, IBZ, RILM.
Published by: Lira Editorial S.A., Isabel Colbrand 10, Madrid, 28050, Spain. TEL 34-91-3588945, FAX 34-91-3588944, correo@ritmo.es. **Dist. by:** Asociacion de Revistas Culturales de Espana, C Covarruvias 9 2o. Derecha, Madrid 28010, Spain. TEL 34-91-3086066, FAX 34-91-3199267, info@arce.es, http://www.arce.es/.

783 ITA ISSN 0394-6282
ML2999
RIVISTA INTERNAZIONALE DI MUSICA SACRA/INTERNATIONAL CHURCH MUSIC REVIEW/INTERNATIONALE ZEITSCHRIFT FUER KIRCHENMUSIK/REVISTA INTERNACIONAL DE MUSICA SAGRADA/REVUE INTERNATIONALE DE MUSIQUE SACREE; the international church music review. Text in English, French, German, Italian. 1979. s-a. adv. bk.rev. **Document type:** *Journal, Academic/Scholarly.* **Description:** Collects contributions from the world's leading authorities on the study and practice of liturgical music throughout the world and thoughout time.
Indexed: DIP, IBR, IBZ, IIMP, M11, MusicInd, PCI, RILM.
Published by: LIM Editrice Srl, Via di Arsina 296/f, Lucca, LU 55100, Italy. TEL 39-0583-394464, FAX 39-0583-394469, lim@lim.it, http://www.lim.it. Ed. Giacomo Baroffio. Adv. contact Paola Borriero.

780.01 ITA ISSN 0035-6867
ML5
RIVISTA ITALIANA DI MUSICOLOGIA. Text in Italian. 1966. s-a. EUR 80 foreign to individuals; EUR 104 combined subscription foreign to institutions (print & online eds.) (effective 2009). adv. bk.rev. **Document type:** *Journal, Academic/Scholarly.*
Related titles: Online - full text ed.: ISSN 2036-5586.
Indexed: A01, A20, A22, ASCA, ArtHuCI, CA, CurCont, DIP, IBR, IBZ, IIMP, M11, MusicInd, PCI, RASB, RILM, T02, W07.
—IE.
Published by: (Societa Italiana di Musicologia), Casa Editrice Leo S. Olschki, Viuzzo del Pozzetto 8, Florence, 50126, Italy. TEL 39-055-6530684, FAX 39-055-6530214, celso@olschki.it, http://www.olschki.it. Ed. Paola Besutti. Circ: 1,000.

780.01 ITA ISSN 0394-4395
RIVISTA ITALIANA DI MUSICOLOGIA. QUADERNI. Text in Italian. 1966. irreg., latest vol.33, 1996. price varies. **Document type:** *Monographic series, Academic/Scholarly.*
Indexed: MLA-IB.
Published by: Casa Editrice Leo S. Olschki, Viuzzo del Pozzetto 8, Florence, 50126, Italy. TEL 39-055-6530684, FAX 39-055-6530214, celso@olschki.it, http://www.olschki.it.

781.642 USA
ROADHOUSE MAGAZINE. Text in English. m. adv. **Document type:** *Magazine, Consumer.*
Published by: Shooting Wilde Entertainment, PO Box 100272, San Antonio, TX 78201. TEL 210-804-0025, FAX 210-832-9922, shootnwild@wireweb.net. Pub. Hank Murray.

780 GBR
ROBOTS AND ELECTRONIC BRAINS. Text in English. 1995. irreg. **Document type:** *Magazine, Consumer.*
Formerly: Jimmy's Riddle (Print)
Media: Online - full text.
Published by: Jimmy's Riddle, c/o R & E B, 133 Green End Rd, Cambridge, CB4 1RW, United Kingdom. Ed. Jimmy Possession.

781 FRA ISSN 0048-8445
ROCK & FOLK. Text in French. 1966. m. EUR 51 (effective 2009). adv. bk.rev.; film rev. charts; illus. **Document type:** *Magazine, Consumer.*
Indexed: PdeR.
Published by: Editions Lariviere, 6 Rue Olof Palme, Clichy, 92587, France. TEL 33-1-47565400, http://www.editions-lariviere.fr. Ed. Philippe Manoeuvre. Pub. Fabien Darmon. Adv. contact Thierry Solal. Circ: 115,000.

784.5 USA ISSN 1068-7653
ML3533.8
ROCK & RAP CONFIDENTIAL. Text in English. 1983. m. USD 24. bk.rev. back issues avail. **Document type:** *Magazine, Consumer.* **Description:** Exposes rock and roll as an industry whose chief aim is profit.
Former titles (until 1992): Rock and Roll Confidential (0891-9372); Dave Marsh's Rock and Roll Confidential (0740-2058)
Related titles: Online - full text ed.
Indexed: IIMP, M11, MusicInd, T02.
Address: PO Box 341305, Los Angeles, CA 90034. Circ: 6,000.

780.42 USA
ROCK FEVER. Text in English. 5/yr. USD 2.95.
Published by: Comic World Corp., 475 Park Ave S, New York, NY 10016. TEL 212-689-2830.

781.45 DEU ISSN 1437-8140
ROCK HARD. Text in German. 1983. m. EUR 63 domestic; EUR 79 in Europe; EUR 89 elsewhere; EUR 6.90 newsstand/cover (effective 2011). adv. **Document type:** *Magazine, Consumer.*
Published by: Rock Hard Verlags- und Handels-GmbH, Paderborner Str 17, Dortmund, 44143, Germany. TEL 49-231-5620140, FAX 49-231-56201413. Ed. Goetz Kuehnemund. Adv. contact Dani Lipka.

781.64 DEU ISSN 1433-8114
ROCK 'N' ROLL; Musikmagazin. Text in German. 1977. bi-m. EUR 30 domestic; EUR 36 foreign; EUR 3.50 newsstand/cover (effective 2005). adv. **Document type:** *Magazine, Consumer.*
Address: Zweigstr 5, Oldenburg, 26135, Germany. TEL 49-441-9250600, FAX 49-441-9250601. Ed., Pub. Heinz-Guenther Hartig.

780 USA
ROCK 'N ROLL EXPERIENCE. Text in English. 1992. m. USD 27. adv. bk.rev.; film rev.; music rev. back issues avail. **Document type:** *Magazine, Consumer.* **Description:** Covers local and national rock and roll artists.
Published by: R J S Entertainment, PO Box 87, White Marsh, MD 21162. TEL 410-335-0092, FAX 410-335-0098. Ed., R&P Bob Suehs. Adv. contact John Gonzalez. B&W page USD 250. Circ: 20,000.

781.66 NLD ISSN 2211-2650
ROCK 'N' ROLL HIGH SCHOOL. Text in English. 2007. a. EUR 10 (effective 2011). **Document type:** *Magazine, Trade.* **Description:** Provides information on the European music industry to young music professionals and semi-professionals.
Formerly (until 2009): Sex, Drugs & Rock 'n' Roll Highschool (1877-4954)
Published by: Rock 'n' Roll Highschool BV, Haringvliet 78, Rotterdam, 3011 TG, Netherlands. TEL 31-10-2067230, FAX 31-10-2067239, info@rocknrollhighschool.nl, http://www.rocknrollhighschool.nl. Ed. Minke Weeda.

781.66 FRA ISSN 1773-570X
ROCK ONE. Text in French. 2004. m. EUR 65.45 domestic; EUR 68.95 in Europe; EUR 70.45 elsewhere (effective 2008). **Document type:** *Magazine, Consumer.*
Published by: B & B Media, 40 Rue de Paradis, Paris, 75010, France. TEL 33-1-53249970, FAX 33-1-53249979, info@bandbmedia.com.

781.64 GBR
ROCK SOUND; music with attitude. Text in English. 1999. m. GBP 34.97 domestic; GBP 46 in US, Canada and Europe countries; GBP 66 elsewhere; GBP 7.97 per issue (effective 2009). adv. back issues avail. **Document type:** *Magazine, Consumer.* **Description:** Covers music with attitude - everything from indie to hard rock.
Related titles: Online - full text ed.
Published by: Freeway Press, Unit 22, Jack's Pl, 6 Corbet Pl, London, E1 6NN, United Kingdom. Ed. Darren Taylor. **Dist. by:** MarketForce UK Ltd, The Blue Fin Bldg, 3rd Fl, 110 Southwark St, London SE1 0SU, United Kingdom. TEL 44-20-31483300, FAX 44-20-31488105.

781.64 FRA ISSN 1241-1337
ROCK SOUND. Text in French. 1992. m. **Document type:** *Magazine, Consumer.*
Related titles: Supplement(s): Rock Sound. Hors Serie. ISSN 1285-1442. 1997.
Address: B.P. 29, Montreuil, Cedex 93104, France. rock-sound.fr.

781.64 ITA ISSN 1127-1337
ROCK SOUND; music with attitude. Text in Italian. 1998. m. (11/yr.). **Document type:** *Magazine, Consumer.* **Description:** Contains articles on the contemporary international rock music scene. Includes interviews, news releases, reviews, and a calendar of rock events in Italy.
Published by: Acacia Edizioni, Via Copernico 3, Binasco, MI 20082, Italy. http://www.acaciaedizioni.com.

781.66 USA
ROCKBITES. Text in English. 1999. d. adv. back issues avail. **Document type:** *Newsletter.* **Description:** Covers rock and related music genres.
Media: Online - full text. Ed. Principal M Jason.

781.66 RUS ISSN 0132-8964
ROCKCOR. Text in Russian. 1991. bi-m. RUR 150 per issue (effective 2004). adv. bk.rev. **Document type:** *Magazine, Consumer.* **Description:** Presents rock music from around the world.
Published by: Barock'Co, B Tishinskii per 41, Moscow, 123577, Russian Federation. TEL 7-095-1932824. Ed. Alexei Boldov.

781.542 ITA ISSN 1129-0803
ROCKERILLA; mensile di musica e cinema. Text in Italian. 1978. m. (11/yr.). EUR 38 domestic; EUR 70 foreign (effective 2009). adv. bk.rev.; music rev.; film rev.; Website rev. 84 p./no.; back issues avail. **Document type:** *Magazine, Consumer.*
Related titles: Online - full text ed.
Published by: Edizioni Rockerilla s.n.c., Via Pighini, 24, Cairo Montenotte, SV 17014, Italy. TEL 39-019-599516, FAX 39-019-501054, rockerilla@tiscalinet.it, isrivera@tin.it. Circ: 30,000.

781.64 DEU
ROCKET. Text in German. 1989. m. EUR 50 (effective 2009). **Document type:** *Magazine, Consumer.*
Media: Braille.
Published by: Bayerischer Blinden- und Sehbehindertenbund e.V., Arnulfstr 22, Munich, 80335, Germany. TEL 49-89-55988134, FAX 49-89-55988334, bit-bestellservice@bbsb.org, http://www.bbsb.org.

781.64 USA
ROCKET FUEL. Text in English. irreg. adv. **Document type:** *Magazine, Consumer.* **Description:** Covers all aspects of independent music from interviews and reviews to features and stories.
Address: 4129, Austin, TX 78765-4129. Eds. Daniel Reed, Monika Bustamante.

780.904 USA ISSN 0738-7717
ROCKIN' 50S; dedicated to the true rock 'n' roll era. Text in English. 1976. bi-m. USD 30; USD 42 foreign (effective 1999). adv. bk.rev.; film rev.; play rev. stat. back issues avail. **Document type:** *Magazine, Consumer.* **Description:** For 1950s record collectors. Covers the music, artists and fads of the 1950's rock and roll era.
Formerly (until June 1986): Reminiscing
Published by: (Buddy Holly Memorial Society), William F. Griggs, Ed. & Pub., PO Box 6123, Lubbock, TX 79493-6123. TEL 806-799-4299. Ed. Bill Griggs. Circ: 5,450 (paid).

780 745.1 USA ISSN 1052-8768
ML156.4.P6
ROCKIN' RECORDS; buyers - sellers reference book and price guide. Text in English. 1986. a. USD 42.95. adv. **Document type:** *Catalog, Trade.* **Description:** Covers music and the hobby of record collecting, with price information for all size records.
Published by: Antique Trader Publications, c/o Sun Ripe Promotions, Box 29, Boyne Falls, MI 49713. TEL 616-582-6852, FAX 616-582-9713. Ed. Jerry Osborne. Adv. contact Linda Osborne. Circ: 10,000.

780 USA ISSN 0738-5382
ROCKPILE. Text in English. m. USD 15 domestic; USD 20 in Canada & Mexico; USD 25 elsewhere (effective 2002). **Document type:** *Magazine, Consumer.*
Published by: Rockpile Magazine, 409 South St., # 2, Philadelphia, PA 19147-1520. TEL 215-885-7625, FAX 215-885-7161, mike@rockpile.net. **Subscr. to:** 63967, Philadelphia, PA 19147-7967.

780.42 USA ISSN 1086-5985
ML3533.8
ROCKRGRL; supporting a women's right to rock. Text in English. 1995. bi-m. USD 25 domestic; USD 50 foreign; USD 4.99 newsstand/cover (effective 2005). adv. bk.rev. illus. back issues avail.; reprints avail. **Document type:** *Magazine, Consumer.* **Description:** For and about women rock musicians. Profiles a variety of artists plus legal tips, equipment reviews, and sound advice.
Related titles: Online - full text ed.
Indexed: DYW, GW.
Address: 3220 1st Ave S, #203, Seattle, WA 98134. TEL 206-230-4280, FAX 206-230-4288. Ed., Pub. Carla A Desantis. Adv. contact Kristy Smith. page USD 400. Circ: 10,000. **Dist. by:** Big Top Publisher Services, 833 Market St, Ste 602, San Francisco, CA 64103. TEL 415-447-4284, FAX 415-974-1328, info@bigtoppubs.com.

781.642 USA
ROCKY MOUNTAIN HIGH: THE JOHN DENVER FAN CLUB. Text in English. 1994. m. USD 20 (effective 2000). adv. **Document type:** *Newsletter.* **Description:** Contains news on the life and career of John Denver and related topics.
Related titles: E-mail ed.
Address: 608 E 96th St, Kansas City, MO 64131. TEL 816-943-0330. Ed., Pub., R&P Emily M Parris. Adv. contact Emily Parris. Circ: 8,000.

780.42 USA
ROCTOBER. Text in English. 1992. 3/yr. USD 10 domestic; USD 15 in Canada & Mexico; USD 20 elsewhere; USD 2 newsstand/cover. adv. bk.rev.; film rev.; music rev.; video rev. illus. back issues avail. **Document type:** *Magazine, Consumer.* **Description:** Reviews and comments on the non-mainstream rock 'n' roll scene of yesterday and today.
Address: 1507 E 53rd St, 617, Chicago, IL 60615. TEL 312-288-5448, FAX 773-288-5443. Ed., Adv. contact Jake A Austen. Circ: 3,500. **Dist. by:** Ubiquity Distributors Inc., 607 DeGraw St, Brooklyn, NY 11217. TEL 718-875-5491.

786 POL ISSN 0208-5992
ML410.C54
➤ **ROCZNIK CHOPINOWSKI.** Text in Polish. 1956. a., latest vol.25, 2001. PLZ 40 per issue domestic; USD 50 per issue foreign (effective 2002). adv. bk.rev. bibl.; illus. Index. back issues avail. **Document type:** *Journal, Academic/Scholarly.* **Description:** Covers Fryderyk Chopin's life and work. Publishes essays by the most prominent chopinologists from all over the world. Also contains Chopin's bibliography and chronicle.
Former titles (until 1965): Annales Chopin (0493-6221); (until 1958): Rocznik Chopinowski (1230-865X)
Related titles: ◆ English ed.: Chopin Studies. ISSN 0239-8567.
Indexed: RILM.
Published by: Towarzystwo im. F. Chopina/Frederick Chopin Society, Ul Okolnik 1, Warsaw, 00368, Poland. TEL 48-22-8265935, FAX 48-22-8279599, muzeum@chopin.pl, http://www.chopin.pl. Adv. contact Grazyna Michniewicz. Circ: 150 (controlled).

➤ **RODMAN HALL BULLETIN.** *see* ART

780 DEU ISSN 0944-0291
ML929
ROHRBLATT; Die Zeitschrift fuer Oboe, Klarinette, Fagott und Saxaphon. Text in German. 1986. q. EUR 32; EUR 28.80 to students; EUR 9 newsstand/cover (effective 2010). adv. bk.rev. index. **Document type:** *Magazine, Consumer.*
Former titles (until 1993): Oboe - Klarinette - Fagott (0179-8170); (until 1989): Klarinette
Indexed: RILM.
Published by: Finkenkruger Musikverlag, Bachstelzenstr 23, Falkensee, 14612, Germany. TEL 49-3322-230381, FAX 49-3322-230380. Ed., Pub. Heike Fricke.

780 USA
ROLLING BLUNDER REVIEW. Variant title: Arlo Guthrie's Rolling Blunder Review. Text in English. 1988 (no.7). 4/yr. illus. **Document type:** *Newsletter, Consumer.* **Description:** Includes the philosophical meanderings of the folksinger, current happenings of the Church, and the "Get-Stuff" mail order catalogue.

Published by: Guthrie Center, 4 Van Deusenville Rd, Great Barrington, MA 01230. TEL 413-528-1955, FAX 413-528-1958, gchq@bcn.net, http://www.guthrie.org. Ed. Arlo Guthrie. R&P Annie Guthrie TEL 413-445-6403. Circ: 5,000.

778.164 ARG ISSN 0329-5656
ML385
ROLLING STONE. Text in Spanish. 1998. m. USD 5.90 newsstand/cover (effective 2002). adv. **Document type:** *Magazine, Consumer.*
Published by: S.A. La Nacion, Leandro N. Alem 628, Piso 3, Buenos Aires, Buenos Aires 1001, Argentina. TEL 54-11-4514-4080, FAX 54-11-4514-4075, revistas@zonarevistas.com.ar, http://www.zonarevistas.com.ar.

781.5 DEU ISSN 1612-9563
ROLLING STONE. Text in German. 1994. m. EUR 5.50 newsstand/cover (effective 2011). adv. **Document type:** *Magazine, Consumer.*
—CCC.
Published by: Axel Springer Mediahouse Berlin GmbH (Subsidiary of: Axel Springer Verlag AG), Mehringdamm 33, Berlin, 10961, Germany. TEL 49-30-30881880, FAX 49-30-3088188223, info@axel-springer-mediahouse-berlin.de, http://www.asmm.de. Ed. Rainer Schmidt. Adv. contact Oliver Horn. Circ: 55,388 (paid).

781.5 ESP ISSN 1575-1554
ROLLING STONE. Text in Spanish. 1999. m. EUR 30.60 (effective 2010). adv. **Document type:** *Magazine, Consumer.*
Published by: Promotora General de Revistas S.A. (P R O G R E S A) (Subsidiary of: Grupo Prisa), C Fuencarral 6, Madrid, 28004, Spain. TEL 34-91-5386104, FAX 34-91-5222291, correo@progresa.es, http://www.progresa.es.

781.5 USA ISSN 0035-791X
ROLLING STONE. Text in English. 1967. 26/yr. USD 14.97 domestic; USD 38 in Canada; USD 65 elsewhere (effective 2009). adv. bk.rev.; rec.rev. illus. back issues avail.; reprints avail. **Document type:** *Magazine, Consumer.* **Description:** Contains articles describes interviews and reviews covering all aspects of the pop-rock music industry. Includes features on politics, movies and fashion.
Related titles: Braille ed.; CD-ROM ed.; Microform ed.: (from PQC); Online - full text ed.
Indexed: A01, A02, A03, A08, A09, A10, A11, A21, A22, A25, A26, A33, ARG, AcaI, B04, BRD, C03, C05, C12, CBCARef, CBRI, CLFP, CPerI, ChPerI, Chicano, E08, F01, F02, G05, G06, G07, G08, G09, I05, I07, IIMP, IIPA, JHMA, L07, M01, M02, M06, M11, MASUSE, MRD, MagInd, MusicInd, P02, P10, P13, P30, P48, P53, P54, PMR, PPI, PQC, R03, R04, R06, RGAb, RGPR, RI-1, RI-2, RILM, S08, S09, T02, TOM, U01, V02, V03, V04, W03, WBA, WMB.
—IE, Infotrieve, Ingenta.
Published by: Rolling Stone LLC, 1290 Ave. of the Americas, 2nd Fl, New York, NY 10104. TEL 212-484-1616, letters@rollingstone.com. Ed. Jann S Wenner. adv.: B&W page USD 149,220, color page USD 165,775; trim 8 x 10.875. Circ: 1,469,213 (paid).

781.542 AUS ISSN 1320-0615
ROLLING STONE. Text in English. 1967. m. adv. **Document type:** *Magazine, Consumer.* **Description:** Focuses on both global and Australian popular culture with passion, honesty and attitude.
Related titles: Online - full text ed.
Indexed: A11, A33, RILM, T02, WBA, WMB.
Published by: A C P Magazines Ltd. (Subsidiary of: P B L Media Pty Ltd.), 54-58 Park St, Sydney, NSW 2000, Australia. TEL 61-2-92828000, FAX 61-2-91263769, http://www.acp.com.au. Ed. Matthew Coyte TEL 61-2-8114 9487. Circ: 30,518.

780 ITA ISSN 1824-2162
ROLLING STONE MAGAZINE. Text in Italian. 2003. m. EUR 30.70 (effective 2011). **Document type:** *Magazine, Consumer.*
Formerly (until 2004): Rolling Stone (1724-0166)
Published by: Editrice Quadratum SpA (Subsidiary of: Arnoldo Mondadori Editore SpA), Piazza Aspromonte 15, Milan, MI 20131, Italy. TEL 39-02-70642242, FAX 39-02-2665555, quadratum@quadratum.it, http://www.quadratum.it.

780 FIN ISSN 0355-5054
ML5
RONDO. Text in Finnish. 1962. m. EUR 62 (effective 2005). adv. bk.rev. charts; illus. **Document type:** *Magazine.*
Incorporates (1992-2003): Classica (1236-0325)
Indexed: MLA-IB.
Published by: Musiikkikustannus Rondo Oy, Tallberginkatu 1 C 129, Helsinki, 00180, Finland. TEL 358-9-6931307, toimitus@rondolehti.fi. Ed. Harri Kuusisaari. adv.: B&W page EUR 1,250, color page EUR 1,550; 195 x 250. Circ: 5,000.

781.65 DEU
RONDO; das Klassik- und Jazz-Magazin. Text in German. 1992. bi-m. EUR 19 domestic; EUR 42 foreign (effective 2007). adv. **Document type:** *Magazine, Consumer.* **Description:** Contains articles, features and reviews of classical and jazz music and musicians.
Related titles: Online - full text ed.: 1997.
Published by: INMEDIA Verlag GmbH, Lucile-Grahn-Str. 37, Munich, 81675, Germany. TEL 49-89-4572610, FAX 49-89-45726150. Ed. Wolfgang Halder. Pub. Guenter F. Bereiter. Adv. contact Eva Kluge. B&W page EUR 5,360, color page EUR 5,940; trim 210 x 285. Circ: 107,509 (paid).

780 621.389 USA
ROOTS & RHYTHM NEWSLETTER. Text in English. 1978. irreg. (approx. 6/yr.). adv. bk.rev.; rec.rev.; video rev. 40 p./no. 4 cols./p.; back issues avail. **Document type:** *Bulletin, Trade.* **Description:** Features reviews of blues, country and jazz music, also folk & world music.
Formerly: Down Home Music Newsletter
Published by: American Music Sales, Inc., PO Box 837, El Cerrito, CA 94530. TEL 510-526-8373, FAX 510-526-9001. Ed. Franklyn Scott. Circ: 13,000 (paid and controlled).

781.623981 DNK ISSN 1902-8547
ROOTS ZONE (ONLINE). Text in Danish. 2007. 3/yr. **Document type:** *Magazine, Consumer.*
Media: Online - full text.
Published by: Folkemusikkens Faelles Sekretariat, Saltholmsgade 22, Aarhus C, 8000, Denmark. TEL 45-70-225070, FAX 45-86-761147, ffs@folkemusik.dk, http://www.folkemusik.dk. Ed. Martin Blom Hansen. Adv. contact Charlotte Dalgas.

780 398 USA
ROOTSWORLD. Text in English. 1994. w. USD 20; USD 25 foreign (effective 1999). adv. bk.rev. **Description:** Dedicated to roots music from around the world, music that has ties to the culture it comes from, whether it is folk, pop or experimental.
Media: Online - full content. **Related titles:** E-mail ed.
Address: PO Box 1285, New Haven, CT 06505. TEL 203-624-6423. Ed. Cliff Furnald.

780 RUS
ROSSIISKAYA MUZYKAL'NAYA GAZETA. Text in Russian. m. USD 95 in United States. **Document type:** *Newspaper, Consumer.*
Published by: Izdatel'stvo Ob'edinenie Kompozitor, Pogodinskaya 2-3, kv 151, Moscow, 119121, Russian Federation. TEL 7-095-2461454. Ed. S Yu Rumyantsev. **Dist. by:** East View Information Services, 10601 Wayzata Blvd, Minneapolis, MN 55305. TEL 952-252-1201, 800-477-1005, FAX 952-252-1202, info@eastview.com, http://www.eastview.com.

780 USA
ROUNDER MAIL ORDER; the roots of real music. Text in English. 1970. bi-m. USD 5. music rev. **Document type:** *Catalog.* **Description:** Reviews new albums available from Rounder Records.
Formerly: Record Roundup
Published by: Rounder Records, One Camp St, Cambridge, MA 02140. TEL 617-661-6308, 800-443-4727, FAX 617-868-8769. Ed., R&P Gail McIntosh TEL 617-354-0700 ext.244.

786.5 CAN ISSN 1701-7440
ROYAL CANADIAN COLLEGE OF ORGANISTS. YEARBOOK & DIRECTORY OF MEMBERS. Text in English. 1973. a. 80 p./no.; back issues avail.
Former titles (until 200?): Royal Canadian College of Organists. Yearbook & Annual Directory of Members (1701-7394); (until 1978): Royal Canadian College of Organists. Yearbook (0228-9539); Supersedes in part: Royal Canadian College of Organists Quarterly (0380-8424); Which was formed by the 1973 merger of: R C C O Newsletter (0557-8159); Royal Canadian College of Organists. Year Book (0225-0349)
Indexed: CMPI.
Published by: Royal Canadian College of Organists, 204 St. George St, Ste 202, Toronto, ON M5R 2N5, Canada. TEL 416-929-6400, FAX 416-929-2265, http://www.rcco.ca.

780 IRL
ROYAL IRISH ACADEMY OF MUSIC. PROSPECTUS. Text in English. 1973. a. free.
Published by: Royal Irish Academy of Music, 36-38 Westland Row, Dublin, 2, Ireland. Circ: 1,000.

780.01 GBR ISSN 0269-0403
ML28.L8
➤ **ROYAL MUSICAL ASSOCIATION. JOURNAL.** Text in English. 1875. s-a. GBP 132 combined subscription in United Kingdom to institutions (print & online eds.); EUR 211, USD 263 combined subscription to institutions (print & online eds.) (effective 2012). adv. bk.rev. cum.index: vols.1-99. 184 p./no.; back issues avail.; reprint service avail. from PSC. **Document type:** *Journal, Academic/Scholarly.* **Description:** Addresses new research into all branches of musical scholarship - historical musicology and ethnomusicology, theory and analysis, textual criticism, archival research, organology and performing practice.
Former titles (until 1987): Royal Musical Association. Proceedings (0080-4452); (until 1945): Musical Association. Proceedings (0958-8442)
Related titles: Microfilm ed.: (from BHP); Online - full text ed.: ISSN 1471-6933. GBP 119 in United Kingdom to institutions; EUR 190, USD 237 to institutions (effective 2012) (from IngentaConnect).
Indexed: A20, A22, A26, A27, ASCA, AmHI, ArtHuCI, B04, BRD, BrHumI, CA, CurCont, E01, E08, G08, H07, H08, HAb, HumInd, IIMP, M11, MLA-IB, MusicInd, P10, P48, P53, P54, PCI, PQC, RASB, RILM, S09, SCOPUS, T02, W03, W07.
—BLDSC (4862.125000), IE, Infotrieve, Ingenta. **CCC.**
Published by: (Royal Musical Association), Routledge (Subsidiary of: Taylor & Francis Group), 4 Park Sq, Milton Park, Abingdon, Oxon OX14 4RN, United Kingdom. TEL 44-20-70176000, FAX 44-20-70176336, subscriptions@tandf.co.uk, http://www.routledge.com. Ed. Dr. Rachel Cowgill. Adv. contact Linda Hann TEL 44-1344-779945. **Subscr. to:** Taylor & Francis Ltd., Journals Customer Service, Sheepen Pl, Colchester, Essex CO3 3LP, United Kingdom. TEL 44-20-70175544, FAX 44-20-70175198, tf.enquiries@tfinforma.com.

780 GBR ISSN 1461-9717
ML27.G7
ROYAL MUSICAL ASSOCIATION. NEWSLETTER. Text in English. 1998 (Mar.). s-a. free to members (effective 2009). back issues avail. **Document type:** *Newsletter, Academic/Scholarly.* **Description:** Contains a calendar of events, conference announcements and reports, calls for papers, and news of the Association itself.
—CCC.
Published by: Royal Musical Association, c/o Dr. Jeffrey Dean, 4 Chandos Rd, Chorlton-cum-Hardy, Manchester, M21 0ST, United Kingdom. jeffrey.dean@stingrayoffice.com. Ed. Michael Byde.

780 GBR ISSN 1472-3808
ML5
➤ **ROYAL MUSICAL ASSOCIATION RESEARCH CHRONICLE.** Text in English. 1961. a. GBP 45 per issue to non-members (effective 2009). 120 p./no.; back issues avail. **Document type:** *Journal, Academic/Scholarly.* **Description:** Comprises articles on the history of music, reviews and musicological documentation.
Formerly (until 1978): R M A Research Chronicle (0080-4460)
Indexed: A22, AmHI, BrHumI, H07, IIMP, M11, MusicInd, RILM, SCOPUS, T02.
—BLDSC (7734.780000), IE, Ingenta. **CCC.**
Published by: Royal Musical Association, Department of Music, University of York, Heslington, Yorks YO10 5DD, United Kingdom. TEL 44-1904-434748, FAX 44-1904-432450, jeffrey.dean@stingrayoffice.com. Ed. Jonathan Wainwright. **Dist. by:** Rosemary Dooley, 3 Kendal Green, Kendal, Cumbria LA9 5PN, United Kingdom. TEL 44-1539-740049, FAX 44-1539-737744, rsd@booksonmusic.co.uk, http://www.booksonmusic.co.uk/.

783 POL ISSN 1428-5983
RUAH; magazyn muzyczny. Text in Polish. 1997. q. PLZ 44 (effective 2003). **Document type:** *Magazine, Consumer.*
Published by: Paganini s.c., Malgorzata i Janusz Kotarba, ul Batorego 25/11, Krakow, 31135, Poland. firma@paganini.com.pl, http://www.paganini.com.pl. Ed. Janusz Kotarba.

780 GBR ISSN 0952-6609
RUBBERNECK. Text in English. 1985. s-a. GBP 5 to individuals; GBP 10 to institutions. adv. bk.rev.; film rev.; music rev. **Document type:** *Journal, Consumer.* **Description:** Devoted to promoting various experimental musics with a particular emphasis on improvised music.
Address: 21 Denham Dr, Basingstoke, Hamps RG22 6LT, United Kingdom. Ed., Pub., R&P, Adv. contact Chris Blackford. Circ: 1,500.

780 POL ISSN 0035-9610
ML5
RUCH MUZYCZNY; a musical review. Text in Polish. 1957. fortn. EUR 108 foreign (effective 2007). bk.rev.; music rev.; rec.rev. illus. index. **Document type:** *Magazine, Consumer.*
Indexed: IIMP, M11, MusicInd, RASB, RILM.
Published by: Biblioteka Narodowa, Dzial Wydawniczy Czasopism Patronackich, Al Niepodleglosci 213, Warsaw, 00-973, Poland. TEL 48-22-6082374, FAX 48-22-6082488. Ed. Ludwik Erhardt. Circ: 5,000. **Dist. by:** Ars Polona, Obroncow 25, Warsaw 03933, Poland. TEL 48-22-5098609, FAX 48-22-5098610, arspolona@arspolona.com.pl, http://www.arspolona.com.pl.

782.421 USA ISSN 1556-8687
RUCKUS. Text in English. 2006. bi-m. free (effective 2007). **Document type:** *Magazine, Consumer.* **Description:** Covers the hip-hop culture worldwide and in the Bay Area.
Address: 1317 N. Carolan Ave., Burlingame, CA 94010. TEL 650-340-8100, FAX 650-340-1818.

781.64 USA
RUDE INTERNATIONAL. Text in English. q. USD 12 domestic; USD 18 in Canada; USD 26 elsewhere; USD 3.50 newsstand/cover (effective 2001). **Document type:** *Magazine, Consumer.* **Description:** Brings together content and reviews of various music scenes such as punk, ska, oi!, mod and reggae.
Address: PO Box 391302, Cambridge, MA 02139. rude@rudeinternational.com, http://www.rudeinternational.com. **Dist. by:** International Publishers Direct, 27500 Riverview Center Blvd, Bonita Springs, FL 34134. TEL 858-320-4563, FAX 858-677-3220.

▼ **RUKUS.** *see* LIFESTYLE

780 SWE ISSN 1650-089X
RUMBA. Text in Swedish. 2000. q. SEK 100 membership (effective 2004). **Document type:** *Magazine, Trade.*
Supersedes in part: Musikant (0345-8210)
Published by: Riksfoerbundet Unga Musikanter (RUM)/Swedish Federation of Young Musicians, Isafjoerdursgatan 4 d, Linkoeping, 58231, Sweden. TEL 46-13-137134, FAX 46-13-149590. Ed. Bertil Haakansson. Circ: 28,000.

781.64 FIN ISSN 0781-0326
RUMBA; rockin ajankohtaislehti. Text in Finnish. 1984. 20/yr. adv. **Document type:** *Consumer.*
Published by: Pop Media oy, Malminkatu 24, Helsinki, 00100, Finland. TEL 358-9-43692407, FAX 358-9-43692409, http://www.popmedia.fi. Ed. Viljami Puustinen. Adv. contact Oskari Anttonen TEL 358-40-5630642. page EUR 1,950; 260 x 3030. Circ: 10,000.

780 ITA ISSN 1121-3523
RUMORE. Text in Italian. 1992. m. (11/yr.). EUR 49 domestic; EUR 79 in Europe (effective 2009). adv. **Document type:** *Magazine, Consumer.*
Published by: Edizioni Apache, Via Dei Mille 178, Pavia, 27100, Italy. TEL 39-0382-303612, FAX 39-0382-566856. Ed. Massimo Stefani. Circ: 40,000.

780 FIN ISSN 1239-1204
RYTMI. Text in Finnish. 1992. 8/yr. EUR 43.50 (effective 2007). adv. back issues avail. **Document type:** *Magazine, Consumer.*
Formerly (until 1996): Rytmimusiikki (0789-7200); Which was formed by the merger of (1987-1992): Musiikkiuutiset (0783-9502); (1934-1992): Rytmi (0789-1962)
Related titles: Online - full text ed.
Published by: Pop Media oy, Malminkatu 24, Helsinki, 00100, Finland. TEL 358-9-43692407, FAX 358-9-43692409, http://www.popmedia.fi. Ed. Mikko Aaltonen. Adv. contact Oskari Anttonen TEL 358-40-5630642. page EUR 1,400; 210 x 285. Circ: 8,000.

786 USA ISSN 0744-0200
M2062
THE S A B CHOIR. (Soprano, Alto, Bass) Text in English. 1981. q. USD 14.95 (effective 2008). adv. **Document type:** *Magazine, Consumer.* **Description:** Provides a steady source of well-crafted seasonal and general three-part music for soprano, alto and baritone.
Published by: Lorenz Publishing Co., 501 E 3rd St, Box 802, Dayton, OH 45402. TEL 937-228-6118, 800-444-1144, FAX 937-223-2042, info@lorenz.com, http://www.lorenz.com. Ed. David Sarandon.

780 USA ISSN 1059-7921
M1
S C I JOURNAL OF MUSIC SCORES. Variant title: Journal of Music Scores. Text in English. 1973. irreg. (2-3/yr.), latest vol.23. price varies. **Description:** Anthology of music scores written by members of SCI.
Formerly: A S U C Journal of Music Scores (0196-1438)
Published by: (Society of Composers Inc.), European American Music Corporation, PO Box 850, Valley Forge, PA 19482-0850. TEL 610-648-0506, FAX 610-889-0242. Ed. Bruce Taub. Circ: 175.

708.89 USA
S E M NEWSLETTER. Text in English. 1966. q. membership. back issues avail.; reprints avail. **Document type:** *Newsletter, Consumer.* **Description:** Covers society news, announces forthcoming conferences and events and profiles noteworthy persons.
Former titles: Ethnomusicology Newsletter; Society for Ethnomusicology Newsletter; S E M Newsletter (Milwaukee, 1967) (0036-1291); Which incorporated: Society for Ethnomusicology. Membership List (0731-1583)
Related titles: Microform ed.: (from PQC).
Indexed: A22, AICP, MAG, RASB, RILM.
—BLDSC (8237.350000), INIST.
Published by: Society for Ethnomusicology, Morrison Hall 005, Indiana University, 1165 E 3rd St, Bloomington, IN 47405. TEL 812-855-6672, FAX 812-855-6673, sem@indiana.edu, http://webdb.iu.edu/sem/. Ed. Tong Soon Lee. Circ: 2,000.

780 USA
S P MUSIC MAGAZINE. Text in English. 2000. bi-m. USD 16.95; USD 3 newsstand/cover (effective 2001). adv. **Document type:** *Magazine, Consumer.*
Published by: S P Magazine, South Santa Fe Ave, Los Angeles, CA 90021. TEL 213-489-5993, joshu@spmag.com, http://www.spmag.com. Ed. Joshua Harris.

780 CAN ISSN 1480-1132
ML5
S Q R M. CAHIERS. Text in French. 1983. a. CAD 18 to individuals; CAD 36 to institutions (effective 2004).
Formerly (until 1997): Cahiers de l'ARMuQ (0821-1817)
Indexed: CMPI, RILM.
Published by: Societe Quebecoise de Recherche en Musique, 300 Blvd de Maissoneuve Est, Montreal, PQ H2X 3X6, Canada. TEL 514-843-9305, FAX 514-843-3167, info@sqrm.qc.ca. Ed. Sylvia L'Ecuyer.

780 SWE ISSN 2000-5628
S T I M - MAGASINET. (Svenska Tonsaettares Internationalla Musikbyraa) Text in Swedish. 1970. q. free. adv. charts; illus. **Document type:** *Magazine, Consumer.*
Former titles (until 2010): S T I M - Nytt (0283-3190); (until 1986): Ord och Ton (0345-8938)
Published by: S T I M/Swedish Performing Rights Society, Sandhamnsgatan 79, PO Box 27327, Stockholm, 10254, Sweden. TEL 46-8-7838800, FAX 46-8-6626275, info@stim.se. Ed. Christina Bild.

783 USA ISSN 0036-2255
CODEN: OIJRD5
SACRED MUSIC. Text in English. 1874. q. free to members (effective 2009). adv. bk.rev. charts. index. back issues avail.; reprints avail. **Document type:** *Journal, Academic/Scholarly.* **Description:** Provides every Church musician, professional or amateur, who is interested in the restoration of the sacred in Catholic liturgical life.
Formed by the merger of (1915-1965): The Catholic Choirmaster (0197-551X); (1874-1965): Caecilia
Related titles: Microform ed.: (from PQC); Online - full text ed.
Indexed: A20, A22, ASCA, ArtHuCI, CPL, CurCont, G06, G07, G08, I05, IIMP, M11, MAG, MLA-IB, MusicInd, RILM, SCOPUS, T02, W07.
—BLDSC (8062.740000), IE, Ingenta.
Published by: Church Music Association of America, 12421 New Point Dr, Richmond, VA 23233. FAX 334-460-9924, contact@musicasacra.com. Ed. William Mahrt.

786 USA ISSN 0036-2263
M6
THE SACRED ORGAN JOURNAL. Text in English. 1966. bi-m. USD 39.95 domestic; USD 44.95 in Canada; USD 75.95 elsewhere (effective 2008). adv. 32 p./no.; **Document type:** *Magazine, Consumer.* **Description:** Features gems from the baroque, classical and romantic periods, as well as works by today's leading composers of sacred music.
Published by: Lorenz Publishing Co., 501 E 3rd St, Box 802, Dayton, OH 45402. TEL 937-228-6118, 800-444-1144, FAX 937-223-2042, info@lorenz.com, http://www.lorenz.com.

SADLER'S WELLS THEATRE PROGRAMME. *see* THEATER

781.7 DEU ISSN 0036-2328
ML5
SAENGER- UND MUSIKANTENZEITUNG; Zeitschrift fuer musikalische Volkskultur. Text in German. 1958. bi-m. EUR 32.50 domestic; EUR 34.60 foreign (effective 2009). adv. bk.rev. illus. **Document type:** *Newspaper, Consumer.*
Indexed: DIP, IBR, IBZ, RILM.
—CCC.
Published by: Deutscher Landwirtschaftsverlag GmbH, Lothstr 29, Munich, 80797, Germany. TEL 49-89-127051, FAX 49-89-12705335, dlv.muenchen@dlv.de, http://www.dlv.de. Ed. Josef Focht. Adv. contact Claudia Sen. B&W page EUR 767, color page EUR 2,071; trim 176 x 246. Circ: 8,516 (controlled).

780 ITA ISSN 1973-1574
SAGGI E MONOGRAFIE. Text in Italian. 2000. irreg. **Document type:** *Monographic series, Academic/Scholarly.*
Published by: Fondazione Donizzetti, Piazza Cavour 15, Bergamo, 24121, Italy. fondazione@donizzetti.org, http://www.donizzetti.org.

780 ITA ISSN 1123-8615
ML5
IL SAGGIATORE MUSICALE; rivista semestrale di musicologia. Text in Italian. 1994. s-a. EUR 120 combined subscription foreign to institutions (print & online eds.) (effective 2012). bk.rev. **Document type:** *Journal, Academic/Scholarly.*
Related titles: Online - full text ed.: ISSN 2035-6706.
Indexed: A01, CA, DIP, IBR, IBZ, IIMP, M11, T02.
Published by: (Universita degli Studi di Bologna, Dipartimento di Musica e Spettacolo), Casa Editrice Leo S. Olschki, Viuzzo del Pozzetto 8, Florence, 50126, Italy. TEL 39-055-6530684, FAX 39-055-6530214, celso@olschki.it, http://www.olschki.it. Ed. Giuseppina La Face Bianconi.

780 DEU ISSN 0036-3308
SAITENSPIEL. Text in German. 1961. 6/yr. adv. bk.rev. **Document type:** *Magazine, Consumer.* **Description:** All about the zither: composition, instruction, recordings.
Published by: Deutscher Zithermusik-Bund e.V., Helene-Weber-Str 1, Troisdorf, 53844, Germany. TEL 49-228-88621715, info@zitherbund.de, http://www.zitherbund.de. Circ: 2,000.

781 DEU
SALLY'SCOUT. Text in German. 10/yr. adv. **Document type:** *Magazine, Consumer.*
Published by: Uncle Sally's GmbH & Co. KG, Waldemarstr 37, Berlin, 10999, Germany. TEL 49-30-69409663, FAX 49-30-6913137, sallys@sallys.net, http://www.sallys.net. adv.: B&W page EUR 870, color page EUR 1,050. Circ: 49,000 (controlled).

780 CUB ISSN 1024-946X
SALSA CUBANA. Text in Spanish. 1997. q.
Related titles: Online - full text ed.: ISSN 1682-6183.
Published by: Instituto Cubano del Libro, Palacio del Segundo Cabo, Calle 21, 459 esq. E y F, Havana, Cuba. TEL 53-78-323487. Ed. Elizabeth Gonzalez Munoz.

781.642 USA
SALT FOR SLUGS; contemporary literature for the random reader. Text in English. 1997. q. USD 12; USD 3 newsstand/cover (effective 2001). adv. **Document type:** *Magazine, Consumer.* **Description:** Contains contemporary literature covering music, art, recreation, leisure, politics, humor, and more.
Address: PO Box 4754, Chapel Hill, NC 27515-4754. TEL 512-481-1365. Ed., Pub., R&P, Adv. contact James Bernard White. Circ: 4,000 (paid).

780 792.8 CHE ISSN 1660-8690
SALZBURGER BEITRAEGE ZUR MUSIK- UND TANZFORSCHUNG. Text in German. 2003. irreg., latest vol.3, 2008. price varies. **Document type:** *Monographic series, Academic/Scholarly.*
Published by: Peter Lang AG (Subsidiary of: Peter Lang Publishing Group), Hochfeldstr 32, Postfach 746, Bern 9, 3000, Switzerland. TEL 41-31-3061717, FAX 41-31-3061727, info@peterlang.com. Ed. Peter Maria Krakauer.

780.01 DEU ISSN 0085-588X
➤ **SAMMLUNG MUSIKWISSENSCHAFTLICHER ABHANDLUNGEN/ COLLECTION D'ETUDES MUSICOLOGIQUES.** Text in English, French, German. 1932. irreg., latest vol.97, 2006. price varies. back issues avail. **Document type:** *Monographic series, Academic/ Scholarly.* **Description:** Monographs on musicological studies.
Published by: Verlag Valentin Koerner GmbH, Postfach 100164, Baden-Baden, 76482, Germany. TEL 49-7221-22423, FAX 49-7221-38697, info@koernerverlag.de, http://www.koernerverlag.de.

781.64 DEU ISSN 1612-8001
ML3469
SAMPLES. Text in German, English. 2002. a. free (effective 2011). **Document type:** *Journal, Academic/Scholarly.* **Description:** Contains articles and research on various forms of popular music.
Media: Online - full text.
—CCC.
Published by: Arbeitskreis Studium Populaere Musik e.V., Ahornweg 154, Halstenbek, 25469, Germany. TEL 49-4101-44840, fk8a003@uni-hamburg.de, http://www.aspm-online.de.

SAN DIEGO SOUND POST. *see* LABOR UNIONS

SAN FRANCISCO ARTS MONTHLY. *see* MUSEUMS AND ART GALLERIES

780 792 IND ISSN 0036-4339
SANGEET NATAK. Text in English. 1965. q. INR 100 domestic to individuals; INR 150 domestic to institutions; USD 15 foreign; INR 30 per issue domestic to individuals; INR 40 per issue domestic to institutions; USD 5 per issue foreign (effective 2011). bk.rev. illus. 50 p./no. 1 cols./p.; back issues avail. **Document type:** *Journal, Academic/Scholarly.* **Description:** Publishes articles, reviews, and reports dealing chiefly Indian music, dance, theatre, culture. Aims to promote and disseminate knowledge in these subjects.
Indexed: BAS, RILM.
—Ingenta.
Published by: Sangeet Natak Akademi/National Academy of Music, Dance and Drama, Rabindra Bhavan, Feroze Shah Rd, New Delhi, 110 001, India. TEL 91-11-23387246, FAX 91-11-23385715, mail@sangeetnatak.gov.in. Ed. Abhijit Chatterjee. **Subscr. to:** I N S I O Scientific Books & Periodicals.

917.309 USA
SANGER-HILSEN/SINGERS' GREETINGS. Text in English, Norwegian. 1910. bi-m. USD 20 (effective 2008). **Document type:** *Newsletter.* **Description:** Aims to promote Scandinavian male chorus music, to create friendship among its members, and to assist and encourage Scandinavian musicians.
Related titles: Online - full content ed.
Published by: Norwegian Singers Association of America, Inc., 407 Leif Erikson Dr, Decorah, IA 52101-1038. Ed. Donald Berg.

780.71 CAN
THE SASKATCHEWAN BAND ASSOCIATION JOURNAL; a smooth connection between notes. Text in English. 1983. s-a. free. adv. **Description:** Contains articles and events pertaining to instrumental music programs in Saskatchewan.
Formerly: Slur
Published by: Saskatchewan Band Association, 34 Sunset Dr N, Yorkton, SK S3N 3K9, Canada. TEL 306-783-2263, FAX 306-565-2177, sask.band@sk.sympatico.ca. Ed. Ian Cochran. Circ: 300.

780 CAN
SASKATCHEWAN MUSIC FESTIVAL ASSOCIATION. ANNUAL DIRECTORY; featuring all competition regulations and scholarships. Text in English. a. CAD 5 (effective 2003). **Description:** Lists 49 local music festivals, provincial competitions and concerto competitions.
Published by: Saskatchewan Music Festival Association, 207 2314 11th Ave, Regina, SK S4P 0K1, Canada. TEL 306-757-1722, FAX 306-347-7789. Circ: 2,500.

780 CAN
SASKATCHEWAN MUSIC FESTIVAL ASSOCIATION OFFICIAL SYLLABUS. Text in English. 1909. triennial. CAD 10 (effective 2003). adv.
Published by: Saskatchewan Music Festival Association, 207 2314 11th Ave, Regina, SK S4P 0K1, Canada. TEL 306-757-1722, FAX 306-347-7789. Ed. Doris Covey Lazecki. Circ: 2,500.

780 USA
SASSAFRAS. Text in English. 1986. s-a. membership. **Document type:** *Newsletter.* **Description:** News and events for singers, songwriters, musicians and others interested in the links between musical expression and progressive social and political change.
Published by: People's Music Network for Songs of Freedom and Struggle, c/o Sarah Underhill, 1150 Berme Rd, Kerhonkson, NY 12446. TEL 617-641-2530. Ed. Julius Gordon.

SAVAGE UNDERGROUND. *see* MOTION PICTURES

780 FIN ISSN 0788-804X
SAVELLYS JA MUSIIKINTEORIA. Text in Finnish. 1991. biennial. **Document type:** *Journal, Academic/Scholarly.*
Related titles: Online - full text ed.: ISSN 1796-1599.
Indexed: RILM.
Published by: Sibelius-Akatemia/The Sibelius Academy, PO Box 86, Helsinki, 00251, Finland. TEL 358-20-75390, FAX 358-20-7539600, info@siba.fi, http://www.siba.fi.

780 SRB
SAVEZ ORGANIZACIJA KOMPOZITORA JUGOSLAVIJE. PISMO. Text in Serbian. 1972. q. free. adv. **Document type:** *Bulletin.* **Description:** Publishes news on SOKOJ-MIC activities: copyright protection, international cooperation, major music events in the country, news on first performances, awards, competitions, festival, courses.
Former titles: Savez Organizacija Kompozitora Jugoslavije. Pismo. Bilten; (until 1998): Savez Organizacija Kompozitora Jugoslavije. Bilten
Related titles: English ed.: Union of Yugoslav Composers' Organizations. Letter. Bulletin.
Published by: Savez Organizacija Kompozitora Jugoslavije (SOKOJ), Music Information Centre/Union of Yugoslav Composers' Organizations, Misarska 12-14, Belgrade, 11000. TEL 381-11-3224056, FAX 381-11-3245192. Ed. Anna Kotevska. Adv. contact Dragana Pantic.

781.65 USA ISSN 0276-4768
ML929
SAXOPHONE JOURNAL. Text in English. 1980. bi-m. USD 25 domestic; USD 35 foreign; USD 35 domestic with CD; USD 45 foreign with CD. back issues avail. **Document type:** *Journal, Trade.* **Description:** Provides news to improve playing with regular columns on jazz improvisation, techniques, doubling, career management, new publications, writing and teaching ideas, and reviews.
Formerly: Saxophone Sheet
Indexed: IIMP, M11, MAG, MusicInd, RILM, T02.
—Ingenta.
Published by: Dorn Publications, Inc., PO Box 206, Medfield, MA 02052.

781.65 USA ISSN 0271-3705
➤ **THE SAXOPHONE SYMPOSIUM.** Text in English. 1970. a. free to members (effective 2011). adv. back issues avail. **Document type:** *Journal, Academic/Scholarly.* **Description:** Features articles submitted for publication are reviewed by an editorial board consisting of professional performers, scholars, and teachers.
Formerly (until 1976): World Saxophone Congress. Newsletter
Indexed: RILM.
—Ingenta.
Published by: North American Saxophone Alliance, c/o Jennifer Turpen, University of Wyoming, Department 3037, 1000 E University Ave, Department of Music, Laramie, WY 82071. Ed. Jennifer Turpen.

➤ **SCALA (MANNHEIM)**; Kultur im Rhein-Neckar-Dreieck. *see* LIFESTYLE

780 CAN ISSN 1486-0317
LA SCENA MUSICALE. Text in French. 1996. m. CAD 40 domestic to individuals; CAD 69 in United States to individuals; CAD 99 elsewhere to individuals; CAD 53 domestic to institutions; CAD 79 in United States to institutions (effective 2007). music rev. **Document type:** *Journal, Academic/Scholarly.* **Description:** Contains a calendar of concerts, CD reviews, interviews with musicians as well as feature articles on the local, national and international classical music scenes.
Former titles (until 1997): Scena Musicale & Vocale (1206-9965); (until 1997): Scena Vocale (1483-5401)
Related titles: Online - full text ed.: ISSN 1206-9973; English ed.: Music Scene. ISSN 1703-8189.
Indexed: CMPI.
Published by: La Scena Musicale, 5409 rue Waverly, Montreal, PQ H2T 2X8, Canada. TEL 514-274-9456, FAX 514-274-9456.

SCENARIA. *see* THEATER

SCENES MAGAZINE; mensuel suisse d'information culturelle. *see* ART

780 ESP ISSN 0213-4802
ML5
SCHERZO. Text in Spanish. 1985. m. (10/yr.). EUR 70 domestic; EUR 105 in Europe; EUR 150 in the Americas; EUR 125 elsewhere (effective 2010). adv. bk.rev.; rec.rev.; music rev. 140 p./no.; back issues avail. **Document type:** *Magazine, Consumer.* **Description:** Presents the world of so-called "serious music" (classical, jazz) in Spain. Covers national and foreign events.
Related titles: Online - full text ed.
Indexed: IIMP, IIPA, M11, MusicInd, P09, PCI, RILM.
Published by: Scherzo Editorial S.A., Cartagena 10, 1o C, Madrid, 28028, Spain. TEL 34-91-3567622, FAX 34-91-7261864. Ed., R&P Tomas Martin de Vidales. Adv. contact Arantza Quintanilla. B&W page EUR 1,140, color page EUR 1,500; 200 x 280. Circ: 15,000 (controlled). **Dist. by:** Asociacion de Revistas Culturales de Espana, C Covarruvias 9 2o. Derecha, Madrid 28010, Spain. TEL 34-91-3086066, FAX 34-91-3199267, info@arce.es, http://www.arce.es/.

780.65 USA
ML427.S27
SCHIRMER NEWS (ONLINE). Text in English. 1987. irreg. (1-4/yr.). free (effective 2005). **Document type:** *Newsletter.* **Description:** Contains articles, calendars, and announcements of interest to performers, conductors, and the classical music business.
Formerly: Schirmer - News (Print) (1060-4111)
Published by: G. Schirmer Inc., 257 Park Ave S, 20th Fl, New York, NY 10010. TEL 212-254-2013, FAX 212-254-2100. Ed. Deborh Horne.

780 CHE
▼ **SCHOLA CANTORUM BASILIENSIS SCRIPTA.** Text in German. 2009. irreg., latest vol.2, 2010. price varies. **Document type:** *Monographic series, Academic/Scholarly.*
Published by: Schwabe und Co. AG, Steinentorstr 13, Basel, 4010, Switzerland. TEL 41-61-2789565, FAX 41-61-2789566, verlag@schwabe.ch, http://www.schwabe.ch.

784 USA ISSN 1098-3694
MT733
SCHOOL BAND AND ORCHESTRA. Abbreviated title: S B O. Text in English. 1998. m. free to qualified personnel (effective 2009). adv. back issues avail. **Document type:** *Magazine, Trade.* **Description:** Provides directors with the information and tools to help build and strengthen their overall music program.
Related titles: Supplement(s): Annual College Search & Career Guide; Music Parents America.
Indexed: E03, E07, G06, G07, G08, I05, P16, P48, P53, P54, PQC.
Published by: Symphony Publishing LLC, 21 Highland Cir, Ste One, Needham, MA 02494. TEL 781-453-9310, 800-964-5150, FAX 781-453-9389, http://www.symphonypublishing.com. Ed. Christian Wissmuller TEL 781-453-9310 ext 16. Pub. Richard E Kessel TEL 781-453-9310 ext 14. Adv. contact Iris Fox TEL 954-973-3555. page USD 2,200; bleed 8.25 x 11.125. Circ: 20,000 (paid).

791 DEU
SCHOTT AKTUELL; the journal. Text in German. 1961. bi-m. free (effective 2011). **Document type:** *Magazine, Consumer.*
Formerly: Schott-Kurier (0036-6919)
Published by: Schott Musik International GmbH, Weihergarten 5, Mainz, 55116, Germany. TEL 49-6131-2460, FAX 49-6131-246211, info@schott-musik.de, http://www.schott-musik.de.

780 158 DEU ISSN 0930-3820
SCHRIFTEN ZUR MUSIKPSYCHOLOGIE UND MUSIKAESTHETIK. Text in German. 1986. irreg., latest vol.17, 2006. price varies. **Document type:** *Monographic series, Academic/Scholarly.*
Published by: Peter Lang GmbH (Subsidiary of: Peter Lang Publishing Group), Eschborner Landstr 42-50, Frankfurt Am Main, 60489, Germany. TEL 49-69-7807050, FAX 49-69-78070550, zentrale.frankfurt@peterlang.com. Ed. Helga de la Motte Haber.

781.62 AUT
SCHRIFTEN ZUR VOLKSMUSIK. Text in German. 1969. irreg., latest vol.24, 2011. price varies. **Document type:** *Monographic series, Academic/Scholarly.*
Published by: Boehlau Verlag GmbH & Co.KG., Wiesingerstr 1, Vienna, W 1010, Austria. TEL 43-1-3302427, FAX 43-1-3302432, boehlau@boehlau.at, http://www.boehlau.at. Ed. Gerlinde Haid.

780 DEU ISSN 1617-6340
ML410.S3
➤ **SCHUBERT: PERSPEKTIVEN.** Text in German. 2001. 2/yr. EUR 66.40; EUR 42 newsstand/cover (effective 2012). adv. reprint service avail. from SCH. **Document type:** *Journal, Academic/Scholarly.*
Indexed: DIP, IBR, IBZ, RILM.
Published by: Franz Steiner Verlag GmbH, Birkenwaldstr 44, Stuttgart, 70191, Germany. TEL 49-711-25820, FAX 49-711-2582290, service@steiner-verlag.de. Eds. Hans Joachim Hinrichsen, Till Gerrit Waidelich. Circ: 450 (paid).

780 DEU ISSN 0174-2345
ML410.S35
SCHUETZ-JAHRBUCH. Text in German. 1966. a. **Document type:** *Journal, Academic/Scholarly.*
Formerly (until 1973): Sagittarius (0080-5408)
Indexed: DIP, IBR, IBZ, IIMP, M11, MusicInd, PCI, RILM.
Published by: (Internationale Heinrich Schuetz-Gesellschaft e.V.), Baerenreiter Verlag, Heinrich-Schuetz-Allee 35, Kassel, 34131, Germany. TEL 49-561-3105154, FAX 49-561-3105195, order@baerenreiter.com, http://www.baerenreiter.com.

780 DEU ISSN 0863-2340
ML410.S4
SCHUMANN STUDIEN. Text in German. 1988. irreg.
Indexed: RILM.
Published by: (Robert Schumann Gesellschaft), Studio Verlag Dr. Gisela Schewe, Zehnthofstr. 2, Sinzig, 53489, Germany. TEL 49-2642-5919, FAX 49-2642-5917, mail@studiopunktverlag.de, http://www.MUUT.de/studio. Ed. Dr. Gerd Nauhaus.

780 CHE ISSN 0259-3165
ML5
SCHWEIZER JAHRBUCH FUER MUSIKWISSENSCHAFT/ANNALES SUISSES DE MUSICOLOGIE. Text in French, German. 1997. a. CHF 65 (effective 2010). **Document type:** *Monographic series, Academic/Scholarly.*
Formerly (until 1981): Schweizerische Musikforschende Gesellschaft. Publikationen. Serie 3: Schweizer Beitraege zur Musikwissenschaft (1012-845X)
Published by: (Schweizerische Musikforschende Gesellschaft), Peter Lang AG (Subsidiary of: Peter Lang Publishing Group), Hochfeldstr 32, Postfach 746, Bern 9, 3000, Switzerland. TEL 41-31-3061717, FAX 41-31-3061727, info@peterlang.com, http://www.peterlang.com. Circ: 500 (paid).

780 CHE ISSN 1422-4674
SCHWEIZER MUSIKZEITUNG/REVUE MUSICALE SUISSE. Text in French, German. 1998. 11/yr. CHF 55 domestic; EUR 45 foreign; CHF 6 newsstand/cover (effective 2008). adv. bk.rev. bibl.; charts; illus. index. reprint service avail. from PSC. **Document type:** *Newspaper, Trade.*
Formed by the merger of (1975-1998): Musique Information (1422-5646); (1939-1998): Sinfonia (1422-5611); (1947-1998): Schweizerischer Musikpaedagogischer Verband. Mitteilungsblatt (1421-5217); Which was formerly (1943-1947): Monatsblaetter fuer Musikerziehung (1421-5241); (1940-1943): Schweizerischer Musikpaedagogischer Verband. Mitteilungsblatt (1421-5233); (1912-1940): Schweizerische Musikpaedagogische Blaetter (1421-5330); (1989-1998): Animato (1422-5603); Which was formerly (1977-1989): V M S - Bulletin (1422-562X); (1985-1998): Presto (1422-5638); Which was formerly (1915-1985): Schweizer Musiker-Blatt (1422-5654); (1984-1998): Schweizer Musikpaedagogische Blaetter (1421-5292); Which superseded in part (in 1984): Schweizerische Musikzeitung - Schweizer Musikpaedagogische Blaetter (1421-5349); Which was formed by the merger of (1949-1959): Schweizer Musikpaedagogische Blaetter (0559-0558); (1861-1959): Schweizerische Musikzeitung (0036-7710); Which superseded in part (in 1937): Schweizerische Musikzeitung und Saengerblatt (1421-5314); Which was formerly (until 1879): Schweizerisches Saengerblatt (1421-5322)
Indexed: A20, M11, RILM.
—CCC.
Published by: (Schweizerischer Musikerverband), Schweizer Musikzeitung, Bellariastr 82, Zuerich, 8038, Switzerland. TEL 41-44-2812321, FAX 41-44-2812353. Ed. Katrin Spelinova. Adv. contact Ida Schmieder. page CHF 2,068; trim 208 x 290. Circ: 22,000 (paid and controlled).

780 CHE
SCHWEIZER VOLKSMUSIK. Text in German. 6/yr.
Address: Riedstr., Postfach 34, Schlosswil, 3082, Switzerland. TEL 031-7111639. Ed. Werner Reber. Circ: 10,000.

784 CHE
SCHWEIZERISCHE CHORZEITUNG/REVUE SUISSE DES CHORALES. Text in French, German, Italian. 1978. m. CHF 32; CHF 38 foreign (effective 1998). adv. **Document type:** *Bulletin.*
Published by: Union Suisse des Chorales/Schweizerische Chorvereinigung, Haus der Musik, Goenhardweg 32, Aarau, 5001, Switzerland. TEL 41-62-8245404, FAX 41-62-8245406. Ed. Theres Ursula Beiner. Circ: 6,500.

780 CHE ISSN 1012-8441
SCHWEIZERISCHE MUSIKFORSCHENDE GESELLSCHAFT. PUBLIKATIONEN. SERIE 2. Text in German. 1952. irreg., latest vol.51, 2009. price varies. **Document type:** *Monographic series, Academic/Scholarly.*
—CCC.
Published by: (Schweizerische Musikforschende Gesellschaft), Peter Lang AG (Subsidiary of: Peter Lang Publishing Group), Hochfeldstr 32, Postfach 746, Bern 9, 3000, Switzerland. TEL 41-31-3061717, FAX 41-31-3061727, info@peterlang.com, http://www.peterlang.com.

780 FRA ISSN 1625-8738
SCIENCES DE LA MUSIQUE. Text in French. 2000. irreg. price varies. **Document type:** *Monographic series, Academic/Scholarly.*
Published by: Centre National de la Recherche Scientifique, Campus Gerard-Megie, 3 Rue Michel-Ange, Paris, 75794, France.

780 USA ISSN 1066-5447
ML2074
THE SCORE. Text in English. 3/yr.
Indexed: F01, F02, T02.
Published by: Society of Composers & Lyricists, 400 S Beverly Dr, Ste 214, Beverly Hills, CA 90212. http://www.thescl.com/site/scl/.

780 GBR
➤ **SCOTTISH JOURNAL OF MUSIC RESEARCH.** Text in English. 2001. s-a. bk.rev.; rec.rev. **Document type:** *Journal, Academic/Scholarly.* **Description:** Includes articles on all aspects of music, with special focus on Scottish music.
Related titles: Online - full text ed.
Published by: University of Aberdeen, Music Research Group, MacRobert Bldg, Aberdeen, AB24 5AU, United Kingdom. TEL 44-1224-272570, music@abdn.ac.uk, https://www.abdn.ac.uk/music/.

781.64 USA ISSN 1092-7352
SCREAMING IN DIGITAL. Text in English. 1991. irreg. **Description:** Focuses primarily on the lives, works and activities of the band Queensryche, their contemporaries and their listeners.
Media: Online - full text.
Address: editor@scream.org, http://www.scream.org/. Ed. Dan Birchall.

SEATTLE FOLKLORE SOCIETY NEWSLETTER. *see* FOLKLORE

782.81 USA
SEATTLE OPERA MAGAZINE. Text in English. q. adv. **Document type:** *Magazine, Consumer.*
Published by: Seattle Opera, 1020 John St, Seattle, WA 98109. Ed. Tina Ryker. Adv. contact Paul Heppner TEL 206-443-0445.

781.57 USA ISSN 0037-0576
ML1
SECOND LINE. Text in English. 1950. q. USD 25 to members. adv. bk.rev. bibl.; charts; illus.; stat. index, cum.index.
Indexed: IIMP, M11, MusicInd, RILM.
Published by: New Orleans Jazz Club, 828 Royal St, Ste 265, New Orleans, LA 70116. TEL 504-455-6847. Ed. Carolyn Stafford. Circ: 1,000.

780 791.4375 CAN ISSN 1196-5347
SEE MAGAZINE. Text in English. 1992. w. free. adv. **Description:** Covers the entertainment scene in the Edmonton area.
Related titles: Online - full text ed.
Address: 8625 109th St., Ste. 222, Edmonton, AB T6G 1E7, Canada. TEL 780-430-9003, FAX 780-432-1102, info@see.greatwest.ca, http://www.greatwest.ca/see. Ed. Andrew Hanon.

780 370 USA
SEGUE (LITTLE ROCK). Text in English. 3/yr. (Oct., Feb. & May). adv. **Document type:** *Magazine, Trade.*
Related titles: Online - full content ed.
Published by: Arkansas Music Educators Association, c/o Mary Zies, Editor, 1503 Scott St, Apt 3, Little Rock, AR 72202. TEL 501-447-5178, FAX 501-375-2054. Ed. Mary Zies. adv.: page USD 190; trim 8.5 x 11. Circ: 1,200.

781.7 USA ISSN 0361-6622
ML3799
➤ **SELECTED REPORTS IN ETHNOMUSICOLOGY.** Text in English. 1966. irreg., latest vol.12, 2005. price varies. illus. back issues avail. **Document type:** *Report, Academic/Scholarly.* **Description:** Contains essays around a central theme concerning ethnomusicological theory and method, particular world music areas, comparative analysis, or specific aspects of ethnomusicological research.
Formerly (until 1974): University of California, Los Angeles. Institute of Ethnomusicology. Selected Reports (0575-4712)
Indexed: A01, AICP, AnthLit, CA, FR, IIMP, M11, MLA, MLA-IB, MusicInd, RILM, T02.
—Ingenta, INIST.
Published by: University of California, Los Angeles, Department of Ethnomusicology, 2539 Schoenberg Music Bldg, Los Angeles, CA 90095. trice@arts.ucla.edu.

781.71 USA ISSN 1046-4158
SENIOR MUSICIAN. Text in English. 1970. q. price varies. back issues avail. **Document type:** *Magazine, Consumer.* **Description:** Contains four new titles in a variety of styles, along with articles, short stories, helps and trivia for senior adult groups.
Published by: LifeWay Christian Resources, 1 Lifeway Plz, Nashville, TN 37234. TEL 615-251-2000, 800-458-2772, FAX 615-251-5933, customerservice@lifeway.com, http://www.lifeway.com.

781.66 FRA ISSN 2109-0335
▼ **SERGE.** Text in French. 2010. bi-m. EUR 29; EUR 5 newsstand/cover (effective 2011). adv. **Document type:** *Magazine, Consumer.*
Published by: Detroit Media, 6, Rue Desargues, Paris, 75011, France. TEL 33-1-42471825. Eds. Didier Varrod, Patrice Bardot.

SEVENTEENTH CENTURY FRENCH STUDIES. *see* LITERATURE

780.6 920 USA ISSN 1054-6022
ML194
SEVENTEENTH CENTURY MUSIC. Text in English. 1984. 2/yr. USD 10 to non-members. adv. bk.rev. **Document type:** *Newsletter.* **Description:** Deals with all aspects of the study and performance of music in the seventeenth century.
Former titles: Schutz Society Reports; Archer
Indexed: RILM.
Published by: Society for Seventeenth - Century Music, c/o Steven Saunders, Dept of Music, Colby College, Waterville, ME 04901. TEL 717-299-2116, FAX 717-299-2116, http://www.arts.uci.edu/sscm/. Ed., R&P, Adv. contact Massimo Ossi. Circ: 120.

SEVENTH SKY AND SEVENTH SKY PEOPLE. *see* SPORTS AND GAMES

783 USA
SHALSHELET: THE CHAIN. Text in English. 1976 (vol.11). irreg. membership.
Published by: Hebrew Union College - Jewish Institute of Religion (New York), One W Fouth St, New York, NY 10012. TEL 212-674-5300. Ed. B Ostfeld Horowitz. Circ: 200.

780 USA ISSN 1548-9108
SHEET MUSIC MAGAZINE. Text in English. 1977. bi-m. USD 22.97 (effective 2006). adv. bk.rev.; music rev.; software rev. back issues avail. **Document type:** *Magazine, Consumer.* **Description:** Contains feature articles on various aspects of musical performance and interest for various types of musicians.
Former titles (until 1999): Sheet Musinc Magazine (Easy Edition) (1521-5563); Sheet Music Magazine. Easy Play (1045-3911); Which was formed by the merger of: Sheet Music Magazine. Easy Organ (0197-3487); Which supersedes in part: Sheet Music Magazine. Standard - Easy Organ (0197-3509); Sheet Music Magazine. Easy Piano - Guitar (0273-6470); Which was formerly: Sheet Music Magazine. Easy Piano (0197-3517)
Indexed: M11, T02.
Published by: Sheet Music Magazine, Inc, PO Box 58629, Boulder, CO 80323. TEL 800-759-3036. adv.: B&W page USD 2,750, color page USD 4,140; trim 10 x 7. Circ: 100,000 (paid).

780.42 USA ISSN 0273-6462
ML1
SHEET MUSIC MAGAZINE. STANDARD PIANO - GUITAR EDITION. Text in English. 1977. bi-m. USD 22.97 domestic; USD 27.97 in Canada (effective 2006). adv. bk.rev. **Document type:** *Magazine, Consumer.* **Description:** Contains articles and features of interest to musicians, amateur and professional, together with instructional material and sheet music for several songs.
Former titles: Sheet Music Magazine. Standard Piano (0197-3525); Sheet Music Magazine. Standard Edition (0164-386X)
Indexed: IIMP.
—Ingenta.
Published by: Shacor, Inc., 2 depot Plaza, Ste 301, Bedford Hills, NY 10507. TEL 914-244-8500, FAX 914-244-8560, http://www.yestermusic.com. Ed., Pub. Edward Shanaphy. adv.: page USD 2,750. Circ: 40,000 (paid and free).

780 USA
SHEMP!; the low-life culture magazine. Text in English. 1993. bi-m. USD 1 per issue (effective 2000). adv. bk.rev.; film rev.; music rev. illus. **Description:** Reviews underground movies, music, and zines.
Address: 593 Waikala St, Kahului, HI 96732-1736. Ed., Pub., R&P Larry Yoshida. Circ: 400.

781.64 USA
SHOCKWAVES (LOS ANGELES). Text in English. 1996. q. USD 18 domestic; USD 25 foreign; USD 3.95 newsstand/cover (effective 2006). adv. bk.rev.; music rev. illus. **Document type:** *Magazine, Consumer.* **Description:** Contains interviews and reviews with rock and metal musicians.
Published by: Shockwaves Publications, PO Box 28391, Los Angeles, CA 90093-0213. TEL 800-715-4690, FAX 714-847-9975. Ed., Pub., Adv. contact Bob Nalbandian. page USD 400; trim 11.88 x 8. Circ: 20,000 (controlled).

781.64 808.8 USA
SHOELACE FANZINE. Text in English. 1990. s-a. USD 3 domestic; USD 5 foreign; USD 1 newsstand/cover. adv. bk.rev.; music rev.; video rev. back issues avail. **Document type:** *Newsletter.* **Description:** Covers all matters concerning underground music, along with poetry, fiction, and artwork. Discusses books, films, and 'zines.
Published by: Shoelace Publishing, PO Box 7952, West Trenton, NJ 08628. Eds. Eric Szantai, Robert Conrad. Adv. contact Rob Conrad. page USD 15; trim 11 x 8.5. Circ: 350 (paid).

780.65 DEU ISSN 0949-9229
SHOW; independent music media service. Text in German. 1968. 48/yr. looseleaf. bk.rev. back issues avail. **Document type:** *Newsletter, Trade.*
Published by: Show Organisation Dieter Liffers GmbH, Stumpf 15, Lohmar, 53797, Germany. TEL 49-2205-6869, FAX 49-2205-6879. Ed., Pub. Dieter Liffers. R&P Kim Liffers. Adv. contact Ursula Maylahn. Circ: 1,600.

SHOWBIZ MAGAZINE. *see* MOTION PICTURES

780.42 BRA ISSN 0104-1649
SHOWBIZZ. Text in Portuguese. 1985. m. USD 60. adv. music rev.; rec.rev. illus.; stat. **Document type:** *Consumer.* **Description:** Covers all aspects of the pop-rock music industry. Contains articles, interviews and reviews.
Formerly (until Sep. 1995): Bizz
Related titles: ◆ Supplement(s): Letras Traduzidas. ISSN 0104-2289.
Published by: Editora Azul, S.A., Ave. NACOES UNIDAS, 5777, Sao Paulo, SP 05479-900, Brazil. TEL 55-11-8673000, FAX 55-11-8673311, TELEX 55-11-83178-EDAZ. Ed. Felipe Zobaran. R&P Benjamin Goncalvez TEL 55-11-8673304. Adv. contact Enio Vergeiro. color page USD 12,900; 299 x 227. Circ: 59,041 (paid).

SHOWCALL. *see* THEATER

780 GBR ISSN 1475-8814
SHOWCASE. Variant title: Showcase International. The Music Business Guide. Text in English. 1965. a. GBP 75 per issue (effective 2009). adv. **Document type:** *Directory, Trade.* **Description:** Contains over 9,000 music industry contacts, including over 10,000 acts and artists.
Former titles (until 2002): Showcase International Music Book (1362-4741); (until 1995): Kemps International Music Book (0963-8490); (until 1989): Kemps International Music and Recording Industry Yearbook; Kemps International Music and Recording Yearbook; (until 1983): Kemps Music and Record Industry Year Book International (0305-7100); (until 1980): Kemps Music and Record Industry Year Book (0075-5451)
Related titles: Online - full content ed.
—BLDSC (8270.353050). **CCC.**

Published by: Hollis Publishing Ltd. (Subsidiary of: Wilmington Group Plc), Paulton House, 8 Shepherdess Walk, London, N1 7LB, United Kingdom. TEL 44-20-75498666, FAX 44-20-75498668, orders@hollis-pr.co.uk, http://www.hollis-pr.co.uk. Adv. contact Sarah Keegan TEL 44-20-75492596.

781.64 USA
SHREDDING PAPER. Text in English. irreg., latest vol.7, 2000. USD 5 newsstand/cover. **Document type:** *Magazine, Consumer.*
Description: Contains articles and reviews on independent label punk and indiepop singles and albums.
Address: PO Box 2271, San Rafael, CA 94912. spzine@excite.com, http://members.home.net/shredding/sp.html.

780 GBR ISSN 2041-2118
▼ **SICK SOUNDS.** Text in English. 2010. m. GBP 38 domestic; GBP 45 in Europe; GBP 57 elsewhere; GBP 4.99 per issue (effective 2010). back issues avail. **Document type:** *Magazine, Consumer.*
Published by: Dark Arts Ltd., Unit 36, 10-50 Willow St, London, EC2A 4BH, United Kingdom. TEL 44-20-77297666.

781 BEL
SIDE-LINE MAGAZINE. Text in English, French. 1989. 4/yr. USD 26.75 (effective 2001).
Related titles: Online - full text ed.: Side-Line Music Magazine.
Published by: Side-Line Fao Seba Dolimont, 90 Rue Charles Degroux, Brussels, 1040, Belgium. TEL 32-2-732-1481, FAX 32-2-732-1481, sideline@ping.be. Ed. Bernard Van Isacker.

780 USA
SIGNAL TO NOISE; the journal of improvised and experimental music. Text in English. q. USD 15 domestic; USD 30 foreign; USD 4 newsstand/cover (effective 2002). **Document type:** *Journal, Consumer.* **Description:** Covers improvised and experimental music, artists, news and trends, placing music in a historical or sociological context.
Address: 416 Pine St, Burlington, VT 05401. TEL 802-658-4267, editor@signaltonoisemagazine.org, http://www.signaltonoisemagazine.org/. Ed., Pub. Pete Gershon.

780 AUT ISSN 1436-3623
SIGNALE AUS KOELN; Beitraege zur Musik der Zeit. Text in German. 1998. irreg., latest vol.15, 2009. price varies. **Document type:** *Monographic series, Academic/Scholarly.*
Published by: Verlag der Apfel, Schottenfeldgasse 24/13, Vienna, 1070, Austria. TEL 43-1-5266152, FAX 43-1-5228718, office@verlagderapfel.at, http://www.verlagderapfel.at.

782.3 FRA ISSN 0338-2052
SIGNES D'AUJOURD'HUI; la revue de l'animation liturgique. Text in French. 1975. bi-m. EUR 39 domestic; EUR 47 in the European Union; EUR 47 DOM-TOM; EUR 48 elsewhere (effective 2009 & 2010). **Document type:** *Magazine, Consumer.* **Description:** Rich in practical elements to aid in making the liturgy more lively.
Published by: Bayard Presse, 3-5 rue Bayard, Paris, 75393 Cedex 08, France. TEL 33-1-44356060, FAX 33-1-44356161, redactions@bayard-presse.com, http://www.bayardpresse.com. Ed. Charles-Eric Hauguel. Circ: 34,000.

782.3 FRA ISSN 1151-4051
SIGNES MUSIQUES; la revue du chant liturgique. Text in French. 1990. bi-m. EUR 39 domestic; EUR 47 DOM-TOM; EUR 47 in the European Union; EUR 48 elsewhere (effective 2009 & 2010). **Document type:** *Magazine, Consumer.* **Description:** The magazine of religious songs, offers a rich selection of liturgical songs.
Published by: Bayard Presse, 3-5 rue Bayard, Paris, 75393 Cedex 08, France. TEL 33-1-44356060, FAX 33-1-44356161, redactions@bayard-presse.com, http://www.bayardpresse.com. Ed. Charles-Eric Hauguel. Circ: 12,000.

781.7 230 NLD ISSN 1871-2770
SIGNS. Text in Dutch. 2005. bi-m. EUR 30 (effective 2008).
Formed by the merger of (2002-2005): Bottomline (1571-1447); (1979-2005): Music en Art (0922-1948); Which was formerly (until 1987): Gospel Music en Art Magazine (0922-193X); (until 1985): Gospel Music Magazine (0167-4374); Which incorporated: Sjofar (0166-7017)
Published by: C N V-Kunstenbond, Robert Kochplaats 342, Rotterdam, 3068 JD, Netherlands. TEL 31-10-4568688, FAX 31-10-4559022, info@continentalart.org, http://www.continentalart.org.

780 AUS ISSN 0810-5200
SINATRA INTERNATIONAL. Text in English. 1974. q. bk.rev.; film rev. stat. back issues avail.
Former titles (until 1982): Newsletter - International Sinatra Society (0810-5219); (until 1980): Newsletter - Sinatra Society of Australia (0810-5227)
Published by: International Sinatra Society, 4 Warwick Court, Dandenong North, VIC 3175, Australia.

THE SINFONIAN. *see* COLLEGE AND ALUMNI

784 USA ISSN 0037-5624
ML1
SING OUT!; folk music - folk songs. Text in English. 1950. q. USD 30 domestic to non-members; USD 35 in Canada to non-members; USD 48 elsewhere to non-members; free to members (effective 2010). adv. bk.rev.; music rev. illus. cum.index. 200 p./no.; back issues avail.; reprints avail. **Document type:** *Magazine, Consumer.* **Description:** Presents a selection of songs and articles reflecting a diversity of folk music styles: blues, blue grass, country, gospel, contemporary, folk, Celtic, traditional, women's, topical, children's, and seasonal.
Related titles: Microform ed.: (from PQC); Online - full text ed.: USD 7.50 per issue domestic; USD 8 per issue in Canada; USD 10 per issue elsewhere (effective 2010); subscr. includes CD Supplement.
Indexed: A01, A20, A22, A26, CA, E08, G06, G07, G08, I05, I07, IIMP, M11, MAG, MLA-IB, MagInd, MusicInd, NPI, PCI, RASB, RILM, S09, S23, T02.
—Ingenta. **CCC.**
Published by: Sing Out Corp., 512 E Fourth St, PO Box 5460, Bethleham, PA 18015. TEL 610-865-5366, FAX 215-895-3052. Ed. Mark D Moss TEL 610-865-5366 ext 203. Adv. contact Blaine Q Waide TEL 610-865-5366 ext 202. B&W page USD 684, color page USD 1,200; trim 7.75 x 10.

SING TO THE LORD. *see* RELIGIONS AND THEOLOGY—Protestant

780 DEU ISSN 1864-242X
SINGEN. Text in German. 1952. m. EUR 22.80 (effective 2009). adv. **Document type:** *Newsletter, Trade.*
Formerly (until 2007): Schwaebische Saengerzeitung (0340-3661)
Published by: (Schwaebischer Saengerbund 1879 e.V.), Edition Omega Wolfgang Layer, Eschweg 12, Kirchlinteln-Otersen, 27308, Germany. TEL 49-4238-943642, FAX 49-4238-943613, info@edition-omega.de. adv.: page EUR 1,200; trim 186 x 259. Circ: 11,300 (paid).

782.3 AUT ISSN 0037-5721
ML5
SINGENDE KIRCHE; Zeitschrift fuer katholische Kirchenmusik. Text in German. 1953. q. EUR 16.50; EUR 5 newsstand/cover (effective 2005). adv. bk.rev. abstr.; bibl.; illus. **Document type:** *Magazine, Consumer.*
Indexed: IIMP, M11, MusicInd, RILM.
Published by: Oesterreichische Bischofskonferenz, Oesterreichische Kirchenmusikkommission, Stock-im-Eisen Platz 3-IV, Vienna, W 1010, Austria. TEL 43-1-5131864, FAX 43-1-515523640. Ed. Karl Dorneger. Circ: 3,500.

782.81 GBR ISSN 0969-9686
THE SINGER. Text in English. 1993. bi-m. GBP 21.50 domestic; GBP 25.50 in Europe; GBP 30 elsewhere; GBP 3.75 per issue (effective 2009). music rev. **Document type:** *Magazine, Consumer.*
Description: Covers all forms of singing: opera, cabaret, folk, gospel, theatrical, barbershop, and choral.
Indexed: IIMP, M11, MusicInd, T02.
—BLDSC (8285.561000). **CCC.**
Published by: Rhinegold Publishing Ltd., 239-241 Shaftesbury Ave, London, WC2H 8TF, United Kingdom. TEL 44-20-73331720, FAX 44-20-73331765, enquiries@rhinegold.co.uk. Ed. Antonia Couling. Adv. contact Neil Cording TEL 44-20-73331733.

782 USA ISSN 1555-9831
ML3795
SINGER & MUSICIAN. Text in English. 2000. bi-m. USD 23 domestic; USD 33 in Canada; USD 60 elsewhere (effective 2006).
Former titles (until 2005): Singer Magazine (1535-2145); (until 2001): Karaoke Singer (1535-0495)
Published by: L A Communications, Inc., PO Box 309, East Rochester, NY 14445. TEL 585-385-9920, FAX 585-385-3637. Ed. Robert A Lindquist.

784 USA ISSN 1060-3956
SINGING NEWS; the voice of southern gospel music. Text in English. 1969. m. USD 25 domestic (effective 2009). adv. bk.rev. bibl.; illus. **Document type:** *Magazine, Consumer.*
Formerly (until 1983): The Singing News
Related titles: Online - full text ed.: USD 15 (effective 2009).
Published by: Salem Publishing, 104 Woodmont Blvd, Ste 300, Nashville, TN 37205. TEL 615-312-4250, 800-527-5226, FAX 615-312-4266, customerservice@salempublishing.com, http://www.salempublishing.com. Ed. Jerry Kirksey. Adv. contact Dede Donatelli-Tarrant TEL 805-987-5072.

051 USA
SLAMM. Text in English. 1994. 24/yr. USD 40 (effective 2000). adv. **Document type:** *Magazine, Consumer.* **Description:** Contains music and lifestyle articles and features for the San Diego area.
Address: 3550 Camino Del Rio N., Ste. 207, San Diego, CA 92108-1739. slammsd@slammsd.com, http://www.slammsd.com. Ed. Andrew Altschul. Pub. Kevin Hellman. Circ: 36,000 (free).

781.64 AUS
A SLICE OF STALE PIZZA. Text in English. 1995. m. **Description:** A punk rock zine from Melbourne, Australia.
Media: Online - full text.
Published by: Slice of Stale Pizza, 17 Kneen St, Fitzroy, VIC 3065, Australia.

781.7 SVK
SLOVAK MUSIC. Text in English. 1969. s-a. USD 40. bk.rev. **Document type:** *Bulletin.* **Description:** Contains information on new compositions, composers, musical history and musical education.
Related titles: ◆ Slovak ed.: Slovenska Hudba. ISSN 1335-2458.
Indexed: IIMP.
Published by: (Hudobny Fond/Music Fund, Hudobne Informacne Stredisko/Music Information Center), Vydavatel'stvo S A P, s.r.o./ Slovak Academic Press Ltd., Medena 29, Bratislava, 81102, Slovakia. TEL 42-7-211728. Ed. Olga Smetanova. Circ: 4,000.

780 SVK ISSN 1335-2458
ML5
SLOVENSKA HUDBA. Text in Slovak. 1957. q. EUR 30 (effective 2009). adv. bk.rev.; film rev.; play rev.; rec.rev.; music rev. abstr.; illus. index. 250 p./no. 2 cols./p.; **Document type:** *Journal, Academic/Scholarly.*
Related titles: ◆ English ed.: Slovak Music.
Indexed: RILM.
Published by: Slovenska Muzikologicka Asociacia, Michalska 10, Bratislava, 81536, Slovakia. FAX 421-2-54430188, http://www.shu.szm.sk/sma.html. Ed. Hana Urbancova. Circ: 2,500. **Dist. by:** Slovart G.T.G. s.r.o., Krupinska 4, PO Box 152, Bratislava 85299, Slovakia. TEL 421-2-63839472, FAX 421-2-63839485, info@slovart-gtg.sk, http://www.slovart-gtg.sk.

780.42 USA
SLUG & LETTUCE. Text in English. 1986. bi-m. USD 3.30 domestic; USD 1 per issue foreign (effective 2000). adv. music rev.; bk.rev. illus.
Description: For punk rockers, zine makers, and do-it-yourselfers.
Address: PO Box 26632, Richmond, VA 23261-6632. FAX 804-236-0705. Ed., Pub., Adv. contact Christine Boarts Larson. Circ: 8,000.

781.65 USA ISSN 1557-3400
ML3505.8
SMOOTH JAZZ MAGAZINE. Text in English. 2002 (July/Aug.). bi-m. USD 18.95 (effective 2006).
Formerly (until 2005): Smooth Jazz Travel Guide (1539-6991)
Address: 3748 Keystone Ave Ste 406, Los Angeles, CA 90034.

780 ARG ISSN 1852-4451
▼ **SOCIEDAD ARGENTINA PARA CIENCIAS COGNITIVAS DE LA MUSICA. BOLETIN.** Text in Spanish. 2009. bi-m. back issues avail. **Document type:** *Journal, Academic/Scholarly.*
Media: Online - full text.
Published by: Sociedad Argentina para Ciencias Cognitivas de la Musica info@saccom.org.ar, http://www.saccom.org.ar/. Eds. Alejandro Pereira, Paz Jacquier.

780 BRA
SOCIEDADE BRASILEIRA DE MUSICOLOGIA. BOLETIM. Text in Portuguese. bi-m.
Published by: Sociedade Brasileira de Musicologia, Rua Paulo Orozimbo 766, Aclimacao, Sao Paulo, 01535-001, Brazil. http://www.musicologia.art.br.

780 700 ITA ISSN 0391-6952
DG401
SOCIETA ROMANA DI STORIA PATRIA. ARCHIVIO. Text in Italian. 1878. a. price varies. **Document type:** *Journal, Academic/Scholarly.*
Former titles (until 1946): Deputazione Romana di Storia Patria. Archivio (0393-6872); (until 1945): Reale Deputazione Romana di Storia Patria. Archivio (0393-6864); (until 1934): Reale Societa Romana di Storia Patria. Archivio (0393-6856); (until 1883): Societa Romana di Storia Patria. Archivio (0393-6848)
Indexed: B24.
Published by: Societa Romana di Storia Patria, Piazza Chiesa Nuova 18, Rome, 00186, Italy. TEL 39-06-6547513, http://www.srsp.it.

780 BEL
SOCIETE LIEGEOISE DE MUSICOLOGIE. BULLETIN. Text in French. a.
Published by: Societe Liegeoise de Musicologie, Universite de Liege, 3 Place Cockerill, Liege, 4000, Belgium. TEL 32-4-3665700.

780 USA
SOCIETY FOR AMERICAN MUSIC. BULLETIN. Text in English. 1975. 3/yr. free to members (effective 2010). adv. bk.rev. bibl. back issues avail.; reprints avail. **Document type:** *Journal, Academic/Scholarly.*
Description: Contains brief articles of current interest, essays, and performance news.
Former titles (until 2000): Sonneck Society Bulletin; (until 1987): Sonneck Society Newsletter (0196-7967)
Related titles: Online - full text ed.: (from PQC).
Indexed: A01, IIMP, M11, MAG, MusicInd, RILM, T02.
—Ingenta.
Published by: Society for American Music, Stephen Foster Memorial, University of Pittsburgh, Pittsburgh, PA 15260. TEL 412-624-3031, sam@american-music.org, http://www.american-music.org/. Ed. Kendra Preston Leonard. Adv. contact Mariana Whitmer.

780 GBR ISSN 1752-1963
➤ **SOCIETY FOR AMERICAN MUSIC. JOURNAL.** Abbreviated title: J S A M. Text in English. 2007. q. GBP 113, USD 208 combined subscription to institutions (print & online eds.) (effective 2012). adv. back issues avail.; reprints avail. **Document type:** *Journal, Academic/Scholarly.* **Description:** Deals with all aspects of American music and music in the Americas.
Related titles: Online - full text ed.: ISSN 1752-1971. GBP 108, USD 197 to institutions (effective 2012).
Indexed: A01, A20, A22, ArtHuCI, CA, E01, IIMP, M11, MLA-IB, RILM, T02, W07.
—IE. **CCC.**
Published by: (Society for American Music USA), Cambridge University Press, The Edinburgh Bldg, Shaftesbury Rd, Cambridge, CB2 8RU, United Kingdom. TEL 44-1223-312393, FAX 44-1223-315052, journals@cambridge.org, http://www.cambridge.org/uk. Ed. Leta Miller. R&P Linda Nicol TEL 44-1223-325702. Adv. contact Rebecca Roberts TEL 44-1223-325083. page GBP 445, page USD 845.

780 USA ISSN 1944-0650
ML27.U5
SOCIETY FOR AMERICAN MUSIC. MEMBERSHIP DIRECTORY. Text in English. 1977. a. free to members (effective 2010). back issues avail. **Document type:** *Directory, Trade.*
Former titles (until 2006): Society for American Music. Membership Directory and Handbook (1944-2173); (until 1999): Sonneck Society for American Music. Membership Directory and Handbook (1944-0669); (until 1996): Sonneck Society. Membership Directory (0270-3726)
Published by: Society for American Music, Stephen Foster Memorial, University of Pittsburgh, Pittsburgh, PA 15260. TEL 412-624-3031, sam@american-music.org, http://www.american-music.org/. Ed. Mariana Whitmer.

780 USA
SOCIETY FOR ETHNOMUSICOLOGY. SPECIAL SERIES. Text in English. 1971 (no.3). irreg., latest vol.6, 1989. price varies. bibl. back issues avail. **Document type:** *Monographic series.* **Description:** Explores the ethnic study of music throughout the world.
Published by: Society for Ethnomusicology, Morrison Hall 005, Indiana University, 1165 E 3rd St, Bloomington, IN 47405. TEL 812-855-6672, FAX 812-855-6673, sem@indiana.edu, http://webdb.iu.edu/sem/.

780 IRL ISSN 1649-7341
ML5
➤ **SOCIETY FOR MUSICOLOGY IN IRELAND. JOURNAL.** Text in English. 2005. irreg. free (effective 2011). bk.rev.; music rev. **Document type:** *Journal, Academic/Scholarly.* **Description:** It exists to promote Irish musicological scholarship.
Media: Online - full text.
Indexed: A39, C27, C29, D03, D04, E13, R14, S14, S15, S18.
Published by: Society for Musicology in Ireland, c/o Department of Music, University College Cork, Cork, Ireland. TEL 353-21-4904530, http://www.musicologyireland.com.

780 USA ISSN 1088-033X
ML27.U5
SOCIETY OF COMPOSERS NEWSLETTER. Variant title: S C I Newsletter. Text in English. 1968. 6/yr. membership. bk.rev. bibl. **Document type:** *Newsletter.*
Former titles (until 1994): The S C I Newsletter (1088-081X); American Society of University Composers News Bulletin; American Society of University Composers Newsletter
Published by: Society of Composers, Inc., PO Box 296, New York, NY 10011-9998. Ed. Ting Ho. Circ: 900.

SOCIOLOGY AND SOCIAL HISTORY OF MUSIC. *see* SOCIOLOGY

781.62 SWE ISSN 0346-2595
SOERMLANDSLAATEN. Text in Swedish. 1968. irreg. (3-4/yr.). SEK 80 (effective 1994). adv. bk.rev.
Published by: Soedermanlands Spelmansfoerbund, c/o Nils Haeggbom, Blidvagen 6, Vasterhaninge, 13757, Sweden. TEL 468-500-312-88. Ed. Nils Haeggbom.

780 CHE
SOLOTHURNISCHES SAENGERBULLETIN. Text in German. 4/yr. **Document type:** *Bulletin.*
Formerly: Solothurnisches Saengerblatt
Address: Buehlweg 2, Messen, 3254, Switzerland. TEL 41-31-7655521. Ed. Heinz Iseli. Circ: 3,200.

780 792 GBR ISSN 1470-2401
SONDHEIM NEWS. Text in English. 1993. bi-m. free to members (effective 2009). film rev.; music rev.; play rev.; video rev. index. **Document type:** *Newsletter.* **Description:** Promotes the work of Stephen Sondheim by providing educational and academic material relating to his work, developing the widening interest in Sondheim, and collecting and disseminating news and listings of major professional and amateur productions in the UK.
Former titles (until 2009): Sondheim Magazine; (until 2005): Sondheim News; (until 1997): Stephen Sondheim Society. Newsletter (1352-6340)
Published by: Stephen Sondheim Society, 265 Wollaton Vale, Wollaton, Notts NG8 2PX, United Kingdom. TEL 44-115-9281613, FAX 44-115-9162960, administrator@sondheim.org.

THE SONDHEIM REVIEW; dedicated to the work of the musical theater's foremost composer and lyricist. *see* THEATER

783 USA ISSN 0273-2920
BX8685
SONG OF ZION; newsletter for LDS musicians. Text in English. 1980. 4/yr. free. adv. bk.rev. bibl.; illus.; tr.lit.
Published by: Jackman Music Corp., PO Box 1900, Orem, UT 84059-5900. TEL 801-225-0859, FAX 801-225-0851. Ed. Jerry R Jackman. Adv. contact Virginia King. Circ: 17,000 (controlled).

780 GBR ISSN 1464-8113
ML156.4.W63
SONGLINES. Text in English. 1999. 8/yr. GBP 29.75 domestic; GBP 36 in Europe; GBP 44 elsewhere; GBP 6 per issue domestic; GBP 8 per issue in Europe; GBP 10 per issue elsewhere (effective 2009). adv. **Document type:** *Magazine, Consumer.* **Description:** Covers music from traditional and popular to contemporary and fusion, features artists from all around the globe.
Indexed: M11, MusicInd.
Address: PO Box 54209, London, W14 0WU, United Kingdom. TEL 44-20-73712777, FAX 44-20-73712220, info@songlines.co.uk. Eds. Jo Frost, Simon Broughton. Pub. Paul Geoghegan. adv.: color page GBP 1,524, B&W page GBP 1,152; trim 220 x 297.

780.65 USA ISSN 0161-5971
MT67
SONGWRITER'S MARKET. Text in English. 1979. a. USD 29.99 (effective 2009). 432 p./no.; back issues avail.; reprints avail. **Document type:** *Directory, Trade.* **Description:** Lists 2000 listings of music publishers, record companies, producers, AD/AV firms, managers, booking agents.
Published by: F + W Media Inc., 4700 E Galbraith Rd, Cincinnati, OH 45236. TEL 513-531-2690, 800-283-0963, FAX 513-531-0798, wds@fwpubs.com, http://www.fwpublications.com.

781.64 781.66 782.421 ITA ISSN 1828-6186
SONIC. Text in Italian. 2006. bi-m. **Document type:** *Magazine, Consumer.*
Published by: Life Edizioni, Via Stazione 2, Baveno, VB 28831, Italy. TEL 39-0323-924644, FAX 39-0323-925197, http://www.lifed.it.

784.18 DEU ISSN 1613-4451
SONIC; Wood & Brass. Text in German. 2001. bi-m. EUR 20.45 (effective 2005). adv. **Document type:** *Magazine, Consumer.*
Published by: P N P Verlag, Ringstr 33, Neumarkt, 92318, Germany. TEL 49-9181-463730, FAX 49-9181-463732, info@pnp-verlag.de, http://www.pnp-verlag.de. Ed. Thomas Kaufhold. Adv. contact Andrea Iven.

781.64 DEU
SONIC SEDUCER; Musik Magazin. Text in German. 1994. 10/yr. EUR 45 domestic; EUR 55 in Europe; EUR 67 elsewhere; EUR 4.95 newsstand/cover (effective 2007). adv. **Document type:** *Magazine, Consumer.*
Related titles: Online - full text ed.
Published by: Thomas Vogel Musikzeitschriften Verlag, Schmachtendorfer Str. 5, Oberhausen, 46147, Germany. TEL 49-208-69937-0, FAX 49-208-69937-15. Ed. Thomas Clausen. Pub., Adv. contact Thomas Vogel. B&W page EUR 2,390, color page EUR 3,890. Circ: 37,753 (paid).

781 MEX
SONIKA; el papel de la musica. Text in Spanish. m.
Related titles: Online - full text ed.
Published by: Grupo Alce, Donato Guerra No. 9, Col. Juarez, Mexico, D.F., 06600, Mexico. TEL 52-55-7030172, FAX 52-55-7030180, http://www.grupo-alce.com/. Ed. Madela Bada. Circ: 50,000.

780 ESP
SONOGRAMA. Text in Spanish, Catalan, English. 2008. irreg. free (effective 2011). **Document type:** *Journal, Academic/Scholarly.*
Media: Online - full text.
Published by: Webdemusica Ed. Maria Ivanovna.

781.64 DEU
THE SOUL. Text in German. bi-m. EUR 4.35 newsstand/cover (effective 2002). adv. **Document type:** *Magazine, Consumer.*
Published by: Piranha Media GmbH, Rolandstr 69, Cologne, 50677, Germany. TEL 49-221-5797800, FAX 49-221-5797879. adv.: page EUR 2,500. Circ: 35,000 (paid and controlled).

781.57 FRA ISSN 0398-9089
ML5
SOUL BAG. Text in French. 1970. q. EUR 24 domestic; EUR 28 in Africa; EUR 28 in Europe; EUR 30 in North America; EUR 34 elsewhere (effective 2009). adv. bk.rev.; rec.rev. back issues avail. **Document type:** *Magazine, Consumer.*
Published by: Comite de Liaison des Amateurs de Rhythm et Blues, 25 rue Trezel, Levallois Perret, 92300, France. TEL 33-1-47308416, FAX 33-1-47308418. Ed. Jacques Perin. Circ: 3,000.

SOUND & VISION; home theater - audio - video - multimedia - movies - music. *see* SOUND RECORDING AND REPRODUCTION

780.7 NZL ISSN 1177-4371
SOUND ARTS. Variant title: M E N Z A Magazine. Text in English. 2005. 3/yr. free membership (effective 2009). back issues avail. **Document type:** *Magazine, Trade.* **Description:** Provides ideas for teaching the sound arts in kura, early childhood, primary and secondary schools, for itinerant and private studies, music therapy, and tertiary and community settings.
Published by: Music Education New Zealand Aotearoa, PO Box 24-173, Manners Street, Wellington, New Zealand. TEL 64-4-4726692, admin@menza.org.nz. Ed. Stephen Gibbs.

780 USA ISSN 8756-6176
ML3469
SOUND CHOICE. Text in English. 1985. s-a. USD 20. adv. bk.rev. back issues avail. **Document type:** *Magazine, Consumer.* **Description:** Features reviews and news relating to alternative and independent audio, video, multi-media and print.
Published by: Audio Evolution Network, PO Box 1125, Oceano, CA 93445-1125. Ed. David Ciaffardini. Circ: 20,000.

781.64 USA ISSN 1523-4851
ML3469
SOUND COLLECTOR. Text in English. 1997. irreg., latest vol.7, 2002. USD 7.50 newsstand/cover. **Document type:** *Magazine, Consumer.* **Description:** Contains reviews and features on alternative music and artists.
Address: PO Box 2056, New York, NY 10013.

780 MYS
SOUND OF MALAYSIAN'S MUSICIAN/TA MA KO YU CHIH SHENG. Text in Chinese. 1971. s-a. MYR 0.30 per issue. illus.
Address: 18 Dato Koyah Rd, Penang, Malaysia.

780 621.389 GBR ISSN 0951-6816
TK7881.7
SOUND ON SOUND. Text in English. 1985. m. GBP 48 (effective 2009). adv. bk.rev. index. back issues avail. **Document type:** *Magazine, Consumer.* **Description:** Provides reviews and information on musicians and record producers, modern music-making instruments and recording gear.
Related titles: Online - full text ed.; International ed.: ISSN 1473-5326. 2001. USD 60 (effective 2007).
—BLDSC (8330.518000), IE. **CCC.**
Published by: S O S Publications Ltd., Media House, Trafalgar Way, Bar Hill, Cambridge, CB23 8SQ, United Kingdom. TEL 44-1954-789888, FAX 44-1954-789895. Ed. Paul White. Pub. Dave Lockwood. Adv. contact Robert Cottee. Circ: 28,200.

381.7 USA ISSN 0749-0755
ML1
SOUND POST; dedicated to Norwegian folk music and dance. Text in English. 1984. q. USD 30 domestic to individual members; USD 40 foreign to individual members; USD 35 domestic to institutional members; USD 45 foreign to institutional members (effective 2008). adv. bk.rev.; dance rev.; music rev. illus. index, cum.index: 1984-1988. back issues avail. **Document type:** *Newsletter, Consumer.* **Description:** Presents Scandinavian folk music and dance with emphasis on the Norwegian Hardanger fiddle.
Indexed: IIMP.
Published by: Hardanger Fiddle Association of America, PO Box 23046, Minneapolis, MN 55423-0046. info@hfaa.org, membership@hfaa.org. Ed. Karin Loeberg Code. Circ: 360.

780 DEU
SOUND STUDIES. Text in German. 2008. irreg., latest vol.2, 2009. price varies. **Document type:** *Monographic series, Academic/Scholarly.*
Published by: Transcript, Muehlenstr 47, Bielefeld, 33607, Germany. TEL 49-521-63454, FAX 49-521-61040, live@transcript-verlag.de.

780.904 USA
SOUND VIEWS; subterranean music and politics. Text in English. m. free. adv. rec.rev. illus. back issues avail.
Published by: Soundviews, PO Box 23523, Brooklyn, NY 11202. TEL 718-797-5350. Ed. Lee Greenfeld. adv.: B&W page USD 235; trim 9.88 x 7.44.

787 USA ISSN 0145-6237
ML1
SOUNDBOARD. Variant title: Guitar Foundation of America. Soundboard. Text in English. 1974. q. free to members (effective 2011). adv. bk.rev. bibl.; illus. back issues avail. **Document type:** *Magazine, Consumer.* **Description:** Features articles, interviews with some of the guitar's foremost personalities, CD and book reviews, publications, guitar community news, and much more.
Indexed: CA, IIMP, M11, MAG, MusicInd, T02.
—Ingenta.
Published by: Guitar Foundation of America, PO Box 171269, Austin, TX 78717. TEL 877-570-1651, FAX 877-570-3409. Adv. contact Kim Horlick Kanoy.

780.7 DEU ISSN 0936-0689
SOUNDCHECK; das Fachblatt fuer Musiker. Text in German. 1984. m. EUR 53; EUR 4.90 newsstand/cover (effective 2007). adv. **Document type:** *Magazine, Consumer.*
Published by: P P V Medien GmbH, Postfach 57, Bergkirchen, 85230, Germany. TEL 49-8131-56550, FAX 49-8131-565510, ppv@ppvmedien.de, http://www.ppvmedien.de. Ed. Michael van Almsick. adv.: B&W page EUR 2,445, color page EUR 3,890. Circ: 6,633 (paid).

780 FIN ISSN 0785-0891
SOUNDI. Text in Finnish. 1975. 11/yr. EUR 65.80 domestic; EUR 68 in Europe; EUR 77.90 elsewhere (effective 2005). adv. **Document type:** *Magazine, Consumer.* **Description:** Covers and analyzes rock music and happenings in the rock culture.
Published by: A-Lehdet Oy, Risto Rytin tie 33, Helsinki, 00081, Finland. TEL 358-9-75961, FAX 358-9-7598600, a-tilaus@a-lehdet.fi. Ed. Timo Kanerva. Adv. contact Matti Sahravuo TEL 358-9-7596385. color page EUR 1,800; 203 x 266. Circ: 25,000 (paid and controlled).

787 USA ISSN 1940-3399
ML1015.L89
SOUNDINGS; a lyre review. Text in English. 2007 (Nov.). s-a. USD 35 membership; USD 75 to institutions (effective 2008). **Document type:** *Journal, Consumer.* **Description:** Includes articles, poetry, reviews, performance advice and music relating to the lyre as well as theories of listening to and playing music.
Published by: Lyre Association of North America, 1603 Tilton Dr, Silver Spring, MD 20802. TEL 301-681-6546, info@lyreamerica.net, http://www.lyreamerica.net. Eds. Catherine Read, Jean Anderberg.

780 DEU
SOUNDS; Das Themenmagazin zur populaeren Musik. Variant title: Sounds by Rolling Stone. Text in German. 2008. q. EUR 5.90 newsstand/cover (effective 2010). adv. **Document type:** *Magazine, Consumer.*
Published by: Axel Springer Mediahouse Berlin GmbH (Subsidiary of: Axel Springer Verlag AG), Mehringdamm 33, Berlin, 10961, Germany. TEL 49-30-30881880, FAX 49-30-3088188223, info@axel-springer-mediahouse-berlin.de, http://www.asmm.de. Ed. Rainer Schmidt. Adv. contact Oliver Horn. page EUR 7,000; trim 200 x 259. Circ: 20,000 (paid and controlled).

781.64 USA
SOUNDS OF DEATH MAGAZINE. Text in English. 1991. s-a. USD 15. adv. film rev.; music rev. illus. back issues avail. **Document type:** *Magazine, Consumer.* **Description:** Covers the death metal subgenre of heavy metal rock.
Published by: Independent Media International, Inc., 731 Heatherstone Dr., High Ridge, MO 63049-1447. TEL 314-966-0976, FAX 314-822-2721. Ed., R&P, Adv. contact David Horn. page USD 900; trim 10.75 x 8.25. Circ: 10,000.

780 GBR ISSN 2045-6824
▼ **SOUNDSPHERE MAGAZINE**; the guide to Northern England's alternative culture. Text in English. 2010. 3/yr. GBP 3.50 per issue (effective 2011). adv. back issues avail. **Document type:** *Magazine, Consumer.*
Published by: Dom Smith, Ed., The Phoenix Ctr, York St John University, York, YO31 7QZ, United Kingdom.

781.64 CAN
SOUNDSTAGE. Text in English. 1995. m. free. **Document type:** *Magazine, Consumer.*
Media: Online - full content.
Published by: Schneider Publishing, 390 Rideau St, Box 20068, Ottawa, ON K1N 9N5, Canada. FAX 208-248-4735. Ed. Marc Mickelson. Pub. Doug Schneider.

780 621.389 USA ISSN 1042-0649
SOUNDTRACK; the journal for music & media. Text in English. 1988. bi-m. USD 29 (effective 2000). adv. bk.rev. back issues avail. **Document type:** *Magazine, Consumer.* **Description:** Contains information on sound technology and applications for: internet audio, computer sound, film/DVD sound, new digital music formats, musical acoustics, soundtracks, and new music and film.
Indexed: IIPA.
Published by: Soundtrack Publishing, 687 Alderman Rd, no 218, Palm Harbor, FL 34683. TEL 727-938-0571, FAX 727-934-5991. Ed., Pub., R&P Don Kulak. Adv. contact Mark Wilkins. Circ: 10,000.

THE SOUNDTRACK. *see* MOTION PICTURES

780 USA ISSN 1063-2085
ML3531
THE SOURCE (NEW YORK, 1988); the magazine of hip-hop music, culture & politics. Text in English. 1988. m. USD 25 domestic; USD 40.95 in Canada; USD 65.95 foreign (effective 2010). music rev. illus. **Document type:** *Magazine, Consumer.* **Description:** Reports on hip-hop music, culture, and politics, covering trends and styles.
Related titles: Spanish ed.: The Source Latino. ISSN 1554-7825. 2005 (Oct.).
Indexed: IIMP, IIPA.
Published by: Northstar Group Publishers, 11 Broadway, 3d Fl, New York, NY 10004. Ed. Amy Andrieux. Circ: 370,700 (paid).

780.01 ZAF ISSN 0258-509X
ML5
➤ **SOUTH AFRICAN JOURNAL OF MUSICOLOGY/SUID-AFRIKAANSE TYDSKRIF VIR MUSIEKWETENSKAP.** Summaries in English. 1981. a. free to members. adv. bk.rev.; music rev. cum.index. back issues avail. **Document type:** *Journal, Academic/Scholarly.* **Description:** Includes articles on South African and other music, conference reports, and other news.
Related titles: Online - full text ed.
Indexed: IIBP, IIMP, ISAP, M11, MusicInd, RILM.
Published by: Musicological Society of Southern Africa, PO Box 3452, Matieland, 7602, South Africa. TEL 27-21-808-2338, FAX 27-21-808-2340, the@maties.sun.ac.za. Ed., R&P, Adv. contact Beverly Parker. Circ: 225 (paid).

780 ZAF ISSN 1815-3623
SOUTH AFRICAN MUSIC. Text in English. 2005. m.
Published by: Sound Issue Media, PO Box 60243, Pierre van Ryneveld, Gauteng 0045, South Africa. TEL 27-82-2331414, FAX 27-12-6621070. Ed. Robin Moorby. **Co-publisher:** S A Music, Theatre, Arts & Entertainment.

780.7 ZAF ISSN 0038-2493
ML5
SOUTH AFRICAN MUSIC TEACHER/SUID-AFRIKAANSE MUSIEKONDERWYSER. Text in Afrikaans, English. 1931. s-a. ZAR 30 domestic to non-members; USD 30, GBP 20 foreign to non-members (effective 2003). adv. bk.rev.; music rev.; rec.rev. Index. back issues avail.; reprints avail. **Document type:** *Magazine, Trade.* **Description:** Presents information and articles of interest and use to music teachers in South Africa.
Indexed: IIMP, ISAP, M11, MusicInd, RILM.
Published by: South African Society of Music Teachers/Suid-Afrikaanse Vereniging van Musiekonderwysers, PO Box 20573, Noordbrug, 2522, South Africa. TEL 27-18-299-1699, FAX 27-18-299-1707, muspjvdm@puknet.puk.ac.za, samt@intekom.co.za. Pub., R&P, Adv. contact Mr. Jaco van der Merwe. Circ: 1,500 (controlled).

788.32 AUS
SOUTH AUSTRALIAN FLUTE NEWS. Text in English. 197?. q. free to members (effective 2009). music rev.; rec.rev.; bk.rev. 36 p./no.; **Document type:** *Newsletter.* **Description:** Provides in-depth news about flute and flute players in South Australia.
Formerly (until 1979): Flute Society of South Australia. Newsletter
Published by: Flute Society of South Australia Inc., PO Box 3208, Norwood, SA 5067, Australia. http://saflutesociety.asn.au.

780 USA ISSN 1545-2271
➤ **SOUTH CENTRAL MUSIC BULLETIN.** Text in English. 2002 (Fall). s-a. free (effective 2011). back issues avail. **Document type:** *Journal, Academic/Scholarly.* **Description:** Publishes articles on all aspects of music and music research.
Media: Online - full text.
Indexed: A39, C27, C29, D03, D04, E13, R14, S14, S15, S18.
Published by: College Music Society, South Central Chapter, c/o Christopher K.Thompson, Department of Music, PO Box 3664, Walnut Ridge, AR 72476. cthompson@wbcoll.edu, http://www.music.org/cgi-bin/showpage.pl?tmpl=/profactiv/conf/reg/sc/schome&h=53. Ed. Nico Schuler.

780.71 USA ISSN 0038-3341
SOUTH DAKOTA MUSICIAN. Text in English. 1970. 3/yr. free to members. adv. **Document type:** *Magazine, Trade.* **Description:** Columns are from all presidents of organizations who are membered: SD-MEA, SD-ACDA, SD-STA, SD-BA as well as columns from choral, band, elementary, special music teachers, orchestra and general music chairmen.
Related titles: Online - full text ed.
Indexed: CA, M01, M02, M11, S22, T02.
Published by: South Dakota Music Educators Association, Northern State University, Music Department, Aberdeen, SD 57401. TEL 605-626-2519, FAX 605-626-2263. Ed. Alexander Fokkens. R&P Janis Pearson. Adv. contact Lonn Sweet. B&W page USD 150; trim 11 x 8.5. Circ: 1,300; 1,300 (paid).

784 USA ISSN 1522-5879
SOUTHEASTERN HISTORICAL KEYBOARD SOCIETY. NEWSLETTER. Text in English. 1981. s-a. free to members (effective 2010). rec.rev. 8 p./no.; back issues avail. **Document type:** *Newsletter, Academic/Scholarly.*
Indexed: IIMP, M11, T02.
Published by: Southeastern Historical Keyboard Society, c/o Elaine Dykstra, PO Box 50092, Dallas, TX 78763. khjacob@gmail.com, http://www.sehks.org.

781.57 USA
SOUTHWEST BLUES MAGAZINE. Text in English. 1997. m. USD 24; free newsstand/cover (effective 2001). adv. **Document type:** *Magazine, Consumer.* **Description:** Focuses on blues artists of the Southwest.
Published by: Bluestronomical Publishing Inc., PO Box 710475, Dallas, TX 75371. TEL 214-887-1188, FAX 972-642-6999. Ed. Joanna Iz. Pub., Adv. contact Patti Coghill. R&Ps Joanna Iz, Patti Coghill. B&W page USD 690; 10.5 x 12. Circ: 13,000 (paid and controlled).

780.71 USA ISSN 0162-380X
SOUTHWESTERN MUSICIAN. Text in English. 1935. m. (Aug.-May). USD 15 (effective 2005). adv. bk.rev. illus. index. 63 p./no.; back issues avail. **Document type:** *Magazine, Trade.* **Description:** Serves the music educators in Texas. Reports on significant research in music education and pedagogy.
Formerly: Southwestern Musician (0038-4895); Incorporates: Texas Music Educator
Related titles: Microfiche ed.
Indexed: A22, M11, MusicInd, T02.
—Ingenta.
Published by: Texas Music Educators Association, 7900 Centre Park Dr., Austin, TX 78754. TEL 512-452-0710, FAX 512-451-9213. Pub. Dennis Bros. Adv. contact Tesa Harding. B&W page USD 450, color page USD 690. Circ: 9,500 (paid).

781.542 CAN
SPANK! YOUTH CULTURE ONLINE. Text in English. 1995. m. **Description:** Covers music, film, interesting people, events and issues for readers 14 to 28.
Media: Online - full text.
Published by: Ububik New Media Research, #505, 300 Meredith Rd NE, Calgary, AB T2E 7A8, Canada. TEL 403-217-0468. Ed. Robin Thompson.

780 USA ISSN 2161-3486
▼ **SPEAK LOUD MAGAZINE.** Text in English. 2011. m. adv. back issues avail. **Document type:** *Magazine, Consumer.*
Related titles: Online - full text ed.: ISSN 2161-3494.
Published by: God Ink Music & Publications, PO Box 12144, Jackson, TN 38308.

SPEX. *see* GENERAL INTEREST PERIODICALS—Germany

789.9 USA ISSN 0886-3032
ML3533.8
SPIN. Text in English. 1985. 11/yr. USD 9.95 domestic; USD 24 in Canada; USD 40 elsewhere (effective 2011). adv. bk.rev. illus. **Document type:** *Magazine, Consumer.* **Description:** Features interviews and interesting articles on music along with magnificent photography.
Related titles: Microform ed.: (from PQC); Online - full text ed.: free (effective 2009).
Indexed: A22, ASIP, IIMP, IIPA, M11, MusicInd, RILM.
—Ingenta. **CCC.**
Published by: Hartle Media Ventures LLC, 408 Broadway, 4th Fl, New York, NY 10013. TEL 212-231-7400, FAX 212-231-7300, http://www.hartlemedia.com/. Ed. Steve Kandell. Pub. Mike Albanese. Adv. contact Dan O'Conor TEL 312-994-2606. Circ: 467,503 (paid).
Co-publisher: McEvoy Group LLC.

780 USA
SPLENDID. Text in English. 1996. w. music rev.
Formerly: Independent Music Reviews
Media: Online - full text.
Published by: Splendid WebMedia, 1202 Curtiss St., 2nd Fl., Downers Grove, IL 60515. Ed. George Zahora.

780 GBR ISSN 1747-0781
SPLINTER MAGAZINE. Text in English. 2005. bi-m. GBP 15 domestic; GBP 25 foreign; GBP 2.75 per issue domestic; GBP 4.50 per issue foreign (effective 2005). adv. **Document type:** *Magazine, Consumer.* **Description:** Covers anything from indie to post-rock to heavy metal to pure pop, past or present.
Related titles: Online - full text ed.
Published by: Splinter Magazine LLP, PO Box 2482, Bristol, BS5 5AB, United Kingdom. enquiries@splintermag.com. adv.: page GBP 175.

780 POL
SPOTKANIA (KRAKOW). Text in Polish. 1985. irreg. price varies. adv. **Description:** Literary text connected with music, engravings and musical text.
Published by: Polskie Wydawnictwo Muzyczne, Al Krasinskiego 11 a, Krakow, 31111, Poland. TEL 48-12-4227044, FAX 48-12-4220174. Ed. Leszek Polony. R&P Janina Warzecha. Adv. contact Elzbieta Widlak.

780 NLD ISSN 2210-9870
▼ **SPREAD.** Text in Dutch. 2010. 5/yr. free (effective 2010). **Document type:** *Magazine, Consumer.*
Published by: Stichting Friesland Pop, Achter de Hoven 21, Leeuwarden, 8933 AG, Netherlands. TEL 31-58-2330700, FAX 31-58-2330709, fripop@keunstwurk.nl. Ed. Inge Heslinga. Circ: 5,000.

780 SRB ISSN 0352-6720
NX571.Y8
SRPSKA AKADEMIJA NAUKA I UMETNOSTI. ODELJENJE LIKOVNE I MUZICKE UMETNOSTI. GLAS/ACADEMIE SERBE DES SCIENCES ET DES ARTS. SECTION DES BEAUX-ARTS ET DE LA MUSIQUE. BULLETIN. Text in Serbo-Croatian. 1961. irreg.
Indexed: ABM, IBR, IBZ.
Published by: Srpska Akademija Nauka i Umetnosti/Serbian Academy of Arts and Sciences, Knez Mihailova 35, Belgrade, 11000. TEL 381-11-2027154, FAX 381-11-2027178, izdavacka@sanu.ac.rs, http://www.sanu.ac.rs.

780 SRB ISSN 0490-6659
SRPSKA AKADEMIJA NAUKA I UMETNOSTI. ODELJENJE LIKOVNE I MUZICKE UMETNOSTI. MUZICKA IZDANJA. Text in Serbo-Croatian. 1953. irreg., latest vol.65, 2002. price varies. **Document type:** *Monographic series, Academic/Scholarly.*
Published by: (Srpska Akademija Nauka i Umetnosti, Odeljenje Likovne i Muzicke Umetnosti), Srpska Akademija Nauka i Umetnosti/Serbian Academy of Arts and Sciences, Knez Mihailova 35, Belgrade, 11000. TEL 381-11-2027154, FAX 381-11-2027178, izdavacka@sanu.ac.rs, http://www.sanu.ac.rs. Circ: 300.

SRPSKA AKADEMIJA NAUKA I UMETNOSTI. ODELJENJE LIKOVNE I MUZICKE UMETNOSTI. POSEBNA IZDANJA. *see* ART

781.62 793.3 IND ISSN 0970-7816
ML5
SRUTI. Text in English. 1983 (Oct.). m. INR 5 per issue to non-members; free to members (effective 2011). dance rev.; music rev.; bk.rev. **Document type:** *Magazine, Trade.* **Description:** Aims to preserve valued traditions and encourage innovation in regard to Indian music and dance.
Related titles: CD-ROM ed.; Microfiche ed.
Indexed: RILM.
Published by: Sruti Foundation, 9 Cathedral Rd, Chennai, 600 086, India. TEL 91-44-28128070, FAX 91-44-28111902, shrutifoundation.info@gmail.com, http://www.shrutifoundation.org/home.

780 NLD ISSN 1879-5684
DE STAARBODE. Text in Dutch. 1945. q. EUR 18 (effective 2010). **Document type:** *Magazine, Consumer.*
Published by: Koninklijke Zangvereniging Mastreechter Staar, Postbus 15, Maastricht, 6200 AA, Netherlands. info@mastreechterstaar.nl, http://www.mastreechterstaar.nl. Ed. Eric Kerkhofs. Circ: 750.

782.1 DEU
STAATSOPER JOURNAL. Text in German. 1997. bi-m. adv. **Document type:** *Magazine, Consumer.*
Published by: Hamburgische Staatsoper GmbH, Grosse Theaterstr 25, Hamburg, 20354, Germany. TEL 49-40-35680, FAX 49-40-3568610, http://www.staatsoper-hamburg.de. adv.: color page EUR 1,950. Circ: 30,000 (controlled).

STADTFUEHRER MOENCHENGLADBACH; Gastronomie & Freizeit. *see* HOTELS AND RESTAURANTS

780 USA ISSN 1042-9409
ML3469
STAGE & STUDIO. Text in English. 1980. m. USD 18. adv.
Formerly (until 1989): Music and Sound Output (0273-8902)
Published by: Testa Communications, Inc., 25 Willowdale Ave, Port Washington, NY 11050. TEL 516-767-2500, FAX 516-767-9335. Ed. Robert Seidenberg. Circ: 78,000.

STAGEBILL. *see* THEATER

783 USA ISSN 0196-2337
ML1
THE STANZA. Text in English. 1978 (vol.2). s-a. free to members (effective 2009). illus. back issues avail. **Document type:** *Newsletter, Academic/Scholarly.* **Description:** Presents news of Hymn Society events and of members activities as well as provides a forum for opinions and requests for information, and advance announcements of contests, programs, lectures, and hymn festivals.
Indexed: IIMP, M11, T02.
Published by: Hymn Society in the United States and Canada, 745 Commonwealth Ave, Boston, MA 02215. TEL 800-843-4966, FAX 617-353-7322, hymnsoc@bu.edu, http://www.thehymnsociety.org.

781.64 910.2 700 800 USA ISSN 1093-5940
STARGREEN; the magazine for the modern sentimentalist. Text in English. 1993. irreg. (approx. 4 times a yr.), latest vol.7. USD 10 (effective 1997). adv. bk.rev.; music rev. back issues avail. **Description:** Independently published zine that features poetry, fiction, travel, music etc.
Published by: Stargreen Productions, PO Box 380406, Cambridge, MA 02238. TEL 617-627-9774. Ed., Adv. contact Patrick Smith. page USD 50. Circ: 1,000.

781.62 DEU
STARS UND MELODIEN; fuer Volksmusik- und Schlagerfreunde. Text in German. 1998. bi-m. EUR 1.95 newsstand/cover (effective 2011). adv. **Document type:** *Magazine, Consumer.*
Published by: Klambt Verlag GmbH, Im Neudeck 1, Speyer, 67346, Germany. TEL 49-6232-3100, FAX 49-6232-310226, info@klambt.de, http://www.klambt.de. Ed. Barbara Jung. Circ: 54,084 (paid).

782.421 USA ISSN 1934-0532
STASH. Text in English. 2007. bi-m. USD 14.99 (effective 2008). **Document type:** *Magazine, Consumer.* **Description:** Features news about new artists, culture, politics, music, business & lifestyle of the Hip-Hop community in the San Francisco Bay Area.
Related titles: Online - full text ed.: ISSN 1934-0540.
Published by: Stash Magazine, 554 Clayton St, PO Box 170646, San Francisco, CA 94117. TEL 415-283-8591, info@stashonline.com. Circ: 50,000.

781.64 IRL ISSN 2009-0897
STATE. Text in English. 2008. m. EUR 48; EUR 4 newsstand/cover (effective 2008). bk.rev.; film rev.; music rev. **Document type:** *Magazine, Consumer.* **Description:** Reflects the best of established music, both in Ireland and internationally.
Published by: State Magazine, 4th Flr, Equity House, 16/17 Upper Ormond Quay, Dublin, 7, Ireland. info@state.ie, http://www.state.ie. Eds. John Walshe, Phil Udell. Pub. Roger Woolman. Adv. contact Susan Maher.

STATE OF THE ARTS. *see* MUSEUMS AND ART GALLERIES

780 SWE ISSN 0282-6534
STATENS MUSIKSAMLINGAR. MUSIKMUSEET. RAPPORTER. Text in Swedish. 1984. irreg. price varies. back issues avail. **Document type:** *Monographic series.*
Published by: Statens Musiksamlingar, Musikmuseet/Swedish National Collections of Music. The Museum of Music, Sibyllegatan 2, PO Box16326, Stockholm, 10326, Sweden. TEL 46-8-51955490, FAX 46-8-6639181. Ed. Krister Malm.

780 SWE ISSN 0282-8952
STATENS MUSIKSAMLINGAR. MUSIKMUSEET. SKRIFTER. Text in Multiple languages. 1964-1982; resumed 1985. irreg. price varies. back issues avail. **Document type:** *Monographic series.*
Formerly (until 1982): Musikhistoriska Museets. Skrifter (0081-5675)
Published by: Statens Musiksamlingar, Musikmuseet/Swedish National Collections of Music. The Museum of Music, Sibyllegatan 2, PO Box16326, Stockholm, 10326, Sweden. TEL 46-8-51955490, FAX 46-8-6639181. Ed. Krister Malm. Circ: 1,000.

780 SWE ISSN 0081-9824
STATENS MUSIKSAMLINGAR. SVENSKT VISARKIV. HANDLINGAR. Text in Swedish. 1967. irreg. price varies. **Document type:** *Monographic series.*
Published by: Statens Musiksamlingar, Svenskt Visarkiv/Swedish National Collections of Music. Swedish Centre for Folk Song and Folk Music Research and Swedish Jazz History, PO Box 16326, Stockholm, Sweden. TEL 46-8-34-09-35, FAX 46-8-31-47-56.

780 SWE ISSN 0081-9832
GR225
STATENS MUSIKSAMLINGAR. SVENSKT VISARKIV. MEDDELANDEN. Text in English, Swedish. 1954. irreg. price varies. **Document type:** *Monographic series.*
Published by: Statens Musiksamlingar, Svenskt Visarkiv/Swedish National Collections of Music. Swedish Centre for Folk Song and Folk Music Research and Swedish Jazz History, PO Box 16326, Stockholm, Sweden. TEL 46-8-34-09-35, FAX 46-8-31-47-56.

780 SWE ISSN 0081-9840
STATENS MUSIKSAMLINGAR. SVENSKT VISARKIV. SKRIFTER. Text in Swedish. 1958. irreg. price varies. **Document type:** *Monographic series.*
Published by: Statens Musiksamlingar, Svenskt Visarkiv/Swedish National Collections of Music. Swedish Centre for Folk Song and Folk Music Research and Swedish Jazz History, PO Box 16326, Stockholm, Sweden. TEL 46-8-34-09-35, FAX 46-8-31-47-56.

780.6 HRV ISSN 1331-2251
STATUS. Text in Croatian. 1993. bi-m. **Document type:** *Magazine, Trade.*
Related titles: Online - full text ed.: ISSN 1332-6554. 1997.
Published by: Hrvatska Glazbena Unija, Rackoga 11-II, Zagreb, 10000, Croatia. TEL 385-1-4550297, FAX 385-1-4550297, hgu@hgu.hr. Ed. Drazen Buhin.

780 AUS ISSN 1443-0401
STEALTH. Text in English. 1999. bi-m. AUD 9.95 per issue (effective 2009); c/w CD-ROM containing 8 songs & 7 videos. bk.rev.; music rev.; software rev.; Website rev.; film rev.; rec.rev.; video rev. illus. 84 p./no.; back issues avail. **Document type:** *Magazine, Consumer.* **Description:** Covers the hip hop scene with features, interviews with artists, and reviews of new music.
Related titles: Online - full content ed.
Address: GPO BOX 666, SYDNEY, NSW 1043, Australia. TEL 61-2-82602921, FAX 61-2-82602821, subscriptions@stealthmag.com.

069 USA ISSN 1046-4387
ML462.A5
STEARNS NEWSLETTER; the Stearns collection of musical instruments at the University of Michigan. Text in English. 1986-1997; resumed 1998. 2/yr. USD 30 (effective 1998). back issues avail. **Document type:** *Newsletter.* **Description:** Contains articles about the Stearns lectures and research on its holdings of over 2,000 instruments worldwide.
Published by: University of Michigan, School of Music, 1100 Baits Dr, Ann Arbor, MI 48109-2085. TEL 734-764-0583, FAX 734-763-5097. Ed. Joseph S C Lam. Circ: 400.

786.2 USA ISSN 1930-1618
ML424.S76
STEINWAY & SONS OFFICIAL MAGAZINE; exclusively for owners and artists. Text in English. 2004. a. **Document type:** *Magazine, Consumer.*
Published by: Faircount Media Group, 701 N. Westshore Blvd., Tampa, FL 33609. TEL 813-639-1900, 888-960-1300, FAX 813-639-4344, rjobson@faircount.com, http://www.faircount.com.

781.64 USA ISSN 1092-2679
STEPPIN' OUT; weekly entertainment magazine. Text in English. w. USD 75; USD 2 newsstand/cover (effective 2005). adv. bk.rev.; film rev.; music rev.; play rev.; software rev.; tel.rev.; video rev. back issues avail. **Document type:** *Magazine, Consumer.* **Description:** Covers entertainment news and celebrities.
Related titles: Online - full text ed.
Indexed: CMPI.
Published by: Collins Communications, Inc., 21-07 Maple Ave, Fair Lawn, NJ 07410-1524. TEL 201-703-0911, FAX 201-703-0211. Ed. Chaunce Hayden. Pub., Adv. contact Lawrence Collins. B&W page USD 455, color page USD 605; trim 10 x 8. Circ: 85,000 (paid).

STEREO. *see* SOUND RECORDING AND REPRODUCTION

STEREOPHILE. *see* SOUND RECORDING AND REPRODUCTION

780 DEU ISSN 0172-388X
STEREOPLAY; Die technische Dimension von HiFi. Text in German. 1979. m. EUR 61.90; EUR 5.30 newsstand/cover (effective 2011). adv. charts; illus. **Document type:** *Magazine, Consumer.*
Incorporates (1963-1983): HiFi Stereophonie (0018-1382); (1976-1982): HiFi Stereophonie. Schallplattenkritik (0343-3609); (197?-1983): HiFi Stereophonie. Test (0343-3617); Which was formerly (1971-197?): HiFi Stereophonie. Testjahrbuch (0343-3765)
Related titles: Online - full text ed.
Indexed: IIMP, M11, MusicInd.
Published by: W E K A Media Publishing GmbH, Gruberstr 46a, Poing, 85586, Germany. TEL 49-8121-950, FAX 49-8121-951199, online@wekanet.de, http://www.weka-media-publishing.de. Ed. Holger Biermann. Adv. contact Michael Hackenberg. Circ: 23,361 (paid).

786.9 DEU ISSN 0934-3865
STICKS; Magazin fuer Schlagzeug und Perkussion. Text in German. 1988. m. EUR 50 domestic; EUR 53.50 foreign; EUR 4.90 newsstand/ cover (effective 2011). adv. back issues avail. **Document type:** *Magazine, Consumer.*
Related titles: Online - full text ed.
Published by: Musik - Media Verlag GmbH (Subsidiary of: Ebner Verlag GmbH), Emil-Hoffmann-Str 13, Cologne, 50996, Germany. TEL 49-2236-962170, FAX 49-2236-962175, info@musikmedia.de, http://www.musikmedia.de. Ed. Axel Mikolajczak. R&P Gerald Dellmann. Adv. contact Christiane Weyres. Circ: 5,414 (paid and controlled). **Dist. by:** ASV Vertriebs GmbH, Suederstr 77, Hamburg 20097, Germany. TEL 49-40-34724857, FAX 49-40-23786715.

781 DEU ISSN 0572-6239
ML5
➤ **STIFTUNG PREUSSISCHER KULTURBESITZ. STAATLICHES INSTITUT FUER MUSIKFORSCHUNG. JAHRBUCH.** Variant title: Jahrbuch des Staatlichen Instituts fuer Musikforschung Preussischer Kulturbesitz. Text in German. 1969. a. **Document type:** *Journal, Academic/Scholarly.*
Indexed: DIP, IBR, IBZ, RILM.
Published by: Stiftung Preussischer Kulturbesitz, Staatliches Institut fuer Musikforschung, Tiergartenstr 1, Berlin, 10785, Germany. TEL 49-30-254810, FAX 49-30-25481172, http://www.sim.spk-berlin.de.

780 GBR
STIRRINGS; folk roots and acoustic music in south yorks and beyond. Text in English. 1974. q. GBP 6.50 (effective 2009). adv. back issues avail. **Document type:** *Magazine, Consumer.* **Description:** Covers regional folk song and dance.
Published by: Stirrings Folk and Acoustic Music, 11 Ratcliffe Rd, Sheffield, S11 8YA, United Kingdom. TEL 44-114-2661158, ads@stirrings.org.uk. Ed., Adv. contact Raymond Greenoaken. page GBP 30; bleed 148 x 210.

780 SWE ISSN 0348-3223
STOCKHOLMS UNIVERSITET. INSTITUTIONEN FOER LINGVISTIK. PAPERS. Text in English, Swedish. 1993. irreg., latest vol.15, 2004. SEK 100 per issue. back issues avail. **Document type:** *Monographic series, Academic/Scholarly.*
Published by: Stockholms Universitet, Institutionen foer Lingvistik/ Stockholm University, Department of Linguistics, Universitetsvagen 10 C, Frescati, Stockholm, 10691, Sweden. TEL 46-8-162347, FAX 46-8-155389, exp@ling.su.se, http://www.ling.su.se/.

780 USA
STOMP AND STAMMER. Text in English. m. **Description:** Contains local music news, features and reviews in the Atlanta area.
Address: PO Box 55233, Atlanta, GA 30308.

787.01 GBR ISSN 0039-2049
ML5
THE STRAD; a monthly journal for professionals and amateurs of all stringed instruments played with the bow. Text in English. 1890. m. GBP 49.95 domestic & Ireland; EUR 109.95 in Europe; USD 109.95 in US & Canada; GBP 99.95 elsewhere (effective 2009). adv. bk.rev.; music rev.; rec.rev.; video rev. illus. reprints avail. **Document type:** *Magazine, Consumer.* **Description:** Aimed at all strings enthusiasts including violinists, violists and cellists; and offers practical advice on technique, profiles of leading performers, in-depth articles on violins, violas, cellos, viols, double basses, bows, orchestras, music schools and more.
Incorporates (1996-2008): The Double Bassist (1362-0835)
Related titles: Microfilm ed.: (from WMP); Microform ed.: (from PQC); Online - full text ed.
Indexed: A01, A02, A03, A08, A20, A22, ASCA, AmHI, ArtHuCI, BrHumI, C12, CA, CurCont, DIP, H07, H20, IBR, IBZ, IIMP, M01, M02, M11, MusicInd, RASB, RILM, SCOPUS, T02, U01, W07.
—BLDSC (8467.600000), IE, Infotrieve, Ingenta. **CCC.**
Published by: Newsquest Media Group (Subsidiary of: Gannett Company, Inc.), Falmouth Business Park, Bickland Water Rd, Falmouth, Cornwall, TR11 4SZ, United Kingdom. TEL 44-1326-213333, FAX 44-1326-212108, http://www.newsquest.co.uk/. Circ: 17,000 (paid).

780 GBR ISSN 2041-7845
▼ **THE STRAD. SPECIAL EDITION.** Text in English. 2009. a. **Document type:** *Trade.*
Published by: Newsquest Specialist Media Ltd., 30 Cannon St, London, EC4M 6YJ, United Kingdom. TEL 44-20-76183456, FAX 44-20-76183459, info@newsquestspecialistmedia.com, http://www.newsquestspecialistmedia.com.

STRANDGUT; Stadtmagazin Frankfurt am Main. *see* MOTION PICTURES

STREET. *see* LIFESTYLE

STREET ARTISTS' NEWSLETTER. *see* ART

781.57 USA
STRICTLY NOTHING BUT; the blues. Text in English. 1989. m. effective 1991. adv. bk.rev.; play rev. bibl.; illus.; tr.lit. **Document type:** *Magazine, Consumer.* **Description:** Focuses on American blues music and related topics.
Published by: J & M Publishing, PO Box 2077, Benton, AR 72018. TEL 501-658-0385, mike@bluesguitarnews.com. Eds. Jo Ann Dollins, Michael Dollins. Circ: 1,000.

780.7 374 AUS ISSN 1327-6808
➤ **STRINGENDO.** Text in English. 1976. s-a. free to members (effective 2008). adv. bk.rev. back issues avail. **Document type:** *Journal, Academic/Scholarly.* **Description:** Provides information and articles that deal with all aspects of performance, teaching, conducting and making of stringed instruments.
Formerly (until 1996): Australian String Teacher (0312-9950)
Published by: Australian Strings Association, PO Box 187, East Brunswick, VIC 3057, Australia. admin@austa.asn.au. Ed. John Reynolds. Adv. contact Leonie Conolan. Circ: 1,000 (paid).

787 USA ISSN 0888-3106
ML749.5
STRINGS; the magazine for players and makers of bowed instruments. Text in English. 1986. 12/yr. USD 42 domestic; USD 54 in Canada; USD 72 elsewhere (effective 2009). adv. bk.rev. back issues avail. **Document type:** *Magazine, Consumer.* **Description:** Directed to the practicing and performing musician who wants to play with greater knowledge and craft.
Related titles: Online - full text ed.
Indexed: A22, A27, IIMP, M11, MAG, MusicInd, P10, P48, P53, P54, PQC, RILM.
—Ingenta.
Published by: String Letter Publishing, 255 West End Ave, San Rafael, CA 94901. TEL 415-485-6946, FAX 415-485-0831, http://www.stringletter.com. Pub. David A Lusterman. Adv. contact Dan Gabel TEL 415-485-6946 ext 627. Circ: 13,957 (paid).

STRINGS AND SQUARES; bladet for traditionel amerikansk dans og musik i Danmark. *see* DANCE

781.91 ITA ISSN 0039-260X
STRUMENTI & MUSICA; periodico degli strumenti musicali e della musica. Text in Italian. 1947. m. EUR 30 (effective 2008). adv. **Document type:** *Magazine, Consumer.*
Published by: Berben Editore, Via Redipuglia 65, Ancona, AN 60122, Italy. Ed. Davide Fabrizi.

780 ITA ISSN 1591-7045
STRUMENTI MUSICALI. Text in Italian. 1979. m. (11/yr.). EUR 53 domestic; EUR 105 in Europe; EUR 125 elsewhere (effective 2011). adv. **Document type:** *Magazine, Consumer.* **Description:** Offers special reports, audiotests, reviews and monographs about acoustic and electronic instruments. Also includes interviews with famous musicians.
Formerly (until 1990): Gli Strumenti Musicali (0392-890X)
Published by: Tecniche Nuove SpA, Via Eritrea 21, Milan, MI 201, Italy. TEL 39-02-390901, FAX 39-02-7570364, info@tecnichenuove.com. Ed. Giuseppe "Pippo" Panenero.

780 CAN
STRUTTER MAGAZINE. Text in English. 2006. m. CAD 18 domestic; USD 18 in United States; USD 32 elsewhere (effective 2007). music rev. **Document type:** *Magazine, Consumer.* **Description:** Covers hardrock & punk, with interviews, profiles, reviews and lifestyle articles.
Published by: ZMag Publishing Inc., 4001 Bayview Ave. Ste 214, Toronto, ON M2M 3Z7, Canada. TEL 416-985-6609.

780 RUS
STUDENT CHOIR DIRECTOR'S LIBRARY. Text in Russian. 1951. a.
Published by: Izdatel'stvo Muzyka, Petrovka 26, Moscow, 127051, Russian Federation. TEL 7-095-9215170, FAX 7-095-9283304, muz-sekretar@yandex.ru, jvolk@mail.ru.

780 ITA ISSN 0394-4417
ML410.V82
STUDI DI MUSICA VENETA. Text in Multiple languages. 1968. irreg., latest vol.27, 2000. price varies. **Document type:** *Monographic series, Academic/Scholarly.*
Related titles: ◆ Series: Studi di Musica Veneta. Quaderni Vivaldiani; ◆ Studi di Musica Veneta. Archivio Nino Rota. Studi. ISSN 1973-8552; ◆ Studi di Musica Veneta. Archivio Luigi Nono. Studi. ISSN 1973-8560.
Published by: (Fondazione Giorgio Cini), Casa Editrice Leo S. Olschki, Viuzzo del Pozzetto 8, Florence, 50126, Italy. TEL 39-055-6530684, FAX 39-055-6530214, celso@olschki.it, http://www.olschki.it.

780 ITA
STUDI DI MUSICA VENETA. ARCHIVIO ALFREDO CASELLA. STUDI. Text in Italian. 1991. irreg.
Published by: (Fondazione Giorgio Cini), Casa Editrice Leo S. Olschki, Viuzzo del Pozzetto 8, Florence, 50126, Italy. TEL 39-055-6530684, FAX 39-055-6530214, celso@olschki.it, http://www.olschki.it.

780.01 ITA ISSN 1973-8579
STUDI DI MUSICA VENETA. ARCHIVIO CAMILLO TOGNI. STUDI. Text in Italian. 2001. irreg. price varies. **Document type:** *Monographic series, Academic/Scholarly.*
Published by: (Fondazione Giorgio Cini), Casa Editrice Leo S. Olschki, Viuzzo del Pozzetto 8, Florence, 50126, Italy. TEL 39-055-6530684, FAX 39-055-6530214, celso@olschki.it, http://www.olschki.it.

780.01 ITA ISSN 1973-8560
STUDI DI MUSICA VENETA. ARCHIVIO LUIGI NONO. STUDI. Text in Italian. 1999. irreg. price varies. **Document type:** *Monographic series, Academic/Scholarly.*
Related titles: ◆ Series of: Studi di Musica Veneta. ISSN 0394-4417.
Published by: (Fondazione Giorgio Cini), Casa Editrice Leo S. Olschki, Viuzzo del Pozzetto 8, Florence, 50126, Italy. TEL 39-055-6530684, FAX 39-055-6530214, celso@olschki.it, http://www.olschki.it.

780.01 ITA ISSN 1973-8552
STUDI DI MUSICA VENETA. ARCHIVIO NINO ROTA. STUDI. Text in Italian. 1999. irreg., latest vol.3, 2001. price varies. **Document type:** *Monographic series, Academic/Scholarly.*
Related titles: ◆ Series of: Studi di Musica Veneta. ISSN 0394-4417.
Published by: (Fondazione Giorgio Cini), Casa Editrice Leo S. Olschki, Viuzzo del Pozzetto 8, Florence, 50126, Italy. TEL 39-055-6530684, FAX 39-055-6530214, celso@olschki.it, http://www.olschki.it.

780 ITA
STUDI DI MUSICA VENETA. QUADERNI VIVALDIANI. Text in Italian. 1980. irreg., latest vol.11, 2001. price varies. **Document type:** *Monographic series, Academic/Scholarly.*
Related titles: ◆ Series of: Studi di Musica Veneta. ISSN 0394-4417.
Published by: (Fondazione Giorgio Cini), Casa Editrice Leo S. Olschki, Viuzzo del Pozzetto 8, Florence, 50126, Italy. TEL 39-055-6530684, FAX 39-055-6530214, celso@olschki.it, http://www.olschki.it.

780.903 ITA ISSN 1122-0686
STUDI E TESTI PER LA STORIA DELLA MUSICA. Text in Italian. 1979. irreg., latest vol.13, 1999. price varies. **Document type:** *Monographic series, Academic/Scholarly.*
Published by: Casa Editrice Leo S. Olschki, Viuzzo del Pozzetto 8, Florence, 50126, Italy. TEL 39-055-6530684, FAX 39-055-6530214, celso@olschki.it, http://www.olschki.it.

780 ITA ISSN 0391-7789
ML5
STUDI MUSICALI. Text in Italian. 1972. s-a. EUR 80 foreign to individuals; EUR 104 combined subscription foreign to institutions (print & online eds.) (effective 2009). bk.rev. **Document type:** *Journal, Academic/Scholarly.*
Related titles: Online - full text ed.: ISSN 2037-6413.
Indexed: A01, A20, A22, ASCA, ArtHuCI, CA, CurCont, DIP, IBR, IBZ, IIMP, M11, MusicInd, RILM, SCOPUS, T02, W07.
—IE, Infotrieve.
Published by: (Accademia Nazionale di Santa Cecilia), Casa Editrice Leo S. Olschki, Viuzzo del Pozzetto 8, Florence, 50126, Italy. TEL 39-055-6530684, FAX 39-055-6530214, celso@olschki.it, http://www.olschki.it. Ed. Agostino Ziino. Circ: 1,000.

780 ITA ISSN 1826-8021
STUDI PERGOLESIANI. Text in Italian. 1986. irreg. **Document type:** *Journal, Academic/Scholarly.*
Related titles: ◆ English ed.: Pergolesi Studies. ISSN 0898-8722.
Published by: La Nuova Italia Editrice S.p.A (Subsidiary of: R C S Libri), Via Ernesto Codignola 1, Florence, 50018, Italy. TEL 39-055-75901, FAX 39-055-7590208, redazione@lanuovaitalia.it, http://www.lanuovaitalia.it.

780 ITA ISSN 1724-2401
ML410.P89
STUDI PUCCINIANI. Text in Italian. 1998. biennial. **Document type:** *Journal, Academic/Scholarly.*
Published by: Centro Studi Giacomo Puccini, Casermetta San Colombano 1, Mura Urbane, Lucca, 55100, Italy. TEL 39-0583-469225, FAX 39-0583-958324, info@puccini.it, http://www.puccini.it.

782.1 ITA ISSN 0393-2532
ML410.V4
STUDI VERDIANI. Text in English, German, Italian. 1982. a. price varies. **Document type:** *Monographic series, Academic/Scholarly.*
Indexed: IBR, IBZ, IIMP, M11, MusicInd, PCI, RILM.
Published by: Istituto Nazionale di Studi Verdiani, Strada della Repubblica 56, Parma, PR 43100, Italy. TEL 39-0521-385275, FAX 39-0521-287949, amministrazione@studiverdiani.it, http://www.studiverdiani.it.

STUDI VIVALDIANI. *see* BIOGRAPHY

780 FIN ISSN 0788-3757
STUDIA MUSICA. Text in Multiple languages. 1990. irreg. back issues avail. **Document type:** *Monographic series, Academic/Scholarly.*
Published by: Sibelius-Akatemia/The Sibelius Academy, PO Box 86, Helsinki, 00251, Finland. TEL 358-20-75390, FAX 358-20-7539600, info@siba.fi, http://www.siba.fi.

780.01 HUN ISSN 1788-6244
ML5
STUDIA MUSICOLOGICA. Text in English, French, German. 1961. q. EUR 360, USD 500 combined subscription (print & online eds.) (effective 2012). adv. bk.rev. bibl.; charts; abstr. index. 120 p./no.; back issues avail. **Document type:** *Journal, Academic/Scholarly.* **Description:** Publishes papers on Hungarian musicology, including topics of music history. Includes reports on congresses, musical notes and records.
Formerly (until 2007): Studia Musicologica Academiae Scientiarum Hungaricae (0039-3266)
Related titles: Online - full text ed.: ISSN 1588-2888. EUR 316, USD 428 (effective 2012).
Indexed: A20, A22, ArtHuCI, DIP, IBR, IBZ, IIMP, M11, MLA-IB, MusicInd, RASB, RILM, SCOPUS, W07.
—IE, Ingenta. **CCC.**
Published by: (Studia Musicologica USA), Akademiai Kiado Rt. (Subsidiary of: Wolters Kluwer N.V.), Prielle Kornelia u 19/D, Budapest, 1117, Hungary. TEL 36-1-4648222, FAX 36-1-4648221, journals@akkrt.hu. Ed. Laszlo Somfai.

780.9481 NOR ISSN 0332-5024
ML3797.1
➤ **STUDIA MUSICOLOGICA NORVEGICA.** Text in English, German, Norwegian; Summaries in English. 1968. a. NOK 395; NOK 260 to students (effective 2010). back issues avail. **Document type:** *Journal, Academic/Scholarly.* **Description:** Music studies, both general and Norwegian, including the history of music, ethnomusicology, analysis and theory.
Related titles: Online - full text ed.: ISSN 1504-2960. 2004. NOK 495 (effective 2010).
Indexed: DIP, IBR, IBZ, IIMP, M11, MusicInd, PCI, RILM.
—**CCC.**
Published by: (Universitetet i Oslo, Institutt for Musikkvitenskap/ University of Oslo, Department of Musicology), Universitetsforlaget AS/Scandinavian University Press (Subsidiary of: Aschehoug & Co.), Sehesteds Gate 3, P O Box 508, Sentrum, Oslo, 0105, Norway. TEL 47-24-147500, FAX 47-24-147501, post@universitetsforlaget.no, http://www.universitetsforlaget.no. Ed. Petter Stigar.

780 SWE ISSN 0081-6744
STUDIA MUSICOLOGICA UPSALIENSIA. NOVA SERIES. Text in Swedish. 1952. irreg., latest vol.21, 2002. price varies. back issues avail. **Document type:** *Monographic series, Academic/Scholarly.*
Related titles: ◆ Series of: Acta Universitatis Upsaliensis. ISSN 0346-5462.
Published by: Uppsala Universitet, Acta Universitatis Upsaliensis/ University Publications from Uppsala, PO Box 256, Uppsala, 75105, Sweden. TEL 46-18-4716804, FAX 46-18-4716804, acta@ub.uu.se, http://www.ub.uu.se/upu/auu/index.html. Ed. Bengt Landgren. **Dist. by:** Almqvist & Wiksell International.

780 ROM ISSN 1844-4369
➤ **STUDIA UNIVERSITATIS BABES-BOLYAI. MUSICA.** Text in English, French, German; Abstracts in English. 2008. s-a. exchange basis. **Document type:** *Journal, Academic/Scholarly.*
Related titles: Online - full text ed.: ISSN 2065-9628.
Indexed: CA, M11, T02.
Published by: Universitatea "Babes-Bolyai", Studia/Babes-Bolyai University, Studia, 51 Hasdeu Str, Cluj-Napoca, 400371, Romania. TEL 40-264-405352, FAX 40-264-591906, office@studia.ubbcluj.ro, http://www.studia.ubbcluj.ro. Ed. Gabriela Coca. **Dist by:** "Lucian Blaga" Central University Library, International Exchange Department, Clinicilor st no 2, Cluj-Napoca 400371, Romania. TEL 40-264-597092, FAX 40-264-597633, iancu@bcucluj.ro.

780 DEU ISSN 0941-9403
STUDIEN UND MATERIALEN ZUR MUSIKWISSENSCHAFT. Text in German. 1984. irreg., latest vol.56, 2010. price varies. **Document type:** *Monographic series, Academic/Scholarly.*
Formerly (until 198?): Studien zur Musikwissenschaft (0176-0033)
Published by: Georg Olms Verlag, Hagentorwall 7, Hildesheim, 31134, Germany. TEL 49-5121-15010, FAX 49-5121-150150, info@olms.de.

780.01 DEU
STUDIEN ZUR GESCHICHTE DER MUSIKTHEORIE. Text in German. 2001. irreg., latest vol.6, 2007. price varies. **Document type:** *Monographic series, Academic/Scholarly.*

Published by: Stiftung Preussischer Kulturbesitz, Staatliches Institut fuer Musikforschung, Tiergartenstr 1, Berlin, 10785, Germany. TEL 49-30-254810, FAX 49-30-25481172, http://www.sim.spk-berlin.de.

780 DEU ISSN 0177-7904
STUDIEN ZUR MUSIK. Text in German. 1982. irreg., latest vol.17, 2007. price varies. **Document type:** *Monographic series, Academic/ Scholarly.*
Published by: Wilhelm Fink Verlag, Juehenplatz 1-3, Paderborn, 33098, Germany. TEL 49-5251-1275, FAX 49-5251-127860, kontakt@fink.de, http://www.fink.de.

780 DEU ISSN 0081-7341
STUDIEN ZUR MUSIKGESCHICHTE DES NEUNZEHNTEN JAHRHUNDERTS. Text in German. 1965. irreg., latest vol.60, 1989. price varies. **Document type:** *Monographic series, Academic/ Scholarly.*
Published by: Gustav Bosse Verlag, Heinrich-Schuetz-Allee 35, Kassel, 34131, Germany. TEL 49-561-3105140, FAX 49-561-3105240, info@bosse-verlag.de, http://www.bosse-verlag.de.

780.01 DEU ISSN 0930-9578
STUDIEN ZUR MUSIKWISSENSCHAFT; Beihefte der Denkmaeler der Tonkunst in Oesterreich. Text in German. biennial. price varies. **Document type:** *Journal, Academic/Scholarly.*
Indexed: DIP, IBR, IBZ, MLA-IB, RILM.
Published by: (Gesellschaft zur Herausgabe von Denkmaelern der Tonkunst in Oesterreich AUT), Verlag Dr. Hans Schneider GmbH, Mozartstr 6, Tutzing, 82323, Germany. TEL 49-815-83050, FAX 49-815-87636, Musikbuch@aol.com, http://www.schneider-musikbuch.de. Ed. Othmar Wessely.

780 DEU ISSN 1613-1185
STUDIEN ZUR MUSIKWISSENSCHAFT (HAMBURG). Text in German. 2004. irreg., latest vol.18, 2009. price varies. **Document type:** *Monographic series, Academic/Scholarly.*
Published by: Verlag Dr. Kovac, Leverkusenstr 13, Hamburg, 22761, Germany. TEL 49-40-3988800, FAX 49-40-39888055, info@verlagdrkovac.de.

781.62 DEU
STUDIEN ZUR TRADITIONELLEN MUSIK JAPANS. Text in German. 1977. irreg., latest vol.13, 2007. price varies. **Document type:** *Monographic series, Academic/Scholarly.*
Published by: Florian Noetzel Verlag, Heinrichshofen Buecher, Holtermannstr 32, Wilhelmshaven, 26384, Germany. TEL 49-4421-43003, FAX 49-4421-42985, florian.noetzel@t-online.de.

STUDIEN ZUR VOLKSLIEDFORSCHUNG. *see* FOLKLORE

780 USA
STUDIES IN CZECH MUSIC. Text in Czech. 1992. irreg., latest vol.4, 2007. price varies. back issues avail. **Document type:** *Monographic series, Trade.*
Published by: Pendragon Press, PO Box 190, Hillsdale, NY 12529. TEL 518-325-6100, FAX 518-325-6102, orders@pendragonpress.com. Ed. Michael Beckerman.

781 GBR ISSN 1479-9294
STUDIES IN MEDIEVAL AND RENAISSANCE MUSIC. Text in English. 2003. irreg., latest vol.11, 2011. price varies. **Document type:** *Monographic series, Academic/Scholarly.*
—BLDSC (8491.106800).
Published by: Boydell & Brewer Ltd., Whitwell House, St Audrys Park Rd, Melton, Woodbridge, IP12 1SY, United Kingdom. TEL 44-1394-610600, FAX 44-1394-610316, editorial@boydell.co.uk, http://www.boydell.co.uk.

780 CAN ISSN 0703-3052
ML5
➤ **STUDIES IN MUSIC.** Text in English. 1976. irreg. free (effective 2004). back issues avail. **Document type:** *Monographic series, Academic/ Scholarly.* **Description:** Articles in musicology and analysis-theory.
Indexed: CMPI, IIMP, MusicInd, PCI, RILM.
—CCC.
Published by: University of Western Ontario, Don Wright Faculty of Music, Talbot College, London, ON N6A 3K7, Canada. TEL 519-661-2043, FAX 519-661-3531, jgrier@uwo.ca. Ed. James Grier. Circ: 350.

➤ **STUDIES IN MUSICAL THEATRE.** *see* THEATER

780 USA ISSN 1097-5977
MT92
STUDIES IN PENDERECKI. Text in English. 1998. irreg. USD 34.95 per vol. (effective 2006). **Document type:** *Monographic series, Consumer.*
Indexed: RILM.
Published by: Hinshaw Music, Inc., PO Box 470, Chapel Hill, NC 27514. TEL 919-933-1691, 800-568-7805, FAX 919-967-3399, http://www.hinshawmusic.com/index.php. Eds. Nola Reed Knouse, Ray Robinson.

780 USA ISSN 0898-0144
➤ **STUDIES IN THE HISTORY AND INTERPRETATION OF MUSIC.** Text in English. 1986. irreg., latest vol.118, 2005. price varies. back issues avail. **Document type:** *Monographic series, Academic/Scholarly.*
—IE, Ingenta.
Published by: Edwin Mellen Press, 415 Ridge St, PO Box 450, Lewiston, NY 14092. TEL 716-754-2266, FAX 716-754-4056, cservice@mellenpress.com.

780 USA ISSN 0743-9822
STUDIES IN THE HISTORY OF MUSIC. Short title: S H M. Text in English. 1983. irreg.
Published by: Broude Brothers Ltd, 141 White Oaks Rd, Williamstown, MA 01267-2257. TEL 413-458-8131.

STUDII SI CERCETARI DE ISTORIA ARTEI. SERIA TEATRU, MUZICA, CINEMATOGRAFIE/STUDIES AND RESEARCH IN ART HISTORY. SERIES: THEATRE, MUSIC, CINEMATOGRAPHY. *see* THEATER

THE STUDIO (OATLEY). *see* EDUCATION—Teaching Methods And Curriculum

780 JPN
STUDIO VOICE; multi-media mix magazine. Text in Japanese. m. JPY 8,160; JPY 680 newsstand/cover (effective 2005). **Document type:** *Magazine, Consumer.*
Published by: Infas Publications, 7-17-14 Roppongi, Minato-ku, Tokyo, 106-0032, Japan. TEL 81-3-57861002, FAX 81-3-57860736. Ed. Haruyuki Kato. **Subscr. to:** Fujisan.co.jp, Shinsen Bldg. 5F, 10-10 Shinsen-cho, Shibuya-ku, Tokyo 150-0045, Japan. TEL 81-3-54597072, FAX 81-3-54597073, pubmail@fujisan.co.jp, http://www.fujisan.co.jp.

STYLE & THE FAMILY TUNES. *see* LIFESTYLE

781.64 USA
STYLUS MAGAZINE. Text in English. 2001. d. **Document type:** *Magazine, Consumer.* **Description:** Aims to provide music reviews, articles and features that are always fair, direct, informative and well written.
Media: Online - full content.
Address: c/o Todd Burns, 81 E 15th Ave, Columbus, OH 43201. Ed. Todd Burns.

781.64 DEU
SUB CULTURE FREIBURG; Trendmagazin fuer Popkultur & Freizeitgestaltung. Text in German. 1996. m. free newsstand/cover (effective 2009). adv. **Document type:** *Magazine, Consumer.*
Related titles: Online - full text ed.
Published by: C. Gimbel und T. Leucht GbR, Zaehringer Str 13b, Freiburg, 79108, Germany. TEL 49-761-55737820, FAX 49-761-55737888. Ed. Thorsten Leucht. Adv. contact Christian Gimbel. color page EUR 650; trim 111 x 154. Circ: 20,000 (controlled).

781.64 DEU
SUB CULTURE KOELN - FRANKFURT. Text in German. 2002. m. free newsstand/cover. adv. **Document type:** *Magazine, Consumer.*
Related titles: Online - full text ed.
Published by: Nightflight Productions, Barbarossastr. 33, Sinzig, 53489, Germany. TEL 49-2642-993638, FAX 49-2642-991945, info@nightflight-productions.de. Ed. Dirk Gemein. Adv. contact Ulf Weber. page EUR 614. Circ: 30,000 (controlled).

781.64 DEU
SUB CULTURE RHEIN-NECKAR. Text in German. m. free newsstand/ cover (effective 2007). adv. **Document type:** *Magazine, Consumer.*
Published by: Sub Culture Rhein-Neckar-Saar, Hafenstr 49, Mannheim, 68159, Germany. TEL 49-621-1568071, FAX 49-621-1568072, info@scrn.de. Ed., Adv. contact Sven Hartmueller. color page EUR 640, B&W page EUR 580; trim 111 x 154. Circ: 19,250 (controlled).

781.64 DEU
SUB CULTURE STUTTGART. Text in German. m. free newsstand/cover (effective 2007). adv. **Document type:** *Magazine, Consumer.*
Related titles: Online - full text ed.
Published by: Sub Culture Stuttgart Verlag, Theodor-Heuss-Str 23, Stuttgart, 70174, Germany. TEL 49-711-22932729, FAX 49-711-22932723. Ed. Martin Elbert. Adv. contact Vladimir Alagic. color page EUR 750, B&W page EUR 680; trim 111 x 154. Circ: 24,300 (controlled).

781.64 DEU
SUB CULTURE ULM. Text in German. 2000. m. free newsstand/cover (effective 2007). adv. **Document type:** *Magazine, Consumer.*
Published by: Sub Culture Ulm Verlag, Kirchweg 41, Elchingen, 89275, Germany. TEL 49-731-26400127, FAX 49-731-26400128. Ed., Adv. contact Juergen Diebold. color page EUR 450, B&W page EUR 410; trim 111 x 154. Circ: 14,400 (controlled).

780 USA
SUBURBAN VOICE. Text in English. 1982. q. USD 4 per issue. adv. bk.rev.; music rev.; rec.rev. **Document type:** *Magazine, Consumer.* **Description:** Provides coverage of punk rock and other energetic musical forms. Includes interviews and editorial commentary.
Published by: Al Quint, Ed. & Pub., PO Box 2746, Lynn, MA 01903. TEL 978-532-7705. Adv. contact Al Quint. Circ: 4,000.

781.64 DEU ISSN 1618-6370
SUBWAY. Text in German. 1987. m. adv. bk.rev.; music rev.; play rev.; software rev.; tel.rev.; video rev. back issues avail. **Document type:** *Magazine, Consumer.*
Related titles: Online - full text ed.
Published by: Subway Werbe und Verlagsgesellschaft mbH, Kohlmarkt 2, Braunschweig, 38100, Germany. TEL 49-531-243200, FAX 49-190-161190, anzeigen@subway.de, http://www.subway.de. Ed. Olaf Stelter. R&P, Adv. contact Thomas Knigge. color page EUR 2,580; trim 210 x 286. Circ: 25,013 (controlled).

780 ESP ISSN 1697-6886
ML5
SUL PONTICELLO; revista online de estudios musicales. Text in Spanish. 2004. m. free (effective 2011). **Document type:** *Journal, Academic/ Scholarly.* **Description:** Aims at teaching and popularizing music.
Media: Online - full text.
Indexed: RILM.
Published by: Conservatorio Virtual, C/ Alcala 319, Madrid, 28027, Spain. TEL 34-91-4042658, FAX 34-91-4050186, secretaria@conservatoriovirtual.com, http://www.conservatoriovirtual.com. Ed. Francisco Villarubia.

780 USA
SUNDAZED TYMES. Text in English. irreg., latest vol.8, 1997. **Document type:** *Magazine, Consumer.* **Description:** Covers neglected and underappreciated rock bands and music from the past.
Published by: Sundazed Music Inc., PO Box 85, Coxsackie, NY 12051. TEL 800-295-8079, FAX 518-731-9492.

780 020 FIN ISSN 0784-0322
SUOMEN MUSIIKKIKIRJASTOYHDISTYS. JULKAISUSARJA. Text in Finnish. 1987. irreg., latest vol.123, 2005. price varies. **Document type:** *Monographic series.*
Published by: Suomen Musiikkikirjastoyhdistys ry/Finnish Music Library Association, PO Box 148, Vantaa, 01301, Finland. TEL 358-9-83923473, FAX 358-9-8736471, musakir@kaapeli.fi, http://www.kaapeli.fi/~musakir.

SUOSIKKI. *see* CHILDREN AND YOUTH—For

781.64 DEU ISSN 1433-8122
SUPERSTAR. Text in German. 1996. q. EUR 3.10 newsstand/cover (effective 2002). adv. **Document type:** *Magazine, Consumer.*
Published by: Superstar GbR, Im Seegarten 8, Bad Nauheim, 61231, Germany. adv.: B&W page EUR 465, color page EUR 716. Circ: 7,400 (paid and controlled).

367 781.7 USA
SUZI DEVERAUX INTERNATIONAL FAN CLUB. Text in English. 1975. q. USD 5. back issues avail. **Description:** For country music fans interested in Suzi Deveraux's career.
Address: 201 Waters Ave, Watertown, TN 37184. TEL 615-237-3020. Ed. Cheryl Ellison. Circ: 2,000.

780 SWE
SVENSK MUSIK (ONLINE). Text in English. 1986. q. free. **Document type:** *Newsletter, Consumer.* **Description:** Newsletter from the Swedish Music Information Center concentrating on the contemporary Swedish music scene.
Formerly (until 2004): Svensk Musik (Print) (0283-2526)
Media: Online - full content.
Indexed: RILM.
Published by: S T I M/ Svensk Music/Swedish Performing Rights Society. Swedish Music Information Centre, Sandhamnsgatan 79, PO Box 27327, Stockholm, 10254, Sweden. TEL 46-8-7838800, FAX 46-8-7839510, swedmic@stim.se. Eds. Karin Heurling, Roland Sandberg.

780.01 SWE ISSN 0081-9816
ML5
➤ **SVENSK TIDSKRIFT FOER MUSIKFORSKNING/SCHWEDISCHE ZEITSCHRIFT FUER MUSIKFORSCHUNG/SWEDISH JOURNAL OF MUSICOLOGY.** Abbreviated title: S T M. Text in Swedish; Text occasionally in English, German; Summaries in English. 1919. a. SEK 200 domestic to individuals; SEK 265 in Europe to individuals; SEK 290 elsewhere to individuals; SEK 250 domestic to institutions; SEK 290 in Europe to institutions; SEK 315 elsewhere to institutions (effective 2006). adv. bk.rev.; music rev. abstr. index, cum.index: 1919-68 (vols. 1-50). back issues avail. **Document type:** *Academic/ Scholarly.* **Description:** Consists of articles covering various fields of musicology. Reports are given of unpublished theses in musicology, of research projects and congresses. Also a review section on literature and scholarly editions of music.
Related titles: Online - full content ed.: S T M-online. ISSN 1403-5715. 1998. free (effective 2011).
Indexed: A20, ASCA, IIMP, M11, MusicInd, PCI, RILM.
Published by: Svenska Samfundet foer Musikforskning/Swedish Society for Musicology, PO Box 7448, Stockholm, 10391, Sweden. Ed. Anders Carlsson TEL 46-31-7734338. Circ: 900.

780 HRV ISSN 1330-2531
➤ **SVETA CECILIJA**; casopis za duhovnu glazbu. Text in Croatian. 1877. bi-m. HRK 120 domestic; EUR 35 in Europe; USD 40 elsewhere (effective 2006). adv. bk.rev. illus. 36 p./no. 2 cols./p.; **Document type:** *Journal, Academic/Scholarly.*
Indexed: A26, RILM.
Published by: (Hrvatsko Drustvo Crkvenih Glazbenika), Sveuciliste u Zagrebu, Katolicki Bogoslovni Fakultet, Institut za Crkvenu Glazbu, Vlaska 38, pp 432, Zagreb, 10000, Croatia. Ed. Duro Tomasic. Circ: 1,200.

785.5 AUS ISSN 1832-5963
SWARA BENDHE. Text in English. 2003. 3/yr. **Document type:** *Magazine, Consumer.* **Description:** Features information linking gamelan and related music around Australia and New Zealand.
Published by: Melbourne Community Gamelan Inc., University of Melbourne, PO Box 4412, Parkville, VIC 3052, Australia. melgamelan@hotmail.com.

780 700 USA
SWINDLE. Text in English. 2004. q. **Document type:** *Magazine, Consumer.*
Published by: Swindle Magazine, 3780 Wilshire Blvd., Ste 210, Los Angeles, CA 90010. http://www.swindlemagazine.com/. Ed. Roger Gastman.

781.57 JPN ISSN 0039-744X
SWING JOURNAL. Text in Japanese. 1947. m. JPY 18,000. adv. bk.rev.; rec.rev. illus.
Published by: Swing Journal Co. Ltd., 3-6-24 Shibakoen, Minato-ku, Tokyo, 105-0011, Japan. FAX 03-3432-7758. Ed. Kiyoshi Koyama. Circ: 250,000.

781.64 MEX
SWITCH. Text in Spanish. m. adv. **Document type:** *Magazine, Consumer.*
Published by: Grupo Editorial Premiere, Horacio no 804, Colonia Polanco, Mexico DF, 11550, Mexico. TEL 52-55-11011300, FAX 52-55-55528051, reginasb@gepremiere.com, http://www.gepremiere.com. adv.: color page MXN 49,891; trim 215 x 275. Circ: 50,000 (paid).

782.1 792 AUS
SYDNEY OPERA HOUSE. EVENTS. Text in English. 1973. bi-m. back issues avail. **Document type:** *Bulletin, Trade.* **Description:** Calendar of events containing performance details and information on all Sydney Opera House events and facilities.
Former titles (until 2002): Sydney Opera House. Diary (0811-0050); (until 1983): Sydney Opera House. Monthly Diary (0311-9246)
Related titles: Online - full text ed.
Published by: Sydney Opera House Trust, Royal Exchange, GPO Box R239, Sydney, NSW 1225, Australia. TEL 61-2-92507111, FAX 61-2-92513843, infodesk@sydneyoperahouse.com, http://www.sydneyoperahouse.nsw.gov.au. Circ: 50,000.

786 AUS ISSN 0817-2285
➤ **THE SYDNEY ORGAN JOURNAL.** Abbreviated title: S O J. Text in English. 1970. q. AUD 35 to non-members; free to members (effective 2009). music rev.; rec.rev.; bk.rev. 56 p./no.; back issues avail. **Document type:** *Magazine, Academic/Scholarly.* **Description:** Provides information for the pipe organ players, listeners, and members of the Organ Music Society of Sydeny.
Formerly (until 1970): Australian Organ Quarterly
Related titles: Diskette ed.
Indexed: RILM.
Published by: Organ Music Society of Sydney Inc., GPO Box 2348, Sydney, NSW 2001, Australia. Ed. Peter Meyer.

780 331.8 SWE ISSN 1104-9723
SYMFONI. Text in Swedish. 1984. 4/yr. adv. **Document type:** *Magazine, Trade.*
Published by: Sveriges Yrkesmusikerfoerbund, PO Box 49144, Stockholm, 10029, Sweden. TEL 46-8-6930330, FAX 46-8-5060555, symf@symf.se, http://www.symf.se. Ed. Jonas Nyberg TEL 46-8-6930335. Adv. contact Marie Olausson TEL 46-90-125570.

785.066 USA
ML1
SYMPHONY (NEW YORK). Text in English. 1948. bi-m. USD 22 (effective 2010). adv. bk.rev.; rec.rev. bibl.; charts; illus.; stat.; tr.lit. index. back issues avail.; reprints avail. **Document type:** *Magazine, Trade.* **Description:** Reports on the critical issues, trends, personalities, and developments of the orchestra world.
Former titles: Symphony (Washington) (1046-3232); (until 1989): Symphony Magazine (0271-2687); (until 1980): Symphony News (0090-5380)
Related titles: Online - full text ed.
Indexed: A22, IIMP, M11, MAG, MusicInd, RILM, T02.
—Ingenta.
Published by: League of American Orchestras, 33 W 60th St, New York, NY 10023. TEL 212-262-5161, FAX 212-262-5198. Ed. Robert Sandla. Circ: 35,000.

780 FIN ISSN 0356-9691
SYNKOOPPI. Text in Finnish. 1976. q. EUR 16 (effective 2006). **Document type:** *Journal, Academic/Scholarly.*
Formerly (until 1978): Aanitorvi
Indexed: RILM.
Published by: Synkooppi ry, University of Helsinki, PO Box 35, Helsinki, 00014, Finland. TEL 358-46-8101976. Ed. Miika Lauriala.

780 POL
SYNTEZY. Text in Polish. 1972. irreg. price varies. adv. **Document type:** *Monographic series.* **Description:** Covers history of music, composers.
Published by: Polskie Wydawnictwo Muzyczne, Al Krasinskiego 11 a, Krakow, 31111, Poland. TEL 48-12-4227044, FAX 48-12-4220174. Ed. Leszek Polony. R&P Janina Warzecha. Adv. contact Elzbieta Widlak.

788 ITA ISSN 1120-7612
SYRINX. Text in Italian. 1989. q. free to qualified personnel (effective 2008). **Document type:** *Magazine, Trade.*
Indexed: RILM.
Published by: Accademia Italiana del Flauto, Via Ferruccio 32/b, Rome, 00187, Italy. http://www.accademiaitalianadelflauto.it.

780 DEU ISSN 1867-7630
SYSTEMATISCHE MUSIKWISSENSCHAFT UND MUSIKKULTUREN DER GEGENWART. Text in German. 2008. irreg. price varies. **Document type:** *Monographic series, Academic/Scholarly.*
Published by: Tectum Wissenschaftsverlag Marburg, Biegenstr 4, Marburg, 35037, Germany. TEL 49-6421-481523, FAX 49-6421-43470, email@tectum-verlag.de. Ed. Claudia Bullerjahn.

780 DEU ISSN 1436-4441
SYSTEMISCHE MUSIKWISSENSCHAFT. Text in German. 1998. irreg., latest vol.9, 2008. price varies. **Document type:** *Monographic series, Academic/Scholarly.*
Published by: Peter Lang GmbH (Subsidiary of: Peter Lang Publishing Group), Eschborner Landstr 42-50, Frankfurt Am Main, 60489, Germany. TEL 49-69-7807050, FAX 49-69-78070550, zentrale.frankfurt@peterlang.com.

781.64 DEU
SZENE KOELN/BONN. Text in German. 1978. m. adv. **Document type:** *Magazine, Consumer.*
Formerly: Szene Bonn
Related titles: Online - full text ed.: 1997.
Published by: Verlag Eberhard A. Breinlinger, Rheinallee 71, Bonn, 53173, Germany. TEL 49-228-363433, FAX 49-228-363401. adv.: B&W page EUR 575.95, color page EUR 1,213.45; trim 135 x 190. Circ: 10,000 (controlled).

781.64 DEU
SZENE KULTUR. Text in German. 1993. m. adv. **Document type:** *Magazine, Consumer.*
Related titles: Online - full text ed.
Published by: Szene Kultur Verlag, Postfach 1462, Wangen, 88230, Germany. TEL 49-7522-795030, FAX 49-7522-795050. adv.: B&W page EUR 700, color page EUR 1,346. Circ: 12,417 (controlled).

781.64 DEU
SZENE LUEBECK. Text in German. 1980. m. adv. **Document type:** *Magazine, Consumer.*
Published by: Szene Verlag GmbH, Langenfelde 11, Bad Schwartau, 23611, Germany. TEL 49-451-21047, FAX 49-451-26039. adv.: B&W page EUR 1,140, color page EUR 1,650. Circ: 14,762 (paid and controlled).

781.64 DEU
SZENE ROSTOCK. Text in German. m. adv. **Document type:** *Magazine, Consumer.* **Description:** Provides listings and reviews of cultural and social events in and around the Rostock city area.
Published by: Szene Verlag GmbH, Langenfelde 11, Bad Schwartau, 23611, Germany. TEL 49-451-21047, FAX 49-451-26039. adv.: B&W page EUR 1,100, color page EUR 1,600; trim 210 x 297. Circ: 13,953 (controlled).

781.64 DEU
SZENE SCHWERIN. Text in German. 1992. m. adv. **Document type:** *Magazine, Consumer.*
Published by: Szene Verlag GmbH, Langenfelde 11, Bad Schwartau, 23611, Germany. TEL 49-451-21047, FAX 49-451-26039. adv.: B&W page EUR 655, color page EUR 1,010; trim 210 x 297. Circ: 9,800 (controlled).

781.64 DEU
SZENE WISMAR. Text in German. 1992. m. adv. **Document type:** *Magazine, Consumer.*
Published by: Szene Verlag GmbH, Langenfelde 11, Bad Schwartau, 23611, Germany. TEL 49-451-21047, FAX 49-451-26039. adv.: B&W page EUR 655, color page EUR 1,010. Circ: 9,800 (controlled).

T N T MAGAZINE. *see* MOTION PICTURES

790.2 USA
TACOMA REPORTER. Text in English. 1996. w. USD 29. adv. bk.rev.; dance rev.; film rev.; music rev.; play rev.; video rev. charts; stat. back issues avail. **Document type:** *Newspaper.* **Description:** Covers music, theatre, art and other aspects of entertainment industry.
Formerly (until 1998): Tacoma Voice
Related titles: Online - full text ed.
Address: 1517 S. Fawcett Ave., Ste. 250, Tacoma, WA 98402-1807. TEL 253-593-3931, FAX 253-272-8824. Ed. Lara Ramsey. Pub. Jeff Daniel. Adv. contact Chris Helm. page USD 1,478; trim 13 x 10. Circ: 20,000.

780 USA
TAIL SPINS; underground music and alternative culture. Text in English. 1991. 2/yr. USD 8; USD 4 newsstand/cover (effective 2002). adv. **Document type:** *Magazine, Consumer.* **Description:** Contains articles and features on music (punk, indie, hardcore, garage) plus bizarre phenomena, public denial of reality, detailed histories of alternative culture, and events with large-scale human casualties.
Published by: Tail Spins Magazine, 908 N. Oakley, Ste 2, Chicago, IL 60622. TEL 773-269-2918, FAX 773-269-2584. Ed., Pub., R&P, Adv. contact Brent Ritzel. B&W page USD 350, color page USD 750. Circ: 9,000 (paid).

TALENT IN MOTION. *see* LIFESTYLE

786.4 USA ISSN 1558-9706
ML649.8
TANGENTS; the bulletin of the Boston Clavichord Society. Text in English. 2004. s-a. USD 3 per issue (effective 2007). **Document type:** *Bulletin.*
Published by: Boston Clavichord Society, PO Box 540515, Waltham, MA 02454. TEL 781-891-0814, http://www.bostonclavichord.org. Ed. Beverly Woodward.

TAPE OP; the creative music recording magazine. *see* SOUND RECORDING AND REPRODUCTION

780 USA ISSN 1547-5530
TARAB; the Arabic and Eastern music newsletter. Text in English. 2003 (Aug.). bi-m. free (effective 2003). **Document type:** *Newsletter.*
Published by: Xauen Music, Inc., 60072, Chicago, IL 60660-0072.

780 DEU ISSN 0082-1969
TASCHENBUECHER ZUR MUSIKWISSENSCHAFT. Text in German. 1969. irreg., latest vol.120, 1993. price varies. **Document type:** *Monographic series.*
Published by: Florian Noetzel Verlag, Heinrichshofen Buecher, Holtermannstr 32, Wilhelmshaven, 26384, Germany. Ed. Richard Schaal. **Dist. in U.S. by:** C. F. Peters Corporation, 373 Park Ave S, New York, NY 10016.

786.2 DEU ISSN 0946-3658
TASTENWELT; Magazin fuer Keyboards und Mehr. Text in German. 1994. bi-m. EUR 26.40; EUR 4.90 newsstand/cover (effective 2007). adv. **Document type:** *Magazine, Consumer.* **Description:** Contains articles and features on all aspects of keyboard musical instruments and accessories.
Related titles: Online - full text ed.
Published by: P P V Medien GmbH, Postfach 57, Bergkirchen, 85230, Germany. TEL 49-8131-56550, FAX 49-8131-565510, ppv@ppvmedien.de, http://www.ppvmedien.de. Ed. Karl Stechl. adv.: B&W page EUR 2,805, color page EUR 4,675. Circ: 16,000 (paid and controlled).

780 USA ISSN 1069-7446
MT1
TEACHING MUSIC. Text in English. 1993. 5/yr. USD 90 combined subscription domestic includes Teaching Music; USD 96 combined subscription foreign includes Teaching Music (effective 2007). adv. **Document type:** *Journal, Trade.* **Description:** Presents association news and brief, practical features for the classroom.
Related titles: Microform ed.: (from PQC); Online - full text ed.
Indexed: A01, A02, A03, A08, A22, A26, B04, B14, BRD, BRI, CA, CBRI, CPE, DIP, E02, E03, E07, E09, ERI, ERIC, EdA, EdI, G05, G06, G07, G08, I05, I06, I07, IBR, IBZ, IIMP, M01, M02, M06, M11, MusicInd, P04, P07, P10, P18, P48, P53, P54, P55, PQC, RILM, S23, T02, W03, W05.
—BLDSC (8614.289430), IE, Ingenta.
Published by: M E N C: National Association for Music Education, 1806 Robert Fulton Dr, Reston, VA 20191-4348. TEL 703-860-4000, FAX 703-860-9443. Adv. contact James Wonsetler. Circ: 80,000 (paid and free). **Subscr. to:** EBSCO Information Services, PO Box 1584, Birmingham, AL 35201. TEL 205-995-1567, 800-633-4931, FAX 205-995-1588.

TEATER. MUUSIKA. KINO. *see* THEATER

TEATRO E STORIA. *see* THEATER

780 600 DEU
TECHNO ONLINE. Text in German. 1994. d.
Media: Online - full text.
Published by: R A N X, Oderbruchstr 10, Berlin, 10369, Germany. TEL 040-441-98-341, FAX 030-25-55-55-99.

787 USA ISSN 1948-1977
TEEN STRINGS; for the next generation of violin, viola, cello, bass, and fiddle players. Text in English. 2005. q. USD 12.95 (effective 2009). adv. back issues avail. **Document type:** *Magazine, Consumer.* **Description:** For both students and string teachers and includes articles on young players and school string programs, as well as practical advice on technique, performance, and instrument care written specifically for this unique audience.
Published by: String Letter Publishing, PO Box 767, San Anselmo, CA 94979. TEL 415-485-6946, FAX 415-485-0831, http://www.stringletter.com. Pub. David A Lusterman. Adv. contact Kara Reagan TEL 415-485-6946 ext 608.

781.57 CHE ISSN 1420-0090
TELEJAZZ (YEAR); Schweizer Jazz Handbuch. Text in German. 1986. a. CHF 20 (effective 2001). **Document type:** *Directory, Consumer.*
Published by: Jazztime Verlag AG, Taefernstr 37, Baden, 5405, Switzerland. TEL 41-56-4833737, FAX 41-56-4833739, verlag@jazztime.com, http://www.jazztime.com. Ed. Eduard Keller.

780.902 DEU ISSN 1613-6039
TELEMANN-KONFERENZBERICHTE. Text in German. 19??. irreg., latest vol.14, 2004. price varies. **Document type:** *Monographic series, Academic/Scholarly.*
Published by: Georg Olms Verlag, Hagentorwall 7, Hildesheim, 31134, Germany. TEL 49-5121-15010, FAX 49-5121-150150, info@olms.de.

TELLUS; the audio magazine series of experimental and innovative sound. *see* LITERARY AND POLITICAL REVIEWS

TEMENOS ACADEMY REVIEW. *see* LITERATURE

780 370 USA ISSN 0040-3016
TEMPO. Text in English. 1960. q. **Document type:** *Magazine, Trade.*
Published by: New Jersey Music Educators Association, 998 Ridge Ave, Manasquan, NJ 08736. Ed. Thomas A Mosher. Circ: 3,800.

780 GBR ISSN 0040-2982
ML5
TEMPO (LONDON, 1939); a quarterly review of modern music. Text in English. 1939. q. GBP 80, USD 130 to institutions; GBP 87, USD 145 combined subscription to institutions (print & online eds.) (effective 2012). adv. bk.rev.; rec.rev. charts; illus. back issues avail.; reprint service avail. from PSC. **Document type:** *Journal, Academic/Scholarly.* **Description:** Contains literate and scholarly articles, often illustrated with music examples, explore many aspects of the work of composers throughout the world.
Related titles: Online - full text ed.: ISSN 1478-2286. GBP 74, USD 126 to institutions (effective 2012).
Indexed: A20, A22, A27, AmHI, ArtHuCI, BrHumI, CA, CurCont, E01, H07, HistAb, IBRH, IIMP, M02, M11, MusicInd, P10, P48, P53, P54, PCI, PQC, RASB, RILM, SCOPUS, T02, U01, W07.
—BLDSC (8790.042000), IE, Infotrieve, Ingenta. **CCC.**
Published by: Cambridge University Press, The Edinburgh Bldg, Shaftesbury Rd, Cambridge, CB2 8RU, United Kingdom. TEL 44-1223-312393, FAX 44-1223-315052, journals@cambridge.org, http://www.cambridge.org/uk. Ed. Calum MacDonald. R&P Linda Nicol TEL 44-1223-325702. Adv. contact Rebecca Roberts TEL 44-1223-325083. page GBP 275, page USD 520. **Subscr. to:** Cambridge University Press, 32 Ave of the Americas, New York, NY 10013. TEL 212-337-5000, FAX 212-691-3239, journals_subscriptions@cup.org.

780 FRA ISSN 2106-5128
▼ **TEMPO FLUTE**; revue de l'association d'histoire de la flute francaise. Text in French. 2009. s-a.
Address: 7, Rue Louis Pasteur, Saint-Clair-sur-Epte, 95770, France. tempoflute@live.fr, http://www.tempoflute.com.

781.64 DEU
TEN DANCE. Text in German. 10/yr. **Document type:** *Consumer.* **Description:** Covers the contemporary dance music scene.
Related titles: Online - full text ed.
Published by: Ten Dance Media, Frankfurter Allee 91, Berlin, 10247, Germany.

780.71 USA ISSN 0040-3334
TENNESSEE MUSICIAN. Text in English. 1948. q. USD 6 to non-members. adv. bk.rev.
Indexed: CA, M11, T02.
Published by: Tennessee Music Educators Association, 3000 Ticonderoga Lane, Knoxville, TN 37920. TEL 865-573-2994, FAX 865-577-9584. Ed. F Michael Combs. adv.: page USD 195; 8 x 10.5. Circ: 1,600.

781.64 GBR ISSN 1350-6978
TERRORIZER. Text in English. 1993. m. GBP 31.20 domestic; GBP 37.50 in Europe; GBP 44.50 elsewhere; GBP 2.60 newsstand/cover. adv. back issues avail. **Document type:** *Magazine, Consumer.*
Published by: Scantec Publishing Ltd., Falmouth Business Park, Falmouth, Cornwall TR11 4SZ, United Kingdom. TEL 44-1326-312619, FAX 44-1326-211721. Ed. Nick Terry. Adv. contact Anna Austin. **Subscr. to:** PO Box 324, Aylesbury, Bucks HP19 3BP, United Kingdom. **Dist. by:** M M C Ltd., Octagon House, White Hart Meadows, Ripley, Woking, Surrey GU23 6HR, United Kingdom. TEL 44-1483-211222, FAX 44-1483-224541.

781.542 DEU
TESTCARD; Beitraege zur Popgeschichte. Text in German. 1996. s-a. EUR 14.50 newsstand/cover (effective 2006). adv. bk.rev.; music rev. illus. back issues avail. **Document type:** *Magazine, Consumer.* **Description:** Covers all aspects of the current and past music scenes. Also includes analysis of motion pictures.
Published by: Ventil Verlag, Augustinerstr 18, Mainz, 55116, Germany. TEL 49-6131-226078, FAX 49-6131-226079, mail@ventil-verlag.de, http://www.ventil-verlag.de. Ed., R&P Martin Buesser.

781.64 USA
TEXAS MUSIC. Text in English. 2000. q. USD 15; USD 3.95 newsstand/cover (effective 2000). adv. **Document type:** *Magazine, Consumer.* **Description:** Showcases the amazing contributions Texans have made and are making to the music scene.
Related titles: ♦ Online - full content ed.: Texas Music Online.
Address: 50273, Austin, TX 78763-0273. TEL 877-358-3927. Ed., Pub. Stewart Ramser. Adv. contact Jon Schultz.

781.64 USA
TEXAS MUSIC ONLINE. Text in English. 2000. q. adv. **Document type:** *Magazine, Consumer.*
Media: Online - full content. **Related titles:** ♦ Print ed.: Texas Music.
Published by: Texas Music, 50273, Austin, TX 78763-0273. TEL 877-358-3927. Ed., Pub. Stewart Ramser. Adv. contact Jon Schultz.

789.9 DEU
TEXTE ZUR POPULAEREN MUSIK. Text in German. 2003. irreg., latest vol.6, 2010. price varies. **Document type:** *Monographic series, Academic/Scholarly.*
Published by: (Arbeitskreis Studium Populaere Musik e.V.), Transcript, Muehlenstr 47, Bielefeld, 33607, Germany. TEL 49-521-63454, FAX 49-521-61040, live@transcript-verlag.de.

THEATER HEUTE. *see* THEATER

THEATER IN GRAZ. *see* THEATER

THEATRE BUSINESS. *see* THEATER

786.6 USA ISSN 0040-5531
ML1
THEATRE ORGAN. Text in English. 1970. bi-m. USD 30 to members. adv. bk.rev.; rec.rev. illus. index. **Document type:** *Newsletter, Trade.*
—Ingenta.
Published by: American Theatre Organ Society, 5327, Fullerton, CA 92838-0327. FAX 831-443-5826. Ed. Vern P Bickel. Pub. Bob Maney. Adv. contact Michael Fellenzer. Circ: 6,200.

780 USA ISSN 1062-4139
THEMATIC CATALOGUES SERIES. Text in English, French, German. 1977. irreg. price varies. back issues avail. **Document type:** *Monographic series, Trade.*
Published by: Pendragon Press, PO Box 190, Hillsdale, NY 12529. TEL 518-325-6100, FAX 518-325-6102, orders@pendragonpress.com. Ed. Eleanor McCrickard.

M

781 USA ISSN 1554-1312
ML1
➤ **THEORIA (DENTON)**; historical aspects of music theory. Text in English. 1985. a. USD 22 per issue (effective 2010). **Document type:** *Journal, Academic/Scholarly.* **Description:** Includes critical articles representing the current stage of research, and editions of newly discovered or mostly unknown theoretical texts with translation and commentary.
Published by: University of North Texas, College of Music, 1155 Union Cir 311367, P O Box 311367, Denton, TX 76203. TEL 940-565-2791, FAX 940-565-2002, music.information@unt.edu. Ed. Frank Heidlberger.

780 USA ISSN 0741-6156
ML1
➤ **THEORY AND PRACTICE.** Text in English. 1975. a. free to members (effective 2011). bk.rev. bibl. back issues avail. **Document type:** *Journal, Academic/Scholarly.*
Indexed: A01, CA, IIMP, M11, MusicInd, PCI, RILM, T02.
—Ingenta.
Published by: Music Theory Society of New York State, Inc., Eastman School of Music, 26 Gibbs St, Rochester, NY 14604. jdunsby@esm.rochester.edu, http://www.ithaca.edu/music/mtsnys/about.html. Eds. Matthew BaileyShea, Seth Monahan.

➤ **THIRST.** *see* LITERATURE

781.1 NLD ISSN 1877-6949
▼ **THIRTY-ONE.** Text in English. 2009. irreg. **Document type:** *Journal, Academic/Scholarly.* **Description:** Aims to promote interest in and knowledge about microtonality.
Media: Online - full text.
Published by: Huygens-Fokker Foundation, Piet Heinkade 5, Amsterdam, 1019 BR, Netherlands. TEL 31-20-7882195, FAX 31-20-7882196, info@huygens-fokker.org, http://www.huygens-fokker.org.

781.542 USA ISSN 1083-0057
ML421.S678
THIS IS THE SPINAL TAP ZINE. Text in English. a. USD 4.95. **Description:** Provides an A-to-Z guide to one of England's loudest bands.
Published by: Chip Rowe, Ed. & Pub., PO Box 11967, Chicago, IL 60611-0967. Circ: 800 (paid).

781.62 USA ISSN 1055-436X
THE THISTLE & SHAMROCK. Text in English. 1987. bi-m. USD 20. music rev. **Document type:** *Newsletter.* **Description:** Informs afficianados of Celtic music on music festivals and workshops worldwide. Provides a playlist for the Thistle & Shamrock radio show featured on National Public Radio.
Published by: Thistle & Shamrock, PO Box 560646, Charlotte, NC 28256-0646.

780 CHN ISSN 1008-2530
TIANJIN YINYUE XUEYUAN XUEBAO (TIANLAI)/TIANJIN CONSERVATORY OF MUSIC. JOURNAL (SOUNDS OF NATURE). Text in Chinese. 1985. q. **Document type:** *Journal, Academic/Scholarly.*
Related titles: Online - full text ed.
Indexed: RILM.
Published by: Tianjin Yinyue Xueyuan, 57, 11-Jing Lu, Tianjin, 300171, China. TEL 86-22-24160056, FAX 86-22-24313950.

780 DEU ISSN 0176-6511
ML929
TIBIA; Magazin fuer Holzblaeser. Text in German. 1976. 4/yr. EUR 20 domestic; EUR 22.50 foreign; EUR 7 newsstand/cover (effective 2006). adv. bk.rev. back issues avail. **Document type:** *Magazine, Consumer.*
Indexed: DIP, IBR, IBZ, IIMP, M11, MusicInd, PCI, RILM.
—CCC.
Published by: Moeck Music Instrumente und Verlag, Postfach 3131, Celle, 29231, Germany. TEL 49-5141-88530, FAX 49-5141-885342, info@moeck.com, http://www.moeck.com. Ed., R&P Sabine Haase-Moeck. Adv. contact Renate Szentpali. B&W page EUR 420, color page EUR 525; trim 140 x 186. Circ: 3,500 (paid and controlled).

780.42 SWE ISSN 1400-5123
TIDIG MUSIK/SWEDISH EARLY MUSIC; magasinet foer musik fraan medeltid, renaessans och barock. Text in Swedish. 1979. q. SEK 295 domestic; SEK 395 foreign; SEK 150 domestic to students; SEK 250 foreign to students (effective 2011). adv. bk.rev.; rec.rev. back issues avail. **Document type:** *Magazine, Trade.* **Description:** Publishes articles and essays on the early music field - Mediaeval, Renaissance, Baroque - in Sweden and other countries; composers, artists, instruments and performance practice.
Formerly (until 1995): Tidskrift foer Tidig Musik (0280-6177)
Indexed: RILM.
Published by: Foereningen foer Tidig Musik/Swedish Early Music Society, PO Box 16344, Stockholm, 10326, Sweden. TEL 46-8-4071723, FAX 46-8-4071727, kansli@tidigmusik.com.

782.1 SWE ISSN 1651-3770
TIDSKRIFTEN OPERA. Variant title: Opera. Text in Swedish. 1978. 5/yr. SEK 400 domestic; SEK 475 elsewhere (effective 2011). adv. bk.rev. **Document type:** *Magazine, Consumer.* **Description:** Covering the contemporary and the past, OPERA features articles on opera, interviews with artists, performance criticism and reviews of recordings.
Former titles (until 2002): M D - Musikdramatik (0283-5754); (until 1984): Tidskriften Musikdramatik (0281-8884); (until 1981): Musikdramatik (0349-7259)
Indexed: IBT&D, IIMP, IIPA, MusicInd, RILM.
Published by: Foereningen MusikDramatik, PO Box 4038, Stockholm, 10261, Sweden. TEL 46-8-6439544. Ed. Soeren Tranberg. Adv. contact Mia Lagerbaeck TEL 46-8-54516070. Circ: 4,000.

780 790.1 USA ISSN 1948-8238
▼ **TIFFANY'Z MAGAZINE.** Text in English. forthcoming 2011. m. USD 1 per issue (effective 2011). **Document type:** *Magazine, Consumer.* **Description:** Features new and upcoming artists, including musicians, singers, writers, actors, filmmakers and fashion designers.
Related titles: Online - full text ed.: ISSN 1948-8246. forthcoming 2010 (Jan.).
Published by: Tiffany Belcher, Ed. & Pub., 400 Alderston Way, Columbia, SC 29229. TEL 404-396-6154, tiffanyzmagazine@yahoo.com.

780 NLD ISSN 1385-3066
MT6
TIJDSCHRIFT VOOR MUZIEKTHEORIE/DUTCH JOURNAL OF MUSIC THEORY. Text in Dutch, English, German. 1996. 3/yr. EUR 51.50 combined subscription to individuals (print & online eds.); EUR 83 combined subscription to institutions (print & online eds.) (effective 2011). bk.rev. **Document type:** *Journal, Academic/Scholarly.* **Description:** Provides a forum for the discussion of music theory and music analysis.
Incorporates (1958-1997): Key Notes (0166-0020); Which was formerly (until 1975): Sonorum Speculum (0038-1438)
Related titles: Online - full text ed.: ISSN 1876-2824. EUR 41 to individuals; EUR 67.50 to institutions (effective 2011).
Indexed: A22, M11, MusicInd, RILM.
—BLDSC (8843.120000), IE, Ingenta.
Published by: Amsterdam University Press, Herengracht 221, Amsterdam, 1016 BG, Netherlands. TEL 31-20-4200050, FAX 31-20-4203214, info@aup.nl, http://www.aup.nl. Ed. Michiel Schuijer.

780.9031 NLD ISSN 0920-0649
➤ **TIJDSCHRIFT VOOR OUDE MUZIEK.** Text in Dutch. 1986. q. EUR 30 membership (effective 2010). adv. bk.rev.; music rev. back issues avail. **Document type:** *Journal, Academic/Scholarly.* **Description:** Covers topics in early music, including historical articles, interviews with performers, and listings of concerts and performances.
Formed by the merger of (1978-1986): Cornemuse (0920-3494); (1972-1986): Stimulus (0166-7386)
Indexed: IIMP, M11.
—IE, Infotrieve.
Published by: Organisatie Oude Muziek, Postbus 19267, Utrecht, 3501 DG, Netherlands. TEL 31-30-2329000, FAX 31-30-2329001, info@oudemuziek.nl. adv.: B&W page EUR 500, color page EUR 1,125; 170 x 240.

786.61 NLD ISSN 1873-121X
TIMBRES. Text in Dutch. 2006. q. EUR 33; EUR 9 newsstand/cover (effective 2010).
Published by: Stichting Het Orgelpark, Gerard Brandstraat 26, Amsterdam, 1054 JK, Netherlands. TEL 31-20-5158111, FAX 31-20-5158119, info@orgelpark.nl. Ed. Hans Fidom TEL 31-595-571885.

TIMEOFF. *see* GENERAL INTEREST PERIODICALS—Australia

780 JPN ISSN 0385-5627
TOHO GAKUEN DAIGAKU KENKYU KIYO/TOHO GAKUEN SCHOOL OF MUSIC FACULTY BULLETIN. Text in Japanese. 1962. a. **Document type:** *Journal, Academic/Scholarly.*
Formerly (until 1962): Toho Gakuen Daigaku Ongaku Gakubu Kiyo (0563-6477)
Indexed: RILM.
Published by: Toho Gakuen Daigaku, Ongaku Gakubu/Toho Gakuen, School of Music, 1-41-1 Wakaba-Cho, Chofu-shi, Tokyo, 182-8510, Japan. TEL 81-3-33074101, FAX 81-3-33074354, http://www.tohomusic.ac.jp/collegeSite/collegeIndex.html.

780 FRA ISSN 2109-0904
TOHU BOHU. Text in French. 200?. irreg. **Document type:** *Magazine, Trade.*
Published by: Trempolino, 51 Bd de l'Egalite, Nantes, 44100, France. TEL 33-2-40466699, FAX 33-2-40466757, lucie@trempo.com, http://www.trempo.com.

781.66 AUS ISSN 1833-9034
TOMATRAX. Text in English. 2003. q. back issues avail. **Document type:** *Magazine, Trade.*
Formerly (until 2006): Tomato Records Monthly (1448-3602)
Media: Online - full text.
Published by: Richard Rowe, Ed. & Pub., PO Box 1054, Belconnen, ACT 2616, Australia. Ed., Pub. Richard Rowe.

TON - VIDEO REPORT. *see* SOUND RECORDING AND REPRODUCTION

TONE (AUCKLAND); technology to change your life. *see* ELECTRONICS

780 USA
TONES & NOTES. Text in English. 2004 (May). a. USD 1 newsstand/cover (effective 2004). 12 p./no.; **Document type:** *Guide, Consumer.* **Description:** Provides information on making music, composing, arranging, playing, notating, recording, etc.
Published by: Light Living Library, c/o Lisa Ahne, POB 181, Alsea, OR 97324.

780 920 GBR ISSN 0260-7425
ML410.S587
TONIC. Text in English. 1980. irreg. adv. bk.rev. back issues avail. **Document type:** *Bulletin.* **Description:** Discusses the music of Robert Simpson.
Published by: Robert Simpson Society, 24 Regent Close, Fleet, Hants GU13 9NS, United Kingdom. TEL 44-1252-614548. Ed. Simon Phillippo. Circ: 200.

781.64 DEU ISSN 1613-4435
TONIQ; music trends tools styles. Text in German. 2002. q. free. **Document type:** *Magazine, Consumer.*
Published by: P N P Verlag, Ringstr 33, Neumarkt, 92318, Germany. TEL 49-9181-463730, FAX 49-9181-463732, info@pnp-verlag.de, http://www.pnp-verlag.de. Eds. Christoph Rocholl, Kai Schwirzke.

TONOVI; casopis glazbenih i plesnih pedagoga. *see* EDUCATION

▼ **TOP.** *see* ART

780 GBR
TOP. Text in English. 1987. m. free. adv. bk.rev. back issues avail. **Document type:** *Magazine, Consumer.*
Published by: Tower Records, 62-64 Kensington High St, London, W8 4PE, United Kingdom. TEL 44-171-938-5388, FAX 44-171-937-5024. Ed. Hugh Fielder. Pub., Adv. contact Kevin Miller. color page GBP 2,295. Circ: 70,129.

780 NLD ISSN 2210-8076
TOP 2000. Variant title: Top Two Thousand. Text in Dutch. 2008. a. EUR 19.90 (effective 2010).
Published by: L.J. Veen Uitgeversgroep, Herengracht 481, Amsterdam, 1017 BT, Netherlands. TEL 31-20-5249800, FAX 31-20-6276851, info@ljveen.nl, http://www.ljveen.nl.

TOP DIVKY. *see* CHILDREN AND YOUTH—For

780 GBR ISSN 1356-4633
TOP OF THE POPS; more gossip! more scandal! more you!. Text in English. 1995. m. GBP 2.85 newsstand/cover (effective 2009). adv. **Document type:** *Magazine, Consumer.* **Description:** Features the best interviews, gossip, facts and features about the artists and music bands.
Published by: B B C Worldwide Ltd., Media Centre, 201 Wood Ln, London, W12 7TQ, United Kingdom. TEL 44-20-84333847, bbcworldwide@bbc.co.uk, http://www.bbcmagazines.com. Adv. contact Claire Stidwell TEL 44-20-84332446. page GBP 9,050. Circ: 119,739. **Dist. by:** Frontline, Midgate House, Midgate, Peterborough PE1 1TN, United Kingdom. TEL 44-1733-555161, FAX 44-1733-562788.

784 NLD ISSN 1574-5627
TOP 40 HITDOSSIER SCHEURKALENDER. Text in Dutch. 2004. triennial. EUR 16.90 per issue (effective 2009).
Published by: Uitgeverij Becht, Postbus 317, Haarlem, 2000 AH, Netherlands. TEL 31-23-5411190, FAX 31-23-5274404, info@gottmer.nl, http://www.gottmer.nl/becht.

780.65 ESP
TOPMUSIC. Text in Spanish. m. EUR 1.95 newsstand/cover (effective 2009). adv. **Document type:** *Magazine, Consumer.*
Published by: Grupo V, C Valportillo Primera, 11, Alcobendas, Madrid, 28108, Spain. TEL 34-91-6622137, FAX 34-91-6622654, secretaria@grupov.es. Ed. Silvia Rueda-Fernandez. Adv. contact Amador Moreno. page EUR 6,500; trim 20 x 25.5. Circ: 78,333.

TOPP. *see* CHILDREN AND YOUTH—For

787.87 GBR ISSN 1355-5049
TOTAL GUITAR. Text in English. 1994. 13/yr. GBP 51.87 domestic; GBP 78 in Europe; GBP 90 elsewhere; GBP 4.99 newsstand/cover (effective 2010). adv. back issues avail. **Document type:** *Magazine, Consumer.*
—CCC.
Published by: Future Publishing Ltd., Beauford Ct, 30 Monmouth St, Bath, Avon BA1 2BW, United Kingdom. TEL 44-1225-442244, FAX 44-1225-73253, customerservice@subscription.co.uk, http://www.futureplc.com. Ed. Stephen Lawson. Adv. contact Matt King. **Subscr. to:** Tower House, Sovereign Park, Market Harborough, Leicestershire LE16 9EF, United Kingdom. TEL 44-844-8481602, FAX 44-1858-438795, future@subscription.co.uk.

780.7 305.8956 JPN ISSN 1340-5578
TOYO ONGAKU GAKKAI KAIHO/SOCIETY FOR RESEARCH IN ASIATIC MUSIC. NEWSLETTER. Text in Japanese. 1984. 3/yr. back issues avail. **Document type:** *Newsletter, Academic/Scholarly.*
Published by: Toyo Ongaku Gakkai/Society for Research in Asiatic Music, Dai2 Hachiko House 201, 5-9-25 Yanaka, Taito-ku, Tokyo, 110-0001, Japan. TEL 81-3-38235173, FAX 81-3-38235174, len03210@nifty.com, http://wwwsoc.nii.ac.jp/tog/.

781.7 JPN ISSN 0039-3851
ML5
TOYO ONGAKU KENKYU/SOCIETY FOR RESEARCH IN ASIATIC MUSIC. JOURNAL. Text in Japanese; Summaries in English. 1937. a. price varies. adv. bk.rev. illus. **Document type:** *Journal, Academic/Scholarly.*
Indexed: M11, MusicInd, RILM.
Published by: Toyo Ongaku Gakkai/Society for Research in Asiatic Music, Dai2 Hachiko House 201, 5-9-25 Yanaka, Taito-ku, Tokyo, 110-0001, Japan. TEL 81-3-38235173, FAX 81-3-38235174, len03210@nifty.com, http://wwwsoc.nii.ac.jp/tog/. Ed. Masao Tanabe. Circ: 4,000. **Dist. by:** Japan Publications Trading Co., Ltd., Book Export II Dept, PO Box 5030, Tokyo International, Tokyo 101-3191, Japan.

781.64 659.152 GBR ISSN 1366-1752
TRACE (LONDON, 1995). Text in English. 1995. 10/yr. adv. **Document type:** *Magazine, Consumer.* **Description:** Covers the worlds of hip-hop and fashion.
Formerly (until 1996): True (1359-5083)
Indexed: AIAP.
—BLDSC (8876.853500). **CCC.**
Published by: Trace Magazine, 18-20 St John St, Farringdon, London, EC1M 4NX, United Kingdom. TEL 44-20-74909357, FAX 44-20-72518051, info@trace44.com, http://www.trace44.com/. Ed. Graham Brown-Martin. Pub. Andrew McAngus. Adv. contact Ivor Placca. page GBP 4,000, page EUR 6,040; 230 x 300.

TRACE (NEW YORK, 1998); transcultural styles & ideas. *see* LIFESTYLE

786.63 USA ISSN 0041-0330
ML1
THE TRACKER. Text in English. 1956. q. free to members (effective 2010). adv. bk.rev. charts; illus.; stat. index. back issues avail. **Document type:** *Journal, Academic/Scholarly.* **Description:** Contains news and articles about the organ and its history, organbuilders, exemplary organs, regional surveys of instruments, and the music played on the organ.
Related titles: Microfilm ed.: (from PQC); Online - full text ed.: free (effective 2010).
Indexed: A01, A22, CA, IIMP, M11, MAG, MusicInd, P48, PQC, RILM, T02.
—Ingenta.
Published by: Organ Historical Society, Inc., PO Box 26811, Richmond, VA 23261. TEL 804-353-9226, FAX 804-353-9266, mail@organsociety.org. Ed. Rollin Smith TEL 516-334-2789. Adv. contact Jason J McHale.

781.64 USA ISSN 1547-6979
TRACKS; music built to last. Text in English. 2003 (Nov.). bi-m. USD 24.95 domestic; USD 30.95 in Canada; USD 36.95 elsewhere (effective 2006). adv. illus. **Document type:** *Magazine, Consumer.* **Description:** Contains articles and features on a variety of musical genres and generations for music fans over 30 years of age.
Related titles: Online - full text ed.
Published by: Sub Rosa Communications, 304 Park Ave. S., 8th Fl., New York, NY 10010. TEL 212-219-7400, FAX 212-219-4697. Ed. Alan Light. Pub. John Rollins TEL 917-690-5974. Adv. contact Jay Adams TEL 212-219-4622. B&W page USD 11,125, color page USD 12,360; trim 8.125 x 10.75. Circ: 150,000 (paid).

781.62 GBR
TRACKS (CARDIFF); traditional music from Wales. Text in English. s-a. free (effective 2001). **Document type:** *Newsletter.*

M

Published by: British Council Wales (Subsidiary of: British Council), 28 Park Pl, Cardiff, CF1 3QE, United Kingdom. TEL 44-2920-397346, FAX 44-2920-237494, http://www.britishcouncil.org/wales/.

780.01 FRA ISSN 0995-3280
ML3620
TRAD MAGAZINE; le monde des musiques et danses traditionnelles. Text in French. 1981. bi-m. EUR 34 domestic; EUR 40 in Europe; EUR 44 elsewhere (effective 2009). **Document type:** *Magazine, Consumer.* **Description:** Covers traditional music from around the world.
Formerly (until 1988): Le Tambourineur (0290-9545)
Indexed: RILM.
Address: 1 bis, Impasse du Vivier, Etampes, 91150, France. TEL 33-1-69587224, FAX 33-1-60832146, tradmag@orange.fr.

780 USA
TRADE REVIEW. Text in English. m. USD 15 (effective 2004). adv. **Document type:** *Magazine, Consumer.*
Address: 330 University Hall Dr, PO Box 2810, Boone, NC 28607. TEL 704-264-3700, FAX 704-264-4621. Eds. Danny Jones, Jerry Kirksey. Pub. Maurice Templeton. Adv. contact Pam Slaney.

780 ITA ISSN 1721-8683
LA TRADIZIONE MUSICALE. Text in Italian. 1999. irreg. **Document type:** *Monographic series, Academic/Scholarly.*
Published by: S I S M E L Edizioni del Galluzzo, Casella Postale 90, Tavarnuzze, FI 50023, Italy. TEL 39-055-2374537, FAX 39-055-2373454, http://www.sismel.it.

780.72 ESP ISSN 1697-0101
ML5
➤ **TRANS - TRANSCULTURAL MUSIC REVIEW/TRANS - REVISTA TRANSCULTURAL DE MUSICA.** Text in English, Spanish. 1995. a. free (effective 2011). **Document type:** *Journal, Academic/Scholarly.* **Description:** Explores all kinds of music from transcultural and inter/transdisciplinary perspectives.
Media: Online - full text.
Indexed: IIMP.
Published by: Sociedad de Etnomusicologia, Apartado 33035, Barcelona, 08080, Spain. TEL 34-657-854731, edicion@sibetrans.com. Ed. Ruben Lopez Cano. Pub. Silvia Martinez. R&P Inigo Sanchez.

786.9 USA ISSN 1942-6054
ML1035
TRAPS. Text in English. 2006. q. USD 19.95 domestic; USD 25 in Canada & Mexico; USD 40 elsewhere (effective 2008). adv. **Document type:** *Magazine, Consumer.* **Description:** Features songs, interviews with drummers in-depth lessons and instruments from the past fifty years of popular, rock and jazz music for serious amateurs and professional drummers.
Published by: Enter Music Publishing, Inc., 95 S Market St, Ste 200, San Jose, CA 95113. TEL 408-971-9794, 888-378-6624, FAX 408-971-0382, http://drummagazine.americommerce.com. Ed. Andy Doerschuk. Pub. Phil Hood.

781.65 BEL ISSN 1379-2725
TRAVERS EMOTION PRESSE. Text in French. 1978. m. adv. back issues avail. **Document type:** *Newsletter, Consumer.*
Formerly (until 2001): Travers (0779-133X)
Published by: Travers, Rue Traversiere 5, Bruxelles, 1210, Belgium. TEL 32-2-217-4800, FAX 32-2-223-1021, info@travers.be info@travers.be. Ed., Pub. Jules Imberechts. Adv. contact Katy Saudmont.

788.32 FRA ISSN 0764-8804
TRAVERSIERES MAGAZINE; la revue officielle de l'Association Francaise de la Flute. Text in French. 1983. q. EUR 40 domestic to members; EUR 49 foreign to members (effective 2008). **Document type:** *Journal.*
Indexed: C05, M11, MusicInd, RILM.
Published by: Association Francaise de la Flute, 132 Bd Vincent Auriol, Paris, 75013, France. TEL 33-1-46718516, http://www.traversieres.eu. Ed. Denis Verroust.

780 USA ISSN 1041-7494
ML935
TRAVERSO; historical flute newsletter. Text in English. 1989. q. USD 18 domestic to individuals; USD 21 foreign to individuals; USD 50 to libraries (effective 2007). bk.rev.; music rev. bibl.; illus. 4 p./no.; back issues avail. **Document type:** *Newsletter.* **Description:** Covers news, information and ideas for all interested in the history of the flute and its music.
Indexed: RILM.
Published by: Folkers Flute Co. Ltd., c/o Ardal Powell, Ed, PO Box 148, Hillsdale, NY 12529. TEL 518-828-9779, traverso@baroqueflute.com, http://www.baroqueflute.com/traverso. Ed. Ardal Powell.

781.64 FRA ISSN 1284-862X
TRAX. Text in French. 1997. m. **Document type:** *Magazine, Consumer.*
Related titles: Supplement(s): Trax. Hors Serie. ISSN 1293-0458. 1998.
Published by: Pole Media Urbain, 91 Rue de Monceau, Paris, 75017, France. Circ: 20,000 (paid). **Subscr. to:** Dipresse. abo@dipinfo.fr.

780.42 USA
TRAX D J MUSIC GUIDE. Text in English. 1985. bi-m. USD 7. adv. **Document type:** *Newsletter.* **Description:** Contains new dance music charts and related news bits.
Related titles: Online - full text ed.
Published by: American Record Pool, 3540 Wilshire Blvd, Ste 834, Los Angeles, CA 90010. TEL 310-659-7852, FAX 310-659-7856, amrecpool@aol.com, http://www.americanrecordpool.com. Ed. Michael Love. Circ: 1,000 (controlled).

781.7 IRL ISSN 0790-004X
ML5
TREOIR; the book of traditional music, song, and dance. Text in English, Irish. 1968. q. EUR 12 in Ireland; GBP 9 in United Kingdom; EUR 12 in Europe; USD 20 in Australia & New Zealand; USD 20 in US & Canada (effective 2005). adv. bk.rev.; music rev. illus. index. **Document type:** *Journal, Consumer.* **Description:** Features articles on traditional Irish music, song, dance, folklore and heritage.
Published by: Comhaltas Ceoltoiri Eireann, 32 Belgrave Sq., Monkstown, Co. Dublin, Ireland. TEL 353-1-2800295, FAX 353-1-2803759. Ed., Pub., Adv. contact Labhras O'Murchu. Circ: 14,000.

780 USA
TRI - M NEWS. Text in English. 1952. s-a. membership. **Document type:** *Newsletter.* **Description:** Features articles for and about student members of the association. Distributed to over 20,000 secondary student members of more than 3,700 chapters with a listing of awards, chapter activities, and accomplishments of outstanding students.
Related titles: Online - full content ed.
Published by: (M E N C: National Association for Music Education), Tri - M Music Honor Society, 1806 Robert Fulton Dr, Reston, VA 22901-4348. TEL 703-860-4000, 800-336-3768, FAX 703-860-2652. Ed., R&P Michelle Caswell. Circ: 15,000.

781.7 USA
TRI-SON NEWS; biggest little news sheet in country music. Text in English. 1963. m. looseleaf. USD 18 (effective 1999). illus.; tr.lit. **Document type:** *Newsletter, Consumer.* **Description:** Covers entertainment with a strong emphasis on country music.
Published by: Tri-Son, Inc., PO Box 40328, Nashville, TN 37204-0328. TEL 615-371-9596, FAX 615-371-9597. Ed. Loudilla Johnson. Circ: 1,200.

785 USA ISSN 0735-4711
ML19
TRI-STATE BLUEGRASS ASSOCIATION BAND AND FESTIVAL GUIDE. Text in English. 1981. a. USD 10 membership (effective 2004). adv. back issues avail. **Document type:** *Magazine, Consumer.* **Description:** Contains information on bluegrass music bands and related materials.
Published by: Tri-State Bluegrass Association, R R 1, Box 71, Kahoka, MO 63445. TEL 573-853-4344. Ed., Adv. contact Erma Spray. Circ: 5,000.

780.71 USA ISSN 0041-2511
ML1
TRIAD (DAYTON). Text in English. 1933. 3/yr. free to members (effective 2010). adv. illus. **Document type:** *Journal, Academic/Scholarly.* **Description:** Addresses issues and concerns relevant to music education.
Indexed: E03, ERI, M11, T02.
Published by: Ohio Music Education Association, 1806 Robert Fulton Dr, Reston, VA 20191. FAX 888-275-6362, mbrserv@menc2.org. Ed. Lisa Hanson TEL 216-227-5981. Adv. contact David N Adamson TEL 440-552-6983. Circ: 6,800.

780 USA
ML1
THE TRIANGLE. Text in English. 1905. q. USD 20 (effective 2008). bk.rev. illus. **Document type:** *Magazine, Trade.*
Formerly (until 2001): Triangle of Mu Phi Epsilon (0041-2600)
Indexed: A01, IIMP, M11, MusicInd.
—Ingenta.
Published by: Mu Phi Epsilon International Professional Music Fraternity, c/o Gloria Debatin, 4705 N Sonora Ave Ste 114, Fresno, CA 93722-3947. TEL 888-259-1471, executiveoffice@muphiepsilon.org, http://home.muphiepsilon.org/index.htm. Ed. Melissa Eddy. Circ: 10,000.

781.64 FRA ISSN 1768-1456
TRIBU ROCK. Text in French. 2004. q. EUR 3.90 newsstand/cover (effective 2009). **Document type:** *Magazine, Consumer.*
Published by: Panini France S A, Z.I. Secteur D, Quartiers des Iscles, Saint-Laurent-du-Var, 06700, France. TEL 33-4-92125757, http://www.paninionline.com/collectibles/institutional/fr/fr/index.asp.

780 ARG ISSN 0041-2767
TRIBUNA MUSICAL. Text in Spanish. 1965. s-a. ARS 20,000. adv. illus.
Published by: Pablo Luis Bardin Ed. & Pub., Av. Libertador 3576, Buenos Aires, Argentina. Circ: 1,500.

780 CHE ISSN 1013-6835
ML5
TRIBUNE DE L'ORGUE. Text in French. 1948. q. CHF 33; (Europe 39 SFr.; elsewhere 45 SFr.) (effective 1999). adv. bk.rev. **Document type:** *Academic/Scholarly.* **Description:** Devoted to the organ and its music.
Indexed: IIMP, M11, MusicInd, RILM.
Published by: Maison du Prieur, Romainmotier, 1323, Switzerland. TEL 41-24-531446, FAX 41-24-4531150. Ed. Guy Bovet. Circ: 2,000.

▼ **TRILL MAGAZINE.** *see* LIFESTYLE

TRIN & TONER. *see* DANCE

780 SWE
TRITONUS. Text in Swedish. 2002. irreg. adv. **Document type:** *Magazine, Consumer.*
Supersedes in part (in 2004): N M - T. Nutida Musik - Tritonus (Print) (1652-005X); Which was formed by the merger of (1957-2002): Nutida Musik (0029-6597); (2001-2002): Tritonus (Online)
Media: Online - full text. **Related titles:** ◆ Print ed.: Nutida Musik. ISSN 1652-6082.
Published by: Tritonus Magazin, Maria Skolgata 46, Stockholm, 11853, Sweden. red@tritonus.se. Eds. Magnus Bunnskog, Per Magnusson.

782.81 POL ISSN 1642-3399
TRUBADUR. Text in Polish. 1996. q. free membership. 52 p./no.; **Document type:** *Magazine, Consumer.* **Description:** Contains reviews of performances and recordings, impressions and discussions on operatic composers, librettis, characters, etc.
Former titles (until 2001): Ogolnopolski Klub Milosnikow Opery Trubadur. Biuletyn (1509-4987); (until 1997): Biuletyn Informacyjny Trubadur (1509-5029)
Related titles: Online - full text ed.
Published by: Ogolnopolski Klub Milosnikow Opery Trubadur, ul Brzozowa 12/23, Warsaw, 00286, Poland. TEL 48-22-8319906. Circ: 350.

780.42 DEU ISSN 1615-4347
TRUST; Hardcore Magazin. Text in German. 1986. bi-m. adv. music rev.; Website rev.; bk.rev. 68 p./no. 3 cols./p.; back issues avail. **Document type:** *Magazine, Consumer.*
Published by: Trust Verlag, Postfach 110762, Bremen, 28087, Germany. TEL 49-421-4915880, FAX 49-421-4915881. Ed. Dolf Hermannstaedter. Circ: 2,200.

781.66 FRA ISSN 1959-8564
TSUGI. Text in French. 2007. 11/yr. EUR 55 domestic; EUR 80 in Europe; EUR 85 elsewhere; EUR 5.95 newsstand/cover (effective 2011). adv. **Document type:** *Magazine, Consumer.*
Published by: Detroit Media, 6, Rue Desargues, Paris, 75011, France. TEL 33-1-42471825.

TUITION, ENTERTAINMENT, NEWS, VIEWS. *see* ART

781.7 USA ISSN 0161-3081
ML1
TUNE UP. Text in English. m. (except July-Sep.). membership. **Document type:** *Newsletter.* **Description:** Covers community news, membership information, and concert and event listings.
Published by: Philadelphia Folksong Society, 7113 Emlen St, Philadelphia, PA 19119. TEL 215-247-1300. Ed., R&P Edward Halpern. Circ: 1,575.

780 DEU ISSN 1439-524X
DER TURNERMUSIKER. Text in German. 1988. 6/yr. adv. **Document type:** *Newsletter, Trade.*
Published by: (Deutscher Turnerbund e.V.), Druck und Verlag Obermayer GmbH, Bahnhofstr 33, Buchloe, 86807, Germany. TEL 49-8241-500816, FAX 49-8241-500846, info@dvo-verlag.de, http://www.dvo-verlag.de. adv.: B&W page EUR 482, color page EUR 1,340; trim 185 x 262. Circ: 1,200 (controlled).

780.43 USA ISSN 1052-3170
ML156.9
TUROK'S CHOICE; the insider's review of new classical recordings. Text in English. 1990. 11/yr. looseleaf. USD 14.95 domestic; USD 16 in Canada & Mexico; USD 23 elsewhere (effective 2007). 4 p./no. 2 cols./p.; back issues avail. **Document type:** *Newsletter, Trade.* **Description:** Examines new classical recordings (on video cassette or CD-ROM) with information about the artist, format, and commentary.
Indexed: RILM.
Published by: Paul Turok, Ed. & Pub., 105 W 13th St, Ste 2C, New York, NY 10011-7838. TEL 212-691-9229, FAX 646-225-7165. Ed., Pub. Paul Turok. Circ: 1,000 (paid and controlled).

780.42 028.5 ITA
TUTTO DISCOTECA DANCE. Text in Italian. 1990. m. **Document type:** *Magazine, Consumer.*
Formerly (until 1995): Tuttodiscoteca
Published by: Edizioni Juvenis, Viale Lunigiana 7, Milan, 20125, Italy. TEL 39-02-66711016, FAX 39-02-92445. Ed. Enrico Cammarota. Adv. contact Vera Risi. Circ: 95,000.

780 GBR ISSN 1478-5722
ML197
➤ **TWENTIETH CENTURY MUSIC.** Text in English. 2004 (Mar.). s-a. GBP 89, USD 145 to institutions; GBP 93, USD 158 combined subscription to institutions (print & online eds.) (effective 2012). adv. bk.rev. back issues avail.; reprint service avail. from PSC. **Document type:** *Journal, Academic/Scholarly.* **Description:** Explores Western art music, music from non-Western traditions, popular music, film music, jazz, improvised music and performance practice.
Related titles: Online - full text ed.: ISSN 1478-5730. GBP 82, USD 140 to institutions (effective 2012).
Indexed: A22, E01, M11, MusicInd, RILM, SCOPUS.
—IE. **CCC.**
Published by: Cambridge University Press, The Edinburgh Bldg, Shaftesbury Rd, Cambridge, CB2 8RU, United Kingdom. TEL 44-1223-312393, FAX 44-1223-315052, journals@cambridge.org, http://www.cambridge.org/uk. Ed. Charles Wilson. R&P Linda Nicol TEL 44-1223-325702. Adv. contact Rebecca Roberts TEL 44-1223-325083. page GBP 415, page USD 785. **Subscr. to:** Cambridge University Press, 32 Ave of the Americas, New York, NY 10013. TEL 212-337-5000, FAX 212-691-3239, journals_subscriptions@cup.org.

▼ ➤ **TWISTED SOUTH.** *see* LIFESTYLE

781.66 POL ISSN 1230-2317
TYLKO ROCK; jedyny pismo rockowe w Polsce. Text in Polish. 1991. m. USD 115 (effective 1998). adv. bk.rev.; music rev. abstr.; charts; illus. back issues avail. **Description:** Covers all kinds of rock music.
Published by: Res Publica Press International Ltd., Ul Grazyny 13, Warsaw, 02548, Poland. TEL 48-22-455292, FAX 48-22-454216. Ed. Wieslaw Weiss. Pub. Andrzej Lubomirski. Adv. contact Agata Wojtczak. page PLZ 2,450; trim 297 x 210. Circ: 75,000.

781.64 810 USA
U.S. ROCKER MAGAZINE. Text in English. 1989. m. USD 20 (effective 1998). adv. music rev.; video rev.; play rev. index. back issues avail. **Document type:** *Newspaper.*
Address: 4758 Ridge Rd, 279, Cleveland, OH 44144. TEL 216-426-8341, FAX 216-426-8342. Ed., Pub., R&P, Adv. contact Sean Carney. B&W page USD 565; 16 x 16.

289.9 USA ISSN 1047-6601
U U M N NOTES. Text in English. 1983. 3/yr. USD 10. adv. bk.rev. back issues avail.
Published by: Unitarian Universalist Musician's Network, c/o D L Jackson, 1234 Oak Knoll Dr, Cincinnati, OH 34224. TEL 513-729-4183. Ed. Betty Wylder. Circ: 1,000.

780 DEU ISSN 0174-6065
MT3.G3
UEBEN & MUSIZIEREN; Zeitschrift fuer Instrumentalpaedagogik und musikalisches Lernen. Text in German. 1983. 6/yr. EUR 46; EUR 9.50 newsstand/cover (effective 2011). adv. bk.rev. bibl.; charts; illus. index. **Document type:** *Magazine, Trade.*
Indexed: DIP, IBR, IBZ, RILM.
Published by: Schott Musik International GmbH, Weihergarten 5, Mainz, 55116, Germany. TEL 49-6131-2460, FAX 49-6131-246211, info@schott-musik.de, http://www.schott-musik.de. Ed. Ruediger Behschnitt. Adv. contact Dieter Schwarz. Circ: 6,000 (paid and controlled).

780 NLD
UITGIDS. Text in Dutch. s-a. adv.
Published by: Amsterdams Uit Buro, Kleine Gartmanplantsoen 21, Amsterdam, 1017 RP, Netherlands. TEL 31-20-6211311, FAX 31-20-6211312, aub@aub.nl, http://www.amsterdamsuitburo.nl. adv.: page EUR 2,750; bleed 210 x 297.

780 UKR
UKRAINS'KA MUZICHNA GAZETA. Text in Ukrainian. q. USD 85 in United States.
Published by: Vseukrains'ka Muzychna Spilka, Ul Pushkinskaya 32, Kiev, Ukraine. TEL 224-22-60. **Dist. by:** East View Information Services, 10601 Wayzata Blvd, Minneapolis, MN 55305. TEL 952-252-1201, 800-477-1005, FAX 952-252-1202, info@eastview.com, http://www.eastview.com.

781.62 GBR ISSN 2045-6425
▼ **THE ULSTER FOLK**; grassroots arts & culture. Text in English. 2010. q. GBP 1 per issue (effective 2010). adv. **Document type:** *Newspaper, Consumer.* **Description:** Focuses on folk music-traditional Ulster-Scots, Irish singers/songwriters and aspects of country, rock, gospel, blues, or any genre that reflects on the culture of the region.
Related titles: Online - full text ed.: ISSN 2045-6433. free (effective 2010).
Published by: ClickNI, 8 Mount Davys Rd, Cullybackey, Ballymena, Antrim BT42 1HE, United Kingdom. TEL 44-28-25002000, info@clickni.co.uk, http://www.clickni.co.uk.

ULTIMATE AUDIO; defining excellence. *see* SOUND RECORDING AND REPRODUCTION

ULTIMO (MUENSTER); Muensters Stadtmagazin. *see* LITERARY AND POLITICAL REVIEWS

781.542 BEL
ULTRA W W W MAGAZINE. Text in English. 1993. irreg. bk.rev.; dance rev.; film rev.; music rev.; rec.rev.; tel.rev.; video rev.; Website rev. 12 p./no.; **Document type:** *Magazine, Consumer.* **Description:** Contains independent music reviews, movie reviews and travel guides.
Media: E-mail.
Address: PO Box 19, Kontich, 2550, Belgium. TEL 32-3-2269779, FAX 32-3-2269779, ultra@yucom.be. Ed. Kris Fagot. Circ: 1,700.

780 700 EGY ISSN 1110-7804
ULUM WA-FUNUN AL-MUSIQA/MUSIC SCIENCE AND ART. Text in Arabic. 1994; N.S. 1994. a. **Document type:** *Academic/Scholarly.*
Published by: Helwan University, Faculty of Music Education, 27 Esmaeil Muhammad Str, Zamalek, Cairo, Egypt. TEL 20-2-3402010, FAX 20-2-3403750, http://web.helwan.edu.eg/musiceduen/index.html. Ed. Dr. Kamal Shafiq Rezq.

781 DEU
UNCLE SALLY'S MAGAZIN. Text in German. 1995. m. EUR 15 (effective 2007). adv. **Document type:** *Magazine, Consumer.*
Published by: Uncle Sally's GmbH & Co. KG, Waldemarstr 37, Berlin, 10999, Germany. TEL 49-30-69409663, FAX 49-30-6913137, sallys@sallys.net, http://www.sallys.net. adv.: color page EUR 1,950. Circ: 130,233 (controlled).

781.542 GBR ISSN 1368-0722
ML5
UNCUT. Text in English. 1997. m. GBP 35.10 domestic; USD 75 in United States; USD 112 in Canada; EUR 73 in Europe; GBP 68 elsewhere (effective 2010). adv. illus. back issues avail. **Document type:** *Magazine, Consumer.* **Description:** Features articles on all types of music including rock and film, both new and old, cult and classic.
Published by: I P C ignite! Ltd. (Subsidiary of: I P C Media Ltd.), Blue Fin Bldg, Southwark St, 4th Fl, London, SE1 0SU, United Kingdom. TEL 44-20-31486985, http://www.ipcmedia.com/about/ignite/. Ed. Allan Jones TEL 44-20-31486985. Pub. Faith Hill TEL 44-20-31486833. Adv. contact Neil McSteen TEL 44-20-31486707. color page GBP 4,190, B&W page GBP 3,020; trim 210 x 297. Circ: 75,518. **Subscr. to:** Rockwood House, Perrymount Rd, Haywards Heath RH16 3DH, United Kingdom. TEL 44-845-1231231, IPCsubs@quadrantsubs.com, http://www.magazinesdirect.co.uk. **Dist. by:** MarketForce UK Ltd, The Blue Fin Bldg, 3rd Fl, 110 Southwark St, London SE1 0SU, United Kingdom.

781.64 USA ISSN 1553-2305
ML3533.8
UNDER THE RADAR; the solution to music pollution. Text in English. q. USD 16 domestic; USD 30 in Canada & Mexico; USD 50 elsewhere; USD 4.50 newsstand/cover (effective 2005). adv. **Document type:** *Magazine, Consumer.*
Address: 238 S Tower Dr, Ste 204, Beverly Hills, CA 90211. TEL 323-653-8705, FAX 323-658-5738. Ed. Mark Redfern. Pubs. Mark Redfern, Wendy Lynch. Adv. contact Robert Gleim TEL 310-306-6168.

780 USA
UNDER THE VOLCANO. Text in English. bi-m. USD 2.95 newsstand/cover (effective 2002). **Document type:** *Magazine, Consumer.* **Description:** Fanzine focuses on punk rock music.
Address: PO Box 236, Nesconset, NY 11767. TEL 631-585-7471, RBlackUTV@aol.com. Ed., Pub. Richard Black. Adv. contact Scott Hafflon TEL 617-623-5319.

785 CHE
UNISONO; die Schweizer Zeitschrift fuer Blasmusik. Text in French, German, Italian. 24/yr. CHF 30.50 (effective 2010). adv. back issues avail. **Document type:** *Magazine, Consumer.*
Former titles (until 2000): Blasmusikzeitung; (until 1988): Schweizerische Blasmusikzeitung; (until 1950): Schweizerische Instrumentalmusik; (until 1935): Schweizerische Zeitschrift fuer Instrumentalmusik; (until 1912): Die Instrumentalmusik
Published by: (National Society of Music from Switzerland), Zollikofer AG, Fuerstenlandstr 122, St. Gallen, 9001, Switzerland. TEL 41-71-2727370, FAX 41-71-2727586, leserservice@zollikofer.ch, http://www.zollikofer.ch.

THE UNIT CIRCLE; a magazine. *see* LITERARY AND POLITICAL REVIEWS

780.01 URY
UNIVERSIDAD DE LA REPUBLICA. FACULTAD DE HUMANIDADES Y CIENCIAS. REVISTA. SERIE MUSICOLOGIA. Text in Spanish. irreg. per issue exchange basis.
Supersedes in part: Universidad de la Republica. Facultad de Humanidades y Ciencias. Revista
Published by: Universidad de la Republica, Facultad de Humanidades y Ciencias de la Educacion, Magallanes 1577, Montevideo, 11200, Uruguay. Ed. Beatriz Martinez Osorio.

UNIVERSIDAD NACIONAL DE COLOMBIA. CENTRO DE ESTUDIOS FOLKLORICOS. MONOGRAFIAS. *see* FOLKLORE

786.5 DEU
UNIVERSITAET MUENSTER. ORGELWISSENSCHAFTLICHE FORSCHUNGSSTELLE. VEROEFFENTLICHUNGEN. Text in German. 1965. irreg., latest vol.22, 2002. price varies. **Document type:** *Monographic series, Academic/Scholarly.*
Published by: (Westfaelische Wilhelms-Universitaet Muenster, Orgelwissenschaftliche Forschungsstelle), Baerenreiter Verlag, Heinrich-Schuetz-Allee 35, Kassel, 34131, Germany. TEL 49-561-3105154, FAX 49-561-3105195, order@baerenreiter.com, http://www.baerenreiter.com.

780.71 AUS ISSN 0726-3929
UNIVERSITY OF WESTERN AUSTRALIA. SCHOOL OF MUSIC. MUSIC MONOGRAPH. Key Title: Music Monograph. Text in English. 1971. irreg., latest vol.6. price varies. **Document type:** *Monographic series, Academic/Scholarly.* **Description:** Contains a scholarly monograph of articles dealing with music education.
Published by: The Callaway Centre, University of Western Australia, School of Music, 35 Stirling Hwy, Crawley, W.A. 6009, Australia. TEL 61-8-64882051, FAX 61-8-64881076, callaway@uwa.edu.au, http://www.callaway.uwa.edu.au/. Ed. Frank Callaway. R&P Joanne Todd.

UNIVERZITA KOMENSKEHO. FILOZOFICKA FAKULTA. ZBORNIK: MUSAICA. *see* ART

780 GBR
UNKNOWN PUBLIC. Text in English. 1995. q. GBP 60 in Europe to individuals; GBP 75 elsewhere to individuals; GBP 100 in Europe to institutions; GBP 125 elsewhere to institutions (effective 2009). illus. **Document type:** *Journal, Consumer.*
Address: P O Box 354, Reading, RG1 5TX, United Kingdom. TEL 44-20-77068484, FAX 44-20-77063434. Ed. John L Walters.

781.64 CAN
UNRESTRAINED!. Text in English. q. USD 3.99 newsstand/cover (effective 2001). music rev. **Document type:** *Magazine, Consumer.* **Description:** Contains interviews, record reviews, zine reviews, demo reviews and concert reviews on various forms of metal music.
Address: 5625 Glen Erin Dr, Unit 57, Mississauga, ON L5M 6V2, Canada. TEL 416-483-3715, FAX 416-483-0698. Ed. Adam Wasylyk. **Dist. by:** International Publishers Direct, 27500 Riverview Center Blvd, Bonita Springs, FL 34134. TEL 858-320-4563, FAX 858-677-3220.

780 791.43 USA
UNSIGNED THE MAGAZINE. Text in English. 2007. bi-m. **Document type:** *Magazine, Consumer.* **Description:** Features indie music, movies, fashion and artists.
Published by: Unsigned The Magazine, Inc., 100 Crescent Court-7th Fl Ste 700, Dallas, TX 75201. Eds. Mut Asheru, Robbie Wilcox. Pub. Robbie Wilcox.

781.66 NLD
UP MAGAZINE. Text in Dutch. 2001. 10/yr. EUR 30.95 (effective 2009). adv. **Document type:** *Magazine, Consumer.*
Address: Postbus 4269, Eindhoven, 5604 EG, Netherlands. TEL 31-40-2221922. Adv. contact Serge van Uden. Circ: 4,100.

785.06 USA
UPBEAT. Text in English. 1965. 5/yr. free. adv. bk.rev. **Document type:** *Newsletter.* **Description:** Contains organization news.
Formerly: Lexington Philharmonic Society Newsletter (0024-161X)
Media: Duplicated (not offset).
Published by: Lexington Philharmonic Society, 161 N Mill St, Lexington, KY 40507-1125. Circ: 6,000.

780.7 GBR
ML5
UPBEAT (LONDON, 1904). Text in English. 1904. 3/yr. adv. bk.rev.; music rev. illus. back issues avail. **Document type:** *Magazine, Consumer.* **Description:** Journal of general musical interest for undergraduate and graduate students and professional musicians and musicologists.
Former titles (until 2006): Royal College of Music Magazine (0961-3609); (until 1990): R C M Magazine (0033-684X)
Indexed: M11, MusicInd.
—BLDSC (8029.500000).
Published by: Royal College of Music, Prince Consort Rd, London, SW7 2BS, United Kingdom. TEL 44-20-75893643, FAX 44-20-75897740, info@rcm.ac.uk.

781.6 362.41 GBR
UPBEAT (LONDON). Text in English. 19??. m. GBP 0.70 per issue domestic; GBP 3.34 per issue foreign (effective 2009). music rev. **Document type:** *Magazine, Consumer.* **Description:** Covers the worlds of rock, pop, jazz, and folk music, with interviews, reviews, and concert diaries.
Media: Braille. **Related titles:** CD-ROM ed.; E-mail ed.
Published by: Royal National Institute of Blind People, 105 Judd St, London, WC1H 9NE, United Kingdom. TEL 44-20-73881266, FAX 44-20-73882034, helpline@rnib.org.uk. **Subscr. to:** Customer Services, PO Box 173, Peterborough PE2 6WS, United Kingdom. TEL 44-303-1239999, FAX 44-1733-375001.

780 GBR ISSN 1479-7380
UPDATE; the UK's most upfront dance music review. Text in English. 198?. w. adv. back issues avail. **Document type:** *Magazine, Consumer.* **Description:** Covers all aspects of the dance and D J scenes.
Former titles (until Oct.2002): 7 Update (1477-6375); (until May 2002): 7 (1466-2663); (until 1999): Mixmag Update (0968-2643)
Related titles: Online - full text ed.: free (effective 2009).
Published by: D M C Publishing Ltd., PO Box 89, Slough, SL1 8NA, United Kingdom. TEL 44-1628-667124, FAX 44-1628-605246, info@dmcworld.com, http://www.dmcworld.com. Adv. contact Martin Madigan.

780.7 USA ISSN 1945-0109
➤ **UPDATE (ONLINE)**; applications of research in music education. Text in English. s-a. USD 58, GBP 34 to institutions (effective 2011). **Document type:** *Magazine, Academic/Scholarly.*
Media: Online - full content.
—CCC.
Published by: (M E N C: National Association for Music Education), Sage Publications, Inc., 2455 Teller Rd, Thousand Oaks, CA 91320. TEL 805-499-9774, 800-818-7243, FAX 805-499-0871, 800-583-2665, info@sagepub.com, http://www.sagepub.com. Ed. Ruth Brittin. **Subscr. outside the Americas to:** Sage Publications Ltd., 1 Oliver's Yard, 55 City Rd, London EC1Y 1SP, United Kingdom. TEL 44-20-73248701, FAX 44-20-73248733, subscription@sagepub.co.uk.

781.542 USA ISSN 1081-9924
ML3469
URB; Future Music Culture. Text in English. 1990. 10/yr. USD 17.95 domestic; USD 40 in Canada; USD 85 elsewhere Europe & S. America; USD 3.95 newsstand/cover (effective 2003). adv. bk.rev.; film rev.; music rev. illus. back issues avail. **Document type:** *Magazine, Consumer.* **Description:** Covers the urban entertainment scene: music, clubs and modern primitive culture for readers 16-30. Includes interviews.
Indexed: M11, MusicInd.
Address: 24 Hyperion Ave, Los Angeles, CA 90027. TEL 323-344-1207, FAX 323-258-0626, word2urb@aol.com. Ed. Daniel Chamberlin. Pub., R&P Raymond Roker. Adv. contact Gabriel Sanchez. B&W page USD 2,490, color page USD 3,270; trim 10 x 12. Circ: 75,000. **Dist. by:** 1200 Eagle Rock Blvd, Los Angeles, CA 90065.

URBAN DESIRES. *see* ART

780 700 USA
USELESS. Text in English. 2005. q. USD 5 newsstand/cover (effective 2005). **Document type:** *Magazine, Consumer.*
Published by: Useless Magazine, 85 North Thrid St., Ste 4B, Brooklyn, NY 11211. info@uselessmagazine.com. Ed. Larry Tee.

780 USA ISSN 0506-306X
ML1
V D G S A NEWS. Text in English. 1964. q. free to members (effective 2010). bk.rev. **Document type:** *Newsletter, Academic/Scholarly.* **Description:** Contains a letter from the president, Society announcements, chapter news, workshop reports, coming events (North America and overseas), reviews, pictures, and classified and commercial advertisements.
Indexed: A01, IIMP, M11, RILM, T02.
Published by: Viola da Gamba Society of America, Inc., c/o Alice Renken, 4440 Trieste Dr, Carlsbad, CA 92010. http://vdgsa.org/. Ed. Janet Scott.

781.57 GBR ISSN 1360-8924
V J M'S JAZZ & BLUES MART. Text in English. 1953. q. GBP 25 domestic; GBP 30 in Europe; USD 48 in the Americas; GBP 32 elsewhere (effective 2009). bk.rev. **Document type:** *Magazine, Consumer.* **Description:** Covers information about jazz record trading.
Former titles (until 1994): Vintage Jazz Mart (0042-6369); (until 1963): Palaver
Published by: Vintage Jazz Mart, PO Box 78, Belper, Derbys DE56 9AR, United Kingdom. Eds. Mark Berresford, Russ Shor.

VANDERBILT JOURNAL OF ENTERTAINMENT AND TECHNOLOGY LAW. *see* LAW

780 CHE ISSN 1660-8666
VARIA MUSICOLOGICA. Text in German. 2002. irreg., latest vol.20, 2010. price varies. **Document type:** *Monographic series, Academic/Scholarly.*
Published by: Peter Lang AG (Subsidiary of: Peter Lang Publishing Group), Hochfeldstr 32, Postfach 746, Bern 9, 3000, Switzerland. TEL 41-31-3061717, FAX 41-31-3061727, info@peterlang.com, http://www.peterlang.com. Ed. Peter Maria Krakauer.

780 USA
VEGAS REPORT. Text in English. 2004 (Jun.). m. adv. **Document type:** *Magazine, Consumer.*
Address: 7251 W Lake Mead, Ste 300, Las Vegas, NV 89128. TEL 702-257-2350, FAX 702-257-9078. Pubs. Alex Karvounis, Nicholas Karvounis.

780 ITA ISSN 1971-8241
VENEZIA MUSICA E DINTORNI. Text in Italian. 2004. bi-m. EUR 15 domestic (effective 2008). **Document type:** *Magazine, Consumer.*
Published by: Euterpe Venezia, Dorsoduro 3488, Venice, 30123, Italy. TEL 39-041-715188, info@euterpevenezia.it, http://www.euterpevenezia.it.

780 USA ISSN 1938-9302
VENUS ZINE; emerging creativity. Text in English. 1995. q. USD 15; USD 4.50 newsstand/cover (effective 2008). adv. **Document type:** *Magazine, Consumer.* **Description:** Covers women in music, art, film, fashion, and DIY culture. It feature interviews with legendary artists (Yoko Ono, Patti Smith, and Kim Deal) in addition to edgy and up-and-coming musicians, designers, writers, actresses, and DIY entrepreneurs.
Related titles: Online - full text ed.
Published by: Venus Media LLC, 2000 N Racine, #3400, Chicago, IL 60614. TEL 773-296-6025, FAX 773-296-6103. Ed. Amy Schroeder. Pub. Anne Brindle. adv.: color page USD 2,300; trim 8.375 x 10.875. Circ: 800 (controlled); 19,200 (paid).

780 700 USA
VERBICIDE. Text in English. q. USD 12; USD 3.95 newsstand/cover domestic; USD 4.95 newsstand/cover in Canada (effective 2004).
Published by: Scissor Press, 32 Alfred St, New Haven, CT 06512. http://www.scissorpress.com. Ed., Pub. Jackson Ellis.

780 ITA ISSN 0042-3734
ML410.V4
VERDI. Text in English, Italian. 1960. irreg. price varies. illus. index, cum.index every 3 nos. **Document type:** *Journal, Academic/Scholarly.* **Description:** Discusses origin, musical aspects, libretto, staging, performances and singers of a single opera.
Published by: Istituto Nazionale di Studi Verdiani, Strada della Repubblica 56, Parma, PR 43100, Italy. TEL 39-0521-385275, FAX 39-0521-287949, amministrazione@studiverdiani.it, http://www.studiverdiani.it.

780 920 USA ISSN 1943-7056
VERDI FORUM. Text in English, Italian. 1976. a. bk.rev. bibl.; charts; illus. back issues avail. **Document type:** *Newsletter, Trade.* **Description:** Research into the music, life and times of Giuseppe Verdi.
Former titles (until 2000): Verdi Newsletter (0160-2667); (until 1977): A I V S Newsletter (0148-0383)
Indexed: RILM.
Published by: (American Institute for Verdi Studies), New York University, Department of Music, 24 Waverly Pl, New York, NY 10003. TEL 212-998-8300, FAX 212-995-4147, michael.beckerman@nyu.edu, http://music.as.nyu.edu/page/home. Ed. David Rosen. R&P, Adv. contact Martin Chusid TEL 212-998-2587.

780 DEU ISSN 0942-1246
VERDRAENGTE MUSIK. Text in German. 1991. irreg., latest vol.19, 2005. price varies. **Document type:** *Monographic series, Academic/Scholarly.*
Published by: Musica Reanimata - Foerderverein zur Wiederentdeckung NS-Verfolgter Komponisten und Ihrer Werke e.V., c/o Peter Sarkar, Steubenstr 35, Weimar, 99423, Germany. TEL 49-3643-400156. Ed., Pub. Albrecht Duemling.

780 DEU ISSN 0941-7370
VERGLEICHENDE MUSIKWISSENSCHAFT. Text in German. 1994. irreg., latest vol.5, 2008. price varies. **Document type:** *Monographic series, Academic/Scholarly.*
Published by: Peter Lang GmbH (Subsidiary of: Peter Lang Publishing Group), Eschborner Landstr 42-50, Frankfurt Am Main, 60489, Germany. TEL 49-69-7807050, FAX 49-69-78070550, zentrale.frankfurt@peterlang.com, http://www.peterlang.com.

780 DEU ISSN 0543-1735
VEROEFFENTLICHUNGEN DES MAX-REGER-INSTITUTES. Text in German. 1966. irreg., latest vol.18. price varies. **Document type:** *Monographic series, Academic/Scholarly.*
Published by: (Max-Reger-Institut), Carus-Verlag GmbH, Sielminger Str 51, Leinfelden-Echterdingen, 70771, Germany. TEL 49-711-7973300, FAX 49-711-79733029, info@carus-verlag.com, http://www.carus-verlag.com.

780 DEU
VEROEFFENTLICHUNGEN ZUR MUSIKFORSCHUNG. Text in German. 1973. irreg., latest vol.11, 1992. price varies. **Document type:** *Monographic series.*
Published by: Florian Noetzel Verlag, Heinrichshofen Buecher, Holtermannstr 32, Wilhelmshaven, 26384, Germany. Ed. Richard Schaal. **Dist. in US by:** C. F. Peters Corporation, 373 Park Ave S, New York, NY 10016.

VI-FI. *see* ELECTRONICS

781.64 USA ISSN 1070-4701
ML3469
VIBE. Text in English. 1993-2009 (Jun.); resumed 2009 (Nov.). m. USD 11.95 domestic; USD 24 in Canada; USD 40 elsewhere (effective 2008). adv. bk.rev.; film rev.; music rev. illus. back issues avail.; reprints avail. **Document type:** *Magazine, Consumer.* **Description:** Chronicles the celebrities, sounds, fashion, lifestyle, new media, and business born of urban music.
Related titles: Online - full text ed.
Indexed: ASIP, B04, BRD, IIMP, IIPA, M02, M11, MusicInd, P34, R03, RGAb, RGPR, T02, W03.
—CCC.
Published by: Vibe Media Group, LLC., 113 E 125th St, 2nd Fl, New York, NY 10035. TEL 212-448-7300, 800-477-3974, FAX 212-448-7400. adv.: B&W page USD 74,277, color page USD 82,530; trim 8.25 x 10.875. Circ: 862,933 (paid).

781.65 CHE ISSN 1022-873X
VIBRATIONS. Text in French. 1991. m. CHF 75 domestic; CHF 85 in Europe; CHF 106 elsewhere; CHF 20 newsstand/cover (effective 2001). adv. back issues avail. **Document type:** *Magazine, Consumer.*
Published by: Consart S.A., 24 Cotes de Montbenon, Lausanne, 1003, Switzerland. TEL 41-21-3117722, FAX 41-21-3117717. Eds. Elisabeth Stoudmann, Pierre Jean Crittin. R&P Pierre Jean Crittin. Adv. contact Elisabeth Stoudmann.

VICE; art and entertainment newsmagazine. *see* ART

780 USA
VICTORY REVIEW. Text in English. 1976. m. USD 20; USD 32 foreign (effective 1999). adv. bk.rev.; rec.rev. **Document type:** *Magazine, Trade.* **Description:** Covers folk, jazz, new acoustic, songwriter, children's, women's, old time dance, blues, and other acoustic music. Includes columns, events, and 100 reviews.
Formerly: Victory Music Review
Published by: Victory Music, PO Box 2254, Tacoma, WA 98401. TEL 253-428-0832, FAX 253-428-8056. Ed. Rachel Papadopoulos. Pub., R&P Patrice O'Neill. Adv. contact Patrick O'Neill. page USD 195; trim 10 x 7.5. Circ: 4,000.

VIDEO FILM MUSIC. *see* COMMUNICATIONS—Video

780 FRA ISSN 0083-6109
VIE MUSICALE EN FRANCE SOUS LES ROIS BOURBONS. SERIE 1: ETUDES. Text in English, French; Summaries in French. 1954. irreg. price varies. adv. **Document type:** *Monographic series, Academic/Scholarly.*
Published by: Editions A. et J. Picard, 82 rue Bonaparte, Paris, 75006, France. TEL 33-1-43269778, FAX 33-1-43264264. Ed. Benoit. Adv. contact Pasini.

780 FRA ISSN 0080-0139
ML270
VIE MUSICALE EN FRANCE SOUS LES ROIS BOURBONS. SERIE 2: RECHERCHES SUR LA MUSIQUE FRANCAISE CLASSIQUE. Text in English, French; Summaries in French. 1960. a. price varies. adv. **Document type:** *Monographic series, Academic/Scholarly.*
Indexed: MusicInd, PCI, RILM.
Published by: Editions A. et J. Picard, 82 rue Bonaparte, Paris, 75006, France. TEL 33-1-43269778, FAX 33-1-43264264. Ed. Benoit. Adv. contact Pasini.

780 GBR ISSN 1475-1062
VIENNA MUSIC. Text in English. 1966. s-a. free to members (effective 2009). **Document type:** *Magazine, Trade.* **Description:** Life and works of the Strauss family.
Formerly (until 2000): Tritsch - Tratsch (0300-3086)
Published by: Johann Strauss Society of Great Britain, 12 Bishams Ct, Church Hill, Caterham, Surrey CR3 6SE, United Kingdom. TEL 44-1883-349681, jss@johann-strauss.org.uk, http://www.johann-strauss.org.uk.

787.87 USA ISSN 1067-2605
VINTAGE GUITAR MAGAZINE. Text in English. 1986. m. USD 24.95; USD 4.95 newsstand/cover (effective 2001). adv. bk.rev.; music rev.; video rev.; software rev. illus.; mkt.; stat.; tr.lit. 188 p./no. 4 cols./p.; back issues avail. **Document type:** *Magazine, Consumer.* **Description:** Focuses on guitar collecting. Includes articles on repair and histories, and interviews with players and builders. Thousands of instruments are offered for sale in each issue.
Indexed: M11.
Published by: Vintage Guitar, Inc., PO Box 7301, Bismarck, ND 58507. TEL 701-255-1197, FAX 701-255-0250. Ed., R&P Ward Meeker. Pub. Cleo Greenwood. Adv. contact James Jiskra TEL 701-255-1197. page USD 715; trim 13 x 11. Circ: 23,000 (paid).

VINTAGE RECORD MART. *see* SOUND RECORDING AND REPRODUCTION

787 DEU ISSN 0172-9098
ML900
DIE VIOLA. Text in German. 1979. irreg. price varies. **Document type:** *Monographic series, Academic/Scholarly.*
Indexed: MusicInd.
Published by: (Internationale Viola Gesellschaft), Baerenreiter Verlag, Heinrich-Schuetz-Allee 35, Kassel, 34131, Germany. TEL 49-561-3105154, FAX 49-561-3105195, order@baerenreiter.com, http://www.baerenreiter.com. Ed. Wolfgang Sawodny.

780 GBR
ML749.5
➤ **THE VIOLA DA GAMBA SOCIETY JOURNAL.** Text in English. 1969. a. bk.rev. **Document type:** *Journal, Academic/Scholarly.* **Description:** Contains articles on early bowed string instruments, their performance and music.
Formerly (until 2007): Chelys (0952-8407)
Media: Online - full text.
Indexed: AmHI, BrHumI, IIMP, M11, MusicInd, PCI, SCOPUS.
—Ingenta.
Published by: The Viola da Gamba Society, 56 Hunters Way, Dringhouses, York, Y024 1JJ, United Kingdom.

780 USA ISSN 0507-0252
ML1
➤ **VIOLA DA GAMBA SOCIETY OF AMERICA. JOURNAL.** Text in English. 1964. a. free to members (effective 2010). bk.rev. bibl.; illus. back issues avail. **Document type:** *Journal, Academic/Scholarly.* **Description:** Contains histories, scholarly articles, translations, reviews of books, music publications and recordings - all relating to the viol.
Indexed: A01, CA, IIMP, M11, T02.
—Ingenta.
Published by: Viola da Gamba Society of America, Inc., c/o Alice Renken, 4440 Trieste Dr, Carlsbad, CA 92010. Ed. Robert Green.

787 USA
VIOLA D'AMORE SOCIETY OF AMERICA. NEWSLETTER. Text in English; Summaries in German. 1977. s-a. free (effective 2011). bk.rev.; music rev. bibl.; tr.lit. back issues avail. **Document type:** *Newsletter, Trade.* **Description:** Furthers the research, history and performance of the Viola d'Amore.
Published by: Viola d'Amore Society of America, 39-23 47th St, Sunnyside, NY 11104. TEL 718-729-3138, roseviola20@gmail.com.

787 USA ISSN 0148-6845
ML1
VIOLIN SOCIETY OF AMERICA. JOURNAL. Key Title: Journal of the Violin Society of America. Text in English. 1976. irreg. (1-2/yr). free to members (effective 2010). adv. bk.rev. illus. back issues avail. **Document type:** *Journal, Academic/Scholarly.* **Description:** Contains articles on all aspects of bowed stringed instruments, auctions and appraisals, history of the violin and performers, playing technique and performance practice, making and restoration, tools, varnish, wood, graduation and acoustics.
Former titles (until 1976): Violin Society of America. News Bulletin (0193-6352); (until 197?): American Society for the Advancement of Violin Making. News Bulletin (0193-6360); Incorporates (in 2005): V S A Papers (1556-5092); Which was formerly (until 2004): C A S Journal (1053-7694); (until 1990): Catgut Acoustical Society. Journal (0882-2212); (until 1984): Catgut Acoustical Society. Newsletter (0576-9280)
Indexed: A20, A22, CA, IIMP, M11, MAG, MusicInd, RILM, T02.
—BLDSC (4912.520000), IE, Ingenta.
Published by: Violin Society of America, 341 N Maitland Ave, Ste 130, Maitland, FL 32751. TEL 407-647-8839, office@vsa.to. Ed. Brian Newnam.

780 ZAF ISSN 1999-3412
VIR DIE MUSIEKLEIER. Variant title: Suid-Afrikaanse Kerkorrelistevereniging. Jaarblad. Text in Afrikaans. 1980. a.
Published by: Suid-Afrikaanse Kerkorrelistevereniging, Posbus 6448, Uniedal, 7612, South Africa. TEL 27-83-4128166, FAX 27-86-6273930, bassonwd@gmail.com.

780 USA ISSN 1932-1384
VIRTUAL INSTRUMENTS. Text in English. 200?. bi-m. USD 16.95 domestic; USD 30 in Canada; USD 36 elsewhere (effective 2007). adv. **Document type:** *Magazine, Trade.*
Published by: Virtual Instruments, Inc., 3849 Ventura Canyon, Sherman Oaks, CA 91423. TEL 877-846-2496, http://www.virtualinstrumentsmag.com/index.html. Ed., Pub. Nick Batzdorf TEL 818-905-9101.

781.64 DEU
VISIONS. Text in German. 1991. m. adv. **Document type:** *Magazine, Consumer.* **Description:** Contains the latest news and reviews on current popular music and musicians.
Related titles: Online - full text ed.
Published by: Visions Verlag und Werbeagentur, Maerkische Strasse 115 - 117, Dortmund, 44141, Germany. TEL 49-231-5571310, FAX 49-231-55713131. Ed. Dennis Plauk. Pub., Adv. contact Michael Lohrmann. B&W page EUR 4,100, color page EUR 5,490. Circ: 31,895 (paid and controlled).

780 USA ISSN 1938-2065
MT1
➤ **VISIONS OF RESEARCH IN MUSIC EDUCATION.** Text in English. 2001. s-a. free (effective 2009). back issues avail. **Document type:** *Journal, Academic/Scholarly.* **Description:** Contains articles of a philosophical, historical, or scientific nature that contribute to an understanding of music teaching and learning at any level.
Media: Online - full content.
Published by: New Jersey Music Educators Association, 998 Ridge Ave, Manasquan, NJ 08736. http://www.njmea.org. Ed. Frank Abrahams.

781.64 DEU
▼ **VIVA**; Das Magazin. Text in German. 2009 (Feb.). m. EUR 2 newsstand/cover (effective 2009). adv.
Published by: Panini Verlags GmbH, Ravensstr 48, Nettetal, 41334, Germany. TEL 49-2157-81750, FAX 49-2157-81484528, info@panini.de, http://www.paninionline.com. Adv. contact Tina Gnauk. page EUR 10,500; trim 210 x 297. Circ: 300,000 (paid and controlled).

VIVA VOCE. *see* WOMEN'S STUDIES

780 AUS
VIVACE!. Text in English. 1949. 3/yr. adv. back issues avail. **Document type:** *Newsletter.* **Description:** Provides information about Musica Viva's activities throughout Australia and internationally - concerts, countrywide touring, export touring, in schools concerts.
Former titles (until 1991): Musica Viva Bulletin (1035-1892); (until 1986): Musica Viva Australia Bulletin (0810-9362); (until 1973): Musica Viva Society of Australia Bulletin
Published by: Musica Viva Australia, PO Box 1687, Strawberry Hills, NSW 2012, Australia. TEL 61-2-83946666, FAX 61-2-96983878, musicaviva@mva.org.au, http://musicaviva.com.au.

780 POL ISSN 1232-9665
VIVO; magazyn muzyczny. Text in Polish. 1991. q. **Document type:** *Magazine, Consumer.*
Published by: Towarzystwo Muzyczne Koryfeusz, ul Starowislna 3, Krakow, 31038, Poland. TEL 48-12-4220455 ext141, FAX 48-12-4222343. Ed. Andrzej Kosowski. Circ: 750.

VLAANDEREN; tijdschrift voor kunst en cultuur. *see* ART

780 ESP ISSN 1134-6272
VOICE. Text in Spanish. 1994. bi-m. USD 64 in United States. **Document type:** *Magazine, Consumer.* **Description:** Covers all genres of music, new and old.
Formerly (until 1994): Vox (1134-6159)
Related titles: Online - full text ed.
Published by: Hi-Tech S.L., C Roca I Batlle 5, entlo. 1a, Barcelona, 08023, Spain. TEL 34-93-4184724, FAX 34-93-4184312, hitech@musicspain.com, http://www.musicspain.com. Ed. Carles P Illa.

784 USA ISSN 1074-0805
ML1499
VOICE OF CHORUS AMERICA. Text in English. 1978. q. membership. adv. bk.rev. illus. reprints avail. **Document type:** *Magazine, Consumer.*
Formerly (until 1999): Voice
Related titles: Online - full text ed.
Indexed: A01, IIMP, M11, MAG, MusicInd, T02.
Published by: Chorus America, 1156 15th St, NW, Ste 310, Washington, DC 20005. TEL 202-331-7577, FAX 202-331-7599, service@chorusamerica.org, http://www.chorusamerica.org. Ed. Fred Leise. R&P Maurice Staples. Circ: 7,000.

780.7 USA ISSN 0147-4367
ML1
VOICE OF WASHINGTON MUSIC EDUCATORS. Variant title: Voice Magazine. Text in English. 1956. q. membership. illus. **Document type:** *Magazine, Trade.*
Supersedes: Washington Music Educator (0043-065X)
Indexed: MAG.
—Ingenta.
Published by: Washington Music Educator's Association, Box 1117, Edmonds, WA 98020-1117. TEL 425-771-7859, 800-324-9632, FAX 425-776-1795, office@wmea.org, http://www.wmea.org/. Ed., Pub. Jo Caldwell. R&P, Adv. contact Bruce Caldwell. Circ: 1,500.

780 NOR ISSN 1504-1611
ML3919
VOICES; a world forum for music therapy. Text in English. 2001. 3/yr. free (effective 2011). back issues avail. **Document type:** *Journal, Academic/Scholarly.* **Description:** Provides a forum for the development of music therapy practice, theory, discussion, and debate.
Media: Online - full content.
Indexed: A39, C27, C29, D03, D04, E-psyche, E13, R14, S14, S15, S18.
—CCC.
Published by: Uni Health, The Grieg Academy Music Therapy Research Centre/Uni Helse, Griegakademiets Senter for Musikkterapiforsking (GAMUT), c/o Grieg Academy, Dept of Music, University of Bergen, Lars Hilles gt 3, Bergen, 5015, Norway. http://helse.uni.no/Default.aspx?site=4&lg=2. Eds. Brynjulf Stige, Carolyn Kenny. Pub., R&P Rune Rolvsjord.

780 USA ISSN 2153-0203
ML1
➤ **VOICEXCHANGE.** Text in English. 2004. s-a. free (effective 2010). back issues avail. **Document type:** *Journal, Academic/Scholarly.*
Media: Online - full text.
Published by: University of Chicago, Department of Music, 1010 E 59th St, Chicago, IL 60637. TEL 773-702-8484, FAX 773-753-0558, musicdept@uchicago.edu, http://music.uchicago.edu/. Ed. Jonathan De Souza.

783 200 FRA ISSN 1277-2895
VOIX NOUVELLES; chants liturgiques et musiques sacrees. Text in French. 1996. bi-m. (5/yr). EUR 46 domestic; EUR 53 foreign (effective 2009). adv. charts. index. **Document type:** *Magazine, Consumer.*
Formed by the merger of (1957-1996): Eglise Qui Chante (0013-2357); (1965-1996): Choristes (0577-9731)
Related titles: CD-ROM ed.
Published by: G I E - Voix Nouvelles, 34 Rue Paul Bert, Lyon, 69003, France. TEL 33-4-72775762, FAX 33-4-72611764, info@voix-nouvelles.com, http://voixnouvelles.online.fr.

780.89 DEU ISSN 1617-0555
VOLKSLIEDSTUDIEN. Text in German. 2001. irreg., latest vol.10, 2010. price varies. **Document type:** *Monographic series, Academic/Scholarly.*
Published by: (Deutsches Volksliedarchiv), Waxmann Verlag GmbH, Steinfurter Str 555, Muenster, 48159, Germany. TEL 49-251-265040, FAX 49-251-2650426, info@waxmann.com. Ed. Max Matter.

784 USA ISSN 1064-8933
M2023
THE VOLUNTEER CHOIR. Text in English. 199?. bi-m. USD 17.95 (effective 2008). adv. **Document type:** *Magazine, Consumer.* **Description:** Contains well-chosen, easy anthems and choral responses for use throughout the church year.

Published by: Lorenz Publishing Co., 501 E 3rd St, Box 802, Dayton, OH 45402. TEL 937-228-6118, 800-444-1144, FAX 937-223-2042, info@lorenz.com, http://www.lorenz.com. Ed. Eugene McCluskey. R&P Joe Sengl.

780.42 920 USA
VOODOO CHILD. Text in English. 1985. q. USD 15 domestic; USD 20 foreign (effective 2001). adv. bk.rev.; film rev.; music rev.; rec.rev.; video rev. stat. back issues avail. **Document type:** *Newsletter.* **Description:** Accumulates and disseminates information regarding the legend and legacy of rock guitarist Jimi Hendrix.
Formerly (until 1997): Jimi
Published by: Jimi Hendrix Information Management Institute, 4219 Winding Way, PO Box 20361, Indianapolis, IN 46220-5513. TEL 317-257-JIMI, FAX 317-255-4476, kenvoss@iquest.net. Ed. Ken Voss. Circ: 1,200 (paid).

VOUS; le mag' des nouveaux talents. *see* ART

780 AUS
VOX. Text in English. 1960. m. free to members (effective 2009). adv. bk.rev. **Document type:** *Magazine, Trade.*
Indexed: CMPI, IIMP.
Published by: Theater Organ Society of Australia, Victorian Division, Southland Ctr, PO Box 172, Cheltenham, VIC 3192, Australia. TEL 61-2-98917227, djmusic@netspace.net.au, http://home.vicnet.net.au/~organ/. Ed. Eric Wicks. Circ: 850.

780 791.4375 CAN
VUE WEEKLY. Text in English. w. free. adv. **Description:** Covers entertainment news and events in the Edmonton area.
Related titles: Online - full content ed.
Address: 10303 108 St, Edmonton, AB T5J 1L7, Canada. TEL 780-426-1996, FAX 780-426-2889, http://www.vueweekly.com.

W A D. (We'ar Different) *see* CHILDREN AND YOUTH—For

780 AUS ISSN 1837-8846
W A M ENEWS. (West Australian Music) Text in English. 2008. m. free to members (effective 2010). adv. back issues avail. **Document type:** *Magazine, Trade.* **Description:** Contains WAM news, events and music industry information.
Media: Online - full text.
Published by: West Australian Music Association, PO Box 171, Northbridge, W.A. 6865, Australia. TEL 61-8-92277962, 800-007-962, FAX 61-8-93287711, wam@wam.asn.au, http://www.wam.asn.au/.

W A S I. *see* ART

790.2 USA ISSN 0092-4113
ML28.W2
W P A S MUSELETTER; Membership Newsletter of Washington Performing Arts Society. Text in English. 1970. q. USD 50 for membership (effective 2001). 8 p./no.; **Document type:** *Newsletter.* **Description:** Contains membership events, development updates, WPAS news, and a calendar of programs and performances.
Published by: Washington Performing Arts Society, 2000 L St, N W, Ste 510, Washington, DC 20036-4907. TEL 202-833-9800, FAX 202-331-7678. Ed. Susan Sandler. Circ: 5,000.

780 534 GRC ISSN 1109-9577
W S E A S TRANSACTIONS ON ACOUSTICS AND MUSIC. Text in English. 2004. q. EUR 300 to individuals; EUR 400 to institutions (effective 2005). **Document type:** *Journal, Academic/Scholarly.*
Indexed: A28, APA, BrCerAb, C&ISA, CA/WCA, CIA, CerAb, CivEngAb, CorrAb, E&CAJ, E11, EEA, EMA, H15, Inspec, M&TEA, M09, MBF, METADEX, SolStAb, T04, WAA.
—BLDSC (9364.916200), Linda Hall.
Published by: World Scientific and Engineering Academy and Society, Ag Ioannou Theologou 17-23, Zographou, Athens 15773, Greece. TEL 30-210-7473313, FAX 30-210-7473314, http://www.wseas.org.

780 USA
W - WEEKLY. Text in English. 2006. w. free. adv. **Document type:** *Magazine, Consumer.* **Description:** Covers the arts and entertainment offerings of Lexington, Kentucky from local musicians to artists and provides a palette of other stories.
Published by: Smiley Pete Publishing, LLC, 434 Old Vine St, Lexington, KY 40507. TEL 859-266-6537, info@bizlex.com, http://www.smileypete.com. Pub. Chuck Creacy. Adv. contact Ann Staton. B&W page USD 1,200, color page USD 1,500; trim 10.5 x 11.25. Circ: 12,000 (free).

782.1 920 GBR ISSN 0963-3332
WAGNER. Text in English. 1980. 3/yr. GBP 20 (effective 2000). adv. bk.rev. **Document type:** *Journal, Academic/Scholarly.* **Description:** Contains items of a scholarly nature about the life and works of the composer Richard Wagner.
Indexed: RILM.
Published by: Wagner Society, c/o Michael Bousfield, Flat 1, Ascot House, Third Ave, Hove, E Sussex BN23 2PD, United Kingdom. Eds. Claudia Kalay, Gurhan Kalay. Circ: 1,100.

THE WAGNER JOURNAL. *see* LITERATURE

782.1 920 GBR ISSN 0261-3468
ML410.W1
WAGNER NEWS. Text in English. 1980. bi-m. free to members (effective 2009). bk.rev.; rec.rev. **Document type:** *Newsletter.* **Description:** Includes news of forthcoming events, reviews and articles of general interest about the works of Richard Wagner.
Indexed: RILM.
Published by: Wagner Society, 16 Doran Dr, Redhill, Surrey, RH1 6AX, United Kingdom. wagnerring@aol.com. Ed. Raymond Browne.

782.1 DEU ISSN 1614-9459
WAGNERSPECTRUM. Text in German. 2005. s-a. EUR 13.50 (effective 2011). **Document type:** *Journal, Academic/Scholarly.*
Published by: Verlag Koenigshausen und Neumann GmbH, Leistenstr 7, Wuerzburg, 97082, Germany. TEL 49-931-3298700, FAX 49-931-83620, info@koenigshausen-neumann.de, http://koenigshausen-neumann.gebhardt-riegel.de.

781.64 HRV ISSN 1332-019X
WAM; webzin o audiju i muzici. Text in Croatian. 1999. q. HRK 95 (effective 2006).
Related titles: Online - full content ed.: ISSN 1332-0181.
Indexed: RILM.
Published by: Dvis d.o.o., Rubeticeva 10, Zagreb, 10000, Croatia.

780 792 USA ISSN 0196-3236
ML1699
WASHINGTON OPERA MAGAZINE. Text in English. 1974. 5/yr. free to members. adv. **Description:** Information about opera productions at the Kennedy Center by the Washington Opera. Includes interviews with guest artists, synopsis of the operas, and a calendar of events.
Published by: Washington Opera, 2600 Virginia Ave NW,104, Washington, DC 20037. TEL 202-295-2476, FAX 202-295-2479. Ed. Eleanor Forrer. Pub. Lance Tucker. Circ: 60,000 (paid); 60,000 (controlled).

781 USA ISSN 1537-8241
WAX POETICS. Text in English. 2002. q. USD 38 domestic; USD 75 in Canada; USD 95 elsewhere (effective 2010). **Document type:** *Magazine, Consumer.*
Published by: Wax Poetics Inc., 45 Main St, Ste 224, Brooklyn, NY 11201. Ed. Andre Torres.

▼ **WEBS**; dedicated to Georgia students' writing, artwork, and music. *see* LITERATURE

781.62 POL ISSN 1643-8590
WEDROWIEC. Text in Polish. 2001. q. PLZ 20 (effective 2003). **Document type:** *Magazine, Consumer.*
Published by: Stowarzyszenie na Rzecz Kultury Tradycyjnej Dom Tanca, ul. Raszynska 56/14, Warsaw, 02033, Poland. TEL 48-22-6686955, wedrowiec4@wp.pl, http://domtanca.art.pl. Ed. Remigiusz Mazur-Hanaj.

WEEKLY PIA. *see* LEISURE AND RECREATION

780.902 DEU ISSN 1863-2882
WEGZEICHEN MUSIK. Text in German. 2006. irreg., latest vol.4, 2009. price varies. **Document type:** *Monographic series, Academic/Scholarly.*
Published by: Georg Olms Verlag, Hagentorwall 7, Hildesheim, 31134, Germany. TEL 49-5121-15010, FAX 49-5121-150150, info@olms.de.

781.7 GBR ISSN 0043-244X
ML289
WELSH MUSIC/CERDDORIAETH CYMRU. Text mainly in English. 1959. 2/yr. GBP 3 per issue. adv. bk.rev.; music rev.; rec.rev. charts; illus.
Indexed: PCI, RILM.
—BLDSC (9294.685000).
Published by: Guild for the Promotion of Welsh Music, 94 Walter Rd, Swansea, SA1 5QE, United Kingdom. Ed. A J Heward Rees. Circ: 450.

780 GBR ISSN 1362-0681
ML289
WELSH MUSIC HISTORY JOURNAL. Text in English, Welsh. 1996. irreg., latest vol.7, 2007. GBP 25 per vol. (effective 2009). back issues avail. **Document type:** *Journal, Academic/Scholarly.* **Description:** Covers all aspects of Welsh music and music in Wales.
Indexed: IBR, IBZ, RILM.
—CCC.
Published by: (University of Wales, Centre for Advanced Welsh Music Studies), University of Wales Press, 10 Columbus Walk, Brigantine Pl, Cardiff, CF10 4UP, United Kingdom. TEL 44-29-20496899, FAX 44-29-20496108, press@press.wales.ac.uk.

WENDY HILTON DANCE & MUSIC SERIES. *see* DANCE

WEST COAST LINE; a journal of contemporary writing and criticism. *see* LITERATURE

781.642 DEU ISSN 0944-0658
WESTERN MAIL; Fachzeitung fuer Country & Western Kultur. Text in German. 1987. 11/yr. EUR 26 domestic; EUR 38 in Europe; EUR 45 elsewhere (effective 2009). adv. bk.rev. **Document type:** *Magazine, Consumer.*
Related titles: Online - full text ed.
Indexed: PQC.
—CCC.
Published by: Ber Verlag, Scharnweberstr 118, Berlin, 13405, Germany. TEL 49-30-41702970, FAX 49-30-41702971. Ed. Iris Paech. Pub. Kai Ulatowski. Adv. contact Wolfgang Retzlaff. Circ: 12,000.

784 USA
WESTERN PENNSYLVANIA BLUEGRASS COMMITTEE. NEWSLETTER. Text in English. 1969. m. USD 10 (effective 1999). adv. bk.rev. **Document type:** *Newsletter.*
Published by: Western Pennsylvania Bluegrass Committee, PO Box 5372, Pittsburgh, PA 15206-0372. Ed., Pub. George P Corey. R&P, Adv. contact George Corey. Circ: 2,000.

786.071 USA
ML549.8
WESTFIELD CENTER. NEWSLETTER (EMAIL). Text in English. 1984. m. membership. adv. bk.rev. illus. back issues avail. **Document type:** *Newsletter, Consumer.* **Description:** Fosters appreciation and understanding of keyboard music from the Renaissance through the Baroque, Classical, and Romantic eras. Emphasis is on historical performance practices and circumstances.
Former titles: Westfield Center. Newsletter (Print); (until Sept.1996): Early Keyboard Studies (0882-0201)
Media: E-mail.
Published by: Westfield Center, PO Box 505, Orcas, WA 98280. TEL 888-544-0619, FAX 360-376-4158, info@westfield.org. Circ: 750.

WESTWIND (LOS ANGELES). *see* ART

780.42 USA
WHARF RATS NEWSLETTER. Text in English. 1996. a. **Document type:** *Newsletter, Consumer.* **Description:** Focuses on Greatful Dead fans and concert goers in recovery.
Related titles: Online - full text ed.: 1996.
Published by: Wharf Rats, c/o Lynn Kravitz, PO Box 405, Mt. Hermon, CA 95041. Groovylynn@hotmail.com. Eds. Randy Cook, Steve Enright.

787 CAN
WHAT WAVE. Text in English. 1984. irreg. (approx. a.). CAD 7 in North America; CAD 8 elsewhere. adv. **Document type:** *Newsletter.* **Description:** Covers 50s rockabilly, 60s and 70s punk, 80s garage music.
Address: 17 Erie Ave, London, ON N6J 1H9, Canada. TEL 519-672-0971, FAX 519-672-0971. Ed. Dave O'Halloran. Circ: 1,000 (paid).

780.5 CAN ISSN 0838-4312
WHAT'S IN A N A M E?. (New Art Music Editions) Text in English. 1987. 2/yr. **Document type:** *Newsletter.*
Indexed: CMPI.
Published by: New Art Music Editions, 799 Beach Ave, Winnipeg, MB R2L 1E1, Canada.

WHAT'S ON AT THE STATE THEATRE. *see* THEATER

780 USA ISSN 0043-4752
ML27.U5
THE WHEEL OF DELTA OMICRON. Variant title: The Wheel: Educational Journal of Delta Omicron. Text in English. 1915. q. illus. back issues avail. **Document type:** *Journal, Academic/Scholarly.* **Description:** Contains organization news and music articles.
Related titles: Online - full text ed.
Published by: Delta Omicron International Music Fraternity, c/o Debbie Beckner, Exec Sec, 910 Church St, PO Box 752, Jefferson, TN 37760. TEL 865-471-6155, FAX 865-475-9716, DOExecSec@att.net, http://www.delta-omicron.org.

780 USA
WHILE YOU WERE SLEEPING; live the life. Text in English. bi-m. USD 19.99 domestic; USD 30 in Canada; USD 50 elsewhere; USD 4.98 newsstand/cover domestic; USD 7.30 newsstand/cover in Canada (effective 2001).
Address: P O Box 34843, Bethesda, MD 20827. TEL 301-493-6920, FAX 301-530-9289. Ed. Roger Gastman. Pub. Marty Gudelsky. Adv. contact Tracy Brumfield TEL 513-751-9997.

781.63 USA
THE WHOLE POP MAGAZINE ONLINE. Text in English. irreg. adv. **Description:** Publishes articles and short stories about popular music.
Media: Online - full text.
Published by: Maxima Multimedia, 2472 Broadway, Ste 195, New York, NY 10025. TEL 212-439-4177, 800-231-3070. Ed. Jack Mingo. Pub. Aron Trauring. Adv. contact Simpha StStull.

780 370.1 HUN ISSN 1727-3307
WHO'S WHO (YEAR). Text in English. 2003. triennial. USD 25 per issue (effective 2003).
Published by: International Kodaly Society, PO Box 67, Budapest, H-1364, Hungary. Ed. Ms. Marta Vandulek.

780 POL
WIEDZA O MUZYCE. Text in Polish. 1983. irreg. price varies. adv. **Document type:** *Academic/Scholarly.* **Description:** Series of text-books for students; it covers various fields of music.
Published by: Polskie Wydawnictwo Muzyczne, Al Krasinskiego 11 a, Krakow, 31111, Poland. TEL 48-12-4227044, FAX 48-12-4220174. Ed. Leszek Polony. R&P Janina Warzecha. Adv. contact Elzbieta Widlak.

WIENER BEITRAEGE ZUR MUSIKTHERAPIE. *see* PSYCHOLOGY

780.01 AUT
WIENER SCHRIFTEN ZUR STILKUNDE UND AUFFUEHRUNGSPRAXIS. Text in German. 1997. irreg., latest vol.6, 2010. price varies. **Document type:** *Monographic series, Academic/Scholarly.*
Published by: (Institut fuer Musikalische Stilforschung), Boehlau Verlag GmbH & Co.KG., Wiesingerstr 1, Vienna, W 1010, Austria. TEL 43-1-3302427, FAX 43-1-3302432, boehlau@boehlau.at.

780 AUT
WIENER SCHRIFTEN ZUR STILKUNDE UND AUFFUEHRUNGSPRAXIS. WIEN MODERN. Text in German. 2001. irreg., latest vol.4, 2008. price varies. **Document type:** *Monographic series, Academic/Scholarly.*
Published by: (Institut fuer Musikalische Stilforschung), Boehlau Verlag GmbH & Co.KG., Wiesingerstr 1, Vienna, W 1010, Austria. TEL 43-1-3302427, FAX 43-1-3302432, boehlau@boehlau.at.

780 AUT ISSN 1817-0412
WIENER VEROEFFENTLICHUNGEN ZUR MUSIKGESCHICHTE. Text in German. 1996. irreg., latest vol.10, 2010. price varies. **Document type:** *Monographic series, Academic/Scholarly.*
Published by: Boehlau Verlag GmbH & Co.KG., Wiesingerstr 1, Vienna, W 1010, Austria. TEL 43-1-3302427, FAX 43-1-3302432, boehlau@boehlau.at.

780.43 943 USA
WILHELM FURTWAENGLER SOCIETY OF AMERICA. NEWSLETTER. Text in English. 1989. q. USD 30; USD 35 foreign (effective 1999). bk.rev.; music rev. back issues avail. **Document type:** *Newsletter.* **Description:** Devoted to the furthering of knowledge about Wilhelm Furtwaengler, the late German conductor and composer, and his unique and interpretative art.
Published by: Wilhelm Furtwaengler Society of America, c/o Hans Raillard, 6400 Lone Pine Rd, Sebastopol, CA 95472-5623. TEL 650-851-3808, FAX 650-851-3151. Ed., Pub. Dade Thieriot. R&P Dade Thierot. Circ: 400.

780 GBR ISSN 0952-0686
ML5
THE WIRE; adventures in modern music. Text in English. 1982. m. GBP 39 combined subscription domestic; GBP 55 combined subscription in North America & Europe; GBP 65 combined subscription elsewhere; GBP 3.90 newsstand/cover (effective 2009). bk.rev.; film rev. charts; illus. back issues avail. **Document type:** *Magazine, Consumer.*
Related titles: Online - full text ed.: GBP 29.50 (effective 2009).
Indexed: A22, M11, MusicInd, RILM, T02.
—IE.
Published by: Wire Magazine Ltd., 23 Jack's Pl, 6 Corbet Pl, London, E1 6NN, United Kingdom. TEL 44-20-74225010, FAX 44-20-74225011, subs@thewire.co.uk. Eds. Chris Bohn, Tony Herrington. Pub. Tony Herrington. **Dist. addr. in UK & Europe:** Comag Specialist Division; **Dist. addr. in US:** Source Interlink Fulfillment Division.

780.71 USA ISSN 0043-6658
ML1
WISCONSIN SCHOOL MUSICIAN. Abbreviated title: W S M. Text in English. 1930. q. USD 15 to non-members; free to members (effective 2011). bk.rev. illus. **Document type:** *Journal, Academic/Scholarly.*
Related titles: Online - full text ed.
Indexed: MAG.
—Ingenta.
Published by: Wisconsin School Music Association, Inc., 1005 Quinn Dr, Waunakee, WI 53597. TEL 608-850-3566, 800-589-9762, FAX 608-850-3515, info@wsmamusic.org. Ed. Kevin Thays. Adv. contact Michelle Dietz.

780.01 CAN ISSN 1942-9126
WISSENSCHAFTLICHE ABHANDLUNGEN. Text in English, German, French. 1955. irreg.
Published by: Institute of Mediaeval Music, 1270 Lampman Crescent, Lions Bay, BC V0N 2E0, Canada. TEL 604-912-0258, medievalmusic@shaw.ca.

780 DEU ISSN 1861-7549
WISSENSCHAFTLICHE BEITRAEGE AUS DEM TECTUM-VERLAG. REIHE MUSIKWISSENSCHAFT. Text in German. 1999. irreg., latest vol.3, 2009. price varies. **Document type:** *Monographic series, Academic/Scholarly.*
Published by: Tectum Wissenschaftsverlag Marburg, Biegenstr 4, Marburg, 35037, Germany. TEL 49-6421-481523, FAX 49-6421-43470, email@tectum-verlag.de.

780 AUT
WISSENSCHAFTSZENTRUM ARNOLD SCHOENBERG. SCHRIFTEN. Text in German. 2005. irreg., latest vol.6, 2010. price varies. **Document type:** *Monographic series, Academic/Scholarly.*
Published by: (Wissenschaftszentrum Arnold Schoenberg), Boehlau Verlag GmbH & Co.KG., Wiesingerstr 1, Vienna, W 1010, Austria. TEL 43-1-3302427, FAX 43-1-3302432, boehlau@boehlau.at.

THE WOMAN CONDUCTOR. *see* EDUCATION—Teaching Methods And Curriculum

300 780 USA ISSN 1090-7505
ML82
➤ **WOMEN AND MUSIC**; a journal of gender and culture. Text in English. 1997. a. USD 33 combined subscription per issue domestic to individuals (print & online eds.); USD 48 combined subscription per issue foreign to individuals (print & online eds.); USD 58 combined subscription per issue domestic to institutions (print & online eds.); USD 73 combined subscription per issue foreign to institutions (print & online eds.); USD 28 per issue to individuals; USD 53 per issue to institutions (effective 2011). adv. back issues avail. **Document type:** *Journal, Academic/Scholarly.* **Description:** Explores on a wide range of disciplines and approaches, and seeks to further understanding of the relationships among gender, music, and culture, with special attention being given to the concerns of women.
Related titles: Online - full text ed.: ISSN 1553-0612.
Indexed: A22, A26, CA, CWI, E01, E08, FemPer, G08, G10, GW, H08, HAb, HumInd, I05, I06, I07, IBR, IBZ, IIMP, M11, MLA-IB, MusicInd, RILM, S09, S23, T02, W03, W05.
—IE. **CCC.**
Published by: (International Alliance for Women in Music), University of Nebraska Press, 1111 Lincoln Mall, Lincoln, NE 68588. TEL 402-472-3581, FAX 402-472-6214, pressmail@unl.edu. Ed. Suzanne G Cusick. Adv. contact Joyce Gettman TEL 402-472-8330. Circ: 300. **Subscr. to:** PO Box 84555, Lincoln, NE 68501. TEL 402-472-8536, 800-848-6224, FAX 800-272-6817, journals@unlnotes.unl.edu.

780 305.4 USA ISSN 1068-2724
ML82
➤ **WOMEN OF NOTE QUARTERLY**; a quarterly journal focused on information and research on women composers. Text in English. 1993. q. USD 20 domestic to individuals; USD 25 to institutions; USD 6 per issue (effective 2011). bk.rev.; music rev. back issues avail. **Document type:** *Journal, Academic/Scholarly.* **Description:** Profiles female composers and songwriters and discusses their work.
Indexed: FemPer, IIMP, M11, MLA-IB, MusicInd, RILM, T02.
Published by: Vivace Press, One University Blvd, 265 Gerneral Services Bldg, Saint Louis, MO 63121. TEL 314-516-4990, FAX 314-516-4992, vivacepress@umsl.edu.

780 USA
WOMEN'S MUSIC PLUS; directory of resources in women's music & culture. Text in English. 1977. a. USD 20 to institutions. **Document type:** *Directory.* **Description:** Contact information (more than 6,000 names, addresses, phone numbers, descriptions) for women's music and culture industry (performers, writers, publishers, festivals, film, video, radio, concert producers, theatre, bookstores, and periodicals).
Published by: Empty Closet Enterprises, Inc., 5210 N Wayne, Chicago, IL 60640. TEL 312-769-9009, FAX 312-728-7002. Ed. Toni Armstrong Jr. Circ: 2,000.

WOMEN'S NETWORK; national newsletter for women. *see* WOMEN'S INTERESTS

780 700 USA
WONKA VISION; your source for independent art, music & thoughts. Text in English. q. USD 10; USD 2.95 newsstand/cover (effective 2004). **Document type:** *Magazine, Consumer.*
Published by: Wonka Vision Magazine, P O Box 63680, Philadelphia, PA 19147. TEL 215-413-2136, FAX 775-261-5247, justin@wonkavisionmagazine.com. Ed., Pub. Justin Luczejko.

780 JPN
WOOFIN'. Text in Japanese. m. back issues avail. **Document type:** *Magazine, Consumer.*
Published by: Shinko Music Publishing Co. Ltd., 2-1 Kanda-Ogawa-Machi, Chiyoda-ku, Tokyo, 101-0052, Japan. TEL 81-3-32922865, FAX 81-3-32915135, http://www.shinko-music.co.jp.

780 GBR ISSN 1479-1498
WORD (LONDON). Text in English. 2003. m. GBP 38 (effective 2010). back issues avail. **Document type:** *Magazine, Consumer.* **Description:** Covers rock music, films, books and television.
Related titles: Online - full text ed.
Published by: Development Hell Ltd., 90-92, Pentonville Rd, London, N1 9HS, United Kingdom. TEL 44-20-70788400, FAX 44-20-78339900, info@developmenthell.co.uk, http://www.developmenthell.co.uk/. Ed. Mark Ellen. Pub. Jerry Perkins.

780.01 NLD ISSN 1566-0958
WORD AND MUSIC STUDIES. Cover title: W M S. Text in English. 1999. a. price varies. **Document type:** *Monographic series, Academic/ Scholarly.*
Related titles: Online - full text ed.: ISSN 1875-8134. 2002 (from IngentaConnect).
Indexed: M11, MusicInd, P02, P10, P48, P53, P54, PQC, RILM, T02.
—Ingenta.
Published by: (International Association for Word and Music Studies AUT), Editions Rodopi B.V., Tijnmuiden 7, Amsterdam, 1046 AK, Netherlands. TEL 31-20-6114821, FAX 31-20-4472979, orders@rodopi.nl. Ed. Walter Bernhart. **Dist. by:** Rodopi - USA, 295 North Michigan Avenue, Suite 1B, Kenilworth, NJ 07033. TEL 908-298-9071, 800-225-3998, FAX 908-298-9075.

780.42 028.5 USA ISSN 1056-4691
WORD UP! (PARAMUS). Text in English. 1987. m. USD 27 (effective 2011). adv. bk.rev. back issues avail. **Document type:** *Magazine, Consumer.* **Description:** Entertainment guide for Black teens, covering the hottest music and personalities of today.
Related titles: Online - full text ed.: USD 29; USD 4.99 per issue (effective 2011).
Published by: Enoble Media Group, 210 Rte 4 E, Ste 401, Paramus, NJ 07652. TEL 201-843-4004, FAX 201-843-8775, mpuntus@magnapublishing.com, http://www.enoblemedia.com.

780 791.43 USA
WORDLY REMAINS. Text in English. 2000. 5/yr. USD 20; USD 4.50 newsstand/cover (effective 2001). **Document type:** *Guide, Consumer.*
Address: 6658 Wilkinson Ave., Apt. 4, N Hollywood, CA 91606-1345. WorldlyRemains@aol.com. Ed. Ron Garmon. Pub. Jessie Lilley.

781.6 CAN ISSN 1195-8316
ML5
WORDS & MUSIC. Text in English. 1994. 6/yr. CAD 15, USD 20 (effective 1999). bk.rev. **Document type:** *Magazine, Trade.*
Related titles: CD-ROM ed.; Microfiche ed.: (from MML); Microform ed.: (from MML); Online - full text ed.; French ed.: Paroles and Musique. ISSN 1195-8324.
Indexed: C03, CBCARef, CMPI, CPerI, G08, M11, MusicInd, P48, PQC, PdeR.
—CIS.
Published by: Society of Composers, Authors and Music Publishers of Canada (SOCAN)/Societe Canadienne des Auteurs, Compositeurs et Editeurs de Musique, 41 Valleybrook Dr., Don Mills, ON M3B 2S6, Canada. TEL 416-445-8700, FAX 416-442-3829, macmillanr@socan.ca. R&P Arlene Stacey. Circ: 21,000.

782 USA ISSN 2151-0741
ML3531
➤ **WORDS.BEATS.LIFE**; the global journal of hip-hop culture. Abbreviated title: W B L. Text in English. 2002. s-a. USD 20 domestic to individuals; USD 30 foreign to individuals; USD 100 to institutions; USD 10 per issue in US & Canada; USD 20 per issue elsewhere (effective 2009). back issues avail. **Document type:** *Journal, Trade.* **Description:** Features scholarly, creative and alternative perspectives of hip-hop culture.
Related titles: Online - full text ed.: ISSN 2151-0989.
Indexed: AmHI, H07, T02.
Published by: Words, Beats, Life, Inc., St. Stephens Church, 3rd Fl, 1525 Newton St NW, Washington, DC 20010. Ed. Jared A Ball.

782.1 USA ISSN 1938-4556
ML423.G334
WORDS WITHOUT MUSIC; the Ira Gershwin newsletter. Text in English. 2007. irreg. **Document type:** *Newsletter, Consumer.* **Description:** Includes news and events from the Ira and Lenore Gershwin Trusts, as well as information about performances and recordings of Gershwin's music.
Published by: Ira and Lenore Gershwin Trusts, 101 Natoma St, San Francisco, CA 94105. info@gershwin.com, www.gershwin.com. Ed. Abigail Kimball.

780 GBR ISSN 1466-1500
THE WORKS. Text in English. 1999. 3/yr. free to members. adv. **Document type:** *Newsletter, Trade.* **Description:** Contains a range of specially commissioned articles, industry updates, interviews and writing opportunities.
—BLDSC (9351.299850).
Published by: British Academy of Composers & Songwriters, British Music House, 26 Berners St, London, W1T 3LR, United Kingdom. TEL 44-20-76362929, FAX 44-20-76362212, info@basca.org.uk, http://www.basca.org.uk/. Circ: 3,500 (controlled).

781.7 JPN
WORKS BY JAPANESE COMPOSERS (YEAR). Text in Japanese. biennial. **Document type:** *Catalog.*
Published by: Suntory Music Foundation, Shin-Nihon Bldg, 3-21-3 Akasaka, Minato-ku, Tokyo, 107-0052, Japan. TEL 81-3-3589-3694, FAX 81-3589-5344.

784 USA
WORLD CHORAL CENSUS. Text in English, French, German. 1984. a. USD 25; free with membership (effective 2000). **Document type:** *Bulletin.* **Description:** Attempts to list all choral organizations in the world.
Published by: International Federation for Choral Music, c/o Michael J Anderson, University of Illinois at Chicago, Dept of Performing Arts (M/C 255), 1040 West Harrison St, L042, Chicago, IL 60607-7130. TEL 312-996-8744, FAX 312-996-0954. Ed. Michael J Anderson. Circ: 2,500.

787.9 USA ISSN 1542-9415
ML1005
WORLD HARP CONGRESS REVIEW. Text in English. 1984. s-a. free to members World Harp Congress (effective 2002). adv.
Indexed: A01, CA, M11, MusicInd, T02.
Published by: World Harp Congress, c/o Kimberly Rowe, 2101 Brandywine St. Ste. 200B, Philadelphia, PA 19130. http://www.worldharpcongress.org. Ed. Ann Yeung. Adv. contact Claire Happel.

781.62 ITA ISSN 1121-5844
ML3469
WORLD MUSIC. Key Title: World Music Magazine. Text in Italian. 1991. bi-m. EUR 50 domestic; EUR 70 foreign (effective 2003). adv. bk.rev.; music rev. back issues avail. **Document type:** *Magazine, Consumer.*
Published by: E D T Srl, Via Pianezza 17, Torino, 10149, Italy. TEL 39-011-5591811, FAX 39-011-2307034. Ed. Pietro Carfi. Pub. Enzo Peruccio. R&P Claudia Peruccio. Adv. contact Antonietta Sortino. Circ: 9,000.

780 DEU ISSN 1019-7117
ML197
WORLD NEW MUSIC MAGAZINE. Text in English. 1991. a. EUR 10 per issue (effective 2009). **Document type:** *Magazine, Consumer.*
Indexed: RILM.
Published by: (International Society of Contemporary Music), Verlag MusikTexte, Postfach 190155, Cologne, 50498, Germany. TEL 49-221-9520215, FAX 49-221-9520216. Ed., Pub. Reinhard Dehlschlaegel. Circ: 1,200.

WORLD OF FANDOM. *see* LITERATURE—Science Fiction, Fantasy, Horror

780 DEU ISSN 0043-8774
ML5
➤ **THE WORLD OF MUSIC.** Text in English. 1959. 3/yr. EUR 64 domestic; EUR 78 foreign; EUR 24 newsstand/cover (effective 2010). adv. bk.rev.; music rev.; rec.rev. illus. reprints avail. **Document type:** *Journal, Academic/Scholarly.* **Description:** Promotes research and study in the field of ethnomusicology.
Indexed: A20, A22, AICP, ASCA, ArtHuCI, BAS, CA, CurCont, DIP, FR, IBR, IBSS, IBZ, IIMP, M11, MLA-IB, MusicInd, PCI, RASB, RILM, SCOPUS, T02, W07.
—BLDSC (9356.730000), IE, Infotrieve, Ingenta, INIST. **CCC.**
Published by: (Department of Ethnomusicology), V W B - Verlag fuer Wissenschaft und Bildung, Postfach 110368, Berlin, 10833, Germany. TEL 49-30-2510415, FAX 49-30-2511136, info@vwb-verlag.com, http://www.vwb-verlag.com.

780 DEU ISSN 0177-6487
ML5
WUERTTEMBERGISCHE BLAETTER FUER KIRCHENMUSIK. Text in German. 1927. bi-m. EUR 15.50 (effective 2009). adv. bk.rev. back issues avail. **Document type:** *Magazine, Consumer.*
Indexed: DIP, IBR, IBZ, RILM.
Published by: Verband Evangelische Kirchenmusik in Wuerttemberg e.V., Gerokstr 19, Stuttgart, 70184, Germany. TEL 49-711-237193410, FAX 49-711-237193411, info@kirchenmusik-wue.de. Ed. Michael Bender. adv.: page EUR 318; trim 145 x 197. Circ: 2,900 (paid and controlled).

780.7 DEU ISSN 1861-2792
WUERZBURGER HEFTE ZUR MUSIKPAEDAGOGIK. Text in German. 2005. irreg. price varies. **Document type:** *Monographic series, Academic/Scholarly.*
Published by: Margraf Publishers, Kanalstr 21, Weikersheim, 97990, Germany. TEL 49-79-343071, FAX 49-79-348156, info@margraf-verlag.de, http://www.margraf-verlag.de.

780 792.8 792 CHN ISSN 1009-766X
PN1609.C6
WUTAI YISHU/STAGECRAFT. Text in Chinese. 2001. bi-m. USD 36 (effective 2009). **Document type:** *Journal, Academic/Scholarly.*
Formed by the merger of (1978-2001): Yinyue Wudao Yanjiu (1001-330X); (1980-2001): Xiju Xiqu Yanjiu (1005-4197); Which was formerly (until 1994): Xiqu Yanjiu (1001-2923)
Published by: Zhongguo Renmin Daxue Shubao Ziliao Zhongxin/Renmin University of China, Information Center for Social Sciences, Dongcheng-qu, 3, Zhangzizhong Lu, Beijing, 100007, China. TEL 86-10-64039458, FAX 86-10-64015080, center@zlzx.org, http://www.zlzx.org/. **Dist. in the US by:** China Publications Service, PO Box 49614, Chicago, IL 60649. TEL 312-288-3191, FAX 312-288-8570; **Dist. by:** China International Book Trading Corp, 35 Chegongzhuang Xilu, Haidian District, PO Box 399, Beijing 100044, China. TEL 86-10-68412045, FAX 86-10-68412023, cibtc@mail.cibtc.com.cn, http://www.cibtc.com.cn.

780.7 POL
➤ **WYCHOWANIE MUZYCZNE.** Text in Polish. 1956. 5/yr. PLZ 60 domestic; PLZ 12 per issue domestic (effective 2011). **Document type:** *Journal, Academic/Scholarly.* **Description:** For music teachers who take care of vocal and instrumental groups in schools and other educational institutions. Publishes articles dealing with music and related fields of knowledge, such as psychology, sociology, music pedagogy, aesthetics, including both Polish and foreign traditions and ideas of music education.
Formerly (until 2011): Wychowanie Muzyczne w Szkole (0512-4255)
Related titles: Online - full text ed.
Indexed: RASB.
Published by: Stowarzyszennie Nauczycieli Muzyki, al Krasnicka 2a, Lublin, 20718, Poland. TEL 48-601-395404, FAX 48-81-5335172, sekretariat@snmuzyki.pl, http://www.snmuzyki.pl. Ed. Halina Koszowska-Kot.

780.42 305.896 USA ISSN 1093-0647
ML3531
X X L; hip-hop on a higher level. Text in English. 1997. 9/yr. USD 19.97 domestic (effective 2010). adv. music rev. illus. **Document type:** *Magazine, Consumer.* **Description:** Includes articles and reviews of hip-hop music and features on other aspects of African American and hip-hop culture.
Published by: Harris Publications, Inc., 1115 Broadway, New York, NY 10010. TEL 212-807-7100, FAX 212-610-7787, subscriptions@harris-pub.com, http://www.harris-pub.com. Pubs. Dennis S Page, Stanley R Harris. Adv. contact Ronnie Zeidel. **Dist. in the UK by:** Comag, Tavistock Rd, W Drayton, Middlesex UB7 7QE, United Kingdom. TEL 44-1895-444055, FAX 44-1895-433602.

782.421 USA ISSN 2152-1867
▼ **X X L PRESENTS: JUICY.** Variant title: Juicy. Text in English. 2010 (May). q. USD 4.99 per issue (effective 2010). **Document type:** *Magazine, Consumer.* **Description:** Special edition of XXL Magazine, featuring hip-hop artists.
Published by: Harris Publications, Inc., 1115 Broadway, New York, NY 10010. TEL 212-807-7100, FAX 212-610-7787, subscriptions@harris-pub.com, http://www.harris-pub.com.

780.65 781.64 USA
X X L PRESENTS: SCRATCH; the blueprint of hip-hop. Text in English. 2005. bi-m. adv. back issues avail. **Document type:** *Magazine, Consumer.*
Formerly (until Mar./Apr., 2007): Scratch Magazine (1548-2421)
Published by: Harris Publications, Inc., 1115 Broadway, New York, NY 10010. TEL 212-807-7100, FAX 212-610-7787, subscriptions@harris-pub.com, http://www.harris-pub.com/. Ed. Brenden Frederick. Pub. Dennis S Page. adv.: B&W page USD 9,450, color page USD 10,670; trim 8 x 10.875. Circ: 100,000 (paid).

780 USA ISSN 0098-3330
ML1
XENHARMONIKON. Text in English. s-a.
Published by: Frog Peak Music, P O Box 1052, Lebanon, NH 03755. fp@frogpeak.org, http://www.frogpeak.org. Ed. Dr. John H Chalmers.

781.46 CZE ISSN 1214-0619
XMAG. Text in Czech. 1996. 10/yr. CZK 390 (effective 2009). **Document type:** *Magazine, Consumer.*
Former titles (until 2002): Tripmag (1212-8805); (until 2000): Trip (1212-4958); (until 1988): Trip2House (1211-9598)

Published by: X Publishing s.r.o., Bartoskova 26, Prague, 140 00, Czech Republic. TEL 420-2-22510517, FAX 420-2-22510761. Ed. Pavel Cejka.

780.42 CHN

XMUSIC MAGAZINE; no.1 rock music magazine in China. Text in Chinese. 1987. m. USD 79.20 (effective 2009). bk.rev.; music rev.; film rev.; rec.rev.; video rev.; Website rev. Index. 80 p./no.; back issues avail. **Document type:** *Magazine, Consumer.* **Description:** Provides information for the Chinese young people who care for rock music and other new fashion and subculture.
Formerly: Tongsu Gequ (1003-7322)
Published by: Hebei Sheng Yishu Yanjiusuo/Hebei Art Research Institute, 41 Tiyu Middle St, Shijiazhuang, Hebei 050021, China. TEL 86-311-8635267, FAX 86-311-5815028, cheizak@hotmail.com. Ed. Hongjie Lee. Pub. Xianbang Cao. **Dist. by:** China International Book Trading Corp, 35 Chegongzhuang Xilu, Haidian District, PO Box 399, Beijing 100044, China. TEL 86-10-68412045, FAX 86-10-68412023, cibtc@mail.cibtc.com.cn, http://www.cibtc.com.cn/.

XPRESS. *see* LIFESTYLE

780 051 USA ISSN 1083-8538
ML3469
YAKUZA. Text in English. 1992. q. USD 29.95; USD 5 newsstand/cover. adv. bk.rev. **Document type:** *Newsletter.* **Description:** Covers travel diaries, interviews of avant garde musicians, humor, lifestyle and zine reviews.
Address: PO Box 26039, Wilmington, DE 19899-6039. TEL 302-651-0203, FAX 302-651-0206. Ed., Pub., R&P, Adv. contact Dave McGurgan. Circ: 4,000.

YAM!. *see* CHILDREN AND YOUTH—For

780 AUS ISSN 0740-1558
ML1
➤ **YEARBOOK FOR TRADITIONAL MUSIC.** Text in English, French, German. 1949. a. USD 150 combined subscription to institutions (print & online eds.) (effective 2012). bk.rev.; rec.rev.; video rev. back issues avail.; reprints avail. **Document type:** *Journal, Academic/Scholarly.* **Description:** Contains essays, reviews and reports in the area of music and dance research.
Former titles (until 1981): International Folk Music Council. Yearbook (0316-6082); (until 1969): International Folk Music Council. Journal (0950-7922)
Related titles: Online - full text ed.: USD 100 to institutions (effective 2012).
Indexed: A20, ABS&EES, AICP, ASCA, ArtHuCI, CurCont, DIP, FR, IBR, IBZ, IDP, IIMP, M11, MLA, MLA-IB, MusicInd, PCI, RILM, SCOPUS, T02, W07.
—Ingenta, INIST.
Published by: International Council for Traditional Music, ICTM Secretariat, Australian National University, School of Music, Bldg 100, Canberra, ACT 0200, Australia. TEL 61-2-61255700, FAX 61-2-61259775, secretariat@ictmusic.org, http://www.ictmusic.org. Ed. Don Niles.

➤ **YES!**, your entertainment source. *see* MOTION PICTURES

780 USA ISSN 1931-3438
NX1
YETI. Text in English. 2005. s-a. USD 12.95 newsstand/cover (effective 2006). **Document type:** *Magazine, Consumer.*
Published by: Yeti Publishing, P O Box 14806, Portland, OR 97293. http://www.yetipublishing.com. Ed. Mike McGonigal.

▼ **YINFUSHE (ONLINE).** *see* LITERATURE—Poetry

780 CHN ISSN 1005-7749
ML5
YINYUE AIHAOZHE/MUSIC LOVER. Text in Chinese. 1979. m. USD 96 (effective 2009). **Document type:** *Magazine, Consumer.* **Description:** Presents popular music knowledge with illustrations.
—East View.
Published by: Shanghai Wenyi Chubanshe/Shanghai Literature & Art Publishing Group, 74 Shaoxing Lu, Shanghai, 200020, China. TEL 86-21-64372608, FAX 86-21-64459916, http://www.shwenyi.com/. Circ: 50,000.

780 CHN ISSN 0513-2436
YINYUE CHUANGZUO/MUSICAL WORKS. Text in Chinese. 1955. q. USD 48 (effective 2009). **Document type:** *Journal, Academic/Scholarly.*
Indexed: RILM.
—East View.
Published by: Zhongguo Yinyuejia Xiehui/Chinese Musicians Association, 10, Nongzhanguan Nanli, Beijing, 100026, China. TEL 86-10-65389294. **Dist. by:** China International Book Trading Corp, 35 Chegongzhuang Xilu, Haidian District, PO Box 399, Beijing 100044, China. TEL 86-10-68412045, FAX 86-10-68412023, cibtc@mail.cibtc.com.cn, http://www.cibtc.com.cn.

780 CHN ISSN 0512-7920
YINYUE SHENGHUO/MUSIC LIFE. Text in Chinese. 1957. m. USD 62.40 (effective 2009). **Document type:** *Journal, Academic/Scholarly.*
—East View.
Published by: (Zhongguo Yinyuejia Xiehui/Chinese Musicians Association), Yinyue Shenghuo Bianjibu, 74 Bajing Jie, Heping-qu, Shenyang, Liaoning 110003, China. TEL 86-24-22710575, FAX 86-24-22712986. **Dist. by:** China International Book Trading Corp, 35 Chegongzhuang Xilu, Haidian District, PO Box 399, Beijing 100044, China. TEL 86-10-68412045, FAX 86-10-68412023, cibtc@mail.cibtc.com.cn, http://www.cibtc.com.cn.

780 CHN ISSN 1003-6784
ML3502.C5
YINYUE SHIJIE/WORLD OF MUSIC. Variant title: Easy Yinyue Shijie. Text in Chinese. 1963. m. USD 98.40 (effective 2009). **Document type:** *Journal, Academic/Scholarly.*
Related titles: Online - full text ed.
Published by: Yiyue Shijie Zazahishe, 85 Hongxing Zhonglu Erduan, Chengdu, Sichuan 610012, China. TEL 86-28-86512204, 86-28-86485547, FAX 86-28-86782650. **Dist. by:** China International Book Trading Corp, 35 Chegongzhuang Xilu, Haidian District, PO Box 399, Beijing 100044, China. TEL 86-10-68412045, FAX 86-10-68412023, cibtc@mail.cibtc.com.cn, http://www.cibtc.com.cn.

780.7 CHN ISSN 1004-2172
YINYUE TANSUO/EXPLORATIONS IN MUSIC; the academic periodical of Sichuan Conservatory. Variant title: Sichuan Yinyue Xueyuan Xuebao. Text in Chinese; Contents page in English. q. USD 16.40 (effective 2009). **Document type:** *Academic/Scholarly.*
Related titles: Online - full text ed.
Indexed: RILM.
—East View.
Published by: Sichuan Yinyue Xueyuan/Sichuan Conservatory of Music, 2, Xinsheng Lu, Xinnan Menwai, Chengdu, Sichuan 610012, China. TEL 552181. Ed. Song Daneng.

780 CHN ISSN 1003-4218
YINYUE TIANDI/WORLD OF MUSIC. Text in Chinese. 1949. m. USD 43.20 (effective 2009). **Document type:** *Journal, Academic/Scholarly.*
Related titles: Online - full text ed.
—East View.
Published by: Shaanxi Sheng Yinyuejia Xiehui, 19, Tiyue Lu, Xi'an, 710054, China. TEL 86-29-87889044, FAX 86-29-87804457, http://www.yyjxh.com/. **Dist. by:** China International Book Trading Corp, 35 Chegongzhuang Xilu, Haidian District, PO Box 399, Beijing 100044, China. TEL 86-10-68412045, FAX 86-10-68412023, cibtc@mail.cibtc.com.cn, http://www.cibtc.com.cn.

780.7 CHN ISSN 0512-7939
ML5
YINYUE YANJIU/MUSIC RESEARCH. Text in Chinese. 1958. q. USD 37.20 (effective 2009). **Document type:** *Journal, Academic/Scholarly.*
Related titles: Online - full text ed.
Indexed: RILM.
—East View.
Published by: Renmin Yinyue Chubanshe/People's Music Publishing House, Haidian-qu, 2, Cuiwei Lu, Beijing, 100036, China. TEL 86-10-68152605, FAX 86-10-68210291, http://www.rymusic.com.cn/. **Dist. by:** China International Book Trading Corp, 35 Chegongzhuang Xilu, Haidian District, PO Box 399, Beijing 100044, China. TEL 86-10-68412045, FAX 86-10-68412023, cibtc@mail.cibtc.com.cn, http://www.cibtc.com.cn.

780 CHN ISSN 1000-4270
ML5
➤ **YINYUE YISHU/ART OF MUSIC.** Variant title: Shanghai Conservatory of Music. Journal. Text in Chinese. 1979. q. USD 24.80 (effective 2009). bk.rev.; music rev. Index. **Document type:** *Journal, Academic/Scholarly.* **Description:** Covers Chinese and western music, musicology, composition, organology and history.
Related titles: Online - full text ed.
Indexed: RILM.
—East View.
Published by: Shanghai Yinyue Xueyuan/Shanghai Conservatory of Music, 20 Fenyang Lu, Shanghai, 200031, China. TEL 86-21-64319166. Circ: 7,000. **Dist. by:** China International Book Trading Corp, 35 Chegongzhuang Xilu, Haidian District, PO Box 399, Beijing 100044, China. TEL 86-10-68412045, FAX 86-10-68412023, cibtc@mail.cibtc.com.cn, http://www.cibtc.com.cn.

780 CHN
YINYUE ZHOUBAO/MUSIC WEEKLY. Text in Chinese. 1979. w. CNY 49.80 (effective 2004). **Document type:** *Newspaper.*
Related titles: Online - full content ed.
Address: 7, Xichangan Jie, Beijing, 100031, China. TEL 86-10-66071623. **Dist. by:** China International Book Trading Corp, 35 Chegongzhuang Xilu, Haidian District, PO Box 399, Beijing 100044, China. TEL 86-10-68412045, FAX 86-10-68412023, cibtc@mail.cibtc.com.cn, http://www.cibtc.com.cn.

780 JPN
YOUNG AUDIO NOW. Text in Japanese. 1974. a. price varies.
Published by: Gakken Co. Ltd., 1-17-15, Nakaikegami, Otaku, Tokyo, 145-0064, Japan. Ed. Akira Ohuchi.

780 JPN
YOUNG GUITAR. Text in Japanese. 1969. m. JPY 33,000.
Published by: Shinko Music Publishing Co. Ltd., 2-1 Kanda-Ogawa-Machi, Chiyoda-ku, Tokyo, 101-0052, Japan. Ed. Takashi Yamamoto.

286.132 USA ISSN 0044-0841
ML1
YOUNG MUSICIANS. Text in English. 1970. q. USD 14.35 (effective 2007). **Document type:** *Magazine, Consumer.* **Description:** Provides children in grades 4-6 with choir music and activities.
Formerly: Junior Musician
Published by: LifeWay Christian Resources, 1 Lifeway Plz, Nashville, TN 37234. TEL 615-251-2000, 800-458-2772, FAX 615-251-5933, customerservice@lifeway.com, http://www.lifeway.com.

780.42 700 810 USA ISSN 1089-8514
ML3533.8
YOUR FLESH QUARTERLY. Text in English. 1981. q. USD 15; USD 4.95 newsstand/cover; USD 35 foreign (effective 1999). adv. bk.rev.; film rev.; music rev.; play rev.; software rev.; tel.rev.; video rev. bibl.; illus.; stat. back issues avail. **Document type:** *Magazine, Consumer.*
Indexed: IIMP, IIPA.
Published by: Creature Talent & Publishers, P O Box 583264, Minneapolis, MN 55458-3264. Ed. Cindy Jaeger. Pub., R&P, Adv. contact Peter Davis. B&W page USD 800, color page USD 1,500; trim 10.88 x 8.38. Circ: 30,000.

780 CHN ISSN 1001-5736
➤ **YUEFU XIN SHENG.** Variant title: Shenyang Yinyue Xueyuan Xuebao. Text in Chinese. 1983. q. USD 14.40 (effective 2009). music rev. back issues avail. **Document type:** *Academic/Scholarly.* **Description:** Covers music theory, music education, theory of composition technique, music history, music science and technology, research on performance art and ethnomusicology.
Related titles: Online - full text ed.
—East View.
Published by: Shenyang Yinyue Xueyuan/Shenyang Conservatory of Music, No 61 Sanhao St, Heping-qu, Shenyang, Liaoning 110003, China. FAX 86-24-2390-3761. Ed. Pan Zhaohe. Circ: 10,000.

780 POL ISSN 0084-442X
Z DZIEJOW MUZYKI POLSKIEJ. Text in Polish. 1960. irreg.
Published by: Bydgoskie Towarzystwo Naukowe, Jezuicka 4, Bydgoszcz, Poland. **Dist. by:** Ars Polona, Obroncow 25, Warsaw 03933, Poland.

ZBORNIK MATICE SRPSKE ZA SCENSKE UMETNOSTI I MUZIKU/ MATICA SRPSKA REVIEW OF STAGE ART AND MUSIC. *see* THEATER

780 ESP ISSN 1133-844X
ZEHAR. Text in Spanish, Basque. 1989. bi-m. back issues avail. **Document type:** *Newsletter, Consumer.*
Indexed: SCOPUS.
Published by: Diputacion Foral de Guipuzcoa, Departamento de Cultura, Arteleku - Kristobaldegi, 14, Loiola, Donostia-San Sebastian, 20014, Spain. TEL 34-943-444669, kml@kultura.gipuzkoa.net, http://www.gipuzkoa.net/kultura/01index.htm. Ed. Miren Eraso Iturrioz.

780 DEU ISSN 1862-6750
ML5
ZEITSCHRIFT DER GESELLSCHAFT FUER MUSIKTHEORIE. Text in German. 2003. irreg., latest vol.6, 2009. price varies. **Document type:** *Monographic series, Academic/Scholarly.*
Media: Online - full content.
Published by: Gesellschaft fuer Musiktheorie, Postfach 120954, Berlin, 10599, Germany. Ed. Ludwig Holtmeier.

780 DEU ISSN 1619-8301
ML5
➤ **ZEITSCHRIFT FUER KRITISCHE MUSIKPAEDAGOGIK.** Text in German, English. 2002. irreg. free (effective 2011). **Document type:** *Journal, Academic/Scholarly.*
Media: Online - full text.
Indexed: RILM.
Address: Prof. Dr. Juergen Vogt, Universitaet Hamburg, Fakultaet 4, Sektion 4, Von-Melle-Park 8, Hamburg, 20146, Germany. Ed. Juergen Vogt.

780 DEU
ZEITSCHRIFT FUER SPIELMUSIK. Text in German. 1932. m. EUR 21.50 domestic; EUR 23.75 foreign (effective 2006). **Document type:** *Journal, Consumer.*
Formerly (until 1940): Zeitschrift fuer Spielmusik auf Allerlei Instrumenten
Published by: Moeck Music Instrumente und Verlag, Postfach 3131, Celle, 29231, Germany. TEL 49-5141-88530, FAX 49-5141-885342, info@moeck.com, http://www.moeck.com.

780 HUN ISSN 0139-0732
ML55
ZENETUDOMANYI DOLGOZATOK. Text in Hungarian. 1978. a. **Document type:** *Journal, Academic/Scholarly.*
Indexed: RILM.
Published by: Magyar Tudomanyos Akademia, Zenetudomanyi Intezet/Hungarian Academy of Sciences, Institute of Musicology, Tancsics M u 7, Budapest, 1014, Hungary. TEL 36-1-2146770, FAX 36-1-3759282, info@zti.hu, http://www.zti.hu.

780.65 DEU
ZENTRALNERV; das Magazin fuer Musiker in Bayern. Text in German. 1985. 5/yr. EUR 15 (effective 2002). adv. **Document type:** *Magazine, Trade.*
Published by: Musikzentrale Nuernberg e.V., Kernstr. 32, Nuernberg, 90429, Germany. TEL 49-911-266622, FAX 49-911-263121. Ed. Rick Roth. adv.: B&W page EUR 490, color page EUR 1,290. Circ: 20,000 (controlled).

781.7 CHN ISSN 1002-9923
ML5
ZHONGGUO YINYUE/CHINESE MUSIC. Text in Chinese. 1981. q. USD 35.60 (effective 2009). **Document type:** *Journal, Academic/Scholarly.*
Indexed: RILM.
—East View, Ingenta.
Published by: Zhongguo Yinyue Xueyuan/China Conservatory, No.1 AnXiang Road, ChaoYang District, Beijing, 100101, China. TEL 86-10-64874884, FAX 86-10-64872695, http://www.ccmusic.edu.cn/. **Dist. by:** China International Book Trading Corp, 35 Chegongzhuang Xilu, Haidian District, PO Box 399, Beijing 100044, China. TEL 86-10-68412045, FAX 86-10-68412023, cibtc@mail.cibtc.com.cn, http://www.cibtc.com.cn.

780.01 CHN ISSN 1003-0042
ML5
ZHONGGUO YINYUEXUE/MUSICOLOGY IN CHINA. Text in Chinese; Abstracts and contents page in English. 1985. q. USD 26.80 (effective 2009). bk.rev. **Document type:** *Journal, Academic/Scholarly.*
Related titles: Online - full text ed.
Indexed: RILM.
Published by: (Yinyue Yanjiusuo), Zhongguo Yishu Yanjiuyuan, Yiyuan Yanjiusuo, 1, Huixin Beilijia, Beijing, 100029, China. TEL 86-10-64933343, FAX 86-10-64813314.

780.7 CHN ISSN 1002-7580
ZHONGXIAOXUE YINYUE JIAOYU/MUSIC EDUCATION FOR ELEMENTARY AND HIGH SCHOOLS. Text in Chinese. 19??-1979; resumed 1983 (no. 121). bi-m. USD 36 (effective 2009). **Description:** Features comprehensive coverage of China's music education.
—East View.
Published by: Zhongguo Yinyuejia Xiehui, Zhejiang Fenhui, 9 Jiande Lu, Hangzhou, Zhejiang 310006, China. TEL 86-571-7065570. **Dist. overseas by:** China International Book Trading Corp, 35 Chegongzhuang Xilu, Haidian District, PO Box 399, Beijing 100044, China.

780.904 CHN ISSN 1001-9871
ML5
ZHONGYANG YINYUE XUEYUAN XUEBAO/CENTRAL CONSERVATORY OF MUSIC. JOURNAL. Text in Chinese; Contents page in English. 1980. q. USD 24.80 (effective 2009). bk.rev. **Document type:** *Journal, Academic/Scholarly.* **Description:** Publishes research papers on music history, theory of ethnomusicology, composition and conducting, and vocal and instrumental performance; articles on music teaching; selected foreign papers on music; and reviews of performances. Also includes recent vocal and instrumental composition scores.
Related titles: Online - full text ed.
Indexed: RILM.
—East View.
Published by: Zhongyang Yinyue Xueyuan/Central Conservatory of Music, 43 Baojia Jie, Xi Cheng-qu, Beijing, 100031, China. TEL 86-1-66417541, FAX 86-1-66413138. Ed. Wang Cizhao. **Dist. by:** China International Book Trading Corp, 35 Chegongzhuang Xilu, Haidian District, PO Box 399, Beijing 100044, China. TEL 86-10-68412045, FAX 86-10-68412023, cibtc@mail.cibtc.com.cn, http://www.cibtc.com.cn.

781.64 DEU
ZILLO. Text in German. m. EUR 45 domestic; EUR 55 in Europe; EUR 68 elsewhere; EUR 4.50 newsstand/cover (effective 2010). adv.
Document type: *Magazine, Consumer.*
Published by: Zillo MusicMedia Verlag GmbH, Sereetzer Weg 20, Ratekau, 23626, Germany. TEL 49-4504-606680, FAX 49-4504-6066810. Ed. Joerg Grieger TEL 49-4504-6066811. Adv. contact Jutta Grieger. B&W page EUR 2,130, color page EUR 3,430. Circ: 40,000 (paid).

780 700 GBR
ZINE-ON-THE-WEB. Text in English. 1999. m. free. bk.rev.; dance rev.; film rev.; music rev.; play rev.; software rev.; tel.rev. **Description:** An online magazine of poetry, music, art and reviews.
Media: E-mail. **Related titles:** Audio cassette/tape ed.
Published by: Lovely Ivor's Triumphant Temple of Wonders, 35 Kearsley Rd, Sheffield, S Yorks S2 4TE, United Kingdom. Ed. Andy Savage. Pub. Lovely Ivor.

782 NLD ISSN 1871-4560
ZING MAGAZINE. Text in Dutch. 1998. bi-m. EUR 32.50 domestic; EUR 28.50 in Europe; EUR 42.50 elsewhere; EUR 4.50 newsstand/cover (effective 2009). adv. **Document type:** *Magazine, Consumer.*
Formerly (until 2005): Zing (1389-0956); Which was formed by the merger of (1986-1998): Dechorum (0929-0796); Koorvenster (0165-4330); Which was formerly (until 1974): Koninklijke Bond van Zang- en Oratoriumverenigingen in Nederland. Tijdschrift
Published by: (Unisono), Uitgeverij de Inzet, Postbus 11497, Amsterdam, 1001 GL, Netherlands. TEL 31-20-6755308, FAX 31-20-5312019. Ed. Martje Lamme. Pub. Gilles Graafland.

057.85 POL ISSN 1732-7857
ZOOM (LUBLIN). Text in Polish. 2004. m. free newsstand/cover (effective 2007). **Document type:** *Magazine, Consumer.*
Published by: Centrum Kultury w Lublinie, ul Peowiakow 12, Lublin, 20007, Poland. TEL 48-81-5360311, FAX 48-81-5360312, sekretariat@ck.lublin.pl, http://www.ck.lublin.pl.

780 POL ISSN 0084-571X
ZRODLA DO HISTORII MUZYKI POLSKIEJ. Text in Polish. 1960. irreg. price varies. adv.
Published by: Polskie Wydawnictwo Muzyczne, Al Krasinskiego 11 a, Krakow, 31111, Poland. TEL 48-12-4227044, FAX 48-12-4220174. R&P Janina Warzecha. Adv. contact Elzbieta Widlak.

780 CHE ISSN 1660-8739
ZUERCHER MUSIKSTUDIEN. Text in German. 2002. irreg., latest vol.6, 2007. price varies. **Document type:** *Monographic series, Academic/Scholarly.*
Published by: Peter Lang AG (Subsidiary of: Peter Lang Publishing Group), Hochfeldstr 32, Postfach 746, Bern 9, 3000, Switzerland. TEL 41-31-3061717, FAX 41-31-3061727, info@peterlang.com, http://www.peterlang.com. Ed. Dominik Sackmann.

ZUGABE. *see* THEATER

780 DEU
ZWISCHEN - TOENE. Text in German. 2001. irreg., latest vol.5, 2006. price varies. **Document type:** *Monographic series, Academic/Scholarly.*
Published by: Weidler Buchverlag Berlin, Luebecker Str 8, Berlin, 10559, Germany. TEL 49-30-3948668, FAX 49-30-3948698, weidler_verlag@yahoo.de. Ed. Hanns-Werner Heister.

780 USA ISSN 8756-7717
ML3809
1/1. Text in English. 1985. irreg. (approx. 2/yr.). USD 19 domestic to institutional members; USD 25 in Canada & Mexico to individual members; USD 30 elsewhere to individual members; USD 35 to institutional members (effective 2006). adv. bk.rev. **Document type:** *Journal, Academic/Scholarly.* **Description:** Covers music theory and practice, and instrument construction and modification relating specifically to just intonation.
Indexed: IIMP, M11, MusicInd, RILM.
Published by: Just Intonation Network, 535 Stevenson St, San Francisco, CA 94103. TEL 415-864-8123 415-864-8123, FAX 415-864-8726, info@JustIntonation.net. Ed. David B Doty. Adv. contact Henry S Rosenthal. Circ: 500.

780 USA
7 BALL MAGAZINE; modern music on cue. Variant title: Seven Ball Magazine. Text in English. 1995. bi-m.
Published by: Vox Publishing, 3670 Central Pike, Ste J, Hermitage, TN 37076. TEL 615-872-8080, FAX 615-872-9786, editorial@voxcorp.com, http://www.releasemagazine.com. Ed. Chris Well. Circ: 60,000.

780 USA ISSN 1534-3219
21ST-CENTURY MUSIC. Text in English. 1994. m. USD 72 (effective 2005).
Formerly (until 2000): 20th-century Music (1085-5505)
Indexed: IIMP, M11, MusicInd, RILM, SCOPUS, T02.
Address: Box 2842, San Anselmo, CA 94960. mus20thc@aol.com.

781.6 745.1 USA
78 QUARTERLY. Text in English. 1994. a. USD 39 4 issues; USD 12 1 issues. adv. bk.rev. 140 p./no. 6 cols./p.; back issues avail. **Document type:** *Magazine, Consumer.* **Description:** Appeals to collectors of blues and jazz 78-RPM phonograph records from the 1920s and 1930s.
Address: PO Box 283, Key West, FL 33041. TEL 305-294-2653, sales@78quarterly.com, http://www.78quarterly.com. Ed., Adv. contact Pete Whelan. page USD 500. Circ: 3,500.

MUSIC—Abstracting, Bibliographies, Statistics

780 USA ISSN 0893-1305
ML1
ABSTRACTS OF PAPERS READ AT THE ANNUAL MEETING OF THE AMERICAN MUSICOLOGICAL SOCIETY. Variant title: American Musicological Society. Annual Meeting. Abstracts of Papers Read. Text in English. a. USD 7.50 domestic; USD 13.50 foreign (effective 2000). **Document type:** *Abstract/Index.* **Description:** Presents short abstracts of about 120 presentations made at annual meeting.
Published by: American Musicological Society, 201 S 34th St, Philadelphia, PA 19104-6316. TEL 215-898-8698, 888-611-4267, FAX 215-573-3673. R&P Robert Judd. Circ: 1,100 (paid).

780.42 GBR ISSN 0968-008X
B P I STATISTICAL HANDBOOK. Text in English. 1976. a. GBP 65 to non-members; free to members (effective 2009). stat. back issues avail. **Document type:** *Handbook/Manual/Guide, Trade.*
Description: Covers the growing links between music and games as well as provides a look at patterns of music consumption.
Formerly (until 1993): B P I Year Book (0142-7636)
—CCC.
Published by: British Phonographic Industry, Riverside Bldg, County Hall, Westminster Bridge Rd, London, SE1 7JA, United Kingdom. TEL 44-20-78031300, FAX 44-20-78031310.

780 USA
A BASIC MUSIC LIBRARY. Text in English. 19??. irreg., latest vol.3, 1997. **Document type:** *Bibliography.* **Description:** Lists about 7,000 sound recordings and 3,000 printed scores from around the world, all of which are coded for various levels of collecting.
Published by: Music Library Association, 8551 Research Way, Ste 180, Middleton, WI 53562. TEL 608-836-5825, FAX 608-831-8200, mla@areditions.com, http://www.musiclibraryassoc.org.
Co-sponsor: American Library Association.

015 780 FRA ISSN 1765-288X
Z2165
BIBLIOGRAPHIE NATIONALE FRANCAISE. MUSIQUE (ONLINE EDITION). Text in French. 2004. 3/yr. **Document type:** *Bibliography.*
Former titles (until 2000): Bibliographie Nationale Francaise. Musique (Print Edition) (1142-3285); (until 1990): Bibliographie de la France. Supplement 3. Musique (0150-5971); (until 1977): Bibliographie de la France. 1ere Partie, Bibliographie Officielle. Supplement 3. Musique (1149-6916); (until 1975): Bibliographie de la France. Supplement C. Oeuvres Musicales (1147-6974); Which superseded in part (in 1946): Bibliographie de la France (0006-1344)
Media: Online - full content.
—Linda Hall.
Published by: Bibliotheque Nationale de France, Site Francois Mitterand, Quai Francois Mauriac, Paris, 75706, France. TEL 33-1-53795950, FAX 33-1-53795045. Ed. P A Berend. **Subscr. to:** Mereau, 175 bd. Anatole France, BP 189, Saint-Denis Cedex 93208, France. TEL 33-1-48133858, FAX 33-1-48130908.

016.78 ESP ISSN 1138-0861
ML120.S6
BIME. BIBLIOGRAFIA MUSICAL ESPANOLA. Text in Spanish. 1997. irreg. **Document type:** *Bulletin, Bibliography.*
Published by: Asociacion Espanola de Documentacion Musical, Torregalindo No.10, Madrid, 28016, Spain. TEL 34-91-3508600, FAX 34-91-3591579, aedom1@teledine.es, http://www.aedom.org/. Ed. Jose Carlos Gonzalvez.

780.01 DEU
BONNER KATALOG/BONN CATALOGUE; Verzeichnis reversgebundener musikalischer Auffuehrungsmateriale. Text in German, English. a. EUR 188 (effective 2009). **Document type:** *Catalog, Abstract/Index.* **Description:** Provides an index of musical performance materials whose rights are owned by German publishers.
Media: CD-ROM.
Published by: De Gruyter Saur (Subsidiary of: Walter de Gruyter GmbH & Co. KG), Mies-van-der-Rohe-Str 1, Munich, 80807, Germany. TEL 49-89-769020, FAX 49-89-76902150, info@degruyter.com.

780 CAN
CADENCE ALL-YEARS INDEX. Text in English. 1988. a. CAD 35 (effective 1999). **Document type:** *Directory.*
Published by: Lord Music Reference Inc., 1540 Taylor Way, West Vancouver, BC V7S 1N4, Canada. Ed. Tom Lord. **Dist. by:** North Country-Cadence, Cadence Bldg, Redwood, NY 13679. TEL 315-287-2852, FAX 315-287-2860.

016.780 780 CAN ISSN 1709-7096
CANADIAN MUSIC PERIODICAL INDEX. Abbreviated title: C M P I. Text in English. 1996. base vol. plus m. updates. free (effective 2005). **Document type:** *Database, Abstract/Index.* **Description:** Provides bibliographic sources for information on all aspects of musical activity in Canada, including more than 25,000 entries indexed from 475 Canadian music journals, newsletters and magazines.
Media: Online - full content.
Published by: National Library of Canada, Marketing and Publishing Services/Bibliotheque Nationale du Canada, 395 Wellington St, Ottawa, ON K1A 0N4, Canada. TEL 613-996-5115, 866-578-7777, FAX 613-995-6274.

780 310 USA
COST OF DOING BUSINESS REPORT: OPERATING PERFORMANCE COMPARISONS FOR MUSIC PRODUCT DEALERS. Text in English. a. USD 35 to members; USD 50 to non-members. **Document type:** *Report, Trade.* **Description:** Reports statistical data supplied by music products retailers on sales volume and product line.
Former titles: Cost of Doing Business Survey: Operating Performance Comparisons for Music Product Dealers; Survey of Operating Performance for Music Dealers
Published by: N A M M - International Music Products Association, 5790 Armada Dr, Carlsbad, CA 92008. TEL 760-438-8001.

784 DNK
DANSK SANGINDEKS (ONLINE); register til sange for boern og voksne. Text in Danish. 1982. irreg. **Document type:** *Abstract/Index.* **Description:** Index to Danish songs.
Formerly (until 2003): Dansk Sangindeks (Print) (0108-2272)
Media: Online - full content.
Published by: D B C A/S, Tempovej 7-11, Ballerup, 2750, Denmark. TEL 45-44-867777, FAX 45-44-867693, dbc@dbc.dk, http://www.dbc.dk.

780 016 USA ISSN 0070-3885
DETROIT STUDIES IN MUSIC BIBLIOGRAPHY. Text in English. 1961. irreg., latest vol.87, 2006. price varies. back issues avail. **Document type:** *Monographic series, Academic/Scholarly.*
Published by: Harmonie Park Press, Liberty Professional Ctr, 35675 Mound Rd, Sterling Heights, MI 48310. TEL 586-979-2077, 800-422-4880, FAX 586-979-1786, djankowski@harmonieparkpress.com.

780 015 DEU ISSN 1613-8937
DEUTSCHE NATIONALBIBLIOGRAPHIE. REIHE M: MUSIKALIEN UND MUSIKSCHRIFTEN. Text in German. 1991. m. EUR 460 (effective 2006). **Document type:** *Bibliography.* **Description:** Bibliography that lists music scores from German-speaking countries available at the Music Archive.
Former titles (until 2004): Deutsche Nationalbibliographie. Reihe M, Musikalien und Musikschriften (Print Edition) (0939-0596); Which was formed by the merger of (1943-1990): Deutsche Musikbibliographie (0012-0502); (1976-1990): Deutsche Bibliographie: Musikalien-Verzeichnis (0170-124X)
Media: CD-ROM.
Published by: (Deutsche Bibliothek, Deutsches Musikarchiv), M V B - Marketing- und Verlagsservice des Buchhandels GmbH, Postfach 100442, Frankfurt Am Main, 60004, Germany. TEL 49-69-13060, FAX 49-69-1306201, info@mvb-online.de, http://www.mvb-online.de.

015 789.91 BGR ISSN 1310-9154
DISKOGRAFIA. Text in Bulgarian. 1974. a. BGL 1.40 per issue (effective 2003). bibl. **Document type:** *Bulletin, Bibliography.*
Formerly: Bulgarski Gramofonii Plochi (0323-9365)
Published by: Narodna Biblioteka Sv. sv. Kiril i Metodii/Cyril and Methodius National Library, 88 Levski Blvd, Sofia, 1504, Bulgaria. TEL 359-2-9881600, FAX 359-2-435495, dipchikova@nationallibrary.bg. R&P A Kasabov TEL 359-2-9882811 ext 226. Circ: 300.

780 016 USA ISSN 0015-6191
ML5
FONTES ARTIS MUSICAE. Text in English, French, German. 1953. q. free to members (effective 2009). bk.rev. bibl.; illus. index. back issues avail.; reprints avail. **Document type:** *Journal, Trade.* **Description:** Features the purposes of IAML, music librarianship and documentation, bibliography and musicology.
Related titles: Online - full text ed.
Indexed: A01, A03, A08, A20, A22, A26, ASCA, ArtHuCI, B04, BRD, BrHumI, CA, CurCont, FR, H14, I05, IBR, IBZ, IIMP, L04, L07, L08, L09, LISTA, LibLit, M11, MLA-IB, MusicInd, P02, P10, P48, P53, P54, PCI, PQC, RASB, RILM, SCOPUS, T02, W03, W05, W07.
—BLDSC (3976.850000), IE, Ingenta, INIST.
Published by: International Association of Music Libraries, Archives and Documentation Centres (U.S. Branch), 8551 Research Way, Ste 180, Middleton, WI 53562. Ed. Maureen Buja TEL 852-2146-8047. Adv. contact David Day. **Subscr. outside US to:** Pamela Thompson, IAML Treasurer, Royal College of Music, Prince Consort Rd, London SW7 2BS, United Kingdom; **Subscr. to:** Robert Follet, Music Library, University of Arizona, Tucson, AZ 85721.

INDEX DES PERIODIQUES DE MUSIQUE CANADIENS. *see* LIBRARY AND INFORMATION SCIENCES—Abstracting, Bibliographies, Statistics

780.01 DEU
INTERNATIONAL BIBLIOGRAPHY OF PRINTED MUSIC, MUSIC MANUSCRIPTS AND RECORDINGS/BIBLIOGRAPHIE INTERNATIONALE DES IMPRIMES, MANUSCRITS ET ENREGISTREMENTS MUSICAUX/INTERNATIONALE BIBLIOGRAPHIE DER MUSIKDRUCKE, MUSIKHANDSCHRIFTEN UND MUSIKAUFNAHMEN. Text in English, French, German. irreg., latest vol.2, 2003. EUR 1,520 base vol(s). (effective 2009). **Document type:** *Catalog, Abstract/Index.*
Related titles: CD-ROM ed.
Published by: De Gruyter Saur (Subsidiary of: Walter de Gruyter GmbH & Co. KG), Mies-van-der-Rohe-Str 1, Munich, 80807, Germany. TEL 49-89-769020, FAX 49-89-76902150, info@degruyter.com.

780 USA ISSN 1528-3135
ML1
INTERNATIONAL INDEX TO MUSIC PERIODICALS. Abbreviated title: I I M P. Text in English. 1996. base vol. plus m. updates. back issues avail. **Document type:** *Database, Abstract/Index.* **Description:** Contains over 600,000 records, with complete runs of over ten important titles, such as the Journal of the American Musicological Society and notes.
Media: Online - full text.
Published by: ProQuest (Subsidiary of: Cambridge Information Group), 789 E Eisenhower Pky, PO Box 1346, Ann Arbor, MI 48106. TEL 734-761-4700, 800-521-0600, FAX 734-997-4040, 888-241-5612, info@proquest.com.

INTERNATIONAL INDEX TO THE PERFORMING ARTS. *see* THEATER—Abstracting, Bibliographies, Statistics

780 016 JPN
JAPAN FEDERATION OF COMPOSERS. CATALOGUE OF PUBLICATIONS. Text in Japanese, English. 1970. a. free. **Document type:** *Catalog.*
Published by: Japan Federation of Composers, No 307 5th Sky Bldg, 3-3-8 Sendagaya, Shibuya-ku, Tokyo, 151-0051, Japan. TEL 81-3-5474-1853, FAX 81-3-5474-1854. Circ: 1,000.

789.91 USA
LASERLOG REPORTER; CD reporter. Text in English. 1985. fortn. looseleaf. USD 228. **Description:** Provides a list of CD albums by title and artist.
Published by: Phonolog Publishing (Subsidiary of: Trade Service Corporation), 10996 Torreyana Rd, Box 85007, San Diego, CA 92138. TEL 619-457-5920. Ed. Bonnie J Dudley.

LITOPYS NOT. *see* PUBLISHING AND BOOK TRADE—Abstracting, Bibliographies, Statistics

780 016 HUN ISSN 0133-5782
ML120.H9
MAGYAR NEMZETI BIBLIOGRAFIA. ZENEMUVEK BIBLIOGRAFIAJA. Text in Hungarian. 1977. q. HUF 800. **Document type:** *Bibliography.* **Description:** Bibliography of musical compositions and recordings published in Hungary and officially deposited in the National Szechenyi Library.
Supersedes in part (in 1977): Magyar Nemzeti Bibliografia (0373-1766); Also supersedes (1970-1977): Magyar Zenemuvek Bibliografiaja (0200-0679)
Published by: Orszagos Szechenyi Konyvtar/National Szechenyi Library, Budavari Palota F epulet, Budapest, 1827, Hungary. TEL 36-1-2243788, FAX 36-1-2020804, kint@oszk.hu, http://www.ki.oszk.hu. Ed. Eva Kelemen. Circ: 200. **Subscr. to:** Nemzetkozi es Kulturalis Kapcsolatok Irodaja, Public Relations and Cultural Affairs, Budavari Palota F epulet, Budapest 1827, Hungary.

782.1 USA
MELLEN OPERA REFERENCE INDEX. Text in English. 1986. irreg., latest 2008. price varies. back issues avail. **Document type:** *Monographic series, Bibliography.*
Published by: Edwin Mellen Press, 415 Ridge St, PO Box 450, Lewiston, NY 14092. TEL 716-754-2266, FAX 716-754-4056, cservice@mellenpress.com.

780 016 USA
MONOGRAPHS AND BIBLIOGRAPHIES IN AMERICAN MUSIC. Text in English. 1974. irreg. price varies. back issues avail. **Document type:** *Monographic series, Bibliography.* **Description:** Provides monographs and bibliographies in the field of American music.
Formerly (until 1995): Bibliographies in American Music
Published by: College Music Society, 312 E Pine St, Missoula, MT 59802. TEL 406-721-9616, FAX 406-721-9419, cms@music.org, http://www.music.org.

780 USA ISSN 1083-1258
ML113
MUSIC IN PRINT MASTER TITLE INDEX. Text in English. 1988. irreg.
Published by: Musicdata, Inc., PO Box 112, Lansdale, PA 19446. TEL 215-855-0181, FAX 215-855-0182.

780 USA
MUSIC-IN-PRINT SERIES (ONLINE). Text in English. 1974. irreg. price varies. adv. bibl. **Document type:** *Catalog.* **Description:** Goal is to locate and catalog all printed music published throughout the world, and to keep the information current by publishing supplements and revised editions.
Formerly (until 2000): Music-in-Print Series (Print) (0146-7883)
Media: Online - full content. **Related titles:** CD-ROM ed.
Published by: eMusicquest, PO Box 112, Lansdale, PA 19446. TEL 215-855-0181, 866-387-7639, FAX 215-855-0182, info@music-in-print.com, http://www.emusicinprint.com. Circ: 2,000.

016.78 USA ISSN 1537-0410
ML118
MUSIC INDEX (ONLINE). Text in English. 1999. q. free (effective 2011). **Document type:** *Database, Abstract/Index.* **Description:** Music Index indexing and abstracts of articles about music. Areas covered include music history, musicology and ethnomusicology. .
Media: Online - full text.
Published by: EBSCO Publishing (Subsidiary of: EBSCO Industries, Inc.), 10 Estes St, PO Box 682, Ipswich, MA 01938. TEL 978-356-6500, 800-653-2726, FAX 978-356-6565, information@ebscohost.com.

780 USA ISSN 0094-6478
MUSIC LIBRARY ASSOCIATION. INDEX AND BIBLIOGRAPHY SERIES. Variant title: M L A Index and Bibliography Series(Music Library Association). Text in English. 1964. irreg., latest vol.34, 2007. price varies. 336 p./no.; back issues avail. **Document type:** *Monographic series, Bibliography.* **Description:** Analytical indexes to music serials and music materials.
Formerly (until 1975): Music Library Association. Index Series (0077-2445)
Published by: (Music Library Association), Scarecrow Press, Inc. (Subsidiary of: Rowman & Littlefield Publishers, Inc.), 4501 Forbes Blvd, Ste 200, Lanham, MD 20706. TEL 301-459-3366, 800-462-6420, FAX 301-429-5748, 800-338-4550, custserv@rowman.com, http://www.scarecrowpress.com. Ed., Pub. Mr. Edward Kurdyla TEL 301-459-3366 ext 5604. R&P Clare Cox TEL 212-529-3888 ext 308. **Subscr. to:** Scarecrow Subscriptions Dept., 15200 NBN Way, Blue Ridge Summit, PA 17214. TEL 717-794-3800, FAX 717-794-3803, tmiller@rowman.com.

780.01 DEU
MUSIC MANUSCRIPTS AFTER 1600/MANUSCRITS MUSICAUX APRES 1600/MUSIKHANDSCHRIFTEN NACH 1600. Text in English, French, German. a. EUR 998 (effective 2009). **Document type:** *Catalog, Abstract/Index.*
Media: CD-ROM.
Published by: De Gruyter Saur (Subsidiary of: Walter de Gruyter GmbH & Co. KG), Mies-van-der-Rohe-Str 1, Munich, 80807, Germany. TEL 49-89-769020, FAX 49-89-76902150, info@degruyter.com.

780 USA ISSN 0736-7740
MUSIC REFERENCE COLLECTION. Text in English. 1983. irreg., latest 2005. price varies. back issues avail. **Document type:** *Monographic series, Academic/Scholarly.*
—BLDSC (5990.401500), IE, Ingenta.
Published by: Greenwood Publishing Group Inc. (Subsidiary of: A B C - C L I O), 88 Post Rd W, PO Box 5007, Westport, CT 06881. TEL 203-226-3571, 800-225-5800, FAX 877-231-6980, sales@greenwood.com, http://www.greenwood.com. Eds. Adrienne Block, Donald Hixon.

MUSIC TECHNOLOGY BUYER'S GUIDE. *see* MUSIC

016.780 RUS ISSN 0208-3086
MUZYKA; referativno-bibliograficheskaya informatsiya. Text in Russian. 1974. bi-m. USD 197 foreign (effective 2010). **Document type:** *Bibliography.* **Description:** Includes abstracts of Russian and foreign publications on different issues in music.
Indexed: RASB.
—East View.
Published by: (Rossiiskaya Gosudarstvennaya Biblioteka/Russian State Library), Idatel'stvo Rossiiskoi Gosudarstvennoi Biblioteki Pashkov Dom/Pashkov Dom, Russian State Library Publishing House, Vozdizhenka 3/5, Moscow, 101000, Russian Federation. TEL 7-495-6955953, FAX 7-495-6955953, pashkov_dom@rsl.ru, http://www.rsl.ru/pub.asp. Ed. Tamara Lapteva. **Dist. by:** East View Information Services, 10601 Wayzata Blvd, Minneapolis, MN 55305. TEL 952-252-1201, 800-477-1005, FAX 952-252-1202, info@eastview.com, http://www.eastview.com.

016.78026 NOR
ML120.N6
NORSK MUSIKKFORTEGNELSE. NOTETRYKK/NORWEGIAN NATIONAL BIBLIOGRAPHY OF PRINTED MUSIC. Text in Norwegian. a. free. **Document type:** *Bibliography.*
Formerly (until 1993): Norsk Bokfortegnelse. Musiktrykk (0800-9805)
Media: Online - full text.
Indexed: RASB.
Published by: Nasjonalbiblioteket, Samlinger og Bibliografiske Tjenester/National Library of Norway, Bibliographic Services Department, PO Box 2674, Solli, Oslo, 0203, Norway. TEL 47-23-27-61-19, FAX 47-23-27-60-50.

016.78 RUS ISSN 0130-7746
NOTNAYA LETOPIS'. Text in Russian. 1931. q. RUR 2,266 domestic; USD 70 foreign (effective 2004). bibl. quarterly index. 80 p./no.; back issues avail. **Document type:** *Bibliography.* **Description:** Informs readers about musical compositions published in books and magazines in Russia.
Media: Large Type. **Related titles:** Diskette ed.; E-mail ed.; Microfiche ed.: (from EVP); Online - full text ed.
Indexed: RASB.
—East View.
Published by: Rossiiskaya Knizhnaya Palata/Book Chamber International, Ostozhenka 4, Moscow, 119034, Russian Federation. TEL 7-095-2911278, FAX 7-095-2919630, bookch@postman.ru. Ed. E Belaeva. Circ: 500.

780 016 JPN
ONGAKU BUNKEN MOKUROKU. Text in Japanese. 1973. a. JPY 3,150 (effective 2001). adv. bk.rev. **Document type:** *Bibliography.* **Description:** Bibliography of music literature in Japan.
Former titles (until 1993, no.21): Ongaku Bunken Yoshi Mokuroku; Nihon Ongaku Bunken Yoshi Mokuroku
Published by: R I L M National Committee of Japan, Musashino Music College, 1-13-1 Hazawa, Nerima-ku, Tokyo, 176-0003, Japan. TEL 81-3-3991-3018, FAX 81-3-3991-3018. Ed. Toshiko Sekine. Adv. contact Ryuichi Higuchi. Circ: 12,000.

789.91 USA
PHONOLOG REPORTER; all-in-one-reporter. Text in English. 1948. w. looseleaf. USD 486. **Description:** Lists pre-recorded music in all formats. Indexed by album, artist, and song title.
Related titles: CD-ROM ed.; Diskette ed.
Published by: Trade Service Corporation, 15445 Innovation Dr., San Diego, CA 92128-3432. TEL 619-457-5920, FAX 619-457-1320. Ed. Bonnie J Dudley.

016.78 USA
RILM ABSTRACTS OF MUSIC LITERATURE. (Repertoire International de Litterature Musicale) Text in English. base vol. plus d. updates. reprints avail. **Document type:** *Database, Abstract/Index.* **Description:** Provides broad, international coverage and concise abstracts from the scholarly literature of music, as well as from other related fields.
Media: Online - full text. **Related titles:** ◆ CD-ROM ed.: M U S E, MUsic SEarch. ISSN 1054-2639.
Published by: R I L M Abstracts, City University of New York, 365 Fifth Ave, New York, NY 10016-4309. TEL 212-817-1990, FAX 212-817-1569, rilm@rilm.org. Circ: 1,500 (controlled). **Co-sponsors:** International Musicological Society; International Association of Music Libraries, Archives and Documentation Centres (U.S. Branch).

780 011 USA
ML156.4.J3
SCHWANN C D REVIEW DIGEST - JAZZ, POPULAR, ETC.; the international indexing service - a guide with excerpts to English language reviews of all music recorded on compact and video laser discs. Text in English. 1983-199?; resumed. irreg. back issues avail. **Document type:** *Abstract/Index.*
Formerly: C D Review Digest - Jazz, Popular, Etc. (1045-0122); Which superseded in part (in 1988): C D Review Digest (0890-0213)
Published by: Peri Press (Subsidiary of: Schwann Publications), 20 Shad Way, Voorheesville, NY 12186-4940. TEL 518-765-3163, 800-513-5898, FAX 518-765-3158. Ed. Janet Grimes.

U.S. LIBRARY OF CONGRESS. CATALOGING FILES - MUSIC. *see* BIBLIOGRAPHIES

MUSIC—Computer Applications

see also COMPUTERS—Computer Music

780 USA
A T M I INTERNATIONAL NEWSLETTER. Text in English. 1977. q. USD 30 domestic; USD 40 foreign; includes Technology Directory. bk.rev. **Document type:** *Newsletter.*
Former titles: Association for Technology in Music Instruction Newsletter; National Consortium for Computer-Based Music Instruction. Newsletter
Published by: Association for Technology in Music Instruction, c/o Peter R Webster, Pres, School of Music, Northwestern University, Evanston, IL 60208. TEL 847-491-5740. Ed. Barbara Murphy. Circ: 325.

780 USA
A T M I TECHNOLOGY DIRECTORY. Text in English. a. USD 30; USD 40 foreign; includes Newsletter. bk.rev. **Document type:** *Directory.* **Description:** Includes listings and information about hardware, software, video discs, and other materials related to technology-based music instruction.
Published by: Association for Technology in Music Instruction, c/o Peter R Webster, Pres, School of Music, Northwestern University, Evanston, IL 60208. TEL 847-491-5740.

780 USA
AFTERTOUCH; new music discoveries. Text in English. 1991. q. free (effective 2005). adv. back issues avail. **Document type:** *Magazine, Consumer.* **Description:** Features write-ups about new music and video art and the artists. Includes articles, feature columns, resource material, a directory, reviews and interviews, and a unique dialogue between artists and listeners.
Published by: Creative Musicians Coalition, Music Discovery Network, PO Box 6205, Peoria, IL 61601-6205. TEL 309-685-4843, 800-882-4262, FAX 309-685-4879, aimcmc@aol.com. Ed., Pub., Adv. contact Ronald Wallace. R&P Ronand Wallace. Circ: 7,000.

786.76 USA
B U G MAGAZINE; the magazine for the electronic musician. (Boss Users Group) Text in English. s-a. USD 3 newsstand/cover (effective 2005). adv. illus. **Document type:** *Magazine, Consumer.* **Description:** News, product reviews, information and technical tips for musicians using Roland equipment.
Formerly: Roland Users Group Magazine
Published by: Roland Corporation U S, 5100 S Eastern Ave, Los Angeles, CA 90091. TEL 323-890-3700, FAX 323-890-3780, http://www.rolandus.com. Ed., R&P Lachlan Westfall. Pub. Dennis Houlihan.

C D AUSTRIA. (Compact Disc) *see* COMPUTERS—Computer Graphics

786.76 620.2 USA ISSN 0148-9267
ML1 CODEN: CMUJDY
➤ **COMPUTER MUSIC JOURNAL.** Abbreviated title: C M J. Text in English. 1977. q. USD 328 combined subscription in US & Canada to institutions (print & online eds.); USD 82 per issue in US & Canada to institutions (effective 2012). adv. bk.rev. illus. back issues avail.; reprints avail. **Document type:** *Journal, Academic/Scholarly.* **Description:** Offers a resource for musicians, composers, scientists, engineers and computer enthusiasts interested in contemporary and electronic music and computer-generated sound.
Related titles: CD-ROM ed.: USD 50 per issue in US & Canada to institutions (effective 2012); Microfilm ed.: (from PQC); Online - full text ed.: ISSN 1531-5169. USD 283 in US & Canada to institutions (effective 2012).
Indexed: A01, A02, A03, A08, A20, A22, A26, A27, A28, APA, ASCA, AcoustA, ArtHuCI, BrCerAb, C&ISA, C10, C23, CA, CA/WCA, CIA, CMCI, CPEI, CerAb, CivEngAb, CompD, CompLI, CompR, CorrAb, CurCont, DIP, E&CAJ, E01, E08, E11, EEA, EMA, ESPM, EngInd, EnvEAb, G01, G08, H15, I05, IBR, IBZ, IIMP, ISR, Inspec, L04, LAMP, LISTA, M&TEA, M09, M11, MAG, MBF, METADEX, MusicInd, P02, P10, P48, P49, P53, P54, PCI, PQC, RASB, RILM, S01, S09, SCI, SCOPUS, SolStAb, T02, T04, W07, WAA.
—BLDSC (3394.113000), AskIEEE, IE, Infotrieve, Linda Hall. **CCC.**
Published by: (Computer Music Journal), M I T Press, 55 Hayward St, Cambridge, MA 02142. TEL 617-253-2889, FAX 617-577-1545, journals-cs@mit.edu, http://mitpress.mit.edu. Ed. Douglas Keislar.

780 USA ISSN 1057-9478
ML73
COMPUTING IN MUSICOLOGY; an international directory of applications. Text in English. 1985. biennial. USD 35 per issue (effective 2010). back issues avail. **Document type:** *Directory, Trade.* **Description:** Covers applications involving both textual and musical information.
Formerly (until 1989): Directory of Computer Assisted Research in Musicology
Related titles: Online - full text ed.
Indexed: A01, CA, IIMP, M11, MusicInd, RILM, T02.
Published by: Center for Computer Assisted Research in the Humanities, Braun Music Ctr, Stanford No. 129, 541 Lasuen Mall, Stanford University, Stanford, CA 94305. TEL 650-725-9240, FAX 650-725-9290, ccarh@ccrma.stanford.edu.

DIGITAL LIFESTYLE MAGAZIN; basics for digital lifestyle. *see* COMMUNICATIONS—Television And Cable

780 ITA ISSN 1824-4173
DIGITAL MUSIC. Text in Italian. 2004. m. adv. **Document type:** *Magazine, Consumer.*
Published by: Edizioni Master SpA, Contrada Lecco 64, Zona Industriale, Roges di Rende, CS 87036, Italy. TEL 39-0984-831900, FAX 39-0984-8319225, contact@edmaster.it.

DIGITALSTUFF. *see* COMMUNICATIONS—Telephone And Telegraph

780 DEU
▼ **EINSNULL**; Das Magazin fuer digitalen Musikgenuss. Text in German. 2009. bi-m. EUR 4.80 newsstand/cover (effective 2011). adv. **Document type:** *Magazine, Consumer.*
Published by: Michael E. Brieden Verlag GmbH, Gartroper Str 42, Duisburg, 47138, Germany. TEL 49-203-42920, FAX 49-203-4292149, info@brieden.de, http://www.brieden.de. Ed. Christian Rechenbach.

781.64 GBR ISSN 0967-0378
FUTURE MUSIC; technique and technology for making music. Text in English. 1992. 13/yr. GBP 59.95 domestic; GBP 65 in Europe; GBP 85 elsewhere; GBP 5.99 newsstand/cover (effective 2010). adv. back issues avail. **Document type:** *Magazine, Consumer.* **Description:** Contains news, reviews of music equipment, and profiles of musicians. Covers all aspects of computer music.
Related titles: Online - full text ed.
—**CCC.**
Published by: Future Publishing Ltd., Beauford Ct, 30 Monmouth St, Bath, Avon BA1 2BW, United Kingdom. TEL 44-1225-442244, FAX 44-1225-446019, customerservice@subscription.co.uk, http://www.futureplc.com. **Subscr. to:** Tower House, Sovereign Park, Market Harborough, Leicestershire LE16 9EF, United Kingdom. TEL 44-844-8481602, FAX 44-1858-438795, future@subscription.co.uk.

INTERFACE (AMSTERDAM, 1995). *see* SOUND RECORDING AND REPRODUCTION

780 SWE
IPLAY; for dig som alskar ipod. Text in Swedish. 3/yr. adv. **Document type:** *Magazine, Consumer.*
Published by: I D G AB (Subsidiary of: I D G Communications Inc.), Karlbergsvaegen 77-81, Stockholm, 10678, Sweden. TEL 46-8-4536000, FAX 46-8-4536005, kundservice@idg.se, http://www.idg.se. Ed. Andreas Leijon TEL 47-8-4536248. Circ: 20,000 (paid and controlled).

KEYS; Magazin fur Musik und Computer. *see* MUSIC

780 GRC
MOUSIKI. Text in Greek. m. USD 40. music rev. back issues avail.
Published by: Epsilon, 176 Septembriou 3, Athens, 112 51, Greece. TEL 30-1-8640845, FAX 30-1-8643533. Ed. Nick Grammatikas.

780 BRA
MP3 MAGAZINE. Text in Portuguese. m. BRL 9.90 newsstand/cover (effective 2006). adv. **Document type:** *Magazine, Consumer.*
Published by: Editora Escala Ltda., Av Prof Ida Kolb, 551, Casa Verde, Sao Paulo, 02518-000, Brazil. TEL 55-11-38552100, FAX 55-11-38579643, escala@escala.com.br, http://www.escala.com.br. Ed. Alessandro Treguer.

MULTIMEDIA. *see* COMMUNICATIONS—Television And Cable

780 DEU
MUSIK UND NEUE TECHNOLOGIE. Text in German. 1999. irreg., latest vol.3, 2000. price varies. **Document type:** *Monographic series, Academic/Scholarly.*
Published by: V & R Unipress GmbH (Subsidiary of: Vandenhoeck und Ruprecht), Robert-Bosch-Breite 6, Goettingen, 37079, Germany. TEL 49-551-5084303, FAX 49-551-5084333, info@vr-unipress.de, http://www.v-r.de/en/publisher/unipress. Ed. Bernd Enders.

ORGANISED SOUND; an international journal of music and technology. *see* MUSIC

780 USA

PLAYLIST; digital music for PC & Mac. Text in English. 2004 (Aug.). irreg. software rev.; music rev. **Document type:** *Magazine, Consumer.* **Description:** Provides a guide to digital music for PC and Mac with all the digital lifestyle essentials, including reviews of the latest digital music products and how-to articles.

Published by: Mac Publishing, L.L.C. (Subsidiary of: I D G Communications Inc.), 501 Second St, 5th Fl, San Francisco, CA 94107. TEL 415-243-0505, FAX 415-243-3544, customer_service@macworld.com, http://www.macworld.com.

780 USA

SIREN'S SONG. Text in English. 2003. w. free. **Document type:** *Magazine, Consumer.* **Description:** Showcases the latest unsigned, independent and MP3-savvy musicians online.

Media: Online - full content.

MYSTERY AND DETECTIVE

see LITERATURE—Mystery And Detective

M

▼ **new title** ➤ **refereed** ♦ **full entry avail.**

NATIVE AMERICAN STUDIES

see also HISTORY—History Of North And South America

970.1 USA
A I C H COMMUNITY BULLETIN. Text in English. 1969. q. price varies. **Document type:** *Bulletin.*
Published by: American Indian Community House, 708 Broadway, Fl 8, New York, NY 10003-9508. TEL 212-598-0100, FAX 212-598-4909. Ed., R&P Carrese P Gullo.

970.1 USA
A I S NEWSLETTER. (American Indian Society) Text in English. 1966. m. looseleaf. USD 8 (effective 1999). adv. bk.rev. back issues avail. **Document type:** *Newsletter.* **Description:** Reports on happenings in the nation's capitol which affect Native Americans or involve the local community.
Published by: American Indian Society of Washington D.C., PO Box 6431, Falls Church, VA 22040-6531. TEL 804-448-3707, FAX 804-448-2493. Ed. Mitchell Bush. Circ: 650 (controlled).

ABORIGINAL POLICING UPDATE. *see* CRIMINOLOGY AND LAW ENFORCEMENT

ALASKA NATIVE LANGUAGE CENTER. RESEARCH PAPERS. *see* LINGUISTICS

ALBERTA SWEETGRASS. *see* ETHNIC INTERESTS

970.1 CAN
ALLIANCE AUTOCHTONE DU QUEBEC. Text in English. m.
Published by: Native Alliance of Quebec, 21 Brodeur, Hull, PQ J8Y 2P6, Canada. TEL 819-770-7763, FAX 819-770-6070.

970 USA ISSN 1528-0640
E51
AMERICAN INDIAN. Text in English. 2000. q. free to members (effective 2010). adv. **Document type:** *Magazine, Academic/Scholarly.* **Description:** Features diverse articles such as American Indian firefighting traditions, the enduring presence of Native peoples in the U.S. military, stunning Native travel destinations, and the modern-day challenges facing Native communities in western Mexico.
Indexed: AICP, BNNA, T02.
Published by: National Museum of the American Indian (Subsidiary of: Smithsonian Institution), 4220 Silver Hill Rd, Suitland, MD 20746. TEL 800-242-6624.

305.897 USA ISSN 1533-7731
➤ **AMERICAN INDIAN AND ALASKA NATIVE MENTAL HEALTH RESEARCH (ONLINE).** Text in English. 1978 (vol.8, no.2). irreg. free (effective 2010). back issues avail. **Document type:** *Journal, Academic/Scholarly.* **Description:** Contains empirical research, program evaluations, case studies, unpublished dissertations, and other articles in the behavioral, social, and health sciences which clearly relate to the mental health status of American Indians and Alaska Natives.
Media: Online - full text.
Indexed: A01, A03, A08, A26, BNNA, CA, E-psyche, E03, E07, EMBASE, ENW, ERI, ERIC, ExcerpMed, IndMed, MEDLINE, P04, P25, P30, P43, P48, PQC, R10, Reac, S02, S03, SCOPUS, T02.
—CCC.
Published by: National Center for American Indian Mental Health Research, Nighthorse Campbell Native Health Bldg, 13055 E 17th Ave, Aurora, CO 80045. TEL 303-724-1414, FAX 303-724-1474, http://aianp.uchsc.edu/ncaianmhr/ncaianmhr_index.htm. Ed. Spero M Manson.

➤ **AMERICAN INDIAN ART MAGAZINE.** *see* ART

➤ **AMERICAN INDIAN BASKETRY AND OTHER NATIVE ARTS.** *see* ARTS AND HANDICRAFTS

016.97000497 USA
AMERICAN INDIAN BIBLIOGRAPHIC SERIES. Text in English. 1977. a. reprints avail. **Document type:** *Bibliography.*
Published by: University of California, Los Angeles, American Indian Studies Center, 3220 Campbell Hall, PO Box 951548, Los Angeles, CA 90095. TEL 310-825-7514, FAX 310-206-7060, aisc@ucla.edu. Ed. Duane Champagne. Circ: 500.

970.1 USA ISSN 0161-6463
E75
➤ **AMERICAN INDIAN CULTURE AND RESEARCH JOURNAL.** Abbreviated title: A I C R J. Text in English. 1971. q. USD 40 domestic to individuals; USD 245 domestic to institutions; USD 265 foreign to institutions; USD 195 combined subscription to individuals (print & online eds.) (effective 2010). adv. bk.rev. illus. cum.index: 1977-1982. back issues avail.; reprints avail. **Document type:** *Journal, Academic/ Scholarly.* **Description:** Provides an interdisciplinary look at the indigenous people of North America.
Formerly (until 1974): American Indian Culture Center. Journal
Related titles: Microfilm ed.; Online - full text ed.
Indexed: A01, A02, A03, A08, A20, A22, A25, A26, A33, AICP, ASCA, AbAn, AltPI, AmH&L, AmHI, AnthLit, ArtHuCI, B04, B14, BNNA, BRD, BRI, BibLing, CA, CBRI, CurCont, DIP, E07, E08, ERIC, FR, G08, H07, H08, HAb, HistAb, HumInd, I05, IBR, IBZ, L&LBA, M08, MLA-IB, P02, P10, P27, P30, P42, P48, P53, P54, PAIS, PCI, PQC, PSA, RILM, S02, S03, S08, S09, SCOPUS, SOPODA, SRRA, SSA, SSAI, SSAb, SSI, SociolAb, T02, W01, W02, W03, W05, W07, W09.
—BLDSC (0819.650000), CIS, IE, Infotrieve, Ingenta, INIST. **CCC.**
Published by: University of California, Los Angeles, American Indian Studies Center, 3220 Campbell Hall, PO Box 951548, Los Angeles, CA 90095. TEL 310-825-7315, FAX 310-206-7060, aisc@ucla.edu, http://www.aisc.ucla.edu/. Adv. contact Christine Dunn. B&W page USD 150. Circ: 1,000.

970.1 USA
AMERICAN INDIAN DEFENSE NEWS. Text in English. 1984. q. USD 10 for 6 issues; USD 1 newsstand/cover. adv. bk.rev. **Document type:** *Newsletter.*
Published by: Big Chief International, PO Box 48193, Wichita, KS 67201-8193. TEL 316-665-3614. Ed. M. L. Webber. Circ: 2,000.

970.1 USA
AMERICAN INDIAN HORSE NEWS. Text in English. 1979. q. USD 15 (effective 2000). adv. bk.rev. **Document type:** *Newsletter.*
Published by: American Indian Horse Registry, 9028 State Park Rd, Lockhart, TX 78644. TEL 512-398-6642. Ed., R&P, Adv. contact Nanci Falley. Circ: 500.

AMERICAN INDIAN LAW REVIEW. *see* LAW

027.97 USA ISSN 2152-3525
Z711.8
AMERICAN INDIAN LIBRARY ASSOCIATION. NEWSLETTER. Abbreviated title: A I L A Newsletter. Text in English. 1976. s-a. free to members (effective 2010). adv. bk.rev. illus. back issues avail.; reprints avail. **Document type:** *Newsletter, Consumer.* **Description:** Covers American Indian interests with news, resources and information of importance to American Indian librarians.
Formerly (until 2009): American Indian Libraries Newsletter (0193-8207)
Published by: American Indian Library Association, c/o Kelly Webster, Membership Coordinator, 12 Highfield Rd, 2, Roslindale, MA 02131. ailawebsite@gmail.com. Ed., Adv. contact Mary Johnson.

AMERICAN INDIAN LITERATURE AND CRITICAL STUDIES SERIES. *see* LITERATURE

970.1 USA ISSN 0095-182X
E75 CODEN: AIQUEW
➤ **AMERICAN INDIAN QUARTERLY.** Text in English. 1974. q. USD 189 combined subscription domestic to institutions (print & online eds.); USD 221 combined subscription foreign to institutions (print & online eds.) (effective 2012). adv. bk.rev. bibl.; abstr.; illus. Index. back issues avail.; reprint service avail. from PSC. **Document type:** *Journal, Academic/Scholarly.* **Description:** Brings out work that contributes to the development of American Indian studies as a field and to the sovereignty and continuance of American Indian nations and cultures.
Related titles: Microform ed.: (from PQC); Online - full text ed.: ISSN 1534-1828. USD 135 to institutions (effective 2012).
Indexed: A01, A02, A03, A08, A21, A22, A25, A26, A33, AFS, AICP, AbAn, AltPI, AmH&L, AmHI, AnthLit, B04, B14, BNNA, BRD, BibLing, C12, CA, CBRI, ChLitAb, DIP, E01, E03, E07, E08, ENW, ERI, ERIC, G05, G06, G07, G08, H05, H07, H08, H09, H10, HAb, HistAb, HumInd, I05, I06, I07, IBR, IBZ, L&LBA, L05, L06, M01, M02, M06, M08, MASUSE, MLA, MLA-IB, P02, P10, P13, P18, P30, P34, P48, P53, P54, PAIS, PCI, PQC, R05, RI-1, RI-2, RILM, S02, S03, S08, S09, S23, SCOPUS, SD, SOPODA, SociolAb, T02, W03, W04, W05, W09.
—BLDSC (0819.800000), CIS, IE, Infotrieve, Ingenta. **CCC.**
Published by: University of Nebraska Press, 1111 Lincoln Mall, Lincoln, NE 68588. TEL 402-472-3581, FAX 402-472-6214, journals@unlnotes.unl.edu, pressmail@unl.edu. Ed. Amanda J Cobb-Greetham. Adv. contact Joyce Gettman TEL 402-472-8330. Circ: 600. **Subscr. to:** PO Box 84555, Lincoln, NE 68501. TEL 402-472-8536, 800-848-6224, FAX 800-272-6817.

970.1 USA
E75
AMERICAN INDIAN REPORT (ONLINE). Text in English. 1985. m. free (effective 2008). adv. bk.rev. 30 p./no. 3 cols./p.; back issues avail.; reprints avail. **Document type:** *Magazine, Consumer.* **Description:** Covers news, events, and Federal Register announcements affecting the Indian community.
Formerly (until May 2008): American Indian Report (Print) (0894-4040)
Indexed: BNNA, T02.
—CIS.
Published by: Falmouth Institute, Inc., 3702 Pender Dr, Ste 300, Fairfax, VA 22030-6066. TEL 703-352-2250, FAX 703-352-2323. Ed., Pub. Marguerite Carroll.

970.1 USA ISSN 1058-563X
AMERICAN INDIAN STUDIES. Text in English. 1993. irreg., latest vol.17, 2008. price varies. **Document type:** *Monographic series, Academic/ Scholarly.* **Description:** Covers all aspects of American Indian history and culture, with an emphasis on contemporary ideas and issues.
Indexed: BNNA.
Published by: Peter Lang Publishing, Inc. (Subsidiary of: Peter Lang Publishing Group), 29 Broadway, New York, NY 10006. TEL 212-647-7700, 212-647-7706, 800-770-5264, FAX 212-647-7707, customerservice@plang.com.

917.106 CAN ISSN 1486-9926
KE7703.9
ANNOTATED INDIAN ACT AND ABORIGINAL CONSTITUTIONAL PROVISIONS. Text in English. 1999. a. CAD 70, USD 59.32 per issue (effective 2005).
Formerly (until 1998): Annotated Indian Act (1197-852X)
Published by: Carswell (Subsidiary of: Thomson Reuters Corp.), One Corporate Plz, 2075 Kennedy Rd, Toronto, ON M1T 3V4, Canada. TEL 416-609-8000, 800-387-5164, FAX 416-298-5094, carswell.customerrelations@thomson.com, http://www.carswell.com.

APPALACHIAN VOICE. *see* HISTORY—History Of North And South America

ASSOCIATION OF AMERICAN INDIAN PHYSICIANS NEWSLETTER. *see* MEDICAL SCIENCES

970.1 371.82 CAN ISSN 0823-9231
AWASIS JOURNAL. Text in English. 1981. irreg. CAD 25 (effective 2000). **Document type:** *Journal, Academic/Scholarly.*
Published by: (Indian and Metis Education Council), Saskatchewan Teachers' Federation, 2317 Arlington Ave., Saskatoon, SK S7J 2H8, Canada. stf@stf.sk.ca.

970.1 371.82997 CAN
AWASIS NEWSLETTER. Text in English. irreg. CAD 25. **Document type:** *Newsletter.*
Published by: (Indian and Native Education Council), Saskatchewan Teachers' Federation, 2317 Arlington Ave., Saskatoon, SK S7J 2H8, Canada. stf@stf.sk.ca.

305.897 DEU
BIRKENRINDE. Text in German. 1999. irreg. **Document type:** *Newsletter, Consumer.*
Published by: Ametas Verlag, Postfach 166, Hamburg, 22401, Germany. TEL 49-40-5276452, renko@freenet.de, http://freenet-homepage.de/niqel/ametas/ametas.htm#impressum. Eds. Henry Kammler, Rene Senenko.

BUILDING ABORIGINAL AND NORTHERN ECONOMIES/ BATISSEURS DE L'ECONOMIE AUTOCHTONE ET DU NORD. *see* BUSINESS AND ECONOMICS

305.897 330 USA
BUSINESS ALERT (FREDERICKSBURG). Text in English. 1985. bi-m. USD 12 (effective 2001); free to native Americans. illus. **Description:** Contains information on topics from marketing to trust fund management and other latest economic news that affect Indian tribes and individuals.
Published by: First Nations Development Institute, The Stores Bldg, 11917 Main St, Fredericksburg, VA 22408. TEL 540-371-5615, FAX 540-371-3505, http://www.firstnations.org. Ed. Jerry Reynolds. Circ: 2,000.

970.1 USA
C E R A NEWS; many cultures, one people, one law. Text in English. m. USD 35 membership (effective 2002).
Published by: Citizens Equal Rights Alliance, P O Box 93, Roman, MT 59864. TEL 605-374-5836, feedback@citizensalliance.org, http://www.citizensalliance.org.

970.1 CAN ISSN 1704-927X
E92
CANADA. PARLIAMENT. HOUSE OF COMMONS. STANDING COMMITTEE ON ABORIGINAL AFFAIRS, NORTHERN DEVELOPMENT AND NATURAL RESOURCES. MINUTES OF PROCEEDINGS. Text in English. 1986. irreg.
Former titles (until 2001): Canada. Standing Committee on Aboriginal Affairs and Northern Development. Minutes of Proceedings (1204-6094); (until 1995): Canada. Standing Committee on Aboriginal Affairs and Northern Development. Minutes of Proceedings and Evidence (1200-0531); (until 1994): Canada. Standing Committee on Aboriginal Affairs. Proceedings and Evidence. Minutes (0844-8582); (until 1989): Canada. Standing Committee on Aboriginal Affairs and Northern Development. Minutes of Proceedings and Evidence (0833-367X); (until 1986): Canada. Standing Committee on Indian Affairs and Northern Development. Minutes of Proceedings and Evidence (0576-3355)
Published by: Supply and Services Canada, Printing and Publishing, 270 Albert St, Ottawa, ON K1A 0S9, Canada.

CANADIAN NATIVE LAW REPORTER. *see* LAW

305.897 USA ISSN 1067-5639
THE CIRCLE; Native American news and arts. Text in English. 1979. m. USD 35 domestic; USD 40 foreign (effective 2005). adv. bk.rev.; film rev.; music rev. 24 p./no.; back issues avail. **Document type:** *Newspaper, Consumer.*
Related titles: Online - full content ed.; Online - full text ed.
Indexed: ENW.
Published by: The Circle, 3355 36th Avenue S, Minneapolis, MN 55406. TEL 612-722-3686, FAX 612-722-3773. Pub. Catherine Whipple. adv.: page USD 1,035. Circ: 15,000 (paid).

970.1 USA ISSN 0069-4304
CIVILIZATION OF THE AMERICAN INDIAN. Text in English. 1932. irreg., latest vol.268, 2010. price varies. back issues avail. **Document type:** *Monographic series, Academic/Scholarly.*
Published by: University of Oklahoma Press, 2800 Venture Dr, Norman, OK 73069. TEL 405-325-2000, 800-627-7377, FAX 405-364-5798, 800-735-0476, kbenson@ou.edu.

305.897 USA
CONFEDERATED UMATILLA JOURNAL. Abbreviated title: C U J. Text in English. 1975. m. USD 15 (effective 2010). adv. back issues avail. **Document type:** *Newspaper, Consumer.* **Description:** Covers news and events of interest to the Umatilla Tribes.
Former titles (until 1993): C T U I R News; (until 1992): Confederated Umatilla Journal
Related titles: Online - full text ed.: free (effective 2010).
Published by: Confederated Tribes of the Umatilla Indian Reservations, PO Box 638, Pendleton, OR 07801. TEL 541-966-2034, FAX 541-966-2043, info@ctuir.com. Ed. Wil Phinney. Pub. Debra Croswell. adv.: page USD 229.50.

333.72 USA
COUNTRY ROAD CHRONICLES. Text in English. 1993. m. USD 27 domestic (effective 2001). adv. bk.rev.; music rev.; video rev. 24 p./no.; back issues avail. **Document type:** *Newspaper, Consumer.* **Description:** Dedicated to Native American Culture. Deals with Mother Earth news, about living with her animals, environment, universe and her people.
Formerly: Country Road Gazette
Indexed: ENW.
Published by: Van Raper Productions, 101 Meadow Ridge Ct, Dingmans Ferry, PA 18328. TEL 570-828-1778, FAX 570-828-7959. Ed., Pub. Elaine V Raper. Adv. contact Lenny Raper. B&W page USD 963.97; trim 15 x 11.5. Circ: 27,135 (paid).

305.897 DEU ISSN 0939-4362
COYOTE. Text in German. 1990. q. EUR 22 domestic; EUR 24 in Europe; EUR 4.50 newsstand/cover (effective 2008). adv. bk.rev.; film rev.; music rev. 48 p./no.; back issues avail. **Document type:** *Magazine, Consumer.* **Description:** Covers current and historical aspects and situations of Native Americans.
Published by: Aktionsgruppe Indianer & Menschenrechte, Frohschammerstr 14, Munich, 80807, Germany. TEL 49-89-35651836, FAX 49-89-35651837, post@aktionsgruppe.de, http://www.aktionsgruppe.de.

970.1 CAN ISSN 0046-1296
EDMONTON NATIVE NEWS. Text in English. 1963. bi-m. membership. **Document type:** *Newsletter.* **Description:** Contains items of local interest and information on programs and services provided.
Published by: Canadian Native Friendship Centre, 11205 101st St, Edmonton, AB T5G 2A4, Canada. TEL 403-479-1999. Ed. Val Kaufman. Circ: 700.

305.89712 CAN ISSN 0318-7551
E99.E8
ESKIMO. Text in English. 1944. s-a. CAD 6 (effective 2000). bk.rev. back issues avail. **Document type:** *Monographic series, Academic/ Scholarly.* **Description:** Information about Inuit culture and religious activities.
Related titles: ◆ French ed.: Eskimo. Edition Francaise. ISSN 0318-756X.
Indexed: A33, AICP.
—BLDSC (3811.230000).
Published by: Diocese of Churchill Hudson Bay, P O Box 10, Churchill, MB R0B 0E0, Canada. TEL 204-675-2252, FAX 204-675-2140. Ed. Lorraine Brandson. Circ: 4,000.

305.89712 CAN ISSN 0318-756X
E99.E7
ESKIMO. EDITION FRANCAISE. Text in French. 1944. s-a.
Related titles: ◆ English ed.: Eskimo. ISSN 0318-7551.
Published by: Diocese of Churchill Hudson Bay, P O Box 10, Churchill, MB R0B 0E0, Canada.

970.1 AUT ISSN 0238-1486
CODEN: JAAHEO

➤ **EUROPEAN REVIEW OF NATIVE AMERICAN STUDIES.** Text in English. 1987. s-a. EUR 20.45, USD 29 (effective 2004). adv. bk.rev. illus. 65 p./no. 3 cols./p.; back issues avail.; reprints avail. **Document type:** *Journal, Academic/Scholarly.*
Indexed: AICP, AmH&L, AnthLit, BNNA, BibLing, CA, DIP, HistAb, IBR, IBZ, MLA-IB, RILM, T02.
Address: c/o Christian Feest, Ed., Linzerstr. 281/1/17, Vienna, 140, Austria. TEL 43-1-9442317, FAX 43-1-52524230, cff.ssk@t-online.de. Ed. Christian Feest. Circ: 600.

➤ **FOREST VOICE.** *see* ENVIRONMENTAL STUDIES

➤ **GILCREASE.** *see* MUSEUMS AND ART GALLERIES

970.1 USA ISSN 0046-8967
E77
INDIAN AFFAIRS. Text in English. 1949. 3/yr. USD 10. bk.rev. reprints avail. **Document type:** *Newsletter.*
Related titles: Microform ed.: 1949 (from PQC).
Indexed: BNNA, CA, T02.
Published by: Association on American Indian Affairs, Inc., Executive Office, 966 Hungerford Dr, Suite 12-B, Rockville, MD 20850. TEL 240-314-7155, FAX 240-314-7159, aaia@sbtc.net, general.aaia@verizon.net, http://www.indian-affairs.org/index.htm. Ed. Merrill O'Connor. Circ: 40,000.

970.1 USA
INDIAN BUSINESS AND MANAGEMENT. Text in English. 1990. q. free. adv. illus. **Document type:** *Journal, Trade.*
Published by: National Center for American Indian Enterprise Development, 953 E Juanita Ave, Mesa, AZ 85204. TEL 602-545-1298, FAX 602-545-4208. Ed. Kenneth E Robbins.

917.106 CAN ISSN 1195-3586
KE7718.A49
INDIAN CLAIMS COMMISSION PROCEEDINGS. Text in English. 1994. irreg.
Published by: Indian Claims Commission, Box 1750, Station B, Ottawa, ON K1P 1A2, Canada. TEL 613-943-2737, FAX 613-943-0157, http://www.indianclaims.ca.

970.1 USA ISSN 1526-8985
E75
INDIAN CRUSADER. Text in English. 1954. q. USD 10 (effective 2000 - 2001). **Document type:** *Newsletter.* **Description:** Chronicles the outreach and relief programs to the reservation Indian by their non-profit organization.
Published by: American Indian Liberation Crusade, Inc., 4009 Halldale Ave, Los Angeles, CA 90062. TEL 323-299-1810. Ed. Basil M Gaynor Jr. R&P Basil Gaynor. Circ: 2,000 (controlled).

INDIAN LAW REPORTER. *see* LAW

970.1 USA
INSTITUTE FOR AMERICAN INDIAN STUDIES. OCCASIONAL PAPER AND BOOKS. Text in English. 1974. irreg. adv. **Document type:** *Newsletter, Consumer.*
Formerly: American Indian Archaeological Institute. Occasional Paper
Published by: Institute for American Indian Studies, 38 Curtis Rd., Box 1260, Washington, CT 06793. TEL 860-868-0518, FAX 203-868-1649. Ed., R&P Alberto C Meloni. Adv. contact Mary L Fletcher. Circ: 2,000.

IO. *see* ART

JAILS IN INDIAN COUNTRY. *see* CRIMINOLOGY AND LAW ENFORCEMENT—Abstracting, Bibliographies, Statistics

305.897 CAN ISSN 1710-0720
JOURNAL DE LA SANTE AUTOCHTONE. Text in French. 2004. s-a. **Document type:** *Journal, Academic/Scholarly.*
Related titles: Online - full content ed.: ISSN 1713-5443; ◆ English ed.: Journal of Aboriginal Health. ISSN 1710-0712.
Published by: National Aboriginal Health Organization (N A H O)/Organisation Nationale de la Sante Autochtone (O N S A), 220 Laurier Ave W. Ste 1200, Ottawa, ON K1P 5Z9, Canada. TEL 613-237-9462, 877-602-4445, FAX 613-237-1810, naho@naho.ca, http://www.naho.ca/english.

305.897 CAN ISSN 1710-0712
➤ **JOURNAL OF ABORIGINAL HEALTH.** Text in English. 2004. s-a. **Document type:** *Journal, Academic/Scholarly.* **Description:** Contains in-depth analysis on emerging issues in the Aboriginal health field, including original research and editorials by health scholars, academics and Aboriginal community members.
Related titles: Online - full text ed.: ISSN 1713-5435. free (effective 2011); ◆ French ed.: Journal de la Sante Autochtone. ISSN 1710-0720.
Indexed: BNNA, SD, T02.
Published by: National Aboriginal Health Organization (N A H O)/Organisation Nationale de la Sante Autochtone (O N S A), 220 Laurier Ave W. Ste 1200, Ottawa, ON K1P 5Z9, Canada. TEL 613-237-9462, 877-602-4445, FAX 613-237-1810, naho@naho.ca.

970.1 370 USA ISSN 0021-8731
E97
➤ **JOURNAL OF AMERICAN INDIAN EDUCATION.** Abbreviated title: J A I E. Text in English. 1961. 3/yr. (Oct., Jan. & May). USD 30 domestic to individuals; USD 33.50 foreign to individuals; USD 65 domestic to institutions; USD 68.50 foreign to institutions; USD 8 per issue (effective 2010). bk.rev. illus. cum.index. back issues avail.; reprints avail. **Document type:** *Journal, Academic/Scholarly.* **Description:** Features papers directly related to the education of North American Indians and Alaska Natives, with an emphasis on basic and applied research.
Related titles: Microfiche ed.; Microfilm ed.; Microform ed.: (from PQC); Online - full text ed.
Indexed: A22, A26, AbAn, B04, BNNA, BRD, CA, CPE, E02, E03, E06, E07, E15, ERA, ERI, ERIC, EdA, EdI, HEA, L&LBA, M12, MLA-IB, PCI, S02, S03, S19, SCOPUS, SOPODA, SociolAb, T02, W03, W05. —BLDSC (4927.290000), Ingenta.
Published by: Arizona State University, Center for Indian Education, c/o Laura Williams, PO Box 871311, Tempe, AZ 85287. TEL 480-965-6292, FAX 480-965-8115, http://coe.asu.edu/cie/index.html. Eds. Bryan Brayboy, Teresa L McCarty.

970.1 929 USA ISSN 0730-6148
JOURNAL OF AMERICAN INDIAN FAMILY RESEARCH. Text in English. 1980. q. USD 29.95. adv. bk.rev. index, cum.index. back issues avail. **Document type:** *Monographic series.*
—Ingenta.
Published by: Histree, PO Box 5982, Yuma, AZ 85366-5982. TEL 520-343-2755. Ed. Larry S Watson. Adv. contact Louis J Simone. Circ: 600.

970.1 929 USA ISSN 1040-6581
E98.G44
JOURNAL OF AMERICAN INDIAN FAMILY RESEARCH MONTHLY NEWSLETTER. Text in English. 1988. m. USD 65. adv. back issues avail. **Document type:** *Newsletter.* **Description:** Covers events and activities that are of interest to Native Americans. Includes calendar of events for the upcoming month.
Published by: Histree, PO Box 5982, Yuma, AZ 85366-5982. TEL 520-343-2755. Ed. Larry S Watson. Adv. contact Louis J Simone. Circ: 100.

JOURNAL OF INDIGENOUS STUDIES. *see* ANTHROPOLOGY

JUSTICE AS HEALING. *see* LAW

970.1 CAN ISSN 1193-3372
KAHTOU NEWS; voice of B C's First Nations. Text in English. 1982. m. CAD 30 domestic (effective 2004). adv. bk.rev. **Document type:** *Newspaper.* **Description:** Covers aboriginal issues impacting British Columbia's First Nations.
Former titles: Kahtou Native News; Kahtou (0827-2077)
Related titles: Microfilm ed.: (from MML); Microform ed.: (from MML).
Indexed: C03, CBCARef, CBPI, P48, PQC.
Published by: K'watamus Publications Inc., 5526 Sinku Dr, P O Box 192, Sechelt, BC V0N 3A0, Canada. TEL 604-885-7391, FAX 604-885-7397. Ed., R&P Stan Dixon. Adv. contact Lauren Dixon. B&W page CAD 1,197. Circ: 15,561.

973.82 USA ISSN 0459-5866
E83.876
LITTLE BIG HORN ASSOCIATES. NEWSLETTER. Text in English. 1967. m. (10/yr.). USD 3 to non-members; USD 2 to members (effective 2010). **Document type:** *Newsletter, Academic/Scholarly.* **Description:** Provides information about Little Big Horn Associates.
Incoporates (1969-1975): Little Big Horn Associates. Research Review
Published by: Little Big Horn Associates, c/o Joan Croy, 6200 Blanchett Rd, Newport, MI 48166. TEL 734-586-2916, jcroy@centurytel.net.

973.82 USA ISSN 0195-8224
E83.876
LITTLE BIG HORN ASSOCIATES. RESEARCH REVIEW. Text in English. 1977. s-a. USD 12.50 per issue to non-members; USD 10 per issue to members (effective 2010). back issues avail. **Document type:** *Journal, Academic/Scholarly.*
Supersedes in part (in 1977): Little Big Horn Associates. Newsletter (0459-5866); Which incorporated (1969-1975): Little Big Horn Associates. Research Review
Published by: Little Big Horn Associates, c/o Joan Croy, 6200 Blanchett Rd, Newport, MI 48166. TEL 734-586-2916, jcroy@centurytel.net.

970.1 CAN ISSN 0229-012X
MAL-I-MIC NEWS. Text in English. 1973. m. CAD 12. **Description:** Covers aboriginal and treaty rights, land claims, education, native economic development.
Formerly (until 1979): Nouvelles Mal-I-Mic (0708-9708)
Published by: (New Brunswick Aboriginal Peoples Council), Daily Gleaner, P O Box 3370, Fredericton, NB E3B 5A2, Canada. TEL 506-452-6671. Ed. Jennifer Sappier. Circ: 1,200. **Subscr. to:** 320 St Mary s St, Fredericton, NB E3A 2S4, Canada.

305.897 USA
MAZINA'IGAN; a chronicle of the Lake Superior Ojibwe. Text in English. 1984. q. free (effective 2010). charts; maps; illus. back issues avail. **Document type:** *Newspaper, Consumer.*
Formerly (until 2002): Masinaigan
Related titles: Online - full text ed.
Published by: Great Lakes Indian Fish & Wildlife Commission, 100 Maple St., Odanah, WI 54861. Ed. Susan Erickson.

610 CAN
MEDICINE BUNDLE. Text in English. 2006. q. adv. **Document type:** *Magazine, Consumer.*
Address: 55 Braintree Crescent, Winnipeg, MB R3J 1E1, Canada. TEL 866-485-2380. Ed. Gilles Pinette. adv.: B&W page USD 3,600, color page USD 4,500; 7.5625 x 10.0625.

970.1 USA
MEETING GROUND. Text in English. 1973. 2/yr. USD 10. bk.rev. **Document type:** *Newsletter.*
Published by: (D'Arcy McNickle Center for American Indian History), Newberry Library, 60 W Walton St, Chicago, IL 60610. TEL 312-943-9090. Ed. Harvey Markowitz. R&P Craig Howe TEL 312-255-3563. Circ: 4,000.

N A J A NEWS. *see* JOURNALISM

970.1 USA ISSN 0739-862X
KF8201.A3
N A R F LEGAL REVIEW. Text in English. 1972. s-a. contribution. bk.rev. back issues avail. **Document type:** *Newsletter.* **Description:** Provides an update on the legal cases, legislation and issues that the fund is involved in on behalf of Native Americans.
Formerly (until 1983): Native American Rights Fund. Announcements
Indexed: BNNA, CA, T02.
—Ingenta.
Published by: Native American Rights Fund, 1506 Broadway, Boulder, CO 80302-6296. TEL 303-447-8760, FAX 303-443-7776, http://www.narf.org. Ed., R&P Ray Ramirez. Circ: 34,000.

305.897 USA ISSN 2151-8165
THE NAHUA NEWSLETTER (ONLINE). Text in English. 1986. s-a. free (effective 2009). back issues avail. **Document type:** *Newsletter, Consumer.*
Media: Online - full text.
Published by: Indiana University, Center for Latin American & Caribbean Studies, 1125 E Atwater Ave, Bloomington, IN 47401. TEL 812-855-9097, FAX 812-855-5345, clacs@indiana.edu, http://www.indiana.edu/~clacs/. Ed. Alan R Sandstrom.

NATIVE AMERICA: YESTERDAY AND TODAY. *see* HISTORY—History Of North And South America

NATIVE AMERICAN BIBLIOGRAPHY SERIES. *see* ETHNIC INTERESTS—Abstracting, Bibliographies, Statistics

NATIVE AMERICAN CONNECTIONS. *see* HISTORY—History Of North And South America

970.1 340 USA ISSN 1067-019X
KF8203.1
NATIVE AMERICAN LAW DIGEST. Text in English. 1991. m.
Indexed: BNNA, CA, T02.
Published by: Falmouth Institute, Inc., 3702 Pender Dr, Ste 300, Fairfax, VA 22030-6066. TEL 703-352-2250, FAX 703-352-2323, http://www.falmouthinstitute.com.

305.897 USA ISSN 1556-682X
KF8201.A3
NATIVE AMERICAN RIGHTS FUND. ANNUAL REPORT. Text in English. a.
Published by: Native American Rights Fund, 1506 Broadway, Boulder, CO 80302-6296. TEL 303-447-8760, FAX 303-443-7776, http://www.narf.org.

305.897 USA ISSN 1542-4928
NATIVE AMERICAN TIMES. Text in English. 1995. w. (Thu.). USD 65 (effective 2010). adv. illus. **Document type:** *Newspaper, Consumer.*
Formerly (until 2001): Oklahoma Indian Times
Related titles: Online - full text ed.: free (effective 2010).
Indexed: BNNA, ENW.
Published by: Oklahoma Indian Times Inc., PO Box 411, Tahlequah, OK 74465. TEL 918-708-5838, FAX 918-431-0213. Ed., Pub., Adv. contact Lisa Snell TEL 918-708-5838. B&W page USD 2,100, color page USD 2,300; 11 x 21. Circ: 60,000.

NO

305.897 USA ISSN 1555-7073
NATIVE AMERICANS OF THE NORTHEAST; culture, history, and the contemporary. Text in English. 200?. irreg., latest 2010. price varies. back issues avail. **Document type:** *Monographic series, Academic/Scholarly.* **Description:** Explores the cultures and histories of the Indian peoples of New England, the Middle Atlantic states, the Great Lakes region, and eastern Canada.
Published by: University of Massachusetts Press, PO Box 429, Amherst, MA 01004. TEL 413-545-2217, FAX 413-545-1226, info@umpress.umass.edu. Eds. Barry O'Connell, Colin G Calloway. **Dist. by:** Hopkins Fulfillment Service, PO Box 50370, Baltimore, MD 21211-4370. TEL 410-516-6965, 800-537-5487, FAX 410-516-6998, hfscustserv@mail.press.jhu.edu.

970.1 USA ISSN 1092-3527
NATIVE AMERICAS; hemispheric journal of indigenous issues. Text in English. 1984. q. USD 75 to individuals members; USD 100 to institutions members (effective 2004). adv. bk.rev. illus. reprints avail. **Document type:** *Journal, Consumer.* **Description:** A multi-disciplinary journal dedicated to the coverage of Indian issues, such as politics, indigenous economics, Native intellectual traditions, eco-systemic thinking and systems, history and art, both from a community perspective and through the writing of nationally respected Native and non-Native authors.
Former titles (until 1992): Akwe Kon Journal; Northeast Indian Quarterly (0897-2354); Indian Times
Related titles: Online - full text ed.
Indexed: AICP, AltPI, BNNA, DYW, ENW, MLA-IB, WildRev.
—Ingenta.
Published by: First Nations Development Institute, 2300 Fall Hill Ave, Ste 412, Fredericksburg, VA 22401. TEL 540-371-5615, FAX 540-371-3505, info@firstnations.org, http://www.firstnations.org. Circ: 8,500.

970.1 USA ISSN 1070-8014
E75
NATIVE NORTH AMERICAN ALMANAC. Text in English. 1993. irreg., latest 2001, 2nd Ed. USD 168 per vol. (effective 2006). charts; illus.; maps. **Document type:** *Monographic series, Academic/Scholarly.* **Description:** Covers all major aspects of the civilization and culture of the indigenous peoples of the U.S. and Canada.
Formerly: North American Indian Almanac
Indexed: CPerI.
Published by: Gale (Subsidiary of: Cengage Learning), 27500 Drake Rd, Farmington Hills, MI 48331. TEL 248-699-4253, 800-877-4253, FAX 877-363-4253, gale.galeord@thomson.com, http://gale.cengage.com. Ed. Duane Champagne.

305.897 USA ISSN 0895-7606
E75
NATIVE PEOPLES. Text in English. 1987. bi-m. USD 19.95 domestic; USD 28 in Canada; USD 40 elsewhere; USD 4.95 newsstand/cover domestic; USD 5.95 newsstand/cover in Canada (effective 2010). adv. bk.rev. illus. Index. back issues avail.; reprints avail. **Document type:** *Magazine, Consumer.* **Description:** Focuses on the arts, culture and lifeways of native people of the Americas.
Incorporates (in 1999): Native Artists (1525-5182)
Related titles: Online - full text ed.
Indexed: A07, A30, A31, AA, ArtInd, B04, BNNA, BRD, BRI, CBRI, E03, M02, MLA-IB, P05, T02, W03, W05.
—Ingenta.
Published by: (Smithsonian Institution, National Museum of the American Indian), Media Concepts Group, Inc., 5333 N 7th St, Ste C224, Phoenix, AZ 85014. TEL 602-265-4855, 888-262-8483, FAX 602-265-3113, info@mediaconceptsgroupinc.com, http://www.mediaconceptsgroupinc.com. Ed. Daniel Gibson. Pub. Stephen Phillips. **Subscr. to:** NMAI.

897 USA
NATIVE REALITIES. Text in English. 2001. irreg., latest 2003, Winter. **Document type:** *Magazine, Consumer.*
Media: Online - full content.
Published by: Wordcraft Circle of Native Writers and Storytellers, 200 Rio Grande Blvd SW, # 218, Albuquerque, NM 87104-1455. nativerealities@comcast.net.

305.897 USA ISSN 1943-2569
E78.S65
➤ **NATIVE SOUTH.** Text in English. 2008. a. USD 33 combined subscription per issue domestic to individuals (print & online eds.); USD 48 combined subscription per issue foreign to individuals (print & online eds.); USD 55 combined subscription per issue domestic to institutions (print & online eds.); USD 70 combined subscription per issue foreign to institutions (print & online eds.); USD 23 per issue to individuals; USD 50 per issue to institutions (effective 2011). adv. back issues avail. **Document type:** *Journal, Academic/Scholarly.* **Description:** Focuses on the investigation of Southeastern Indian history with the goals of encouraging study and exposing the influences of Indian people on the wider South.
Related titles: Online - full text ed.: ISSN 2152-4025.
Indexed: A22, E01, MLA-IB.
Published by: University of Nebraska Press, 1111 Lincoln Mall, Lincoln, NE 68588. TEL 402-472-3581, FAX 402-472-6214, pressmail@unl.edu. Eds. Greg O'Brien, James T Carson, Robbie Ethridge. Circ: 100. **Subscr. to:** PO Box 84555, Lincoln, NE 68501. TEL 402-472-8536, 800-848-6224, FAX 800-272-6817, journals@unlnotes.unl.edu.

970.1 CAN ISSN 0831-585X
➤ **NATIVE STUDIES REVIEW.** Text in English; Abstracts in English, French. 1984. s-a. CAD 31.50 to individuals; CAD 47.25 to institutions (effective 2010). bk.rev. illus.; abstr.; maps. back issues avail. **Document type:** *Journal, Academic/Scholarly.* **Description:** Feature original scholarly research on aboriginal perspectives and issues in contemporary and historical contexts.
Related titles: Online - full text ed.
Indexed: A01, A03, A08, AmH&L, BNNA, C03, CA, CBCARef, E03, I02, P48, PQC, T02.
—CCC.
Published by: University of Saskatchewan, Department of Native Studies, 125 Kirk Hall, 117 Science Pl, Saskatoon, SK S7N 5C8, Canada. TEL 306-966-6209, FAX 306-966-6242, native.studies@usask.ca, http://www.usask.ca/nativestudies/. Ed. Robert Alexander Innes.

➤ **NATIVE TITLE NEWS.** *see* LAW

➤ **NATIVE VOICE.** *see* FISH AND FISHERIES

305.897 USA
NEW VOICES (MINNEAPOLIS); news and arts from a Native youth perspective. Text in English. 2002. 3/yr. USD 15 (effective 2004). **Document type:** *Magazine, Consumer.* **Description:** Contains articles and features on culture, history and heritage written by and for Native American youth.
Published by: The Circle, 3355 36th Avenue S, Minneapolis, MN 55406. TEL 612-722-3686, FAX 612-722-3773, info@thecirclenews.org, http://www.thecirclenews.org/. Ed. Jenn Torres. Circ: 6,000 (paid and controlled).

970.00497 979.4 USA ISSN 1040-5437
E78.C15
NEWS FROM NATIVE CALIFORNIA. Text in English. 1987. q. USD 22.50 domestic; USD 42.50 foreign; USD 5.95 per issue (effective 2010). adv. bk.rev.; film rev. illus. index. 48 p./no.; back issues avail.; reprints avail. **Document type:** *Magazine, Consumer.* **Description:** Features articles ranging from ceremonial regalia and traditional use of tobacco to environmental issues and California archaeology, all emphasizing Native Californian points of view, historic and contemporary.
Related titles: Online - full text ed.
Indexed: A01, A02, A03, A08, AICP, APW, BNNA, CalPI, ENW, M02, MASUSE, T02.
—CIS, Ingenta.
Published by: Heyday Books, 1633 University Ave, Berkeley, CA 94703. TEL 510-549-3564, FAX 510-549-1889, heyday@heydaybooks.com. Pub. Malcom Margolin. Adv. contact Margaret Dubin. page USD 750; 7.5 x 10.

305.897 USA
NIPMUC INDIAN ASSOCIATION OF CONNECTICUT. HISTORICAL SERIES. Text in English. irreg., latest vol.3. **Document type:** *Monographic series.*
Published by: Nipmuc Indian Association of Connecticut, PO Box 411, Thompson, CT 06277-0411.

970.1 CAN ISSN 1194-708X
NORTHERN STAR. Text in English. 1971. w. CAD 32.10; CAD 50 in United States; CAD 75 elsewhere. adv. bk.rev.; music rev.; video rev. illus. back issues avail. **Document type:** *Newspaper.* **Description:** News and features from the western Northwest Territories, especially of interest to the Indian and Metis communities.
Former titles (until 1993): Press Independent (1182-9931); Native Press (0833-093X)
Related titles: Microfilm ed.: (from MML); Microform ed.: (from MML).
Published by: D M Communications Ltd., P O Box 1919, Yellowknife, NT X1A 2P4, Canada. TEL 403-873-2661, FAX 403-920-4205. Ed. Lee Selleck. Circ: 5,600.

305.897 USA
ON INDIAN LAND; support for native sovereignty. Text in English. 1992. q. USD 12 to individuals; USD 20 to institutions.
Published by: Support for Native Sovereignty, Box 2104, Seattle, WA 98111. Circ: 3,000.

305.897 USA
PEQUOT TIMES. Text in English. 1992. bi-m. free subscr - mailed (effective 2008). **Document type:** *Newspaper, Consumer.*
Indexed: ENW.
Address: 4 Ann Wampey Dr, Mashantucket, CT 06339-3130. TEL 860-396-6572, FAX 860-396-6570. Ed. Bruce MacDonald.

305.897 USA
QUINNEHTUKQUT NIPMUC NEWS. Text in English. 1970. q. USD 12 to members. **Document type:** *Newsletter.* **Description:** Reports on the association's efforts to honor and publicize the culture and achievements of the Nipmuc.
Published by: Nipmuc Indian Association of Connecticut, PO Box 411, Thompson, CT 06277-0411.

RAVEN'S EYE. *see* ETHNIC INTERESTS

970.1 USA
RED INK; a Native American student publication. Text in English. 1992. s-a. USD 20. adv. illus.
Published by: University of Arizona, American Indian Studies Programs, 1615 E Seventh St, Tucson, AZ 85719.

970.1 305.897 USA ISSN 1071-3204
E76.2
REFERENCE ENCYCLOPEDIA OF THE AMERICAN INDIAN. Text in English. 1967. biennial. USD 125 per issue (effective 2010). **Document type:** *Directory, Trade.* **Description:** Provides annotated listings of individuals and organizations involved in Native American affairs. Includes tribes, associations, schools and colleges, museums, periodicals, books, and individuals.
Published by: Todd Publications, PO Box 1752, Boca Raton, FL 33429. TEL 561-910-0440, FAX 561-910-0440, toddpub@aol.com.

330 USA
REZ BIZ. Text in English. m. **Document type:** *Magazine, Trade.* **Description:** Covers tribal business with a sensitivity to cultural norms of tribal communities.
Published by: REZ BIZ RB Publications, Inc., TOAS Tohatchi Advanced Business Solutions, PO Box 460, Tohatchi, NM 87325. TEL 505-733-2226. Pub. George Joe TEL 505-979-1216.

305.897 CAN ISSN 1482-3802
SAHTU DENE AND METIS COMPREHENSIVE LAND CLAIM AGREEMENT. IMPLEMENTATION COMMITTEE. ANNUAL REPORT. Text in English. 1995. a.
Published by: Department of Justice, Legislative Services Branch, 284 Wellington St SAT-4, Ottawa, ON K1A 0H8, Canada. TEL 613-957-4222, FAX 613-954-0811.

SASKATCHEWAN SAGE. *see* ETHNIC INTERESTS

SEEDHEAD NEWS. *see* AGRICULTURE

STUDIES IN AMERICAN INDIAN LITERATURES. *see* LITERATURE

305.897 USA ISSN 1079-5308
SYCAMORE ROOTS; new Native Americans. Text in English. 1994. q. USD 8 (effective 1998). adv. bk.rev. back issues avail. **Document type:** *Newsletter.*
Published by: Ice Cube Press, 205 N Front St, North Liberty, IA 52317. TEL 319-626-2055. Ed., Pub. Steven H Semken. Adv. contact Steve Semken. page USD 100; trim 10.5 x 8. Circ: 600.

TERRES EN VUES/ASSI NUKUAN. *see* ARTS AND HANDICRAFTS—Abstracting, Bibliographies, Statistics

THINK CANADA!. *see* EDUCATION—Higher Education

TLALOCAN; revista de fuentes para el conocimiento de las culturas indigenas de Mexico. *see* ANTHROPOLOGY

TRIBAL COLLEGE; journal of American Indian higher education. *see* EDUCATION—Higher Education

305.897 347 USA ISSN 1548-887X
KF8224.C6
TRIBAL JUSTICE TODAY; the newsletter of the National Tribal Justice Resource Center. Text in English. 2001 (Sum.). q. free (effective 2004).
Related titles: Online - full text ed.: ISSN 1548-8888.
Published by: National Tribal Justice Resource Center, 4410 Arapahoe Ave Ste 135, Boulder, CO 80303. TEL 303-245-0786, 877-976-8572, FAX 303-245-0785, mail@ntjrc.org, http://www.ntjrc.org.

TYUONYI. *see* LITERATURE

362.1021 USA ISSN 1095-2896
RA448.5.I5
U.S. DEPARTMENT OF HEALTH AND HUMAN SERVICES. INDIAN HEALTH SERVICE. TRENDS IN INDIAN HEALTH. Text in English. 1989. biennial. stat. **Document type:** *Government.*
Published by: U.S. Department of Health and Human Services, Indian Health Service, Clinical Support Center, 801 Thompson Ave Ste 400, Rockville, MD 20852-1627. TEL 301-443-1083, http://www.ihs.gov/AboutIHS/index.asp.

305.897 USA ISSN 2160-424X
▼ **UPTOWN PROFESSIONAL;** promise position purpose performance. Text in English. 2011. q. **Document type:** *Magazine, Trade.* **Description:** Covers diverse talent in America's workforce today.
Published by: Robert Ingram, Ed. & Pub., 113 E 125th St, Second Fl, Harlem, NY 10035. TEL 212-360-5073, FAX 212-360-0944.

THE VISION MAKER. *see* COMMUNICATIONS—Television And Cable

305.897 CAN ISSN 1480-7815
CA1FR12-37
WAPAHKE. Text in English. 1998. s-a.
Published by: First Nations Forestry Program, 10 Wellington St, Hull, PQ K1A 0H4, Canada. TEL 819-953-9557, FAX 819-953-1885, CrevierD@INAC.gc.ca.

WAWATAY NEWS. *see* ETHNIC INTERESTS

970.1 305.8 USA ISSN 0749-6427
E96
➤ **WICAZO SA REVIEW/RED PENCIL REVIEW;** a journal of Native American studies. Text in English. 1985. s-a. USD 75 combined subscription domestic to institutions (print & online eds.); USD 82.50 foreign to institutions (print & online eds.) (effective 2012). adv. bk.rev. bibl.; illus. 250 p./no.; back issues avail.; reprints avail. **Document type:** *Journal, Academic/Scholarly.* **Description:** Provides inquiries into the Indian past and its relationship to the present. Aims to be an interdisciplinary instrument to assist indigenous peoples of the Americas to take possession of their intellectual and creative pursuits.
Related titles: Online - full text ed.: ISSN 1533-7901. 2000. USD 50 (effective 2012).
Indexed: A01, A02, A03, A08, A22, A26, AICP, AltPI, AmH&L, AmHI, B04, BNNA, BRD, CA, E01, E07, E08, G08, H07, H08, HAb, HumInd, I05, MLA-IB, PCI, RILM, S09, T02, W03, W05.
—IE, Ingenta. CCC.
Published by: University of Minnesota Press, Ste 290, 111 Third Ave S, Minneapolis, MN 55401. TEL 612-627-1970, FAX 612-627-1980, ump@umn.edu. Ed. James Riding In. Adv. contact Anne Klingbeil TEL 612-627-1938. B&W page USD 150; 4.75 x 7.875. **Co-sponsor:** Association for American Indian Research.

970.1 370 USA ISSN 0888-8612
E97
WINDS OF CHANGE; empowering native Americans through higher education and careers. Text in English. 1986. q. USD 24 domestic to non-members; USD 34 in Canada to non-members; USD 48 elsewhere to non-members; free to members (effective 2010). adv. bk.rev. illus. Index. back issues avail.; reprints avail. **Document type:** *Magazine, Trade.* **Description:** Features articles oriented toward career development and enhancement, plus topics covering contemporary native issues.
Related titles: Online - full text ed.
Indexed: E03, ERI, T02.
—Ingenta.
Published by: (American Indian Science & Engineering Society), A I S E S Publishing, 4450 Arapahoe Ave, Ste 100, Boulder, CO 80303. TEL 303-448-8853, FAX 303-444-6607, info@aises.org. Adv. contact Barbra Wakshul TEL 303-448-8853. B&W page USD 2,825, color page USD 3,110; bleed 8.75 x 11.25. Circ: 60,000 (paid).

WINDSPEAKER. *see* ETHNIC INTERESTS

305.8974 USA
WOTANGING IKCHE/NATIVE AMERICAN NEWS. Text in English. 1993. w. free (effective 2008). **Document type:** *Newsletter.* **Description:** Provides information for brothers and sisters who share the Spirit and keep informed about current events within the lives of those who walk the Red Road.
Related titles: Online - full text ed.
Published by: Wolfstar LLC, PO Box 10052, Danville, VA 24543-5001. Pub. Gary Night Owl.

WOTANIN WOWAPI. *see* ETHNIC INTERESTS

NEEDLEWORK

see also ARTS AND HANDICRAFTS ; HOBBIES

746 FRA ISSN 2107-2396
A PETITS POINTS. Text in French. 2008. irreg. **Document type:** *Monographic series, Consumer.*
Formerly (until 2009): La France a Petits Points (1962-7513)
Published by: Mango Pratique (Subsidiary of: Editions Fleurus), 15-27, Rue Moussorgski, Paris Codex 18, 75895, France. http://www.fleuruseditions.com/mango.

746.4 DNK ISSN 0107-9611
AARETS KORSSTING/CROSS STITCH OF THE YEAR/KREUZSTICHE DES JAHRES/YEAR IN CROSS STITCH. Text in Danish, English, German. 1960. a. price varies. back issues avail. **Document type:** *Monographic series, Consumer.* **Description:** 12 patterns for annual theme in crosstich.
Former titles (until 1978): Haandarbejdets Fremme. Kalender (0107-9603); (until 1965): Aarets Korssting (0436-5216)
Published by: Haandarbejdets Fremme's Production ApS, Hennebjergvej 31, Nr. Nebel, 6830, Denmark. TEL 45-75-256066, FAX 45-75-256166, hf@haandarbejdetsfremme.dk, http://www.haandarbejdetsfremme.dk.

746.43 ARG ISSN 1669-1598
ALBUM DE FAMILIA. TEJIDOS. Text in Spanish. 2005. q. **Document type:** *Magazine, Consumer.*
Published by: Editorial Patagonica Argentina, Uruguay 266 P.2, Buenos Aires, C1015ABF, Argentina. TEL 54-11-43714947, redaccion@patagoniaediciones.com.ar, http://ww.patagoniaediciones.com.ara.

ALT OM HAANDARBEIDE. *see* HOME ECONOMICS

746.4 USA ISSN 1066-758X
TT835
AMERICAN PATCHWORK & QUILTING. Text in English. 1993. bi-m. USD 25 for 2 yrs. domestic; USD 30 for 2 yrs. in Canada; USD 5.95 per issue (effective 2009). adv. **Document type:** *Magazine, Consumer.* **Description:** Inspires and instructs quilters of all skill levels with valuable tips, new techniques, and creative ideas.
Published by: Meredith Corporation, 1716 Locust St, Des Moines, IA 50309. TEL 515-284-3000, 800-678-8091, FAX 515-284-3058, patrick.taylor@meredith.com, http://www.meredith.com. Pub. Mark J Josephson TEL 212-551-7109. Adv. contact Amy Gates TEL 515-284-3960. B&W page USD 61,080, color page USD 88,760; trim 8 x 10.5. Circ: 250,000.

746 USA ISSN 8756-6591
TT835
AMERICAN QUILTER. Text in English. 1985. q. USD 19.95 membership (effective 2007). adv. bk.rev. 100 p./no.; **Document type:** *Magazine, Consumer.* **Description:** Serves today's quilters with articles on quilt designing techniques, study, exhibition, issues, events.
Published by: American Quilter's Society, 5801 Kentucky Dam Rd, PO Box 3290, Paducah, KY 42002-3290. TEL 270-898-7903, FAX 270-898-1173, http://www.aqsquilt.com. Circ: 56,000 (paid).

305.4 746 UKR
ANNA. Text in Russian. m. UAK 28.98 for 6 mos. domestic (effective 2004). **Document type:** *Magazine, Consumer.*
Published by: Burda Ukraina, Zhyljanskaja ul. 29, Kiev, 01033, Ukraine. TEL 38-044-4908363, FAX 38-044-4908364, zhestkov@burda.ua, http://www.burda.ua.

746 RUS ISSN 1560-5507
ANNA. Text in Russian. 1996. m. RUR 636 domestic; RUR 53 newsstand/cover domestic (effective 2004). adv. **Document type:** *Magazine, Consumer.* **Description:** Presents various handicraft techniques and shows how things can be created individually and attractively.
Published by: Izdatel'skii Dom Burda, ul Pravdy 8, Moscow, 125040, Russian Federation. TEL 7-095-7979849, FAX 7-095-2571196, vertrieb@burda.ru, http://www.burda.ru. adv.: page USD 600. Circ: 30,000 (paid and controlled).

746 USA
▼ **ANNA;** for the creative and curious multi-crafter. Variant title: Burda Anna. Text in English. 2009. q. USD 14.95 domestic (effective 2011). adv. **Document type:** *Magazine, Consumer.*
Related titles: Online - full text ed.
Published by: Vikant Crafts Publishing, Inc., 6577 Windham Lane, Long Grove, IL 60047. TEL 888-670-6869. Ed. Margery Winter.

746 FRA ISSN 0243-3672
ANNA. Text in French. 1980. m. EUR 54.60 (effective 2009). **Document type:** *Magazine, Consumer.*
Published by: Editions DIPA Burda, 26 Avenue de l'Europe, Strasbourg, 67013, France. TEL 33-3-88192525, FAX 33-3-88621646, contactlecteurs@burda.fr, http://www.burda.fr.

746 USA ISSN 1936-4946
TT820
ANNIE'S HOOKED ON CROCHET!. Text in English. 1987. bi-m. USD 4.99 per issue domestic (effective 2008). back issues avail. **Document type:** *Magazine, Consumer.*

Formed by the merger of: Hooked on Crochet! (0893-1879); Annie's Favorite Crochet (1525-5107); Which was formerly (until 199?): Annie's Crochet Newsletter (0745-6360)
Indexed: H20, T02.
Published by: Dynamic Resource Group (D R G), 306 E Parr Rd, Berne, IN 46711. TEL 260-589-4000, FAX 260-589-8093, http://www.drgnetwork.com. Ed. Brenda Stratton. Circ: 80,000.

746 USA ISSN 2152-9299
▼ **ANTIQUE QUILTS: THEN AND NOW.** Text in English. 2010. a. USD 12.99 per issue (effective 2010). **Document type:** *Magazine, Consumer.* **Description:** Features antique and vintage quilts and patterns.
Published by: Meredith Corporation, 1716 Locust St, Des Moines, IA 50309. TEL 515-284-3000, FAX 515-284-3058, patrick.taylor@meredith.com, http://www.meredith.com.

746 USA
APPLIQUE QUILTS. Variant title: Quilt Magazine Presents: Applique Quilts. Text in English. 2000. a. adv. **Document type:** *Magazine, Consumer.*
Published by: Harris Publications, Inc., 1115 Broadway, New York, NY 10010. TEL 212-807-7100, FAX 212-924-2352, subscriptions@harris-pub.com, http://www.harris-pub.com. Ed. Jean Ann Eitel. Pub. Stanley R Harris.

746.4 GBR ISSN 1746-6350
THE ART OF KNITTING. Text in English. 2005. w. GBP 0.99 per issue (effective 2009). back issues avail. **Document type:** *Magazine, Consumer.* **Description:** Provides new techniques in knitting.
Related titles: ◆ Italian ed.: Facilmente Maglia. ISSN 1970-1659; Ed.: Eycolo Pleximo. ISSN 1971-1360.
Published by: Hachette Partworks Ltd. (Subsidiary of: Hachette Livre), 4th Fl, Jordan House, 47 Brunswick Pl, London, N1 6EB, United Kingdom. http://www.hachettepartworks.co.uk. **Subscr. to:** PO Box 77, Jarrow NE32 3YJ, United Kingdom. TEL 44-871-4724240, FAX 44-871-4724241, hachettepw@jacklinservice.com.

746.4 GBR ISSN 2045-6530
▼ **THE ART OF QUILTING;** discover the rewarding & relaxing art of knitting. Text in English. 2011. w. **Document type:** *Magazine, Consumer.*
Published by: Hachette Partworks Ltd. (Subsidiary of: Hachette Livre), 4th Fl, Jordan House, 47 Brunswick Pl, London, N1 6EB, United Kingdom. http://www.hachettepartworks.co.uk.

746 AUS
AUSTRALIAN COUNTRY THREADS. Text in English. 2001 (Sep.). 14/yr. AUD 75.18 domestic; AUD 142.98 in New Zealand; AUD 163.98 elsewhere; AUD 8.95 newsstand/cover (effective 2008). back issues avail. **Document type:** *Magazine, Consumer.* **Description:** Focuses projects from Australia's leading craft talents - including patchwork, applique, stitchery, dolls and cross stitch.
Published by: Express Publications Pty. Ltd., 2-4 Stanley St, Locked Bag 111, Silverwater, NSW 2168, Australia. TEL 61-2-97413800, 800-801-647, FAX 61-2-97378017, subs@magstore.com.au, http://www.expresspublications.com.au. Ed. Lynelle Slade. Adv. contact Natalie Stanic TEL 61-2-97413832. **Subscr. to:** ISubscribe Pty Ltd., 25 Lime St, Ste 303, Level 3, Sydney, NSW 2000, Australia. TEL 61-2-92621722, FAX 61-2-92625044, info@isubscribe.com.au, http://www.isubscribe.com.au.

746 AUS ISSN 1446-2958
AUSTRALIAN EMBROIDERY AND CROSS STITCH. Text in English. 1995. 12/yr. AUD 77.61; AUD 9.95 newsstand/cover (effective 2008). adv. illus. **Document type:** *Magazine, Consumer.* **Description:** Covers techniques and offers ideas in embroidery and cross-stitching.
Formerly (until 2000): Embroidery and Cross Stitch (1324-1559)
Published by: Express Publications Pty. Ltd., 2-4 Stanley St, Locked Bag 111, Silverwater, NSW 2168, Australia. TEL 61-2-97480599, 800-801-647, FAX 61-2-97481956, subs@magstore.com.au, http://www.expresspublications.com.au. **Dist. by:** Quilters' Resource Inc., PO Box 148850, Chicago, IL 60614-8850. TEL 773-278-1348, FAX 773-278-5695.

746 AUS ISSN 1322-1159
AUSTRALIAN PATCHWORK AND QUILTING. Abbreviated title: A P & Q. Text in English. 1994. 14/yr. AUD 75.18 domestic; AUD 142.98 in New Zealand; AUD 163.98 elsewhere; AUD 8.95 newsstand/cover (effective 2008). adv. illus. back issues avail. **Document type:** *Magazine, Consumer.* **Description:** Discusses techniques in patchwork and quilting.
Published by: Express Publications Pty. Ltd., 2-4 Stanley St, Locked Bag 111, Silverwater, NSW 2168, Australia. TEL 61-2-97413800, 800-801-647, FAX 61-2-97378017, subs@magstore.com.au, http://www.expresspublications.com.au. Ed. Marianne Roberts TEL 61-2-97413800. Adv. contact Sonia Spiteri TEL 61-2-97413827. **Subscr. to:** ISubscribe Pty Ltd., 25 Lime St, Ste 303, Level 3, Sydney, NSW 2000, Australia. TEL 61-2-92621722, FAX 61-2-92625044, info@isubscribe.com.au, http://www.isubscribe.com.au.

746 AUS ISSN 1322-5464
AUSTRALIAN STITCHES; the fashion magazine for people who sewing. Text in English. 1994. m. AUD 67.18 domestic; AUD 123.40 in New Zealand; AUD 142.90 elsewhere; AUD 7.95 newsstand/cover (effective 2008). adv. illus. back issues avail. **Document type:** *Magazine, Consumer.* **Description:** Contains latest fabrics and patterns, foolproof fitting advice, historical dressmaking/fashion features, creative sewing ideas from clothing to machine embroidery etc.
Published by: Express Publications Pty. Ltd., 2-4 Stanley St, Locked Bag 111, Silverwater, NSW 2168, Australia. TEL 61-2-97413800, 800-801-647, FAX 61-2-97378017, subs@magstore.com.au, http://www.expresspublications.com.au. **Subscr. to:** ISubscribe Pty Ltd., 25 Lime St, Ste 303, Level 3, Sydney, NSW 2000, Australia. TEL 61-2-92621722, FAX 61-2-92625044, info@isubscribe.com.au, http://www.isubscribe.com.au.

746 USA ISSN 1945-9106
▼ **BAGS, PILLOWS & PINCUSHIONS.** Variant title: Better Homes and Gardens Creative Collection Bags, Pillows & Pincushions. Text in English. 2009 (Mar.). a. USD 16.99 per issue (effective 2011). **Document type:** *Magazine, Consumer.*
Published by: Meredith Corporation, 1716 Locust St, Des Moines, IA 50309. TEL 515-284-3000, FAX 515-284-3058, patrick.taylor@meredith.com, http://www.meredith.com. **Dist. by:** John Wiley & Sons, Inc., 111 River St, Hoboken, NJ 07030. TEL 201-748-6000, FAX 201-748-6088, info@wiley.com, http://www.wiley.com.

746.4 ARG ISSN 1852-3757
BARBARA HOY. BEBES + NINOS. Text in Spanish. 2008. m. **Document type:** *Magazine, Consumer.*
Published by: Grupo Buenos Aires, S.R.L., Ave Velez Sarsfield, 1572, Buenos Aires, 1285, Argentina. TEL 54-11-43024049.

746.4 ARG ISSN 1666-5058
BARBARA HOY. CROCHET BEBE. Text in Spanish. 2002. m. **Document type:** *Magazine, Consumer.*
Published by: Grupo Buenos Aires, S.R.L., Ave Velez Sarsfield, 1572, Buenos Aires, 1285, Argentina. TEL 54-11-43024049.

746.4 ARG ISSN 1851-2712
BARBARA HOY. CROCHET HOGAR. Text in Spanish. 2007. m. **Document type:** *Magazine, Consumer.*
Published by: Grupo Buenos Aires, S.R.L., Ave Velez Sarsfield, 1572, Buenos Aires, 1285, Argentina. TEL 54-11-43024049.

746.4 ARG ISSN 1666-5066
BARBARA HOY. CROCHET MUJER. Text in Spanish. 2000. m. **Document type:** *Magazine, Consumer.*
Published by: Grupo Buenos Aires, S.R.L., Ave Velez Sarsfield, 1572, Buenos Aires, 1285, Argentina. TEL 54-11-43024049.

746.4 ARG ISSN 1852-2955
BARBARA HOY. ESPECIAL CROCHET. Text in Spanish. 2008. m. ARS 7 newsstand/cover. **Document type:** *Magazine, Consumer.*
Published by: Grupo Buenos Aires, S.R.L., Ave Velez Sarsfield, 1572, Buenos Aires, 1285, Argentina. TEL 54-11-43024049.

746.4 ARG ISSN 1668-2920
BARBARA HOY. GANCHILLO BEBE. Text in Spanish. 2004. m. **Document type:** *Magazine, Consumer.*
Published by: Grupo Buenos Aires, S.R.L., Ave Velez Sarsfield, 1572, Buenos Aires, 1285, Argentina. TEL 54-11-43024049.

746.4 ARG ISSN 1668-2912
BARBARA HOY. GANCHILLO MUJER. Text in Spanish. 2004. m. **Document type:** *Magazine, Consumer.*
Published by: Grupo Buenos Aires, S.R.L., Ave Velez Sarsfield, 1572, Buenos Aires, 1285, Argentina. TEL 54-11-43024049.

746.4 ARG ISSN 1851-6823
BARBARA HOY. MANUAL DE PUNTOS. Text in Spanish. 2008. q. **Document type:** *Magazine, Consumer.*
Published by: Grupo Buenos Aires, S.R.L., Ave Velez Sarsfield, 1572, Buenos Aires, 1285, Argentina. TEL 54-11-43024049.

746.4 ARG ISSN 1853-0281
▼ **BARBARA HOY TALLERES ESPECIALES.** Text in Spanish. 2010. m. **Document type:** *Magazine, Consumer.*
Published by: Grupo Buenos Aires, S.R.L., Ave Velez Sarsfield, 1572, Buenos Aires, 1285, Argentina. TEL 54-11-43024049.

746.4 ARG ISSN 1852-3552
BARBARA HOY. TEJIDOS. Text in Spanish. 2008. m. **Document type:** *Magazine, Consumer.*
Published by: Grupo Buenos Aires, S.R.L., Ave Velez Sarsfield, 1572, Buenos Aires, 1285, Argentina. TEL 54-11-43024049.

746.4 ARG ISSN 1668-477X
BARBARA HOY. TEJIDOS DOS AGUJAS. Text in Spanish. 2004. m. **Document type:** *Magazine, Consumer.*
Published by: Grupo Buenos Aires, S.R.L., Ave Velez Sarsfield, 1572, Buenos Aires, 1285, Argentina. TEL 54-11-43024049.

746.4 ARG ISSN 1851-1872
BARBARA HOY. TEJIDOS NINO. Text in Spanish. 2007. m. **Document type:** *Magazine, Consumer.*
Published by: Grupo Buenos Aires, S.R.L., Ave Velez Sarsfield, 1572, Buenos Aires, 1285, Argentina. TEL 54-11-43024049.

746.4 USA ISSN 1072-4931
BEAD & BUTTON; creative ideas and profjects for the art of beads and jewelry. Text in English. 1994. bi-m. USD 28.95 domestic; USD 36.95 in Canada; USD 42.95 elsewhere; USD 5.95 per issue (effective 2009). adv. illus. back issues avail.; reprints avail. **Document type:** *Magazine, Trade.* **Description:** Includes extensive how-to projects, for beginning and experienced crafters, as well as a gallery of work by readers and profiles of leading beaders.
Related titles: Online - full text ed.
Indexed: H20, IHTDI, T02.
Published by: Kalmbach Publishing Co., 21027 Crossroads Circle, PO Box 1612, Waukesha, WI 53187. TEL 262-796-8776, 800-533-6644, FAX 262-796-1615, customerservice@kalmbach.com, http://www.kalmbach.com. Ed. Ann Dee Allen. Pub. Kevin P Keefe. Adv. contact Debbie Simon TEL 888-558-1544 ext 546. B&W page USD 3,839, color page USD 5,375; bleed 8.5 x 11. Circ: 119,042 (paid).

746.43 ARG ISSN 1668-2874
BEBE AJUAR TEJIDO. Text in Spanish. 2004. bi-m. **Document type:** *Magazine, Consumer.*
Published by: Editorial Patagonica Argentina, Uruguay 266 P.2, Buenos Aires, C1015ABF, Argentina. TEL 54-11-43714947, redaccion@patagoniaediciones.com.ar, http://ww.patagoniaediciones.com.ara.

746.4 USA
BETTER HOMES AND GARDENS QUILTING IDEAS. Variant title: Quilting Ideas. Text in English. 2001. a. USD 12.95 per issue (effective 2009). **Document type:** *Magazine, Consumer.* **Description:** Provides advice and decorating ideas for quilters of various skill levels.
Published by: Meredith Corporation, 1716 Locust St, Des Moines, IA 50309. TEL 515-284-3000, 800-678-8091, FAX 515-284-3058, patrick.taylor@meredith.com, http://www.meredith.com.

746 973 USA ISSN 1547-9595
TT835
BLANKET STATEMENTS. Text in English. 1984. q. free to members (effective 2010). illus. 20 p./no.; **Document type:** *Newsletter, Academic/Scholarly.* **Description:** Brings out research articles, AQSG information, research notes and queries, quilt world news.
Published by: American Quilt Study Group, 1610 L St, Lincoln, NE 68508. TEL 402-477-1181, FAX 402-477-1181, aqsg2@americanquiltstudygroup.org. Ed. Paula Pahl.

746.4 NLD ISSN 1574-7034
BORDUURBLAD. Text in Dutch. 2004. bi-m. EUR 23.95; EUR 4.25 newsstand/cover (effective 2009). adv. **Document type:** *Magazine, Consumer.*
Published by: Uitgeverij Rielies Timmer, Tuinbouwweg 23, Maarssen, 3602 AT, Netherlands. TEL 31-346-578869, FAX 31-346-678365.

746 ITA ISSN 1120-4362
BRAVA CASA; mensile di arredamento. Text in Italian. 1974. bi-m. EUR 20.80; EUR 3.50 newsstand/cover (effective 2011). adv. illus. back issues avail. **Document type:** *Magazine, Consumer.* **Description:** Offers practical do-it-yourself advice and techniques for decorating and enhancing the home. Covers both interior decorating and furnishings.
Formerly (until 1985): Brava (0392-3193)
Published by: R C S Periodici (Subsidiary of: R C S Mediagroup), Via San Marco 21, Milan, 20121, Italy. TEL 39-2-25844111, FAX 39-2-25845444, info@periodici.rcs.it, http://www.rcsmediagroup.it/siti/periodici.php.

746.4 FRA ISSN 2108-243X
BRODERIE CREATIVE MAINS & MERVEILLES. Text in French. 200?. bi-m. EUR 39.50 (effective 2010). **Document type:** *Magazine, Consumer.*
Formerly (until 2009): Mains & Merveilles. Broderie Creative (1779-4137)
Related titles: Supplement(s): Broderie Creative Mains & Merveilles. Hors-Serie. ISSN 2108-2448. 2009.
Published by: Editions de Saxe, 20 Rue Croix Barret, Lyon, 69358 Cedex 7, France. TEL 33-4-78728323, FAX 33-4-78726418, http://www.edisaxe.com.

746.4 FRA ISSN 1766-6317
BURDA PATCHWORK. Text in French. 2002. q. EUR 43.90 for 2 yrs. (effective 2009). **Document type:** *Magazine, Consumer.*
Formerly (until 2004): Burda Patchwork et Appliques (1761-1253)
Published by: Editions DIPA Burda, 26 Avenue de l'Europe, Strasbourg, 67013, France. TEL 33-3-88192525, FAX 33-3-88621646, contactlecteurs@burda.fr, http://www.burda.fr.

BURDA. SZYCIE KROK PO KROKU. *see* CLOTHING TRADE—Fashions

746 ITA ISSN 1721-8322
I CAPOLAVORI. Variant title: I Capolavori del Punto Croce. Text in Italian. 2002. q. **Document type:** *Magazine, Consumer.*
Published by: Edizioni Idea Donna, Via Milano 39-41, Cesano Boscone, MI 20090, Italy. TEL 39-02-4584844, FAX 39-02-48600357, http://www.edizioniideadonna.com.

746 USA ISSN 1557-573X
CAST ON. Text in English. 1984. 4/yr. free to members (effective 2010). adv. bk.rev. bibl.; charts; illus.; tr.lit. back issues avail. **Document type:** *Magazine, Consumer.* **Description:** Provides education and communication for hand and machine knitters wishing to advance the quality of workmanship and creativity in their knitting endeavors.
Indexed: IHTDI.
Published by: Knitting Guild of America, 1100H, Brandywine Blvd, Zanesville, OH 43701. TEL 740-452-4541, FAX 740-452-2552, tkga@tkga.com. Ed. Marrijane Jones TEL 740-452-4541 ext 3131. Adv. contact Jane Miller TEL 740-452-4541 ext 3202.

746 JPN
CHARM. Text in Japanese. 1975. bi-m. JPY 2,320.
Published by: Shufu-to-Seikatsu Sha Ltd., 3-5-7 Kyobashi, Chuo-ku, Tokyo, 104-8357, Japan. Ed. Tsuguo Nakamura.

793 USA
CHRISTMAS CRAFTS. Text in English. 1973. a. USD 4.99 newsstand/cover (effective 2007). adv. bk.rev. charts; illus.; tr.lit. back issues avail. **Document type:** *Magazine, Consumer.* **Description:** Offers advice and ideas for persons who enjoy making crafts for the holidays, including sewing, embroidery, cross-stitching, quilting, and knitting.
Former titles: Woman's Day Holiday Craft and Granny Square; Granny Square and Craft Ideas; Woman's Day Granny Squares
Published by: Hachette Filipacchi Media U.S., Inc. (Subsidiary of: Hachette Filipacchi Medias S.A.), 1633 Broadway, New York, NY 10019. TEL 212-767-6000, FAX 212-767-5600, saleshfmbooks@hfmus.com, http://www.hfmus.com. Ed. Olivia Monjo. adv.: B&W page USD 15,980, color page USD 22,250; trim 7.88 x 10.5. Circ: 450,000 (paid).

746.4 GBR ISSN 1352-9730
CLASSIC STITCHES; for friends, family & home. Text in English. 1994. bi-m. GBP 21; GBP 4.20 per issue (effective 2009). adv. back issues avail. **Document type:** *Magazine, Consumer.* **Description:** Covers a wide variety of creative needlework to inspire readers.
Published by: D.C. Thomson & Co. Ltd., 80 Kingsway E, Dundee, Angus, Scotland DD4 8SL, United Kingdom. TEL 44-1382-223131, FAX 44-1382-462097, circulation@dcthomson.co.uk, http://www.dcthomson.co.uk. Ed. Bea Neilson. Adv. contact Pauline Nicolson. B&W page GBP 1,390, color page GBP 1,970; trim 225 x 295. Circ: 7,730.

746 USA ISSN 8755-2655
THE CLOTH DOLL; the voice of cloth dollmaking worldwide. Text in English. 1982. q. USD 19.95 domestic; USD 26.95 in Canada; USD 31.95 elsewhere (effective 2000). adv. bk.rev. illus. **Document type:** *Magazine, Consumer.* **Description:** Contains how-to articles, supply sources, features on doll makers, and patterns.
Indexed: IHTDI.
Published by: Beswick Publishing, PO Box 2167, Lake Oswego, OR 97035-0051. TEL 503-244-3539, 800-695-7005. Ed., Pub. Judy Beswick. R&P, Adv. contact Rose M Darke. Circ: 16,000.

746 USA ISSN 1548-6931
CLOTILDE'S SEWING SAVVY. Text in English. 2001. bi-m. USD 19.97 domestic; USD 29.97 in Canada (effective 2007). **Document type:** *Magazine, Consumer.*
Formerly (until 2004): Sewing Savvy (1531-7226)
Indexed: H20, T02.
Published by: Clotilde (Subsidiary of: Dynamic Resource Group (D R G)), 306 E Parr Rd, Berne, IN 46711-1100. TEL 800-538-5354, FAX 260-589-4000, customer_service@clotilde.com, http://www.clotilde.com/cl/. Ed. Barbara Weiland.

746 ITA ISSN 1123-850X
COLLANA PRESTIGIO. Text in Italian. 1995. m. (11/yr.). EUR 49.92 (effective 2008). **Document type:** *Magazine, Consumer.*

NO

Published by: Alexandra Editrice, Largo Lanciani 1, Roma, 00162, Italy. TEL 39-06-86320393, FAX 39-06-86320481, alexandra@alexandra.it, http://www.alexandra.it.

746.7 GBR ISSN 2045-1334
▼ **COLLECT.** Text in English. 2010. 3/yr. back issues avail. **Document type:** *Magazine, Consumer.*
Published by: The Rug Company, 124 Holland Park Ave, London, W11 4UE, United Kingdom. TEL 44-20-72295148, FAX 44-20-77923384.

746.9 GBR ISSN 2045-0230
THE COSTUME SOCIETY OF SCOTLAND. BULLETIN. Text in English. 1968. a. free to members (effective 2010). **Document type:** *Bulletin, Trade.* **Description:** Contains articles,exhibition reviews,book reviews,details of museums displaying costumes,notices of exhibitions, conferences etc.
Published by: The Costume Society of Scotland, 18 Grierson Cres, Edinburgh, EH 5 2 AX, United Kingdom. costumescotland@hotmail.co.uk.

746 USA
COUNTRY QUILT. Text in English. s-a. adv. **Document type:** *Magazine, Consumer.*
Published by: Harris Publications, Inc., 1115 Broadway, New York, NY 10010. TEL 212-807-7100, FAX 212-924-2352, subscriptions@harris-pub.com, http://www.harris-pub.com/.

746.7 GBR ISSN 2042-7069
COVER (LONDON, 2009). Text in English. 2005. q. GBP 32 in the UK & US; GBP 38 elsewhere (effective 2010). adv. **Document type:** *Magazine, Consumer.* **Description:** Contains market trends, innovations and the creative process in the modern carpet and textile industry.
Former titles (until 2009): Modern Carpets & Textiles for Interiors; (until 200?): Modern Carpets & Textiles (1749-3226)
Related titles: Online - full text ed.: ISSN 2042-7077.
Indexed: ABM, D05.
Published by: Hali Publications Ltd. (Subsidiary of: Centaur Communications Ltd.), Studio 30, Liddell Rd, W Hampstead, London, NW6 2EW, United Kingdom. TEL 44-20-75787201, FAX 44-20-75787221, info@hali.com, http://www.hali.com. Pub. Sebastian Ghandchi. Adv. contact David Young.

746 745.5 GBR ISSN 2040-4689
▼ ➤ **CRAFT RESEARCH.** Text in English. 2010. a. GBP 36, USD 68 per issue to individuals; GBP 110, USD 154 per issue to institutions (effective 2012). adv. **Document type:** *Journal, Academic/Scholarly.* **Description:** Aims to promote current and emerging craft research.
Related titles: Online - full text ed.: ISSN 2040-4697. GBP 75, USD 105 per issue (effective 2012).
Indexed: A30, A31, T02.
Published by: Intellect Ltd., The Mill, Parnall Rd, Fishponds, Bristol, BS16 3JG, United Kingdom. TEL 44-117-9589910, FAX 44-117-9589911, info@intellectbooks.com. Eds. Katherine Townsend, Kristina Niedderer. Pub. Masoud Yazdani. **Dist. by:** Turpin Distribution Services Ltd., Pegasus Dr, Stratton Business Park, Biggleswade, Bedfordshire SG18 8QB, United Kingdom. TEL 44-1767-604951, FAX 44-1767-601640, custserv@turpin-distribution.com, http://www.turpin-distribution.com/.

746 USA ISSN 1527-5973
CRAZY FOR CROSS STITCH. Text in English. 1990. bi-m. USD 19.97 domestic; USD 29.97 foreign (effective 2007). back issues avail. **Document type:** *Magazine, Consumer.* **Description:** Presents cross stitch patterns and instructions for home decorating and clothing.
Formerly (until 2000): Cross Stitch! Magazine (1056-7542)
Published by: Dynamic Resource Group (D R G), 306 E Parr Rd, Berne, IN 46711. TEL 260-589-4000, FAX 260-589-8093, http://www.drgnetwork.com. Ed. Brenda Stratton. Circ: 59,000.

746 ESP ISSN 2171-8997
▼ **CREATION POINT DE CROIX.** Text in Spanish. 2010. bi-m. **Document type:** *Magazine, Consumer.*
Published by: Cesar Editions, Ave Pastor, s-n, Rosas, Girona, 17480, Spain. TEL 34-972-459736.

746 FRA ISSN 2106-8933
▼ **CREATIONS FACILES AU CROCHET.** Text in French. 2010. bi-m. **Document type:** *Magazine, Consumer.*
Published by: Euro Services Internet, 60 rue Vitruve, Paris, 75020, France. FAX 33-1-55253101.

746.43 USA ISSN 1551-6512
CREATIVE KNITTING; easy knitting for everyone. Text in English. 197?. bi-m. USD 19.97 domestic; USD 24.97 in Canada (effective 2008). adv. bk.rev. charts; illus. back issues avail. **Document type:** *Magazine, Consumer.* **Description:** Features 12 to 15 patterns including afghans, clothing, holiday items, dolls and toys all knitted with familiar stitches and a variety of readily available yarns.
Former titles (until 2004): Knitting Digest (1072-7167); (until 1993): Knitting World (0194-8083)
Related titles: Online - full text ed.: USD 14.97 (effective 2008).
Indexed: H20, T02.
Published by: Dynamic Resource Group (D R G), 306 E Parr Rd, Berne, IN 46711. TEL 260-589-4000, FAX 260-589-8093, http://www.drgnetwork.com. Eds. Barb Bettegnies, Bobbie Matela. adv.: color page USD 3,217; trim 8.625 x 10.875.

746 USA ISSN 1060-0493
CREATIVE MACHINE. Text in English. 1990. q. USD 20 domestic (effective 1999); USD 26 foreign; includes guide to resources. adv. bk.rev.; video rev. illus. **Document type:** *Magazine, Consumer.* **Description:** Projects and advice for sewing machine lovers. Also highlights new products.
Published by: Open Chain Publishing, PO Box 2634, Menlo Park, CA 94026-2634. TEL 650-366-4440, FAX 650-366-4455. Ed., Pub., R&P Robbie Fanning. Adv. contact Mora Dewey. Circ: 10,000 (paid).

746.44 USA ISSN 1541-5414
CREATIVE MACHINE EMBROIDERY; ideas inspections & techniques. Abbreviated title: C M E. Text in English. 2001. bi-m. USD 24.95 domestic; USD 30.95 in Canada; USD 36.95 elsewhere (effective 2009). adv. **Document type:** *Magazine, Consumer.*
Published by: C K Media LLC, 1450 Pony Express Rd, Bluffdale, UT 84065. TEL 801-816-8300, 800-815-3538, FAX 801-816-8302, info@ckmedia.com, http://www.ckmedia.com. Adv. contact Madalene Becker TEL 303-215-5607. B&W page USD 2,285, color page USD 3,530; trim 8 x 10.875. Circ: 65,000 (paid).

746 AUS ISSN 1838-6695
CREATIVE MACHINE EMBROIDERY & TEXTILE ART. Text in English. 1996. m. AUD 107.40 (effective 2011). back issues avail. **Document type:** *Magazine, Consumer.* **Description:** Contains projects, design suggestions, patterns and tips related to embroidery.
Former titles (until 2009): Machine Embroidery & Textile Art; (until 2004): Machine Embroidery; (until 1998): Machine Embroidery & Textile Art (1325-8419)
Published by: Express Publications Pty. Ltd., 2 Stanley St, Silverwater, NSW 2128, Australia. TEL 61-2-97413800, 800-801-647, subs@magstore.com.au, http://www.emgroup.com.au/.

746.4 USA ISSN 0887-2384
CREATIVE NEEDLE. Text in English. bi-m. USD 32.95 domestic; USD 43.60 in Canada & Mexico; USD 80.95 elsewhere (effective 2004). back issues avail.
Related titles: Online - full text ed.
Published by: Needle Publishing, 1 Apollo Rd, Lockout Mountain, GA 30750. FAX 800-443-3127, info@creativeneedle.com. Ed. Ann Henderson.

746 USA ISSN 1539-011X
CROCHET!. Text in English. 2002. bi-m. USD 19.97 domestic; USD 24.97 in Canada (effective 2008). adv. back issues avail. **Document type:** *Magazine, Consumer.* **Description:** Crochet patterns and instructions for home decorating, toys, and clothing for the beginner and experienced stitcher alike.
Formed by the merger of (199?-2002): Annie's Crochet to Go! (1522-9440); Which was formerly (199?-199?): Annie's Quick & Easy Crochet to Go! (1096-4541); (199?-199?): Annie's Quick & Easy Pattern Club (1051-3337); (1980-199?): Annie's Pattern Club Newsletter (0199-7106); (1999-2002): Crochet Home & Holiday (1527-1382); Which was formerly (1989-1999): Crochet Home (1046-719X); (1987-1989): Crochet Fun (0897-3490)
Indexed: H20, T02.
Published by: Dynamic Resource Group (D R G), 306 E Parr Rd, Berne, IN 46711. TEL 260-589-4000, FAX 260-589-8093, http://www.drgnetwork.com. Eds. Carol Alexander, Donna Robertson. adv.: color page USD 2,542; trim 8 x 10.75. Circ: 68,000.

746.4 FRA ISSN 1961-3741
CROCHET. Text in French. 2007. bi-m. EUR 4.90 newsstand/cover (effective 2008). **Document type:** *Magazine, Consumer.*
Published by: Societe Francaise de Revues, 60 rue Greneta, Paris, 75002, France. TEL 33-1-44769831, http://www.michel-buh.com/catalogue/index.php.

746 FRA ISSN 0395-6997
CROCHET D'ART. Text in French. 1974. m. **Document type:** *Consumer.*
Formerly: Tout le Tricot - Le Crochet et le Tricot d'Art (0183-3898)
Published by: Editions de Saxe, 20 Rue Croix Barret, Lyon, 69358 Cedex 7, France. TEL 33-4-78728323, FAX 33-4-78726418, http://www.edisaxe.com. Circ: 66,000.

746 USA ISSN 8750-8877
CROCHET FANTASY. Text in English. 1983. 9/yr. USD 20 (effective 2005). adv. bk.rev. illus. reprints avail. **Document type:** *Magazine, Consumer.* **Description:** Publication for crochet enthusiasts featuring photographs, instructions, and diagrams for traditional and contemporary garments, accessories, and home decor.
Published by: Fiber Circle Publishing, PO Box 552, Farmersville, TX 75442. TEL 800-628-8047, FAX 972-782-6631. Ed. Diane Piwko. Circ: 40,000 (paid).

746 USA ISSN 1932-3832
TT820
CROCHET TODAY; be creative your way. Text in English. 2006 (Aug.). bi-m. USD 17.97 (effective 2011). adv. back issues avail. **Document type:** *Magazine, Consumer.*
Published by: Soho Publishing Company, 4000 Shoreline Ct, Ste 400, S San Francisco, CA 94080. TEL 800-865-7240, FAX 646-292-3570. Ed. Theresa Gonzalez.

746 USA ISSN 0164-7962
CROCHET WORLD. Text in English. 1978. bi-m. USD 19.97 domestic; CAD 24.97 in Canada (effective 2008). adv. illus.; charts. back issues avail. **Document type:** *Magazine, Consumer.* **Description:** Contains 15 to 25 patterns for afghans and doilies, plus contests and questions and answers.
Related titles: Online - full text ed.
Indexed: H20, T02.
Published by: Dynamic Resource Group (D R G), 306 E Parr Rd, Berne, IN 46711. TEL 260-589-4000, FAX 260-589-8093, http://www.drgnetwork.com. Ed. Susan Hankins Tullis. adv.: color page USD 2,246; trim 8 x 10.75. Circ: 70,000 (paid).

746.44 USA ISSN 1932-2720
TT740
CROSS-STITCH AND NEEDLEWORK. Text in English. 1995. bi-m. USD 19.99 domestic; USD 21.99 in Canada; USD 35.99 elsewhere; USD 5.95 per issue (effective 2010). back issues avail. **Document type:** *Magazine, Consumer.* **Description:** Contains articles on stitching techniques and designs from around the world.
Former titles (until 2006): Stitcher's World (1524-4466); (until 1999): The Stitchery Magazine (1084-8630)
Published by: Baywood Publishing, 26 Austin Ave, PO Box 337, Amityville, NY 11701. TEL 631-691-1270, 800-638-7819, FAX 631-691-1770, info@baywood.com, http://www.baywood.com.

746.44305 GBR ISSN 1462-3595
CROSS STITCH CARD SHOP. Text in English. 1998. bi-m. GBP 22.95 domestic; GBP 31.50 in Europe; GBP 35.50 elsewhere; GBP 3.99 newsstand/cover (effective 2010). adv. back issues avail. **Document type:** *Magazine, Consumer.* **Description:** Provides designs for readers to stitch and sent to their friends and family and contains designs for every imaginable occasion, as well as more general greetings and notes.
Published by: Origin Publishing Ltd. (Subsidiary of: B B C Worldwide Ltd.), Tower House, Fairfax St, Bristol, BS1 3BN, United Kingdom. TEL 44-117-9279009, FAX 44-117-9349008, info@originpublishing.co.uk, http://www.originpublishing.co.uk. Ed. Charlotte Lyon. Adv. contact Melanie Harris TEL 44-117-3148367. **Subscr. to:** PO Box 326, Sittingbourne ME9 8FA, United Kingdom. origin@servicehelpline.co.uk.

746.4 USA ISSN 1081-468X
TT778.C76
A CROSS STITCH CHRISTMAS. Text in English. 1955. a. **Document type:** *Magazine, Consumer.*
Formerly (until 1995): Merry Christmas in Cross Stitch
Published by: Better Homes and Gardens, Special Interest Publications (Subsidiary of: Meredith Corporation), 125 Park Ave, 18th Fl, New York, NY 10017. TEL 212-551-7193, FAX 212-551-7192, support@bhg.com. Ed. Barbara Hickey.

745.5 GBR
CROSS STITCH COLLECTION; the most beautiful cross stitch designs. Text in English. 1992. 13/yr. GBP 48.07 domestic; GBP 55 in Europe; GBP 60 in United States; GBP 65 elsewhere; GBP 6.25 per issue domestic; GBP 7.25 per issue in Europe; GBP 8.25 per issue elsewhere; GBP 4.25 newsstand/cover (effective 2010). bk.rev. back issues avail. **Document type:** *Magazine, Consumer.* **Description:** Contains a selection of charted designs for experienced cross-stitchers.
Formerly (until 1997): Needlecraft's Cross Stitch Collection (0965-8602)
Related titles: Online - full text ed.
—CCC.
Published by: Future Publishing Ltd., Beauford Ct, 30 Monmouth St, Bath, Avon BA1 2BW, United Kingdom. TEL 44-1225-442244, FAX 44-1225-446019, customerservice@subscription.co.uk, http://www.futureplc.com. Ed. Catherine Hood. **Subscr. to:** Tower House, Sovereign Park, Market Harborough, Leicestershire LE16 9EF, United Kingdom. TEL 44-844-8481602, FAX 44-1858-438795, future@subscription.co.uk.

746.44305 GBR ISSN 1467-6907
CROSS STITCH CRAZY. Text in English. 1997. 13/yr. GBP 31.12 domestic; GBP 40 in Europe; GBP 48 elsewhere; GBP 3.75 newsstand/cover (effective 2010). adv. back issues avail. **Document type:** *Magazine, Consumer.* **Description:** Contains technical information, money-saving tips and the latest news from the world of stitching.
Related titles: Online - full text ed.
Published by: Origin Publishing Ltd. (Subsidiary of: B B C Worldwide Ltd.), Tower House, Fairfax St, Bristol, BS1 3BN, United Kingdom. TEL 44-117-9279009, FAX 44-117-9349008, info@originpublishing.co.uk, http://www.originpublishing.co.uk. Ed. Emma Roberts. Adv. contact Melanie Harris TEL 44-117-3148367. Circ: 19,225. **Subscr. to:** PO Box 326, Sittingbourne ME9 8FA, United Kingdom. TEL 44-1795-414676, FAX 44-1795-414555, origin@servicehelpline.co.uk.

746.44305 GBR ISSN 1471-3667
CROSS STITCH GOLD. Text in English. 2000. 9/yr. GBP 24.30 domestic; GBP 40.40 in Europe; GBP 53.28 elsewhere; GBP 4.50 newsstand/cover (effective 2010). adv. back issues avail. **Document type:** *Magazine, Consumer.* **Description:** Contains seven projects including designs for cards to appeal to the experienced stitcher, as well as advice from the experts and reviews of chart and kits of larger designs.
Published by: Origin Publishing Ltd. (Subsidiary of: B B C Worldwide Ltd.), Tower House, Fairfax St, Bristol, BS1 3BN, United Kingdom. TEL 44-117-9279009, FAX 44-117-9349008, info@originpublishing.co.uk, http://www.originpublishing.co.uk. Ed. Charlotte Lyon. Adv. contact Melanie Harris TEL 44-117-3148367. **Subscr. to:** PO Box 326, Sittingbourne ME9 8FA, United Kingdom. TEL 44-1795-414676, FAX 44-1795-414555, origin@servicehelpline.co.uk.

745.5 GBR ISSN 0966-811X
CROSS-STITCHER; packed with fresh ideas. Text in English. 1992. 13/yr. GBP 41.50 domestic; GBP 55 in Europe; GBP 65 elsewhere; GBP 5.99 per issue domestic; GBP 6.99 per issue in Europe; GBP 7.99 per issue elsewhere; GBP 3.99 newsstand/cover (effective 2010). adv. back issues avail. **Document type:** *Magazine, Consumer.* **Description:** Filled with projects from the country's best designers, ranging from small and fun beginners' projects to larger, intermediate projects aimed at more experienced stitchers.
Related titles: Online - full text ed.: GBP 87.10; GBP 6.70 per issue (effective 2010).
—CCC.
Published by: Future Publishing Ltd., Beauford Ct, 30 Monmouth St, Bath, Avon BA1 2BW, United Kingdom. TEL 44-1225-442244, FAX 44-1225-446019, customerservice@subscription.co.uk, http://www.futureplc.com. Ed. Cathy Lewis. Adv. contact Amanda Haughey TEL 44-1225-442244. **Subscr. to:** Tower House, Sovereign Park, Market Harborough, Leicestershire LE16 9EF, United Kingdom. TEL 44-844-8481602, FAX 44-1858-438795, future@subscription.co.uk.

746 USA ISSN 1055-2871
THE CROSS STITCHER. Text in English. 1984. bi-m. adv. back issues avail. **Document type:** *Magazine, Consumer.*
Related titles: Online - full text ed.
Published by: Amos Publishing, Craft (Subsidiary of: Amos Publishing), 911 S Vandemark Rd, P.O. Box 828, Sidney, OH 45365. TEL 800-572-6885, FAX 937-498-0807, 800-488-5349, cuserv@amospress.com, https://www.amosadvantage.com.

D A T A PRACTICE; the design amd technology curriculum publication for the profession. (Design and Technology Association) *see* EDUCATION—Teaching Methods And Curriculum

746 USA
DEBBIE BLISS KNITTING MAGAZINE. Text in English. 2008. s-a. **Document type:** *Magazine, Consumer.* **Description:** Contains interviews, book reviews on knitting. It also includes patterns for things like baby blankets and socks.
Published by: Knitting Fever Inc., 315 Bayview Ave, P O Box 336, Amityville, NY 11701. TEL 516-546-3600, FAX 516-546-6871, admin@knittingfever.com.

746.4 DEU ISSN 1433-9137
DEKORATIVES HAEKELN. Text in German. 1992. bi-m. EUR 13.20; EUR 2.20 newsstand/cover (effective 2011). adv. **Document type:** *Magazine, Consumer.*
Published by: OZ Verlag GmbH, Roemerstr 90, Rheinfelden, 79618, Germany. TEL 49-7623-9640, FAX 49-7623-964200, info@oz-verlag.de, http://www.oz-verlag.com. Adv. contact Veronika Mainka.

746.4 CZE
DIANA - BABY. Text in Czech. 200?. q. CZK 316; CZK 79 newsstand/cover (effective 2009). **Document type:** *Magazine, Consumer.*
Published by: Rolino, spol. s.r.o., Bratri Capku 10, Prague 10, 101 00, Czech Republic. TEL 420-2-67311358, FAX 420-2-67315529, info@rolino.cz, http://www.rolino.cz.

746.4 CZE ISSN 1860-1146
DIANA - FILETOVE HACKOVANI. Text in Czech. 2005. 2/yr. CZK 170; CZK 85 newsstand/cover (effective 2009). **Document type:** *Magazine, Consumer.*
Published by: Rolino, spol. s.r.o., Bratri Capku 10, Prague 10, 101 00, Czech Republic. TEL 420-2-67311358, FAX 420-2-67315529, info@rolino.cz, http://www.rolino.cz.

746.4 CZE ISSN 1433-9188
DIANA - HACKOVANA MODA. Text in Czech. 2004. bi-m. CZK 270; CZK 45 newsstand/cover (effective 2009). **Document type:** *Magazine, Consumer.*
Published by: Rolino, spol. s.r.o., Bratri Capku 10, Prague 10, 101 00, Czech Republic. TEL 420-2-67311358, FAX 420-2-67315529, info@rolino.cz, http://www.rolino.cz.

746.4 CZE
DIANA - HACKOVANI. Text in Czech. 200?. bi-m. CZK 270; CZK 45 newsstand/cover (effective 2009). **Document type:** *Magazine, Consumer.*
Published by: Rolino, spol. s.r.o., Bratri Capku 10, Prague 10, 101 00, Czech Republic. TEL 420-2-67311358, FAX 420-2-67315529, info@rolino.cz, http://www.rolino.cz.

746.4 CZE ISSN 1613-3226
DIANA - HACKOVANI SPECIAL. Text in Czech. 2004. s-a. CZK 49 newsstand/cover (effective 2009). **Document type:** *Magazine, Consumer.*
Published by: Rolino, spol. s.r.o., Bratri Capku 10, Prague 10, 101 00, Czech Republic. TEL 420-2-67311358, FAX 420-2-67315529, info@rolino.cz, http://www.rolino.cz.

746.4 DEU ISSN 1862-0183
DIANA HORGOLT DIVAT. Variant title: Horgolt Divat. Text in Hungarian. 2006. irreg. HUF 550 newsstand/cover (effective 2010). adv. **Document type:** *Magazine, Consumer.*
Published by: BPV Medien Vertrieb GmbH & Co. KG, Roemerstr 90, Rheinfelden, 79618, Germany. TEL 49-7623-9640, FAX 49-7623-964149, info@bpv-medien.de, http://www.bpv-medien.com.

746 DEU ISSN 1613-1819
DIANA KEZIMUNKA. Variant title: Kezimunka. Text in Hungarian. 2004. 2/yr. HUF 550 newsstand/cover (effective 2010). adv.
Published by: BPV Medien Vertrieb GmbH & Co. KG, Roemerstr 90, Rheinfelden, 79618, Germany. TEL 49-7623-9640, FAX 49-7623-964149, info@bpv-medien.de, http://www.bpv-medien.com.

746.4 CZE ISSN 1864-5844
DIANA - KRAJKOVE HACKOVANI. Text in Czech. 2007. bi-m. CZK 65 newsstand/cover (effective 2009). **Document type:** *Magazine, Consumer.*
Published by: Rolino, spol. s.r.o., Bratri Capku 10, Prague 10, 101 00, Czech Republic. TEL 420-2-67311358, FAX 420-2-67315529, info@rolino.cz, http://www.rolino.cz.

746.4 RUS ISSN 1683-0997
DIANA KREATIV. Text in Russian. 2000. m. **Document type:** *Magazine, Consumer.* **Description:** Provides original patterns using all types of needlecraft techniques.
Published by: Edipresse-Konliga ZAO, ul Bakuninskaya 71, Bldg 10, Fl 6, Moscow, 107082, Russian Federation. TEL 7-495-7751435, FAX 7-495-7751434, n.filkina@konliga.ru, http://www.konliga.ru. Ed. Galina Mednikova. Adv. contact Lyudmila Soldalova. Circ: 20,715 (paid and controlled).

646.4 CZE ISSN 1865-7168
DIANA - KREATIVNI MODA. Text in Czech. 2008. q. CZK 49 newsstand/cover (effective 2009). **Document type:** *Magazine, Consumer.*
Published by: Rolino, spol. s.r.o., Bratri Capku 10, Prague 10, 101 00, Czech Republic. TEL 420-2-67311358, FAX 420-2-67315529, info@rolino.cz, http://www.rolino.cz.

746.4 FRA ISSN 2108-1379
DIANA LE CROCHET FACILE. Text in French. 2008. q. **Document type:** *Magazine, Consumer.*
Published by: B P V Media, 21 Rue de l'Altenbach, Michelbach le Bas, 68730, France.

746 DEU
DIANA MODEN. Text in German. 1995. 4/yr. EUR 20; EUR 5 newsstand/cover (effective 2010). adv. **Document type:** *Magazine, Consumer.*
Published by: OZ Verlag GmbH, Roemerstr 90, Rheinfelden, 79618, Germany. TEL 49-7623-9640, FAX 49-7623-964200, info@oz-verlag.de, http://www.oz-verlag.com. Adv. contact Veronika Mainka.

746 POL ISSN 1732-5277
DIANA MODEN. Text in Polish. 2004. bi-m. EUR 53.40; EUR 9.90 newsstand/cover (effective 2010). adv. **Document type:** *Magazine, Consumer.*
Published by: BPV Polska Sp. z o.o., ul Rybacka 11, Wroclaw, 53-656, Poland. TEL 48-71-3518077, FAX 48-71-3518079.

746.4 CZE ISSN 1861-8693
DIANA - PLETENA MODA PRO DETI. Text in Czech. 2006. s-a. CZK 55 newsstand/cover (effective 2009). **Document type:** *Magazine, Consumer.*
Published by: Rolino, spol. s.r.o., Bratri Capku 10, Prague 10, 101 00, Czech Republic. TEL 420-2-67311358, FAX 420-2-67315529, info@rolino.cz, http://www.rolino.cz.

746.4 CZE ISSN 1865-7176
DIANA - PLETENA MODA PRO ZENY. Text in Czech. 2008. q. CZK 59 newsstand/cover (effective 2009). **Document type:** *Magazine, Consumer.*
Published by: Rolino, spol. s.r.o., Bratri Capku 10, Prague 10, 101 00, Czech Republic. TEL 420-2-67311358, FAX 420-2-67315529, info@rolino.cz, http://www.rolino.cz.

746.4 CZE ISSN 1865-9047
DIANA - SKOLA HACKOVANI. Text in Czech. 2008. s-a. CZK 59 newsstand/cover (effective 2009). **Document type:** *Magazine, Consumer.*
Published by: Rolino, spol. s.r.o., Bratri Capku 10, Prague 10, 101 00, Czech Republic. TEL 420-2-67311358, FAX 420-2-67315529, info@rolino.cz, http://www.rolino.cz.

746.4 CZE
DIANA - VYSIVANI. Text in Czech. 2008. s-a. CZK 59 newsstand/cover (effective 2009). **Document type:** *Magazine, Consumer.*
Published by: Rolino, spol. s.r.o., Bratri Capku 10, Prague 10, 101 00, Czech Republic. TEL 420-2-67311358, FAX 420-2-67315529, info@rolino.cz, http://www.rolino.cz.

746 ITA ISSN 1591-2604
DISNEY A PUNTO CROCE. Text in Italian. 2000. m. EUR 37.40 (effective 2010). **Document type:** *Magazine, Consumer.*
Published by: Walt Disney Company Italia SpA (Subsidiary of: Arnoldo Mondadori Editore SpA), Via Sandro Sandri 1, Milan, MI 20121, Italy. TEL 39-02-29085150, FAX 39-02-29085162, pubblicita@disney.it, http://www.disney.it.

DOWN UNDER QUILTS. *see* ARTS AND HANDICRAFTS

746.4 USA ISSN 1938-6893
EASY KNIT & CROCHET IDEAS. Text in English. 2006. a. USD 4.50 per issue (effective 2007). adv. **Document type:** *Magazine, Consumer.* **Description:** Contains over 60 original designs with complete instructions for scarves, afghans, sweaters, holiday home decor, fashions for babies, kids and teens, and more.
Published by: Hachette Filipacchi Media U.S., Inc. (Subsidiary of: Hachette Filipacchi Medias S.A.), 1633 Broadway, New York, NY 10019. TEL 212-767-6000, FAX 212-767-5600, saleshfmbooks@hfmus.com, http://www.hfmus.com. Pub. James Fraquela TEL 212-767-6817. adv.: B&W page USD 17,375, color page USD 21,350; trim 7.875 x 10.5. Circ: 400,000.

746.44 GBR ISSN 1477-3724
EMBROIDERY. Text in English. 1932. bi-m. GBP 29.40 domestic; GBP 36 in Europe; GBP 42.30 in the Americas; GBP 43.50 elsewhere; GBP 4.90 per issue domestic; GBP 6 per issue in Europe; GBP 7.05 per issue in the Americas; GBP 7.25 per issue elsewhere (effective 2009). adv. bk.rev. illus. index. back issues avail.; reprints avail. **Document type:** *Magazine, Consumer.* **Description:** Features current embroidery, both amateur and professional techniques, historical, and ethnographic subjects and design.
Former titles (until 2002): World of Embroidery (1351-9603); (until 1993): Embroidery (0013-6611)
Indexed: ABM, D05, SCOPUS, WTA.
—Ingenta. **CCC.**
Published by: Embroiderers' Guild, PO Box 42B, East Molesey, Surrey KT8 9BB, United Kingdom. TEL 44-20-89431229, FAX 44-20-89779882, administrator@embroiderersguild.com, http://www.embroiderersguild.org.uk. Ed. Joanne Hall. Adv. contact Carly Brown TEL 44-20-73060300.

746.4 DEU ISSN 1863-9550
EMILY-MAUSEZAHN; Stricken fuer Babys und Kleinkinder. Text in German. 2006. 2/yr. EUR 4.95 newsstand/cover (effective 2010). adv. **Document type:** *Magazine, Consumer.*
Published by: Emily-Mausezahn GbR, Fuenfhausen 6, Jesteburg, 21266, Germany. TEL 49-4183-4504. Eds. Florence Buggenthin, Gisela Witt.

746.4 FRA ISSN 1772-662X
EWA CROCHET. Text in French. 2005. q. EUR 15.50 domestic (effective 2009). back issues avail. **Document type:** *Magazine, Consumer.*
Published by: Editions de la Rose, 37 Rue de Lauterbourg, Schiltigheim, 67300, France. TEL 33-3-88790400, FAX 33-3-88797210, info@editionsdelarose.com, http://www.editionsdelarose.com/.

746 FRA ISSN 1772-1067
EWA PATCH. Text in French. 2005. q. EUR 18 domestic (effective 2009). back issues avail. **Document type:** *Magazine, Consumer.*
Published by: Editions de la Rose, 37 Rue de Lauterbourg, Schiltigheim, 67300, France. TEL 33-3-88790400, FAX 33-3-88797210, info@editionsdelarose.com, http://www.editionsdelarose.com/.

746 USA ISSN 1531-3573
FABRIC SHOWCASE SPECIAL. Text in English. 1998. a. USD 4.99 newsstand/cover domestic; USD 5.99 newsstand/cover in Canada (effective 2003). 64 p./no. 3 cols./p.; back issues avail. **Document type:** *Magazine, Consumer.*
Published by: Chitra Publications, 2 Public Ave, Montrose, PA 18801. TEL 570-278-1984, FAX 570-278-2223, chitra@epix.net, http://www.quilttownusa.com. Adv. contact Sandra Babuka TEL 570-278-1984.

746 ITA ISSN 1970-1659
FACILMENTE MAGLIA. Text in Italian. 2006. w. adv. **Document type:** *Magazine, Consumer.*
Related titles: ◆ English ed.: The Art of Knitting. ISSN 1746-6350; Ed.: Eycolo Pleximo. ISSN 1971-1360.
Published by: Hachette Rusconi SpA (Subsidiary of: Hachette Filipacchi Medias S.A.), Viale Sarca 235, Milan, 20126, Italy. TEL 39-02-66192629, FAX 39-02-66192469, dirgen@rusconi.it, http://portale.hachettepubblicita.it.

FAIT MAIN (PARIS, 1997). *see* CLOTHING TRADE—Fashions

FASHION POETRY PATTERNS & RECITALS NEWS. *see* WOMEN'S INTERESTS

746.4 DEU ISSN 1862-7374
FILATI. HANDKNITTING. Text in English. 1999. 2/yr. **Document type:** *Magazine, Consumer.*
Published by: Lana Grossa GmbH, Ingolstaedter Str 86, Gaimersheim, 85080, Germany. TEL 49-8458-610, FAX 49-8458-6136, office@lanagrossa.de, http://www.lanagrossa.de.

746.4 DEU ISSN 2190-233X
▼ **FILATI-INFANTI.** Text in German. 2010. a. EUR 4 newsstand/cover (effective 2010). **Document type:** *Magazine, Consumer.*
Published by: Lana Grossa GmbH, Ingolstaedter Str 86, Gaimersheim, 85080, Germany. TEL 49-8458-610, FAX 49-8458-6136, office@lanagrossa.de, http://www.lanagrossa.de.

746.4 DEU ISSN 2105-7370
FILATI. TRICOT. Text in French. 2003. irreg. **Document type:** *Magazine, Consumer.*
Published by: Lana Grossa GmbH, Ingolstaedter Str 86, Gaimersheim, 85080, Germany. TEL 49-8458-610, FAX 49-8458-6136, office@lanagrossa.de, http://www.lanagrossa.de.

746 ITA ISSN 1824-5986
FILET FACILE. Text in Italian. 2004. m. **Document type:** *Magazine, Consumer.*
Published by: Edizioni Mimosa, Piazza E de Angeli 9, Milan, 20146, Italy. TEL 39-02-3650507, FAX 39-02-48110494, segreteria@edizionimimosa.it, http://www.edizionimimosa.it.

746.4 DEU ISSN 0947-1456
FILETHAEKELN LEICHT GEMACHT. Text in German. 1991. bi-m. EUR 13.20; EUR 2.20 newsstand/cover (effective 2011). adv. **Document type:** *Magazine, Consumer.*
Published by: OZ Verlag GmbH, Roemerstr 90, Rheinfelden, 79618, Germany. TEL 49-7623-9640, FAX 49-7623-964200, info@oz-verlag.de, http://www.oz-verlag.com. Adv. contact Susanne Weis.

746.4 USA ISSN 1525-1284
FONS AND PORTER'S LOVE OF QUILTING. Variant title: Love of Quilting. Text in English. 1996. bi-m. USD 20.97; USD 5.99 newsstand/cover (effective 2009). adv. bk.rev. back issues avail. **Document type:** *Magazine, Consumer.* **Description:** Provides quilt patterns and instructions for quiltmakers.
Former titles (until 1999): Fons and Porter's Sew Many Quilts (1523-1984); (until 1998): Sew Many Quilts (1085-5734)
Published by: Love of Quilting, Inc. (Subsidiary of: New Track Media LLC), PO Box 171, Winterset, IA 50273. TEL 515-462-1020, 888-985-1020, FAX 515-462-5856. Pub. Kristi Loeffelholz TEL 513-462-5416. Adv. contact Cristy Adamski TEL 715-824-4546. color page USD 7,172; trim 8 x 10.5. Circ: 319,424 (paid).

746 USA ISSN 1040-3965
FOR THE LOVE OF CROSS STITCH. Text in English. 1986. 6/yr. USD 12.95. adv.
Published by: Leisure Arts, PO Box 420126, Palm Coast, FL 32142. TEL 501-868-8800. Ed. Anne Van Wagner Young.

746.432 ARG ISSN 1851-3484
GANCHILLO PASO A PASO. Text in Spanish. 2008. m.
Published by: Producciones Publiexpress, Magallanes 1346, Buenos Aires, C1288ABB, Argentina. TEL 54-11-43031484, FAX 54-11-43031280, rrhh@publiexpress.com.ar, http://www.publiexpress.com.ar/.

746.41 USA ISSN 1932-9601
TT876
GLEANINGS (BUHLER). Text in English. 1988. q. free to members (effective 2007). **Document type:** *Newsletter, Consumer.* **Description:** Provides information about the history of weaving with straw, supplier information, tips and hints, and articles about straw work in other countries.
Published by: National Association of Wheat Weavers, PO Box 344, Buhler, KS 67522. http://www.nawwstrawart.org. Eds. Jan Huss, Veronica Main.

746.4 AUS ISSN 1832-8121
GREAT AUSTRALIAN QUILTS. Text in English. 2004. a. **Document type:** *Magazine, Consumer.*
Published by: Universal Magazines Pty. Ltd., Unit 5, 6-8 Byfield St, Private Bag 154, North Ryde, NSW 2113, Australia. TEL 61-2-98870300, FAX 61-2-98050714, info@universalmagazines.com.au, http://www.universalmagazines.com.au.

746 DNK ISSN 1397-5315
HAANDARBEJDETS FREMME/DANISH HANDCRAFT GUILD. Text in Danish; Text occasionally in English, German. 1934. 3/yr. DKK 325 domestic; DKK 375 in Europe; DKK 450 elsewhere (effective 2009). adv. bk.rev. **Document type:** *Magazine, Consumer.*
Formerly (until 1996): Haandarbejdets Fremme (0107-1769)
Published by: Foreningen Haandarbejdets Fremme/Danish Handcraft Guild, c/o Lise Lind Jensen, Soendervangs Alle 44, Valby, 2500, Denmark. TEL 45-36-464639, http://www.hf-forening.dk. Ed. Birgitte Eskildsen TEL 45-75-857236. Adv. contact Anita Joergensen TEL 45-73-670470. B&W page DKK 3,500, color page DKK 5,200.

746 AUS
HANDMADE; craft - decorating - sewing. Text in English. 14/yr. AUD 75.18 domestic; AUD 132.90 in New Zealand; AUD 153.90 elsewhere; AUD 8.95 newsstand/cover (effective 2008). back issues avail. **Document type:** *Magazine, Consumer.* **Description:** Covers patchwork, sewing, knitting, stamping, scrapbooking and card-making etc.
Published by: Express Publications Pty. Ltd., 2-4 Stanley St, Locked Bag 111, Silverwater, NSW 2168, Australia. TEL 61-2-97413800, 800-801-647, FAX 61-2-97378017, subs@magstore.com.au, http://www.expresspublications.com.au. Ed. Sharon Hawkins. Adv. contact Chris Middleton TEL 61-2-97413829. **Subscr. to:** ISubscribe Pty Ltd., 25 Lime St, Ste 303, Level 3, Sydney, NSW 2000, Australia. TEL 61-2-92621722, FAX 61-2-92625044, info@isubscribe.com.au, http://www.isubscribe.com.au.

746.4 FRA ISSN 1639-2280
IDEAL TRICOT. Text in French. 2003. q. EUR 16 domestic (effective 2009). back issues avail. **Document type:** *Magazine, Consumer.*
Published by: Editions de la Rose, 37 Rue de Lauterbourg, Schiltigheim, 67300, France. TEL 33-3-88790400, FAX 33-3-88797210, info@editionsdelarose.com, http://www.editionsdelarose.com/.

746.4 FRA ISSN 1959-2442
IDEES 100% BRODERIE. Variant title: Idees Cent pour Cent Broderie. Text in French. 200?. irreg. EUR 5.90 newsstand/cover (effective 2008). **Document type:** *Magazine, Consumer.*
Published by: Societe Francaise de Revues, 60 rue Greneta, Paris, 75002, France. TEL 33-1-44769831.

746.4 FRA ISSN 1960-7903
IDEES LAYETTE. Text in French. 2007. bi-m. EUR 5.90 newsstand/cover (effective 2008). **Document type:** *Magazine, Consumer.*
Published by: Societe Francaise de Revues, 60 rue Greneta, Paris, 75002, France. TEL 33-1-44769831.

INGELISE; alt om haandarbejde, mode, ideer, sy, strik. *see* HOME ECONOMICS

746 GBR ISSN 2040-1051
▼ **INSIDE CROCHET.** Text in English. 2009. m. GBP 48; GBP 4.99 per issue (effective 2011). adv. **Document type:** *Magazine, Consumer.*
Published by: Kal Media, Hatfield Broad Oak Rd, Takley, Herts CM22 6TD, United Kingdom. http://www.kalmedia.co.uk/.

746 USA ISSN 1095-1938
INSPIRATIONAL CRAFTS. Text in English. 1997. q. USD 19.80; USD 4.95 newsstand/cover; CAD 5.95 newsstand/cover in Canada; GBP 2.50 newsstand/cover in United Kingdom (effective 1999). **Document type:** *Magazine, Consumer.*
Published by: All American Crafts, Inc., 7 Waterloo Rd, Stanhope, NJ 07874-2621. TEL 973-347-6900, FAX 973-347-6909, dcohen@allamericancrafts.com, http://www.allamericancrafts.com. Ed. Marie Arnold TEL 973-347-6900 ext 141. Pub. Jerry Cohen. Adv. contact Lee Jaworski TEL 973-383-8080 ext 114. **Dist. by:** Curtis CIRC Company.

N
O

746 USA ISSN 0740-6746
INTERNATIONAL OLD LACERS, INC. BULLETIN. Text in English. 1981. q. USD 15 membership; USD 22 foreign membership. adv. bk.rev.; video rev. **Document type:** *Bulletin.* **Description:** Provides current news of lace activities, improvement of skills and inspiration for new ventures. Includes features about the history and study of old lace or the preservation and expansion of the crafts of lace, regular tatting column, illustrations of members' work, patterns and ideas.
Published by: International Old Lacers, Inc., PO Box 265, Camden, ME 04843. TEL 207-236-0755. Ed., Adv. contact Susan Penner. B&W page USD 150; trim 11 x 8.5. Circ: 2,000.

746.434 USA ISSN 1937-0008
TT820
INTERWEAVE CROCHET. Text in English. 2005. q. USD 21.95 domestic; USD 25.95 in Canada; USD 28.95 elsewhere; USD 7.99 newsstand/cover (effective 2008). adv. back issues avail. **Document type:** *Magazine, Consumer.* **Description:** Contains crochet news, ideas, articles and patterns.
Published by: Interweave Press, LLC., 201 E Fourth St, Loveland, CO 80537. TEL 970-613-4658, 800-272-2193, FAX 970-667-8317, customerservice@interweave.com, http://www.interweave.com. Ed. Kim Werker. Adv. contact Tiffany Ball-Zerges TEL 970-669-7455. **Subscr. to:** Publishers Creative Systems, PO Box 469076, Escondido, CA 92046. TEL 760-291-1531, 888-403-5986, FAX 760-291-1567, interweavecrochet@pcspublink.com, http://www.pcspublink.com.

746.43 USA ISSN 1088-3622
TT740
INTERWEAVE KNITS. Text in English. 1996. q. USD 24 domestic; USD 28 in Canada; USD 31 elsewhere; USD 6.99 newsstand/cover (effective 2008). adv. illus.; charts. 128 p./no. 2 cols./p.; back issues avail.; reprints avail. **Document type:** *Magazine, Consumer.* **Description:** Features captivating smart designs, step-by-step instructions, easy-to-understand illustrations, plus well-written, lively articles sure to inspire.
Published by: Interweave Press, LLC., 201 E Fourth St, Loveland, CO 80537. TEL 970-613-4658, 800-272-2193, FAX 970-667-8317, customerservice@interweave.com, http://www.interweave.com. Ed. Pam Allen. Pub. Maryln Murphy. Adv. contact Tiffany Ball-Zerges TEL 970-669-7455. Circ: 51,500 (paid and controlled). **Subscr. to:** Publishers Creative Systems, PO Box 469117, Escondido, CA 92046. TEL 760-291-1531, 800-835-6187, FAX 760-291-1567, interweaveknits@pcspublink.com, http://www.pcspublink.com.

746 USA ISSN 2160-6838
INTERWEAVE STITCH. Text in English. 2001 (Jan.). q. USD 14.99 per issue (print or online ed.) (effective 2011). adv. back issues avail. **Document type:** *Magazine, Consumer.* **Description:** Covers a wide range of skills, includes exceptional how-to articles, answers readers' questions, features guest teachers and artists, and explores contemporary textile works, surface design, embellishments, and motifs.
Formerly (until 2011): Quilting Arts (1538-4950)
Related titles: Online - full text ed.
Published by: Interweave Press, LLC., 201 E Fourth St, Loveland, CO 80537. TEL 970-613-4658, 800-272-2193, FAX 970-667-8317, customerservice@interweave.com. Adv. contact Barbara Staszak.

746 RUS ISSN 1728-8584
IREN. Text in Russian. 2003. bi-m. USD 40 in United States (effective 2010). **Document type:** *Magazine, Consumer.*
Published by: Edipresse-Konliga ZAO, ul Bakuninskaya 71, Bldg 10, Fl 6, Moscow, 107082, Russian Federation. TEL 7-495-7751435, FAX 7-495-7751434, n.filkina@konliga.ru, http://www.konliga.ru. **Subscr. to:** Unicont Enterprises Inc., 1340 Centre St, Ste 209, Newton, MA 02459. TEL 800-763-7475, FAX 617-964-8753, podpiska@unipressa.com, http://www.podpiska.us.

746.4 GBR ISSN 1463-5461
JANE GREENOFF'S CROSS STITCH; original designs from Britain's best-loved stitcher. Text in English. 1998. 7/yr. GBP 19.99 in United Kingdom; GBP 3.99 newsstand/cover; GBP 26 in Europe; GBP 35 rest of world (effective 2000). adv. **Document type:** *Journal, Consumer.* **Description:** Offers cross stitch projects aimed at hobbyists.
—CCC.
Published by: Future Publishing Ltd., Beauford Ct, 30 Monmouth St, Bath, Avon BA1 2BW, United Kingdom. TEL 44-1225-442244, FAX 44-1225-446019, customerservice@subscription.co.uk, http://www.futureplc.com. Ed. Jenny Dixon.

746.4 AUS
JILL OXTON'S CROSS STITCH & BEADING. Text in English. 1990. 3/yr. AUD 40.50 domestic; AUD 44.85 in New Zealand; AUD 56 elsewhere; AUD 13.50 per issue (effective 2009). adv. charts; illus. 51 p./no.; back issues avail. **Document type:** *Magazine, Consumer.* **Description:** Provides charts and designs for cross-stitch and tapestry. Designs include native flora and fauna, people, landscapes, jewelry and buildings.
Formerly (until 2001): Jill Oxton's Cross Stitch Australia (1037-339X)
Published by: Jill Oxton Publications Pty. Ltd., PO Box 283, Park Holme, SA 5043, Australia. TEL 61-8-82762722, FAX 61-8-83743494, jill@jilloxtonxstitch.com. Ed., Pub., Adv. contact Jill Oxton. **Dist. in UK by:** M M C Ltd.

746 USA ISSN 0883-0797
TT778.C76
JUST CROSS STITCH. Text in English. 1983. bi-m. USD 19.98 domestic; USD 29.98 in Canada; USD 39.98 elsewhere; USD 4.99 newsstand/cover (effective 2009). adv. illus. back issues avail.; reprints avail. **Document type:** *Magazine, Consumer.* **Description:** Contains articles that shed light on the world in which the hand-wrought wonders of the past were produced; needlework projects that challenge and build the skills of the contemporary needleworker; and photographs of antique needlework and sewing tools.
Related titles: Online - full text ed.
Published by: Hoffman Media, LLC., 149 Old Big Cove Rd, Brownsboro, AL 35741. TEL 800-547-4176 ext 147, publicrelations@hoffmanmedia.com, http://www.hoffmanmedia.com. Eds. Elizabeth Pugh, Lorna Reeves TEL 205-262-2125, Phyllis Hoffman. Pub. Gary Johnson TEL 205-262-2165. Adv. contact Robyn Brown Hoglan TEL 205-262-2137. page USD 4,285; bleed 8.125 x 10.75. Circ: 50,000.

746 USA
KEEPSAKE CALENDAR; (year) cross-stitch collection. Text in English. 1988. a. USD 11.95. adv. charts. **Description:** Cross-stitch patterns, articles and instructions themed to each month for the needlework hobbyist.
Published by: Craftways Corp., 1716 Locust St, Des Moines, IA 50309-3023. TEL 515-284-3971, FAX 515-284-2568. Ed. Beverly Rivers. Pub. William Reed. Adv. contact Maureen Ruth. **Subscr. to:** PO Box 10670, Des Moines, IA 50336-0670.

746.4 DEU ISSN 0946-4395
DIE KLEINE DIANA. Text in German. 1983. 10/yr. EUR 16.50; EUR 2.20 newsstand/cover (effective 2011). adv. **Document type:** *Magazine, Consumer.*
Related titles: ◆ International ed.: Malen'kaya Diana. ISSN 1683-0970.
Published by: OZ Verlag GmbH, Roemerstr 90, Rheinfelden, 79618, Germany. TEL 49-7623-9640, FAX 49-7623-964200, info@oz-verlag.de, http://www.oz-verlag.com. Adv. contact Veronika Mainka.

746.22 DNK ISSN 0900-8799
KNIPLEBREVET. Text in Danish; Text occasionally in English. 1985. 3/yr. DKK 225 domestic to members; EUR 44 in Europe (effective 2009). adv. bk.rev. illus. index. back issues avail. **Document type:** *Magazine, Consumer.* **Description:** Devoted to lacemaking and lacemakers. Includes patterns.
Published by: Foreningen Knipling i Danmark/Danish Lace Association, PO Box 94, Toender, 6270, Denmark. k-i-d@webspeed.dk, http://www.knipling-i-danmark.dk. Ed. Karen Vontillius.

745 GBR ISSN 2046-388X
KNIT. Text in English. 2006. m. GBP 4.99 per issue (effective 2011). adv. **Document type:** *Magazine, Consumer.*
Formerly (until 2011): Yarn Forward (1757-5192)
Published by: Kal Media, Ground Fl, The Chestnuts Brewers End, Takeley, Herts CM22 6QJ, United Kingdom. TEL 44-1279-879038, http://www.kalmedia.co.uk/.

746.4 USA ISSN 1940-2058
KNIT 1. Text in English. 2006. q. adv. back issues avail. **Document type:** *Magazine, Consumer.*
Published by: Soho Publishing Company, 161 Ave Of the Americas, Ste 1301, New York, NY 10013. TEL 212-937-2555, http://www.sohopub.com/.

746.4 USA ISSN 1541-1990
KNIT IT!. Text in English. 2001. a.
Published by: Meredith Corporation, 1716 Locust St, Des Moines, IA 50309. TEL 515-284-3000, 800-678-8091, FAX 515-284-3058, patrick.taylor@meredith.com, http://www.meredith.com.

746 USA ISSN 1096-5408
KNIT 'N STYLE; real fashion for real knitters. Text in English. 1981. bi-m. USD 24.97 domestic; USD 36.97 in Canada; USD 42.97 elsewhere; USD 6.99 per issue (effective 2008). adv. illus. back issues avail. **Document type:** *Magazine, Consumer.* **Description:** Features contemporary knitted garment designs, photographs, instructions, diagrams and more.
Formerly (until 1997): Fashion Knitting (8750-8869)
Published by: All American Crafts, Inc., 7 Waterloo Rd, Stanhope, NJ 07874-2621. TEL 973-347-6900, FAX 973-347-6909, dcohen@allamericancrafts.com, http://www.allamericancrafts.com. Ed. Penelope Taylor. Pub. Jerry Cohen. Adv. contacts Jennifer Schwesinger TEL 973-347-6900 ext 121, Lee Jaworski TEL 973-383-8080 ext 114. B&W page USD 1,470, color page USD 2,045. Circ: 55,000 (paid).

746 USA ISSN 1932-1325
TT820
KNIT SIMPLE; yarn-life-fun. Text in English. 1993. q. USD 19.97; USD 6.99 per issue domestic; USD 7.99 per issue in Canada (effective 2011). adv. back issues avail. **Document type:** *Magazine, Consumer.* **Description:** Contains new ideas and patterns for knitting enthusiasts.
Formerly (until 2005): Family Circle Easy Knitting
Published by: Soho Publishing Company, PO Box 421558, Palm Coast, FL 32142. TEL 814-942-3186, 877-860-6164. Adv. contact Doreen Conners TEL 212-937-2554.

746.9 RUS
KNIT&MODE. Text in Russian. m. USD 60 in United States (effective 2010). **Document type:** *Magazine, Consumer.*
Published by: Edipresse-Konliga ZAO, ul Bakuninskaya 71, Bldg 10, Fl 6, Moscow, 107082, Russian Federation. TEL 7-495-7751435, FAX 7-495-7751434, n.filkina@konliga.ru, http://www.konliga.ru. Circ: 50,000 (paid and controlled). **Subscr. to:** Unicont Enterprises Inc., 1340 Centre St, Ste 209, Newton, MA 02459. TEL 800-763-7475, FAX 617-964-8753, podpiska@unipressa.com, http://www.podpiska.us.

746.4 CAN
KNITNET; the online knitting magazine. Text in English. 6/yr. USD 12; USD 25 combined subscription online & CD-ROM eds. (effective 2005). adv. back issues avail. **Document type:** *Magazine, Consumer.* **Description:** Provides information about knitting patterns and techniques.
Media: Online - full content. **Related titles:** CD-ROM ed.
Published by: e.o.b. inc., Ste 688, 2938 Dundas St W, Toronto, ON M6P 4E7, Canada. TEL 416-410-9880, FAX 416-410-9880. Ed., R&P Ms. Sharon Airhart. Pub., Adv. contact Mr. Dougal Bichan.

746.43 DEU
▼ **THE KNITTER**; Das Magazin fuer kreatives Stricken. Text in German. 2010. q. EUR 17.70; EUR 5.90 newsstand/cover (effective 2011). adv. **Document type:** *Magazine, Consumer.*
Published by: OZ Verlag GmbH, Roemerstr 90, Rheinfelden, 79618, Germany. TEL 49-7623-9640, FAX 49-7623-964200, info@oz-verlag.de, http://www.oz-verlag.com.

746.43 GBR ISSN 1759-1031
▼ **THE KNITTER.** Text in English. 2009. m. adv. **Document type:** *Magazine, Consumer.*
Published by: Future Publishing Ltd., Beauford Ct, 30 Monmouth St, Bath, Avon BA1 2BW, United Kingdom. TEL 44-1225-442244, FAX 44-1225-446019, customerservice@subscription.co.uk, http://www.futureplc.com.

746.43 USA ISSN 0747-9026
TT825
KNITTER'S MAGAZINE. Text in English. 1984. q. USD 20 domestic; USD 25 in Canada; USD 29 elsewhere; USD 5.95 newsstand/cover domestic; USD 7.95 newsstand/cover in Canada (effective 2007). adv. bk.rev. charts; illus.; tr.lit. back issues avail.; reprints avail. **Document type:** *Magazine, Consumer.* **Description:** Features techniques and instructions for innovative fashion knitting projects, plus interviews with designers and craftspeople.
Published by: X R X, Inc., 132C S Minnesota Ave, PO Box 1525, Sioux Falls, SD 57105. TEL 605-338-2450, 800-232-5648, FAX 605-338-2994, http://www.knittinguniverse.com. Ed. Rick L Mondragon. Pub. Alexis Viorgos Xenakis. Adv. contact Molly Vagle. Circ: 30,000 (paid).

746.43 DNK ISSN 1903-2099
KREATIV STRIK. Text in Danish. 2008. q. adv. back issues avail. **Document type:** *Magazine, Consumer.*
Published by: Forlaget Ingelise Sy og Strik, Ved Soen 1, Jels, Roedding, 6630, Denmark. TEL 45-70-117080, FAX 45-73-996622, http://www.ingelise.dk.

746 745.5 DNK ISSN 1902-2298
KREATIVE KVINDER. Text in Danish. 2006. m. DKK 477 (effective 2008). adv. **Document type:** *Magazine, Consumer.*
Incorporates (1999-2007): Hobby Ideer (1601-0434)
Related titles: Norwegian ed.: Kreative Kvinner. ISSN 1902-7427. 2007; Swedish ed.: Kreativa Kvinnor. ISSN 1902-7435. 2007.
Published by: Audio Media A-S, Sejroegade 7-9, Copenhagen OE, 2100, Denmark. TEL 45-33-912833, FAX 45-33-747191, forlaget@audio.dk, http://www.audio.dk. Ed. Louise Simonsen. adv.: color page DKK 29,500; 210 x 297. Circ: 41,000.

746 ESP ISSN 0047-3863
LABORES DEL HOGAR. Text in Spanish. 1926. m. EUR 39.60 domestic; EUR 78.95 in Europe; EUR 269.80 elsewhere; EUR 3.60 newsstand/cover (effective 2008). adv. bk.rev. charts; illus. **Document type:** *Magazine, Consumer.*
Related titles: ◆ Supplement(s): Punto de Cruz. ISSN 1576-5873; Labores del Hogar Coleccion.
Published by: R B A Edipresse, Perez Galdos 36, Barcelona, 08012, Spain. TEL 34-93-4157374, FAX 34-93-2177378, http://www.rbaedipresse.es. Circ: 78,400 (paid and controlled).

746 DEU ISSN 1433-4151
LACE EXPRESS. Text in English, German. 1997. q. EUR 60 (effective 2009). **Document type:** *Magazine, Consumer.*
Address: Rosenstr 56, Papenburg, 26871, Germany. TEL 49-4961-982618, FAX 49-4961-982619.

746 ITA ISSN 1828-6097
I LAVORI DI BEATRICE. Text in Italian. 2006. m. EUR 2.90 newsstand/cover (effective 2009). **Document type:** *Magazine, Consumer.* **Description:** Italian version of the Australian magazine Smocking & Embroidery, specializing in needlework for young girls.
Published by: Edizioni Mimosa, Piazza E de Angeli 9, Milan, 20146, Italy. TEL 39-02-3650507, FAX 39-02-48110494, segreteria@edizionimimosa.it, http://www.edizionimimosa.it. Circ: 35,000.

746 ITA ISSN 1828-6089
I LAVORI DI CAROLINA. Text in Italian. 2005. m. EUR 2.90 newsstand/cover (effective 2009). **Document type:** *Magazine, Consumer.* **Description:** Italian version of the Australian needlework magazine Inspirations.
Formerly (until 2006): I Capolavori di Arte Femminile (1825-0475)
Published by: Edizioni Mimosa, Piazza E de Angeli 9, Milan, 20146, Italy. TEL 39-02-3650507, FAX 39-02-48110494, segreteria@edizionimimosa.it, http://www.edizionimimosa.it. Circ: 35,000.

746 POL ISSN 1898-0252
LENA. Text in Polish. 2007. 2/yr. PLZ 7.90 newsstand/cover (effective 2010). adv. **Document type:** *Magazine, Consumer.*
Published by: BPV Polska Sp. z o.o., ul Rybacka 11, Wroclaw, 53-656, Poland. TEL 48-71-3518077, FAX 48-71-3518079.

746.4 DEU ISSN 1431-1097
LENA; die besten Ideen zum selbermachen. Text in German. 1995. m. EUR 45.60; EUR 3.80 newsstand/cover (effective 2011). adv. **Document type:** *Magazine, Consumer.*
Published by: OZ Verlag GmbH, Roemerstr 90, Rheinfelden, 79618, Germany. TEL 49-7623-9640, FAX 49-7623-964200, info@oz-verlag.de, http://www.oz-verlag.com. Adv. contact Susanne Weis.

746.4 DEU
LENA CREATIV. Text in German. 2003. 4/yr. EUR 14.50; EUR 4.80 newsstand/cover (effective 2011). adv. **Document type:** *Magazine, Consumer.*
Published by: OZ Verlag GmbH, Roemerstr 90, Rheinfelden, 79618, Germany. TEL 49-7623-9640, FAX 49-7623-964200, info@oz-verlag.de, http://www.oz-verlag.com. Adv. contact Susanne Weis.

LENA - RUKODELIE. *see* ARTS AND HANDICRAFTS

746.4 DEU
LENA'S PATCHWORK UND APPLIKATIONEN. Text in German. 2004. 8/yr. EUR 35; EUR 5.50 newsstand/cover (effective 2011). adv. **Document type:** *Magazine, Consumer.*
Formerly (until 2010): Lena Special Handarbeiten
Published by: OZ Verlag GmbH, Roemerstr 90, Rheinfelden, 79618, Germany. TEL 49-7623-9640, FAX 49-7623-964200, info@oz-verlag.de, http://www.oz-verlag.com. Adv. contact Susanne Weis.

746.432 GBR ISSN 1753-4895
LET'S KNIT; your knitting your style. Text in English. 2007. m. GBP 49.99 domestic; GBP 71.50 in Europe; GBP 82 elsewhere (effective 2010). adv. **Document type:** *Magazine, Consumer.*
—CCC.
Published by: Aceville Publications Ltd., 21-23 Phoenix Ct, Hawkins Rd, Colchester, Essex CO2 8JY, United Kingdom. TEL 44-1206-505962, FAX 44-1206-505915, aceville@servicehelpline.co.uk, http://www.aceville.com. Ed. Sarah Neal TEL 44-1206-508622. Adv. contact Emily Richardson TEL 44-1206-505117. **Subscr. to:** 800 Guillat Ave, Kent Science Park, Sittingbourne, Kent ME9 8GU, United Kingdom. TEL 44-844-8440381, FAX 44-845-4567143.

746.4 DEU ISSN 1869-9715
▼ **LINEA PURA.** Text in German. 2009. 2/yr. **Document type:** *Magazine, Consumer.*

Published by: Lana Grossa GmbH, Ingolstaedter Str 86, Gaimersheim, 85080, Germany. TEL 49-8458-610, FAX 49-8458-6136, office@lanagrossa.de, http://www.lanagrossa.de.

LIVING CRAFTS; craft your whole life. *see* ARTS AND HANDICRAFTS

LOOK. *see* CLOTHING TRADE—Fashions

746 ROM ISSN 1841-5296
LUCRU DE MANA. Text in Romanian. 2005. s-a. ROL 30 domestic; EUR 30 foreign (effective 2007). adv. **Document type:** *Magazine, Consumer.*
Published by: Edipresse A.S. SRL, 50-52 Buzesti Str, Fl 1, Sector 1, Bucharest, Romania. TEL 40-21-3193559, FAX 40-21-3193568, office@edipresse.ro, http://www.edipresse.ro. adv.: color page EUR 1,500.

746 GBR ISSN 0269-9761
MACHINE KNITTING MONTHLY. Text in English. 1986. m. GBP 39; GBP 3.25 newsstand/cover (effective 2009). adv. bk.rev. 64 p./no. 4 cols./p.; back issues avail. **Document type:** *Magazine, Consumer.* **Description:** The latest patterns, features and news for all machine knitters.
Incorporates (1978-1998): To and Fro Machine Knitting (0968-2511); Incorporates (1989-1997): Modern Machine Knitting (0957-6673)
Published by: R P A Publishing Ltd., PO Box 1479, Maidenhead, Berks SL6 8DP, United Kingdom. TEL 44-1628-783080, FAX 44-1628-633250. **Dist. by:** Seymour Distribution Ltd, 86 Newman St, London W1T 3EX, United Kingdom. TEL 44-20-73968000, FAX 44-20-73968002.

746 FRA ISSN 0246-5957
MAGIC CROCHET. Text in French. 1979. bi-m. USD 17.50. **Document type:** *Consumer.*
Published by: Editions de Saxe, 20 Rue Croix Barret, Lyon, 69358 Cedex 7, France.

746 ITA ISSN 1590-8410
MAGIC PATCH. Text in Italian. 2000. q. EUR 20.66 (effective 2008). **Document type:** *Magazine, Consumer.*
Published by: Alexandra Editrice, Largo Lanciani 1, Roma, 00162, Italy. TEL 39-06-86320393, FAX 39-06-86320481, alexandra@alexandra.it, http://www.alexandra.it.

746 ITA ISSN 1121-8525
MAGICO UNCINETTO. Variant title: Magico Uncinetto di Tricot Selezione. Text in Italian. 1980. m. EUR 28.80 (effective 2008). **Document type:** *Magazine, Consumer.*
Published by: Alexandra Editrice, Largo Lanciani 1, Roma, 00162, Italy. TEL 39-06-86320393, FAX 39-06-86320481, alexandra@alexandra.it, http://www.alexandra.it.

746 ITA ISSN 1974-8604
LA MAGLIA DI RAKAM. Text in Italian. 2008. bi-m. **Document type:** *Magazine, Consumer.*
Published by: Edizioni Mimosa, Piazza E de Angeli 9, Milan, 20146, Italy. TEL 39-02-3650507, FAX 39-02-48110494, segreteria@edizionimimosa.it, http://www.edizionimimosa.it.

746 FRA ISSN 1962-4050
MAILLES. Text in French. bi-m. EUR 24 (effective 2009). **Document type:** *Magazine, Consumer.*
Formerly (until 2008): 1000 Mailles (0339-3445)
Published by: Editions de Saxe, 20 Rue Croix Barret, Lyon, 69358 Cedex 7, France. TEL 33-4-78728323, FAX 33-4-78726418.

746 POL ISSN 0945-6678
MALA DIANA. Text in Polish. 199?. m. PLZ 54; PLZ 5.50 newsstand/cover (effective 2010). adv. **Document type:** *Magazine, Consumer.*
Published by: BPV Polska Sp. z o.o., ul Rybacka 11, Wroclaw, 53-656, Poland. TEL 48-71-3518077, FAX 48-71-3518079.

746 RUS ISSN 1683-0970
MALEN'KAYA DIANA. Text in Russian. 1993. m. USD 56 in United States (effective 2010). **Document type:** *Magazine, Consumer.*
Related titles: ◆ International ed. of: Die Kleine Diana. ISSN 0946-4395.
Published by: Edipresse-Konliga ZAO, ul Bakuninskaya 71, Bldg 10, Fl 6, Moscow, 107082, Russian Federation. TEL 7-495-7751435, FAX 7-495-7751434, n.filkina@konliga.ru, http://www.konliga.ru. Circ: 130,000 (paid and controlled). **Subscr. to:** Unicont Enterprises Inc., 1340 Centre St, Ste 209, Newton, MA 02459. TEL 800-763-7475, FAX 617-964-8753, podpiska@unipressa.com, http://www.podpiska.us.

746 RUS ISSN 1815-543X
MALEN'KAYA DIANA. SPETSYAL'NYI VYPUSK. Text in Russian. 2005. m. **Document type:** *Magazine, Consumer.*
Published by: Edipresse-Konliga ZAO, ul Bakuninskaya 71, Bldg 10, Fl 6, Moscow, 107082, Russian Federation. TEL 7-495-7751435, FAX 7-495-7751434, n.filkina@konliga.ru. Circ: 60,000 (paid and controlled).

MANEQUIM. *see* CLOTHING TRADE—Fashions

746.3 BRA ISSN 1414-4972
MANEQUIM PONTO CRUZ. Text in Portuguese. 1996. m. adv. **Document type:** *Magazine, Consumer.*
Published by: Editora Abril, S.A., Avenida das Nacoes Unidas 7221, Pinheiros, Sao Paulo, SP 05425-902, Brazil. TEL 55-11-50872112, FAX 55-11-50872100, abrilsac@abril.com.br, http://www.abril.com.br.

746 USA ISSN 1940-3097
MARK LIPINSKI'S QUILTER'S HOME; for the new generation of quilters. Abbreviated title: Q H. Variant title: Quilter's Home. Text in English. 2006. bi-m. USD 29.99 domestic; USD 35.99 in Canada; USD 41.99 elsewhere (effective 2009). adv. back issues avail. **Document type:** *Magazine, Consumer.*
Published by: C K Media LLC, 1450 Pony Express Rd, Bluffdale, UT 84065. TEL 801-816-8300, 800-815-3538, FAX 801-816-8302, info@ckmedia.com, http://www.ckmedia.com. Adv. contacts Lisa O'Bryan TEL 303-215-5641, Lisa Rankin TEL 719-539-7410. B&W page USD 2,445, color page USD 3,155; trim 8.375 x 10.875. Circ: 130,000.

746.4 USA ISSN 1549-7631
TT835
MCCALL'S QUICK QUILTS. Text in English. 1996. bi-m. USD 19.98 domestic; USD 25.98 in Canada; USD 31.98 elsewhere (effective 2009). adv. back issues avail. **Document type:** *Magazine, Consumer.* **Description:** Provides the right kind of information and inspiration for those newly interested in quilting and those more experienced quilters looking for a quick, fun project.
Formerly (until 2004): McCall's Quilting Quick Quilts (1092-3438)
Published by: C K Media LLC, 1450 Pony Express Rd, Bluffdale, UT 84065. TEL 801-816-8300, 800-815-3538, FAX 801-816-8302, info@ckmedia.com, http://www.ckmedia.com. Adv. contacts Lisa O'Bryan TEL 303-215-5641, Lisa Rankin TEL 719-539-7410. B&W page USD 1,795, color page USD 2,395; trim 8 x 10.875. Circ: 105,000.

746.4 USA ISSN 1072-8295
MCCALL'S QUILTING. Variant title: Quilting. Text in English. 1993. bi-m. USD 19.98 domestic; USD 25.98 in Canada; USD 31.98 elsewhere (effective 2008). adv. back issues avail. **Document type:** *Magazine, Consumer.* **Description:** Provides patterns that speak to tradition and heritage, as well as celebrity interviews, techniques and tips.
—CCC.
Published by: C K Media LLC, 1450 Pony Express Rd, Bluffdale, UT 84065. TEL 801-816-8300, 800-815-3538, FAX 801-816-8302, info@ckmedia.com, http://www.ckmedia.com. Ed. Beth Hayes. Adv. contact Lisa O'Bryan TEL 303-215-5641. B&W page USD 2,705, color page USD 3,690; trim 8.875 x 10.875. Circ: 175,000.

MEYERS MODEBLATT. *see* CLOTHING TRADE—Fashions

746 USA ISSN 1933-5997
MINI TEDDY HUGS. Text in English. 2006. m. **Document type:** *Magazine, Consumer.* **Description:** Deals with the art of miniature teddy bears.
Media: Online - full text.
Published by: Mary Robinson editor@miniteddyhugs.com, http://www.miniteddyhugs.com/index.htm. Ed. Mary Robinson.

746 USA ISSN 1065-0245
MINIATURE QUILTS. Text in English. 6/yr. USD 19.98 worldwide; USD 4.99 newsstand/cover domestic; CAD 5.99 newsstand/cover in Canada (effective 2003). adv. bk.rev. 64 p./no. 3 cols./p.; back issues avail. **Document type:** *Magazine, Consumer.* **Description:** Covers miniature quilting.
Indexed: IHTDI.
Published by: Chitra Publications, 2 Public Ave, Montrose, PA 18801. TEL 570-278-1984, FAX 570-278-2223. Ed. Joyce Libal. Pub. Christiane Meunier. R&P Phyllis Montanye. Adv. contact Sandra Babuka TEL 570-278-1984.

746 DEU ISSN 2192-1237
▼ **MIT SPINNRAD UND SPINDEL.** Text in German. 2011. 2/yr. EUR 24 membership (effective 2011). **Document type:** *Journal, Trade.*
Published by: Handspinngilde e.V., Am Herrnberg 110, Prien, 83209, Germany. http://www.handspinngilde.org.

746 FIN ISSN 1459-692X
MODA. Text in Finnish. 1984. 6/yr. EUR 40.70 (effective 2005). adv. **Document type:** *Magazine, Consumer.* **Description:** Handicraft magazine with patterns and directions for knitting, sewing and decorating.
Former titles (until 2004): Novita Neuleet (1238-9374); Which incorporated (1995-2000): Moda Muotikaavat (1238-5646); (1989-2001): Uudet Kasiyut (0788-3471); (until 1996): Novita Kasityot (1236-1860); (until 1993): Novitakerho
Published by: Yhtyneet Kuvalehdet Oy/United Magazines Ltd., Maistraatinportti 1, Helsinki, 00015, Finland. TEL 358-9-15661, FAX 358-9-145650, http://www.kuvalehdet.fi. Ed. Heidi Laaksonen. adv.: color page EUR 2,750; trim 280 x 217.

646 BRA ISSN 0104-1983
MODA MOLDES. Text in Portuguese. m. (13/yr.). adv. illus. **Document type:** *Magazine, Consumer.* **Description:** Each issue includes 70 patterns of the latest fashions.
Related titles: Supplement(s): Moda Moldes Especial Infantil. ISSN 0104-2319. 1987; Moda Moldes Superfacil; Moda Moldes Especial Tamanhos Grandes. ISSN 1413-3083. 1996; Moda Moldes Especial Lingerie. ISSN 1413-2702. 1996; Moda Moldes Especial Maios e Biquinis. ISSN 1413-3091. 1996; Moda Moldes Especial Homem. ISSN 1413-3067. 1996.
Published by: Editora Globo S.A., Av. Jaguare 1487, Sao Paulo, SP 05346 902, Brazil. TEL 55-11-37677400, FAX 55-11-37677870, atendimento@edglobo.com.br, http://editoraglobo.globo.com. adv.: color page USD 11,300. Circ: 229,000 (paid).

646.4 MEX ISSN 0188-817X
MODA MOLDES. Text in Spanish. 1992. bi-m. adv. **Document type:** *Consumer.* **Description:** Covers women's fashion. Includes patterns and instructions.
Published by: Editorial Television S.A. de C.V., Licio Blanco 435, Azcapotzalco, Mexico City, DF 02070, Mexico. TEL 352-32-66. Ed. Aida Contreras de Pagano.

646.4 746.4 USA ISSN 1946-5629
MODERN SEAMSTER; sewing - style - culture. Text in English. 2008. q. USD 17.95 combined subscription domestic (print & online eds.); USD 27.95 combined subscription foreign (print & online eds.); USD 6.99 per issue; CAD 8.99 per issue in Canada (effective 2009). adv. back issues avail. **Document type:** *Magazine, Consumer.* **Description:** Provides information on fashion sewing.
Related titles: Online - full text ed.: ISSN 1946-5610.
Address: Fort Mason, Bldg 240, San Francisco, CA 94123. Ed., Pub. Devi B Luna. Adv. contact Lee Toulmy.

746 RUS ISSN 1683-3228
NATAL'YA. Text in Russian. 1994. bi-m. **Document type:** *Magazine, Consumer.*
Published by: Edipresse-Konliga ZAO, ul Bakuninskaya 71, Bldg 10, Fl 6, Moscow, 107082, Russian Federation. TEL 7-495-7751435, FAX 7-495-7751434, n.filkina@konliga.ru, http://www.konliga.ru. Circ: 50,000 (paid and controlled).

746.0284 GBR ISSN 1754-6745
NEEDLE & HANDICRAFTS. Variant title: Needle & Handy Crafts. Text in English. 1959. bi-m. GBP 20 domestic; GBP 48 foreign (effective 2009). adv. bk.rev. back issues avail. **Document type:** *Magazine, Trade.* **Description:** Contains informative articles aimed at all aspects of running a retail outlet and early advice of events happening within the trade - exhibitions, product launches etc.
Incorporates (in 2008): Needle & HandiCrafts Buyers' Guide (1755-2605); Which was formerly (1998-2006): Needle & Hobby Crafts Buyers' Guide (1749-8147); (1996-1997): Needlecrafts Review Buyers' Guide (1367-8906); Formerly (until 2007): Needle & Hobby Crafts (1479-2842); (until 1998): Needle & Hobby Crafts Review (1479-2834); (until 1997): Knitting & Haberdashery (1479-2826); (until 1992): Knitting and Haberdashery Review (0023-2327); Knitting and Needle Trade; Knitting Wool Review
—BLDSC (5100.357000).
Address: 1 Castle Close, Romford, Essex RM3 7LN, United Kingdom. TEL 44-1708379897, FAX 44-1708-379804, sales@needlehandicrafts.co.uk. Ed. Arthur Damery. Pubs. Peter J Damery, Susan Damery. Adv. contact Peter J Damery. B&W page GBP 840, color page GBP 1,260; trim 210 x 297.

746.44 USA ISSN 0047-925X
NEEDLE ARTS. Text in English. 1970. q. USD 24 membership. adv. bk.rev. charts; illus.; tr.lit. reprints avail.
Indexed: A&ATA, A30, A31, T01, T02, TTI.
Published by: Embroiderers Guild of America, 335 W Broadway, Ste 100, Louisville, KY 40202. TEL 502-589-6956, FAX 502-584-7900. Ed. Jody Jeroy. Adv. contact Carolyn Deutsch. Circ: 21,000.

746.4 CAN ISSN 1715-4650
A NEEDLE PULLING THREAD. Text in English. 5/yr. CAD 40.45 in New Brunswick, Newfoundland, or Nova Scotia; CAD 37.59 except New Brunswick, Newfoundland, or Nova Scotia; USD 37.95 in United States; CAD 35.80 elsewhere (effective 2008). **Document type:** *Magazine, Consumer.*
Published by: A Needle Pulling Thread, 219 Savage Rd, Newmarket, ON L3X 1R7, Canada. TEL 905-898-4838, 866-969-2678, carla@aneedlepullingthread.com, john@aneedlepullingthread.com. Ed. Carla A Canonico.

746.6 GBR ISSN 0961-4540
NEEDLECRAFT; the magazine for people who just love to stitch. Text in English. 1991. 13/yr. GBP 30.50 in United Kingdom; GBP 38 in Europe; GBP 53 rest of world; GBP 2.99 newsstand/cover (effective 2004). adv. **Document type:** *Magazine, Consumer.* **Description:** Covers all areas of the needle-and-thread hobby, including cross stitch, needlepoint, embroidery and patchwork.
—CCC.
Published by: Future Publishing Ltd., Beauford Ct, 30 Monmouth St, Bath, Avon BA1 2BW, United Kingdom. TEL 44-1225-442244, FAX 44-1225-446019, customerservice@subscription.co.uk, http://www.futureplc.com. Ed. Vivienne Wells. Circ: 33,350 (paid).

746 USA
NEEDLEPOINT BULLETIN. Text in English. 1973. m. USD 12. bk.rev.
Published by: Needlepoint, Inc., 336 Golfview Rd., Apt. 216, N Palm Beach, FL 33408-3521. Ed. Sharlene Weldon.

746 USA
NEEDLEWORK RETAILER. Text in English. 1992. bi-m. USD 12; USD 18 in Canada; USD 25 elsewhere. adv. bk.rev. **Document type:** *Magazine, Trade.*
Published by: Yarn Tree Design, Inc., 117 Alexander Ave, Ames, IA 50010. TEL 515-232-3121, 800-247-3952, FAX 515-232-0789. Ed. Pamela B Chaplin. Pub. Larry R Johnson. R&P Larry Johnson. adv.: B&W page USD 1,135, color page USD 1,585; trim 10.88 x 8.13. Circ: 15,000.

746 GBR ISSN 0967-5884
NEW STITCHES. Text in English. 1992. m. GBP 37.88 domestic; GBP 57 in Europe includes Eire; GBP 69 elsewhere (effective 2009). back issues avail. **Document type:** *Magazine, Consumer.* **Description:** Provides tips and tricks for those interested in creating and improving stitching techniques and patterns.
Published by: Creative Crafts Publishing Ltd., Well Oast, Brenley Ln, Brenley, Faversham, Kent ME13 9LY, United Kingdom. TEL 44-1227-750215, FAX 44-1227-751813, enquiries@ccpuk.co.uk. Adv. contact David Jones. **Dist. by:** Comag.

746.46 FRA ISSN 1956-7480
LES NOUVELLES PATCHWORK ET CREATION TEXTILE. Text in French. 1984. q. EUR 42 domestic; EUR 50 DOM-TOM; EUR 50 in Europe; EUR 52 elsewhere (effective 2007). back issues avail. **Document type:** *Magazine, Consumer.*
Former titles (until 2007): Les Nouvelles du Patchwork (0991-2118); (until 1985): La Lettre du Patchwork (0762-3453)
Published by: Association France Patchwork, B P 214-07, Paris, cedex 7, France. auteur@francepatchwork.com.

746.4 FRA ISSN 0771-7571
TT800
O I D F A BULLETIN. (Organisation Internationale de la Dentelle au Fuseau et a l'Aiguille) Text in English, French. 1983. q. free to members (effective 2009). adv. **Document type:** *Magazine, Consumer.* **Description:** Bulletin of the International Bobbin and Needle Lace Organization, a world-wide lace organization established in 1982.
Indexed: SCOPUS, WTA.
Published by: O I D F A, c/o Sophie Robert, 3 Rue Canteduc, Nimes, 30000, France. http://www.oidfa.com. Ed. Josephine Groeneveld.

746 USA ISSN 1557-2676
$100,000 QUILTING CHALLENGE. Text in English. 2005. q. USD 19.97 domestic; USD 23.97 in Canada; USD 27.97 elsewhere (effective 2007). **Document type:** *Magazine, Consumer.*
Published by: Reality Publishing, LLC, 7 Waterloo Rd, Stanhope, NJ 07874. TEL 973-347-6900, FAX 973-347-6909. Ed. Lisa Swenson Ruble. Pub. Jerry Cohen. **Dist. by:** Kable Media Services, Inc, 505 Park Ave., New York, NY 10022. FAX 212-705-4667, https://www.kable.com.

746.43 ARG ISSN 1852-2335
▼ **PATAGONIA TEJIDO BEBE NINOS. ANUARIO.** Text in Spanish. 2009. m. **Document type:** *Magazine, Consumer.*
Published by: Editorial Patagonica Argentina, Uruguay 266 P.2, Buenos Aires, C1015ABF, Argentina. TEL 54-11-43714947, redaccion@patagoniaediciones.com.ar, http://www.patagoniaediciones.com.ara.

746.43 ARG ISSN 1852-2327
▼ **PATAGONIA TEJIDO BEBE NINOS. ARGENTINA.** Text in Spanish. 2009. m. **Document type:** *Magazine, Consumer.*
Published by: Editorial Patagonica Argentina, Uruguay 266 P.2, Buenos Aires, C1015ABF, Argentina. TEL 54-11-43714947, redaccion@patagoniaediciones.com.ar, http://ww.patagoniaediciones.com.ara.

746 GBR ISSN 0268-5620
PATCHWORK & QUILTING. Text in English. 1985. bi-m. GBP 47.40 domestic; USD 119.88 in US & Canada; GBP 65.40 elsewhere; EUR 3.95, USD 9.99 newsstand/cover (effective 2009). adv. index. back issues avail. **Document type:** *Magazine, Consumer.* **Description:** Describes and reviews quilting and patchwork projects; provides useful hints and advice. Covers exhibitions and profiles noteworthy craftspersons.
Published by: Traplet Publications Ltd, Traplet House, Pendragon Close, Malvern, Worcs WR14 1GA, United Kingdom. TEL 44-1684-588500, FAX 44-1684-578558, general@traplet.com, http://www.traplet.com. Ed. Dianne Huck. Adv. contact Steph Hill TEL 44-1684-588534. **Dist. in Australia & N Zealand:** Traplet Publications Australia, PO Box 501, Engadine, NSW 2233, Australia. TEL 61-2-9520-0933, FAX 61-2-9520-0032, aus@traplet.com; **Dist. in US & Canada:** Traplet Distribution USA Ltd., PO Box 6178, Champaign, IL 61826. usa@traplet.com.

746 AUS ISSN 1838-6687
PATCHWORK & STITCHING. Text in English. 2001 (Aug.). 13/yr. AUD 76 domestic; AUD 115 in New Zealand; AUD 167 elsewhere (effective 2011). adv. back issues avail. **Document type:** *Magazine, Consumer.* **Description:** Provides tips and advice for the first time or a seasoned stitcher with decorating ideas.
Formerly (until 2010): Simply Patchwork & Stitching
Published by: Express Publications Pty. Ltd., 2 Stanley St, Silverwater, NSW 2128, Australia. TEL 61-2-97413800, 800-801-647, subs@magstore.com.au, http://www.emgroup.com.au/.

746 USA
PATCHWORK PATTER. Text in English. 1973. q. adv. bk.rev. **Description:** Furthers the understanding of quilts, quilting, and the history of this particular craft.
Published by: National Quilting Association, Inc., 12190, Columbus, OH 43212-0190. TEL 301-461-5733.

746 ARG ISSN 1851-3565
PATRONES PASO A PASO. Text in Spanish. 2008. m.
Published by: Producciones Publiexpress, Magallanes 1346, Buenos Aires, C1288ABB, Argentina. TEL 54-11-43031484, FAX 54-11-43031280, rrhh@publiexpress.com.ar, http://www.publiexpress.com.ar/.

746 JPN
PICHI. Text in Japanese. 1977. bi-m. JPY 2,340.
Published by: Gakken Co. Ltd., 1-17-15, Nakaikegami, Otaku, Tokyo, 145-0064, Japan. Ed. Junko Horibe.

746 USA ISSN 1067-2249
TT740
PIECEWORK; needlework's living legacy. Text in English. 1993. bi-m. USD 24 domestic; USD 29 in Canada; USD 34 elsewhere; USD 5.99 newsstand/cover (effective 2008). adv. bk.rev. charts; illus. back issues avail.; reprints avail. **Document type:** *Magazine, Consumer.* **Description:** Celebrates and expresses historic and ethnic fabric-related handwork in stories and selected projects on quillting, knitting and other traditional crafts.
Related titles: Online - full text ed.
Indexed: A07, A30, A31, AA, AICP, ArtInd, B04, BRD, W03, W05.
—Ingenta.
Published by: Interweave Press, LLC., 201 E Fourth St, Loveland, CO 80537. TEL 970-613-4658, 800-272-2193, FAX 970-667-8317, customerservice@interweave.com, http://www.interweave.com. Ed. Jeane Hutchins. Pub. Marilyn Murphy. Adv. contact Vicki Yost. Circ: 47,000 (paid and controlled). **Subscr. to:** Publishers Creative Systems, PO Box 469107, Escondido, CA 92046. TEL 760-291-1531, 800-340-7496, FAX 760-291-1567, piecework@pcspublink.com, http://www.pcspublink.com.

746 FRA ISSN 1634-9768
PIQUAGES DE PROVENCE. Text in French. 2002. irreg. back issues avail. **Document type:** *Monographic series, Consumer.*
Published by: Editions Edisud, 30 Av. des Ecoles Militaires, Le Vieux Lavoir, Aix-en-Provence, 13100, France. TEL 33-4-42216144, FAX 33-4-42215620, info@edisud.com.

746.4 FRA ISSN 2108-5706
▼ **POINT DE CROIX ET COMPAGNIE.** Text in French. 2009. irreg. EUR 9.90 per issue (effective 2010). 62 p./no.; **Document type:** *Monographic series, Consumer.*
Published by: Mango Pratique (Subsidiary of: Editions Fleurus), 15-27, Rue Moussorgski, Paris Codex 18, 75895, France. http://www.fleuruseditions.com/mango.

746 BRA ISSN 0104-4052
PONTO DE CRUZ. Text in Portuguese. 199?. m. illus. **Document type:** *Magazine, Consumer.* **Description:** Presents craft projects to make by cross-stitch.
Published by: Editora Globo S.A., Av. Jaguare 1487, Sao Paulo, SP 05346 902, Brazil. TEL 55-11-37677400, FAX 55-11-37677870, http://editoraglobo.globo.com. Pub. Jose Francisco Queiroz. adv.: B&W page USD 2,160, color page USD 2,700; trim 274 x 208. Circ: 40,000 (paid).

PRAKTIKI. *see* WOMEN'S INTERESTS

PROFESSIONAL QUILTER; the business journal for professional quilters. *see* BUSINESS AND ECONOMICS—Small Business

746 ITA ISSN 1724-3998
PUNTO CROCE FACILE E VELOCE. Text in Italian. 2003. m. EUR 1.90 newsstand/cover (effective 2009). **Document type:** *Magazine, Consumer.*
Published by: Edizioni Mimosa, Piazza E de Angeli 9, Milan, 20146, Italy. TEL 39-02-3650507, FAX 39-02-48110494, segreteria@edizionimimosa.it, http://www.edizionimimosa.it.

746 ITA ISSN 1970-8289
PUNTO CROCE. LA GRANDE BIBLIOTECA DELLE IDEE. Text in Italian. 2006. w. **Document type:** *Magazine, Consumer.*
Published by: R C S Libri (Subsidiary of: R C S Mediagroup), Via Mecenate 91, Milan, 20138, Italy. TEL 39-02-5095-2248, FAX 39-02-5095-2975, http://rcslibri.corriere.it/libri/index.htm.

746 ESP ISSN 1576-5873
PUNTO DE CRUZ. Text in Spanish. 2000. 3/yr. **Document type:** *Magazine, Consumer.*
Related titles: ◆ Supplement to: Labores del Hogar. ISSN 0047-3863.
Published by: R B A Edipresse, Perez Galdos 36, Barcelona, 08012, Spain. TEL 34-93-4157374, FAX 34-93-2177378, http://www.rbaedipresse.es.

746 USA ISSN 0885-0631
QUICK AND EASY CROCHET. Text in English. 1985. bi-m. USD 34.75; USD 5.95 newsstand/cover (effective 2004). adv. **Document type:** *Magazine, Consumer.* **Description:** Features the latest crochet fashions, contemporary home decor projects; detailed, easy-to-follow instructions; designs for everyone from beginner to the experienced crocheter.
Published by: Grass Roots Publishing Co., Inc., 908 Oak Tree Ave, Ste H, South Plainfield, NJ 07080-5100. customerservice2@mycomcast.com, http://www.grassrootsmag.com/. Ed. Diane Simpson. Pub. Harry Hochman. Adv. contact Lisa Allmendinger TEL 734-433-1052. B&W page USD 800, color page USD 2,800; trim 8.375 x 10.875. Circ: 32,000 (paid).

746 USA ISSN 1525-7029
TT835
QUICK QUILTS. Text in English. 1996. q. USD 6.95 domestic; USD 8.95 in Canada (effective 2009). adv. back issues avail. **Document type:** *Magazine, Consumer.* **Description:** Features a variety of lap-size quilts and smaller projects, such as totes, table runners, wall hangings and pillows.
Published by: Harris Publications, Inc., 1115 Broadway, New York, NY 10010. TEL 212-807-7100, FAX 212-610-7787, subscriptions@harris-pub.com, http://www.harris-pub.com. Ed. Lisa Swenson Ruble. Pub. Elaine Sexton. Adv. contact Jim Coen. B&W page USD 1,695, color page USD 2,295; trim 8 x 10.875. Circ: 70,000 (paid).

746.4 NLD ISSN 2210-9080
▼ **QUILT & ZO.** Text in Dutch. 2009. q. EUR 23 (effective 2010). adv. **Document type:** *Magazine, Consumer.*
Published by: Uitgeverij Marken, Kaldenkerkerweg 223, Venlo, 5915 PP, Netherlands. TEL 31-77-3207001, FAX 31-77-3207008, info@uitgeverijmarken.nl, http://www.uitgeverijmarken.nl.

746 USA ISSN 1946-0635
TT835
QUILT IT FOR KIDS. Text in English. 2000. a. USD 5.99 per issue (effective 2008). adv. back issues avail. **Document type:** *Magazine, Consumer.* **Description:** Features both contemporary and traditional quilting patterns and designs that appeal to many tastes and skill levels.
Formerly (until 2000): Quilter's Newsletter Magazine's Quilt It for Kids
Published by: C K Media LLC, 741 Corporate Circle, Ste A, Golden, CO 80401. TEL 303-277-0370, FAX 303-278-1010, info@ckmedia.com, http://www.ckmedia.com. Ed. Vivian Ritter. Adv. contact Lisa Rankin TEL 719-539-7410.

746 USA ISSN 2150-248X
TT835
▼ **THE QUILT LIFE.** Text in English. 2010 (Apr.). bi-m. USD 24.99 (effective 2010). **Document type:** *Magazine, Consumer.* **Description:** Features quilt artists revealing sources for their creativity and sharing their techniques, patterns and what "the quilt life" means to them.
Published by: American Quilter's Society, 5801 Kentucky Dam Rd, PO Box 3290, Paducah, KY 42002-3290. TEL 270-898-7903, FAX 270-898-1173, AQSquilt@apex.net, http://www.aqsquilt.com. Ed. Jan Magee.

746.46 USA ISSN 1939-8050
QUILT PINK. Text in English. 2007 (Oct.). a. USD 34.95 per issue (effective 2009). **Document type:** *Magazine, Consumer.*
Published by: Meredith Corporation, 1716 Locust St, Des Moines, IA 50309. TEL 515-284-3000, 800-678-8091, FAX 515-284-3058, patrick.taylor@meredith.com, http://www.meredith.com. Ed. John Riha.

746.4 USA ISSN 1939-2354
TT835
QUILT SAMPLER. Text in English. 1995. s-a. USD 4.99 newsstand/cover (effective 2009). adv. **Document type:** *Magazine, Consumer.* **Description:** Features profiles of ten quilt shops in North America, a distinctive quilt pattern from each shop, and a directory of other shops.
Formerly (until 2007): Better Homes and Gardens Quilt Sampler
Published by: Meredith Corporation, 1716 Locust St, Des Moines, IA 50309. TEL 515-284-3000, 800-678-8091, FAX 515-284-3058, patrick.taylor@meredith.com, http://www.meredith.com. adv.: color page USD 14,954.

746 677 GBR ISSN 0954-4933
THE QUILTER. Text in English. 1979. q. free to members (effective 2009). adv. bk.rev. illus. **Document type:** *Journal, Trade.* **Description:** Provides information for members of guild events and news, as well as features instructive articles.
Formerly (until 1987): Quilters Guild. Newsletter (0261-7420)
Related titles: Supplement(s): Textile Perspectives.
Indexed: ABM, D05, SCOPUS.
Published by: The Quilters Guild of the British Isles, St Anthony's Hall, York, YO1 7PW, United Kingdom. TEL 44-1904-613242, FAX 44-1904-632394, info@quiltersguild.org.uk. Ed. Anne Williams. Adv. contact Carmen Walton.

746 USA ISSN 1531-5630
THE QUILTER MAGAZINE; for yesterday, today, and tomorrow. Text in English. 1989. 7/yr. USD 24.97 domestic; USD 38.97 in Canada; USD 45.97 elsewhere; USD 6.99 per issue (effective 2009). adv. bk.rev. illus. back issues avail. **Document type:** *Magazine, Consumer.* **Description:** Provides quilters a wide variety of projects ranging from small and easy quilts to full-size traditional and contemporary designs.
Formerly (until 2000): Traditional Quilter (1050-0073)
Published by: All American Crafts, Inc., 7 Waterloo Rd, Stanhope, NJ 07874-2621. TEL 973-347-6900, FAX 973-347-6909, dcohen@allamericancrafts.com, http://www.allamericancrafts.com. Ed. Laurette Koserowski TEL 973-347-6900 ext 135. Pub. Jerry Cohen. Adv. contact Carol Newman TEL 570-395-3196. Circ: 65,000 (paid).

746 677 USA ISSN 0274-712X
TT835
QUILTER'S NEWSLETTER MAGAZINE; the magazine for quilt lovers. Text in English. 1969. 10/yr. USD 19.95 domestic; USD 25.95 in Canada; USD 31.95 elsewhere (effective 2008). adv. bk.rev. charts; illus. cum.index: 1969-1988. back issues avail.; reprints avail. **Document type:** *Magazine, Consumer.* **Description:** Presents what is new and news in quilting around the world.
Indexed: IHTDI.
—CCC.
Published by: C K Media LLC, 1450 Pony Express Rd, Bluffdale, UT 84065. TEL 801-816-8300, 800-815-3538, FAX 801-816-8302, info@ckmedia.com, http://www.ckmedia.com. Ed. Angie Hodapp. adv.: B&W page USD 4,770, color page USD 5,640; trim 8.375 x 10.875. Circ: 180,000.

746 USA ISSN 1543-1819
TT835
QUILTER'S WORLD. Text in English. 2003. bi-m. USD 19.97 domestic; USD 24.97 in Canada (effective 2008). adv. bk.rev.; software rev. charts; illus. back issues avail. **Document type:** *Magazine, Consumer.* **Description:** Contains patterns and a directory of quilt shows.
Formed by the merger of (1976-2002): Quilt World (0149-8045); (1989-2002): Quick & Easy Quilting (1045-5965); Which was formerly (1979-1989): Quilt World Omnibook (0199-0985)
Related titles: Online - full text ed.: USD 14.97 (effective 2008).
Indexed: H20, T02.
Published by: Dynamic Resource Group (D R G), 306 E Parr Rd, Berne, IN 46711. TEL 260-589-4000, FAX 260-589-8093, http://www.drgnetwork.com. Ed. Sandra L Hatch.

746 677 USA ISSN 1047-1634
CODEN: DBGEDJ
QUILTMAKER; step-by-step patterns, tips & techniques. Text in English. 1982. bi-m. USD 17.97 domestic; USD 23.97 in Canada; USD 29.97 elsewhere (effective 2008). adv. illus. cum.index: 1982-1986. back issues avail.; reprints avail. **Document type:** *Magazine, Consumer.* **Description:** Features quilts made from appealing new fabrics in patterns geared toward all skill levels—easy, intermediate and challenging.
Indexed: IHTDI.
—CCC.
Published by: C K Media LLC, 1450 Pony Express Rd, Bluffdale, UT 84065. TEL 801-816-8300, 800-815-3538, FAX 801-816-8302, info@ckmedia.com, http://www.ckmedia.com. Eds. Brenda Bauermeister Groelz, June Dudley. Adv. contact Lisa O'Bryan TEL 303-215-5641. B&W page USD 2,705, color page USD 3,690; trim 8.375 x 10.875. Circ: 175,000.

746 USA ISSN 2154-9184
QUILTMAKER'S QUILTING & EMBROIDERY. Variant title: Quilting & Embroidery. Text in English. 2008. irreg. **Description:** Features tips and patterns for quilting and embroidery.
Published by: C K Media LLC, 741 Corporate Circle, Ste A, Golden, CO 80401. TEL 303-215-5600, FAX 303-215-5601, info@ckmedia.com, http://www.ckmedia.com.

746.4 FRA ISSN 1282-3767
QUILTMANIA; le magazine du patchwork. Text in French. 1997. bi-m. EUR 40 (effective 2009). **Document type:** *Magazine, Consumer.*
Published by: Quiltmania Editions, La Butte Gaillard, St-Etienne-de-Montluc, 44360, France. TEL 33-2-40868686, FAX 33-2-40859201. Ed. Martine Redor. Pub. Carol Veillon.

746.4 USA ISSN 1939-2362
TT835
QUILTS & MORE; simple, fresh & fun!. Text in English. 2005. q. USD 6.95 per issue (effective 2009). adv. back issues avail. **Document type:** *Magazine, Consumer.*
Published by: Meredith Corporation, 1716 Locust St, Des Moines, IA 50309. TEL 515-284-3000, 800-678-8091, FAX 515-284-3058, patrick.taylor@meredith.com, http://www.meredith.com. Adv. contact Michelle Thorpe TEL 515-284-3428. color page USD 14,954; trim 8 x 10.5.

746 JPN
QUILTS JAPAN. Text in Japanese. 1986. bi-m. JPY 6,000 domestic; JPY 10,392 foreign; JPY 1,000 newsstand/cover (effective 2001). adv. 170 p./no.; back issues avail. **Document type:** *Magazine, Consumer.* **Description:** Contains articles for quilt enthusiasts, from amateurs to semi-professionals.
Published by: Nihon Vogue Co. Ltd., 3-23 Ichigaya-Honmura-cho, Shinjuku-ku, Tokyo, 162-0845, Japan. TEL 81-3-5261-5489, FAX 81-3-5261-5298, http://www.tezukuritown.com. Ed. Hiroko Koyama. Pub. Nobuaki Seto. adv.: page JPY 500,000; trim 235 x 297. Circ: 150,000.

746 USA ISSN 1543-1606
QUILTS WITH STYLE. Text in English. 1996. bi-m. USD 29.95 domestic; USD 38.95 foreign (effective 2003).
Formerly (until 2002): The Foundation Piecer (1089-0475)
Published by: Zippy Designs Publishing, Inc., R. R. 1 Box 187M, Newport, VA 24128. TEL 540-544-7153, FAX 540-544-7071, zdesigns@swva.net, http://www.zippydesigns.com. Ed. Liz Schwartz.

746 USA
QUILTWORKS TODAY. Text in English. 2003. bi-m. USD 21.98 domestic; USD 27.98 foreign; USD 4.99 newsstand/cover domestic; USD 5.99 newsstand/cover in Canada (effective 2003). **Document type:** *Magazine, Consumer.*
Formed by the merger of (1987-2003): Quilting Today (1040-4457); (1988-2003): Traditional Quiltworks (1050-4435)
Published by: Chitra Publications, 2 Public Ave, Montrose, PA 18801. TEL 570-278-1984, FAX 570-278-2223. Ed. Joyce Libal. Pub. Christiane Meunier. R&P Connie Ellsworth. Adv. contact Sandra Babuka TEL 570-278-1984.

746.9 SWE
RIKSTAECKET. Text in Swedish. 1995. q. SEK 200; SEK 240 foreign (effective 1996).
Published by: Kviltfoereningen Rickstaecket, Fack 27, Sollentuna, 19121, Sweden. TEL 46-8-766-33-36.

746.4 GBR ISSN 2045-340X
ROWAN KNITTING & CROCHET MAGAZINE. Text in English. 1987. s-a. free to members (effective 2010). back issues avail. **Document type:** *Magazine, Consumer.*
Former titles (until 2003): Rowan Knitting Magazine (1365-5264); (until 199?): Rowan (0955-2642)
Published by: Rowan Yarns, Green Ln Mill, Holmfirth, W Yorkshire HD9 2DX, United Kingdom. TEL 44-1484-681881.

746 UKR ISSN 1814-9367
RUKODELIE. Text in Russian. 2005. bi-m. **Document type:** *Magazine, Consumer.*

Published by: Edipress Ukraina LLC, vul Dymytrova, 5, Bldg 10A, 3-i poverkh, Kiev, 03680, Ukraine. TEL 380-44-4907140, FAX 380-44-4907141, edipresse-info@edipresse.com.ua. Ed. Elena Senina. Pub. Inna Ryk. Circ: 20,000 (controlled).

S A G A NEWS. *see* ARTS AND HANDICRAFTS

338.47687 USA
S Q E PROFESSIONAL. (Sewing Quilting & Embroidery) Text in English. 1965. m. USD 100 membership (effective 2006). adv. bk.rev. **Document type:** *Magazine, Trade.* **Description:** Provides business, marketing, and other information of relevance to dealers in the sewing, quilting and embroidery industries.
Former titles: Sewing & Embroidery Professional; Round Bobbin (1076-058X)
Published by: V D T A/S D T A, 2724 2nd Ave, Des Moines, IA 50313. TEL 515-282-9101, 800-367-5651, FAX 515-282-4483, mail@vdta.com. Ed. Beth Vitiritto. Adv. contact Joe Burklund. Circ: 10,000 (controlled).

746 053.1 DEU ISSN 0946-4379
SABRINA; Strickjournal. Text in German. 1991. m. EUR 33.60; EUR 2.80 newsstand/cover (effective 2011). adv. **Document type:** *Magazine, Consumer.* **Description:** Contains patterns and advice on various knitting and needlework projects.
Related titles: Hungarian ed.: ISSN 1863-8686. 2007; Supplement(s): Sabrina Special. ISSN 1434-0046.
Published by: OZ Verlag GmbH, Roemerstr 90, Rheinfelden, 79618, Germany. TEL 49-7623-9640, FAX 49-7623-964200, info@oz-verlag.de, http://www.oz-verlag.com. Adv. contact Veronika Mainka.

746 POL ISSN 1732-792X
SABRINA. Text in Polish. 2006. q. PLZ 27.60; PLZ 6.90 newsstand/cover (effective 2010). adv. **Document type:** *Magazine, Consumer.*
Published by: BPV Polska Sp. z o.o., ul Rybacka 11, Wroclaw, 53-656, Poland. TEL 48-71-3518077, FAX 48-71-3518079.

746.4 RUS ISSN 1683-0954
SABRINA. Text in Russian. 1997. m. USD 74 in United States (effective 2010). **Document type:** *Magazine, Consumer.* **Description:** Filled with knitting tips and advice, including tips for beginning knitters and knitting pattern help.
Published by: Edipresse-Konliga ZAO, ul Bakuninskaya 71, Bldg 10, Fl 6, Moscow, 107082, Russian Federation. TEL 7-495-7751435, FAX 7-495-7751434. Ed. Galina Mednikova. Adv. contact Lyudmila Soldalova. Circ: 74,880 (paid and controlled). **Subscr. to:** Unicont Enterprises Inc., 1340 Centre St, Ste 209, Newton, MA 02459. TEL 800-763-7475, FAX 617-964-8753, podpiska@unipressa.com, http://www.podpiska.us.

746.4 CZE
SABRINA. Text in Czech. bi-m. CZK 414; CZK 69 newsstand/cover (effective 2009). **Document type:** *Magazine, Consumer.*
Published by: Rolino, spol. s.r.o., Bratri Capku 10, Prague 10, 101 00, Czech Republic. TEL 420-2-67311358, FAX 420-2-67315529, info@rolino.cz, http://www.rolino.cz.

746 RUS ISSN 1811-8097
SABRINA. BABY. Text in Russian. 1997. bi-m. **Document type:** *Magazine, Consumer.*
Published by: Edipresse-Konliga ZAO, ul Bakuninskaya 71, Bldg 10, Fl 6, Moscow, 107082, Russian Federation. TEL 7-495-7751435, FAX 7-495-7751434, n.filkina@konliga.ru, http://www.konliga.ru. Circ: 82,000 (paid and controlled).

746.4 FRA ISSN 2108-1352
SABRINA CROCHET ACTUEL. Text in French. 2003. bi-m. **Document type:** *Magazine, Consumer.*
Published by: B P V Media, 21 Rue de l'Altenbach, Michelbach le Bas, 68730, France.

746.4 CZE ISSN 1614-6956
SABRINA - DEKORATIVNI HACKOVANI. Text in Czech. 2005. bi-m. CZK 270; CZK 45 newsstand/cover (effective 2009). **Document type:** *Magazine, Consumer.*
Published by: Rolino, spol. s.r.o., Bratri Capku 10, Prague 10, 101 00, Czech Republic. TEL 420-2-67311358, FAX 420-2-67315529, info@rolino.cz, http://www.rolino.cz.

646.4 FRA ISSN 2108-1328
SABRINA FILET AU CROCHET. Text in French. 2007. q. **Document type:** *Magazine, Consumer.*
Related titles: Supplement(s): Sabrina Filet au Crochet. Hors-serie. ISSN 2106-8275. 200?.
Published by: B P V Media, 21 Rue de l'Altenbach, Michelbach le Bas, 68730, France.

746.4 CZE
SABRINA - HACKOVANI SPECIAL. Text in Czech. s-a. CZK 65 newsstand/cover (effective 2009). **Document type:** *Magazine, Consumer.*
Published by: Rolino, spol. s.r.o., Bratri Capku 10, Prague 10, 101 00, Czech Republic. TEL 420-2-67311358, FAX 420-2-67315529, info@rolino.cz, http://www.rolino.cz.

746.4 CZE
SABRINA - KREATIVNI. Text in Czech. 2005. 5/yr. CZK 245; CZK 49 newsstand/cover (effective 2009). **Document type:** *Magazine, Consumer.*
Published by: Rolino, spol. s.r.o., Bratri Capku 10, Prague 10, 101 00, Czech Republic. TEL 420-2-67311358, FAX 420-2-67315529, info@rolino.cz, http://www.rolino.cz.

746.4 CZE
SABRINA - KREATIVNI SPECIAL. Text in Czech. 5/yr. CZK 55 newsstand/cover (effective 2009). **Document type:** *Magazine, Consumer.*
Published by: Rolino, spol. s.r.o., Bratri Capku 10, Prague 10, 101 00, Czech Republic. TEL 420-2-67311358, FAX 420-2-67315529, info@rolino.cz, http://www.rolino.cz.

746 FRA ISSN 2108-1336
▼ **SABRINA PATCHWORK.** Text in French. 2009. q. **Document type:** *Magazine, Consumer.*
Published by: B P V Media, 21 Rue de l'Altenbach, Michelbach le Bas, 68730, France.

746.4 CZE
SABRINA - SPECIAL. Text in Czech. 2005. q. CZK 59 newsstand/cover (effective 2009). **Document type:** *Magazine, Consumer.*
Published by: Rolino, spol. s.r.o., Bratri Capku 10, Prague 10, 101 00, Czech Republic. TEL 420-2-67311358, FAX 420-2-67315529, info@rolino.cz, http://www.rolino.cz.

746 RUS ISSN 1815-5464
SABRINA. SPETSIAL'NYI VYPUSK. Text in Russian. 2005. m. **Document type:** *Magazine, Consumer.*
Published by: Edipresse-Konliga ZAO, ul Bakuninskaya 71, Bldg 10, Fl 6, Moscow, 107082, Russian Federation. TEL 7-495-7751435, FAX 7-495-7751434, n.filkina@konliga.ru. Circ: 10,000 (paid and controlled).

746 RUS ISSN 1815-5456
SABRINA. VYAZANIE DLYA DETEI. Text in Russian. 2005. bi-m. USD 40 in United States (effective 2010). **Document type:** *Magazine, Consumer.*
Published by: Edipresse-Konliga ZAO, ul Bakuninskaya 71, Bldg 10, Fl 6, Moscow, 107082, Russian Federation. TEL 7-495-7751435, FAX 7-495-7751434, n.filkina@konliga.ru. Circ: 70,000 (paid and controlled). **Subscr. to:** Unicont Enterprises Inc., 1340 Centre St, Ste 209, Newton, MA 02459. TEL 800-763-7475, FAX 617-964-8753, podpiska@unipressa.com, http://www.podpiska.us.

746 USA ISSN 1061-6756
SAMPLER & ANTIQUE NEEDLEWORK QUARTERLY. Text in English. 1991. q. USD 24.95 domestic; USD 34.95 in Canada; USD 44.95 elsewhere; USD 6.99 per issue (effective 2009). adv. **Document type:** *Magazine, Consumer.* **Description:** Features needlework projects that challenge and build the skills of the contemporary needleworker and also lavish photographs of antique needlework and sewing tools.
Related titles: Online - full text ed.
Published by: Hoffman Media, LLC., 1900 International Park Dr, Ste 50, Birmingham, AL 35243. TEL 205-995-8860, 888-411-8995, FAX 205-991-0071, publicrelations@hoffmanmedia.com, http://www.hoffmanmedia.com. Ed. Lorna Reeves TEL 205-262-2125. Pub. Gary Johnson TEL 205-262-2165. Adv. contact Robyn Brown Hoglan TEL 205-262-2137. page USD 2,000; bleed 8.25 x 11.125. Circ: 7,900.

746.4 USA ISSN 1553-0876
SAMPLINGS; a selected offering of antique samplers and needlework. Text in English. 1992. s-a. USD 45 domestic; USD 55 foreign (effective 2005). **Document type:** *Catalog.*
Published by: M. Finkel & Daughter, Inc., 936 Pine St, Philadelphia, PA 19107-6128. TEL 215-627-7797, 800-598-7432, FAX 215-627-8199, mailbox@finkelantiques.com.

646 DEU ISSN 1863-9720
SANDRA; stricken. Text in German. 1994. q. EUR 17.60; EUR 4.40 newsstand/cover (effective 2011). adv. **Document type:** *Magazine, Consumer.*
Formerly (until 2003): Stricken Aktuell (0948-4035)
Published by: OZ Verlag GmbH, Roemerstr 90, Rheinfelden, 79618, Germany. TEL 49-7623-9640, FAX 49-7623-964200, info@oz-verlag.de, http://www.oz-verlag.com. Adv. contact Veronika Mainka.

746 POL ISSN 1895-2496
SANDRA EXTRA. Text in Polish. 2006. bi-m. PLZ 36; PLZ 6.90 newsstand/cover (effective 2010). adv. **Document type:** *Magazine, Consumer.*
Published by: BPV Polska Sp. z o.o., ul Rybacka 11, Wroclaw, 53-656, Poland. TEL 48-71-3518077, FAX 48-71-3518079.

746.4 FRA ISSN 2106-7945
▼ **SANDRA MODE AU CROCHET.** Text in French. 2009. q. **Document type:** *Magazine, Consumer.*
Published by: B P V Media, 21 Rue de l'Altenbach, Michelbach le Bas, 68730, France.

746.4 FRA ISSN 2106-7678
SARAH FILET AU CROCHET. Text in French. 2008. q. **Document type:** *Magazine, Consumer.*
Related titles: Supplement(s): Sabrina Filet au Crochet. Hors-serie. ISSN 2106-8275. 200?.
Published by: B P V Media, 21 Rue de l'Altenbach, Michelbach le Bas, 68730, France.

746.4 FRA ISSN 2106-7686
SARAH HARDANGER. Text in French. 2008. q. **Document type:** *Magazine, Consumer.*
Published by: B P V Media, 21 Rue de l'Altenbach, Michelbach le Bas, 68730, France.

746.22 GBR ISSN 1742-254X
SELVEDGE. Text in English. 2004. bi-m. GBP 45 domestic; EUR 75 in Europe; USD 115 in United States; CAD 135 in Canada; AUD 160 in Australasia; JPY 10,500 in Japan; GBP 75 elsewhere; GBP 8.50 newsstand/cover (effective 2009). adv. back issues avail. **Document type:** *Magazine, Consumer.* **Description:** Contains information about textiles in fine art, interiors, fashion, travel, textile photography and shopping.
Related titles: Online - full text ed.: GBP 20 (effective 2006).
Indexed: D05, SCOPUS, WTA.
—CCC.
Published by: Selvedge Magazine, P O Box 40038, London, N6 5UW, United Kingdom. subeditor@selvedge.org. Ed. Polly Leonard. adv.: color page GBP 1,500, color page EUR 2,000, color page USD 3,000; 238 x 238. Circ: 25,000.

746 646.4 USA ISSN 1063-9160
SEW BEAUTIFUL. Text in English. 1987. bi-m. USD 24.99 (effective 2005). adv. bk.rev. back issues avail. **Document type:** *Magazine, Consumer.* **Description:** How-to articles and patterns. Features include heirloom sewing, smocking, embroidery, applique and cross stitch designs, with emphasis on sewing for children and women.
Related titles: E-mail ed.; Fax ed.
Published by: Martha Pullen Co., Inc. (Subsidiary of: Hoffman Media, LLC.), 149 Old Big Cove Rd., Brownsboro, AL 35741. TEL 256-533-9586 ext 115, 800-547-4176 ext 115, http://www.marthapullen.com/index.html. Ed. Kathy Bernard. adv.: B&W page USD 1,300, color page USD 525; trim 10.88 x 8.13. Circ: 57,000 (paid); 3,300 (controlled).

SEW NEWS; the fashion how-to magazine. *see* CLOTHING TRADE—Fashions

SEW NEWS HOLIDAYS. *see* CLOTHING TRADE

746 GBR ISSN 1352-013X
SEWING WORLD; the sewing magazine for sewing machine enthusiasts. Text in English. 1995. m. GBP 47.40 domestic; USD 119.88 in US & Canada; GBP 65.40 elsewhere; GBP 3.95, USD 9.99 newsstand/cover (effective 2009). adv. **Document type:** *Magazine, Consumer.* **Description:** Describes sewing projects to make clothing, as well as quilts, placemats, and upholstery. Reviews sewing machines and other products of interest.
Published by: Traplet Publications Ltd, Traplet House, Pendragon Close, Malvern, Worcs WR14 1GA, United Kingdom. TEL 44-1684-588500, FAX 44-1684-578558, general@traplet.com, http://www.traplet.com. Ed. Wendy Gardiner. R&P Tony Stephenson. Adv. contact Steph Hill TEL 44-1684-588534. **Dist. addr. in Australia & New Zealand:** Traplet Publications Australia, PO Box 501, Engadine, NSW 2233, Australia. TEL 61-2-9520-0933, FAX 61-2-9520-0032, aus@traplet.com; **Dist. addr. in US & Canada:** Traplet Distribution USA Ltd., PO Box 6178, Champaign, IL 61826. usa@traplet.com.

746.4 USA ISSN 1935-8482
SEWSTYLISH. Variant title: Sew Stylish. Text in English. 2007 (Apr.). 5/yr. USD 6.99 per issue (effective 2011). adv. back issues avail. **Document type:** *Magazine, Consumer.* **Description:** Teaches sewing secrets, improves sewing confidence and creates the latest styles.
Published by: The Taunton Press, Inc., 63 South Main St, PO Box 5506, Newtown, CT 06470. TEL 203-426-8171, 800-477-8727, FAX 203-426-3434, publicrelations@taunton.com, http://www.taunton.com.

746 USA
SIMPLE CREATIVE CROCHET. Text in English. q.
Published by: Meredith Corporation, 1716 Locust St, Des Moines, IA 50309. TEL 515-284-3000, 800-678-8091, FAX 515-284-3058, patrick.taylor@meredith.com, http://www.meredith.com. **Subscr. to:** PO Box 37341, Boone, IA 50337.

746 USA ISSN 1061-3234
SIMPLY CROSS STITCH. Text in English. 1990. bi-m. USD 19.97 domestic; USD 29.97 foreign (effective 2007). back issues avail. **Document type:** *Magazine, Consumer.* **Description:** Presents cross stitch patterns and instructions for home decorating, toys and clothing.
Published by: Dynamic Resource Group (D R G), 306 E Parr Rd, Berne, IN 46711. TEL 260-589-4000, FAX 260-589-8093, http://www.drgnetwork.com. Ed. Brenda Stratton. Circ: 32,500.

746.4 GBR ISSN 1745-7793
SIMPLY KNITTING. Text in English. 2005. 13/yr. GBP 44.76 domestic; GBP 55 in Europe; GBP 60 in United States; GBP 65 elsewhere; GBP 4.99 newsstand/cover (effective 2010). adv. back issues avail. **Document type:** *Magazine, Consumer.* **Description:** Covers designer interviews, club news, competitions and terrific technical advice, not forgetting exclusive reader offers and the most stylish new designs from famous names on the UK knitting scene.
Published by: Future Publishing Ltd., Beauford Ct, 30 Monmouth St, Bath, Avon BA1 2BW, United Kingdom. TEL 44-1225-442244, FAX 44-1225-446019, customerservice@subscription.co.uk, http://www.futureplc.com. Ed. Debora Bradley. Adv. contact Amanda Haughey. **Subscr. to:** Tower House, Sovereign Park, Market Harborough, Leicestershire LE16 9EF, United Kingdom. TEL 44-844-8481602, FAX 44-1858-438795, future@subscription.co.uk.

SLOEJDFORUM. *see* ARTS AND HANDICRAFTS

746.4 USA
SPINCRAFT PATTERN NEWSLETTER; the handspinner's craft pattern newsletter. Text in English. 3/yr. USD 12 (effective 2000). index. **Document type:** *Newsletter, Consumer.* **Description:** For handspinners, knitters, crocheters and weavers. Contains patterns for handspun or exotic yarn.
Published by: Connie Delaney, Ed. & Pub., 300 Monroe St, Salmon, ID 83467-3313. TEL 208-756-3076, FAX 801-741-8489. Circ: 600 (paid).

746.4 USA ISSN 2155-8043
▼ **SPOOL.** Text in English. 2010 (Sept.). q. USD 18 domestic; USD 26 in Canada; USD 34 elsewhere (effective 2011). **Document type:** *Magazine, Consumer.* **Description:** Features knitting, crochet, needlepoint, cross stitch, embroidery and punch needle.
Published by: Selby & Selby, LLC, 120 Crown Ct, Nicholasville, KY 40356. TEL 859-492-8244, dvselby@yahoo.com.

746.4 NLD ISSN 1879-7563
STITCH & PRINT INTERNATIONAL. Text in German, English. 2008. q. EUR 59 (effective 2010). adv. **Document type:** *Magazine, Consumer.*
Formerly (until 2009): Eurostitch Magazine (English/German Edition) (1878-1845); Which was formed by the merger of (1999-2008): Eurostitch Magazine (English Edition) (1387-0076); (199?-2008): Eurostitch Magazine (Deutsche Ausgabe) (1389-1413)
Indexed: SCOPUS, TM, WTA.
Published by: Eisma Businessmedia bv, Celsiusweg 41, Postbus 340, Leeuwarden, 8901 BC, Netherlands. TEL 31-58-2954854, FAX 31-58-2954875, businessmedia@eisma.nl. Ed. Marijke Kuypers. adv.: color page EUR 2,365; 202 x 268. Circ: 13,000.

746 NLD ISSN 1877-8658
STITCH AT HOME. Text in Dutch. 200?. q. EUR 20; EUR 5.95 newsstand/cover (effective 2010). adv. **Document type:** *Magazine, Consumer.*
Related titles: Online - full text ed.: ISSN 2212-2745.
Published by: Uitgeverij Blad Apart, Kerkstraat 63, Giesbeek, 6987 AB, Netherlands. Eds. Judith Schol, Bea Demmers. Pub. Judith Schol.

746.4 GBR ISSN 1467-6648
STITCH WITH THE EMBROIDERERS GUILD. Text in English. 1999. bi-m. GBP 23.70 domestic; GBP 28.80 in Europe; GBP 35.70 in the Americas; GBP 38.10 elsewhere; GBP 3.95 per issue domestic; GBP 4.80 per issue in Europe; GBP 5.95 per issue in the Americas; GBP 6.35 per issue elsewhere (effective 2009). adv. back issues avail. **Document type:** *Magazine, Consumer.* **Description:** Covers a wide range of stitches through their history, step by step instructions, contemporary design ideas and projects.
—CCC.
Published by: E G Enterprises Ltd., PO Box 42B, East Molesey, Surrey KT8 9BB, United Kingdom. TEL 44-20-89431229, FAX 44-20-89779882. Ed. Kathy Troup.

STITCHES. *see* CLOTHING TRADE

N O

746 DEU
STRICKTRENDS. Text in German. q. EUR 15; EUR 5 newsstand/cover (effective 2011). adv. **Document type:** *Magazine, Consumer.*
Formerly (until 2008): Sabrina Strick-Trends
Published by: OZ Verlag GmbH, Roemerstr 90, Rheinfelden, 79618, Germany. TEL 49-7623-9640, FAX 49-7623-964200, info@oz-verlag.de, http://www.oz-verlag.com.

SUSANNA - RUKODELIE. *see* ARTS AND HANDICRAFTS

746 RUS ISSN 1729-8660
SUSANNA - VYAZANIE. Text in Russian. 2004. m. USD 74 in United States (effective 2010). **Document type:** *Magazine, Consumer.*
Published by: Edipresse-Konliga ZAO, ul Bakuninskaya 71, Bldg 10, Fl 6, Moscow, 107082, Russian Federation. TEL 7-495-7751435, FAX 7-495-7751434, n.filkina@konliga.ru, http://www.konliga.ru. Circ: 75,000 (paid and controlled). **Subscr. to:** Unicont Enterprises Inc., 1340 Centre St, Ste 209, Newton, MA 02459. FAX 617-964-8753, podpiska@unipressa.com, http://www.podpiska.us.

746 FIN ISSN 1236-3855
SUURI KASITYOLEHTI. Text in Finnish. 1974. 10/yr. EUR 92 (effective 2009). adv. **Document type:** *Magazine, Consumer.* **Description:** Dispenses advice on various hobby handicrafts such as sewing, knitting, home decoration, and other do-it-yourself crafts.
Formerly (until 1993): Suuri Kasityokerho (0355-2098)
Published by: Sanoma Magazines Finland Corporation, Lapinmaentie 1, Helsinki, 00350, Finland. TEL 358-9-1201, FAX 358-9-1205171, info@sanomamagazines.fi, http://www.sanomamagazines.fi. Circ: 68,042 (paid).

646.26 POL ISSN 1898-5807
SZYDELKOWANIE. Text in Polish. 2008. bi-m. PLZ 36; PLZ 6.90 newsstand/cover (effective 2010). adv. **Document type:** *Magazine, Consumer.*
Published by: BPV Polska Sp. z o.o., ul Rybacka 11, Wroclaw, 53-656, Poland. TEL 48-71-3518077, FAX 48-71-3518079.

TAITO. *see* ARTS AND HANDICRAFTS

746.43 ARG ISSN 1852-1797
▼ **TEJDIOS PATAGONICA ARGENTINA.** Text in Spanish. 2009. m. **Document type:** *Magazine, Consumer.*
Published by: Editorial Patagonica Argentina, Uruguay 266 P.2, Buenos Aires, C1015ABF, Argentina. TEL 54-11-43714947, redaccion@patagoniaediciones.com.ar, http://ww.patagoniaediciones.com.ara.

746.43 ARG ISSN 1851-6068
TEJIDOS PASO A PASO. Text in Spanish. 2008. m.
Published by: Producciones Publiexpress, Magallanes 1346, Buenos Aires, C1288ABB, Argentina. TEL 54-11-43031484, FAX 54-11-43031280, rrhh@publiexpress.com.ar, http://www.publiexpress.com.ar/.

746 DEU
TEXTILSTUNDE; Lehrblaetter fuer Textiles Gestalten und Werken. Text in German. 1977. s-a. looseleaf. EUR 14 (effective 2008). cum.index: 1977-1999. back issues avail. **Document type:** *Journal, Academic/Scholarly.*
Published by: A L S Verlag GmbH, Voltastr 3, Dietzenbach, 63128, Germany. TEL 49-6074-82160, FAX 49-6074-27322, info@als-verlag.de, http://www.als-verlag.de.

746 DEU
TEXTILSTUNDE II. Text in German. 1992. s-a. looseleaf. EUR 14.50 (effective 2008). cum.index: 1992-1999. back issues avail. **Document type:** *Journal, Academic/Scholarly.*
Published by: A L S Verlag GmbH, Voltastr 3, Dietzenbach, 63128, Germany. TEL 49-6074-82160, FAX 49-6074-27322, info@als-verlag.de, http://www.als-verlag.de.

746 USA ISSN 0882-7370
TT697
THREADS; for people who love to sew. Variant title: Taunton's Threads. Text in English. 1985. bi-m. USD 32.95 in US & Canada; USD 38.95 elsewhere; USD 6.99 per issue (effective 2009). adv. bk.rev. illus. index. back issues avail.; reprints avail. **Document type:** *Magazine, Trade.* **Description:** Covers the design, materials and techniques of fashion sewing, embellishment and other needle arts.
Related titles: Online - full text ed.
Indexed: ASIP, G05, G06, G07, G08, I05, IHTDI, MagInd, SCOPUS, T01, T02, TTI.
—BLDSC (8820.317800), IE, Ingenta.
Published by: The Taunton Press, Inc., 63 South Main St, PO Box 5506, Newtown, CT 06470. TEL 203-426-8171, FAX 203-426-3434, publicrelations@taunton.com, http://www.taunton.com. Pub. Kathleen Davis. adv.: B&W page USD 6,155, color page USD 8,615; trim 8.88 x 10.88. Circ: 130,000 (paid).

746 ITA ISSN 1121-8533
TRICOT CASA; nuove idee. Text in Italian. 1975. m. EUR 20.50 (effective 2008). **Document type:** *Magazine, Consumer.*
Published by: Alexandra Editrice, Largo Lanciani 1, Roma, 00162, Italy. TEL 39-06-86320393, FAX 39-06-86320481, alexandra@alexandra.it, http://www.alexandra.it.

746.4 FRA ISSN 1959-7819
TRICOT MAGAZINE. Text in French. 2008. bi-m. EUR 24 (effective 2008). **Document type:** *Magazine, Consumer.*
Published by: Editions de Saxe, 20 Rue Croix Barret, Lyon, 69358 Cedex 7, France. TEL 33-4-78728323, FAX 33-4-78726418, http://www.edisaxe.com.

746 ITA ISSN 1121-8541
TRICOT SELEZIONE; uncinetto d'arte. Text in Italian. 1973. m. EUR 25 (effective 2008). **Document type:** *Magazine, Consumer.*
Published by: Alexandra Editrice, Largo Lanciani 1, Roma, 00162, Italy. TEL 39-06-86320393, FAX 39-06-86320481, alexandra@alexandra.it, http://www.alexandra.it.

746 ITA ISSN 1971-9353
UNCINETTO FACILE FACILE. Text in Italian. 2007. w. adv. **Document type:** *Magazine, Consumer.*
Published by: Fabbri Editori (Subsidiary of: R C S Libri), Via Mecenate 91, Milan, 20138, Italy.

746 305.4 USA ISSN 0277-0628
TT835
➤ **UNCOVERINGS.** Text in English. 1980. a., latest vol.23, 2002. USD 20 per issue to non-members; free to members (effective 2010). illus. Index. back issues avail.; reprints avail. **Document type:** *Journal, Academic/Scholarly.* **Description:** Contains essays that represent the recent advances in quilt and related research.
Indexed: A07, A30, A31, AA, ABM, AmH&L, ArtInd, B04, B24, CA, D05, FemPer, MLA-IB, SCOPUS, T02, W03, W05.
—Ingenta.
Published by: American Quilt Study Group, 1610 L St, Lincoln, NE 68508. TEL 402-477-1181, FAX 402-477-1181, aqsg2@americanquiltstudygroup.org. Ed. Laurel Horton.

746 SWE ISSN 0281-3343
VAEVMAGASINET; Scandinavian weaving magazine. Text in Swedish. 1982. q. SEK 220 domestic; SEK 240 in Nordic countries; SEK 260 in Europe; SEK 340 elsewhere (effective 2007). adv. **Document type:** *Magazine, Consumer.*
Related titles: English ed.: ISSN 1653-9141.
Indexed: IHTDI.
Published by: T B Ignell AB, Vestmansgatan 37, Linkoeping, 58216, Sweden. TEL 46-13-138460, FAX 46-13-133617. Ed. Kristina Ignell. Pubs. Bengt Arne Ignell, Kristina Ignell. adv.: B&W page SEK 8,700, color page SEK 12,000; 220 x 290. Circ: 13,000.

746 RUS ISSN 1560-5388
VERENA. Text in Russian. 1997. m. RUR 660 domestic; RUR 55 newsstand/cover domestic (effective 2004). adv. **Document type:** *Magazine, Consumer.*
Published by: Izdatel'skii Dom Burda, ul Pravdy 8, Moscow, 125040, Russian Federation. TEL 7-095-7979849, FAX 7-095-2571196, vertrieb@burda.ru, http://www.burda.ru. adv.: page USD 2,000. Circ: 80,000 (paid and controlled).

746.92 UKR
VERENA. Text in Russian. m. UAK 24.35 for 6 mos. domestic (effective 2004). **Document type:** *Magazine, Consumer.*
Published by: Burda Ukraina, Zhyljanskaja ul. 29, Kiev, 01033, Ukraine. TEL 38-044-4908363, FAX 38-044-4908364, zhestkov@burda.ua, http://www.burda.ua.

746 USA ISSN 1938-0534
VERENA KNITTING. Text in English. 2008. q. USD 24.97 domestic; USD 47.47 in Canada; USD 52.47 elsewhere (effective 2011). adv. **Document type:** *Magazine, Consumer.*
Related titles: Online - full text ed.
Published by: Vikant Crafts Publishing, Inc., 6577 Windham Lane, Long Grove, IL 60047. TEL 888-670-6869. Ed. Margery Winter.

746 DEU ISSN 1865-6951
VERENA STRICKEN. Variant title: Verena. Text in German. 1986. 4/yr. EUR 25 domestic (effective 2011). adv. **Document type:** *Magazine, Consumer.*
Formerly (until 2002): Verena (0940-9297)
Published by: Vikant Crafts Publishing GmbH, Bahnhofstr 50, Suderburg, 29556, Germany. TEL 49-5826-958950, FAX 49-5826-9589520. adv.: B&W page EUR 3,000, color page EUR 5,000. Circ: 180,000 (paid and controlled).

746 USA ISSN 1067-702X
TT900.C4
VICTORIAN CHRISTMAS. Text in English. 1990. 10/yr. USD 1.25 per issue (effective 2008). back issues avail. **Document type:** *Magazine, Consumer.*
Related titles: Online - full text ed.
Published by: Goodman Media Group, Inc., 250 W 57th St, Ste 710, New York, NY 10107. TEL 212-262-2247, FAX 212-400-8620, info@goodmanmediagroup.com, http://www.goodmanmediagroup.com. Eds. Haug Priscilla, Haug Rebecca.

746.4 CZE ISSN 1804-221X
VLNIKA. Text in Czech. 2007. q. CZK 196; CZK 49 newsstand/cover (effective 2010). adv. **Document type:** *Magazine, Consumer.*
Published by: Vlnika s.r.o., Dolni Pena 5, J. Hradec, 377 01, Czech Republic. TEL 420-774-844836.

746 USA ISSN 0890-9237
TT820
VOGUE KNITTING INTERNATIONAL. Text in English. 1982. q. USD 21.97 domestic; USD 25.97 in Canada; USD 6.99 per issue domestic; USD 8.50 per issue in Canada (effective 2009). adv. illus. back issues avail.; reprints avail. **Document type:** *Magazine, Consumer.*
Formerly (until 198?): Vogue Knitting
—CCC.
Published by: Soho Publishing Company, 233 Spring St, 3rd Fl, New York, NY 10013. FAX 646-336-3960, http://www.sohopub.com/. Adv. contact Doreen Connors TEL 212-937-2554. B&W page USD 6,263, color page USD 8,386; trim 8.25 x 10.75. **Subscr. to:** G M C Publications Ltd., 166 High St, Lewes, East Sussex BN7 1XU, United Kingdom. TEL 44 -1273-488005, craigj@thegmcgroup.com, http://www.thegmcgroup.com.

746 RUS ISSN 1681-844X
VYAZANIE - VASHE HOBBI. Text in Russian. 2002. m. USD 68 in United States (effective 2010). **Document type:** *Magazine, Consumer.*
Published by: Edipresse-Konliga ZAO, ul Bakuninskaya 71, Bldg 10, Fl 6, Moscow, 107082, Russian Federation. TEL 7-495-7751435, FAX 7-495-7751434, n.filkina@konliga.ru, http://www.konliga.ru. Circ: 100,000 (paid and controlled). **Subscr. to:** Unicont Enterprises Inc., 1340 Centre St, Ste 209, Newton, MA 02459. TEL 800-763-7475, FAX 617-964-8753, podpiska@unipressa.com, http://www.podpiska.us.

746.4 RUS ISSN 1681-8431
VYSHITYE KARTINY. Text in Russian. 2002. m. **Document type:** *Magazine, Consumer.*
Published by: Edipresse-Konliga ZAO, ul Bakuninskaya 71, Bldg 10, Fl 6, Moscow, 107082, Russian Federation. TEL 7-495-7751435, FAX 7-495-7751434, n.filkina@konliga.ru, http://www.konliga.ru. Circ: 75,000 (paid and controlled).

746 USA
WOOL GATHERING. Text in English. 1959. s-a. USD 20 domestic; USD 25 foreign (effective 2001). bk.rev.; video rev. 12 p./no.; back issues avail. **Document type:** *Newsletter.* **Description:** Aimed at handknitters; includes complete instructions for an original Meg Swansen or Elizabeth Zimmermann designs.
Former titles: Elizabeth Zimmermann's Wool Gathering; Wool Gathering
Published by: Schoolhouse Press, 6899 Cary Bluff, Pittsville, WI 54466. TEL 715-884-2799, FAX 715-884-2829. Ed., R&P Meg Swansen TEL 715-884-2799. Circ: 3,000 (paid).

746 GBR ISSN 1360-0699
WORKBOX; embroidery - textiles - needlecrafts - today and through history. Text in English. 1984. bi-m. USD 17 domestic; USD 49 in United States (effective 2009). adv. bk.rev. illus. back issues avail. **Document type:** *Magazine, Consumer.* **Description:** For needlecraft enthusiasts: news about embroidery, dollmaking, patchwork and quilting.
Formerly (until 1995): Audrey Babington's Workbox (0268-5175)
Published by: Ebony Media Ltd., PO Box 25, Liskeard, Cornwall PL14 6XX, United Kingdom. TEL 44-1579-340100, FAX 44-1579-340400. Ed. Carole D'Silva. Adv. contact Paul Elkin. **Dist. by:** Comag, Tavistock Rd, W Drayton, Middlesex UB7 7QE, United Kingdom.

745.5 GBR ISSN 1460-1974
THE WORLD OF CROSS STITCHING. Text in English. 1997. 13/yr. GBP 39.99 domestic; GBP 50 in Europe; GBP 65 elsewhere; GBP 3.99 newsstand/cover (effective 2010). adv. back issues avail. **Document type:** *Magazine, Consumer.* **Description:** Contains designs, ideas, hints, patterns and advice for those interested in cross stitching.
Published by: Origin Publishing Ltd. (Subsidiary of: B B C Worldwide Ltd.), Tower House, Fairfax St, Bristol, BS1 3BN, United Kingdom. TEL 44-117-9279009, FAX 44-117-9349008, info@originpublishing.co.uk, http://www.originpublishing.co.uk. Ed. Hannah Bellis. Adv. contact Melanie Harris TEL 44-117-3148367. Circ: 42,022. **Subscr. to:** PO Box 326, Sittingbourne ME9 8FA, United Kingdom. TEL 44-1795-414676, FAX 44-1795-414555, origin@servicehelpline.co.uk.

NEW AGE PUBLICATIONS

see also ASTROLOGY ; PARAPSYCHOLOGY AND OCCULTISM

133 USA
ABSURD ORG. Text in English. irreg. back issues avail. **Description:** Presents miscellaneous projects cutting the edge of common sense, new age and high-pressure.
Media: Online - full text.

299 USA
ABUNDANT LIVING (PRESCOTT). Text in English. 1991. m. USD 18 domestic (effective 2011). bk.rev.; Website rev. abstr. back issues avail. **Document type:** *Newsletter, Consumer.* **Description:** Promotes uplifting and inspiring thoughts through poetry, humor and other ways to a wide audience. Includes excerpts from books by famous authors of spiritual and motivational literature.
Published by: Delia Sellers Ministries, Inc., PO Box 12525, Prescott, AZ 86304-2525. abundantnow@juno.com. Ed., Pub., R&P Dr. Delia Sellers. Circ: 2,500 (paid); 2,500 (controlled).

299 USA ISSN 1552-9827
ABUNDANT WELLNESS. Text in English. 2004. m. **Document type:** *Newsletter, Consumer.*
Media: Online - full text.
Published by: Open The Gift, Inc. http://www.openthegift.org. Ed. Dr. Ray Pope.

158 NOR ISSN 1504-4343
ACEM-MAGASINET. Text in Norwegian. 1973. bi-m. NOK 200 membership (effective 2006). **Document type:** *Magazine, Consumer.*
Formerly (until 2005): Acem-Nytt (0805-6676)
Published by: Acem International School of Meditation, PO Box 2559, Solli, Oslo, 0202, Norway. TEL 47-23-118708, FAX 47-23-831831, acem@acem.no.

299 USA ISSN 2152-436X
▼ **ALIGN YOUR LIFE.** Text in English. 2009. w. free (effective 2010). back issues avail. **Document type:** *Newsletter, Consumer.*
Media: Online - full text.
Published by: Inner Alignment Living

299 USA ISSN 1946-0538
▼ ➤ **ALTERNATIVE SPIRITUALITY AND RELIGION REVIEW.** Abbreviated title: A S R R. Text in English. 2009 (May). s-a. USD 65 to individuals; USD 225 to institutions (effective 2011). **Document type:** *Journal, Academic/Scholarly.* **Description:** Publishes book reviews, review essays, and literature surveys in the New Religious Movements field.
Media: Online - full text.
Published by: Academic Publishing, PO Box 102, Stevens Point, WI 54481. admin@academicpublishing.org, http://www.academicpublishing.org. Ed. James R Lewis.

051 USA
AMERICAN SPIRIT (BERKELEY). Text in English. 1992. bi-m. USD 12; USD 25 foreign (effective 1998). **Document type:** *Newspaper, Consumer.* **Description:** Educates people about what is going on behind the scenes in all areas of their life, especially finances, the economy, spirituality, medicine and health.
Published by: Sterling Rose Press, Inc., PO Box 14341, Berkeley, CA 94712. TEL 510-848-7673.

110 MEX
ANO CERO. Text in Spanish. 1990. m. MXN 4,500.
Published by: Editorial Samra S.A. de C.V., Lucio Blanco 435, Azcapotzalco, Mexico City, DF 02400, Mexico. TEL 525-3523266. Ed. Enrique de Vicente.

APPLIED PSYCHOPHYSIOLOGY AND BIOFEEDBACK. *see* PSYCHOLOGY

133.9 NLD ISSN 1567-9896
BF1001
➤ **ARIES**; journal for the study of western esotericism. Text in English. 2001. 2/yr. EUR 130, USD 180 to institutions; EUR 141, USD 197 combined subscription to institutions (print & online eds.) (effective 2012). back issues avail.; reprint service avail. from PSC. **Document type:** *Journal, Academic/Scholarly.* **Description:** Covers all aspects of the study of esoteric currents in modern and contemporary western culture.
Incorporates (1983-199?): A R I E S (0752-2452)
Related titles: Online - full text ed.: ISSN 1570-0593. EUR 118, USD 164 to institutions (effective 2012) (from IngentaConnect).
Indexed: A01, A03, A08, A21, A22, AmHI, CA, E01, H07, IZBG, RI-1, T02.

—IE, Ingenta. **CCC.**
Published by: Brill, PO Box 9000, Leiden, 2300 PA, Netherlands. TEL 31-71-5353500, FAX 31-71-5317532, cs@brill.nl. Eds. Antoine Faivre, Roland Edighoffer, Wouter J Hanegraaff. **Dist. by:** Turpin Distribution Services Ltd., Pegasus Dr, Stratton Business Park, Biggleswade, Bedfordshire SG18 8QB, United Kingdom. TEL 44-1767-604954, FAX 44-1767-601640, custserv@turpin-distribution.com, http://www.turpin-distribution.com/.

133.9 NLD ISSN 1871-1405
➤ **ARIES BOOK SERIES.** Text in English. 2005. irreg., latest vol.12, 2011. price varies. **Document type:** *Monographic series, Academic/Scholarly.*
Indexed: IZBG.
Published by: Brill, PO Box 9000, Leiden, 2300 PA, Netherlands. TEL 31-71-5353500, FAX 31-71-5317532, cs@brill.nl. Ed. Marco Pasi.

051 USA
ARIZONA NETWORKING NEWS. Text in English. 1981. bi-m. USD 15 domestic; USD 30 foreign (effective 2000). adv. bk.rev. back issues avail. **Document type:** *Newspaper.* **Description:** Focuses on holistic health.
Published by: Tri-Pyramids, Inc., PO Box 5477, Scottsdale, AZ 85261-5477. TEL 480-951-1275, FAX 480-951-1295. Ed. Joanne Henning Tedesco. adv.: page USD 725; trim 15.75 x 10.25. Circ: 50,000.

133 100 BEL ISSN 0778-5437
ATLANTIDE. Text in French. 1990. q. free (effective 2005). 24 p./no. 2 cols./p.; **Document type:** *Newsletter.*
Address: Rue Bois Paris 16, Lasne, 1380, Belgium. info@atlantideasbl.org, http://www.atlantideasbl.org/index.htm. Ed., Pub. Huguette Declercq. Circ: 5,000.

110 USA
AURORA RISING; the magazine for a new world. Text in English. q. USD 26.65; USD 20 in Canada. adv. illus. **Document type:** *Magazine, Consumer.* **Description:** Human potential forum for issues of heart, mind and soul with focuses on healing and the arts.
Formerly (until 1994): Aurora
Address: PO Box 33459, Decatur, GA 30033. TEL 404-315-8040, FAX 404-315-8050, aurorarising@earthlink.net. Ed., Pub., R&P Karen Willis. Adv. contact Karen Adler.

613.05 AUS ISSN 1446-1056
AUSTRALIAN YOGA LIFE. Text in English. 2001. 3/yr. AUD 20.85 domestic; AUD 55 foreign (effective 2007). **Document type:** *Magazine, Consumer.*
Indexed: PEI.
Address: PO Box 399, Moorooka, QLD 4105, Australia. TEL 61-7-3397-6699, FAX 61-7-3397-5288, ay@ayl.com.au, http://www.ayl.com.au/subs1.html. Ed. Mike Sullivan. Pub. Judith Clements.

110 USA
AVATAR JOURNAL; on the trail of spiritual enlightenment. Text in English. q.?. USD 3.95 newsstand/cover. illus. **Description:** Covers a specific approach to the study of spiritual enlightenment with articles and interviews.
Published by: Star's Edge International, 237 North Westmonte Dr., Altomonte Springs, FL 32714. TEL 407-788-3090. Ed. Miken Chappell.

THE AZRAEL PROJECT NEWSLETTER; 25 years of researching anthropomorphic death encounters. *see* PARAPSYCHOLOGY AND OCCULTISM

133 USA
B P M CULTURE ONLINE; the electronic renaissance. Text in English. irreg. USD 18 (effective 2001). adv. music rev. **Description:** Covers new age and underground rave culture, its music, fashion and events.
Media: Online - full text.
Published by: Djmixed.com, 8517 Santa Monica Blvd, West Hollywood, CA 90069. TEL 310-360-7170, 800-471-3291, FAX 310-360-7171. Ed. David Ireland.

110 GBR ISSN 1355-1876
BAELDER; the pan-European fraternity of knowledge. Text in English. 1990. q. GBP 15, EUR 25, USD 25 in Europe; GBP 18, EUR 31, USD 31 elsewhere (effective 2003). adv. bk.rev. 92 p./no.; back issues avail. **Document type:** *Journal, Academic/Scholarly.* **Description:** Contains articles on the occult, mythology, folklore, ethnography, pagan history, religion and spirituality. Covers the European traditions and heritage as they exist on the continent and worldwide. Includes membership directory and reports of coming events.
Published by: (European Cultural Centre for Appreciation and Advancement of Regions, Traditions and Heritage), Order of the Jarls of Baelder / Arktion, Arktion Foundation, Ground Fl, 60, Elmhurst Rd, Reading, Berkshire RG1 5HY, United Kingdom. heritage-school@ntlworld.com. Circ: (controlled).

158 CAN ISSN 1920-9207
BE-INSPIRED. Text in English. 2004. w. free (effective 2010). back issues avail. **Document type:** *Newsletter, Consumer.* **Description:** Contains inspirational messages, inspirational stories and quotes that have empowered.
Media: Online - full text.
Published by: Joshua M. Zuchter, Pub, 4243C Dundas St, W, Ste 153, Toronto, ON, Canada. TEL 416-388-1135, info@joshuazuchter.com.

133 110 USA
THE BEACON (MIAMI). Text in English. 1974. m. USD 5. adv. bk.rev.
Published by: Roundtable of the Light Centers, Inc., 1801 S W 82nd Pl, Miami, FL 33155. TEL 305-261-0722. Ed. Larry Cuttler. Circ: 450.

158 NLD ISSN 1877-1440
BEWUST ZIJN MAGAZINE. Text in Dutch. 2008. q. EUR 22.50 domestic; EUR 29.50 in Belgium (effective 2011). adv. bk.rev. **Document type:** *Magazine, Consumer.*
Published by: Idrie, Bernhardsteeg 2a, Zutphen, 7201 DB, Netherlands. TEL 31-575-548159.

181.45 158.12 SWE ISSN 1104-1722
BINDU; magazine on yoga, tantra and meditation. Text in Danish, English, German, Swedish. 1993. s-a. back issues avail. **Document type:** *Journal, Consumer.*
Published by: Skandinavisk Yoga och Meditationskola/Scandinavian Yoga and Meditation School, Haa Course Center, Hamneda, 34013, Sweden. TEL 46-372-55063, FAX 46-372-55036, haa@scand-yoga.org.

THE BLESSED BEE; a pagan family newsletter. *see* RELIGIONS AND THEOLOGY—Other Denominations And Sects

391.65 CAN
BODY MODIFICATION EZINE. Text in English. irreg. **Document type:** *Magazine, Consumer.* **Description:** Focuses on body piercing, scarification, subincision, castration, body art, and all other forms of body modification.
Media: Online - full text.
Address: c/o Shannon Larratt, 247 Bathurst St, Toronto, ON M4T 2B4, Canada. Pub. Shannon Larratt.

051 USA ISSN 2150-9786
▼ **BODY STORIES.** Text in English. 2009. w.
Media: Online - full content.
Published by: The Missing Thread, 55 Graystone Terr, San Francisco, CA 94114. TEL 415-440-1561, info@themissingthread.com, http://www.themissingthread.com.

299 USA
BOING BOING. Text in English. 1988. 4/yr. USD 14; USD 25 foreign. adv. bk.rev. **Description:** Includes cyberpunk, fringe technology, psychedelia, altered consciousness, high weirdness, and subculture curiosities.
Address: 11288 Ventura Blvd, 818, Studio City, CA 91604. http://www.well.com/user/mark. Circ: 15,000 (paid).

133 USA ISSN 0006-8233
BOTH SIDES NOW; a journal of spiritual, cultural and political alternatives. Text in English. 1969. irreg., latest no.34-35. USD 9; USD 15 foreign (effective 1999). adv. bk.rev. **Document type:** *Newsletter.* **Description:** Covers spiritual and political alternatives with emphasis on New Age,lightworking and peacemaking.
Related titles: Microform ed.: (from PQC).
Published by: Free People, 10547 State Hwy 110 N, Tyler, TX 75704-3731. TEL 903-592-4263. Ed., Pub. Elihu Edelson. adv.: page USD 50; 11 x 8.5. Circ: 200.

181.45 USA
BREATH SERIES; a progression of pranayama practices. Text in English. irreg., latest vol.4. adv. **Document type:** *Magazine, Consumer.* **Description:** Helps readers learn the importance of proper breathing.
Indexed: E-psyche.
Published by: Himalayan International Institute (HII), 952 Bethany Turnpike, Honesdale, PA 18431- 9706. TEL 570-253-4929, FAX 570-253-9078, info@himalayaninstitute.org, http://www.himalayaninstitute.org. Ed. Deborah Willoughby. R&P Irene Petryszak. Adv. contact Jim McGinley.

181.45 USA
BREATHE (NEW YORK). Text in English. 2004. bi-m. USD 19.95 domestic; USD 33.58 in Canada; USD 3.95 newsstand/cover (effective 2004). adv. **Document type:** *Magazine, Consumer.* **Description:** Covers the people, places, art forms and styles that shape yoga, including modern philosophy and practices as well as ancient traditions.
Published by: Breathe Media, Inc., 141 Fifth Ave, 11th Fl, New York, NY 10010. TEL 212-358-4010, FAX 212-505-6899, info@breathemag.com. Ed. Danielle Claro. Pub. Lisa Haines. adv.: B&W page USD 7,875, color page USD 10,500; trim 9 x 10.75. Circ: 150,000 (paid and controlled).

133.90135 USA
BRIDGING REALITIES. Text in English. m. free. **Document type:** *Newsletter.* **Description:** Provides information for anyone aspiring to empower the self-creation of reincarnation experience and the answers to the questions of life and death.
Media: Online - full text.
Published by: Pure Mind Foundation, 1228 Westloop, 320, Manhattan, KS 66502. TEL 573-858-3222. Ed. Stan Stitz.

299 NLD ISSN 1874-6691
BRILL HANDBOOKS ON CONTEMPORARY RELIGION. Text in English. 2007. irreg., latest vol.3, 2010. price varies. **Document type:** *Monographic series, Academic/Scholarly.*
Indexed: IZBG.
Published by: Brill, PO Box 9000, Leiden, 2300 PA, Netherlands. TEL 31-71-5353500, FAX 31-71-5317532, cs@brill.nl. Ed. James R Lewis.

158 613.7 GBR ISSN 2043-9393
▼ ➤ **BRITISH JOURNAL OF WELLBEING**; a new approach to mental and physical health. Text in English. 2010. m. GBP 90 (effective 2010). adv. back issues avail.; reprints avail. **Document type:** *Journal, Academic/Scholarly.* **Description:** Addresses ways in which practitioners can support people to take care of their own mental and physical needs.
Related titles: Online - full text ed.
Indexed: C06, T02.
Published by: MA Healthcare Ltd., St Jude's Church, Dulwich Rd, London, SE24 0PB, United Kingdom. TEL 44-20-75016762, FAX 44-20-79788319, conferences@markallengroup.com, http://www.mahealthcareevents.co.uk. Adv. contact Stacy Schwarz TEL 44-20-75016734. **Subscr. to:** Jesses Farm, Snow Hill, Dinton, Salisbury SP3 5HN, United Kingdom. TEL 44-1722-716997.

299.93 AUS ISSN 1326-4311
BROADSWORD. Text in English. 1995. bi-m. AUD 6 domestic; AUD 12 foreign (effective 2000).
Address: 153 Wardell Rd, Dulwich Hill, NSW 2203, Australia. http://www.broadsword.org/about.htm.

133 PRY ISSN 1017-2777
BUHARDILLA. Text in Spanish. 1990. m. adv.
Published by: Distribuidor Internacional Publicaciones Paraguayas, Ayoreos e-4a y 5a, PO Box 2507, Asuncion, Paraguay. TEL 595-21-495367, FAX 595-21-447460. Circ: 1,000.

299 USA ISSN 1931-6917
C I H S JOURNAL; subtle energy and spiritual evolution. Text in English. 2006. a. free (effective 2009). **Document type:** *Journal, Academic/Scholarly.* **Description:** Aims to enhance the integration of science and religion.
Media: Online - full text. **Related titles:** Print ed.: ISSN 1942-5945. 2008.
Published by: California Institute for Human Science, 701 Garden View Ct, Encinitas, CA 92024. TEL 760-634-1771, FAX 760-634-1772, info@cihs.edu. Ed. Elizabeth Newby-Fraser. Adv. contact Hideki Baba.

133 VEN
CABALA; la magia de saber insolito. Text in Spanish. 1977. m. adv.
Published by: Editorial Elite, Publicaciones Capriles (Subsidiary of: Publicaciones Capriles), Torre de la Prensa, Plaza del Panteon, Apartado Postal 2976, Caracas, DF 1010-A, Venezuela. TEL 81-49-31-832399, FAX 83-88-35, TELEX 21173 ULTIN VC. Ed. J P Leroy. Circ: 80,000.

299 TWN ISSN 1992-6944
CAOBENFENG/HERBAIR. Text in Chinese. 2006. q. **Document type:** *Journal, Academic/Scholarly.*
Formerly (until 2007): Caoben Xinjiankang Lu/Herb & Health (1817-6356)
Published by: Caobenfeng Wenhua Youxian Gongsi/HerbAir Culture, Funan Lu, no.1, 9/F, Taipei, Taiwan. TEL 886-2-27489639, FAX 886-2-27470022, info@HerbAir.com.

133 USA
CATALYST (MARIETTA); a publication resource of New Age newsletters, book reviews, personals, holistic health, UFO's and psychic connections. Text in English. 1985. a. USD 9.95; USD 14.95 foreign. bk.rev. **Document type:** *Directory.*
Formerly: Psychic Connections
Published by: Catalyst, 2384 Forest Green Dr., Marietta, GA 30062-2505. Ed., Pub., R&P Irene Serra.

658 USA
CATALYST DIRECTORY NEWSLETTER. Text in English. 1985. a. USD 9.95. adv. bk.rev. **Document type:** *Directory, Trade.* **Description:** Lists metaphysical, New Age UFO, psychtronics newsletters; resources, back to earth, holistic health.
Formerly: Catalyst Perspective (0899-000X)
Related titles: Online - full text ed.
Indexed: B11, CWI, G05, G06, G07, G08, I05.
Published by: Catalyst, 2384 Forest Green Dr., Marietta, GA 30062-2505. Circ: 2,000.

CHOICE; health & wellbeing. *see* ALTERNATIVE MEDICINE

CHRISTIAN*NEW AGE QUARTERLY; a bridge supporting dialogue. *see* RELIGIONS AND THEOLOGY

158 USA
CHRYSALIS (OMAHA). Text in English. 1995. bi-w. **Description:** Includes personal stories of interest to addictions recovery, personal growth, coping skills for medical conditions and abuse survivors.
Media: Online - full text.
Published by: Transformations Forum, SIS, Inc., 4524 Shirley St, Omaha, NE 68106. Ed. Terre Seuss.

110 133.5 USA ISSN 0009-6520
CHURCH OF LIGHT QUARTERLY. Text in English. 1925. q. USD 20 domestic; USD 35 foreign (effective 2000). adv. bk.rev. charts; illus. **Document type:** *Newsletter, Consumer.* **Description:** Provides astrological analysis of topical personalities and events, current cycle charts and weather data. Covers mental and spiritual alchemy, sacred tarot, and the hermetic tradition of the Brotherhood of Light.
Published by: Church of Light Inc., 111 South Kraemer Blvd, Suite A, Brea, CA 92821. TEL 714-255-9218, FAX 714-255-9121. Ed. Paul Brewer. R&P Vicki Brewer. Circ: 1,000 (paid).

COLOURAMA; world's premier colour magazine & directory. *see* ALTERNATIVE MEDICINE

110 USA
COMMON GROUND (MILL VALLEY); bay area's magazine for conscious community since 1974. Text in English. 1973. q. free local. adv. bk.rev. illus. **Document type:** *Magazine, Consumer.* **Description:** Lists resources for personal growth, with interviews and feature articles on topics relating to personal development.
Related titles: Online - full text ed.
Indexed: E-psyche.
Published by: Common Ground Publishing Inc., 775 East Blithesdale Ave. #222, Mill Valley, CA 94941. TEL 415-459-4900, FAX 415-505-1410. Ed., Pub. Rob Sidon. adv.: B&W page USD 1,390, color page USD 2,060; trim 13.25 x 10.5. Circ: 105,000.

133 AUS ISSN 1834-4267
COMPASS BEARINGS. Text in English. 2002. m. **Document type:** *Newsletter, Consumer.*
Media: Online - full text.
Published by: Inner Compass http://www.innercompass.com.au/content/blogcategory/13/35.

100 DEU ISSN 1863-0758
CONNECTION SPIRIT; Bewusstsein, Vision, Lebenskunst. Text in German. 1985. bi-m. EUR 47 domestic; EUR 49 foreign (effective 2009). adv. music rev.; bk.rev. back issues avail. **Document type:** *Magazine, Consumer.*
Formerly (until 2005): Connection (0932-5565)
Related titles: Online - full text ed.
Published by: Connection Medien GmbH, Hauptstr 5, Niedertaufkirchen, 84494, Germany. TEL 49-8639-98340, FAX 49-8639-1219, schneider@connection-medien.de, http://www.connection-medien.de. Ed., Pub., R&P Wolf Schneider TEL 49-8639-600970. Adv. contact Birgit Roeser. page EUR 1,680; trim 216 x 303. Circ: 14,000.

299.9 NZL ISSN 1177-3189
CONTACT (CHRISTCHURCH). Text in English. 2006. bi-m. **Document type:** *Magazine, Consumer.*
Published by: Time Will Tell Spiritual Resource Centre, 13 Beaumont St, Beckenham, Christchurch, 8002, New Zealand. contact@timewilltell.co.nz.

299 GBR ISSN 2042-7298
CONTAKT. Text in English. 2007. q. GBP 15; GBP 1.50 per issue (effective 2010). adv. back issues avail. **Document type:** *Magazine, Consumer.* **Description:** Features issues that impact on our lives.
Related titles: Online - full text ed.: free (effective 2010).
Published by: Black Development Agency, 5, Russell Town Ave, Redfield, Bristol, BS5 9LT, United Kingdom. TEL 44-117-9396645, FAX 44-117-9396646. Ed. Marvin Rees. Adv. contact Seniz Ismet. page GBP 300; 210 x 297.

158 USA
CONTINUUM MAGAZINE; many paths, one voice. Text in English. q. USD 24; USD 6.95 newsstand/cover (effective 2001). adv. **Document type:** *Magazine, Consumer.* **Description:** Offered as a high vibration tool to aid in the evolution of the human consciousness.
Address: Rr 2 Box 32a., Tyler, MN 56178-9797. TEL 507-476-8283. **Dist. by:** International Publishers Direct, 27500 Riverview Center Blvd, Bonita Springs, FL 34134. TEL 858-320-4563, FAX 858-677-3220.

CORPORATE STATEMENT; the organ of the United Fascist Union. *see* POLITICAL SCIENCE

133 USA ISSN 1058-4196
COSMIC VOICE; cosmic revelations for the New Age. Text in English. 1955. q. USD 20 (effective 2000). adv. illus. back issues avail. **Document type:** *Newsletter.* **Description:** Provides latest information about cosmic activities for ecological balance and spiritual upliftment. Contains cosmic transmissions given by extraterrestrials through yogic medium, George King.
Supersedes: Aetherius Society Newsletter; Cosmic Voice
Published by: Aetherius Society, 6202 Afton Pl., Hollywood, CA 90028-8298. TEL 323-465-9652, FAX 323-462-5165. Ed., R&P Brian Keneipp. Circ: 1,000.

133 GBR ISSN 0269-8773
BL300
COSMOS (EDINBURGH). Text in English. 1984. s-a. free to members (effective 2009). **Document type:** *Journal, Academic/Scholarly.* **Description:** Examines myth, religion and cosmology across cultural and disciplinary boundaries and with increasing understanding of world views in the past and present.
Incorporates (in 1985): Shadow (0266-8599)
Indexed: AICP, MLA-IB.
Published by: Traditional Cosmology Society, School of Scottish Studies, University of Edinburgh, 27 George Sq., Edinburgh, Scotland EH8 9LD, United Kingdom. TEL 44-131-6504152, E.Lyle@ed.ac.uk.

299 CAN ISSN 1910-703X
BV4000P37
➤ **COUNSELING ET SPIRITUALITE/COUNSELLING AND SPIRITUALITY.** Text in English, French. 1981. s-a. CAD 40 domestic to individuals; USD 38 foreign to individuals; CAD 75 domestic to institutions; USD 70 foreign to institutions (effective 2007). **Document type:** *Journal, Academic/Scholarly.* **Description:** Provides a forum for dialogue among researchers, trainers and practitioners in the vast area of pastoral studies.
Formerly (until 2006): Pastoral Sciences (0713-3383)
Indexed: A21, DIP, FR, IBR, IBZ, P03, PsycInfo, R&TA, RI-1.
—INIST. **CCC.**
Published by: Saint Paul University, Faculty of Human Sciences (Subsidiary of: Saint Paul University/Universite Saint-Paul), 223 Main St, Ottawa, ON K1S 1C4, Canada. TEL 613-236-1393, humansciences@ustpaul.ca, http://web.ustpaul.uottawa.ca/HumanSciences/index_e.asp. Ed. Terry L Gall. Circ: 250 (paid and controlled).

158 USA ISSN 1945-9300
CREATING TRUE WEALTH. Text in English. 2008. s-m. free (effective 2009). back issues avail. **Document type:** *Newsletter, Consumer.* **Description:** Offers advice on self improvement and how to be successful.
Media: Online - full content.
Published by: Books2Wealth, PO Box 3151, Albany, OR 97321. info@books2wealth.com. Pub. Daniel R Murphy.

110 USA
CREATIONS; a showcase of Long Island's creative spirit. Text in English. 1987. 6/yr. USD 20 (effective 1999). adv. bk.rev. **Document type:** *Magazine, Consumer.* **Description:** Contains articles, poems and photography on spirituality, alternative health, the environment and mental and emotional health.
Published by: The InnerLight Center, Inc., P O Box 970, Black Mountain, NC 28711. TEL 516-674-3051, FAX 516-674-2117, ilcreations@earthlink.net. Eds. Constance Burns, Vijay Director. Pub., Adv. contact Vijay Director. R&P Constance Burns. Circ: 55,000.

CRONE; women coming of age. *see* WOMEN'S INTERESTS

299.93 USA
CURIOSITY'S ESCAPE. Text in English. 1997. irreg. free. adv. bk.rev. back issues avail. **Document type:** *Newsletter.* **Description:** Publishes unkowns, fiction, essay and general columns on new age.
Media: Online - full text. Eds. Bryan Nelson, Joshua Schulman. Pub. Jimmy Lo.

DAGOBERT'S REVENGE (ONLINE EDITION). *see* CLUBS

613.2 USA ISSN 2155-708X
▼ **DELCIOUS BYTE EZINE.** Text in English. 2009. m. free (effective 2010). **Document type:** *Magazine, Consumer.* **Description:** Provides holistic health information, recipes and nutrition and lifestyle tips.
Media: Online - full text.
Published by: Delicious Health, Inc., 1504 Lyon St, San Francisco, CA 94115. TEL 415-595-5775.

DIRECTORY TO CANADIAN PAGAN RESOURCES. *see* RELIGIONS AND THEOLOGY—Other Denominations And Sects

135.3 154.63 USA ISSN 1054-6707
BF1074
DREAM NETWORK JOURNAL; a quarterly publication exploring dreams and myth. Text in English. 1982. q. USD 25 in US & Canada; USD 35 elsewhere (effective 2007). adv. film rev.; music rev.; tel.rev.; video rev.; Website rev.; bk.rev. illus. cum.index: 1982-1991. 52 p./no.; back issues avail.; reprints avail. **Document type:** *Journal, Consumer.* **Description:** Provides a forum for exchange of ideas among individuals interested in understanding the symbologic language of dreams, with a focus on dream sharing and exploring relationships between dream and mythology.
Related titles: Online - full text ed.
Indexed: E-psyche.
Published by: Dream Network, P O Box 1026, Moab, UT 84532-1026. TEL 435-259-5936, FAX 435-259-5936. Ed., Pub., Adv. contact H Roberta Ossana. page USD 380; 7.25 x 9.5. Circ: 4,000.

E F T WITH KIYA. (Emotional Freedom Techniques) *see* PSYCHOLOGY

299 631 AUS ISSN 0310-222X
EARTH GARDEN; sustainable living with country or city alternatives. Abbreviated title: E G. Text in English. 1972. q. AUD 27 domestic; AUD 43 foreign; AUD 6.95 per issue (effective 2008). adv. bk.rev. back issues avail. **Document type:** *Magazine, Consumer.* **Description:** Provides practical ideas, shared knowledge, sources and a guide to alternatives to high-consumption lifestyles.
Indexed: A11, GardL, Gdlns, M01, M02, Pinpoint, T02, WBA, WMB.
Published by: Earth Garden Pty. Ltd., PO Box 2, Trentham, VIC 3458, Australia. TEL 61-3-54241819, FAX 61-3-54241743, info@earthgarden.com.au. Ed. Alan T Gray. Pub. Judith K Gray. Adv. contact Doug Falconer TEL 61-3-54241399. B&W page AUD 1,400, color page AUD 1,500; 173 x 232. Circ: 17,500.

133 USA
EARTHSPIRIT. Text in English. 1988. q. USD 8.50. adv. bk.rev. back issues avail. **Document type:** *Newsletter.* **Description:** Devoted to magic and nature spirituality and to exploring various traditions such as Wicca, Paganism, Shamanism and New Age spirituality.
Formerly (until 1994): FireHeart (1046-6029)
Published by: EarthSpirit Community, PO Box 723-UI, Willimsburg, MA 01096. TEL 413-238-4240. Ed. A Arther. Circ: 3,000.

EASY FENG SHUI. *see* INTERIOR DESIGN AND DECORATION

133 USA
EKLECTIQUE. Text in English. s-a. USD 2. bk.rev.; music rev. **Description:** Covers the underground scene.
Related titles: Online - full text ed.
Address: PO Box 616, Salt Lake City, UT 84110. Ed. Alicia Poter.

100 USA ISSN 0890-538X
EMERGING. Text in English. 1969. s-a. USD 50 contribution (effective 2011). illus. **Document type:** *Magazine, Consumer.* **Description:** Essays and commentary on spiritual consciousness and evolution, stressing the importance of universal and unconditional love, the study of wisdom teachings, and living life with purpose.
Supersedes (in 1987): Seeker Magazine (0886-1285); (in 1982): Seeker Newsletter (0145-8361); (in 1972): New Focus (0047-9683)
Published by: Teleos Institute, 7119 E Shea Blvd, Ste 109, PMB 418, Scottsdale, AZ 85254. TEL 480-948-1800, FAX 480-948-1870, Teleosinst@aol.com, http://www.consciousnesswork.com. Circ: 150 (paid).

133 100 USA
EMSHOCK LETTER. Text in English. 1977. irreg. (7-12/yr.). USD 25 (effective 2000). bk.rev. back issues avail. **Document type:** *Newsletter.* **Description:** Provides an "experiment in consciousness," with no limit on variables.
Published by: Vongrutnorv Og Press, Inc., Randall Flat Rd, PO Box 411, Troy, ID 83871-0411. TEL 208-835-4902. Ed., Pub., R&P Steven E Erickson. Circ: 1,000.

ENCHANTING NEWS. *see* PARAPSYCHOLOGY AND OCCULTISM

299 AUT
ENGELMAGAZIN. Text in German. 2008. bi-m. EUR 25.80; EUR 4.30 newsstand/cover (effective 2011). adv. **Document type:** *Magazine, Consumer.*
Published by: Mondhaus Medien GmbH, Wieningerstr 1, Schaerding, 4780, Austria. TEL 43-7712-358500, FAX 43-7712-3585011, info@mh-medien.at.

ENLIGHTENNEXT; the magazine for evolutionaries. *see* RELIGIONS AND THEOLOGY

299.93 USA ISSN 1523-1224
➤ **ESOTERICA.** Text in English. 1999. irreg., latest 2010. bk.rev. back issues avail. **Document type:** *Journal, Academic/Scholarly.* **Description:** Devoted to the study of the Western esoteric traditions, such as alchemy, magic and mysticism.
Media: Online - full text.
Published by: Michigan State University, College of Arts & Letters, 116 Morrill Hall, East Lansing, MI 48824. wurst@msu.edu, http://www.cal.msu.edu/. Ed. Arthur Versluis.

133 ITA
L'ETA DELL'ACQUARIO. Text in Italian. 1971. bi-m. bk.rev. back issues avail. **Document type:** *Newsletter, Consumer.* **Description:** Presents writings from all of the world's different philosophies and religions.
Published by: Edizioni L' Eta dell'Acquario, Corso Re Umberto 37, Turin, 10128, Italy. TEL 39-011-5175324, FAX 39-011-6693929, etadellacquario@etadellacquario.it, http://www.etadellacquario.it.

100 USA
EVERGREEN MONTHLY. Text in English. 1985. m. USD 33 in US & Canada (effective 2004). adv. bk.rev.; music rev.; Website rev. illus. 44 p./no. 4 cols./p.; back issues avail. **Document type:** *Magazine, Consumer.* **Description:** Focuses on personal growth, spirituality, and holistic approaches to living, blending the mystical and the pragmatic.
Formerly (until 2003): The New Times (1044-2782); Incorporates (in 1991): Inner Woman; Which was formerly: Spiritual Women's Times
Published by: Dragonfly Media Group, 3600 15th Ave W, Ste 200, Seattle, WA 98119-3110. TEL 206-320-7788, FAX 206-320-7717, http://www.dragonflymedia.com. Ed., R&P David A Young TEL 206-320-7788. Pub. Deverick Martin. Adv. contact Penny Cooke TEL 206-320-7788. B&W page USD 1,165, color page USD 1,665; trim 10.2 x 12.5. Circ: 50,000.

299 USA ISSN 1942-5627
EVOLVE!. Text in English. 2003. q. USD 5 (effective 2008). **Document type:** *Magazine, Consumer.*
Published by: New Leaf Distributing Company, 401 Thornton Rd, Lithia Springs, GA 30122. TEL 770-948-7845, FAX 770-944-2313, http://www.newleaf-dist.com, http://www.newleafvendors.com. Ed. Wesley Morris.

181.45 USA
EXPANDING LIGHT PROGRAM GUIDE. Text in English. 1981. 2/yr. free. **Document type:** *Catalog.* **Description:** Describes retreat programs in yoga, meditation, and spiritual growth offered at Ananda Village.
Former titles: Ananda Program Guide; Ananda
Published by: Ananda Church of Self-Realization, 14618 Tyler Foote Rd, Nevada City, CA 95959. TEL 530-478-7518, FAX 530-478-7519. Ed., R&P Anandi Cornell. Circ: 50,000.

133 USA ISSN 1524-0452
THE FEDERATION FLASH; exploring the frontiers of miraculous probability. Text in English. 1990. q. USD 12; USD 3 newsstand/cover (effective 2000). illus. back issues avail. **Document type:** *Newsletter.* **Description:** Covers various New Age topics, including spirituality, truth, unity, technologies of consciousness, other dimensions, community, and reality.
Related titles: E-mail ed.; Fax ed.; Online - full text ed.
Published by: Starbuilders, PO Box 220964, Hollywood, FL 33022-0964. TEL 954-927-7900, FAX 954-927-7659. Ed., Pub., R&P Evin O'Ryan. Circ: 5,000.

FINDHORN FOUNDATION. GUEST PROGRAMME. *see* RELIGIONS AND THEOLOGY—Other Denominations And Sects

299 GBR ISSN 2044-3072
▼ **THE FIRMINIST.** Text in English. 2010. s-a. GBP 5 per issue domestic; GBP 7 per issue in Europe; GBP 8 per issue elsewhere (effective 2011). **Document type:** *Magazine, Academic/Scholarly.*
Published by: University of Bradford, c/o Mark Goodall, Bradford Media School, Richmond Rd, Bradford, W Yorkshire BD7 1DP, United Kingdom. TEL 44-1274-236071, m.goodall@bradford.ac.uk, http://www.bradford.ac.uk/.

234 USA ISSN 1947-0444
FORGIVENESS AND FREEDOM EZINE WITH BRENDA ADELMAN; out of shame, into forgiveness, onward to freedom. Text in English. 200?. m. free (effective 2009). back issues avail. **Document type:** *Newsletter, Consumer.* **Description:** Provides articles, ideas, tips, and strategies designed to help our journey of forgiving and freedom.
Formerly (until 2008): Forgiveness and Freedom News
Media: Online - full content.
Published by: Brenda Adelman, Pub. http://www.forgivenessandfreedomnews.com. Pub. Brenda Adelman.

FORMSANTE. *see* ALTERNATIVE MEDICINE

261.513 USA
FOUR CORNERS. Text in English. bi-m. USD 24 domestic; USD 45 foreign (effective 2007). adv. illus. back issues avail. **Document type:** *Magazine, Consumer.* **Description:** Provide readers with inspiring features and tools to incorporate the power and beauty of the southwest into their daily life, regardless of where they reside.
Address: PO Box 1776, Sedona, AZ 86339. TEL 928-282-7233, badger@sedona.net. Ed., Pub. Lane Badger. adv.: color page USD 2,000; 9.25 x 12.

FREE SPIRIT (BROOKLYN); a directory and journal of new realities. *see* PHILOSOPHY

158 NLD ISSN 1569-7983
FRONTIER MAGAZINE. Text in Dutch. 2001. bi-m. EUR 28.95 domestic; EUR 36 in Europe; EUR 50 elsewhere (effective 2009). adv. **Document type:** *Magazine, Consumer.*
Published by: Frontier Sciences Foundation, Postbus 10681, Amsterdam, 1015 DH, Netherlands. TEL 31-20-3309151, FAX 31-20-3309150, info@fsf.nl, http://www.fsf.nl.

158 AUS ISSN 1837-9109
▼ **GODDESS.** Text in English. 2010. m. AUD 8.95, NZD 9.95 newsstand/cover (effective 2011). adv. back issues avail. **Document type:** *Magazine, Trade.* **Description:** Assist in anchoring spiritual concepts into everyday life.
Related titles: Online - full text ed.: free (effective 2011).
Published by: BlackRose Magazine Pty Ltd., 14 Kennedy Parade, Golden Beach, QLD 4551, Australia. TEL 44-7-54922551. Ed. S'Roya Rose. Adv. contact Dean England.

133 USA ISSN 1068-2457
GOLDEN ISIS. Text in English. 1980. biennial. USD 10 (effective 1999). adv. bk.rev. **Document type:** *Magazine, Trade.* **Description:** Contains pagan art, Wiccan news, reviews, white magic and goddess-inspired poetry. Networking forum for contemporary pagans and witches. Includes a catalogue of new age products and services.
Published by: Golden Isis Press, PO Box 4263, Chatsworth, CA 91313-4263. FAX 775-417-0737, witchywoman13@paganpoet.com, http://www.iamawitch.com/. Ed., Pub. Gerina Dunwich. Circ: 3,600.

299 USA ISSN 1553-3239
HM1106
GREATER GOOD; magazine of the center for the development of peace and well-being. Text in English. s-a. USD 9.95 domestic; USD 15.95 foreign; USD 5.95 newsstand/cover (effective 2005). **Description:** Collects, synthesizes, and interprets groundbreaking scientific research into the roots of compassion, altruism, and peaceful human relationships. It fuses this cutting edge science with inspiring stories, promoting dialogue between social scientists and parents, teachers, community leaders and policy makers. Dedicated to studying the roots of benevolent relationships between individuals, within families and across communities.
Indexed: N06, S02, S03.
Address: 1113 Tolman Hall #1690, UC-Berkeley, Berkeley, CA 94720-1690. TEL 510-643-8965, greater@berkeley.edu, http://peacecenter.berkeley.edu. Eds. Dacher Keltner, Jason Marsh.

299 FRA ISSN 1959-4275
GUETTEUR DE L'AUBE. Text in French. 2007. bi-m. **Document type:** *Magazine, Consumer.*
Published by: Scop Guetteur de l'Aube, La Scop, Carla-Bayle, 09130, France. TEL 33-5-61603930.

613.7 135 CAN ISSN 1187-502X
LE GUIDE RESSOURCES/RESOURCES GUIDE; sante, psychologie, spiritualite. Text in English. 1985. m. (10/yr.). CAD 34.49 domestic; CAD 39.95 foreign (effective 2005). adv. bk.rev. **Document type:** *Handbook/Manual/Guide, Consumer.* **Description:** Devoted to New Age topics: nutrition, environmental issues, psychology, health and spirituality.
Former titles (until 1991): Guide Ressources pour une Conscience Globale (1184-1818); (until 1990): Guide Ressources, Santes, Psychologies, Spiritualites (0842-1943); (until 1988): Guide Ressources pour le Corps, le Coeur et l'Esprit (0838-8997); (until 1987): Guide Ressources (0838-8989); (until 1987): Resources Guide (0827-7982)
Indexed: PdeR.
—**CCC.**
Published by: S W A A Communications Inc., 600 Blvd Roland Therrien, Lonjueuil, PQ G4H 3V9, Canada. TEL 450-646-0060, 800-463-4961, FAX 450-646-2070. Ed., R&P Denys Lavigne. Pub. Francois Charles Gauthier. Adv. contact Yves Brunette. Circ: 17,184 (paid). **Subscr. to:** 525, rue Louis-Pasteur, Boucherville, PQ J4B 8E7, Canada. TEL 514-875-4444, 800-667-4444, FAX 514-523-4444.

181.45 613.704 USA
GUIDE TO YOGA TEACHERS AND CLASSES. Text in English. a. free. adv. **Document type:** *Guide, Consumer.* **Description:** Lists teachers and classes by state and city with some international listings. Includes listings of organizations that provide yoga teacher certification.

Published by: Himalayan International Institute (HII), 952 Bethany Turnpike, Honesdale, PA 18431-9706. TEL 570-253-4929, FAX 570-253-9078, info@himalayaninstitute.org, http://www.himalayaninstitute.org. Ed. Deborah Willoughby. R&P Irene Petryszak. Adv. contact Jim McGinley.

299 GBR ISSN 1759-457X
▼ **GWYDION'S MOON DIARY.** Text in English. 2009. a. GBP 4.75 per issue (effective 2011). **Document type:** *Consumer.* **Description:** Features the understanding of natural spirituality and the concepts behind the quaint and beautiful myths, deities and ceremonies.
Published by: Pandimensional Publishing, 11 Summerhouse Orchard Cottages, Bove Town, Glastonbury, Somerset BA6 8JA, United Kingdom. http://www.pandimensional.co.uk.

HAKOMI FORUM. *see* PSYCHOLOGY

135 180 FRA ISSN 1961-5973
LES HAUTS LIEUX DE LA FRANCE MYSTERIEUSE. Text in French. 2008. bi-m. **Document type:** *Magazine, Consumer.*
Published by: S P H, 31 Rue de Paris, Nice, 06000, France.

THE HEALER. *see* RELIGIONS AND THEOLOGY

299 USA
HIGHER CHOICE; Sharing Truth from the Heart of Source. Text in English. 1992. m. USD 12; USD 17 foreign.
Address: Heart of the Soul, Box 65, Neotsu, OR 97364. TEL 503-994-3887. Ed. Salanda. Circ: 500.

133.9 USA
HOLISTIC HEALTH SOURCEBOOK. Text in English. 1997. irreg. USD 39.95. **Document type:** *Directory.* **Description:** Provides source information on holistic health related topics.
Published by: Reference Press International, PO Box 4126, Greenwich, CT 06830. TEL 203-629-4900, FAX 203-622-5983. Ed., Pub., R&P Cheryl Klein Lacoff.

299 IRL ISSN 2009-4035
▼ **HUGINN.** Text in English. 2010. s-a. free (effective 2011). **Document type:** *Journal, Consumer.*
Media: Online - full text.
Published by: Talas Pai & Maris Pai, Eds. & Pubs.

179.3 USA ISSN 1097-6051
I AM NATION NEWS. Text in English. 1960. bi-m. USD 25 domestic; USD 30 foreign; USD 5 newsstand/cover (effective 2004). bk.rev.; film rev.; play rev. illus. back issues avail. **Document type:** *Magazine, Consumer.* **Description:** Contains news, educational articles and guidelines for linking of light workers and groups as preparation for the Second Coming and New Age of Aquarius.
Formerly: M A I N (0147-1201)
Published by: Mark-Age, Inc., PO Box 10, Pioneer, TN 37847. TEL 423-784-3269, http://www.thenewearth.org/markage.html. Ed. Pauline Sharpe. R&P Philip J Jacobs TEL 423-784-6904. Circ: 1,000.

299 USA ISSN 1549-4314
IMAGINE (SPOKANE). Text in English. 2004. q. USD 7 per issue (effective 2007). adv. **Document type:** *Newsletter.*
Published by: Little River Publishing, PO Box 28490, Spokane, WA 99228-8490. info@imaginemagazine.net.

158 CAN ISSN 1492-7519
IMPRINT MAGAZINE; mind, body, soul. Text in English. 2000. q. CAD 24, USD 20; CAD 6.95 newsstand/cover. back issues avail. **Document type:** *Magazine, Consumer.* **Description:** Covers the philosophy of connecting the mind, body and soul. Presents information pertaining to beliefs beyond our ordinary lives.
Published by: Imprint Magazine Inc., 5004 - 48 Ave., Red Deer, AB T4N 3T6, Canada. TEL 403-309-0008, FAX 403-309-4449. Ed. Sheri Bourne. Pub. Gary Layden. Circ: 3,000 (paid); 7,000 (controlled).

181.45 USA ISSN 0149-6026
BL624
INNER PATHS; a magazine of eastern and western spiritual teaching. Text in English. 1977. m. USD 15 (effective 2001). adv. bk.rev. **Document type:** *Magazine, Academic/Scholarly.*
Published by: Inner Paths Publications, Inc., 26 Reichert Circle, Westport, CT 06880. Ed., Pub. Louis Rogers. Circ: 33,500.

158 USA
INNER SELF; rediscovering wisdom, peace and joy. Text in English. 1985. m. USD 28.50. adv. bk.rev.; film rev.; music rev. **Description:** Provides an opportunity for increased well-being on all levels - body, mind and spirit.
Formerly (until 1985): Mighty Natural Magazine
Related titles: E-mail ed.
Published by: Innerself Publications, 965 Francis ST, Altamante Springs, FL 32701. TEL 407-331-8556, FAX 407-331-9680, editor@innerself.com. adv.: B&W page USD 570; 9.25 x 7.25. Circ: 10,000.

100 NGA ISSN 0794-7968
INSIGHT MAGAZINE; a magazine for spiritual development. Text in English. 1987. m. USD 2 per issue. adv. back issues avail.
Related titles: Online - full text ed.
Published by: O A L Research Publications Ltd., Cleanjohn House, 90 Ladipo House, PO Box 9802, Lagos, Nigeria. TEL 234-1-523420, TELEX 27358. Ed. O A Lawal. Circ: 25,000.

158 USA
THE INTEGRITY JOURNAL. Text in English. s-m. **Document type:** *Newsletter.* **Description:** Contains articles, quotes and commentary on the value and benefits of basing one's life on time-proven principles and values.
Media: Online - full text.
Published by: Integrity Network Ed., Pub. Roger Montgomery.

INTENSITIES; the journal of cult media. *see* MOTION PICTURES

299 USA ISSN 1093-1104
INTER-STATE HIGH WAY. Text in English. 1989. irreg. looseleaf. USD 20; USD 25 foreign (effective 1999). bk.rev.; film rev.; music rev.; software rev.; video rev. back issues avail. **Document type:** *Newsletter, Consumer.* **Description:** Contains articles, humor and reviews relating to shamanism for practitioners and students.
Formerly: Shaman Papers
Published by: Whole Health, Inc., Denali Center, HC89 Box 451, Willow, AK 99688-9705. TEL 907-495-6853. Ed. Kathy Lynn Douglass. Pub. Wade Greyfox. Circ: 205.

INTERSPACE - LINK CONFIDENTIAL NEWSLETTER; the link. *see* AERONAUTICS AND SPACE FLIGHT

INTUITIVE FLASH; forecasting environmental, economic, and societal trends. *see* EARTH SCIENCES

181.45 USA ISSN 1541-5910
J O Y; investigating the philosophy, science, and spirituality of yoga. (Journal of Yoga) Text in English. 2002. q. bk.rev.; Website rev. back issues avail. **Document type:** *Journal, Academic/Scholarly.* **Description:** Dedicated to serving the global community and educational institutions throughout the world in furthering understanding of yoga.
Media: Online - full text.
Indexed: A04, C11, CA, T02.
Published by: GodConsciousness.com, 4002 Lincoln St, SE, Port Salerno, FL 34997. TEL 772-341-3797, service@godconsciousness.com, http://www.godconsciousness.com.

JINGSHEN WENMING DAOKAN/GUIDE TO SPIRITUAL CIVILIZATION. *see* PHILOSOPHY

299 USA ISSN 1048-8715
BF1442.S49
JOURNAL OF ESOTERIC PSYCHOLOGY. Text in English. 198?. s-a. **Document type:** *Journal, Consumer.*
Related titles: Online - full text ed.: ISSN 1557-5543. 2005.
Published by: The Seven Ray Institute, 128 Manhattan Ave., Jersey City Heights, NJ 07307-3812. TEL 201-798-7777, 877-738-36729, FAX 201-659-3263, sevenray@sevenray.com, http://sevenray.net.

JOURNAL OF REGRESSION THERAPY. *see* PSYCHOLOGY

110 GBR ISSN 0955-7067
HM73
KINDRED SPIRIT; bringing you health and happiness. Text in English. 1987. bi-m. GBP 21 domestic; GBP 25.50 in North America & Europe; GBP 31.50 elsewhere (effective 2009). adv. bk.rev.; music rev.; video rev.; Website rev. 102 p./no.; back issues avail. **Document type:** *Magazine, Consumer.* **Description:** Covers a range of diverse subjects such as spiritual growth, personal development, complementary therapies, travel, health and much more.
Related titles: Online - full text ed.
Indexed: AmHI, CCR, CPerI.
Address: Unit 101, The Purfume Factory, 140 Wales Farm Rd, London, W3 6UG, United Kingdom. TEL 44-208-7528172, FAX 44-208-7528185. **Dist. by:** Diamond Distribution Ltd., Unit 7, Ironworks, Fishmarket Rd, Rye, E Sussex TN31 7LP, United Kingdom. TEL 44-1797-225229; **Dist. in US by:** Ingram Periodicals Inc., 1240 Heil Quaker Blvd, Box 7000, La Vergne, TN 37086. TEL 800-627-6247, FAX 615-793-6043.

L O H A S JOURNAL; tracking the lifestyles of health and sustainability. *see* BUSINESS AND ECONOMICS

158 USA ISSN 1930-0778
LEADING EDGE LIVING. Text in English. 2002. w. **Document type:** *Magazine, Consumer.*
Media: Online - full text.
Published by: Leading Edge Coaching and Training Eva@LeadingEdgeCoaching.com, http://www.leadingedgecoaching.com.

158 DEU
LEBENSWERT; Koerper - Geist - Seele. Text in German. 2000. 2/yr. free (effective 2011). adv. **Document type:** *Magazine, Consumer.*
Published by: Rossipaul Kommunikation GmbH, Menzinger Str 37, Munich, 80638, Germany. TEL 49-89-1791060, FAX 49-89-17910622, info@rossipaul.de. Ed. Carola Feddersen. Adv. contact Ursula Rossipaul. Circ: 400,000 (controlled).

158 USA ISSN 1943-8133
▼ **THE LEGACY JOURNAL.** Text in English. 2009. s-w. free (effective 2010). back issues avail. **Document type:** *Newsletter, Consumer.* **Description:** Contains legacy stories with their examples of making a positive difference in a sustainable way.
Media: Online - full text.
Published by: Thrive dmgarlo@AllThrive.com, http://www.allthrive.com. Ed. Dolly M Garlo.

158 DEU
LICHTFOKUS. Text in German. 2003. q. EUR 30; EUR 7.50 newsstand/cover (effective 2009). adv. **Document type:** *Magazine, Consumer.*
Published by: Elraanis Verlag, Baderpoint 3a, Seeon, 83370, Germany. TEL 49-8624-8795944, FAX 49-8624-8795945, info@elraanis.de, http://www.elraanis.de. Ed. Herbert Reinig. Adv. contact Tom Gross. color page EUR 880; trim 210 x 284. Circ: 12,000 (paid and controlled).

200 100 USA ISSN 1040-7448
BP605.T78
LIGHT OF CONSCIOUSNESS; journal of spiritual awakening. Text in English. 1988. q. USD 19.95 domestic; USD 27.95 foreign (effective 2010). adv. bk.rev.; music rev.; video rev. illus. 80 p./no.; back issues avail. **Document type:** *Magazine, Consumer.* **Description:** Presents classical spirituality applicable to today's world.
Formerly (until vol.1, no.1, 1988): Truth Consciousness Journal (0191-5207)
Related titles: Online - full text ed.
Published by: Truth Consciousness at Desert Ashram, 3403 W Sweetwater Dr, Tucson, AZ 85745-9301. TEL 520-743-8821, FAX 520-743-3394. Ed. Sita Stuhlmiller. Circ: 20,000. **Dist. by:** International Publishers Direct, 27500 Riverview Center Blvd, Bonita Springs, FL 34134. TEL 858-320-4563, FAX 858-677-3220, cbaum@ucsinc.com.

133 USA ISSN 2150-8666
▼ **LILLIAN TOO'S MANDALA.** Text in English. 2009. w. free (effective 2009). **Document type:** *Newsletter, Consumer.* **Description:** Weekly advice on feng shui.
Media: E-mail.
Published by: Lillian Too, Ed. & Pub., 3840 Blackhawk Rd, Ste 100, Danville, CA 94506. TEL 925-736-6696, lnoon@noon-intl.com.

299 USA ISSN 1521-1924
LIVING WITH CRYSTALS. Text in English. 1998. m. **Document type:** *Newsletter.* **Description:** Covers subjects including working with crystals for the achievement of goals, to help develop and enhance creativity, deepen meditation and chakra.
Media: Online - full content. **Related titles:** E-mail ed.
Published by: Beyond the Rainbow, PO Box 110, Ruby, NY 12475. rainbow@ulster.net. Ed., Pub., R&P, Adv. contact Constance Barrett TEL 845-336-4609.

133 299 USA
LLEWELLYN'S NEW WORLDS OF MIND & SPIRIT; new age resources for human potential and magical living. Text in English. 1980. bi-m. USD 10 (effective 1997 & 1998). adv. bk.rev. **Document type:** *Catalog, Consumer.*
Former titles: Llewellyn New Worlds; Llewellyn New Times (0893-1534)
Published by: Llewellyn Worldwide, 84 S Wabasha, St. Paul, MN 55107. TEL 612-291-1970, FAX 612-291-1908. Ed. Wendy Crowe. R&P Maria Bloomberg. Adv. contact Lee Briske. B&W page USD 1,610, color page USD 2,010; trim 10.75 x 8.25. Circ: 150,000.

101 USA
LOVE; the journal of the human spirit. Text in English. 1978. irreg. free.
Address: PO Box 9, Prospect Hill, NC 27314-0009. Eds. Bob Love, Pat Warren. Circ: 100.

299 133 SWE ISSN 1654-1618
LYZTRAN; tidskriften foer spiritualism, mediumskap, healing, haelsa och andlig filosofi. Text in Swedish. 2007. q. SEK 350 (effective 2007). **Document type:** *Magazine, Consumer.*
Related titles: Online - full text ed.
Published by: Jane's Energi Oas, c/o Skolan Lyztran, Finnvaegen 6, Ramsberg, 71198, Sweden. TEL 46-581-660901, info@janesenergioas.com. Eds. Joel Strandberg, Jane Lyzell.

700 USA ISSN 1073-5879
MAGICAL BLEND; a transformative journey. Text in English. 1980. 5/yr. USD 9 (effective 2005). adv. bk.rev.; music rev.; software rev.; video rev. illus. back issues avail.; reprints avail. **Document type:** *Magazine, Trade.* **Description:** Contains articles on metaphysics, healing, ancient mysticism, human potentials, transformational psychology, holistic health, interspecies communication as well as philosophy, cyberspace, art, world music, and technology.
Formerly (until 1989): Magical Blend Magazine (1040-4287)
Related titles: Online - full text ed.
Indexed: BRI, CBRI.
Published by: M B Media, 55 Independence Circle, #202, Chico, CA 95973. TEL 530-893-9037, 888-296-2442, FAX 530-893-9076, editor@magicalblend.com. Ed. Finnuala Barrett. Pub., R&P Michael Langevin. Adv. contact Victor Cahtu. B&W page USD 2,250, color page USD 2,775. Circ: 85,000.

133 USA ISSN 1069-1057
MANY HANDS; resources for personal and social transformation. Text in English. 1979. q. USD 24 (effective 2008). adv. bk.rev.; film rev. illus.
Address: PO Box 299, Northampton, MA 01061. TEL 413-585-5290, FAX 413-585-5293, http://www.manyhands.com. Ed. Polly S Baumer. Circ: 20,000.

MEDITATOR'S NEWSLETTER. *see* RELIGIONS AND THEOLOGY—Hindu

057.86 CZE ISSN 1212-1738
MEDIUM. Text in Czech. 1991. m. CZK 216; CZK 20 newsstand/cover (effective 2010). adv. **Document type:** *Magazine, Consumer.*
Address: Vietnamska 1490, PO Box 112, Ostrava, 708 00, Czech Republic. TEL 420-596-965848, FAX 420-596-965848. Ed., Pub. Miluse Bajgerova.

299 CZE ISSN 1214-4932
MEDUNKA. Text in Czech. 2004. m. adv. **Document type:** *Magazine, Consumer.*
Published by: Prazska Vydavatelska Spolecnost, s.r.o., Olsanska 3, Prague 3, 13000, Czech Republic. TEL 420-222-317812, info@pvsp.cz, http://www.pvsp.cz. Ed. Zuzana Paulusova. Adv. contact Gabriela Proksova.

156 DEU ISSN 0177-3852
MERIDIAN; Fachzeitschrift fuer Astrologie. Text in German. 1979. 6/yr. EUR 38 domestic; EUR 43 foreign; EUR 7 newsstand/cover (effective 2007). adv. **Document type:** *Magazine, Consumer.*
Formed by the merger of (1949-1979): Kosmobiologie (0023-4214); (1952-1979): Kosmischer Beobachter (0177-3844)
Indexed: E-psyche.
Published by: Jehle und Garms OHG, Hochfirstweg 12, Lenzkirch-Saig, 79853, Germany. TEL 49-7653-960277, FAX 49-7653-960276. Ed. Markus Jehle. Adv. contact Martin Garms. B&W page EUR 990, color page EUR 1,390; trim 169 x 257. Circ: 3,700 (paid and controlled).

158 NZL ISSN 1177-9624
METAMORETALK. Text in English. 1998. m. NZD 65 (effective 2008). **Document type:** *Magazine, Consumer.*
Media: Online - full text.
Published by: MetaMorphosis Ltd, PO Box 17476, Greenlane, Auckland, 1546, New Zealand. TEL 64-9-6363133, FAX 64-9-6363155.

METAPSICHICA; rivista italiana di parapsicologia. *see* PARAPSYCHOLOGY AND OCCULTISM

299 GBR ISSN 2044-3218
▼ ➤ **THE MICHAELIAN.** Text in English. 2009. a. free (effective 2010). back issues avail. **Document type:** *Journal, Academic/Scholarly.* **Description:** Aims to publish articles on Michael field's works and the lives of Katharine Bradley and Edith Cooper, and the writers, artists, decadents and new women associated with them.
Media: Online - full text.
Published by: Rivendale Press, PO Box 85, High Wycombe, Bucks HP14 4WZ, United Kingdom. TEL 44-1494-562266, sales@rivendalepress.com, http://www.rivendalepress.com. Eds. Michelle Lee, Sharon Bickle.

➤ **MIND - MAGIC.** *see* PARAPSYCHOLOGY AND OCCULTISM

133 USA
MIND TOOLS. Text in English. 1984. bi-m. USD 15. adv.
Formerly: Green Light News
Published by: (Crystal Research Foundation), Kryolux, Inc., 27 Hickory St, Box 467, Ellenville, NY 12428-1307. TEL 914-647-3111. Ed. Steven Krulick.

110 USA
MINDQUEST RECOMMENDATIONS. Text in English. 1996. 7/yr. free. adv. bk.rev.; film rev.; music rev.; video rev. **Document type:** *Newsletter.* **Description:** Contains metaphysical and New Age reviews.
Formerly (until 1999): Mindquest Reviews (1097-5586)
Published by: Lightword Publishing, 525 S Main, Ste 309A, Del Rio, TX 78840. TEL 830-774-3141. Ed., Pub., Adv. contact Bernie P Nelson. Circ: 5,000 (controlled).

NO

131 612.022 571.77 USA
MINI EXAMINER. Text in English. 1979. bi-w. looseleaf. USD 21 (effective 1998). back issues avail. **Document type:** *Newsletter.* **Description:** Applies biorhythm character and compatibility analysis to relationships to determine whether they will work.
Published by: Irene Hamlen Stephenson, Ed. & Pub., PO Box 3893, Chatsworth, CA 91313. TEL 818-347-6949.

MINSTREL. *see* PARAPSYCHOLOGY AND OCCULTISM

100 USA
MIRACLES MAGAZINE; miracles, mysticism, metaphysics & mirth. Text in English. 1983. bi-m. USD 29 (effective 2008). adv. bk.rev. bibl.; illus. back issues avail. **Document type:** *Magazine, Consumer.* **Description:** A course in miracles orientation and attitudinal healing helps bring people of different faiths together. Includes daily meditations, quotations, jokes, parables, prayers, poems, and seasonal perspectives.
Former titles: On Course (1098-4372); Mustard Seed
Address: PO Box 1000, Washingtonville, NY 10992. TEL 845-496-9089, jon@miraclesmagazine.org. Ed., Pub. Jon Mundy. Circ: 9,000.

299 USA ISSN 1941-3319
BP605.N46
MODERN WITCH. Text in English. 2008. q. USD 24 (effective 2010). adv. illus. **Document type:** *Magazine, Consumer.* **Description:** Present the information about green technologies, health, life and family for pagan community.
Published by: Modern Witch Magazine, PO Box 2854, Ramona, CA 92065. editor@modernwitchmagazine.com. Ed. Sandy Lareau. adv.: page USD 390.

700 780 USA ISSN 0892-2721
MUSIC OF THE SPHERES; a quarterly magazine of art and music for the New Age. Text in English. 1988. q. USD 14. adv. bk.rev.; film rev.; play rev. illus. **Description:** Focuses on promoting and networking the art and music of the New Age, and to promote world peace.
Published by: Music of the Spheres Publishing, PO Box 1751, Taos, NM 87571. TEL 505-758-0405. Ed. John Patrick Lamkin. Circ: 10,000.

301 ARG ISSN 0326-0666
MUTANTIA; cuadernos eco-espirituales. Text in Spanish. 1980. q. USD 30. adv. bk.rev. illus. back issues avail. **Document type:** *Trade.* **Description:** Covers documents exploring the building of the 21st century's society, transformational education, and eco-villages, focusing on human potentials and alternative ways of living.
Related titles: Microfilm ed.
Published by: Ediciones Mutantia, Casilla 260, Sucursal 12, 1412, Buenos Aires, Argentina. TEL 54-114-38560366, FAX 54-114-3433768. Ed. Miguel Grinberg. Circ: 9,000 (paid).

381.45002 USA ISSN 1098-4364
N A P R A REVIEW; for retailers serving the body/mind/spirit marketplace. Variant title: NaPRA ReView. Text in English. 1987. bi-m. USD 75 domestic; USD 125 foreign (effective 2002). adv. bk.rev.; video rev. illus.; tr.lit. **Document type:** *Journal, Trade.* **Description:** Reports on issues and developments of interest in new consciousness publishing and retailing.
Formerly (until 1995): N A P R A Trade Journal
Published by: Networking Alternatives for Publishers, Retailers, and Artists, Inc., 109 North Beach Rd, PO Box 9, Eastsound, WA 98245. TEL 360-376-2702, FAX 360-376-2704, napra@napra.con, http://www.napra.com. Ed. Michael Weaver. Pub., R&P Marilyn McGuire. Adv. contact Erin Johnson. B&W page USD 1,512, color page USD 2,079. Circ: 10,500 (controlled).

133 USA
N H N E NEWS BRIEF. Text in English. 1994. w. USD 104; USD 130 foreign.
Related titles: Online - full text ed.
Published by: New Heaven New Earth, PO Box 10627, Sedona, AZ 10627. TEL 888-293-1833. Ed. James Gregory.

NATURAL HEALTH. *see* ALTERNATIVE MEDICINE

NATURE & HEALTH; the holistic journal of wellbeing. *see* ALTERNATIVE MEDICINE

299 USA ISSN 2151-8718
THE NETER LETTER. Text in English. 2006. m. free to qualified personnel (effective 2009). back issues avail. **Document type:** *Newsletter, Academic/Scholarly.*
Media: Online - full content.
Published by: Hanford Mead Publishers, Inc., PO Box 8051, Santa Cruz, CA 95065. TEL 831-459-6855, info@hanfordmead.com, http://www.hanfordmead.com.

053.1 DEU ISSN 1617-8769
DIE NEUE ESOTERA; Das Fachmagazin fuer neues Denken und spirituelles Leben. Text in German. 2001. bi-m. EUR 43.20 domestic; EUR 52.38 in Europe; EUR 54.95 elsewhere; EUR 7.50 newsstand/cover (effective 2010). adv. **Document type:** *Magazine, Consumer.*
Formed by the merger of (1991-2001): Dao (0939-950X); (1959-2001): Esotera (0003-2921); Which was formerly (until 1970): Die Andere Welt (0174-8637)
Published by: Hoks Medien Dienst, Postfach 730023, Berlin, 13062, Germany. TEL 49-30-47469225, FAX 49-30-47469226, hk@esotera.de. Ed., Adv. contact Holger Karstens.

133 USA
NEW AGE DIGEST. Text in English. 1983. irreg. per issue exchange basis.
Published by: New Age Press, PO Box 1373, Kealakekua, HI 96750. TEL 808-328-8013. Ed. Jim Butler. Circ: 400.

158 USA ISSN 1084-0931
NEW AGE PATRIOT. Text in English. 1989. q. back issues avail. **Description:** For drug, environmental, and social activists.
Address: PO Box 419, Dearborn, MI 48127. TEL 313-563-3192.

028.1 USA ISSN 1042-6566
NEW AGE RETAILER; products for a better world, ideas for better business. Text in English. 1987. 7/yr. USD 92 domestic; USD 155 foreign; USD 10 newsstand/cover; free to qualified personnel (effective 2005). adv. bk.rev. tr.lit. back issues avail. **Document type:** *Magazine, Trade.* **Description:** Trade journal focusing on quality material for retailers of new age books, music, videos and sidelines. Includes articles and reviews.
Formerly (until 1989): Monthly Report to Booksellers
Published by: Continuity Publishing, Inc., 1300 N State St, Ste 105, Bellingham, WA 98225-4730. TEL 360-676-0789, 800-463-9243, FAX 360-676-0932. Ed. Ray Hemachandra. Adv. contact Patty Rodgers. B&W page USD 1,150, color page USD 1,645; 7.5 x 10. Circ: 5,800 (controlled).

133.9 USA
NEW AGE SOURCEBOOK. Text in English. 1993. irreg. USD 39.95. **Document type:** *Directory.* **Description:** Resource and information on association, schools, retreats, events, museums, distributors, stores relating to holistic health, spirituality, parapsychology, astrology, and New Age topics.
Formerly: Parapsychology, New Age and the Occult (1065-3031)
Published by: Reference Press International, PO Box 4126, Greenwich, CT 06830. TEL 203-629-4900, FAX 203-622-5983. Ed., Pub., R&P Cheryl Klein Lacoff.

NEW AGE TEACHINGS. *see* RELIGIONS AND THEOLOGY—Other Denominations And Sects

133.5 AUS ISSN 1036-8035
THE NEW DAWN. Text in English. 1991. bi-m. AUD 39 domestic; USD 55 in US & Canada; EUR 42 in Europe; GBP 38 in United Kingdom; NZD 70 in New Zealand; AUD 60 in Asia & the Pacific; AUD 85 elsewhere (effective 2009). back issues avail. **Document type:** *Magazine, Consumer.*
Related titles: Online - full text ed.
Published by: New Gnosis Communications International Pty Ltd, GPO Box 3126, Melbourne, NSW 3001, Australia. FAX 61-7-33196293.

100 USA ISSN 1040-2047
NEW DAY HERALD. Text in English. 1975. bi-m. USD 25 (effective 2002). adv. back issues avail. **Document type:** *Newspaper.*
Formerly (until 1988): Movement Newspaper
Published by: (Church of the Movement of Spiritual Inner Awareness), Mandeville Press, PO Box 513935, Los Angeles, CA 90051. FAX 213-737-5680. Ed. John Roger. R&P Stede Barber. Circ: 5,000.

301 USA
NEW ENVIRONMENT BULLETIN. Text in English. 1974. m. USD 10 in North America; USD 14 elsewhere (effective 2001). bk.rev. 6 p./no.; **Document type:** *Newsletter.* **Description:** Articles, reviews and announcements dealing with a wide range of ecological and social topics; includes reports on activities of the New Environment Association.
Published by: New Environment Association, 270 Fenway Dr, Syracuse, NY 13224. TEL 315-446-8009. Ed. Harry Schwarzlander. Circ: 140.

100 USA ISSN 0886-4616
NEW FRONTIER; magazine of transformation. Text in English. 1981. m. adv. bk.rev.; film rev.; music rev. back issues avail. **Document type:** *Magazine, Consumer.* **Description:** Presents informative articles by, and interviews with, internationally respected leaders in the New Age field. Covers holistic health, metaphysics, yoga, natural foods, astrology and latest world news.
Related titles: Online - full text ed.: 1981.
Published by: New Frontier Education Society, PO Box 17397, Asheville, NC 28816-7397. advertising@newfrontier.com. Ed. Swami Nostradamus Virato. adv.: B&W page USD 1,180. Circ: 60,000.

613 USA ISSN 1088-1441
NEW LIFE; America's guide to a healthy life, body, spirit. Text in English. bi-m. USD 40 (effective 2008). illus. **Document type:** *Magazine, Consumer.* **Description:** Reference and resource guide for holistic health, environment and New Age. Examines consciousness and the human potential, and provides information on products and services.
Formerly: Serenity's New Life (1051-2195)
Related titles: Online - full content ed.
Published by: Serenity Health Organization, Inc., 168 W Park Ave, Long Beach, NY 11561-3334. TEL 516-897-0900, 800-928-6208, FAX 516-897-0585. Pub. Mark Becker. Circ: 60,000.

234 USA ISSN 1930-370X
NEW SPIRIT JOURNAL. Text in English. 2005. m. adv. **Document type:** *Magazine, Consumer.*
Address: 14911 Chain Lake Rd, Ste 431, Monroe, WA 98272. TEL 425-356-7237. Eds., Pubs. Krysta Gibson, Rhonda Dickson. adv.: page USD 900; trim 7.5 x 10. Circ: 35,000 (controlled).

NEXUS (BOULDER); Colorado's holistic journal. *see* ALTERNATIVE MEDICINE

133 DNK ISSN 0108-3503
NYT ASPEKT; magazine for alternative living and thinking. Variant title: Nyt Aspekt og Guiden. Text in Danish. 1983. 6/yr. DKK 198 (effective 2009). adv. bk.rev. back issues avail. **Document type:** *Magazine, Consumer.* **Description:** Covers spiritual science, personal growth, health, parapsychology and alternative thinking and living.
Formed by the merger of (1969-1982): Psykisk Forum (0108-7800); (1954-1982): U F O Aspekt (0107-0258)
Address: Bjelkes Alle 17 A, Copenhagen N, 2200, Denmark. TEL 45-35-868670, FAX 45-35-868651, info@nytaspekt.dk, http://www.nytaspekt.dk. Eds. Iben Gaarde Nissen, Steen Landsy. Adv. contact Benny DeMolade. B&W page DKK 4,175, color page DKK 4,775; 175 x 233.

133 USA
O R A C L E NEWSLETTER. Text in English. 1975. 6/yr. USD 15 (effective 1998). adv. bk.rev. **Document type:** *Newsletter.* **Description:** News and information regarding psychic phenomena, research and educational activities of interest to members.
Formerly: O P R A Newsletter
Published by: Oklahoma Educational Research Association, PO Box 720366, Norman, OK 73070-4271. TEL 405-364-3912. Ed., R&P, Adv. contact Joane Fogel. Circ: 240 (paid).

ODYSSEY (TOKAI); an adventure in more conscious living. *see* PHILOSOPHY

OMEGA NEW AGE DIRECTORY. *see* RELIGIONS AND THEOLOGY—Other Denominations And Sects

299 NZL ISSN 1179-6529
ONERAHI ORBIT. Text in English. 2007. 5/yr. free (effective 2010). back issues avail. **Document type:** *Newsletter, Trade.*
Related titles: Online - full text ed.: ISSN 1179-6537. free (effective 2010).
Published by: Onerahi Community Association, PO Box 3031, Onerahi, 0142, New Zealand. TEL 64-9-4363203, onerahi.mail@gmail.com. Ed. Barry Tetley TEL 64-9-4360757.

133 615.5 NLD ISSN 0165-5027
ONKRUID; voor aarde, lichaam en geest. Text in Dutch. 1978. bi-m. EUR 24.95 Netherlands and Belgium; EUR 43.50 in Europe (effective 2010). adv. bk.rev. illus. back issues avail. **Document type:** *Magazine, Consumer.* **Description:** Covers alternative health, environmental and spiritual concerns.
Related titles: Online - full text ed.
Published by: Stichting Onkruid, Postbus 167, Vianen, 4130 ED, Netherlands. TEL 31-347-351089, FAX 31-347-351066. adv.: B&W page EUR 875; trim 170 x 240. Circ: 30,000 (paid).

299.93 USA
ONLINE NOETIC NETWORK. Text in English. 1995. 3/w. USD 25 to members (effective 1999). bk.rev. back issues avail. **Document type:** *Newsletter.* **Description:** Distributes articles by e-mail and interviews experts in noetic topics, highlighting spirituality and conscious experience.
Media: Online - full text.
Published by: LightSpeed Publishing, 105 W. Ashland St., # A, Doylestown, PA 18901-4152. Ed. Joel Metzger. Circ: 2,500.

ORGANICA; a magazine of arts & activism. *see* LITERATURE

110 DEU ISSN 1869-6678
OYA; anders denken, anders leben. Text in German. 1988. 6/yr. EUR 36 (effective 2011). adv. back issues avail. **Document type:** *Magazine, Consumer.*
Formerly (until 2010): KursKontakte (1435-7518)
Published by: Oya Medien eG, Am See 1, Klein Jasedow, 17440, Germany. TEL 49-38374-75210, FAX 49-38374-75223. Ed. Lara Mallien.

299 USA
PAN-LIME; the newsletter of the Pan Community. Text in English. m. USD 15; USD 16 in Canada & Mexico; USD 18 elsewhere. **Document type:** *Newsletter.* **Description:** Informs readers of news and events concerning the Pan community throughout the U.S. and around the world.
Published by: Pen & Pan Publishing, 800 W Drayton, Ferndale, MI 48220. TEL 810-543-0565.

PARA; Zeitschrift fuer alternative Heilkunde und spirituelles Leben. *see* ALTERNATIVE MEDICINE

133 USA
PARADIGM SHIFT (KINGSTON); magick, music, media. Text in English. 1998. q. back issues avail. **Description:** An eclectic, independent zine for just about anyone who hopes for something new and challenging, with a bit of an esoteric twist.
Media: Online - full text.
Published by: Paradigm Shift, PO Box 4431, Kingston, NY 12402. Ed. Phillip H Forber.

299 GBR ISSN 1757-1758
PAST TIMES (CARLUKE AND LANARK EDITION). Text in English. 2008. a. **Document type:** *Magazine, Consumer.*
Published by: Johnston (Falkirk) Ltd., Unit 4A, Gateway Business Park, Beancross Rd, Grangemouth, FK3 8WX, United Kingdom. TEL 44-1324-690222, FAX 44-1324-690214, http://www.johnstonpress.co.uk.

299 USA ISSN 2161-6116
PENSAMIENTOS. Text in English. 1975. irreg., latest 2002. USD 3 per issue (effective 2011). back issues avail. **Document type:** *Journal, Trade.*
Published by: Rational Island Publishers, PO Box 2081, Main Office Station, Seattle, WA 98111. TEL 206-284-0311, FAX 206-284-8429, litsales@rc.org, http://www.rationalisland.com.

110 USA
PHENOMENEWS; exploring human potential, holistic health and living. Text in English. 1978. m. USD 14. adv. bk.rev. **Document type:** *Newspaper.*
Published by: PhenomeNEWS Inc., 18444 W 10 Mile Rd, 105, Southfield, MI 48075-2626. TEL 248-569-3888, FAX 248-569-4512. Ed., Pub. Cindy Saul. R&P, Adv. contact Gerri Magee. B&W page USD 555; 12.88 x 9.75. Circ: 50,000.

158 USA
THE PHOENIX (ST. PAUL). Text in English. 1981. m. USD 18; USD 2 newsstand/cover (effective 2000). adv. bk.rev. back issues avail. **Document type:** *Newspaper.* **Description:** For people actively working on their physical, mental, emotional, and spiritual well-being. Committed to providing them articles and advertising a broad spectrum of recovery, renewal, and growth information to assist in their journey toward peace and serenity.
Related titles: Online - full text ed.
Published by: Phoenix, 447 Marshall Ave, Ste, St Paul, MN 55102. TEL 651-291-2691, 800-983-9887, FAX 651-291-0553. Ed. Pat Samples. Pub., R&P Fran Jackson. Adv. contact Leni Zumas. page USD 1,392. Circ: 130,000.

PILGRIMAGE. *see* RELIGIONS AND THEOLOGY

299 GBR ISSN 2041-5524
PLAIN ENGLISH (ONLINE); the voice of plain english campaign. Text in English. 1979. 3/yr. free (effective 2010). back issues avail. **Document type:** *Magazine, Consumer.*
Formerly (until 2009): Plain English (Print) (0143-6252)
Media: Online - full text.
Published by: Plain English Campaign, PO Box 3, New Mills, High Peak SK22 4QP, United Kingdom. TEL 44-1663-744409, FAX 44-1663-747038, info@plainenglish.co.uk.

299 USA ISSN 2152-6958
▼ **PLESSET'S PRINCIPLES FOR TODAY'S HOME.** Text in English. 2009. w. free (effective 2010). **Document type:** *Newsletter, Consumer.* **Description:** Features tips and informative articles on home renovation.
Media: Online - full text.
Published by: DP Design, PO Box 1132, Oregon City, OR 97045. TEL 503-632-8801. Ed., Pub. Diane Plesset.

299 GBR ISSN 2040-3704
▼ ➤ **THE POSTER.** Text in English. 2010. s-a. GBP 36, USD 68 to individuals; GBP 132, USD 185 to institutions (effective 2012). adv. back issues avail. **Document type:** *Journal, Academic/Scholarly.* **Description:** Aims to sway the popular heart and mind through visual public interventions.
Related titles: Online - full text ed.: ISSN 2040-3712. GBP 99, USD 140 (effective 2012).

Indexed: A30, A31, T02.
Published by: Intellect Ltd., The Mill, Parnall Rd, Fishponds, Bristol, BS16 3JG, United Kingdom. TEL 44-117-9589910, FAX 44-117-9589911, info@intellectbooks.com. Pub. Masoud Yazdani. **Dist. by:** Turpin Distribution Services Ltd., Pegasus Dr, Stratton Business Park, Biggleswade, Bedfordshire SG18 8QB, United Kingdom. TEL 44-1767-604951, FAX 44-1767-601640, custserv@turpin-distribution.com, http://www.turpin-distribution.com/.

110 910.202 CAN ISSN 1206-8152
POWER TRIPS. Text in English. 1997. bi-m. CAD 27, USD 19.95 (effective 1999). adv. bk.rev. **Document type:** *Magazine, Consumer.* **Description:** Devoted to the sacred places of Mother Earth.
Related titles: Online - full text ed.
Published by: Cedar Cottage Media Inc., 6282 Kathleen Ave, Ste 502, Burnaby, BC V5H 4J4, Canada. TEL 604-431-2917, FAX 604-431-2918. Ed., Pub., Adv. contact Robert Scheer. Circ: 2,000.

100 BEL ISSN 0777-9909
PRESSE-INTER. Text in French. 1981. q. adv. bk.rev. **Description:** Examines peace and non-violence in culture and spirituality.
Formerly (until 1988): Alternatives (0770-4437)
Published by: Centre d'Inter-Action Culturelle, Rue de la Procession 4, Rosieres, 1331, Belgium. TEL 32-2-653-53-24, FAX 32-2-654-19-08. Ed. Pierre Houart.

PRIMARY POINT. *see* RELIGIONS AND THEOLOGY—Buddhist

135 RUS
PRIVOROT. Text in Russian. m. RUR 95.40 for 6 mos. domestic (effective 2004). illus. **Document type:** *Newspaper, Consumer.*
Published by: Izdatel'stvo S-Info, A-ya 42, Moscow, 125284, Russian Federation. TEL 7-095-7969294, FAX 7-095-2520920, s-info@si.ru. **Subscr. to:** Unicont Enterprises Inc., 1340 Centre St, Ste 209, Newton, MA 02459. TEL 800-763-7475, FAX 617-964-8753, podpiska@unipressa.com.

PSYCHIC READER. *see* PARAPSYCHOLOGY AND OCCULTISM

PULSAR; Zeitschrift fuer Gesundheit, Therapie und Innere Entwicklung. *see* ALTERNATIVE MEDICINE

299 USA ISSN 1936-8682
PURE INSPIRATION. Text in English. 2006. q. USD 19.97 domestic; USD 27.97 in Canada; USD 31.97 elsewhere (effective 2008). adv. **Document type:** *Magazine, Consumer.*
Published by: Lightstream Publishing, 7 Waterloo Rd, Stanhope, NJ 07874. TEL 973-347-6900, FAX 973-347-6909, http://www.lightstreampublishing.com. Ed. Robert Becker.

RADIANCE TECHNIQUE JOURNAL. *see* ALTERNATIVE MEDICINE

100 USA
RAINBOW RAY FOCUS. Text in English. 6/yr. USD 12.
Formerly: Ruby Focus
Published by: Magnificent Consummation Inc., PO Box 1188, Sedona, AZ 86336. Ed. Angel Violet.

RAINBOW REFLECTIONS. *see* PARAPSYCHOLOGY AND OCCULTISM

RELIGION, HEALTH, AND HEALING. *see* RELIGIONS AND THEOLOGY

299 CAN ISSN 1705-3773
THE RENEWAL TIMES. Text in English. 2003. m. **Document type:** *Newsletter, Consumer.*
Media: Online - full text.
Published by: Renewal Technologies Inc., 5423 North Dr, Ottawa, ON K4M 1G5, Canada. TEL 613-692-1424, FAX 613-692-1790, info@renewal.ca, http://www.renewal.ca/index.html. Ed. Roger Ellerton.

100 USA
REVELATIONS OF AWARENESS; the cosmic newsletter. Text in English. 1972. 12/yr. USD 42 to members (effective 1999). bk.rev. on internet. 20 p./no. 2 cols./p.; back issues avail. **Document type:** *Newsletter.* **Description:** Explains UFOs, the alien presence, other mysteries, plus spiritual philosophy, and life-after-death.
Published by: Cosmic Awareness Communications, PO Box 115, Olympia, WA 98507. FAX 360-352-6294. Circ: 3,100.

301 USA ISSN 0275-6935
BF309
➤ **REVISION**; a journal of consciousness and transformation. Text in English. 1978. q. USD 48 combined subscription domestic (print & online eds.); USD 84 combined subscription foreign (print & online eds.) (effective 2011). adv. bk.rev. abstr.; bibl.; charts; stat.; tr.lit.; illus. Index. back issues avail.; reprint service avail. from PSC. **Document type:** *Journal, Academic/Scholarly.*
Related titles: Online - full text ed.: ISSN 1940-3038. USD 47 to individuals; USD 103 to institutions (effective 2008).
Indexed: A01, A02, A03, A08, A21, A22, A26, APW, AltPI, AmHI, BRD, C12, CA, E-psyche, E08, G08, H07, H08, H14, HAb, HumInd, I05, I07, M01, M02, P10, P43, P48, P53, P54, PQC, PsycholAb, R05, RI-1, RI-2, S09, T02, W03, W05.
—BLDSC (7800.565000), IE, Ingenta. **CCC.**
Published by: (Helen Dwight Reid Education Foundation), Revision Publishing, PO Box 1855, Sebastopol, CA 95473. Ed. Juergen Werner Kremer.

➤ **S C P JOURNAL.** *see* RELIGIONS AND THEOLOGY

➤ **SACRED HOOP.** *see* ETHNIC INTERESTS

299 USA ISSN 1068-1698
HQ1101
SAGEWOMAN; celebrating the goddess in every woman. Text in English. 1983. q. USD 21 domestic; USD 26 foreign; USD 6.95 newsstand/cover domestic; USD 8.95 newsstand/cover in Canada (effective 2004). adv. video rev.; Website rev.; film rev.; music rev.; rec.rev.; bk.rev. illus. 96 p./no. 3 cols./p.; reprints avail. **Document type:** *Magazine, Consumer.* **Description:** Celebrates the spirituality of women through articles and artworks created by women, special interest in Goddess spirituality.
Related titles: Online - full text ed.
Indexed: FemPer, GW, WSI.
—Ingenta.
Published by: B B I Media, Inc., PO Box 641, Point Arena, CA 95468. TEL 707-882-2052, FAX 707-882-2793, bbimedia@mcn.org. Ed. Anne Newkirk Niven. adv.: B&W page USD 625; trim 7.25 x 9. Circ: 21,000 (paid).

100 USA
THE SEARCHER (HUALAPAI). Text in English. 1968. bi-m. USD 25 domestic; USD 35 foreign (effective 2001). bk.rev.; music rev. illus.; mkt. back issues avail. **Document type:** *Newsletter.* **Description:** Contains information about New Age ideas and believes discussing a variety of subjects such as UFO's, spiritualism, life after death, vegetarianism, astral travel, crystal power and I-Ching.
Formerly: Faithist Journal
Published by: Kosmon Publishing, Inc., PO Box 4670, Hualapai, AZ 86412-4670. Ed. Kasandra Kares. Circ: 2,000.

299 USA ISSN 1530-3365
SEDONA JOURNAL OF EMERGENCE. Text in English. 1989. m. **Document type:** *Magazine, Consumer.*
Formerly (until 199?): Emergence (Sedona) (1040-8975)
Related titles: Online - full text ed.: USD 43 (effective 2006).
Published by: Light Technology Publishing, PO Box 3870, Flagstaff, AZ 86003. TEL 928-526-1345, 800-450-0985, FAX 928-714-1132, 800-393-7017. Ed. Melody O'Ryin Swanson.

SELF & SOCIETY; a forum for contemporary psychology. *see* PSYCHOLOGY

158 USA ISSN 1941-6083
SELF IMPROVEMENT MAGAZINE. Text in English. 2008. q. free to members (effective 2009). **Document type:** *Magazine, Consumer.* **Description:** Provides practical education in the areas of life success like wealth & abundance, personal growth, well-being, personal effectiveness and relationships.
Published by: Self Improvement Association, 7982 Westbury Ave, Ste A, San Diego, CA 92126. TEL 760-203-2252, FAX 760-466-7564, info@sia-hq.com.

SELF-REALIZATION. *see* RELIGIONS AND THEOLOGY—Other Denominations And Sects

150 USA ISSN 1947-0606
SERENITY MATTERS. Text in English. 2008. bi-w. free (effective 2009). **Document type:** *Newsletter, Trade.* **Description:** Features inspiring articles for a better living including information on classes, seminars and workshops for self development.
Media: Online - full content.
Published by: Serenity Matters, LLC, 2875 Ashley River Rd, Ste 6-34, Charleston, SC 29414. TEL 843-991-5089.

299 USA ISSN 2151-1977
▼ **SHAPE YOUR SUCCESS.** Text in English. 2009. w. free (effective 2009). **Document type:** *Newsletter, Consumer.*
Media: Online - full content.
Published by: Changing Lanes, 595 Forest Ave, Plymouth, MI 48170. TEL 734-956-2925, info@changing-lanes.com. Ed. Amy Hale.

299 338.91 USA ISSN 0169-1341
SHARE INTERNATIONAL. Text in English. 1982. m. USD 32.50 (effective 2004). bk.rev. back issues avail. **Document type:** *Magazine, Consumer.* **Description:** Offers a global perspective on positive developments transforming every field of human endeavor throughout the world. Source of latest information on Maitreya, the World Teacher.
Related titles: Dutch ed.; French ed.; Spanish ed.; Japanese ed.; German ed.
Published by: Share International Foundation, U.S. Office, PO Box 971, North Hollywood, CA 91603. TEL 818-785-6300, FAX 818-904-9132. Ed. Benjamin Creme. R&P Lynne Girdlestone. Circ: 5,000 (paid).

SKEPTIC; promoting science and critical thinking. *see* PARAPSYCHOLOGY AND OCCULTISM

THE SKEPTIC; a journal of fact and opinion. *see* PARAPSYCHOLOGY AND OCCULTISM

110 DEU ISSN 0936-9244
➤ **SKEPTIKER**; Zeitschrift fuer Wissenschaft und kritisches Denken. Text in German. 1987. q. EUR 19.60 domestic; EUR 23 foreign; EUR 4.90 newsstand/cover (effective 2003). adv. bk.rev. back issues avail. **Document type:** *Journal, Academic/Scholarly.*
Published by: Gesellschaft zur Wissenschaftlichen Untersuchung von Parawissenschaften e.V., Arheilger Weg 11, Rossdorf, 64380, Germany. TEL 49-6154-695023, FAX 49-6154-695022, info@gwup.org. Ed. Inge Huesgen.

100 USA
SOARING SPIRIT. Text in English. 1976. q. free (effective 2005). adv. bk.rev. **Document type:** *Catalog, Consumer.* **Description:** Offers articles and research reports on reincarnation and psychic development, plus over 300 books, tapes and CD's on self help and Eastern metaphysics.
Former titles: Master of Life; Self - Help Update
Published by: Valley of the Sun Publishing Co., PO Box 38, Malibu, CA 90265. TEL 818-706-0963, FAX 818-706-3606. Ed., Pub. Richard Sutphen. R&P Jason McKean. Circ: 100,000.

SOMATICS; magazine - journal of the mind - body arts and sciences. *see* PHYSICAL FITNESS AND HYGIENE

133 USA
SOMNIAL TIMES. Text in English. 1988. 6/yr. USD 12 domestic; USD 20 foreign; USD 10 domestic by e-mail; USD 12 foreign by e-mail. adv. bk.rev. **Document type:** *Newsletter.* **Description:** Shares dreamland adventures dreams, reveries, dream programming and explores the dream state.
Related titles: Online - full text ed.
Published by: American Mensa Ltd., Dreamers Special Interest Group, c/o Gloria Reiser, Box 561, Quincy, IL 62306-0561. TEL 217-222-9082. Ed., Pub., Adv. contact Gloria Reiser. Circ: 100 (paid).

158 GBR ISSN 1754-0186
SOUL & SPIRIT; your spiritual life coach. Text in English. 2008. m. GBP 35 domestic; GBP 50 in Europe; GBP 55 elsewhere; GBP 3.50 newsstand/cover (effective 2010). adv. **Document type:** *Magazine, Consumer.*
—**CCC.**
Published by: Aceville Publications Ltd., 21-23 Phoenix Ct, Hawkins Rd, Colchester, Essex CO2 8JY, United Kingdom. TEL 44-1206-505962, FAX 44-1206-505915, aceville@servicehelpline.co.uk, http://www.aceville.com. Ed. Katy Evans TEL 44-1206-508628. Adv. contact Joy Mitchell TEL 44-1206-505944. **Subscr. to:** 800 Guillat Ave, Kent Science Park, Sittingbourne, Kent ME9 8GU, United Kingdom. TEL 44-844-8440381, FAX 44-845-4567143.

299 CAN ISSN 1922-1657
SOURCES (MONTREAL). Text in English. s-a. **Document type:** *Newsletter, Academic/Scholarly.*
Published by: Concordia University, Multi-Faith Chaplaincy, 2090 Mackay Z Annex, Montreal, PQ, Canada. TEL 514-848-2424.

300 USA
SPECTRUM QUARTERLY UPDATE; celebrating the unity and diversity of all races, religions and cultures. Text in English. 1965. q. USD 10; USD 25 membership; USD 15 to students & senior citizens (effective 2000). adv. bk.rev. **Document type:** *Newsletter.* **Description:** Aims to foster a new type of person and new civilization based on the dynamic integration of diversity among all peoples and all life.
Formerly: Spectrum Monthly Update
Indexed: AES.
Published by: Unity-and-Diversity World Council, 5521 Grosvenor Blvd, Los Angeles, CA 90066-6915. TEL 310-577-1968, FAX 310-578-1028, udcworld@gte.net, http://udcworld.org/. R&P Leland P Stewart. Circ: 500.

133.52 CZE ISSN 0862-6405
SPIRIT. Text in Czech. 1990. w. CZK 758; CZK 14 newsstand/cover (effective 2010). adv. **Document type:** *Magazine, Consumer.*
Published by: Victory Media, a.s., Ve Stromkach 10, Usti nad Labem, 400 21, Czech Republic. TEL 420-472741989, FAX 420-472741989.

SPIRIT & DESTINY; for women who want the best possible future. *see* WOMEN'S INTERESTS

299 USA ISSN 2154-6851
▼ **SPIRITUAL ENTHUSIAST.** Text in English. 2010 (June). m. free (effective 2011). **Document type:** *Magazine, Consumer.* **Description:** For holistic networking, spiritual seekers, life enthusiast and those who respect universal love and the evolution of the soul.
Media: Online - full text.
Published by: Spiritual Enthusiast, Inc., PO Box 4321, Grapevine, TX 76099. TEL 214-418-7433.

299 AUS ISSN 1838-8914
▼ **SPIRITUAL SPACE ONLINE MAGAZINE.** Variant title: Spiritual Space Magazine. Text in English. 2011. m. AUD 3.50 per issue (effective 2011). back issues avail. **Document type:** *Magazine, Consumer.* **Description:** Covers topics such as spiritual meditation, spiritual development. spiritual healing, multicultural spiritual insights and much more.
Media: Online - full text.
Published by: Spiritual Space Publishing, Chapel Hill, Brisbane, QLD 4069, Australia. info@spiritualspace.com.au.

SPIRITUALITY & HEALTH; the soul body connection. *see* ALTERNATIVE MEDICINE

133 CHE ISSN 1424-0041
SPUREN; Magazin fuer neues Bewusstsein. Text in German. 1986. q. CHF 25; CHF 30 foreign (effective 1999). adv. bk.rev.; music rev. back issues avail. **Document type:** *Newsletter, Consumer.*
Related titles: Online - full text ed.
Published by: Herausgeberverein Spuren, Wartstr 3, Winterthur, 8400, Switzerland. TEL 41-52-2123361, FAX 41-52-2123371, spuren@compuserve.com, http://www.access.ch/spuren. Ed., Pub. Martin Frischknecht. Adv. contact Rita Lenz. B&W page CHF 1,500; trim 280 x 210. Circ: 10,000 (paid).

SQUIFFY ETHER JAG; words, wings, canivals, and victorial electronics. *see* LITERARY AND POLITICAL REVIEWS

133.5 USA ISSN 1081-5171
STAR BEACON. Text in English. 1987. m. looseleaf. USD 20; USD 28 foreign (effective 2001). adv. bk.rev. 12 p./no. 3 cols./p.; back issues avail.; reprints avail. **Document type:** *Newsletter.* **Description:** For UFO percipients offering a wide variety of metaphysical information and promoting spiritual awareness.
Published by: (U F O Contact Center International, Delta County), Earth Star Publications, PO Box 117, Paonia, CO 81428. TEL 970-527-3257, FAX 970-527-2433, ulrichac@tds.net, http://www.earthstarpublications.com. Ed., Pub., R&P, Adv. contact Ann Ulrich. Circ: 500.

STAR TECH; the real cosmic connection. *see* ASTRONOMY

100 GBR
STARFIRE. Text in English. 19??. irreg. GBP 20 per issue (effective 2009). illus. **Document type:** *Monographic series, Trade.*
Published by: B C M Starfire, London, WC1N 3XX, United Kingdom. starfire.books@btinternet.com. Ed. Michael Staley.

299 GBR ISSN 0308-4531
STELLA POLARIS. Text in English. 1950. bi-m. GBP 11.60 domestic; GBP 2 per issue (effective 2009). bk.rev. Index. Supplement avail.; back issues avail. **Document type:** *Magazine, Consumer.* **Description:** Provides articles on healing, astrology, and other topics of interest to followers of the teaching, such as the ancient spiritual centers. Includes stories and articles for children.
Related titles: German ed.: ISSN 1613-8562.
Published by: White Eagle Publishing Trust, White Eagle Lodge, New Lands, Brewells Ln, Rake, Liss, Hants GU33 7HY, United Kingdom. TEL 44-1730-893300, FAX 44-1730-892235, info@whiteagle.org, http://www.whiteagle.org. Ed. Ylana Hayward. R&P Stuart Neil.

299 USA
SUB ROSA; where science and magic, myth and history meet. Text in English. 2005 (Jun.). q. free. adv. **Document type:** *Magazine, Consumer.* **Description:** Contains stories on the supernatural, mythical beliefs, revision history, and UFO in PFD file format.
Media: Online - full content. Ed. Greg Taylor. adv.: page USD 100.

135 USA ISSN 1045-4942
CODEN: ENTOF7
SUBCONSCIOUSLY SPEAKING; you can change your life through the power of your mind. Text in English. 1985. bi-m. USD 14 domestic; USD 18 in Canada; USD 25 elsewhere (effective 2006). bk.rev.; video rev. 12 p./no. 2 cols./p.; **Document type:** *Newsletter, Consumer.* **Description:** To elevate the consciousness of all who read through current information regarding hypnosis, imagery, and healing of body, mind and spirit.
Related titles: Online - full content ed.; Online - full text ed.
Indexed: A04, CA, D02, G05, G06, G07, G08, I05, T02.
Published by: Infinity Institute International Inc., 4110 Edgeland, Dept. 800, Royal Oak, MI 48073-2285. TEL 248-549-5594, FAX 248-549-5421, aspencer@infinityinstitute.com, http://www.infinityinstitute.com. Circ: 4,500 (paid and free).

158 USA ISSN 1935-4886
THE SUCCESSFUL DILETTANTE. Text in English. 2006. s-a. **Document type:** *Magazine, Consumer.*
Published by: Susan Henderson coach@susanhenderson.com, http://www.thesuccessfuldilettante.com.

299 GBR ISSN 2045-1849
'SUP MAGAZINE. Text in English. 1998. s-a. back issues avail. **Document type:** *Magazine, Consumer.*
Published by: Sup Magazine, 11 Chance St, London, E2 7JB, United Kingdom. Eds. Josh Jones, Laura Martin, Marisa Brickman.

158 USA ISSN 1948-917X
BF309
SUPERCONSCIOUSNESS MAGAZINE. Abbreviated title: S C. Text in English. 2007. bi-m. USD 38 domestic; USD 29 in Mexico; USD 50 in Canada; USD 65 elsewhere (effective 2009). adv. back issues avail. **Document type:** *Magazine, Consumer.* **Description:** Acts as forum for this emerging knowledge base, exploring and exposing the extraordinary abilities innate in every human being.
Related titles: Online - full text ed.: ISSN 1948-9188.
Published by: Editora La Voz del Istmos, USA Inc., 305 Van Trump Ave, NE, PO Box 2903, Yelm, WA 98597. TEL 360-400-2383, FAX 360-400-2531. Ed. Heidi Smith. Pub. Jair B Robles. adv.: color page USD 1,250; bleed 7.5 x 10.125.

100 USA
SUPPORTIVE LIFESTYLES NEWS. Text in English. 1972. 12/yr. USD 25. adv. bk.rev.
Published by: Fellowship of the Inner Light, 620 14 St, Virginia Beach, VA 23451. TEL 703-896-3673, FAX 804-428-6648. Ed. Myrrh Haslam.

158 CAN ISSN 1198-760X
SYNCHRONICITY; the magazine. Text in English. 1993. bi-m. CAD 20; CAD 3.75 newsstand/cover (effective 2005). **Document type:** *Magazine, Consumer.* **Description:** Provides information for people interested in holistic living, healthier relationships, complementary therapies, alternative spirituality and personal healing.
Published by: Synchronicity Publishing Ltd, 2604 Kensington Rd, NW, PO Box 63118, Calgary, AB T2N 2S5, Canada. TEL 403-270-9544, FAX 403-270-7407.

299 USA ISSN 1938-5056
TAROT WORLD MAGAZINE. Text in English. 2008. q. USD 32 domestic; USD 52 foreign (effective 2008). adv. **Document type:** *Magazine, Consumer.*
Related titles: Online - full text ed.: ISSN 1938-2278.
Published by: T W M Publishing, 2509 Richmond Rd, Ste 112, Texarkana, TX 75503. TEL 877-253-2755, FAX 214-594-7273, info@tarotworldmag.com. Ed. Heidi Snelgrove.

THEOSOPHICAL HISTORY; a quarterly journal of research. *see* RELIGIONS AND THEOLOGY—Other Denominations And Sects

TO YOUR HEALTH!; the magazine of healing and hope. *see* PHYSICAL FITNESS AND HYGIENE

051.4 USA ISSN 1937-6502
THE TOM MONTE MONTHLY; healing the body, mind and spirit. Text in English. 2008. m. free to members (effective 2010). **Document type:** *Newsletter, Consumer.* **Description:** Designed to provide help for restoring health, enhance mental and emotional well-being, and show how to bring love and harmony to most important relationships.
Media: Online - full text.
Published by: Tom Monte, Ed. & Pub., 120 High Point Dr, Amherst, MA 01002. TEL 413-253-0514, http://www.tommonte.com/.

133 USA
TOTAL ECLIPSE. Text in English. 6/yr. USD 12; USD 14 in Canada; USD 17 elsewhere. **Document type:** *Magazine, Consumer.*
Address: PO Box 1055, Suisun, CA 94585. Ed. J Taylor Black.

158 USA
TRANSFORMATION TIMES; new age journal. Text in English. 1982. 10/yr. USD 8 (effective 2001). adv. bk.rev. **Document type:** *Newspaper.*
Published by: (Christ Light Community Church), Life Resources Unlimited, PO Box 425, Beavercreek, OR 97004. TEL 503-632-7141. Ed. Connie L Faubel. Circ: 8,000.

299 292 GBR
TUATHA. Text in English. 1998. s-m. free to members (effective 2003). adv. bk.rev. back issues avail. **Document type:** *Newsletter.* **Description:** Contains Pagan calendar of fests, sports training events, exchanges and accomodation, study holiday abroad, zine listings, and reviews of members only rituals, courses and training manuals. Directory of Pagan facts, body training notes, Pagan Etymology, guide to Western magick, Pagan world news, etc.
Related titles: Diskette ed.; E-mail ed.; Fax ed.
Published by: Order of the Jarls of Baelder / Arktion, Arktion Foundation, Ground Fl, 60, Elmhurst Rd, Reading, Berkshire RG1 5HY, United Kingdom. heritage-school@ntlworld.com, http://www.arktion.org/. Ed., Pub. Stephen B Cox.

U F O DIGEST; online webzine. (Unidentified Flying Object) *see* AERONAUTICS AND SPACE FLIGHT

001.942 AUS
U F O ENCOUNTER. (Unidentified Flying Object) Text in English. 1966. bi-m. AUD 30 domestic; AUD 40 foreign; free to members (effective 2009). bk.rev.; video rev. illus.; maps; stat. back issues avail. **Document type:** *Journal, Academic/Scholarly.* **Description:** Contains Australian and international articles, as well as up-to-date information on local and global UFO sightings, UFO-related news and developments in science.
Former titles (until 1977): Queensland U.F.O. Research Bureau. Contact; (until 1973): Flying Saucer Research Bureau, Queensland. Newsletter
Published by: U F O Research (Queensland), PO Box 15222, City East, QLD 4002, Australia. TEL 61-7-33761780, info@uforq.asn.au. Ed. Lee Paqui.

299 AUS ISSN 1833-4962
U F O LOGIST MAGAZINE; beyond imagination lies the truth. (Unidentified Flying Object) Text in English. 1997. bi-m. AUD 38 domestic; EUR 42 in Europe excluding UK; GBP 29 in United Kingdom; USD 57 in United States; CAD 61 in Canada; AUD 21 combined subscription domestic (print & online eds.); EUR 12.50 combined subscription in Europe (print & online eds.); excluding UK; GBP 11 combined subscription in United Kingdom (print & online eds.) (effective 2009). adv. back issues avail. **Document type:** *Magazine, Consumer.*
Former titles (until 2006): Australasian U F Ologist (1441-9173); (until 1999): Australian U F Ologist (1441-9165); (until 1998): U F Ologist (1326-6942)
Related titles: CD-ROM ed.; Online - full text ed.; Optical Disk - DVD ed.
Published by: Earthlink Publishing Aust Pty Ltd, PO Box 738, Jimboomba, QLD 4280, Australia. TEL 61-7-55487205. Ed. Robert Frola. adv.: B&W page AUD 480, color page AUD 650; 175 x 270. Circ: 10,000.

U S P S JOURNAL. *see* PARAPSYCHOLOGY AND OCCULTISM

THE UNABRIDGED LIFE EZINE. *see* LITERATURE

100 USA
UNIVERSAL PROUTIST. Text in English. 1985. m. membership. bk.rev. illus. back issues avail. **Description:** Informs members of developments in the PROUT (Progressive Utilization Theory) movement, social projects, and activities of other progressive organizations.
Formerly: New Waves (Washington) (1040-8185)
Indexed: EnvAb.
Published by: Proutist Universal, Inc., PO Box 56466, Washington, DC 20040. TEL 202-829-2278, FAX 202-829-0462. Ed. D Dhruva. Circ: 4,000.

UNKNOWN MAGAZINE; real experiences of unusual phenomena. *see* PARAPSYCHOLOGY AND OCCULTISM

299 USA ISSN 1543-3463
BJ1131
V I A (MISSION VIEJO); the quarterly journal of Vision-In-Action. (Vision In Action) Text in English. 2003. q. USD 30 in US & Canada; USD 43 in Mexico; USD 56 elsewhere (effective 2003).
Published by: Vision in Action, 27882 Calle Marin, Mission Viejo, CA 92692. TEL 949-454-1349, 800-509-1955, FAX 949-206-9602, think@via-visioninaction.org, http://www.via-visioninaction.org. Ed., Pub. Yasuhiko Genku Kimura.

158 USA
VIEWS FROM OFF CENTER. Text in English. 1991. bi-m. **Document type:** *Newsletter.*
Published by: Ethical Humanist Society, 38 Old Country Rd, Garden City, NY 11530. TEL 516-739-0042. Eds. Graceann V Inyard, Scott Allison.

VITALITY MAGAZINE; Toronto's monthly wellness journal. *see* ALTERNATIVE MEDICINE

VOX FEMINARUM. *see* WOMEN'S INTERESTS

299 GBR ISSN 2046-3979
▼ **WATKINS REVIEW.** Text in English. 2010. 3/yr. GBP 4.99 per issue (effective 2011). back issues avail. **Document type:** *Magazine, Consumer.*
Published by: Watkins Books, 19-21 Cecil Ct, London, WC2N 4EZ, United Kingdom.

WELCOME TO PLANET EARTH; journal of new astrology in the contemporary world. *see* ASTROLOGY

299 USA ISSN 2161-590X
WELL-BEING (SEATTLE, WASH.). Text in English. 1975. irreg., latest 2008. USD 3 per issue (effective 2011). back issues avail. **Document type:** *Journal, Trade.*
Published by: Rational Island Publishers, PO Box 2081, Main Office Station, Seattle, WA 98111. TEL 206-284-0311, FAX 206-284-8429, litsales@rc.org, http://www.rationalisland.com.

170 CHE
WENDEZEIT. Text in German. 1989. bi-m. CHF 48 domestic; CHF 50 foreign (effective 2000). adv. bk.rev. back issues avail. **Document type:** *Magazine, Consumer.*
Formerly: Wassermann Zeitalter
Published by: Fatema, Parkstr 14, Matten B. Interl, 3800, Switzerland. TEL 41-33-8235667, FAX 41-33-8265653. Ed., R&P Orith Tempelman.

158 USA ISSN 1935-4827
WHAT COULD BE BETTER?. Text in English. 2006. m. **Document type:** *Newsletter, Consumer.*
Media: Online - full text.
Published by: Better Than Ever Coaching, PO Box 391, Brewster, MA 02631. TEL 508-896-5779, 888-294-5779, http://www.betterthanevercoaching.com/index.html. Ed. Helen F Kosinski.

051 USA ISSN 2155-2371
BP605.N48
WHOLE LIVING; body + soul in balance. Variant title: Body & Soul. Text in English. 1974. 10/yr. USD 12 domestic (print or online ed.); USD 15 in Canada (print or online ed.) (effective 2010). adv. bk.rev. illus. back issues avail.; reprints avail. **Document type:** *Magazine, Consumer.* **Description:** Serves as a discerning chronicle of America's spiritual reawakening, examing such topics as holistic medicine, natural foods, self-help psychology, contemporary mysticism, and green politics.
Former titles (until 2010): Body + Soul (1539-0004); (until 2002): New Age (1098-447X); (until 1998): New Age Journal (0746-3618); (until 1983): New Age Magazine (0164-3967); (until 1976): New Age Journal; (until 19??): New Journal
Related titles: Online - full text ed.: (from PQC).
Indexed: A22, AltPI, BRI, CBRI, CCR, NPI.
—Ingenta.
Published by: Martha Stewart Living Omnimedia LLC, 11 W 42nd St, 25th Fl, New York, NY 10036. TEL 212-827-8000, 800-357-7060, FAX 212-827-8204, help@mstewart.customersvc.com, http://www.marthastewart.com. adv.: B&W page USD 30,100, color page USD 38,250. Circ: 200,000 (paid).

WICCAN CANDLES. *see* PARAPSYCHOLOGY AND OCCULTISM

WINGSPAN (NORTH LAKE); journal of the male spirit. *see* MEN'S STUDIES

133 USA ISSN 0740-6754
THE WORD (ROCHESTER, NY). Text in English. 1986. q. USD 25 associate membership; USD 50 contributing membership; USD 100 sponsoring membership (effective 2003); subscr. included with membership. bk.rev. 20 p./no. 2 cols./p.; back issues avail. **Document type:** *Monographic series.* **Description:** Sheds light on problems of human living for individuals seeking to make progress through self-improvement.
Published by: The Word Foundation, Inc., PO Box 17510, Rochester, NY 14617. TEL 585-544-6790, FAX 585-544-6975, http://www.word-foundation.org. Ed., Pub., R&P John L Coiro. Adv. contact Dante Di Prosa TEL 585-288-3515.

133 USA
WORLD FREE INTERNET. Text in English. 1981. q. free. back issues avail. **Document type:** *Bulletin.*
Formerly (until 1996): Territorial Herald
Published by: Central News Service, RP 200 0203, Box 7075, Laguna Niguel, CA 92607. TEL 714-240-8472, http://www.web2010.com/marcerlc/. Ed. Marc Ely Chaitlin. Circ: 7,000.

181.45 USA
B132.Y6
YOGA INTERNATIONAL. Text in English. 1991. q. USD 15 (effective 2010). adv. bk.rev.; video rev. illus. 116 p./no.; back issues avail. **Document type:** *Magazine, Consumer.* **Description:** Brings information on the practice of yoga and yoga' sister science Ayurveda.
Former titles (until 2010): Yoga Plus Joyful Living (1935-2158); (until 2006): Yoga International (1055-7911); Which superseded (in Jul.1991): Dawn (0277-4461)
Related titles: Online - full text ed.
Indexed: C11, E-psyche, SD.
—CCC.
Published by: Himalayan International Institute (HII), 952 Bethany Turnpike, Honesdale, PA 18431- 9706. TEL 570-253-5551, 800-822-4547, FAX 570-253-9078, info@himalayaninstitute.org. Ed. Shannon Sexton. R&P Irene Petryszak. Adv. contact Jim McGinley. Circ: 24,500 (controlled).

613 USA ISSN 0191-0965
YOGA JOURNAL. Text in English. 1975. 9/yr. USD 15.95 domestic; USD 22.95 in Canada; USD 37.95 elsewhere (effective 2008). bk.rev. illus. 180 p./no. 3 cols./p.; back issues avail.; reprints avail. **Document type:** *Magazine, Consumer.* **Description:** Covers yoga, holistic health, psychology, New Age consciousness, meditation and Eastern and Western spirituality.
Related titles: CD-ROM ed.; Microform ed.: (from PQC); Online - full text ed.; Russian ed.: 2005.
Indexed: A04, A22, APW, B04, C06, C07, C11, CA, NPI, R03, R09, RGAb, RGPR, SD, T02, W03, W05.
—Ingenta.
Address: 475 Sansome St, Ste 850, San Francisco, CA 94111. TEL 415-591-0555, FAX 415-591-0733. Ed. Kaitlin Quistgaard. Pub. Andrew W Clurman TEL 310-356-4129. Circ: 325,000 (paid).

YOGA JOURNAL. *see* PHYSICAL FITNESS AND HYGIENE

613.05 GBR ISSN 1478-9671
YOGA MAGAZINE. Text in English. 2003. m. GBP 26.50 domestic; GBP 50 in Europe; GBP 70 elsewhere (effective 2009). back issues avail. **Document type:** *Magazine, Consumer.* **Description:** Contains informative articles on a wide variety of yoga topics from positions and philosophy to food and fashion.
—CCC.
Address: 26 York St, London, W1U 6PZ, United Kingdom. TEL 44-20-77295454, FAX 44-20-77390181. Ed. Dr. Yogi Malik. Adv. contact Lesley Wigham TEL 44-2073-060300. **Subscr. to:** Warners Group Publications Plc., The Maltings, Manor Ln, Bourne, Lincs PE10 9PH, United Kingdom. TEL 44-1778-392043, FAX 44-1778-421706, subscriptions@warnersgroup.co.uk, http://www.warnersgroup.co.uk.

158 USA ISSN 2161-5985
YOUNG AND POWERFUL. Text in English. 19??. irreg., latest 2003. USD 3 per issue (effective 2011). back issues avail. **Document type:** *Journal, Trade.*
Formerly (until 1978): Upcoming
Published by: Rational Island Publishers, PO Box 2081, Main Office Station, Seattle, WA 98111. TEL 206-284-0311, FAX 206-284-8429, litsales@rc.org, http://www.rationalisland.com.

158 USA ISSN 1947-1890
YOUR NEXT QUEST CHRONICLES; starting you on the journey to where you want to be. Text in English. 2008. m. free (effective 2009). back issues avail. **Document type:** *Newsletter, Consumer.* **Description:** Features inspiring articles, stories and interviews for a better way of life.
Media: Online - full content.
Published by: Michele M. Meagher, Pub., 131 Franklin St, Arlington, MA 02474. TEL 781-583-7185, mmm@yournextquest.com.

133.323 DEU
ZEITSCHRIFT FUER RADIAESTHESIE UND HARMONIEFINDUNG. Text in German. 1949. q. EUR 25 (effective 2010). adv. bk.rev. bibl.; charts; illus. index, cum.index: 1950-1961. 56 p./no.; **Document type:** *Journal, Academic/Scholarly.*
Formerly: Zeitschrift fuer Radiaesthesie (0044-3425)
Published by: (Zentrum fuer Radiaesthesie), Herold Verlag Dr. Franz Wetzel und Co. KG, Kirchbachweg 16, Munich, 81479, Germany. TEL 49-89-7915774. Circ: 2,500.

NEW AGE PUBLICATIONS—Abstracting, Bibliographies, Statistics

299 USA ISSN 2161-8119
JONATHAN BUYS. Text in English. 2007. w. back issues avail. **Document type:** *Consumer.*
Media: Online - full text.
Published by: Jonathan Buys, Ed.

NUCLEAR ENERGY

see ENERGY—*Nuclear Energy*

NUCLEAR PHYSICS

see PHYSICS—Nuclear Physics

NUMISMATICS

see also HOBBIES

737 CZE ISSN 0862-1195
HG970.3.Z9
ACTA MUSEI MORAVIAE. SUPPLEMENTUM: FOLIA NUMISMATICA. Text in Czech; Summaries in English, French, German, Russian. 1986. a. EUR 24 per vol. (effective 2009). illus. index. **Document type:** *Journal, Academic/Scholarly.*
Incorporates: Moravskie Numismaticke Zpravy (0077-152X)
Related titles: ◆ Supplement to: Acta Musei Moraviae. Scientiae Sociales. ISSN 0323-0570.
Indexed: RASB.
Published by: (Moravske Zemske Muzeum, Numismaticke Oddeleni), Moravske Zemske Muzeum, Zelny trh 6, Brno, 65937, Czech Republic. TEL 420-5-42321205, FAX 420-5-42212792, mzm@mzm.cz. Ed. Dagmar Kasparova. Circ: 100.

737 ESP ISSN 0211-8386
CJ9
ACTA NUMISMATICA. Text in Multiple languages. 1971. a. EUR 40 (effective 2008). **Document type:** *Journal, Academic/Scholarly.*
Related titles: Online - full text ed.: ISSN 2013-3928. 1971.
Published by: Institut d'Estudis Catalans, Carrer del Carme 47, Barcelona, 08001, Spain. TEL 34-932-701620, FAX 34-932-701180, informacio@iecat.net, http://www2.iecat.net.

737.4 USA ISSN 1053-8356
CJ1
AMERICAN JOURNAL OF NUMISMATICS. Text in English. 1866. a. price varies. bk.rev. charts; illus. back issues avail. **Document type:** *Journal, Academic/Scholarly.* **Description:** Academic analysis of numismatic objects contributing to the understanding and interpretation of history, political science, archaeology, and art history.
Formerly (1945-1989): Museum Notes (New York) (0145-1413)
Indexed: IBR, IBZ, NumL, PCI.
Published by: American Numismatic Society, 75 Varick St, 11th Fl, New York, NY 10013. TEL 212-571-4470, FAX 212-571-4479. Ed. Peter van Alfen TEL 212-571-4470 ext 153. Circ: 2,400.

737 USA
AMERICAN NUMISMATIC SOCIETY. MAGAZINE. Abbreviated title: A N S Magazine. Text in English. 1955. 3/yr. USD 50 to non-members; USD 18 per issue to non-members; free to members (effective 2010). illus. **Document type:** *Magazine, Consumer.* **Description:** Covers study of coins from all periods and countries.
Former titles (until 2002): American Numismatic Society. Newsletter; (until 199?): A N S Newsletter
Related titles: Online - full text ed.
Published by: American Numismatic Society, 75 Varick St, 11th Fl, New York, NY 10013. TEL 212-571-4470, FAX 212-571-4479, orders@numismatics.org, http://www.numismatics.org. Ed. Ute Wartenberg Kagan TEL 212-571-4470 ext 110. Adv. contact Joanne Isaac TEL 212-571-4470 ext 112.

737.4 USA ISSN 0271-4019
ANCIENT COINS IN NORTH AMERICAN COLLECTIONS. Text in English. 1969. irreg., latest vol.9, 2007. price varies. back issues avail.; reprints avail. **Document type:** *Monographic series, Academic/Scholarly.* **Description:** Covers public and private collections not generally available for inspection.
Formerly (until 1979): Greek Coins in North American Collections
Published by: American Numismatic Society, 75 Varick St, 11th Fl, New York, NY 10013. TEL 212-571-4470, FAX 212-571-4479, orders@numismatics.org.

737 954 IND
ANDHRA PRADESH, INDIA. DEPARTMENT OF ARCHAEOLOGY AND MUSEUMS. MUSEUM SERIES. Text in English. 1961. irreg., latest vol.27. price varies. back issues avail. **Document type:** *Monographic series, Government.*
Former titles: Andhra Pradesh, India. Department of Archaeology and Museums. Museum Objects and Numismatics Series; Andhra Pradesh, India. Department of Archaeology. Museum Series (0066-166X)
Published by: Department of Archaeology and Museums, Gunfoundry, Hyderabad, 500 001, India. TEL 91-40-23234942, FAX 91-40-23234942, chennareddyp@gmail.com.

737 ITA ISSN 1121-7464
ANNOTAZIONI NUMISMATICHE. Text in Italian. 1991. 6/yr. EUR 32 (effective 2008). bk.rev. bibl. Supplement avail. **Document type:** *Magazine, Consumer.* **Description:** Contains news, reviews, discussions and bibliographic notes.
Published by: Edizioni/Ennerre s.r.l., Via San Rocco 8, Milan, MI 20135, Italy. FAX 39-02-58309185, http://www.edizioniennerre.it.

737 USA ISSN 0884-0180
CJ3481
ARMENIAN NUMISMATIC JOURNAL. Key Title: Hay Dramagitakan Handes. Text in English. 1975. q. USD 30 (effective 2000). bk.rev. charts; illus. cum.index: vols.1-15. back issues avail.
Indexed: NumL.
Published by: Armenian Numismatic Society, 8511 Beverly Park Place, Pico Rivera, CA 90660-1920. TEL 562-695-0380, armnumsoc@aol.com, nercessian@aol.com. Ed. Y T Nercessian. R&P W Gewenian. Circ: 225.

737 BEL
ASSOCIATION INTERNATIONALE DES NUMISMATES PROFESSIONNELS. PUBLICATION. Text in English, French. irreg., latest vol.13. price varies. back issues avail. **Document type:** *Monographic series, Trade.* **Description:** Publishes news from the community of people interested in numismatics.
Published by: International Association of Professional Numismatists, Rue de la Bourse 14, Brussels, 1000, Belgium. TEL 32-2-513-3400, FAX 32-2-512-2528. Ed. J L Van der Scheuren. Circ: 110.

737 CAN ISSN 0708-3181
ATLANTIC NUMISMATIST. Text in English. 1965. m. free to members. **Document type:** *Newsletter.* **Description:** Publishes research articles and information that further the cause of Numismatics in general and Maritime Numismatics in particular.
Formerly (until 1979): Atlantic Provinces Numismatic Association. Newsletter (0044-9903)
Published by: Atlantic Provinces Numismatic Association, c/o The Dartmouth Seniors Service Center, 45 Ochterloney St, Dartmouth, NS B2Y 4M7, Canada. chalmers@apnaonline.ca, http://www.apnaonline.ca.

737 AUS ISSN 1440-4508
AUSTRALASIAN COIN AND BANKNOTE MAGAZINE. Text in English. 1996. m. (11/yr. plus yearbook). AUD 77 domestic; AUD 114 in New Zealand; AUD 116 in SE Asia; AUD 144 in Europe & the Americas (effective 2009). back issues avail. **Document type:** *Magazine, Consumer.*
Incorporates (in 19??): Australian Coin Review
Published by: Greg McDonald Publishing and Numismatics Pty Ltd, PO Box 6313, North Ryde, NSW 2113, Australia. TEL 61-2-98893799, FAX 61-2-98893766. Ed. John Mulhall.

737 AUS ISSN 0004-9875
➤ **AUSTRALIAN NUMISMATIC JOURNAL;** devoted to the study of coins, tokens, paper money and medals, particularly the issues of Australia. Text in English. 1949. irreg. bk.rev. index, cum.index. **Document type:** *Journal, Academic/Scholarly.*
Formerly (until 1958): South Australian Numismatic Journal
Indexed: NumL, PCI.
Published by: Numismatic Society of South Australia Inc., 3 Graves St, Kadina, SA 5554, Australia. TEL 61-8-88212906, FAX 61-8-88212901. Ed., Pub., R&P, Adv. contact Mick Vort-Ronald.

737 USA ISSN 0164-0828
BANK NOTE REPORTER; complete monthly guide for paper money collectors. Text in English. 1973. m. USD 39.98; USD 4.99 newsstand/cover (effective 2012). adv. bk.rev. illus. back issues avail.; reprints avail. **Document type:** *Magazine, Trade.* **Description:** Contains news on market values, "Bank Note Clinic" (a collector Q&A), an up-to-date foreign exchange chart, "Fun Notes" (interesting, odd, & unusual notes), a price guide, a world currency section, historical features on paper money worldwide (emphasizing U.S. issues), & hundreds of display & classified ads offering to buy, sell, & trade bank notes of all kinds.
Related titles: Online - full text ed.
Indexed: G08, I05, NumL.
—CCC.
Published by: F + W Media Inc., 4700 E Galbraith Rd, Cincinnati, OH 45236. TEL 513-531-2690, contact_us@fwmedia.com, http://www.fwmedia.com/. Ed. Bob Van Ryzin TEL 715-445-2214 ext 13306. Pub. Scott Tappa TEL 715-445-2214 ext 13428.

737.4 NLD ISSN 0165-8654
BEELDENAAR; munt- en penningkundig nieuws. Text in Dutch. 1977. bi-m. EUR 25 domestic; EUR 30 in Belgium & Luxembourg; EUR 37.50 in Europe; EUR 40 elsewhere (effective 2010). adv. bk.rev. illus.
Indexed: B24.
—IE, Infotrieve.
Published by: (Koninklijk Nederlands Genootschap voor Munt- en Penningkunde/Royal Dutch Society of Numismatics), Stichting de Beeldenaar, Postbus 11, Utrecht, 3500 AA, Netherlands. Ed. Janjaap Luijt. **Co-sponsor:** Vereniging voor Penningkunst.

737 DEU ISSN 0233-0148
BERLINER NUMISMATISCHE FORSCHUNGEN. Text in German. 1987. irreg., latest vol.9, 2004. price varies. back issues avail. **Document type:** *Monographic series, Academic/Scholarly.*
Published by: (Staatliche Museen zu Berlin, Preussischer Kulturbesitz), Gebr. Mann Verlag, Berliner Str 53, Berlin, 10713, Germany. TEL 49-30-70013880, FAX 49-30-700138811, vertrieb-kunstverlage@reimer-verlag.de, http://www.reimer-mann-verlag.de.

737 POL ISSN 0006-4017
BIULETYN NUMIZMATYCZNY/NUMISMATIC BULLETIN. Text in Polish. 1965. q. EUR 55 foreign (effective 2006). adv. bk.rev. abstr.; bibl.; illus. cum.index. 80 p./no. 1 cols./p.; **Document type:** *Bulletin.*
Indexed: NumL.
Published by: Polskie Towarzystwo Numizmatyczne, ul Jezuicka 6, PO Box 2, Warsaw, 00281, Poland. zpptn@interia.pl, http://www.ptn.pl. Ed. Wieslaw Kopicki. Adv. contact Lech Kokocinski. Circ: 1,000. **Dist. by:** Ars Polona, Obroncow 25, Warsaw 03933, Poland. TEL 48-22-5098609, FAX 48-22-5098610, arspolona@arspolona.com.pl, http://www.arspolona.com.pl.

737 ITA ISSN 0392-971X
CJ2900
BOLLETTINO DI NUMISMATICA. Text in Italian. 1983. s-a. EUR 62 domestic; EUR 75 foreign (effective 2009). **Document type:** *Magazine, Trade.*
Published by: (Italy. Ministero per i Beni e le Attivita Culturali), Istituto Poligrafico e Zecca dello Stato, Piazza Verdi 10, Rome, 00198, Italy. TEL 39-06-85082147, editoriale@ipzs.it, http://www.ipzs.it.

THE BOUTONNEUR. *see* HOBBIES

737 GBR ISSN 0143-8956
CJ2470
BRITISH NUMISMATIC JOURNAL. Abbreviated title: B N J. Text in English. 1903. a. free to members (effective 2009). bk.rev. bibl.; charts; illus. index, cum.index every 10 vols. back issues avail. **Document type:** *Journal, Academic/Scholarly.* **Description:** Contains the numismatic articles and notes, obituaries, reviews of new publications and an annual register of single coin finds, together with supporting photographic plates.
Related titles: Online - full text ed.
Indexed: BrArAb, NumL, PCI.
—BLDSC (2331.300000).
Published by: British Numismatic Society, c/o The Warburg Institute, Woburn Sq, London, WC1H 0AB, United Kingdom. secretary@britnumsoc.org. Eds. M Delme Radcliffe, N J Mayhew.

737 CAN ISSN 1922-8872
CJ1860
THE C N JOURNAL. (Canadian Numismatic) Text in English. 1950. 10/yr. free to members (effective 2010). adv. bk.rev. bibl.; illus.; stat. index. back issues avail. **Document type:** *Journal, Academic/Scholarly.* **Description:** Aims to encourage and promotes the science of numismatics by study of coins, paper money, medals, tokens and all other numismatic items, with emphasis on material pertaining to Canada.
Former titles (until 2004): Canadian Numismatic Association. Journal (0008-4573); (until 1994): Canadian Numismatic Journal (1207-1870); (until 1956): C N A Bulletin (0315-4882)
Related titles: Microfiche ed.: (from MML); Online - full text ed.: (from MML).
Indexed: C03, CBCARef, CBPI, NumL, PQC.
Published by: The Royal Canadian Numismatic Association, 5694 Hwy #7 E, Ste 432, Markham, ON L3P 1B4, Canada. TEL 647-401-4014, FAX 905-472-9645, info@rcna.ca. Ed. Dan Gosling TEL 780-922-5743. Adv. contact Paul Fiocca.

737 USA ISSN 0010-1443
C N L. (Colonial Newsletter) Text in English. 1960. 3/yr. USD 50 to non-members; USD 35 to members; USD 20 per issue to non-members (effective 2010). bk.rev. charts; illus.; stat. back issues avail. **Document type:** *Newsletter, Academic/Scholarly.* **Description:** Focuses on the study of the coinages produced by the states during the Confederation period of the United States. Brings out scholarly and seminal studies in the area of numismatics.
Related titles: CD-ROM ed.: USD 50 domestic; USD 58 foreign (effective 2010).
Indexed: NumL.
Published by: American Numismatic Society, 75 Varick St, 11th Fl, New York, NY 10013. TEL 212-571-4470, FAX 212-571-4479, orders@numismatics.org. Ed. Oliver Hoover.

CAESARAUGUSTA. *see* ARCHAEOLOGY

CAHIERS ERNEST - BABELON. *see* ARCHAEOLOGY

737 FRA ISSN 0008-0373
CAHIERS NUMISMATIQUES. Text in French. 1964. q. EUR 8.50 per issue (effective 2009). adv. bk.rev. bibl.; charts; illus.; stat. **Document type:** *Consumer.*
Indexed: NumL.
Published by: Societe d'Etudes Numismatiques et Archeologiques, 4 rue Jean-Jacques Rousseau, Paris, 75001, France. tresorier@sena.fr. Ed. Dominique Hollard. Circ: 380.

737 USA
THE CALIFORNIA NUMISMATIST. Text in English. q. free to members (effective 2008). **Document type:** *Magazine, Consumer.*
Related titles: Online - full text ed.
Published by: California State Numismatic Association, c/o Greg Burns, P O Box 1181, Claremont, CA 91711-1181. gburns@adelphia.net, http://www.calcoin.org.

769.55 CAN
CANADIAN BANK NOTES. Text in English. 1980. irreg. (4th ed). CAD 74.95, USD 49.95, GBP 49.95 per vol. (effective 2004).
Former titles: Charlton Standard Catalogue of Canadian Government Paper Money (0835-3573); (until 1984): Charlton Standard Catalogue of Canadian Paper Money (0706-0432)
Published by: Charlton Press, 2040 Yonge St, Ste 208, Toronto, ON M4S 1Z9, Canada. http://www.charltonpress.com.

737 CAN ISSN 0702-3162
CANADIAN COIN NEWS. Text in English. 1963. 26/yr. CAD 37.40 domestic; USD 37.40 in United States; CAD 149 elsewhere (effective 2004). adv. bk.rev. illus.; stat. **Document type:** *Magazine, Consumer.* **Description:** Offers news, auction results, show listings, and price trends for the most popular Canadian coins.
Formerly: Coin, Stamp, Antique News (0010-0439)
Related titles: Microfilm ed.: (from MML); Microform ed.: (from MML).
Indexed: C03, CBCARef, CBPI, NumL, P48, PQC.
Published by: Trajan Publishing Corp., 103 Lakeshore Rd, Ste 202, St Catharines, ON L2N 2T6, Canada. TEL 905-646-7744, FAX 905-646-0995, office@trajan.com, http://www.trajan.com. Ed. Bret Evans. Circ: 18,500.

737 CAN ISSN 1716-0782
CANADIAN COINS. Text in English. 1946. a. (61st ed), latest 2006. CAD 19.95 per issue domestic; USD 19.95, GBP 14.95 per issue foreign (effective 2006). **Document type:** *Catalog, Trade.*
Former titles (until 2005): Charlton's Standard Catalogue of Canadian Coins (0706-0424); (until 1980): Standard Catalogue of Canadian Coins (0845-5708); Which superseded in part (in 1979): Standard Catalogue of Canadian Coins Tokens and Paper Money (0585-038X); Which was formerly (until 1960): Standard Catalogue of Canadian & Newfoundland Coins, Tokens and Fractional Currency (0380-383X); (until 1958): Catalogue of Canadian Coins, Tokens & Fractional Currency (0700-4672)
Published by: Charlton Press, 2040 Yonge St, Ste 208, Toronto, ON M4S 1Z9, Canada. chpress@charltonpress.com. Eds. Jean Dale, W K Cross.

737 CAN ISSN 0045-5202
CJ1860
CANADIAN NUMISMATIC RESEARCH SOCIETY. TRANSACTIONS. Text mainly in English; Text occasionally in French. 1965. a. CAD 15, USD 15 (effective 1998). bk.rev. **Document type:** *Journal, Academic/Scholarly.*
Indexed: NumL.
Published by: Canadian Numismatic Research Society, Elmwood Sq, P O Box 22022, St Thomas, ON N5R 6A1, Canada. TEL 519-631-1884. Ed., R&P Harry N James. Circ: 50.

737 CAN ISSN 1914-6922
HG657
CANADIAN PAPER MONEY SOCIETY JOURNAL. Text in English. 1965. a. membership. adv. bk.rev. illus. **Document type:** *Journal, Consumer.*
Formerly (until 2001): Canadian Paper Money Journal (0045-5237)
Indexed: NumL.
Published by: Canadian Paper Money Society, P.O. Box 562, Pickering, ON L1V 2R7, Canada. TEL 905-509-1146, cpms@idirect.com. Ed. L Wojtiw. Circ: 300 (controlled).

737 CAN ISSN 0703-895X
CANADIAN TOKEN. Text in English. 1972. bi-m. membership. bk.rev.

NO

Indexed: NumL.
Published by: Canadian Association of Token Collectors, 10 Wesanford Place, Hamilton, ON L8P 1N6, Canada. Ed. K A Palmer. Circ: 300.

737.4 700 USA ISSN 1048-0986
CJ201
THE CELATOR; journal of ancient and medieval coinage. Text in English. 1987. m. USD 30 domestic; USD 36 in Canada; USD 60 elsewhere; USD 5 newsstand/cover (effective 2007). adv. bk.rev. bibl.; charts; illus.; tr.lit. 60 p./no.; back issues avail. **Document type:** *Magazine, Trade.* **Description:** Includes articles and features about ancient coins and artifacts, connoisseurship and market news.
Incorporates: Roman Coins and Culture
Indexed: NumL.
Published by: P N P, Inc., PO Box 10607, Lancaster, PA 17605-0607. kerry@celator.com. Ed., Pub., R&P, Adv. contact Kerry K Wetterstrom. page USD 400. Circ: 2,550 (paid and free).

737 BEL ISSN 0009-0344
CERCLE D'ETUDES NUMISMATIQUES. BULLETIN. Text in French. 1964. q. adv. bk.rev. charts; illus. cum.index. back issues avail. **Document type:** *Bulletin.*
Indexed: NumL.
Published by: Cercle d'Etudes Numismatiques, Bd de l'Empereur 4, Brussels, 1000, Belgium.

737 BEL
CERCLE D'ETUDES NUMISMATIQUES. DOSSIERS. Text in French. 1986. irreg., latest vol.2. price varies. back issues avail. **Document type:** *Monographic series.*
Published by: Cercle d'Etudes Numismatiques, Bd de l'Empereur 4, Brussels, 1000, Belgium.

737 BEL ISSN 0069-2247
CERCLE D'ETUDES NUMISMATIQUES. TRAVAUX. Text in French. 1964. irreg., latest vol.13, 1996. price varies. back issues avail. **Document type:** *Monographic series.*
Published by: Cercle d'Etudes Numismatiques, Bd de l'Empereur 4, Brussels, 1000, Belgium.

737.4 USA
CERTIFIED COIN DEALER NEWSLETTER. Text in English. 1986. w. USD 117 (effective 2005). adv. back issues avail. **Document type:** *Newsletter, Trade.*
Published by: Coin Dealer Newsletter, PO Box 7939, Torrance, CA 90504. TEL 310-515-7369, FAX 310-515-7534. Ed. Keith M Zaner. Pub. Shane Downing. adv.: page USD 750.

737.4 CAN ISSN 0706-0459
CHARLTON COIN GUIDE. Text in English. 1961. a. CAD 6.95 domestic; GBP 5.95 in United Kingdom; USD 5.95 elsewhere (effective 2006).
Former titles (until 1978): Coin Guide of Canadian, Newfoundland and Maritime Coinage, Tokens, Paper Money with Premium List of U.S. Coins and Bills, Coins of Great Britain (0701-8223); (until 1977): Coin Guide with Premium List of Canadian & U.S. Coins & Bills & Coins of Great Britain (0319-3748); (until 1962): Coin Guide with Premium List of Canadian & U.S. Coins & Bills (0319-3772)
Published by: Charlton Press, PO Box 820, Sta Willowdale B, North York, ON M2K 2R1, Canada. TEL 416-488-1418, FAX 416-488-4656, chpress@charltonpress.com, http://www.charltonpress.com.

737 CAN ISSN 0835-748X
THE CHARLTON STANDARD CATALOGUE OF CANADIAN COLONIAL TOKENS. Text in English. 1988. irreg. CAD 24.95, USD 19.95. **Description:** Guide to the tokens used in Canada between 1794 and 1867.
Published by: Charlton Press, 2040 Yonge St, Ste 208, Toronto, ON M4S 1Z9, Canada. TEL 416-488-1418, FAX 416-488-4656.

737 CAN ISSN 1203-1496
NK4660
THE CHARLTON STANDARD CATALOGUE OF ROYAL DOULTON BESWICK STORYBOOK FIGURINES. Text in English. a. CAD 19.95, USD 17.95. **Description:** Includes over 400 photographs illustrating the Royal Doulton and Beswick figurines based on storybook characters.
Published by: Charlton Press, 2040 Yonge St, Ste 208, Toronto, ON M4S 1Z9, Canada. TEL 416-488-1418, FAX 416-488-4656. Ed. Jean Dale.

737 USA ISSN 1066-3061
CHECK COLLECTOR; devoted to the study of security paper. Text in English. 1974. q. free to members (effective 2011). adv. bk.rev. charts; illus. **Document type:** *Journal, Academic/Scholarly.*
Formerly (until 1987): Check List
Published by: American Society of Check Collectors, PO Box 808, Northfield, MN 55057. Ed. Robert D Hohertz.

737 CAN ISSN 1497-6498
CLASSICAL AND MEDIEVAL NUMISMATIC SOCIETY. JOURNAL. Text in English. 2000. q. **Document type:** *Journal, Academic/Scholarly.*
Formed by the merger of (1991-2000): Anvil (1188-5173); (1992-2000): Picus (1188-519X)
Published by: Classic and Medieval Nunismatic Society, Station B, Box 956, Willowdale, ON M2K 2T6, Canada. TEL 416-494-8670, billmcd@idirect.com, http://www.cmns.ca/.

737 USA ISSN 1064-1181
CJ1
CLASSICAL NUMISMATIC REVIEW. Text in English. 1936. 3/yr. USD 75 domestic; USD 100 foreign (effective 2005). bk.rev. illus.; tr.lit. index. **Document type:** *Catalog.*
Formerly: Seaby's Coin and Medal Bulletin (0037-0053)
Indexed: BrArAb, NumL, RASB.
Published by: Classical Numismatic Group Inc., PO Box 479, Lancaster, PA 17608-0479. TEL 717-390-9194, FAX 717-390-9978. Ed. Kerry K Wetterstrom. Circ: 6,000. **U.K. subscr. to:** Seaby Coins, 14 Old Bond St, London W1X 3DB, United Kingdom. TEL 44-171-495-1888.

737.4 USA ISSN 1062-8169
CJ1
COIN DEALER NEWSLETTER. Text in English. 1963. w. USD 98 (effective 2000). adv. back issues avail. **Document type:** *Newsletter.*
Address: PO Box 7939, Torrance, CA 90504. TEL 310-515-7369, FAX 310-515-7534. Ed. Keith M Zaner. Pub., Adv. contact Shane Downing.

737 GBR ISSN 0140-1149
CJ153.A2
COIN HOARDS. Text in English. 1975. irreg., latest vol.8. GBP 20 per issue (effective 2009). **Document type:** *Bulletin.*
Indexed: BrArAb, NumL.
Published by: Royal Numismatic Society, British Museum, Dept. of Coins and Medals, Great Russell St, London, WC1B 3DG, United Kingdom. info@numismatics.org.uk. **Subscr. to:** Spink, 69 Southampton Row, Bloomsbury, London WC1B 4ET, United Kingdom. TEL 44-20-75634000, FAX 44-20-75634066, info@spink.com, http://www.spink.com.

737.4 GBR
COIN MONTHLY. Text in English. 1966. m. adv. bk.rev. charts; illus.; mkt.; stat. **Document type:** *Magazine, Consumer.*
Former titles: Coin (0143-5485); Coin Monthly (0010-0390)
Indexed: NumL.
Published by: Numismatic Publishing Co., Sovereign House, Brentwood, Essex CM14 4SE, United Kingdom. Circ: 10,534.

737 GBR ISSN 0958-1391
CJ1
COIN NEWS. Text in English. 1979. m. GBP 34 domestic; GBP 42 foreign (effective 2010). adv. bk.rev. index. back issues avail. **Document type:** *Magazine, Consumer.* **Description:** Provides information for collectors of coins and banknotes.
Supersedes in part (in 1989): Coin and Medal News (0955-4386); Which was formed by the merger of (1981-198?): Coin News (0261-7072); Which was formerly (until 1981): Coins and Medals (0142-5641); (until 1974): Coins (0010-048X); (1981-198?): Medal News (0262-3625); Which was formerly (until 1981): Medals International (0143-3687); (until 1979): Medals Magazine
Indexed: NumL.
Published by: Token Publishing Ltd., Orchard House, Duchy Rd, Heathpark, Honiton, Devon EX14 1YD, United Kingdom. TEL 44-1404-46972, FAX 44-1404-44788, info@tokenpublishing.com. Adv. contact Carol Hartman.

737 332.6 USA
COIN PREVIEWER; numismatic investment newsletter. Text in English. 1974. m. USD 19.95. adv. bk.rev. back issues avail.
Address: 500 N.W. 101st Ave., Coral Springs, FL 33071. TEL 305-755-7930. Ed. Robert J Leuchten. Circ: 200. **Subscr. to:** PO Box 8655, Coral Springs, FL 33075.

737.4 USA ISSN 0010-0412
CJ1
COIN PRICES. Text in English. 1967. bi-m. USD 24.98; USD 4.99 newsstand/cover (effective 2012). adv. illus. back issues avail.; reprints avail. **Document type:** *Magazine, Trade.* **Description:** Complete guide to retail values for collectible U.S. coins. A market update section (value guide) begins each issue. Rotating special sections provide values for Canadian and Mexican coins, Colonial coins, territorial coins, errors and varieties and selected issues of U.S. paper money. Regular departments include a guide to grading U.S. coins.
Indexed: G08, I05.
—CCC.
Published by: F + W Media Inc., 4700 E Galbraith Rd, Cincinnati, OH 45236. TEL 513-531-2690, contact_us@fwmedia.com, http://www.fwmedia.com/. Ed. Bob Van Ryzin TEL 715-445-2214 ext 13306. Pub. Scott Tappa TEL 715-445-2214 ext 13428.

737.4 USA ISSN 0010-0447
CJ1
COIN WORLD. Text in English. 1960. w. USD 5.99 newsstand/cover; USD 19.99, USD 59.99 (effective 2011). adv. bk.rev. illus.; stat. reprints avail. **Document type:** *Magazine, Trade.* **Description:** Reports breaking news of major importance to coin collectors, covering new coin issues, auctions, coin shows, as well as values for all US coins in each grade. Profiles prominent collectors, dealers, and numismatic experts to discuss the value and history of coins, as well as how to store and care for a coin collection.
Formerly: Numismatic Scrapbook (0029-6058)
Related titles: Microform ed.: (from PQC); Online - full text ed.: ISSN 1542-5363.
Indexed: A22, B01, B07, BRI, NumL, P30.
Published by: Amos Publishing, Hobby (Subsidiary of: Amos Publishing), PO Box 29, Sidney, OH 45365-0029. TEL 937-498-0850, FAX 937-498-0812, http://www.amospress.com.

737 332.6 USA
COIN WORLD ANNUAL PRICE GUIDE. Text in English. 1989. a. USD 5.99. **Document type:** *Guide, Consumer.*
Published by: Signet Books, Penguin USA, 375 Hudson St, New York, NY 10014. TEL 212-366-2594. Ed. Michaela Hamilton. Pub. Elaine Koster. R&P Leigh Butler.

737.4 USA ISSN 1545-5319
CJ1826
COIN WORLD'S COIN VALUES. Text in English. 2003 (Dec.). m. free (effective 2011). adv. **Document type:** *Magazine, Trade.* **Description:** Provides retail values for more than 65,000 U.S. coins. It is updated weekly to provide you with the most comprehensive and current retail pricing information available in the marketplace.
Related titles: Online - full text ed.
Indexed: G06, G07, G08, I05.
Published by: Amos Publishing, Hobby (Subsidiary of: Amos Publishing), PO Box 29, Sidney, OH 45365-0029. TEL 937-498-0850, FAX 937-498-0812, http://www.amospress.com.

737.4 GBR ISSN 0307-6571
CJ2471
COIN YEARBOOK. Text in English. 1968. a. GBP 9.95 per issue (effective 2010). illus. **Document type:** *Yearbook, Consumer.* **Description:** Offers a comprehensive guide to the coins of England, Scotland, Ireland, the Channel Islands, and the Isle of Man.
Formerly (until 1970): Coin Monthly Year Book
Published by: Token Publishing Ltd., Orchard House, Duchy Rd, Heathpark, Honiton, Devon EX14 1YD, United Kingdom. TEL 44-1404-46972, FAX 44-1404-44788, info@tokenpublishing.com, http://www.tokenpublishing.com. Adv. contact Carol Hartman.

737.4 USA ISSN 0010-0455
CJ1
COINAGE. Text in English. 1964. m. USD 29.95 domestic; USD 44.95 foreign; USD 4.99 per issue (effective 2009). adv. illus. back issues avail.; reprints avail. **Document type:** *Magazine, Trade.* **Description:** Features the latest updates on U.S. coin prices with an insider's guide to market trends.
Related titles: CD-ROM ed.; Microform ed.: (from PQC); Online - full text ed.
Indexed: A22, NumL.
Published by: Miller Magazines, Inc, 290 Maple Ct, Ste 232, Ventura, CA 93003. TEL 805-644-3824, FAX 805-644-3875, http://www.millermags.com. Ed. Ed Reiter. Adv. contact Mike Gumpel TEL 805-644-3824 ext 114. Circ: 150,000 (paid).

737.4 USA
COINAGE MAGAZINE'S QUARTER COLLECTOR (YEAR). Text in English. 2001. a. **Document type:** *Magazine, Consumer.*
Published by: Miller Magazines, Inc, 290 Maple Ct, Ste 232, Ventura, CA 93003. TEL 805-644-3824, FAX 805-644-3875, http://www.millermags.com.

737.4 USA ISSN 8756-6265
COINAGE OF THE AMERICAS CONFERENCE. PROCEEDINGS. Text in English. 1985. irreg., latest vol.16, 2009. price varies. charts; illus. back issues avail. **Document type:** *Proceedings, Academic/Scholarly.*
Published by: American Numismatic Society, 75 Varick St, 11th Fl, New York, NY 10013. TEL 212-571-4470, FAX 212-571-4479, orders@numismatics.org.

737 332.6 USA
THE COINFIDENTIAL REPORT. Text in English. 1963. bi-m. USD 6.95; USD 19.95 for 3 yrs.; USD 99 for life (effective 2001). adv. bk.rev.; film rev. charts; illus.; mkt.; stat.; tr.lit. back issues avail. **Document type:** *Newsletter, Trade.* **Description:** Features in-depth market analyses of coins and stocks, market forecasts, and best coin and stock buys.
Media: Duplicated (not offset).
Published by: Bale Publications, 5121 St Charles Ave, New Orleans, LA 70115. TEL 504-895-5750. Ed., Pub., R&P, Adv. contact Don Bale Jr. Circ: 300 (paid).

737.4 USA
COINLINK.COM; numismatic news and resources. Text in English. 1995. irreg. free (effective 2010). adv. **Document type:** *Directory, Trade.* **Description:** Provides the numismatic community with information and features on rare coins.
Media: Online - full text.
Published by: (American Numismatic Association, The Royal Canadian Numismatic Association CAN), CoinLink Inc, PO Box 916909, Longwood, FL 32791. TEL 407-786-5555, 800-579-5225, FAX 866-778-3908, 800-784-8504. Ed. Scott Purvis.

737.4 USA ISSN 0010-0471
CJ1
COINS. Text in English. 1955. m. USD 39.98; USD 4.99 newsstand/cover (effective 2012). adv. bk.rev. illus. back issues avail.; reprints avail. **Document type:** *Magazine, Trade.* **Description:** Covers market trends, buying tips, and historical perspectives on all aspects of numismatic. The news section, "Bits and Pieces," wraps up the latest happenings in numismatic. Regular columns and departments include "Basics & Beyond," "Budget Buyer," "Coin Clinic" (Q&A), the editors column, coin finds, a calendar of upcoming shows nationwide, "Coin Value Guide" and "Market Watch.".
Former titles (until 1961): Coin Press Magazine; (until 19??): Coin News Magazine
Related titles: Online - full text ed.
Indexed: A22, G08, I05, NumL.
—CCC.
Published by: F + W Media Inc., 4700 E Galbraith Rd, Cincinnati, OH 45236. TEL 513-531-2690, contact_us@fwmedia.com, http://www.fwmedia.com/. Ed. Bob Van Ryzin TEL 715-445-2214 ext 13306. Pub. David Blansfield TEL 212-447-1400 ext 12261.

COLLECTORS' SHOWCASE; America's premier entertainment collectors' magazine . *see* ANTIQUES

737 ITA ISSN 1973-0721
COLLEZIONE MONETE. Text in Italian. 2007. bi-w. **Document type:** *Magazine, Consumer.*
Published by: De Agostini Editore, Via G da Verrazzano 15, Novara, 28100, Italy. TEL 39-0321-4241, FAX 39-0321-424305, info@deagostini.it, http://www.deagostini.it.

737 AUT ISSN 1562-6377
COMPTE RENDU. Text in English, French, German. 1951. a. **Document type:** *Journal, Trade.*
Published by: International Numismatic Commission/Commission Internationale de Numismatique, c/o Michael Alram, Kunsthistorisches Museum Wien, Muenzkabinett, Burgring 5, Vienna, 1010, Austria. TEL 43-1-525244201, FAX 43-1-525244299, michael.alram@khm.at, http://www.muenzgeschichte.ch/inc/4801.html.

737 ITA ISSN 1594-901X
CRONACA NUMISMATICA; mensile di monete, cartamoneta, medaglie e titoli antichi. Text in Italian. 1989. m. (11/yr.). EUR 42 (effective 2008). adv. **Document type:** *Magazine, Consumer.*
Formerly (until 2002): C N. Cronaca Numismatica (1591-1039)
Published by: Gruppo Editoriale Olimpia SpA, Via E Fermi 24, Loc Osmannoro, Sesto Fiorentino, FI 50129, Italy. TEL 39-055-30321, FAX 39-055-3032280, info@edolimpia.it, http://www.edolimpia.it. Circ: 14,600.

737.4 USA
CURRENCY DEALER NEWSLETTER; a monthly report on the currency market. Text in English. 1979. m. USD 44 (effective 2005). adv. back issues avail. **Document type:** *Newsletter, Trade.* **Description:** Wholesale price guide to old US paper money.
Published by: Coin Dealer Newsletter, PO Box 7939, Torrance, CA 90504. TEL 310-515-7369, FAX 310-515-7534. Ed. Keith M Zaner. Pub. Shane Downing. adv.: page USD 500.

737 POL ISSN 1509-1317
CZESTOCHOWSKI MAGAZYN NUMIZMATYCZNY. Text in Polish. 1989. q. PLZ 14 domestic; USD 50 foreign (effective 2001). adv. bibl.; illus. cum.index every 5 yrs. **Document type:** *Bulletin.* **Description:** Covers scientific, historial as well as popular information about numismatics.
Formerly: Magazyn Numizmatyczny
Published by: Stowarzyszenie Archeologiczno-Numizmatyczne, Ul Kossaka 26, Czestochowa, 42200, Poland. TEL 48-34-3658699. Ed. Tadeusz Saczek. adv.: page USD 100;.

737.49489 769.559489 DNK ISSN 0908-0317
DANMARKS MOENTER OG PENGESEDLER. Text in Danish. 1974. a. DKK 49 (effective 2008). **Document type:** *Catalog, Consumer.* **Description:** Register of all Denmarks coins and bills since 1873.
Formerly (until 1993): Danmarks Moenter

Published by: A F A - Forlaget (Subsidiary of: Nordfrim A/S), Kvindevadet 42, Otterup, 5450, Denmark. TEL 45-64-821256, FAX 45-64-821056, afa@afa.dk, http://www.afa.dk. **Dist. by:** Nordfrim A/S, Kvindevadet 42, Otterup 5450, Denmark. mail@nordfrim.dk, http://www.nordfrim.dk.

737.4 332.6 USA
DAVID HALL'S INSIDE VIEW. Text in English. 1979. bi-m. USD 97. **Document type:** *Newsletter.*
Published by: David Hall's Rare Coins and Collectibles, 1936 E Deere Ave, Ste 102, Santa Ana, CA 92705-5723. TEL 714-261-0509, FAX 714-252-0541. Ed. David Hall.

DEUTSCHE BRIEFMARKEN - REVUE. *see* PHILATELY

737 DEU ISSN 0933-8527
DEUTSCHES MUENZEN MAGAZIN. Text in German. 1987. bi-m. EUR 22.80; EUR 4.50 newsstand/cover (effective 2009). adv. **Document type:** *Magazine, Consumer.*
Published by: E M S Verlag GmbH, Bientzlestr 3, Stuttgart, 70599, Germany. TEL 49-711-45999222, FAX 49-711-45999210. Ed., Pub. Wolfgang Erzinger. adv.: B&W page EUR 945, color page EUR 1,650; trim 185 x 246.

737 SRB ISSN 1450-5185
CJ9
DINAR; numizmaticki casopis. Text in Serbian. 1996. s-a. USD 30 (effective 2007). **Document type:** *Journal.*
Related titles: Online - full content ed.
Published by: Srpsko Numizmaticko Drustvo/Serbian Association of Numismatists, Narodni Muzej, Trg Republike 1a, Belgrade, 11000. TEL 381-11-3034595, FAX 381-11-3282262, snd@snd.org.yu.

EL ECO FILATELICO Y NUMISMATICO. *see* PHILATELY

737 USA
ENGRAVINGS. Text in English. 1993 (vol.3, no.1). q.
Published by: American Bank Note Commemoratives, Inc., 7 High St, Ste 412, Huntington, NY 11743. TEL 800-533-2262.

737 USA
ERROR TRENDS COIN MAGAZINE. Text in English. 1968. m. USD 16 (effective 2007). adv. bk.rev. illus. 40 p./no.; back issues avail. **Document type:** *Magazine, Consumer.* **Description:** Devoted entirely to coin collectors who specialize in numismatic error coins.
Address: PO Box 158, Oceanside, NY 11572. TEL 516-764-8063. Ed. Arnold Margolis. adv.: page USD 350. Circ: 2,000.

737 USA
ERRORSCOPE. Text in English. 1963. bi-m. USD 25 domestic includes membership; USD 37.50 foreign includes membership (effective 2008). adv. bk.rev. **Document type:** *Magazine, Consumer.*
Formerly: Errorgram
Related titles: Supplement(s): Errorscope Online Supplement. 2007 (July).
Published by: Combined Organizations of Numismatic Error Collectors of America, c/o Robert Neff, 321 Kingslake Dr, Debary, FL 32713. flrc@aol.com, coneca@gmail.com, wavysteps2003@aol.com. Ed. Stella Teiglang. Circ: 550.

737.6 NOR ISSN 1504-4386
ETT TRYKK; ideblad for stempelblad. Variant title: 1 Trykk. Text in Norwegian. 2005. q. NOK 600; NOK 120 per issue (effective 2005). **Document type:** *Magazine, Consumer.*
Published by: Norsk Stempelblad AS, Kvennhusvegen 13, Fjerdingby, Norway.

EUROPHIL NEWS. *see* PHILATELY

737 USA ISSN 0014-7745
FARE BOX. Text in English. 1947. m. USD 22 domestic membership; USD 25 in Canada & Mexico membership; USD 33 elsewhere membership (effective 2006). adv. bk.rev. charts; stat. **Document type:** *Newsletter, Consumer.* **Description:** For collectors of transportation fare tokens and those interested in urban transportation history.
Indexed: NumL.
Published by: American Vecturist Association, c/o Karl Gabsch, 2820 Scenic Meadow, Waldorf, MD 20603. info@vecturist.com, http://vecturist.com. Ed. John M Coffee Jr. Adv. contact Robert M Butler. Circ: 825.

737.4 USA ISSN 1541-8022
CJ1826
FELL'S OFFICIAL KNOW-IT-ALL GUIDE. COINS. Variant title: Fell's United States Coin Book. Text in English. 1949. a. USD 18.95 per issue (effective 2011). **Document type:** *Catalog, Trade.* **Description:** For collectors and investors. Highlights numismatic news and expands upon basic beginner information for the advanced collector.
Formerly (until 2000): Fell's U S Coins Quarterly Investment Guide (1041-6951)
Published by: Frederick Fell Publishers, Inc., 2131 Hollywood Blvd, Ste 305, Hollywood, CA 33020. TEL 954-455-4243, fellpub@aol.com. Pub. Donald L Lessne.

THE FORECASTER. *see* BUSINESS AND ECONOMICS

FRIMERKER OG MYNTER. *see* PHILATELY

737 ESP ISSN 0210-2137
GACETA NUMISMATICA. Text in Spanish. 1966. q. membership. adv. bk.rev. cum.index in vol.101. back issues avail. **Document type:** *Bulletin, Academic/Scholarly.*
Indexed: NumL.
—INIST.
Published by: Asociacion Numismatica Espanola, Gran Via de Les Corts Catalanes, 627, Barcelona, 08010, Spain. TEL 34-93-3188245, FAX 34-93-3189062. Ed. Josep Pellicer I Bru. Circ: 2,000.

737 CHE ISSN 0016-5565
GAZETTE NUMISMATIQUE SUISSE/SCHWEIZER MUENZBLAETTER. Text in English, French, German. 1949. q. CHF 100 membership. adv. illus. cum.index every 5 yrs. **Document type:** *Newsletter.*
Indexed: NumL.
Published by: Societe Suisse de Numismatique/Schweizerische Numismatische Gesellschaft, c/o Regie de Fribourg, 24 SA rue de Romont, Fribourg, 1701, Switzerland. Circ: 1,000. **Subscr. to:** Alexander Wild, Rathausgasse 30, Bern 3011, Switzerland.

GELDGESCHICHTLICHE NACHRICHTEN. *see* HOBBIES

737 DEU ISSN 0931-0681
DER GELDSCHEINSAMMLER; Zeitschrift fuer Papiergeld. Text in German. 1986. 11/yr. EUR 47 (effective 2005). adv. bk.rev. index. back issues avail. **Document type:** *Magazine, Consumer.*
Indexed: NumL.
Published by: H. Gietl Verlag & Publikationsservice GmbH, Pfaelzer Str 11, Regenstauf, 93128, Germany. TEL 49-9402-93370, FAX 49-9402-933724, info@gietl-verlag.de, http://www.gietl-verlag.de. Pubs. Heinrich Gietl, Josef Roidl. Adv. contact Kurt Fischer. Circ: 3,000.

737 POL
GROSZ; magazyn numizmatyczny. Text in Polish. 1985. q. PLZ 3.50 newsstand/cover. bibl.; illus.; mkt. 20 p./no. 1 cols./p.; back issues avail. **Document type:** *Bulletin.*
Published by: Polskie Towarzystwo Numizmatyczne, Oddzial w Jastrzebiu Zdroju, ul. Malchera 21/3, PO Box 21, Jastrzebie Zdroj, 44330, Poland. TEL 48-32-4707006. Eds. A. Muzial, K. Grabinski, S. Lastowka.

737.4 USA ISSN 0072-8829
CJ1826
GUIDEBOOK OF UNITED STATES COINS. Text in English. 1946. a. USD 16.95 (effective 2008). illus. index. **Document type:** *Directory, Consumer.* **Description:** Presents a retail guide of all U.S. coins from 1616 to the present.
Published by: Whitman Publishing, LLC, 3101 Clairmont Rd, Ste C, Atlanta, GA 30329. TEL 800-546-2995, info@WhitmanBooks.com, http://www.whitmanbooks.com.

737.4 USA ISSN 0072-9949
HANDBOOK OF UNITED STATES COINS. Text in English. 1941. a. USD 9.95 (effective 2008). illus. index. **Document type:** *Directory, Consumer.* **Description:** Contains up-to-date wholesale values for all U.S. coins from 1616 to the present.
Published by: Whitman Publishing, LLC, 3101 Clairmont Rd, Ste C, Atlanta, GA 30329. TEL 800-546-2995, info@WhitmanBooks.com, http://www.whitmanbooks.com.

737 GRC
HELLENIC NUMISMATIC SOCIETY. BIBLIOTECA. Text in English, Greek. 1993. irreg., latest vol.6, 1999. price varies. **Document type:** *Monographic series, Academic/Scholarly.* **Description:** Covers various topics in Greek numismatics and related issues.
Published by: Hellenic Numismatic Society/Elleniki Nomismatiki Etaireia, 28 Andrea Metaxa St, Athens, 106 81, Greece. TEL 30-1-330-5080, FAX 30-1-3934-296, hellenum@hotmail.com, http://www.helicon.gr/hellenum. Ed. Anastasios P Tzamalis.

737 USA
I B N S JOURNAL. Text in English. 1961. q. USD 20 to members (effective 2001). adv. bk.rev.; Website rev. bibl.; illus. **Document type:** *Bulletin.*
Supersedes: International Bank Note Society Magazine (0020-6121)
Indexed: NumL.
Published by: International Bank Note Society, c/o Milan Alusic, Sec -Gen, Box 1642, Racine, WI 53401. TEL 414-554-6255. Ed. Steve Feller. Circ: 2,200 (paid).

737 AUT
INTERNATIONAL NUMISMATIC NEWSLETTER. Text in English, French, German. 1980. a. **Document type:** *Newsletter, Trade.*
Formerly (until 1986): C I N Newsletter (1562-6512)
Related titles: Online - full text ed.: ISSN 1662-1220. 2005.
Published by: International Numismatic Commission/Commission Internationale de Numismatique, c/o Michael Alram, Kunsthistorisches Museum Wien, Muenzkabinett, Burgring 5, Vienna, 1010, Austria. TEL 43-1-525244201, FAX 43-1-525244299, michael.alram@khm.at, http://www.muenzgeschichte.ch/inc/4801.html.

737 ISR
ISRAEL NUMISMATIC RESEARCH. Text in English. 1963; N.S. 1980. irreg. (approx. a.). price varies. bk.rev. bibl.; charts; illus.; stat. **Document type:** *Monographic series, Academic/Scholarly.*
Formerly (until 2006): Israel Numismatic Journal (0021-2288)
Indexed: IHP, NumL.
Published by: Israel Numismatic Society, P O Box 750, Jerusalem, Israel. FAX 972-2-249779, TELEX 26598. Circ: 300.

737 ITA ISSN 0578-9923
CJ23
ISTITUTO ITALIANO DI NUMISMATICA. ANNALI. Text in Italian. 1954. a., latest vol.54, 2008. adv. bk.rev. back issues avail. **Document type:** *Journal, Academic/Scholarly.* **Description:** Presents research on numismatic subjects.
Indexed: B24, IBR, IBZ, NumL.
Published by: Istituto Italiano di Numismatica, Palazzo Barberini, Via Quattro Fontane 13, Rome, RM 00184, Italy. TEL 39-6-4743603, FAX 39-6-4743603.

737.4 NLD ISSN 0920-380X
CJ2930
JAARBOEK VOOR MUNT- EN PENNINGKUNDE. Text in Dutch; Text occasionally in English, French, German; Summaries in English. 1914. a. EUR 45 domestic; EUR 55 in Europe; EUR 60 elsewhere (effective 2009). cum.index. **Document type:** *Academic/Scholarly.*
Formerly (until 1954): Koninklijk Nederlandsch Genootschap voor Munt- en Penningkunde. Jaarboek
Indexed: A22, B24.
—IE.
Published by: Koninklijk Nederlands Genootschap voor Munt- en Penningkunde/Royal Dutch Society of Numismatics, c/o Geldmuseum, Postbus 2407, Utrecht, 3500 GK, Netherlands. info@munt-penningkunde.nl, http://www.munt-penningkunde.nl/.

737.0994 AUS ISSN 0815-998X
JOURNAL OF NUMISMATIC ASSOCIATION OF AUSTRALIA. Abbreviated title: J N A A. Text in English. 1985. a. free to members (effective 2009). back issues avail. **Document type:** *Journal, Trade.*
Indexed: AusPAIS.
Published by: Numismatic Association of Australia, PO Box 3664, Norwood, SA 5067, Australia. janislane@aapt.net.au.

KOLEKCJONER LOMZYNSKI. *see* ANTIQUES

737 USA ISSN 0308-8677
L A N S A. (Latin American Notaphilic Society) Text in English, Spanish. 1973. 3/yr. USD 10 (effective 2001). bk.rev. illus. index. back issues avail. **Document type:** *Bulletin, Directory.* **Description:** Covers articles on paper money and related items of Latin America and Iberia for the collector.
Published by: Latin American Paper Money Society/Sociedad Latinoamericana de Papel Moneda, 3304 Milford Mill Rd, Baltimore, MD 21244. TEL 410-655-3109, http://members.spree.com/whiteknigh49/. Ed., Adv. contact Arthur C Matz. Circ: 400.

LANDESMUSEUM FUER KAERNTEN. BUCHREIHE. *see* MUSEUMS AND ART GALLERIES

737 POL ISSN 0024-5771
LODZKI NUMIZMATYK. Text in Polish. 1961. q. membership. bk.rev. abstr.; bibl.; charts; illus.; stat. index, cum.index.
Indexed: NumL.
Published by: Polskie Towarzystwo Numizmatyczne, Oddzial w Lodzi, ul Wypoczynkowa 2, Lodz, 91614, Poland. TEL 48-42-6597673, copernicusorest@bajt.net, http://ptnlodz.w.interia.pl. Ed. Anatol Gupieniec.

737 POL ISSN 1233-9695
LUBELSKIE WIADOMOSCI NUMIZMATYCZNE. Text in Polish. 1992. a. PLZ 6 domestic; USD 4 foreign (effective 2002). bk.rev. illus. back issues avail. **Document type:** *Bulletin, Consumer.* **Description:** Presents scientific articles on numismatics.
Published by: Polskie Towarzystwo Numizmatyczne, Oddzial w Lublinie, c/o Prof. Dr. Edward Soczewinski, Ul Staszica 6, Lublin, 20081, Poland. TEL 48-81-5320413, FAX 48-81-5328903, TELEX AM 642345, rysio@eskulap.am.lublin.pl. Ed. Zbigniew Nestorowicz. Circ: 500 (paid). **Co-sponsor:** Lubelski Klub Kolekcjonerow.

M R I BANKERS' GUIDE TO FOREIGN CURRENCY. *see* BUSINESS AND ECONOMICS—Banking And Finance

737 730 GBR ISSN 0263-7707
CJ5501
➤ **THE MEDAL.** Text in English. 1982. s-a. free to members (effective 2009). adv. bk.rev. index every 10 issues. **Document type:** *Journal, Academic/Scholarly.* **Description:** Contains articles on both the history of the medal and on contemporary medals, reviews of exhibitions, and news about new medallic work.
Indexed: ABM, B24, D05, FR, IBR, IBZ, NumL, SCOPUS.
—BLDSC (5424.628800), IE, Ingenta, INIST.
Published by: British Art Medal Trust, c/o Philip Attwood, Editor, Department of Coins and Medals, British Museum, London, WC1B 3DG, United Kingdom. TEL 44-20-73238260, FAX 44-20-73238171. Ed. Philip Attwood. Adv. contact Janet Larkin TEL 44-20-73238568.

355 ZAF
MILITARY MEDAL SOCIETY OF SOUTH AFRICA. JOURNAL. Text in English. 1974. s-a. ZAR 90 domestic; USD 23 foreign (effective 2001). bk.rev. cum.index. back issues avail. **Document type:** *Newsletter.*
Indexed: ISAP.
Published by: Military Medal Society of South Africa, 1 Jacqueline Ave, Northcliff, Johannesburg 2195, South Africa. TEL 27-11-888-5797. Ed. Gordon T Bickley. Circ: 200.

737.4 CAN ISSN 1922-4885
MONETA. Text in English. 1960. m. USD 1 per issue to non-members; free to members (effective 2010). adv. **Document type:** *Magazine, Trade.*
Former titles (until 2010): Ottawa Coin Club. Newsletter (1922-4877); (until 2009): City of Ottawa Coin Club. Journal (1184-6798); (until 1986): City of Ottawa Coin Club. Bulletin (0045-7019); (until 1976): City of Ottawa Coin Club. Monthly Bulletin (0831-9162); (until 1969): City of Ottawa Institute of Numismatics (0319-4833); (until 1968): Ottawa Coin Club. Bulletin (0831-9154)
Published by: City of Ottawa Coin Club, RPO St, Laurent Blvd, PO Box 42004, Ottawa, ON K1K 4L8, Canada.

737 AUT ISSN 1012-6562
MONETA IMPERII ROMANI. Text in German. 1984. irreg., latest vol.14, 2010. price varies. **Document type:** *Monographic series, Academic/Scholarly.*
Published by: Verlag der Oesterreichischen Akademie der Wissenschaften, Postgasse 7/4, Vienna, W 1011, Austria. TEL 43-1-515813402, FAX 43-1-515813400, verlag@oeaw.ac.at.

737 VGB ISSN 0958-1545
MONETA INTERNATIONAL; coins and treasures monthly. Text in English. 1988. m. USD 20. adv. bk.rev. index. back issues avail. **Description:** Covers coin collecting and numismatic research from ancient to modern coins.
Address: c/o Vernon W. Pickering, P.O. Box 704, Road Town, Tortola, Virgin Isl., UK. TEL 809-49-43510, FAX 809-494-4540. Ed. Giorgio Migliavacca. Circ: 6,000.

737 ITA ISSN 1824-1468
MONETE STORICHE DA COLLEZIONE. Text in Italian. 2004. w. **Document type:** *Magazine, Consumer.*
Published by: R C S Libri (Subsidiary of: R C S Mediagroup), Via Mecenate 91, Milan, 20138, Italy. TEL 39-02-5095-2248, FAX 39-02-5095-2975, http://rcslibri.corriere.it/libri/index.htm.

737 769.55 FRA
MONNAIES FRANCAISES. Text in French. a. illus.; mkt. **Document type:** *Catalog, Consumer.* **Description:** Covers the collecting of French coins.
Published by: Echo de la Timbrologie, 37 rue des Jacobins, Amiens, Cedex 1 80036, France. TEL 33-3-22717180, FAX 33-3-22717189.

737 DEU ISSN 0254-461X
MUENZEN-REVUE; international coin trend journal. Text in English, German. 1969. 11/yr. EUR 70; EUR 5.90 per issue (effective 2009). adv. bk.rev. bibl. **Document type:** *Magazine, Trade.* **Description:** Features news, history, values, new coins, trade as well as reports of events and auctions for coin hobbyists.
Indexed: DIP, IBR, IBZ.
Published by: H. Gietl Verlag & Publikationsservice GmbH, Pfaelzer Str 11, Regenstauf, 93128, Germany. TEL 49-9402-93370, FAX 49-9402-933724, info@gietl-verlag.de. Ed. Helmut Kahnt. Pub. Heinrich Gietl. adv.: B&W page EUR 920; trim 210 x 290. Circ: 20,000 (paid and controlled).

737 CHE ISSN 0027-3007
MUENZEN UND MEDAILLEN/MONNAIES ET MEDAILLES. Text in German. 1942. m. free. illus. **Document type:** *Trade.*

N O

Published by: Muenzen und Medaillen AG, Malzgasse 25, Basel, 4002, Switzerland. Circ: 12,500.

737 DEU ISSN 0947-8116
MUENZEN UND PAPIERGELD. Text in German. 10/yr. EUR 47 domestic; EUR 58 foreign; EUR 4.70 newsstand/cover (effective 2007). adv. **Document type:** *Magazine, Consumer.*
Published by: H. Gietl Verlag & Publikationsservice GmbH, Pfaelzer Str 11, Regenstauf, 93128, Germany. TEL 49-9402-93370, FAX 49-9402-933724, info@gietl-verlag.de. Ed. Helmut Kahnt. Pubs. Heinrich Gietl, Josef Roidl. Adv. contact Kurt Fischer. B&W page EUR 870; trim 210 x 290. Circ: 20,000 (paid and controlled).

737 NLD ISSN 0165-5442
MUNTKOERIER. Text in Dutch. 1972. m. EUR 44.50 domestic; EUR 46.50 in Belgium; EUR 60 in Europe; EUR 73 elsewhere (effective 2009). adv. bk.rev. index. 60 p./no. 3 cols./p.; back issues avail. **Document type:** *Magazine, Consumer.* **Description:** For collectors and investors in coins, medals, banknotes, and foreign currency.
Published by: Uitgeverij Omni-Trading b.v., Postbus 1044, Apeldoorn, 7301 BG, Netherlands. TEL 31-55-5216629, FAX 31-55-5223963.

737.4 NLD
MUNTPERS CATALOGUS. Text in Dutch. 1989. a. free (effective 2009). illus. **Document type:** *Catalog, Consumer.* **Description:** Describes in detail new and antique coins from the Netherlands and her former colonies, available to the collector.
Formerly (until 2006): Muntpers (0924-0039)
Published by: Nederlandse Munt NV, Leidseweg 90, Postbus 2407, Utrecht, 3500 GK, Netherlands. TEL 31-30-2910410, FAX 31-30-2946179, info@coins.nl, http://nl.knm.nl.

737 ROM ISSN 0256-0844
MUZEUL NATIONAL DE ISTORIE A ROMANIEI. CERCETARI NUMISMATICE. Key Title: Cercetari Numismatice. Text in Romanian; Summaries in English, French. 1978. irreg. **Document type:** *Academic/Scholarly.*
Formerly: Muzeul de Istorie al Republicii Socialiste Romania. Cercetari Numismatice
Indexed: NumL.
Published by: Muzeul National de Istorie a Romaniei, Calea Victoriei 12, Bucharest, Romania. TEL 40-1-6149078.

737.4 POL ISSN 0208-5062
MUZEUM ARCHEOLOGICZNE I ETNOGRAFICZNE, LODZ. PRACE I MATERIALY. SERIA NUMIZMATYCZNA I KONSERWATORSKA. Text in Polish; Summaries in English. 1981. a. price varies. **Document type:** *Academic/Scholarly.*
Published by: Muzeum Archeologiczne i Etnograficzne w Lodzi, Pl Wolnosci 14, Lodz, 91415, Poland. TEL 48-42-6328440, FAX 48-42-6329714. Eds. Jerzy Pininski, Ryszard Grygiel. Circ: 600.

737 SWE ISSN 0347-2922
MYNTBOKEN. Text in Swedish. 1971. a., latest vol.34, 2004. SEK 120 (effective 2004). **Document type:** *Catalog, Consumer.* **Description:** Lists appraised value of Swedish coins and bills starting in1521.
Published by: Tonkin AB, Gjutformsgatan 9, Ljungsbro, 59074, Sweden. TEL 46-13-66647, FAX 46-13-66771, tonkin@tonkin.se. Ed. Archie Tonkin.

737 SWE ISSN 1652-2303
MYNTSTUDIER. Text in Swedish. 2003. irreg. **Document type:** *Magazine, Trade.* **Description:** Contributes research and guiding mainly within viking-age and medieval coinage and coin circulation.
Media: Online - full text.
Published by: Stockholms Universitet, Institutionen foer Archaeologi och Antikens Kultur. Numismatiska Forskningsgruppen/Stockholm University, Stockholm Numismatic Institute, c/o Gunnar Ekstroem, Stockholms Universitet, Stockholm, 10691, Sweden. TEL 46-8-6747750, archeology.su.se/numismatiska. Ed. Kenneth Jonsson.

737 SWE ISSN 1104-4233
MYNTTIDNINGEN. Text in Swedish. 1994. 10/yr. SEK 240 (effective 1994).
Published by: Myntinformatoeren, Stureplatsen 1, Goeteborg, 41139, Sweden.

737 USA ISSN 0027-6006
CJ15
N A S C QUARTERLY. Text in English. 1959. q. USD 15 membership (effective 2001). adv. bk.rev. charts; illus.; stat. **Document type:** *Magazine, Consumer.* **Description:** Contains articles, coin club and association news.
Published by: Numismatic Association of Southern California, PO Box 4159, Panorama City, CA 91412-4159. Ed. Greg Burns. Circ: 700.

737 DEU ISSN 0937-6488
N N B - NUMISMATISCHES NACHRICHTENBLATT. Text in German. 1952. m. EUR 25; EUR 2.50 newsstand/cover (effective 2007). adv. bk.rev. abstr.; bibl.; illus. index. 40 p./no. 3 cols./p.; back issues avail. **Document type:** *Newsletter, Consumer.*
Formerly (until 1978): Numismatisches Nachrichtenblatt (0029-6082)
Indexed: NumL.
Published by: (Deutsche Numismatische Gesellschaft), H. Gietl Verlag & Publikationsservice GmbH, Pfaelzer Str 11, Regenstauf, 93128, Germany. TEL 49-9402-93370, FAX 49-9402-933724, info@gietl-verlag.de, http://www.gietl-verlag.de. Ed. Rainer Albert. adv.: B&W page EUR 440; trim 140 x 200. Circ: 4,500 (paid and controlled).

737 USA
NEW JERSEY NUMISMATIC JOURNAL. Text in English. 1975. q. membership. adv. bk.rev. bibl.; illus.
Published by: Garden State Numismatic Association, Inc., PO Box 787, Pearl River, NY 10965. TEL 201-827-2482. Ed. James K Brandt. Circ: 1,000. **Subscr. to:** Judith Kessler, Correspondence Sec., P O Box 331, Millville, NJ 08332; **Subscr. to:** PO Box 3462, Toms River, NJ 08756-3462.

737 NZL ISSN 0028-8527
NEW ZEALAND NUMISMATIC JOURNAL. Text in English. 1931. irreg. free membership. adv. bk.rev. illus. cum.index: 1947-1966. **Document type:** *Journal, Consumer.*
Indexed: NumL.
Published by: Royal Numismatic Society of New Zealand, Inc., PO Box 2023, Wellington, 6140, New Zealand. Circ: 500.

737 GRC ISSN 1105-8579
CJ9
NOMISMATIKA KHRONIKA. Text in English, Greek. 1972. a., latest vol.19, 1999. USD 30 (effective 1999). adv. bk.rev. **Document type:** *Monographic series, Academic/Scholarly.* **Description:** Covers Greek and related numismatics of all periods.
Indexed: NumL.
Published by: Hellenic Numismatic Society/Elleniki Nomismatiki Etaireia, 28 Andrea Metaxa St, Athens, 106 81, Greece. TEL 30-1-330-5080, FAX 30-1-3934-296, 30-1-330-5080, hellenum@hotmail.com. Ed. Anastasios P Tzamalis. Circ: 1,000.

NORDISK FILATELI. *see* PHILATELY

737 DNK ISSN 0078-107X
NORDISK NUMISMATISK AARSSKRIFT/NORDIC NUMISMATIC JOURNAL/SCANDINAVIAN NUMISMATIC JOURNAL. Text in Multiple languages; Summaries in Multiple languages. 1936. a. price varies. cum.index: 1936-1970 in vol.1971. back issues avail. **Document type:** *Yearbook, Consumer.*
Indexed: NumL.
Published by: Nordisk Numismatisk Union/Scandinavian Numismatic Union, c/o Preben Nielsen, Galionsvej 12, Copenhagen K, 1437, Denmark. TEL 45-43-521918, formand@numismatik.dk.

737 DNK ISSN 0025-8539
NORDISK NUMISMATISK UNIONS MEDLEMSBLAD. Text in Danish, Norwegian, Swedish. 1916. 8/yr. adv. bk.rev. illus. cum.index: 1936-1970, 1971-1980, 1981-1990. 20 p./no.; back issues avail. **Document type:** *Journal, Consumer.*
Formerly (until 1936): Numismatisk Forenings Medlemsbladd
Indexed: NAA, NumL, RASB.
Published by: Nordisk Numismatisk Union/Scandinavian Numismatic Union, c/o Preben Nielsen, Galionsvej 12, Copenhagen K, 1437, Denmark. TEL 45-43-521918, formand@numismatik.dk, http://www.nnunion.net. Circ: 2,000.

737.4 USA ISSN 1935-0562
CJ1826
NORTH AMERICAN COINS & PRICES. Text in English. 1992. a. USD 13.59 per issue (effective 2012). 624 p./no.; back issues avail. **Document type:** *Directory, Consumer.* **Description:** Covers prices and identifying details for coins of the United States, Canada and Mexico.
Published by: Krause Publications, Inc. (Subsidiary of: F + W Media Inc.), 700 E State St, Iola, WI 54990. TEL 715-445-2214, 800-258-0929, FAX 715-445-4087, info@krause.com, http://www.krause.com. Ed. David C Harper.

737 COL
NOTAS NUMISMATICAS. Text in Spanish. 1976 (Sep., no.4). irreg. COP 30,000 (effective 2007).
Formerly (until 2007): Numis-Notas
Published by: Circulo Numismatico Antioqueno, Apdo Postal 54708, Medellin, ANT, Colombia. http://www.numismaticacolombiana.com/. Ed. Jorge Emilio Restrepo.

737.4 CHE ISSN 1424-9383
NUMIS-POST UND H M ZEITUNG; das Schweizer Magazin fuer Muenzen. Text in German. 2002. 11/yr. CHF 48; CHF 5 newsstand/cover (effective 2010). adv. **Document type:** *Magazine, Consumer.*
Formed by the merger of (1966-2002): Helvetische Muenzen-Zeitung (1013-350X); (1968-2002): Numis-Post (1424-0181)
Indexed: NumL.
Published by: Numis-Post & H M Z, Postfach, Bad Ragaz, 7310, Switzerland. TEL 49-81-5110404, FAX 49-81-5110403. Circ: 6,000 (paid).

737 FIN ISSN 0355-5615
NUMISMAATIKKO. Text in Finnish. 1965. 6/yr. adv. bk.rev. cum.index: 1965-1974. **Document type:** *Magazine, Consumer.*
Indexed: NumL.
Published by: Suomen Numismaatikkoliitto, PO Box 5, Tampere, 33701, Finland. Ed. Petri Virolainen. Circ: 2,500.

737 900 GBR ISSN 0078-2696
CJ1
➤ **NUMISMATIC CHRONICLE.** Text in English. 1839. a. GBP 40 per issue; free to members (effective 2009). adv. bk.rev. illus.; maps. back issues avail. **Document type:** *Journal, Academic/Scholarly.*
Formerly (until 1966): Royal Numismatic Society. Numismatic Chronicle and Journal (0267-7504)
Indexed: BrArAb, DIP, I14, IBR, IBZ, NAA, NumL, RASB, SCOPUS.
—BLDSC (6184.719000).
Published by: Royal Numismatic Society, British Museum, Dept. of Coins and Medals, Great Russell St, London, WC1B 3DG, United Kingdom. info@numismatics.org.uk. Ed. Marcus Phillips. **Subscr. to:** Spink, 69 Southampton Row, Bloomsbury, London WC1B 4ET, United Kingdom. TEL 44-20-75634000, FAX 44-20-75634066, info@spink.com, http://www.spink.com.

737 GBR ISSN 0029-6023
NUMISMATIC CIRCULAR. Text in English. 1892. bi-m. GBP 20 domestic; GBP 25 in Europe; GBP 40 elsewhere (effective 2009). bk.rev. bibl.; tr.lit. index. back issues avail. **Document type:** *Catalog.* **Description:** Features books and banknotes for sale at fixed prices and features articles of diverse numismatic interest.
Related titles: Online - full text ed.
Indexed: BrArAb, NumL, RASB.
Published by: Spink, St James, Spink & Son Ltd, 5 King St, London, SW1Y 6QS, United Kingdom. info@spink.com.

737 USA ISSN 0029-6031
Z6866
NUMISMATIC LITERATURE. Text in English. 1947. a. USD 50 (effective 2005). abstr.; bibl.; illus. index. back issues avail.; reprints avail. **Document type:** *Monographic series, Bibliography.* **Description:** Brings out work in all fields of numismatics.
Indexed: ABS&EES, RASB.
Published by: American Numismatic Society, 75 Varick St, 11th Fl, New York, NY 10013. TEL 212-571-4470, FAX 212-571-4479, orders@numismatics.org. Ed. Oliver Hoover.

737 USA ISSN 0029-604X
CJ1
NUMISMATIC NEWS; the complete information source for coin collectors. Text in English. 1952. 52/yr. USD 79.99; USD 2.99 newsstand/cover (effective 2012). adv. bk.rev. bibl.; charts; illus.; mkt.; stat.; tr.lit. back issues avail.; reprints avail. **Document type:** *Newsletter, Consumer.* **Description:** Reports on market happenings and news concerning collectible coins. Sections include the weekly Coin Clinic Q&A column, Coin Market section provides comprehensive pricing monthly, with additional pricing of the most popular coin types offered weekly in Coin Market at a Glance. Each issue also includes columns with practical how-to advice and historical features by some of the top experts in the field.
Formerly (until 19??): Numismatic News Weekly
Related titles: Online - full text ed.
Indexed: NumL.
—CCC.
Published by: F + W Media Inc., 4700 E Galbraith Rd, Cincinnati, OH 45236. TEL 513-531-2690, contact_us@fwmedia.com, http://www.fwmedia.com/. Ed. Dave Harper TEL 715-445-2214 ext 13344. Pub. Scott Tappa TEL 715-445-2214 ext 13428.

737 USA ISSN 0078-2718
NUMISMATIC NOTES AND MONOGRAPHS. Text in English. 1921. irreg., latest vol.169, 2009. price varies. back issues avail.; reprints avail. **Document type:** *Monographic series, Academic/Scholarly.* **Description:** Covers all aspects of numismatic studies.
Indexed: NumL.
Published by: American Numismatic Society, 75 Varick St, 11th Fl, New York, NY 10013. TEL 212-571-4470, FAX 212-571-4479, orders@numismatics.org.

737 AUS ISSN 1326-8775
NUMISMATIC SOCIETY OF SOUTH AUSTRALIA, INC. NEWSLETTER. Text in English. 1986. q. **Document type:** *Newsletter.* **Description:** Contains proceedings, reports on meetings, occassional articles and news.
Published by: Numismatic Society of South Australia Inc., 3 Graves St, Kadina, SA 5554, Australia. TEL 61-8-88212906, FAX 61-8-88212901.

737 USA ISSN 0517-404X
NUMISMATIC STUDIES. Text in English. 1938. irreg., latest vol.24, 2001. price varies. back issues avail.; reprints avail. **Document type:** *Monographic series, Academic/Scholarly.* **Description:** Features studies where extended illustration is necessary or where flanned coins of considerable number are involved.
Indexed: NumL.
Published by: American Numismatic Society, 75 Varick St, 11th Fl, New York, NY 10013. TEL 212-571-4470, FAX 212-571-4479, orders@numismatics.org. Circ: 800.

737 CHE ISSN 1420-1739
CJ201
➤ **NUMISMATICA E ANTICHITA CLASSICHE**; quaderni ticinesi. Text in English, French, German, Italian. 1972. a., latest vol.31, 2002. CHF 175 per issue (effective 2003). index. Supplement avail.; back issues avail. **Document type:** *Monographic series, Academic/Scholarly.*
Indexed: IBR, IBZ, NumL.
Published by: Amici dei Quaderni Ticinesi di Numismatica e Antichita Classiche, Secretariat, Case Postale 3157, Lugano, 6901, Switzerland. TEL 41-91-6061606, erarslan@tin.it, http://www.quaderniticinesi.com. Circ: 500.

737 BEL
NUMISMATICA LOVANIENSIA. Text in French. 1977. irreg., latest vol.18, 1997. price varies. illus. **Document type:** *Monographic series, Academic/Scholarly.*
Published by: Association Belge de Numismatique Professeur Marcel Hoc, Place Blaise Pascal 1, Louvain-la-Neuve, 1348, Belgium. TEL 32-10-474882, FAX 32-10-474972, moucharte@fltr.ucl.ac.be, http:numismatica.fltr.ucl.ac.be. R&P Ghislaine Moucharte.

737 CZE ISSN 0029-6074
CJ9
➤ **NUMISMATICKE LISTY.** Text in Czech; Summaries in English. 1945. bi-m. EUR 65, USD 98 foreign (effective 2009). bk.rev. abstr.; bibl.; illus. index. **Document type:** *Journal, Academic/Scholarly.*
Indexed: CA, NumL, RASB, T02.
Published by: Narodni Muzeum, Vaclavske nam 68, Prague 1, 11579, Czech Republic. TEL 420-22-4497111, nm@nm.cz. Ed. Lubos Polansky. Circ: 7,500. **Subscr. to:** Myris Trade Ltd., V Stihlach 1311, PO Box 2, Prague 4 14201, Czech Republic. TEL 420-2-34035200, FAX 420-2-34035207, myris@myris.cz, http://www.myris.cz.

737 FRA ISSN 0335-1971
CJ2454
NUMISMATIQUE & CHANGE. Text in French. 1972. 11/yr. adv. bk.rev. charts; stat.
Indexed: NumL, RASB.
Published by: S E P S, 12 rue Raymond Poincare, Revigny-sur-Ornain, 55800, France. TEL 33-3-29705633, FAX 33-3-29705744. Ed. Rene Louis Martin. Circ: 15,000.

737 SWE ISSN 0078-2734
CJ9
NUMISMATISKA MEDDELANDEN/NUMISMATIC ESSAYS. Variant title: Communications Numismatique. Text in Swedish; Summaries in English, French, German. 1874. irreg., latest vol.42, 2004. price varies. cum index: 1874-1995. back issues avail. **Document type:** *Monographic series, Academic/Scholarly.*
Indexed: NAA, NumL.
Published by: Svenska Numismatiska Foereningen/Swedish Numismatic Society, Banergatan 17 nb, Stockholm, 11522, Sweden. TEL 46-8-6675598, FAX 46-8-6670771, info@numismatik.se, http://www/numismatik.se. Circ: 1,000.

737 USA ISSN 0029-6090
CJ1
NUMISMATIST; for collectors of coins, medals, tokens and paper money. Text in English. 1888. m. free to members (print & online eds.) (effective 2010). bk.rev. charts; illus.; stat. index, cum.index: vols.1-51, 52-71. reprints avail. **Document type:** *Magazine, Trade.* **Description:** Designed for collectors of coins, medals, tokens and paper money.
Incorporates (1987-1994): First Strike (0896-4432); (1951-1981): A N A Club Bulletin (0001-1991)
Related titles: Microfiche ed.; Online - full text ed.

Indexed: A06, ABS&EES, NumL.
—Ingenta.
Published by: American Numismatic Association, 818 N Cascade Ave, Colorado Springs, El Paso, CO 80903. TEL 719-632-2646, 800-367-9723, FAX 719-634-4085. Ed. Barbara Gregory TEL 719-632-2646 ext.131.

737 SRB ISSN 0350-9397
NUMIZMATICAR. Text in Serbo-Croatian. 1978. a. **Document type:** *Bulletin, Academic/Scholarly.* **Description:** Focuses on various numismatic themes and issues, from the beginnings of the coin minting and paper bills emitting to this day.
Published by: Narodni Muzej Beograd, Trg. Republike 1a, Belgrade. TEL 381-11-624322, FAX 381-11-627721, narodnimuzej@narodnimuzej.org.yu. **Co-sponsor:** Srpsko Numizmaticko Drustvo/Serbian Association of Numismatists.

737 RUS
NUMIZMATICHESKII AL'MANAKH. Text in Russian. q. USD 79 in United States.
Published by: Finansovaya Gruppa Nika, Ul Narvskaya 23, k 306, 113, Moscow, 125493, Russian Federation. TEL 7-095-1557135, FAX 7-095-4521720. **Dist. by:** East View Information Services, 10601 Wayzata Blvd, Minneapolis, MN 55305. TEL 952-252-1201, 800-477-1005, FAX 952-252-1202, info@eastview.com, http://www.eastview.com.

737 BGR ISSN 0861-8313
NUMIZMATIKA I SFRAGISTIKA. Text in Bulgarian; Summaries in English, French, German. 1969. s-a. USD 32 foreign (effective 2002).
Formerly (until 1991): Numizmatika (0204-4064)
Published by: Bulgarska Akademiya na Naukite, Etnografski Institut/ Bulgarian Academy of Sciences, Ethnographic Institute, 6a Moskovska St, Sofia, 1000, Bulgaria. FAX 359-2-9801162. **Dist. by:** Sofia Books, ul Silivria 16, Sofia 1404, Bulgaria. TEL 359-2-9586257, info@sofiabooks-bg.com, http://www.sofiabooks-bg.com.

737 PRT ISSN 0871-2743
NUMMUS. Text in English, French, Portuguese; Summaries in English, French. 1952. a. USD 25. bk.rev. bibl.; charts; illus. cum.index: 1968-1972. **Document type:** *Journal, Academic/Scholarly.*
Formerly: Numus - Numismatica, Medalhistica, Arqueologia (0085-364X)
Indexed: NumL.
Published by: Sociedade Portuguesa de Numismatica, Rua Costa Cabral, 664, Porto, 4200, Portugal. TEL 596029. Circ: 2,000.

737 ESP ISSN 0029-6015
CJ9
NVMISMA. Text in English, French, Spanish. 1951. a. bk.rev. bibl.; charts; illus.; stat. **Document type:** *Magazine, Consumer.*
Indexed: NumL.
Published by: Sociedad Ibero-Americana de Estudios Numismaticos (S I A E N), Calle Jorge Juan 106, Madrid, 28009, Spain. TEL 34-91-5666536, siaen@fnmt.es, http://www.siaen.org.

737 AUT
OESTERREICHISCHE AKADEMIE DER WISSENSCHAFTEN. NUMISMATISCHE KOMMISSION. VEROEFFENTLICHUNGEN. Text in German. 1973. irreg. price varies. illus. 208 p./no.; back issues avail. **Document type:** *Monographic series, Academic/Scholarly.*
Related titles: ♦ Series of: Oesterreichische Akademie der Wissenschaften. Philosophisch-Historische Klasse. Sitzungsberichte. ISSN 0029-8832.
Published by: (Oesterreichische Akademie der Wissenschaften, Numismatische Kommission), Verlag der Oesterreichischen Akademie der Wissenschaften, Postgasse 7/4, Vienna, W 1011, Austria. TEL 43-1-515813402, FAX 43-1-515813400, verlag@oeaw.ac.at, http://www.verlag.oeaw.ac.at. Ed. Rika Gyselen.

737 AUT ISSN 0029-9359
OESTERREICHISCHE NUMISMATISCHE GESELLSCHAFT. MITTEILUNGEN. Text in German. 1883. 6/yr. adv. bk.rev. abstr.; illus. cum.index. **Document type:** *Bulletin, Consumer.*
Indexed: NumL, RASB.
Published by: Oesterreichische Numismatische Gesellschaft, Burgring 5, Vienna, W 1010, Austria. TEL 43-1-52524380, FAX 43-1-52524353, office@oeng.at, http://www.oeng.at. Ed., Adv. contact Karl Schulz. Circ: 700.

737 CAN ISSN 0048-1815
ONTARIO NUMISMATIST. Text in English. 1961. m.
Published by: Ontario Numismatic Association, 75 King St, S, P O Box 40033, Waterloo Square PO, Waterloo, ON N2J 4V1, Canada. Ed. Bruce H Raszmann.

737.4 DEU ISSN 1613-9682
ORIENTALISCHES MUENZKABINETT JENA. Text in German. 2004. irreg. price varies. **Document type:** *Monographic series, Academic/ Scholarly.*
Published by: Harrassowitz Verlag, Kreuzberger Ring 7b-d, Wiesbaden, 65205, Germany. TEL 49-611-5300, FAX 49-611-530560, verlag@harrassowitz.de, http://www.harrassowitz.de. Ed. Norbert Nebes.

737 ITA ISSN 1126-8689
PANORAMA NUMISMATICO; mensile di numismatica - medaglistica e carta moneta. Text in Italian. 1984. m. (11/yr.). adv. bk.rev. back issues avail. **Document type:** *Magazine, Consumer.* **Description:** Covers ancient and Italian numismatics for collectors and scholars.
Published by: Nomisma, Via Olivella 88, Serravalle, RSM 47899, Italy. TEL 39-0549-904012 x378, FAX 39-0549-904042, info@nomismaweb.com, http://www.nomismaweb.com.

737 ESP ISSN 2174-016X
▼ **PANORAMANUMISMATICO.COM.** Text in Spanish. 2009. w. back issues avail. **Document type:** *Magazine, Consumer.*
Media: Online - full text.
Published by: Asociacion Espanola de Numismaticos Profesionales, Paseo de ka /castelana, 201-2, Madrid, 28046, Spain. info@aenp.org, http://www.aenp.org/.

737 USA ISSN 0031-1162
HG353
PAPER MONEY. Text in English. 1962. bi-m. free to members (effective 2010). bk.rev. bibl.; charts; illus.; mkt.; tr.lit. Index. 80 p./no.; reprints avail. **Document type:** *Magazine, Consumer.* **Description:** Designed for anyone interested in paper money or related areas such as checks, stocks, engravings, and other fiscal ephemera.
Indexed: NumL.
Published by: Society of Paper Money Collectors, Inc., c/o Frank Clark, PO Box 117060, Carrollton, TX 75011. frank_clark@spmc.org. Ed. Fred L Reed.

THE PHILATELIC EXPORTER; the World stamp trade journal. *see* PHILATELY

737.6 CAN ISSN 1922-5512
PHILATELIC MAIL AUCTION. Text in English. 2008. irreg. **Document type:** *Monographic series, Consumer.*
Published by: Lex De Ment Ltd., PO Box 1836, Niagara-on-the-Lake, ON LOS 1J0, Canada. TEL 905-468-2917, FAX 905-468-2787, lex.dement@sympatico.ca, http://web.me.com/ohnoglo/lexdement/ HOME.html.

737.2 PRT ISSN 1647-8258
▼ **PRO PHALARIS.** Text in Portuguese. 2010. q. **Document type:** *Magazine, Consumer.*
Published by: Academia Faleristica de Portugal, Rua 2, Bairro Quinta do Jacinto 1, Lisbon, 1300-494, Portugal. faleristica.pt@gmail.com, http://www.acd-faleristica.com.

737 USA
PROOF COLLECTORS CORNER. Text in English. 1964. bi-m. USD 15 domestic; USD 20 foreign (effective 2000). bk.rev. 36 p./no.; back issues avail. **Document type:** *Catalog, Trade.* **Description:** Provides current coverage of numismatic issues, with information on the history and background of coins. Seeks to educate both the advanced and beginning numismatist.
Published by: World Proof Numismatic Association, PO Box 4094, Pittsburgh, PA 15201-0094. TEL 412-782-4477, FAX 412-782-0227. Ed., Pub. Edward J Moschetti. Circ: 1,500; 2,500 (paid).

793 USA ISSN 0095-263X
CJ1
RARE COIN REVIEW. Text in English. 1969. bi-m. USD 29 (effective 1998). adv. bk.rev. bibl.; illus. **Document type:** *Catalog.*
Published by: Bowers and Merena Galleries, Inc., PO Box 1224, Wolfeboro, NH 03894. TEL 603-569-5095, 800-458-4646, FAX 603-569-5319. Ed. Q David Bowers. R&P, Adv. contact Chris Karstedt. Circ: (controlled).

RECOGNITION REVIEW. *see* ART

737 BEL ISSN 0774-5885
REVUE BELGE DE NUMISMATIQUE ET DE SIGILLOGRAPHIE. Text in French. 1842. a. EUR 55 (effective 2003). adv. bk.rev. cum.index. 250 p./no.; **Document type:** *Consumer.*
Former titles (until 1908): Revue Belge de Numismatique (0774-5877); (until 1875): Revue de la Numismatique Belge (0774-5869)
Indexed: MLA-IB, NumL, RASB.
Published by: Societe Royale de Numismatique de Belgique, c/o JA Schoonheyt, Treas, Av G van Nerom 1, Brussels, 1160, Belgium. TEL 32-2-6728904, FAX 32-2-6728904. Circ: 550.

737 FRA ISSN 0484-8942
CJ3
REVUE NUMISMATIQUE. Text in French. 1836. a. EUR 54 (effective 2008). bk.rev. **Document type:** *Magazine, Trade.*
Related titles: Online - full text ed.: ISSN 1963-1693.
Indexed: FR, IBR, IBZ, NumL, P30, RASB, SCOPUS.
—BLDSC (7938.600000), INIST.
Published by: Societe Francaise de Numismatique, 58 rue de Richelieu, Paris, 75002, France. secretariat@sfnum.asso.fr, http://www.sfnum.asso.fr/pages/accueil.php.

737 CHE ISSN 0035-4163
REVUE SUISSE DE NUMISMATIQUE/SCHWEIZERISCHE NUMISMATISCHE RUNDSCHAU. Text in English, French, German. 1890. a. CHF 60 (effective 2001). adv. illus. **Document type:** *Bulletin, Consumer.*
Indexed: NumL.
Published by: Societe Suisse de Numismatique/Schweizerische Numismatische Gesellschaft, c/o Regie de Fribourg, 24 SA rue de Romont, Fribourg, 1701, Switzerland. TEL 41-26-3505511, FAX 41-26-3505599, regiedefribourg@rfsa.ch, http://www.rfsa.ch. Circ: 1,000. **Subscr. to:** Alexander Wild, Rathausgasse 30, Bern 3011, Switzerland.

737 ITA ISSN 1126-8700
RIVISTA ITALIANA DI NUMISMATICA E SCIENZE AFFINI. Text in Italian. 1888. a. **Document type:** *Magazine, Consumer.*
Formerly (until 1897): Rivista Italiana di Numismatica (1126-8719)
Indexed: B24.
Published by: Societa Numismatica Italiana, Via degli Orti 3, Milan, 20122, Italy. TEL 39-02-55194970, segreteria@socnumit.org, http://www.socnumit.org.

737 GBR ISSN 0080-4487
CODEN: SPRSD5
ROYAL NUMISMATIC SOCIETY. SPECIAL PUBLICATIONS. Text in English. 1956. irreg., latest vol.43. Price varies. back issues avail. **Document type:** *Monographic series, Academic/Scholarly.*
—BLDSC (8380.400000), CASDDS, IE, Ingenta.
Published by: Royal Numismatic Society, British Museum, Dept. of Coins and Medals, Great Russell St, London, WC1B 3DG, United Kingdom. info@numismatics.org.uk. Ed. Richard Ashton. **Subscr. to:** Spink, 69 Southampton Row, Bloomsbury, London WC1B 4ET, United Kingdom. TEL 44-20-75634000, FAX 44-20-75634066, info@spink.com, http://www.spink.com.

737 USA ISSN 0036-4053
SAN DIEGO NUMISMATIC SOCIETY. BULLETIN. Text in English. 1947. m. membership. charts; illus. **Document type:** *Bulletin.*
Published by: San Diego Numismatic Society Inc., 611 Oakwood Way, El Cajon, CA 92021. Ed. Dorothy Baber. Circ: 150. **Subscr. to:** PO Box 6909, San Diego, CA 92112.

737.296 USA
SHEKEL. Text in English. 1968. 6/yr. USD 18 in US & Canada; USD 25 elsewhere (effective 2008). bk.rev. back issues avail. **Document type:** *Magazine, Consumer.* **Description:** Presents collection of Israel and Judaic coins, medals and currency, from antiquity to the present.
Indexed: NumL.
Published by: American Israel Numismatic Association, PO Box 13063, Silver Spring, MD 20911-3063. Ed. Edward Schuman TEL 305-466-2833. Circ: 3,000.

737.4 DNK ISSN 0586-4496
SIEG'S MOENTKATALOG. DANMARK, DANSK VESTINDIEN, TRANKEBAR, FAEROERNE, GROENLAND, ISLAND. Cover title: Sieg's Moentkatalog. Danmark, Groenland, Faeroeerne, Island, Dansk Vestindien, Trankebar. Text in Danish. 1968. a. price varies. illus. **Document type:** *Catalog, Consumer.*
Published by: Pilegaards Forlag, Algade 65, Aalborg, 9000, Denmark. TEL 45-98-139000, FAX 45-98-139221, http://www.antikvar.dk/ pilegaard.

737.4 DNK ISSN 0900-9310
SIEG'S MOENTKATALOG. NORDEN. Text in Danish. 1969. a. price varies. **Document type:** *Catalog, Consumer.*
Published by: Pilegaards Forlag, Algade 65, Aalborg, 9000, Denmark. TEL 45-98-139000, FAX 45-98-139221, http://www.antikvar.dk/ pilegaard.

737 SVK ISSN 0081-0088
SLOVENSKA NUMIZMATIKA. Text in Slovak; Summaries in German. 1970. biennial.
Indexed: NumL, RASB.
Published by: (Slovenska Akademia Vied/Slovak Academy of Sciences), Vydavatel'stvo Slovenskej Akademie Vied Veda/Veda, Publishing House of the Slovak Academy of Sciences, Dubravska cesta 9, PO Box 106, Bratislava 45, 84005, Slovakia. Ed. Eva Kolnikova. **Dist. by:** Slovart G.T.G. s.r.o., Krupinska 4, PO Box 152, Bratislava 85299, Slovakia. TEL 421-2-63839472, FAX 421-2-63839485, http:// www.slovart-gtg.sk.

737 ROM ISSN 1012-0890
CJ3330
SOCIETATEA NUMISMATICA ROMANA. BULETINUL. Text in Romanian; Summaries in French, Romanian. 1904. a.
Related titles: Online - full text ed.
Published by: Editura Academiei Romane/Publishing House of the Romanian Academy, Calea 13 Septembrie 13, Sector 5, Bucharest, 050711, Romania. TEL 40-21-3188146, FAX 40-21-3182444, edacad@ear.ro, http://www.ear.ro. Ed. Constantin Preda. **Dist. by:** Rodipet S.A., Piata Presei Libere 1, sector 1, PO Box 33-57, Bucharest 3, Romania. TEL 40-21-2226407, 40-21-2224126, rodipet@rodipet.ro.

737 FRA ISSN 0037-9344
CJ17
SOCIETE FRANCAISE DE NUMISMATIQUE. BULLETIN. Text in French. 1946. 10/yr. EUR 54 domestic membership; EUR 51 foreign membership (effective 2009). bk.rev. charts; illus. cum.index every 5 yrs. **Document type:** *Bulletin, Consumer.*
Formerly (until 1948): Societe Francaise de Numismatique (1958-6566)
Indexed: NumL, RASB.
Published by: Societe Francaise de Numismatique, 58 rue de Richelieu, Paris, 75002, France. secretariat@sfnum.asso.fr, http:// www.sfnum.asso.fr/pages/accueil.php. Circ: 950.

STAMP AND COIN AUCTION. *see* PHILATELY

STAMP & COIN MART. *see* HOBBIES

737.4 USA ISSN 1939-814X
CJ1755
STANDARD CATALOG OF WORLD COINS. 1901-2000. Variant title: World Coins. Text in English. 1972. a. USD 60 (effective 2008). **Document type:** *Magazine, Consumer.*
Supersedes in part (in 2006): Standard Catalog of World Coins. 1901-Present (1556-2263); Which was formerly (until 200?): Standard Catalog of World Coins. 1701-1800 (1078-8816); Which superseded in part (in 1993): Standard Catalog of World Coins (0190-7689)
—BLDSC (8430.255551).
Published by: Krause Publications, Inc. (Subsidiary of: F + W Media Inc.), 700 E State St, Iola, WI 54990. TEL 715-445-2214, 888-457-2873, FAX 715-445-2164, info@krause.com, http://www.krause.com.

737 790.13 USA ISSN 1935-4339
CJ1756
STANDARD CATALOG OF WORLD COINS. 2001-DATE. Text in English. 2007. a. USD 26.40 per issue (effective 2012). back issues avail. **Document type:** *Catalog, Consumer.*
Supersedes in part (in 2006): Standard Catalog of World Coins. 1901-Present (1556-2263); Which was formerly (until 200?): Standard Catalog of World Coins. 1701-1800 (1078-8816); Which superseded in part (in 1993): Standard Catalog of World Coins (0190-7689)
—BLDSC (8430.255550).
Published by: Krause Publications, Inc. (Subsidiary of: F + W Media Inc.), 700 E State St, Iola, WI 54990. TEL 715-445-2214, 800-258-0929, FAX 715-445-4087, info@krause.com, http://www.krause.com. Ed. George S Cuhaj.

737.4 GBR
STANDARD CATALOGUE OF BRITISH COINS. Text in English. 1929. a., latest 44th ed. GBP 25 per issue (effective 2009). illus. back issues avail. **Document type:** *Catalog.* **Description:** Designed to be a guide for beginners, serious numismatists and anyone interested in British Coinage.
Former titles (19??): Seaby's Standard Catalogue of British Coins; (until 1973): Seaby's Standard Catalogue: British Coins, England and the United Kingdom; (until 1971): Standard Catalogue of British Coins; (until 1962): Standard Catalogue of the Coins of Great Britain and Ireland
Published by: Spink, 69 Southampton Row, Bloomsbury, London, WC1B 4ET, United Kingdom. TEL 44-20-75634000, FAX 44-20-75634066, info@spink.com.

737.4942 GBR ISSN 1756-4840
STUDIES IN EARLY MEDIEVAL COINAGE. Text in English. 2008. irreg., latest vol.2, 2011. price varies. **Document type:** *Monographic series, Academic/Scholarly.*
Published by: Boydell & Brewer Ltd., Whitwell House, St Audrys Park Rd, Melton, Woodbridge, IP12 1SY, United Kingdom. TEL 44-1394-610600, FAX 44-1394-610316, editorial@boydell.co.uk, http:// www.boydell.co.uk.

737.4 SWE ISSN 0283-071X
SVENSK NUMISMATISK TIDSKRIFT. Text in Swedish. 1972. 8/yr. SEK 200 (effective 2007). adv. bk.rev. illus. cum.index: 1972-1982, 1983-1992, 1993-2002. back issues avail. **Document type:** *Magazine, Consumer.*
Formerly (until 1986): Myntkontakt (0345-8245)

Related titles: Online - full text ed.
Indexed: NAA, NumL.
Published by: (Kungliga Myntkabinettet/Royal Coin Cabinet), Svenska Numismatiska Foereningen/Swedish Numismatic Society, Banergatan 17 nb, Stockholm, 11522, Sweden. TEL 46-8-6675598, FAX 46-8-6670771, info@numismatik.se, http://www/numismatik.se. Ed. Monica Golabiewski TEL 46-8-51955300. Adv. contact Carin Hirsch-Lundborg. page SEK 2,000; 151 x 214. **Co-publisher:** Kungliga Myntkabinettet/Royal Coin Cabinet.

737 USA ISSN 0271-3993
SYLLOGE NUMMORUM GRAECORUM. Short title: S N G A N S. Text in English. 1961. irreg., latest vol.9, 1998. price varies. charts; illus. reprints avail. **Document type:** *Monographic series, Academic/Scholarly.* **Description:** Describes and illustrates coins in the Society's Greek collection.
Published by: American Numismatic Society, 75 Varick St, 11th Fl, New York, NY 10013. TEL 212-571-4470, FAX 212-571-4479, orders@numismatics.org.

737 USA ISSN 0039-8233
T A M S JOURNAL. Text in English. 1961. bi-m. USD 20 in US & Canada; USD 25 elsewhere (effective 2000). adv. bk.rev. charts; illus. index, cum.index.
Formerly: Token and Medal Society. Journal
Indexed: NumL.
Published by: Token and Medal Society, PO Box 366, Bryantown, MD 20617. TEL 301-274-3441. Ed., R&P, Adv. contact David E Schenkman. Pub. Paul Cunningham. Circ: 1,600 (paid).

737 AUS ISSN 0817-4075
TASMANIAN NUMISMATIST. Text in English. 1964. m. bk.rev. **Document type:** *Newsletter.* **Description:** Contains numismatic news, particularly Australian society news.
Former titles (until 1985): Tasmanian Numismatic Society. Journal (0157-9088); (until 1979): Tasmanian Numismatic Society. Newsletter; (until 1965): Tasmanian Numismatic Society. Journal
Related titles: Online - full text ed.
Published by: Tasmanian Numismatic Society Inc., GPO Box 8845, Hobart, TAS 7001, Australia. pwood@vision.net, http://www.vision.net.au/~pwood/tns.html.

737 USA
TIPSICO BULLETIN. Text in English. 1972. bi-m. USD 6. adv. bk.rev. illus. **Document type:** *Catalog.*
Formerly: Collector's Choice Bulletin
Published by: Tipsico Coin LLC, 2141 Broadway, N, PO Box 1128, Bend, OR 97459. TEL 541-756-7111. Ed. Alex A Pancheco. Circ: 1,000 (controlled).

737 FRA ISSN 0223-4300
CJ3
TRESORS MONETAIRES. Text in French. 1979. a. **Document type:** *Monographic series, Academic/Scholarly.*
Published by: Bibliotheque Nationale de France, Site Francois Mitterand, Quai Francois Mauriac, Paris, 75706, France. TEL 33-1-53795959, http://www.bnf.fr.

TRIDENT - VISNYK. *see* PHILATELY

TRIERER ZEITSCHRIFT FUER GESCHICHTE UND KUNST DES TRIERER LANDES UND SEINER NACHBARGEBIETE. *see* ARCHAEOLOGY

737 USA
U S COIN COLLECTOR. Text in English. 1990. bi-m. USD 18.
Published by: National Coin Collectors Association, PO Box 1150, Murphysboro, IL 62966. Ed. William Atkinson.

UKRAINIAN PHILATELIST. *see* PHILATELY

737.4 USA
UNITED STATES MINT. WORLD COINAGE REPORT. Text in English. biennial?. illus. **Document type:** *Government.* **Description:** Contains photographs, sketches, and descriptions of coins from all over the world.
Published by: United States Mint, 1500 Pennsylvania Ave, N W, Washington, DC 20220. **Subscr. to:** U.S. Government Printing Office, Superintendent of Documents.

069.9 737 BRA
UNIVERSIDADE DE SAO PAULO. MUSEU PAULISTA. COLECAO. SERIE DE NUMISMATICA. Text in Portuguese. 1975. irreg.
Supersedes in part (in 1975): Museu Paulista. Colecao (0080-6382)
Published by: Universidade de Sao Paulo, Museu Paulista, Ipiranga, Caixa Postal 42503, Sao Paulo, SP 04299-970, Brazil. Ed. Antonio Rocha Penteado.

769.5 CAN ISSN 1922-477X
VAN DAM'S REVENEWS. Text in English. 1970. m. CAD 28.75 in state includes Maritimes; CAD 26.75 out of state; CAD 36 in United States; CAD 50 elsewhere (effective 2010). **Document type:** *Newsletter, Consumer.*
Related titles: Online - full text ed.
Published by: E S J van Dam Ltd., PO Box 300, Bridgenorth, ON K0L 1H0, Canada. TEL 705-292-7013, 866-382-6326, FAX 705-292-6311, 866-820-9542, esvandam@esjvandam.com.

737 CAN ISSN 0049-5824
VANCOUVER NUMISMATIC SOCIETY. NEWS BULLETIN. Text in English. 1961. m. (except July-Aug.). CAD 15 to members. adv. bk.rev. **Document type:** *Newsletter.*
Media: Duplicated (not offset).
Published by: Vancouver Numismatic Society, 4645 W 6th Ave, Vancouver, BC IV6R 1V6, Canada. Ed. Peter N Moogk. Circ: 225.

737 USA ISSN 1933-561X
CJ89
WARMAN'S COINS & PAPER MONEY; identification and price guide. Text in English. 1999. triennial, latest 2008, 4th Ed. USD 16.49 per issue (effective 2011). **Document type:** *Guide, Consumer.*
Published by: Krause Publications, Inc. (Subsidiary of: F + W Media Inc.), 700 E State St, Iola, WI 54990. TEL 715-445-2215, 800-258-0929, FAX 715-445-4087, info@krause.com, http://www.krause.com. Ed. Allen G Berman.

737 POL ISSN 0043-5155
WIADOMOSCI NUMIZMATYCZNE/NUMISMATIC NEWS. Text in Polish. 1957. s-a. EUR 39 foreign (effective 2011). charts; illus. index. **Document type:** *Journal, Academic/Scholarly.*
Formerly: Wiadomosci Numizmatyczno-Archeologiczne
Indexed: NumL, RASB.
Published by: (Polska Akademia Nauk, Komitet Nauk Historycznych/Polish Academy of Sciences, Historical Sciences Committee), Polska Akademia Nauk, Instytut Archeologii i Etnologii, Al Solidarnosci 105, Warsaw, 00140, Poland. TEL 48-22-6202881, FAX 48-22-6240100, director@iaepan.edu.pl, http://www.iaepan.edu.pl. Ed. Borys Paszkiewicz. Circ: 740. **Dist. by:** Ars Polona, Obroncow 25, Warsaw 03933, Poland. TEL 48-22-5098609, FAX 48-22-5098610, arspolona@arspolona.com.pl, http://www.arspolona.com.pl.

737.4 USA ISSN 0145-9090
WORLD COIN NEWS. Text in English. 1973. m. USD 39.99; USD 4.99 newsstand/cover (effective 2012). adv. bk.rev. bibl.; charts; illus. back issues avail.; reprints avail. **Document type:** *Magazine, Trade.* **Description:** Reports on new issues, auctions and other coin news from around the world. Features by some of the top experts in the field provide in-depth historical information on coins and the countries that issued them. Each issue also provides a calendar of upcoming shows worldwide.
Related titles: Online - full text ed.
Indexed: NumL.
—CCC.
Published by: F + W Media Inc., 4700 E Galbraith Rd, Cincinnati, OH 45236. Ed. Maggie Stigsell TEL 715-445-2214 ext 13623. Pub. Scott Tappa TEL 715-445-2214 ext 13428.

737.4 CHN ISSN 1001-8638
CJ3490
ZHONGGUO QIANBI/CHINA NUMISMATICS. Text in Chinese. 1983. q. USD 20.80 (effective 2009). 80 p./no.; **Document type:** *Journal, Academic/Scholarly.* **Description:** Publishes research on numismatics or the history of money, news of excavations, and interesting anecdotes about coins. Introduces historic coins, presents the experiences of money collectors, and reports related events in China and the world.
Related titles: Online - full text ed.
—East View.
Published by: (Zhongguo Qianbi Xuehui/China Numismatic Society), Zhongguo Qianbi Bianjibu, 22 Xi Jiaomin Xiang, Xicheng-qu, Beijing, 100031, China. TEL 86-10-66053042. Circ: 20,000. **Dist. by:** China International Book Trading Corp, 35 Chegongzhuang Xilu, Haidian District, PO Box 399, Beijing 100044, China. TEL 86-10-68412045, FAX 86-10-68412023, cibtc@mail.cibtc.com.cn, http://www.cibtc.com.cn. **Co-sponsor:** Zhongguo Qianbi Bowuguan/China Numismatic Museum.

NUMISMATICS—Abstracting, Bibliographies, Statistics

011 737.4 USA
NUMISMATIC BOOKS IN PRINT. Text in English. 1975. a. USD 3 (effective 2000). **Document type:** *Bibliography.*
Published by: Sanford J. Durst Numismatic Publications, Ltd., 11 Clinton Ave, Rockville Centre, NY 11570. TEL 516-766-4444, FAX 516-766-4520. Ed., R&P Sanford J Durst. Circ: 10,000.

NURSES AND NURSING

see MEDICAL SCIENCES—Nurses And Nursing

NUTRITION AND DIETETICS

see also FOOD AND FOOD INDUSTRIES ; HEALTH FACILITIES AND ADMINISTRATION ; PHARMACY AND PHARMACOLOGY ; PHYSICAL FITNESS AND HYGIENE

613.2 USA ISSN 1545-3871
A D A TIMES. (American Dietetic Association) Text in English. 2004. q. free to members (effective 2010). adv. **Document type:** *Magazine, Trade.* **Description:** Emphasizes current nutrition, legal and financial issues; professional development and personal growth; public policy issues, and Association news and events.
Published by: American Dietetic Association, 120 S Riverside Plz, Ste 2000, Chicago, IL 60606. TEL 312-899-0040, 800-877-1600, FAX 312-899-4899, sales@eatright.org, http://www.eatright.org.

613.2 USA ISSN 1932-6211
A MOTHER'S GIFT. Text in English. 2006. q. USD 15.99 (effective 2008). **Document type:** *Magazine, Consumer.* **Description:** Provides education and support to new mothers who wish to breastfeed their babies. Includes advice for working with healthcare providers, nutrition informaiton, encouraging stories and useful information for those new to breastfeeding.
Published by: Breastfeeding America, 7609 Roosevelt Rd, Forest Park, IL 60130. TEL 877-541-6962, FAX 708-689-0215, info@breast-feedingamerica.com, http://www.breast-feedingamerica.com. Ed., Pub. Mishawn Purnell-O'Neal.

A N D I NEWS. *see* MEDICAL SCIENCES—Psychiatry And Neurology

613.2 FRA ISSN 1951-8285
ACTIF'S. Text in French. 2006. q. EUR 165 (effective 2009). **Document type:** *Magazine, Trade.*
Published by: Editions Business Group Media, 12 rue Frederic Soddy, ZAC Des Coteaux Sarrazins, Creteil, 94044 Cedex, France. TEL 33-1-56711840, FAX 33-1-43396709, http://www.editionsbgm.fr.

613.25 ESP ISSN 1138-0322
ACTIVIDAD DIETETICA. Text in Spanish. 1997. q. EUR 78.97 combined subscription to individuals print & online eds.; EUR 199.93 combined subscription to institutions print & online eds. (effective 2009). back issues avail. **Document type:** *Journal, Academic/Scholarly.*
Related titles: Online - full text ed.: EUR 65,378 (effective 2009) (from ScienceDirect).
Indexed: EMBASE, ExcerpMed, SCOPUS.
—CCC.
Published by: Elsevier Doyma (Subsidiary of: Elsevier Health Sciences), Traversa de Gracia 17-21, Barcelona, 08021, Spain. TEL 34-932-418800, FAX 34-932-419020, editorial@elsevier.com. Ed. N. Schinca. Circ: 2,500.

615.854 DEU ISSN 1865-1739
ADIPOSITAS; Ursachen, Klinik und Folgeerkrankungen. Text in German. 2007. q. EUR 96 to individuals; EUR 136 to institutions; EUR 48 to students; EUR 34 newsstand/cover (effective 2011). adv. **Document type:** *Journal, Academic/Scholarly.*
Published by: (Deutsche Adipositas-Gesellschaft), Schattauer GmbH, Hoelderlinstr 3, Stuttgart, 70174, Germany. TEL 49-711-229870, FAX 49-711-2298750, info@schattauer.de, http://www.schattauer.com. Eds. H Hauner, Wieland Kiess. Adv. contact Jasmin Thurner.

613.2 DNK ISSN 1602-6780
ADIPOSITASFORENINGEN. NYHEDSBREV. Text in Danish. 1999. q. DKK 200 to individual members; DKK 400 to institutional members; DKK 100 to students (effective 2008). back issues avail. **Document type:** *Newsletter, Consumer.* **Description:** News and advice for people with weight problems.
Formerly (until 2001): Landsforeningen af Overvaegtige i Danmark. Nyhedsbrev (1600-8995)
Related titles: Online - full text ed.
Published by: Adipositasforeningen, c/o Nina Frahm, Stroeby Bygade 21, Stroeby, 4671, Denmark. TEL 45-56-570277, info@adipositasforeningen.dk. Ed. Nina Frahm.

613.2 500 600 GBR ISSN 2042-4868
▼ ➤ **ADVANCE JOURNAL OF FOOD SCIENCE AND TECHNOLOGY.** Abbreviated title: A J F S T. Text in English. 2009. bi-m. back issues avail.; reprints avail. **Document type:** *Journal, Academic/Scholarly.*
Related titles: Online - full text ed.: ISSN 2042-4876. free (effective 2011).
—CCC.
Published by: Maxwell Science Publications, 74 Kenelm Rd, Birmingham, B10 9AJ, United Kingdom. admin@maxwellsci.com.

613.2 USA ISSN 1043-4526
TX537 CODEN: AFNREL
ADVANCES IN FOOD AND NUTRITION RESEARCH. Text in English. 1948. irreg., latest vol.58, 2009. USD 166 per vol. (effective 2010). index. back issues avail.; reprints avail. **Document type:** *Monographic series, Academic/Scholarly.* **Description:** Provides the integral relationship between the food and nutritional sciences and brings together comprehensive reviews that highlight this relationship.
Formerly (until 1989): Advances in Food Research (0065-2628)
Related titles: Online - full text ed.
Indexed: A20, A22, Agr, B&AI, B&BAb, B04, B10, B19, B21, C06, C07, CA, CIN, ChemAb, ChemTitl, ChemoAb, EMBASE, ESPM, ExcerpMed, FS&TA, I10, IBR, IBZ, IndMed, MEDLINE, P30, R10, Reac, SCOPUS, T02.
—BLDSC (0706.850000), CASDDS, GNLM, IE, Infotrieve, Ingenta, INIST, Linda Hall. **CCC.**
Published by: Academic Press (Subsidiary of: Elsevier Science & Technology), 3251 Riverport Ln, Maryland Heights, MO 63043. TEL 314-447-8010, FAX 314-447-8030, JournalCustomerService-usa@elsevier.com, http://www.elsevierdirect.com/imprint.jsp?iid=5. Ed. Steve Taylor.

613.2 USA ISSN 2161-8313
QP141.A1
▼ **ADVANCES IN NUTRITION.** Text in English. 2010. bi-m. USD 150 to individuals; USD 345 to institutions; free to members (effective 2012). **Document type:** *Journal, Trade.*
Related titles: Online - full text ed.: ISSN 2156-5376. free (effective 2011).
Published by: American Society for Nutrition, 9650 Rockville Pike, Bethesda, MD 20814. TEL 301-634-7050, FAX 301-634-7892, info@nutrition.org. Ed. John W Suttie.

613.2 USA ISSN 0149-9483
QP141.A1 CODEN: ANURD9
➤ **ADVANCES IN NUTRITIONAL RESEARCH.** Text in English. 1977. irreg., latest vol.10, 2002. price varies. back issues avail. **Document type:** *Monographic series, Academic/Scholarly.* **Description:** Provides accounts of the current state of knowledge regarding topics of research in the nutritional sciences.
Indexed: A22, ASCA, BIOSIS Prev, CIN, ChemAb, ChemTitl, EMBASE, ExcerpMed, ISR, IndMed, MEDLINE, MycolAb, P30, R10, Reac, SCI, SCOPUS, W07.
—BLDSC (0709.510000), CASDDS, GNLM, Ingenta, INIST, Linda Hall. **CCC.**
Published by: Springer New York LLC (Subsidiary of: Springer Science+Business Media), 233 Spring St, New York, NY 10013. TEL 212-460-1500, FAX 212-460-1575, service-ny@springer.com.

613.2 KEN ISSN 1684-5358
TX360.A35
➤ **AFRICAN JOURNAL OF FOOD, AGRICULTURE, NUTRITION AND DEVELOPMENT/JOURNAL AFRICAIN DE L'ALIMENTATION, L'AGRICULTURE, NUTRITION ET LE DEVELOPPEMENT.** Text in English. 2001. q. back issues avail. **Document type:** *Journal, Academic/Scholarly.* **Description:** Enables the dissemination and sharing of food and nutrition information issues on the continent. Covers both social science and biochemical food and nutrition related research and information. Addresses issues in nutrition and food security that affect Africa's development.
Formerly (until 2003): African Journal of Food & Nutritional Sciences Print Edition) (1681-7303)
Related titles: Online - full text ed.: ISSN 1684-5374. free (effective 2011).
Indexed: A01, A26, B21, ChemoAb, ESPM, F10, FS&TA, G05, G06, G07, G08, I05, I10, IIBP, T02.
Published by: Rural Outreach Program, PO Box 29086, Nairobi, 00625, Kenya. TEL 254-20-2737989, FAX 254-20-2734039. Ed. Ruth Oniango TEL 254-20-2737989.

613.2 KEN ISSN 1608-1366
HD9017.A1
AFRICAN JOURNAL OF FOOD AND NUTRITIONAL SECURITY. Text in English. 2001. s-a. KES 500 domestic to individuals; USD 50 in Africa to individuals; USD 100 elsewhere to individuals; KES 1,000 domestic to institutions; USD 100 in Africa to institutions; USD 200 elsewhere to institutions (effective 2004). back issues avail. **Document type:** *Journal, Academic/Scholarly.* **Description:** Covers nutritional security issues in Africa and the Third World in wide range perspectives.
Related titles: Online - full content ed.; Online - full text ed.
Published by: (Friends-of-the Book Foundation), Quest and Insight Publishers, PO Box 39624, Nairobi, Kenya. TEL 251-490-812313.

613.2 NGA ISSN 1996-0794
AFRICAN JOURNAL OF FOOD SCIENCE. Variant title: A J F S. Text in English. 2007. m. free (effective 2007). **Document type:** *Journal, Academic/Scholarly.*
Media: Online - full text.
Indexed: A34, A35, A37, A38, AgrForAb, B&BAb, B19, B21, B23, C25, C30, CABA, ChemoAb, D01, E12, ESPM, F08, FCA, GH, H16, I10, ImmunAb, LT, MaizeAb, N02, N03, N04, P32, P33, P40, R07, R08, R11, S13, S16, SoyAb, T05, W10, W11.
Published by: Academic Journals, PO Box 73023, Victoria Island, Lagos, Nigeria. service@academicjournals.org. Ed. Mamoudou H Dicko.

613 613.2 FRA ISSN 1158-0259
AGE ET NUTRITION. Text in Multiple languages. 1990. 3/yr.
Indexed: A34, A36, CABA, D01, F08, FR, GH, N02, N03, N04, P37, VS.
—BLDSC (0736.081070), IE, Ingenta, INIST.
Published by: Editions Hervas, 123 Av Philippe Auguste, Paris, 75011, France. TEL 33-01-43791095.

AGENDA DELLA SALUTE. *see* PHYSICAL FITNESS AND HYGIENE

613.2 363.7 630 VEN ISSN 1690-4745
➤ **AGROALIMENTACION & DESARROLLO SUSTENTABLE**; revista de educacion agroalimentare. Text in Spanish, Portuguese; Summaries in English. 2003. 3/yr. **Document type:** *Journal, Academic/Scholarly.*
Published by: Centro de Investigacion y Reproduccion de Especies Silvestres, Apartado Postal 397, Merida, 5101, Venezuela. cires@ciens.ula.ve, http://www.ciens.ula.ve/~cires.

➤ **AGROALIMENTARIA.** *see* SOCIOLOGY

613.26 051 USA ISSN 1521-1118
AHIMSA. Text in English. 1960. 4/yr. USD 18 domestic; USD 25 foreign (effective 2000). bk.rev. index, cum.index. **Document type:** *Newsletter.* **Description:** Presents Vegan (total-vegetarian) diet, lifestyle, and philosophies.
Published by: American Vegan Society, 56 Dinshah Ln., P O Box 369, Malaga, NJ 08328-0908. TEL 856-694-2887, FAX 856-694-2288. Ed. H Jay Dinshah. R&P Jay Dinshah.

612.3 DEU ISSN 0341-0501
RM214 CODEN: AEKPDQ
➤ **AKTUELLE ERNAEHRUNGSMEDIZIN**; Zeitschrift fuer Stoffwechselforschung, klinische Ernaehrung und Diaetetik. Text in German. 1976. bi-m. EUR 218 to institutions; EUR 290 combined subscription to institutions (print & online eds.); EUR 48 newsstand/cover (effective 2011). adv. index. reprints avail. **Document type:** *Journal, Academic/Scholarly.*
Related titles: Online - full text ed.: ISSN 1438-9916. EUR 280 to institutions (effective 2011).
Indexed: A22, A34, A36, CABA, ChemAb, D01, E12, EMBASE, ExcerpMed, FR, G11, GH, H16, H17, LT, MaizeAb, N02, N03, N04, P30, P33, PN&I, R10, R11, RRTA, Reac, S12, SCOPUS, SoyAb, T05, VS, W11.
—BLDSC (0785.735000), CASDDS, GNLM, IE, Infotrieve, Ingenta, INIST. **CCC.**
Published by: (Deutsche Gesellschaft fuer Ernaehrungsmedizin), Georg Thieme Verlag, Ruedigerstr 14, Stuttgart, 70469, Germany. TEL 49-711-8931421, FAX 49-711-8931410, leser.service@thieme.de. Ed. Guenther Wolfram. Adv. contact Ulrike Bradler. Circ: 4,100 (paid and controlled). **Co-sponsors:** Oesterreichischen Arbeitsgemeinschaft fuer klinische Ernaehrung; Deutsche Akademie fuer Ernaehrungsmedizin; Gesellschaft fuer klinische Ernaehrung der Schweiz.

613.2 ESP ISSN 1136-1336
LA ALIMENTACION EN ESPANA. Text in Spanish. 1989. a. **Document type:** *Government.*
Related titles: CD-ROM ed.: ISSN 1885-8376. 2000.
Published by: Ministerio de Agricultura Pesca y Alimentacion, Secretaria General Tecnica, Centro de Publicaciones, Paseo Infanta Isabel 1, Madrid, 28071, Spain. TEL 34-91-3475550, FAX 34-91-3475722, http://www.mapya.es.

613.2 ESP ISSN 1136-4815
ALIMENTACION, NUTRICION Y SALUD. Text in Spanish. 1994. q. free domestic to qualified personnel (effective 2008). **Document type:** *Journal, Academic/Scholarly.*
Indexed: A22, FS&TA, IECT.
—BLDSC (0787.866000), IE, Ingenta. **CCC.**
Published by: (Instituto Danone), Aran Ediciones, Castello 128, 1o, Madrid, 28006, Spain. TEL 34-91-7820030, FAX 34-91-5615787, edita@grupoaran.com, http://www.grupoaran.com. Pub. Jose Jimenez Marquez. R&P Maria Dolores Linares TEL 34-91-7820035.

613.2 FRA ISSN 1629-1212
ALIMENTATION ET PRECARITE. Text in French. 2000. q. **Document type:** *Bulletin.*
Related titles: Online - full content ed.: ISSN 1777-5973.
Published by: Centre de Recherche et d'Information Nutritionnelles (C E R I N), 45 rue Saint Lazare, Paris Cedex 09, 75314, France. TEL 33-1-49707220, FAX 33-1-42806413, nutrition-fr@cerin.org, http://www.cerin.org/.

613.2 FRA ISSN 1955-5911
ALIMENTATION NUTRITION. Text in French. 2004. bi-m. **Document type:** *Newsletter, Trade.*
Published by: Association Nationale des Industries Alimentaires (A N I A), 21 Rue Leblanc, Paris, 75015, France. TEL 33-1-53838600, FAX 33-1-53839237.

613.2 ITA ISSN 2039-6155
▼ **ALIMENTI FUNZIONALI.** Text in Italian. 2009. s-a. **Document type:** *Magazine, Consumer.*
Published by: Chiriotti Editori S p A, Viale Rimembranza 60, Pinerolo, TO 10064, Italy. TEL 39-0121-393127, FAX 39-0121-794480, info@chiriottieditori.it, http://www.chiriottieditori.com.

613.2 BRA ISSN 0103-4235
QP141.A1 CODEN: ALNUE4
➤ **ALIMENTOS E NUTRICAO.** Text in Portuguese, Spanish, English; Abstracts in English, Portuguese. 1989. q. abstr.; bibl.; charts. back issues avail. **Document type:** *Journal, Academic/Scholarly.*
Related titles: Print ed.: ISSN 2179-4448. free (effective 2011).
Indexed: A26, A34, A35, A36, A37, A38, AgBio, AgrForAb, BA, BP, C01, C25, C30, CABA, CIN, ChemAb, ChemTitl, D01, E12, F05, F06, F07, F08, F11, F12, FCA, FS&TA, GH, H12, H16, H17, I06, IndVet, N02, N03, N04, OR, P32, P33, P37, P38, P40, PGegResA, PHN&I, PN&I, R07, R08, R11, R12, R13, RA&MP, RM&VM, S12, S13, S16, S17, SoyAb, T05, TAR, TriticAb, VS, W11.
—CASDDS, INIST.
Published by: (Universidade Estadual Paulista "Julio de Mesquita Filho", Faculdade de Ciencias Farmaceuticas), Universidade Estadual Paulista, Fundacao Editora U N E S P, Praca da Se 108, Sao Paulo, SP 01001-900, Brazil. TEL 55-11-32427171, cgb@marilia.unesp.br, http://www.unesp.br. Ed. Joao Bosco Faria.

➤ **ALIVE**; Canada's natural health & wellness magazine. *see* PHYSICAL FITNESS AND HYGIENE

613.2 USA ISSN 0731-5724
RC620.A1 CODEN: JONUDL
➤ **AMERICAN COLLEGE OF NUTRITION. JOURNAL.** Abbreviated title: J A C N. Text in English. 1982. bi-m. free to members (effective 2009). adv. bk.rev. abstr.; illus. index. back issues avail.; reprints avail. **Document type:** *Journal, Academic/Scholarly.* **Description:** Covers nutrition research as it applies to patient care.
Related titles: Microform ed.; Online - full text ed.: ISSN 1541-1087.
Indexed: A22, A35, A36, A37, A38, ASCA, AgBio, Agr, AgrForAb, B21, B25, BIOBASE, BIOSIS Prev, BibAg, C06, C07, C25, CA, CABA, CIN, ChemAb, ChemTitl, CurCont, D01, E12, EMBASE, ESPM, ExcerpMed, F05, F06, F07, F08, F09, FR, FS&TA, Faml, GH, H16, H17, IABS, ISR, IndMed, Inpharma, LT, MEDLINE, MaizeAb, MycolAb, N02, N03, NRN, NSA, P30, P33, P35, P38, P39, PEI, PHN&I, PN&I, R08, R10, R11, R12, RA&MP, RRTA, Reac, S12, SCI, SCOPUS, SD, SoyAb, T02, T05, THA, ToxAb, TriticAb, VITIS, VS, W07, W11.
—BLDSC (4685.780000), CASDDS, GNLM, IE, Infotrieve, Ingenta, INIST, Linda Hall. **CCC.**
Published by: American College of Nutrition, 300 S Duncan Ave, Ste 225, Clearwater, FL 33755. TEL 727-446-6086, FAX 727-446-6202, office@amcollnutr.org, http://www.am-coll-nutr.org/jacn/jacn.htm. Ed. John J Cunningham. adv.: B&W page USD 1,000, color page USD 1,500; 8.25 x 10.875.

613.26 USA ISSN 0002-8223
RM214 CODEN: JADAAE
➤ **AMERICAN DIETETIC ASSOCIATION. JOURNAL.** Variant title: A D A Journal. Text in English. 19??. 12/yr. USD 479 in United States to institutions; USD 494 elsewhere to institutions (effective 2012). adv. bk.rev. abstr.; bibl.; charts; illus. Index. back issues avail.; reprints avail. **Document type:** *Journal, Academic/Scholarly.* **Description:** Publishes reports of original research and other papers covering all aspects of dietetics, including nutrition and diet therapy, community nutrition, education, and administration.
Formerly (until 1925): American Dietetic Association. Bulletin
Related titles: Microform ed.: (from PMC, PQC); Online - full text ed.: ISSN 1878-3570. 200? (from IngentaConnect, ScienceDirect).
Indexed: A01, A03, A20, A22, A25, A26, A33, A34, A35, A36, A37, A38, AHCMS, AIM, ASCA, AgBio, Agr, B&AI, B04, B10, B21, BRD, BibAg, C06, C07, C08, C25, CA, CABA, CIN, CINAHL, CISA, CTA, ChPerI, ChemAb, ChemTitl, Chicano, CurCont, D01, DentInd, DokArb, E04, E05, E08, E12, EMBASE, ESPM, ExcerpMed, F05, F06, F07, F08, F09, F10, F12, FR, FS&TA, Faml, G03, G08, G10, GH, GSA, GSI, H&SSA, H&TI, H06, H11, H12, H13, H16, HlthInd, HospLI, I05, I06, I07, INI, ISR, IndMed, IndVet, Inpharma, LT, M06, MEDLINE, MaizeAb, N02, N03, N04, NRN, OR, P02, P10, P11, P20, P22, P24, P26, P30, P34, P35, P37, P38, P48, P50, P52, P53, P54, P56, PEI, PHN&I, PN&I, PQC, PsycholAb, R10, R11, R12, RA&MP, RRTA, Reac, S02, S03, S08, S09, S12, S13, S16, S23, SCI, SCOPUS, SWR&A, SoyAb, T02, T05, TAR, THA, TriticAb, VS, W03, W07, W09, W11.
—BLDSC (4686.130000), CASDDS, GNLM, IE, Infotrieve, Ingenta, INIST. **CCC.**
Published by: (American Dietetic Association), Elsevier Inc. (Subsidiary of: Elsevier Science & Technology), 360 Park Ave S, New York, NY 10010. TEL 212-989-5800, FAX 212-633-3990, JournalCustomerService-usa@elsevier.com, usinfo-f@elsevier.com. Eds. Jason T Switt, Ryan Lipscomb, Linda van Horn. adv.: B&W page USD 6,500, color page USD 8,710; trim 8 x 10.5. Circ: 70,000 (paid). **Subscr. to:** 6277 Sea Harbor Dr, Orlando, FL 32887. TEL 407-563-6022, 877-839-7126, FAX 407-363-1354.

➤ **AMERICAN INSTITUTE FOR CANCER RESEARCH. NEWSLETTER**; on diet, nutrition and cancer prevention. *see* MEDICAL SCIENCES—Oncology

613.2 USA ISSN 0002-9165
RC584 CODEN: AJCNAC
➤ **THE AMERICAN JOURNAL OF CLINICAL NUTRITION.** Text in English. 1952. m. USD 205 combined subscription domestic to individuals (print & online eds.); USD 230 combined subscription in Canada & Mexico to individuals (print & online eds.); USD 255 combined subscription elsewhere to individuals (print & online eds.); USD 510 combined subscription domestic to institutions (print & online eds.); USD 535 combined subscription in Canada & Mexico to institutions (print & online eds.); USD 560 combined subscription elsewhere to institutions (print & online eds.); USD 40 combined subscription domestic to members (print & online eds.); USD 80 combined subscription foreign to members (print & online eds.) (effective 2011). adv. bk.rev. bibl.; charts; illus. Index. Supplement avail.; back issues avail.; reprints avail. **Document type:** *Journal, Academic/Scholarly.* **Description:** Brings out research contributed by scientists throughout the world, editorials, reviews, special articles, meeting reports.
Formerly (until 1954): Journal of Clinical Nutrition (0095-9871); Incorporates (1950-1958): National Vitamin Foundation, Nutrition Symposium Series (0547-003X)
Related titles: Microfilm ed.: (from PMC, PQC); Online - full text ed.: ISSN 1938-3207. USD 180 to individuals; USD 490 to institutions (effective 2011).
Indexed: A20, A22, A23, A24, A26, A34, A35, A36, A37, A38, ABS&EES, AIIM, AIM, AMED, ASCA, AgBio, Agr, AgrForAb, B&AI, B04, B10, B13, B21, B25, BDM&CN, BIOBASE, BIOSIS Prev, BP, BibAg, C06, C07, C08, C13, C25, C33, CA, CABA, CIN, CINAHL, CTA, ChemAb, ChemTitl, Chicano, CurCont, D01, DBA, DokArb, E04, E05, E08, E12, EMBASE, ESPM, EnerRev, ExcerpMed, F05, F06, F07, F08, F09, F10, F12, FR, FS&TA, Faml, G08, G10, GH, H11, H12, H13, H16, H17, I05, I10, IABS, IDIS, INI, ISR, IndMed, IndVet, Inpharma, Kidney, LT, MEDLINE, MaizeAb, MycolAb, N02, N03, N04, N05, NRN, OR, P02, P10, P11, P13, P20, P24, P26, P30, P33, P35, P37, P38, P39, P48, P50, P52, P53, P54, P56, PEI, PHN&I, PN&I, PQC, PsycholAb, R08, R10, R11, R12, R13, RA&MP, RM&VM, RRTA, Reac, S09, S12, S13, S16, SCI, SCOPUS, SPPI, SoyAb, T02, T05, TAR, TriticAb, VITIS, VS, W07, W09, W11.
—BLDSC (0823.000000), CASDDS, GNLM, IE, Infotrieve, Ingenta, INIST, Linda Hall. **CCC.**
Published by: American Society for Nutrition, 9650 Rockville Pike, Bethesda, MD 20814. TEL 301-634-7050, FAX 301-634-7892, info@nutrition.org, http://www.nutrition.org. Ed. Dennis M Bier. Adv. contact Veronica Purvis TEL 301-634-7791. Circ: 3,350. **Dist. by:** Turpin Distribution Services Ltd., The Bleachery, 143 W St, New Milford, CT 06776. TEL 860-350-0041, FAX 860-350-0036, turpinna@turpin-distribution.com; Turpin Distribution Services Ltd., Pegasus Dr, Stratton Business Park, Biggleswade, Bedfordshire SG18 8QB, United Kingdom. TEL 44-1767-604951, FAX 44-1767-601640, custserv@turpin-distribution.com, http://www.turpin-distribution.com/.

➤ **AMERICAN JOURNAL OF HEALTH PROMOTION.** *see* PHYSICAL FITNESS AND HYGIENE

613.2 USA ISSN 1521-4524
RM258.5
➤ **AMERICAN NUTRACEUTICAL ASSOCIATION. JOURNAL.** Variant title: J A N A. Text in English. 1998. q. free to members (effective 2010). adv. back issues avail. **Document type:** *Journal, Academic/Scholarly.* **Description:** Contains original research articles, comprehensive review articles, timely editorials, opinion articles, book reviews and interviews with leaders in the fields of nutraceuticals, MD's, researchers and others that are involved in the clinical use of nutraceuticals.
Related titles: Online - full text ed.: free (effective 2010).
Indexed: F05, F06, F07, I12.
—BLDSC (4689.250000).
Published by: American Nutraceutical Association, 5120 Selkirk Dr, Ste 100, Birmingham, AL 35242. TEL 205-980-5710, FAX 205-991-9302, info@ana-jana.org. Ed. Dr. Mark Houston.

N O

613.2 VEN ISSN 0798-0752
TX360.V4
ANALES VENEZOLANOS DE NUTRICION. Text in Spanish. 1988. q.
Related titles: Online - full text ed.: free (effective 2011).
Indexed: A01, CA, F03, F04, F10, SCOPUS, T02.
Published by: Fundacion Bengoa, Apdo. Postal 7840, Caracas, 1010, Venezuela.

ANIMAL NUTRITION ASSOCIATION OF CANADA. EASTERN NUTRITION CONFERENCE. PROCEEDINGS. *see* AGRICULTURE—Poultry And Livestock

612.3 CHE ISSN 0250-6807
RM214 CODEN: ANUMDS
➤ **ANNALS OF NUTRITION AND METABOLISM**; European journal of nutrition, metabolic diseases and dietetics. Text in English, French, German. 1981. 8/yr. CHF 3,304, EUR 2,640, USD 3,236 to institutions; CHF 3,628, EUR 2,900, USD 3,550 combined subscription to institutions (print & online eds.) (effective 2012). adv. bibl.; charts; illus. index. back issues avail.; reprints avail. **Document type:** *Journal, Academic/Scholarly.* **Description:** Reports of basic research, primarily on the biochemical and physiological aspects of nutrition.
Formed by the merger of (1947-1981): Annales de la Nutrition et de l'Alimentation (0003-4037); (1970-1981): Nutrition and Metabolism (0029-6678); Which was formerly (1959-1969): Nutritio et Dieta (0550-4031)
Related titles: Microform ed.; Online - full text ed.: ISSN 1421-9697. CHF 3,236, EUR 2,588, USD 3,142 to institutions (effective 2012); Supplement(s): ISSN 1018-9688. 1982.
Indexed: A01, A03, A08, A22, A34, A35, A36, A37, A38, AgBio, Agr, AgrForAb, B21, B25, BIOBASE, BIOSIS Prev, BibAg, C06, C07, C25, C33, CA, CABA, CIN, Cadscan, ChemAb, ChemTitl, CurCont, D01, DBA, DentInd, E01, E12, EMBASE, ExcerpMed, F08, F10, FR, FS&TA, GH, H13, H16, IABS, IBR, IBZ, ISR, IndMed, Inpharma, LT, LeadAb, MEDLINE, MaizeAb, MycolAb, N02, N03, N04, NRN, OR, P10, P11, P19, P20, P22, P24, P26, P30, P33, P37, P38, P39, P48, P50, P52, P53, P54, P56, PHN&I, PN&I, PQC, R10, R11, R12, RA&MP, RRTA, Reac, S12, SCI, SCOPUS, SoyAb, T02, T05, TriticAb, VITIS, VS, W07, W10, W11, Zincscan.
—BLDSC (1043.250000), CASDDS, GNLM, IE, Infotrieve, Ingenta, INIST, Linda Hall. **CCC.**
Published by: (Federation of European Nutrition Societies), S. Karger AG, Allschwilerstr 10, Basel, 4055, Switzerland. TEL 41-61-3061111, FAX 41-61-3061234, karger@karger.ch, http://www.karger.ch. Ed. Ibrahim Elmadfa. adv.: page CHF 1,730; trim 210 x 280. Circ: 1,200.

613.2 USA ISSN 1055-6990
TX341
➤ **ANNUAL EDITIONS: NUTRITION.** Text in English. 1988. a. USD 22.25 per issue (effective 2010). illus. back issues avail. **Document type:** *Journal, Academic/Scholarly.*
Related titles: Online - full text ed.
Published by: McGraw-Hill, Contemporary Learning Series (Subsidiary of: McGraw-Hill Companies, Inc.), 1221 Ave of the Americas, New York, NY 10020. TEL 212-904-2000, FAX 212-512-2000, customer.service@mcgraw-hill.com, http://www.mcgraw-hill.com.

613.2 USA ISSN 0199-9885
QP141.A1 CODEN: ARNTD8
➤ **ANNUAL REVIEW OF NUTRITION.** Text in English. 1981. a. USD 251 combined subscription per issue to institutions (print & online eds.); USD 209 per issue to institutions (print or online ed.) (effective 2012). bibl.; charts; abstr. index, cum.index. back issues avail.; reprint service avail. from PSC. **Document type:** *Journal, Academic/Scholarly.* **Description:** Synthesizes and filters primary research to identify the principal contributions in the field of physiology.
Related titles: Microform ed.: (from PQC); Online - full text ed.: ISSN 1545-4312.
Indexed: A01, A02, A03, A08, A22, A26, A34, A35, A36, A37, A38, ASCA, AgBio, Agr, B&AI, B04, B10, B21, BIOBASE, BIOSIS Prev, BRD, C06, C07, C08, C11, C13, C33, CA, CABA, CIN, CINAHL, CTA, ChemAb, ChemTitl, CurCont, D01, DentInd, E-psyche, E08, E12, EMBASE, ESPM, ExcerpMed, F10, FS&TA, GH, H04, H11, H16, I05, I10, IABS, IBR, IBZ, ISR, IndMed, IndVet, Inpharma, LT, MEDLINE, MycolAb, N02, N03, N04, P10, P11, P15, P19, P20, P22, P24, P26, P30, P33, P37, P48, P50, P52, P53, P54, P56, PHN&I, PN&I, PQC, R08, R09, R10, R12, R13, RA&MP, RM&VM, RRTA, Reac, S01, S04, S12, SCI, SCOPUS, SD, SoyAb, T02, T05, VITIS, VS, W03, W05, W07.
—BLDSC (1524.300000), CASDDS, GNLM, IE, Infotrieve, Ingenta, INIST, Linda Hall. **CCC.**

Published by: Annual Reviews, PO Box 10139, Palo Alto, CA 94303. TEL 650-493-4400, FAX 650-424-0910, 800-523-8635, service@annualreviews.org. Eds. Robert Cousins TEL 352-392-2133, Samuel Gubins.

➤ **ANTHROPOLOGY OF FOOD AND NUTRITION.** *see* FOOD AND FOOD INDUSTRIES

613.26 NLD ISSN 0195-6663
QP136 CODEN: APPTD4

➤ **APPETITE.** Text in English. 1980. 6/yr. EUR 1,371 in Europe to institutions; JPY 148,300 in Japan to institutions; USD 1,220 elsewhere to institutions (effective 2012). adv. bk.rev. illus. Index. reprint service avail. from PSC. **Document type:** *Journal, Academic/Scholarly.* **Description:** Specializes in behavioral nutrition and the cultural, sensory, and physiological influences on choices and intakes of foods and drinks.
Related titles: Online - full text ed.: ISSN 1095-8304. USD 893 (effective 2002) (from IngentaConnect, ScienceDirect).
Indexed: A01, A03, A08, A20, A22, A26, A34, A35, A36, A37, A38, ASCA, AgBio, Agr, AnBeAb, B21, B25, BIOSIS Prev, C06, C07, C25, CA, CABA, CIN, ChemAb, ChemTitl, ChemoAb, CurCont, D01, DentInd, E-psyche, E01, E12, EMBASE, ExcerpMed, F05, F06, F07, F08, F09, F10, FR, FS&TA, FamI, GH, H16, I05, ISR, IndMed, Inpharma, LT, MEDLINE, MaizeAb, MycolAb, N02, N03, N04, NRN, OR, P03, P30, P33, P37, P38, PEI, PHN&I, PN&I, PsycInfo, PsycholAb, R10, R11, R12, R13, RA&MP, RM&VM, RRTA, Reac, S12, S13, S16, SCI, SCOPUS, SoyAb, T02, T05, TAR, THA, TriticAb, VITIS, VS, W07, W11.
—BLDSC (1570.200000), CASDDS, GNLM, IE, Infotrieve, Ingenta, INIST. **CCC.**
Published by: Elsevier BV (Subsidiary of: Elsevier Science & Technology), Radarweg 29, PO Box 211, Amsterdam, 1000 AE, Netherlands. TEL 31-20-4853911, FAX 31-20-4852457, JournalsCustomerServiceEMEA@elsevier.com, http://www.elsevier.nl.

➤ **APPETITT**; magasinet for mat og drikke. *see* HOME ECONOMICS

613.2 VEN ISSN 0004-0622
TX341 CODEN: ALANBH

➤ **ARCHIVOS LATINOAMERICANOS DE NUTRICION.** Abbreviated title: A L A N. Text in English, French, Portuguese, Spanish. 1950. q. USD 20 domestic to individuals; USD 50 in the Americas to individuals; USD 80 in Europe to individuals; USD 140 in the Americas to institutions; USD 160 in the European Union to institutions (effective 2005). adv. bk.rev. abstr.; bibl.; charts. index. 90 p./no.; back issues avail.; reprints avail. **Document type:** *Journal, Academic/Scholarly.* **Description:** Presents results of research in the fields of food and nutrition.
Formerly (until 1966): Archivos Venezolanos de Nutricion (0365-8260)
Related titles: Online - full text ed.: free (effective 2011).
Indexed: A22, A29, A34, A35, A36, A38, ASCA, AgBio, AgrForAb, B20, B21, C01, C25, CA, CABA, CIN, CTA, ChemAb, ChemTitl, CurCont, D01, DentInd, E12, EMBASE, ESPM, ExcerpMed, F08, F10, FS&TA, GH, H16, H17, I10, IBR, IBZ, INI, INIS AtomInd, IndMed, LT, MEDLINE, MaizeAb, N02, N03, N04, NRN, OR, P30, P32, P33, P37, P38, P39, P40, PGegResA, PHN&I, PN&I, R07, R08, R10, R11, R12, RA&MP, RM&VM, RRTA, Reac, S12, S17, SCI, SCOPUS, SoyAb, T02, T05, TAR, TriticAb, VITIS, VS, VirolAbstr, W07, W11.
—BLDSC (1655.300000), CASDDS, GNLM, IE, Infotrieve, Ingenta, INIST, Linda Hall. **CCC.**
Published by: Sociedad Latinoamericana de Nutricion/Latin American Nutrition Society, Apartado Postal 62778, Caracas, Chaco DF 1060, Venezuela. TEL 58-212-2831429, FAX 58-212-2860061, josefelixchavez@cantv.net. Ed. Dr. Jose Felix Chavez P. Circ: 1,000.

613.2 AUS ISSN 0964-7058
QP141.A1 CODEN: APJNFQ

➤ **ASIA PACIFIC JOURNAL OF CLINICAL NUTRITION.** Abbreviated title: A P J C N. Text in English. 1992. q. AUD 195 combined subscription to individuals (print & online eds.); AUD 450 combined subscription to institutions (print & online eds.); AUD 50 per issue (effective 2009). adv. bk.rev. back issues avail.; reprints avail. **Document type:** *Journal, Academic/Scholarly.* **Description:** Promotes the education and training of clinical nutritionists in the region and enhances the practice of human nutrition and related disciplines in their application to health and the prevention of disease.
Incorporates (1976-2000): Nutrition Society of Australia. Proceedings (0314-1004)
Related titles: CD-ROM ed.: AUD 170, USD 100 (effective 2004); for vol.1-11; Online - full text ed.: ISSN 1440-6047. AUD 150 to individuals; USD 300 to institutions (effective 2009).
Indexed: A01, A02, A03, A08, A20, A22, A26, A34, A35, A36, A38, AgBio, AgrForAb, BA, C06, C07, C25, C30, CA, CABA, CurCont, D01, E01, E12, EMBASE, ExcerpMed, F08, F10, F12, FS&TA, GH, H04, H16, H17, Inpharma, LT, MEDLINE, MaizeAb, N02, N03, N04, O01, OR, P20, P22, P30, P32, P33, P34, P37, P38, P39, P40, P48, P50, P54, PGegResA, PGrRegA, PHN&I, PN&I, PQC, R07, R08, R10, R11, R12, R13, RA&MP, RM&VM, RRTA, Reac, S12, S13, S16, SCI, SCOPUS, SD, SoyAb, T02, T05, TAR, TriticAb, VS, W07, W11.
—BLDSC (1742.260680), CASDDS, IE, Infotrieve, Ingenta. **CCC.**
Published by: (Asia Pacific Clinical Nutrition Society), H E C Press, PO Box 4121, McKinnon, VIC 3204, Australia. TEL 61-4-08551702, FAX 61-3-95154544, info@healthyeatingclub.org, http://www.healthyeatingclub.com/. Ed. Dr. Mark Wahlqvist.

➤ **ASIAN CONFERENCE ON DIARRHOEAL DISEASES AND NUTRITION.** *see* MEDICAL SCIENCES

613.2 PAK ISSN 1992-1470
RC620.A1

➤ **ASIAN JOURNAL OF CLINICAL NUTRITION.** Text in English. 2006. 4/yr. **Document type:** *Journal, Academic/Scholarly.* **Description:** Covers all aspect of human nutrition. It promotes the research activities and training of clinical nutritionists in the region and to enhance the practice of human nutrition and related disciplines in their application to health and the prevention of disease. It publishes original research reports, reviews and short communications.
Related titles: Online - full text ed.: ISSN 2077-2033. free (effective 2011).
Indexed: A01, A34, A36, C25, CABA, D01, E12, F10, GH, H16, MaizeAb, N02, N03, N04, P32, PHN&I, RA&MP, SCOPUS, SoyAb, T02, T05, VS.
Published by: A N S I Network, 308 Lasani Town, Sargodha Rd, Faisalabad, 38090, Pakistan. TEL 92-41-8787087, FAX 92-41-8815544, sarwarm@ansimail.org, http://ansinet.com.

615.854 USA

ATKINS: A PASSION FOR HEALTHY LIVING. Text in English. 2000 (June). q. free. illus. **Document type:** *Magazine, Consumer.* **Description:** Offers advice on better health through nutrition. Includes articles, news, and recipes.
Published by: Atkins Center for Complementary Medicine, 152 E 55th St, New York, NY 10022. TEL 212-758-2110, 888-ATKINS8, http://atkinscenter.com.

AUSTRALASIAN COLLEGE OF NUTRITIONAL AND ENVIRONMENTAL MEDICINE. JOURNAL. *see* MEDICAL SCIENCES

AUSTRALIAN TABLE. *see* FOOD AND FOOD INDUSTRIES

613.7 DEU ISSN 1618-9833

B & B AGRAR; die Zeitschrift fuer Bildung und Beratung. (Bildung und Beratung) Text in German. 1948. 6/yr. EUR 18 combined subscription domestic (print & online eds.); EUR 21 combined subscription foreign (print & online eds.); EUR 3.60 newsstand/cover (effective 2010). **Document type:** *Magazine, Trade.*
Former titles (until 2002): Ausbildung und Beratung im Agrarbereich (1618-9825); (until 1995): Ausbildung und Beratung in Land- und Hauswirtschaft (0045-0049); (until 1955): Ausbildung und Beratung in der Landwirtschaft; (until 1952): Nachrichten fuer Beratung und Ausbildung in der Landwirtschaft
Related titles: Online - full text ed.: EUR 15 (effective 2010).
Indexed: IBR, IBZ.
—**CCC.**
Published by: Aid Infodienst - Ernaehrung, Landwirtschaft, Verbraucherschutz e.V., Heilsbachstr 16, Bonn, 53123, Germany. TEL 49-228-84990, FAX 49-228-8499177, aid@aid.de. Ed. Britte Ziegler.

613.2 GBR ISSN 1350-6854

B N F BRIEFING PAPERS. Text in English. 1980. irreg., latest 2009. price varies. back issues avail. **Document type:** *Monographic series, Academic/Scholarly.* **Description:** Covers nutrition during pregnancy, salt intake, obesity, dental health, sports nutrition, food labeling, food fortification, heart disease, cancer, vegetarianism, nutrition in older people, nutrition in infancy, food processing, meat in the diet, and related topics.
—**CCC.**
Published by: British Nutrition Foundation, High Holborn House, 52-54 High Holborn, London, WC1V 6RQ, United Kingdom. TEL 44-20-74046504, FAX 44-20-74046747, postbox@nutrition.org.uk.

613.2 GBR

B N F TASK FORCE REPORTS. Text in English. 1983. irreg., latest 2005. price varies. back issues avail. **Document type:** *Monographic series, Academic/Scholarly.* **Description:** Provide a comprehensive and authoritative review of a particular area of nutrition science and are aimed at researchers, teachers and their students, health professionals, the food industry and government.
Published by: British Nutrition Foundation, High Holborn House, 52-54 High Holborn, London, WC1V 6RQ, United Kingdom. TEL 44-20-74046504, FAX 44-20-74046747, postbox@nutrition.org.uk.

613.2 NZL ISSN 1177-8849

BALANCED NUTRITION INDEX/INDICE DE NUTRICION EQUILIBRADA. Text in English. 2007. irreg. free (effective 2009). **Document type:** *Monographic series, Academic/Scholarly.*
Media: Online - full text.
Published by: Jose D Pergonomas, Pub. Ed. Jose D Perezgonzalez. **Dist. by:** Lulu Press Inc., 3131 RDU Center Dr, Ste 210, Morrisville, NC 27560. TEL 919-459-5858, orders@lulu.com, http://www.lulu.com.

613.2 USA ISSN 1551-3572

➤ **BARIATRIC TIMES**; clinical developments and relevant news in total bariatric patient care. Text in English. 2004 (Sept./Oct.). m. free to qualified personnel (effective 2010). adv. back issues avail. **Document type:** *Journal, Academic/Scholarly.* **Description:** Offers a wide spectrum of multidisciplinary technologies and insights impacting all areas of bariatrics.
Related titles: Online - full text ed.; Spanish ed.: ISSN 1939-4829.
Indexed: A01.
Published by: Matrix Medical Communications, LLC, 1595 Paoli Pike, Ste 103, West Chester, PA 19380. TEL 484-266-0702, 866-325-9907, FAX 484-266-0726, editorial@matrixmedcom.com, http://www.matrixmedcom.com. Pub. Robert L Dougherty TEL 610-325-9905 ext 12.

➤ **BE WELL (MILFORD).** *see* PHYSICAL FITNESS AND HYGIENE

613.26 USA

BETTER HOMES AND GARDENS LIFESTYLE. Text in English. 1982. q. USD 3.99 newsstand/cover; CAD 4.99 newsstand/cover in Canada (effective 2007). adv. illus. **Document type:** *Magazine, Consumer.* **Description:** Compiles recipes for nutritious, low-calorie and low-fat dishes. Provides easy-to-follow diet plans and special tips for cutting calories from everyday favorite foods.
Former titles: Better Homes and Gardens Low Calorie, Low Fat Recipes; Better Homes and Gardens Low Calorie Recipes; Diet and Exercise (0163-0334)
Published by: Meredith Corporation, 1716 Locust St, Des Moines, IA 50309. TEL 515-284-3000, 800-678-8091, FAX 515-284-3058, patrick.taylor@meredith.com, http://www.meredith.com. Pub. Steve Levinson. Adv. contact Diane Claude. B&W page USD 20,925, color page USD 28,560; trim 8 x 10.5. Circ: 400,000 (paid).

613.2 USA ISSN 0405-668X
TX341

BETTER NUTRITION; the shopping magazine for natural living. Text in English. 1938. m. adv. illus. reprints avail. **Document type:** *Magazine, Trade.* **Description:** Educates consumers on the latest industry research and on natural methods for achieving optimal health and enhanced longevity.
Former titles: Better Nutrition for Today's Living; (until 1990): Better Nutrition; Incorporates (in 1990): Today's Living (0743-7285)
Related titles: Microform ed.: (from PQC); Online - full text ed.: ISSN 2162-2655.
Indexed: A01, A02, A03, A04, A08, A26, C06, C07, C08, CINAHL, E08, F10, G05, G06, G07, G08, H03, H11, H12, H13, HlthInd, I05, I06, I07, M01, M02, P02, P10, P19, P20, P24, P34, P48, P53, P54, PMR, PQC, S09, S23, T02.
—BLDSC (1947.085000). **CCC.**
Published by: Active Interest Media, 300 Continental Blvd, Ste 650, El Segundo, CA 90245. TEL 310-356-4100, FAX 310-356-4110, mleighland@aimmedia.com, http://www.aimmedia.com/. Ed. Nicole Brechka TEL 707-604-7531. Pub. Joanna Shaw TEL 800-443-4974.

BEYOND CHANGE; information regarding obesity and obesity surgery. *see* MEDICAL SCIENCES

BIEN-ETRE; le magazine de toute la famille. *see* PHYSICAL FITNESS AND HYGIENE

613.2 631.5 FRA ISSN 1968-0597

BIO & NATURE MAGAZINE. Text in French. 2008. q. EUR 32 for 2 yrs. (effective 2010). **Document type:** *Magazine, Consumer.*
Published by: Lafont Presse, 53 Rue du Chemin Vert, Boulogne-Billancourt, 92100, France. TEL 33-1-46102121, FAX 33-1-45792211, http://www.lafontpresse.fr.

631.5 613.2 FRA ISSN 1963-2169

BIO LINEAIRES. Text in French. 200?. bi-m. EUR 50 (effective 2008). back issues avail. **Document type:** *Magazine, Consumer.*
Related titles: Online - full text ed.: free.
Published by: Karre Vert, 6 Rue Thomas Edison, Saint Medard, 33160, France. TEL 33-5-56054224, FAX 33-5-56700697, biolineaires@wanadoo.fr.

BIO NACHRICHTEN; Zeitschrift fur oekologischen Landbau und gesunde Ernaehrung. *see* AGRICULTURE—Crop Production And Soil

612.3 DEU

BIOHANDEL; das Fachmagazin fuer den Naturkostfachhandel. Text in German. m. EUR 35; EUR 55 combined subscription (print & online eds.) (effective 2009). adv. **Document type:** *Magazine, Consumer.*
Related titles: Online - full text ed.: EUR 40 (effective 2009).
Published by: bio verlag gmbH, Magnolienweg 23, Aschaffenburg, 63741, Germany. TEL 49-6021-44890, FAX 49-6021-4489499, info@bioverlag.de, http://www.bioverlag.de. Ed. Horst Fiedlke. Adv. contact Silvia Michna. B&W page EUR 1,550, color page EUR 2,770; trim 210 x 280. Circ: 7,600 (controlled).

▼ **BIOMEDICINE & PREVENTIVE NUTRITION.** *see* MEDICAL SCIENCES

613.262 USA

BOVINE VETERINARIAN. Text in English. 1993. 8/yr. **Document type:** *Magazine, Trade.* **Description:** Focuses on business management information for bovine veterinarians so they can better assist their beef and dairy clients.
Published by: Vance Publishing Corp., 400 Knightsbridge Pkwy, Lincolnshire, IL 60069. TEL 847-634-2600, 866-647-0918, FAX 847-634-4379, info@vancepublishing.com, http://www.vancepublishing.com.

BRAZILIAN JOURNAL OF FOOD TECHNOLOGY. *see* FOOD AND FOOD INDUSTRIES

612.3 AUS ISSN 0729-2759
RJ216

➤ **BREASTFEEDING REVIEW.** Text in English. 1982. 3/yr. AUD 50 domestic; AUD 56 foreign (effective 2008). adv. bk.rev.; video rev. back issues avail. **Document type:** *Journal, Academic/Scholarly.* **Description:** Provides articles and information on human lactation and its management, including research papers, scientific findings, case studies, articles on social and ethical aspects of lactation, reviews and letters.
Indexed: A26, C06, C07, C08, CA, CINAHL, EMBASE, ExcerpMed, F09, FamI, H12, I05, INI, MEDLINE, P20, P22, P24, P30, P48, P54, PQC, R10, Reac, SCOPUS, T02.
—Ingenta. **CCC.**
Published by: Australian Breastfeeding Association, PO Box 4000, Glen Iris, VIC 3146, Australia. TEL 61-3-98850855, FAX 61-3-98850866, info@breastfeeding.asn.au. adv.: B&W page AUD 600. Circ: 1,500 (paid).

612.3 GBR ISSN 0007-1145
TX501 CODEN: BJNUAV

➤ **THE BRITISH JOURNAL OF NUTRITION**; an international journal of nutritional science. Text in English. 1947. 24/yr. GBP 1,060, EUR 1,723, USD 2,067 to institutions; GBP 1,113, EUR 1,782, USD 2,169 combined subscription to institutions (print & online eds.) (effective 2012). adv. bk.rev. bibl.; charts; illus.; abstr. index. back issues avail.; reprint service avail. from PSC. **Document type:** *Journal, Academic/Scholarly.* **Description:** Devoted to the advancement of the scientific study of nutrition and its application to the maintenance of human and animal health. Includes papers on clinical and human nutrition, as well as general nutrition.
Related titles: Microform ed.: (from PMC, PQC, SWZ); Online - full text ed.: ISSN 1475-2662. GBP 877, EUR 1,401, USD 1,710 to institutions (effective 2012); ◆ Supplement(s): Nutrition Research Reviews. ISSN 0954-4224.
Indexed: A20, A22, A34, A35, A36, A37, A38, ASCA, AgBio, Agr, AgrForAb, B&AI, B04, B10, B21, B25, BA, BIOBASE, BIOSIS Prev, BRD, BibAg, C06, C07, C08, C25, C33, CABA, CIN, CINAHL, CTA, ChemAb, ChemTitl, CurCont, D01, DBA, DentInd, E01, E04, E05, E12, EMBASE, ExcerpMed, F05, F06, F07, F08, F09, F11, F12, FCA, FR, FS&TA, FamI, G11, GH, H13, H16, H17, IABS, ISR, ImmunAb, IndMed, IndVet, Inpharma, LT, MEDLINE, MaizeAb, MycolAb, N02, N03, N04, NRN, O01, OR, P02, P10, P11, P20, P22, P24, P30, P32, P33, P35, P37, P38, P39, P40, P48, P50, P52, P53, P54, P56, PGegResA, PHN&I, PN&I, PQC, R07, R08, R10, R11, R12, R13, RA&MP, RM&VM, RRTA, Reac, S&MA, S04, S12, S13, S16, S17, SAA, SCI, SCOPUS, SoyAb, T05, THA, TriticAb, VITIS, VS, W03, W05, W07, W11.
—BLDSC (2312.000000), CASDDS, GNLM, IE, Infotrieve, Ingenta, INIST, Linda Hall. **CCC.**
Published by: (Nutrition Society), Cambridge University Press, The Edinburgh Bldg, Shaftesbury Rd, Cambridge, CB2 8RU, United Kingdom. TEL 44-1223-312393, FAX 44-1223-315052, journals@cambridge.org, http://www.cambridge.org/uk. Ed. P C Calder. R&P Linda Nicol TEL 44-1223-325702. Adv. contact Rebecca Roberts TEL 44-1223-325083. page GBP 610, page USD 1,160. Circ: 1,500.

▼ ➤ **C I D E S D BOLETIM INFORMATIVO DA SAUDE.** (Centro de Investigacao em Desporto, Saude e Desenvolvimento Humano) *see* PHYSICAL FITNESS AND HYGIENE

➤ **C M U JOURNAL OF SCIENCE.** *see* AGRICULTURE

➤ **(YEARS) C N DAILY PLANNER.** (Child Nutrition) *see* EDUCATION—School Organization And Administration

642.5 613.2 USA
C N SOLUTIONS. (Child Nutrition) Text in English. 2002. q. adv.
Document type: *Newsletter, Trade.* **Description:** Contains recipes for menu planning, informative topics hosted and written by child nutrition professionals and menu promotions designed to increase participation.
Published by: Carroll Services, Inc., 2171 E Francisco Blvd, Ste M, San Rafael, CA 94901. TEL 415-485-5588, FAX 415-485-3825, advertising@CSIfoodpro.com, http://www.csifoodpro.com/. adv.: B&W page USD 3,995; trim 8.5 x 11. Circ: 17,488.

616.39 USA ISSN 0192-6241
RC620
C R C HANDBOOK SERIES IN NUTRITION AND FOOD. Variant title: Handbook Series in Nutrition and Food. Text in English. 1978. irreg., latest 2007, 2nd ed. USD 309.95 per issue (effective 2010). back issues avail. **Document type:** *Handbook/Manual/Guide, Academic/Scholarly.*
—CCC.
Published by: C R C Press, LLC (Subsidiary of: Taylor & Francis Group), 6000 Broken Sound Pky, NW, Ste 300, Boca Raton, FL 33487. TEL 800-272-7737, FAX 800-374-3401, orders@crcpress.com. Eds. Carolyn D Berdanier, Elaine B Feldman, Johanna Dwyer.

CAB REVIEWS: PERSPECTIVES IN AGRICULTURE, VETERINARY SCIENCE, NUTRITION AND NATURAL RESOURCES. *see* AGRICULTURE

613.2 FRA ISSN 0007-9960
TX551 CODEN: CNDQA8
CAHIERS DE NUTRITION ET DE DIETETIQUE. Text in French. 1966. 6/yr. EUR 187 in Europe to institutions; EUR 163.57 in France to institutions; JPY 31,800 in Japan to institutions; USD 257 elsewhere to institutions (effective 2012). adv. bk.rev. charts; illus. **Document type:** *Journal, Academic/Scholarly.* **Description:** Establishes a relationship between the medical world and the food industry. Publishes original articles and general reviews.
Related titles: Online - full text ed.: (from ScienceDirect).
Indexed: A22, A34, A35, A36, A38, C25, CABA, CIN, ChemAb, ChemTitl, D01, E12, EMBASE, ExcerpMed, FR, FS&TA, GH, H16, LT, MaizeAb, N02, N03, N04, P32, P33, PHN&I, PN&I, R12, R13, RA&MP, RM&VM, RRTA, S12, SCOPUS, SoyAb, T05, VS, W11.
—BLDSC (2950.200000), CASDDS, GNLM, IE, Infotrieve, Ingenta, INIST, Linda Hall. **CCC.**
Published by: Elsevier Masson (Subsidiary of: Elsevier Health Sciences), 62 Rue Camille Desmoulins, Issy les Moulineaux, Cedex 92442, France. TEL 33-1-71165500, infos@elsevier-masson.fr. Ed. Cyrille Costa. Circ: 3,500 (controlled).

613.2 JAM ISSN 0376-7655
TX360.C35
CAJANUS. Text in English. 1968. q. USD 6 in developing nations; USD 12 in United States (effective 1999). bk.rev. bibl.; charts. index. **Document type:** *Newsletter.* **Description:** Research articles on nutrition and dietary intake, focusing on the population of the Caribbean.
Indexed: FS&TA, REE&TA.
Published by: Caribbean Food and Nutrition Institute, University of the West Indies, U.W.I. Mona Campus, PO Box 140, Kingston, 7, Jamaica. TEL 876-927-1540-1, FAX 876-927-1927, TELEX 3705. Ed. Clare A Forrester. Circ: 2,028. **Co-sponsor:** Pan American Health Organization/Organizacion Panamericana de la Salud.

613.26 USA ISSN 1049-1791
CALORIE CONTROL COMMENTARY. Text in English. 1979. 2/yr. free in United States; USD 10 foreign (effective 2000). charts; illus.; stat. back issues avail. **Document type:** *Newsletter.* **Description:** Newsletter summarizing scientific, regulatory and other developments relating to sweeteners, fat replacers, dieting, weight control and low-calorie - reduced fat foods and beverages.
Published by: Calorie Control Council, 5775 Peachtree Dunwoody Rd, Ste 500 G, Atlanta, GA 30342. TEL 404-252-3663, FAX 404-252-0774. Ed. Keith C Keeney. R&P Keith Keeney. Circ: 12,000 (controlled).

613.2 CAN ISSN 1486-3847
CODEN: JCDTAH
➤ **CANADIAN JOURNAL OF DIETETIC PRACTICE AND RESEARCH/ REVUE CANADIENNE DE LA PRACTIQUE ET DE LA RECHERCHE EN DIETETIQUE.** Text in English, French. 1939. q. CAD 85 domestic; USD 85 foreign; CAD 25 per issue domestic; USD 25 per issue foreign (effective 2004). adv. bk.rev. abstr.; charts; illus. index. **Document type:** *Journal, Academic/Scholarly.* **Description:** Publishes articles and research reports in nutrition, dietetics, food administration and management.
Formerly (until 1998): Canadian Dietetic Association. Journal (0008-3399)
Related titles: Microfilm ed.: (from PQC); Online - full text ed.
Indexed: A22, A34, A36, A38, ASCA, Agr, C03, C06, C07, C08, CA, CABA, CBCARef, CINAHL, ChemAb, CurCont, D01, EMBASE, ExcerpMed, FS&TA, GH, LT, MEDLINE, N02, N03, N04, NRN, P11, P19, P20, P22, P24, P26, P30, P37, P48, P50, P52, P54, P56, PHN&I, PQC, R10, R11, RRTA, Reac, SCI, SCOPUS, SD, T02, T05, W07, W11.
—BLDSC (3031.138000), CASDDS, GNLM, IE, Infotrieve, Ingenta. **CCC.**
Published by: Dietitians of Canada, 480 University Ave, Ste 604, Toronto, ON M5G 1V2, Canada. TEL 416-596-0857, FAX 416-596-0603. Ed. Dawna Royall. Adv. contact Joan Embury. Circ: 6,000.

➤ **CAPITAL SANTE.** *see* PHYSICAL FITNESS AND HYGIENE

613.25 USA ISSN 1544-497X
CARBHEALTH MAGAZINE. Text in English. 2002 (Oct.). m. USD 19.99 domestic; USD 29.99 in Canada; USD 49.99 in United Kingdom (effective 2003). **Document type:** *Magazine, Consumer.* **Description:** Covers the low-carb diet, including features in recipes, health, dieting tips and tricks, and articles by experienced writers.
Address: PO Box 604, Wappingers Falls, NY 12590. Ed. Tiffany Anthony.

613.2 641.5 BEL ISSN 1782-0162
LA CERISE. Text in French. 2005. m. free. **Document type:** *Magazine, Consumer.*
Related titles: Dutch ed.: De Kers. ISSN 1782-0154.
Published by: Sciences Today, 18-17 Rue Rixensart, Genval, 1332, Belgium.

613.2 CHN ISSN 1007-810X
CHANGWAI YU CHANGNEI YINGYANG/PARENTERAL & ENTERAL NUTRITION. Text in Chinese. 1994. bi-m. CNY 10 newsstand/cover (effective 2006). **Document type:** *Journal, Academic/Scholarly.*
Related titles: Online - full text ed.
Address: 305, Zhongshan Dong Lu, Nanjing, 210002, China. TEL 86-25-80860942, FAX 86-25-84803956.

CHINESE MARKETS FOR FATTY ACIDS. *see* BUSINESS AND ECONOMICS—Marketing And Purchasing

CHINESE MARKETS FOR FATTY ALCOHOL. *see* BUSINESS AND ECONOMICS—Marketing And Purchasing

613.2 FRA ISSN 1639-2558
CHOLE-DOC. Text in French. 1990. bi-m. **Document type:** *Journal, Trade.*
Published by: Centre de Recherche et d'Information Nutritionnelles (C E R I N), 45 rue Saint Lazare, Paris Cedex 09, 75314, France. TEL 33-1-49707220, FAX 33-1-42806413, nutrition-fr@cerin.org, http://www.cerin.org/.

▼ **CHOLESTEROL.** *see* MEDICAL SCIENCES

CLICK! SANATATE. *see* PHYSICAL FITNESS AND HYGIENE

613.2 NLD ISSN 0261-5614
CODEN: CLNUDP
➤ **CLINICAL NUTRITION.** Text in English. 1982. 6/yr. EUR 1,418 in Europe to institutions; JPY 153,100 in Japan to institutions; USD 1,321 elsewhere to institutions (effective 2012). adv. bk.rev. back issues avail. **Document type:** *Journal, Academic/Scholarly.* **Description:** Provides essential scientific information on nutritional and metabolic care and the relationship between nutrition and disease both in the setting of basic science and clinical practice.
Related titles: Microform ed.: (from PQC); Online - full text ed.: ISSN 1532-1983 (from ScienceDirect); Supplement(s): ISSN 1744-1161.
Indexed: A20, A22, A26, A34, A35, A36, A37, A38, ASCA, AgBio, AgrForAb, B21, BIOBASE, C06, C07, C08, CA, CABA, CIN, CINAHL, CTA, ChemAb, ChemTitl, CurCont, D01, E01, E12, EMBASE, ExcerpMed, F08, F12, FS&TA, GH, H12, H16, H17, I05, IABS, IBR, IBZ, INI, IndMed, IndVet, Inpharma, LT, MEDLINE, MaizeAb, N02, N03, N04, NRN, P30, P32, P33, P35, PHN&I, PN&I, R10, R11, R12, R13, RA&MP, RRTA, Reac, RefZh, S12, SCI, SCOPUS, SoyAb, T02, T05, TriticAb, VITIS, VS, W07.
—BLDSC (3286.314500), CASDDS, GNLM, IE, Infotrieve, Ingenta, INIST. **CCC.**
Published by: (European Society for Clinical Nutrition and Metabolism CHE), Elsevier BV (Subsidiary of: Elsevier Science & Technology), Radarweg 29, PO Box 211, Amsterdam, 1000 AE, Netherlands. TEL 31-20-4853911, FAX 31-20-4852457, JournalsCustomerServiceEMEA@elsevier.com, http://www.elsevier.nl. Ed. N E P Deutz.

613.2 USA ISSN 1938-8640
CLINICAL NUTRITION INSIGHT; evidence-based reports for improved patient care. Text in English. 1974. m. USD 254 domestic to institutions; USD 345 foreign to institutions (effective 2011). back issues avail. **Document type:** *Newsletter, Academic/Scholarly.* **Description:** Covers developments in nutritional research, recommendations, and guidelines affecting every type of patient.
Formerly (until 2007): Nutrition & the M D (0732-0167)
Related titles: Online - full text ed.: USD 175.50 domestic for academic site license; USD 195.50 foreign for academic site license; USD 195.75 domestic for corporate site license; USD 215.75 foreign for corporate site license (effective 2002).
Indexed: A22, Agr, C06, C07, C08, CINAHL, P50.
—IE. **CCC.**
Published by: Lippincott Williams & Wilkins (Subsidiary of: Wolters Kluwer N.V.), 530 Walnut St, Philadelphia, PA 19106. TEL 215-521-8300, FAX 215-521-8902, customerservice@lww.com. Ed. Kevin Lomangino.

616.39 GBR ISSN 1758-8103
▼ ➤ **CLINICAL OBESITY.** Text in English. 2011. bi-m. **Document type:** *Journal, Academic/Scholarly.*
Related titles: Online - full text ed.: ISSN 1758-8111.
Published by: (International Association for the Study of Obesity), Wiley-Blackwell Publishing Ltd. (Subsidiary of: John Wiley & Sons, Inc.), 9600 Garsington Rd, Oxford, OX4 2DQ, United Kingdom. TEL 44-1865-776868, FAX 44-1865-714591, customerservices@blackwellpublishing.com, http://www.wiley.com/WileyCDA/.

➤ **CO-OP NEWS (HANOVER).** *see* FOOD AND FOOD INDUSTRIES—Grocery Trade

➤ **COCINA LIGERA EXTRA.** *see* HOME ECONOMICS

➤ **COCINA LIGERA Y VIDA SANA.** *see* HOME ECONOMICS

➤ **COMPARATIVE EXERCISE PHYSIOLOGY;** the international journal of exercise physiology, biomechanics and nutrition. *see* SPORTS AND GAMES—Horses And Horsemanship

613.2 GBR
THE COMPOSITION OF FOODS. Variant title: McCance and Widdowson's The Composition of Foods. Text in English. 19??. irreg., latest 2002, Sept. price varies. Supplement avail.; back issues avail. **Document type:** *Monographic series, Academic/Scholarly.* **Description:** Contains revised and updated nutrient data on nearly 1,200 foods.
Published by: Royal Society of Chemistry, Burlington House, Piccadilly, London, W1J 0BA, United Kingdom. TEL 44-20-74378656, FAX 44-20-74378883, http://www.rsc.org.

CONSCIOUS CHOICE; the journal of ecology and natural living. *see* ENVIRONMENTAL STUDIES

CONSCIOUS LIVING FREMANTLE. *see* ENVIRONMENTAL STUDIES

COOKING LIGHT; the magazine of food and fitness. *see* HOME ECONOMICS

CORRIERE SALUTE. *see* PHYSICAL FITNESS AND HYGIENE

613.2 GBR ISSN 1746-0034
COUNTRY KITCHEN; cooking with traditional, seasonal and fresh food. Text in English. 2005. m. GBP 35.76 domestic; GBP 41.28 in Europe; GBP 46.80 elsewhere; GBP 3.25 per issue domestic; GBP 4.25 per issue in Europe; GBP 4.75 per issue elsewhere (effective 2010). adv. back issues avail. **Document type:** *Magazine, Consumer.* **Description:** Aimed at people who either grow their own food or buy from farmer's markets or want to buy the best quality foods from supermarkets. Contains seasonal recipes.
Related titles: Online - full text ed.
Published by: Kelsey Publishing Ltd., Cudham Tithe Barn, Berry's Hill, Cudham, Kent TN16 3AG, United Kingdom. TEL 44-1959-541444, FAX 44-1959-541400, info@kelsey.co.uk, http://www.kelsey.co.uk. Ed. Rachel Graham. Pub. Stephen Curtis. Adv. contact Sue Loome TEL 44-1342-301731.

613.2 FRA ISSN 1959-2388
CROQUER LA VIE DANS SON ASSIETTE. Text in French. 2007. q. back issues avail. **Document type:** *Newsletter, Consumer.*
Published by: Institut Europeen de Dietetique et Micronutrition (I E D M), 20 Rue Emeriau, Paris, 75015, France. TEL 33-1-53860081, FAX 33-1-53860082.

613.2 MEX ISSN 0186-3274
➤ **CUADERNOS DE NUTRICION.** Text in Spanish. 1981. bi-m. MXN 150, USD 50; MXN 25 newsstand/cover (effective 2002). adv. bk.rev. illus. cum.index: 1992-1997. **Document type:** *Journal, Academic/Scholarly.* **Description:** Includes articles on basic nutrition, economics, production, food technology, and social aspects like food habits and traditions.
Indexed: C01, P30.
Published by: (Fomento de Nutricion y Salud), Cuadernos de Nutricion A.C., ALTATA 51 P.B., Col Hipodromo de la Condesa, Mexico City, DF 06170, Mexico. TEL 52-5-5151939, FAX 52-5-2726207. Ed., R&P Dr. Hector Bourges Rodriguez. Adv. contact Enrique Rios. page MXN 11,500; trim 275 x 210. Circ: 10,000 (controlled). **Dist. by:** Publicaciones CITEM, S.A. de C. V. Mier y Pesado 126 y 128, Col Del Valle, Mexico City, DF 03100, Mexico. TEL 52-5-6874699.

613.2 ITA ISSN 1974-000X
CURARSI MANGIANDO. Variant title: Riza Curarsi Mangiando. Text in Italian. 2008. m. EUR 33 (effective 2010). **Document type:** *Magazine, Consumer.*
Published by: Edizioni Riza, Via Luigi Anelli 1, Milan, 20122, Italy. TEL 39-02-5845961, info@riza.it, http://www.riza.it.

613.2 NLD ISSN 1573-4013
RC584
➤ **CURRENT NUTRITION & FOOD SCIENCE.** Text in English. 2005 (Jan). q. USD 480 to institutions (print or online ed.) (effective 2012). back issues avail.; reprints avail. **Document type:** *Journal, Academic/Scholarly.* **Description:** Publishes frontier reviews on all the latest advances on basic and clinical nutrition and food sciences.
Related titles: Online - full text ed.: (from IngentaConnect).
Indexed: A01, B&BAb, B19, B21, C06, C07, CA, CTA, EMBASE, ESPM, ExcerpMed, F05, F06, F07, F10, I10, ImmunAb, NSA, P30, SCOPUS, T02.
—IE, Ingenta. **CCC.**
Published by: Bentham Science Publishers Ltd., PO Box 294, Bussum, 1400 AG, Netherlands. TEL 31-35-6923800, FAX 31-35-6980150, sales@bentham.org, http://www.bentham.org. Ed. Fidel Toldra. **Subscr. to:** Bentham Science Publishers Ltd., c/o Richard E Morrissy, PO Box 446, Oak Park, IL 60301. TEL 312-413-5867, FAX 312-996-7107, subscriptions@bentham.org.

612.3 USA ISSN 1363-1950
RM214 CODEN: COCMF3
➤ **CURRENT OPINION IN CLINICAL NUTRITION AND METABOLIC CARE.** Text in English. 1998. bi-m. USD 1,254 domestic to institutions; USD 1,346 foreign to institutions (effective 2011). adv. back issues avail.; reprints avail. **Document type:** *Journal, Academic/Scholarly.* **Description:** Covers key subjects such as protein and amino acid metabolism, biology and nutrition, nutrition and the intensive care unit, lipid metabolism and therapy, anabolic and catabolic signals etc.
Related titles: Online - full text ed.: ISSN 1473-6519. USD 273 to individuals (effective 2011).
Indexed: A34, A35, A36, A37, A38, AgBio, C06, C07, CABA, CurCont, D01, E-psyche, E12, EMBASE, ExcerpMed, GH, H16, IndMed, LT, MEDLINE, N02, N03, N04, P30, P33, P39, PN&I, R10, R12, RA&MP, RM&VM, RRTA, Reac, S12, SCI, SCOPUS, SoyAb, T05, VS, W07, W11.
—BLDSC (3500.773530), CASDDS, IE, Infotrieve, Ingenta, INIST. **CCC.**
Published by: Lippincott Williams & Wilkins (Subsidiary of: Wolters Kluwer N.V.), 530 Walnut St, Philadelphia, PA 19106. TEL 215-521-8300, FAX 215-521-8902, customerservice@lww.com, http://www.lww.com. Eds. Luc A Cynober, Yvon A Carpentier. Circ: 250.

613.28 USA ISSN 1540-7535
QP144.F85 CODEN: CTNRC3
➤ **CURRENT TOPICS IN NUTRACEUTICAL RESEARCH;** an international scientific journal for decision makers in nutraceutical industry. Text in English. 2003 (Feb.). q. USD 264 to individuals; USD 484 to institutions (effective 2010). adv. **Document type:** *Journal, Academic/Scholarly.* **Description:** Aims to provide scientific data to students, researchers, healthcare providers, and the decision makers in the nutraceutical industry to help make informed choices about nutraceuticals.
Indexed: A01, A34, A35, A36, A38, AgBio, B01, B07, B25, BIOSIS Prev, C25, C30, CA, CABA, CurCont, D01, E12, EMBASE, ExcerpMed, F05, F06, F07, F08, F10, F12, FS&TA, GH, H16, IndVet, LT, MaizeAb, MycolAb, N02, N03, N04, P30, P32, P33, P37, P40, P48, P50, P52, P56, PGegResA, PHN&I, PN&I, PQC, R10, R11, R12, R13, RA&MP, RM&VM, RRTA, Reac, S12, S13, S16, SCI, SCOPUS, SoyAb, T02, T05, TriticAb, VS, W07.
—BLDSC (3504.893600), IE, Ingenta. **CCC.**
Published by: New Century Health Publishers, LLC, PO Box 175, Coppell, TX 75019. FAX 940-565-8148, nchpjournals@gmail.com, http://www.newcenturyhealthpublishers.com.

613.2 NZL ISSN 1176-1210
D A S H. (Diet, Adventure, Sport and Health) Text in English. 2003. bi-m. NZD 50 (effective 2008). adv. **Document type:** *Magazine, Consumer.*
Published by: Dash Magazine, PO Box 9392, Newmarket, Auckland, New Zealand. TEL 64-9-3070208. Adv. contact Phil Clode.

D N O NIEUWS. (Diabetes and Nutrition Organization) *see* MEDICAL SCIENCES—Endocrinology

613.2 USA
CODEN: DACDAK
DAIRY COUNCIL DIGEST; an interpretive review of recent nutrition research. Text in English. 1929. bi-m. free (effective 2010). illus. index. back issues avail.; reprints avail. **Document type:** *Newsletter, Academic/Scholarly.* **Description:** Covers recent research information for nutrition professionals.
Media: Online - full text. **Related titles:** Microform ed.: (from PQC).
Indexed: B16, CHNI, G08, H11, H12, HlthInd, P10, P11, P16, PQC.
—CASDDS.
Published by: National Dairy Council, O'Hare International Center, 10255 W Higgins Rd, Ste 900, Rosemont, IL 60018. TEL 847-803-2000, FAX 847-803-2077, ndc@dairyinformation.com. Ed. Lois D McBean.

613.2 JPN ISSN 1344-4050
CODEN: DTKKEE
DAIZU TAMPAKUSHITSU KENKYU/NUTRITIONAL SCIENCE OF SOY PROTEIN, JAPAN. Text in Japanese; Summaries in English. 1980. a. **Document type:** *Academic/Scholarly.*
Former titles (until 1997): Daizu Tanpakushitsu Kenkyukai Kaishi/Soy Protein Research Committee. Report (0919-9535); (until 1993): Daizu Tanpakushitsu Eiyo Kenkyukai Kaishi/Nutritional Science of Soy Protein (0288-6219)
Indexed: A34, A35, A36, AgBio, C25, C30, CABA, ChemAb, D01, E12, F08, FCA, FS&TA, GH, H16, MaizeAb, N02, N03, N04, N05, O01, P32, P40, PGegResA, PHN&I, R13, S17, SoyAb, TriticAb, VS, W10.
—BLDSC (8360.730000), CASDDS.
Published by: Fuji Tanpakushitsu Kenkyu Shinko Zaidan/Fuji Foundation for Protein Research, 1 Sumiyoshi-cho, Izumisano, Osaka 598-8540, Japan. TEL 81-72-4631764, FAX 81-72-4631756, foundation@fujioil.co.jp, http://www.fujioil.co.jp/daizu/.

▼ **DELCIOUS BYTE EZINE.** *see* NEW AGE PUBLICATIONS

613.2 USA
DESK REFERENCES. Text in English. 200?. irreg. **Document type:** *Handbook/Manual/Guide, Trade.* **Description:** Guides for nutrition and health issues.
Related titles: Online - full text ed.: ISSN 2154-4530.
Published by: C R C Press, LLC (Subsidiary of: Taylor & Francis Group), 6000 Broken Sound Pky, NW, Ste 300, Boca Raton, FL 33487. TEL 561-994-0555, FAX 561-989-9732, journals@crcpress.com, http://www.crcpress.com.

DIABETES CARE AND EDUCATION NEWSLETTER. *see* MEDICAL SCIENCES—Endocrinology

613.2 AUS ISSN 1839-0587
DIABETIC LIVING. Text in English. 200?. bi-m. AUD 35 (effective 2011). adv. **Document type:** *Magazine, Consumer.* **Description:** Provides information on recipes for people with diabetes. It offers lifestyle articles, exersice tips and information.
Published by: Pacific Magazines Pty Ltd., Media City, 8 Central Ave, Eveleigh, NSW 2015, Australia. TEL 61-2-93942000, subscriptions@pacpubs.com.au. Eds. Erica Goatly TEL 61-2-94643335, Julia Zaetta TEL 61-2-94642649. Adv. contact Rhonda Maunder TEL 61-2-94643250. Circ: 57,387. **Subscr. to:** Subscribe Today, GPO Box 4983, Sydney, NSW 2001, Australia. TEL 61-2-82965425, FAX 61-2-92793161, subscriptions@pacificmags.com.au, http://www.subscribetoday.com.au.

DIABETIC LIVING. *see* MEDICAL SCIENCES—Endocrinology

613.2 DEU ISSN 1862-0620
DIAET UND INFORMATION. Text in German. 19??. bi-m. adv. **Document type:** *Magazine, Trade.*
Published by: Karl F. Haug Verlag in MVS Medizinverlage Stuttgart GmbH & Co. KG (Subsidiary of: Georg Thieme Verlag), Oswald-Hesse-Str 50, Stuttgart, 70469, Germany. TEL 49-711-89310, FAX 49-711-8931706, kunden.service@thieme.de, http://www.haug-verlag.de. adv.: B&W page EUR 1,390, color page EUR 2,387. Circ: 4,300 (controlled).

612.23 ARG ISSN 0328-1310
DIAETA. Text in Spanish. 1981. q. ARS 200 (effective 2010). back issues avail. **Document type:** *Journal, Academic/Scholarly.*
Related titles: Online - full text ed.: ISSN 1852-7337. 2002.
Published by: Asociación Argentina de Dietistas y Nutricionistas Dietistas, Viamonte, 1328 Piso 7 Ofic. 25, Buenos Aires, C1053ACB, Argentina. TEL 54-11-43743090, FAX 54-11-43743301, aadyn@aadynd.org.ar. Ed. Marina Wallinger.

613.2 DEU ISSN 1861-955X
DIAITA. Text in German. 2005. q. EUR 29.95 (effective 2007). adv. **Document type:** *Magazine, Trade.*
Published by: Fachgesellschaft fuer Ernaehrungstherapie und Praevention e.V., Mariahilfstr 9, Aachen, 52062, Germany. TEL 49-241-961030, FAX 49-241-9610322, baumbach@fet-ev.de, http://www.fet-ev.de. adv.: color page EUR 1,000. Circ: 3,480 (paid).

613.2 JPN
DIET & BEAUTY/DAIETTO & BYUUTI. Text in Japanese. m. JPY 10,000 (effective 2008). **Document type:** *Magazine, Consumer.*
Related titles: Online - full content ed.
Published by: C M P Japan Co.,Ltd. (Subsidiary of: C M P Asia Ltd.), Kanda 91 Bldg. 2F, 1-8-3, Kaji-cho, Chiyoda-ku, Tokyo, 101-0044, Japan. info@cmpjapan.com, http://www.cmpjapan.com/.

613.2 613.7 USA
DIET & NUTRITION SOURCEBOOK. Text in English. 1996. irreg., latest 2006, 3rd ed. USD 84 3rd ed. (effective 2008). charts; illus.; stat. master index. **Document type:** *Magazine, Consumer.* **Description:** Offers consumers advice on nutrition and weight control.
Related titles: ◆ Series of: Omnigraphics Health Reference Series.
Published by: Omnigraphics, Inc., PO Box 31-1640, Detroit, MI 48231. TEL 313-961-1340, 800-234-1340, FAX 313-961-1383, 800-875-1340, info@omnigraphics.com. Eds. Joyce Brennfleck Shannon, Karen Bellenir. Pub. Frederick G Ruffner Jr.

613.26 CZE ISSN 1214-8784
DIETA. Text in Czech. 2004. m. CZK 390 (effective 2011). adv. **Document type:** *Magazine, Consumer.*
Published by: Mlada Fronta, Mezi Vodami 1952/9, Prague 4, 14300, Czech Republic. TEL 420-2-25276201, FAX 420-2-25276222, online@mf.cz. Ed. Petra Lamschova. Adv. contact Daniela Caplicka.

613.26 USA ISSN 1062-1121
DIETARY MANAGER MAGAZINE. Text in English. 1992. 10/yr. USD 40 (effective 2005). adv. bk.rev. **Document type:** *Magazine, Trade.* **Description:** A valuable management and training tool for professionals in non-commercial food service.
Published by: Dietary Managers Association, 406 Surrey Woods Dr., St. Charles, IL 60174-2386. TEL 630-587-6336, 800-323-1908, FAX 630-587-6308. Ed. Diane Everett. Adv. contact Susan Wrona. page USD 647; trim 10.88 x 8.13. Circ: 16,750.

THE DIETARY SUPPLEMENT. *see* PHARMACY AND PHARMACOLOGY

613.26 ITA ISSN 1974-5354
DIETE. Text in Italian. 2008. bi-m. **Document type:** *Magazine, Consumer.*
Published by: Sprea Editori Srl, Via Torino 51, Cernusco sul Naviglio, MI 20063, Italy. TEL 39-02-92432222, FAX 39-02-92432236, editori@sprea.it, http://www.sprea.it.

613.26 CAN ISSN 0834-3160
DIETETIQUE EN ACTION. Text in English, French. 1986. 3/yr. CAD 58.85 (effective 1998). bk.rev. **Document type:** *Bulletin.*
Indexed: PdeR.
Published by: Ordre Professionel des Dietetistes du Quebec, 1425 bd Rene Levesque O, Bur 703, Montreal, PQ H3G 1T7, Canada. TEL 514-393-3733, FAX 514-393-3582. Ed. Annie Langlois. adv.: B&W page CAD 615, color page CAD 1,345; trim 11 x 8.5. Circ: 2,500.

613.2 USA
DIETITIAN'S EDGE. Text in English. bi-m. USD 20; USD 5 newsstand/cover (effective 2001). adv.
Published by: Dietitian's Edge LLC, 70 Hilltop Rd, 3rd fl, Ramsey, NJ 07446. TEL 201-825-2552, FAX 201-825-0553. Ed. Tamara Schryver. Adv. contact Heather Shanley.

613.2 USA ISSN 1542-8214
DIGESTION & DIET HEALTH MONITOR. Text in English. 2000. q. free. **Document type:** *Magazine, Consumer.*
Published by: Data Centrum Communications, Inc., 650 From Rd, 2nd Fl, Paramus, NJ 07652. TEL 201-391-1911, FAX 201-225-1440, info@healthmonitor.com, http://www.healthmonitor.com.

613.2 ITA ISSN 1594-719X
DIMAGRIRE. Variant title: Riza Dimagrire. Text in Italian. 2002. m. EUR 32 (effective 2010). **Document type:** *Magazine, Consumer.*
Published by: Edizioni Riza, Via Luigi Anelli 1, Milan, 20122, Italy. TEL 39-02-5845961, info@riza.it, http://www.riza.it.

613.2 POL ISSN 1643-6202
DOBRE RADY. DIETY ODCHUDZAJACE. Variant title: Diety Odchudzajace. Text in Polish. 2002. 2/yr. adv. **Document type:** *Magazine, Consumer.*
Published by: Hubert Burda Media, ul Warecka 11a, Warsaw, 00034, Poland. TEL 48-22-4488000, FAX 48-22-4488001, kontakt@burdamedia.pl, http://www.burdamedia.pl.

613.2 CHN ISSN 1672-5018
DONGFANG SHILIAO YU BAOJIAN/ORIENTAL DIET, THERAPY & HEALTHCARE. Text in Chinese. 1976. m. CNY 69.60 (effective 2009). **Document type:** *Magazine, Consumer.*
Related titles: Online - full text ed.
Published by: Dongfang Shiliao yu Baojian Zazhishe, 113, Shaoshan Zhong Lu, Changsha, 410007, China. TEL 86-731-5540052, FAX 86-731-5556807.

DONGFANG YANGSHENG. *see* PHYSICAL FITNESS AND HYGIENE

DOSSIER MEDICINA; rivista medica su benessere e salute. *see* PHYSICAL FITNESS AND HYGIENE

613.2 NLD ISSN 1751-4991
RM214
E - S P E N; the European e-journal of clinical nutrition and metabolism. Text in English. 2006. bi-m. EUR 527 in Europe to institutions; JPY 76,800 in Japan to institutions; USD 670 elsewhere to institutions (effective 2011). **Document type:** *Journal, Academic/Scholarly.* **Description:** Addresses the educational aspects of nutritional and metabolic care and the relationship between nutrition and disease in the setting of basic science and clinical practice.
Media: Online - full content. **Related titles:** Online - full text ed.: (from ScienceDirect).
Indexed: A26, EMBASE, ExcerpMed, I05, SCOPUS.
—BLDSC (3638.675000), IE, Ingenta. **CCC.**
Published by: (European Society for Clinical Nutrition and Metabolism CHE), Elsevier BV (Subsidiary of: Elsevier Science & Technology), Radarweg 29, PO Box 211, Amsterdam, 1000 AE, Netherlands. TEL 31-20-4853911, FAX 31-20-4852457, JournalsCustomerServiceEMEA@elsevier.com, http://www.elsevier.nl. Ed. N E P Deutz.

613.2 NLD ISSN 1567-651X
E-ZINE VOEDINGONLINE. Text in Dutch. 2001. m. free (effective 2011).
Media: Online - full text.
Published by: VoedingOnline, Broeksloot 10, Zegveld, 3474 HP, Netherlands. TEL 31-348-421593, FAX 31-348-691114, info@voedingonline.nl, http://www.voedingonline.nl. Ed. Manon A Verheul-Koot.

613.2 CAN ISSN 1719-8291
EAT YOUR WAY TO HEALTH. Text in English. 2006. q. **Document type:** *Magazine, Consumer.*
Published by: Sun Media Corp./Corporation Sun Media, 333 King St. East, Toronto, ON M5A 3X5, Canada. TEL 416-947-2222, http://www.sunmedia.ca, http://www.quebecor.com/NewspapersWeeklies/Dailies.aspx?Culture=en.

EATING AND WEIGHT DISORDERS (ONLINE); studies on anorexia, bulimia and obesity. *see* MEDICAL SCIENCES—Psychiatry And Neurology

EATING DISORDERS REVIEW; current clinical information for the professional treating eating disorders. *see* MEDICAL SCIENCES—Psychiatry And Neurology

EATING WELL; where good taste meets good health. *see* FOOD AND FOOD INDUSTRIES

613.2 USA ISSN 0367-0244
TX341 CODEN: ECFNBN
➤ **ECOLOGY OF FOOD AND NUTRITION.** Text in French. 1971. bi-m. GBP 962 combined subscription in United Kingdom to institutions (print & online eds.); EUR 994, USD 1,250 combined subscription to institutions (print & online eds.) (effective 2012). adv. bk.rev. bibl.; charts; illus.; stat. index. back issues avail.; reprint service avail. from PSC. **Document type:** *Journal, Academic/Scholarly.* **Description:** Emphasizes foods and their utilization in satisfying the nutritional needs of mankind, but also extends to nonfood contributions, to obesity and leanness, malnutrition, vitamin requirements, and mineral needs.
Related titles: Microform ed.; Online - full text ed.: ISSN 1543-5237. GBP 866 in United Kingdom to institutions; EUR 895, USD 1,125 to institutions (effective 2012) (from IngentaConnect).
Indexed: A20, A22, A34, A35, A36, A38, AICP, ARDT, ASCA, ASFA, AbAn, AgBio, Agr, AgrForAb, B07, B21, BA, BibAg, C25, CA, CABA, Cadscan, ChemAb, Chicano, CurCont, D01, DIP, E01, E04, E05, E12, EIA, EMBASE, ESPM, EnerInd, F08, F10, FR, FS&TA, FamI, GEOBASE, GH, H16, I10, IBR, IBZ, ISR, LT, LeadAb, MEDLINE, MaizeAb, N02, N03, N04, NRN, O01, OR, P30, P32, P33, P37, P38, P40, P50, PGegResA, PHN&I, PN&I, R08, R11, R12, RA&MP, RM&VM, RRTA, S12, SCI, SCOPUS, SPPI, SoyAb, T02, T05, TAR, TriticAb, VS, W07, W11, Zincscan.
—IE, Infotrieve, Ingenta, INIST, Linda Hall. **CCC.**
Published by: Taylor & Francis Inc. (Subsidiary of: Taylor & Francis Group), 325 Chestnut St, Ste 800, Philadelphia, PA 19106. TEL 215-625-2940, 800-354-1420, orders@taylorandfrancis.com, http://www.taylorandfrancis.com. Ed. Sunil Khanna. Adv. contact Linda Hann TEL 44-1344-779945.

613.2 EGY ISSN 1110-6360
EGYPTIAN JOURNAL OF NUTRITION AND FEED. Text in English. 1970. irreg. **Document type:** *Journal, Academic/Scholarly.*
Formerly (until 1998): Egyptian Journal of Nutrition (1687-1235)
Indexed: A34, A35, A38, AgBio, AgrForAb, C25, C30, CABA, D01, E12, F08, F11, F12, G11, GH, H16, IndVet, MaizeAb, N02, N04, P33, P37, P38, R07, R08, R11, R12, R13, RA&MP, RM&VM, S12, S13, S16, SoyAb, TAR, TriticAb, VS, W11.
Published by: Egyptian Society of Nutrition and Feed, 16 El-Qasr El-Aini Str, Cairo, Egypt. TEL 20-2-3645322, FAX 20-2-3647476. Ed. Dr. Mohamed Abdel-Monim El-Ashry.

613.2 EGY ISSN 1687-7950
EGYPTIAN JOURNAL OF NUTRITION AND HEALTH/MAGALLAT AL-MISRIYYAT LI-L-TAGHZIYYAT WA-AL-SIHHAT/MAJALLAT AL-MISRIYYAT LI-L-TAGHZIYYAT WA-AL-SIHHAT. Text in English. 2006. s-a. **Document type:** *Journal, Academic/Scholarly.*
Published by: Society of Feeding Mind, Combating Malnutrition, 6 Shatr El-Asher, New Maadi, Cairo, Egypt. Ed. Dr. Muhammad Amr Hussein.

613.2 JPN ISSN 0013-6492
EIYO NIPPON/NUTRITION OF JAPAN. Text in Japanese. 1958. m. **Document type:** *Journal, Academic/Scholarly.*
Published by: Nihon Eiyoshikai/Japan Dietetic Association, 1-39 Kanda-Jinbo-cho, Chiyoda-ku, Tokyo, 101-0051, Japan. TEL 81-3-32955151, FAX 81-3-32955165.

613.2 JPN ISSN 0021-5147
RA784 CODEN: EYGZAD
EIYOGAKU ZASSHI/JAPANESE JOURNAL OF NUTRITION AND DIETETICS. Text in Japanese. 1941. bi-m. free to members. adv. bk.rev. **Document type:** *Academic/Scholarly.*
Indexed: A34, A36, AgrForAb, C25, CABA, CIN, ChemAb, ChemTitl, D01, E12, F08, FS&TA, GH, H16, LT, N02, N03, P38, PN&I, R11, R12, RRTA, S12, SoyAb, T05, TriticAb, VS, W11.
—BLDSC (4656.752000), CASDDS, Ingenta, INIST, Linda Hall.
Published by: Japanese Society of Nutrition and Dietetics, 1-23-1 Toyama, Shinjuku-ku, Tokyo, 162-8636, Japan. TEL 81-3-5287-5580, FAX 81-3-5287-5585, kaizen@jade.dti.ne.jp, http://www.jade.dti.ne.jp/~kaizen/.

613.2 JPN ISSN 0915-759X
CODEN: EHCHES
EIYOU HYOKA TO CHIRYO/JAPANESE JOURNAL OF NUTRITIONAL ASSESSMENT. Text in Japanese. 1987. q. JPY 10,860 (effective 2005). **Document type:** *Journal, Academic/Scholarly.*
—CASDDS.
Published by: Medikaru Rebyusha/Medical Review Co., Ltd., 1-7-3 Hirano-Machi, Chuo-ku, Yoshida Bldg., Osaka-shi, 541-0046, Japan. TEL 81-6-62231468, FAX 81-6-62231245.

614.8 613.7 NLD ISSN 1574-7352
ELEMENT. Text in Dutch. 2004. s-a. free (effective 2009). **Document type:** *Magazine, Consumer.*
Published by: Drs. Hans Schreuder Products, Bergseweg 28b, Vreeland, 3633 AK, Netherlands. TEL 31-294-237981, FAX 31-294-237982, http://www.drshansschreuder.com.

ENCYCLOPEDIE MEDICO-CHIRURGICALE. ENDOCRINOLOGIE - NUTRITION. *see* MEDICAL SCIENCES—Endocrinology

613.2 051 USA ISSN 1073-1369
ENERGY TIMES; enhancing your life through proper nutrition. Text in English. 10/yr. adv. **Document type:** *Magazine, Consumer.* **Description:** Educates consumers looking to lead a healthy lifestyle. Includes information on nutrition, natural foods, herbs, natural products, recipes, fitness, alternative health care and more.
Published by: Energy Times Inc, 548 Broadhollow Rd, Melville, NY 11747. TEL 631-777-7773, FAX 631-755-1064. Ed., Pub. Stephen Hanks. Adv. contact Corina Diaz.

613.2 USA ISSN 0893-4452
ENVIRONMENTAL NUTRITION; the newsletter of food, nutrition and health. Abbreviated title: E N. Text in English. 1977. m. looseleaf. USD 39 domestic; USD 49 in Canada; USD 59 elsewhere (effective 2010). bk.rev. illus. Index. 8 p./no.; back issues avail.; reprints avail. **Document type:** *Newsletter, Consumer.* **Description:** Contains the reports about food, nutrition, health, and their connection to the environment.
Formerly (until 1986): Environmental Nutrition Newsletter (0195-4024)
Related titles: Online - full text ed.
Indexed: A01, A02, A03, A04, A08, A22, A26, Agr, BiolDig, C06, C07, C08, C11, C12, CHNI, CINAHL, E08, F10, G06, G07, G08, H03, H04, H11, H12, H13, HlthInd, I05, I07, M01, M02, P02, P10, P20, P24, P48, P52, P53, P54, P56, PQC, S06, S09, S23, T02.
—BLDSC (3791.527600), IE, Ingenta.

Published by: Belvoir Media Group, LLC, PO Box 5656, Norwalk, CT 06856. TEL 203-857-3100, 800-424-7887, FAX 203-857-3103, customer_service@belvoir.com, http://www.belvoir.com. Eds. Sharon Palmer, Susan Male Smith. **Subscr. to:** Palm Coast Data, LLC, 11 Commerce Blvd, Palm Coast, FL 32164. TEL 386-445-4662, http://www.palmcoastdata.com.

ENVIRONMENTAL OPPORTUNITIES NEWSLETTER. *see* ENVIRONMENTAL STUDIES

613.2 ITA ISSN 1721-5676
ERBORISTERIA DOMANI. Text in Italian. 1978. m. (11/yr.). adv. **Document type:** *Magazine, Consumer.*
Indexed: ApicAb.
Published by: Studio Edizioni, Piazza Wagner 1, Milan, 20145, Italy. TEL 39-02-24818684, FAX 39-02-24817843. Circ: 20,000.

613.2 AUT
ERNAEHRUNG AKTUELL. Text in German. 4/yr. EUR 15 domestic; EUR 20 foreign (effective 2005). **Document type:** *Journal, Academic/Scholarly.*
Published by: Oesterreichische Gesellschaft fuer Ernaehrung, Zaunergasse 1-3, Vienna, 1030, Austria. TEL 43-1-7147193, FAX 43-1-7186146, info@oege.at, http://gerda.univie.ac.at/oege/.

613.2 DEU ISSN 1617-4518
HC290.5.C6
➤ **ERNAEHRUNG IM FOKUS**; Zeitschrift fuer Fach-, Lehr- und Beratungskraefte im Bereich Ernaehrung. Text in German. 1956. m. EUR 30 combined subscription domestic (print & online eds.); EUR 36 combined subscription foreign (print & online eds.); EUR 3 newsstand/cover (effective 2010). bk.rev.; video rev.; Website rev. **Document type:** *Journal, Academic/Scholarly.*
Former titles (until 2001): A I D Verbraucherdienst (0720-7522); (until 1979): Verbraucherdienst (0720-650X); (until 1978): Verbraucherdienst. Ausgabe B (0505-2432)
Related titles: Online - full text ed.: EUR 24 (effective 2010).
Indexed: FS&TA, IBR, IBZ.
—BLDSC (3810.640000), IE, Ingenta.
Published by: Aid Infodienst - Ernaehrung, Landwirtschaft, Verbraucherschutz e.V., Heilsbachstr 16, Bonn, 53123, Germany. TEL 49-228-84990, FAX 49-228-8499177, aid@aid.de. Ed. Birgit Jaehnig. Circ: 8,500.

613.2 DEU ISSN 1439-1635
➤ **ERNAEHRUNG UND MEDIZIN.** Text in German; Summaries in English. 1986. 4/yr. EUR 84 to institutions; EUR 116 combined subscription to institutions (print & online eds.); EUR 27.50 newsstand/cover (effective 2011). adv. bk.rev.; software rev.; Website rev. abstr.; bibl.; charts; illus. back issues avail. **Document type:** *Journal, Academic/Scholarly.*
Former titles (until 2001): Vitaminspur (0943-3163); (until 1992): Vitamine, Mineralstoffe, Spurenelemente in Medizin, Ernaehrung und Umwelt (0930-4827)
Related titles: Online - full text ed.: ISSN 1438-9002. EUR 112 to institutions (effective 2011).
Indexed: A22, A36, C25, CABA, D01, E12, GH, N02, N03, S12, TAR, TriticAb, W11.
—GNLM, IE. **CCC.**
Published by: (Verband fuer Ernaehrung und Diaetetik e.V.), Hippokrates Verlag in MVS Medizinverlage Stuttgart GmbH & Co.KG (Subsidiary of: Georg Thieme Verlag), Oswald-Hesse-Str 50, Stuttgart, 70469, Germany. TEL 49-711-89310, FAX 49-711-8931706, kunden.service@thieme.de, http://www.hippokrates.de. Ed. Hanno Kretschmer. Adv. contact Kathrin Thomas. Circ: 14,199 (paid).

613.2 DEU ISSN 0367-0899
ERNAEHRUNGS - LEHRE UND PRAXIS. Text in German. 1964. m.
Related titles: ◆ Supplement(s): Ernaehrungs Umschau. ISSN 0174-0008.
Published by: Umschau Zeitschriftenverlag Breidenstein GmbH, Otto-Volger-Str 15, Sulzbach, 65843, Germany. TEL 49-69-2600621, FAX 49-69-2600609. Ed. Werner Stark.

613.2 DEU ISSN 0174-0008
CODEN: ERUMAT
ERNAEHRUNGS UMSCHAU; Forschung und Praxis. Text in German. 1977. m. EUR 89.40 domestic; EUR 95 foreign; EUR 67.80 to students; EUR 8.10 newsstand/cover (effective 2007). adv. bk.rev. charts; illus.; stat. index. 48 p./no. 3 cols./p.; back issues avail. **Document type:** *Magazine, Consumer.*
Formed by the merger of (1964-1977): Ernaehrungs - Umschau. Ausgabe B (0340-2371); (1954-1977): Ernaehrungs - Umschau. Ausgabe M (0340-2320); Which was formerly (until 1964): Ernaehrungs - Umschau (0014-021X)
Related titles: ◆ Supplement to: Ernaehrungs - Lehre und Praxis. ISSN 0367-0899.
Indexed: A20, A22, CABA, CIN, ChemAb, ChemTitl, CurCont, DIP, FS&TA, GH, IBR, IBZ, N02, OR, SCI, SCOPUS, SoyAb, VITIS, VS, W07.
—CASDDS, GNLM, IE, Ingenta, INIST. **CCC.**
Published by: (Deutsche Gesellschaft fuer Ernaehrung), Umschau Zeitschriftenverlag Breidenstein GmbH, Otto-Volger-Str 15, Sulzbach, 65843, Germany. TEL 49-6196-76670, FAX 49-6196-7667269, info@uzv.de, http://www.uzv.de. Ed. Sabine Fankhaenel. Adv. contact Barbara Goerlach. B&W page EUR 2,822, color page EUR 4,412; trim 176 x 257. Circ: 10,708 (paid and controlled). **Co-sponsor:** Guetegemeinschaft Diaetverpflegung.

ERNAEHRUNGSDIENST; unabhaengige Handels- und Boersenzeitung. *see* AGRICULTURE—Feed, Flour And Grain

612.3 DEU ISSN 0721-5118
ERNAEHRUNGSRUNDBRIEF. Text in German. 1970. q. EUR 18 domestic; EUR 20 foreign; EUR 4.50 newsstand/cover (effective 2008). adv. bk.rev. index. 64 p./no. 1 cols./p.; back issues avail. **Document type:** *Journal, Academic/Scholarly.*
Published by: Arbeitskreis fuer Ernaehrungsforschung e.V., Niddastr 14, Bad Vilbel, 61118, Germany. TEL 49-6101-521875, FAX 49-6101-521886, info@ak-ernaehrung.de. Ed., Adv. contact Petra Kuehne. Circ: 4,000.

ERTONG YU JIANKANG/HEALTHY FOR BABY. *see* CHILDREN AND YOUTH—About

613.2 GBR ISSN 0954-3007
CODEN: EJCNEQ
➤ **EUROPEAN JOURNAL OF CLINICAL NUTRITION.** Abbreviated title: E J C N. Text in English. 1982. m. EUR 1,061 in Europe to institutions; USD 1,335 in the Americas to institutions; JPY 181,500 in Japan to institutions; GBP 685 to institutions in the UK & elsewhere (effective 2011). adv. bk.rev. charts; stat.; illus. back issues avail.; reprints avail. **Document type:** *Journal, Academic/Scholarly.* **Description:** Covers all aspects of human and clinical nutrition.
Formerly (until 1988): Human Nutrition. Clinical Nutrition (0263-8290); Which superseded in part (in 1982): Journal of Human Nutrition (0308-4329); Which was formerly (until 1976): Nutrition (0029-6600)
Related titles: Online - full text ed.: ISSN 1476-5640.
Indexed: A01, A02, A03, A08, A20, A22, A26, A34, A35, A36, A37, A38, ASCA, AgBio, Agr, B07, B21, B25, B28, BIOBASE, BIOSIS Prev, BRD, BibAg, C06, C07, C11, C25, CA, CABA, CTA, CurCont, D01, E01, E08, E12, EMBASE, ESPM, ExcerpMed, F05, F06, F07, F08, F09, F10, FR, FS&TA, G03, G08, G10, GH, GSA, GSI, GeoRef, H04, H13, H16, H17, I05, IABS, IBR, IBZ, ISR, IndMed, Inpharma, LT, MEDLINE, MaizeAb, MycolAb, N02, N03, N04, NRN, NSA, OR, P02, P10, P11, P20, P22, P24, P30, P33, P35, P37, P38, P48, P50, P52, P53, P54, P56, PHN&I, PN&I, PQC, R08, R10, RA&MP, RRTA, Reac, RiskAb, S09, S12, S13, S17, SCI, SCOPUS, SoyAb, T02, T05, TriticAb, VITIS, VS, W03, W07, W09, W10, W11.
—CASDDS, GNLM, IE, Infotrieve, Ingenta, INIST, Linda Hall. **CCC.**
Published by: Nature Publishing Group (Subsidiary of: Macmillan Publishers Ltd.), The MacMillan Bldg, 4 Crinan St, London, N1 9XW, United Kingdom. TEL 44-20-78334000, FAX 44-20-78334640. Ed. Prakash S Shetty. Adv. contact Ben Harkinson TEL 617-475-9222. **Subscr. to:** Brunel Rd, Houndmills, Basingstoke, Hamps RG21 6XS, United Kingdom. TEL 44-1256-329242, FAX 44-1256-812358, subscriptions@nature.com.

613.2 DEU ISSN 1436-6207
QP141.A1 CODEN: EJNUFZ
➤ **EUROPEAN JOURNAL OF NUTRITION.** Text and summaries in English, German. 1960. bi-m. EUR 856, USD 1,073 combined subscription to institutions (print & online eds.) (effective 2012). adv. bk.rev. charts; illus.; abstr. index. back issues avail.; reprint service avail. from PSC. **Document type:** *Journal, Academic/Scholarly.* **Description:** Publishes original papers, invited reviews, and short communications in nutritional sciences.
Formerly (until 1999): Zeitschrift fuer Ernaehrungswissenschaft (0044-264X)
Related titles: Microform ed.: (from PQC); Online - full text ed.: ISSN 1436-6215. 1998 (from IngentaConnect).
Indexed: A01, A02, A03, A08, A22, A26, A34, A35, A36, A37, A38, ASCA, AgBio, Agr, B25, BA, BIOSIS Prev, C06, C07, C08, C11, C25, CA, CABA, CIN, CINAHL, ChemAb, ChemTitl, CurCont, D01, E01, E12, EMBASE, ExcerpMed, F05, F06, F07, F08, F10, FR, FS&TA, GH, H04, H12, H16, IBR, IBZ, INI, IndMed, LT, MEDLINE, MaizeAb, MycolAb, N02, N03, N04, OR, P19, P20, P22, P24, P30, P33, P38, P48, P50, P54, PEI, PHN&I, PN&I, PQC, R09, R10, R11, R12, RA&MP, RM&VM, RRTA, Reac, S12, S13, S16, SCI, SCOPUS, SD, SoyAb, T02, T05, TriticAb, VITIS, VS, W07, W11.
—BLDSC (3829.731900), CASDDS, GNLM, IE, Infotrieve, Ingenta, INIST, Linda Hall. **CCC.**
Published by: Dr. Dietrich Steinkopff Verlag (Subsidiary of: Springer Science+Business Media), Tiergartenstr 17, Heidelberg, 69121, Germany. TEL 49-6221-4878821, FAX 49-6221-4878830, info.steinkopff@springer.com, http://www.steinkopff.com. Ed. Gerhard Rechkemmer TEL 49-721-6625200. adv.: B&W page EUR 740, color page EUR 1,780; trim 210 x 279. Circ: 173 (paid). **Subscr. in the Americas to:** Springer New York LLC, Journal Fulfillment, PO Box 2485, Secaucus, NJ 07096. TEL 201-348-4033, FAX 201-348-4505, journals-ny@springer.com; **Subscr. to:** Springer Distribution Center, Kundenservice Zeitschriften, Haberstr 7, Heidelberg 69126, Germany. TEL 49-6221-3454303, FAX 49-6221-3454229, subscriptions@springer.com.

613.2 GBR ISSN 1751-6730
EUROPEAN NUTRIGENOMICS ORGANISATION. EXECUTIVE SUMMARY. Text in English. 2005. a. back issues avail. **Document type:** *Trade.* **Description:** Aims to develop strategies for disease prevention and health optimisation based on the relationship between diet and health.
Formerly (until 2007): European Nutrigenomics Organisation. Periodic Activity Report Summary (1751-6722)
Related titles: Online - full text ed.
Published by: NuGO, Institute of Food Research, Norwich Research Park, Colney, Norwich, NR4 7UA, United Kingdom. TEL 44-1603-255219, FAX 44-1603-255168, sian.astley@bbsrc.ac.uk, http://www.nugo.org.

EVE; Ernaehrung - Vitalitaet - Erleben. *see* PHYSICAL FITNESS AND HYGIENE

EVEAN PLUS. *see* PHYSICAL FITNESS AND HYGIENE

EVERYDAY HEALTHY FOOD. *see* HOME ECONOMICS

614 FIN ISSN 1796-9182
EVIRAN KAARI. Text in Finnish. 2002. q. EUR 20; EUR 5 per issue (effective 2007). back issues avail. **Document type:** *Magazine, Consumer.*
Formerly (until 2007): Kaari Pellolta Poytaan (1458-7041)
Related titles: Online - full text ed.: ISSN 1796-9190.
Published by: Elintarviketurvallisuusvirasto/The Finnish Food Safety Authority, Mustialankatu 3, Helsinki, 00790, Finland. TEL 358-20-772003, FAX 358-20-7724350, info@evira.fi. Ed. Jaana Husu-Kallio.

EXERCISE PHYSIOLOGY: CURRENT SELECTED RESEARCH. *see* PHYSICAL FITNESS AND HYGIENE

F A O FOOD AND NUTRITION PAPER. (Food and Agriculture Organization of the United Nations) *see* FOOD AND FOOD INDUSTRIES

613.2 USA ISSN 1014-3181
F A O FOOD AND NUTRITION SERIES. Text in English, French, Spanish. 1948. irreg., latest vol.29, 2004. price varies. back issues avail. **Document type:** *Monographic series, Academic/Scholarly.*
Formerly: F A O Nutritional Study (0071-7088)
Related titles: French ed.: Collection F A O, Alimentation et Nutrition. ISSN 0253-2549; Spanish ed.: Coleccion F A O, Alimentacion y Nutricion. ISSN 1014-3173.
Indexed: FS&TA, IndMed, P30.
Published by: Food and Agriculture Organization of the United Nations, c/o Bernan Associates, 4501 Forbes Blvd, Ste 200, Lanham, MD 20706. TEL 301-459-7666, 800-865-3457, FAX 301-459-0056, 800-865-3450, customercare@bernan.com.

613.26 USA
F A R M REPORT. Text in English. 1981. irreg. (3-4/yr.). USD 20 to members (effective 2000). bk.rev. **Document type:** *Newsletter, Trade.* **Description:** Promotes vegetarianism and exposes the adverse impacts of factory farming. Includes articles on eating trends and developments in the meat industry.
Published by: Farm Animal Report Movement, PO Box 30654, Bethesda, MD 20824. TEL 301-530-1737, FAX 301-530-5747, farm@farmusa.org, http://www.farmusa.org. Ed., Pub. Alex Hershaft. Circ: 12,000 (controlled).

THE FAMILY DOCTOR. *see* MEDICAL SCIENCES

613.2 USA
FARMACIST TIMES. Text in English. 2006 (Sep.). m. free in S. California region. **Document type:** *Newspaper, Consumer.*
Published by: Benacquista Publishing Corp., 12707 High Bluff Dr Ste.140, San Diego, CA 92130 .

FIELD & FEAST; the magazine of food, agriculture, & health. *see* FOOD AND FOOD INDUSTRIES

613.2 USA
FIT / LOW CARB. Text in English. 2004. q. USD 14.95; USD 4.99 newsstand/cover domestic; USD 5.99 newsstand/cover in Canada (effective 2004).
Published by: Kalish, Quiley & Rosen, 242 West 27th St., #3A, New York, NY 10001. Ed. Donna Raskin.

613.2 641.5 NLD ISSN 0929-1822
FIT MET VOEDING. Text in Dutch. 1993. 8/yr. EUR 29.50 (effective 2010). adv. **Document type:** *Magazine, Consumer.*
Published by: Ortho Communications & Science b.v., Anholtseweg 36, Gendringen, 7081 CM, Netherlands. TEL 31-315-695211, FAX 31-315-695215, ortho@orthoeurope.com, http://www.orthoeurope.com. Ed. Dr. G E Schuitemaker. adv.: page EUR 1,730; trim 210 x 280.

613.2 NLD ISSN 2211-6990
FOLIA ORTHICA. Text in Dutch. 1993. s-a. **Document type:** *Magazine, Trade.*
Published by: Stichting Folia Orthica, Postbus 10295, Almere, 1301 AG, Netherlands. TEL 31-36-5460911, info@foliaorthica.nl, http://www.foliaorthica.nl. Eds. Rene de Vos, Ivonne Pappot.

664 613.2 IRL ISSN 1029-8614
FOOD ADDITIVE INTAKE STUDIES. Text in English. irreg.
Published by: Trinity College, Institute of European Food Studies, Dublin, Ireland. TEL 353-1-6709175, FAX 353-1-6709176, iefs@iefs.ie, http://www.iefs.org.

FOOD & DRINK NEWS REVIEW. *see* FOOD AND FOOD INDUSTRIES

613.2 USA ISSN 0740-9710
TX341 CODEN: FOFWEC
➤ **FOOD AND FOODWAYS**; explorations in the history and culture of human nutrition. Text in English. 1985. q. GBP 836 combined subscription in United Kingdom to institutions (print & online eds.); EUR 838, USD 1,054 combined subscription to institutions (print & online eds.) (effective 2012). adv. back issues avail.; reprint service avail. from PSC. **Document type:** *Journal, Academic/Scholarly.* **Description:** Explores the powerful but often subtle ways in which food has shaped and continues to shape our lives socially, economically, politically, mentally, and morally.
Related titles: Microform ed.; Online - full text ed.: ISSN 1542-3484. GBP 753 in United Kingdom to institutions; EUR 754, USD 948 to institutions (effective 2012) (from IngentaConnect).
Indexed: A01, A03, A08, A22, A36, AmH&L, C25, CA, CABA, D01, DIP, E01, F10, FS&TA, Faml, GH, H16, HistAb, IBR, IBSS, IBZ, MLA-IB, MaizeAb, N02, N03, OR, P11, P30, P32, P40, P50, P52, P56, PCI, PGegResA, PHN&I, PQC, R12, S12, SCOPUS, T02, T05, TAR, W11.
—IE, Infotrieve, Ingenta. **CCC.**
Published by: Routledge (Subsidiary of: Taylor & Francis Group), 325 Chestnut St, Ste 800, Philadelphia, PA 19106. TEL 800-354-1420, FAX 215-625-2940, journals@routledge.com, http://www.routledge.com. Ed. Carole Counihan TEL 717-872-3575. Adv. contact Linda Hann TEL 44-1344-779945.

613.2 USA ISSN 0379-5721
TX341 CODEN: FNBPDV
➤ **FOOD AND NUTRITION BULLETIN.** Text in English. 1971. q. adv. bk.rev. cum.index: vols.1-3. back issues avail. **Document type:** *Journal, Academic/Scholarly.* **Description:** Covers problems of world hunger and malnutrition.
Supersedes (in 1978): Protein-Calorie Advisory Group of the United Nations System. P A G Bulletin; Incorporates (in 197?): P A G Bulletin (0377-760X)
Related titles: Microfiche ed.: (from CIS); Online - full text ed.: ISSN 1564-8265 (from IngentaConnect).
Indexed: A22, A34, A35, A36, A38, AgBio, Agr, AgrForAb, B25, BA, BIOSIS Prev, C06, C07, C25, C30, CA, CABA, ChemAb, CurCont, D01, E12, EMBASE, ExcerpMed, F05, F06, F07, F08, F09, F10, FS&TA, GEOBASE, GH, H16, H17, IIS, LT, MEDLINE, MaizeAb, MycolAb, N02, N03, N04, P30, P32, P33, P37, P38, P39, P40, PHN&I, R08, R10, R11, R12, R13, RA&MP, RASB, RM&VM, RRTA, Reac, S&MA, S12, S13, S16, S17, SCI, SCOPUS, SoyAb, T02, T05, TAR, TriticAb, VS, W07, W10, W11.
—BLDSC (3977.043200), IE, Infotrieve, Ingenta, Linda Hall.
Published by: (United Nations System Standing Committee on Nutrition CHE), International Nutrition Foundation, 150 Harrison Ave, Rm 243, Boston, MA 02111. TEL 617-636-3771, FAX 617-636-3781, infoperations@inffoundation.org, http://www.inffoundation.org/.

612.3 SWE ISSN 1654-6628
CODEN: SJNUEI
➤ **FOOD & NUTRITION RESEARCH.** Text in English; Summaries in English. 1957. a. GBP 31 in United Kingdom to libraries; EUR 42 to libraries rest of Europe; USD 62 elsewhere to libraries (effective 2008). bk.rev. 48 p./no.; back issues avail.; reprint service avail. from PSC. **Document type:** *Journal, Academic/Scholarly.* **Description:** Directed to present state of the art in the various fields within nutrition. Provides readers with information through original and review articles and reports.

NO

Former titles (until 2008): Scandinavian Journal of Food and Nutrition (1748-2976); (until 2006): Scandinavian Journal of Nutrition (1102-6480); (until vol.36, 1992): Naeringsforskning (0027-7878)
Related titles: Online - full text ed.: ISSN 1654-661X. 2002. free (effective 2011) (from IngentaConnect); Supplement(s): ISSN 2000-6039. 2009.
Indexed: A01, A03, A08, A22, A34, A36, ASG, C06, C07, C08, C25, CA, CABA, CINAHL, D01, E01, F05, F06, F07, F10, FS&TA, GH, N02, N03, R09, SCOPUS, SD, SoyAb, T02.
—GNLM, IE, Infotrieve, Ingenta, Linda Hall. **CCC.**
Published by: (Swedish Nutrition Foundation), Co-Action Publishing, Ripvaegen 7, Jaerfaella, 17564, Sweden. TEL 46-18-4951150, FAX 46-18-4951138, info@co-action.net, http://www.co-action.net. Ed. Nils-Georg Asp. Circ: 2,500 (controlled).

613.2 USA
FOOD & NUTRITION RESEARCH BRIEFS. Abbreviated title: F N R B. Text in English. 1995. q. free (effective 2010). back issues avail. **Document type:** *Bulletin, Government.*
Media: Online - full text. **Related titles:** Spanish ed.
Indexed: CA.
Published by: U.S. Department of Agriculture, Agricultural Research Service, Jamie L Whitten Bldg, Room 302A, 1400 Independence Ave, SW, Washington, DC 20250. TEL 202-720-3656, FAX 202-720-5427, Mark.Hughes@ars.usda.gov.

613.2 USA ISSN 2157-944X
TX545
▼ ➤ **FOOD AND NUTRITION SCIENCES.** Text in English. 2010. q. back issues avail. **Document type:** *Journal, Academic/Scholarly.* **Description:** Aims to keep a record of the state-of-the-art research and to promote study, research and improvement within its various specialties.
Related titles: Online - full text ed.: ISSN 2157-9458. free (effective 2011).
Indexed: A34, A35, A36, A38, C25, CABA, D01, E12, F08, GH, H16, N02, N03, N04, P32, P33, R07, T05, W11.
Published by: Scientific Research Publishing, Inc., PO Box 54821, Irvine, CA 92619. TEL 408-329-4591, service@scirp.org. Ed. Micheal A Kontominas.

613.2 DEU ISSN 0721-6912
TX551
FOOD COMPOSITION AND NUTRITION TABLES/ ZUSAMMENSETZUNG DER LEBENSMITTEL, NAEHRWERT TABELLEN. Text in English, French, German. 1962. irreg. (2-3/yr.). price varies. **Document type:** *Monographic series, Trade.*
Published by: Wissenschaftliche Verlagsgesellschaft mbH, Postfach 101061, Stuttgart, 70009, Germany. TEL 49-711-2582-0, FAX 49-711-2582-290, service@wissenschaftliche-verlagsgesellschaft.de, http://www.wissenschaftliche-verlagsgesellschaft.de.

FOOD, CULTURE, AND SOCIETY; an international journal of multidisciplinary research. *see* HOME ECONOMICS

▼ **FOOD DIGESTION.** *see* MEDICAL SCIENCES—Gastroenterology

FOOD INSIGHT. *see* FOOD AND FOOD INDUSTRIES

FOOD SCIENCE & TECHNOLOGY BULLETIN; functional foods. *see* FOOD AND FOOD INDUSTRIES

FOOD SURVEY INFORMATION SHEET. *see* FOOD AND FOOD INDUSTRIES

FOODNOTE NIEUWS. *see* ADVERTISING AND PUBLIC RELATIONS

613.2 GBR
FOODS MATTER (ONLINE). Text in English. 200?. m. free (effective 2009). adv. **Document type:** *Magazine, Trade.* **Description:** Features articles and research reports on the causes and management allergy and intolerance and the many health conditions related to them.
Media: Online - full text.
Published by: Berrydales Publishers, 5 Lawn Rd, London, NW3 2XS, United Kingdom. TEL 44-20-77222866, FAX 44-20-77227685. Ed. Michelle Berriedale-Johnson.

613.2 USA ISSN 2157-9156
▼ **FOODSMART FOCUS.** Text in English. 2010. bi-w. USD 20 (effective 2010). **Document type:** *Newsletter, Trade.* **Description:** Covers a wide array of nutrition topics and provides with nutrient information, recalls, health tips, healthy recipes, food reviews, Q and A section, member news and views.
Media: Online - full text.
Published by: Consumer Press, 13326 SW 28th St, Suite 102, Fort Lauderdale, FL 33330. TEL 954-370-9153, info@consumerpress.com, http://www.consumerpress.com/. Ed. Diana Hunter.

613.04244 RUS
FORMULA ZDOROV'YA. Text in Russian. m. USD 20.20 domestic; USD 119 foreign (effective 2005). **Document type:** *Magazine, Consumer.*
Published by: Independent Media (Moscow), 3 Polkovaya Ul, Bldg 1, Moscow, 127018, Russian Federation. TEL 7-095-2323200, FAX 7-095-2321761, podpiska@imedia.ru, http://www.independent-media.ru. Ed. Yevgeniya Killikh.

613.2 CHE ISSN 1660-0347
CODEN: FNOUA6
➤ **FORUM OF NUTRITION.** Text in English. 1960. irreg., latest vol.61, 2009. price varies. back issues avail.; reprints avail. **Document type:** *Monographic series, Academic/Scholarly.* **Description:** Reports on the latest progress in nutrition research and evaluates its impact on medical, economical and social issues.
Formerly (until 2001): Bibliotheca Nutritio et Dieta (0067-8198)
Related titles: Online - full text ed.: ISSN 1662-2987.
Indexed: A22, ASCA, BioDAb, ChemAb, EMBASE, ExcerpMed, FS&TA, IndMed, MEDLINE, P30, R10, Reac, SCI, SCOPUS, W07.
—BLDSC (4024.094535), CASDDS, GNLM, IE, Ingenta, INIST. **CCC.**
Published by: S. Karger AG, Allschwilerstr 10, Basel, 4055, Switzerland. TEL 41-61-3061111, FAX 41-61-3061234, karger@karger.ch, http://www.karger.ch. Ed. Ibrahim Elmadfa.

➤ **FRANCE NATURE.** *see* ALTERNATIVE MEDICINE

➤ **FRISCH GEKOCHT**; ist halb gewonnen. *see* HOME ECONOMICS

613.2 GBR
FRONTIERS IN NUTRITIONAL SCIENCE SERIES (NO.). Text in English. 2002. irreg., latest no.4, 2009. price varies. back issues avail. **Document type:** *Monographic series, Academic/Scholarly.*
Published by: CABI (Subsidiary of: CAB International), Nosworthy Way, Wallingford, Oxfordshire OX10 8DE, United Kingdom. TEL 44-1491-832111, FAX 44-1491-829292, enquiries@cabi.org.

613.2 JPN
FUKUYAMA AKENOHOSHI GAKUIN EIYO SENMON GAKKO. KENKYU KIYO/FUKUYAMA AKENOHOSHI GAKUIN SCHOOL OF DIETETICS. BULLETIN. (3 issues published: 1973, 1988, 1997) Text in Japanese. 1973. irreg., latest 1997.
Formerly: Fukuyama Akenohoshi Gakuin Eiyo Senmon Gakko Kenkyu Kiyo (0385-5880)
Published by: Fukuyama Akenohoshi Gakuin Eiyo Senmon Gakko, 3-4-1 Nishi-Fukatsu-cho, Fukuyama-shi, Hiroshima-ken 721-0975, Japan.

613.2 CAN ISSN 1947-5799
QP144.F85
▼ ➤ **FUNCTIONAL FOOD REVIEWS.** Text in English. 2009. q. CAD 318 domestic to institutions; USD 254.40 in United States to institutions; USD 339.20 elsewhere to institutions; CAD 381.60 combined subscription domestic to institutions (print & online eds.); USD 302.25 combined subscription in United States to institutions (print & online eds.); USD 407 combined subscription elsewhere to institutions (print & online eds.) (effective 2010). adv. back issues avail. **Document type:** *Journal, Academic/Scholarly.* **Description:** Publishes articles by leading scientists in the field of nutrition studies.
Related titles: Online - full text ed.: ISSN 1947-5802. CAD 318 domestic to institutions; USD 254.40 foreign to institutions (effective 2010).
Published by: B.C. Decker Inc., 50 King St E, 2nd Fl, Hamilton, ON L8N 2A1, Canada. TEL 905-522-7017, 800-568-7281, FAX 905-522-7839, info@bcdecker.com. Eds. Philip M Sherman, W Allan Walker. Adv. contact Jennifer Coates TEL 905-522-7017 ext 291. B&W page USD 1,050, color page USD 2,150; trim 8.125 x 10.875. Circ: 2,500.

613.2 USA ISSN 2160-3855
▼ ➤ **FUNCTIONAL FOODS IN HEALTH AND DISEASE.** Abbreviated title: F F H D. Text in English. 2010. m. free (effective 2011). **Document type:** *Journal, Academic/Scholarly.* **Description:** Covers various aspects of functional foods and chronic diseases such as cardiovascular, obesity, diabetes, cancer and/or scientific policies related to functional foods.
Media: Online - full text.
Published by: Functional Food Center, Inc., 1212 Hampshire Ln, Ste 213, Richardson, TX 75080. TEL 866-464-6955, FAX 972-234-8182, ffc_usa@sbcglobal.net. Ed. Danik M Martirosyan.

613.2 USA
QP144.F85
FUNCTIONAL INGREDIENTS; the magazine for the global supply market. Text in English. 1998. 11/yr. USD 110 (effective 2011). adv. **Document type:** *Magazine, Trade.* **Description:** Focused on delivery of strategic, innovative and scientific news and information related to functional ingredients and their applications.
Former titles (until Sep., 2007): Functional Foods and Nutraceuticals (1470-0336); (until 1999): Functional Foods (1462-0286)
Related titles: Online - full text ed.
Indexed: A15, A26, ABIn, B01, B02, B03, B07, B15, B17, B18, C06, C07, F10, FS&TA, G04, H11, H12, I05, P16, P19, P24, P53, P54, PQC, T02.
—CIS. **CCC.**
Published by: New Hope Natural Media (Subsidiary of: Penton Media, Inc.), 1401 Pearl St, Boulder, CO 80302. TEL 303-939-8440, 888-721-4321, FAX 303-998-9020, customerservice@newhope.com, http://www.newhope.com. Ed. Tod L Runestad. Circ: 12,500 (controlled).

613.2 GBR ISSN 2042-3721
▼ **FUNCTIONAL SPORTS NUTRITION JOURNAL.** Text in English. 2010. bi-m. GBP 15 (effective 2011). adv. **Document type:** *Magazine, Trade.*
—**CCC.**
Published by: Target Publishing Ltd., The Old Dairy, Hudsons Farm, Fieldgate Ln, Ugley Green, Bishops Stortford, Essex CM22 6HJ, United Kingdom. TEL 44-1279-810080, FAX 44-1279-810081, info@targetpublishing.com, http://www.targetpublishing.com. Ed. Simon Martin. Adv. contact Sally-Ann Dobson TEL 44-1279-810060.

612.3 USA ISSN 0890-507X
G I G NEWSLETTER. Text in English. 1974. q. looseleaf. USD 35 domestic membership; USD 50 in Canada & Mexico membership; USD 60 elsewhere membership (effective 2008). bk.rev. index. back issues avail. **Document type:** *Newsletter, Consumer.* **Description:** Contains research reports, food product and drug information, seminar-meeting announcements, activities of national and local interest, and recipes.
Published by: Gluten Intolerance Group of North America, 31214 124th Ave SE, Auburn, WA 98092-3667. TEL 253-833-6655, FAX 253-833-6675, info@gluten.net, http://www.gluten.net. Ed., R&P, Adv. contact Cynthia R Kupper. Circ: 2,000.

612.3 NCL ISSN 1022-9221
GARDEN TO KITCHEN NEWSLETTER. Text in French. 1992. s-a. **Document type:** *Newsletter.*
Published by: Secretariat of the Pacific Community, PO Box D5, Noumea, Cedex 98848, New Caledonia. TEL 687-262000, FAX 687-263818, spc@spc.int, http://www.spc.int.

GATHERED VIEW. *see* MEDICAL SCIENCES

GENES & NUTRITION; a journal devoted to study of relationship between genetics & nutrition for improvement of human health. *see* BIOLOGY—Genetics

GESUND ESSEN IM ERSTEN JAHR. *see* CHILDREN AND YOUTH—About

613.2 664 TUR ISSN 1300-3070
➤ **GIDA**; journal of food. Text in Turkish, English. 1976. bi-m. **Document type:** *Journal, Academic/Scholarly.*
Related titles: Online - full text ed.: ISSN 1309-6273. free (effective 2011).
Indexed: A01, A34, A36, AgrForAb, C25, CA, CABA, D01, E12, F08, GH, H16, MaizeAb, N02, N03, N04, P33, SoyAb, T05, TAR, W11.
Published by: Gida Teknolojisi Dernegi/The Association of Food Technology, Ankara University, Ankara, Turkey.

613.2 IDN ISSN 0436-0265
GIZI INDONESIA. Text in English, Indonesian. q. IDR 1,200. adv. bk.rev. illus.
Published by: (Indonesian Nutrition Association), Akedemi Gizi, J1. Hang Jebat III/F3, Kebayoran Baru, P.O. Box 8 KBB, Jakarta, Indonesia. Ed. Ig Tarnotjo.

613.2 USA
GLYCOHEALTH NEWS. Text in English. w. **Document type:** *Newsletter.* **Description:** Presents notes and news articles on glyconutrients for optimal health.
Media: Online - full text.
Published by: Glycohealth News, PO Box 584, Reading, MI 49274. TEL 512-283-2075. Pub. Hal Mesler.

▼ **GOCCE DI BENESSERE.** *see* PHYSICAL FITNESS AND HYGIENE

613.2 616.462 USA
GOOD EATING, GOOD LIVING. Text in English. 2007. s-a. **Document type:** *Magazine, Consumer.* **Description:** Contains expert advice, recipes and tips for people with diabetes and their families.
Published by: Kraft Foods Global, Inc., Three Lakes Dr., Northfield, IL 60093. http://www.kraftfoods.com/.

GOOD HEALTH & MEDICINE. *see* PHYSICAL FITNESS AND HYGIENE

GOUR-MED; Das Magazin fuer Aerzte. *see* MEDICAL SCIENCES

▼ **IL GRANDE ATLANTE DELLA SALUTE.** *see* PHYSICAL FITNESS AND HYGIENE

GREAT HEALTH. *see* MEDICAL SCIENCES

GUIA PREVENIR SALUD. *see* PHYSICAL FITNESS AND HYGIENE

612.3 371.025 USA ISSN 1040-2616
THE GUIDE TO COOKING SCHOOLS. Text in English. 1989. a.
Published by: ShawGuides, Box 231295, Ansonia Station, New York, NY 10023. TEL 212-799-6464, FAX 212-724-9287, info@shawguides.com.

613.2 SWE ISSN 0345-4797
HAELSA; foer kropp och sjael i balans. Variant title: Tidskrift foer Haelsa. Text in Swedish. 1940. 11/yr. SEK 400 (effective 2007). adv. bk.rev. back issues avail. **Document type:** *Magazine, Consumer.* **Description:** Focuses on health, physical fitness, hygiene, consumer education and protection.
Former titles (until vol.10, 1971): Tidskrift Foer Haelsa; (until 1956): Waerlands Maanads-Magasin; (until vol.5, 1944): Solvikingen
Related titles: Audio cassette/tape ed.
Published by: Haelsa & Helhet Foerlags AB, Turistvaegen 544, PO Box 33, Orsa, 79421, Sweden. TEL 46-250-552010, FAX 46-25043191. Ed., Pub. Per Frisk. Adv. contact Renee Linden. color page SEK 31,500; trim 190 x 265. Circ: 51,600 (paid and controlled). **Subscr. to:** Titeldata AB.

613.2 664 USA ISSN 1532-351X
HALAL CONSUMER. Text in English. q. **Document type:** *Magazine, Consumer.* **Description:** Promotes Halal food and the institution of Halal. Objectives include making Halal food conveniently available, introducing Halal to food companies and institutions, creating awareness of Halal among consumers and providing Halal solutions to consumer needs.
Address: C/o Dr. Muhammad Munir Chaudry, 5901 N Cicero Ave., Ste 309, Chicago, IL 60646. TEL 773-283-3708, FAX 773-283-3973, mchaudry@ifanca.org, http://www.ifanca.org. Ed. Roger M Othman.

613.2 PAK ISSN 0259-3734
HAMDARD NAUNEHAL. Text in English. 1952. m. USD 30 (effective 2000). **Document type:** *Journal, Academic/Scholarly.*
Published by: Hamdard Foundation, Nazimabad No.3, Karachi, 74600, Pakistan. TEL 92-21-6616001, FAX 92-21-6611755. Ed. Masood Ahmed Barakaatee.

613.2 KOR ISSN 1226-3311
TX341 CODEN: HSYHFB
➤ **HAN'GUG SIGPUM YEONG'YANG GWAHAG HOEJI/KOREAN SOCIETY OF FOOD SCIENCE AND NUTRITION. JOURNAL.** Text in Korean; Summaries in English. 1972. q. adv. 200 p./no.; reprints avail. **Document type:** *Journal, Academic/Scholarly.*
Formerly (until 1996): Han'gug Yeong'yang Sigryang Haghoeji/Korean Society of Food and Nutrition. Journal (0253-3154)
Media: Large Type (10 pt.). **Related titles:** CD-ROM ed.; Online - full content ed.
Indexed: A22, FS&TA, SCOPUS.
—BLDSC (4812.344700), IE, Ingenta.
Published by: Korean Society of Food Science and Nutrition, Yeonsan 4-dong, Yeonje-gu, 587-8 SK View, 103-1307, Busan, 611-820, Korea, S. TEL 86-51-8663693, FAX 86-51-8663695, kfn@kfn.or.kr, http://www.kfn.or.kr/. Eds. Kwang-Soo Oh, Mihyang Kim, Woo-Po Park, Young-Jun Cha. Pub. Eul-Sang Kim. adv.: page KRW 500,000; 210 x 280.

➤ **HEALING GARDEN JOURNAL.** *see* ALTERNATIVE MEDICINE

▼ ➤ **HEALTH (IRVINE).** *see* MEDICAL SCIENCES

613.2 THA ISSN 1513-7589
HEALTH & CUISINE. Text in Thai. 2001. m. THB 960 (effective 2006). adv. **Document type:** *Magazine, Consumer.* **Description:** Focuses on healthy and nutritious cooking secrets and recipes.
Published by: Amarin Printing & Publishing Public Co. Ltd., 65/101-103 Chaiyaphruk Rd., Taling Chan, Bangkok, 10700, Thailand. TEL 66-2-4229999, FAX 66-2-4343555, info@amarin.co.th, http://www.amarin.co.th.

HEALTH AND FITNESS; all you need for life!. *see* PHYSICAL FITNESS AND HYGIENE

613.2 BEL ISSN 1374-626X
HEALTH AND FOOD (FRENCH EDITION). Text in French. 1994. bi-m. back issues avail. **Document type:** *Magazine, Trade.*
Related titles: Dutch ed.: Health and Food (Dutch Edition). ISSN 1374-3600.
Indexed: F05, F06, F07.
Published by: Sciences Today, 18-17 Rue Rixensart, Genval, 1332, Belgium. Circ: 15,000.

HEALTH & NUTRITION. *see* PHYSICAL FITNESS AND HYGIENE

613.2 IND ISSN 0970-8685
RA529
HEALTH FOR THE MILLIONS. Abbreviated title: H F M. Text in English. 1975. bi-m. adv. bk.rev. bibl.; illus. **Document type:** *Magazine, Consumer.* **Description:** Aims to influence decision making and disseminates practical information on health policies and programs affecting the public.
Indexed: F09, P30, PAA&I, SCOPUS.

Published by: Health for the Millions Trust, Voluntary Health Association of India, B-40, Qutab Institutional Area, S of I.I.T. Delhi, New Delhi, 110 016, India. TEL 91-11-47004300, vhai@vsnl.com. Circ: 1,200.

613.7 USA ISSN 0883-8216
RA776.5
HEALTH SCIENCE; living in harmony with nature. Text in English. 1978. bi-m. USD 35 in US & Canada; USD 55 foreign (effective 2005). adv. bk.rev. charts; illus. cum.index: 1978-1983. back issues avail.
Former titles (until vol.8, no.2): Vegetarian Health Science (8750-1643); Health Science (0161-5874)
Related titles: Online - full text ed.
Indexed: A26, E08, G08, H11, H12, I05, I07, S06, S09, S23.
Published by: American Natural Hygiene Society, Inc., PO Box 30630, Tampa, FL 33630. TEL 813-855-6607. Circ: 7,500.

HEALTHNEWS. *see* PUBLIC HEALTH AND SAFETY

613.2 USA ISSN 1539-1205
HEALTHSMART TODAY. Text in English. 2002 (Spring). q. USD 12 in United States; USD 18 in Canada (effective 2002). adv.
Published by: Impakt Health, LLC, PO Box 12496, Green Bay, WI 54307-2496. Eds. Frances E Fitzgerald, Maura Heardon. Pub. Karolyn A Gazella.

HEALTHSPAN. *see* HEALTH FACILITIES AND ADMINISTRATION

613.2 USA ISSN 0897-9251
HEALTHWAYS. Text in English. 1987. 3/yr. USD 25 domestic; USD 30 foreign (effective 2000). bk.rev. **Document type:** *Newsletter.*
Published by: International Macrobiotic Shiatsu Society, 1410 Oneco Avenue, Winter Park, FL 32789. TEL 707-444-8620, FAX 707-445-2391. Ed. Patrick McCarty. Circ: 600.

613.2 641.5 613.7 USA ISSN 1559-2871
HEART-HEALTHY LIVING. Variant title: Better Homes and Gardens Heart Healthy Living. Text in English. 2006 (Spr.). q. USD 5.99 newsstand/cover domestic; USD 7.99 newsstand/cover in Canada (effective 2006). adv. back issues avail. **Document type:** *Magazine, Consumer.* **Description:** Provides information for an audience of consumers interested in treating various types of heart disease, Heart-Healthy Living guides readers of all ages on how to live a healthy and active lifestyle.
Published by: Better Homes and Gardens, Special Interest Publications (Subsidiary of: Meredith Corporation), 125 Park Ave, 18th Fl, New York, NY 10017. TEL 212-551-7193, FAX 212-551-7192, support@bhg.com, http://www.bhg.com. Pub. Mark Josephson TEL 212-551-7109. Adv. contact Josh Dammers TEL 212-551-7051. B&W page USD 61,080, color page USD 88,760; bleed 8.5 x 11.125. Circ: 270,000.

613.2 JPN
HERUSUKEA RESUTORAN/HEALTHCARE RESTAURANT. Text in Japanese. m. JPY 13,200 (effective 2007). **Document type:** *Magazine, Trade.*
Published by: Nihon Iryo Kikaku/Japan Medical Planning, 4-14 Kanda-Iwamoto-cho, Chiyoda-ku, Tokyo, 101-0033, Japan. TEL 81-3-32562861, FAX 81-3-32562865.

613.2 USA
HIGH PERFORMANCE MAGAZINE. Text in English. 2003. 3/yr. USD 24.95 (effective 2006). **Document type:** *Magazine, Consumer.* **Description:** Keeps you abreast of the latest Physique Altering and Performance Enhancing training, sports supplementation, pharmaceuticals and nutrition strategies.
Published by: Vital Pharmaceuticals, Inc, 15751 SW 41 St, Ste 300, Fort Lauderdale, FL 33331. TEL 954-641-0570, FAX 954-641-4960, info@vpxsports.com, http://www.vpxsports.com/. Ed. Jack Owoc.

613.2 664 HRV ISSN 1847-3423
HRVATSKI CASOPSIS ZA PREHRAMBENU TEHNOLOGIJU, BIOTEHNOLOGIJU I NUTRICIONIZAM/CROATIAN JOURNAL OF FOOD TECHNOLOGY, BIOTECHNOLOGY AND NUTRITION. Text in Croatian, English. 2002. q. **Document type:** *Journal, Academic/Scholarly.*
Formerly (until 2006): P B N Revija (1334-0719)
Related titles: Online - full text ed.: ISSN 1847-7461. free (effective 2011).
Indexed: A34, A36, C25, CABA, D01, E12, GH, MaizeAb, N02, N03, P33, PQC, S13, SoyAb, W11.
Published by: Hrvatsko Drustvo Prehrambenih Tehnologa, Biotehnologa i Nutricionista/Croatian Society of Food Technology, Food Biotechnology and Nutritionists, Kaciceva 23, Zagreb, 10000, Croatia. TEL 385-1-4605223, FAX 385-1-4605200. Ed. Damir Karlovic.

HUNGER NOTES (ONLINE). *see* SOCIAL SERVICES AND WELFARE

HYGIENE AND NUTRITION IN FOOD SERVICE AND CATERING; an international journal. *see* FOOD AND FOOD INDUSTRIES

613.2 USA ISSN 1941-4064
▼ ➤ **I C A N**; infant, child & adolescent nutrition. (Infant, Child & Adolescent Nutrition) Text in English. 2009 (Jan.). bi-m. USD 165, GBP 98 combined subscription to institutions (print & online eds.); USD 162, GBP 96 to institutions (effective 2011). **Document type:** *Journal, Academic/Scholarly.* **Description:** Serves as a resource and forum for health care professionals involved in the nutritional care of children from birth through adolescence, providing practical information derived from research and practice.
Related titles: Online - full text ed.: ISSN 1941-4072. USD 149, GBP 88 to institutions (effective 2011).
Indexed: A22, A36, CABA, D01, E01, GH, N02, N03, P33, R12, RA&MP, S12, SoyAb, T05, W11.
—CCC.
Published by: Sage Publications, Inc., 2455 Teller Rd, Thousand Oaks, CA 91320. TEL 805-499-9774, 800-818-7243, FAX 805-499-0871, 800-583-2665, info@sagepub.com. Ed. Linda Heller.

613.2 USA ISSN 1432-0010
➤ **I L S I MONOGRAPH.** Text in German. 1988. irreg. price varies. back issues avail. **Document type:** *Monographic series, Academic/Scholarly.*
Published by: International Life Sciences Institute, 1156 Fifteenth St, NW, Ste 200, Washington, DC 20005. TEL 202-659-0074, FAX 202-659-3859, ilsi@ilsi.org.

613.2 IND ISSN 0022-3174
TX341 CODEN: IJNDAN
➤ **INDIAN JOURNAL OF NUTRITION AND DIETETICS.** Text in English. 1964. m. INR 950 domestic; USD 80, GBP 40 foreign (effective 2011). bk.rev. bibl.; charts; stat. index. **Document type:** *Journal, Academic/Scholarly.* **Description:** Contains research papers and review articles in the fields of nutrition and dietetics.
Formerly (until vol.7, 1970): Journal of Nutrition and Dietetics (0368-3257)
Related titles: CD-ROM ed.
Indexed: A34, A35, A36, AgrForAb, BA, C25, C30, CABA, ChemAb, D01, E12, ExtraMED, F08, F09, FS&TA, GH, H16, H17, LT, MaizeAb, N02, N03, N04, OR, P30, P32, P33, P37, P38, P39, P40, PGegResA, PHN&I, R08, R11, R12, R13, RA&MP, RM&VM, RRTA, S&MA, S12, S13, S16, SoyAb, T05, TAR, TOSA, TriticAb, VS, W11.
—CASDDS, GNLM, Ingenta, INIST, Linda Hall.
Published by: Avinashilingam Institute for Home Science and Higher Education for Women, Deemed university for women, Mettupalayam Rd, coimbatore, Tamil Nadu 641 043, India. TEL 91-422-2440241, FAX 91-422-2438786, info_adu@avinuty.ac.in. Eds. S Premakumari, Meenakshi T S K Sundaram. **Subscr. to:** I N S I O Scientific Books & Periodicals.

612.3 CAN ISSN 1194-6180
INFANT FEEDING ACTION COALITION. NEWSLETTER. Text in English. 1981. q. USD 55; USD 25 to students (effective 2006). **Document type:** *Newsletter, Consumer.*
Indexed: P30.
Published by: Infant Feeding Action Coalition, 6 Trinity Square, Toronto, ON M5G 1B1, Canada. TEL 416-595-9819, FAX 416-591-9355, info@infactcanada.ca.

613.2 USA ISSN 1542-4413
INFORMED EATING. Text in English. 2002 (Sept./Oct.). bi-m.
Related titles: Online - full text ed.: ISSN 1542-4421.
Published by: Center for Informed Food Choices, P. O. Box 16053, Oakland, CA 94610. TEL 510-465-0322, FAX 510-238-8228, info@informedeating.org. Eds. Michele Simon, Rich Ganis.

613.2 GTM ISSN 0533-4179
INSTITUTO DE NUTRICION DE CENTRO AMERICA Y PANAMA (I N C A P). INFORME ANUAL. Text in English. 1950. a. **Document type:** *Newsletter, Consumer.*
Related titles: Spanish ed.
Published by: Instituto de Nutricion de Centroamerica y Panama (I N C A P)/Institute of Nutrition of Central America and Panama, Calzada Roosevelt, Zona 11, Guatemala, Guatemala. TEL 502-24723762, FAX 502-24736529, http://www.incap.org.gt.

613.2 ITA ISSN 1127-6320
L'INTEGRATORE NUTRIZIONALE. Text in Italian. 1998. q. **Document type:** *Magazine, Consumer.*
Published by: C E C Editore, Viale Legioni Romane 55, Milan, 20147, Italy. TEL 39-02-4152943, FAX 39-02-416737, http://www.cecpublisher.com. Pub. Anna Lebovich.

613.2 MYS ISSN 1985-4668
➤ **INTERNATIONAL FOOD RESEARCH JOURNAL.** Text in English. 1985. 3/yr. MYR 60 domestic; USD 75 foreign (effective 2009). **Document type:** *Journal, Academic/Scholarly.* **Description:** Contains original research in all areas of food science, food technology, and food biotechnology.
Formerly (until 2008): A S E A N Food Journal (0127-7324)
Related titles: Online - full content ed.: ISSN 1505-5337.
Indexed: A22, ASFA, Agr, B21, ESPM, F05, F06, F07, SCOPUS.
—BLDSC (4540.304350), IE, Ingenta.
Published by: (Agricultural University of Malaysia/Universiti Pertanian Malaysia), Universiti Putra Malaysia, Faculty of Food Science and Technology, 43400 UPM, Serdang, Selangor, Malaysia. TEL 60-3-89468419, FAX 60-3-89423552. Ed. Jinap Selamat.

➤ **INTERNATIONAL JOURNAL FOR VITAMIN AND NUTRITION RESEARCH.** *see* PHARMACY AND PHARMACOLOGY

➤ **THE INTERNATIONAL JOURNAL OF BEHAVIORAL NUTRITION AND PHYSICAL ACTIVITY.** *see* PSYCHOLOGY

➤ **INTERNATIONAL JOURNAL OF BODY COMPOSITION RESEARCH.** *see* MEDICAL SCIENCES

616.39 155.633 616.852 USA ISSN 0276-3478
RC552.A72 CODEN: INDIDJ
➤ **INTERNATIONAL JOURNAL OF EATING DISORDERS.** Text in English. 1981. 8/yr. GBP 1,522 in United Kingdom to institutions; EUR 1,922 in Europe to institutions; USD 2,813 in United States to institutions; USD 2,925 in Canada & Mexico to institutions; USD 2,981 elsewhere to institutions; GBP 1,751 combined subscription in United Kingdom to institutions (print & online eds.); EUR 2,212 combined subscription in Europe to institutions (print & online eds.); USD 3,235 combined subscription in United States to institutions (print & online eds.); USD 3,347 combined subscription in Canada & Mexico to institutions (print & online eds.); USD 3,403 combined subscription elsewhere to institutions (print & online eds.) (effective 2012). adv. bk.rev. bibl.; stat. Cum. Index. back issues avail.; reprint service avail. from PSC. **Document type:** *Journal, Academic/Scholarly.* **Description:** Covers basic research, clinical and theoretical articles of scholarly substance on a variety of aspects of anorexia nervosa, bulimia, obesity and other atypical patterns of eating behavior and body weight regulation.
Related titles: Microform ed.: (from PQC); Online - full text ed.: ISSN 1098-108X. GBP 1,436 in United Kingdom to institutions; EUR 1,814 in Europe to institutions; USD 2,813 elsewhere to institutions (effective 2012).
Indexed: A01, A02, A03, A08, A20, A22, A26, A36, AMHA, ASCA, AbAn, Agr, B04, B21, B25, BIOSIS Prev, BRD, C06, C07, C08, CA, CABA, CINAHL, CurCont, D01, E-psyche, E08, E12, EMBASE, ESPM, ExcerpMed, F09, FR, FS&TA, FamI, G08, GH, H&SSA, H12, H13, I05, IndMed, Inpharma, JW-P, LT, MEDLINE, MycolAb, N02, N03, NRN, P02, P03, P10, P12, P20, P27, P30, P35, P43, P48, P50, P53, P54, PEI, PQC, PsycInfo, PsycholAb, R10, R12, RA&MP, RRTA, Reac, RiskAb, S02, S03, S09, S12, SCI, SCOPUS, SSAI, SSAb, SSCI, SSI, T02, T05, THA, W03, W07.
—BLDSC (4542.195500), GNLM, IE, Infotrieve, Ingenta, INIST. **CCC.**

Published by: John Wiley & Sons, Inc., 111 River St, Hoboken, NJ 07030. TEL 201-748-6000, FAX 201-748-6088, info@wiley.com, http://www.wiley.com/WileyCDA/. Ed. Dr. Michael Strober. Pub., Adv. contact Kim Thompkins TEL 212-850-6921. B&W page USD 1,241, color page USD 1,576; trim 6.875 x 10. **Subscr. outside the Americas to:** John Wiley & Sons Ltd., The Atrium, Southern Gate, Chichester, West Sussex PO19 8SQ, United Kingdom. TEL 44-1243-779777, 800-243407, FAX 44-1243-775878, cs-journals@wiley.com.

▼ ➤ **INTERNATIONAL JOURNAL OF FOOD, NUTRITION AND PUBLIC HEALTH.** *see* PUBLIC HEALTH AND SAFETY

612.3 GBR ISSN 0963-7486
TX341 CODEN: IJFNEH
➤ **INTERNATIONAL JOURNAL OF FOOD SCIENCES AND NUTRITION.** Text in English. 1973. 8/yr. GBP 1,090, EUR 1,475, USD 1,850 combined subscription to institutions (print & online eds.); GBP 2,200, EUR 2,980, USD 3,725 combined subscription to corporations (print & online eds.) (effective 2010). adv. back issues avail.; reprint service avail. from PSC. **Document type:** *Journal, Academic/Scholarly.* **Description:** Aims to integrate food science with nutrition. It contains impact of nutritional science on food product development.
Former titles (until 1992): Food Sciences and Nutrition (0954-3465); (until 1988): Human Nutrition. Food Sciences and Nutrition (0952-8954); (until 1987): Journal of Plant Foods (0142-968X); (until 1978): Plant Foods for Man (0306-2686)
Related titles: Online - full text ed.: ISSN 1465-3478 (from IngentaConnect).
Indexed: A01, A02, A03, A08, A22, A26, A34, A35, A36, A37, A38, AMED, ASCA, ASFA, AgBio, Agr, AgrForAb, B&BAb, B07, B19, B21, B25, BA, BIOBASE, BIOSIS Prev, BP, BRD, C06, C07, C11, C25, C30, CA, CABA, CIN, ChemAb, ChemTitl, CurCont, CurPA, D01, E01, E08, E12, EMBASE, ESPM, ExcerpMed, F05, F06, F07, F08, F09, F10, F11, F12, FCA, FR, FS&TA, G03, G08, GH, GSA, GSI, H04, H11, H12, H13, H16, I05, I10, IABS, IBR, IBZ, IPackAb, IndMed, IndVet, LT, MEDLINE, MaizeAb, MycolAb, N02, N03, N04, O01, OR, P02, P10, P11, P20, P26, P30, P32, P33, P37, P38, P40, P48, P52, P53, P54, P56, PEI, PGegResA, PGrRegA, PHN&I, PN&I, PQC, R07, R08, R09, R11, R12, R13, RA&MP, RM&VM, RRTA, RefZh, S09, S10, S12, S13, S16, S17, SCI, SCOPUS, SD, SoyAb, T02, T05, TAR, TriticAb, VITIS, VS, W03, W07, W10, W11.
—CASDDS, GNLM, IE, Infotrieve, Ingenta, INIST, Linda Hall. **CCC.**
Published by: Informa Healthcare (Subsidiary of: T & F Informa plc), Telephone House, 69-77 Paul St, London, EC2A 4LQ, United Kingdom. TEL 44-20-70175000, FAX 44-20-70176792, healthcare.enquiries@informa.com. Ed. C J K Henry. Adv. contact Per Sonnerfeldt. **Subscr. in N. America to:** Taylor & Francis Inc., Customer Services Dept, 325 Chestnut St, 8th Fl, Philadelphia, PA 19106. TEL 215-625-8900, 800-354-1420, FAX 215-625-8914, customerservice@taylorandfrancis.com; **Subscr. outside N. America to:** Taylor & Francis Ltd., Journals Customer Service, Sheepen Pl, Colchester, Essex CO3 3LP, United Kingdom. TEL 44-20-70175544, FAX 44-20-70175198, tf.enquiries@tfinforma.com.

613.2 IND
➤ **INTERNATIONAL JOURNAL OF NUTRITION.** Text in English. s-a. USD 425 (effective 2011). **Document type:** *Journal, Academic/Scholarly.*
Related titles: Online - full text ed.: free (effective 2011).
Published by: Bioinfo Publications, 49/F-72, Vighnahar Complex, Front of Overseas Bank, Sector 12, Kharghar, Navi Mumbai, 410 210, India. TEL 91-22-27743967, FAX 91-22-66736413, editor@bioinfo.in, subscription@bioinfo.in.

612.3 572.4 NGA
➤ **INTERNATIONAL JOURNAL OF NUTRITION AND METABOLISM.** Text in English. m. free (effective 2010). adv. **Document type:** *Journal, Academic/Scholarly.*
Media: Online - full text.
Published by: Academic Journals, PO Box 73023, Victoria Island, Lagos, Nigeria. service@academicjournals.org. Eds. Dr. Kedar N Mohanta, Malay Chatterjee, Dr. Wei Wang.

613.25 GBR ISSN 0307-0565
RC628 CODEN: IJOBDP
➤ **INTERNATIONAL JOURNAL OF OBESITY.** Abbreviated title: I J O. Cover title: International Journal of Obesity and Related Metabolic Disorders. Text in English. 1977. m. EUR 1,391 in Europe to institutions; USD 1,751 in the Americas to institutions; JPY 238,100 in Japan to institutions; GBP 898 to institutions in the UK & elsewhere (effective 2011). adv. bk.rev. cum.index. back issues avail.; reprints avail. **Document type:** *Journal, Academic/Scholarly.* **Description:** Describes basic clinical and applied studies in biochemistry, physiology, genetics and nutrition, molecular, metabolic, psychological and epidemiological aspects of obesity and related disorders.
Related titles: Online - full text ed.: ISSN 1476-5497; Supplement(s): International Journal of Obesity. Supplement. ISSN 1359-6373.
Indexed: A01, A02, A03, A08, A20, A22, A26, A34, A35, A36, A37, A38, AgBio, Agr, B21, B25, BIOBASE, BIOSIS Prev, C06, C07, CA, CABA, CIN, ChemAb, ChemTitl, CurCont, D01, DentInd, E01, E12, EMBASE, ESPM, ExcerpMed, F09, F10, FR, FS&TA, FamI, GH, H&SSA, H12, H16, I05, IABS, IBR, IBZ, ISR, IndMed, Inpharma, LT, MEDLINE, MaizeAb, MycolAb, N02, N03, N04, NRN, NSA, OR, P03, P11, P20, P22, P25, P30, P32, P35, P37, P38, P48, P50, P52, P54, P56, PEI, PGrRegA, PN&I, PQC, PsycInfo, PsycholAb, R10, R11, R12, RA&MP, RRTA, Reac, RefZh, RiskAb, S12, S17, S21, SCI, SCOPUS, SoyAb, T02, T05, THA, VITIS, VS, W07, W11.
—BLDSC (4542.410000), CASDDS, GNLM, IE, Infotrieve, Ingenta, INIST. **CCC.**
Published by: (International Association for the Study of Obesity), Nature Publishing Group (Subsidiary of: Macmillan Publishers Ltd.), The MacMillan Bldg, 4 Crinan St, London, N1 9XW, United Kingdom. TEL 44-20-78334000, FAX 44-20-78334640. Eds. Ian Macdonald TEL 44-115-8230119, Richard L Atkinson TEL 301-663-0658. Adv. contact Ben Harkinson TEL 617-475-9222. **Subscr. to:** Brunel Rd, Houndmills, Basingstoke, Hants RG21 6XS, United Kingdom. TEL 44-1256-329242, FAX 44-1256-812358, subscriptions@nature.com.

N O

613.2 USA ISSN 1526-484X
RC1235 CODEN: ISNUE5

➤ **INTERNATIONAL JOURNAL OF SPORT NUTRITION & EXERCISE METABOLISM.** Abbreviated title: I J S N E M. Short title: I J S N. Text in English. 1991. bi-m. USD 468 domestic to individuals; USD 483 foreign to individuals; USD 552 combined subscription domestic to institutions (print & online eds.); USD 567 combined subscription foreign to institutions (print & online eds.) (effective 2012). adv. bk.rev. abstr.; bibl.; charts; stat.; illus. index. back issues avail.; reprint service avail. from PSC. **Document type:** *Journal, Academic/ Scholarly.* **Description:** Provides original research in the fields of sport nutrition and exercise metabolism.
Formerly (until 2000): International Journal of Sport Nutrition (1050-1606)
Related titles: Online - full text ed.: ISSN 1543-2742. USD 468 to institutions (effective 2012).
Indexed: A01, A02, A03, A08, A22, A26, ASCA, Agr, B04, BIOBASE, BRD, C06, C07, C08, CA, CIN, CINAHL, ChemAb, ChemTitl, CurCont, DIP, E08, EMBASE, ExcerpMed, F10, FoSS&M, G03, G08, GSA, GSI, H04, H12, IABS, IBR, IBZ, ISR, IndMed, Inpharma, MEDLINE, P30, PEI, R09, R10, Reac, S09, SCI, SCOPUS, SD, SportS, T02, W03, W07.
—BLDSC (4542.680900), CASDDS, GNLM, IE, Ingenta, INIST. **CCC.**
Published by: Human Kinetics, 1607 N Market St, Champaign, IL 61820. TEL 800-747-4457, FAX 217-351-2674, info@hkusa.com, http://www.humankinetics.com. Pub. Rainer Martens. R&P Martha Gullo TEL 217-403-7534. Adv. contact Amy Bleich TEL 217-403-7803.

▼ ➤ **INTERNATIONAL JOURNAL OF WINE RESEARCH.** *see* MEDICAL SCIENCES

➤ **INTERNATIONAL SEMINARS IN PAEDIATRIC GASTROENTEROLOGY AND NUTRITION.** *see* MEDICAL SCIENCES—Gastroenterology

613.7 613.2 GBR ISSN 1550-2783

➤ **INTERNATIONAL SOCIETY OF SPORTS NUTRITION. JOURNAL.** Abbreviated title: J I S S N. Text in English. 2004. irreg. free (effective 2011). adv. back issues avail.; reprints avail. **Document type:** *Journal, Academic/Scholarly.* **Description:** Covers various aspects of sports nutrition, supplementation, exercise metabolism, and/or scientific policies related sports nutrition.
Formerly (vol.1, no.1, 2004): Sports Nutrition Review Journal
Media: Online - full text.
Indexed: A26, A34, A36, AgrForAb, BP, CA, CABA, D01, F08, FoSS&M, G03, GH, GSA, GSI, H12, H16, I05, LT, N02, N03, N04, P30, P33, PEI, R08, R13, RA&MP, RM&VM, RRTA, S12, SCI, SCOPUS, SD, SoyAb, T05, VS, W03, W05, W07, W11.
—**CCC.**
Published by: (International Society of Sports Nutrition USA), BioMed Central Ltd. (Subsidiary of: Springer Science+Business Media), 236 Gray's Inn Rd, London, WC1X 8HB, United Kingdom. TEL 44-20-31922000, FAX 44-20-31922010, info@biomedcentral.com, http://www.biomedcentral.com. Eds. Douglas S Kalman, Jose Antonio, Richard B Kreider.

613.2 USA ISSN 1937-8297
RA776

➤ **THE INTERNET JOURNAL OF NUTRITION AND WELLNESS.** Text in English. 2005. s-a. free (effective 2011). **Document type:** *Journal, Academic/Scholarly.*
Media: Online - full text.
Indexed: A26, A36, A39, C06, C07, C11, C27, C29, CA, CABA, D03, D04, E08, E12, E13, F08, F10, G08, GH, H11, H12, H16, I05, N02, N03, P33, R14, S06, S09, S14, S15, S18, SoyAb, T02, T05.
Published by: Internet Scientific Publications, Llc., 23 Rippling Creek Dr, Sugar Land, TX 77479. TEL 832-443-1193, FAX 281-240-1533, wenker@ispub.com. Ed. Olivier Wenker TEL 832-754-0335.

▼ ➤ **INVENTI IMPACT NUTRACEUTICALS.** *see* PHARMACY AND PHARMACOLOGY

▼ ➤ **INVENTI RAPID NUTRACEUTICALS.** *see* PHARMACY AND PHARMACOLOGY

613.262 GBR ISSN 0021-681X

JEWISH VEGETARIAN. Text in English. 1965. q. free to members (effective 2009). bk.rev. **Document type:** *Magazine, Trade.*
Published by: International Jewish Vegetarian Society, Membership Secretary, 855 Finchley Rd, London, NW11 8LX, United Kingdom. http://www.ivu.org/jvs/.

613.262 USA
TX392

JEWISH VEGETARIAN NEWSLETTER. Text in English. 1983. q. bk.rev. **Document type:** *Newsletter, Consumer.* **Description:** Discusses Judaism and vegetarianism. Topics include health, ecology, world hunger, animal rights and Jewish holidays.
Formerly (until 1990): Jewish Vegetarians of North America (0883-1904)
Related titles: Online - full text ed.: free.
Published by: Jewish Vegetarians of North America, 6938 Reliance Rd, Federalsburg, MD 21632. TEL 410-754-5550, mail@jewishveg.com, http://www.jewishveg.com/. Ed. Eva R Mossman. R&P Israel Mossman. Circ: 600; 900 (paid); 520 (controlled).

JIANKANG BAO/HEALTH NEWSPAPER. *see* PHYSICAL FITNESS AND HYGIENE

JIANKANG ZHONGGAO/HEALTH ADVICE. *see* PHYSICAL FITNESS AND HYGIENE

613.2 362.1 KOR ISSN 1226-0983

JIYEOG SAHOE YEONG-YANG HAG-HOEJI/KOREAN JOURNAL OF COMMUNITY NUTRITION. Text in Korean. 1996. bi-m. **Document type:** *Journal, Academic/Scholarly.*
Related titles: Online - full text ed.
Indexed: A35, A36, C25, CABA, D01, E12, GH, H16, LT, N02, N03, OR, P32, P37, PHN&I, PN&I, R11, R12, RA&MP, RRTA, S12, SoyAb, T05, TriticAb, VS, W11.
—BLDSC (5113.526800).
Published by: Korean Society of Community Nutrition/Daehan Jiyeog Sahoe Yeong-yang Hag-hoe, #612 Daewoo The Oville, 312-4 Hangangno2-ga, Youngsan-gu, Seoul, 140-871, Korea, S. TEL 82-2-7490745, FAX 82-2-7490746, koreajcn@daum.net, http://www.koscom.or.kr/. Ed. Hong Seok Ahn.

613.2 JPN ISSN 1344-4980

JOMYAKU, KEICHO EIYO/JAPANESE SOCIETY FOR PARENTERAL AND ENTERAL NUTRITION. JOURNAL. Text in English, Japanese. 1986. a. JPY 10,000 (effective 2007). **Document type:** *Journal, Academic/Scholarly.*
Formerly (until 1998): Nihon Jomyaku Keicho Eiyo Kenkyukaishi (0912-9405)
Related titles: Online - full text ed.
Published by: Nihon Jomyaku Keicho Eiyo Kenkyukai/Japanese Society for Parenteral and Enteral Nutrition, Jikeikai Ika Daigaku Dai 2 Geka, 377-2, Ohno-Higashi, Osaka-Sayama, Osaka 589-8511, Japan. TEL 81-723-660221, FAX 81-723-683382, info@jeff.co.jp, http://www.jspen.jp/.

613.2 JPN ISSN 0286-0511
CODEN: JEDKD7

➤ **JOSHI EIYO DAIGAKU KIYO/KAGAWA NUTRITION UNIVERSITY. JOURNAL.** Text in English, Japanese. 1970. a. adv. **Document type:** *Journal, Academic/Scholarly.* **Description:** Contains reviews and original papers on natural sciences, humanities and social sciences.
Related titles: Online - full text ed.
Indexed: CIN, ChemAb, ChemTitl, JPI.
—CASDDS.
Published by: Joshi Eiyo Daigaku/Kagawa Nutrition University, 3-9-21 Chiyoda, Sakado, Saitama 350-0288, Japan. TEL 81-49-2846410, FAX 81-49-2846245, knuintlo@eiyo.ac.jp. Circ: 900.

613.2 AUT ISSN 1563-2873
RC620.A1

➤ **JOURNAL FUER ERNAEHRUNGSMEDIZIN**; interdisziplinaeres Organ fuer Praevention und Therapie von Krankheiten durch Ernaehrung. Text in German. 1999. q. EUR 36 (effective 2005). bk.rev. abstr.; bibl. 32 p./no. 3 cols./p.; back issues avail. **Document type:** *Journal, Academic/Scholarly.* **Description:** Presents an interdisciplinary forum for research into the prevention of nutritional deficiencies and diseases.
Related titles: Online - full text ed.: ISSN 1680-9432. 2001. free (effective 2011).
Indexed: R10, Reac, SCOPUS.
—BLDSC (4979.544000), IE, Ingenta. **CCC.**
Published by: Krause & Pachernegg GmbH, Mozartgasse 10, Gablitz, 3003, Austria. TEL 43-2231-612580, FAX 43-2231-6125810, k_u_p@eunet.at, http://www.kup.at/verlag.htm. Ed. Dr. Kurt Widhalm. Circ: 6,500 (paid).

➤ **JOURNAL OF CLINICAL BIOCHEMISTRY AND NUTRITION.** *see* BIOLOGY—Biochemistry

613.2 USA ISSN 1542-8052
TX341 CODEN: JNMDFS

➤ **JOURNAL OF CULINARY SCIENCE & TECHNOLOGY.** Text in English. 1994. q. GBP 230 combined subscription in United Kingdom to institutions (print & online eds.); EUR 298, USD 306 combined subscription to institutions (print & online eds.) (effective 2012). adv. bk.rev. back issues avail.; reprint service avail. from PSC. **Document type:** *Journal, Academic/Scholarly.* **Description:** Addresses the issues of science and technology behind the meal planning, preparation, processing, and service for a global consuming public.
Formerly (until 2005): Journal of Nutrition in Recipe & Menu Development (1055-1379)
Related titles: Microfiche ed.: (from PQC); Microform ed.; Online - full text ed.: ISSN 1542-8044. GBP 207 in United Kingdom to institutions; EUR 268, USD 276 to institutions (effective 2012).
Indexed: A01, A03, A10, A22, A29, A34, A36, A37, Agr, B20, B21, C25, CA, CABA, D01, E01, E12, ESPM, F08, F10, F11, FR, FS&TA, GH, H&TI, H06, H14, H16, I10, LT, M02, MaizeAb, N02, N03, P02, P10, P37, P48, P53, P54, PN&I, PQC, PerIslam, R12, RRTA, S10, S12, S13, SCOPUS, SoyAb, T02, T05, TAR, TriticAb, V03, VS, VirolAbstr, W11.
—IE, Ingenta, INIST. **CCC.**
Published by: Taylor & Francis Inc. (Subsidiary of: Taylor & Francis Group), 325 Chestnut St, Ste 800, Philadelphia, PA 19106. TEL 800-354-1420, FAX 215-625-8914, customerservice@taylorandfrancis.com, http://www.taylorandfrancis.com. Eds. John M Antun, Joseph A Hegarty.

➤ **JOURNAL OF DIETARY SUPPLEMENTS.** *see* PHARMACY AND PHARMACOLOGY

➤ **JOURNAL OF FOOD AND DRUG ANALYSIS/YAOWU SHIPIN FENXI.** *see* FOOD AND FOOD INDUSTRIES

612.2 664 SVK ISSN 1336-8672
TP368

➤ **JOURNAL OF FOOD AND NUTRITION RESEARCH/BULLETIN OF FOOD RESEARCH.** Text in English. 1962. q. EUR 80 (effective 2009). **Document type:** *Journal, Academic/Scholarly.*
Former titles (until 2006): Bulletin Potravinarskeho Vyskumu (0231-9950); (until 1981): Vyskumny Ustav Potravinarsky. Bulletin (0322-8320)
Related titles: Microfiche ed.
Indexed: A01, A34, A35, A36, A37, AgBio, AgrForAb, B21, B23, BA, BP, C25, CA, CABA, ChemoAb, CurCont, D01, E12, ESPM, F05, F06, F07, F08, F10, F11, F12, FCA, FS&TA, GH, H&SSA, H16, I10, INIS AtomInd, IndVet, MaizeAb, N02, N03, N04, OR, P32, P33, P37, P38, P39, P40, PGegResA, PHN&I, PN&I, R11, R12, R13, RA&MP, RM&VM, RiskAb, S12, S13, S16, SCI, SCOPUS, SoyAb, T02, T05, TAR, TriticAb, VS, W07, W11.
—BLDSC (4984.539500), IE, Ingenta.
Published by: Vyskumny Ustav Potravinarsky, Priemyselna 4, PO Box 25, Bratislava 26, 824 75, Slovakia. TEL 42-12-50237135, FAX 42-12-55571417. Ed. Dr. Peter Simko. **Dist. by:** Slovart G.T.G. s.r.o., Krupinska 4, PO Box 152, Bratislava 85299, Slovakia. TEL 421-2-63839472, FAX 421-2-63839485, info@slovart-gtg.sk, http://www.slovart-gtg.sk.

613.2 KOR

➤ **JOURNAL OF FOOD SCIENCE AND NUTRITION.** Text in English. 1996. q. adv. 80 p./no.; reprints avail. **Document type:** *Journal, Academic/Scholarly.*
Former titles (until 2003): Nutraceuticals and Food (1598-6195); (until 2002): Journal of Food Science and Nutrition (1226-332X)
Related titles: CD-ROM ed.; Online - full content ed.
Indexed: FS&TA.
—IE, Ingenta.
Published by: Korean Society of Food Science and Nutrition, Yeonsan 4-dong, Yeonje-gu, 587-8 SK View, 103-1307, Busan, 611-820, Korea, S. TEL 86-51-8663693, FAX 86-51-8663695, kfn@kfn.or.kr, http://www.kfn.or.kr/. Ed. Kun-Young Park. Pub. Dr. Kwang-su Kim. adv.: page KRW 500,000; 210 x 280.

▼ ➤ **JOURNAL OF FUNCTIONAL FOODS.** *see* FOOD AND FOOD INDUSTRIES

613.2 GBR ISSN 0952-3871
QP141.A1 CODEN: JHNDEO

➤ **JOURNAL OF HUMAN NUTRITION AND DIETETICS.** Text in English. 1982. bi-m. GBP 558 in United Kingdom to institutions; EUR 708 in Europe to institutions; USD 1,029 in the Americas to institutions; USD 1,198 elsewhere to institutions; GBP 642 combined subscription in United Kingdom to institutions (print & online eds.); EUR 815 combined subscription in Europe to institutions (print & online eds.); USD 1,183 combined subscription in the Americas to institutions (print & online eds.); USD 1,378 combined subscription elsewhere to institutions (print & online eds.) (effective 2012). adv. bk.rev. abstr.; bibl.; illus. index. back issues avail.; reprint service avail. from PSC. **Document type:** *Journal, Academic/Scholarly.* **Description:** Aims to meet the changing needs of those concerned with human nutrition and dietetics.
Formerly (until 1988): Human Nutrition. Applied Nutrition (0263-8495); Which superseded in part (in 1982): Journal of Human Nutrition (0308-4329); Which was formerly (until 1976): Nutrition (0029-6600); (until 1951): Nutrition, Dietetics, Catering
Related titles: Microform ed.: (from PQC); Online - full text ed.: ISSN 1365-277X. GBP 558 in United Kingdom to institutions; EUR 708 in Europe to institutions; USD 1,029 in the Americas to institutions; USD 1,198 elsewhere to institutions (effective 2012) (from IngentaConnect); Supplement(s): Journal of Human Nutrition and Dietetics (Supplement). ISSN 1465-8178. 1999.
Indexed: A01, A02, A03, A08, A22, A26, A34, A35, A36, A37, A38, ASCA, AgBio, Agr, B21, B25, BIOSIS Prev, C06, C07, C08, C11, C25, CA, CABA, CINAHL, CurCont, D01, DiabCont, E01, E12, EMBASE, ESPM, ExcerpMed, F05, F06, F07, F08, F09, F10, FR, FS&TA, GH, H04, H12, H16, I10, ISR, Inpharma, LT, MEDLINE, MaizeAb, MycolAb, N02, N03, N04, P03, P30, P33, P34, P37, PN&I, PsycInfo, PsycholAb, R09, R10, R11, R12, RA&MP, RM&VM, RRTA, Reac, S12, SCI, SCOPUS, SD, SoyAb, T02, T05, VS, W07, W11.
—BLDSC (5003.419300), CASDDS, GNLM, IE, Infotrieve, Ingenta, INIST, Linda Hall. **CCC.**
Published by: (British Dietetic Association), Wiley-Blackwell Publishing Ltd. (Subsidiary of: John Wiley & Sons, Inc.), 9600 Garsington Rd, Oxford, OX4 2DQ, United Kingdom. TEL 44-1865-776868, FAX 44-1865-714591, customerservices@blackwellpublishing.com. Ed. Joan Gandy TEL 44-20-84290892. Adv. contact Craig Pickett TEL 44-1865-476267.

613.2 363.8 USA ISSN 1932-0248
TX341

➤ **JOURNAL OF HUNGER AND ENVIRONMENTAL NUTRITION.** Text in English. 2006 (Spring). q. GBP 243 combined subscription in United Kingdom to institutions (print & online eds.); EUR 316, USD 326 combined subscription to institutions (print & online eds.) (effective 2012). adv. reprint service avail. from PSC. **Document type:** *Journal, Academic/Scholarly.*
Related titles: Online - full text ed.: ISSN 1932-0256. 2006. GBP 219 in United Kingdom to institutions; EUR 285, USD 293 to institutions (effective 2012).
Indexed: A22, A28, A34, A36, APA, B&BAb, BrCerAb, C&ISA, C25, CA, CA/WCA, CABA, CIA, CerAb, CivEngAb, CorrAb, D01, E&CAJ, E01, E04, E05, E11, E12, EEA, EMA, EMBASE, ESPM, EnvEAb, ExcerpMed, F10, FS&TA, FamI, GH, H15, H17, Inspec, LT, M&TEA, M02, M09, MBF, METADEX, MaizeAb, N02, N03, OR, P30, P33, PAIS, PHN&I, R11, R12, RRTA, S13, S16, SCOPUS, SociolAb, SolStAb, SoyAb, T02, T04, T05, TAR, TriticAb, W11, WAA.
—IE, Ingenta. **CCC.**
Published by: Taylor & Francis Inc. (Subsidiary of: Taylor & Francis Group), 325 Chestnut St, Ste 800, Philadelphia, PA 19106. TEL 215-625-8900, 800-354-1420, FAX 215-625-8914, 215-625- 8914, customerservice@taylorandfrancis.com, http://www.taylorandfrancis.com. Ed. Dr. Marie Boyle Struble.

➤ **JOURNAL OF MUSCLE FOODS.** *see* FOOD AND FOOD INDUSTRIES

➤ **JOURNAL OF NATURAL REMEDIES**; dedicated to medicinal plant research. *see* ALTERNATIVE MEDICINE

➤ **JOURNAL OF NUTRIGENETICS AND NUTRIGENOMICS.** *see* BIOLOGY—Genetics

613.2 USA ISSN 0022-3166
RM214 CODEN: JONUAI

➤ **THE JOURNAL OF NUTRITION.** Abbreviated title: J N. Text in English. 1928. m. USD 205 combined subscription domestic to individuals (print & online eds.); USD 255 combined subscription foreign to individuals (print & online eds.); USD 710 combined subscription domestic to institutions (print & online eds.); USD 760 combined subscription foreign to institutions (print & online eds.); USD 40 combined subscription domestic to members (print & online eds.); USD 80 combined subscription foreign to members (print & online eds.) (effective 2011). adv. bk.rev. abstr.; bibl.; charts; illus. Index. back issues avail.; reprints avail. **Document type:** *Journal, Academic/ Scholarly.* **Description:** Covers all aspects of experimental nutrition, critical reviews, commentaries, and symposia and workshop proceedings.
Related titles: Microform ed.: (from PMC, PQC); Online - full text ed.: ISSN 1541-6100. USD 180 to individuals; USD 670 to institutions (effective 2011).
Indexed: A01, A02, A03, A08, A20, A22, A23, A24, A25, A26, A34, A35, A36, A37, A38, ASCA, ASFA, AbAn, AgBio, Agr, AgrForAb, B&AI, B04, B10, B13, B21, B25, BA, BIOBASE, BIOSIS Prev, BP, BRD, C06, C07, C13, C25, C30, C33, CA, CABA, CIN, CRFR, CTA, Cadscan, ChemAb, ChemTitl, CurCont, D01, DBA, DentInd, E04, E05, E08, E12, EMBASE, ESPM, ExcerpMed, F05, F06, F07, F08, F09, F10, F12, FR, FS&TA, FamI, G03, G08, G10, G11, GH, GSA, GSI, H04, H11, H12, H13, H16, H17, I05, IABS, INI, ISR, IndMed, IndVet, Inpharma, LT, LeadAb, M01, M02, MEDLINE, MaizeAb, MycolAb, N02, N03, N04, NRN, P02, P10, P11, P13, P15, P19, P20, P22, P24, P26, P30, P32, P33, P34, P37, P38, P39, P40, P48, P50, P52, P53, P54, P56, PGegResA, PHN&I, PN&I, PQC, R07, R08, R10, R11, R12, R13, RA&MP, RM&VM, RRTA, Reac, S&MA, S08, S09, S12, S13, S16, S17, SCI, SCOPUS, SoyAb, T02, T05, THA, TOSA, ToxAb, TriticAb, VITIS, VS, W03, W07, W11, WildRev, Zincscan.
—BLDSC (5024.000000), CASDDS, GNLM, IE, Infotrieve, Ingenta, INIST, Linda Hall. **CCC.**

Published by: American Society for Nutrition, 9650 Rockville Pike, Bethesda, MD 20814. TEL 301-634-7050, FAX 301-634-7892, info@nutrition.org, http://www.nutrition.org. Ed. Dr. A Catherine Ross. Adv. contact Veronica Purvis TEL 301-634-7791. Circ: 1,850. **Dist. by:** Turpin Distribution Services Ltd., The Bleachery, 143 W St, New Milford, CT 06776. TEL 860-350-0041, FAX 860-350-0036, turpinna@turpin-distribution.com; Turpin Distribution Services Ltd., Pegasus Dr, Stratton Business Park, Biggleswade, Bedfordshire SG18 8QB, United Kingdom. TEL 44-1767-604951, FAX 44-1767-601640, custserv@turpin-distribution.com, http://www.turpin-distribution.com/.

613.2 USA ISSN 2155-9600
QP141.A1

▼ ➤ **JOURNAL OF NUTRITION & FOOD SCIENCES.** Text in English. 2010 (Oct.). bi-m. free (effective 2011). **Document type:** *Journal, Academic/Scholarly.* **Description:** Covers all aspects of experimental nutrition and various sub-disciplines of food science, diet and health.
Media: Online - full text.
Published by: Omics Publishing Group, 5716 Corse Ave, Ste 110, Westlake, Los Angeles, CA 91362. TEL 650-268-9744, 800-216-6499, info@omicsonline.com, http://www.omicsonline.com.

613.2 USA ISSN 2090-0724

▼ ➤ **JOURNAL OF NUTRITION AND METABOLISM.** Text in English. 2010. irreg. USD 595 (effective 2011). **Document type:** *Journal, Academic/Scholarly.* **Description:** Publishes original research articles, review articles, case reports, and clinical studies in all areas of nutrition and metabolism.
Related titles: Online - full text ed.: ISSN 2090-0732. 2010. free (effective 2011).
Indexed: A01, A35, A36, AgrForAb, B21, CABA, CTA, D01, F08, F10, GH, H16, MaizeAb, N02, N03, NSA, P30, T02, T05.
Published by: Hindawi Publishing Corporation, 410 Park Ave, 15th Fl, PMB 287, New York, NY 10022. FAX 215-893-4392, 866-446-3294, info@hindawi.com.

613.2 USA ISSN 1499-4046
QP141.A1

➤ **JOURNAL OF NUTRITION EDUCATION AND BEHAVIOR.** Abbreviated title: J N E B. Text in English. 1969. 6/yr. USD 403 in United States to institutions; USD 448 elsewhere to institutions (effective 2012). adv. bk.rev. abstr.; bibl.; charts; illus. Index. 64 p./no. 2 cols./p.; back issues avail.; reprints avail. **Document type:** *Journal, Academic/Scholarly.* **Description:** Designed to stimulate interest and research in applied nutritional sciences and to disseminate information to educators and others concerned about positive nutritional practices and policies.
Formerly (until 2002): Journal of Nutrition Education (0022-3182)
Related titles: Online - full text ed.: ISSN 1708-8259. CAD 282 domestic to individuals; USD 209 foreign to individuals (effective 2006) (from ScienceDirect).
Indexed: A01, A02, A03, A08, A20, A22, A25, A26, A34, A36, A37, ASCA, Agr, AgrForAb, B04, BRD, C03, C05, C06, C07, C08, C25, CA, CABA, CBCARef, CINAHL, CPE, CPerI, ChPerI, CurCont, D01, E02, E03, E06, E07, E08, E09, E12, EMBASE, ERI, ERIC, EdA, EdI, ExcerpMed, F08, F09, F10, FR, FS&TA, FamI, G03, G08, GH, GSA, GSI, H&TI, H04, H06, H11, H12, H13, H16, I05, LT, M01, M02, MEDLINE, MLA-IB, MaizeAb, N02, N03, N04, NRN, OR, P02, P03, P04, P07, P10, P11, P18, P20, P24, P26, P30, P34, P38, P48, P50, P52, P53, P54, P55, P56, PHN&I, PQC, PsycInfo, PsycholAb, R09, R10, R12, RA&MP, RRTA, Reac, S02, S03, S08, S09, S12, SCI, SCOPUS, SD, SoyAb, T02, T05, TAR, W03, W07, W11.
—BLDSC (5024.705000), GNLM, IE, Ingenta, INIST. **CCC.**
Published by: (Society for Nutrition Education), Elsevier Inc. (Subsidiary of: Elsevier Science & Technology), 360 Park Ave S, New York, NY 10010. TEL 212-989-5800, FAX 212-633-3990, usinfo-f@elsevier.com. Ed. Karen Chapman-Novakofski. Adv. contact Roxana Aldea TEL 212-633-3160. B&W page USD 1,380, color page USD 2,480; trim 8.125 x 10.675. Circ: 2,856.

➤ **JOURNAL OF NUTRITION, HEALTH AND AGING.** *see* MEDICAL SCIENCES—Internal Medicine

➤ **JOURNAL OF NUTRITION IN GERONTOLOGY AND GERIATRICS.** *see* GERONTOLOGY AND GERIATRICS

612.3 USA ISSN 0955-2863
QP141.A1 CODEN: JNBIEL

➤ **THE JOURNAL OF NUTRITIONAL BIOCHEMISTRY.** Abbreviated title: J N B. Text in English. 1970. 12/yr. USD 1,968 in United States to institutions; USD 2,235 elsewhere to institutions (effective 2012). adv. charts; illus. index. back issues avail.; reprints avail. **Document type:** *Journal, Academic/Scholarly.* **Description:** Provides a forum for advances and issues in nutrition, nutritional biochemistry and food sciences.
Supersedes (in 1990): Nutrition Reports International (0029-6635)
Related titles: Microfilm ed.: (from PQC); Online - full text ed.: ISSN 1873-4847 (from IngentaConnect, ScienceDirect).
Indexed: A01, A03, A08, A22, A26, A34, A35, A36, A37, A38, ASCA, AgBio, Agr, AgrForAb, B21, B25, B27, BIOBASE, BIOSIS Prev, BP, BibAg, C06, C07, C25, C33, CA, CABA, CIN, CTA, Cadscan, ChemAb, ChemTitl, CurCont, D01, E04, E05, E12, EMBASE, ESPM, ExcerpMed, F08, F10, FS&TA, GH, GenetAb, H&SSA, H16, I05, IABS, ISR, IndVet, Inpharma, LT, MEDLINE, MaizeAb, MycolAb, N02, N03, N04, NRN, NSA, P30, P32, P33, P37, P40, PGegResA, PGrRegA, PHN&I, PN&I, R07, R08, R10, R11, R13, RA&MP, RM&VM, RRTA, Reac, S&MA, S12, SCI, SCOPUS, SoyAb, T02, T05, TOSA, ToxAb, TriticAb, VITIS, VS, W07, W11, WildRev, Zincscan.
—BLDSC (5024.730000), CASDDS, GNLM, IE, Infotrieve, Ingenta, INIST, Linda Hall. **CCC.**
Published by: Elsevier Inc. (Subsidiary of: Elsevier Science & Technology), 360 Park Ave S, New York, NY 10010. TEL 212-989-5800, FAX 212-633-3990, usinfo-f@elsevier.com. Ed. Dr. Bernhard Hennig. Adv. contact John Marmero Jr. TEL 212-633-3657. B&W page USD 1,675, color page USD 2,990; trim 8.25 x 11. Circ: 1,000 (paid).

613.2 JPN ISSN 0301-4800
QP141.A1 CODEN: JNSVA5

➤ **JOURNAL OF NUTRITIONAL SCIENCE AND VITAMINOLOGY.** Text in Japanese. 1954. bi-m. bk.rev. bibl.; charts; illus. Index. **Document type:** *Journal, Academic/Scholarly.*
Formerly (until 1972): Journal of Vitaminology (0022-5398)
Related titles: Online - full text ed.: ISSN 1881-7742; ◆ Japanese ed.: Nippon Eiyo Shokuryo Gakkaishi. ISSN 0287-3516.
Indexed: A22, A34, A35, A36, A38, ASCA, AgBio, AgrForAb, B21, B25, BIOBASE, BIOSIS Prev, BP, C06, C07, C25, C33, CABA, CIN, CTA, ChemAb, ChemTitl, CurCont, D01, DBA, E12, EMBASE, ESPM, ExcerpMed, F08, F11, F12, FS&TA, GH, H16, I10, IABS, IBR, IBZ, ISR, IndMed, Inpharma, LT, MEDLINE, MaizeAb, MycolAb, N02, N03, N04, NRN, NSA, O01, P30, P32, P33, P37, P38, P40, PGegResA, PN&I, R07, R08, R10, R11, R12, RA&MP, RM&VM, RRTA, Reac, S12, S17, SCI, SCOPUS, SoyAb, T05, TAR, TriticAb, VS, W07.
—BLDSC (5024.750000), CASDDS, GNLM, IE, Infotrieve, Ingenta, INIST, Linda Hall. **CCC.**
Published by: (Nippon Eiyo Shokuryo Gakkai/Japanese Society of Nutrition and Food Science), Center for Academic Publications Japan, 4-16, Yayoi 2-chome, Bunkyo-ku, Tokyo, 113-0032, Japan. FAX 81-3-38175830, http://www.capj.or.jp/. Circ: 1,500. **Co-sponsor:** Nihon Bitamin Gakkai/Vitamin Society of Japan.

612.3 USA ISSN 0148-6071
RM224 CODEN: JPENDU

➤ **JOURNAL OF PARENTERAL AND ENTERAL NUTRITION.** Key Title: J P E N: Journal of Parenteral and Enteral Nutrition. Text in English. 1979. bi-m. USD 353, GBP 208 combined subscription to institutions (print & online eds.); USD 346, GBP 204 to institutions (effective 2011). adv. bk.rev. 80 p./no. 2 cols./p.; back issues avail.; reprint service avail. from PSC. **Document type:** *Journal, Academic/Scholarly.* **Description:** Research on nutritional deficiency and its treatment, including administration, risks and complications.
Related titles: Microform ed.: (from PQC); Online - full text ed.: ISSN 1941-2444. USD 318, GBP 187 to institutions (effective 2011); Supplement(s): Guidelines in the Use of Parenteral and Enteral Nutrition in Adult and Pediatric Patients.
Indexed: A22, A35, A36, A37, ASCA, AgBio, B25, B28, BA, BIOSIS Prev, C06, C07, C08, CABA, CINAHL, CurCont, D01, E01, E12, EMBASE, ExcerpMed, FR, GH, H16, I12, IDIS, ISR, IndMed, Inpharma, JW-G, MEDLINE, MaizeAb, MycolAb, N02, N03, NRN, OR, P11, P20, P22, P24, P30, P33, P48, P54, PN&I, PQC, R10, R12, RA&MP, RM&VM, Reac, S12, SCI, SCOPUS, SoyAb, T05, VS, W07.
—BLDSC (5029.100000), CASDDS, GNLM, IE, Infotrieve, Ingenta, INIST. **CCC.**
Published by: (American Society for Parenteral and Enteral Nutrition), Sage Publications, Inc., 2455 Teller Rd, Thousand Oaks, CA 91320. TEL 805-499-9774, FAX 805-499-0871, info@sagepub.com, http://www.sagepub.com/. Ed. Paul Wischmeyer. adv.: B&W page USD 1,450; 8.5 x 11. Circ: 7,300.

612.3 USA ISSN 0277-2116
CODEN: JPGND6

➤ **JOURNAL OF PEDIATRIC GASTROENTEROLOGY AND NUTRITION.** Text in English. 1982. 10/yr. USD 1,380 domestic to institutions; USD 1,544 foreign to institutions (effective 2011). adv. bk.rev. charts; illus. index. back issues avail.; reprints avail. **Document type:** *Journal, Academic/Scholarly.* **Description:** Provides a forum for papers and reviews dealing with nutrition in normal and abnormal functions of the alimentary tract and its associated organs, including the salivary glands, pancreas, gallbladder, and liver.
Related titles: Online - full text ed.: ISSN 1536-4801. USD 880.10 domestic for academic site license; USD 966.10 foreign for academic site license; USD 981.65 domestic for corporate site license; USD 1,067.65 foreign for corporate site license (effective 2002).
Indexed: A22, A34, A36, A38, ASCA, Agr, B25, BIOBASE, BIOSIS Prev, BP, BibAg, C06, C07, CABA, CCIP, CIN, ChemAb, ChemTitl, CurCont, D01, DentInd, E12, EMBASE, ExcerpMed, F09, FR, FS&TA, FamI, GH, H16, H17, IABS, IDIS, ISR, IndMed, IndVet, Inpharma, JW-G, LT, MEDLINE, MycolAb, N02, N03, N04, NRN, OR, P30, P33, P35, P39, PHN&I, PN&I, R08, R10, R11, R12, RA&MP, RM&VM, RRTA, Reac, S12, SCI, SCOPUS, SoyAb, T05, TriticAb, VS, W07, W10, W11.
—BLDSC (5030.175000), CASDDS, GNLM, IE, Infotrieve, Ingenta, INIST. **CCC.**
Published by: (North American Society for Pediatric Gastroenterology and Nutrition), Lippincott Williams & Wilkins (Subsidiary of: Wolters Kluwer N.V.), Two Commerce Sq, 2001 Market St, Philadelphia, PA 19103. TEL 215-521-8300, FAX 215-521-8902, customerservice@lww.com, http://www.lww.com. Eds. David Branski, Eric Sibley. Pub. David Myers. Circ: 1,753. **Co-sponsors:** European Society for Pediatric Gastroenterology and Nutrition; North American Society for Pediatric Gastroenterology and Nutrition.

616.39 USA ISSN 1051-2276

➤ **JOURNAL OF RENAL NUTRITION.** Text in English. 1991. bi-m. USD 339 in United States to institutions; USD 389 elsewhere to institutions (effective 2012). adv. bk.rev. back issues avail.; reprints avail. **Document type:** *Journal, Academic/Scholarly.* **Description:** Includes review, original research, articles on the clinical management and education of patients, a current literature review, and nutritional analysis of food products that have clinical relevance.
Related titles: Online - full text ed.: ISSN 1532-8503 (from ScienceDirect).
Indexed: A22, A36, AgrForAb, C06, C07, C08, C25, CABA, CINAHL, CurCont, D01, E01, EMBASE, ExcerpMed, F08, GH, H16, IndMed, LT, MEDLINE, N02, N03, O01, OR, P30, P37, P38, R10, R12, RRTA, Reac, S12, SCI, SCOPUS, SoyAb, T05, VS, W07, W10, W11.
—BLDSC (5049.460000), GNLM, IE, Infotrieve, Ingenta, INIST. **CCC.**
Published by: (National Kidney Foundation, Inc., Council on Renal Nutrition), W.B. Saunders Co. (Subsidiary of: Elsevier Health Sciences), Elsevier, Health Sciences Division, Order Fulfillment, 3251 Riverport Ln, Maryland Heights, MO 63043. TEL 314-872-8370, 800-325-4177, FAX 314-432-1380, JournalCustomerService-usa@elsevier.com, http://www.us.elsevierhealth.com. Eds. Dr. D Jordi Goldstein-Fuchs TEL 775-828-4311, Denis Fouque. Pub. Sarah Kane. Circ: 1,970.

➤ **JOURNAL OF SENSORY STUDIES.** *see* MEDICAL SCIENCES—Psychiatry And Neurology

613.262 USA

JUST EAT AN APPLE. Text in English. bi-m. USD 30 domestic; USD 40 in Canada & Mexico; USD 45 elsewhere (effective 2001). adv. back issues avail. **Document type:** *Magazine, Consumer.* **Description:** Features articles on raw food & natural living.
Published by: Nature's First Law, PO Box 900202, San Diego, CA 92190. TEL 619-645-7282, 888-729-3663, nature@rawfood.com, http://www.rawfood.com. Ed. Frederic Patenaude.

613.2 USA

K D A COMMUNICATOR. Text in English. 1946. 6/yr. free to members. bk.rev. **Document type:** *Newsletter.* **Description:** Covers professional and educational activities of the association's members.
Formerly: Sunflower (0039-5382)
Published by: Kansas Dietetic Association, 3133 U Ave, Herington, KS 67449-5027. TEL 785-258-3337, eatrightks@tctelco.net, http://www.dietetics.com/kda/index.html. Ed. Kathy Chambers. Circ: 750.

KEY NOTE MARKET ASSESSMENT. DIET FOODS. *see* BUSINESS AND ECONOMICS—Production Of Goods And Services

KEY NOTE MARKET ASSESSMENT. HEALTHY EATING. *see* FOOD AND FOOD INDUSTRIES

KEY NOTE MARKET ASSESSMENT. VEGETARIAN FOODS. *see* BUSINESS AND ECONOMICS—Production Of Goods And Services

KEY NOTE PLUS MARKET REPORT. HEALTH FOODS. *see* FOOD AND FOOD INDUSTRIES

613.2 GBR ISSN 1744-5450

KID'S NUTRITION REPORT. Abbreviated title: K N R. Text in English. 2004 (June). bi-m. GBP 675 combined subscription in UK& Ireland, (print & online eds.); EUR 795 combined subscription in Europe (print & online eds.); AUD 1,330 combined subscription in Asia & the Pacific (print & online eds.); CAD 1,150 combined subscription in Canada (print & online eds.); USD 1,050 combined subscription elsewhere (print & online eds.) (effective 2009). **Document type:** *Newsletter, Consumer.* **Description:** Focuses on youth-oriented food products, strategies, policies and politics around the globe.
Related titles: Online - full text ed.
Indexed: FS&TA.
Published by: Centre for Food & Health Studies, Crown House, 72 Hammersmith Rd, London, W14 8TH, United Kingdom. TEL 44-20-76177032, FAX 44-20-79001937, miranda.mills@new-nutrition.com. Ed. Julian Mellentin.

613.2 USA ISSN 1933-2920
TX369

KIWI; growing families the natural and organic way. Text in English. 2006. bi-m. USD 11.95; USD 3.99 newsstand/cover domestic; USD 4.99 newsstand/cover in Canada (effective 2011). adv. **Document type:** *Magazine, Consumer.*
Related titles: Online - full text ed.: ISSN 1933-2912.
Indexed: F10, G05, G06, G07, I05, M02.
Published by: May Media Group, Llc., 152 Madison Ave, Ste 700, New York, NY 10016. TEL 212-532-0010, FAX 212-683-1333.

613.2 641.5 NOR ISSN 0332-9046

KJOEKKENSKRIVEREN; tidsskrift for matomsorg. Text in Norwegian. 1960. 7/yr. NOK 480 (effective 2011). adv. bk.rev. **Document type:** *Magazine, Trade.*
Related titles: Online - full text ed.
Published by: Kost- og Naeringsforbundet, Lakkegata 3, PO Box 9202, Groenland, Oslo, 0134, Norway. TEL 47-21-013650, matomsorg@delta.no. Ed. Elisabeth Stroem TEL 47-91-155994. Adv. contact Rolf Lundberg.

613.2 JPN ISSN 0911-565X

KOBE GAKUIN DAIGAKU EIYOGAKUBU RONBUNSHU/KOBE GAKUIN UNIVERSITY. FACULTY OF NUTRITION. JOURNAL. Text in English, German, Japanese; Summaries in English. 1969. a.
Published by: Kobe Gakuin Daigaku, Eiyogakubu, 518 Ikawadanichoarise, Nishi-ku, Kobe-shi, Hyogo-ken 651-2113, Japan.

KOEKKENLIV. *see* HEALTH FACILITIES AND ADMINISTRATION

612.3 JPN ISSN 0916-5800
TX341

KOKURITSU KENKO, EIYO KENKYUJO KENKYU HOKOKU/NATIONAL INSTITUTE OF HEALTH AND NUTRITION. ANNUAL REPORT. Text in Japanese; Summaries in English. 1949. a. per issue exchange basis. **Document type:** *Government.*
Formerly (until 1988): Kokuritsu Kenko Eiyo Kenkyujo Hokoku (0368-5209); Which incorporated (1949-1971): Kokuritsu Eiyo Kenkyujo Hokoku/National Institute of Nutrition. Annual Report (0452-3148)
—GNLM, INIST, Linda Hall.
Published by: Kose-sho, Kokuritsu Kenko Eiyo Kenkyujo/National Institute of Health and Nutrition, 1-23-1 Toyama, Shinjuku-ku, Tokyo, 162-8636, Japan. TEL 81-3-32035721, FAX 81-3-32023278.

613.2 JPN ISSN 0913-5537
CODEN: KDKAEH

KOSHIEN DAIGAKU KIYO. A, EIYOGAKUBU HEN/KOSHIEN UNIVERSITY. BULLETIN. A. Text in Japanese; Summaries in English, Japanese. 1970. a. **Document type:** *Journal, Academic/Scholarly.*
Supersedes in part (in 1985): Koshien Daigaku Kiyo/Koshien University. Bulletin (0286-5548)
Published by: Koshien Daigaku/Koshien University, 10-1 Momijigaoka, Takarazuka, Hyogo 665-0006, Japan. http://www.koshien.ac.jp/. Circ: 500.

613.2 JPN

KOUSEI ROUDOUSHOU. KOKUMIN KENKO - EIYO CHOSA HOKOKU/JAPAN. MINISTRY OF HEALTH, LABOUR AND WELFARE, NATIONAL HEALTH AND NUTRITION SURVEY IN JAPAN. Text in Japanese. 1947. s-a. JPY 3,360 (effective 1999). **Document type:** *Government.*
Formerly (until 2004): Kokumin Eiyo no Genjo/Report of National Nutritive Conditions
Published by: (Japan. Koseisho, Japan. Hoken Iryokyoku), Daiichi Shuppan K.K., 1-39 Kanda-Jinbo-cho, Chiyoda-ku, Tokyo, 101-0051, Japan. TEL 81-3-32914576, FAX 81-3-32914579, http://www.daiichi-shuppan.co.jp.

KRAUT UND RUEBEN; Magazin fuer biologisches Gaertnern und naturgemaesses Leben. *see* GARDENING AND HORTICULTURE

613.2 POL ISSN 1734-5960

LECZENIE ZYWIENIOWE I METABOLICZNE/NUTRITION & METABOLIC THERAPY. Text in Polish. 2005. q. **Document type:** *Journal, Academic/Scholarly.* **Description:** Publishes Polish and international papers and exchange experiences on clinical nutrition and metabolic diseases related to nutrition or its lack.
Related titles: Online - full text ed.
Published by: Blackhorse Scientific Publishers, Ltd., Zeganska 16, Warsaw, 04713, Poland. TEL 48-22-4999099, FAX 48-22-4995081, blackhorse@blackhorse.pl, http://blackhorse.pl/blackhorse. Ed. Marian Grzymislawski.

LEGISLATION PROFESSIONNELLE. PRODUITS DIETETIQUES. *see* LAW

028.5 613.2 641 NLD ISSN 1875-1571
LEKKER BELANGRIJK!. Text in Dutch. 2007. s-a.
Published by: Voedingscentrum, Postbus 85700, The Hague, 2508 CK, Netherlands. TEL 31-70-3068888, FAX 31-70-3504259, http://www.voedingscentrum.nl.

613.2 NLD ISSN 1879-8926
▼ **LEKKER SLANK SCHEURKALENDER.** Text in Dutch. 2009. a. EUR 8.95 (effective 2010).
Published by: Mix Media, Postbus 16, Lelystad, 8200 AA, Netherlands. TEL 31-320-265080, FAX 31-320-259199, http://www.mixmedia.nl.

613.26 NLD ISSN 1567-3502
LEVEN. Text in Dutch. q. EUR 24.50 domestic; EUR 36.50 in Europe; EUR 39.50 elsewhere (effective 2010). adv. bk.rev. **Document type:** *Magazine, Consumer.* **Description:** Covers topics relating to vegetarianism, nutrition, animal welfare and related matters.
Former titles (until 2000): Leven en Laten Leven (0166-0802); (until 1971): Vegetische Bode
Published by: Nederlandse Vegetariersbond, Nieuwezijds Voorburgwal 153, Amsterdam, 1012 RK, Netherlands. TEL 31-20-3300044, FAX 31-20-4203737, info@vegetariers.nl.

613.2 USA
LIFELINELETTER. Text in English. 1977. bi-m. USD 35 (effective 2000). bk.rev. back issues avail. **Document type:** *Newsletter.* **Description:** Provides support, education and information on research in the field of home parenteral or enteral nutrition.
Published by: Oley Foundation for Home Parenteral & Enteral Nutrition, 214 Hun Memorial A 28, Albany Medical Center, Albany, NY 12208-3478. TEL 518-262-5079, FAX 518-262-5528. Ed., Adv. contact Roslyn Scheib Dahl. Circ: 4,500.

613.262 CAN ISSN 0834-3543
LIFELINES (TORONTO); the voice of Toronto's vegetarian community. Text in English. 1987. bi-m. CAD 20 (effective 2002). adv. bk.rev. illus. 16 p./no.; back issues avail. **Document type:** *Newsletter, Consumer.* **Description:** Publishes a range of articles and news items geared toward vegetarian lifestyles. Includes recipes. Target audience is Toronto and vegetarians, however the publications aims at broader appeal to vegetarians and would-be vegetarians around the world.
Formerly: Toronto Vegetarian Association. Newsletter (0049-4232)
Published by: Toronto Vegetarian Association, 2300 Yonge St, Ste 1101, P O Box 2307, Toronto, ON M4P 1E4, Canada. TEL 416-544-9800, FAX 416-544-9094, lifelines@veg.on.ca. Circ: 3,000.

613.2 DEU
LISA DIAET. Text in German. 2/yr. EUR 1.95 newsstand/cover (effective 2003). adv. **Document type:** *Magazine, Consumer.*
Published by: Medien Innovation GmbH (Subsidiary of: Hubert Burda Media Holding GmbH & Co. KG), Am Kestendamm 1, Offenburg, 77652, Germany. TEL 49-89-92500, FAX 49-89-92502745, info@hubert-burda-media.com, http://www.hubert-burda-media.com. adv.: color page EUR 6,000. Circ: 250,000 (paid and controlled).

LONG LIFE. *see* PHYSICAL FITNESS AND HYGIENE

613.2 641.5 USA
LOW CARB RECIPES. Text in English. bi-m. adv. **Document type:** *Magazine, Consumer.* **Description:** Contains recipes, cooking tips, product reviews, culinary news, and information focused on a low carb lifestyle that is easy to follow.
Published by: Roxbury Media, LLC, 27 Glen Rd, PO Box 140, Sandy Hook, CT 06482. TEL 203-270-8572 ext 119, FAX 203-426-9522. Pubs. John Damboragian TEL 203-270-8572 ext 114, Kevin Montanaro. adv.: B&W page USD 2,500, color page USD 3,125; trim 8.125 x 10.875. Circ: 200,000 (free).

613.25 USA ISSN 1549-991X
LOWCARB LIVING; smart choices for living well. Text in English. 2004 (Jan./Feb.). bi-m. USD 17.97 domestic; USD 27.97 in Canada; USD 35.97 elsewhere (effective 2004). adv. **Document type:** *Magazine, Consumer.*
Published by: CappMedia, Inc., 1563 Solano Ave, Ste 379, Berkeley, CA 94707. TEL 510-525-5223, 800-669-1559. Pub. James Capparell. Adv. contact Steve Randall.

MAA BRA; specialtidningen foer kropp & sjael. *see* PHYSICAL FITNESS AND HYGIENE

613.2 USA
MACROBIOTICS TODAY. Text in English. 1960. 6/yr. USD 30 domestic to non-members; USD 40 foreign to non-members (effective 2007). adv. bk.rev. 40 p./no.; **Document type:** *Magazine, Consumer.* **Description:** Contains articles, interviews and news events concerning macrobiotics and alternative health care.
Formerly (until 1984): G O M F News
Indexed: A04, CA.
Published by: George Ohsawa Macrobiotic Foundation, PO Box 3998, Chico, CA 95927-3998. TEL 530-566-9765, FAX 530-566-9768, gomf@2earthlink.net. Ed., Adv. contact Carl Ferre. Circ: 5,000.

613.2 BHR ISSN 1608-8352
TX360.A65
AL-MAGALLAT AL-'ARABIYYAT LI-L-GIDA WA-AL-TAGDIYAT/ARAB JOURNAL OF FOOD AND NUTRITION. Text in Arabic; Abstracts in Arabic, English. 2000. q. bk.rev. **Document type:** *Journal, Academic/Scholarly.* **Description:** Publishes articles and scientific reports, reports on conferences and scientific seminars, reviews and studies on: Nutrition in the community and applied nutrition, food analysis, food safety, food processing and its effect on nutritional value, the social and economic factors that affect psychological and behavioral attitudes to food, the economics of food and food-related diseases.
Published by: Markaz al-Bahrayn Li-l-dirasat Wa-al-buhut/Bahrain Center for Studies and Research, PO Box 496, Manama, Bahrain. TEL 973-17-754757, FAX 973-17-754678, Info@bcsr.gov.bh.

LE MAGAZINE. *see* HOME ECONOMICS

613.2 649 GBR ISSN 1740-8695
RG559
➤ **MATERNAL AND CHILD NUTRITION.** Text in English. 2004. q. GBP 317 in United Kingdom to institutions; EUR 403 in Europe to institutions; USD 591 in the Americas to institutions; USD 686 elsewhere to institutions; GBP 365 combined subscription in United Kingdom to institutions (print & online eds.); EUR 464 combined subscription in Europe to institutions (print & online eds.); USD 680 combined subscription in the Americas to institutions (print & online eds.); USD 789 combined subscription elsewhere to institutions (print & online eds.) (effective 2011). adv. back issues avail.; reprint service avail. from PSC. **Document type:** *Journal, Academic/Scholarly.* **Description:** Carries research findings and information on new initiatives and innovative ways of responding to changes in public attitudes. Targets health professionals, academic and service users.
Related titles: Online - full text ed.: ISSN 1740-8709. 2004. GBP 317 in United Kingdom to institutions; EUR 403 in Europe to institutions; USD 591 in the Americas to institutions; USD 686 elsewhere to institutions (effective 2011) (from IngentaConnect).
Indexed: A01, A20, A22, A26, A36, AgrForAb, C06, C07, CA, CABA, CurCont, D01, E01, E12, EMBASE, ExcerpMed, F05, F06, F07, F08, F10, FS&TA, GH, H17, MEDLINE, MaizeAb, N02, N03, P30, P33, P38, P39, PN&I, R08, R10, R11, R12, RA&MP, Reac, SCI, SCOPUS, SoyAb, T02, T05, VS, W07, W11.
—BLDSC (5399.272550), IE, Ingenta. **CCC.**
Published by: Wiley-Blackwell Publishing Ltd. (Subsidiary of: John Wiley & Sons, Inc.), 9600 Garsington Rd, Oxford, OX4 2DQ, United Kingdom. TEL 44-1865-776868, FAX 44-1865-714591, customerservices@blackwellpublishing.com. Eds. Peter Aggett, Victoria Hall Moran. Adv. contact Craig Pickett TEL 44-1865-476267.

➤ **MEALEY'S LITIGATION REPORT: FEN-PHEN - REDUX.** *see* PHARMACY AND PHARMACOLOGY

613.2 FRA ISSN 0398-7604
CODEN: MENUDI
MEDECINE ET NUTRITION. Text in French; Abstracts in English. 1965. 4/yr. EUR 200 combined subscription in the European Union (print & online eds.); EUR 221 combined subscription elsewhere (print & online eds.) (effective 2012). adv. bibl.; charts; illus. **Document type:** *Journal, Academic/Scholarly.* **Description:** Publishes original studies on the fundamental and applied aspects of food and nutrition.
Former titles (until 1975): Annales d'Hygiene de Langue Francaise. Medecine et Nutrition (0398-7582); Annales d'Hygiene de Langue Francaise (0003-4363)
Related titles: Online - full text ed.: EUR 150 (effective 2011).
Indexed: A22, CISA, ChemAb, ChemTitl, FR, FS&TA, SCOPUS.
—BLDSC (5487.732500), CASDDS, GNLM, IE, Infotrieve, Ingenta, INIST. **CCC.**
Published by: (Societe d'Hygiene de Langue Francaise), E D P Sciences, 17 Ave du Hoggar, Parc d'Activites de Courtaboeuf, BP 112, Cedex A, Les Ulis, F-91944, France. TEL 33-1-69187575, FAX 33-1-69860678, http://www.edpsciences.org.

612.3 ITA ISSN 1973-798X
➤ **MEDITERRANEAN JOURNAL OF NUTRITION AND METABOLISM.** Text in English. 2008. 3/yr. EUR 248, USD 334 combined subscription to institutions (print & online eds.) (effective 2012). reprint service avail. from PSC. **Document type:** *Journal, Academic/Scholarly.* **Description:** Publishes original research on dietary and nutritional practices and management and their impact on health from prevention to treatment.
Related titles: Online - full text ed.: ISSN 1973-7998. 2008 (from IngentaConnect).
Indexed: A22, A26, E01, E08, EMBASE, ExcerpMed, H12, S09, SCOPUS.
—IE. **CCC.**
Published by: Springer Italia Srl (Subsidiary of: Springer Science+Business Media), Via Decembrio 28, Milan, 20137, Italy. TEL 39-02-54259722, FAX 39-02-55193360, springer@springer.it. Ed. Samir G Sukkar.

➤ **MEDITSINSKI PREGLED. DETSKI BOLESTI/MEDICAL REVIEW. CHILDREN'S DISEASES.** *see* MEDICAL SCIENCES—Pediatrics

➤ **MELK;** meieriprodukter, ernaering, livsstil, kunnskap. *see* HOME ECONOMICS

➤ **MEMPHIS HEALTH CARE NEWS.** *see* PHYSICAL FITNESS AND HYGIENE

613.2 USA ISSN 0271-1893
SF95 CODEN: MNCPDB
MINNESOTA NUTRITION CONFERENCE. PROCEEDINGS. Text in English. 1972. a. back issues avail. **Document type:** *Proceedings, Academic/Scholarly.*
Related titles: CD-ROM ed.
—BLDSC (5810.413000).
Published by: University of Minnesota, College of Continuing Education, CCE Information Center, 1420 Eckles Avenue, St. Paul, MN 55108. TEL 612-624-4000, 800-234-6564, FAX 612-625-1511, info@cce.umn.edu, http://www.cce.umn.edu/.

616.39 CHE ISSN 1424-1307
RA421 CODEN: MGLHAE
MITTEILUNGEN AUS LEBENSMITTELUNTERSUCHUNG UND HYGIENE/TRAVAUX DE CHIMIE ALIMENTAIRE ET D'HYGIENE. Text mainly in French, German; Text occasionally in English, Italian. 1910. 6/yr. adv. bk.rev. bibl.; illus. index. **Document type:** *Journal, Trade.*
Formerly (until 1998): Mitteilungen aus der Gebiete der Lebensmitteluntersuchung und Hygiene (0026-6841)
Indexed: A22, B25, BIOSIS Prev, ChemAb, ChemTitl, DBA, F05, F06, F07, FS&TA, GeoRef, IndMed, MycolAb, P30, PST, SpeleolAb, VITIS.
—CASDDS, IE, Infotrieve, Ingenta, INIST, Linda Hall.
Published by: Bundesamt fuer Gesundheit, Bern, 3003, Switzerland. TEL 41-31-3222111, FAX 41-31-3233772, http://www.bag.admin.ch. Circ: 1,700. **Co-sponsors:** Schweizerische Gesellschaft fuer Lebensmittelhygiene; Schweizerische Gesellschaft fuer Lebensmittel- und Umweltchemie.

613.2 DEU ISSN 1613-4133
➤ **MOLECULAR NUTRITION & FOOD RESEARCH (ONLINE).** Text in English. 1998. m. GBP 1,147 in United Kingdom to institutions; EUR 1,740 in Europe to institutions; USD 2,245 elsewhere to institutions (effective 2012). **Document type:** *Journal, Academic/Scholarly.* **Description:** Devoted to health, safety and all aspects of molecular nutrition such as nutritional biochemistry, nutrigenomics and metabolomics aiming to link the information arising from related disciplines.
Former titles (until 2004): Food (Online) (1611-6070); (until 2003): Nahrung (Online) (1521-3803)
Media: Online - full text. **Related titles:** ◆ Print ed.: Molecular Nutrition & Food Research (Print). ISSN 1613-4125.
—BLDSC (5900.817992). **CCC.**
Published by: Wiley - V C H Verlag GmbH & Co. KGaA (Subsidiary of: John Wiley & Sons, Inc.), Postfach 101161, Weinheim, 69451, Germany. TEL 49-6201-606400, FAX 49-6201-606184, info@wiley-vch.de, http://www.wiley-vch.de. Ed. Peter Schreier.

613.2 DEU ISSN 1613-4125
TX341 CODEN: MNFRCV
➤ **MOLECULAR NUTRITION & FOOD RESEARCH (PRINT).** Text in English, German. 1957. m. GBP 1,147 in United Kingdom to institutions; EUR 1,740 in Europe to institutions; USD 2,245 elsewhere to institutions; GBP 1,319 combined subscription in United Kingdom to institutions (print & online eds.); EUR 2,002 combined subscription in Europe to institutions (print & online eds.); USD 2,582 combined subscription elsewhere to institutions (print & online eds.) (effective 2012). adv. charts; illus.; abstr.; bibl. index. back issues avail.; reprint service avail. from PSC. **Document type:** *Journal, Academic/Scholarly.* **Description:** Devoted to health, safety and all aspects of molecular nutrition such as nutritional biochemistry, nutrigenomics and metabolomics aiming to link the information arising from related disciplines.
Formerly (until 2004): Nahrung/Food (0027-769X)
Related titles: ◆ Online - full text ed.: Molecular Nutrition & Food Research (Online). ISSN 1613-4133.
Indexed: A20, A22, A34, A35, A36, A37, A38, ASCA, AgBio, Agr, AgrForAb, ApicAb, B&BAb, B19, B21, B23, B25, B27, BA, BIOSIS Prev, BP, BioEngAb, C25, C33, CABA, CIN, CTA, Cadscan, ChemAb, ChemTitl, CurCont, CurPA, D01, E12, EMBASE, ESPM, ExcerpMed, F05, F06, F07, F08, F11, F12, FCA, FS&TA, GH, H16, H17, I10, I11, ISR, ImmunAb, IndMed, IndVet, LT, LeadAb, MEDLINE, MaizeAb, MycolAb, N02, N03, N04, NSA, O01, OR, P30, P32, P33, P37, P38, P39, P40, PGegResA, PGrRegA, PHN&I, PN&I, R07, R08, R11, R12, R13, RA&MP, RM&VM, RRTA, S12, S13, S16, S17, SCI, SCOPUS, SoyAb, T05, TriticAb, VITIS, VS, W07, W10, W11, Zincscan.
—BLDSC (5900.817992), CASDDS, GNLM, IE, Infotrieve, Ingenta, INIST, Linda Hall. **CCC.**
Published by: Wiley - V C H Verlag GmbH & Co. KGaA (Subsidiary of: John Wiley & Sons, Inc.), Postfach 101161, Weinheim, 69451, Germany. TEL 49-6201-606400, FAX 49-6201-606184, info@wiley-vch.de. Ed. Peter Schreier. Circ: 450. **Subscr. in the Americas to:** John Wiley & Sons, Inc., 111 River St, Hoboken, NJ 07030. TEL 201-748-6645, subinfo@wiley.com; **Subscr. outside Germany, Austria & Switzerland to:** John Wiley & Sons Ltd., The Atrium, Southern Gate, Chichester, West Sussex PO19 8SQ, United Kingdom. TEL 44-1243-779777, FAX 44-1243-775878, cs-agency@wiley.com.

➤ **MUSCLE MEDIA;** training guide. *see* PHYSICAL FITNESS AND HYGIENE

➤ **LE MUST ALIMENTAIRE.** *see* HOME ECONOMICS

613.2 USA
N A A F A NEWSLETTER. Text in English. 1969. 6/yr. adv. bk.rev. back issues avail. **Document type:** *Newsletter.* **Description:** Provides information regarding obesity research, size discrimination, and advances in the size acceptance movement.
Published by: National Association to Advance Fat Acceptance, Inc., PO Box 22510, Oakland, CA 94609-5110. TEL 916-558-6880, naafa@naafa.org.com, http://www.naafa.org/. Ed. Sally E Smith. Circ: 5,000.

N A F A S. (Nutrition, Aliments Fonctionnels, Aliments Sante) *see* MEDICAL SCIENCES

613.2 IND ISSN 0971-2720
N F I BULLETIN. Text in English. 1980. q. free to qualified personnel (effective 2011). back issues avail. **Document type:** *Bulletin, Trade.*
Related titles: Online - full text ed.: free (effective 2011).
Indexed: P30.
—BLDSC (6109.073500), IE, Infotrieve, Ingenta.
Published by: Nutrition Foundation of India, C-13, Qutab Institutional Area, New Delhi, 110 016, India. TEL 91-11-26962615, FAX 91-11-26857814, nfi@nutritionfoundationofindia.res.in.

N N F A TODAY. *see* FOOD AND FOOD INDUSTRIES

613.2 USA
N O H A NEWS. Text in English. 1976. q. USD 10 to non-members; free to members (effective 2000). bk.rev. back issues avail. **Document type:** *Newsletter.* **Description:** Reports on nutritional information and research findings culled from a wide range of scientific sources; includes a column written by members of the professional advisory board.
Published by: Nutrition for Optimal Health Association, PO Box 380, Winnetka, IL 60093. TEL 708-786-5326, 847-604-3258, FAX 847-604-3358. Ed. Marjorie Fisher. Circ: 700.

613.2 CAN
N P I DAILY. Text in English. d. free. **Document type:** *Newsletter, Trade.* **Description:** Designed for for professionals in the nutraceutical, nutritional, dietary supplement, cosmetic, and food industries.
Media: Online - full content.
Published by: N P Icenter (Subsidiary of: New Hope Natural Media), 16 Main St, Georgetown, ON L7G 3G5, Canada. TEL 877-463-0110, FAX 905-877-0468, sales@npicenter.com.

613.2 CAN
N P I WATCH. Text in English. w. **Document type:** *Newsletter, Trade.*
Media: Online - full content.
Published by: N P Icenter (Subsidiary of: New Hope Natural Media), 16 Main St, Georgetown, ON L7G 3G5, Canada. TEL 877-463-0110, FAX 905-877-0468, sales@npicenter.com.

613.26 SWE ISSN 1653-8137
NAERINGSVAERT; om kost och naering. Text in Swedish. 1949. 6/yr. adv. **Document type:** *Magazine, Trade.*
Former titles (until 2006): Dietisten (0348-0674); (until vol.3, 1977): Svenska Ekonomifoerestaandares Tidskrift (0346-2293); (until vol.3, 1968): Svenska Ekonomifoerestaandarinnors Tidskrift; (until vol.7, 1950): Meddelande fraan Svenska Ekonomifoerestaandarinnors Foerening
Published by: Kost och Naering/Swedish Association of Dietitians, c/o Ledarna, PO Box 12069, Stockholm, 10222, Sweden. info@kostochnaring.se. Ed. Inger K Lagerman TEL 46-8-383821. Adv. contact Joakim Lind TEL 46-8-55696010.

613.2 IND ISSN 0377-3744
NATIONAL INSTITUTE OF NUTRITION. ANNUAL REPORT. Text in English. 1946. a. back issues avail. **Document type:** *Report, Academic/Scholarly.*
Formerly: Nutrition Research Laboratories. Annual Report
Published by: National Institute of Nutrition, Indian Council of Medical Research, Jamai-Osmania PO, Hyderabad, Andhra Pradesh 500 007, India. TEL 91-40-27197345, FAX 91-40-27019074, nin@ap.nic.in, http://www.ninindia.org.

613.2 USA ISSN 0732-7013
QP141.A1
NATIONAL INSTITUTES OF HEALTH. PROGRAM IN BIOMEDICAL AND BEHAVIORAL NUTRITION RESEARCH AND TRAINING. ANNUAL REPORT. Text in English. 1977. a.
Published by: U.S. National Institutes of Health, Division of Nutrition Research Coordination, 2 Democracy Plaza, 6707 Democracy Blvd, Rm. 679, MSC 5461,, Bethesda, MD 20892-5450. TEL 301-594-8822, http://dnrc.niddk.nih.gov/index.htm. Ed. Dr. Jean A Pennington TEL 301-594-8824.

613.262 DEU ISSN 1437-0735
NATUERLICH VEGETARISCH. Text in German. 1949. bi-m. EUR 21 domestic; EUR 29 foreign (effective 2003). bk.rev. 54 p./no.; back issues avail. **Document type:** *Magazine, Consumer.* **Description:** Contains information on all aspects of vegetarianism.
Formerly: Vegetarier (0178-9104)
Published by: Vegetarier Bund Deutschlands e.V., Blumenstr 3, Hannover, 30159, Germany. TEL 49-511-3632050, FAX 49-511-3632007, info@vegetarierbund.de, http://www.vegetarierbund.de. R&P Hildegund Scholvien TEL 49-6305-993108. Adv. contact Norbert Moch. Circ: 5,000.

613.2 DEU ISSN 0932-3503
NATUR UND HEILEN; die Monatszeitschrift fuer gesundes Leben. Text in German. 1924. m. EUR 45.60 domestic; EUR 54 foreign (effective 2011). adv. bk.rev. back issues avail. **Document type:** *Magazine, Consumer.* **Description:** For people who are interested in healthy life and natural healing.
Formerly (until 1986): Volksgesundheit (0042-8493); Incorporates (in 1995): Modernes Leben, Natuerliches Heilen (0340-577X); Which was formerly (1953-1975): Homoeopaethische Monatsblaetter (0018-4497)
Indexed: AMED, P30.
—BLDSC (6033.868000), GNLM, IE, Ingenta.
Published by: Verlag Natur und Heilen, Nikolaistr 5, Munich, 80802, Germany. TEL 49-89-38015910, FAX 49-89-38015912. Ed. Anne Devillard. Pub. Hansjoerg Volkhardt. adv.: B&W page EUR 2,300, color page EUR 3,680; trim 124 x 224. Circ: 62,342 (paid and controlled).

NATURAL FOODS MERCHANDISER; new ideas, trends, products for the natural and organic foods industry. *see* BUSINESS AND ECONOMICS—Marketing And Purchasing

613.262 AUS
NATURAL HEALTH AND VEGETARIAN LIFE. Text in English. 1996. q. AUD 6.95 newsstand/cover (effective 2009). adv. back issues avail. **Document type:** *Magazine, Consumer.* **Description:** Provides information about vegeterian and natural health life.
Formerly (until 2006): New Vegetarian and Natural Health (1328-2131); Which was formed by the merger of (1991-1996): New Vegetarian (1325-0310); Which was formerly (1948-1991): Australian Vegetarian; (1975-1996): Natural Health (0816-2751); Which was formerly (1973-1975): Natural Health News
Related titles: Online - full text ed.
Indexed: A04, C11, F10, T02.
Published by: Natural Health Society of Australia, Inc., Skiptons Arcade Ste, 28/541 High St, Penrith, NSW 2750, Australia. TEL 61-2-47215068, FAX 61-2-47311174, info@health.org.au. adv.: B&W page AUD 800, color page AUD 1,100; 186 x 265.

613.2 572 DEU ISSN 2192-2209
▼ ➤ **NATURAL PRODUCTS AND BIOPROSPECTING.** Text in English. 2011. irreg. free (effective 2011). **Document type:** *Journal, Academic/Scholarly.* **Description:** Provides an international forum for essential research on natural products.
Media: Online - full text.
Published by: SpringerOpen (Subsidiary of: Springer Science+Business Media), Tiergartenstr 17, Heidelberg, 69121, Germany. info@springeropen.com, http://www.springeropen.com. Ed. Ji-Kai Liu.

➤ **NATURAL PRODUCTS ASSOCIATION. NEWSLETTER.** *see* FOOD AND FOOD INDUSTRIES

613.2 658 USA ISSN 1525-5301
NATURAL PRODUCTS INDUSTRY INSIDER. Text in English. 1996. 13/yr. USD 249 domestic; USD 349 foreign (effective 2008). adv. back issues avail. **Document type:** *Magazine, Trade.* **Description:** Contains coverage of marketing, manufacturing, regulatory and financial news that affects the dietary supplement industry.
Formerly: H S R's Supplement Industry Insider
Related titles: E-mail ed.; Online - full text ed.; Supplement(s): Buyer's Guide.
Published by: Virgo Publishing, Llc, PO Box 40079, Phoenix, AZ 85067. TEL 480-990-1101, FAX 480-990-0819, jsiefert@vpico.com, http://www.vpico.com. adv.: B&W page USD 2,960, color page USD 4,035; bleed 8.375 x 11.125. Circ: 9,000 (paid and controlled).

613.2 615 USA
NATURAL PRODUCTS MARKETPLACE. Text in English. 1995. m. USD 27.50 domestic; USD 80 in Canada; USD 120 elsewhere (effective 2008). adv. charts; pat.; tr.lit. back issues avail. **Document type:** *Magazine, Trade.* **Description:** Serves the dietary supplement industry with news, market information, analyses, and new product information. Aimed at owners of retail stores and manufacturers.
Formerly (until Oct.2006): H S R: Health Supplement Retailer (1097-7961)
Related titles: Online - full text ed.
Published by: Virgo Publishing, Llc, PO Box 40079, Phoenix, AZ 85067. TEL 480-990-1101, FAX 480-990-0819, jsiefert@vpico.com, http://www.vpico.com. Pub. Jodi Rich TEL 480-990-1101 ext 1038. adv.: B&W page USD 2,860, color page USD 3,935; trim 7 x 10. Circ: 19,570.

613.2 FRA ISSN 1952-577X
NATURE GOURMANDE. Text in French. 2006. irreg. back issues avail. **Document type:** *Monographic series, Consumer.*
Published by: Anagramme Editions, 48 Rue des Ponts, Croissy sur Seine, 78290, France. TEL 33-1-39769943, FAX 33-1-39764587, info@anagramme-editions.fr, http://www.anagramme-editions.fr/. **Dist. by:** Volumen, 69 bis Rue de Vaugirard, Paris 75006, France. TEL 33-1-44107575, FAX 33-1-44107580.

613.26 NLD ISSN 1875-9955
NEDERLANDS TIJDSCHRIFT VOOR VOEDING EN DIETETIEK. Text in Dutch. 1947. bi-m. EUR 63 to individuals; EUR 76 to institutions; EUR 47 to students (effective 2009). adv. bk.rev. **Document type:** *Journal, Academic/Scholarly.* **Description:** Informs society members of developments in the field of dietetics.
Formerly (until 2007): Nederlands Tijdschrift voor Dietisten (0166-7203)
—IE, Infotrieve.
Published by: Nederlandse Vereniging voor Dietisten, Postbus 526, Houten, 3990 GH, Netherlands. TEL 31-30-6346222, FAX 31-30-6346211, bureau@nvdietist.nl, http://www.nvdietist.nl. Ed. Lara van Aalst. Adv. contact Ria Bosman.

613.2 CHE
NESTLE FOUNDATION. ANNUAL REPORT. Text in English. 1969. a. free. **Document type:** *Corporate.*
Published by: Nestle Foundation, 4 Place de la Gare, Lausanne, 1003, Switzerland. FAX 41-21-3203392. Ed. B Schuerch. Circ: 1,500.

613.2 CHE ISSN 1664-2147
CODEN: NNWSAQ
➤ **NESTLE NUTRITION INSTITUTE WORKSHOP SERIES.** Text in English. 1982. irreg., latest vol.69, 2011. price varies. reprints avail. **Document type:** *Monographic series, Academic/Scholarly.* **Description:** Aims to improve and disseminate knowledge on health and nutrition.
Former titles (until 2011): Nestle Nutrition Workshop Series Pediatric Program (1661-6677); (until 1999): Nestle Nutrition Workshop Series (0742-2806)
Related titles: Online - full text ed.: ISSN 1664-2155.
Indexed: A22, Agr, C06, CA, CIN, ChemAb, ChemTitl, EMBASE, ExcerpMed, MEDLINE, P30, R10, Reac, T02.
—BLDSC (6076.609000), CASDDS, IE, Ingenta. **CCC.**
Published by: S. Karger AG, Allschwilerstr 10, Basel, 4055, Switzerland. TEL 41-61-3061111, FAX 41-61-3061234, karger@karger.ch, http://www.karger.ch.

613.2 CHE ISSN 1422-7584
CODEN: CEMLBA
NESTLE NUTRITION WORKSHOP SERIES CLINICAL AND PERFORMANCE PROGRAMME. Text in English. 1999. irreg., latest vol.13, 2009. price varies. **Document type:** *Monographic series, Academic/Scholarly.* **Description:** Covers topics related to clinical nutrition or performance nutrition.
Related titles: Online - full text ed.: ISSN 1662-386X.
Indexed: ChemAb, ChemTitl, EMBASE, ExcerpMed, MEDLINE, P30, R10, Reac, SCOPUS.
—BLDSC (6076.609500), IE, Infotrieve, Ingenta. **CCC.**
Published by: S. Karger AG, Allschwilerstr 10, Basel, 4055, Switzerland. TEL 41-61-3061111, FAX 41-61-3061234, karger@karger.ch, http://www.karger.ch.

NEW MEXICO STATE UNIVERSITY. COOPERATIVE EXTENSION SERVICE. GUIDE E. *see* HOME ECONOMICS

613.2 GBR ISSN 1464-3308
NEW NUTRITION BUSINESS; the journal for the business of food, nutrition and health. Abbreviated title: N N B. Text in English. 1995. 11/yr. GBP 675, EUR 795, USD 1,050, CAD 1,150, AUD 1,330, NZD 1,550, JPY 90,000 combined subscription (print & online eds.) (effective 2009). back issues avail. **Document type:** *Journal, Academic/Scholarly.* **Description:** Provides an unrivalled collection of news analysis and case studies from around the world on.
Formerly (until 1998): Low & Lite Digest (1360-3558)
Related titles: Online - full text ed.
Indexed: FS&TA.
—IE.
Published by: Centre for Food & Health Studies, Crown House, 72 Hammersmith Rd, London, W14 8TH, United Kingdom. TEL 44-20-76177032, FAX 44-20-79001937, miranda.mills@new-nutrition.com. Ed. Julian Mellentin.

613.2 NZL ISSN 1176-8746
NEW ZEALAND HEALTHY FOOD GUIDE. Variant title: Healthy Food Guide. Text in English. 2005. m. NZD 49.50 domestic; NZD 121.50 in Australia & the Pacific (effective 2008); NZD 193.50 elsewhere (effective 2007). adv. **Document type:** *Magazine, Consumer.*
Published by: Healthy Food Media Limited, PO Box 47177, Ponsonby, Auckland, New Zealand. TEL 64-9-3600582, FAX 64-9-3766856. Ed. Niki Bezzant TEL 64-9-3611984. Adv. contact Pip Mehrtens.

613.2 JPN ISSN 0286-8202
CODEN: NREZEN
➤ **NIHON RINSHO EIYO GAKKAI ZASSHI/JAPANESE SOCIETY OF CLINICAL NUTRITION. JOURNAL.** Text in Japanese; Summaries in English. 1982. 3/yr. JPY 1,000 newsstand/cover (effective 2007). adv. **Document type:** *Journal, Academic/Scholarly.*
—BLDSC (6113.480900).
Published by: Nihon Rinsho Eiyo Gakkai, 4-2-6 Kojimachi, Chiyoda-ku, 5F, Dai 2 Izumi-Shoji Bldg, Tokyo, 102-0083, Japan. TEL 81-3-35561216, FAX 81-3-52751192, info@jscn.gr.jp.

613.2 JPN ISSN 1882-4773
NIHON SHOKUIKU GAKKAISHI/JOURNAL OF JAPANESE SOCIETY OF SHOKUIKU. Text in Japanese. 2007. q. **Document type:** *Journal, Academic/Scholarly.*
—**CCC.**
Published by: Nihon Shokuiku Gakkai/Japanese Society of Shokuiku, Sakuragaoka 1-1-1, Setagaya-ku, Tokyo, 156-8502, Japan. shokuiku@nodai.ac.jp, http://www.shokuiku-gakkai.jp.

613.2 JPN ISSN 0029-0572
NINGEN IGAKU/HUMAN MEDICINE. Text in Japanese. 1938. m. JPY 3,120 domestic; USD 4,000 (effective 2005). adv. bk.rev. illus.; tr.lit. **Document type:** *Journal, Academic/Scholarly.*
Published by: Ningen Igakusha, 1-1-25 Shibata, Kita-ku, Osaka 530-0012, Japan. TEL 81-6-63720441, FAX 81-6-63723482, http://www.ningen-igaku.co.jp/. Ed. Takaaki Oura. Circ: 20,000.

613.2 JPN ISSN 0287-3516
RM214 CODEN: NESGDC
NIPPON EIYO SHOKURYO GAKKAISHI/JAPANESE SOCIETY OF NUTRITION AND FOOD SCIENCE. JOURNAL. Text in Japanese; Summaries in English. 1947. 6/yr. JPY 8,000 membership (effective 2004). adv. bk.rev. **Document type:** *Journal, Academic/Scholarly.*
Former titles (until 1982): Eiyo to Shokuryo/Food and Nutrition (0021-5376); (until 1949): Eiyo Shokuryo Gakkaishi/Japanese Society of Food and Nutrition. Journal (0367-0554)
Related titles: ◆ Japanese ed.: Journal of Nutritional Science and Vitaminology. ISSN 0301-4800.
Indexed: A22, A35, A36, AgBio, B21, C25, CABA, CIN, ChemAb, ChemTitl, ChemoAb, D01, E12, ESPM, F08, FS&TA, GH, H16, N02, N03, P30, P33, P37, PHN&I, PN&I, R08, R11, RA&MP, S12, SPPI, SoyAb, TAR, VS.
—BLDSC (4809.474000), CASDDS, IE, Ingenta, INIST, Linda Hall. **CCC.**
Published by: Nippon Eiyo Shokuryo Gakkai/Japanese Society of Nutrition and Food Science, 3-60-5 Ikebukuro, Toshima-ku, Hueivuahuirudo Ikebukuro 203, Tokyo, 171-0014, Japan. TEL 81-3-5814-5801, FAX 81-3-5814-5820, eishokujimu@nifty.com, http://plaza.umin.ac.jp/~eishoku/. Ed. Yousuke Seyama. Circ: 4,300.

613.2 SWE ISSN 1654-8337
NORDISK NUTRITION. Text in Danish, Norwegian, Swedish. 2008 (Apr.). q. SEK 275 to individuals; SEK 450 to institutions (effective 2008). **Document type:** *Journal, Academic/Scholarly.*
Published by: Swedish Nutrition Foundation, Ole Roemersvej 5, Ideon Science Park, Lund, 22370, Sweden. TEL 46-46-2862282, FAX 46-46-2862281, info@snf.ideon.se, http://www.snf.ideon.se. Ed. Susanne Bryngelsson TEL 46-46-2862284.

613.2 NOR ISSN 1503-5034
NORSK TIDSSKRIFT FOR ERNAERING. Text in Norwegian. 2003. q. NOK 250 (effective 2004). adv. **Document type:** *Trade.*
Formed by the merger of (1992-2003): Eutrophia (0803-5946); (1990-2003): Ernaeringsfysiologen (0800-0972)
Published by: Kliniske Ernaeringsfysiologers Forening tilsluttet Forskerforbundet, c/o Rina Lilje, Arnulf Oeverlandsvej 19, Oslo, 50763, Norway. TEL 47-23-074528, rina.lilje@rikshospitales.no. Ed. Vibeke Landaas. Adv. contact Roger Mathisen. color page NOK 6,000; 184 x 272.

613.2 USA ISSN 2153-6198
NUTRACEUTICAL DIRECT MARKETING LETTER. Text in English. 2006. m. free (effective 2010). **Document type:** *Newsletter, Trade.* **Description:** Contains articles about and for the nutraceutical industry.
Media: Online - full text.
Published by: Pam Magnuson Copywriting, 19710 SW Cascadia St, Aloha, OR 97007. TEL 503-848-4047, pam@pammagnusoncopywriting.com, http:// www.pammagnusoncopywriting.com.

613.2 615 USA
NUTRACEUTICAL SCIENCE AND TECHNOLOGY. Text in English. 200?. irreg., latest vol.10, 2010. price varies. **Document type:** *Monographic series, Trade.* **Description:** Features monographs on nutraceuticals, nutrition, and related techologies.
Related titles: Online - full text ed.: ISSN 2154-7394.
Published by: C R C Press, LLC (Subsidiary of: Taylor & Francis Group), 6000 Broken Sound Pky, NW, Ste 300, Boca Raton, FL 33487. TEL 561-994-0555, FAX 561-989-9732, journals@crcpress.com, http://www.crcpress.com.

613.2 GBR ISSN 1478-6605
NUTRACEUTICALS NOW. Text in English. 2001. q. GBP 120 domestic (print or CD-ROM ed.); GBP 140 in Europe (print or CD-ROM ed.); GBP 150 elsewhere (print or CD-ROM ed.); GBP 160 combined subscription domestic (print & CD-ROM eds.); GBP 180 combined subscription in Europe (print & CD-ROM eds.); GBP 190 combined subscription elsewhere (print & CD-ROM eds.) (effective 2009). adv. back issues avail. **Document type:** *Magazine, Trade.* **Description:** Provides the latest information on functional products and ingredients which are defined as having a disease preventing and/or health promoting benefit in addition to their nutritional value.
Related titles: CD-ROM ed.
Indexed: A01, F05, F06, F07, F10, FS&TA.
—BLDSC (6187.223000). **CCC.**
Published by: Script Publishing Ltd., 106 Church St, Inverness, IV1 1EP, United Kingdom. TEL 44-1463-223568, FAX 44-1463-242058, info@nutraceuticalsnow.com. Ed. Charles Faulkner.

362.176 USA ISSN 1531-0671
NUTRACEUTICALS WORLD; serving the dietary supplement, functional food and nutritional beverage industries. Text in English. 1998. 10/yr. USD 100; free to qualified personnel (effective 2008). adv. back issues avail. **Document type:** *Magazine, Trade.* **Description:** Showcases the latest products and trends and tracks the global nutraceuticals industry. Also covers market and technology developments, dissects regulatory issues and provides new product and market sourcing information as well as covering all the major trade shows and conferences in the nutritional supplement and food and beverage industries.
Related titles: Online - full text ed.: free to qualified personnel (effective 2008).
Indexed: A26, B01, B03, CWI, F05, F06, F07, F10, G06, G07, G08, H11, H12, I05.
—BLDSC (6187.225000). **CCC.**

Published by: Rodman Publishing, Corp., 70 Hilltop Rd, 3rd Fl, Ramsey, NJ 07446. TEL 201-825-2552, FAX 201-825-0553, info@rodpub.com, http://www.rodmanpublishing .com. Ed. Rebecca Wright. Pub. Matthew Montgomery TEL 201-825-2552 ext 355. Adv. contact Stephen Lipscomb. B&W page USD 3,165, color page USD 4,290; trim 178 x 253. Circ: 12,005 (controlled).

613.2 668.5 ITA ISSN 1827-8590
NUTRAFOODS. Text in Italian. 2002. q. EUR 110, USD 146 combined subscription to institutions (print & online eds.) (effective 2012).
Document type: *Magazine, Consumer.*
Indexed: F05, F06, F07.
—BLDSC (6187.227500).
Published by: C E C Editore, Viale Legioni Romane 55, Milan, 20147, Italy. TEL 39-02-4152943, FAX 39-02-416737, http://www.cecpublisher.com. Pub. Anna Lebovich.

613.2 NLD ISSN 0167-4587
CODEN: NUSYD8
➤ **NUTRICIA SYMPOSIA.** Text in English. 1964. irreg., latest vol.9, 1996. price varies. **Document type:** *Proceedings, Academic/Scholarly.*
—CASDDS.
Published by: Springer Netherlands (Subsidiary of: Springer Science+Business Media), Van Godewijckstraat 30, Dordrecht, 3311 GX, Netherlands. TEL 31-78-6576050, FAX 31-78-6576474.

613.2 AUS
NUTRIDATE (ONLINE); class room support for teachers since 1990. Text in English. 1990. q. AUD 60 (effective 2008). back issues avail.
Document type: *Journal, Academic/Scholarly.* **Description:** Presents recent developments in nutrition, health and physical education for 12th grade students.
Formerly (until 2006): Nutridate (Print) (1320-9701)
Media: E-mail.
Indexed: A01, A02, A03, A08, A11, C05, C11, C12, F10, H03, M01, M02, T02, U01, WBA, WMB.
Published by: Warringal Publications, PO Box 166, East Kew, VIC 3121, Australia. TEL 61-3-93834233, 800-334-641, FAX 61-3-93834288, 800-629-559, warringalpublications@edassist.com.au, http://www.warringalpublications.com.au. Circ: 1,500.

613.2 CHE ISSN 2072-6643
▼ **NUTRIENTS.** Text in English. 2009. q. free (effective 2011). **Document type:** *Journal, Academic/Scholarly.*
Media: Online - full text.
Indexed: A34, A35, A36, A38, AgBio, AgrForAb, C06, C07, C25, C30, CABA, D01, E12, F05, F06, F07, F08, F10, F11, F12, FCA, GH, H16, LT, N02, N03, N04, P30, P32, P33, P40, R07, R12, R13, S12, SoyAb, T02, T05, W10, W11.
Published by: M D P I AG, Postfach, Basel, 4005, Switzerland. TEL 41-61-6837734, FAX 41-61-3028918, http://www.mdpi.org/. Ed. Peter Howe.

NUTRIFORM' MAGAZINE. *see* PHARMACY AND PHARMACOLOGY

613.2 IND ISSN 0550-404X
NUTRITION. Text in English. 1966. q. INR 8 (effective 2011). **Document type:** *Journal, Trade.* **Description:** Popular magazine concerning food and nutrition.
Related titles: Telugu ed.: Poshana. INR 8 (effective 2007); Hindi ed.: Poshan. INR 8 (effective 2007).
Indexed: ISR.
—Ingenta.
Published by: National Institute of Nutrition, Indian Council of Medical Research, Jamai-Osmania PO, Hyderabad, Andhra Pradesh 500 007, India. TEL 91-40-27197345, FAX 91-40-27019074, nin@ap.nic.in.

616.39 USA ISSN 0899-9007
QP141.A1 CODEN: NUTRER
➤ **NUTRITION**; an international journal of applied and basic nutritional science. Text in English. 1985. 12/yr. USD 891 in United States to institutions; USD 965 elsewhere to institutions (effective 2012). adv. back issues avail.; reprints avail. **Document type:** *Magazine, Academic/Scholarly.* **Description:** Publishes news of current research and practice in the field of applied and basic nutrition.
Formerly (until 1987): Nutrition International (0888-1294)
Related titles: Online - full text ed.: ISSN 1873-1244 (from IngentaConnect, ScienceDirect).
Indexed: A01, A03, A08, A22, A26, A34, A35, A36, A37, A38, ASCA, AgBio, Agr, AgrForAb, B21, BA, C06, C07, C08, C25, CA, CABA, CINAHL, ChemAb, ChemTitl, CurCont, D01, E12, EMBASE, ESPM, ExcerpMed, F05, F06, F07, F08, F10, F11, F12, FR, FS&TA, Faml, GH, H12, H16, I05, INI, ISR, IndMed, Inpharma, LT, MEDLINE, MaizeAb, N02, N03, N04, NRN, P30, P33, P37, P38, P39, PEI, PN&I, R08, R10, R11, R12, R13, RA&MP, RM&VM, RRTA, Reac, S12, S17, SCI, SCOPUS, SoyAb, T02, T05, ToxAb, TriticAb, VS, W07, W11.
—BLDSC (6187.930000), CASDDS, GNLM, IE, Infotrieve, Ingenta, INIST. **CCC.**
Published by: Elsevier Inc. (Subsidiary of: Elsevier Science & Technology), 360 Park Ave S, New York, NY 10010. TEL 212-989-5800, FAX 212-633-3990, usinfo-f@elsevier.com. Ed. Dr. Michael M Meguid. Adv. contact John Marmero Jr. TEL 212-633-3657. B&W page USD 2,010, color page USD 3,510; trim 8 x 10.75. Circ: 650 (paid).

➤ **NUTRITION ABSTRACTS AND REVIEWS. SERIES A: HUMAN AND EXPERIMENTAL**; an excellent gateway to all current research on human and experimental nutrition. *see* NUTRITION AND DIETETICS—Abstracting, Bibliographies, Statistics

613.2 USA ISSN 0885-7792
CODEN: NAHLED
NUTRITION ACTION HEALTH LETTER. Text in English. 1974. 10/yr. USD 10 domestic; CAD 15 in Canada; USD 25 elsewhere; USD 2.50 newsstand/cover (effective 2009). bk.rev. abstr.; bibl.; charts; illus. Index. 16 p./no. 2 cols./p.; back issues avail.; reprints avail.
Document type: *Newsletter, Consumer.* **Description:** Deals with news, commentary, features, letters, and advocacy on nutrition and food policy, in order to promote good health.
Formerly (until 1985): Nutrition Action (0199-5510); Incorporating (1976-1980): Intake (New Hyde Park) (0732-6920)
Related titles: Microform ed.: (from PQC); Online - full text ed.: ISSN 1930-6431.
Indexed: A01, A02, A03, A04, A08, A22, A25, A26, Agr, AltPI, B04, BRD, BiolDig, C06, C07, C08, C11, C12, CHNI, CINAHL, ConsI, E07, E08, F10, G05, G06, G07, G08, H03, H04, H11, H12, H13, HlthInd, I05, I07, M01, M02, M06, MASUSE, MagInd, P02, P07, P10, P11, P19, P20, P24, P48, P50, P52, P53, P54, P56, PQC, R03, RGAb, RGPR, S06, S08, S09, S23, T02, W03, W05.
—BLDSC (6188.025100), IE, Ingenta. **CCC.**
Published by: Center for Science in the Public Interest, 1875 Connecticut Ave, NW, Ste 300, Washington, DC 20009. TEL 202-332-9110, FAX 202-265-4954, cspi@cspinet.org.

613.2 USA ISSN 0163-5581
RC261.A1 CODEN: NUCADQ
➤ **NUTRITION AND CANCER**; an international journal. Text in English. 1978. 8/yr. GBP 1,255 combined subscription in United Kingdom to institutions (print & online eds.); EUR 1,673, USD 2,104 combined subscription to institutions (print & online eds.) (effective 2012). adv. bk.rev. charts; illus. back issues avail.; reprint service avail. from PSC.
Document type: *Journal, Academic/Scholarly.* **Description:** Reports and reviews current findings on the effect of nutrition on the etiology, therapy, and prevention of cancer.
Related titles: Online - full text ed.: ISSN 1532-7914. GBP 1,129 in United Kingdom to institutions; EUR 1,506, USD 1,894 to institutions (effective 2012) (from IngentaConnect).
Indexed: A01, A03, A04, A08, A22, A34, A35, A36, ASCA, AgBio, Agr, AgrForAb, B21, B25, BA, BIOBASE, BIOSIS Prev, BibAg, C06, C07, C08, C11, C25, CA, CABA, CIN, CINAHL, ChemAb, ChemTitl, CurCont, D01, DentInd, E-psyche, E01, E12, EMBASE, ESPM, ExcerpMed, F08, F10, F12, FR, FS&TA, Faml, GH, H&SSA, H16, IABS, ISR, IndMed, Inpharma, MEDLINE, MaizeAb, MycolAb, N02, N03, N04, NRN, P26, P30, P32, P33, P37, P38, P40, P50, P54, PGegResA, PHN&I, PN&I, PQC, R08, R10, R11, R13, RA&MP, RM&VM, Reac, RiskAb, S12, SCI, SCOPUS, SoyAb, T02, T05, THA, ToxAb, TriticAb, VITIS, VS, W07.
—BLDSC (6188.045000), CASDDS, GNLM, IE, Infotrieve, Ingenta, INIST. **CCC.**
Published by: Routledge (Subsidiary of: Taylor & Francis Group), 325 Chestnut St, Ste 800, Philadelphia, PA 19106. TEL 800-354-1420, FAX 215-625-2940, journals@routledge.com, http://www.routledge.com. Ed. Dr. Leonard A Cohen.

613.2 AUS ISSN 1446-6368
RM216
➤ **NUTRITION AND DIETETICS.** Text in English. 1944. q. GBP 135 combined subscription in United Kingdom to institutions (print & online eds.); EUR 172 combined subscription in Europe to institutions (print & online eds.); USD 233 combined subscription in the Americas to institutions (print & online eds.); USD 265 combined subscription elsewhere to institutions (print & online eds.) (effective 2012). adv. bk.rev. abstr. back issues avail.; reprint service avail. from PSC.
Document type: *Journal, Academic/Scholarly.* **Description:** Scientific journal specialising in nutrition and dietetics.
Incorporates (1951-2005): New Zealand Dietetic Association. Journal; Which was formerly: New Zealand Dietetic Association. Bulletin; Former titles (until 2002): Australian Journal of Nutrition and Dietetics (1032-1322); (until 1989): Journal of Food and Nutrition (0728-4713); (until 1981): Food and Nutrition Notes and Reviews (0015-6329)
Related titles: Online - full text ed.: ISSN 1747-0080. GBP 117 in United Kingdom to institutions; EUR 150 in Europe to institutions; USD 203 in the Americas to institutions; USD 231 elsewhere to institutions (effective 2012) (from IngentaConnect).
Indexed: A01, A02, A03, A04, A08, A11, A20, A22, A26, A34, A36, A37, AEI, ASFA, Agr, C06, C07, C08, C11, C12, C25, CA, CABA, CINAHL, D01, E01, E08, E12, F05, F06, F07, F08, F10, FS&TA, G08, GH, H04, H11, H12, H16, I05, IndVet, LT, M01, M02, MaizeAb, N02, N03, N04, OR, P37, P50, PHN&I, PN&I, R09, R12, RA&MP, RRTA, S09, S12, SCI, SCOPUS, SD, SoyAb, T02, T05, VS, W07, W11, WBA, WMB.
—BLDSC (6188.057000), IE, Ingenta. **CCC.**
Published by: (Dietitians Association of Australia, New Zealand Dietetic Association Inc. NZL), Wiley-Blackwell Publishing Asia (Subsidiary of: Wiley-Blackwell Publishing Ltd.), 155 Cremorne St, Richmond, VIC 3121, Australia. TEL 61-3-92743100, FAX 61-3-92743101, subs@blackwellpublishingasia.com, http://www.wiley.com/WileyCDA/. Ed. Dr. Linda Tapsell. Adv. contact Yasemin Caglar TEL 61-3-83591071. Circ: 2,700.

613.2 610 USA
NUTRITION AND DISEASE PREVENTION. Text in English. 200?. irreg.
Document type: *Monographic series, Trade.* **Description:** Monograph series on special topics in nutrition and disease prevention, including cancer, genomics, and perinatal health.
Related titles: Online - full text ed.: ISSN 2154-7408.
Published by: C R C Press, LLC (Subsidiary of: Taylor & Francis Group), 6000 Broken Sound Pky, NW, Ste 300, Boca Raton, FL 33487. TEL 561-994-0555, FAX 561-989-9732, journals@crcpress.com, http://www.crcpress.com.

613.2 GBR ISSN 0034-6659
TX341 CODEN: NFSCD7
NUTRITION & FOOD SCIENCE. Abbreviated title: N F S. Text in English. 1966. bi-m. EUR 6,189 combined subscription in Europe (print & online eds.); USD 7,419 combined subscription in the Americas (print & online eds.); GBP 4,369 combined subscription in the UK & elsewhere (print & online eds.); AUD 8,569 combined subscription in Australasia (print & online eds.) (effective 2012). adv. bk.rev. abstr.; charts; stat. index. back issues avail.; reprint service avail. from PSC.
Document type: *Journal, Academic/Scholarly.* **Description:** Keeps you informed about new initiatives, the latest research findings and innovative ways of responding to changes in public attitudes.
Formerly (until 1971): Review of Nutrition and Food Science (0486-6126)
Related titles: Online - full text ed.: ISSN 1758-6917 (from IngentaConnect).
Indexed: A01, A03, A08, A22, A26, A28, A34, A35, A36, APA, ASFA, AgBio, Agr, AgrForAb, B21, B23, BA, BP, BrCerAb, BrTechI, C&ISA, C25, CA, CA/WCA, CABA, CIA, CTA, CerAb, ChemAb, CivEngAb, CorrAb, D01, E&CAJ, E01, E07, E11, E12, EEA, EMA, ESPM, EnerIntel, EnvEAb, F05, F06, F07, F08, F10, F11, F12, FCA, FS&TA, G08, G09, G11, GH, H&TI, H06, H11, H12, H15, H16, I05, LT, M&TEA, M09, MBF, METADEX, MaizeAb, N02, N03, N04, O01, P02, P07, P10, P11, P16, P24, P32, P33, P37, P38, P40, P48, P50, P52, P53, P54, P56, PHN&I, PQC, R11, R12, RA&MP, RM&VM, RRTA, S12, S17, SCOPUS, SolStAb, SoyAb, T02, T04, T05, TAR, TriticAb, VS, W11, WAA.
—BLDSC (6188.070000), CASDDS, IE, Infotrieve, Ingenta, Linda Hall. **CCC.**
Published by: Emerald Group Publishing Ltd., Howard House, Wagon Ln, Bingley, W Yorks BD16 1WA, United Kingdom. TEL 44-1274-777700, FAX 44-1274-785201, information@emeraldinsight.com. Ed. Dr. Mabel Blades. Pub. Kate Snowden. Circ: 3,500. **Subscr. in Australia to:** Emerald Group Publishing Limited, PO Box 1441, Fitzroy North, VIC 3068, Australia. TEL 61-3-90781748, FAX 61-3-90781748; **Subscr. in the Americas to:** Emerald Group Publishing, One Mifflin Pl, Ste 400, Harvard Sq, Cambridge, MA 02138. TEL 617-576-5782, 888-309-7810, FAX 617-576-5883

613.2 USA
➤ **NUTRITION AND HEALTH.** Text in English. 1997. irreg., latest 2010. price varies. illus. back issues avail.; reprints avail. **Document type:** *Monographic series, Academic/Scholarly.* **Description:** Examines a wide variety of topics in the ways in which good nutrition can maintain health. Also covers procedures physicians can take to ensure the good nutrition of their patients, including managing obesity and eating disorders.
Published by: Humana Press, Inc. (Subsidiary of: Springer Science+Business Media), 233 Spring St, New York, NY 10013. TEL 212-460-1500, FAX 212-460-1575, service-ny@springer.com. Ed. Adrianne Bendich.

613.2 GBR ISSN 0260-1060
CODEN: NUHEDT
➤ **NUTRITION AND HEALTH.** Text in English. 1982. 4/yr. GBP 169, USD 335 to non-members; free to members (effective 2010). bk.rev.
Document type: *Journal, Academic/Scholarly.* **Description:** Covers preventive medical and nutrition education.
Related titles: Microform ed.
Indexed: A22, A35, A36, ASSIA, AgBio, AgrForAb, B21, B25, BIOSIS Prev, C06, C07, C25, CA, CABA, CTA, ChemAb, ChemTitl, D01, E04, E05, EMBASE, ESPM, ExcerpMed, F05, F06, F07, F08, FR, FS&TA, GH, H16, I10, IBR, IBZ, IndMed, MEDLINE, MycolAb, N02, N03, NRN, NSA, P30, P33, P39, PEI, R10, R12, R13, RA&MP, Reac, S02, S03, SCOPUS, SOPODA, SociolAb, SoyAb, T02, T05, VS, W11.
—BLDSC (6188.073000), CASDDS, GNLM, IE, Infotrieve, Ingenta, INIST. **CCC.**
Published by: (The Mccarrison Society for Nutrition and Health), Sage Publications Ltd. (Subsidiary of: Sage Publications, Inc.), 1 Oliver's Yard, 55 City Rd, London, EC1Y 1SP, United Kingdom. TEL 44-20-73248500, FAX 44-20-73248600, info@sagepub.co.uk, http://www.uk.sagepub.com/home.nav.

613.2 NZL ISSN 1178-6388
▼ **NUTRITION AND METABOLIC INSIGHTS.** Text in English. 2010. irreg. free (effective 2011). **Document type:** *Journal, Academic/Scholarly.*
Media: Online - full text.
—**CCC.**
Published by: Libertas Academica Ltd., PO Box 300-874, Mairangi Bay, Auckland, 0751, New Zealand. TEL 64-9-4763930, FAX 64-9-3531397, enquiries@la-press.com. Ed. Dexter Canoy.

NUTRITION & METABOLISM. *see* MEDICAL SCIENCES

613.26 USA
NUTRITION AND YOUR HEALTH: DIETARY GUIDELINES FOR AMERICANS. Text in English. 1980. every 5 yrs., latest 2010. back issues avail. **Document type:** *Monographic series, Consumer.*
Formerly: U S D A Dietary Guidelines
Published by: U.S. Department of Agriculture, Center for Nutrition Policy and Promotion, 3101 Park Ctr Dr, 10th Fl, Ste 1034, Alexandria, VA 22302. TEL 703-305-7600, FAX 703-305-3300, Support@cnpp.usda.gov. **Subscr. to:** U.S. Government Printing Office, Superintendent of Documents. **Co-publisher:** U.S. Department of Health and Human Services.

613.2 USA
NUTRITION ASSESSMENT. Text in English. 200?. irreg. **Document type:** *Monographic series, Trade.* **Description:** Monograph series featuring nutrition, drug and dietetic assessments.
Related titles: Online - full text ed.: ISSN 2154-7416.
Published by: C R C Press, LLC (Subsidiary of: Taylor & Francis Group), 6000 Broken Sound Pky, NW, Ste 300, Boca Raton, FL 33487. TEL 561-994-0555, FAX 561-989-9732, journals@crcpress.com, http://www.crcpress.com.

613.2 GBR ISSN 1471-9827
CODEN: BNUBD6
➤ **NUTRITION BULLETIN.** Text in English. 1968. q. GBP 419 in United Kingdom to institutions; EUR 533 in Europe to institutions; USD 774 in the Americas to institutions; USD 904 elsewhere to institutions; GBP 483 combined subscription in United Kingdom to institutions (print & online eds.); EUR 613 combined subscription in Europe to institutions (print & online eds.); USD 891 combined subscription in the Americas to institutions (print & online eds.); USD 1,039 combined subscription elsewhere to institutions (print & online eds.) (effective 2012). adv. index. back issues avail.; reprint service avail. from PSC. **Document type:** *Journal, Academic/Scholarly.* **Description:** Contains overview articles and covers the current state of knowledge in clinical nutrition, food processing, and food policy. Highlights areas of controversy and debate, summarizes concepts and methods, and discusses recently published scientific papers and newsworthy issues.
Former titles (until 1993): B N F Nutrition Bulletin (0141-9684); (until 1977): B N F Bulletin (0307-3548); (until 1972): British Nutrition Foundation. Information Bulletin (0142-0151)
Related titles: Online - full text ed.: ISSN 1467-3010. 2000. GBP 419 in United Kingdom to institutions; EUR 533 in Europe to institutions; USD 774 in the Americas to institutions; USD 904 elsewhere to institutions (effective 2012) (from IngentaConnect).
Indexed: A01, A03, A08, A22, A26, A34, A35, A36, AgBio, Agr, B21, BA, BIOBASE, C06, C07, C08, C25, CA, CABA, CINAHL, CTA, ChemAb, D01, E01, E12, F05, F06, F07, F10, FS&TA, GH, H12, H16, H17, IABS, IT, N02, N03, N04, NSA, P33, P34, PEI, PHN&I, PST, R12, RM&VM, RRTA, RefZh, S12, S17, SoyAb, T02, T05, TriticAb, VS, W11.
—BLDSC (6188.120000), CASDDS, IE, Infotrieve, Ingenta. **CCC.**
Published by: (British Nutrition Foundation), Wiley-Blackwell Publishing Ltd. (Subsidiary of: John Wiley & Sons, Inc.), 9600 Garsington Rd, Oxford, OX4 2DQ, United Kingdom. TEL 44-1865-776868, FAX 44-1865-714591, customerservices@blackwellpublishing.com. Eds. Claire Williamson, Judith Buttriss, Sara Stanner.

613.2 USA ISSN 1548-6168
RA784 CODEN: NBJOF6

NUTRITION BUSINESS JOURNAL; strategic information for the nutrition industry. Abbreviated title: N B J. Text in English. 1996. m. USD 1,295 domestic; USD 1,345 foreign (effective 2011). adv. back issues avail. **Document type:** *Journal, Trade.* **Description:** Provides a strategic business overview of the nutrition, natural health and natural products for executives within the industry.
Related titles: Online - full text ed.
Indexed: B01, B07, CA, F10, G08, I05, T02.
—BLDSC (6188.122000), IE, Ingenta.
Published by: New Hope Natural Media (Subsidiary of: Penton Media, Inc.), 1401 Pearl St, Boulder, CO 80302. TEL 303-939-8440, FAX 303-998-9020, info@newhope.com, http://newhope360.com. Adv. contact Emma Chanin TEL 303-998-9536.

613.2 572 USA ISSN 1548-4327
NUTRITION BYTES. Text in English. 1995 (Spr.). a. back issues avail. **Document type:** *Journal, Academic/Scholarly.* **Description:** Covers topics such as biochemical, psycho-social, epidemiological, clinical and public health issues of nutrition.
Related titles: Online - full text ed.: ISSN 1548-601X. free (effective 2011).
Published by: (University of California, Los Angeles, Department of Biological Chemistry), eScholarship (Subsidiary of: California Digital Library), 300 Lakeside Dr, 7th Fl, Oakland, CA 94612. TEL 510-587-6439, FAX 510-987-0243, info@escholarship.org, http://www.escholarship.org. Eds. Eryn Ujita Lee, Lenore Arab.

613.2 CAN ISSN 1491-8536
NUTRITION FACTOR. Text in English. 1994. q.
Formerly (until 1998): Nutrition Post (1483-5207)
Indexed: C03, CBCARef, PQC.
Published by: Medical Post, Maclean Hunter Bldg, 777 Bay St, Toronto, ON M5W 1A7, Canada. TEL 416-596-5722, FAX 416-593-3177.

NUTRITION FOCUS. *see* CHILDREN AND YOUTH—About

613.2 CAN ISSN 0318-4501
NUTRITION FORUM/FORUM DE NUTRITION. Text in English. 1966. s-a. membership. bk.rev.
Formerly (until 1973): Newsletter - Nutrition (0318-4498)
Related titles: Online - full text ed.
—CCC.
Published by: Canadian Society for Nutritional Sciences, Department of Foods and Nutrition, University of Manitoba, Winnipeg, MB R3T 2N2, Canada. TEL 613-993-4484. Ed. Vivian Bruce. Circ: (controlled).
Dist. by: Department de Nutrition, Universite de Manitoba, Montreal, PQ H30 3J7, Canada.

613.2 USA ISSN 0892-1474
THE NUTRITION FUNDING REPORT; a monthly guide to locating resources. Text in English. 1986. m. USD 65 combined subscription in North America for print & online eds.; USD 75 combined subscription elsewhere for print & online eds. (effective 2003). **Document type:** *Newsletter.* **Description:** A monthly report of available resources for your food, nutrition, and health programs/projects, from the private sector (corporations, foundations, etc) and public sector (US Federal Government department/agencies): grant awards, scholarships/fellowships/internships, policy documents and publications and relevant information.
Related titles: Online - full text ed.: USD 65 includes print ed. (effective 2000).
Published by: Nutrition Legislation Services, PO Box 75035, Washington, DC 20013. TEL 202-488-8879, FAX 202-554-3116. Ed., Pub., R&P Lenora Moragne.

613.2 USA ISSN 0164-7202
NUTRITION HEALTH REVIEW; the consumer's medical journal. Text in English. 1975. q. USD 24 for 2 yrs. domestic; USD 36 for 2 yrs. in Canada; USD 66 for 2 yrs. foreign; USD 3 newsstand/cover (effective 2006). bk.rev.; video rev. charts; illus.; stat. **Document type:** *Magazine, Consumer.* **Description:** Provides information on nutrition, health and medicine for consumers and related health professionals.
Related titles: CD-ROM ed.; Microfilm ed.; Microform ed.: (from PQC); Online - full text ed.
Indexed: A01, A02, A03, A04, A08, A22, A26, C06, C07, C08, C11, C12, CINAHL, E-psyche, F10, G05, G06, G07, G08, H03, H04, H12, H13, HlthInd, I05, I07, M01, M02, MASUSE, P02, P10, P19, P20, P24, P48, P53, P54, PQC, S23, T02.
Published by: Vegetus Publications, PO Box 406, Haverford, PA 19041. TEL 610-896-1853, FAX 610-896-1857. Eds. Andrew Rifkin, William Renaurd. Pub. Frank Ray Rifkin. R&P Andrew Rifkin. Circ: 280,800 (controlled).

613.2 USA ISSN 0884-5336
RM225 CODEN: NCPREH

➤ **NUTRITION IN CLINICAL PRACTICE.** Short title: N C P. Text in English. 1986. bi-m. USD 314, GBP 184 combined subscription to institutions (print & online eds.); USD 308, GBP 180 to institutions (effective 2011). adv. bk.rev. 80 p./no.; back issues avail.; reprint service avail. from PSC. **Document type:** *Journal, Academic/Scholarly.* **Description:** Multidisciplinary clinical journal providing information on clinical nutrition for health care personnel. Publishes articles, clinical observations, case reports, techniques and procedures.
Related titles: Microform ed.: (from PQC); Online - full text ed.: ISSN 1941-2452. USD 283, GBP 166 to institutions (effective 2011).
Indexed: A22, A36, C06, C07, C08, CA, CABA, CINAHL, CurCont, D01, E01, E12, EMBASE, ExcerpMed, F09, GH, I12, IDIS, LT, MEDLINE, N02, N03, P24, P30, P33, P48, PQC, R10, R12, RA&MP, Reac, SCI, SCOPUS, SoyAb, T02, T05, W07, W11.
—BLDSC (6188.130000), GNLM, IE, Infotrieve, Ingenta, INIST. **CCC.**
Published by: (American Society for Parenteral and Enteral Nutrition), Sage Publications, Inc., 2455 Teller Rd, Thousand Oaks, CA 91320. TEL 805-499-9774, FAX 805-499-0871, info@sagepub.com. Ed. Jeanette Hasse. adv.: B&W page USD 1,060. Circ: 6,800.

613.2 GBR ISSN 1470-4730
NUTRITION IN PRACTICE. Text in English. 2000. 3/yr. free to qualified personnel (effective 2009). back issues avail. **Document type:** *Bulletin, Trade.* **Description:** Features informative articles on balanced nutrition.
Incorporates (2000-2006): Dental Digest (1470-4722); Which was formerly (1990-2000): Good Dietary Practice News (0964-4091); Formed by the merger of (1992-2000): Practice Nutrition (0965-9722); (1990-2000): C - H - O (0961-7728)
Related titles: Online - full text ed.: free (effective 2009).
—BLDSC (6188.595000). **CCC.**
Published by: Advisa Media, c/o The Sugar Bureau, 25 Floral St, London, WC2E 9DS, United Kingdom. TEL 44-20-71898301, FAX 44-20-70318101, info@sugar-bureau.co.uk. Ed. Jonathan Levy.

613.2 USA
NUTRITION INDUSTRY EXECUTIVE; the business magazine for dietary supplement industry manufacturers. Text in English. 1996. 10/yr. USD 50 domestic; USD 80 in Canada & Mexico; USD 175 elsewhere (effective 2004). adv. **Document type:** *Magazine, Trade.* **Description:** Provides dietary supplement manufacturers with useful and timely information that they can utilize and benefit from.
Formerly: Supplement Industry Executive
Published by: Vitamin Retailer Magazine, Inc, 431 Cranbury Rd, East Brunswick, NJ 08816. TEL 732-432-9600, FAX 732-432-9288, info@vitaminretailer.com. Ed. Paul Bubny TEL 732-432-9600 ext 105. Pub. Daniel McSweeney TEL 805-646-2921. Adv. contact Russ Fields TEL 732-432-9600 ext 102. B&W page USD 2,695, color page USD 3,875; trim 8.125 x 10.875. Circ: 4,000.

613.2 GBR ISSN 1475-2891
➤ **NUTRITION JOURNAL.** Text in English. 2002 (Sep.). irreg. free (effective 2011). adv. back issues avail. **Document type:** *Journal, Academic/Scholarly.* **Description:** Covers on all aspects of human and clinical nutrition, as well as research articles and animal studies in the field of nutrition.
Media: Online - full text.
Indexed: A01, A02, A03, A08, A26, A34, A36, A37, A38, Agr, AgrForAb, BP, C06, C07, CA, CABA, CurCont, D01, E12, EMBASE, ExcerpMed, F08, F10, F12, FS&TA, GH, H16, I05, LT, MEDLINE, N02, N03, N04, P20, P22, P30, P33, P37, P38, P39, PEI, PHN&I, PN&I, PQC, R08, R10, R11, R12, RA&MP, RRTA, Reac, S06, S12, SCI, SCOPUS, SoyAb, T02, T05, TAR, TriticAb, VS, W07, W11.
—CCC.
Published by: BioMed Central Ltd. (Subsidiary of: Springer Science+Business Media), 236 Gray's Inn Rd, London, WC1X 8HB, United Kingdom. TEL 44-20-31922000, FAX 44-20-31922010, info@biomedcentral.com, http://www.biomedcentral.com. Ed. Nehme Gabriel.

613.2 USA
NUTRITION LEGISLATION AND REGULATORY NEWS; a twice-monthly report of United States legislative, executive, and regulatory activities. Text in English. 1985. s-m. USD 150 combined subscription in North America for print & online eds.; USD 175 combined subscription elsewhere for print & online eds. (effective 2003). bk.rev. **Document type:** *Newsletter.* **Description:** Provides an unedited report of US government legislative and regulatory initatives pertaining to nutrition including nutrition research, nutrition education, food assistance, international nutrition, nutrition monitoring, nutrition manpower training, food quality and food safety.
Formerly: Nutrition Legislation News (8756-6060)
Related titles: Online - full text ed.: USD 175 in North America includes print ed.; USD 200 elsewhere includes print ed. (effective 2000).
Published by: Nutrition Legislation Services, PO Box 75035, Washington, DC 20013. TEL 202-488-8879, FAX 202-554-3116. Pub. Lenora Moragne. R&P Nora Champion.

612.3 GBR ISSN 0939-4753
RC666 CODEN: NMCDEE

➤ **NUTRITION, METABOLISM & CARDIOVASCULAR DISEASES.** Variant title: N M C D. Text in English. 1991. 10/yr. EUR 599 in Europe to institutions; JPY 81,100 in Japan to institutions; USD 774 elsewhere to institutions (effective 2012). adv. bk.rev. back issues avail.; reprints avail. **Document type:** *Journal, Academic/Scholarly.* **Description:** Designed to address the many unanswered questions raised by the interplay between nutritional and metabolic alterations and cardiovascular disorders.
Related titles: Online - full text ed.: ISSN 1590-3729 (from ScienceDirect).
Indexed: A22, A26, A36, ASCA, C06, C07, CA, CABA, CIN, ChemAb, ChemTitl, CurCont, D01, E12, EMBASE, ExcerpMed, F08, FS&TA, GH, I05, ISR, IndMed, Inpharma, MEDLINE, N02, N03, P30, P35, R10, R12, RA&MP, Reac, SCI, SCOPUS, SoyAb, T02, T05, TriticAb, VITIS, VS, W07.
—BLDSC (6188.440000), CASDDS, GNLM, IE, Infotrieve, Ingenta, INIST. **CCC.**
Published by: (Italian Society of Diabetology ITA, Italian Society for the Study of Atherosclerosis ITA, Italian Society of Human Nutrition ITA), Elsevier Ltd (Subsidiary of: Elsevier Science & Technology), The Blvd, Langford Ln, Kidlington, Oxford, OX5 1GB, United Kingdom. TEL 44-1865-843434, FAX 44-1865-843970, journalscustomerserviceemea@elsevier.com. Ed. P Rubba.

613.2 IND
NUTRITION NEWS. Text in English. 19??. q. INR 20 domestic; USD 4 foreign (effective 2011). **Document type:** *Journal, Trade.*
Published by: National Institute of Nutrition, Indian Council of Medical Research, Jamai-Osmania PO, Hyderabad, Andhra Pradesh 500 007, India. TEL 91-40-27197345, FAX 91-40-27019074, nin@ap.nic.in.

613.2 613.71 USA ISSN 8756-5919
NUTRITION NEWS (RIVERSIDE). Text in English; Some issues in Spanish. 1976 (Apr.). m. USD 24 domestic; USD 29 in Canada & Mexico; USD 39 elsewhere (effective 2007). bk.rev. back issues avail.; reprints avail. **Document type:** *Newsletter, Consumer.* **Description:** Creates a nutritional context that empowers consumers to make healthy choices.
Related titles: CD-ROM ed.; Online - full text ed.
Indexed: A04, C06, C07.
Published by: Siri & Gurumantra Khalsa, 4108 Watkins Dr, Riverside, CA 92507-4701. TEL 951-784-7500, 800-784-7550, FAX 951-784-7555. Ed., R&P Siri Khalsa. Pub. Gurumantra Khalsa. Circ: 50,000 (paid).

613.2 USA
NUTRITION NEWS FOCUS. Text in English. d. free. **Document type:** *Newsletter, Consumer.* **Description:** Offers non-experts unbiased information on nutrition, enabling them to make sense of the huge amount of information on the subject published in the news media.
Media: Online - full text.
Published by: Nutrition News Focus Inc., 4426 St. Clair Ave, Studio City, CA 91604. TEL 818-761-8074, FAX 818-761-7025, ken@nutritionnewsfocus.com, http://www.nutritionnewsfocus.com/. Ed. Dr. David Klurfeld. Adv. contact Ken Deifik.

NUTRITION NEWS IN ZAMBIA. *see* FOOD AND FOOD INDUSTRIES

613.2 USA
NUTRITION NOTES. Text in English. 1965. q. USD 30 to non-members; free to members (effective 2010). adv. back issues avail. **Document type:** *Newsletter, Trade.* **Description:** Provides news of member activities, future and annual meetings, course offerings, NIH grant opportunities, student news, possible job opportunities, and available relevant publications.
Related titles: Online - full text ed.: free (effective 2010).
Published by: American Society for Nutrition, 9650 Rockville Pike, Bethesda, MD 20814. TEL 301-634-7050, FAX 301-634-7892, info@nutrition.org. Ed. Neil Shay.

613.2 USA ISSN 1556-1895
RA784

NUTRITION NOTEWORTHY. Text in English. 1998. irreg., latest vol.7, no.1, 2005. free (effective 2011). back issues avail. **Document type:** *Journal, Academic/Scholarly.* **Description:** Covers topics such as biochemical, psycho-social, epidemiological, clinical and public health issues of nutrition.
Media: Online - full text. **Related titles:** Print ed.
Published by: (University of California, Los Angeles, Department of Biological Chemistry), eScholarship (Subsidiary of: California Digital Library), 300 Lakeside Dr, 7th Fl, Oakland, CA 94612. TEL 510-587-6439, FAX 510-987-0243, info@escholarship.org, http://www.escholarship.org.

N
O

613.2 028.5 USA ISSN 1935-4630
NUTRITION NUGGETS. Text in English. 2006. m. (Sep-May). **Document type:** *Newsletter.*
Related titles: Online - full text ed.: ISSN 1935-4649; Spanish ed.: ISSN 1935-4673. 2006.
Published by: Resources for Educators (Subsidiary of: Aspen Publishers, Inc.), 3035 Valley Ave, Ste 103, Winchester, VA 22601. TEL 540-723-0322.

613.2 USA ISSN 0271-5317
QP141.A1 CODEN: NTRSDC

➤ **NUTRITION RESEARCH**; an international publication for nutrition to advance food and life science research. Text in English. 1981. 12/yr. USD 2,052 in United States to institutions; USD 2,297 elsewhere to institutions (effective 2012). adv. bk.rev. illus. index. back issues avail.; reprints avail. **Document type:** *Journal, Academic/Scholarly.* **Description:** Presents reports on basic and applied research on all aspects of food and nutrition, including relevant topics from the social sciences.
Incorporates (1975-1993): Progress in Food and Nutrition Science (0306-0632); Which was formerly: International Encyclopedia of Food and Nutrition (0074-4700)
Related titles: Online - full text ed.: ISSN 1879-0739 (from IngentaConnect, ScienceDirect).
Indexed: A01, A03, A08, A20, A22, A26, A32, A34, A35, A36, A37, A38, ASCA, ASFA, AgBio, Agr, AgrForAb, B&AI, B10, B21, B25, BIOBASE, BIOSIS Prev, BP, BibAg, C06, C07, C25, C33, CA, CABA, CTA, ChemAb, ChemTitl, CurCont, D01, E12, EIA, EMBASE, ESPM, EnerInd, ExcerpMed, F05, F06, F07, F08, F10, F12, FR, FS&TA, FamI, GH, H&SSA, H16, H17, I05, IABS, IBR, IBZ, ISR, IndMed, Inpharma, LT, MEDLINE, MaizeAb, MycolAb, N02, N03, N04, NRN, NSA, O01, P30, P32, P33, P37, P38, P40, PHN&I, PN&I, R08, R10, R11, R12, RA&MP, RRTA, Reac, RiskAb, S01, S12, S13, S16, S17, SCI, SCOPUS, SoyAb, T02, T05, TOSA, TriticAb, VITIS, VS, W07, W10, W11.
—BLDSC (6188.950000), CASDDS, GNLM, IE, Infotrieve, Ingenta, INIST, Linda Hall. **CCC.**
Published by: Elsevier Inc. (Subsidiary of: Elsevier Science & Technology), 360 Park Ave S, New York, NY 10010. TEL 212-989-5800, FAX 212-633-3990, usinfo-f@elsevier.com. Ed. Bruce A Watkins TEL 765-496-7849. Circ: 580 (paid).

613.2 KOR ISSN 1976-1457
PP141.A1

NUTRITION RESEARCH AND PRACTICE. Text in English. 2007. q. USD 30 in Asia to individuals; USD 60 elsewhere to individuals; USD 60 in Asia to institutions; USD 100 elsewhere to institutions (effective 2008). **Document type:** *Journal, Academic/Scholarly.*
Incorporated (1999-2007): Journal of Community Nutrition (1229-540X)
Related titles: Online - full text ed.
Indexed: A34, A36, A38, AgrForAb, C25, CABA, D01, F08, F11, F12, GH, H16, MaizeAb, N02, N03, N04, P30, P32, P33, P40, PGegResA, PN&I, R08, R11, R12, RA&MP, S12, SCI, SoyAb, T05, VS, W07, W11.
—BLDSC (6188.960000), IE.
Published by: Korean Nutrition Society/Han'gug Yeong'yang Haghoe, #804 The Korean Science and Technology Center, 635-4 Yeogsam-dong, Kangnam-Ku, Seoul, 135-703, Korea, S. TEL 82-2-34520449, FAX 82-2-34523018, kns@kns.or.kr, http://www.kns.or.kr/. Eds. Hye-Ryeon Park, Rina Yu, Young-Hee Kang. **Co-publisher:** Korean Society of Community Nutrition/Daehan Jiyeog Sahoe Yeong-yang Hag-hoe.

613.2 USA ISSN 0736-0037
TX350.8 CODEN: GTNEEA

NUTRITION RESEARCH NEWSLETTER. Text in English. 1983. m. abstr. index. back issues avail.; reprints avail. **Document type:** *Newsletter, Trade.* **Description:** Presents an overview of all aspects of nutrition. Aims to provide a broad-based knowledge of the role that food and food supplements can play in health.
Incorporates (1990-1998): Food Safety Notebook (1050-1843)
Related titles: Online - full text ed.
Indexed: A01, A02, A03, A08, A26, C12, CA, E08, F10, G08, H11, H12, I05, I07, M01, M02, M06, P34, S06, S09, S23, T02.
—CASDDS.
Published by: Technical Insights (Subsidiary of: Frost & Sullivan), 7550 IH 10 W, Ste 400, San Antonio, TX 78229. TEL 210-348-1000, 877-463-7678, FAX 888-690-3329, myfrost@frost.com, http://www.frost.com/prod/servlet/ti-home.pag.

612.3 GBR ISSN 0954-4224
QP141.A1 CODEN: NREREX

➤ **NUTRITION RESEARCH REVIEWS.** Text in English. 1988. s-a. GBP 204, EUR 311, USD 395 to institutions; GBP 217, EUR 337, USD 423 combined subscription to institutions (print & online eds.) (effective 2012). adv. back issues avail.; reprint service avail. from PSC. **Document type:** *Journal, Academic/Scholarly.* **Description:** Reviews research on a variety of nutritional problems.

Related titles: Microform ed.: (from PQC); Online - full text ed.: ISSN 1475-2700. GBP 161, EUR 241, USD 298 to institutions (effective 2012); ◆ Supplement to: The British Journal of Nutrition. ISSN 0007-1145.
Indexed: A01, A22, A34, A35, A36, A38, AgBio, Agr, B&AI, B&BAb, B10, B19, B21, BIOSIS Prev, BRD, C06, C07, C08, CA, CABA, CIN, CINAHL, CTA, ChemAb, ChemTitl, CurCont, D01, E01, E04, E05, E12, EMBASE, ExcerpMed, F05, F06, F07, F08, F10, FR, FS&TA, GH, H16, ISR, IndVet, LT, MEDLINE, MaizeAb, MycolAb, N02, N03, N04, NSA, P02, P10, P11, P24, P30, P33, P37, P39, P48, P50, P52, P53, P54, P56, PN&I, PQC, R10, R12, RA&MP, RRTA, Reac, S04, S10, S12, SCI, SCOPUS, SoyAb, T02, T05, TriticAb, VITIS, VS, W03, W05, W07, W11.
—BLDSC (6188.975000), CASDDS, GNLM, IE, Infotrieve, Ingenta, INIST, Linda Hall. **CCC.**
Published by: (Nutrition Society), Cambridge University Press, The Edinburgh Bldg, Shaftesbury Rd, Cambridge, CB2 8RU, United Kingdom. TEL 44-1223-312393, FAX 44-1223-315052, journals@cambridge.org, http://www.cambridge.org/uk. Ed. Kate Younger TEL 353-1-4024662. R&P Linda Nicol TEL 44-1223-325702. Adv. contact Rebecca Roberts TEL 44-1223-325083. page GBP 610, page USD 1,160.

613.2 CAN
NUTRITION RESOURCES BULLETIN. Text in English. 1996. bi-m. **Description:** Covers normal nutrition such as healthy eating, life cycle nutrition, sports nutrition, vegetarianism, and cultural and ethnic resources; medical nutrition, including special diets; quantity food preparation; food service management; food safety; food science and food security.
Media: Online - full content.
Published by: Simon Fraser University, 8888 University Dr, Burnaby, BC V5A 1S6, Canada.

612.3 USA ISSN 0029-6643
CODEN: NUREA8
➤ **NUTRITION REVIEWS.** Text in English. 1942. m. GBP 295 combined subscription in United Kingdom to institutions (print & online eds.); EUR 375 combined subscription in Europe to institutions (print & online eds.); USD 467 combined subscription in the Americas to institutions (print & online eds.); USD 576 combined subscription elsewhere to institutions (print & online eds.) (effective 2012). bk.rev. abstr.; bibl.; illus. index. back issues avail.; reprint service avail. from PSC. **Document type:** *Journal, Academic/Scholarly.* **Description:** International journal of authoritative and critical reviews of significant developments in all areas of nutrition science and policy.
Related titles: Microfilm ed.: (from PQC); Online - full text ed.: ISSN 1753-4887. GBP 256 in United Kingdom to institutions; EUR 326 in Europe to institutions; USD 405 in the Americas to institutions; USD 501 elsewhere to institutions (effective 2012) (from IngentaConnect).
Indexed: A01, A02, A03, A04, A08, A22, A25, A26, A34, A35, A36, A37, A38, ASCA, AcaI, AgBio, Agr, B&AI, B04, B10, B21, BIOBASE, BP, BRD, BibAg, C06, C07, C08, C11, CA, CINAHL, Cadscan, ChemAb, ChemoAb, CurCont, D01, DentInd, E01, E04, E05, E08, E12, EMBASE, ESPM, ExcerpMed, F05, F06, F07, F08, F09, F10, FR, FS&TA, FamI, G03, G08, GH, GSA, GSI, H&TI, H03, H04, H06, H12, H13, H16, H17, HlthInd, I05, IABS, ISR, IndMed, Inpharma, LT, LeadAb, M01, M02, MEDLINE, MaizeAb, N02, N03, N04, NRN, P02, P10, P11, P13, P19, P20, P22, P24, P26, P30, P32, P33, P37, P39, P40, P48, P50, P52, P53, P54, P56, PHN&I, PN&I, PQC, PollutAb, R08, R09, R10, R12, RA&MP, RM&VM, RRTA, Reac, S08, S09, S12, S17, SCI, SCOPUS, SD, SoyAb, T02, T05, TriticAb, VITIS, VS, W03, W07, W11.
—BLDSC (6189.000000), CASDDS, GNLM, IE, Infotrieve, Ingenta, INIST, Linda Hall. **CCC.**
Published by: International Life Sciences Institute, One Thomas Cir, NW 9th Fl, Washington, DC 20005. TEL 202-659-0074, FAX 202-659-3859, ilsi@ilsi.org. Ed. Naomi Fukagawa. **Subscr. to:** Wiley-Blackwell Publishing, Inc., Commerce Pl, 350 Main St, Malden, MA 02148. TEL 781-388-8598, 800-835-6770, cs-journals@wiley.com, http://www.wiley.com/WileyCDA.

613.2 NLD ISSN 0924-4557
CODEN: NUTSDT
NUTRITION SCIENCES. Text in English. 1982. irreg., latest vol.2, 1983. price varies. **Document type:** *Monographic series, Academic/Scholarly.*
—CCC.
Published by: Springer Netherlands (Subsidiary of: Springer Science+Business Media), Van Godewijckstraat 30, Dordrecht, 3311 GX, Netherlands. TEL 31-78-6576050, FAX 31-78-6576474.

613.2 IND ISSN 0253-7567
NUTRITION SOCIETY OF INDIA. PROCEEDINGS. Text in English. 1967. a. INR 150 per issue (effective 2011). back issues avail. **Document type:** *Proceedings, Trade.*
Indexed: P30, TOSA.
—BLDSC (6779.600000).
Published by: Nutrition Society of India, Jamai Osmania P.O., Hyderabad, Andhra Pradesh 500 007, India. TEL 91-40-27002008, FAX 91-40-27019074, info@nutritionsocietyindia.org.

613.2 GBR ISSN 0029-6651
TX501 CODEN: PNUSA4
➤ **NUTRITION SOCIETY. PROCEEDINGS.** Variant title: Proceedings of the Nutrition Society. Text in English. 1941. 5/yr. GBP 497, EUR 795, USD 970 to institutions; GBP 523, EUR 834, USD 1,019 combined subscription to institutions (print & online eds.) (effective 2012). adv. abstr.; bibl.; charts. index. back issues avail.; reprints avail. **Document type:** *Proceedings, Academic/Scholarly.* **Description:** Publishes papers presented by invitation at symposia of the society, and abstracts of original communications presented at other meetings.
Related titles: Microform ed.: (from PMC, PQC, SWZ); Online - full text ed.: ISSN 1475-2719. GBP 407, EUR 637, USD 794 to institutions (effective 2012).
Indexed: A20, A22, A34, A35, A36, A37, A38, ASCA, AgBio, Agr, AgrForAb, B&AI, B04, B10, B21, B25, BIOSIS Prev, BP, BibAg, C06, C07, C08, C25, C30, CABA, CIN, CINAHL, Cadscan, ChemAb, ChemTitl, CurCont, D01, DBA, E01, E04, E05, E12, EIA, EMBASE, EnerInd, ExcerpMed, F05, F06, F07, F08, F09, F11, F12, FS&TA, G11, GH, H16, H17, IBR, IBZ, ISR, ImmunAb, IndMed, IndVet, Inpharma, LT, LeadAb, MEDLINE, MaizeAb, MycolAb, N02, N03, N04, NRN, NSA, OR, P11, P20, P22, P24, P30, P32, P33, P37, P40, P48, P50, P52, P54, P56, PHN&I, PN&I, PQC, R08, R10, R11, R12, R13, RA&MP, RM&VM, RRTA, Reac, S13, S16, SCI, SCOPUS, SoyAb, T05, TriticAb, VITIS, VS, W07, W11, Zincscan.
—BLDSC (6780.000000), CASDDS, GNLM, IE, Infotrieve, Ingenta, INIST, Linda Hall. **CCC.**
Published by: (Nutrition Society), Cambridge University Press, The Edinburgh Bldg, Shaftesbury Rd, Cambridge, CB2 8RU, United Kingdom. TEL 44-1223-312393, FAX 44-1223-315052, journals@cambridge.org, http://www.cambridge.org/uk. Ed. C J Newbold. R&P Linda Nicol TEL 44-1223-325702. Adv. contact Rebecca Roberts TEL 44-1223-325083. page GBP 610, page USD 1,160.

613.2 USA ISSN 0029-666X
RA784
➤ **NUTRITION TODAY.** Abbreviated title: N T. Text in English. 1966. bi-m. USD 297 domestic to institutions; USD 415 foreign to institutions (effective 2011). adv. bk.rev. illus. Index. back issues avail.; reprints avail. **Document type:** *Journal, Academic/Scholarly.* **Description:** Presents articles on developments in nutrition for dieticians, nutritionists, and physicians.
Related titles: Online - full text ed.: ISSN 1538-9839.
Indexed: A01, A03, A05, A22, A23, A24, A25, A26, A36, AS&TA, AS&TI, Agr, B04, B13, BRD, BibAg, C06, C07, C08, C10, CA, CABA, CHNI, CINAHL, D01, E04, E05, E07, E08, E12, F10, FS&TA, FamI, G03, G05, G06, G07, G08, GH, GSA, GSI, H11, H12, H13, HlthInd, I05, I07, LT, MaizeAb, N02, N03, NRN, OR, P02, P07, P10, P13, P20, P26, P30, P34, P48, P50, P53, P54, PEI, PQC, RRTA, S04, S08, S09, S12, S23, SCOPUS, T02, W03, W05, W11.
—BLDSC (6190.100000), GNLM, IE, Infotrieve, Ingenta, Linda Hall. **CCC.**
Published by: Lippincott Williams & Wilkins (Subsidiary of: Wolters Kluwer N.V.), 530 Walnut St, Philadelphia, PA 19106. TEL 215-521-8300, FAX 215-521-8902, customerservice@lww.com, http://www.lww.com. Ed. Johanna T Dwyer. Pub. Kathleen M Phelan. adv.: B&W page USD 1,255, color page USD 2,670; trim 7.75 x 10.75. Circ: 1,732.

613.2 USA ISSN 0736-0096
NUTRITION WEEK. Text in English. 1970. w. (48/yr.). USD 85. bk.rev. bibl. index. **Document type:** *Newsletter.* **Description:** Offers an independent up-to-date examination of events in food and nutrition policy, be they specific reports on congressional action, or in-depth analyses about the trends shaping nutrition policymaking.
Former titles: C N I Weekly Report (0191-0833); C N I Report
Indexed: A26, Agr, BibAg, H12, I05, P21, P48, PQC.
—CCC.
Published by: Community Nutrition Institute, 910 17th St NW, Ste. 800, Washington, DC 20006-2606. TEL 202-776-0595, FAX 202-776-0599. Ed., R&P Pam Muha. Pub. Rodney E Leonard. Circ: 2,000.

NUTRITIONAL NEUROSCIENCE (ONLINE). *see* MEDICAL SCIENCES—Psychiatry And Neurology

612.3 USA ISSN 1098-1179
RM217 CODEN: NOUUAT
NUTRITIONAL OUTLOOK; the manufacturers resource for dietary supplements & healthy foods and beverages. Text in English. 1998. 9/w. free in US & Canada to qualified personnel (effective 2008). adv. back issues avail. **Document type:** *Magazine, Consumer.* **Description:** Designed to be the manufacturer's resource for dietary supplements and healthy foods and beverages.
Related titles: Online - full text ed.
Indexed: B02, G04, G08, I05.
—CCC.
Published by: Canon Communications LLC (Subsidiary of: Apprise Media LLC), 11444 W Olympic Blvd, Ste 900, Los Angeles, CA 90064. TEL 310-445-4200, FAX 310-445-4299, info@cancom.com, http://www.cancom.com. Ed. Daniel Schatzman. Pub. James Wagner. Adv. contact Tim Baudler. color page USD 3,100, B&W page USD 3,950; trim 7.875 x 10.75. Circ: 13,040.

613.2 USA ISSN 0160-3922
RM214
NUTRITIONAL PERSPECTIVES. Text in English. 1978. q.
Indexed: C06, C07, C08, CA, CINAHL, F10, T02.
Published by: American Chiropractic Association Council on Nutrition, c/o Bonnie Sealock, Corresponding Secretary, 6855 Browntown Rd, Front Royal, VA 22630. TEL 540-635-8844, FAX 540-635-3669, info@councilonnutrition.com, http://www.councilonnutrition.com.

613.2 KOR ISSN 1229-232X
CODEN: NSUCC5
NUTRITIONAL SCIENCES. Text in English. 1997. s-a. **Document type:** *Journal, Academic/Scholarly.*
Formerly (until 1998): Korean Journal of Nutrition (1226-4687); Which superseded in part: Han'guk Yongyang Hakhoechi (0367-6463)
Related titles: Online - full text ed.
Indexed: A34, A36, AgrForAb, BP, C25, C30, CABA, D01, E12, F08, F11, F12, GH, H16, LT, MaizeAb, N02, N03, P32, P33, P37, P38, P40, PGegResA, PHN&I, PN&I, R07, R08, R11, R12, RA&MP, RRTA, S12, SoyAb, T05, TriticAb, VS, W11.
—BLDSC (5113.568000), IE.
Published by: Korean Nutrition Society/Han'gug Yeong'yang Haghoe, #804 The Korean Science and Technology Center, 635-4 Yeogsam-dong, Kangnam-Ku, Seoul, 135-703, Korea, S. TEL 82-2-34520449, FAX 82-2-34523018, kns@kns.or.kr, http://www.kns.or.kr/.

613.2 ITA ISSN 1828-6232
NUTRITIONAL THERAPY & METABOLISM. Text in English. 1983. 4/yr. EUR 148 combined subscription in Europe to institutions (print & online eds.); EUR 176 combined subscription elsewhere to institutions (print & online eds.) (effective 2009). adv. abstr.; bibl.; charts; illus. 64 p./no.; back issues avail.; reprints avail. **Document type:** *Journal, Academic/Scholarly.*
Formerly (until 2006): Rivista Italiana di Nutrizione Parenterale ed Enterale (0393-5582)
Related titles: Online - full text ed.: ISSN 1724-5982.
Indexed: C06, C07, CA, F10, FR, R10, Reac, RefZh, SCOPUS, T02.
—BLDSC (6190.421500), GNLM, INIST. **CCC.**
Published by: Wichtig Editore Srl, Via Friuli 72, Milan, MI 20135, Italy. TEL 39-02-55195443, FAX 39-02-55195971, info@wichtig-publisher.com. Ed. Francesco William Guglielmi. Circ: 1,000 (paid); 1,200 (controlled).

362 USA ISSN 1559-8705
NUTRITIONAL WELLNESS. Text in English. 2006. q. free with subsc. to Dynamic Chiropractic magazine. adv. **Document type:** *Magazine, Trade.* **Description:** Designed so doctors learn about nutrition (whole foods, herbs, homeopathy, and other natural nutritional products), understand how it philosophically fits within the scope of their profession, and can therefore help improve the health of their patients while expanding the services they offer.
Related titles: Online - full text ed.: ISSN 1559-887X; ◆ Supplement to: Dynamic Chiropractic. ISSN 1076-9684.
Indexed: I05, S23.
Published by: M P A Media, PO Box 4139, Huntington Beach, CA 92605-4139. TEL 714-230-3150, 800-324-7758, FAX 714-899-4273, editorial@mpamedia.com, http://www.mpamedia.com. Ed. Ramon McLeod. adv.: color page USD 3,711; trim 10 x 14.5. Circ: 36,149.

613.2 JAM ISSN 0255-8203
TX360.C35
NYAM NEWS. Text in English. 1975. m. free. **Document type:** *Newsletter, Academic/Scholarly.* **Description:** Feature service directed mainly at students, teachers and the mass media in the English-speaking Caribbean, giving sample information on topical and pertinent food and nutrition issues.
Published by: Caribbean Food and Nutrition Institute, University of the West Indies, U.W.I. Mona Campus, PO Box 140, Kingston, 7, Jamaica. TEL 876-927-1540-1, FAX 876-927-1927. Ed. Clare A Forrester. R&P Clare Forrester. Circ: 700. **Co-sponsor:** Pan American Health Organization/Organizacion Panamericana de la Salud.

613.26 JPN ISSN 0910-7258
NYU DAIETTO SERAPI/NEW DIET THERAPY. Text in Japanese. 1985. q. **Document type:** *Journal, Academic/Scholarly.*
Formerly (until 1984): Diet Therapy (0910-724X)
Published by: Nihon Rinsho Eiyo Kyokai/Japanese Clinical Nutrition Association, Toho University Ohashi Medical Center, Department of Nutrition, 2-17-6 Ohashi Meguro-ku, Tokyo, 153-8515, Japan. TEL 81-3-34817322, FAX 81-3-34686192, jcna1979@agate.plala.or.jp, http://www.jcna.jp/.

613.2 DEU ISSN 1611-5562
➤ **O M**; Zeitschrift fuer Orthomolekulare Medizin. (Orthomolekulare Medizin) Text in German. 2003. q. EUR 52 to institutions; EUR 102 combined subscription to institutions (print & online eds.); EUR 17.50 newsstand/cover (effective 2011). adv. **Document type:** *Journal, Academic/Scholarly.*
Related titles: Online - full text ed.: ISSN 1864-2470. 2007. EUR 102 to institutions (effective 2011).
Indexed: A22, A36, CABA, E12, F08, GH, LT, N02, N03, RefZh.
—BLDSC (6256.419000), IE. **CCC.**
Published by: Hippokrates Verlag in MVS Medizinverlage Stuttgart GmbH & Co.KG (Subsidiary of: Georg Thieme Verlag), Oswald-Hesse-Str 50, Stuttgart, 70469, Germany. TEL 49-711-89310, FAX 49-711-8931706, kunden.service@thieme.de, http://www.hippokrates.de. Ed. Dr. Claudia Mueller. Adv. contact Kathrin Thomas. Circ: 22,300 (paid).

613.2 FRA ISSN 1951-5995
RC628
OBESITE; revue francophone pour l'etude de l'obesite. Text in French. 2006. q. EUR 302, USD 364 combined subscription to institutions (print & online eds.) (effective 2012). reprint service avail. from PSC. **Document type:** *Journal, Academic/Scholarly.*
Related titles: Online - full text ed.: ISSN 1951-6002 (from IngentaConnect).
Indexed: A22, A26, E01, I05, SCOPUS.
—IE, Ingenta, INIST. **CCC.**
Published by: Springer France (Subsidiary of: Springer Science+Business Media), 22 Rue de Palestro, Paris, 75002, France. TEL 33-1-53009860, FAX 33-1-53009861, sylvie.kamara@springer.com. Ed. O Ziegler.

OBESITY AND METABOLISM. *see* MEDICAL SCIENCES

613.2 CHE ISSN 1662-4025
➤ **OBESITY FACTS**; the European journal of obesity. Text in English. 2008. bi-m. CHF 305, EUR 195, USD 333.50 to institutions; CHF 377, EUR 245, USD 408.50 combined subscription to institutions (print & online eds.) (effective 2012). adv. **Document type:** *Journal, Academic/Scholarly.* **Description:** Covers all aspects of obesity, in particular epidemiology, etiology and pathogenesis, treatment, and the prevention of adiposity.
Related titles: Online - full text ed.: ISSN 1662-4033. CHF 254, EUR 175, USD 263 to institutions (effective 2012).
Indexed: A22, B21, CurCont, E01, EMBASE, ESPM, ExcerpMed, H&SSA, MEDLINE, P30, RiskAb, SCI, SCOPUS, W07.
—IE. **CCC.**
Published by: S. Karger AG, Allschwilerstr 10, Basel, 4055, Switzerland. TEL 41-61-3061111, FAX 41-61-3061234, karger@karger.ch, http://www.karger.ch. Ed. Johannes Hebebrand. adv.: page EUR 2,300. Circ: 3,000 (controlled).

➤ **OBESITY, FITNESS, AND WELLNESS WEEK.** *see* PHYSICAL FITNESS AND HYGIENE

613.2 GBR ISSN 1467-7881
RC628 CODEN: ORBEBL
➤ **OBESITY REVIEWS.** Text in English. 2000. bi-m. GBP 493 in United Kingdom to institutions; EUR 627 in Europe to institutions; USD 903 in the Americas to institutions; USD 1,055 elsewhere to institutions; GBP 568 combined subscription in United Kingdom to institutions (print & online eds.); EUR 721 combined subscription in Europe to institutions (print & online eds.); USD 1,038 combined subscription in the Americas to institutions (print & online eds.); USD 1,214 combined subscription elsewhere to institutions (print & online eds.) (effective 2012). adv. back issues avail.; reprint service avail. from PSC. **Document type:** *Journal, Academic/Scholarly.* **Description:** Provides a forum for publishing updated reviews in all disciplines related to obesity.

Related titles: Online - full text ed.: ISSN 1467-789X. GBP 493 in United Kingdom to institutions; EUR 627 in Europe to institutions; USD 903 in the Americas to institutions; USD 1,055 elsewhere to institutions (effective 2012) (from IngentaConnect); Supplement(s): Obesity Reviews. Supplement. ISSN 1743-7008.
Indexed: A01, A03, A08, A20, A22, A26, A34, A36, A37, Agr, B21, BIOBASE, CA, CABA, CurCont, D01, E01, E12, EMBASE, ESPM, ExcerpMed, F08, F10, FS&TA, GH, H&SSA, H12, H16, I14, IABS, LT, MEDLINE, MaizeAb, N02, N03, N04, P30, P34, P38, PEI, R10, R12, RA&MP, RRTA, Reac, RiskAb, S12, SCI, SCOPUS, SoyAb, T02, T05, VS, W07, W11.
—BLDSC (6196.952700), IE, Infotrieve, Ingenta, INIST. **CCC.**
Published by: (International Association for the Study of Obesity), Wiley-Blackwell Publishing Ltd. (Subsidiary of: John Wiley & Sons, Inc.), 9600 Garsington Rd, Oxford, OX4 2DQ, United Kingdom. TEL 44-1865-776868, FAX 44-1865-714591, customerservices@blackwellpublishing.com. Ed. Arne Astrup TEL 45-3533-2507.

613.262 GBR ISSN 1759-2607
OFF THE HOOF; going veggie for a greener planet. Text in English. 2008. q. GBP 15; GBP 3.95 per issue (effective 2010). adv. back issues avail. **Document type:** *Magazine, Consumer.* **Description:** Covers vegan veggie friendly businesses, places to stay, eat and shop as well as products.
Related titles: Online - full text ed.: free (effective 2010).
Published by: Yaoh, PO Box 333, Bristol, BS99 1NF, United Kingdom. TEL 44-117-9239053, info@yaoh.co.uk, http://www.yaoh.co.uk. Ed. Al Slurry. Adv. contact Charlie Chang TEL 44-117-9239053.

THE OILY PRESS LIPID LIBRARY. *see* BIOLOGY—Biochemistry

613.2 FRA ISSN 1958-1718
OK SANTE. Text in French. 2007. bi-m. **Document type:** *Magazine, Consumer.*
Published by: Mix Book, 34 Bd des Italiens, Paris, 75009, France.

ONCOLOGY NUTRITION CONNECTION. *see* MEDICAL SCIENCES—Oncology

613.2 615.32 NLD ISSN 1876-3960
QP144.F85
➤ **THE OPEN NUTRACEUTICALS JOURNAL.** Text in English. 2008. irreg. free (effective 2011). **Document type:** *Journal, Academic/Scholarly.*
Media: Online - full text.
Indexed: F05, F06, F07, F10, T02.
Published by: Bentham Open (Subsidiary of: Bentham Science Publishers Ltd.), PO Box 294, Bussum, AG 1400, Netherlands. TEL 31-35-6923800, FAX 31-35-6980150, subscriptions@bentham.org. Ed. Ram B Singh.

613.2 NLD ISSN 1874-2882
QP141.A1
➤ **THE OPEN NUTRITION JOURNAL.** Text in English. 2007. irreg. free (effective 2011). **Document type:** *Journal, Academic/Scholarly.* **Description:** Covers all areas of experimental and clinical nutrition research.
Media: Online - full text.
Indexed: CABA, CTA, D01, E12, F05, F06, F07, F10, GH, N02, N03, NSA, P30, T02.
Published by: Bentham Open (Subsidiary of: Bentham Science Publishers Ltd.), PO Box 294, Bussum, AG 1400, Netherlands. TEL 31-35-6923800, FAX 31-35-6980150, subscriptions@bentham.org. Ed. Akio Inui.

613.2 GBR ISSN 2046-2328
OPTIMUM NUTRITION I-MAG. Text in English. 1987. q. GBP 18 to non-members; free to members (effective 2011). **Document type:** *Magazine, Consumer.* **Description:** Contains articles releated to the field of nutrition.
Formerly (until 2010): Optimum Nutrition (1475-8725)
Media: Online - full text.
Published by: (The Institute for Optimum Nutrition), Target Publishing Ltd., The Old Dairy, Hudsons Farm, Fieldgate Ln, Ugley Green, Bishops Stortford, Essex CM22 6HJ, United Kingdom. TEL 44-1279-816300, FAX 44-1279-810081, info@targetpublishing.com, http://www.targetpublishing.com.

OPTIMUM WELLNESS. *see* PHYSICAL FITNESS AND HYGIENE

612.3 CAN
ORGANIC LIVING. Text in English. 1997 (Dec.). bi-m. free. **Document type:** *Newsletter.*
Media: Online - full text.
Published by: Pro Organics Marketing Inc., 4535 Still Creek Ave., Burnaby, BC V5C 5V1, Canada. Ed. Steve Boyle.

ORGANIC PRODUCTS RETAILER. *see* FOOD AND FOOD INDUSTRIES

613.2 USA ISSN 0748-8394
CODEN: SBLAES
OUTPOST EXCHANGE; Milwaukee's food and wellness magazine. Text in English. 1971. 20/yr. USD 12 (effective 2005). adv. bk.rev. 60 p./no. 3 cols./p.; **Document type:** *Magazine, Consumer.*
Published by: Outpost Natural Foods, 205 W Highland Ave, Milwaukee, WI 53203. TEL 414-431-3377, FAX 414-431-4522, exchange@execpc.com. Ed. Malcolm Woods. R&P Kristine Lorentzsen. Adv. contact Margee Foulke. B&W page USD 680. Circ: 35,000; 13,000 (paid).

613.2 640.73 USA
P C C SOUND CONSUMER. Text in English. 1974. m. free to members. adv. bk.rev. illus. back issues avail. **Document type:** *Newsletter.*
Formerly: Puget Consumers Co-op Newsletter
Published by: Puget Consumers Co-op, 4201 Roosevelt Way, NE, Seattle, WA 98105-6008. TEL 206-547-1222, FAX 206-545-7131, http://www.pugetcoop.com. Ed. Kim Runciman. Adv. contact Nancy Gagnat. Circ: 36,000.

613.2 USA ISSN 1534-3642
RM258.5
P D R FOR NUTRITIONAL SUPPLEMENTS. (Physicians' Desk Reference) Text in English. 2001. irreg. **Document type:** *Handbook/Manual/Guide, Trade.* **Description:** Covers vitamins, minerals, amino acids, probiotics, metabolites, hormones, enzymes, cartilage products, including sections on relevant contraindications, precautions, side effects, and potential interactions with prescription and OTC drugs.
Published by: Thomson P D R, 3 Times Sq, New York, NY 10036. TEL 646-223-4000, TH.customerservice@thomson.com, http://www.pdr.net.

613.26 NCL ISSN 1023-9197
PACIFIC DIET ADVISORY LEAFLET. Text in English. 1995. irreg., latest vol.8, 1995. **Document type:** *Monographic series.*
Related titles: French ed.: Fiches Techniques sur l'Alimentation et la Sante dans le Pacifique.
Published by: Secretariat of the Pacific Community, PO Box D5, Noumea, Cedex 98848, New Caledonia. TEL 687-262000, FAX 687-263818, spc@spc.int, http://www.spc.int.

612.3 NCL ISSN 1022-2782
RA601
PACIFIC ISLANDS NUTRITION. Text in English. 1989. q. **Document type:** *Newsletter.*
Related titles: French ed.: Nutrition en Oceanie. ISSN 1022-2790.
Indexed: A11.
Published by: Secretariat of the Pacific Community, PO Box D5, Noumea, Cedex 98848, New Caledonia. TEL 687-262000, FAX 687-263818, spc@spc.int, http://www.spc.int.

613.2 PAK ISSN 1680-5194
QP141.A1
➤ **PAKISTAN JOURNAL OF NUTRITION.** Text in English. 2001. bi-m. **Document type:** *Journal, Academic/Scholarly.* **Description:** Covers all aspects of nutritional sciences.
Related titles: Online - full text ed.: free (effective 2011).
Indexed: A01, A34, A35, A36, A37, A38, AgBio, AgrForAb, B23, BA, BP, C25, C30, CABA, D01, E12, EMBASE, ExcerpMed, F08, F10, F11, F12, FCA, G11, GH, H16, H17, I11, IndVet, LT, MaizeAb, N02, N03, N04, O01, OR, P32, P33, P37, P38, P39, P40, PGegResA, PGrRegA, PHN&I, PN&I, R07, R08, R10, R11, R12, R13, RA&MP, RM&VM, RRTA, Reac, S12, S13, S16, S17, SCOPUS, SoyAb, T02, T05, TAR, TriticAb, VS, W10, W11, Z01.
—BLDSC (6341.610000), IE, Ingenta.
Published by: A N S I Network, 308 Lasani Town, Sargodha Rd, Faisalabad, 38090, Pakistan. TEL 92-41-8787087, FAX 92-41-8815544, sarwarm@ansimail.org, http://ansinet.com.

➤ **PEDIATRIC ENDOCRINOLOGY REVIEWS**; diabetes, nutrition, metabolism. *see* MEDICAL SCIENCES—Endocrinology

613.2 649 GBR ISSN 2047-3087
RJ399.C6
➤ **PEDIATRIC OBESITY.** Abbreviated title: I J P O. Text in English. 2006 (Jan.). q. GBP 415, EUR 550, USD 685 combined subscription to institutions (print & online eds.); GBP 830, EUR 1,100, USD 1,370 combined subscription to corporations (print & online eds.) (effective 2010). adv. back issues avail.; reprint service avail. from PSC. **Document type:** *Journal, Academic/Scholarly.* **Description:** Devoted to research into obesity during childhood and adolescence.
Formerly (until 2012): International Journal of Pediatric Obesity (1747-7166)
Related titles: Online - full text ed.: ISSN 1747-7174 (from IngentaConnect).
Indexed: A01, A36, C06, C07, CA, CABA, CurCont, D01, EMBASE, ExcerpMed, GH, LT, MEDLINE, N02, N03, P03, P30, PsycInfo, R10, R12, RRTA, Reac, S12, SCI, SCOPUS, T02, T05, W07, W11.
—IE, Ingenta. **CCC.**
Published by: (International Association for the Study of Obesity), Wiley-Blackwell Publishing Ltd. (Subsidiary of: John Wiley & Sons, Inc.), 9600 Garsington Rd, Oxford, OX4 2DQ, United Kingdom. TEL 44-1865-776868, FAX 44-1865-714591, customerservices@blackwellpublishing.com, http://www.wiley.com/WileyCDA/. Ed. Michael I Goran.

612 USA ISSN 1063-8822
CODEN: PCNSEW
PENNINGTON CENTER NUTRITION SERIES. Text in English. 1991. irreg. price varies. **Document type:** *Monographic series, Academic/Scholarly.* **Description:** Addresses topics in nutrition and health.
Related titles: Online - full text ed.
Indexed: Agr.
—BLDSC (6421.689000), Ingenta.
Published by: (Pennington Biomedical Research Center), Louisiana State University Press, 3990 W Lakeshore Dr, Baton Rouge, LA 70808. TEL 225-578-6294, 800-848-6224, FAX 225-578-6461, 800-272-6817, customerservice@longleafservices.org, http://www.lsu.edu/lsupress/.

PERSONAL CARE NEWS. *see* PHYSICAL FITNESS AND HYGIENE

613.2 COL ISSN 0124-4108
➤ **PERSPECTIVAS EN NUTRICION HUMANA.** Text in Spanish. 1999. s-a. bk.rev. Index. back issues avail. **Document type:** *Journal, Academic/Scholarly.*
Related titles: Online - full text ed.: free (effective 2011).
Indexed: A26, A34, A35, A36, AgBio, C01, C25, CABA, D01, E12, GH, H11, H12, H16, H17, I04, I05, LT, MaizeAb, N02, N03, N04, OR, P33, P37, P38, P39, R11, R12, RRTA, S12, T05, VS, W11.
Published by: Universidad de Antioquia, Escuela de Nutricion y Dietetica, Cra 75 No. 65-87, Medellin, Colombia. TEL 57-4-4259222, FAX 57-4-4259235, dirnutricion@arhuaco.udeaedu.co, http://www.pijas.udea.edu.co/revista.

➤ **PHARMA UND FOOD**; Hygiene - Produktion - Ausruestung. *see* PHARMACY AND PHARMACOLOGY

613.2 PHL
PHILIPPINES. FOOD AND NUTRITION RESEARCH INSTITUTE. ANNUAL REPORT. Text in English. 1950. a. **Document type:** *Corporate.* **Description:** Offers a detailed compilation of the institute's various projects and activities. Includes completed research, research in progress, public services, staff papers and publications, staff development, cooperative activities, foreign visitors, financial resources, and technical staff.
Formerly: Philippines. Food and Nutrition Research Center. Annual Report (0071-7142)
Published by: Food and Nutrition Research Institute, Science Complex, Bicutan, Tagiug Mm, 1631, Philippines. TEL 63-2-837-2071, FAX 63-2-837-2934. Ed., R&P Catherine Q Castaneda TEL 837-81-13. Circ: (controlled).

PHYSICAL. *see* PHYSICAL FITNESS AND HYGIENE

▼ **PIU SALUTE MAGAZINE.** *see* PHYSICAL FITNESS AND HYGIENE

613.2 USA
PLANETARY HEALTH. Text in English. 1989. 4/yr. USD 30 to individuals; USD 50 families (effective 2000). adv. bk.rev. **Document type:** *Magazine, Consumer.*
Former titles: One Peaceful World; Return to Paradise
Published by: One Peaceful World, Inc., PO Box 10, Becket, MA 01223. TEL 413-623-2322, FAX 413-623-6042. Ed., Pub., R&P Alex Jack. Adv. contact Laura Wepman. Circ: 10,000.

612.3 USA ISSN 0921-9668
TX341 CODEN: PFHNE8
➤ **PLANT FOODS FOR HUMAN NUTRITION.** Text in English. 1952. q. EUR 676, USD 631 combined subscription to institutions (print & online eds.) (effective 2012). adv. bk.rev. bibl.; charts; illus. reprint service avail. from PSC. **Document type:** *Journal, Academic/Scholarly.* **Description:** Publishes reports of original research concerned with the improvement and evaluation of the nutritional quality of plant foods for humans, as they are influenced by biotechnology, plant breeding, cooking and processing, plant and soil ecology, and plant production practices.
Formerly (until 1987): Qualitas Plantarum (0377-3205); Which was formed by the 1972 merger of: Qualitas Plantarum et Materiae Vegetabiles (0033-5134); Which was formerly (1952-1957): Materiae Vegetabiles (0369-2698); (1968-1972): Plant Foods for Human Nutrition (0554-2723)
Related titles: Microform ed.: (from PQC); Online - full text ed.: ISSN 1573-9104 (from IngentaConnect).
Indexed: A22, A26, A34, A35, A36, ASCA, AgBio, Agr, AgrForAb, B25, BA, BIOBASE, BIOSIS Prev, BP, BibAg, BibLing, C06, C07, C25, C30, CA, CABA, CIN, ChemAb, ChemTitl, CurCont, D01, E01, E04, E05, E08, E12, EMBASE, ExcerpMed, F08, F10, F11, F12, FCA, FS&TA, G08, GH, H11, H16, I05, IABS, IndMed, MEDLINE, MaizeAb, MycolAb, N02, N03, N04, O01, OR, P30, P32, P33, P38, P40, PGegResA, PGrRegA, PHN&I, PN&I, PlantSci, R11, R13, RA&MP, RM&VM, S09, S12, S17, SCI, SCOPUS, SoyAb, T02, T05, TAR, TOSA, TriticAb, VITIS, VS, W07, W10.
—BLDSC (6517.500000), CASDDS, GNLM, IE, Ingenta, INIST, Linda Hall. **CCC.**
Published by: Springer New York LLC (Subsidiary of: Springer Science+Business Media), 233 Spring St, New York, NY 10013. TEL 212-460-1500, FAX 212-460-1575, journals-ny@springer.com, http://www.springer.com. Ed. O Paredes-Lopez.

➤ **POSITIVE HEALTH (ONLINE).** *see* PHYSICAL FITNESS AND HYGIENE

▼ ➤ **POTRAVINARSTVO.** *see* FOOD AND FOOD INDUSTRIES

613.2 FRA ISSN 1766-7305
➤ **PRATIQUES EN NUTRITION**; sante et alimentation. Text in French. 2005. 4/yr. EUR 89 in Europe to institutions; EUR 78.35 in France to institutions; JPY 13,300 in Japan to institutions; USD 116 elsewhere to institutions (effective 2012). **Document type:** *Journal, Academic/Scholarly.*
Related titles: Online - full text ed.
Indexed: SCOPUS.
—**CCC.**
Published by: Elsevier Masson (Subsidiary of: Elsevier Health Sciences), 62 Rue Camille Desmoulins, Issy les Moulineaux, Cedex 92442, France. TEL 33-1-71165500, FAX 33-1-71165600, infos@elsevier-masson.fr.

➤ **PREVENIR ES SALUD.** *see* PHYSICAL FITNESS AND HYGIENE

➤ **PRIMAL PARENTING.** *see* CHILDREN AND YOUTH—About

613.2 AUT ISSN 0301-7656
CODEN: PELEDR
PROBLEME DER ERNAEHRUNGS- UND LEBENSMITTELWISSENSCHAFT. Text in German. 1973. irreg., latest vol.6, 1979. price varies. adv. bk.rev. **Document type:** *Monographic series, Academic/Scholarly.*
Indexed: ChemAb.
—CASDDS.
Published by: Oesterreichische Gesellschaft fuer Ernaehrung, Zaunergasse 1-3, Vienna, 1030, Austria. TEL 43-1-7147193, FAX 43-1-7186146, info@oege.at, http://gerda.univie.ac.at/oege/.

612.3 UKR
➤ **PROBLEMY KHARCHUVANNYA.** Text in Ukrainian, Russian. 1932. q. **Document type:** *Journal, Academic/Scholarly.*
Related titles: Online - full text ed.
Published by: (Instytut Ekohihieny i Toksykolohii), Vydavnytsvo Medytsyna Ukrainy, vul Popudrenka, 34, Kyiv, Ukraine. TEL 380-44-5740756, FAX 380-44-5529502. Ed. V I Smolyar.

➤ **PROFESSIONE ALLEVATORE.** *see* AGRICULTURE—Poultry And Livestock

613.2 ITA ISSN 1129-8723
PROGRESS IN NUTRITION; giornale italiano del metabolismo e della nutrizione. Text in Italian, English. 1999. q. EUR 86 in Europe to institutions; EUR 97 elsewhere to institutions (effective 2009). **Document type:** *Journal, Academic/Scholarly.* **Description:** The primary goal of this magazine is to bring together the various disciplines involved in the world of nutrition.
Indexed: EMBASE, ExcerpMed, R10, Reac, SCI, SCOPUS, W07.
—BLDSC (6871.230000), IE, Ingenta.
Published by: Mattioli 1885 SpA, Via Coduro 1, Fidenza, PR 43036, Italy. TEL 39-0524-84547, FAX 39-0524-84751, http://www.mattioli1885.com. Ed. Massimo Cocchi. Circ: 5,000.

613.2 GBR ISSN 1368-9800
RA784 CODEN: PHNUF6
➤ **PUBLIC HEALTH NUTRITION.** Text in English. 1998. m. GBP 770, EUR 1,219, USD 1,453 to institutions; GBP 813, EUR 1,303, USD 1,559 combined subscription to institutions (print & online eds.) (effective 2012). adv. back issues avail.; reprint service avail. from PSC. **Document type:** *Journal, Academic/Scholarly.* **Description:** Focuses on the promotion of good health through nutrition and the primary prevention of nutrition related illness in the population.
Related titles: Online - full text ed.: ISSN 1475-2727. GBP 643, EUR 1,022, USD 1,219 to institutions (effective 2012).

Indexed: A01, A03, A08, A20, A22, A34, A35, A36, ASG, AgBio, Agr, AgrForAb, B21, C06, C07, C08, C25, CA, CABA, CINAHL, CurCont, D01, E01, E12, EMBASE, ESPM, ExcerpMed, F05, F06, F07, F08, F09, F10, FS&TA, GH, H&SSA, H16, H17, IndMed, IndVet, LT, MEDLINE, MaizeAb, N02, N03, N04, P11, P20, P22, P24, P30, P32, P33, P34, P37, P38, P39, P40, P48, P50, P52, P54, P56, PHN&I, PN&I, PQC, R08, R10, R11, R12, RA&MP, RRTA, Reac, RiskAb, S12, SCI, SCOPUS, SoyAb, T02, T05, TriticAb, VS, W07, W11.
—BLDSC (6964.770000), IE, Infotrieve, Ingenta, INIST. **CCC.**
Published by: (Nutrition Society), Cambridge University Press, The Edinburgh Bldg, Shaftesbury Rd, Cambridge, CB2 8RU, United Kingdom. TEL 44-1223-326070, FAX 44-1223-325150, journals@cambridge.org. Ed. Agneta Yngve. R&P Linda Nicol TEL 44-1223-325702. Adv. contact Rebecca Roberts TEL 44-1223-325083. page GBP 610, page USD 1,160.

➤ **PUBLIC HEALTH REVIEWS (PRINT)**; an international quarterly. *see* PUBLIC HEALTH AND SAFETY

613.2 ESP
PUNTEX HERBOLISTERIA Y DIETETICA. Text in Spanish. 2001. a. adv. back issues avail. **Document type:** *Yearbook, Consumer.*
Formerly: Guia Puntex. Anuario Espanol de Herboristeria y Dietetica (1576-5571)
Published by: Publicaciones Nacionales Tecnicas y Extranjeras (PUNTEX), Padilla 323, Barcelona, 08025, Spain. TEL 34-934-462820, FAX 34-934-462064, puntex@puntex.es, http://www.puntex.es. Ed. Raul Sanahuja. adv.: color page EUR 2,615; trim 170 x 240. Circ: 5,000.

613.2 USA
PURE FACTS. Text in English. 1978. 10/yr. free to members. back issues avail. **Document type:** *Newsletter, Consumer.* **Description:** Non-profit support group helping children with learning or behavior problems and chemically-sensitive adults.
Indexed: E-psyche.
Published by: Feingold Association of the United States, 554 E Main St, Ste 301, Riverhead, NY 11901-2671. TEL 631-369-9340, FAX 631-369-2988, orders@feingold.org. Circ: 6,000.

PURE POWER; when training + science = peak performance. *see* PHYSICAL FITNESS AND HYGIENE

613.2 ITA ISSN 1828-9029
I QUADERNI DEL MANGIAR SANO. Text in Italian. 2006. bi-m. **Document type:** *Magazine, Consumer.*
Published by: Vallecchi Editore, Viale Giovanni Milton 7, Florence, 50129, Italy. TEL 39-055-290765, FAX 39-055-293477, http://www.vallecchi.it.

RADIUS; for health, healing, happiness. *see* PHYSICAL FITNESS AND HYGIENE

613.2 616.3 FRA ISSN 1958-1084
REALITES EN NUTRITION. Text in French. 2007. m. EUR 52 domestic to qualified personnel; EUR 42 domestic to students; EUR 65 foreign (effective 2008). **Document type:** *Journal, Trade.*
Published by: Performances Medicales, 91 Av. de la Republique, Paris, 75011, France. TEL 33-1-47006714, FAX 33-1-47006999.

▼ **RECENT PATENTS ON FOOD, NUTRITION & AGRICULTURE.** *see* PATENTS, TRADEMARKS AND COPYRIGHTS

613.2 BRA ISSN 0103-7196
REVISTA BRASILEIRA DE NUTRICAO CLINICA. Text in Portuguese. 1984. 3/yr. **Document type:** *Journal, Academic/Scholarly.*
Formerly (until 1989): Sociedade Brasileira de Nutricao Parenteral. Revista (0102-9754)
Published by: Sociedade Brasileira de Nutricao Parenteral e Enteral (S B N P E), Rua Abilio Soares 233 Cj 144, Paraiso, Sao Paulo, 04005-000, Brazil. TEL 55-11-38899909, FAX 55-11-38898770, sbnpe@terra.com.br, http://www.sbnpe.com.br.

REVISTA CHILENA DE DOCENCIA E INVESTIGACION EN SALUD. *see* EDUCATION

613.2 CHL ISSN 0716-1549
REVISTA CHILENA DE NUTRICION. Text in Spanish; Summaries in English, Spanish. 1980. 3/yr. CLP 16 domestic; USD 50 foreign. **Document type:** *Journal, Academic/Scholarly.*
Supersedes (1961-1968): Nutricion, Bromatologia y Toxicologia (0550-4023)
Related titles: Online - full text ed.: ISSN 0717-7518. 2002. free (effective 2011) (from SciELO).
Indexed: A22, C01, FS&TA, IBR, IBZ, P30, SCOPUS.
—BLDSC (7848.910000), IE, Infotrieve, Ingenta.
Published by: Sociedad Chilena de Nutricion Bromatologia y Toxicologia, Universidad de Chile, Fac. de Medicina Depto. Nutricion, Independencia, 1027, Santiago, Chile. Ed. Hector Araya.

613.2 CHL ISSN 0716-6931
REVISTA CHILENA DE OBESIDAD. Text in Spanish. 1989. 3/yr.
Published by: Sociedad Chilena de Obesidad, Esmeralda 678, 2o Piso, Santiago, Chile. TEL 56-2-6327537, FAX 56-2-6391085, sochob@entelchile.net, http://www.sochob.cl.

REVISTA DE DERECHO ALIMENTARIO. *see* LAW

REVISTA DE INVESTIGACION CLINICA. *see* MEDICAL SCIENCES

363.8 BRA ISSN 1415-5273
➤ **REVISTA DE NUTRICAO**; Brazilian journal of nutrition. Text in Portuguese, English, Spanish; Summaries in Portuguese, English, Spanish. 1988. 3/yr. BRL 70 domestic; BRL 120 foreign (effective 2008). bk.rev. abstr. 95 p./no.; back issues avail. **Document type:** *Journal, Academic/Scholarly.* **Description:** Publishes research and works that deal with the study and development of nutritional science for academics and professionals.
Supersedes (in 1998): Revista de Nutricao da PUCCAMP (0103-1627)
Related titles: Online - full text ed.: ISSN 1678-9865. 2000. free (effective 2011).
Indexed: A34, A35, A36, AgBio, C25, CABA, D01, E12, F08, F09, F12, FS&TA, GH, H16, H17, LT, MaizeAb, N02, N03, N04, P32, P33, P40, PHN&I, PN&I, R11, R12, R13, RA&MP, RM&VM, RRTA, S12, SCI, SCOPUS, SoyAb, T05, TAR, TriticAb, VS, W07, W11.
—BLDSC (7868.492000), IE, Ingenta.
Published by: Pontificia Universidade Catolica de Campinas, Centro de Ciencias da Vida, Av. John Boyd Dunlop, s/n, Bloco B, Jd. Ipaussurama, Campinas, SP 13059-000, Brazil. TEL 55-19-37298349, FAX 55-19-37298576, revistas.ccv@puc-campinas.edu.br, http://www.puccamp.edu.br/ccv. Eds., Pubs. Rosa Wanda Diez Garcia, Semiramis Martins Alvares Domene. Adv. contact Maria Cristina Matoso. Circ: 1,200.

613.262 BRA ISSN 1980-0630
REVISTA DOS VEGETARIANOS. Text in Portuguese. 2006. m. BRL 104.50; BRL 9.90 newsstand/cover (effective 2007). adv. **Document type:** *Magazine, Consumer.*
Published by: Editora Europa Ltda., Rua MMDC 121, Butanta, Sao Paulo, SP 05510-021, Brazil. TEL 55-11-30385050, FAX 55-11-38190538.

613.2 ESP ISSN 1135-3074
REVISTA ESPANOLA DE NUTRICION COMUNITARIA. Text in Spanish. 1995. q. EUR 70 to institutions (effective 2009). back issues avail. **Document type:** *Journal, Academic/Scholarly.*
Related titles: Online - full text ed.: (from ScienceDirect).
Indexed: BIOBASE, EMBASE, ExcerpMed, IABS, R10, Reac, SCI, SCOPUS, W07.
—**CCC.**
Published by: Nexus Medica Editores, C/ Passeig d'Amunt 38, Barcelona, 08024, Spain. TEL 34-93-5510260, FAX 34-93-2136672, redaccion@nexusmedica.com.

613.2 ESP ISSN 1696-6112
REVISTA ESPANOLA DE OBESIDAD. Text in Multiple languages. 1998. q. adv. **Document type:** *Journal, Trade.*
Formerly (until 2002): Formacion Continuada en Nutricion y Obesidad (1575-409X)
Indexed: EMBASE, ExcerpMed, R10, Reac, SCOPUS.
—BLDSC (7854.128000). **CCC.**
Published by: (Sociedad Espanola de Nutricion Basica y Aplicada), Sociedad Espanola para el Estudio de la Obesidad, Paseo de la Bonanua, 47, Barcelona, 08017, Spain. contacto@seedo.es. Ed. J A Fernandez Lopez. Circ: 4,000.

REVISTA SALUD PUBLICA Y NUTRICION. *see* PUBLIC HEALTH AND SAFETY

613.2 664 VEN ISSN 2218-4384
▼ ➤ **REVISTA VENEZOLANA DE CIENCIA Y TECNOLOGIA DE ALIMENTOS.** Summaries in English, Spanish; Text in Spanish. 2010 (Jul.). s-a. free (effective 2011). Index. back issues avail. **Document type:** *Journal, Academic/Scholarly.* **Description:** Publishes research results dealing with Food Science and Technology and related areas, including food engineering, human and animal nutrition, agriculture, food biotechnology, and others.
Media: Online - full text.
Indexed: A34, A37, C25, CABA, D01, F08, FCA, GH, H16, MaizeAb, N02, N03, N04, P32, P33, R08, S13, SoyAb, T05, W11.
Published by: Asociacion Revista Venezolana de Ciencia y Tecnologia de Alimentos, Avenida Andres Bello No 101-79, Municipio Valencia, Ciudad Valencia, Estado Carabobo, Venezuela. TEL 58-241-8573187, asociacion@rvcta.org, http://www.rvcta.org/Asociacion/Asociacion.html. Ed., Pub., R&P, Adv. contact Carlos Alberto Padron Pereira.

613.2 JPN ISSN 0485-1412
CODEN: RNEYAW
RINSHO EIYO/JAPANESE JOURNAL OF CLINICAL NUTRITION. Text in Japanese. 1952. m. JPY 1,260 newsstand/cover (effective 2007). adv. bk.rev. charts; illus. **Document type:** *Magazine, Trade.*
Indexed: ChemAb.
—CASDDS.
Published by: Ishiyoku Shuppan K.K./Ishiyaku Publishers Inc., 1-7-10 Honkomagome, Bunkyo-ku, Tokyo, 113-0021, Japan. Circ: 16,500.

ROSEMARY CONLEY DIET & FITNESS. *see* PHYSICAL FITNESS AND HYGIENE

613.2 618.92 USA ISSN 0557-3467
RJ21 CODEN: RRRCAP
ROSS CONFERENCE ON PEDIATRIC RESEARCH. REPORT. Key Title: Report of the Ross Conference on Pediatric Research. Text in English. 1958. irreg.
Published by: Ross Laboratories, 625 Cleveland Ave, Columbus, OH 43215-1724. TEL 800-986-8510, http://www.ross.com.

636.085 GBR ISSN 0969-4560
➤ **ROWETT RESEARCH INSTITUTE ANNUAL REPORT.** Text in English. 1922. a. free. **Document type:** *Journal, Academic/Scholarly.*
Former titles (until 1988): Rowett Research Institute. Report (0952-7222); (until 1987): Rowett Research Institute. Annual Report of Studies in Animal Nutrition and Allied Sciences (0307-8035); (until 1966): Rowett Research Institute. Annual Report on Animal Nutrition and Allied Studies; Which incorporated (1925-1961): Rowett Research Institute. Collected Papers
—BLDSC.
Published by: Rowett Research Institute, Greenburn Rd, Bucksburn, Aberdeen, AB21 9SB, United Kingdom. TEL 44-1224-712751, FAX 44-1224-715349, enquiries@rowett.ac.uk, http://www.rowett.ac.uk/. Circ: 2,000 (controlled).

➤ **RUNNING & FITNEWS.** *see* PHYSICAL FITNESS AND HYGIENE

362.176 ZAF ISSN 1607-0658
➤ **S A J C N.** (South African Journal of Clinical Nutrition) Text in English. 1988. q. back issues avail. **Document type:** *Journal, Academic/Scholarly.* **Description:** Publishes clinical and experimental research in nutrition.
Related titles: Online - full text ed.: free (effective 2011); ◆ Supplement to: S A M J South African Medical Journal. ISSN 0256-9574.
Indexed: A26, BIOBASE, C06, C07, CA, EMBASE, ExcerpMed, H12, I05, IABS, ISAP, P30, R10, Reac, SCOPUS, T02.
—INIST. **CCC.**
Published by: (Association for Dietetics in Southern Africa, Nutrition Society of Southern Africa, South African Society of Parenteral and Enteral Nutrition), Medpharm Publications (Pty) Ltd, PO Box 14804, Lyttelton, 0140, South Africa. TEL 27-12-6647460, FAX 27-12-6646276, reception@medpharm.co.za, http://www.medpharm.co.za. Ed. Demetre Lapadarios.

➤ **S I I CSALUD.** (Sociedad Iberoamericana de Informacion Cientifica) *see* MEDICAL SCIENCES

➤ **SALUD(I)CIENCIA.** *see* MEDICAL SCIENCES

613.2 CAN ISSN 1719-9263
LA SANTE C'EST ALIMENTAIRE. Text in French. 2006. q. **Document type:** *Newsletter, Consumer.*
Published by: Sun Media Corp./Corporation Sun Media, 465 Rue McGill, 3e Etage, Montreal, PQ H2Y 4B4, Canada. http://www.sunmedia.ca.

SANTE ZEN. *see* PHYSICAL FITNESS AND HYGIENE

613.2 USA ISSN 1528-5707
SCAN'S PULSE. Text in English. 1982. q. USD 50 to individuals; USD 100 to institutions; free to members (effective 2010). back issues avail. **Document type:** *Newsletter, Trade.*
Related titles: Online - full text ed.: free (effective 2010).
Indexed: SD.
Published by: (American Dietetic Association, Sports, Cardiovascular, and Wellness Nutrition), American Dietetic Association, 120 S Riverside Plz, Ste 2000, Chicago, IL 60606. TEL 312-899-0040, 800-877-1600, FAX 312-899-4899, http://www.nutrifit.org. Ed. Mark Kern TEL 619-594-1834.

613.2 DEU ISSN 0931-1068
SCHROT UND KORN. Text in German. 1985. m. EUR 20 domestic; EUR 26 foreign; EUR 1.65 newsstand/cover (effective 2009). adv. **Document type:** *Magazine, Consumer.*
Published by: bio verlag gmbH, Magnolienweg 23, Aschaffenburg, 63741, Germany. TEL 49-6021-44890, FAX 49-6021-4489499, info@bioverlag.de, http://www.bioverlag.de. Ed. Barbara Gruber. Adv. contact Ellen Heil. B&W page EUR 8,050, color page EUR 11,750. Circ: 682,285 (controlled).

613.2 ITA ISSN 1824-1824
SCIENTIFIC NUTRITION TODAY (ONLINE). Text in Multiple languages. 1995. q. **Document type:** *Journal, Academic/Scholarly.*
Formerly (until 2003): Scientific Nutrition Today (Print) (1127-8714)
Published by: Nutricia Italia SpA, Via Bonnet 6 A, Milan, 20154, Italy. TEL 39-02-636951.

SEMEINYI DOKTOR/FAMILY DOCTOR; prakticheskie sovety po meditsine. *see* MEDICAL SCIENCES

613.2 USA ISSN 0898-5995
SEMINARS IN NUTRITION. Text in English. 1983. bi-m. USD 99 domestic; USD 144 in Canada; USD 120 elsewhere (effective 2004). **Description:** Addresses current topics in medical and nutrition research.
Indexed: Agr.
Address: PO Box 261126, Littleton, CO 80163-1126. TEL 303-346-7145, FAX 720-344-6945, http://www.seminarsinnutrition.com. Pub. Therese Beaudette.

613.2 CHN ISSN 1005-9989
SHIPIN KEJI/FOOD SCIENCE AND TECHNOLOGY. Text in Chinese. 1994. m. USD 80.40 (effective 2009).
Related titles: Online - full text ed.
Indexed: A28, APA, B21, BrCerAb, C&ISA, CA/WCA, CIA, CerAb, CivEngAb, CorrAb, E&CAJ, E11, EEA, EMA, ESPM, EnvEAb, FS&TA, H15, M&TEA, M09, MBF, METADEX, OceAb, SolStAb, T04, WAA.
—BLDSC (3983.052000), East View.
Published by: Beijing Shi Liangshi Kexue Yanjiusuo/Beijing Grain Science Research Institute, Xuanwu-qu, 11, Caishikuo Shizidian, Beijing, 100053, China. TEL 86-10-63173840, FAX 86-10-63016390, bgsrikg@95777.com. **Dist. by:** China International Book Trading Corp, 35 Chegongzhuang Xilu, Haidian District, PO Box 399, Beijing 100044, China. TEL 86-10-68412045, FAX 86-10-68412023, cibtc@mail.cibtc.com.cn, http://www.cibtc.com.cn.

613.2 JPN ISSN 1343-4594
SHISHITSU EIYOUGAKU/JOURNAL OF LIPID NUTRITION. (Former parallel English title: Japan Society for Lipid Nutrition. Proceedings) Text in Japanese. s-a. **Document type:** *Journal, Academic/Scholarly.*
—**CCC.**
Published by: Nihon Shishitsu Eiyou Gakkai/Japan Society for Lipid Nutrition, c/o National Institute of Agrobiological Resources, 2-1-2 Kannondai, Tsukuba, Ibaraki 305-0856, Japan. TEL 81-298-388089, FAX 81-298-387996, http://wwwsoc.nii.ac.jp/jsln/index.html.

613.2 JPN ISSN 1343-7844
SHOKU NI KANSURU JOSEI KENKYU CHOSA HOKOKUSHO/SKYLARK FOOD SCIENCE INSTITUTE. STUDY FOR FOOD UNDER THE SUPPORTING PROGRAM. ANNUAL REPORT. Text in Japanese; Summaries in English, Japanese. 1992. s-a. **Document type:** *Corporate.*
Published by: Sukairaku Fudo Saiensu Kenkyujo/Skylark Food Science Institute, 6-14-1, Nishi-Shinjuku, Shinjuku-ku, 16F, Shinjuku Green Tower, Tokyo, 160-0023, Japan. TEL 81-3-53226345, FAX 81-3-53226346, inst.skylark-food-sc@helen.ocn.ne.jp, http://www9.ocn.ne.jp/~food-sc/.

SHOKUHIN EISEIGAKU ZASSHI/FOOD HYGIENIC SOCIETY OF JAPAN. JOURNAL. *see* PUBLIC HEALTH AND SAFETY

613.2 KOR ISSN 1226-3338
SIGPUM SAN'EOB GWA YEONG'YANG/FOOD INDUSTRY AND NUTRITION. Text in Korean. 1996. s-a. **Document type:** *Journal, Academic/Scholarly.*
Related titles: Online - full text ed.
Indexed: FS&TA.
Published by: Korean Society of Food Science and Nutrition, Yeonsan 4-dong, Yeonje-gu, 587-8 SK View, 103-1307, Busan, 611-820, Korea, S. TEL 86-51-8663693, FAX 86-51-8663695, kfn@kfn.or.kr, http://www.kfn.or.kr/.

613.2 GBR ISSN 1753-0245
SLIM AT HOME. Text in English. 198?. 10/yr. GBP 20.80 domestic; GBP 40 in Europe; GBP 45 elsewhere (effective 2010). adv. **Document type:** *Magazine, Consumer.* **Description:** Provides readers with information on how to achieve and maintain a healthy lifestyle with proper nutrition along with exercise and beauty tips.
Formerly (until 2007): Slimmer (0955-758X)
—**CCC.**
Published by: Aceville Publications Ltd., 21-23 Phoenix Ct, Hawkins Rd, Colchester, Essex CO2 8JY, United Kingdom. TEL 44-1206-505962, FAX 44-1206-505915, aceville@servicehelpline.co.uk, http://www.aceville.com. Ed. Naomi Abeykoon TEL 44-1206-505960. Adv. contact Joy Mitchell TEL 44-1206-505944. Circ: 90,000 (paid).
Subscr. to: 800 Guillat Ave, Kent Science Park, Sittingbourne, Kent ME9 8GU, United Kingdom. TEL 44-844-8150041, FAX 44-845-4567143.

613.2 GBR ISSN 0144-8129
SLIMMING. Text in English. 1969. 11/yr. GBP 31.20 (effective 2006). adv. bk.rev. **Document type:** *Magazine, Consumer.* **Description:** Encourages safe and steady weight loss and weight maintenance through healthy eating and an active lifestyle. Provides practical guide to individuals to help them reach and maintain their target weight.
Formerly (until Mar. 1979): Slimming and Nutrition (0049-075X)
—CCC.
Published by: Emap Esprit Ltd. (Subsidiary of: Emap Consumer Media), Greater London House, Hampstead, London, NW1 7EJ, United Kingdom. TEL 44-20-73471912, FAX 44-20-78740580, gill.mond@emap.com, http://www.emapesprit.com. Ed. Juliette Kellow. adv.: B&W page GBP 4,450, color page GBP 4,450; trim 210 x 297. Circ: 98,489.

052 AUS
SLIMMING & HEALTH. Text in English. 1992. m. AUD 49.95 domestic; AUD 59.95 in New Zealand; AUD 77.95 elsewhere; AUD 5.95 newsstand/cover (effective 2008). adv. **Document type:** *Magazine, Consumer.* **Description:** Covers healthy lifestyles for people on diets, exercising the fun way, and eating fabulously tasty foods.
Former titles (until 2005): Slimming (1321-8824); (until 1993): Slimming Australia (1321-8840)
Published by: A C P Magazines Ltd. (Subsidiary of: P B L Media Pty Ltd.), 54-58 Park St, Sydney, NSW 2000, Australia. TEL 61-2-92828000, FAX 61-2-91263769, research@acpaction.com.au. Ed. Kate Fitzpatrick. Adv. contact Nicole Dixon TEL 61-2-81149413. page AUD 3,118; bleed 215 x 285. Circ: 30,088.

SMAK. *see* CHILDREN AND YOUTH—About

613.25 USA ISSN 1553-5509
THE SOUTH BEACH DIET NEWSLETTER. Text in English. 2005. m. USD 29.95 (effective 2007). **Document type:** *Newsletter, Consumer.* **Description:** Features recipes, vitamin supplement, nutrition, health and lifestyle information for individuals following the South Beach Diet program.
Related titles: Online - full text ed.
Published by: Waterfront Media, 45 Main St, Ste 400, Brooklyn, NY 11201. TEL 718-797-0722, FAX 718-797-0582, info@waterfrontmedia.com, http://www.waterfrontmedia.com/. Ed. Arthur Agatston.

SOUTH PACIFIC FOODS. *see* FOOD AND FOOD INDUSTRIES

613.2 USA
SPOTLIGHT ON FOOD. Text in English. 1986. m.
Media: Online - full content.
Address: 604 E Pitkin, Fort Collins, CO 80524. Ed. Kathrynne Holden.

613.26 USA ISSN 0744-9860
SPROUTLETTER; superfoods from Amazonia and the Klamath Basin. Variant title: Stemenhance. Text in English. 1980. q. USD 18 (effective 2007). adv. bk.rev. charts; illus.; tr.lit. cum.index. 16 p./no. 2 cols./p.; back issues avail. **Document type:** *Newsletter, Trade.* **Description:** Explores nutrition and superfoods, holistic health, vegetarianism, sprouting, live foods, blue-green algae, probiotics, enzymes, Amazonian healing herbs, indoor food gardening. Also includes recipes and product listings.
Published by: Sprouting Publications, PO Box 62, Ashland, OR 97520. TEL 541-488-8010, emailml@mac.com, http://www.urbantribefoods.com. Ed., Pub. Michael Linden. R&P, Adv. contact Mark Nobel. Circ: 3,000 (paid and controlled).

613.2 USA ISSN 1559-8268
THE STEP-POWER WEIGH. Text in English. 2005. m. **Document type:** *Newsletter, Consumer.* **Description:** Nutrition and health tips.
Media: Online - full text.
Published by: HealthSteps Rx TEL 866-281-9406, StepPower@HealthStepsRx.com, http://www.healthstepsrx.com/index.htm. Pub. Cheryl Winter.

613.2 DEU CODEN: KLEREQ
➤ **STOFFWECHSELMANAGEMENT.** Text in German. 1980. irreg., latest vol.39, 2000. price varies. **Document type:** *Monographic series, Academic/Scholarly.*
Formerly (until 2000): Klinische Ernaehrung (0174-2469)
Indexed: ChemAb, ChemTitl.
—BLDSC (5099.366000), CASDDS.
Published by: W. Zuckschwerdt Verlag GmbH, Industriestr 1, Germering, 82110, Germany. TEL 49-89-8943490, FAX 49-89-89434950, post@zuckschwerdtverlag.de, http://www.zuckschwerdtverlag.de.

➤ **STUDIES IN EATING DISORDERS: AN INTERNATIONAL SERIES.** *see* MEDICAL SCIENCES—Psychiatry And Neurology

613.26 USA ISSN 1067-3768
SUPPORT LINE. Text in English. 1984. bi-m. USD 60 to individuals; USD 120 to institutions; free to members (effective 2010). adv. back issues avail. **Document type:** *Newsletter, Consumer.*
Former titles (until 1992): Dietitians in Nutritional Support (0892-5879); (until 1987): Dietitians in Critical Care (0892-5860)
Indexed: C06, C07, C08, CINAHL, P24, P48, PQC.
—BLDSC (8547.638310), IE, Ingenta. **CCC.**
Published by: (Dietitians in Nutrition Support), American Dietetic Association, 120 S Riverside Plz, Ste 2000, Chicago, IL 60606. TEL 312-899-0040, 800-877-1600, FAX 312-899-4899, sales@eatright.org, http://www.eatright.org. Ed. Susan Roberts TEL 214-820-6751.

613.2 USA ISSN 1547-1802
RA784
TAKING SIDES: CLASHING VIEWS ON CONTROVERSIAL ISSUES IN FOOD AND NUTRITION. Text in English. 2003. irreg., latest 2004, 1st ed. **Document type:** *Catalog, Academic/Scholarly.* **Description:** Presents current issues in a debate-style format designed to stimulate student interest and develop critical thinking skills.
Published by: McGraw-Hill, Contemporary Learning Series (Subsidiary of: McGraw-Hill Companies, Inc.), 1221 Ave of the Americas, New York, NY 10020. TEL 212-904-2000, 800-243-6532, FAX 212-512-2000, customer.service@mcgraw-hill.com, http://www.mhhe.com/cls/.

TASTE OF HOME'S DIABETIC COOKBOOK. *see* HOME ECONOMICS

613.2 USA ISSN 1935-8865
TEEN FOOD & FITNESS. Text in English. 2007 (Jul.). 9/yr. USD 198 (effective 2007). **Document type:** *Newsletter, Consumer.*
Related titles: Online - full text ed.: ISSN 1935-8873. 2007 (July); Spanish ed.: Teen Food & Fitness (Spanish Edition). ISSN 1935-889X.
Published by: Resources for Educators, 3035 Valley Ave, Ste 103, Winchester, VA 22601. TEL 800-394-5052, FAX 540-723-0321, rfecustomer@aspenpublishers.com, http://www.rfeonline.com.

TETSU TAISHA KENKYUKAI PUROGURAMU SHOROKUSHU/ CONFERENCE ON CURRENT TOPICS FOR IRON METABOLISM. PROGRAM AND ABSTRACTS. *see* BIOLOGY—Biochemistry

612.3 NLD ISSN 1570-6680
TIJDSCHRIFT VOOR ORTHOMOLECULAIRE GENEESKUNDE. Text and summaries in Dutch. 1986. bi-m. EUR 33.60 domestic; EUR 38.40 in Belgium; EUR 50.40 foreign (effective 2008). adv. back issues avail. **Document type:** *Bulletin.* **Description:** Covers orthomolecular medicine and nutrition, micronutrients and food supplementation.
Formerly (until 2007): De Orthomoleculaire Koerier (0920-9166)
Published by: (Stichting Orthomoleculaire Educatie), Orthos Media B.V., Koperslager 17, Nootdorp, 2631 RK, Netherlands. TEL 31-70-3520074, FAX 31-70-3587504, http://www.aov.nl. Circ: 2,250.

613.2 USA
TODAY'S DIET & NUTRITION (ONLINE). Text in English. 2005 (Fall). m. USD 9.99 (effective 2010). **Document type:** *Magazine, Consumer.* **Description:** Covers various aspects of food & fitness.
Formerly (until 2010): Today's Diet & Nutrition (Print) (1559-5110)
Media: Online - full text.
Indexed: C11.
Published by: Great Valley Publishing Company, Inc., 3801 Schuylkill Rd, Spring City, PA 19475. TEL 610-948-9500, 800-278-4400, FAX 610-948-4202, Sales@gvpub.com, http://www.gvpub.com. Ed. Kate Jackson.

613.26 USA ISSN 1540-4269
TODAY'S DIETITIAN. Text in English. 1999 (Jan.). m. USD 12 domestic; USD 48 in Canada; USD 95 elsewhere; USD 5 per issue (effective 2010). adv. back issues avail.; reprints avail. **Document type:** *Magazine, Trade.* **Description:** Provides the news source for dietitians and nutritionists, covering topics such as diabetes management, long-term care etc.
Related titles: Online - full text ed.: free (effective 2010).
Indexed: C06, C07.
Published by: Great Valley Publishing Company, Inc., 3801 Schuylkill Rd, Spring City, PA 19475. TEL 610-948-9500, 800-278-4400, FAX 610-948-4202, Sales@gvpub.com, http://www.gvpub.com. Ed. Heather Gurk. Pub., Adv. contact Mara E Honicker. Circ: 40,000.

613.2 USA ISSN 0883-5691
QP141.A1
➤ **TOPICS IN CLINICAL NUTRITION**; changing the face of dietetics. Abbreviated title: T I C N. Text in English. 1986. q. USD 349 domestic to institutions; USD 442 foreign to institutions (effective 2011). adv. back issues avail.; reprints avail. **Document type:** *Journal, Academic/Scholarly.* **Description:** Addresses topics of interest primarily to dietitians and nutritionists, students and interns in professional training programs and other health care personnel involved in the nutritional care of patients.
Incorporates (1986-1991): Nutrition Clinics (0888-3483)
Related titles: Online - full text ed.: ISSN 1550-5146.
Indexed: A22, A26, A34, A36, A38, AMED, Agr, C06, C07, C08, CA, CABA, CINAHL, D01, E08, E12, EMBASE, ExcerpMed, F08, FS&TA, G08, GH, H11, H12, H16, I05, LT, N02, N03, N04, P11, P24, P30, P33, P52, P56, PHN&I, PQC, R10, R11, RA&MP, RM&VM, RRTA, Reac, S09, S12, SCOPUS, SoyAb, T02, T05, TriticAb, VS, W11.
—BLDSC (8867.432800), GNLM, IE, Ingenta. **CCC.**
Published by: Lippincott Williams & Wilkins (Subsidiary of: Wolters Kluwer N.V.), Two Commerce Sq, 2001 Market St, Philadelphia, PA 19103. TEL 215-521-8300, FAX 215-521-8902, customerservice@lww.com, http://www.lww.com. Ed. Judith A Gilbride. Pub. Kathleen M Phelan.

➤ **TOPS NEWS.** *see* PHYSICAL FITNESS AND HYGIENE

613.2 USA ISSN 0274-6743
RA421 CODEN: BLPEEB
TOTAL HEALTH; for longevity. Text in English. 1979. bi-m. USD 16.95 domestic; USD 23.95 foreign (effective 2005). adv. bk.rev. **Document type:** *Magazine, Consumer.* **Description:** Presents preventive health care life-style articles covering nutrition, diet, fitness, travel, psychological-spiritual health encompassing mind, body, and spirit. Emphasis on anti-aging.
Formerly (until 1980): Trio (0196-2191)
Related titles: Microform ed.: (from PQC); Online - full text ed.
Indexed: A01, A02, A03, A04, A08, A11, A26, C06, C07, C08, C12, CINAHL, E-psyche, E07, G05, G06, G07, G08, H03, H11, H12, H13, HlthInd, I05, I07, M01, M02, MASUSE, P02, P07, P10, P19, P20, P24, P26, P48, P53, P54, PQC, T02, U01.
Published by: Total Health Holdings LLC, 165 N 100 St E, Ste 2, Saint George, UT 84770-2505. TEL 435-673-1789, 888-316-6051. Ed., Pub., R&P Lyle Hurd Jr. Adv. contact Richard Hurd. B&W page USD 2,615, color page USD 2,835; 7.25 x 9.75. Circ: 95,000.

613 ESP ISSN 1887-2778
TRASTORNOS DE LA CONDUCTA ALIMENTICIA. Text in Spanish. 2007. a. back issues avail. **Document type:** *Monographic series, Academic/Scholarly.*
Related titles: Online - full text ed.: ISSN 1699-7611. 2005.
Published by: Instituto de Ciencias de la Conducta, C Virgen del Monte 31, Sevilla, 41011, Spain. TEL 34-954-280789, FAX 34-954-277647, revista@casevilla.com, http://www.tcasevilla.com/default.aspx.

613.2 USA ISSN 1526-0143
CODEN: TUDLET
TUFTS UNIVERSITY HEALTH & NUTRITION LETTER. Text in English. 1983. m. USD 24 domestic (effective 2011). bk.rev. illus. back issues avail.; reprints avail. **Document type:** *Newsletter, Consumer.* **Description:** Aims to provide the consumer with reliable and scientific authoritative health and nutrition advice.
Formerly (until 1997): Tufts University Diet and Nutrition Letter (0747-4105)
Related titles: Microfilm ed.; Microform ed.: (from PQC); Online - full text ed.
Indexed: A01, A02, A03, A04, A08, A25, A26, Agr, BRD, BiolDig, C06, C07, C08, C11, C12, CA, CHNI, CINAHL, Consl, E07, E08, F10, G05, G06, G07, G08, H03, H04, H11, H12, H13, HlthInd, I05, I07, M01, M02, M06, MASUSE, MagInd, P02, P07, P10, P11, P19, P20, P24, P48, P50, P53, P54, PQC, R03, R09, RGAb, RGPR, S08, S09, S23, SD, T02, W03, W05.
—**CCC.**
Published by: Tufts University, PO Box 5656, Norwalk, CT 06856. healthletterhelp@tufts.edu. Ed. Irwin H Rosenberg. Pub. David B Lee.

TURNING OVER A NEW LEAF; your heart-healthy living guide. *see* MEDICAL SCIENCES—Cardiovascular Diseases

613.2 CHE ISSN 1564-3743
TX360.5
UNITED NATIONS SYSTEM STANDING COMMITTEE ON NUTRITION. NEWS. Variant title: S C N News. Text in English. 1988. s-a. free. **Document type:** *Newsletter, Academic/Scholarly.* **Description:** Provides periodic review of developments in international nutrition compiled from information available to the SCN.
Related titles: Online - full content ed.: ISSN 1564-3751. 1997.
Indexed: A36, C25, CABA, D01, E12, GH, H16, N02, N03, R12, S13, S16, T05, TAR, W11.
—BLDSC (8205.451010).
Published by: United Nations System Standing Committee on Nutrition, SCN Secretariat, c/o World Health Organization, 20, Avenue Appia, Geneva 27, CH-1211, Switzerland. TEL 41-22-7910456, FAX 41-22-7988891, scn@who.int.

UNIVERSIDAD DE ZARAGOZA. ESCUELA UNIVERSITARIA DE CIENCIAS DE LA SALUD. ANALES. *see* PHYSICAL FITNESS AND HYGIENE

UNIVERSITY OF CALIFORNIA, BERKELEY. WELLNESS LETTER; the newsletter of nutrition, fitness, and stress management. *see* PHYSICAL FITNESS AND HYGIENE

613.2 664 ROM ISSN 1843-5157
UNIVERSITY OF GALATI "DUNAREA DE JOS". FASCICLE VI. FOOD TECHNOLOGY. ANNALS. Text in English. 1978. a. **Document type:** *Journal, Academic/Scholarly.*
Former titles (until 2006): Universitatea "Dunarea de Jos" din Galati. Fascicula VI. Tehnologia Produselor Alimentare. Analele (1221-4574); (until 1989): Universitatea din Galati. Fascicula VI. Tehnologia si Chimia Produselor Alimentare. Analele (1011-4025); (until 1982): Universitatea din Galati. Fascicula VI. Tehnologia si Chimia Produselor Alimentare. Buletinul (0254-5608)
Related titles: Online - full text ed.: ISSN 2068-259X. free (effective 2011).
Indexed: A28, A34, A36, A38, APA, BA, C25, C30, CA/WCA, CABA, CIA, CivEngAb, D01, E11, E12, EEA, EMA, F08, GH, H15, H16, MBF, MaizeAb, N02, N03, P33, P48, P50, P51, P53, P54, PQC, R08, T04, W11.
Published by: Universitatea "Dunarea de Jos" din Galati, Str Domneasca Nr 111, Galati, 6200, Romania. TEL 40-36-460328, FAX 40-36-461353, http://www.ugal.ro.

N
O

613.262 NLD ISSN 1879-5714
V. Text in Dutch. 1986. q. EUR 15 (effective 2010). **Document type:** *Magazine, Consumer.*
Former titles (until 2009): Vega (1573-6199); (until 2004): Gezond Idee! (0929-4570); (until 1992): Veganismen (0920-7635)
Published by: Nederlandse Vereniging voor Veganisme, Herenweg 59, Utrecht, 3513 CC, Netherlands. TEL 31-6-52433931, http://www.veganisme.org.

613.2 DEU
V F E D AKTUELL. Text in German. 1992. 7/yr. adv. **Document type:** *Magazine, Trade.*
Published by: Verband fuer Ernaehrung und Diaetetik e.V., Roermonder Str 594, Aachen, 52072, Germany. TEL 49-241-507300, FAX 49-241-507311, info@vfed.de, http://www.vfed.de. Ed. Margret Morlo. adv.: B&W page EUR 200, color page EUR 300. Circ: 3,000 (controlled).

613.2 ZAF
V I C MEDICAL UPDATE. (Vitamin Information Centre) Text in English. 3/yr. free to qualified personnel. **Document type:** *Bulletin, Consumer.* **Description:** Provides an accurate, scientific, timely review of current vitamin related issues and research.
Published by: Vitamin Information Centre, PO Box 182, Isando, Transvaal 1600, South Africa. TEL 27-11-3934794, FAX 27-11-3934790. R&P Mrs. H L Robertson. **Co-sponsor:** Roche Products (Pty) Ltd.

613.2 SWE ISSN 0042-2657
TX341 CODEN: VAFOAS
VAAR FOEDA. Text in Swedish; Summaries in English. 1949. 6/yr. SEK 325; SEK 150 to students (effective 2004). adv. bk.rev. charts; illus. cum.index: 1994-1998, 1999-2002. **Document type:** *Government.* **Description:** Covers activities in food control projects, new regulations and current research.
Indexed: A22, CIN, ChemAb, F05, F06, F07, FS&TA.
—BLDSC (9146.020000), CASDDS, IE, Ingenta, Linda Hall.
Published by: Livsmedelsverket/National Food Administration, PO Box 622, Uppsala, 75126, Sweden. TEL 46-18-175500, FAX 46-18-105848, livsmedelverket@slv.se. Eds. Anne-Marie Svedin, Jerker Soerenson. Circ: 5,500.

▼ **VAK M. SECTOR VOEDING.** *see* LABOR UNIONS

613.262 USA ISSN 1544-8495
VEG NEWS. Text in English. 2000. bi-m. USD 20 (effective 2007). adv. **Document type:** *Magazine, Consumer.* **Description:** Covers the latest vegetarian news, interviews, travel, food & health, recipes, new products, events, advise and more.
Published by: VegNews, PO Box 320130, San Francisco, CA 94132. TEL 415-665-6397, FAX 415-665-6398. adv.: page USD 1,979; 8.625 x 10.875.

613.26 GBR ISSN 0307-4811
THE VEGAN. Text in English. 19??. q. GBP 10 domestic; GBP 15 in Europe; GBP 17 elsewhere; GBP 2.50 newsstand/cover; free to members (effective 2009). adv. bk.rev. illus. back issues avail.; reprints avail. **Document type:** *Magazine, Consumer.* **Description:** Supplies information on animal rights, vegan nutrition, health and ecology.
Formerly (until 1946): Vegan News
Published by: Vegan Society, Donald Watson House, 21 Hylton St, Hockley, Birmingham, B18 6HJ, United Kingdom. TEL 44-121-5231730, FAX 44-121-5231749, info@vegansociety.com. Circ: 7,000.

613.262 179.3 USA ISSN 1084-9289
THE VEGAN NEWS. Text in English. 1993. q. free (effective 2004). adv. bk.rev. back issues avail. **Document type:** *Newsletter.* **Description:** Reports organization news and covers vegetarian diets and lifestyles.
Formerly (until Oct. 1994): East Bay Vegan News

Media: Online - full content.
Published by: Vegan Action, PO Box 4288, Richmond, VA 23220-8288. TEL 804-502-8736, FAX 703-832-1050, information@vegan.org, http://www.vegan.org. Ed., Adv. contact Leor Jacobi. page USD 300. Circ: 10,000 (controlled).

613.262 GBR ISSN 1759-5460
VEGAN VIEWS; a forum for vegan opinion. Text in English. 1975. 3/yr. GBP 5 (print or online ed.) (effective 2011). back issues avail. **Document type:** *Magazine, Consumer.* **Description:** Designed for young vegans living in London, who want to make contact with others who are interested in creating a more harmonious way of living based on veganism.
Formerly (until 1977): Vegan Newsletter
Related titles: Online - full text ed.
Address: 1 Church Hill, Woodlands, Dorset BH21 8LW, United Kingdom. TEL 44-845-4589595.

613.262 DNK ISSN 1397-7989
VEGETAREN. Text in Danish. 1907. q. DKK 150 (effective 2009). adv. illus. **Document type:** *Magazine, Consumer.*
Former titles (until 1997): Vegetarisk Forum (0909-7740); (1983-1994): Groen-Sagen (0907-9394); Vegetarisk Forum incorporates (in 1994): Vegetarisk Tidsskrift (0109-8861); Which was formerly (until 1983): V F (0109-8845); (until 1967): Vegetarisk Tidsskrift (0909-5292); (until 1924): Solblink (0909-5306)
Published by: Dansk Vegetarforening/Danish Vegetarian Society, Gribskovvej 21, Copenhagen OE, 2100, Denmark. TEL 45-70-224001. adv.: B&W page DKK 1,500, color page DKK 2,600; trim 207 x 268.

613.262 GBR ISSN 1475-3413
TX392
THE VEGETARIAN. Text in English. 1977. q. free to members (effective 2009). bk.rev. charts; illus. index. **Document type:** *Magazine, Consumer.* **Description:** Covers all aspects of vegetarianism, diet, health and ethics.
Former titles (until 1995): Vegetarian Living (0965-1780); (until 1992): Vegetarian (0260-3233); (until 1980): Alive (0141-8440); (until 1978): New Vegetarian (0309-9253); (until 1977): Vegetarian; (until 19??): British Vegetarian (0007-1927)
—CCC.
Published by: Vegetarian Society, Parkdale, Dunham Rd, Altrincham, Ches WA14 4QG, United Kingdom. TEL 44-161-9252000, FAX 44-161-9269182, info@vegsoc.org. Ed. Jane Bowler.

613.262 USA ISSN 0885-7636
VEGETARIAN JOURNAL. Text in English. 1982. q. USD 25 in Canada & Mexico to non-members; USD 42 elsewhere to non-members; free to members (effective 2011). bk.rev.; film rev. illus. Index. 36 p./no.; reprints avail. **Document type:** *Journal, Consumer.* **Description:** Covers various aspects of vegetarianism and veganism, including health, recipes, ethics, ecology, world hunger, and animal rights. Contains information about restaurants, new products carried by supermarkets, and results of the latest medical research. Aims to present nutritional information based on current scientific literature in an easy and practical fashion.
Formerly (until 198?): Baltimore Vegetarians (0883-1165)
Related titles: CD-ROM ed.; Online - full text ed.
Indexed: A04, A26, B04, B14, BRD, BRI, C06, C07, C08, C11, CA, CINAHL, E07, F10, G05, G06, G07, G08, H11, H12, H20, I05, I07, P07, R03, RGAb, RGPR, S23, T02, W03, W05.
Published by: Vegetarian Resource Group, PO Box 1463, Baltimore, MD 21203. TEL 410-366-8343, FAX 410-366-8804, vrg@vrg.org. Ed. Keryl Cryer.

613.262 USA ISSN 1072-0820
VEGETARIAN JOURNAL'S FOODSERVICE UPDATE; healthy tips and recipes for institutions. Text in English. 1993. q. USD 10 (effective 2006). bk.rev. back issues avail. **Document type:** *Newsletter.* **Description:** For food service personnel and others working for healthier food in schools, restaurants, hospitals and other institutions. Contains quantity recipes, tips, product reviews, and educational resources. Spotlights leaders in the industry who are providing healthy options.
Related titles: Online - full text ed.
Indexed: A04, F10, H&TI, H06.
Published by: Vegetarian Resource Group, PO Box 1463, Baltimore, MD 21203. TEL 410-366-8343, vrg@vrg.org, http://www.vrg.org. Ed. Keryl Cryer.

VEGETARIAN JOURNAL'S GUIDE TO NATURAL FOODS RESTAURANTS IN THE U S AND CANADA. *see* HOTELS AND RESTAURANTS

613.2 NZL ISSN 1176-9335
VEGETARIAN LIVING NEW ZEALAND. Text in English. 1947. q. free to members. **Document type:** *Magazine, Consumer.*
Formerly (until 2004): New Zealand Vegetarian (1173-0919)
Published by: New Zealand Vegetarian Society, PO Box 26664, Epsom, Auckland, New Zealand. http://www.vegetarian.org.nz.

613.26 USA ISSN 0164-8497
TX392 CODEN: VETIFB
VEGETARIAN TIMES. Text in English. 1974. m. USD 14.95 domestic; USD 26.95 in Canada; USD 38.95 elsewhere (effective 2009). adv. bk.rev. illus.; tr.lit. reprints avail. **Document type:** *Magazine, Consumer.* **Description:** Contains vegetarian recipes, dietary information, advice on buying whole foods and preparing foods for maximum nutritional value, and articles on nutritional approaches to disease, information for travelers and profiles of prominent vegetarians.
Incorporates: Vegetarian World
Related titles: Microform ed.: (from PQC); Online - full text ed.
Indexed: A01, A02, A03, A04, A08, A11, A22, A26, Agr, B04, C05, C06, C07, C12, CHNI, CPerI, F10, G05, G06, G07, G08, H03, H11, H12, H13, H20, HlthInd, I05, I07, M01, M02, MASUSE, MagInd, NPI, P02, P10, P11, P19, P20, P24, P48, P50, P53, P54, PQC, R03, RGPR, S23, T02, U01, W03, W05, WBA, WMB.
—Ingenta.
Published by: Active Interest Media, 300 Continental Blvd, Ste 650, El Segundo, CA 90245. TEL 310-356-4100, FAX 310-356-4110, mleighland@aimmedia.com, http://www.sabot.net. Ed. Elizabeth Turner. **Subscr. to:** PO Box 420235, Palm Coast, FL 32142. TEL 877-717-8923.

613.26 USA ISSN 0271-1591
TX392.A1
VEGETARIAN VOICE. Text in English. 1974. q. USD 22 domestic to individuals membership; USD 29 foreign to individuals membership (effective 2011). bk.rev. illus. **Document type:** *Magazine, Consumer.* **Description:** Information on nutrition, cooking, health, animal and environmental protection for people interested in vegetarianism, with organization news and reports on annual conferences.
Indexed: AltPI, T02.
Published by: North American Vegetarian Society, PO Box 72, Dolgeville, NY 13329. TEL 518-568-7970, FAX 518-568-7979, navs@telenet.net, http://www.navs-online.org. Circ: 11,000.

613.262 DEU ISSN 1614-2128
VEGETARISCH FIT!; Das gesunde Magazin. Text in German. 1994. bi-m. EUR 19.90; EUR 3.90 newsstand/cover (effective 2011). adv. **Document type:** *Magazine, Consumer.*
Published by: Marken Verlag GmbH, Hansaring 97, Cologne, 50670, Germany. TEL 49-221-9574270, FAX 49-221-95742777, marken-info@markenverlag.de, http://www.markenverlag.de. Circ: 50,000 (paid and controlled).

179.3 613.262 FRA ISSN 2107-3023
VEGMAG. Text in French. 2006. bi-m. EUR 35 (effective 2009). back issues avail. **Document type:** *Magazine, Consumer.*
Formerly (until 2010): Vegetariens Magazine (1953-6909)
Published by: Valian Editions, 34 Bd Solferino, Poitiers, 86000, France.

VETERINARY FOCUS; the worlwide journal for the companion animal veterinarian. *see* PETS

VIBRANT LIFE; a magazine for healthful living. *see* PHYSICAL FITNESS AND HYGIENE

663.2 613.2 FRA ISSN 1955-8104
VINS ET SANTE. Text in French. 199?. a. EUR 20 newsstand/cover (effective 2009).
Published by: Dubos N'Co Editions, 34 avenue des Colibris, Hyeres, 83400, France. TEL 33-8-75322477, FAX 33-4-94975816.

613.2 FRA ISSN 2101-8308
VITAFORM'. Text in French. 200?. s-a. **Document type:** *Magazine, Trade.*
Related titles: ◆ Supplement to: Nutriform' Magazine. ISSN 1772-7553.
Published by: Editions Business Group Media, 12 rue Frederic Soddy, ZAC Des Coteaux Sarrazins, Creteil, 94044 Cedex, France. TEL 33-1-56711840, FAX 33-1-43396709.

613.2 ITA ISSN 1120-4591
VITALITY. Text in Italian. 1989. 10/yr. adv. back issues avail. **Document type:** *Magazine, Consumer.*
Published by: Hachette Rusconi SpA (Subsidiary of: Hachette Filipacchi Medias S.A.), Viale Sarca 235, Milan, 20126, Italy. TEL 39-02-66192629, FAX 39-02-66192469, http://portale.hachettepubblicita.it. Ed. M Picollo. Adv. contact Eduardo Giliberti. Circ: 121,000.

VITAMIN RETAILER; the dietary supplement industry's leading magazine. *see* PHARMACY AND PHARMACOLOGY

646.7 BRA ISSN 1516-9723
VIVER LIGHT. Text in Portuguese. 1999. irreg. BRL 2.50 newsstand/cover (effective 2006). **Document type:** *Magazine, Consumer.*
Published by: Editora Escala Ltda., Av Prof Ida Kolb, 551, Casa Verde, Sao Paulo, 02518-000, Brazil. TEL 55-11-38552100, FAX 55-11-38579643, escala@escala.com.br, http://www.escala.com.br.

613.2 ARG ISSN 1515-8519
VIVIR MEJOR. Text in Spanish. 2001. m. ARS 3.90 newsstand/cover (effective 2008).
Published by: Producciones Publiexpress, Magallanes 1346, Buenos Aires, C1288ABB, Argentina. TEL 54-11-43031484, FAX 54-11-43031280, rrhh@publiexpress.com.ar, http://www.publiexpress.com.ar/. Circ: 60,345.

613.2 NLD ISSN 1389-7608
TX341
VOEDING NU; Netherlands journal of nutrition. Text in Dutch; Text occasionally in English. 1998. 11/yr. EUR 57.75 domestic; EUR 63.25 in Belgium; EUR 74.25 elsewhere; EUR 33.75 domestic to students; EUR 46.75 in Belgium to students (effective 2009). adv. bk.rev. charts; illus. index. back issues avail. **Document type:** *Journal, Trade.* **Description:** Reviews research and information in all areas of nutrition.
Formed by the merger of (1939-1998): Voeding (0042-7926); (1990-1998): Voeding en Voorlichting (0924-6045); Which was formed by the merger of (1978-1989): Voedingsinformatie (0165-7496); (1985-1989): Groepsvoeding Informatie (0923-1099); Which was formerly (1974-1985): Groepsvoeding Informatiekrant (0923-1080)
Indexed: A22, CIN, ChemAb, F05, F06, F07, FS&TA, IndMed, P30.
—BLDSC (9251.100000), CASDDS, GNLM, IE, Ingenta, INIST.
Published by: (Voedingscentrum), Keesing Noordervliet BV (Subsidiary of: Keesing International Publishers N.V.), De Molen 82, Houten, 3995 AX, Netherlands. TEL 31-30-6358585, FAX 31-30-6358500, http://www.keesing.nl. Eds. Annemarie de Graaf, Marianne van der Wooning, Hans Kraak. Pub. P T Both. adv.: color page EUR 2,630; bleed 210 x 297. **Subscr. to:** Postbus 325, Houten 3990 GC, Netherlands. klantenservice@keesing.nl.

613.2 NLD ISSN 0922-8012
VOEDINGSMAGAZINE. Text in Dutch. 1988. bi-m. free (effective 2010). back issues avail. **Document type:** *Magazine, Trade.* **Description:** Contains information on nutrition and health matters for general practitioners, registered dieticians, medical specialists in food-related disciplines, and educators in nutrition and health.
Indexed: A34, A35, A36, A38, AgBio, CABA, D01, E12, GH, LT, N02, N03, N04, R12, RRTA, T05, VS, W11.
Published by: Nederlandse Zuivel Organisatie, Postbus 165, Zoetermeer, 2700 AD, Netherlands. Eds. Ria van de Pol, Wim Swart, Gert Jan Hiddink.

612.3 RUS ISSN 0042-8833
QP141.A1 CODEN: VPITAR
➤ **VOPROSY PITANIYA/PROBLEMS OF NUTRITION.** Text in Russian. 1932. bi-m. USD 153 foreign (effective 2005). adv. index. 48 p./no.; **Document type:** *Journal, Academic/Scholarly.* **Description:** Publishes original and survey articles that reflect joint work done by physiologists, biochemists, hygienists, pathophysiologists, clinicians and technologists dealing with nutrition problems.
Indexed: A34, A35, A36, A37, A38, ASFA, AgBio, B21, B25, BIOSIS Prev, C25, CABA, CIN, ChemAb, D01, DentInd, DokArb, E12, EMBASE, ESPM, ExcerpMed, F08, F11, F12, FCA, FS&TA, GH, H16, H17, IndMed, LT, MEDLINE, MaizeAb, MycolAb, N02, N03, N04, O01, P30, P32, P33, P37, P38, P40, PHN&I, R07, R08, R10, R11, R13, RA&MP, RASB, RM&VM, RRTA, Reac, S12, S13, S16, SCOPUS, SoyAb, T05, TriticAb, VS, W10, W11.
—CASDDS, East View, GNLM, INIST, Linda Hall. **CCC.**
Published by: (Rossiiskaya Akademiya Nauk/Russian Academy of Sciences, Institut Pitaniya), Nutritec, Dmitrovskoe shosse 46-2, Moscow, 127238, Russian Federation. TEL 7-095-4824118, FAX 7-095-4844312. Ed. V A Tutelyan. Pub. M N Solovova. Adv. contact G O Marchik. Circ: 1,700. **Dist. by:** East View Information Services, 10601 Wayzata Blvd, Minneapolis, MN 55305. TEL 952-252-1201, 800-477-1005, FAX 952-252-1202, info@eastview.com, http://www.eastview.com. **Co-sponsor:** Ministerstvo Zdravookhraneniya Rossiiskoi Federatsii/Ministry of Public Health of Russian Federation.

613.2 CZE ISSN 1211-846X
TX341
VYZIVA A POTRAVINY. Text in Czech; Summaries in English. 1946. bi-m. CZK 534; CZK 89 per issue (effective 2010). adv. bk.rev. 32 p./no.; back issues avail. **Document type:** *Journal, Trade.* **Description:** Provides nutrition news, recommendations, nutrition and food policy, new raw materials and food, catering, food processing, market information, food safety and food security, hygienic standards, etc.
Former titles (until 1994): Vyziva; (until 1991): Vyziva Lidu (0042-9414)
Indexed: ChemAb, FS&TA, P30.
—CCC.
Published by: Spolecnost pro Vyzivu/Czech Nutrition Society, Slezska 32, Prague 2, 12000, Czech Republic. TEL 420-2-67311280, FAX 420-2-71732669, vyziva.spv@volny.cz. Ed. Ctibor Perlin. Pub., R&P Jan Susta. Adv. contact Marie Voldanova. Circ: 5,500 (controlled).

WALTHAM FOCUS (JAPANESE EDITION). *see* PETS

613.2 340 BEL ISSN 1374-8637
WARENWETGEVING INFO. Text in Dutch. 1998. q. EUR 103 (effective 2008). **Document type:** *Journal, Trade.*
Published by: Die Keure NV, Kleine Pathoekeweg 3, Bruges, 8000, Belgium. TEL 32-50-471272, FAX 32-50-335154, juridische.uitgaven@diekeure.be, http://www.diekeure.be.

WARM EARTH; organic gardening. *see* GARDENING AND HORTICULTURE

WARSAW AGRICULTURAL UNIVERSITY. S G G W. ANNALS. FOOD TECHNOLOGY AND NUTRITION. *see* FOOD AND FOOD INDUSTRIES

613.26 DEU ISSN 1868-5269
WEIGHT WATCHERS; das schlanke Frauenmagazin. Text in German. 2001. bi-m. EUR 19.20; EUR 3.50 newsstand/cover (effective 2011). adv. **Document type:** *Magazine, Consumer.*
Published by: Marken Verlag GmbH, Hansaring 97, Cologne, 50670, Germany. TEL 49-221-9574270, FAX 49-221-95742777, marken-info@markenverlag.de, http://www.markenverlag.de. Circ: 103,930 (paid and controlled).

613.2 AUS ISSN 1327-5267
WEIGHT WATCHERS (SYDNEY). Text in English. 1991. bi-m. AUD 37.30 domestic; NZD 37.30 in New Zealand (effective 2008). **Document type:** *Magazine, Consumer.* **Description:** Contains weight-loss ideas, health advice, successful slimmers, exercise tips, recipe and food ideas.
Published by: Weight Watchers Australia, PO Box 1961, North Sydney, NSW 2059, Australia. FAX 61-2-99232526, editor@weightwatchers.com.au, http://www.weightwatchers.com.au.

613.26 USA ISSN 0043-2180
RM222.2
WEIGHT WATCHERS MAGAZINE. Text in English. 1968. bi-m. USD 14.95 domestic; USD 24.95 in Canada; USD 3.95 newsstand/cover (effective 2009). adv. bk.rev. illus. Index. reprints avail. **Document type:** *Magazine, Consumer.* **Description:** Provides "how-to" tips on smart eating, beauty, fashion, fitness, health and nutrition.
Related titles: Microfiche ed.: (from PQC); Microform ed.: (from PQC); Online - full text ed.
Indexed: A22, Agr, CHNI, G05, G06, G07, G08, H11, H12, H13, I05, MagInd, P02, P10, P20, P50, P53, P54, PQC.
—Ingenta.
Published by: Weight Watchers Publishing Group, 175 Crossways Park W, New York, NY 11797.

WELL MAGAZINE. *see* PHYSICAL FITNESS AND HYGIENE

WELLBEING MAGAZINE; personal and planetary healing. *see* PHYSICAL FITNESS AND HYGIENE

613 DEU ISSN 1612-247X
WELLNESS FOODS EUROPE. Text in English. 2003. 3/yr. EUR 51 domestic; EUR 63 foreign (effective 2011). adv. **Document type:** *Magazine, Trade.*
Indexed: C06, C07, FS&TA.
—CCC.
Published by: Dr. Harnisch Verlagsgesellschaft GmbH, Blumenstr 15, Nuernberg, 90402, Germany. TEL 49-911-20180, FAX 49-911-2018100, service@harnisch.com. Ed. Silke Watkins TEL 49-911-2018115. Adv. contact Benno Keller TEL 49-911-2018200. Circ: 6,150 (paid and controlled).

613.2 303 663.2 ITA ISSN 2039-4446
▼ ➤ **WINE STUDIES.** Text in English. 2010. irreg. **Document type:** *Journal, Academic/Scholarly.*
Media: Online - full text.
Published by: Pagepress, Via Giuseppe Belli 4, Pavia, 27100, Italy. TEL 39-0382-1751762, FAX 39-0382-1750481, http://www.pagepress.org. Ed. Maurizio Trevisan.

613.2 DEU ISSN 1431-0201
WISSENSCHAFTLICHE SCHRIFTENREIHE BIOLOGISCHE CHEMIE UND ERNAEHRUNGSWISSENSCHAFT. Text in German. 1994. irreg. price varies. **Document type:** *Monographic series, Academic/Scholarly.*
Published by: Verlag Dr. Koester, Rungestr 22-24, Berlin, 10179, Germany. TEL 49-30-76403224, FAX 49-30-76403227, verlag-koester@t-online.de, http://www.verlag-koester.de.

613.2 ITA ISSN 1010-9099
HV696.F6
WORLD FOOD PROGRAMME JOURNAL. Text in Italian. 1963. 6/yr. free. **Document type:** *Journal, Trade.*
Formerly (until 1987): World Food Programme News (0049-8084)
Related titles: Spanish ed.: Programe Mundial de Alimentos. ISSN 1010-9102; French ed.: Programme Alimentaire Mondial. Journal. ISSN 1010-9110.
Indexed: EnvAb, IIS, SCOPUS.
Published by: Food and Agriculture Organization of the United Nations (F A O), Viale delle Terme di Caracalla, Rome, RM 00153, Italy. TEL 39-06-5705-1, FAX 39-06-5705-3360, publications-sales@fao.org, http://www.fao.org.

613.2 CHE ISSN 0084-2230
QP141.A1 CODEN: WRNDAT
➤ **WORLD REVIEW OF NUTRITION AND DIETETICS.** Text in English. 1964. irreg., latest vol.102, 2011. price varies. reprints avail. **Document type:** *Monographic series, Academic/Scholarly.* **Description:** Contains reviews on topics selected as either fundamental to improved understanding of human and animal nutrition, useful in resolving present controversies, or relevant to problems of social and preventive medicine that depend for their solution on progress in nutrition.
Related titles: Online - full text ed.: ISSN 1662-3975.
Indexed: A22, Agr, C06, C07, CIN, ChemAb, ChemTitl, DentInd, EMBASE, ExcerpMed, FS&TA, IBR, IBZ, IndMed, MEDLINE, P30, R10, Reac, SCOPUS, VITIS.
—BLDSC (9359.180000), CASDDS, GNLM, IE, Infotrieve, Ingenta, INIST. **CCC.**
Published by: S. Karger AG, Allschwilerstr 10, Basel, 4055, Switzerland. TEL 41-61-3061111, FAX 41-61-3061234, karger@karger.ch, http://www.karger.ch. Ed. A P Simopoulos.

➤ **Y M C A WEEKLY NEWS.** (Young Men's Christian Association) *see* PHYSICAL FITNESS AND HYGIENE

613.2 CHN ISSN 0512-7955
QP141 CODEN: YYHPA4
YINGYANG XUEBAO/ACTA NUTRIMENTA SINICA. Text in Chinese. 1956-1958; resumed 1982. bi-m. USD 48 (effective 2009). **Document type:** *Journal, Academic/Scholarly.*
Related titles: Online - full text ed.
Indexed: A34, A35, A36, A38, AgBio, AgrForAb, B25, BIOSIS Prev, C25, C30, CABA, CIN, ChemAb, ChemTitl, D01, E12, F08, F11, F12, GH, H16, H17, IndVet, LT, MaizeAb, MycolAb, N02, N03, N04, O01, P30, P32, P33, P37, P38, P40, PGegResA, PHN&I, PN&I, R07, R08, R11, R12, RA&MP, RRTA, S12, S17, SoyAb, T05, TAR, TriticAb, VITIS, VS, W11.
—BLDSC (0641.500000), CASDDS, East View.
Published by: Junshi Yixue Kexueyuan, Weishengxue Huanjing Yixue Yanjiusuo/Academy of Military Medical Sciences, Institute of Hygiene & Environmental Medicine, 1 Dali Dao, Heping-qu, Tianjin, 300050, China. **Dist. by:** China International Book Trading Corp, 35 Chegongzhuang Xilu, Haidian District, PO Box 399, Beijing 100044, China. TEL 86-10-68412045, FAX 86-10-68412023, cibtc@mail.cibtc.com.cn, http://www.cibtc.com.cn. **Co-sponsor:** Zhongguo Yingyang Xuehui/Chinese Nutrition Society.

YOGA AND HEALTH. *see* PHYSICAL FITNESS AND HYGIENE

ZA OBE SHCHECHKI; zhurnal o pitanii i zdorovie malyshei. *see* MEDICAL SCIENCES—Pediatrics

ZAMBIA. NATIONAL FOOD AND NUTRITION COMMISSION. ANNUAL REPORT. *see* FOOD AND FOOD INDUSTRIES

613.2 CHN ISSN 1004-7484
ZHONGGUO BAOJIAN YINGYANG/CHINA HEALTH NUTRITION. Text in Chinese. 1989. m. USD 80.40 (effective 2009). **Document type:** *Academic/Scholarly.*
Related titles: Online - full text ed.
Address: 62, Xichui Lu, Haidian-qu, Beijing, 100036, China. TEL 86-10-68270613. **Dist. by:** China International Book Trading Corp, 35 Chegongzhuang Xilu, Haidian District, PO Box 399, Beijing 100044, China. TEL 86-10-68412045, FAX 86-10-68412023, cibtc@mail.cibtc.com.cn, http://www.cibtc.com.cn.

613.2 CHN ISSN 1674-635X
ZHONGHUA LINCHUANG YINGYANG ZAZHI/CHINESE JOURNAL OF CLINICAL NUTRITION. Text in Chinese. 1993. bi-m. **Document type:** *Journal, Academic/Scholarly.*
Formerly (until 2009): Zhongguo Linchuang Yingyang Zazhi (1008-5882)
Related titles: Online - full text ed.
Indexed: B&BAb, B19, B21, CTA, EMBASE, ExcerpMed, ImmunAb, NSA, NucAcAb, R10, Reac, SCOPUS.
—BLDSC (9512.776500).
Published by: Zhongguo Yixue Kexueyuan/Chinese Academy of Medical Sciences, 9 Dongdan Santiao, Beijing, 100730, China. TEL 86-10-65105998, FAX 86-10-65133074.

613.2 TWN ISSN 1011-6958
CODEN: ZMYZEG
ZHONGHUA MINGUO YINGYANG XUEHUI ZAZHI/CHINESE NUTRITION SOCIETY. JOURNAL. Text in Chinese. 1976. irreg. membership. **Document type:** *Journal, Academic/Scholarly.*
Indexed: A22, A34, A36, AgrForAb, BP, C25, CABA, D01, EMBASE, ExcerpMed, F08, GH, H16, LT, N02, N03, PHN&I, R10, R11, R12, RA&MP, Reac, S12, SCOPUS, SoyAb, T05, TAR, TriticAb, VS, W11.
—BLDSC (6190.411000), CASDDS, IE, Ingenta.
Published by: Zhonghua Minguo Yingyang Xuehui/Nutrition Society of Taiwan, c/o Department of Biochemical Science & Technology, National Taiwan University, No.1, Sec. 4, Roosevelt Road, Taipei, 10617, Taiwan. http://www.nutrition.org.tw/.

612.3 POL ISSN 0209-164X
CODEN: ZCMEDQ
ZYWIENIE CZLOWIEKA I METABOLIZM/POLISH JOURNAL OF HUMAN NUTRITION AND METABOLISM. Text in Polish; Summaries in English. 1973. 4/yr. EUR 80 foreign (effective 2006). bk.rev. **Document type:** *Journal, Academic/Scholarly.* **Description:** Contains articles on physiology and biochemistry of nutrition, assessment of dietary habits and nutritional status of different population groups.
Formerly (until 1983): Zywienie Czlowieka (0303-7851)
Indexed: A22, A34, A35, A36, A37, A38, AgBio, AgrAg, AgrForAb, AgrLib, B23, C25, C30, CABA, CIN, ChemAb, ChemTitl, D01, E12, F08, F12, FCA, FS&TA, G11, GH, H16, LT, MaizeAb, N02, N03, N04, OR, P32, P33, P37, P38, P40, PHN&I, PN&I, R11, R12, R13, RA&MP, RM&VM, RRTA, S12, S13, S16, S17, SCOPUS, SoyAb, T05, TAR, TriticAb, VS, W11.
—BLDSC (9538.941000), CASDDS, GNLM, IE, Ingenta, INIST.
Published by: Instytut Zywnosci i Zywienia/National Food and Nutrition Institute, ul Powsinska 61-63, Warsaw, 02903, Poland. TEL 48-22-8422171, http://www.izz.waw.pl. Ed. Miroslaw Jarosz. Circ: 500. **Dist. by:** Ars Polona, Obroncow 25, Warsaw 03933, Poland. TEL 48-22-5098609, FAX 48-22-5098610, arspolona@arspolona.com.pl, http://www.arspolona.com.pl.

NUTRITION AND DIETETICS—Abstracting, Bibliographies, Statistics

613.2021 AUS
AUSTRALIA. BUREAU OF STATISTICS. INFORMATION PAPER: NATIONAL NUTRITION SURVEY, CONFIDENTIALISED UNIT RECORD FILE (ONLINE). Text in English. 1995. irreg. free (effective 2009). **Document type:** *Government.* **Description:** Provides information about the data content of the national nutrition survey, confidentialised unit record sample file, along with conditions of issue and how to order the file.
Formerly: Australia. Bureau of Statistics. Information Paper: National Nutrition Survey, Confidentialised Unit Record File (Print) (0817-9344)
Media: Online - full text.
Published by: Australian Bureau of Statistics, Locked Bag 10, Belconnen, ACT 2616, Australia. TEL 61-2-92684909, 61-2-62527037, 300-135-070, FAX 61-2-62528103, client.services@abs.gov.au.

613.2021 AUS
AUSTRALIA. BUREAU OF STATISTICS. NATIONAL NUTRITION SURVEY: FOODS EATEN, AUSTRALIA (ONLINE). Text in English. 1995. irreg., latest 1995. free (effective 2009). **Document type:** *Government.* **Description:** Presents detailed information on food intake of Australians aged two years and over.
Formerly: Australia. Bureau of Statistics. National Nutrition Survey: Foods Eaten, Australia (Print)
Media: Online - full text.
Published by: Australian Bureau of Statistics, Locked Bag 10, Belconnen, ACT 2616, Australia. TEL 61-2-92684909, 61-2-62527037, 300-135-070, FAX 61-2-62528103, client.services@abs.gov.au. **Co-sponsor:** Australia. Department of Health and Ageing.

613.2021 AUS
AUSTRALIA. BUREAU OF STATISTICS. NATIONAL NUTRITION SURVEY: NUTRIENT INTAKES AND PHYSICAL MEASUREMENTS, AUSTRALIA (ONLINE). Text in English. 1995. irreg., latest 1995. free (effective 2009). **Document type:** *Government.* **Description:** Presents detailed information on energy, water and nutrient intake of Australians aged two years and over.
Formerly: Australia. Bureau of Statistics. National Nutrition Survey: Nutrient Intakes and Physical Measurements, Australia (Print)
Media: Online - full text.
Published by: Australian Bureau of Statistics, Locked Bag 10, Belconnen, ACT 2616, Australia. TEL 61-2-92684909, 61-2-62527037, 300-135-070, FAX 61-2-62528103, client.services@abs.gov.au. **Co-sponsor:** Australia. Department of Health and Ageing.

613.2021 AUS
AUSTRALIA. BUREAU OF STATISTICS. QUEENSLAND OFFICE. SAFETY IN THE HOME, QUEENSLAND (ONLINE). Text in English. 1996. quinquennial. free (effective 2009). **Document type:** *Government.* **Description:** Summarises the results of a survey on safety in the home.
Formerly: Australia. Bureau of Statistics. Queensland Office. Safety in the Home, Queensland (Print)
Media: Online - full text.
Published by: Australian Bureau of Statistics, Queensland Office, GPO Box 9817, Brisbane, QLD 4001, Australia. TEL 61-2-92684909, 300-135-070, client.services@abs.gov.au.

HEALTH MODULE. *see* MEDICAL SCIENCES—Abstracting, Bibliographies, Statistics

016.6132 USA
HOUSEHOLD FOOD SECURITY IN THE UNITED STATES. Text in English. 1999. a., latest 2009. free (effective 2011). back issues avail. **Document type:** *Report, Government.*
Related titles: Online - full text ed.
Published by: U.S. Department of Agriculture, Economic Research Service, 1800 M St NW, Washington, DC 20036. TEL 202-694-5050, 800-999-6779, FAX 202-694-5638, ersinfo@ers.usda.gov.

016.6132 GBR ISSN 0309-1295
QP141.A1
NUTRITION ABSTRACTS AND REVIEWS. SERIES A: HUMAN AND EXPERIMENTAL; an excellent gateway to all current research on human and experimental nutrition. Abbreviated title: N A R A. Text in English. 1977. m. adv. bk.rev. illus. index, cum.index: vols.1-10 (in 2 vols.). **Document type:** *Abstract/Index.* **Description:** Covers the latest information on all issues related to food and health from food composition and safety to obesity, parenteral nutrition and allergies.
Supersedes in part (in 1977): Nutrition Abstracts and Reviews (0029-6619); Incorporates: Reviews in Clinical Nutrition
Indexed: P30.
—GNLM. **CCC.**
Published by: CABI (Subsidiary of: CAB International), Nosworthy Way, Wallingford, Oxfordshire OX10 8DE, United Kingdom. TEL 44-1491-832111, FAX 44-1491-829292, enquiries@cabi.org.

016.6132 016.664 GBR
NUTRITION AND FOOD SCIENCES DATABASE. Text in English. base vol. plus w. updates. **Document type:** *Database, Abstract/Index.*
Media: Online - full text.
Published by: CABI (Subsidiary of: CAB International), Nosworthy Way, Wallingford, Oxfordshire OX10 8DE, United Kingdom. TEL 44-1491-832111, FAX 44-1491-829292.

50 TITRES SUR.. *see* POPULATION STUDIES—Abstracting, Bibliographies, Statistics

OBSTETRICS AND GYNECOLOGY

see MEDICAL SCIENCES—Obstetrics And Gynecology

OCCUPATIONAL HEALTH AND SAFETY

A M I - RAPPORT. *see* BUSINESS AND ECONOMICS—Labor And Industrial Relations

613.62 USA ISSN 1059-1753
A O T A SELF STUDY SERIES. Text in English. 1990. irreg. price varies. **Document type:** *Monographic series, Academic/Scholarly.*
—CCC.
Published by: American Occupational Therapy Association, Inc., 4720 Montgomery Ln, PO Box 31220, Bethesda, MD 20824. TEL 301-652-2682, 800-377-8555, FAX 301-652-7711, ajotsis@aota.org, http://www.aota.org.

658.31244 DEU ISSN 0938-7226
ABWEHR BETRIEBLICHER STOERFAELLE. Text in German. 1990. 5 base vols. plus a. updates. looseleaf. EUR 118 base vol(s).; EUR 32 updates per issue (effective 2009). **Document type:** *Monographic series, Trade.*
Published by: Erich Schmidt Verlag GmbH & Co. (Berlin), Genthiner Str 30 G, Berlin, 10785, Germany. TEL 49-30-2500850, FAX 49-30-250085305, vertrieb@esvmedien.de, htttp://www.erich-schmidt-verlag.de.

363.11 CAN ISSN 0044-5878
HV675
ACCIDENT PREVENTION. Text in English. 1952. bi-m. CAD 18 domestic; CAD 24 in United States; CAD 33 elsewhere. bk.rev. abstr.; illus.; charts. **Document type:** *Journal, Trade.*
Indexed: CISA, CSNB, L12.
—BLDSC (0573.200000), IE, Ingenta.
Published by: Industrial Accident Prevention Association, 250 Yonge St, 28th Fl, Toronto, ON M5B 2N4, Canada. TEL 416-506-8888, FAX 416-506-8880. Circ: 35,000.

613.62 658 USA ISSN 1093-720X
ADMINISTRATION & MANAGEMENT SPECIAL INTEREST SECTION QUARTERLY. Text in English. 1985. q. free to members (effective 2010). adv. **Document type:** *Newsletter, Trade.* **Description:** Focuses on diverse administration and management issues. Participants include occupational therapy professionals who have administrative or managerial responsibilities as part of their daily jobs, or who wish to gain knowledge and skills in these areas.
Formerly (until 1997): Administration and Management Special Interest Section Newsletter (8756-629X)
Related titles: Online - full text ed.: free to members (effective 2010); ◆ Series: Gerontology Special Interest Section Quarterly. ISSN 1093-717X; ◆ Mental Health Special Interest Section Quarterly. ISSN 1093-7226; ◆ Technology Special Interest Section Quarterly. ISSN 1093-7137; ◆ Work & Industry Special Interest Section Quarterly; ◆ Education Special Interest Section Quarterly. ISSN 1093-7188; ◆ Physical Disabilities Special Interest Section Quarterly. ISSN 1093-7234; ◆ Developmental Disabilities Special Interest Section Quarterly. ISSN 1093-7196; ◆ Sensory Integration Special Interest Section Quarterly. ISSN 1093-7250.
Indexed: C06, C07, C08, CINAHL, P21, P24, P48, P50, P52, P56, PQC.
—CCC.
Published by: American Occupational Therapy Association, Inc., 4720 Montgomery Ln, PO Box 31220, Bethesda, MD 20824. TEL 301-652-2682, 800-377-8555, FAX 301-652-7711, ajotsis@aota.org. Ed. Sharon Kurfuerst.

ADVANCE FOR OCCUPATIONAL THERAPY PRACTITIONERS. *see* MEDICAL SCIENCES—Physical Medicine And Rehabilitation

363.11 NLD ISSN 1384-2269
ADVANCES IN OCCUPATIONAL ERGONOMICS AND SAFETY. Text in English. 1997. irreg., latest vol.4, 2001. price varies. back issues avail. **Document type:** *Monographic series, Academic/Scholarly.* **Description:** Disseminates research in the field of occupational health and safety; covers ergonomics.
—CCC.
Published by: I O S Press, Nieuwe Hemweg 6B, Amsterdam, 1013 BG, Netherlands. TEL 31-20-6883355, FAX 31-20-6870039, info@iospress.nl. **Subscr. to:** I O S Press, Inc, 4502 Rachael Manor Dr, Fairfax, VA 22032-3631. sales@iospress.com. **Dist. by:** Ohmsha Ltd, 3-1 Kanda-Nishiki-cho, Tokyo 101-0054, Japan. TEL 81-3-32330641, FAX 81-3-32332426, http://www.ohmsha.co.jp.

613.62 FIN ISSN 0788-4877
T55.A1
AFRICAN NEWSLETTER ON OCCUPATIONAL HEALTH AND SAFETY. Text in English. 1987. 3/yr. free (effective 2005). 28 p./no.; Supplement avail.; back issues avail. **Document type:** *Newsletter, Trade.*
Formerly (until 1991): East African Newsletter on Occupational Health and Safety (0783-6201)
Related titles: Online - full text ed.: African Newsletter on Occupational Health and Safety - Online. ISSN 1239-4386. 1995.
Indexed: A34, A36, A37, CABA, E12, F08, F11, GH, H16, N02, O01, P33, R07, R08, R12, S13, S16, T05, TAR, W11.
—BLDSC (0732.902500), IE, Ingenta.
Published by: Tyoterveyslaitos/Finnish Institute of Occupational Health, Topeliuksenkatu 41a A, Helsinki, 00250, Finland. TEL 358-30-4741, FAX 358-30-4742779. Ed. Suvi Lehtinen.

658.31244 ITA ISSN 2035-5149
AMBIENTE E SICUREZZA. Text in Italian. 1999. s-m. **Document type:** *Magazine, Trade.*
Published by: Il Sole 24 Ore Business Media, Via Monte Rosa 91, Milan, 20149, Italy. TEL 39-02-30221, FAX 39-02-312055, info@ilsole24ore.com, http://www.gruppo24ore.com.

658.31244 ITA ISSN 0393-7054
AMBIENTE E SICUREZZA SUL LAVORO. Text in Italian. 1985. m. (11/yr.). EUR 160 domestic print & online eds. (effective 2009). adv. illus. 130 p./no.; **Document type:** *Trade.*
Related titles: Online - full text ed.
Published by: Insic, Via dell' Acqua Traversa 189, Rome, 00135, Italy. TEL 39-06-3313000, FAX 39-06-33111043, info@insic.it, http://www.insic.it. Circ: 10,000.

613.62 USA ISSN 0271-3586
CODEN: AJIMD8
➤ **AMERICAN JOURNAL OF INDUSTRIAL MEDICINE.** Text in English. 1980. m. GBP 3,349 in United Kingdom to institutions; EUR 4,233 in Europe to institutions; USD 6,307 in United States to institutions; USD 6,475 in Canada & Mexico to institutions; USD 6,559 elsewhere to institutions; GBP 3,852 combined subscription in United Kingdom to institutions (print & online eds.); EUR 4,870 combined subscription in Europe to institutions (print & online eds.); USD 7,254 combined subscription in United States to institutions (print & online eds.); USD 7,422 combined subscription in Canada & Mexico to institutions (print & online eds.); USD 7,506 combined subscription elsewhere to institutions (print & online eds.) (effective 2012). adv. bk.rev. bibl.; charts; illus. index. back issues avail.; reprint service avail. from PSC. **Document type:** *Journal, Academic/Scholarly.* **Description:** Presents both clinical and laboratory findings, as well as general academic and scientific contributions in the fundamental or applied study of occupational disease.
Related titles: Microform ed.: (from PQC); Online - full text ed.: ISSN 1097-0274. GBP 3,220 in United Kingdom to institutions; EUR 4,070 in Europe to institutions; USD 6,307 elsewhere to institutions (effective 2012); Supplement(s): American Journal of Industrial Medicine Supplement.
Indexed: A20, A22, A34, A36, A37, A38, AESIS, ASCA, AcoustA, B21, B25, BIOSIS Prev, C&ISA, CA, CABA, CIN, CSNB, Cadscan, ChPerl, ChemAb, ChemTitl, CorrAb, CurCont, D01, DentInd, E&CAJ, E04, E05, E12, EMBASE, ESPM, ErgAb, ExcerpMed, F08, F11, FR, GH, GeoRef, H&SSA, INI, INIS AtomInd, ISR, IndMed, Inpharma, L12, LT, LeadAb, MEDLINE, MS&D, MycolAb, N02, N03, NRN, P30, P33, P37, P38, PHN&I, PN&I, PollutAb, R07, R08, R10, R12, RILM, RM&VM, RRTA, Reac, RiskAb, SCI, SCOPUS, SolStAb, T02, T05, THA, ToxAb, TriticAb, VITIS, VS, W07, W09, W10, W11, WAA, Zincscan.
—BLDSC (0826.750000), CASDDS, GNLM, IE, Infotrieve, Ingenta, INIST. **CCC.**
Published by: John Wiley & Sons, Inc., 111 River St, Hoboken, NJ 07030. TEL 201-748-6000, FAX 201-748-6088, info@wiley.com, http://www.wiley.com/WileyCDA/. Ed. Steven B Markowitz. Adv. contact Kim Thompkins TEL 212-850-6921. B&W page USD 772, color page USD 1,009; trim 8.25 x 11. **Subscr. outside the Americas to:** John Wiley & Sons Ltd., The Atrium, Southern Gate, Chichester, West Sussex PO19 8SQ, United Kingdom. TEL 44-1243-779777, FAX 44-1243-775878, cs-journals@wiley.com.

615.851 USA ISSN 0272-9490
RM735.A1 CODEN: AJOTAM
➤ **AMERICAN JOURNAL OF OCCUPATIONAL THERAPY.** Abbreviated title: A J O T. Text in English. 1947. bi-m. USD 114 domestic to individuals; USD 159.75 in Canada to individuals; USD 285 elsewhere to individuals; USD 182.50 domestic to institutions; USD 214 in Canada to institutions; USD 310 elsewhere to institutions; free to members (effective 2010). adv. bk.rev. abstr.; bibl.; charts; illus. index. back issues avail.; reprints avail. **Document type:** *Journal, Academic/Scholarly.* **Description:** Focuses on research, practice, and health care issues in the field of occupational therapy.
Former titles (until 1980): A J O T: The American Journal of Occupational Therapy (0161-326X); (until 1977): The American Journal of Occupational Therapy (0002-9386)
Related titles: Microform ed.: (from PQC); Online - full text ed.: ISSN 1943-7676. free (effective 2010).
Indexed: A20, A22, A26, AMED, ASCA, ASSIA, AgeL, BDM&CN, C06, C07, C08, CA, CINAHL, CurCont, DentInd, DokArb, E-psyche, E08, ECER, EMBASE, ExcerpMed, F09, FamI, H12, HospLI, I05, INI, IndMed, MEDLINE, P03, P18, P20, P22, P24, P27, P30, P48, P53, P54, PQC, PsycInfo, PsycholAb, R10, RILM, Reac, RehabLit, S09, SCOPUS, SSCI, T02, W07.
—BLDSC (0828.750000), GNLM, IE, Infotrieve, Ingenta, INIST. **CCC.**
Published by: American Occupational Therapy Association, Inc., 4720 Montgomery Ln, PO Box 31220, Bethesda, MD 20824. TEL 301-652-2682, 800-377-8555, FAX 301-652-7711, members@aota.org. Ed. Sharon Gutman.

613.62 USA
AMERICAN OCCUPATIONAL THERAPY ASSOCIATION. ANNUAL REPORT (ONLINE). Text in English. 1972. a. free (effective 2010). **Document type:** *Report, Trade.*
Formerly (until 1994): American Occupational Therapy Association. Annual Report (Print) (0145-8922)
—CCC.
Published by: American Occupational Therapy Association, Inc., 4720 Montgomery Ln, PO Box 31220, Bethesda, MD 20824. TEL 301-652-2682, 800-377-8555, FAX 301-652-7711, members@aota.org, http://www.aota.org.

AMERISURE SAFETY NEWS. *see* PUBLIC HEALTH AND SAFETY

614.85 DEU ISSN 1610-2835
ANLAGEN- UND BETRIEBSSICHERHEIT. Text in German. 2003. 4 base vols. plus updates 2/yr. EUR 186 base vol(s).; EUR 48 updates per issue (effective 2009). **Document type:** *Monographic series, Trade.*
Published by: Erich Schmidt Verlag GmbH & Co. (Berlin), Genthiner Str 30 G, Berlin, 10785, Germany. TEL 49-30-2500850, FAX 49-30-250085305, esv@esvmedien.de, http://www.esv.info.

613.62 GBR ISSN 0003-4878
RC963 CODEN: AOHYA3
➤ **ANNALS OF OCCUPATIONAL HYGIENE**; an international scientific journal on the causation and control of work-related ill-health. Text in English. 1958. 9/yr. GBP 868 in United Kingdom to institutions; EUR 1,302 in Europe to institutions; USD 1,737 in US & Canada to institutions; GBP 868 elsewhere to institutions; GBP 948 combined subscription in United Kingdom to institutions (print & online eds.); EUR 1,420 combined subscription in Europe to institutions (print & online eds.); USD 1,895 combined subscription in US & Canada to institutions (print & online eds.); GBP 948 combined subscription elsewhere to institutions (print & online eds.) (effective 2012). adv. bk.rev. charts; illus. index. 72 p./no.; back issues avail.; reprint service avail. from PSC. **Document type:** *Journal, Academic/Scholarly.* **Description:** Aims to promote a healthy working environment through publication of research papers and reviews on health hazards and risks resulting from work, especially their recognition, quantification, management and control.
Related titles: Microfilm ed.: (from PQC); Online - full text ed.: ISSN 1475-3162. GBP 704 in United Kingdom to institutions; EUR 1,055 in Europe to institutions; USD 1,408 in US & Canada to institutions; GBP 704 elsewhere to institutions (effective 2012) (from IngentaConnect).
Indexed: A01, A03, A08, A22, A34, A36, A37, A38, ASCA, AcoustA, Agr, B21, B25, BA, BIOBASE, BIOSIS Prev, C&ISA, C06, C07, C25, CA, CABA, CIN, CISA, CMCI, CPEI, CSNB, ChemAb, ChemTitl, CorrAb, CurCont, D01, E&CAJ, E01, E04, E05, E12, EMBASE, ESPM, EngInd, ErgAb, ExcerpMed, F08, F11, F12, FR, GH, H&SSA, H16, IABS, IHD, IMMAb, ISMEC, ISR, IndMed, Inpharma, Inspec, L12, LT, MEDLINE, MS&D, MycolAb, N02, N03, NPPA, OR, P30, P33, P37, PHN&I, PollutAb, R07, R08, R10, R12, R13, R18, RM&VM, RRTA, Reac, RiskAb, S13, S16, SCI, SCOPUS, SolStAb, SoyAb, T02, T05, TAR, THA, ToxAb, TriticAb, VS, W07, W10, W11, WAA.
—BLDSC (1043.300000), CASDDS, GNLM, IE, Infotrieve, Ingenta, INIST. **CCC.**
Published by: (British Occupational Hygiene Society), Oxford University Press, Great Clarendon St, Oxford, OX2 6DP, United Kingdom. TEL 44-1865-556767, FAX 44-1865-556646, enquiry@oup.co.uk, http://www.oxfordjournals.org. Ed. Trevor L Ogden. Pub. Mandy Sketch. adv.: B&W page GBP 320, B&W page USD 575, color page GBP 570, color page USD 1,025; bleed 268 x 296. Circ: 1,545.

613.62 CHN ISSN 1002-3631
ANQUAN/SAFETY. Text in Chinese. 1980. m. CNY 120; CNY 10 per issue (effective 2011). back issues avail. **Document type:** *Magazine, Trade.*
Formerly (until 1983): Laodong Baohu Jishu
Related titles: Online - full text ed.
Published by: Beijingshi Laodong Baohu Kexue Yanjiusuo/Beijing Municipal Institute of Labour Protection, 55, Taoranting Lu, Beijing, 100054, China. TEL 86-10-63524191, FAX 86-10-63524191. Ed. Kaili Zhang.

363.11 363.7 CHN ISSN 1672-7932
ANQUAN JIANKANG HE HUANJING/SAFETY HEALTH & ENVIRONMENT. Text in Chinese. 1999. m. CNY 120 (effective 2009). **Document type:** *Journal, Academic/Scholarly.*
Former titles (until 2002): Anquan Huanjing he Jiankang/Safety Environment & Health; (until 2001): Huagong Laodong Baohu; Which was formed by the merger of (1983-1999): Huagong Laodong Baohu (Anquan Jishu yu Guanli Fence); (1983-1999): Huagong Laodong Baohu (Gongye Weisheng yu Zhiyebing Fence); Both of which superseded in part (in 1982): Huagong Laodong Baohu
Related titles: Online - full text ed.
Published by: Zhongguo Shiyou Huagong Jituan Gongsi Anquan Gongcheng Yanjiuyuan/S I N O P E C Reserach Institute of Safety Engineering, 218, Yanan San Lu, Qingdao, 266071, China. TEL 86-532-83786257, FAX 86-532-83786260, yuanban@qdrise.com.cn, http://www.qdrise.com.cn/default.aspx.

613.62 363.11 JPN ISSN 0911-0011
ANZEN EISEI NO HIROBA/SAFETY AND HEALTH. Text in Japanese. 1960. m. JPY 24,000 membership (effective 2007). **Document type:** *Magazine, Trade.*
Formerly (until 1965): Anzen no Hiroba (0518-1119)
Published by: Boira Kuren Anzen Kyokai/Boiler and Crane Safety Association, 6-41-20, Kameido, Koto-ku, Tokyo, 136-0071, Japan. TEL 81-3-36852141, FAX 81-3-36852189, http://www.bcsa.or.jp/.

AOMORIKEN SAGYO RYOHO KENKYU/BULLETIN OF AOMORI OCCUPATIONAL THERAPY. *see* MEDICAL SCIENCES—Physical Medicine And Rehabilitation

613.62 331.5 NLD ISSN 1872-3535
ARBEID IN ZORG EN WELZIJN (UTRECHT). Text in Dutch. 2005. a. free (effective 2010).
Published by: Prismant, Papendorpseweg 65, Utrecht, 3528 BJ, Netherlands. TEL 31-30-2345678, FAX 31-30-2345677, prismant@prismant.nl, http://www.prismant.nl.

614.85 NOR ISSN 0806-3648
ARBEID OG HELSE. Text in Norwegian. 1995. a. back issues avail. **Document type:** *Magazine, Government.*
Related titles: Online - full text ed.
Published by: Statens Arbeidsmiljoeinstitutt/National Institute of Occupational Health, PO Box 8149, Dep, Oslo, 0033, Norway. TEL 47-23-195100, FAX 47-23-195200, stami@stami.no. Ed. Sture Len Bye. Circ: 5,000.

614.8 NOR ISSN 0332-7124
HD7200
ARBEIDERVERN; working environment journal. Text in Norwegian. 1973. 6/yr. NOK 250 (effective 2011). adv. illus. **Document type:** *Journal, Trade.*
Indexed: CISA, INIS AtomInd.
—CCC.
Published by: Direktoratet for Arbeidstilsynet/Directorate of Labour Inspection, Statens hus, PO Box 4720, Trondheim, 7468, Norway. TEL 47-81-548222, FAX 47-73-199701, post@arbeidstilsynet.dep.no. Circ: 28,300.

363.1 NOR ISSN 0800-2088
ARBEIDSMILJOE. Text in Norwegian. 1951. 8/yr. NOK 455 (effective 2007). adv. bk.rev. **Document type:** *Magazine, Academic/Scholarly.* **Description:** Concentrates on work environment, occupational health and safety. Contains research articles and general information about safety and health.
Former titles (until 1982): Vern og Velferd Arbejdsmiljoe (0332-9127); (until 1980): Vern og Velferd (0049-5964)
Related titles: Online - full text ed.: ISSN 1504-6311. 200?.
—CCC.
Published by: Arbeidsmiljoesenteret, Postboks 9326, Groenland, Oslo, 0135, Norway. TEL 47-815-9750, FAX 46-22-057839. Ed. Paul Norberg TEL 47-22-057807. Adv. contact Jan Jensen TEL 47-99-439009. B&W page NOK 10,300, color page NOK 14,900; 185 x 260. Circ: 8,200.

613.62 DEU ISSN 0946-7602
ARBEIT UND GESUNDHEIT; Zeitschrift fuer Sicherheit und Gesundheit bei der Arbeit. Text in German. 1949. m. EUR 9.72 (effective 2006). adv. **Document type:** *Magazine, Trade.*
Formerly (until 1994): Blickpunkt Arbeitssicherheit (0930-8156)
Related titles: Special ed(s).: Arbeit und Gesundheit. Ausgabe fuer Sicherheitsfachkraefte und Sicherheitsbeauftragte. ISSN 0946-7599.
—IE.

Published by: (Hauptverband der gewerblichen Berufsgenossenschaften e.V.), Universum Verlagsanstalt GmbH KG, Taunusstr 54, Wiesbaden, 65183, Germany. TEL 49-611-90300, FAX 49-611-9030183, info@universum.de, http://www.universum.de. adv.: page EUR 9,585. Circ: 392,792 (controlled).

ARBEITSMEDIZIN, SOZIALMEDIZIN, UMWELTMEDIZIN; Zeitschrift fuer Praxis, Klinik, Forschung, Begutachtung. *see* PUBLIC HEALTH AND SAFETY

363.11 DEU ISSN 1611-5694
ARBEITSSICHERHEIT IM BAUWESEN. Text in German. 2003. irreg., latest vol.5, 2006. price varies. **Document type:** *Monographic series, Academic/Scholarly.*
Published by: Logos Verlag Berlin, Comeniushof, Gubener Str 47, Berlin, 10243, Germany. TEL 49-30-42851090, FAX 49-30-42851092, redaktion@logos-verlag.de. Ed. Karl-Dieter Roebenack.

614.85 DEU ISSN 1862-8087
ARBEITSSICHERHEIT IN GEWERBE UND INDUSTRIE AKTUELL. Text in German. 2005. 16/yr. **Document type:** *Newsletter, Trade.*
Formerly (until 2006): Gefahren Erkennen und Beseitigen (1861-2326)
Published by: V N R Verlag fuer die Deutsche Wirtschaft AG, Theodor-Heuss-Str 2-4, Bonn, 53095, Germany. TEL 49-228-9550555, FAX 49-228-3696001, info@vnr.de, http://www.vnr.de.

363.11 DEU ISSN 1868-6109
▼ **ARBEITSSICHERHEIT.JOURNAL**; das Fachmagazin fuer Arbeitssicherheit im Unternehmen. Text in German. 2009. 8/yr. EUR 106.40; EUR 15.90 newsstand/cover (effective 2011). adv. **Document type:** *Journal, Trade.*
Related titles: Online - full text ed.
Published by: Wolters Kluwer Deutschland GmbH (Subsidiary of: Wolters Kluwer N.V.), Luxemburger Str 449, Cologne, 50939, Germany. TEL 49-221-943737000, FAX 49-221-943737201, info@wolterskluwer.de, http://www.wolters-kluwer.de. Ed. Monika Schaake. Adv. contact Joerg Walter. Circ: 9,700 (paid).

613.62 DEU ISSN 0720-1699
ARBEITSWISSENSCHAFTLICHE ERKENNTNISSE. Text in German. 1979. irreg. EUR 52 per vol. (effective 2010). **Document type:** *Monographic series, Academic/Scholarly.*
Published by: (Germany. Bundesanstalt fuer Arbeitsschutz und Arbeitsmedizin), Wirtschaftsverlag N W - Verlag fuer Neue Wissenschaft GmbH, Buergermeister-Smidt-Str 74-76, Bremerhaven, 27568, Germany. TEL 49-471-945440, FAX 49-471-9454477, info@nw-verlag.de, http://www.nw-verlag.de.

363.11 DNK ISSN 0900-291X
ARBEJDSMILJOE. Added title page title: Magasinet Arbejdsmiljoe. Variant title: Arbejdsmiljoe, Udvikling og Forskning. Text in Danish. 1972. 11/yr. DKK 595; DKK 47 per issue (effective 2008). adv. back issues avail. **Document type:** *Magazine, Consumer.*
Formerly (until 1985): Pas Paa! (0105-6239)
Related titles: Online - full text ed.
Published by: Videncenter for Arbejdsmiljoe/The Working Environment Information Centre, Lersoe Parkalle 105, Copenhagen OE, 2100, Denmark. TEL 45-39-165307, FAX 45-39-165201, videncenter@vfa.dk, http://www.arbejdsmiljoviden.dk. Ed. Hannah Maimin Weil TEL 45-39-16-5494. Adv. contact Lasse Nielsen TEL 45-33-707696. page DKK 17,400; 173 x 243. Circ: 8,553.

363.11 SWE ISSN 0346-7805
ARBETARSKYDD. Text in Swedish. 1972. 14/yr. SEK 490 (effective 2004). adv. 20 p./no. 5 cols./p.; **Document type:** *Newspaper, Trade.*
Former titles (until 1975): Aktuell Information (0345-0244); (until 1974): Aktuellt fraan Arbetarskyddsverket (0345-0252); A I Aktuellt
Published by: Talentum Sweden AB (Subsidiary of: Talentum Media Oyj), Maester Samuelsgatan 56, Stockholm, 10612, Sweden. TEL 46-8-7966650, FAX 46-8-202157, info@talentum.se, http://www.talentum.se. Ed. Johanna Kronlid TEL 46-8-7966447. Adv. contact Susanne Webb. B&W page SEK 25,000, color page SEK 27,000; trim 252 x 360. Circ: 25,000 (controlled).

363.11 SWE ISSN 1654-4277
ARBETARSKYDDSREGLER FOER BYGGSEKTORN. Text in Swedish. 1982-1984; N.S. 1985. a. SEK 990 (effective 2006). **Document type:** *Trade.*
Former titles (until 2007): Arbetarskyddsregler Byggarbete (0282-910X); (until 1984): Arbetsmiljoens Foerfatterhandbok Byggplatser (0281-0875)
Published by: Svensk Byggtjaenst/Swedish Building Centre, Sankt Eriksgatan 117, 9, Stockholm, 11387, Sweden. TEL 46-8-4571000, FAX 46-8-4571199.

658.31244 SWE ISSN 1650-3163
ARBETSMILJOEVERKETS FOERFATTNINGSSAMLING. Variant title: A F S. Text in Swedish. 1978. irreg. price varies. back issues avail. **Document type:** *Monographic series, Government.*
Formerly (until 2001): Arbetarskyddsstyrelsens Foerfattningssamling (0348-2138); Which was formed by the merger of (196?-1978): Arbetarskyddsstyrelsens Meddelanden; (1921-1978): Arbetarskyddsstyrelsens Anvisningar (0491-7448)
Related titles: Online - full text ed.
Published by: Arbetsmiljoeverket/National Swedish Board of Occupational Safety and Health, Ekelundsvaegen 16, Solna, 17184, Sweden. TEL 46-8-7309000, FAX 46-8-7301967, arbetsmiljoverket@av.se.

363.11 NLD ISSN 1571-4152
HD7262
ARBO. Text in Dutch. 1927. 10/yr. EUR 175; EUR 23 newsstand/cover (effective 2009). adv. bk.rev. bibl.; illus.; stat. **Document type:** *Journal, Trade.*
Formed by the merger of (1993-2003): Arbo en Milieu (0928-1290); Which was formerly (1990-1993): Arbo Reporter (0929-0087); (1987-2003): Arbeidsomstandigheden (0920-119X); Which was formerly (1986-1987): Maandblad voor Arbeidsomstandigheden (0929-6115); (1927-1986): De Veiligheid - Safety (0042-3149); Which incorporated (1993-1997): Arbeidsomstandigheden Concreet (0929-1105); Which was formerly (1992-1993): Arbeidsomstandigheden-Actueel (0927-4480)
Related titles: ◆ Supplement(s): Arbo. Special. ISSN 1572-3658; ◆ Arbeidsomstandigheden Concreet. ISSN 0929-1105.
Indexed: CISA, ChemAb.
—IE, Infotrieve. **CCC.**
Published by: Kluwer B.V. (Subsidiary of: Wolters Kluwer N.V.), Postbus 23, Deventer, 7400 GA, Netherlands. TEL 31-570-673555, FAX 31-570-691555, info@kluwer.nl, http://www.kluwer.nl. Ed. Jacqueline Joosten. adv.: B&W page EUR 1,425, color page EUR 2,320. Circ: 4,876.

363.11 NLD ISSN 1568-1513
ARBO ACTUEEL. Text in Dutch. 2001. 22/yr. EUR 158; EUR 18 newsstand/cover (effective 2009). adv. **Document type:** *Bulletin, Trade.*
Formed by the merger of (1986-2001): Arbo Bulletin (0169-9237); (1994-2001): Arbo Actueel (1384-5055)
—IE, Infotrieve.
Published by: (Nederlands Instituut voor Arbeidsomstandigheden), Kluwer B.V. (Subsidiary of: Wolters Kluwer N.V.), Postbus 23, Deventer, 7400 GA, Netherlands. TEL 31-570-673555, FAX 31-570-691555, juridisch@kluwer.nl, http://www.kluwer.nl. Ed. Thea Rijsewijk.

363.11 NLD ISSN 1567-4843
T55.A1
ARBO JAARBOEK. Text in Dutch. 1959. a. EUR 102 (effective 2009). adv. bk.rev. **Document type:** *Trade.* **Description:** Constitutes a yearbook for those professionally occupied with the working environment.
Formerly (until 1984): Veiligheidsjaarboek (0083-534X)
Published by: (Nederlands Instituut voor Arbeidsomstandigheden), Kluwer B.V. (Subsidiary of: Wolters Kluwer N.V.), Postbus 23, Deventer, 7400 GA, Netherlands. TEL 31-570-673555, FAX 31-570-691555, juridisch@kluwer.nl, http://www.kluwer.nl.

ARBO RENDEMENT. *see* BUSINESS AND ECONOMICS—Personnel Management

362.1 613.6 FRA ISSN 1775-8785
CODEN: AMPMAR
ARCHIVES DES MALADIES PROFESSIONNELLES ET DE L'ENVIRONNEMENT. Text in French; Summaries in English. 1938. 6/yr. EUR 407 in Europe to institutions; EUR 358.47 in France to institutions; JPY 68,800 in Japan to institutions; USD 552 elsewhere to institutions (effective 2012). adv. bk.rev. illus. index. reprints avail. **Document type:** *Journal, Academic/Scholarly.* **Description:** Supplies technical, scientific and practical information to practitioners devoted to occupational medicine or professional pathology.
Former titles (until 2005): Archives des Maladies Professionnelles et de Medecine du Travail (1250-3274); (until 1992): Archives des Maladies Professionnelles de Medecine du Travail et de Securite Sociale (0003-9691)
Related titles: Microform ed.: (from PQC); Online - full text ed.: ISSN 1778-4190 (from ScienceDirect).
Indexed: A22, A34, A36, CABA, CISA, CSNB, ChemAb, D01, E12, ErgAb, F08, F11, F12, FR, GH, H16, H17, IBR, IBZ, IndMed, L12, LT, N02, N03, P30, P32, P33, P37, P39, PHN&I, R07, R08, R11, R12, R13, RRTA, S13, S16, SCI, SCOPUS, T05, W07, W10, W11.
—BLDSC (1637.380000), CASDDS, GNLM, IE, Infotrieve, Ingenta, INIST. **CCC.**
Published by: (Societes de Medecine du Travail), Elsevier Masson (Subsidiary of: Elsevier Health Sciences), 62 Rue Camille Desmoulins, Issy les Moulineaux, Cedex 92442, France. TEL 33-1-71165500, infos@elsevier-masson.fr. Ed. Patrick Hadengue. Circ: 3,500.

ARCHIVES OF PUBLIC HEALTH. *see* PUBLIC HEALTH AND SAFETY

613.62 620.8 ESP ISSN 1138-9672
➤ **ARCHIVOS DE PREVENCION DE RIESGOS LABORALES.** Text in Spanish. 1963. q. back issues avail.; reprints avail. **Document type:** *Journal, Academic/Scholarly.*
Formerly (until 1998): Medicina de Empresa (0378-6668)
Related titles: Online - full text ed.: ISSN 1578-2549. 1998.
Published by: Societat Catalana de Medicina i Securetat en el Treball, Tapineria, 10 Pral, Barcelona, 08002, Spain. TEL 34-93-3101144, FAX 34-93-3105230, scsmt@scsmt.cat. Ed. Ana M. Garcia. Circ: 1,000 (paid).

➤ **ARHIV ZA HIGIJENU RADA I TOKSIKOLOGIJU/ARCHIVES OF INDUSTRIAL HYGIENE AND TOXICOLOGY.** *see* ENVIRONMENTAL STUDIES—Toxicology And Environmental Safety

363.11 613.62 FIN ISSN 1237-0843
RC963.A1
ASIAN - PACIFIC NEWSLETTER ON OCCUPATIONAL HEALTH AND SAFETY. Text in English. 1994. 3/yr. free (effective 2006). back issues avail. **Document type:** *Newsletter, Trade.*
Related titles: Online - full text ed.: ISSN 1458-5944.
Indexed: A34, A36, C06, C07, CABA, D01, E12, GH, IndVet, N02, N03, P33, P37, R08, R12, RefZh, T05, VS, W11.
Published by: Tyoterveyslaitos/Finnish Institute of Occupational Health, Topeliuksenkatu 41a A, Helsinki, 00250, Finland. TEL 358-30-4741, FAX 358-30-4742779. Ed. Inkeri Haataja.

658.31244 ESP ISSN 1132-6255
CODEN: RAEEFM
ASOCIACION ESPANOLA DE ESPECIALISTAS EN MEDICINA DEL TRABAJO. REVISTA. Text in Spanish. 1989. bi-m. **Document type:** *Journal, Academic/Scholarly.*
Formerly (until 1991): Medicina del Trabajo (0214-6037)
Indexed: SCOPUS.
—**CCC.**
Published by: Grupo Accion Medica, Fernandez de la Hoz 61, Madrid, 28003, Spain. TEL 34-91-5360814, FAX 34-91-5360607, info@accionmedica.es, http://www.accionmedica.es.

613.62 CAN ISSN 1491-7971
ASSOCIATION OF CANADIAN ERGONOMISTS. COMMUNIQUE. Text in English. 1971. bi-m. **Document type:** *Newsletter.*
Formerly (until 1999): Human Factors Association of Canada. Communique (0712-936X)
Indexed: ErgAb.
Published by: Association Canadienne d'Ergonomie/Association of Canadian Ergonomists, 1304-2 Carlton St, Toronto, ON M5B 1J3, Canada. TEL 416-979-3946, 888-432-2223, FAX 416-979-1144, info@ace.ergonomist.ca, http://www.ace.ergonomist.ca.

613.62 POL ISSN 1230-4700
ATEST; ochrona pracy. Text in Polish; Summaries in English, Russian. 1947. m. PLZ 239.40 domestic; EUR 135 foreign (effective 2011). adv. bk.rev. bibl.; illus.; pat. index. 52 p./no.; **Document type:** *Journal, Trade.* **Description:** Covers work safety and hygiene, and labor medicine.
Former titles (until 1992): Ochrona Pracy (0029-8220); (until 1952): Bezpieczenstwo i Higiena Pracy (1230-4727)
Related titles: Online - full text ed.
Indexed: AgrLib, CISA, ChemAb.
Published by: (Naczelna Organizacja Techniczna), Wydawnictwo SIGMA - N O T Sp. z o.o., ul Ratuszowa 11, PO Box 1004, Warsaw, 00950, Poland. TEL 48-22-8180918, FAX 48-22-6192187, sekretariat@sigma-not.pl, http://www.sigma-not.pl. Ed. Zofia Lejko. adv.: B&W page PLZ 1,500, color page PLZ 3,300. Circ: 7,000. **Dist. by:** Ars Polona, Obroncow 25, Warsaw 03933, Poland. TEL 48-22-5098609, FAX 48-22-5098610, arspolona@arspolona.com.pl, http://www.arspolona.com.pl. **Co-sponsor:** Panstwowa Inspekcja Pracy.

658.31244 AUS ISSN 1328-9071
AUSTRALIAN OCCUPATIONAL HEALTH & SAFETY FILE. Variant title: Australian O H S File. Text in English. 1993. q. price varies. **Document type:** *Directory, Trade.* **Description:** Provides a comprehensive research tool covering Occupational Health and Safety information from over 130 Australian and relevant overseas organisations.
Formerly (until 1997): A C E L Occupational Health and Safety Plus (1039-141X)
Related titles: CD-ROM ed.; Online - full text ed.
Published by: I H S Australian Pty. Ltd., Level 3, 33 Rowe St, Locked Bag 7, Eastwood, NSW 2122, Australia. TEL 61-2-98041200, FAX 61-2-98040200, ihsinfo@ihs.com.

NO

658.31244 DEU
B A U A: AKTUELL. Text in German. 1996. 4/yr. free (effective 2009). bk.rev. 20 p./no. 2 cols./p.; **Document type:** *Bulletin, Trade.*
Formerly (until 2004): Bundesanstalt fuer Arbeitsschutz und Arbeitsmedizin. Amtliche Mitteilungen (1434-9701); Which was formed by the merger of (1984-1996): Bundesanstalt fuer Arbeitsschutz. Amtliche Mitteilungen (0177-3062); (1993-1996): Bundesanstalt fuer Arbeitsmedizin. Informationen (0944-2278)
Related titles: Online - full text ed.
Indexed: DIP, IBR, IBZ.
Published by: Bundesanstalt fuer Arbeitsschutz und Arbeitsmedizin, Postfach 170202, Dortmund, 44061, Germany. TEL 49-231-90710, FAX 49-231-90712454, info-zentrum@baua.bund.de. Eds. Angelika Limbach, Wolfgang Dicke.

658.31244 USA
B C S P NEWSLETTER. Text in English. 1975. 2/yr. membership only. back issues avail. **Document type:** *Newsletter.* **Description:** Professional certification in safety, demographics of safety professionals and credentialling activities.
Published by: Board of Certified Safety Professionals, 208 Barwash Ave, Savoy, IL 61874. TEL 217-359-9263, http://www.bcsp.org. Ed. Roger L Brauer.

B F S - BERICHTE. (Bundesamt fuer Strahlenschutz) *see* ENERGY—Nuclear Energy

B F S - S E. (Bundesamt fuer Strahlenschutz - Fachbereich Sicherheit Nuklearer Entsorgung) *see* ENERGY—Nuclear Energy

B F S - S G. (Bundesamt fuer Strahlenschutz - Fachbereich Strahlenschutz und Gesundheit) *see* ENERGY—Nuclear Energy

B F S - S K. (Bundesamt fuer Strahlenschutz - Sicherheit in der Kerntechnik) *see* ENERGY—Nuclear Energy

658.31244 DEU
B G I A HANDBUCH. Text in German. 1985. 2 base vols. plus updates 2/yr. EUR 98 base vol(s).; EUR 38.60 updates per issue (effective 2009). **Document type:** *Monographic series, Trade.*
Formerly: B I A Handbuch (0933-4629)
Published by: (Berufsgenossenschaftliches Institut fuer Arbeitssicherheit), Erich Schmidt Verlag GmbH & Co. (Berlin), Genthiner Str 30 G, Berlin, 10785, Germany. TEL 49-30-2500850, FAX 49-30-250085305, esv@esvmedien.de, http://www.erich-schmidt-verlag.de.

613.62 DEU
B G W JAHRESBERICHT. Text in German. 1986. a. **Document type:** *Journal, Trade.*
Formerly (until 1996): B G W Verwaltungsbericht
Published by: Berufsgenossenschaft fuer Gesundheitsdienst und Wohlfahrtspflege, Pappelallee 35-37, Hamburg, 22089, Germany. TEL 49-40-202070, FAX 49-40-202072495, webmaster@bgw-online.de, http://www.bgw-online.de.

658.3 USA ISSN 1091-2894
KF3563
B N A'S SAFETYNET. (Bureau of National Affairs) Text in English. 1996 (Oct.). bi-w. looseleaf. USD 396 (effective 2010 - 2011). index. 8 p./no.; back issues avail. **Document type:** *Newsletter, Trade.* **Description:** Features reviews of workplace safety and health regulations, policies and trends.
Related titles: Online - full text ed.: ISSN 1533-337X. USD 448 (effective 2010 - 2011); ◆ Series of: B N A Policy and Practice Series. ISSN 0005-3228.
—**CCC.**
Published by: The Bureau of National Affairs, Inc., 1801 S Bell St, Arlington, VA 22202. TEL 703-341-3000, 800-372-1033, FAX 703-341-4634, bnaplus@bna.com.

658.31244 CZE ISSN 1801-3724
B O Z P & P O AKTUALNE. (Bezpecnost a Ochrana Zdravi pri Praci a Pozarni Ochrana) Text in Czech. 2005. base vol. plus m. updates. CZK 3,190 base vol(s). (effective 2009). **Document type:** *Trade.*
Related titles: Online - full text ed.: CZK 5,940 (effective 2009).
Published by: Verlag Dashoefer s.r.o., Na Prikope 18, PO Box 756, Prague 1, 11121, Czech Republic. TEL 420-224-197333, FAX 420-224-197555, info@dashofer.cz.

617.03 CAN ISSN 1206-6826
BACK TO WORK. Text in English. 1997. m. CAD 249 domestic; USD 249 foreign (effective 2008). adv. **Document type:** *Newsletter, Trade.* **Description:** Dedicated to providing cost-effective strategies for managing employee rehabilitation and return-to-work.
Related titles: Online - full content ed.

Published by: Business Information Group, 12 Concorde Pl, Ste 800, Toronto, ON M3C 4J2, Canada. TEL 416-442-2122, 800-668-2374, FAX 416-442-2191.

363.11 613.62 FIN ISSN 1455-8459
RC963.A1
BARENTS NEWSLETTER ON OCCUPATIONAL HEALTH AND SAFETY. Text in English, Russian. 1998. 3/yr. free (effective 2005). back issues avail. **Document type:** *Newsletter, Trade.* **Description:** Reports on issues of concern to persons involved in occupational safety and health.
Related titles: Online - full text ed.: ISSN 1458-5952. 1998.
Indexed: C06, C07.
Published by: Tyoterveyslaitos/Finnish Institute of Occupational Health, Topeliuksenkatu 41a A, Helsinki, 00250, Finland. TEL 358-30-4741, FAX 358-30-4742779. Eds. Marjanna Mattila, Suvi Lehtinen.

658.31244 DEU ISSN 1615-0333
BAU - B G AKTUELL (HANNOVER). (Berufsgenossenschaft) Text in German. 1976. q. free to members (effective 2009). adv. bk.rev. back issues avail. **Document type:** *Newspaper, Trade.*
Former titles (until 2000): Sicher Bauen (0944-7784); (until 1993): Bau-Berufsgenossenschaft Hannover. Mitteilungsblatt (0931-2862)
Published by: Bau-Berufsgenossenschaft Hannover, Hildesheimer Str 309, Hannover, 30519, Germany. TEL 49-511-9870, FAX 49-511-9872440, info-2@bgbau.de, http://www.bgbau.de/d/pages/wir/region/hochbau/hannover/index.html. Circ: 76,000.

613.62 DEU ISSN 1615-3804
BAU - B G AKTUELL (WUPPERTAL). (Berufsgenossenschaft) Text in German. 1949. q. free to members (effective 2009). **Document type:** *Magazine, Trade.*
Formerly (until 2000): Bau (0341-096X)
Published by: Bau-Berufsgenossenschaft Rheinland und Westfalen, Viktoriastr 21, Wuppertal, 42115, Germany. TEL 49-202-3980, FAX 49-202-3981404, info-3@bgbau.de, http://www.bgbau.de.

BERUFSGENOSSENSCHAFT FUER GESUNDHEITSDIENST UND WOHLFAHRTSPFLEGE. MITTEILUNGEN. *see* INSURANCE

613.62 DEU ISSN 0933-4289
BERUFSKRANKHEITENVERORDNUNG. Text in German. 1977. base vol. plus updates 2/yr. looseleaf. EUR 68 base vol(s).; EUR 34.80 updates per issue (effective 2009). **Document type:** *Monographic series, Trade.*
Published by: Erich Schmidt Verlag GmbH & Co. (Berlin), Genthiner Str 30 G, Berlin, 10785, Germany. TEL 49-30-2500850, FAX 49-30-250085305, vertrieb@esvmedien.de, http://www.erich-schmidt-verlag.de.

613.62 CAN
BEST OF HEALTH IN THE WORKPLACE. Text in English. 1988. a. CAD 40 per issue domestic; USD 33.89 per issue foreign (effective 2005). 60 p./no.; **Description:** Presents a national perspective on topical workplace health and safety issues; helps to learn how some of the top manufacturing and service companies handle them. Methods and strategies that can be put to work to protect personal and corporate interests.
Formerly: Health in the Workplace (0842-2559)
Published by: Carswell (Subsidiary of: Thomson Reuters Corp.), One Corporate Plz, 2075 Kennedy Rd, Toronto, ON M1T 3V4, Canada. TEL 416-609-8000, 800-387-5164, FAX 416-298-5094, carswell.customerrelations@thomson.com, http://www.carswell.com. Ed. Laurie Blake.

BETRIEBSPRAXIS & ARBEITSFORSCHUNG. *see* BUSINESS AND ECONOMICS—Labor And Industrial Relations

613.62 RUS ISSN 0409-2961
TN295 CODEN: BZTPAM
➤ **BEZOPASNOST' TRUDA V PROMYSHLENNOSTI/LABOUR SAFETY IN INDUSTRY.** Text in Russian. 1932. m. USD 200 foreign (effective 2007). adv. **Document type:** *Journal, Academic/Scholarly.* **Description:** Covers a wide variety of themes relevant to industrial production and safety.
Indexed: CIN, ChemAb, ChemTitl, GeoRef, RASB, RefZh, SCOPUS, SpeleolAb.
—CASDDS, East View, INIST. **CCC.**
Published by: Promyshlennaya Bezopasnost', Luk'yanova ul 4, korp 8, kom 310, Moscow, 105066, Russian Federation. Ed. S N Buinovskii. Pub. V I Sidorov. Adv. contact N Yu Solenikova. Circ: 25,000 (paid and controlled). **Dist. by:** East View Information Services, 10601 Wayzata Blvd, Minneapolis, MN 55305. TEL 952-252-1201, 800-477-1005, FAX 952-252-1202, info@eastview.com, http://www.eastview.com.

658.31244 SVK ISSN 0322-8347
BEZPECNA PRACA. Text in Czech, Slovak; Summaries in English, German, Russian. 1969. bi-m. EUR 45 (effective 2010). **Document type:** *Journal, Academic/Scholarly.* **Description:** Deals with theory and praxis of occupational safety.
Related titles: CD-ROM ed.; E-mail ed.; Fax ed.
Indexed: CISA, RASB.
Published by: Ministerstvo Prace, Socialnych Veci a Rodiny Slovenskej Republiky, Vyskumny a Vzdelavaci Ustav Bezpecnosti Prace/Ministry of Labor, Social Affairs and Family of the Slovak Republic, Research Institute of Work Security, Trnavska cesta 57, Bratislava, 81435, Slovakia. TEL 421-2-57291109, FAX 421-2-57291171. Ed. Anastazia Bezakova. **Dist. by:** Slovart G.T.G. s.r.o., Krupinska 4, PO Box 152, Bratislava 85299, Slovakia. TEL 421-2-63839472, FAX 421-2-63839485, info@slovart-gtg.sk, http://www.slovart-gtg.sk.

613.62 CZE ISSN 0006-0453
BEZPECNOST A HYGIENA PRACE/SAFETY AND HYGIENE OF WORK. Text in Czech. 1951. m. CZK 1,026 (effective 2008). adv. bk.rev. **Document type:** *Magazine, Consumer.*
Indexed: CISA.
Published by: ASPI, a. s., U Nakladoveho nadrazi 6, Prague 3, 13000, Czech Republic. TEL 420-246040400, FAX 420-246040401, obchod@aspi.cz, http://www.aspi.cz. Circ: 48,000.

613.62 POL ISSN 0137-7043
HD7727.7
➤ **BEZPIECZENSTWO PRACY;** nauka i praktyka. Text in Polish; Summaries in English, Polish. 1971. m. EUR 91 per quarter foreign (effective 2006). adv. Website rev.; bk.rev. abstr.; bibl.; charts; illus. 32 p./no. 2 cols./p.; back issues avail.; reprints avail. **Document type:** *Journal, Academic/Scholarly.* **Description:** Covers occupational safety and ergonomics.
Indexed: AgrLib.
Published by: Centralny Instytut Ochrony Pracy/Central Institute for Labour Protection, Ul Czerniakowska 16, Warsaw, 00701, Poland. TEL 48-22-6234601, FAX 48-22-6233693, oinip@ciop.pl, http://www.ciop.pl. Ed. Wiktor Zawieska. Adv. contact Barbara Szczepankowska. Circ: 2,500 (controlled). **Dist. by:** Ars Polona, Obroncow 25, Warsaw 03933, Poland. TEL 48-22-5098609, FAX 48-22-5098610, arspolona@arspolona.com.pl, http://www.arspolona.com.pl.

613.62 DEU ISSN 0930-195X
BIOLOGISCHE ARBEITSSTOFF TOLERANZ WERTE UND EXPOSITIONSAEQUIVALENTE FUER KREBSERZEUGENDE ARBEITSSTOFFE. Text in German. 1983. irreg., latest vol.16, 2009. price varies. **Document type:** *Monographic series, Academic/Scholarly.*
Published by: (Deutsche Forschungsgemeinschaft), Wiley - V C H Verlag GmbH & Co. KGaA (Subsidiary of: John Wiley & Sons, Inc.), Postfach 101161, Weinheim, 69451, Germany. TEL 49-6201-606400, FAX 49-6201-606184, subservice@wiley-vch.de, http://www.wiley-vch.de. Ed. Hans Drexler. Circ: 600 (controlled).

BOIRA KUREN YOUSETSU NO JITSU TEN. *see* MACHINERY

BOLETIN TECNICO DE ERGONOMIA. *see* ENGINEERING—Engineering Mechanics And Materials

613.62 GBR ISSN 0266-6936
BRITISH OCCUPATIONAL HYGIENE SOCIETY. TECHNICAL GUIDE SERIES. Text in English. 1984. irreg., latest vol.15, 2009. back issues avail. **Document type:** *Monographic series, Academic/Scholarly.*
Related titles: Online - full text ed.
Published by: British Occupational Hygiene Society, 5/6 Melbourne Business Ct, Millennium Way, Pride Park, Derby, DE24 8LZ, United Kingdom. TEL 44-1332-298101, FAX 44-1332-298099, admin@bohs.org.

658.382 GBR
BRITISH SAFETY COUNCIL GUIDES. Text in English. 19??. m. (11/yr.). GBP 60 to non-members; GBP 40 to members (effective 2010). **Document type:** *Handbook/Manual/Guide, Consumer.* **Description:** Designed to help maintain safety attitudes and develop a safety culture in the workplace.
Published by: British Safety Council, 70 Chancellors Rd, London, W6 9RS, United Kingdom. TEL 44-20-87411231, FAX 44-20-87414555, mail@britsafe.org.

BRUECKE; Informationen fuer Arbeitssicherheit und Gesundheitsschutz. *see* TEXTILE INDUSTRIES AND FABRICS

BUNDESAMT FUER STRAHLENSCHUTZ. SCHRIFTEN. *see* ENERGY—Nuclear Energy

613.82 DEU ISSN 1433-2086
BUNDESANSTALT FUER ARBEITSSCHUTZ UND ARBEITSMEDIZIN. SCHRIFTENREIHE FORSCHUNG. Text in German. 1997. a. EUR 22.50 per issue (effective 2010). **Document type:** *Monographic series, Academic/Scholarly.*
Formed by the merger of (199?-1997): Bundesanstalt fuer Arbeitsmedizin. Schriftenreihe Forschung (0944-9191); (19??-1997): Bundesanstalt fuer Arbeitsschutz. Schriftenreihe Forschung (0932-3856); Which was formerly (until 1985): Bundesanstalt fuer Arbeitsschutz. Forschungsbericht (0932-3813); (until 1983): Bundesanstalt fuer Arbeitsschutz und Unfallforschung. Forschungsbericht (0340-5915)
Indexed: TM.
Published by: (Germany. Bundesanstalt fuer Arbeitsschutz und Arbeitsmedizin), Wirtschaftsverlag N W - Verlag fuer Neue Wissenschaft GmbH, Buergermeister-Smidt-Str 74-76, Bremerhaven, 27568, Germany. TEL 49-471-945440, FAX 49-471-9454477, info@nw-verlag.de, http://www.nw-verlag.de.

613.62 DEU
BUNDESANSTALT FUER ARBEITSSCHUTZ UND ARBEITSMEDIZIN. SCHRIFTENREIHE FORSCHUNGSANWENDUNG. Text in German. 1985. irreg., latest vol.61, 2005. price varies. **Document type:** *Monographic series, Academic/Scholarly.*
Formerly: Bundesanstalt fuer Arbeitsschutz. Schriftenreihe Forschungsanwendung (0932-4836)
Published by: (Germany. Bundesanstalt fuer Arbeitsschutz und Arbeitsmedizin), Wirtschaftsverlag N W - Verlag fuer Neue Wissenschaft GmbH, Buergermeister-Smidt-Str 74-76, Bremerhaven, 27568, Germany. TEL 49-471-945440, FAX 49-471-9454477, info@nw-verlag.de, http://www.nw-verlag.de.

613.62 DEU
BUNDESANSTALT FUER ARBEITSSCHUTZ UND ARBEITSMEDIZIN. SCHRIFTENREIHE GEFAEHRLICHE ARBEITSSTOFFE. Text in German. 1981. irreg., latest vol.66, 2006. price varies. **Document type:** *Monographic series, Academic/Scholarly.*
Former titles: Bundesanstalt fuer Arbeitsschutz. Schriftenreihe Gefaehrliche Arbeitsstoffe (0932-4712); (until 1984): Schriftenreihe Gefaehrliche Arbeitsstoffe (0932-4704)
Related titles: Online - full text ed.
Published by: (Germany. Bundesanstalt fuer Arbeitsschutz und Arbeitsmedizin), Wirtschaftsverlag N W - Verlag fuer Neue Wissenschaft GmbH, Buergermeister-Smidt-Str 74-76, Bremerhaven, 27568, Germany. TEL 49-471-945440, FAX 49-471-9454477, info@nw-verlag.de, http://www.nw-verlag.de.

613.62 DEU
BUNDESANSTALT FUER ARBEITSSCHUTZ UND ARBEITSMEDIZIN. SCHRIFTENREIHE REGELWERKE. Text in German. 1976. irreg., latest vol.31, 2005. price varies. **Document type:** *Monographic series, Academic/Scholarly.*
Former titles: Bundesanstalt fuer Arbeitsschutz. Schriftenreihe Regelwerke (0932-478X); (until 1987): Schriftenreihe Regelwerke Arbeitsschutz (0173-2013)
Related titles: Online - full text ed.
Published by: (Germany. Bundesanstalt fuer Arbeitsschutz und Arbeitsmedizin), Wirtschaftsverlag N W - Verlag fuer Neue Wissenschaft GmbH, Buergermeister-Smidt-Str 74-76, Bremerhaven, 27568, Germany. TEL 49-471-945440, FAX 49-471-9454477, info@nw-verlag.de, http://www.nw-verlag.de.

613.62 DEU
BUNDESANSTALT FUER ARBEITSSCHUTZ UND ARBEITSMEDIZIN. SCHRIFTENREIHE SONDERSCHRIFTEN. Text in German. 1977. irreg., latest vol.87, 2007. price varies. **Document type:** *Monographic series, Academic/Scholarly.*
Former titles: Bundesanstalt fuer Arbeitsschutz. Schriftenreihe Sonderschrift (0932-481X); (until 1985): Bundesanstalt fuer Arbeitsschutz. Sonderschrift (0932-4976); (until 1984): Bundesanstalt fuer Arbeitsschutz und Unfallforschung. Sonderschrift (0932-4984)
Published by: (Germany. Bundesanstalt fuer Arbeitsschutz und Arbeitsmedizin), Wirtschaftsverlag N W - Verlag fuer Neue Wissenschaft GmbH, Buergermeister-Smidt-Str 74-76, Bremerhaven, 27568, Germany. TEL 49-471-945440, FAX 49-471-9454477, info@nw-verlag.de, http://www.nw-verlag.de.

613.62 DEU
BUNDESANSTALT FUER ARBEITSSCHUTZ UND ARBEITSMEDIZIN. SCHRIFTENREIHE TAGUNGSBERICHT. Text in German. 1973. irreg., latest vol.143, 2005. price varies. **Document type:** *Monographic series, Academic/Scholarly.*
Former titles: Bundesanstalt fuer Arbeitsschutz. Schriftenreihe Tagungsbericht (0932-4828); (until 1984): Schriftenreihe Arbeitsschutz (0341-9819)
Related titles: Online - full text ed.
Published by: (Germany. Bundesanstalt fuer Arbeitsschutz und Arbeitsmedizin), Wirtschaftsverlag N W - Verlag fuer Neue Wissenschaft GmbH, Buergermeister-Smidt-Str 74-76, Bremerhaven, 27568, Germany. TEL 49-471-945440, FAX 49-471-9454477, info@nw-verlag.de, http://www.nw-verlag.de.

613 IRL ISSN 1393-8797
BUSINESS HEALTH. Text in English. m. **Document type:** *Magazine, Trade.*
Former titles (until 2000): Health & Safety (0791-8380); (until 1988): Sciath (0791-1602)
Published by: Jude Publications Ltd., 9 Nth Frederick St, Dublin, 2, Ireland. TEL 353-1-6713500, FAX 353-1-6713074. Pub. Anne-Marie Moran.

613 USA ISSN 2153-0270
▼ **C A O W I NEWS.** Text in English. 2009 (Jan.). m. free to members (effective 2011). **Document type:** *Newsletter, Trade.* **Description:** Features news and information from the California Association of Workplace Investigators.
Formerly announced: C A O W I Quarterly
Related titles: Online - full text ed.: free (effective 2011).
Published by: California Association of Workplace Investigators, 770 L St, Ste 950, Sacramento, CA 95814. TEL 916-760-2442, info@caowi.org.

C K C REPORT. *see* HOME ECONOMICS

613.62 BEL ISSN 1780-7867
C N A C INFO. (Comite Nationale d'Action pour la Securite et l'Hygiene dans la Construction) Text in French. 1967. q.
Former titles (until 2004): Securite Construction (1780-7239); (until 1977): Objectif Prevention (0771-2634); (until 1970): Attention Feu Rouge (0771-923X)
Related titles: ◆ Dutch ed.: N A V B Info. ISSN 1780-7875.
Published by: Nationaal Actiecomite voor Veiligheid en Hygiene in het Bouwbedrijf (NAVB)/Comite National d'Action pour la Securite et l'Hygiene dans la Construction (CNAC), Rue Saint-Jean 4, Bruxelles, 1000, Belgium. TEL 32-2-552-0500, FAX 32-2-552-0505, publications@cnac.be. Circ: 27,000.

613.62 620 USA
C S P DIRECTORY AND INTERNATIONAL REGISTRY OF CERTIFIED SAFETY PROFESSIONALS. Text in English. 1975. biennial. USD 60 (effective 2000). adv. **Document type:** *Directory.* **Description:** Lists certified individuals by location, examination passed, services offered and areas of expertise.
Formerly: C S P Directory
Related titles: CD-ROM ed.: USD 250 (effective 2000).
Published by: Board of Certified Safety Professionals, 208 Barwash Ave, Savoy, IL 61874. TEL 217-359-9263. Circ: 13,000.

CAIKUANG YU ANQUAN GONGCHENG XUEBAO/JOURNAL OF MINING AND SAFETY ENGINEERING. *see* MINES AND MINING INDUSTRY

613.62 USA ISSN 1054-1209
KFC579.A6
CAL - O S H A REPORTER; credible authoritative trustworthy. (Occupational Safety and Health Administration) Text in English. 1973. w. (48/yr.). looseleaf. USD 427 (effective 2010). adv. bk.rev. index. back issues avail. **Document type:** *Newsletter, Trade.* **Description:** Written for occupational safety and health practitioners primarily in California. Covers job safety and health, workers' compensation, toxics, risk management and other related issues. Provides detailed coverage of laws, regulations and complete summaries of all related court cases.
Former titles: California - O S H A Reporter; Cal - O S H A Reporter
Related titles: Online - full text ed.
Published by: Providence Publications, LLC, PO Box 2610, Granite Bay, CA 95746. TEL 916-774-4000, FAX 916-780-0600, http://www.provpubs.com. Ed. Kevin Thompson.

344 613.62 CAN
CANADIAN EMPLOYMENT SAFETY AND HEALTH GUIDE. Text in English. m. CAD 1,550 (effective 2008). **Document type:** *Handbook/Manual/Guide, Trade.* **Description:** Reports on federal and provincial legislation on employment safety and health plus relevant case law.
Related titles: CD-ROM ed.: CAD 1,550 (effective 2008); Online - full text ed.: ISSN 1910-1694. CAD 1,550 (effective 2008).
Published by: C C H Canadian Ltd. (Subsidiary of: Wolters Kluwer N.V.), 90 Sheppard Ave E, Ste 300, North York, ON M2N 6X1, Canada. TEL 416-224-2248, 800-268-4522, FAX 416-224-2243, 800-461-4131, cservice@cch.ca.

CANADIAN MINING JOURNAL. *see* MINES AND MINING INDUSTRY

614.8 CAN ISSN 0709-5252
CANADIAN OCCUPATIONAL HEALTH & SAFETY NEWS. Abbreviated title: C O H S N. Text in English. 1978. w. (50/yr.). CAD 399 domestic; USD 399 foreign (effective 2008). adv. q. index. back issues avail. **Document type:** *Newsletter, Trade.* **Description:** Contains the latest legislative and regulatory changes, new techniques and technology, calendars of forthcoming conferences and workshops and WHMIS updates.
Formerly: Canadian Industrial Health and Safety News (0701-8983)
Related titles: Online - full text ed.

Published by: Business Information Group, 12 Concorde Pl, Ste 800, Toronto, ON M3C 4J2, Canada. TEL 416-442-2122, 800-668-2374, FAX 416-442-2191, http://www.businessinformationgroup.ca. Ed. Angela Stelmakowich TEL 416-510-5121. Pub. Peter Boxer TEL 416-510-5102. Adv. contact Sheila Hemsley TEL 416-510-5105.

658.31244 CAN ISSN 0008-4611
CANADIAN OCCUPATIONAL SAFETY. Text in English. 1963. 6/yr. CAD 64 domestic; USD 64 in United States; USD 96 elsewhere (effective 2008). adv. **Document type:** *Magazine, Trade.* **Description:** Informs and educates Canadian safety professionals on a wide variety of safety topics, practices and concerns in today's workplace.
Formerly (until 1964): Canadian Occupational Safety Magazine (0315-1611)
Related titles: Online - full text ed.
Indexed: A22, C03, C06, CBCABus, CSNB, L12, P48, PQC.
—BLDSC (3043.140000), CIS, IE, Ingenta. **CCC.**
Published by: C L B Media, Inc. (Subsidiary of: Canada Law Book Inc.), 240 Edward St, Aurora, ON L4G 3S9, Canada. TEL 905-727-0077, FAX 905-727-0017, http://www.clbmedia.ca. Ed. Todd Phillips. Pub. Cocoe Horsley. Circ: 13,500 (controlled).

CESKE PRACOVNI LEKARSTVI/CZECH JOURNAL OF OCCUPATIONAL MEDICINE. *see* MEDICAL SCIENCES

CHEMIEKAARTEN; gegevens voor veilig werken met chemicalien. *see* CHEMISTRY

CHILD LABOR MONITOR (ONLINE). *see* CHILDREN AND YOUTH—About

614.8 CHL ISSN 0718-0306
➤ **CIENCIA & TRABAJO.** Variant title: C & T. Text in English, Spanish, Portuguese. 1999. q. free (effective 2011). bibl.; charts; illus. Index. back issues avail. **Document type:** *Journal, Academic/Scholarly.* **Description:** The purpose of this journal is to spread scientific knowledge on working conditions among occupational health related professionals and workers. The journal receives educational, review and research articles on occupational health and safety, industrial hygiene, environmental health, ergonomy, and other sciences related to work.
Formerly (until 2003): Asociacion Chilena de Seguridad. Boletin Cientifico (0717-4586)
Related titles: Online - full text ed.: ISSN 0718-2449. 2001.
Indexed: F04, T02.
Published by: Fundacion Cientifica y Tecnologica de la Asociacion Chilena de Seguridad, Vicuna Mackenna 210, piso 6, Providencia, Chile. Ed. Victor Olivares. Circ: 1,000 (controlled).

➤ **CLEANROOM TECHNOLOGY.** *see* ENGINEERING

➤ **COLLANA DI DIRITTO COMPARATO E COMUNITARIO DEL LAVORO E DELLA SICUREZZA SOCIALE.** *see* LAW

658.31244 CAN ISSN 1715-4189
CONFINED SPACE ENTRY PROGRAM. Text in English. 2005. irreg. **Document type:** *Monographic series, Trade.*
Published by: WorkSafeB C, PO Box 5350, Stn Terminal, Vancouver, BC V6B 5L5, Canada. TEL 604-276-3100, 888-621-7233, http://www.worksafebc.com/default.asp.

613.62 USA
CONN - O S H A QUARTERLY (EMAIL). Text in English. 1994. q. free (effective 2008). **Document type:** *Magazine, Government.*
Formerly (until 2003): CONN - O S H A Quarterly (Print)
Media: E-mail.
Published by: Connecticut Department of Labor, Division of Occupational Safety and Health, 200 Folly Brook Blvd, Wethersfield, CT 06109. TEL 860-263-6000, dol.webhelp@ct.gov, http://www.ctdol.state.ct.us/osha/osha.htm.

658.31244 654 USA ISSN 1533-4759
THE CONSTRUCTION FOREMAN'S GUIDE TO O S H A REGULATIONS. (Occupational Health and Safety Administration) Text in English. 2000. bi-w. USD 195 (effective 2008). back issues avail. **Document type:** *Newsletter, Trade.* **Description:** Assists construction job-site foremen in the understanding of and compliance with over 500 OSHA regulations covering the construction business.
Published by: Clement Communications, Inc., 10 LaCrue Ave, PO Box 36, Concordville, PA 19331. TEL 610-459-4200, 888-358-5858, FAX 610-459-4582, 800-459-1933, customerservice@clement.com. Pub. George Y Clement.

CRONER'S DANGEROUS SUBSTANCES. *see* ENGINEERING—Chemical Engineering

613.62 363.11 340.5 GBR
CRONER'S HEALTH AND SAFETY CASE LAW. Text in English. 1984. base vol. plus q. updates. looseleaf. **Document type:** *Handbook/Manual/Guide, Trade.* **Description:** Deals with all areas of U.K. health and safety case law. Compiles and interprets recent and important legal decisions in the health and safety field.
Related titles: CD-ROM ed.: GBP 585 combined subscription (online & CD-ROM eds.) (effective 2010); Online - full text ed.; ◆ Supplement(s): Health and Safety Case Law Newsletter. ISSN 2042-2253.
Published by: Croner C C H Group Ltd. (Subsidiary of: Wolters Kluwer UK Ltd.), 145 London Rd, Kingston upon Thames, Surrey KT2 6SR, United Kingdom. TEL 44-20-85473333, FAX 44-20-85472638, info@croner.co.uk.

613.62 363.11 GBR ISSN 1352-5611
CRONER'S HEALTH & SAFETY MANAGER. Variant title: Health & Safety Manager. Text in English. 1994. base vol. plus updates 3/yr. looseleaf. GBP 487; GBP 778.99 combined subscription (print, online & CD-ROM eds.) (effective 2010). **Document type:** *Handbook/Manual/Guide, Trade.* **Description:** Provides information to assist with building and maintaining an effective safety culture within organizations.
Related titles: CD-ROM ed.: GBP 640 (effective 2010); Online - full text ed.: GBP 585 (effective 2010).
Published by: Croner C C H Group Ltd. (Subsidiary of: Wolters Kluwer UK Ltd.), 145 London Rd, Kingston upon Thames, Surrey KT2 6SR, United Kingdom. TEL 44-20-85473333, FAX 44-20-85472638, info@croner.co.uk.

613.62 658.31244 GBR
CRONER'S OFFICE HEALTH & SAFETY. Text in English. base vol. plus s-a. updates. looseleaf. GBP 585 combined subscription (print & CD-ROM eds.) (effective 2010). **Document type:** *Handbook/Manual/Guide, Trade.* **Description:** Provides information on health and safety legislation within the office environment, giving necessary practical advice.
Former titles: Office Health & Safety Briefing (0968-6606); Croner's Health and Safety at Work
Related titles: CD-ROM ed.; Diskette ed.
Indexed: WSCA.
Published by: Croner C C H Group Ltd. (Subsidiary of: Wolters Kluwer UK Ltd.), 145 London Rd, Kingston upon Thames, Surrey KT2 6SR, United Kingdom. TEL 44-20-85473333, FAX 44-20-85472638, info@croner.co.uk.

613.62 GBR
CRONER'S SUBSTANCES HAZARDOUS TO HEALTH. Text in English. 1986. base vol. plus q. updates. looseleaf. GBP 610; GBP 980.01 combined subscription (print & CD-ROM eds.) (effective 2010). **Document type:** *Handbook/Manual/Guide, Trade.* **Description:** Provides a practical guide to the assessment, measurement, and control of specific hazardous substances.
Related titles: CD-ROM ed.: GBP 927 (effective 2010).
Published by: Croner C C H Group Ltd. (Subsidiary of: Wolters Kluwer UK Ltd.), 145 London Rd, Kingston upon Thames, Surrey KT2 6SR, United Kingdom. TEL 44-20-85473333, FAX 44-20-85472638, info@croner.co.uk.

613.62 USA
RC963.A1
CURRENT OCCUPATIONAL & ENVIRONMENTAL MEDICINE. Text in English. 1990. triennial, latest 2006, 4th ed. USD 72.95 per vol. (effective 2010). **Document type:** *Monographic series, Trade.* **Description:** Offers the definitive overview of common occupational and environmental illnesses, covering their diagnosis and treatment-plus preventive and remedial measures in the workplace and community.
Former titles (until 2004): Occupational & Environmental Medicine (1097-9212); (until 1997): Occupational Medicine (1047-4498)
Indexed: GeoRef.
Published by: McGraw-Hill Education (Subsidiary of: McGraw-Hill Companies, Inc.), 148 Princeton-Hightstown Rd, Hightstown, NJ 08520. TEL 609-426-5793, FAX 609-426-7917, customer.service@mcgraw-hill.com, http://www.mheducation.com/.

613.62 362.1 AUS ISSN 1832-8016
CUSTOMER CIRCULAR. Text in English. 1995. irreg. free (effective 2008). back issues avail. **Document type:** *Bulletin, Consumer.* **Description:** Provides advice on changes to the Safety, Rehabilitation and Compensation Act 1988 (SRC Act).
Media: Online - full text.
Published by: Comcare, GPO Box 9905, Canberra, ACT 2601, Australia. TEL 300-366-979, FAX 61-2-62575634, ohs.help@comcare.gov.au.

371.42 CHN ISSN 1009-6353
DATONG ZHIYE JISHU XUEYUAN XUEBAO/DATONG VOCATIONAL COLLEGE. JOURNAL. Text in Chinese. 1987. q. CNY 7 newsstand/cover (effective 2006). **Document type:** *Journal, Academic/Scholarly.*
Formerly (until 2000): Datong Gaodeng Zhuanke Xuexiao Xuebao/Datong College. Journal (1009-2110)
Published by: Datong Zhiye Jishu Xueyuan, 1, Xiangyang Dong Jie, Datong, 037008, China. TEL 86-352-5102501.

DELO + VARNOST; revija za varstvo pri delu. *see* BUSINESS AND ECONOMICS—Labor And Industrial Relations

613.62 DEU ISSN 0177-7580
CODEN: RCHFEJ
DEUTSCHE FORSCHUNGSGEMEINSCHAFT, COMMISSION FOR THE INVESTIGATION OF HEALTH HAZARDS OF CHEMICAL COMPOUNDS IN THE WORK AREA. REPORT. Variant title: Maximum Concentrations at the Workplace and Biological Tolerance Values for Working Materials. Text in English. 1979. a. EUR 37.90 (effective 2009). **Document type:** *Monographic series, Trade.*
Related titles: German ed.: Deutsche Forschungsgemeinschaft. Senatskommission zur Pruefung Gesundheitsschaedlicher Arbeitsstoffe. Mitteilungen. ISSN 0417-1810.
—**CCC.**
Published by: (Deutsche Forschungsgemeinschaft), Wiley - V C H Verlag GmbH & Co. KGaA (Subsidiary of: John Wiley & Sons, Inc.), Postfach 101161, Weinheim, 69451, Germany. TEL 49-6201-606400, FAX 49-6201-606184, info@wiley-vch.de, http://www.wiley-vch.de.

DEUTSCHE GESELLSCHAFT FUER ARBEITSMEDIZIN UND UMWELTMEDIZIN. DOKUMENTATION. *see* PUBLIC HEALTH AND SAFETY

DEVELOPMENTAL DISABILITIES SPECIAL INTEREST SECTION QUARTERLY. *see* PSYCHOLOGY

DICTIONNAIRE PERMANENT: SECURITE ET CONDITIONS DE TRAVAIL. *see* BUSINESS AND ECONOMICS—Labor And Industrial Relations

658.31244 616.9803 FRA ISSN 0339-6517
DOCUMENTS POUR LE MEDECIN DU TRAVAIL. Text in French. 1973. q. free domestic to qualified personnel (effective 2010). bk.rev. index, cum.index. **Document type:** *Bulletin, Government.* **Description:** Scientific and medical publication for occupational medical practitioners.
Indexed: A22, CISA.
—BLDSC (3609.113080), GNLM, IE, Ingenta, INIST.
Published by: (France. France. Ministere de la Sante et de la Securite Sociale), Institut National de Recherche et de Securite pour la Prevention des Accidents du Travail et des Maladies Professionnelles, 30 rue Olivier Noyer, Paris, 75680 Cedex 14, France. TEL 33-1-40443000, FAX 33-1-40443099, thanh@inrs.fr, http://www.inrs.fr. Ed. Anne Delepine. Circ: 12,000.

658.31244 SWE ISSN 1403-9710
DU & JOBBET. Text in Swedish. 1912. 10/yr. SEK 845 (effective 2011). bk.rev. charts; illus. back issues avail. **Document type:** *Magazine, Consumer.*
Former titles (until 1999): Arbetsmiljoe (0003-7834); (until 1970): Arbetarskyddet
Related titles: Online - full text ed.
Indexed: CISA.
—BLDSC (3630.577000).
Published by: Arbetsmiljoeforum i Sverige AB/Swedish Work Environment Association, Laangholmsgatan 34, PO Box 17550, Stockholm, 11891, Sweden. TEL 46-8-4424600, FAX 46-8-4424608, http://www.arbetsmiljoforum.se. Ed. Eva Berlin TEL 46-8-4424624. Circ: 17,800 (controlled).

613.62 363.73 USA
E H & S PRODUCTS. (Environmental, Health & Safety) Text in English. s-a. **Document type:** *Magazine, Trade.* **Description:** Publishes new product information for environmental, health and safety professionals.
Related titles: Online - full content ed.
Published by: 1105 Media Inc., 9121 Oakdale Ave, Ste 101, Chatsworth, CA 91311. TEL 818-734-1520, FAX 818-734-1522, info@1105media.com, http://www.1105media.com.

613.6 363.7 USA ISSN 1546-9026
E H S GLOBAL ALERT. (Environmental Health Safety) Text in English. 2003 (Oct.). m. USD 1,604 2 users (effective 2010 - 2011). **Document type:** *Newsletter, Trade.*
Media: E-mail. **Related titles:** Online - full text ed.
—**CCC.**
Published by: The Bureau of National Affairs, Inc., 1801 S Bell St, Arlington, VA 22202. TEL 703-341-3000, 800-372-1033, FAX 703-341-4634, bnaplus@bna.com.

363.7 USA ISSN 1945-9599
HD7260 CODEN: OCHAAZ
E H S TODAY; the magazine of safety, health and loss prevention. (Environment, Health and Safety Leaders) Text in English. 1938. m. USD 59 domestic; USD 67 in Canada; USD 84 elsewhere; free domestic to qualified personnel (effective 2011). adv. bk.rev. charts; illus.; stat.; tr.lit. index. reprints avail. **Document type:** *Magazine, Trade.* **Description:** News on industrial safety, occupational health, environmental control, insurance, first aid, medical care, and hazardous material control.
Formerly (until 2008): Occupational Hazards (0029-7909)
Related titles: Microform ed.: (from PQC); Online - full text ed.: ISSN 1931-6739.
Indexed: A09, A10, A12, A13, A14, A17, A22, A26, ABIn, ASFA, B01, B02, B04, B06, B07, B08, B09, B11, B15, B16, B17, B18, BPI, BPIA, BRD, BusI, CISA, CSNB, CWI, ChemAb, E04, E05, E07, ESPM, G04, G06, G07, G08, H01, H11, H12, H13, HlthInd, I05, I07, IHD, L12, M01, M02, M06, P02, P05, P07, P10, P13, P16, P19, P20, P21, P26, P34, P48, P52, P53, P54, P56, PMA, PQC, S22, T&II, T02, ToxAb, V02, V03, V04, W01, W02, W03, W05, WorkRelAb.
—BLDSC (3664.730400), IE, Ingenta, Linda Hall. **CCC.**
Published by: Penton Media, Inc., 1300 E 9th St, Cleveland, OH 44114. TEL 216-696-7000, FAX 216-696-3432, information@penton.com, http://www.penton.com. Ed. Sandy Smith TEL 216-931-9464. Pub. Joseph M DiFranco. adv.: B&W page USD 8,890. Circ: 65,000 (paid and controlled).

613.62 USA ISSN 1070-4027
E M F HEALTH REPORT. (Electric and Magnetic Field) Text in English. 1993. bi-m. USD 285 domestic; USD 315 foreign (effective 2010). back issues avail. **Document type:** *Report, Academic/Scholarly.* **Description:** Covers health effects of powerlines, cell phones and medical applications of electric and magnetic field.
Published by: Information Ventures, Incorporated, 42 S 15th St, Ste 700, Philadelphia, PA 19102. TEL 215-569-2300, FAX 215-569-2575, ivi@infoventures.com, http://www.infoventures.com.

E-MAIL NOVINY PRO BEZPECNOST PRACE A POZARNI OCHRANU. *see* FIRE PREVENTION

658.31244 DEU ISSN 1619-5299
EDITION PROFESSIONELL. AUSGABE A: ARBEITSSCHUTZ, GESUNDHEIT, UMWELT. Text in German. 2002. q. adv. **Document type:** *Magazine, Trade.*
Published by: Edition Professionell Chantal Albrecht, Im Ried 4, Malsburg, 79429, Germany. TEL 49-7626-977410, FAX 49-7626-977419, info@ed-pro.de, http://www.ed-pro.de. Ed. Rolf Albrecht. adv.: color page EUR 3,200, B&W page EUR 2,000. Circ: 12,000 (paid and controlled).

EDUCATION SPECIAL INTEREST SECTION QUARTERLY. *see* EDUCATION—Adult Education

EGYPTIAN JOURNAL OF OCCUPATIONAL MEDICINE. *see* MEDICAL SCIENCES

613.62 613.85 USA
EMPLOYER HEALTH REGISTER. Text in English. 2000. a. USD 125 per issue (effective 2000). **Description:** Guide to products and services for employers to improve the health and productivity of their employees.
Published by: Work - Loss Data Institute LLC, 169 Saxony Rd., Ste. 210, Encinitas, CA 92024-6780. Ed. Philip L Denniston.

363.11 346.086 CAN ISSN 1910-3824
EMPLOYERS' GUIDE TO ONTARIO WORKPLACE SAFETY & INSURANCE. Text in English. 1999. irreg. looseleaf. CAD 240 per issue domestic; USD 224.30 per issue in United States (effective 2006). **Document type:** *Handbook/Manual/Guide, Trade.*
Published by: Carswell (Subsidiary of: Thomson Reuters Corp.), One Corporate Plz, 2075 Kennedy Rd, Toronto, ON M1T 3V4, Canada. TEL 416-609-8000, 800-387-5164, FAX 416-298-5094, carswell.customerrelations@thomson.com. Ed. Richard Anstruther.

613 CAN
EMPLOYER'S HEALTH AND SAFETY MANUAL - ONTARIO. Text in English. 1989. 6/yr. looseleaf. CAD 265 domestic; USD 224.58 foreign (effective 2005). back issues avail. **Description:** Provides a complete text of the Occupational Health and Safety Act and amendments, as well as vital information on how to meet its responsibilities and obligations. Includes checklists and sample forms for supervisors and front-line managers.
Published by: Carswell (Subsidiary of: Thomson Reuters Corp.), One Corporate Plz, 2075 Kennedy Rd, Toronto, ON M1T 3V4, Canada. TEL 416-609-8000, 800-387-5164, FAX 416-298-5094, carswell.customerrelations@thomson.com, http://www.carswell.com. Eds. Charles Humphrey, Cheryl Edwards. Circ: 2,800.

N O

331 USA ISSN 0093-1535
KF3568.4
EMPLOYMENT SAFETY AND HEALTH GUIDE. Text in English. 1971. 5 base vols. plus m. updates. looseleaf. USD 1,439 base vol(s). print or online or CD-ROM ed. (effective 2005). **Description:** Provides comprehensive coverage of the legal and practical aspects of job safety and health. Full text of standards, regulations, laws, and executive orders issued by OSHA and MSHA. Includes analysis, official forms and OSHA Field Inspection Reference Manual.
Related titles: CD-ROM ed.; Online - full text ed.
—CCC.
Published by: C C H Inc. (Subsidiary of: Wolters Kluwer N.V.), 2700 Lake Cook Rd, Riverwoods, IL 60015. TEL 847-267-7000, 800-449-6439, cust_serv@cch.com, http://www.cch.com. Ed. Paul Gibson. Pub. Catherine Wolfe.

613.62 GBR ISSN 0142-2979
ENCYCLOPEDIA OF HEALTH & SAFETY AT WORK: LAW AND PRACTICE. Text in English. 1962. 4 base vols. plus updates 3/yr. looseleaf. GBP 609 base vol(s). (effective 2009). **Document type:** *Handbook/Manual/Guide, Trade.* **Description:** Authoritative guide to every aspect of the law relating to the safety, health and welfare of employees.
Formerly (until 1978): Encyclopedia of Factories, Shops and Offices Law and Practice (0142-2960)
Related titles: Supplement(s): Encyclopedia of Health & Safety at Work: Law and Practice. Bulletin.
Published by: Sweet & Maxwell Ltd. (Subsidiary of: Thomson Reuters Corp.), 100 Avenue Rd, London, NW3 3PF, United Kingdom. TEL 44-20-73937000, FAX 44-20-74491144, sweetandmaxwell.customer.services@thomson.com, http://www.sweetandmaxwell.co.uk. Ed. Michael J Goodman. **Subscr. to:** PO Box 1000, Andover SP10 9AF, United Kingdom. TEL 44-20-73938051, sweetandmaxwell.international.queries@thomson.com.

ENCYCLOPEDIE MEDICO-CHIRURGICALE. PATHOLOGIE PROFESSIONNELLE ET DE L'ENVIRONNEMENT. *see* ENVIRONMENTAL STUDIES—Toxicology And Environmental Safety

363.17 GBR ISSN 1470-4439
ENVIRONMENTAL HAZARDS BRIEFING. Text in English. 2000. m. **Document type:** *Journal, Trade.*
Formerly (until 2000): Croner Environmental Hazards Briefing (1362-1874)
—CCC.
Published by: Croner C C H Group Ltd. (Subsidiary of: Wolters Kluwer UK Ltd.), 145 London Rd, Kingston upon Thames, Surrey KT2 6SR, United Kingdom. TEL 44-20-85473333, FAX 44-20-85472638, info@croner.co.uk, http://www.croner.co.uk/.

ERGA. *see* PUBLIC HEALTH AND SAFETY

ERGONOMICS AUSTRALIA. *see* ENGINEERING—Engineering Mechanics And Materials

ERGONOMICS, HUMAN FACTORS AND SAFETY. *see* ENGINEERING

ERGONOMICS NEW ZEALAND. *see* ENGINEERING—Engineering Mechanics And Materials

620 USA
ERGONOMICS NEWS (ONLINE). Text in English. 1995. bi-m. free. **Document type:** *Newsletter, Trade.* **Description:** Designed to help Ergonomists and Safety Managers find the right solutions to a host of ergonomic-related challenges, from manual material handling to office ergonomics.
Formerly: Ergonomics News (Print) (1089-0548)
Media: Online - full text.
—CIS. **CCC.**
Published by: Penton Media, Inc., 1300 E 9th St, Cleveland, OH 44114. TEL 216-696-7000, FAX 216-696-3432, information@penton.com, http://www.penton.com. Ed. Sandy Smith TEL 216-931-9464.

613.62 ZAF ISSN 1010-2728
➤ **ERGONOMICS S A.** Text in English. 1987. s-a. **Document type:** *Journal, Academic/Scholarly.* **Description:** Publishes material relevant to occupational conditions and needs in Southern Africa.
Indexed: C06, C07, CA, ErgAb, ISAP, P20, P24, P48, P50, P52, P54, PQC, T02.
Published by: Ergonomics Society of South Africa, c/o Jon James, Department of Human Kinetics and Ergonomics, Rhodes University, PO Box 94, Grahamstown, 6140, South Africa. TEL 27-46-6038472, FAX 27-46-6223803. Ed. P A Scott.

613.62 FRA ISSN 2108-2650
ETAT DE LA PREVENTION DES RISQUES TECHNOLOGIQUES EN CHAMPAGNE-ARDENNE. Text in French. 199?. a., latest 2009. **Document type:** *Government.*
Formerly (until 2009): Etat de l'Environnement Industriel en Champagne-Ardenne (1289-480X)
Published by: France. Ministere de l'Ecologie, du Developpement Durable, des Transports et du Logement, 40 Boulevard Anatole France, BP 80556, Chalons-en-Champagne, 51022, France. TEL 33-3-51416200, FAX 33-3-51416201, http://www.developpement-durable.gouv.fr.

658.31244 ESP ISSN 1681-0155
T55.A1
EUROPEAN AGENCY FOR SAFETY AND HEALTH AT WORK. ANNUAL REPORT. Text in English. 1997. a. back issues avail. **Document type:** *Yearbook, Government.*
Related titles: CD-ROM ed.: ISSN 1681-6536; Online - full text ed.: ISSN 1681-2611; Finnish ed.: ISSN 1681-0201. 2000; Swedish ed.: ISSN 1681-0228. 2000; German ed.: ISSN 1681-0120. 1999; Greek ed.: ISSN 1681-0139. 1999; Italian ed.: ISSN 1681-0171. 2000; Portuguese ed.: ISSN 1681-0198. 2000; Spanish ed.: ISSN 1681-0090. 1997; Danish ed.: ISSN 1681-0104. 1999; Dutch ed.: ISSN 1681-018X. 2000; French ed.: ISSN 1681-0163. 1997.
—BLDSC (1245.285000).
Published by: European Agency for Safety and Health at Work, Gran Via 33, Bilbao, E-48009, Spain. TEL 34-94-4794360, FAX 34-94-4794383, information@osha.eu.int, http://agency.osha.eu.int/.

658.31244 ESP
EUROPEAN AGENCY FOR SAFETY AND HEALTH AT WORK. CONFERENCE PROCEEDINGS. Text in English. irreg. **Document type:** *Proceedings, Consumer.*
Related titles: Online - full content ed.
Published by: European Agency for Safety and Health at Work, Gran Via 33, Bilbao, E-48009, Spain. TEL 34-94-4794360, FAX 34-94-4794383, information@osha.eu.int.

658.31244 ESP ISSN 1681-2123
T55.A1
EUROPEAN AGENCY FOR SAFETY AND HEALTH AT WORK. FACTS. Variant title: European Agency for Safety and Health at Work. Fact Sheets. Text in English. 1999. irreg. **Document type:** *Newsletter, Consumer.*
Related titles: Online - full content ed.: ISSN 1681-2239. 1999; Danish ed.: ISSN 1681-2093; German ed.: ISSN 1681-2107; Greek ed.: ISSN 1681-2115; Swedish ed.: ISSN 1681-2182; Italian ed.: ISSN 1681-214X; Dutch ed.: ISSN 1681-2158; Portuguese ed.: ISSN 1681-2166; Finnish ed.: ISSN 1681-2174; Spanish ed.: ISSN 1681-2085; French ed.: ISSN 1681-2131.
Indexed: CSNB, L12.
—BLDSC (3864.107593).
Published by: European Agency for Safety and Health at Work, Gran Via 33, Bilbao, E-48009, Spain. TEL 34-94-4794360, FAX 34-94-4794383, information@osha.eu.int.

658.31244 ESP ISSN 1681-4398
HD7694
EUROPEAN AGENCY FOR SAFETY AND HEALTH AT WORK. FORUM. Text in English. 2001. a. back issues avail. **Document type:** *Newsletter, Government.*
Related titles: Online - full content ed.: ISSN 1681-4444; German ed.: ISSN 1681-438X; French ed.: ISSN 1681-4401; Spanish ed.: ISSN 1681-4371.
—CCC.
Published by: European Agency for Safety and Health at Work, Gran Via 33, Bilbao, E-48009, Spain. TEL 34-94-4794360, FAX 34-94-4794383, information@osha.eu.int.

658.31244 ESP ISSN 1608-4144
HD7694
EUROPEAN AGENCY FOR SAFETY AND HEALTH AT WORK. MAGAZINE. Text in English. 2000. s-a. back issues avail. **Document type:** *Monographic series, Trade.* **Description:** Acts as a new forum for discussions on issues of major importance to health and safety at work in the EU.
Related titles: Online - full content ed.; Spanish ed.: ISSN 1608-4152; German ed.: ISSN 1608-4160; French ed.: ISSN 1608-4136.
Indexed: ErgAb.
—BLDSC (5332.703570). **CCC.**
Published by: European Agency for Safety and Health at Work, Gran Via 33, Bilbao, E-48009, Spain. TEL 34-94-4794360, FAX 34-94-4794383, information@osha.eu.int.

EVERYONE'S BACKYARD; the journal of the grassroots environmental movement. *see* ENVIRONMENTAL STUDIES—Waste Management

658.31244 621.3 DEU ISSN 0176-0920
CODEN: EXMADW
EX MAGAZINE. Text in English. 1975. a. free. **Document type:** *Magazine, Trade.* **Description:** For installers and operators of explosion protected electrical installations.
Related titles: Online - full text ed.
Indexed: Inspec.
—Linda Hall.
Published by: R. Stahl Schaltgeraete GmbH, Am Bahnhof 30, Waldenburg, 74638, Germany. TEL 49-7942-9430, FAX 49-7942-9434333, info@stahl.de, http://www.stahl.de.

614.85 NOR ISSN 1890-2677
FAKTA OM ARBEID & HELSE. Text in Norwegian. 2006. 4/yr. free. back issues avail. **Document type:** *Monographic series, Government.*
Related titles: Online - full text ed.: ISSN 1890-2685.
Published by: Statens Arbeidsmiljoeinstitutt/National Institute of Occupational Health, PO Box 8149, Dep, Oslo, 0033, Norway. TEL 47-23-195100, FAX 47-23-195200, stami@stami.no. Ed. Sture Len Bye.

363.11 DNK ISSN 1396-9455
FAKTA OM ARBEJDSMILJOE. Text in Danish. 1969. a. DKK 175 per issue (effective 2008). adv. back issues avail. **Document type:** *Consumer.*
Former titles (until 1996): Arbejdsmiljoe (0905-5010); (until 1989): Sikkerhed (0902-7696); (until 1984): Sikkerhedshaandbogen (0902-770X)
Published by: A O F Danmark/The Workers' Educational Association in Denmark, Teglvaerksgade 27, Copenhagen Oe, 2100, Denmark. TEL 45-39-296066, FAX 45-39-294996, aof@aof-danmark.dk, http://www.aofforlag.dk, http://www.aof-danmark.dk.

FAKTOR ARBEITSSCHUTZ. *see* INSURANCE

622.8 USA ISSN 0193-7987
KF3574.M5
FEDERAL MINE SAFETY AND HEALTH REVIEW COMMISSION DECISIONS. Text in English. 1979. m. USD 116 domestic; USD 162.40 foreign (effective 2005). **Document type:** *Government.*
Related titles: Online - full content ed.: ISSN 1555-1253.
Indexed: MEDOC.
Published by: U.S. Federal Mine Safety and Health Review Commission, 601 New Jersey Ave, NW, Washington, DC 20001. TEL 202-434-9900, FAX 202-434-9944, info@fmshrc.gov. Circ: 300. **Subscr. to:** U.S. Government Printing Office, Superintendent of Documents, PO Box 371954, Pittsburgh, PA 15250. TEL 202-512-1800, FAX 202-512-2250, orders@gpo.gov, http://www.access.gpo.gov.

613.62 FIN ISSN 1237-9263
FINNISH INSTITUTE OF OCCUPATIONAL HEALTH. REVIEWS. Text in English. 1976. irreg. back issues avail. **Document type:** *Monographic series, Trade.*
Formerly (until 1994): Institute of Occupational Health. Reviews (0357-5993)
Related titles: ◆ Finnish ed.: Tyoterveyslaitos. Katsauksia. ISSN 0357-4296.
Published by: Tyoterveyslaitos/Finnish Institute of Occupational Health, Topeliuksenkatu 41a A, Helsinki, 00250, Finland. TEL 358-30-4741, FAX 358-30-4742779.

613 USA
FOCUS ON FEDERAL EMPLOYEE WORK/LIFE AND WELLNESS PROGRAMS. Text in English. 1989. bi-m. **Document type:** *Newsletter, Government.* **Description:** Provides news and developments in federal employee health and fitness programs, counseling, work and family AIDS and drug-free workplace programs.
Formerly (until 2000): Focus on Federal Employee Health and Assistance Programs (1057-994X)
Published by: (U.S. Office of Personnel Management, Office of Public Policy), U.S. Office of Personnel Management, Employee Health Services Branch, 1900 E St, NW, No 7412, Washington, DC 20415. TEL 202-606-1638, FAX 202-606-0967. Ed. Tracey Long. Circ: 2,900 (paid). **Subscr. to:** U.S. Government Printing Office, Superintendent of Documents, PO Box 371954, Pittsburgh, PA 15250. TEL 202-512-1800, FAX 202-512-2250, orders@gpo.gov, http://www.access.gpo.gov.

613.62 363.11 HUN ISSN 1417-1015
FOGLALKOZAS-EGESZSEGUGY. Text in Hungarian. 1997. q. **Document type:** *Journal.*
—BLDSC (3964.276800).
Published by: Munkavedelmi Kutatasi Kozalapitvany/Public Foundation for Research on Occupational Safety, Postafiok 7, Budapest 27, 1281, Hungary. TEL 36-1-3942922, FAX 36-1-3942932, mkk@mkk.org.hu, http://www.mkk.org.hu.

658.31244 DEU ISSN 1013-4506
FORTSCHRITTE IM STRAHLENSCHUTZ. Text in German. 1973. irreg., latest vol.152, 2010. price varies. **Document type:** *Monographic series, Trade.*
Indexed: GeoRef.
—CCC.
Published by: (Fachverband fuer Strahlenschutz e.V.), T Ue V Media GmbH, Am Grauen Stein 1, Cologne, 51105, Germany. TEL 49-221-8063535, FAX 49-221-8063510, tuev-media@de.tuv.com, http://www.tuev-media.de.

658.31244 DEU ISSN 0948-9487
G I T SICHERHEIT UND MANAGEMENT. (Glas und Instrumenten Technik) Variant title: Sicherheit & Management. Text in German. 1992. 10/yr. EUR 102; EUR 14 newsstand/cover (effective 2010). adv. **Document type:** *Journal, Trade.*
Formerly (until 1995): G I T Spezial Arbeitsschutz - Arbeitssicherheit (0942-2374)
Published by: G I T Verlag GmbH (Subsidiary of: Wiley - V C H Verlag GmbH & Co. KGaA), Roesslerstr 90, Darmstadt, 64293, Germany. TEL 49-6151-80900, FAX 49-6151-8090146, info@gitverlag.com. Ed. Steffen Ebert. Adv. contact Claudia Vogel. Circ: 28,281 (paid and controlled).

613.62 JPN
GENERAL GUIDEBOOK ON INDUSTRIAL SAFETY. Text in Japanese. a. JPY 520 (effective 2000). **Description:** Educational and promotional booklet for Japan's annual National Safety Week.
Formerly: Guidebook on Industrial Safety
Published by: Japan Industrial Safety and Health Association, Publishing and Sales Department, 5-35-1 Shiba, Minato-ku, Tokyo, 108-0014, Japan. TEL 81-3-3452-6841, FAX 81-3-3454-8043. Ed. Toru Sasaki.

GERONTOLOGY SPECIAL INTEREST SECTION QUARTERLY. *see* GERONTOLOGY AND GERIATRICS

363.12 NLD ISSN 1389-0050
GEVAARLIJKE LADING. Text in Dutch. 1998. bi-m. EUR 102.50 domestic; EUR 123 foreign; EUR 51.25 to students (effective 2010). adv. **Document type:** *Magazine, Trade.*
Published by: Media Business Press BV, Postbus 8632, Rotterdam, 3009 AP, Netherlands. TEL 31-10-2894075, FAX 31-10-2894076, info@mbp.nl, http://www.mbp.nl/. Ed. Tjitske Gijzen. Pub. Suzanne Wanders. Adv. contact Lian Gebhardt. color page EUR 2,735; trim 210 x 297. Circ: 1,264.

614.85 NLD ISSN 1573-9813
GIDS BEDRIJFSHULPVERLENING. Text in Dutch. 2004. a. EUR 151.50 (effective 2009).
Published by: Kluwer B.V. (Subsidiary of: Wolters Kluwer N.V.), Postbus 4, Alphen aan den Rijn, 2400 MA, Netherlands. TEL 31-172-466633, info@kluwer.nl, http://www.kluwer.nl.

616.98 ITA ISSN 1592-7830
CODEN: GIMLDG
GIORNALE ITALIANO DI MEDICINA DEL LAVORO ED ERGONOMIA. Text in English, Italian; Summaries in English. 1979. q. adv. bk.rev. index, cum.index. back issues avail. **Document type:** *Journal, Academic/Scholarly.* **Description:** Features research papers on various topics of occupational health.
Formerly (until 1997): Giornale Italiano di Medicina del Lavoro (0391-9889)
Related titles: Online - full text ed.
Indexed: A22, ChemAb, DentInd, EMBASE, ErgAb, ExcerpMed, IHD, IndMed, MEDLINE, P30, R10, Reac, SCOPUS.
—BLDSC (4178.231000), CASDDS, GNLM, IE, Ingenta, INIST.
Published by: (Fondazione Salvatore Maugeri), PI-ME Editrice, Via Vigentina 136, Pavia, 27100, Italy. TEL 39-0382-572169, FAX 39-0382-572102, tipografia@pime-editrice.it. Circ: 1,500.

631.62 CHN ISSN 1000-7164
CODEN: GWZHEW
GONGYE WEISHENG YU ZHIYEBIN/INDUSTRIAL HEALTH AND OCCUPATIONAL DISEASES. Text in Chinese. 1983. bi-m. USD 22.80 (effective 2009). **Document type:** *Journal, Trade.*
Related titles: Online - full text ed.
Indexed: A22, CIN, ChemAb, ChemTitl.
—BLDSC (4454.740000), CASDDS, East View, IE, Ingenta.
Published by: (Angang Laodong Weisheng Yanjiusuo), Gongye Weisheng yu Zhiyebin Zazhi Bianweihui, 42, Qianshan Lu, Anshan, 114001, China. TEL 86-412-5537140, FAX 86-412-5513701. **Dist. by:** China International Book Trading Corp, 35 Chegongzhuang Xilu, Haidian District, PO Box 399, Beijing 100044, China. TEL 86-10-68412045, FAX 86-10-68412023, cibtc@mail.cibtc.com.cn, http://www.cibtc.com.cn.

658.3124 USA ISSN 1550-1566
T55.A1
THE GREY HOUSE SAFETY AND SECURITY DIRECTORY. Text in English. 1943. irreg., latest 2008. USD 165 per issue (effective 2008). adv. 1600 p./no.; **Document type:** *Directory, Trade.* **Description:** Provides OSHA Content and support materials for the safety professional.

Former titles (until 2002): Best's Safety and Security Directory (1099-3584); (until 1998): Best's Safety Directory (0090-7480); (until 1973): Best's Environmental Control and Safety Directory (0067-6322); Best's Safety Directory of Safety-Maintenance-Security Products
Related titles: Online - full text ed.
—CCC.
Published by: Grey House Publishing, 4919 Rte 22, PO Box 56, Amenia, NY 12501. TEL 518-789-8700, 800-562-2139, FAX 518-789-0556, customerservice@greyhouse.com. adv.: B&W page USD 4,235, color page USD 4,835; trim 8.375 x 10.875.

613.62 614.85 FRA ISSN 1964-583X
GUIDE DU RESPONSABLE HSE. (Hygiene, Securite et Environnement) Text in French. 2008. base vol. plus updates 2/yr. looseleaf. EUR 501 base vol(s). print & CD-ROM eds. (effective 2010). **Document type:** *Trade.*
Related titles: CD-ROM ed.: ISSN 1954-7196.
Published by: Lamy S.A. (Subsidiary of: Wolters Kluwer France), 1 Rue Eugene et Armand Peugeot, Rueil-Malmaison, 92856 Cedex, France. TEL 33-1-76733000, FAX 33-1-76734809.

613.62 BEL ISSN 1815-3615
HD7260
H E S A NEWSLETTER. (Health and Safety) Text in English. 1996. 3/yr. **Document type:** *Newsletter, Trade.*
Formerly (until 2004): T U T B Newsletter (1027-4693)
Related titles: Online - full content ed.; French ed.: ISSN 1815-3550.
Indexed: CSNB, L12.
Published by: European Trade Union Institute - Research, Education, Health and Safety, Health and Safety Department, 5 Bd du Roi Albert II, Brussels, B-1210, Belgium. TEL 32-2-2240560, FAX 32-2-224-0561, hesa@etui-rehs.org.

658.31244 NOR ISSN 1501-9144
H M S - MAGASINET; bladet for helse, miljoe og sikkerhet. Text in Norwegian. 1999. 6/yr. NOK 540 domestic; NOK 630 elsewhere (effective 2011). **Document type:** *Magazine, Consumer.*
Related titles: Online - full text ed.
Published by: Ask Media AS, PO Box 130, Kirkenaer, 2261, Norway. TEL 47-62-941000, FAX 47-62-948705, http://www.askmedia.no. Ed. Jan Tveita TEL 47-91-123330. Adv. contact Lena Oerbog TEL 47-93-090509.

H S E INFORMATION SHEET. CONSTRUCTION INFORMATION SHEET. *see* BUILDING AND CONSTRUCTION

363.11 GBR ISSN 1471-0463
H S M. (Health and Safety Matters) Text in English. 2000. bi-m. free (effective 2010). **Document type:** *Journal, Trade.* **Description:** Provides information about health and safety.
Related titles: Online - full text ed.
—CCC.
Published by: Western Business Publishing, 33-35 Cantelupe Rd, East Grinstead, RH19 3BE, United Kingdom. TEL 44-1342-314300, FAX 44-1342-333700, ipe.sales@western-bp.co.uk. Ed. Georgina Bisby. Pub. Neill Western.

613.62 NLD ISSN 1874-818X
HANDBOEK ARBEIDSHYGIENE. Text in Dutch. 1994. a. EUR 111.50 (effective 2009).
Formerly (until 2004): Jaarboek Arbo en Binnenmilieu (1381-0030)
Published by: Kluwer B.V. (Subsidiary of: Wolters Kluwer N.V.), Postbus 4, Alphen aan den Rijn, 2400 MA, Netherlands. TEL 31-172-466633, info@kluwer.nl, http://www.kluwer.nl. Ed. H P Pennekamp.

658.31244 USA
HAZARD CONTROL MANAGER. Text in English. s-a. adv. **Document type:** *Newsletter, Trade.* **Description:** Covers the management of safety programs.
Published by: Board of Certified Hazard Control Management, 11900 Parklawn Dr, Ste 451, Rockville, MD 20852. TEL 301-770-2540, FAX 301 770-2183, info@chcm-chsp.org, http://www.chcm-chsp.org/index.html. Ed., Pub., R&P, Adv. contact Harold M Gordon.

658.31244 331.8 GBR ISSN 0267-7296
HAZARDS MAGAZINE. Text in English. 1976. q. GBP 15 domestic to individuals; GBP 20 foreign to individuals; GBP 28 in Europe to institutions; GBP 32 elsewhere to institutions (effective 2009). adv. bk.rev. abstr.; charts; illus.; stat. index. back issues avail. **Document type:** *Magazine, Trade.* **Description:** Aims to help workers organize health and safety concerns through their unions.
Formerly (until 1984): Hazards Bulletin (0140-0525)
Indexed: CSNB, L12.
—BLDSC (4274.451570). **CCC.**
Published by: Hazards Publications Ltd., PO Box 4042, Sheffield, S Yorks S8 2DG, United Kingdom. TEL 44-114-2014265. Ed. Rory O'Neill.

363.11 GBR ISSN 1464-1569
HEALTH AND SAFETY AT WORK. Text in English. 1993. 10/yr. GBP 159 domestic; GBP 189 foreign (effective 2011). **Document type:** *Newsletter, Trade.* **Description:** Covers the latest changes and developments in this ever-changing area, including new legislation in force, important case law and HSE guidance etc. Regular features include health and safety Q&A, and key news items.
Former titles (until 1996): Health & Safety at Work Newsletter (1365-652X); Tolley's Office Health & Safety Practice (1350-1488)
—CCC.
Published by: Bloomsbury Professional Ltd. (Subsidiary of: Bloomsbury Publishing plc), 41-43 Boltro Rd, Haywards Heath, West Sussex RH16 1BJ, United Kingdom. TEL 44-1444-416119, FAX 44-1444-440426, customerservices@bloomsburyprofessional.com. Ed. Susan Ghaiwal.

613.62 363.11 GBR ISSN 1745-2864
HEALTH & SAFETY@ WORK. Text in English. 200?. q. **Document type:** *Magazine, Trade.* **Description:** Contains up-to-date with new/pending legislation and topical employment issues.
—CCC.
Published by: Associa Ltd., North Gate, Northgate, Uppingham, Rutland LE15 9PL, United Kingdom. TEL 44-870-2640202, FAX 44-1572-824651, info@associaemployment.co.uk, http://www.associaemployment.co.uk/.

614 GBR ISSN 0141-8246
HEALTH & SAFETY AT WORK (CROYDON). Abbreviated title: H S W. Text in English. 1978. m. GBP 129 (effective 2010). adv. bk.rev. reprints avail. **Document type:** *Magazine, Trade.* **Description:** Provides incisive news reports and insight into topical occupational health and safety issues.
Related titles: Microform ed.: (from PQC); Online - full text ed.
Indexed: A12, A17, ABIn, ADPA, BMT, BldManAb, BrRB, C&ISA, CBNB, CISA, CSNB, Cadscan, CorrAb, E&CAJ, ErgAb, G08, H11, H12, I05, Inspec, L12, LeadAb, M&MA, P48, P51, P53, P54, PQC, R18, SolStAb, WAA, WSCA, Zincscan.
—BLDSC (4274.869800), GNLM, IE, Infotrieve, Ingenta. **CCC.**
Published by: LexisNexis Butterworths, Halsbury House, 35 Chancery Ln, London, Mddx WC2A 1EL, United Kingdom. TEL 44-20-74002500, FAX 44-20-74002842, customer.services@lexisnexis.co.uk, http://www.lexisnexis.co.uk. Ed. Sarah Grainger TEL 44-20-74002581. Adv. contact Daniel Wild TEL 44-20-82121995. color page GBP 2,125, B&W page GBP 1,580; trim 225 x 297. Circ: 23,051.

613.62 GBR
HEALTH AND SAFETY AT WORK (KINGSTON). Variant title: Croner's Health and Safety at Work. Text in English. 19??. base vol. plus q. updates. looseleaf. GBP 520; GBP 805 combined subscription (print, online & CD-ROM eds.) (effective 2010). **Document type:** *Newsletter, Trade.* **Description:** Contains the health and safety information.
Related titles: CD-ROM ed.: GBP 625.01 (effective 2010); Online - full text ed.: GBP 583 (effective 2010).
Published by: Croner C C H Group Ltd. (Subsidiary of: Wolters Kluwer UK Ltd.), 145 London Rd, Kingston upon Thames, Surrey KT2 6SR, United Kingdom. TEL 44-20-85473333, FAX 44-20-85472638, info@croner.co.uk.

344.204 GBR ISSN 0966-8365
HEALTH & SAFETY AT WORK ACT NEWSLETTER. Short title: H A S W A Newsletter. Text in English. 1992. m. GBP 220 to non-members; GBP 200 to members (effective 2010); subscr. includes British Safety Council Guide. **Document type:** *Newsletter.* **Description:** Provides information for directors, managers and anyone with responsibility for workplace health and safety.
Published by: British Safety Council, 70 Chancellors Rd, London, W6 9RS, United Kingdom. TEL 44-20-87411231, FAX 44-20-87414555, mail@britsafe.org.

613.62 363.11 ZAF ISSN 1742-6928
KTL1430.A15
HEALTH & SAFETY AT WORK IN S A. Text in English. 2003. q. ZAR 175.54 (effective 2006). **Document type:** *Journal, Trade.* **Description:** Covers the latest issues in workplace health and safety.
Published by: LexisNexis Butterworths South Africa (Subsidiary of: LexisNexis Europe and Africa), PO Box 792, Durban, KwaZulu-Natal 4000, South Africa. TEL 27-31-2683266, FAX 27-31-2683116, http://global.lexisnexis.com/za.

613.62 GBR ISSN 0963-5351
HEALTH AND SAFETY BRIEFING. Variant title: Croner's Health and Safety Briefing. Text in English. 1991. fortn. included with subscr. to Health and Safety at Work. **Document type:** *Newsletter, Trade.* **Description:** Provides timely information on issues affecting health and safety at work.
Published by: Croner C C H Group Ltd. (Subsidiary of: Wolters Kluwer UK Ltd.), 145 London Rd, Kingston upon Thames, Surrey KT2 6SR, United Kingdom. TEL 44-20-85473333, FAX 44-20-85472638, info@croner.co.uk.

344.104465 GBR ISSN 2042-2253
HEALTH AND SAFETY CASE LAW NEWSLETTER. Text in English. 1996. m. Included with subscr. to Health & Safety Case Law. **Document type:** *Newsletter, Trade.* **Description:** Covers range of cases heard at Crown or magistrates' court level which are often 'six pack' prosecutions.
Formerly (until 2009): Croner's Health and Safety Case Law Special Report (1362-1831)
Related titles: ◆ Supplement to: Croner's Health and Safety Case Law.
Published by: Croner C C H Group Ltd. (Subsidiary of: Wolters Kluwer UK Ltd.), 145 London Rd, Kingston upon Thames, Surrey KT2 6SR, United Kingdom. TEL 44-20-85473333, FAX 44-20-85472638, info@croner.co.uk.

363.11094105 GBR ISSN 0956-4977
HEALTH AND SAFETY EXECUTIVE. NEWS BULLETIN SERVICE. Text in English. 1985. w. GBP 50 (effective 2010). adv. **Document type:** *Bulletin, Trade.* **Description:** Provides a weekly compilation of all press releases issued by HSE's Press Office on a variety of subjects relating to health and safety in the workplace.
Formerly (until 1987): Health and Safety Executive. News Bulletin (0956-4969)
—CCC.
Published by: Health and Safety Executive, Redgrave Court, Merton Rd, Bootle, Merseyside, L20 7HS, United Kingdom. TEL 44-151-9514000, http://www.hse.gov.uk.

613.62 363.11 GBR ISSN 2046-1062
HEALTH AND SAFETY MANAGEMENT NEWSLETTER (ONLINE). Text in English. 1994. m. **Document type:** *Newsletter, Trade.* **Description:** Covers news and information about health and safety regulations, plus the requirements of risk assessment, training and health surveillance.
Former titles (until 2011): Health and Safety Management Newsletter (Print) (2042-2261); (until 2009): Health & Safety Manager (1352-5611)
Media: Online - full text.
Published by: Croner C C H Group Ltd. (Subsidiary of: Wolters Kluwer UK Ltd.), 145 London Rd, Kingston upon Thames, Surrey KT2 6SR, United Kingdom. TEL 44-20-85473333, FAX 44-20-85472638, info@croner.co.uk.

340 613.62 GBR ISSN 0140-8534
KD3168.A13 CODEN: HSMOE5
HEALTH & SAFETY MONITOR. Text in English. 1977. m. GBP 316 combined subscription (print & online eds.) (effective 2009). back issues avail. **Document type:** *Newsletter, Trade.* **Description:** Advisory service on Codes of Practice and the changing legal and technical requirements of Health and Safety at Work.
Incorporates: Accident and Incident Investigation Part 2; Health and Safety Court Report
Related titles: Online - full text ed.; Supplement(s): In Focus (Sudbury). ISSN 1368-6666. 1992.
Indexed: A22, Cadscan, ELJI, LJI, LeadAb, M&MA, Zincscan.
—BLDSC (4274.865500), IE, Infotrieve, Ingenta. **CCC.**
Published by: Schofield Publishing, Ste 10, Intwood Rd, Cringleford Business Ctr, Norwich, Norfolk NR4 6AU, United Kingdom. TEL 44-1603-274130, FAX 44-1603-274131, hcannell@schofieldpublishing.co.uk, http://www.schofieldmediagroup.com/.

HEALTH & SAFETY RESOURCE. *see* FORESTS AND FORESTRY

613.62 IRL
HEALTH & SAFETY REVIEW. Text in English. 1996. 10/yr. EUR 145 (effective 2001). **Document type:** *Journal, Trade.* **Description:** Covers all aspects of health, safety and environmental issues which impact on the workplace.
Related titles: Online - full content ed.
Published by: IRN Publishing, 123 Ranelagh, Dublin, 6, Ireland. TEL 353-1-4972711, FAX 353-1-4972799, irn@irn.ie, http://www.irn.ie. Ed. Herbert Mulligan. Pub. Martin Macdonnell. Adv. contact Orla McAleer.

HEALTH & SAFETY SPECIFIERS; health, safety and environmental safety. *see* PUBLIC HEALTH AND SAFETY

613.62 NLD
HEALTH IN BEDRIJF. Text in Dutch. 4/yr.
Published by: (Groene Land Achmea, Zilveren Kruis Achmea), Axioma Communicatie BV/Axioma Communications BV (Subsidiary of: Springer Science+Business Media), Lt Gen Van Heutszlaan 4, Postbus 176, Baarn, 3740 AD, Netherlands. TEL 31-35-5488140, FAX 31-35-5425820, informatie@axioma.nl, http://www.axioma.nl. Circ: 20,000.

HEALTHCARE HAZARD MANAGEMENT MONITOR. *see* MEDICAL SCIENCES

658.31244 USA ISSN 0897-7615
RC969.H43
HEALTHY COMPANIES. Text in English. 1984. q. **Document type:** *Journal, Consumer.*
Formerly (until 1987): Corporate Commentary (0749-4335)
Indexed: P30.
Published by: National Business Group on Health, 50 F St, N W Ste 600, Washington, DC 20001. TEL 202-628-9320, FAX 202-628-9244, info@businessgrouphealth.org, http://www.wbgh.org.

HELSEJOB. *see* PHYSICAL FITNESS AND HYGIENE

613.62 363.11 622 USA ISSN 0271-3888
TN295
HOLMES SAFETY ASSOCIATION. BULLETIN. Text in English. m. free to members (effective 2009). **Document type:** *Bulletin, Government.*
Formerly (until 1979): Holmes Safety Association Monthly Safety Topic (0272-3190)
Related titles: Online - full text ed.
Published by: (U.S. Department of Labor, Mine Safety and Health Administration), Joseph A. Holmes Safety Association, PO Box 9375, Arlington, VA 22219. TEL 703-235-0249, FAX 202-693-9571, mail@holmessafety.org.

HOPE HEALTH LETTER. *see* PHYSICAL FITNESS AND HYGIENE

HOSPITAL EMPLOYEE HEALTH. *see* HEALTH FACILITIES AND ADMINISTRATION

HOSPITAL SAFETY CONNECTION. *see* HEALTH FACILITIES AND ADMINISTRATION

HUANJING YU ZHIYE YIXUE/JOURNAL OF ENVIRONMENTAL & OCCUPATIONAL MEDICINE. *see* MEDICAL SCIENCES

HUMAN FACTORS AND AEROSPACE SAFETY; an international journal. *see* AERONAUTICS AND SPACE FLIGHT

HUMAN FACTORS AND ERGONOMICS IN MANUFACTURING. *see* ENGINEERING—Industrial Engineering

331 USA
HUMAN RESOURCES MANAGEMENT - O S H A COMPLIANCE. Text in English. 2 base vols. plus m. updates. looseleaf. USD 529 base vol(s). print or online or CD-ROM ed. (effective 2004). **Description:** Provides practical guidance on compliance issues arising under federal OSHA and state OSHA Acts. Offers the guidelines and examples needed to establish an effective company safety program.
Formerly: C C H - O S H A Compliance Guide
Related titles: CD-ROM ed.; Online - full text ed.
Published by: C C H Inc. (Subsidiary of: Wolters Kluwer N.V.), 2700 Lake Cook Rd, Riverwoods, IL 60015. TEL 847-267-7000, 800-449-6439, cust_serv@cch.com, http://www.cch.com. Ed. Paul Gibson.

613.62 150 USA
HUMAN SYSTEMS I A C GATEWAY. (Information Analysis Center) Text in English. q. **Description:** Addresses current issues in human factors and ergonomics.
Formerly: C S E R I A C Gateway
Related titles: Online - full text ed.
Indexed: ErgAb.
Published by: Human Systems Immigration Information Analysis Center, AFRL/HEC/HSIAC, 2245 Monahan Way, Bldg 29, Wright-Patterson AFB, OH 454337008. TEL 937-255-4842, FAX 937-255-4823, http://iac.dtic.mil/hsiac/. Ed. Roseann Venis.

363.11 613.6 FRA ISSN 1776-9272
CODEN: CNDIBJ
HYGIENE ET SECURITE DU TRAVAIL. Text in French. 1956. q. EUR 71 domestic; EUR 81.10 in Europe; EUR 81.10 DOM-TOM; EUR 90.20 elsewhere (effective 2010). abstr.; charts; illus. index, cum.index. **Document type:** *Journal, Academic/Scholarly.* **Description:** Scientific and technical publication in the field of occupational safety and health.
Formerly (until 2004): Cahiers de Notes Documentaires (0007-9952)
Indexed: A22, CIN, CISA, ChemAb, FR, INIS AtomInd.
—BLDSC (4352.240500), CASDDS, GNLM, IE, Infotrieve, Ingenta, INIST. **CCC.**
Published by: Institut National de Recherche et de Securite pour la Prevention des Accidents du Travail et des Maladies Professionnelles, 30 rue Olivier Noyer, Paris, 75680 Cedex 14, France. TEL 33-1-40443000, FAX 33-1-40443099, thanh@inrs.fr, http://www.inrs.fr. Circ: 10,000.

N O

614.8 628 331.8 CHE ISSN 0376-9410
I Z A. Text and summaries in German. 1953. 6/yr. CHF 67 domestic; EUR 49 in Europe; CHF 10 newsstand/cover (effective 2007). adv.
Document type: *Journal, Trade.*
Former titles (until 1965): Illustrierte Zeitschrift fuer Arbeitsschutz (1423-3045); (until 1958): Illustrierte Betriebszeitschrift (1423-3037)
Published by: Binkert Publishing GmbH, Postfach 112, Dornach 2, 4143, Switzerland. TEL 41-61-7031435, FAX 41-61-7031439, ludwigbinkert@binkertpublishing.ch, http://www.binkertpublishing.ch. Ed. Ludwig Binkert. adv.: B&W page CHF 1,200, color page CHF 1,520; trim 185 x 265. Circ: 5,500.

363.11 658.31244 USA
INCIDENT PREVENTION; providing safety information to utilities, municipalities and telcom. Text in English. 2004. bi-m. adv.
Document type: *Magazine, Trade.* **Description:** Provides utility safety professionals with job specific safety information.
Published by: Incident Prevention, Inc., 2615 Three Oaks Rd, Ste 2B, Cary, IL 60013. TEL 847-639-7035, FAX 847-620-0662, carla@incident-prevention.com. Ed. Seth Skydel. Pub. Carla Housh. adv.: color page YER 2,599; trim 8.125 x 10.875.

INDIAN JOURNAL OF OCCUPATIONAL AND ENVIRONMENTAL MEDICINE. *see* MEDICAL SCIENCES

658.31244 CAN ISSN 0712-774X
INDUSTRIAL ACCIDENT PREVENTION ASSOCIATION. ANNUAL REVIEW. Text in English. 1918. a. **Document type:** *Corporate.*
Formerly: Industrial Accident Prevention Association. Annual Report (0073-7305)
Published by: Industrial Accident Prevention Association, 250 Yonge St, 28th Fl, Toronto, ON M5B 2N4, Canada. TEL 416-506-8888. Circ: 7,500.

613.62 JPN ISSN 0019-8366
RC963 CODEN: INHEAO
➤ **INDUSTRIAL HEALTH.** Text in English. 1958. q. free (effective 2009). charts; illus. Index. reprints avail. **Document type:** *Journal, Academic/Scholarly.* **Description:** Contains original articles, review articles, short communications, case reports, and field reports in scientific researches in the fields of occupational health and industrial hygiene.
Formerly (until 1962): Rodo Eisei Kenkyujo Kenkyu Hokoku/National Institute of Industrial Health. Bulletin (0557-2304)
Related titles: Online - full text ed.: ISSN 1880-8026. free (effective 2011).
Indexed: A&ATA, A22, A36, A37, ASCA, AcoustA, B21, B25, BIOBASE, BIOSIS Prev, CA, CABA, CISA, CSNB, ChemAb, DentInd, E04, E05, E12, EMBASE, ESPM, ErgAb, ExcerpMed, F08, F11, F12, GH, H&SSA, H17, IABS, IHD, INI, INIS AtomInd, IndMed, L12, LT, MEDLINE, MS&D, MycolAb, N02, N03, OR, P30, P33, P37, PEI, PHN&I, PN&I, PollutAb, R07, R08, R10, R11, R12, RM&VM, RRTA, Reac, RiskAb, S13, SCI, SCOPUS, SD, T02, T05, ToxAb, VS, W07, W10, W11.
—BLDSC (4454.700000), CASDDS, GNLM, IE, Infotrieve, Ingenta, INIST.
Published by: Roudou Anzen Eisei Sougou Kenkyujo/National Institute of Occupational Safety and Health, Japan, Nagao 6-21-1, Tama-Ku, Kawasaki, 214-8585, Japan. TEL 81-44-865-6111, FAX 81-44-865-6124. Ed. Shunichi Araki. Circ: 1,100.

613.62 340 USA ISSN 0890-3018
INDUSTRIAL HEALTH & HAZARDS UPDATE. Text in English. 1984. m. USD 369 domestic; USD 409 in Canada; USD 479 elsewhere (effective 2001). back issues avail.; reprints avail. **Document type:** *Newsletter.* **Description:** Covers occupational health, safety, hazards, and related subjects. Designed for busy executives in the health, medical, environmental, legal, management, and technological fields of industry, government, commerce, and academia.
Incorporates (1994-200?): Environmental Problems & Remediation (1077-1395)
Related titles: Online - full text ed.
Indexed: PROMT.
Published by: Merton Allen Associates, InfoTeam Inc., PO Box 15640, Plantation, FL 33318-5640. TEL 954-473-9560, FAX 954-473-0544. Eds. David R Allen, Merton Allen.

331 USA ISSN 0147-5401
INDUSTRIAL HYGIENE NEWS. Text in English. 1978. 7/yr. free to qualified personnel (effective 2005). adv. bk.rev. tr.lit. back issues avail. **Document type:** *Magazine, Trade.* **Description:** Information on occupational health and safety. Persons responsible for the industrial hygiene function, nurses and physicians, management, insurance executives, industrial hygienists, safety directors, plant engineers.
Related titles: Online - full text ed.
Indexed: E04, E05.
—IE, Infotrieve.
Published by: Rimbach Publishing, Inc., 8650 Babcock Blvd, Pittsburgh, PA 15237-5821. TEL 412-364-5366, FAX 412-369-9720, info@rimbach.com. Eds. David C Lavender, Raquel Rimbach. Pub. Norberta Rimbach. Adv. contact Raquel Rimbach. page USD 4,450; trim 11 x 16. Circ: 62,000 (controlled).

614.85 USA
INDUSTRIAL PREVENTION AND RESPONSE. Text in English. 2007 (Aug.). bi-m. **Document type:** *Magazine, Trade.* **Description:** Covers industrial safety and security, including fire and emergency response, hazards, internal and external plant security, laws and regulations, terrorism, and liability.
Related titles: Online - full text ed.
Published by: The TradeFair Group, Inc. (Subsidiary of: Access Intelligence, LLC), 11000 Richmond, Ste 500, Houston, TX 77042. TEL 832-242-1969, FAX 832-242-1971, info@tradefairgroup.com, http://www.tradefairgroup.com/.

658.31244 USA
CODEN: CIHNEM
INDUSTRIAL SAFETY AND HYGIENE NEWS; news of safety, health and hygiene, environmental, fire, security and emergency protection equipment. Abbreviated title: I S H N. Text in English. 1967. m. USD 104 domestic; USD 137 in Canada; USD 154 elsewhere; free to qualified personnel (print or online ed.) (effective 2009). charts; illus.; tr.lit. back issues avail.; reprints avail. **Document type:** *Newspaper, Trade.* **Description:** Focuses on high hazard industry worksites in manufacturing, construction, health, facilities and service industries and keeps readers up-to-date on changing trends and quick how-to guides on everyday work situations.
Former titles (until 199?): Chilton's Industrial Safety and Hygiene News (8755-2566); (until 1982): Industrial Safety and Hygiene News; (until 1981): Industrial Safety Product News (0192-8325); (until 1978): Safety Products News (0278-8217)
Related titles: Microform ed.: (from PQC); Online - full text ed.
Indexed: A10, A15, A28, ABIn, APA, B01, B02, B03, B06, B07, B09, B11, B15, B17, B18, B21, BrCerAb, C&ISA, CA/WCA, CIA, CerAb, CivEngAb, CorrAb, CurPA, E&CAJ, E11, EEA, EMA, ESPM, EnvEAb, G04, G06, G07, G08, H&SSA, H15, I05, IHD, M&TEA, M09, MBF, P19, P26, P48, P50, P51, P52, P54, P56, PQC, S22, SolStAb, T02, T03, T04, V03, WAA.
—Linda Hall. **CCC.**
Published by: B N P Media, 2401 W Big Beaver Rd, Ste 700, Troy, MI 48084. TEL 248-244-6499, FAX 248-244-2925, portfolio@bnpmedia.com, http://www.bnpmedia.com. Ed. Dave Johnson TEL 610-666-0261. Pub. Randy Green TEL 248-244-6498. Circ: 62,000.

613.62 NZL ISSN 1179-996X
INDUSTRIAL SAFETY NEWS. Abbreviated title: I S N. Text in English. 2006. q. USD 30 (effective 2010). adv. **Document type:** *Magazine, Trade.* **Description:** Features the news and information about safety legislation, products and services to make industrial businesses throughout New Zealand safer.
Former titles (until 2010): National Safety News; (until 2009): Industrial Safety News (1177-3219)
Published by: Hayleymedia, PO Box 33 146, Takapuna, North Shore City, 0740, New Zealand. TEL 64-9-4860077, FAX 64-9-4860078, info@hayleymedia.com. Ed. Lisa Gossage. Adv. contact Jeff Singleton TEL 64-9-4841311. Circ: 19,000.

628.5 NLD ISSN 0921-9110
➤ **INDUSTRIAL SAFETY SERIES.** Text in Dutch. 1987. irreg., latest vol.6, 1998. price varies. back issues avail. **Document type:** *Monographic series, Academic/Scholarly.*
Related titles: Online - full text ed.
Indexed: SCOPUS.
—BLDSC (4462.440000), IE, Ingenta. **CCC.**
Published by: Elsevier BV (Subsidiary of: Elsevier Science & Technology), Radarweg 29, PO Box 211, Amsterdam, 1000 AE, Netherlands. TEL 31-20-4853911, FAX 31-20-4852457, JournalsCustomerServiceEMEA@elsevier.com, http://www.elsevier.nl.

➤ **INDUSTRIAL VENTILATION**; a manual of recommended practice. *see* HEATING, PLUMBING AND REFRIGERATION

613 AUS ISSN 1441-8886
INSIDE O H S. (Occupational Health Safety) Text in English. 1987. bi-m. included with subscr. to Occupational Health News. adv. **Document type:** *Newsletter, Trade.* **Description:** Provides information service on occupational health and safety. Alerts employers and unions to key developments in workplace safety and health from Australia and throughout the world.
Former titles (until 1999): Occupational Health Magazine (1032-0989); (until 1988): Occupational Health and Safety Products and Services (1032-0970); (until 1987): Products and Services (1032-0962)
Related titles: Online - full text ed.: ISSN 1446-5825. 2002.
Published by: Thomson C P D (Subsidiary of: Thomson Reuters (Professional) Australia Limited), Level 5, 100 Harris St, Pyrmont, NSW 2009, Australia. TEL 61-2-85877000, FAX 61-2-85877100, LRA.Service@thomson.com, http://www.thomsonreuters.com.au.

363.11 USA
INSIDE O S H A. (Occupational Safety and Health Administration) Text in English. 1994. bi-w. USD 675 (effective 2008). back issues avail.
Document type: *Newsletter, Trade.* **Description:** Contains information on the occupational safety and health administration.
Related titles: E-mail ed.; Online - full text ed.: USD 300; USD 25 per issue (effective 2008).
Published by: Inside Washington Publishers, 1919 South Eads St, Ste 201, Arlington, VA 22202. TEL 703-416-8500, 800-424-9068, custsvc@iwpnews.com, http://www.iwpnews.com. Ed. Bob Cusack. Pub. Donna Haseley.

658.31244 USA ISSN 2153-2265
INSIDE O S H A REGULATIONS. (Occupational Health and Safety Administration) Text in English. 1998. bi-w. USD 247 (effective 2010). back issues avail. **Document type:** *Newsletter, Trade.* **Description:** Assists supervisors in training their employees on important safety issues to help prevent safety violations and accidents.
Formerly (until 2010): The Supervisor's Guide to O S H A Regulations (1522-8711)
Related titles: Online - full text ed.: ISSN 2153-2273.
Published by: Clement Communications, Inc., 10 LaCrue Ave, PO Box 36, Concordville, PA 19331. TEL 610-459-4200, 888-358-5858, FAX 610-459-4582, 800-459-1933, customerservice@clement.com. Pub. George Y Clement.

363.11 613.62 CAN ISSN 1701-4700
CA2PQTM880 A56
INSTITUT DE RECHERCHE EN SANTE ET SECURITE DU TRAVAIL. RAPPORT D'ACTIVITE. Text in French. 2000. a.
Formerly (until 1999): Institut de Recherche en Sante et Securite du Travail du Quebec. Rapport Annuel (0820-8409)
Related titles: English ed.: I R S S T. Activity Report. ISSN 1701-4697.
Published by: Institut de Recherche en Sante et Securite du Travail (I R S S T), 505, boul. De Maisonneuve Ouest, Montreal, PQ H3A 3C2, Canada. TEL 514-288-1551, FAX 514-288-7636, Publications@irsst.qc.ca, http://www.irsst.qc.ca/fr/accueil.html.

INSTITUTUL POLITEHNIC DIN IASI. BULETINUL. SECTIA STIINTA SI INGINERIA MATERIALELOR/POLYTECHNIC INSTITUTE OF IASI. BULLETIN. MATERIAL SCIENCE AND ENGINEERING. *see* ENGINEERING—Engineering Mechanics And Materials

INTERFACHES (ENGLISH EDITION). *see* ENVIRONMENTAL STUDIES

613.62 DEU ISSN 0340-0131
RC963.A1 CODEN: IAEHDW
➤ **INTERNATIONAL ARCHIVES OF OCCUPATIONAL AND ENVIRONMENTAL HEALTH.** Text in English. 1930. 8/yr. EUR 3,492, USD 4,146 combined subscription to institutions (print & online eds.) (effective 2012). adv. bibl.; charts; illus. index. back issues avail.; reprint service avail. from PSC. **Document type:** *Journal, Academic/Scholarly.* **Description:** Covers occupational, environmental, and social medicine, and their subdisciplines.
Former titles (until 1975): International Archives of Occupational Health (0020-5923); (until 1969): Internationales Archiv fuer Gewerbepathologie und Gewerbehygiene (0367-9977); (until 1961): Archiv fuer Gewerbepathologie und Gewerbehygiene (0365-2564)
Related titles: Microform ed.: (from PQC); Online - full text ed.: ISSN 1432-1246 (from IngentaConnect); Supplement(s): ISSN 1431-5777.
Indexed: A01, A03, A08, A20, A22, A26, A34, A36, A37, ASCA, ASFA, AcoustA, B21, B25, BIOBASE, BIOSIS Prev, CA, CABA, CIN, CISA, Cadscan, ChemAb, ChemTitl, CurCont, DentInd, E01, E04, E05, E12, EMBASE, ESPM, ErgAb, ExcerpMed, F08, F11, F12, FR, GH, H&SSA, H12, H16, IABS, INI, ISR, IndMed, IndVet, Inpharma, LT, LeadAb, MEDLINE, MS&D, MycolAb, N02, N03, NRN, O01, OR, P20, P22, P26, P30, P33, P34, P37, P48, P50, P52, P54, P56, PN&I, PQC, PollutAb, R07, R08, R10, R11, R12, R13, RM&VM, RRTA, Reac, RefZh, S13, S16, SCI, SCOPUS, T02, T05, ToxAb, VITIS, VS, W07, W10, W11, Zincscan.
—BLDSC (4536.128000), CASDDS, GNLM, IE, Infotrieve, Ingenta, INIST. **CCC.**
Published by: Springer (Subsidiary of: Springer Science+Business Media), Tiergartenstr 17, Heidelberg, 69121, Germany. TEL 49-6221-4870, FAX 49-6221-345229. Ed. Dr. Hans Drexler. adv.: B&W page EUR 700, color page EUR 1,740. Circ: 470 (paid and controlled). **Subscr. in the Americas to:** Springer New York LLC, Journal Fulfillment, PO Box 2485, Secaucus, NJ 07096. TEL 800-777-4643, 201-348-4033, FAX 201-348-4505, journals-ny@springer.com, http://www.springer.com; **Subscr. to:** Springer Distribution Center, Kundenservice Zeitschriften, Haberstr 7, Heidelberg 69126, Germany. TEL 49-6221-3454303, FAX 49-6221-3454229, subscriptions@springer.com.

➤ **INTERNATIONAL COMMISSION ON RADIOLOGICAL PROTECTION. ANNALS.** *see* MEDICAL SCIENCES—Radiology And Nuclear Medicine

613.62 AUS ISSN 0074-3828
➤ **INTERNATIONAL CONGRESS OF OCCUPATIONAL THERAPY. PROCEEDINGS.** Text in English. 1974. irreg. **Document type:** *Proceedings, Academic/Scholarly.*
Published by: World Federation of Occupational Therapists, PO Box 30, Forrestfield, W.A. 6058, Australia. FAX 61-8-94539746, admin@wfot.org.au, http://www.wfot.org.au.

613.62 USA ISSN 1077-3525
RC963.A1 CODEN: IOEHFU
➤ **INTERNATIONAL JOURNAL OF OCCUPATIONAL AND ENVIRONMENTAL HEALTH.** Abbreviated title: I J O E H. Text in English. 1995. q. USD 150 combined subscription domestic to individuals; USD 165 combined subscription foreign to individuals; USD 285 combined subscription domestic to institutions; USD 315 combined subscription foreign to institutions (effective 2010). adv. charts; illus. Index. back issues avail.; reprints avail. **Document type:** *Journal, Academic/Scholarly.* **Description:** Provides up-to-date clinical and research information on promotion of health in the workplace and the wider issue of the relationship between human health and the environment.
Related titles: Online - full text ed.: USD 135 to individuals (effective 2010).
Indexed: C06, C07, C08, CINAHL, CSNB, CurCont, EMBASE, ErgAb, ExcerpMed, F09, H13, IndMed, L12, MEDLINE, P10, P11, P20, P21, P22, P24, P26, P30, P48, P50, P52, P53, P54, P56, PQC, RILM, SCI, SCOPUS, SSCI, W07.
—BLDSC (4542.410800), GNLM, IE, Infotrieve, Ingenta, INIST.
Published by: Abel Publication Services, Inc., 8 N Main St, Ste 404A, Attleboro, MA 02703. Eds. Andrew Watterson, Ken Takahashi, David S Egilman.

613.62 IRN ISSN 2008-5109
▼ ➤ **INTERNATIONAL JOURNAL OF OCCUPATIONAL HYGIENE.** Text in English. 2009. s-a. free. bk.rev. Index. back issues avail.
Document type: *Journal, Academic/Scholarly.* **Description:** Publishes original research, field and case reports, review articles, short communications and letters to the editor, covering multidisciplinary researches concerning factors influencing quality of life in any environment and workplaces.
Related titles: Online - full text ed.: ISSN 2008-5435.
Published by: (Iranian Occupational Health Association), Danishgah-i Ulum-i Pizishki-i Tihran/Tehran University of Medical Sciences, Department of Occupational Health, School of Public Health, Tehran University of Medical Sciences, PO Box 13155-119, Tehran, Iran. TEL 98-21-88992664, FAX 98-21-88992665. Ed. Seyed Jamoldin Shahtaheri. Pub. Fariba Golbabaei.

613.85 POL ISSN 1232-1087
➤ **INTERNATIONAL JOURNAL OF OCCUPATIONAL MEDICINE AND ENVIRONMENTAL HEALTH.** Text in English. 1988. q. EUR 288, USD 355 combined subscription to institutions (print & online eds.) (effective 2012). adv. bk.rev. abstr.; bibl.; illus. index. 90 p./no. 2 cols./p.; back issues avail.; reprints avail. **Document type:** *Journal, Academic/Scholarly.* **Description:** Publishes papers concerning industrial hygiene, preventive medicine, diagnosis and treatment of occupational diseases, physiology and psychology of work, toxicological research, environmental toxicology, environmental epidemiology, and epidemiological studies devoted to occupational problems.
Former titles (until 1993): Polish Journal of Occupational Medicine and Environmental Health (0867-8383); (until 1991): Polish Journal of Occupational Medicine (0860-6536)
Related titles: CD-ROM ed.: USD 12.20 (effective 2005); Online - full text ed.: ISSN 1896-494X.

Indexed: A01, A03, A08, A36, ASFA, B21, B25, BIOSIS Prev, C06, C07, CA, CABA, E04, E05, E12, EMBASE, ESPM, ErgAb, ExcerpMed, F08, GH, H&SSA, INIS AtomInd, IndMed, LT, MEDLINE, MycolAb, N02, N03, P03, P20, P22, P30, P33, P48, P50, P52, P54, P56, PQC, PollutAb, PsycInfo, PsycholAb, R07, R08, R10, RM&VM, RRTA, Reac, RefZh, RiskAb, SCI, SCOPUS, T02, T05, ToxAb, TriticAb, W07, W10.
—BLDSC (4542.412000), GNLM, IE, Infotrieve, Ingenta.
Published by: Instytut Medycyny Pracy im. Jerzego Nofera/Nofer Institute of Occupational Medicine, ul Sw Teresy 8, PO Box 199, Lodz, 90950, Poland. TEL 48-42-6314718, FAX 48-42-6314719, redakcja@imp.lodz.pl, http://www.imp.lodz.pl. Ed. Konrad Rydzynski. Circ: 400. **Co-publishers:** Springer; Polskie Towarzystwo Medycyny Pracy/Polish Association of Occupational Medicine. **Co-sponsor:** Polska Akademia Nauk, Komitet Badan Naukowych/Polish Academy of Sciences, Committee for Scientific Research.

363.11 620.8 613.62 POL ISSN 1080-3548
T59.7 CODEN: IJOEF2
➤ **INTERNATIONAL JOURNAL OF OCCUPATIONAL SAFETY AND ERGONOMICS.** Variant title: J O S E. Text in English. 1995. q. USD 50 domestic to individuals; USD 70 foreign to individuals; USD 170 domestic to institutions; USD 190 foreign to institutions; USD 40 to members (effective 2005). adv. bk.rev. index. 120 p./no. 1 cols./p.; back issues avail.; reprints avail. **Document type:** *Journal, Academic/Scholarly.* **Description:** Covers occupational safety and ergonomics for research workers from experts in the United States, Canada, Central and Eastern Europe. Includes studies of hazardous chemicals, physical and biological agents, new technologies for protection, criteria and requirements of occupational safety and ergonomics as well as the information about seminars and conferences organized in Poland and abroad.
Related titles: Online - full text ed.
Indexed: B21, EMBASE, ESPM, ErgAb, ExcerpMed, H&SSA, IndMed, Inspec, MEDLINE, P30, RiskAb, SCOPUS, SSCI, W07.
—BLDSC (4542.414000), AskIEEE, GNLM, IE, Infotrieve, Ingenta. **CCC.**
Published by: Centralny Instytut Ochrony Pracy/Central Institute for Labour Protection, Ul Czerniakowska 16, Warsaw, 00701, Poland. TEL 48-22-6234601, FAX 48-22-6233693, oinip@ciop.pl. Ed. Danuta Koradecka. Circ: 200. **Co-sponsor:** International Ergonomics Association.

613.62 628.92 GBR ISSN 2041-9031
▼ **INTERNATIONAL JOURNAL OF SAFETY AND SECURITY ENGINEERING.** Text in English. 2011. q. EUR 340, USD 480 combined subscription (print & online eds.) (effective 2011). **Document type:** *Journal, Trade.* **Description:** Aims to provide a forum for publication of papers on the most recent developments in the theoretical and practical aspects of these important fields.
Related titles: Online - full text ed.: ISSN 2041-904X.
Published by: W I T Press, Ashurst Lodge, Ashurst, Southampton, Hants SO40 7AA, United Kingdom. TEL 44-238-0293223, FAX 44-238-0292853, marketing@witpress.com, http://www.witpress.com.

613.62 GBR ISSN 1753-8351
➤ **INTERNATIONAL JOURNAL OF WORKPLACE HEALTH MANAGEMENT.** Text in English. 2008. 3/yr. EUR 339 combined subscription in Europe (print & online eds.); USD 479 combined subscription in the Americas (print & online eds.); GBP 239 combined subscription in the UK & elsewhere (print & online eds.); AUD 639 combined subscription in Australasia (print & online eds.) (effective 2012). reprint service avail. from PSC. **Document type:** *Journal, Academic/Scholarly.* **Description:** Publishes current research and debate on all aspects of health in the workplace, from both the wider public health perspective and the perspective of the individual organization.
Related titles: Online - full text ed.: ISSN 1753-836X (from IngentaConnect).
Indexed: A12, A17, ABIn, B21, EMBASE, ESPM, ExcerpMed, H&SSA, P48, P51, P53, P54, PQC, RiskAb, SCOPUS.
—BLDSC (4542.701855), IE. **CCC.**
Published by: Emerald Group Publishing Ltd., Howard House, Wagon Ln, Bingley, W Yorks BD16 1WA, United Kingdom. TEL 44-1274-777700, information@emeraldinsight.com. Ed. Dr. Lydia Makrides.

363.11 USA
INTERNATIONAL SOCIETY FOR OCCUPATIONAL ERGONOMICS AND SAFETY. NEWSLETTER. Text in English. 1997. s-a. free to members (effective 2011); membership. back issues avail. **Document type:** *Newsletter, Trade.* **Description:** Informs members of important news and events.
Related titles: Online - full text ed.: free (effective 2011).
Published by: International Society for Occupational Ergonomics and Safety, c/o JFAssociates, 9609 Scotch Haven Dr, Vienna, VA 22181. TEL 703-989-3996, anilk@jfa-inc.com. Ed. Gabriel Ibarra-Mejia.

INTERNATIONAL SOCIETY FOR RESPIRATORY PROTECTION. JOURNAL. *see* MEDICAL SCIENCES—Respiratory Diseases

▼ **THE INTERNET JOURNAL OF OCCUPATIONAL HEALTH.** *see* MEDICAL SCIENCES

615.851 IRL ISSN 0791-8437
THE IRISH JOURNAL OF OCCUPATIONAL THERAPY. Text in English. 1973. bi-m. adv. **Document type:** *Journal, Academic/Scholarly.*
Formerly (until 1992): O.T. Ireland (1393-0621)
Indexed: C06, C07, CA, T02.
—BLDSC (4572.050000), IE, Ingenta.
Published by: Association of Occupational Therapists of Ireland, 29 Gardiner Pl, Dublin, 1, Ireland. http://www.aoti.ie/. adv.: page EUR 255.

613.62 363.11 JPN
JAPAN INDUSTRIAL SAFETY AND HEALTH ASSOCIATION. ANNUAL REPORT. Text in Japanese. a.
Indexed: L12.
Published by: Japan Industrial Safety and Health Association, International Cooperation Department, 5-35-1, Shiba, Minato-ku, Tokyo, 108-0014, Japan. TEL 81-3-3452-6841, FAX 81-3-3454-4596.

JIANZHU ANQUAN/CONSTRUCTION SAFETY. *see* BUILDING AND CONSTRUCTION

613.62 363.11 USA
JOB SAFETY AND HEALTH. Text in English. 1977. m. looseleaf. USD 898 (effective 2005 - 2006); includes SafetyNet newsletter. **Document type:** *Magazine, Trade.* **Description:** Covers workplace safety and health regulations, policies, practices and trends.
Published by: The Bureau of National Affairs, Inc., 1801 S Bell St, Arlington, VA 22202. TEL 800-372-1033.

613.62 FRA ISSN 1775-0318
JOURNAL DES PROFESSIONNELS DE LA SANTE AU TRAVAIL. Abbreviated title: J S T. Text in French. 1961. bi-m. EUR 60 (effective 2010). adv. bk.rev. **Document type:** *Newspaper, Trade.* **Description:** Publishes articles on occupational medicine, industrial health, hygienics, and safety at work.
Former title (until 2005): Journal des Medecins du Travail (1632-2428); (until 2002): Medecine et Travail (0025-6757)
Indexed: CISA.
—BLDSC (5042.728000).
Published by: Syndicat National des Professionnels de la Sante au Travail (S N P S T), 12 Impasse Mas, Toulouse, 31000, France. TEL 33-5-61992077, FAX 33-5-61627566, courrier@snpst.org, http://snpst.org/index2.html. Eds. Dr. F Blanc, M C Remesy. Circ: 1,250.

613.62 USA ISSN 1059-924X
RC965.A5
➤ **JOURNAL OF AGROMEDICINE;** interface of human health & agriculture. Abbreviated title: J A. Text in English. 1994. q. GBP 243 combined subscription in United Kingdom to institutions (print & online eds.); EUR 316, USD 326 combined subscription to institutions (print & online eds.) (effective 2012). adv. bk.rev. 120 p./no. 1 cols./p.; back issues avail.; reprint service avail. from PSC. **Document type:** *Journal, Academic/Scholarly.* **Description:** Focuses on the health effects of agricultural operations on workers and their families, consumers, and the environment.
Related titles: Microfiche ed.: (from PQC); Microform ed.; Online - full text ed.: ISSN 1545-0813. GBP 219 in United Kingdom to institutions; EUR 285, USD 293 to institutions (effective 2012).
Indexed: A01, A03, A22, A34, A35, A36, A37, A38, ASFA, AbAn, AgBio, Agr, AgrForAb, B21, BA, BP, Biostat, C06, C07, C08, CA, CABA, CINAHL, D01, E01, E04, E05, E12, EMBASE, ESPM, EnvAb, EnvInd, ExcerpMed, F08, F12, FS&TA, GH, GardL, H&SSA, H16, H17, IndVet, LT, M02, MEDLINE, N02, N03, N04, N05, OR, P30, P33, P37, P50, PGrRegA, PN&I, PollutAb, R07, R08, R12, R13, RRTA, RefZh, RiskAb, S13, S16, SCOPUS, SoyAb, T02, T05, TAR, ToxAb, VS, W10, W11.
—BLDSC (4926.240000), IE, Infotrieve, Ingenta. **CCC.**
Published by: Routledge (Subsidiary of: Taylor & Francis Group), 325 Chestnut St, Ste 800, Philadelphia, PA 19106. TEL 800-354-1420, FAX 215-625-2940, journals@routledge.com, http://www.routledge.com. Ed. Steven R Kirkhorn. Adv. contact Linda Hann TEL 44-1344-779945.

➤ **JOURNAL OF ECOPHYSIOLOGY AND OCCUPATIONAL HEALTH.** *see* ENVIRONMENTAL STUDIES

➤ **JOURNAL OF ENVIRONMENTAL HEALTH RESEARCH.** *see* ENVIRONMENTAL STUDIES

613 AUS ISSN 1837-9362
RC963.A1
➤ **JOURNAL OF HEALTH, SAFETY AND ENVIRONMENT.** Text in English. 1978. bi-m. AUD 737 (effective 2008). adv. bk.rev.; film rev. illus. cum.index: 1985-1995. back issues avail. **Document type:** *Journal, Academic/Scholarly.* **Description:** Provides information on occupational health and safety. Contains articles by OHS professionals and academics.
Former titles (until 2010): The Journal of Occupational Health and Safety: Australia and New Zealand (0815-6409); (until 1984): Occupational Health: Australian and New Zealand (0159-303X)
Related titles: Online - full text ed.
Indexed: A15, A22, ABIn, AESIS, CSNB, ErgAb, GeoRef, L12, P21, P48, P51, P52, P56, PQC, SCOPUS.
—BLDSC (4996.870150), GNLM, IE, Infotrieve, Ingenta. **CCC.**
Published by: C C H Australia Ltd. (Subsidiary of: Wolters Kluwer), GPO Box 4072, Sydney, NSW 2001, Australia. TEL 61-2-98571300, 300-300-224, FAX 61-2-98571601, 300-306-224, support@cch.com.au. adv.: page AUD 440; 180 x 240.

➤ **THE JOURNAL OF MENTAL HEALTH, TRAINING, EDUCATION AND PRACTICE;** issues for workforce development. *see* MEDICAL SCIENCES—Psychiatry And Neurology

613.62 USA ISSN 1545-9624
RC963.A1 CODEN: JOEHA2
➤ **JOURNAL OF OCCUPATIONAL AND ENVIRONMENTAL HYGIENE.** Abbreviated title: J O E H. Text in English. 2004. m. GBP 549 combined subscription in United Kingdom to institutions (print & online eds.); EUR 726, USD 907 combined subscription to institutions (print & online eds.) (effective 2012). adv. bk.rev. abstr.; charts; illus. Index. 2 cols./p.; back issues avail.; reprint service avail. from PSC. **Document type:** *Journal, Academic/Scholarly.* **Description:** Features articles of interest to the occupational and environmental safety and health professional.
Formed by the merger of (1990-2003): Applied Occupational and Environmental Hygiene (1047-322X); Which was formerly (until 1990): Applied Industrial Hygiene (0882-8032); (1940-2004): A I H A Journal (1542-8117); Which was formerly (until 2002): A I H A J (1529-8663); (until 2000): American Industrial Hygiene Association. Journal (0002-8894); (until 1958): American Industrial Hygiene Association. Quarterly (0096-820X); (until 1946): Industrial Hygiene; (until 1945): Industrial Medicine. Industrial Hygiene Section
Related titles: ◆ Online - full text ed.: Journal of Occupational and Environmental Hygiene (Online). ISSN 1545-9632.
Indexed: A01, A02, A03, A08, A12, A13, A20, A22, A28, A34, A36, A37, A38, ABIn, APA, APIAb, B21, B25, BIOBASE, BIOSIS Prev, BP, BrCerAb, C&ISA, C06, C07, C24, CA, CA/WCA, CABA, CIA, CIN, CSNB, CerAb, ChemAb, ChemTitl, CivEngAb, CorrAb, CurCont, D01, E&CAJ, E01, E04, E05, E11, E12, EEA, EMA, EMBASE, ESPM, EnvAb, EnvEAb, EnvInd, ErgAb, ExcerpMed, F08, F11, F12, GH, H&SSA, H04, H13, H15, H16, IABS, IHD, ISR, IndMed, Inspec, L12, M&TEA, M09, MBF, MEDLINE, METADEX, MycolAb, N02, N03, N04, OR, P10, P20, P24, P26, P30, P33, P34, P39, P48, P50, P51, P52, P53, P54, P56, PHN&I, PN&I, PQC, PollutAb, R07, R08, R10, R13, RA&MP, RM&VM, Reac, RiskAb, S13, S16, SCI, SCOPUS, SolStAb, SoyAb, T02, T04, T05, TAR, TM, ToxAb, VS, W07, W10, WAA, WSCA.
—CASDDS, GNLM, IE, Infotrieve, Ingenta, INIST, Linda Hall. **CCC.**
Published by: (American Industrial Hygiene Association, American Conference of Governmental Industrial Hygienists, Inc.), Taylor & Francis Inc. (Subsidiary of: Taylor & Francis Group), 325 Chestnut St, Ste 800, Philadelphia, PA 19106. TEL 215-625-8900, 800-354-1420, FAX 215-625-8914, orders@taylorandfrancis.com, http://www.taylorandfrancis.com. Ed. Dr. Michael S Morgan. **Subscr. to:** Taylor & Francis Ltd., Journals Customer Service, Sheepen Pl, Colchester, Essex CO3 3LP, United Kingdom. TEL 44-20-70175544, FAX 44-20-70175198, subscriptions@tandf.co.uk.

613.62 USA ISSN 1545-9632
JOURNAL OF OCCUPATIONAL AND ENVIRONMENTAL HYGIENE (ONLINE). Text in English. 2003. m. GBP 494 in United Kingdom to institutions; EUR 653, USD 816 to institutions (effective 2012). **Document type:** *Journal, Academic/Scholarly.*
Formed by the meger of (1990-2003): Applied Occupational and Environmental Hygiene (Online) (1521-0898); (2002-2003): A I H A Journal (Online) (1542-8125); Which was formerly (until 2002): A I H A J (Online)
Media: Online - full text (from IngentaConnect). **Related titles:** ◆ Print ed.: Journal of Occupational and Environmental Hygiene. ISSN 1545-9624.
—BLDSC (5026.080500). **CCC.**
Published by: (American Conference of Governmental Industrial Hygienists, Inc.), Taylor & Francis Inc. (Subsidiary of: Taylor & Francis Group), 325 Chestnut St, Ste 800, Philadelphia, PA 19106. TEL 215-625-8900, 800-354-1420, FAX 215-625-8914, orders@taylorandfrancis.com, http://www.taylorandfrancis.com. Ed. Dr. Michael S Morgan.

JOURNAL OF OCCUPATIONAL AND ENVIRONMENTAL MEDICINE. *see* MEDICAL SCIENCES

613.6 JPN ISSN 1341-9145
RC963 CODEN: JOCHFV
➤ **JOURNAL OF OCCUPATIONAL HEALTH.** Text in English. 1996. q. **Document type:** *Journal, Academic/Scholarly.* **Description:** Features original contributions relevant to occupational and environmental health, including fundamental toxicological studies of industrial chemicals and other related studies.
Related titles: Online - full text ed.: ISSN 1348-9585. free (effective 2011); ◆ Japanese ed.: Sangyo Eiseigaku Zasshi. ISSN 1341-0725.
Indexed: A20, B21, B25, BIOSIS Prev, C06, C07, CIN, ChemAb, ChemTitl, EMBASE, ESPM, ExcerpMed, H&SSA, MEDLINE, MycolAb, P30, R10, Reac, RiskAb, SCI, SCOPUS, ToxAb, W07.
—BLDSC (5026.088000), CASDDS, GNLM, IE, Ingenta. **CCC.**
Published by: Nihon Sangyo Eisei Gakkai/Japan Society for Occupational Health, Public Health Bldg, 1-29-8 Shinjuku, Shinjuku-ku, Tokyo, 160-0022, Japan. Ed. Kazuyuki Omae. Pub. Yukio Fujiki. Circ: 8,000. **Subscr. to:** International Press Editing Center, 1-2-3 Sugamo, Toshima-ku, Tokyo 170-0002, Japan. TEL 81-3-5978-467, FAX 81-3-5978-4068.

158.7 USA ISSN 1076-8998
RC967.5 CODEN: JOHPFC
➤ **JOURNAL OF OCCUPATIONAL HEALTH PSYCHOLOGY.** Text in English. 1996. q. USD 98 domestic to individuals; USD 125 foreign to individuals; USD 410 domestic to institutions; USD 455 foreign to institutions (effective 2011). adv. back issues avail.; reprint service avail. from PSC. **Document type:** *Journal, Academic/Scholarly.* **Description:** Publishes research, theory, and public policy articles that concern the application of psychology to improving the quality of worklife and to protecting and promoting the safety, health and well-being of workers.
Related titles: Online - full text ed.: ISSN 1939-1307. free (effective 2010) (from ScienceDirect).
Indexed: A22, B01, B06, B07, B09, B21, C06, C07, CA, CurCont, EMBASE, ESPM, ErgAb, ExcerpMed, H&SSA, INI, IndMed, MEDLINE, P03, P30, PsycInfo, PsycholAb, R10, RILM, Reac, S02, S03, SCOPUS, SSCI, SWR&A, T02, W07.
—BLDSC (5026.095000), IE, Infotrieve, Ingenta. **CCC.**
Published by: American Psychological Association, 750 First St, NE, Washington, DC 20002. TEL 202-336-5500, 800-374-2721, journals@apa.org. Ed. Joseph J Hurrell. Adv. contact Doug Constant TEL 202-336-5574. Circ: 400.

➤ **JOURNAL OF OCCUPATIONAL PSYCHOLOGY, EMPLOYMENT AND DISABILITY (ONLINE).** *see* PSYCHOLOGY

615.8 USA ISSN 1053-0487
RC964 CODEN: JOCTEW
➤ **JOURNAL OF OCCUPATIONAL REHABILITATION.** Text in English. 1991. q. EUR 1,095, USD 1,138 combined subscription to institutions (print & online eds.) (effective 2012). adv. bk.rev. back issues avail.; reprint service avail. from PSC. **Document type:** *Journal, Academic/Scholarly.* **Description:** Provides a forum for the publication of papers on the rehabilitation of the disabled worker.
Related titles: Online - full text ed.: ISSN 1573-3688 (from IngentaConnect).
Indexed: A12, A17, A20, A22, A26, ABIn, AMED, ASCA, B21, BibLing, C06, C07, C08, CA, CINAHL, CurCont, E-psyche, E01, EMBASE, ESPM, ErgAb, ExcerpMed, FamI, H&SSA, H12, H13, HRA, IBR, IBZ, MEDLINE, P03, P10, P20, P22, P24, P25, P27, P30, P48, P50, P51, P52, P53, P54, P56, PQC, PsycInfo, PsycholAb, R09, R10, Reac, SCOPUS, SD, SSCI, T02, W07.
—BLDSC (5026.125000), IE, Infotrieve, Ingenta. **CCC.**
Published by: Springer New York LLC (Subsidiary of: Springer Science+Business Media), 233 Spring St, New York, NY 10013. TEL 212-460-1500, FAX 212-460-1575, service-ny@springer.com, http://www.springer.com/. Ed. Michael Feuerstein.

➤ **JOURNAL OF PESTICIDE SAFETY EDUCATION.** *see* AGRICULTURE—Crop Production And Soil

363.7 GBR ISSN 0022-4375
HV675.A1 CODEN: JSFRAV
➤ **JOURNAL OF SAFETY RESEARCH.** Text in English. 1969. 6/yr. EUR 1,038 in Europe to institutions; JPY 137,300 in Japan to institutions; USD 1,159 elsewhere to institutions (effective 2012). adv. bk.rev. illus. Index. back issues avail.; reprints avail. **Document type:** *Journal, Academic/Scholarly.* **Description:** Provides a forum for the exchange of ideas and data developed through research experience in all areas of safety including traffic, industry, farm, home, school and public.
Related titles: Microfilm ed.: (from PQC); Online - full text ed.: ISSN 1879-1247 (from IngentaConnect, ScienceDirect).

N O

Indexed: A01, A02, A03, A08, A22, A25, A26, ASCA, B21, CA, CIS, CISA, CPEI, CurCont, E-psyche, E04, E05, E08, EMBASE, ESPM, EngInd, ErgAb, ExcerpMed, FamI, G01, G08, H&SSA, H13, HRIS, I05, MEDLINE, MycolAb, P02, P03, P10, P20, P30, P48, P50, P52, P53, P54, P56, PQC, PsycInfo, PsycholAb, R10, Reac, RefZh, RiskAb, S01, S02, S03, S08, S09, SCOPUS, SSCI, T02, W07.
—BLDSC (5052.130000), IE, Infotrieve, Ingenta, Linda Hall. **CCC.**
Published by: (National Safety Council USA), Pergamon (Subsidiary of: Elsevier Science & Technology), The Blvd, Langford Ln, East Park, Kidlington, Oxford OX5 1GB, United Kingdom. TEL 44-1865-843000, FAX 44-1865-843010, JournalsCustomerServiceEMEA@elsevier.com. Eds. Mei-Li Lin, Thomas Planek. **Subscr. to:** Elsevier BV, Radarweg 29, PO Box 211, Amsterdam 1000 AE, Netherlands. TEL 31-20-4853757, FAX 31-20-4853432, http://www.elsevier.nl.

➤ **JOURNALEN**; nyhetsbrev fraan yrkes-och miljoemedicin i Goeteborg. *see* MEDICAL SCIENCES

658.31244 USA ISSN 1087-853X
KELLER'S COMPLIANCE FOCUS; workplace safety, environment, transportation, and more. Variant title: Compliance Focus. Text in English. 1992. s-m. looseleaf. USD 194 (effective 2008). **Document type:** *Newsletter, Trade.* **Description:** Provides OSHA, EPA, DOT, EEOC, and SBA developments. Includes how-to articles on topics such as: hazmat training, driver safety and confined spaces.
Formerly (until 199?): Keller's Regulatory Update (1063-4479)
—CCC.
Published by: J.J. Keller & Associates, Inc., 3003 W Breezewood Ln, PO Box 368, Neenah, WI 54957. TEL 877-564-2333, FAX 800-727-7516, kellersoft@jjkeller.com. Ed. Tricia S Hodkiewicz.

658.31244 USA ISSN 1077-7008
KELLER'S O S H A SAFETY TRAINING NEWSLETTER. (Occupational Safety & Health Administration) Variant title: O S H A Safety Training Newsletter. Text in English. 1994. m. looseleaf. USD 189 (effective 2008). **Document type:** *Newsletter, Trade.* **Description:** Contains ideas and advice that can improve training techniques and help meet OSHA requirements.
Formerly: Keller's O S H A Safety Training Guide
—CCC.
Published by: J.J. Keller & Associates, Inc., 3003 W Breezewood Ln, PO Box 368, Neenah, WI 54957. TEL 877-564-2333, FAX 800-727-7516, kellersoft@jjkeller.com. Ed. Judie Smithers.

658.31244 USA ISSN 1090-3445
KELLER'S SAFETY MANAGEMENT TODAY NEWSLETTER. Variant title: Safety Management Today. Text in English. 1996. m. looseleaf. USD 189 (effective 2008). **Document type:** *Newsletter, Trade.* **Description:** Includes articles on ways to improve worker safety, selling safety, and what to do when employees bring problems to work. Included are questions and answers on how to save time and money.
—CCC.
Published by: J.J. Keller & Associates, Inc., 3003 W Breezewood Ln, PO Box 368, Neenah, WI 54957. TEL 877-564-2333, FAX 800-727-7516, kellersoft@jjkeller.com. Ed. Jennifer Stroschein.

KELLER'S TRANSPORTATION SAFETY TRAINING NEWSLETTER. *see* TRANSPORTATION

658.31244 USA ISSN 1931-7638
KELLER'S WORKPLACE SAFETY ADVISOR. Variant title: Workplace Safety Advisor. Text in English. 1980. m. USD 189; USD 249 combined subscription (print & online eds.) (effective 2008). back issues avail. **Document type:** *Newsletter, Trade.* **Description:** Reports on state and federal regulations dealing with the manufacture, distribution, disposal, transport of and exposure to hazardous substances.
Former titles (until Jan. 2006): Keller's Industrial Safety Report (1053-3826); Hazardous Substance Advisor
Related titles: Online - full text ed.: USD 239 (effective 2008).
—CCC.
Published by: J.J. Keller & Associates, Inc., 3003 W Breezewood Ln, PO Box 368, Neenah, WI 54957. TEL 877-564-2333, FAX 800-727-7516, kellersoft@jjkeller.com. Ed. Julie A Nussbaum.

616 CHE
LABOR FLASH. Text in German. 9/yr. adv. **Document type:** *Journal, Trade.*
Published by: Kretz AG, General Wille-Str 147, Postfach, Feldmeilen, 8706, Switzerland. TEL 41-44-9255060, FAX 41-44-9255077, info@kretzag.ch, http://www.kretzag.ch. Ed. H Zullinger. Adv. contact Esther Kretz. B&W page CHF 2,410, color page CHF 3,470; trim 265 x 185. Circ: 6,400.

658.31244 CAN ISSN 0831-5604
CODEN: LIAIE3
LIAISON (HAMILTON). Text in English. 1986. q. **Document type:** *Newsletter, Trade.* **Description:** Provides articles on current occupational health and safety news and trends.
Related titles: Online - full text ed.; French ed.: ISSN 0838-553X.
Published by: Canadian Centre for Occupational Health and Safety (C C O H S)/Centre Canadien d'Hygiene et de Securite au Travail, 135 Hunter St E, Hamilton, ON L8N 1M5, Canada. TEL 905-572-4400, FAX 905-572-4500.

LINYE LAODONG ANQUAN/FORESTRY LABOUR SAFETY. *see* FORESTS AND FORESTRY

LOSS PREVENTION BULLETIN. *see* ENGINEERING—Chemical Engineering

613.62 DEU ISSN 1860-496X
RA1229.5
THE M A K - COLLECTION FOR OCCUPATIONAL HEALTH AND SAFETY. PART 1: M A K VALUE DOCUMENTATIONS. (Maximale Arbeitsplatzkonzentrationen) Text in English. 1991. irreg., latest vol.26, 2010. price varies. **Document type:** *Monographic series, Academic/Scholarly.*
Formerly (until 200?): Occupational Toxicants (0944-4459)
—BLDSC (5353.694903).
Published by: (Deutsche Forschungsgemeinschaft), Wiley - V C H Verlag GmbH & Co. KGaA (Subsidiary of: John Wiley & Sons, Inc.), Postfach 101161, Weinheim, 69451, Germany. TEL 49-6201-606400, FAX 49-6201-606184, info@wiley-vch.de, http://www.wiley-vch.de. Ed. Helmut Greim.

613.62 USA
M I O S H A NEWS. (Michigan Occupational Safety and Health Act) Text in English. 1952. q. free. charts; illus. **Document type:** *Newsletter, Government.* **Description:** Contains articles pertaining to occupational safety and health, engineering controls and interpretations of federal and state occupational health standards.
Formerly (until 1997): Michigan's Health (0026-2501)
Related titles: Online - full text ed.
—Linda Hall.
Published by: Department of Consumer and Industry Services, Bureau of Safety and Regulation, PO Box 30643, Lansing, MI 48909-8143. TEL 517-322-1791, FAX 517-372-1374. Ed., R&P Judith Simons. Circ: 8,500.

613.62 USA
MAINE. BUREAU OF LABOR STANDARDS. SAFETY WORKS; quarterly news for a safer workplace. Text in English. 1994. q. free (effective 2011). **Document type:** *Newsletter, Government.* **Description:** Contains articles concerning safety and health issues in Maine.
Formerly (until 1998): Maine. Bureau of Labor Standards. Safety and Health Monitor
Related titles: Online - full text ed.
Published by: Department of Labor, Bureau of Labor Standards, 45 State House Sta, Augusta, ME 04333. TEL 207-623-7900, 800-794-1110, FAX 207-624-6449, http://www.maine.gov/labor/bls/.

363.11 USA ISSN 0733-8384
MAINE. DEPARTMENT OF LABOR. BUREAU OF LABOR STANDARDS. CHARACTERISTICS OF WORK-RELATED INJURIES & ILLNESSES. Text in English. 19??. a., latest 2006. back issues avail. **Document type:** *Report, Government.* **Description:** Summary of data collected from workers' compensation reports of injury or illness.
Related titles: Online - full text ed.; Series of: Maine. Department of Labor. Bureau of Labor Standards. BLS Bulletin.
Published by: (Maine. Technical Services Division), Department of Labor, Bureau of Labor Standards, 45 State House Sta, Augusta, ME 04333. TEL 207-623-7900, 800-794-1110, FAX 207-624-6449, http://www.maine.gov/labor/bls/.

613.62 CAN ISSN 1912-3000
MATERIAL SAFETY DATA SHEETS. Short title: M S D S. Text in English. 1996. triennial. **Document type:** *Report, Consumer.*
Former titles (until 2006): M S D S + CHEMINFO (1494-0019); (until 1998): M S D S (1494-0000)
Media: CD-ROM. **Related titles:** French ed.: F S T S. ISSN 1494-0027.
—CCC.
Published by: Canadian Centre for Occupational Health and Safety (C C O H S)/Centre Canadien d'Hygiene et de Securite au Travail, 250 Main St., E., Hamilton, ON L8N 1H6, Canada.

MEALEY'S LITIGATION REPORT: MOLD. *see* LAW—Civil Law

MEDICALSPAS; the healthy aging business review. *see* PHYSICAL FITNESS AND HYGIENE

613.62 ITA ISSN 0025-7818
RC963 CODEN: MELAAD
LA MEDICINA DEL LAVORO; rivista di medicina del lavoro ed igiene industriale. Text in Italian, English. 1901. bi-m. EUR 90 in Europe to institutions; EUR 101 elsewhere to institutions (effective 2009). adv. bk.rev. illus.; stat. index. **Document type:** *Journal, Academic/Scholarly.*
Formerly (until 1925): Il Lavoro (1125-3460)
Related titles: Online - full text ed.
Indexed: A22, A34, A35, A36, AgBio, BA, CABA, CISA, CSNB, ChemAb, ChemTitl, D01, E12, EMBASE, ErgAb, ExcerpMed, F08, F11, F12, GH, IHD, INI, IndMed, IndVet, L12, MEDLINE, N02, N03, P30, P32, P33, P37, R07, R08, R10, R12, R13, RM&VM, Reac, S13, S16, SCI, SCOPUS, T05, VS, W07, W10, W11.
—BLDSC (5533.600000), CASDDS, GNLM, IE, Infotrieve, Ingenta, INIST.
Published by: (Istituti Clinici di Perfezionamento), Mattioli 1885 SpA, Via Coduro 1, Fidenza, PR 43036, Italy. TEL 39-0524-84547, FAX 39-0524-84751, http://www.mattioli1885.com. Ed. Vito Foa. Circ: 2,500.

616.9803 ESP ISSN 0465-546X
RC963 CODEN: MSTRAW
MEDICINA Y SEGURIDAD DEL TRABAJO. Text in Spanish. 1952. q. EUR 12 domestic; EUR 24 foreign (effective 2010). back issues avail. **Document type:** *Journal, Academic/Scholarly.*
Incorporated (in 1994): Notas y Documentos sobre Prevencion de Riesgos Profesionales (1132-4422)
Related titles: Online - full text ed.: free (effective 2011).
Indexed: ErgAb, IBR, IBZ, P30.
—CCC.
Published by: Escuela Nacional de Medicina del Trabajo, Pabellon, 8, Ciudad Universitaria, Madrid, 28040, Spain. TEL 34-91-8224031, FAX 34-91-5432466, revistaenmt@isciii.es, http://www.inmst.es/.

613.6 RUS ISSN 1026-9428
CODEN: GTPZAB
➤ **MEDITSINA TRUDA I PROMYSHLENNAYA EKOLOGIYA.** Text in Russian; Summaries in English. 1957. m. USD 156 foreign (effective 2005). adv. bk.rev. index. 48 p./no. 2 cols./p.; back issues avail.; reprints avail. **Document type:** *Journal, Academic/Scholarly.* **Description:** Covers hygiene in industry and agriculture, physiology of labor, industrial toxicology, clinical picture of occupational diseases.
Formerly (until 1993): Gigiena Truda i Professional'nye Zabolevaniya (0016-9919)
Indexed: B25, BIOSIS Prev, CEABA, CIN, CISA, ChemAb, ChemTitl, DentInd, EMBASE, ExcerpMed, IHD, IndMed, MEDLINE, MycolAb, P30, R10, RASB, Reac, RefZh, SCOPUS, WBSS.
—BLDSC (0103.294000), CASDDS, East View, GNLM, IE, Infotrieve, INIST. **CCC.**
Published by: Rossiiskaya Akademiya Meditsinskikh Nauk, Institut Meditsiny Truda, Pr-t Budennogo 31, Moscow, 105275, Russian Federation. TEL 7-095-3661110, FAX 7-095-3660588, izmerov@rinet.ru. Ed., Pub. N F Izmerov. R&P G A Suvorov. Adv. contact N A Kalashnikova. Circ: 600. **Dist. by:** M K - Periodica, ul Gilyarovskogo 39, Moscow 129110, Russian Federation. TEL 7-095-2845008, FAX 7-095-2813798, info@periodicals.ru, http://www.mkniga.ru.

➤ **MEDYCYNA PRACY.** *see* MEDICAL SCIENCES

➤ **MENTAL HEALTH OCCUPATIONAL THERAPY.** *see* PSYCHOLOGY

➤ **MENTAL HEALTH SPECIAL INTEREST SECTION QUARTERLY.** *see* PSYCHOLOGY

658.31244 DEU ISSN 0936-1197
MERKBLAETTER GEFAEHRLICHE ARBEITSSTOFFE. Text in German. 1974. 3 base vols. plus updates 8/yr. looseleaf. EUR 198 (effective 2009). **Document type:** *Bulletin, Trade.*
Published by: Ecomed Verlagsgesellschaft AG & Co. KG (Subsidiary of: Verlagsgruppe Huethig Jehle Rehm GmbH), Justus-von-Liebig-Str 1, Landsberg, 86899, Germany. TEL 49-8191-1250, FAX 49-8191-125492, info@ecomed.de, http://www.ecomed.de. Ed. K Birett. Circ: 10,500 (controlled).

MINE SAFETY DIGEST. *see* MINES AND MINING INDUSTRY

MINE VENTILATION SOCIETY OF SOUTH AFRICA. JOURNAL. *see* MINES AND MINING INDUSTRY

658.31244 690 NLD ISSN 1876-2190
MONITOR ARBEIDSONGEVALLEN IN DE BOUW. Text in Dutch. 199?. a.
Formerly (until 2006): Arbeidsongevallen in de Bouw (1872-1214)
Published by: (Economisch Instituut voor de Bouw), Stichting Arbouw, Postbus 8114, Amsterdam, 1005 AC, Netherlands. TEL 31-20-5805580, FAX 31-20-5805555, info@arbouw.nl, http://www.arbouw.nl.

614.85 NLD ISSN 1874-7418
MONITOR ARBEIDSONGEVALLEN IN NEDERLAND. Text in Dutch. 2004. a. EUR 20 (effective 2010).
Published by: (Netherlands. Nederlandse Organisatie voor Toegepast Natuurwetenschappelijk Onderzoek (TNO)/Netherlands Organization for Applied Scientific Research, Ministerie van Sociale Zaken en Werkgelegenheid, Stichting Consument en Veiligheid), T N O, Kwaliteit van Leven, Postbus 718, Hoofddorp, 2132 JJ, Netherlands. TEL 31-23-5549393, FAX 31-23-5549394, info-arbeid@tno.nl, http://www.tno.nl/arbeid.

MOTOR CARRIER SAFETY REPORT. *see* TRANSPORTATION

363.11 GBR ISSN 2046-6277
MOUNTAIN ACCIDENTS. Text in English. 1973. a. GBP 2 per issue (effective 2011). back issues avail. **Document type:** *Report, Trade.* **Description:** Covers the accidents in mountain rescue operations.
Related titles: Online - full text ed.: ISSN 2046-6285. free (effective 2011).
Published by: Lake District Search & Mountain Rescue Association, c/o Simeon Leech, Rowan Cottage, The Gill, Ulverston, Cumbria LA12 7BN, United Kingdom. TEL 44-1229-480768, sim.leech@virgin.net.

613.62 GBR ISSN 2046-6307
MOUNTAIN RESCUE ENGLAND & WALES. INCIDENT REPORT. Text in English. 200?. a. free (effective 2011). back issues avail. **Document type:** *Report, Trade.*
Related titles: Online - full text ed.: free (effective 2011).
Published by: Mountain Rescue (England & Wales), c/o Ged Feeney, 57 Castlesteads Dr, Carlisle, Cumbria CA2 7XD, United Kingdom. TEL 44-1228-525709, ged@gfeeney.demon.co.uk, http://www.mountain.rescue.org.uk.

613.62 USA
N I O S H MANUAL OF ANALYTICAL METHODS. Variant title: N M A M. Text in English. 19??. irreg. free (effective 2011). **Document type:** *Handbook/Manual/Guide, Trade.* **Description:** A compilation of methods for sampling and analysis of the contaminants in workplace air, and in the blood and urine of workers who are occupationally exposed to that air.
Related titles: Online - full text ed.
Published by: U.S. National Institute for Occupational Safety and Health, 1600 Clifton Rd, Atlanta, GA 30333. TEL 888-232-6348, cdcinfo@cdc.gov.

615.902 USA
N I O S H POCKET GUIDE TO CHEMICAL HAZARDS. (National Institute for Occupational Safety and Health) Variant title: N P G. Text in English. 19??. irreg. free (effective 2011). **Document type:** *Handbook/Manual/Guide, Government.* **Description:** Intended as a source of general industrial hygiene information for workers, employers, and occupational health professionals. Aims to help users recognize and control occupational chemical hazards. Includes information about substances found in the work environment including chemical structures or formulas, properties, measurement methods, signs and symptoms of exposure, and procedures for emergency treatment.
Related titles: CD-ROM ed.; Online - full text ed.
Published by: U.S. National Institute for Occupational Safety and Health, 1600 Clifton Rd, Atlanta, GA 30333. TEL 888-232-6348, cdcinfo@cdc.gov.

658.31244 613.62 USA
N I O S H T I C. (National Institute for Occupational Safety and Health - Technical Information Center) Text in English. 19??. base vol. plus q. updates. free (effective 2011). bibl. **Document type:** *Database, Government.* **Description:** Contains information from a wide variety of sources in addition to those with a primary occupational safety and health orientation in order to aid the examination of all aspects of adverse effects experienced by workers.
Media: Online - full text. **Related titles:** CD-ROM ed.
Published by: (Technical Information Center), U.S. National Institute for Occupational Safety and Health, 1600 Clifton Rd, Atlanta, GA 30333. TEL 888-232-6348, cdcinfo@cdc.gov.

658.31244 NZL ISSN 1177-2239
N O H S A C TECHNICAL REPORT. Text in English. 2004. irreg., latest vol.4, 2006. **Document type:** *Monographic series.*
Published by: National Occupational Health and Safety Advisory Commission, Level 4, Unisys House, 56 The Terrace, PO Box 3705, Wellington, New Zealand. TEL 64-4-9154463, FAX 64-4-9154329, info@nohsac.govt.nz.

N P R A NATIONAL SAFETY CONFERENCE. PROCEEDINGS. *see* PETROLEUM AND GAS

363.11 NLD ISSN 0928-4923
N V V K INFO. Text in Dutch. 1987. 5/yr. adv. **Document type:** *Journal, Trade.*
Formerly (until 1992): N V V K Nieuws (0929-1245)
Published by: Nederlandse Vereniging voor Veiligheidskunde, Postbus 1342, Eindhoven, 5602 BH, Netherlands. TEL 31-40-2480323, nvvk@veiligheidskunde.nl, http://www.veiligheidskunde.nl.

615.8 JPN ISSN 0917-3617
NAGANOKEN SAGYO RYOHOSHIKAI GAKUJUTSUSHI/NAGANO ASSOCIATION OF OCCUPATIONAL THERAPISTS. JOURNAL. Text in Japanese. 1982. a. adv. **Document type:** *Journal, Academic/ Scholarly.*
Published by: Naganoken Sagyo Ryohoshikai/Nagano Association of Occupational Therapists, c/o Suwa Red Cross Hospital, 5-11-50 Kogan-dori, Suwa, 392-8510, Japan. http://www.ot-nagano.org/ index.html.

658.31244 616.2 ZAF ISSN 0374-9800
NATIONAL CENTRE FOR OCCUPATIONAL HEALTH. ANNUAL REPORT. Text in English. 1957. irreg. free. **Document type:** *Report, Trade.*
Formerly: National Institute for Occupational Diseases. Annual Report
Published by: Department of Health, National Centre for Occupational Health, PO Box 4788, Johannesburg, 2000, South Africa. TEL 27-11-7124600, FAX 27-11-7206608, sesokn@health.gov.za, http://www.doh.gov.za/department/ncoh.html. Ed. Dr. A C Cantrell. Circ: 400 (controlled).

613.62 AUS ISSN 0813-1694
NATIONAL SAFETY COUNCIL OF AUSTRALIA. ANNUAL REPORT. Text in English. 1947. a.
Formerly (until 1982): National Safety Council of Australia. Report to the Nation (0156-7241)
Published by: National Safety Council of Australia, Bldg 4, Brandon Office Park, 540 Springvale Rd, Glen Waverley, VIC 3150, Australia. TEL 61-3-85621555, FAX 61-3-85621590, natsafe@nsca.org.au.

363.7 USA ISSN 1048-2911
RA566.3 CODEN: NESLES
➤ **NEW SOLUTIONS**; a journal of environmental and occupational health policy. Abbreviated title: N S. Text in English. 1990. q. USD 103 combined subscription to individuals (print & online eds.); USD 263 combined subscription to institutions (print & online eds.) (effective 2011). back issues avail.; reprints avail. **Document type:** *Journal, Academic/Scholarly.* **Description:** Covers investigated problems of occupational and environmental health with the people at risk - the workers and the community.
Related titles: Online - full text ed.: ISSN 1541-3772. USD 90 to individuals; USD 250 to institutions (effective 2011).
Indexed: AltPI, B21, C06, C07, CA, E-psyche, E04, E05, EMBASE, ESPM, EnvAb, EnvInd, ErgAb, ExcerpMed, H&SSA, IBR, IBZ, LeftInd, MEDLINE, P30, P34, PAIS, PollutAb, RefZh, RiskAb, S02, S03, SCOPUS, SSA, SSciA, SWRA, SociolAb, T02.
—BLDSC (6088.645000), GNLM, IE, Ingenta. **CCC.**
Published by: (Oil, Chemical & Atomic Workers Union), Baywood Publishing Co., Inc., 26 Austin Ave, PO Box 337, Amityville, NY 11701. TEL 631-691-1270, 800-638-7819, FAX 631-691-1770, Baywood@baywood.com, http://www.baywood.com. Eds. Beth Rosenberg, Carlos Eduardo Siqueira, Craig Slatin TEL 978-934-3291. **Co-publisher:** University of Massachusetts Lowell.

363.11 NLD ISSN 2211-1743
NIEUWE ARBOAANPAK. Text in Dutch. 2007. a. EUR 46 (effective 2010).
Published by: Gelling Publishing, Postbus 249, Nieuwerkerk aan den IJssel, 2910 AE, Netherlands. TEL 31-180-319298, FAX 31-180-320069, secretariaat@gelling.nl, http://www.gelling.nl.

363.11 BEL ISSN 1378-8450
NIEUWSBRIEF ARBEIDSVEILIGHEID. Text in Flemish. 1982. s-m. EUR 285.28 (effective 2005). index. **Document type:** *Newsletter.* **Description:** Focuses on latest developments in workers' safety.
Formerly (until 2002): Arbeidsveiligheid (0770-7649)
Published by: C E D Samsom (Subsidiary of: Wolters Samsom Belgie n.v.), Kouterveld 14, Diegem, 1831, Belgium. TEL 32-2-7231111, http://www.kluwer.be/kluwer/home.asp.

NIHON HOUSHASEN ANZEN KANRI GAKKAISHI/JAPANESE JOURNAL OF RADIATION SAFETY MANAGEMENT. *see* PHYSICS—Nuclear Physics

NOISE & HEALTH; a bimonthly inter-disciplinary international journal. *see* MEDICAL SCIENCES—Otorhinolaryngology

613.620711 NOR
NORWAY. DIREKTORATET FOR ARBEIDSTILSYNET. FORSKRIFTER/ REGULATIONS. Text in Norwegian. irreg. price varies. charts; illus. **Document type:** *Monographic series, Trade.*
Formerly: Norway. Statens Arbeidstilsyn Direktoratet. Verneregler
Related titles: Online - full text ed.
Published by: Direktoratet for Arbeidstilsynet/Directorate of Labour Inspection, Statens hus, PO Box 4720, Trondheim, 7468, Norway. TEL 47-81-548222, FAX 47-73-199701, post@arbeidstilsynet.dep.no. **Subscr. to:** Tiden Norsk Forlag, Youngstorget, Postboks 8813, Oslo 0181, Norway.

613.62 GBR
O E D A NEWSLETTER. Text in English. 1996. irreg. GBP 10 domestic; GBP 25 foreign (effective 2001). bk.rev. illus. back issues avail.; reprints avail. **Document type:** *Newsletter.* **Description:** Discusses cases of individuals and groups of workers who have been exposed to asbestos on the job. Provides support for families affected by the disease.
Formerly (until 1996): S P A I D News (0144-4301)
Published by: Occupational and Environmental Diseases Association, Bush Hill Park, Mitre House, 66 Abbey Rd, Enfield, Mddx EN1 2QN, United Kingdom. TEL 44-20-8360-8490, http:// www.oeda.demon.co.uk. Eds. John Griffiths, Nancy Tait. Circ: 2,000.

613.6 616.9 362 USA ISSN 0894-2811
THE O E M REPORT. (Occupational and Environmental Medicine) Text in English. 1987. m. looseleaf. USD 195 in US & Canada; USD 215 elsewhere (effective 2002). bk.rev. back issues avail.; reprints avail. **Document type:** *Newsletter, Trade.* **Description:** Provides scientific information and opinion to occupational and environmental health professionals in a timely fashion.
Published by: O E M Health Information Inc., 8 West St, Beverly, MA 01915. TEL 978-921-7300, FAX 978-921-0304. Ed. Dr. Robert J McCunney. Pub., R&P Curtis R Vouwie.

613.62 AUS ISSN 1443-9832
O H S BULLETIN. (Occupational Health and Safety) Text in English. 1992. fortn. AUD 450 domestic (print or email ed.); AUD 409.09 foreign (print or email ed.) (effective 2008). **Document type:** *Newsletter, Trade.* **Description:** Covers health and safety issues. Keeps up to date with expert commentary, compliance updates and detailed case studies from across Australia.
Formerly (until 19??): Insurance Record
Related titles: CD-ROM ed.; E-mail ed.; Online - full text ed.
Published by: Crown Content, Level 2, 141 Capel St, North Melbourne, VIC 3051, Australia. TEL 61-3-93299800, FAX 61-3-93299698, online@crowncontent.com.au. Ed. Suzannah Pearce.

613.62 363.11 CAN ISSN 0827-4576
O H S CANADA MAGAZINE. (Occupational Health & Safety) Text in English. 1985. m. CAD 90 domestic; USD 90 foreign (effective 2008). adv. bk.rev. charts; illus.; stat.; tr.lit. index. back issues avail. **Document type:** *Magazine, Trade.* **Description:** Provides information on accident prevention, occupational hygiene, laws and standards, workers' compensation.
Related titles: Online - full text ed.
Indexed: A12, A17, A22, ABIn, C03, CBCABus, CBPI, CPerI, G08, H13, I05, P10, P19, P20, P21, P48, P50, P51, P52, P53, P54, P56, PQC.
—BLDSC (6247.585000), IE, Ingenta. **CCC.**
Published by: Business Information Group, 12 Concorde Pl, Ste 800, Toronto, ON M3C 4J2, Canada. TEL 416-442-2122, 800-668-2374, FAX 416-442-2191, orders@businessinformationgroup.ca, http://www.businessinformationgroup.ca. Ed. Angela Stelmakowich TEL 416-510-5121. Pub. Peter Boxer TEL 416-510-5102. Circ: 7,000.

363.1 340 CAN ISSN 1910-7994
O H S COMPLIANCE.CA. (Occupational Health and Safety) Text in English. 1984. m. CAD 329 domestic; USD 329 foreign (effective 2007). **Document type:** *Journal, Trade.* **Description:** Keeps up with new draft legislation, judicial decisions and enforcement activities.
Former titles (until 2006): Occupational Health & Safety Compliance Report (1485-0818); (until 1998): Canadian Occupational Safety and Health Law Monthly Report (0825-608X)
Related titles: E-mail ed.
Published by: EcoLog Environmental Resources Group, 12 Concorde Pl. Ste 800, Toronto, ON M3C 4J2, Canada. TEL 416-442-2122, 800-668-2374, http://www.ecolog.com.

O O H N A JOURNAL. *see* MEDICAL SCIENCES—Nurses And Nursing

613.62 NLD ISSN 1875-7685
O S B TODAY. Text in Dutch. 2006. 4/yr. adv. **Document type:** *Magazine, Trade.*
Published by: (Ondernemersorganisatie Schoonmaak- en Bedrijfsdiensten), A P P R, Postbus 5135, Naarden, 1410 AC, Netherlands. TEL 31-35-6942878, FAX 31-35-6947427, info@appr.nl, http://www.appr.nl. adv.: color page EUR 1,824; bleed 210 x 297. Circ: 3,500.

363.11 USA ISSN 1948-7924
▼ **O S H A COMPLIANCE MANUAL**; application of key O S H A topics insight. (Occupational Safety and Health Administration) Variant title: Insight. Text in English. 2009 (Jul). q. USD 229 per issue (effective 2009). **Document type:** *Magazine, Trade.* **Description:** Provides information on OSHA compliance regulations.
Related titles: Online - full text ed.: ISSN 1948-7932. 2009.
Published by: J.J. Keller & Associates, Inc., 3003 W Breezewood Ln, PO Box 368, Neenah, WI 54957. TEL 877-564-2333, FAX 800-727-7516, kellersoft@jjkeller.com, http://www.jjkeller.com.

O S H A ENVIRONMENTAL COMPLIANCE HANDBOOK. (Occupational Safety and Health Administration) *see* ENVIRONMENTAL STUDIES

363.11 USA ISSN 0740-1418
O S H A NEWS. (Occupational Safety and Health Administration) Text in English. 1996. bi-w. **Document type:** *Newsletter.* **Description:** Contains information and news about developments in the field of occupational safety and health, with a focus on developments regarding OSHA and CFR 1910 and 1926 regulations.
Formed by the 1996 merger of: O S H A News for Construction; O S H A News for General Industry
Published by: U.S. Department of Labor, Occupational Safety and Health Administration, 200 Constitution Ave N W, Washington, DC 20210. TEL 800-321-6742, http://www.osha-slc.gov. Circ: 4,000.

613.62 363.11 USA ISSN 1065-9277
HD7654
O S H A REGULATIONS, DOCUMENTS, AND TECHNICAL INFORMATION ON CD-ROM. (Occupational Safety and Health Administration) (CD-ROM can be used with both Windows and Macintosh systems) Text in English. 1991. q. USD 45 (effective 2001). **Document type:** *Government.* **Description:** Contains the text of all OSHA regulations (standards), selected documents, and technical information from the OSHA Computerized Information System. Includes Mine Safety and Health Regulations.
Media: CD-ROM.
Published by: U.S. Occupational Safety and Health Administration, Office of Public Affairs, Rm N3647, 200 Constitution Ave, N W, Washington, DC 20210. **Subscr. to:** U.S. Government Printing Office, Superintendent of Documents, PO Box 371954, Pittsburgh, PA 15250. TEL 202-512-1800, FAX 202-512-2250, orders@gpo.gov, http://www.access.gpo.gov.

O S H A REQUIRED TRAINING FOR SUPERVISORS. (Occupational Safety and Health Administration) *see* ENVIRONMENTAL STUDIES

613.62 USA
O S H A UP TO DATE NEWSLETTER. (Occupational Safety & Health Administration) Text in English. 19??. m. USD 40 to non-members (print or online ed.); USD 30.80 to members (print or online ed.) (effective 2009). **Document type:** *Newsletter, Trade.* **Description:** Provides a quick update on federal safety initiatives and on state-based and regional OSHA programs.
Related titles: Online - full text ed.
Published by: National Safety Council, 1121 Spring Lake Dr, Itasca, IL 60143. TEL 630-775-2056, 800-621-7619, FAX 630-285-0797, customerservice@nsc.org, http://www.nsc.org.

614.85 USA ISSN 1944-6772
O S H A WATCH. (Occupational Safety and Health Administration) Text in English. 19??. bi-m. USD 99 (effective 2011). adv. back issues avail. **Document type:** *Newsletter, Trade.* **Description:** Focuses on OSHA compliance and general safety needs for smaller practices such as physician and dental offices and ambulatory care centers.
Related titles: Online - full text ed.: ISSN 1944-6780.
Indexed: A26, G06, G07, G08, H12, I05.
Published by: H C Pro, Inc., 200 Hoods Ln, PO Box 1168, Marblehead, MA 01945. TEL 800-650-6787, FAX 781-639-7857, 800-639-8511, customerservice@hcpro.com. Adv. contact Margo Padios TEL 781-639-1872 ext 3145.

613.62 344.04 USA ISSN 1529-9791
O S H A WEEK. (Occupational Safety and Health Administration) Text in English. 1989. w. **Document type:** *Newsletter, Trade.* **Description:** Discusses government policy on occupational health and safety, OSHA Commission review, legislative updates, and tips on workplace health.
Former titles (until 2000): Occupational Health & Safety Week (1524-0622); (until 19??): O S H A Week (1057-1485)
—**CCC.**
Published by: 1105 Media Inc., 9121 Oakdale Ave, Ste 101, Chatsworth, CA 91311. TEL 818-734-1520, FAX 818-734-1522, info@1105media.com, http://www.1105media.com.

363.11 613.62 GBR
O S H BRIEFING (ONLINE). (Occupational Safety and Health) Text in English. 19??. 51/yr. **Document type:** *Bulletin, Trade.* **Description:** Provides concise summaries of newly published U.K. and E.C. legislation, reports, and other documents of an official and authoritative nature. Covers health, safety, fire safety, and related topics.
Media: Online - full text.
Published by: Barbour (Subsidiary of: C M P Information Ltd.), Building B, Kingswood, Kings Ride, Ascot, Berks SL5 8AJ, United Kingdom. TEL 44-1344-884121, FAX 44-1344-899332, barbour-cmc@cmpi.biz.

615.851 USA ISSN 1084-4902
O T PRACTICE. (Occupational Therapy) Text in English. 1986. bi-w. USD 142.50 domestic to individuals; USD 205.25 in Canada to individuals; USD 310 elsewhere to individuals; USD 216.50 domestic to institutions; USD 262.50 in Canada to institutions; USD 365 elsewhere to institutions; free to members (effective 2010). adv. bk.rev.; software rev. charts; illus.; stat.; tr.lit. index. back issues avail. **Document type:** *Magazine, Trade.* **Description:** Covers professional information on all aspects of occupational therapy practice today.
Formerly (until 1995): O T Week (0893-1712)
Related titles: Online - full text ed.: free (effective 2010).
Indexed: A22, C06, C07, C08, CINAHL, P24, P48, PQC, SCOPUS.
—BLDSC (6313.177000), IE, Ingenta. **CCC.**
Published by: American Occupational Therapy Association, Inc., 4720 Montgomery Ln, PO Box 31220, Bethesda, MD 20824. TEL 301-652-2682, 800-377-8555, FAX 301-652-7711, members@aota.org. Ed. Laura Farr Collins. Adv. contact Tracy Hammond.

613.62 616.98 GBR ISSN 1351-0711
RC963 CODEN: OEMEEM
➤ **OCCUPATIONAL AND ENVIRONMENTAL MEDICINE**; an international peer-reviewed journal in all aspects of occupational & environmental medicine. Abbreviated title: O E M. Text in English. 1944. m. GBP 382 to institutions; GBP 495 combined subscription to institutions small FTE (print & online eds.) (effective 2011). adv. bk.rev. abstr.; charts; illus. index, cum.index: 1944-1960. back issues avail.; reprints avail. **Document type:** *Journal, Academic/Scholarly.* **Description:** Focuses on current interest in the whole field of occupational medicine.
Formerly (until 1994): British Journal of Industrial Medicine (0007-1072)
Related titles: CD-ROM ed.; Microform ed.: (from PQC); Online - full text ed.: O E M Online. ISSN 1470-7926. GBP 391 to institutions small FTE (effective 2011).
Indexed: A20, A22, A26, A28, A34, A35, A36, A37, AESIS, APA, APIAb, APICat, APIH&E, APIOC, APIPR, APIPS, APITS, ASCA, AcoustA, B21, B25, BA, BCIRA, BIOBASE, BIOSIS Prev, BrCerAb, C&ISA, C06, C07, C08, CA, CA/WCA, CABA, CADCAM, CIA, CINAHL, CISA, CSNB, CTFA, Cadscan, CerAb, ChemAb, ChemTitl, CivEngAb, CorrAb, CurCont, DentInd, E&CAJ, E01, E04, E05, E08, E11, E12, EEA, EMA, EMBASE, ESPM, EnerRev, EnvAb, EnvEAb, ErgAb, ExcerpMed, F08, F11, F12, FR, G08, GH, GeoRef, H&SSA, H11, H12, H15, H16, I05, IABS, IHD, ISR, IndMed, Inpharma, L12, LT, LeadAb, M&TEA, M09, MBF, MEDLINE, METADEX, MS&D, MycolAb, N02, N03, NRN, OR, P20, P21, P22, P24, P30, P33, P48, P50, P52, P54, P56, PHN&I, PN&I, PQC, PollutAb, R07, R08, R12, R13, RA&MP, RILM, RM&VM, RRTA, RefZh, RiskAb, S09, S13, S16, SCI, SCOPUS, SSCI, SolStAb, SoyAb, SpeleolAb, T02, T04, T05, THA, ToxAb, VS, VirolAbstr, W07, W10, W11, WAA, WSCA, WTA, Zincscan.
—BLDSC (6227.833000), CASDDS, GNLM, IE, Infotrieve, Ingenta, INIST, Linda Hall. **CCC.**
Published by: (Faculty of Occupational Medicine, Royal College of Physicians of London), B M J Group, BMA House, Tavistock Sq, London, WC1H 9JR, United Kingdom. TEL 44-20-73836373, FAX 44-20-73836668, http://group.bmj.com. Ed. Dana Loomis. Pub. Allison Lang TEL 44-20-73836212. Adv. contact Nick Gray TEL 44-20-73836386. Circ: 2,325.

613.62 USA ISSN 0362-4064
RC963 CODEN: OHSADQ
OCCUPATIONAL HEALTH & SAFETY. Abbreviated title: O H & S. Text in English. 1932. m. USD 79 domestic; USD 149 in Canada; USD 189 elsewhere; free domestic to qualified personnel (print or online ed.) (effective 2009). adv. bk.rev. charts; illus. Index. 108 p./no. 3 cols./p.; Supplement avail.; back issues avail.; reprints avail. **Document type:** *Magazine, Trade.* **Description:** Helps professionals understand and control injury, illness and hazardous exposures in the workplace.
Former titles (until 1976): The International Journal of Occupational Health & Safety (0093-2205); (until 1974): International Industrial Medicine and Surgery (0163-934X); (until 1969): The International Journal of Industrial Medicine & Surgery (0093-2191); (until 1967): Industrial Medicine and Surgery (0019-8536); (until 1949): Industrial Medicine and Surgery Trauma (0163-9331); Industrial Medicine (0093-2183)
Related titles: Microform ed.: (from PQC); Online - full text ed.: ISSN 1938-3851.

N O

Indexed: A01, A02, A03, A08, A12, A13, A14, A17, A22, A23, A24, ABIn, B01, B04, B06, B07, B08, B09, B13, B21, BPI, BRD, C06, C07, C08, C12, CA, CINAHL, CISA, ChemAb, DentInd, E04, E05, EMBASE, ESPM, ErgAb, ExcerpMed, FR, H&SSA, H13, HospLI, IHD, IndMed, Inspec, M01, M02, MEDLINE, NPPA, P06, P10, P13, P16, P19, P20, P21, P22, P24, P26, P30, P34, P47, P48, P51, P52, P53, P54, P56, PAIS, PQC, PersLit, RiskAb, S02, S03, SCOPUS, T&DA, T02, V02, W01, W02, W03.
—BLDSC (6228.858000), GNLM, IE, Infotrieve, Ingenta, INIST, Linda Hall. **CCC.**
Published by: 1105 Media Inc., 14901 Quorum Dr, Ste 425, Dallas, TX 75254. TEL 972-687-6700, FAX 972-687-6799, info@1105media.com, http://www.1105media.com. Ed. Jerry Laws TEL 972-687-6701. Pub. Russell Lindsay TEL 254-829-3003. adv.: B&W page USD 10,245, color page USD 11,925; bleed 7.675 x 10.75. Circ: 80,100. **Subscr. to:** PO Box 2087, Skokie, IL 60076. TEL 847-763-9688, FAX 972-687-6769.

344.01 CAN
OCCUPATIONAL HEALTH AND SAFETY IN ONTARIO EDUCATION; a risk and compliance manual. Text in English. base vol. plus updates 3/yr. looseleaf. CAD 210 base vol(s). (effective 2010). **Document type:** *Handbook/Manual/Guide, Trade.*
Published by: LexisNexis Canada Inc. (Subsidiary of: LexisNexis North America), 123 Commerce Valley Dr E, Ste 700, Markham, ON L3T 7W8, Canada. TEL 905-479-2665, 800-668-6481, FAX 905-479-3758, 800-461-3275, info@lexisnexis.ca. Ed. Sandra Glasbeek.

340 CAN ISSN 1719-9522
OCCUPATIONAL HEALTH AND SAFETY IN ONTARIO HEALTH CARE; a risk and compliance manual. Text in English. 2002. base vol. plus updates 3/yr. looseleaf. CAD 210 base vol(s).; CAD 125 updates per issue (effective 2010). **Document type:** *Handbook/Manual/Guide, Trade.*
Published by: LexisNexis Canada Inc. (Subsidiary of: LexisNexis North America), 123 Commerce Valley Dr E, Ste 700, Markham, ON L3T 7W8, Canada. TEL 905-479-2665, 800-668-6481, FAX 905-479-3758, 800-461-3275, info@lexisnexis.ca, http://global.lexisnexis.com/ca. Eds. Fred Campbell, Nora Rock.

OCCUPATIONAL HEALTH AND SAFETY LAW. *see* LAW

OCCUPATIONAL HEALTH AND SAFETY LAW NEW SOUTH WALES. *see* LAW

OCCUPATIONAL HEALTH AND SAFETY LIBRARY. *see* BUSINESS AND ECONOMICS—Labor And Industrial Relations

613.62029 USA ISSN 0896-3835
CODEN: OHSDE2
OCCUPATIONAL HEALTH & SAFETY NEWS. Text in English. 1985. 48/yr. USD 399 (effective 2009). adv. reprints avail. **Document type:** *Newsletter, Trade.* **Description:** Discusses industry news and legislative updates, ergonomics, drug testing, corporate liability and O S H A compliance. Includes case studies and checklists.
—CCC.
Published by: 1105 Media Inc., 14901 Quorum Dr, Ste 425, Dallas, TX 75254. TEL 972-687-6700, FAX 972-687-6799, info@1105media.com, http://www.1105media.com. Pub. Russell Lindsay TEL 254-829-3003. **Subscr. to:** PO Box 2087, Skokie, IL 60076. TEL 847-763-9688, FAX 972-687-6769.

613.62 658.31244 GBR ISSN 1744-2265
OCCUPATIONAL HEALTH [AT WORK]; the multidisciplinary journal that examines the science, law and practice of occupational health at work. Text in English. 2004. bi-m. GBP 189 domestic; GBP 199 foreign (effective 2009). back issues avail. **Document type:** *Journal, Academic/Scholarly.* **Description:** Aims to keep professionals up-to-date with the science, law and practice of occupational health.
Related titles: Online - full text ed.
Published by: The At Work Partnership Ltd., 19 Bishops Ave, Elstree, Herts WD6 3LZ, United Kingdom. TEL 845-017-6986, FAX 208-275-8469, info@atworkpartnership.co.uk. Ed. John Ballard.

613.62 USA ISSN 1082-5339
OCCUPATIONAL HEALTH MANAGEMENT. Text in English. 1991. m. USD 499 combined subscription (print & online eds.); USD 82 per issue (effective 2010). **Document type:** *Newsletter, Trade.* **Description:** Delivers the expert advice, news, and latest regulations that will help you successfully manage your occupational health program, build loyalty in the community, and expand market share for your facility.
Incorporates (1979-2000): Employee Health & Fitness (0199-6304)
Related titles: Online - full text ed.: ISSN 1945-0389.
Indexed: A01, A26, G08, H11, H12, I05, P50.
—CCC.
Published by: A H C Media LLC (Subsidiary of: Thomson Corporation, Healthcare Information Group), 3525 Piedmont Rd, NE, Bldg 6, Ste 400, Atlanta, GA 30305. TEL 404-262-7436, 800-688-2421, FAX 404-262-7837, 800-284-3291, customerservice@ahcmedia.com, http://www.ahcmedia.com/. Pub. Brenda L Mooney TEL 404-262-5403. **Subscr. to:** PO Box 105109, Atlanta, GA 30348. TEL 404-262-5476, FAX 404-262-5560.

613 AUS ISSN 1441-144X
OCCUPATIONAL HEALTH NEWS. Text in English. 1984. w. AUD 922 (effective 2009). **Document type:** *Newsletter, Trade.* **Description:** Provides information on occupational health and safety. Alerts employers and unions to key developments in work place safety and health from Australia and throughout the world.
Formerly (until 1998): Occupational Health Newsletter (1320-1514)
Related titles: Online - full text ed.: ISSN 1446-5787. AUD 929 (effective 2009).
Published by: Thomson C P D (Subsidiary of: Thomson Reuters (Professional) Australia Limited), Level 5, 100 Harris St, Pyrmont, NSW 2009, Australia. TEL 61-2-85877000, FAX 61-2-85877100, LRA.Service@thomson.com, http://www.thomsonreuters.com.au.

613.62 340 GBR
OCCUPATIONAL ILLNESS LITIGATION. Text in English. 2002. base vol. plus updates 2/yr. looseleaf. GBP 326 base vol(s). domestic; EUR 431 base vol(s). in Europe; USD 561 base vol(s). elsewhere (effective 2011). **Document type:** *Handbook/Manual/Guide, Trade.* **Description:** Offers comprehensive and authoritative guidance on all aspects of occupational illness litigation, including exposure to hazardous substances and stress.
Published by: Sweet & Maxwell Ltd. (Subsidiary of: Thomson Reuters Corp.), 100 Avenue Rd, London, NW3 3PF, United Kingdom. TEL 44-20-73937000, FAX 44-20-74491144, sweetandmaxwell.customer.services@thomson.com. Eds. Allan Gore, Andrew McDonald. **Subscr. to:** PO Box 1000, Andover SP10 9AF, United Kingdom. TEL 44-20-73938051, sweetandmaxwell.international.queries@thomson.com.

363.11 USA
OCCUPATIONAL INJURIES AND ILLNESSES. Text in English. 1992. 3 base vols. plus a. updates. looseleaf. USD 623 base vol(s). (effective 2008). **Document type:** *Handbook/Manual/Guide, Trade.* **Description:** Provides information on the medical analysis that is required to prove, refute or prevent allegations of occupational injury and illness.
Related titles: CD-ROM ed.
Published by: Matthew Bender & Co., Inc. (Subsidiary of: LexisNexis North America), 1275 Broadway, Albany, NY 12204. TEL 518-487-3000, 800-424-4200, FAX 518-487-3083, international@bender.com, http://bender.lexisnexis.com. Ed. Daniel Stone.

363.11 USA
HD7262.5.U62
OCCUPATIONAL INJURIES & ILLNESSES IN MAINE (ONLINE). Text in English. 19??. a. free (effective 2011). back issues avail. **Document type:** *Report, Government.* **Description:** Data collected from the survey of occupational injuries and illnesses.
Formerly: Occupational Injuries & Illnesses in Maine (Print) (0198-7771)
Related titles: Series of: Maine. Department of Labor. Bureau of Labor Standards. BLS Bulletin.
Published by: (Maine. Techical Services Division), Department of Labor, Bureau of Labor Standards, 45 State House Sta, Augusta, ME 04333. TEL 207-623-7900, 800-794-1110, FAX 207-624-6449, http://www.maine.gov/labor/bls/.

613.62 616.98 GBR ISSN 0962-7480
CODEN: OCMEE8
➤ **OCCUPATIONAL MEDICINE.** Text in English. 1951. 8/yr. GBP 537 in United Kingdom to institutions; EUR 805 in Europe to institutions; USD 1,020 in US & Canada to institutions; GBP 537 elsewhere to institutions; GBP 586 combined subscription in United Kingdom to institutions (print & online eds.); EUR 878 combined subscription in Europe to institutions (print & online eds.); USD 1,112 combined subscription in US & Canada to institutions (print & online eds.); GBP 586 combined subscription elsewhere to institutions (print & online eds.) (effective 2012). adv. bk.rev. illus. index. 72 p./no.; back issues avail.; reprint service avail. from PSC. **Document type:** *Journal, Academic/Scholarly.* **Description:** Covers original and review articles on all aspects of occupational health.
Former titles (until 1992): Society of Occupational Medicine. Journal (0301-0023); (until 1973): Society of Occupational Medicine. Transactions (0037-9972); (until 1966): Association of Industrial Medical Officers. Transactions (0371-5205)
Related titles: Microform ed.: (from PQC); Online - full text ed.: ISSN 1471-8405. GBP 474 in United Kingdom to institutions; EUR 711 in Europe to institutions; USD 901 in US & Canada to institutions; GBP 474 elsewhere to institutions (effective 2012) (from IngentaConnect).
Indexed: A01, A03, A08, A20, A22, A34, A36, ASCA, B21, BIOBASE, CA, CABA, CISA, ChemAb, CurCont, D01, E01, E04, E05, E12, EMBASE, ESPM, ErgAb, ExcerpMed, F08, F11, F12, FR, GH, H&SSA, IABS, INI, IndMed, IndVet, Inpharma, LT, MEDLINE, N02, N03, N04, P03, P20, P21, P22, P30, P33, P39, P48, P50, P52, P54, P56, PQC, PollutAb, PsycInfo, R07, R08, R10, R12, RM&VM, RRTA, Reac, RiskAb, S02, S03, S12, SCI, SCOPUS, T02, T05, ToxAb, VS, W07, W10, W11.
—BLDSC (6229.610000), CASDDS, GNLM, IE, Infotrieve, Ingenta, INIST. **CCC.**
Published by: (The Society of Occupational Medicine), Oxford University Press, Great Clarendon St, Oxford, OX2 6DP, United Kingdom. TEL 44-1865-556767, FAX 44-1865-556646, enquiry@oup.co.uk, http://www.oxfordjournals.org. Ed. Dr. John Hobson.

658.31244 JPN ISSN 1345-2649
OCCUPATIONAL SAFETY & HEALTH. Text in Japanese. 1950. m. **Description:** Magazine for occupational safety managers, specialists and practitioners.
Formerly (until 2000): Safety (0385-6836)
Published by: Japan Industrial Safety and Health Association, Publishing and Sales Department, 5-35-1 Shiba, Minato-ku, Tokyo, 108-0014, Japan. TEL 81-3-3452-6841, FAX 81-3-3453-8034. Ed. Noriyuki Okano.

613.62 363.11 USA
OCCUPATIONAL SAFETY AND HEALTH ACT. Abbreviated title: O S H A. Text in English. 1977. irreg. (in 5 vols.). looseleaf. USD 793 vols.1-5 (effective 2008). Index. **Document type:** *Monographic series, Trade.* **Description:** Designed for those responsible for the health and safety of employees and who represent injured employees and includes tips on approaching OSHA cases, employer defenses to OSHA enforcement and guide to state OSHA regulations.
Related titles: CD-ROM ed.
Published by: Matthew Bender & Co., Inc. (Subsidiary of: LexisNexis North America), 1275 Broadway, Albany, NY 12204. TEL 518-487-3000, 800-424-4200, FAX 518-487-3083, international@bender.com, http://bender.lexisnexis.com. Ed. John M Hament.

613.62 USA ISSN 0095-5515
OCCUPATIONAL SAFETY AND HEALTH CASES. Text in English. 1974. irreg. USD 719 (effective 2004).
—CCC.
Published by: The Bureau of National Affairs, Inc., 1801 S Bell St, Arlington, VA 22202. TEL 703-341-3000, 800-372-1033, FAX 703-341-4634, 800-253-0332, bnaplus@bna.com, http://www.bna.com.

613.62 346.066 USA ISSN 1535-1602
OCCUPATIONAL SAFETY & HEALTH DAILY. Text in English. 2001. d. USD 1,991 (effective 2010 - 2011). back issues avail. **Document type:** *Newsletter, Trade.* **Description:** Covers legislative, regulatory, and judicial developments affecting job safety and health.
Media: Online - full text.
—CCC.
Published by: The Bureau of National Affairs, Inc., 1801 S Bell St, Arlington, VA 22202. TEL 703-341-3000, 800-372-1033, FAX 703-341-4634, bnaplus@bna.com.

344.043 USA
OCCUPATIONAL SAFETY AND HEALTH HANDBOOK; an employer's guide to OSHA laws, regulations, and practices. Text in English. 1993. latest 4th ed., base vol. plus irreg. updates. looseleaf. USD 128 base vol(s). (effective 2008). **Document type:** *Handbook/Manual/Guide, Trade.* **Description:** Contains laws, regulations and practices.
Related titles: Online - full text ed.
Published by: Michie Company (Subsidiary of: LexisNexis North America), 701 E Water St, Charlottesville, VA 22902. TEL 434-972-7600, 800-446-3410, FAX 434-972-7677, customer.support@lexisnexis.com, http://www.michie.com.

613.62 AUS
OCCUPATIONAL SAFETY AND HEALTH HANDBOOK. Text in English. base vol. plus irreg. updates. looseleaf. AUD 483 to non-members; AUD 261.45 to members (effective 2008). stat. **Document type:** *Journal, Trade.* **Description:** Contains model policies that can be adapted to most workplaces with ready-to-use standard forms, checklists and reports.
Published by: Chamber of Commerce and Industry of Western Australia, 180 Hay St, East Perth, W.A. 6004, Australia. TEL 61-8-93657555, FAX 61-8-93657550, info@cciwa.com.

613.62 AUS
OCCUPATIONAL SAFETY AND HEALTH PROCEDURES MANUAL. Text in English. base vol. plus irreg. updates. looseleaf. AUD 1,650 to non-members; AUD 1,100 to members (effective 2008). **Document type:** *Journal, Trade.* **Description:** Provides details and assists employers to integrate OSH into their policies, procedures and daily business.
Related titles: CD-ROM ed.; Online - full text ed.
Published by: Chamber of Commerce and Industry of Western Australia, 180 Hay St, East Perth, W.A. 6004, Australia. TEL 61-8-93657555, FAX 61-8-93657550, info@cciwa.com.

331 USA ISSN 0095-3237
KF3570.A1
OCCUPATIONAL SAFETY & HEALTH REPORTER. Text in English. 1971. w. looseleaf. USD 2,008 (effective 2010 - 2011). charts; stat. index. 30 p./no.; back issues avail. **Document type:** *Journal, Trade.* **Description:** Provides information on federal and state regulation of occupational safety and health, standards, legislation, enforcement activities, research, and legal decisions.
Related titles: Online - full text ed.: ISSN 1522-4082. USD 1,700 (effective 2010 - 2011); ◆ Optical Disk - DVD ed.: Safety Library. ISSN 1936-6752.
Indexed: EnvAb, IHD.
—BLDSC (6231.205000). **CCC.**
Published by: The Bureau of National Affairs, Inc., 1801 S Bell St, Arlington, VA 22202. TEL 703-341-3000, 800-372-1033, FAX 703-341-4634, bnaplus@bna.com.

613.62 CHE ISSN 0078-3129
CODEN: OSHSDY
OCCUPATIONAL SAFETY AND HEALTH SERIES. Text in English. 1963. irreg., latest vol.72, 1998. price varies. **Document type:** *Monographic series, Trade.*
Related titles: Microform ed.; Spanish ed.; French ed.
Indexed: IMMAb.
—GNLM, Linda Hall. **CCC.**
Published by: I L O, 4 Route des Morillons, Geneva, 1211, Switzerland. TEL 41-22-7996111, FAX 41-22-7988655, ilo@ilo.org, http://www.ilo.org.

363.11 GBR ISSN 1758-2687
▼ **OCCUPATIONAL SAFETY ASIA.** Abbreviated title: O S A. Text in English. 2010. q. GBP 80 (effective 2010). adv. back issues avail. **Document type:** *Magazine, Consumer.* **Description:** Dedicated one-stop resource for commercially unbiased, high quality articles about personal protective equipment.
Published by: Bay Publishing, 1 Oxford Ct, The Granby, Weymouth, Dorset DT4 9GH, United Kingdom. TEL 44-1305-785199, FAX 44-1305-772722, http://www.bay-publishing.com. Ed. Jenny Hardy. Pub. Nick Limm. Adv. contact Chantelle McCrystal.

615.851 GBR ISSN 0966-7903
RM735.A1 CODEN: OTICAT
➤ **OCCUPATIONAL THERAPY INTERNATIONAL.** Text in English. 1994. q. GBP 264 in United Kingdom to institutions; EUR 332 in Europe to institutions; USD 515 elsewhere to institutions; GBP 305 combined subscription in United Kingdom to institutions (print & online eds.); EUR 382 combined subscription in Europe to institutions (print & online eds.); USD 592 combined subscription elsewhere to institutions (print & online eds.) (effective 2012). adv. abstr. back issues avail.; reprint service avail. from PSC. **Document type:** *Journal, Academic/Scholarly.* **Description:** Covers clinical research, current practices, technology, professional issues, education, trends in health care, industrial health and other areas of interest to occupational therapists throughout the world.
Related titles: Online - full text ed.: ISSN 1557-0703. GBP 264 in United Kingdom to institutions; EUR 332 in Europe to institutions; USD 515 elsewhere to institutions (effective 2012).
Indexed: A01, A02, A03, A08, A22, AMED, ASSIA, C06, C07, C08, C11, CA, CINAHL, CurCont, EMBASE, ExcerpMed, H04, MEDLINE, P03, P24, P30, P48, PQC, PsycInfo, PsycholAb, R10, Reac, SCI, SCOPUS, SSCI, T02, W07.
—BLDSC (6231.254800), IE, Infotrieve, Ingenta. **CCC.**
Published by: John Wiley & Sons Ltd. (Subsidiary of: John Wiley & Sons, Inc.), 1-7 Oldlands Way, PO Box 808, Bognor Regis, West Sussex PO21 9FF, United Kingdom. TEL 44-1865-778315, FAX 44-1243-843232, cs-journals@wiley.com, http://eu.wiley.com/WileyCDA/. Ed. Franklin Stein. **Subscr. to:** 1-7 Oldlands Way, PO Box 809, Bognor Regis, West Sussex PO21 9FG, United Kingdom. TEL 44-1865-778054, cs-agency@wiley.com. **Dist. by:** Turpin Distribution Services Ltd., Pegasus Dr, Stratton Business Park, Biggleswade, Bedfordshire SG18 8QB, United Kingdom. TEL 44-1767-604800, FAX 44-1767-601640, custserv@turpin-distribution.com, http://www.turpin-distribution.com/.

613.62 613.85 USA
OFFICIAL DISABILITY GUIDELINES. Text in English. 1996. a., latest 2003, 8th Ed. USD 195 per issue (effective 2003). **Description:** Provides length of disability data with codes from CDC and OSHA. Audience includes case managers, physical therapists, nurses, risk managers, and insurance personnel.
Related titles: CD-ROM ed.: USD 195 per issue (effective 2003).

Published by: Work - Loss Data Institute LLC, 169 Saxony Rd., Ste. 210, Encinitas, CA 92024-6780. Ed. Philip L Denniston.

OMNIGRAPHICS' SECURITY REFERENCE SERIES. *see* CRIMINOLOGY AND LAW ENFORCEMENT—Security

ONTARIO HEALTH AND SAFETY LAW; a complete guide to the law and procedures, with digest of cases. *see* LAW

613.62 CAN ISSN 1719-931X
ONTARIO OCCUPATIONAL HEALTH & SAFETY ACT. Text in English. 2004. a. CAD 65, USD 61.90 per issue (effective 2006). 760 p./no.; **Document type:** *Handbook/Manual/Guide, Trade.*
Published by: Carswell (Subsidiary of: Thomson Reuters Corp.), One Corporate Plz, 2075 Kennedy Rd, Toronto, ON M1T 3V4, Canada. TEL 416-609-8000, 800-387-5164, FAX 416-298-5094, carswell.customerrelations@thomson.com.

613.6 368.41 CAN ISSN 1487-1955
ONTARIO. WORKPLACE SAFETY & INSURANCE BOARD. ANNUAL REPORT. Text in English. 19??. a. **Document type:** *Government.*
Former titles (until 1997): Ontario. Workers' Compensation Board. Annual Report (0822-2150); (until 1982): Ontario. Workmen's Compensation Board. Annual Report (0706-3040); (until 1955): Workmen's Compensation Board. Report (0706-3059)
Published by: The Workplace Safety & Insurance Board, 200 Front St W, Toronto, ON M5V 3J1, Canada. TEL 416-344-1000, FAX 416-344-4684.

613.62 658 USA ISSN 1086-0266
HD49 CODEN: ORENFX
➤ **ORGANIZATION & ENVIRONMENT**; international journal of ecosocial research. Text in English. 1987. q. adv. bk.rev. back issues avail.; reprint service avail. from PSC. **Document type:** *Journal, Academic/Scholarly.* **Description:** Provides an international forum featuring work on the social causes and consequences of environmental damage, restoration, and sustainability, centering on patterns of organizing human production and consumption.
Former titles (until 1996): Industrial and Environmental Crisis Quarterly (1087-0172); (until 1993): Industrial Crisis Quarterly (0921-8106)
Related titles: Microfilm ed.: (from PQC); Online - full text ed.: ISSN 1552-7417. USD 649, GBP 382 to institutions (effective 2011); Special ed(s).: The Organization Dimensions of Global Environmental Change.
Indexed: A12, A13, A17, A20, A22, A28, ABIn, APA, AltPI, B01, B06, B07, B08, B09, BrCerAb, C&ISA, CA/WCA, CIA, CerAb, CivEngAb, CorrAb, CurCont, DIP, E&CAJ, E01, E04, E05, E11, EEA, EMA, ESPM, EconLit, EnvAb, EnvEAb, EnvInd, FR, G02, GEOBASE, GSS&RPL, H04, H15, HPNRM, IBR, IBSS, IBZ, IPsyAb, JEL, LeftInd, M&TEA, M09, MBF, METADEX, P30, P42, P48, P51, P52, P53, P54, P56, PQC, PSA, PollutAb, S02, S03, SCOPUS, SOPODA, SSA, SSCI, SSciA, SUSA, SociolAb, SolStAb, T02, T04, V02, W07, W08, WAA, WildRev.
—BLDSC (6289.122000), IE, Infotrieve, Ingenta, INIST, Linda Hall. **CCC.**
Published by: (Industrial Crisis Institute Inc., New York), Sage Publications, Inc., 2455 Teller Rd, Thousand Oaks, CA 91320. TEL 805-499-9774, 800-818-7243, FAX 805-499-0871, 800-583-2665, info@sagepub.com. Ed. John M Jermier. Circ: 250. **Subscr. outside the Americas to:** Sage Publications Ltd., 1 Oliver's Yard, 55 City Rd, London EC1Y 1SP, United Kingdom. TEL 44-20-73248701, FAX 44-20-73248733, subscription@sagepub.co.uk.

613.62 DEU ISSN 1619-7305
PERSONAL PROTECTION AND FASHION. Abbreviated title: P P F. Text in German. 2001. 4/yr. EUR 38 (effective 2011). adv. **Document type:** *Magazine, Trade.*
Indexed: TM.
Published by: Verlagshaus Gruber GmbH, Max-Planck-Str 2, Eppertshausen, 64859, Germany. TEL 49-6071-39410, FAX 49-6071-394111, info@verlagshaus-gruber.de, http://www.verlagshaus-gruber.de. Ed. Moritz Matthes. adv.: B&W page EUR 2,100, color page EUR 2,800; trim 210 x 297. Circ: 10,500 (paid and controlled).

PERSPECTIVES INTERDISCIPLINAIRES SUR LE TRAVAIL ET LA SANTE. *see* PUBLIC HEALTH AND SAFETY

613.62 CAN ISSN 1910-6904
LE PETIT REPERTOIRE DES RESSOURCES EN SANTE ET SECURITE DU TRAVAIL. Text in French. 1997. irreg.
Formerly (until 2002): Petit Repertoire, Sante et Securite du Travail (1484-2025)
Published by: Commission de la Sante et de la Securite du Travail du Quebec, Direction de la Comptabilite et de la Gestion de l'Information. Service de la Statistique, CP 4900, Succursale Terminus, Quebec, PQ G1K 7S6, Canada. TEL 418-266-4000, 800-668-6811, FAX 418-266-4015, http://www.csst.qc.ca/Portail/fr/index.htm.

PHYSICAL DISABILITIES SPECIAL INTEREST SECTION QUARTERLY. *see* HANDICAPPED

628.5 USA ISSN 1541-2407
PLANT SAFETY & MAINTENANCE. Text in English. 1999. m. free domestic (effective 2002). adv. **Document type:** *Magazine, Trade.*
Published by: Grand View Media Group, Inc. (Subsidiary of: EBSCO Industries, Inc.), 200 Croft St, Ste 1, Birmingham, AL 35242. TEL 888-431-2877, FAX 205-408-3797, webmaster@grandviewmedia.com, http://www.gvmg.com. Ed. Dan Cannon. adv.: color page USD 5,000; bleed 8.375 x 11.

363.11 613.62 GBR ISSN 1477-3996
T55.A1
POLICY AND PRACTICE IN HEALTH AND SAFETY. Text in English. 1997. s-a. GBP 115, EUR 169, USD 175 to institutions; GBP 40, EUR 58, USD 60 to non-members; GBP 20, EUR 29, USD 30 to members (effective 2009). **Document type:** *Journal, Academic/Scholarly.* **Description:** Aimed at those who practice, tutor, research or study health and safety management.
Formerly (until 2003): Institution of Occupational Safety and Health. Journal (1366-1965)
Related titles: Online - full text ed.: ISSN 1477-4003 (from IngentaConnect).
—BLDSC (6543.322480), IE, Ingenta. **CCC.**
Published by: I O S H Publishing Ltd. (Subsidiary of: Institution of Occupational Safety and Health), The Grange, Highfield Dr, Wigston, Leics LE18 1NN, United Kingdom. TEL 44-116-2573100, FAX 44-116-2573101.

363.11 613.62 671.2 POL ISSN 1642-4670
PRACA, ZDROWIE, BEZPIECZENSTWO. Text in Polish. 1958. q. PLZ 100 (effective 2009). **Document type:** *Magazine, Trade.*
Former titles (until 2001): Ochrona Zdrowia Pracownika (1425-1000); (until 1993): Ochrona Zdrowia Hutnika (0208-6913)
Published by: Stowarzyszenie Inzynierow i Technikow Przemyslu Hutniczego w Polsce, ul Podgorna 4, skr poczt 361, Katowice, 40954, Poland. TEL 48-32-2561065, FAX 48-32-2564585, sitphzg@wp.pl, http://www.sitph.republika.pl. Ed. Adam Beluch.

614.85 SVK ISSN 1336-7668
PRAKTICKA PRIRUCKA PRE BEZPECNOSTNYCH TECHNIKOV. Text in Slovak. 2005. q. EUR 128.64 (effective 2009). **Document type:** *Journal, Trade.*
Related titles: CD-ROM ed.; Online - full text ed.: ISSN 1336-8346. 2006.
Published by: Verlag Dashoefer, s.r.o., Zelezniciarska 13, PO Box 323, Bratislava, 814 99, Slovakia. TEL 421-2-33005555, FAX 421-2-33005550, info@dashofer.sk.

613.62 331.11 NLD ISSN 1876-4223
PRAKTIJKBLAD PREVENTIE; het magazine voor arbeid en gezondheid. Text in Dutch. 2007. m. EUR 104; EUR 15 newsstand/cover (effective 2008).
Formed by the merger of (2001-2007): Arbo Informatie (1568-1505); (1995-2007): Verzuim en Reintegratie (1570-0534); Which was formerly (until 2002): Nieuwsbrief Verzuimmanagement (1566-3949)
Published by: Kluwer B.V. (Subsidiary of: Wolters Kluwer N.V.), Postbus 4, Alphen aan den Rijn, 2400 MA, Netherlands. info@kluwer.nl, http://www.kluwer.nl. Eds. Inge Mulder, Jacqueline Joosten.

620.8 USA ISSN 0099-0027
T55.A1 CODEN: PRSAD5
➤ **PROFESSIONAL SAFETY.** Text in English. 1956. m. USD 60 in North America to individuals; USD 70 elsewhere to individuals; USD 51 in North America to institutions; USD 60 elsewhere to institutions (effective 2011). adv. bk.rev. charts; illus.; tr.lit. index. back issues avail.; reprints avail. **Document type:** *Journal, Academic/Scholarly.* **Description:** Features information on developments in the research and technology of accident prevention, safety management and program development.
Former titles (until 1970): A S S E Journal (0884-0776); (until 1969): American Society of Safety Engineers. Journal (0003-1208)
Related titles: Online - full text ed.
Indexed: A01, A02, A03, A05, A08, A12, A13, A17, A22, A23, A24, A36, A37, ABIn, AS&TA, AS&TI, B01, B04, B06, B07, B08, B09, B10, B11, B13, BRD, C10, C12, CA, CABA, CISA, E04, E05, ErgAb, GH, H01, H02, H13, Inspec, M&MA, M01, M02, P10, P13, P19, P20, P21, P26, P30, P34, P48, P50, P51, P52, P53, P54, P56, PQC, R12, S04, SCOPUS, T02, T05, W03, W05.
—BLDSC (6864.215000), IE, Infotrieve, Ingenta, Linda Hall. **CCC.**
Published by: American Society of Safety Engineers, 1800 E Oakton St, Des Plaines, IL 60018. TEL 847-699-2929, FAX 847-768-3434, customerservice@asse.org. Ed. Sue Trebswether. Adv. contact Cathy Wegener TEL 847-768-3414. Circ: 30,500 (paid).

613.62 NLD ISSN 1569-4968
PROFESSIONEEL SCHOONMAKEN. Variant title: P S. Text in Dutch. 2002. 10/yr. EUR 35 (effective 2008). adv. **Document type:** *Magazine, Trade.*
Published by: (Vereniging Schoonmaak Research), A P P R, Postbus 5135, Naarden, 1410 AC, Netherlands. TEL 31-35-6942878, FAX 31-35-6947427, info@appr.nl, http://www.appr.nl. adv.: color page EUR 2,414; bleed 210 x 297. Circ: 5,076.

658.31244 POL ISSN 1426-6660
PROMOTOR; bezpieczenstwo, komfort, praca. Text in Polish. 1996. q. PLZ 140 domestic (effective 2011). **Document type:** *Magazine, Trade.* **Description:** Deals with all aspects of health and safety. Designed for professionals who care about the safety of workers - the owners and managers of companies, labor services, purchasers, wholesalers, and retailers and fire safety equipment.
Related titles: Online - full text ed.
Published by: Wydawnictwo Elamed, Al Rozdzienskiego 188, Katowice, 40203, Poland. TEL 48-32-2580361, FAX 48-32-2039356, elamed@elamed.com.pl, http://www.elamed.com.pl. Ed. Malgorzata Podplomyk.

613.62 ESP
PROTECCION LABORAL. Variant title: Gaceta de la Proteccion Laboral. Text in Spanish, English. 1993. q. EUR 53 domestic; EUR 205 in Europe; EUR 226 elsewhere (effective 2010). **Document type:** *Magazine, Trade.*
Related titles: Online - full text ed.
Published by: Prensa Tecnica S.A., Caspe 118-120, 6o, Barcelona, 08013, Spain. TEL 34-93-2455190, FAX 34-93-2322773, http://www.prensa-tecnica.com.

QUEENSLAND MINES AND QUARRIES SAFETY PERFORMANCE AND HEALTH REPORT. *see* MINES AND MINING INDUSTRY

636.11 GBR
R O S P A OCCUPATIONAL SAFETY & HEALTH BULLETIN. Text in English. 1971. m. GBP 48 domestic to non-members; GBP 56.40 foreign to non-members; GBP 42 domestic to members; GBP 49.35 foreign to members (effective 2009). adv. **Document type:** *Bulletin, Academic/Scholarly.* **Description:** Contains news of all forthcoming relevant legislation, HSC/E discussion documents, guidance notes, approved codes of practice, drafts for development, British and European Standards, EU Directives, research work as well as details of important conferences and publications.
Former titles (until 2001): O S & H Bulletin (1462-4958); (until 1997): R O S P A Bulletin (0143-3377); Which incorporated (in 1979): O S & H Bulletin (0309-1155); Which was formerly (until 1976): Occupational Safety & Health. Supplement (0029-7992); (until 1971): Occupational Safety Bulletin; Which incorporated: Industrial Safety Bulletin; Commerce Safety Bulletin; (until 1966): Industrial Accident Prevention Bulletin
Indexed: BrTechI.
—Linda Hall. **CCC.**
Published by: Royal Society for the Prevention of Accidents, Edgbaston Park, 353 Bristol Rd, Edgbaston, Birmingham, Worcs B5 7ST, United Kingdom. TEL 44-121-2482000, FAX 44-121-2482001, help@rospa.co.uk. Adv. contact Sue Philo TEL 44-1367-820949. B&W page GBP 800; trim 210 x 297.

363.11 613.6 GBR ISSN 1474-7952
T55.A1
R O S P A OCCUPATIONAL SAFETY & HEALTH JOURNAL. Abbreviated title: O S H. Text in English. 1946. m. GBP 91 domestic to non-members; GBP 106.93 foreign to non-members; GBP 77 domestic to members; GBP 90.48 foreign to members (effective 2009). adv. bk.rev.; Website rev. abstr.; charts; illus.; tr.lit. Index. **Document type:** *Journal, Trade.* **Description:** Contains occupational safety and health news and comment, in depth feature articles and series, details of RoSPA affiliated groups' events, details of new products and services plus analysis of policy issues.
Former titles (until 2001): Occupational Safety and Health (0143-5353); (until 1971): British Journal of Occupational Safety (0366-080X); (until 1967): British Journal of Industrial Safety
Related titles: Online - full text ed.
Indexed: A22, A26, A28, ADPA, APA, B01, B07, BCIRA, BMT, BrCerAb, BrRB, BrTechI, C&ISA, CA/WCA, CIA, CISA, Cadscan, CerAb, CivEngAb, CorrAb, E&CAJ, E11, EEA, EMA, Emerald, G08, H&TI, H06, H11, H12, H15, I05, LeadAb, M&MA, M&TEA, M09, MBF, METADEX, P07, P34, Repind, SolStAb, T02, T04, WAA, Zincscan.
—BLDSC (8024.690000), IE, Infotrieve, Ingenta, Linda Hall. **CCC.**
Published by: Royal Society for the Prevention of Accidents, Edgbaston Park, 353 Bristol Rd, Edgbaston, Birmingham, Worcs B5 7ST, United Kingdom. TEL 44-121-2482000, FAX 44-121-2482001, help@rospa.co.uk, http://www.rospa.co.uk. Adv. contact Sue Philo TEL 44-1367-820949. B&W page GBP 950, color page GBP 1,260; trim 210 x 297.

363.11 USA ISSN 1086-6353
R S O MAGAZINE. (Radiation Safety Officer) Text in English. 1996. bi-m. USD 39 in North America to individuals; USD 74 elsewhere to individuals; USD 125 in North America to institutions; USD 160 elsewhere to institutions (effective 2001). adv. bk.rev.; software rev. tr.lit. 32 p./no. 2 cols./p.; back issues avail. **Document type:** *Journal, Trade.* **Description:** Presents practical, work-related information to licensed users of radioactive materials, including training topics, NRC and other guidelines and procedures, and topics relating to the use, storage and disposal of nuclear materials. For radiation safety officers at laboratories, medical facilities, in industry, and at power plants.
Published by: R S A Publications, 19 Pendleton Dr, Box 19, Hebron, CT 06248. TEL 860-228-0824, FAX 860-228-4402. Ed. K Paul Steinmeyer. R&P, Adv. contact Sharyn Mathews TEL 860-228-0487. Circ: 1,200 (paid).

614.8 539.2 USA ISSN 0740-0640
R895.A1 CODEN: RPMAEI
RADIATION PROTECTION MANAGEMENT; the journal of applied health physics. Text in English. 1983. bi-m. USD 54 in North America (effective 2004). adv. bk.rev.; Website rev.; software rev. index. Supplement avail.; back issues avail. **Document type:** *Magazine, Trade.* **Description:** Presents practical, work-related information on applied radiation protection programs at nuclear power plants, fuel facilities, laboratories and waste disposal facilities. Covers the entire spectrum of industrial health physics topics, as well as respiratory protection, technical management, and relevant computer applications.
Indexed: A22, CIN, ChemAb, ChemTitl.
—CASDDS, IE, Ingenta.
Published by: R S A Publications, 19 Pendleton Dr, Box 19, Hebron, CT 06248. TEL 860-228-0824, FAX 860-228-4402, publish@radpro.com, http://www.radpro.com. Ed. K Paul Steinmeyer. R&P, Adv. contact Sharyn Mathews TEL 860-228-0487. Circ: 1,200 (paid).

RADIATION SAFETY MANAGEMENT. *see* PHYSICS—Nuclear Physics

362.104 NOR ISSN 0805-5238
RAMAZZINI/NORWEGIAN JOURNAL OF OCCUPATIONAL MEDICINE. Text in Norwegian. 1969. 4/yr. adv. bk.rev. **Document type:** *Bulletin, Academic/Scholarly.* **Description:** Covers industrial and occupational medicine, as well as general preventive medicine.
Former titles (until 1994): Norsk Tidsskrift for Arbeidsmedisin (0803-2394); (until 1991): Norsk Bedriftshelsetjeneste (0333-0249); (until 1980): Norsk Fretagshaelsovaerd (0332-8910); (until 1978): N I R - Nytt (0358-4909)
—**CCC.**
Published by: Norsk Arbeidsmedisinsk Forening, c/o Den Norske Legeforening, Postboks 1152, Sentrum, Oslo, 0107, Norway. TEL 47-23-109000, legeforeningen@legeforeningen, http://www.legeforeningen.no/index.db2?id=8058. Eds. Bente Moen, Petter Kristensen. Circ: 1,783.

▼ **REDUCING HEALTHCARE COSTS FOR EMPLOYERS.** *see* HEALTH FACILITIES AND ADMINISTRATION

REFERATIVNYI SBORNIK. MEDITSINA TRUDA. NOVOSTI NAUKI I TEKHNIKI. *see* MEDICAL SCIENCES—Abstracting, Bibliographies, Statistics

REPETITIVE STRESS INJURY LAW BULLETIN. *see* LAW

363.11 622.8 676 674 CAN ISSN 1198-1237
RESSOURCE EN SANTE ET EN SECURITE. Text in French. 1955. bi-m. free. bk.rev. back issues avail. **Document type:** *Journal, Trade.* **Description:** For the mining, forestry, and pulp and paper industries of Ontario.
Supersedes in part (in 1994): Tallyboard (0712-3094)
Related titles: ◆ English ed.: Health & Safety Resource. ISSN 1198-1229.
Published by: Ontario Natural Resource Safety Association, 690 Mc Keown Ave, P O Box 2050, North Bay, ON P1B 9P1, Canada. TEL 705-474-SAFE, FAX 705-472-5800. Ed. Susan Haldane. Circ: 10,000 (controlled).

620.82 621.3984 USA ISSN 1557-234X
TA166
REVIEW OF HUMAN FACTORS AND ERGONOMICS. Text in English. 2006. a. USD 118 to institutions; USD 90 to non-members (print or online ed.); USD 80 to members (print or online ed.); USD 140 combined subscription to institutions (print & online eds.); USD 120 combined subscription to non-members (print & online eds.); USD 105 combined subscription to members (print & online eds.) (effective 2010). adv. back issues avail. **Document type:** *Journal, Academic/Scholarly.* **Description:** Provides an excellent overview of some of today's top research topics, including cockpit automation, human performance modeling, and augmented cognition.
Related titles: Online - full text ed.: USD 108 to institutions (effective 2010) (from IngentaConnect).
—BLDSC (7790.769725), IE. **CCC.**

N O

Published by: Human Factors and Ergonomics Society, PO Box 1369, Santa Monica, CA 90406. TEL 310-394-1811, FAX 310-394-2410, info@hfes.org. Ed. Francis T Durso.

613.62 BRA ISSN 0303-7657
RC963.7.B6 CODEN: RBSOEQ
REVISTA BRASILEIRA DE SAUDE OCUPACIONAL. Text in Portuguese, Spanish. 1973. q. BRL 20 per issue domestic (effective 2007). adv. bk.rev. **Document type:** *Journal, Academic/Scholarly.* **Description:** Presents articles on occupational health, hygiene and safety.
Related titles: Online - full text ed.: free (effective 2011).
Indexed: A34, A35, A36, AgBio, C01, CABA, CISA, E12, F08, GH, H16, IndMed, LT, N02, N03, R12, RRTA, Repind, S13, S16, T05.
Published by: Fundacao Jorge Duprat Figueiredo de Seguranca e Medicina do Trabalho, Rua Capote Valente 710, Pinheiros, Sao Paulo, SP 05409-002, Brazil. www.fundacentro.gov.br.

658.31244 ZAF ISSN 1817-6585
RISK MANAGEMENT. Text in English. 2005. m. ZAR 227.40; ZAR 20.50 newsstand/cover (effective 2006). adv. **Document type:** *Magazine, Trade.* **Description:** For the occupational health, safety, environmental and quality management professions.
Published by: 3S Shorten Publications, Pentad House, 55 Andries St N, Wyndberg, Sandton, 2090, South Africa. TEL 27-11-4459404, FAX 27-11-8851594. Ed. Edmond Furter. adv.: page ZAR 6,710; 210 x 297.

301 614.85 ITA ISSN 1825-5396
RIVISTA AMBIENTE E LAVORO. Text in Italian. 2000. m. **Document type:** *Magazine, Consumer.*
Formerly (until 2004): RivistAmbiente (1593-9642)
Published by: Associazione Ambiente e Lavoro, Viale Marelli 497, Sesto San Giovanni, MI 20099, Italy. TEL 39-02-26223130, FAX 39-02-26223130, http://www.amblav.it.

613.62 368 363 ITA ISSN 0035-5836
HD7816.I8 CODEN: RIMPAA
RIVISTA DEGLI INFORTUNI E DELLE MALATTIE PROFESSIONALI. Text in Italian. 1914. bi-m. EUR 60 domestic; EUR 65 foreign (effective 2008). adv. bk.rev. abstr.; bibl.; charts; illus.; stat. index, cum.index. **Document type:** *Magazine, Consumer.*
Indexed: CISA, ChemAb, DoGi, P30, WBSS.
—CASDDS.
Published by: Istituto Nazionale per l'Assicurazione Contro gli Infortuni sul Lavoro (I N A I L), Piazzale G Pastore 6, Rome, 00144, Italy. TEL 39-06-54872014, FAX 39-06-54872050, dccomunicazione@inail.it, http://www.inail.it.

610 JPN
HD4811 CODEN: ROKAAV
RODO KAGAKU/JOURNAL OF SCIENCE OF LABOUR. PART 1. Text in English, Japanese. 1924. m. adv. bk.rev. abstr.; bibl. Index. **Document type:** *Journal, Academic/Scholarly.*
Former titles: Rodo Kagaku. Part 1 (0022-443X); Sangyo Igaku; Incorporated: Institute for Science of Labour. Reports
Related titles: Microfilm ed.
Indexed: A22, A36, CABA, CISA, ChemAb, ChemTitl, E12, ErgAb, F08, F12, GH, IHD, INIS AtomInd, LT, N02, P30, P37, PsycholAb, R12, T05, VS, W11.
—BLDSC (5056.230000), CASDDS, GNLM, IE, Ingenta.
Published by: Institute for Science of Labour/Rodo Kagaku Kenkyujo, 2-8-14 Sugao, Miyamae-ku, Kawasaki, Kanagawa 216-8501, Japan. TEL 81-44-9772121, FAX 81-44-9777504, http://www.isl.or.jp/top.html. Circ: 2,500.

610 JPN ISSN 0035-7774
CODEN: ROKAAV
RODO NO KAGAKU/DIGEST OF SCIENCE OF LABOUR. Text in Japanese. 1946. m. adv. bk.rev. **Document type:** *Academic/Scholarly.*
Indexed: ChemAb, RASB.
Published by: Institute for Science of Labour/Rodo Kagaku Kenkyujo, 2-8-14 Sugao, Miyamae-ku, Kawasaki, Kanagawa 216-8501, Japan. TEL 81-44-9772121, FAX 81-44-9777504, http://www.isl.or.jp/top.html. Circ: 3,000.

620.8 JPN
ROUDOU ANZEN EISEI SOUGOU KENKYUJO GIJUTSU SHISHIN/NATIONAL INSTITUTE OF OCCUPATIONAL SAFETY AND HEALTH. TECHNICAL RECOMMENDATION. Text in Japanese. 1972. irreg. back issues avail. **Document type:** *Academic/Scholarly.*
Formerly (until 2006): Sangyo Anzen Kenkyujo Gijutsu Shishin/National Institute of Industrial Safety. Technical Recommendation (0911-8063)
Published by: Roudou Anzen Eisei Sougou Kenkyujo/National Institute of Occupational Safety and Health, Japan, 1-4-6.Umezono, Kiyose, Tokyo 204-0024, Japan. TEL 86-42-4914512, FAX 81-42-4917846. Circ: 450.

613.62 343.097 USA ISSN 1539-9273
S C S I SAFETY MONITOR. (Southern California Safety Institute) Text in English. 2002. q.
Related titles: Online - full text ed.: ISSN 1539-9893.
Published by: Southern California Safety Institute, 3521 Lomita Blvd., Ste. 103, Torrance, CA 90505. TEL 310-517-8844, http://www.scsi-inc.com.

613.62 363.11 USA
CODEN: SSJOFA
➤ **S E S H A E-JOURNAL.** Text in English. 2002 (vol.15, vol.3, March). s-a. free to members (effective 2011). bk.rev. back issues avail. **Document type:** *Journal, Academic/Scholarly.* **Description:** Provides industry solutions via education and development of our members, and promotes sharing of ESH information and experience.
Media: Online - full text.
Published by: Semiconductor Environmental Safety Health Association, c/o Brett Burk, 1313 Dolley Madison Blvd, Ste 402, McLean, VA 22101. TEL 703-790-1745, FAX 703-790-2672, BBurk@BurkInc.com. Ed. Mary Majors.

658.31244 DEU ISSN 1612-765X
S I FA TIPP; Praxiszeitung fuer Sicherheitsfachkraefte. (Sicherheitsfachkraft) Text in German. 2003. 4/yr. EUR 29 (effective 2008). adv. **Document type:** *Magazine, Trade.*
Published by: W E K A Media GmbH & Co. KG, Roemerstr 16, Kissing, 86438, Germany. TEL 49-8233-239490, FAX 49-8233-237400, service@weka.de, http://www.weka.de. Ed. Christiane Deppe. Adv. contact Stefan-Andreas Schaefer. B&W page EUR 2,600, color page EUR 3,380; trim 215 x 315. Circ: 20,120 (controlled).

613.6 FIN ISSN 1795-9926
RC963.A1
S J W E H SUPPLEMENTS. (Scandinavian Journal of Work, Environment & Health) Text in English. 2005. a. **Document type:** *Journal, Academic/Scholarly.*
Related titles: Online - full text ed.: ISSN 1795-9918. free (effective 2011).
Indexed: SD.
Published by: Tyoterveyslaitos/Finnish Institute of Occupational Health, Topeliuksenkatu 41a A, Helsinki, 00250, Finland. TEL 358-30-4742694, FAX 358-9-241-4634, http://www.occupahealth.fi.

613.62 NOR ISSN 1890-131X
S T A M I-RAPPORT (ONLINE). (Statens Arbeidsmiljoeinstitutt) Text mainly in Norwegian; Text occasionally in English. 2000. irreg. price varies. back issues avail. **Document type:** *Monographic series.*
Formerly (until 2005): S T A M I-Rapport (Print) (1502-0932)
Media: Online - full content.
Published by: Statens Arbeidsmiljoeinstitutt/National Institute of Occupational Health, PO Box 8149, Dep, Oslo, 0033, Norway. TEL 47-23-195100, FAX 47-23-195200, stami@stami.no.

613.62 AUS ISSN 1838-0581
▼ **SAFE WORK AUSTRALIAN.** Text in English. 2009. q. free (effective 2011). back issues avail. **Document type:** *Newsletter, Government.* **Description:** Focuses on the key issues in work health and safety and workers' compensation matters and provides an update on the work of safe work Australia.
Media: Online - full text.
Published by: Safe Work Australia, GPO Box 641, Canberra, ACT 2601, Australia. TEL 61-2-61215317, info@safeworkaustralia.gov.au.

331 USA ISSN 0896-9051
HD7262
SAFE WORKER. Text in English. 1928. m. illus. **Description:** On-the-job safety information for non-supervisory personnel.
Published by: National Safety Council, 1121 Spring Lake Dr, Itasca, IL 60143. TEL 630-775-2056, 800-621-7619, FAX 630-285-0797, customerservice@nsc.org, http://www.nsc.org.

363.11 613.62 658.31244 NZL ISSN 0113-9533
SAFEGUARD (AUCKLAND); the magazine for better safety and health at the workplace. Text in English. 1992. bi-m. NZD 85 (effective 2008). adv. bk.rev.; video rev. illus.; stat.; tr.lit. 74 p./no.; back issues avail. **Document type:** *Magazine, Trade.* **Description:** Explores all aspects of workplace health and safety in New Zealand and includes profiles of organisations and people with progressive and inspirational OHS ideas, features on technical topics to help sharpen your practice, commentary on law changes, and summaries of all OHS prosecutions.
Related titles: ◆ Supplement(s): Safeguard - Buyers Guide. ISSN 1172-9872.
Indexed: INZP.
Published by: Safeguard Publications Ltd., Ponsonby, PO Box 147-245, Auckland, New Zealand. TEL 64-4-4998178, service@brookers.co.nz. Ed. Peter Bateman TEL editor@safeguard.co.nz. Pub. Terry Barnett. Adv. contact Angela M J Kilikolly. Circ: 7,000 (paid).

363.11 613.62 658.31244 NZL ISSN 1172-9872
SAFEGUARD - BUYERS GUIDE. Text in English. 1994. a. adv. 128 p./no.; back issues avail. **Document type:** *Directory, Trade.* **Description:** Covers health, safety products and services directory.
Related titles: Online - full content ed.; ◆ Supplement to: Safeguard (Auckland). ISSN 0113-9533.
Published by: Safeguard Publications Ltd., Ponsonby, PO Box 147-245, Auckland, New Zealand. TEL 64-4-4998178, http://www.safeguard.co.nz.

613.6 USA ISSN 1547-1098
SAFETY ALERT FOR SUPERVISORS. Text in English. 2003 (Jul.). s-m. USD 117 (effective 2011). **Document type:** *Newsletter, Trade.* **Description:** Designed as a training tool for supervisors.
Formerly (until 2003): Manager's Security Alert (1541-7379)
Published by: Institute of Business Publications, 748 Springdale Dr, Exton, PA 19341. TEL 484-876-0223, FAX 484-876-0230, iobp@comcast.net. Ed. Jim McCanney.

363.72 USA ISSN 0891-1797
SAFETY & HEALTH. Abbreviated title: S H. Variant title: Safety + Health. Text in English. 1917. m. USD 67.50 to non-members (effective 2011). adv. bk.rev. abstr.; bibl.; charts; illus.; stat.; tr.lit. index, cum.index. reprints avail. **Document type:** *Magazine, Trade.* **Description:** Provides national coverage of occupational safety news and analysis of industry trends.
Former titles (until 1987): National Safety and Health News (8756-5366); (until May 1985): National Safety News (0028-0100)
Related titles: Microform ed.: (from PQC); Online - full text ed.
Indexed: A01, A02, A03, A08, A22, A23, A24, A25, A26, ABIPC, ASFA, B02, B04, B11, B13, B15, B17, B18, BPI, BRD, BusI, C12, CISA, CSNB, ChemAb, E04, E05, E06, E08, ESPM, EngInd, G04, G06, G07, G08, H11, H12, H13, HlthInd, I05, IHD, L12, M01, M02, P02, P06, P07, P10, P20, P30, P34, P48, P52, P53, P54, P56, PQC, S08, S09, SCOPUS, SSciA, T&DA, T&II, T02, W01, W02, W03.
—IE, Infotrieve, Ingenta, Linda Hall.
Published by: National Safety Council, 1121 Spring Lake Dr, Itasca, IL 60143. TEL 630-775-2056, 800-621-7619, FAX 630-285-0797, customerservice@nsc.org, http://www.nsc.org.

363.11 613.6 JPN
SAFETY & HEALTH IN JAPAN. Text in English. irreg., latest vol.27, 1999. **Document type:** *Newsletter.* **Description:** Provides information about the Association's activities, including awards, conferences and conventions relating to occupational health and safety. Also covers government activities and initiatives, and information from recent papers on topics such as disaster prevention, traffic safety, and public health.
Indexed: L12.
Published by: Japan Industrial Safety and Health Association, International Cooperation Department, 5-35-1, Shiba, Minato-ku, Tokyo, 108-0014, Japan. TEL 81-3-3452-6841, FAX 81-3-3454-4596.

363 USA ISSN 1069-4943
SAFETY AND THE SUPERVISOR. Text in English. 1993. bi-w. USD 208 (effective 2008). back issues avail. **Document type:** *Newsletter, Trade.* **Description:** Contains information and advice on how to protect employees from accidents and injuries.

Published by: Clement Communications, Inc., 10 LaCrue Ave, PO Box 36, Concordville, PA 19331. TEL 610-459-4200, 888-358-5858, FAX 610-459-4582, 800-459-1933, customerservice@clement.com. Pub. George Y Clement.

331 AUS ISSN 1444-6995
SAFETY AT WORK. Text in English. 2000. bi-m. back issues avail. **Document type:** *Magazine, Trade.*
Related titles: Online - full text ed.: 2000. AUD 171.60 domestic; AUD 156 foreign (effective 2009).
Published by: Workplace Safety Services, 849 High St, Regent, VIC 3073, Australia. TEL 61-3-9478-9484, FAX 61-3-9442-3607, jones@worksafety.com.au, http://www.worksafety.com.au/.

363.11 613.62 USA ISSN 1546-9247
SAFETY.BNA.COM. Text in English. 2002. bi-w. **Document type:** *Journal, Trade.* **Description:** Covers thousands of worker safety and health topics.
Media: Online - full text.
—CCC.
Published by: The Bureau of National Affairs, Inc., 1801 S Bell St, Arlington, VA 22202. TEL 703-341-3000, 800-372-1033, FAX 703-341-4634, bnaplus@bna.com, http://www.bna.com.

363.11 658.31244 USA ISSN 1077-9787
SAFETY COMPLIANCE ALERT. Abbreviated title: S C A. Text in English. 1994. s-m. USD 299 (effective 2008). charts. 8 p./no.; **Document type:** *Newsletter, Trade.* **Description:** Aims to keep safety professionals current on safety rules and worker compliance.
Published by: Progressive Business Publications, 370 Technology Dr, Malvern, PA 19355. TEL 610-695-8600, 800-220-5000, FAX 610-647-8089, customer_service@pbp.com. Ed. Maureen Hennessy. R&P Curt Brown. Circ: 18,114 (paid).

614.8 USA ISSN 1556-6900
HD7653
SAFETY COMPLIANCE LETTER. Text in English. 19??. m. USD 399; USD 40 per issue (effective 2011). index. **Document type:** *Newsletter, Trade.* **Description:** Features include analysis from industry, labor, and government officials on current issues and trends.
Incorporates (1975-200?): Safety Management (1069-2118); Former titles (until 2002): Safety (1069-2037); (until 1986): O S H A Compliance Letter (0092-5799)
Related titles: Online - full text ed.
Indexed: A15, ABIn, B01, B02, B06, B07, B09, B15, B17, B18, G04, G06, G07, G08, I05, PQC, T02.
—CCC.
Published by: Aspen Publishers, Inc. (Subsidiary of: Wolters Kluwer N.V.), 76 Ninth Ave, 7th Fl, New York, NY 10011. TEL 212-771-0600, 800-317-3113, FAX 212-771-0885, Aspen-InternationalS@wolterskluwer.com, https://www.aspenpublishers.com. **Subscr. to:** 7201 McKinney Cir, Frederick, MD 21704. TEL 301-698-7100, FAX 301-695-7931. **Dist. by:** Turpin Distribution Services Ltd. kluwerlaw@turpin-distribution.com, http://www.turpin-distribution.com/.

SAFETY DIGEST (OTTAWA)/DIGEST DE SECURITE. *see* MILITARY

636.11 GBR ISSN 1359-9313
SAFETY EXPRESS. Text in English. 1995. bi-m. GBP 29 domestic to non-members; GBP 34.08 foreign to non-members; GBP 25 domestic to members; GBP 29.38 foreign to members (effective 2009). adv. video rev. stat.; tr.lit. back issues avail. **Document type:** *Newspaper.* **Description:** Covers health and safety in the workplace aimed at the non-specialist. Contains extensive coverage of court cases, new publications and videos, training courses, news from the trade unions plus features and a monthly competition and topical cartoon guide.
—BLDSC (8065.783000). **CCC.**
Published by: Royal Society for the Prevention of Accidents, Edgbaston Park, 353 Bristol Rd, Edgbaston, Birmingham, Worcs B5 7ST, United Kingdom. TEL 44-121-2482000, FAX 44-121-2482001, help@rospa.co.uk. Adv. contact Sue Philo TEL 44-1367-820949. B&W page GBP 850.

613.62 363.11 USA ISSN 1936-6752
KF3568
SAFETY LIBRARY. Text in English. 1994 (Sept.). m. USD 1,943 (effective 2010 - 2011). **Document type:** *Newsletter, Trade.* **Description:** Collection of resources including the laws, regulations, related documents and analysis covering occupational safety and health issues.
Formerly (until 2007): B N A's Safety Library on C D (1084-9599)
Media: Optical Disk - DVD. **Related titles:** Online - full text ed.: ISSN 1522-4082. USD 1,700 (effective 2010 - 2011); ◆ Print ed.: Occupational Safety & Health Reporter. ISSN 0095-3237.
—CCC.
Published by: The Bureau of National Affairs, Inc., 1801 S Bell St, Arlington, VA 22202. TEL 703-341-3000, 800-372-1033, FAX 703-341-4634, bnaplus@bna.com.

363.11 354.7 ZAF ISSN 0377-8592
T55.A1
SAFETY MANAGEMENT; the bigger picture in occupational safety, health and environmental risk management. Text in English. 1958. m. (11/yr.). ZAR 130 domestic; USD 200 foreign (effective 2001 - 2002). adv. bk.rev.; Website rev.; software rev.; video rev. illus.; stat.; tr.lit.; pat.; abstr. Supplement avail. **Document type:** *Magazine, Trade.* **Description:** Explores the various echelons of management and the workforce in industrial, commercial, financial and governmental undertakings. Emphasis on all aspects of occupational health, safety, and environment.
Formerly: Safety in Industry (0036-2484); Incorporates: Safety Digest (0036-2468)
Indexed: CISA, INIS AtomInd.
—Linda Hall.
Published by: National Occupational Safety Association, PO Box 26434, Arcadia, Pretoria 0007, South Africa. TEL 27-12-3039700, FAX 27-12-3039870, taniam@nosa.co.za, http://www.nosa.co.za. Ed. Ed Furter. Adv. contact Eugene Howell TEL 27-12-3039717. B&W page ZAR 170, color page ZAR 980. Circ: 6,300 (paid and controlled).
Co-sponsor: Association of Societies for Occupational Safety and Health.

658.382 GBR ISSN 0951-2624
HD7261
SAFETY MANAGEMENT MAGAZINE. Key Title: Safety Management. Text in English. 1983. m. (11/yr.). GBP 60; GBP 55 to members (effective 2010). bk.rev.; video rev. **Document type:** *Magazine, Trade.* **Description:** Aims to provide objective reporting on news, as well as in-depth features on issues in the field of occupational health and safety. Includes listings of forthcoming events, an information section, and important helplines.
Former titles (until 1987): Safety & Risk Management (0267-8624); (until 1985): Safety & Fire News (0953-1157); Which was formed by the merger of (1981-1983): Fire News (0262-4451); (1978-1983): Safety
Indexed: A28, APA, B21, BrCerAb, BrTechI, C&ISA, CA/WCA, CIA, CSNB, CerAb, CivEngAb, CorrAb, E&CAJ, E11, EEA, EMA, ESPM, EnvEAb, H&SSA, H15, L12, M&TEA, M09, MBF, METADEX, RefZh, SolStAb, T04, WAA.
—IE, Infotrieve, Ingenta, Linda Hall.
Published by: British Safety Council, 70 Chancellors Rd, London, W6 9RS, United Kingdom. TEL 44-20-87411231, FAX 44-20-87414555, mail@britsafe.org. Ed. Robert Jarvis. R&P Ian Fraser. Adv. contact Brian Carter.

613.62 362.1 USA
SAFETY MEETING REPROS. Text in English. q. USD 295 (effective 2009). **Document type:** *Handbook/Manual/Guide, Trade.* **Description:** Contains 50 safety training meetings on OSHA-required safety topics.
Published by: Business & Legal Reports, Inc., 141 Mill Rock Rd E, Old Saybrook, CT 06475. TEL 860-510-0100, 800-727-5257, FAX 860-510-7225, service@blr.com. Ed. Peggy Carter Ward. Pub. Robert L Brady.

SAFETY NEWS. *see* WATER RESOURCES

363.11 USA ISSN 1078-0114
SAFETY NOW; putting safety into practice. Text in English. 1994. m. USD 325; USD 33 per issue (effective 2011). index. **Document type:** *Newsletter, Trade.* **Description:** Features training tips and techniques for the supervisor.
Incorporates: Safety Dates and Deadlines
Related titles: Online - full text ed.
Indexed: A15, ABIn, B02, B15, B17, B18, G04, G06, G07, G08, I05, P52, PQC.
—CCC.
Published by: Aspen Publishers, Inc. (Subsidiary of: Wolters Kluwer N.V.), 76 Ninth Ave, 7th Fl, New York, NY 10011. TEL 212-771-0600, 800-317-3113, FAX 212-771-0885, ASPEN-CustomerService@wolterskluwer.com, https://www.aspenpublishers.com. Eds. Elaine Stattler, Joyce Anne Grabel. Pub. Paul Gibson. **Subscr. to:** 7201 McKinney Cir, Frederick, MD 21704. TEL 301-698-7100, FAX 301-695-7931.

613 USA
SAFETY ONLINE; virtual community for the safety industry. Text in English. d.
Media: Online - full text.
Address: 1287 W 108th St, Cleveland, OH 44102. Ed. Sandy Smith.

614.8 USA
SAFETY REMINDER. Text in English. 1973. m. price varies. **Document type:** *Newsletter, Trade.* **Description:** Includes safety checklists, case decisions covering the legal problems of safety and security, "Questions and Answers" that probe all aspects of industrial safety and security, and safety and security ideas that work.
Formerly: Safety & Security for Supervisors (1040-4236)
Published by: Business & Legal Reports, Inc., 141 Mill Rock Rd E, Old Saybrook, CT 06475. TEL 860-510-0100, 800-727-5257, FAX 860-510-7225, service@blr.com, http://www.blr.com. Ed. Judith A Ruddy.

331 NLD ISSN 0925-7535
HD7262 CODEN: SSCIEO
➤ **SAFETY SCIENCE.** Text in English, French, German. 1977. 10/yr. EUR 1,329 in Europe to institutions; JPY 176,600 in Japan to institutions; USD 1,486 elsewhere to institutions (effective 2012). adv. bk.rev. charts; illus. index. reprints avail. **Document type:** *Journal, Academic/Scholarly.* **Description:** For safety engineers and inspectors, industrial engineers, research scientists, industrial psychologists and ergonomists. Presents research papers on aspects of work-related risks of various occupations.
Formerly (until 1992): Journal of Occupational Accidents (0376-6349)
Related titles: Microform ed.: (from PQC); Online - full text ed.: (from IngentaConnect, ScienceDirect).
Indexed: A01, A03, A08, A22, A26, A28, A35, A36, A37, AESIS, APA, ASCA, AgBio, B21, BrCerAb, C&ISA, CA, CA/WCA, CABA, CIA, CISA, CPEI, CSNB, CerAb, CivEngAb, CorrAb, CurCont, E&CAJ, E04, E05, E11, E12, EEA, EMA, EMBASE, ESPM, EngInd, EnvEAb, ErgAb, ExcerpMed, F08, F12, FR, GH, GeoRef, H&SSA, H15, H16, HRIS, I05, L12, LT, M&TEA, M09, MBF, METADEX, N02, P03, P30, PAIS, PsycInfo, PsycholAb, R10, R12, RRTA, Reac, RiskAb, S01, S13, S16, SCI, SCOPUS, SolStAb, T02, T04, T05, TAR, W07, W11, WAA.
—BLDSC (8069.124900), GNLM, IE, Infotrieve, Ingenta, INIST, Linda Hall. **CCC.**
Published by: Elsevier BV (Subsidiary of: Elsevier Science & Technology), Radarweg 29, PO Box 211, Amsterdam, 1000 AE, Netherlands. TEL 31-20-4853911, FAX 31-20-4852457, JournalsCustomerServiceEMEA@elsevier.com, http://www.elsevier.nl. Ed. K Mearns.

363.1 AUS ISSN 1443-8844
➤ **SAFETY SCIENCE MONITOR.** Abbreviated title: S S M. Text in English. 1997. a., latest vol.12, 2008. free (effective 2011). back issues avail. **Document type:** *Journal, Academic/Scholarly.* **Description:** Focuses on different aspects of the management of safety - in fire fighting, in medical care and in off-shore oil production.
Media: Online - full text.
Indexed: AusPAIS, B21, ESPM, H&SSA, RiskAb.
Published by: I P S O Australia, PO Box 516, Mt Eliza, VIC 3930, Australia. Ed. Tore J Larsson TEL 61-3-99051890.

614 USA
SAFETY SIGNALS. Text in English. 1974. bi-m. free. bk.rev. **Document type:** *Newsletter, Trade.* **Description:** Contains information about the safety equipment industry, member companies, association activities and upcoming meetings and events.
Published by: International Safety Equipment Association, 1901 N Moore St, Ste 808, Arlington, VA 22209. TEL 703-525-1695, FAX 703-528-2148, isea@safetyequipment.org. Ed., Pub., R&P Bruce R Clash. Circ: 450 (controlled).

614.85 AUS ISSN 1447-8277
SAFETY SOLUTIONS. Text in English. 2003. bi-m. free to qualified personnel (effective 2008). adv. **Document type:** *Magazine, Trade.* **Description:** Provides vital information on safety products and services in the industrial, construction, utilities and mining sectors.
Related titles: Online - full text ed.; Supplement(s): Industrial Workwear Solutions.
Published by: Westwick-Farrow Pty. Ltd., Locked Bag 1289, Wahroonga, NSW 2076, Australia. TEL 61-2-94872700, FAX 61-2-94891265, admin@westwick-farrow.com.au. Eds. Paul Stathis, Janette Woodhouse. Pub. Adrian Farrow. adv.: color page AUD 4,526, B&W page AUD 4,076. Circ: 10,158.

658.31244 AUS ISSN 1321-9553
SAFETY W A; West Australian journal of occupational safety and health. (West Australia) Text in English. 1972. bi-m. free to members (effective 2008). bk.rev. charts; stat.; tr.lit. back issues avail. **Document type:** *Magazine, Trade.* **Description:** Provides details on the latest occupational safety and health issues on a local, national and international level.
Former titles (until 1987): I F A P Bulletin (0813-0035); (until 1982): I F A P News (0311-0311)
Related titles: Online - full text ed.: free (effective 2008).
Published by: Industrial Foundation for Accident Prevention, PO Box 339, Willetton, W.A. 6955, Australia. TEL 61-8-93103760, FAX 61-8-93323511, ifap@ifap.asn.au. Eds. David Leith, Ray Thomas TEL 61-8-93671921. R&P Arianne George TEL 61-9-4306611. Circ: 1,700.

614.85 AUS ISSN 1834-4151
SAFETYLINE NEWSLETTER FOR O S H PROFESSIONALS. (Occupational Safety and Health) Text in English. 2006. q. **Document type:** *Newsletter, Trade.*
Media: Online - full text.
Published by: Western Australia, Department of Consumer and Employment Protection. Worksafe Division, 1260 Hay St, West Perth, W.A. 6005, Australia. TEL 61-8-9327-8777, 1300-307-877, FAX 61-8-9321-8973, safety@docep.wa.gov.au, http://www.worksafe.wa.gov.au. Ed. Rhonda Husdon.

614.85 AUS ISSN 1834-4135
SAFETYLINE NEWSLETTER FOR SAFETY AND HEALTH REPRESENTATIVES. Text in English. 2006. q. **Document type:** *Newsletter, Trade.*
Media: Online - full text. **Related titles:** Print ed.: ISSN 1834-4127.
Published by: Western Australia, Department of Consumer and Employment Protection. Worksafe Division, 1260 Hay St, West Perth, W.A. 6005, Australia. TEL 61-8-9327-8777, 1300-307-877, FAX 61-8-9321-8973, safety@docep.wa.gov.au, http://www.worksafe.wa.gov.au. Ed. Rhonda Husdon.

614.85 AUS ISSN 1834-4143
SAFETYLINE NEWSLETTER FOR SMALL BUSINESS. Text in English. 2006. q. **Document type:** *Newsletter, Trade.*
Media: Online - full text.
Published by: Western Australia, Department of Consumer and Employment Protection. Worksafe Division, 1260 Hay St, West Perth, W.A. 6005, Australia. TEL 61-8-9327-8777, 1300-307-877, FAX 61-8-9321-8973, safety@docep.wa.gov.au, http://www.worksafe.wa.gov.au. Ed. Rhonda Husdon.

613.62 JPN ISSN 0915-1354
SAGYO RYOHO JANARU/JAPANESE JOURNAL OF OCCUPATIONAL THERAPY. Text in Japanese. 1967. m. JPY 22,785; JPY 1,628 newsstand/cover (effective 2007).
Supersedes in part (in 1988): Rigaku Ryoho to Sagyo Ryoho/Japanese Journal of Physical Therapy and Occupational Therapy (0386-9849)
—BLDSC (4656.765000).
Published by: Miwa-Shoten Ltd., 6-17-9 Hongo, Bunkyo-ku, Hongou Tsuna Bldg. 4F, Tokyo, 113-0033, Japan. TEL 81-3-38167796, FAX 81-3-38167756, info@miwapubl.com, http://www.miwapubl.com/.

613.62 IRN ISSN 1735-5133
➤ **SALAMAT-I KAR-I IRAN/IRAN OCCUPATIONAL HEALTH.** Text in Persian, Modern; Abstracts in English, Persian, Modern. 2004. q. software rev. abstr.; charts; illus.; stat. back issues avail.; reprints avail. **Document type:** *Journal, Academic/Scholarly.* **Description:** Publishes original research papers and case reports, review articles and technical reports related to the fields of public health and occupational health particularly.
Related titles: Online - full text ed.
Published by: Danishgah-i Ulum-i Pizishki-i Tihran/Tehran University of Medical Sciences, Faculty of Public Health, No.60, Alvand St., Argentina Sq., Tehran, Iran. TEL 98-21-88779118, FAX 98-21-88779487. Ed., R&P Ali-Asghar Farshad.

613.62 CAN ISSN 1912-0818
SAMPLING GUIDE FOR AIR CONTAMINANTS IN THE WORKPLACE. Text in English. 1990. irreg., latest 2005. CAD 16 per issue (effective 2007). 200 p./no.; **Document type:** *Handbook/Manual/Guide, Trade.*
Published by: Institut de Recherche en Sante et Securite du Travail (I R S S T), 505, boul. De Maisonneuve Ouest, Montreal, PQ H3A 3C2, Canada. TEL 514-288-1551, FAX 514-288-7636, Publications@irsst.qc.ca, http://www.irsst.qc.ca/fr/accueil.html.

613.6 JPN ISSN 1341-0725
RC963.A1 CODEN: SEZAFI
SANGYO EISEIGAKU ZASSHI. Text in Japanese; Summaries in English. 1959. 6/yr. free to members. adv. bk.rev. illus. Index. **Document type:** *Journal, Academic/Scholarly.* **Description:** Publishes original contributions relevant to occupational and environmental health, including fundamental toxicological studies of industrial chemicals and other related studies.
Formerly (until 1995): Sangyo Igaku/Japanese Journal of Industrial Health (0047-1879)
Related titles: Online - full text ed.: ISSN 1349-533X. free (effective 2011); ◆ English ed.: Journal of Occupational Health. ISSN 1341-9145.
Indexed: A22, B21, CISA, ChemAb, ChemTitl, EMBASE, ESPM, ExcerpMed, FR, H&SSA, IHD, INIS AtomInd, IndMed, MEDLINE, P30, PollutAb, RiskAb, SCOPUS.
—BLDSC (8073.242000), CASDDS, GNLM, IE, Infotrieve, Ingenta, INIST. **CCC.**
Published by: Nihon Sangyo Eisei Gakkai/Japan Society for Occupational Health, Public Health Bldg, 1-29-8 Shinjuku, Shinjuku-ku, Tokyo, 160-0022, Japan. TEL 81-3-3356-1536, FAX 81-3-3356-1536. Ed. Akio Koizumi. Circ: 5,300.

613.62 JPN ISSN 0387-821X
CODEN: JOUOD4
SANGYO IKA DAIGAKU ZASSHI. Key Title: Journal of U O E H. Text in English, Japanese; Summaries in English. 1979. q. bk.rev. back issues avail. **Document type:** *Journal, Academic/Scholarly.* **Description:** Focuses on occupational and environmental health sciences, but includes articles in other fields of medicine and humanities.
Indexed: A22, A34, A36, B25, BIOSIS Prev, C25, CABA, CISA, E12, EMBASE, ExcerpMed, GH, INIS AtomInd, IndMed, IndVet, MEDLINE, MycolAb, N02, N03, P30, P32, P33, P40, PGegResA, R08, R10, R11, R12, RA&MP, Reac, S12, S13, S16, SCOPUS, T05, VS.
—BLDSC (4912.250000), CASDDS, GNLM, IE, Infotrieve, Ingenta, INIST.
Published by: University of Occupational and Environmental Health Japan, Association of Health Sciences, Iseigaoka 1-1, Yahatanishi-ku, Kitakyushu, 807-8555, Japan. Ed. U. Yamashita. Circ: 900 (controlled).

613.6 FIN ISSN 0355-3140
RC963.A1 CODEN: SWEHDO
➤ **SCANDINAVIAN JOURNAL OF WORK, ENVIRONMENT & HEALTH.** Text in English. 1975. bi-m. EUR 180 in Scandinavia to individuals; EUR 200 elsewhere to individuals; EUR 210 in Scandinavia to institutions; EUR 230 elsewhere to institutions; EUR 360 combined subscription in Scandinavia print and online eds; EUR 880 combined subscription elsewhere print and online eds (effective 2006). bk.rev. abstr.; illus. index. back issues avail.; reprints avail. **Document type:** *Journal, Academic/Scholarly.*
Formed by the merger of (1962-1974): Work - Environment - Health (0300-3221); (1920-1974): Nordisk Hygienisk Tidskrift (0029-1374); Which superseded in part (1908-1920): Hygienisk Tidskrift; (1904-1920): Maanedsskrift for Sundhedspleje
Related titles: Online - full text ed.: ISSN 1795-990X; Supplement(s): Scandinavian Journal of Work, Environment and Health. Supplement. ISSN 0356-6528. 1976.
Indexed: A20, A22, A34, A36, A37, A38, ASCA, B21, B25, BIOBASE, BIOSIS Prev, CA, CABA, CIS, CISA, CSNB, ChemAb, ChemTitl, CurCont, D01, DentInd, E-psyche, E12, EMBASE, ESPM, EnvAb, EnvInd, ErgAb, ExcerpMed, F08, F11, F12, FR, GEOBASE, GH, H&SSA, IABS, IHD, INI, ISR, IndMed, IndVet, Inpharma, L12, LT, MEDLINE, MycolAb, N02, N03, N04, NRN, P03, P20, P22, P25, P27, P30, P33, P48, P50, P52, P54, P56, PEI, PN&I, PQC, PollutAb, PsycholAb, R07, R08, R12, RM&VM, RRTA, RiskAb, S13, S16, SCI, SCOPUS, SD, SSCI, T02, T05, THA, TM, ToxAb, TriticAb, VS, W07, W11, WSCA.
—BLDSC (8087.568000), CASDDS, GNLM, IE, Infotrieve, Ingenta, INIST. **CCC.**
Published by: (Det Nationale Forskningscenter for Arbejdsmiljoe/The National Research Centre for the Working Environment DNK, Statens Arbeidsmiljoeinstituttt/National Institute of Occupational Health NOR), Tyoterveyslaitos/Finnish Institute of Occupational Health, Topeliuksenkatu 41a A, Helsinki, 00250, Finland. TEL 358-30-4742694, FAX 358-9-878-3326, http://www.occuphealth.fi/eng/dept/sjweh/index.htm. Eds. Eira Viikari-Juntura, Dr. Mikko Harma TEL 358-9-304742729. Circ: 1,100. **Co-sponsor:** National Institutes of Occupational Health for Sweden, Norway and Denmark.

613.62 GBR
SCIENCE & RESEARCH OUTLOOK. Text in English. 2004. q. free (effective 2009). back issues avail. **Document type:** *Newsletter, Trade.* **Description:** Provides information on specific research projects on the wider impact of the HSE's science and research portfolio, across all industry sectors.
Incorporates (in 2004): Offshore Research Focus (Online)
Media: E-mail. **Related titles:** Online - full text ed.
Published by: Health & Safety Executive, 1G Redgrave Ct, Merton Rd, Bootle, Merseyside L20 7HS, United Kingdom. TEL 44-151-9514000, http://www.hse.gov.uk/.

614 FRA ISSN 0755-2386
SECURITE ET MEDECINE DU TRAVAIL. Text in French. 1969. q. EUR 94 domestic; EUR 110 foreign (effective 2007). adv. bibl.; charts; illus. **Document type:** *Magazine, Trade.*
Indexed: CISA, FR.
Published by: Association Francaise des Techniciens et Ingenieurs de Securite et des Medecins du Travail (A F T I M), 1 Place Uranie, Joinville le Pont, 94340, France. TEL 33-1-48857059.

614.85 DEU ISSN 2190-4367
SECURITY. Text in English. 1992. 6/yr. EUR 70; EUR 14 newsstand/cover (effective 2010). adv. **Document type:** *Magazine, Trade.*
Formerly (until 2009): G I T Security & Management (1865-3782); Which superseded in part (in 2007): G I T Sicherheit und Management (0948-9487); Which was formerly (until 1995): G I T Spezial Arbeitsschutz, Arbeitssicherheit (0942-2374)
Related titles: Online - full text ed.
Published by: G I T Verlag GmbH (Subsidiary of: Wiley - V C H Verlag GmbH & Co. KGaA), Roesslerstr 90, Darmstadt, 64293, Germany. TEL 49-6151-80900, FAX 49-6151-8090146, info@gitverlag.com. Circ: 20,000 (paid and controlled).

363.11 NLD ISSN 1386-0941
SECURITY MANAGEMENT. Text in Dutch. 1975. 10/yr. EUR 114.50; EUR 49 to students; EUR 15 newsstand/cover (effective 2009). adv. **Document type:** *Journal, Trade.*
Former titles (until 1997): Preventie (0169-0884); (until 1983): Stip (0166-3259); (until 1977): Beveiliging (0920-0991)
—IE.
Published by: (Stichting Informatie Preventie), Kluwer B.V. (Subsidiary of: Wolters Kluwer N.V.), Postbus 4, Alphen aan den Rijn, 2400 MA, Netherlands. TEL 31-172-466633, info@kluwer.nl, http://www.kluwer.nl. adv.: B&W page EUR 1,220, color page EUR 1,805. Circ: 2,715 (paid and controlled).

614.8 ESP ISSN 1888-5438
SEGURIDAD Y MEDIO AMBIENTE. Text in Spanish; Summaries in English. 1981. q. free to qualified personnel (effective 2009). adv. cum.index: 1981-1991. back issues avail. **Document type:** *Journal, Trade.* **Description:** Covers accident and fire prevention, industrial hygiene, occupational medicine, and safety at work.
Formerly (until 2007): Mapfre Seguridad (0212-1050)

N O

Indexed: IECT, WSCA.
Published by: Fundacion Mapfre, Paseo de Recoletos, 23, Madrid, 28004, Spain. TEL 34-91-5812353, FAX 34-91-5816070, fundacion.informacion@mafre.com. Adv. contact Javier Delbusto. Circ: 21,226 (controlled).

620.8 NLD
SERIES IN PHYSICAL ERGONOMICS. Variant title: Physical Ergonomics Series. Text in English. 1993. irreg., latest vol.6, 2000. price varies. back issues avail. **Document type:** *Monographic series, Academic/Scholarly.* **Description:** Discusses ways in which products can be made to better accommodate the human body.
Published by: Delft University Press (Subsidiary of: I O S Press), Nieuwe Hemweg 6B, Amsterdam, 1013 BG, Netherlands. TEL 31-20-6883355, FAX 31-20-6870039, info.dupress@iospress.nl.

SHEPARD'S FEDERAL O S H A CITATIONS. (Occupational Safety and Health) *see* LAW—Judicial Systems

613.6 DEU ISSN 1613-1223
SICHER IST SICHER - ARBEITSSCHUTZ AKTUELL; Fachzeitschrift fuer Sicherheitstechnik, Gesundheitsschutz und menschengerechte Arbeitsgestaltung. Text in German. 2004. m. EUR 74.40; EUR 7.40 newsstand/cover (effective 2012). adv. **Document type:** *Magazine, Trade.*
Formed by the merger of (1949-2004): Sicher ist Sicher (0037-4504); (1990-2004): Arbeitsschutz Aktuell (0863-3924)
Related titles: Online - full text ed.: ISSN 1865-195X. EUR 74.40 (effective 2012).
Published by: Erich Schmidt Verlag GmbH & Co. (Berlin), Genthiner Str 30 G, Berlin, 10785, Germany. TEL 49-30-2500850, FAX 49-30-250085305, esv@esvmedien.de, http://www.esv.info. Ed. Ralf Pieper. Adv. contact Peter Taprogge. Circ: 2,450 (paid and controlled).

613.6 368.5 AUT ISSN 0037-4512
SICHERE ARBEIT; Zeitschrift fuer Arbeitsschutz. Text in German. 1947. bi-m. EUR 46 domestic; EUR 61.60 foreign (effective 2004). adv. bk.rev. charts; illus.; stat. index. **Document type:** *Magazine, Trade.*
Indexed: A22, CISA, TM.
—IE, Infotrieve.
Published by: (Allgemeine Unfallversicherungsanstalt), Bohmann Druck und Verlag GmbH & Co. KG, Leberstr 122, Vienna, W 1110, Austria. TEL 43-1-740950, FAX 43-1-74095183, office.gl@bohmann.at, http://www.bohmann.at. Ed. Christian Klobucsar. Adv. contact Christoph Jenschke TEL 43-1-74095476. B&W page EUR 2,430, color page EUR 3,340; trim 185 x 250. Circ: 13,000.

613.62 DEU ISSN 1438-9398
SICHERHEIT AM ARBEITSPLATZ. Text in German. 1971. q. free to members (effective 2007). adv. **Document type:** *Bulletin, Trade.*
Formerly (until 199?): Sicherheit am Arbeitsplayz. Ausgabe LE (0172-8342)
Published by: Lederindustrie-Berufsgenossenschaft, Lortzingstr 2, Mainz, 55127, Germany. libg@lpz-bg.de.

613.6 AUT ISSN 1016-0515
SICHERHEITSMAGAZIN. Variant title: Neue Betriebs Sicherheit. Text in German. 1965. 10/yr. adv. bk.rev. abstr.; illus.; stat. index. **Document type:** *Magazine, Consumer.*
Formerly (until 1988): Betriebssicherheit - B S (0005-3287)
Indexed: CISA.
Published by: Allgemeine Unfallversicherungsanstalt, Adalbert-Stifter-Str 65, Vienna, 1200, Austria. TEL 43-1-331110, FAX 43-1-33111855, http://www.auva.at. Ed. Wilfried Friedl. Adv. contact Margot Weidner. Circ: 250,000 (controlled).

363.1 CAN ISSN 0228-9091
SIGNAL. Text in English, French. 1989. q. free. adv. **Document type:** *Newsletter.* **Description:** Covers road safety, home and occupational safety, accident prevention instructions and research data.
Related titles: Online - full text ed.
Published by: Ligue Securite du Quebec/Quebec Safety League, 533, rue Ontario Est, bureau 206, Montreal, PQ H2L 1N8, Canada. TEL 514-595-9110, FAX 514-595-3398. Ed., R&P Diane Des Autels. Circ: 10,000.

SIMPLY BETTER. *see* LIFESTYLE

363.11 GBR ISSN 1360-7103
SITE SAFE NEWS. Text in English. 1981. irreg., latest 2008. back issues avail. **Document type:** *Newsletter, Trade.*
Related titles: Online - full text ed.: free (effective 2009).
—CCC.
Published by: Health and Safety Executive, Rose Court, 2 Southwark Bridge, London, SE1 9HS, United Kingdom. TEL 44-845-3450055, FAX 44-20-75562102, public.enquiries@hse.gov.uk.

658.31244 GBR ISSN 1757-8205
SKILLS PLEDGE. Text in English. 2008. q. back issues avail. **Document type:** *Magazine, Trade.* **Description:** Provides leading expert analysis, reviews, discussions and opinions, while giving valuable case studies and insights on the personal development initiative that assist in driving forward business and commerce within the English market place, ensuring the enhancement of future competitiveness.
Related titles: Online - full text ed.: free (effective 2010).
Published by: Distinctive Publishing Ltd., 7th Fl, Aidan House, Sunderland Rd, Gateshead, NE8 3HU, United Kingdom. TEL 44-191-4788300, production@distinctivepublishing.co.uk, http://www.distinctivepublishing.co.uk.

614 USA ISSN 1043-1721
RA399.A1
SOCIETY FOR HEALTH SYSTEMS. JOURNAL. Key Title: Journal of the Society for Health Systems. Text in English. q. USD 35 membership (effective 2004). **Document type:** *Journal, Trade.*
Formerly (until 1989): I E News: Health Services
Indexed: INI, IndMed, P30, SCOPUS.
—GNLM. **CCC.**
Published by: Institute of Industrial Engineers, Society for Health Systems, 3577 Pkwy Ln Ste 200, Norcross, GA 30092. TEL 770-449-0460, 800-494-0460, FAX 770-441-3295, http://shs.iienet.org/index.cfm. Circ: 1,000.

616.980 FRA ISSN 1775-9595
SOINS ET PREVENTION EN ENTREPRISE. Text in French. 2003. irreg. **Document type:** *Monographic series, Trade.*
Related titles: ◆ Series of: Collection Etude Pratique. ISSN 1289-8368; ◆ Supplement to: Collection Etude Pratique. ISSN 1289-8368.
Published by: Gereso Editions, 26 rue Xavier-Bichat, Le Mans, 72018 Cedex 2, France. TEL 33-2-43230353, FAX 33-2-43284067, edition@gereso.fr, http://www.gereso.com.

658.31244 DEU ISSN 0935-4905
STRAHLENSCHUTZ; Radioaktive Stoffe - Roentgengeraete - Beschleuniger. Text in German. 1973. 2 base vols. plus a. updates. looseleaf. EUR 98 base vol(s).; EUR 49.80 updates per issue (effective 2009). **Document type:** *Monographic series, Trade.*
Published by: Erich Schmidt Verlag GmbH & Co. (Berlin), Genthiner Str 30 G, Berlin, 10785, Germany. TEL 49-30-2500850, FAX 49-30-250085305, vertrieb@esvmedien.de, http://www.erich-schmidt-verlag.de.

615.849 DEU ISSN 0081-5888
CODEN: STFPAT
STRAHLENSCHUTZ IN FORSCHUNG UND PRAXIS. Text in German. 1961. irreg. **Document type:** *Monographic series, Academic/Scholarly.*
Indexed: P30.
—CCC.
Published by: (Vereinigung Deutscher Strahlenschutzaerzte), Urban und Fischer Verlag (Subsidiary of: Elsevier GmbH), Loebdergraben 14a, Jena, 07743, Germany. TEL 49-3641-6263, FAX 49-3641-626500, journals@urbanfischer.de, http://www.urbanundfischer.de.

658.31244 DEU ISSN 0947-434X
TK9152 CODEN: STPRFM
STRAHLENSCHUTZPRAXIS; Zeitschrift fuer den sicheren Umgang mit ionisierender und nichtionisierender Strahlung. Text in German. 1995. q. EUR 52; EUR 17 newsstand/cover (effective 2010). adv. **Document type:** *Magazine, Trade.*
Indexed: CIN, ChemAb, ChemTitl, GeoRef, INIS AtomInd, SpeleolAb, TM.
—CASDDS. **CCC.**
Published by: (Fachverband fuer Strahlenschutz e.V.), T Ue V Media GmbH, Am Grauen Stein 1, Cologne, 51105, Germany. TEL 49-221-8063535, FAX 49-221-8063510, tuev-media@de.tuv.com, http://www.tuev-media.de. Ed. Dr. Rupprecht Maushart. Adv. contact Gudrun Karafiol.

613.62 USA ISSN 1945-4503
THE SUPER ADVISOR; real world solutions for employee management and supervisor success. Text in English. 2008 (Nov.). m. USD 199 (effective 2011). **Document type:** *Newsletter, Trade.* **Description:** Provides HR pros with expert insight and advice to strengthen and reinforce supervisors' employee management skills.
Published by: J.J. Keller & Associates, Inc., 3003 W Breezewood Ln, PO Box 368, Neenah, WI 54957. TEL 877-564-2333, 800-558-5011, FAX 800-727-7516.

363.11 USA ISSN 2150-6639
SUPERSAFEMARK GUIA DE REFERENCIA RAPIDA LAS MEJORES PRACTICAS DE SEGURIDAD E HIGIENE EN LA VENTA DIRECTA DE ALIMENTOS AL CONSUMIDOR. Text in Spanish. 2007. a. USD 14.99 per issue to non-members; USD 9.74 per issue to members (effective 2009). **Document type:** *Guide, Consumer.* **Description:** Focuses on the key areas of personal hygiene, time and temperature management, preventing cross contamination, cleaning and sanitizing practices, and accident prevention and safety.
Published by: Food Marketing Institute, 2345 Crystal Dr, Ste 800, Arlington, VA 22202. TEL 202-452-8444, FAX 202-429-4519, fmi@fmi.org.

613.62 USA ISSN 1548-002X
SUPERVISOR SAFETY ALERT; what line supervisors need to know about safety. Text in English. 2004 (Mar.). m. USD 189; free to qualified personnel (effective 2008). **Document type:** *Newsletter, Trade.* **Description:** Addresses safety-related issues affecting supervisors and their employees.
Related titles: Online - full text ed.
—CCC.
Published by: J.J. Keller & Associates, Inc., 3003 W Breezewood Ln, PO Box 368, Neenah, WI 54957. TEL 877-564-2333, FAX 800-727-7516, kellersoft@jjkeller.com. Ed. Travis Rhoden.

363.11 SWE
SWEDISH WORK ENVIRONMENT AUTHORITY. NEWSLETTER. Text in English, Swedish. 1975. biennial. free. back issues avail. **Document type:** *Newsletter.* **Description:** Provides articles on specific work environment issues.
Former titles (until 2000): National Board of Occupational Safety and Health. Newsletter (Online) (1403-9672); (until 1996): National Board of Occupational Safety and Health. Newsletter (Print) (0348-7598)
Media: Online - full content.
Indexed: ErgAb, R18.
Published by: Swedish Work Environmental Authority, Solna, 17184, Sweden. TEL 46-8-730-9000, FAX 46-8-730-1967. Ed. Elisabet Delang. Pub. Bertil Remaeus.

613.62 USA ISSN 1066-7660
SYNERGIST (FAIRFAX). Text in English. 1989. m. charts; stat.; tr.lit. back issues avail. **Description:** Provides information on issues affecting the profession and the association. Includes meeting announcements and conference updates.
Indexed: CSNB, EnvAb, EnvInd, L12.
—CCC.
Published by: American Industrial Hygiene Association, 2700 Prosperity Ave, Ste 250, Fairfax, VA 22031-4307. TEL 703-849-8888, FAX 703-207-3561, infonet@aiha.org, http://www.aiha.org. Ed. Debbie Williams. Circ: 11,000.

613 GBR
SYSTEM CONCEPTS LTD; ergonomics in practice. Text in English. m.
Media: Online - full text.
Address: 2 Savoy Court, The Strand, London, WC2R 0EZ, United Kingdom. helpdesk@system-concepts.com, http://www.system-concepts.com.

T O G; revista terapia ocupacional Galicia. (Terapia Ocupacional Galicia) *see* MEDICAL SCIENCES—Physical Medicine And Rehabilitation

613.6 DEU ISSN 1434-9728
CODEN: TUSZA6
TECHNISCHE UEBERWACHUNG. Text in German. 1960. 9/yr. EUR 207.50 domestic; EUR 226 foreign; EUR 25 per issue (effective 2010). adv. bk.rev. charts; illus.; pat.; tr.mk. index. back issues avail.; reprints avail. **Document type:** *Magazine, Trade.*
Former titles (until 1996): T Ue - Technische Ueberwachung. Sicherheit Zuverlaessigkeit und Umweltschutz in Wirtschaft und Verkehr (0376-1185); (until 1970): Technische Ueberwachung (0372-2457); Which was formed by the merger of (1955-1960): Technische Ueberwachung (Munich) (0173-9883); (1955-1960): B T U - Betrieb und Technische Ueberwachung (0404-5696); Which was formerly (until 1956): Betrieb und Technische Ueberwachung (0173-9891)
Related titles: Online - full text ed.: ISSN 1436-4948. 1999.
Indexed: A22, CEABA, ChemAb, DIP, IBR, IBZ, INIS AtomInd, Inspec, SCOPUS, TM.
—BLDSC (8753.500000), CASDDS, IE, Ingenta, INIST, Linda Hall. **CCC.**
Published by: (Verband der Technischen Ueberwachungsvereine e.V.), Springer V D I Verlag GmbH & Co. KG, VDI-Platz 1, Duesseldorf, 40468, Germany. TEL 49-211-61030, FAX 49-211-6103300, info@technikwissen.de. Ed. Elisabeth Zimmermann TEL 49-211-6103343. Adv. contact Gabriele Jahn TEL 49-211-6103378. B&W page EUR 2,424, color page EUR 3,414; trim 210 x 297. Circ: 4,447 (paid and controlled).

TECHNOLOGY SPECIAL INTEREST SECTION QUARTERLY. *see* TECHNOLOGY: COMPREHENSIVE WORKS

363.11 CHN ISSN 1674-1390
TEZHONG SHEBEI ANQUAN JISHU/SAFETY TECHNOLOGY OF SPECIAL EQUIPMENT. Text in Chinese. 1979. bi-m.
Former titles (until 2004): Guolu Yali Rongqi Anquan Jishu; (until 1979): Guolu Anquan Jishu
Address: 352, Xudong Dajie, Wuhan, 430077, China. TEL 86-27-86787767, gjsbjb@hotmail.com.

TIDSSKRIFT FOR ARBEJDSLIV. *see* BUSINESS AND ECONOMICS—Labor And Industrial Relations

TIEDAO LAODONG ANQUAN WEISHENG YU HUAN-BAO/RAILWAY OCCUPATIONAL SAFETY HEALTH & ENVIRONMENTAL PROTECTION. *see* TRANSPORTATION—Railroads

620.1 NLD ISSN 0921-4348
TIJDSCHRIFT VOOR ERGONOMIE. Text in Dutch. 1976. 6/yr. EUR 75 (effective 2009). adv. **Document type:** *Trade.*
Formerly (until 1981): Ergonomie (0921-4402)
Indexed: ErgAb.
—IE, Infotrieve.
Published by: Nederlandse Vereniging voor Ergonomie, Postbus 1145, Eindhoven, 5602 BC, Netherlands. TEL 31-40-2566596, FAX 31-40-2480711, nvve@planet.nl. Ed. Jorrit Jansen. Circ: 1,500.

658.31244 USA ISSN 0734-3302
HD7260
TODAY'S SUPERVISOR. Text in English. 1935. m. USD 30 to non-members; USD 23.10 to members (effective 2009). illus. 15 p./no. 2 cols./p.; **Document type:** *Newsletter, Trade.* **Description:** Addresses the many safety and health problems and issues that first-line supervisors face.
Formerly (until 1982): Industrial Supervisor (0019-879X)
Related titles: Microform ed.: (from PQC).
Indexed: A22.
Published by: (Periodicals Department), National Safety Council, 1121 Spring Lake Dr, Itasca, IL 60143. TEL 630-775-2056, 800-621-7619, FAX 630-285-0797, customerservice@nsc.org, http://www.nsc.org.

363.11 613.6 GBR ISSN 1366-2856
TOLLEY'S HEALTH AND SAFETY AT WORK HANDBOOK. Text in English. 1983. a. GBP 110 per issue (effective 2010). back issues avail. **Document type:** *Handbook/Manual/Guide, Trade.* **Description:** Covers key aspects of health and safety as well as related environmental and employment information.
—BLDSC (8863.686350).
Published by: (Royal Society for the Prevention of Accidents), LexisNexis Butterworths, Halsbury House, 35 Chancery Ln, London, Mddx WC2A 1EL, United Kingdom. TEL 44-20-74002500, FAX 44-20-74002842, customer.services@lexisnexis.co.uk.

613.62 USA
TOPHEALTH; the health promotion and wellness letter. Text in English. 1987. m. price varies per number of employees. **Document type:** *Newsletter.* **Description:** Promotes the good health of members and employees of organizations and corporations.
Related titles: Online - full text ed.: TopHealth Online; Spanish ed.: 1987.
Published by: Oakstone Publishing. LLC, 100 Corporate Pkwy, Ste 600, Birmingham, AL 35242. TEL 800-871-9525, FAX 205-437-3084, servicewellness@oakstonepub.com.

613.62 381.3 NLD ISSN 1566-0443
➤ **TOPICS IN SAFETY, RISK, RELIABILITY AND QUALITY.** Text in English. 1991. irreg., latest vol.14, 2008. price varies. **Document type:** *Monographic series, Academic/Scholarly.* **Description:** Publishes studies covering the spectrum of disciplines required to deal with safety, quality and reliability of products, processes and services.
Formerly (until vol.4, 1995): Topics in Safety, Reliability and Quality (0927-1015)
Indexed: CIS.
—BLDSC (8867.487050).
Published by: Springer Netherlands (Subsidiary of: Springer Science+Business Media), Van Godewijckstraat 30, Dordrecht, 3311 GX, Netherlands. TEL 31-78-6576050, FAX 31-78-6576474. Ed. Adrian V Gheorghe.

➤ **TOXICOLOGY AND INDUSTRIAL HEALTH**; an international journal. *see* ENVIRONMENTAL STUDIES—Toxicology And Environmental Safety

➤ **TRANSPORTATION SAFETY REFLEXIONS. RAIL.** *see* TRANSPORTATION

➤ **TRAUMA UND BERUFSKRANKHEIT.** *see* MEDICAL SCIENCES—Orthopedics And Traumatology

➤ **TRAVAIL & CHANGEMENT.** *see* BUSINESS AND ECONOMICS—Labor And Industrial Relations

613.62 CAN ISSN 0829-0369
TRAVAIL ET SANTE; revue francophone pour la sante du travail et de l'environnement. Text in French. 1985. q. CAD 35 domestic; CAD 80 in United States; CAD 95 elsewhere (effective 2004). adv.
Indexed: ErgAb, PdeR.
—CCC.

Published by: Le Groupe de Communication Sansectra Inc., PO Box 1089, Napierville, PQ J0J 1L0, Canada. TEL 450-245-7285, FAX 450-245-0593, travail.sante@sympatico.ca. Ed. Robert Richards. Adv. contact Jean Yves Martel. Circ: 1,904.

614 331 FRA ISSN 0373-1944
HD7262
TRAVAIL ET SECURITE. Text in French. 1949. m. (11/yr.). EUR 45 domestic; EUR 67 in Europe; EUR 72 elsewhere (effective 2010). bk.rev.; film rev. bibl.; illus. cum.index. **Document type:** *Magazine, Government.*
Indexed: A22, CISA, FR, WSCA.
—BLDSC (9027.000000), IE, Infotrieve, Ingenta, INIST.
Published by: Institut National de Recherche et de Securite pour la Prevention des Accidents du Travail et des Maladies Professionnelles, 30 rue Olivier Noyer, Paris, 75680 Cedex 14, France. TEL 33-1-40443000, FAX 33-1-40443099, thanh@inrs.fr, http://www.inrs.fr. Ed. Delphine Vaudoux. Circ: 65,000.

TREEWORKER. *see* FORESTS AND FORESTRY

363.11 345.0242 USA ISSN 1081-4140
TRIODYNE SAFETY BULLETIN. Text in English. 1995. irreg., latest vol.10, no.1, 2002. back issues avail. **Document type:** *Bulletin, Trade.*
Related titles: Online - full text ed.
Published by: Triodyne Inc., 450 Skokie Blvd, Northbrook, IL 60062. TEL 847-677-4730, FAX 847-647-2047, infoserv@triodyne.com.

613.62 FIN ISSN 0041-4816
TYO, TERVEYS, TURVALLISUUS/WORK - HEALTH - SAFETY. Text in Finnish; Summaries in English. 1936. 12/yr. adv. bk.rev. illus. **Document type:** *Magazine, Academic/Scholarly.*
Formerly (until 1971): Varokeino
Related titles: Online - full text ed.
Indexed: CISA, ErgAb.
Published by: Tyoterveyslaitos/Finnish Institute of Occupational Health, Topeliuksenkatu 41a A, Helsinki, 00250, Finland. TEL 358-30-4741, FAX 358-30-4742779. Ed., R&P Matti Tapiainen. Adv. contact Ingmar Qvist TEL 358-9-2213-246. B&W page EUR 3,100, color page EUR 4,950; 209 x 266. Circ: 70,000.

613.62 FIN ISSN 0359-1255
HD7727.3
TYOETERVEISET. Text in Finnish; Text occasionally in English. 1973. q. free (effective 2005). **Document type:** *Newsletter, Trade.*
Formerly (until 1981): Tiedotuslehti (0355-9947)
Related titles: Online - full content ed.: ISSN 1239-4378.
Published by: Tyoterveyslaitos/Finnish Institute of Occupational Health, Topeliuksenkatu 41a A, Helsinki, 00250, Finland. TEL 358-30-4741, FAX 358-30-4742779.

613.62 FIN ISSN 0357-4296
TYOTERVEYSLAITOS. KATSAUKSIA. Text in Finnish. 1976. irreg. **Document type:** *Monographic series, Trade.*
Related titles: ◆ English ed.: Finnish Institute of Occupational Health. Reviews. ISSN 1237-9263.
Published by: Tyoterveyslaitos/Finnish Institute of Occupational Health, Topeliuksenkatu 41a A, Helsinki, 00250, Finland. TEL 358-30-4741, FAX 358-30-4742779.

613.62 FIN ISSN 1459-7373
TYOTERVEYSLAITOS. TOIMINTAOHJELMAT - SARJA. Text in Finnish. 2003. irreg. **Document type:** *Monographic series, Trade.*
Published by: Tyoterveyslaitos/Finnish Institute of Occupational Health, Topeliuksenkatu 41a A, Helsinki, 00250, Finland. TEL 358-30-4741, FAX 358-30-4742779.

363.1 USA
RC965.R25
U.S. NUCLEAR REGULATORY COMMISSION. OCCUPATIONAL RADIATION AT COMMERCIAL NUCLEAR POWER REACTORS AND OTHER FACILITIES. ANNUAL REPORT. Key Title: Occupational Radiation Exposure, Annual Report. Text in English. 1970. a. **Document type:** *Report, Trade.*
Former titles: U.S. Nuclear Regulatory Commission. Occupational Radiation Exposure. Annual Report (0198-8360); U.S. Nuclear Regulatory Commission. Annual Occupational Radiation Exposure Report
Published by: U.S. Nuclear Regulatory Commission, Office of Nuclear Regulatory Research, Washington, DC 20555. TEL 301-415-8200, 800-368-5642, opa@nrc.gov, http://www.nrc.gov. Circ: 2,000.

613.62 UKR
UKRAINS'KYI ZHURNAL Z PROBLEM MEDYTSYNY PRATSI. Text in Ukrainian. 2005. q. USD 110 foreign (effective 2006). **Document type:** *Journal, Academic/Scholarly.*
Published by: Akademiya Medychnykh Nauk Ukrainy, Instytut Medytsyny Pratsi, vul Saksahans'koho, 75, Kyiv, 01033, Ukraine. TEL 380-44-2897088, yik@nanu.kiev.ua. Ed. Yu. Kundiev. **Dist. by:** East View Information Services, 10601 Wayzata Blvd, Minneapolis, MN 55305. TEL 952-252-1201, 800-477-1005, FAX 952-252-1202, info@eastview.com, http://www.eastview.com.

UMWELTMEDIZIN IN FORSCHUNG UND PRAXIS. *see* MEDICAL SCIENCES

DER UNFALLCHIRURG. *see* MEDICAL SCIENCES—Orthopedics And Traumatology

UNION MATTERS. *see* LABOR UNIONS

658.31244 690 NLD ISSN 1573-2169
V C A NIEUWS. (Veiligheids Checklist Aannemers) Text in Dutch. 2004. q. EUR 27 (effective 2009). adv.
—IE.
Published by: Uitgeverij Kerckebosch bv, Julianalaan 59, Postbus 122, Zeist, 3700 AC, Netherlands. TEL 31-30-6984222, FAX 31-30-6984223, uitgeverij@kerckebosch.nl, http://www.kerckebosch.nl. Eds. Daan Speetjens, Siep Slager, Wilbert Timp. adv.: B&W page EUR 620, color page EUR 1,400; bleed 210 x 297. Circ: 800.

613.62 NLD ISSN 1387-2419
VEILIGHEID. Text in Dutch. 1997. q. EUR 33.40 (effective 2010). adv. **Document type:** *Magazine, Trade.*
Formed by the merger of (1995-1996): Nieuwsbrief Veiligheid (Praktijkgids Arbeidsveiligheid Edition) (1383-8822); (1995-1996): Nieuwsbrief Veiligheid (Handboek Persoonlijke Beschermingsmiddelen Edition) (1383-8830)
—IE.
Published by: Nederlands Instituut voor Bedrijfshulpverlening, Postbus 8714, Rotterdam, 3009 AS, Netherlands. TEL 31-10-2892888, FAX 31-10-2892880, bhv@nibhv.nl. adv.: color page EUR 1,761; trim 225 x 295. Circ: 10,000.

613.62 AUS ISSN 1837-7386
▼ **VIREO VIEWS.** Text in English. 2010. m. free to qualified personnel (effective 2010). **Document type:** *Newsletter, Trade.* **Description:** Aims to designing, implementing and evaluating workplace health promotion programs.
Published by: Vireo Health Promotions, 12 Kooyalee St, Deception Bay, QLD 4508, Australia. TEL 61-7-31023183, FAX 61-7-30366948, info@vireohealthpromotions.com.

613.62 CAN ISSN 1703-0935
T55.3.H3
W H M I S AT WORK. (Workplace Hazardous Materials Information System) Text in English. 1999. irreg. **Document type:** *Monographic series, Trade.*
Published by: Workers' Compensation Board of British Columbia, PO Box 5350, Stn Terminal, Vancouver, BC V6B 5L5, Canada. TEL 604-232-9704, 866-319-9704, FAX 604-232-9703, http://www.worksafebc.com/default.asp.

658.31244 CAN
W H M I S COMPLIANCE MANUAL. (Workplace Hazardous Materials Information Systems) Text in English. 1989. 3/yr. CAD 265 domestic; USD 224.58 foreign (effective 2005). **Description:** For companies developing and maintaining a program to comply with WHMIS requirements throughout Canada.
Published by: Carswell (Subsidiary of: Thomson Reuters Corp.), One Corporate Plz, 2075 Kennedy Rd, Toronto, ON M1T 3V4, Canada. TEL 416-609-8000, 800-387-5164, FAX 416-298-5094, carswell.customerrelations@thomson.com, http://www.carswell.com. Ed. Reg Ferguson.

658.31244 353.12 DEU ISSN 0343-1525
DAS WARNKREUZ; Zeitschrift fuer Sicherheit und Gesundheit in Verkehrsunternehmen. Text in German. 1949. 4/yr. EUR 2.05 newsstand/cover (effective 2009). adv. **Document type:** *Magazine, Trade.*
Published by: Christian Killinger Verlags GmbH, Tuebinger Str 24, Reutlingen, 72762, Germany. TEL 49-7121-34880, FAX 49-7121-348899, info@killinger-druck.de, http://www.killinger-druck.de. Ed. Alfons Groesbrink. adv.: B&W page EUR 1,450. Circ: 40,500 (paid and controlled).

363.11 NLD ISSN 1051-9815
RM735.A1 CODEN: WORKFK
➤ **WORK;** a journal of prevention, assessment & rehabilitation. Text in English. 1990. m. USD 1,413 combined subscription in North America (print & online eds.); EUR 1,010 combined subscription elsewhere (print & online eds.) (effective 2012). back issues avail. **Document type:** *Journal, Academic/Scholarly.* **Description:** Each issue is devoted to one topic within the scope of work practice, such as injury prevention, work assessment, and the older worker.
Related titles: Online - full text ed.: ISSN 1875-9270 (from IngentaConnect).
Indexed: A12, A13, A14, A17, A20, A22, ABIn, AMED, B01, B06, B07, B09, B21, C06, C07, C08, CA, CINAHL, CurCont, E01, E04, E05, EMBASE, ESPM, ErgAb, ExcerpMed, H&SSA, Inspec, MEDLINE, P03, P30, P48, P50, P51, P52, P53, P54, P56, PQC, PsycInfo, PsycholAb, SCOPUS, SSCI, T02, W07.
—BLDSC (9348.040100), GNLM, IE, Infotrieve, Ingenta. **CCC.**
Published by: I O S Press, Nieuwe Hemweg 6B, Amsterdam, 1013 BG, Netherlands. TEL 31-20-6883355, FAX 31-20-6870019, info@iospress.nl. Ed. Karen Jacobs TEL 617-353-7516. Circ: 400. **Subscr. to:** I O S Press, Inc, 4502 Rachael Manor Dr, Fairfax, VA 22032-3631. iosbooks@iospress.com; Globe Publication Pvt. Ltd., C-62 Inderpuri, New Delhi 100 012, India. TEL 91-11-579-3211, 91-11-579-3212, FAX 91-11-579-8876, custserve@globepub.com, http://www.globepub.com; Kinokuniya Co Ltd., Shinjuku 3-chome, Shinjuku-ku, Tokyo 160-0022, Japan. FAX 81-3-3439-1094, journal@kinokuniya.co.jp, http://www.kinokuniya.co.jp.

➤ **WORK & INDUSTRY SPECIAL INTEREST SECTION QUARTERLY.** *see* OCCUPATIONS AND CAREERS

➤ **WORK AND STRESS.** *see* PSYCHOLOGY

➤ **WORKERS' COMP EXECUTIVE;** credible authoritative trustworthy. *see* BUSINESS AND ECONOMICS—Labor And Industrial Relations

➤ **WORKERS' COMPENSATION - BUSINESS MANAGEMENT GUIDE NEWSLETTER.** *see* INSURANCE

➤ **WORKER'S COMPENSATION GUIDE.** *see* BUSINESS AND ECONOMICS—Personnel Management

613.62 GBR ISSN 1351-4792
WORKERS' HEALTH INTERNATIONAL NEWSLETTER. Text in English. s-a. adv. **Document type:** *Newsletter, Trade.* **Description:** Aims to highlight the problems facing working people as a result of the globalization of trade and globalization of capital. It also aims to provide trade unions and safety activists with the resources and information they need to expose and challenge threats to workplace health and safety.
Related titles: Spanish ed.: W H I N en Espanol. ISSN 1130-8575.
—**CCC.**
Published by: Hazards Publications Ltd., PO Box 4042, Sheffield, S Yorks S8 2DG, United Kingdom. TEL 44-114-2014265, editor@hazards.org. Ed. Rory O'Neill. Adv. contact Jawad Qasrawi.

363.11 ZAF
WORKERS LIFE (PRETORIA). Text in English, Sotho, Northern, Sotho, Southern, Zulu; Summaries in English. 1985. m. ZAR 660 per month domestic for 10 copies; USD 200 per month foreign for 1 copy (effective 2001 - 2002). adv. bk.rev.; Website rev.; video rev.; software rev. abstr.; pat.; stat.; tr.lit. **Document type:** *Magazine, Government.*
Published by: National Occupational Safety Association, PO Box 26434, Arcadia, Pretoria 0007, South Africa. TEL 27-12-3039700, FAX 27-12-3039870, taniam@nosa.co.za, http://www.nosa.co.za. Ed. Sipho Siso. R&P Ed Furter. Adv. contact Eugene Howell TEL 27-12-3039717. page ZAR 640; 297 x 418. Circ: 13,800 (paid and controlled).

WORKLIFE (KINGSTON). *see* BUSINESS AND ECONOMICS—Labor And Industrial Relations

614.85 USA ISSN 1528-8013
WORKPLACE ERGONOMICS NEWS. Text in English. 1999. m. **Document type:** *Newsletter, Trade.* **Description:** Publishes information on government regulations, prevention and treatment strategies and trends within the industry.
Published by: 1105 Media Inc., 14901 Quorum Dr, Ste 425, Dallas, TX 75254. TEL 972-687-6700, FAX 972-687-6799, info@1105media.com, http://www.1105media.com.

658.31244 GBR ISSN 2046-6463
WORKPLACE LEARNING AND SKILLS BULLETIN. WEEKLY BRIEFING. Text in English. 200?. w. GBP 75 includes Workplace Learning and Skills Bulletin (effective 2011). **Document type:** *Report, Academic/Scholarly.*
Media: Online - full text.
Published by: The Education Publishing Co. Ltd., Woodbury House, Green Ln, Exton, Exeter, EX3 0PW, United Kingdom. TEL 44-1363-774455, info@educationpublishing.com, http://www.educationpublishing.com. Ed. Ian Nash.

363.11 CAN ISSN 1494-7412
WORKSAFE MAGAZINE. Text in English. 1995. 6/yr. free. back issues avail. **Document type:** *Newspaper, Government.* **Description:** Provides information on workplace health and safety in BC, as well as information on policies and operations of the WCB.
Formerly (until 2000): Prevention at Work (1208-882X); Which was formed by the merger of (1958-1995): W C B News (0709-9428); Which was formerly (until 1974): Workmen's Compensation Board of British Columbia. News Bulletin (0524-5621); (1967-1995): Your Workplace Health & Safety (1191-1263); Which was formerly (until 1991): Health and Safety Digest (0714-8429); (until 1975): Safety Digest (Vancouver) (0714-8488)
Related titles: Online - full text ed.
Published by: Workers' Compensation Board, Communications Department, PO Box 5350, Sta Terminal, Vancouver, BC V6B 5L5, Canada. TEL 604-279-7572, FAX 604-279-7406, http://www.wcb.bc.ca. Ed. Diane Bentley. R&P Dawn Knoll. Circ: 25,000.

613.62 363.11 CAN ISSN 1203-3774
WORKSITE NEWS. Text in English. 1992. 10/yr. CAD 65 domestic (effective 2001). adv. **Document type:** *Magazine, Trade.* **Description:** Covers occupational safety, health and environmental issues for the industrial and commericial sectors across North America.
Published by: Morrow Communications, Inc., 3216-108A St, Edmonton, AB T6J 3E2, Canada. TEL 888-430-6405, worksite@worldgate.com, http://www.worksite-news.com.

658.31244 AUS ISSN 1834-2213
WORKWISE WORK RELATED DEATH PREVENTION: THE CORONIAL APPROACH. Text in English. 2006. q. **Document type:** *Newsletter, Trade.*
Media: Online - full text.
Published by: Victorian Institute of Forensic Medicine, 57-83 Kavanagh St, Southbank, VIC 3006, Australia. TEL 61-3-96844444, FAX 61-3-96827353, assist@vifm.org.

614.8 CHE ISSN 0084-165X
WORLD CONGRESS ON THE PREVENTION OF OCCUPATIONAL ACCIDENTS AND DISEASES. PROCEEDINGS. (Proceedings published by national organizing committee) Text in Multiple languages. 1955. triennial. **Document type:** *Proceedings, Trade.* **Description:** Presents issues concerning concepts, scope, organization, financing and implementation of occupational health services, with the aim of education and training.
Published by: International Social Security Association (I S S A)/Association Internationale de la Securite Sociale, 4 Rte des Morillons, Geneva, 1211, Switzerland. TEL 41-22-7996617, FAX 41-22-7998509, issa@ilo.org, http://www.issa.int.

614.85 USA ISSN 1944-4192
Q183.A1
WORLDWIDE SURVEY OF L I M S USERS. (Laboratory Information Management Systems) Text in English. 199?. irreg. USD 5,195 per issue (effective 2008). **Document type:** *Report, Trade.*
Published by: Strategic Directions International, Inc., 6242 Westchester Pkwy, Ste 100, Los Angeles, CA 90045. TEL 310-641-4982, FAX 310-641-8851, sdi@strategic-directions.com, http://www.strategic-directions.com/.

658.31244 JPN
YEARBOOK OF INDUSTRIAL SAFETY AND HEALTH. Text in Japanese. a. JPY 4,000 (effective 2001). **Description:** Covers activities and relevant information in the field of industrial safety and health in Japan.
Formerly: Yearbook of Industrial Safety
Published by: Japan Industrial Safety and Health Association, Publishing and Sales Department, 5-35-1 Shiba, Minato-ku, Tokyo, 108-0014, Japan. TEL 81-3-3452-6841, FAX 81-3-3453-8034. Ed. Toru Sasaki.

363.11 EGY ISSN 1687-8671
➤ **ZAGAZIG JOURNAL OF OCCUPATIONAL HEALTH AND SAFETY/ MAGALAT AL-ZAQAZIQ LI-L-SIHHAT WA-AL-SALAMAT AL-MIHANIYYAT/MAJALAT AL-ZAQAZIQ LI-L-SIHHAT WA-AL-SALAMAT AL-MIHANIYYAT.** Text in Egyptian. 2008. s-a. Index. back issues avail. **Document type:** *Journal, Academic/Scholarly.* **Description:** Covers diagnosis, prevention, management and scientific analysis of occupational, environmental and safety health problems, including the promotion of health of workers, their families, and communities.
Related titles: Online - full text ed.
Indexed: B21, ESPM, H&SSA, RiskAb.
Published by: Zagazig University, Faculty of Medicine. Occupational and Environmental Health Services Center, Zagazig, Egypt. TEL 20-55-2302809, FAX 20-55-2307830. Ed. Ahmed-Refat AG Ahmed-Refat.

331.45 SRB ISSN 0044-1880
ZASTITA RADA; casopis za bezbednost i zdravlje na radu i zastitu radne i zivotne sredine. Text in Serbo-Croatian. 1959. m. YUN 40, USD 2.67. **Document type:** *Newspaper, Consumer.*
Published by: Zastita Press, Jelene Cetkovic 3, Belgrade. Ed. Veroljub Micic.

N O

613.62 DEU ISSN 0944-2502
CODEN: ZAAEE
ZENTRALBLATT FUER ARBEITSMEDIZIN, ARBEITSSCHUTZ UND ERGONOMIE. Text in German. 1976. m. EUR 160.20 (effective 2011). adv. bk.rev. abstr.; bibl.; charts; illus.; pat. index. **Document type:** *Magazine, Trade.*
Former titles (until 1992): Zentralblatt fuer Arbeitsmedizin, Arbeitsschutz, Prophylaxe und Ergonomie (0173-3338); (until 1980): Zentralblatt fuer Arbeitsmedizin, Arbeitsschutz und Prophylaxe (0340-7047); Which was formed by the merger of (1965-1976): Prophylaxe (Heidelberg) (0033-1368); (1920-1976): Zentralblatt fuer Arbeitsmedizin und Arbeitsschutz (0044-4049); Which was formerly (until 1951): Zentralblatt fuer Gewerbehygiene und Unfallverhuetung (0372-8773); Which was formed by the merger of (1907-1920): Sozial-Technik (0931-8461); (1910-1920): Institut fuer Gewerbehygiene zu Frankfurt. Mitteilungen (0931-8488); (1911-1920): Gewerbehygiene und Gewerbekrankheiten (0931-847X); (1913-1920): Zentralblatt fuer Gewerbehygiene (0931-8372)
Indexed: A22, CIN, CISA, ChemAb, ChemTitl, DIP, ErgAb, IBR, IBZ, IndMed, P30, R10, Reac, SCOPUS, TM.
—BLDSC (9500.799500), CASDDS, GNLM, IE, Infotrieve, Ingenta, INIST. **CCC.**
Published by: Dr. Curt Haefner Verlag GmbH (Subsidiary of: Konradin Verlag Robert Kohlhammer GmbH), Dischingerstr 8, Heidelberg, 69123, Germany. TEL 49-6221-64460, FAX 49-6221-644640, info@haefner-verlag.de, http://www.haefner-verlag.de. Ed. Bernd Wilfing. Adv. contact Sandra Rink. Circ: 1,000 (paid and controlled).

613.62 CHN ISSN 1003-3033
ZHONGGUO ANQUAN KEXUE XUEBAO/CHINESE SAFETY SCIENCE JOURNAL. Text in Chinese. 1991. bi-m. CNY 10 per issue domestic (effective 2000). back issues avail. **Document type:** *Academic/Scholarly.*
Related titles: Online - full text ed.
Indexed: A28, APA, B21, BrCerAb, C&ISA, CA/WCA, CIA, CerAb, CivEngAb, CorrAb, E&CAJ, E11, EEA, EMA, ESPM, EnvEAb, H&SSA, H15, M&TEA, M09, MBF, METADEX, RiskAb, SolStAb, T04, WAA.
—BLDSC (9830.239000).
Published by: Zhongguo Laodong Baohu Kexue Jishu Xuehui Bianji Chubanbu, Zhaoyang-qu, Huixin Xi Jie 17 Hao, Beijing, 100029, China. TEL 86-1-64915566 ext 2717, 86-1-64915341. Ed. Deshu Xu.

363.11 620.86 CHN ISSN 1673-193X
CODEN: ZASKBO
➤ **ZHONGGUO ANQUAN SHENGCHAN KEXUE JISHU/JOURNAL OF SAFETY SCIENCE AND TECHNOLOGY.** Abstracts and contents page in English; Text in Chinese. bi-m. CNY 114, USD 60; CNY 19 newsstand/cover (effective 2009). **Document type:** *Journal, Academic/Scholarly.* **Description:** Covers the development with the occupational safety in China, and reports advanced theories in occupational safety research, technologies, achievements and experiences, including the treatises about state-level research projects, such as original treatises, important reviews, argument upon major scientific problem or discussing treatises.
Former titles (until 2005): Zhongguo Zhiye Anquan Weisheng Guanli Tixi Renzheng (1671-4245); (until 2001): Laodong Baohu Kexue Jishu
Related titles: Online - full text ed.
Indexed: B21, ESPM, H&SSA.
Published by: Zhongguo Anquan Shengchan Kexue Yanjiuyuan/China Academy of Safety Science and Technology, Rm. 1210, No.17, Huixin W. St., Chaoyang District, Beijing, 100029, China. TEL 86-10-64941258, FAX 86-10-64914634, oshms@chinasafety.ac.cn, http://www.chinasafety.ac.cn/. Ed. Juan-Juan Xing. Circ: 4,000.

613.62 362.1 CHN ISSN 1671-0312
ZHONGGUO GETI FANGHU ZHUANGBEI/CHINA PERSONAL PROTECTION EQUIPMENT. Text in Chinese. 1993. bi-m. CNY 10 newsstand/cover (effective 2006).
Formerly (until 2000): Zhongguo Laodong Fanghu Yongpin/China Labor Protection Equipments (1009-3052)
Related titles: Online - full text ed.
Address: 28, Xizhimen Bei Dajie, Beijing, 100088, China. TEL 86-10-62251204, FAX 86-10-62251206.

613.62 CHN ISSN 1002-221X
ZHONGGUO GONGYE YIXUE ZAZHI/CHINESE JOURNAL OF INDUSTRIAL MEDICINE. Text in Chinese. 1988 (Oct.). bi-m. USD 21.60 (effective 2009). adv. bk.rev. illus.; abstr.; charts; stat. 64 p./no.; back issues avail. **Document type:** *Journal, Academic/Scholarly.*
Related titles: Online - full content ed.; Online - full text ed.
Indexed: A22.
—BLDSC (3180.354500), East View, IE, Ingenta.
Published by: (Zhonghua Yufang Yixuehui/China Preventive Medicine Association), Shenyang Institute of Occupational Health and Medicine, Tiexi-qu, Nan 11 Xi Lu 18 Hao, Shenyang, 110024, China. TEL 86-24-25731414, FAX 86-24-25731482, sycpcc@pub.sy.ln.cn. Eds. He Wang Chao, Lin Zhang Shou, Feng Sheng He, Jin Duo Zhao. Adv. contacts Xin Yuan Li, Ying Ll Dan. Circ: 2,000 (paid). **Dist. by:** China International Book Trading Corp, 35 Chegongzhuang Xilu, Haidian District, PO Box 399, Beijing 100044, China. TEL 86-10-68412045, FAX 86-10-68412023, cibtc@mail.cibtc.com.cn, http://www.cibtc.com.cn.

ZHONGGUO HAISHI/CHINA MARITIME SAFETY. *see* TRANSPORTATION—Ships And Shipping

613.62 CHN ISSN 1001-9391
CODEN: ZLWZEX
➤ **ZHONGHUA LAODONG WEISHENG ZHIYEBING ZAZHI/CHINESE JOURNAL OF INDUSTRIAL HYGIENE AND OCCUPATIONAL DISEASES.** Text in Chinese; Abstracts in English. 1983. bi-m. USD 62.40 (effective 2009). adv. abstr.; charts. 80 p./no.; **Document type:** *Journal, Academic/Scholarly.* **Description:** Contains epidemiological investigation on industrial hygiene and occupational medicine, and studies on prevention, diagnosis and treatment of occupational diseases.
Related titles: Online - full content ed.; Online - full text ed.
Indexed: CIN, ChemAb, ChemTitl, EMBASE, ExcerpMed, MEDLINE, P30, R10, Reac, SCOPUS.
—BLDSC (3180.354000), CASDDS, East View.
Published by: (Zhonghua Yixuehui/Chinese Medical Association), Zhonghua Laodong Weisheng Zhiyebing Zazhi, Hedong District, Hualong-Dao, Tiajin, 300011, China. Circ: 4,000 (paid); 400 (controlled). **Dist. by:** China International Book Trading Corp, 35 Chegongzhuang Xilu, Haidian District, PO Box 399, Beijing 100044, China. TEL 86-10-68412045, FAX 86-10-68412023, cibtc@mail.cibtc.com.cn, http://www.cibtc.com.cn.

614.85 USA ISSN 1932-1937
KF3567.19
29 C F R 1910 O S H A GENERAL INDUSTRY REGULATIONS BOOK. (Code of Federal Regulations / Occupational Safety and Health Administration) Text in English. 200?. irreg. USD 59.98 per issue (effective 2011). **Document type:** *Handbook/Manual/Guide, Trade.*
Formerly: 29 C F R Code of Federal Regulations. Part 1910, General Industry
Related titles: CD-ROM ed.: USD 59.98 per issue (effective 2011).
Published by: Mangan Communications, Inc, 315 W 4th St, Davenport, IA 52801. TEL 563-323-6245, 877-626-2666, FAX 888-398-6245, safetyinfo@mancomm.com.

614.85 USA ISSN 1932-216X
KF3574.C65
29 C F R 1926 O S H A CONSTRUCTION INDUSTRY REGULATIONS. (Code of Federal Regulations / Occupational Safety and Health Standards) Text in English. 200?. irreg. USD 89.95 combined subscription per issue (print & CD-ROM eds.); USD 49.98 per issue (effective 2011). **Document type:** *Handbook/Manual/Guide, Trade.*
Formerly: 29 C F R Code of Federal Regulations, Part 1926, Construction
Related titles: CD-ROM ed.: USD 59.98 per issue (effective 2011).
Published by: Mangan Communications, Inc, 315 W 4th St, Davenport, IA 52801. TEL 563-323-6245, 877-626-2666, FAX 888-398-6245, safetyinfo@mancomm.com.

OCCUPATIONAL HEALTH AND SAFETY—
Abstracting, Bibliographies, Statistics

613.62 USA
AMERICAN INDUSTRIAL HYGIENE ASSOCIATION. CONFERENCE ABSTRACTS. Text in English. bi-m. free conference attendees (effective 2007). **Document type:** *Proceedings.* **Description:** Abstracts of papers presented at the annual meeting of the American Industrial Hygiene Conference.
Media: Online - full text.
Published by: American Industrial Hygiene Association, 2700 Prosperity Ave, Ste 250, Fairfax, VA 22031-4307. TEL 703-849-8888, FAX 703-207-3561, infonet@aiha.org, http://www.aiha.org. **Subscr. to:** AIHA Journal, Dept 796, Alexandria, VA 22334-0796.

658.31244021 CAN ISSN 1910-7366
ASSOCIATIONS SECTORIELLES PARITAIRES, LESIONS PROFESSIONNELLES, STATISTIQUES. TOME 1. ASSOCIATION PARITAIRE POUR LA SANTE ET LA SECURITE DU TRAVAIL DU SECTEUR AFFAIRES SOCIALES. Text in French. 2004. a. **Document type:** *Government.*
Published by: Commission de la Sante et de la Securite du Travail du Quebec, Direction de la Comptabilite et de la Gestion de l'Information. Service de la Statistique, CP 4900, Succursale Terminus, Quebec, PQ G1K 7S6, Canada. TEL 418-266-4000, 800-668-6811, FAX 418-266-4015, http://www.csst.qc.ca/Portail/fr/index.htm.

613.62021 CAN ISSN 1910-7315
ASSOCIATIONS SECTORIELLES PARITAIRES, LESIONS PROFESSIONNELLES, STATISTIQUES. TOME 11. ASSOCIATION PARITAIRE POUR LA SANTE ET LA SECURITE DU TRAVAIL DU SECTEUR MINIER. Text in French. 2004. a. **Document type:** *Government.*
Published by: Commission de la Sante et de la Securite du Travail du Quebec, Direction de la Comptabilite et de la Gestion de l'Information. Service de la Statistique, CP 4900, Succursale Terminus, Quebec, PQ G1K 7S6, Canada. TEL 418-266-4000, 800-668-6811, FAX 418-266-4015, http://www.csst.qc.ca/Portail/fr/index.htm.

613.62021 CAN ISSN 1910-7323
ASSOCIATIONS SECTORIELLES PARITAIRES, LESIONS PROFESSIONNELLES, STATISTIQUES. TOME 12. ASSOCIATION PARITAIRE POUR LA SANTE ET LA SECURITE DU TRAVAIL DU SECTEUR DES AFFAIRES MUNICIPALES. Text in French. 2004. a. **Document type:** *Government.*
Published by: Commission de la Sante et de la Securite du Travail du Quebec, Direction de la Comptabilite et de la Gestion de l'Information. Service de la Statistique, CP 4900, Succursale Terminus, Quebec, PQ G1K 7S6, Canada. TEL 418-266-4000, 800-668-6811, FAX 418-266-4015, http://www.csst.qc.ca/Portail/fr/index.htm.

613.62021 CAN ISSN 1910-734X
ASSOCIATIONS SECTORIELLES PARITAIRES, LESIONS PROFESSIONNELLES, STATISTIQUES. TOME 13. ASSOCIATION PARITAIRE POUR LA SANTE ET LA SECURITE DU TRAVAIL DU SECTEUR DE L'HABILLEMENT. Text in French. 2004. a. **Document type:** *Government.*
Published by: Commission de la Sante et de la Securite du Travail du Quebec, Direction de la Comptabilite et de la Gestion de l'Information. Service de la Statistique, CP 4900, Succursale Terminus, Quebec, PQ G1K 7S6, Canada. TEL 418-266-4000, 800-668-6811, FAX 418-266-4015, http://www.csst.qc.ca/Portail/fr/index.htm.

613.62021 CAN ISSN 1910-7374
ASSOCIATIONS SECTORIELLES PARITAIRES, LESIONS PROFESSIONNELLES, STATISTIQUES. TOME 2. PREVENTEX - ASSOCIATION PARITAIRE DU TEXTILE. Text in French. 2004. a. **Document type:** *Government.*
Published by: Commission de la Sante et de la Securite du Travail du Quebec, Direction de la Comptabilite et de la Gestion de l'Information. Service de la Statistique, CP 4900, Succursale Terminus, Quebec, PQ G1K 7S6, Canada. TEL 418-266-4000, 800-668-6811, FAX 418-266-4015, http://www.csst.qc.ca/Portail/fr/index.htm.

613.62021 CAN ISSN 1910-7382
ASSOCIATIONS SECTORIELLES PARITAIRES, LESIONS PROFESSIONNELLES, STATISTIQUES. TOME 3. ASSOCIATION PARITAIRE POUR LA SANTE ET LA SECURITE DU TRAVAIL DU SECTEUR TRANSPORT ET ENTREPOSAGE. Text in French. 2004. a. **Document type:** *Government.*
Published by: Commission de la Sante et de la Securite du Travail du Quebec, Direction de la Comptabilite et de la Gestion de l'Information. Service de la Statistique, CP 4900, Succursale Terminus, Quebec, PQ G1K 7S6, Canada. TEL 418-266-4000, 800-668-6811, FAX 418-266-4015, http://www.csst.qc.ca/Portail/fr/index.htm.

613.62021 CAN ISSN 1910-7390
ASSOCIATIONS SECTORIELLES PARITAIRES, LESIONS PROFESSIONNELLES, STATISTIQUES. TOME 4. ASSOCIATION PARITAIRE POUR LA SANTE ET LA SECURITE DU TRAVAIL DU SECTEUR DE L'IMPRIMERIE ET ACTIVITES CONNEXES. Text in French. 2004. a. **Document type:** *Government.*
Published by: Commission de la Sante et de la Securite du Travail du Quebec, Direction de la Comptabilite et de la Gestion de l'Information. Service de la Statistique, CP 4900, Succursale Terminus, Quebec, PQ G1K 7S6, Canada. TEL 418-266-4000, 800-668-6811, FAX 418-266-4015, http://www.csst.qc.ca/Portail/fr/index.htm.

613.62021 CAN ISSN 1910-7404
ASSOCIATIONS SECTORIELLES PARITAIRES, LESIONS PROFESSIONNELLES, STATISTIQUES. TOME 5. ASSOCIATION PARITAIRE POUR LA SANTE ET LA SECURITE DU TRAVAIL DU SECTEUR ADMINISTRATION PROVINCIALE. Text in French. 2004. a. **Document type:** *Government.*
Published by: Commission de la Sante et de la Securite du Travail du Quebec, Direction de la Comptabilite et de la Gestion de l'Information. Service de la Statistique, CP 4900, Succursale Terminus, Quebec, PQ G1K 7S6, Canada. TEL 418-266-4000, 800-668-6811, FAX 418-266-4015, http://www.csst.qc.ca/Portail/fr/index.htm.

613.62021 621.9 CAN ISSN 1910-7277
ASSOCIATIONS SECTORIELLES PARITAIRES, LESIONS PROFESSIONNELLES, STATISTIQUES. TOME 6. ASSOCIATION PARITAIRE POUR LA SANTE ET LA SECURITE DU TRAVAIL DU SECTEUR FABRICATION D'EQUIPEMENT DE TRANSPORT ET DE MACHINES. Text in French. 2004. a. **Document type:** *Government.*
Published by: Commission de la Sante et de la Securite du Travail du Quebec, Direction de la Comptabilite et de la Gestion de l'Information. Service de la Statistique, CP 4900, Succursale Terminus, Quebec, PQ G1K 7S6, Canada. TEL 418-266-4000, 800-668-6811, FAX 418-266-4015, http://www.csst.qc.ca/Portail/fr/index.htm.

613.62021 CAN ISSN 1910-7285
ASSOCIATIONS SECTORIELLES PARITAIRES, LESIONS PROFESSIONNELLES, STATISTIQUES. TOME 7. ASSOCIATION PARITAIRE POUR LA SANTE ET LA SECURITE DU TRAVAIL DU SECTEUR DE LA FABRICATION DE PRODUITS EN METAL ET DE PRODUITS ELECTRIQUES. Text in French. 2004. a. **Document type:** *Government.*
Published by: Commission de la Sante et de la Securite du Travail du Quebec, Direction de la Comptabilite et de la Gestion de l'Information. Service de la Statistique, CP 4900, Succursale Terminus, Quebec, PQ G1K 7S6, Canada. TEL 418-266-4000, 800-668-6811, FAX 418-266-4015, http://www.csst.qc.ca/Portail/fr/index.htm.

613.62021 629.286 CAN ISSN 1910-7293
ASSOCIATIONS SECTORIELLES PARITAIRES, LESIONS PROFESSIONNELLES, STATISTIQUES. TOME 8. ASSOCIATION PARITAIRE POUR LA SANTE ET LA SECURITE DU TRAVAIL DU SECTEUR DES SERVICES AUTOMOBILES. Text in French. 2004. a. **Document type:** *Government.*
Published by: Commission de la Sante et de la Securite du Travail du Quebec, Direction de la Comptabilite et de la Gestion de l'Information. Service de la Statistique, CP 4900, Succursale Terminus, Quebec, PQ G1K 7S6, Canada. TEL 418-266-4000, 800-668-6811, FAX 418-266-4015, http://www.csst.qc.ca/Portail/fr/index.htm.

613.62021 690 CAN ISSN 1910-7307
ASSOCIATIONS SECTORIELLES PARITAIRES, LESIONS PROFESSIONNELLES, STATISTIQUES. TOME 9. ASSOCIATION PARITAIRE POUR LA SANTE ET LA SECURITE DU TRAVAIL DU SECTEUR DE LA CONSTRUCTION. Text in French. 2004. a. **Document type:** *Government.*
Published by: Commission de la Sante et de la Securite du Travail du Quebec, Direction de la Comptabilite et de la Gestion de l'Information. Service de la Statistique, CP 4900, Succursale Terminus, Quebec, PQ G1K 7S6, Canada. TEL 418-266-4000, 800-668-6811, FAX 418-266-4015, http://www.csst.qc.ca/Portail/fr/index.htm.

613.62 011 USA ISSN 1047-8124
CODEN: CSOHE7
C A SELECTS. OCCUPATIONAL EXPOSURE & HAZARDS. Text in English. 1988. s-w. USD 385 to non-members; USD 115 to members; USD 575 combined subscription to individuals (print & online eds.) (effective 2011). **Document type:** *Abstract/Index.* **Description:** Covers occupational exposure and related hazards. Includes epidemiological studies on workplace exposure of humans to chemicals, biological agents, radiation, and noise.
Formerly (until 1989): BIOSIS CAS Selects: Occupational Exposure
Related titles: Online - full text ed.: USD 380 to non-members; USD 114 to members (effective 2011).
Published by: Chemical Abstracts Service (Subsidiary of: American Chemical Society), 2540 Olentangy River Rd, Columbus, OH 43210-0012. TEL 614-447-3600, FAX 614-447-3713, help@cas.com, http://caselects.cas.org. **Subscr. to:** PO Box 3012, Columbus, OH 43210. TEL 800-753-4227, FAX 614-447-3751.

613.62 USA ISSN 1083-2769
CODEN: CSPSFC

C A SELECTS PLUS. CHEMICAL HAZARDS, HEALTH & SAFETY. Text in English. s-w. USD 385 to non-members; USD 115 to members; USD 575 combined subscription to individuals (print & online eds.) (effective 2011). **Document type:** *Abstract/Index.* **Description:** Covers safety in chemical laboratories and in the chemical and nuclear industries; health and safety of personnel working in these areas or working with hazardous substances.
Formerly: C A Selects. Chemical Hazards, Health and Safety (0190-9398)
Related titles: Online - full text ed.: USD 380 to non-members; USD 114 to members (effective 2011).
Published by: Chemical Abstracts Service (Subsidiary of: American Chemical Society), 2540 Olentangy River Rd, Columbus, OH 43210-0012. TEL 614-447-3600, FAX 614-447-3713, help@cas.com, http://caselects.cas.org. **Subscr. to:** PO Box 3012, Columbus, OH 43210. TEL 800-753-4227, FAX 614-447-3751.

016.61362 GBR ISSN 0265-5721
TP149 CODEN: CHINEK

CHEMICAL HAZARDS IN INDUSTRY. Text in English. 1984. m. GBP 3,243, USD 6,054 combined subscription (print & online eds.) (effective 2012). adv. abstr. back issues avail.; reprints avail. **Document type:** *Journal, Abstract/Index.* **Description:** Provides current awareness of such topics as health and safety, chemical and biological hazards, plant safety, legislation, protective equipment and storage relating to the chemical and allied industries.
Related titles: CD-ROM ed.; E-mail ed.; Online - full text ed.: ISSN 1476-3907. GBP 3,081, USD 5,751 (effective 2012).
—CCC.
Published by: Royal Society of Chemistry, Thomas Graham House, Science Park, Milton Rd, Cambridge, CB4 0WF, United Kingdom. TEL 44-1223-420066, FAX 44-1223-423623, sales@rsc.org. Adv. contact Emma Clements TEL 44-1223-432683.

016.61362 GBR

CHEMICAL SAFETY NEWSBASE. Abbreviated title: C S N B. Text in English. 19??. base vol. plus m. updates. abstr. back issues avail. **Document type:** *Database, Abstract/Index.* **Description:** Provides information on the hazards of chemicals used, and all health and safety matters relevant to the laboratory and office environment.
Media: Online - full text. **Related titles:** ♦ CD-ROM ed.: Dialog OnDisc Environmental Chemistry, Health and Safety.
Published by: Royal Society of Chemistry, Thomas Graham House, Science Park, Milton Rd, Cambridge, CB4 0WF, United Kingdom. TEL 44-1223-420066, FAX 44-1223-423623. Pub. Dr. Graham McCann.

EXCERPTA MEDICA. SECTION 35: OCCUPATIONAL HEALTH AND INDUSTRIAL MEDICINE. *see* MEDICAL SCIENCES—Abstracting, Bibliographies, Statistics

613.62 USA

FATAL OCCUPATIONAL INJURIES AND ILLNESSES IN CALIFORNIA. Text in English. 1993. a. **Document type:** *Government.*
Related titles: Online - full content ed.
Published by: Department of Industrial Relations, Division of Labor Statistics & Research, PO Box 420603, San Francisco, CA 94142-0603. http://www.dir.ca.gov/dlsr/statistics_research.html.

616.7021 USA

FATAL OCCUPATIONAL INJURIES IN MAINE. Text in English. 1991. a., latest 2008. back issues avail. **Document type:** *Report, Government.* **Description:** Provides statistics concerning work-related fatalities in Maine.
Formerly (until 1996): Report of Fatal Occupational Injuries in Maine
Related titles: Online - full text ed.; Series of: Maine. Bureau of Labor Standards. B L S Bulletin.
Published by: Department of Labor, Bureau of Labor Standards, 45 State House Sta, Augusta, ME 04333. TEL 207-623-7900, 800-794-1110, FAX 207-624-6449, http://www.maine.gov/labor/bls/.

HEALTH AND SAFETY SCIENCE ABSTRACTS (ONLINE). *see* PUBLIC HEALTH AND SAFETY—Abstracting, Bibliographies, Statistics

614.85 ITA ISSN 1970-5654

I N A I L DATI. (Istituto Nazionale per l'Assicurazione Contro gli Infortuni sul Lavoro) Text in Italian. 1995. m. **Document type:** *Newsletter, Trade.*
Related titles: Online - full text ed.: ISSN 2035-5645.
Published by: Istituto Nazionale per l'Assicurazione Contro gli Infortuni sul Lavoro (I N A I L), Piazzale G Pastore 6, Rome, 00144, Italy. TEL 39-06-54872014, FAX 39-06-54872050, dccomunicazione@inail.it, http://www.inail.it.

658.31244021 ITA ISSN 1592-6818

I N A I L NOTIZIARIO STATISTICO. (Istituto Nazionale per l'Assicurazione Contro gli Infortuni sul Lavoro) Text in Italian. 1951. q. charts. index. **Document type:** *Bulletin, Trade.* **Description:** Contains statistics of injuries and diseases obtained during professional activities.
Related titles: Supplement(s): Statistiche per la Prevenzione. Serie Dati Globali. ISSN 0391-5638. 1975; Statistiche per la Prevenzione. Serie Monografica. ISSN 0393-4047. 1974.
Published by: Istituto Nazionale per l'Assicurazione Contro gli Infortuni sul Lavoro (I N A I L), Piazzale G Pastore 6, Rome, 00144, Italy. TEL 39-06-54872014, FAX 39-06-54872050, dccomunicazione@inail.it, http://www.inail.it. Circ: 2,500 (paid).

622.8021 USA ISSN 0270-2053
TN295

INJURY EXPERIENCE IN SAND AND GRAVEL MINING. Text in English. a. free. charts; stat. **Document type:** *Government.* **Description:** Reviews in detail the occupational injury and illness experience of mining, by category, in the United States in the given year.
Former titles (until 1978): Injury Experience in the Sand and Gravel Industry (0191-6645); (until 1973): Injury Experience and Worktime Data for the Sand and Gravel Industry (0364-3131)
—Linda Hall.
Published by: U.S. Department of Labor, Mine Safety and Health Administration, 1100 Wilson Blvd, 21st Fl, Arlington, VA 22209-2249. TEL 202-693-9400, FAX 202-693-9401. **Subscr. to:** U.S. Government Printing Office, Superintendent of Documents.

016.61485 016.661 GBR ISSN 0261-2917
CODEN: LHBUD2

LABORATORY HAZARDS BULLETIN. Text in English. 1981. m. GBP 1,896, USD 3,540 combined subscription (print & online eds.) (effective 2012). adv. index. cum.index. back issues avail. **Document type:** *Bulletin, Abstract/Index.* **Description:** Reports on safety measures, potential hazards and new legislation affecting the well-being of employees working in laboratories.
Related titles: CD-ROM ed.; Online - full text ed.: ISSN 1476-3915. GBP 1,801, USD 3,363 (effective 2012).
—CCC.
Published by: Royal Society of Chemistry, Thomas Graham House, Science Park, Milton Rd, Cambridge, CB4 0WF, United Kingdom. TEL 44-1223-420066, FAX 44-1223-423623, sales@rsc.org. Adv. contact Emma Clements TEL 44-1223-432683.

613.62 ESP

LANEKO LESIOEN ESTATISTIKAK (YEAR)/ESTADISTICAS DE LA LESIONES PROFESIONALES. Text in Spanish. a., latest 1996. **Document type:** *Monographic series, Government.*
Published by: (Basque Region. Lan eta Gizarte Segurantza Saila/ Departamento de Trabajo y Seguridad Social), Eusko Jaurlaritzaren Argitalpen-Zerbitzu Nagusia/Servicio Central de Publicaciones del Gobierno Vasco, Donostia-San Sebastian, 1, Vitoria-gasteiz, Alava 01010, Spain. TEL 34-945-018561, FAX 34-945-189709, hac-sabd@ej-gv.es, http://www.ej-gv.net/publicaciones. Circ: 2,000.

338.47665 USA

N P R A STATISTICAL REPORT. ANNUAL SURVEY OF OCCUPATIONAL INJURIES & INJURIES. Text in English. a. back issues avail. **Document type:** *Report, Trade.* **Description:** Provides a statistical overview of injuries at petrochemical plants and refineries.
Published by: National Petrochemical & Refiners Association, 1667 K St, N W, Ste 700, Washington, DC 20006. TEL 202-457-0480, FAX 202-457-0486, info@npra.org, http://www.npradc.org.

658.31244 USA

N R C REGULATORY GUIDES. OCCUPATIONAL HEALTH (DIVISION 8). (Nuclear Regulatory Commission) Text in English. 1973. irreg. free (effective 2011). **Document type:** *Government.*
Published by: U.S. Nuclear Regulatory Commission, Washington, DC 20555. TEL 301-415-7000, 800-368-5642.

613.62 USA

NONFATAL OCCUPATIONAL INJURIES AND ILLNESSES IN CALIFORNIA. Text in English. a. **Document type:** *Government.*
Related titles: Online - full content ed.
Published by: Department of Industrial Relations, Division of Labor Statistics & Research, PO Box 420603, San Francisco, CA 94142-0603. http://www.dir.ca.gov/dlsr/statistics_research.html.

016.61362 AUS ISSN 1324-8715

OCCUPATIONAL HEALTH & SAFETY CURRENT CONTENTS. Short title: O H & S Current Contents. Text in English. 1986. bi-m. back issues avail. **Document type:** *Abstract/Index.* **Description:** Includes listing of all new publications in OH&S received in VIOSH Australia and the E.J. Barker University Library.
Published by: V I O S H Australia, c/o University of Ballarat, University Dr, Mt. Helen, PO Box 663, Ballarat, VIC 3353, Australia. TEL 61-3-53279000, FAX 61-3-53279704.

658.31244021 USA ISSN 0092-8712
JK850.A3

OCCUPATIONAL SAFETY AND HEALTH STATISTICS OF THE FEDERAL GOVERNMENT. Text in English. 1972. a.
Published by: U.S. Occupational Safety and Health Administration, Office of Public Affairs, Rm N3647, 200 Constitution Ave, N W, Washington, DC 20210. TEL 202-523-8148, http://www.osha-slc.gov/html/jshq-index.html.

658.31244 310 USA ISSN 0195-9344

WESTERN WOOD PRODUCTS ASSOCIATION. QUARTERLY INJURY & ILLNESS INCIDENCE REPORT. Text in English. 19??. q. USD 18 (effective 2009). back issues avail. **Document type:** *Report, Trade.* **Description:** Supplies a year-to-date injury-control index and annual summary of injuries sustained by lumberjacks in Western timber forests.
Published by: Western Wood Products Association, 522 SW Fifth Ave, Ste 500, Portland, OR 97204. TEL 503-224-3930, FAX 503-224-3934, info@wwpa.org.

613.62021 USA ISSN 1932-085X
HD7262.5.U6

WORKPLACE INJURIES AND ILLNESSES IN (YEAR). Text in English. 1992. a., latest 2007. free (effective 2009). back issues avail. **Document type:** *Government.*
Former titles (until 1992): News. B L S Reports on Survey of Occupational Injuries and Illnesses in (Year); (until 1985): News. Occupational Injuries and Illnesses in (Year); (until 1979): News. B L S Reports on Occupational Injuries and Illnesses for (Year); (until 1975): News. B L S Reports Results of Survey of Occupational Injuries and Illneses for (Year)
Related titles: Online - full text ed.: ISSN 1932-0884.
Published by: U.S. Department of Labor, Bureau of Labor Statistics, 2 Massachusetts Ave, NE, Rm 2860, Washington, DC 20212. TEL 202-691-5200, FAX 202-691-7890, blsdata_staff@bls.gov.

OCCUPATIONS AND CAREERS

see also BUSINESS AND ECONOMICS—Labor And Industrial Relations

A A C E CAREERS UPDATE; connecting careers, education and work. *see* EDUCATION—Adult Education

331.1 610.7365 USA ISSN 1521-7558
HV1454.2.U6

▼ **A A H S A CONTINUING CARE RETIREMENT COMMUNITY SALARY & BENEFITS REPORT.** Variant title: Continuing Care Retirement Community Salary & Benefits Report. Text in English. 2009. a. USD 155 per issue participant; USD 295 per issue non-participant (effective 2010). **Document type:** *Report, Trade.* **Description:** Provides salary and benefits information for employees of retirement communities, including management, nursing, therapy, dietary, and clerical positions.
Related titles: CD-ROM ed.: ISSN 2151-3759. 2010.
Published by: (American Association of Homes and Services for the Aging), Hospital & Healthcare Compensation Service, PO Box 376, Oakland, NJ 07436. TEL 201-405-0075, FAX 201-405-2110, allinfo@hhcsinc.com.

331.1 610.7365 USA ISSN 1523-8164

A A H S A NURSING HOME SALARY & BENEFITS REPORT. Variant title: Nursing Home Salary & Benefits Report. Text in English. 1998. a. USD 155 per issue participant; USD 295 per issue non-participant (effective 2010). **Document type:** *Report, Trade.* **Description:** Provides salary and bonus data on management, nursing, therapy, dietary, and clerical positions in nursing homes.
Related titles: CD-ROM ed.: ISSN 2151-3694. 2010.
Published by: (American Association of Homes and Services for the Aging), Hospital & Healthcare Compensation Service, PO Box 376, Oakland, NJ 07436. TEL 201-405-0075, FAX 201-405-2110, allinfo@hhcsinc.com.

371.42 BRA ISSN 1414-8889

A B O P. REVISTA. (Associacao Brasileira de Orientadores Profissionais) Text in Portuguese. 1997. s-a. **Document type:** *Magazine, Consumer.*
Published by: Associacao Brasileira de Orientadores Profissionais, Av Lucas de Oliveira 1873, Porto Alegre, RS, Brazil. TEL 55-51-30287816, http://www.abopbrasil.org.br.

A C J S EMPLOYMENT BULLETIN; for criminal justice - criminology positions. *see* BUSINESS AND ECONOMICS—Personnel Management

371.42 150 GBR

A E P APPOINTMENTS BROADSHEET. Text in English. 1978. w. free to members (effective 2009). adv. back issues avail. **Document type:** *Newsletter, Trade.* **Description:** Contains advertisements for vacant positions in educational psychology.
Indexed: E-psyche.
Published by: Association of Educational Psychologists, 4 The Riverside Ctr, Frankland Ln, Durham, DH1 5TA, United Kingdom. TEL 44-191-3849512, FAX 44-191-3865287, info@aep.org.uk, http://www.aep.org.uk.

331.11 NLD ISSN 2210-6219

A I A S NEWSLETTER/AMSTERDAM INSTITUUT VOOR ARBEIDSSTUDIES. NEWSLETTER. Text in English. 1998. s-a.
Formerly (until 2009): A I A S Nieuwsbrief (1567-1119)
Published by: Amsterdam Institute for Advanced Labour Studies/ Amsterdam Instituut voor Arbeidsstudies, University of Amsterdam, Plantage Muidergracht 12, Amsterdam, 1018 TV, Netherlands. TEL 31-20-5254199, FAX 31-20-5254301, aias@uva.nl, http://www.uva-aias.net. Circ: 2,500.

371.42 AUT

A P A - JOURNAL. BILDUNG. Text in German. w. EUR 380 combined subscription for print & online eds. (effective 2003). **Document type:** *Journal, Trade.*
Related titles: Online - full text ed.
Published by: Austria Presse Agentur, Gunoldstr 14, Vienna, W 1190, Austria. TEL 43-1-360600, FAX 43-1-360603099, kundenservice@apa.at, http://www.apa.at.

331.1 AUS ISSN 1833-4520

A P E S M A / F A S T S PROFESSIONAL SCIENTIST REMUNERATION SURVEY REPORT. (Association of Professional Engineers, Scientists and Managers - Federation of Australian Scientific) Text in English. 2006. a. AUD 85 per issue to members; AUD 275 per issue to non-members (effective 2008). **Document type:** *Yearbook, Trade.* **Description:** Contains salary information based on the results of APESMA's annual survey of professional scientists.
Related titles: Online - full text ed.
Published by: (Federation of Australian Scientific and Technological Societies), Association of Professional Engineers, Scientists and Managers, GPO Box 1272, Melbourne, VIC 8060, Australia. TEL 61-3-96958800, FAX 61-3-96958902, info@apesma.asn.au.

A P S JOBS. (Australian Public Service) *see* PUBLIC ADMINISTRATION

331.1 USA ISSN 0361-5669
Z682.3

A R L ANNUAL SALARY SURVEY. Text in English. 1973. a. USD 170 per issue to non-members; USD 85 per issue to members (effective 2010). charts. 126 p./no.; back issues avail. **Document type:** *Report, Trade.* **Description:** Covers salary reports of more than 12,000 professional positions in ARL member libraries on an annual basis.
Related titles: Microfiche ed.: (from CIS); Online - full text ed.: ISSN 1930-367X.
Indexed: SRI.
—Linda Hall.
Published by: Association of Research Libraries, 21 Dupont Cir NW, Ste 800, Washington, DC 20036. TEL 202-296-2296, FAX 202-872-0884. Circ: 500. **Subscr. to:** ARL Publications Distribution Ctr, PO Box 531, Annapolis Junction, MD 20701. TEL 301-362-8196, FAX 301-206-9789.

A S C E SALARY SURVEY (ONLINE). *see* ENGINEERING—Civil Engineering

A S P B NEWS. *see* BIOLOGY—Botany

371.42 USA ISSN 1930-8620
HF5549.5.T7

THE A S T D TRAINING & PERFORMANCE SOURCEBOOK. (American Society for Training & Development) Text in English. 1996. a. USD 69.95 per issue to non-members; USD 59.95 per issue to members (effective 2009). **Document type:** *Handbook/Manual/Guide, Consumer.* **Description:** Contains organization development and leadership training tools that focus on the hottest topics facing organizations today.
Former titles (until 2005): The.. Training and Performance Sourcebook; (until 1998): The.. McGraw-Hill Training and Performance Sourcebook (1084-1342)
Published by: American Society for Training & Development, 1640 King St, PO Box 1443, Alexandria, VA 22313. TEL 703-683-8100, 800-628-2783, FAX 703-683-8103, customercare@astd.org, http://www.astd.org. Ed. Mel Silberman.

371.42 808.02 USA

A W P JOB LIST. Text in English. 7/yr. membership. adv. **Description:** Lists jobs for teaching creative writing in universities.

Published by: Association of Writers & Writing Programs, Tallwood House, Mail Stop 1E3, George Mason University, Fairfax, VA 22030. TEL 703-993-4301, FAX 703-993-4302, awp@awpwriter.org, http://www.awpwriter.org. Ed. David W Fenza. Adv. contact Katherine Peppy. Circ: 5,000.

371.42 USA

ACADEMIC JOBS DIGEST. Text in English. 19??. a. (plus q. updates). **Document type:** *Directory, Trade.* **Description:** Provides information on positions available to managers, administrators, staff, and faculty. Includes current job possibilities, an employment directory of colleges and universities, and Job Hot Line telephone numbers.
Published by: Career Advancement Publications, 460 Thornridge Dr, Rochester Hls, MI 48307. TEL 716-483-3454, FAX 716-664-2417.

610.711 USA ISSN 1093-1139

ACADEMIC PHYSICIAN AND SCIENTIST; the most comprehensive single source for recruitment in academic medicine. Abbreviated title: A P S. Text in English. 19??. 10/yr. USD 150 domestic to individuals; USD 190 foreign to individuals; USD 208 domestic to institutions; USD 243 foreign to institutions (effective 2010). adv. back issues avail. **Document type:** *Magazine, Trade.* **Description:** Features news from the world of medical education along with more than 30 pages of listings for open faculty, administrative, and fellowship positions throughout academic medicine.
Formerly (until 1993): Academic Physician
Related titles: Online - full text ed.
Indexed: CA, E-psyche, T02.
—CCC.
Published by: (Association of American Medical Colleges), Lippincott Williams & Wilkins (Subsidiary of: Wolters Kluwer N.V.), 333 7th Ave, 19th Fl, New York, NY 10001. TEL 646-674-6530, FAX 646-674-6500, customerservice@lww.com, http://www.lww.com. Ed. Debra Wenger. Pub. David Myers. Adv. contact Martha McGarity TEL 646-674-6535.

371.42 LBN ISSN 1816-3513

ACADEMIX; Middle East - your career guide magazine. Text in English. 2005. m. USD 55 in Arab countries; USD 110 elsewhere; USD 4 newsstand/cover (effective 2006). adv. **Document type:** *Magazine, Trade.* **Description:** Provides career guidance detailing academic paths to a specific career in five major education systems: American, British, Canadian, Australian and French, as well as a list of universities offering related courses in the Arab world and abroad.
Published by: International Graphic Arts, Al Mubashir Bldg, 1st Fl, Hamra, Beirut, Lebanon. TEL 961-1-736168, FAX 961-1-736168, iga@inco.com.lb. Ed. Nada Tabbakh. R&P Dima Raouda Casutt. adv.: color page USD 4,500. Circ: 70,000 (paid).

331.1 USA
HF5382.5.U5

ACCESS (WASHINGTON); the national non-profit employment clearinghouse. Text in English. 1977. bi-w. USD 109; USD 5 newsstand/cover (effective 1999). adv. **Document type:** *Newspaper.* **Description:** Offers a national resource on employment, internships, volunteering and career development for non-profit organizations.
Formerly (until 1998): Community Jobs (0195-1157)
Published by: ACCESS: Networking in the Public Interest, 1001 Connecticut Ave, Ste 838, Washington, DC 20036. TEL 202-785-4233, FAX 202-785-4212. Ed., Pub. Ryan Dryden. R&P Diana Sevillano. Adv. contact Zeus Allen. Circ: 10,000 (paid).

331.1 USA

ADAMS COVER LETTER ALMANAC. Text in English. 1995. irreg., latest 2006, 2nd ed. USD 17.95 per issue (effective 2009). **Description:** Contains sample cover letters that can be easily customized to match the needs of any job seeker.
Related titles: Diskette ed.
Published by: Adams Media (Subsidiary of: F + W Media Inc.), 4700 E Galbraith Rd, Cincinnati, OH 45236. TEL 513-531-2690, FAX 800-258-0929, deskcopies@adamsmedia.com, http://www.adamsmedia.com.

331.1 USA

ADAMS JOB INTERVIEW ALMANAC. Text in English. 1996. irreg., latest 2005, 2nd ed. USD 17.95 per issue (effective 2009).
Related titles: CD-ROM ed.
Published by: Adams Media (Subsidiary of: F + W Media Inc.), 4700 E Galbraith Rd, Cincinnati, OH 45236. TEL 513-531-2690, FAX 800-258-0929, deskcopies@adamsmedia.com, http://www.adamsmedia.com.

371.42 USA ISSN 1072-592X
HF5382.75.U6

ADAMS JOBS ALMANAC. Variant title: Jobs Almanac. Text in English. 1994. irreg., latest 2006, 9th ed. USD 10 per issue (effective 2009). adv. **Document type:** *Guide, Trade.* **Description:** Provides job market developments in every major industry, 7,000 major employers, and job search strategies.
Published by: Adams Media (Subsidiary of: F + W Media Inc.), 4700 E Galbraith Rd, Cincinnati, OH 45236. TEL 513-531-2690, FAX 800-258-0929, deskcopies@adamsmedia.com, http://www.adamsmedia.com.

331.1 USA

ADAMS RESUME ALMANAC. Text in English. 1994. irreg., latest 2005, 2nd ed. USD 17.95 per issue (effective 2009). **Description:** Contains everything a candidate needs to know in order to craft a job-winning resume.
Related titles: Diskette ed.
Published by: Adams Media (Subsidiary of: F + W Media Inc.), 4700 E Galbraith Rd, Cincinnati, OH 45236. TEL 513-531-2690, FAX 800-258-0929, deskcopies@adamsmedia.com, http://www.adamsmedia.com.

ADVANCES IN DEVELOPING HUMAN RESOURCES. *see* BUSINESS AND ECONOMICS—Personnel Management

▼ **ADVANCES IN MEDICAL EDUCATION AND PRACTICE.** *see* EDUCATION—Higher Education

AFFAIRES PLUS. *see* BUSINESS AND ECONOMICS—Investments

371.42 305.89607305 USA

AFRICAN-AMERICAN CAREER WORLD; the diversity employment magazine. Text in English. 2001. s-a. USD 18; free to qualified personnel (effective 2010). adv. 48 p./no. 3 cols./p.; **Document type:** *Magazine, Trade.* **Description:** Aims to be the recruitment link between the students and professionals who are African American and the major corporations that seeks to hire them.
Published by: Equal Opportunity Publications, Inc., 445 Broad Hollow Rd, Ste 425, Melville, NY 11747. TEL 631-421-9421, FAX 631-421-1352, info@eop.com. Ed. James Schneider TEL 631-421-9421 ext 12. Pub., Adv. contact Tamara Flaum-Dreyfuss TEL 631-421-9421 ext 21.

305.896 371.42 USA ISSN 1540-1324
E185.5

AFRICAN AMERICAN YEARBOOK; a resource and referral guide for and about African Americans. Variant title: African-American Yearbook. Text in English. 2001. a. USD 29.95 per vol. (effective 2010). **Document type:** *Yearbook.* **Description:** Features information in the area of employment, business, education, and health, as well as a tool for organizations seeking to reach the large African-American market.
Related titles: CD-ROM ed.: USD 895 per issue for 1 user (effective 2007); Online - full text ed.
Published by: T I Y M Publishing Co., Inc., 6718 Whittier Ave, Ste 130, McLean, VA 22101. TEL 703-734-1632, FAX 703-356-0787, tiym@tiym.com, http://www.tiym.com/.

AGENDA. *see* ART

AIR JOBS DIGEST. *see* AERONAUTICS AND SPACE FLIGHT

371.42 DEU ISSN 0944-582X

AKADEMIE. Text in German. 1979. q. EUR 2.80 newsstand/cover (effective 2007). adv. **Document type:** *Magazine, Consumer.*
Formerly (until 1993): Die Fortbildung (0173-9042); Which was formed by the merger of (1955-1979): Die Fortbildung. Ausgabe B D I V W A (0344-421X); Which was formerly (until 1977): Die Fortbildung. Ausgabe B (0341-1311); (1955-1979): Die Fortbildung. Ausgabe V W A (0173-9034); Which was formerly (until 1977): Die Fortbildung. Ausgabe A (0341-1303); Both of which superseded in part (in 1967): Die Fortbildung (0427-0207)
Published by: Schuermann & Klagges GmbH & Co. KG, Industriestr 34, Bochum, 44894, Germany. TEL 49-234-92140, FAX 49-234-9214100, sk@skala.de, http://www.skala.de. adv.: page EUR 894. Circ: 15,979 (controlled).

371.42 DEU

AKADEMIKER-STELLENMARKT.DE. Text in German. 2000. irreg. adv. **Document type:** *Magazine, Trade.* **Description:** Contains information and advice for students on how to prepare for entering the job market.
Media: Online - full content.
Published by: Evoluzione Media AG, Dillwaechterstr 4, Munich, 80686, Germany. TEL 49-89-7690030, FAX 49-89-76900329, info@evoluzione.de, http://www.evoluzionemedia.de.

370.15 USA ISSN 1546-2781
BF637.C6

ALABAMA COUNSELING ASSOCIATION. JOURNAL. Text in English. 1974. s-a. USD 60 to members; USD 30 students & retired members (effective 2007). bk.rev. charts; abstr.; stat. **Document type:** *Magazine, Trade.*
Former titles: Alabama Association for Counseling and Development Journal; Alabama Personnel and Guidance Journal
Related titles: Online - full text ed.: free (effective 2007).
Indexed: E-psyche.
Published by: Alabama Counseling Association, c/o Dr Ervin L Wood, 217 Daryle St, Livingston, AL 35470. TEL 205-652-1712, 888-655-5460, FAX 205-652-1576, alca@alabamacounseling.org. Ed. Dr. Debbie Grant. R&P Dr. Ervin L Wood. Circ: 2,000.

371.42 DEU ISSN 0938-7250

ALLGEMEINER HOCHSCHUL-ANZEIGER; Zeitung fuer den Fach- und Fuehrungsnachwuchs. Variant title: Hochschulanzeiger. Text in German. 1989. 6/yr. EUR 8.40; EUR 1.40 newsstand/cover (effective 2010). adv. **Document type:** *Newspaper, Consumer.*
—CCC.
Published by: Frankfurter Allgemeine Zeitung GmbH, Hellerhofstr 2-4, Frankfurt Am Main, 60327, Germany. TEL 49-69-75910, FAX 49-69-75911743, info@faz.net. Ed. Josef Krief. Circ: 241,067 (controlled).

THE ALMANAC OF AMERICAN EMPLOYERS. *see* BUSINESS AND ECONOMICS—Labor And Industrial Relations

331.1 USA ISSN 1075-0355

AMERICAN CAREERS. Text in English. 1990. 2/yr. price varies. adv. **Document type:** *Guide, Trade.* **Description:** publishes American careers programs for high school, middle school and elementary classrooms that integrate academics and careers.
Published by: Career Communications, Inc., 6701 W 64th St, Ste 210, Overland Park, KS 66202. TEL 800-669-7795, FAX 913-362-4864, ccinfo@carcom.com.

331.1 CAN

AMERICAN EMPLOYER DIGEST. Text in English. a. CAD 44.95 (effective 2003). **Document type:** *Directory, Trade.* **Description:** Helps job-seekers quickly locate great employers in hundreds of major industries in the United States.
Published by: Mediacorp Canada Inc., 21 New St, Toronto, ON M5R 1P7, Canada. TEL 416-964-6069, FAX 416-964-3202, info@mediacorp2.com, http://www.mediacorp2.com.

667.1 USA ISSN 1047-9090

AMERICAN WINDOW CLEANER; voice of the professional window cleaner. Text in English. 1986. bi-m. USD 35 domestic; USD 40 in Canada; USD 60 elsewhere (effective 2005). adv. bk.rev. back issues avail. **Document type:** *Magazine, Trade.* **Description:** Provides an industry-wide communication link on new products, techniques, association news, interviews, business advice, and upcoming events.
Formerly: American Window Cleaner Newsletter
Published by: (International Window Cleaning Association), 12 Twelve Publishing Corp., 750-B NW Broad St, Southern Pines, NC 28387. TEL 910-246-1681, FAX 910-693-2644. Ed., Pub. Norman J Finegold. adv.: B&W page USD 1,250, color page USD 1,625; trim 8.5 x 11. Circ: 8,000 (paid).

371.42 USA

AMERICA'S TOP 101 JOBS FOR COLLEGE GRADUATES. Text in English. 1994. biennial. USD 15.95 newsstand/cover (effective 2006).
Formerly (until 2005): America's Top Jobs for College Graduates (1088-3924)
Published by: JIST Publishing, 7321 Shadeland Station, Ste 200, Indianapolis, IN 46256. TEL 800-648-5478, FAX 800-547-8329, info@jist.com, http://www.jist.com.

371.42 USA ISSN 1931-017X
HD5724

AMERICA'S TOP 101 JOBS FOR PEOPLE WITHOUT A FOUR-YEAR DEGREE. Text in English. 19??. biennial (7th ed.). **Document type:** *Guide, Trade.*
Former titles (until 2003): America's Top Jobs for People Without a Four-Year Degree (1931-1567); (until 1999): America's Top Jobs for People Without College Degrees (1088-3894)
Published by: JIST Publishing, 7321 Shadeland Station, Ste 200, Indianapolis, IN 46256. TEL 800-648-5478, FAX 800-547-8329, info@jist.com, http://www.jist.com. Ed. Michael Farr.

ANNUAL REPORT OF LABOR MARKET INFORMATION. *see* BUSINESS AND ECONOMICS—Economic Situation And Conditions

371.42 975.3 USA ISSN 1067-330X
HD2346.U52

ANUARIO HISPANO/HISPANIC YEARBOOK. Text in English, Spanish. 1985. a. USD 29.95 per issue (effective 2007). adv. **Document type:** *Yearbook, Trade.* **Description:** Resource in the areas of employment, business, education and health, as well as a tool for organizations seeking to reach the rapidly growing Hispanic American market.
Related titles: CD-ROM ed.: ISSN 2154-0012. USD 895 per issue (effective 2007); Online - full text ed.
Published by: T I Y M Publishing Co., Inc., 6718 Whittier Ave, Ste 130, McLean, VA 22101. TEL 703-734-1632, FAX 703-356-0787, tiym@tiym.com, http://www.tiym.com/. Ed. Angela E. Zavala. Pub. Joan Ovidio Zavala. Adv. contact Jordan Dansby. B&W page USD 11,000, color page USD 14,500; trim 8.375 x 10.875. Circ: 200,000 (paid).

331.1 GBR ISSN 1366-6932

THE APPOINTMENT; the careers magazine for retail, fashion and hospitality. Text in English. 1997. m. GBP 30 (effective 2010). adv. back issues avail. **Document type:** *Magazine, Trade.* **Description:** Describes career opportunities in retail, fashion and hospitality.
Published by: The Appointment Ltd., Northcliffe House, 2 Derry St, London, W8 5TT, United Kingdom. TEL 44-20-83403366, FAX 44-20-83408866.

315.8927 371.42 USA ISSN 1940-1000

ARAB-AMERICAN YEARBOOK; the resource and referral guide for and about Arab Americans. Text in English. 2007. a. USD 29.95 per issue (effective 2007). adv. **Document type:** *Yearbook.* **Description:** Resource in the areas of employment, business, education and health, as well as a tool for organizations seeking to reach the rapidly growing Arab-American market.
Related titles: CD-ROM ed.: USD 895 per issue (effective 2007); Online - full text ed.
Published by: T I Y M Publishing Co., Inc., 6718 Whittier Ave, Ste 130, McLean, VA 22101. TEL 703-734-1632, FAX 703-356-0787, tiym@tiym.com, http://www.tiym.com/. adv.: B&W page USD 7,452, color page USD 9,950; trim 8.375 x 10.875.

331.1 NLD ISSN 1873-8796

ARBEIDSMARKTANALYSE. Text in Dutch. 2003. a.
Published by: Raad voor Werk en Inkomen, Postbus 93048, The Hague, 2509 AA, Netherlands. TEL 31-70-7890789, FAX 31-70-7890790, info@rwi.nl, http://www.rwi.nl.

371.42 DEU ISSN 1869-9073
Q3

▼ **ARBEITSTITEL**; Forum fuer Leipziger Promovierende. Text in Multiple languages. 2009. irreg. free (effective 2011). **Document type:** *Journal, Academic/Scholarly.*
Media: Online - full text.
Published by: Meine Verlag OHG, Werner-Heisenberg-Str 3, Magdeburg, 39106, Germany. TEL 49-391-5446964, FAX 49-1803-62222910031, post@meine-verlag.de, http://www.meine-verlag.de. Ed. Enrico Thomas.

331.1 USA

ARKANSAS. EMPLOYMENT SECURITY DEPARTMENT. ANNUAL REPORT. Text in English. 194?. a. free. charts; stat. **Document type:** *Government.*
Formerly: Arkansas. Department of Labor. Employment Security Division. Annual Report
Published by: Employment Security Department, PO Box 2981, Little Rock, AR 72203-2981. TEL 501-682-2121. Ed., R&P Stacy A Hoover TEL 501-682-3125. Circ: (controlled).

ARTMATTERS!. *see* ART

ARTSEARCH (ONLINE). *see* THEATER

305.895 371.42 USA ISSN 1551-0867
E184.A75

ASIAN-AMERICAN YEARBOOK; a resource and referral guide for and about Asian Americans. Text in English. 2004. a. USD 24.95 per issue (effective 2007). adv. **Document type:** *Yearbook.* **Description:** Resource in the areas of employment, business, education and health, as well as a tool for organizations seeking to reach the rapidly growing Asian Pacific American market.
Related titles: CD-ROM ed.: USD 895 per academic year (effective 2007); Online - full text ed.
Published by: T I Y M Publishing Co., Inc., 6718 Whittier Ave, Ste 130, McLean, VA 22101. TEL 703-734-1632, FAX 703-356-0787, tiym@tiym.com, http://www.tiym.com/. Ed. Angela E. Zavala. Pub. Joan Ovidio Zavala. Adv. contact Jordan Dansby. B&W page USD 7,452, color page USD 9,950; trim 8.375 x 10.875. Circ: 44,000.

371.42 USA ISSN 1931-4388

ASSOCIATION IMPACT. Text in English. bi-m. **Document type:** *Magazine, Trade.*
Formerly (until 2006): Association News
Published by: Michigan Society of Association Executives, 1350 Haslett Rd, E Lansing, MI 48823. TEL 517-332-6723, FAX 517-332-6724, info@msae.org, http://www.msae.org/Default.aspx?tabid=149.

331.1 USA ISSN 0888-4870

ATHLETICS EMPLOYMENT WEEKLY. Text in English. 1986. 46/yr. USD 80 (effective 2000). adv. **Document type:** *Newsletter.* **Description:** Lists job openings for athletic directors, coaches, assistant coaches and graduate assistants. Covers all sports and all sizes of colleges throughout the United States.
Published by: R D S T Enterprises, 1775 E County Rd 1300, Carthage, IL 62321. TEL 217-357-3615, FAX 217-357-3615. Eds., Pubs. Duane Fugate, Ruth Fugate. R&P Ruth Fugate. Adv. contact Duane Fugate. Circ: 1,600 (paid).

371.42 DEU
AUD!MAX REIFEPRUEFUNG. Text in German. 2002. 2/yr. EUR 2.50 newsstand/cover (effective 2008). adv. **Document type:** *Magazine, Consumer.*
Published by: Audimax Verlag GmbH, Hauptmarkt 6-8, Nuernberg, 90403, Germany. TEL 49-911-2377956, FAX 49-911-204939. Ed. Nicole Hoppe. Adv. contact Josefine Lorenz. B&W page EUR 4,076, color page EUR 6,318. Circ: 225,000 (paid and controlled).

371.42 DEU
AUSBILDUNG, FORTBILDUNG, PERSONALENTWICKLUNG. Text in German. 1972. irreg., latest vol.38, 1997. price varies. **Document type:** *Monographic series, Academic/Scholarly.*
Formerly (until 1987): Ausbildung und Fortbildung (0340-9740)
Published by: Erich Schmidt Verlag GmbH & Co. (Berlin), Genthiner Str 30 G, Berlin, 10785, Germany. TEL 49-30-2500850, FAX 49-30-250085305, vertrieb@esvmedien.de.

371.42 370 AUS ISSN 1038-4162
➤ **AUSTRALIAN JOURNAL OF CAREER DEVELOPMENT.** Variant title: A J C D. Text in English. 1992. 3/yr. AUD 94.95 domestic; AUD 120 foreign (effective 2009). **Document type:** *Journal, Academic/Scholarly.* **Description:** Contains articles on career planning and guidance, labour market trends, latest research, vocational training and case studies of innovative programs.
Indexed: A10, A12, A17, A26, ABIn, AEI, CA, DRIE, E03, ERI, ERIC, ERO, I05, IBR, IBZ, P48, P51, P53, P54, PQC, T02, V03.
—BLDSC (1805.300000), Ingenta. **CCC.**
Published by: Australian Council for Educational Research, 19 Prospect Hill Rd, Private Bag 55, Camberwell, VIC 3124, Australia. TEL 61-3-98357447, 1800-338-402, FAX 61-3-98357499, sales@acer.edu.au. Ed. Peter McIlveen.

➤ **AVIATIONCAREER.NET.** *see* AERONAUTICS AND SPACE FLIGHT

➤ **AZUR;** Karrieremagazin fuer junge Juristen. *see* LAW

331 DEU
B D B - ARGUMENTE. (Bundesverband der Berufsbetreuer/-innen) Text in German. 2003. irreg., latest vol.6, 2007. price varies. **Document type:** *Monographic series, Trade.*
Published by: Bundesverband der Berufsbetreuer/-innen e.V., Brodschrangen 3-5, Hamburg, 20457, Germany. TEL 49-40-38629030, FAX 49-40-38629032, info@bdb-ev.de, http://www.bdb-ev.de.

331.1 DEU ISSN 1611-0404
B D B - ASPEKTE. (Bundesverband der Berufsbetreuer/-innen) Text in German. 2002. q. EUR 5 newsstand/cover (effective 2009). adv. **Document type:** *Journal, Trade.*
Incorporates (2005-2008): Betreuungsrechtliche Plus (1860-8027)
Published by: Bundesverband der Berufsbetreuer/-innen e.V., Brodschrangen 3-5, Hamburg, 20457, Germany. TEL 49-40-38629030, FAX 49-40-38629032, info@bdb-ev.de, http://www.bdb-ev.de. Adv. contact Susanne Harder. B&W page EUR 900; trim 210 x 297. Circ: 8,000 (controlled).

331.1 DEU ISSN 1865-0821
B I B B REPORT. Text in German. 2000. q. **Document type:** *Journal, Trade.*
Formerly (until 2007): B I B B Forschung
Related titles: Online - full text ed.: ISSN 1866-7279.
—CCC.
Published by: (Germany. Bundesinstitut fuer Berufsbildung), W. Bertelsmann Verlag GmbH & Co. KG, Postfach 100633, Bielefeld, 33506, Germany. TEL 49-521-911010, FAX 49-521-9110179, service@wbv.de, http://www.wbv.de.

331.1 GBR ISSN 1742-6774
B M J CAREER FOCUS (ONLINE). Text in English. 2002. irreg. free. **Document type:** *Monographic series, Trade.*
Media: Online - full text. **Related titles:** ◆ Print ed.: B M J Career Focus (Print).
—CCC.
Published by: B M J Group, BMA House, Tavistock Sq, London, WC1H 9JR, United Kingdom. TEL 44-20-73836373, FAX 44-20-73836668, support@bmjgroup.com, http://group.bmj.com. Ed. Edward Davies.

331.4 GBR
B P W NEWS INTERNATIONAL. (Business and Professional Women) Text in English, French, Spanish. m. GBP 30. **Document type:** *Newsletter.*
Published by: International Federation of Business and Professional Women, Studio Sixteen, 8 Cloisters House, Cloisters Business Centre, 8 Battersea Park Rd, London, SW8 4BG, United Kingdom. TEL 0171-738-8323, FAX 0171-622-0528.

658.3 FRA ISSN 2116-6110
B R E F DU C E R E Q. (Bulletin de Recherches sur l'Emploi et la Formation du Centre d'Etudes et de Recherches sur les Qual) Text in French. 1972. m. free (effective 2011). **Document type:** *Newsletter, Consumer.*
Former titles (until 2011): B R E F (0758-1858); Formerly (until 1983): Note d'Information - Centre d'Etudes et de Recherches sur les Qualifications (0291-8064)
Related titles: Online - full text ed.: ISSN 2107-0822. 19??.
Indexed: FR.
Published by: Centre d'Etudes et de Recherches sur les Qualifications, BP 21321, Marseille, 13567, France. http://www.cereq.fr.

331.1 CAN ISSN 1922-1835
BANKING REVIEW. Text in English. 2008. 3/yr. free to qualified personnel (effective 2010). back issues avail. **Document type:** *Journal, Trade.* **Description:** Shares a Canadian perspective on the challenges and opportunities facing the banking and capital markets sector.
Related titles: Online - full text ed.
Published by: Pricewaterhouse Coopers, Royal Trust Tower, Toronto-Dominion Ctr, 77 King St W, Ste 3000, PO Box 82, Toronto, ON M5K 1G8, Canada. TEL 416-863-1133, FAX 416-365-8178.

371.42 DNK ISSN 0901-313X
BARTENDEREN. Text in Danish. 1950. 6/yr. free. adv. **Document type:** *Magazine, Trade.*
—CCC.
Published by: Dansk Bartender Laug, P O Box 230, Copenhagen V, 1502, Denmark. TEL 45-39-290076, freddy@bartenderen.dk, http://www.bartenderen.dk. Ed. Nick Kobbernagel.

057.1 DEU ISSN 1618-047X
BEI UNS IN HAMBURG; Information - Werbung - Integration. Text in Russian. 2000. m. free newsstand/cover (effective 2006). adv. **Document type:** *Magazine, Consumer.* **Description:** Contains job listings and other information for Russian immigrants living in the Hamburg region.
Published by: Informbuero Verlag, Muehlenkamp 29, Hamburg, 22303, Germany. TEL 49-40-2799812, FAX 49-40-27881843. Ed., Adv. contact Elena Stroiakovski.

371.42 DEU ISSN 0721-2917
BEITRAEGE ZUR ARBEITS-, BERUFS- UND WIRTSCHAFTSPAEDAGOGIK. Text in German. 1979. irreg., latest vol.28, 2010. price varies. **Document type:** *Monographic series, Academic/Scholarly.*
Published by: Peter Lang GmbH (Subsidiary of: Peter Lang Publishing Group), Eschborner Landstr 42-50, Frankfurt Am Main, 60489, Germany. TEL 49-69-7807050, FAX 49-69-78070550, zentrale.frankfurt@peterlang.com. Ed. Andreas Schelten.

331.1 DEU ISSN 0173-6574
HD5777
BEITRAEGE ZUR ARBEITSMARKT- UND BERUFSFORSCHUNG. Text in German. 1970. irreg. (approx. 10-12/yr.). EUR 12.50 per issue (effective 2005). abstr. back issues avail. **Document type:** *Journal, Academic/Scholarly.*
—CCC.
Published by: Institut fuer Arbeitsmarkt- und Berufsforschung, Regensburger Str 104, Nuernberg, 90478, Germany. TEL 49-911-1793206, FAX 49-911-1793736, martina.dorsch@iab.de, http://www.iab.de. R&P Gerd Peters. Circ: 1,800.

331.1 GBR ISSN 1745-8129
BENCHMARK OF SALARIES AND EMPLOYMENT TRENDS IN I T. BUSINESS REPORT (YEAR). (Information Technology) Text in English. 1982. a. GBP 330 per issue to non-members (print or online ed.); GBP 220 per issue to members (print or online ed.); free to qualified personnel (effective 2009); subscr. includes Research Report. back issues avail. **Document type:** *Journal, Trade.* **Description:** Provides a comprehensive analysis of IT salary levels, and IT employment trends.
Formely (until 2005): Salaries and Staff Issues in I T. Business Report (1473-0537)
Related titles: Online - full text ed.
—BLDSC (1891.288000).
Published by: National Computing Centre Ltd., Oxford House, Oxford Rd, Manchester, Lancs M1 7ED, United Kingdom. TEL 44-161-2286333, FAX 44-161-2422499, info@ncc.co.uk, http://www.ncc.co.uk.

331.1 GBR ISSN 1745-8110
BENCHMARK OF SALARIES AND EMPLOYMENT TRENDS IN I T. RESEACH REPORT (YEAR). (Information Technology) Text in English. 19??. a. GBP 330 per issue to non-members (print or online ed.); GBP 220 per issue to members (print or online ed.); free to qualified personnel (effective 2009); subscr. includes Business Report. back issues avail. **Document type:** *Journal, Trade.* **Description:** Provides a comphrehensive analysis of IT salary levels, and IT employment trends in the UK.
Former titles (until 2005): Salaries and Staff Issues in I T (1469-1345); (until 1999): Salaries and Staff Issues in Computing
Related titles: Online - full text ed.
—BLDSC (1891.288500).
Published by: National Computing Centre Ltd., Oxford House, Oxford Rd, Manchester, Lancs M1 7ED, United Kingdom. TEL 44-161-2286333, FAX 44-161-2422499, info@ncc.co.uk, http://www.ncc.co.uk.

371.42 DEU ISSN 0931-8895
BERUFLICHE REHABILITATION. Text in German. 1987. bi-m. EUR 27; EUR 7.20 newsstand/cover (effective 2006). adv. bk.rev. **Document type:** *Journal, Trade.*
Published by: (Bundesarbeitsgemeinschaft der Berufsbildungswerke), Lambertus-Verlag GmbH, Mitscherlichstr 56, Freiburg Im Breisgau, 79108, Germany. TEL 49-761-368250, FAX 49-761-3682533, info@lambertus.de, http://www.lambertus.de. Ed. Philibert Magin. Circ: 1,600.

371.42 DEU
BERUFS- UND KARRIERE-PLANER. I T UND E-BUSINESS. Text in German. a. EUR 19.90 per issue (effective 2011). **Document type:** *Magazine, Trade.*
Published by: Betriebswirtschaftlicher Verlag Dr. Th. Gabler GmbH (Subsidiary of: Springer Fachmedien Wiesbaden GmbH), Abraham-Lincoln-Str 46, Wiesbaden, 65189, Germany. TEL 49-611-78780, FAX 49-611-7878400, springerfachmedien-wiesbaden@springer.com, http://www.gabler.de. Circ: 4,000 (paid and controlled).

371.42 DEU
BERUFS- UND KARRIERE-PLANER. TECHNIK. Text in German. 1999. a. EUR 24.95 per issue (effective 2011). **Document type:** *Journal, Trade.*
Published by: Betriebswirtschaftlicher Verlag Dr. Th. Gabler GmbH (Subsidiary of: Springer Fachmedien Wiesbaden GmbH), Abraham-Lincoln-Str 46, Wiesbaden, 65189, Germany. TEL 49-611-78780, FAX 49-611-7878400, springerfachmedien-wiesbaden@springer.com. Circ: 10,000 (controlled).

371.42 DEU
BERUFS- UND KARRIERE-PLANER. WIRTSCHAFT. Text in German. 1998. a. EUR 24.95 per issue (effective 2011). **Document type:** *Journal, Trade.*
Published by: Betriebswirtschaftlicher Verlag Dr. Th. Gabler GmbH (Subsidiary of: Springer Fachmedien Wiesbaden GmbH), Abraham-Lincoln-Str 46, Wiesbaden, 65189, Germany. TEL 49-611-78780, FAX 49-611-7878400, springerfachmedien-wiesbaden@springer.com, http://www.gabler.de. Circ: 10,000 (paid and controlled).

371.42 CHE
BERUFSBILDER. Text in French, German. s-a.
Address: Muehlirain, Ruemlang, 8153, Switzerland. TEL 01-8173055, FAX 01-8170406. Ed. A Amacher.

371.42 DEU ISSN 0933-4505
BERUFSBILDUNG IM OEFFENTLICHEN DIENST. Text in German. 1976. 3 base vols. plus updates 2/yr. looseleaf. EUR 138 base vol(s).; EUR 34.80 updates per issue (effective 2009). **Document type:** *Monographic series, Trade.*
Published by: Erich Schmidt Verlag GmbH & Co. (Berlin), Genthiner Str 30 G, Berlin, 10785, Germany. TEL 49-30-2500850, FAX 49-30-250085305, vertrieb@esvmedien.de, http://www.erich-schmidt-verlag.de.

371.42 DEU ISSN 0341-4515
BERUFSBILDUNG IN WISSENSCHAFT UND PRAXIS. Text in German. 1972. bi-m. EUR 39.70 domestic; EUR 44.40 foreign; EUR 7.90 per issue (effective 2011). adv. **Document type:** *Journal, Trade.*
Indexed: DIP, IBR, IBZ.
—IE, Infotrieve. **CCC.**
Published by: (Germany. Bundesinstitut fuer Berufsbildung), W. Bertelsmann Verlag GmbH & Co. KG, Postfach 100633, Bielefeld, 33506, Germany. TEL 49-521-911010, FAX 49-521-9110179, service@wbv.de, http://www.wbv.de. Ed. Christiane Jaeger. Circ: 2,550 (paid and controlled).

371.42 DEU
BERUFSPLANUNG FUER DEN I T NACHWUCHS. Text in German. 1999. irreg., latest vol.5, 2004. adv. **Document type:** *Directory, Trade.*
Published by: Staufenbiel Institut fuer Studien- und Berufsplanung GmbH, Maria-Hilf-Str 15, Cologne, 50677, Germany. TEL 49-221-9126630, FAX 49-221-9126639, info@staufenbiel.de, http://www.staufenbiel.de. adv.: B&W page EUR 2,450, color page EUR 3,380. Circ: 10,000 (paid and controlled).

371.42 DEU
BERUFSSTART TECHNIK. Text in German. 1961. 2/yr. adv. **Document type:** *Magazine, Consumer.*
Published by: Klaus Resch Verlag OHG, Moorbeker Str 31, Grossenkneten, 26197, Germany. TEL 49-4435-96120, FAX 49-4435-961296. adv.: B&W page EUR 2,370, color page EUR 3,720. Circ: 40,000 (controlled).

371.42 DEU
BERUFSSTART WIRTSCHAFT. Text in German. 1961. 2/yr. adv. **Document type:** *Magazine, Consumer.*
Published by: Klaus Resch Verlag OHG, Moorbeker Str 31, Grossenkneten, 26197, Germany. TEL 49-4435-96120, FAX 49-4435-961296. adv.: B&W page EUR 2,370, color page EUR 3,720. Circ: 40,000 (controlled).

371.42 CHE
BERUFSWAHL UND AUSBILDUNG. Text in German. s-a.
Address: Buchholzstr 47, Postfach, Zuerich, 8053, Switzerland. TEL 01-555075. Circ: 5,000.

331.1 USA ISSN 1930-5605
BEST ENTRY-LEVEL JOBS; paying your dues without losing your mind. Text in English. 2004. a., latest 2008. USD 16.95 per issue (effective 2008). 400 p./no.; **Document type:** *Guide, Consumer.* **Description:** Details the top job opportunities at more than 100 for profit and not-for-profit organizations and reveals what graduates need to do to land their dream jobs.
Published by: Random House Inc. (Subsidiary of: W. Bertelsmann Verlag GmbH & Co. KG), 1745 Broadway, New York, NY 10019. TEL 212-782-9000, 800-733-3000, FAX 212-572-6066.

BETRIEBLICHE PERSONALENTWICKLUNG UND WEITERBILDUNG IN FORSCHUNG UND PRAXIS. *see* EDUCATION—Teaching Methods And Curriculum

BIG DREAMS. *see* BUSINESS AND ECONOMICS—Small Business

BIJ DE LES; magazine voor leerlingbegeleiding en schooldecanaat. *see* EDUCATION—Higher Education

371.42 DEU ISSN 0935-8269
BILDUNGSBRIEF. Text in German. 1985. bi-m. **Document type:** *Bulletin, Trade.*
Published by: Deutscher Wirtschaftsdienst (Subsidiary of: Wolters Kluwer Deutschland GmbH), Luxemburger Str 449, Cologne, 50939, Germany. TEL 49-221-943737000, FAX 49-221-943737201, box@dwd-verlag.de, http://www.dwd-verlag.de.

371.42 AUS ISSN 1837-5731
▼ **BIZMOJO;** your work. your passion. your world: BizMojo the webzine. take control. Text in English. 2009. q. adv. **Document type:** *Magazine, Trade.* **Description:** Provides support, advice and information on the Australian working landscape to people who are working, wish to work, or are taking extended time from the workforce such as stay-at-home parents, full-time students or semi-retirees.
Media: Online - full text.
Published by: Clayton Jan, Ed. & Pub., Level 1, 530 Little Collins St, Melbourne, VIC 3000, Australia. cjan@BizMojo.com.au.

371.42 305.896 USA ISSN 0192-3757
THE BLACK COLLEGIAN. Text in English. 1970. s-a. USD 15; free to qualified personnel (effective 2010). adv. bk.rev. illus. back issues avail.; reprints avail. **Document type:** *Magazine, Consumer.* **Description:** Provides information on careers, job opportunities, graduate or professional school, internships or co-ops and study abroad programs for students.
Related titles: Microform ed.: (from PQC); ◆ Online - full text ed.: Black Collegian Online.
Indexed: A01, A02, A03, A08, A09, A10, A22, A25, A26, C05, C12, CA, CPerI, E02, E03, E07, E08, E09, ENW, ERI, EdA, EdI, G05, G06, G07, G08, I05, I07, IIBP, M01, M02, M06, M08, MASUSE, P02, P04, P07, P10, P13, P18, P48, P53, P54, PCI, PQC, S08, S09, S23, T02, TOM, V03, V04, W03, W05.
—Ingenta.
Published by: Black Collegian, 140 Carondelet St, New Orleans, LA 70130. TEL 504-523-0154, FAX 504-598-3894. **Subscr. to:** PO Box 17035, N Hollywood, CA 91615. TEL 818-286-3163.

371.42 305.896 USA
BLACK COLLEGIAN ONLINE; the career site for students of color. Text in English. 1995 (Nov.). irreg. adv. bk.rev. illus. **Document type:** *Magazine, Consumer.* **Description:** Provides information on career resources for Black collegians, including job search strategies, graduate school opportunities, career and industry reports.
Incorporates: Expressions, a National Review of the Black Arts
Media: Online - full text. **Related titles:** Microform ed.: (from PQC); Online - full text ed.; ◆ Print ed.: The Black Collegian. ISSN 0192-3757.

NO

Indexed: Acal.
Published by: Black Collegian, 909 Poydras St, 36th Fl, New Orleans, LA 70112. TEL 504-523-0154, FAX 504-523-0271. Ed. Robert G Miller. Circ: 106,000.

331 USA
THE BLACK PERSPECTIVE. Text in English. 1980. a. adv. back issues avail. **Document type:** *Magazine, Consumer.* **Description:** Dedicated to informing the African-American community about opportunities in the worlds of business, technology, and education.
Related titles: Online - full text ed.: free (effective 2011).
Published by: (The Black Perspective), E M Publishing Enterprises, Inc, 13351 Riverside Dr, Ste 514, Sherman Oaks, CA 91423. TEL 818-654-0870, http://www.equalitymagazines.com. Ed. Lyndon Conrad Bell.

371.42 CAN ISSN 1712-8137
BRITISH COLUMBIA. INDUSTRY TRAINING AUTHORITY. SERVICE PLAN. Text in English. 200?. a. **Document type:** *Government.*
Published by: British Columbia, Industry Training Authority, 1223-13351 Commerce Pkwy, Richmond, BC V6V 2X7, Canada. TEL 604-214-8700, FAX 604-214-8701, info@itabc.ca.

371.4 GBR ISSN 0306-9885
LB1027.5 CODEN: BJGCDD
➤ **BRITISH JOURNAL OF GUIDANCE AND COUNSELLING.** Text in English. 19??. q. GBP 501 combined subscription in United Kingdom to institutions (print & online eds.); EUR 717, USD 900 combined subscription to institutions (print & online eds.) (effective 2012). adv. bk.rev. abstr. index. back issues avail.; reprint service avail. from PSC. **Document type:** *Journal, Academic/Scholarly.* **Description:** Provides to communicate theoretical and practical writing of high quality in the guidance and counselling field.
Formerly (until 1973): Guidance and Counselling (0085-1345)
Related titles: Microfiche ed.; Online - full text ed.: ISSN 1469-3534. GBP 451 in United Kingdom to institutions; EUR 645, USD 810 to institutions (effective 2012) (from IngentaConnect).
Indexed: A01, A02, A03, A08, A20, A22, ASSIA, B28, B29, C06, C07, CA, CPE, CurCont, DIP, E-psyche, E01, E03, E09, ERI, ERIC, FAMLI, Faml, H13, HECAB, IBR, IBZ, IPsyAb, P02, P03, P10, P12, P18, P20, P25, P30, P43, P48, P53, P54, PQC, PsycInfo, PsycholAb, S02, S03, SCOPUS, SFSA, SOPODA, SSCI, SociolAb, T02, W07, WBA, WMB.
—BLDSC (2308.700000), IE, Infotrieve, Ingenta. **CCC.**
Published by: (Careers Research and Advisory Centre), Routledge (Subsidiary of: Taylor & Francis Group), 4 Park Sq, Milton Park, Abingdon, Oxon OX14 4RN, United Kingdom. TEL 44-20-70176000, FAX 44-20-70176336, subscriptions@tandf.co.uk, http://www.routledge.com. Eds. Jennifer M Kidd, Paul Wilkins. Adv. contact Linda Hann TEL 44-1344-779945. Circ: 750. **Subscr. to:** Taylor & Francis Ltd., Journals Customer Service, Sheepen Pl, Colchester, Essex CO3 3LP, United Kingdom. TEL 44-20-70175544, FAX 44-20-70175198.

371.42 DEU ISSN 1619-2583
DIE BUEROBERUFE; Zeitschrift fuer die erfolgreiche Aus- und Weiterbildung. Text in German. 1990. m. EUR 55.80; EUR 46.80 to students (effective 2010). adv. back issues avail. **Document type:** *Magazine, Trade.*
Published by: Friedrich Kiehl Verlag GmbH (Subsidiary of: Verlag Neue Wirtschafts-Briefe GmbH & Co. KG), Eschstr 22, Herne, 44629, Germany. TEL 49-2323-141700, FAX 49-2323-141123, service@kiehl.de. Circ: 4,234 (paid and controlled).

BUND UND BERUF. *see* MILITARY

371.42 330 USA
BUSINESS EDGE. Text in English. 1992. 2/yr.
Published by: Media Passage Holdings, Inc., 401 Second Ave W, Seattle, WA 98119. TEL 206-282-8111, FAX 206-282-1280. adv.: B&W page USD 12,120; trim 10.88 x 8.25. Circ: 250,000.

371.42 GBR ISSN 1473-1053
BUSINESS RATIO REPORT. EMPLOYMENT AGENCIES (YEAR). Text in English. 1980. a. GBP 365 per issue (effective 2010). charts; stat. back issues avail. **Document type:** *Report, Trade.*
Former titles (until 2001): Business Ratio. Employment Agencies (1469-7327); (until 2000): Business Ratio Plus: Employment Agencies (1357-8820); (until 1994): Business Ratio Report: Employment Agencies (0261-8052)
Published by: Key Note Ltd. (Subsidiary of: Bonnier Business Information), Harlequin House, 5th Fl, 7 High St, Teddington, Richmond upon Thames, TW11 8EE, United Kingdom. TEL 44-845-5040452, FAX 44-845-5040453, sales@keynote.co.uk.

371.42 CAN ISSN 1912-0206
C H R P NATIONAL KNOWLEDGE EXAM. STUDY GUIDE. (Canadian Human Resources Press) Text in English. 2004. a. **Document type:** *Handbook/Manual/Guide, Consumer.*
Published by: Canadian H R Press, 14845-6 Yonge St. Ste 165, Aurora, ON L4G 6H8, Canada. TEL 416-410-4593, 866-607-0876, info@canadianhrpress.ca, http://www.canadianhrpress.ca.

371.42 GBR
C R A C ANNUAL REPORT. Text in English. 19??. a. free (effective 2010). **Document type:** *Corporate.* **Description:** Features reports on the work and achievements of CRAC over the previous year, including industry-education link activities and teacher-development programs.
Related titles: Online - full text ed.: free (effective 2010).
Published by: (Careers Research and Advisory Centre), Hobsons PLC, IDT House, 44 Featherstone St, London, EC1Y 8RN, United Kingdom. Enquiries@hobsons.co.uk, http://www.hobsons.com. **Dist. by:** Biblios Publishers' Distribution Services Ltd.

331 USA ISSN 0892-6395
CALIFORNIA JOB JOURNAL. Text in English. w. free (effective 2004).
Indexed: A10, M02, V03.
Address: 2033 Howe Ave Ste 100, Sacramento, CA 95825. TEL 916-925-0800, 800-655-5627, FAX 916-925-0101.

CAMPUS EKONOMI. *see* EDUCATION—Higher Education

CAMPUS TEKNIK. *see* EDUCATION—Higher Education

371.42 CAN ISSN 1204-6191
HF5382.5.C2
CANADA STUDENT EMPLOYMENT GUIDE. Text in English. 1995. a. **Document type:** *Handbook/Manual/Guide, Trade.*
Formerly (until 1995): Ontario Student Employment Guide (1189-2668)
Published by: Student Employment Network, 117 Gerrard St., E., Suite 1002, Toronto, ON M5B 2L4, Canada. TEL 416-977-3782, FAX 416-971-5090, sen@studentjobs.com, http://www.studentjobs.com.

371.42 CAN ISSN 1719-2234
HF5382.5 .C2 S95
THE CANADIAN SUMMER JOB DIRECTORY. Text in English. 2004. a. (3rd ed.). CAD 19.95 per issue (effective 2007). **Document type:** *Directory, Consumer.*
Formerly (until 2006): Summer Jobs in Canada (1711-8999)
Published by: Sentor Media Inc., 285 Mutual St., Ste 2401, Toronto, ON M4Y 3C5, Canada. TEL 416-924-4832, FAX 416-924-6979, info@sentormedia.com, http://www.sentormedia.com.

331.1 USA ISSN 1049-1767
CAPITOL WEEKLY; the newspaper of record for California state government. Text in English. 1989. w.
Published by: Capitol Weekly Corp. http://www.capitolweekly.com/.

371.42 GBR ISSN 1747-6720
CARE APPOINTMENTS SCOTLAND. Variant title: Care Appointments. Text in English. 2005. m. GBP 30 (effective 2009). adv. back issues avail. **Document type:** *Magazine, Consumer.* **Description:** Provides the latest news, views and opportunities across the industry.
Related titles: Online - full text ed.: free (effective 2009).
—CCC.
Published by: Career Media Ltd, Regent Ct, 70 West Regent St, Glasgow, G2 2QZ, United Kingdom. TEL 44-141-3336665, FAX 44-141-3331116, enquiries@careermedia.co.uk, http://www.careermedia.co.uk. Ed. Laura McKellar. adv.: B&W page GBP 3,295, color page GBP 4,495; 180 x 254. **Subscr. to:** Nile St, Glasgow G1 2RN, United Kingdom. subscriptions@careappointments.co.uk.

370.113 USA ISSN 1930-5524
CAREER AND TECHNICAL EDUCATION ADVISOR. Text in English. 1984. m. looseleaf. USD 195 (effective 2008). charts; stat. s-a. index. **Document type:** *Newsletter, Trade.* **Description:** Provides current reports on the federal Job Training Partnership Act and the Carl D. Perkins Vocational Education Act. Includes coverage of adult literacy, dropout prevention, and state education and training initiatives.
Formerly (until 2006): Vocational Training News (1553-4065); Which was formed by the merger of (1970-1984): Manpower and Vocational Education Weekly (0047-5785); (1975-1984): Education and Work (0194-231X)
Indexed: A09, A10, A15, ABIn, B01, B06, B07, B09, E03, ERI, P04, P16, P21, P48, P51, P53, P54, PQC, V02, V03, V04.
—CCC.
Published by: L R P Publications, Inc., 747 Dresher Rd, Ste 500, PO Box 980, Horsham, PA 19044. TEL 215-784-0860, 800-341-7874, FAX 215-784-9639, custserve@lrp.com, http://www.lrp.com.

371.42 USA ISSN 2150-6299
▼ **CAREER & WORK LIFE MATTERS.** Text in English. 2009. bi-m. free (effective 2009). **Document type:** *Newsletter, Trade.*
Media: Online - full content.
Published by: Jennifer Bradley, Pub., PO Box 59272, Dallas, TX 75229. TEL 800-339-7701.

658.3 USA ISSN 1940-8935
THE CAREER CHAMPION. Text in English. 2008. bi-w. (Tue.). free (effective 2009). **Document type:** *Journal, Consumer.* **Description:** Offers proven strategies for leadership professionals targeting high-powered careers.
Media: Online - full content.
Published by: Laura Smith-Proulx, Pub., c/o An Expert Resume, 15400 West 64th Ave, Ste E9 164, Arvadac, CO 80007. TEL 877-258-3517, laura@thecareerchampion.com.

371.42 790.1 USA
CAREER CONNECTIONS (CHANDLER). Text in English. 1990. s-m. USD 149 (effective 2000). back issues avail. **Document type:** *Newsletter, Trade.* **Description:** Contains job listings in sports media, sports telemarketing, sales, health and fitness, facility management, sporting goods, event management, college athletics, sports law, professional sports, and leisure and recreation.
Published by: Franklin Covey Co., Sports Division, 1620 S. Stapley Dr., Ste. 224, Mesa, AZ 85204-6656. TEL 602-954-4882, FAX 602-943-4544. Ed., Pub. Duke Little. R&P Kim Janz. Circ: 1,800 (paid).

641.14 USA
CAREER CONNECTIONS (SOMESWORTH). Text in English. 1997. m. free. back issues avail. **Document type:** *Newsletter.* **Description:** Helps job-seekers market themselves more effectively in a changing and ever-increasing job market. Provides ongoing support, encouragement, and ideas to job-seekers worldwide.
Related titles: Online - full text ed.
Published by: Distinctive Documents, 146 Blackwater Rd, Somersworth, NH 03878. TEL 603-742-3983, FAX 603-743-6720. Ed. Michelle Dumas.

CAREER DEVELOPMENT FOR EXCEPTIONAL INDIVIDUALS. *see* EDUCATION—Special Education And Rehabilitation

371.42 GBR ISSN 1362-0436
HF5549.5.C35
➤ **CAREER DEVELOPMENT INTERNATIONAL.** Abbreviated title: C D I. Text in English. 1996. 7/yr. EUR 10,489 combined subscription in Europe (print & online eds.); USD 12,079 combined subscription in the Americas (print & online eds.); GBP 7,039 combined subscription in the UK & elsewhere (print & online eds.); AUD 15,429 combined subscription in Australasia (print & online eds.) (effective 2012). bk.rev. charts; illus. index. reprint service avail. from PSC. **Document type:** *Journal, Academic/Scholarly.* **Description:** Publishes scholarly research relating to career and development.
Formed by the merger of (1989-1996): International Journal of Career Management (0955-6214); Which incorporated (1992-1994): Recruitment Selection and Retention (0965-5980); (1988-1995): Executive Development (0953-3230)
Related titles: Online - full text ed.: ISSN 1758-6003 (from IngentaConnect).
Indexed: A12, A17, A22, ABIn, B01, B06, B07, B09, CA, CPE, CurCont, E01, E03, ERA, ERI, ERIC, ESPM, EmerIntel, Emerald, EnvEAb, M&MA, P03, P10, P18, P21, P48, P51, P53, P54, PQC, PsycInfo, S21, SCOPUS, SSCI, T&DA, T02, V05, W07.
—BLDSC (3051.705000), IE, Infotrieve, Ingenta. **CCC.**
Published by: Emerald Group Publishing Ltd., Howard House, Wagon Ln, Bingley, W Yorks BD16 1WA, United Kingdom. TEL 44-1274-777700, FAX 44-1274-785201, information@emeraldinsight.com. Eds. Hetty Van Emmerik, Jim M Jawahar. Pub. Nancy Rolph. **Subscr. addr. in N America:** Emerald Group Publishing Limited, One Mifflin Pl, Ste 400, Harvard Sq, Cambridge, MA 02138. TEL 617-576-5782, 888-309-7810, FAX 617-576-5883.

371.42 USA ISSN 0889-4019
➤ **THE CAREER DEVELOPMENT QUARTERLY.** Abbreviated title: C Q D. Text in English. 1952. q. GBP 141 in United Kingdom to institutions; EUR 163 in Europe to institutions; USD 200 elsewhere to institutions; GBP 163 combined subscription in United Kingdom to institutions (print & online eds.); EUR 188 combined subscription in Europe to institutions (print & online eds.); USD 230 combined subscription elsewhere to institutions (print & online eds.) (effective 2012). adv. bibl.; charts; abstr.; illus. Index. 96 p./no.; back issues avail. **Document type:** *Journal, Academic/Scholarly.* **Description:** Provides foster career development through the design and use of career interventions and to publish articles on career counseling, individual and organizational career development, work and leisure, career education, career coaching, and career management.
Formerly (until 1986): Vocational Guidance Quarterly (0042-7764)
Related titles: Microform ed.: 1952 (from PQC); Online - full text ed.: ISSN 2161-0045. 1952. GBP 141 in United Kingdom to institutions; EUR 163 in Europe to institutions; USD 200 elsewhere to institutions (effective 2012).
Indexed: A01, A02, A03, A08, A09, A10, A12, A20, A22, A26, ABIn, ABS&EES, ASCA, B01, B02, B04, B06, B07, B08, B09, B15, B17, B18, BPIA, BRD, CA, CPE, CurCont, E-psyche, E02, E03, E06, E07, E08, E09, ERI, ERIC, EdA, EdI, Faml, G04, G06, G07, G08, H01, HEA, HECAB, I05, I07, ILD, L09, M01, M02, P02, P03, P04, P06, P07, P10, P13, P18, P21, P25, P30, P48, P51, P53, P54, P55, PQC, PsycInfo, PsycholAb, S02, S03, S09, S23, SCOPUS, SSCI, SWR&A, T&DA, T02, V02, V03, V04, W03, W05, W07, YAE&RB.
—BLDSC (3051.706000), IE, Infotrieve, Ingenta.
Published by: (National Career Development Association), American Counseling Association, 5999 Stevenson Ave, Alexandria, VA 22304. TEL 800-347-6647, FAX 703-823-0252, 800-473-2329. Ed. Jerry Trusty TEL 814-863-7536. Adv. contact Kathy Maguire TEL 703-823-9800 ext 207.

371.42 USA ISSN 1056-5558
CAREER DIRECTIONS. Text in English. 1989. q. adv. **Description:** Publishes articles directed to college juniors, seniors and graduate students.
Related titles: Regional ed(s).: Career Directions (Great Lake Edition).
Published by: Directions Publishing, Inc., 21 N Henry St, Edgerton, WI 53534. TEL 608-884-3367. Circ: 112,000.

371.42 629.286 GBR ISSN 1749-3277
CAREER DRIVEN. Text in English. 2004. s-a. adv. back issues avail. **Document type:** *Magazine, Consumer.* **Description:** Dedicated to illustrating the many diverse career opportunities open to young people within the automotive industry. Contains editorial on a range of careers available as well as interesting lifestyle pieces on the Industry itself.
Related titles: Online - full content ed.
Published by: (Institute of the Motor Industry), Independent Educational Publishing Ltd., Independent House, 191 Marsh Wall, London, E14 9RS, United Kingdom. TEL 44-20-70052000, FAX 44-20-70052292, http://www.independent.co.uk/student/. Ed. Dan Poole. Adv. contact Richard Morshead TEL 44-20-70052174.

658.3 AUS ISSN 1838-8523
CAREER EDGE; for young professionals. Text in English. 2008. a. free to members (effective 2011). adv. back issues avail. **Document type:** *Magazine, Trade.* **Description:** Provides practical information, representation, support and advice on employment and career advancement to APESMA members.
Published by: Association of Professional Engineers, Scientists and Managers, GPO Box 1272, Melbourne, VIC 8060, Australia. TEL 61-3-96958800, FAX 61-3-96958902, info@apesma.asn.au.

331.1 NLD ISSN 1574-3527
CAREER&CO. Text in Dutch. 2005. bi-m. EUR 20 (effective 2009). adv. **Document type:** *Magazine, Consumer.*
Published by: Uitgeverij VWBmedia, Zandstr 5, Voorst, 7383 AH, Netherlands. TEL 31-575-503245, FAX 31-575-503285, media@vwb.nl, http://www.vwb.nl. adv.: color page EUR 2,350; trim 190 x 260. Circ: 30,000.

658.3 USA ISSN 1946-1135
CAREER EXPERTS. Text in English. 2008. bi-w. free (effective 2009). **Document type:** *Journal, Trade.* **Description:** Features inspiring articles from experts essential for a better career.
Media: Online - full content.
Published by: Maria Hebda, Pub., 4580 Dolores Dr, Trenton, MI 48183. TEL 734-676-9170, mhebda@careerexpertsonline.com, http://www.certifiedcareercoaches.com/careerexpertsonline.htm.

CAREER EXPOSURE'S WHAT'S NEWS E-ZINE. *see* BUSINESS AND ECONOMICS—Labor And Industrial Relations

371.42 USA ISSN 1049-9946
CAREER FOCUS. Text in English. 1988. bi-m. USD 29.95 for 2 yrs.; USD 3 per issue (effective 2009). bk.rev. illus.; tr.lit. back issues avail.; reprints avail. **Document type:** *Magazine, Consumer.* **Description:** Aims to inform and motivate Black and Hispanic young adults, ages 21-45, on preparing, developing and advancing their careers.
Related titles: Online - full text ed.: free (effective 2009).
Published by: (National Eagle Leadership Institute), C P G Publications, 660 Penn Tower, 3100 Broadway St. Ste 660, Kansas City, MO 64111-2413. info@cpgpublications.com, http://www.cpgpublications.com/. Ed., Pub. Georgia L Clark.

371.42 CAN ISSN 1718-2964
CAREER INSIDER FINANCE. Text in English. 2005. a. CAD 3.95 (effective 2006). **Document type:** *Magazine, Consumer.*
Related titles: Online - full text ed.: ISSN 1718-2972.
Published by: Career Insider Magazines, 727 Dufferin St., Toronto, ON M6K 2B6, Canada. http://www.careerinsider.ca. Ed. Richard Terry.

371.42 USA
CAREER MAGAZINE. Text in English. 1994. w. (plus d. updates). **Description:** Contains job listings, resumes, articles, employer profiles, and relocation resources.
Media: Online - full text.

Address: C/O Beyond.com, Inc., 1060 First Ave Ste 100, King of Prussia, PA 19406. TEL 610-878-2800. Ed. Gary Resnikoff.

371.42 USA
CAREER OPPORTUNITIES FOR MINORITY COLLEGE GRADUATES. Text in English. 1991. a. USD 11.95. adv. **Document type:** *Directory.* **Description:** Guide for minorities seeking employment from major US employers. Lists employment opportunities in accounting, advertising, banking and finance, communications, computer sciences, consulting, continuing education, government agencies, engineering, health care, nursing, retail and teaching.
Published by: Paoli Publishing, Inc., 1708 E Lancaster Ave, Ste 287, Paoli, PA 19301. TEL 215-640-9889. Ed. J W Wrigley. Pub. J.W. Wrigley. Adv. contact Pat Wrigley.

371.42 USA ISSN 0739-5043
HF5381.A1
CAREER OPPORTUNITIES NEWS. Short title: C News. Text in English. 1983. bi-m. bk.rev. charts. Index. 16 p./no.; reprints avail. **Document type:** *Newsletter, Trade.* **Description:** Provides news about colleges & the job market. Perfect for high school students, guidance counselors and career professionals.
Published by: Ferguson Publishing Co. (Subsidiary of: Facts on File, Inc.), 132 W 31st St, 17th Fl, New York, NY 10001. TEL 800-322-8755, FAX 800-678-3633, CustServ@factsonfile.com, http://www.fergpubco.com/.

331.1 CAN ISSN 0835-3913
CAREER OPTIONS. Text in English. 1970. a. USD 3.95 per issue. adv. **Description:** Includes trends and market conditions, issues in the workplace, tips on the job search process, writing resumes and filling out applications, a list of employers who recruit on campus and the educational background required of recruits.
Related titles: French ed.
Published by: A C C I S, 1209 King St W, Ste 205, Toronto, ON M6K 1G2, Canada. TEL 416-535-8126, FAX 416-532-0934. Circ: 145,000.

331.1 USA
CAREER PILOT JOB REPORT (ONLINE). Text in English. m. USD 50 (effective 2005). **Document type:** *Newsletter, Trade.*
Formerly: Career Pilot Job Report (Print) (0891-0855)
Media: Online - full content.
Published by: Berliner Aviation Group, 102 S. 6th St., Geneva, IL 60134. TEL 630-865-4668.

CAREER PLANNING AND ADULT DEVELOPMENT JOURNAL. *see* EDUCATION—Adult Education

CAREER PLANNING AND ADULT DEVELOPMENT NETWORK NEWSLETTER; the network is a non-profit association of professionals who work with adults in career transition. *see* EDUCATION—Adult Education

331.70205 GBR ISSN 1472-6564
CAREER RESEARCH & DEVELOPMENT; making practice thoughtful and theory practical. Variant title: The N I C E C Journal. Text in English. 199?. 3/yr. GBP 34 domestic; GBP 50 foreign (effective 2009). **Document type:** *Journal, Academic/Scholarly.* **Description:** Aimed at those working in all sectors of education and in work and community settings.
Formerly (until 2000): N I C E C Bulletin (1355-767X)
—BLDSC (3051.766000).
Published by: National Institute for Careers Education and Counselling, Sheraton House, Castle Park, Cambridge, CB3 0AX, United Kingdom. TEL 44-1223-460277, FAX 44-1223-311708, http://www.crac.org.uk/crac_new/Research_&_Publications/Index.asp.

371.42 GBR ISSN 1465-475X
THE CAREER STEPS GUIDE; your guide to private and public sector careers. Text in English. 1999. a. GBP 110 combined subscription per issue (print & CD-ROM eds.); GBP 60 per issue (effective 2009). adv. **Document type:** *Directory, Trade.* **Description:** Provides a valuable reference source for all seeking a career or further education: school leavers; college students; graduates; post-graduates; mature students and others looking for employment; training or gap year positions.
Formed by the merger of (1997-1999): First Steps Guide (1369-9695); (1997-1999): Next Steps Guide (1460-0269)
Related titles: CD-ROM ed.: GBP 70 per issue (effective 2009).
—CCC.
Published by: Carlton Publishing & Printing Ltd., Maple House, Maple View, Steeds Ln, Kingsnorth, TN26 1NQ, United Kingdom. TEL 44-1923-800801, FAX 44-1923-800802, info@carlton-group.co.uk.

331.128 USA
CAREER WIRE. Text in English. 1999. bi-m. free. adv. **Document type:** *Newsletter.* **Description:** Covers career advice, placement and tips on how to get and keep a job.
Media: Online - full text.
Published by: College Central Network, Inc., 141 W 28th St 9th Fl, New York, NY 10001. TEL 212-714-1731, FAX 212-714-1688. Ed. Jim Brown.

371.42 USA ISSN 0744-1002
HF5381.A1
CAREER WORLD. Text in English. 1981. 3/yr. USD 17.25 per academic year; USD 5.13 per academic year (per student for 10 or more subscr.) (effective 2008 - 2009). bk.rev. illus. Index. back issues avail.; reprints avail. **Document type:** *Magazine, Academic/Scholarly.* **Description:** Contains informational articles, essays, and photographs on job markets, job search techniques, and prospective business trends pertaining to college, career and vocational choices for high school students. Includes a teachers guide.
Formed by the merger of (1977-1981): Career World 1 (0198-7615); (1977-1981): Career World 2 (0198-7623); Which was formerly (1972-1977): Career World (0361-8994); Incorporates: Real World
Related titles: Online - full text ed.
Indexed: A01, A02, A03, A08, A11, A22, A25, A26, ARG, B04, BRD, C05, C12, CPerl, E03, E07, E08, ERI, G05, G06, G07, G08, I05, I06, I07, I09, ICM, M01, M02, M04, MASUSE, P02, P04, P10, P16, P48, P53, P54, PQC, R03, R06, RGAb, RGPR, RGYP, S08, S09, S11, S23, T02, V02, W03, W05.
—Ingenta.
Published by: Weekly Reader Corporation (Subsidiary of: W R C Media Inc.), 3001 Cindel Dr, PO Box 8037, Delran, NJ 08075. TEL 800-446-3355, FAX 856-786-3360, customerservice@weeklyreader.com. Eds. Charles Piddock, Carole Rubenstein. Pub. Peter Esposito. R&P Cathy Pekai TEL 203-705-3426. Adv. contact Jeannie DeLeonardo. Circ: 120,000 (paid).

378.0025 USA
CAREERS & COLLEGES (ONLINE). Text in English. 2007. q. free to qualified personnel (effective 2009). back issues avail. **Document type:** *Magazine, Consumer.* **Description:** Covers college and career preparation for teens, including higher education, career awareness, financial aid, getting a job, and personal development.
Media: Online - full text.
Published by: Alloy Education, 2 LAN Dr, Ste 100, Westford, MA 01886. TEL 978-692-5092, FAX 978-692-4174, information@alloyeducation.com, http://www.alloyeducation.com/.

CAREERS AND THE DISABLED. *see* HANDICAPPED

371.42 GBR ISSN 0969-6431
CAREERS GUIDANCE TODAY. Text in English. 19??. q. free to members (effective 2009). adv. bk.rev. **Document type:** *Journal, Trade.* **Description:** Covers news, labour market information, professional practice, research and articles from ICG members.
Former titles (until 1992): Careers Officer (0958-7489); (until 1989): Careers Journal (0260-5694); (until 1980): Careers Quarterly
Indexed: HECAB.
—BLDSC (3051.781950), IE, Ingenta.
Published by: I C G, Ground Fl, Copthall House, 1 New Rd, Stourbridge, DY8 1PH, United Kingdom. TEL 44-1384-376464. Adv. contact Kathryn Keay TEL 44-1384-445627.

331.1 AUS ISSN 1832-0635
CAREERS IN ASIA. Text in English. 2000. a. **Document type:** *Journal, Consumer.*
Published by: Hobsons Australia, Level 12, OCBC House, 565 Bourke St, Melbourne, VIC 3000, Australia. TEL 61-3-96274845, info@hobsons.com.au, http://www.gradcareers.com.au/.

371.42 580 USA
CAREERS IN BOTANY. Text in English. 1965. irreg. **Document type:** *Guide, Consumer.*
Former titles: Botany as a Profession (0068-0397); Botanical Society of America. Miscellaneous Publications
Related titles: Online - full text ed.
Indexed: SpeleolAb.
Published by: Botanical Society of America, Inc., PO Box 299, St. Louis, MO 63166-0299. TEL 314-577-9566, FAX 314-577-9515.

641.2 371.42 664 GBR
CAREERS IN FOOD & DRINK INDUSTRY. Text in English. 19??. a. adv. **Document type:** *Directory, Trade.* **Description:** A guide for graduates looking for jobs within the food and drink industry. Offers an industry overview from leading sources including case studies and advice on graduate opportunities.
Related titles: Online - full text ed.
Published by: William Reed Directories (Subsidiary of: William Reed Business Media Ltd.), Broadfield Park, Crawley, W Sussex RH11 9RT, United Kingdom. TEL 44-1293-610488, FAX 44-1293-610322, directories@william-reed.co.uk, http://www.william-reed.co.uk.

331.7 AUS
CAREERS INFORMATION LEAFLET SERIES. Text in English. irreg. **Description:** Provides information on different careers in various fields and industries.
Published by: Graduate Careers Australia Ltd., A'Beckett St, PO Box 12103, Melbourne, VIC 8006, Australia. TEL 61-3-96053700, FAX 61-3-96705752, info@graduatecareers.com.au, http://www.graduatecareers.com.au.

331.1291378 GBR
CAREERSCOPE (ONLINE). Text in English. 19??. 3/yr. free (effective 2010). back issues avail. **Document type:** *Magazine, Consumer.* **Description:** Deals with careers of all kinds and developments in higher education.
Media: Online - full text.
Published by: The Inspiring Futures Foundation, St. George's House, Knoll Rd, Camberley, Surrey GU15 3SY, United Kingdom. TEL 44-1276-687500, FAX 44-1276-28258, http://www.inspiringfutures.org.uk.

331.12 USA
CAREERSOURCE. Text in English. m. USD 20 domestic (effective 2001); Free throughout San Francisco Bay area. adv. **Document type:** *Magazine, Consumer.* **Description:** Contains career related editorial and recruitment advertising from employers and career training services in the greater San Francisco Bay area.
Related titles: Online - full text ed.
Published by: CareerSource Magazine, 221 F Mt Hermon Rd, Scotts Valley, CA 95066. TEL 408-295-1438, FAX 408-295-8026, http://www.careersource-magazine.com/.

371.42 CHE
CAREERSTEP; das Karrieremagazin fuer High Potentials. Text in German. q. free. adv. **Document type:** *Magazine, Consumer.* **Description:** Contains articles and advice on career and occupation opportunities and choices for young people.
Published by: Mediax AG, Schneebergstr 7, Sankt Gallen, 9000, Switzerland. TEL 41-71-2264040, FAX 41-71-2264045, info@mediaxag.ch, http://www.mediaxag.ch. adv.: page CHF 4,500; trim 235 x 310. Circ: 15,000 (controlled).

371.42 USA ISSN 1074-3642
THE CARETAKER GAZETTE; number 1 source for caretaker jobs!. Text in English. 1983. bi-m. looseleaf. USD 29.95 domestic; USD 35.95 foreign (effective 2007). adv. bk.rev.; Website rev. illus.; stat. 16 p./no.; back issues avail. **Document type:** *Newsletter, Consumer.* **Description:** Provides information on property caretaker positions available in the US and abroad, includes caretaker classified ads, reader correspondence and profiles of successful property caretakers. Provides free ads for landowners seeking to hire caretakers.
Related titles: Online - full text ed.
Published by: Caretaker Publishing, Inc, PO Box 4005, Bergheim, TX 78004-4005. TEL 830-336-3939, FAX 636-246-9267. Ed. Thea K Dunn. Pub., R&P, Adv. contact Gary C Dunn TEL 830-336-3939. Circ: 12,000 (paid).

331.1 CAN ISSN 1911-2823
LA CARRIERE A 50 ANS ET PLUS. Variant title: Carriere a Cinquante Ans et Plus. Text in French. 2007. biennial. **Document type:** *Journal, Consumer.*
Published by: Editions Jobboom, 300 Av. Viger Est, 3eme Etage, Montreal, PQ H2X 3W4, Canada. TEL 514-871-0222, 877-796-8266, http://www.jobboom.com.

331.1 658.0029 340 NLD ISSN 2211-0011
HET CARRIERE JAARBOEK. ECONOMISCHE EN JURIDISCHE EDITIE; de top van advocatenkantoren en andere juridische werkgevers. Text in Dutch. 1999. a. **Document type:** *Directory.*
Published by: Memory Publications, Keizersgracht 424, Amsterdam, 1016 GC, Netherlands. TEL 31-20-6382146, FAX 31-20-6386380, info@memory.nl, http://www.memory.nl. Ed. Sandra Veltmaat-Herklots. Circ: 125,000.

331.1 371.4 CAN ISSN 1702-3300
CARRIERES D'AVENIR. Text in French. 1999. a. **Document type:** *Journal, Consumer.*
Former titles (until 200?): Carrieres d'Avenir au Quebec (1488-9552); (until 2000): Guide Pratique des Carrieres d'Avenir au Quebec (1493-2032)
Published by: Editions Jobboom, 300 Av. Viger Est, 3eme Etage, Montreal, PQ H2X 3W4, Canada. TEL 514-871-0222, 877-796-8266, http://www.jobboom.com.

331.1 794.8 CAN ISSN 1911-2831
LES CARRIERES DU JEU ELECTRONIQUE. Text in French. 2006. biennial. CAD 12.95 newsstand/cover (effective 2007). **Document type:** *Journal, Consumer.*
Published by: Editions Jobboom, 300 Av. Viger Est, 3eme Etage, Montreal, PQ H2X 3W4, Canada. TEL 514-871-0222, 877-796-8266, http://www.jobboom.com.

N O

371.42 GBR
CAS LONDON. Text in English. 2005 (Apr.). bi-m. GBP 18 (effective 2009). adv. **Document type:** *Magazine, Trade.* **Description:** Covers global talent industry for various media outlets such as film, television, art, theatre, and music.
Published by: Afro Universe Media, 25B Admiral St., London, SE8 4HY, United Kingdom. TEL 44-20-86946680, FAX 44-20-86922454.

331.1 690 NLD ISSN 1875-4899
CASCO. Text in Dutch. 1977. 8/yr. EUR 20; free to qualified personnel (effective 2010). adv. **Document type:** *Magazine, Trade.*
Supersedes in part (in 2008): F N V Bouw Magazine (1570-1395); Which was formerly (until 2002): F N V Magazine. F N V Bouw (1567-682X); (until 2000): F N V Magazine. Bouw- en Houtbond F N V (0924-204X); (until 1988): F N V Magazine. Profiel (0169-5045); (until 1985): Profiel (Woerden) (0166-7548); Which was formed by the merger of (1972-1976): Steiger (Woerden) (0926-6739); Which was formed by the merger of (1921-1972): Op de Steiger (0926-6747); (1911-1972): Bondsblad (Utrecht) (0926-6755); (1920-1976): Bouwer (Amsterdam) (0926-6720); Which was formed by the merger of (1890-1920): Timmerman (Amsterdam) (0926-6704); (1908-1920): Bouwvakarbeider (Amsterdam) (0926-6712)
Published by: (F N V Bouw en Infra), F N V Bouw, Postbus 520, Woerden, 3440 AM, Netherlands. TEL 31-348-575575, FAX 31-348-423610, info@fnvbouw.nl. Ed. Peter van der Aa. adv.: color page EUR 2,550; trim 230 x 300. Circ: 100,000.

CASS RECRUITMENT MEDIA. *see* BUSINESS AND ECONOMICS—Personnel Management

CATHOLIC TEACHERS GAZETTE. *see* EDUCATION

CHAMBER JOBWATCH. *see* BUSINESS AND ECONOMICS—Chamber Of Commerce Publications

331.702 CAN
CHANGING TIMES; the labour market information webzine for the career practitioner. Text in English. 1997. w. **Description:** Developed by and for practitioners and providers in the educational, career and employment services.
Media: Online - full text.
Published by: Labour Market and Career Information Association of British Columbia, Ste 600 Kingsway, Burnaby, BC 5H 4C2, Canada. TEL 604-435-5548, FAX 604-435-5548, changing@lmcia.bc.ca. Ed. JudyLynn Archer TEL 780-462-1451.

371.42 305.4 CAN ISSN 1715-9393
CHAPEAU LES FILLES! CONCOURS. Text in French. 1999. a. **Document type:** *Journal, Consumer.*
Related titles: Online - full text ed.: ISSN 1715-9407.
Published by: Quebec, Ministere de l'Education, du Loisir et du Sport, 1035, rue De La Chevrotiere, Quebec, PQ G1R 5A5, Canada. http://www.mels.gouv.qc.ca.

CHEERS; Kuaile Gongzuoren Zazhi. *see* BUSINESS AND ECONOMICS—Labor And Industrial Relations

371.42 USA ISSN 1042-7848
UB357
CIVILIAN CAREER GUIDE. Text in English. 1987. a. USD 14.95 (effective 1993). adv. back issues avail. **Document type:** *Directory.* **Description:** For former military personnel entering the civilian job market. Offers economic analyses of the industries most likely to hire former military personnel.
Published by: Grant's Guides, Inc., PO Box 613, Lake Placid, NY 12946. TEL 800-922-1923, FAX 518-523-2974. Ed. James Grant. Circ: 10,000.

331.1 USA
CIVILIAN JOB NEWS. Text in English. 2006. bi-m. dist. free at military bases. adv. **Document type:** *Newspaper, Consumer.* **Description:** Features practical information for the military person transitioning from the military and seeking a civilian job.
Related titles: Online - full content ed.
Published by: Bradley-Morris, Inc.,, 1825 Barrett Lakes Blvd., Ste. 300, Kennesaw, GA 30144. TEL 866-801-4418, FAX 678-819-5161. Pub. George Bernloehr. adv.: B&W page USD 1,400; trim 15.25 x 11.5. Circ: 45,000 (free).

CIVVY STREET. *see* MILITARY

371.42 CAN ISSN 1708-9026
THE COACHING NEWS. Text in English. 2002. q. free (effective 2010). adv. back issues avail. **Document type:** *Newsletter, Trade.* **Description:** Provides information about emerging trends, critical issues, and essential resources to persons involved in or considering coaching as a career.
Related titles: Online - full text ed.
Published by: Peer Systems Consulting Group, 1052 Davie St, Victoria, BC V8S 4E3, Canada. TEL 250-595-3503, 800-567-3700, info@peer.ca.

331.1 AUS ISSN 1833-6949
COFFEE WORKING PAPERS. (Centre of Full Employment and Equity) Text in English. 1997. irreg. free (effective 2009). back issues avail.
Document type: *Monographic series, Academic/Scholarly.*
Description: Provides papers that constitute the basis of our research effort.
Media: Online - full text.
Published by: University of Newcastle, Centre of Full Employment and Equity, The University of Newcastle, Callaghan, NSW 2308, Australia. TEL 61-2-49217283, FAX 61-2-49218731, http://www.newcastle.edu.au/index.html.

371.42 ESP ISSN 1885-7493
COL - LECIO FORMACIO. Text in Spanish, Catalan. 2006. irreg.
Document type: *Monographic series, Trade.*
Published by: Fundacio Rafael Campalans, Trafalgar, 12 entresol 1a, Barcelona, 08010, Spain. TEL 34-93-3195412, FAX 34-93-3199844, fundacio@fcampalans.cat.

658.3 CAN ISSN 1920-7301
▼ **COLLAR TO COLLAR.** Text in English. 2010. s-a. CAD 7.50 newsstand/cover (effective 2010). **Document type:** *Magazine, Trade.*
Published by: Outridge Enterprises Inc., 47 Salt Dr, Ajax, ON L1S 7P5, Canada. TEL 289-314-1018, consulting@outridge.ca, http://www.outridgeenterprises.ca/.

331.281 FRA ISSN 1775-9331
COLLECTIVITES TERRITORIALES. GUIDE DE LA REMUNERATION; fonctionnaire, non-titulaires, emplois aides, elus locaux, personnels participants a l'action de l'administration. Text in French. 2002. irreg.
Document type: *Bulletin, Trade.*
Published by: Editions Weka, 249 Rue de Crimee, Paris, 75935 Cedex 19, France.

371.42 USA
COLLEGE OUTLOOK (FALL EDITION). Text in English. 1977. a. adv. bk.rev. illus. **Document type:** *Magazine, Academic/Scholarly.*
Description: Provides high school counselors and college bound students with information about higher educational opportunities.
Related titles: Online - full text ed.: free (effective 2009); Alternate Frequency ed(s).: College Outlook (Spring Edition). a.
Published by: Townsend Outlook Publishing Co., Inc., 20 E Gregory Blvd, Kansas City, MO 64114. TEL 816-361-0616, 800-274-8867, FAX 816-361-6164, production@collegeoutlook.net. Ed. Kellie Houx. Pub. H Guyon Townsend III.

331 351 CAN ISSN 1912-0729
COMMISSION DE LA FONCTION PUBLIQUE DU CANADA. RAPPORT ANNUEL. POINTS SAILLANTS. Text in French. 200?. a. **Document type:** *Report, Trade.*
Media: Online - full text.
Published by: Public Service Commission of Canada/Commission de la Fonction Publique du Canada, 300 Laurier Ave W, Ottawa, ON K1A OM7, Canada. TEL 613-992-9562, FAX 613-992-9352, info-com@psc-cfp.gc.ca.

344.106664 GBR ISSN 0964-8445
COMPANY SECRETARY. Text in English. 1991. m. free to members (effective 2010). back issues avail. **Document type:** *Magazine, Trade.*
Related titles: Online - full text ed.: ISSN 2042-986X.
—CCC.
Published by: Institute of Chartered Secretaries and Administrators, 16 Park Crescent, London, W1B 1AH, United Kingdom. TEL 44-20-75804741, FAX 44-20-73231132, info@icsa.co.uk, http://www.icsa.org.uk/. Ed. Andrew Hamer.

371.42 USA ISSN 1930-2010
HF5549.A2
THE COMPLETE DO-IT-YOURSELF HUMAN RESOURCES DEPARTMENT. Text in English. 19??. irreg. USD 159 per issue (effective 2010). **Document type:** *Handbook/Manual/Guide, Trade.*
Formerly (until 2001): Complete Do-it-Yourself Personnel Department
Published by: Aspen Publishers, Inc. (Subsidiary of: Wolters Kluwer N.V.), 111 Eighth Ave., 7th Fl, New York, NY 10011. TEL 212-771-0600, FAX 212-771-0885, ASPEN-CustomerService@wolterskluwer.com, https://www.aspenpublishers.com. Ed. Mary F Cook.

331.1 ESP ISSN 2171-4746
▼ **COMUNIDAD VALENCIANA. ENCUESTA SEMESTRAL SOBRE EL MERCADO DE TRABAJO.** Text in Spanish. 2009. s-a. **Document type:** *Bulletin, Consumer.*
Published by: Fundacion Servicio Valenciano de Empleo, San Vicente, 16 5o. 1a., Valencia, 46002, Spain. TEL 34-902-200302, clientes@sve.es, http://www.sve.es/.

331 FRA ISSN 1767-3356
HD4807
CONNAISSANCE DE L'EMPLOI. Text in French. 1994. m. free,
Document type: *Bulletin.*
Formerly (until 2004): France. Centre d'Etudes de l'Emploi. Quatre pages (1251-8107)
Related titles: Online - full text ed.: ISSN 1776-2715.
Indexed: IBSS.
Published by: Centre d'Etudes de l'Emploi, Le Descartes I, 29 promenade Michel Simon, Noisy-le-Grand, Cedex 93166, France. TEL 33-1-45926800, FAX 33-1-49310244, cee@mail.enpc.fr.

CONSULTING OPPORTUNITIES JOURNAL. *see* BUSINESS AND ECONOMICS—Management

331.1 330 USA
CONSULTING RATES AND BUSINESS PRACTICES. ANNUAL SURVEY. Text in English. 1979. biennial. USD 25. **Document type:** *Directory, Trade.*
Published by: Professional and Technical Consultants Association, 849 B Independence Ave, Mountain View, CA 94043. TEL 650-903-8305, FAX 650-967-0995. R&P Catherine Tornbom. Adv. contact Jeff Shelton. Circ: 2,000.

CONTACT POINT BULLETIN. *see* SOCIAL SERVICES AND WELFARE

CONTACT TORONTO. *see* BUSINESS AND ECONOMICS

371.42 CAN ISSN 1924-6544
CONTINUING STUDIES GUIDE. Text in English. 200?. s-a. **Document type:** *Magazine, Trade.* **Description:** Helps to increase self-confidence, self-esteem and personal motivation, income potential, new operational and management techniques and then apply these techniques to the real world.
Former titles (until 2009): The Centre of Continuing Studies (1915-2566); (until 2008): Continuing Education (1719-5098)
Related titles: Online - full text ed.: free (effective 2011).
Published by: Assiniboine Community College, Centre of Continuing Studies, 1430 Victoria Ave E, Brandon, MB R7A 2A9, Canada. TEL 204-725-8725, 800-862-6307, FAX 204-725-8740, info@assiniboine.net.

CONTRACT EMPLOYMENT WEEKLY. *see* BUSINESS AND ECONOMICS—Trade And Industrial Directories

COUNSELING TODAY. *see* PSYCHOLOGY

331.1 FRA ISSN 0220-6994
COURRIER CADRES; le magazine de l'emploi des cadres. Text in French. w. **Document type:** *Magazine, Trade.* **Description:** Offers vocational guidance and training and presents a clear picture of job availability in France.
Published by: Association pour l'Emploi des Cadres (A P E C), B.P. 91, Paris, Cedex 14 75662, France. TEL 33-1-40522000. Ed. Dominique Cornet. Pub. Jean Claude Merlin.

▼ **CREATE YOUR FASHION CAREER.** *see* CLOTHING TRADE—Fashions

371.42 USA
HF5382.5.U5
D & B EMPLOYMENT OPPORTUNITIES DIRECTORY - CAREER GUIDE. Text in English. 1984. a. **Document type:** *Directory, Trade.*
Description: Describes career opportunities and hiring practices of 5,000 companies actively seeking resumes.
Former titles (until 19??): The Career Guide (0891-0596); (until 1985): Dun's Employment Opportunities Directory (0740-7289)
Published by: Dun & Bradstreet (Subsidiary of: Dun & Bradstreet Corporation), 103 JFK Pky, Short Hills, NJ 07078. TEL 973-921-5500, 800-234-3867, custserv@dnb.com, http://www.dnb.com.

371.42 CHN ISSN 1674-9154
▼ **DANGDAI ZHIYE JIAOYU/CONTEMPORARY VACATIONAL EDUCATION.** Text in Chinese. 2009. m. **Document type:** *Journal, Academic/Scholarly.*
Published by: Sichuan Guangbo Dianshi Daxue/Sichuan Radio and T V University, 3, Yihuan Lu Xi 3-duan, Chengdu, 610073, China. TEL 86-28-87769491, FAX 86-28-87769920.

DATA WAREHOUSING CAREER NEWSLETTER. *see* BUSINESS AND ECONOMICS—Management

371.42 DEU ISSN 0936-000X
DEUTSCHE HANDWERKSORDNUNG; Kommentar, Mustersatzungen und Materialien. Text in German. 1967. base vol. plus updates 2/yr. looseleaf. EUR 86 base vol(s).; EUR 42 updates per issue (effective 2009). **Document type:** *Monographic series, Trade.*
Published by: Erich Schmidt Verlag GmbH & Co. (Berlin), Genthiner Str 30 G, Berlin, 10785, Germany. TEL 49-30-2500850, FAX 49-30-250085305, vertrieb@esvmedien.de, http://www.erich-schmidt-verlag.de.

371.42 DEU ISSN 0938-3301
DAS DEUTSCHE SCHORNSTEINFEGERWESEN. Text in German. 1969. base vol. plus a. updates. looseleaf. EUR 49.80 base vol(s).; EUR 33.95 updates per issue (effective 2009). **Document type:** *Monographic series, Trade.*
Published by: Erich Schmidt Verlag GmbH & Co. (Berlin), Genthiner Str 30 G, Berlin, 10785, Germany. TEL 49-30-2500850, FAX 49-30-250085305, vertrieb@esvmedien.de, http://www.erich-schmidt-verlag.de.

371.42 FRA ISSN 1951-7459
DEVELOPPEMENT PROFESSIONNEL. Text in French. 2006. irreg. back issues avail. **Document type:** *Monographic series, Consumer.*
Published by: Editions Flammarion, 87 Quai Panhard et Levassor, Paris, 75647 Cedex 13, France. TEL 33-1-40513100, http://www.flammarion.com.

371.42 USA
DIRECT AIM; for today's career strategies. Text in English. 1994. q. USD 9.95; USD 3 per issue (effective 2009). adv. back issues avail.; reprints avail. **Document type:** *Magazine, Consumer.* **Description:** Assists vocational-technical graduates in their search for career opportunities.
Formed by the merger of (1985-1994): Aim (Black Sudents Edition) (1050-7191); (1985-1994): Aim (Hispanic Students Edition) (1050-7183)
Related titles: Online - full text ed.: free (effective 2009).
Published by: C P G Publications, 7300 W 110th St, 7th Fl, Overland Park, KS 66210. TEL 913-317-2888, FAX 913-317-1505, info@cpgpublications.com, http://www.cpgpublications.com/. Ed. Georgia L Clark. Pub. Georgia Lee Clark.

DIRECTORY OF OSTEOPATHIC POSTDOCTORAL EDUCATION. *see* MEDICAL SCIENCES—Chiropractic, Homeopathy, Osteopathy

371.42 USA ISSN 1941-7675
DISCOVER THE EDGE. Text in English. 2008. w. free (effective 2009). back issues avail. **Document type:** *Newsletter, Consumer.*
Description: Provides leadership skills, advice, and training articles.
Media: Online - full content.
Published by: Karen J. Keller, Ed. & Pub. info@TheExecutiveCoach.com. Ed. Karen J Keller.

371.42 USA
DIVERSITY: ALLIED HEALTH CAREERS. Text in English. 2002 (Summer). q. free to qualified personnel. adv. **Document type:** *Magazine, Trade.* **Description:** Focuses on the career and educational issues affecting allied health professionals, including career and salary outlook, job search advice, graduate school information, news & stats, cross cultural care issues, allied health professional organizations, networking and more.
Published by: Career Recruitment Media, Inc., 211 W Wacker Dr, Ste 900, Chicago, IL 60606. TEL 312-525-3099, FAX 312-429-3312, info@careermedia.com. Ed. Vicki Chung. Pub. Tim Clancy. Adv. contact Peter Fuhrman TEL 609-689-1033.

371.42 USA
DIVERSITY/CAREERS IN ENGINEERING & INFORMATION TECHNOLOGY. Text in English. 1994. bi-m. Free to qualified subscribers. adv. back issues avail. **Document type:** *Magazine, Trade.* **Description:** Covers technical and career issues of interest to engineers and information technology professionals who are women, members of minority groups or people with disabilities.
Related titles: Online - full text ed.
Published by: Renard Communications, Inc., P O Box 557, Springfield, NJ 07081-0557. TEL 973-912-8527, FAX 973-912-8599, editor@diversitycareers.com, http://www.diversitycareers.com. Pub. Roberta Renard TEL 973-912-8552. Adv. contact Janet O. Penn TEL 973-912-8555.

DOSSIER OR RENDEMENT. (OndernemingsRaad) *see* BUSINESS AND ECONOMICS—Labor And Industrial Relations

DRAMATISTS SOURCEBOOK. *see* THEATER

331.1 USA ISSN 2153-4004
E A CONNECTIONS. (Employers' Association) Text in English. m. free to members (effective 2010). back issues avail. **Document type:** *Newsletter, Trade.* **Description:** Provides news and information for a not-for-profit membership organization serving the employer community in 60 counties throughout Illinois and bordering communities in Iowa, Missouri, and Wisconsin.
Related titles: Online - full text ed.
Published by: A A I M Employers' Association, 401 NE Jefferson Ave, Peoria, IL 61603. TEL 309-637 3333, 800-948 5700, FAX 309-637 3300, kpopadziuk@eaconnect.com.

361.73 371.42 USA
E S S EMPLOYMENT OPPORTUNITIES. (Executive Search Service) Text in English. 1963. m. USD 25 to non-members. adv. **Description:** Information on career opportunities in fund-raising.
Former titles: Executive Search Service News; E S S Employment Newsletter
Published by: Association of Fundraising Professionals, 4300 Wilson Blvd, Ste 300, Arlington, VA 22203. TEL 703-684-0410, FAX 703-684-0540, http://www.afpnet.org. Ed. Scott Rall. Circ: 19,000 (controlled).

371.42 658.3 ZAF ISSN 1998-7250
E T D ONLINE. Key Title: ETDonline. Text in English. 2008. m. ZAR 575 (effective 2008).
Media: Online - full text.
Published by: Knowledge Resources, PO Box 3954, Randburg, 2125, South Africa. TEL 27-11-8808540, FAX 27-11-8808700, mail@knowres.co.za.

371.42 USA
EDITOR & PUBLISHER'S EMPLOYMENT LINE NEWSLETTER. Variant title: Employment Line. Text in English. w. **Document type:** *Newsletter, Trade.*
Media: E-mail.
Published by: Editor & Publisher Co., Inc. (Subsidiary of: Duncan McIntosh Co. Inc.), 17782 Cowan, Ste A, Irvine, CA 92614 . TEL 949-660-6150, FAX 949-660-6172, http://www.editorandpublisher.com.

EDUCATION + TRAINING. *see* EDUCATION—Adult Education

EDUCATOR SUPPLY AND DEMAND IN THE UNITED STATES. *see* EDUCATION—School Organization And Administration

371.42 DEU
EINBLICK (BERLIN). Text in German. 1998. fortn. free (effective 2009). adv. **Document type:** *Magazine, Trade.*
Published by: Graewis Verlag GmbH, Wallstr 60, Berlin, 10179, Germany. TEL 49-30-3088240, FAX 49-30-30882420. Ed. Anne Graef. Adv. contact Bettina Muetzel. B&W page EUR 2,547, color page EUR 3,081; trim 210 x 297. Circ: 12,323 (controlled).

658.3 CAN ISSN 1910-6866
EMPLOI - QUEBEC. C A M O - P I. RAPPORT ANNUEL DE GESTION. Text in French. 2002. a. **Document type:** *Report, Trade.*
Formerly (until 2005): Emploi - Quebec. C A M O - P I. Rapport Annuel (1707-1151)
Published by: Emploi - Quebec, C A M O - P I (Subsidiary of: Emploi - Quebec), 4560b, boule Saint-Laurent, bureau 201, Montreal, PQ H2T 1R3, Canada. TEL 514-845-3939, FAX 514-845-3256, http://www.camo-pi.qc.ca/index.shtml.

331.1 USA
EMPLOYMENT BULLETIN. Text in English. 1954. m. free. **Description:** Covers RI labor force trends, consumer price index and labor market info.
Published by: RI Dept of Labor & Training, 1511 Pontiac Ave., Cranston, RI 02920-4407. TEL 401-222-3706, FAX 401-222-2731. Eds. Joyce D'Orsi, Maria Ferrerra.

331.1 CAN ISSN 1912-2489
EMPLOYMENT EQUITY. A YEAR-END REVIEW. Text in English. 2000. a. **Document type:** *Report, Trade.*
Formerly (until 2002): Employment Equity Report (1498-2994)
Media: Online - full text. **Related titles:** Print ed.: ISSN 1711-3881.
Published by: Canadian Human Rights Commission/Commission Canadienne des Droits de la Personne, 344 Slater St, 8th Flr, Ottawa, ON K1A 1E1, Canada. TEL 613-995-1151, 888-214-1090, FAX 613-996-9661, info.com@chrc-ccdp.ca, http://www.chrc-ccdp.ca.

371.42 USA
EMPLOYMENT MARKETPLACE. Text in English. 1982. q. USD 26 (effective 2001). adv. back issues avail. **Document type:** *Magazine, Trade.*
Address: 12015 Robyn Park Dr., St. Louis, MO 63131. TEL 314-569-3095, FAX 636-458-4955, info@eminfo.com, http://www.eminfo.com. Ed., Adv. contact Pat Turner. Pub. A P Mueller.

331.1 IND
EMPLOYMENT NEWS. Text in English. 1975. w. INR 350; INR 8 per issue (effective 2011). **Document type:** *Journal, Government.*
Description: Strives to upgrade the awareness of the job seeking fraternity about suitable openings in public and private sector and provides a useful component of guidance material designed to assist them in coping with the prescribed tests.
Related titles: Urdu ed.; Hindi ed.
Published by: Ministry of Information & Broadcasting, Publications Division, Soochna Bhawan, C.G.O Complex, Lodi Rd, New Delhi, 110 003, India. http://publicationsdivision.nic.in/. Ed. Hasan Zia TEL 91-11-26195165. **Subscr. to:** Assistant Business Manager.

331.1 USA
EMPLOYMENT OPPORTUNITIES (NEW YORK). Text in English. m. free to members. **Document type:** *Newsletter, Consumer.* **Description:** Announcements of administrative openings in the field of community arts education.
Related titles: Online - full text ed.

Published by: National Guild for Community Arts Education, 520 Eighth Ave, 3rd Fl, Ste 302, New York, NY 10018. TEL 212-268-3337, FAX 212-268-3995, info@nationalguild.org, http://www.nationalguild.org. Circ: 400.

331.1 USA
EMPLOYMENT PRACTICE GUIDE. Text in English. 1965. 4 base vols. plus fortn. updates. looseleaf. USD 1,359 base vol(s). (effective 2004).
Related titles: CD-ROM ed.: USD 1,479 (effective 2004).
Published by: C C H Inc. (Subsidiary of: Wolters Kluwer N.V.), 2700 Lake Cook Rd, Riverwoods, IL 60015. TEL 847-267-7000, 800-449-6439, FAX 800-224-8299, cust_serv@cch.com, http://www.cch.com. Pub. Catherine Wolfe.

331.12 USA
EMPLOYMENT REVIEW (JUPITER). Text in English. m. **Document type:** *Magazine, Consumer.* **Description:** Provides job search information through pages of recruitment advertisements and editorials about workplace trends and employment issues.
Related titles: Online - full content ed.
Published by: Recourse Communications, Incorporated, 550 Heritage Dr., Ste. 200, Jupiter, FL 33458-3030. TEL 561-686-6800, FAX 561-686-8043, rci@bestjobusa.com, http://www.bestjobsusa.com.

368.44 USA
EMPLOYMENT SERVICE AND UNEMPLOYMENT INSURANCE OPERATIONS; a monthly summary. Text in English. m. **Document type:** *Government.*
Published by: Employment Security Commission, Labor Market Information Division, 532 Kendal Bldg, 700 Wade Ave, Box 25903, Raleigh, NC 27611. TEL 919-733-2936.

371.42 GBR ISSN 1366-8188
END OF TERM. Abbreviated title: E O T. Text in English. 1995. q. adv. **Document type:** *Magazine, Consumer.* **Description:** Highlights and promotes the opportunities available to young people. Aimed at school leavers, the editorial mixes both career and lifestyle features.
—CCC.
Published by: Craven Publishing Ltd, 15-39 Durham St, Kinning Park, Glasgow, G41 1BS, United Kingdom. TEL 44-141-4190044, FAX 44-141-4190077, http://www.cravenpublishing.com/. Adv. contact Neil Millar TEL 44-7717-842215. color page GBP 3,495; bleed 216 x 303.

ENTREPRISE ET CARRIERES. *see* BUSINESS AND ECONOMICS

ENVIRONMENTAL CAREERS ORGANIZATION. CONNECTIONS. *see* ENVIRONMENTAL STUDIES

EQUAL OPPORTUNITY; the career magazine for minority graduates. *see* ETHNIC INTERESTS

331.1 CAN ISSN 1912-2497
L'EQUITE EN MATIERE D'EMPLOI. BILAN. Text in French. 2000. a. **Document type:** *Journal, Trade.*
Formerly (until 2002): L' Equite en Matiere d'Emploi. Rapport (1498-3001)
Media: Online - full text.
Published by: Canadian Human Rights Commission/Commission Canadienne des Droits de la Personne, 344 Slater St, 8th Flr, Ottawa, ON K1A 1E1, Canada. TEL 613-995-1151, 888-214-1090, FAX 613-996-9661, info.com@chrc-ccdp.ca.

371.42 GRC
EUROPEAN CENTRE FOR THE DEVELOPMENT OF VOCATIONAL TRAINING. ANNUAL REPORT. Text in English. a. **Document type:** *Corporate.*
Published by: European Centre for the Development of Vocational Training, 123 Europis, Thessaloniki, 55102, Greece. TEL 30-2310-490111, FAX 30-2310-490102, info@cedefop.eu.int, http://www.cedefop.eu.int.

331.128 USA
THE EVERYTHING GET A JOB BOOK; the tools and strategies you need to land the job of your dreams. Text in English. 2000. irreg., latest 2007, 2nd ed. USD 14.95 per issue (effective 2009). illus. **Document type:** *Handbook/Manual/Guide, Trade.* **Description:** Focuses on all aspects of a job hunt including job offers and much more. Includes many examples of what to do and what not to do and includes sample resumes and cover letters.
Related titles: E-mail ed.; Fax ed.; Online - full text ed.
Published by: Adams Media (Subsidiary of: F + W Media Inc.), 4700 E Galbraith Rd, Cincinnati, OH 45236. TEL 513-531-2690, FAX 800-258-0929, deskcopies@adamsmedia.com, http://www.adamsmedia.com.

371.42 USA
EXECUTIVE'S GUIDE TO INTERIM POSITIONS. Text in English. 19??. a. (plus q. updates). **Document type:** *Guide, Trade.* **Description:** Provides details on search firms that specialize in temporary project assignments for top executives and mid level managers.
Published by: Career Advancement Publications, 460 Thornridge Dr, Rochester Hls, MI 48307. TEL 716-483-3454, FAX 716-664-2417.

051 USA
EXPERIENCE. Text in English. 1999. q. adv. **Document type:** *Magazine, Consumer.* **Description:** Targets students and young professionals who are beginning their careers.
Published by: The Pohly Co., 99 Bedford St, Fl 5, Boston, MA 02111. TEL 617-451-1700, 800-383-0888, FAX 617-338-7767, info@pohlyco.com, http://www.pohlyco.com.

"EXTRA" WORK FOR BRAIN SURGEONS. *see* MOTION PICTURES

371.42 FRA ISSN 2106-8704
F A P E. LA LETTRE. (Fondation Agir pour l'Emploi) Text in French. 1997. bi-m. **Document type:** *Consumer.*
Former titles (until 2009): La Lettre d'Information de la F A P E (1771-3781); (until 2003): Lettre aux Donateurs (1631-431X)
Published by: Fondation Agir pour l'Emploi, 10 Rue Mercoeur, Paris, 75011, France. http://www.webfape.net/spip.php.

331.1 NLD ISSN 2210-805X
F N V SPOOR. (Federatie Nederlandse Vakbeweging) Text in Dutch. 1961. bi-m.
Formerly (until 2010): Recht Spoor (0166-5138)
Published by: (F N V Bondgenoten), Stichting F N V Pers, Postbus 9354, Amsterdam, 1006 AJ, Netherlands. TEL 31-20-5816300, FAX 31-20-6151091. Circ: 7,500.

371.42 USA ISSN 1931-647X
FAST TRACK TRANSITIONS. Text in English. 2006. m. **Document type:** *Newsletter, Consumer.*
Published by: Front Line Success Systems coach@frontlinetransitions.com, http://www.frontlinetransitions.com/EZine.html. Pub. Kathy Malone.

331.1 USA ISSN 0279-2230
JK765
FEDERAL CAREER OPPORTUNITIES. Text in English. 1974. bi-w. USD 175; USD 19.97 per month online (effective 2001). adv. illus. reprints avail. **Document type:** *Directory, Government.* **Description:** Updated listings of federal government job vacancies. Includes articles on how to get a federal job.
Related titles: Online - full text ed.: 1974.
Published by: Federal Research Service, Inc., PO Box 1708, Annandale, VA 22003-1708. TEL 703-281-0200, FAX 703-281-7639. Ed., Pub. Judelle A McArdle. R&P Sandy Harris. Adv. contact Sharon Patterson.

371.42 USA ISSN 0739-1684
FEDERAL JOBS DIGEST. Abbreviated title: F J D. Text in English. 1977. bi-w. USD 125 (effective 2010). adv. illus. 32 p./no. 5 cols./p.; back issues avail.; reprints avail. **Document type:** *Newspaper, Consumer.* **Description:** Presents Federal recruitment information and job database. Each issue contains more than 5,000 current openings with the Federal government in the United States and overseas, including all occupations and career levels.
Related titles: Online - full text ed.: USD 7.95 per month (effective 2010).
Published by: HYR LLC, PO Box 89, Edgemont, PA 19028. TEL 610-725-1769.

FEDERAL PERSONNEL GUIDE; employment, pay, benefits, postal service, civil service. *see* BUSINESS AND ECONOMICS—Personnel Management

371.42 332 USA ISSN 1088-9531
FINANCE AND ACCOUNTING JOBS REPORT. Text in English. 19??. m. **Document type:** *Report, Trade.* **Description:** Offers a forum where corporate recruiters, personnel consultants, search firms and direct hiring companies list positions that are currently available.
Published by: Career Advancement Publications, 460 Thornridge Dr, Rochester Hls, MI 48307. TEL 716-483-3454, FAX 716-664-2417.

331.1 NZL ISSN 1177-6331
FOCUS; career planning guide. Variant title: Career Planning Guide. Text in English. 2007. biennial. **Document type:** *Handbook/Manual/Guide, Academic/Scholarly.* **Description:** Aimed at penultimate and final year students, the guide is packed with information to help you consider life and a career after university.
Published by: University of Auckland, University Careers Centre, Clock Tower, Room 001, 22 Princes St, Auckland, New Zealand. TEL 64-9-3737599 ext. 88727, careers@auckland.ac.nz.

FORDYCE LETTER; commentary and information provided exclusively for those involved in the personnel, search, employment, recruiting and outplacement professions. *see* LAW—Corporate Law

371.42 ITA ISSN 1973-4778
FORMAZIONE & INSEGNAMENTO; rivista quadrimestrale di ricerca, documentazione, critica. Text in Italian. 1999. 3/yr. EUR 25 domestic; EUR 45 foreign (effective 2010). **Document type:** *Journal, Academic/Scholarly.*
Formerly (until 2002): Formazione (1970-8408)
Published by: Pensa MultiMedia, Via A M Caprioli 8, Lecce, 73100, Italy. TEL 39-0832-230435, FAX 39-0832-230896, http://www.pensamultimedia.it. Ed. Umberto Margiotta.

371.42 ITA ISSN 1824-2782
FORMAZIONE PERMANENTE. Text in Italian. 1999. irreg. **Document type:** *Magazine, Trade.*
Published by: Franco Angeli Edizioni, Viale Monza 106, Milan, 20127, Italy. TEL 39-02-2837141, FAX 39-02-26144793, redazioni@francoangeli.it, http://www.francoangeli.it.

FORMER; revista para formadores. *see* BUSINESS AND ECONOMICS—Personnel Management

331.1 DEU
FORUM PRAXISFUEHRER. Text in German. 1988. a. EUR 10 (effective 2003). **Document type:** *Directory, Consumer.*
Published by: Forum Verlag GmbH, Bleicherstr 10, Konstanz, 78467, Germany. TEL 49-7531-98250, FAX 49-7531-982555, online-redaktion@forum-jobline.de, http://www.forum.de. Circ: 25,000 (controlled).

331.115 SWE ISSN 1402-2397
FRAMTIDEN DIREKT. Text in Swedish. 1996. 8/yr. adv. **Document type:** *Magazine, Trade.*
Published by: Framtidslaenken Media, Box 3348, Stockholm, 10367, Sweden. TEL 46-8-10-66-00, FAX 46-8-10-25-04, http://www.framtidslanken.se. Ed., Pub. Tobias Oestberg. Adv. contact Oskar Lindholm. page SEK 39,000; trim 250 x 370. Circ: 50,000 (controlled).

331.1 USA
FREELANCE NEW YORK; marketplace for the new workforce. Text in English. 1998. m. USD 19.95 (effective 1999). **Document type:** *Newsletter.* **Description:** Provides news, features, opinion, and humor on the financial, legal, and personal aspects of working for oneself.
Published by: Magazinedata Ltd., 111 E 14th St, Ste 324, New York, NY 10003. TEL 212-598-4820, FAX 212-598-1802. Ed. Daniel D'Arezzo. Pub. William Duke. Circ: 60,000 (paid).

331.1 AUS ISSN 1832-7044
FUTURE WORLD OF WORK SERIES. Text in English. 2005. irreg. free to qualified personnel (effective 2009). **Document type:** *Monographic series, Trade.* **Description:** Provides Australian HR practitioners with important data on what is happening in the Australian workforce.
Published by: Manpower Services (Australia) Pty Ltd., Level 22, Darling Park, Tower 2, 201 Sussex St, Sydney, NSW 2000, Australia. TEL 61-2-92638500, FAX 61-2-92638600, marketing@manpower.com.au, http://www.manpower.com.au.

331.1 NLD ISSN 1877-2188
G B I O. (Gemeenschappelijk BegeleidingsInstituut Ondernemingsraden) Text in Dutch. 1988. s-a.
Former titles (until 2007): Het Gemeenschappelijk BegeleidingsInstituut Ondernemingsraden en de Ondernemingsraad (1871-8442); (until 2002): De G B I O Krant (1381-0073)
Published by: Stichting Gemeenschappelijk BegeleidingsInstituut Ondernemingsraden, Postbus 19306, Utrecht, 3501 DH, Netherlands. TEL 31-30-2318800, FAX 31-30-2342267, info@gbio.nl. Ed. Jaap Rodenburg.

331.702 GBR ISSN 2040-0179
G E T : DIRECTORY OF GRADUATE EMPLOYMENT AND TRAINING. Variant title: G E T Directory. Text in English. 19??. a. **Document type:** *Directory, Trade.* **Description:** Guides graduates through the various avenues to the career of their choice. Indexed by degree subject, occupation, and employer type. Details the latest developments in several private- and public-sector industries.
Former titles (until 2006): Hobsons Directory; (until 2003): Hobsons Graduate Career Directory (1747-3047); (until 2001): G E T: Graduate Employment and Training (Year) (0309-894X); (until 1976): Careers Beyond a Degree
Published by: (Careers Research and Advisory Centre), Hobsons PLC, Bateman St, Cambridge, Cambs CB2 1LZ, United Kingdom. Enquiries@hobsons.co.uk, http://www.hobsons.com. **Dist. by:** Biblios Publishers' Distribution Services Ltd. TEL 44-1403-710851, FAX 44-1403-711143.

650.14 USA ISSN 1545-9527
G I JOBS; get hired. Text in English. 2002 (Jan.). m. USD 19.95 (effective 2005). adv. **Document type:** *Magazine, Trade.* **Description:** Provides information on careers and companies looking for employees with military experience.
Published by: Victory Media, Inc., PO Box 26, Sewickley, PA 15143. TEL 412-269-1663, FAX 412-291-2772, info@victorymediainc.com, http://www.victorymediainc.com. Pub. Chris Hale. Adv. contact Scott Shaw TEL 717-832-3038. B&W page USD 3,490; trim 8.375 x 10.875. Circ: 360,000.

▼ **G O MAGAZINE.** (Gemeenschappelijke Opleiding) *see* EDUCATION—Adult Education

GAODENG ZHIYE JIAOYU - TIANJIN ZHIYE DAXUE XUEBAO/ HIGHER VOCATIONAL EDUCATION - JOURNAL OF TIANJIN PROFESSIONAL COLLEGE. *see* EDUCATION—Higher Education

371.42 ITA ISSN 1825-7631
GENERAZIONI. Text in Italian. 2004. 3/yr. EUR 40 domestic; EUR 70 foreign (effective 2010). **Document type:** *Journal, Academic/Scholarly.*
Published by: (Universita degli Studi del Salento, Facolta di Scienze della Formazione), Pensa MultiMedia, Via A M Caprioli 8, Lecce, 73100, Italy. TEL 39-0832-230435, FAX 39-0832-230896, http://www.pensamultimedia.it. Ed. Luciano Galliani.

371.42 BRA ISSN 1808-4060
GESTAO E NEGOCIOS HOJE. Text in Portuguese. 2005. m. BRL 106.80 (effective 2006). **Document type:** *Magazine, Consumer.*
Published by: Editora Escala Ltda., Av Prof Ida Kolb, 551, Casa Verde, Sao Paulo, 02518-000, Brazil. TEL 55-11-38552100, FAX 55-11-38579643, escala@escala.com.br, http://www.escala.com.br.

GOAL IX. *see* POLITICAL SCIENCE—Civil Rights

GODT I GANG/GOOD START. *see* EDUCATION

371.42 CAN
GOODWILL DIMENSIONS. Text in English. 195?. s-a. free. back issues avail. **Description:** Informs clients, customers, donors, corporations about job training programs, retail news, donation needs.
Published by: Goodwill Industries of Toronto, 234 Adelaide St E, Toronto, ON M5A 1M9, Canada. TEL 416-362-4711, FAX 416-362-0720. Ed. Marylou Frazer.

331.1 IRL ISSN 1649-5446
GRADIRELAND. Text in English. 2003. a. GBP 8 to individuals; free to students (effective 2006). **Description:** Includes information on job opportunities, as well as advice on job searching.
Published by: GTI Ireland, 9-11 Upper Baggot St, Dublin, 4, Ireland. TEL 353-1-6603422, FAX 353-1-6606623.

331.7 AUS ISSN 1037-8553
GRADUATE DESTINATION SURVEY. Text in English. 1976. a. **Document type:** *Government.* **Description:** Reviews activities of graduates who have recently completed the requirements for their qualification.
Former titles (until 1991): Australian Graduates (0810-8145); (until 1981): Destinations of .. University and College Graduates (0727-5269); (until 1979): First Destinations of .. University and College Graduates (0727-5250)
Published by: Graduate Careers Australia Ltd., A'Beckett St, PO Box 12103, Melbourne, VIC 8006, Australia. TEL 61-3-96053700, FAX 61-3-96705752, info@graduatecareers.com.au, http://www.graduatecareers.com.au.

371.42 AUS ISSN 1834-3465
GRADUATE OPPORTUNITIES. Text in English. 2007. a., latest 2007. AUD 22 per issue (effective 2007). **Document type:** *Directory, Consumer.* **Description:** The official annual directory of graduate employers in Australia and New Zealand. It contains editorial articles offering advice to students and a comprehensively indexed guide to employers.
Published by: Graduate Careers Australia Ltd., PO Box 28, Parkville, VIC 3052, Australia. TEL 61-3-8344-9333, FAX 61-3-9347-7298, info@graduatecareers.com.au.

371.42 AUS ISSN 1834-3422
GRADUATE OPPORTUNITIES IN ACCOUNTING, BUSINESS, FINANCE. Text in English. 2007. a., latest 2007. **Document type:** *Directory, Consumer.*
Related titles: Online - full text ed.: ISSN 1834-3430.
Published by: Graduate Careers Australia Ltd., PO Box 28, Parkville, VIC 3052, Australia. TEL 61-3-8344-9333, FAX 61-3-9347-7298, info@graduatecareers.com.au, http://www.graduatecareers.com.au.

371.42 AUS ISSN 1834-3449
GRADUATE OPPORTUNITIES IN ENGINEERING & INFORMATION TECHNOLOGY. Text in English. 2007. a., latest 2007. **Document type:** *Directory, Consumer.*
Related titles: Online - full text ed.: ISSN 1834-3457.
Published by: Graduate Careers Australia Ltd., PO Box 28, Parkville, VIC 3052, Australia. TEL 61-3-8344-9333, FAX 61-3-9347-7298, info@graduatecareers.com.au, http://www.graduatecareers.com.au.

331.28 AUS
GRADUATE SALARIES. Text in English. 1986. a. AUD 33 per issue to non-members; free to members (effective 2009). **Document type:** *Report, Consumer.* **Description:** Provides detailed information on the earnings of new graduates in their first full time employment in Australia.
Formerly (until 2005): Graduate Starting Salaries (1030-7311)
Published by: Graduate Careers Australia Ltd., A'Beckett St, PO Box 12103, Melbourne, VIC 8006, Australia. TEL 61-3-96053700, FAX 61-3-96705752, info@graduatecareers.com.au.

620 USA ISSN 2154-9702
TA157
GRADUATING ENGINEER & COMPUTER CAREERS (PRINT). Text in English. 1979. 3/yr. USD 50.70 (effective 2006). adv. illus. reprints avail. **Document type:** *Magazine, Trade.* **Description:** Covers recruitment and career development for engineering and computer science students.
Formerly (until 1997): Graduating Engineer (0193-2276)
Related titles: Online - full text ed.
Indexed: CADCAM.
—Ingenta, Linda Hall.
Published by: Career Recruitment Media, Inc., 211 W Wacker Dr, Ste 900, Chicago, IL 60606. TEL 312-525-3099, FAX 312-429-3312, info@careermedia.com, http://www.careermedia.com/. Ed. Valerie Anderson. adv.: B&W page USD 9,000, color page USD 9,875; trim 8 x 10.75. Circ: 64,000 (controlled).

GRADX. *see* EDUCATION

331.1 334 USA ISSN 1071-0590
HD28
GRASSROOTS ECONOMIC ORGANIZING NEWSLETTER. Short title: G E O. Text in English. 1991. bi-m. USD 10 domestic; USD 25.95 foreign (effective 2001). adv. bk.rev.; film rev.; play rev. illus. back issues avail. **Document type:** *Newsletter, Consumer.* **Description:** Consists of news articles, interviews, departments, and informational documents in pursuit of democratizing the workplace and effecting worker-community ownership.
Formered by the merger of (1984-1991): Changing Work (0883-1416); (1981-1991): Workplace Democracy (0738-6044)
Related titles: Online - full text ed.
Indexed: AESIS, APW, AltPI, P48, PQC, PdeR.
Published by: GEO, R R 1, Box 124A, Stillwater, PA 17878. TEL 800-240-9721. Ed., Pub. Wade Wright. Adv. contact Berta Nelson. Circ: 1,200 (paid).

371.42 GBR ISSN 2044-0669
▼ **THE GUARDIAN UK 300.** Text in English. 2010. a. GBP 19.99 (effective 2011). adv. **Document type:** *Magazine, Trade.* **Description:** Presents a survey of UK employers and what students want from their graduate careers.
Related titles: Online - full text ed.: free (effective 2011).
Published by: G T I Media Ltd, The Fountain Bldg, Howbery Park, Benson Ln, Wallingford, Oxon OX10 8BA, United Kingdom. TEL 44-1491-826262, FAX 44-1491-833146, http://groupgti.com/gtimedia.

331.1 USA ISSN 1931-5937
JK692
GUIDE TO AMERICA'S FEDERAL JOBS. Text in English. 2001. irreg. USD 18.95 per issue (effective 2007). **Document type:** *Guide, Consumer.*
Published by: JIST Publishing, 7321 Shadeland Station, Ste 200, Indianapolis, IN 46256. TEL 800-648-5478, FAX 800-547-8329, info@jist.com.

371.42 362.82 CAN ISSN 1924-0392
A GUIDE TO WINNIPEG FOR ABORIGINAL NEWCOMERS. Text in English. 200?. s-a. free to qualified personnel (effective 2010). **Document type:** *Handbook/Manual/Guide, Consumer.* **Description:** Provides employment, education and training opportunities in Winnipeg.
Published by: Partners for Careers, 510 Selkirk Ave, Winnipeg, MB R2W 2M7, Canada. TEL 204-945-0447, 800-883-0398, FAX 204-948-2714, roberta.hewson@gov.mb.ca.

331.7 USA ISSN 1097-6418
GUIDE TO YOUR CAREER. Variant title: Princeton Review Guide to Your Career. Text in English. 1997. irreg., latest 2006. USD 19.95 per issue (effective 2010). back issues avail. **Document type:** *Handbook/Manual/Guide, Academic/Scholarly.* **Description:** Contains descriptions of 240 professions in a wide range of fields, including business, law, design, sports, entertainment, and more.
Published by: Princeton Review Publishing, L.L.C. (Subsidiary of: Random House Inc.), 111 Speen St, Ste 550, Framingham, MA 01701. TEL 800-273-8439, ses@review.com, http://www.princetonreview.com.

371.42 IRL
GUIDELINE. Text in English. 5/yr. adv. **Document type:** *Journal, Academic/Scholarly.*
Published by: Institute of Guidance Counsellors, 17 Herbert St., Dublin, 2, Ireland. TEL 353-1-6761975, FAX 353-1-6612551, igc@indigo.ie, http://www.igc-edu.ie. adv.: B&W page EUR 380. Circ: 750 (controlled).

371.42 362.11068 USA
H F M A CAREER OPPORTUNITIES. Text in English. bi-w. free (effective 2008). **Document type:** *Newsletter, Trade.* **Description:** Developed specifically for healthcare finance professionals who are always looking to take their careers to the next level.
Media: E-mail.
Published by: Healthcare Financial Management Association, 2 Westbrook Corporate Ctr, Ste 700, Westchester, IL 60154. TEL 708-531-9600, 800-252-4362, FAX 708-531-0032.

371.42 USA ISSN 1540-0697
H F M A WANTS YOU TO KNOW. Text in English. 1999. bi-w. free (effective 2008). back issues avail. **Document type:** *Newsletter, Trade.* **Description:** Provides practical career and professional development insights.
Media: E-mail.
Published by: Healthcare Financial Management Association, 2 Westbrook Corporate Ctr, Ste 700, Westchester, IL 60154. TEL 708-531-9600, 800-252-4362, FAX 708-531-0032. Eds. Laura Noble, Maxine Harrison.

658.3 GBR ISSN 1755-3520
THE H R & TRAINING JOURNAL. (Human Resources) Text in English. 2007. s-a. GBP 30 (effective 2011). adv. back issues avail. **Document type:** *Journal, Trade.* **Description:** Covers issues pertinent to developing skills and leadership in the public sector.
Related titles: Online - full text ed.: ISSN 2046-6145. free (effective 2011).
Published by: P S C A International Ltd., Ebenezer House, Rycroft, Newcastle-under-Lyme, Staffs ST5 2UB, United Kingdom. TEL 44-1782-630200, FAX 44-1782-625533, mailbox@publicservice.co.uk. Ed. Laura Evans. Adv. contact Gerrod Mellor TEL 44-1782-630200.

371.42 USA ISSN 1933-3064
TT958
THE HAIR, MAKEUP & FASHION STYLING CAREER GUIDE. Text in English. irreg., latest 4th ed. 400 p./no.; **Document type:** *Guide, Consumer.*
Published by: Set The Pace Publishing Group, 4237 Los Nietos Dr, Los Angeles, CA 90027-2911. TEL 323-913-0773, FAX 323-913-0900, info@setthepacepubgroup.com, http://www.setthepacepubgroup.com. Pub. Crystal A. Wright.

371.42 DEU
HANDFEST. Text in German. 2000. bi-m. EUR 10.75 (effective 2010). adv. **Document type:** *Magazine, Consumer.*
Published by: Westdeutscher Handwerkskammertag e.V., Sternwartstr 27-29, Duesseldorf, 40547, Germany. TEL 49-211-3007700, FAX 49-211-3007900, whkt@handwerk-nrw.de, http://www.handwerk-nrw.de. Ed. Rolf Goebels. adv.: page EUR 3,950; trim 210 x 280. Circ: 97,236 (controlled).

HEALTH CAREER POST. *see* HEALTH FACILITIES AND ADMINISTRATION

371.42 DEU
HIGH POTENTIAL. Text in German. 1999. q. adv. **Document type:** *Magazine, Consumer.*
Published by: Evoluzione Media AG, Dillwaechterstr 4, Munich, 80686, Germany. TEL 49-89-7690030, FAX 49-89-76900329, info@evoluzione.de, http://www.evoluzionemedia.de. adv.: page EUR 7,780; trim 210 x 297. Circ: 86,000 (controlled).

331.1 USA ISSN 0749-2960
HIGH TECHNOLOGY CAREERS. Text in English. 1984. 10/yr. USD 43 domestic; USD 52 in Canada; USD 135 elsewhere (effective 2000). adv. bk.rev. tr.lit. back issues avail.; reprints avail. **Document type:** *Magazine, Trade.* **Description:** Covers information relevant to the development and growth of high technology. It addresses topics including emerging technologies, US trade issues, future trends, business development, regional and national technological growth, professional advancement, and employment trends.
Related titles: Online - full text ed.
Published by: Central Newspapers, Inc. (Subsidiary of: Gannett Company, Inc.), 4701 Patrick Henry Dr, Ste 1901, Santa Clara, CA 95054. TEL 408-970-8800, FAX 408-567-0242. Ed., R&P Cathy Mickelson. Pub. Paul Burrowes. Adv. contact Claudia Herrera. B&W page USD 7,575, color page USD 8,475; trim 12.13 x 10.75. Circ: 160,000.

371.42 305.868 USA
HISPANIC CAREER WORLD; the diversity employment magazine. Text in English. 2001. s-a. USD 18; free to qualified personnel (effective 2008). adv. 48 p./no. 3 cols./p.; **Document type:** *Magazine, Trade.* **Description:** Aims to be the recruitment link between the students and professionals who are Hispanic and the major corporations that seeks to hire them.
Published by: Equal Opportunity Publications, Inc., 445 Broad Hollow Rd, Ste 425, Melville, NY 11747. TEL 631-421-9421, FAX 631-421-1352, info@eop.com. Ed. James Schneider TEL 631-421-9421 ext 12. Pub., Adv. contact Tamara Flaum-Dreyfuss TEL 631-421-9421 ext 21.

HISPANIC ENGINEER & INFORMATION TECHNOLOGY. *see* ENGINEERING

HISPANIC NETWORK MAGAZINE; a Latino lifesyle, business and employment magazine. *see* ETHNIC INTERESTS

HISPANIC TODAY. *see* ETHNIC INTERESTS

HOME BUSINESS MAGAZINE; the home-based entrepreneur's magazine. *see* BUSINESS AND ECONOMICS—Small Business

610.73 331.1 USA ISSN 1058-7934
RA645.35
HOME CARE SALARY & BENEFITS REPORT. Text in English. 1992. a. USD 295 per issue (effective 2012). **Document type:** *Report, Trade.* **Description:** Includes salary data for nursing, therapy, and clerical jobs in home care.
Related titles: CD-ROM ed.: ISSN 2151-0792. 2009 (Oct.).
Published by: (National Association for Home Care & Hospice), Hospital & Healthcare Compensation Service, PO Box 376, Oakland, NJ 07436. TEL 201-405-0075, FAX 201-405-2110, allinfo@hhcsinc.com, http://www.hhcsinc.com.

HOSPICE SALARY & BENEFITS REPORT. *see* HEALTH FACILITIES AND ADMINISTRATION

HUMAN RESOURCE DEVELOPMENT REVIEW. *see* BUSINESS AND ECONOMICS—Personnel Management

371.42 USA ISSN 1089-8158
HUMAN RESOURCES JOBS REPORT. Text in English. 1996. m. **Document type:** *Report, Trade.*
Published by: Career Advancement Publications, 460 Thornridge Dr, Rochester Hls, MI 48307. TEL 716-483-3454, FAX 716-664-2417.

371.42 USA
I LOVE MY JOB!. Text in English. 1997. bi-w.
Media: Online - full text.
Published by: Herbelin Publishing, 3836 Kentucky Ave., Riverbank, CA 95367. TEL 209-869-6389, FAX 209-869-6389, herbelin@worldnet.att.net, http://www.riverbankbooks.com. Ed. Steve Herbelin. Circ: 545.

I T EMPOWERMENT PROGRAMME FOR THE UNEMPLOYED. (Information Technology) *see* COMPUTERS

331 SVK ISSN 1337-0774
I T KARIERA. Text in Slovak. 2006. m. adv. **Document type:** *Magazine, Trade.*
Related titles: Online - full text ed.: ISSN 1337-0375.
Published by: I C T, s.r.o., Bebravska 9, Bratislava, 821 07, Slovakia. TEL 421-905-777628, FAX 421-220-777628, office@ict.sk, http://www.ict.sk. Ed. Renata Jaloviarova.

331 SVK ISSN 1336-9318
I T PROFESIA. Text in Slovak. 2006. d. **Document type:** *Trade.*
Media: Online - full content.
Published by: I C T, s.r.o., Bebravska 9, Bratislava, 821 07, Slovakia. TEL 421-905-777628, FAX 421-220-777628, office@ict.sk, http://www.ict.sk.

371.42 FRA ISSN 1959-6766
IDEES - JOB. Text in French. 2007. q. **Document type:** *Magazine, Consumer.*
Published by: Lafont Presse, 53 Rue du Chemin Vert, Boulogne-Billancourt, 92100, France. FAX 33-1-45792211, http://www.lafontpresse.fr.

INDIAN JOURNAL OF TRAINING & DEVELOPMENT. *see* BUSINESS AND ECONOMICS—Personnel Management

331.1 AUS ISSN 1834-5352
INDIGENOUS EMPLOYMENT IN ACTION. Text in English. 2006. q. **Document type:** *Journal, Trade.* **Description:** Focuses on what is required to develop and implement actions and strategies to help Indigenous Australians and their communities succeed in employment, business ownership and management.
Related titles: Online - full text ed.: ISSN 1834-5360.
Published by: Australia. Department of Employment and Workplace Relations, GPO Box 9879, Canberra, ACT 2601, Australia. TEL 61-2-61216000, FAX 61-2-61217542, http://www.dewrsb.gov.au. Ed. Alex Bellis.

371.42 DEU
INDIVIDUELL BEWERBEN. Text in German. 1994. irreg. **Document type:** *Directory, Trade.*
Published by: Staufenbiel Institut fuer Studien- und Berufsplanung GmbH, Maria-Hilf-Str 15, Cologne, 50677, Germany. TEL 49-221-9126630, FAX 49-221-9126639, info@staufenbiel.de, http://www.staufenbiel.de. Ed. Joerg Staufenbiel.

INFO ALSO. *see* SOCIAL SERVICES AND WELFARE

331.1 USA ISSN 1532-1169
HD5723
INFORMATION PLUS REFERENCE SERIES. CAREERS & OCCUPATIONS; looking to the future. Text in English. 1998. biennial. USD 49 per issue (effective 2008). back issues avail. **Document type:** *Monographic series, Abstract/Index.* **Description:** Provides a compilation of current and historical statistics, with analysis, on aspects of one contemporary social issue.
Related titles: Online - full text ed.; ◆ Series: Information Plus Reference Series.
Published by: Gale (Subsidiary of: Cengage Learning), 27500 Drake Rd, Farmington Hills, MI 48331. TEL 248-699-4253, 800-347-4253, FAX 248-699-8035, 800-414-5043, gale.customerservice@cengage.com, http://gale.cengage.com.

DAS INGENIEURSTUDIUM. *see* EDUCATION—Guides To Schools And Colleges

371.42 790.1 USA ISSN 1085-6218
THE INSIDER (PHOENIX). Text in English. 1996. s-m. USD 149 for 6 mos. **Document type:** *Newsletter, Trade.*
Formerly: Sports Careers Newsletter
Published by: Franklin Covey Co., Sports Division, 1620 S. Stapley Dr., Ste. 224, Mesa, AZ 85204-6656. TEL 480-539-3800, FAX 480-539-3811, sportscareers@timemanagement.com. Ed., Pub. Duke Little. R&P Kim Janz.

371.42 USA
INSIDER JOBS REVIEW. Text in English. 19??. m. **Document type:** *Journal, Trade.* **Description:** Offers a forum where corporate recruiters, personnel consultants, search firms, and direct hiring companies list positions that are currently available.
Published by: Career Advancement Publications, 460 Thornridge Dr, Rochester Hls, MI 48307. TEL 716-483-3454, FAX 716-664-2417.

331.133 658.3 USA ISSN 2154-0349
INSIGHT INTO DIVERSITY. Text in English. 1974. m. (except July). free (effective 2010). adv. illus. back issues avail.; reprints avail. **Document type:** *Magazine, Trade.* **Description:** Features in-depth news, reports and commentary on issues surrounding all aspects of diversity and inclusion practices in the workplace and in the world.
Formerly (until 2009): Affirmative Action Register (0146-2113)
Related titles: Online - full text ed.: ISSN 2154-0454. free (effective 2010).
Indexed: RehabLit.
Published by: Potomac Publishing, Inc, 225 S Meramec Ave Ste 400, St. Louis, MO 63105. TEL 314-863-2900, 800-537-0655, FAX 314-863-2905, http://www.potomacpub.com/. Ed. Michael Rainey. Pub. Lenore Pearlstein. Adv. contact Sarah Zeveski. B&W page USD 2,730, color page USD 3,060; 7 x 9.75.

371.42 GBR ISSN 1749-4567
INSPIRE (SHEFFIELD). Text in English. 2004. 3/yr. free (effective 2009). back issues avail. **Document type:** *Magazine, Consumer.* **Description:** Designed for those who are looking for their first job, thinking about returning to work or considering a change in career.
Formerly (until 2004): Outlook
Related titles: Audio cassette/tape ed.; Braille ed.; Online - full text ed.: ISSN 1749-4575.
Published by: Jobcentre Plus, Level 1, Steel City House, W St, Sheffield, S1 2GQ, United Kingdom. contact-us@jobcentreplus.gsi.gov.uk.

371.42 LKA
INSTITUTE OF BANKERS OF SRI LANKA. JOURNAL. Text in English. 1981. s-a. LKR 50; LKR 100 foreign. adv.
Formerly (until 1981): Bankers' Training Institute (Sri Lanka). Bulletin
Published by: Institute of Bankers of Sri Lanka, No. 5 Milepost Ave., Colombo, 3, Sri Lanka. TEL 573625. Ed. H B Illankone. Circ: 5,000.

371.42 IRL ISSN 0332-3641
INSTITUTE OF GUIDANCE COUNSELLORS. JOURNAL. Text in English. 1981 (vol.4). a. bk.rev. cum.index: vols.1-14. **Document type:** *Journal, Trade.* **Description:** The chief aim of the journal is to disseminate both practical and theoretical ideas among guidance counselors and others involved in education, careers and counselling.
Formerly: Career Guidance and Counselling

Published by: Institute of Guidance Counsellors, 17 Herbert St., Dublin, 2, Ireland. TEL 353-1-6761975, 353-1-6761975, FAX 353-1-6612551, igc@indigo.ie. Ed. Finian Buckley. Circ: 750.

331.1 NLD ISSN 1879-8675
INTERMEDIAIR CARRIERGIDS VOOR STARTERS. Text in Dutch. 1971. a. EUR 4.95 (effective 2010).
Formerly (until 2009): Intermediair Orientatiegids. Editie Starters (1876-9330); Which superseded in part (in 2005): Intermediair Jaarboek (1876-9322)
Published by: Nielsen Business Publications, Postbus 37040, Amsterdam, 1030 AA, Netherlands. TEL 31-20-2042000, FAX 31-20-2042001. Ed. Alex Beishuizen TEL 31-23-5463531. Pub. Masha Kodden.

331.125 USA
HD4802
INTERNATIONAL CAREER EMPLOYMENT WEEKLY. Text in English. 1980. m. looseleaf. USD 140 (effective 2005). adv. **Document type:** *Newsletter, Consumer.* **Description:** Reports on developments in the international job market, covering a wide range of overseas job openings for US citizens.
Former titles: International Employment Hotline (0748-8890); International Career Employment Opportunities (1065-0105)
Published by: Carlyle Corp., PO Box 6729, Charlottesville, VA 22906-6729. TEL 434-985-6444, FAX 434-985-6828, lisa@internationaljobs.org, http://www.internationaljobs.org/. Ed. Keeby Ipsan. Pub. Lisa L Law. Circ: 15,000 (paid).

658 USA ISSN 1079-9508
INTERNATIONAL DIRECTORY OF BUSINESS AND MANAGEMENT SCHOLARS AND RESEARCH. Text in English. 1996. biennial.
Related titles: CD-ROM ed.: ISSN 1079-9516.
Published by: Harvard Business School Publishing, 60 Harvard Way, Boston, MA 02163. TEL 617-783-7500, 800-988-0886, FAX 617-783-7555, corpcustserv@hbsp.harvard.edu, http://www.hbsp.harvard.edu.

THE INTERNATIONAL EDUCATOR. *see* EDUCATION—International Education Programs

INTERNATIONAL JOURNAL FOR EDUCATIONAL AND VOCATIONAL GUIDANCE. *see* EDUCATION—Adult Education

THE INTERNET WEB SOURCE. *see* COMPUTERS—Internet

331.1021 IRL ISSN 1649-8445
HD5768
IRELAND. CENTRAL STATISTICS OFFICE. NATIONAL EMPLOYMENT SURVEY. Text in English. 2006. a., latest 2006, for the year 2003. EUR 10 (effective 2006).
Published by: Ireland. Central Statistics Office/Eire, An Phriomh-Oifig Staidrimh, Skehard Rd, Cork, Ireland. TEL 353-21-4535000, FAX 353-21-4535555, information@cso.ie.

ITRECRUITERMAG.COM; employment opportunities and career news for information technology professionals. *see* COMPUTERS—Information Science And Information Theory

IT'S FOR REAL. *see* CHILDREN AND YOUTH—For

371.42 362.7 USA
J A C S VOLUNTEER. Text in English. 1968. q. free. **Document type:** *Newsletter.* **Description:** Directed to volunteers across the U.S. providing help for ex-Job Corps (disadvantaged youth 16-24 yrs.) students.
Published by: Joint Action in Community Service, Inc., 5225 Wisconsin Ave N W, Ste 404, Washington, DC 20015. TEL 202-537-0996, FAX 202-363-0239. Ed. Ana M Gomez. Circ: 6,000.

JAPANESE NURSING ASSOCIATION RESEARCH REPORT. *see* MEDICAL SCIENCES—Nurses And Nursing

371.42 CHN
JI'NAN ZHEYE XUEYUAN XUEBAO/JINAN VOCATIONAL COLLEGE. JOURNAL. Text in Chinese. 1999. bi-m. CNY 8 newsstand/cover (effective 2006). **Document type:** *Journal, Academic/Scholarly.*
Formerly: Ji'nan Jiaoyu Xueyuan Xuebao/Ji'nan Education College. Journal (1009-7732)
Related titles: Online - full text ed.
Published by: Jinan Zheye Xueyuan, 37, Gannan Dong Jie, Ji'nan, 250001, China. TEL 86-531-2052413.

371.42 600 CHN ISSN 1671-3699
JINHUA ZHIYE JISHU XUEYUAN XUEBAO/JINHUA COLLEGE OF PROFESSION AND TECHNOLOGY. JOURNAL. Text in Chinese. 2001. q. CNY 8 newsstand/cover (effective 2006). **Document type:** *Journal, Academic/Scholarly.*
Related titles: Online - full text ed.
Published by: Jinhua Zhiye Jishu Xueyuan, 1188, Wuzhou Jie, Jinhua, 321007, China. TEL 86-579-2265046, FAX 86-579-2265004.

331.7 USA
HF5382.5.U5
JOB CHOICES (YEAR). Text in English. 1996. a. (in 3 vols.). illus. **Document type:** *Directory.* **Description:** Contains information on career planning, the job search, work-related education, graduate schools; administration, business and other nontechnical career options; engineering, sciences, computer field and other technical career options; medical, nursing, and allied health career options.
Formerly (until 2000): Planning Job Choices (1520-8893)
Related titles: Online - full text ed.
Published by: National Association of Colleges and Employers, 62 Highland Ave, Bethlehem, PA 18017. TEL 610-868-1421, 800-544-5272, FAX 610-868-0208, customer_service@naceweb.org, http://www.naceweb.org.

331.7 USA ISSN 1944-6918
JOB CHOICES. DIVERSITY EDITION (YEAR). Key Title: Planning Job Choices. Minority Edition. Text in English. 1996. a. USD 13.95 per issue to non-members; USD 12.95 per issue to members (effective 2009). reprints avail. **Document type:** *Magazine, Consumer.* **Description:** Provides information for job-search, plus articles focusing on diversity in the workplace, including how to find a mentor, communicate in the culturally diverse work environment, adapt to corporate culture, and more.
Formerly (until 2000): Planning Job Choices (1520-8893)
Published by: National Association of Colleges and Employers, 62 Highland Ave, Bethlehem, PA 18017. TEL 610-868-1421, 800-544-5272, FAX 610-868-0208, customer_service@naceweb.org. Circ: 154,575.

331.7 USA ISSN 1946-9314
JOB CHOICES IN BUSINESS & LIBERAL ARTS STUDENTS (YEAR). Text in English. 1994. a. USD 12.95 per issue to members; USD 13.95 per issue to non-members (effective 2009). reprints avail. **Document type:** *Magazine, Consumer.* **Description:** Contains information on career planning for persons entering business professions.
Formerly (until 2004): Job Choices in Business; Which superseded in part (in 1994): C P C Annual (0749-7474); Which was formerly (until 1984): College Placement Annual (0069-5734)
Published by: National Association of Colleges and Employers, 62 Highland Ave, Bethlehem, PA 18017. TEL 610-868-1421, 800-544-5272, FAX 610-868-0208, customer_service@naceweb.org. Circ: 374,150.

331.7 USA ISSN 1534-2301
JOB CHOICES IN SCIENCE, ENGINEERING, AND TECHNOLOGY (YEAR). Text in English. 1994. a. USD 13.95 per issue to non-members; USD 12.95 per issue to members (effective 2009). reprints avail. **Document type:** *Magazine, Consumer.* **Description:** Contains information on career planning for college graduates about to enter engineering or scientific professions.
Incorporates (in 1999): Job Choices in Health Care (1945-9173); Formerly (until 1999): Job Choices in Science and Engineering; Which superseded in part (in 1994): C P C Annual (0749-7474); Which was formerly (until 1984): College Placement Annual (0069-5734)
Published by: National Association of Colleges and Employers, 62 Highland Ave, Bethlehem, PA 18017. TEL 610-868-1421, 800-544-5272, FAX 610-868-0208, customer_service@naceweb.org. Circ: 201,700.

JOB FUTURES. *see* BUSINESS AND ECONOMICS—Labor And Industrial Relations

371.42 USA ISSN 1053-1874
HF5382.75.U6
JOB HUNTER'S SOURCEBOOK; where to find employment leads and other job search resources. Text in English. 1991. biennial, latest 2008. USD 187 per issue (effective 2008). back issues avail. **Document type:** *Directory, Consumer.* **Description:** Lists sources of help wanted ads, employer directories, employment agencies, placement services, and electronic resources for 228 specific careers.
Published by: Gale (Subsidiary of: Cengage Learning), 27500 Drake Rd, Farmington Hills, MI 48331. TEL 248-699-4253, 800-877-4253, FAX 877-363-4253, gale.customerservice@cengage.com, http://gale.cengage.com. Ed. Michelle Lecompte.

JOB LINE AND NEWS FROM C P R S. *see* LEISURE AND RECREATION

331 330 USA
JOB OPENINGS FOR ECONOMISTS (ONLINE). Text in English. 1974. m. (except Jan. & Jul.). tr.lit. back issues avail. **Document type:** *Newsletter, Trade.* **Description:** Lists job vacancies.
Formerly (until 2001): Job Openings for Economists (0196-1551)
Media: Online - full text.
—CCC.
Published by: American Economic Association, 2014 Broadway, Ste 305, Nashville, TN 37203. TEL 615-322-2595, FAX 615-343-7590, aeainfo@vanderbilt.edu, http://www.vanderbilt.edu/AEA/.

331.1 USA ISSN 1070-8952
THE JOB SEEKER. Text in English. 1987. s-m. USD 85 to individuals; USD 110 to institutions (effective 2005). adv. illus. reprints avail. **Document type:** *Newsletter, Consumer.* **Description:** Covers the employment opportunities nation wide in the ecology/environment field.
Related titles: Online - full content ed.: USD 60 to individuals; USD 110 to institutions (effective 2005).
Published by: Job Seeker, 403 Oakwood St., Warrens, WI 54666. TEL 608-378-4450, FAX 267-295-2005. Ed. William Oakes. Circ: 2,850 (controlled and free).

331.7 CAN ISSN 1492-9031
HD5729 Q3J63
JOBBOOM LE MAGAZINE. Variant title: jobboom mag. Text in French. 2000. 10/yr. CAD 29.95; free newsstand/cover (effective 2007). **Document type:** *Magazine, Consumer.*
Related titles: Online - full text ed.
Published by: Editions Jobboom, 300 Av. Viger Est, 3eme Etage, Montreal, PQ H2X 3W4, Canada. TEL 514-871-0222, 877-796-8266, http://www.jobboom.com.

331.1 ZAF ISSN 1028-3307
JOBMAIL. Text in English. 1997. fortn.
Published by: Junkmail Publishing, 1312 Pretorius St, Hatfield, Pretoria, South Africa. TEL 27-12-3423840, FAX 822-305-100.

331.1 USA ISSN 0826-788X
JOBMART. Text in English. 1980. 22/yr. USD 80 domestic to non-members; USD 95 in Canada to non-members; USD 130 elsewhere to non-members; USD 35 domestic to members; USD 50 in Canada to members; USD 85 elsewhere to members (effective 2000). adv. reprints avail. **Document type:** *Directory, Trade.* **Description:** Lists employment opportunities available in the field of planning and related areas.
Published by: American Planning Association, 122 S Michigan Ave, Ste 1600, Chicago, IL 60603. TEL 312-431-9100, FAX 312-431-9985. Ed. Grace Williams. Circ: 5,000 (paid).

331.125 GBR ISSN 1479-0300
JOBS & CAREERS (OXFORDSHIRE & WILTSHIRE EDITION). Text in English. 1994. w. GBP 130 (effective 2008). **Document type:** *Newsletter, Consumer.*
Formerly (until 2003): Appointments (1353-0763)
Published by: Newsquest (Oxford) Ltd. (Subsidiary of: Newsquest Media Group), Osney Mead, Oxford, OX2 OEJ, United Kingdom. TEL 44-1865-425262, FAX 44-1865-425554, http://www.oxfordmail.net/.

JOBS CLEARINGHOUSE ONLINE. *see* EDUCATION

331.1 GBR
JOBS DIRECT. Text in English. 1999. fortn. adv. **Document type:** *Journal, Trade.* **Description:** Covers the latest company news and job vacancies within regions in the United Kingdom.
Address: 18 Brock St, Bath, BA1 2LW, United Kingdom. TEL 44-1225-426600, FAX 44-1225-337051, info@jobs-web.co.uk, http://www.jobs-web.co.uk. adv.: B&W page GBP 2,500, color page GBP 2,754; trim 290 x 390. Circ: 50,000 (free).

331.1 100 USA
JOBS FOR PHILOSOPHERS. Abbreviated title: J F P. Text in English. 1973. q. free to members (effective 2011). adv. **Document type:** *Bulletin, Trade.* **Description:** Contains current academic and non-academic job openings of interest to philosophers.
Related titles: Online - full text ed.
Published by: American Philosophical Association, c/o University of Delaware, 31 Amstel Ave, Newark, DE 19716. TEL 302-831-1112, FAX 302-831-8690, apaonline@udel.edu. Adv. contact Lindsay Palkovitz TEL 302-831-4298. Circ: 7,000.

371.42 USA
JOBS FROM RECYCLABLES POSSIBILITY NEWSLETTER. Text in English. 1991. a. looseleaf. USD 15.95 (effective 2007). adv. **Document type:** *Newsletter, Trade.* **Description:** Presents ideas on creating jobs from recyclables.
Published by: Prosperity & Profits Unlimited, PO Box 416, Denver, CO 80201. TEL 303-575-5676, FAX 303-575-1187, starsuccess@excite.com. Ed. A C Doyle. adv.: page USD 1,000. Circ: 2,000 (paid and controlled).

331.1 USA ISSN 1053-654X
JOBS IN RECESSIONARY TIMES POSSIBILITY NEWSLETTER. Text in English. 1990. a. looseleaf. USD 15.95 (effective 2007). adv. 7 p./no.; **Document type:** *Newsletter, Trade.*
—CCC.
Published by: Prosperity & Profits Unlimited, PO Box 416, Denver, CO 80201. TEL 303-575-5676, FAX 303-575-1187, starsuccess@excite.com, http://www.prosperityandprofitsunlimited.com. Ed. A C Doyle. adv.: page USD 900. Circ: 1,500 (paid).

371.2 GBR
JOBS NORTH WEST; helping you find your way through the job market. Text in English. 1987. w. GBP 19 (effective 1999). adv. **Document type:** *Newspaper, Consumer.* **Description:** Lists job and career and training opportunities throughout northwestern England.
Formerly: Northwest Job Car and Bargain Mart
Published by: Guardian Media Group plc, 164 Deansgate, Manchester, Lancs M60 6DS, United Kingdom. TEL 44-161-211-2638, FAX 44-161-839-2618. Ed., Pub. Jaqui Pacey. Adv. contact Karen Brosh. Circ: 25,000.

371.42 GBR ISSN 0962-9742
JOBSEARCH U K. Text in English. 1991. w. GBP 22.50 for 18 mos.; GBP 1.20 newsstand/cover. adv. back issues avail. **Document type:** *Newspaper, Consumer.* **Description:** Lists jobs and vacancies nationwide.
Published by: Trinity Newspapers Southern Ltd., 50-56 Portman Rd, Reading, Berks RG30 1EA, United Kingdom. TEL 44-118-949-0060, FAX 44-118-949-0061. Pub. Peter Thorp. Adv. contact Martin Gardner. **Subscr. to:** Customer Interface Ltd., Bradley Pavilions, Bradley Stoke, N Bristol BS32 0PP, United Kingdom. TEL 44-1454-620070. **Dist. by:** M M C Ltd., Octagon House, White Hart Meadows, Ripley, Woking, Surrey GU23 6HR, United Kingdom. TEL 44-1483-211222, FAX 44-1483-211731.

371.42 DEU
JOBTIPP. Text in German. 1998. 2/yr. adv. **Document type:** *Magazine, Consumer.*
Published by: Hutt Verlag, Unterhaeuser Str 1, Stuttgart, 70597, Germany. TEL 49-711-767150, FAX 49-711-7671511, info@hutt-verlag.de, http://www.hutt-verlag.de. adv.: B&W page EUR 2,750, color page EUR 3,290. Circ: 60,000 (controlled).

331.1 NZL ISSN 1176-9319
JOBWEEK. Text in English. 2005. bi-w. free (effective 2009). **Document type:** *Newspaper, Consumer.*
Address: Beckenham, PO Box 12-106, Christchurch, 8242, New Zealand. TEL 64-3-3316310, FAX 64-3-3316272, admin@jobweek.co.nz, http://jobweek.co.nz.

JONG EN AMBTENAAR. *see* PUBLIC ADMINISTRATION

JOURNAL FOR THE PROFESSIONAL COUNSELOR. *see* EDUCATION

JOURNAL OF CAREER ASSESSMENT. *see* PSYCHOLOGY

371.42 USA ISSN 0894-8453
LC1037.5
➤ **JOURNAL OF CAREER DEVELOPMENT.** Text in English. 1972. bi-m. USD 654, GBP 385 combined subscription to institutions (print & online eds.); USD 641, GBP 377 to institutions (effective 2011). adv. bk.rev. bibl.; charts; illus.; stat. index. reprint service avail. from PSC. **Document type:** *Journal, Academic/Scholarly.* **Description:** Covers career education, adult career development, career development of special-needs population, and career and leisure, focusing on impact of theory and research on practice.
Formerly (until 1984): Journal of Career Education (0164-2502)
Related titles: Microform ed.: (from PQC); Online - full text ed.: ISSN 1573-3548. USD 589, GBP 347 to institutions (effective 2011) (from IngentaConnect).
Indexed: A12, A13, A20, A22, A26, ABIn, ABS&EES, ASCA, B01, B02, B04, B07, B17, B18, BRD, BibLing, BusEdI, CA, CPE, CurCont, E-psyche, E01, E02, E03, E07, E08, E09, E10, EAA, ERI, ERIC, EdA, EdI, FamI, G04, G08, HEA, HRA, I05, IBR, IBZ, P03, P10, P18, P21, P25, P30, P48, P51, P53, P54, PQC, PsycInfo, PsycholAb, S02, S03, S09, SCOPUS, SSCI, SWR&A, T&DA, T02, W03, W05, W07.
—BLDSC (4954.876000), IE, Infotrieve, Ingenta. **CCC.**
Published by: Sage Publications, Inc., 2455 Teller Rd, Thousand Oaks, CA 91320. TEL 805-499-9774, FAX 805-499-0871, info@sagepub.com. Ed. Lisa Y Flores. adv.: B&W page USD 385, color page USD 775; 4.5 x 7.5. **Subscr. to:** Sage Publications Ltd., 1 Oliver's Yard, 55 City Rd, London EC1Y 1SP, United Kingdom. TEL 44-20-73248701, FAX 44-20-73248733, subscription@sagepub.co.uk.

▼ ➤ **THE JOURNAL OF CAREER EDUCATION PRINCIPLES AND PRACTICES.** *see* EDUCATION—Adult Education

331 USA ISSN 1544-0893
HF5549.5.E42
JOURNAL OF EMPLOYEE ASSISTANCE. Text in English. 1973. q. **Document type:** *Journal, Trade.*
Formerly (until 2003): E A P Association Exchange (1085-0856)
Related titles: Online - full text ed.
Indexed: A26, B02, B11, B15, B17, B18, CWI, E08, G04, G06, G07, G08, I05, S09.

N O

Published by: Employee Assistance Professionals Association, 2101 Wilson Blvd, Ste 500, Arlington, VA 22201-3062. TEL 703-387-1000, FAX 703-522-4585.

JOURNAL OF EMPLOYMENT COUNSELING. *see* PSYCHOLOGY

371.42 RUS
KAR'ERA. Text in Russian. m.
Related titles: Online - full text ed.: ISSN 1684-8365.
Published by: Izdatel'skii Dom Rodionova, ul B Andron'evskaya 17, Moscow, 109544, Russian Federation. Ed. Andrei Moskalenko. Pub. Aleksandr Zotikov. Circ: 80,000.

371.42 RUS
KAR'ERA - KAPITAL. Text in Russian. w.
Address: Ul Vyborgskaya 16, Moscow, 152212, Russian Federation. TEL 7-095-9563461, FAX 7-095-9560716. Ed. Aleksandr Gubskii.

371.42 DEU
KARRIERE; das junge Job- und Wirtschaftsmagazin. Text in German. 1987. m. EUR 32.40 (effective 2011). adv. **Document type:** *Magazine, Consumer.* **Description:** Contains articles and features on occupations and careers available to young professionals.
Formerly: Junge Karriere (1436-1469)
Published by: Verlagsgruppe Handelsblatt GmbH, Grafenberger Allee 293, Duesseldorf, 40237, Germany. TEL 49-211-8870, FAX 49-211-371792, leser-service@vhb.de, http://www.fachverlag.de. Ed. Joern Huesgen. adv.: page EUR 14,024; trim 210 x 280. Circ: 121,494 (paid and controlled).

331.1 DEU ISSN 1435-327X
KARRIEREFUEHRER BAUINGENIEURE; Berufseinstieg fuer Hochschulabsolventen. Text in German. 1987. a. adv. **Document type:** *Magazine, Trade.*
Published by: Transmedia Verlagsgesellschaft mbH, Weyertal 59, Cologne, 50937, Germany. TEL 49-221-4722300, FAX 49-221-4722370, info@karrierefuehrer.de, http://www.karrierefuehrer.de. adv.: color page EUR 4,444; trim 185 x 268. Circ: 12,000 (controlled).

331.1 DEU ISSN 1435-3261
KARRIEREFUEHRER FINANZDIENSTLEISTUNGEN; Berufseinstieg fuer Hochschulabsolventen. Text in German. 1987. a. adv. **Document type:** *Magazine, Trade.*
Published by: Transmedia Verlagsgesellschaft mbH, Weyertal 59, Cologne, 50937, Germany. TEL 49-221-4722300, FAX 49-221-4722370, info@karrierefuehrer.de, http://www.karrierefuehrer.de. adv.: color page EUR 4,444; trim 185 x 268. Circ: 20,000 (controlled).

331.1 DEU ISSN 1435-1978
KARRIEREFUEHRER HOCHSCHULEN; Berufseinstieg fuer Hochschulabsolventen. Text in German. 1987. a. adv. **Document type:** *Magazine, Trade.*
Formerly (until 1993): Karrierefuehrer Fachhochschulen (0934-4039)
Published by: Transmedia Verlagsgesellschaft mbH, Weyertal 59, Cologne, 50937, Germany. TEL 49-221-4722300, FAX 49-221-4722370, info@karrierefuehrer.de, http://www.karrierefuehrer.de. adv.: color page EUR 4,444; trim 140 x 200. Circ: 35,000 (paid and controlled).

331.1 DEU ISSN 1436-2139
KARRIEREFUEHRER INFORMATIONSTECHNOLOGIE; Berufseinstieg fuer Hochschulabsolventen. Text in German. 1998. a. adv. **Document type:** *Magazine, Trade.*
Published by: Transmedia Verlagsgesellschaft mbH, Weyertal 59, Cologne, 50937, Germany. TEL 49-221-4722300, FAX 49-221-4722370, info@karrierefuehrer.de, http://www.karrierefuehrer.de. adv.: color page EUR 4,444; trim 185 x 268. Circ: 20,000 (paid and controlled).

331.1 DEU
KARRIEREFUEHRER LIFE SCIENCES; Berufseinstieg fuer Hochschulabsolventen. Text in German. a. adv. **Document type:** *Magazine, Trade.*
Published by: Transmedia Verlagsgesellschaft mbH, Weyertal 59, Cologne, 50937, Germany. TEL 49-221-4722300, FAX 49-221-4722370, info@karrierefuehrer.de, http://www.karrierefuehrer.de. adv.: color page EUR 4,444; trim 185 x 268. Circ: 20,000 (paid and controlled).

331.1 DEU
KARRIEREFUEHRER RECHT; Berufseinstieg fuer Hochschulabsolventen. Text in German. 1987. a. adv. **Document type:** *Magazine, Trade.*
Published by: Transmedia Verlagsgesellschaft mbH, Weyertal 59, Cologne, 50937, Germany. TEL 49-221-4722300, FAX 49-221-4722370, info@karrierefuehrer.de, http://www.karrierefuehrer.de. adv.: color page EUR 4,444; trim 185 x 268. Circ: 20,000 (paid and controlled).

KEY NOTE MARKET ASSESSMENT. E-RECRUITMENT. *see* BUSINESS AND ECONOMICS—Production Of Goods And Services

KEY NOTE MARKET ASSESSMENT. I T RECRUITMENT. *see* BUSINESS AND ECONOMICS—Production Of Goods And Services

KIDS' ACTING FOR BRAIN SURGEONS; the insiders guide for kids in the industry. *see* CHILDREN AND YOUTH—For

331.1 SVK ISSN 1337-0367
KNIHA INFORMATIKOV. Text in Slovak. 2006. s-a. **Document type:** *Trade.*
Media: Online - full content.
Published by: Jobagent.sk, s.r.o., Bojnicka 10, Bratislava, 823 65, Slovakia. TEL 421-903-197179, obchod@jobagent.sk, http://www.jobagent.sk.

331.1 USA
KNOW: THE MAGAZINE FOR PARALEGALS. Text in English. 2008. bi-m. USD 35 (effective 2008). **Document type:** *Magazine, Trade.* **Description:** Carries information on how to balance work and related responsibilities with lifestyle. Aims to help with responsibility for purchasing decisions in such areas as depositions, e-discovery, litigation support, office supplies, travel and electronics and software.
Published by: Knowledge Networks, Inc., 11271 Ventura Blvd, Ste 411, Studio City, CA 91604. TEL 888-803-8807. Circ: 10,000 (paid).

331.1 694 684 NLD ISSN 1875-4880
KRUL. Text in Dutch. 1977. 8/yr. EUR 20; free to qualified personnel (effective 2010). adv. **Document type:** *Magazine, Trade.*
Supersedes in part (in 2008): F N V Bouw Magazine (1570-1395); Which was formerly (until 2002): F N V Magazine. F N V Bouw (1567-682X); (until 2000): F N V Magazine. Bouw- en Houtbond F N V (0924-204X); (until 1988): F N V Magazine. Profiel (0169-5045); (until 1985): Profiel (Woerden) (0166-7548); Which was formed by the merger of (1972-1976): Steiger (Woerden) (0926-6739); Which was formed by the merger of (1921-1972): Op de Steiger (0926-6747); (1911-1972): Bondsblad (Utrecht) (0926-6755); (1920-1976): Bouwer (Amsterdam) (0926-6720); Which was formed by the merger of (1890-1920): Timmerman (Amsterdam) (0926-6704); (1908-1920): Bouwvakarbeider (Amsterdam) (0926-6712)
Published by: (F N V Meubel en Hout), F N V Bouw, Postbus 520, Woerden, 3440 AM, Netherlands. TEL 31-348-575575, FAX 31-348-423610, info@fnvbouw.nl, http://www.fnvbouw.nl. Ed. Peter van der Aa. adv.: color page EUR 1,600; trim 230 x 300. Circ: 12,000.

331.1 CAN ISSN 1910-2887
LABOUR FORCE STATISTICS. ABORIGINAL POPULATION OFF-RESERVE PACKAGE. Text in English. 200?. m. **Document type:** *Report, Trade.*
Media: Online - full text.
Published by: Alberta Human Resources and Employment, 324 Legislature Bldg, 10800 - 97 Ave, Edmonton, AB T5K 2B6, Canada. TEL 780-415-4800, FAX 780-422-9556, ahre.communications@gov.ab.ca, http://www.hre.gov.ab.ca/cps/rde/xchg/hre/hs.xsl/563.html.

331.1 CAN ISSN 1910-2828
LABOUR MARKET BULLETIN. NEW BRUNSWICK REGION. Text in English, French. 2001. bi-m. **Document type:** *Newsletter, Trade.*
Formerly (until 2005): Labour Market Bulletin. Pan-Canadian Activities, New Brunswick Region (1910-281X)
Published by: Public Works and Government Services Canada/Travaux Publics et Services Gouvernementaux Canada, Place du Portage, Phase III, 11 Laurier St, Gatineau, PQ K1A 0S5, Canada. TEL 800-622-6232, Questions@pwgsc.gc.ca, http://www.pwgsc.gc.ca/text/home-e.html.

331.1 CAN ISSN 1718-5521
LABOUR MARKET MONTHLY. Text in English. 2002. m. **Document type:** *Newsletter, Trade.*
Formed by the 2006 merger of: Nova Scotia Labour Market (1716-673X); (2002-2006): Employment Situation (1910-863X)
Published by: Nova Scotia, Department of Finance, PO Box 187, Halifax, NS B3J 2N3, Canada. TEL 902-424-5554, FAX 902-434-0635.

658.3 USA ISSN 2154-5804
▼ **LAMP LIGHTER.** Text in English. 2009. bi-m. free (effective 2010). back issues avail. **Document type:** *Newsletter, Trade.* **Description:** Provides information on landing jobs and finding business opportunities.
Media: Online - full text.
Published by: Empowering Today's Professionals Press, PO Box 1213, Jackson, NJ 08527. TEL 732-367-5580, info@etpnetwork.com, http://www.etpnetwork.com. Ed. Adelaida Rodriguez.

371.42 GBR ISSN 1752-2765
LEARNING AND DEVELOPMENT. Text in English. 2006. q. GBP 439.24 domestic to non-members; GBP 490 foreign to non-members; GBP 394.32 domestic to members; GBP 445 foreign to members (effective 2010); includes online access. back issues avail. **Document type:** *Journal, Trade.* **Description:** Covers every area of training, learning and development, suitable for all industry sectors and sizes.
Related titles: Online - full text ed.: ISSN 1752-2773.
Published by: Chartered Institute of Personnel and Development, 151 The Broadway, London, SW19 1JQ, United Kingdom. TEL 44-20-86126200, FAX 44-20-86126201.

331.1 SWE ISSN 0024-0230
LEDIGA PLATSER. Text in Swedish. 1961. 40/yr. SEK 220 (effective 1991). adv. bk.rev.
Former titles (until vol.17, 1962): Lediga Platser foer Ingenjoerer och Administratoerer; (until vol.16, 1961): Lediga Platser foer Tekniker och Ingenjoerer
Address: Fack 1335, Orebro, 70113, Sweden. Ed. John H Larsson. Circ: 12,500.

371.42 CAN ISSN 1718-3545
LEXPERT LAW STUDENT AND ASSOCIATE RECRUITMENT GUIDE. Text in English. 2006. a. **Document type:** *Handbook/Manual/Guide, Trade.*
Published by: Carswell (Subsidiary of: Thomson Reuters Corp.), One Corporate Plz, 2075 Kennedy Rd, Toronto, ON M1T 3V4, Canada. TEL 416-609-8000, 800-387-5164, FAX 416-298-5094, carswell.customerrelations@thomson.com, http://www.carswell.com.

371.42 DEU ISSN 1612-927X
LIFE AND SCIENCE. Text in German. 2003. q. EUR 12.50; EUR 3.50 newsstand/cover (effective 2010). adv. **Document type:** *Journal, Academic/Scholarly.*
Published by: Klett MINT GmbH, Rotebuehlstr 77, Stuttgart, 70178, Germany. TEL 49-711-66720, http://www.klett-mint.de. Ed. Angelika Mathes. Circ: 199,878 (paid and controlled).

LIFESTYLES & CAREER CHOICES. *see* LIFESTYLE

331.1 NLD ISSN 1879-9663
▼ **LOOPBAANVISIE.** Text in Dutch. 2010. q. EUR 28.50 (effective 2010). adv. **Document type:** *Magazine, Trade.*
Published by: Uitgeverij Kloosterhof Acquisitie Services, Napoleonsweg 128a, Neer, 6086 AJ, Netherlands. TEL 31-475-597151, FAX 31-475-597153, info@kloosterhof.nl, http://www.kloosterhof.nl. adv.: color page EUR 895.

371.42 USA ISSN 2161-2307
HF5382.5.U5
LOVICK MINORITY CAREER JOURNAL. Text in English. 19??. bi-m. USD 25 (effective 2011). **Document type:** *Journal, Trade.*
Related titles: Online - full text ed.: free (effective 2011).
Published by: Calvin Lovick, Ed. & Pub., PO Box 91262, Los Angeles, CA 90009. TEL 424-227-8318, lovickcareer1@aol.com.

M I E. JOURNAL. (Montigny Initiative Emploi) *see* BUSINESS AND ECONOMICS—Labor And Industrial Relations

331.1 410 USA
M L A JOB INFORMATION LISTS. Abbreviated title: J I L. Text in English. 1971. q. free to members (effective 2010). reprints avail. **Document type:** *Directory, Trade.* **Description:** Lists available college teaching positions in English, comparative literature, linguistics and foreign languages.
Related titles: Online - full text ed.
Published by: Modern Language Association of America, 26 Broadway, 3rd Fl, New York, NY 10004. TEL 646-576-5000, FAX 646-458-0030, execdirector@mla.org. Circ: 6,000.

M U F A C E. *see* PUBLIC ADMINISTRATION—Municipal Government

331.1 USA
MANAGING YOUR CAREER. Text in English. q. **Document type:** *Bulletin.*
Published by: Dow Jones & Company (Subsidiary of: News Corporation), 1 World Financial Ctr, 200 Liberty St, New York, NY 10281. TEL 212-416-2000, http://www.dowjones.com. Ed. Robert Thomson.

331.1 NZL ISSN 1176-905X
MANPOWER EMPLOYMENT OUTLOOK SURVEY. NEW ZEALAND. Text in English. 2004. q. **Document type:** *Report, Trade.* **Description:** Measure employers' intentions to increase or decrease the number of employees in their workforces during the next quarter.
Related titles: Online - full text ed.: free.
Published by: Manpower Inc., Level 5, 8 Willis St, Wellington, New Zealand. TEL 64-4-4941000, FAX 64-4-4941009, wellington@manpowerprofessional.co.nz.

MARKT UND CHANCE - BEWERBERPROFILE. *see* SOCIAL SERVICES AND WELFARE

MASTER THE CIVIL SERVICE EXAMS. *see* EDUCATION—Adult Education

371.42 363.2 USA ISSN 1939-6988
HV8143
MASTER THE POLICE OFFICER EXAM. Text in English. 1981. irreg., latest 17th ed. USD 10.87 per issue (effective 2009). **Document type:** *Handbook/Manual/Guide, Trade.*
Formerly (until 2005): Police Officer (1530-003X)
Published by: Thomson Peterson's (Subsidiary of: Thomson Reuters Corp.), Princeton Pike Corporate Center, 2000 Lenox Dr, 3rd Fl, PO Box 67005, Lawrenceville, NJ 08648. TEL 609-896-1800, 800-338-3282 ext 54229, FAX 609-896-4531, custsvc@petersons.com, http://www.petersons.com.

371.42 USA ISSN 1930-4803
HE6499
MASTER THE POSTAL EXAMS. Text in English. 19??. irreg. (7th ed.). USD 12.71 per issue (effective 2008). **Document type:** *Handbook/Manual/Guide, Trade.* **Description:** Provides guidance for those considering a career with the U.S. postal service.
Former titles (until 2005): Postal Exams; (until 2000): Everything You Need to Score High on Postal Exams
Published by: Thomson Peterson's (Subsidiary of: Thomson Reuters Corp.), Princeton Pike Corporate Center, 2000 Lenox Dr, 3rd Fl, PO Box 67005, Lawrenceville, NJ 08648. TEL 609-896-1800, 800-338-3282 ext 54229, FAX 609-896-4531, custsvc@petersons.com, http://www.petersons.com.

371.42 USA ISSN 1930-6512
HV8143
MASTER THE STATE TROOPER EXAMS. Text in English. 2006. irreg., latest 15th ed. USD 12.91 per issue (effective 2008). **Document type:** *Handbook/Manual/Guide, Trade.* **Description:** Designed to help aspiring state troopers to prepare for the qualifying exams.
Former titles (until 2006): State Trooper Exam; (until 2001): State Trooper, Highway Patrol Officer/State Traffic Officer; (until1988): State Trooper, Highway Patrolman, Ranger
Published by: Thomson Peterson's (Subsidiary of: Thomson Reuters Corp.), Princeton Pike Corporate Center, 2000 Lenox Dr, 3rd Fl, PO Box 67005, Lawrenceville, NJ 08648. TEL 609-896-1800, 800-338-3282 ext 54229, FAX 609-896-4531, custsvc@petersons.com, http://www.petersons.com.

MATERIALIEN ZUR BERUFS- UND ARBEITSPAEDAGOGIK. *see* EDUCATION

MEDICAL INDUSTRY E-MAIL NEWS SERVICE. *see* MEDICAL SCIENCES

331.1 NLD ISSN 2210-4992
▼ **MINKS MAGAZINE.** Text in Dutch. 2010. q.
Published by: Minks Groep, W M Dudokweg 27, Heerhugowaard, 1703 DA, Netherlands. TEL 31-72-5728371, FAX 31-72-5728372, info@minksgroep.nl, http://www.minksgroep.nl.

371.42 610.73 USA
MINORITY NURSE; the career and education resource for minority nursing professionals, students and faculty. Text in English. 1993. q. USD 19.95; free to qualified personnel (effective 2010). adv. **Document type:** *Magazine, Trade.* **Description:** Addresses career concerns of minority nursing professionals and the unique challenges and opportunities for these professionals.
Former titles (until 1999): M N; (until 1998): Minority Nurse (1076-7223)
Related titles: Online - full text ed.
Indexed: C06, C07, C08, CINAHL.
—BLDSC (5810.553734).
Published by: Career Recruitment Media, Inc., 211 W Wacker Dr, Ste 900, Chicago, IL 60606. TEL 312-525-3100, info@careermedia.com, http://www.careermedia.com/. Ed. Pam Chwedyk. Adv. contact Peter Fuhrman TEL 609-689-1033.

371.42 GBR ISSN 1748-9202
MINT (LONDON). Text in English. 2004. s-a. GBP 11.50; GBP 6.50 per issue (effective 2009). **Document type:** *Magazine, Consumer.* **Description:** Careers and opportunities magazine for female students aged between 16-19 years old.
—CCC.
Published by: Arberry Pink, 57 Poland St, London, W1F 7NW, United Kingdom. TEL 44-20-74399100, FAX 44-20-74399101, media@arberrypink.co.uk, http://www.arberrypink.co.uk/.

371.42 659.152 USA ISSN 1061-4737
MODEL CALL. Text in English. 1991. q. USD 14. adv. **Document type:** *Journal, Trade.* **Description:** Covers the business activities of professional models and talents who work in advertising print media.
Published by: Richard Poirier Model and Talent Agency, 3575 Cahuenga Blvd W, 254, Los Angeles, CA 90068-1341. TEL 213-969-9990, FAX 213-850-3382. Circ: 20,000.

MODEL SCENE MAGAZINE; models, entertainment & lifestyles. *see* CLOTHING TRADE—Fashions

331 SVK ISSN 1336-9687
MOJA KARIERA. Text in Slovak. 2006. d. adv. **Document type:** *Trade.*

Media: Online - full content.
Published by: Infokariera, Kpt Nalepku 13, Kosice, 040 01, Slovakia. TEL 421-911-251883. Ed., Pub. Marian Jalc.

331.1 NLD ISSN 1872-6569
MR MAGAZINE. Text in Dutch. 1985. 10/yr. EUR 88.50 (effective 2009). adv. **Document type:** *Magazine, Trade.*
Formerly (until 2006): School en Medezeggenschap (0921-2914)
Published by: Kluwer B.V. (Subsidiary of: Wolters Kluwer N.V.), Postbus 23, Deventer, 7400 GA, Netherlands. TEL 31-570-673555, FAX 31-570-691555, info@kluwer.nl. Ed. Leonie de Bruin. adv.: page EUR 1,275; bleed 210 x 297. Circ: 5,200.

371.42 ZAF ISSN 0027-5425
MY CAREER; biennial publication on employment and skills development information. Text in English. 1950. biennial. free. abstr.; bibl.; charts. index, cum.index. **Document type:** *Government.* **Description:** Intended for juvenile counseling agents in the field of employment and skills development.
Indexed: ISAP.
Published by: Department of Labour/Departement van Arbeid, Private Bag X117, Pretoria, 0001, South Africa. TEL 27-12-309-4246, FAX 27-12-309-4247. Ed. L Dumon. Circ: 45,000 (controlled).

N A C E JOURNAL. *see* BUSINESS AND ECONOMICS—Labor And Industrial Relations

371.42 USA
LB2343.5
N A C E NATIONAL DIRECTORY. Text in English. 1985. a. **Document type:** *Directory, Trade.* **Description:** Contains information on 2,200 colleges, 2,100 employers and 9,400 personnel people in the field. Includes names, addresses, phone numbers, interview schedules, and minority enrollments.
Formerly: C P C National Directory (8755-8378)
Published by: National Association of Colleges and Employers, 62 Highland Ave, Bethlehem, PA 18017. TEL 610-868-1421, 800-544-5272, FAX 610-868-0208, customer_service@naceweb.org, http://www.naceweb.org.

▼ **N C V E R MONOGRAPH SERIES.** (National Centre for Vocational Education Research) *see* EDUCATION—Adult Education

N S B E BRIDGE. *see* ENGINEERING

371.42 USA ISSN 1093-5738
BF318.5
N S E E QUARTERLY. Text in English. 1973. q. free to members (effective 2005). adv. bk.rev. back issues avail. **Document type:** *Magazine, Consumer.* **Description:** Covers college and K-12 programs for experiential education, internships, community-service learning, field education, cooperative education, community-based learning, and action research.
Formerly (until 199?): Experiential Education (0739-2338)
Published by: National Society for Experiential Education, c/o Talley Management Group, Inc, 19 Mantua Rd, Mt Royal, NJ 08061. TEL 856-423-3427, FAX 856-423-3420, info@nsee.org, http://www.nsee.org. Ed. Mark Andrew Clark. Circ: 2,000.

371.42 CHN ISSN 1008-5327
NANTONG ZHIYE DAXUE XUEBAO/NANTONG VOCATIONAL COLLEGE. JOURNAL. Text in Chinese. 1987. q. CNY 5 newsstand/cover (effective 2006). **Document type:** *Journal, Academic/Scholarly.*
Published by: Nantong Zhiye Daxue, 28, Jiaoyu Lu, Nantong, 226007, China. TEL 86-513-3560064 ext 8065.

331.1 USA ISSN 1051-4872
HF5382.5.U5
THE NATIONAL JOBBANK. Text in English. 1983. a. USD 475 per issue (effective 2009). adv. back issues avail. **Document type:** *Directory, Trade.* **Description:** Aims job seekers. Contains profiles over 21,000 companies nationwide.
Related titles: CD-ROM ed.
Published by: Adams Media (Subsidiary of: F + W Media Inc.), 4700 E Galbraith Rd, Cincinnati, OH 45236. TEL 513-531-2690, FAX 800-258-0929, deskcopies@adamsmedia.com, http://www.adamsmedia.com. Pub. Bob Adams.

371.42 378.02 USA ISSN 1524-7473
THE NEXT STEP MAGAZINE; college - careers - life. Text in English. 1995. 5/yr. USD 15.95 (effective 2006). adv. **Document type:** *Magazine, Consumer.* **Description:** Offers high-school students advice on planning for college, career, and life.
Related titles: Online - full text ed.
Indexed: B04, BRD, DYW, ENW, R03, RGAb, RGPR, W03, W05.
—CCC.
Published by: Next Step Magazine, 86 W Main St, Victor, NY 14564-0405. TEL 716-742-1260, FAX 716-742-1263, feedback@nextstepmag.com. Ed. Luisa Cordaro. Adv. contact Dave Mammano.

371.42 JPN
NIKKEI PLACEMENT GUIDE. Text in Japanese. a. **Document type:** *Directory.* **Description:** Provides detailed information for college seniors on job opportunities by corporation.
Published by: Nihon Keizai Shimbun Inc., 1-9-5 Ote-Machi, Chiyoda-ku, Tokyo, 100-0004, Japan. TEL 81-3-32700251, FAX 81-3-52552661.

NO LIMITS; life after high school in Wisconsin. *see* CHILDREN AND YOUTH—About

371.42 331.259 NLD ISSN 1879-4890
DE NOBILES CARRIERE- EN TRAINEESHIPGIDS. Text in Dutch. 2007. a.
Formerly (until 2009): Nobiles Carrieregids (1876-732X); Which was formed by the merger of (1993-2007): Nobiles Ingenieursgids (1385-075X); Which was formerly (until 1992): Toekomstperspectief. Ingenieurs (0927-040X); (1991-1991): Toekomstperspectief. Technici (0927-4154); (1992-2007): Nobiles Economengids (1385-0687); Which was formerly (1990-1992): Toekomstperspectief. Academici (0926-5562)
Published by: Nobiles Media, Postbus 1542, Amsterdam, 1000 BM, Netherlands. TEL 31-20-6231800, info@nobiles.nl, http://www.nobiles.nl.

NOTA WERKEN IN HET ONDERWIJS. *see* EDUCATION

371.42 CAN ISSN 1914-1394
NOVA SCOTIA. APPRENTICESHIP TRAINING AND SKILL DEVELOPMENT. ANNUAL REPORT. Text in English. 199?. a.
Formerly (until 2003): Nova Scotia. Department of Education. Apprenticeship Training Division. Annual Report (1914-1386)
Published by: Nova Scotia, Apprenticeship Training and Skill Development Division, PO Box 578, Halifax, NS B3J 2S9, Canada. TEL 902-424-5168, FAX 902-424-0511.

371.4 340 USA ISSN 1059-6445
KF299.G6
NOW HIRING; government jobs for lawyers. Text in English. 1984. a. USD 19.95 to non-members; USD 14.95 to members. adv. **Document type:** *Magazine, Trade.*
Published by: American Bar Association, Law Student Division, 321 N Clark St, Chicago, IL 60610. TEL 312-988-5522. Ed. Stephanie Johnston. R&P Richard Vittenson TEL 312-988-6101. Adv. contact Michael Loquercio.

371.42 GBR ISSN 1740-5998
NUMBER TEN; inspiring careers for women. Text in English. 199?. s-a. GBP 11.50; GBP 6.50 per issue (effective 2009). adv. back issues avail. **Document type:** *Magazine, Consumer.* **Description:** Contains career advice and opportunities, humor and graduate lifestyle concerns.
Related titles: Online - full text ed.: free to members (effective 2009).
—CCC.
Published by: Arberry Pink, 57 Poland St, London, W1F 7NW, United Kingdom. TEL 44-20-74399100, FAX 44-20-74399101, media@arberrypink.co.uk, http://www.arberrypink.co.uk/. Ed. Laura Sheed. Pub. Chris Hollins.

O-HAYO SENSEI; the newsletter of English teaching jobs in Japan. *see* EDUCATION—International Education Programs

371.42 RUS
OBRAZOVANIE I KAR'ERA. Text in Russian. 26/yr. USD 145 in United States.
Published by: Rabota dlya Vas, Krasnokholmskaya nab 13-15, Moscow, 109172, Russian Federation. TEL 7-095-9111538, FAX 7-095-9113815. Ed. V A Grigorov. **Dist. by:** East View Information Services, 10601 Wayzata Blvd, Minneapolis, MN 55305. TEL 952-252-1201, 800-477-1005, FAX 952-252-1202, info@eastview.com, http://www.eastview.com.

OCCUPATIONAL PROGRAMS IN CALIFORNIA PUBLIC COMMUNITY COLLEGES. *see* EDUCATION—Guides To Schools And Colleges

OFFENDER EMPLOYMENT REPORT. *see* CRIMINOLOGY AND LAW ENFORCEMENT

OFFICIAL GUIDE TO DENTAL SCHOOLS. *see* MEDICAL SCIENCES—Dentistry

331 384.5443 USA
ON-AIR JOB TIPSHEET. Text in English. w. USD 35 per month domestic; USD 85 per quarter domestic (effective 2001). **Document type:** *Journal, Trade.* **Description:** Lists current job openings in the radio broadcasting industry.
Related titles: E-mail ed.
Address: 542 Ingalton Ave, West Chicago, IL 60185. TEL 630-231-7937, 800-231-7940, info@onairjobtipsheet.com, http://onairjobtipsheet.com.

ONDERNEMEN IN DE SECTOREN. *see* BUSINESS AND ECONOMICS—Management

371.42 USA ISSN 1550-347X
➤ **ONLINE JOURNAL FOR WORKFORCE EDUCATION AND DEVELOPMENT.** Text in English. 2003. 3/yr. free (effective 2010). back issues avail. **Document type:** *Journal, Academic/Scholarly.* **Description:** Contains original papers from practitioners and researchers on current research, promising practices, and significant issues and problems in workforce education. Also provides a forum for discourse on critical issues in workforce, career, and technical education, including training and development. Audience includes: faculty and students in schools, colleges, and universities; human resource developers in corporate, military and professional fields; researchers; and other specialists in workforce, career, and technical education, including training and development.
Media: Online - full text.
Published by: Southern Illinois University Carbondale. Department of Workforce Education and Development, 475 Clocktower Dr., Pulliam Hall, Rm.212, Mailcode 4605, Carbondale, IL 62901-4605. TEL 618-453-3321, FAX 618-453-1909, http://wed.siu.edu/public1/.

➤ **OPPORTUNITIES FOR MINORITY STUDENTS IN THE U S DENTAL SCHOOLS.** *see* EDUCATION—Higher Education

351 USA ISSN 1065-0121
JK716
OPPORTUNITIES IN PUBLIC AFFAIRS. Text in English. 1990. bi-m. USD 129 to individuals; USD 189 to institutions (effective 2005). **Document type:** *Directory, Consumer.*
Published by: Brubach Enterprises Inc., PO Box 34949, Bethesda, MD 20827. TEL 800-315-9777, FAX 434-984-2331, http://www.brubach.com.

331.1 658 NLD ISSN 1572-4840
OR RENDEMENT. (OndernemingsRaad) Text in Dutch. 2004. m. (11/yr.). EUR 239; EUR 24 newsstand/cover (effective 2010). adv.
Related titles: ◆ Supplement(s): Dossier OR Rendement. ISSN 1871-6350.
Published by: Rendement Uitgeverij BV (Subsidiary of: Springer Netherlands), Postbus 27020, Rotterdam, 3003 LA, Netherlands. TEL 31-10-2433933, FAX 31-10-2439028. Pub. Marnix Hoogerwerf. Adv. contact Ralph Pennenburg. B&W page EUR 2,100; trim 210 x 297. Circ: 8,000.

371.42 658.3 USA ISSN 0734-1776
ORGANIZE YOUR LUCK!. Text in English. 1976. 10/yr. free. adv. bk.rev. **Document type:** *Newsletter, Consumer.* **Description:** Assists people in finding, getting and keeping their jobs through self-marketing methods.
Related titles: Talking Book ed.
—CCC.
Published by: Behavioral Images, Inc., 302 Leland St, Ste 101, Bloomington, IL 61701-5646. TEL 309-829-3931, FAX 309-829-9677. Ed. Stephen C Johnson. Circ: 3,000 (paid).

371.42 CAN ISSN 0833-0530
L'ORIENTATION. Text in English, French. 1964. 3/yr. CAD 30 to individuals; CAD 40 to institutions. adv. bk.rev. charts. cum.index.
Formerly (until 1987): Orientation Professionnelle - Vocational Guidance (0030-5413)
Indexed: ISAP, PdeR.
Published by: Ordre Professionnel des Conseillers et Conseilleres d'Orientation du Quebec, 1100 ave, Beaumont, PQ H3P 3H5, Canada. TEL 514-737-4717. Ed. Louise Landry. Circ: 2,500.

331.1 NLD
OTTO WORK FORCE. Text in Dutch. s-a.
Published by: (OTTO Work Force), EFKA Uitgevers bv, Postbus 155, Weert, 6000 AD, Netherlands. TEL 31-495-450105, FAX 31-495-539485, info@efka-uitgevers.nl, http://www.efka-uitgevers.nl. Circ: 10,000.

371.42 AUS ISSN 1838-6679
OZSTARS. Text in English. 19??. m. **Document type:** *Bulletin, Consumer.*
Formerly (until 2010): ReEmploy Resolutions
Related titles: Online - full text ed.
Published by: Ostara P R A Employment Service, Level 11, 1 Lawson Sq, Redfern, NSW 2016, Australia. TEL 61-2-96908900, FAX 61-2-96995188, info@pra.org.au, http://www.pra.org.au/services/employment.html.

371.42 658 USA
P B L BUSINESS LEADER. Text in English. 1991. 3/yr. membership. adv. **Document type:** *Magazine, Trade.*
Published by: (Phi Beta Lambda), Future Business Leaders of America - Phi Beta Lambda, 1912 Association Dr, Reston, VA 20191-1591. TEL 703-860-3334. Ed. Betty Penzer. Pub. Jean M Buckley. Circ: 15,500.

331.125 ESP ISSN 1138-8722
PAPELES DE FORMACION; revista divulgativa de formacion continua. Text in Spanish. 1997. m. **Document type:** *Magazine, Trade.*
Published by: Planificacion y Formacion, San Ignacio 2, Seville, 41080, Spain. TEL 34-95-4574434, FAX 34-95-4576237, planiform@interbook.net.

PARENTHOOD & CAREERS. *see* LIFESTYLE

331.1 658.3 GBR ISSN 1465-3796
PAY MAGAZINE. Text in English. 1990. m. GBP 118 domestic; GBP 120 foreign; GBP 28.75 per issue (effective 2010). adv. software rev. illus.; stat.; tr.lit. back issues avail. **Document type:** *Journal, Trade.* **Description:** Publishes information concerning employment in the United Kingdom.
Former titles (until 1998): Gee's Pay Monthly (1358-9873); (until 1994): Pay (1356-708X)
Related titles: Online - full text ed.
—CCC.
Published by: Croner C C H Group Ltd. (Subsidiary of: Wolters Kluwer UK Ltd.), 145 London Rd, Kingston upon Thames, Surrey KT2 6SR, United Kingdom. TEL 44-20-85473333, FAX 44-20-85472638, info@croner.co.uk, http://www.croner.co.uk. Ed. Cathy Heys TEL 44-1903-219131. Pub. Mark Cleeve TEL 44-20-82471427. Adv. contact Nick Pye TEL 44-20-82471350.

PERSONA. *see* BUSINESS AND ECONOMICS

658.3 SWE
PERSONALAKTUELLT. Text in Swedish. 5/yr. adv. **Document type:** *Magazine, Trade.*
Formerly (until 2004): LoeneAktuellt
Published by: Anne Faelldin Personalkonsult AB, Sandvaktaregatan 21, Aahus, 29635, Sweden. TEL 46-44-247780, FAX 46-44-247786. Ed., Pub. Anne Faelldin. Adv. contact Christina Eliasson. page SEK 9,600.

PHOENIX (MANCHESTER). *see* EDUCATION—Higher Education

658.2 USA ISSN 1087-7983
THE PHYSICIAN RECRUITER. Text in English. 1995. q. adv. **Document type:** *Magazine, Trade.*
—CCC.
Published by: Professional Publishing, Inc., PO Box 698, Portland, OR 97207-0698. TEL 503-221-1260, FAX 503-221-1545.

331.1 610 USA
PHYSICIAN SALARY SURVEY REPORT, HOSPITAL-BASED, GROUP PRACTICE, AND H M O. Short title: Physician Salary Survey Report. Text in English. 1977. a. USD 295 per issue (effective 2009). **Document type:** *Report, Trade.* **Description:** Annual salary and benefits reports for physicians.
Former titles (until 1995): Physician Salary Survey Report, Hospital-Based and Group Practice; (until 1991): Compensation Report on Hospital-Based and Group Practice Physicians (1046-9435); (until 1986): Compensation Report on Hospital-Based Physicians (0275-5211)
Related titles: CD-ROM ed.: Physician Salary & Benefits Report. ISSN 2153-9324. 2010.
Published by: Hospital & Healthcare Compensation Service, PO Box 376, Oakland, NJ 07436. TEL 201-405-0075, FAX 201-405-2110, allinfo@hhcsinc.com.

331.7020866094 GBR ISSN 1756-7734
PINK'S. Text in English. 2007. s-a. GBP 11.50; GBP 6.50 per issue (effective 2009). adv. **Document type:** *Magazine, Trade.*
Related titles: Online - full text ed.
—CCC.
Published by: Arberry Pink, 57 Poland St, London, W1F 7NW, United Kingdom. TEL 44-20-74399100, FAX 44-20-74399101, media@arberrypink.co.uk, http://www.arberrypink.co.uk/. Ed. Laura Sheed. Pub. Chris Hollins. Adv. contact Vanessa Pardoe.

331.1 CAN ISSN 1492-3726
PLAN D'ACTION REGIONAL. MONTEREGIE. Text in French. 2000. a. **Document type:** *Government.*
Related titles: Online - full text ed.: ISSN 1496-8878. 2006.
Published by: Emploi - Quebec, 600, blvd Casavant Est, Saint-Hyacinthe, PQ J2S 7T2, Canada. TEL 450-773-7463, 866-740-2135, FAX 450-773-3614, http://emploiquebec.net/francais/index.htm.

331.1 690 NLD ISSN 1875-4864
PLEIN. Text in Dutch. 1977. 8/yr. EUR 20 membership (effective 2011). adv. **Document type:** *Magazine, Trade.*

NO

Supersedes in part (in 2008): F N V Bouw Magazine (1570-1395); Which was formerly (until 2002): F N V Magazine. F N V Bouw (1567-682X); (until 2000): F N V Magazine. Bouw- en Houtbond F N V (0924-204X); (until 1988): F N V Magazine. Profiel (0169-5045); (until 1985): Profiel (Woerden) (0166-7548); Which was formed by the merger of (1972-1976): Steiger (Woerden) (0926-6739); Which was formed by the merger of (1921-1972): Op de Steiger (0926-6747); (1911-1972): Bondsblad (Utrecht) (0926-6755); (1920-1976): Bouwer (Amsterdam) (0926-6720); Which was formed by the merger of (1890-1920): Timmerman (Amsterdam) (0926-6704); (1908-1920): Bouwvakarbeider (Amsterdam) (0926-6712)
Published by: (F N V Woondiensten), Stichting F N V Pers, Postbus 9354, Amsterdam, 1006 AJ, Netherlands. TEL 31-20-5816300, FAX 31-20-6844541, http://www.fnv.nl. Ed. Peter van der Aa. Circ: 7,500.

PLUNKETT'S COMPANION TO THE ALMANAC OF AMERICAN EMPLOYERS: MID-SIZE FIRMS. *see* BUSINESS AND ECONOMICS—Labor And Industrial Relations

930.1 USA
POSITIONS FOR CLASSICISTS & ARCHAEOLOGISTS. Text in English. 19??. m. looseleaf. USD 25 (effective 2010). adv. back issues avail. **Document type:** *Journal, Academic/Scholarly.*
Published by: American Philological Association, University of Pennsylvania, 220 S 40th St, Ste 201E, Philadelphia, PA 19104. TEL 215-898-4975, FAX 215-573-7874, apaclassics@sas.upenn.edu, http://www.apaclassics.org. **Co-sponsor:** Archaeological Institute of America.

331.1 IRL ISSN 1649-8070
POSTGRADIRELAND. Text in English. 2003. a. GBP 5 to individuals; free to students (effective 2006).
Supersedes in part (in 2006): Gradireland (1649-5446)
Published by: GTI Ireland, 9-11 Upper Baggot St, Dublin, 4, Ireland. TEL 353-1-6603422, FAX 353-1-6606623.

331.1 POL ISSN 1425-4794
PRACA. Text in Polish. 1994. w. PLZ 54 per month domestic; EUR 15 per month in Europe; USD 23 per month in North America (effective 2011). **Document type:** *Newspaper, Consumer.*
Formerly (until 1995): Gazeta o Pracy (1232-1710)
Related titles: ◆ Supplement to: Gazeta Wyborcza. ISSN 0860-908X.
Published by: Agora S.A., ul Czerska 8/10, Warsaw, 00732, Poland. TEL 48-22-5556000, FAX 48-22-5554850, prenumerata@gazeta.pl, http://www.agora.pl.

371.42 NLD ISSN 1872-485X
PRO-KRANT. Text in Dutch. 200?. 10/yr. EUR 56 (effective 2008).
Published by: (Referentiegroep Praktijkonderwijs in de Steigers), Eenvoudig Communiceren, Postbus 10208, Amsterdam, 1001 EE, Netherlands. TEL 31-20-5206070, FAX 31-20-5206061, info@eenvoudigcommuniceren.nl, http://www.eenvoudigcommuniceren.nl. Ed. Nicolet Oost Lievense. Pub. Ralf Beekveldt.

331 SVK ISSN 1336-1228
PROFESIA. Text in Slovak. 2002. w. adv. **Document type:** *Newspaper, Trade.* **Description:** Provides timely information on the job market and economic situation in Slovakia.
Related titles: Online - full text ed.: ISSN 1336-3166.
Published by: Profesia, spol. s.r.o., Vajnorska cesta 7, Bratislava, 851 01, Slovakia. TEL 421-2-64211663, FAX 421-2-64211681, obchod@profesia.sk. Ed. Iveta Schaefferova.

371.42 CHE ISSN 1661-6251
PROFESSION UND FALLVERSTEHEN. Text in German. 2007. irreg., latest vol.2, 2009. price varies. **Document type:** *Monographic series, Academic/Scholarly.*
Published by: Peter Lang AG (Subsidiary of: Peter Lang Publishing Group), Hochfeldstr 32, Postfach 746, Bern 9, 3000, Switzerland. TEL 41-31-3061717, FAX 41-31-3061727, info@peterlang.com. Eds. Roland Becker, Thomas Ley.

658.3 RUS ISSN 0869-4761
PROFESSIONAL. Text in Russian. 10/yr. USD 125 in United States. —East View.
Published by: Ministerstvo Obshchego i Professional'nogo Obrazovaniya Rossiiskoi Federatsii, Ul Chernyakhovskogo 9, Moscow, 125319, Russian Federation. TEL 7-095-1527879, FAX 7-095-2145006. Ed. E D Guseva. **Dist. by:** East View Information Services, 10601 Wayzata Blvd, Minneapolis, MN 55305. TEL 952-252-1201, 800-477-1005, FAX 952-252-1202, info@eastview.com, http://www.eastview.com.

371.42 USA ISSN 1045-9863
HF5382.5.U5
PROFESSIONAL CAREERS SOURCEBOOK. Text in English. 1989. irreg., latest vol.7, 2002. **Document type:** *Directory, Trade.* **Description:** Provides profiles on 129 professional and technical occupations, ranging from account and architect to visual artist and writer.
Published by: Gale (Subsidiary of: Cengage Learning), 27500 Drake Rd, Farmington Hills, MI 48331. TEL 248-699-4253, 800-877-4253, FAX 248-699-8035, gale.customerservice@cengage.com, http://gale.cengage.com. Eds. Joseph M Palmisano, Kathleen M Savage.

371.42 USA ISSN 1548-0704
HD8038.A1
➤ **PROFESSIONAL STUDIES REVIEW.** Abbreviated title: P S R. Text in English. 2004. s-a. bk.rev. back issues avail. **Document type:** *Journal, Academic/Scholarly.* **Description:** Devoted to the pedagogic needs and research interests of those working within career-oriented disciplines.
Indexed: A10, CA, MLA-IB, T02, V03.
Published by: St. John's University, College of Professional Studies, 8000 Utopia Pky, Queens, NY 11439. TEL 718-990-2000, admhelp@stjohns.edu.

371.42 USA ISSN 0190-1796
HD6278.U5 CODEN: PWMIDY
PROFESSIONAL WOMEN AND MINORITIES; a total human resources data compendium. Text in English. 1975. biennial. USD 101.25 to non-members; USD 75 to members; USD 325 combined subscription (effective 2008). bibl.; charts. index. reprints avail. **Description:** Comprehensive reference book of data on human resources presented in approximately 400 tables and charts, and broken down by sex and or minority status categories.
Related titles: Online - full text ed.: USD 93.75 to non-members; USD 67.50 to members (effective 2008).
Indexed: SRI.
—CASDDS. **CCC.**
Published by: (Commission on Professionals in Science and Technology), C P S T Publications, 1200 New York Ave, NW Ste 113, Washington, DC 20005. TEL 202-326-7080, FAX 202-842-1603, info@cpst.org, http://www.cpst.org. Eds. Betty M Vetter, Eleanor L Babco. Circ: 1,000.

371.42 RUS
PROFESSIYA. Text in Russian. w.
Address: Ul Tallinskaya 6b, Petersburg, 195196, Russian Federation. TEL 7-812-4442043, FAX 7-812-4442152. Ed. Nataliya Mironenko.

371.42 420 USA
PROMOTE YOURSELF WITH BETTER GRAMMAR. Text in English. a. USD 10 newsstand/cover (effective 2006). **Document type:** *Handbook/Manual/Guide, Trade.*
Published by: Manpower Education Institute, 715 Ladd Rd, Bronx, NY 10471-1203. TEL 718-548-4200, FAX 718-548-4202, meiready@aol.com, http://www.manpower-education.org.

371.42 GBR ISSN 1360-9084
PROSPECTS DIRECTORY. Text in English. 1978. a. GBP 21.99 per issue (effective 2010). adv. index. **Document type:** *Directory, Academic/Scholarly.* **Description:** Contains recruitment plans and training policies of organizations that employ graduates.
Formerly (until 1993): R O G E T (0962-4082)
Published by: Graduate Prospects Ltd (Subsidiary of: Higher Education Careers Services Unit), Prospects House, Booth St E, Manchester, Lancs M13 9EP, United Kingdom. TEL 44-161-2775200, FAX 44-161-2775210, csd-feedback@prospects.ac.uk. adv.: page GBP 4,660.

371.42 GBR
PROSPECTS FINALIST. Text in English. 1976. 8/yr. GBP 14.99 (effective 2010). adv. **Document type:** *Magazine, Academic/Scholarly.* **Description:** Aimed at students in their final year of study; lists vacancies for which applications can be made in advance of exams.
Former titles (until 1996): Prospect Plus; (until 19??): Future Vacancies for the Finalist: Jobs for Those Graduating in (Year)
Published by: Graduate Prospects Ltd (Subsidiary of: Higher Education Careers Services Unit), Prospects House, Booth St E, Manchester, Lancs M13 9EP, United Kingdom. TEL 44-161-2775200, FAX 44-161-2775210, csd-feedback@prospects.ac.uk.

371.42 340 GBR
PROSPECTS LAW. Text in English. 199?. a. GBP 9.99 per issue (effective 2010). charts; stat. **Document type:** *Directory, Trade.* **Description:** Contains recruitment plans and training policies of organizations employing trainee solicitors and barristers.
Formerly (until 2004): Prospects Focus on Law
Published by: Graduate Prospects Ltd (Subsidiary of: Higher Education Careers Services Unit), Prospects House, Booth St E, Manchester, Lancs M13 9EP, United Kingdom. TEL 44-161-2775200, FAX 44-161-2775210, csd-feedback@prospects.ac.uk.

331.1 GBR
PROSPECTS TODAY (ONLINE). Text in English. 1972. 37/yr. free (effective 2010). adv. **Document type:** *Journal, Academic/Scholarly.* **Description:** Contains lists immediate vacancies for graduates, featuring jobs, career opportunities, and vocational training.
Former titles (until 19??): Prospects Today (Print) (1471-6690); (until 1993): Clearing House Bulletin
Published by: Graduate Prospects Ltd (Subsidiary of: Higher Education Careers Services Unit), Prospects House, Booth St E, Manchester, Lancs M13 9EP, United Kingdom. TEL 44-161-2775200, FAX 44-161-2775210, csd-feedback@prospects.ac.uk, http://www.prospects.ac.uk. adv.: color page GBP 1,800. Circ: 50,000.

PSYCHOLOGIST APPOINTMENT. *see* PSYCHOLOGY

331.1 698 NLD ISSN 1875-4872
PUNT (AMSTERDAM). Text in Dutch. 1977. 8/yr. EUR 20 membership (effective 2011). adv. **Document type:** *Magazine, Trade.*
Supersedes in part (in 2008): F N V Bouw Magazine (1570-1395); Which was formerly (until 2002): F N V Magazine. F N V Bouw (1567-682X); (until 2000): F N V Magazine. Bouw- en Houtbond F N V (0924-204X); (until 1988): F N V Magazine. Profiel (0169-5045); (until 1985): Profiel (Woerden) (0166-7548); Which was formed by the merger of (1972-1976): Steiger (Woerden) (0926-6739); Which was formed by the merger of (1921-1972): Op de Steiger (0926-6747); (1911-1972): Bondsblad (Utrecht) (0926-6755); (1920-1976): Bouwer (Amsterdam) (0926-6720); Which was formed by the merger of (1890-1920): Timmerman (Amsterdam) (0926-6704); (1908-1920): Bouwvakarbeider (Amsterdam) (0926-6712)
Published by: (F N V Afbouw en Onderhoud), Stichting F N V Pers, Postbus 9354, Amsterdam, 1006 AJ, Netherlands. TEL 31-20-5816300, FAX 31-20-6844541, http://www.fnv.nl. Ed. Peter van der Aa. Circ: 20,500.

331.1 CAN ISSN 1912-0931
QUEBEC PROVINCE. MINISTERE DE L'EMPLOI ET DE LA SOLIDARITE SOCIALE. RAPPORT ANNUEL DE GESTION. Text in French. 2004. a. **Document type:** *Government.*
Formed by the 2004 merger of part of: Quebec Province. Ministere de l'Emploi, de la Solidarite Sociale et de la Famille. Rapport Annuel de Gestion (1912-0826); Which was formed by the merger of (2002-2003): Quebec Province. Ministere de l'Emploi et de la Solidarite Sociale. Rapport Annuel de Destion (1706-9580); Which was formerly (until 2001): Quebec. Ministere de l'Emploi et de la Solidarite Sociale. Rapport Annuel (1701-2074); (until 2000): Quebec. Ministere de la Solidarite Sociale. Rapport Annuel (1495-0499); (1998-1999): Quebec. Ministere de l'Mploi et de la Solidarite. Rapport Annuel (1490-294X); (2002-2003): Quebec Province. Ministere de la Famille et de l'Enfance. Rapport Annuel de Gestion (1706-8827); Which was formerly (until 2002): Quebec. Ministere de la Famille et de l'Enfance. Rapport Annuel (1481-837X); (until 1998): Quebec. Office des Services de Garde a l'Enfance. Rapport Annuel (0838-097X); (until 1987): Office des Services de Garde a l'Enfance. Rapport d'Activite (0837-5992); (1981-1984): Office des Services de Garde a l'Enfance. Rapport Annuel (0229-9488); (2002-2004): Quebec Province. Securite du Revenu. Rapport Annuel de Gestion (1705-0316); (1999-2004): Emploi-Quebec. Rapport Annuel de Gestion (1488-6812); Which was formerly (1993-1999): Societe Quebecoise de Developpement de la Main-d'oeuvre. Rapport Annuel (1195-5546); (2002-2004): Quebec Province. Centre de Recouvrement. Rapport Annuel de Gestion (1703-8294); Which was formerly (until 2002): Quebec. Centre de Recouvrement. Rapport de Gestion (1707-0198); (until 2000): Centre de Recouvrement. Rapport Annuel (1707-018X); (until 1997): Centre de Recouvrement en Securite du Revenu. Rapport Annuel (1707-0171)
Published by: Quebec, Ministere de l'Emploi et de la Solidarite Sociale, 425, rue Saint-Amable, RC, Quebec, PQ G1R 4Z1, Canada. TEL 418-643-4721, 888-643-4721, http://www.mess.gouv.qc.ca/index.asp.

371.42 340 USA
RAISING THE BAR. Text in English. q. USD 100 to non-members (effective 2000). adv. **Document type:** *Newsletter.*
Former titles: W B A Newsletter and Career Opportunities Bulletin; Career Opportunities Bulletin
Published by: Women's Bar Association of D.C., 815 15th St, N W, Ste 815, Washington, DC 20005-2201. TEL 202-639-8880, FAX 202-639-8889, http://www.wbadc.org. Ed. Calvert Thomas Cynthia, R&P, Adv. contact Julie Almacy TEL 202-639-8880. Circ: 1,700.

658.3 AUS
READY; career, workplace & you. Text in English. a. free to members (effective 2008). adv. back issues avail. **Document type:** *Magazine, Academic/Scholarly.* **Description:** Features stories and information to help students achieve the best possible outcome in their transition from university to the workforce.
Related titles: Online - full text ed.
Published by: Association of Professional Engineers, Scientists and Managers, GPO Box 1272, Melbourne, VIC 8060, Australia. TEL 61-3-96958800, FAX 61-3-96958902, info@apesma.asn.au. adv.: color page AUD 2,400;. Circ: 15,000.

READY OR NOT; retirement guide. *see* EDUCATION—Adult Education

370.113 CAN
REALM; creating work you want. Text in English. 1991. q. CAD 10.69 domestic; CAD 14.98 foreign (effective 2001). **Description:** Provides career advice to the twentysomething audience.
Related titles: Online - full content ed.
Published by: YES Canada-BC Publishing Division, 5172 Kingsway, Ste 310, Burnaby, BC V5H 2E8, Canada. TEL 604-412-4137, 877-REALM-99, info@realm.net, http://realm.net. Ed. Lisa Manfield. Pub. Elisa Hendricks. Circ: 200,000.

331.1 FRA ISSN 1243-6267
REBONDIR; travailler autrement. Text in French. 1993. 11/yr. EUR 44 (effective 2009). bk.rev. bibl.; charts; illus.; maps. back issues avail. **Document type:** *Magazine, Consumer.* **Description:** Explores the different aspects of unemployment, the job search, and the training available in the work place.
Related titles: Online - full text ed.
Published by: Groupe Touati, 1 Rue des Entrepreneurs, Saint Ouen, 93400, France. TEL 33-1-40114444, FAX 33-1-40115550, info@groupetouati.com. Circ: 160,000 (paid).

RECRUIT!. *see* INSURANCE

RECRUITER. *see* BUSINESS AND ECONOMICS—Personnel Management

658.3 USA ISSN 2152-8543
▼ **RECRUITER BENCHMARKING SURVEY.** Text in English. 2009. a. USD 75 per issue to non-members; USD 50 per issue to members (effective 2010). **Document type:** *Report, Trade.*
Published by: Medical Group Management Association, 104 Inverness Terr E, Englewood, CO 80112. TEL 303-799-1111, 877-275-6462, FAX 303-643-4439, support@mgma.com.

331.3 USA ISSN 0163-5611
HD6278.U5
RECRUITING TRENDS (EAST LANSING). Text in English. 19??. a. USD 50 (effective 2007). **Document type:** *Journal, Trade.*
—**CCC.**
Published by: Michigan State University, Collegiate Employment Research Institute, 113 Student Services, East Lansing, MI 48824. TEL 517-355-2211, FAX 517-353-2597, gardnerp@msu.edu, http://www.ceri.msu.edu/home.html.

371.42 613 USA
RECRUITMENT DIRECTIONS. Variant title: N A H C R Directions. Text in English. 1985. 6/yr. USD 135 to individual members; USD 1,100 to institutional members (effective 2007). adv. bk.rev. **Document type:** *Newsletter, Trade.* **Description:** Provides regional information on a host of topics and center spread articles on a number of important topics of interest to health care recruiters.
Published by: National Association for Health Care Recruitment, 1401 S Primrose Dr, Orlando, FL 32806. TEL 407-481-2893, 407-843-6981, FAX 407-481-2825, amy@nahcr.com, http://www.nahcr.com/. Ed. Cathy Allman. R&P Karen Hart. Circ: 1,600.

REHABILITATION COUNSELING BULLETIN. *see* HANDICAPPED

331.1 USA
RESEARCH DOCTORATE PROGRAMS IN THE UNITED STATES: CONTINUITY AND CHANGE. Text in English. 1973. irreg., latest 2010. USD 99.95 per issue (effective 2010). charts; stat.; tr.lit. **Document type:** *Monographic series, Academic/Scholarly.* **Description:** Reports the results of an extensive study of U.S. research-doctorate programs in five broad fields: physical sciences and mathematics, engineering, social and behavioral sciences, biological sciences, and the humanities.
Formerly (until 199?): Doctoral Scientists and Engineers in the United States (Year) Profile; Which superseded in part (in 198?): Science, Engineering, and Humanities Doctorates in the United States: Profile (0732-5924); Which was formerly (until 1977): Doctoral Scientists and Engineers in the United States. Profile (0095-0750)
Published by: National Academy Press, 500 Fifth Street NW, Lockbox 285, Washington, DC 20055. TEL 202-334-3313, 888-624-8373, customer_service@nap.edu, http://www.nap.edu. Circ: 3,000.

RESEARCH PROGRAMME ON HUMAN RESOURCES DEVELOPMENT. RESEARCH MONOGRAPH. *see* BUSINESS AND ECONOMICS—Personnel Management

RESPONSIBILITY. *see* BUSINESS AND ECONOMICS

371.42 BRA ISSN 1679-3390
REVISTA BRASILEIRA DE ORIENTACAO PROFISSIONAL. Text in Multiple languages. 2003. s-a. **Document type:** *Magazine, Trade.*

Published by: Associacao Brasileira de Orientadores Profissionais, Av Lucas de Oliveira 1873, Porto Alegre, RS, Brazil. TEL 55-51-30287816, http://www.abopbrasil.org.br.

658.3 BRA ISSN 1806-8405
LA558
REVISTA BRASILEIRA DE POS - GRADUACAO. Abbreviated title: R B P G. Text in Portuguese. 2004. 3/yr. **Document type:** *Magazine, Consumer.*
Indexed: A01.
Published by: Ministerio da Educacao, Coordenacao de Aperfeicoamento de Pessoal de Nivel Superior (C A P E S), Coordenacao de Estudos e Divulgacao Cientifica, Bl.L Anexo II, 2o Andar, Brasilia, DF 70047-900, Brazil. TEL 55-61-21048866.

331.1 FRA ISSN 1167-3656
RHONE METIERS. Text in French. 1965. bi-m. EUR 12 (effective 2009). adv. bk.rev. **Document type:** *Magazine, Trade.*
Formerly (until 1991): Carrefour des Metiers (1167-3664)
Published by: Chambre de Metiers, 58 av. Marechal Foch, Lyon, Cedex 6 69453, France. TEL 33-4-72434300, FAX 33-4-72434301. Eds. M Laroche, Nathalie Beroujon. Circ: 25,000.

371.42 USA
RUSSIAN - KOREAN INTERNATIONAL SYMPOSIUM ON SCIENCE AND TECHNOLOGY. Text in English. 19??. a., latest 2005. adv. back issues avail.; reprints avail. **Document type:** *Proceedings, Trade.*
Related titles: Online - full text ed.
Published by: I E E E, 445 Hoes Ln, Piscataway, NJ 08854. TEL 732-981-0060, 800-678-4333, FAX 732-562-6380, customer.service@ieee.org, http://www.ieee.org.

371.4 CAN ISSN 0845-244X
S C W E A NEWSLETTER. Text in English. 1981. irreg. (2-3/yr.). CAD 20 (effective 2000). **Document type:** *Newsletter.*
Published by: (Saskatchewan Career - Work Education Association), Saskatchewan Teachers' Federation, 2317 Arlington Ave., Saskatoon, SK S7J 2H8, Canada. stf@stf.sk.ca. Ed. Anna Marie Donovan.

371.42 USA ISSN 1948-1195
S T E MTRENDS; science, technology, engineering, mathematics. (Science, Technology, Engineering, Mathematics) Text in English. 1963. bi-m. USD 75 domestic to non-members; USD 85 foreign to non-members; free to members (effective 2009). bk.rev. back issues avail. **Document type:** *Newsletter, Trade.* **Description:** A digest of current developments affecting the recruitment, training, and utilization of scientists and engineers. Special sections profile information on supply and demand, salaries, women and minorities, education, federal agency activities, and new publications and resources of interest.
Formerly (until 2009): C P S T Comments (1540-8892); Which superseded (in 1994): Scientific, Engineering, Technical Manpower Comments (0036-8768)
Related titles: Microform ed.; Online - full content ed.
Published by: (Commission on Professionals in Science and Technology), C P S T Publications, 1200 New York Ave, NW Ste 113, Washington, DC 20005. TEL 202-326-7080, FAX 202-842-1603, info@cpst.org.

331.1 500 USA ISSN 0146-5015
Q149.U5
SALARIES OF SCIENTISTS, ENGINEERS AND TECHNICIANS; a summary of salary surveys. Text in English. 1965. biennial. USD 100 to non-members; USD 80 to members; USD 175 combined subscription print & online eds. (effective 2008). charts; illus.; stat. back issues avail.; reprints avail. **Document type:** *Report, Trade.* **Description:** Provides information from more than 50 salary surveys on starting and advance salaries in industry, government and educational institutions, with further breakdowns by field, highest degree, years since first degree, age group, category of employment, work activity, type of employer, geographic area, academic rank, civil service grade and grade distribution, and level of responsibility.
Related titles: Microfiche ed.: 1965 (from CIS); Online - full text ed.: USD 90 to non-members; USD 70 to members (effective 2008).
Indexed: SRI.
—CCC.
Published by: (Commission on Professionals in Science and Technology), C P S T Publications, 1200 New York Ave, NW Ste 113, Washington, DC 20005. TEL 202-326-7080, FAX 202-842-1603, http://www.cpst.org. Ed. Eleanor L Babco. Circ: 1,000.

331.21 USA
SALARY INCREASE SURVEY REPORT. Text in English. a.
Published by: Hewitt Associates, 100 Half Day Rd, Lincolnshire, IL 60069-9971. TEL 708-295-5000.

371.42 USA ISSN 1088-9523
SALES AND MARKETING JOBS REPORT. Abbreviated title: S M J R. Text in English. 19??. m. **Document type:** *Report, Trade.* **Description:** Offers a forum where corporate recruiters, personnel consultants, search firms, and direct hiring companies list their best positions that are currently available.
Published by: Career Advancement Publications, 460 Thornridge Dr, Rochester Hls, MI 48307. TEL 716-483-3454, FAX 716-664-2417.

371.42 CHE
SCHWEIZERISCHE ZEITSCHRIFT FUER KAUFMAENNISCHES BILDUNGSWESEN. Text in French, German, Italian. 1906. 6/yr. CHF 50 (effective 1998). adv. bk.rev. **Document type:** *Bulletin.*
Address: Guisanstr 9, St. Gallen, 9010, Switzerland. TEL 41-71-2242630, FAX 41-71-2242619. Ed. Rolf Dubs. Circ: 1,000.

THE SECURITY EXECUTIVE'S JOB REPORT. *see* CRIMINOLOGY AND LAW ENFORCEMENT—Security

331.1 NLD ISSN 1871-9090
SENIOREN CONTACT. Variant title: F N V Senioren Contact. Text in Dutch. 2005. 3/yr.
Published by: Federatie Nederlandse Vakbeweging, Postbus 8456, Amsterdam, 1005 AL, Netherlands. TEL 31-20-5816300, FAX 31-20-6844541. Ed. Isabel Coenen. Circ: 220,000.

▼ **SHISHI BAOGAO (ZHIJIAO BAN).** *see* EDUCATION—Adult Education

331.1 SWE ISSN 1653-7750
SHORTCUT. Text in Swedish. 1999. 6/yr. SEK 449 (effective 2006). adv. **Document type:** *Magazine, Consumer.*
Related titles: Online - full text ed.
Published by: Universum International AB, Karlavaegen 108, Stockholm, 11526, Sweden. TEL 46-8-56202700, FAX 46-8-56202070. Ed. Andreas Dahlin. Adv. contact Niclas Richtner. page SEK 37,200; trim 225 x 298. Circ: 25,000.

370 USA ISSN 1949-0771
SINGLES SUCCESS. Text in English. 2008. m. USD 179; free to qualified personnel (effective 2009). **Document type:** *Newsletter, Consumer.* **Description:** Designed for singles who want to achieve and maintain an above average lifestyle at home and work.
Media: Online - full content.
Published by: Singles Career Coaching, LLC, 1937 W Palmetto St, #136, Florence, SC 29501. TEL 888-267-4140, FAX 888-257-0253, info@singlescareercoaching.com, http://www.singlescareercoaching.com.

SMART CONNECTIONS. *see* EDUCATION—Higher Education

371.42 AUS ISSN 1035-1116
SMART START. Text in English. 1967. a. adv. **Document type:** *Journal, Consumer.*
Former titles (until 1990): Jobs, Careers and Further Studies (1031-0886); Australian School Leavers Yearbook; (until 1981): Opportunities for School Leavers in Australia
Published by: A P N Educational Media Pty. Ltd., Level 1, 2 Elizabeth Plaza, PO Box 6097, North Sydney, NSW 2060, Australia. TEL 61-2-99368666, FAX 61-2-99368631, http://www.apn.com.au. Ed. Paul Dagarin. Adv. contact Bruce Jenner TEL 61-2-99368639. page AUD 5,000; trim 206 x 276. Circ: 15,000.

331.1 360 USA
SOCIAL SERVICE JOBS. Text in English. 1975. fortn. USD 118; USD 142 foreign (effective 1999). adv. back issues avail. **Document type:** *Newsletter.* **Description:** List current jobs nationally in the areas of social work, psychology, and counseling.
Published by: Employment Listings for the Social Services, 10 Angela Dr, Framingham, MA 01701. TEL 508-626-8644, FAX 508-626-9389. Ed., R&P, Adv. contact M.B. Sack. Pub. M B Sack. Circ: 5,250 (paid).

SOZIALGESETZBUCH: GRUNDSICHERUNG FUER ARBEITSUCHENDE. *see* LAW—Civil Law

650.14 GBR
SPACE CAREERS. Text in English. w. **Document type:** *Newsletter.* **Description:** Aims to be a resource for employment in the space industry.
Media: E-mail.
Published by: Space Links Limited, Willow House, Winterbrook, Wallingford, OX10 9EQ, United Kingdom. TEL 44-1491-832671. Ed. Pierre Oppetit. Circ: 1,700.

371.42 GBR ISSN 1748-9199
SPECTRUM (LONDON). Text in English. 1996. s-a. GBP 11.50; GBP 6.50 per issue (effective 2009). **Document type:** *Magazine, Trade.* **Description:** Careers and opportunities magazine for ethnic minority students aged between 16-19 years old. Keeps pace with youth issues and addresses subjects that meet the needs of ethnic minority groups.
—CCC.
Published by: Arberry Pink, 57 Poland St, London, W1F 7NW, United Kingdom. TEL 44-20-74399100, FAX 44-20-74399101, media@arberrypink.co.uk, http://www.arberrypink.co.uk/.

STAFFING MANAGEMENT. *see* BUSINESS AND ECONOMICS—Personnel Management

THE STANDARDS FUND. *see* EDUCATION

371.42 620 DEU
STAUFENBIEL-INGENIEURE. Text in German. 1981. a. adv. **Document type:** *Directory, Trade.*
Formerly (until 2006): Berufsplanung fuer Ingenieure
Published by: Staufenbiel Institut fuer Studien- und Berufsplanung GmbH, Maria-Hilf-Str 15, Cologne, 50677, Germany. TEL 49-221-9126630, FAX 49-221-9126639, info@staufenbiel.de, http://www.staufenbiel.de.

371.42 DEU ISSN 1860-7667
STAUFENBIEL KARRIEREMAGAZIN; Das Magazin fuer Ihre Karriereplanung. Text in German. 2001. 4/yr. adv. **Document type:** *Magazine, Trade.*
Formerly (until 2005): Staufenbiel-Newsletter fuer Berufseinstieg & Karriere (1618-4521)
Published by: Staufenbiel Institut fuer Studien- und Berufsplanung GmbH, Maria-Hilf-Str 15, Cologne, 50677, Germany. TEL 49-221-9126630, FAX 49-221-9126639, info@staufenbiel.de. Circ: 130,000 (controlled).

371.42 DEU
STAUFENBIEL WIRTSCHAFTSWISSENSCHAFTLER. Text in German. 1974. a. adv. **Document type:** *Directory, Trade.*
Former titles (until 2008): Staufenbiel Management-Nachwuchs; (until 2006): Berufsplanung fuer den Management Nachwuchs
Published by: Staufenbiel Institut fuer Studien- und Berufsplanung GmbH, Maria-Hilf-Str 15, Cologne, 50677, Germany. TEL 49-221-9126630, FAX 49-221-9126639, info@staufenbiel.de, http://www.staufenbiel.de.

DER STELLENREPORT; fuer Schulabsolventen, Hochschulabsolventen und Professionals. *see* EDUCATION—Higher Education

DER STELLENREPORT - FUER HOCHSCHULABSOLVENTEN. *see* EDUCATION—Higher Education

STREET ARTISTS' NEWSLETTER. *see* ART

371.42 CAN ISSN 1719-4180
STUDENT CAREER SKILLS DEVELOPMENT PROGRAM. JOB CATALOGUE. Text in English. a. **Document type:** *Catalog, Consumer.*
Formerly (until 2005): Nova Scotia Employment Program for Students Job Catalogue (1207-1226)
Published by: Nova Scotia Economic Development, PO Box 2311, halifax, NS B3J 3C8, Canada. TEL 902-424-0377, FAX 902-424-7008, comm@gov.ns.ca.

371.42 DEU ISSN 1866-7244
STUDIEN ZUR BERUFS- UND PROFESSIONSFORSCHUNG. Text in German. 2008. irreg., latest vol.3, 2009. price varies. **Document type:** *Monographic series, Academic/Scholarly.*
Published by: Verlag Dr. Kovac, Leverkusenstr 13, Hamburg, 22761, Germany. TEL 49-40-3988800, FAX 49-40-39888055, info@verlagdrkovac.de.

371.42 DEU ISSN 1610-1006
STUTTGARTER BEITRAEGE ZUR BERUFS- UND WIRTSCHAFTSPAEDAGOGIK. Text in German. 1984. irreg., latest vol.30, 2007. price varies. **Document type:** *Monographic series, Academic/Scholarly.*
Published by: Shaker Verlag GmbH, Kaiserstr 100, Herzogenrath, 52134, Germany. TEL 49-2407-95960, FAX 49-2407-95969, info@shaker.de.

650 150 USA ISSN 0745-2489
BF637.S8 CODEN: SUCSEY
SUCCESS (NEW YORK); what achievers read. Text in English. 1895-1999 (May); resumed 2000 (Jun.)-2001 (Apr.); resumed 2006 (May)-2007; resumed 2008 (Mar.). bi-m. USD 19.99 domestic; USD 29.99 in Canada; USD 39.99 elsewhere (effective 2008). adv. bk.rev.; software rev. stat.; illus. back issues avail.; reprints avail. **Document type:** *Magazine, Consumer.* **Description:** Brings business news, how-to articles and profiles of inspiring businessmen and women to up-and-coming entrepreneurs.
Formerly (until 1981): Success Unlimited (0039-4424)
Indexed: A12, A13, A14, A17, A22, A26, ABIn, B01, B02, B03, B04, B06, B07, B08, B09, B11, B15, B17, B18, BPI, BRD, C12, E07, G04, G06, G07, G08, G09, I05, Inspec, M01, M02, M06, P02, P07, P10, P18, P48, P51, P53, P54, P55, PQC, R03, RGAb, RGPR, S23, W01, W02, W03.
—AskIEEE, CASDDS, IE, Ingenta.
Published by: VideoPlus, LLC, 200 Swisher Rd, Lake Dallas, TX 75065. http://www.videoplus.com/. adv.: B&W page USD 11,660, color page USD 13,840; trim 8.375 x 10.875. Circ: 668,000 (paid).

371.42 USA ISSN 1947-5152
▼ **SUCCESS WITH PURPOSE.** Text in English. 2009. w. free (effective 2009). **Document type:** *Newsletter, Consumer.* **Description:** Provides tips, tools and advice for you to learn, grow and share.
Media: Online - full content.
Published by: Karen L. Keeney, Ed. & Pub., 2351 Sunset Blvd, Ste 170-108, Rocklin, CA 95765. TEL 916-402-6024, info@karenlkeeney.com. Ed. Karen L Keeney.

371.42 CAN ISSN 1912-1636
SUMMER WORK EXPERIENCE. Text in English. 1999. a. **Document type:** *Journal, Consumer.*
Formerly (until 2004): Student Summer Job Action (1494-7838)
Media: CD-ROM. **Related titles:** Print ed.: ISSN 1912-1628.
Published by: Human Resources and Skills Development Canada, 140 Promenade du Portage, Phase IV, Gatineau, PQ K1A 0J9, Canada. FAX 819-953-8700, http://www.hrsdc.gc.ca/en/home.shtml.

331.1 USA
Q148
SUPPLY & DEMAND INDICATORS FOR NEW SCIENCE AND ENGINEERING DOCTORATES. Text in English. 1977. irreg. USD 5 domestic; USD 10 foreign (effective 2008). charts. **Document type:** *Monographic series, Trade.* **Description:** Presents results of a pilot study conducted by CPST in collaboration with professional societies to develop a system to monitor the supply of and demand for recent doctorates in science and engineering.
Formerly: Supply and Demand for Scientists and Engineers (0732-2631)
—CCC.
Published by: (Commission on Professionals in Science and Technology), C P S T Publications, 1200 New York Ave, NW Ste 113, Washington, DC 20005. TEL 202-326-7080, FAX 202-842-1603, info@cpst.org, http://www.cpst.org. Ed. Betty M Vetter.

SUPPORTED EMPLOYMENT INFOLINES. *see* SOCIAL SERVICES AND WELFARE

371.42 AUS ISSN 1839-1044
▼ **SYDNEY UNIVERSITY LAW SOCIETY CAREERS GUIDE.** Text in English. 2010. a. back issues avail. **Document type:** *Handbook/Manual/Guide, Academic/Scholarly.* **Description:** Explains the ins and outs of applying, qualifying and practising.
Related titles: Online - full text ed.: ISSN 1839-1052. free (effective 2011).
Published by: Sydney University Law Society, Rm 103, New Law Bldg F10, Camperdown, NSW 2006, Australia. TEL 61-2-93510204, secretary@suls.org.au.

331.1 CAN ISSN 1719-5543
TABLEAU SYNTHESE SUR LES PROFESSIONS ET METIERS EN DEMANDE. Text in French. 2005. a. **Document type:** *Journal, Trade.*
Media: Online - full text.
Published by: Emploi - Quebec, 600, blvd Casavant Est, Saint-Hyacinthe, PQ J2S 7T2, Canada. TEL 450-773-7463, 866-740-2135, FAX 450-773-3614, http://emploiquebec.net/francais/index.htm.

TALBOT'S STUDENT PLANNING BOOK. *see* EDUCATION—Higher Education

658.3 GBR ISSN 2045-0001
▼ **TALENT ENGAGEMENT REVIEW.** Abbreviated title: T E R. Text in English. 2010. q. GBP 295 (effective 2010). adv. back issues avail. **Document type:** *Trade.* **Description:** Covers HR case studies, workshops and articles from the distinguished leaders in the industry.
Formed by the merger of (2007-2010): Talent Management Review (1754-5102); (2007-2010): Employee Engagement Today (1755-5078)
Related titles: Online - full text ed.: ISSN 2045-001X.
Published by: Osney Media, Ground Fl Churchill House, 142-146 Old St, London, EC1V 9BW, United Kingdom. TEL 44-20-73364600, FAX 44-20-73364601, info@osneymedia.com, http://www.osneymedia.com. Pub. Uday Singh. Adv. contact Lynne Martin.

371.42 GBR ISSN 2046-1429
TARGETJOBS.CO.UK. Text in English. 2001. irreg. adv. **Document type:** *Magazine, Consumer.* **Description:** Contains information about jobs, graduate recruitment, and careers advice for students and graduates.
Former titles (until 2010): Targetjobs (1757-420X); (until 2007): Doctorjob (1476-9174); (until 2002): Wanted Now! (1474-3450)
Related titles: Online - full text ed.
Published by: G T I Media Ltd, The Fountain Bldg, Howbery Park, Benson Ln, Wallingford, Oxon OX10 8BA, United Kingdom. TEL 44-1491-826262, FAX 44-1491-833146, http://groupgti.com/gtimedia.

657.4602341 GBR ISSN 1743-713X
TAX CAREERS. Text in English. 2004. m. free (effective 2010). **Document type:** *Magazine, Trade.*
—CCC.

Published by: Croner C C H Group Ltd. (Subsidiary of: Wolters Kluwer UK Ltd.), 145 London Rd, Kingston upon Thames, Surrey KT2 6SR, United Kingdom. TEL 44-20-85473333, FAX 44-20-85472638, info@croner.co.uk.

331.1241658153 GBR ISSN 1746-1359
TAXATION 2. Text in English. 2005. fortn. free (effective 2010).
Document type: *Journal, Trade.* **Description:** Contains practical advice, profiles of leading firms and interviews with top tax specialists plus pages of all the latest tax vacancies.
Related titles: Online - full text ed.
—CCC.
Published by: LexisNexis Butterworths, Halsbury House, 35 Chancery Ln, London, Mddx WC2A 1EL, United Kingdom. TEL 44-20-74002500, FAX 44-20-74002842, customer.services@lexisnexis.co.uk, http://www.lexisnexis.co.uk. Eds. Allison Plager, Richard Curtis. Adv. contact Daniel Wild TEL 44-20-82121995. **Subscr. to:** 2 Addiscombe Rd, Croydon, Surrey CR9 5AF, United Kingdom. TEL 44-845-3701234, FAX 44-28-90344215.

371.42 USA
TECHJOBS MAGAZINE. Text in English. bi-m. adv.
Published by: 1st Communications, PO Box 409, Wickliffe, OH 44092-0409. TEL 216-901-8000, FAX 216-901-8181. Pub. Paul Raihle.

TECHLINKS. *see* TECHNOLOGY: COMPREHENSIVE WORKS

331.7 USA
TEMP SLAVE. Text in English. irreg. USD 2 per issue. bk.rev. illus.
Description: Offers stories, graphics, scams and rants about temp work.
Published by: Jeff Kelly, Ed. & Pub., PO Box 8284, Madison, WI 53708-8284.

TENDANCES DE LA MAIN-D'OEUVRE DES INFIRMIERES ET INFIRMIERS AUTORISES AU CANADA (ONLINE). *see* MEDICAL SCIENCES—Nurses And Nursing

TENDANCES DE LA MAIN-D'OEUVRE DES INFIRMIERES ET INFIRMIERS AUTORISES AU CANADA (PRINT). *see* MEDICAL SCIENCES—Nurses And Nursing

TENDANCES DE LA MAIN-D'OEUVRE DES INFIRMIERES ET INFIRMIERS PSYCHIATRIQUES AUTORISES AU CANADA. *see* MEDICAL SCIENCES—Nurses And Nursing

658.3 CAN ISSN 1715-0132
TENDANCES R H. (Ressources Humaines) Text in French. 2003. a.
Document type: *Journal, Trade.*
Published by: Observatoire Interministeriel en Ressources Humaines, 888, rue Saint-Jean, 4e etage, Quebec, PQ G1R 5H6, Canada. TEL 418-643-5173, FAX 418-528-9803, http://www.ccgp.gouv.qc.ca/pages_htm/Observatoire.htm.

TERTIARY EDUCATION AND TRAINING VICTORIA. *see* EDUCATION—Adult Education

371.42 USA ISSN 0279-9685
TOMORROW'S BUSINESS LEADER. Text in English. 1969. q. membership. adv. bk.rev.
Published by: Future Business Leaders of America - Phi Beta Lambda, 1912 Association Dr, Reston, VA 20191-1591. Ed. Betty Penzer. Pub. Jean M Buckley. Circ: 220,000.

371.42 USA ISSN 1093-6238
TOMORROW'S CHRISTIAN GRADUATE. Text in English. 1998. a.
Published by: WIN Press, Box 1357, Oak Park, IL 60304. TEL 708-524-5070, FAX 708-524-5174, WINPress@aol.com, http://www.christiangraduate.com. Circ: 150,000.

TOOLKIT MEDEZEGGENSCHAP. *see* BUSINESS AND ECONOMICS—Personnel Management

371.42 USA
TRAINING MEDIA REVIEW. Text in English. 1994. m. USD 229 worldwide membership (effective 2007). **Document type:** *Magazine, Trade.* **Description:** Provides hands-on reviews of business training content, technology, and tools as well as independent commentary.
Media: Online - full text.
Indexed: A10, V03.
—CCC.
Published by: T M R Publications, P.O. Box 381822, Cambridge, MA 02238-1822. TEL 617-489-9120, 877-532-1838, FAX 617-489-3437, CustomerService@tmreview.com. Ed. Bill Ellet.

371.42 FRA ISSN 2107-2418
▼ TRAVAILLER EFFICACEMENT EN .. Text in French. 2010. irreg.
Document type: *Magazine, Consumer.*
Published by: Association Francaise de Normalisation (A F N O R), 11 av Francis-de-Pressense, La Plaine, Saint Denis, 93571 Cedex, France. TEL 33-1-41628000, FAX 33-1-49179000, http://www.afnor.org.

331.1 USA
TRENDLINES. Text in English. 19??. bi-m. free (effective 2011). back issues avail. **Document type:** *Newsletter, Government.* **Description:** Covers the Utah economy.
Related titles: Online - full text ed.
Indexed: A10, V03.
Published by: Utah Department of Workforce Services, PO Box 45249, Salt Lake City, UT 84145. TEL 801-526-9675, FAX 801-526-9211, dwscontactus@utah.gov.

371.42 GBR ISSN 2045-3000
▼ THE U C D CAREER GUIDE. (University College Dublin) Text in English. 2010. a. **Document type:** *Newsletter, Trade.*
Related titles: Online - full text ed.: free (effective 2011).
Published by: (University College Dublin IRL), G T I Media Ltd, The Fountain Bldg, Howbery Park, Benson Ln, Wallingford, Oxon OX10 8BA, United Kingdom. TEL 44-1491-826262, FAX 44-1491-833146, http://groupgti.com/gtimedia.

U I DATA SUMMARY. (Unemployment Insurance) *see* INSURANCE—Abstracting, Bibliographies, Statistics

U K EMPLOYMENT ALERT. (United Kingdom) *see* LAW

331.1 USA
U R I S A MARKETPLACE. Text in English. 19??. m. free (effective 2010).
Document type: *Newsletter, Trade.* **Description:** Contains comprehensive listings of GIS & IT job openings.
Related titles: Online - full text ed.
Published by: Urban and Regional Information Systems Association, 701 Lee St, Ste 680, Des Plaines, IL 60016. TEL 847-824-6300, FAX 847-824-6363, info@urisa.org.

U.S. DEPARTMENT OF LABOR. EMPLOYMENT & TRAINING ADMINISTRATION. TRAINING AND EMPLOYMENT REPORT OF THE SECRETARY OF LABOR. *see* BUSINESS AND ECONOMICS—Labor And Industrial Relations

371.42 DEU ISSN 0943-5913
UNFALLSACHBEARBEITER. Text in German. 1968. base vol. plus updates 2/yr. looseleaf. EUR 96 base vol(s).; EUR 38.80 updates per issue (effective 2009). **Document type:** *Monographic series, Trade.*
Published by: Erich Schmidt Verlag GmbH & Co. (Berlin), Genthiner Str 30 G, Berlin, 10785, Germany. TEL 49-30-2500850, FAX 49-30-250085305, vertrieb@esvmedien.de, http://www.erich-schmidt-verlag.de.

371.42 DEU
UNICOMPACT - START. Text in German. 1999. 2/yr. adv. **Document type:** *Magazine, Consumer.*
Formerly (until 2008): High Potential Chances
Published by: Evoluzione Media AG, Dillwaechterstr 4, Munich, 80686, Germany. TEL 49-89-7690030, FAX 49-89-76900329, info@evoluzione.de, http://www.evoluzionemedia.de. adv.: B&W page EUR 4,207, color page EUR 6,783. Circ: 119,000 (controlled).

UNIQUE OPPORTUNITIES; the physician's resource. *see* MEDICAL SCIENCES

331.1 DEU
UNTERNEHMEN STELLEN SICH VOR. Text in German. 1988. a. EUR 4.20 (effective 2007). **Document type:** *Directory, Trade.*
Published by: Klaus Resch Verlag OHG, Moorbeker Str 31, Grossenkneten, 26197, Germany. TEL 49-4435-96120, FAX 49-4435-961296. Circ: 10,300 (controlled).

371.42 RUS
UPRAVLENIE SHKOLOI. Text in Russian. w.
Published by: Chistye Prudy, Ul Platovskaya 4, Moscow, 121165, Russian Federation. Ed. A Adamskii. Circ: 8,000.

331.1 USA
UTAH CAREERS. Text in English. 2005. a. free (effective 2011).
Document type: *Magazine, Government.*
Related titles: Online - full text ed.; ◆ Supplement(s): Utah Careers for Older Workers; ◆ Utah Careers for Women.
Indexed: A10, V03.
Published by: Utah Department of Workforce Services, PO Box 45249, Salt Lake City, UT 84145. TEL 801-526-9675, FAX 801-526-9211, dwscontactus@utah.gov.

331.1 USA
UTAH CAREERS FOR OLDER WORKERS. Text in English. 19??. a. free (effective 2011). **Document type:** *Government.*
Related titles: Online - full text ed.; ◆ Supplement to: Utah Careers.
Indexed: A10, V03.
Published by: Utah Department of Workforce Services, PO Box 45249, Salt Lake City, UT 84145. TEL 801-526-9675, FAX 801-526-9211, dwscontactus@utah.gov.

331.1 USA
UTAH CAREERS FOR WOMEN. Text in English. 2005 (Dec.). a. free (effective 2011). **Document type:** *Government.* **Description:** Addresses topics such as work, family, salary, mistakes, work from home, legal issues, job market, education and benefits.
Related titles: Online - full text ed.; ◆ Supplement to: Utah Careers.
Published by: Utah Department of Workforce Services, PO Box 45249, Salt Lake City, UT 84145. TEL 801-526-9675, FAX 801-526-9211, dwscontactus@utah.gov.

UWMAGAZINE. *see* LABOR UNIONS

VACATURES IN NEDERLAND. *see* BUSINESS AND ECONOMICS—Labor And Industrial Relations

371.42 SWE ISSN 1101-9611
VAEGLEDAREN I UTBILDNING OCH ARBETSLIV. Text in Swedish. 1975. 4/yr. SEK 350 (effective 2011). adv. **Document type:** *Magazine, Trade.*
Formerly (until 1990): Studie- och Yrkesorientering Bulletinen (0347-4771)
Published by: Sveriges Vaegledarfoerening/Swedish Association of Guidance Counsellors, Vaevstuguvaegen 12, Njurunda, 86241, Sweden. TEL 46-60-31089, http://www.vagledarforeningen.org. Ed. Agneta Soederlund.

331.1 340 USA ISSN 1549-8484
KF301
VAULT GUIDE TO THE TOP 100 LAW FIRMS. Text in English. 2004. a., latest 2009. USD 39.95 (print or online ed.) (effective 2009). adv. 756 p./no.; **Document type:** *Handbook/Manual/Guide, Trade.*
Description: Provides a glimpse of more than 60 additional firms, with contact and salary information, office locations, notable perks, major practice areas and includes the "Buzz" section, in which associates offer observations about firms other than their own.
Former titles (until 2000): Vault.com Guide to the Top 50 Law Firms (1540-1901); (until 1999): VaultReports.com Guide to America's Top 50 Law Firms (1535-4296); Vault Reports Guide to America's Top 50 Law Firms
Related titles: Online - full text ed.: free to qualified personnel (effective 2008).
Published by: Vault, Inc., 75 Varick St, 8th Fl, New York, NY 10013. TEL 212-366-4212. Ed. Brian Dalton.

331.1 338 USA ISSN 1557-4199
HD9720.1
VAULT GUIDE TO THE TOP MANUFACTURING EMPLOYERS. Text in English. 2005. a., latest 2009. USD 19.95 (print or online ed.) (effective 2009). adv. **Document type:** *Directory, Trade.* **Description:** Provides information on the most important manufacturing employers, with company overviews, recent company news and info on the hiring process.
Related titles: Online - full text ed.: free (effective 2008).
Published by: Vault, Inc., 75 Varick St, 8th Fl, New York, NY 10013. TEL 212-366-4212.

331.1 340 USA ISSN 1557-4172
KF190
VAULT GUIDE TO THE TOP MID-ATLANTIC LAW FIRMS. Text in English. 2006. a. USD 29.95 (print or online ed.) (effective 2008). adv. **Document type:** *Directory, Trade.* **Description:** Provides information on the work, lifestyle, hours, compensation and jobs in the area.
Related titles: Online - full text ed.: free to qualified personnel (effective 2008).
Published by: Vault, Inc., 75 Varick St, 8th Fl, New York, NY 10013.

331.1 340 USA ISSN 1557-4180
KF190
VAULT GUIDE TO THE TOP NORTHWEST & GREAT PLAINS LAW FIRMS. Variant title: Northwest & Great Plains Law Firms. Text in English. 2006. a. USD 29.95 (print or online ed.) (effective 2008). **Document type:** *Directory, Trade.* **Description:** Ranks law firms for prospective associates on hours, compensation, treatment by partners, training and office space.
Related titles: Online - full text ed.: free to qualified personnel (effective 2008).
Published by: Vault, Inc., 75 Varick St, 8th Fl, New York, NY 10013. TEL 212-366-4212.

371.42 USA ISSN 1559-3681
VAULT - INROADS GUIDE TO DIVERSITY INTERNSHIP, CO-OP AND ENTRY-LEVEL PROGRAMS. Text in English. 2005. irreg., latest 2007. USD 34.95 per issue (effective 2007). 756 p./no.; **Document type:** *Guide, Consumer.*
Published by: (Inroads, Inc.), Vault, Inc., 75 Varick St, 8th Fl, New York, NY 10013. http://www.vault.com.

371.42 USA ISSN 1559-3673
VAULT - S E O GUIDE TO INVESTMENT BANK DIVERSITY PROGRAMS. (Sponsors for Educational Opportunity) Text in English. 2005. a. USD 39.95 (print or online ed.) (effective 2009). adv. 309 p./no.; **Document type:** *Handbook/Manual/Guide, Trade.*
Description: Designed to provide students with the information necessary to evaluate investment banks' diversity initiatives and programs, as well as to allow investment banks to benchmark their efforts against their peer firms.
Related titles: Online - full text ed.: free to qualified personnel (effective 2009).
Published by: (Sponsors for Educational Opportunity (S E O)), Vault, Inc., 75 Varick St, 8th Fl, New York, NY 10013. TEL 212-366-4212.

371.42 RUS
VESTNIK OBRAZOVANIYA. Text in Russian. m. USD 135 in United States.
Published by: Izdatel'stvo Progress, Chistoprudnyi bulv 6, Moscow, 101856, Russian Federation. TEL 7-095-9236453, FAX 7-095-9253692. **Dist. by:** East View Information Services, 10601 Wayzata Blvd, Minneapolis, MN 55305. TEL 952-252-1201, 800-477-1005, FAX 952-252-1202, info@eastview.com, http://www.eastview.com.

371.42 355 USA ISSN 1524-282X
VETERAN'S ENTERPRISE; the military and veteran's business network. Text in English. 1980. q. adv. **Document type:** *Magazine, Consumer.* **Description:** Provides veterans with information about educational, vocational, and professional opportunities available to our veteran community.
Related titles: Online - full text ed.: free (effective 2011).
Published by: E M Publishing Enterprises, Inc, 13351 Riverside Dr, Ste 514, Sherman Oaks, CA 91423. TEL 818-654-0870, http://www.equalitymagazines.com. Ed. Richard Chudy.

371.42 305 USA
VETERAN'S VISION. Text in English. 1993. q. back issues avail.
Document type: *Magazine, Consumer.* **Description:** Discusses employment issues as they pertain to American veterans.
Address: 210 E Broad St, Ste 202, Falls Church, VA 22046.

371.42 DEU
VIGO! JOBFIT BLEIBGESUND. Variant title: Jobfit. Text in German. bi-m. free. adv. **Document type:** *Magazine, Consumer.*
Published by: (AOK-Bundesverband), W D V Gesellschaft fuer Medien & Kommunikation mbH & Co. OHG, Siemensstr 6, Bad Homburg, 61352, Germany. TEL 49-6172-6700, FAX 49-6172-670144, info@wdv.de, http://www.wdv.de. adv.: page EUR 15,000; trim 190 x 260. Circ: 1,177,239 (controlled).

371.42 USA ISSN 1948-1497
▼ VISIONS (KENTWOOD). Text in English. 2009. s-m. **Document type:** *Magazine, Consumer.*
Media: Online - full content.
Published by: Micheal J. Hillsey, Pub. michael@successfulpathways.com, http://www.successfulpathways.com.

371.42 AUS ISSN 1445-5080
VOCAL JOURNAL. Text in English. 1998. biennial, latest vol.6, 2006-2007. free to members. **Document type:** *Journal, Academic/Scholarly.* **Description:** Provides information for vocational teachers and coordinators in schools, including features, analyses of contemporary issues and range of best-practice case studies helped foster interest, discussion and debate.
Related titles: Online - full text ed.
Published by: Vocational Education and Training Network Australia Inc., 13/75 Welsby St, PO Box 1029, New Farm, QLD 4005, Australia. TEL 61-7-32541431, FAX 61-7-33585881, vetnetwork@vetnetwork.org.au.

VOCATION SAGE - FEMME. *see* MEDICAL SCIENCES—Obstetrics And Gynecology

371.42 USA ISSN 1060-5630
Z7164.V6
VOCATIONAL CAREERS SOURCEBOOK. Text in English. 1992. biennial. **Document type:** *Directory, Trade.* **Description:** Provides profiles describing 139 vocational occupations.
Related titles: Diskette ed.; Magnetic Tape ed.
Published by: Gale (Subsidiary of: Cengage Learning), 27500 Drake Rd, Farmington Hills, MI 48331. TEL 248-699-4253, 800-877-4253, FAX 877-363-4253, gale.customerservice@cengage.com, http://gale.cengage.com. Eds. Karen Hill, Kathleen M Savage.

370.113 USA
HD7256.U5
➤ **VOCATIONAL EVALUATION AND CAREER ASSESSMENT PROFESSIONALS. JOURNAL.** Text in English. 1968; N.S. 2004. q. USD 35 domestic to non-members; USD 45 foreign to non-members; free to members (effective 2011). Index. back issues avail. **Document type:** *Journal, Academic/Scholarly.* **Description:** Provides practitioners, consumers, and educators with an understanding of critical information in vocational assessment and therapeutic adjustment services.
Former titles (until 2004): Vocational Evaluation and Work Adjustment Journal (Colorado Springs, 2002); (until 2001): National Vocational Evaluation and Work Adjustment Journal (1544-9718); Vocational Evaluation and Work Adjustment Journal; Vocational Evaluation and Work Adjustment Bulletin (0160-8312)
Indexed: A10, A22, CA, E-psyche, V03.
—IE, Ingenta.
Published by: Vocational Evaluation and Career Assessment Professionals, PO Box 26273, Colorado Springs, CO 80936. http://www.vecap.org/. Eds. Cari Schmidt, Steven Sligar.

371.42 LUX
VOCATIONAL TRAINING INFORMATION BULLETIN. Text in English. 3/yr. USD 20.
Published by: European Commission, Office for Official Publications of the European Union, 2 Rue Mercier, Luxembourg, L-2985, Luxembourg. **Dist. in the U.S. by:** Bernan Associates, Bernan, 4611-F Assembly Dr., Lanham, MD 20706-4391. TEL 301-459-0056, 800-274-4447.

371.42 NLD ISSN 1874-785X
VOCATIONS AND LEARNING. Text in English. 2008. 3/yr. EUR 239 combined subscription to institutions (print & online eds.) (effective 2011). bk.rev. reprint service avail. from PSC. **Document type:** *Journal, Academic/Scholarly.* **Description:** Provides an international forum for papers on the broad field of vocational learning, across a range of settings: vocational colleges, schools, universities, workplaces, domestic environments, voluntary bodies, etc.
Related titles: Online - full text ed.: ISSN 1874-7868. 2008 (from IngentaConnect).
Indexed: A22, A26, B29, CurCont, E01, E08, S09, SCOPUS, SSCI, W07.
—IE. **CCC.**
Published by: Springer Netherlands (Subsidiary of: Springer Science+Business Media), Van Godewijckstraat 30, Dordrecht, 3311 GX, Netherlands. TEL 31-78-6576050, FAX 31-78-6576474. Ed. Stephen Billett.

371.42 DEU ISSN 1868-3908
▼ **WANDLUNGSPROZESSE IN INDUSTRIE- UND DIENSTLEISTUNGSBERUFEN UND MODERNE LERNWELTEN.** Text in German. 2009. irreg., latest vol.5, 2011. price varies. **Document type:** *Monographic series, Academic/Scholarly.*
Published by: Verlag Dr. Kovac, Leverkusenstr 13, Hamburg, 22761, Germany. TEL 49-40-3988800, FAX 49-40-39888055, info@verlagdrkovac.de.

371.42 USA ISSN 0740-8501
WASHINGTON COUNSELETTER. Abbreviated title: W C L. Text in English. 1963. 8/yr. (Oct.-May). looseleaf. bk.rev.; film rev. **Document type:** *Newsletter, Trade.* **Description:** Publishes articles, events, programs, activities, and reviews of the professional literature of interest to counselors and educators.
Related titles: Online - full text ed.: free (effective 2011).
Indexed: A09, A10, V03.
Published by: Chronicle Guidance Publications, Inc., PO Box 1190, Moravia, NY 13118.

331.1 USA ISSN 1067-0769
HF5382.75.U62
WASHINGTON JOB SOURCE. Text in English. 1993. irreg., latest vol.3, 1996. USD 16.95. **Document type:** *Directory.* **Description:** Offers a comprehensive and up-to-date guide to finding internships and entry-level jobs in Washington, DC. Includes northern Virginia and suburban Maryland.
Published by: Metcom, Inc., 2700 Q St NW, Apt. 323, Washington, DC 20007-5013. TEL 202-337-7800, FAX 202-337-3121. Ed. Faith Regan. Pub. Ben Psillas. Circ: 10,000.

331.1 USA ISSN 2155-3335
HD4461
▼ **WATER WORKFORCE TRENDS.** Text in English. 2009. a. **Document type:** *Report, Trade.* **Description:** Features statistics and information on waterworks occupations and employees.
Published by: American Water Works Association, 6666 W Quincy Ave, Denver, CO 80235. TEL 303-347-6100, FAX 303-730-0851, custsvc@awwa.org, http://www.awwa.org.

331.1 NLD ISSN 1874-6462
WERK!. Text in Dutch. 2002. a. EUR 25 (effective 2009). adv.
Published by: Uitgeverij Tweesprong, Koopmanslaan 3, Doetinchem, 7005 BK, Netherlands. TEL 31-314-373607, info@tweesprong.nl, http://www.tweesprong.nl. Ed. Nolan Groenland. Pub. Erwin Visser.

371.42 USA ISSN 8755-4658
HF5382.7
WHAT COLOR IS YOUR PARACHUTE? (YEAR); a practical manual for job-hunters and career-changers. Text in English. 1971. a. USD 27.95, CAD 45 per vol. hard cover; USD 17.95, CAD 27.95 per vol. paper (effective 2004). **Document type:** *Handbook/Manual/Guide, Consumer.*
—BLDSC (9309.670000).
Published by: Ten Speed Press, PO Box 7123, Berkeley, CA 94707. TEL 510-559-1600, 800-841-2665, FAX 510-559-1629, http://www.tenspeed.com/index.php3.

371.42 GBR ISSN 1759-0973
WHAT DO GRADUATES DO? (YEAR). Text in English. 1984. a. GBP 14.95 per issue (effective 2010). stat. back issues avail. **Document type:** *Handbook/Manual/Guide, Academic/Scholarly.* **Description:** Provides career guidance articles aimed at graduates, teachers and parents.
Published by: (Association of Graduate Careers Advisory Services, U C A S), Graduate Prospects Ltd (Subsidiary of: Higher Education Careers Services Unit), Prospects House, Booth St E, Manchester, Lancs M13 9EP, United Kingdom. TEL 44-161-2775200, FAX 44-161-2775210, csd-feedback@prospects.ac.uk. Ed. Maureen Tibby.

WINDS OF CHANGE; empowering native Americans through higher education and careers. *see* NATIVE AMERICAN STUDIES

371.42 DEU ISSN 0341-339X
➤ **WIRTSCHAFT UND BERUFSERZIEHUNG.** Text in German. 1949. m. EUR 109; EUR 14.80 newsstand/cover (effective 2010). adv. reprint service avail. from SCH. **Document type:** *Journal, Academic/Scholarly.*
Indexed: DIP, IBR, IBZ, RASB.
—IE. **CCC.**
Published by: ZIEL Verlag, Zeuggasse 7-9, Augsburg, 86150, Germany. TEL 49-821-4209977, FAX 49-821-4209978, verlag@ziel.org, http://www.ziel-verlag.de. Ed., Pub. Rainer Kieslinger.

➤ **WOMEN IN PUBLIC SERVICE BULLETIN.** *see* WOMEN'S INTERESTS

331.1 613.62 USA
WORK & INDUSTRY SPECIAL INTEREST SECTION QUARTERLY. Text in English. 1987. q. free to members (effective 2010). adv. **Document type:** *Newsletter, Trade.*
Former titles (until 2008): Work Programs Special Interest Section Quarterly (1093-7145); (until 1997): Work Programs Special Interest Section Newsletter (1043-1462)
Related titles: Online - full text ed.; ◆ Series: Developmental Disabilities Special Interest Section Quarterly. ISSN 1093-7196; ◆ Gerontology Special Interest Section Quarterly. ISSN 1093-717X; ◆ Technology Special Interest Section Quarterly. ISSN 1093-7137; ◆ Sensory Integration Special Interest Section Quarterly. ISSN 1093-7250; ◆ Education Special Interest Section Quarterly. ISSN 1093-7188; ◆ Physical Disabilities Special Interest Section Quarterly. ISSN 1093-7234; ◆ Administration & Management Special Interest Section Quarterly. ISSN 1093-720X; ◆ Mental Health Special Interest Section Quarterly. ISSN 1093-7226.
Indexed: C06, C07, C08, CINAHL, P21, P24, P48, PQC.
—**CCC.**
Published by: American Occupational Therapy Association, Inc., 4720 Montgomery Ln, PO Box 31220, Bethesda, MD 20824. TEL 301-652-2682, 800-377-8555, FAX 301-652-7711, members@aota.org. Ed. Jeff Snodgrass.

640 338 USA
WORK-AT-HOME SOURCEBOOK; how to find "at-home" work that's right for you. Text in English. 1987. a. USD 19.95 (effective 1999). illus. index. **Document type:** *Directory.* **Description:** Provides names, addresses and complete information on over 1,000 companies that have work-at-home programs, plus contact information for hundreds of home business opportunities.
Published by: Live Oak Publications, PO Box 2193, Boulder, CO 80306. TEL 303-448-1169, FAX 303-447-8684. Ed., Pub., R&P Tom Ellison.

371.42 910.09 USA ISSN 0895-3678
WORKAMPER NEWS; America's guide to working while camping. Text in English. 1987. bi-m. USD 25 domestic; USD 30 foreign (effective 2005). adv. bk.rev. 52 p./no.; back issues avail. **Document type:** *Magazine, Trade.* **Description:** Provides information on seasonal and year-round employment opportunities in parks and resort areas and information on full-time and part-time RVing.
Published by: Workamper Inc., 709 W. Searcy St., Heber Springs, AR 72543-3761. TEL 501-362-2637, FAX 501-362-6769, info@workamper.com. Ed. Greg Robus. Pub. Debbie Robus. Circ: 14,000 (paid).

WORKFORCE TRENDS OF REGISTERED NURSES IN CANADA. *see* MEDICAL SCIENCES—Nurses And Nursing

WORKFORCE TRENDS OF REGISTERED PSYCHIATRIC NURSES IN CANADA. *see* MEDICAL SCIENCES—Nurses And Nursing

371.42 USA
WORKING NIGHTS; improving the health, safety and quality of life of people who work non-traditional hours. Text in English. m. USD 44 domestic; USD 52 in Canada; USD 60 elsewhere (effective 2004). **Document type:** *Newsletter, Trade.*
Published by: Circadian Technologies, Inc., 24 Hartwell Ave, Lexington, MA 02421. TEL 781-676-6900, 800-284-5001.

WORKING WOMEN. *see* WOMEN'S STUDIES

371.42 CHN ISSN 1008-6129
XINGTAI ZHIYE JISHU XUEYUAN XUEBAO/XINGTAI VOCATIONAL AND TECHNICAL COLLEGE. JOURNAL. Text in Chinese. 1984. bi-m. CNY 6 newsstand/cover (effective 2006). **Document type:** *Journal, Academic/Scholarly.*
Related titles: Online - full text ed.
Published by: Xingtai Zhiye Jishu Xueyuan, 552, Gangtie Lu, Xingtai, 054035, China. TEL 86-319-2273031, FAX 86-319-2272074.

374 371.42 CHN ISSN 1674-8689
XINJIANG ZHIYE JIAOYU YANJIU/VOCATIONAL EDUCATION RESEARCH IN XINJIANG. Text in Chinese. 1993. q. CNY 8 newsstand/cover (effective 2006). **Document type:** *Journal, Academic/Scholarly.*
Former titles (until 2010): Wulumuqi Chengren Jiaoyu Xueyuan Xuebao/Urumqi Adult Education Institute. Journal (1671-5179); (until 1993): Wulumuqi Jiaoyu Xueyuan Xuebao
Related titles: Online - full text ed.
—BLDSC (9365.256200).
Published by: Wulumuqi Zhiye Daxue/Urumqi vocational University, 723, Xingfu Lu, Urumqi, Xinjiang 830002, China. TEL 86-991-8812161, FAX 86-991-2617156, http://www.uvu.edu.cn/.

331.7 AUS
YOUR CAREER AND YOU. Abbreviated title: Y C & Y. Text in English. 2000. a. AUD 5.50 per issue to non-members; free to members (effective 2009). **Document type:** *Handbook/Manual/Guide, Consumer.* **Description:** Helps the readers to consider their goals, values, attributes and skills as a basis for their career exploration.
Published by: Graduate Careers Australia Ltd., A'Beckett St, PO Box 12103, Melbourne, VIC 8006, Australia. TEL 61-3-96053700, FAX 61-3-96705752, info@graduatecareers.com.au.

375 SWE ISSN 0513-6261
HF5382.5.S8
YRKE OCH FRAMTID; din vaegvisare till yrken och utbildninger. Text in Swedish. 1966. a. illus.
Formerly: Skola och Yrke
Published by: Arbetsmarknadsstyrelsen/National Labour Market Board, Kungstensgatan 5, Stockholm, 11399, Sweden. TEL 46-8-58606000, FAX 46-8-58606499.

371.42 CHN ISSN 1009-6329
YUEYANG ZHIGONG GAODENG ZHUANKE XUEXIAO XUEBAO/YUEYANG HIGHER VOCATIONAL AND TECHNICAL COLLEGE. JOURNAL. Text in Chinese. 1986. q. CNY 8 newsstand/cover (effective 2006). **Document type:** *Journal, Academic/Scholarly.*
Related titles: Online - full text ed.
Published by: Yueyang Zhigong Gaodeng Zhuanke Xuexiao, Baling Zhong Lu, Yueyang, 414000, China. TEL 86-730-8258317, FAX 86-730-8219387.

354.689 ZMB ISSN 0514-5457
ZAMBIA. EDUCATIONAL AND OCCUPATIONAL ASSESSMENT SERVICE. ANNUAL REPORT. Text in English. a. ZMK 200. stat. **Document type:** *Government.* **Description:** Annual report on the selection process of talent for Zambia's secondary schools.
Published by: (Zambia. Educational and Occupational Assessment Service), Government Printing Department, PO Box 30136, Lusaka, Zambia.

371.42 USA ISSN 2160-4398
▼ **ZHAOSHENG YU JIUYE/COLLEGE AND JOB.** Text in Chinese; Abstracts in English. forthcoming 2011. q. **Document type:** *Journal, Academic/Scholarly.*
Related titles: Online - full text ed.: ISSN 2160-4401. forthcoming. free.
Published by: Hansi Chubanshe/Hans Publishers, 40 E. Main St., Box 275, Newark, DE 19711. TEL 926408-329-4591.

1ST STEPS IN THE HUNT. *see* COMPUTERS—Internet

OCCUPATIONS AND CAREERS—Abstracting, Bibliographies, Statistics

331.1 CAN
ADMINISTRATIVE AND SUPPORT STAFF COMPENSATION SURVEY (YEAR). Text in English. a. CAD 419 to non-members; CAD 335.20 to members. **Document type:** *Bulletin.*
Former titles: Clerical Compensation Survey (Year) (1206-145X); Administrative and Support Compensation Survey (Year)
Published by: Toronto Board of Trade, PO Box 60, Toronto, ON M5X 1C1, Canada. TEL 416-366-6811.

AMERICAN SALARIES AND WAGES SURVEY. *see* BUSINESS AND ECONOMICS—Abstracting, Bibliographies, Statistics

ARKANSAS. EMPLOYMENT SECURITY DEPARTMENT. STATISTICAL REVIEW. *see* BUSINESS AND ECONOMICS—Abstracting, Bibliographies, Statistics

331.021 USA ISSN 1943-4030
ARTIST EMPLOYMENT IN (YEAR). Text in English. 19??. a. **Document type:** *Government.*
Formerly (until 1997): Artist Employment in America
Media: Online - full content.
Published by: National Endowment for the Arts, Nancy Hanks Center, 1100 Pennsylvania Ave NW, Washington, DC 20506. TEL 202-682-5400, http://www.arts.gov.

371.42021 AUS
AUSTRALIA. BUREAU OF STATISTICS. AUSTRALIAN AND NEW ZEALAND STANDARD CLASSIFICATION OF OCCUPATIONS. Abbreviated title: A N Z S C O. Text in English. 1997. irreg., latest 2006. AUD 125 per issue (effective 2009). back issues avail. **Document type:** *Government.* **Description:** Comprises an explanation of the conceptual basis of the classification, the classification structure and definitions for all levels of the classification (Major, sub-major, minor and unit groups and occupations).
Formerly (until 2006): Australian Standard Classification of Occupations
Related titles: CD-ROM ed.; Online - full text ed.: free (effective 2008).
Published by: Australian Bureau of Statistics, Locked Bag 10, Belconnen, ACT 2616, Australia. TEL 61-2-62527037, 61-2-92684909, 300-135-070, FAX 61-2-62528103, client.services@abs.gov.au.

371.42021 AUS
AUSTRALIA. BUREAU OF STATISTICS. AUSTRALIAN STANDARD CLASSIFICATION OF OCCUPATION, LINK FILE. Text in English. 1996. irreg. **Document type:** *Government.*
Related titles: Diskette ed.
Published by: Australian Bureau of Statistics, Locked Bag 10, Belconnen, ACT 2616, Australia. TEL 61-2-62527037, 61-2-92684909, 300-135-070, FAX 61-2-62528103, client.services@abs.gov.au, http://www.abs.gov.au.

371.42021 AUS
AUSTRALIA. BUREAU OF STATISTICS. AUSTRALIAN STANDARD CLASSIFICATION OF OCCUPATIONS - MANUAL CODING SYSTEM: OCCUPATION LEVEL. Text in English. 1993. irreg. **Document type:** *Government.* **Description:** Provides information on personnel management information systems, job vacancy specifications, or responses collected from special purpose statistical collections.
Published by: Australian Bureau of Statistics, Locked Bag 10, Belconnen, ACT 2616, Australia. TEL 61-2-92684909, 300-135-070, FAX 61-2-62528103, client.services@abs.gov.au, http://www.abs.gov.au.

371.42021 AUS
AUSTRALIA. BUREAU OF STATISTICS. CAREER EXPERIENCE, AUSTRALIA (ONLINE). Text in English. 1993. irreg., latest 2002. free (effective 2009). back issues avail. **Document type:** *Government.* **Description:** Presents information on the career experiences of wage and salary earners including details of current job, changes in job such as promotions and transfers, and training opportunities.
Formerly (until 2002): Australia. Bureau of Statistics. Career Experience, Australia (Print) (1326-9046)
Media: Online - full text.
Published by: Australian Bureau of Statistics, Locked Bag 10, Belconnen, ACT 2616, Australia. TEL 61-2-92684909, 61-2-62527037, 300-135-070, FAX 61-2-62528103, client.services@abs.gov.au.

378.0021 AUS
AUSTRALIA. BUREAU OF STATISTICS. EDUCATION AND WORK, AUSTRALIA (ONLINE). Text in English. 1964. a., latest 2008. free (effective 2009). **Document type:** *Government.* **Description:** Contains statistics on the level of education and work status for people ages 15 to 64.

Former titles (until 2005): Australia. Bureau of Statistics. Education and Work, Australia (Print) (1446-4586); (until 2001): Australia. Bureau of Statistics. Transition from Education to Work, Australia (0729-2902)
Media: Online - full text.
Published by: Australian Bureau of Statistics, Locked Bag 10, Belconnen, ACT 2616, Australia. TEL 61-2-92684909, 61-2-62527037, 300-135-070, FAX 61-2-62528103, client.services@abs.gov.au.

371.42021 AUS
AUSTRALIA. BUREAU OF STATISTICS. INFORMATION PAPER: A N Z S C O - AUSTRALIAN AND NEW ZEALAND STANDARD CLASSIFICATION OF OCCUPATIONS. Text in English. 1986. irreg. free (effective 2009). **Document type:** *Government.* **Description:** Contains the updated classification structure at the most detailed level.
Former titles (until 2005): Information Paper: Australian Standard Classification of Occupations; (until 1996): Australia. Bureau of Statistics. Information Paper: A S C O - Australian Standard Classification of Occupations (Print)
Media: Online - full text.
Published by: Australian Bureau of Statistics, Locked Bag 10, Belconnen, ACT 2616, Australia. TEL 61-2-62527037, 61-2-92684909, 300-135-070, FAX 61-2-62528103, client.services@abs.gov.au.

331.1021 AUS
AUSTRALIA. BUREAU OF STATISTICS. JOB SEARCH EXPERIENCE, AUSTRALIA (ONLINE). Text in English. 1982. a. free (effective 2009). back issues avail. **Document type:** *Government.* **Description:** Presents statistical information about the experiences of unemployed people in seeking work, in terms of the steps they have taken to find work and the difficulties they have encountered in finding work.
Former titles: Australia. Bureau of Statistics. Job Search Experience, Australia (Print) (1832-164X); (until 2003): Australia. Bureau of Statistics. Job Search Experience of Unemployed Persons, Australia (1832-1631); (until 1985): Australia. Bureau of Statistics. Job Search Experience of Unemployed Persons Excluding Persons Who Were Stood Down Australia (0815-9971); (until 1984): Australia. Bureau of Statistics. Characteristics of Persons Looking for Work, Australia (0814-141X); (until 1982): Australia. Bureau of Statistics. Persons Looking for Work, Australia
Media: Online - full text.
Published by: Australian Bureau of Statistics, Locked Bag 10, Belconnen, ACT 2616, Australia. TEL 61-2-92684909, 61-2-62527037, 300-135-070, FAX 61-2-62528103, client.services@abs.gov.au.

016.37142 AUS ISSN 1838-0530
AUSTRALIAN VOCATIONAL EDUCATION AND TRAINING STATISTICS. APPRENTICES AND TRAINEES. EARLY TREND ESTIMATES TO .. Text in English. q. free (effective 2011). back issues avail. **Document type:** *Catalog, Academic/Scholarly.*
Media: Online - full text.
Published by: National Centre for Vocational Education Research Ltd., Level 11, 33 King William St., PO Box 8288, Station Arcade, Adelaide, SA 5000, Australia. TEL 61-8-82308400, FAX 61-8-82123436, ncver@ncver.edu.au.

331.1 CAN
BENEFITS & EMPLOYMENT PRACTICES REPORT (YEAR). Text in English. a. CAD 250 to non-members; CAD 200 to members.
Published by: Toronto Board of Trade, PO Box 60, Toronto, ON M5X 1C1, Canada. TEL 416-366-6811.

331.1 317.2 MEX
CLASIFICACION MEXICANA DE OCUPACIONES. Text in Spanish. 1990. irreg.
Published by: Instituto Nacional de Estadistica, Geografia e Informatica, Secretaria de Programacion y Presupuesto, Prol. Heroe de Nacozari 2301 Sur, Puerta 11, Acceso, Aguascalientes, 20270, Mexico. TEL 52-4-918-19488, FAX 52-4-918-0739.

371.021 ITA ISSN 1826-2600
I DIPLOMATI UNIVERSITARI E IL MERCATO DEL LAVORO. Text in Italian. 2002. a.
Published by: Istituto Nazionale di Statistica (I S T A T), Via Cesare Balbo 16, Rome, 00184, Italy. TEL 39-06-46731, http://www.istat.it.

331.1 CAN ISSN 1197-5806
EXECUTIVE COMPENSATION SURVEY (YEAR). Text in English. a. CAD 512 to non-members; CAD 409.60 to members.
Published by: Toronto Board of Trade, PO Box 60, Toronto, ON M5X 1C1, Canada. TEL 416-366-6811.

FINLAND. TILASTOKESKUS. SIJOITTUMISCD. *see* EDUCATION—Abstracting, Bibliographies, Statistics

371.42 310 GBR ISSN 1467-3312
GRADUATE MARKET TRENDS. Abbreviated title: G M T. Text in English. 1979. q. GBP 50; GBP 15 per issue (effective 2010). back issues avail. **Document type:** *Newsletter, Trade.* **Description:** Contains reviews of trends in the U.K. graduate-employment market.
Formerly (until 1997): Statistical Information Package; Incorporates (1987-1996): Statistical Quarterly (1352-0075); Which was formerly (19??-1987): Statistical Quarterly Salary Survey
Related titles: Online - full text ed.: free (effective 2010).
Published by: Graduate Prospects Ltd (Subsidiary of: Higher Education Careers Services Unit), Prospects House, Booth St E, Manchester, Lancs M13 9EP, United Kingdom. TEL 44-161-2775200, FAX 44-161-2775210, csd-feedback@prospects.ac.uk. Ed., Pub. Kathrine Jensen.

HONG KONG ANNUAL DIGEST OF STATISTICS. *see* POPULATION STUDIES—Abstracting, Bibliographies, Statistics

HONG KONG MONTHLY DIGEST OF STATISTICS. *see* POPULATION STUDIES—Abstracting, Bibliographies, Statistics

331 HKG
HONG KONG SPECIAL ADMINISTRATIVE REGION OF CHINA. CENSUS AND STATISTICS DEPARTMENT. EMPLOYMENT AND VACANCIES STATISTICS (DETAILED TABLES) SERIES A. SERVICES SECTORS. Text in Chinese, English. 1981. a. HKD 64 (effective 2002). stat. back issues avail. **Document type:** *Bulletin, Government.* **Description:** Contains detailed employment and vacancies statistics in respect of the services sectors, viz. the transport, storage and communications sector; the financing, insurance, real estate and business services sector; and the community, social and personal services sector. The statistics are analysed by District Council district and size of establishment.
Former titles: People's Republic of China. Census and Statistics Department. Hong Kong Special Administrative Region. Employment and Vacancies Statistics. Series A: Services Sector; Employment and Vacancies Statistics in: Transport, Storage and Communication Financing, Insurance, Real Estate and Business Services, Community, Social and Personal Services
Related titles: Online - full content ed.
Published by: Census and Statistics Department/Zhengfu Tongjichu, Employment Statistics Section, 20/F Wanchai Tower, 12 Harbour Rd, Wan Chai, Hong Kong. TEL 852-2582-5076, FAX 852-2827-2296, es_2@censtatd.gov.hk, http://www.statisticalbookstore.gov.hk. **Subscr. to:** Information Services Department, Publications Sales Unit, Rm 402, 4th Fl, Murray Bldg, Garden Rd, Hong Kong, Hong Kong. TEL 852-2842-8844, FAX 852-2598-7482, puborder@isd.gcn.gov.hk, http://www.info.gov.hk/isd/book_e.htm. **Dist. by:** Government Publications Centre, Low Block, Ground Fl, Queensway Government Offices, 66 Queensway, Hong Kong, Hong Kong. TEL 852-2537-1910, FAX 852-2523-7195.

331.1 HKG
HONG KONG SPECIAL ADMINISTRATIVE REGION OF CHINA. CENSUS AND STATISTICS DEPARTMENT. EMPLOYMENT AND VACANCIES STATISTICS (DETAILED TABLES) SERIES B. WHOLESALE AND RETAIL TRADES, RESTAURANTS AND HOTELS. Text in Chinese, English. 1981. a. USD 32 (effective 2002). stat. **Document type:** *Bulletin, Government.* **Description:** Contains detailed employment and vacancies statistics in respect of the wholesale and retail trades, restaurants and hotels. The statistics are analysed by District Council district and size of establishment.
Formerly: Employment and Vacancies Statistics in: Wholesale, Retail and Import / Export Trades, Restaurants and Hotels
Related titles: Online - full text ed.
Published by: Census and Statistics Department/Zhengfu Tongjichu, Employment Statistics Section, 20/F Wanchai Tower, 12 Harbour Rd, Wan Chai, Hong Kong. TEL 852-2582-5076, FAX 852-2827-2296, es_2@censtatd.gov.hk, http://www.statisticalbookstore.gov.hk. **Subscr. to:** Information Services Department, Publications Sales Unit, Rm 402, 4th Fl, Murray Bldg, Garden Rd, Hong Kong, Hong Kong. TEL 852-2842-8844, FAX 852-2598-7482, puborder@isd.gcn.gov.hk, http://www.info.gov.hk/isd/book_e.htm. **Dist. by:** Government Publications Centre, Low Block, Ground Fl, Queensway Government Offices, 66 Queensway, Hong Kong, Hong Kong. TEL 852-2537-1910, FAX 852-2523-7195.

331.1 CAN ISSN 1206-1468
INFORMATION TECHNOLOGY COMPENSATION SURVEY (YEAR). Text in English. a. CAD 470 to non-members; CAD 376 to members.
Formerly: Data Procession Salary Survey and Employment Practices (Year)
Published by: Toronto Board of Trade, PO Box 60, Toronto, ON M5X 1C1, Canada. TEL 416-366-6811.

IRELAND. CENTRAL STATISTICS OFFICE. NATIONAL EMPLOYMENT SURVEY. *see* OCCUPATIONS AND CAREERS

331.1 JPN
HB1481
KOUSEIROUDOUSHOU. JINKOU DOUTAI SHOKUGUON. SANGYOUTOUKEI: JINKOU DOUTAI TOUKEI TOKUSHU HOUKOKU/JAPAN. MINISTRY OF HEALTH, LABOUR AND WELFARE. OCCUPATIONAL AND INDUSTRIAL ASPECTS: SPECIAL REPORT OF VITAL STATISTICS IN (YEAR). Text in English, Japanese. 1951. quinquennial. JPY 5,775. **Document type:** *Government.*
Formerly: Shokugyo, Sangyobetsu Jinko Dotai Tokei/Japan. Ministry of Health and Welfare. Special Report of Vital Statistics. Occupational and Industrial Aspects (0911-8527)
Published by: Kouseiroudoushou/Ministry of Health, Labour and Welfare, 1-2-2 Kasumigaseki Chiyoda-ku, Tokyo, 100-8916, Japan. TEL 81-3-52531111, http://www.mhlw.go.jp/. R&P Yoke Kanegae.

331.1 CAN ISSN 1197-5857
MIDDLE MANAGEMENT COMPENSATION SURVEY (YEAR). Text in English. a. CAD 512 to non-members; CAD 409.60 to members.
Formerly: Middle Management and Professional Compensation Survey (Year)
Published by: Toronto Board of Trade, PO Box 60, Toronto, ON M5X 1C1, Canada. TEL 416-366-6811.

331.1 USA
NONTRADITIONAL OCCUPATIONS FOR WOMEN IN (YEAR). Text in English. a. stat. **Document type:** *Government.*
Media: Online - full content.
Published by: U.S. Department of Labor, Women's Bureau, Frances Perkins Bldg, 200 Constitution Ave, N W, Washington, DC 20210. TEL 800-827-5335.

371.42 331.2 330.9 USA ISSN 0082-9072
HD8051
OCCUPATIONAL OUTLOOK HANDBOOK. Abbreviated title: O O H. Text in English. 1946. biennial. USD 39 per issue (effective 2009). charts; illus.; stat. reprints avail. **Document type:** *Bulletin, Government.* **Description:** Reports on trends in all professions with a standard industry classification. Discusses what the work entails, working conditions, education and training needed, earnings, job outlook, advancement potential, and related occupations.
Related titles: CD-ROM ed.: ISSN 1076-7681; Online - full text ed.; ♦ Series of: U.S. Bureau of Labor Statistics. Bulletin. ISSN 0082-9021; Supplement(s): Occupational Projections and Training Data. ISSN 0273-382X. 1971.
Indexed: A09, A10, A12, ABIn, B01, B07, H01, P16, P21, P48, P51, P53, P54, PQC, T02, V03, V04.
Published by: U.S. Department of Labor, Bureau of Labor Statistics, 2 Massachusetts Ave, NE, Rm 2860, Washington, DC 20212. TEL 202-691-5200, FAX 202-691-7890, blsdata_staff@bls.gov. **Subscr. to:** U.S. Government Printing Office, Superintendent of Documents, PO Box 371954, Pittsburgh, PA 15250. TEL 202-512-1800, FAX 202-512-2250, ContactCenter@gpo.gov, http://bookstore.gpo.gov.

371.42 331.1 330.9 USA ISSN 0199-4786
HF5382.5.U5 CODEN: OOQUAK
OCCUPATIONAL OUTLOOK QUARTERLY. Abbreviated title: O O Q. Variant title: The (Year) Job Outlook in Brief. Text in English. 1957. q. (Sep.-June). USD 15 domestic; USD 21 foreign; USD 6 per issue domestic; USD 8.40 per issue foreign (effective 2009). bibl.; charts; illus. Index. back issues avail.; reprints avail. **Document type:** *Bulletin, Trade.* **Description:** Helps job seekers, career counselors, guidance counselors and others to evaluate the prospects of occupations by examining trends and developments.
Formerly (until 1958): The Occupational Outlook (0029-7968)
Related titles: CD-ROM ed.; Microfiche ed.: (from CIS, NBI, PQC); Online - full text ed.: ISSN 1555-0559.
Indexed: A01, A02, A03, A08, A09, A10, A12, A13, A14, A17, A22, A25, A26, ABIn, ARG, AmStI, B01, B02, B04, B06, B07, B08, B09, B11, B15, B16, B17, B18, BPI, BRD, BusI, C05, C12, CA, CPerI, E02, E03, E07, E08, ERI, EdA, EdI, G04, G05, G06, G07, G08, H01, H02, I05, I07, IUSGP, M01, M02, M05, M06, MASUSE, MagInd, P02, P04, P06, P07, P10, P13, P16, P18, P21, P30, P34, P47, P48, P51, P53, P54, P55, PAIS, PQC, PersLit, R03, RASB, RGAb, RGPR, S08, S09, S22, S23, SCOPUS, T&II, T02, V02, V03, V04, W01, W02, W03, W05, WorkRelAb.
—BLDSC (6229.700000), IE, Infotrieve, Ingenta.
Published by: U.S. Department of Labor, Bureau of Labor Statistics, 2 Massachusetts Ave, NE, Rm 2860, Washington, DC 20212. TEL 202-691-5200, FAX 202-691-7890, blsdata_staff@bls.gov. **Subscr. to:** U.S. Government Printing Office, Superintendent of Documents, PO Box 371954, Pittsburgh, PA 15250. TEL 202-512-1800, FAX 202-512-2250, ContactCenter@gpo.gov, http://bookstore.gpo.gov.

331.1 CAN
PROFESSIONAL, SUPERVISORY & SALES COMPENSATION SURVEY (YEAR). Text in English. a. CAD 470 to non-members; CAD 376 to members.
Published by: Toronto Board of Trade, PO Box 60, Toronto, ON M5X 1C1, Canada. TEL 416-366-6811.

331.1 USA ISSN 0083-0526
HD4903.5.U58
U.S. EQUAL EMPLOYMENT OPPORTUNITY COMMISSION. EQUAL OPPORTUNITY REPORT. JOB PATTERNS FOR MINORITIES AND WOMEN IN PRIVATE INDUSTRY. Variant title: Job Patterns for Minorities & Women in Private Industry. Minorities and Women in Private Industry. Text in English. 1966. a.
Published by: U.S. Equal Employment Opportunity Commission, 1801 L St, N W, Washington, DC 20507. TEL 202-663-4900, FAX 202-663-4494, info@ask.eeoc.gov.

016.37142 USA
VOCATIONAL & CAREER COLLECTION. Text in English. base vol. plus updates 2/m. **Document type:** *Database, Abstract/Index.*
Media: Online - full text.
Published by: EBSCO Publishing (Subsidiary of: EBSCO Industries, Inc.), 10 Estes St, PO Box 682, Ipswich, MA 01938. TEL 978-356-6500, 800-653-2726, FAX 978-356-6565, information@ebscohost.com.

WASHINGTON LABOR MARKET QUARTERLY REVIEW. *see* BUSINESS AND ECONOMICS—Abstracting, Bibliographies, Statistics

331.1021 AUS ISSN 1834-6545
WOMEN IN THE PROFESSIONS SURVEY REPORT. Text in English. 2000. biennial. free (effective 2008). **Document type:** *Report, Trade.* **Description:** Contains information about employment status, hours of work, family and working life, career development and equal pay.
Media: Online - full text. **Related titles:** Print ed.: ISSN 1834-6537.
Published by: Association of Professional Engineers, Scientists and Managers, GPO Box 1272, Melbourne, VIC 8060, Australia. TEL 61-3-96958800, FAX 61-3-96958902, info@apesma.asn.au.

331.1021 USA ISSN 0162-0592
HD5723
WORK EXPERIENCE OF THE POPULATION. Text in English. 19??. a. free (effective 2009). **Document type:** *Government.*
Related titles: Online - full text ed.
Published by: U.S. Department of Labor, Bureau of Labor Statistics, 2 Massachusetts Ave, NE, Rm 2860, Washington, DC 20212. TEL 202-691-5200, FAX 202-691-7890, blsdata_staff@bls.gov. **Subscr. to:** U.S. Government Printing Office, Superintendent of Documents, PO Box 371954, Pittsburgh, PA 15250. TEL 202-512-1800, FAX 202-512-2250, ContactCenter@gpo.gov, http://bookstore.gpo.gov.

331.1 USA
20 LEADING OCCUPATIONS OF EMPLOYED WOMEN. Text in English. a. free. stat. back issues avail. **Document type:** *Government.*
Media: Online - full content.
Published by: U.S. Department of Labor, Women's Bureau, Frances Perkins Bldg, 200 Constitution Ave, N W, Washington, DC 20210. TEL 800-827-5335.

OCEANOGRAPHY

see EARTH SCIENCES—Oceanography

OFFICE EQUIPMENT AND SERVICES

see BUSINESS AND ECONOMICS—Office Equipment And Services

ONCOLOGY

see MEDICAL SCIENCES—Oncology

OPHTHALMOLOGY AND OPTOMETRY

see MEDICAL SCIENCES—Ophthalmology And Optometry

OPTICS

see PHYSICS—Optics

ORGANIC CHEMISTRY

see CHEMISTRY—Organic Chemistry

ORIENTAL STUDIES

see ASIAN STUDIES

ORNITHOLOGY

see BIOLOGY—Ornithology

ORTHOPEDICS AND TRAUMATOLOGY

see MEDICAL SCIENCES—Orthopedics And Traumatology

OTORHINOLARYNGOLOGY

see MEDICAL SCIENCES—Otorhinolaryngology

OUTDOOR LIFE

see SPORTS AND GAMES—Outdoor Life

799.2 FRA ISSN 2104-4937

LE CHASSEUR DE LA LOIRE. Text in French. 1968. q. **Document type:** *Consumer.*

Published by: Maison de la Chasse et de la Nature, Hotel de Guenegaud, Paris, France. http://www.chassenature.org.

N O

PACKAGING

658.788 GBR ISSN 2040-2821
ACTIVE & INTELLIGENT PACKAGING WORLD. Text in English. 2002. 10/yr. GBP 750 (effective 2010). adv. **Document type:** *Newsletter, Trade.* **Description:** Provides coverage of all new active and intelligent packaging concepts and devices, new materials and technical developments.
Former titles (until 2008): Active & Intelligent Packaging (1758-1710); Active & Intelligent Pack News (1478-7059)
Media: Online - full text.
—CCC.
Published by: IntertechPira, Cleeve Rd, Leatherhead, Surrey KT22 7RU, United Kingdom. TEL 44-1372-802000, FAX 44-1372-802238, info@pira-international.com.

660.29 658.7 DEU ISSN 0943-4798
TS198.A3 CODEN: AEEUEC
AEROSOL EUROPE; the European magazine for the international aerosol industry. Text in English, German. 1993. 11/yr. EUR 135; EUR 13 per issue (effective 2009). adv. Website rev. back issues avail.; reprints avail. **Document type:** *Magazine, Trade.* **Description:** Discusses in details topics relevant to the European market, individual products and fairs and congresses.
Related titles: Online - full text ed.
Indexed: IPackAb, SCOPUS.
Published by: Media Service International, Am Grundwassersee 1, Seeshaupt, 82402, Germany. TEL 49-8801-914682, FAX 49-8801-914683. Ed. Guenter Vogel. Pub. Heinz Melcher. Adv. contact Dagmar Melcher. B&W page EUR 1,900, color page EUR 3,130; trim 183 x 256. Circ: 5,050 (paid).

688.8 HRV ISSN 1331-0224
AMBALAZA. Text in Croatian. 1996. q. **Document type:** *Journal, Trade.* **Description:** Contains information about packaging technology, transportation and storage.
Published by: Tectus, Ul grada Vukovara 224, Zagreb, 10000, Croatia. TEL 385-1-6151649, FAX 385-1-6155590, tectus@ambalaza.hr.

ANNUAL BOOK OF A S T M STANDARDS. VOLUME 15.09 PAPER; BUSINESS IMAGING PRODUCTS. (American Society for Testing and Materials) *see* ENGINEERING—Engineering Mechanics And Materials

658.7884 USA
ANNUAL CAN SHIPMENTS REPORT. Text in English. 1972. a. USD 79.50 (effective 2000). **Document type:** *Report, Trade.* **Description:** Covers domestic can shipments by market, product, technology and material used.
Formerly: Can Manufacturers Institute. Annual Metal Can Shipments Report (0068-7014)
Published by: Can Manufacturers Institute, 1625 Massachusetts Ave, N W, Washington, DC 20036. TEL 202-232-4677. Ed. Sean Reilly. R&P Robert Budway. Circ: 500.

ANUARIO DEL EMPAQUE. *see* BUSINESS AND ECONOMICS—Trade And Industrial Directories

A+CS. *see* TRANSPORTATION—Ships And Shipping

ARTES GRAFICAS. *see* PRINTING

688.8 AUS
ASIA PACIFIC PACKAGING. Text in English. 200?. bi-m. AUD 48 domestic; AUD 60 in New Zealand; AUD 78 elsewhere (effective 2009). adv. back issues avail. **Document type:** *Magazine, Trade.* **Description:** Contains source of all information for the region's packaging industry - overseeing the entire value-added chain in the dynamic package printing and converting industry.
Related titles: Online - full text ed.: free (effective 2009).
Published by: Printer Magazines Pty Ltd., 3/7 Parkes St, PO Box 3665, Parramatta, NSW 2150, Australia. TEL 61-2-96356059, FAX 61-2-96357683, info@i-grafix.com, http://www.printermags.com.au/. Eds. Wayne Robinson, Brian Moore. Pub. Anders Oqvist. Circ: 3,000.

ASIA PACIFIC PERSONAL CARE. *see* BEAUTY CULTURE

658.7 AUT ISSN 0005-0563
AUSTROPACK; Zeitschrift fuer alle Gebiete des Verpackungswesens fuer Transport und Verkehr. Text in German. 1964. m. EUR 60 domestic; EUR 130 foreign (effective 2006). adv. bk.rev. abstr.; charts; illus.; stat. **Document type:** *Magazine, Trade.*
Indexed: IPackAb.
Published by: Verlag Dr. A. Schendl GmbH & Co. KG, Geblergasse 95, Vienna, 1170, Austria. TEL 43-1-906801124, FAX 43-1-9068091124. adv.: B&W page EUR 1,075, color page EUR 2,149; trim 175 x 257. Circ: 2,700.

676.3 USA ISSN 1752-167X
B C N; fortnightly newsletter serving the European corrugated & folding carton industry. (Board Converting News) Text in English. 1987. w. USD 199 in US & Canada; USD 310 elsewhere (effective 2008). adv. 2 cols./p.; back issues avail. **Document type:** *Newsletter, Trade.* **Description:** Covers the corrugated and folding carton converting industry. Features products and current news, transacted board prices for the U.S. and Canada.
Indexed: IPackAb, P&BA.
—CCC.
Published by: N.V. Business Publishers Corp., 43 Main St, Avon By The Sea, NJ 07717. TEL 732-502-0500, FAX 732-502-9606, aschiffenhaus@nvpublications.com. Ed. Jim Curley. Pub., Adv. contact Tom Vilardi TEL 732-502-0500 ext 304. B&W page USD 850, color page USD 1,010; bleed 8.25 x 11.25. Circ: 3,028 (paid and free).

658.788 FRA
B I C - CODE. Text in English. 1970. a. charts. **Document type:** *Magazine, Trade.*
Related titles: Online - full text ed.
Published by: Bureau International des Containers/International Container Bureau, 38 Rue des Blancs Manteaux, Paris, 75004, France. TEL 33-1-47660390, FAX 33-1-47660891. Ed. P Fournier.

BAOXIAN YU JIAGONG/STORAGE AND PROCESS. *see* AGRICULTURE

688.8 CHN ISSN 1001-3563
BAOZHUANG GONGCHENG/PACKAGING ENGINEERING. Text in Chinese. 1972. m. CNY 312 (effective 2009). **Document type:** *Journal, Academic/Scholarly.*
Formerly (until 1980): Fangfu Baozhuang
Related titles: Online - full text ed.
Indexed: A28, APA, BrCerAb, CA/WCA, CIA, CerAb, CivEngAb, E11, EEA, EMA, ESPM, EnvEAb, H15, M&TEA, M09, MBF, METADEX, T04.
—BLDSC (1863.123000).
Published by: Zhongguo Bingqi Gongye Di-59 Yanjiusuo/No.59 Institute of China Ordnance Industry, 33, Shiqiaopuyuzhou Lu, Chongqing, 400039, China. TEL 86-23-68792836, FAX 96-23-68793154, http://www.cq59.com/.

688.8 CHN ISSN 1003-9929
BAOZHUANG SHIJIE/PACKAGING WORLD. Text in Chinese. 1982. bi-m. **Document type:** *Magazine, Trade.*
Related titles: Online - full text ed.
Published by: Baozhuang Shijie Zazhishe, 99-1, Gulou 15 Kuixiang, Hangzhou, 310002, China. TEL 86-571-85330153, FAX 86-571-85330821, bzsj18@yahoo.com.cn. **Co-sponsors:** Zhongguo Baozhuang Jishu Xiehui; Zhejiang Sheng Baozhuang Jishu Xiehui/Zhejianng Packaging Technology Association.

688.8 664 621.9 CHN ISSN 1005-1295
BAOZHUANG YU SHIPIN JIXIE/PACKAGING AND FOOD MACHINERY. Text in Chinese; Abstracts in Chinese, English. 1983. bi-m. CNY 60, USD 60 (effective 2009). adv. **Document type:** *Magazine, Trade.* **Description:** Covers the latest developments of theoretical and applied researches in the fields of packaging and food machinery.
Related titles: Online - full text ed.
Published by: Zhongguo Jixie Gongcheng Xuehui Baozhuang Yu Shipin Gongcheng Fenhui, No.29, Tian Hu Rd, High & New Technology Development Zone, Hefei, 230088, China. TEL 86-551-5311880, FAX 86-551-5335818. Ed. Zhi-yong Zhang. adv.: page CNY 100; 210 x 285. Circ: 4,000.

658.788 JPN
BEST OF PACKAGING IN JAPAN. Text in Japanese. 1990. a. JPY 16,000. **Description:** Information on packaged goods: food, drugs, cosmetics, confectioneries and daily necessities.
Published by: Nippo Co. Ltd., 1-19 Misaki-cho 3-chome, Chiyoda-ku, Tokyo, 101-0061, Japan. TEL 03-3262-3461, FAX 03-3263-2560.

BEVERAGE DIGEST. *see* BEVERAGES

658.788 GBR ISSN 2040-283X
BIOPACKAGING WORLD. Text in English. 2007. 10/yr. GBP 750 (effective 2010). **Document type:** *Journal, Trade.* **Description:** Covers all the trends, launches and developments in the biopackaging industry.
Formerly (until 2008): Biopack (1752-8089); Which incorporated (2005-2008): Biopack News (1749-7892)
Media: Online - full text.
Published by: IntertechPira, Cleeve Rd, Leatherhead, Surrey KT22 7RU, United Kingdom. TEL 44-1372-802000, FAX 44-1372-802238, info@pira-international.com.

676.3 GBR
BOARD CONVERTING NEWS INTERNATIONAL. Text in English. 1988. fortn. GBP 65 domestic; EUR 135 in Europe; USD 160 in US & Canada; GBP 85 elsewhere (effective 2010). adv. back issues avail. **Document type:** *Newsletter, Trade.* **Description:** Covers feature articles, product news and current news for the completed and carton markets in Europe.
Related titles: Online - full text ed.: free (effective 2010).
Published by: Brunton Business Publications Ltd., 1 Salisbury Office Park, London Rd, Salisbury, Wiltshire SP1 3HP, United Kingdom. TEL 44-1722-337038, publications@brunton.co.uk. Pub. Michael Brunton. Adv. contact Dan Brunton. page GBP 980, page EUR 1,080; 183 x 247. Circ: 8,250.

676.3 GBR ISSN 1358-0701
BOARD MARKET DIGEST. Text in English. 1987. m. looseleaf. GBP 350; GBP 45 per issue (effective 2009). bk.rev. mkt.; stat. back issues avail. **Document type:** *Journal, Trade.* **Description:** Provides up-to-date information on prices, market trends, company information and future prospects for the professional buyer of packaging papers and boards.
Related titles: E-mail ed.; Supplement(s): Fantasy Futures. ISSN 1366-381X.
—CCC.
Published by: P P L Research Ltd., PO Box 2002, Watford, Herts WD25 9JQ, United Kingdom. TEL 44-1923-894777, FAX 44-1923-894888, enquiries@pplresearch.co.uk.

676.3 GBR ISSN 1758-1702
HF5770.A1
BRAND (ONLINE). Text in English. 200?. 10/yr. GBP 750 to non-members; free to members (effective 2010). charts; stat. 50 p./no.; **Document type:** *Journal, Trade.* **Description:** Dedicated to the research needs of business managers in the global pulp, paper and packaging industries.
Formed by the merger of (2001-2006): Brand (Print) (1475-0929); (2003-2008): Brand Protection News (1740-1607)
Media: Online - full text.
Indexed: A22, ABIPC, B02, B15, CPEI, EngInd, G04, G08, I05, IPackAb, KES, P&BA, P31, SCOPUS.
—Ingenta. **CCC.**
Published by: IntertechPira, Cleeve Rd, Leatherhead, Surrey KT22 7RU, United Kingdom. TEL 44-1372-802080, FAX 44-1372-802079, info@pira-international.com.

688.8 USA ISSN 1558-3570
TS195.A1 CODEN: BRANB2
BRAND PACKAGING; elevating packaging in the marketing mix. Text in English. 1997. bi-m. USD 104 domestic; USD 137 in Canada; USD 154 elsewhere; free to qualified personnel (print or online ed.) (effective 2009). adv. back issues avail.; reprints avail. **Document type:** *Magazine, Trade.* **Description:** Focuses on the role of packaging in the consumer product marketing mix.
Related titles: Online - full text ed.: ISSN 1558-3589.
Indexed: A10, A12, A13, A15, A17, ABIn, B01, B02, B07, B15, B17, B18, F10, G04, G08, I05, P41, P48, P51, P52, P53, P54, PQC, S22, V03.
—CCC.
Published by: B N P Media, 155 Pfingsten Rd, Ste 205, Deerfield, IL 60015. TEL 847-405-4000, FAX 847-405-4100, portfolio@bnpmedia.com, http://www.bnpmedia.com. Eds. Pauline Tingas Hammerbeck, Jennifer Acevedo. Pub. Gerri Brownstein TEL 973-243-9624. adv.: B&W page USD 5,520, color page USD 7,700; trim 8.875 x 10.75. Circ: 35,000 (paid). **Subscr. to:** PO Box 1080, Skokie, IL 60076.

676.3 658.8 GBR ISSN 1474-0907
BUSINESS RATIO REPORT. PAPER & BOARD PACKAGING MANUFACTURERS. Text in English. 1976. a. GBP 365 per issue (effective 2010). charts; stat. back issues avail. **Document type:** *Report, Trade.* **Description:** Covers companies active as paper and board packaging manufacturers.
Former titles (until 2001): Business Ratio. Paper & Board Packaging Manufacturers (1470-7020); (until 2000): Business Ratio Plus. Paper and Board Packaging Manufacturers (1354-3415); (until 1994): Business Ratio Report. Paper and Board Packaging Manufacturers (1465-5969); (until 1992): Business Ratio Report. Paper & Board Packaging (0261-9334)
Published by: Key Note Ltd. (Subsidiary of: Bonnier Business Information), Harlequin House, 5th Fl, 7 High St, Teddington, Richmond upon Thames, TW11 8EE, United Kingdom. TEL 44-845-5040452, FAX 44-845-5040453, sales@keynote.co.uk.

658.788 668.4 658.8 GBR ISSN 1474-6018
BUSINESS RATIO REPORT. PLASTICS PACKAGING MANUFACTURERS. Text in English. 1978. a. GBP 365 per issue (effective 2010). charts; stat. back issues avail. **Document type:** *Report, Trade.* **Description:** Covers companies active as plastic packaging manufacturers.
Former titles (until 2001): Business Ratio. Plastics Packaging Manufacturers (1467-4491); (until 1999): Business Ratio Plus: Plastics Packaging Manufacturers (1356-5079); (until 1994): Business Ratio Report. Plastics Packaging Manufacturers (1466-027X); (until 1992): Business Ratio Report. Plastics Packaging (0261-9385)
Published by: Key Note Ltd. (Subsidiary of: Bonnier Business Information), Harlequin House, 5th Fl, 7 High St, Teddington, Richmond upon Thames, TW11 8EE, United Kingdom. TEL 44-845-5040452, FAX 44-845-5040453, sales@keynote.co.uk.

688.8 668.5 GBR ISSN 1465-2986
C H P PACKER INTERNATIONAL. (Cosmetics, Healthcare, Pharmaceuticals) Text in English. 1994. bi-m. GBP 40 domestic; BRL 48 foreign (effective 2009). adv. **Document type:** *Journal, Trade.* **Description:** Targeted at individuals in the cosmetics, healthcare and pharmaceutical industries. Reports on new machinery and materials, issues affecting packaging, industry events, company news and market trends.
Indexed: R18.
—BLDSC (3181.754250). **CCC.**
Published by: Binsted Group Plc, Attwood House, Mansfield Park, Four Marks, Alton, Hants GU34 5PZ, United Kingdom. TEL 44-1420-568900, FAX 44-1420-565994, info@binstedgroup.com, http://www.binsteadgroup.com. Ed., Pub. Edward C Binsted. Adv. contact Andrew Flew.

658.788 USA
CAN SHIPMENTS REPORT. (Annual edition avail.) Text in English. 1975. q. USD 265 (effective 2000). back issues avail. **Document type:** *Report, Trade.* **Description:** Lists domestic (US and US controlled territories) shipment by market, product, material used and technology.
Related titles: Cumulative ed(s).: Can Shipments Report (Annual Edition); Special ed(s).
Published by: Can Manufacturers Institute, 1625 Massachusetts Ave, N W, Washington, DC 20036. TEL 202-232-4677. Ed. Sean Reilly. R&P Robert Budway. Circ: 750.

658.7 670 CAN ISSN 0008-4654
CODEN: CPAKAN
CANADIAN PACKAGING. Text in English, French. 1948. m. (11/yr.). adv. illus. **Document type:** *Magazine, Trade.* **Description:** Provides information on the packaged goods industry in Canada, with special attention paid to packaging materials, the conversion of such materials, the use of new machinery, and marketing-related issues.
Related titles: Microfiche ed.: (from MML); Microform ed.: (from MML, PQC); Online - full text ed.
Indexed: A&ATA, A15, A22, ABIPC, ABIn, C03, CBCABus, CBPI, CPerI, ChemAb, CurPA, EngInd, FS&TA, G06, G07, G08, I05, IPackAb, KES, P52, PQC, PST, SCOPUS, TM.
—BLDSC (3043.350000), CIS, IE, Ingenta. **CCC.**
Published by: Business Information Group, 80 Valleybrook Dr., Toronto, ON M3B 2S9, Canada. TEL 416-442-5600, FAX 416-510-5140, orders@businessinformationgroup.ca, http://www.businessinformationgroup.ca. Ed. George Guidoni TEL 416-442-5600 ext 3209. Pub. Stephen Dean TEL 416-442-5600 ext 5198. Adv. contact Munira Khan TEL 416-510-5199. B&W page USD 3,830, color page USD 5,280; 8.138 x 10.88. Circ: 13,000.

688.8 GBR ISSN 1354-5396
THE CANMAKER. Text in English. 1988. m. free to members (effective 2009). adv. bk.rev. back issues avail. **Document type:** *Magazine, Trade.* **Description:** Provides latest news and developments in the manufacture and application of aluminum and steel cans.
Formerly (until 1994): Canmaker and Canner (0953-8690)
Indexed: IPackAb.
—BLDSC (3047.240000), IE, Infotrieve, Ingenta.
Published by: Sayers Publishing Group, Durand House, Manor Royal, Crawley, W Sussex RH10 2PY, United Kingdom. TEL 44-1293-435100, FAX 44-1293-619988, info@sayers-publishing.com, http://www.sayers-publishing.com/. Eds. Monica Higuera TEL 44-1293-435133, John Nutting TEL 44-1293-435128. Pub. Allan J Sayers TEL 44-1293-435124.

664.09 GBR
CANTECH INTERNATIONAL. Text in English. 200?. bi-m. EUR 165 in Europe; USD 185 elsewhere (effective 2010). adv. back issues avail. **Document type:** *Magazine, Trade.* **Description:** Covers the latest developments in the global metal packaging market.
Published by: Bell Publishing Ltd., 57 Bath St, Gravesend, Kent, DA11 0DF, United Kingdom. TEL 44-1474-532202, FAX 44-1474-532203, info@bellpublishing.com, http://www.bellpublishing.com. Adv. contact Victoria Deakins. Circ: 3,628.

676.2 ESP
CARTIFLEX; revista informativa del cartonaje y envase flexible. Text in Spanish. 1988. bi-m. EUR 30 domestic; EUR 42 in Europe; EUR 54 elsewhere (effective 2009). **Document type:** *Magazine, Trade.*
Published by: Alabrent Ediciones S.L., Rbla Josep Tarradellas 1 1s. 4a., Granollers, Barcelona, 08402, Spain. TEL 34-93-8603162, FAX 34-93-8795301, http://www.alabrent.com/. Circ: 4,000.

658.7 676.3 FRA ISSN 0247-8390
CARTONNAGES & EMBALLAGES MODERNES. Text in French. 1940. 7/yr. EUR 96 domestic; EUR 160 foreign (effective 2009). adv. charts; illus. **Document type:** *Magazine, Trade.* **Description:** Deals with paper and board packaging.
Formed by the merger of: Emballage Moderne (0013-6565); Cartonnages
Indexed: ABIPC, CPEI, Englnd, GALA, IPackAb, KES, P&BA, P31, RefZh, SCOPUS.
—CCC.
Published by: Presse Communication International, 176 Rue du Temple, Paris, 75003, France. TEL 33-1-44593838, FAX 33-1-44593839, pci@editions-pci.fr. adv.: color page EUR 3,500. Circ: 3,300.

CHINESE MARKETS FOR PACKAGING MATERIALS. *see* BUSINESS AND ECONOMICS—Marketing And Purchasing

688.8 CHN ISSN 1672-4380
CHUKOU SHANGPIN BAOZHUANG/EXPORT COMMODITIES PACKAGING. Text in Chinese. 1975. bi-m. adv. **Document type:** *Magazine, Trade.*
Formerly (until 1981): Waimao Baozhuang Dongtai
Published by: Zhongguo Chukou Shangpin Baozhuang Yanjiusuo/China National Export Commodities Packaging Research Institute, 28, Donghouxiang, An Ding men Wai, Dongcheng District, Beijing, 100710, China. TEL 86-10-84241043, FAX 86-10-84241040, cepi@cepi-china.com. Ed. Zhu Tong.

688.8 USA
CONTRACT PACKAGING. Text in English. 2005. 3/yr. free to qualified personnel (effective 2011). **Document type:** *Magazine, Trade.* **Description:** Includes news, trends, analysis and information for buyers and sellers of contract packaging.
Related titles: ♦ Supplement to: Packaging World. ISSN 1073-7367.
Published by: (Contract Packaging Association), Summit Publishing Co., 330 N Wabash Ave, Ste 2401, Chicago, IL 60611. TEL 312-222-1010, FAX 312/527-1890. Ed. Bob Sperber. Pub. Joseph L Angel.

CONVERTING TODAY. *see* PAPER AND PULP

676.32 USA ISSN 1934-497X
CORRUGATED TODAY. Text in English. 2005 (Jan/Feb). bi-m. USD 35 domestic; USD 45 in Canada; USD 95 in Europe (effective 2008). adv. **Document type:** *Magazine, Trade.* **Description:** Features information on corrugated industry in the U.S. and Canada.
Published by: N.V. Business Publishers Corp., 43 Main St, Avon By The Sea, NJ 07717. TEL 732-502-0500, FAX 732-502-9606, aschiffenhaus@nvpublications.com, http://www.nvpublications.com. Ed. Jackie Schultz. Pub., Adv. contact Tom Vilardi TEL 732-502-0500 ext 304. page USD 1,990; trim 8.25 x 11. **Co-publisher:** Brunton Business Publications Ltd.

COSMETIC - PERSONAL CARE PACKAGING. *see* BEAUTY CULTURE—Perfumes And Cosmetics

688.8 DEU ISSN 1433-8750
CREATIV VERPACKEN; Marken, Design, Erfolge. Text in German. 1996. 8/yr. EUR 110 domestic; EUR 128.40 in Europe; EUR 145 elsewhere; EUR 16 newsstand/cover (effective 2007). adv. bk.rev. **Document type:** *Magazine, Trade.* **Description:** Provides information about pertinent current and future demands concerning packaging trends. The publication aims to offer support in design, marketing, technology and ecological aspects of packaging.
Published by: Lindenhaus Verlagsgesellschaft mbH & Co. KG, Wilmersdorfer Str 6, Wilmersdorf, 16278, Germany. TEL 49-33334-85200, FAX 49-33334-852029. Ed., Pub., R&P Ute von Buch. Adv. contact Dietrich von Buch. B&W page EUR 2,520, color page EUR 3,870; trim 210 x 297. Circ: 10,000 (paid).

688.8 USA ISSN 1547-9803
HD9839.B683
DAVISON'S BOX & CARTON BLUE BOOK. Variant title: Box & Carton Blue Book. Text in English. 1866. a. USD 125 (print or online ed.) (effective 2008). adv. 350 p./no. 3 cols./p.; back issues avail. **Document type:** *Directory, Trade.* **Description:** Contains profiles of virtually all box and carton manufacturing plants in North America as well as the companies who supply them.
Formerly (until 2003): Official Sourcebook for Corrugated Box and Folding Carton Converters
Related titles: Online - full text ed.
Published by: Davison Publishing Co., LLC (Subsidiary of: Simmons-Boardman Publishing Corp.), 3452 Lake Lynda Dr, Ste 363, Orlando, FL 32817. TEL 407-380-8900, 800-328-4766, FAX 407-380-5222, info@davisonpublishing.com, http://www.davisonpublishing.com. adv.: color page USD 950, B&W page USD 800; 6.5 x 9.5. Circ: 3,000 (paid and controlled).

688.8 621.381 CHN ISSN 1681-1070
DIANI YU FENGZHUANG/ELECTRONICS AND PACKAGING. Text in Chinese. 2001. m. **Document type:** *Magazine, Trade.*
Related titles: Online - full text ed.
Published by: Zhongguo Dianzi Keji Jituan Gongsi Di-58 Yanjiusuo/China Electronics Technology Group Corp. (CETC) No.58 Research Institute, 5, Huihe Lu, Wuxi, 214035, China. TEL 86-510-85860386, FAX 86-510-85802157, cetc58@cetc58.com, cyfz@cetc58.com, http://www.ep.org.cn/.

688.8 GBR ISSN 2044-0685
DIGITAL LABELS & PACKAGING. Text in English. 19??. q. GBP 80, EUR 105 domestic; GBP 130, EUR 170 in Europe; GBP 180, EUR 235 elsewhere (effective 2011). adv. **Document type:** *Magazine, Trade.* **Description:** Provides labels and packaging information to world's paper and printing industries.
Formerly (until 2010): Digital Packaging Strategies Newsletter
Related titles: Online - full text ed.: ISSN 2044-0693. free (effective 2010).
Published by: Whitmar Publications Ltd., 30 London Rd, Southborough, Tunbridge Wells, Kent TN4 0RE, United Kingdom. TEL 44-1892-542099, FAX 44-1892-546693, rob.m@whitmar.co.uk. Ed. Sean Smith. Pub. Marie Rushton.

658.7 USA
EL EMPAQUE. Text in Spanish. 1995. q. free to qualified personnel (print or online ed.) (effective 2009). adv. **Document type:** *Magazine, Trade.*
Formerly (until 2004): Industria del Empaque (1076-8173)
Related titles: Online - full text ed.
Published by: B2B Portales, Inc. (Subsidiary of: Carvajal International, Inc.), 6505 Blue Lagoon Dr, Ste 430, Miami, FL 33126. TEL 305-448-6875, FAX 305-448-9942, contactenos@b2bportales.com, http://www.b2bportales.com. Ed. Lilian Robayo TEL 57-1-4106355 ext 12659. Pub. Terry Beirne TEL 305-448-6875 ext 47311. adv.: color page USD 6,160; trim 8.0625 x 10.8437. Circ: 20,050.

ELECTRONICS PACKAGING TECHNOLOGY CONFERENCE. PROCEEDINGS. *see* ELECTRONICS

676.3 PRT
EMBALAGEM. Text in Portuguese. 6/yr.
Address: Praca das Industrias, Lisbon, 1300, Portugal.

658.7 670 FRA ISSN 0013-6557
EMBALLAGE DIGEST. Text in English, French, German, Italian. 1958. m. (10/yr). EUR 100 domestic; EUR 120 foreign (effective 2009). adv. illus. **Document type:** *Magazine, Trade.*
Indexed: ABIPC, Englnd, IPackAb, P&BA, PST, SCOPUS.
—BLDSC (3732.970000), IE, Ingenta.
Address: 60 bis Rue de Bellevue, Boulogne-Billancourt, 92100, France. TEL 31-1-55203030, FAX 31-1-55203013, ed@emballagedigest.fr, http://www.emballagedigest.fr. Ed. Francoise Albasini TEL 33-1-55203010. Circ: 11,000.

658.7 FRA ISSN 0754-0590
TS158
EMBALLAGES MAGAZINE. Text in French. 1932. 10/yr. EUR 131 domestic (effective 2009). adv. bk.rev. bibl.; illus.; pat.; stat. **Document type:** *Magazine, Trade.*
Formerly (until 1983): Emballages (0013-6573)
Related titles: Online - full text ed.
Indexed: A22, ABIPC, CurPA, Englnd, FS&TA, IPackAb, KES, P&BA, PROMT, SCOPUS.
—BLDSC (3733.001000), IE, INIST, Linda Hall. **CCC.**
Published by: Groupe Industrie Services Info, Antony Parc II, 10 Av. du General de Gaulle, Antony, 92160, France. TEL 33-1-77929775, http://www.librairie-gisi.fr. Circ: 10,000.

663 ARG ISSN 0325-0415
ENVASAMIENTO. Text in Spanish. 1969. m. (11/yr.). USD 150 (effective 1998). adv. bk.rev. bibl.; stat. **Description:** Raw materials, machines, design and confections, analysis of markets, regulations, adhesion and events.
Published by: Today S.A., Talcahuano, 342 Pb 4, Buenos Aires, 1013, Argentina. TEL 54-114-3754458, FAX 54-114-3754458. Ed. Graciela Pancotto. Circ: 5,000.

676.3 ESP ISSN 0211-2965
ENVASPRES; revista profesional del envase y embalaje. Text in Spanish. 1980. 10/yr. EUR 87 domestic; EUR 155 in Europe; EUR 218 elsewhere (effective 2009). **Document type:** *Magazine, Trade.*
Indexed: IPackAb.
Published by: TPI Edita, Ave Manoteras, 26 3a Planta, Madrid, 28050, Spain. TEL 34-91-3396807, FAX 34-91-3396096, info@grupotpi.es, http://www.tpiedita.es. Circ: 7,000.

676 ESP ISSN 0212-5226
EQUIPACK; revista de los equipos y tecnologias del envase y el embalaje. Text in Spanish. 1983. q. EUR 57.04 domestic; EUR 67.92 foreign. **Document type:** *Trade.* **Description:** Offers solutions to the industry in packaging, bottling, and specialized packaging.
Published by: Reed Business Information SA (Subsidiary of: Reed Business Information International), Zancoeta 9, Bilbao, 48013, Spain. TEL 34-944-285600, FAX 34-944-425116, rbi@rbi.es, http://www.rbi.es. Ed. Cristina Garcia. Circ: 6,000.

688.8 JPN ISSN 1343-9677
➤ **EREKUTORONIKUSU JISSO GAKKAISHI/JAPAN INSTITUTE OF ELECTRONICS PACKAGING. JOURNAL.** Text in Japanese. 1998. bi-m. back issues avail. **Document type:** *Journal, Academic/Scholarly.*
Formed by the merger of (1985-1998): S H M Kaishi/Society for Hybrid Microelectronics. Journal (0919-4398); Which was formerly (until 1992): Hybrids (0914-2568); (1986-1998): Kairo Jisso Gakkaishi/Japan Institute for Interconnecting and Packaging Electronic Circuits. Journal (1341-0571); Which was formerly (until 1994): Sakitto Tekunoroji/Japan Institute of Printed Circuit. Journal (0914-8299)
Related titles: Online - full text ed.
Indexed: CPEI.
—BLDSC (4805.165000).
Published by: Erekutoronikusu Jisso Gakkai/Japan Institute of Electronics Packaging, 3-12-2 NIshiogikita, Suginami-ku, Tokyo, 167-0042, Japan. TEL 81-3-53102010, FAX 81-3-53102011, jiep-info@jiep.or.jp.

➤ **ETIKETTERING VAN LEVENSMIDDELEN.** *see* PUBLIC HEALTH AND SAFETY

688.8 FRA ISSN 1951-0330
ETIQ ET PACK. Text in French. 2006. m. EUR 100 domestic; EUR 130 foreign (effective 2010). **Document type:** *Magazine, Trade.*
Published by: M P Medias, L'Admiral, Face au 9 Quai du 4 Septembre, Boulogne, 92100, France. TEL 33-1-46048612.

ETIQUETTES PLUS. *see* PAPER AND PULP

688.8 DEU
EUROPAEISCHER WIRTSCHAFTSDIENST. VERPACKUNG. Text in German. 1978. fortn. EUR 450 (effective 2009). adv. **Document type:** *Bulletin, Trade.*
Formerly (until 1989): Europaeischer Wirtschaftsdienst. Verpackungs-Dienst
Published by: (Europaeischer Wirtschaftsdienst), E U W I D - Europaeischer Wirtschaftsdienst GmbH, Bleichstr 20-22, Gernsbach, 76593, Germany. TEL 49-7224-9397572, FAX 49-7224-9397901, service@euwid.com, http://www.euwid.de. Adv. contact Sven Roth. B&W page EUR 1,220, color page EUR 2,120; trim 189 x 260. Circ: 2,340 (paid and controlled).

EUROPEAN CONVERTING INDUSTRY DIRECTORY. *see* PAPER AND PULP

EUROPEAN ENVIRONMENT & PACKAGING LAW WEEKLY. *see* ENVIRONMENTAL STUDIES—Waste Management

688.8 687 NLD ISSN 2212-0483
F I N A T YEARBOOK. (Federation Internationale des Fabricants Transformateurs d'Adhesifs et Thermocollants) Text in English. 1964. a.
Formerly (until 2011): F I N A T Labelling News (0925-7152); Which superseded in part (in 1990): F I N A T News (0925-7144)
Published by: F I N A T, PO Box 85612, The Hague, 2508 CH, Netherlands. TEL 31-70-3123920, FAX 31-70-3636348, info@finat.com, http://www.finat.com.

688.8 664 USA ISSN 1535-0797
TS195.A1 CODEN: FLPAFA
FLEXIBLE PACKAGING. Text in English. 1999. m. USD 161 domestic; USD 198 in Canada; USD 211 elsewhere; free to qualified personnel (effective 2009). adv. back issues avail.; reprints avail. **Document type:** *Magazine, Trade.* **Description:** Features the latest in business, flexible packaging industry news, original research, technology, operations and new product development.
Related titles: Online - full text ed.
Indexed: A10, A12, A13, A15, A17, ABIn, B01, B07, F10, P41, P48, P51, P52, P53, P54, PQC, S22, V03.
—CCC.
Published by: (Flexible Packaging Association), B N P Media, 155 Pfingsten Rd, Ste 205, Deerfield, IL 60015. TEL 847-405-4000, FAX 847-405-4100, http://www.bnpmedia.com. Ed. Brendan O'Neill. Pub., Adv. contact Mike Barr TEL 630-499-7392. B&W page USD 5,000, color page USD 1,410; trim 8 x 10.75.

343.075 USA
FLEXIBLE PACKAGING ASSOCIATION. REGULATORY REVIEW. Text in English. q. membership. **Document type:** *Magazine, Trade.* **Description:** Covers regulatory activity affecting the flexible packaging industry.
Published by: Flexible Packaging Association, 971 Corporate Blvd, Ste 403, Linthicum, MD 21090. TEL 410-694-0800, FAX 410-694-0900. R&P Mark Wygonik. Circ: (controlled).

688.8 USA
FLEXIBLE PACKAGING ASSOCIATION. UPDATE NEWSLETTER; issues and activities affecting the flexible packaging industry. Text in English. m. membership. **Document type:** *Newsletter, Trade.* **Description:** Covers government policy, public relations, marketing, business and economic research, technology and regulatory affairs, and legal issues affecting flexible packaging products.
Published by: Flexible Packaging Association, 971 Corporate Blvd, Ste 403, Linthicum, MD 21090. TEL 410-694-0800, FAX 410-694-0900. Ed., R&P Mimi Pappas. Circ: 1,000 (controlled).

688.8 GBR ISSN 2040-2880
FLEXIBLE PLASTICS PACKAGING WORLD. Text in English. 2004. m. (10/yr). GBP 750 (effective 2010). **Document type:** *Newsletter, Trade.*
Former titles (until 2008): Flexible and Plastic Packaging Innovation News (1758-1699); (until 2007): Plastic Packaging Innovation News (1745-6819)
Media: Online - full text.
—CCC.
Published by: IntertechPira, Cleeve Rd, Leatherhead, Surrey KT22 7RU, United Kingdom. TEL 44-1372-802080, FAX 44-1372-802079, info@pira-international.com.

676.3 GBR ISSN 0306-168X
TS1200.A1
FOLDING CARTON INDUSTRY. Text in English. 1974. bi-m. GBP 35 domestic; EUR 110 in Europe; USD 130 in US & Canada; GBP 75 elsewhere; GBP 5 per issue (effective 2010); subscr. includes Board Mill. adv. **Document type:** *Magazine, Trade.* **Description:** Covers all technical aspects of folding-carton production.
Indexed: ABIPC, Englnd, IPackAb, P&BA, PST, RefZh, SCOPUS.
—BLDSC (3964.570000), IE, Ingenta. **CCC.**
Published by: Brunton Business Publications Ltd., 1 Salisbury Office Park, London Rd, Salisbury, Wiltshire SP1 3HP, United Kingdom. TEL 44-1722-337038, publications@brunton.co.uk. Pub. Michael Brunton. Adv. contact Dan Brunton. page GBP 1,680, page EUR 1,850; trim 280 x 210. Circ: 8,798.

658.7 664.09 USA ISSN 1941-8531
FOOD & BEVERAGE PACKAGING; market insights to packaging solutions. Text in English. 1959. 11/yr. USD 128 domestic; USD 159 in Canada; USD 172 elsewhere; free to qualified personnel (effective 2008). adv. charts; illus.; tr.lit. index. **Document type:** *Magazine, Trade.* **Description:** Industry journal covering new products, marketing trends and regulatory developments in packaging for the food, drug, pharmaceutical and cosmetic industries.
Former titles (until 2007): Food & Drug Packaging (1085-2077); (until 1995): New Food and Drug Packaging (1075-3028); (until 1993): Food and Drug Packaging (0015-6272)
Related titles: Microform ed.; Online - full text ed.; Supplement(s): Design Gallery. ISSN 1939-7100.
Indexed: A10, B02, B03, B11, B15, B17, B18, F10, G04, G06, G07, G08, H01, I05, IPackAb, PROMT, S22, V03.
—BLDSC (3977.026815). **CCC.**
Published by: B N P Media, 2401 W Big Beaver Rd, Ste 700, Troy, MI 48084. TEL 248-244-6499, FAX 248-244-2925, http://www.bnpmedia.com. Ed. Lisa McTigue Pierce. Pub. Pete Giannakopoulos. adv.: B&W page USD 6,080, color page USD 7,950. Circ: 73,615 (controlled).

658.788 GBR ISSN 2040-2856
FOOD CONTACT WORLD. Text in English. 2006. 10/yr. GBP 750 (effective 2010). **Document type:** *Newsletter, Trade.* **Description:** Contains news and developments directly affecting regulatory and compliance experts in food packaging.
Former titles (until 2008): Global Food Contact (1758-1753); Global Food Contact News (1750-2624)
Media: Online - full text.
Published by: IntertechPira, Cleeve Rd, Leatherhead, Surrey KT22 7RU, United Kingdom. TEL 44-1372-802000, FAX 44-1372-802238, info@pira-international.com.

FOOD MAGAZINE. *see* FOOD AND FOOD INDUSTRIES

688.8 664 GBR ISSN 1355-0497
FOOD PACKAGING BULLETIN; the bulletin for regulatory and packaging safety advisers. Text in English. 1992. 10/yr. GBP 450, USD 900; free to qualified personnel (effective 2010). adv. back issues avail. **Document type:** *Newsletter, Trade.* **Description:** Covers all aspects of regulatory affairs in food packaging.
Related titles: Online - full text ed.: ISSN 2045-2500.
Published by: Research Information Ltd., Grenville Ct, Britwell Rd, Burnham, Bucks SL1 8DF, United Kingdom. TEL 44-1628-600499, FAX 44-1628-600488, info@researchinformation.co.uk.

FOOD PACKER & PROCESSOR DIRECTORY (YEAR). *see* BUSINESS AND ECONOMICS—Trade And Industrial Directories

P

670.29 MEX
GUIA DEL ENVASE Y EMBALAJE/CONTAINER AND PACKAGING GUIDE. Text in English, Spanish. 1975. a. USD 80. adv. index avail. on the Internet. **Document type:** *Directory.* **Description:** Lists more than 1,400 suppliers in Mexico. Lists 800 products, containers, materials, accessories, tools and services. Includes English-Spanish product index.
Formerly: Envase y Embalaje
Published by: Informatica Cosmos, S.A. de C.V., Calz. del Hueso 122-A1, Col. Ex-Hacienda Coapa, Mexico City, DF 14300, Mexico. TEL 52-5-677-48-68, FAX 52-5-679-3575. Ed., Pub. Raul Macazaga. Adv. contact Mary Christen. B&W page USD 1,000; trim 274 x 211. Circ: 5,000. **Dist. in US by:** Schnell Publishing Co. Inc., 2 Rector St, 26th Fl, New York, NY 10006-1819. TEL 212-791-4311, 212-791-4251.

688.8 USA ISSN 2154-3666
HEALTHCARE PACKAGING. Text in English. 2005 (Jan.). bi-m. USD 180 domestic; USD 260 in Canada & Mexico; USD 430 in Europe; USD 650 elsewhere; free to qualified personnel (effective 2010). **Document type:** *Magazine, Trade.* **Description:** Provides information for manufacturers of pharmaceutical, nutraceutical, medical device or biotech products.
Related titles: Online - full text ed.: free (effective 2010).
Published by: Summit Publishing Co., 330 N Wabash Ave, Ste 2401, Chicago, IL 60611. TEL 312-222-1010, FAX 312/527-1890. Pub., Adv. contact Jim Chrzan.

658.564 HKG ISSN 1026-6720
HONG KONG PACKAGING. Text in Chinese, English. 1996. s-a. adv. **Document type:** *Magazine, Trade.* **Description:** Source guide to Hong Kong's packaging industry.
Related titles: Ed.
Published by: Hong Kong Trade Development Council, 38th Fl Office Tower, Convention Plaza, 1 Harbour Rd, Wanchai, Hong Kong. TEL 852-1830668, FAX 852-28240249, hktdc@tdc.org.hk, publications@tdc.org.hk. adv.: color page HKD 1,300; 213 x 280.

688.8 JPN ISSN 0385-728X
HOSO GIJUTSU/JAPAN PACKAGING INSTITUTE. JOURNAL. Text in Japanese; Summaries in English. 1963. m. JPY 2,000 newsstand/cover (effective 2006). **Document type:** *Magazine, Trade.*
—BLDSC (5073.684000).
Published by: Nihon Hoso Gijutsu Kyokai/Japan Packaging Institute, 10F Togeki Bldg. 4-1-1, Tsukiji, Chuo-ku, Tokyo, 104-0045, Japan. TEL 81-3-35431189, FAX 81-3-35438970, http://www.jpi.or.jp/.

688.8 621.9 JPN
HOSO KIKAI SHINBUN/PACKAGING MACHINERY NEWS. Text in Japanese. 1969. m. JPY 2,000.
Indexed: IPackAb.
Published by: Nihon Hoso Kikai Kogyokai/Japan Packaging Machinery Manufactures Association, 5-5 Asakusa-Bashi 5-chome, Taito-ku, Tokyo, 111-0053, Japan.

HOUSEHOLD & PERSONAL PRODUCTS INDUSTRY; the magazine for the detergent, soap, cosmetic and toiletries, wax, polish and aerosol industries. *see* BUSINESS AND ECONOMICS—Marketing And Purchasing

658.788 389.1 USA
I S T A RESOURCE BOOK. Text in English. 1998. a. USD 150 to non-members; USD 75 to members (effective 2000). **Document type:** *Directory, Trade.* **Description:** Contains a membership directory, laboratory directory and ISTA procedures and projects.
Published by: International Safe Transit Association, 1400 Abbott Rd., Ste. 160, East Lansing, MI 48823-1900. TEL 517-333-3437, FAX 517-333-3813.

663.19 ITA ISSN 0392-792X
IMBOTTIGLIAMENTO. Text in Italian. 1978. m. (9/yr.). EUR 40 domestic; EUR 80 in Europe; EUR 100 elsewhere (effective 2011). adv. **Document type:** *Magazine, Trade.* **Description:** Various technologies for the production of alcoholic and non-alcoholic beverages.
Related titles: Online - full text ed.
Indexed: A22, FS&TA, IPackAb.
—BLDSC (4369.057000), IE, Ingenta.
Published by: Tecniche Nuove SpA, Via Eritrea 21, Milan, MI 201, Italy. TEL 39-02-390901, FAX 39-02-7570364, info@tecnichenuove.com. Ed. Maria Grazia Cassinerio. Circ: 6,500.

658.823 DNK ISSN 0106-9403
IN-PAK; packaging and handling: from process to shelf. Text in Danish. 1980. m. DKK 675 (effective 2010). adv. **Document type:** *Magazine, Trade.*
Related titles: Online - full text ed.: 2007.
Indexed: IPackAb.
Published by: TechMedia A/S, Naverland 35, Glostrup, 2600, Denmark. TEL 45-43-242628, FAX 45-43-242626, info@techmedia.dk. Ed. Allan Malmberg TEL 45-43-242681. Adv. contact Anne-Mette Broedsgaard TEL 45-43-242677. color page DKK 29,800; 185 x 265. Circ: 4,476.

INDUSTRIE ALIMENTARI. *see* FOOD AND FOOD INDUSTRIES

INDUSTRIE DELLE BEVANDE. *see* BEVERAGES

688.8 ESP ISSN 1136-3053
INFOPACK E & E; ciencia, tecnologia y diseno del envase y embalaje. Text in Spanish. 1993. 10/yr. adv. **Document type:** *Trade.*
Former titles (until 1996): Embalajes Modernos Packaging (1136-3266); (until 1995): Embalajes Modernos (1136-3258)
Indexed: IPackAb.
Published by: Ediciones Press Graph S.L., Joanot Martorell 4-10, Sabedell, Barcelona, 08203, Spain. TEL 34-93-7205230, FAX 34-93-7205249, info@pressgraph.es. Ed. Francisco Javier Romero. Circ: 7,000 (controlled).

688.8 JPN
INNOVATIVE NEW PACKAGING IN JAPAN. Text in English. 1997. m. USD 595 (effective 2003). **Document type:** *Report, Trade.* **Description:** Provides current news and patent information on the packaging industry in Japan. The first half of the report covers current awareness news on the packaging industry; the second half covers packaging-related patents filed and published in Japan during the previous month.
Indexed: A15, P14, P51, P52.
Published by: Pacific Research Consulting, 4-18-2, Shikahama, Adachi-ku, Tokyo, 123-0864, Japan. TEL 212-532-8815, 81-3-38999953, FAX 81-3-38999968, prc@abelia.ocn.ne.jp, prcnyrep@hotmail.com.

688.8 DEU ISSN 1860-9708
INTELLIGENT VERPACKEN; Magazin fuer Verpackungstechnik. Text in German. 2005. q. EUR 12 newsstand/cover (effective 2007). adv. **Document type:** *Magazine, Trade.*
Published by: Lindenhaus Verlagsgesellschaft mbH & Co. KG, Wilmersdorfer Str 6, Wilmersdorf, 16278, Germany. TEL 49-33334-85200, FAX 49-33334-852029. Ed., Adv. contact Dietrich von Buch. B&W page EUR 1,680, color page EUR 2,880. Circ: 7,000 (paid and controlled).

INTERNATIONAL BOTTLER AND PACKER. *see* BEVERAGES

676 USA ISSN 0020-8191
TS1135
INTERNATIONAL PAPER BOARD INDUSTRY. Text in English. 1956. m. USD 60 in North America; GBP 38 in United Kingdom; GBP 75 elsewhere (effective 2008). adv. charts; illus.; tr.lit. **Document type:** *Magazine, Trade.* **Description:** Provides news, technical articles and in-plant reports from boxmakers all over the world.
Related titles: Online - full text ed.
Indexed: ABIPC, CPEI, EngInd, IPackAb, KES, P&BA, P31, PROMT, RefZh, SCOPUS.
—BLDSC (4544.860000), IE, Ingenta.
Published by: N.V. Business Publishers Corp., 43 Main St, Avon By The Sea, NJ 07717. TEL 732-502-0500, FAX 732-502-9606, aschiffenhaus@nvpublications.com. Ed. Jim Curley. Pub., Adv. contact Tom Vilardi TEL 732-502-0500 ext 304. B&W page USD 2,550, color page USD 3,550; trim 8.25 x 11. Circ: 7,688. **Dist. in UK & Europe:** Brunton Business Publications Ltd., 1 Salisbury Office Park, London Rd, Salisbury, Wiltshire SP1 3HP, United Kingdom. TEL 44-1722-337038, publications@brunton.co.uk.

688.8 USA
INTERNATIONAL SYMPOSIUM ON ADVANCED PACKAGING MATERIALS: PROCESSES, PROPERTIES AND INTERFACES. PROCEEDINGS. Text in English. 19??. a. adv. back issues avail.; reprints avail. **Document type:** *Proceedings, Academic/Scholarly.*
Former titles (until 2005): International Symposium on Advanced Packaging Materials. Proceedings (1727-4842); (until 2002): International Symposium on Advanced Packaging Materials: Processes, Properties and Interfaces. Proceedings; (until 1999): International Symposium on Advanced Packaging Materials. Proceedings (1550-5723)
Related titles: Online - full text ed.
Published by: I E E E, 445 Hoes Ln, Piscataway, NJ 08854. TEL 732-981-0060, 800-678-4333, FAX 732-562-6380, customer.service@ieee.org, http://www.ieee.org.

688.8 ITA
ITALIA IMBALLAGGIO; the voice of Italian packaging. Text in Italian, English. 1994. m. EUR 60 domestic; EUR 96 foreign (effective 2009). adv. illus. back issues avail. **Document type:** *Magazine, Trade.*
Indexed: FS&TA, IPackAb, R18.
Published by: Istituto Italiano Imballaggio Servizi Srl, Via Cosimo del Fante 10, Milan, 20122, Italy. TEL 39-02-58319624, FAX 39-02-58319677, http://www.istitutoimballaggio.it. Circ: 12,000 (paid).

ITALIAN FOOD AND BEVERAGE TECHNOLOGY. *see* FOOD AND FOOD INDUSTRIES

688.8 ITA ISSN 1970-9684
ITALIAN FOOD MATERIALS AND MACHINERY. Text in English. 1993. 5/yr. EUR 20 domestic; EUR 40 in Europe; EUR 35 elsewhere (effective 2011). adv. **Document type:** *Magazine, Trade.*
Formerly (until 2006): Packaging and Bottling International (1128-5990)
Related titles: Online - full text ed.
Indexed: R18.
Published by: Tecniche Nuove SpA, Via Eritrea 21, Milan, MI 201, Italy. TEL 39-02-390901, FAX 39-02-7570364, info@tecnichenuove.com, http://www.tecnichenuove.com. Ed. Antonio Ratti.

688.8 ITA
ITALY CONVERTING. Text in Italian. 4/yr. EUR 24 domestic (effective 2008); Includes subscription to Label World. **Document type:** *Magazine, Trade.*
Related titles: Online - full text ed.
Published by: BE-MA Editrice Srl, Via Teocrito 50, Milan, MI 20128, Italy. TEL 39-02-252071, FAX 39-02-27000692, segreteria@bema.it.

688.8 JPN ISSN 1883-3365
➤ **JAPAN INSTITUTE OF ELECTRONICS PACKAGING. TRANSACTIONS.** Text in English. 2008. a. back issues avail. **Document type:** *Journal, Academic/Scholarly.* **Description:** Publishes papers on Jisso technology, including assembling, packaging, mounting and interconnection, and new ideas for future devices.
—BLDSC (8973.695000), IE.
Published by: Erekutoronikusu Jisso Gakkai/Japan Institute of Electronics Packaging, 3-12-2 NIshiogikita, Suginami-ku, Tokyo, 167-0042, Japan. TEL 81-3-53102010, FAX 81-3-53102011, jiep-info@jiep.or.jp. Ed. Hajime Tomokage.

660.29 658.7 670 GBR ISSN 0021-8502
QC882 CODEN: JALSB7
➤ **JOURNAL OF AEROSOL SCIENCE.** (Also contains selected translations from: Journal of Aerosol Research, Japan) Text in English. 1970. 12/yr. EUR 2,916 in Europe to institutions; JPY 386,900 in Japan to institutions; USD 3,260 elsewhere to institutions (effective 2012). adv. bk.rev. back issues avail.; reprints avail. **Document type:** *Journal, Academic/Scholarly.* **Description:** Features original papers in basic and applied aerosol research.
Related titles: Microfilm ed.: (from PQC); Online - full text ed.: ISSN 1879-1964 (from IngentaConnect, ScienceDirect).
Indexed: A01, A03, A08, A22, A26, A34, A36, A37, ASCA, AgrForAb, ApMecR, BA, C&ISA, C10, C24, C25, C33, CA, CABA, CEA, CEABA, CIN, CISA, CPEI, Cadscan, ChemAb, ChemTitl, CurCont, DBA, E&CAJ, E12, EMBASE, ESPM, EngInd, EnvAb, EnvInd, ExcerpMed, F08, F11, F12, FR, G11, GEOBASE, GH, GeoRef, I05, I11, ISR, Inspec, LeadAb, M&GPA, P30, P33, P37, PN&I, PollutAb, R08, R10, R11, RM&VM, Reac, RefZh, S01, S12, S13, S16, SCI, SCOPUS, SolStAb, SoyAb, T02, T05, TCEA, VS, W07, W10, Zincscan.
—BLDSC (4919.060000), AskIEEE, CASDDS, IE, Infotrieve, Ingenta, INIST, Linda Hall. **CCC.**
Published by: (Gesellschaft fuer Aerosolforschung), Pergamon (Subsidiary of: Elsevier Science & Technology), The Blvd, Langford Ln, East Park, Kidlington, Oxford OX5 1GB, United Kingdom. TEL 44-1865-843000, FAX 44-1865-843010, JournalsCustomerServiceEMEA@elsevier.com. Eds. E J Davis TEL 206-543-0298, G Kasper, M Choi TEL 82-2-8807128.

688.8 USA ISSN 1557-7244
TS195.A1
➤ **JOURNAL OF APPLIED PACKAGING RESEARCH.** Text in English. 2006 (Sep.). q. USD 319 (print or online ed.); USD 344 combined subscription (print & online eds.); USD 95 per issue (effective 2011). adv. abstr.; bibl. Index. back issues avail.; reprints avail. **Document type:** *Journal, Academic/Scholarly.* **Description:** Brings out referred papers, review articles, and tutorial papers on technologies for the packaging industry.
Related titles: Online - full text ed.
—BLDSC (4943.725000). **CCC.**
Published by: DEStech Publications, Inc., 439 N Duke St, Lancaster, PA 17602. TEL 717-290-1660, 877-500-4337, FAX 717-509-6100, info@destechpub.com. Eds. Bruce A Welt, Changfeng Ge.

688.8 GBR
KEY NOTE MARKET REPORT: PACKAGING (GLASS). Variant title: Packaging (Glass) Market Report. Text in English. 19??. irreg., latest 2008, Jun. GBP 460 per issue (effective 2010). **Document type:** *Report, Trade.* **Description:** Provides an overview of a specific UK market segment and includes executive summary, market definition, market size, industry background, competitor analysis, current issues, forecasts, company profiles, and more.
Formerly (until 1995): Key Note Report: Packaging (Glass) (0268-4462)
Related titles: CD-ROM ed.; Online - full text ed.
Published by: Key Note Ltd. (Subsidiary of: Bonnier Business Information), Harlequin House, 5th Fl, 7 High St, Teddington, Richmond upon Thames, TW11 8EE, United Kingdom. TEL 44-845-5040452, FAX 44-845-5040453, info@keynote.co.uk.

KEY NOTE MARKET REPORT: PACKAGING (METALS & AEROSOLS). *see* BUSINESS AND ECONOMICS—Production Of Goods And Services

KEY NOTE MARKET REPORT: PACKAGING (PAPER & BOARD). *see* BUSINESS AND ECONOMICS—Production Of Goods And Services

688.8 GBR
KEY NOTE MARKET REPORT: PACKAGING (PLASTICS). Variant title: Packaging (Plastics) Market Report. Text in English. 19??. irreg., latest 2010, Feb. GBP 460 per issue (effective 2010). **Document type:** *Report, Trade.* **Description:** Provides an overview of a specific UK market segment and includes executive summary, market definition, market size, industry background, competitor analysis, current issues, forecasts, company profiles, and more.
Formerly (until 1995): Key Note Report: Packaging (Plastics) (0954-4364)
Related titles: CD-ROM ed.; Online - full text ed.
Published by: Key Note Ltd. (Subsidiary of: Bonnier Business Information), Harlequin House, 5th Fl, 7 High St, Teddington, Richmond upon Thames, TW11 8EE, United Kingdom. TEL 44-845-5040452, FAX 44-845-5040453, info@keynote.co.uk.

688.8 DEU ISSN 0171-2713
KOMMENTAR FERTIGPACKUNGSRECHT. Text in German. 1974. 2 base vols. plus irreg. updates. EUR 199.50 base vol(s).; EUR 99.50 updates (effective 2011). **Document type:** *Directory, Trade.*
Published by: B. Behr's Verlag GmbH & Co. KG, Averhoffstr 10, Hamburg, 22085, Germany. TEL 49-40-2270080, FAX 49-40-2201091, info@behrs.de, http://www.behrs.de.

688.8 AUT
KOMPACK; Magazin fuer Verpackung, Umwelt und Gemeinde. Text in German. 1990. bi-m. **Document type:** *Magazine, Trade.*
Formerly (until 1993): Compack
Published by: Werbeagentur Harald Eckert, Landstrasser Hauptstr 141/3a/5, Vienna, N 1030, Austria. TEL 43-1-7122036, FAX 43-1-7122070, werbeagentur.harald.eckert@chello.at, http://www.packlist.at. Ed., Pub. Harald Eckert. Circ: 12,000.

688.8 DEU ISSN 1619-8662
L V T LEBENSMITTEL - INDUSTRIE. (Lebensmittel- und Verpackungs-Technik) Text in German. 1954. 8/yr. GBP 50 in United Kingdom to institutions; EUR 98 in Europe to institutions; USD 98 elsewhere to institutions (effective 2012). adv. **Document type:** *Magazine, Trade.*
Former titles (until 2001): L V T (0946-7726); (until 1994): Lebensmittelindustrie (0024-0028); Which was formed by the merger of (1953-1954): Deutsche Obst-, Gemuese-, Zucker-, und Suesswaren-Zeitschrift (0323-6250); (1953-1954): Deutsche Genussmittel Zeitschrift (0323-780X)
Indexed: A34, A35, A37, AgBio, BA, C25, CABA, D01, E12, F08, FS&TA, GH, H16, N02, N03, P32, P33, P40, R11, R13, RM&VM, S12, S13, S16, W11.
—INIST, Linda Hall. **CCC.**
Published by: (Industrievereinigung fuer Lebensmitteltechnologie und Verpackung e.V., Forschungskreises der Ernaehrungsindustrie e.V.), G I T Verlag GmbH (Subsidiary of: Wiley - V C H Verlag GmbH & Co. KGaA), Roesslerstr 90, Darmstadt, 64293, Germany. TEL 49-6151-80900, FAX 49-6151-8090146, info@gitverlag.com. Adv. contact Kerstin Kunkel. Circ: 9,820 (paid and controlled).

688.8 686.2 ITA
LABEL WORLD. Text in English, Italian. 2/yr. EUR 24 domestic (effective 2008); Includes subscription to Italy Converting. **Document type:** *Magazine, Trade.*
Published by: BE-MA Editrice Srl, Via Teocrito 50, Milan, MI 20128, Italy. TEL 39-02-252071, FAX 39-02-27000692, segreteria@bema.it, http://www.bema.it.

676.2 658.7 686.2 GBR ISSN 1478-7520
HD9999.L17
LABELS AND LABELING; the wider world of narrow web. Text in English. 1979. bi-m. GBP 72 (effective 2009). bk.rev. back issues avail. **Document type:** *Magazine, Trade.* **Description:** Contains in-depth technology features, converter profiles and news items on almost every conceivable area of labelling.
Fomerly (until 2002): Labels and Labeling International (0143-2192)
Indexed: A22, ABIPC, IPackAb, P&BA, PST, SCOPUS.
—BLDSC (5137.891800), IE, Ingenta.

Published by: Tarsus Publishing Ltd., Metro Bldg, 4th Fl, 1 Butterwick, London, W6 8DL, United Kingdom. TEL 44-20-88462700, FAX 44-20-88462801, http://www.worldoflabels.com. Ed. Mr. Andy Thomas TEL 44-20-88462835.

688.8 GBR
LABELS & LABELING YEARBOOK. Text in English. 200?. a. free to members. back issues avail. **Document type:** *Yearbook, Trade.* **Description:** Designed to give the label industry the information it needs to grow to the next level of global growth.
Incorporates: Labels & Labelling Annual Directory
Related titles: Online - full text ed.
Published by: Tarsus Publishing Ltd., Metro Bldg, 4th Fl, 1 Butterwick, London, W6 8DL, United Kingdom. TEL 44-20-88462700, FAX 44-20-88462801, subs@labelsandlabeling.com, http://www.worldoflabels.com. Ed. Mr. Andy Thomas TEL 44-20-88462835.

688.8 CHE ISSN 1420-5939
TX341 CODEN: LEINAQ
LEBENSMITTELINDUSTRIE. Text in German. 1992. 6/yr. CHF 80 domestic; CHF 100 foreign (effective 2001). adv. bk.rev. bibl.; charts; illus.; stat.; tr.lit. index. back issues avail. **Document type:** *Magazine, Trade.* **Description:** Publishes articles concerning the management of the food industry.
Formerly (until 1995): Schweizer Lebensmittelindustrie (1021-5484)
Related titles: Online - full text ed.
Indexed: ChemAb, FS&TA, IPackAb.
—CASDDS.
Published by: Verlag Lebensmittelindustrie, Spielhof 14a, Glarus, 8750, Switzerland. TEL 41-55-645-37-50, FAX 41-55-640-21-71, verlag@lebensmittelindustrie.com. Ed. Peter Laternser. Pub. Marie Anne Laternser. Adv. contact Marie-Anne Laternser. B&W page CHF 3,700, color page CHF 5,320; trim 184 x 256. Circ: 7,000.

LEVNEDSMIDDELBLADET/FOODSTUFF MAGAZINE - THE SUPERMARKET. *see* FOOD AND FOOD INDUSTRIES—Grocery Trade

658.788 GBR ISSN 2044-0529
LIGHTING, IMAGING & DISPLAYS WORLD. Text in English. 2004. m. free to members (effective 2010). **Document type:** *Newsletter, Trade.*
Former titles (until 2010): Organic Electronics World (2040-2872); (until 2008): Printed and Disposable Electronics News (1743-5293); Which incorporated: Smart Fabrics
Media: Online - full text.
Published by: IntertechPira, Cleeve Rd, Leatherhead, Surrey KT22 7RU, United Kingdom. TEL 44-1372-802000, FAX 44-1372-802079, publications@pira-international.com.

LINK (SAN ANTONIO). *see* FOOD AND FOOD INDUSTRIES

LOGISTYKA. *see* MACHINERY

676.3 COL ISSN 0121-6554
M A R I; papel y corrugado para America Latina. (Magazine of the Americas Revista Interamericana) Text in Portuguese, Spanish. 1988. bi-m. USD 65 (effective 2005). adv. bk.rev. **Document type:** *Magazine, Trade.* **Description:** Covers the corrugated folding carton industry in Latin America. Offers country-by-country production reports, plant operation stories, personnel interviews, supplier profiles and productivity articles.
Indexed: ABIPC, IPackAb, P&BA.
Published by: (Association of Corrugators of the Caribbean, Central and South America), Latin Press Inc., Apartado Postal 67 252, Medellin, ANT, Colombia. TEL 57-4-4140169, FAX 57-4-2506990, http://www.latinpressinc.com. Ed. Victor Alarcon. Pub. Max Jaramillo. Adv. contact Manuela Jaramillo. color page USD 2,135; trim 8 x 10.5. Circ: 2,000.

676 USA
M A R I - BOARD CONVERTING NEWS ESPANOL. Text in Spanish. 1989. 7/yr. adv. **Document type:** *Magazine, Trade.*
Formerly: Board Converting News Espanol
Published by: N.V. Business Publishers Corp., 43 Main St, Avon By The Sea, NJ 07717. TEL 732-502-0500, FAX 732-502-9606, jcurley@nvpublications.com. Pub., Adv. contact Tom Vilardi TEL 732-502-0500 ext 304. B&W page USD 1,775. Circ: 2,234.

688.8 628.5 GBR ISSN 0969-4145
MACHINERY UPDATE. Text in English. 1989. bi-m. GBP 35 domestic; GBP 50 in Europe; GBP 65 elsewhere (effective 2009). adv. **Document type:** *Magazine, Trade.* **Description:** Provides clear technical and market information for the processing and packaging machinery industry.
Indexed: IPackAb.
Published by: (Processing and Packaging Machinery Association), P P M A Publications ., New Progress House, 34 Stafford Rd, Wallington, Surrey SM6 9AA, United Kingdom. TEL 44-20-87738111, FAX 44-20-87730022, publishing@ppma.co.uk. Ed. Mary Murphy TEL 44-1424-777783.

688.8 USA ISSN 0121-618X
MARI BOARD CONVERTING NEWS. Text in Spanish. 1990. bi-m. **Document type:** *Magazine, Trade.* **Description:** The premier Spanish language publication for the corrugated and folding carton converting industries of Latin America.
Indexed: CPEI, EngInd, P31, SCOPUS.
Published by: N.V. Business Publishers Corp., 43 Main St, Avon By The Sea, NJ 07717. TEL 732-502-0500, FAX 732-502-9606, jcurley@nvpublications.com, http://www.nvpublications.com. Circ: 2,100 (controlled). **Co-publisher:** Edinalco Sa.

MATERIAL HANDLING & LOGISTICS. *see* MACHINERY

MATERIALS K T N FOCUS. (Knowledge Trasnfer Network) *see* PLASTICS

MAZON PLUS/FOOD. *see* FOOD AND FOOD INDUSTRIES

MEIERIPOSTEN. *see* AGRICULTURE—Dairying And Dairy Products

688.8 NLD ISSN 1873-9334
N V C ACTUEEL. Text in Dutch. 1993. 3/yr.
Former titles (until 2005): Nieuwsbrief N V C Actueel (1383-4940); (until 1995): N V C Actueel (1380-8702)
Published by: Nederlands Verpakkingscentrum, Postbus 164, Gouda, 2800 AD, Netherlands. TEL 31-182-512411, FAX 31-182-512769, http://www.nvc.nl.

658.788 DEU ISSN 0341-0390
TS195.A1
N V - NEUE VERPACKUNG; Technik - Marketing - Design. Text in German. 1947. m. EUR 246.40 (effective 2010). adv. **Document type:** *Magazine, Trade.* **Description:** Package engineering in both food and non-food areas.
Formerly (until 1952): Neue Verpackung (0028-3428)
Indexed: A22, ABIPC, EngInd, FS&TA, IPackAb, P&BA, SCOPUS, TM.
—BLDSC (6077.820000), IE, Infotrieve, Ingenta, INIST. **CCC.**
Published by: Huethig GmbH & Co. KG, Postfach 102869, Heidelberg, 69018, Germany. TEL 49-6221-4890, FAX 49-6221-489279, aboservice@huethig.de, http://www.huethig.de. Ed. Matthias Mahr. Adv. contact Anja Breuer. Circ: 14,309 (paid and controlled).

658.788 GBR ISSN 2040-2864
NANOMATERIALS WORLD. Text in English. 2004. m. (10/yr). GBP 750 (effective 2010). **Document type:** *Newsletter, Trade.*
Former titles (until 2008): Nanomaterials (1758-1745); Nanomaterials News (1758-1680); (until 2006): Nanotechnology in Paper & Packaging News (1745-6800)
Media: Online - full text.
—**CCC.**
Published by: IntertechPira, Cleeve Rd, Leatherhead, Surrey KT22 7RU, United Kingdom. TEL 44-1372-802080, FAX 44-1372-802238, publications@pira-international.com.

NATIONAL PACKING NEWS. *see* FOOD AND FOOD INDUSTRIES

NEW DESIGN. *see* TECHNOLOGY: COMPREHENSIVE WORKS

688.8 NZL ISSN 1177-3979
NEW ZEALAND PACKAGING ACCORD (YEAR). Text in English. 2005. a.
Published by: Packaging Council of New Zealand, Accord Secretariat, PO Box 58899, Greenmount, Auckland, New Zealand. TEL 64-9-2714044, FAX 64-9-2714041.

NIEUWSBLAD TRANSPORT. *see* TRANSPORTATION

688.8 JPN ISSN 0918-5283
NIHON HOSO GAKKAISHI/JOURNAL OF PACKAGING SCIENCE & TECHNOLOGY, JAPAN. Text in Japanese. 1992. bi-m. JPY 8,000 membership (effective 2005). **Document type:** *Journal, Academic/Scholarly.* **Description:** Contains information on contribution, explanation of technical terms, event information, etc.
—BLDSC (5027.768000). **CCC.**
Published by: Society of Packaging Science & Technology, Japan, c/o Secretariat, Ballade Heim No.703, 20-3 Hyakunincho-1chome, Shinjuku-ku, Tokyo, 169-0073, Japan. TEL 81-3-53378717, FAX 81-3-53378718, housou@oak.ocn.ne.jp, http://wwwsoc.nii.ac.jp/spstj/.

658.7 SWE ISSN 0039-6494
TS195.A1
NORD-EMBALLAGE; foerpackning, lager, transport, materialhantering. Text in Swedish. 1934. 10/yr. SEK 500; SEK 50 newsstand/cover (effective 2000). adv. bk.rev. bibl.; charts; illus.; mkt.; pat.; stat.; tr.lit.; tr.mk. index. 3 cols./p.; **Document type:** *Magazine, Trade.* **Description:** Directed toward the five Nordic countries. Covers developments in consumer packaging, aerosols, printing and design techniques, as well as transport handling. The editorial features also cover important business events within the industry and other organizations in Sweden and internationally.
Former titles (until 1970): Svensk Emballagetidskrift; (until 1962): Svensk Emballage- och Foerpackningstidskrift
Indexed: IPackAb, P&BA.
Published by: AB Thorsten Fahlskog, Fack 25, Vallingby, 16211, Sweden. TEL 46-8-87-02-80, FAX 46-8-87-48-15, nord.emballage@swipnet.se. Ed., Pub. Kerstin Fahlskog. adv.: B&W page SEK 16,500, color page SEK 21,000; trim 178 x 263. Circ: 4,100 (controlled).

658.7 AUT
O V Z - MITTEILUNGEN. (Oesterreichisches Verpackungszentrum) Text in German. 1956. bi-m. membership. bk.rev. illus.; stat. **Document type:** *Trade.*
Formerly (until Oct. 1976): Besser Verpacken (0005-9595)
Indexed: IPackAb, PST.
Published by: Wirtschaftskammer W I F I Oesterreich, Oesterreichisches Verpackungszentrum, Gumpendorfer Strasse 6, Vienna, W 1060, Austria. TEL 43-1-5869233, FAX 43-1-58886267. Circ: 4,500.

676 USA ISSN 0030-0284
OFFICIAL BOARD MARKETS; "the yellow sheet". Abbreviated title: O B M. Text in English. 1925. w. USD 85 domestic to qualified personnel (effective 2008). adv. charts; mkt.; stat. 20 p./no. 2 cols./p.; back issues avail.; reprints avail. **Document type:** *Magazine, Trade.* **Description:** Covers paperboard, converted paperboard products, waste paper prices and all related news from the board converting industry.
Related titles: Online - full text ed.
Indexed: A15, ABIPC, ABIn, B01, B02, B07, B15, B17, B18, EngInd, G04, G06, G07, G08, I05, P11, P34, P48, P51, P52, P56, PQC, SCOPUS, T02.
—**CCC.**
Published by: Questex Media Group Inc., 275 Grove St, Bldg 2, Ste 130, Newton, MA 02466. TEL 617-219-8300, 888-552-4346, FAX 617-219-8310, questex@sunbeltfs.com, http://www.questex.com. Ed. Mark Arzoumanian TEL 773-880-2234. Adv. contact Dan Weist TEL 216-706-3757. B&W page USD 980, color page USD 1,100; trim 7.75 x 10.75. Circ: 3,527 (paid).

658.7 POL ISSN 0030-3348
OPAKOWANIE. Text in Polish; Summaries in English. 1955. m. PLZ 226.80 domestic; EUR 143 foreign (effective 2011). adv. bk.rev. abstr.; bibl.; charts; illus.; stat. index. 88 p./no.; **Document type:** *Journal, Trade.*
Related titles: Online - full text ed.
Indexed: AgrAg, AgrLib, FS&TA, PST.
Published by: (Federacja Stowarzyszen' Naukowo-Technicznych NOT), Wydawnictwo SIGMA - N O T Sp. z o.o., ul Ratuszowa 11, PO Box 1004, Warsaw, 00950, Poland. TEL 48-22-8180918, FAX 48-22-6192187. Ed. Tadeusz Romanowicz TEL 48-22-8266131. adv.: B&W page PLZ 1,700, color page PLZ 3,200. Circ: 4,500. **Dist. by:** Ars Polona, Obroncow 25, Warsaw 03933, Poland. TEL 48-22-5098609, FAX 48-22-5098610, arspolona@arspolona.com.pl, http://www.arspolona.com.pl.

658.7 GBR
P A C. (Pallett and Case Industry) Text in English. q.
Indexed: IPackAb.
Address: Nelton House, 46A High St, Gravesend, Kent DA11 0AY, United Kingdom. TEL 0474-536535, FAX 0474-536552. Ed. N H Smith.

658.788 USA
P H L BULLETIN. (Packaging, Handling, Logistics) Text in English. 1956. m. USD 50. adv. bk.rev. bibl.
Published by: National Institute of Packaging, Handling and Logistic Engineers, 6902 Lyle St, Lanham, MD 20706-3454. TEL 301-459-9105, FAX 301-459-4925. Ed. James A Russell. Circ: 850.

658.7 AUS
P K N. PACKAGING NEWS. Text in English. 1961. 11/yr. AUD 88 domestic; AUD 105 in New Zealand; AUD 120 in Asia; AUD 160 elsewhere (effective 2008). adv. **Document type:** *Magazine, Trade.* **Description:** Provides news, views, industry analysis, user reports and new product information for Australia's packaging industry.
Former titles (until 1999): Packaging News (0048-2676); (until 1967): Australian Packaging News; (until 1965): Pakit
Related titles: Online - full text ed.
Indexed: ABIX, EngInd, IPackAb, KES, SCOPUS.
Published by: Yaffa Publishing Group Pty Ltd., 17-21 Bellevue St, Surry Hills, NSW 2010, Australia. TEL 61-2-92812333, FAX 61-2-92812750, info@yaffa.com.au. Ed. Lindy Hughson TEL 61-2-92138249. Adv. contact Brian Gent TEL 61-3-96908199. B&W page AUD 3,060, color page AUD 4,250; trim 220 x 297. Circ: 5,194.
Subscr. to: GPO Box 606, Sydney, NSW 2001, Australia.

688.8 628.5 GBR ISSN 1356-0212
P P M A MACHINERY DIRECTORY. Text in English. 1989. a. GBP 45 domestic; GBP 55 in Europe; GBP 65 elsewhere (effective 2009). adv. **Document type:** *Directory, Trade.* **Description:** Features information on machinery for processing and packaging.
Published by: (Processing and Packaging Machinery Association), P P M A Publications ., New Progress House, 34 Stafford Rd, Wallington, Surrey SM6 9AA, United Kingdom. TEL 44-20-87738111, FAX 44-20-87730022, publishing@ppma.co.uk.

688.8 CHE
PACK AKTUELL; Fachmagazin fuer Verpackungstechnik und -design. Text in German. 1983. 20/yr. CHF 97 domestic; CHF 120 foreign (effective 2001). adv. **Document type:** *Magazine, Trade.*
Published by: Profi Press Fachverlag AG, Maihofstr 76, Luzern, 6002, Switzerland. TEL 41-41-4295252, FAX 41-41-4295222. Eds. Irene Jung, Joachim Kreuter. Adv. contact Franziska Birchler TEL 41-1-7671739. Circ: 5,300.

688.8 629.8 BEL ISSN 1370-2491
PACK NEWS & MECHANICAL HANDLING NEWS/PACK NEWS & VERPAKKINGSGIDS. Text in Dutch, French. 1983. 8/yr. EUR 89.31 (effective 2003). **Document type:** *Trade.*
Formerly (until 1986): Pack News (0774-2061)
Indexed: IPackAb.
Published by: Editions Kluwer (Subsidiary of: Wolters Kluwer Belgique), Avenue Louise 326, Brussels, 1050, Belgium. TEL 32-800-16868, FAX 32-2-3003003, customer@editionskluwer.be, http://www.editionskluwer.be/ek/home.asp. Ed., Pub. Bernard Lefevre. Circ: 11,325 (controlled).

688.8 DNK ISSN 1602-1436
PACK + PLAST. Variant title: Pack plus Plast. Text in Swedish. 1997. 11/yr. adv. **Document type:** *Magazine, Trade.*
Formerly (until 2000): T F S Pack + Plast (1403-0217)
Related titles: Online - full text ed.: 2007.
Published by: TechMedia A/S, Naverland 35, Glostrup, 2600, Denmark. TEL 45-43-242628, FAX 45-43-242626, info@techmedia.dk. Eds. Kenneth Bengtsson, Boerje Aahgren TEL 45-43-242683. Adv. contact Thomas Liljeroth TEL 46-70-5445945. B&W page SEK 24,400, color page SEK 27,400; 190 x 265. Circ: 5,300 (controlled).

688.8 USA ISSN 1554-6772
PACKAGE DESIGN MAGAZINE. Text in English. 2003. 10/yr. USD 48 domestic; USD 129 foreign; free domestic to qualified personnel (effective 2008). adv. **Document type:** *Magazine, Trade.* **Description:** Targets professional package designers. Includes information on new materials and new technologies and profiles of design projects and processes.
Indexed: ESPM, SSciA.
Published by: Lyons Media, Inc. (Subsidiary of: S T Media Group International, Inc.), 20 Valley Stream Pkwy Ste 265, Malvern, PA 19355. TEL 610-296-3001, FAX 610-296-1553. Ed. Ron Romanik TEL 610-296-3001 ext 102. Pub. Christopher Lyons TEL 610-296-3001 ext 100. adv.: page USD 4,250; trim 8.125 x 10.875. Circ: 30,000.

658.7 AUS ISSN 1328-3847
CODEN: AUPAEH
PACKAGING; the business - the issues - the solutions. Text in English. 1952. bi-m. AUD 70; free domestic to qualified personnel; AUD 7 per issue (effective 2008). adv. bk.rev. charts; illus.; pat.; tr.lit.; tr.mk. back issues avail. **Document type:** *Magazine, Trade.* **Description:** Focuses on packaging technology and its applications, overseas packaging developments and industry corporate news.
Formerly (until 1995): Australian Packaging (0004-9921)
Indexed: A15, ABIPC, ABIX, ABIn, B01, B07, C10, CurPA, IPackAb, M01, M02, P48, P51, P52, PQC, PST.
—**CCC.**
Published by: Reed Business Information Pty Ltd. (Subsidiary of: Reed Business Information International), Tower 2, 475 Victoria Ave, Locked Bag 2999, Chatswood, NSW 2067, Australia. TEL 61-2-94222999, FAX 61-2-94222922, customerservice@reedbusiness.com.au, http://www.reedbusiness.com.au. Ed. Anna Game-Lopata TEL 61-2-94222645. Pub. Chris Williams TEL 61-2-94222957. Adv. contact Agnes Beugnon TEL 61-2-99872914. color page AUD 3,410; trim 235 x 297. Circ: 5,658.

688.8 GBR ISSN 1743-4882
PACKAGING (FOOD & DRINK) INDUSTRY. Variant title: Packaging (Food & Drink) Industry Market Review. Text in English. 1996. irreg., latest 2003, Nov. GBP 595 per issue (effective 2010). **Document type:** *Report, Trade.* **Description:** Provides an overview of a specific UK market segment and includes executive summary, market definition, market size, industry background, competitor analysis, current issues, forecasts, company profiles, and more.

P

Formerly (until 2003): Key Note Market Report: Packaging (Food & Drink) (1363-3295)
Published by: Key Note Ltd. (Subsidiary of: Bonnier Business Information), Harlequin House, 5th Fl, 7 High St, Teddington, Richmond upon Thames, TW11 8EE, United Kingdom. TEL 44-845-5040452, FAX 44-845-5040453, info@keynote.co.uk.

676.3 GBR ISSN 2041-2371
PACKAGING & CONVERTING INTELLIGENCE. Text in English. 2004 (Aug.). s-a. GBP 5.95 per issue domestic; EUR 8 per issue in Europe; USD 8.95 per issue in United States; free to qualified personnel (effective 2010). adv. back issues avail. **Document type:** *Magazine, Trade.* **Description:** Provides expert insight, advice and information on the latest developments in the FMCG packaging industry today including independent analyses of current trends, technological advances and industry success stories that can be implemented in an organization.
Related titles: Online - full text ed.
Published by: S P G Media Ltd. (Subsidiary of: Sterling Publishing Group Plc.), Brunel House, 55-57 N Wharf Rd, London, W2 1LA, United Kingdom. TEL 44-20-79159660, FAX 44-20-77242089, info@spgmedia.com, http://www.spgmedia.com/. Eds. Lucy Schwerdtfeger TEL 44-20-79159714, John Lawrence. Pub. William Crocker.

658.788 USA
PACKAGING AND CONVERTING TECHNOLOGY SERIES. Text in English. 1987. irreg., latest 2005. price varies. back issues avail. **Document type:** *Monographic series, Academic/Scholarly.*
Formerly: Packaging Technology Series
Published by: C R C Press, LLC (Subsidiary of: Taylor & Francis Group), 6000 Broken Sound Pky, NW, Ste 300, Boca Raton, FL 33487. TEL 800-272-7737, FAX 800-374-3401, orders@crcpress.com.

THE PACKAGING AND DESIGN DIRECTORY. *see* BUSINESS AND ECONOMICS—Trade And Industrial Directories

658.7 670 USA ISSN 0030-9117
PACKAGING DIGEST. Text in English. 1963. m. free to qualified personnel (print or online ed.) (effective 2010). adv. illus.; tr.lit. back issues avail.; reprints avail. **Document type:** *Magazine, Trade.* **Description:** Features reports on the most successful applications of packaging materials, machinery and technologies.
Incorporates (in 1985): Packaging (0746-3820); Which was formerly (until 1985): Package Engineering Including Modern Packaging (0747-9999); Which was formed by the merger of (1927-1979): Modern Packaging (0026-8224); (1956-1979): Package Engineering (0030-9044); Which incorporated (in 1974): Package Engineering New Products (0160-8258); Which was formerly (until 1973): Package Engineering New Products News (0300-6735)
Related titles: Microform ed.: (from PQC); Online - full text ed.; ◆ Spanish ed.: Packaging Digest Edicion Latino Americana.
Indexed: A05, A09, A10, A12, A13, A17, A22, A23, A24, ABIn, AS&TA, AS&TI, B01, B02, B03, B06, B07, B08, B09, B11, B13, B15, B17, B18, BPI, BRD, CurPA, EngInd, G04, G06, G07, G08, GALA, I05, IPackAb, P&BA, P48, P51, P52, P53, P54, PQC, PROMT, R18, SCOPUS, T&II, T02, V02, V03, V04, W01, W02, W03, W05.
—BLDSC (6332.651000), IE, Infotrieve, Ingenta, INIST, Linda Hall. **CCC.**
Published by: Canon Communications LLC (Subsidiary of: Apprise Media LLC), 1200 Jorie Blvd., Ste.230, Oak Brook, IL 60523. TEL 630-990-2371, FAX 630-990-8894, info@cancom.com, http://www.cancom.com. Ed. John Kalkowski. adv.: B&W page USD 12,340, color page USD 14,360; trim 15.75 x 11. Circ: 91,681.

658.7 USA
PACKAGING DIGEST EDICION LATINO AMERICANA. Text in Spanish. 1994. s-a. illus.; tr.lit. back issues avail.; reprints avail. **Document type:** *Magazine, Trade.* **Description:** Publishes articles for makers and prime users of packaging in Latin America.
Related titles: ◆ English ed.: Packaging Digest. ISSN 0030-9117.
Published by: Canon Communications LLC (Subsidiary of: Apprise Media LLC), 1200 Jorie Blvd., Ste.230, Oak Brook, IL 60523. TEL 630-990-2371, FAX 630-990-8894, info@cancom.com, http://www.cancom.com.

676 621.9 USA
PACKAGING DIGEST MACHINERY - MATERIALS GUIDE. Text in English. 1979. a. **Document type:** *Directory.*
Published by: Canon Communications LLC (Subsidiary of: Apprise Media LLC), 1200 Jorie Blvd., Ste.230, Oak Brook, IL 60523. TEL 630-990-2371, FAX 630-990-8894, info@cancom.com, http://www.cancom.com.

658.788 USA
PACKAGING HOTLINE; connecting buyers and sellers of packaging equipment, materials, services and suppliers. Text in English. 1990. m. free to qualified personnel (print or online ed.) (effective 2009). adv. back issues avail. **Document type:** *Magazine, Trade.* **Description:** Designed to keep packaging professionals current on equipment, machinery, materials and business services.
Related titles: Online - full text ed.
Published by: Industry Marketing Solutions, 809 Central Ave, 2nd Fl, PO Box 893, Fort Dodge, IA 50501. TEL 515-574-2248, 888-247-2007, FAX 515-574-2237, http://www.industrymarketingsolutions.com/. Pub. Steve Scanlan. adv.: B&W page USD 618, color page USD 751; trim 7.625 x 10.75. Circ: 60,000 (controlled).

658.7 IND ISSN 0030-9125
CODEN: PINDDS
PACKAGING INDIA. Text in English. 1968. bi-m. INR 1,200 domestic to non-members; USD 150 foreign to non-members; INR 1,500 SAARC to non-members; free to members (effective 2011). adv. bk.rev. 100 p./no. 3 cols./p.; back issues avail. **Document type:** *Journal, Academic/Scholarly.* **Description:** Covers technical and economic aspects of the packaging industry as well as new product information.
Formed by the 1968 merger of: Packaging Digest; Packaging Update; Packaging India
Indexed: IPackAb.
—BLDSC (6332.750000), IE, Ingenta, INIST.
Published by: Indian Institute of Packaging, E-2 MIDC Area, Andheri E, Mumbai, Maharashtra 400 093, India. TEL 91-22-28219803, iip@iip-in.com.

658.7 JPN ISSN 0288-3864
TS195.A1 CODEN: PAJAEC
PACKAGING JAPAN. Text in Japanese. 1980. bi-m. USD 90 in Asia; USD 158 in Europe. adv. bk.rev. charts; illus. **Document type:** *Trade.*
Formerly: New Packaging (0004-6469)
Indexed: A22.
Published by: Nippo Co. Ltd., 1-19 Misaki-cho 3-chome, Chiyoda-ku, Tokyo, 101-0061, Japan. FAX 81-3-3263-2560, TELEX 2322348 PJNIPOJ. Ed. Katsushi Kawamura. Circ: 10,000. **Dist. by:** International Marketing Corp., I.P.O. Box 5056, Tokyo 100-30, Japan. TEL 81-3-3661-7458, FAX 81-3-3667-9646.

688.8 DEU
PACKAGING JOURNAL; Technologie - Logistik - Marketing - Produkte. Text in German. 2001. 8/yr. EUR 70 domestic; EUR 94 foreign; EUR 10.50 newsstand/cover (effective 2009). adv. **Document type:** *Magazine, Trade.*
Published by: Ella Verlag, Emil-Hoffmann-Str 55-59, Cologne, 50996, Germany. TEL 49-2236-84880, FAX 49-2236-848824, info@ella-verlag.de, http://www.ella-verlag.de. Pub., Adv. contact Elke Latuperisa. B&W page EUR 2,575, color page EUR 3,850; trim 216 x 303. Circ: 10,712 (paid and controlled).

658.7884 USA
PACKAGING MACHINERY MANUFACTURERS INSTITUTE. OFFICIAL PACKAGING MACHINERY DIRECTORY (CD-ROM). Cover title: Packaging Machinery Directory. Text in English. 1954. biennial. index. **Document type:** *Directory.* **Description:** Contains information on all 500+ PMMI member companies, who are committed to producing quality products and providing world-class service to their customers.
Formerly: Packaging Machinery Manufacturers Institute. Official Packaging Machinery Directory (Print) (0078-7698)
Media: CD-ROM.
Published by: Packaging Machinery Manufacturers Institute, 4350 Fairfax Dr, Ste 600, Arlington, VA 22203-1619. TEL 703-243-8555, 888-275-7664, FAX 703-243-8556, pmmi@pmmi.org, http://www.pmmi.org/. Ed. Jerry Welcome. Circ: 50,000.

688.8 658 USA ISSN 1556-1658
PACKAGING MACHINERY TECHNOLOGY. Text in English. 2003. bi-m. adv. **Document type:** *Magazine, Trade.* **Description:** Covers precisely what packaging machinery buyers and management teams need to know to do their jobs better.
Related titles: Online - full text ed.
Published by: Packaging Machinery Manufacturers Institute, 4350 Fairfax Dr, Ste 600, Arlington, VA 22203-1619. TEL 703-243-8555, 888-275-7664, FAX 703-243-8556, pmmi@pmmi.org, http://www.pmmi.org/. Pub. Stephen G Osborne. adv.: B&W page USD 3,996; trim 8.375 x 10.875. Circ: 35,000 (controlled).

658.7 GBR ISSN 0030-9133
HF5770.A1 CODEN: PKGNAY
PACKAGING NEWS. Abbreviated title: P N. Text in English. 1954. m. GBP 95 (effective 2009). adv. bk.rev. charts; illus.; tr.lit. reprints avail. **Document type:** *Magazine, Trade.* **Description:** Covers the very latest in industry news, product/brand design, materials, printing, machinery, labels and labelling.
Incorporates (in May.2006): Packaging Magazine (1461-4200); (1983-199?): Converting World (0266-0350)
Related titles: Online - full text ed.
Indexed: A10, ABIPC, B01, B07, CurPA, F10, IPackAb, P&BA, PST, V03.
—BLDSC (6332.840000). **CCC.**
Published by: Haymarket Publishing Ltd. (Subsidiary of: Haymarket Media Group), 174 Hammersmith Rd, London, W6 7JP, United Kingdom. TEL 44-20-82674210, info@haymarket.com, http://www.haymarket.com. Ed. Josh Brooks TEL 44-20-82678096. Adv. contacts James Fleetham TEL 44-20-82678098, Susan Moffat TEL 44-20-82674256. Circ: 15,081. **Subscr. to:** 12-13 Cranleigh Gardens Industrial Estate, Southall UB1 2DB, United Kingdom. TEL 44-84-51557355, FAX 44-20-86067503, subscriptions@haymarket.com, http://www.haymarketbusinesssubs.com.

688.8 HKG
PACKAGING PRO. Text mainly in Chinese; Contents page in English, Chinese. 1994. 4/yr. HKD 305 domestic; USD 60 in Asia; USD 65 elsewhere (effective 2003). adv. back issues avail. **Document type:** *Trade.*
Formerly: China P F P (1024-8633)
Published by: (China Packaging Technology Association CHN), Yashi Chuban Gongsi/Adsale Publishing Ltd., 4-F, Stanhope House, 734 King's Rd, North Point, Hong Kong. TEL 852-2811-8897, FAX 852-2516-5119. Ed. Mabel Tang. Pub. Annie Chu. Adv. contact Janet Tong TEL 852-2516-3380. B&W page USD 1,116, color page USD 2,831; trim 280 x 215. Circ: 24,200. **Co-sponsors:** China Food and Packaging Machinery Industry Association; Guangzhou Printing Technology Association; Printing and Printing Equipment Association of China.

688.8099105 GBR ISSN 1477-8467
THE PACKAGING PROFESSIONAL. Text in English. 1977. bi-m. GBP 214 to institutions; USD 405 in United States to institutions (effective 2012). adv. back issues avail. **Document type:** *Magazine, Trade.* **Description:** Focuses on technology, innovation and design in packaging, the magazine serves a community of industry professionals, from packaging technologists to product designers and marketing specialists. Includes a news section, innovation pages, an events diary, and updates on training courses run by the Institute.
Formerly (until 2002): Panorama
Related titles: Online - full text ed.
—CCC.
Published by: (The Packaging Society), I O M Communications Ltd. (Subsidiary of: Institute of Materials, Minerals and Mining), 1 Carlton House Terr, London, SW1Y 5DB, United Kingdom. TEL 44-20-74517300, FAX 44-20-78392289. Ed. Katherine Williams TEL 44-20-74517314. **Subscr. in N. America to:** Maney Publishing, 875 Massachusetts Ave, 7th Fl, Cambridge, MA 02139. TEL 866-297-5154, FAX 617-354-6875, maney@maneyusa.com; **Subscr. to:** Maney Publishing, Ste 1C, Joseph's Well, Hanover Walk, Leeds, W Yorks LS3 1AB, United Kingdom. TEL 44-113-3868168, FAX 44-113-3868178, subscriptions@maney.co.uk.

658.788 ZAF ISSN 1014-8280
PACKAGING REVIEW SOUTH AFRICA. Text in English. 1975. m. ZAR 260 (effective 2006). adv. illus. **Document type:** *Magazine, Trade.* **Description:** Covers new equipment, processes and materials, market trends and legislative developments affecting raw materials suppliers, converters and users of packaging products.
Indexed: FS&TA, IPackAb, ISAP, PST, R18.
Published by: (Institute of Packaging, South Africa), National Publishing (Pty) Ltd., IHS Bldg., Cnr. Northern Parkway & Handel Rd., Ormonde, Johannesburg, 2091, South Africa. TEL 27-11-8352221, FAX 27-11-8352631, info@natpub.co.za, http://www.natpub.co.za/. Ed. Gill Loubser TEL 27-21-6711140. Circ: 3,000. **Co-sponsor:** Packaging Council.

658.7 GBR ISSN 0952-4495
PACKAGING SCOTLAND. Text in English. 1987. q. GBP 32 domestic; GBP 40 foreign (effective 2009). adv. **Document type:** *Magazine, Trade.*
Indexed: IPackAb, R18.
—CCC.
Published by: Peebles Media Group, Bergius House, Clifton St, Glasgow, G3 7LA, United Kingdom. TEL 44-141-5676000, FAX 44-141-3311395, info@peeblesmedia.com, http://www.peeblesmedia.com/. Ed. Kim McAllister TEL 44-141-5676028. Adv. contact Linda Scott TEL 44-141-5676027. color page GBP 1,475; trim 210 x 297. Circ: 4,219.

658.564 USA
(YEAR) PACKAGING SOURCEBOOK (INTERNATIONAL EDITION). Text in English. 1997. a. USD 375 (effective 1998). **Document type:** *Directory.* **Description:** Guide to the international packaging industry including contact information for manufacturers, suppliers, and buyers as well as country overviews and market reports.
Related titles: CD-ROM ed.
Published by: North American Publishing Co., 1500 Spring Garden St., 12th Fl, Philadelphia, PA 19130. TEL 215-238-5300, FAX 215-238-5213, magazinecs@napco.com, http://www.napco.com.

658.564 USA ISSN 1076-1659
HF5770.A1
(YEAR) PACKAGING SOURCEBOOK (NORTH AMERICAN EDITION). Text in English. 1995. a. USD 375 (effective 1998). **Document type:** *Directory.* **Description:** Includes information on contacts at packaging manufacturers, suppliers, and buyers.
Related titles: CD-ROM ed.: ISSN 1529-3688.
Published by: North American Publishing Co., 1500 Spring Garden St., 12th Fl, Philadelphia, PA 19130. TEL 215-238-5300, FAX 215-238-5457, http://www.napco.com.

670 USA ISSN 8755-6189
CODEN: PASTEC
PACKAGING STRATEGIES; an exclusive intelligence service on critical trends and new developments in packaging materials, containers, and machinery. Text in English, Japanese. 1983. 22/yr. looseleaf. USD 497 domestic (effective 2009). charts; illus. 8 p./no. 2 cols./p.; back issues avail. **Document type:** *Newsletter, Trade.* **Description:** Focuses on emerging trends, technologies and business issues pertaining to the packaging industries. Reports on materials, containers and equipment.
Related titles: E-mail ed.: USD 497 (effective 2009); Online - full text ed.: USD 497 (effective 2007).
Indexed: B02, B03, B11, B15, B17, B18, G04, G06, G07, G08, I05, IPackAb, T03.
—Infotrieve. **CCC.**
Published by: B N P Media, 600 Willowbrook Ln, Ste 610, West Chester, PA 19382. TEL 610-436-4220, 800-524-7225, FAX 610-436-6277, portfolio@bnpmedia.com, http://www.bnpmedia.com.

688.8 USA
PACKAGING TECHNOLOGY AND ENGINEERING (ONLINE). Text in English. irreg.
Media: Online - full text.
Published by: Institute of Packaging Professionals, 1601 North Bond St, Ste 101, Naperville, IL 60563. TEL 630-544-5050, FAX 630-544-5055, info@iopp.org, http://www.iopp.org.

676 335 GBR ISSN 0894-3214
TS195.A1 CODEN: PTSCEQ
PACKAGING TECHNOLOGY AND SCIENCE. Text in English. 1988. 8/yr. GBP 1,265 in United Kingdom to institutions; EUR 1,600 in Europe to institutions; USD 2,478 elsewhere to institutions; GBP 1,455 combined subscription in United Kingdom to institutions (print & online eds.); EUR 1,841 combined subscription in Europe to institutions (print & online eds.); USD 2,850 combined subscription elsewhere to institutions (print & online eds.) (effective 2012). adv. back issues avail.; reprint service avail. from PSC. **Document type:** *Journal, Academic/Scholarly.* **Description:** Provides an international forum for the rapid publication of articles about developments in this field.
Related titles: Microform ed.: (from PQC); Online - full text ed.: ISSN 1099-1522. 1997. GBP 1,265 in United Kingdom to institutions; EUR 1,600 in Europe to institutions; USD 2,478 elsewhere to institutions (effective 2012) (from IngentaConnect).
Indexed: A20, A22, A28, A34, A37, ABIPC, APA, B21, BA, BP, BrCerAb, C&ISA, C25, C30, CA/WCA, CABA, CIA, CIN, CPEI, CerAb, ChemAb, ChemTitl, CivEngAb, CorrAb, CurCont, D01, E&CAJ, E04, E05, E11, E12, EEA, EMA, ESPM, EngInd, EnvEAb, F05, F06, F07, F08, F11, F12, FR, FS&TA, GH, H&SSA, H15, H16, IPackAb, ISMEC, Inspec, M&TEA, M09, MBF, METADEX, MaizeAb, N02, N03, OR, P31, P33, P37, PHN&I, PN&I, R18, RA&MP, RM&VM, S12, S13, S16, SCI, SCOPUS, SolStAb, SoyAb, T04, TAR, TM, TriticAb, VS, W07, W11, WAA.
—CASDDS, IE, Infotrieve, Ingenta, INIST, Linda Hall. **CCC.**
Published by: John Wiley & Sons Ltd. (Subsidiary of: John Wiley & Sons, Inc.), 1-7 Oldlands Way, PO Box 808, Bognor Regis, West Sussex PO21 9FF, United Kingdom. TEL 44-1865-778315, FAX 44-1243-843232, cs-journals@wiley.com, http://eu.wiley.com/WileyCDA/. Ed. David Shires. **Subscr. in the Americas to:** John Wiley & Sons, Inc., 111 River St, Hoboken, NJ 07030. TEL 201-748-6645, subinfo@wiley.com; **Subscr. to:** 1-7 Oldlands Way, PO Box 809, Bognor Regis, West Sussex PO21 9FG, United Kingdom. TEL 44-1865-778054, cs-agency@wiley.com.

614.7 AUS ISSN 0159-1843
PACKAGING TODAY. Text in English. 1979. q. **Document type:** *Newsletter, Trade.* **Description:** Provides packaging news, headlines, and feature stories of interest to packaging companies, packaging suppliers, and the packaging industry 24 hours a day, every day.
Supersedes: Packaging Council of Australia. Legislation and Metrication Newsletter
Indexed: FS&TA, IPackAb.
Published by: Packaging Council of Australia, Level 3, 15-17 Park St, South Melbourne, VIC 3205, Australia. TEL 61-3-96901955, FAX 61-3-96903514, info@pca.org.au, http://www.pca.org.au. Circ: 4,000.

658.7 670 GBR ISSN 1747-7468
PACKAGING TODAY. Text in English. 1979. m. GBP 114 domestic; EUR 283 in Europe; USD 279 in US & Canada; USD 335 elsewhere (effective 2010). adv. back issues avail. **Document type:** *Magazine, Trade.* **Description:** Provides Europe's packaging professionals with news and features on key factors affecting the packaging industry - everything from corporate developments to news on machinery, packaging materials and packs.
Incorporates: Packaging Today Europe (1369-1198); Former titles (until 2004): Packaging Today International (1470-6008); (until 2000): Packaging Today (0268-0920)
Related titles: Online - full text ed.: GBP 89.22 domestic; EUR 124.90 in Europe; USD 179.33 elsewhere (effective 2010).
Indexed: B02, B15, B17, B18, FS&TA, G04, G06, G07, G08, I05, IPackAb, R18.
—BLDSC (6333.019550), IE, Infotrieve, Ingenta. **CCC.**
Published by: Global Trade Media Ltd. (Subsidiary of: Progressive Media Group), Progressive House, 2 Maidstone Rd, Footscray, Sidcup, Kent DA14 5HZ, United Kingdom. TEL 44-20-82697700, FAX 44-20-82697880, info@globaltrademedia.com, http://www.globaltrademedia.com/. Ed. Maureen Byrne. Pub. Maria Wallace TEL 44-20-79159646. adv.: page GBP 3,350. Circ: 15,122 (controlled).

PACKAGING, TRANSPORT, STORAGE & SECURITY OF RADIOACTIVE MATERIAL. *see* TRANSPORTATION

688.8 USA ISSN 1073-7367
CODEN: PWORE4
PACKAGING WORLD; packaging news, trends & innovations. Text in English. 1994. m. USD 200 domestic; USD 285 in Canada & Mexico; USD 475 in Europe; USD 715 elsewhere; free to qualified personnel (effective 2011). **Document type:** *Magazine, Trade.*
Related titles: Online - full text ed.: free (effective 2011); ◆ Supplement(s): Contract Packaging.
—Linda Hall.
Published by: Summit Publishing Co., 330 N Wabash Ave, Ste 2401, Chicago, IL 60611. TEL 312-222-1010, FAX 312/527-1890. Pub. Joseph L Angel.

658.564 DNK ISSN 1395-4652
PACKMARKEDET. Text in Danish. 1995. 11/yr. DKK 390 (effective 2009). adv. **Document type:** *Magazine, Trade.*
Related titles: Online - full text ed.
Published by: Odsgard A/S, Stationsparken 25, Glostrup, 2600, Denmark. TEL 45-43-432900, FAX 45-43-431328, odsgard@odsgard.dk, http://www.odsgard.dk. Ed. Jacob Kestner TEL 45-46-936636. Adv. contact Preben Reinholdt Andersen. page DKK 14,900; 184 x 270.

658.788 SWE ISSN 1404-8477
PACKMARKNADEN NORDICA. Text in Swedish. 1999. 11/yr. SEK 924 domestic print ed.; SEK 1,155 domestic print & online eds.; SEK 1,355 foreign print & online eds.; SEK 1,124 foreign print ed.; SEK 613 online ed. (effective 2007). adv. **Document type:** *Magazine, Trade.*
Formed by the merger of (1991-1999): Pack Nordica (1102-7584); (1978-1999): Packmarknaden Scandinavia (0348-260X)
Related titles: Online - full text ed.
Indexed: IPackAb.
Published by: Mentor Online AB, Landskronawaegen 1, PO Box 601, Helsingborg, 25106, Sweden. info@mentoronline.se, http://www.mentoronline.se. Ed. Marcus Petersson TEL 46-42-4901911. Adv. contact Pernilla Sandberg TEL 46-42-4901915. page SEK 28,600; trim 202 x 302. Circ: 3,800.

658.7 NOR ISSN 1890-7903
PACKNEWS. Text in Norwegian. 1939. bi-m. NOK 692 (effective 2011). adv. illus. **Document type:** *Magazine, Trade.*
Former titles (until 2008): Emballering (0013-6581); (until 1970): Norske Esker (0333-4597); Incorporates (in 2003): Mat & Pack (1503-0938); Which was formerly (1996-2001): Mat & Pack Markedet (0807-7665)
Related titles: Online - full text ed.
Indexed: ABIPC, IPackAb, P&BA.
—CCC.
Published by: Skarland Press A-S, P O Box 2843, Toeyen, Oslo, 0608, Norway. TEL 47-22-708300, FAX 47-22-708301, firmapost@skarland.no, http://www.skarland.no. Ed. Per Oeyvind Nordberg. Adv. contact Arne Jensen TEL 47-22-708309. Circ: 3,000.

658.7 GBR
PACKPLAS INTERNATIONAL. Text in Arabic. q. GBP 42. bk.rev. **Document type:** *Handbook/Manual/Guide, Trade.* **Description:** Provides technology guides, in-depth features and analysis for the packaging, plastics, converting and allied industries in the Arab world.
Published by: International Printing Communications Ltd., Crownhill Industry, PO Box 923, Milton Keynes, Bucks MK8 0AY, United Kingdom. TEL 44-1908-561444, FAX 44-1908-569564. Ed. A Zahra. Pub. R Ghozzi. adv.: B&W page GBP 1,675, color page GBP 1,975; trim 186 x 272. Circ: 14,000 (controlled).

670 NLD ISSN 1389-7381
PAKBLAD. Text in Dutch. 1970. 10/yr. EUR 245 (effective 2009). adv. bk.rev. charts; illus. **Document type:** *Trade.* **Description:** Offers information on packaging for managers of selfpacking industries, product and marketing managers, designers and product engineers.
Former titles (until 1997): Missets Pakblad (0165-294X); Industrieel Verpakken; Incorporates (1981-1985): N V C Berichten
Related titles: ◆ Supplement(s): Snack Koerier. ISSN 1383-4126.
Indexed: IPackAb, KES, PST.
—IE.
Published by: Reed Business bv (Subsidiary of: Reed Business), Postbus 4, Doetinchem, 7000 BA, Netherlands. TEL 31-314-349911, FAX 31-314-343991, info@reedbusiness.nl, http://www.reedbusiness.nl. Ed. Jack Kwakman. Pub. Ivo de Wit. adv.: B&W page EUR 5,160, color page EUR 7,039; trim 307 x 465. Circ: 4,742.

658.7 FIN ISSN 0031-0131
PAKKAUS. Text in Finnish; Summaries in English. 1964. 10/yr. EUR 65 domestic to individuals; EUR 100 foreign to individuals; EUR 32.50 educational institutions (effective 2005). adv. bk.rev. charts; illus.; mkt. **Document type:** *Magazine, Trade.* **Description:** Contains news, reviews and articles on all topics related to packaging. Also introduces readers to new products.
Related titles: Supplement(s): Packaging Directory.
Indexed: IPackAb, P&BA, PST.
Published by: Suomen Pakkausyhdistys/Finnish Packaging Association, Ritarikatu 3 b A, Helsinki, 00170, Finland. TEL 358-9-6840340, FAX 358-9-68403410, http://www.pakkaus.com. Ed. Jorma Hamalainen TEL 358-9-6840-3421. Adv. contact Kaisu Vahamaki TEL 358-9-6840-3426. B&W page EUR 1,460, color page EUR 2,335; 210 x 297. Circ: 2,800.

676 USA ISSN 0031-1138
TS195.A1 CODEN: PFFCAT
PAPER, FILM AND FOIL CONVERTER. Text in English. 1927. m. USD 59 domestic; USD 67 in Canada; USD 84 elsewhere; free domestic to qualified personnel (effective 2011). adv. bk.rev. charts; illus.; stat.; tr.lit. index. reprints avail. **Document type:** *Magazine, Trade.* **Description:** Coverage provides problem-solving information and assists readers in managing operations and expanding into new markets.
Former titles (until 1953): American Paper Converter (0096-090X); (until 1944): Converter (0097-4080)
Related titles: Microfilm ed.: (from PQC); Online - full text ed.
Indexed: A&ATA, A09, A10, A15, A22, ABIPC, ABIn, B01, B02, B03, B06, B07, B09, B11, B15, B17, B18, BPI, BRD, CPEI, ChemAb, CurPA, EngInd, G04, G06, G07, G08, GALA, I05, IPackAb, KES, P&BA, P26, P31, P52, P54, PQC, PST, R18, SCOPUS, T02, V03, V04, W01, W02, W03, W05.
—BLDSC (6362.000000), IE, Infotrieve, Ingenta, INIST, Linda Hall. **CCC.**
Published by: Penton Media, Inc., 330 N Wabash Ave, Ste 2300, Chicago, IL 60611. TEL 312-595-1080, FAX 312-595-0295, information@penton.com, http://www.penton.com. Ed. Yolanda Simonsis. Pub. Scott Bieda TEL 312-840-8406. adv.: B&W page USD 3,973, color page USD 5,377; trim 10.88 x 8.13. Circ: 42,500 (controlled).

PAPER TECHNOLOGY. *see* PAPER AND PULP

676 658.7 USA
HF5770
PAPERBOARD PACKAGING. Text in English. 1916. m. free to qualified personnel (effective 2008). adv. charts; illus.; mkt.; stat. index. back issues avail.; reprints avail. **Document type:** *Magazine, Trade.* **Description:** Edited for management and other key personnel involved in the manufacturing and marketing segments of the paperboard packaging industry.
Incorporates: Paperboard Packaging Resource Directory; Which was formerly: Official Container Directory (0198-8867); Former titles (until 2003): Paperboard Packaging Worldwide; (until 1997): Paperboard Packaging (0031-1227); (until 1959): Fibre Containers and Paperboard Mills (0097-2770)
Related titles: Online - full text ed.: free to qualified personnel (effective 2008).
Indexed: A09, A10, A15, A22, A23, ABIPC, ABIn, B01, B02, B03, B06, B07, B08, B09, B11, B13, B15, B18, BusI, C12, ChemAb, CurPA, EngInd, G04, G06, G07, G08, GALA, I05, IPackAb, M01, M02, P&BA, P06, P48, P51, PQC, PST, S22, SCOPUS, SRI, T&II, T02, V02, V03, V04.
—IE. **CCC.**
Published by: Questex Media Group Inc., 275 Grove St, Bldg 2, Ste 130, Newton, MA 02466. TEL 617-219-8300, 888-552-4346, FAX 617-219-8310, questex@sunbeltfs.com, http://www.questex.com. Adv. contact Dan Weist TEL 216-706-3757. B&W page USD 4,635; 7 x 9.75. Circ: 7,500.

PAPERPRINTPACK INDIA. *see* PAPER AND PULP

688.8 615 USA ISSN 1081-5481
CODEN: PMPNAP
PHARMACEUTICAL & MEDICAL PACKAGING NEWS. Abbreviated title: P M P News. Text in English. 1993. m. free in US & Canada to qualified personnel; USD 150 elsewhere (effective 2008). adv. 88 p./no.; back issues avail. **Document type:** *Magazine, Trade.* **Description:** Designed for the medical and pharmaceutical manufacturing professionals who need focused, reliable and timely information to make intelligent packaging decisions.
Related titles: Online - full text ed.
Indexed: IPackAb.
—BLDSC (6442.755000), IE. **CCC.**
Published by: Canon Communications LLC (Subsidiary of: Apprise Media LLC), 11444 W Olympic Blvd, Ste 900, Los Angeles, CA 90064. TEL 310-445-4200, FAX 310-445-4299, info@cancom.com, http://www.cancom.com. Eds. Daphne Allen, David Vaczek. adv.: B&W page USD 4,750, color page USD 6,000; trim 7.125 x 10. Circ: 20,000.

PHARMACEUTICAL MANUFACTURING & PACKING SOURCER. *see* PHARMACY AND PHARMACOLOGY

658.788 USA
PHARMACEUTICAL SOLUTIONS; the nation's marketplace serving buyers and sellers of pharmaceutical, processing, chemical, packaging, equipment, services and supplies. Text in English. 2004. q. free to qualified personnel (print or online ed.) (effective 2009). adv. back issues avail. **Document type:** *Magazine, Trade.* **Description:** Provides the pharmaceutical industry with a quality low cost medium for reaching active buyers of new and used pharmaceutical manufacturing and packaging equipment, materials and supplies.
Related titles: Online - full text ed.
Published by: Industry Marketing Solutions, 809 Central Ave, 2nd Fl, PO Box 893, Fort Dodge, IA 50501. TEL 515-574-2354, 888-247-2007, FAX 515-574-2237, http://www.industrymarketingsolutions.com/. Pub. Steve Scanlan. adv.: color page USD 900; trim 7.625 x 10.75. Circ: 30,000 (controlled).

THE PLACE. *see* PAPER AND PULP

PLASTICS RECYCLING UPDATE. *see* ENVIRONMENTAL STUDIES—Waste Management

658.788 380.5 USA ISSN 1043-2841
PRESHIPMENT TESTING. Text in English. 1977. q. membership. adv. bk.rev. **Document type:** *Newsletter.* **Description:** Discusses packaging and transportation issues such as preshipment testing of packaged products, transport damage, quality control and customer service.
Published by: International Safe Transit Association, 1400 Abbott Rd., Ste. 160, East Lansing, MI 48823-1900. TEL 517-333-3437, FAX 517-333-3813. Circ: 3,200 (controlled).

688.8 USA ISSN 1532-8899
PRIVATE LABEL BUYER. Abbreviated title: P L B. Variant title: P L Buyer. Text in English. 1987. m. USD 161 domestic; USD 198 in Canada; USD 211 elsewhere; free to qualified personnel (effective 2009). adv. back issues avail.; reprints avail. **Document type:** *Magazine, Trade.* **Description:** Geared toward supermarkets and other retail chains selling store-brand products.
Former titles (until 2000): Private Label News (1080-5214); (until 1994): Private Label Product News (0892-6727)
Related titles: Online - full text ed.
Indexed: A10, ATI, B01, B02, B03, B07, B11, B15, B17, B18, G04, G06, G07, G08, I05, I07, P41, P48, P52, P53, P54, PQC, S22, S23, V03.
—CCC.
Published by: B N P Media, 155 Pfingsten Rd, Ste 205, Deerfield, IL 60015. TEL 847-405-4000, FAX 847-405-4100, portfolio@bnpmedia.com, http://www.bnpmedia.com. Ed. Kathie Canning TEL 847-405-4105. Pub. Steven T Lichtenstein TEL 201-576-9370. Adv. contact Janet Blaney TEL 630-364-1566. B&W page USD 4,810, color page USD 6,270; trim 10 x 13. Circ: 24,575.

658.788 USA ISSN 1932-9334
HD9999.C743
PROTECTIVE PACKAGING. Text in English. 19??. irreg. USD 4,800 per issue (print or online ed.) (effective 2011). back issues avail. **Document type:** *Monographic series, Trade.*
Related titles: Online - full text ed.
Published by: The Freedonia Group, Inc., 767 Beta Dr, Cleveland, OH 44143. TEL 440-684-9600, 800-927-5900, FAX 440-646-0484, info@freedoniagroup.com.

658.78 ESP ISSN 1575-3662
PUNTOMARKET. Text in Spanish. 1997. fortn. adv. mkt.; stat.; charts; tr.mk. Index. **Document type:** *Bulletin, Trade.*
Related titles: CD-ROM ed.; Fax ed.; Online - full text ed.
Published by: Publicaciones Alimarket S.A., Albasanz 14 3o, Madrid, 28037, Spain. TEL 34-91-3274340, FAX 34-91-3274522, informa@alimarket.es, http://www.alimarket.es.

R C O UPDATE. *see* ENVIRONMENTAL STUDIES—Waste Management

688.8 DEU ISSN 0935-2295
R G V HANDBUCH VERPACKUNG. (Rationalisierungs Gemeinschaft Verpackung) Text in German. 1978. base vol. plus a. updates. looseleaf. EUR 68 base vol(s).; EUR 24.80 updates per issue (effective 2009). **Document type:** *Monographic series, Trade.*
Published by: Erich Schmidt Verlag GmbH & Co. (Berlin), Genthiner Str 30 G, Berlin, 10785, Germany. TEL 49-30-2500850, FAX 49-30-250085305, vertrieb@esvmedien.de, http://www.erich-schmidt-verlag.de.

658.788 ITA ISSN 1971-5463
RASSEGNA DELL'IMBALLAGGIO. Text in Italian. 1980. fortn. (16/yr.). EUR 51 domestic (effective 2008). adv. **Document type:** *Magazine, Trade.* **Description:** Provides information on packaging equipment, machines and materials.
Formerly (until 2001): Rassegna dell'Imballaggio e Confezionamento (1120-6136)
Related titles: Online - full text ed.
Indexed: FS&TA, IPackAb.
—IE, Ingenta.
Published by: BE-MA Editrice Srl, Via Teocrito 50, Milan, MI 20128, Italy. TEL 39-02-252071, FAX 39-02-27000692, segreteria@bema.it, http://www.bema.it. Circ: 9,500 (controlled).

628.4458 GBR ISSN 1740-0635
RECOVERED FIBRE NEWS. Text in English. 1989. m. GBP 45 domestic; USD 100 in US & Canada; EUR 95 in Europe; GBP 55 elsewhere (effective 2010). adv. bk.rev. **Document type:** *Magazine, Trade.* **Description:** Covers methods and technology developments for processing and recycling waste paper.
Formerly (until 2003): Waste Paper News (0956-4683)
Indexed: WasteInfo.
—CCC.
Published by: Brunton Business Publications Ltd., 1 Salisbury Office Park, London Rd, Salisbury, Wiltshire SP1 3HP, United Kingdom. TEL 44-1722-337038, publications@brunton.co.uk. Ed. Michael Brunton. Adv. contact Dan Brunton. page GBP 525; 176 x 250.

RESEARCH & DEVELOPMENT ASSOCIATES FOR MILITARY FOOD AND PACKAGING SYSTEMS. ACTIVITIES REPORT. *see* MILITARY

338.476888 GBR ISSN 1362-1009
RETAIL PACKAGING (COLCHESTER). Text in English. 1996-suspended; N.S. 2003 (Jan.). bi-m. GBP 20 domestic; GBP 45 foreign; GBP 4 per issue; free to qualified personnel (effective 2010). **Document type:** *Magazine, Trade.* **Description:** Features retail packaging industry news, product news and interviews of key business officials.
Indexed: R18.
—CCC.
Published by: M S Publications, 2nd Fl, Ewer House, 44-46 Crouch St, Colchester, CO3 3HH, United Kingdom. TEL 44-1206-506249, FAX 44-1206-500180. Ed. Mike Hall. Adv. contact Bonnie Howard TEL 44-1206-506249.

688.8 PRT ISSN 0870-7553
REVIPACK. Text in Portuguese. 1980. q. EUR 28.65 (effective 2011). **Document type:** *Magazine, Trade.*
Related titles: Online - full text ed.: EUR 17.64 (effective 2011).
Published by: Oditecnica, Apartado 30, Odivelas, 2676-901, Portugal. http://www.oditecnica.wordpress.com.

670 CHE
SCHWEIZER VERPACKUNGSKATALOG. Text in French, German. 1942. a. CHF 37 (effective 2001). adv. **Document type:** *Catalog, Trade.*
Published by: Binkert Medien AG, Baslerstr 15, Laufenburg, 5080, Switzerland. TEL 41-62-8697900, FAX 41-62-8697901, binkertmedien@binkert.ch, http://www.binkertmedien.ch. Ed. Peter Suter. Adv. contact Bruno Schwaninger. Circ: 4,200.

SCRAP PLASTICS MARKETS DIRECTORY. *see* BUSINESS AND ECONOMICS—Trade And Industrial Directories

688.8 DEU ISSN 1431-5556
SEIBT VERPACKUNGSTECHNIK. Text in English, German. 1996. a. **Document type:** *Directory, Trade.* **Description:** Provides a guide to all fields of packaging technology and logistics.
Related titles: CD-ROM ed.; E-mail ed.; Fax ed.; Online - full text ed.

P

Published by: Seibt Verlag GmbH (Subsidiary of: Hoppenstedt Publishing GmbH), Havelstr 9, Darmstadt, 64295, Germany. TEL 49-6151-380120, FAX 49-6151-380468, info@seibt.com, http://www.seibt.com. Circ: 5,000 (paid).

676.3 CHN ISSN 1005-9423
SHANGHAI BAOZHUANG/SHANGHAI PACKAGING. Text in Chinese. 1976. bi-m. CNY 10 newsstand/cover (effective 2006). **Document type:** *Journal, Academic/Scholarly.*
Related titles: Online - full text ed.
Published by: (Zhongguo Chukou Shangpin Baozhuang Yanjiusuo, Shanghai Fensuo/Chinese Institute of Export Commodities Packaging, Shanghai Branch), Shanghai Baozhuang Zazhishe, 1111, Zhennan Lu, 12/F, Shanghai, 021-66081291, China.

688.8 USA
SHELFIMPACT!; strategies for successful package design and marketing. Text in English. 2005 (Jan.). m. free to qualified personnel (effective 2011). **Document type:** *Magazine, Trade.* **Description:** Covers all aspects of package design, function and branding.
Media: Online - full text.
Published by: Summit Publishing Co., 330 N Wabash Ave, Ste 2401, Chicago, IL 60611. TEL 312-222-1010, FAX 312/527-1890.

SOUTH AFRICAN FOOD REVIEW. *see* FOOD AND FOOD INDUSTRIES

660.29 658.7 USA ISSN 1055-2340
TS198.P7 CODEN: STEMEJ
SPRAY TECHNOLOGY & MARKETING; the magazine of spray pressure packaging. Text in English. 1956. 12/yr. USD 40; USD 50 in Canada & Mexico; USD 120 elsewhere; free to qualified personnel (effective 2005). adv. charts; illus.; pat.; tr.mk. reprints avail. **Document type:** *Magazine, Trade.*
Formerly (until Apr. 1991): Aerosol Age (0001-9291)
Related titles: Microform ed.: (from PQC); Online - full text ed.
Indexed: A22, A23, B13, ChemAb, CurPA, IPackAb, KES, PROMT.
—IE, Infotrieve, Ingenta, INIST, Linda Hall.
Published by: Industry Publications, Inc., 3621 Hill Rd, Parsippany, NJ 07054. TEL 973-331-9545, FAX 973-331-9547, http://members.aol.com/spraytec/index.htm. Ed. Michael L SanGiovanni. Pub., Adv. contact Cynthia Hundley. R&P Marie Ferraro. Circ: 7,000 (controlled and free).

STATIONERY TRENDS. *see* PAPER AND PULP

688.8 CHE
SWISSPACK INTERNATIONAL. Text in German. 1995. q. CHF 28 (effective 2000). adv. **Document type:** *Magazine, Trade.*
Address: Stampfenbachstr 61, Postfach, Zuerich, 8048, Switzerland. TEL 41-1-4316445, FAX 41-1-4316497. Ed. Peter Senecky. adv.: B&W page CHF 1,850, color page CHF 2,950; trim 175 x 254. Circ: 3,700 (paid).

T A P P I INTERNATIONAL CORRUGATED CONTAINERS CONFERENCE AND TRADE FAIR. PROCEEDINGS. (Technical Association of the Pulp and Paper Industry) *see* PAPER AND PULP

688.8 CHE
TARA. Text in German. m. CHF 89; CHF 115 foreign. adv. **Document type:** *Trade.*
Indexed: ABIPC, FS&TA, IPackAb.
Published by: Tara Verlag AG, Postfach 1012, Rapperswil Sg, 8640, Switzerland. TEL 41-55-272874, FAX 41-55-274524. Ed. Claude Buerki. Adv. contact Susan Brenner. B&W page CHF 2,097; trim 264 x 180. Circ: 4,130.

658.788 RUS ISSN 0131-6907
TARA I UPAKOVKA. Text in Russian. 1972. bi-m. USD 185 in United States (effective 2011). **Document type:** *Journal, Trade.* **Description:** Contains information on economics of containers and packing, machinery and equipment, packing materials, packing methods, design and printing.
Published by: Redaktsiya Zhurnala Tara i Upakovka, ul Suvorovskaya dom 6, Moscow, 107023, Russian Federation. TEL 7-495-6440402, FAX 7-495-6440403. Ed. Igor' Smirennyi. Circ: 10,000. **Dist. by:** East View Information Services, 10601 Wayzata Blvd, Minneapolis, MN 55305. TEL 952-252-1201, 800-477-1005, FAX 952-252-1202, info@eastview.com, http://www.eastview.com.

676 USA ISSN 0892-7146
CODEN: TEPAEC
TECHPAK. Text in English. 1955. bi-w. back issues avail. **Document type:** *Newsletter, Trade.*
Former titles (until 1986): Packaging Letter (0277-9722); (until 198?): Packascope-U S A (0094-016X)
—CCC.
Published by: McGraw-Hill Companies, Inc., 1221 Ave of the Americas, 43rd fl, New York, NY 10020. TEL 212-512-2000, customer.service@mcgraw-hill.com, http://www.mcgraw-hill.com.

688.8 USA
TOPICAL MEETINGS ON ELECTRICAL PERFORMANCE OF ELECTRONIC PACKAGING. Text in English. 1992. a. adv. back issues avail.; reprints avail. **Document type:** *Proceedings, Trade.*
Related titles: Online - full text ed.
Published by: I E E E, 445 Hoes Ln, Piscataway, NJ 08854. TEL 732-981-0060, 800-678-4333, FAX 732-562-6380, customer.service@ieee.org, http://www.ieee.org.

658.7 670 DEU ISSN 0341-7131
CODEN: VVRUEJ
V R - VERPACKUNGS-RUNDSCHAU. Text in German; Contents page in English, German. 1950. m. EUR 185 domestic; EUR 220 foreign (effective 2006). adv. bk.rev. charts; illus.; pat. index, cum.index. **Document type:** *Journal, Trade.*
Formerly (until 1974): Verpackungs-Rundschau (0042-4307)
Indexed: A22, ABIPC, ChemAb, CurPA, FS&TA, IPackAb, KES, P&BA, RefZh, SCOPUS, TM.
—BLDSC (9194.740000), IE, Infotrieve, Ingenta, INIST, Linda Hall. **CCC.**
Published by: P. Keppler Verlag GmbH und Co. KG, Industriestr 2, Heusenstamm, 63150, Germany. TEL 49-6104-6060, FAX 49-6104-606333, info@kepplermediengruppe.de, http://www.kepplermediengruppe.de. Ed. Norbert Sauermann. Pub. Eckhart Thomas. R&P Sabine Thomas. Adv. contact Marion Neckaermann. B&W page EUR 2,700, color page EUR 3,975. Circ: 12,429 (controlled).

668.8 CHL ISSN 0716-9698
VAS; revista del packaging. Text in Spanish; Summaries in English. 1980. bi-m. CLP 35,000 domestic; USD 140 in Latin America; USD 180 elsewhere; CLP 6,200 newsstand/cover domestic (effective 2001). adv. Website rev.; bk.rev. tr.lit.; abstr.; bibl.; charts; illus.; mkt.; maps; pat.; stat. 80 p./no.; back issues avail. **Document type:** *Magazine, Trade.* **Description:** Presents national and international information on products, machinery, regulations, POS, marketing, design, processes, events and more.
Published by: Ediciones Vas S.A., Merced, 346, Of. F3,, Santiago Centro, Chile. TEL 56-2-6325440, FAX 56-2-6382622, vas@terra.cl. Ed., R&P Maria Loreto Valdes. Adv. contact Gloria Emaldia. color page USD 2,100; trim 210 x 275. Circ: 2,500 (controlled).

658.7 CHE ISSN 0042-4277
DIE VERPACKUNG; schweizerische Fachzeitschrift fuer Verpackung, Technologie, Verpackungspsychologie, Package Design, Marketing. Text in German. 1945. 10/yr. CHF 88 domestic; CHF 98 foreign (effective 2001). adv. bk.rev. charts; illus.; stat. **Document type:** *Magazine, Trade.*
Indexed: IPackAb, KES.
Published by: HandelsZeitung Fachverlag AG, Foerrlibuckstr 70, Zurich, 8021, Switzerland. TEL 41-1-2889414, FAX 41-1-2889301, verlag@handelszeitung.ch, http://www.handelszeitung.ch. Ed. Werner Ruedi. Adv. contact Jean-Claude Page TEL 41-1-2889410. Circ: 4,650.

658.7 NLD ISSN 0167-9686
VERPAKKEN; magazine voor verpakkingsprofessionals. Text in Dutch. 1981. q. EUR 95 (effective 2010). adv. **Document type:** *Magazine, Trade.* **Description:** Surveys the packaging industry.
Formed by the merger of (1948-1980): Verpakking (0042-4315); (1975-1978): Pak Aktueel (0165-4500); Incorporates (1988-1990): Verpakken Nieuwsbrief (1383-3758); (1981-1985): N V C Berichten (0920-8135)
Indexed: IPackAb, P&BA, PST.
—IE.
Published by: ManagementMedia B.V., PO Box 1932, Hilversum, 1200 BX, Netherlands. TEL 31-35-6232756, info@managementmedia.nl, http://www.managementmedia.nl.

658.7 NLD ISSN 1382-0583
VERPAKKINGSMANAGEMENT. Text in Dutch. 1985. m. (11/yr.). EUR 146 (effective 2010). adv. **Document type:** *Magazine, Trade.* **Description:** Surveys the packaging industry.
Indexed: IPackAb.
—BLDSC (9194.780000), Infotrieve.
Published by: ManagementMedia B.V., PO Box 1932, Hilversum, 1200 BX, Netherlands. TEL 31-35-6232756, FAX 31-35-6232401, info@managementmedia.nl, http://www.managementmedia.nl.

677.7 USA ISSN 0740-1809
WIRE ROPE NEWS AND SLING TECHNOLOGY. Text in English. 1979. bi-m. USD 20 domestic; USD 25 in Canada; USD 30 foreign (effective 2000). adv. **Document type:** *Magazine, Trade.* **Description:** Aimed at persons who manufacture, distribute, or use wire rope, chain, cordage, and related products and services.
Indexed: A28, APA, BrCerAb, C&ISA, CA/WCA, CIA, CerAb, CivEngAb, CorrAb, E&CAJ, E11, EEA, EMA, ESPM, EnvEAb, H15, M&TEA, M09, MBF, METADEX, SolStAb, T04, WAA.
—Ingenta, Linda Hall.
Address: PO Box 871, Clark, NJ 07066. TEL 908-486-3221, FAX 732-396-4215. Ed. Conrad Miller. Pub. Edward J Bluvias. R&P, Adv. contact Edward Bluvias. Circ: 3,640 (paid and controlled).

688.8 CHN ISSN 1865-6382
XIANDAI BAOZHUAN/PROCESS PACKAGING. Text in Chinese. 2004. m. free. **Document type:** *Magazine, Trade.*
Published by: Deguo Fuge Gongye Meiti Jituan/Vogel Media Group (Subsidiary of: Vogel Business Media GmbH & Co.KG), 11/F, 1, Baiyue Lu, Xicheng-qu, Beijing, 100045, China. TEL 86-10-63326090, FAX 86-10-63326099, http://www.vogel.com.cn/.

658.788 CHN ISSN 1003-062X
ZHONGGUO BAOZHUANG/CHINA PACKAGING. Text in Chinese. 1981. bi-m. USD 31.20 (effective 2009). **Document type:** *Magazine, Trade.*
Related titles: Online - full content ed.; Online - full text ed.
—East View.
Published by: (Zhongguo Baozhuang Yishu Xuehui/China Packaging Technology Association), Zhongguo Baozhuang Zazhishe, Donghuangchenggen Beijiejia, Beijing, 100010, China. **Dist. by:** China International Book Trading Corp, 35 Chegongzhuang Xilu, Haidian District, PO Box 399, Beijing 100044, China. TEL 86-10-68412045, FAX 86-10-68412023, cibtc@mail.cibtc.com.cn, http://www.cibtc.com.cn.

ZHONGGUO SHIPIN XUEBAO/CHINESE INSTITUTE OF FOOD SCIENCE AND TECHNOLOGY. JOURNAL. *see* FOOD AND FOOD INDUSTRIES

ZHONGGUO YINSHUA YU BAOZHUANG YANJIU/CHINA PRINTING AND PACKAGING STUDY. *see* PRINTING

PACKAGING—Abstracting, Bibliographies, Statistics

ANYAGMOZGATASI ES CSOMAGOLASI SZAKIRODALMI TAJEKOZTATO/ABSTRACT JOURNAL FOR MATERIALS HANDLING AND PACKAGING. *see* TRANSPORTATION—Abstracting, Bibliographies, Statistics

658.788 016 GBR ISSN 1475-598X
PACKAGING MONTH. Text in English. 1981. bi-m. GBP 950 (effective 2010). bk.rev. abstr. index. 100 p./no.; **Document type:** *Journal, Abstract/Index.* **Description:** Examines over 1,000 sources and pick out the most important global business and technical developments across the packaging industry.
Formerly (until 2001): International Packaging Abstracts (0260-7409); Which was formed by the merger of (1944-1981): Packaging Abstracts (0030-9087); (1976-1981): Referatedienst Verpackung (0342-2674)
Related titles: CD-ROM ed.; Microform ed.; Online - full text ed.: 1975.
Indexed: F05, F06, F07.
—CCC.
Published by: IntertechPira, Cleeve Rd, Leatherhead, Surrey KT22 7RU, United Kingdom. TEL 44-1372-802000, FAX 44-1372-802238, info@pira-international.com.

PAINTS AND PROTECTIVE COATINGS

667.6 SWE ISSN 0346-9182
AKTUELLT MAALERI; tidskrift foer faerg, yta och miljoe. Text in Swedish. 1911. 6/yr. SEK 330 (effective 2007). adv. **Document type:** *Magazine, Trade.*
Incorporates (1978-1979): Branchaktuellt (0348-5145); Incorporates (in 1975): Maalaren; Which was formerly (until 1926): Tidning foer Sveriges Maalaremaestarefoerening
Published by: Maalarmaestarnas Riksfoerening/Swedish Painting Contractors' Association, Skeppsbron 40, PO Box 16286, Stockholm, 10325, Sweden. TEL 46-8-4539000, FAX 46-8-4539001, info@maleri.se. Ed. Ann-Charlotte Borgoe TEL 46-8-4539037. Adv. contact Leslie Spenner TEL 46-42-147040. color page SEK 22,900; trim 172 x 250. Circ: 3,800 (controlled).

698 USA ISSN 0003-0325
TT300
AMERICAN PAINTING CONTRACTOR. Abbreviated title: A P C. Text in English. 1924. 9/yr. free to qualified personnel (effective 2011). adv. illus.; tr.lit. index. 48 p./no. 3 cols./p.; back issues avail.; reprints avail. **Document type:** *Magazine, Trade.* **Description:** Offers industrial, commercial, and residential painting contractors well-researched technical articles, business and management advice, and reviews of equipment.
Formerly (until 1963): American Painter and Decorator (0096-0918)
Related titles: Online - full text ed.: free to qualified personnel (effective 2011).
Indexed: A10, V03.
—Linda Hall. **CCC.**
Published by: Briefings Media Group, PO Box 787, Williamsport, PA 17703. TEL 570-567-1982, 800-791-8699, FAX 570-320-2079, info@briefingsmediagroup.com, http://www.briefingsmediagroup.com. Ed. Emily Howard TEL 850-936-0200. Pub. Andrew Dwyer TEL 719-471-7230. Circ: 26,000.

ANNUAL BOOK OF A S T M STANDARDS. VOLUME 06.01. PAINT - TESTS FOR CHEMICAL, PHYSICAL AND OPTICAL PROPERTIES; APPEARANCE. (American Society for Testing and Materials) *see* ENGINEERING—Engineering Mechanics And Materials

ANNUAL BOOK OF A S T M STANDARDS. VOLUME 06.02. PAINT - PRODUCTS AND APPLICATIONS; PROTECTIVE COATINGS; PIPELINE COATINGS. (American Society for Testing and Materials) *see* ENGINEERING—Engineering Mechanics And Materials

ANNUAL BOOK OF A S T M STANDARDS. VOLUME 06.03. PAINT - PIGMENTS, DRYING OILS, POLYMERS, RESINS, NAVAL STORES, CELLULOSIC ESTERS, AND INK VEHICLES. (American Society for Testing and Materials) *see* ENGINEERING—Engineering Mechanics And Materials

698 CHE ISSN 1422-4194
APPLICA; Zeitschrift fuer das Maler- und Gipsergewerbe. Text in German. 1893. 19/yr. CHF 115; CHF 150 foreign. adv. **Document type:** *Trade.*
Indexed: CISA, WSCA.
—BLDSC (1570.430000), IE, Ingenta.
Published by: Schweizerischer Maler und Gipsermeister Verband, Grindelstr 2, Wallisellen, 8304, Switzerland. TEL 41-1-8305959, FAX 41-1-8301176. Ed. Juergen Hildebrandt. Adv. contact Nelly Temperli.

667.6 686 GBR ISSN 1468-1412
CODEN: PIINFZ
ASIA PACIFIC COATINGS JOURNAL. Abbreviated title: A P C J. Text in English. 1988. bi-m. GBP 127 domestic; GBP 145 foreign (effective 2010). adv. reprints avail. **Document type:** *Journal, Trade.* **Description:** Covers worldwide developments in the paint and printing ink industries, from raw materials to manufacturing processes, equipment, and applications.
Formerly (until 2000): Paint and Ink International (0953-9891)
Related titles: Online - full text ed.
Indexed: A22, A28, APA, B01, B02, B06, B07, B08, B09, B15, B17, B18, BrCerAb, C&ISA, C12, CA, CA/WCA, CBNB, CIA, CerAb, ChemAb, ChemTitl, CivEngAb, CorrAb, E&CAJ, E11, EEA, EMA, G04, G06, G07, G08, H15, I05, M&TEA, M09, MBF, METADEX, R18, SolStAb, T02, T04, WAA, WSCA.
—BLDSC (1742.257920), CASDDS, IE, Ingenta. **CCC.**
Published by: D M G Business Media Ltd. (Subsidiary of: D M G World Media Ltd.), Equitable House, Lyon Rd, Harrow, Middlesex HA1 2EW, United Kingdom. TEL 44-20-85152080, http://www.dmgworldmedia.com. Eds. Elit Kane, Elit Rowland TEL 44-1737-855328. adv.: B&W page GBP 2,909, color page GBP 4,952; trim 210 x 297. Circ: 4,860.

698 AUS ISSN 0816-3596
AUSTRALASIAN PAINT & PANEL. Text in English. 1982. bi-m. AUD 71.50 domestic; AUD 85 in New Zealand; AUD 100 in Asia; AUD 130 elsewhere (effective 2008). adv. **Document type:** *Magazine, Trade.* **Description:** Provides latest news, reviews and issues affecting the collision repair industry; offers new product information available in paint and panel shop industries.
Related titles: Supplement(s): Smash Repairers' Directory.
Published by: Yaffa Publishing Group Pty Ltd., 17-21 Bellevue St, Surry Hills, NSW 2010, Australia. TEL 61-2-92812333, FAX 61-2-92812750, info@yaffa.com.au. Ed. Will Tuck TEL 61-2-92138334. Adv. contact Max Yaffa TEL 61-2-92138246. color page AUD 4,090; trim 210 x 297. Circ: 7,499. **Subscr. to:** GPO Box 606, Sydney, NSW 2001, Australia.

667.6 DEU ISSN 1439-409X
TT300 CODEN: ILBEAE
BESSER LACKIEREN. Text in German. 1933. fortn. EUR 97 domestic; EUR 138.57 foreign (effective 2010). adv. bk.rev. abstr.; bibl.; charts; illus.; pat. **Document type:** *Magazine, Trade.*
Formerly (until 1999): Industrie Lackierbetrieb (0019-9109)
Indexed: A22, CIN, CISA, ChemAb, ChemTitl, PST, TM, WSCA.
—CASDDS, IE, Infotrieve, INIST, Linda Hall. **CCC.**

Published by: (European Coil Coating Association GBR), Vincentz Verlag, Plathnerstr 4c, Hannover, 30175, Germany. TEL 49-511-9910000, FAX 49-511-9910099, info@vincentz.de, http://www.vincentz.de. Ed. Franziska Moennig TEL 49-511-9910320. adv.: B&W page EUR 3,240, color page EUR 4,800. Circ: 12,069 (paid and controlled).

679.6 DEU ISSN 0178-4412
BROSSA PRESS; Nachrichtenblatt fuer die Buersten- und Pinselindustrie. Text in English, French, German, Italian. 1925. bi-m. EUR 180, USD 235 (effective 2009). adv. bk.rev. charts; illus.; pat.; stat.; tr.lit. 90 p./no.; **Document type:** *Magazine, Trade.* **Description:** Designed for the brush and paintbrush manufacturing industry, hair and fibre processing industries, specialized machinery industry, importers and exporters of branch related articles.
Formerly: Nachrichtenblatt fuer die Buersten- und Pinselindustrie (0027-7487)
Address: Hexentalstr 31, Bollschweil, 79283, Germany. TEL 49-7633-4066054, FAX 49-7633-4067093. Ed. B U Wagner. adv.: B&W page EUR 749.86, color page EUR 1,302.06. Circ: 4,500 (paid and controlled).

BRUSHWARE. *see* BUILDING AND CONSTRUCTION—Hardware

667.6 686.2 GBR ISSN 1473-4443
BUSINESS RATIO REPORT. PAINT & PRINTING INK MANUFACTURERS (YEAR). Text in English. 1973. a., latest no.37, 2008, Oct. GBP 365 per issue (effective 2010). charts; stat. back issues avail. **Document type:** *Report, Trade.*
Former titles (until 2000): Business Ratio. Paint & Printing Ink Manufacturers (1469-2686); (until 1999): Business Ratio Plus. Paint and Printing Ink Manufacturers (1358-233X); (until 1994): Business Ratio Report. Paint and Printing Ink Manufacturers (0261-930X)
Published by: Key Note Ltd. (Subsidiary of: Bonnier Business Information), Harlequin House, 5th Fl, 7 High St, Teddington, Richmond upon Thames, TW11 8EE, United Kingdom. TEL 44-845-5040452, FAX 44-845-5040453, sales@keynote.co.uk.

667.6 ARG ISSN 0325-4186
CENTRO DE INVESTIGACION Y DESARROLLO EN TECNOLOGIA DE PINTURAS. ANALES. Variant title: C I D E P I N T. Anales. Text in Multiple languages. 1977. a.
Indexed: A22, C01.
—INIST.
Published by: Centro de Investigacion y Desarrollo en Tecnologia de Pinturas, Calle 52 entre 121 y 122 s/n, La Plata, BA B1900AYB, Argentina. TEL 54-0221-4831142, FAX 54-0221-4271537, secretaria@cidepint.gov.ar, http://www.cidepint.gov.ar.

667.6 DEU
CHEMIE UND LACK; Das aktuelle Kennziffern-Fachjournal. Text in German. 1973. m. EUR 241; EUR 22 newsstand/cover (effective 2010). adv. **Document type:** *Magazine, Trade.*
Published by: Fachverlag Chemie und Lack GmbH, Am Hechenberg 15, Mainz, 55129, Germany. TEL 49-6131-593766, FAX 49-6131-593768, chemie.u.lack@t-online.de, http://www.fachverlag-chemie-lack.de.

667.6 HKG ISSN 1682-4636
CHINA COATINGS JOURNAL/ZHONGGUO TULIAO GONGYE. Text in Chinese, English. 1996. 5/yr. (Jan., Mar., May, Jul. & Oct.). HKD 50 domestic; USD 10 foreign (effective 2006); free domestic to qualified personnel. **Document type:** *Magazine, Trade.*
—BLDSC (9512.825132).
Published by: Sinostar International Ltd., 2101-2 Connaught Commercial Bldg., 185 Wanchai Rd., Wanchai, Hong Kong. http://www.sinostar-intl.com.hk/.

CHINESE MARKETS FOR AUTOMOTIVE COATINGS. *see* BUSINESS AND ECONOMICS—Marketing And Purchasing

CHINESE MARKETS FOR PRINTING INKS. *see* BUSINESS AND ECONOMICS—Marketing And Purchasing

667.6 CHE ISSN 2079-6412
▼ ➤ **COATINGS.** Text in English. 2011. q. free (effective 2011). **Document type:** *Journal, Academic/Scholarly.* **Description:** Publishes research involving coatings and surface engineering.
Media: Online - full text.
Published by: M D P I AG, Postfach, Basel, 4005, Switzerland. TEL 41-61-6837734, FAX 41-61-3028918, http://www.mdpi.org/. Ed. Ugo Bardi.

698 CAN ISSN 0225-6363
CODEN: CMOACA
COATINGS. Text in English. 1979. bi-m. free domestic to qualified personnel; CAD 65 foreign; CAD 75 combined subscription foreign print & online eds. (effective 2007). adv. bk.rev. back issues avail. **Document type:** *Magazine, Trade.* **Description:** Serving Canada's $2 billion paint, coatings and industrial finishing markets. Each issue highlights topics of interest to each of these market segments; every report reflects the current business situation in the industry.
Related titles: Online - full text ed.
Indexed: A15, A22, ABIn, C03, CBCABus, CPerI, G08, I05, P52, PQC, SCOPUS.
—BLDSC (3292.580000), IE, Ingenta, Linda Hall. **CCC.**
Published by: Rogers Publishing Ltd./Les Editions Rogers Limitee, One Mount Pleasant Rd, 11th Fl, Toronto, ON M4Y 2Y5, Canada. TEL 416-764-2000, 800-268-9119, FAX 416-764-1740, http://www.rogerspublishing.ca. Ed. Mary Scianna TEL 416-764-1540. Pub. Larry Bonikowsky TEL 416-464-2918. Circ: 7,600.

338.476679 DEU ISSN 1463-3647
COATINGS AGENDA NEW PRODUCTS. Text in English. 1998. m. **Document type:** *Journal, Trade.*
—**CCC.**
Published by: Vincentz Verlag, Plathnerstr 4c, Hannover, 30175, Germany. TEL 49-511-9910000, FAX 49-511-9910099, info@vincentz.de, http://www.vincentz.de.

667.6 628.5 ITA ISSN 1123-9123
CODEN: RMCOFO
COATINGS AND COMPOSITE MATERIALS/RIVESTIMENTI & MATERIALI COMPOSITI. Text in English, Italian. 1993. bi-m. adv. **Document type:** *Magazine, Trade.*
Indexed: R18.
—CASDDS. **CCC.**
Published by: Cada Communications, Via Mario Pagano 23, Salerno, SA 84135, Italy. TEL 39-089-481834, FAX 39-089-481617, editor@cada.it, http://www.cada.it. Circ: 8,500 (paid).

667.6 330.9 GBR ISSN 0968-7149
COATINGS C O M E T. (Companies Markets Economic Trends) Text in English. 1993. m. GBP 460 to non-members (print or online ed.); GBP 345 to members (print or online ed.); GBP 575 combined subscription to non-members (print & online eds.); GBP 430 combined subscription to members (print & online eds.) (effective 2009). abstr.; stat. back issues avail. **Document type:** *Magazine, Trade.* **Description:** Contains information on coatings, adhesives, inks, and their raw materials worldwide.
Related titles: CD-ROM ed.; E-mail ed.; Online - full text ed.: C O M E T Search. GBP 860 to non-members; GBP 650 to members (effective 2009).
—**CCC.**
Published by: P R A Coatings Technology Centre, 14 Castle Mews, High St, Hampton, Mddlx. TW12 2NP, United Kingdom. TEL 44-20-84870800, FAX 44-20-84870801, publications@pra-world.com. Ed. Glenda Thisdell TEL 44-20-84870807.

698 667.6 USA
COATINGS PRO. Text in English. 2001. bi-m. free domestic to qualified personnel (effective 2006). adv. **Document type:** *Magazine, Trade.* **Description:** Features a broad base of articles edited for applicators and specifying engineers of industrial and commercial coatings.
Published by: Four Point Publishing, LLC (Subsidiary of: N A C E International), PO Box 507112, San Diego, CA 92150. TEL 858-490-2708, FAX 858-272-0622, info@coatingspromag.com. Ed. Michele Ostgrove TEL 858-490-2708 ext 5. Pub. Lou Frank TEL 858-490-2708 ext 7. adv.: B&W page USD 2,529, color page USD 3,775; bleed 8.125 x 10.875. Circ: 22,000 (controlled).

667.6 USA ISSN 1527-1129
COATINGS WORLD; covering the paints, coatings, adhesives and sealants industries. Text in English. 1996. m. USD 75; free to qualified personnel (effective 2008). adv. back issues avail. **Document type:** *Magazine, Trade.* **Description:** Provides information on new technologies, production and marketing aspects of the worldwide paint and coatings industry.
Related titles: Online - full text ed.: free to qualified personnel (effective 2008).
Indexed: A28, APA, B01, B02, B03, B11, B15, B17, B18, BrCerAb, C&ISA, CA/WCA, CIA, CWI, CerAb, CivEngAb, CorrAb, E&CAJ, E11, EEA, EMA, G04, G06, G07, G08, H15, I05, M&TEA, M09, MBF, METADEX, R18, S22, SolStAb, T04, WAA.
—BLDSC (3292.625000), IE, Ingenta, Linda Hall. **CCC.**
Published by: Rodman Publishing, Corp., 70 Hilltop Rd, 3rd Fl, Ramsey, NJ 07446. TEL 201-825-2552, FAX 201-825-0553, info@rodpub.com, http://www.rodmanpublishing .com. Eds. Christine Esposito, Tim Wright. Pub. Dale Pritchett. Adv. contact Robert Frederick. B&W page USD 3,650, color page USD 5,150; trim 178 x 253. Circ: 17,114 (controlled).

COLOR RESEARCH AND APPLICATION. *see* ENGINEERING—Chemical Engineering

667.6 IND ISSN 0588-5094
TP934 CODEN: COSJAZ
COLOUR SOCIETY. JOURNAL. Text in English. 1962. q. adv. bk.rev. abstr. index. **Document type:** *Journal, Academic/Scholarly.*
Indexed: A&ATA, ChemAb, WSCA.
—CASDDS, INIST, Linda Hall.
Published by: Colour Society, c/o P.A.Mahanwar, Polymer Engineering and Paints Section, Institute of Chemical Technology, N.M.Parekh Marg, Matunga, Mumbai, Maharastra, India. TEL 91-22-33612413, contact@coloursociety.com, coloursociety@yahoo.com.

660 FRA ISSN 0430-2222
CODEN: FAPVAP
CONGRES F A T I P E C. Variant title: Federation d'Associations de Techniciens des Industries des Peintures, Vernis, Emaux et Encres d'Imprimerie de l'Europe Continentale. Congress Proceedings. Text in Dutch. 1951. biennial. price varies. **Document type:** *Proceedings, Trade.*
Indexed: CIN, ChemAb, ChemTitl.
—CASDDS, Ingenta. **CCC.**
Published by: F A T I P E C/European Organisation of Paint Scientists and Engineers, 5 Rue Etex, Paris, 75018, France. TEL 33-1-42634591, FAX 33-1-42633150, http://www.aftpva.org/fatipec.asp.

667.6 ZAF ISSN 0377-8711
TA418.74 CODEN: CCSADT
CORROSION AND COATINGS. Text in English. 1973. bi-m. ZAR 134.52; ZAR 152 in Africa; ZAR 176 elsewhere. adv. **Document type:** *Magazine, Trade.* **Description:** Covers the corrosion prevention and surface coatings industry in South Africa.
Indexed: A22, CIN, ChemAb, ChemTitl, ISAP, SCOPUS, WSCA.
—CASDDS, IE.
Published by: (South African Corrosion Institute), George Warman Publications (Pty.) Ltd., Rondebosch, PO Box 705, Cape Town, 7701, South Africa. info@gwarmanpublications.co.za, http://www.gwarmanpublications.co.za. Ed. John Kench. Circ: 2,149.

667.6 ZAF
CORROSION AND COATINGS BUYER'S GUIDE. Text in English. 1984. a. ZAR 110. **Document type:** *Handbook/Manual/Guide, Trade.* **Description:** Lists suppliers, services, manufacturers, corrosion related products and services.
Published by: George Warman Publications (Pty.) Ltd., Rondebosch, PO Box 705, Cape Town, 7701, South Africa. info@gwarmanpublications.co.za, http://www.gwarmanpublications.co.za.

667.6 USA ISSN 2158-8090
CURRENT INDUSTRIAL REPORTS. MQ325F - PAINT, VARNISH, AND LACQUER. Text in English. 19??. q. free (effective 2011). back issues avail. **Document type:** *Report, Government.*
Formerly (until 2000): Current Industrial Reports. MQ28F, Paint and Allied Products
Media: Online - full text.
Published by: U.S. Census Bureau (Subsidiary of: U.S. Department of Commerce), 4600 Silver Hill Rd, Washington, DC 20233. TEL 301-763-4673.

698.1 DNK ISSN 0905-6440
DANSKE MALERMESTRE. Text in Danish. 1990. every 3 wks. adv. bk.rev. **Document type:** *Magazine, Trade.* **Description:** Provides technical, political and legal information for members of the Danish Federation of Printing Contractors.
Formed by the merger of (1907-1990): Malertidende (0900-4564); (1963-1990): Malermesteren (0025-1364)
Address: Islands Brygge 26, PO Box 1989, Copenhagen S, 2300, Denmark. TEL 45-32-630370, FAX 45-32-630399, http://www.malermestre.dk.

698 DEU ISSN 1866-4059
DEUTSCHES TASCHENBUCH FUER MALER UND LACKIERER. BAND 1: CHEFINFO. Text in German. 1952. a. EUR 15 (effective 2011). **Document type:** *Directory, Trade.*
Supersedes in part (in 2006): Deutsches Taschenbuch fuer Maler und Lackierer (Year) (0343-3722)
Published by: Callwey Verlag, Streitfeldstr 35, Munich, 81673, Germany. TEL 49-89-4360050, FAX 49-89-436005113, a.hagenkord@callwey.de, http://www.callwey.de. Ed. Klaus Halmburger. Circ: 15,000.

698 DEU ISSN 1866-4067
DEUTSCHES TASCHENBUCH FUER MALER UND LACKIERER. BAND 2: BAUSTELLENINFO. Text in German. 1953. a. **Document type:** *Directory, Trade.*
Formerly (until 2006): Deutsches Taschenbuch fuer Maler und Lackierer (0343-3722)
Published by: Callwey Verlag, Streitfeldstr 35, Munich, 81673, Germany. TEL 49-89-4360050, FAX 49-89-436005113, a.hagenkord@callwey.de, http://www.callwey.de.

DIRECTORY OF CUSTOM COASTERS (YEAR). *see* ENGINEERING—Engineering Mechanics And Materials

667.6 GBR ISSN 1750-2438
DISPERSION POLYMERS; technology and applications. Text in English. 1989. m. GBP 460 to non-members (print or online ed.); GBP 345 to members (print or online ed.); GBP 575 combined subscription to non-members (print & online eds.); GBP 430 combined subscription to members (print & online eds.) (effective 2009). **Document type:** *Bulletin, Trade.* **Description:** Provides critical reviews of developments in dispersion polymer technology, covering new latex compositions, polymer processes, physical properties and applications of dispersion polymers in paints adhesives, membranes, non-woven fabrics, textiles and paper.
Former titles (until 2006): Emulsion Polymer Technologies (1364-9353); (until 1996): Emulsion Polymerisation and Polymer Emulsions (0955-2804); Which was formed by the merger of (1970-1989): Emulsion Polymerisation (0143-7151); (1971-1989): Applications of Polymer Emulsions (0143-716X)
Related titles: E-mail ed.; Online - full text ed.
—**CCC.**
Published by: P R A Coatings Technology Centre, 14 Castle Mews, High St, Hampton, Mddlx. TW12 2NP, United Kingdom. TEL 44-20-84870800, FAX 44-20-84870801, publications@pra-world.com. Ed. Peter Jones.

667.6 FRA ISSN 1166-4398
TP934
DOUBLE LIAISON. Text in French. 1973. bi-m. **Document type:** *Journal, Trade.* **Description:** Contains information on economic and technical aspects of the paint, varnish, printing ink, glue and adhesive market.
Formerly (until 1988): Double Liaison, Chimie des Peintures (0291-8412); Which was formed by the merger of (1954-1973): Double Liaison (0012-5709); (1966-1973): Chimie des Peintures (0772-3474)
Indexed: A22, FR.
—BLDSC (3619.890000), IE, Infotrieve, Ingenta, INIST, Linda Hall. **CCC.**
Published by: Editions Techniques pour l'Automobile et l'Industrie (E T A I), 20 rue de la Saussiere, Boulogne-Billancourt, 92641, France. TEL 33-1-46992424, FAX 33-1-48255692.

667.6 USA
THE DROP CLOTH. Text in English. 6/yr. membership. adv. **Document type:** *Newsletter.* **Description:** Discusses paints and protective coatings, as well as building and construction.
Published by: Texas Council of Painting and Decorating Contractors of America, 823 Congress Ave, Ste 1300, Austin, TX 78701-2429. TEL 512-479-0425, FAX 512-495-9031. Ed., R&P, Adv. contact Lisa Fry. Circ: 200.

698 NLD ISSN 1567-1852
EISMA'S SCHILDERSBLAD. Text in Dutch. 1899. fortn. EUR 198.50 (effective 2009). adv. bk.rev. illus. index. **Document type:** *Trade.*
Former titles (until 2000): Eisma's Vakpers (0920-2099); (until 1986): Eisma's Schildersblad (0013-287X)
—IE, Infotrieve.
Published by: Eisma Businessmedia bv, Celsiusweg 41, Postbus 340, Leeuwarden, 8901 BC, Netherlands. TEL 31-58-2954854, FAX 31-58-2954875, businessmedia@eisma.nl, http://www.eisma.nl/businessmedia/index.asp. Eds. Broer Feenstra, Marijke Kuypers, Wouter Mooij TEL 31-58-3954853. adv.: color page EUR 3,032; 185 x 262.

EQUIPMENT PROTECTION. *see* MACHINERY

667.6 DEU ISSN 0930-3847
CODEN: ECJOEF
EUROPEAN COATINGS JOURNAL. Text in English, French. 1985. m. EUR 173.34 (effective 2009). adv. bk.rev. bibl.; charts; illus. reprints avail. **Document type:** *Magazine, Trade.* **Description:** Serves Europe as indispensable source of information for the coatings, printing inks, construction chemicals, adhesives and sealants industry.
Indexed: A22, A28, APA, B01, BioDAb, BrCerAb, C&ISA, CA/WCA, CEABA, CIA, CIN, CPEI, CerAb, ChemAb, ChemTitl, CivEngAb, CorrAb, E&CAJ, E11, EEA, EMA, EngInd, FLUIDEX, H15, M&TEA, M09, MBF, METADEX, P&BA, PhysBer, R18, SCOPUS, SolStAb, T04, WAA, WSCA.
—BLDSC (3829.609000), CASDDS, IE, Infotrieve, Ingenta, INIST, Linda Hall. **CCC.**
Published by: Vincentz Verlag, Plathnerstr 4c, Hannover, 30175, Germany. TEL 49-511-9910000, FAX 49-511-9910099, info@vincentz.de, http://www.vincentz.de. Ed. Kirsten Wrede. Pub. Juergen Nowak. adv.: B&W page EUR 2,660, color page EUR 4,220; trim 175 x 250. Circ: 9,194 (paid and controlled).

P

667.6 GBR ISSN 0266-7800
EUROPEAN PAINT AND RESIN NEWS. Abbreviated title: E P R N. Text in English. 1957. m. GBP 365 to non-members (print or online ed.); GBP 295 to members (print or online ed.); GBP 456 combined subscription to non-members (print & online eds.); GBP 370 combined subscription to members (print & online eds.) (effective 2009). pat.; tr.lit. **Document type:** *Newsletter, Trade.* **Description:** Covers industry developments, marketing news and statistics, technology developments, symposia and exhibition news of the European paint and resin industry.
Former titles (until 1984): Continental Paint and Resin News (0010-7735); (until 1963): Continental Paints and Resins; Incorporates: Phosphating News
Related titles: E-mail ed.; Online - full text ed.
Indexed: CBNB, WSCA.
—BLDSC (3829.768400). **CCC.**
Published by: P R A Coatings Technology Centre, 14 Castle Mews, High St, Hampton, Mddlx. TW12 2NP, United Kingdom. TEL 44-20-84870800, FAX 44-20-84870801, publications@pra-world.com. Ed. Glenda Thisdell TEL 44-20-84870807.

667.6 SWE ISSN 0427-9107
FAERG OCH FERNISSA; tidskrift foer industriell produktmaalning. Text in Swedish. 1937. s-a. free. adv. charts; illus.; tr.lit. cum.index every 5 yrs. **Document type:** *Trade.*
Related titles: Supplement(s): Industrial Coatings.
Indexed: WSCA.
Published by: Becker Industrifaerg AB, Fack 2041, Marsta, 19502, Sweden. TEL 8-590-790-00, FAX 8-591-16949. Ed. Birgitta Karlsson. Circ: 10,000.

667.6 667.7 DNK ISSN 0106-7559
CODEN: FLSCDT
FAERG OCH LACK SCANDINAVIA. Text in English, Danish, Norwegian, Swedish. 1955. 6/yr. adv. bk.rev. charts; illus. index. **Document type:** *Magazine, Trade.*
Formerly (until 1980): Skandinavisk Tidskrift foer Faerg och Lack (0037-6094)
Indexed: A22, CIN, ChemAb, ChemTitl.
—BLDSC (3869.520000), CASDDS, IE, Ingenta, INIST. **CCC.**
Published by: Skandinaviska Lackteknikers Foerbund/Federation of Scandinavian Paint and Varnish Technologists, c/o Simon Greve, R2ChemTech A/S, Odinsvej 25, Hedehusene, 8722, Denmark. http://www.slf.cc. Eds. Anders G Kjellin TEL 46-8-7317780, Simon Greve TEL 45-30-947421. Circ: 2,000 (controlled).

620.11223 TWN ISSN 1016-2356
FANGSHI GONGCHENG/JOURNAL OF CHINESE CORROSION ENGINEERING. Text in Chinese. 1984. q. free to members (effective 2005). **Document type:** *Journal, Academic/Scholarly.*
Indexed: APA, C&ISA, CorrAb, E&CAJ, EEA, EngInd, ISMEC, Inspec, SolStAb, TM, WAA.
—BLDSC (2087.813000), Ingenta, Linda Hall.
Published by: Zhonghua Minguo Fangshi Gongcheng Xuehui/Corrosion Engineering Association of the Republic of China, no.14, Section 1, Alley 147, 1st Fl., Jialong Road, Taipei, Taiwan. TEL 86-2-27567098, FAX 86-2-87878784, anticorr@seed.net.tw, http://cubic.mat.ncku.edu.tw/~anticorr/.

667.6 DEU ISSN 0014-7699
CODEN: FALAAA
FARBE UND LACK. Text in German. 1894. m. EUR 101 domestic; EUR 169.06 foreign; EUR 16.50 per issue (effective 2010). adv. bk.rev. abstr.; bibl.; charts; illus.; pat. reprints avail. **Document type:** *Magazine, Trade.*
Former titles (until 1945): Lack- und Farben-Zeitschrift (0368-7678); (until 1943): Farben-Zeitung (0367-1755)
Related titles: Microform ed.: (from PQC); Online - full text ed.
Indexed: A&ATA, A22, B01, B03, BioDAb, CBNB, CEABA, CIN, CISA, Cadscan, ChemAb, ChemTitl, EngInd, IPackAb, KES, LeadAb, PROMT, PST, R18, SCOPUS, TM, WSCA, Zincscan.
—BLDSC (3869.000000), CASDDS, IE, Infotrieve, Ingenta, INIST, Linda Hall. **CCC.**
Published by: (Gesellschaft Deutscher Chemiker), Vincentz Verlag, Plathnerstr 4c, Hannover, 30175, Germany. TEL 49-511-9910000, FAX 49-511-9910099, info@vincentz.de, http://www.vincentz.de. Ed. Barbara Brune. adv.: B&W page EUR 2,510, color page EUR 4,010; trim 175 x 250. Circ: 4,806 (paid and controlled). **Co-sponsor:** Schweizerische Vereinigung der Lack- und Farbenchemiker (SVLFC).

667.6 AUT ISSN 0014-7737
FARBENKREIS; oesterreichisches Magazin fuer Gewerbe und Handel. Text in German. 10/yr. EUR 60.50 domestic; EUR 87.80 foreign (effective 2005). adv. **Document type:** *Magazine, Trade.*
Published by: (Landesinnung Wien der Maler und Lackierer), Oesterreichischer Wirtschaftsverlag GmbH (Subsidiary of: Sueddeutscher Verlag GmbH), Wiedner Hauptstr 120-124, Vienna, W 1051, Austria. TEL 43-1-546640, FAX 43-1-54664406, office@wirtschaftsverlag.at. Ed. Wolfgang Biedermann. adv.: B&W page EUR 1,680, color page EUR 2,400; trim 185 x 255. Circ: 3,600.

698.1 DNK ISSN 0908-9926
DE FARVER/COLORS. Text in Danish. 1994. q. DKK 230 (effective 2009). adv. **Document type:** *Magazine, Trade.* **Description:** Features work by painters and architects with respect to colors and surface coating.
Published by: Danske Malermestre, Islands Brygge 26, PO Box 1989, Copenhagen S, 2300, Denmark. TEL 45-32-630370, FAX 45-32-630399. Ed. Adam Pade. Adv. contact Peter Graah. Circ: 7,352.

667.6 667.7 FRA ISSN 1026-1923
FEDERATION D'ASSOCIATIONS DE TECHNICIENS DES INDUSTRIES DES PEINTURES, VERNIS, EMAUX ET ENCRES D'IMPRIMERIE DE L'EUROPE CONTINENTALE. ANNUAIRE OFFICIEL. OFFICIAL YEARBOOK. AMTLICHES JAHRBUCH/AMTLICHES JAHRBUCH/OFFICIAL YEARBOOK. Text in English, French, German. 1955. biennial. adv. **Document type:** *Proceedings, Trade.*
Published by: Federation d'Associations de Techniciens des Industries des Peintures Vernis Emaux et Encres d'Imprimerie de l'Europe Continentale (F A T I P E C), c/o AFTPVA, 5 Rue Etex, Paris, 75018, France. TEL 33-1-42634591, FAX 33-1-42633150, aftpva-mob@wanadoo.fr, http://www.fatipec.com. Circ: 3,000.

667.6 USA ISSN 0099-801X
CODEN: FSCTCE
FEDERATION SERIES ON COATINGS TECHNOLOGY. Text in English. 1964. irreg., latest vol.28, 1998. USD 30 per vol. (effective 2005). **Document type:** *Monographic series.*
—Linda Hall. **CCC.**
Published by: Federation of Societies for Coatings Technology, 492 Norristown Rd, Blue Bell, PA 19422-2350. TEL 610-940-0777, FAX 610-940-0292, publications@coatingstech.org, http://www.coatingstech.org.

698 GBR ISSN 0264-2506
TS670.A1 CODEN: FINIE2
FINISHING. Text in English. 1948. bi-m. GBP 121 domestic; GBP 136 foreign (effective 2009). adv. bk.rev. **Document type:** *Magazine, Trade.* **Description:** Covers both in-house and trade finishing operations for metals and plastics, whether electro-plated, organic or inorganic coatings are being applied. It features technical advances in both plant and materials, major installations, commercial and company news.
Formerly (until 1982): Finishing Industries (0309-3018); Which was formed by the merger of (1970-1977): Industrial Finishing and Surface Coatings (0039-6001); (1947-1977): Electroplating and Metal Finishing (0013-5305); Which incorporated (1955 -1974): Metal finishing Journal (0026-0592)
Related titles: Online - full text ed.: Finishing Online. 2006.
Indexed: A22, A28, APA, B02, B15, B17, B18, BrCerAb, C&ISA, CA/WCA, CIA, Cadscan, CerAb, ChemAb, CivEngAb, CorrAb, E&CAJ, E11, EEA, EMA, ESPM, EngInd, EnvAb, EnvEAb, G04, G08, H15, I05, IPackAb, Inspec, LeadAb, M&TEA, M09, MBF, METADEX, SCOPUS, SolStAb, T04, WAA, WSCA, Zincscan.
—BLDSC (3928.204000), CASDDS, IE, Infotrieve, Ingenta, INIST, Linda Hall. **CCC.**
Published by: Turret Group Ltd., 173 High St, Rickmansworth, Herts WD3 1AY, United Kingdom. TEL 44-1923-692660, FAX 44-1923-692679, http://www.turretgroup.com. Ed. John Hatcher TEL 44-1923-692670. Adv. contact Stewart Freshwater TEL 44-1923-692663. color page GBP 1,250; trim 210 x 297. **Subscr. to:** PO Box 371, Chesham, Bucks HPS 2BF, United Kingdom. FAX 44-1494-794024.

FINISHING INDUSTRY YEARBOOK. *see* BUSINESS AND ECONOMICS—Trade And Industrial Directories

698 ITA
FINITURE & COLORE; verniciatura, decorazione e restauro leggero. Text in Italian. 1993. 8/yr. EUR 32 domestic (effective 2008). Supplement avail. **Document type:** *Magazine, Trade.*
Related titles: Online - full text ed.
Indexed: WSCA.
Published by: BE-MA Editrice Srl, Via Teocrito 50, Milan, MI 20128, Italy. TEL 39-02-252071, FAX 39-02-27000692, segreteria@bema.it. Ed. Dario Marabelli. Circ: 25,000.

FOREST CHEMICALS REVIEW. *see* PAPER AND PULP

FUSHI YU FANGHU/CORROSION AND PROTECTION. *see* CHEMISTRY—Electrochemistry

667.6 FRA ISSN 0982-7870
CODEN: GAOREN
GALVANO-ORGANO - TRAITEMENTS DE SURFACE. Text in French; Summaries in English. 1980. 9/yr. EUR 125 domestic; EUR 136 in the European Union; EUR 163 elsewhere (effective 2009). adv. bk.rev. abstr.; bibl.; charts; illus. index. **Document type:** *Magazine, Trade.*
Incorporates (1963-2004): Surfaces (0585-9840); Formed by the merger of (1960-1980): Traitements de Surface (0397-4596); (1973-1980): Galvano-Organo (0302-6477); Which was formerly (1932-1973): Galvano (0016-4224)
Indexed: A22, A28, APA, BrCerAb, C&ISA, CA/WCA, CIA, Cadscan, CerAb, ChemAb, CivEngAb, CorrAb, E&CAJ, E11, EEA, EMA, ESPM, EnvEAb, H15, LeadAb, M&TEA, M09, MBF, METADEX, SCOPUS, SolStAb, T04, WAA, Zincscan.
—CASDDS, IE, Ingenta, INIST, Linda Hall. **CCC.**
Published by: Societe Galvano, 10 rue Saint Nicolas, Paris, 75012, France. Circ: 4,500.

667.6 676.284 GBR ISSN 1470-4811
HOME DECOR & FURNISHINGS. Text in English. 1955. bi-m. adv. bk.rev. 4 cols./p.; back issues avail. **Document type:** *Magazine, Trade.*
Former titles (until 1999): Home Decor (1470-1839); W P W Home Decor; (until 1986): W P W Decor; (until 1980): Wallpaper, Paint and Wallcovering (0043-0153)
Indexed: WSCA.
Published by: Indices Publications Ltd., First Fl, Entrance B, Salamander Quay W, Park Ln, Harefield, UB9 6NZ, United Kingdom. TEL 44-870-2052924, FAX 44-870-2052934. Ed. Michael I Weedon. Adv. contact Simon Green TEL 44-121-4466688.

667.6 COL
I N P R A LATINA. (Industrias de Pinturas, Revestimientos, Adhesivos y Tintas) Text in Portuguese, Spanish. 1996. bi-m. USD 30. adv. **Document type:** *Trade.* **Description:** Serves the Latin American paint and protective coating, ink and adhesive manufacturing industries. Offers country-by-country production reports, plant operation stories, personnel interviews, supplier profiles and productivity articles.
Published by: (Anafapyt (The Mexican Paint and Ink Manufacturers' Association)), Latin Press Inc., Apartado Postal 67 252, Medellin, ANT, Colombia. TEL 57-4-4140169, FAX 57-4-2506990, http://www.latinpressinc.com. Ed. Victor Alarcon. Pub. Max Jaramillo. adv.: page USD 1,890. Circ: 9,500.

THE INTERNATIONAL DIRECTORY OF PAINT, PAINT SUPPLIES AND ALLIED PRODUCTS IMPORTERS. *see* BUSINESS AND ECONOMICS—Trade And Industrial Directories

698 DEU
INTERSTANDOX; information for the world of the car repair painter. Text in German. 1978. s-a. free. back issues avail. **Document type:** *Trade.*
Related titles: Multiple languages ed.
Published by: Herberts GmbH, Christbusch 25, Wuppertal, 42285, Germany. TEL 0202-529-0, FAX 0202-529-2809.

698 DEU
INTERSTANDOX EXTRA. Text in German. 1978. 4/yr. free. back issues avail. **Document type:** *Trade.* **Description:** Information for body shops and car repair painters.
Published by: Herberts GmbH, Christbusch 25, Wuppertal, 42285, Germany. TEL 0202-529-0, FAX 0202-529-2809. Circ: 22,000.

667.6 USA ISSN 1547-0083
TP934 CODEN: JCCOBW
J C T COATINGSTECH. (Journal of Coatings Technology) Text in English. 1923. m. USD 180 in US & Canada to individuals; USD 250 in Europe to individuals; USD 210 elsewhere to individuals; USD 400 to institutions; USD 400 to libraries (effective 2005); includes subscr. to J C T Research. **Document type:** *Journal, Trade.* **Description:** Provides practical articles that are applications, manufacturing, and business related. Highlights industry and product news as well as updates on new materials and technology in practice.
Supersedes in part (in 2004): J C T: Journal of Coatings Technology (0361-8773); Which was formerly (until 1976): Journal of Paint Technology (0022-3352); (until 1966): Federation of Societies for Paint Technology. Official Digest (0097-2835); (until 1960): Federation of Paint and Varnish Production Clubs. Official Digest (0097-2827)
Related titles: Online - full text ed.
Indexed: A05, A20, A28, APA, AS&TA, AS&TI, ASFA, B04, BRD, BrCerAb, C&ISA, C10, CA, CA/WCA, CIA, CerAb, CivEngAb, CorrAb, CurCont, E&CAJ, E11, EEA, EMA, ESPM, EngInd, EnvEAb, G06, G07, G08, H15, I05, ISR, M&TEA, M09, MBF, METADEX, MSCI, OceAb, PollutAb, RefZh, S04, SCI, SCOPUS, SSciA, SWRA, SolStAb, T02, T04, W03, W05, W07, WAA.
—BLDSC (4663.443920), IE, Ingenta, INIST, Linda Hall. **CCC.**
Published by: Federation of Societies for Coatings Technology, 492 Norristown Rd, Blue Bell, PA 19422-2350. TEL 610-940-0777, FAX 610-940-0292, subscriptions@coatingstech.org, http://www.coatingstech.org.

667.6 DEU ISSN 1616-4539
JAHRBUCH BESSER LACKIEREN!. Text in German. 1943. a. EUR 36.50 per issue (effective 2010). **Document type:** *Trade.*
Former titles (until 2000): Jahrbuch fuer Lackierbetriebe (1434-5269); (until 1997): Taschenbuch fuer Lackierbetriebe (0340-8167)
Published by: Vincentz Verlag, Plathnerstr 4c, Hannover, 30175, Germany. TEL 49-511-9910000, FAX 49-511-9910099, info@vincentz.de, http://www.vincentz.de. Ed. Dieter Ondratschek. Circ: 7,000.

JOURNAL OF ARCHITECTURAL COATINGS. *see* ARCHITECTURE

667.6 USA ISSN 1945-9645
TP934 CODEN: JCTRCP
➤ **JOURNAL OF COATINGS TECHNOLOGY AND RESEARCH.** Abbreviated title: J C T R. Text in English. 2007. q. EUR 553, USD 664 combined subscription to institutions (print & online eds.) (effective 2012). reprint service avail. from PSC. **Document type:** *Journal, Academic/Scholarly.* **Description:** Publishes original research papers, which highlight the advances in coatings science and innovations in materials and processes.
Formed by the merger of (2001-2006): Surface Coatings International. Part B, Coatings Transactions (1476-4865); Which superseded in part (in 2001): Surface Coatings International (1356-0751); Which was formerly (1918-1991): Oil and Colour Chemists' Association. Journal (0030-1337); (2004-2006): J C T Research (1547-0091); Which superseded in part (in 2004): J C T: Journal of Coatings Technology (0361-8773); Which was formerly (until 1976): Journal of Paint Technology (0022-3352); (until 1966): Federation of Societies for Paint Technology. Official Digest (0097-2835); (1923-1960): Federation of Societies and Varnish Production Clubs. Official Digest (0097-2827)
Related titles: Online - full text ed.: ISSN 1935-3804 (from IngentaConnect).
Indexed: A05, A22, A26, A28, APA, AS&TA, AS&TI, ASFA, BRD, BrCerAb, C&ISA, C10, C24, C33, CA, CA/WCA, CIA, CPEI, CerAb, CivEngAb, CorrAb, CurCont, E&CAJ, E01, E11, EEA, EMA, ESPM, EngInd, EnvEAb, G06, G07, G08, H15, I05, ISR, M&TEA, M09, MBF, METADEX, MSCI, OceAb, PollutAb, RefZh, S04, SCI, SCOPUS, SolStAb, T02, T04, W03, W05, W07, WAA.
—BLDSC (4663.443970), IE, Ingenta, INIST, Linda Hall. **CCC.**
Published by: (Federation of Societies for Coatings Technology, Oil & Colour Chemists' Association GBR), Springer New York LLC (Subsidiary of: Springer Science+Business Media), 233 Spring St, New York, NY 10013. TEL 212-460-1500, FAX 212-460-1575, service-ny@springer.com. Ed. Ray A Dickie.

➤ **THE JOURNAL OF CORROSION SCIENCE AND ENGINEERING.** *see* METALLURGY

➤ **JOURNAL OF INDUSTRIAL TEXTILES.** *see* TEXTILE INDUSTRIES AND FABRICS

667.6 USA ISSN 8755-1985
TP934
JOURNAL OF PROTECTIVE COATINGS & LININGS. Abbreviated title: J P C L. Text in English. 1984. m. USD 80 in North America; USD 100 elsewhere (effective 2005). adv. bk.rev. 100 p./no.; back issues avail.; reprints avail. **Document type:** *Journal, Trade.* **Description:** Provides technical and regulatory information about the use of heavy-duty corrosion protective coatings for maintaining steel and concrete industrial structures and ships.
Related titles: CD-ROM ed.; Microfilm ed.: (from PQC); Online - full text ed.
Indexed: A22, A28, ABIPC, APA, B01, BrCerAb, C&ISA, C24, CA/WCA, CIA, CPEI, CTE, CerAb, CivEngAb, ConcrAb, CorrAb, E&CAJ, E11, EEA, EMA, ESPM, EngInd, EnvEAb, H15, HRIS, ISMEC, M&TEA, M09, MBF, P26, P48, P52, P54, PQC, RefZh, SCOPUS, SolStAb, T04, WAA, WSCA.
—BLDSC (5042.940000), IE, Infotrieve, Ingenta, INIST, Linda Hall.
Published by: (Society for Protective Coatings), Technology Publishing Co., 2100 Wharton St, Ste 310, Pittsburgh, PA 15203. TEL 412-431-8300, FAX 412-431-5428, http://www.paintsquare.com/. Ed., R&P Karen Kapsanis. Pub. Harold Hower. Adv. contact Gina Fleitman. B&W page USD 2,540. Circ: 15,000 (paid and controlled).

KINKI ARUMINYUMU HYOMEN SHORI KENKYUKAI KAISHI. *see* METALLURGY

667.6 JPN ISSN 0286-6943
HD9999.C646 CODEN: KTOSDW
KOGYO TOSO/INDUSTRIAL COATING. Text in Japanese. 1972. bi-m. **Document type:** *Journal, Trade.*
—BLDSC (4448.335400).

Published by: Toryo Hochi Shinbunsha Co., Ltd., 3, Yarai-cho, Shinjuku-ku, Tokyo, 162-0805, Japan. TEL 81-3-32606111, FAX 81-3-32606116, toryohochi@nifty.com, http://web01.cpi-media.co.jp/toryo/.

667.6 JPN ISSN 0288-4534
➤ **KONA**; powder and particle journal. Text in English. 1983. s-a.
Related titles: Online - full text ed.: free (effective 2011).
Indexed: CurCont, SCI, SCOPUS, W07.
—BLDSC (5105.897400), IE, Linda Hall.
Published by: Hosokawa Powder Technology Foundation, c/o Hosokawa Micron Corporation, 1-9, Shodai Tajika, Hirakata-shi, Osaka 573-1132, Japan. TEL 81-72-8671686, FAX 81-72-8671658, info@kona.or.jp, http://www.kona.or.jp/.

667.6 540 HUN ISSN 0133-2546 CODEN: KOFIDO
KORROZIOS FIGYELO/CORROSION OBSERVER. Text in Hungarian; Summaries in English. 1961. bi-m. HUF 3,808 domestic; USD 40 foreign (effective 2001). adv. bk.rev. abstr.; bibl.; illus. index. back issues avail. **Document type:** *Bulletin, Trade.* **Description:** Deals with corrosion and corrosion prevention, corrosion science and technology.
Indexed: A28, APA, BrCerAb, C&ISA, CA/WCA, CIA, CIN, CTE, CerAb, ChemAb, ChemTitl, CivEngAb, CorrAb, E&CAJ, E11, EEA, EMA, ESPM, EnvEAb, FLUIDEX, H15, M&TEA, M09, MBF, METADEX, MSCI, RefZh, SCI, SCOPUS, SWRA, SolStAb, T04, W07, WAA.
—CASDDS, Linda Hall.
Published by: V E K O R Ltd./Corrosion Protection from Veszprem, Wartha V utca 1, Veszprem, 8200, Hungary. TEL 36-88-428514, FAX 36-88-428514, vekor@informax.hu, kofi-vekor@posta.net. Ed., Pub., Adv. contact I Bozso. R&P M Horvatth. Circ: 600.

667.6 DEU ISSN 1434-0526
LACKIERERBLATT. Text in German. 1992. bi-m. EUR 69.30 domestic; EUR 74.90 foreign (effective 2011). adv. **Document type:** *Magazine, Trade.*
Formerly (until 1997): Deutsche Lackiererblatt (0949-4650)
Published by: (Bundesfachgruppe Fahrzeuglackierer), Konradin Verlag Robert Kohlhammer GmbH, Ernst Mey Str 8, Leinfelden-Echterdingen, 70771, Germany. TEL 49-711-75940, FAX 49-711-7594390, info@konradin.de, http://www.konradin.de. Ed. Michael Rehm. Adv. contact Carola Gayda. Circ: 5,896 (paid).

677.6 RUS ISSN 0130-9013 CODEN: LAMAAD
LAKOKRASOCHNYE MATERIALY I IKH PRIMENENIE. Text in Russian; Abstracts in English, Russian. 1960. m. USD 170 foreign (effective 2005). adv. bk.rev. bibl. index. **Document type:** *Journal, Trade.* **Description:** Provides information on paints and coatings in the former USSR (CIS). Covers scientific and production achievements in the paint industry and finishing technology. Also includes a section trade, economy, firm presentation, and advertising.
Indexed: A&ATA, CIN, ChemAb, ChemTitl, RefZh, SCOPUS, WSCA.
—BLDSC (0095.300000), CASDDS, East View, IE, Ingenta, INIST, Linda Hall. **CCC.**
Address: 2-ya Zvenigorodskaya, 12, Moscow, 123100, Russian Federation. TEL 7-095-2596835, FAX 7-0-95-2596488. Ed. Vladimir V Menshikov. Adv. contact Olga M Androutskaya. color page USD 700. Circ: 5,000. **Dist. by:** East View Information Services, 10601 Wayzata Blvd, Minneapolis, MN 55305. TEL 952-252-1201, 800-477-1005, FAX 952-252-1202, info@eastview.com, http://www.eastview.com.

698 SWE ISSN 0280-8226
MAALARMAESTAREN. Text in Swedish. 1960. bi-m. adv. **Document type:** *Magazine, Trade.*
Formerly (until 1981): Maaleri (0025-1232)
Published by: Maalerifoeretagarna, Vaestbergs Alle 1, Haegersten, 12630, Sweden. TEL 46-8-7446370, FAX 46-8-7446371, info@maleriforetagarna.org, http://www.maleriforetagarna.org. Circ: 7,000.

698 SWE ISSN 0345-7710
MAALARNAS FACKTIDNING. Text in Swedish. 1887. 9/yr. SEK 159; SEK 17 newsstand/cover (effective 2004). adv. 4 cols./p.; **Document type:** *Trade.*
Published by: Svenska Maalarefoerbundet/Swedish Painters' Union, Olof Palmes Gata 31, PO Box 1113, Stockholm, 11181, Sweden. TEL 46-8-58727400, FAX 46-8-58727499, post@malareforbundet.a.se. Ed. Lars-Aake Lundin. Adv. contact Dan Svard. B&W page SEK 22,000, color page SEK 29,000. Circ: 25,000.

667.6 DEU ISSN 1614-6158
MALER UND LACKIERER. Text in German. 2005. m. **Document type:** *Magazine, Trade.*
Published by: Directa Buldt Fachverlag, Luebecker Str 8, Bad Schwartau, 23611, Germany. TEL 49-451-499990, FAX 49-451-4999940, info@directa-verlag.de, http://www.directa-verlag.de.

698 DEU ISSN 0947-7489
DER MALER UND LACKIERERMEISTER. Text in German. 1950. m. EUR 28; EUR 3 per issue (effective 2011). adv. charts; illus.; tr.lit. **Document type:** *Magazine, Trade.*
Published by: Verlag W. Sachon GmbH & Co., Schloss Mindelburg, Mindelheim, 87714, Germany. TEL 49-8261-999457, FAX 49-8261-999491, info@sachon.de. Ed. Peter Schmid. Adv. contact Anita Elsaesser. B&W page EUR 4,750, color page EUR 7,045. Circ: 21,745 (paid and controlled).

698 DEU ISSN 1434-1360
TT300
MALERBLATT. Text in German. 1928. m. EUR 114 domestic; EUR 120 foreign (effective 2011). adv. bk.rev. charts; illus.; tr.lit. index. Supplement avail. **Document type:** *Magazine, Trade.*
Formerly (until 1996): Deutsche Malerblatt (0012-0448); Which incorporated (1951-1982): Malerzeitung Drei Schilde (0025-1372)
Indexed: A&ATA, BioDAb, WSCA.
—BLDSC (5356.087400). **CCC.**
Published by: (Hauptverband Farbe, Gestaltung, Bautenschutz), Konradin Verlag Robert Kohlhammer GmbH, Ernst Mey Str 8, Leinfelden-Echterdingen, 70771, Germany. TEL 49-711-75940, FAX 49-711-7594390, info@konradin.de, http://www.konradin.de. Ed. Ulrich Schweizer. Adv. contact Carola Gayda. Circ: 21,844 (paid and controlled).

698 NOR ISSN 0333-3531
MALEREN; organ for malermestrenes landsforbund. Text in Norwegian. 1908. 10/yr. NOK 890 (effective 2011). adv. bk.rev. **Document type:** *Journal, Trade.* **Description:** Articles about the construction industry and painting as a trade.
Formerly (until 1909): Fagblad for Malermestrenes Landsforbund (0804-4422)
Related titles: Online - full text ed.
Indexed: CISA.
Published by: (Malermestrenes Landsforbund), Skarland Press A-S, P O Box 2843, Toeyen, Oslo, 0608, Norway. TEL 47-22-708300, FAX 47-22-708301, firmapost@skarland.no, http://www.skarland.no. Ed. Georg Mathisen TEL 47-90-932897. Adv. contact Trine Fredheim TEL 47-22-708316.

698 747 FRA ISSN 0755-1533
MANUEL GENERAL DE LA PEINTURE ET DE LA DECORATION. Text in French. 1961. 10/yr. EUR 87 domestic; EUR 109 foreign (effective 2010). **Document type:** *Magazine, Trade.*
Address: 77 Rue des Archives, Paris, 75003, France. TEL 33-1-40270104, FAX 33-1-40279082.

698 DEU ISSN 0025-2697
NK1700
DIE MAPPE; Deutsche Maler- und Lackierer-Zeitschrift. Text in German. 1881. m. EUR 117 domestic to individuals; EUR 126 foreign to individuals; EUR 69 domestic to students; EUR 78 foreign to students; EUR 10.50 newsstand/cover (effective 2011). adv. bk.rev. bibl.; illus.; stat. index. **Document type:** *Magazine, Trade.*
Incorporates (1954-1991): Farbe und Raum (0014-7702); Which was formerly (until 1955): Farbe und Glas (0323-5238)
Indexed: A&ATA, A22, DIP, IBR, IBZ, WSCA.
—BLDSC (5369.350000), IE, Ingenta. **CCC.**
Published by: Callwey Verlag, Streitfeldstr 35, Munich, 81673, Germany. TEL 49-89-4360050, FAX 49-89-436005113, a.hagenkord@callwey.de, http://www.callwey.de. Ed. Matthias Heilig. Adv. contact Elmar Grosse. Circ: 20,254 (paid).

380.1029 USA ISSN 0090-5402
TP934.5
MODERN PAINT & COATINGS PAINT RED BOOK; directory of the paint and coatings industry. Text in English. 1968. a. USD 58.95. **Document type:** *Directory.*
—**CCC.**
Published by: Cygnus Business Media, Inc., 1233 Janesville Ave, PO Box 803, Fort Atkinson, WI 53538. TEL 920-563-6388, FAX 920-563-1702, http://www.cygnusb2b.com. Circ: 18,712.

MUR + BETONG; arkitektur og byggeteknikk. *see* ARCHITECTURE

698 CHE ISSN 1422-3511 CODEN: OBSUA7
OBERFLAECHEN/POLYSURFACES. Text in French, German. 1959. bi-m. CHF 30 domestic; CHF 50 foreign (effective 2005). adv. bk.rev. illus. index. **Document type:** *Journal, Trade.*
Former titles (until 1997): Oberflaechen - Werkstoffe (1024-0624); (until 1993): Oberflaeche (0048-1270); (until 1968): Galvanotechnik und Oberflaechenschutz (0433-1427)
Indexed: A&ATA, A22, A28, APA, BrCerAb, C&ISA, CA/WCA, CEABA, CIA, CIN, CerAb, ChemAb, ChemTitl, CivEngAb, CorrAb, E&CAJ, E11, EEA, EMA, ESPM, EnvEAb, H15, M&TEA, M09, MBF, METADEX, SolStAb, T04, WAA, WSCA.
—BLDSC (6196.765000), CASDDS, IE, Infotrieve, INIST, Linda Hall.
Published by: (Schweizerische Gesellschaft fuer Oberflaechentechnik), Polymedia Meichtry SA, Chemin de la Caroline 26, Petit-Lancy, 1213, Switzerland. TEL 41-22-8798820, FAX 41-22-8798825, info@polymedia.ch, http://www.polymedia.ch. adv.: B&W page CHF 2,590, color page CHF 3,690; trim 185 x 265. Circ: 6,000. **Co-sponsor:** Verband Galvano Betriebe der Schweiz.

667.6 GBR ISSN 1357-731X
TP934 CODEN: EPPJEJ
P P C J. (Polymers Paint Colour Journal) Text in English. 1879. q. adv. bk.rev. abstr.; charts; mkt.; pat. s-a. index. back issues avail. **Document type:** *Journal, Trade.* **Description:** Contains information of value to those in the paint, printing inks, and allied industries.
Incorporates (2002-2004): European Adhesives & Sealants (1478-9574); Which was formerly (until 2002): Adhesive Technology (1462-0146); (until 1998): European Adhesives & Sealants (0264-9047); Former titles (until 1995): European Polymers Paint Colour Journal (0963-8474); (until 1990): Polymers Paint Colour Journal (0370-1158); (until 1971): Paint, Oil and Colour Journal (0030-9516); (until 1950): Oil & Colour Trades Journal (0369-7088); (until 1906): Oil & Colour Trades Journal
Related titles: Online - full text ed.; ◆ Supplement(s): Polymers Paint Colour Journal Yearbook (Year). ISSN 1472-8885; ◆ European Adhesives and Sealants. ISSN 1478-9574; Ink Review; Middle East Directory; European Powder Coatings.
Indexed: A&ATA, A22, B02, B15, B17, B18, BMT, C&ISA, CBNB, CEA, CEABA, CPEI, ChemAb, CorrAb, E&CAJ, EngInd, G04, G06, G07, G08, I05, KES, R18, RefZh, SCOPUS, SolStAb, TCEA, TM, WAA, WSCA.
—BLDSC (6547.743000), CASDDS, IE, Ingenta, INIST, Linda Hall. **CCC.**
Published by: Quartz Business Media Ltd., Westgate House, 120/130 Station Rd, Redhill, Surrey RH1 1ET, United Kingdom. TEL 44-1737-855000, FAX 44-1737-855475, http://www.quartzltd.co.uk/business. Ed. Sue Tyler TEL 44-1737-855161. Adv. contact Ranjeet Sandhu TEL 44-1737-855570. B&W page GBP 2,637, color page GBP 4,585; trim 210 x 297. Circ: 8,600.

667.6 USA ISSN 0884-3848
TP934
PAINT & COATINGS INDUSTRY; globally serving liquid and powder manufacturers and formulators. Abbreviated title: P C I. Text in English. 1914. m. USD 104 domestic; USD 137 in Canada; USD 154 elsewhere; free to qualified personnel (print or online ed.) (effective 2009). adv. bk.rev. illus.; pat.; stat.; tr.lit. index. back issues avail.; reprints avail. **Document type:** *Magazine, Trade.* **Description:** Serves manufacturers, suppliers, distributors in the paint and coatings field with industry news, technology and product coverage.
Former titles (until 1985): Industry Section of Western Paint and Decorating; Decorative Products World; Paint and Decorating; Western Paint and Decorating; Supersedes in part (in 198?): Western Paint & Decorating (0274-8703); Which was formerly (until 1980): Western Paint Industry (0164-839X); (until 1978): Western Paint Review (0043-4027)
Related titles: Online - full text ed.; Chinese ed.; Supplement(s): Raw Material & Equipment Directory & Buyers Guide.
Indexed: A09, A10, A15, A22, A28, ABIn, APA, B01, B02, B06, B07, B08, B09, B15, B17, B18, BrCerAb, C&ISA, C12, CA/WCA, CBNB, CIA, CerAb, ChemAb, CivEngAb, CorrAb, E&CAJ, E11, EEA, EMA, ESPM, EnvEAb, G04, G06, G07, G08, H15, I05, M&TEA, M01, M02, M09, MBF, METADEX, P48, P51, P52, PQC, S22, SCOPUS, SolStAb, T02, T04, V02, V03, V04, WAA, WSCA.
—BLDSC (6334.249900), IE, Ingenta, Linda Hall. **CCC.**
Published by: B N P Media, 2401 W Big Beaver Rd, Ste 700, Troy, MI 48084. TEL 248-244-6499, FAX 248-244-2925, portfolio@bnpmedia.com, http://www.bnpmedia.com. Ed. Darlene R Brezinski TEL 906-779-9498. Pub. Donna Campbell TEL 610-650-4050. adv.: B&W page USD 4,250, color page USD 5,850; trim 8 x 10.75. Circ: 20,030.

PAINT & DECORATING RETAILER. *see* INTERIOR DESIGN AND DECORATION

PAINT & DECORATING RETAILER'S DECORATING REGISTRY. *see* INTERIOR DESIGN AND DECORATION

667.6 GBR ISSN 1476-0274
TP934 CODEN: PRTAC9
PAINT AND RESIN TIMES; the newsletter for the paint and surface treatment industry. Text in English. 1931. bi-m. adv. bk.rev. abstr.; bibl.; charts; illus.; stat. index. **Document type:** *Newsletter, Trade.* **Description:** Presents relevant information for the production, technical, and research and development management in paint, ink, resins, varnishes and lacquers manufacturers and colour chemists/paint formulators in the processing sector.
Former titles (until 2002): Paint and Resin International (1464-0139); (until 1993): Paint and Resin (0261-5746); (until 1981): Paint Manufacture (0030-9508)
Related titles: Online - full text ed.
Indexed: A&ATA, A22, CBNB, CEABA, CIN, CISA, Cadscan, ChemAb, ChemTitl, G08, LeadAb, SCOPUS, WSCA, Zincscan.
—CASDDS, IE, INIST. **CCC.**
Published by: Complete Circulation and Marketing Ltd., Unit 8, Netherhall Yard, Mill Ln, Newick, E Sussex BN8 4JL, United Kingdom. TEL 44-1825-724623, FAX 44-1825-724623, http://www.completecircmktg.co.uk. Pub., Adv. contact Colin C Dann. page GBP 588; trim 210 x 297. Circ: 2,000.

667.6 USA
PAINT CONSUMER RESEARCH PROGRAM. Abbreviated title: P C R P. Text in English. 19??. q. **Document type:** *Trade.* **Description:** Provides information on consumer paint purchases by brand, geographic area, distribution channel, and purchase price.
Published by: National Paint and Coatings Association, 1500 Rhode Island Ave, NW, Washington, DC 20005. TEL 202-462-6272, FAX 202-462-8549, npca@paint.org.

667.6 USA
▼ **THE PAINT CONTRACTOR.** Text in English. 2009 (Jan.). m. free to qualified personnel (effective 2009). adv. **Document type:** *Magazine, Trade.*
Published by: Mugler Publications, Inc., 111-A N Kirkwood Rd, St Louis, MO 63122. TEL 314-984-0800, FAX 314-984-0866, http://www.paintdealer.com. Pub. Hans Mugler. adv.: color page USD 3,000; trim 8 x 10.75.

667.6 381.1 USA ISSN 1067-1110
THE PAINT DEALER; dedicated to the retail paint market. Text in English. 1992. m. USD 36 domestic; USD 100 foreign; free to qualified personnel (effective 2007). adv. bk.rev. illus.; tr.lit. 72 p./no.; **Document type:** *Magazine, Trade.* **Description:** Covers product innovations, merchandising ideas, store management and industry news.
Published by: Mugler Publications, Inc., 111-A N Kirkwood Rd, St Louis, MO 63122. TEL 314-984-0800, 800-984-0801, FAX 314-984-0866, primecoat@aol.com. Ed., R&P John F D Taff. Pub. Hans Mugler. adv.: page USD 3,600; trim 10.75 x 8. Circ: 23,000 (controlled).

667.6 IND ISSN 0556-4409
TP934 CODEN: PIDABZ
PAINTINDIA. Text in English. 1951. m. INR 500 (effective 2011). adv. bk.rev. abstr.; illus.; stat. reprints avail. **Document type:** *Magazine, Trade.*
Related titles: Microfilm ed.: (from PQC); Alternate Frequency ed(s).: ISSN 0030-9540. a.
Indexed: A&ATA, A22, B01, B07, CTE, ChemAb, ChemTitl, WSCA.
—BLDSC (6340.000000), CASDDS, IE, Ingenta, INIST, Linda Hall.
Published by: Colour Publications Pvt. Ltd., Dhuruwadi 126-A, A.V. Nagveka Marg, Prabhadevi, Mumbai, Maharashtra 400 025, India. TEL 91-22-24306319, FAX 91-22-24300601, paintindia.2010@gmail.com. Ed. R V Raghavan. Circ: 5,096. **Subscr. to:** I N S I O Scientific Books & Periodicals, PO Box 7234, Indraprastha HPO, New Delhi 110 002, India. iihm@ap.nic.in, http://iihm.ap.nic.in/.

698 GBR
PAINTING AND DECORATING ASSOCIATION. MEMBERS REFERENCE HANDBOOK. Text in English. 1932. a. free to members (effective 2009). abstr.; charts. **Document type:** *Handbook/Manual/Guide, Trade.* **Description:** Aims to bring together all the latest information relevant to the industry.
Formerly (until 2002): British Decorators Association. Members Reference Handbook
Published by: Painting and Decorating Association, 32 Coton Rd, Nuneaton, Warks CV11 5TW, United Kingdom. TEL 44-24-76353776, FAX 44-24-76354513, info@paintingdecoratingassociation.co.uk, http://www.paintingdecoratingassociation.co.uk/.

698 USA ISSN 0735-9713
TT300
PAINTING AND WALLCOVERING CONTRACTOR. Short title: P W C. Text in English. 1938. bi-m. adv. stat. 100 p./no. 3 cols./p.; back issues avail. **Document type:** *Magazine, Trade.* **Description:** Covers all phases of the painting, decorating and wallcovering industry.
Former titles (until 1983): Professional Decorating and Coating Action (0099-0310); (until 1975): P D C A; P D C A 74 (0038-8416); Spotlights
Related titles: Microform ed.: (from PQC); Online - full text ed.; Supplement(s): Printing Contractor Resource Guide.
Indexed: A15, A22, ABIn, G09, P10, P13, P16, P48, P51, P52, P53, P54, PQC.

P

Published by: (Painting & Decorating Contractors of America), Finan Publishing Company, Inc., 2100 Wharton St, ste 310, Pittsburgh, PA 15203. TEL 800-837-8303, FAX 412-431-5428.

667.6 NZL ISSN 0113-8685
PANELTALK. Text in English. 1984. bi-m. NZD 42 domestic; NZD 50 Australia & Pacific Islands; NZD 55 in North America; NZD 60 in Europe (effective 2009). adv. **Document type:** *Magazine, Trade.* **Description:** Covers all aspects of interest to the panelbeating and spray painting (refinish) trade for the New Zealand automobile industry.
Published by: NZ Collision Repair Association, Waikato Mail Centre, PO Box 9208, Hamilton, 3240, New Zealand. TEL 64-7-8470216, FAX 64-7-8470217, info@collisionrepair.co.nz. Circ: 800 (paid); 500 (controlled).

667.6 DEU
PHAENOMEN FARBE. Text in German. 1980. 10/yr. EUR 108 domestic; EUR 142 foreign (effective 2011). adv. **Document type:** *Magazine, Trade.*
Published by: Verlag Phaenomen Farbe, Noerdlinger Str 15, Duesseldorf, 40597, Germany. TEL 49-211-7182314, FAX 49-211-7182366, pf-verlag@t-online.de. adv.: page EUR 1,840. Circ: 1,950 (paid).

667.6 GBR ISSN 0369-9420
TP934 CODEN: PGRTBC
➤ **PIGMENT & RESIN TECHNOLOGY**; the international journal of colorants, polymers and colour applications. Abbreviated title: P R T. Text in English. 1936. bi-m. EUR 4,519 combined subscription in Europe (print & online eds.); USD 4,579 combined subscription in the Americas (print & online eds.); GBP 3,259 combined subscription in the UK & elsewhere (print & online eds.); AUD 6,249 combined subscription in Australasia (print & online eds.) (effective 2012). bk.rev. abstr.; charts; illus.; tr.lit. index. back issues avail.; reprint service avail. from PSC. **Document type:** *Journal, Academic/Scholarly.* **Description:** Provides coverage of the materials and techniques used in paint and resin technology.
Formerly (until 1972): Paint Technology (0030-9524); Which was formerly (until 1936): British Plastics and Moulded Product Trader (0366-2853); Paint Technology incorporated (in 1936): Synthetic and Applied Finishes (0371-4829)
Related titles: Microfilm ed.: (from PMC); Online - full text ed.: ISSN 1758-6941 (from IngentaConnect).
Indexed: A01, A03, A08, A15, A22, A26, A28, ABIn, APA, B02, B15, B17, B18, BrCerAb, BrTechI, C&ISA, C24, CA, CA/WCA, CBNB, CCI, CIA, CIN, CPEI, Cadscan, CerAb, ChemAb, ChemTitl, CivEngAb, CorrAb, CurCont, E&CAJ, E01, E11, EEA, EMA, ESPM, EmerIntel, EngInd, EnvEAb, G04, G08, GALA, H15, I05, Inspec, LeadAb, M&TEA, M09, MBF, METADEX, MSCI, P26, P48, P51, P52, P54, PQC, R18, RefZh, SCI, SCOPUS, SolStAb, T01, T02, T04, TTI, W07, WAA, WSCA, Zincscan.
—BLDSC (6500.145000), CASDDS, IE, Infotrieve, Ingenta, INIST, Linda Hall. **CCC.**
Published by: Emerald Group Publishing Ltd., Howard House, Wagon Ln, Bingley, W Yorks BD16 1WA, United Kingdom. TEL 44-1274-777700, FAX 44-1274-785201, information@emeraldinsight.com. Ed. Long Lin. Pub. Harry Colson.

667.5 ESP ISSN 0031-9945
PINTORES. Text in Spanish. 1961. bi-m. adv. illus.; stat.
Published by: Asociacion de Maestros Pintores de Barcelona, Diputacio, 297, Barcelona, 08009, Spain. TEL 34-93-4881288. Ed. A Palat Ullastres. Circ: 6,000.

698 ITA
CODEN: PIVEAY
PITTURE E VERNICI EUROPEAN COATINGS. Text in Italian. 1924. fortn. EUR 155 (effective 2009). adv. bk.rev. abstr. **Document type:** *Magazine, Trade.*
Former titles: Pitture e Vernici (0048-4245); (until 1945): Vernici (0372-5634)
Indexed: A&ATA, A22, BioDAb, CIN, ChemAb, ChemTitl, FR, WSCA.
—BLDSC (6506.000000), CASDDS, IE, Ingenta, INIST.
Published by: Gi.Bi.Pi. Editrice Srl, Via Ponte Nuovo 26, Milan, MI 20128, Italy. TEL 39-02-26305505, FAX 39-02-26305621, http://www.gbp.it. Circ: 5,000.

698 747 ZAF ISSN 1994-148X
PLASCON COLOUR. Text in English. 2002. s-a. adv. **Document type:** *Magazine, Consumer.*
Formerly (until 2004): VISI Colour (1684-7067)
Published by: (Plascon), New Media Publishing, PO Box 440, Green Point, 8051, South Africa. TEL 27-21-4171111, FAX 27-21-4171112, newmedia@newmediapub.co.za, http://www.newmediapub.co.za. Ed. Sumien Brink. Pub. Hannerie Visser. Adv. contact Heidi Finestone. Circ: 9,778.

667.6029 GBR ISSN 1472-8885
TP934.5
POLYMERS PAINT COLOUR JOURNAL YEARBOOK (YEAR). Variant title: Polymers Paint Colour Journal Directory. Text in English. 1961. a. GBP 160 per issue domestic; GBP 168, USD 333 per issue foreign (effective 2009). adv. **Document type:** *Directory, Trade.* **Description:** Lists manufacturers of paint, printing ink, and raw materials used in the printing process.
Former titles (until 2000): Polymers Paint Color Yearbook (Year) (0078-7817); (until 1973): Paint, Oil, Colour Year Book
Related titles: ◆ Supplement to: P P C J. ISSN 1357-731X.
—CCC.
Published by: Quartz Business Media Ltd., Westgate House, 120/130 Station Rd, Redhill, Surrey RH1 1ET, United Kingdom. TEL 44-1737-855000, FAX 44-1737-855475, http://www.quartzltd.co.uk/business. Adv. contact Ranjeet Sandhu TEL 44-1737-855570.

698 USA ISSN 0032-9940
TS200 CODEN: PRFCAB
PRODUCTS FINISHING. Abbreviated title: P F. Text in English. 1936. m. USD 89 domestic; USD 99 in Canada; USD 200 elsewhere; free in North America to qualified personnel (effective 2008). adv. bibl.; illus.; tr.lit. back issues avail.; reprints avail. **Document type:** *Magazine, Trade.* **Description:** Covers the application of both organic coatings, such as paint and powder coating, and inorganic coatings, like electroplating, electroless plating and conversion coatings, including anodizing, phosphating and chromating.
Related titles: Online - full text ed.; ◆ Supplement(s): Products Finishing Directory. ISSN 0478-4251.
Indexed: A05, A09, A10, A15, A22, A28, ABIn, APA, AS&TA, AS&TI, B01, B02, B06, B07, B09, B15, B17, B18, BRD, BrCerAb, C&ISA, C10, CA/WCA, CIA, CIN, CTE, Cadscan, CerAb, ChemAb, ChemTitl, CivEngAb, CorrAb, E&CAJ, E11, EEA, EMA, ESPM, EngInd, EnvEAb, G04, G06, G07, G08, H15, I05, LeadAb, M&TEA, M09, MBF, METADEX, P34, P48, P51, P52, PQC, S22, SCOPUS, SolStAb, T02, T04, V03, V04, W03, W05, WAA, WSCA, Zincscan.
—BLDSC (6854.000000), CASDDS, IE, Infotrieve, Ingenta, INIST, Linda Hall. **CCC.**
Published by: Gardner Publications, Inc., 6915 Valley Ave, Cincinnati, OH 45244. TEL 513-527-8800, 800-950-8020, FAX 513-527-8801, skline2@gardnerweb.com. Ed. Jim Destefani. Pub. Don Kline. adv.: B&W page USD 3,900, color page USD 5,750; trim 7.5 x 10.5. Circ: 40,162.

698 USA ISSN 0478-4251
PRODUCTS FINISHING DIRECTORY. Abbreviated title: P F D. Variant title: Products Finishing Directory and Technology Guide. Text in English. a. USD 15 per issue (effective 2009); free with subscr. to Products Finishing. adv. **Document type:** *Directory, Trade.* **Description:** Designed to be the finishing industry's single best resource for practical finishing knowledge and supplier information.
Related titles: ◆ Supplement to: Products Finishing. ISSN 0032-9940.
Indexed: CTE.
—CCC.
Published by: Gardner Publications, Inc., 6915 Valley Ave, Cincinnati, OH 45244. TEL 513-527-8800, 800-950-8020, FAX 513-527-8801, skline2@gardnerweb.com, http://www.gardnerweb.com. Ed. Jim Destefani. Pub. Don Kline. Adv. contact Donald Kline. B&W page USD 3,650; trim 5.3125 x 7.125. Circ: 30,000 (paid).

698 USA
PROFESSIONAL SPRAYING. Text in English. q. free.
Published by: Graco Inc., PO Box 1441, Minneapolis, MN 55440. TEL 612-623-6000. Ed. Mick Lee.

698 ITA ISSN 1825-1196
PROGETTO COLORE. Text in Italian. 1966. bi-m. EUR 25 domestic; EUR 70 in Europe; EUR 80 elsewhere (effective 2011). adv. index. back issues avail. **Document type:** *Magazine, Trade.*
Former titles (until 2004): Il Giornale del Colore (1594-9311); (until 2002): La Bottega del Colore (1591-8769)
Related titles: Online - full text ed.
Published by: (Federcolori - Federazione Nazionale dei Commercianti di Colori), Tecniche Nuove SpA, Via Eritrea 21, Milan, MI 201, Italy. TEL 39-02-390901, FAX 39-02-7570364, info@tecnichenuove.com. Ed. Veronica Mulinello. Circ: 14,000.

547 698 NLD ISSN 0300-9440
CODEN: POGCAT
➤ **PROGRESS IN ORGANIC COATINGS.** Text in English, French, German. 1973. 12/yr. EUR 2,421 in Europe to institutions; JPY 321,600 in Japan to institutions; USD 2,721 elsewhere to institutions (effective 2012). adv. bk.rev. charts; illus. Index. **Document type:** *Journal, Academic/Scholarly.* **Description:** Analyzes and publicizes the progress and current state of knowledge in the field of organic coatings and related materials.
Related titles: Microform ed.: (from PQC); Online - full text ed.: ISSN 1873-331X (from IngentaConnect, ScienceDirect).
Indexed: A01, A03, A08, A20, A22, A26, A28, APA, ASCA, BrCerAb, C&ISA, C24, C33, CA, CA/WCA, CIA, CPEI, CTE, CerAb, ChemAb, ChemTitl, CivEngAb, CorrAb, CurCont, E&CAJ, E11, EEA, EMA, ESPM, EngInd, EnvEAb, H15, I05, ISR, M&TEA, M09, MBF, METADEX, MSCI, PhysBer, R16, RefZh, S01, SCI, SCOPUS, SolStAb, T02, T04, TM, W07, WAA, WSCA.
—BLDSC (6872.200000), CASDDS, IE, Infotrieve, Ingenta, INIST, Linda Hall. **CCC.**
Published by: Elsevier BV (Subsidiary of: Elsevier Science & Technology), Radarweg 29, PO Box 211, Amsterdam, 1000 AE, Netherlands. TEL 31-20-4853911, FAX 31-20-4852457, JournalsCustomerServiceEMEA@elsevier.com, http://www.elsevier.nl. **Subscr. to:** Radarweg 29, PO Box 211, Amsterdam 1000 AE, Netherlands. TEL 31-20-4853757, FAX 31-20-4853432.

667.6 RUS
PROMYSHLENNAYA OKRASKA. Text in Russian. 2003. bi-m. **Document type:** *Journal, Trade.*
Published by: Lakokrasochnye Materialy i ikh Primenenie, 2-ya Zvenigorodskaya, 12, Moscow, 123100, Russian Federation. TEL 7-095-2596835, FAX 7-0-95-2596488, journal-lkm@mtu-net.ru.

667.6 USA ISSN 1085-5645
PROTECTIVE COATINGS EUROPE. Text in English. m. USD 80 (effective 2004). adv. back issues avail. **Document type:** *Magazine, Trade.*
Indexed: A28, APA, BrCerAb, C&ISA, CA/WCA, CIA, CerAb, CivEngAb, CorrAb, E&CAJ, E11, EEA, EMA, ESPM, EnvEAb, H15, M&TEA, M09, MBF, METADEX, SolStAb, T04, WAA.
—BLDSC (6935.789000), IE, Ingenta, Linda Hall.
Published by: PaintSquare, Inc., 2100 Wharton Street, Ste 310, Pittsburgh, PA 15203. TEL 412-431-8300, 800-837 8303, FAX 412-431-5428, webmaster@paintsquare.com. Ed. Brian Goldie TEL 44-20-82880077. Adv. contacts Bernadette Landon TEL 412-922-0522, Jan Lagrand TEL 31-78-6180588. color page USD 2,270; trim 206 x 276.

QUICK AND EASY PAINTING. *see* HOBBIES

667.6 CHN ISSN 1002-7432
REGUXING SHUZHI/THERMOSETTING RESIN. Text in Chinese; Abstracts in English. 1986. q. USD 48 (effective 2009). **Document type:** *Academic/Scholarly.* **Description:** Contains reports and reviews on the research, development, production and application of various thermosetting resins such as epoxy resin, unsaturated polyester resin, polyurethane, and phenolic resin.
Formerly (until vol.2, 1987): Huanyang Shuzhi - Epoxy Resin
Related titles: Online - full text ed.
Indexed: A28, APA, BrCerAb, C&ISA, CA/WCA, CIA, CIN, CerAb, ChemAb, ChemTitl, CivEngAb, CorrAb, E&CAJ, E11, EEA, EMA, ESPM, EnvEAb, H15, M&TEA, M09, MBF, METADEX, SolStAb, T04, WAA.
—BLDSC (8814.892300), East View, Linda Hall.
Published by: (Tianjin Shi Hecheng Cailiao Gongye Yanjiusuo), Reguxing Shuzhi Bianjibu, 29 Dongting Lu, Hexi-qu, Tianjin 300220, China. TEL 81-22-834-1651, FAX 22-834-0113. Ed. Jinfen Xue. R&P, Adv. contact Qi Zhang. Circ: 2,500. **Dist. overseas by:** China International Book Trading Corp, 35 Chegongzhuang Xilu, Haidian District, PO Box 399, Beijing 100044, China.

667 FIN ISSN 0780-086X
RUTER COATING. Text in Swedish. 1980. a. free. **Document type:** *Trade.*
Related titles: ◆ Finnish ed.: Ruutu. ISSN 0780-0851.
Published by: Tikkurila Oy, Kuninkaalantie 1, PL 53, Vantaa, 01301, Finland. TEL 358-9-857-721, FAX 358-9-8577-6900.

667 FIN ISSN 0780-0851
RUUTU. Text in Finnish. 1980. a. free. **Document type:** *Trade.*
Related titles: ◆ Swedish ed.: Ruter Coating. ISSN 0780-086X.
Published by: Tikkurila Oy, Kuninkaalantie 1, PL 53, Vantaa, 01301, Finland. TEL 358-9-857-721, FAX 358-0-8577-6900. Ed. Tapio Kaar.

363.7 GBR ISSN 1741-475X
S H E ALERT. (Safety Health Environment) Text in English. 1993. m. GBP 655 to non-members (print or online ed.); GBP 490 to members (print or online ed.); GBP 820 combined subscription to non-members (print & online eds.); GBP 610 combined subscription to members (print & online eds.) (effective 2009). **Document type:** *Bulletin, Trade.* **Description:** Provides an alerting service on safety, health and environmental issues of relevance to the coatings industry.
Related titles: E-mail ed.; Online - full text ed.: S H E Alert Online. GBP 925 to non-members; GBP 690 to members (effective 2009).
Indexed: CSNB, L12.
—CCC.
Published by: P R A Coatings Technology Centre, 14 Castle Mews, High St, Hampton, Mddlx. TW12 2NP, United Kingdom. TEL 44-20-84870800, FAX 44-20-84870801, publications@pra-world.com. Ed. Dr. Tina Walton.

S V C NEWS BULLETIN. *see* ENGINEERING—Engineering Mechanics And Materials

SCAFFOLD INDUSTRY. *see* BUILDING AND CONSTRUCTION

667.6 USA
SEALANTS; the professional's guide. Text in English. a. USD 40 to non-members; USD 30 to members (effective 1999). adv. charts; illus.; stat. **Document type:** *Handbook/Manual/Guide, Trade.* **Description:** Covers joints, sealants, and specifications for the industry.
Published by: Sealant, Waterproofing and Restoration Institute, 2841 Main St, Kansas City, MO 64108. TEL 816-472-7974, FAX 816-472-7765, info@swrionline.org, http://www.swrionline.org. Pub. Ken Bowman. Adv. contact Sheila Navis.

621.885 GBR ISSN 1350-4789
SEALING TECHNOLOGY. Text in English. 1994. m. EUR 1,157 in Europe to institutions; JPY 153,700 in Japan to institutions; USD 1,297 elsewhere to institutions (effective 2010). adv. back issues avail.; reprints avail. **Document type:** *Newsletter, Trade.* **Description:** Covers new developments in seals, including innovative design, new materials, applications in all industries, environmental and standards issues.
Related titles: Microform ed.: (from PQC); Online - full text ed.: ISSN 1879-100X (from IngentaConnect, ScienceDirect).
Indexed: A15, A22, A26, B01, B06, B07, B09, CA, CPEI, EngInd, FLUIDEX, I05, PQC, R18, SCOPUS, T02.
—IE, Infotrieve, Ingenta. **CCC.**
Published by: Elsevier Advanced Technology (Subsidiary of: Elsevier Science & Technology), The Blvd, Langford Ln, Kidlington, Oxon OX5 1GB, United Kingdom. TEL 44-1865-843434, FAX 44-1865-843970, eatsales@elsevier.co.uk. Ed. R K Flitney TEL 44-1799-501659. **Subscr. to:** Elsevier BV, Radarweg 29, PO Box 211, Amsterdam 1000 AE, Netherlands. TEL 31-20-4853757, FAX 31-20-4853432, JournalsCustomerServiceEMEA@elsevier.com, http://www.elsevier.nl.

667.6 CHN ISSN 1009-1696
SHANGHAI TUKE/SHANGHAI COATINGS. Text in Chinese. 1962. bi-m. CNY 48 (effective 2003). **Document type:** *Magazine, Trade.*
Related titles: Online - full text ed.
—BLDSC (8254.588820).
Published by: Shanghai-shi Tuke Yanjiusuo/Shanghai Coatings Research Institute, 345, Yunling Dong Lu, Shanghai, 200062, China. TEL 86-21-52808959, FAX 86-21-52806562.

382 IND ISSN 0304-8179
HD9769.L33
SHELLAC EXPORT PROMOTION COUNCIL. ANNUAL REPORT. Text in English. 1944. a., latest 2006. stat. **Document type:** *Report, Trade.*
Related titles: Online - full text ed.
Published by: Shellac Export Promotion Council, 1-1 Wood St, 2nd Fl, Kolkata, West Bengal 700 016, India. TEL 91-33-22834417, FAX 91-33-22834699, sepc@vsnl.net.

667.6 JPN ISSN 0010-180X
TP934 CODEN: SKYOAO
SHIKIZAI KYOKAISHI/JAPAN SOCIETY OF COLOUR MATERIAL. JOURNAL. (0371-0777) Text in English, Japanese; Summaries in English. 1927. m. JPY 50,400 (effective 2004). adv. illus.; pat.; tr.lit. Index. **Document type:** *Journal, Academic/Scholarly.* **Description:** Contains research papers, reviews, lecture notes, abstracts from domestic and overseas publications and information on various activites of related societies.
Indexed: A22, CIN, ChemAb, ChemTitl, JTA, RefZh, WSCA.
—BLDSC (4807.050000), CASDDS, IE, Ingenta, INIST. **CCC.**
Published by: Shikizai Kyokai/Japan Society of Colour Material, Tokyo Toryo Kaikan, 3-12-8, Ebisu, Shibuya-ku, Tokyo, 150-0013, Japan. Ed. Takeshi Amari.

667.6 665.5 CHN ISSN 1007-015X
TS200
SHIYOU HUAGONG FUSHI YU FANGHU/CORROSION & PROTECTION IN PETROCHEMICAL INDUSTRY. Text in Chinese. 1984. bi-m. **Document type:** *Magazine, Trade.*
Related titles: Online - full text ed.
—BLDSC (8267.299153).
Published by: (Zhongguo Shi-hua Jituan Fangfushi Yanjiu Zhongxin), Zhongguo Shi-hua Jituan Luoyang Shi-hua Gongcheng Gongsi/S I N O P E C, Luoyang Petrochemical Engineering Corporation, 27, Zhongzhou Western Rd., Luoyang, 471003, China. TEL 86-379-64885572, http://www.lpec.com.cn/. Ed. Zhongqiang Chui.

667.6 GBR ISSN 1362-9905
SIF NEWS. (Silicon and Fluorine) Text in English. 1996. bi-m. GBP 190 to non-members; GBP 170 to members. **Document type:** *Bulletin.*
Description: Contains information on silicon and fluorine in coatings and allied products.
Published by: Chemical and Polymers, 38 Lomond Rd, Hemel Hempstead, Herts HP2 6PA, United Kingdom. TEL 44-1442-249113, FAX 44-1442-249113.

658 620.1 USA ISSN 0737-5921
TS695 CODEN: PASVBF
SOCIETY OF VACUUM COATERS. ANNUAL TECHNICAL CONFERENCE PROCEEDINGS. Text in English. 1957. a. adv. bk.rev. abstr.; charts; illus.; stat. 500 p./no.; back issues avail.; reprints avail. **Document type:** *Proceedings, Academic/Scholarly.*
Description: Contains full text and abstracts of more than 100 papers presented at the Annual Technical Conference.
Formerly (until 1982): Society of Vacuum Coaters. Technical Conference. Proceedings (0731-1699)
Related titles: CD-ROM ed.: Society of Vacuum Coaters. Technical Conference Proceedings (Years). ISSN 1099-4718; Online - full text ed.: ISSN 1539-2236.
Indexed: Englnd, SCOPUS.
—BLDSC (6842.380000), IE, Ingenta, Linda Hall. **CCC.**
Published by: Society of Vacuum Coaters, 71 Pinon Hill Pl NE, Alberquerque, NM 87122. TEL 505-856-7188, FAX 505-856-6716.

667.6 AUS ISSN 0815-709X
CODEN: SCAUE6
SURFACE COATINGS AUSTRALIA. Text in English. 1964. 11/yr. AUD 150 to non-members; free to members (effective 2009). adv. bk.rev. 32 p./no.; back issues avail. **Document type:** *Journal, Trade.*
Description: Covers association activities, news and technical papers of interest and relevance to the surface coatings industries of Australia and New Zealand.
Formerly (until 1984): Australian O C C A Proceedings and News (0045-0774)
Indexed: ASI, CIN, ChemAb, ChemTitl, WSCA.
—BLDSC (8547.793000), CASDDS, IE, Ingenta, Linda Hall.
Published by: Surface Coatings Association Australia Inc., PO BOX 563, Toorak, VIC 3142, Australia. TEL 61-3-98278921, 800-803-378, FAX 61-3-98240258, scaa@unite.com.au. adv.: B&W page AUD 670, color page AUD 1,320; trim 210 x 297. Circ: 700 (controlled).
Co-sponsor: Surface Coatings Association New Zealand Inc.

667.9 GBR ISSN 1754-0925
TP934 CODEN: JOCCAB
SURFACE COATINGS INTERNATIONAL; the journal of the oil and colour chemists' association. Text in English. 2007. bi-m. USD 150 in North America; USD 80 elsewhere (effective 2010). bk.rev. illus. index. back issues avail. **Document type:** *Journal, Trade.* **Description:** Contains articles on technology, news of the industry and news of the Oil and Colour Chemists' Association.
Formed by the merger of (2001-2007): Surface Coatings International. Part A, Coatings Journal (1476-4857); (2001-2007): Surface Coatings International. Part B, Coatings Transactions (1476-4865); Both of which superseded in part (in 2001): Surface Coatings International (1356-0751); Which was formerly (1918-1991): Oil and Colour Chemists' Association. Journal (0030-1337)
Indexed: A&ATA, A28, APA, ASCA, BMT, BrCerAb, C&ISA, C24, CA/WCA, CIA, CIN, CPEI, CTE, Cadscan, CerAb, ChemAb, ChemTitl, CivEngAb, CorrAb, CurCR, CurCont, E&CAJ, E11, EEA, EMA, ESPM, Englnd, EnvEAb, GALA, H15, LeadAb, M&TEA, M09, MBF, METADEX, RICS, RefZh, SCI, SCOPUS, SolStAb, T04, W07, WAA, WSCA, Zincscan.
—BLDSC (8547.797050), CASDDS, IE, Ingenta, INIST, Linda Hall.
Published by: Oil & Colour Chemists' Association, The Membership Secretary, 1st Fl, 3 Eden Ct, Eden Way, Leighton Buzzard, Bedfordshire LU7 4FY, United Kingdom. TEL 44-1525-372530, FAX 44-1525-372600, publications@occa.org.uk.

SURFACE WORLD. *see* CHEMISTRY—Analytical Chemistry

TI02 WORLDWIDE UPDATE. *see* CHEMISTRY—Inorganic Chemistry

667 FIN
TIKKURILA COATINGS & PAINTS JOURNAL. Text in English. 1994. a. free. back issues avail. **Document type:** *Journal, Trade.*
Formerly: Tikkurila Coatings Journal (1237-4113)
Published by: Tikkurila Oy, Kuninkaalantie 1, PL 53, Vantaa, 01301, Finland. TEL 358-9-857-721, FAX 358-9-8577-6900. Ed. Tapio Kaar. Circ: 15,000.

TIKKURILAN VIESTI. *see* BUILDING AND CONSTRUCTION

667.6 JPN ISSN 0372-0365
TS653. A1 CODEN: TOGIBO
TOSO GIJUTSU. Abbreviated title: Japan Finishing. Text in Japanese. 1962. m. JPY 16,700 (effective 2003).
—BLDSC (4648.268000), Linda Hall.
Published by: Riko Shuppansha/Riko Publishing Company, 3-11-22 Iidabashi, Chiyoda-ku, Tokyo, 102-0072, Japan. TEL 81-3-32634021, FAX 81-3-32634022, info@rrikou.co.jp, http://www.rrikou.co.jp/.

667.6 FRA ISSN 1767-9419
TRAITEMENT DES SURFACES DE L'ANTICORROSION ET DES TRAITEMENTS THERMIQUES. Text in French. 1963. a. adv. **Document type:** *Directory, Trade.* **Description:** Covers the entire French market of surface coatings.
Formerly (until 2003): Catalogue National du Traitement des Surfaces de l'Anticorrosion et des Traitements Thermiques (0396-1214)
Published by: Editions Techniques pour l'Automobile et l'Industrie (E T A I), 20 rue de la Saussiere, Boulogne-Billancourt, 92641, France. TEL 33-1-46992424, FAX 33-1-48255692, http://www.groupe-etai.com. Circ: 10,000.

669 698 ITA ISSN 0041-1833
TRATTAMENTI E FINITURE. Text in English, Italian. 1961. bi-m. (7/yr.). EUR 35 domestic; EUR 70 in Europe; EUR 90 elsewhere (effective 2011). adv. bk.rev. charts; illus.; tr.lit. index. back issues avail.
Document type: *Magazine, Trade.* **Description:** Technical review concerning treatment processing, protection and finishing of metals as well as processes for treating the metal surface, finishing, protection and paintings.
Related titles: Online - full text ed.
Indexed: A28, APA, BrCerAb, C&ISA, CA/WCA, CIA, CerAb, CivEngAb, CorrAb, E&CAJ, E11, EEA, EMA, H15, M&TEA, M09, MBF, METADEX, SolStAb, T04, WAA, WSCA.
—INIST.
Published by: Tecniche Nuove SpA, Via Eritrea 21, Milan, MI 201, Italy. TEL 39-02-390901, FAX 39-02-7570364, info@tecnichenuove.com. Ed. Paola Pagani. Circ: 9,000.

667.6 CHN ISSN 0253-4312
CODEN: TLKYD5
TULIAO GONGYE/PAINT & COATINGS INDUSTRY. Text in Chinese; Summaries in English. 1959. m. USD 80.40 (effective 2009). adv. charts; illus.; tr.lit. index. 64 p./no.; back issues avail. **Document type:** *Journal, Trade.* **Description:** Contains reports and technical papers relating to paints and pigments industry; as well as brief news from domestic and foreign front.
Related titles: Fax ed.; Online - full text ed.
Indexed: A22, CIN, ChemAb, ChemTitl.
—BLDSC (6334.250000), CASDDS, East View, IE, Ingenta, Linda Hall.
Published by: (Changzhou Tuliao Huagong Yanjiuyuan/Changzhon Paint and Coatings Research Institute), Tuliao Gongye Bianjibu, Jichang Lu, Changzhou, Jiangsu 213016, China. TEL 86-519-3274974, FAX 86-519-3273017. Ed. Xie Daoli. R&P Yushu Zhu. Adv. contact Sujing Ga. B&W page CNY 2,000, color page CNY 10,000; trim 215 x 285. Circ: 10,000 (paid). **Dist. overseas by:** China International Book Trading Corp, 35 Chegongzhuang Xilu, Haidian District, PO Box 399, Beijing 100044, China. TEL 86-10-68412045, FAX 86-10-68412023, cibtc@mail.cibtc.com.cn, http://www.cibtc.com.cn.

667.9 GBR ISSN 1353-8942
TP934.5
U K SURFACE COATINGS HANDBOOK. Text in English. 1994. a. GBP 80 per issue (effective 2010). adv. **Document type:** *Directory, Academic/Scholarly.* **Description:** Contains detailed information on the products of and supplies to the Surface coatings industry, including full contact information.
Related titles: Online - full text ed.
Published by: Oil & Colour Chemists' Association, The Membership Secretary, 1st Fl, 3 Eden Ct, Eden Way, Leighton Buzzard, Bedfordshire LU7 4FY, United Kingdom. TEL 44-1525-372530, FAX 44-1525-372600, publications@occa.org.uk.

698 FIN ISSN 1459-4994
VAERI JA PINTA. Text in Finnish; Summaries in Swedish. 1917. 6/yr. adv. abstr.; charts; illus.; stat. index, cum.index. **Document type:** *Magazine, Trade.*
Formerly (until 2003): Maalarilehti (0024-8568)
Published by: Suomen Maalarimestariliitto/Master Painters' Association of Finland, Unioninkatu 14, Helsinki, 00130, Finland. TEL 358-9-1299503, FAX 358-9-1299509, info@smml.fi, http://www.smml.fi. Ed. Laakkonen Pertti TEL 358-9-72062680. Circ: 6,000.

VERNICIATURA DEL LEGNO. *see* BUILDING AND CONSTRUCTION—Carpentry And Woodwork

698 ITA ISSN 0048-8348
CODEN: RCLRA3
VERNICIATURA INDUSTRIALE. Text in Italian. 1968. m. (11/yr.). EUR 100 domestic; EUR 200 foreign (effective 2009). adv. bk.rev. abstr.; tr.lit. index. **Document type:** *Magazine, Trade.*
Formerly (until 1974): La Rivista del Colore (1974-7160)
Indexed: ChemAb, ChemTitl, RefZh, WSCA.
—BLDSC (9173.100000), CASDDS, INIST.
Published by: Rivista del Colore SpA, Palazzo Larice Edificio M, Via Torri Bianche 3, Vimercate, MI 20059, Italy. TEL 39-039-629041, FAX 39-039-62904208, info@larivistadelcolore.com, http://www.larivistadelcolore.com. Circ: 3,000.

667.6 GBR ISSN 0140-8798
WATERBORNE & HIGH SOLIDS COATINGS. Text in English. 1978. m. GBP 390 to non-members (print or online ed.); GBP 295 to members (print or online ed.); GBP 490, GBP 370 combined subscription to non-members (print & online eds.) (effective 2009). bk.rev. charts; pat.; stat. back issues avail. **Document type:** *Bulletin, Trade.*
Description: Features all aspects of waterborne and high-solids coatings technology.
Formerly (until 1990): Waterborne & High Solids Coatings Bulletin
Related titles: E-mail ed.; Online - full text ed.
—CCC.
Published by: P R A Coatings Technology Centre, 14 Castle Mews, High St, Hampton, Mddlx. TW12 2NP, United Kingdom. TEL 44-20-84870800, FAX 44-20-84870801, publications@pra-world.com. Ed. Richard Kennedy TEL 44-20-84870835.

667.6 DEU
WELT DER FARBEN; Branchen-Magazin. Text in German. 1981. 11/yr. EUR 70; EUR 9.20 newsstand/cover (effective 2006). adv. **Document type:** *Magazine, Trade.*
Formerly (until 1993): Phaenomen Farbe
Indexed: WSCA.
Published by: R L - Press Eva Elisabeth Berger, Ostlandstr 1, Cologne, 50858, Germany. TEL 49-2234-73488, FAX 49-2234-73598. Ed. Eva Elsiabeth Berger. Pub. Renate Wittsack. Adv. contact Sabine Esener. B&W page EUR 1,450, color page EUR 2,500; trim 175 x 250. Circ: 1,500 (paid and controlled).

671.7 JPN ISSN 0916-6076
TS655
YOSHA/JAPAN THERMAL SPRAYING SOCIETY. JOURNAL. Text in Japanese. 1964. q. **Document type:** *Journal, Academic/Scholarly.*
Formerly (until 1989): Nihon Yosha Kyokaishi (0288-5522)
Indexed: A22, A28, APA, BrCerAb, C&ISA, CA/WCA, CIA, CerAb, CivEngAb, CorrAb, E&CAJ, E11, EEA, EMA, H15, M&TEA, M09, MBF, METADEX, SolStAb, T04, WAA.
—BLDSC (4808.368000), IE, Ingenta, Linda Hall.
Published by: Nihon Yosha Kyokai/Japan Thermal Spraying Society, 2-2-29 Eiwa, Higashi-Osaka-shi, 577-0809, Japan. TEL 81-6-67220096, FAX 81-6-67220092, jtss@mb8.seikyou.ne.jp, http://wwwsoc.nii.ac.jp/jtss/.

667.6 JPN ISSN 0289-422X
CODEN: YOGIEE
YOSHA GIJUTSU. Text in Japanese. 1979. q. JPY 3,150 (effective 2008). **Document type:** *Journal, Academic/Scholarly.*
Published by: (Nihon Yosha Kyokai/Spray Coating Society of Japan), Sanpo Shuppan K.K./Sanpo Publications, Inc., 1-11 Kanda Sakuma-cho Chiyoda-ku, Tokyo, 101-0025, Japan. sanpo@sanpo-pub.co.jp, http://www.sanpo-pub.co.jp/.

698 SRB ISSN 0351-9465
ZASTITA MATERIJALA/MATERIALS PROTECTION. Text in Serbian, English. 1953. q. **Document type:** *Journal, Academic/Scholarly.*
Indexed: RefZh.
—INIST.
Published by: (Inzenjersko Drustvo za Koroziju/Engineers Society for Corrosion), Savez Inzenjera i Tehnicara za Zasitu Materijala Srbije, Kneza Milosa 9/I, Belgrade, 11000. TEL 381-11-3241614, sitzams@eunet.yu. Ed. Milan M Antonijevic. **Co-publisher:** Inzenjersko Drustvo za Koroziju/Engineers Society for Corrosion.

620.12223 CHN ISSN 1005-4537
TA462
ZHONGGUO FUSHI YU FANGHU XUEBAO/CHINESE SOCIETY OF CORROSION AND PROTECTION. JOURNAL. Text in Chinese. 1981. bi-m. USD 37.20 (effective 2009). **Document type:** *Journal, Academic/Scholarly.*
Related titles: Online - full content ed.; Online - full text ed.
Indexed: A22, A28, APA, BrCerAb, C&ISA, CA/WCA, CIA, CerAb, CivEngAb, CorrAb, E&CAJ, E11, EEA, EMA, ESPM, EnvEAb, FLUIDEX, H15, M&TEA, M09, MBF, METADEX, RefZh, SCOPUS, SolStAb, T04, WAA.
—BLDSC (4729.330330), IE, Ingenta, Linda Hall. **CCC.**
Published by: Zhongguo Kexueyuan Jinshu Yanjiusuo/Chinese Academy of Sciences, Institute of Metal Research, 72, Wenhua Lu, Shenyang, Liaoning 110015, China. TEL 86-24-23971318, FAX 86-24-23891320, http://www.imr.ac.cn/index.jsp.

667.6 CHN ISSN 1006-2556
ZHONGGUO TULIAO/CHINA PAINT. Text in Chinese. 1986. m. **Document type:** *Journal, Academic/Scholarly.*
Related titles: Online - full text ed.: (from WanFang Data Corp.).
—BLDSC (9512.825125).
Published by: Zhongguo Tuliao Gongye Xiehui/China National Coatings Industry Association, Rm. B-093, Bldg.1, No.99, Lianhui Rd., Haidian District, Beijing, 100082, China. TEL 86-10-62252368, FAX 86-10-62252368.

PAINTS AND PROTECTIVE COATINGS— Abstracting, Bibliographies, Statistics

667.6 USA ISSN 0275-7036
CODEN: CCIPDO
C A SELECTS. COATINGS, INKS, & RELATED PRODUCTS. Text in English. s-w. USD 385 to non-members; USD 115 to members; USD 575 combined subscription to individuals (print & online eds.) (effective 2011). **Document type:** *Abstract/Index.* **Description:** Covers the chemistry, chemical and physical properties, and analysis of decorative and protective coatings.
Related titles: Online - full text ed.: USD 380 to non-members; USD 114 to members (effective 2011).
Published by: Chemical Abstracts Service (Subsidiary of: American Chemical Society), 2540 Olentangy River Rd, Columbus, OH 43210-0012. TEL 614-447-3600, FAX 614-447-3713, help@cas.com, http://caselects.cas.org. **Subscr. to:** PO Box 3012, Columbus, OH 43210. TEL 800-753-4227, FAX 614-447-3751.

667.6 USA ISSN 0749-7296
CODEN: CASCEM
C A SELECTS. CORROSION - INHIBITING COATINGS. Text in English. s-w. USD 385 to non-members; USD 115 to members; USD 575 combined subscription to individuals (print & online eds.) (effective 2011). **Document type:** *Abstract/Index.* **Description:** Covers the formulation and application of coatings intended to prevent corrosion of metallic surfaces.
Related titles: Online - full text ed.: USD 380 to non-members; USD 114 to members (effective 2011).
Published by: Chemical Abstracts Service (Subsidiary of: American Chemical Society), 2540 Olentangy River Rd, Columbus, OH 43210-0012. TEL 614-447-3600, FAX 614-447-3713, help@cas.com, http://caselects.cas.org. **Subscr. to:** PO Box 3012, Columbus, OH 43210. TEL 800-753-4227, FAX 614-447-3751.

667.6 USA ISSN 0734-8762
CODEN: CAPADY
C A SELECTS. PAINT ADDITIVES. Text in English. s-w. USD 385 to non-members; USD 115 to members; USD 575 combined subscription to individuals (print & online eds.) (effective 2011).
Document type: *Abstract/Index.* **Description:** Covers materials added to paints (pigmented coatings) other than the basic polymeric binder, solvents, pigments.
Related titles: Online - full text ed.: USD 380 to non-members; USD 114 to members (effective 2011).
Published by: Chemical Abstracts Service (Subsidiary of: American Chemical Society), 2540 Olentangy River Rd, Columbus, OH 43210-0012. TEL 614-447-3600, FAX 614-447-3713, help@cas.com, http://caselects.cas.org. **Subscr. to:** PO Box 3012, Columbus, OH 43210. TEL 800-753-4227, FAX 614-447-3751.

667 USA ISSN 0749-7369
CODEN: CSWCEW
C A SELECTS. WATER - BASED COATINGS. Text in English. s-w. USD 385 to non-members; USD 115 to members; USD 575 combined subscription to individuals (print & online eds.) (effective 2011).
Document type: *Abstract/Index.* **Description:** Covers formulation, application, and performance of water-borne coatings, water-soluble coatings, latex coatings, and aqueous coatings.
Related titles: Online - full text ed.: USD 380 to non-members; USD 114 to members (effective 2011).
Published by: Chemical Abstracts Service (Subsidiary of: American Chemical Society), 2540 Olentangy River Rd, Columbus, OH 43210-0012. TEL 614-447-3600, FAX 614-447-3713, help@cas.com, http://caselects.cas.org. **Subscr. to:** PO Box 3012, Columbus, OH 43210. TEL 800-753-4227, FAX 614-447-3751.

667.6016 USA ISSN 0891-1886
C P I DIGEST; key to world literature serving the coatings, plastics, fibers, adhesives, and related industries. (Chemical Process Industries) Text in English. 1974. m. USD 397 (effective 1999). abstr.; pat. back issues avail.; reprints avail. **Document type:** *Abstract/Index.*
Formerly: Coatings Adlibra (0146-9290)
Related titles: CD-ROM ed.
—CCC.
Published by: C P I Information Services, 108 W. Main St., Springfield, KY 40069-1227. TEL 502-456-6288, FAX 502-454-4808. Ed. George S Mattingly.

P

016.667 USA ISSN 0969-6210
FOCUS ON PIGMENTS. Text in English. 1994. m. EUR 1,090 in Europe to institutions; JPY 145,400 in Japan to institutions; USD 1,230 elsewhere to institutions (effective 2012). back issues avail. **Document type:** *Newsletter, Academic/Scholarly.* **Description:** Provides report on business and technical developments across the pigments industry with a brief editorial and a series of concise summaries on business, market and technical developments from a global perspective.
Related titles: Online - full text ed.: ISSN 1873-7021 (from IngentaConnect, ScienceDirect).
Indexed: CBNB, WSCA.
—BLDSC (3964.233300), IE, Ingenta. **CCC.**
Published by: Elsevier Engineering Information, Inc. (Subsidiary of: Elsevier Science & Technology), 360 Park Ave S, New York, NY 10010. TEL 314-447-8070, 800-221-1044, FAX 212-633-3680, eicustomersupport@elsevier.com, http://www.ei.org/. Ed. R Adams. **Subscr. to:** Elsevier BV.

016.667 USA ISSN 1364-5439
FOCUS ON POWDER COATINGS. Text in English. 1978. m. EUR 1,090 in Europe to institutions; JPY 145,400 in Japan to institutions; USD 1,230 elsewhere to institutions (effective 2012). bk.rev. charts; pat.; stat. back issues avail. **Document type:** *Newsletter, Academic/ Scholarly.* **Description:** Covers all aspects of the powder coatings industry, including growth of the business, market, new product development, and company news.
Formerly (until 1996): Powder Coatings Bulletin (0140-8445)
Related titles: Online - full text ed.: ISSN 1873-7048 (from IngentaConnect, ScienceDirect).
Indexed: CBNB, WSCA.
—BLDSC (3964.234030), IE, Ingenta. **CCC.**
Published by: Elsevier Engineering Information, Inc. (Subsidiary of: Elsevier Science & Technology), 360 Park Ave S, New York, NY 10010. TEL 314-447-8070, 800-221-1044, FAX 212-633-3680, eicustomersupport@elsevier.com, http://www.ei.org/. Ed. S T Harris. **Subscr. to:** Elsevier BV.

667.6 016 GBR ISSN 0144-4425
PAINT TITLES; ultra-rapid alerting for the coatings industry. Text in English. 1971. w. GBP 620 to non-members (print or online ed.); GBP 775 combined subscription to non-members (print & onlin eds.); free to members (effective 2009). bibl. **Document type:** *Abstract/Index.* **Description:** Covers scientific, technical, health and safety, and market information relevant to coatings, adhesives and inks.
Related titles: E-mail ed.; Online - full text ed.
—CCC.
Published by: P R A Coatings Technology Centre, 14 Castle Mews, High St, Hampton, Mddlx. TW12 2NP, United Kingdom. TEL 44-20-84870800, FAX 44-20-84870801, publications@pra-world.com. Eds. Catherine Haworth, Norman Morgan TEL 44-20-84870814.

667.6 GBR
RAPRA ABSTRACTS. ADDITIVES. Text in English. 19??. bi-m. price varies. **Document type:** *Abstract/Index.*
Media: CD-ROM.
Published by: iSmithers, Shawbury, Shrewsbury, Shrops SY4 4NR, United Kingdom. TEL 44-1939-250383, FAX 44-1939-251118, info@ismithers.net, http://www.ismithers.net.

667.6 GBR
RAPRA ABSTRACTS. ADHESIVES, SEALANTS AND COATINGS. Text in English. bi-m. price varies. **Document type:** *Abstract/Index.*
Media: CD-ROM.
Published by: iSmithers, Shawbury, Shrewsbury, Shrops SY4 4NR, United Kingdom. TEL 44-1939-250383, FAX 44-1939-251118, info@ismithers.net, http://www.ismithers.net.

667.6 GBR
RAPRA ABSTRACTS. POLYURETHANES. Text in English. 19??. bi-m. price varies. **Document type:** *Abstract/Index.*
Media: CD-ROM.
Published by: iSmithers, Shawbury, Shrewsbury, Shrops SY4 4NR, United Kingdom. TEL 44-1939-250383, FAX 44-1939-251118, info@ismithers.net, http://www.ismithers.net.

REFERATIVNYI ZHURNAL. KORROZIYA I ZASHCHITA OT KORROZII; otdel'nyi vypusk. *see* METALLURGY—Abstracting, Bibliographies, Statistics

667.6 016 GBR ISSN 0043-9088
Z7914.P15
WORLD SURFACE COATING ABSTRACTS. Abbreviated title: W S C A. Text in English. 1928. m. (13/yr). GBP 1,440 to non-members; GBP 980 to members (effective 2009). a.index. **Document type:** *Journal, Abstract/Index.* **Description:** Contains articles abstracts on all aspects of paints, from raw materials to formulations, and their uses.
Formerly (until 1969): Review of Current Literature on the Paint and Allied Industries
Related titles: CD-ROM ed.; Magnetic Tape ed.; Online - full text ed.
Indexed: IPackAb.
—Linda Hall. **CCC.**
Published by: P R A Coatings Technology Centre, 14 Castle Mews, High St, Hampton, Mddlx. TW12 2NP, United Kingdom. TEL 44-20-84870800, FAX 44-20-84870801, publications@pra-world.com. Ed. Norman Morgan TEL 44-20-84870814.

PALEONTOLOGY

A A S P NEWSLETTER. *see* EARTH SCIENCES—Geology

560 FRA ISSN 1631-0683
QE701
➤ **ACADEMIE DES SCIENCES. COMPTES RENDUS. PALEVOL.** Text in English, French. 2002. 12/yr. EUR 321 in Europe to institutions; EUR 225.17 in France to institutions; JPY 32,200 in Japan to institutions; USD 317 elsewhere to institutions (effective 2012). **Document type:** *Journal, Academic/Scholarly.* **Description:** Covers the fields of palaeontology, prehistory and evolution. Articles presented are original notes describing briefly an important discovery, short review papers, or historic chronicles.
Supersedes in part: Academie des Sciences. Comptes Rendus. Series IIA. Earth and Planetary Science
Related titles: Online - full text ed.: ISSN 1777-571X (from IngentaConnect, ScienceDirect).
Indexed: A01, A03, A08, A20, A22, A26, A28, APA, ASFA, B21, B25, BIOSIS Prev, BrCerAb, C&ISA, CA, CA/WCA, CIA, CerAb, CivEngAb, CorrAb, CurCont, E&CAJ, E11, EEA, EMA, ESPM, EnvEAb, FLUIDEX, GEOBASE, GeoRef, H15, I05, ISR, M&TEA, M09, MBF, METADEX, SCI, SCOPUS, SolStAb, T02, T04, W07, WAA, Z01.
—BLDSC (3384.866000), IE, Ingenta, INIST, Linda Hall. **CCC.**
Published by: (Academie des Sciences), Elsevier Masson (Subsidiary of: Elsevier Health Sciences), 62 Rue Camille Desmoulins, Issy les Moulineaux, Cedex 92442, France. TEL 33-1-71165500, FAX 33-1-71165600, infos@elsevier-masson.fr. Eds. Armand De Ricqles, Kevin Padian, Philippe Taquet, Yves Coppens.

561 POL ISSN 0001-6594
QE901 CODEN: APBCAG
➤ **ACTA PALAEOBOTANICA**; international journal of palaeobotany and palynology. Text in English. 1960. s-a. EUR 60 (effective 2011). bk.rev. bibl.; charts; illus. back issues avail. **Document type:** *Journal, Academic/Scholarly.* **Description:** Contains original papers concerned with all topics of paleobotany, palaeoecology, palynology and palaeophytogeography.
Related titles: Online - full text ed.: ISSN 2082-0259. free (effective 2011); Supplement(s): Acta Palaeobotanica. Supplementum. ISSN 1427-6402. 1994.
Indexed: AgrAg, AgrLib, B25, BIOSIS Prev, C25, CABA, E12, F08, GEOBASE, GeoRef, IBR, IBZ, MycolAb, P32, RefZh, S13, SCOPUS, SpeleolAb, Z01.
—BLDSC (0642.480000), IE, Ingenta, INIST.
Published by: Polska Akademia Nauk, Instytut Botaniki im. W. Szafera/ Polish Academy of Sciences, W. Szafer Institute of Botany, ul Lubicz 46, Krakow, 31512, Poland. TEL 48-12-4241700, FAX 48-12-4219790, ibpan@botany.pl. Ed. Leon Stuchlik.

560 POL ISSN 0567-7920
QE755.P7 CODEN: APGPAC
➤ **ACTA PALAEONTOLOGICA POLONICA.** Text in English; Summaries in Polish. 1956. q. EUR 194 foreign (effective 2006). adv. bk.rev. bibl.; illus. 160 p./no. 2 cols./p.; back issues avail. **Document type:** *Journal, Academic/Scholarly.* **Description:** Publishes original research papers and articles on all areas of paleontology. Includes paper reviews, short communications, brief reports.
Related titles: Online - full text ed.: ISSN 1732-2421. 2002. free (effective 2011).
Indexed: A22, AgrAg, AgrLib, B21, B25, BIOSIS Prev, CurCont, GEOBASE, GeoRef, IBR, IBZ, MycolAb, P30, PetrolAb, RefZh, SCI, SCOPUS, SpeleolAb, W07, Z01.
—BLDSC (0642.500000), IE, Infotrieve, Ingenta, INIST, Linda Hall, PADDS.
Published by: Polska Akademia Nauk, Instytut Paleobiologii, ul Twarda 51-55, Warsaw, 00-818, Poland. TEL 48-22-6978850, FAX 48-22-6206225. Ed. Zofia Kielan-Jaworowska. Pub. Andrzej Balinski. R&P Marcin Machalski. Adv. contact Jaroslaw Stolarski TEL 48-22-6978879. Circ: 500. **Dist. by:** Ars Polona, Obroncow 25, Warsaw 03933, Poland. TEL 48-22-5098609, FAX 48-22-5098610, arspolona@arspolona.com.pl, http://www.arspolona.com.pl.

➤ **ADVANCES IN ARCHAEOLOGICAL AND MUSEUM SCIENCE.** *see* ARCHAEOLOGY

➤ **AFRICAN NATURAL HISTORY/SUID-AFRIKAANSE MUSEUM. ANNALE.** *see* BIOLOGY

➤ **ALAVESIA.** *see* BIOLOGY—Entomology

560 CAN ISSN 1497-2018
ALBERTA PALEONTOLOGICAL SOCIETY BULLETIN. Text in English. 1986. q.
Published by: Alberta Palaeontological Society, Box 35111, Sarcee, Calgary, AB T3E 7C7, Canada. info@albertapaleo.org, http://www.albertapaleo.org/. Ed. Howard Allen.

560 551 NLD ISSN 0169-4324
ALBERTIANA. Text in English. 1983. s-a. **Document type:** *Newsletter.*
Related titles: Online - full text ed.: E-Albertiana.
Indexed: GeoRef, Z01.
Published by: (International Union of Geological Sciences, Subcommission on Triassic Stratigraphy), Utrecht University, Laboratory of Palaeobotany and Palynology, Budapestlaan 4, Utrecht, 3584 CD, Netherlands. TEL 31-30-2532629, FAX 31-30-2535096, http://www.bio.uu.nl/~palaeo/. Ed. Wolfram M Kuerschner.

560 GBR ISSN 0311-5518
QE758.A1 CODEN: ALCHDB
➤ **ALCHERINGA**; an Australasian journal of palaeontology. Text in English. 1975. q. GBP 179 combined subscription in United Kingdom to institutions (print & online eds.); EUR 239, AUD 458, USD 298 combined subscription to institutions (print & online eds.) (effective 2012). adv. bk.rev. illus. back issues avail.; reprint service avail. from PSC. **Document type:** *Journal, Academic/Scholarly.* **Description:** Covers all aspects of palaeontology and its ramifications into the earth and biological sciences.
Related titles: Online - full text ed.: ISSN 1752-0754. GBP 161 in United Kingdom to institutions; EUR 215, AUD 412, USD 268 to institutions (effective 2012) (from IngentaConnect).
Indexed: A01, A02, A03, A08, A11, A20, A22, A33, AESIS, ASCA, B07, B25, BIOSIS Prev, CA, CurCont, E01, E04, E05, GEOBASE, GeoRef, ISR, MycolAb, PetrolAb, SCI, SCOPUS, SpeleolAb, T02, W07, Z01.
—BLDSC (0786.752000), IE, Ingenta, INIST, Linda Hall, PADDS. **CCC.**
Published by: (Geological Society of Australia Inc. AUS, Association of Australasian Palaeontologists AUS), Taylor & Francis Ltd. (Subsidiary of: Taylor & Francis Group), 4 Park Sq, Milton Park, Abingdon, Oxfordshire OX14 4RN, United Kingdom. TEL 44-20-70176000, FAX 44-20-70176336, subscriptions@tandf.co.uk, http://www.taylorandfrancis.com. Ed. Tony Wright. Adv. contact Linda Hann. **Subscr. to:** Journals Customer Service, Sheepen Pl, Colchester, Essex CO3 3LP, United Kingdom. TEL 44-20-70175544, FAX 44-20-70175198, tf.enquiries@tfinforma.com.

➤ **ALTENBURGER NATURWISSENSCHAFTLICHE FORSCHUNGEN.** *see* BIOLOGY

560 RUS
AMBER & FOSSILS. Text in English. s-a. USD 65 in United States. **Document type:** *Journal, Academic/Scholarly.*
Published by: Museum of World Ocean, Nab Petra Velikogo, Kaliningrad, 236006, Russian Federation. TEL 234-02-00. **Dist. by:** East View Information Services, 10601 Wayzata Blvd, Minneapolis, MN 55305. TEL 952-252-1201, 800-477-1005, FAX 952-252-1202, info@eastview.com, http://www.eastview.com.

560 ARG ISSN 0002-7014
QE752.A7 CODEN: AMGHB2
➤ **AMEGHINIANA.** Text and summaries in English, Spanish, Portuguese. 1957. q. USD 55 in Latin America; USD 60 elsewhere (effective 2005). adv. bk.rev. bibl. index. 128 p./no.; back issues avail.; reprints avail. **Document type:** *Journal, Academic/Scholarly.* **Description:** Publishes papers on all aspects of palaeontology and related areas, such as biostratigraphy and palaeobiology.
Related titles: E-mail ed.; Fax ed.; Online - full text ed.: ISSN 1851-8044. 2006 (from SciELO).
Indexed: AESIS, B25, BIOSIS Prev, C01, CurCont, GEOBASE, GeoRef, MycolAb, RefZh, SCI, SCOPUS, SpeleolAb, W07, Z01.
—INIST, Linda Hall, PADDS. **CCC.**
Published by: Asociacion Paleontologica Argentina, Maipu 645 1o Piso, Buenos Aires, 1006, Argentina. secretaria@apaleontologica.org.ar, http://www.apaleontologia.org.ar/. Ed., Pub., R&P Dr. Susana E Damborenea. Adv. contact Nora Cabaleri. page USD 1,500. Circ: 550 (paid).

551 USA ISSN 0160-8843
CODEN: ASPLCY
➤ **AMERICAN ASSOCIATION OF STRATIGRAPHIC PALYNOLOGISTS. CONTRIBUTIONS SERIES.** Text in English. 1970. irreg., latest vol.43, 2006. price varies. back issues avail. **Document type:** *Monographic series, Academic/Scholarly.*
Indexed: GeoRef, SCOPUS, SpeleolAb, Z01.
—BLDSC (3461.370000), Ingenta.
Published by: American Association of Stratigraphic Palynologists Foundation, c/o Vaughn M Bryant, Jr, Palynology Laboratory, Texas A & M Univ, College Station, TX 77843. FAX 979-845-4070, vbryant@tamu.edu.

560 USA ISSN 0192-737X
QE77
AMERICAN ASSOCIATION OF STRATIGRAPHIC PALYNOLOGISTS FOUNDATION. FIELD TRIP GUIDE. Text in English. 1971. irreg., latest 1998. price varies. back issues avail. **Document type:** *Guide, Trade.*
Indexed: GeoRef, SpeleolAb.
Published by: American Association of Stratigraphic Palynologists Foundation, c/o Vaughn M Bryant, Jr, Palynology Laboratory, Texas A & M Univ, College Station, TX 77843. FAX 979-845-4070, vbryant@tamu.edu.

AMERICAN MUSEUM NOVITATES. *see* BIOLOGY—Zoology

AMERICAN MUSEUM OF NATURAL HISTORY. BULLETIN. *see* BIOLOGY—Zoology

560 USA ISSN 1066-8772
QE701
AMERICAN PALEONTOLOGIST; a newsmagazine of earth sciences. Abbreviated title: A P. Text in English. 1992. q. USD 30; USD 5 per issue (effective 2010). adv. bk.rev. illus. reprints avail. **Document type:** *Magazine, Trade.* **Description:** Features news, essays and announcements of interest to paleontologists at all levels and every specialty.
Indexed: GeoRef, SpeleolAb, Z01.
—BLDSC (0849.300000), Linda Hall.
Published by: Paleontological Research Institution, 1259 Trumansburg Rd, Ithaca, NY 14850. TEL 607-273-6623, FAX 607-273-6620, publications@museumoftheearth.org.

ANARTIA. *see* BIOLOGY

560 FRA ISSN 0753-3969
QE701
➤ **ANNALES DE PALEONTOLOGIE.** Text in French, English. 1905. 4/yr. EUR 627 in Europe to institutions; EUR 568.72 in France to institutions; JPY 70,900 in Japan to institutions; USD 814 elsewhere to institutions (effective 2012). illus. back issues avail.; reprints avail. **Document type:** *Journal, Academic/Scholarly.* **Description:** Contains original articles on paleobotany, paleozoology, and human paleontology.
Formed by the 1982 merger of: Annales de Paleontologie: Vertebres (0570-1627); Annales de Paleontologie: Invertebres (0570-1619); Both of which superseded in part (in 1964): Annales de Paleontologie (0003-4142)
Related titles: Microform ed.: (from PQC); Online - full text ed.: (from IngentaConnect, ScienceDirect).
Indexed: A01, A03, A08, A22, A26, AESIS, ASFA, B21, B25, BIOSIS Prev, BrGeoL, CA, CurCont, GEOBASE, GeoRef, I05, MycolAb, SCI, SCOPUS, SpeleolAb, T02, W07, Z01.
—BLDSC (0991.000000), IE, Ingenta, INIST, Linda Hall. **CCC.**
Published by: Elsevier Masson (Subsidiary of: Elsevier Health Sciences), 62 Rue Camille Desmoulins, Issy les Moulineaux, Cedex 92442, France. TEL 33-1-71165500, FAX 33-1-71165600, infos@elsevier-masson.fr. Ed. Philippe Taquet. Circ: 430.

599.9 CZE ISSN 0003-5572
GN4 CODEN: ATHRAH
ANTHROPOS; studies in anthropology, palaeoethnology, palaeonthology and quaternary geology. Text in English, German. 1958. irreg., latest vol.27, 2009. price varies. **Document type:** *Monographic series, Academic/Scholarly.*
Indexed: A22, CCA, CERDIC, EI, GeoRef, MLA-IB, RI-1, SpeleolAb.
—INIST.
Published by: (Moravske Zemske Muzeum, Ustav Anthropos/Moravian Museum, Anthropos Institute), Moravske Zemske Muzeum, Zelny trh 6, Brno, 65937, Czech Republic. TEL 420-5-42321205, FAX 420-5-42212792, mzm@mzm.cz, http://www.mzm.cz. Ed. Martin Oliva.

560 ROM
APLICATIILE IN ARHEOLOGIE. Text in Romanian; Summaries in English, French. 1994. a. **Document type:** *Academic/Scholarly.*
Published by: Muzeul National de Istorie a Romaniei, Calea Victoriei 12, Bucharest, Romania. TEL 614-90-78.

930.1 DEU ISSN 0933-288X
ARCHAEOPTERYX. Text in German, English. 1983. a. EUR 20 (effective 2011). **Document type:** *Journal, Academic/Scholarly.*
Indexed: GeoRef, SpeleolAb, Z01.

—CCC.
Published by: (Freunde des Jura-Museums Eichstaett), Verlag Dr. Friedrich Pfeil, Wolfratshauser Str 27, Munich, 81379, Germany. TEL 49-89-7428270, FAX 49-89-7242772, info@pfeil-verlag.de. Ed. Peter Wellnhofer.

560 DEU ISSN 0936-2967
ARCHIV FUER GESCHIEBEKUNDE. Text in English, German; Summaries in English. 1990. irreg., latest vol.5, 2006. price varies. adv. bk.rev. index. back issues avail. **Document type:** *Journal, Academic/Scholarly.*
Indexed: GeoRef, RefZh, SpeleolAb, Z01.
Published by: Gesellschaft fuer Geschiebekunde, Friedrich-Ludwig-Jahn-Str 17a, Greifswald, 17487, Germany. TEL 49-3834-864550, FAX 49-3834-864572, ihinz-s@uni-greifswald.de, http://www.geschiebekunde.de. R&P R Schallreuter. Circ: 200 (paid).

ARGENTINA. MUSEO PROVINCIAL DE CIENCIAS NATURALES. COMUNICACIONES. *see* BIOLOGY

ARKEOMETRI SONUCLARI TOPLANTISI. *see* ARCHAEOLOGY

560 JPN ISSN 1345-5044
ASHORO DOUBUTSU KASEKI HAKUBUTSUKAN KIYOU/ASHORO MUSEUM OF PALEONTOLOGY. BULLETIN. Text in Japanese. 2000. a. **Document type:** *Journal, Academic/Scholarly.*
Published by: Ashoro Doubutsu Kaseki Hakubutsukan/Ashoro Museum of Paleontology, Konan 1-chome, Ashoro-cho, Ashoro-gun, Hokkaidou 089-3727, Japan. TEL 81-156-25-9100, FAX 81-156-25-9101, http://www.museum.ashoro.hokkaido.jp/.

560 ARG ISSN 0328-347X
ASOCIACION PALEONTOLOGICA ARGENTINA. PUBLICACIONES ESPECIALES. Text in Spanish. 1981. irreg., latest vol.6, 1999. USD 30 per issue (effective 2010). **Document type:** *Academic/Scholarly.* **Description:** Publishes articles on paleontology and related fields. Includes lectures and conferences from symposiums and scientific meetings.
Indexed: GeoRef, SpeleolAb.
Published by: Asociacion Paleontologica Argentina, Maipu 645 1o Piso, Buenos Aires, 1006, Argentina. Ed. Dr. Ana Baez. Pub., R&P Dr. Susana E Damborenea. Adv. contact Nora Cabaleri. Circ: 500 (paid).

500 AUS ISSN 0810-8889
QE701
➤ **ASSOCIATION OF AUSTRALASIAN PALAEONTOLOGISTS. MEMOIRS.** Text in English. 1983. irreg., latest vol.30, 2004. price varies. back issues avail. **Document type:** *Monographic series, Academic/Scholarly.* **Description:** Presents publications on all aspects of palaeontology, targeted to professional palaeontologists.
Indexed: AESIS, GeoRef, SpeleolAb.
—BLDSC (5577.283000), IE, Ingenta. **CCC.**
Published by: (Association of Australasian Palaeontologists), Geological Society of Australia Inc., Ste 706, 301 George St, Sydney, NSW 2000, Australia. TEL 61-2-92902194, FAX 61-2-92902198, info@gsa.org.au, http://www.gsa.org.au. Ed. John R. Laurie. Circ: 200 (paid).

➤ **ATTI TICINENSI DI SCIENZE DELLA TERRA.** *see* EARTH SCIENCES

560 FRA ISSN 2116-9632
▼ **AUX ORIGINES DE L'HOMME.** Text in French. 2011. q. EUR 8 newsstand/cover (effective 2011). **Document type:** *Magazine, Consumer.*
Published by: Export Press, 91 Rue de Turenne, Paris, 75003, France. TEL 33-1-40291451, FAX 33-1-42720743, dir@exportpress.com, http://www.exportpress.com.

560 ESP ISSN 0214-7831
BATALLERIA; revista de paleontologia. Text in Spanish. 1988. a. adv. back issues avail. **Document type:** *Journal, Academic/Scholarly.*
Indexed: ASFA, B21, ESPM, GEOBASE, GeoRef, IECT, SCOPUS, SpeleolAb, Z01.
Published by: Museo Geologico Seminario de Barcelona, Diputacio, 231, Barcelona, 08007, Spain. TEL 34-93-4541600, FAX 34-93-4525538.

BEITRAEGE ZUR ARCHAEOZOOLOGIE UND PRAEHISTORISCHEN ANTHROPOLOGIE. *see* ANTHROPOLOGY

560 DEU ISSN 1024-4727
QE755.A8 CODEN: BPOEDX
➤ **BEITRAEGE ZUR PALAEONTOLOGIE.** Text and summaries in English, German. 1976. a. EUR 169 (effective 2011). back issues avail. **Document type:** *Monographic series, Academic/Scholarly.*
Formerly (until 1993): Beitraege zur Palaeontologie von Oesterreich (1017-5563)
Indexed: GeoRef, SpeleolAb, VITIS.
—Linda Hall.
Published by: (Institut fuer Palaeontologie AUT), E. Schweizerbart'sche Verlagsbuchhandlung, Johannesstr 3A, Stuttgart, 70176, Germany. TEL 49-711-3514560, FAX 49-711-35145699, order@schweizerbart.de. Ed., R&P Doris Nagel. Pub. Gernot Rabeder. Circ: 200.

560 551 DEU ISSN 0937-0242
QE1
➤ **BERINGERIA;** Wuerzburger geowissenschaftliche Mitteilungen. Text in English, German. 1989. 2/yr. free to members. back issues avail. **Document type:** *Journal, Academic/Scholarly.* **Description:** Contains articles and reports on systematic paleontology, sedimentology, and paleoecology.
Related titles: Supplement(s): Beringeria. Special Issue. ISSN 1432-4180.
Indexed: GeoRef, RASB, SpeleolAb, Z01.
Published by: Freunde der Wuerzburger Geowissenschaften e.V./Society of Friends of Geosciences in Wuerzburg, Pleicherwall 1, Wuerzburg, 97070, Germany.

560 DEU ISSN 1612-0361
BERLINER PALAEOBIOLOGISCHE ABHANDLUNGEN. Text in German. 1992. irreg., latest vol.9, 2006. price varies. **Document type:** *Monographic series, Academic/Scholarly.*
Formerly (until 2002): Berliner Geowissenschaftliche Abhandlungen. Reihe E, Palaeobiologie (0941-7338)
Indexed: GeoRef, Z01.
—**CCC.**
Published by: Freie Universitaet Berlin, Institut fuer Geologische Wissenschaften, Malteserstr 74-100, Berlin, 12249, Germany. TEL 49-30-83870575, FAX 49-30-83870723, plansec@zedat.fu-berlin.de, http://www.geo.fu-berlin.de/geol/index.html.

BOREAS; an international journal of quaternary research. *see* EARTH SCIENCES—Geology

BUDOWA GEOLOGICZNA POLSKI. *see* EARTH SCIENCES—Geology

560 USA ISSN 0007-5779
CODEN: BAPLAJ
➤ **BULLETINS OF AMERICAN PALEONTOLOGY.** Abbreviated title: B A P. Text in English. 1895. s-a. USD 185 combined subscription domestic (print & online eds.); USD 205 combined subscription foreign (print & online eds.) (effective 2010). illus. back issues avail.; reprint service avail. from PSC. **Document type:** *Monographic series, Academic/Scholarly.* **Description:** Features high quality monographs in paleontology or in neontological subjects that impact paleontology.
Related titles: Online - full text ed.: USD 165 (effective 2010).
Indexed: A22, AESIS, B25, BIOSIS Prev, GEOBASE, GeoRef, MycolAb, PetrolAb, SCOPUS, SpeleolAb, Z01.
—BLDSC (2827.750000), IE, Infotrieve, Ingenta, INIST, Linda Hall, PADDS.
Published by: (Cornell University), Paleontological Research Institution, 1259 Trumansburg Rd, Ithaca, NY 14850. TEL 607-273-6623, FAX 607-273-6620, publications@museumoftheearth.org. Ed. Paula M Mikkelsen.

560 FRA ISSN 0760-2766
CAHIERS DE PALEOANTHROPOLOGIE. Text in French. 1981. a. price varies. adv. bk.rev. index. **Document type:** *Monographic series, Academic/Scholarly.*
Formerly (until 1983): Cahiers de Paleontologie. Paleoanthropologie (0293-1176)
Indexed: FR, GeoRef, SpeleolAb.
—INIST.
Published by: Centre National de la Recherche Scientifique, Campus Gerard-Megie, 3 Rue Michel-Ange, Paris, 75794, France. TEL 33-1-44964000, FAX 33-1-44965390, http://www.cnrseditions.fr. Circ: 1,250 (controlled).

CAINOZOIC RESEARCH. *see* EARTH SCIENCES—Geology

560 570 GBR
CAMBRIDGE PALEOBIOLOGY SERIES. Text in English. 1994. irreg. price varies. back issues avail.; reprints avail. **Document type:** *Monographic series, Academic/Scholarly.* **Description:** Covers the multidisciplinary area of modern paleobiology.
Indexed: SpeleolAb.
Published by: Cambridge University Press, The Edinburgh Bldg, Shaftesbury Rd, Cambridge, CB2 8RU, United Kingdom. TEL 44-1223-312393, FAX 44-1223-315052, journals@cambridge.org, http://www.cambridge.org/uk. Eds. B J Macfadden, J J Sepkoski, P Dodson.

560 CAN
CANADIAN PALAEOBIOLOGY. Text in English, French. s-a.
Published by: Canadian Museum of Nature, Publishing Division, P O Box 3443, Sta D, Ottawa, ON K1P 6P4, Canada. TEL 613-566-4292, FAX 613-566-4763.

CARNEGIE MUSEUM OF NATURAL HISTORY. ANNALS. *see* SCIENCES: COMPREHENSIVE WORKS

CARNEGIE MUSEUM OF NATURAL HISTORY. BULLETIN. *see* SCIENCES: COMPREHENSIVE WORKS

560 AUT ISSN 0375-6084
CATALOGUS FOSSILIUM AUSTRIA. Text in German. 1965. irreg., latest 2005. price varies. **Document type:** *Monographic series, Academic/Scholarly.* **Description:** Catalogs all fossil remains discovered in Austria.
Indexed: GeoRef, SpeleolAb, Z01.
Published by: Verlag der Oesterreichischen Akademie der Wissenschaften, Postgasse 7/4, Vienna, W 1011, Austria. TEL 43-1-515813402, FAX 43-1-515813400, verlag@oeaw.ac.at.

CAVE ARCHAEOLOGY AND PALAEONTOLOGY RESEARCH ARCHIVE. *see* ARCHAEOLOGY

COLLANA DI STUDI PALEONTOLOGICI. *see* ANTHROPOLOGY

560 ESP ISSN 1132-1660
CODEN: CLPAB7
COLOQUIOS DE PALEONTOLOGIA. Text in Multiple languages. 1964. a., latest vol.52, 2001. EUR 18 domestic; EUR 21 in Europe; EUR 25 elsewhere (effective 2009). **Document type:** *Journal, Academic/Scholarly.* **Description:** Publishes articles and summaries of conferences on paleontology.
Formerly (until 1990): Col-Pa (0210-7236)
Related titles: CD-ROM ed.; Online - full text ed.: ISSN 1988-2580. free.
Indexed: A26, GeoRef, I04, I05, IECT, P02, P10, P26, P48, P52, P53, P54, P56, PQC, S10, SpeleolAb, Z01.
Published by: (Universidad Complutense de Madrid, Facultad de Ciencias Geologicas), Universidad Complutense de Madrid, Servicio de Publicaciones, C/ Obispo Trejo 2, Ciudad Universitaria, Madrid, 28040, Spain. TEL 34-91-3941127, FAX 34-91-3941126, servicio.publicaciones@rect.ucm.es, http://www.ucm.es/publicaciones. Ed. Maria Jose Comas Rengifo.

CONTRIBUTIONS IN BIOLOGY AND GEOLOGY. *see* BIOLOGY

CURRENT RESEARCH IN THE PLEISTOCENE. *see* ARCHAEOLOGY

563 USA ISSN 0070-2242
CODEN: SPCFAO
CUSHMAN FOUNDATION FOR FORAMINIFERAL RESEARCH. SPECIAL PUBLICATION. Text in English. 1928. irreg., latest vol.42, 2010. price varies. back issues avail. **Document type:** *Monographic series, Academic/Scholarly.*
Formerly (until 1952): Cushman Laboratory for Foraminiferal Research. Special Publication (0197-548X)
Related titles: Online - full text ed.
Indexed: B25, BIOSIS Prev, GeoRef, MycolAb, SpeleolAb, Z01.
—Ingenta, Linda Hall. **CCC.**
Published by: Cushman Foundation for Foraminiferal Research, MRC 121, Department of Paleobiology, Smithsonian Institution, PO Box 37012, Washington, DC 20013. jbernhard@whoi.edu.

595.33 591 USA ISSN 0886-3806
CYPRIS; international ostracoda newsletter. Text in English. 1983. a. membership. bk.rev. bibl. **Document type:** *Newsletter.* **Description:** To improve international contacts between ostracode workers.
Related titles: Online - full text ed.
Indexed: GeoRef, SpeleolAb.
Published by: International Research Group on Ostracoda, U S Geological Survey, Federal Center, MS 300, PO Box 25046, Denver, CO 80225. TEL 303-236-5440, FAX 303-236-5448, http://ncgmp.cr.usgs.gov/ncgmp/ostracodes. Ed. Elizabeth Brouers. Circ: 400 (controlled).

DAIYONKI KENKYU/QUATERNARY RESEARCH. *see* EARTH SCIENCES—Geology

DENVER MUSEUM OF NATURAL HISTORY. PROCEEDINGS. *see* BIOLOGY—Zoology

560 551.7 NLD ISSN 0920-5446
QE701 CODEN: DPSTEJ
➤ **DEVELOPMENTS IN PALAEONTOLOGY AND STRATIGRAPHY.** Text in Dutch. 1975. irreg., latest vol.19, 2001. price varies. back issues avail. **Document type:** *Monographic series, Academic/Scholarly.* **Description:** Publishes research in the geologic study of stratigraphy and palaeontology.
Related titles: Online - full text ed.
Indexed: B21, ESPM, GeoRef, SCOPUS, SWRA, SpeleolAb, Z01.
—BLDSC (3579.085500), CASDDS. **CCC.**
Published by: Elsevier BV (Subsidiary of: Elsevier Science & Technology), Radarweg 29, PO Box 211, Amsterdam, 1000 AE, Netherlands. TEL 31-20-4853911, FAX 31-20-4852457, JournalsCustomerServiceEMEA@elsevier.com, http://www.elsevier.nl. Ed. P Wignall.

560 USA
DIATOMS. Text in English. 19??. a. USD 300 to non-profit organizations; USD 600 government; USD 1,200 to corporations (effective 2010). **Document type:** *Journal, Academic/Scholarly.*
Media: Online - full text. **Related titles:** CD-ROM ed.
Published by: Micropress Inc., 6530 Kissena Blvd, Flushing, NY 11367. TEL 718-570-0505, FAX 718-570-0506, http://www.micropress.org.

567.91 USA
DINO - SOURCE NEWSLETTER. Text in English. 1998. m. back issues avail. **Document type:** *Newsletter.* **Description:** Provides news about dinosaurs and paleontology.
Media: Online - full text.
Published by: Dinotreker, 2005 Palo Verde Ave, PMB 171, Long Beach, CA 90815. Ed., Pub., R&P, Adv. contact Michael Rusher TEL 562-595-8034.

567.91 USA
THE DINOSAUR INTERPLANETARY GAZETTE (ONLINE EDITION). Text in English. 1996. w. free. adv. back issues avail. **Document type:** *Magazine, Consumer.* **Description:** Focuses on how science works in paleontology.
Formerly (until 200?): The Dinosaur Interplanetary Gazette (Print Edition)
Media: Online - full text.
Published by: Laser Publishing Group, Planetarium Station, PO Box 502 LPG, New York, NY 10024-0502. Circ: 25,000.

560 USA ISSN 1540-8736
THE DINOSAUR MUSEUM JOURNAL. Text in English. 2002 (Aug.). a.
Published by: The Dinosaur Museum, 754 S. 200 West, Blanding, UT 84511. TEL 435-678-3454, FAX 435-587-2094, dinos@dinosaur-museum.org, http://www.dinosaur-museum.org. Ed. Sylvia J. Czerkas.

567.9 USA ISSN 1091-3661
DINOSAUR WORLD. Text in English. 1997. 3/yr. USD 16.50 domestic; USD 20 foreign; USD 7.50 newsstand/cover (effective 2000). adv. bk.rev. illus. back issues avail. **Document type:** *Magazine, Consumer.* **Description:** Includes articles and interviews on all aspects of palaeontology, as well as the depiction of dinosaurs in popular literature, art, and film.
Published by: (Maverick Films), Hell Creek Creations, 1208 Nashua Ln, Bartlett, IL 60103. TEL 630-289-7018. Ed., R&P, Adv. contact Allen A Debus. Pub. Gary R Williams. B&W page USD 50, color page USD 125. Circ: 300.

567.9 DEU
▼ **DINOSAURIER;** Die Welt der Urzeit-Giganten erleben!. Text in German. 2010. bi-m. EUR 2.99 newsstand/cover (effective 2011). adv. **Document type:** *Magazine, Consumer.*
Published by: Blue Ocean Entertainment AG, Breitscheidstr 6, Stuttgart, 70174, Germany. TEL 49-711-22021790, FAX 49-711-22021799, leserservice@blue-ocean-ag.de. Adv. contact Simone Grenz. Circ: 36,911 (paid).

560 551 JPN ISSN 0912-0823
DOJIN/ASSOCIATION OF JAPANESE CAVERS. JOURNAL. Text in Japanese. 1978. irreg.
Published by: Nihon Dokutsu Kyokai/Association of Japanese Cavers, Akiyoshidai Kagaku Hakubutsukan, Shuho-cho, Mine-gun, Akiyo-shi, Yamaguchi-ken 754-0511, Japan.

DORTMUNDER BEITRAEGE ZUR LANDESKUNDE. *see* BIOLOGY

560 DEU ISSN 0424-7116
QE696 CODEN: EZGWAB
➤ **EISZEITALTER UND GEGENWART: E & G;** quarternary science journal. Text in English. 1951. 4/yr. EUR 27 per issue (effective 2011). back issues avail. **Document type:** *Journal, Academic/Scholarly.*
Related titles: Online - full text ed.: free (effective 2011).
Indexed: BrArAb, FR, GeoRef, IBR, IBZ, NumL, SpeleolAb.
—Linda Hall. **CCC.**
Published by: Deutsche Quartaervereinigung, Stilleweg 2, Hannover, 30655, Germany. TEL 49-511-6433613, deuqua@lbeg.niedersachsen.de, http://www.deuqua.org. Ed. Holger Freund.

➤ **ERDGESCHICHTE MITTELEUROPAEISCHER REGIONEN.** *see* EARTH SCIENCES—Geology

➤ **ERRATICA;** Monographien zur Geschiebekunde. *see* EARTH SCIENCES—Geology

P

560 579 DEU ISSN 0932-4739
QH274 CODEN: EJPREZ
➤ **EUROPEAN JOURNAL OF PROTISTOLOGY.** Text in English. 1964. 4/yr. EUR 761 in Europe to institutions; EUR 588 to institutions in Germany, Austria and Switzerland; JPY 104,500 in Japan to institutions; USD 846 elsewhere to institutions (effective 2012). adv. abstr.; bibl.; charts; illus. **Document type:** *Journal, Academic/ Scholarly.* **Description:** Covers the structure of protists, unicellular organisms, their development, ecology, molecular biology, and physiology.
Formerly: Protistologica (0033-1821)
Related titles: Online - full text ed.: ISSN 1618-0429 (from IngentaConnect, ScienceDirect).
Indexed: A20, A22, A26, A29, A33, A34, ASCA, ASFA, B21, B23, B25, BIOBASE, BIOSIS Prev, C25, CA, CABA, ChemAb, CurCont, E01, E12, E17, EMBASE, ESPM, ExcerpMed, F08, F12, GH, GeoRef, H17, I05, I11, IABS, IBR, IBZ, ISR, IndVet, MEDLINE, MycolAb, N02, N04, OR, P20, P22, P30, P32, P33, P39, P48, P52, P54, P56, PQC, PlantSci, R07, R08, R10, R11, Reac, RefZh, S13, S16, SCI, SCOPUS, SpeleolAb, T02, T05, TAR, VS, W07, Z01.
—BLDSC (3829.737600), CASDDS, IE, Infotrieve, Ingenta, INIST, Linda Hall. **CCC.**
Published by: (France. Centre National de la Recherche Scientifique FRA), Urban und Fischer Verlag (Subsidiary of: Elsevier GmbH), Loebdergraben 14a, Jena, 07743, Germany. TEL 49-3641-6263, FAX 49-3641-626500, info@urbanfischer.de, http://www.urbanundfischer.de. Ed. Thomas Weisse. Adv. contact Eva Kraemer TEL 49-89-5383704. Circ: 150. **Non-German speaking countries subscr. to:** Nature Publishing Group, Brunel Rd, Houndmills, Basingstoke, Hamps RG21 6XS, United Kingdom. TEL 44-1256-302629, FAX 44-1256-476117, subscriptions@nature.com

➤ **FACIES**; international journal of paleontology, sedimentology and geology. *see* EARTH SCIENCES

560 GBR ISSN 0962-5321
➤ **FIELD GUIDE TO FOSSILS.** Text in English. 1983. irreg., latest vol.2, 2002, 2nd ed. price varies. back issues avail. **Document type:** *Monographic series, Academic/Scholarly.* **Description:** Provides informations about amateur and professional palaeontologists.
Indexed: GeoRef, Z01.
—BLDSC (3920.310000).
Published by: Palaeontological Association, c/o Dr. Tim Palmer, I G E S, University of Wales, Aberystwyth, Wales SY23 3DB, United Kingdom. TEL 44-1970-627107, FAX 44-1970-622659, secretary@palass.org. Ed. David J Batten.

➤ **FLORIDA MUSEUM OF NATURAL HISTORY. BULLETIN.** *see* BIOLOGY

➤ **FOLDTANI KOZLONY**; bulletin of the Hungarian Geological Society. *see* EARTH SCIENCES—Geology

560 POL ISSN 0015-573X
QE696 CODEN: FOQUAN
FOLIA QUATERNARIA. Text in English, German. 1960. irreg., latest vol.79, 2010. price varies. **Document type:** *Monographic series, Academic/Scholarly.* **Description:** Paleography of the Quaternary, mainly of Poland. Papers concern geomorphology, stratigraphy, paleobotany and paleozoology, archaeology of Quaternary sediments.
Indexed: B22, B25, BIOSIS Prev, GeoRef, MycolAb, NAA, SpeleolAb, Z01.
—INIST, Linda Hall.
Published by: Polska Akademia Nauk, Oddzial w Krakowie/Polish Academy of Sciences, Krakow Branch, ul sw Jana 28, Krakow, 31018, Poland. TEL 48-12-4224853, FAX 48-12-4222791, paniec@zdp.pan.krakow.pl, http://www.instytucja.pan.pl. Ed. Elzbieta Szychowska-Krapiec.

560 USA ISSN 0140-0010
FORAMINIFERA. Text in English. 1974. a. USD 725 per issue to non-profit organizations; USD 1,450 per issue government; USD 2,900 per issue to corporations (effective 2010). **Document type:** *Journal, Academic/Scholarly.*
Media: Online - full text. **Related titles:** CD-ROM ed.
Published by: Micropress Inc., 6530 Kissena Blvd, Flushing, NY 11367. TEL 718-570-0505, FAX 718-570-0506, http://www.micropress.org.

901 CHL ISSN 0717-9235
FOSIL; revista de paleontologia. Text in Spanish. 2000. m. **Document type:** *Journal, Academic/Scholarly.*
Media: Online - full text.
Indexed: Z01.
Address: sodil@fosil.cl, http://www.fosil.org/. Ed. Jose Yanez.

562 DEU ISSN 0943-1829
FOSSIL CNIDARIA UND PORIFERA. Text in German. 1984. irreg. **Document type:** *Monographic series, Academic/Scholarly.*
Formerly (until 1991): Fossil Cnidaria (0177-123X)
Indexed: GeoRef.
Published by: Westfaelische Wilhelms-Universitaet Muenster, Geologisch-Palaeontologisches Institut. Forschungsstelle fuer Korallenpalaeozoologie, Pferdegasse 3, Muenster, 48143, Germany. TEL 49-251-8323938, FAX 49-251-8324891, oekentorp@korallen.de, http://www.korallen.de.

560 AUS ISSN 1037-2997
THE FOSSIL COLLECTOR. Text in English. 1980. 3/yr. **Document type:** *Bulletin, Consumer.*
Published by: Fossil Collectors' Association of Australasia, c/o Mr. Frank Holmes, 15 Kenbry Rd, Heathmont, VIC 3135, Australia.

560 USA ISSN 1522-6859
QE701
FOSSIL NEWS; journal of avocational paleontology. Text in English. 1995. m. USD 33 domestic; USD 45 foreign (effective 2001). adv. bk.rev. illus. cum.index: 1995-1998. back issues avail. **Document type:** *Newsletter, Trade.* **Description:** Covers all facets of paleontology, including field experiences, flora and fauna of type or region, paleoart, and evolutionary theory.
Related titles: Online - full text ed.: USD 10 (effective 2001).
Indexed: BiolDig.
Address: 1185 Claremont Dr, Boulder, CO 80303-6601. TEL 303-499-5337, lmclos@netone.com, http://www.fossilnews.com/. Ed., R&P, Adv. contact Lynne M Clos. B&W page USD 120; trim 11 x 8.5. Circ: 450 (paid).

560 FRA ISSN 2108-2138
▼ **FOSSILES.** Text in French. 2010. q. EUR 40 domestic to individuals; EUR 60 domestic to institutions; EUR 50 in Europe to individuals; EUR 60 elsewhere to individuals (effective 2011). back issues avail.
Published by: Editions du Piat, Glavenas, Saint-Julien-du-Pinet, 43200, France. TEL 33-4-71665467, baylelrm@wanadoo.fr baylelrm@wanadoo.fr, http://www.leregnemineral.fr. Ed. Patrice Lebrun.

560 DEU ISSN 0175-5021
QE701
FOSSILIEN; Zeitschrift fuer Hobbypalaeontologen. Text in German. 1984. bi-m. EUR 8.70 newsstand/cover (effective 2007). adv. bk.rev. 64 p./no.; back issues avail. **Document type:** *Magazine, Consumer.* **Description:** For collectors and amateur fossil hunters.
Indexed: Z01.
Published by: Goldschneck Verlag, Industriepark 3, Wiebelsheim, 56291, Germany. TEL 49-6766-903140, FAX 49-6766-903320, http://www.goldschneck.de. Ed., Adv. contact Werner Karl Weidert. B&W page EUR 705, color page EUR 881.25. Circ: 5,000 (paid and controlled).

590 560 NLD ISSN 1572-6525
➤ **FOSSILIUM CATALOGUS: ANIMALIA.** Text in English. 1911. irreg., latest vol.144, 2007. price varies. illus. back issues avail. **Document type:** *Monographic series, Academic/Scholarly.* **Description:** Compiles complete records of palaeontological finds of animal remains in a monographic catalog format.
Indexed: SpeleolAb, Z01.
Published by: Backhuys Publishers BV, Postbus 321, Leiden, 2300 AH, Netherlands. TEL 31-71-5170208, FAX 31-71-5171856, backhuys@backhuys.com, http://www.backhuys.com.

➤ **FOSSILIUM CATALOGUS: PLANTAE.** *see* BIOLOGY—Botany

560 GBR ISSN 0960-8664
FOSSILS ILLUSTRATED. Text in English. 1991. irreg., latest vol.1, 1991. USD 105, GBP 55 per vol. (effective 2010). **Document type:** *Monographic series, Academic/Scholarly.*
Indexed: GeoRef.
—BLDSC (4024.380500).
Published by: Boydell Press (Subsidiary of: Boydell & Brewer Ltd.), Whitwell House, St Audry's Park Rd, Melton, Woodbridge, Suffolk IP12 1SY, United Kingdom. TEL 44-1394-610600, FAX 44-1394-610316, trading@boydell.co.uk.

560 549 HUN ISSN 1586-930X
FRAGMENTA PALEONTOLOGICA HUNGARICA. Text in English. 1969. s-a. illus. 100 p./no.; back issues avail. **Document type:** *Journal, Academic/Scholarly.* **Description:** Contains papers written by museum staff members or based on material deposited there.
Formerly (until 1997): Fragmenta Mineralogica et Paleontologica (0367-2697)
Indexed: B25, BIOSIS Prev, GeoRef, MycolAb, Z01.
—INIST, Linda Hall.
Published by: Magyar Termeszettudomanyi Muzeum, Baross utca 13, Budapest, 1088, Hungary. TEL 36-1-3130035, FAX 36-1-3171669. Ed. J Szabo. R&P, Adv. contact I Matskasi TEL 36-1-2677100. Circ: 200 (paid).

560 DEU ISSN 0942-5845
FREUNDE DER BAYERISCHEN STAATSSAMMLUNG FUER PALAEONTOLOGIE UND HISTORISCHE GEOLOGIE MUENCHEN. JAHRESBERICHT UND MITTEILUNGEN. Text in German. 1973. a. EUR 5 (effective 2011). **Document type:** *Journal, Academic/Scholarly.*
Published by: Verlag Dr. Friedrich Pfeil, Wolfratshauser Str 27, Munich, 81379, Germany. TEL 49-89-7428270, FAX 49-89-7242772, info@pfeil-verlag.de, http://www.pfeil-verlag.de.

560 JPN ISSN 1347-5622
FUKUI KENRITSU KYOURYUU HAKUBUTSUKAN KIYOU/FUKUI PREFECTURAL DINOSAUR MUSEUM. MEMOIR. Text in Japanese. 2002. a.
Indexed: GEOBASE, GeoRef, RefZh, SCOPUS, Z01.
—BLDSC (5605.290000), IE, Ingenta.
Published by: Fukui Kenritsu Kyouryuu Hakubutsukan/Fukui Prefectural Dinosaur Museum, 51-11, Muroko, Katsuyama, Fukui 911-8601, Japan. TEL 81-779-880001, FAX 81-779-888700, http://www.dinosaur.pref.fukui.jp/.

560 AUT ISSN 1824-7741
QE285
GEO.ALP. Text in German. 19??. a. **Document type:** *Monographic series, Academic/Scholarly.*
Formerly (until 2004): Geologisch-Palaeontologische Mitteilungen Innsbruck (0378-6870)
Indexed: GeoRef, RefZh, Z01.
Published by: Universitaet Innsbruck, Institut fuer Geologie und Palaeontologie, Innrain 52, Innsbruck, 6020, Austria. TEL 43-512-5075581, FAX 43-512-5072914, geologie@uibk.ac.at, http://www.uibk.ac.at/geologie/.

560 DEU
GEO BIO NANO. Text in German. 2003. irreg. price varies. **Document type:** *Monographic series, Academic/Scholarly.*
Published by: Herbert Utz Verlag GmbH, Adalbertstr 57, Munich, 80799, Germany. TEL 49-89-27779100, FAX 49-89-27779101, utz@utzverlag.com. Ed. Wolfgang Heckl.

560.17 FRA ISSN 0016-6995
QE701 CODEN: GEBSAJ
➤ **GEOBIOS.** Text and summaries in English, French. 1968. 6/yr. EUR 273 in Europe to institutions; EUR 257.59 in France to institutions; JPY 35,400 in Japan to institutions; USD 343 elsewhere to institutions (effective 2012). adv. bk.rev. illus. index. reprints avail. **Document type:** *Journal, Academic/Scholarly.*
Related titles: Online - full text ed.: (from IngentaConnect, ScienceDirect); Supplement(s): Geobios. Memoire Speciale. ISSN 0293-843X. 1977.
Indexed: A01, A03, A08, A20, A22, A26, B25, BIOSIS Prev, CA, CurCont, E&PHSE, GEOBASE, GP&P, GeoRef, I05, ISR, MycolAb, OffTech, PetrolAb, S01, SCI, SCOPUS, SpeleolAb, T02, W07, Z01.
—BLDSC (4116.902000), IE, Ingenta, INIST, PADDS. **CCC.**
Published by: (Association Eurolypal, Universite Lyon 1 (Claude-Bernard), Sciences de la Terre), Elsevier Masson (Subsidiary of: Elsevier Health Sciences), 62 Rue Camille Desmoulins, Issy les Moulineaux, Cedex 92442, France. TEL 33-1-71165500, FAX 33-1-71165600, infos@elsevier-masson.fr. Ed. Gilles Escarguel. Circ: 850.

➤ **GEOLOGICA ET PALAEONTOLOGICA.** *see* EARTH SCIENCES—Geology

560 HUN ISSN 0374-1893
➤ **GEOLOGICA HUNGARICA. SERIES PALAEONTOLOGICA.** Text in English. 1928. irreg., latest vol.56, 2005. price varies. **Document type:** *Monographic series, Academic/Scholarly.*
Supersedes in part (in 1928): Geologica Hungarica
Indexed: GeoRef, Z01.
—INIST, Linda Hall.
Published by: Magyar Allami Foldtani Intezet/Geological Institute of Hungary, Stefania ut 14, Budapest, 1143, Hungary. TEL 36-1-2510999, FAX 36-1-2510703, geo@mafi.hu, http://www.mafi.hu.

➤ **GEOLOGISCHE ABHANDLUNGEN HESSEN.** *see* EARTH SCIENCES—Geology

➤ **GEOLOGISCHE BUNDESANSTALT. JAHRBUCH.** *see* EARTH SCIENCES—Geology

➤ **GEOLOGISCHES JAHRBUCH HESSEN.** *see* EARTH SCIENCES—Geology

➤ **GEOLOGISCHES JAHRBUCH. REIHE A: ALLGEMEINE UND REGIONALE GEOLOGIE B.R. DEUTSCHLAND UND NACHBARGEBIETE, TEKTONIK, STRATIGRAPHIE, PALAEONTOLOGIE.** *see* EARTH SCIENCES—Geology

➤ **GEOLOGISCHES JAHRBUCH. REIHE G: INFORMATIONEN AUS DEN BUND - LAENDER-ARBEITSGRUPPEN DER GEOLOGISCHEN DIENSTE.** *see* EARTH SCIENCES—Geology

➤ **GEOLOGISCHES JAHRBUCH. REIHE H: WIRTSCHAFTSGEOLOGIE, BERICHTE ZUR ROHSTOFFWIRTSCHAFT.** *see* EARTH SCIENCES—Geology

561.05 IND ISSN 0376-5156
QE901 CODEN: GPHTAR
➤ **GEOPHYTOLOGY.** Text in English. 1971. s-a. bk.rev. illus. back issues avail. **Document type:** *Journal, Academic/Scholarly.*
Indexed: AESIS, ApicAb, B21, GeoRef, SpeleolAb, VirolAbstr.
—INIST.
Published by: (Palaeobotanical Society), Scientific Publishers, 5-A, New Pali Rd, PO Box 91, Jodhpur, Rajasthan 342 001, India. TEL 91-291-2433323, FAX 91-291-2624154, info@scientificpub.com, http://www.scientificpub.com.

560 DEU ISSN 0178-1731
GESCHIEBEKUNDE AKTUELL. Text in German; Summaries in English. 1985. q. EUR 30 membership (effective 2005). index. back issues avail. **Document type:** *Journal, Academic/Scholarly.*
Indexed: GeoRef, RefZh, SpeleolAb, Z01.
Published by: Gesellschaft fuer Geschiebekunde, Friedrich-Ludwig-Jahn-Str 17a, Greifswald, 17487, Germany. TEL 49-3834-864550, ihinz-s@uni-greifswald.de, http://www.geschiebekunde.de. Ed. Roger Schallreuter. R&P R Schallreuter. Circ: 500 (paid).

DER GESCHIEBESAMMLER. *see* EARTH SCIENCES—Geology

GESELLSCHAFT DER GEOLOGIE- UND BERGBAUSTUDENTEN IN OESTERREICH. MITTEILUNGEN. *see* EARTH SCIENCES—Geology

GLACIOLOGY AND QUATERNARY GEOLOGY. *see* EARTH SCIENCES—Geology

GORTANIA. GEOLOGIA PALEONTOLOGIA PALETNOLOGIA; atti del Museo Friulano di Storia Naturale. *see* EARTH SCIENCES—Geology

560 KOR ISSN 1225-0929
GO'SAENGMUL HAGHOEJI/PALEONTOLOGICAL SOCIETY OF KOREA. JOURNAL. Text in Korean. s-a. USD 30 to individuals; USD 100 to institutions (effective 2009). **Document type:** *Journal, Academic/Scholarly.*
Indexed: Z01.
—BLDSC (4839.505000), IE.
Published by: Han'gug Go'saengmul Haghoe/Paleontological Society of Korea, c/o Korea Dinosaur Research Center, Chonnam National University, Gwangju, 500-757, Korea, S. minhuh@chonnam.ac.kr. Ed. Sangheon Yi.

GREEK SPELEOLOGICAL SOCIETY. DELTION/SOCIETE SPELEOLOGIQUE DE GRECE. BULLETIN TRIMESTRIEL; Bulletin of Hellenic Speleological Society. *see* EARTH SCIENCES—Geology

GUDILI XUEBAO/JOURNAL OF PALAEOGEOGRAPHY. *see* GEOGRAPHY

560 CHN ISSN 0001-6616
QE701 CODEN: KSWHAT
➤ **GUSHENGWU XUEBAO/ACTA PALAEONTOLOGICA SINICA.** Text in Chinese; Summaries in English. 1953. q. CNY 40 per issue (effective 2011). adv. bk.rev. **Document type:** *Journal, Academic/ Scholarly.* **Description:** Contains theses on paleontology, academic discussions, and comments. Introduces new methodology and techniques.
Related titles: Online - full text ed.
Indexed: A22, GeoRef, SpeleolAb, Z01.
—BLDSC (0643.000000), IE, Ingenta, INIST, Linda Hall.
Published by: (Zhongguo Kexueyuan Nanjing Dizhi Gushengwu Yanjiusuo/Chinese Academy of Sciences, Nanjing Institute of Geology and Palaeontology), Kexue Chubanshe/Science Press, 16 Donghuang Cheng Genbei Jie, Beijing, 100717, China. TEL 86-10-64000246, FAX 86-10-64030255. Circ: 7,000.

560 HUN ISSN 1219-3933
QE701
HANTKENIANA. Text in English. 1995. a. **Document type:** *Journal, Academic/Scholarly.*
Indexed: GEOBASE, GeoRef, SCOPUS, Z01.
—Linda Hall.
Published by: Eotvos Lorand Tudomanyegyetem, Department of Paleontology/Eotvos Lorand University, Ludovika ter 2, Budapest, 1083, Hungary.

570.9 GBR ISSN 0891-2963
QE701 CODEN: HIBIEW
➤ **HISTORICAL BIOLOGY**; an international journal of paleobiology. Text in English. 1988. a. GBP 957 combined subscription in United Kingdom to institutions (print & online eds.); EUR 998, USD 1,254 combined subscription to institutions (print & online eds.) (effective 2012). adv. bk.rev. illus. back issues avail.; reprint service avail. from PSC. **Document type:** *Journal, Academic/Scholarly.* **Description:** Provides a vehicle for developments in the sciences concerned with the history of life through geological time and the biology of past organism.
Related titles: CD-ROM ed.: ISSN 1026-7980; Microform ed.; Online - full text ed.: ISSN 1029-2381. GBP 861 in United Kingdom to institutions; EUR 898, USD 1,128 to institutions (effective 2012) (from IngentaConnect).
Indexed: A01, A03, A08, A22, A26, AnBeAb, B04, B21, B25, BIOSIS Prev, BRD, CA, CurCont, E01, E08, E17, EMBASE, ESPM, ExcerpMed, G01, G03, G08, GEOBASE, GSA, GSI, GeoRef, I05, MEDLINE, P30, P52, P56, S01, S09, SCI, SCOPUS, SpeleolAb, T02, W03, W07, Z01.
—IE, Infotrieve, Ingenta. **CCC.**
Published by: Taylor & Francis Ltd. (Subsidiary of: Taylor & Francis Group), 4 Park Sq, Milton Park, Abingdon, Oxfordshire OX14 4RN, United Kingdom. TEL 44-20-70176000, FAX 44-20-70176336, subscriptions@tandf.co.uk, http://www.taylorandfrancis.com. Ed. Gareth Dyke. Adv. contact Linda Hann. **Subscr. in N. America to:** Taylor & Francis Inc., Customer Services Dept, 325 Chestnut St, 8th Fl, Philadelphia, PA 19106. TEL 215-625-8900, 800-354-1420, FAX 215-625-2940, customerservice@taylorandfrancis.com; **Subscr. to:** Journals Customer Service, Sheepen Pl, Colchester, Essex CO3 3LP, United Kingdom. TEL 44-20-70175544, FAX 44-20-70175198, tf.enquiries@tfinforma.com.

560 CHN ISSN 1000-3185
QE701
HUASHI/FOSSILS. Text in Chinese. 1972. q. USD 13.60 (effective 2009). adv. **Document type:** *Academic/Scholarly.* **Description:** For popular reading. Covers the evolution of living things from a paleontological point of view: evolution of plants, invertebrates, vertebrates, and mankind. Also reports on activities, museums, primitive clan customs, and interesting tidbits.
Related titles: Online - full content ed.; Online - full text ed.
—Linda Hall.
Published by: (Zhongguo Kexueyuan Gujizhui Dongwu Yu Gurenlei Yanjiusuo/Chinese Academy of Sciences, Institute of Vertebrate Paleontology and Paleoanthropology), Kexue Chubanshe/Science Press, 16 Donghuang Cheng Genbei Jie, Beijing, 100717, China. TEL 86-10-64000246, FAX 86-10-64030255. Circ: 100,000. **Dist. by:** China International Book Trading Corp, 35 Chegongzhuang Xilu, Haidian District, PO Box 399, Beijing 100044, China. TEL 86-10-68412045, FAX 86-10-68412023, cibtc@mail.cibtc.com.cn, http://www.cibtc.com.cn.

560 USA ISSN 1042-0940
QE720.5 CODEN: ICHSER
➤ **ICHNOS**; an international journal of plant and animal traces. Text in English. 1990. q. GBP 766 combined subscription in United Kingdom to institutions (print & online eds.); EUR 943, USD 1,185 combined subscription to institutions (print & online eds.) (effective 2012). adv. reprint service avail. from PSC. **Document type:** *Journal, Academic/Scholarly.* **Description:** Promotes research on ichnologic with primary emphases center upon the ethologic and ecologic significance of tracemaking organisms; organism-substrate interrelationships; and the role of biogenic processes in environmental reconstruction, sediment dynamics, sequence or event stratigraphy, biogeochemistry, and sedimentary diagenesis.
Related titles: CD-ROM ed.; Microform ed.; Online - full text ed.: ISSN 1563-5236. GBP 690 in United Kingdom to institutions; EUR 849, USD 1,066 to institutions (effective 2012) (from IngentaConnect).
Indexed: A01, A03, A08, A20, A22, A29, AESIS, B20, B21, B25, BIOSIS Prev, CA, CurCont, E01, ESPM, EntAb, GEOBASE, GenetAb, GeoRef, I10, MycolAb, NucAcAb, S01, SCI, SCOPUS, SpeleolAb, T02, VirolAbstr, W07, Z01.
—IE, Infotrieve, Ingenta. **CCC.**
Published by: Taylor & Francis Inc. (Subsidiary of: Taylor & Francis Group), 325 Chestnut St, Ste 800, Philadelphia, PA 19106. TEL 215-625-2940, 800-354-1420, orders@taylorandfrancis.com, http://www.taylorandfrancis.com. Eds. Murray Gingras, S George Pemberton. Adv. contact Linda Hann TEL 44-1344-779945.

560 JPN
IGA BONCHI KASEKISHU/ATLAS OF FOSSILS FROM IGA BASIN. Text in Japanese. 1981. a.
Published by: Shigemi Okuyama Pub., 1096-27 Tateoka-Shijukucho, Ueno-shi, Mie-ken 518-0000, Japan.

INSTITUTE FOR THE STUDY OF EARTH AND MAN NEWSLETTER. *see* ARCHAEOLOGY

INSTITUTUL GEOLOGIC AL ROMANIEI. MEMOIRE. *see* EARTH SCIENCES

560 GBR ISSN 1879-9817
▼ **INTERNATIONAL JOURNAL OF PALEOPATHOLOGY.** Text in English. forthcoming 2011. q. EUR 244 in Europe to institutions; JPY 27,400 in Japan to institutions; USD 300 elsewhere to institutions (effective 2012). **Document type:** *Journal, Academic/Scholarly.*
Related titles: Online - full text ed.: forthcoming (from ScienceDirect).
—CCC.
Published by: Elsevier Ltd (Subsidiary of: Elsevier Science & Technology), The Blvd, Langford Ln, Kidlington, Oxford, OX5 1GB, United Kingdom. TEL 44-1865-843434, FAX 44-1865-843970, journalscustomerserviceemea@elsevier.com. Ed. Jane Buikstra.

JOANNEA GEOLOGIE UND PALAEONTOLOGIE. *see* EARTH SCIENCES—Geology

567.9 USA
JOURNAL OF DINOSAUR PALEONTOLOGY. Text in English. 19??. irreg. free (effective 2010). **Document type:** *Journal, Academic/Scholarly.* **Description:** Contains articles and discussions from enthusiasts and actual paleontologists on various dinosaur topics.
Media: Online - full text.
Published by: Dinosauria On-Line, PO Box 3402, Dublin, OH 43016. TEL 614-718-9432.

560 USA ISSN 0096-1191
QL368.F6 CODEN: JFARAH
➤ **JOURNAL OF FORAMINIFERAL RESEARCH.** Abbreviated title: J F R. Text in English. 1925. q. free to members (effective 2010). adv. bk.rev. charts; illus. index. back issues avail.; reprints avail. **Document type:** *Journal, Academic/Scholarly.*
Former titles (until 1970): Cushman Foundation for Foraminiferal Research. Contributions (0011-409X); (until 1949): Contributions from the Cushman Laboratory for Foraminiferal Research (0271-7530)
Related titles: Online - full text ed.: ISSN 1943-264X.
Indexed: A22, AESIS, ASCA, ASFA, B21, B25, BIOSIS Prev, BrGeoL, CurCont, E&PHSE, GEOBASE, GP&P, GSW, GeoRef, ISR, MycolAb, OffTech, PetrolAb, SCI, SCOPUS, SpeleolAb, W07, Z01.
—BLDSC (4984.575000), IE, Infotrieve, Ingenta, INIST, Linda Hall, PADDS. **CCC.**
Published by: Cushman Foundation for Foraminiferal Research, MRC 121, Department of Paleobiology, Smithsonian Institution, PO Box 37012, Washington, DC 20013. Ed. Kenneth L Finger.

560 GBR ISSN 0262-821X
QE719
➤ **JOURNAL OF MICROPALAEONTOLOGY.** Abbreviated title: J M. Text in English. 1982. s-a. GBP 243.85 combined subscription in the UK & European Union (print & online eds.); GBP 207, USD 413 combined subscription elsewhere (print & online eds.) (effective 2012). bk.rev. index. back issues avail. **Document type:** *Journal, Academic/Scholarly.* **Description:** Shows the application of microfossils for solving geological problems, with an emphasis on taxonomy. Also covers biostratigraphy, evolution, palaeobiology, palaeoenvironment, reviews and taxonomic studies.
Related titles: Online - full text ed.: ISSN 2041-4978. GBP 220.80 in the UK & European Union; GBP 184, USD 368 elsewhere (effective 2012).
Indexed: A22, B25, BIOSIS Prev, CurCont, GEOBASE, GeoRef, PetrolAb, SCI, SCOPUS, SpeleolAb, W07, Z01.
—BLDSC (5019.675000), IE, Ingenta, PADDS. **CCC.**
Published by: (The Micropalaeontological Society, Geological Society of London, Geological Society), Geological Society Publishing House Ed. Alan Lord. Circ: 900. **Co-sponsor:** British Micropalaeontological Society.

561.1 NLD ISSN 0921-2728
CODEN: JOUPE8
➤ **JOURNAL OF PALEOLIMNOLOGY.** Text in English. 8/yr. EUR 1,876, USD 1,970 combined subscription to institutions (print & online eds.) (effective 2012). adv. bk.rev. illus. Index. back issues avail.; reprint service avail. from PSC. **Document type:** *Journal, Academic/Scholarly.* **Description:** Publishes papers concerned with all aspects of the reconstruction and interpretation of lake histories, including paleoenvironmental studies of rivers and wetlands, and research contributions from biological, chemical and geological perspectives.
Related titles: Microform ed.: (from PQC); Online - full text ed.: ISSN 1573-0417 (from IngentaConnect).
Indexed: A20, A22, A26, A29, A33, ASCA, ASFA, B20, B21, B25, BIOBASE, BIOSIS Prev, BibLing, ChemAb, CurCont, E01, E04, E05, ESPM, EntAb, GEOBASE, GeoRef, I05, I10, IABS, IBR, IBZ, ISR, M&GPA, MycolAb, P30, P52, P56, PQC, PollutAb, RefZh, SCI, SCOPUS, SWRA, SpeleolAb, T02, VirolAbstr, W07, Z01.
—BLDSC (5027.995500), IE, Infotrieve, Ingenta. **CCC.**
Published by: Springer Netherlands (Subsidiary of: Springer Science+Business Media), Van Godewijckstraat 30, Dordrecht, 3311 GX, Netherlands. TEL 31-78-6576050, FAX 31-78-6576474, http://www.springer.com. Eds. Mark Brenner, Thomas J Whitmore.

560 USA ISSN 0022-3360
QE701 CODEN: JPALAZ
➤ **JOURNAL OF PALEONTOLOGY.** Text in English. 1927. bi-m. adv. bk.rev. bibl.; charts; illus.; maps; stat. index, cum.index. back issues avail.; reprints avail. **Document type:** *Journal, Academic/Scholarly.* **Description:** Features original articles and notes on the systematics, phylogeny, paleoecology, paleogeography, and evolution of fossil organisms. It emphasizes specimen-based research and features high quality illustrations.
Related titles: Microform ed.: (from PQC); Online - full text ed.: ISSN 1937-2337.
Indexed: A01, A02, A03, A08, A20, A22, A26, A33, AESIS, ASCA, ASFA, AbAn, B&AI, B04, B10, B21, B25, BIOBASE, BIOSIS Prev, BrGeoL, CA, CurCont, E&PHSE, E01, E08, G01, G08, GEOBASE, GP&P, GSW, GeoRef, H09, H10, I05, IABS, IBR, IBZ, ISR, MycolAb, OceAb, OffTech, P02, P10, P15, P26, P30, P48, P52, P53, P54, P56, PQC, PetrolAb, S01, S05, S09, S10, SCI, SCOPUS, SPPI, SpeleolAb, T02, W07, W08, WildRev, Z01.
—BLDSC (5028.000000), IE, Infotrieve, Ingenta, INIST, Linda Hall, PADDS. **CCC.**
Published by: Paleontological Society, c/o Roger D. K. Thomas, Secretary, Department of Earth and Environment, Franklin and Marshall College, PO Box 3003, Lancaster, PA 17604. TEL 717-291-4135, FAX 717-291-4186, roger.thomas@fandm.edu, http://www.paleosoc.org/. Eds. Richard Lupia, Steve Westrop.

560 ITA ISSN 1120-0200
R134.8
JOURNAL OF PALEOPATHOLOGY. Text in English. 1987. 3/yr. bk.rev. **Document type:** *Journal, Academic/Scholarly.*
—BLDSC (5028.100000), GNLM, IE, Ingenta.
Published by: Universita degli Studi di Chieti e Pescara "Gabriele d'Annunzio", Facolta di Medicina e Chirurgia, Campus Universitario, Via dei Vestini 31, Chieti, Italy. http://www.unich.it.

JOURNAL OF QUATERNARY SCIENCE. *see* EARTH SCIENCES—Geology

560 ESP ISSN 1696-0815
➤ **JOURNAL OF TAPHONOMY.** Text in English. 2003. q. EUR 400 to institutions; EUR 590 combined subscription to institutions (print & online eds.) (effective 2008). **Document type:** *Journal, Academic/Scholarly.* **Description:** Covers all aspects of taphonomic research in all its diversity, from the analysis of burial processes affecting micro-organisms to the study of processes conditioning the modification and preservation of macro-organisms in natural and/or human-created settings.
Related titles: Online - full text ed.: ISSN 1696-2648. 2003.
Indexed: B25, BIOSIS Prev, GeoRef, MycolAb, Z01.
—CCC.
Published by: Palaeontological Network Foundation, Avenida de Sagunto s/n (Edificio Dinopolis), Teruel, 44002, Spain. Ed. Luis Alcala.

560 USA ISSN 0272-4634
QE841 CODEN: JVPADK
➤ **JOURNAL OF VERTEBRATE PALEONTOLOGY.** Abbreviated title: J V P. Text in English. 1980. bi-m. GBP 305 combined subscription in United Kingdom to institutions (print & online eds.); EUR 404, USD 505 combined subscription to institutions (print & online eds.) (effective 2012). adv. bk.rev. illus. Index. 200 p./no.; back issues avail.; reprint service avail. from PSC. **Document type:** *Journal, Academic/Scholarly.* **Description:** Publishes original contributions on all aspects of the subject, including vertebrate origins, evolution, functional morphology, taxonomy, biostratigraphy, paleoecology, paleobiogeography and paleoanthropology.
Related titles: Online - full text ed.: ISSN 1937-2809. GBP 275 in United Kingdom to institutions; EUR 363, USD 454 to institutions (effective 2012) (from IngentaConnect); ◆ Supplement(s): Society of Vertebrate Paleontology Memoir. ISSN 1062-161X.
Indexed: A01, A22, ASCA, ASFA, B21, B25, BIOSIS Prev, CA, CurCont, E01, GEOBASE, GeoRef, ISR, MycolAb, SCI, SCOPUS, SpeleolAb, T02, W07, W08, WildRev, Z01.
—BLDSC (5072.320000), IE, Infotrieve, Ingenta, INIST, Linda Hall. **CCC.**
Published by: (Society of Vertebrate Paleontology), Taylor & Francis Inc. (Subsidiary of: Taylor & Francis Group), 325 Chestnut St, Ste 800, Philadelphia, PA 19106. TEL 215-625-2940, 800-354-1420, FAX 215-625-8914, customerservice@taylorandfrancis.com, http://www.taylorandfrancis.com. Adv. contact Kristen Way TEL 802-244-1457 ext 356. page USD 500; 7 x 9.

560 JPN ISSN 0022-9202
QE701 CODEN: KASKAS
KASEKI/FOSSILS. Text in Japanese. 1960. s-a. JPY 85,000 combined subscription for Kaseki & Paleontological Research (effective 2007). adv. bk.rev. **Document type:** *Proceedings, Academic/Scholarly.*
Indexed: B25, BIOSIS Prev, GEOBASE, GeoRef, JPI, MycolAb, SCOPUS, SpeleolAb, Z01.
—INIST. **CCC.**
Published by: The Paleontological Society of Japan, TohShin Bldg. 3F, Hongo 2-27-2, Bunkyo-ku, Tokyo, 113-0033, Japan. TEL 81-3-38145490, FAX 81-3-38146216, psj-office@world.ocn.ne.jp, http://ammo.kueps.kyoto-u.ac.jp/palaeont/. Circ: 400.

560 JPN ISSN 0387-1924
➤ **KASEKI KENKYUKAI KAISHI/JOURNAL OF FOSSIL RESEARCH.** Text in Japanese; Summaries in English, Japanese. 1968. s-a. JPY 4,000 membership (effective 2003). **Document type:** *Academic/Scholarly.*
Indexed: GeoRef, JPI, SpeleolAb.
Published by: Kaseki Kenkyukai/Fossil Research Society of Japan, c/o Dr. Hidetoshi Kamiya, Dept. of Geology & Mineral, Kyoto University, Sakyo-ku, Kyoto, 606-8502, Japan. TEL 81-75-753-4166, FAX 81-75-753-4189, fossiljim@mlgw.dino.or.jp. Eds. H Kodera, M Goto, M Shimamoto, Y Fukuda.

560 JPN ISSN 0389-3847
QE756.J29
KASEKI NO TOMO/TOKAI FOSSIL SOCIETY. JOURNAL. Text in Japanese. 1969. irreg.
Published by: Toukai Kaseki Kenkyukai/Tokai Fossil Society, 9-21 Sawashita-cho, Atsuta-ku, Nagoya-shi, Aichi-ken 456-0006, Japan.

KAUPIA; Darmstaedter Beitraege zur Naturgeschichte. *see* SCIENCES: COMPREHENSIVE WORKS

KAZI SONUCLARI TOPLANTISI. *see* ARCHAEOLOGY

LANDESAMT FUER GEOLOGIE, ROHSTOFFE UND BERGBAU BADEN-WUERTTEMBERG. ABHANDLUNGEN. *see* EARTH SCIENCES

560 622 551 AUT
LANDESMUSEUM JOANNEUM. REFERAT FUER GEOLOGIE UND PALAEONTOLOGIE. MITTEILUNGEN. Text in German. 1937. irreg. (approx. 1/yr.). price varies. illus. **Document type:** *Bulletin.*
Former titles: Landesmuseum Joanneum. Abteilung fuer Geologie, Palaeontologie und Bergbau. Mitteilungen; (until 1972): Joanneum. Museum fuer Bergbau, Geologie und Technik. Mitteilungen
Published by: Landesmuseum Joanneum, Abteilung fuer Geologie und Palaeontologie, Raubergasse 10, Graz, St 8010, Austria. http://www.museum-joanneum.steiermark.at.

560.17 GBR ISSN 0024-1164
QE701 CODEN: LETHAT
➤ **LETHAIA**; an international journal of palaeontology and stratigraphy. Text in English. 1968. q. GBP 257 combined subscription in United Kingdom to institutions (print & online eds.); EUR 328 combined subscription in Europe to institutions (print & online eds.); USD 433 combined subscription in the Americas to institutions (print & online eds.); USD 505 combined subscription elsewhere to institutions (print & online eds.) (effective 2012). bk.rev. illus. Index. back issues avail.; reprint service avail. from PSC. **Document type:** *Journal, Academic/Scholarly.* **Description:** Focuses on geology, especially the fields of palaeontology, stratigraphy and fossils.
Related titles: Microform ed.: (from PQC); Online - full text ed.: ISSN 1502-3931. 2000. GBP 223 in United Kingdom to institutions; EUR 286 in Europe to institutions; USD 377 in the Americas to institutions; USD 439 elsewhere to institutions (effective 2012) (from IngentaConnect).
Indexed: A01, A03, A08, A20, A22, AESIS, ASCA, ASFA, AbAn, B21, B25, BIOSIS Prev, BrGeoL, CA, CIS, CTO, CurCont, E&PHSE, E01, GEOBASE, GP&P, GeoRef, IBR, IBZ, ISR, MycolAb, OffTech, P30, PetrolAb, SCI, SCOPUS, SpeleolAb, T02, W07, Z01.
—BLDSC (5184.950000), IE, Infotrieve, Ingenta, INIST, Linda Hall, PADDS. **CCC.**
Published by: (International Palaeontological Association USA), Wiley-Blackwell Publishing Ltd. (Subsidiary of: John Wiley & Sons, Inc.), 9600 Garsington Rd, Oxford, OX4 2DQ, United Kingdom. TEL 44-1865-776868, FAX 44-1865-714591, customerservices@blackwellpublishing.com. Ed. Peter Doyle. **Co-sponsor:** International Commission on Stratigraphy.

➤ **MAINZER GEOWISSENSCHAFTLICHE MITTEILUNGEN.** *see* EARTH SCIENCES—Geology

➤ **MALAKOLOGIAI TAJEKOZTATO/MALACOLOGICAL NEWSLETTER.** *see* BIOLOGY—Zoology

➤ **MAMMOTH TRUMPET.** *see* ARCHAEOLOGY

P

➤ **MAN & ENVIRONMENT.** *see* ANTHROPOLOGY

560 NLD ISSN 0377-8398
QE719 CODEN: MAMIDH
➤ **MARINE MICROPALEONTOLOGY.** Text in Dutch. 1976. 16/yr. EUR 1,654 in Europe to institutions; JPY 219,400 in Japan to institutions; USD 1,849 elsewhere to institutions (effective 2012). bk.rev. illus. reprints avail. **Document type:** *Journal, Academic/Scholarly.*
Description: Publishes results of research in all fields of marine micropalaentology of the ocean basins and continents, including paleoceanography, evolution, ecology and paleoecology, biology and paleobiology, biochronology, paleoclimatology, taphonomy, and the systematic relationships of higher taxa.
Related titles: Microform ed.: (from PQC); Online - full text ed.: ISSN 1872-6186 (from IngentaConnect, ScienceDirect).
Indexed: A01, A03, A08, A22, A26, A29, A33, AESIS, ASCA, ASFA, B20, B21, B25, BIOBASE, BIOSIS Prev, CA, CurCont, E&PHSE, ESPM, GEOBASE, GP&P, GeoRef, I05, I10, IABS, ISR, MSCT, MycolAb, OceAb, OffTech, PetrolAb, RefZh, S01, SCI, SCOPUS, SPPI, SpeleolAb, T02, VirolAbstr, W07, Z01.
—BLDSC (5376.400000), IE, Infotrieve, Ingenta, INIST, Linda Hall, PADDS. **CCC.**
Published by: Elsevier BV (Subsidiary of: Elsevier Science & Technology), Radarweg 29, PO Box 211, Amsterdam, 1000 AE, Netherlands. TEL 31-20-4853911, FAX 31-20-4852457, JournalsCustomerServiceEMEA@elsevier.com, http://www.elsevier.nl. Eds. A Mackensen, E Thomas.

➤ **MEDICON VALLEY**; nordic life sciences. *see* ENGINEERING—Chemical Engineering

562 FRA ISSN 1561-0799
MEGANEURA. Text in English. 1997. s-a. **Document type:** *Journal, Academic/Scholarly.*
Published by: European Science Foundation, 1 Quai Lezay Marnesia, Strasbourg, 67080 Cedex, France. TEL 33-3-88767100, FAX 33-3-88370532, esf@esf.org, http://www.esf.org.

563 USA ISSN 0026-2803
QE701 CODEN: MCPLAI
➤ **MICROPALEONTOLOGY.** Text in English. 1947. 6/yr. USD 780 combined subscription to institutions (print & online eds.); USD 450 combined subscription to members (print & online eds.) (effective 2010); Subscription includes Stratigraphy. bk.rev. charts; illus. back issues avail.; reprints avail. **Document type:** *Journal, Academic/Scholarly.* **Description:** Contains international research on stratigraphy, systematics, morphology, paleobiology and paleoecology of all microorganisms with fossilized hard parts.
Formerly (until 1955): The Micropaleontologist (1050-0960)
Related titles: Microfilm ed.; Microform ed.: (from MIM, PQC); Online - full text ed.: ISSN 1937-2795. USD 660 to institutions; USD 330 to members (effective 2010); Subscription includes Stratigraphy.
Indexed: A01, A03, A08, A22, A33, AESIS, ASCA, ASFA, B21, B25, BIOSIS Prev, CA, ChemAb, CurCont, E01, GEOBASE, GSW, GeoRef, IBR, IBZ, ISR, MycolAb, OceAb, PetrolAb, SCI, SCOPUS, SpeleolAb, T02, W07, Z01.
—BLDSC (5759.500000), IE, Infotrieve, Ingenta, INIST, Linda Hall, PADDS. **CCC.**
Published by: American Museum of Natural History, Central Park West at 79th St, New York, NY 10024-5192. TEL 212-769-5656, FAX 212-769-5653, scipubs@amnh.org, http://www.amnh.org. Ed. John A Van Couvering. Circ: 900.

563 USA ISSN 0160-2071
CODEN: MSPUDO
MICROPALEONTOLOGY SPECIAL PAPERS. Text in English. 1970-1997; resumed. irreg. price varies. charts; illus.; maps. reprints avail. **Document type:** *Monographic series.* **Description:** Contains monographs on micropaleontology, including biostratigraphy, paleo-ecology, and systematics in all microfossil groups.
Indexed: GeoRef, SpeleolAb.
—CCC.
Published by: American Museum of Natural History, Central Park West at 79th St, New York, NY 10024-5192. TEL 212-769-5656, FAX 212-769-5653, scipubs@amnh.org, http://www.amnh.org. Circ: 625.

560 622 FRA ISSN 0335-6566
MINERAUX ET FOSSILES; le guide du collectionneur. Text in French. 1975. 4/yr. EUR 60 to institutions (effective 2010). adv. bk.rev. index. **Document type:** *Magazine, Consumer.*
Related titles: Supplement(s): Mineraux et Fossiles. Hors-Serie. ISSN 1298-2938. 199?.
Indexed: GeoRef, SpeleolAb, Z01.
Address: 6 Ave Rene Cassin, Carry-le-Rouet, 13620, France. TEL 33-4-42449930, FAX 33-4-42453733.

MISSISSIPPI GEOLOGY. *see* EARTH SCIENCES—Geology

560 JPN ISSN 0385-0900
QE756.J29 CODEN: MKHKEZ
MIZUNAMISHI KASEKI HAKUBUTSUKAN KENKYU HOKOKU/ MIZUNAMI FOSSIL MUSEUM. BULLETIN. Text in English, Japanese. 1974. a., latest vol.29. JPY 2,000 newsstand/cover (effective 2003). adv. 200 p./no.; back issues avail.; reprints avail. **Document type:** *Journal, Academic/Scholarly.*
Indexed: GeoRef, RefZh, SpeleolAb, Z01.
Published by: Mizunamishi Kaseki Hakubutsukan/Mizunami Fossil Museum, Yamanouchi, Akeyocho, Mizunami-shi, Gifu-ken 509-6132, Japan. TEL 81-572-68-7710, FAX 81-572-66-1122, hkarasawa@mbh.nifty.com. Ed. H. Karasawa. R&P H Karasawa.

560 JPN
➤ **MIZUNAMISHI KASEKI HAKUBUTSUKAN SENPO/MIZUNAMI FOSSIL MUSEUM. MONOGRAPH.** Text in Japanese. 1980. irreg., latest vol.9. JPY 1,000 newsstand/cover (effective 2003). back issues avail.; reprints avail. **Document type:** *Monographic series, Academic/Scholarly.*
Indexed: SpeleolAb.
Published by: Mizunamishi Kaseki Hakubutsukan/Mizunami Fossil Museum, Yamanouchi, Akeyocho, Mizunami-shi, Gifu-ken 509-6132, Japan. TEL 81-572-68-7710, FAX 81-572-66-1122, hkarasawa@mbh.nifty.com. Ed. Y Okumura. R&P H Karasawa.

560 USA ISSN 0736-3907
QE701.M68
THE MOSASAUR. Text in English. 1983. irreg., latest vol.7, 2004. USD 15 per issue to non-members; free to members (effective 2010). back issues avail. **Document type:** *Journal, Academic/Scholarly.*
Description: Contains articles on fossils and geology related topics, especially those of local interest.
Related titles: CD-ROM ed.
Indexed: GeoRef, SpeleolAb, Z01.
—Linda Hall.
Published by: Delaware Valley Paleontological Society, c/o Ned Gilmore, Dept of Vertebrate Zoology, The Academy of Natural Sciences, 1900 Benjamin Franklin Pky, Philadelphia, PA 19103. EGilmore@acnatsci.org.

560 551 DEU ISSN 0177-0950
QE1
MUENCHNER GEOWISSENSCHAFTLICHE ABHANDLUNGEN. REIHE A: GEOLOGIE UND PALAEONTOLOGIE. Text in English, French, German. 1984. irreg., latest vol.41, 2008. EUR 60 per vol. (effective 2011). **Document type:** *Monographic series, Academic/Scholarly.*
Description: Covers geology and paleontology.
Indexed: GeoRef, IBR, IBZ, SpeleolAb, Z01.
—CCC.
Published by: Verlag Dr. Friedrich Pfeil, Wolfratshauser Str 27, Munich, 81379, Germany. TEL 49-89-7428270, FAX 49-89-7242772, info@pfeil-verlag.de. Circ: 500.

MUENSTERSCHE FORSCHUNGEN ZUR GEOLOGIE UND PALAEONTOLOGIE. *see* EARTH SCIENCES—Geology

560 551 JPN ISSN 1882-5249
MUKAWA CHOURITSU HOBETSU HAKUBUTSUKAN KENKYUU HOUKOKU/HOBETSU MUSEUM. BULLETIN. Text in English, Japanese; Summaries in English. 1984. a. free to institutions. back issues avail. **Document type:** *Bulletin, Academic/Scholarly.*
Description: Contains mainly paleontological and geological studies of the Hobetsu area of Hokkaido. Includes studies on late Cretaceous-Neogene vertebrate and invertebrate fossils.
Formerly (until 2007): Hobetsu-choritsu Hakubutsukan Kenkyu Hokoku/Hobetsu Museum. Bulletin (0912-7798)
Indexed: Z01.
Published by: Hobetsu Museum/Hobetsu-choritsu Hakubutsukan, 80-6 Hobetsu, Hobetsu-cho, Yufutsu-gun, Hokkaido, 054-0211, Japan. TEL 86-145-453141, FAX 86-145-453141. Circ: 550.

MUSEO CIVICO DI STORIA NATURALE DI FERRARA. ANNALI. *see* EARTH SCIENCES—Geology

560 URY ISSN 0374-7123
QE752.A1 CODEN: CPMHA6
MUSEO DE HISTORIA NATURAL DE MONTEVIDEO. COMUNICACIONES PALEONTOLOGICAS. Text in Spanish. 1970. irreg.
Indexed: ASFA, B21, C01, ESPM, GeoRef.
—Linda Hall.
Published by: Museo de Historia Natural de Montevideo, Casilla de Correo 399, Montevideo, 11000, Uruguay.

560 ARG ISSN 0325-2256
QE701 CODEN: UPMPAO
MUSEO DE LA PLATA. NOTAS. PALEONTOLOGIA. Text in Spanish. 1935. irreg. **Document type:** *Monographic series, Academic/Scholarly.*
Indexed: C01.
Published by: Universidad Nacional de La Plata, Facultad de Ciencias Naturales y Museo, Paseo el Bosque s-n, La Plata, 1900, Argentina. FAX 54-221-4259161, http://www.fcnym.unlp.edu.ar/museo/.

560 ARG ISSN 0373-3823
QE701
MUSEO DE LA PLATA. REVISTA. SECCION PALEONTOLOGIA. Text in Spanish. 1936. irreg.
Supersedes in part (in 1936): Museo de La Plata. Revista (0375-1147)
Indexed: C01, GeoRef, Z01.
—INIST.
Published by: Universidad Nacional de La Plata, Facultad de Ciencias Naturales y Museo, Avenidas 60 y 122, La Plata, Buenos Aires, Argentina. TEL 54-221-4258252, facultad@museo.fcnym.unlp.edu.ar.

MUSEO DI STORIA NATURALE DELLA MAREMMA. ATTI. *see* BIOLOGY

560 URY ISSN 0797-6828
MUSEO NACIONAL DE HISTORIA NATURAL DE MONTEVIDEO. ANALES. Text in English. 1894. irreg.
Former titles (until 1965): Museo de Historia Natural de Montevideo. Anales (0797-8774); (until 1925): Museo Nacional de Montevideo. Anales (0797-3780)
Indexed: Z01.
Published by: Museo de Historia Natural de Montevideo, Casilla de Correo 399, Montevideo, 11000, Uruguay.

MUSEU DE GEOLOGIA DE BARCELONA. TREBALLS. *see* EARTH SCIENCES

MUSEUM VICTORIA. MEMOIRS. *see* BIOLOGY—Zoology

NATURAL HISTORY CONTRIBUTIONS. *see* BIOLOGY

NATURAL HISTORY MUSEUM IN BELGRADE. BULLETIN. *see* EARTH SCIENCES—Geology

560 ESP ISSN 1138-8013
QH7
NATURALEZA ARAGONESA. Text in Spanish. 1997. s-a. EUR 6 (effective 2009). back issues avail. **Document type:** *Journal, Academic/Scholarly.*
Indexed: GeoRef, Z01.
Published by: (Universidad de Zaragoza, Sociedad de Amigos del Museo Paleontologico), Prensas Universitarias de Zaragoza, C/ Pedro Cerbuna 12, Edificio de Ciencias Geologicas, Zaragoza, 50009, Spain. TEL 34-976-761330, FAX 34-976-761063, puz@posta.unizar.es, http://puz.unizar.es.

NATURHISTORISCHES MUSEUM BASEL. VEROEFFENTLICHUNGEN. *see* SCIENCES: COMPREHENSIVE WORKS

NATURHISTORISCHES MUSEUM IN WIEN. ANNALEN. SERIE A, MINERALOGIE UND PETROGRAPHIE, GEOLOGIE UND PALAEONTOLOGIE, ANTHROPOLOGIE UND PRAEHISTORIE. *see* SCIENCES: COMPREHENSIVE WORKS

NATURWISSENSCHAFTLICHER VEREIN IN HAMBURG. ABHANDLUNGEN. *see* BIOLOGY—Zoology

NATURWISSENSCHAFTLICHER VEREIN IN HAMBURG. VERHANDLUNGEN. *see* BIOLOGY—Zoology

NATURWISSENSCHAFTLICHER VEREIN WUERZBURG. ABHANDLUNGEN. *see* BIOLOGY

NATURWISSENSCHAFTLICHER VEREIN ZU BREMEN. ABHANDLUNGEN. *see* BIOLOGY

NATUURHISTORISCH GENOOTSCHAP IN LIMBURG. PUBLICATIES. *see* BIOLOGY

560 DEU ISSN 0948-0331
NEUE PALAEONTOLOGISCHE ABHANDLUNGEN. Text in German, English. 1996. irreg., latest vol.5, 2002. price varies. **Document type:** *Monographic series, Academic/Scholarly.*
Indexed: GeoRef, Z01.
Published by: CPress Verlag, Postfach 192409, Dresden, 01282, Germany. FAX 49-3212-1007315, info@cp-v.de. Ed. Hannes Loeser.

NEUES JAHRBUCH FUER GEOLOGIE UND PALAEONTOLOGIE. ABHANDLUNGEN. *see* EARTH SCIENCES—Geology

560 USA ISSN 1524-4156
J87
NEW MEXICO MUSEUM OF NATURAL HISTORY AND SCIENCE. BULLETIN. Text in English. 1992. s-a. **Document type:** *Bulletin, Academic/Scholarly.*
Indexed: B25, BIOSIS Prev, GeoRef, MycolAb, Z01.
Published by: New Mexico Museum of Natural History and Science, 1801 Mountain Rd NW, Albuquerque, NM 87104. TEL 505-841-2800, FAX 505-841-2866, nmmnhs.info@state.nm.us.

560 AUS ISSN 0077-8699
NEW SOUTH WALES. GEOLOGICAL SURVEY. MEMOIRS: PALAEONTOLOGY. Text in English. 1888. irreg., latest vol.19, 1982. price varies. **Document type:** *Monographic series, Government.*
Indexed: GeoRef, SpeleolAb.
—Linda Hall.
Published by: Department of Primary Industries, Mineral Resources Division, PO Box 344, Hunter Region Mail Centre, NSW 2310, Australia. TEL 61-2-49316666, FAX 61-2-49316790, mineralpublication.orders@dpi.nsw.gov.au.

560 551 JPN ISSN 0913-6746
NIHON DOKETSUGAKU KENKYUJO HOKOKU/SPELEOLOGICAL RESEARCH INSTITUTE OF JAPAN. ANNUAL. Text in Japanese. 1969. a. JPY 1,500 (effective 2000). **Document type:** *Bulletin.*
Published by: Nihon Doketsugaku Kenkyujo/Speleological Research Institute of Japan, c/o Ryusendo Jimusho, Shimohei-gun, Iwaizumicho, Iwate-ken 027-05, Japan. TEL 81-194-22-2566, FAX 81-194-22-5005. Ed. Kiyohumi Sasaki.

561 JPN ISSN 0387-1851
NIHON KAFUN GAKKAI KAISHI/JAPANESE JOURNAL OF PALYNOLOGY. Text in English, Japanese. 1965. s-a. **Document type:** *Bulletin.*
—CCC.
Published by: Nihon Kafun Gakkai/Palynological Society of Japan, Toho Daigaku Yakugakubu Shoyakugaku Kyoshitsu, 2-1 Miyama 2-chome, Funabashi-shi, Chiba-ken 274-0072, Japan.

560 AUS ISSN 1447-4662
QE701
NOMEN NUDUM (ONLINE). Text in English. 1972. a. free to members (effective 2008). **Document type:** *Newsletter, Trade.*
Formerly (until 1999): Nomen Nudum (Print) (0159-818X)
Media: Online - full text.
Indexed: AESIS, GeoRef, SpeleolAb.
—Linda Hall.
Published by: (Association of Australasian Palaeontologists), Geological Society of Australia Inc., Ste 706, 301 George St, Sydney, NSW 2000, Australia. TEL 61-2-92902194, FAX 61-2-92902198, info@gsa.org.au, http://www.gsa.org.au. Eds. Andrew Simpson TEL 61-2-98508183, James Valentine TEL 61-2-98507484, Peter Molloy. Circ: 600.

560 ESP ISSN 1134-5209
QE701
NOTICIAS PALEONTOLOGICAS. Text in Spanish. 1982. s-a. free membership (effective 2005). **Document type:** *Newsletter, Trade.*
Indexed: GeoRef, Z01.
Published by: Sociedad Espanola de Paleontologia, C Jose Gutierrez Abascal, 2, Madrid, 28006, Spain. http://www.sepaleontologia.es.

OESTERREICHISCHE GEOLOGISCHE GESELLSCHAFT. MITTEILUNGEN. *see* EARTH SCIENCES—Geology

560 NLD ISSN 1874-4257
QE701
➤ **THE OPEN PALEONTOLOGY JOURNAL.** Text in English. 2008. irreg. free (effective 2011). **Document type:** *Journal, Academic/Scholarly.*
Media: Online - full text.
Indexed: A01, Z01.
Published by: Bentham Open (Subsidiary of: Bentham Science Publishers Ltd.), PO Box 294, Bussum, AG 1400, Netherlands. TEL 31-35-6923800, FAX 31-35-6980150, subscriptions@bentham.org. Ed. Jean-Paul Colin.

567.9 FRA ISSN 1290-4805
➤ **ORYCTOS.** Text in French. 1998. a. **Document type:** *Journal, Academic/Scholarly.*
Indexed: Z01.
Published by: (European Association of Vertebrate Palaeontologists DEU), Musee des Dinosaures, Esperaza, 11260, France. TEL 33-4-68742688, FAX 33-4-68740575, contact@dinosauria.org. Ed. Dr. Lionel Cavin.

560 USA
OSTRACODA. Text in English. 1965. a. USD 525 to non-profit organizations; USD 1,050 government; USD 2,100 to corporations (effective 2010). **Document type:** *Journal, Academic/Scholarly.*
Media: Online - full text. **Related titles:** CD-ROM ed.

Published by: Micropress Inc., 6530 Kissena Blvd, Flushing, NY 11367. TEL 718-570-0505, FAX 718-570-0506, subs@micropress.org, http://www.micropress.org.

560 PAK ISSN 0078-8155
PAKISTAN. GEOLOGICAL SURVEY. MEMOIRS; PALEONTOLOGIA PAKISTANICA. Text in English. 1956. irreg. price varies.
Indexed: GeoRef, SpeleolAb.
Published by: Geological Survey of Pakistan, c/o Chief Librarian, P O Box 15, Quetta, 87550, Pakistan. TEL 92-81-9211038. Circ: 1,500.

560 DEU ISSN 1867-1594
QE701 CODEN: SLETAE
➤ **PALAEOBIODIVERSITY AND PALAEOENVIRONMENTS**; international journal of palaeontology and stratigraphy. Text and summaries in English, French, German. 1919. 4/yr. EUR 96, USD 145 combined subscription to institutions (print & online eds.) (effective 2012). bibl.; charts; illus.; maps. index. back issues avail.; reprint service avail. from PSC. **Document type:** *Journal, Academic/ Scholarly.* **Description:** Contains papers on paleozoology (including micropaleontology) and paleobotany with references to biofacies, biostratigraphy and paleobiogeography.
Formerly (until 2009): Senckenbergiana Lethaea (0037-2110)
Related titles: Online - full text ed.: ISSN 1867-1608.
Indexed: A22, A29, ASFA, B20, B21, B25, BIOSIS Prev, BrGeoL, ChemAb, ESPM, EntAb, GEOBASE, GeoRef, I10, IBR, IBZ, MycolAb, SCOPUS, SWRA, SpeleolAb, VirolAbstr, Z01.
—IE, Ingenta, INIST, Linda Hall. **CCC.**
Published by: (Senckenbergische Naturforschende Gesellschaft/ Senckenberg Nature Research Society, Deutsche Forschungsgemeinschaft), Springer (Subsidiary of: Springer Science+Business Media), Tiergartenstr 17, Heidelberg, 69121, Germany. TEL 49-6221-4870, FAX 49-6221-345229, subscriptions@springer.com. Ed. Peter Koenigshof. Circ: 850.

560 550 NLD ISSN 0031-0182
QE500 CODEN: PPPYAB
➤ **PALAEOGEOGRAPHY, PALAEOCLIMATOLOGY, PALAEOECOLOGY.** Text in English, French, German. 1965. 56/yr. EUR 4,524 in Europe to institutions; JPY 601,600 in Japan to institutions; USD 5,060 elsewhere to institutions (effective 2012). adv. bk.rev. abstr.; bibl.; charts; illus. index. back issues avail.; reprints avail. **Document type:** *Journal, Academic/Scholarly.* **Description:** Publishes original studies and comprehensive reviews in the field of palaeo-environmental geology.
Related titles: Microform ed.: (from PQC); Online - full text ed.: ISSN 1872-616X (from IngentaConnect, ScienceDirect); ◆ Supplement(s): Global and Planetary Change. ISSN 0921-8181.
Indexed: A01, A03, A08, A20, A22, A26, A33, A34, A37, A38, AESIS, ASCA, ASFA, AbAn, AgrForAb, B21, B25, BA, BIOBASE, BIOSIS Prev, BrArAb, BrGeoL, C25, C30, CA, CABA, ChemAb, CurCont, E04, E05, E12, E17, ESPM, EnvAb, F08, F11, F12, FR, G11, GEOBASE, GH, GeoRef, H16, H17, HPNRM, I05, I10, I11, IABS, IBR, IBZ, ISR, IndVet, Inspec, M&GPA, MycolAb, O01, OR, OceAb, P30, P32, P33, P39, P40, PGegResA, PN&I, PetrolAb, R07, R08, RefZh, S01, S12, S13, S16, SCI, SCOPUS, SSciA, SWRA, SpeleolAb, T02, TAR, VS, W07, W10, W11, Z01.
—BLDSC (6343.450000), CASDDS, IE, Infotrieve, Ingenta, INIST, Linda Hall, PADDS. **CCC.**
Published by: Elsevier BV (Subsidiary of: Elsevier Science & Technology), Radarweg 29, PO Box 211, Amsterdam, 1000 AE, Netherlands. TEL 31-20-4853911, FAX 31-20-4852457, JournalsCustomerServiceEMEA@elsevier.com, http://www.elsevier.nl. Eds. D J Bottjer, P Kershaw, T Correge.

560 ITA ISSN 0373-0972
QE701 CODEN: PLITAZ
PALAEONTOGRAPHIA ITALICA. Text in Italian. 1895. irreg. price varies. **Document type:** *Monographic series, Academic/Scholarly.*
Related titles: Online - full text ed.
Indexed: FR, GeoRef, SpeleolAb, Z01.
—INIST.
Published by: Edizioni Plus - Universita di Pisa (Pisa University Press), Lungarno Pacinotti 43, Pisa, Italy. TEL 39-050-2212056, FAX 39-050-2212945, http://www.edizioniplus.it.

551 DEU ISSN 0375-0442
QE701 CODEN: PGABA8
➤ **PALAEONTOGRAPHICA. ABT. A: PALAEOZOOLOGIE - STRATIGRAPHIE.** Text in English, German; Summaries in English, French, German. 1846. irreg. (2-3 vol./yr., each vol. contains 2 double issues), latest vol.286, 2008. USD 513 per vol. (effective 2011). illus. back issues avail. **Document type:** *Journal, Academic/Scholarly.*
Indexed: A22, AESIS, B25, BIOSIS Prev, BrGeoL, CurCont, GeoRef, H09, H10, IBR, IBZ, MycolAb, S05, SCI, SCOPUS, SpeleolAb, W07, Z01.
—BLDSC (6343.603000), IE, Ingenta, INIST. **CCC.**
Published by: E. Schweizerbart'sche Verlagsbuchhandlung, Johannesstr 3A, Stuttgart, 70176, Germany. TEL 49-711-3514560, FAX 49-711-35145699, order@schweizerbart.de.

560 DEU ISSN 0375-0299
QE701 CODEN: PABPAD
➤ **PALAEONTOGRAPHICA. ABT. B: PALAEOPHYTOLOGIE.** Text in English, French, German. 1846. irreg. (2-3 vols./yr. 1 vol. consists of 2 double issues), latest vol.283, 2010. USD 513 per vol. (effective 2011). bibl.; charts; illus. index. back issues avail. **Document type:** *Journal, Academic/Scholarly.*
Indexed: A22, AESIS, B25, BIOSIS Prev, BrGeoL, CurCont, GEOBASE, GeoRef, IBR, IBZ, MycolAb, SCI, SCOPUS, SpeleolAb, W07, Z01.
—BLDSC (6343.605000), IE, Infotrieve, Ingenta, INIST. **CCC.**
Published by: E. Schweizerbart'sche Verlagsbuchhandlung, Johannesstr 3A, Stuttgart, 70176, Germany. TEL 49-711-3514560, FAX 49-711-35145699, order@schweizerbart.de.

560 USA ISSN 0078-8546
QE701 CODEN: PALAAI
➤ **PALAEONTOGRAPHICA AMERICANA.** Abbreviated title: P A. Text in English. 1916. irreg., latest vol.63, 2009. price varies. bibl.; charts; illus.; stat. back issues avail. **Document type:** *Monographic series, Academic/Scholarly.* **Description:** Features high quality monographs in paleontology or in neontological subjects that impact paleontology.
Indexed: AESIS, B25, BIOSIS Prev, GeoRef, MycolAb, SpeleolAb, Z01.
—Linda Hall.
Published by: Paleontological Research Institution, 1259 Trumansburg Rd, Ithaca, NY 14850. TEL 607-273-6623, FAX 607-273-6620, publications@museumoftheearth.org. Ed. Paula M Mikkelsen.

➤ **PALAEONTOGRAPHICAL SOCIETY. MONOGRAPHS (LONDON).** see EARTH SCIENCES—Geology

560 ZAF ISSN 0078-8554
QE701 CODEN: PBPRAS
➤ **PALAEONTOLOGIA AFRICANA.** Text in English. 1953. a., latest vol.38, 2002. price varies. bk.rev. cum.index: vols.1-34 (1953-1998). back issues avail. **Document type:** *Monographic series, Academic/ Scholarly.* **Description:** Publishes original research relating to any aspect of palaeontology.
Indexed: B25, BIOSIS Prev, GEOBASE, GeoRef, IBR, IBZ, ISAP, MycolAb, SCOPUS, SpeleolAb, Z01.
—Ingenta, INIST, Linda Hall.
Published by: University of the Witwatersrand Johannesburg, Bernard Price Institute for Palaeontological Research, Editorial, Wits, 2050, South Africa. TEL 27-11-717-6685, FAX 27-11-403-1423, 106GAR@cosmos.wits.ac.za. Ed. Marion Banford. R&P Bruce S Rubidge TEL 27-11-717-6685. Circ: 600 (controlled).

560 CHN
➤ **PALAEONTOLOGIA CATHAYANA/HUAXIA GUSHENGWU.** Text in English. 1983. irreg., latest vol.4, 1989. price varies. illus. **Document type:** *Monographic series, Academic/Scholarly.* **Description:** Publishes papers on all aspects of paleontology, stratigraphy, and paleobiogeography. Includes review articles, short papers of description or discussion of important flora and fauna, news of current research, and occasional translations.
Indexed: SpeleolAb.
Published by: Kexue Chubanshe/Science Press, 16 Donghuang Cheng Genbei Jie, Beijing, 100717, China. TEL 86-10-64000246, FAX 86-10-64030255. Ed. Lu Yan Hao.

560 USA ISSN 1094-8074
QE701
➤ **PALAEONTOLOGIA ELECTRONICA.** Text in English. 1998. s-a. free (effective 2011). back issues avail. **Document type:** *Journal, Academic/Scholarly.*
Media: Online - full text. **Related titles:** CD-ROM ed.: ISSN 1532-3056; Print ed.: ISSN 1935-3952.
Indexed: A39, ASFA, C27, C29, CurCont, D03, D04, E13, GEOBASE, GeoRef, PetrolAb, R14, S14, S15, S18, SCI, SCOPUS, SpeleolAb, W07, Z01.
—Linda Hall, PADDS.
Published by: Coquina Press, PO Box 577, Columbia, CA 95310. TEL 386-931-3076, coquinapress@mac.com, http://www.coquinapress.com.

560 IND ISSN 0971-2844
PALAEONTOLOGIA INDICA/PAILIOMTOLOJIYA INDIKA. Text in English. 1961. irreg., latest vol.52, 2006. price varies. back issues avail. **Document type:** *Monographic series, Academic/Scholarly.*
Formerly (until 1984): Geological Survey of India. Palaeontologia Indica. Memoirs (0970-0528)
Indexed: GeoRef, Z01.
Published by: Geological Survey of India, 29 Jawaharlal Nehru Rd, Kolkata, West Bengal 700 016, India. TEL 91-33-22861676, FAX 91-33-22861656, dg-gsi@gsi.gov.in.

560 POL ISSN 0078-8562
QE701 CODEN: PLPOAL
PALAEONTOLOGIA POLONICA. Text in English, French; Summaries in Polish. 1929. irreg., latest vol.64, 2007. price varies. charts; illus. **Document type:** *Monographic series, Academic/Scholarly.* **Description:** Devoted to publishing data which emphasise both morphologic and time dimensions of the evolution, that is detailed descriptions of fossils and precise stratigraphic co-ordinates.
Indexed: AgrAg, B25, BIOSIS Prev, GEOBASE, GeoRef, MycolAb, RefZh, SCOPUS, SpeleolAb, Z01.
—INIST, Linda Hall.
Published by: Polska Akademia Nauk, Instytut Paleobiologii, ul Twarda 51-55, Warsaw, 00-818, Poland. TEL 48-22-6978850, FAX 48-22-6206225, paleo@twarda.pan.pl, http://www.paleo.pan.pl. Ed. Jerzy Dzik. Circ: 560.

560 IND ISSN 0552-9360
QE756.I4 CODEN: PLSIBJ
PALAEONTOLOGICAL SOCIETY OF INDIA. JOURNAL. Text in English. 1956. s-a. **Document type:** *Journal, Academic/Scholarly.*
Related titles: Online - full text ed.: free (effective 2011).
Indexed: B25, BIOSIS Prev, GeoRef, MycolAb, SpeleolAb, Z01.
—Ingenta, INIST.
Published by: University of Lucknow, Department of Geology, Badshaw Bagh, Lucknow, Uttar Pradesh, India.

560 JPN ISSN 0549-3927
QE701 CODEN: PSJSAI
PALAEONTOLOGICAL SOCIETY OF JAPAN. SPECIAL PAPERS. Text in English. 1951. irreg. **Document type:** *Monographic series, Academic/Scholarly.*
Indexed: GeoRef, SpeleolAb, Z01.
—Linda Hall. **CCC.**
Published by: Nihon Kodansei Gakkai/Japan Society for Photoelasticity, Nihon Gakkai Jimu Senta, 16-9 Honkomagome 5-chome, Bunkyo-ku, Tokyo, 113-0021, Japan. Ed. Yukimitsu Tomida.

560 DEU ISSN 0031-0220
QE701 CODEN: PAZEAW
➤ **PALAEONTOLOGISCHE ZEITSCHRIFT.** Text in English, German; Summaries in English, French. 1914. q. EUR 336, USD 506 combined subscription to institutions (print & online eds.) (effective 2012). adv. bibl.; charts; illus. back issues avail.; reprint service avail. from PSC. **Document type:** *Journal, Academic/Scholarly.* **Description:** Dedicated to the promotion of palaeontology as a scientific discipline. Publishes research and review papers on all aspects of this field.
Related titles: Online - full text ed.: ISSN 1867-6812.
Indexed: A22, B25, BIOSIS Prev, BrGeoL, CurCont, E01, GeoRef, IBR, IBZ, MycolAb, RefZh, SCI, SCOPUS, SpeleolAb, W07, Z01.
—BLDSC (6345.250000), IE, Ingenta, INIST, Linda Hall. **CCC.**
Published by: (Palaeontologische Gesellschaft e.V.), Springer (Subsidiary of: Springer Science+Business Media), Tiergartenstr 17, Heidelberg, 69121, Germany. TEL 49-6221-4870, FAX 49-6221-345229, subscriptions@springer.com. Ed. Oliver Rauhut.

560 GBR ISSN 0031-0239
QE701 CODEN: PONTAD
➤ **PALAEONTOLOGY.** Text in English. 1957. bi-m. GBP 655 in United Kingdom to institutions; EUR 833 in Europe to institutions; USD 1,209 in the Americas to institutions; USD 1,412 elsewhere to institutions; GBP 719 combined subscription in United Kingdom to institutions (print & online eds.); EUR 916 combined subscription in Europe to institutions (print & online eds.); USD 1,330 combined subscription in the Americas to institutions (print & online eds.); USD 1,553 combined subscription elsewhere to institutions (print & online eds.) (effective 2012). adv. illus. cum.index: 1989-1999. back issues avail.; reprint service avail. from PSC. **Document type:** *Journal, Academic/ Scholarly.* **Description:** Publishes a wide variety of papers on palaeontological topics covering palaeozoology, palaeobotany, systematic studies, palaeoecology, micropalaeontology, palaeobiogeography, functional morphology, stratigraphy, taxonomy, taphonomy, palaeoenvironmental reconstruction, palaeoclimate analysis and biomineralization studies.
Related titles: Online - full text ed.: ISSN 1475-4983. GBP 655 in United Kingdom to institutions; EUR 833 in Europe to institutions; USD 1,209 in the Americas to institutions; USD 1,412 elsewhere to institutions (effective 2012) (from IngentaConnect); ◆ Supplement(s): Special Papers in Palaeontology. ISSN 0038-6804.
Indexed: A01, A03, A08, A22, A26, AESIS, ASCA, ASFA, B21, B25, BIOSIS Prev, CA, CurCont, E01, EntAb, GEOBASE, GenetAb, GeoRef, HGA, ISR, MycolAb, OceAb, P02, P10, P30, P48, P52, P53, P54, P56, PQC, PetrolAb, RefZh, S01, S10, SCI, SCOPUS, SpeleolAb, T02, W07, Z01.
—BLDSC (6345.200000), IE, Infotrieve, Ingenta, INIST, Linda Hall, PADDS. **CCC.**
Published by: (Palaeontological Association), Wiley-Blackwell Publishing Ltd. (Subsidiary of: John Wiley & Sons, Inc.), 9600 Garsington Rd, Oxford, OX4 2DQ, United Kingdom. TEL 44-1865-776868, FAX 44-1865-714591, customerservices@blackwellpublishing.com. Ed. S Stouge. Adv. contact Craig Pickett TEL 44-1865-476267.

560 GBR ISSN 0954-9900
QE701
PALAEONTOLOGY NEWSLETTER. Text in English. 19??. 3/yr. free to members (effective 2009). bk.rev. back issues avail. **Document type:** *Newsletter, Academic/Scholarly.* **Description:** Contains palaeontological news, book reviews, reviews of past meetings, details of forthcomming meetings as well as a series of regular discussion features.
Formerly (until 1988): Palaeontological Association. Circular
Related titles: Online - full text ed.: free (effective 2009).
Indexed: GeoRef, Z01.
—Linda Hall. **CCC.**
Published by: Palaeontological Association, c/o Dr. Tim Palmer, I G E S, University of Wales, Aberystwyth, Wales SY23 3DB, United Kingdom. TEL 44-1970-627107, FAX 44-1970-622659, secretary@palass.org. Ed. Richard Twitchett.

560 NLD ISSN 1871-174X
QE701
➤ **PALAEOWORLD.** Text in English. 2006. 4/yr. EUR 458 in Europe to institutions; JPY 62,200 in Japan to institutions; USD 575 elsewhere to institutions (effective 2012). **Document type:** *Journal, Academic/ Scholarly.* **Description:** Dedicated to studies on palaeontology and stratigraphy centered in China and the neighboring regions, encouraging original works of fossils and strata, comparative studies worldwide, and interdisciplinary approaches in related disciplines.
Related titles: Online - full text ed.: ISSN 1875-5887 (from ScienceDirect).
Indexed: B21, B25, BIOBASE, BIOSIS Prev, GEOBASE, IABS, MycolAb, PetrolAb, SCOPUS, Z01.
—BLDSC (6345.210500), IE, Ingenta, PADDS. **CCC.**
Published by: (Zhongguo Kexueyuan Nanjing Dizhi Gushengwu Yanjiusuo/Chinese Academy of Sciences, Nanjing Institute of Geology and Palaeontology CHN), Elsevier BV (Subsidiary of: Elsevier Science & Technology), Radarweg 29, PO Box 211, Amsterdam, 1000 AE, Netherlands. TEL 31-20-4853911, FAX 31-20-4852457, JournalsCustomerServiceEMEA@elsevier.com. Eds. Douglas Erwin, Qun Yang.

560 CHN ISSN 1671-2412
PALAEOWORLD. Text mainly in Chinese; Text occasionally in English. irreg. **Document type:** *Monographic series, Academic/Scholarly.*
Indexed: Z01.
Published by: Zhongguo Kexueyuan Nanjing Dizhi Gushengwu Yanjiusuo/Chinese Academy of Sciences, Nanjing Institute of Geology and Palaeontology, 39 Beijing Donglu, Nanjing, Jiangsu 210008, China. ngb@nigpas.ac.cn, http://www.nigpas.ac.cn.

560 USA ISSN 0883-1351
QE701 CODEN: PALAEM
➤ **PALAIOS**; emphasizing the impact of life on earth's history. Text in English. 1986. bi-m. USD 415 combined subscription domestic to non-members (print, online & CD-ROM eds.); USD 425 combined subscription foreign to non-members (print, online & CD-ROM eds.); free to members (effective 2010). adv. bk.rev. illus. Index. 2 cols./p.; back issues avail. **Document type:** *Journal, Academic/Scholarly.* **Description:** Contains comprehensive articles, short papers, invited editorials, and essays devoted to the applications of paleontology in solving geologic problems.
Related titles: CD-ROM ed.; Online - full text ed.: ISSN 1938-5323. USD 315 combined subscription to non-members (online & CD-ROM eds.); free to members (effective 2010).
Indexed: A20, A22, A33, AESIS, ASCA, ASFA, B21, B25, BIOSIS Prev, CurCont, E01, E17, ESPM, GEOBASE, GSW, GeoRef, ISR, M&GPA, MycolAb, P30, PetrolAb, SCI, SCOPUS, SpeleolAb, W07, Z01.
—BLDSC (6345.214500), CASDDS, IE, Infotrieve, Ingenta, INIST, Linda Hall, PADDS. **CCC.**
Published by: Society for Sedimentary Geology (S E P M), 4111 S Darlington, Ste 100, Tulsa, OK 74135. TEL 918-610-3361, 800-865-9765, FAX 918-621-1685, foundation@sepm.org, http://www.sepm.org. Eds. Edith L Taylor, Stephen T Hasiotis.

560 930.1 NLD ISSN 1872-4582
PALARCH FOUNDATION'S NEWSLETTER. Text in English. 2004. q. **Document type:** *Newsletter, Trade.*
Media: Online - full text.
Indexed: A01.
Published by: PalArch Foundation, Mezquitalaan 23, Amsterrdam, 1064 NS, Netherlands.

P

566 NLD ISSN 1567-2158
PALARCH'S JOURNAL OF VERTEBRATE PALAEONTOLOGY. Text in English. 2003. free (effective 2011). bk.rev. **Document type:** *Journal, Trade.*
Media: Online - full text.
Indexed: A01, CA, SCOPUS.
Published by: PalArch Foundation, Mezquitalaan 23, Amsterdram, 1064 NS, Netherlands.

560 NLD ISSN 0168-6208
QE993 CODEN: PLEABR
➤ **PALAEOECOLOGY OF AFRICA**; and the surrounding islands. Text in Dutch. 1966. irreg. (approx. a.), latest vol.28, 2007. price varies. illus.; maps. back issues avail. **Document type:** *Academic/Scholarly.*
Description: Provides comprehensive and up-to-date information on research in many disciplines, offering a broad insight into the environmental history of Africa.
Former titles: Paleoecology of Africa and the Surrounding Islands; Palaeoecology of Africa and the Surrounding Islands and Antarctica (0078-8538)
Indexed: AnthLit, FR, GeoRef, SpeleolAb.
—BLDSC (6343.430000). **CCC.**
Published by: A A Balkema (Subsidiary of: Taylor & Francis Ltd.), Postbus 447, Leiden, 2300 AK, Netherlands. TEL 31-71-5243080, pub.nl@tandf.co.uk, http://www.balkema.nl. **Dist. in US by:** Ashgate Publishing Co, Old Post Rd, Brookfield, VT 05036. TEL 802-276-3837, 802-276-3162.

560 570 NLD ISSN 1572-6622
PALEO-AKTUEEL. Text in Dutch. 1989. irreg., latest vol.18, 2006. price varies. **Document type:** *Monographic series, Academic/Scholarly.*
Published by: (Rijksuniversiteit Groningen, Groninger Instituut voor Archeologie/Groningen Institute of Archaeology), Barkhuis Publishing, Zuurstukken 37, Eelde, 9761 KP, Netherlands. TEL 31-50-3080936, FAX 31-50-3080934, info@barkhuis.nl, http://www.barkhuis.nl.

560 USA ISSN 0094-8373
QE701 CODEN: PALBBM
➤ **PALEOBIOLOGY.** Variant title: Journal of Paleobiology. Text in English. 1975. q. adv. bk.rev. abstr.; bibl.; charts; illus.; pat.; stat. index. back issues avail.; reprints avail. **Document type:** *Journal, Academic/Scholarly.* **Description:** Features original contributions of any length (but normally 10-50 manuscript pages) dealing with any aspect of biological paleontology.
Related titles: Microform ed.: (from PQC); Online - full text ed.: ISSN 1938-5331.
Indexed: A20, A22, A29, AESIS, ASCA, ASFA, AbAn, B20, B21, B25, BIOSIS Prev, BrArAb, C25, C30, CA, CABA, CurCont, E01, E12, E17, ESPM, F08, F11, F12, GEOBASE, GSW, GeoRef, I10, I11, IBR, IBZ, ISR, MycolAb, P15, P30, P32, P40, P48, P52, P56, PGegResA, PQC, PetrolAb, R07, S13, S16, SCI, SCOPUS, SPPI, SpeleolAb, T02, VirolAbstr, W07, W08, WildRev, Z01.
—BLDSC (6345.280000), IE, Infotrieve, Ingenta, INIST, Linda Hall, PADDS. **CCC.**
Published by: Paleontological Society, Department of Paleobiology, National Museum of Natural History, Smithsonian Institution, PO Box 37012, Washington, DC 20013. TEL 202-633-1345, FAX 202-786-2832, roger.thomas@fandm.edu. Eds. Matthew Carrano TEL 202-633-1314, Peter J Wagner. adv.: page USD 150.

560 551 USA ISSN 0031-0298
QE701 CODEN: PLBIA
➤ **PALEOBIOS.** Text in English. 1967. 3/yr. USD 25; USD 7.50 per issue (effective 2010). bibl.; charts; illus. back issues avail. **Document type:** *Journal, Academic/Scholarly.* **Description:** Publishes scholarly articles on all paleontological topics.
Indexed: B25, BIOSIS Prev, GeoRef, MycolAb, SpeleolAb, WildRev, Z01.
—BLDSC (6345.285000), Ingenta, INIST, Linda Hall.
Published by: University of California, Berkeley, Museum of Paleontology, 1101 Valley Life Sciences Bldg, Berkeley, CA 94720. TEL 510-642-1821, FAX 510-642-1822, crmarshall@berkeley.edu. Ed. Mark Goodwin.

560 PRT ISSN 1647-2756
▼ **PALEOLUSITANA.** Text in Portuguese. 2009. a. **Document type:** *Journal, Academic/Scholarly.*
Indexed: Z01.
Published by: Associacao Leonel Trindade, Rua Cavaleiros da Espoura Dourada 27A, Torres Vedras, 2564-909, Portugal. http://www.alt-shn.org.

560 GBR
PALEONET FORUM. Text in English. 1994. m. free (effective 2009). back issues avail. **Document type:** *Journal, Academic/Scholarly.*
Description: Designed as a resource for paleontological professionals and graduate students.
Media: Online - full text.
Published by: PaleoNet, c/o Norman MacLeod, Natural History Museum, Cromwell Rd, London, SW7 5BD, United Kingdom. N.MacLeod@nhm.ac.uk.

560 ITA ISSN 1121-3361
PALEONTOLOGIA LOMBARDA. Text in Italian. 1993. irreg. price varies. back issues avail. **Document type:** *Monographic series, Academic/Scholarly.*
Indexed: GeoRef, SpeleolAb.
Published by: Societa Italiana di Scienze Naturali, Corso Venezia 55, Milan, MI 20121, Italy. TEL 39-02-795965, FAX 39-02-795965, http://www.scienzenaturali.org. Circ: 1,000.

560 MEX ISSN 0543-7652
PALEONTOLOGIA MEXICANA. Text in Spanish. 1954. irreg., latest vol.61, 1993. MXN 25, USD 10 (effective 1998 & 1999). **Document type:** *Monographic series, Academic/Scholarly.*
Indexed: SpeleolAb.
—Linda Hall.
Published by: Universidad Nacional Autonoma de Mexico, Instituto de Geologia, Circuito de la Investigacion Cientifica s-n, Ciudad Universitaria, Del. Coyoacan, Mexico, D.F., DF 04510, Mexico. TEL 52-5-622-4304, FAX 52-5-622-4318, alcayde@servidor.unam.mx, publigl@geologia.unam.mx.

560 USA ISSN 1946-0279
CODEN: UKPCE3
➤ **PALEONTOLOGICAL CONTRIBUTIONS.** Text in English. 1947. irreg. abstr.; bibl.; illus. back issues avail.; reprints avail. **Document type:** *Journal, Academic/Scholarly.* **Description:** Publishes results of research in paleontology done by workers at the University of Kansas or with close ties to the university, based on Kansas materials, or related to scientific projects sponsored by the university.
Formerly (until 2009): University of Kansas. Paleontological Contributions. New Series (1046-8390); Which was formed by the merger of (1982-1992): University of Kansas. Paleontological Contributions. Monographs (0278-9744); (1969-1992): University of Kansas. Paleontological Contributions. Articles (0075-5044); (1965-1992): University of Kansas. Paleontological Contributions. Papers (0075-5052)
Related titles: Online - full text ed.: free (effective 2011).
Indexed: AESIS, B25, BIOSIS Prev, GeoRef, MycolAb, SpeleolAb, Z01.
—CASDDS, INIST, Linda Hall.
Published by: University of Kansas, Paleontological Institute, 121 Lindley Hall, Lawrence, KS 66045. paleo@ku.edu.

560 RUS ISSN 0031-0301
QE701 CODEN: PJOUA
➤ **PALEONTOLOGICAL JOURNAL.** Text in English. 1959. bi-m. EUR 5,649, USD 6,839 combined subscription to institutions (print & online eds.) (effective 2012). adv. bk.rev. illus. reprints avail. **Document type:** *Journal, Academic/Scholarly.* **Description:** Deals with the anatomy, morphology and taxonomy of extinct animals and plants.
Related titles: Microform ed.: (from PQC); Online - full text ed.: ISSN 1555-6174 (from IngentaConnect); ◆ Translation of: Paleontologicheskii Zhurnal. ISSN 0031-031X.
Indexed: A22, A26, A33, A34, ASFA, B21, B25, BIOSIS Prev, CABA, CurCont, E01, E12, ESPM, EntAb, F08, F11, F12, GH, GeoRef, I05, IndVet, MycolAb, P32, P33, P40, PGegResA, R07, R08, S13, S16, SCI, SCOPUS, SWRA, SpeleolAb, T05, VS, W07, WildRev.
—BLDSC (0416.675000), East View, IE, Ingenta, INIST. **CCC.**
Published by: (Rossiiskaya Akademiya Nauk/Russian Academy of Sciences), M A I K Nauka - Interperiodica (Subsidiary of: Pleiades Publishing, Inc.), Profsoyuznaya ul 90, Moscow, 117997, Russian Federation. TEL 7-095-3347420, FAX 7-095-3360666, compmg@maik.ru, http://www.maik.ru. Ed. A Y Rozanov. R&P Vladimir I Vasil'ev. Circ: 425. **Distr. in the Americas by:** Springer New York LLC, Journal Fulfillment, PO Box 2485, Secaucus, NJ 07096. TEL 212-460-1500, FAX 201-348-4505; **Distr. outside of the Americas by:** Springer, Haber Str 7, Heidelberg 69126, Germany. TEL 49-6221-3454303, FAX 49-6221-3454229. **Co-sponsor:** American Geological Institute.

560 JPN ISSN 1342-8144
QE756.J29
➤ **PALEONTOLOGICAL RESEARCH.** Text in English. 1935. q. JPY 6,000 to individuals; USD 75 to institutions (effective 2007). bk.rev. illus. back issues avail. **Document type:** *Journal, Academic/Scholarly.* **Description:** Publishes articles to disseminate knowledge in all areas of paleontological research.
Formerly (until 1996): Nihon Koseibutsu Gakkai Hokoku, Kiji/Palaeontological Society of Japan. Transactions and Proceedings (0031-0204)
Related titles: Online - full text ed.
Indexed: B21, B25, BIOSIS Prev, GEOBASE, GeoRef, IBR, IBZ, MycolAb, PetrolAb, SCI, SCOPUS, SpeleolAb, W07, Z01.
—BLDSC (6345.326070), IE, Ingenta, INIST, Linda Hall, PADDS. **CCC.**
Published by: The Paleontological Society of Japan, TohShin Bldg. 3F, Hongo 2-27-2, Bunkyo-ku, Tokyo, 113-0033, Japan. TEL 81-3-38145490, FAX 81-3-38146216, psj-office@world.ocn.ne.jp, http://ammo.kueps.kyoto-u.ac.jp/palaeont/. Ed. Kenshiro Ogasawara. Circ: 1,200.

560 USA ISSN 0078-8597
CODEN: PSMECR
PALEONTOLOGICAL SOCIETY. MEMOIR. Text in English. 1968. irreg. included with Journal of Paleontology subscr. **Document type:** *Monographic series, Academic/Scholarly.*
Related titles: Online - full text ed.: ISSN 1937-2833.
Indexed: B25, BIOSIS Prev, GeoRef, MycolAb, SpeleolAb, Z01.
Published by: Paleontological Society, c/o Roger D. K. Thomas, Secretary, Department of Earth and Environment, Franklin and Marshall College, PO Box 3003, Lancaster, PA 17604. TEL 717-291-4135, FAX 717-291-4186, roger.thomas@fandm.edu, http://www.paleosoc.org/.

560 USA ISSN 1089-3326
THE PALEONTOLOGICAL SOCIETY. PAPERS. Text in English. 1996. s-a. **Document type:** *Monographic series, Academic/Scholarly.*
Formed by the merger of (1984-19??): Paleontological Society. Special Publication; (1988-1996): Short Courses in Paleontology
Indexed: GeoRef, SpeleolAb, Z01.
—BLDSC (6345.326150), IE, Ingenta. **CCC.**
Published by: Paleontological Society, c/o Roger D. K. Thomas, Secretary, Department of Earth and Environment, Franklin and Marshall College, PO Box 3003, Lancaster, PA 17604. TEL 717-291-4135, FAX 717-291-4186, roger.thomas@fandm.edu, http://www.paleosoc.org/.

560 RUS ISSN 0031-031X
QE701 CODEN: PAZHA7
➤ **PALEONTOLOGICHESKII ZHURNAL.** Text in Russian. 1959. q. USD 224 foreign (effective 2005). index. **Document type:** *Journal, Academic/Scholarly.* **Description:** Deals with the anatomy, morphology and taxonomy of extinct animals and plants.
Incorporates: Akademiya Nauk S.S.S.R. Institut Paleontologii. Trudy
Related titles: ◆ English Translation: Paleontological Journal. ISSN 0031-0301.
Indexed: ASCA, GeoRef, RefZh, SCOPUS, SpeleolAb, Z01.
—East View, INIST, Linda Hall. **CCC.**
Published by: (Rossiiskaya Akademiya Nauk, Institut Paleontologii), Izdatel'stvo Nauka, Profsoyuznaya ul 90, Moscow, 117864, Russian Federation. TEL 7-095-3347151, FAX 7-095-4202220, secret@naukaran.ru, http://www.naukaran.ru. Circ: 1,200. **Dist. by:** M K - Periodica, ul Gilyarovskogo 39, Moscow 129110, Russian Federation. TEL 7-095-2845008, FAX 7-095-2813798, info@periodicals.ru, http://www.mkniga.ru.

560 BGR ISSN 0204-7217
QE755.B8 CODEN: PSLIDZ
PALEONTOLOGIIA, STRATIGRAFIIA I LITOLOGIIA. Text in Multiple languages; Summaries in Bulgarian, English, French, German. 1975. irreg. price varies. illus. reprint service avail. from IRC.
Supersedes in part: Bulgarska Akademiia na Naukite. Geologicheski Institut. Izvestiia
Indexed: BSLGeo, GeoRef, SpeleolAb.
—INIST, Linda Hall.
Published by: (Bulgarska Akademiya na Naukite/Bulgarian Academy of Sciences, Geologicheski Institut), Sofiiski Universitet Sv. Kliment Ohridski, Universitetsko Izdatelstvo/Sofia University St. Kliment Ohridski University Press, Akad G Bonchev 6, Sofia, 1113, Bulgaria. Ed. C Spasov. Circ: 470.

560 BEL ISSN 1377-4654
PALEONTOS. Text in Multiple languages. 2001. irreg. price varies. **Document type:** *Monographic series, Academic/Scholarly.*
Indexed: GeoRef, Z01.
—PADDS.
Published by: Paleo Publishing & Library vzw, Minervastraat 23, Mortsel, 2640, Belgium. FAX 32-3-2903653.

560 USA ISSN 0148-4737
R135
PALEOPATHOLOGY NEWSLETTER. Text in English. 1972. q. USD 30; USD 20 to students (effective 2006).
Indexed: EMBASE, ExcerpMed, MEDLINE, P30, SCOPUS.
Published by: Paleopathology Association, c/o Anne L Grauer, Loyola University of Chicago, Department of Anthropology, 6525 N Sheridan Rd, Chicago, IL 60626. TEL 773-508-3480, FAX 773-508-3383. Ed. Mary Lucas Powell.

560 FRA ISSN 0153-9345
GN855.M628 CODEN: PALEDX
➤ **PALEORIENT.** Text in French. 1973. s-a. price varies. adv. bk.rev. bibl. index. back issues avail. **Document type:** *Journal, Academic/Scholarly.*
Related titles: Online - full text ed.: ISSN 1957-701X.
Indexed: AICP, AnthLit, BAS, DIP, FR, GeoRef, IBR, IBZ, MEA&I, RASB, SpeleolAb, Z01.
—IE, Ingenta, INIST. **CCC.**
Published by: (Universite de Paris I (Pantheon-Sorbonne), Laboratoire de Paleontologie Humaine et de Paleontologie des Vertebres), Centre National de la Recherche Scientifique, 15 Rue Malebranche, Paris, 75005, France. TEL 33-1-53102700, FAX 33-1-53102727. Ed. S Renimel. Circ: 1,500 (controlled).

560 FRA ISSN 2108-6532
PALETHNOLOGIE; revue bilingue de prehistoire. Text in French, English. 200?. irreg. **Document type:** *Journal, Academic/Scholarly.*
Media: Online - full text.
Published by: Revue Palethnologie http://www.palethnologie.org/revue.php.

566 USA ISSN 1091-0263
QE841
PALUDICOLA. Text in English. 1996. s-a. USD 20 to individuals (print or online ed.); USD 30 to institutions (effective 2011). back issues avail. **Document type:** *Journal, Academic/Scholarly.*
Related titles: Online - full text ed.
Indexed: Z01.
Published by: Rochester Institute of Vertebrate Paleontology, 265 Carling Rd, Rochester, NY 14610. http://vortex.weather.brockport.edu/~jmassare/rivp/info.htm. Eds. Judy A Massare, Dr. William W Korth.

561 560 USA ISSN 0191-6122
QE993 CODEN: PALYDP
➤ **PALYNOLOGY.** Text in English. 1975. s-a. GBP 93 combined subscription in United Kingdom to institutions (print & online eds.); EUR 122, USD 152 combined subscription to institutions (print & online eds.) (effective 2012). illus. Index. back issues avail.; reprint service avail. from PSC. **Document type:** *Journal, Academic/Scholarly.*
Supersedes (in 1977): Geoscience and Man (0072-1395); Incorporates (1970-1976): American Association of Stratigraphic Palynologists. Proceedings of the Annual Meeting (0270-1316)
Related titles: Online - full text ed.: ISSN 1558-9188. GBP 83 in United Kingdom to institutions; EUR 109, USD 136 to institutions (effective 2012).
Indexed: A01, A20, A22, AESIS, AnthLit, B21, B25, BIOSIS Prev, BrGeoL, CA, CurCont, GEOBASE, GSW, GeoRef, M&GPA, MycolAb, PetrolAb, SCI, SCOPUS, SpeleolAb, T02, W07, Z01.
—BLDSC (6345.580000), IE, Ingenta, Linda Hall, PADDS. **CCC.**
Published by: (American Association of Stratigraphic Palynologists Foundation), Taylor & Francis Inc. (Subsidiary of: Taylor & Francis Group), 325 Chestnut St, Ste 800, Philadelphia, PA 19106. TEL 215-625-8900, 800-354-1420, FAX 215-625-8914, customerservice@taylorandfrancis.com, http://www.taylorandfrancis.com.

560 551 USA ISSN 1936-1718
PALYNOS (ONLINE). Text in English. 1978. s-a. free to members (effective 2011). back issues avail. **Document type:** *Newsletter, Academic/Scholarly.*
Former titles (until 200?): Palynos (Print) (0256-1670); (until 1984): I C P Newsletter (0737-5786)
Media: Online - full text.
Indexed: GeoRef.
Published by: International Federation of Palynological Societies, Department of Geosciences, University of Arizona, Tucson, AZ 85721. TEL 520-621-7953, FAX 520-621-2672, palynolo@geo.arizona.edu. Ed. Jean Nicolas Haas.

PANSTWOWY INSTYTUT GEOLOGICZNY. PRACE. *see* EARTH SCIENCES—Geology

560 DEU ISSN 0724-9012
PISCIUM CATALOGUS. Text in German. 1993. irreg., latest vol.2, 1999. price varies. **Document type:** *Monographic series, Academic/Scholarly.*
Published by: Verlag Dr. Friedrich Pfeil, Wolfratshauser Str 27, Munich, 81379, Germany. TEL 49-89-7428270, FAX 49-89-7242772, info@pfeil-verlag.de. Ed. Werner Schwarzhans.

PREHISTORIC TIMES. *see* HOBBIES

Q R A TECHNICAL GUIDE. (Quaternary Research Association) *see* EARTH SCIENCES—Geology

560 ITA ISSN 1123-2676
GN700
QUATERNARIA NOVA. Text and summaries in English, French, German, Italian, Spanish. N.S. 1954. a. bk.rev. bibl.; charts; illus. cum.index.
Document type: *Monographic series, Academic/Scholarly.*
Description: Contains articles on quaternary prehistory, paleontology and geology.
Formerly (until 1981): Quaternaria (0085-5235)
Indexed: AnthLit, BrArAb, BrGeoL, GeoRef, SpeleolAb, Z01.
Published by: Istituto Italiano di Paleontologia Umana, Piazza Mincio 2, Rome, 00198, Italy. TEL 39-06-8557598, info@isipu.org, http://www.isipu.org.

QUATERNARY NEWSLETTER. *see* EARTH SCIENCES—Geology

QUATERNARY PERSPECTIVE. *see* EARTH SCIENCES—Geology

QUATERNARY RESEARCH. *see* EARTH SCIENCES—Geology

QUATERNARY RESEARCH ASSOCIATION. FIELD GUIDE SERIES. *see* EARTH SCIENCES—Geology

QUATERNARY SCIENCE REVIEWS. *see* EARTH SCIENCES—Geology

RENLEIXUE XUEBAO/ACTA ANTHROPOLOGICA SINICA. *see* ANTHROPOLOGY

561 NLD ISSN 0034-6667
CODEN: RPPYAX
➤ **REVIEW OF PALAEOBOTANY AND PALYNOLOGY.** Text in English, French, German. 1967. 20/yr. EUR 2,616 in Europe to institutions; JPY 347,200 in Japan to institutions; USD 2,924 elsewhere to institutions (effective 2012). adv. bk.rev. abstr.; bibl.; charts; illus. index. reprints avail. **Document type:** *Journal, Academic/Scholarly.*
Description: Aims to stimulate wide interdisciplinary cooperation and understanding among workers in the fields of palaeobotany and palynology.
Related titles: Microform ed.: (from PQC); Online - full text ed.: (from IngentaConnect, ScienceDirect).
Indexed: A01, A03, A08, A20, A22, A26, A34, A35, AESIS, ASCA, ASFA, AbAn, AgBio, Agr, AgrForAb, B21, B25, BA, BIOBASE, BIOSIS Prev, BrGeoL, C25, C30, CA, CABA, CurCont, E12, ESPM, F08, F11, F12, FCA, FR, G11, GEOBASE, GH, GeoRef, H16, I05, I11, IABS, ISR, LT, MaizeAb, MycolAb, N02, N04, O01, P30, P32, P33, P39, P40, PGegResA, PetrolAb, PlantSci, R07, R13, RA&MP, RRTA, RefZh, S01, S13, S16, S17, SCI, SCOPUS, SWRA, SpeleolAb, T02, TAR, TriticAb, VITIS, VS, W07, W10, Z01.
—BLDSC (7793.830000), IE, Infotrieve, Ingenta, INIST, Linda Hall, PADDS. **CCC.**
Published by: Elsevier BV (Subsidiary of: Elsevier Science & Technology), Radarweg 29, PO Box 211, Amsterdam, 1000 AE, Netherlands. TEL 31-20-4853911, FAX 31-20-4852457, JournalsCustomerServiceEMEA@elsevier.com, http://www.elsevier.nl. Eds. A F Lotter, H Kerp, M Stephenson. **Subscr. to:** Radarweg 29, PO Box 211, Amsterdam 1000 AE, Netherlands. TEL 31-20-4853757, FAX 31-20-4853432.

560 BRA ISSN 1519-7530
QE752.B8
REVISTA BRASILEIRA DE PALEONTOLOGIA. Text in Portuguese. 2001. s-a. **Document type:** *Journal, Academic/Scholarly.*
Related titles: Online - full text ed.: free (effective 2011).
Indexed: B25, BIOSIS Prev, CurCont, GeoRef, MycolAb, SCI, SCOPUS, W07, Z01.
Published by: Sociedade Brasileira de Paleontologia, Avenida Pasteur 404, Rio de Janeiro, Brazil. http://acd.ufrj.br/geologia/sbp/sbp2.htm. Ed. Maria Claudia Malabarba.

560 ESP ISSN 0556-655X
QE719 CODEN: RTEMB5
REVISTA ESPANOLA DE MICROPALEONTOLOGIA. Text in Spanish. 1969. 3/yr. EUR 59 domestic; EUR 72 foreign (effective 2009). adv. bk.rev. **Document type:** *Journal, Academic/Scholarly.*
Indexed: A22, B25, BIOSIS Prev, GeoRef, IBR, IBZ, IECT, MycolAb, RefZh, SpeleolAb, Z01.
—BLDSC (7854.110000), IE, Infotrieve, Ingenta, INIST, Linda Hall. **CCC.**
Published by: Ministerio de Ciencia e Innovacion, Instituto Geologico y Minero de Espana, Rios Rosas 23, Madrid, 28003, Spain. TEL 34-91-3495819, FAX 34-91-3495830, publicaciones@igme.es, http://www.igme.es/internet/principal.asp. Ed. Isabel Rabano. Circ: 700.

560 ESP ISSN 0213-6937
QE755.S6 CODEN: RESAE5
➤ **REVISTA ESPANOLA DE PALEONTOLOGIA.** Text in Spanish, English. 1986. s-a. bk.rev. 150 p./no.; **Document type:** *Journal, Academic/Scholarly.* **Description:** Publishes original papers in any paleontological field of research. Contributions related to Spain and neighboring areas are favored.
Indexed: B25, BIOSIS Prev, GeoRef, IECT, MycolAb, P30, SpeleolAb, Z01.
—BLDSC (7854.170000). **CCC.**
Published by: Sociedad Espanola de Paleontologia, C Jose Gutierrez Abascal, 2, Madrid, 28006, Spain.

563 FRA ISSN 0035-1598
QE701 CODEN: RMCPAM
➤ **REVUE DE MICROPALEONTOLOGIE.** Text in English, French. 1958. 4/yr. EUR 199 in Europe to institutions; EUR 182.17 in France to institutions; JPY 26,500 in Japan to institutions; USD 259 elsewhere to institutions (effective 2012). adv. bk.rev. bibl.; charts; illus.
Document type: *Journal, Academic/Scholarly.* **Description:** Publishes original scientific contributions, review papers, short communications, and congress and symposium reports dealing with any micropaleontological theme.
Related titles: Online - full text ed.: ISSN 1873-4413 (from IngentaConnect, ScienceDirect).
Indexed: A22, A26, B21, B25, BIOSIS Prev, BrGeoL, CA, GEOBASE, GeoRef, I05, IBR, IBZ, MycolAb, PetrolAb, SCOPUS, SpeleolAb, T02, Z01.
—BLDSC (7933.500000), IE, Ingenta, INIST, Linda Hall, PADDS. **CCC.**
Published by: Elsevier Masson (Subsidiary of: Elsevier Health Sciences), 62 Rue Camille Desmoulins, Issy les Moulineaux, Cedex 92442, France. TEL 33-1-71165500, FAX 33-1-71165600, infos@elsevier-masson.fr. Ed. Taniel Danelian. Circ: 500.

➤ **REVUE DE PALEOBIOLOGIE.** *see* EARTH SCIENCES—Geology

560.17 ITA ISSN 0035-6883
QE701 CODEN: RPLSAT
➤ **RIVISTA ITALIANA DI PALEONTOLOGIA E STRATIGRAFIA.** Text in English; Abstracts in English, Italian. 1895. q. EUR 200 (effective 2010). bk.rev. abstr.; bibl.; charts; illus.; maps. index, cum.index. back issues avail. **Document type:** *Journal, Academic/Scholarly.*
Description: Articles dealing with palaeontology and stratigraphy aimed at scholars and university students as well as amateurs.
Formerly (until 1946): Rivista Italiana di Paleontologia (0393-8689)
Related titles: Online - full text ed.: ISSN 2039-4942.
Indexed: B25, BIOSIS Prev, CurCont, GEOBASE, GeoRef, IBR, IBZ, MycolAb, PetrolAb, SCI, SCOPUS, SpeleolAb, W07, Z01.
—BLDSC (7987.480000), IE, Ingenta, INIST, PADDS.
Published by: Universita degli Studi di Milano, Dipartimento di Scienze della Terra, Via Luigi Mangiagalli, 34, Milan, MI 20133, Italy. TEL 39-2-23698232, FAX 39-2-70638261, renesto@mailserver.unimi.it, http://www.gp.terra.unimi.it/rivista.html. Ed., R&P Maurizio Gaetani TEL 39-2-23698229.

➤ **ROCKY MOUNTAIN GEOLOGY.** *see* EARTH SCIENCES—Geology

560 ROM ISSN 1220-5656
QE755.R6
ROMANIAN JOURNAL OF PALEONTOLOGY. Text in English. 1910. a. USD 35. **Document type:** *Journal, Academic/Scholarly.*
Former titles (until 1991): Institutul de Geologie si Geofizica. Dari de Seama ale Sedintelor. 3. Paleontologie (0254-7295); (until 1974): Institutul Geologie. Dari de Seama ale Sedintelor. 3. Paleontologie (1010-9439); Supersedes in part (in 1967): Comitetul de Stat al Geologiei. Dari de Seama ale Sedintelor (0366-9726)
Indexed: GeoRef, SpeleolAb.
—INIST, Linda Hall.
Published by: Institutul Geologic al Romaniei, Str. Caransebes 1, Bucharest, 78344, Romania. TEL 40-1-2242091, FAX 40-1-2240404. Ed. Gheorghe Udubasa. R&P Serban Veliciu TEL 40-1-2242093. Circ: 550.

560 USA ISSN 0731-759X
CODEN: SERSDU
S E P M REPRINT SERIES. Text in English. 1976. irreg., latest 1990. price varies. back issues avail. **Document type:** *Monographic series, Academic/Scholarly.*
Indexed: GeoRef.
—**CCC.**
Published by: Society of Economic Paleontologists and Mineralogists, 4111 S Darlington, Ste 100, Tulsa, OK 74135. TEL 918-610-3361, 800-865-9765, FAX 918-621-1685, jcurtis@sepm.org.

560 CZE ISSN 0036-5297
QE755.C95 CODEN: SGPABC
➤ **SBORNIK GEOLOGICKYCH VED: PALEONTOLOGIE/JOURNAL OF GEOLOGICAL SCIENCES: PALEONTOLOGY.** Text in English, French, German; Summaries in Czech. 1949. irreg., latest vol.34, 1998. price varies. charts; illus. 200 p./no. 2 cols./p.; back issues avail. **Document type:** *Journal, Academic/Scholarly.* **Description:** Papers by Czech and foreign specialists on paleontology and biostratigraphy.
Indexed: GeoRef, SCOPUS, SpeleolAb.
—INIST, Linda Hall.
Published by: Ceska Geologicka Sluzba/Czech Geological Survey, Klarov 3, Prague, 11821, Czech Republic. TEL 420-2-57089439, http://www.geology.cz. Ed. Ivo Chlupac. Circ: 600.

576 ESP ISSN 1135-0105
SCRIPTA MUSEI GEOLOGICI SEMINARII BARCINONENSIS. Text in Spanish. 193?. irreg. back issues avail. **Document type:** *Journal, Academic/Scholarly.*
Formerly (unitl 1993): Museo Geologico del Seminario de Barcelona. Trabajos (1135-0091)
Indexed: GeoRef, IECT, SpeleolAb, Z01.
Published by: Museo Geologico Seminario de Barcelona, Diputacio, 231, Barcelona, 08007, Spain. TEL 34-93-4541600, FAX 34-93-4525538. Ed. Sebastian C Calzada.

560 ZAF
SIDNEY HAUGHTON MEMORIAL LECTURES. Text in English. 1984. biennial. price varies. illus. back issues avail. **Document type:** *Monographic series, Academic/Scholarly.* **Description:** Publishes lectures delivered by invited speakers. Honors Sidney Haughton and his contribution to palaeontology and geology of southern Africa.
Indexed: SpeleolAb.
Published by: South African Museum, PO Box 61, Cape Town, 8000, South Africa. TEL 27-21-4243330, FAX 27-21-4246716. Ed. Elizabeth Louw. R&P Elizabeth Lou. Circ: 450 (controlled).

560 USA ISSN 0081-0266
QE701 CODEN: SPBYA8
SMITHSONIAN CONTRIBUTIONS TO PALEOBIOLOGY. Text in English. 1969. irreg., latest vol.94, 2002. price varies. back issues avail.; reprints avail. **Document type:** *Monographic series, Academic/Scholarly.*
Related titles: Online - full text ed.: ISSN 1943-6688.
Indexed: A29, AESIS, ASFA, B20, B21, B25, BIOSIS Prev, ESPM, GeoRef, I10, MycolAb, RefZh, SpeleolAb, VirolAbstr, WildRev, Z01.
—BLDSC (8311.610000), INIST, Linda Hall. **CCC.**
Published by: Smithsonian Institution Press, SI Bldg, Rm 153, MRC 010, PO Box 37012, Washington, DC 20013. TEL 202-633-3017, FAX 202-633-6877, schol.press@si.edu, http://www.si.edu.

560 ITA ISSN 0375-7633
QE755.I8 CODEN: BSPIAY
SOCIETA PALEONTOLOGICA ITALIANA. BOLLETTINO. Text in English, Italian. 1960. 3/yr. free to members (effective 2008). cum.index: 1960-1983. **Document type:** *Bulletin, Consumer.*
Indexed: A22, B25, BIOSIS Prev, GEOBASE, GeoRef, MycolAb, RefZh, SCI, SCOPUS, SpeleolAb, W07, Z01.
—BLDSC (2231.700000), IE, Ingenta, INIST, Linda Hall.
Published by: (Consiglio Nazionale delle Ricerche (C N R)/Italian National Research Council), Societa Paleontologica Italiana, Civico Museo di Storia Naturale, Corso Venezia 55, Milan, Italy. TEL 39-02-88463280, http://www.spi.unimo.it. Circ: 700.

560 ITA ISSN 2037-4267
SOCIETA PALEONTOLOGICA ITALIANA. RENDICONTI. Text in Multiple languages. 2002. irreg. **Document type:** *Monographic series, Academic/Scholarly.*
Published by: Societa Paleontologica Italiana, Civico Museo di Storia Naturale, Corso Venezia 55, Milan, Italy. TEL 39-02-88463280, http://www.spi.unimo.it.

560 ESP ISSN 1135-7665
SOCIETAT PALEONTOLOGICA D'ELX. SECCION PALEONTOLOGICA. REVISTA. Text in Spanish, Catalan. 1995. a.
Document type: *Monographic series, Academic/Scholarly.*
Indexed: GeoRef, IECT, Z01.
Published by: Societat Paleontologica d'Elx, Llano de San Jose, P1-134, Elche, Alicante 03293, Spain.

596 ESP ISSN 1576-9550
SOCIETAT PALEONTOLOGICA D'ELX. SECCION VERTEBRADOS ACTUALES. REVISTA. Text in Multiple languages. 2000. irreg.
Document type: *Monographic series, Academic/Scholarly.*
Indexed: IECT, Z01.
Published by: Societat Paleontologica d'Elx, Llano de San Jose, P1-134, Elche, Alicante 03293, Spain. TEL 34-965-434078.

560 USA ISSN 1062-161X
SOCIETY OF VERTEBRATE PALEONTOLOGY MEMOIR. Text in English. 1991. irreg., latest 2007. USD 85 per issue (effective 2009). back issues avail. **Document type:** *Monographic series.*
Related titles: ◆ Supplement to: Journal of Vertebrate Paleontology. ISSN 0272-4634.
Indexed: A01, GeoRef, T02.
—Linda Hall. **CCC.**
Published by: Society of Vertebrate Paleontology, 111 Deer Lake Rd, Ste 100, Deerfield, IL 60015 . TEL 847-480-9095, FAX 847-480-9282, svp@vertpaleo.org. Ed. Nicholas C Fraser TEL 131-247-4007.

560 USA
QE701 CODEN: SVPNAJ
SOCIETY OF VERTEBRATE PALEONTOLOGY. NEWS BULLETIN (ONLINE). Abbreviated title: S V P News Bulletin. Text in English. 1941. s-a. free to members (effective 2009). adv. back issues avail.
Document type: *Bulletin, Trade.* **Description:** Contains minutes of annual business meetings, news from members around the world, address changes, new members, job advertisements, and obituaries.
Formerly (until 200?): Society of Vertebrate Paleontology. News Bulletin (Print) (0096-9117)
Media: Online - full text.
Indexed: GeoRef, SpeleolAb.
—Linda Hall.
Published by: Society of Vertebrate Paleontology, 111 Deer Lake Rd, Ste 100, Deerfield, IL 60015 . TEL 847-480-9095, FAX 847-480-9282, svp@vertpaleo.org. Ed. David S Berman. Adv. contact Brent H Breithaupt TEL 307-766-4218.

560 USA ISSN 0160-4937
QE701
SOUTHERN CALIFORNIA PALEONTOLOGICAL SOCIETY. BULLETIN. Text in English. bi-m.
Indexed: GeoRef, Z01.
Published by: Southern California Paleontological Society, 2608 El Dorado Street, Torrance, CA 90503 . scpaleo@aol.com, http://members.aol.com/scpaleo/.

560 GBR ISSN 0038-6804
CODEN: SPPAB7
➤ **SPECIAL PAPERS IN PALAEONTOLOGY.** Text in English. 1967. 2/yr. GBP 80 to institutions; GBP 25 to students (effective 2009). back issues avail. **Document type:** *Monographic series, Academic/Scholarly.*
Related titles: ◆ Supplement to: Palaeontology. ISSN 0031-0239.
Indexed: AESIS, BIOSIS Prev, GeoRef, MycolAb, SCI, SCOPUS, SpeleolAb, W07, Z01.
—BLDSC (8370.500000), IE, Ingenta. **CCC.**
Published by: (Palaeontological Association), Wiley-Blackwell Publishing Ltd. (Subsidiary of: John Wiley & Sons, Inc.), 9600 Garsington Rd, Oxford, OX4 2DQ, United Kingdom. TEL 44-1865-776868, FAX 44-1865-714591, customerservices@blackwellpublishing.com, http://www.wiley.com/. Ed. David J Batten.

➤ **SPELEOLOGICAL SOCIETY OF JAPAN. JOURNAL.** *see* EARTH SCIENCES

560 ITA ISSN 0587-1239
QE736
STUDI E RICERCHE SUI GIACIMENTI TERZIARI DI BOLCA. Text and summaries in English, French, Italian. 1969. irreg., latest vol.8, 1999. back issues avail. **Document type:** *Monographic series, Academic/Scholarly.*
Indexed: GeoRef, RefZh, SpeleolAb, Z01.
—INIST.
Published by: Museo Civico di Storia Naturale di Verona, Lungadige Porta Vittoria 9, Verona, VR 37129, Italy. TEL 39-045-8079400, FAX 39-045-8035639, mcsnat@comune.verona.it, http://www.museostorianaturaleverona.it. Circ: 600.

STUDI PER L'ECOLOGIA DEL QUATERNARIO. *see* ANTHROPOLOGY

560 NLD ISSN 1876-6129
STUIFMAIL. Text in English, Dutch. 200?. q. **Document type:** *Magazine, Trade.*
Media: Online - full text.
Published by: Paleobotanisch Palynologisch Genootschap Utrecht/Palaeobotanical Palynological Society of Utrecht, Budapestlaan 4, Utrecht, 3584 CD, Netherlands. TEL 31-30-2532629, FAX 31-30-2535096, http://www.bio.uu.nl/~palaeo/ppgu.

560 CHE ISSN 1664-2376
QE701 CODEN: SPAAAX
➤ **SWISS JOURNAL OF PALEONTOLOGY/MEMOIRES SUISSE DE PALEONTOLOGIE.** Text in English, French, German, Italian. 1874. s-a. EUR 298, USD 367 combined subscription to institutions (print & online eds.) (effective 2012). index. **Document type:** *Journal, Academic/Scholarly.*
Formerly (until 2011): Schweizerische Palaeontologische Abhandlungen (0080-7389)
Related titles: Online - full text ed.: ISSN 1664-2384.
Indexed: B25, BIOSIS Prev, GeoRef, MycolAb, SpeleolAb, Z01.
—INIST, Linda Hall. **CCC.**
Published by: (Kommission der Schweizerischen Palaeontologischen Abhandlungen), Birkhaeuser Verlag AG (Subsidiary of: Springer Science+Business Media), Viaduktstr 42, Postfach 133, Basel, 4051, Switzerland. TEL 41-61-2050707, FAX 41-61-2050799, info@birkhauser.ch, http://www.birkhauser.ch. Ed. L Costeur.

P

560 USA ISSN 0738-2464
TEXAS PALEONTOLOGY SERIES. Text in English. 1977. irreg., latest vol.10. price varies. back issues avail. **Document type:** *Monographic series, Academic/Scholarly.*
Related titles: CD-ROM ed.
Indexed: GeoRef, Z01.
Published by: Houston Gem and Mineral Society, 10805 Brooklet, Houston, TX 77099. TEL 281-530-0942, paleo@hgms.org.

TOHOKU DAIGAKU RIGAKUBU CHISHITSUGAKU KOSEIBUTSUGAKU KYOSHITSU KENKYU HOBUN HOKOKU/ TOHOKU UNIVERSITY. FACULTY OF SCIENCE. INSTITUTE OF GEOLOGY AND PALEONTOLOGY. CONTRIBUTIONS. *see* EARTH SCIENCES—Geology

562 USA
TREATISE ON INVERTEBRATE PALEONTOLOGY. Text in English. 1952. irreg. **Document type:** *Monographic series, Academic/ Scholarly.* **Description:** Presents a comprehensive yet compact statement of knowledge concerning groups of invertebrate fossils. Issued in print both as monographs and chapters.
Related titles: CD-ROM ed.; Online - full text ed.: ISSN 2153-621X. 2010 (Apr.). free (effective 2010); ◆ Special ed(s).: Treatise Online. ISSN 2153-4012.
Published by: University of Kansas, Paleontological Institute, 1475 Jayhawk Blvd, Rm 119, Lawrence, KS 66045. TEL 785-864-3338, paleo@ku.edu, http://paleo.ku.edu/.

560 USA ISSN 2153-4012
▼ ➤ **TREATISE ONLINE.** Text in English. 2011. irreg. **Document type:** *Journal, Academic/Scholarly.*
Media: Online - full text. **Related titles:** ◆ Special ed. of: Treatise on Invertebrate Paleontology.
Published by: University of Kansas, Paleontological Institute, 1475 Jayhawk Blvd, Rm 119, Lawrence, KS 66045. TEL 785-864-3338, paleo@ku.edu, http://paleo.ku.edu/.

560 DEU ISSN 0937-373X
TUEBINGER MIKROPALAEONTOLOGISCHE MITTEILUNGEN. Text in German. 1983. irreg. **Document type:** *Monographic series, Academic/Scholarly.*
Indexed: GeoRef, Z01.
Published by: Eberhard Karls Universitaet Tuebingen, Institut fuer Geowissenschaften, Sigwartstr 10, Tuebingen, 72076, Germany. TEL 49-7071-2972489, FAX 49-7071-295727, gregor.markl@uni-tuebingen.de, http://www.uni-tuebingen.de/geo/ifg/.

560 ESP ISSN 0214-2023
UNIVERSIDAD DE ZARAGOZA. MUSEO PALEONTOLOGICO. MEMORIAS. Text in Spanish. 1986. a. back issues avail. **Document type:** *Monographic series, Academic/Scholarly.*
Indexed: GeoRef, Z01.
Published by: Universidad de Zaragoza, Museo Paleontologico, C. Pedro Cerbuna, 12, Zaragoza, 50009, Spain. TEL 34-976-762122, mpznavas@unizar.es, http://museo-paleo.unizar.es/.

560 ITA ISSN 0071-4542
UNIVERSITA DI FERRARA. ANNALI. SEZIONE 15: PALEONTOLOGIA UMANA E PALETNOLOGIA. Text and summaries in English, French, Italian. 1936. a. price varies. **Document type:** *Journal, Academic/ Scholarly.*
Formerly (until19??): Universita degli Studi di Ferrara. Istituto di Geologia, Paleontologia e Paletnologia Umana. Annali. Sezione 15. Paleontologia Umana e Paleontologia; Which superseded in part (in 1951): Universita di Ferrara. Annali (0365-7833)
Indexed: GeoRef, SpeleolAb.
—Linda Hall.
Published by: Universita degli Studi di Ferrara, Via Savonarola 9, Ferrara, 44100, Italy. TEL 39-0532-293111, FAX 39-0532-293031, http://www.unife.it. Circ: 450.

UNIVERSITAET HAMBURG. GEOLOGISCH-PALAEONTOLOGISCHES INSTITUT. MITTEILUNGEN (ONLINE). *see* EARTH SCIENCES—Geology

560 USA ISSN 0148-3838
QE701 CODEN: PPUMD3
➤ **UNIVERSITY OF MICHIGAN. MUSEUM OF PALEONTOLOGY. PAPERS ON PALEONTOLOGY.** Text in English. 1972. irreg., latest vol.34, 2004. price varies. **Document type:** *Monographic series, Academic/Scholarly.*
Indexed: B25, BIOSIS Prev, GeoRef, MycolAb, SpeleolAb, Z01.
—Linda Hall.
Published by: University of Michigan, Museum of Paleontology, 1109 Geddes Ave, Ann Arbor, MI 48109. TEL 734-764-0489, FAX 734-936-1380.

➤ **UNIVERSITY OF NEBRASKA STATE MUSEUM. BULLETIN.** *see* BIOLOGY

566 USA ISSN 1877-9077
VERTEBRATE PALEOBIOLOGY AND PALEOANTHROPOLOGY. Text in English. 1998. irreg., latest 2010. price varies. illus. back issues avail. **Document type:** *Monographic series, Academic/Scholarly.* **Description:** Examines all aspects of vertebrate paleontology, with topics including comparative morphology, phylogeny reconstruction, historical biogeography, paleoecology, and biostratigraphy.
Formerly: Advances in Vertebrate Paleobiology
Published by: Springer New York LLC (Subsidiary of: Springer Science+Business Media), 233 Spring St, New York, NY 10013. TEL 212-460-1500, FAX 212-460-1575, service-ny@springer.com. Eds. Eric Delson TEL 212-769-5992, Eric Sargis.

560 RUS
QE701 CODEN: EVPOA4
VSEROSSIISKOE PALEONLOLOGICESKOE OBSHCHESTVO. EZHEGODNIK. Text in Russian. 1916. irreg.
Former titles (until 1992): Vsesouznoe Paleonlologiceskoe Obshchestvo. Ezhegodnik (0201-9280); (until 1953): Vserossiiskoe Paleonlologiceskoe Obshchestvo. Ezhegodnik (1561-6576); (until 1931): Russkoe Paleonlologiceskoe Obshchestvo. Ezhegodnik (1561-6568)
Indexed: GeoRef.
—INIST, Linda Hall. **CCC.**
Published by: Izdatel'skii Dom Sankt-Peterburgskogo Gosudarstvennogo Universiteta, V.O., 6-ya liniya, dom 11/21, komn 319, St Petersburg, 199004, Russian Federation. TEL 7-812-3252604, press@unipress.ru, http://www.unipress.ru.

560 JPN ISSN 0387-5784
YAMAGUCHI KEIBINGU KURABU KAIHO/YAMAGUCHI CAVING CLUB. REPORT. Text in Japanese. a.
Published by: Yamaguchi Keibingu Kurabu/Yamaguchi Caving Club, Akiyoshidai Kagaku Hakubutsukan, Akiyoshi, Mine-gun, Shuho-cho, Yamaguchi-ken 754-0511, Japan.

560 551 DEU ISSN 1612-412X
QE701 CODEN: BSPGBT
➤ **ZITTELIANA. REIHE A. MITTEILUNGEN DER BAYERISCHEN STAATSSAMMLUNG FUR PALAEONTOLOGIE UND GEOLOGIE.** Text and summaries in English, German. 1961. a. **Document type:** *Proceedings, Academic/Scholarly.*
Formerly (until 2003): Bayerische Staatssammlung fuer Palaeontologie und Historische Geologie. Mitteilungen (0077-2070)
Indexed: B25, BIOSIS Prev, GEOBASE, GeoRef, IBR, IBZ, MycolAb, RefZh, SCOPUS, SpeleolAb, Z01.
—INIST, Linda Hall.
Published by: Bayerische Staatssammlung fuer Palaeontologie und Geologie, Richard-Wagner-Str 10, Munich, 80333, Germany. TEL 49-89-21806630, FAX 49-89-21806601, pal.biblio@lrz.uni-muenchen.de, http://www.palmuc.de/staatssammlung/.

560 551 DEU ISSN 1612-4138
QE701 CODEN: ZTLAAN
ZITTELIANA. REIHE B: ABHANDLUNGEN DER BAYERISCHEN STAATSSAMMLUNG FUR PALAEONTOLOGIE UND GEOLOGIE. Text in German. 1969. irreg., latest vol.26, 2005. price varies. **Document type:** *Proceedings, Academic/Scholarly.*
Formerly (until 2003): Zitteliana (0373-9627)
Indexed: B25, BIOSIS Prev, GEOBASE, GeoRef, MycolAb, RefZh, SCOPUS, SpeleolAb, Z01.
—INIST, Linda Hall. **CCC.**
Published by: Bayerische Staatssammlung fuer Palaeontologie und Geologie, Richard-Wagner-Str 10, Munich, 80333, Germany. TEL 49-89-21806630, FAX 49-89-21806601, pal.biblio@lrz.uni-muenchen.de, http://www.palmuc.de/staatssammlung/.

PALEONTOLOGY—Abstracting, Bibliographies, Statistics

016.56 GBR ISSN 0969-1111
BIBLIOGRAPHY OF EUROPEAN PALAEOBOTANY & PALYNOLOGY. Text in English. 1976. biennial. bibl. **Document type:** *Bibliography.* **Description:** Reports on work in progress and recently published works on palaeobotany and palynology in Europe.
Formerly (until 1990): Report on British Palaeobotany and Palynology (0266-4755)
Indexed: GeoRef, SpeleolAb.
Published by: National Museum Wales/Amgueddfa Genedlaethol Cymru, Cathays Park, Cardiff, CF10 3NP, United Kingdom. TEL 44-29-20397951, FAX 44-29-20573321, biosyb@nmgw.ac.uk, http://www.nmgw.ac.uk.

560 JPN
NIHON KOSEIBUTSU GAKKAI NENKAI KOEN YOKOSHU/ PALAEONTOLOGICAL SOCIETY OF JAPAN. ABSTRACTS OF THE ANNUAL MEETING. Text in English, Japanese. a. **Document type:** *Abstract/Index.*
Published by: Nihon Kodansei Gakkai/Japan Society for Photoelasticity, Nihon Gakkai Jimu Senta, 16-9 Honkomagome 5-chome, Bunkyo-ku, Tokyo, 113-0021, Japan.

016.56 RUS ISSN 0202-9421
REFERATIVNYI ZHURNAL. STRATIGRAFIYA. PALEONTOLOGIYA; vypusk svodnogo toma. Text in Russian. m. USD 500.40 foreign (effective 2011). **Document type:** *Journal, Abstract/Index.*
Related titles: CD-ROM ed.; Online - full text ed.
—East View.
Published by: VINITI RAN, ul Usievicha 20, Moscow, 125190, Russian Federation. TEL 7-499-1526113, FAX 7-499-9430060, dir@viniti.ru, http://www.viniti.ru. **Dist. by:** Informnauka Ltd., Ul Usievicha 20, Moscow 125190, Russian Federation. alfimov@viniti.ru.

560 016 DEU ISSN 0044-4189
CODEN: ZGPGA4
ZENTRALBLATT FUER GEOLOGIE UND PALAEONTOLOGIE. TEIL II: PALAEONTOLOGIE. Text in German. 1807. irreg. (5-7/yr.). USD 275 per issue (effective 2011). adv. bk.rev. abstr.; bibl.; illus. index. reprints avail. **Document type:** *Journal, Academic/Scholarly.*
Indexed: ChemAb, GeoRef, IBR, IBZ, SpeleolAb.
—Linda Hall. **CCC.**
Published by: E. Schweizerbart'sche Verlagsbuchhandlung, Johannesstr 3A, Stuttgart, 70176, Germany. TEL 49-711-3514560, FAX 49-711-35145699, order@schweizerbart.de. Eds. C. Schmitt-Riegraf, W. Riegraf.

PAPER AND PULP

see also FORESTS AND FORESTRY—Lumber And Wood ; PACKAGING

A P A - JOURNAL. HOLZ - PAPIER. *see* FORESTS AND FORESTRY—Lumber And Wood

676 DEU ISSN 0002-5917
CODEN: AAPRDT
A P R. (Allgemeine Papier-Rundschau) Text in German. 1966. m. EUR 190 domestic; EUR 220 foreign; EUR 6 newsstand/cover (effective 2007). adv. bk.rev. abstr.; bibl.; charts; illus.; pat.; stat. index. **Document type:** *Magazine, Trade.*
Formed by the merger of (1947-1966): A P R - Allgemeine Papier-Rundschau. Technische Ausgabe (0343-5415); (1947-1966): A P R - Allgemeine Papier-Rundschau. M - Marketing Papier, Papierwaren (0171-1369); Both of which superseded in part (in 1965): A P R - Allgemeine Papier-Rundschau (0343-5407); Which was formerly (until 1959): Allgemeine Papier-Rundschau (0342-989X); (until 1949): Neue Deutsche Papier-Zeitung (0369-3619); (until 1948): Deutsche Papier-Zeitung (0366-9548)
Related titles: Online - full text ed.
Indexed: A22, ABIPC, B03, IPackAb, P&BA, PROMT, PST, RefZh, SCOPUS.
—BLDSC (0791.900000), CASDDS, IE, Ingenta. **CCC.**
Published by: P. Keppler Verlag GmbH und Co. KG, Industriestr 2, Heusenstamm, 63150, Germany. TEL 49-6104-6060, FAX 49-6104-606333, info@kepplermediengruppe.de, http://www.kepplermediengruppe.de. Ed. Gerhard Brucker. Pub. Eckhart Thomas. Adv. contact Marion Apitz. B&W page EUR 2,345, color page EUR 3,725; trim 188 x 257. Circ: 4,984 (paid and controlled).

676.1 MEX
A T C P. Text in Spanish. 1960. bi-m. MXN 1,012; USD 115 foreign. adv. **Description:** Features news, announcements, reports, international events on topics related to pulp, cellulose, and paper industry.
Published by: G S A de C.V., Av. Insurgentes Sur No. 3493, Poseidon No. 4-504, Mexico City, DF 14020, Mexico. TEL 52-5-665-0368, FAX 52-5-665-0368. Ed., Adv. contact Octavio Tirado. color page USD 1,000; trim 270 x 210. Circ: 2,500 (controlled).

676 MEX
A T C P REVISTA. Text in Spanish; Summaries in English. 1960. bi-m. MXN 64.50, USD 45 (effective 1998). adv. bk.rev. bibl.; charts; illus.; stat.; tr.lit. back issues avail. **Document type:** *Trade.* **Description:** Information on the technology, manufacture and business administration of the pulp and paper trade industry worldwide.
Related titles: Microform ed.
Indexed: ABIPC.
Published by: (Asociacion Mexicana de Tecnicos de las Industrias de la Celulosa y del Papel, A.C.), Gas de C.V., Av. Insurgentes No. 3493, Poseidon No. 504, Mexico City, DF 14020, Mexico. TEL 52-5-665-0368, FAX 52-5-665-0368, TELEX 1773608 CNCPME. Ed. Virgilio Gonzalez. Pub., Adv. contact Octavio Tirado. B&W page USD 600, color page USD 1,000. Circ: 2,530.

676 FRA ISSN 0997-7554
CODEN: ATIPBH
A T I P. Text in French. 1947. irreg. adv. bk.rev. charts; illus. **Document type:** *Journal, Trade.* **Description:** Disseminates information on innovations and new technologies, research and applications developed in France, in Europe and throughout the world in relation to the pulp, paper, and allied industries.
Former titles (until 1989): Revue A T I P (0750-7666); (until 1982): A T I P (0004-5896); (until 1966): Association Technique de l'Industrie Papetiere. Bulletin (0403-7383)
Indexed: ABIPC, CISA, CPEI, ChemAb, ChemTitl, EngInd, P&BA, P31, RefZh, SCOPUS.
—BLDSC (7874.723000), CASDDS, IE, Ingenta, INIST. **CCC.**
Published by: Association Technique de l'Industrie Papetiere, 154 bd. Haussmann, Paris, 75008, France. TEL 33-1-45621191, FAX 33-1-45635309, atip@wanadoo.fr. Ed. E Devos. Circ: 1,850 (controlled).

676 ARG ISSN 1851-5053
AFCP NOTICIAS. Text in Spanish. 2007. s-m.
Media: E-mail.
Published by: Asociacion de Fabricantes de Celulosa y Papel, Ave Belgrano 2852, Buenos Aires, C1209AAN, Argentina. TEL 54-11-49310051, FAX 54-11-49310053, afcpnoticias@afcparg.org.ar, http://www.afcparg.org.ar/. Ed. Hernan Murua.

676.2 CHN
ALMANAC OF CHINA'S PAPER INDUSTRY. Text in Chinese; Summaries in English. 1986. triennial. CNY 150; USD 120 foreign. adv. bk.rev. back issues avail. **Document type:** *Directory.* **Description:** An up-to-date factbook on Chinese paper industry. Covers production and construction, market trends, technological advances, fibrous and chemical materials, equipments and accessories, and more.
Related titles: Fax ed.; Online - full text ed.
Published by: China Technical Association of the Paper Industry, 12 Guanghua Rd, Beijing, 100020, China. TEL 86-10-658-626-53. Ed. Huang Run Bin. R&P Yiji Yu. Adv. contact Li Wan. Circ: 6,500 (paid).

676 USA
AMERICAN FOREST & PAPER ASSOCIATION. CAPACITY SURVEY. Text in English. 1958. a., latest 2008. **Document type:** *Report, Trade.*
Formerly: American Paper Institute. Capacity Survey
Related titles: Microfiche ed.: (from CIS).
Indexed: SRI.
Published by: American Forest & Paper Association, 1111 19th St, NW, Ste 800, Washington, DC 20036. TEL 202-463-2700, 800-878-8878, info@afandpa.org, http://www.afandpa.org.

676 FRA ISSN 1274-4662
ANNUAIRE DU PAPIER. Text in French. 1975. a. adv. **Document type:** *Directory.* **Description:** Identifies participants, partners and companies in all involved sectors of activity.
Former titles (until 1994): Annuaire des 3000 Grandes Entreprises Europeennes de la Filiere Papier (1242-2398); (until 1992): Annuaire Papier, Carton et Cellulose (1147-8373); (until 1988): Annuaire du Papier (0337-4971)
Published by: Michel Burton Communication (M B C), 16 Rue Saint Fiacre, Paris, 75002, France. TEL 33-1-42365102, FAX 33-1-42338324, diffusion@groupembc.com, http://www.pnpapetier.com/. Circ: 3,000.

ANNUAL BOOK OF A S T M STANDARDS. VOLUME 15.09 PAPER; BUSINESS IMAGING PRODUCTS. (American Society for Testing and Materials) *see* ENGINEERING—Engineering Mechanics And Materials

676 USA
ANNUAL PROFITABILITY REPORT: A BENCHMARK STUDY OF PAPER & PLASTICS WHOLESALE PERFORMANCE. Text in English. 1935. a. USD 350. charts; stat.
Formerly: Paper Merchant Performance
Indexed: SRI.
Published by: National Paper Trade Association, Inc., 500 Bi-County Blvd., Ste. 200E, Farmingdale, NY 11735. TEL 631-777-2223, 800-355-6785, FAX 631-777-2224, http://www.gonpta.com/. Ed. Frank Fell. Circ: 2,500.

676.05 AUS ISSN 1443-5454
APPITA. ANNUAL CONFERENCE PROCEEDINGS. Text in English. 19??. a. AUD 135 per vol. domestic; AUD 148 per vol. in New Zealand; AUD 156 per vol. in Asia; AUD 164 per vol. in N. America & Middle East; AUD 170 per vol. in Europe, Africa & Latin America (effective 2008). **Document type:** *Proceedings, Academic/Scholarly.* **Description:** Provides technical papers presented at the Annual Conference conducted by the Australian Pulp and Paper Industry Technical Association.

Formerly (until 1998): Appita. Annual General Conference Proceedings (1443-5446)
Related titles: CD-ROM ed.: AUD 135 per vol. domestic; AUD 130.50 per vol. in New Zealand; AUD 131.50 per vol. in Asia; AUD 132.50 per vol. in North America & Middle East; AUD 133.50 per vol. in Europe, Africa & Latin America (effective 2008).
Indexed: Englnd, P31, SCOPUS.
—**CCC.**
Published by: Appita, Inc., Ste 47 Level 1, Carlton Clocktower, 255 Drummond St, Carlton, VIC 3053, Australia. TEL 61-3-93472377, FAX 61-3-93481206, info@appita.com.au.

676 AUS ISSN 1038-6807 CODEN: APJOES
➤ **APPITA JOURNAL.** Text in English. 1957. bi-m. AUD 155 (effective 2009). adv. bk.rev. charts; illus. Index. 80 p./no.; back issues avail.; reprints avail. **Document type:** *Journal, Academic/Scholarly.* **Description:** Covers industry news, articles, peer-reviewed papers, technical notes, supplier notes, conference calendar, section reports, membership information and corporate news and industry developments related to Australian paper and pulp industry.
Formerly (until 1986): A P P I T A (0365-5660); Which was formed by the merger of (1947-1956): Australian Pulp and Paper Industry Technical Association. Proceedings (0365-5334); Australian Pulp and Paper Industry Technical Association. Newsletter
Related titles: Microform ed.: (from PQC); Online - full text ed.
Indexed: A20, A22, A32, A37, ABIPC, ABIX, AgrForAb, BA, C25, C30, CABA, CEA, CEABA, CIN, CPEI, ChemAb, ChemTitl, CurCont, E11, E12, EIA, ESPM, EnerInd, Englnd, F08, F11, F12, H16, I11, ISR, M&MA, P&BA, P31, PollutAb, R11, R12, S12, S13, S16, SCI, SCOPUS, SWRA, T04, TCEA, W07, W11.
—BLDSC (1570.303000), CASDDS, IE, Infotrieve, Ingenta, INIST, Linda Hall.
Published by: Appita, Inc., Ste 47 Level 1, Carlton Clocktower, 255 Drummond St, Carlton, VIC 3053, Australia. TEL 61-3-93472377, FAX 61-3-93481206, info@appita.com.au. Ed., R&P Ralph S Coghill. Adv. contact Jan Henderson TEL 61-3-97230922. B&W page AUD 1,378, color page AUD 2,704; 184 x 265. Circ: 1,800.

676 COL ISSN 0122-9052
ASOCIACION COLOMBIANA DE TECNICOS DE LA INDUSTRIA DE LA PULPA, PAPEL Y CARTON. REVISTA. Text in Spanish. 1987. q. **Document type:** *Magazine, Trade.*
Published by: Asociacion Colombiana de Tecnicos de la Industria de la Pulpa, Papel y Carton (A C O T E P A C), Calle 94 No 25-70, Medellin, Colombia. TEL 57-6-3200392, FAX 57-6-3200392, http://www.acotepacolombia.com.

676.2 AUS ISSN 1449-7018
AUSTRALIAN PAPER CRAFTS; easy to follow instructions. Text in English. 2000. m. AUD 8.95 per issue domestic; USD 8.95 per issue foreign (effective 2008). adv. back issues avail. **Document type:** *Magazine, Trade.* **Description:** Covers projects from beginner to advanced and a masterclass to extend skills, Australian paper crafts features inspirational projects for every paper crafter.
Formerly (until 2003): Australian Paper Arts (1444-2671)
Published by: Creative Living Publications Pty. Ltd., PO Box 645, Rozelle, NSW 2039, Australia. TEL 61-2-95559322, FAX 61-2-95556188, info@creativelivingmedia.com.au, http://www.creativelivingmedia.com.au. Pub. Deborah Segaert. adv.: color page AUD 1,595; trim 210 x 275.

B C N; fortnightly newsletter serving the European corrugated & folding carton industry. (Board Converting News) *see* PACKAGING

634.9 676 USA
B C NEWS. Text in English. 1986. bi-m. free to qualified personnel. **Document type:** *Newsletter.* **Description:** Provides news and information for employees and retirees of Boise Cascade Corporation.
Former titles (until 1992): Boise Cascade Insight; Boise Cascade Quarterly
Published by: Boise Cascade Corporation, 1111 W Jefferson St, Box 50, Boise, ID 83728-0001. TEL 208-384-7294, FAX 208-384-7224. Ed. Ralph Poore. Circ: 25,000 (controlled).

BERITA SELULOSA. *see* FORESTS AND FORESTRY

676 SWE ISSN 1652-6503
BEYOND; science, research, application. Text in English. 2004. q. free (effective 2009). **Document type:** *Journal, Trade.*
Published by: S T F I - Packforsk/Swedish Pulp and Paper Research Institute - Packforsk, Drottning Kristinas Vaeg 61, PO Box 5604, Stockholm, 11486, Sweden. TEL 46-8-6767000, FAX 46-8-4115518, info@stfi.se, http://www.stfi-packforsk.se. Ed. Veronica Rudheim. Pub. Thomas Johannesson.

676 USA ISSN 1930-2126
TP248.65.L54 CODEN: BIORCM
➤ **BIORESOURCES.** Text in English. 2006. q. free (effective 2011). **Document type:** *Journal, Academic/Scholarly.* **Description:** Covers sustainable manufacture involving lignocellulosic or woody biomass resources, including agricultural residues with emphasis on bioproducts, bioenergy, papermaking technology, new manufacturing materials, composite structures, and chemicals derived from lignocellulosic biomass.
Media: Online - full content.
Indexed: A01, A34, A35, A36, A37, A38, A39, AgBio, Agr, AgrForAb, B23, BA, C25, C27, C29, C30, C33, CA, CABA, CPEI, CurCont, D01, D03, D04, E12, E13, F08, F11, F12, FCA, G11, GH, H16, I11, MSCI, MaizeAb, N02, N03, N04, OR, P32, P33, P40, PHN&I, PN&I, R07, R11, R12, R13, R14, RA&MP, S12, S13, S14, S15, S16, S17, S18, SCI, SCOPUS, SoyAb, T02, TAR, TriticAb, VS, W07, W10, W11.
—BLDSC (2089.495050), IE.
Published by: North Carolina State University, College of Natural Resources, Dept. of Wood & Paper Science, Campus Box 8005, Raleigh, NC 27695-8005. TEL 919-515-7707, FAX 919-515-6302. Eds. Lucian Lucia, Martin Hubbe.

676 DEU
BIRKNER (YEAR) - EUROPEAN AND INTERNATIONAL PAPERWORLD. Text in English, French, German, Italian, Portuguese, Spanish. 2005. a. EUR 274; EUR 440 combined subscription (print & online eds.) (effective 2008). adv. **Document type:** *Directory, Trade.*
Formed by the merger of (1907-2005): Europa Birkner; (1991-2005): Birkner PaperWorld
Related titles: CD-ROM ed.: EUR 197 (effective 2005); Online - full text ed.: EUR 319 (effective 2005).
Published by: Birkner GmbH & Co. KG, Winsbergring 38, Hamburg, 22525, Germany. TEL 49-40-85308502, FAX 49-40-85308381, info@birkner.de, http://www.birkner.de. Ed., Pub. Stephan Otto. Adv. contact Peter Junker. Circ: 4,500.

BOARD CONVERTING NEWS INTERNATIONAL. *see* PACKAGING

676 CUB ISSN 0138-8940
BOLETIN TECNICO PULPA Y PAPEL. Text in Spanish. 1984. s-a. per issue exchange basis. bk.rev. **Document type:** *Trade.* **Description:** Offers updated information on pulp, paper and converting issues from both domestic and international industries.
Published by: Union del Papel, Departamento Tecnico, Calle Perla y Primera,, Los Pinos, La Habana 11800, Cuba. TEL 448651, TELEX 512121. Ed. Francisco Cabrera. Circ: 2,000.

676 658.8 GBR ISSN 1473-7426
BUSINESS RATIO REPORT. PAPER AND BOARD MANUFACTURERS. Text in English. 1973. a., latest no.36, 2008, Apr. GBP 365 per issue (effective 2010). charts; stat. back issues avail. **Document type:** *Report, Trade.* **Description:** Covers companies active as paper and board manufacturers.
Former titles (until 2001): Business Ratio. Paper and Board Manufacturers (1470-6911); (until 2000): Business Ratio Plus: Paper & Board Manufacturers (1358-8443); (until 1995): Business Ratio Report. Paper and Board Manufacturers (0261-9326)
Published by: Key Note Ltd. (Subsidiary of: Bonnier Business Information), Harlequin House, 5th Fl, 7 High St, Teddington, Richmond upon Thames, TW11 8EE, United Kingdom. TEL 44-845-5040452, FAX 44-845-5040453, sales@keynote.co.uk.

BUSINESS RATIO REPORT. PAPER & BOARD PACKAGING MANUFACTURERS. *see* PACKAGING

676 658.8 GBR ISSN 1473-5261
BUSINESS RATIO REPORT. PAPER MERCHANTS. Text in English. 1973. a. GBP 365 per issue (effective 2010). charts; stat. back issues avail. **Document type:** *Report, Trade.* **Description:** Covers companies active as paper merchants.
Former titles (until 2001): Business Ratio. Paper Merchants (1470-3416); (until 2000): Business Ratio Plus: Paper Merchants (1358-4243); (until 1995): Business Ratio Report. Paper Merchants (0261-9318)
Published by: Key Note Ltd. (Subsidiary of: Bonnier Business Information), Harlequin House, 5th Fl, 7 High St, Teddington, Richmond upon Thames, TW11 8EE, United Kingdom. TEL 44-845-5040452, FAX 44-845-5040453, sales@keynote.co.uk.

676 384 CAN
C E P JOURNAL/JOURNAL S C E P. Text in English, French. 1977. q. free. **Document type:** *Newspaper.*
Formerly: C P U Journal (0711-1053); Formed by the 1981 merger of: Intercom (English Edition) (0229-9402); Intercom (French Edition) (0229-9410); Which superseded in part (in 1980): C P U Journal (0705-0763)
Published by: Communications, Energy and Paperworkers Union of Canada/Syndicat Canadien des Communications, de l'Energie et du Papier, 350 Albert St, Ste 1900, Ottawa, ON K1R 1A4, Canada. TEL 613-230-5200, FAX 613-230-5801. Ed. Michelle Walsh. Circ: 145,000.

676.021 CAN ISSN 0709-602X
HD9820.1
CANADIAN PULP AND PAPER ASSOCIATION. MONTHLY NEWSPRINT STATISTICS/ASSOCIATION CANADIENNE DES PATES ET PAPIERS. STATISTIQUES MENSUELLES SUR LE PAPIER JOURNAL. Text in English, French. m. looseleaf. charts; stat. **Description:** Reviews pulp and paper production, stocks, exports, and consumption.
Indexed: ABIPC.
Published by: Canadian Pulp and Paper Association/Association Canadienne des Pates et Papiers, Sun Life Bldg, 19th Fl, 1155 Metcalfe St, Ste 1900, Montreal, PQ H3B 4T6, Canada. TEL 514-866-6621, FAX 514-866-3035.

676 CHL ISSN 0716-2308
CELULOSA Y PAPEL. Text in Spanish. 1985. q. USD 100 foreign (effective 2005). **Document type:** *Magazine, Trade.*
Indexed: CPEI, Englnd, P31, SCOPUS.
Published by: Asociacion Tecnica de la Celulosa y el Papel, Anibal Pinto 372, Concepcion, Chile. TEL 56-41-732210, FAX 56-41-218845, atcpchile@atcp.cl, http://www.atcp.cl.

676 FRA ISSN 1280-5572
CENTRE TECHNIQUE DU PAPIER. FEUILLETS BIBLIOGRAPHIQUES. Text in French. 1969. m. bibl. **Document type:** *Bulletin, Trade.*
Formerly: Association Technique de l'Industrie Papetiere. Feuillets Bibliographiques (0004-5888)
Published by: Centre Technique du Papier, Domaine Universitaire, B.P. 251, Grenoble, Cedex 9 38044, France. Circ: 200.

676 GBR ISSN 0010-8189
TS195.A1
CONVERTER. Text in English. 1964. m. adv. bk.rev. charts; illus.; stat.; tr.lit. index. reprints avail. **Document type:** *Magazine, Trade.* **Description:** Covers the paper, paperboard, foil, and film converters market.
Related titles: ◆ Supplement(s): Converter Directory. ISSN 0309-2143.
Indexed: A&ATA, ABIPC, B01, B07, CPEI, CurPA, Englnd, IPackAb, P&BA, P31, R18, SCOPUS.
—BLDSC (3463.600000), Linda Hall. **CCC.**
Published by: Faversham House Group Ltd., Faversham House, 232a Addington Rd, South Croydon, Surrey CR2 8LE, United Kingdom. TEL 44-20-86517100, FAX 44-20-86517117, info@fav-house.com. Ed. David Callinan TEL 44-1452-760900. Adv. contact Ruth Feather TEL 44-20-86517103.

380.1029 GBR ISSN 0309-2143
CONVERTER DIRECTORY; suppliers and services to the U.K. converting industry. Text in English. 1976. a. reprints avail. **Document type:** *Directory, Trade.*
Related titles: ◆ Supplement to: Converter. ISSN 0010-8189.
—BLDSC (3463.603000).
Published by: Faversham House Group Ltd., Faversham House, 232a Addington Rd, South Croydon, Surrey CR2 8LE, United Kingdom. TEL 44-20-86517100, FAX 44-20-86517117, info@fav-house.com.

676.3 GBR ISSN 0264-715X
CONVERTING TODAY. Text in English. 1981. m. GBP 84 domestic; EUR 215 in Europe; USD 221 in US & Canada; USD 249 elsewhere (effective 2010). adv. back issues avail. **Document type:** *Magazine, Trade.* **Description:** Contains up-to-date information and news for users and buyers of converting machinery, materials and services.
Related titles: Online - full text ed.: GBP 65.74 domestic; EUR 92.03 in Europe; USD 132.14 elsewhere (effective 2010).
Indexed: B02, B03, B11, B15, B17, B18, Englnd, G04, G06, G07, G08, I05, IPackAb, P&BA, SCOPUS.
—BLDSC (3463.614500), IE, Ingenta. **CCC.**
Published by: Progressive Media Group, Progressive House, 2 Maidstone Rd, Sidcup, DA14 5HZ, United Kingdom. TEL 44-20-82697747, FAX 44-20-82697881, pmg@progressivemediagroup.com, http://www.progressivemediagroup.com/. Ed. Maureen Byrne TEL 44-1255-424611. adv.: page EUR 3,550. Circ: 7,044.

DEUTSCHER DRUCKER. *see* PRINTING

DRUCK UND PAPIER. *see* PRINTING

676 GBR ISSN 0247-3372
ECONOMIE PAPETIERE. Text in French. 1980. m. GBP 442 domestic; GBP 419 in Europe; GBP 447 elsewhere (effective 2003). **Description:** French language report for the international pulp and paper markets with a special focus on the printing market in France. Offers unique expertise in market cycle analysis and forecasting, ensuring you stay up-to-date with industry developments; includes regular reports on Asia.
Published by: Agra Europe (London) Ltd. (Subsidiary of: Agra Informa Ltd.), 80 Calverley Rd, Tunbridge Wells, Kent TN1 2UN, United Kingdom. TEL 44-1892-533813, FAX 44-1892-544895, marketing@agra-net.com, http://www.agra-net.com.

676.2 FRA ISSN 1765-4602
ETIQUETTES PLUS. Text in French. 2004. q. **Document type:** *Magazine, Trade.*
Related titles: ◆ Supplement to: Transfoplus. ISSN 1954-2534.
Published by: Michel Burton Communication (M B C), 16 Rue Saint Fiacre, Paris, 75002, France. TEL 33-1-42365102, FAX 33-1-42338324, diffusion@groupembc.com, http://www.pnpapetier.com/.

676 DEU
EUROPAEISCHER WIRTSCHAFTSDIENST. PAPIER UND ZELLSTOFF. Text in German. 1926. w. EUR 490 (effective 2009). adv. **Document type:** *Magazine, Trade.*
Former titles (until 2000): E U W I D Papier (1439-4782); (until 1989): Europaeischer Wirtschaftsdienst. Papier- und Zellstoff-Dienst (0171-1458)
Published by: (Europaeischer Wirtschaftsdienst), E U W I D - Europaeischer Wirtschaftsdienst GmbH, Bleichstr 20-22, Gernsbach, 76593, Germany. TEL 49-7224-9397572, FAX 49-7224-9397901, service@euwid.com, http://www.euwid.de. Adv. contact Sven Roth. B&W page EUR 1,490, color page EUR 2,390; trim 189 x 260. Circ: 2,910 (paid and controlled).

676 DEU
EUROPAEISCHER WIRTSCHAFTSDIENST. PULP AND PAPER. Text in English. 1926. w. EUR 560 (effective 2009). adv. back issues avail. **Document type:** *Bulletin, Trade.* **Description:** Covers the latest developments throughout the pulp and paper industry.
Related titles: Online - full text ed.
Published by: (Europaeischer Wirtschaftsdienst), E U W I D - Europaeischer Wirtschaftsdienst GmbH, Bleichstr 20-22, Gernsbach, 76593, Germany. TEL 49-7224-9397572, FAX 49-7224-9397901, service@euwid.com, http://www.euwid.de. Ed. Bernd Hecht. adv.: B&W page EUR 570, color page EUR 1,470; trim 189 x 260. Circ: 1,250 (paid and controlled).

676 DEU
EUROPAEISCHER WIRTSCHAFTSDIENST. SERVICE PAPIER ET PATE. Text in French. 1998. w. EUR 560 (effective 2009). adv. **Document type:** *Bulletin, Trade.*
Published by: E U W I D - Europaeischer Wirtschaftsdienst GmbH, Bleichstr 20-22, Gernsbach, 76593, Germany. TEL 49-7224-9397572, FAX 49-7224-9397901, service@euwid.com, http://www.euwid.de. Adv. contact Sven Roth. B&W page EUR 570, color page EUR 1,470; trim 189 x 260. Circ: 560 (paid).

676 658.7 GBR ISSN 0961-7507
EUROPEAN CONVERTING INDUSTRY DIRECTORY. Text in English. 1990. a. GBP 33. **Document type:** *Directory.*
Formerly (until 1991): Converting Today Directory (0959-261X)
Related titles: CD-ROM ed.
Address: Kingland House, 361 City Rd, London, EC1V 1LR, United Kingdom. TEL 44-171-417-7400, FAX 44-171-417-7500. Ed. R Gormally.

676 CHE ISSN 1661-1748
L'EVENEMENT SYNDICAL. ED. UNIA. Text in French. 1998. m. **Document type:** *Journal, Trade.*
Formerly (until 2004): L' Evenement Syndical (1422-6022); Which was formed by the merger of (1920-1998): La Lutte Syndicale (1422-3945); (1993-1998): Le Nouveau Syndicat (1422-6030); Which was formed by the merger of (1980-1993): Germinal (1422-6057); (1991-1993): F O B B - L'Ouvrier (1422-6049); Which was formerly (1983-1991): F O B B (1422-6146); (1921-1983): L' Ouvrier sur Bois et du Batiment (1422-6154)
Published by: Unia - Societe l'Evenement Syndical, Weltpoststr 20, Bern 15, 3000, Switzerland. TEL 41-31-3502111, info@unia.ch, http://www.unia.ch. Ed. Alfio Guardo. Circ: 3,000.

F R A BULLETIN. *see* FORESTS AND FORESTRY

667.6 645 USA ISSN 1520-0191
TP977 CODEN: FCREF3
FOREST CHEMICALS REVIEW. Text in English. 1953. bi-m. USD 110 domestic; USD 145 foreign (effective 2005). adv. bk.rev. charts; illus.; mkt.; stat. **Document type:** *Magazine, Trade.* **Description:** Includes statistical information for international naval stores imports and exports.
Former titles (until 1999): Naval Stores Review (0164-4580); (until 1979): Naval Stores Review and Terpene Chemicals (0028-1468)
Indexed: ABIPC, Agr, CPEI, ChemAb, Englnd, P06, P31, PAIS, SCOPUS, SRI.
—BLDSC (3989.475000), CASDDS, IE, Ingenta.

P

Published by: Kriedt Enterprises, Ltd., 129 S Cortez St, New Orleans, LA 70119-6118. TEL 504-482-3914, FAX 504-482-4205. Eds. Alan Hodges, Patricia Danflous. Pubs. Romney Kriedt-Richard, Romney Richard. R&P Romney Richard. Adv. contact Romney Kriedt-Richard. B&W page USD 380, color page USD 780; trim 11 x 8.5. Circ: 350 (paid).

676 FRA
LA FRANCE PAPETIERE. Text in French. 1993. triennial. adv.
Published by: Michel Burton Communication (M B C), 16 Rue Saint Fiacre, Paris, 75002, France. TEL 33-1-42365102, FAX 33-1-42338324, diffusion@groupembc.com, http://www.pnpapetier.com/. Circ: 6,500.

676 JPN ISSN 0286-0988
FUSHOKUFU JOHO. Text in Japanese. 1972. m. JPY 31,500 (effective 2003). **Document type:** *Trade.*
—BLDSC (4648.381000).
Address: 1-6-6 Higashitenma Kita-ku, Osaka, 530-0044, Japan. TEL 81-6-63585081, FAX 81-6-63585028. Circ: 3,600.

676 JPN
FUTURE. Text in Japanese. w. JPY 126,000 (effective 2008). **Document type:** *Magazine, Trade.*
Published by: Tekku Taimusu/Tec Times Co. Ltd., 3-13-7 Kanda-Nishikicho, Chiyoda-ku, Tokyo, 101-0054, Japan. TEL 81-3-32332580, FAX 81-3-32332523, http://www.st-times.co.jp/.

676 USA ISSN 0364-1260
Z247
GOVERNMENT PAPER SPECIFICATION STANDARDS. Text in English. 19??. base vol. plus irreg. updates. looseleaf. **Document type:** *Government.* **Description:** Prescribes standards for paper stock for printing. Contains detailed standard specifications, standards to be used in testing, and color standards. For paper manufacturers, printers, and others concerned wtih paper standards.
Published by: U.S. Government Printing Office, 732 N Capitol St, NW, Washington, DC 20401. TEL 202-512-1800, 866-512-1800, FAX 202-512-2104, ContactCenter@gpo.gov.

676 658.7 FRA
GUIDE DU PAPIER ARTS GRAPHIQUES. Text in French. 1988. biennial. adv. **Document type:** *Trade.* **Description:** Describes the characteristics of papers used for graphic arts.
Formerly (until 1992): Papier, Carton et Cellulose. Guide du Papier (0995-5771)
Published by: Michel Burton Communication (M B C), 16 Rue Saint Fiacre, Paris, 75002, France. TEL 33-1-42365102, FAX 33-1-42338324, diffusion@groupembc.com, http://www.pnpapetier.com/. Circ: 3,000.

676 FRA
GUIDE DU PAPIER CARTON POUR LA TRANSFORMATION. Text in French. 1997. biennial. adv.
Published by: Michel Burton Communication (M B C), 16 Rue Saint Fiacre, Paris, 75002, France. TEL 33-1-42365102, FAX 33-1-42338324, diffusion@groupembc.com, http://www.pnpapetier.com/. Circ: 3,000.

676.2 CHN ISSN 1006-2599
TS1171
GUOJI ZAOZHI/WORLD PULP AND PAPER. Text in Chinese. 1982. bi-m. USD 31.20 (effective 2009). adv. bk.rev. 96 p./no.; **Document type:** *Journal, Trade.* **Description:** Covers news and technological achievements in global pulp and paper industry.
Formerly (until 1994): Guowai Zaozhi (1001-3911)
Related titles: Online - full text ed.
Indexed: ABIPC, SCOPUS.
—East View.
Published by: Zhongguo Zaozhi Xuehui/China Technical Association of the Paper Industry, 12 Guanghua Lu, Chaoyang-qu, Beijing, 100020, China. FAX 86-10-65810022 ext 2128, 86-10-65817480, http://www.piric.com.cn/. Ed. Shijun Kuang. Adv. contact Heqin Li TEL 86-10-65831284. Circ: 8,000. **Co-publisher:** Zhongguo Shijiang Zaozhi Yanjiuyuan/China National Pulp and Paper Research Institute. **Co-sponsor:** China Paper Association, Pulp and Paper Industrial Research Institute of China.

676.2 745.5 USA ISSN 0887-1418
TS1124.5
HAND PAPERMAKING. Text in English. 1986. s-a. USD 45 domestic; USD 50 in Canada & Mexico; USD 55 elsewhere (effective 2005). adv. bk.rev. back issues avail. **Document type:** *Magazine, Trade.* **Description:** Devoted to advancing traditional and contemporary ideas in the art of Eastern and Western papermaking by hand. Provides information for readers at all levels of expertise and from all perspectives of interest.
Indexed: A07, A30, A31, AA, ABIPC, ABM, ArtInd, B04, D05, IHTDI, P&BA, SCOPUS.
—BLDSC (4241.594000), Ingenta.
Address: PO Box 77027, Washington, DC 20013-7027. TEL 301-220-2393, 800-821-6604, FAX 301-220-2394, handpapermaking@bookarts.com. Ed. Michael Durgin. R&P, Adv. contact Tom Bannister. B&W page USD 275; 9 x 12. Circ: 1,400 (paid).

676.12 USA ISSN 1075-1319
TS1080
HAND PAPERMAKING NEWSLETTER. Text in English. 1988. q.
—BLDSC (4241.595000).
Published by: Hand Papermaking, PO Box 77027, Washington, DC 20013-7027. TEL 800-821-6604, handpapermaking@bookarts.com, http://www.handpapermaking.org.

676 CHN ISSN 1672-3066
HUNAN ZAOZHI/HUNAN PAPERMAKING. Text in Chinese. 1982. q. CNY 6 newsstand/cover (effective 2006). **Document type:** *Journal, Academic/Scholarly.*
Related titles: Online - full text ed.
Published by: Hunan Sheng Zaozhi Yanjiusuo Youxian Gongsi/Hunan Technical Association of Paper Industry, 7, Jianshe Zhong Lu, Xiangtan, 411104, China. TEL 86-732-8523295, FAX 86-732-8561602, http://www.hnprc.com/.

676 DEU ISSN 1815-669X
TS1090
I P H CONGRESS BOOK/ANNUAIRE I P H/I P H - JAHRBUCH. Text in English, French, German. 1980. a. EUR 60 per issue to non-members (effective 2009). **Document type:** *Handbook/Manual/Guide, Trade.*
Formerly (until 200?): I P H Yearbook (1010-4054)
Published by: International Association of Paper Historians/ Internationalen Arbeitsgemeinschaft der Papierhistoriker, c/o Dr. Sabine Schachtner, IPH Secretary, Rheinisches Industriemuseum, Alte Dombach, Bergisch Gladbach, 51465, Germany. TEL 49-2202-936680, sabine.schachtner@lvr.de, http://www.paperhistory.org.

676 IND ISSN 0379-5462
CODEN: IPPTDO
I P P T A. Text in English. 1964. q. free to members (effective 2011). adv. back issues avail. **Document type:** *Journal, Academic/Scholarly.*
Related titles: Online - full text ed.: free (effective 2011).
Indexed: A22, CPEI, EngInd, P31, SCOPUS.
—BLDSC (4567.464000), IE, Ingenta.
Published by: Indian Pulp and Paper Technical Association, CPPRI Campus, Paper Mill Rd, Near Himmat Nagar, P O Box 47, Saharanpur, Uttar Pradesh 247 001, India. ipptaonline@ipptaonline.org ipptaonline@ipptaonline.org.

676 700 ESP ISSN 0211-2876
IMPREMPRES; revista tecnica de la industria grafica. Text in Spanish. 1973. 11/yr. EUR 69 domestic; EUR 118 in Europe; EUR 163 elsewhere (effective 2009). **Document type:** *Bulletin, Trade.* **Description:** Includes sections on technology, products, companies, and a buyers' guide.
Related titles: Online - full text ed.: free.
Published by: TPI Edita, Ave Manoteras, 26 3a Planta, Madrid, 28050, Spain. TEL 34-91-3396807, FAX 34-91-3396096, info@grupotpi.es, http://www.tpiedita.es. Circ: 7,000.

676 ITA ISSN 0019-7548
HD9820.1 CODEN: ICAMA4
INDUSTRIA DELLA CARTA. Text in Italian; Summaries in English, Italian. 1934. 7/yr. EUR 60 domestic; EUR 120 in Europe; EUR 140 elsewhere (effective 2011). adv. bk.rev. illus.; stat. index. **Document type:** *Magazine, Trade.*
Incorporates (1899-1933): Industria della Carta e Arti Grafiche (0367-7117); (1922-1933): Regia Stazione Sperimentale per l'Industria della Carta e lo Studio delle Fibre Tessili Vegetali. Bollettino (0366-2233)
Related titles: Online - full text ed.
Indexed: A22, ABIPC, CIN, ChemAb, ChemTitl, EngInd, P&BA, SCOPUS.
—BLDSC (4438.466000), CASDDS, IE, Ingenta, INIST, Linda Hall.
Published by: Tecniche Nuove SpA, Via Eritrea 21, Milan, MI 201, Italy. TEL 39-02-390901, FAX 39-02-7570364, info@tecnichenuove.com. Ed. Chiara Italia. Circ: 5,000.

INFORMACION TECNICO ECONOMICA. *see* BUSINESS AND ECONOMICS

676 FIN ISSN 1455-5794
INSIGHT. Text in English. 1997. q.
Related titles: Finnish ed.: ISSN 1458-4182.
Published by: M-Real Corporation, Revontulentie 6, PO Box 20, Metsa, 02020, Finland. TEL 358-10-4611, FAX 358-10-4694562, atyourservice@m-real.com, http://www.m-real.com. Ed. Veli-Matti Mynttinen.

THE INTERNATIONAL DIRECTORY OF PAPER, PAPER GOODS AND STATIONERY PRODUCTS IMPORTERS. *see* BUSINESS AND ECONOMICS—Trade And Industrial Directories

INTERNATIONAL PAPER BOARD INDUSTRY. *see* PACKAGING

676 DEU ISSN 1615-1720
CODEN: DPAWA2
INTERNATIONAL PAPERWORLD. Short title: I P W. Text in English, German. 1958. 10/yr. EUR 150 domestic; EUR 170 foreign; EUR 15 newsstand/cover (effective 2009). adv. bk.rev. illus.; stat. reprints avail. **Document type:** *Magazine, Trade.* **Description:** Covers economy and technology of the manufacturing, finishing and converting of pulp, paper and substitution products of the printing world.
Former titles (until 1999): Internationale Papierwirtschaft (0949-8303); (until 1995): Deutsche Papierwirtschaft (0070-4296)
Indexed: ABIPC, CPEI, ChemAb, EngInd, P&BA, P31, RefZh, SCOPUS, TM.
—BLDSC (4567.497000), CASDDS, IE, INIST, Linda Hall. **CCC.**
Published by: D P W Verlagsgesellschaft mbH, Industriestr 2, Heusenstamm, 63150, Germany. TEL 49-6104-6060, FAX 49-6104-606317, info@kepplermediengruppe.de, http://www.kepplermediengruppe.de. Ed. Susanne Haase. Pub. Sabine Walser. Adv. contact Jean-Pierre Ferreira. B&W page EUR 3,070, color page EUR 4,660; trim 216 x 303. Circ: 7,185 (paid and controlled).

676.12 USA ISSN 1076-2043
TS1176.6.B6
INTERNATIONAL PULP BLEACHING CONFERENCE. PROCEEDINGS. Text in English. 1970. triennial. **Document type:** *Proceedings, Trade.* **—CCC.**
Published by: T A P P I Press, 15 Technology Pkwy S, Norcross, Fulton, GA 30092. TEL 770-446-1400, FAX 770-446-6947, memberconnection@tappi.org.

676 USA
INTERNATIONAL WOODFIBER REPORT. Abbreviated title: I W R. Text in English. 1995. m. USD 597 (effective 2009). adv. back issues avail. **Document type:** *Newsletter.* **Description:** Covers and analyzes woodfiber markets throughout North and South America, Europe and Asia. Provides the latest news/information concerning woodfiber prices, supply and demand, timberland sales, environmental legislation affecting timber rights, and regional as well as global news.
Formerly (until 1996): Pulp and Paper Wood Report
Related titles: Online - full text ed.: USD 507 (effective 2005).
Published by: R I S I, Inc., 4 Alfred Cir, Bedford, MA 01730. TEL 781-734-8900, 866-271-8525, FAX 781-271-0337, info@risiinfo.com. Ed. Chris Lyddan TEL 804-358-0144. Adv. contact Misty Belser TEL 415-947-3605.

676 ESP ISSN 0368-0789
CODEN: IVTPA3
INVESTIGACION Y TECNICA DEL PAPEL. Text in Spanish; Summaries in English, French, German, Spanish. 1964. q. USD 105. adv. bk.rev. bibl.; stat. index. back issues avail. **Document type:** *Magazine, Consumer.*
Indexed: ABIPC, ChemAb, IECT, P&BA, SCOPUS.
—CASDDS. **CCC.**
Published by: (Asociacion de Investigacion Tecnica de la Industria Papelera Espanola), Instituto Papelero Espanol, Ave de Baviera, 15, Madrid, 28028, Spain. TEL 34-91-5763003, FAX 34-91-5774710, http://www.ipe.es/. Circ: 1,000.

676 CAN ISSN 0826-6220
TS1080 CODEN: JPUSDN
➤ **JOURNAL OF PULP & PAPER SCIENCE.** Text in English, French. 1975. m. CAD 251.04 domestic; CAD 268.84, USD 188 in United States; CAD 305.57, USD 213.68 elsewhere (effective 2005). charts; illus. index. 40 p./no. 3 cols./p.; back issues avail.; reprints avail. **Document type:** *Journal, Academic/Scholarly.*
Formerly: Canadian Pulp and Paper Association. Technical Section. Transactions (0317-882X)
Related titles: Microform ed.: (from MML); Online - full text ed.; ◆ Supplement(s): Pulp and Paper Technical Association of Canada. News Bulletin. ISSN 1493-017X.
Indexed: A22, ABIPC, ASCA, C&ISA, C03, C33, CBCARef, CIN, CPEI, ChemAb, ChemTitl, CurCont, E&CAJ, EngInd, EnvAb, ISMEC, ISR, Inspec, MSCI, P&BA, P11, P31, P48, P52, P56, PQC, RefZh, SCI, SCOPUS, SolStAb, W07.
—BLDSC (5043.660000), AskIEEE, CASDDS, IE, Infotrieve, Ingenta, INIST, Linda Hall. **CCC.**
Published by: Pulp and Paper Technical Association of Canada/ Association Technique des Pates et Papiers du Canada, 740 rue Notre Dame ouest, Ste 1070, Montreal, PQ H3C 3X6, Canada. TEL 514-392-0265, FAX 514-392-0369, pubs@paptac.ca. Ed. D H Page. Circ: 14,000.

676 668.4 338.476 686.2 JPN ISSN 1349-4643
KAMI INSATSU PURASUCHIKKU GOMU SEIHIN TOUKEI GEPPOU/ MONTHLY REPORT OF PAPER, PRINTING, PLASTICS PRODUCTS AND RUBBER PRODUCTS STATISTICS. Text in Japanese. 2001. m. **Document type:** *Government.*
Formerly (until 2004): Kami Parupu Purasuchikku Gomu Seihin Toukei Geppou (1347-1163); Which was formed by the merger of (1952-2001): Kami, Parupu Tokei Geppo (0022-8168); (1968-2002): Purasuchikku Seihin Tokei Geppo (0916-3980); Which was formerly: Purasuchikku Tokei Geppo; (1968-2001): Gomu Seihin Tokei Geppo (1342-6974); Which was formerly (until 1968): Gomu Tokei Geppo (0432-0654); (until 1954): Zakka Tokei Geppo
Published by: Keizai Sangyoushou. Keizai Sangyou Seisakukyoku. Chousa Toukeibu/Ministry of Economy, Trade and Industry. Economic and Industrial Policy Bureau. Research and Statistics Department, 1-3-1 Kasumigaseki, Chiyoda-ku, Tokyo, 100-8902, Japan. http://www.meti.go.jp/.

676 JPN ISSN 0022-815X
TS1171 CODEN: KAGIAU
KAMI PA GIKYOSHI/JAPAN T A P P I JOURNAL. Text in Japanese; Summaries in English. 1947. m. price varies. adv. bk.rev. abstr.; bibl.; charts; illus.; pat.; stat. **Document type:** *Journal, Trade.*
Formerly (until 1954): Parupu Kami Kogyo Zasshi/Japanese Technical Association of Pulp and Paper Industry. Journal (0370-0313)
Indexed: A22, ABIPC, CIN, CPEI, ChemAb, ChemTitl, ESPM, EngInd, INIS AtomInd, P&BA, P31, SCOPUS.
—BLDSC (4650.260000), CASDDS, IE, Ingenta, Linda Hall. **CCC.**
Published by: Kami Paupu Gijutsu Kyokai/Japan Technical Association of Pulp and Paper Industry, Kami Pulp Kaikan Bldg 11th Fl, 9-11 Ginza 3-chome, Chuo-ku, Tokyo, 104-8139, Japan. TEL 81-3-32484841, FAX 81-3-32484843, info@japantappi.org. Circ: 4,500.

676 JPN ISSN 0453-1507
KAMI PARUPU GIJUTSU TAIMUSU/JAPANESE JOURNAL OF PAPER TECHNOLOGY. Text in Japanese. 1958. m. JPY 31,500 (effective 2008). **Document type:** *Magazine, Trade.*
Indexed: EngInd, SCOPUS.
—BLDSC (4656.890000).
Published by: Tekku Taimusu/Tec Times Co. Ltd., 3-13-7 Kanda-Nishikicho, Chiyoda-ku, Tokyo, 101-0054, Japan. TEL 81-3-32332580, FAX 81-3-32332690, http://www.st-times.co.jp/.

338.4 JPN ISSN 0453-1515
KAMI PARUPU TOKEI NENPO/YEARBOOK OF PULP AND PAPER STATISTICS. Text in Japanese. 1947. a. JPY 6,120.
Published by: International Trade and Industry Statistics Association, Kobikikan Ginza Bldg, 8-9 Ginza 2-chome, Chuo-ku, Tokyo, 104-0061, Japan. TEL 81-3-3561-2974, FAX 81-3-3561-5212.

676 JPN
KAMI PAUPU GIJUTSU KYOKAI. NENJI TAIKAI. KOUEN YOKOSHU/ JAPAN TECHNICAL ASSOCIATION OF PULP AND PAPER INDUSTRY. ANNUAL MEETING. PROCEEDINGS. Text in Japanese. a. **Document type:** *Proceedings.*
Published by: Kami Paupu Gijutsu Kyokai/Japan Technical Association of Pulp and Paper Industry, Kami Pulp Kaikan Bldg 11th Fl, 9-11 Ginza 3-chome, Chuo-ku, Tokyo, 104-8139, Japan. TEL 81-3-32484841, FAX 81-3-32484843, info@japantappi.org, http://www.japantappi.org/.

676 338 GBR ISSN 1460-3152
KEY NOTE MARKET REPORT: DISPOSABLE PAPER PRODUCTS. Variant title: Disposable Paper Products Market Report. Text in English. 19??. irreg., latest 2009, Oct. GBP 460 per issue (effective 2010). **Document type:** *Report, Trade.* **Description:** Provides an overview of the UK disposable paper products market, including industry structure, market size and trends, developments, prospects, and major company profiles.
Formerly (until 1997): Key Note Report: Disposable Paper Products (0269-9028)
Related titles: CD-ROM ed.; Online - full text ed.
Published by: Key Note Ltd. (Subsidiary of: Bonnier Business Information), Harlequin House, 5th Fl, 7 High St, Teddington, Richmond upon Thames, TW11 8EE, United Kingdom. TEL 44-845-5040452, FAX 44-845-5040453, info@keynote.co.uk.

KEY NOTE MARKET REPORT: PAPER & BOARD MANUFACTURING. *see* BUSINESS AND ECONOMICS—Production Of Goods And Services

676 JPN ISSN 0288-5867
KINOSHI KENKYUKAISHI/HIGH PERFORMANCE PAPER SOCIETY, JAPAN. ANNALS. Text in Japanese. 1962. a. **Document type:** *Academic/Scholarly.*
Formerly (until 1982): Kasenshi Kenkyukaishi (0288-5859)
Indexed: EngInd, SCOPUS.
—BLDSC (1026.050000).

Published by: Kinoshi Kenkyukai/High Performance Paper Society, Japan, 4084-1,Kawanoe,Kawanoe, Ehime, 799-0101, Japan. TEL 81-896-58-2055, FAX 81-896-58-6240.

676 659.1 DEU
KOEHLER RUNDSCHAU. Text in German. 1963. 3/yr. **Document type:** *Consumer.*
Published by: Papierfabrik August Koehler AG, Postfach 1245, Oberkirch, 77696, Germany. TEL 49-7802-81340, FAX 49-7802-81330. Ed. Ruth Karcher. Circ: 3,500.

676 FRA ISSN 1279-5577
LA LETTRE DU PAPIER. Text in French. 1996. s-m. EUR 340 (effective 2009). adv. **Document type:** *Newsletter, Trade.*
Published by: Michel Burton Communication (M B C), 16 Rue Saint Fiacre, Paris, 75002, France. TEL 33-1-42365102, FAX 33-1-42338324, diffusion@groupembc.com, http://www.pnpapetier.com/.

LOCKWOOD - POST'S DIRECTORY AMERICAN TRAVELER'S EDITION. see BUSINESS AND ECONOMICS—Trade And Industrial Directories

676 382.029 USA
LOCKWOOD - POST'S DIRECTORY ASIAN TRAVELER'S EDITION (ONLINE). Text in English. irreg. USD 795 (effective 2009). **Document type:** *Directory, Trade.*
Published by: R I S I, Inc., 4 Alfred Cir, Bedford, MA 01730. TEL 781-734-8900, 866-271-8525, FAX 781-271-0337, info@risiinfo.com.

676 382.029 USA
LOCKWOOD - POST'S DIRECTORY EUROPEAN TRAVELER'S EDITION (ONLINE). Text in English. irreg. USD 795 (effective 2009). **Document type:** *Directory, Trade.*
Media: Online - full text.
Published by: R I S I, Inc., 4 Alfred Cir, Bedford, MA 01730. TEL 781-734-8900, 866-271-8525, FAX 781-271-0337, info@risiinfo.com.

LOCKWOOD - POST'S DIRECTORY GLOBAL EDITION. see BUSINESS AND ECONOMICS—Trade And Industrial Directories

M A R I; papel y corrugado para America Latina. (Magazine of the Americas Revista Interamericana) see PACKAGING

M A R I - BOARD CONVERTING NEWS ESPANOL. see PACKAGING

676 CAN ISSN 1484-4672
MILL PRODUCT NEWS. Text in English. 1990. bi-m. adv. **Document type:** *Magazine, Trade.* **Description:** Contains a useful mix of industry news, articles on new mills and upgrades, technical articles, new product and technology news.
Formerly (until 1993): Canadian Mill Product News (1186-2033)
Indexed: Englnd, SCOPUS.
—CCC.
Published by: Baum International Media, 1625 Ingleton Ave, Burnaby, BC V5C 4L8, Canada. TEL 604-298-3004, FAX 604-291-1906. Ed. Toni Dabbs. Pub. Heri R Baum. Adv. contact Kevin Cook. Circ: 18,639.

N L K MONITOR. MARKET PULP. see BUSINESS AND ECONOMICS—Production Of Goods And Services

NONWOVENS INDUSTRY; the international magazine for the nonwoven fabrics and disposable soft goods industry. see TEXTILE INDUSTRIES AND FABRICS

NONWOVENS REVIEW. see TEXTILE INDUSTRIES AND FABRICS

676 338.4 SWE ISSN 1652-7259
NORDIC PAPER & PULP MAKERS' DIRECTORY. Variant title: Brusewitz Nordisk Papperskalender. Text in English. 1902. a., latest 2004. price varies. adv. index. **Document type:** *Directory, Trade.* **Description:** Covers paper and pulp production sites in Sweden, Norway, Denmark and Finland. Gives information about capacity and key personnel.
Formerly (until 2004): Nordisk Papperskalender (0281-7241); Which incorporates (1958-1981): Paper & Pulp Makers' Directory (0281-725X)
Published by: Mentor Online AB, Tryffelslingan 10, PO Box 72001, Lidingoe, 18172, Sweden. TEL 46-8-6704100, FAX 46-8-6616455, info@mentoronline.se, http://www.mentoronline.se.

676 SWE ISSN 1651-2995
NORDISK PAPPER & MASSA. Variant title: Papper och Massa. Text in Swedish. 2000. 7/yr. SEK 699 (effective 2007). adv. **Document type:** *Journal, Trade.*
Published by: Conventus Communication AB, PO Box 24053, Stockholm, 10450, Sweden. TEL 46-8-50624400, FAX 46-8-50624499, http://www.branschnyheter.se. Ed. Michael Novotny TEL 46-8-50624416. adv.: B&W page SEK 19,900, color page SEK 24,700; 194 x 260.

676 SWE ISSN 1651-9515
TS1080
NORDISK PAPPERSTIDNING/NORDIC PAPER JOURNAL. Text in Swedish. 2003. 11/yr. SEK 924 domestic print ed.; SEK 1,155 domestic print & online eds.; SEK 1,124 foreign print ed.; SEK 1,355 foreign print & online eds.; SEK 693 online ed. (effective 2007). adv. bk.rev. abstr.; bibl.; charts; illus.; pat.; stat. index. **Document type:** *Magazine, Trade.* **Description:** Covers trade information and products for the pulp and paper industries.
Supersedes in part (1999-2002): Svensk Papperstidning (1403-9605); Which was formerly (until 1999): Svensk Papperstidning - Nordisk Cellulosa (1101-766X); Which was formed by the merger of (1975-1990): Nordisk Cellulosa (0281-6733); Which was formerly (until 1984): Cellulosa (0346-6302); (1934-1990): Svensk Papperstidning (0283-6831); Which was formerly (until 1981): Svensk Papperstidning och Svensk Pappersforadlingstidskrift (0346-2188); Which was formed by the merger of (1898-1934): Svensk Papperstidning (0039-6680); (19??-1934): Svensk Pappersforadlingstidskrift (0371-4519)
Related titles: Online - full text ed.
Indexed: A20, A22, ABIPC, ASCA, ChemAb, CurPA, P&BA.
—BLDSC (6122.535000), CASDDS, IE, Ingenta, INIST, Linda Hall.
Published by: Mentor Online AB, Tryffelslingan 10, PO Box 72001, Lidingoe, 18172, Sweden. TEL 46-8-6704100, FAX 46-8-6616455, info@mentoronline.se, http://www.mentoronline.se. Ed. Allan Almegaard. Adv. contact Ing-Marie Matsson TEL 46-8-6704185. B&W page SEK 19,100, color page SEK 28,900; trim 185 x 267. Circ: 6,200 (controlled).

676 BRA ISSN 0031-1057
TS1080 CODEN: PAPLA3
O PAPEL. Text in Portuguese; Summaries in English. 1939. m. USD 250 (effective 2001). adv. illus.; stat.; tr.lit. 100 p./no.; back issues avail. **Document type:** *Trade.*
Indexed: A22, A28, APA, BrCerAb, C&ISA, C01, CA/WCA, CIA, CPEI, CerAb, ChemAb, CivEngAb, CorrAb, E&CAJ, E11, EEA, EMA, ESPM, Englnd, EnvEAb, H15, M&TEA, M09, MBF, METADEX, P&BA, P31, SCOPUS, SolStAb, T04, WAA.
—BLDSC (6358.400000), CASDDS, IE, Ingenta, Linda Hall.
Published by: Associacao Tecnica Brasileira de Celulose e Papel, Rua Ximbo, 165, Aclimacao, Sao Paulo, SP 04108-040, Brazil. TEL 55-11-5574-0166, FAX 55-11-5571-6485, abtcp@abtcp.com.br. Ed., Pub., R&P Patricia Capo TEL 55-11-5574-0166 ext 229. Adv. contact Selma Ugolini Azevedo TEL 55-11-5574-0166 ext 233. Circ: 4,000.

OFFICIAL BOARD MARKETS; "the yellow sheet". see PACKAGING

676 USA
OUTLOOK FOR GLOBAL RECOVERED PAPER MARKETS. Text in English. irreg.
Published by: R I S I, Inc., 4 Alfred Cir, Bedford, MA 01730. TEL 781-734-8900, FAX 781-271-0337, info@risiinfo.com, http://www.risiinfo.com.

676 USA
OUTLOOK FOR THE WORLD TISSUE BUSINESS. Text in English. a. USD 6,200 (effective 2009). back issues avail.; reprints avail. **Document type:** *Report, Trade.* **Description:** Provides thorough analysis and extensive detail about regional/country markets and identifies medium to long-term trends.
Published by: R I S I, Inc., 4 Alfred Cir, Bedford, MA 01730. TEL 781-734-8900, 866-271-8525, FAX 781-271-0337, info@risiinfo.com.

676 AUT
P B S - SPIEL MAGAZIN. (Papier Buero Schreibwaren) Text in German. 1985. 11/yr. **Document type:** *Magazine, Trade.*
Former titles: P B S Magazin; Papierhandelsfachblatt
Published by: Verlag Heymann und Jahn, Holochergasse 45, Vienna, W 1150, Austria. TEL 43-1-9827191, FAX 43-1-982347117. Ed. Helmut Herz.

676 USA ISSN 1531-1902
TS1080 CODEN: APPAFH
P I M A'S ASIA PACIFIC PAPERMAKER. (Paper Industry Management Association) Text in English. 1997. 8/yr. USD 170 in Asia & the Pacific; USD 200 elsewhere (effective 2001). adv. bk.rev. abstr.; charts; illus.; stat. index. **Document type:** *Magazine, Trade.* **Description:** Articles on operations and management, training and staff development written in non-technical language, including interviews with industry executives. Columns focus on management issues or key mill technical processes. Departments focus on news and trends, new products, application stories and personnel changes.
Supersedes in part: P I M A's International Papermaker (1093-670X); Which was formed by the merger of (1993-1997): European Papermaker (1103-6966); (1993-1997): Asia Pacific Papermaker (1320-9787); (1938-1997): P I M A Magazine (1046-4352); Which was formerly (until 1986): P I M A (0161-1364); (until 1978): Paper Industry (0197-3991); (until 1977): American Paper Industry (0003-0333); (until 1965): The Paper Industry (0360-6031); (until 1950): Paper Industry and Paper World (0096-1787)
Related titles: Microfiche ed.: (from PQC); Online - full text ed.; Chinese ed.
Indexed: P&BA, SCOPUS.
—IE, Ingenta, Linda Hall. **CCC.**
Published by: Paper Industry Management Association, 4700 W Lake Ave, Glenview, IL 60025-1468. TEL 847-375-6860, FAX 877-527-5973, alan@pima-online.org, http://www.papermaker.net, http://www.pima-online.org. Eds. Diana Ward, Alan Rooks. Pub. Lindsay Beddingfield. Adv. contact Carolyn Benedict. B&W page USD 6,475, color page USD 8,955; trim 10.88 x 8.13. Circ: 6,500.

676 GBR
P I T A ANNUAL REVIEW & MEMBERSHIP DIRECTORY (YEARS). Text in English. 1988. a. free to members (effective 2010). adv. illus.; stat.; charts; tr.lit. 128 p./no.; **Document type:** *Directory, Trade.* **Description:** Contains industry information and statistics as well as a full listing of individual and corporate members with contact details.
Former titles (until 2009): P I T A Year Book (1367-6199); (until 1996): Paper Industry Technical Association. Membership and Year Book; (until 1991): British Paper and Board Industry Federation Technical Section. Handbook and Membership List
—BLDSC (6504.141500).
Published by: Paper Industry Technical Association, 5 Frecheville Ct, Bury, Lancs BL9 0UF, United Kingdom. TEL 44-161-7645858, FAX 44-161-7645353, info@pita.co.uk, http://www.pita.co.uk.

676 USA
P P I ASIA. (Pulp and Paper Industry) Text in English. 24/yr. USD 897 (effective 2009). **Document type:** *Newsletter, Trade.* **Description:** Covers all the latest business developments in paper industry throughout the Asia-Pacific region.
Formerly: P P I Asia News
Related titles: Online - full text ed.: USD 707 (effective 2005); ◆ Regional ed(s).: Pulp & Paper. ISSN 0033-4081.
Published by: R I S I, Inc., 4 Alfred Cir, Bedford, MA 01730. TEL 781-734-8900, FAX 781-271-0337, info@risiinfo.com. Ed. Joanne Potter.

676 USA
P P I EUROPE. (Paper & Pulp Industry) Text in English. 1986. 48/yr. EUR 930 (effective 2009). back issues avail. **Document type:** *Newsletter, Trade.* **Description:** Contains a concise report detailing market conditions and current prices for all the major pulp, paper and paperboard grades, plus all the latest industry and corporate news.
Formerly (until 2008): P P I This Week
Related titles: Fax ed.: EUR 1,327 (effective 2005); Ed.
Indexed: ABIPC, P&BA.
Published by: R I S I, Inc., 4 Alfred Cir, Bedford, MA 01730. TEL 781-734-8900, FAX 781-271-0337, info@risiinfo.com. Ed. Michael Dixon.

676 USA
P P I GLOBAL FACT & PRICE BOOK. (Pulp & Paper Industry) Text in English. 1980. a. **Document type:** *Handbook/Manual/Guide, Trade.*
Former titles: P P I International Fact & Price Book; Pulp and Paper International Factbook
Published by: R I S I, Inc., 4 Alfred Cir, Bedford, MA 01730. TEL 781-734-8900, FAX 781-271-0337, info@risiinfo.com, http://www.risiinfo.com.

676 USA
P P I'S EUROPEAN COMPANY PROFILES. (Pulp & Paper International) Cover title: European Company Profiles. Variant title: Pulp and Paper Internaitonal European Company Profiles. Text in English. 1999. a., latest 2001. **Document type:** *Monographic series, Trade.* **Description:** Provides comprehensive examination of the operations, finances, and marketing strategies of major European pulp, paper, and board companies.
Published by: R I S I, Inc., 4 Alfred Cir, Bedford, MA 01730. TEL 781-734-8900, FAX 781-271-0337, info@risiinfo.com, http://www.risiinfo.com.

P R N NIEUWSBRIEF. (Papier Recycling Nederland) see ENVIRONMENTAL STUDIES—Waste Management

676 DEU ISSN 1864-1482
PACKMITTEL; Das Fachmagazin fuer Entwicklung, Produktion und Veredelung. Text in German. 1965. bi-m. EUR 126.80 domestic; EUR 130.70 in the European Union; EUR 135 elsewhere; EUR 25 newsstand/cover (effective 2009). adv. **Document type:** *Journal, Trade.*
Former titles: Papier und Folien; Papier und Kunststoff Verarbeiter (0048-2897); Papier Verarbeiter
Related titles: Online - full text ed.
Indexed: ABIPC, IPackAb, P&BA, PST, SCOPUS.
—CCC.
Published by: Deutscher Fachverlag GmbH, Mainzer Landstr 251, Frankfurt Am Main, 60326, Germany. TEL 49-69-75952052, FAX 49-69-75952999, info@dfv.de, http://www.dfv.de. Ed. Thomas Roehl. Adv. contact Sabine Strauss TEL 49-69-75951224. B&W page EUR 2,825, color page EUR 3,445; trim 185 x 270. Circ: 4,400 (paid and controlled).

676 USA ISSN 0031-1081
PAPER AGE. Text in English. 1884. 10/yr. USD 140 foreign (effective 2004); free to qualified personnel. adv. bk.rev. charts; illus. **Document type:** *Magazine, Trade.* **Description:** For global manufacturers and converters of paper, pulp and paperboard products. Provides information about corporate strategies, and plant operations. Profiles the world's pulp and paper companies and suppliers to the industry.
Related titles: Online - full text ed.
Indexed: A22, ABIPC, Englnd, GALA, IPackAb, P&BA, PROMT, SCOPUS.
—BLDSC (6358.850000), IE, Ingenta.
Published by: O'Brien Publications, Inc., 185 Lincoln St, Ste 200B, Hingham, MA 02043. TEL 781-749-5255, FAX 781-749-5896. Ed. John O'Brien. Pub., Adv. contact Michael O'Brien. Circ: 31,400 (controlled).

676 USA ISSN 1931-8278
PAPER & PACKAGING. Text in English. 1959. bi-m. free to members; USD 49 to non-members. adv. bk.rev. charts; stat. **Document type:** *Magazine, Trade.*
Former titles (until 2006?): Distribution Sales & Management (1092-8073); (until 1997): Distribution Management (1080-7160); Which incorporates (1903-1997): Who's Who in the Paper, Packaging, and Allied Products Distribution Channel; Which was formerly: Who's Who in Paper Distribution; Former titles (until 1995): N P T A Management News (0739-2214); Current (Great Neck) (0737-0067); Who's Who in Paper Distribution and Factbook; Who's Who in Paper Distribution
Indexed: ABIPC, CPEI, Englnd, P31, SCOPUS, SRI.
Published by: National Paper Trade Association, Inc., 500 Bi-County Blvd., Ste. 200E, Farmingdale, NY 11735. TEL 631-777-2223, 800-355-6785, FAX 631-777-2224. Pub. Debra Ray. Adv. contacts Mary Jo Becker, J.F. Purcell. Circ: 21,000 (paid).

676 MYS ISSN 0218-4540
HD9836.A1
PAPER ASIA; for the Asia-Pacific pulp, paper & converting industries. Text in English. 1985. m. (10/yr.). MYR 193 domestic; USD 141 foreign (effective 2005). adv. **Document type:** *Magazine, Trade.* **Description:** Covers major happenings, developments, and issues of interest to persons in the paper industry.
Related titles: ◆ Chinese ed.: Yazhou Zhi.
Indexed: ABIPC, CPEI, Englnd, P&BA, P31, SCOPUS.
—BLDSC (6359.970000), IE.
Published by: S H P Media Sdn Bhd., C-17-1, 17th Fl., Block C, Megan Phileo Ave., 12, Jalan Yap Kwan Seng, PO Box 10836, Kuala Lumpur, 50726, Malaysia. TEL 60-3-21660852 ext 5175, FAX 60-3-2161-0541, info@shpmedia.com. Ed. Anders Julin. adv.: B&W page USD 3,010, color page USD 4,080; trim 275 x 210. Circ: 5,287.

676.3 USA
PAPER BUYERS' ENCYCLOPEDIA. Text in English. 1968. a. USD 125 domestic; USD 160 foreign (effective 2000). adv. **Document type:** *Directory, Trade.* **Description:** Provides information on paper, sources, distribution channels and grades.
Published by: Grade Finders, Inc., 662 Exton Commons, Box 944, Exton, PA 19341. TEL 610-524-7070, FAX 610-524-8912. Ed., Adv. contact Mark Subers. Pub., R&P Phyllis Subers.

PAPER, FILM AND FOIL CONVERTER. see PACKAGING

676 DEU
PAPER HISTORY. Text in English, French, German. 1962. s-a. EUR 20 per vol. (effective 2009). **Document type:** *Newsletter, Trade.* **Description:** Present general information about activities of the international as well as the national associations of paper historians, shorter notes, personals, literature, call for papers, agenda for the IPH general assembly, congress invitations, programs and reports.
Former titles (until 2009): International Paper History (1561-2104); (until 1991): I P H Information (0250-8338)
Related titles: Online - full text ed.
Indexed: P&BA.
—CCC.
Published by: International Association of Paper Historians/ Internationalen Arbeitsgemeinschaft der Papierhistoriker, c/o Dr. Sabine Schachtner, IPH Secretary, Rheinisches Industriemuseum, Alte Dombach, Bergisch Gladbach, 51465, Germany. TEL 49-2202-936680, sabine.schachtner@lvr.de, http://www.paperhistory.org. Ed. Anna-Grethe Rischel TEL 45-45-816803.

P

676 USA ISSN 1048-8251
PAPER INDUSTRY. Text in English. 1984. bi-m. adv. reprints avail. **Document type:** *Magazine, Trade.*
Formerly: Paper Industry Equipment (0889-731X)
Indexed: ABIPC, Englnd, SCOPUS.
—CCC.
Published by: Paper Industry Magazine, PO Box 5675, Montgomery, AL 36103-5675. TEL 888-224-6611, FAX 604-264-1367. Ed., R&P Peter N Williamson TEL 514-458-4571. Pub. Tim Shaddick. Adv. contact John Robertson. B&W page USD 2,480, color page USD 3,485; 14.5 x 11. Circ: 19,000 (controlled). **Subscr. to:** PO Box 2268, Montgomery, AL 36102-2268.

676 GBR ISSN 1358-0671
PAPER MARKET DIGEST. Text in English. 1983. m. looseleaf. GBP 350; GBP 45 per issue (effective 2009). mkt.; stat. back issues avail. **Document type:** *Journal, Trade.* **Description:** Provides information on prices, market trends, company information and future prospects for the professional buyer of graphic papers and boards.
Related titles: E-mail ed.; Supplement(s): Fantasy Futures. ISSN 1366-381X.
Indexed: ABIPC, Englnd, P&BA, SCOPUS.
—CCC.
Published by: P P L Research Ltd., PO Box 2002, Watford, Herts WD25 9JQ, United Kingdom. TEL 44-1923-894777, FAX 44-1923-894888, enquiries@pplresearch.co.uk.

PAPER RECYCLING MARKETS DIRECTORY. *see* ENVIRONMENTAL STUDIES—Waste Management

676 ZAF ISSN 0254-3494
PAPER SOUTHERN AFRICA; devoted exclusively to the pulp, paper & board industries in Southern Africa. Text in English. 1980. bi-m. ZAR 98.04 domestic; ZAR 124 in Africa; ZAR 140 elsewhere. adv. **Document type:** *Magazine, Trade.* **Description:** Technical journal on pulp, paper and board production and processing.
Indexed: ABIPC, ISAP, P&BA, SCOPUS.
Published by: (Technical Association of the Pulp and Paper Industry of Southern Africa), George Warman Publications (Pty.) Ltd., Rondebosch, PO Box 705, Cape Town, 7701, South Africa. info@gwarmanpublications.co.za, http://www.gwarmanpublications.co.za. Ed. John Kench. Circ: 1,362.

676.142 USA ISSN 1064-1432
THE PAPER STOCK REPORT. Text in English. 1990. bi-m. USD 115 domestic; USD 135 in Canada & Mexico; USD 225 elsewhere (effective 2005). adv. stat. back issues avail. **Document type:** *Newsletter.* **Description:** Covers the latest news and trends about the waste paper markets and industry from waste-paper generation at residential, commercial-industrial and office settings to end-use at paper mills, etc. and includes weekly market prices for various grades of waste paper. Focus is on the end-use market trends for various grades of waste paper, legislation and regulations impacting scrap market.
Related titles: Online - full text ed.
Published by: McEntee Media Corp., 9815 Hazelwood Ave, Strongsville, OH 44149-2305. TEL 440-238-6603, FAX 440-238-6712. Ed., Pub. Ken McEntee. Adv. contact Richard Downing. page USD 700. Circ: 2,000 (paid).

676 686.2 688.8 GBR ISSN 0958-6024
TS1080.B73 CODEN: PATEE6
PAPER TECHNOLOGY. Text in English. 1960. 10/yr. GBP 100 to non-members; free to members (effective 2009). adv. bk.rev. pat.; stat.; tr.lit.; mkt.; abstr.; bibl.; charts; illus. index, cum.index. back issues avail.; reprints avail. **Document type:** *Journal, Trade.* **Description:** Aims to keep readers aware of new technology through technical articles, abstracts, news and latest developments of the pulp, papermaking, non-woven and converting industries.
Incorporates: Pira News; Former titles (until 1989): Paper Technology and Industry (0306-252X); (until 1975): Paper Technology (0031-1189); Which was formed by the merger of (1950-1960): British Paper and Board Makers' Association. Technical Section. Proceedings (0366-2942); Which was formerly (1921-1949): Paper Makers' Association of Great Britain and Ireland. Technical Section. Proceedings (0370-0518); (1950-1960): British Paper and Board Makers' Association. Technical Section. Technical Bulletin (0371-5442); Which was formerly (until 1950): Paper Makers' Association of Great Britain and Ireland. Technical Section. Technical Bulletin
Indexed: A22, ABIPC, CIN, CISA, CPEI, ChemAb, ChemTitl, Englnd, FR, GALA, IBR, IBZ, Inspec, P&BA, P31, SCOPUS.
—BLDSC (6364.750000), CASDDS, IE, Ingenta, INIST, Linda Hall. **CCC.**
Published by: Paper Industry Technical Association, 5 Frecheville Ct, Bury, Lancs BL9 0UF, United Kingdom. TEL 44-161-7645858, FAX 44-161-7645353, info@pita.co.uk. Ed. Margaret Marley TEL 44-20-76229269. Adv. contact Barry Read. color page GBP 1,310; 175 x 260. Circ: 1,500.

676 USA ISSN 1933-3684
TS1080 CODEN: TAJODT
PAPER360. Text in English. 1920. m. free to members (effective 2008). adv. bk.rev. charts; illus.; mkt.; pat.; tr.lit. index. back issues avail.; reprints avail. **Document type:** *Magazine, Trade.* **Description:** Explores the links within the pulp and paper industry, from forest resource to finished product; from superintendent to CEO; around the industry and around the world.
Formerly (until 2006): Solutions! (1537-0275); Which was formed by the merger of (1982-2001): T A P P I Journal (0734-1415); Which was formerly (until 1982): T A P P I (0039-8241); (until 1949): Technical Association Papers (0096-4557); Technical Papers and Addresses; (1997-2001): P I M A's .. Papermaker (1093-670X)
Related titles: Online - full text ed.: free to qualified personnel (effective 2008); Chinese ed.: China Paper360.
Indexed: A&ATA, A05, A10, A20, A22, A23, A24, A28, ABIPC, APA, AS&TA, AS&TI, ASCA, Agr, B01, B04, B07, B13, BibAg, BrCerAb, C&ISA, C10, C33, CA, CA/WCA, CADCAM, CBTA, CEA, CEABA, CIA, CIN, CIS, CerAb, ChemAb, ChemTitl, CivEngAb, CorrAb, CurCont, CurPA, E&CAJ, E04, E05, E11, EEA, EIA, EMA, Englnd, EnvAb, EnvInd, FLUIDEX, G08, GALA, H15, I05, IPackAb, ISR, M&TEA, M09, MBF, METADEX, MSCI, P&BA, PST, PhotoAb, R18, RefZh, RoboAb, SCI, SCOPUS, SolStAb, T01, T02, T04, TCEA, TM, TTI, V03, W07, WAA, WSCA, WasteInfo.
—BLDSC (6366.160000), CASDDS, IE, Ingenta, INIST, Linda Hall. **CCC.**
Published by: (Paper Industry Management Association, T A P P I), Questex Media Group Inc., 275 Grove St, Bldg 2, Ste 130, Newton, MA 02466. TEL 617-219-8300, 888-552-4346, FAX 617-219-8310, questex@sunbeltfs.com, http://www.questex.com. Ed. Jan Bottiglieri TEL 847 466-3891. adv.: page USD 7,831; trim 7.75 x 10.5. Circ: 28,679.

676 FIN ISSN 0031-1243
HD9765.F4 CODEN: PAPUAU
PAPERI JA PUU/PAPER AND TIMBER. Text in English, Finnish. 1919. 8/yr. EUR 100 domestic; EUR 144 elsewhere (effective 2007); incl. supplements. adv. bibl.; charts; illus.; stat. index. back issues avail. **Document type:** *Journal, Trade.*
Formerly (until 1952): Paperi ja Puu. B Painos (0370-1360); Which superseded in part (1921-1950): Suomen Paperi- ja Puutavaralehti (0371-2273)
Indexed: A20, A22, ABIPC, ASCA, CISA, ChemAb, ChemTitl, CurCont, Englnd, GALA, ISR, MSCI, P&BA, RefZh, SCI, SCOPUS, W07.
—BLDSC (6366.500000), CASDDS, IE, Infotrieve, Ingenta, INIST.
Published by: (Suomen Metsateollisuuden Keskusliitto/Finnish Forest Industries Federation), Paperi ja Puu Oy/Paper and Timber, Snellmaninkatu 13, PO Box 155, Helsinki, 00171, Finland. TEL 358-9-132-6688, FAX 358-9-630-365, http://www.paperijapuu.fi. Ed. Marja Korpivaara TEL 358-9-2785230. Adv. contact Tom Forsman TEL 358-40-5770385. B&W page EUR 1,900, color page EUR 2,900; 184 x 271. Circ: 4,000. **Co-sponsor:** Finnish Paper Engineers' Association.

676 IND ISSN 0048-2862
PAPERPRINTPACK INDIA. Text in English. 1963. m. USD 20 (effective 2011). charts; illus. **Document type:** *Magazine, Trade.* **Description:** Devoted to developments in the paper, printing, packaging, and other affiliated industries in India. Includes calendar of relevant events.
Indexed: PST.
Published by: (Shantarani Sons & Co.), Smt. S. Tikku Pub., Prabhadevi P O, 7-104 Nariman Passage, Mumbai, Maharashtra 400 025, India.

676 CAN
PAPERWEEK INTERNATIONAL REPORTER/REPORTER DE LA SEMAINE INTERNATIONALE DU PAPIER. Text in English. a.
Published by: (Pulp & Paper Technical Association of Canada), Southam Magazine Group (St. Laurent), 1 Holiday St, East Tower, Ste 705, Pointe Claire, PQ H9R 5N3, Canada. TEL 514-630-5955, FAX 514-630-5980. Ed. Graeme Rodden.

PAPERWORKER. *see* LABOR UNIONS

676 CHE ISSN 1423-7016
PAPETERIE UND BUERO. Text in French, German. 1919. 11/yr. CHF 45 (effective 2008). adv. illus.; mkt. **Document type:** *Magazine, Trade.*
Former titles (until 1999): Papeterist (0031-1316); (until 1921): Verband Schweizerischer Papeterien. Korrespondenzblatt (1421-8232)
Published by: Verband Schweizerischer Papeteristen, Laupenstr 2, Postfach 8524, Bern, 3001, Switzerland. TEL 41-31-3816611, FAX 41-31-3816614, info@papeterie.ch. Ed. Juerg Kuehni. adv.: color page CHF 2,960; trim 191 x 267. Circ: 6,400 (paid and controlled).

676.2 CAN ISSN 0048-2889
PAPETIER. Text in French. 1964. q. free. **Document type:** *Journal, Trade.*
Indexed: PdeR.
Published by: Association des Industries Forestieres du Quebec, 1200 Ave Germain des Pres, Ste 102, Ste Foy, PQ G1V 3M7, Canada. TEL 418-651-9352, FAX 418-651-4622. Ed. Andre Duchesne. Circ: 13,000.

676 CAN ISSN 0847-2645
TS1080 P36
LES PAPETIERES DU QUEBEC. Text in French. 1990. 5/yr. CAD 34 domestic; USD 53 in United States; USD 81 elsewhere (effective 2008). adv. bk.rev. **Document type:** *Magazine, Trade.* **Description:** Addresses the scientific and technical information needs of the pulp and paper industry.
Indexed: Englnd, SCOPUS.
—CCC.
Published by: Business Information Group, 12 Concorde Pl, Ste 800, Toronto, ON M3C 4J2, Canada. TEL 416-442-2122, 800-668-2374, FAX 416-442-2191, orders@businessinformationgroup.ca. Ed. Anya Orzechowska. Pub. Jim Bussiere TEL 514-630-5955. Circ: 4,500.

676 AUT ISSN 1011-0186
TS1080 CODEN: POESF4
PAPIER AUS OESTERREICH. Text in English, German. 1964. 10/yr. EUR 75 domestic; EUR 99 foreign (effective 2010). adv. bk.rev. illus.; stat. index. **Document type:** *Magazine, Trade.*
Formerly: Oesterreichische Papier (0473-8322)
Indexed: A22, ABIPC, IPackAb, P&BA, SCOPUS.
—BLDSC (6403.080000), IE, Ingenta.
Published by: Austropapier - Vereinigung der Oesterreichischen Papierindustrie, Gumpendorfer Str 6, Vienna, W 1061, Austria. TEL 43-1-58886294, FAX 43-1-58886222, austropapier@austropapier.at. Adv. contact Lydia Fuchs. B&W page EUR 1,630, color page EUR 2,700; trim 192 x 257. Circ: 5,000 (paid and controlled).

676 DEU ISSN 1862-7579
PAPIER + TECHNIK. Text in German. 1996. 7/yr. **Document type:** *Magazine, Trade.*
Former titles (until 2005): Papiermacher (1611-2407); (until 2002): Papiermacher Magazin (1435-2753); Which was formed by the 1996 merger of: Papiermacher (0031-1405); Magazin fuer Mitarbeiter (1435-277X); Which was formerly: Magazin fuer Mitarbeiter - Werk und Leben (0344-0257); (1951-1975): Werk und Leben (0049-7142)
Related titles: Online - full text ed.
Indexed: ABIPC, IBR, IBZ, P&BA.
—CCC.
Published by: (Vereinigung der Arbeitgeberverbaende der Deutschen Papierindustrie e.V.), Dr. Curt Haefner Verlag GmbH (Subsidiary of: Konradin Verlag Robert Kohlhammer GmbH), Dischingerstr 8, Heidelberg, 69123, Germany. TEL 49-6221-64460, FAX 49-6221-644640, info@haefner-verlag.de, http://www.haefner-verlag.de. Ed. Verena Manek. Adv. contact Sandra Rink. Circ: 40,000 (controlled).

676 POL ISSN 1426-1456
PAPIERNICZY SWIAT. Text in Polish. 1996. 8/yr. PLZ 50 (effective 2011). adv. **Document type:** *Magazine, Trade.*
Published by: Unit Wydawnictwo Informacje Branzowe Sp. z o.o., ul Kierbedzia 4, Warsaw, 00-728, Poland. TEL 48-22-3201500, FAX 48-22-3201506, info@unit.com.pl.

676 SVN ISSN 0350-6614
PAPIR. Text in Slovenian. 1973. 3/yr. **Document type:** *Journal, Trade.*
Related titles: Online - full text ed.: ISSN 1581-4041. 2001.
Indexed: SCOPUS.
Published by: Institut za Celulozo in Papir, Bogisiceva 8, Ljubljana, 1000, Slovenia. TEL 386-1-2002800, FAX 386-1-4265639, info@icp-lj.si, http://www.icp-lj.si.

676 CZE ISSN 0031-1421
TS1080 CODEN: PCELAU
PAPIR A CELULOZA/PAPER AND PULP. Text in Czech, Slovak; Summaries in English, German, Russian. 1946. m. CZK 600 domestic; EUR 58 foreign (effective 2009). adv. bk.rev. illus.; mkt.; stat.; tr.lit. 32 p./no.; back issues avail. **Document type:** *Journal, Trade.* **Description:** Contains technical, economical, trade, market and general information from the Czech paper, printing and packaging industries.
Indexed: ABIPC, CIN, CISA, ChemAb, ChemTitl, P&BA, RASB, SCOPUS.
—BLDSC (6403.200000), CASDDS, INIST, Linda Hall.
Published by: Svaz Prumyslu Papiru a Celulozy/Czech Pulp & Paper Association, K Hrusovu 4, Prague 10, 10223, Czech Republic. TEL 420-2-71081133, FAX 420-2-71081136, acpp@acpp.cz. Ed. Milos Lesikar. adv.: B&W page CZK 20,000, color page CZK 35,000; bleed 215 x 310. Circ: 2,000.

676 HUN ISSN 0031-1448
CODEN: PAPIBT
PAPIRIPAR. Text in Hungarian; Summaries in English, German. 1957. bi-m. USD 60 (effective 1999). adv. bk.rev. abstr.; bibl.; charts; illus. index. **Document type:** *Trade.*
Indexed: A22, ABIPC, ChemAb, ChemTitl, GALA, P&BA, SCOPUS.
—BLDSC (6403.290000), CASDDS, IE, Ingenta.
Published by: Papir- es Nyomdaipari Mueszaki Egyesuelet, Fo utca 68, PF 433, Budapest, 1371, Hungary. Ed. Eva Polyanszky. Adv. contact Sandor Pesti. Circ: 1,200.

PAPIRIPARI ES NYOMDAIPARI SZAKIRODALMI TAJEKOZTATO/ PAPER INDUSTRY & PRINTING ABSTRACTS. *see* PAPER AND PULP—Abstracting, Bibliographies, Statistics

676 KOR ISSN 0253-3200
TS1080 CODEN: PCGIDY
PEOLPEU JONG'I GI'SUL/TECHNICAL ASSOCIATION OF THE PULP AND PAPER INDUSTRY OF KOREA. JOURNAL. Text in English. 1969. q. **Document type:** *Journal, Trade.*
Indexed: CPEI, Englnd, P31, SCOPUS.
—BLDSC (4905.660000), IE, Ingenta. **CCC.**
Published by: Han'gug Pulp Jong'i Gi'sul Haghoe/Korean Technical Association of the Pulp and Paper Industry, 701. InYong Bldg., 44-13, Yuido-Dong, Youngdeungpo-Gu, Seoul, 150-890, Korea, S. TEL 82-2-786-8620.

676.3 USA
THE PLACE. Text in English. 2000. m. free to members (effective 2011). **Document type:** *Journal, Trade.* **Description:** Covers polymers, laminations, coatings, and corrugating technology.
Media: Online - full text.
Published by: T A P P I Press, 15 Technology Pkwy S, Norcross, Fulton, GA 30092. TEL 770-446-1400, FAX 770-446-6947, memberconnection@tappi.org.

676 GBR ISSN 1746-7179
PRINT & PAPER MONTHLY. Text in English. 1989. m. GBP 130 domestic; GBP 180 in Europe; GBP 225 elsewhere (effective 2009). back issues avail. **Document type:** *Magazine, Trade.* **Description:** Features concerning print & paper based topics.
Former titles (until 2004): Print & Paper Europe (1471-3063); (until 2000): Paper Europe (0955-7806)
Related titles: Online - full text ed.: free (effective 2009).
Indexed: ABIPC, B03, P&BA, SCOPUS.
—IE, Ingenta. **CCC.**
Published by: Whitmar Publications Ltd., 30 London Rd, Southborough, Tunbridge Wells, Kent TN4 0RE, United Kingdom. TEL 44-1892-542099, FAX 44-1892-546693. Pub. Rob Mulligan.

676 FRA ISSN 0989-1889
PROFESSION NOUVEAU PAPETIER. Text in French. 1988. m. (11/yr.). adv. **Document type:** *Magazine, Trade.*
Published by: Michel Burton Communication (M B C), 16 Rue Saint Fiacre, Paris, 75002, France. TEL 33-1-42365102, FAX 33-1-42338324, diffusion@groupembc.com, http://www.pnpapetier.com/. Circ: 11,000.

676 DEU ISSN 1612-0485
PROFESSIONAL PAPERMAKING; stock preparation - paper manufacturing - paper finishing. Text in English. 2003. q. EUR 111.30 domestic; EUR 112.40 in the European Union; EUR 116 elsewhere; EUR 35 newsstand/cover (effective 2009). adv. **Document type:** *Journal, Trade.* **Description:** Presents scientific and technological reports and company notices concerning innovations for higher productivity, better quality and cost reduction in the manufacturing of pulp, paper and board.
Indexed: CPEI, P31, RefZh, SCOPUS.
—BLDSC (6864.108700), INIST. **CCC.**
Published by: Deutscher Fachverlag GmbH, Mainzer Landstr 251, Frankfurt Am Main, 60326, Germany. TEL 49-69-75952052, FAX 49-69-75952999, info@dfv.de, http://www.dfv.de. Ed. Dr. Manhart Schlegel. Adv. contact Dagmar Henning. Circ: 5,400.

628.4458 USA ISSN 1061-1452
TS1120.5 CODEN: PPREFY
➤ **PROGRESS IN PAPER RECYCLING.** Abbreviated title: P P R. Text in English. 1991. q. USD 357 to non-members; free to members (effective 2011). bk.rev. abstr.; pat. back issues avail. **Document type:** *Journal, Academic/Scholarly.* **Description:** Publishes articles on science, technology, and economics of paper recycling.
Related titles: Online - full text ed.
Indexed: ABIPC, CIN, CPEI, ChemAb, ChemTitl, Englnd, P&BA, P31, SCOPUS.
—BLDSC (6872.350000), CASDDS, IE, Infotrieve, Ingenta, Linda Hall. **CCC.**
Published by: T A P P I, 15 Technology Pky S, Norcross, GA 30092. TEL 770-446-1400, 800-332-8686, FAX 770-446-6947, memberconnection@tappi.org.

676 POL ISSN 0033-2291
TS1080 CODEN: PRZPAE
PRZEGLAD PAPIERNICZY/POLISH PAPER REVIEW. Text in Polish. 1945. m. PLZ 245.70 domestic; EUR 136 foreign (effective 2011). adv. bk.rev. abstr.; charts; illus.; stat. index. 72 p./no.; **Document type:** *Journal, Trade.*
Related titles: Online - full text ed.
Indexed: A22, ABIPC, AgrLib, B22, CIN, CPEI, ChemAb, ChemTitl, Englnd, P&BA, P31, PST, SCOPUS.
—BLDSC (6944.000000), CASDDS, IE, Ingenta, INIST.
Published by: (Stowarzyszenie Papiernikow Polskich), Wydawnictwo SIGMA - N O T Sp. z o.o., ul Ratuszowa 11, PO Box 1004, Warsaw, 00950, Poland. TEL 48-22-8180918, FAX 48-22-6192187, sekretariat@sigma-not.pl. Ed. Pawel Wandelt. adv.: B&W page PLZ 1,200, color page PLZ 2,640. Circ: 1,400. **Dist. by:** Ars Polona, Obroncow 25, Warsaw 03933, Poland. TEL 48-22-5098609, FAX 48-22-5098610, arspolona@arspolona.com.pl, http://www.arspolona.com.pl.

676.1029 USA
PULP & PAPER BUYERS GUIDE. Text in English. 1976. a. reprints avail. **Document type:** *Handbook/Manual/Guide, Trade.*
Related titles: Microfilm ed.
Published by: R I S I, Inc., 4 Alfred Cir, Bedford, MA 01730. TEL 781-734-8900, FAX 781-271-0337, info@risiinfo.com, http://www.risiinfo.com. Circ: 41,000.

676.12 674 CAN ISSN 0316-4004
TS1080 CODEN: PPCAAA
PULP & PAPER CANADA. Text in English. 1903. m. CAD 88 domestic; USD 93 in United States; USD 197 elsewhere (effective 2008). adv. bk.rev. charts; illus.; mkt.; stat.; tr.lit. index. **Document type:** *Magazine, Trade.* **Description:** Addresses the scientific and technical information needs of the pulp and paper industry.
Former titles (until 1974): Pulp & Paper Magazine of Canada (0033-4103); Which incorporated (1932-1967): Woodlands Review (0380-2493); (until 1936): Pulp and Paper of Canada (0380-2507); (until 1932): Pulp and Paper Magazine of Canada (0380-2515)
Related titles: Microfiche ed.: (from MML, PQC); Microfilm ed.: (from MML); Microform ed.: (from MML); Online - full text ed.
Indexed: A20, A22, A23, A24, A35, A37, ABIPC, ASCA, AgBio, Agr, AgrForAb, B03, B11, B13, BA, BibAg, C03, C25, CABA, CADCAM, CBCABus, CBPI, CIN, CMCI, CPEI, CWI, ChemAb, ChemTitl, CurCont, E12, EIA, Englnd, EnvAb, F08, F11, F12, GALA, GH, I11, Inspec, MSCI, MaizeAb, P&BA, P11, P31, P32, P40, P48, P52, P56, PQC, S12, S13, S16, SCI, SCOPUS, W07, W11.
—BLDSC (7157.050000), CASDDS, CIS, IE, Infotrieve, Ingenta, INIST, Linda Hall. **CCC.**
Published by: (Pulp & Paper Technical Association of Canada), Business Information Group, 12 Concorde Pl, Ste 800, Toronto, ON M3C 4J2, Canada. TEL 416-442-2122, 800-668-2374, FAX 416-442-2191, orders@businessinformationgroup.ca, http://www.businessinformationgroup.ca. Ed. Anya Orzechowska. Pub. Jim Bussiere TEL 514-630-5955. adv.: B&W page USD 4,045, color page USD 5,495; 10.88 x 8.13. Circ: 10,300.

676 CAN ISSN 0709-2563
TS1088
PULP & PAPER CANADA ANNUAL DIRECTORY. Text in English. 1930. a. CAD 165 domestic; USD 165 foreign; CAD 325 combined subscription domestic (print & CD-ROM eds.); USD 325 combined subscription foreign (print & CD-ROM eds.) (effective 2008). adv. index. **Document type:** *Directory, Trade.* **Description:** Gives corporate and technical information (equipment lists and flow charts) of Canada's pulp and paper companies and their mills. Lists suppliers and products plus complete address information. Also lists allied and related organizations.
Formed by the merger of: Pulp & Paper Canada's Reference Manual and Buyers' Guide (0316-6716); Which was formerly: Pulp & Paper Magazine of Canada's Reference Manual and Buyers' Guide (0316-6708); Pulp & Paper Canada Directory (0708-501X); Which was formerly: Pulp & Paper Canada Business Directory (0317-3550)
Related titles: CD-ROM ed.
Published by: Business Information Group, 12 Concorde Pl, Ste 800, Toronto, ON M3C 4J2, Canada. TEL 416-442-2122, 800-668-2374, FAX 416-442-2191, orders@businessinformationgroup.ca. Circ: 1,086.

676 USA
PULP & PAPER COMPANY PROFILES (YEAR). Text in English. 199?. a. (in 2 vols.). back issues avail.; reprints avail. **Document type:** *Monographic series, Trade.* **Description:** Helps to understand today's market activity in the North American and European pulp and paper industry.
Published by: R I S I, Inc., 4 Alfred Cir, Bedford, MA 01730. TEL 781-734-8900, FAX 781-271-0337, info@risiinfo.com, http://www.risiinfo.com.

676 AUS ISSN 1449-9711
PULP & PAPER EDGE (ONLINE). Text in English. m. AUD 900 (effective 2010).
Media: Online - full text.
Published by: IndustryEdge, GPO Box 77, Hobart, TAS, Australia. TEL 613-6224-7166, FAX 613-6224-7322, info@industryedge.com.au, http://www.industryedge.com.au.

676 USA ISSN 1041-7249
TS1109 CODEN: CRCFDZ
PULP AND PAPER INDUSTRY TECHNICAL CONFERENCE. CONFERENCE RECORD. Variant title: Annual Pulp and Paper Industry Technical Conference. Conference Record. Text in English. 19??. a. adv. back issues avail.; reprints avail. **Document type:** *Proceedings, Trade.* **Description:** Examines development and application of electrical systems related to the manufacture and fabrication of products.
Former titles (until 1985): I E E E. Pulp and Paper Industry Technical Conference. Conference Record (0190-2172); (until 1971): I E E E. Pulp and Paper Industry Technical Conference. Record
Related titles: CD-ROM ed.; Microfiche ed.; Online - full text ed.
Indexed: A22, Agr, Englnd, Inspec, P31, SCOPUS.
—IE, Ingenta. **CCC.**
Published by: I E E E, 445 Hoes Ln, Piscataway, NJ 08854. TEL 732-981-0060, 800-678-4333, FAX 732-562-6380, customer.service@ieee.org, http://www.ieee.org. **Co-sponsor:** Industry Applications Society.

676 USA ISSN 0033-409X
TS1080 CODEN: PUPIAW
PULP & PAPER INTERNATIONAL. Short title: P P I. Text in English. 1876. m. free to qualified personnel (effective 2010). adv. bk.rev. charts; illus.; stat. index. back issues avail.; reprints avail. **Document type:** *Magazine, Trade.* **Description:** Covers worldwide developments in management issues, new technologies, and mill operations for the pulp, paper, and paperboard industry.
Incorporates (in 2009): Pulp & Paper (0033-4081); Which was formerly (until 1947): Pulp & Paper Industry (0096-4816); (1927-1944): Pacific Pulp & Paper Industry (0096-4999); Pulp & Paper incorporated (1872-1986): Paper Trade Journal (0031-1197); (1941-1964): Paper Mill News (0096-1892); Which was formerly (1876-1941): Paper Mill and Wood Pulp News (0096-2120)
Related titles: Online - full text ed.; ◆ International ed. of: Pulp & Paper. ISSN 0033-4081.
Indexed: A09, A10, A12, A15, A17, A22, ABIPC, ABIn, B01, B02, B03, B04, B06, B07, B08, B09, B15, B17, B18, BPI, BusI, C&ISA, C10, C12, CBNB, CPEI, ChemAb, CurPA, E&CAJ, Englnd, G04, G06, G07, G08, I05, KES, M01, M02, P&BA, P11, P31, P34, P48, P51, P52, P53, P54, P56, PQC, RefZh, S22, SCOPUS, SolStAb, T02, V02, V03, V04, W01, W02, W03.
—BLDSC (7157.700000), IE, Infotrieve, Ingenta, INIST, Linda Hall. **CCC.**
Published by: R I S I, Inc., 4 Alfred Cir, Bedford, MA 01730. TEL 781-734-8900, FAX 781-271-0337, info@risiinfo.com. Ed. Mark Rushton. Adv. contact Misty Belser TEL 415-947-3605. B&W page USD 5,350, color page USD 10,195; trim 210 x 297. Circ: 15,000.

676 USA
HD9821
PULP & PAPER NORTH AMERICAN FACTBOOK. Text in English. 1980. a. reprints avail. **Document type:** *Handbook/Manual/Guide, Trade.* **Description:** Provides information on the pulp and paper industry in the US, Canada, and Mexico, including features such as economic analysis, profiles, statistics and analysis, financial data, and North American overview.
Formerly: Pulp & Paper North American Industry Factbook (0273-3781)
Indexed: SRI.
—CCC.
Published by: R I S I, Inc., 4 Alfred Cir, Bedford, MA 01730. TEL 781-734-8900, FAX 781-271-0337, info@risiinfo.com, http://www.risiinfo.com. Circ: 600.

676.2 USA
PULP & PAPER PROJECT UPDATE. Text in English. 1982. w. reprints avail. **Document type:** *Newsletter.* **Description:** Provides industry producers, suppliers and financial analysts with the up-to-date project development news and information as it breaks.
Formerly (until 2001): Pulp & Paper Project Report (0748-1608)
Media: Online - full content.
Indexed: SCOPUS.
—IE. **CCC.**
Published by: R I S I, Inc., 4 Alfred Cir, Bedford, MA 01730. TEL 781-734-8900, FAX 781-271-0337, info@risiinfo.com, http://www.risiinfo.com.

676 CAN ISSN 0079-7960
TS1080
PULP AND PAPER RESEARCH INSTITUTE OF CANADA. ANNUAL REPORT. Text in English. 1968. a. free.
Published by: Pulp and Paper Research Institute of Canada, 570 blvd St Jean, Pointe Claire, PQ H9R 3J9, Canada. TEL 514-630-4100, FAX 514-630-4134, TELEX 05-821541. Ed. J M MacLeod. Circ: 3,000.

676 CAN ISSN 1494-7722
PULP AND PAPER TECHNICAL ASSOCIATION OF CANADA. ANNUAL MEETING. PREPRINTS A/ASSOCIATION TECHNIQUE DES PATES ET PAPIERS DU CANADA. CONGRES ANNUEL. PRETIRES A. Text in English, French. a. CAD 75, USD 51 to non-members; CAD 60, USD 40.80 to members (effective 2005). **Document type:** *Proceedings, Academic/Scholarly.*
Formerly (until 1999): Canadian Pulp and Paper Association. Technical Section. Preprints A (0822-5206); Which superseded in part (in 1982): Canadian Pulp and Paper Association. Technical Section. Annual Meeting. Preprints (0316-6732)
Related titles: CD-ROM ed.: Pulp and Paper Technical Association of Canada. Annual Meeting Preprints CD. ISSN 1910-0515. 2004.
Indexed: Englnd, P31, SCOPUS.
—IE. **CCC.**
Published by: Pulp and Paper Technical Association of Canada/ Association Technique des Pates et Papiers du Canada, 740 rue Notre Dame ouest, Ste 1070, Montreal, PQ H3C 3X6, Canada. TEL 514-392-0265, FAX 514-392-0369, pubs@paptac.ca.

676 CAN
PULP AND PAPER TECHNICAL ASSOCIATION OF CANADA. ANNUAL MEETING. PREPRINTS B/ASSOCIATION TECHNIQUE DES PATES ET PAPIERS DU CANADA. CONGRES ANNUEL. PRETIRES B. Text in English, French. a. CAD 75, USD 51 to non-members; CAD 60, USD 40.80 to members (effective 2005).
Formerly (until 1999): Canadian Pulp and Paper Association. Technical Section. Preprints B (0822-5214); Which superseded in part (in 1982): Canadian Pulp and Paper Association. Technical Section. Annual Meeting. Preprints (0316-6732)
—IE. **CCC.**
Published by: Pulp and Paper Technical Association of Canada/ Association Technique des Pates et Papiers du Canada, 740 rue Notre Dame ouest, Ste 1070, Montreal, PQ H3C 3X6, Canada. TEL 514-392-0265, FAX 514-392-0369, pubs@paptac.ca.

676.05 CAN ISSN 1494-4138
PULP AND PAPER TECHNICAL ASSOCIATION OF CANADA. MEETING. PREPRINT BOOK C. Text in English, French. 1998. a. **Document type:** *Journal, Trade.*
—CCC.
Published by: Pulp and Paper Technical Association of Canada/ Association Technique des Pates et Papiers du Canada, 740 rue Notre Dame ouest, Ste 1070, Montreal, PQ H3C 3X6, Canada. TEL 514-392-0265, FAX 514-392-0369, pubs@paptac.ca, http://www.paptac.ca.

676 CAN ISSN 1493-017X
PULP AND PAPER TECHNICAL ASSOCIATION OF CANADA. NEWS BULLETIN. Text in English, French. bi-m. membership. **Document type:** *Bulletin, Trade.*
Former titles (until 1999): Canadian Pulp and Paper Association. Technical Section. News (1207-8328); (until 1995): Canadian Pulp and Paper Association. Technical Section. News Bulletin (0834-0234); (until 1985): Canadian Pulp and Paper Association. Technical Section. News Letter (0319-6445)
Related titles: ◆ Supplement to: Journal of Pulp & Paper Science. ISSN 0826-6220.
—BLDSC (6404.280000).
Published by: Pulp and Paper Technical Association of Canada/ Association Technique des Pates et Papiers du Canada, 740 rue Notre Dame ouest, Ste 1070, Montreal, PQ H3C 3X6, Canada. TEL 514-392-0265, FAX 514-392-0369, pubs@paptac.ca, http://www.paptac.ca.

676 USA ISSN 0738-0917
HD9820.1 CODEN: PPWEFP
PULP & PAPER WEEK. Text in English. 1979. w. looseleaf. USD 1,297 (print & online eds.) (effective 2009). stat. index. back issues avail.; reprints avail. **Document type:** *Newsletter, Trade.* **Description:** Helps you keep up with the latest pricing information, supply-demand conditions, financial news, mill projects, and market trends in the paper industry.
Incorporates (1990-1998): Paper Recycler (1072-1223)
Related titles: Fax ed.: USD 1,067 (effective 2005); Online - full text ed.: USD 1,297 (effective 2008).
Indexed: ABIPC, Englnd, P&BA, SCOPUS.
—CCC.
Published by: R I S I, Inc., 4 Alfred Cir, Bedford, MA 01730. TEL 781-734-8900, FAX 781-271-0337, info@risiinfo.com.

676 ZAF
PULP & PAPER YEARBOOK. Text in English. a. adv. illus. **Document type:** *Directory.* **Description:** Buyers guide for the southern African paper industry.
Published by: George Warman Publications (Pty.) Ltd., Rondebosch, PO Box 705, Cape Town, 7701, South Africa. info@gwarmanpublications.co.za, http://www.gwarmanpublications.co.za.

RECYCLED PAPER NEWS; independent coverage of recycled paper issues. *see* ENVIRONMENTAL STUDIES—Waste Management

REPRODUCTION BULLETIN. *see* PRINTING

RESSOURCE EN SANTE ET EN SECURITE. *see* OCCUPATIONAL HEALTH AND SAFETY

676 FIN ISSN 1798-0933
RESULTS PULP & PAPER. Text in English. 1985. 3/yr. free to qualified personnel (effective 2012). charts; illus. **Document type:** *Magazine, Trade.* **Description:** Covers a wide range of solutions and services for the pulp and paper industry, including process automation and power generation technologies.
Formed by the merger of (2008-2009): Fiber & Paper & Power Express (1797-271X); (2008-2009): Fiber & Paper & Power (1797-2698); Both of which superseded in part (in 2008): Fiber & Paper (1457-1234); Which was formerly (until 1999): Valmet Paper News (0784-722X)
Related titles: Online - full text ed.
—BLDSC (7783.233500).
Published by: Metso Paper, Inc., PO Box 587, Jyvaskyla, 40101, Finland. TEL 358-20-482150, FAX 358-20-482151, pulpandpaper@metso.com, http://www.metsopaper.com. Eds. Riitta Raisanen, Riitta-Maija Peltovuori.

REVISTA FORESTAL BARACOA. *see* FORESTS AND FORESTRY—Lumber And Wood

676 FRA ISSN 1279-0958
CODEN: RPRCFG
REVUE DU PAPIER CARTON; production - distribution - transformation. Text in French. 1952. m. (10/yr.). EUR 110 per quarter domestic; EUR 126 per quarter in Europe; EUR 143 per quarter elsewhere (effective 2009). adv. bk.rev. abstr.; bibl.; charts; illus.; stat. **Document type:** *Magazine, Trade.* **Description:** Includes producers in Europe, suppliers, converters, merchants and agents.
Formed by the merger of: Papier, Carton et Cellulose (0031-1367); Transformation Papier Carton (1249-6464)
Indexed: ABIPC, ChemAb, ChemTitl, FR, P&BA, SCOPUS.
—CASDDS. **CCC.**
Published by: Michel Burton Communication (M B C), 16 Rue Saint Fiacre, Paris, 75002, France. TEL 33-1-42365102, FAX 33-1-42338324, diffusion@groupembc.com, http://www.pnpapetier.com/. Circ: 6,002.

676 SWE ISSN 1104-3377
S C A INVESTOR REPORT. (Svenska Cellulosa Aktiebolaget) Text in English. 1990. q. free (effective 2004).
Formerly (until 1992): Concern (English Edition) (1102-3155)
Related titles: Online - full content ed.
Published by: Svenska Cellulosa Aktiebolaget, Stureplan 3, Stockholm, 10397, Sweden. TEL 46-8-7885100, FAX 46-8-6607430.

S I A. (Skogsindustriarbetaren) *see* FORESTS AND FORESTRY—Lumber And Wood

676 SWE ISSN 0280-6800
S P C I. MEDDELANDE. Text in Swedish. 1954. irreg., latest vol.78, 2005. price varies. **Document type:** *Monographic series, Trade.*
Published by: Svenska Pappers- och Cellulosaingenioersfoereningen/ Swedish Association of Pulp and Paper Engineers, PO Box 5515, Stockholm, 11485, Sweden. TEL 46-8-7938400, FAX 46-8-6617344, spci@spci.se, http://www.spci.se.

676 SWE ISSN 1651-9981
S P C I SVENSK PAPPERSTIDNING. (Svenska Pappers- och Cellulosaingenioersfoereningen) Text in Swedish. 1999. 10/yr. SEK 850 domestic; SEK 1,300 foreign (effective 2007). adv. back issues avail. **Document type:** *Magazine, Trade.*
Supersedes in part (in 2003): Svensk Papperstidning (1403-9605)
Related titles: Online - full text ed.
—Ingenta, INIST.
Published by: Svenska Pappers- och Cellulosaingenioersfoereningen/ Swedish Association of Pulp and Paper Engineers, PO Box 5515, Stockholm, 11485, Sweden. TEL 46-8-7938400, FAX 46-8-6617344, spci@spci.se, http://www.spci.se. Ed. Ewa Arve TEL 46-8-7838482. Adv. contact Camilla Sinivaara TEL 46-8-7838254. B&W page SEK 19,100, color page SEK 29,900; 185 x 267.

P

676 SWE
S T F I ANNUAL REVIEW. (Skogsindustrins Tekniska Forskningsinstitut) Text in English. a. **Document type:** *Journal, Trade.* **Description:** Covers the activities and performance of the Swedish Pulp and Paper Research Institute.
Published by: S T F I - Packforsk/Swedish Pulp and Paper Research Institute - Packforsk, Drottning Kristinas Vaeg 61, PO Box 5604, Stockholm, 11486, Sweden. TEL 46-8-6767000, FAX 46-8-4115518, info@stfi.se, http://www.stfi-packforsk.se.

676 SWE
S T F I - KONTAKT (ENGLISH EDITION); current awareness of pulp and paper research. (Skogsindustrins Tekniska Forskningsinstitut) Text in English. 1969. q. **Document type:** *Magazine, Trade.* **Description:** Contains information and articles geared towards customers of the Swedish paper and pulp industry.
Formerly (until 1997): S T F I - Kontakt (Svensk utg.) (0347-0504)
Related titles: Online - full text ed.
Indexed: ABIPC, SCOPUS.
Published by: S T F I - Packforsk/Swedish Pulp and Paper Research Institute - Packforsk, Drottning Kristinas Vaeg 61, PO Box 5604, Stockholm, 11486, Sweden. TEL 46-8-6767000, FAX 46-8-4115518, info@stfi.se, http://www.stfi-packforsk.se.

676 SWE ISSN 1650-4607
SD1
S T F I REPORT. PUB. (Skogsindustrins Tekniska Forskningsinstitut) Text in English, Swedish. 1969. irreg. illus. cum.index: 1969-1983. back issues avail. **Document type:** *Monographic series, Trade.*
Former titles (until 2001): S T F I Rapport. P (1400-4305); (until 1995): S T F I Meddelande. Series A (0348-2650); (until 1976): Svenska Traeforskningsinstitutet. Meddelande. Series A (0085-6983)
Indexed: ABIPC.
Published by: S T F I - Packforsk/Swedish Pulp and Paper Research Institute - Packforsk, Drottning Kristinas Vaeg 61, PO Box 5604, Stockholm, 11486, Sweden. TEL 46-8-6767000, FAX 46-8-4115518, info@stfi.se, http://www.stfi-packforsk.se.

SCRIPT (DUTCH EDITION); vakblad voor de kantoorvakhandel. *see* BUSINESS AND ECONOMICS—Office Equipment And Services

SEKUNDAER-ROHSTOFFE; Fachzeitschrift fuer Rohstoffhandel, Kreislaufwirtschaft und Recycling-Technik. *see* MACHINERY

676 JPN ISSN 0912-5019
SHIGYO TAIMUSU/PAPER INDUSTRY. Text in Japanese. s-m. **Document type:** *Trade.*
Published by: Tekku Taimusu/Tec Times Co. Ltd., 3-13-7 Kanda-Nishikicho, Chiyoda-ku, Tokyo, 101-0054, Japan. TEL 81-3-32332580, FAX 81-3-32332523, http://www.st-times.co.jp/.

676 NOR ISSN 0800-8582
SKOGINDUSTRI; tidsskriftet for masse, papir, trelast og bioenergi. Text in Norwegian. 1945. 8/yr. NOK 512 (effective 2007). adv. stat. index. **Document type:** *Journal, Trade.* **Description:** Journal for the Norwegian paper, pulp, timber and wallboard industries.
Former titles (until 1985): Norsk Skogindustri (0029-2095); (until 1947): Papir-Journalen (1501-7214)
Indexed: ABIPC, ChemAb, P&BA, SCOPUS.
—INIST. **CCC.**
Published by: Media Oslo As, Storgata 14, Postboks 151, Sentrum, Oslo, 0102, Norway. TEL 47-23-158500, FAX 47-22-171279, http://www.mediaoslo.no. Ed. Karl Joergen Gurandsrud TEL 47-23-158503. Adv. contact Uno Dahl Henriksen. B&W page NOK 10,000, color page NOK 13,000; 210 x 297. Circ: 2,600.

676 676.3 USA ISSN 2159-7448
STATIONERY TRENDS. Text in English. 2008. q. USD 15 domestic; USD 56 in Canada; USD 100 elsewhere; USD 6 per issue (effective 2011). adv. back issues avail. **Document type:** *Magazine, Trade.* **Description:** Provides retailers with a peek at some of the industry's hottest designers and most sought-after products.
Related titles: Online - full text ed.: ISSN 2159-7456.
Published by: Great American Publishing Co., 75 Applewood Dr, Ste A, PO Box 128, Sparta, MI 49345. TEL 616-887-9008, FAX 616-887-2666, http://greatamericanpublish.com. Ed. Sarah Schwartz TEL 216-464-0709. Pub. Matt McCallum TEL 616-887-9008 ext 101. Adv. contact Brian Virgona TEL 570-223-9190.

676 686.2 USA
T A P P I COATING & GRAPHIC ARTS CONFERENCE PROCEEDINGS. (Technical Association of the Pulp and Paper Industry) Text in English. a., latest 2004. back issues avail. **Document type:** *Proceedings, Trade.*
Formerly: Technical Association of the Pulp and Paper Industry. Graphic Arts Conference Proceedings
Media: CD-ROM.
Published by: T A P P I, 15 Technology Pky S, Norcross, GA 30092. TEL 770-446-1400, 800-332-8686, FAX 770-446-6947, memberconnection@tappi.org.

676.3 USA
TS198.3. P3
T A P P I INTERNATIONAL CORRUGATED CONTAINERS CONFERENCE AND TRADE FAIR. PROCEEDINGS. (Technical Association of the Pulp and Paper Industry) Text in English. 196?. a. price varies. back issues avail. **Document type:** *Proceedings, Academic/Scholarly.*
Former titles (until 1995): T A P P I International Corrugated Containers Conference. Proceedings (1079-2899); (until 1993): T A P P I Corrugated Containers Conference. Proceedings (1079-3143); (until 1992): T A P P I Corrugated Conference. Proceedings (1079-2902); (until 1991): T A P P I Corrugated Containers Conference (1058-0883); (until 1983): T A P P I Corrugated / Testing Conference. Proceedings; (until 1982): T A P P I Corrugated Containers Conference; (until 1976): T A P P I Corrugated Containers / Papermakers Conference. Proceedings; (until 1975): T A P P I Corrugated Containers Conference
—CCC.
Published by: T A P P I, 15 Technology Pky S, Norcross, GA 30092. TEL 770-446-1400, 800-332-8686, FAX 770-446-6947, memberconnection@tappi.org, http://www.tappi.org.

676 USA
➤ **T A P P I JOURNAL (ONLINE).** (Technical Association of the Pulp and Paper Industry) Abbreviated title: T J. Text in English. 19??. m. free to members (effective 2010). back issues avail. **Document type:** *Journal, Academic/Scholarly.*
Formerly (until 2009): T A P P I Journal (Print)
Media: Online - full text.
Published by: T A P P I, 15 Technology Pky S, Norcross, GA 30092. TEL 770-446-1400, 800-332-8686, FAX 770-446-6947, memberconnection@tappi.org. Ed. Monica Shaw.

676 USA ISSN 1549-3539
TS1088
T A P P I MEMBERSHIP DIRECTORY. (Technical Association of the Pulp and Paper Industry) Text in English. 1919. a. free to members (effective 2010). back issues avail. **Document type:** *Directory, Trade.*
Former titles (until 2000): T A P P I Membership Directory and Company Guide; (until 1994): T A P P I Membership Directory; (until 1993): T A P P I Membership Directory and Company Guide; (until 1987): T A P P I Directory of Members, Products, and Services; (until 1985): T A P P I Membership Directory; (until 1982): T A P P I Directory (0091-7737); (until 1973): Technical Association of the Pulp and Paper Industry. Yearbook (0092-3737)
Related titles: Online - full text ed.
Published by: T A P P I, 15 Technology Pky S, Norcross, GA 30092. TEL 770-446-1400, 800-332-8686, FAX 770-446-6947, memberconnection@tappi.org, http://www.tappi.org.

676 USA
TS1176.6.M4 CODEN: PTAIDL
(YEAR) T A P P I RECYCLING SYMPOSIUM. (Technical Association of the Pulp and Paper Industry) Text in English. 1985. irreg., latest 2000. price varies. back issues avail. **Document type:** *Proceedings, Academic/Scholarly.*
Former titles (until 2000): T A P P I Proceedings (Year) (1046-4166); (until 1988): Technical Association of the Pulp and Paper Industry. Annual Meeting Proceedings (0272-7269)
Indexed: A22.
—CASDDS, Ingenta. **CCC.**
Published by: T A P P I, 15 Technology Pky S, Norcross, GA 30092. TEL 770-446-1400, 800-332-8686, FAX 770-446-6947, memberconnection@tappi.org.

676 USA
T A P P I TECHNICAL INFORMATION PAPERS. (Technical Association of the Pulp and Paper Industry) Text in English. 1989. biennial. USD 700 to non-members; USD 475 to members (effective 2011). **Document type:** *Journal, Trade.*
Formerly (until 1996): T A P P I Technical Information Sheets (1056-9022)
—CCC.
Published by: (T A P P I), T A P P I Press, 15 Technology Pkwy S, Norcross, Fulton, GA 30092. TEL 770-446-1400, FAX 770-446-6947, memberconnection@tappi.org.

676 USA ISSN 1045-618X
TS1109
➤ **T A P P I TEST METHODS.** (Technical Association of the Pulp and Paper Industry) Text in English. 1926. biennial. USD 383 per issue (effective 2010). index. **Document type:** *Journal, Academic/Scholarly.*
Former titles: T A P P I Standards and Provisional Methods; T A P P I Standards and Suggested Methods
Related titles: Online - full text ed.
—CCC.
Published by: T A P P I, 15 Technology Pky S, Norcross, GA 30092. TEL 770-446-1400, 800-332-8686, FAX 770-446-6947, memberconnection@tappi.org, http://www.tappi.org.

676 ZAF ISSN 1029-0109
T A P P S A JOURNAL. Text in English. 1998. bi-m. USD 90 (effective 2007). adv.
Published by: Technical Association of the Pulp and Paper Industry of Southern Africa, PO Box 1633, Kloof, 3640, South Africa. TEL 27-31-7642494, FAX 27-31-7640676, secretary@tappsa.co.za. Ed. Jane Molony. Circ: 1,200.

676 FIN ISSN 1797-4496
T K K REPORTS IN FOREST PRODUCTS TECHNOLOGY. SERIES A. (Teknillinen Korkeakoulu) Text mainly in English. 1994. irreg. back issues avail. **Document type:** *Monographic series, Academic/Scholarly.*
Former titles (until 2008): Helsinki University of Technology. Laboratory of Paper and Printing Technology. Reports. Series A (1796-7414); (until 2006): Helsinki University of Technology. Laboratory of Paper Technology. Reports. Series A (1456-7172); (until 1998): Laboratory of Paper Technology. Reports. Series A (1237-6248)
Related titles: Online - full text ed.: ISSN 1797-5093. 1999.
Published by: Teknillinen Korkeakoulu, Puunjalostustekniikan Laitos/Helsinki University of Technology. Department of Forest Products Technology, Vuorimiehentie 1 A, Espoo, 02150, Finland. TEL 358-9-4511, FAX 358-9-4514259, http://puu.tkk.fi.

676 FIN ISSN 1797-450X
T K K REPORTS IN FOREST PRODUCTS TECHNOLOGY. SERIES B. (Teknillinen Korkeakoulu) Text in Multiple languages. 1993. irreg. **Document type:** *Monographic series, Academic/Scholarly.*
Former titles (until 2008): Helsinki University of Technology. Laboratory of Paper and Printing Technology. Reports. Series B (1797-0008); (until 2007): Helsinki University of Technology. Laboratory of Paper Technology. Reports. Series B (1456-7180); (until 1999): Laboratory of Paper Technology. Reports. Series B (1236-4568)
Related titles: Online - full text ed.
Published by: Teknillinen Korkeakoulu, Puunjalostustekniikan Laitos/Helsinki University of Technology. Department of Forest Products Technology, Vuorimiehentie 1 A, Espoo, 02150, Finland. TEL 358-9-4511, FAX 358-9-4514259.

TAIWAN LINYE KEXUE/TAIWAN JOURNAL OF FOREST SCIENCE. *see* FORESTS AND FORESTRY

676 CHN ISSN 1674-5469
TIANJIN ZAOZHI/TIANJIN PAPER MAKING. Text in Chinese. 1970. q.
Formerly (until 1979): Tianjin Zaozhi Tongxun
Related titles: Online - full text ed.
Published by: Tianjin Shi Qinggongye Zaozhi Jishu Yanjiusuo/Tianjin Paper Making Technological Research Institute of Light Industry, 1069, Dagu Nan Lu, Hexi-qu, Tianjin, 300222, China. TEL 86-22-88823001, FAX 86-22-28162543. **Co-sponsor:** Tianjin Shi Zaozhi Xuehui.

676 USA
TISSUE MONITOR. Text in English. 11/yr. USD 3,700 (effective 2007). **Description:** Provides coverage of bath tissue, napkins, facial tissue and toweling markets.
Related titles: Online - full text ed.
Published by: R I S I, Inc., 4 Alfred Cir, Bedford, MA 01730. TEL 781-734-8900, FAX 781-271-0337, info@risiinfo.com, http://www.risiinfo.com.

676 USA ISSN 1379-0668
TISSUE WORLD. Abbreviated title: T W. Text in English. 2002. bi-m. **Document type:** *Magazine, Trade.* **Description:** Covers the entire tissue supply chain from raw materials and manufacturing technology to converting, packaging and distribution.
Indexed: Englnd, SCOPUS.
Published by: R I S I, Inc., 4 Alfred Cir, Bedford, MA 01730. TEL 781-734-8900, FAX 781-271-0337, info@risiinfo.com, http://www.risiinfo.com.

676 SGP
TISSUE WORLD ASIA. Text in English. bi-m. free to qualified personnel. back issues avail. **Document type:** *Magazine, Trade.*
Related titles: Online - full content ed.
Published by: C M P Asia Trade Fairs Ptd Ltd. (Subsidiary of: C M P Asia Ltd.), 111 Somerset Rd, #09-07, Singapore Power Bldg, Singapore, 238164, Singapore. TEL 65-6735-3366, FAX 65-6738-9057. Ed. Martin Bayliss. Pub. Jean Oh.

676 FRA ISSN 1954-2534
TRANSFOPLUS; le magazine de la transformation papier, carton et film. Text in French. 2006. q. EUR 101 domestic; EUR 116 in Europe; EUR 132 elsewhere (effective 2009). **Document type:** *Magazine, Trade.*
Related titles: ◆ Supplement(s): Etiquettes Plus. ISSN 1765-4602.
Published by: Michel Burton Communication (M B C), 16 Rue Saint Fiacre, Paris, 75002, France. TEL 33-1-42365102, FAX 33-1-42338324, diffusion@groupembc.com, http://www.pnpapetier.com/.

676 RUS ISSN 0869-4923
CODEN: TBKAEY
TSELLYULOZA, BUMAGA, KARTON. Text in English, Russian. m. USD 99.95 in United States.
Indexed: ABIPC, ChemAb, Englnd, P&BA, SCOPUS.
—BLDSC (0396.495000), CASDDS, East View.
Published by: Torgovyi Dom Bumaga, Ul Krzhizhanovskogo 24-35, k 3, Moscow, 117218, Russian Federation. TEL 7-095-3312511, FAX 7-095-3322811. **Dist. by:** East View Information Services, 10601 Wayzata Blvd, Minneapolis, MN 55305. TEL 952-252-1201, 800-477-1005, FAX 952-252-1202, info@eastview.com, http://www.eastview.com.

338.476 GBR ISSN 1473-5989
U K PREVIEW. (United Kingdom) Text in English. 1996. a. GBP 799 per issue (effective 2009). back issues avail. **Document type:** *Journal, Trade.* **Description:** Provides annual demand and price forecasts for the main paper and board sectors.
Related titles: Online - full text ed.
Published by: P P L Research Ltd., PO Box 2002, Watford, Herts WD25 9JQ, United Kingdom. TEL 44-1923-894777, FAX 44-1923-894888, enquiries@pplresearch.co.uk.

VORWAERTS. *see* LABOR UNIONS

676.029 USA
TS1088
WALDEN'S A B C GUIDE. Text in English. 1885. a. USD 245 combined subscription per issue (print & online eds.) (effective 2011). index. **Document type:** *Directory, Trade.* **Description:** Lists U.S. and Canadian paper manufacturers and merchants.
Former titles (until 1998): Walden's A B C Guide and Paper Production Yearbook (0731-2571); (until 19??): Walden's A B C Guide (0083-7024); Walden's A B C Pocket Guide
Related titles: Online - full text ed.
Published by: Walden-Mott Corporation, 225 N Franklin Tpke, Ramsey, NJ 07446. TEL 201-818-8630, FAX 201-818-8720, walden@walden-mott.com.

676 USA
WALDEN'S PAPER CATALOG. Text in English. 19??. s-a. USD 85 (effective 2011). **Document type:** *Catalog, Trade.* **Description:** Lists paper distributors, mills, manufacturers, converters, and merchants. Provides a condensed review of U.S. Government Paper Specification Standards. Includes listings of mill brand papers arranged according to grade.
Published by: Walden-Mott Corporation, 225 N Franklin Tpke, Ramsey, NJ 07446. TEL 201-818-8630, FAX 201-818-8720, walden@walden-mott.com.

676 USA
WALDEN'S PAPER HANDBOOK. Text in English. 19??. irreg. USD 25 per issue (effective 2011). charts. **Document type:** *Handbook/Manual/Guide, Trade.* **Description:** Serves as a reference source of practical data on paper. Includes facts, figures, tables, charts and references relevant when introducing new sales and marketing people to the language and customs of paper and allied industries.
Published by: Walden-Mott Corporation, 225 N Franklin Tpke, Ramsey, NJ 07446. TEL 201-818-8630, FAX 201-818-8720, walden@walden-mott.com.

676 USA
WALDEN'S PAPER REPORT. Text in English. 1971. s-m. USD 240 (effective 2011). bk.rev. charts; stat. **Document type:** *Newsletter, Trade.* **Description:** Reviews news of the North American paper industry.
Formerly: Walden-Mott Paper Report
Published by: Walden-Mott Corporation, 225 N Franklin Tpke, Ramsey, NJ 07446. TEL 201-818-8630, FAX 201-818-8720, walden@walden-mott.com, http://www.walden-mott.com/.

WEYERHAEUSER TODAY. *see* FORESTS AND FORESTRY—Lumber And Wood

676.32029 GBR
WHO'S WHO IN CORRUGATED, FOLDING CARTONS AND THE RECOVERED FIBRE SECTOR FOR THE U K & EIRE: ANNUAL DIRECTORY. Text in English. 1974. a. GBP 125 per issue (effective 2010). **Document type:** *Directory, Trade.* **Description:** Provides information for the corrugated board industry.
Formerly (until 2009): Who's Who in Corrugated (0307-6040)
—CCC.
Published by: (International Paper Board Industry), Brunton Business Publications Ltd., 1 Salisbury Office Park, London Rd, Salisbury, Wiltshire SP1 3HP, United Kingdom. TEL 44-1722-337038, publications@brunton.co.uk. Pub. Michael Brunton.

676 DEU ISSN 0043-7131
TS1080 CODEN: WBPFAZ
WOCHENBLATT FUER PAPIERFABRIKATION; Fachzeitschrift fuer die Papier-, Pappen- und Zellstoff-industrie. Text in German. 1871. 18/yr. EUR 123.10 domestic; EUR 127.30 in the European Union; EUR 132.70 elsewhere; EUR 9 newsstand/cover (effective 2009). adv. bk.rev. abstr.; charts; illus.; pat.; stat.; tr.lit. index. reprints avail. **Document type:** *Journal, Trade.*
Related titles: Online - full text ed.
Indexed: A20, A22, ABIPC, ASCA, ASFA, CIN, CPEI, ChemAb, ESPM, Englnd, FR, MSCI, P&BA, P31, PROMT, RefZh, SCI, SCOPUS, SWRA, TM, W07.
—BLDSC (9342.000000), CASDDS, IE, Infotrieve, Ingenta, INIST. **CCC.**
Published by: Deutscher Fachverlag GmbH, Mainzer Landstr 251, Frankfurt Am Main, 60326, Germany. TEL 49-69-75952052, FAX 49-69-75952999, info@dfv.de, http://www.dfv.de. Ed. Dr. Manhart Schlegel. Adv. contact Dagmar Henning. B&W page EUR 2,080, color page EUR 2,850; trim 190 x 270. Circ: 2,815 (paid and controlled). **Co-sponsors:** Akademischer Papieringenieur-Verein an der TH Darmstadt; Vereinigter Papierfachverband Munchen e.V.; Papiertechnische Stiftung Muenchen; Vereinigung Gernsbacher Papiermacher e.V.; Papiermacher-Berufsgenossenschaft Mainz.

WOODWORKING INTERNATIONAL. *see* FORESTS AND FORESTRY—Lumber And Wood

676 USA
WORLD TISSUE BUSINESS MONITOR. Text in English. 19??. q. USD 2,400 (effective 2009). back issues avail. **Document type:** *Newsletter, Trade.* **Description:** Features industry news, in-depth regional reports, updates on investment projects, and statistics on demand, supply and trade for the global tissue industry.
Related titles: Online - full text ed.
Published by: R I S I, Inc., 4 Alfred Cir, Bedford, MA 01730. TEL 781-734-8900, 866-271-8525, FAX 781-271-0337, info@risiinfo.com. Adv. contact Misty Belser TEL 415-947-3605.

676 USA
WORLD TISSUE FORECAST. Text in English. 4/yr. USD 5,300 per issue (effective 2007). **Document type:** *Report, Trade.* **Description:** Covers the key concepts of apparent consumption, production, capacity, operating rates and trade, the forecast also includes a macroeconomic overview, executive summary and fiber cost outlook.
Media: Online - full content.
Published by: R I S I, Inc., 4 Alfred Cir, Bedford, MA 01730. TEL 781-734-8900, FAX 781-271-0337, info@risiinfo.com, http://www.risiinfo.com.

676.2 CHN ISSN 1004-8405
CODEN: XKYJFZ
XIANWEISU KEXUE YU JISHU/JOURNAL OF CELLULOSE SCIENCE AND TECHNOLOGY. Text in Chinese; Abstracts in English. 1993. q. USD 20 (effective 2003). **Document type:** *Journal, Academic/Scholarly.* **Description:** Covers achievements in the fields of cellulose chemistry and lignocellulosic chemistry.
Related titles: Online - full text ed.
—BLDSC (4955.051000), CASDDS.
Published by: Zhongguo Kexueyuan Guangzhou Huaxue Yanjiusuo/Chinese Academy of Sciences, Guangzhou Institute of Chemistry, PO Box 1122, Guangzhou, 510650, China. TEL 86-20-85231297, FAX 86-20-85231119. Ed. Shulin Cao. Circ: 1,000 (controlled). **Dist. by:** China Publications International Trading Corporation, P.O. Box 782, Beijing, China.

676.2 CHN ISSN 1007-2225
ZAOZHI HUAXUEPIN/PAPER CHEMICALS. Text in Chinese. 1988. bi-m. USD 60 (effective 2008). adv. **Document type:** *Journal.* **Description:** Covers R&D and technological achievements in the field of pulp and paper chemicals both in China and abroad.
Related titles: Online - full text ed.
Published by: China Papermaking Chemicals Industry Association, 7 Shihuiba, Changbanxiang, Hangzhou, Zhejiang Province 310014, China. TEL 86-571-8315561. Ed. Fulin Wang. R&P, Adv. contact Genrong Chen. Circ: 5,000.

676 CHN ISSN 1671-4571
ZAOZHI KEXUE YU JISHU/PAPER SCIENCE & TECHNOLOGY. Text in Chinese. 1982. bi-m. CNY 7.50 newsstand/cover (effective 2006). **Document type:** *Journal, Academic/Scholarly.*
Formerly (until 2000): Guangdong Zaozhi/Guangdong Pulp & Paper (1008-7397)
Related titles: Online - full text ed.
Published by: Huanan Ligong Daxue/South China Unversity of Technology, Guangzhou, 510640, China.

672 CHN ISSN 1006-8791
ZAOZHI XINXI/CHINA PAPERMAKING NEWS. Text in English. 1995. m. USD 62.40 (effective 2009). 80 p./no.; **Document type:** *Newsletter, Trade.* **Description:** Focuses on the latest news of the Chinese pulp and paper industry.
Published by: Zhongguo Zaozhi Xiehui/China Paper Association, 22 B FuWai Street, Beijing, 100833, China. TEL 86-10-65831256, FAX 86-10-65817480. Adv. contact Heqin Li TEL 86-10-65831284. **Co-sponsors:** Zhongguo Shijiang Zaozhi Yanjiuyuan/China National Pulp and Paper Research Institute; Zhongguo Zaozhi Xuehui/China Technical Association of the Paper Industry.

676 CHN ISSN 1001-6309
TS1080
ZHI HE ZAOZHI/PAPER AND PAPERMAKING. Text in Chinese. 1982. bi-m. USD 24.60 (effective 2009). adv. bk.rev. abstr.; charts; illus.; mkt.; stat. 72 p./no.; back issues avail. **Document type:** *Magazine, Academic/Scholarly.*
Related titles: Online - full text ed.; Cumulative ed(s).
Indexed: ABIPC.
—East View.
Published by: Zhongguo Zaozhi Xuehui/China Technical Association of the Paper Industry, 12 Guanghua Lu, Chaoyang-qu, Beijing, 100020, China. TEL 86-10-65812880, FAX 86-10-65812653. Eds. Wending Li, Yiji Yu. Adv. contact Wanping Chen TEL 86-28-87284769. Circ: 11,000. **Dist. by:** China International Book Trading Corp, 35 Chegongzhuang Xilu, Haidian District, PO Box 399, Beijing 100044, China. TEL 86-10-68412045, FAX 86-10-68412023, cibtc@mail.cibtc.com.cn, http://www.cibtc.com.cn.

676.2 CHN ISSN 0254-508X
TS1080 CODEN: ZHZADC
ZHONGGUO ZAOZHI/CHINA PULP AND PAPER. Text in Chinese; Abstracts in English. 1982. m. USD 62.40 (effective 2009). adv. bibl.; abstr.; charts. 160 p./no.; **Document type:** *Trade.* **Description:** Covers latest development and information on technology and science in China.
Related titles: Online - full text ed.
Indexed: ABIPC, CIN, ChemAb, ChemTitl, Englnd, P&BA, SCOPUS.
—BLDSC (3180.225000), CASDDS, East View.
Published by: Zhongguo Zaozhi Xuehui/China Technical Association of the Paper Industry, 12 Guanghua Lu, Chaoyang-qu, Beijing, 100020, China. TEL 86-10-65810022 ext 2108, FAX 86-10-65817480, cpp.pub2@95777.com. Ed. Shijun Kuang. Adv. contact Li Ping TEL 86-10-65830256. Circ: 9,500. **Co-publisher:** Zhongguo Shijiang Zaozhi Yanjiuyuan/China National Pulp and Paper Research Institute.

676.2 CHN ISSN 1000-6842
➤ **ZHONGGUO ZAOZHI XUEBAO/TRANSACTIONS OF CHINA PULP AND PAPER.** Text in Chinese; Abstracts in English. 1986. s-a. USD 35.60 (effective 2009). 130 p./no.; **Document type:** *Journal, Academic/Scholarly.* **Description:** Covers R&D achievements in China.
Related titles: Online - full text ed.
Indexed: ABIPC, CIN, ChemAb, ChemTitl, Englnd, SCOPUS.
—East View.
Published by: Zhongguo Zaozhi Xuehui/China Technical Association of the Paper Industry, 12 Guanghua Lu, Chaoyang-qu, Beijing, 100020, China. TEL 86-10-65810022 ext 2108, FAX 86-10-65817480, cpp.pub2@95777.com. Ed. Zhu Yince. Circ: 900. **Co-publisher:** Zhongguo Shijiang Zaozhi Yanjiuyuan/China National Pulp and Paper Research Institute.

676 CHN ISSN 1007-9211
HD9836.C6
ZHONGHUA ZHIYE/CHINA PULP & PAPER INDUSTRY. Text in Chinese. 1979. m. USD 98.40 (effective 2009). **Document type:** *Journal, Academic/Scholarly.*
Formerly (until 1997): Beifang Zaozhi/North Paper Making (1005-8745); (until 1993): Shandong Zaozhi
Related titles: Online - full text ed.
—East View.
Published by: Shandong Sheng Zaozhi Gongye Yanjiu Shejiyuan, 101, Gongye Nan Lu, Ji'nan, 250100, China. TEL 86-531-88929286, FAX 86-531-88926310, http://www.cppinet.com.

PAPER AND PULP—Abstracting, Bibliographies, Statistics

676 016 USA ISSN 1523-388X
Z7914.P2 CODEN: ABPCAM
ABSTRACT BULLETIN OF PAPER SCIENCE AND TECHNOLOGY. Text in English. 1930. m. EUR 2,520 in Europe to institutions; JPY 333,700 in Japan to institutions; USD 2,740 elsewhere to institutions (effective 2012). cum.index. back issues avail.; reprints avail. **Document type:** *Bulletin, Abstract/Index.* **Description:** Covers international patent and journal literature related to pulp and paper technology.
Former titles (until 1998): Institute of Paper Science and Technology. Abstract Bulletin (1047-2088); (until Jul.1989): Institute of Paper Chemistry. Abstract Bulletin (0020-3033); (until 1958): Institute of Paper Chemistry. Bulletin (0096-9680)
Related titles: CD-ROM ed.: USD 3,700 (effective 2000); Microform ed.: (from PMC); Online - full text ed.: PaperChem.
—CASDDS. **CCC.**
Published by: Elsevier Engineering Information, Inc. (Subsidiary of: Elsevier Science & Technology), 360 Park Ave S, New York, NY 10010. TEL 314-447-8070, 800-221-1044, FAX 212-633-3680, eicustomersupport@elsevier.com, http://www.ei.org/.

676 USA ISSN 0734-8711
CODEN: CSPAEP
C A SELECTS. PAPER ADDITIVES. Text in English. s-w. USD 385 to non-members; USD 115 to members; USD 575 combined subscription to individuals (print & online eds.) (effective 2011). **Document type:** *Abstract/Index.* **Description:** Covers noncellulosic materials added during papermaking; chemicals used for treating freshly formed sheets.
Related titles: Online - full text ed.: USD 380 to non-members; USD 114 to members (effective 2011).
Published by: Chemical Abstracts Service (Subsidiary of: American Chemical Society), 2540 Olentangy River Rd, Columbus, OH 43210-0012. TEL 614-447-3600, FAX 614-447-3713, help@cas.com, http://caselects.cas.org. **Subscr. to:** PO Box 3012, Columbus, OH 43210. TEL 800-753-4227, FAX 614-447-3751.

676 310 FRA
CONFEDERATION FRANCAISE DE L'INDUSTRIE DES PAPIERS, CARTONS ET CELLULOSES. RAPPORT ANNUEL. Text in French. a. illus.
Former titles: Statistiques de l'Industrie Francaise des Pates, Papiers et Cartons (0997-0991); Donnees Statistiques sur l'Industrie Francaise des Pates, Papiers, Cartons (0481-0112)
Related titles: Online - full text ed.: free.
Published by: Confederation Francaise de l'Industrie des Papiers Cartons & Celluloses, 154 bd. Haussmann, Paris, 75008, France. TEL 33-1-53892400, FAX 33-1-53892401, contact@copacel.fr.

676 BEL
CONFEDERATION OF EUROPEAN PAPER INDUSTRIES. ANNUAL STATISTICS. Text in English. 1992. a. EUR 619.33 (effective 2001). **Description:** Provides statistics relating to the previous year's paper production and consumption.
Published by: Confederation of European Paper Industries, Av Louise 250, Brussels, 1050, Belgium. TEL 32-2-6274917, FAX 32-2-6468137.

676 USA ISSN 0003-0341
HD9824
PAPER, PAPERBOARD, & WOOD PULP; monthly statistical summary. Text in English. 1921. m. USD 435; USD 465 foreign. charts; mkt. Supplement avail. **Document type:** *Newsletter.* **Description:** Reports data such as production, inventories, imports and exports for various grades of pulp, paper and paperboard.
Related titles: Microfiche ed.: (from CIS).
Indexed: ABIPC, Englnd, SCOPUS, SRI.
Published by: American Forest & Paper Institute, 1111 19th St N W, Washington, DC 20036. TEL 202-463-2700, FAX 202-463-2785. Ed. Stan Lancey. Circ: 800.

676 016 GBR ISSN 1359-5156
TS1080
PAPERBASE ABSTRACTS. Text in English. 1968. m. GBP 850 (effective 2010). bk.rev. abstr. index. 200 p./no.; back issues avail. **Document type:** *Journal, Abstract/Index.* **Description:** Provides comprehensive source of information on key pulp and paper topics.
Incorporates (1989-2001): Nonwovens Abstracts (0956-1234); Formerly (until 1995): Paper and Board Abstracts (0307-0778)
Related titles: CD-ROM ed.; Microform ed.; Online - full text ed.
—BLDSC (6366.260000). **CCC.**
Published by: IntertechPira, Cleeve Rd, Leatherhead, Surrey KT22 7RU, United Kingdom. TEL 44-1372-802000, FAX 44-1372-802238, info@pira-international.com.

674 676 016 HUN ISSN 0231-0740
PAPIRIPARI ES NYOMDAIPARI SZAKIRODALMI TAJEKOZTATO/ PAPER INDUSTRY & PRINTING ABSTRACTS. Text in Hungarian. 1949. m. HUF 7,000. abstr. index.
Supersedes (in 1983): Muszaki Lapszemle. Faipar, Papir-es Nyomdaipar - Technical Abstracts. Wood and Paper Industry, Printing (0027-4992)
Published by: Orszagos Muszaki Informacios Kozpont es Konyvtar/ National Technical Information Centre and Library, Muzeum utca 17, PO Box 12, Budapest, 1428, Hungary. Ed. Peter Kalmar. Circ: 230. **Subscr. to:** Kultura, PO Box 149, Budapest 1389, Hungary.

676.1 CAN
PULP & PAPER TECHNICAL ASSOCIATION OF CANADA. INDICES/ ASSOCIATION TECHNIQUE DES PATES ET PAPIERS DU CANADA. LISTES. Text in English, French. a. **Description:** Indexes technical papers, authors and branch and committee papers added to the PAPTAC Database.
Formerly: Canadian Pulp and Paper Association. Technical Section. Indices
Published by: Pulp and Paper Technical Association of Canada/ Association Technique des Pates et Papiers du Canada, 740 rue Notre Dame ouest, Ste 1070, Montreal, PQ H3C 3X6, Canada. TEL 514-392-0265, FAX 514-392-0369, pubs@paptac.ca, http://www.paptac.ca.

016.676 RUS ISSN 0208-1415
REFERATIVNYI ZHURNAL. TEKHNOLOGIYA I OBORUDOVANIE LESOZAGOTOVITEL'NOGO, DEREVOOBRABATYVAYUSHCHEGO I TSELLYULOZNO-BUMAZHNOGO PROIZVODSTVA; otdel'nyi vypusk. Text in Russian. 1958. m. USD 360 foreign (effective 2011). **Document type:** *Journal, Abstract/Index.*
Related titles: CD-ROM ed.; Online - full text ed.
—East View.
Published by: VINITI RAN, ul Usievicha 20, Moscow, 125190, Russian Federation. TEL 7-499-1526113, FAX 7-499-9430060, dir@viniti.ru, http://www.viniti.ru. **Dist. by:** Informnauka Ltd., Ul Usievicha 20, Moscow 125190, Russian Federation. alfimov@viniti.ru.

REFERATIVNYI ZHURNAL. TEKHNOLOGIYA POLIMERNYKH MATERYALOV: PRIRODNYE VYSOKOMOLEKULYARNYE SOEDINENIYA. KHIMIYA I PERERABOTKA DREVESINY. KHIMICHESKIE VOLOKNA. TEKSTIL'NYE MATERIALY. BUMAGA. KOZHA. MEKH; vypusk svodnogo toma. *see* CHEMISTRY—Abstracting, Bibliographies, Statistics

PARAPSYCHOLOGY AND OCCULTISM

see also NEW AGE PUBLICATIONS

133 USA
A A - E V P NEWSLETTER. Text in English. 1982. q. USD 20 to members (effective 2000). bk.rev. illus. 6 p./no. 2 cols./p.; back issues avail. **Document type:** *Newsletter.* **Description:** Evidence of death survival as presented through electronic instruments such as tape recorders, televisions, and computers.
Published by: American Association - Electronic Voice Phenomena, 816 Midship Ct, Annapolis, MD 21401-7387. TEL 410-573-0873, aaevp@prodigy.net. Ed., Pub., R&P Sarah V Estep. Circ: 300; 250 (paid).

133.4 DEU ISSN 2192-1636
A H A - ZEITSCHRIFT. Text in German. 2008. s-a. **Document type:** *Magazine, Consumer.*
Formerly (until 2011): Abrahadabra, The Magickal Observer (2190-1724); Which was formed by the merger of (2007-2008): The Magickal Observer; (1988-2008): A H A - Abrahadabra (0943-4208); Which was formerly (until 1992): Abrahadabra (0936-8841)
Media: Online - full text.
Published by: Event Horizon, Dorfstr 30, Beldorf, 25557, Germany. TEL 49-178-8750981, redaktion@event-horizon.de, http://www.event-horizon.de. Ed., Pub. Olaf Francke.

133.91 USA ISSN 0044-7919
A S P R NEWSLETTER. (American Society for Psychical Research) Text in English. 1968. q. USD 20 to non-members (effective 1999). illus. **Document type:** *Newsletter.*
Published by: American Society for Psychical Research, Inc., 5 W 73rd St, New York, NY 10023. TEL 212-799-5050, FAX 212-496-2497. Circ: 2,000.

133 200 USA
ACADEMY OF SPIRITUALITY AND PARANORMAL STUDIES. PROCEEDINGS. Text in English. 1980. a., latest 2009. USD 12 per issue (effective 2010). abstr.; bibl. 1 cols./p.; back issues avail. **Document type:** *Proceedings, Academic/Scholarly.* **Description:** Interfaces religion and psychical research.
Formerly (until 2004): Academy of Religion and Psychical Research. Proceedings
Published by: Academy of Spirituality and Paranormal Studies, Inc., PO Box 614, Bloomfield, CT 06002. TEL 860-242-4593, admin@aspsi.org. Circ: 200 (paid).

ALIEN HIDEOUT WEEKLY EZINE. *see* AERONAUTICS AND SPACE FLIGHT

001.9 FRA ISSN 2104-1938
▼ **ALIENS.** Text in French. 2009. q. EUR 8 newsstand/cover (effective 2011). **Document type:** *Magazine, Consumer.*

Published by: Export Press, 91 Rue de Turenne, Paris, 75003, France. TEL 33-1-40291451, FAX 33-1-42720743, dir@exportpress.com, http://www.exportpress.com.

133.91 USA ISSN 0003-1070
BF1010

➤ **AMERICAN SOCIETY FOR PSYCHICAL RESEARCH. JOURNAL.** Text in English. 1907. q. free to members (effective 2010). bk.rev. abstr.; charts; stat.; illus. index. back issues avail.; reprints avail. **Document type:** *Journal, Academic/Scholarly.* **Description:** Discusses and reports on studies of clairvoyance, extrasensory perception, precognition, psychokinesis, psychic healing and other subjects related to parapsychology.
Former titles (until 1932): Psychic Research (0092-8259); (until 1928): American Society for Psychical Research. Journal (0093-0318)
Related titles: Microform ed.: (from PQC).
Indexed: A20, A22, ASCA, CIS, E-psyche, H09, IBR, IBZ, MEA&I, P30, PCI, Philind, PsycholAb, S05, SCOPUS.
—BLDSC (4693.050000), IE, Ingenta, INIST.
Published by: American Society for Psychical Research, Inc., 5 W 73rd St, New York, NY 10023. TEL 212-799-5050, FAX 212-496-2497, aspr@aspr.com.

133.9 NLD ISSN 1566-7952
ANCIENT MAGIC AND DIVINATION. Text in English. 1999. irreg., latest vol.8, 2010. price varies. **Document type:** *Monographic series, Academic/Scholarly.*
Indexed: IZBG.
Published by: Brill, PO Box 9000, Leiden, 2300 PA, Netherlands. TEL 31-71-5353500, FAX 31-71-5317532, cs@brill.nl. Eds. Ann K Guinan, Francesca Rochberg, Tzvi Abusch.

001.9 USA
THE ANOMALIST (ONLINE). Text in English. 1994. irreg. USD 12.95 per issue (effective 2010). back issues avail. **Document type:** *Journal, Consumer.* **Description:** Explores the mysteries of science, nature and history.
Formerly (until 2002): The Anomalist (Print) (1076-4208)
Media: Online - full text.
Published by: The Anomalist, PO Box 577, Jefferson Valley, NY 10535. Ed. Patrick Huyghe.

133.91 CAN
ATHAM Z - PSYCHIC NEWS. Text in English. 1999. q. adv. back issues avail. **Description:** Methodologies and philosophies of psychic reading. Topics also touch on the metaphysical and esoteric.
Related titles: Online - full text ed.
Published by: Atham Z, RR 1, Golden lake, ON K0J 1X0, Canada. TEL 613-628-3998. Ed., R&P, Adv. contact Atham Z. Circ: 1,000.

ATHLONE HISTORY OF WITCHCRAFT AND MAGIC IN EUROPE. *see* HISTORY—History Of Europe

133 150 AUS ISSN 1445-2308
➤ **AUSTRALIAN JOURNAL OF PARAPSYCHOLOGY.** Text in English. 1983. 2/yr. AUD 70 (effective 2009). bk.rev. charts; illus. back issues avail. **Document type:** *Journal, Academic/Scholarly.* **Description:** Promotes scientific study of parapsychological and related phenomena. Emphasis on Australian studies.
Former titles (until 2000): Australian Parapsychological Review (1035-9621); Australian Institute of Parapsychological Research Bulletin; Australian Institute of Psychic Research Bulletin (0813-2194)
Indexed: E-psyche.
Published by: Australian Institute of Parapsychological Research Inc., PO Box 295, Gladesville, NSW 2111, Australia. info@aiprinc.org. Ed. Lance Storm. Circ: 400.

133 USA
THE AZRAEL PROJECT NEWSLETTER; 25 years of researching anthropomorphic death encounters. Text in English. s-a. Website rev.; bk.rev. bibl.; tr.lit. back issues avail. **Description:** Puts forth the word of the Angel of Death to conquer fear through understanding. Helps people understand the nature of death and to gain a macrocosmic understanding of it and of life.
Media: Online - full content.
Published by: Westgate Press Ltd., 5219 Magazine St, New Orleans, LA 70115. TEL 504-899-3077. Ed. Lorraine Chandler. R&P Loni Chandler.

THE BEACON (MIAMI). *see* NEW AGE PUBLICATIONS

THE BEACON (NEW YORK, 1922). *see* PHILOSOPHY

133 USA
BEYOND REALITY; the latest discoveries in ESP, UFO's & psychic phenomena. Text in English. 1972. bi-m. USD 18. adv. bk.rev. illus. reprints avail.
Related titles: Microform ed.
Published by: Beyond Reality Magazine, Inc., PO Box 428, Nanuet, NY 10954. Ed. Harry Belil. Circ: 40,000.

BLACK RAVEN. *see* LITERATURE—Science Fiction, Fantasy, Horror

133 FRA ISSN 1955-8368
BULLETIN METAPSYCHIQUE. Text in French. 1920. q. bk.rev. reprints avail. **Document type:** *Bulletin, Consumer.*
Supersedes in part (in 2007): Revue Metapsychique (0180-9636); Which was formerly (until 1976): Revue Metapsychique Parapsychologie (0180-9628); (until 1973): Revue Metapsychique (0484-8934)
Published by: Institut Metapsychique International, 51 Rue de l'Aqueduc, Paris, 75010, France. TEL 33-1-46072385, contact@metapsychique.org. Circ: 500.

133 MEX
CASOS EXTRAORDINARIOS!; el universo de lo oculto. Text in Spanish. 1993. fortn. MXN 3, USD 2 per issue. **Document type:** *Consumer.* **Description:** Contains stories of the occult, phenomena, ghosts, crimes, and mysteries.
Published by: Publicaciones Llergo, Ave. CEYLAN 517, Col Industrial Vallejo, Mexico City, DF 02300, Mexico. TELEX 17620550. Ed. Gilberto Juarez.

CATALYST (MARIETTA); a publication resource of New Age newsletters, book reviews, personals, holistic health, UFO's and psychic connections. *see* NEW AGE PUBLICATIONS

LE CHAUDRON MAGIQUE. *see* CHILDREN AND YOUTH—For

CHURCH OF LIGHT QUARTERLY. *see* NEW AGE PUBLICATIONS

133.4 110 USA
CINCINNATI JOURNAL OF MAGIC. Text in English. 1976. a. USD 6 (effective 2000). bk.rev. **Document type:** *Bulletin, Consumer.* **Description:** Contains a collection of night side magicks.
Published by: Black Moon Publishing, PO Box 622, Logan, OH 43138-0622. TEL 504-897-6567. Ed., Pub. Louis Martinie. Circ: 1,000.

COLLECTION PSY POPULAIRE. *see* PSYCHOLOGY

001.9 FRA ISSN 1969-1122
COMPLOTS & DOSSIERS SECRETS. Text in French. 2008. q. EUR 6.90 newsstand/cover (effective 2011). **Document type:** *Magazine, Consumer.*
Published by: Export Press, 91 Rue de Turenne, Paris, 75003, France. TEL 33-1-40291451, FAX 33-1-42720743, dir@exportpress.com, http://www.exportpress.com.

001.9 FRA
▼ **COMPLOTS & DOSSIERS SECRETS. HORS-SERIE.** Text in French. 2009. a. EUR 12.95 newsstand/cover (effective 2011). **Document type:** *Magazine, Consumer.*
Published by: Export Press, 91 Rue de Turenne, Paris, 75003, France. TEL 33-1-40291451, FAX 33-1-42720743, dir@exportpress.com, http://www.exportpress.com.

133 ARG ISSN 0010-6291
CONOCIMIENTO DE LA NUEVA ERA. Text in Spanish. 1938. m. ARS 2. bk.rev.
Address: Viamonte 1716, Buenos Aires, 1055, Argentina. Ed. Adolfo Bruziks. Circ: 8,000.

COSMIC VOICE; cosmic revelations for the New Age. *see* NEW AGE PUBLICATIONS

133.4 USA ISSN 1945-0621
BF1562.5
THE CROOKED PATH. Text in English. 2008. q. USD 9 per issue (effective 2008). **Document type:** *Magazine, Consumer.*
Published by: Pendraig Publishing, 10546 Jardine Ave, Sunland, CA 91040. http://pendraigpublishing.com. Ed. Peter Paddon.

052 THA
CYBERSTAR. Text in Thai. 1996. irreg. free. **Description:** Aims to be the Internet's first "E-bloid" (electronic tabloid) of "virtual truth and near news from around the world." Includes stories on government conspiracies, extraterrestrial encounters, and other sensational news.
Media: Online - full text.
Published by: J P B Creative Co. Ltd., Sukhumvit 39 Rd, 12-23 Soi Prommitr, Bangkok, 10110, Thailand. TEL 66-2-258-8451, FAX 66-2-261-6679, jeffreyb@jpb.com, cyberstar@jpb.com. Ed. Jeffrey Baumgartner.

133 CAN
DIRECT VOICE. Text in English. 1994. q.
Published by: Inner Quest Foundation, P O Box 934, Depot 3, Victoria, BC V8W 2R9, Canada. TEL 250-383-2293.

133 USA
DIRECTORY OF GHOSTLY WEBSITES. Text in English. 1998. a. looseleaf. back issues avail. **Document type:** *Newsletter, Consumer.* **Description:** Lists Web sites and Web pages on the Internet dealing with ghosts, hauntings and poltergeist phenomena.
Published by: Ghost Research Society, PO Box 205, Oak Lawn, IL 60454. TEL 708-425-5163, FAX 708-425-3969, http://www.ghostresearch.org.

133.902571 CAN ISSN 1187-7227
DIRECTORY OF SPIRITUALIST ORGANIZATIONS IN CANADA. Text in English. 1991. irreg. CAD 5 newsstand/cover (effective 2001). **Document type:** *Directory.* **Description:** Intended to provide useful information to Spiritualists who travel in Canada and to foster contacts and the sharing of ideas by those interested in study of life after death and survival evidence.
Published by: Survival Research Institute of Canada, P O Box 8697, Victoria, BC V8W 3S3, Canada. TEL 250-386-4478, FAX 250-386-4478, http://www.islandnet.com/sric. Ed. Walter J. Meyer zu Erpen. Circ: 550.

DIRECTORY TO CANADIAN PAGAN RESOURCES. *see* RELIGIONS AND THEOLOGY—Other Denominations And Sects

DOWSING TODAY. *see* WATER RESOURCES

133 ISL ISSN 1670-5270
DULRAEN MALEFNI. Text in Icelandic. 2004. 2/yr. **Document type:** *Magazine, Consumer.*
Published by: Umgerd ehf., Tunguhalsi 19, Reykjavik, 110, Iceland. TEL 354-553-8200, dulo@dulo.is. Ed. Anna Kristjansdottir. Adv. contact Gudjon Baldvinsson.

EARTHSPIRIT. *see* NEW AGE PUBLICATIONS

133 USA
ENCHANTING NEWS. Text in English. 4/yr. USD 4.50 per issue. **Description:** Includes practical ritual, formulas for incense.
Published by: Fanscifiaroan Church of Wicca, PO Box 145, Marion, CT 06444.

130 BEL ISSN 0773-7912
ETUDES PHENOMENOLOGIQUES. Text in French; Text occasionally in English. 1985. s-a. EUR 32.20 for 2 yrs. domestic; EUR 40.90 for 2 yrs. foreign; EUR 8.68 newsstand/cover domestic; EUR 11.16 newsstand/cover foreign (effective 2004). **Document type:** *Journal.*
Indexed: FR.
—INIST.
Published by: (Institut Superieur de Philosophie, Centre d'Etudes Phenomenologiques), Editions OUSIA, Rue Bosquet, 37 bte 3, Brussels, 1060, Belgium. TEL 33-2-6471195, FAX 33-2-6473489, ousia@swing.be, http://www.eurorgan.be. Ed. Danielle Lories.

130 GBR ISSN 0168-7263
➤ **EUROPEAN JOURNAL OF PARAPSYCHOLOGY.** Text in English; Abstracts in English, French, German, Italian, Portuguese, Spanish. 1974. s-a. GBP 20 in Europe to individuals; GBP 30 elsewhere to individuals; GBP 60 in Europe to institutions; GBP 70 elsewhere to institutions (effective 2009). bk.rev. back issues avail. **Document type:** *Journal, Academic/Scholarly.* **Description:** Aims to stimulate and enhance activity in parapsychology through articles, research notes, reviews and comments that offer insight into or criticisms of parapsychological research.
Indexed: E-psyche, P03, PsycInfo, PsycholAb.
—BLDSC (3829.733400), IE, Ingenta.

Published by: (Parapsychological Association USA), Koestler Chair of Parapsychology, Department of Psychology, University of Derby, Kedleston Rd, Derby, DE22 1GB, United Kingdom. Ed. Ian Baker.

➤ **EXOPOLITICS JOURNAL.** *see* AERONAUTICS AND SPACE FLIGHT

133.05 USA ISSN 0014-8776
BF1995
FATE; true reports of the strange & unknown. Text in English. 1948. m. USD 32.95 domestic; USD 41.95 in Canada & Mexico; USD 48.95 elsewhere; USD 5.95 newsstand/cover (effective 2007). adv. bk.rev.; Website rev. abstr.; illus. 128 p./no. 2 cols./p.; back issues avail.; reprints avail. **Document type:** *Magazine, Consumer.* **Description:** Presents true stories, personal vignettes, and journalistic reports pertaining to strange, mystical, and parapsychological experiences and occurrences.
Related titles: Microform ed.: (from PQC); Online - full text ed.
Indexed: A22, ASIP, G06, G07, G08, HlthInd, MagInd.
Published by: Fate Magazine, Inc., PO Box 460, Lakeville, MN 55044. TEL 952-431-2050, 800-728-2730, FAX 952-891-6091. Ed., Pub. Phyllis Galde. Adv. contact Diane Coulson. color page USD 850. Circ: 12,000 (paid).

THE FEDERATION FLASH; exploring the frontiers of miraculous probability. *see* NEW AGE PUBLICATIONS

FLYING SAUCER REVIEW. *see* AERONAUTICS AND SPACE FLIGHT

001.94 GBR ISSN 0308-5899
BF1001
FORTEAN TIMES. Abbreviated title: F T. Text in English. 1973. m. GBP 35.10 domestic; GBP 37.50 in Europe; GBP 45 elsewhere; GBP 4.25 newsstand/cover (effective 2009). adv. bk.rev. bibl.; illus. index. back issues avail. **Document type:** *Magazine, Trade.* **Description:** Contains news, reviews and research on strange phenomena and experiences, curiosities, prodigies and portents.
Formerly (until 1976): News (0306-0764)
Published by: John Brown Citrus Publishing, 136-142 Bramley Rd, London, W10 6SR, United Kingdom. TEL 44-20-75653000, FAX 44-20-75653060, http://www.johnbrownmedia.com. Ed. David Sutton. Adv. contact James Clements. **Dist. by:** Comag; **Dist. in the US by:** Eastern News Distributors Inc.

133.9 GBR ISSN 2045-7243
▼ **FOUR WINDS**; social, political, spiritual, ethical. Text in English. 2010. bi-m. GBP 15; GBP 2.80 per issue (effective 2011). adv. **Document type:** *Magazine, Consumer.* **Description:** Features articles on a wide range of topics including spirituality, social justice, activism, witchcraft, sustainability, environment, green living, religion, etc.
Related titles: Online - full text ed.: ISSN 2045-7278. free (effective 2011).
Published by: Court Arcana, 59b Hill Head, Glastonbury, Somerset BA6 8AW, United Kingdom. TEL 44-20-3239202, tower@courtofarcana.co.uk, http://www.courtofarcana.com.

133 USA ISSN 0886-6791
THE GATE; explore the mysteries. Text in English. 1985. q. USD 8. adv. bk.rev. illus. back issues avail. **Document type:** *Newsletter.*
Published by: Gate, PO Box 43518, Richmond, OH 44143. Ed. Beth Robbins. Circ: 200.

133 USA ISSN 1552-7646
GHOST! MAGAZINE. Text in English. 2004 (Oct.). m. USD 22.25 (effective 2004). bk.rev. **Document type:** *Magazine, Consumer.* **Description:** Includes investigative and opinion-based feature articles, short news items pertain to ghost hunting, technology or research, humorous sidebars, and book reviews with occasional excerpts from forthcoming books.
Published by: JusDus Productions, LLC., PO Box 1855, Middleburg, FL 32050. TEL 904-210-8383.

133 004.678 USA
GHOST SITES. Text in English. 1996. irreg. free.
Media: Online - full text.
Address: http://www.isobey.com/ghostsites. Ed. Steve Baldwin.

133 USA
GHOST TRACKERS NEWSLETTER. Text in English. 1982. q. looseleaf. free to members (effective 2011). bk.rev. back issues avail. **Document type:** *Newsletter, Consumer.*
Published by: Ghost Research Society, PO Box 205, Oak Lawn, IL 60454. TEL 708-425-5163, FAX 708-425-3969.

133 ITA ISSN 1122-4940
IL GIORNALE DEI MISTERI; mensile di varia ed insolita cultura. Text in Italian. 1971. m. EUR 44 domestic; EUR 71.50 in Europe; EUR 94 elsewhere (effective 2009). **Document type:** *Magazine, Consumer.* **Description:** Contains articles about parapsychology, shamanism, the occult sciences, esoteric disciplines, astrology and UFO's.
Published by: Edizioni I Libri del Casato, Via Casato di Sopra 19, Siena, 53100, Italy. TEL 39-0577-49748, FAX 39-0577-49759.

133 DEU ISSN 1863-933X
GRENZUEBERSCHREITUNGEN (WUERZBURG); Beitraege zur wissenschaftlichen Erforschung aussergewoehnlicher Erfahrungen und Phaenomene. Text in German. 2003. irreg., latest vol.8, 2009. price varies. **Document type:** *Monographic series, Academic/Scholarly.*
Published by: Ergon Verlag, Keesburgstr 11, Wuerzburg, 97074, Germany. TEL 49-931-280084, FAX 49-931-282872, service@ergon-verlag.de, http://www.ergon-verlag.de.

133.4 GBR ISSN 0966-6427
HARVEST MOON. Text in English. 1987. 6/yr. GBP 4. adv. bk.rev.
Formerly (until 1990): Odinn Magazine
Address: 36 Dawes House, Orb St, London, SE17 1RE, United Kingdom. TEL 071-708-4629.

133 GBR ISSN 2044-5091
▼ **HAUNTED.** Text in English. 2009. bi-m. GBP 16 (effective 2010). adv. **Document type:** *Magazine, Consumer.*
Related titles: Online - full text ed.: GBP 6.66 (effective 2010).
Published by: Anon Publications, 6 Peveril Dr, Sutton in Ashfield, Nottinghamshire NG17 2GT, United Kingdom. TEL 44-1623-511203. Ed. Albert Nonn. Adv. contact Morgan Steele TEL 44-7999-642628. page GBP 1,000; 210 x 297.

133 150 FIN ISSN 1459-3432
HENKIMAAILMA. Text in Finnish. 1997. bi-m. EUR 35 (effective 2007). adv. **Document type:** *Magazine, Consumer.*
Former titles (until 2002): Ilmiot ja Henkimaailma (1456-0364); (until 1998): T T. Tarua vai Totta (1455-4569)

Published by: Karprint Oy, Vanha Turunrie 371, Huhmari, 03150, Finland. TEL 358-9-41397300, FAX 358-9-41397405, http://www.karprint.fi. Ed. Reetta Ahola. Adv. contact Arja Blom. page EUR 1,213. Circ: 11,000.

133 AUT ISSN 1605-6736
HEUREKA!. Text in German. 1998. bi-m. EUR 15 domestic; EUR 25 foreign (effective 2005). **Document type:** *Magazine, Consumer.*
Media: Online - full text.
Published by: Falter Verlag GmbH, Marc-Aurel-Str 9, Wien, W 1011, Austria. TEL 43-1-536600, FAX 43-1-53660935, service@falter.at.

133 ISL ISSN 1024-5502
HUGINN & MUNINN; interstellar messenger. Text in English. 1966-1974; resumed 1987. 4/yr. USD 10. bk.rev. **Document type:** *Bulletin, Consumer.* **Description:** Focuses on philosophy, parapsychology, Old Norse religion and lore.
Former titles: Interstellar Bulletins; Interstellar Communication (0020-9740)
Media: Duplicated (not offset).
Published by: Felag Nyalssinna, PO Box 1159, Reykjavik, 121, Iceland. TEL 354-553-5683, FAX 354-568-9303. Ed. Thorsteinn Gudjonsson. Circ: 400.

IMAGINATION, COGNITION AND PERSONALITY; consciousness in theory, research, clinical practice. *see* PSYCHOLOGY

133 ITA ISSN 1828-4841
INFORMAZIONI PARAPSICOLOGICHE. Abbreviated title: I P. Text in Italian. 1963. s-a. **Document type:** *Magazine, Consumer.*
Formerly (until 1989): Informazioni di Parapsicologia (0046-9491)
Published by: Centro Italiano Parapsicologia (C I P), Via Poggio de' Mari 16, Naples, 80129, Italy. http://www.centroitalianoparapsicologia.org.

133 USA
INTERNATIONAL DIRECTORY OF PSYCHIC SCIENCES. Text in English. 1986. a. looseleaf. **Document type:** *Directory, Consumer.* **Description:** Lists organizations, groups and individuals associated with the occult in general.
Published by: Ghost Research Society, PO Box 205, Oak Lawn, IL 60454. TEL 708-425-5163, FAX 708-425-3969, http://www.ghostresearch.org.

133 USA ISSN 0553-206X
INTERNATIONAL JOURNAL OF PARASYCHOLOGY. Text in English. 2000. s-a.
Published by: Parapsychology Foundation, 1562, New York, NY 10021-0043. TEL 212-628-1550, http://www.parapsychology.org. Ed. Lisette Coly.

001.9 USA ISSN 1099-856X
INTO THE DARK. Text in English. m.
Media: Online - full content.
Published by: Dark Times Publishing

INTUITIVE FLASH; forecasting environmental, economic, and societal trends. *see* EARTH SCIENCES

133 USA
IRIDIS. Text in English. 1959. 10/yr. USD 10 (effective 1999). bk.rev. **Document type:** *Newsletter.*
Published by: California Society for Psychical Study, PO Box 844, Berkeley, CA 94701. TEL 510-530-8564. Ed. Ruth Inge Heinze.

133 USA ISSN 1933-1517
IT'S IN YOUR HANDS. Text in English. 2002. s-m. free (effective 2008). **Document type:** *Magazine, Consumer.*
Media: Online - full text.
Published by: The Hand Analyst, Inc., 5075 N La Canada Dr, Ste 157-304, Tucson, AZ 85704. TEL 520-429-8455, 800-575-8313, FAX 520-844-3400, support@handanalyst.com, http://www.handanalyst.com/index.html. Pub. Beth Davis.

133.4 700.457 398 GBR ISSN 1479-0750
GN475.3
➤ **JOURNAL FOR THE ACADEMIC STUDY OF MAGIC.** Text in English. 2003 (May). a. GBP 19.99, USD 40 per issue (effective 2009). 200 p./no.; back issues avail. **Document type:** *Journal, Academic/Scholarly.* **Description:** Covers all areas of magic, witchcraft, paganism, etc.; all geographical regions and all historical periods.
Indexed: A01, B04, CA, SSAI, SSAb, SSI, T02, W01, W02, W03, W05.
Published by: Mandrake of Oxford, PO Box 250, Oxford, OX1 1AP, United Kingdom. TEL 44-1865-243671, mandrake@mandrake.uk.net. Eds. Dave Green, Susan Johnston.

➤ **JOURNAL OF BORDERLAND RESEARCH.** *see* SCIENCES: COMPREHENSIVE WORKS

130 USA ISSN 0022-3387
BF1001 CODEN: JPRPAU
➤ **JOURNAL OF PARAPSYCHOLOGY.** Text in English. 1937. s-a. free to members (effective 2010). adv. bk.rev. abstr.; bibl.; charts; illus. Index. 430 p./no.; back issues avail.; reprints avail. **Document type:** *Journal, Academic/Scholarly.* **Description:** Designed for anyone interested in the scientific study of paranormal phenomena.
Related titles: Microform ed.: (from PQC); Online - full text ed.
Indexed: A01, A02, A03, A08, A20, A22, A25, A26, ASCA, B04, B14, BRD, BRI, CA, CBRI, DIP, E-psyche, E08, G08, H09, I05, IBR, IBZ, MEA&I, P02, P03, P10, P12, P13, P25, P26, P27, P30, P43, P48, P53, P54, PCI, PQC, PsycInfo, PsycholAb, RASB, S02, S03, S05, S08, S09, SCOPUS, SSAI, SSAb, SSI, T02, W03, W05.
—BLDSC (5028.800000), IE, Infotrieve, Ingenta, INIST. **CCC.**
Published by: Rhine Research Center, 2741 Campus Walk Ave, Bldg 500, Durham, NC 27705. TEL 919-309-4600, FAX 919-309-4700, office@rhine.org. Ed. John A. Palmer.

➤ **JOURNAL OF SCIENTIFIC EXPLORATION.** *see* SCIENCES: COMPREHENSIVE WORKS

133 200 USA ISSN 1932-5770
BL65.P3
JOURNAL OF SPIRITUALITY AND PARANORMAL STUDIES. Text in English. 1979. q. free to members (effective 2010). bk.rev. abstr.; bibl. index. 64 p./no. 1 cols./p.; back issues avail. **Document type:** *Journal, Academic/Scholarly.* **Description:** Features articles that deal with religion, psychical research, and other related topics.
Former titles (until 2006): Journal of Religion & Psychical Research (0731-2148); (until 1981): Academy of Religion and Psychical Research. Journal (0272-7188)
Related titles: Online - full text ed.
Indexed: A01, A02, A03, A08, A21, CA, RI-1, RI-2, T02.
—BLDSC (5066.183175), IE, Ingenta.
Published by: Academy of Spirituality and Paranormal Studies, Inc., PO Box 614, Bloomfield, CT 06002. TEL 860-242-4593. Ed. Dr. Donald R Morse. Circ: 200.

154 GBR
➤ **THE KABBALIST (ONLINE).** Text in English. 1974. irreg. adv. bk.rev. bibl. **Document type:** *Journal, Academic/Scholarly.* **Description:** Covers all aspects of the Kabbalah and related occult/esoteric subjects.
Formerly (until 2001): The Kabbalist (Print)
Media: Online - full text.
Published by: International Order of Kabbalists, A.G. Reed, 6 Oakwood, 62 King Charles Rd, Surbiton, Surrey KT5 8QR, United Kingdom. iokoffice@internationalorderofkabbalists.com, http://internationalorderofkabbalists.com/. Ed. D M Dalton. Adv. contact D.M. Dalton. Circ: 1,500 (paid).

133.91 GRC ISSN 0023-4257
KOSMOS TIS PSYCHIS/WORLD OF SOUL. Text in Greek. 1947. m. USD 3.50. bk.rev. abstr.; bibl.; illus.; tr.mk. index.
Published by: Psychic Society of Athens, 32 Tsiller St, Athens, 905, Greece. Ed. Georgos Sakellaropoulos. Circ: 1,000.

133.91 GBR ISSN 0047-4649
BF1001
➤ **LIGHT (LONDON, 1881)**; a journal of psychic and spiritual studies. Text in English. 1881. s-a. (July & Nov.). free to members (effective 2009). bk.rev. back issues avail. **Document type:** *Journal, Academic/Scholarly.* **Description:** Features new perspectives on psychic and spiritual studies for those wanting to stay in step with what is happening now.
Indexed: AIAP, CCR, Perlslam.
Published by: College of Psychic Studies, 16 Queensberry Pl, London, SW7 2EB, United Kingdom. TEL 44-20-75893292, FAX 44-20-75892824, admin@collegeofpsychicstudies.co.uk. Ed. Nicola Harrod.

133.9 USA
LIGHT - LINES. Text in English. 1982. q. looseleaf. USD 10 (effective 2005); free for prisoners and elderly. back issues avail. **Document type:** *Newsletter.*
Related titles: Online - full text ed.: free.
Published by: Rock Creek Research & Development Labs, Inc., 1504 Hobbs Park Rd, Anchorage, KY 40223-1442. carla.l.rueckert@llresearch.org. Ed. Jim McCarty. R&P James McCarty. Circ: 1,500.

THE LIGHT WITHIN. *see* RELIGIONS AND THEOLOGY—Other Denominations And Sects

LLEWELLYN'S NEW WORLDS OF MIND & SPIRIT; new age resources for human potential and magical living. *see* NEW AGE PUBLICATIONS

133 DEU ISSN 1434-3088
MAGAZIN 2000 PLUS; Kosmos - Erde - Mensch. Text in German. 1979. m. EUR 8 newsstand/cover (effective 2008). adv. bk.rev. **Document type:** *Magazine, Consumer.*
Formerly (until 1997): Magazin 2000 (0177-672X)
—**CCC.**
Published by: Argo Verlag, Sternstr 3, Marktoberdorf, 87616, Germany. TEL 49-8349-920440, FAX 49-8349-9204449. Circ: 22,000.

133 ITA ISSN 1970-8912
MAGIA. Text in Italian. 2004. s-a. EUR 50, EUR 70 (effective 2008). **Document type:** *Magazine, Consumer.*
Published by: Comitato Italiano per il Controllo delle Affermazioni sul Paranormale (C I C A P), Casella Postale 847, Padua, 35100, Italy. http://www.cicap.org.

133.4 USA ISSN 1556-8547
GN474
➤ **MAGIC, RITUAL, AND WITCHCRAFT.** Abbreviated title: M R W. Text in English. 2006 (Sum.). s-a. USD 25 combined subscription to individuals (print & online eds.); USD 47 combined subscription to institutions (print & online eds.); USD 20 to students (effective 2011). adv. bk.rev. back issues avail. **Document type:** *Journal, Academic/Scholarly.* **Description:** Draws from a broad spectrum of perspectives, methods, and disciplines, offering the widest possible geographical scope and chronological range, from prehistory to the modern era and from the old world to the new.
Related titles: Online - full text ed.: ISSN 1940-5111. USD 22 to individuals; USD 42 to institutions (effective 2011).
Indexed: A21, A22, A26, AmHI, B04, BRD, CA, E01, E08, H07, H08, HAb, HumInd, I05, IIPA, L05, L06, MLA-IB, S09, T02, W03, W05.
—IE. **CCC.**
Published by: University of Pennsylvania Press, 3905 Spruce St, Philadelphia, PA 19104. TEL 215-898-6261, FAX 215-898-0404, custserv@pobox.upenn.edu, http://www.pennpress.org. Eds. Brain P Copenhaver, Michael D Bailey.

133 GBR
MAGONIA. Text in English. bi-m. GBP 4 domestic; GBP 5 in Europe; USD 10 in United States; GBP 5.50 elsewhere. **Document type:** *Bulletin.*
Address: John Dee Cottage, Mortlake Churchyard, 5 James Terr, London, SW14 8HB, United Kingdom. Ed. John Rimmer.

MEMORIE. *see* PSYCHOLOGY

133 GBR
METAMORPHIC ASSOCIATION PROGRAMME. Text in English. 1981. s-a. illus. **Document type:** *Newsletter.* **Description:** Lists activities and members of the Association.
Supersedes in part (in 1983): Metamorphic Association Newsletter (0262-1533)
Related titles: Online - full content ed.
Published by: Metamorphic Association, 67 Ritherdon Rd, London, SW17 8QE, United Kingdom. stpierregaston@aol.com, http://www.metamorphicassociation.org.uk/. Ed. Gaston St Pierre. Circ: 7,000.

133 GBR
METAMORPHOSIS. Text in English. 1981. 2/yr. GBP 7. bk.rev. illus. back issues avail. **Document type:** *Newsletter.* **Description:** Articles on the theory and principles behind Metamorphosis and the Metamorphic technique, an approach to self-healing and creative growth.
Supersedes in part (in 1983): Metamorphic Association Newsletter (0262-1533)
Published by: Metamorphic Association, 67 Ritherdon Rd, London, SW17 8QE, United Kingdom. Ed. Gaston St Pierre. Circ: 1,200.

133.91 ITA ISSN 0026-1076
METAPSICHICA; rivista italiana di parapsicologia. Text in Italian. 1946. q. free to members. adv. bk.rev. **Document type:** *Journal, Academic/Scholarly.* **Description:** Journal dealing with parapsychological research from worldwide conferences. Includes articles contributed by Italian authors interested in this field.
Published by: Associazione Italiana Scientifica di Metapsichica, Via San Vittore 19, Milan, MI 20123, Italy. TEL 39-02-4980365. Ed. Pierangelo Garzia. Circ: 1,000.

133 USA
MEZLIM; independent journal for the working magus. Text in English. q. USD 6 per issue.
Address: PO Box 19566, Cincinnati, OH 45219.

133 USA
MIND - MAGIC. Abbreviated title: M - M. Text in English. bi-w. back issues avail. **Document type:** *Newsletter.* **Description:** Devoted to helping find personal power, magic and love.
Media: Online - full text.

133 CAN ISSN 1492-1952
MINSTREL. Text in English. 1987. 4/yr. CAD 10; CAD 18 foreign. adv. bk.rev.; music rev. **Document type:** *Magazine, Consumer.* **Description:** Includes articles on pagan subjects, magick, folkways, local events and a calendar of festivals.
Address: P O Box 3068, Winnipeg, MB R3C 4E5, Canada. TEL 204-942-2881, minstrel@solutions.mb.ca, http://www.pangea.ca/nredking/minstrel/main.htm. Ed., Pub. Glen Hoban. Circ: 160.

MUTANTIA; cuadernos eco-espirituales. *see* NEW AGE PUBLICATIONS

133 GBR
➤ **NEOMETAPHYSICAL DIGEST.** Text in English. 1952. 2/yr. GBP 20 domestic; USD 40 in United States; GBP 22 elsewhere (effective 2005). bk.rev. abstr.; bibl. 40 p./no.; back issues avail. **Document type:** *Journal, Academic/Scholarly.* **Description:** Seeks functional solutions to human problems and an understanding of consciousness and its manifestations in mysticism, esoterica, and psychic phenomena. Presents neometaphysical science applied to all human activity.
Formerly: Metaphysical Digest
Related titles: E-mail ed.; Fax ed.
Published by: Society of Metaphysicians Ltd., Archers' Ct, Stonestile Ln, The Ridge, Hastings, E Sussex TN35 4PG, United Kingdom. TEL 44-1424-751577, FAX 44-1424-722387, http://www.metaphysicians.org.uk. Ed. Desmond Cumberland. R&P J J Williamson. Circ: 60,000 (paid and controlled).

➤ **NEW AGE SOURCEBOOK.** *see* NEW AGE PUBLICATIONS

133 USA
NEW MOON RISING; journal of magick and wicca. Text in English. 1989. bi-m. USD 25; USD 30 in Canada & Mexico; USD 37 elsewhere (effective 2000). adv. bk.rev. **Document type:** *Journal, Consumer.*
Address: PO Box 3587, Duluth, MN 55830-3587. TEL 503-659-1543. Ed., Pub., R&P, Adv. contact Scot Rhoads. Circ: 2,300 (paid).

001.9 AUS ISSN 1039-0170
NEXUS MAGAZINE. Text in English. 1986. bi-m. AUD 35.45 domestic; AUD 38.49 in United Kingdom; AUD 45.40 in United States; AUD 60.56 in Canada; AUD 31.37 in New Zealand; AUD 50 in Asia & the Pacific; AUD 7.23 per issue (effective 2009). adv. bk.rev.; music rev.; video rev. illus. back issues avail.; reprints avail. **Document type:** *Magazine, Consumer.* **Description:** Contains information on the subjects of health, science, world events and history.
Related titles: Online - full text ed.; Supplement(s): ISSN 1833-4180.
Published by: Nexus Magazine Pty Ltd., PO Box 30, Mapleton, QLD 4560, Australia. TEL 61-7-54429280, FAX 61-7-54429381. Ed. Duncan M Roads. Adv. contact Kathy Collins. page AUD 990; 180 x 240. Circ: 45,000 (paid).

O R A C L E NEWSLETTER. *see* NEW AGE PUBLICATIONS

133 133.5 398 200 USA
ORACLE (SIERRA MADRE). Text in English. 1975. 12/yr. USD 10. adv. bk.rev. **Document type:** *Newsletter.*
Formerly: Light Bearer
Published by: Healing Light Center, 261 E Alegria Ave, Ste 12, Sierra Madre, CA 91024. TEL 626-306-2170, FAX 626-355-0996. Ed. Susan Brown. Circ: 1,500.

133 RUS
ORAKUL; gazeta predskazanii. Text in Russian. m. USD 109.95 in United States.
Published by: Logos Media, A-ya 512, Moscow, 107061, Russian Federation. TEL 7-095-2092565. Ed. Yu Ya Gusinskii. **Dist. by:** East View Information Services, 10601 Wayzata Blvd, Minneapolis, MN 55305. TEL 952-252-1201, 800-477-1005, FAX 952-252-1202, info@eastview.com, http://www.eastview.com.

133 220 USA
P L I M REPORT. (Power Latent in Man) Text in English. bi-m. **Description:** Covers metaphysics, the Bible, and psychology. Instructs and encourages readers in a conscious realization of the ever-presence of the Power Latent in Man.
Media: Online - full text.
Published by: P L I M Inc., PO Box 14-6217, Chicago, IL 60614-6217. TEL 773-509-8124, plim@acen.net, http://www.plim.org/indexgraphic.htm.

133.91 GBR ISSN 1369-0426
THE PARANORMAL REVIEW. Text in English. 1981. q. free to members (effective 2010). back issues avail. **Document type:** *Magazine, Consumer.* **Description:** Aims to provide a forum for debate on psychical research, parapsychology and related areas.
Former titles (until 1997): Psi Researcher (0964-9506); (until 1991): S P R Newsletter
Indexed: RefZh.
—**CCC.**
Published by: Society for Psychical Research, 49 Marloes Rd, Kensington, London, W8 6LA, United Kingdom. TEL 44-20-79378984.

133 USA ISSN 0078-9437
PARAPSYCHOLOGICAL MONOGRAPHS. Text in English. 1958. irreg., latest vol.18, 1981. price varies. **Document type:** *Monographic series.*
Indexed: PsycholAb.
Published by: Parapsychology Foundation, 1562, New York, NY 10021-0043. TEL 212-628-1550. Ed. Lisette Coly. R&P Eileen Coly.

P

133 USA
PARAPSYCHOLOGY FOUNDATION. PROCEEDINGS OF INTERNATIONAL CONFERENCES. Text in English. 1953. a. price varies. **Document type:** *Proceedings.*
Published by: Parapsychology Foundation, 1562, New York, NY 10021-0043. TEL 212-628-1550. Ed. Lisette Coly. R&P Eileen Coly.

133 USA
PARAPSYCHOLOGY-PSYCHIC SCIENCE REPORTS; magazine of psychic phenomena. Text in English. 1973. m. adv. bk.rev. **Document type:** *Magazine, Consumer.*
Former titles (until 19??): Parapsychology-Psychic Science Journal; Parapsychology
Published by: Gibbs Publishing Company, PO Box 97, Sylva, NC 28779. gibbsic@aol.com. Ed. James Calvin Gibbs. Circ: 10,000.

133 NOR ISSN 0333-1172
PARAPSYKOLOGISKE NOTISER. Text in Norwegian. 1977. s-a. NOK 350 membership (effective 2011). **Document type:** *Magazine, Consumer.*
Published by: Norsk Parapsykologisk Selskap, PO Box 249, Bekkestua, 1319, Norway. TEL 47-67-534884, FAX 47-67-564377, info@parapsykologi.no, http://www.parapsykologi.no.

133 GBR ISSN 2040-0985
▼ **PHENOMENA.** Text in English. 2009. q. GBP 3.50 per issue to non-members; free to members (effective 2010). **Document type:** *Journal, Consumer.* **Description:** Includes information on the society's activities as well as articles and reports on all aspects of the paranormal by society members and others.
Published by: Chiltern Society for Psychical Research, 43 Neville Rd, Limbury, Luton, Bedfordshire LU3 2JG, United Kingdom. Ed. Paul Adams.

001.9 USA ISSN 1550-7653
PHENOMENA (VENICE). Variant title: Cinescape Presents Phenomena. Text in English. 2003 (Nov./Dec.). bi-m. USD 19.95 domestic; USD 29.95 in Canada; USD 39.95 elsewhere (effective 2004). adv. **Document type:** *Magazine, Consumer.*
Published by: Mania Entertainment LLC, 220 Main St, Ste C, Venice, CA 90291. TEL 310-399-8001, FAX 310-399-2622. Ed. Simon Cox. Adv. contact Dave Young.

POWER PLACES OF CALIFORNIA. *see* EARTH SCIENCES—Geophysics

133 GBR ISSN 0032-7182
PREDICTION. Text in English. 1936. m. GBP 29.99 domestic; USD 73.70 in US & Canada; EUR 58.80 in Europe; GBP 46 elsewhere; GBP 2.95 newsstand/cover (effective 2009). adv. bk.rev. illus. **Document type:** *Magazine, Consumer.* **Description:** Explores astrology, palmistry, tarot, graphology, dream interpretations and methods used to interpret character and events in life including articles, news briefs, questions and answers, and personal advertisements.
Incorporates: Weekly Horoscope
Published by: I P C Country & Leisure Media Ltd. (Subsidiary of: I P C Media Ltd.), Leon House, 233 High St, Croydon, CR9 1HZ, United Kingdom. http://www.ipcmedia.com. Ed. Marion Williamson TEL 44-20-87268255. Pub. Clive Birch TEL 44-20-87268235. Adv. contact Joanne O'Brien TEL 44-20-87268231. B&W page GBP 1,103, color page GBP 1,638; 190 x 278. Circ: 14,646. **Subscr. to:** Rockwood House, Perrymount Rd, Haywards Heath RH16 3DH, United Kingdom. TEL 44-845-1231231, IPCsubs@quadrantsubs.com, http://www.magazinesdirect.co.uk. **Dist. by:** MarketForce UK Ltd, The Blue Fin Bldg, 3rd Fl, 110 Southwark St, London SE1 0SU, United Kingdom. TEL 44-20-31483300, FAX 44-20-31488105, salesinnovation@marketforce.co.uk, http://www.marketforce.co.uk/.

PREDICTION HOROSCOPES. *see* ASTROLOGY

133.91 GBR ISSN 0033-2801
PSYCHIC NEWS. Text in English. 1932. w. GBP 59.95 domestic; GBP 71.70 foreign (effective 2009). adv. bk.rev. bibl.; charts; illus.; tr.lit. back issues avail. **Document type:** *Newspaper, Trade.* **Description:** Contains reports on people and events as well as articles covering all aspects of the psychic and spiritualist scene.
Published by: Psychic Press Ltd., The Coach House, Stansted Hall, Stansted, Essex CM24 8UD, United Kingdom. TEL 44-1279-817050, FAX 44-1279-817051.

133 USA
PSYCHIC READER. Text in English. 1975. m. USD 13.50 domestic; USD 46 foreign (effective 2000). adv. bk.rev. back issues avail. **Document type:** *Newsletter.* **Description:** New age publication that discusses parapsychology, alternative healing, religions and theology.
Formerly: Psychic Life
Published by: (Church of Divine Man), Deja Vu Publishing, 2018 Allston Way, Berkeley, CA 94704-1418. TEL 510-644-1600, FAX 510-644-1686. Ed. Kirstin Miller. Adv. contact Pat King. Circ: 210,000.

500 133 USA
PURSUIT - S I T U. Text in English. 1969 (vol.2). q. USD 12. bk.rev. bibl.; charts; illus. index.
Formerly: Pursuit (0033-4685)
Indexed: AFS, GeoRef, SpeleolAb.
Published by: Society for the Investigation of the Unexplained, PO Box 265, Little Silver, NJ 07739. TEL 201-842-5229. Ed. Robert C Warth. Circ: 1,500.

133 ITA
QUADERNI DI PARAPSICOLOGIA. Text in Italian; Abstracts in English, Italian. 1970. 2/yr. free to members (effective 2008). bk.rev. abstr. back issues avail. **Document type:** *Journal, Academic/Scholarly.*
Incorporates: Centro Studi Parapsicologici. Bollettino
Published by: Centro Studi Parapsicologici, Via Luigi Valeriani 39, Bologna, BO 40134, Italy. centrsp@iperbole.bologna.it. Ed. Brunilde Cassoli. Circ: 450.

133 ITA
QUADERNI GNOSIS. Text in Italian; Summaries in English. 1963. s-a. free to members. adv. bk.rev. bibl.; illus. **Document type:** *Newsletter, Consumer.* **Description:** Presents articles on the frontier of parapsychology, psychology and all elements favorable to the survival hypothesis.
Published by: Associazione Gnosis per la Ricerca sulla Ipotesi della Sopravvivenza, Via Andrea Belvedere 87, Naples, 80127, Italy. TEL 39-081-5603497, gnosis@infinito.it. Ed. Giorgio di Simone. Circ: 500.

133 200 800 FRA ISSN 0246-5434
QUESTION DE. Text in French. 1973. q. adv. bk.rev. bibl.; charts; illus. **Document type:** *Academic/Scholarly.*
Former titles: Question de Racines, Pensees, Sciences Eclairees; Question de Spiritualite, Tradition, Litteratures
Published by: Edition Question de, BP 21, Gordes, 84220, France. FAX 90-72-08-38. Ed. Marc de Smedt. Circ: 12,000.

130 CHE ISSN 1420-4894
RADIAESTHESIE. Text in German. 1950. q. CHF 56 domestic; CHF 61 foreign (effective 2003). adv. bk.rev. maps. 80 p./no. 2 cols./p.; back issues avail. **Document type:** *Journal, Academic/Scholarly.*
Formerly: Radiaesthesie - Geopathie - Strahlenbiologie (0033-7552)
Published by: Verlag R G S, Postfach 2225, St. Gallen, 9001, Switzerland. TEL 41-71-2226621, FAX 41-71-2226621, globuli@smile.ch, http://www.vrgs.ch/verlag.htm. Ed. Egon Minikus. Circ: 2,500.

133 USA ISSN 1521-1916
RAINBOW REFLECTIONS. Text in English. 1996. m. back issues avail. **Document type:** *Newsletter.* **Description:** Discusses issues relating to personal spiritual growth, and to discovering and dissolving beliefs which limit our view of ourselves and our world.
Media: Online - full text.
Published by: Beyond the Rainbow, PO Box 110, Ruby, NY 12475. Ed., Pub., R&P, Adv. contact Constance Barrett TEL 845-336-4609.

133 USA ISSN 0744-432X
BF1623.R7
RAYS FROM THE ROSE CROSS. Text in English. 1915. bi-m. USD 20 domestic; USD 25 foreign (effective 2001). bk.rev. index. 64 p./no. 2 cols./p.; back issues avail. **Description:** Includes Christian esotericism, occult principles of health and healing, spiritual astrology, Western wisdom, and Bible studies.
Published by: Rosicrucian Fellowship, 2222 Mission Ave, Box 713, Oceanside, CA 92054. TEL 760-757-6600, FAX 760-721-3806, rosfshp@rosicrucianfellowship.org, http://www.rosicrucianfellowship.org. Ed., R&P Charles Weber TEL 760-757-6600 ext 203. Circ: 800.

133 USA ISSN 0093-4798
BF1021
RESEARCH IN PARAPSYCHOLOGY. Text in English. 1964. irreg., latest 1996. USD 48 per issue (effective 2009). illus. Index. back issues avail.; reprints avail. **Document type:** *Monographic series, Abstract/Index.* **Description:** Publishes original presentations on empirical, methodological, philosophical, and historical themes.
Formerly (until 1972): Parapsychological Association. Proceedings (0090-5399)
—**CCC.**
Published by: (Parapsychological Association), Scarecrow Press, Inc. (Subsidiary of: Rowman & Littlefield Publishers, Inc.), 4501 Forbes Blvd, Ste 200, Lanham, MD 20706. TEL 301-459-3366, 800-462-6420, FAX 301-429-5748, 800-338-4550, custserv@rowman.com, http://www.scarecrowpress.com. Ed., Pub. Mr. Edward Kurdyla TEL 301-459-3366 ext 5604. R&P Clare Cox TEL 212-529-3888 ext 308.

133 ITA ISSN 1970-8904
SCIENZA & PARANORMALE. Text in Italian. 1993. bi-m. EUR 35 domestic; EUR 40 foreign (effective 2008). **Document type:** *Magazine, Consumer.*
Published by: Comitato Italiano per il Controllo delle Affermazioni sul Paranormale (C I C A P), Casella Postale 847, Padua, 35100, Italy. http://www.cicap.org.

133.4 DEU
SHEKINAH; Schriftreihe fuer Schamanismus, Okkultismus, Parapsychologie und Magie. Text in German. 2007. irreg. **Document type:** *Monographic series, Academic/Scholarly.*
Published by: Edition Roter Drache, Treppendorf 31, Remda-Teichel, 07407, Germany. TEL 49-36743-35303, edition@roterdrache.org.

130 NOR ISSN 1890-1107
SKEPSIS (ONLINE); kritisk undersoegelse av moderne overtro. Text in Norwegian; Text occasionally in English. 1991. 2/yr. bk.rev. **Document type:** *Magazine, Consumer.* **Description:** Devoted to promoting critical examination of paranormal phenomena, pseudo-science and occultism.
Formerly (until 2002): Skepsis (Print) (0803-2718)
Published by: Foreningen Skepsis, St Olavs Gate 27, Oslo, 0166, Norway. kontakt@skepsis.no. Ed. Asbjoern Dyrendal.

133 110 AUS ISSN 0726-9897
THE SKEPTIC; a journal of fact and opinion. Text in English. 1981. q. AUD 44 (effective 2008). bk.rev. back issues avail. **Document type:** *Journal, Consumer.* **Description:** Provides information on scientific articles that deal with paranormal issues: psychics, astrology, UFOs, alternative medicine, creation "science" and new age beliefs.
Related titles: Online - full text ed.: free (effective 2008).
Published by: Australian Skeptics Inc., PO Box 268, Roseville, NSW 2069, Australia. TEL 61-2-94172071, FAX 61-2-94177930, contact@skeptics.com.au. Ed. Barry Williams. Circ: 2,500.

133 110 USA ISSN 1063-9330
Q174
➤ **SKEPTIC**; promoting science and critical thinking. Text in English. 1992. q. USD 30 domestic; USD 40 in Canada & Mexico; USD 50 elsewhere (effective 2010). adv. bk.rev. illus. Index. back issues avail.; reprints avail. **Document type:** *Magazine, Consumer.* **Description:** Features articles that investigate claims by scientists, historians, and controversial figures on a wide variety of theories and conjectures.
Related titles: Online - full text ed.
Indexed: A01, A02, A03, A08, A21, A26, ASIP, AmHI, B04, BRD, CA, CBRI, E07, E08, G03, G05, G06, G07, G08, G09, GSA, GSI, H07, I05, I07, MLA-IB, P02, P05, P10, P18, P25, P26, P48, P53, P54, P55, PQC, R05, RI-1, RI-2, S04, S06, S09, SOPODA, T02, W03, W05.
—**CCC.**
Published by: (Skeptics Society), Millenium Press, PO Box 338, Altadena, CA 91001. TEL 626-794-3119, FAX 626-794-1301. Ed., Pub. Michael Shermer.

133 USA ISSN 1060-216X
SKEPTICAL BRIEFS. Text in English. 1984. q. USD 20 membership (effective 2005). 16 p./no.; **Document type:** *Newsletter, Consumer.*
Published by: Committee for the Scientific Investigation of Claims of the Paranormal, PO Box 703, Buffalo, NY 14226. TEL 716-636-1425, FAX 716-636-1733, info@csicop.org. Eds. Benjamin Radford TEL 716-636-1425 ext 217, Kevin Christopher. Circ: 3,500.

133 USA ISSN 0194-6730
BF1001
SKEPTICAL INQUIRER; the magazine for science and reason. Text in English. 1976. bi-m. USD 19.95 (effective 2010). bk.rev. charts; illus.; stat. cum.index. 72 p./no.; back issues avail.; reprints avail. **Document type:** *Magazine, Consumer.* **Description:** Contains articles, news and comments.
Formerly (until 1978): The Zetetic (0148-1096)
Related titles: Online - full text ed.
Indexed: A21, A22, A25, A26, B04, BRD, CA, CCR, CIS, E08, G05, G06, G07, G08, GeoRef, I05, I07, M02, M06, MLA-IB, MagInd, P02, P10, P12, P13, P25, P48, P53, P54, PQC, PhilInd, R03, RASB, RGAb, RGPR, RI-1, RI-2, S06, S08, S09, S23, SCOPUS, SOPODA, SociolAb, SpeleolAb, T02, W03.
—BLDSC (8295.305000), IE, Infotrieve, Ingenta.
Published by: Committee for the Scientific Investigation of Claims of the Paranormal, PO Box 703, Buffalo, NY 14226. TEL 716-636-1425, 800-634-1610, FAX 716-636-1733, info@csicop.org. Ed. Kendrick Frazier.

133.91 GBR ISSN 0037-9751
BF1011
SOCIETY FOR PSYCHICAL RESEARCH. JOURNAL. Text in English. 1884. q. GBP 40, USD 80 to non-members; free to members (effective 2010); includes subscr. with Society for Psychical Research. Proceedings. adv. bk.rev. charts; illus. index. cum.index published irregularly. back issues avail.; reprints avail. **Document type:** *Journal, Academic/Scholarly.* **Description:** Contains reports of current laboratory and fieldwork research, as well as theoretical, methodological and historical papers with a bearing on the field of parapsychology.
Related titles: Online - full text ed.
Indexed: A01, A22, CA, DIP, E-psyche, IBR, IBZ, IPsyAb, PCI, PsycholAb, RASB, T02.
—BLDSC (4896.000000), IE, Infotrieve, Ingenta, INIST. **CCC.**
Published by: Society for Psychical Research, 49 Marloes Rd, Kensington, London, W8 6LA, United Kingdom. TEL 44-20-79378984. Ed. Chris Roe.

133 GBR ISSN 0081-1475
BF1011 CODEN: PPSRA5
SOCIETY FOR PSYCHICAL RESEARCH. PROCEEDINGS. Text in English. 1882. irreg. free to members (effective 2010); free with subscr. to Society for Psychical Research. Journal. adv. reprints avail. **Document type:** *Proceedings.* **Description:** Contains scholarly papers on particular themes in the field of parapsychology.
Indexed: DIP, H09, H10, IBR, IBZ, PsycholAb, RefZh, S05.
—INIST. **CCC.**
Published by: Society for Psychical Research, 49 Marloes Rd, Kensington, London, W8 6LA, United Kingdom. TEL 44-20-79378984.

133 SWE ISSN 0038-0504
SOEKAREN; tidskrift foer livsfraagor. Text in Swedish. 1964. 6/yr. SEK 250 (effective 1999). adv. bk.rev. illus.
Published by: Sven Magnusson Ed. & Pub., Fack 10, Skoghall, 66321, Sweden. TEL 46-54-51-89-00, FAX 46-54-51-89-02. Circ: 2,000.

SOMNIAL TIMES. *see* NEW AGE PUBLICATIONS

133.9 AUS ISSN 1833-2552
THE SPIRIT GUIDE TO SPELLCRAFT. Text in English. 2006. q. AUD 6.95 per issue (effective 2007). **Document type:** *Magazine, Consumer.*
Published by: Metier Media Pty Ltd, PO Box 6019, Mtchelton, QLD 4053, Australia. TEL 61-7-3353-4666, FAX 61-7-3353-6926, http://www.spellcraft.com.au. Ed. Leela Williams.

133.9 USA ISSN 2160-6625
SPIRIT OF GRACE. Text in English. 19??. q. free (effective 2011). **Document type:** *Newsletter, Trade.*
Formerly (until 2011): Graciously Free Spiritual Formation Group Newsletter
Media: Online - full text.
Published by: Annette F. Brown, Ed. & Pub., PO Box 5757, River Forest, IL 60305. TEL 60305-5757, admin@graciouslyfree.com.

299 USA
SPIRITUAL FRONTIERS FELLOWSHIP INTERNATIONAL JOURNAL. Text in English. bi-m. USD 50 domestic membership; USD 65 foreign membership (effective 2000). back issues avail. **Document type:** *Newsletter.* **Description:** Explores consciousness studies.
Published by: Spiritual Frontiers Fellowship International, PO Box 7868, Philadelphia, PA 19101. TEL 215-222-1991, FAX 215-222-1990. R&P Elizabeth W Fenske. Circ: 1,200.

299 USA
SPIRITUAL FRONTIERS FELLOWSHIP INTERNATIONAL NEWSLETTER. Text in English. m. USD 50 domestic membership; USD 55 foreign membership (effective 2000). back issues avail. **Document type:** *Newsletter.* **Description:** Explores consciousness studies.
Published by: Spiritual Frontiers Fellowship International, PO Box 7868, Philadelphia, PA 19101. TEL 215-222-1991, FAX 215-222-1990. Ed. Elizabeth W Fenske. Circ: 1,500.

133.9 CAN
SPIRITUAL INFORMATION BULLETIN. Text in English. 1991. q.
Published by: Springdale Church, 30 Merritt Rd, Toronto, ON M4B 3K5, Canada. TEL 416-759-3958.

SPIRITUELE SCHEURKALENDER. *see* PSYCHOLOGY

133.9 IND ISSN 0972-5296
SPLENDOUR. Text in English. 2001. m. INR 200 domestic; USD 40 foreign (effective 2011). back issues avail. **Document type:** *Magazine, Consumer.*
Published by: The Alpha Foundation, Flat No 53 Nagarjuna Hills, Panjagutta, Hyderabad, Andhra Pradesh 500 082, India. TEL 91-40-23435353.

STRANGE MAGAZINE. *see* BIOLOGY—Zoology

133 150 GBR
STUDIES IN PSYCHIC RESEARCH. Text in English. 1997. irreg., latest 1999. GBP 34.99 per issue (effective 2010). illus. **Document type:** *Monographic series, Academic/Scholarly.*
Indexed: E-psyche.
Published by: (Society for Psychical Research), Athlone Press Ltd., 44 Bedford Row, London, WC1R 4LL, United Kingdom. info@continuumbooks.com. Ed. John Beloff.

SUBCONSCIOUSLY SPEAKING; you can change your life through the power of your mind. *see* NEW AGE PUBLICATIONS

SUBTLE ENERGIES AND ENERGY MEDICINE; an interdisciplinary journal of energetic and informational interactions. *see* PHYSICS

133 RUS ISSN 1563-3845
TAINAYA VLAST'. Text in Russian. 1995. s-w. USD 125 in United States (effective 2000).
Related titles: Supplement(s): Zigzag Udachy.
Published by: Izdatel'sko-Proizvodsvennoe Ob'edinenie Pisatelei, Tsvetnoi bulv 30, Moscow, 103051, Russian Federation. TEL 7-095-2002323, FAX 7-095-2002323, plife@postman.ru, http://www.privatelife.ru. Ed. V I Shvarts. **Dist. by:** East View Information Services, 10601 Wayzata Blvd, Minneapolis, MN 55305. TEL 952-252-1201, 800-477-1005, FAX 952-252-1202, info@eastview.com, http://www.eastview.com.

133.9 CAN
THAT'S THE SPIRIT MAGAZINE. Text in English. 1988. q.
Published by: Gateway Psychic Center and Spiritualist Church, 1609d Kensington Rd N W, Calgary, AB T2N 3R2, Canada. TEL 403-270-3341.

133.4 GBR
THELEMIC MAGICK; proceedings of the ninth international symposium of Thelemic magick. Text in English. 1986. irreg., latest 1994. price varies. bk.rev. **Document type:** *Monographic series, Consumer.*
Formerly: Nuit - Isis (0269-9850)
Related titles: E-mail ed.
Published by: Mandrake of Oxford, PO Box 250, Oxford, OX1 1AP, United Kingdom. TEL 44-1865-243671, mandrake@mandrake.uk.net. Ed. Mogg Morgan.

THRESHOLDS; counselling with spirit. *see* PSYCHOLOGY

TOTAL ECLIPSE. *see* NEW AGE PUBLICATIONS

TRANSFORMATION TIMES; new age journal. *see* NEW AGE PUBLICATIONS

133 USA
TRENDS & PREDICTIONS ANALYST. Text in English. 1985. s-a. looseleaf. USD 6; USD 3 newsstand/cover (effective 1998). adv. bk.rev. abstr.; bibl.; illus.; maps; tr.lit. back issues avail. **Document type:** *Newsletter.* **Description:** Includes information on Earthchanges, information-sources, safe-areas, social-economic trends, UFOs, innerearth, subterranean worlds, survival strategies, astrology, alternative healing techniques, and alternative energy sources.
Related titles: Online - full text ed.
Published by: Patrick O'Connell Associates, 8505 Rancho Sante Fe Pl, N E, Albuquerque, NM 87113. TEL 505-823-0851. Ed., Pub., R&P, Adv. contact Patrick O'Connell. page USD 100; trim 11 x 8.5.

U F O; brazilian ufo magazine. (Unidentified Flying Object) *see* AERONAUTICS AND SPACE FLIGHT

U F O DIGEST; online webzine. (Unidentified Flying Object) *see* AERONAUTICS AND SPACE FLIGHT

U F O DOCUMENTO. *see* AERONAUTICS AND SPACE FLIGHT

U F O ESPECIAL. *see* AERONAUTICS AND SPACE FLIGHT

001.9 GBR ISSN 2044-365X
▼ **U F O MATRIX MAGAZINE.** Text in English. 2010. bi-m. GBP 29.95 domestic; GBP 50.95 foreign; GBP 5.99 newsstand/cover (effective 2011). back issues avail. **Document type:** *Magazine, Trade.*
Related titles: Online - full text ed.: ISSN 2044-3668.
Published by: Healings of Atlantis, The Maltings, West St, Bourne, Lincolnshire PE10 9PH, United Kingdom. TEL 4-20-86564641, http://www.healingsofatlantis.com.

133.91 GBR
U S P S JOURNAL. Text in English. 1968. s-a. GBP 8 (effective 2003). bk.rev. 40 p./no.; back issues avail. **Document type:** *Journal, Academic/Scholarly.* **Description:** Examines the relation of psychical studies to religion.
Formerly (until 1988): Psychical Studies (0968-6487)
Related titles: Online - full text ed.
Published by: Unitarian Society for Psychical Studies, Waterbarrow, High Cunsey, Via Ambleside, Cumbria LA22 0LT, United Kingdom. TEL 44-1539-446629. Ed., R&P Irene Hornby. Circ: 150 (paid).

001.9 USA ISSN 1096-3790
UNKNOWN MAGAZINE; real experiences of unusual phenomena. Text in English. 1997. q. USD 28 domestic; USD 40 in Canada; USD 50 elsewhere; USD 5.95 newsstand/cover (effective 2001). adv. **Document type:** *Magazine, Consumer.* **Description:** Presents informative and interesting first hand accounts of unusual experiences not covered by the mainstream media.
Related titles: Online - full text ed.
Address: PO Box 59274, Schaumburg, IL 601590274. TEL 847-884-2044, FAX 847-490-0671, http://www.unknownmag.com. Ed., Pub., Adv. contact Christopher Stephen Fleming. Circ: 8,000 (paid). **Dist. by:** International Publishers Direct, 27500 Riverview Center Blvd, Bonita Springs, FL 34134. TEL 858-320-4563, FAX 858-677-3220.

133 DEU ISSN 0174-3538
V T F - POST. Text in German. 1975. q. bk.rev. back issues avail. **Document type:** *Newsletter.* **Description:** Provides members and subscribers with the latest information about the field of electronic voice phenomenon (EVP).
Published by: Verein fuer Tonbandstimmenforschung e.V., Hoehscheider Str 2, Duesseldorf, 40591, Germany. TEL 49-211-786439. Ed. Fidelio Koeberle. Circ: 2,000.

133 USA ISSN 0748-3406
BF1001
VENTURE INWARD. Text in English. 1984. bi-m. USD 20; USD 27 foreign (effective 1999). bk.rev. index. **Document type:** *Bulletin.* **Description:** Publishes articles that relate to the parapsychology, holistic medicine, metaphysical and spiritual concepts contained in the readings of the late psychic Edgar Cayce.
Incorporates (in 1996): Perspective on Consciousness and Psi Research; Formed by the 1984 merger of: A.R.E. Journal; (1979-1984): A.R.E. News
Published by: Association for Research and Enlightenment, Inc., 3777 Fox Creek Rd, Mouth Of Wilson, VA 24363. TEL 757-428-3588, FAX 757-422-4631, are@are-cayce.com, are@webartisans.com. Ed. A Robert Smith. Pub. John Van Avken. Circ: 35,000 (paid).

133 CAN ISSN 1910-7730
VIE & DESTIN. Text in French. 2003. m. **Document type:** *Magazine, Consumer.*
Published by: Editions Colette, 350, rue Regnier, Iberville, PQ J2X 3V9, Canada.

133.9 MEX ISSN 0185-6480
VOZ INFORMATIVA; revista bimestral de filosofia, ciencia y moral. Text in Spanish. 1952. bi-m. MXN 120, USD 6.
Address: Pino 129, Mexico City 4, DF, Mexico. Ed. Jose Castol Gonzalez. Circ: 1,000.

133 USA
WEIRDOLOGY. Text in English. bi-m.
Published by: United Aerial Phenomena Agency, PO Box 347032, Cleveland, OH 44134-7032. Ed. Allan J Manak.

133 CAN ISSN 1480-1744
WICCAN CANDLES. Text in English. 1997. 8/yr. CAD 20 domestic; USD 24 foreign (effective 2000). adv. bk.rev. **Document type:** *Newsletter.* **Description:** Includes scholarly articles on pagan mythologies and history, interviews, profiles, social networking and other information.
Address: P O Box 307, Creemore, ON L0M 1G0, Canada. TEL 705-466-2231, kzworld@lynx.org. Ed., R&P Iris O Bard. Pub. Z Halkewycz. Adv. contact Kate Russell. B&W page CAD 200. Circ: 400 (paid).

133.43 NLD ISSN 1384-0363
WICCAN REDE. Text in Dutch, English. 1980. q. EUR 29 in Europe (effective 2010). adv. bk.rev. **Document type:** *Newsletter.* **Description:** Covers Wicca and modern witchcraft.
Published by: Silver Circle, PO Box 473, Zeist, 3700 AL, Netherlands. merlin@silvercircle.org, http://www.silvercircle.com. Eds. Merlin, Morgana.

THE WISE WOMAN. *see* WOMEN'S INTERESTS

133.4 GBR ISSN 1755-9960
WITCHCRAFT & WICCA. Text in English. 200?. s-a. GBP 6.50, EUR 9.45, USD 12.47 to non-members; GBP 3.25, EUR 4.73, USD 6.24 per issue to non-members; free to members (effective 2010). back issues avail. **Document type:** *Magazine, Consumer.* **Description:** Promotes understanding of the beliefs of Wicca and Witchcraft.
Published by: Children of Artemis Ltd., Media Line, BM Artemis, London, WC1N 3XX, United Kingdom. TEL 870-442-7290.

133.3 IRL ISSN 1649-6426
YOUR DESTINY. Text in English. 2005. q. EUR 3.50 newsstand/cover domestic; EUR 4.50 newsstand/cover in United Kingdom; EUR 5.50 newsstand/cover elsewhere (effective 2006). adv. **Document type:** *Magazine, Consumer.*
Published by: Mac Communications, Taney Hall, Eglinton Terrace, Dundrum, Dublin, Dublin 14, Ireland. TEL 353-1-2960000, FAX 353-1-2960383, info@maccommunications.ie, http://www.maccommunications.ie. Ed. Julian de Burgh. adv.: page EUR 2,000; trim 210 x 297. Circ: 15,000.

133.91 DEU ISSN 0028-3479
BF1003
➤ **ZEITSCHRIFT FUER PARAPSYCHOLOGIE UND GRENZGEBIETE DER PSYCHOLOGIE.** Text in German. 1957. q. EUR 50; EUR 15 per issue (effective 2010). adv. bk.rev. illus. reprints avail. **Document type:** *Journal, Academic/Scholarly.* **Description:** Covers the entire field of parapsychology, including paranormal experiences, field work, experimental research, and theoretical developments. Also includes the history, methods, results, problems and controversies related to the paranormal.
Supersedes: Neue Wissenschaft
Indexed: DIP, IBR, IBZ, PsycholAb.
—GNLM, IE.
Published by: Wissenschaftliche Gesellschaft zur Foederung der Parapsychologie e.V., Hildastr 64, Freiburg Im Breisgau, 79102, Germany. TEL 49-761-77202, info@parapsychologische-beratungsstelle.de. Ed. Walter von Lucadou. Circ: 1,000.

➤ **ZEITSCHRIFT FUER RADIAESTHESIE UND HARMONIEFINDUNG.** *see* NEW AGE PUBLICATIONS

PARAPSYCHOLOGY AND OCCULTISM—Abstracting, Bibliographies, Statistics

133 USA
OCCULT PUBLICATIONS DIRECTORY. Text in English. 19??. a. **Document type:** *Directory, Consumer.* **Description:** Lists newsletters, directories, and tabloids dealing with the occult in general.
Published by: Ghost Research Society, PO Box 205, Oak Lawn, IL 60454. TEL 708-425-5163, FAX 708-425-3969, http://www.ghostresearch.org.

PATENTS, TRADEMARKS AND COPYRIGHTS

A I P L A BULLETIN. *see* LAW

340 AUT
A K M INFORMATIONEN. (Autoren, Komponisten und Musikverleger) Text in German. 1899. 5/yr. membership. adv. illus. index. **Document type:** *Newsletter, Trade.* **Description:** Provides information to members of AKM on various subjects of interest such as composer competitions, workshops, information on music fairs, copyright rules and regulations, etc.
Formerly (until 1995): Oesterreichische Autorenzeitung (0029-8883)
Indexed: RASB.
Published by: Staatlich Genehmigte Gesellschaft der Autoren Komponisten Musikverleger, Baumannstrasse 10, Vienna, W 1030, Austria. TEL 43-1-71714, FAX 43-1-717141107. Ed., R&P Ingrid Waldingbrett. Adv. contact Helmut Neugebauer. Circ: 14,200.

346.73 USA ISSN 1074-8369
KF2995
ADVANCED SEMINAR ON COPYRIGHT LAW. Text in English. 199?. a. USD 199 (effective 2009). back issues avail. **Document type:** *Proceedings, Trade.*
Related titles: Audio CD ed.: USD 497.50 (effective 2009); Online - full text ed.: USD 995 (online or Optical Disk - DVD ed.); for Live webcast, Live seminar (effective 2009); Optical Disk - DVD ed.
Published by: Practising Law Institute, 810 Seventh Ave, 21st Fl, New York, NY 10019. TEL 212-824-5700, info@pli.edu.

346.73 USA ISSN 1543-2416
KF3180.Z9
ADVANCED SEMINAR ON TRADEMARK LAW. Text in English. 1993. a. USD 199 (effective 2009). back issues avail. **Document type:** *Proceedings, Trade.*
Former titles (until 1997): Annual Advanced Seminar on Trademark Law (1543-2440); (until 1996): Advanced Seminar on Trademark Law (1074-9136)
Related titles: Audio CD ed.: USD 497.50 (effective 2009); Online - full text ed.: USD 995 (online or Optical Disk - DVD ed.); for Live webcast, Live seminar (effective 2009); Optical Disk - DVD ed.
Published by: Practising Law Institute, 810 Seventh Ave, 21st Fl, New York, NY 10019. TEL 212-824-5700, info@pli.edu.

ALLEN'S TRADEMARK DIGEST. *see* LAW

340 CAN ISSN 1196-7528
KE2793.9
THE (YEAR) ANNOTATED COPYRIGHT ACT. Text in English. 1991. a. CAD 125 per issue domestic; USD 105.93 per issue foreign (effective 2005).
Published by: Carswell (Subsidiary of: Thomson Reuters Corp.), One Corporate Plz, 2075 Kennedy Rd, Toronto, ON M1T 3V4, Canada. TEL 416-609-8000, FAX 416-298-5094, http://www.carswell.com.

346.14 USA ISSN 1932-1295
KF2972
ANNUAL INTELLECTUAL PROPERTY LAW CONFERENCE. Text in English. 19??. a. **Document type:** *Journal, Trade.*
Formerly (until 2002): Patent, Trademark, and Copyright Law, Litigation and Corporate Practice (1088-5919)
—CCC.
Published by: American Bar Association, Section of Intellectual Property Law, 321 N Clark Street, Chicago, IL 60610-4714. TEL 312-988-5598, FAX 312-988-6800, iplaw@abanet.org.

348 USA ISSN 1947-9867
KF2980
ANNUAL INTELLECTUAL PROPERTY LAW INSTITUTE. Text in English. 2007. a. USD 99 combined subscription (print & CD-ROM eds.) (effective 2009). back issues avail. **Document type:** *Journal, Trade.* **Description:** Designed to meet the needs of practitioners of varied levels of experience in intellectual property law, addresses a wide variety of topics and provides a ready reference when those inevitable IP questions arise.
Formerly (until 2008): Intellectual Property Law Institute
Related titles: CD-ROM ed.: ISSN 1947-864X.
Published by: Pennsylvania Bar Institute, 5080 Ritter Rd, Mechanicsburg, PA 17055. TEL 717-796-0804, 800-247-4724, 800-932-4637, FAX 717-796-2348, info@pbi.org, http://www.pbi.org. Ed. Wendy B McGovern TEL 717-796-0804 ext 2257.

P

341.7582 CHE ISSN 1424-4276
K25
ARCHIV FUER URHEBER- UND MEDIENRECHT. (Archiv fuer Urheber-, Film-, Funk- und Theaterrecht) Text in English, French, German, Italian. 1928. 3/yr. adv. bk.rev. charts. index. **Document type:** *Bulletin, Trade.*
Former titles (until 1999): Archiv fuer Urheber-, Film-, Funk- und Theaterrecht (0003-9454); (until 1944): Archiv fuer Urheber-, Film- und Theaterrecht (0174-822X)
Indexed: DIP, FLP, IBR, IBZ.
—CCC.
Published by: Staempfli Verlag AG (Subsidiary of: LexisNexis Europe and Africa), Woelflistr 1, Bern, 3001, Switzerland. TEL 41-31-3006666, FAX 41-31-3006688, verlag@staempfli.com, http://www.staempfli.com. Ed. Manfred Rehbinder. Circ: 500.

346.04 USA
ATTORNEY'S DICTIONARY OF PATENT CLAIMS. Text in English. 1985. 3 base vols. plus irreg. updates. looseleaf. USD 838 base vol(s). (effective 2008). Supplement avail. **Document type:** *Directory, Trade.* **Description:** For patent drafters, providing invaluable assistance in preparing patent applications, is a lexicon of the language of modern patent claims. Includes terms from all patent arts, culled from thousands of claims accepted by the U.S. Patent and Trademark Office.
Published by: Matthew Bender & Co., Inc. (Subsidiary of: LexisNexis North America), 1275 Broadway, Albany, NY 12204. TEL 518-487-3000, 800-424-4200, FAX 518-487-3083, international@bender.com, http://bender.lexisnexis.com. Ed. Irwin Aisenberg.

608.7 AUS
AU-A WEEKLY UPDATES INCLUDING MASTER INDEX ON CD-ROM. Text in English. 1999. w. AUD 1,500 (effective 2009). back issues avail. **Document type:** *Government.* **Description:** Contains data of AU-A patent specifications as laid open to public inspection, search material.
Media: CD-ROM. **Related titles:** Online - full content ed.
Published by: I P Australia, PO Box 200, Woden, ACT 2606, Australia. TEL 61-2-62832999, FAX 61-2-62837999, assist@ipaustralia.gov.au, http://www.ipaustralia.gov.au.

340 AUS
KU1104.A13
AUSTRALIAN COPYRIGHT COUNCIL. PRACTICAL GUIDES AND DISCUSSION PAPERS. Text in English. 1973. irreg., latest 2009. price varies. **Document type:** *Bulletin.*
Formerly: Australian Copyright Council. Bulletin (0311-2934)
Published by: Australian Copyright Council, 245 Chalmers St, Redfern, NSW 2016, Australia. TEL 61-2-88159777, FAX 61-2-88159799, info@copyright.org.au. Ed. Libby Baulch. Circ: 600.

341.7582 AUS ISSN 1038-1635
K9
➤ **AUSTRALIAN INTELLECTUAL PROPERTY JOURNAL.** Abbreviated title: A I P J. Text in English. 1990. q. AUD 610 (effective 2008). back issues avail. **Document type:** *Journal, Academic/Scholarly.* **Description:** Discusses the developments in intellectual property law in Australia.
Formerly (until 1992): Intellectual Property Journal (1034-3032)
Related titles: Online - full text ed.
Indexed: AusPAIS, P30.
—BLDSC (1801.674300), IE, Infotrieve, Ingenta.

Published by: Lawbook Co. (Subsidiary of: Thomson Reuters (Professional) Australia Limited), PO Box 3502, Rozelle, NSW 2039, Australia. TEL 61-2-85877980, 300-304-195, FAX 61-2-85877981, 300-304-196, LTA.Service@thomsonreuters.com, http://www.thomson.com.au. Ed. Ann Dufty.

608.7 340 AUS ISSN 1832-9942
AUSTRALIAN OFFICIAL JOURNAL OF DESIGNS (ONLINE). Abbreviated title: A O J D. Text in English. 1907. fortn. free (effective 2008). adv. back issues avail. **Document type:** *Journal, Trade.* **Description:** Covers proceedings under the designs act, including design applications lodged and registered.
Formerly (until 2005): Australian Official Journal of Designs (Print) (1038-0671); Which superseded in part: Australian Official Journal of Patents, Trade Marks and Designs (0004-9891)
Media: Online - full text.
Indexed: ChemAb, PetrolAb.
Published by: I P Australia, PO Box 200, Woden, ACT 2606, Australia. TEL 61-2-62832999, FAX 61-2-62837999, assist@ipaustralia.gov.au.

608.7 602.7 AUS ISSN 1832-9950
T321.A2 CODEN: AOJPEO
AUSTRALIAN OFFICIAL JOURNAL OF PATENTS (ONLINE). Abbreviated title: A O J P. Text in English. 1904. w. free (effective 2008). back issues avail. **Document type:** *Journal, Trade.* **Description:** Contains proceedings under the patents act, including applications lodged, applications open to public inspection, complete specifications accepted, and patents renewed.
Formerly (until 2005): Australian Official Journal of Patents (Print) (0819-1794); Supersedes in part (in 1987): Australian Official Journal of Patents, Trade Marks and Designs (0004-9891)
Media: Online - full text.
Indexed: PetrolAb.
—CASDDS.
Published by: I P Australia, PO Box 200, Woden, ACT 2606, Australia. TEL 61-2-62832999, FAX 61-2-62837999, assist@ipaustralia.gov.au, http://www.ipaustralia.gov.au.

608.7 602.7 AUS ISSN 1832-9969
T321.V1
AUSTRALIAN OFFICIAL JOURNAL OF TRADE MARKS (ONLINE). Abbreviated title: A O J T M. Text in English. 1906. w. free (effective 2008). back issues avail. **Document type:** *Journal, Government.* **Description:** Contains proceedings under the trade marks act, including applications lodged, accepted, registered, and renewed.
Formerly (until 2005): Australian Official Journal of Trade Marks (Print) (0819-1808); Which superseded in part (in 1987): Australian Official Journal of Patents, Trade Marks and Designs (0004-9891)
Media: Online - full text.
Published by: I P Australia, PO Box 200, Woden, ACT 2606, Australia. TEL 61-2-62832999, FAX 61-2-62837999, assist@ipaustralia.gov.au, http://www.ipaustralia.gov.au.

346.04 AUS ISSN 1832-1070
AUSTRALIAN PATENT APPLICATIONS SCOREBOARD (YEAR). Text in English. 2004. a. AUD 25 per issue (effective 2009). 32 p./no.; **Document type:** *Journal, Trade.* **Description:** Contains a large amount of information about patent applications in an easily accessible form, the Scoreboard is a useful tool for enterprises that facilitate the commercialisation of research projects.
Published by: (University of Melbourne, Melbourne Institute of Applied Economic and Social Research), The University of Melbourne, Intellectual Property Research Institute of Australia, Alan Gilbert Bldg, Parkville, VIC 3010, Australia. TEL 61-3-83442100, FAX 61-3-83442111, info@ipria.org. Eds. Dr. Alfons Palangkaraya TEL 61-3-83442119, Dr. Paul H Jensen TEL 61-3-83442117.

346.04 USA ISSN 0404-3030
AUTHORS GUILD BULLETIN. Text in English. 1914. q. membership only. bk.rev. **Document type:** *Bulletin, Trade.* **Description:** Covers business and legal matters of interest to authors.
Formerly (until 1956): Author's League Bulletin
Published by: Authors Guild, 31 E 32nd St, 7th Fl, New York, NY 10016. TEL 212-563-5904, FAX 212-564-5363, staff@authorsguild.org. Ed. Martha Fay. R&P John Blesso. Circ: 7,500.

AWISHKARA. *see* SCIENCES: COMPREHENSIVE WORKS

608.7 602.7 USA ISSN 1095-5615
KF2979
B N A'S INTELLECTUAL PROPERTY LIBRARY ON C D. (Bureau of National Affairs) Text in English. 1995. m. USD 4,049 (effective 2010 - 2011). **Document type:** *Magazine, Trade.* **Description:** Covers cases in patents, trademarks, copyrights, unfair competition, trade secrets and computer chip protection.
Media: CD-ROM. **Related titles:** ◆ Online - full text ed.: Intellectual Property Law Resource Center; ◆ Print ed.: United States Patents Quarterly. ISSN 0041-803X.
—CCC.
Published by: The Bureau of National Affairs, Inc., 1801 S Bell St, Arlington, VA 22202. TEL 703-341-3000, 800-372-1033, FAX 703-341-4634, 800-253-0332, bnaplus@bna.com, http://www.bna.com.

340 608.7 USA ISSN 0148-7965
K2
B N A'S PATENT, TRADEMARK & COPYRIGHT JOURNAL. (Bureau of National Affairs) Text in English. 1970. w. looseleaf. USD 2,485 (effective 2010 - 2011). bk.rev. abstr.; pat.; stat. index, cum.index. 20 p./no.; back issues avail. **Document type:** *Journal, Trade.* **Description:** Provides an in-depth review of current developments in the intellectual property field. Covers congressional activity, court decisions, relevant conferences, professional associations, international developments, and actions of the Patent and Trademark Office and the Copyright Office.
Formerly: Patent, Trademark & Copyright Journal
Related titles: Online - full text ed.: ISSN 1522-4325. USD 2,740 (effective 2010 - 2011).
—CCC.
Published by: The Bureau of National Affairs, Inc., 1801 S Bell St, Arlington, VA 22202. TEL 703-341-3000, 800-372-1033, FAX 703-341-4634, bnaplus@bna.com.

608.7 FRA ISSN 0750-7674
T271 CODEN: BOPBEN
B O P I BREVETS D'INVENTION - ABREGES ET LISTES. (Bulletin Officiel de la Propriete Industrielle) Text in French. 1982. w. pat. index. back issues avail. **Document type:** *Bulletin, Trade.* **Description:** Contains bibliographical data and abstracts of French patent applications, lists of French specifications, translations of European patents, supplementary protection certificates, and integrated circuit layout designs.
Which was formed by the merger of (1974-1982): B O P I Abreges (0151-0592); (1970-1982): B O P I Listes (0223-4092)
Related titles: Microfiche ed.
Indexed: PetrolAb.
—CASDDS, INIST.
Published by: Institut National de la Propriete Industrielle, 26 bis rue de St. Petersbourg, Paris, Cedex 8 75800, France. TEL 33-01-53045304, FAX 33-01-42-93-59-30. Circ: 900.

608.7 FRA ISSN 0223-3401
B O P I MARQUES DE FABRIQUE, DE COMMERCE OU DE SERVICE. (Bulletin Officiel de la Propriete Industrielle) Text in French. 1884. w. EUR 450 (effective 2010). tr.mk. index. back issues avail. **Document type:** *Bulletin, Trade.*
Published by: Institut National de la Propriete Industrielle, 26 bis rue de St. Petersbourg, Paris, Cedex 8 75800, France. TEL 33-01-53045304. Circ: 500.

608.7 USA
BASIC FACTS ABOUT TRADEMARKS. Text in English. 1996. irreg., latest 2010. free (effective 2011). **Document type:** *Government.* **Description:** Contains an introduction to general US patent information.
Formerly: General Information Concerning Trademarks (0083-3029)
Related titles: Online - full text ed.
Published by: U.S. Patent and Trademark Office, General Information Services Division, PO Box 1450, Alexandria, VA 22313. TEL 571-272-1000, 800-786-9199, usptoinfo@uspto.gov. **Subscr. to:** U.S. Government Printing Office, Superintendent of Documents.

608.7 NLD ISSN 1571-0017
BENELUX TEKENINGEN- OF MODELLENBLAD (CD-ROM)/RECUEIL DES DESSINS OU MODELES BENELUX. Text in Dutch, French. 1975. m. EUR 79 domestic; EUR 87 foreign (effective 2009).
Formerly (until 2002): Benelux Tekeningen- of Modellenblad (Print) (0165-6023)
Media: CD-ROM.
Published by: Benelux Bureau voor de Intellectuele Eigendom, Bordewijklaan 15, PO Box 90404, The Hague, 2509 LK, Netherlands. TEL 31-70-3491111, FAX 31-70-3475708, info@boip.int, http://www.boip.int.

347.7 NLD ISSN 2211-4815
KKM1194.A48
BERICHTEN INDUSTRIEELE EIGENDOM. Text in Dutch. 1933. m. EUR 165; EUR 15 newsstand/cover (effective 2011). bk.rev. bibl.; charts; stat. index. **Document type:** *Government.*
Former titles (until 2011): Bulletin Industriele Eigendom (1879-954X); (until 2008): Bijblad bij de Industriele Eigendom (0006-2251)
Related titles: Online - full text ed.: ISSN 1879-9558.
Indexed: ELLIS.
Published by: Uitgeverij deLex, Postbus 3564, Amsterdam, 1001 AJ, Netherlands. TEL 31-20-3452212, FAX 31-20-3452213, service@delex.nl, http://www.delex.nl. Pub. Claudia Zuidema.

BERLINER HOCHSCHULSCHRIFTEN ZUM GEWERBLICHEN RECHTSSCHUTZ UND URHEBERRECHT. *see* LAW—Corporate Law

BLAKES REPORT ON INTELLECTUAL PROPERTY. *see* LAW

608.7 602.7 DEU ISSN 0930-2980
T273
BLATT FUER P M Z. (Patent, Muster- und Zeichenwesen) Text in German. 1898. m. EUR 80; EUR 8 newsstand/cover (effective 2011). adv. pat.; stat.; tr.mk. index, cum.index. reprints avail. **Document type:** *Magazine, Trade.*
Formerly (until 1986): Blatt fuer Patent, Muster- und Zeichenwesen (0341-4949)
Indexed: A22.
—IE, Infotrieve.
Published by: (Germany. Deutsches Patent- und Markenamt), Carl Heymanns Verlag KG (Subsidiary of: Wolters Kluwer Deutschland GmbH), Luxemburger Str 449, Cologne, 50939, Germany. TEL 49-221-943730, FAX 49-221-94373901, marketing@heymanns.com, http://www.heymanns.com. Circ: 2,150 (paid and controlled).

346.04 USA ISSN 1948-4186
KF2975.3
BLOOMBERG LAW REPORTS. INTELLECTUAL PROPERTY. Text in English. 2007. w. USD 2,500 to non-members; free to members (effective 2009). **Document type:** *Report, Trade.*
Related titles: Online - full text ed.: ISSN 2152-954X. free (effective 2010).
Published by: Bloomberg Finance L.P., 499 Park Ave, New York, NY 10022. TEL 212-318-2200, FAX 212-980-4585, blaw_us@bloomberg.net, http://www.bloomberg.com.

608.7 VEN ISSN 0006-6338
BOLETIN DE LA PROPIEDAD INDUSTRIAL. Text in Spanish. 1931. m. free. index.
Published by: (Venezuela. Oficina de Registro de la Propiedad Industrial), Ministerio de Fomento, Centro Simon Bolivar, Edificio Sur, Caracas, DF 1060, Venezuela. Ed. Ricardo Pages. Circ: 600.

602.7 608.7 ESP ISSN 1136-3312
BOLETIN DE RESUMENES DE PATENTES. Text in Spanish. 1980. bi-w. **Document type:** *Government.*
Formerly (until 1989): Informacion Tecnologica de Patentes (0211-187X)
Related titles: Online - full text ed.
Indexed: GeoRef, SpeleolAb.
Published by: Ministerio de Industria y Energia, Oficina Espanola de Patentes y Marcas, Panama, 1, Madrid, 28036, Spain. TEL 34-91-3495300, FAX 34-91-4572280, http://www.oepm.es.

346.04 SWE ISSN 1104-4675
BRAND NEWS; varumaerken, brand management, reklamjuridik. Text in Swedish. 1990. 10/yr. **Document type:** *Magazine, Consumer.*
Published by: Brand Eye AB, PO Box 3457, Stockholm, 10369, Sweden. TEL 46-8-4060900, FAX 46-8-203810, input@brandeye.se.

608 NLD ISSN 2211-0429
▼ **BRANDBRIEF.** Text in Dutch. 2011. s-a. **Document type:** *Newsletter, Trade.*
Related titles: Online - full text ed.: ISSN 2211-047X.
Published by: Merkenbureau Merk-Echt B.V., Postbus 1022, Breda, 4801 BA, Netherlands. TEL 31-76-5148403, FAX 31-76-5145616, info@merkecht.com, http://www.merkecht.com. Circ: 8,500.

346.04 SWE ISSN 1654-4846
BRANDMANAGER; affaerer genom varumaerken. Text in Swedish. 2007. q. SEK 340; SEK 87 per issue (effective 2007). **Document type:** *Magazine, Consumer.*
Published by: Brand Eye AB, PO Box 3457, Stockholm, 10369, Sweden. TEL 46-8-4060900, FAX 46-8-203810, input@brandeye.se, http://www.brandeye.se. Circ: 8,500.

602.7 USA ISSN 1047-6407
T223.V4
BRANDS AND THEIR COMPANIES. Text in English. 1990. a. USD 1,292 (effective 2009). Supplement avail.; back issues avail. **Document type:** *Directory, Trade.* **Description:** Identifies more than 339,000 consumer products and their manufacturers. Entries are arranged alphabetically by trade name and include contact information for product inquiries or complaints.
Formed by the merger of (1976-1990): Trade Names Dictionary (0272-8818); (1976-1990): New Trade Names (0272-8826)
Related titles: Online - full text ed.
Published by: Gale (Subsidiary of: Cengage Learning), 27500 Drake Rd, Farmington Hills, MI 48331. TEL 248-699-4253, 800-877-4253, FAX 877-363-4253, gale.customerservice@cengage.com, http://gale.cengage.com. Ed. Christine Kesler.

BRITISH GLASS MANUFACTURERS CONFEDERATION. DIGEST INFORMATION AND PATENT REVIEW (ONLINE). *see* CERAMICS, GLASS AND POTTERY

602.1841 GBR ISSN 1367-2134
BRITISH STANDARDS INSTITUTION. UPDATE STANDARDS. Text in English. 1995. m. free to members (effective 2010). back issues avail. **Document type:** *Magazine, Trade.*
Formerly (until 1996): B S I Update
Related titles: Online - full text ed.: free (effective 2010).
—BLDSC (9121.907900).
Published by: British Standards Institution, 389 Chiswick High Rd, London, W4 4AL, United Kingdom. TEL 44-20-89969001, FAX 44-20-89967001, cservices@bsi-global.com, http://www.bsigroup.com/.

608.7 ROM ISSN 1223-7728
BULETIN OFICIAL DE PROPRIETATE INDUSTRIALA. SECTIUNEA DESENE SI MODELE INDUSTRIALE/OFFICIAL BULLETIN FOR INDUSTRIAL PROPERTY. INDUSTRIAL DESIGN SECTION. Text in Romanian; Summaries in English, French, German. 1993. m. USD 800. adv. back issues avail.; reprints avail. **Document type:** *Bulletin, Trade.*
Related titles: CD-ROM ed.
Published by: Oficiul de Stat pentru Inventii si Marci (OSIM)/State Office for Inventions and Trademarks, Str. Ion Ghica 5, Sector 3, Bucharest, 70418, Romania. TEL 40-01-3151966, FAX 40-01-3123819, office@osim.ro. R&Ps Dan Petcu, Maria Minaescu. **Co-sponsor:** Rumanian Institute for Inventions and Trademarks.

602.7 608.7 ROM ISSN 1220-6105
CODEN: BPSIEW
BULETIN OFICIAL DE PROPRIETATE INDUSTRIALA. SECTIUNEA INVENTII/OFFICIAL BULLETIN FOR INDUSTRIAL PROPERTY. INVENTIONS SECTION. Text in Romanian; Summaries in English, French, German. 1961. m. USD 960; or exchange basis. adv. pat. Supplement avail.; back issues avail.; reprints avail. **Document type:** *Bulletin, Trade.*
Supersedes in part (in 1991): Buletinul de Informare pentru Inventii si Marci - Bulletin for Inventions and Trademarks (1012-8883); Which was formerly (until 1978): Buletin de Informare pentru Inventii si Marci (0254-2269)
Related titles: CD-ROM ed.; Online - full text ed.
—CASDDS.
Published by: Oficiul de Stat pentru Inventii si Marci (OSIM)/State Office for Inventions and Trademarks, Str. Ion Ghica 5, Sector 3, Bucharest, 70418, Romania. TEL 40-01-3151966, FAX 40-01-3123819. R&P Dan Petcu. Adv. contact Mihaela Tarcolea. **Co-sponsor:** Rumanian Institute for Inventions and Trademarks.

602.7 ROM ISSN 1220-6091
CODEN: BINMD3
BULETIN OFICIAL DE PROPRIETATE INDUSTRIALA. SECTIUNEA MARCI/OFFICIAL BULLETIN FOR INDUSTRIAL PROPERTY. TRADEMARKS SECTION. Text in Romanian; Summaries in English, French. 1961. m. USD 800. adv. back issues avail.; reprints avail. **Document type:** *Bulletin, Trade.*
Supersedes in part (in 1991): Buletinul de Informare pentru Inventii si Marci - Bulletin for Inventions and Trademarks (1012-8883); Which was formerly (until 1978): Buletin de Informare pentru Inventii si Marci (0254-2269)
Related titles: CD-ROM ed.
—CASDDS.
Published by: Oficiul de Stat pentru Inventii si Marci (OSIM)/State Office for Inventions and Trademarks, Str. Ion Ghica 5, Sector 3, Bucharest, 70418, Romania. TEL 40-01-3151966, FAX 40-01-3123819, office@osim.ro, http://www.osim.ro. R&P Dan Petcu. Adv. contact Mitrita Bularda.

346.68048 ZAF
BURRELL'S INTELLECTUAL PROPERTY LAW REPORTS. Text in English. irreg. price varies. back issues avail. **Document type:** *Report, Academic/Scholarly.* **Description:** Deals with intellectual property law reports.
Formerly: Burrell's Patent Law Reports
Related titles: CD-ROM ed.: Burrell's Intellectual Property Law Library (CD-ROM Edition). ISSN 1560-4594; Online - full text ed.: Burrell's Intellectual Property Law Library (Online Edition). ISSN 1682-0614. ZAR 1,281 single user; ZAR 641 per additional user (effective 2007).
Published by: Juta & Company Ltd., Juta Law, PO Box 14373, Lansdowne, 7779, South Africa. TEL 27-21-7633500, FAX 27-11-8838169, cserv@juta.co.za. Ed. Timothy D Burrell.

602.7 608.7 ESP ISSN 1138-7211
C D - B O P I. (Boletin Oficial de la Propiedad Industrial) Text in Spanish. 1998. s-m. **Document type:** *Government.* **Description:** Contains judicial, administrative and bibliographic information on Spanish patents and utility models, Spanish trademarks, Spanish industrial designs.
Media: CD-ROM.
Published by: Ministerio de Industria y Energia, Oficina Espanola de Patentes y Marcas, Panama, 1, Madrid, 28036, Spain. TEL 34-91-3495300, FAX 34-91-4572280, http://www.oepm.es.

608.7 ESP ISSN 1889-1284
CODEN: BPMBBC
C D - B O P I. TOMO I. (Boletin Oficial de la Propiedad Industrial) Text in Spanish. 1886. bi-w. charts; illus.; pat. index. **Document type:** *Government.*
Formerly (until 2005): Boletin Oficial de la Propiedad Indistrial. 1: Marcas y Otros Signos Distintivos (0211-0105); Which superseded in part (in 1965): Boletin Oficial de la Propiedad Industrial (0038-6413); Which was formerly (until 1906): Boletin Oficial de la Propiedad Intelectual e Industrial (0211-0148)
Media: CD-ROM. **Related titles:** Online - full text ed.
—CASDDS.
Published by: Ministerio de Industria y Energia, Oficina Espanola de Patentes y Marcas, Panama, 1, Madrid, 28036, Spain. TEL 34-91-3495300, FAX 34-91-4572280, http://www.oepm.es.

608.5 ESP ISSN 1889-1292
C D - B O P I. TOMO II. (Boletin Oficial de la Propriedad Industrial) Text in Spanish. 1886. bi-w. charts; illus.; pat. index. **Document type:** *Government.*
Formerly (until 2005): Boletin Oficial de la Propiedad Industrial. 2: Patentes y Modelos de Utilidad (0211-0121); Which superseded in part (in 1968): Boletin Oficial de la Propiedad Industrial. 2: Patentes, Modelos y Dibujos (0211-0113); Which superseded in part (in 1965): Boletin Oficial de la Propiedad Industrial (0038-6413); Which was formerly (until 1906): Boletin Oficial de la Propiedad Intelectual e Industrial (0211-0148)
Media: CD-ROM. **Related titles:** Online - full text ed.
Published by: Ministerio de Industria y Energia, Oficina Espanola de Patentes y Marcas, Panama, 1, Madrid, 28036, Spain. TEL 34-91-3495300, FAX 34-91-4572280, http://www.oepm.es.

608.5 ESP ISSN 1889-1306
C D - B O P I. TOMO III. (Boletin Oficial de la Propriedad Industrial) Text in Spanish. 1886. bi-w. charts; illus.; pat. index. **Document type:** *Government.*
Formerly (until 2005): Boletin Oficial de la Propiedad Industrial. 3: Modelos y Dibujos Industriales y Artisticos (0211-013X); Which superseded in part (in 1968): Boletin Oficial de la Propiedad Industrial. 2: Patentes, Modelos y Dibujos (0211-0113); Which superseded in part (in 1965): Boletin Oficial de la Propiedad Industrial (0038-6413); Which was formerly (until 1906): Boletin Oficial de la Propiedad Intelectual e Industrial (0211-0148)
Media: CD-ROM. **Related titles:** Online - full text ed.
Published by: Ministerio de Industria y Energia, Oficina Espanola de Patentes y Marcas, Panama, 1, Madrid, 28036, Spain. TEL 34-91-3495300, FAX 34-91-4572280, http://www.oepm.es.

608.7 ESP ISSN 1137-6430
C D - CIBEPAT. Text in Spanish. 1990. q. **Document type:** *Directory, Government.* **Description:** Includes bibliographic information on Spanish patents and utility models since 1968, European patent documents designating Spain, patent applications designating Spain, and patents of 18 Latin-American countries.
Media: CD-ROM. **Related titles:** Online - full text ed.
Published by: Ministerio de Industria y Energia, Oficina Espanola de Patentes y Marcas, Panama, 1, Madrid, 28036, Spain. TEL 34-91-3495300, FAX 34-91-4572280, http://www.oepm.es.

608.7 GBR ISSN 0306-0314
C I P A. Variant title: C I P A Journal. Text in English. 1883. m. GBP 120 domestic to non-members; free to members (effective 2009). adv. bk.rev. back issues avail. **Document type:** *Journal, Academic/Scholarly.* **Description:** Contains information on forthcoming IP events, job advertisements and newsletter.
Former titles (until 1971): Chartered Institute of Patent Agents. Transactions; (until 1891): Institute of Patent Agents. Transactions
—CCC.
Published by: Chartered Institute of Patent Attorneys, 95 Chancery Ln, London, WC2A 1DT, United Kingdom. TEL 44-20-74059450, FAX 44-20-74300471, mail@cipa.org.uk. Ed. Tibor Gold. Adv. contact Iain Ross TEL 44-20-74409368.

C I P REPORT. (Center of Intellectual Property) *see* LAW—Corporate Law

346.04 AUS ISSN 1833-9913
COPYRIGHT NEWS. Text in English. 2006. bi-m. free (effective 2008). **Document type:** *Newsletter, Trade.* **Description:** Keeps government staff informed about copyright matters.
Media: Online - full text.
Published by: Attorney General's Department of New South Wales, Legislation and Policy Division, GPO Box 6, Sydney, NSW 2000, Australia. TEL 61-2-92288028, FAX 61-2-92288563.

346.04 USA
CALIFORNIA INTELLECTUAL PROPERTY LAWS. Text in English. 1991. a., latest 2007. looseleaf. USD 89 (effective 2008). **Document type:** *Handbook/Manual/Guide, Trade.* **Description:** Features updated text provisions of all relevant California and federal intellectual property statutes and include consultant commentary and the full text of California statutes dealing with trademarks, name protection, trade secrets, protection of inventions, sound recordings and films and computers.
Related titles: CD-ROM ed.
Published by: Matthew Bender & Co., Inc. (Subsidiary of: LexisNexis North America), 1275 Broadway, Albany, NY 12204. TEL 518-487-3000, 800-424-4200, FAX 518-487-3083, international@bender.com, http://bender.lexisnexis.com.

602.7 USA
CALLMANN ON UNFAIR COMPETITION, TRADEMARKS AND MONOPOLIES. Text in English. 19??. 10 base vols. plus s-a. updates. looseleaf. USD 2,599 base vol(s). (effective 2010). **Document type:** *Journal, Trade.* **Description:** Provides comprehensive analysis to unfair competition and trademark laws.
Published by: Thomson West (Subsidiary of: Thomson Reuters Corp.), 610 Opperman Dr, Eagan, MN 55123. TEL 651-687-7000, 800-344-5008, west.customer.service@thomson.com.

346.04 CAN
CANADIAN FORMS & PRECEDENTS. INTELLECTUAL PROPERTY. Text in English. base vol. plus a. updates. looseleaf. CAD 265 base vol(s). (effective 2010). **Document type:** *Handbook/Manual/Guide, Trade.* **Description:** Provides extensive coverage of Copyright, Industrial Design, Trademarks, Patents, and Private Sector Privacy laws.
Related titles: CD-ROM ed.
Published by: LexisNexis Canada Inc. (Subsidiary of: LexisNexis North America), 123 Commerce Valley Dr E, Ste 700, Markham, ON L3T 7W8, Canada. TEL 905-479-2665, 800-668-6481, FAX 905-479-3758, 800-461-3275, info@lexisnexis.ca.

346.04 CAN
CANADIAN FORMS & PRECEDENTS. LICENSING. Text in English. base vol. plus a. updates. looseleaf. CAD 265 base vol(s). (effective 2010). **Document type:** *Handbook/Manual/Guide, Trade.* **Description:** Delivers commentary on Licensing Law and practices. Provides the legal context and framework for the licensing forms and precedents.
Related titles: CD-ROM ed.
Published by: LexisNexis Canada Inc. (Subsidiary of: LexisNexis North America), 123 Commerce Valley Dr E, Ste 700, Markham, ON L3T 7W8, Canada. TEL 905-479-2665, 800-668-6481, FAX 905-479-3758, 800-461-3275, info@lexisnexis.ca. Eds. Gord Sustrik, Martin P Kratz, Roger T Hughes.

602.7 608.7 CAN ISSN 0825-7256
CANADIAN INTELLECTUAL PROPERTY REVIEW. Text in English. 1984. s-a. CAD 75. **Document type:** *Journal, Academic/Scholarly.* **Description:** Contains technical papers presented at spring and annual meetings of the institute and submissions to the editor.
Formerly: Patent and Trademark Institute of Canada. Bulletin
Related titles: Online - full text ed.
Indexed: A26, B04, CLI, CPerl, G08, I01, I05, ICLPL, ILP, LRI.
—CCC.
Published by: Intellectual Property Institute of Canada, 60 Queen St, Ste 606, Ottawa, ON K1P 5Y7, Canada. TEL 613-234-0516, FAX 613-234-0671, info@ipic.ca, http://www.ipic.ca. Circ: 1,300.

346.04 CAN ISSN 1712-4034
CANADIAN PATENT OFFICE RECORD/GAZETTE DU BUREAU DES BREVETS. Text in English, French. 1999. w. **Document type:** *Bulletin, Trade.* **Description:** Contains new patents, Canadian applications open to public inspection, and important notices.
Formerly (until 2004): Patent Office Record (1493-6275)
Media: Online - full content.
Indexed: PetrolAb.
Published by: Canadian Intellectual Property Office/Office de la Propriete Intellectuelle du Canada, Place du Portage I, 50 Victoria St., Room C-114, Gatineau, PQ K1A 0C9, Canada. TEL 819-997-1936, FAX 819-953-7620, cipo.contact@ic.gc.ca, http://cipo.gc.ca.

CANADIAN PATENT REPORTER. *see* LAW

CARDOZO ARTS & ENTERTAINMENT LAW JOURNAL. *see* LAW

346.04 USA
CHISUM ON PATENTS. Text in English. 1978. 26 base vols. plus irreg. updates. looseleaf. USD 3,385 base vol(s). (effective 2008). **Document type:** *Handbook/Manual/Guide, Trade.* **Description:** Covers all aspects of patent law and related issues. Thorough coverage of the substantive law - principles, doctrines, rules, and cases - gives you the convenience of one-stop research, written by the leading expert on patent law.
Related titles: CD-ROM ed.: USD 3,385 (effective 2008).
Published by: Matthew Bender & Co., Inc. (Subsidiary of: LexisNexis North America), 1275 Broadway, Albany, NY 12204. TEL 518-487-3000, 800-424-4200, FAX 518-487-3083, international@bender.com, http://bender.lexisnexis.com. Ed. Donald Chisum.

346.04 608.7 USA
CODE OF FEDERAL REGULATIONS, TITLE 37: PATENTS, TRADEMARKS, AND COPYRIGHTS. Text in English. 19??. a. **Document type:** *Government.* **Description:** Compiles Rules of Practice in Patent Cases, Trademark Rules of Practice, and Copyright Rules of Practice.
Related titles: Microfiche ed.; Online - full text ed.: free (effective 2011).
Published by: U.S. Patent and Trademark Office, General Information Services Division, PO Box 1450, Alexandria, VA 22313. TEL 571-272-1000, 800-786-9199, usptoinfo@uspto.gov.

346.04 GBR
COMMUNITY DESIGNS HANDBOOK. Text in English. 2005. base vol. plus updates 1/yr. looseleaf. GBP 460 base vol(s). domestic; EUR 608 base vol(s). in Europe; USD 791 base vol(s). elsewhere (effective 2011). **Document type:** *Handbook/Manual/Guide, Trade.* **Description:** Provides a description of the law and practice relating to designs law in the European Community. Includes procedural checklists and case studies to aid understanding and compliance.
Published by: (Chartered Institute of Patent Attorneys, Institute of Trade Mark Attorneys), Sweet & Maxwell Ltd. (Subsidiary of: Thomson Reuters Corp.), 100 Avenue Rd, London, NW3 3PF, United Kingdom. TEL 44-20-73937000, FAX 44-20-74491144, sweetandmaxwell.customer.services@thomson.com. **Subscr. to:** PO Box 1000, Andover SP10 9AF, United Kingdom. TEL 44-20-73938051, sweetandmaxwell.international.queries@thomson.com.

602.7 GBR
COMMUNITY TRADEMARK HANDBOOK. Text in English. 2001. 2 base vols. plus updates 2/yr. looseleaf. GBP 619 base vol(s). domestic; EUR 818 base vol(s). in Europe; USD 1,064 base vol(s). elsewhere (effective 2011). **Document type:** *Handbook/Manual/Guide, Trade.* **Description:** Offers everything need to know about the CTM system.
Published by: (Chartered Institute of Patent Attorneys, Institute of Trade Mark Attorneys), Sweet & Maxwell Ltd. (Subsidiary of: Thomson Reuters Corp.), 100 Avenue Rd, London, NW3 3PF, United Kingdom. TEL 44-20-73937000, FAX 44-20-74491144, sweetandmaxwell.customer.services@thomson.com. **Subscr. to:** PO Box 1000, Andover SP10 9AF, United Kingdom. TEL 44-20-73938051, sweetandmaxwell.international.queries@thomson.com.

341.7582 USA
COMPENDIUM OF COPYRIGHT OFFICE PRACTICES. Variant title: Compendium II. Text in English. base vol. plus s-a. updates. looseleaf. USD 71 (effective 2001). **Document type:** *Government.* **Description:** Discusses the operating problems and practices for the staff of the Copyright Office.
Published by: U.S. Library of Congress, Copyright Office, First St, N E, Washington, DC 20559. **Subscr. to:** U.S. Government Printing Office, Superintendent of Documents, PO Box 371954, Pittsburgh, PA 15250. TEL 202-512-1800, FAX 202-512-2250, orders@gpo.gov, http://www.access.gpo.gov.

CONTREFACON RIPOSTE; lettre des acteurs et technologies de la lutte anti-contrefacon. *see* BUSINESS AND ECONOMICS—Management

COPYRIGHT. *see* LAW—Corporate Law

341.758 AUS
COPYRIGHT AND DESIGNS. Abbreviated title: I P C. Text in English. 1996. 3 base vols. plus q. updates. looseleaf. AUD 1,567.50 (effective 2008). adv. **Description:** Provides a thorough discussion of all the latest developments and case law, both local and overseas.
Former titles (until 1996): Intellectual Property in Australia - Copyright Law; Intellectual Property in Australia - Copyright
Related titles: CD-ROM ed.; Online - full text ed.: AUD 984.50 (effective 2008).
Published by: LexisNexis Butterworths (Subsidiary of: LexisNexis Asia Pacific), Level 9, Tower 2, 475-495 Victoria Ave, Locked Bag 2222, Chatswood Delivery Ctr, Chatswood, NSW 2067, Australia. TEL 61-2-94222174, FAX 61-2-94222405, academic@lexisnexis.com.au.

602.7 GBR
COPYRIGHT AND DESIGNS LAW. Text in English. 1993. 2 base vols. plus updates 2/yr. looseleaf. GBP 720 base vol(s). domestic; EUR 951 base vol(s). in Europe; USD 1,238 base vol(s). elsewhere (effective 2011). **Document type:** *Handbook/Manual/Guide, Trade.* **Description:** Provides a complete guide to the modern law relating to copyright, including how it relates to the arts, the media (including cable and satellite broadcasting) and the special requirements of new technology.
Published by: Sweet & Maxwell Ltd. (Subsidiary of: Thomson Reuters Corp.), 100 Avenue Rd, London, NW3 3PF, United Kingdom. TEL 44-20-73937000, FAX 44-20-74491144, sweetandmaxwell.customer.services@thomson.com. Eds. Jack Black, Robert Merkin. **Subscr. to:** PO Box 1000, Andover SP10 9AF, United Kingdom. TEL 44-20-73938051, sweetandmaxwell.international.queries@thomson.com.

THE COPYRIGHT & NEW MEDIA LAW NEWSLETTER; for libraries, archives & museums. *see* LAW

346.066 340 USA
COPYRIGHT LAW IN BUSINESS AND PRACTICE. Text in English. 1989. 2 base vols. plus s-a. updates. looseleaf. USD 551 (effective 2008). Supplement avail. **Document type:** *Handbook/Manual/Guide, Trade.*
Published by: (R I A), Thomson West (Subsidiary of: Thomson Reuters Corp.), 610 Opperman Dr, Eagan, MN 55123. TEL 651-687-7000, 800-344-5008, FAX 651-687-6674, west.support@thomson.com, http://west.thomson.com. Ed. John W Hazard Jr.

341.758 USA ISSN 0884-4437
KF2987
COPYRIGHT LAW JOURNAL; an analysis of current cases and developments affecting intellectual property rights. Text in English. 1984. bi-m. USD 495; USD 595 combined subscription (print & online eds.) (effective 2011). index. 12 p./no.; back issues avail.; reprints avail. **Document type:** *Journal, Trade.* **Description:** Presents copyright developments.
Related titles: Online - full text ed.: USD 395 (effective 2011).
Published by: Executive Press, PO Box 21639, Concord, CA 94521. TEL 925-685-1442, FAX 925-930-9284. Ed. Neil Boorstyn.

341.758 USA ISSN 0091-1208
KF2994.A1
COPYRIGHT LAW OF THE UNITED STATES OF AMERICA. Text in English. 1898. irreg., latest 2009.
Published by: U.S. Government Printing Office, 732 N Capitol St, NW, Washington, DC 20401. TEL 202-512-1800, 866-512-1800, FAX 202-512-2104, ContactCenter@gpo.gov, http://www.gpo.gov.

320 USA
COPYRIGHT LAW REPORTS. Text in English. 2 base vols. plus m. updates. looseleaf. USD 1,005 base vol(s). (effective 2004). **Description:** Gives everything on copyright law—the full text of federal laws, precedent-setting court decisions, annotated explanations, Copyright Office forms, official circulars and reference materials.
Published by: C C H Inc. (Subsidiary of: Wolters Kluwer N.V.), 2700 Lake Cook Rd, Riverwoods, IL 60015. TEL 847-267-7000, 800-449-6439, cust_serv@cch.com, http://www.cch.com. Pub. Stacey Caywood.

COPYRIGHT, NEW MEDIA LAW & E-COMMERCE NEWS. *see* LAW

340 AUS ISSN 0725-0509
K3
COPYRIGHT REPORTER. Text in English. 1981. q. AUD 154 domestic; AUD 196 foreign (effective 2008). **Document type:** *Journal, Trade.* **Description:** Contains articles, case notes and information for copyright practitioners.
Published by: Australian Copyright Council, 245 Chalmers St, Redfern, NSW 2016, Australia. TEL 61-2-88159777, FAX 61-2-88159799, info@copyright.org.au. Ed. Libby Baulch.

340 USA ISSN 0886-3520
KF2987 CODEN: JCUSEZ
➤ **COPYRIGHT SOCIETY OF THE U.S.A. JOURNAL.** Text in English. 1953. q. free to members (effective 2009). bk.rev. bibl. index. reprints avail. **Document type:** *Journal, Academic/Scholarly.* **Description:** Covers articles on significant subjects, notes and summaries of domestic and foreign legislative and administrative developments, and news of important court decisions throughout the world. It also publishes bibliographic data on books, articles and other data from law reviews, related periodicals and trade publications, and contains announcements of interest to the copyright field including news and notices from the copyright office.
Formerly (until 1981): Copyright Society of the U S A. Bulletin (0010-8642)
Related titles: Microfilm ed.: (from WSH); Microform ed.: (from WSH); Online - full text ed.

P

Indexed: A20, A22, A26, ASCA, B04, CLI, CurCont, G08, I01, I03, I05, ILP, LRI, PCI, RILM, SCOPUS, SSCI, W07.
—BLDSC (4732.210000), CASDDS, IE, Infotrieve, Ingenta.
Published by: Copyright Society of the U.S.A., c o Amy Nickerson, 352 Seventh Ave, Ste 739, New York, NY 10001. amy@csusa.org. Eds. F Jay Dougherty, Stacey Dugan.

340 AUS ISSN 1328-4908
COPYRIGHT UPDATES. Text in English. 1997. bi-m. AUD 264 (effective 2008). **Document type:** *Magazine, Trade.* **Description:** Contains summaries of recent articles, cases, and news about copyright in Australia and overseas.
Published by: Australian Copyright Council, 245 Chalmers St, Redfern, NSW 2016, Australia. TEL 61-2-88159777, FAX 61-2-88159799, info@copyright.org.au.

340 USA
CORPORATE COUNSEL'S GUIDE TO COPYRIGHT LAW. Text in English. 2001 (Sep). base vol. plus a. updates. USD 207 base vol(s). (effective 2009). **Document type:** *Guide, Trade.* **Description:** Provides a basic, working knowledge of the law of copyright.
Related titles: CD-ROM ed.
Published by: Thomson West (Subsidiary of: Thomson Reuters Corp.), 610 Opperman Dr, Eagan, MN 55123. TEL 651-687-7000, 800-328-4880, FAX 651-687-6674, west.support@thomson.com.

346.04 USA
CORPORATE COUNSEL'S GUIDE TO INTELLECTUAL PROPERTY; patents, copyrights, trademarks, and trade secrets. Text in English. 1993. base vol. plus a. updates. USD 207 base vol(s). (effective 2009). **Document type:** *Guide, Trade.* **Description:** Includes an overview of patents, copyrights, trademarks, and trade secrets, and information on ways to safeguard intellectual property.
Related titles: CD-ROM ed.
Published by: Thomson West (Subsidiary of: Thomson Reuters Corp.), 610 Opperman Dr, Eagan, MN 55123. TEL 651-687-7000, 800-328-4880, FAX 651-687-6674, west.support@thomson.com.

346.04 USA
CORPORATE COUNSEL'S GUIDE TO TECHNOLOGY MANAGEMENT AND TRANSACTIONS. Text in English. 1994. 2 base vols. plus a. updates. USD 340 base vol(s). (effective 2009). **Document type:** *Guide, Trade.* **Description:** Provides overview of the various types of intellectual property rights, as well as advice on how to protect these assets.
Formerly (until 2006): Corporate Counsel's Guide to Technology Transactions
Related titles: CD-ROM ed.
Published by: Thomson West (Subsidiary of: Thomson Reuters Corp.), 610 Opperman Dr, Eagan, MN 55123. TEL 651-687-7000, 800-328-4880, FAX 651-687-6674, west.support@thomson.com.

346.04 USA
CORPORATE COUNSEL'S GUIDE TO TRADEMARK LAW. Text in English. 2001. base vol. plus a. updates. USD 207 base vol(s). (effective 2009). **Document type:** *Guide, Trade.* **Description:** Covers the basics of trademark law to help manage day-to-day legal issues where special trademark counsel is not necessary.
Published by: Thomson West (Subsidiary of: Thomson Reuters Corp.), 610 Opperman Dr, Eagan, MN 55123. TEL 651-687-7000, 800-328-4880, FAX 651-687-6674, west.support@thomson.com.

346.04 USA ISSN 1534-455X
KF3145.A15
CORPORATE COUNSEL'S LICENSING LETTER. Text in English. 2001. m. USD 393 (effective 2009). back issues avail. **Document type:** *Newsletter, Trade.* **Description:** Provides copies and discussions of illustrative licensing agreements covering software licenses of all types.
—**CCC.**
Published by: Thomson West (Subsidiary of: Thomson Reuters Corp.), 610 Opperman Dr, Eagan, MN 55123. TEL 651-687-7000, 800-328-4880, FAX 651-687-6674, west.support@thomson.com.

346.04 USA
COURT OF APPEALS FOR THE FEDERAL CIRCUIT: PRACTICE AND PROCEDURE. Text in English. 1973. 2 base vols. plus irreg. updates. looseleaf. USD 461 base vol(s). (effective 2008). **Document type:** *Handbook/Manual/Guide, Trade.* **Description:** Covers the procedure for patent and trademark cases on review in the court of appeals for the federal circuit from the U.S. patent and trademark office and the U.S. district courts.
Related titles: CD-ROM ed.
Published by: Matthew Bender & Co., Inc. (Subsidiary of: LexisNexis North America), 1275 Broadway, Albany, NY 12204. TEL 518-487-3000, 800-424-4200, FAX 518-487-3083, international@bender.com, http://bender.lexisnexis.com. Eds. Charles Cholz, Donald Dunner.

CRONER'S MODEL BUSINESS CONTRACTS. *see* BUSINESS AND ECONOMICS

608.7 CUB ISSN 1028-1452
CUBA. OFICINA CUBANA DE LA PROPIEDAD INDUSTRIAL. BOLETIN OFICIAL. Text in Spanish. 1906. q. CUP 100 domestic; USD 132 foreign (effective 2001). adv. tr.lit.; pat. index. back issues avail. **Document type:** *Bulletin, Government.* **Description:** Includes scientific inventions, industrial models, trademarks and other forms of industrial ownership, which are granted by the National Office.
Former titles (until no. 141, 1997): Cuba. Oficina Nacional de Invenciones, Informacion Tecnica y Marcas. Boletin Oficial (1010-0865); (until 1973): Cuba. Registro de la Propiedad Industrial. Boletin Oficial (0011-2615); (until 1968): Cuba. Departamento de la Propiedad Industrial. Boletin Oficial (1010-1063)
Related titles: Microfilm ed.
Published by: Oficina Cubana de la Propiedad Industrial, Picota no 15 e Luz y Acosta, Havana Vieja, Havana, 10100, Cuba. TEL 537-610185, FAX 537-335610, TELEX 511290, http://www.ocpi.cu/. Ed. America Santos Rivera. Pub. Carmen Cid. R&P America Santos Rivera TEL 537-624379. Adv. contact William Nunez. Circ: 200.

608.7489 DNK ISSN 1602-6691
DANSK BRUGSMODELTIDENDE (ONLINE). Text in Danish. 1992. bi-w. DKK 150 per issue print ed. (effective 2009). back issues avail. **Document type:** *Government.*
Formerly (until 2003): Dansk Brugsmodeltidende (Print) (0907-4597)
Media: Online - full content.
Published by: Patent- og Varemaerkestyrelsen/Danish Patent and Trademark Office, Helgeshoj Alle 81, Taastrup, 2630, Denmark. TEL 45-43-508000, FAX 45-43-508001, pvs@dkpto.dk.

346.489 DNK ISSN 1601-7366
DANSK DESIGNTIDENDE. Text in Danish. 1971. w. DKK 150 per issue (effective 2009). back issues avail. **Document type:** *Government.*
Former titles (until 2001): Dansk Moenstertidende (0903-8825); (until 1988): Registreringstidende for Moenstre (0106-5246)
Related titles: Online - full text ed.: ISSN 1601-7374. 1997; ◆ Supplement(s): Dansk Designtidende Register.
Published by: Patent- og Varemaerkestyrelsen/Danish Patent and Trademark Office, Helgeshoj Alle 81, Taastrup, 2630, Denmark. TEL 45-43-508000, FAX 45-43-508001, pvs@dkpto.dk. Ed. Keld Nymann Jensen.

346.489 DNK
DANSK DESIGNTIDENDE REGISTER. Text in Danish. a. DKK 200. **Document type:** *Government.*
Formerly: Dansk Moensterregister
Related titles: Online - full text ed.; ◆ Supplement to: Dansk Designtidende. ISSN 1601-7366.
Published by: Patent- og Varemaerkestyrelsen/Danish Patent and Trademark Office, Helgeshoj Alle 81, Taastrup, 2630, Denmark. TEL 45-43-508000, FAX 45-43-508001, pvs@dkpto.dk.

608.7489 DNK ISSN 0011-6416
CODEN: DAPAA8
DANSK PATENTTIDENDE. Text in Danish. 1894. w. DKK 150 per issue (effective 2009). back issues avail. **Document type:** *Government.*
Related titles: Online - full text ed.: ISSN 1602-6667; ◆ Supplement(s): Register over Danske Patenter Udstedt i (Year). ISSN 0107-590X.
—CASDDS.
Published by: Patent- og Varemaerkestyrelsen/Danish Patent and Trademark Office, Helgeshoj Alle 81, Taastrup, 2630, Denmark. TEL 45-43-508000, FAX 45-43-508001, pvs@dkpto.dk. Ed. Keld Nymann Jensen.

346.489 DNK
DANSK VAREMAERKEREGISTER. Text in Danish. a. **Document type:** *Government.*
Related titles: Online - full text ed.
Published by: Patent- og Varemaerkestyrelsen/Danish Patent and Trademark Office, Helgeshoj Alle 81, Taastrup, 2630, Denmark. TEL 45-43-508000, FAX 45-43-508001, pvs@dkpto.dk.

346.489 DNK ISSN 0903-8809
DANSK VAREMAERKETIDENDE. Text in Danish. 1913. w. DKK 150 per issue (effective 2009). back issues avail. **Document type:** *Government.*
Formerly (until 1988): Registreringstidende for Vare- og Faellesmaerker (0106-522X)
Related titles: Online - full text ed.: ISSN 1602-6683. 2000.
Published by: Patent- og Varemaerkestyrelsen/Danish Patent and Trademark Office, Helgeshoj Alle 81, Taastrup, 2630, Denmark. TEL 45-43-508000, FAX 45-43-508001, pvs@dkpto.dk. Ed. Keld Nymann Jensen.

346.04 CHN ISSN 1004-9517
DIANZI ZHISHI CHANQUAN. Text in English. 1991. m. USD 74.40 (effective 2009). **Document type:** *Journal, Academic/Scholarly.*
Related titles: Online - full content ed.; Online - full text ed.
Published by: Xinxi Chanyebu, Dianzi Keji Qingbao Yanjiusuo, Shijingshan-qu, 35, Lugu Lu, Beijing, 100040, China. TEL 86-10-68685460, FAX 86-10-68632927, http://www.etiri.com.cn.

341.7582 ITA ISSN 0012-3420
KKH1160.A15
IL DIRITTO DI AUTORE. Text in French, Italian. 1930. q. EUR 60 in the European Union; EUR 90 elsewhere (effective 2008). adv. bk.rev. abstr.; bibl. index. **Document type:** *Journal, Trade.* **Description:** Covers Italian and foreign legal decisions concerning the rights of authors.
Indexed: A22, DoGi, ELLIS, FLP, IBR, IBZ, RASB.
—IE, Infotrieve.
Published by: (Societa Italiana degli Autori ed Editori (S I A E)), Casa Editrice Dott. A. Giuffre (Subsidiary of: LexisNexis Europe and Africa), Via Busto Arsizio, 40, Milan, MI 20151, Italy. TEL 39-02-380891, FAX 39-02-38009582. Ed. Mario Fabiani. Circ: 900.

609.87 ISL ISSN 1670-0104
E L S TIDINDI. (Einkaleyfastofan) Text in Icelandic. 1984. m. **Document type:** *Government.* **Description:** Patent news from Iceland.
Formerly (until 1996): Vorumerkja & Einkaleyfa Tidindi (1012-6392)
Related titles: Online - full text ed.
Published by: Einkaleyfastofan/Islandic Patent Office, Skulagata 63, Reykjavik, 150, Iceland. TEL 354-580-9400, FAX 354-580-9401, patent@patent.is.

341.758 DEU ISSN 1434-8853
E P I INFORMATION. (Europaeischen Patentamt Institut) Text in German. 1992. q. EUR 52; EUR 20 newsstand/cover (effective 2011). adv. **Document type:** *Journal, Trade.*
Published by: (European Patent Office, Institute of Professional Representatives), Carl Heymanns Verlag KG (Subsidiary of: Wolters Kluwer Deutschland GmbH), Luxemburger Str 449, Cologne, 50939, Germany. TEL 49-221-943730, FAX 49-221-94373901, marketing@heymanns.com, http://www.heymanns.com. Adv. contact Marcus Kipp. Circ: 10,500 (paid).

E P M ENTERTAINMENT MARKETING SOURCEBOOK. *see* BUSINESS AND ECONOMICS—Marketing And Purchasing

346.04 USA
ECKSTROM'S LICENSING IN FOREIGN AND DOMESTIC OPERATIONS. Text in English. 1987. 5 base vols. plus updates 3/yr. looseleaf. USD 2,270 base vol(s). (effective 2010). **Document type:** *Journal, Trade.* **Description:** Covers source for the international licensing of intellectual property rights.
Published by: Thomson West (Subsidiary of: Thomson Reuters Corp.), 610 Opperman Dr, Eagan, MN 55123. TEL 651-687-7000, 800-344-5008, west.customer.service@thomson.com, http://west.thomson.com.

346.01 USA
ECKSTROM'S LICENSING IN FOREIGN AND DOMESTIC OPERATIONS: JOINT VENTURES. Text in English. 19??. 5 base vols. plus updates 3/yr. looseleaf. USD 2,354 base vol(s). (effective 2010). **Document type:** *Journal, Trade.* **Description:** Provides practical guidance on the techniques and considerations involved in forming international joint ventures.
Published by: Thomson West (Subsidiary of: Thomson Reuters Corp.), 610 Opperman Dr, Eagan, MN 55123. TEL 651-687-7000, 800-344-5008, west.customer.service@thomson.com.

346.04 USA
ECKSTROM'S LICENSING IN FOREIGN AND DOMESTIC OPERATIONS: THE FORMS AND SUBSTANCE OF LICENSING. Text in English. 19??. 5 base vols. plus updates 3/yr. looseleaf. USD 2,917 base vol(s). (effective 2010). **Document type:** *Journal, Trade.* **Description:** Provides 'state-of-the-art' forms and agreement for the domestic and international licensing of intellectual property rights.
Published by: Thomson West (Subsidiary of: Thomson Reuters Corp.), 610 Opperman Dr, Eagan, MN 55123. TEL 651-687-7000, 800-344-5008, west.customer.service@thomson.com.

608.7 GBR ISSN 0142-2987
ENCYCLOPEDIA OF UNITED KINGDOM AND EUROPEAN PATENT LAW. Text in English. 1977. 2 base vols. plus updates 2/yr. looseleaf. GBP 1,112 base vol(s). domestic; EUR 1,469 base vol(s). in Europe; USD 1,911 base vol(s). elsewhere (effective 2011). **Document type:** *Handbook/Manual/Guide, Trade.* **Description:** Provides complete coverage of the key issues of substantive patent law including the construction of the patent specification and infringement, validity and amendment.
Published by: Sweet & Maxwell Ltd. (Subsidiary of: Thomson Reuters Corp.), 100 Avenue Rd, London, NW3 3PF, United Kingdom. TEL 44-20-73937000, FAX 44-20-74491144, sweetandmaxwell.customer.services@thomson.com. **Subscr. to:** PO Box 1000, Andover SP10 9AF, United Kingdom. TEL 44-20-73938051, sweetandmaxwell.international.queries@thomson.com.

ENTERTAINMENT MARKETING LETTER. *see* BUSINESS AND ECONOMICS—Marketing And Purchasing

608.7 DEU ISSN 0423-250X
ENTSCHEIDUNGEN DES BUNDESPATENTGERICHTS. Text in German. 1962. irreg., latest vol.47, 2005. price varies. index. **Document type:** *Proceedings, Trade.*
Published by: (Germany. Deutsches Patent- und Markenamt), Carl Heymanns Verlag KG (Subsidiary of: Wolters Kluwer Deutschland GmbH), Luxemburger Str 449, Cologne, 50939, Germany. TEL 49-221-943730, FAX 49-221-94373901, marketing@heymanns.com, http://www.heymanns.com.

608.7 DEU
ERFINDER UND NEUHEITENDIENST. Text in German. 1949. m. adv. bk.rev. **Document type:** *Journal, Trade.*
Formerly (until 1972): Neuheiten und Erfinderdienst (0028-3711)
Published by: Deutscher Erfinderring e.V., Sandstr 7, Nuernberg, 90443, Germany. TEL 49-911-269811, FAX 49-911-269780, dev.ev@t-online.de, http://www.deutscher-erfinder-verband.de. Circ: 1,000.

▼ **L'ESSENTIEL DROIT DE LA PROPRIETE INTELLECTUELLE.** *see* LAW

608.7 DEU ISSN 0170-9291
EUROPAEISCHES PATENTAMT. AMTSBLATT/EUROPEAN PATENT OFFICE. OFFICIAL JOURNAL. Text in English, French, German. m. EUR 147 (effective 2009). adv. **Document type:** *Journal, Trade.*
Related titles: CD-ROM ed.; Online - full text ed.
—IE, Infotrieve. **CCC.**
Published by: European Patent Office/Europaeisches Patentamt, Munich, 80298, Germany. TEL 49-89-23990, FAX 49-89-23994560, bookorder@epo.org. Circ: 3,500.

608.7 DEU
EUROPAEISCHES PATENTBLATT (ONLINE)/BULLETIN EUROPEEN DES BREVETS/EUROPEAN PATENT BULLETIN. Text in German, English, French. w. free (effective 2011). **Document type:** *Bulletin, Trade.*
Media: Online - full text. **Related titles:** Optical Disk - DVD ed.
Published by: European Patent Office/Europaeisches Patentamt, Munich, 80298, Germany. TEL 49-89-23990, FAX 49-89-23994560, bookorder@epo.org, http://www.european-patent-office.org.

341.758 GBR ISSN 1467-6656
EUROPEAN COPYRIGHT AND DESIGNS REPORT. Text in English. 1999. bi-m. GBP 630, EUR 831, USD 1,083 (effective 2012). **Document type:** *Journal, Trade.* **Description:** Brings out all the key copyright and design decisions of the national courts in the EU - as well as cases from key EU accession states such as the Czech Republic and key ECJ and EFTA court decisions.
Published by: Sweet & Maxwell Ltd. (Subsidiary of: Thomson Reuters Corp.), 100 Avenue Rd, London, NW3 3PF, United Kingdom. TEL 44-20-73937000, FAX 44-20-74491144, sweetandmaxwell.customer.services@thomson.com. Ed. Dr. Uma Suthersanen. **Subscr. to:** PO Box 1000, Andover SP10 9AF, United Kingdom. TEL 44-20-73938051, sweetandmaxwell.international.queries@thomson.com.

346.04 USA
EUROPEAN INTELLECTUAL PROPERTY BULLETIN. Variant title: European I P Bulletin. Text in English. 2003 (Apr.). 10/yr. (some combined issues). free (effective 2009). **Document type:** *Bulletin, Trade.*
Media: Online - full content.
Published by: McDermott, Will & Emery, 227 W Monroe St, Chicago, IL 60606. TEL 312-372-2000, FAX 312-984-7700, contactus@mwe.com.

341 GBR ISSN 0142-0461
K5 CODEN: EIPRES
EUROPEAN INTELLECTUAL PROPERTY REVIEW. Abbreviated title: E I P R. Text in English. 1978. m. GBP 1,219, EUR 1,607, USD 2,095 (effective 2012). bk.rev. index. back issues avail. **Document type:** *Journal, Academic/Scholarly.* **Description:** Presents recent developments and news for intellectual property lawyers, patent agents, trade mark agents, music publishers and academics.
Related titles: Online - full text ed.; Supplement(s): E I P R Practice Series. ISSN 1749-5083.
Indexed: A22, A26, B04, CLI, ELJI, ELLIS, FLP, G08, I01, I05, IBR, IBZ, ILP, LJI, LRI, P30.
—BLDSC (3829.720960), IE, Infotrieve, Ingenta. **CCC.**

Published by: Sweet & Maxwell Ltd. (Subsidiary of: Thomson Reuters Corp.), 100 Avenue Rd, London, NW3 3PF, United Kingdom. TEL 44-20-73937000, FAX 44-20-74491144, sweetandmaxwell.customer.services@thomson.com. Ed. Hugh Brett. **Subscr. to:** PO Box 1000, Andover SP10 9AF, United Kingdom. TEL 44-20-73938051, sweetandmaxwell.international.queries@thomson.com.

608.7 GBR
EUROPEAN PATENT DECISIONS. Text in English. 1998. 2 base vols. plus updates 3/yr. looseleaf. GBP 475 base vol(s). domestic; EUR 628 base vol(s). in Europe; USD 817 base vol(s). elsewhere (effective 2011). **Document type:** *Journal, Trade.* **Description:** Contains a digest of substantially all the more important decisions of the European Patent Office.
Published by: Sweet & Maxwell Ltd. (Subsidiary of: Thomson Reuters Corp.), 100 Avenue Rd, London, NW3 3PF, United Kingdom. TEL 44-20-73937000, FAX 44-20-74491144, sweetandmaxwell.customer.services@thomson.com. **Subscr. to:** PO Box 1000, Andover SP10 9AF, United Kingdom. TEL 44-20-73938051, sweetandmaxwell.international.queries@thomson.com.

608.7 DEU ISSN 0724-7729
KJC2732.A13
EUROPEAN PATENT OFFICE. ANNUAL REPORT. Text in English, French, German. 1978. a. free. adv. back issues avail. **Description:** Annual review detailing patent growth, international patent cooperation, new patents and judicial developments.
Related titles: Online - full text ed.
—CCC.
Published by: European Patent Office/Europaeisches Patentamt, Munich, 80298, Germany. TEL 49-89-23990, FAX 49-89-23994560, bookorder@epo.org, http://www.european-patent-office.org. Circ: 7,000.

608.7 341 GBR ISSN 0269-0802
KJE2732.A6
EUROPEAN PATENT OFFICE REPORTS. Text in English. 1986. 8/yr. GBP 990, EUR 1,305, USD 1,702 (effective 2012). bk.rev. back issues avail. **Document type:** *Journal, Trade.* **Description:** Provides lawyers and patent practitioners with a simple way of keeping up to date with the latest decisions from the European Patent Office. The reports are essential reading for anyone advising on patent protection.
—IE, Infotrieve. **CCC.**
Published by: Sweet & Maxwell Ltd. (Subsidiary of: Thomson Reuters Corp.), 100 Avenue Rd, London, NW3 3PF, United Kingdom. TEL 44-20-73937000, FAX 44-20-74491144, sweetandmaxwell.customer.services@thomson.com. Ed. Peter McLean Colley. **Subscr. outside the UK to:** PO Box 1000, Andover SP10 9AF, United Kingdom. TEL 44-20-73938051, sweetandmaxwell.international.queries@thomson.com.

346.04 GBR
EUROPEAN PATENTS HANDBOOK. Text in English. 1990. 3 base vols. plus updates 3/yr. looseleaf. GBP 1,426 base vol(s). domestic; EUR 1,883 base vol(s). in Europe; USD 2,451 base vol(s). elsewhere (effective 2011). **Document type:** *Handbook/Manual/Guide, Trade.* **Description:** Covers organization and procedures of the European Patent Office, patentability classifications and standards, and requirements for filing a European patent.
Published by: (Chartered Institute of Patent Attorneys), Sweet & Maxwell Ltd. (Subsidiary of: Thomson Reuters Corp.), 100 Avenue Rd, London, NW3 3PF, United Kingdom. TEL 44-20-73937000, FAX 44-20-74491144, sweetandmaxwell.customer.services@thomson.com. **Subscr. to:** PO Box 1000, Andover SP10 9AF, United Kingdom. TEL 44-20-73938051, sweetandmaxwell.international.queries@thomson.com.

608.7 GBR
EUROPEAN PATENTS SOURCEFINDER. Text in English. 1988. 2 base vols. plus updates 2/yr. looseleaf. GBP 565 base vol(s). domestic; EUR 746 base vol(s). in Europe; USD 971 base vol(s). elsewhere (effective 2011). **Document type:** *Handbook/Manual/Guide, Trade.* **Description:** Contains over 2,000 fully indexed references, with summaries, as well as the most important material with a bearing on European Patent Convention Law, practice and procedure.
Published by: (Chartered Institute of Patent Attorneys), Sweet & Maxwell Ltd. (Subsidiary of: Thomson Reuters Corp.), 100 Avenue Rd, London, NW3 3PF, United Kingdom. TEL 44-20-73937000, FAX 44-20-74491144, sweetandmaxwell.customer.services@thomson.com. **Subscr. to:** PO Box 1000, Andover SP10 9AF, United Kingdom. TEL 44-20-73938051, sweetandmaxwell.international.queries@thomson.com.

608.7 DEU ISSN 1022-4025
EUROPEAN QUALIFYING EXAMINATION. Text in English, French, German. 1993. a. **Document type:** *Bulletin.* **Description:** Helps to test the candidate's knowledge and aptitude to represent applicants before the European Patent Office.
Related titles: Online - full text ed.
Published by: European Patent Office/Europaeisches Patentamt, Munich, 80298, Germany. TEL 49-89-23990, FAX 49-89-23994560, bookorder@epo.org, http://www.european-patent-office.org.

341.758 GBR ISSN 1363-4542
EUROPEAN TRADE MARK REPORTS. Abbreviated title: E T M R. Text in English. 1996. m. GBP 1,088, EUR 1,434, USD 1,870 (effective 2012). **Document type:** *Report, Trade.* **Description:** Provide timely reports of all important OHIM and relevant CFI and ECJ trade mark decisions.
Published by: Sweet & Maxwell Ltd. (Subsidiary of: Thomson Reuters Corp.), 100 Avenue Rd, London, NW3 3PF, United Kingdom. TEL 44-20-73937000, FAX 44-20-74491144, sweetandmaxwell.customer.services@thomson.com. Eds. Jeremy Phillips, Rebecca Chong. **Subscr. to:** PO Box 1000, Andover SP10 9AF, United Kingdom. TEL 44-20-73938051, sweetandmaxwell.international.queries@thomson.com.

EXPERT OPINION ON THERAPEUTIC PATENTS. *see* PHARMACY AND PHARMACOLOGY

F O G R A PATENTSCHAU. *see* PRINTING

FEDERAL BIO-TECHNOLOGY TRANSFER DIRECTORY. *see* BIOLOGY—Biotechnology

346.04 FIN ISSN 0355-4481
FINLAND. PATENTTI- JA REKISTERIHALLITUS. MALLIOIKEUSLEHTI/ MOENSTER RAETTS TIDNING. Text in Finnish, Swedish. 1971. m. EUR 280 domestic; EUR 298 in Scandinavia and Baltic countries; EUR 310 in Europe; EUR 325 elsewhere (effective 2005). **Document type:** *Magazine, Government.*
Related titles: Online - full content ed.: ISSN 1795-4940.
Published by: (Finland. Patentti- ja Rekisterihallitus/National Board of Patents and Registration), Stellatum Oy, Tyopajankatu 6 A, Helsinki, 00580, Finland. TEL 358-9-8689700, FAX 358-9-86897070, info@stellatum.fi, http://www.stellatum.fi. Ed. Sirkka Liisa Lahtinen. Circ: 134.

346.04 FIN ISSN 0031-2916
CODEN: PATPB2
FINLAND. PATENTTI- JA REKISTERIHALLITUS. PATENTTILEHTI/ PATENTTIDNING. Text in Finnish, Swedish. 1889. s-m. index. **Document type:** *Magazine, Government.*
—CASDDS.
Published by: Patentti- ja Rekisterihallitus/National Board of Patents and Registration, Arkadiankatu 6, PO Box 1140, Helsinki, 00101, Finland. TEL 358-9-6939500, FAX 358-9-69395328, http://www.prh.fi. Ed. Pekka Launis. Circ: 520. **Dist. by:** Oy Edita Ab, PL 260, Edita 00043, Finland.

346.04 608.7 FIN ISSN 0039-9922
FINLAND. PATENTTI- JA REKISTERIHALLITUS. TAVARAMERKKILEHTI/VARUMAERKESTIDNING. Text in Finnish, Swedish. 1889. s-m. charts; tr.mk. **Document type:** *Magazine, Government.*
Former titles: Tavaraleimalehti; Tavaraleimarekisteri Rekisterilehti
Related titles: Online - full content ed.: ISSN 1795-4932.
Published by: (Finland. Patentti- ja Rekisterihallitus/National Board of Patents and Registration), Stellatum Oy, Tyopajankatu 6 A, Helsinki, 00580, Finland. TEL 358-9-8689700, FAX 358-9-86897070, info@stellatum.fi, http://www.stellatum.fi. Ed. Sirkka Liisa Lahtinen. Circ: 135.

346.048 GBR ISSN 0141-9455
KD1365.A2
FLEET STREET REPORTS; cases on intellectual property law. Text in English. 1963. m. GBP 1,226, EUR 1,616, USD 2,107 (effective 2012). index. back issues avail. **Document type:** *Report, Trade.* **Description:** Provides a reference to all major cases on industrial property law.
Formerly (until 1978): Fleet Street Patent Law Reports (0141-9919)
—CCC.
Published by: Sweet & Maxwell Ltd. (Subsidiary of: Thomson Reuters Corp.), 100 Avenue Rd, London, NW3 3PF, United Kingdom. TEL 44-20-73937000, FAX 44-20-74491144, sweetandmaxwell.customer.services@thomson.com. Ed. Mary Vitoria. **Subscr. to:** PO Box 1000, Andover SP10 9AF, United Kingdom. TEL 44-20-73938051, sweetandmaxwell.international.queries@thomson.com.

FORDHAM INTELLECTUAL PROPERTY, MEDIA & ENTERTAINMENT LAW JOURNAL. *see* LAW

346.04 USA
FORMS AND AGREEMENTS ON INTELLECTUAL PROPERTY AND INTERNATIONAL LICENSING. Text in English. 1979. 4 base vols. plus updates 3/yr. looseleaf. USD 2,494 base vol(s). (effective 2010). **Document type:** *Journal, Trade.* **Description:** Covers international licensing and intellectual property rights around the world.
Published by: Thomson West (Subsidiary of: Thomson Reuters Corp.), 610 Opperman Dr, Eagan, MN 55123. TEL 651-687-7000, 800-344-5008, west.customer.service@thomson.com.

608.7 GBR ISSN 1351-3109
FUTURE AND THE INVENTOR. Text in English. 1928. irreg. free to members (effective 2009). bk.rev. bibl. **Document type:** *Journal, Trade.* **Description:** Contains information pertinent to inventors and details the forthcoming activities of the Institute.
Former titles (until 199?): Future (0952-2522); (until 1987): Inventor (0579-8388)
Published by: Institute of Patentees and Inventors, PO Box 39296, London, SE3 7WH, United Kingdom. TEL 44-871-2262091, FAX 44-208-2935920, ipi@invent.org.uk, http://www.invent.org.uk.

346.04 DEU ISSN 1869-3849
▼ **G R U R PRAX;** Praxis im Immaterialgueter- und Wettbewerbsrecht. (Gewerblicher Rechtsschutz und Urheberrecht) Text in German. 2009. s-m. EUR 198; EUR 10 newsstand/cover (effective 2011). **Document type:** *Journal, Trade.*
Related titles: Online - full text ed.
Published by: Verlag C.H. Beck oHG, Wilhelmstr 9, Munich, 80801, Germany. TEL 49-89-381890, FAX 49-89-38189398, bestellung@beck.de, http://www.beck.de.

608.7 DEU ISSN 1616-2277
G R U R - RECHTSPRECHUNGS-REPORT. (Gewerblicher Rechtsschutz und Urheberrecht) Abbreviated title: GRUR-RR. Text in German. 2001. m. EUR 198; EUR 18.60 newsstand/cover (effective 2010). reprint service avail. from SCH. **Document type:** *Journal, Trade.*
Indexed: IBR, IBZ.
Published by: Verlag C.H. Beck oHG, Wilhelmstr 9, Munich, 80801, Germany. TEL 49-89-381890, FAX 49-89-38189398, abo.service@beck.de, http://www.beck.de.

608.7 CHE ISSN 1020-4679
T325
GAZETTE O M P I DES MARQUES INTERNATIONALES. Text in French. 1893. m. adv. charts; tr.mk. index. back issues avail. **Description:** Covers all marks, registered, renewed, modified, transferred, refused or otherwise. Includes countries of origin and destination, with reproduction of the actual trademarks or service marks.
Formerly (until 1996): Marques Internationales (0025-3936)
Related titles: CD-ROM ed.
Published by: World Intellectual Property Organization/Organisation Mondiale de la Propriete Intellectuelle, Publications Sales and Distribution Unit, 34 Chemin des Colombettes, Geneva 20, 1211, Switzerland. TEL 41-22-338-9111, FAX 41-22-740-1812, TELEX 412912-OMPI-CH, publications.mail@ompi.int. Circ: 1,600.

608 USA ISSN 0160-9491
T223.J4
GENERAL INFORMATION CONCERNING PATENTS. Text in English. 1922. a. free (effective 2011). back issues avail. **Document type:** *Government.*
Related titles: Online - full text ed.
—Linda Hall.
Published by: U.S. Patent and Trademark Office, General Information Services Division, PO Box 1450, Alexandria, VA 22313. TEL 571-272-1000, 800-786-9199, usptoinfo@uspto.gov.

608.7 JPN
GEPPO HATSUMEI/MONTHLY REPORT OF INVENTION. Text in Japanese. 1965. m. JPY 1,800. **Document type:** *Newspaper.*
Published by: Hatsumei Kyokai/Japan Institute of Invention and Innovation, 9-14 Toranomon 2-chome, Minato-ku, Tokyo, 105-0001, Japan.

608.7 DEU
GESCHMACKSMUSTERBLATT (ONLINE). Text in German. 1988. s-m. free. **Document type:** *Journal, Trade.*
Formerly (until 2004): Geschmacksmusterblatt (Print) (0934-7062)
Published by: Deutsches Patent- und Markenamt, Zweibrueckenstr 12, Munich, 80331, Germany. TEL 49-89-21950, FAX 49-89-21952221, post@dpma.de, http://www.dpma.de. Circ: 600.

608.7 340 DEU ISSN 0016-9420
GEWERBLICHER RECHTSSCHUTZ UND URHEBERRECHT. Abbreviated title: G R U R. Text in German. 1896. m. EUR 512; EUR 47.50 newsstand/cover (effective 2011). adv. bk.rev. bibl.; pat.; tr.lit. index. reprint service avail. from SCH. **Document type:** *Journal, Academic/Scholarly.* **Description:** Covers industrial property protection and copyright law.
Incorporates (1996-2001): N J W Entscheidungsdienst Wettbewerbsrecht (0949-7102)
Related titles: CD-ROM ed.: ISSN 1618-9574. EUR 1,298 base vol(s).; EUR 496 updates (effective 2006); Online - full text ed.: ISSN 1522-2446; Optical Disk - DVD ed.: G R U R - D V D. ISSN 1618-9582. EUR 298 base vol(s).; EUR 542.64 updates (effective 2008).
Indexed: A22, DIP, ELLIS, FLP, IBR, IBZ.
—IE, Infotrieve. **CCC.**
Published by: (Deutsche Vereinigung fuer Gewerblichen Rechtsschutz und Urheberrecht), Verlag C.H. Beck oHG, Wilhelmstr 9, Munich, 80801, Germany. TEL 49-89-381890, FAX 49-89-38189398, abo.service@beck.de, http://www.beck.de. Circ: 3,200 (paid and controlled).

608.7 340 DEU ISSN 0435-8600
K7
GEWERBLICHER RECHTSSCHUTZ UND URHEBERRECHT. INTERNATIONALER TEIL. Abbreviated title: GRUR Int. Text in German. 1952. m. EUR 504; EUR 46.60 newsstand/cover (effective 2011). adv. reprint service avail. from SCH. **Document type:** *Journal, Academic/Scholarly.* **Description:** Covers the latest information on international and European industrial property protection.
Related titles: CD-ROM ed.; Online - full text ed.: ISSN 1522-2438.
Indexed: A22, DIP, ELLIS, FLP, IBR, IBZ, RASB.
—IE, Infotrieve. **CCC.**
Published by: (Deutsche Vereinigung fuer Gewerblichen Rechtsschutz und Urheberrecht), Verlag C.H. Beck oHG, Wilhelmstr 9, Munich, 80801, Germany. TEL 49-89-381890, FAX 49-89-38189398, abo.service@beck.de, http://www.beck.de. Circ: 2,000 (paid and controlled).

346.04 USA
GILSON, TRADEMARK PROTECTION AND PRACTICE. Text in English. 1974. 13 base vols. plus irreg. updates. looseleaf. USD 1,449 base vol(s). (effective 2006). **Document type:** *Handbook/Manual/Guide, Trade.* **Description:** Analyzes U.S. trademark law, including registration, likelihood of confusion, licensing, and unfair competition.
Related titles: CD-ROM ed.
Published by: Matthew Bender & Co., Inc. (Subsidiary of: LexisNexis North America), 1275 Broadway, Albany, NY 12204. TEL 518-487-3000, 800-424-4200, FAX 518-487-3083, international@bender.com, http://bender.lexisnexis.com. Ed. J Gilson.

346.04 USA
GLOBAL INTELLECTUAL PROPERTY ASSET MANAGEMENT REPORT. Abbreviated title: G I P A M R. Text in English. 1999. m. USD 659 domestic; USD 709 foreign (effective 2005). **Document type:** *Journal, Trade.* **Description:** Covers the legal and financial changes that continue to sweep through the management of intellectual property assets worldwide.
Former titles: Managing Intellectual Property Assets Worldwide; Global eCommerce Law and Business Report
Related titles: Online - full text ed.
Published by: WorldTrade Executive, Inc., 2250 Main St, Ste 100, PO Box 761, Concord, MA 01742. TEL 978-287-0301, FAX 978-287-0302, info@wtexec.com, http://www.wtexec.com. Pub. Gary A Brown. Adv. contact Jay Stanley.

346.04 USA
GLOBAL PATENT LITIGATION; strategy and practice. Text in English. 2006. base vol. plus m. updates. looseleaf. USD 527 base vol(s). (effective 2010). **Document type:** *Handbook/Manual/Guide, Trade.* **Description:** Aims to fulfill the increasing need for information on the strategy and practical aspects of patent litigation in the trading countries of the world.
Published by: Aspen Publishers, Inc. (Subsidiary of: Wolters Kluwer N.V.), 76 Ninth Ave, 7th Fl, New York, NY 10011. TEL 212-771-0600, 800-317-3113, FAX 212-771-0885, Aspen-InternationalS@wolterskluwer.com, https://www.aspenpublishers.com. **Subscr. to:** 7201 McKinney Cir, Frederick, MD 21704. TEL 301-698-7100, 800-234-1660, FAX 301-695-7931, 800-901-9075. **Dist. by:** Turpin Distribution Services Ltd., Pegasus Dr, Stratton Business Park, Biggleswade, Bedfordshire SG18 8QB, United Kingdom. TEL 44-1767-604958, FAX 44-1767-601640, kluwerlaw@turpin-distribution.com, http://www.turpin-distribution.com/.

608.7 GBR
GREAT BRITAIN. PATENT OFFICE. ANNUAL REPORT AND ACCOUNTS. Text in English. a. GBP 14.35 per issue (effective 2010). back issues avail.; reprints avail. **Document type:** *Government.*
Former titles: Great Britain. Department of Trade. Patents, Design and Trade Marks: Annual Report of the Comptroller-General of Patents, Designs and Trade Marks (0072-5706); Great Britain. Patent Office. Comptroller General of Patents, Designs and Trade Marks. Report; Great Britain. Commissioners of Patents. Annual Reports
Related titles: Online - full text ed.

P

Published by: (Great Britain. Intellectual Property Office), The Stationery Office, St Crispins, Duke St, Norwich, NR3 1PD, United Kingdom. TEL 44-1603-622211, FAX 44-870-6005533, customer.services@tso.co.uk, http://www.tso.co.uk. **Subscr. to:** PO Box 29, Norwich NR3 1GN, United Kingdom. TEL 44-870-6005522.

341.7 USA
GRIMES & BATTERSBY REPORT. Text in English. 1988. 4/yr. free.
Document type: *Newsletter.*
Published by: Grimes & Battersby, 488 Main Ave, Norwalk, CT 06851-1008. TEL 203-324-2828, FAX 203-348-2720. Eds. Charles Grimes, Gregory Battersby. Circ: 2,500.

GUIDE TO AVAILABLE TECHNOLOGIES; an annual guide to business opportunities in technology. *see* TECHNOLOGY: COMPREHENSIVE WORKS

GUIDE TO MEDICAL DEVICE REGISTRATION IN JAPAN. *see* MEDICAL SCIENCES

346.048 GBR ISSN 0968-2635
GUIDE TO THE LICENSING WORLD (YEAR). Text in English. 1993. a. GBP 120 combined subscription per issue (print & online eds.) (effective 2010); subscr. includes 2010 guide. adv. **Document type:** *Directory, Trade.* **Description:** Designed to give those involved in the licensing industry as much relevant information as possible under one cover.
Related titles: Online - full text ed.
Published by: D J Publishing Ltd., The Old Stables, School Ln, Crowborough, E Sussex TN6 1PA, United Kingdom. TEL 44-1892-6684444, FAX 44-1892-6685555.

608.7 JPN ISSN 0385-7115
T305.A2
HATSUMEI/INVENTION. Text in Japanese. 1905. m. JPY 700 per issue.
Document type: *Trade.*
Published by: Hatsumei Kyokai/Japan Institute of Invention and Innovation, 9-14 Toranomon 2-chome, Minato-ku, Tokyo, 105-0001, Japan.

608.7 JPN
HATSUMEI KOAN NO SHOKAI/INVENTION AND CONTRIVANCE INFORMATION. Text in Japanese. a. **Document type:** *Government.*
Published by: Japanese Institute of Invention and Innovation (JIII)/ Hatsumei-kyokai, 2-9-14 Toranomon, Minato-ku, Tokyo, 105-0001, Japan. FAX 81-3-3502-3485.

608.7 JPN ISSN 0385-2490
HATSUMEI KYOKAI KOKAI GIHO. HANGETSUKAN/JAPAN INSTITUTE OF INVENTION & INNOVATION JOURNAL OF TECHNICAL DISCLOSURE. Text in Japanese. 1976. s-m. JPY 32,400. **Document type:** *Bulletin, Trade.*
Published by: Hatsumei Kyokai/Japan Institute of Invention and Innovation, 9-14 Toranomon 2-chome, Minato-ku, Tokyo, 105-0001, Japan.

608.7 JPN
HATSUMEI TO SEIKATSU/INVENTION & LIFE. Text in Japanese. 1962. m. JPY 1,800.
Published by: Nihon Hatsumei Shinko Kyokai/Japan Society for the Advancement of Inventions, 4-22 Sakuragaoka-cho, Shibuya-ku, Tokyo, 150-0031, Japan.

608.7 JPN
HATSUMEI TSUSHIN (CD-ROM). Text in Japanese. 1963. m. JPY 21,000 (effective 2007). **Document type:** *Newspaper, Trade.*
Formerly: Hatsumei Tsushin (Print)
Media: CD-ROM.
Published by: Hatsumei Tsushinsha, 1-12-2, Uchi Kanda, Chiyoda, Tokyo, 101-0047, Japan. TEL 81-3-52815511, FAX 81-3-52815512, http://www.hatsumei.co.jp/. Ed. K Kitamura. Pub. K Yamagata.

608.7 JPN
HOKKAIDO HATSUMEI KOAN NENPO/ANNUAL REPORT OF INVENTION IN HOKKAIDO. Text in Japanese. 1955. a.
Published by: Asahikawa Sangyo Gijutsu Joho Senta/Asahikawa Information Center for Industry and Technology, Asahikawa Shiritsu Toshokan, Tokiwa-Koen, Asahikawa-shi, Hokkaido 070-0044, Japan.

608.7 HRV ISSN 1331-6079
HRVATSKI INOVATOR. Text in Croatian. 1997. q. **Document type:** *Journal, Trade.*
Published by: Hrvatski Savez Inovatora, Dalmatinska 12, Zagreb, 10000, Croatia. TEL 385-1-4848755, FAX 385-1-4848766, hsi@hztk.hr, http://www.inovator.hr.

608.7 CAN
HUGHES AND WOODLEY ON PATENTS. Text in English. 2 base vols. plus updates 2/yr. looseleaf. CAD 420 base vol(s). (effective 2010). **Document type:** *Handbook/Manual/Guide, Trade.* **Description:** Commentary and full text of Canadian patent legislation, practice, procedure and case law.
Related titles: CD-ROM ed.: CAD 495.
Published by: LexisNexis Canada Inc. (Subsidiary of: LexisNexis North America), 123 Commerce Valley Dr E, Ste 700, Markham, ON L3T 7W8, Canada. TEL 905-479-2665, 800-668-6481, FAX 905-479-3758, 800-461-3275, info@lexisnexis.ca. Eds. Dino P Clarizio, Roger T Hughes.

340 CAN
HUGHES ON COPYRIGHT AND INDUSTRIAL DESIGN. Text in English. base vol. plus updates 4/yr. looseleaf. CAD 420 base vol(s). (effective 2010). **Document type:** *Handbook/Manual/Guide, Trade.* **Description:** Commentary and full text of Canadian copyright and industrial design legislation, practice, procedure and case law.
Related titles: CD-ROM ed.: CAD 495.
Published by: LexisNexis Canada Inc. (Subsidiary of: LexisNexis North America), 123 Commerce Valley Dr E, Ste 700, Markham, ON L3T 7W8, Canada. TEL 905-479-2665, 800-668-6481, FAX 905-479-3758, 800-461-3275, info@lexisnexis.ca. Eds. Roger T Hughes, Susan J Peacock.

602.7 CAN
HUGHES ON TRADEMARKS. Text in English. base vol. plus updates 4/yr. looseleaf. CAD 420 base vol(s).; CAD 149 updates per issue (effective 2010). **Document type:** *Monographic series, Trade.* **Description:** Covers Canadian trademarks legislation, practice, procedures, and case law.
Published by: LexisNexis Canada Inc. (Subsidiary of: LexisNexis North America), 123 Commerce Valley Dr E, Ste 700, Markham, ON L3T 7W8, Canada. TEL 905-479-2665, 800-668-6481, FAX 905-479-3758, 800-461-3275, info@lexisnexis.ca, http://www.lexisnexis.ca. Ed. Roger T Hughes.

608 DEU
K9 CODEN: IICLDM
➤ **I I C - INTERNATIONAL REVIEW OF INTELLECTUAL PROPERTY AND COMPETITION LAW.** Text in English, German. 1969. 8/yr. EUR 378; EUR 51 newsstand/cover (effective 2011). adv. bk.rev. index. reprint service avail. from SCH. **Document type:** *Journal, Academic/ Scholarly.*
Formerly: I I C - International Review of Industrial Property and Copyright Law (0018-9855)
Related titles: CD-ROM ed.; Microfilm ed.; Online - full text ed.: ISSN 1522-2578.
Indexed: A20, A22, APEL, ASCA, CurCont, DIP, ELJI, ELLIS, FLP, IBR, IBZ, P06, P30, RASB, SCOPUS, SSCI, W07.
—CASDDS, IE, Infotrieve, Ingenta, INIST. **CCC.**
Published by: (Max-Planck-Institut for Intellectual Property, Competition and Tax Law/Max-Planck-Institut fuer Geistiges Eigentum, Wettbewerbs- und Steuerrecht), Verlag C.H. Beck oHG, Wilhelmstr 9, Munich, 80801, Germany. TEL 49-89-381890, FAX 49-89-38189398, abo.service@beck.de, http://www.beck.de. Circ: 825 (paid and controlled).

608.7 HKG ISSN 1011-3649
I P ASIA; intellectual property marketing and communications law. (Intellectual Property) Text in Chinese. 1988. 10/yr. HKD 5,136 domestic; USD 700 foreign (effective 2001). s-a. index. back issues avail. **Description:** Covers intellectual property legal developments and enforcement news in 16 Asian countries.
Related titles: Online - full text ed.
Indexed: B11, HongKongiana.
—**CCC.**
Published by: Asia Law & Practice Ltd. (Subsidiary of: Euromoney Institutional Investor Plc.), 5/F Printing House, 6 Duddell St, Central Hong Kong, Hong Kong. TEL 852-2523-3399, FAX 852-2521-6110, info@euromoneyhk.com, http://www.asialaw.com/. Ed. Chris Hunter.

608.7 346.04 GBR
I P HANDBOOK (YEAR). (Intellectual Property) Text in English. a. **Document type:** *Directory, Trade.* **Description:** Lists experts in intellectual property issues worldwide.
Formerly (until 2008): World I P Contacts Handbook (Year)
Related titles: ◆ Supplement to: Managing Intellectual Property. ISSN 0960-5002.
—BLDSC (4567.171700).
Published by: Euromoney Institutional Investor Plc., Nestor House, Playhouse Yard, London, EC4V 5EX, United Kingdom. TEL 44-20-77798673, information@euromoneyplc.com, http://www.euromoneyplc.com/. Ed. Emma Barraclough TEL 44-20-77798334.

602.7 608.7 CAN ISSN 0849-3154
I P I C BULLETIN. Text in English. 1967. 10/yr. looseleaf. membership. adv. **Document type:** *Newsletter.*
Formerly: P T I C Newsletter (0380-6375)
Published by: Intellectual Property Institute of Canada, 60 Queen St, Ste 606, Ottawa, ON K1P 5Y7, Canada. TEL 613-234-0516. Adv. contact Karen Klingbeil.

340 USA ISSN 1940-3593
KF2972
I P L NEWSLETTER. (Intellectual Property Law Section) Text in English. 1982. q. **Document type:** *Newsletter.* **Description:** Recent developments in intellectual property law, Section activities, calendar of events.
Formerly: P T C Newsletter (0736-8232)
Indexed: A01, A22, A26, I05, LRI.
—**CCC.**
Published by: American Bar Association, Section of Intellectual Property Law, 321 N Clark Street, Chicago, IL 60610-4714. TEL 312-988-5598, FAX 312-988-6800, iplaw@abanet.org, http://www.abanet.org/intelprop/. Ed. Jennifer Mahalingappa.

346.04 USA ISSN 1549-294X
KF2972
I P LAW & BUSINESS. (Intellectual Property) Text in English. 2003. m. USD 199 domestic; USD 285 foreign (effective 2009). adv. back issues avail.; reprints avail. **Document type:** *Magazine, Trade.* **Description:** Updates attorneys and executives on the law and business of intellectual property, including stories about copyrights, patents, trademarks, etc.
Related titles: Online - full text ed.
—**CCC.**
Published by: A L M (Subsidiary of: Incisive Media Plc.), 120 Broadway, 5th Fl, New York, NY 10271. TEL 212-457-9400, FAX 646-417-7705, customerservices@incisivemedia.com, http://www.incisivemedia.com/. Ed. Ed Shanahan. Adv. contact Lilian Mendez. Circ: 17,500.

346.04 USA ISSN 2154-6452
K9
▼ **THE I P LAW BOOK REVIEW.** (Intellectual Property) Text in English. 2010 (May). 3/yr. **Document type:** *Journal, Academic/Scholarly.* **Description:** Features book reviews in the area of intellectual property and copyright law.
Media: Online - full text.
Published by: Golden Gate University, School of Law, 536 Mission St, San Francisco, CA 94105. TEL 415-442-6690, 800-448-4968, FAX 415-442-7807, lawreview@ggu.edu, http://www.ggu.edu. Eds. Chester Chuang, William Gallagher.

346.04 USA ISSN 1086-914X
K9
THE I P LITIGATOR. (Intellectual Property) Text in English. 1995. 10/yr. USD 557; USD 67 per issue (effective 2011). **Document type:** *Journal, Trade.* **Description:** Briefings on the latest thinking and strategies for successful intellectual property litigation and enforcement.
Related titles: Online - full text ed.
Indexed: A01, A12, A17, A26, ABIn, B02, B15, B17, B18, CLI, G04, G06, G07, G08, I05, LRI, P52, P53, P54, PQC.
—Ingenta. **CCC.**
Published by: Aspen Publishers, Inc. (Subsidiary of: Wolters Kluwer N.V.), 76 Ninth Ave, 7th Fl, New York, NY 10011. TEL 212-771-0600, 800-317-3113, FAX 212-771-0885, ASPEN-CustomerService@wolterskluwer.com, https://www.aspenpublishers.com. **Dist. by:** 7201 McKinney Cir, Frederick, MD 21704. TEL 301-698-7100, FAX 301-695-7931.

346.04 FIN ISSN 1456-9914
I P R INFO. (Intellectual and Industrial Property Rights) Text mainly in Finnish; Text occasionally in English. 1999. q. adv. back issues avail. **Document type:** *Magazine, Academic/Scholarly.* **Description:** Contains articles on topical issues of intellectual and industrial property rights.
Related titles: Online - full text ed.
Published by: (I P R University Center - Immateriaalioikeusinstituutti), Unionimedia, Kaupintie 16 A, Helsinki, 00440, Finland. TEL 358-9-41334400, FAX 358-9-41334433, toimitus@unionimedia.fi, http://www.unionimedia.fi. Ed. Marja-Leena Mansala. adv.: page EUR 520; 210 x 297. Circ: 1,000.

346.04 FIN ISSN 1458-9486
I P R UNIVERSITY CENTER. JULKAISIJA. I P R SERIES A. (Intellectual and Industrial Property Rights) Text in English, Finnish. 2006. irreg. **Document type:** *Monographic series, Academic/Scholarly.*
Media: Online - full content.
Published by: I P R University Center - Immateriaalioikeusinstituutti, c/o University of Helsinki, Yliopistonkatu 3, 4, PO Box 4, Helsinki, 00014, Finland. TEL 358-9-19122766, FAX 358-9-19122762, info@iprinfo.com.

346.04 FIN ISSN 1458-9494
I P R UNIVERSITY CENTER. PUBLICATIONS. I P R SERIES B. (Intellectual and Industrial Property Rights) Text in English. 2005. irreg. **Document type:** *Monographic series, Academic/Scholarly.*
Media: Online - full content.
Published by: I P R University Center - Immateriaalioikeusinstituutti, c/o University of Helsinki, Yliopistonkatu 3, 4, PO Box 4, Helsinki, 00014, Finland. TEL 358-9-19122766, FAX 358-9-19122762, info@iprinfo.com.

346.04 FIN ISSN 1796-8194
I P R UNIVERSITY CENTERIN. JULKAISUJA/I P R UNIVERSITY CENTER. PUBLICATIONS. (Intellectual and Industrial Property Rights) Text in Finnish. 2007. irreg., latest vol.2, 2007. price varies. **Document type:** *Monographic series, Academic/Scholarly.*
Published by: I P R University Center - Immateriaalioikeusinstituutti, c/o University of Helsinki, Yliopistonkatu 3, 4, PO Box 4, Helsinki, 00014, Finland. TEL 358-9-19122766, FAX 358-9-19122762, info@iprinfo.com, http://www.iprinfo.com.

346.48 GBR ISSN 1751-0414
I P VALUE. (Intellectual Property) Text in English. 2002. a. GBP 125 per issue (effective 2009). back issues avail. **Document type:** *Yearbook, Trade.*
Formerly (until 2005): Building and Enforcing Intellectual Property Value (1478-8462)
—**CCC.**
Published by: Global White Page Ltd., New Hibernia House, Winchester Walk, London Bridge, London, SE1 9AG, United Kingdom. TEL 44-20-72340606, FAX 44-20-72340808. Pub. Gavin Stewart.

I P WORLDWIDE. (Intellectual Property) *see* LAW

346.043 USA ISSN 0019-1272
K9
IDEA (CONCORD); the intellectual property law review. Text in English. 1957. q. USD 68 domestic; USD 79 foreign; USD 25 to students (effective 2010). bk.rev. abstr.; bibl.; charts; pat.; stat.; tr.mk. back issues avail.; reprint service avail. from WSH. **Document type:** *Journal, Academic/Scholarly.* **Description:** Serves as an outlet for high quality intellectual property practice and scholarship.
Formerly (until 1964): Patent, Trade-mark and Copyright Journal of Research and Education (0893-1429)
Indexed: A22, A26, B04, BPIA, CLI, EnvAb, EnvInd, G06, G07, G08, I01, I03, I05, ILP, LRI, P06, PAIS, TelAb, Telegen.
—BLDSC (4362.355000), IE, Ingenta.
Published by: Franklin Pierce Law Center, 2 White St, Concord, NH 03301. TEL 603-228-1541, FAX 603-228-0386, khennessy@piercelaw.edu. Ed. Eli M Sheets.

IMPACT COMPRESSOR - TURBINE NEWS AND PATENTS. *see* MACHINERY

IMPACT PUMP NEWS AND PATENTS. *see* MACHINERY

IMPACT VALVES NEWS AND PATENTS. *see* MACHINERY

608.7 NLD ISSN 0920-0746
T277 CODEN: INEIAL
DE INDUSTRIELE EIGENDOM. Text in Dutch, English. 1981. m. EUR 220; EUR 19 per issue (effective 2009). index. **Document type:** *Bulletin, Government.*
Formed by the merger of (1964-1981): Industriele Eigendom. Deel I (0166-9737); (1964-1981): Industriele Eigendom. Deel II (0166-9788); Both of which superseded in part (in 1964): Industrieele Eigendom (0019-9249)
Indexed: KES.
—CASDDS.
Published by: Octrooicentrum Nederland/Netherlands Patents Office, Patentlaan 2, Postbus 5820, Rijswijk, 2280 HV, Netherlands. TEL 31-70-3986699, FAX 31-70-3986606, info@octrooicentrum.nl, http://www.octrooicentrum.nl.

602.7 CUB
INFORMACION DE PATENTES. Text in Spanish. fortn.
Published by: Academia de Ciencias de Cuba, Instituto de Documentacion e Informacion Cientifico-Tecnica (I D I C T), Capitolio Nacional, Prado y San Jose, Habana, 2, Cuba.

608.7 DEU
INFORMATION SOURCES IN PATENTS. Text in English. 1992. irreg., latest vol.2, 2006. USD 98 base vol(s). (effective 2008). **Document type:** *Directory, Trade.* **Description:** Enables information professionals and librarians to evaluate information sources on patents.
Published by: De Gruyter Saur (Subsidiary of: Walter de Gruyter GmbH & Co. KG), Mies-van-der-Rohe-Str 1, Munich, 80807, Germany. TEL 49-89-769020, FAX 49-89-76902150, info@degruyter.com. Ed. Peter Auger.

340 AUS
INSTITUTE OF PATENT AND TRADE MARK ATTORNEYS OF AUSTRALIA. ANNUAL PROCEEDINGS. Text in English. 1919. irreg. (every 3-5 yrs.). bk.rev. **Document type:** *Proceedings.*
Formerly (until 1968): Institute of Patent Attorneys of Australia. Annual Proceedings
Published by: Institute of Patent and Trademark Attorneys of Australia, Level 2, 302 Burwood Rd, Hawthorn, VIC 3122, Australia. TEL 61-3-98192004, FAX 61-3-98196002, mail@ipta.com.au, http://www.ipta.com.au.

346.04 BGR
INTELEKTUALNA SOBSTVENOST/INTELLECTUAL PROPERTY. Text in Bulgarian; Summaries in English, Russian, German. m. USD 85 foreign (effective 2002). **Description:** Publishes scientific articles in the field of patent law, intellectual property, trade marks, industrial property rights, Bulgarian copyrights and related rights laws.
Published by: Patentno Vedomstvo na Republika Bulgaria/Patent Office of the Republic of Bulgaria, 52b, Dr G M Dimitrov Blvd, Sofia, 1797, Bulgaria. TEL 359-2-710152, FAX 359-2-717044, http://www.bpo.bg/. **Dist. by:** Sofia Books, ul Silivria 16, Sofia 1404, Bulgaria. TEL 359-2-9586257, info@sofiabooks-bg.com, http://www.sofiabooks-bg.com.

346.04 UKR ISSN 1608-6422
K9
➤ **INTELEKTUAL'NA VLASNIST'.** Text in Ukrainian. 1998. m. USD 297 in United States (effective 2007). **Document type:** *Journal, Academic/Scholarly.*
—East View.
Published by: Aspekt - 2003, vul Bozhenka, 11, ofis 404, Kyiv, 03680, Ukraine. TEL 380-44-2008858. Ed. Iryna Abdulina. **Dist. by:** East View Information Services, 10601 Wayzata Blvd, Minneapolis, MN 55305. TEL 952-252-1201, 800-477-1005, FAX 952-252-1202, info@eastview.com, http://www.eastview.com. **Co-publisher:** Akademiya Pravovykh Nauk Ukrainy, Ukrains'kyi Instytut Promyslovoi Vlasnosti.

➤ **INTELLECTUAL ASSET MANAGEMENT.** *see* BUSINESS AND ECONOMICS—Management

346.04 USA
INTELLECTUAL PROPERTY (BLAINE); answers to your questions about trademarks, copyrights, trade secrets, and patents. Text in English. base vol. plus updates 2/yr. looseleaf. USD 435 base vol(s). loose-leaf (effective 2009). **Document type:** *Handbook/Manual/Guide, Trade.* **Description:** Focuses all four common components of intellectual property, trademarks, copyrights, patents, and trade secrets.
Published by: Specialty Technical Publishers Inc., 1750 Grant Ave, Blaine, WA 98230. TEL 604-983-3434, 800-251-0381, FAX 604-983-3445, custinfo@stpub.com, info@stpub.com, orders@stpub.com. Eds. Martin D Fern, Michael Harris.

341.7 USA
➤ **INTELLECTUAL PROPERTY (SPRINGFIELD).** Text in English. 1961. q. USD 20 to members; USD 6.50 per issue (effective 2009). adv. back issues avail.; reprints avail. **Document type:** *Newsletter, Trade.* **Description:** Designed to improve the professional capabilities of Illinois lawyers who specialize in the practice of patent, trademark and copyright law and associated areas concerning trade secrets, unfair competition and antitrust law.
Former titles (until 1988): Illinois State Bar Association. Patent, Trademark and Copyright; (until 1980): Illinois State Bar Association. Patent, Trademark and Copyright Newsletter (0073-5043)
Related titles: Online - full text ed.: free to members (effective 2008).
Published by: Illinois State Bar Association, Illinois Bar Center, 424 S Second St, Springfield, IL 62701. TEL 217-525-1760, 800-252-8908, FAX 217-525-9063, jfenski@isba.org, http://www.isba.org. Adv. contact Nancy Vonnahmen TEL 217-747-1437. page USD 400; 7 x 9.625. Circ: 1,223.

341.758 USA
INTELLECTUAL PROPERTY AND ANTITRUST LAW. Text in English. 19??. 2 base vols. plus s-a. updates. looseleaf. USD 954 base vol(s). (effective 2010). **Document type:** *Journal, Trade.* **Description:** Covers cases involving patents, trademarks, copyrights, trade secrets, dealer terminations, or when enforcing intellectual property rights against infringers.
Published by: Thomson West (Subsidiary of: Thomson Reuters Corp.), 610 Opperman Dr, Eagan, MN 55123. TEL 651-687-7000, 800-344-5008, west.customer.service@thomson.com.

346.04805 GBR ISSN 1463-7006
INTELLECTUAL PROPERTY AND INFORMATION TECHNOLOGY LAW. Text in English. 1996. bi-m. **Document type:** *Journal, Trade.* **Description:** Offers pertinent summary and comment on key law.
Formerly (until 1998): Intellectual Property (1361-5793)
—**CCC.**
Published by: XPL Publishing, 99 Hatfield Rd, St Albans, Herts AL1 4EG, United Kingdom. TEL 44-870-1432569, FAX 44-845-4566385, info@xplpublishing.com, http://www.xplpublishing.com.

346.04 USA
INTELLECTUAL PROPERTY AND TECHNOLOGY FORUM. Text in English. 1997. a., latest 2006. free (effective 2011). **Document type:** *Journal, Academic/Scholarly.* **Description:** Publishes news and articles relating to intellectual property and technology law.
Media: Online - full text.
Published by: Boston College Law School, 885 Ctr St, Newton, MA 02459. Ed. Patrick Wu.

341.7 USA ISSN 1534-3618
KF2972
INTELLECTUAL PROPERTY AND TECHNOLOGY LAW JOURNAL. Text in English. 1988. m. looseleaf. USD 697; USD 70 per issue (effective 2011). back issues avail.; reprints avail. **Document type:** *Journal, Trade.* **Description:** Contains information on important trends in patent, trade secret, trademark and intellectual property law.
Formerly (until 2000): The Journal of Proprietary Rights (1041-3952)
Related titles: Online - full text ed.
Indexed: A12, A13, A17, A26, ABIn, B01, B02, B06, B07, B09, B15, B17, B18, C10, CA, CLI, CompLI, G04, G08, I05, L03, LRI, P52, P53, P54, PQC, T02.
—Ingenta. **CCC.**
Published by: Aspen Publishers, Inc. (Subsidiary of: Wolters Kluwer N.V.), 76 Ninth Ave, 7th Fl, New York, NY 10011. TEL 212-771-0600, 800-317-3113, FAX 212-771-0885, ASPEN-CustomerService@wolterskluwer.com, https://www.aspenpublishers.com. **Dist. by:** 7201 McKinney Cir, Frederick, MD 21704. TEL 301-698-7100, FAX 301-695-7931.

346.04 USA
INTELLECTUAL PROPERTY COUNSELING AND LITIGATION. Text in English. 1988. 7 base vols. plus irreg. updates. looseleaf. USD 1,490 base vol(s). (effective 2008). **Document type:** *Handbook/Manual/Guide, Trade.* **Description:** A practice guide to both client counseling and dispute resolution in all areas of intellectual property law. Written by a host of U.S. intellectual property attorneys.
Related titles: CD-ROM ed.
Published by: Matthew Bender & Co., Inc. (Subsidiary of: LexisNexis North America), 1275 Broadway, Albany, NY 12204. TEL 518-487-3000, 800-424-4200, FAX 518-487-3083, international@bender.com, http://bender.lexisnexis.com. Eds. Ethan Horwitz, Lester Horwitz.

346.04 346 USA ISSN 1092-5864
KF2972
INTELLECTUAL PROPERTY COUNSELOR. Text in English. 1997. m. USD 663 (effective 2008). **Document type:** *Newsletter, Trade.*
—**CCC.**
Published by: Thomson West (Subsidiary of: Thomson Reuters Corp.), 610 Opperman Dr, Eagan, MN 55123. TEL 651-687-7000, 800-344-5008, FAX 651-687-6674, west.support@thomson.com.

346.048 341.7 AUS ISSN 0815-2098
K9
INTELLECTUAL PROPERTY FORUM. Text in English. 1984. q. AUD 330 domestic; AUD 300 foreign; free to members (effective 2009). **Document type:** *Journal, Academic/Scholarly.* **Description:** Covers intellectual property subjects and related issues dealing with commercial law, trade practices, licensing, innovation and technology transfer.
Related titles: Online - full text ed.
Indexed: B04, I01, ILP.
—BLDSC (4531.823600).
Published by: Intellectual Property Society of Australa and New Zealand, c/o National Secretariat, GPO Box 2491, Melbourne, VIC 3001, Australia. TEL 61-3-97612833, FAX 61-3-97222899, secretariat@ipsanz.com.au. Ed. Christopher Sexton.

INTELLECTUAL PROPERTY JOURNAL. *see* LAW

340 USA ISSN 1554-9607
KF2972
INTELLECTUAL PROPERTY LAW BULLETIN. Abbreviated title: I P L B. Text in English. 1996. s-a. USD 30 domestic; USD 40 foreign (effective 2009). **Document type:** *Bulletin, Academic/Scholarly.* **Description:** Contains articles from students, professors, and practitioners on diverse areas of intellectual property ranging from patents to cyberlaw.
Published by: University of San Francisco, School of Law, Kendrick Hall, 328, 2130 Fulton St, San Francisco, CA 94117. TEL 415-422-6304, FAX 415-422-6433, lawschool@usfca.edu, http://www.usfca.edu/law. Ed. Athena Johns.

346.04 NLD ISSN 1871-6725
INTELLECTUAL PROPERTY LAW LIBRARY. Text in English. 2006. irreg., latest vol.2, 2006. price varies. **Document type:** *Monographic series, Academic/Scholarly.*
Indexed: IZBG.
Published by: Martinus Nijhoff (Subsidiary of: Brill), PO Box 9000, Leiden, 2300 PA, Netherlands. TEL 31-71-5353500, FAX 31-71-5317532, marketing@brill.nl.

341.7 USA
INTELLECTUAL PROPERTY LAW NEWS. Text in English. 1991. irreg., latest 2009. looseleaf. free to members (effective 2010). back issues avail. **Document type:** *Newsletter, Trade.*
Related titles: Online - full text ed.
Published by: (Intellectual Property Law Section), State Bar of Wisconsin, PO Box 7158, Madison, WI 53707. TEL 608-257-3838, 800-728-7788, FAX 608-257-5502, service@wisbar.org. Ed. Adam Gustafson.

608.7 USA ISSN 0193-4864
KF3114.A1
INTELLECTUAL PROPERTY LAW REVIEW. Text in English. 1969. 4 base vols. plus a. updates. USD 638 base vol(s). (effective 2010). index. reprints avail. **Document type:** *Journal, Trade.* **Description:** Covers major developments in patents, trademarks, and copyright, as well as relevant topics affecting practice and procedure.
Formerly (until 1978): Patent Law Review (0079-0168)
Related titles: Online - full text ed.
Indexed: A22, A26, CLI, G08, I05, LRI, PCI.
—BLDSC (4531.824000), IE, Ingenta.
Published by: Thomson West (Subsidiary of: Thomson Reuters Corp.), 610 Opperman Dr, Eagan, MN 55123. TEL 651-687-7000, 800-344-5008, west.customer.service@thomson.com.

346.04 658.8 USA ISSN 1948-0423
INTELLECTUAL PROPERTY MARKETING ADVISOR. Abbreviated title: I P M A. Variant title: I P Marketing Advisor. Text in English. 2008. m. USD 397 (effective 2009). adv. back issues avail. **Document type:** *Newsletter, Trade.* **Description:** Guides to apply detailed, proven marketing tactics and high-level sales techniques to IP portfolio.
Published by: BizWorld, Inc, 4301 Gulfsore Blvd N, Ste 1404, Naples, FL 34103. TEL 877-729-0959, FAX 239-649-5101. Pub. Leslie C Norins. Adv. contact Sara Henderson TEL 877-729-0959 ext 105.

346.04 USA ISSN 1553-6491
KF2975.A2
INTELLECTUAL PROPERTY PLEADINGS. Text in English. 2004. 2/m. USD 1,269 (effective 2007). **Document type:** *Newsletter, Trade.* **Description:** Presents intellectual property law from the unique perspective of the voices of those involved in patent, trademark and copyright battles.
Published by: Mealey Publications & Conferences Group (Subsidiary of: LexisNexis North America), 1018 W 9th Ave, 3rd Fl, King of Prussia, PA 19406. TEL 610-768-7800, 800-632-5397, info@mealeys.com, http://www.mealeys.com.

346.04 GBR ISSN 1364-906X
K9
➤ **INTELLECTUAL PROPERTY QUARTERLY.** Text in English. 1997. q. GBP 519, EUR 684, USD 892 (effective 2012). bk.rev. **Document type:** *Journal, Academic/Scholarly.* **Description:** Publishes interdisciplinary articles on intellectual property law, which covers policy, legal, economic, industrial, technical, managerial and technical issues, including international coverage with focus on common law jurisdiction.
Indexed: A26, CLI, E08, G08, LRI, S09.
—BLDSC (4531.824700), IE, Ingenta. **CCC.**
Published by: (Intellectual Property Institute), Sweet & Maxwell Ltd. (Subsidiary of: Thomson Reuters Corp.), 100 Avenue Rd, London, NW3 3PF, United Kingdom. TEL 44-20-73937000, FAX 44-20-74491144, sweetandmaxwell.customer.services@thomson.com. Ed. Dr. Margaret Llewelyn. **Subscr. outside the UK to:** PO Box 1000, Andover SP10 9AF, United Kingdom. TEL 44-20-73938051, sweetandmaxwell.international.queries@thomson.com.

346.04 AUS ISSN 0812-2024
K1555.4
INTELLECTUAL PROPERTY REPORTS. Abbreviated title: I P R. Text in English. 1983. 9/yr. AUD 2,314.40 (effective 2008). adv. **Document type:** *Report, Trade.* **Description:** Contains the reports of decisions from intellectual property and superior courts and tribunals in Australia, the UK, New Zealand, Hong Kong, Singapore, Malaysia, the USA and Canada.
Related titles: CD-ROM ed.; Online - full text ed.: AUD 2,401.30 (effective 2008).
Published by: LexisNexis Butterworths (Subsidiary of: LexisNexis Asia Pacific), Level 9, Tower 2, 475-495 Victoria Ave, Locked Bag 2222, Chatswood Delivery Ctr, Chatswood, NSW 2067, Australia. TEL 61-2-94222174, FAX 61-2-94222405, academic@lexisnexis.com.au.

346.04 USA
INTELLECTUAL PROPERTY REVIEW. Variant title: I P Review. Text in English. 2003. s-a. **Document type:** *Newsletter, Trade.* **Description:** Contains insights into the various topics of IP while incorporating the authors points of view.
Media: Online - full content.
Published by: McDermott, Will & Emery, 227 W Monroe St, Chicago, IL 60606. TEL 312-372-2000, FAX 312-984-7700, contactus@mwe.com.

346 USA ISSN 1079-2422
KF2972
INTELLECTUAL PROPERTY STRATEGIST. Text in English. 1994. m. looseleaf. USD 459 combined subscription (print & online eds.) (effective 2008). back issues avail.; reprints avail. **Document type:** *Newsletter, Trade.*
Related titles: Online - full text ed.: USD 439 (effective 2008).
Indexed: A26, B02, B15, B17, B18, G04, I05.
—**CCC.**
Published by: Law Journal Newsletters (Subsidiary of: A L M), 1617 JFK Blvd, Ste 1750, Philadelphia, PA 19103. TEL 215-557-2300, 800-722-7670, customercare@incisivemedia.com, http://www.ljnonline.com. Ed. Howard Shire.

346.04 USA
INTELLECTUAL PROPERTY UPDATE. Text in English. m. free (effective 2009). **Document type:** *Newsletter, Trade.*
Media: Online - full content.
Published by: McDermott, Will & Emery, 227 W Monroe St, Chicago, IL 60606. TEL 312-372-2000, FAX 312-984-7700, contactus@mwe.com.

341.7582 NLD
INTELLECTUAL PROPERTY WORLD DESK REFERENCE; a guide to practice by country, state and province. Text in English. 1993. base vol. plus a. updates. looseleaf. USD 427 (effective 2009). **Document type:** *Handbook/Manual/Guide, Trade.* **Description:** Country by country description of the legal protection afforded different categories of intellectual property, including copyright, industrial designs and models, patents, as well as relevant information on matters such as royalties, currency controls, and other issues.
Published by: Kluwer Law International (Subsidiary of: Aspen Publishers, Inc.), PO Box 316, Alphen aan den Rijn, 2400 AH, Netherlands. TEL 31-172-641562, FAX 31-172-641555, sales@kluwerlaw.com, http://www.kluwerlaw.com. Ed. Anthony Prenol.

341.758 NLD ISSN 0169-1074
KKM1155.A15
INTELLECTUELE EIGENDOM & RECLAMERECHT. Short title: I E R. Text in Dutch. 1985. 6/yr. EUR 216; EUR 295.31 combined subscription (print & online eds.); EUR 108 to students; EUR 41 newsstand/cover (effective 2009). adv. **Document type:** *Journal, Trade.*
Related titles: CD-ROM ed.: EUR 219.30 (effective 2009); Online - full text ed.: EUR 242.45 (effective 2009).
Indexed: A22, ELLIS.
—IE, Infotrieve.
Published by: Kluwer B.V. (Subsidiary of: Wolters Kluwer N.V.), Postbus 23, Deventer, 7400 GA, Netherlands. TEL 31-570-673555, FAX 31-570-691555, juridisch@kluwer.nl, http://www.kluwer.nl.

602.7 608.7 340 JPN
K1
INTERNATIONAL ASSOCIATION FOR THE PROTECTION OF INTELLECTUAL PROPERTY. JAPANESE GROUP. JOURNAL (INTERNATIONAL EDITION). Text in English. 1976. bi-m. JPY 12,900 (effective 2003). adv. cum.index: 1976-1986. **Document type:** *Journal, Academic/Scholarly.* **Description:** Presents court decisions, current topics, law and practices concerning industrial and intellectual properties in Japan. Also covers international R&D licensing and technology transfer.
Formerly (until 2001): International Association for the Protection of Industrial Property. Japanese Group. Journal (International Edition) (0385-8863)
Related titles: ♦ Japanese ed.: International Association for the Protection of Intellectual Property. Japanese Group. Journal (Japanese Edition).
Published by: Nihon Kokusai Chiteki Zaisan Hogo Kyokai/International Association for the Protection of Intellectual Property of Japan, Yuseigojokai Kotohira Bldg, 14-1, Toranomon 1-chome, Minato-ku, Tokyo, 105-0001, Japan. TEL 81-3-35915301, FAX 81-3-35911510, japan@aippi.or.jp, http://www.aippi.or.jp/index.htm. Circ: 3,000.

P

608.7 JPN
INTERNATIONAL ASSOCIATION FOR THE PROTECTION OF INTELLECTUAL PROPERTY. JAPANESE GROUP. JOURNAL (JAPANESE EDITION). Text in Japanese. 1956. m. JPY 700 per issue (effective 2003). **Document type:** *Journal, Academic/Scholarly.*
Formerly (until 2001): Shadan Hojin Nihon Kokusai Kogyo Shoyuken Hogo Kyokai Geppo/International Association for the Protection of Industrial Property. Japanese Group. Journal (Japanese Edition) (0385-6909)
Related titles: ◆ English ed.: International Association for the Protection of Intellectual Property. Japanese Group. Journal (International Edition).
—BLDSC (4809.315500).
Published by: Nihon Kokusai Chiteki Zaisan Hogo Kyokai/International Association for the Protection of Intellectual Property of Japan, Yuseigojokai Kotohira Bldg, 14-1, Toranomon 1-chome, Minato-ku, Tokyo, 105-0001, Japan. TEL 81-3-35915301, FAX 81-3-35911510, japan@aippi.or.jp, http://www.aippi.or.jp/index.htm.

341.758 FRA ISSN 1682-9530
K3
INTERNATIONAL CONFEDERATION OF SOCIETIES OF AUTHORS AND COMPOSERS. NEWS. Text in Multiple languages. irreg., latest vol.186, 1976. **Document type:** *Journal.*
Indexed: PAIS.
Published by: International Confederation of Societies of Authors and Composers, 11 rue Keppler, Paris, 75116, France.

341.758 USA
INTERNATIONAL COPYRIGHT AND NEIGHBOURING RIGHTS. Text in English. 1989. latest 1999, update, 2 base vols. plus a. updates. USD 195.
Published by: LexisNexis (Subsidiary of: LexisNexis North America), 701 E Water St, PO Box 7587, Charlottesville, VA 22906. TEL 434-972-7600, 800-446-3410, FAX 800-643-1280, customer.support@lexisnexis.com, http://www.lexisnexis.com/.

608.7 USA
INTERNATIONAL COPYRIGHT LAW AND PRACTICE. Text in English. 1988. base vol. plus a. updates. looseleaf. USD 698 base vol(s). (effective 2008). **Document type:** *Handbook/Manual/Guide, Trade.* **Description:** Provides information on international copyright and national laws.
Related titles: CD-ROM ed.: USD 716 (effective 2008).
Published by: Matthew Bender & Co., Inc. (Subsidiary of: LexisNexis North America), 1275 Broadway, Albany, NY 12204. TEL 518-487-3000, 800-424-4200, FAX 518-487-3083, international@bender.com, http://bender.lexisnexis.com. Ed. Paul Edward Geller.

608.7 CHE ISSN 0250-7730
TS171.A1
INTERNATIONAL DESIGNS BULLETIN; bulletin des dessins et modeles internationaux. Text in English, French. 1979. m. CHF 460; CHF 185 foreign (effective 1999). adv. illus. back issues avail. **Document type:** *Bulletin.*
Formerly: Dessins et Modeles Internationaux (0011-9520)
Indexed: RASB.
Published by: World Intellectual Property Organization/Organisation Mondiale de la Propriete Intellectuelle, Publications Sales and Distribution Unit, 34 Chemin des Colombettes, Geneva 20, 1211, Switzerland. TEL 41-22-338-9111, FAX 41-22-740-1812. Circ: 420.

608.7 GBR ISSN 1478-9647
K1401.A15
➤ **INTERNATIONAL JOURNAL OF INTELLECTUAL PROPERTY MANAGEMENT.** Abbreviated title: I J I P M. Text in English. 2006. 4/yr. EUR 494 to institutions (print or online ed.); EUR 672 combined subscription to institutions (print & online eds.) (effective 2012). back issues avail. **Document type:** *Journal, Academic/Scholarly.* **Description:** Aims to enhance communications between policy makers, organizational agents, academics, and managers on the critical understanding and research on intellectual property; and to promote the development of the newly-cultivated research field.
Related titles: Online - full text ed.: ISSN 1478-9655 (from IngentaConnect).
Indexed: A26, A28, APA, B02, B15, B17, B18, BrCerAb, C&ISA, CA/WCA, CIA, CerAb, CivEngAb, CorrAb, E&CAJ, E11, EEA, EMA, ESPM, EconLit, EnvEAb, G04, H15, I05, Inspec, JEL, LRI, M&TEA, M09, MBF, METADEX, SolStAb, T04, WAA.
—BLDSC (4542.310290), Ingenta. **CCC.**
Published by: Inderscience Publishers, PO Box 735, Olney, Bucks MK46 5WB, United Kingdom. TEL 44-1234-240519, FAX 44-1234-240515, editorial@inderscience.com. Ed. Dr. M A Dorgham. **Subscr. to:** World Trade Centre Bldg, 29 Rte de Pre-Bois, Case Postale 856, Geneva 15 1215, Switzerland. subs@inderscience.com.

608.7 USA
INTERNATIONAL PATENT LITIGATION. SUPPLEMENT. Text in English. 1990. a. USD 250 (effective 2008). **Document type:** *Journal, Trade.*
Related titles: ◆ Supplement to: International Patent Litigation. ISSN 0738-9337.
Published by: The Bureau of National Affairs, Inc., 1801 S Bell St, Arlington, VA 22202. TEL 703-341-3000, 800-372-1033, FAX 703-341-4634, 800-253-0332, bnaplus@bna.com, http://www.bna.com.

INVENTION INTELLIGENCE. *see* SCIENCES: COMPREHENSIVE WORKS

608 FRA ISSN 1959-4631
INVENTION PASSION. Text in French. 2007. q. adv. **Document type:** *Magazine, Consumer.*
Address: 62 Rue Orbe, Rouen, 76000, France. TEL 33-2-35368377. adv.: page EUR 700. Circ: 60,000.

608.7 USA ISSN 0883-9859
T339
INVENTORS' DIGEST. Text in English. 1985. bi-m. USD 27 domestic; USD 32 in Canada; USD 45 elsewhere (effective 2002). adv. bk.rev. back issues avail. **Document type:** *Journal, Trade.* **Description:** Oriented to anyone with ideas for new products, with guidance through the process of new product development.
Related titles: Online - full text ed.
Indexed: A10, B01, B07, M02, T02, V03.
—Ingenta, Linda Hall.
Published by: J M H Publishing Co., 30-31 Union Wharf, 3rd Fl, Boston, MA 02109. TEL 617-367-4540, FAX 617-723-6988, inventorsd@aol.com, http://www.inventorsdigest.com. Ed., Adv. contact Joanne Hayes-Rines. Pub. Joanne M Hayes Rines. R&P Joanne Hayes Rines. B&W page USD 1,166; trim 11 x 8.5. Circ: 20,000.

INZYNIERIA MATERIALOWA. *see* ENGINEERING

608.7 RUS ISSN 0130-1802
T201
IZOBRETATEL' I RATSIONALIZATOR. Text in Russian. 1929. m. USD 84. adv.
—East View, Linda Hall.
Published by: Izdatel'stvo Izobretatel' i Ratsionalizator, Myasnitskaya ul 13, str 18, Moscow, 101000, Russian Federation. TEL 7-095-9258387, FAX 7-095-9258888. Ed. G P Kushner. **Dist. by:** East View Information Services, 10601 Wayzata Blvd, Minneapolis, MN 55305. TEL 952-252-1201, 800-477-1005, FAX 952-252-1202, info@eastview.com, http://www.eastview.com.

608.7 RUS ISSN 1683-2019
T285.A2 CODEN: OTIZDX
IZOBRETENIYA. POLEZNYE MODELI/INVENTIONS; ofitsial'nyi patentnyi byulleten'. Text in Russian. 1924. 3/m. USD 1,499.95. adv. illus.; pat.; tr.mk. index. **Document type:** *Bulletin.* **Description:** Publishes formulas and drawings of scientific inventions and discoveries listed in the Russian Federal Register. Contains information about any changes in their legal status and description.
Supersedes in part (in 2000): Izobreteniya (1021-0865); Which was formerly (until 1992): Otkrytiya, Izobreteniya (0208-287X); Which superseded in part (in 1983): Otkrytiya, Izobreteniya, Promyshlennye Obraztsy, Tovarnye Znaki (0007-4020); Which was formerly: Bulleten' Izobretenii, Promyshlennykh Obraztsov i Tovarnykh Znakov
Related titles: Microfiche ed.; Microfilm ed.
Indexed: ABIPC, ChemAb.
—CASDDS, East View, INIST, Linda Hall. **CCC.**
Published by: Vsesoyuznyi Nauchno-Issledovatel'skii Institut Patentnoi Informatsii (VNIIPI)/Committee of Russian Federation for Patents and Trademarks, Raushskaya nab 4-5, Moscow, 113035, Russian Federation. TEL 7-095-2301805, FAX 7-095-9593307. Ed. E I Daich. Circ: 11,125. **Dist. by:** East View Information Services, 10601 Wayzata Blvd, Minneapolis, MN 55305. TEL 952-252-1201, 800-477-1005, FAX 952-252-1202, info@eastview.com, http://www.eastview.com.

608.7 JPN
JAPANESE PATENT OFFICE. ANNUAL REPORT. Text in English. 1977. a. free to qualified personnel. **Description:** Shows JPO's industrial property statistics and organization, budget etc.
Published by: Tokkyocho/Japanese Patent Office (JPO), 4-3 Kasumigaseki 3-chome, Chiyoda-ku, Tokyo, 100-0013, Japan. TEL 81-3-3581-1898, FAX 81-3-3581-0762.

JOHN MARSHALL JOURNAL OF COMPUTER & INFORMATION LAW. *see* LAW

346.04 USA
JOURNAL OF INTELLECTUAL PROPERTY LAW. Abbreviated title: J I P L. Text in English. 1993. s-a. USD 30 domestic; USD 40 foreign (effective 2009). back issues avail. **Document type:** *Journal, Academic/Scholarly.* **Description:** Features student-written articles on all aspects of intellectual property law, including trademarks, patents, copyright, and unfair trade.
Related titles: Online - full text ed.
Published by: University of Georgia, School of Law, School of Law, Athens, GA 30602. TEL 706-542-7288, FAX 706-542-5556, lawreg@uga.edu. Ed. Delia Gervin.

346.04 GBR ISSN 1747-1532
K1401.A15
➤ **JOURNAL OF INTELLECTUAL PROPERTY LAW & PRACTICE.** Abbreviated title: J I P L P. Text in English. 2005 (Nov.). m. GBP 560 in United Kingdom to institutions; EUR 839 in Europe to institutions; USD 1,065 in US & Canada to institutions; GBP 560 elsewhere to institutions; GBP 611 combined subscription in United Kingdom to institutions (print & online eds.); EUR 916 combined subscription in Europe to institutions (print & online eds.); USD 1,161 combined subscription in US & Canada to institutions (print & online eds.); GBP 611 combined subscription elsewhere to institutions (print & online eds.) (effective 2012). adv. back issues avail.; reprint service avail. from PSC. **Document type:** *Journal, Academic/Scholarly.* **Description:** Designed for intellectual property lawyers, patent attorneys and trademark attorneys both in private practice and working in industry. Covers developments and actions related to the intellectual property of artists, inventors, programmers, web page designers and small business owners, as well as the licenses necessary to distribute and link to the property.
Related titles: Online - full text ed.: ISSN 1747-1540. GBP 509 in United Kingdom to institutions; EUR 763 in Europe to institutions; USD 967 in US & Canada to institutions; GBP 509 elsewhere to institutions (effective 2012).
Indexed: A22, E01.
—BLDSC (5007.538443), IE, Ingenta. **CCC.**
Published by: Oxford University Press, Great Clarendon St, Oxford, OX2 6DP, United Kingdom. TEL 44-1865-556767, FAX 44-1865-556646, enquiry@oup.co.uk, http://www.oxfordjournals.org. Ed. Jeremy Phillips.

346.04 USA ISSN 1948-576X
K10
JOURNAL OF LAW, ETHICS AND INTELLECTUAL PROPERTY. Text in English. 2007. s-a. free (effective 2009). **Document type:** *Journal, Academic/Scholarly.*
Media: Online - full content.
Indexed: CA.
Published by: Scientific Journals International (Subsidiary of: Global Commerce & Communication, Inc), 1407 33rd St S, Saint Cloud, MN 56301. TEL 320-217-6019, info@scientificjournals.org.

346.04 608.7 USA ISSN 1087-6995
K10
JOURNAL OF TECHNOLOGY LAW & POLICY. Text in English. 1996. s-a. USD 35 domestic; USD 40 foreign (effective 2009). back issues avail. **Document type:** *Journal, Academic/Scholarly.* **Description:** Publishes articles concerning legal issues in technology law and policy.
Media: Online - full text.
Indexed: A01, CA, L03, P34, T02.
—CIS.
Published by: University of Florida, Levin College of Law, 218 Bruton-Geer Hall, Gainesville, FL 32611. TEL 352-273-0907, FAX 352-392-3800, flalaw@law.ufl.edu, http://www.law.ufl.edu/. Ed. Matthew Ocksrider.

608.7 341.7 GBR ISSN 1422-2213
K1401.A15
➤ **THE JOURNAL OF WORLD INTELLECTUAL PROPERTY.** Abbreviated title: J W I P. Text in English. 1998. bi-m. GBP 526 combined subscription in United Kingdom to institutions (print & online eds.); EUR 667 combined subscription in Europe to institutions (print & online eds.); USD 885 combined subscription in the Americas to institutions (print & online eds.); USD 1,028 combined subscription elsewhere to institutions (print & online eds.) (effective 2012). adv. 190 p./no.; back issues avail.; reprint service avail. from PSC. **Document type:** *Journal, Academic/Scholarly.* **Description:** Focuses on the intellectual property issues which affect the free flow of capital, goods and services throughout the world.
Related titles: Online - full text ed.: ISSN 1747-1796. GBP 477 in United Kingdom to institutions; EUR 607 in Europe to institutions; USD 804 in the Americas to institutions; USD 935 elsewhere to institutions (effective 2012) (from IngentaConnect).
Indexed: A22, A26, B01, B07, CA, E01, ESPM, FLP, LRI, P30, PAIS, RiskAb, T02.
—BLDSC (5072.681000), IE, Ingenta. **CCC.**
Published by: Wiley-Blackwell Publishing Ltd. (Subsidiary of: John Wiley & Sons, Inc.), 9600 Garsington Rd, Oxford, OX4 2DQ, United Kingdom. TEL 44-1865-776868, FAX 44-1865-714591, customerservices@blackwellpublishing.com. Ed. Daniel Gervais. Adv. contact Craig Pickett TEL 44-1865-476267. B&W page GBP 445, B&W page USD 823; 135 x 205. Circ: 560.

346.04 IND ISSN 0971-7544
JOURNALS OF INTELLECTUAL PROPERTY RIGHTS. Abbreviated title: J I P R. Text in English. 1996. bi-m. USD 600 (effective 2009). adv. bk.rev. Index. back issues avail. **Document type:** *Journal, Academic/Scholarly.* **Description:** Covers: Contributed/ Invited articles, case studies and patent reviews; Literature review - National and International IPR news; Technical notes on current IPR Issues; Book reviews; Conference reports.
Related titles: Online - full text ed.: ISSN 0975-1076. free (effective 2011).
Indexed: L13, SSCI, W07.
Published by: National Institute of Science Communication and Information Resources (N I S C A I R), Dr. K.S. Krishnan Marg, New Delhi, 110 012, India. TEL 91-11-25841647, FAX 91-11-25847062, http://www.niscair.res.in/. Ed. Madhu Sahni.

341.7582 JPN
KANSAI TOKKYU JOHO SENTA SHINKOKAI NYUSU/ASSOCIATION FOR KANSAI PATENT INFORMATION CENTER NEWS. Text in Japanese. 1959. irreg. (2-3/yr.).
Formerly (until May 1997): Kansai Bunken Senta Nyusu - Kansai Literature Center News (0289-1395)
Published by: Kansai Tokkyo Joho Senta Shinkokai/Association for Kansai Patent Information Center, Prefectural Patent Information Center, 2-7 Reinin-cho, Tennoji-ku, Osaka-shi, 543-0061, Japan. TEL 81-6-772-0704.

608.7 FIN ISSN 0789-4767
HF5565
KAUPPAREKISTERILEHTI/HANDELSREGISTERTIDNING. Text in Finnish, Swedish. 1943. w. EUR 420 domestic; EUR 669 in Scandinavia and Baltic region; EUR 775 in Europe; EUR 1,155 elsewhere (effective 2005). index. **Document type:** *Government.*
Formerly (until 1979): Kaupparekisteri (0022-9504)
Indexed: RASB.
Published by: (Finland. Patentti- ja Rekisterihallitus/National Board of Patents and Registration), Stellatum Oy, Tyopajankatu 6 A, Helsinki, 00580, Finland. TEL 358-9-8689700, FAX 358-9-86897070, info@stellatum.fi, http://www.stellatum.fi. Ed. Olli Koikkalainen TEL 358-9-6939500. Circ: 200.

347.78 AUT ISSN 1990-987X
KNOWLEDGE BASE COPYRIGHT LAW. Text in English, German. 2006. irreg. **Document type:** *Journal, Academic/Scholarly.*
Media: Online - full content.
Published by: Institut fuer Technikfolgen-Abschaetzung, Strohgasse 45, Vienna, 1030, Austria. TEL 43-1-515816582, FAX 43-1-7109883, tamail@oeaw.ac.at, http://www.oeaw.ac.at/ita/index.htm.

608.7 JPN ISSN 0287-3125
K11
KOGYO SHOYUKENHO KENKYU/STUDIES ON LAWS OF INDUSTRIAL PROPERTY RIGHTS. Text in Japanese. 1964. q. JPY 600 per issue.
Published by: Hanabusa Kogyo Shoyuken Kenkyujo Shuppanbu/Hanabusa Institute for the Protection of Industrial Property, Ochanomizu Sukuea B Kan, 1-6 Kanda-Surugadai, Chiyoda-ku, Tokyo, 101-0062, Japan.

346.04 DEU ISSN 1437-2355
KUNSTRECHT UND URHEBERRECHT. Abbreviated title: K U R. Text in German. 1999. bi-m. EUR 90; EUR 17.50 newsstand/cover (effective 2007). adv. **Document type:** *Journal, Academic/Scholarly.*
Indexed: RILM.
Published by: Schleuen Verlag OHG, Schwedter Str 9A, Berlin, 10119, Germany. TEL 49-30-40505825, kontakt@schleuen-verlag.de, http://www.schleuen-verlag.de. Ed. Ulf Bischof. Adv. contact Roland Meyer.

L E S NOUVELLES. (Licensing Executives Society) *see* TECHNOLOGY: COMPREHENSIVE WORKS

346.04 FRA ISSN 1954-4073
LAMY DROIT DE L'IMMATERIEL. FORMULAIRE COMMENTE. Text in French. 2006. base vol. plus updates 2/yr. looseleaf. EUR 613 base vol(s). print & CD-ROM eds. (effective 2010). **Document type:** *Trade.*
Related titles: CD-ROM ed.: ISSN 1959-8947; ◆ Series of: ProActa. ISSN 1636-8541.
Published by: Lamy S.A. (Subsidiary of: Wolters Kluwer France), 1 Rue Eugene et Armand Peugeot, Rueil-Malmaison, 92856 Cedex, France. TEL 33-1-76733000, FAX 33-1-76734809.

608.7 ESP ISSN 1139-7152
LICENCIAS ACTUALIDAD. Text in Spanish. 1998. q. EUR 72.89. adv. **Document type:** *Magazine, Trade.*

Published by: Ediciones Just, S.L., Violant d'Hungria, III, Barcelona, 08004, Spain. TEL 34-93-3253287, FAX 34-93-4244460, ejust@app.es, http://www.edicionesjust.com. Ed. Maria Dolores Just. adv.: page EUR 1,323; 210 x 297. Circ: 5,800.

659.1 DEU
LICENSING. Text in German. bi-m. EUR 50 domestic; EUR 66 foreign (effective 2007). adv. **Document type:** *Magazine, Trade.*
Published by: Licensing Press, Maybachstr 4, Roedermark, 63322, Germany. TEL 49-6074-917199, FAX 49-6074-919430. Ed., Pub. Fred Goepfardt. Adv. contact Hannah Kraus-Vetter. B&W page EUR 3,340, color page EUR 4,290. Circ: 14,000 (paid and controlled).

608.7 658 USA ISSN 0741-0107
THE LICENSING BOOK. Text in English. 1983. m. USD 36. adv. **Document type:** *Newsletter.* **Description:** Discusses the commercial use of sports team names.
Published by: Adventure Publishing, 1107 Broadway., Ste. 1204, New York, NY 10010-2891. TEL 212-575-4510, FAX 212-575-4521. Ed. Rich Levitt. Pub. Ernest Lustenring. Circ: 25,000.

602.7 USA ISSN 1040-4023
KF3145.A15
THE LICENSING JOURNAL. Text in English. 1982. 10/yr. USD 523; USD 63 per issue (effective 2011). adv. bk.rev. index. **Document type:** *Journal, Trade.* **Description:** Contains valuable strategies, cautionary tips and creative approaches to structure the secure licensing deals.
Formerly (until 1988): The Merchandising Reporter (0890-135X)
Related titles: Online - full text ed.
Indexed: A12, A13, A17, A26, ABIn, B01, B02, B06, B07, B09, B15, B17, B18, CA, CLI, G04, G06, G07, G08, I05, L03, LRI, P52, P53, P54, PQC, T02.
—**CCC.**
Published by: Aspen Publishers, Inc. (Subsidiary of: Wolters Kluwer N.V.), 76 Ninth Ave, 7th Fl, New York, NY 10011. TEL 212-771-0600, 800-317-3113, FAX 212-771-0885, ASPEN-CustomerService@wolterskluwer.com, https://www.aspenpublishers.com. Circ: 1,000. **Dist. by:** 7201 McKinney Cir, Frederick, MD 21704. TEL 301-698-7100, FAX 301-695-7931.

346.04 352.84 GBR ISSN 1473-706X
LICENSING LAW REPORTS. Text in English. 2001. q. GBP 225 (effective 2010). adv. back issues avail. **Document type:** *Report, Trade.* **Description:** Covers cases arising from disputes about licenses granted in the magistrates courts and by local authorities.
Related titles: Online - full text ed.
Published by: Jordan Publishing Ltd., 21 St Thomas St, Bristol, BS1 6JS, United Kingdom. TEL 44-117-9230600, FAX 44-117-9250486, customerservice@jordanpublishing.co.uk. Ed. Kerry Barker. Adv. contact Sue Reynolds TEL 44-117-9181230.

608 658.8 USA ISSN 8755-6235
HF5429.255
THE LICENSING LETTER. Text in English. 1977. s-m. USD 467 (effective 2008). 12 p./no.; back issues avail. **Document type:** *Newsletter, Trade.* **Description:** News on licensed properties, licensing representatives, manufacturer licenses and statistical data and contact lists.
Incorporates: Licensing Industry Newsletter
Related titles: Online - full text ed.
Indexed: B03, B11, I05, PROMT, T03.
Published by: E P M Communications, Inc., 160 Mercer St, 3rd Fl, New York, NY 10012. TEL 212-941-0099, 888-852-9467, FAX 212-941-1622, 888-852-3899, info@epmcom.com. Ed. Marty Brochstein. Pub. Ira Mayer TEL 212-941-1633 ext 27.

346.04 USA
LITALERT (ONLINE). Text in English. 200?. base vol. plus w. updates. **Document type:** *Database, Trade.* **Description:** Contains records of IP lawsuits filed in the 94 US District Courts since 1973, as reported to the Commissioner of the US Patent and Trademark office.
Media: Online - full content.
Published by: Thomson Reuters (Subsidiary of: Thomson Reuters Corp.), 1500 Spring Garden, 4th Fl, Philadelphia, PA 19130. TEL 215-386-0100, 800-336-4474, FAX 215-386-2911, general.info@thomson.com, http://science.thomsonreuters.com/.

608.7 MWI ISSN 0025-1267
MALAWI PATENT JOURNAL AND TRADE MARKS JOURNAL. Text in English. 1966. m. pat.; tr.mk. **Document type:** *Government.*
Published by: Ministry of Finance, PO Box 30049, Lilongwe, Malawi. TEL 265-782199. **Orders to:** Government Printer, PO Box 37, Zomba, Malawi. TEL 265-50-523155.

341.758 658.575 GBR ISSN 0960-5002
K13
MANAGING INTELLECTUAL PROPERTY. Text in English. 1990. 10/yr. GBP 750 combined subscription domestic (print & online eds.); EUR 940 combined subscription in Europe (print & online eds.); USD 1,465 combined subscription elsewhere (print & online eds.) (effective 2010). **Document type:** *Magazine, Trade.*
Related titles: Online - full text ed.; ◆ Supplement(s): I P Handbook (Year).
Indexed: A09, A10, A12, A17, A22, A26, ABIn, B01, B02, B03, B06, B07, B08, B09, B11, B15, B17, B18, C12, CA, ELJI, G04, G08, I05, LJI, LRI, P21, P34, P48, P51, P53, P54, PQC, T02, T03, V03, V04.
—BLDSC (5359.287960), IE, Ingenta. **CCC.**
Published by: Euromoney Institutional Investor Plc., Nestor House, Playhouse Yard, London, EC4V 5EX, United Kingdom. TEL 44-20-7779-8673, information@euromoneyplc.com, http://www.euromoneyplc.com/. Ed. James Nurton TEL 44-20-77798685. **Dist. in US by:** American Educational Systems, PO Box 246, New York, NY 10024-0246. TEL 800-431-1579.

608.7 NLD ISSN 1568-0703
MARKASSIET/BENELUX MERK REGISTEREN. Variant title: Merkenregister. Text in Dutch, French. 1976. d. EUR 240 (effective 2009).
Formerly (until 2000): Benelux-Merkenblad (0165-8964); Which incorporated (1881-1971): Merkenblad Benelux - Marques Benelux Recueil (0026-007X)
Media: CD-ROM. **Related titles:** CD-ROM ed.
Published by: Benelux Bureau voor de Intellectuele Eigendom, Bordewijklaan 15, PO Box 90404, The Hague, 2509 LK, Netherlands. TEL 31-70-3491111, FAX 31-70-3475708, info@boip.int, http://www.boip.int.

608.7 DEU ISSN 1436-9265
MARKENR; Zeitschrift fuer deutsches, europaeisches und internationales Markenrecht. Text in German. 1999. 10/yr. EUR 178; EUR 24.50 newsstand/cover (effective 2011). adv. **Document type:** *Journal, Trade.*
Indexed: IBR, IBZ.
Published by: Carl Heymanns Verlag KG (Subsidiary of: Wolters Kluwer Deutschland GmbH), Luxemburger Str 449, Cologne, 50939, Germany. TEL 49-221-943730, FAX 49-221-94373901, marketing@heymanns.com, http://www.heymanns.com. Adv. contact Marcus Kipp. Circ: 850 (paid).

346.04 NLD ISSN 1567-8318
MAX PLANK SERIES ON ASIAN INTELLECTUAL PROPERTY LAW. Text in English. irreg. price varies. **Document type:** *Monographic series, Academic/Scholarly.*
Published by: (Max-Planck-Institut for Foreign and International Patent, Copyright and Competition Law DEU), Kluwer Law International (Subsidiary of: Aspen Publishers, Inc.), PO Box 316, Alphen aan den Rijn, 2400 AH, Netherlands. TEL 31-172-641562, FAX 31-172-641555, sales@kluwerlaw.com, http://www.kluwerlaw.com. Ed. Christopher Heath.

341.7588 USA
MCCARTHY ON TRADEMARKS AND UNFAIR COMPETITION. Text in English. 19??. 7 base vols. plus q. updates. looseleaf. USD 3,229 base vol(s). (effective 2010). **Document type:** *Journal, Trade.* **Description:** Explains and analyzes trademark law with clear, concise analyses of cases and statutes; provides advice on registering and protecting trademarks.
Published by: Thomson West (Subsidiary of: Thomson Reuters Corp.), 610 Opperman Dr, Eagan, MN 55123. TEL 651-687-7000, 800-344-5008, west.customer.service@thomson.com.

346.04 USA ISSN 1539-6177
KF2991.3
MEALEY'S LITIGATION REPORT: COPYRIGHT. Text in English. 2001 (Mar.). m. USD 963 (effective 2011). **Document type:** *Report, Trade.* **Description:** Features unbiased news stories, case summaries, attorney listings, and the full text of court documents.
Related titles: Online - full text ed.: ISSN 2159-1369.
—**CCC.**
Published by: LexisNexis (Subsidiary of: Reed Elsevier Group plc), 1016 W Ninth Ave, 1st Fl, King of Prussia, PA 19406. TEL 215 564-1788, 800 448-1515, customer.support@lexisnexis.com. Ed. Melissa Ritti.

346.738 374.3 USA ISSN 1065-9390
KF2972
MEALEY'S LITIGATION REPORT: INTELLECTUAL PROPERTY. Text in English. 1992 (Oct.). s-m. USD 1,440 (effective 2011). index. **Document type:** *Report, Trade.* **Description:** Provides timely information on international developments in intellectual property litigation, including copyright, patent, trademark, trade secret and unfair competition disputes, issues related to the internet and disputes over insurance coverage for intellectual property suits.
Related titles: Diskette ed.; Online - full text ed.: ISSN 2158-9836.
—**CCC.**
Published by: LexisNexis (Subsidiary of: Reed Elsevier Group plc), 1016 W Ninth Ave, 1st Fl, King of Prussia, PA 19406. TEL 215 564-1788, 800 448-1515, customer.support@lexisnexis.com. Ed. Melissa Ritti.

346.73 347.30648 USA ISSN 1070-4043
KF3109
MEALEY'S LITIGATION REPORT: PATENTS. Text in English. 1992 (Nov.). s-m. looseleaf. USD 1,026 (effective 2008). adv. index. **Document type:** *Newsletter, Trade.* **Description:** Covers the highly specialized area of patent litigation, from the district courts to the Federal Circuit to the U.S. Supreme Court. Topics include infringement, claim interpretation, biotechnology issues, affirmative defenses, jurisdiction, discovery, and insurance coverage.
Incorporates (1996-1998): Mealey's Litigation Reports. Biotechnology (1091-8345)
Related titles: Diskette ed.; Online - full text ed.: USD 930 (effective 2002).
—**CCC.**
Published by: Mealey Publications & Conferences Group (Subsidiary of: LexisNexis North America), 1018 W 9th Ave, 3rd Fl, King of Prussia, PA 19406. TEL 610-768-7800, 800-632-5397, info@mealeys.com, http://www.mealeys.com. Ed. Melissa Ritti. Pub. Tom Hagy. R&P Scott M. Jacobs.

MEALEY'S LITIGATION REPORT: TRADEMARKS. *see* LAW—Corporate Law

608 616.027 USA ISSN 2154-9931
KF3827.M4
MEDICAL DEVICE PATENTS. Text in English. 2008. a. USD 219 per issue (effective 2010). **Document type:** *Handbook/Manual/Guide, Trade.* **Description:** Addresses the unique aspects of U.S. medical device patents, specifically durable medical equipment, and examines their grant and enforcement.
Published by: Thomson West (Subsidiary of: Thomson Reuters Corp.), 610 Opperman Dr, Eagan, MN 55123. TEL 651-687-7000, FAX 651-687-6674, west.customer.service@thomson.com.

608 330 USA ISSN 1552-5597
MEDICAL PATENT BUSINESS WEEK. Text in English. 2004. w. USD 2,295 in US & Canada; USD 2,495 elsewhere; USD 2,525 combined subscription in US & Canada (print & online eds.); USD 2,755 combined subscription elsewhere (print & online eds.) (effective 2008). back issues avail. **Document type:** *Newsletter, Trade.*
Related titles: E-mail ed.; Online - full text ed.: ISSN 1552-5600. USD 2,295 combined subscription (online & email eds.); single user (effective 2008).
Indexed: A15, ABIn, B16, H13, P10, P20, P21, P48, P51, P52, P53, P54, PQC.
Published by: NewsRx, 2727 Paces Ferry Rd SE, Ste 2-440, Atlanta, GA 30339. TEL 770-435-8286, 800-726-4550, FAX 770-435-6800, pressrelease@newsrx.com. Pub. Susan Hasty TEL 770-507-7777.

346.04 344.041 USA ISSN 1551-5230
MEDICAL PATENT LAW WEEKLY. Text in English. 2004. w. USD 2,295 in US & Canada; USD 2,495 elsewhere; USD 2,525 combined subscription in US & Canada (print & online eds.); USD 2,755 combined subscription elsewhere (print & online eds.) (effective 2008). back issues avail. **Document type:** *Newsletter, Trade.*
Related titles: E-mail ed.; Online - full text ed.: ISSN 1551-5249. USD 2,295 combined subscription (online & email eds.); single user (effective 2008).
Indexed: L10, P10, P21, P48, P53, P54, PQC.
Published by: NewsRx, 2727 Paces Ferry Rd SE, Ste 2-440, Atlanta, GA 30339. TEL 770-435-8286, 800-726-4550, FAX 770-435-6800, pressrelease@newsrx.com, http://www.newsrx.com. Pub. Susan Hasty TEL 770-507-7777.

608 USA ISSN 1552-5619
MEDICAL PATENT WEEK. Text in English. 2004. w. USD 2,295 in US & Canada; USD 2,495 elsewhere; USD 2,525 combined subscription in US & Canada (print & online eds.); USD 2,755 combined subscription elsewhere (print & online eds.) (effective 2008). back issues avail. **Document type:** *Newsletter, Trade.* **Description:** Covers the latest patent filings for new drugs, genetic discoveries, medical materials and devices.
Related titles: E-mail ed.; Online - full text ed.: ISSN 1552-5627. 2004. USD 2,295 combined subscription (online & email eds.); single user (effective 2008).
Indexed: H13, P10, P20, P21, P48, P52, P53, P54, PQC.
Published by: NewsRx, 2727 Paces Ferry Rd SE, Ste 2-440, Atlanta, GA 30339. TEL 770-435-8286, 800-726-4550, FAX 770-435-6800, pressrelease@newsrx.com. Pub. Susan Hasty TEL 770-507-7777.

346.04 USA
MILGRIM ON LICENSING. Text in English. 1991. 4 base vols. plus irreg. updates. looseleaf. USD 680 base vol(s). (effective 2008). Supplement avail. **Document type:** *Handbook/Manual/Guide, Trade.* **Description:** Covers licensing in all areas of intellectual property and provides practical guidance on drafting agreements and contracts.
Related titles: CD-ROM ed.: USD 687 (effective 2008).
Published by: Matthew Bender & Co., Inc. (Subsidiary of: LexisNexis North America), 1275 Broadway, Albany, NY 12204. TEL 518-487-3000, 800-424-4200, FAX 518-487-3083, international@bender.com, http://bender.lexisnexis.com. Ed. Valri Nesbit.

346.04 USA
MILGRIM ON TRADE SECRETS. Text in English. 1967. 4 base vols. plus irreg. updates. looseleaf. USD 1,659 base vol(s). (effective 2008). **Document type:** *Handbook/Manual/Guide, Trade.* **Description:** Includes information on the protection and utilization of trade secrets and other intangible property.
Related titles: CD-ROM ed.: USD 1,674 (effective 2008).
Published by: Matthew Bender & Co., Inc. (Subsidiary of: LexisNexis North America), 1275 Broadway, Albany, NY 12204. TEL 518-487-3000, 800-424-4200, FAX 518-487-3083, international@bender.com, http://bender.lexisnexis.com. Ed. Roger Milgrim.

608.7 340 DEU ISSN 0026-6884
KK2721.3
MITTEILUNGEN DER DEUTSCHEN PATENTANWAELTE. Text in German. 1909. m. EUR 192; EUR 19 newsstand/cover (effective 2011). adv. bk.rev. abstr.; pat. index. **Document type:** *Bulletin, Trade.*
Indexed: A22.
—IE. **CCC.**
Published by: (Germany. Patentanwaltskammer), Carl Heymanns Verlag KG (Subsidiary of: Wolters Kluwer Deutschland GmbH), Luxemburger Str 449, Cologne, 50939, Germany. TEL 49-221-943730, FAX 49-221-94373901, marketing@heymanns.com, http://www.heymanns.com. Adv. contact Marcus Kipp. Circ: 1,550 (paid and controlled).

MUSIC & COPYRIGHT. *see* MUSIC

602.7 780 USA ISSN 1067-876X
ML1
MUSICOPYRIGHT INTELLIGENCE; a newsletter of financial success through copyright ownership. Text in English. 1993. m. USD 195; USD 220 in Canada; USD 270 elsewhere. adv. bk.rev. charts; illus.; stat. index. back issues avail. **Document type:** *Newsletter.* **Description:** Provides investigative research, news and perspectives on music industry finance, and money-making ideas for success in a growing world of market economy.
Related titles: Online - full text ed.
Published by: E.S. Proteus, Inc., 1657 The Fairway, Ste 123, Jenkintown, PA 19046. jazz@jazzimprov.com. Ed. Eric Nemeyer. Circ: 2,000.

346.048 SWE ISSN 0027-6723
K14
➤ **N I R/NORDIC INTELLECTUAL PROPERTY LAW REVIEW.** (Nordiskt Immateriellt Raettsskydd) Variant title: Nordiskt Immateriellt Raettsskydd. Text in Danish, Norwegian, Swedish; Summaries in English. 1932. 6/yr. SEK 1,190 (effective 2010). adv. bk.rev. index, cum.index: 1932-1955, 1956-1962, 1963-1969, 1970-1976, 1977-1984, 1985-1992. back issues avail. **Document type:** *Journal, Academic/Scholarly.*
Formerly (until 1949): Nordiskt Industriellt Raettsskydd
Related titles: Online - full text ed.
Indexed: FLP.
Published by: (Nordiskt Immateriellt Raettsskydd/Nordic Intellectual Property Law Review), Eddy.se AB, Norra Kyrkogatan 3, Visby, 62155, Sweden. TEL 46-498-253900, FAX 46-498-249789, order@eddy.se, info@eddy.se, http://www.eddy.se. Ed. Per Jonas Nordell TEL 46-8-164078. Adv. contact Adam Weijmers. page SEK 13,500; 110 x 200.

346.04 USA
NEW YORK INTELLECTUAL PROPERTY HANDBOOK. Text in English. 1991. a. looseleaf. USD 131 (effective 2009). **Document type:** *Handbook/Manual/Guide, Trade.* **Description:** Reference to the New York and federal statutes and NYCRR regulations governing intellectual property matters.
Related titles: CD-ROM ed.
Published by: Matthew Bender & Co., Inc. (Subsidiary of: LexisNexis North America), 1275 Broadway, Albany, NY 12204. TEL 518-487-3000, 800-424-4200, FAX 518-487-3083, international@bender.com, http://bender.lexisnexis.com. Ed. Hugh Hansen.

P

608.7 NZL ISSN 1359-9054
K14
NEW ZEALAND INTELLECTUAL PROPERTY JOURNAL. Text in English. 1995. q. **Document type:** *Journal, Academic/Scholarly.* **Description:** Forum in which informed industry experts, leading legal practitioners, legislators and academics air their views and opinions on a whole range of intellectual property matters including copyright, designs, patents, trade marks, confidential information, passing off, Fair Trading Act issues, and plant variety rights.
Indexed: INZP.
—BLDSC (6092.476000), Ingenta.
Published by: Butterworths of New Zealand Ltd. (Subsidiary of: LexisNexis Asia Pacific), PO Box 472, Wellington, 6140, New Zealand. TEL 64-4-3851479, FAX 64-4-3851598, Customer.Service@lexisnexis.co.nz. Ed. Delia Browne. Circ: 200 (paid).

608.7 346.048 328 NZL ISSN 1175-1487
NEW ZEALAND. PATENT OFFICE. JOURNAL (CD-ROM). Text in English. 1998. m. free (effective 2010). **Document type:** *Journal, Government.* **Description:** Contains the official source of New Zealand's patent, trademark and registered design information.
Media: CD-ROM. **Related titles:** Online - full text ed.: Patent Office Journal. ISSN 1179-9714. free (effective 2010).
Published by: Intellectual Property Office of New Zealand (Subsidiary of: Ministry of Economic Development), Marion Sq, PO Box 9241, Wellington, 6141, New Zealand. TEL 64-3-9622607, 508-447-669, info@iponz.govt.nz.

608 GBR ISSN 0967-8565
NEWS EXCHANGE. Text in English. 1986. bi-m. free to members (effective 2010). **Document type:** *Magazine, Trade.*
—BLDSC (6104.010000). **CCC.**
Published by: Licensing Executives Society (Britain and Ireland), c/o Northern Networking Events Ltd, Glenfinnan Suit, Braeview House, 9-11 Braeview Pl, East Kilbride, G74 3XH, United Kingdom. TEL 44-1355-244966, FAX 44-1355-249959, les@northernnetworking.co.uk. Ed. Mary Elson.

346.04 USA
NIMMER ON COPYRIGHT. Text in English. 1963. 11 base vols. plus updates 3/yr. looseleaf. USD 1,885 base vol(s). (effective 2008). **Document type:** *Handbook/Manual/Guide, Trade.* **Description:** Provides copyright law support and includes wide-ranging analysis of: copyright protection of computer software, liability of on-line service providers for copyright infringement and international copyright protection.
Related titles: CD-ROM ed.: USD 1,906 base vol(s). (effective 2008).
Published by: Matthew Bender & Co., Inc. (Subsidiary of: LexisNexis North America), 1275 Broadway, Albany, NY 12204. TEL 518-487-3000, 800-424-4200, FAX 518-487-3083, international@bender.com, http://bender.lexisnexis.com. Ed. David Nimmer.

NONWOVENS PATENT NEWS. *see* TEXTILE INDUSTRIES AND FABRICS

346.048 NOR ISSN 1503-5808
NORSK DESIGNTIDENDE. Text in Norwegian. 1971. s-m. illus. index. **Document type:** *Government.*
Former titles (until 2003): Norsk Moenstertidende (Online) (1503-4941); (until 2002): Norsk Moenstertidende (Print) (0803-6985); (until 1992): Norsk Tidende for det Industrielle Rettsvern. Del 3: Moenstre (0029-2184)
Media: Online - full content.
—Linda Hall.
Published by: Patentstyret/Norwegian Patent Office, Koebenhavngate 10, Postboks 8160, Dep, Oslo, 0033, Norway. TEL 47-22-387300, FAX 47-22-387301.

346.048 NOR ISSN 1503-4933
NORSK PATENTTIDENDE (ONLINE). Text in Norwegian. 2002. w. pat. back issues avail. **Document type:** *Government.*
Media: Online - full content.
Published by: Patentstyret/Norwegian Patent Office, Koebenhavngate 10, Postboks 8160, Dep, Oslo, 0033, Norway. TEL 47-22-387300, FAX 47-22-387301, mail@patentstyret.no.

346.048 NOR ISSN 1503-4925
CODEN: NTAVA
NORSK VAREMERKETIDENDE (ONLINE). Text in Norwegian. 1911. w. illus.; tr.mk. index. back issues avail. **Document type:** *Government.*
Former titles (until 2003): Norsk Varemerketidende (Print) (0803-6977); (until 1992): Norsk Tidende for det Industrielle Rettsvern. Del 2: Varemerker (0029-2192)
Media: Online - full content.
—Linda Hall.
Published by: Patentstyret/Norwegian Patent Office, Koebenhavngate 10, Postboks 8160, Dep, Oslo, 0033, Norway. TEL 47-22-387300, FAX 47-22-387301.

340 AUT ISSN 0029-8921
KJJ1155.A13
OESTERREICHISCHE BLAETTER FUER GEWERBLICHEN RECHTSSCHUTZ UND URHEBERRECHT. Text in German. 1952. bi-m. EUR 251; EUR 50.20 newsstand/cover (effective 2011). adv. bk.rev. index. reprint service avail. from SCH. **Document type:** *Journal, Academic/Scholarly.*
Related titles: Microfiche ed.; Microfilm ed.
Indexed: IBR, IBZ, RASB.
Published by: (Oesterreichische Vereinigung fuer Gewerblichen Rechtsschutz und Urheberrecht), Manz'sche Verlags- und Universitaetsbuchhandlung GmbH, Johannesgasse 23, Vienna, W 1010, Austria. TEL 43-1-531610, FAX 43-1-53161181, verlag@manz.at. Adv. contact Heidrun Engel. Circ: 900 (paid and controlled).

OESTERREICHISCHE SCHRIFTENREIHE ZUM GEWERBLICHEN RECHTSCHUTZ, URHEBER- UND MEDIENRECHT. *see* LAW

602.7 AUT ISSN 0029-9782
OESTERREICHISCHER MARKENANZEIGER. Text in German. 1948. m. EUR 131.82 (effective 2005). tr.mk. index. **Document type:** *Journal, Government.*
Published by: Oesterreichisches Patentamt, Dresdner Str 87, Vienna, 1200, Austria. TEL 43-1-534240, FAX 43-1-53424110, info@patent.bmvit.gv.at, http://www.patentamt.at. Circ: 170.

602.7 AUT
OESTERREICHISCHER MUSTERANZEIGER. Text in German. 1991. m. EUR 117 (effective 2005). **Document type:** *Journal, Government.*
Published by: Oesterreichisches Patentamt, Dresdner Str 87, Vienna, 1200, Austria. TEL 43-1-534240, FAX 43-1-53424110, info@patent.bmvit.gv.at, http://www.patentamt.at. Circ: 100.

608.7 AUT
OESTERREICHISCHES GEBRAUCHSMUSTERBLATT. Text in German. 1994. m. **Document type:** *Journal, Government.*
Published by: Oesterreichisches Patentamt, Dresdner Str 87, Vienna, 1200, Austria. TEL 43-1-534240, FAX 43-1-53424110, info@patent.bmvit.gv.at, http://www.patentamt.at. Circ: 100.

608.7 AUT ISSN 0029-9944
CODEN: ORPBAD
OESTERREICHISCHES PATENTBLATT. Text in German. 1899. m. (in 2 parts). bibl.; charts; illus.; pat. index. **Document type:** *Journal, Government.* **Description:** Decisions and statistics concerning patents, utility models, trademarks and industrial designs.
Published by: Oesterreichisches Patentamt, Dresdner Str 87, Vienna, 1200, Austria. TEL 43-1-534240, FAX 43-1-53424110, info@patent.bmvit.gv.at, http://www.patentamt.at. Circ: 330.

THE ONLINE INVENTOR. *see* BUSINESS AND ECONOMICS—Marketing And Purchasing

▼ **OPEN SOURCE SCIENCE JOURNAL.** *see* PUBLISHING AND BOOK TRADE

346.04 CHE ISSN 1020-6264
P C T GAZETTE (BILINGUAL EDITION). (Patent Cooperation Treaty) Variant title: Patent Cooperation Treaty Gazette. Text in English, French. 1998. m.
Formed by the merger of (1978-1998): Gazette du P C T (Ed. Francaise) (0250-7749); (1978-1998): P C T Gazette (English Edition) (0250-7757)
Related titles: Online - full content ed.: ISSN 1564-796X.
Indexed: PetrolAb.
Published by: World Intellectual Property Organization/Organisation Mondiale de la Propriete Intellectuelle, Publications and Public Information Section, 32 Chemin des Colombettes, Geneva 20, 1211, Switzerland. wipo.mail@wipo.int.

608.7 CHE ISSN 1020-072X
P C T NEWSLETTER. (Patent Cooperation Treaty) Text in English. 1994. m. CHF 70 (effective 2005). back issues avail. **Document type:** *Newsletter, Trade.*
—IE.
Published by: World Intellectual Property Organization/Organisation Mondiale de la Propriete Intellectuelle, Publications Sales and Distribution Unit, 34 Chemin des Colombettes, Geneva 20, 1211, Switzerland. TEL 41-22-338-9111, FAX 41-22-740-1812, wipo.mail@wipo.int. Circ: 3,000 (controlled).

608.7 CAN ISSN 0079-015X
PATENT AND TRADEMARK INSTITUTE OF CANADA. ANNUAL PROCEEDINGS. Text in English. 1928. a. membership. adv. **Document type:** *Proceedings.*
Published by: Intellectual Property Institute of Canada, 60 Queen St, Ste 606, Ottawa, ON K1P 5Y7, Canada. TEL 613-234-0516. Adv. contact Karen Klingbeil. Circ: (controlled).

340 USA
PATENT AND TRADEMARK OFFICE NOTICES. Text in English. 19??. w. USD 430; USD 20 per issue (effective 2011). back issues avail. **Document type:** *Government.* **Description:** Publishes the notices in each weekly edition of the Official Gazette.
Related titles: Online - full text ed.: free (effective 2011).
Published by: U.S. Patent and Trademark Office, Madison Bldgs (E & W), 600 Dulany St, Alexandria, VA 22314. TEL 571 272-1000, 800-786-9199, ebc@uspto.gov.

602.7 USA ISSN 0882-9098
K16
PATENT AND TRADEMARK OFFICE SOCIETY. JOURNAL. Abbreviated title: J P T O S. Text in English. 1918. m. free to members (effective 2010). adv. back issues avail.; reprint service avail. from WSH. **Document type:** *Journal, Academic/Scholarly.* **Description:** Provides a medium for the exchange of information and thought in the intellectual-property field. Discusses technical subjects and other knowledge of the functional attributes of patent, trademark, and copyright law.
Formerly (until 1984): Patent Office Society. Journal (0096-3577)
Related titles: CD-ROM ed.; Microfiche ed.: (from WSH); Microform ed.: (from WSH); Online - full text ed.
Indexed: A20, A22, A26, B02, B04, B11, B15, B17, B18, BRD, CLI, G04, G06, G07, G08, I01, I03, I05, ILP, LRI, P06, P30, SCOPUS, SSCI, W03, W05.
—IE, Infotrieve, Ingenta, Linda Hall. **CCC.**
Published by: Patent and Trademark Office Society, PO Box 2600, Arlington, VA 22202. TEL 703-305-9643, FAX 703-266-1600. Ed. Louis Zarfas. R&P Karin Ferriter. Adv. contact Tariq Hafiz. page USD 300; 6.75 x 4.5. Circ: 5,000 (paid).

346.04 608.7 USA
PATENT APPLICATIONS HANDBOOK. Text in English. 19??. base vol. plus a. updates. USD 791 base vol(s). (effective 2010). **Document type:** *Handbook/Manual/Guide, Trade.* **Description:** Includes information on: exactly what must appear in an application; how information must be prepared and presented to the Patent and Trademark Office; procedures and tips for filing and prosecuting applications; fundamentals of preparing a disclosure and for drafting claims; the proper subject matter for an invention; how and when to submit prior art under the new Rules; information regarding reexamination and reissue.
Published by: Thomson West (Subsidiary of: Thomson Reuters Corp.), 610 Opperman Dr, Eagan, MN 55123. TEL 651-687-7000, 800-344-5008, west.customer.service@thomson.com.

346.73 608.7 USA ISSN 1948-349X
KF3165.A3
PATENT ATTORNEYS - AGENTS SEARCH. Variant title: Patent Attorneys and Agents Registered to Practice before the U.S. Patent and Trademark Office. Text in English. 19??. d. free (effective 2011). **Document type:** *Government.* **Description:** Lists patent attorneys and agents registered to practice before the U.S. Patent and Trademark Office alphabetically and by geographic region.
Former titles (until 200?): Attorneys and Agents Registered to Practice before the U.S. Patent and Trademark Office (Print) (0361-3844); Attorneys and Agents Registered to Practice before the U.S. Patent Office (0092-5934); Roster of Attorneys and Agents Registered to Practice before the U.S. Patent Office; Directory of Registered Patent Attorneys and Agents (0565-9582)
Media: Online - full text.
—Linda Hall.
Published by: U.S. Patent and Trademark Office, General Information Services Division, PO Box 1450, Alexandria, VA 22313. TEL 571-272-1000, 800-786-9199, usptoinfo@uspto.gov, http://www.uspto.gov. **Subscr. to:** U.S. Government Printing Office, Superintendent of Documents.

346.04 USA ISSN 2155-2436
K1501.3
▼ **PATENT CLAIM INTERPRETATION**; global edition. Text in English. 2009. a. USD 239 per issue (effective 2010). **Document type:** *Handbook/Manual/Guide, Trade.* **Description:** Provides an in-depth understanding of international patent claims and the varying interpretations that exist among different cultures.
Published by: Thomson West (Subsidiary of: Thomson Reuters Corp.), 610 Opperman Dr, Eagan, MN 55123. TEL 651-687-7000, FAX 651-687-6674, west.support@thomson.com.

602.7 GBR
PATENT COOPERATION TREATY HANDBOOK. Text in English. 1997. base vol. plus updates 2/yr. looseleaf. GBP 539 base vol(s). domestic; EUR 712 base vol(s). in Europe; USD 927 base vol(s). elsewhere (effective 2011). **Document type:** *Handbook/Manual/Guide, Trade.* **Description:** Provides detailed coverage of the procedures for international applications under the Patent Cooperation Treaty, plus the general principle of national stages.
Published by: Sweet & Maxwell Ltd. (Subsidiary of: Thomson Reuters Corp.), 100 Avenue Rd, London, NW3 3PF, United Kingdom. TEL 44-20-73937000, FAX 44-20-74491144, sweetandmaxwell.customer.services@thomson.com. **Subscr. to:** PO Box 1000, Andover SP10 9AF, United Kingdom. TEL 44-20-73938051, sweetandmaxwell.international.queries@thomson.com.

PATENT FAST-ALERT. *see* PHARMACY AND PHARMACOLOGY

608.7 602.7 ZAF ISSN 0031-286X
T319.S7 CODEN: PASDEW
PATENT JOURNAL INCLUDING TRADEMARKS, DESIGNS AND COPYRIGHT. Key Title: Patentjoernaal Insluitende Handelsmerke, Modelle en Outeursreg. Text in Afrikaans, English. 1948. m. ZAR 28.40 (effective 2006). charts; illus.; pat.; tr.mk. **Document type:** *Journal, Government.*
Indexed: ChemAb.
—CASDDS, PADDS.
Published by: South Africa. Government Printing Works, 149 Bosman St, Private Bag X85, Pretoria, 0001, South Africa. TEL 27-12-3344507, FAX 27-12-323-9574. Ed. J Barton.

340 USA ISSN 0192-8198
KF3114
PATENT LAW HANDBOOK. Text in English. 1978. a. USD 664 per issue (effective 2010). **Document type:** *Handbook/Manual/Guide, Trade.* **Description:** Provides information on inequitable conduct; defenses and counterclaims; infringement; willful infringement; remedies; appeal; pretrial and trial issues; Patent Office proceedings; licensing; patent proceedings in other forms, including ITC proceedings and claims court.
Published by: Thomson West (Subsidiary of: Thomson Reuters Corp.), 610 Opperman Dr, Eagan, MN 55123. TEL 651-687-7000, 800-344-5008, west.customer.service@thomson.com.

346.04 608.7 USA
PATENT LAW: LEGAL AND ECONOMIC PRINCIPLES. Text in English. 1992. 2 base vols. plus a. updates. looseleaf. USD 632 base vol(s). (effective 2010). **Document type:** *Journal, Trade.* **Description:** Describes patent law by explaining how the major rules of patent law relate to the purpose of a patent system. Surveys how a law and economics approach is applied to patent law.
Published by: Thomson West (Subsidiary of: Thomson Reuters Corp.), 610 Opperman Dr, Eagan, MN 55123. TEL 651-687-7000, 800-344-5008, west.customer.service@thomson.com.

346.0496 USA
PATENT LAW PERSPECTIVES. Text in English. 1970. 8 base vols. plus irreg. updates. looseleaf. USD 2,046 base vol(s). (effective 2008). **Document type:** *Journal, Trade.* **Description:** Analysis of developments in patent law and the effects of these developments on current and future practice.
Related titles: CD-ROM ed.: USD 1,370 (effective 2002).
Published by: Matthew Bender & Co., Inc. (Subsidiary of: LexisNexis North America), 1275 Broadway, Albany, NY 12204. TEL 518-487-3000, 800-424-4200, FAX 518-487-3083, international@bender.com, http://bender.lexisnexis.com. Ed. Martin Adelman.

346.04 USA ISSN 1549-9871
KF3091.A3
THE PATENT LAWYER. Text in English. 2004. q. free to qualified personnel. **Document type:** *Magazine, Trade.* **Description:** Aims to raise the profile of the association and its member firms through the timely, thoughtful analysis of current issues in patent law.
Published by: Association of Patent Law Firms, PO Box 7418, Washington, DC 20044-7418. TEL info@aplf.org, http://www.aplf.org. Ed. Robert Ambrogi. Pub. James Kayden. Adv. contact Paul Kuttner.

346.0486 USA
PATENT LICENSING TRANSACTIONS. Text in English. 1968. 2 base vols. plus irreg. updates. looseleaf. USD 807 base vol(s). (effective 2008). **Document type:** *Journal, Trade.* **Description:** Includes coverage of royalty bases and rates, domestic and foreign patent licensing, assignments, territorial limitations and duration, termination of agreeements, antitrust, and U.S. taxation of domestic and foreign patent transactions.
Related titles: CD-ROM ed.
Published by: Matthew Bender & Co., Inc. (Subsidiary of: LexisNexis North America), 1275 Broadway, Albany, NY 12204. TEL 518-487-3000, 800-424-4200, FAX 518-487-3083, international@bender.com, http://bender.lexisnexis.com. Ed. Harold Einhorn.

346.0486 USA
PATENT LITIGATION: PROCEDURES & TACTICS. Text in English. 1971. 3 base vols. plus irreg. updates. looseleaf. USD 472 base vol(s). (effective 2008). Supplement avail. **Document type:** *Handbook/Manual/Guide, Trade.* **Description:** Discusses all stages of patent litigation, contains sample jury instructions and issues checklist and litigation forms.
Related titles: CD-ROM ed.
Published by: Matthew Bender & Co., Inc. (Subsidiary of: LexisNexis North America), 1275 Broadway, Albany, NY 12204. TEL 800-424-4200, FAX 518-487-3083, international@bender.com, http://bender.lexisnexis.com. Eds. Ethan Horwitz, Lester Horwitz.

608.781 SWE ISSN 0347-500X
PATENT- OCH REGISTRERINGSVERKETS FOERFATTNINGSSAMLING; P R V F S. Text in Swedish. 1977-1987; resumed 1991. irreg. SEK 4 per page.
Published by: Patent- och Registreringsverket, Patentverket, Fack 5055, Stockholm, 10242, Sweden.

608.7 USA
PATENT OFFICE RULES AND PRACTICE. Text in English. 1959. 11 base vols. plus q. updates. looseleaf. USD 2,881 combined subscription (print & CD-ROM eds.) (effective 2008). **Document type:** *Handbook/Manual/Guide, Trade.* **Description:** Contains analysis of the patent and trademark office rules of practice.
Related titles: CD-ROM ed.: USD 2,987 (effective 2008).
Published by: Matthew Bender & Co., Inc. (Subsidiary of: LexisNexis North America), 1275 Broadway, Albany, NY 12204. TEL 518-487-3000, 800-424-4200, FAX 518-487-3083, international@bender.com, http://bender.lexisnexis.com. Ed. Lester Horwitz.

PATENT STRATEGY AND MANAGEMENT. *see* LAW

346.04 USA ISSN 1535-1610
PATENT, TRADEMARK & COPYRIGHT LAW DAILY. Text in English. 2001. d. USD 3,073 (effective 2010 - 2011). back issues avail. **Document type:** *Newsletter, Trade.* **Description:** Reports on intellectual property cases, regulatory developments, and trends.
Media: Online - full text. **Related titles:** E-mail ed.
—CCC.
Published by: The Bureau of National Affairs, Inc., 1801 S Bell St, Arlington, VA 22202. TEL 703-341-3000, 800-372-1033, FAX 703-341-4634, bnaplus@bna.com.

346.04 USA ISSN 0741-1219
KF3091.9
PATENT, TRADEMARK AND COPYRIGHT LAWS (YEAR). Text in English. 1983. a., latest 2004. USD 35 (effective 2005). **Document type:** *Handbook/Manual/Guide, Trade.* **Description:** Compiles all the language from federal statutes affecting US intellectual property law. Includes all relevant sections of the USC and other laws relating to intellectual property.
Formerly (until 1985): Patent and Trademark Laws (0736-9670)
—CCC.
Published by: Patent Publishing, LLC, 1919 S. Eads St., Ste. 401, Annandale, VA 22003. TEL 703-521-3230, 866-880-6737, FAX 703-521-1012.

346.04 USA
PATENT, TRADEMARK, AND COPYRIGHT REGULATIONS. Text in English. 1991. base vol. plus s-a. updates. looseleaf. USD 245 base vol(s). (includes most recent Supplement) (effective 2009). back issues avail. **Document type:** *Handbook/Manual/Guide, Trade.* **Description:** Compiles all the intellectual property rules contained in Vol 37 of the US Code of Federal Regulations, along with those of the US Patent and Trademark Office, Copyright Office, and Copyright Arbitration Royalty Panels.
Related titles: ◆ Supplement(s): Patent, Trademark, and Copyright Regulations. Supplement.
Published by: The Bureau of National Affairs, Inc., 1801 S Bell St, Arlington, VA 22202. TEL 703-341-3000, 800-372-1033, FAX 703-341-4634, 800-253-0332, bnaplus@bna.com, http://www.bna.com.

346.04 USA
PATENT, TRADEMARK, AND COPYRIGHT REGULATIONS. SUPPLEMENT. Text in English. a. included into subsc. to Patent, Trademark, and Copyright Regulations. **Document type:** *Handbook/Manual/Guide, Trade.*
Related titles: ◆ Supplement to: Patent, Trademark, and Copyright Regulations.
Published by: The Bureau of National Affairs, Inc., 1801 S Bell St, Arlington, VA 22202. TEL 703-341-3000, 800-372-1033, FAX 703-341-4634, 800-253-0332, bnaplus@bna.com, http://www.bna.com. Ed. James D Crowne.

608.7 DEU CODEN: PATBAR
PATENTBLATT (ONLINE). Text in German. 1877. w. reprints avail. **Document type:** *Bulletin, Trade.*
Formerly (until 2003): Patentblatt (Print) (0031-2894)
Media: Online - full content.
Indexed: ABIPC, ChemAb.
—CASDDS, Linda Hall.
Published by: Deutsches Patent- und Markenamt, Zweibrueckenstr 12, Munich, 80331, Germany. TEL 49-89-21950, FAX 49-89-21952221, post@dpma.de.

346.04 SWE ISSN 1403-2309
PATENTEYE; specialtidningen om patent- och designskydd. Text in Swedish. 1995. 8/yr. **Document type:** *Magazine, Consumer.*
Published by: Brand Eye AB, PO Box 3457, Stockholm, 10369, Sweden. TEL 46-8-4060900, input@brandeye.se. Ed. Christer Loefgren.

608.7 SRB ISSN 0031-2908
T201
PATENTNI GLASNIK; Sluzbeni list Saveznog Zavoda za Patente. Text in Croatian, Macedonian, Serbian, Slovenian. 1921. bi-m. YUN 1,800, USD 106.40; (effective Aug. 1991). adv. illus.; pat. index.
Published by: Savezni Zavod za Patente, Savczni zavod za intelektu, Alnu Svojinu, Bulevar A V N O J a 104, Belgrade, 11070. TEL 011-639-412, FAX 011-639-761, TELEX 12761 SZPAT YU. Adv. contact Blagota Zarkovic. Circ: 900.

346.04 BGR
PATENTNO VEDOMSTVO NA REPUBLIKA BULGARIA. GODISHEN OTCHET/PATENT OFFICE OF THE REPUBLIC OF BULGARIA. ANNUAL REPORT. Text in Bulgarian, English. a.
Published by: Patentno Vedomstvo na Republika Bulgaria/Patent Office of the Republic of Bulgaria, 52b, Dr G M Dimitrov Blvd, Sofia, 1797, Bulgaria. TEL 359-2-710152, FAX 359-2-717044, tivanova@bpo.bg, http://www.bpo.bg/. Adv. contact Elina Sinkova.

346.04 BGR
PATENTNO VEDOMSTVO NA REPUBLIKA BULGARIA. OFITSIALEN BIULETIN/OFFICIAL GAZETTE OF THE PATENT OFFICE OF THE REPUBLIC OF BULGARIA. Text in Bulgarian; Contents page in Russian, French, German, English. m. BGL 120 (effective 2002). **Description:** Contains bibliographical data and abstracts with drawings/chemical formulae of published applications and granted patents for inventions and utility models.
Published by: Patentno Vedomstvo na Republika Bulgaria/Patent Office of the Republic of Bulgaria, 52b, Dr G M Dimitrov Blvd, Sofia, 1797, Bulgaria. TEL 359-2-710152, FAX 359-2-717044, tivanova@bpo.bg, http://www.bpo.bg/. Adv. contact Elina Sinkova.

608.7 607.7 ISR
T313.I75 CODEN: ISPDBT
PATENTS AND DESIGN JOURNAL (ONLINE)/R'SHUMOT. YOMAN HAPPATENTIM W'HAMIDGAMIM. Text in English, Hebrew. 1968. m. free (effective 2008). abstr. **Document type:** *Government.*
Formerly (until 2007): Patents and Design Journal (Print) (0334-3332); Which superseded in part (in 1968): Patents, Designs and Trade Marks Journal (0021-2326)
Media: Online - full text.
Indexed: ChemAb.
Published by: Ministry of Justice, Patent Office, P O Box 34255, Jerusalem, 91341, Israel. Circ: 150. **Subscr. to:** Distribution Service of Government Publications, 29-B St., Hakirya, Tel Aviv, Israel.

608.7 JPN ISSN 0388-7081
PATENTS AND LICENSING. Text in English. 1971. bi-m. JPY 5,000 in Asia; USD 130 in the Middle East; USD 140 elsewhere (effective 2000). adv. **Document type:** *Handbook/Manual/Guide, Trade.* **Description:** Offers the latest information and data concerning intellectual property and licensing.
Formerly: Patents and Engineering
Indexed: JTA.
Published by: I P L Communications Inc., Rm 202, Sun Mansion, 1-11, Azabudai 1-chome, Minato-ku, Tokyo, 106-0041, Japan. TEL 81-3-3589-4749, FAX 81-3-3589-4619. Ed. Osahito Makiyama. adv.: page USD 6,300.

608.7 602.7 IRL ISSN 1393-1415
PATENTS OFFICE JOURNAL. Text in English. 1928. fortn. EUR 203.16 (effective 2005). charts; pat.; tr.mk. index. **Document type:** *Government.*
Formerly (until 1992): Official Journal of Industrial and Commercial Property (0030-0349)
Published by: (Irish Patents Office), Government Supplies Agency, 4-5 Harcourt Rd., Dublin, 2, Ireland.

608.7 346.04 AUS
PATENTS, TRADE MARKS AND RELATED RIGHTS. Text in English. 1996. 4 base vols. plus updates 5/yr. looseleaf. AUD 1,567.50 (effective 2008). **Document type:** *Handbook/Manual/Guide, Trade.* **Description:** Contains detailed commentary on patents, trade marks, confidential information and unfair competition.
Formerly: Intellectual Property in Australia: Patents, Designs and Trademarks
Related titles: CD-ROM ed.; Online - full text ed.: AUD 1,314.50 (effective 2008).
Published by: LexisNexis Butterworths (Subsidiary of: LexisNexis Asia Pacific), Level 9, Tower 2, 475-495 Victoria Ave, Locked Bag 2222, Chatswood Delivery Ctr, Chatswood, NSW 2067, Australia. TEL 61-2-94222174, FAX 61-2-94222405, academic@lexisnexis.com.au.

346.04 RUS
PATENTY I LITSENZII. Text in Russian. m. USD 199.95 in United States.
Published by: Informatsionno-Izdatel'skii Tsentr Rospatenta, Raushskaya nab 4, Moscow, 113035, Russian Federation. TEL 7-095-2307352, FAX 7-095-2307352. Ed. N P Kuznetsova. **Dist. by:** East View Information Services, 10601 Wayzata Blvd, Minneapolis, MN 55305. TEL 952-252-1201, 800-477-1005, FAX 952-252-1202, info@eastview.com, http://www.eastview.com.

608.71 CAN ISSN 1193-1647
PATSCAN NEWS. Text in English. 1988. irreg. CAD 20 (effective 2006). **Description:** Promotes the understanding of patent searching and technology transfer.
Published by: PATEX Research and Consulting Ltd., PATSCAN Service, 5230 Patrick St, Burnaby, BC V5J 3B3, Canada. TEL 604-438-5935, FAX 604-438-5945, ron@patex.ca, http://www.patex.ca.

608.7 PHL
PHILIPPINE INVENTIONS. Text in English. q. PHP 200; USD 50 foreign.
Published by: (Department of Science and Technology), Science and Technology Information Institute, P.O. Box 3596, Manila, Philippines. TEL 822-0954. **Subscr. to:** Dept. of Science and Technology, Bicutan, Taguig, P.O. Box 2131, Manila, Philippines.

346.04 NLD ISSN 2210-9951
▼ **PICTORIGHT.** Text in Dutch. 2009. s-a.
Address: Postbus 15887, Amsterdam, 1001 NJ, Netherlands. TEL 31-20-5891840, FAX 31-20-4124269, info@pictorights.nl, http://www.pictoright.nl. Ed. Marcel van de Graaf.

608.7 CHE ISSN 1660-2307
PLANT VAR/FEUILLE SUISSE DES BREVETS, DESSINS ET MARQUES/FOGLIO SVIZZERO DEI BREVETTI, DISEGNI E MARCHI. Text in French, German; Text occasionally in Italian. 1889. s-m. adv. charts; illus.; pat. index. **Document type:** *Journal, Trade.*
Supersedes in part (in 2002): Schweizerisches Patent-, Muster- und Markenblatt (0036-7974); Which was formerly (until 1968): Schweizerisches Patent- und Muster und Modellblatt (0559-0868); (until 1962): Patent-Liste (1422-061X)
Published by: Eidgenoessisches Institut fuer Geistiges Eigentum/Swiss Federal Institute of Intellectual Property, Einsteinstr 2, Bern, 3003, Switzerland. TEL 41-31-3252525, FAX 41-31-3252526, info@ipi.ch, http://www.ige.ch. Ed. Florian Gruetzner. Circ: 255.

608.7 POL ISSN 0137-8015
POLAND. URZAD PATENTOWY. BIULETYN/POLAND. PATENT OFFICE. BULLETIN. Text in Polish. 1973. bi-w. EUR 367 foreign (effective 2006). illus. **Document type:** *Bulletin.*
Published by: Urzad Patentowy, Al Niepodleglosci 188, Departament Wydawnictw, Warsaw, Poland. TEL 48-22-8258001, FAX 48-22-8750682, wydawnictwa@uprp.pl, http://www.uprp.pl. **Dist. by:** Ars Polona, Obroncow 25, Warsaw 03933, Poland. TEL 48-22-5098609, FAX 48-22-5098610, arspolona@arspolona.com.pl, http://www.arspolona.com.pl.

608.7 POL ISSN 0043-5201
CODEN: WIUPA3
POLAND. URZAD PATENTOWY. WIADOMOSCI/POLAND. PATENT OFFICE. NEWS. Text in Polish; Summaries in English, Russian. 1924. m. PLZ 126 domestic; USD 141 foreign (effective 2000). adv.
—CASDDS.
Published by: Urzad Patentowy, Al Niepodleglosci 188, Departament Wydawnictw, Warsaw, Poland. wydawnictwa@uprp.pl, http://www.uprp.pl. **Dist. by:** Ars Polona, Obroncow 25, Warsaw 03933, Poland.

608.7 RUS
POLEZNYE MODELI. PROMYSHLENNYE OBRAZTSY. Text in Russian. 1924. m. USD 302 (effective 1998). **Document type:** *Bulletin.*
Supersedes in part (in 1994): Promyshlennye Obraztsy. Tovarnye Znaki (0208-2888); Which supersedes in part (in 1983): Otkrytiya, Izobreteniya, Promyshlennye Obraztsy, Tovarnye Znaki (0007-4020)
—Linda Hall.
Published by: Vsesoyuznyi Nauchno-Issledovatel'skii Institut Patentnoi Informatsii (VNIIPI)/Committee of Russian Federation for Patents and Trademarks, Raushskaya nab 4-5, Moscow, 113035, Russian Federation. TEL 7-095-9593313, FAX 7-095-9593304. Ed. E I Daich. **Dist. by:** East View Information Services, 10601 Wayzata Blvd, Minneapolis, MN 55305. TEL 952-252-1201, 800-477-1005, FAX 952-252-1202, info@eastview.com, http://www.eastview.com; M K - Periodica, ul Gilyarovskogo 39, Moscow 129110, Russian Federation. TEL 7-095-2845008, FAX 7-095-2813798, info@periodicals.ru, http://www.mkniga.ru.

346.04 GBR
PRACTICAL INTELLECTUAL PROPERTY. Text in English. 2000. base vol. plus updates 2/yr. looseleaf. GBP 478 base vol(s). domestic; EUR 632 base vol(s). in Europe; USD 822 base vol(s). elsewhere (effective 2011). **Document type:** *Handbook/Manual/Guide, Trade.* **Description:** Shows the practical steps necessary to protect the whole range of 'intellectual property' rights. Specifically designed to be used as a first point of reference, it contains all the information practitioners need for their daily business.
Published by: Sweet & Maxwell Ltd. (Subsidiary of: Thomson Reuters Corp.), 100 Avenue Rd, London, NW3 3PF, United Kingdom. TEL 44-20-73937000, FAX 44-20-74491144, sweetandmaxwell.customer.services@thomson.com. **Subscr. to:** PO Box 1000, Andover SP10 9AF, United Kingdom. TEL 44-20-73938051, sweetandmaxwell.international.queries@thomson.com.

346.04 GBR
PRACTICAL INTELLECTUAL PROPERTY PRECEDENTS. Text in English. 1997. base vol. plus updates 2/yr. looseleaf. GBP 512 base vol(s). domestic; EUR 676 base vol(s). in Europe; USD 880 base vol(s). elsewhere (effective 2011). **Document type:** *Handbook/Manual/Guide, Trade.* **Description:** Covers comprehensive range of intellectual property precedents, from copyright assignments, patent licences, and commissioning and funding agreements, to enforcement and dispute precedents.
Published by: Sweet & Maxwell Ltd. (Subsidiary of: Thomson Reuters Corp.), 100 Avenue Rd, London, NW3 3PF, United Kingdom. TEL 44-20-73937000, FAX 44-20-74491144, sweetandmaxwell.customer.services@thomson.com. **Subscr. to:** PO Box 1000, Andover SP10 9AF, United Kingdom. TEL 44-20-73938051, sweetandmaxwell.international.queries@thomson.com.

346.04 USA ISSN 1523-3979
KF3181
PRACTITIONER'S TRADEMARK MANUAL OF EXAMINING PROCEDURE. Text in English. 1997. a. USD 375 (effective 2008). **Document type:** *Handbook/Manual/Guide, Trade.* **Description:** Provides the U.S. Patent and Trademark Office Manual of Patent Examining Procedure (MPEP) from a practitioner's perspective through a series of author comments, practice references, and other links, thoroughly explaining the practices and procedures of the patent application process.
Related titles: Online - full text ed.
Published by: Thomson West (Subsidiary of: Thomson Reuters Corp.), 610 Opperman Dr, Eagan, MN 55123. TEL 651-687-7000, 800-344-5008, FAX 651-687-6674, west.support@thomson.com.

352.749 GTM
LA PROPIEDAD INTELECTUAL; en la integracion economica de Centroamerica. Text in Spanish. 1997. q.
Published by: Secretaria Permanente del Tratado General de Integracion Economica Centroamericana, 4a Avda. 10-25, ZONA, 14, PO Box 1237, Guatemala City, 01901, Guatemala. TEL 502-3682151, FAX 502-3681071.

381 FRA ISSN 0338-6473
PROPRIETE INDUSTRIELLE BULLETIN DOCUMENTAIRE. Text in French. 1968. 22/yr. EUR 148 (effective 2009). bk.rev. abstr.; pat.; bibl.; stat.; tr.mk. 65 p./no.; back issues avail. **Document type:** *Bulletin, Bibliography.* **Description:** Contains information and reports of French and foreign case law and literature in the field of industrial property.
Related titles: Microfiche ed.
Published by: Institut National de la Propriete Industrielle, 26 bis rue de St. Petersbourg, Paris, Cedex 8 75800, France. TEL 33-01-53045506, FAX 33-01-42934783, http://www.inpi.fr. R&P Marie-Andree Ouret. Circ: 1,300.

RECENT PATENTS ON ANTI-CANCER DRUG DISCOVERY. *see* MEDICAL SCIENCES—Oncology

RECENT PATENTS ON ANTI-INFECTIVE DRUG DISCOVERY. *see* MEDICAL SCIENCES—Allergology And Immunology

608 610.28 NLD ISSN 1874-7647
➤ **RECENT PATENTS ON BIOMEDICAL ENGINEERING.** Text in English. 2008. 3/yr. USD 870 to institutions (effective 2012). adv. back issues avail.; reprints avail. **Document type:** *Journal, Academic/Scholarly.* **Description:** Publishes articles on recent patents in the field of biomedical engineering, including new medical devices and biomaterials.
Media: Online - full text. **Related titles:** Print ed.: ISSN 2211-3320. 2011.
Indexed: A01, CA, CPEI, SCOPUS, T02.

P

—CCC.
Published by: Bentham Science Publishers Ltd., PO Box 294, Bussum, 1400 AG, Netherlands. TEL 31-35-6923800, FAX 31-35-6980150, sales@bentham.org. Eds. Biaoyang Lin, Wei Li. **Subscr. to:** Bentham Science Publishers Ltd., c/o Richard E Morrissy, PO Box 446, Oak Park, IL 60301. TEL 312-413-5867, FAX 312-996-7107, subscriptions@bentham.org.

➤ **RECENT PATENTS ON C N S DRUG DISCOVERY.** (Central Nervous System) *see* MEDICAL SCIENCES—Psychiatry And Neurology

➤ **RECENT PATENTS ON CARDIOVASCULAR DRUG DISCOVERY.** *see* MEDICAL SCIENCES—Cardiovascular Diseases

608 660 NLD ISSN 1874-4788
➤ **RECENT PATENTS ON CHEMICAL ENGINEERING.** Text in English. 2008. 3/yr. USD 870 to institutions (effective 2012). adv. back issues avail.; reprints avail. **Document type:** *Journal, Academic/Scholarly.* **Description:** Covers recent patents in chemical engineering, including oil recovery processes, food processing, hydro-processing technologies, desalination and diesel particulate matter removal.
Media: Online - full text. **Related titles:** Print ed.: ISSN 2211-3347. 2011.
Indexed: CPEI.
—CCC.
Published by: Bentham Science Publishers Ltd., PO Box 294, Bussum, 1400 AG, Netherlands. TEL 31-35-6923800, FAX 31-35-6980150, sales@bentham.org. Eds. Piotr M Slomkiewicz, Yousheng Tao. **Subscr. to:** Bentham Science Publishers Ltd., c/o Richard E Morrissy, PO Box 446, Oak Park, IL 60301. TEL 312-413-5867, FAX 312-996-7107, subscriptions@bentham.org.

608 621.39 NLD ISSN 1874-4796
➤ **RECENT PATENTS ON COMPUTER SCIENCE.** Text in English. 2008. 3/yr. USD 870 to institutions (effective 2012). adv. back issues avail.; reprints avail. **Document type:** *Journal, Academic/Scholarly.* **Description:** Follows recent patents in all areas of computer science, including patents in initial issues covering optical and server networks, land vehicle navigation, epileptic series prediction, civil and structural engineering and programming.
Media: Online - full text.
Indexed: C10, CA, CPEI, T02.
—CCC.
Published by: Bentham Science Publishers Ltd., PO Box 294, Bussum, 1400 AG, Netherlands. TEL 31-35-6923800, FAX 31-35-6980150, sales@bentham.org. Ed. Khurshid Zaman. **Subscr. to:** Bentham Science Publishers Ltd., c/o Richard E Morrissy, PO Box 446, Oak Park, IL 60301. TEL 312-413-5867, FAX 312-996-7107, subscriptions@bentham.org.

608 621.3 NLD ISSN 1874-4761
➤ **RECENT PATENTS ON ELECTRICAL ENGINEERING.** Text in English. 2008. 3/yr. USD 870 to institutions (effective 2012). adv. back issues avail.; reprints avail. **Document type:** *Journal, Academic/Scholarly.* **Description:** Designed for all researchers involved in electrical engineering science. Publishes articles by experts on recent patents in electrical engineering.
Media: Online - full text.
Indexed: A01, C10, CA, CPEI, E14, SCOPUS, T02.
—CCC.
Published by: Bentham Science Publishers Ltd., PO Box 294, Bussum, 1400 AG, Netherlands. TEL 31-35-6923800, FAX 31-35-6980150, sales@bentham.org. Ed. Khurshid Zaman. **Subscr. to:** Bentham Science Publishers Ltd., c/o Richard E Morrissy, PO Box 446, Oak Park, IL 60301. TEL 312-413-5867, FAX 312-996-7107, subscriptions@bentham.org.

608 613.2 630 NLD ISSN 1876-1429
▼ ➤ **RECENT PATENTS ON FOOD, NUTRITION & AGRICULTURE.** Text in English. 2009. 3/yr. USD 800 to institutions (print or online ed.) (effective 2012). adv. back issues avail.; reprints avail. **Document type:** *Journal, Academic/Scholarly.* **Description:** Publishes review articles by experts on recent patents in all fields of food science & technology, nutrition and agricultural science & technology.
Related titles: Online - full text ed.
Indexed: A34, A35, A38, AgBio, C25, CABA, D01, E12, GH, H16, MEDLINE, N02, N03, P30, P32, P40, PGegResA, PN&I, RA&MP, SCOPUS, SoyAb, TAR, VS.
—IE. **CCC.**
Published by: Bentham Science Publishers Ltd., PO Box 294, Bussum, 1400 AG, Netherlands. TEL 31-35-6923800, FAX 31-35-6980150, sales@bentham.org. Ed. Afaf Kamal-Eldin. **Subscr. to:** Bentham Science Publishers Ltd., c/o Richard E Morrissy, PO Box 446, Oak Park, IL 60301. TEL 312-413-5867, FAX 312-996-7107, subscriptions@bentham.org.

620.1 NLD ISSN 1874-4648
RECENT PATENTS ON MATERIALS SCIENCE. Text in English. 2007. 3/yr. USD 870 to institutions (print or online ed.) (effective 2012). adv. back issues avail.; reprints avail. **Document type:** *Journal, Academic/Scholarly.* **Description:** Publishes review articles on recent patents in all areas of materials science.
Related titles: Online - full text ed.: ISSN 1874-4656.
Indexed: A01, A28, APA, BrCerAb, C&ISA, CA, CA/WCA, CIA, CPEI, CerAb, CivEngAb, CorrAb, E&CAJ, E11, EEA, EMA, H15, M&TEA, M09, MBF, METADEX, SCOPUS, SolStAb, T02, T04, WAA.
—CCC.
Published by: Bentham Science Publishers Ltd., PO Box 294, Bussum, 1400 AG, Netherlands. TEL 31-35-6923800, FAX 31-35-6980150, sales@bentham.org. Ed. Khurshid Zaman. **Subscr. to:** Bentham Science Publishers Ltd., c/o Richard E Morrissy, PO Box 446, Oak Park, IL 60301. TEL 312-413-5867, FAX 312-996-7107, subscriptions@bentham.org.

608 621 NLD ISSN 1874-477X
➤ **RECENT PATENTS ON MECHANICAL ENGINEERING.** Text in English. 2008. 3/yr. USD 870 to institutions (effective 2012). adv. back issues avail.; reprints avail. **Document type:** *Journal, Academic/Scholarly.* **Description:** Covers recent patents in mechanical engineering, including CAD, electronics packaging, fuel cells, mechanical tolerances and environmental systems.
Media: Online - full text.
Indexed: C10, CA, CPEI, SCOPUS, T02.
—CCC.
Published by: Bentham Science Publishers Ltd., PO Box 294, Bussum, 1400 AG, Netherlands. TEL 31-35-6923800, FAX 31-35-6980150, sales@bentham.org. Ed. Khurshid Zaman. **Subscr. to:** Bentham Science Publishers Ltd., c/o Richard E Morrissy, PO Box 446, Oak Park, IL 60301. TEL 312-413-5867, FAX 312-996-7107, subscriptions@bentham.org.

608.7 BEL ISSN 0034-1851
T267 CODEN: REBIA8
RECUEIL DES BREVETS D'INVENTION/VERZAMELING DER UITVINDINGSOCTROOIEN. Text in Dutch, French. 1854. 13/yr. illus.; pat. index. **Document type:** *Government.*
Formerly (until 1897): Recueil Special des Brevets d'Invention (0770-4267)
Related titles: Online - full text ed.
Published by: Ministry of Economic Affairs, Office de la Propriete Industrielle/Dienst voor Industriele Eigendom, 16 Bd. du Roi Albert II, Brussels, 1000, Belgium. TEL 32-2-2064111, FAX 32-2-2065750, PIIE_doc@pophost.eunet.be, http://www.european-patent-office.org/patlib.country/belgium. Circ: 1,000.

608.7 GBR ISSN 1358-5355
REGISTER OF PATENT AGENTS. Text in English. 1889. a. GBP 25 to non-members; free to members (effective 2009). adv. **Document type:** *Directory, Trade.* **Description:** Contains name, business address, date of registration of private practice firms.
Related titles: Online - full text ed.: free (effective 2009).
Published by: Chartered Institute of Patent Attorneys, 95 Chancery Ln, London, WC2A 1DT, United Kingdom. TEL 44-20-74059450, FAX 44-20-74300471, mail@cipa.org.uk, http://www.cipa.org.uk. Adv. contact Iain Ross TEL 44-20-74409368.

354.489 DNK ISSN 0107-590X
REGISTER OVER DANSKE PATENTER UDSTEDT I (YEAR). Text in Danish. 1971. a. **Document type:** *Government.*
Related titles: Online - full text ed.; ◆ Supplement to: Dansk Patenttidende. ISSN 0011-6416.
Published by: Patent- og Varemaerkestyrelsen/Danish Patent and Trademark Office, Helgeshoj Alle 81, Taastrup, 2630, Denmark. TEL 45-43-508000, FAX 45-43-508001, pvs@dkpto.dk.

608.7 GBR ISSN 0080-1364
KD1365.A2
REPORTS OF PATENT, DESIGN AND TRADE MARK CASES. Text in English. 1884. m. GBP 429 in United Kingdom to institutions; EUR 650 in Europe to institutions; USD 867 in US & Canada to institutions; GBP 429 elsewhere to institutions; GBP 468 combined subscription in United Kingdom to institutions (print & online eds.); EUR 703 combined subscription in Europe to institutions (print & online eds.); USD 936 combined subscription in US & Canada to institutions (print & online eds.); GBP 468 combined subscription elsewhere to institutions (print & online eds.) (effective 2012). adv. back issues avail.; reprint service avail. from PSC. **Document type:** *Journal, Academic/Scholarly.* **Description:** Contains leading full-text law reports in intellectual property, definitive text of selected key decisions and judgements, along with expert headnotes.
Formerly (1886): Reports of Patent Cases
Related titles: Online - full text ed.: ISSN 1756-1000. GBP 390 in United Kingdom to institutions; EUR 586 in Europe to institutions; USD 780 in US & Canada to institutions; GBP 390 elsewhere to institutions (effective 2012) (from IngentaConnect).
—BLDSC (7661.910000), IE, Ingenta. **CCC.**
Published by: (Great Britain. Intellectual Property Office), Oxford University Press, Great Clarendon St, Oxford, OX2 6DP, United Kingdom. TEL 44-1865-556767, FAX 44-1865-556646, enquiry@oup.co.uk, http://www.oxfordjournals.org. Ed. Mary Vitoria.

346.04 CHE
REPRAX; Zeitschrift zur Handelsregisterpraxis. Text in German. 1999. 3/yr. CHF 128 domestic; CHF 148 foreign (effective 2001). **Document type:** *Journal, Trade.*
Published by: Schulthess Juristische Medien AG, Zwinglilplatz 2, Zuerich, 8022, Switzerland. TEL 41-1-2519336, FAX 41-1-2616394, zs.verlag@schulthess.com, http://www.schulthess.com.

608.7 338 GBR ISSN 0374-4353
CODEN: RSDSBB
RESEARCH DISCLOSURE. Text mainly in English. 1960. m. USD 745 in United States; GBP 495 in UK & elsewhere (effective 2009). **Document type:** *Journal, Trade.* **Description:** Provides an alternative to obtaining a patent at a fraction of the cost and time taken.
Supersedes in part (in 1965): Product Licensing Index (0032-9770); Which was formerly (until 19??): New Products International
Related titles: Online - full content ed.: R D Electronic. EUR 1,490 in Europe for 1 license; USD 1,490 in United States for 1 license; GBP 995 in the UK & elsewhere; for 1 license (effective 2004); Price varies based on number on licenses; please contact publisher.
Indexed: ABIPC, CIN, ChemAb, ChemTitl, EngInd, FS&TA, IPackAb, Inspec, P&BA, PhotoAb, SCOPUS, T01, T02, TTI, WTA.
—BLDSC (7738.873000), CASDDS, IE, Ingenta, INIST, Linda Hall. **CCC.**
Published by: Kenneth Mason Publications Ltd., The Book Barn, White Chimney Row, Westbourne, Hamps PO10 8RS, United Kingdom. TEL 44-1243-377977, FAX 44-1243-379136, bookshop@kennethmason.co.uk, http://www.kennethmason.co.uk/.

346.04 USA ISSN 1944-8422
KF2983
RESOLVING TECHNOLOGY AND MEDIA DISPUTES BEFORE TRIAL. Text in English. 2007. a. **Document type:** *Handbook/Manual/Guide, Trade.*
Published by: Practising Law Institute, 810 Seventh Ave, 21st Fl, New York, NY 10019. TEL 212-824-5700, FAX 800-321-0093, info@pli.edu, http://www.pli.edu.

346.04 COL ISSN 1657-1959
➤ **REVISTA DE LA PROPRIEDAD INMATERIAL.** Text in Spanish. 2001. a. COP 40,000 domestic; USD 40 foreign (effective 2011). Index. back issues avail. **Document type:** *Journal, Academic/Scholarly.* **Description:** Covers legal issues with intellectual property and new technology environment and publishes findings and opinions of scientists and researchers. Audience include students, researchers and professionals interested in new technologies, the digital age, biotechnology, and intellectual property in the Colombian and international issues.
Related titles: Online - full text ed.
Published by: (Universidad Externado de Colombia, Centro de Estudios de la Propiedad Intelectual), Universidad Externado de Colombia, Departamento de Publicaciones, Calle 12, No 1-17 Este, Bogota, Colombia. TEL 57-1-2826066, publicaciones@uexternado.edu.co. Ed. Ernesto Rengifo Garcia. R&P Carolina Esguerra. **Dist. by:** Siglo del Hombre Editores, Cra. 32 No.25-46/50, Bogota, D.C., Colombia. TEL 57-1-3377700, FAX 57-1-3377665, info@siglodelhombre.com, http://www.siglodelhombre.com.

340 608.7 MEX ISSN 0035-0044
REVISTA MEXICANA DE LA PROPIEDAD INDUSTRIAL Y ARTISTICA. Text in Spanish. 1963. s-a. MXN 250, USD 14. bk.rev. illus.; pat.; tr.mk. index.
Indexed: C01.
Published by: David Rangel Medina, Ed. & Pub., Cerrada de Xitle No. 19, Pedregal San Angel, Mexico City 20, DF, Mexico. Circ: 1,000.

340 ROM ISSN 1220-3009
REVISTA ROMANA DE PROPRIETATE INDUSTRIALA/ROMANIAN REVIEW FOR INDUSTRIAL PROPERTY. Text in Romanian; Summaries in English, French, German. 1961. 6/yr. USD 200 or exchange basis. adv. **Document type:** *Government.*
Supersedes in part (in 1991): Buletinul de Inventii si Inovatii - Bulletin for Inventions and Innovations
Related titles: CD-ROM ed.
Published by: Oficiul de Stat pentru Inventii si Marci (OSIM)/State Office for Inventions and Trademarks, Str. Ion Ghica 5, Sector 3, Bucharest, 70418, Romania. TEL 40-01-3151966, FAX 40-01-3123819, office@osim.ro, http://www.osim.ro. R&P Victoria Dancescu. Adv. contact Valeriu Geambazu TEL 40-01-3142746.

608 FRA ISSN 0242-1623
T201
REVUE INTERNATIONALE DE LA PROPRIETE INDUSTRIELLE ET ARTISTIQUE. Text in French. 1883. q. EUR 131 domestic to individuals; EUR 136.50 foreign to individuals; EUR 98 domestic to members; EUR 103.50 foreign to members; EUR 114.50 domestic to institutions; EUR 120 foreign to institutions (effective 2010). bk.rev. illus.; tr.mk. index. **Document type:** *Bulletin.*
Indexed: A22.
—IE, Infotrieve.
Published by: Union des Fabricants pour la Protection de la Propriete Industrielle et Artistique, 16 rue de la Faisanderie, Paris, 75116, France. TEL 33-1-45015111, FAX 33-1-47049122. Ed. Francois Eyssette. Circ: 1,800.

340 070 850 FRA ISSN 0035-3515
K21
REVUE INTERNATIONALE DU DROIT D'AUTEUR. Text in English, French, Spanish. 1953. q. EUR 161 domestic; EUR 200 foreign (effective 2009). bk.rev. abstr. index.
Indexed: A22, DIP, ELLIS, FLP, FR, IBR, IBZ, RASB.
—IE, Infotrieve, INIST.
Address: 225, avenue Charles de Gaulle, Neuilly Sur Seine, 92200, France. TEL 33-1-47154469, FAX 33-1-47154783.

608.7 338 ITA ISSN 0035-614X
K22
RIVISTA DI DIRITTO INDUSTRIALE. Text in Italian. 1952. bi-m. EUR 80 in the European Union; EUR 120 elsewhere (effective 2008). adv. bk.rev. abstr. **Document type:** *Journal, Academic/Scholarly.* **Description:** Presents issues of intellectual and industrial property rights.
Related titles: CD-ROM ed.
Indexed: DoGi, IBR, IBZ.
—CCC.
Published by: Casa Editrice Dott. A. Giuffre (Subsidiary of: LexisNexis Europe and Africa), Via Busto Arsizio, 40, Milan, MI 20151, Italy. TEL 39-02-380891, FAX 39-02-38009582, giuffre@giuffre.it, http://www.giuffre.it. Eds. Giuseppe Sena, Vincenzo Franceschelli. Circ: 1,200.

ROYALTY RATE REPORT FOR THE PHARMACEUTICAL & BIOTECHNOLOGY INDUSTRIES. *see* BUSINESS AND ECONOMICS—Banking And Finance

346.04 DEU
SCHRIFTEN ZUM DEUTSCHEN, EUROPAEISCHEN UND INTERNATIONALEN RECHT DES GEISTIGEN EIGENTUMS UND WETTBEWERBS. Text in German. 2006. irreg., latest vol.14, 2010. price varies. **Document type:** *Monographic series, Academic/Scholarly.*
Published by: JWV Jenaer Wissenschaftliche Verlagsgesellschaft mbH, Magdelstieg 6, Jena, 07745, Germany. kontakt@jwv.de.

346.04 DEU
SCHRIFTEN ZUM EUROPAEISCHEN URHEBERRECHT. Text in German. 2006. irreg., latest vol.10, 2011. price varies. **Document type:** *Monographic series, Academic/Scholarly.*
Media: Large Type.
Published by: Walter de Gruyter GmbH & Co. KG, Genthiner Str 13, Berlin, 10785, Germany. TEL 49-30-260050, FAX 49-30-26005251, info@degruyter.de, http://www.degruyter.de. Eds. Karl Riesenhuber, Karl-Nikolaus Peifer.

346.04 DEU ISSN 1860-076X
SCHRIFTENREIHE ZUM URHEBER- UND KUNSTRECHT. Text in German. 2005. irreg., latest vol.8, 2008. price varies. **Document type:** *Monographic series, Academic/Scholarly.*
Published by: Peter Lang GmbH (Subsidiary of: Peter Lang Publishing Group), Eschborner Landstr 42-50, Frankfurt Am Main, 60489, Germany. TEL 49-69-7807050, FAX 49-69-78070550, zentrale.frankfurt@peterlang.com. Ed. Thomas Hoeren.

346.04 NLD ISSN 1872-1893
SDU WETTENVERZAMELING. INTELLECTUELE EIGENDOM. Text in Dutch. 2006. a. EUR 35.38 (effective 2009).
Published by: Sdu Uitgevers bv, Postbus 20025, The Hague, 2500 EA, Netherlands. TEL 31-70-3789911, FAX 31-70-3854321, sdu@sdu.nl, http://www.sdu.nl/.

608.7 JPN
SHINKETSU KOHO/TRIAL DECISION JOURNAL. Text in Japanese. 1938. 15/m.
Published by: Tokkyocho/Japanese Patent Office (JPO), 4-3 Kasumigaseki 3-chome, Chiyoda-ku, Tokyo, 100-0013, Japan.

346.04 DEU ISSN 1613-3994
STUDIEN ZUM GEWERBLICHEN RECHTSSCHUTZ UND ZUM URHEBERRECHT. Text in German. 2004. irreg., latest vol.68, 2010. price varies. **Document type:** *Monographic series, Academic/Scholarly.*
Published by: Verlag Dr. Kovac, Leverkusenstr 13, Hamburg, 22761, Germany. TEL 49-40-3988800, FAX 49-40-39888055, info@verlagdrkovac.de.

608.781 SWE ISSN 0346-2196
CODEN: SPTGBB
SVENSK PATENTTIDNING/SWEDISH PATENT GAZETTE; tidningen foer kungoerelser om patentansoekningar och patent. Text in Swedish. 1968. w. SEK 500, USD 74 (effective 1998).
Related titles: ◆ Supplement(s): Svensk Patenttidnings Kumulerade Namnregister. ISSN 0347-898X.
—CASDDS.
Published by: Patent- och Registreringsverket, Patentverket, Fack 5055, Stockholm, 10242, Sweden. TEL 46-8-782-25-00, FAX 46-8-783-01-63.

608.781 SWE ISSN 0347-898X
SVENSK PATENTTIDNINGS KUMULERADE NAMNREGISTER/ SWEDISH PATENT GAZETTE'S ACCUMULATED NAME REGISTER. Text in Swedish. 1977. m. SEK 500, USD 74 (effective 1998).
Related titles: ◆ Supplement to: Svensk Patenttidning. ISSN 0346-2196.
Published by: Patent- och Registreringsverket, Patentverket, Fack 5055, Stockholm, 10242, Sweden.

608.7 SWE ISSN 0348-324X
SVENSK VARUMAERKESTIDNING. KUNGOERELSE A. Text in Swedish. 1885. w. SEK 1,250 (effective 1998). illus.; stat.; tr.mk. Supplement avail.
Former titles (until 1978): Registrering foer Varumaerken. A; (until 1934): Registreringstidning foer Varumaerken; (until 1886): Registreringstidning foer Varumaerken. Serien A
Published by: Patent- och Registreringsverket/Patent and Registration Office, Fack 5055, Stockholm, 10242, Sweden. Circ: 640.

608.7 SWE ISSN 0348-3258
SVENSK VARUMAERKESTIDNING. REGISTRERADE VARUMAERKEN. B. Text in Swedish. 1885. w. SEK 1,250 (effective 1998). illus.
Former titles (until 1978): Registreringstidning foer Varumaerken. B; (until 1934): Registreringstidning foer Varumaerken; (until 1886): Registreringstidning foer Varumaerken. Serien B
Related titles: Supplement(s): Varumaerkesstatistik.
Published by: Patent- och Registreringsverket/Patent and Registration Office, Fack 5055, Stockholm, 10242, Sweden. Circ: 640.

608.87 SWE ISSN 0348-3266
SVENSK VARUMAERKESTIDNING. REGISTRERINGSTIDNING FOER VARUMAERKEN. C. Text in Swedish. 1961. w. SEK 1,250 (effective 1998). illus.
Formerly (until 1978): Registreringstidning foer Varumaerken. C (0347-3465)
Related titles: Supplement(s): Varumaerkesstatistik.
Published by: Patent- och Registreringsverket/Patent and Registration Office, Fack 5055, Stockholm, 10242, Sweden. Circ: 480.

602.7 SWE
SVENSKT VARUMAERKESARKIV/SWEDISH TRADEMARK ARCHIVE; computer-indexed microfiche archive including full information about registered trademarks and pending applications. Text in Swedish. 1976. a. (in 2 vols., plus w. updates). SEK 6,400 (effective 1998).
Published by: Patent- och Registreringsverket/Patent and Registration Office, Fack 5055, Stockholm, 10242, Sweden.

608 SWE
SWEDEN. PATENT- OCH REGISTERERINGSVERKET. AARSBERAETTELSE. Text in Swedish. 1965. a. free. pat.; stat.
Published by: Patent- och Registreringsverket/Patent and Registration Office, Fack 5055, Stockholm, 10242, Sweden. Circ: 3,000.

608.7 602.7 HUN ISSN 0039-8071
T265.5
SZABADALMI KOZLONY ES VEDJEGYERTESITO/GAZETTE OF PATENTS AND TRADEMARKS. Text in Hungarian; Summaries in English, French, German, Russian. 1896. m. HUF 43,824 domestic (effective 2008). pat. **Document type:** *Newspaper, Government.*
Formerly (until 1963): Szabadalmi Kozlony (0200-027X)
Related titles: Online - full content ed.: ISSN 1588-0974. free.
Indexed: CRIA, CRICC.
Published by: Magyar Szabadalmi Hivatal/Hungarian Patent Office, Pf 552, Budapest, 1370, Hungary. TEL 36-1-3124400, FAX 36-1-3312596, mszh@hpo.hu.

T M A TRADEMARK REPORT. (Tobacco Merchants Association) *see* TOBACCO

346.04 336.2 USA
TAXATION OF INTELLECTUAL PROPERTY: TAX PLANNING GUIDE. Text in English. 1985. base vol. plus s-a. updates. looseleaf. **Document type:** *Handbook/Manual/Guide, Trade.* **Description:** Includes coverage of topics such as effects of recent tax legislation, patents, trade secrets, trademarks and tradenames, copyrights and computer software, and alternative tax treatments.
Published by: Matthew Bender & Co., Inc. (Subsidiary of: LexisNexis North America), 1275 Broadway, Albany, NY 12204. TEL 518-487-3000, 800-424-4200, FAX 518-487-3083, international@bender.com, http://bender.lexisnexis.com. Ed. Marvin Petry.

TECHNOLOGY COMMERCIALIZATION - EUROPE EDITION. *see* TECHNOLOGY: COMPREHENSIVE WORKS

TECHNOLOGY COMMERCIALIZATION - NORTH AMERICA EDITION. *see* TECHNOLOGY: COMPREHENSIVE WORKS

338.926 343.074 USA
TECHNOLOGY TRANSFERS AND LICENSING. Text in English. 1996. base vol. plus a. updates. USD 60.
Published by: LexisNexis (Subsidiary of: LexisNexis North America), 701 E Water St, PO Box 7587, Charlottesville, VA 22906. TEL 434-972-7600, 800-446-3410, FAX 800-643-1280, customer.support@lexisnexis.com, http://www.lexisnexis.com/.

608.7 JPN ISSN 0285-3353
TOKKYO/PATENTS. Text in Japanese. 1971. m. JPY 160 per issue. **Document type:** *Government.*
Published by: Hatsumei Kyokai/Japan Institute of Invention and Innovation, 9-14 Toranomon 2-chome, Minato-ku, Tokyo, 105-0001, Japan. **Co-sponsor:** Tokkyocho Somubu - Patent Office, General Administration Division.

608.7 JPN ISSN 0385-9142
TOKKYO NYUSU/PATENT NEWS. Text in Japanese. 1961. d.
Published by: Tsusho Sangyo Chosakai/Research Institute on International Trade and Industry, 8-9 Ginza 2-chome, Chuo-ku, Tokyo, 104-0061, Japan.

608.7 JPN
TOKKYOCHO NENPO/PATENT OFFICE. ANNUAL GAZETTE. Text in Japanese. 1948. a. JPY 850. **Document type:** *Government.*
Published by: Tokkyocho/Japanese Patent Office (JPO), 4-3 Kasumigaseki 3-chome, Chiyoda-ku, Tokyo, 100-0013, Japan. TEL 81-3-3581-1898, FAX 81-3-3581-0762. **Subscr. to:** Japanese Institute of Invention and Innovation (JIII), 2-9-14 Toranomon, Minato-ku, Tokyo 105-0001, Japan. TEL 81-3-3502-5421, FAX 81-3-3502-3485.

608.7 JPN
TOKUGIKON/JAPANESE PATENT OFFICE SOCIETY. JOURNAL. Text in Japanese. 1960. bi-m.
Published by: Tokkyocho/Japanese Patent Office (JPO), 4-3 Kasumigaseki 3-chome, Chiyoda-ku, Tokyo, 100-0013, Japan.

608.7 RUS
TOVARNYE ZNAKI, ZNAKI OBSLUZHIVANIYA I NAUMENOVANIYA MEST PROIZVEDENIYA TOVAROV. Text in Russian. 1924. m. USD 652 (effective 1998). adv. **Document type:** *Bulletin.* **Description:** Publishes information about industrial designs, trademarks; contains their graphic representation; also includes information about any relevant changes.
Supersedes in part (in 1994): Promyshlennye Obraztsy. Tovarnye Znaki (0208-2888); Which supersedes in part (in 1983): Otkrytiya, Izobreteniya, Promyshlennye Obraztsy, Tovarnye Znaki (0007-4020)
Related titles: Microfiche ed.; Microfilm ed.
—Linda Hall.
Published by: Vsesoyuznyi Nauchno-Issledovatel'skii Institut Patentnoi Informatsii (VNIIPI)/Committee of Russian Federation for Patents and Trademarks, Raushskaya nab 4-5, Moscow, 113035, Russian Federation. TEL 7-095-9593313, FAX 7-095-9593304. Ed. E I Daich. Circ: 6,375. **Subscr. to:** NPO "Poisk", Raushskaya nab 4, Moscow 113834, Russian Federation.

341.7588 USA
TRADE DRESS PROTECTION. Text in English. 19??. base vol. plus a. updates. looseleaf. USD 438 base vol(s). (effective 2010). **Document type:** *Journal, Trade.* **Description:** Provides comprehensive coverage of trade dress, including protection of colors as trade dress, the importance of image advertising in trade dress cases, registration of trade dress on the federal and state level.
Published by: Thomson West (Subsidiary of: Thomson Reuters Corp.), 610 Opperman Dr, Eagan, MN 55123. TEL 651-687-7000, 800-344-5008, west.customer.service@thomson.com.

608.7 GBR
THE TRADE MARK HANDBOOK. Text in English. 1991. 2 base vols. plus updates 2/yr. looseleaf. GBP 813 base vol(s). domestic; EUR 1,074 base vol(s). in Europe; USD 1,397 base vol(s). elsewhere (effective 2011). **Document type:** *Handbook/Manual/Guide, Trade.* **Description:** Provides a detailed description of the law and practice relating to trademarks, and of the relevant aspects of European and international law.
Published by: Sweet & Maxwell Ltd. (Subsidiary of: Thomson Reuters Corp.), 100 Avenue Rd, London, NW3 3PF, United Kingdom. TEL 44-20-73937000, FAX 44-20-74491144, sweetandmaxwell.customer.services@thomson.com. **Subscr. to:** PO Box 1000, Andover SP10 9AF, United Kingdom. TEL 44-20-73938051, sweetandmaxwell.international.queries@thomson.com.

608.7 602.7 CAN ISSN 0041-0438
TRADE MARKS JOURNAL/JOURNAL DES MARQUES DE COMMERCE; consumer and corporate affairs. Text in English, French. 1954. w. CAD 72, USD 86.40. illus.; tr.mk.
Published by: Supply and Services Canada, Printing and Publishing, 270 Albert St, Ottawa, ON K1A 0S9, Canada. TEL 819-997-2560. Circ: 799.

608.7 602.7 GBR ISSN 0041-0446
TRADE MARKS JOURNAL. Abbreviated title: T M J. Text in English. 1876. w. free (effective 2009). adv. illus. back issues avail. **Document type:** *Journal, Government.* **Description:** Contains details of all trade mark applications accepted in the previous week (Thursday to Wednesday) as well as registrations, renewals, and changes to the register.
Related titles: Online - full content ed.
Indexed: R18.
—CCC.
Published by: Great Britain. Intellectual Property Office, Concept House, Cardiff Rd, Newport, South Wales NP10 8QQ, United Kingdom. TEL 44-1633-814000, FAX 44-1633-817777, enquiries@ipo.gov.uk.

346.0482 GBR
TRADE MARKS, TRADE NAMES AND UNFAIR COMPETITION; world law and practice. Text in English. 1996. 3 base vols. plus updates 3/yr. looseleaf. GBP 668 base vol(s). domestic; EUR 882 base vol(s). in Europe; USD 1,148 base vol(s). elsewhere (effective 2011). **Document type:** *Handbook/Manual/Guide, Trade.* **Description:** Covers the law and practice of trademark applications, registration and enforcement in 200 jurisdictions worldwide.
Related titles: CD-ROM ed.: GBP 1,366.80 base vol(s). domestic to institutions; EUR 1,504 base vol(s). in Europe to institutions; USD 1,958 base vol(s). elsewhere to institutions (effective 2011).
Published by: Sweet & Maxwell Ltd. (Subsidiary of: Thomson Reuters Corp.), 100 Avenue Rd, London, NW3 3PF, United Kingdom. TEL 44-20-73937000, FAX 44-20-74491144, sweetandmaxwell.customer.services@thomson.com. **Subscr. outside the UK to:** PO Box 1000, Andover SP10 9AF, United Kingdom. TEL 44-20-73938051, sweetandmaxwell.international.queries@thomson.com.

341.7588 USA
TRADEMARK LAW PRACTICE FORMS. Text in English. 1996. 4 base vols. plus s-a. updates. looseleaf. USD 2,132 base vol(s). (print & CD-ROM eds.) (effective 2010). **Document type:** *Journal, Trade.* **Description:** Contains trademark litigation forms, including typical responses to pleadings, concise editorial notes to accompany each form, forms tailored to specific situations etc.
Published by: Thomson West (Subsidiary of: Thomson Reuters Corp.), 610 Opperman Dr, Eagan, MN 55123. TEL 651-687-7000, 800-344-5008, west.customer.service@thomson.com.

346.04 USA
TRADEMARK PRACTICE THROUGHOUT THE WORLD. Text in English. 19??. 3 base vols. plus a. updates. looseleaf. USD 765 base vol(s). (effective 2010). **Document type:** *Journal, Trade.* **Description:** Covers international trademark laws.
Published by: Thomson West (Subsidiary of: Thomson Reuters Corp.), 610 Opperman Dr, Eagan, MN 55123. TEL 651-687-7000, 800-344-5008, west.customer.service@thomson.com.

608.7 USA ISSN 0082-5786
T223.V4
TRADEMARK REGISTER OF THE UNITED STATES. Text in English. 1958. a. USD 435 (effective 1999). adv. bk.rev. cum.index: 1881-1997. **Document type:** *Directory, Trade.* **Description:** Lists all trademarks registered with the U.S. Patent and Trademark Office plus owner data and product information.
Related titles: CD-ROM ed.; Online - full text ed.
—Linda Hall.
Published by: Trademark Register, 2100 National Press Bldg, Washington, DC 20045-1000. TEL 202-662-1233, FAX 202-347-4408. Ed. Judith Lefebvre. Pub. Cyril Sernak. Adv. contact Diane Christen.

602.7 USA
TRADEMARK REGISTRATION PRACTICE. Text in English. 19??. latest 2nd ed., 2 base vols. plus s-a. updates. looseleaf. USD 811 base vol(s). (effective 2010). **Document type:** *Handbook/Manual/Guide, Trade.* **Description:** Guides to attorneys through the federal and state trademark registration process, while providing all necessary legal information.
Published by: Thomson West (Subsidiary of: Thomson Reuters Corp.), 610 Opperman Dr, Eagan, MN 55123. TEL 651-687-7000, 800-344-5008, west.customer.service@thomson.com.

P

602.7 USA ISSN 0041-056X
K24
THE TRADEMARK REPORTER. Text in English. 1911. bi-m. free to members (effective 2009). bk.rev. charts. index, cum.index: 1937-1950, 1951-1960; every 5 yrs. thereafter. back issues avail. **Document type:** *Magazine, Trade.* **Description:** Contains articles that explore all aspects of trademark law and practice.
Incorporates (in 19??): United States Trademark Association. Bulletin
Related titles: Microfilm ed.: (from PQC); Online - full text ed.: ISSN 1943-1228.
Indexed: A22, A26, B04, CLI, G08, I01, I03, I05, ILP, LRI.
—Ingenta.
Published by: International Trademark Association, 655 Third Ave, 10th Fl, New York, NY 10017. TEL 212-642-1700, FAX 212-768-7796, info@inta.org. Ed. Cliff Browning.

346.04 USA
TRADEMARK TRIAL AND APPEAL BOARD MANUAL OF PROCEDURE. Text in English. 2003. base vol. plus a. updates. looseleaf. **Document type:** *Government.* **Description:** Provides practitioners with basic information generally useful for litigating cases before the Trademark Trial and Appeal Board.
Related titles: Online - full text ed.: free (effective 2011).
Published by: U.S. Patent and Trademark Office, Madison Bldgs (E & W), 600 Dulany St, Alexandria, VA 22314. TEL 571 272-1000, 800-786-9199, ebc@uspto.gov.

341.7586 USA
TRADEMARKS THROUGHOUT THE WORLD. Text in English. 1977. 3 base vols. plus q. updates. looseleaf. USD 672.96 base vol(s). (effective 2010). **Document type:** *Journal, Trade.* **Description:** Features includes classifications for goods and services. Provides an international directory of trademark law practitioners.
Published by: Thomson West (Subsidiary of: Thomson Reuters Corp.), 610 Opperman Dr, Eagan, MN 55123. TEL 651-687-7000, 800-344-5008, west.customer.service@thomson.com.

608.7 DEU ISSN 0041-1310
TRANSPATENT. Text in German. 1949. 18/yr. adv. bk.rev. pat. **Document type:** *Bulletin.*
Published by: Transpatent GmbH, Gogrevestr 11, Duesseldorf, 40223, Germany. TEL 49-211-9342301, FAX 49-211-319784. Ed. H Jochen Krieger.

341.7582 USA ISSN 0090-2845
KF3002.A86
U.S. COPYRIGHT OFFICE. ANNUAL REPORT OF THE REGISTER OF COPYRIGHTS. Key Title: Annual Report of the Register of Copyrights. Text in English. 1910. a. price varies. **Document type:** *Government.*
Published by: U.S. Library of Congress, Copyright Office, First St, N E, Washington, DC 20559. **Dist. by:** U.S. Government Printing Office, Superintendent of Documents, PO Box 371954, Pittsburgh, PA 15250. TEL 202-512-1800, FAX 202-512-2250, orders@gpo.gov, http://www.access.gpo.gov.

608.7 USA ISSN 0083-3010
U.S. PATENT AND TRADEMARK OFFICE. CLASSIFICATION BULLETINS. Text in English. 19??. irreg., latest 2002. price varies. **Document type:** *Bulletin, Government.*
Published by: U.S. Patent and Trademark Office, Madison Bldgs (E & W), 600 Dulany St, Alexandria, VA 22314. TEL 571 272-1000, 800-786-9199, ebc@uspto.gov.

608.7 USA ISSN 1554-9550
U.S. PATENT AND TRADEMARK OFFICE. ELECTRONIC OFFICIAL GAZETTE. PATENTS. Text in English. 2002. w. (Tue.). free (effective 2011). back issues avail. **Document type:** *Government.*
Media: Online - full text. **Related titles:** CD-ROM ed.
Published by: U.S. Patent and Trademark Office, General Information Services Division, PO Box 1450, Alexandria, VA 22313. TEL 571-272-1000, 800-786-9199, usptoinfo@uspto.gov.

608.7 USA
U.S. PATENT AND TRADEMARK OFFICE. MANUAL OF CLASSIFICATION. Text in English. 19??. 2 base vols. plus s-a. updates. looseleaf. free (effective 2011). **Document type:** *Handbook/Manual/Guide, Government.* **Description:** Presents and lists descriptive titles of about 430 classes and 140,000 subclasses into which patented subject matter is classified.
Related titles: Optical Disk - DVD ed.
Published by: U.S. Patent and Trademark Office, General Information Services Division, PO Box 1450, Alexandria, VA 22313. TEL 571-272-1000, 800-786-9199, usptoinfo@uspto.gov. **Subscr. to:** U.S. Government Printing Office, Superintendent of Documents, PO Box 371954, Pittsburgh, PA 15250. TEL 202-512-1800, FAX 202-512-2250, orders@gpo.gov, http://www.access.gpo.gov.

608.7 USA ISSN 0364-2453
KF3120
U.S. PATENT AND TRADEMARK OFFICE. MANUAL OF PATENT EXAMINING PROCEDURE. Text in English. base vol. plus irreg. updates. looseleaf. **Document type:** *Government.* **Description:** Demonstrates the practices and procedures for prosecuting patent applications.
Related titles: Online - full text ed.: free (effective 2011).
Published by: U.S. Patent and Trademark Office, General Information Services Division, PO Box 1450, Alexandria, VA 22313. TEL 571-272-1000, 800-786-9199, usptoinfo@uspto.gov.

602.7 USA ISSN 0360-5132
T223.V13
U.S. PATENT AND TRADEMARK OFFICE. OFFICIAL GAZETTE. TRADEMARKS. Text in English. 1872. w. back issues avail. **Document type:** *Government.* **Description:** Contains bibliographic information and a representative drawing for each mark published, along with a list of cancelled and renewed registrations.
Supersedes in part (in 1975): U.S. Patent Office. Official Gazette (0041-8021)
Related titles: CD-ROM ed.; Online - full text ed.: ISSN 2157-1775. free (effective 2010).
Indexed: ABIPC, PetrolAb, WTA.
—BLDSC (6239.397000), Linda Hall.
Published by: U.S. Patent and Trademark Office, General Information Services Division, PO Box 1450, Alexandria, VA 22313. TEL 571-272-1000, 800-786-9199, TMPostPubQuery@uspto.gov. **Subscr. to:** U.S. Government Printing Office, Superintendent of Documents.

608.7 USA
U.S. PATENT AND TRADEMARK OFFICE. PERFORMANCE AND ACCOUNTABILITY REPORT. Text in English. 1837. a. free (effective 2011). back issues avail. **Document type:** *Report, Government.*
Former titles (until 2000): U.S. Patent and Trademark Office. Patent and Trademark Office Review; (until 1994): U.S. Patent and Trademark Office. Commissioner of Patents and Trademarks. Annual Report (0162-9735); (until 1975): U.S. Patent and Trademark Office. Annual Report of the Commissioner of Patents (0083-3002)
Related titles: Online - full text ed.
Indexed: SCOPUS.
—Linda Hall.
Published by: U.S. Patent and Trademark Office, Madison Bldgs (E & W), 600 Dulany St, Alexandria, VA 22314. TEL 571 272-1000, 800-786-9199, ebc@uspto.gov.

608 346.048 USA
U.S. PATENT AND TRADEMARK OFFICE. PRODUCTS AND SERVICES. Text in English. 19??. a. **Document type:** *Catalog, Government.*
Published by: U.S. Patent and Trademark Office, General Information Services Division, PO Box 1450, Alexandria, VA 22313. TEL 571-272-1000, 800-786-9199, usptoinfo@uspto.gov.

608.7 USA
U.S. PATENT AND TRADEMARK OFFICE. TECHNOLOGY ASSESSMENT AND FORECAST: PUBLICATIONS. Text in English. irreg. price varies. **Document type:** *Monographic series, Government.* **Description:** Surveys the U.S. patent activity of specific technologies, corporations, and countries.
Published by: U.S. Patent and Trademark Office, Office of Electronic Information Products, C P K 3 Suite 441, Washington, DC 20231. TEL 703-306-2600, FAX 703-306-2737.

602.7 USA
U.S. PATENT AND TRADEMARK OFFICE. TRADEMARK MANUAL OF EXAMINING PROCEDURE. Text in English. 1974. base vol. plus irreg. updates. looseleaf. **Document type:** *Handbook/Manual/Guide, Government.* **Description:** Provides trademark applicants and attorneys with a reference work on the practices and procedures for prosecuting applications to register a trademark at the U.S. Patent and Trademark Office.
Related titles: Online - full text ed.
Published by: U.S. Patent and Trademark Office, General Information Services Division, PO Box 1450, Alexandria, VA 22313. TEL 571-272-1000, 800-786-9199, usptoinfo@uspto.gov.

608.7 USA
U.S. PATENT CLASSIFICATION DEFINITIONS. Text in English. 19??. base vol. plus s-a. updates. **Document type:** *Government.* **Description:** Gives a detailed definition for each class and official subclass in the Manual of Classification.
Former titles: U.S. Patent and Trademark Office. Patent Classification Definitions; (until 1981): United States. Patent Office. Classification Definitions
Published by: U.S. Patent and Trademark Office, General Information Services Division, PO Box 1450, Alexandria, VA 22313. TEL 571-272-1000, 800-786-9199, usptoinfo@uspto.gov.

UNFAIR COMPETITION AND THE I T C. (International Trade Commission) *see* BUSINESS AND ECONOMICS—International Commerce

608.7 USA ISSN 0041-803X
KF2975.3
UNITED STATES PATENTS QUARTERLY. Text in English. 1929. w. looseleaf. USD 3,192 (effective 2010 - 2011). abstr.; pat.; tr.mk. index, cum.index every 5 yrs. back issues avail. **Document type:** *Newsletter, Trade.* **Description:** Contains reports on decisions dealing with patents, trademarks, copyrights, unfair competition, trade secrets, and computer chip protection.
Related titles: ◆ CD-ROM ed.: B N A's Intellectual Property Library on C D. ISSN 1095-5615; ◆ Online - full text ed.: Intellectual Property Law Resource Center.
—CCC.
Published by: The Bureau of National Affairs, Inc., 1801 S Bell St, Arlington, VA 22202. TEL 703-341-3000, 800-372-1033, FAX 703-341-4634, bnaplus@bna.com, http://www.bna.com.

621.9 340 USA ISSN 1081-5058
K25
THE UNIVERSITY OF BALTIMORE INTELLECTUAL PROPERTY LAW JOURNAL. Text in English. 1992. s-a. back issues avail. **Document type:** *Journal, Academic/Scholarly.* **Description:** Serves as a forum for the exchange of ideas and information related to intellectual property. The journal publishes local, regional, national, and international articles.
Related titles: Online - full text ed.
Indexed: A26, BRD, CLI, G08, I01, I05, ILP, LRI, W03, W05.
—CIS.
Published by: University of Baltimore, School of Law, 1415 Maryland Ave, Baltimore, MD 21201. TEL 410-837-4468, FAX 410-837-4450, alumni@ubalt.edu.

346.048 USA
V I P NEWSLETTER. (Virtual Intellectual Property) Variant title: U.S. Intellectual Property & New Media Law Update. Text in English. 1997. w. free. **Document type:** *Newsletter, Trade.* **Description:** Provides a summary of current intellectual property and new media issues, litigation decisions and recently filed complaints.
Media: Online - full text. **Related titles:** E-mail ed.
Published by: Bazerman & Drangel, PC, Intellectual Property and New Media Attorneys, 60 E 42nd St, Ste 1158, New York, NY 10165. TEL 212-292-5390, FAX 212-292-5391. Ed., R&P Steven Bazerman. Circ: 2,000.

340 CHE ISSN 1020-7074
K1401.A15
W I P O MAGAZINE. Text in English. 1995. m. CHF 190; CHF 300 foreign (effective 1999). adv. bk.rev. charts. index. **Document type:** *Magazine, Academic/Scholarly.* **Description:** Gives an overview of the main activities of the Organization and provides in-depth articles on areas of particular interest and concern to the intellectual property community, with emphasis on addressing the conflict between trademarks and domain names.
Supersedes in part (in 1998): Industrial Property and Copyright (1020-2196); Which was formed by the merger of (1965-1995): Copyright (0010-8626); (1962-1995): Industrial Property (0019-8625)
Related titles: Spanish ed.; French ed.
Indexed: FLP.
—BLDSC (9319.962000), CASDDS, Ingenta, Linda Hall.
Published by: World Intellectual Property Organization/Organisation Mondiale de la Propriete Intellectuelle, Publications Sales and Distribution Unit, 34 Chemin des Colombettes, Geneva 20, 1211, Switzerland. TEL 41-22-338-9111, FAX 41-22-740-1812, publications.mail@ompi.int, wipo.mail@wipo.int. Circ: 700.

341.7 USA
WASHINGTON STATE BAR ASSOCIATION. INTELLECTUAL AND INDUSTRIAL PROPERTY SECTION. NEWSLETTER. Text in English. 1983. irreg. free to members (effective 2011). **Document type:** *Newsletter, Trade.*
Published by: (Intellectual and Industrial Property Section), Washington State Bar Association, 1325 Fourth Ave, Ste 600, Seattle, WA 98101. TEL 206-443-9722, 800-945-9722, FAX 206-727-8320, questions@wsba.org, http://www.wsba.org.

346.04 USA ISSN 1942-0250
KF2974 .599
WEST'S CODE OF FEDERAL REGULATIONS ANNOTATED. TITLE 37, PATENTS, TRADEMARKS, AND COPYRIGHTS. Text in English. 2007. a. USD 450 per issue (effective 2010). **Document type:** *Journal, Trade.* **Description:** Contains the code of Federal Regulations, title 37, patents, trademarks, and copyrights, current through amendments published in the Federal Register through April 8, 2009.
Published by: Thomson West (Subsidiary of: Thomson Reuters Corp.), 610 Opperman Dr, Eagan, MN 55123. TEL 651-687-7000, 800-344-5008, west.customer.service@thomson.com.

341.7582 BEL
WETBOEK INTELLECTUELE RECHTEN. Text in Dutch, French. 2 base vols. plus a. updates. looseleaf. EUR 207 (effective 2003). **Document type:** *Trade.* **Description:** Covers intellectual property law in Belgium.
Published by: Kluwer Uitgevers (Subsidiary of: Wolters Kluwer Belgique), Ragheno Business Park, Motstraat 30, Mechelen, B-2800, Belgium. TEL 32-15-800-94571, info@kluwer.be, http://www.kluwer.be.

346.04 DEU ISSN 1616-914X
WETTBEWERBSRECHTLICHE STUDIEN: TECHNOLOGIERECHT - KARTELLRECHT - VERGABERECHT. Text in German. 2001. irreg., latest vol.7, 2009. price varies. **Document type:** *Monographic series, Academic/Scholarly.*
Published by: Peter Lang GmbH (Subsidiary of: Peter Lang Publishing Group), Eschborner Landstr 42-50, Frankfurt Am Main, 60489, Germany. TEL 49-69-7807050, FAX 49-69-78070550, zentrale.frankfurt@peterlang.com, http://www.peterlang.com. Ed. Hanns Ullrich.

346.04 GBR ISSN 1465-2161
WHO'S WHO LEGAL. PATENTS. Text in English. biennial. USD 200 per issue (effective 2011). **Document type:** *Handbook/Manual/Guide, Trade.*
Formerly (until 200?): International Who's Who of Patent Lawyers
Published by: Law Business Research Ltd., 87 Lancaster Rd, London, W11 1QQ, United Kingdom. TEL 44-20-79081188, FAX 44-20-72296910, http://www.lbresearch.com/.

346.04 GBR ISSN 2041-6733
WHO'S WHO LEGAL. TRADEMARKS. Text in English. biennial. USD 200 per issue (effective 2011). **Document type:** *Handbook/Manual/Guide, Trade.*
Formerly (until 200?): International Who's Who of Trademark Lawyers
Published by: Law Business Research Ltd., 87 Lancaster Rd, London, W11 1QQ, United Kingdom. TEL 44-20-79081188, FAX 44-20-72296910, http://www.lbresearch.com/.

602.7 608.7 GBR ISSN 0952-7613
K1401.A13
WORLD INTELLECTUAL PROPERTY REPORT. Text in English. 1987. m. pat. index. back issues avail. **Document type:** *Newsletter, Trade.* **Description:** Provides information on copyright, trademark, and unfair-competition issues worldwide.
Incorporates (1999-2005): World Licensing Law Report (1465-3818)
Related titles: Online - full text ed.: ISSN 1470-6466. USD 1,725 (effective 2010 - 2011).
Indexed: A22.
—CCC.
Published by: B N A International Inc. (Subsidiary of: The Bureau of National Affairs, Inc.), 38 Threadneedle St, London, EC2R 8AY, United Kingdom. TEL 44-20-78475800, 800-372-1033, FAX 44-20-78475848, marketing@bnai.com, http://www.bnai.com. Ed. Derek Tong.

608.7 GBR ISSN 0172-2190
T210 CODEN: WPAID2
➤ **WORLD PATENT INFORMATION.** Text in English. 1979. 4/yr. EUR 844 in Europe to institutions; JPY 112,200 in Japan to institutions; USD 943 elsewhere to institutions (effective 2012). back issues avail.; reprints avail. **Document type:** *Journal, Academic/Scholarly.* **Description:** Provides a worldwide forum for the exchange of information among professionals working in the patents information and documentation field.
Related titles: Microfilm ed.: (from PQC); Online - full text ed.: ISSN 1874-690X (from IngentaConnect, ScienceDirect).
Indexed: A01, A03, A08, A22, A26, BPIA, C10, CA, I05, ISTA, Inspec, L04, L13, LISTA, PAIS, SCOPUS, T02, WSCA.
—BLDSC (9356.973000), AskIEEE, CASDDS, IE, Infotrieve, Ingenta. CCC.
Published by: Pergamon (Subsidiary of: Elsevier Science & Technology), The Blvd, Langford Ln, East Park, Kidlington, Oxford OX5 1GB, United Kingdom. TEL 44-1865-843000, FAX 44-1865-843010, JournalsCustomerServiceEMEA@elsevier.com. Ed. Michael J R Blackman TEL 44-208-6580637. **Subscr. to:** Elsevier BV, Radarweg 29, PO Box 211, Amsterdam 1000 AE, Netherlands. TEL 31-20-4853757, FAX 31-20-4853432, http://www.elsevier.nl. **Co-sponsor:** World Intellectual Property Organization.

608.7 USA
WORLD PATENT LAW AND PRACTICE; patent statutes, regulations and treaties. Text in English. 1975. 16 base vols. plus updates 3/yr. looseleaf. USD 2,336 base vol(s). (effective 2009). index. **Document type:** *Handbook/Manual/Guide, Trade.* **Description:** Compilation of US and foreign patent statutes, regulations and treaties, and European intellectual property decisions.
Published by: Matthew Bender & Co., Inc. (Subsidiary of: LexisNexis North America), 1275 Broadway, Albany, NY 12204. TEL 518-487-3000, 800-424-4200, FAX 518-487-3083, international@bender.com, http://bender.lexisnexis.com.

602.7 USA
WORLD TRADEMARK LAW AND PRACTICE. Text in English. 1982. 5 base vols. plus irreg. updates. looseleaf. USD 1,160 base vol(s). (effective 2008). **Document type:** *Handbook/Manual/Guide, Trade.* **Description:** Features information on world trademark law and practice with detailed coverage of 35 major jurisdictions and summary coverage of another 100.
Related titles: CD-ROM ed.; Online - full text ed.
Published by: Matthew Bender & Co., Inc. (Subsidiary of: LexisNexis North America), 1275 Broadway, Albany, NY 12204. TEL 518-487-3000, 800-424-4200, FAX 518-487-3083, international@bender.com, http://bender.lexisnexis.com. Ed. Ethan Horwitz.

346.04 GBR ISSN 1757-3696
WORLD TRADEMARK REVIEW. YEARBOOK. Text in English. 2005. a. GBP 95 per issue (effective 2010). adv. back issues avail. **Document type:** *Yearbook, Trade.* **Description:** Provides a comparison of some of the important aspects of trademark law around the world.
Former titles (until 2008): World Trademark Yearbook (1751-0635); (until 2005): World Trademark Law Report Yearbook (1748-2844)
Published by: Globe Business Publishing Ltd., New Hibernia House, Winchester Walk, London, SE1 9AG, United Kingdom. TEL 44-20-72340606, FAX 44-20-72340808, globe@gbp.co.uk, http://www.globebusinesspublishing.com. Eds. Trevor Little, Joff Wild. Adv. contact Gavin Stewart.

346.04 341.7 NLD ISSN 2211-4130
ZACCO NIEUWSBRIEF. Text in Dutch. 2008. q. **Document type:** *Newsletter, Trade.*
Former titles (until 2010): ShieldMark Zacco Nieuwsbrief (2211-4149); (until 2009): Shield Mark Nieuwsbrief (2211-4157)
Published by: Zacco Netherlands, Postbus 75683, Amsterdam, 1070 AR, Netherlands. TEL 31-20-5111888, FAX 31-20-5111800, info.amsterdam@zacco.nl.

346.04 DEU ISSN 1867-237X
▼ **ZEITSCHRIFT FUER GEISTIGES EIGENTUM.** Text in German. 2009. q. EUR 129 to individuals; EUR 199 to institutions (effective 2012). reprint service avail. from SCH. **Document type:** *Journal, Academic/Scholarly.*
Related titles: Online - full text ed.: ISSN 1867-2523. 2009 (from IngentaConnect).
Published by: Mohr Siebeck GmbH & Co. KG, Wilhelmstr 18, Tuebingen, 72074, Germany. TEL 49-7071-9230, FAX 49-7071-51104, info@mohr.de.

341.758 CHE
ZEITSCHRIFT FUER IMMATERIALGUETER-, INFORMATIONS- UND WETTBEWERBSRECHT. Text in French, German. 9/yr. CHF 216 domestic; CHF 241 foreign (effective 2001). **Document type:** *Journal, Trade.*
Former titles: Zeitschrift fuer Wettbewerbs-, Immaterialgueter- und Informationsrecht; (until 1997): Schweizerische Mitteilungen ueber Immaterialgueterrecht
Published by: Schulthess Juristische Medien AG, Zwinglipatz 2, Zuerich, 8022, Switzerland. TEL 41-1-2519336, FAX 41-1-2616394, zs.verlag@schulthess.com, http://www.schulthess.com. Circ: 1,100 (paid and controlled).

346.04 CHN
ZHONGGUO PINPAI YU FANGWEI/CHINA BRAND AND ANTI-COUNTERFEITION. Text in Chinese. 1999. m. USD 85.20 (effective 2009). **Document type:** *Journal, Academic/Scholarly.*
Formerly: Zhongguo Fangwei/China Anti Counterfeiting (1008-9098)

—East View.
Published by: (Zhongguo Fangwei Hangwei Xiehui/China Trade Association for Anti-Counterfeiting USA), Zhongguo Pinpai yu Fangwei Zazhishe, Madianguancheng Bei Yuan, No.1 Bldg., 2nd Unit, Rm. 1B, Beijing, 100088, China. TEL 86-10-62373610 ext 809, FAX 86-10-62373608. **Dist. by:** China International Book Trading Corp, 35 Chegongzhuang Xilu, Haidian District, PO Box 399, Beijing 100044, China. TEL 86-10-68412045, FAX 86-10-68412023, cibtc@mail.cibtc.com.cn, http://www.cibtc.com.cn.

346.04 CHN
ZHONGGUO ZHISHI CHANQUAN BAO/CHINA INTELLECTUAL PROPERTY NEWS. Text in Chinese. 1989. 2/w. CNY 52.80 (effective 2004). **Document type:** *Newspaper, Trade.* **Description:** Provides news and coverage of the copyright issues in China.
Formerly (until 1999): Zhongguo Zhuanli Bao
Related titles: Online - full text ed.
Published by: (Zhonghua Renmin Gongheguo Guojia Zhishi Chanquan/State Intellectual Property Office of Peope's Republic of China), Zhongguo Zhishi Chanquan Baoshe, Haidian-qu, Jimen, 6, Xitucheng Lu, Beijing, 100088, China. **Dist. by:** China International Book Trading Corp, 35 Chegongzhuang Xilu, Haidian District, PO Box 399, Beijing 100044, China. TEL 86-10-68412045, FAX 86-10-68412023, cibtc@mail.cibtc.com.cn, http://www.cibtc.com.cn.

PATENTS, TRADEMARKS AND COPYRIGHTS—Abstracting, Bibliographies, Statistics

016.6087 AUS
AUSTRALIAN PATENT ABSTRACTS ON CD-ROM. Text in English. 1981. w. AUD 1,500 (effective 2009). back issues avail. **Document type:** *Government.* **Description:** Abstracts of accepted and unaccepted complete patent specifications as laid open to public inspection; search materials for the public.
Supersedes (in 1997): Patent Abstracts Supplement to the Australian Official Journal of Patents (0819-4831); Which was formerly (until 1987): Patent Abstracts Supplement to the Australian Official Journal of Patents, Trade Marks and Designs (0729-0489)
Media: CD-ROM.
Published by: I P Australia, PO Box 200, Woden, ACT 2606, Australia. TEL 61-2-62832999, FAX 61-2-62837999, assist@ipaustralia.gov.au, http://www.ipaustralia.gov.au. Circ: 44.

016.6087 DEU ISSN 0943-125X
AUSZUEGE AUS DEN EUROPAEISCHEN PATENTANMELDUNGEN. TEIL 1A. CHEMIE UND HUETTENWESEN/EXTRACTS FROM EUROPEAN PATENT APPLICATIONS. PART 1A. CHEMISTRY AND METALLURGY. Text in German. 1985. w. EUR 1,270 (effective 2010). **Document type:** *Journal, Abstract/Index.*
Supersedes in part (in 1993): Auszuege aus den Europaeischen Patentanmeldungen. Teil 1. Grund- und Rohstoffindustrie, Chemie und Huettenwesen, Bauwesen, Bergbau (0177-9621)
Related titles: Online - full text ed.
Published by: Thomson Reuters (Professional) Deutschland (Subsidiary of: Thomson Reuters Corp.), Landsberger Str 191A, Munich, 80687, Germany. TEL 49-89-54756301, FAX 49-89-54756309, info@@thomsonreuters.com, http://www.thomsonreuters.com. Circ: 1,000.

016.6087 DEU ISSN 0943-1268
AUSZUEGE AUS DEN EUROPAEISCHEN PATENTANMELDUNGEN. TEIL 1B. GRUND- UND ROHSTOFFINDUSTRIE, BAUWESEN, BERGBAU/EXTRACTS FROM EUROPEAN PATENT APPLICATIONS. PART 1B. PRIMARY INDUSTRY, FIXED CONSTRUCTIONS, MINING. Text in German. 1985. w. EUR 1,270 (effective 2010). **Document type:** *Journal, Abstract/Index.*
Supersedes in part (in 1993): Auszuege aus den Europaeischen Patentanmeldungen. Teil 1. Grund- und Rohstoffindustrie, Chemie und Huettenwesen, Bauwesen, Bergbau (0177-9621)
Indexed: SCOPUS, WTA.
Published by: Thomson Reuters (Professional) Deutschland (Subsidiary of: Thomson Reuters Corp.), Landsberger Str 191A, Munich, 80687, Germany. TEL 49-89-54756301, FAX 49-89-54756309, info@@thomsonreuters.com, http://www.thomsonreuters.com.

016.6087 DEU ISSN 0943-1276
AUSZUEGE AUS DEN EUROPAEISCHEN PATENTANMELDUNGEN. TEIL 2A. PHYSIK, OPTIK, AKUSTIK, FEINMECHANIK/EXTRACTS FROM EUROPEAN PATENT APPLICATIONS. PART 2A. PHYSICS, PRECISION ENGINEERING, OPTICS, ACOUSTICS. Text in German. 1993. w. EUR 1,865 (effective 2010). **Document type:** *Journal, Abstract/Index.*
Supersedes in part (1985-1993): Auszuege aus den Europaeischen Patentanmeldungen. Teil 2. Elektrotechnik, Physik, Feinmechanik und Optik, Akustik (0177-963X)
Related titles: Online - full text ed.
Published by: Thomson Reuters (Professional) Deutschland (Subsidiary of: Thomson Reuters Corp.), Landsberger Str 191A, Munich, 80687, Germany. TEL 49-89-54756301, FAX 49-89-54756309, info@@thomsonreuters.com, http://www.thomsonreuters.com. Circ: 1,500.

016.6087 DEU ISSN 0943-1284
AUSZUEGE AUS DEN EUROPAEISCHEN PATENTANMELDUNGEN. TEIL 2B. ELEKTROTECHNIK/EXTRACTS FROM EUROPEAN PATENT APPLICATIONS. PART 2B. ELECTRICITY. Text in German. 1993. w. EUR 1,865 (effective 2010). **Document type:** *Journal, Abstract/Index.*
Supersedes in part (1985-1993): Auszuege aus den Europaeischen Patentanmeldungen. Teil 2. Elektrotechnik, Physik, Feinmechanik und Optik, Akustik (0177-963X)
Published by: Thomson Reuters (Professional) Deutschland (Subsidiary of: Thomson Reuters Corp.), Landsberger Str 191A, Munich, 80687, Germany. TEL 49-89-54756301, FAX 49-89-54756309, info@@thomsonreuters.com, http://www.thomsonreuters.com.

016.6087 DEU ISSN 0943-1292
AUSZUEGE AUS DEN EUROPAEISCHEN PATENTANMELDUNGEN. TEIL 3A. UEBRIGE VERARBEITUNGSINDUSTRIE UND ARBEITSVERFAHREN, FAHRZEUGBAU, ERNAEHRUNG, LANDWIRTSCHAFT/EXTRACTS FROM EUROPEAN PATENT APPLICATIONS. PART 3A. MANUFACTURING INDUSTRY, PERFORMING OPERATIONS, VEHICLE CONSTRUCTION, FOOD INDUSTRY, AGRICULTURE. Text in German. 1993. w. EUR 2,625 (effective 2010). **Document type:** *Journal, Abstract/Index.*
Supersedes in part (1985-1993): Auszuege aus den Europaeischen Patentanmeldungen. Teil 3. Uebrige Verarbeitungsindustrie und Arbeitsverfahren, Maschinen- und Fahrzeugbau, Ernaehrung, Landwirtschaft (0177-9648)
Related titles: Online - full text ed.
Published by: Thomson Reuters (Professional) Deutschland (Subsidiary of: Thomson Reuters Corp.), Landsberger Str 191A, Munich, 80687, Germany. TEL 49-89-54756301, FAX 49-89-54756309, info@@thomsonreuters.com, http://www.thomsonreuters.com. Circ: 1,000.

016.6087 DEU ISSN 0943-1306
AUSZUEGE AUS DEN EUROPAEISCHEN PATENTANMELDUNGEN. TEIL 3B. MASCHINENBAU/EXTRACTS FROM EUROPEAN PATENT APPLICATIONS. PART 3B. MECHANICAL ENGINEERING. Text in German. 1993. w. EUR 2,625 (effective 2010). **Document type:** *Journal, Abstract/Index.*
Supersedes in part (1985-1993): Auszuege aus den Europaeischen Patentanmeldungen. Teil 3. Uebrige Verarbeitungsindustrie und Arbeitsverfahren, Maschinen- und Fahrzeugbau, Ernaehrung, Landwirtschaft (0177-9648)
Published by: Thomson Reuters (Professional) Deutschland (Subsidiary of: Thomson Reuters Corp.), Landsberger Str 191A, Munich, 80687, Germany. TEL 49-89-54756301, FAX 49-89-54756309, info@@thomsonreuters.com, http://www.thomsonreuters.com.

016.8107 DEU ISSN 0941-0007
AUSZUEGE AUS DEN EUROPAEISCHEN PATENTSCHRIFTEN. TEIL 1. GRUND- UND ROHSTOFFINDUSTRIE, CHEMIE UND HUETTEN-WESEN, BAUWESEN UND BERGBAU. Text in German. 1992. w. EUR 1,240 (effective 2010). abstr.; pat. **Document type:** *Journal, Abstract/Index.*
Supersedes in part (1981-1992): Auszuege aus den Europaeischen Patentschriften (0720-9339)
Related titles: Online - full text ed.; ◆ English ed.: Extracts from European Patent Specifications. Part 1. Primary Industry, Chemistry and Metallurgy, Fixed Constructions, Mining. ISSN 0940-564X.
Published by: Thomson Reuters (Professional) Deutschland (Subsidiary of: Thomson Reuters Corp.), Landsberger Str 191A, Munich, 80687, Germany. TEL 49-89-54756301, FAX 49-89-54756309, info@@thomsonreuters.com, http://www.thomsonreuters.com. Ed. Michael Lipp. Adv. contact Petra Benesch. Circ: 500.

016.6087 DEU ISSN 0941-0015
AUSZUEGE AUS DEN EUROPAEISCHEN PATENTSCHRIFTEN. TEIL 2. ELEKTROTECHNIK, PHYSIK, FEINMECHANIK UND OPTIK, AKUSTIK. Text in German. 1992. w. EUR 1,240 (effective 2010). **Document type:** *Journal, Abstract/Index.*
Supersedes in part (1980-1992): Auszuege aus den Europaeischen Patentschriften (0720-9339)
Related titles: ◆ English ed.: Extracts from European Patent Specifications. Part 2. Electricity, Physics, Precision Engineering, Optics and Acoustics. ISSN 0941-0031.
Published by: Thomson Reuters (Professional) Deutschland (Subsidiary of: Thomson Reuters Corp.), Landsberger Str 191A, Munich, 80687, Germany. TEL 49-89-54756301, FAX 49-89-54756309, info@@thomsonreuters.com, http://www.thomsonreuters.com. Circ: 500.

016.6087 DEU ISSN 0941-0023
AUSZUEGE AUS DEN EUROPAEISCHEN PATENTSCHRIFTEN. TEIL 3. UEBRIGE VERARBEITUNGSINDUSTRIE UND ARBEITSVERFAHREN, MASCHINEN- UND FAHRZEUGBAU, ERNAEHRUNG, LANDWIRTSCHAFT. Text in German. 1992. w. EUR 1,240 (effective 2010). **Document type:** *Journal, Abstract/Index.*
Supersedes in part (1980-1992): Auszuege aus den Europaeischen Patentschriften (0720-9339)
Related titles: ◆ English ed.: Extracts from European Patent Specifications. Part 3. Manufacturing Industry and Performing Operations, Mechanical Engineering and Vehicle Construction, Food Industry. ISSN 0941-004X.
Published by: Thomson Reuters (Professional) Deutschland (Subsidiary of: Thomson Reuters Corp.), Landsberger Str 191A, Munich, 80687, Germany. TEL 49-89-54756301, FAX 49-89-54756309, info@@thomsonreuters.com, http://www.thomsonreuters.com. Circ: 500.

016.6087 DEU ISSN 0005-0571
AUSZUEGE AUS DEN GEBRAUCHSMUSTERN. AUSGABE A/EXTRACTS FROM GERMAN UTILITY MODELS. EDITION A. Text in German. 1964. w. EUR 1,350 (effective 2010). abstr.; illus.; pat. **Document type:** *Journal, Abstract/Index.*
Related titles: Online - full text ed.
Published by: Thomson Reuters (Professional) Deutschland (Subsidiary of: Thomson Reuters Corp.), Landsberger Str 191A, Munich, 80687, Germany. TEL 49-89-54756301, FAX 49-89-54756309, info@@thomsonreuters.com, http://www.thomsonreuters.com. Ed. Michael Lipp. Adv. contact Petra Benesch. Circ: 1,000.

016.6087 DEU ISSN 0340-2126
AUSZUEGE AUS DEN GEBRAUCHSMUSTERN. AUSGABE B/EXTRACTS FROM GERMAN UTILITY MODELS. EDITION B. Text in German. 1964. w. EUR 1,680 (effective 2010). **Document type:** *Journal, Abstract/Index.*
Published by: Thomson Reuters (Professional) Deutschland (Subsidiary of: Thomson Reuters Corp.), Landsberger Str 191A, Munich, 80687, Germany. TEL 49-89-54756301, FAX 49-89-54756309, info@@thomsonreuters.com, http://www.thomsonreuters.com.

016.6087 DEU ISSN 0340-0816
AUSZUEGE AUS DEN OFFENLEGUNGSSCHRIFTEN. TEIL 1. GRUND- UND ROHSTOFFINDUSTRIE, CHEMIE UND HUETTEN-WESEN, BAUWESEN UND BERGBAU. Text in German. 1968. w. EUR 1,450 (effective 2010). **Document type:** *Journal, Abstract/Index.*
Related titles: Online - full text ed.
Published by: Thomson Reuters (Professional) Deutschland (Subsidiary of: Thomson Reuters Corp.), Landsberger Str 191A, Munich, 80687, Germany. TEL 49-89-54756301, FAX 49-89-54756309, info@@thomsonreuters.com, http://www.thomsonreuters.com.

016.6087 DEU ISSN 0340-0867
AUSZUEGE AUS DEN OFFENLEGUNGSSCHRIFTEN. TEIL 2. ELEKTROTECHNIK, PHYSIK, FEINMECHANIK UND OPTIK, AKUSTIK. Text in German. 1968. w. EUR 1,450 (effective 2010). **Document type:** *Journal, Abstract/Index.*
Related titles: Online - full text ed.
Published by: Thomson Reuters (Professional) Deutschland (Subsidiary of: Thomson Reuters Corp.), Landsberger Str 191A, Munich, 80687, Germany. TEL 49-89-54756301, FAX 49-89-54756309, info@@thomsonreuters.com, http://www.thomsonreuters.com. Circ: 1,500.

016.6087 DEU ISSN 0340-0913
AUSZUEGE AUS DEN OFFENLEGUNGSSCHRIFTEN. TEIL 3. UEBRIGE VERARBEITUNGSINDUSTRIE UND ARBEITSVERFAHREN, MASCHINEN- UND FAHRZEUGBAU, ERNAEHRUNG, LANDWIRTSCHAFT. Text in German. 1968. w. EUR 1,450 (effective 2010). **Document type:** *Journal, Abstract/Index.*
Related titles: Online - full text ed.
Published by: Thomson Reuters (Professional) Deutschland (Subsidiary of: Thomson Reuters Corp.), Landsberger Str 191A, Munich, 80687, Germany. TEL 49-89-54756301, FAX 49-89-54756309, info@@thomsonreuters.com, http://www.thomsonreuters.com. Circ: 1,000.

016.6087 DEU ISSN 0178-4250
AUSZUEGE AUS DEN PATENTSCHRIFTEN. AUSGABE A/EXTRACTS FROM GERMAN PATENT SPECIFICATIONS. EDITION A. Text in German. 1955. w. EUR 1,560 (effective 2010). **Document type:** *Journal, Abstract/Index.*
Former titles: Auszuege aus den Auslegeschriften; Auszuege aus den Patentanmeldungen (0005-058X)
Related titles: Online - full text ed.
—PADDS.
Published by: Thomson Reuters (Professional) Deutschland (Subsidiary of: Thomson Reuters Corp.), Landsberger Str 191A, Munich, 80687, Germany. TEL 49-89-54756301, FAX 49-89-54756309, info@@thomsonreuters.com, http://www.thomsonreuters.com. Circ: 1,500.

016.6087 DEU ISSN 0178-4269
AUSZUEGE AUS DEN PATENTSCHRIFTEN. AUSGABE B/EXTRACTS FROM GERMAN PATENT SPECIFICATIONS. EDITION B. Text in German. 1985. w. EUR 1,870 (effective 2010). **Document type:** *Journal, Abstract/Index.*
Published by: Thomson Reuters (Professional) Deutschland (Subsidiary of: Thomson Reuters Corp.), Landsberger Str 191A, Munich, 80687, Germany. TEL 49-89-54756301, FAX 49-89-54756309, info@@thomsonreuters.com, http://www.thomsonreuters.com.

C A SELECTS. CERAMIC MATERIALS (PATENTS). *see* CERAMICS, GLASS AND POTTERY—Abstracting, Bibliographies, Statistics

540 USA ISSN 0734-8819
CODEN: CAPPEC
C A SELECTS. NOVEL POLYMERS FROM PATENTS. Text in English. s-w. USD 385 to non-members; USD 115 to members; USD 575 combined subscription to individuals (print & online eds.) (effective 2011). **Document type:** *Abstract/Index.* **Description:** Covers patents mentioning newly reported polymeric materials.
Related titles: Online - full text ed.: USD 380 to non-members; USD 114 to members (effective 2011).
Published by: Chemical Abstracts Service (Subsidiary of: American Chemical Society), 2540 Olentangy River Rd, Columbus, OH 43210-0012. TEL 614-447-3600, FAX 614-447-3713, help@cas.com, http://caselects.cas.org. **Subscr. to:** PO Box 3012, Columbus, OH 43210. TEL 800-753-4227, FAX 614-447-3751.

C A SELECTS. PHARMACEUTICAL CHEMISTRY (PATENTS). *see* PHARMACY AND PHARMACOLOGY—Abstracting, Bibliographies, Statistics

COPYRIGHT CATALOGING: MONOGRAPHS AND DOCUMENTS. *see* BIBLIOGRAPHIES

COPYRIGHT CATALOGING: MONOGRAPHS, DOCUMENTS, AND SERIALS. *see* BIBLIOGRAPHIES

016.6087 DEU ISSN 0940-564X
EXTRACTS FROM EUROPEAN PATENT SPECIFICATIONS. PART 1. PRIMARY INDUSTRY, CHEMISTRY AND METALLURGY, FIXED CONSTRUCTIONS, MINING. Text in English. 1992. w. EUR 1,240 (effective 2010). **Document type:** *Journal, Abstract/Index.*
Related titles: ◆ German ed.: Auszuege aus den Europaeischen Patentschriften. Teil 1. Grund- und Rohstoffindustrie, Chemie und Huetten-Wesen, Bauwesen und Bergbau. ISSN 0941-0007.
Published by: Thomson Reuters (Professional) Deutschland (Subsidiary of: Thomson Reuters Corp.), Landsberger Str 191A, Munich, 80687, Germany. TEL 49-89-54756301, FAX 49-89-54756309, info@@thomsonreuters.com, http://www.thomsonreuters.com. Ed. Michael Lipp. Adv. contact Petra Benesch.

016.6087 DEU ISSN 0941-0031
EXTRACTS FROM EUROPEAN PATENT SPECIFICATIONS. PART 2. ELECTRICITY, PHYSICS, PRECISION ENGINEERING, OPTICS AND ACOUSTICS. Text in English. 1992. w. EUR 1,240 (effective 2010). **Document type:** *Journal, Abstract/Index.*
Related titles: ◆ German ed.: Auszuege aus den Europaeischen Patentschriften. Teil 2. Elektrotechnik, Physik, Feinmechanik und Optik, Akustik. ISSN 0941-0015.
Published by: Thomson Reuters (Professional) Deutschland (Subsidiary of: Thomson Reuters Corp.), Landsberger Str 191A, Munich, 80687, Germany. TEL 49-89-54756301, FAX 49-89-54756309, info@@thomsonreuters.com, http://www.thomsonreuters.com.

016.6087 DEU ISSN 0941-004X
EXTRACTS FROM EUROPEAN PATENT SPECIFICATIONS. PART 3. MANUFACTURING INDUSTRY AND PERFORMING OPERATIONS, MECHANICAL ENGINEERING AND VEHICLE CONSTRUCTION, FOOD INDUSTRY. Text in English. 1992. w. EUR 1,240 (effective 2010). **Document type:** *Journal, Abstract/Index.*
Related titles: ◆ German ed.: Auszuege aus den Europaeischen Patentschriften. Teil 3. Uebrige Verarbeitungsindustrie und Arbeitsverfahren, Maschinen- und Fahrzeugbau, Ernaehrung, Landwirtschaft. ISSN 0941-0023.
Published by: Thomson Reuters (Professional) Deutschland (Subsidiary of: Thomson Reuters Corp.), Landsberger Str 191A, Munich, 80687, Germany. TEL 49-89-54756301, FAX 49-89-54756309, info@@thomsonreuters.com, http://www.thomsonreuters.com.

016.6087 DEU ISSN 1436-6894
EXTRACTS FROM INTERNATIONAL PATENT APPLICATIONS. PART 1: PRIMARY INDUSTRY, CHEMISTRY AND METALLURGY, FIXED CONTRUCTIONS, MINING. Text in German. 1998. w. EUR 660 (effective 2010). **Document type:** *Journal, Trade.* **Description:** Provides information on the legal protection of industrial property, including full bibliographic data, an abstract and, where available, a copy of the drawing accompanying the abstract.
Published by: Thomson Reuters (Professional) Deutschland (Subsidiary of: Thomson Reuters Corp.), Landsberger Str 191A, Munich, 80687, Germany. TEL 49-89-54756301, FAX 49-89-54756309, info@@thomsonreuters.com, http://www.thomsonreuters.com.

016.6087 DEU ISSN 1436-6908
EXTRACTS FROM INTERNATIONAL PATENT APPLICATIONS. PART 2: ELECTRICITY, PHYSICS, PRECISION ENGINEERING, OPTICS AND ACOUSTICS. Text in English. 2004. w. EUR 660 (effective 2010). **Document type:** *Journal, Abstract/Index.*
Published by: Thomson Reuters (Professional) Deutschland (Subsidiary of: Thomson Reuters Corp.), Landsberger Str 191A, Munich, 80687, Germany. TEL 49-89-54756301, FAX 49-89-54756309, info@@thomsonreuters.com, http://www.thomsonreuters.com.

016.6087 DEU ISSN 1436-6916
EXTRACTS FROM INTERNATIONAL PATENT APPLICATIONS. PART 3: MANUFACTURING INDUSTRY AND PERFORMING OPERATIONS, MECHANICAL ENGINEERING AND VEHICLE CONSTRUCTION, FOOD INDUSTRY. Text in English. 2005. w. EUR 660 (effective 2010). **Document type:** *Journal, Abstract/Index.*
Published by: Thomson Reuters (Professional) Deutschland (Subsidiary of: Thomson Reuters Corp.), Landsberger Str 191A, Munich, 80687, Germany. TEL 49-89-54756301, FAX 49-89-54756309, info@@thomsonreuters.com, http://www.thomsonreuters.com.

608.7 USA ISSN 0161-9470
T223
INDEX TO THE U.S. PATENT CLASSIFICATION SYSTEM. Text in English. 1956. a. free (effective 2011). back issues avail. **Document type:** *Government.* **Description:** Lists about 67,000 common, informal headings of terms referring to classes or subclasses in the Manual of Classification.
Formerly (until 1977): Index to Classification
Related titles: Online - full text ed.
—Linda Hall.
Published by: U.S. Patent and Trademark Office, General Information Services Division, PO Box 1450, Alexandria, VA 22313. TEL 571-272-1000, 800-786-9199, usptoinfo@uspto.gov.

608.7 CHE ISSN 1013-8374
T201
INDUSTRIAL PROPERTY, STATISTICS B. PART 1 - PATENTS/ PROPRIETE INDUSTRIELLE, STATISTIQUES B. PARTIE 1 - BREVETS. Text in English, French. a. CHF 60 (effective 1999). charts. back issues avail. **Description:** Covers year in question, with complete statistics on patent applications and patents granted to residents and nonresidents.
Supersedes in part (in 1985): Industrial Property, Statistics B (0377-0044)
Indexed: IIS.
Published by: World Intellectual Property Organization/Organisation Mondiale de la Propriete Intellectuelle, Publications Sales and Distribution Unit, 34 Chemin des Colombettes, Geneva 20, 1211, Switzerland. TEL 41-22-338-9111, FAX 41-22-338-1812. Circ: 250.

602.7 608.7 CHE ISSN 1013-8382
INDUSTRIAL PROPERTY, STATISTICS B. PART 2 - TRADEMARKS AND SERVICE MARKS, UTILITY MODELS, INDUSTRIAL DESIGNS, VARIETIES OF PLANTS, MICROORGANISMS/ PROPRIETE INDUSTRIELLE, STATISTIQUES B. PARTIE 2 - MARQUES DE PRODUITS ET DES SERVICES, MODELES D'UTILITE, DESSINS ET MODELES INDUSTRIELS, OBTENTIONS VEGETALES, MICRO-ORGANISMES. Text in English, French. a. CHF 60 (effective 1999). charts. back issues avail. **Description:** Covers year in question with complete statistics on trademark and service mark applications and registrations by residents and nonresidents.
Supersedes in part (in 1985): Industrial Property, Statistics B (0377-0044)
Published by: World Intellectual Property Organization/Organisation Mondiale de la Propriete Intellectuelle, Publications Sales and Distribution Unit, 34 Chemin des Colombettes, Geneva 20, 1211, Switzerland. TEL 41-22-338-9111, FAX 41-22-740-1812.

608.7 RUS
PATENT ABSTRACTS IN ENGLISH. Text in Russian. 1994. 6/yr. USD 1,500. **Document type:** *Bulletin, Abstract/Index.*
Media: CD-ROM.
Published by: Vsesoyuznyi Nauchno-Issledovatel'skii Institut Patentnoi Informatsii (VNIIPI)/Committee of Russian Federation for Patents and Trademarks, Raushskaya nab 4-5, Moscow, 113035, Russian Federation. TEL 7-095-9593313, FAX 7-095-9593304. Ed. E I Daich.

346.04 BGR
PATENT ABSTRACTS OF BULGARIA. Text in English. m. **Description:** Contains English language translations of bibliographical data and abstracts with drawings/chemical formulae of published applications and granted patents for inventions and utility models.
Published by: Patentno Vedomstvo na Republika Bulgaria/Patent Office of the Republic of Bulgaria, 52b, Dr G M Dimitrov Blvd, Sofia, 1797, Bulgaria. TEL 359-2-710152, FAX 359-2-717044, tivanova@bpo.bg, http://www.bpo.bg/. Adv. contact Elina Sinkova.

608.7 JPN
PATENTS ABSTRACTS OF JAPAN. Text in English. 1976. m. JPY 60,408 (effective 2001). abstr.; bibl.; illus. **Document type:** *Abstract/ Index.* **Description:** Provides information on unexamined patent applications. Includes bibliographic data, abstracts, and drawings.
Media: CD-ROM.
Published by: (Japan. Japanese Patent Office), Japan Patent Information Organization, Sato-Dia Bldg, 4-1-7 Toyo, Koto-ku, Tokyo, 135-0016, Japan. TEL 81-3-36155510, FAX 81-3-36155520, service@japio.or.jp.

PEDIATRICS

see MEDICAL SCIENCES—Pediatrics

PERFUMES AND COSMETICS

see BEAUTY CULTURE—Perfumes And Cosmetics

PERSONAL COMPUTERS

see COMPUTERS—Personal Computers

PERSONNEL MANAGEMENT

see BUSINESS AND ECONOMICS—Personnel Management

PETROLEUM AND GAS

666.5 553.282 USA ISSN 0149-1423
TN860 CODEN: AABUD2
➤ **A A P G BULLETIN.** Text in English. 1917. m. free to members (effective 2009). bk.rev. bibl.; illus.; maps; stat. Index. 200 p./no.; back issues avail. **Document type:** *Journal, Academic/Scholarly.* **Description:** Provides information on geoscience and the associated technology of the energy industry.
Former titles (until 1974): The American Association of Petroleum Geologists Bulletin (0002-7464); (until 1967): American Association of Petroleum Geologists. Bulletin (0883-9247); (until 1918): Southwestern Association of Petroleum Geologists. Bulletin
Related titles: CD-ROM ed.: ISSN 1522-1423; Microform ed.: ISSN 0364-9849 (from PMC, PQC); Online - full text ed.: ISSN 1558-9153.
Indexed: A05, A20, A22, A23, A24, ABS&EES, AESIS, AS&TA, AS&TI, ASCA, ASFA, B04, B10, B13, BrGeoL, C&ISA, C10, CA, CIN, CPEI, CTO, ChemAb, ChemTitl, CurCont, E&CAJ, E&PHSE, EIA, ESPM, EngInd, EnvAb, F&EA, GEOBASE, GP&P, GSW, GasAb, GeoRef, GeotechAb, INIS AtomInd, ISMEC, ISR, MinerAb, OceAb, OffTech, P30, PetrolAb, RefZh, SCI, SCOPUS, SWRA, SolStAb, SpeleolAb, T02, W07.
—BLDSC (0537.502000), CASDDS, IE, Infotrieve, Ingenta, INIST, Linda Hall, PADDS. **CCC.**
Published by: American Association of Petroleum Geologists, PO Box 979, Tulsa, OK 74101. TEL 918-584-2555, FAX 918-560-2665, info@aapg.org. Ed. Andrea Sharrer.

666.5 USA ISSN 0195-2986
TN860
A A P G EXPLORER. Text in English. 1979. m. USD 75 to non-members; free to members (effective 2009). adv. charts; illus.; maps; stat. back issues avail. **Document type:** *Newspaper, Trade.* **Description:** Features breaking news stories, features, profiles of personalities, comment columns and Association information with an emphasis on exploration for hydrocarbons and energy minerals.
Related titles: Online - full text ed.
Indexed: A22, A33, AESIS, GeoRef, PetrolAb, SpeleolAb.
—BLDSC (0537.502300), IE, Infotrieve, Ingenta, Linda Hall, PADDS. **CCC.**
Published by: American Association of Petroleum Geologists, PO Box 979, Tulsa, OK 74101. TEL 918-584-2555, 800-364-2274, FAX 918-560-2665, info@aapg.org. Ed. Edward A Ted Beaumont. Adv. contact Brenda Merideth TEL 918-560-2647. Circ: 31,000 (paid).

A A P G MEMOIR. *see* EARTH SCIENCES—Geology

666.5 USA ISSN 0271-8510
CODEN: ASTGD6
➤ **A A P G STUDIES IN GEOLOGY SERIES.** Text in English. 1975. irreg., latest vol.57, 2006. price varies. cum.index: 1971-75, 1976-80, 1981-85. **Document type:** *Monographic series, Academic/Scholarly.* **Description:** Book series that documents current, state-of-the-art advances in research applicable to the geological community.
Related titles: CD-ROM ed.; Online - full text ed.
Indexed: AESIS, CIS, ChemAb, GeoRef, IMMAb, SpeleolAb.
—BLDSC (0537.506000), CASDDS. **CCC.**
Published by: American Association of Petroleum Geologists, PO Box 979, Tulsa, OK 74101. TEL 918-584-2555, 800-364-2274, FAX 918-560-2665, info@aapg.org, http://www.aapg.org.

665.5 UAE
A D N O C NEWS/AKHBAR A D N O C. (Abu Dhabi National Oil Company) Text in Arabic, English. 1978. m. free. adv. **Document type:** *Magazine, Corporate.* **Description:** Discusses ADNOC activities and all petroleum projects in Abu Dhabi and the U.A.E.
Formerly (until Dec. 1988): Petroleum Community - Mujtama' al-Bitrul
Published by: Abu Dhabi National Oil Company, Public Relations Department, PO Box 898, Abu Dhabi, United Arab Emirates. TEL 971-2-6023767, FAX 971-2-6657339, TELEX 22215 EM, adnoc@adnoc.com, http://www.adnoc.com. Ed. Hulaiman Al-Hameli. Adv. contact Mounir Mohamed. Circ: 2,000.

A E S C DIRECTORY. *see* BUSINESS AND ECONOMICS—Trade And Industrial Directories

338.47 665.74 USA
A G A RATE SERVICE. Text in English. 1919. s-a. looseleaf. USD 500 to non-members; USD 250 to members (effective 2008).
Published by: (American Gas Association), AUS Inc, 155 Gaither Dr, Ste A, Mount Laurel, NJ 08054. TEL 856-234-9200, aus@ausinc.com, http://www.ausinc.com. Circ: 500.

665.5 USA ISSN 0271-2253
A P I PUBLICATION. (American Petroleum Institute) Text in English. irreg.
Indexed: APIAb, GeoRef, SCOPUS.
—BLDSC (1567.940000). **CCC.**
Published by: American Petroleum Institute, 2101 L St, NW, Washington, DC 20037.

665.5 AUS
A P P E A ANNUAL REPORT. Text in English. a. (Aug/Sep). free (effective 2008). back issues avail. **Document type:** *Corporate.*
Related titles: Online - full content ed.
Indexed: AESIS.
Published by: Australian Petroleum Production and Exploration Association, GPO Box 2201, Canberra, ACT 2601, Australia. TEL 61-2-62470960, FAX 61-2-62470548, appea@appea.com.au.

553 AUS
TN271.P4 CODEN: APJOFT
THE A P P E A JOURNAL (DVD). Text in English. 1961. a. AUD 242 to non-members; AUD 220 to members (effective 2008). adv. back issues avail. **Document type:** *Proceedings, Academic/Scholarly.* **Description:** Contains all papers presented at the annual APPEA Conference.
Former titles (until 2007): The A P P E A Journal (Print) (1326-4966); (until 1995): A P E A Journal (0084-7534)
Media: Optical Disk - DVD.
Indexed: A22, AESIS, ASI, ChemAb, FR, GeoRef, PetrolAb, SpeleolAb.
—BLDSC (1570.003000), CASDDS, IE, Infotrieve, Ingenta, INIST, Linda Hall, PADDS. **CCC.**
Published by: Australian Petroleum Production and Exploration Association, GPO Box 2201, Canberra, ACT 2601, Australia. TEL 61-2-62470960, FAX 61-2-62470548, appea@appea.com.au. Ed., R&P, Adv. contact Lynda Gordon. Circ: 1,000.

338.47665 CYP
A P S REVIEW DOWNSTREAM TRENDS. Text in English. w. **Document type:** *Journal, Trade.*
Published by: Arab Press Service, PO Box 23896, Nicosia, Cyprus. TEL 357-2-350265, FAX 357-2-351778, apsnews@spidernet.com.cy.

338.47665 CYP
A P S REVIEW GAS MARKET TRENDS. Text in English. w. **Document type:** *Newsletter, Trade.*
Media: Online - full content.
Published by: Arab Press Service, PO Box 23896, Nicosia, Cyprus. TEL 357-2-350265, FAX 357-2-351778, apsnews@spidernet.com.cy.

665.5 GBR ISSN 0263-5054
ABERDEEN PETROLEUM REPORT. Text in English. 1981. w. GBP 540 (effective 2009); subscr. includes Europetroleum Magazine. adv. back issues avail. **Document type:** *Newsletter, Trade.* **Description:** Provides business intelligence on North Sea oil and gas activities.
Related titles: Online - full text ed.: free (effective 2009).
—**CCC.**
Published by: Aberdeen Petroleum Publishing Ltd., 37 Cochrane Park Ave, Newcastle upon Tyne, NE7 7JU, United Kingdom. TEL 44-870-4380001, FAX 44-870-4380002, info@aproil.co.uk, http://www.aproil.co.uk. Ed. Kevin Daley.

ACTA UNIVERSITATIS SZEGEDIENSIS. ACTA MINERALOGICA - PETROGRAPHICA. *see* MINES AND MINING INDUSTRY

665.5 NLD ISSN 1876-0147
ADVANCES IN GAS PROCESSING. Text in English. 2008. a. price varies.
Published by: Elsevier BV (Subsidiary of: Elsevier Science & Technology), Radarweg 29, PO Box 211, Amsterdam, 1000 AE, Netherlands. TEL 31-20-4853911, FAX 31-20-4852457, http://www.elsevier.com.

665.5 CAN ISSN 1925-542X
▼ ➤ **ADVANCES IN PETROLEUM EXPLORATION AND DEVELOPMENT.** Text in English. 2011 (Jun.15th). q. **Document type:** *Journal, Academic/Scholarly.* **Description:** Covers petroleum (natural gas) geology; reservoir sedimentology; integrated exploration technology; oilfield development; reservoir engineering; well logging; mathematical modeling; reservoir simulation; formation evolution.
Related titles: Online - full text ed.: ISSN 1925-5438. free (effective 2011).
Published by: Canadian Research & Development Center of Sciences and Cultures, 3-265 Melrose, Montreal, PQ H4H 1T2, Canada. http://www.cscanada.org. Ed. Jenny Ding.

665.5 USA ISSN 1937-7991
TD196.P4
▼ **ADVANCES IN SUSTAINABLE PETROLEUM ENGINEERING SCIENCE.** Text in English. 2009. q. USD 370 to institutions; USD 555 combined subscription to institutions (print & online eds.) (effective 2012). **Document type:** *Journal, Academic/Scholarly.* **Description:** Aims to demystify the science behind energy sustainability, with particular focus on petroleum engineering.
Related titles: Online - full text ed.: USD 370 to institutions (effective 2012).
Published by: Nova Science Publishers, Inc., 400 Oser Ave, Ste 1600, Hauppauge, NY 11788. TEL 631-231-7269, FAX 631-231-8175, main@novapublishers.com. Ed. Rafiq R Islam.

665.538 549 FRA ISSN 1635-2742
HD9502.A35
AFRICA ENERGY INTELLIGENCE (ENGLISH EDITION). Text in English. 1983. 23/yr. EUR 745, USD 1,045 (effective 2009). adv. **Document type:** *Newsletter, Trade.* **Description:** Pertinent information for energy and mining professionals on what is happening on the African continent.
Formerly (until 2000): Africa Energy and Mining (0994-0235)
Related titles: Online - full text ed.: ISSN 1635-902X; ◆ French ed.: Africa Energy Intelligence (French Edition). ISSN 1635-9003.
—CIS.
Published by: Indigo Publications, 142 rue Montmartre, Paris, 75002, France. TEL 33-1-44882610, FAX 33-1-44882615, http://www.indigo-net.com. Ed., R&P Maurice Botbol.

665.5 621.3 FRA ISSN 1635-9003
AFRICA ENERGY INTELLIGENCE (FRENCH EDITION). Text in French. 1983. 23/yr. EUR 745 (effective 2009). adv. **Document type:** *Newsletter, Trade.* **Description:** Pertinent information for energy and mining professionals on what is happening on the African continent.
Formerly (until 2000): La Lettre Afrique Energies (0754-5215)
Related titles: Online - full text ed.: ISSN 1635-9011; ◆ English ed.: Africa Energy Intelligence (English Edition). ISSN 1635-2742.
Indexed: FR.
—CIS. **CCC.**
Published by: Indigo Publications, 142 rue Montmartre, Paris, 75002, France. TEL 33-1-44882610, FAX 33-1-44882615, info@africaintelligence.com, http://www.africaintelligence.com. Ed., R&P Maurice Botbol.

552 UAE
AKHBAR AL-BUTRUL WAS-SINA'A/PETROLEUM AND INDUSTRY NEWS. Text in Arabic. 1970. m. **Description:** Discusses current developments and news in petroleum and industry, with a focus on the U.A.E.
Published by: Ministry of Petroleum and Mineral Wealth, P O Box 59, Abu Dhabi, United Arab Emirates. TEL 651810, FAX 663414, TELEX 22544 MPMR EM. Ed. Manaa Said Al Otaiba. Circ: 2,000 (controlled).

552 BHR
AKHBAR B A P C O. Text in Arabic; Summaries in English. 1957. w. free. bk.rev. **Document type:** *Newsletter.*
Formerly (until 1981): Weekly Star - An-Najma al-Usbou'
Published by: (Public Relations Department), Bahrain Petroleum Co. Ltd., P O Box 25149, Awali, Bahrain. TEL 973-755055, FAX 973-755047, TELEX 8214 BAPCO BN. Ed. Khalid Fahad Mehmas. Circ: 8,000.

665.5 LBY
AL-FATEH UNIVERSITY. FACULTY OF PETROLEUM. BULLETIN. Text in English. a.
Published by: Al-Fateh University, Faculty of Petroleum, P O Box 13040, Tripoli, Libya. TEL 36010, TELEX 20629.

665.5 USA
ALABAMA PROPANE GAS NEWS. Text in English. 1950. m. adv. **Document type:** *Newsletter.*
Published by: Alabama Propane Gas Association, 173 Medical Center Dr, Prattville, AL 36066. TEL 331-358-9590, 800-242-2742, FAX 334-358-9520, info@alabamapropane.com, http://www.alabamapropane.com. adv.: B&W page USD 280; 11 x 8.5. Circ: 500.

665.5 GBR ISSN 2044-4982
▼ **ALAELA.** Text in English. 2010 (Spr.). s-a. **Document type:** *Magazine, Trade.*
Published by: Aramco Overseas Company UK Ltd., 26th Fl Ctr Pt, 103 New Oxford St, London, WC1A 1DD, United Kingdom. TEL 44-20-76324950, FAX 44-20-73796912.

665.5 CAN ISSN 1912-5291
ALBERTA OIL. Text in English. 200?. bi-m. CAD 29.95 domestic; USD 49.95 in United States; USD 79.95 elsewhere (effective 2008). **Document type:** *Magazine, Trade.* **Description:** Offers an insight into the Canadian energy sector.
Published by: Venture Publishing, 10259-105 St, Edmonton, AB T5J 1E3, Canada. TEL 780-990-0839, 866-227-4276, FAX 780-425-4921, admin@albertaventure.com, http://www.albertaventure.com/. Ed. Gordon Jaremko. Pub. Ruth Kelly. Circ: 60,000 (controlled).

ALBERTA OIL & GAS DIRECTORY. *see* BUSINESS AND ECONOMICS—Trade And Industrial Directories

665.74 333.8 CAN ISSN 0229-8546
TN873.C22 CODEN: ANTEAU
ALBERTA'S RESERVE OF GAS: COMPLETE LISTING. Text in English. 1979. a. CAD 250. **Document type:** *Government.* **Description:** Detailed data on gas reserves in Alberta with individual estimates and reservoir factors, by pools and areas, for all non-confidential established gas reserves.
Media: Microfiche.
Published by: Energy and Utilities Board, 640 5th Ave, S W, Calgary, AB T2P 3G4, Canada. TEL 403-297-8311, FAX 403-297-7040.

661.804 GBR ISSN 1749-2114
ALGERIA PETROCHEMICALS REPORT. Cover title: Algeria Petrochemicals and Chemicals Report. Text in English. 2005. q. EUR 820, USD 1,030 combined subscription (print & email eds.) (effective 2010). **Document type:** *Report, Trade.* **Description:** Covers independent forecasts and competitive intelligence on the Algerian petrochemicals industry.
Related titles: E-mail ed.
Indexed: A15, ABIn, B02, B15, B17, B18, G04, I05, P48, P51, P52, P56, PQC.
Published by: Business Monitor International Ltd., Senator House, 85 Queen Victoria St, London, EC4V 4AB, United Kingdom. TEL 44-20-72480468, FAX 44-20-72480467, subs@businessmonitor.com.

665.5 USA ISSN 1930-4897
HD9575.R8
THE ALMANAC OF RUSSIAN AND CASPIAN PETROLEUM. Text in English. 1993. a. USD 1,295 per issue (effective 2009). **Document type:** *Yearbook, Trade.* **Description:** Provides a recognized as the annual reference work comprising all the competitive data, vital statistics, and market analysis on every aspect of the oil and gas business in one of the industry's most dynamic arenas.
Formerly (until 2001): The Almanac of Russian Petroleum (1528-1221)
Related titles: Online - full text ed.
Published by: Energy Intelligence Group, Inc., 5 E 37th St, 5th Fl, New York, NY 10016. TEL 212-532-1112, FAX 212-532-4479, info@energyintel.com. Eds. David Knapp, John Van Schaik.

662.6 USA ISSN 1521-4648
CODEN: PSADFZ
AMERICAN CHEMICAL SOCIETY. DIVISION OF FUEL CHEMISTRY. PREPRINTS OF SYMPOSIA. Text in English. 19??. s-a. free to members (effective 2009). back issues avail. **Document type:** *Government.* **Description:** Provides a forum for documentation and communication to the international community of research and development results, in order to promote efficient and environmentally acceptable fuel production and use.
Formerly (until 1997): American Chemical Society. Division of Fuel Chemistry. Preprints of Papers Presented (0569-3772)
Indexed: A22, C33, GeoRef, INIS AtomInd, SCOPUS.
—IE, INIST, Linda Hall.
Published by: (American Chemical Society, Division of Fuel Chemistry), American Chemical Society, 1155 16th St, NW, Washington, DC 20036. TEL 202-872-4600, 800-227-5558, http://pubs.acs.org, https://portal.chemistry.org/. Ed. Bahram Fathollahi TEL 858-395-8653. **Subscr. to:** PO Box 3337, Columbus, OH 43210. TEL 614-447-3674, 888-338-0012, FAX 614-447-5475.

AMERICAN CHEMICAL SOCIETY. PETROLEUM CHEMISTRY DIVISION. PREPRINTS. *see* CHEMISTRY—Organic Chemistry

665.7 USA ISSN 1043-0652
TP700 CODEN: AMGLEH
AMERICAN GAS. Text in English. 1918. 11/yr. USD 59 domestic to non-members; USD 110 foreign to non-members; free to members (effective 2006). adv. bk.rev. charts; illus.; maps; stat. index. back issues avail. **Document type:** *Magazine, Trade.* **Description:** Provides gas industry professionals with the information they need to enhance their effectiveness and that of their companies.
Former titles (until 1989): A G A Monthly (0885-2413); American Gas Association Monthly (0002-8584)
Related titles: Microfilm ed.: 1919; Online - full text ed.: 1919.
Indexed: A09, A10, A12, A13, A15, A17, A22, A23, A24, ABIn, B01, B02, B03, B06, B07, B09, B13, B15, B17, B18, ChemAb, E04, E05, E14, EIA, EnvAb, EnvInd, F&EA, G04, G08, GasAb, I05, L09, P34, P48, P51, P52, P53, P54, P56, PQC, PetrolAb, SCOPUS, T02, V03, V04.
—BLDSC (0815.900000), IE, Ingenta, INIST, Linda Hall.
Published by: American Gas Association, 400 N Capitol St N W., 4th Fl, Washington, DC 20001. TEL 202-824-7000, FAX 202-824-7216, amgas@aga.com. Ed. Stacey Bell. Adv. contact Carnie Wosicki. B&W page USD 3,145, color page USD 4,040; 8.5 x 11. Circ: 9,000 (paid and controlled).

665.7 USA ISSN 1553-5711
TN880.A1
AMERICAN GAS ASSOCIATION. OPERATING SECTION. PROCEEDINGS (CD-ROM). Text in English. a. USD 198 (effective 2008).
Media: CD-ROM.
Published by: American Gas Association, 400 N Capitol St N W., 4th Fl, Washington, DC 20001. TEL 202-824-7000, FAX 202-824-7216, amgas@aga.com, http://www.aga.org/.

665.5 USA ISSN 0145-9198
TN872
AMERICAN OIL & GAS REPORTER. Text in English. 1958. 12/yr. USD 50 domestic; USD 125 in Canada & Mexico; USD 250 elsewhere (effective 2005). adv. bk.rev. tr.lit. **Document type:** *Magazine, Trade.* **Description:** For the U.S. oil and gas exploration, drilling and production industry.
Formerly: Mid-America Oil and Gas Reporter
Indexed: E&PHSE, GP&P, OffTech, PetrolAb.
—BLDSC (0847.320000), IE, Ingenta, PADDS. **CCC.**
Published by: National Publishers Group, Inc., PO Box 343, Derby, KS 67037-0343. TEL 316-788-6271. Pub. Charlie Cookson. Adv. contact Karen Holmes. B&W page USD 3,000, color page USD 4,200; 8.25 x 10.875. Circ: 14,000 (paid and controlled).

AMERICAN PETROLEUM INSTITUTE. MONTHLY COMPLETION REPORT. *see* PETROLEUM AND GAS—Abstracting, Bibliographies, Statistics

665.75 USA
AMERICAN PUBLIC GAS ASSOCIATION. PUBLIC GAS NEWS. Text in English. 1962. bi-w. USD 45 (effective 2000). **Document type:** *Newsletter.*
Former titles: American Public Gas Association. Newsletter; American Public Gas Association. Memorandum Bulletins (0065-9894)
Published by: American Public Gas Association, 201 Massachusetts Ave NE, Ste. C4, Washington, DC 20002-4988. TEL 703-352-3890. Ed. Kelly Bardzell. Circ: 1,000.

338.272809705 GBR ISSN 1750-7529
HD9574.A1
AMERICAS OIL AND GAS INSIGHT. Text in English. 2006. m. USD 1,010 combined subscription (print & online eds.) (effective 2010). adv. **Document type:** *Report, Trade.* **Description:** Provides analysis, forecasts and company profiles on a country-by-country basis, covering the key trends impacting oil and gas markets across the Americas.
Related titles: Online - full text ed.
Indexed: A15, ABIn, P48, P51, P52, P56, PQC.
Published by: Business Monitor International Ltd., Senator House, 85 Queen Victoria St, London, EC4V 4AB, United Kingdom. TEL 44-20-72480468, FAX 44-20-72480467, subs@businessmonitor.com, http://www.businessmonitor.com. Adv. contact Leila Scott TEL 44-207-2465131.

ANNUAL BOOK OF A S T M STANDARDS. 05.01 PETROLEUM PRODUCTS AND LUBRICANTS (I): D56 - D3348. *see* ENGINEERING—Engineering Mechanics And Materials

ANNUAL BOOK OF A S T M STANDARDS. 05.04 PETROLEUM PRODUCTS AND LUBRICANTS (4): D6730 - LATEST. (American Society for Testing and Materials) *see* ENGINEERING—Engineering Mechanics And Materials

ANNUAL BOOK OF A S T M STANDARDS. VOLUME 05.02. PETROLEUM PRODUCTS AND LUBRICANTS (II): D2597 - D4927. *see* ENGINEERING—Engineering Mechanics And Materials

ANNUAL BOOK OF A S T M STANDARDS. VOLUME 05.03. PETROLEUM PRODUCTS AND LUBRICANTS (3). (American Society for Testing and Materials) *see* ENGINEERING—Engineering Mechanics And Materials

ANNUAL BOOK OF A S T M STANDARDS. VOLUME 05.06. GASEOUS FUELS; COAL AND COKE. (American Society for Testing and Materials) *see* ENGINEERING—Engineering Mechanics And Materials

665.5 338 NGA ISSN 0189-1529
ANNUAL REPORT ON THE NIGERIAN OIL INDUSTRY. Text in English. 1975. a.
Published by: Nigerian National Petroleum Corporation, PMB 12701, Lagos, Nigeria. TEL 234-1-269-0470.

665.5 USA ISSN 0361-5987
TN863 CODEN: PSPCD3
ANNUAL SOUTHWESTERN PETROLEUM SHORT COURSE. PROCEEDINGS. Text in English. 1964. a. **Document type:** *Proceedings.*
Indexed: A22, EngInd, GeoRef, SCOPUS.
—BLDSC (6842.267000), IE, Ingenta, Linda Hall.
Published by: (Southwestern Petroleum Short Course), Texas Tech University, Department of Petroleum Engineering, PO Box 43111, Lubbock, TX 79409-3111. TEL 806-742-1727, FAX 806-742-3502, http://www.pe.ttu.edu.

APPLIED ENERGY. *see* ENERGY

661.804 DEU ISSN 2190-5525
▼ ➤ **APPLIED PETROCHEMICAL RESEARCH.** Text in German. 2011. free (effective 2011). **Document type:** *Journal, Academic/Scholarly.* **Description:** Contains research on all aspects of the petrochemical industry.
Related titles: Online - full text ed.: ISSN 2190-5533. 2011.
Published by: SpringerOpen (Subsidiary of: Springer Science+Business Media), Tiergartenstr 17, Heidelberg, 69121, Germany. info@springeropen.com, http://www.springeropen.com. Eds. Arno de Klerk, Soliman Al-Khowaiter.

338.476 USA ISSN 0264-259X
AQUANAUT. Text in English. 1982. m. **Document type:** *Newsletter, Trade.* **Description:** Analyzes and comments on the main topics and trends which have emerged in the course of the day-to-day monitoring of the global subsurface support business.
Related titles: E-mail ed.; Online - full text ed.
—**CCC.**
Published by: O D S - Petrodata, 3200 Wilcrest Dr, Ste 170, Houston, TX 77042. TEL 832-463-3000, FAX 832-463-3100, general@ods-petrodata.com, http://www.ods-petrodata.com.

338.2 FRA ISSN 0304-8551
HD9578.A55
ARAB OIL & GAS DIRECTORY. Text in English. 1974. a., latest vol.30. EUR 902.90 (effective 2008). adv. illus.; stat. **Document type:** *Directory.* **Description:** Provides complete coverage of Arab oil and gas exporting countries, new products, investment figures, survey of all oil producing surveys, addresses of oil companies.
Related titles: Online - full text ed.: USD 1,240 (effective 2001).
—**CCC.**
Published by: Arab Petroleum Research Center, 7 avenue Ingres, Paris, Cedex 16 75781, France. TEL 33-01-45243310, FAX 33-01-45201685, aprc@arab-oil-gas.com. Pub. Nicolas Sarkis. Adv. contact Anne Marie Happey. B&W page USD 3,080, color page USD 4,580; trim 245 x 180. Circ: 6,700.

338.2 665.538 FRA ISSN 0378-7184
ARAB OIL & GAS MAGAZINE (MONTHLY). Text in Arabic, English. 1966. fortn. USD 280 (effective 2008). adv. **Document type:** *Magazine, Trade.*
Related titles: Arabic ed.: Magallat al-batrul wa-al-gaz al-'arabi. ISSN 0378-7400; French ed.: Le Petrole et le Gaz Arabes. ISSN 0031-6369. FRF 1,530 (effective 2000).
—BLDSC (1583.255000), IE, Ingenta.
Published by: Arab Petroleum Research Center, 7 avenue Ingres, Paris, Cedex 16 75781, France. TEL 33-01-45243310, FAX 33-01-45201685, aprc@arab-oil-gas.com. Ed. Nicolas Sarkis. Adv. contact Anne Marie Happey. B&W page USD 3,080, color page USD 4,580; trim 250 x 190. Circ: 16,500.

665 LBY ISSN 0003-7435
ARAB OIL REVIEW. Text in English, Arabic. 1964. bi-m. LYD 7. adv. illus.; mkt.; tr.lit. index.
Address: Sharia Omar Ibn Abdulaziz 4, Tripoli, Libya. Ed. Naim El Arady.

665 622 LBY ISSN 0003-7443
ARAB PETROLEUM. Text in English. 1964. m.
Published by: Arab Federation of Petroleum Mining & Chemical Workers, P O Box 1905, Tripoli, Libya.

ARCTIC AND MARINE OILSPILL PROGRAM REPORT. *see* ENVIRONMENTAL STUDIES

ARCTIC AND MARINE OILSPILL PROGRAM TECHNICAL SEMINAR. PROCEEDINGS. *see* ENVIRONMENTAL STUDIES

665.7 CAN ISSN 0849-5416
HD9581.C3
AREAS SERVED BY GAS IN CANADA. Text in English. 1984. biennial. CAD 60 to non-members; CAD 30 to members. **Document type:** *Directory, Trade.* **Description:** Lists distributors and areas served by natural gas, population, number of customers or meters in each area.
Published by: (Economics and Statistics Department), Canadian Gas Association, 243 Consumers Rd, Ste 1200, North York, ON M2J 5E3, Canada. TEL 416-498-1994, FAX 416-498-7465.

661.804 982 338.47665 GBR ISSN 1749-2122
ARGENTINA PETROCHEMICALS REPORT. Text in English. a. EUR 820, USD 1,030 combined subscription per issue (print & email eds.) (effective 2010). **Document type:** *Report, Trade.* **Description:** Provides industry professionals and strategists, sector analysts, trade associations and regulatory bodies with independent forecasts and competitive intelligence on the Argentinian petrochemicals industry.
Related titles: E-mail ed.
Indexed: A15, ABIn, B02, B15, B17, B18, G04, I05, P48, P51, P52, P56, PQC.
Published by: Business Monitor International Ltd., Senator House, 85 Queen Victoria St, London, EC4V 4AB, United Kingdom. TEL 44-20-72480468, FAX 44-20-72480467, subs@businessmonitor.com.

665.5 ITA
ARGOMENTI ESSO. Text in Italian. 1974. m. free. charts; illus.; stat. **Document type:** *Magazine, Trade.* **Description:** House organ of Esso Italia and of ExxonMobil Mediterranea, covers the activities of these two companies.
Formerly (until 1988): Esso Italiana. Informazioni Economiche
Published by: Esso Italiana, Viale Castello della Magliana 25, Rome, 00148, Italy. http://www.esso.com, http://www.esso.it.

662.338 GBR ISSN 2042-9703
▼ **ARGUS BASE OILS.** Text in English. 2010. w. **Document type:** *Report, Trade.* **Description:** Provides weekly prices and market commentary on base oils globally as well as relevant crude oil and petroleum products prices.
Media: Online - full text.
Published by: Argus Media Ltd., Argus House, 175 St. John St, London, EC1V 4LW, United Kingdom. TEL 44-20-77804200, FAX 44-20-77804201, london@argusmedia.com. Ed. Iain Pocock.

662.338 GBR ISSN 2043-0671
▼ **ARGUS BASE OILS. DAILY UPDATE.** Text in English. 2010. d. **Document type:** *Report, Trade.* **Description:** Provides daily prices and market commentary on base oils globally as well as relevant crude oil and petroleum products prices.
Media: Online - full text.
Published by: Argus Media Ltd., Argus House, 175 St. John St, London, EC1V 4LW, United Kingdom. TEL 44-20-77804200, FAX 44-20-77804201, london@argusmedia.com. Ed. Iain Pocock.

338.47665 USA
ARGUS CHINA PETROLEUM. Text in English. 2008. m. **Document type:** *Newsletter, Trade.* **Description:** Supplies data on the oil industry in China. Includes news and analysis of the oil markets, policy and infrastructure in China and surrounding countries.
Published by: Argus Media Inc., 3040 Post Oak Blvd, Ste 550, Houston, TX 77056. TEL 713-968-0000, FAX 713-622-2991, houstoneditorial@argusmediagroup.com, http://www.argusmediagroup.com.

P

ARGUS FREIGHT; daily international freight rates and market commentary. *see* TRANSPORTATION—Ships And Shipping

665.538 658.7 GBR ISSN 0957-039X
ARGUS FUNDAMENTALS. Text in English. 1989. m. **Document type:** *Newsletter, Trade.* **Description:** Provides news and analysis of latest developments in the European natural gas industry.
Related titles: Online - full content ed.
Published by: Argus Media Ltd., Argus House, 175 St. John St, London, EC1V 4LW, United Kingdom. TEL 44-20-77804200, FAX 44-20-77804201, enquiries@argusmedia.com, http://www.argusmedia.com. Ed. Ian Bourne. Pub. Adrian Binks.

665.74 GBR ISSN 1460-695X
ARGUS GAS CONNECTIONS; European supplies, production and transport. Variant title: Petroleum Argus Gas Connections. Text in English. 1997. s-m. **Document type:** *Newsletter, Trade.* **Description:** Contains comprehensive analytical briefs on the latest developments in European gas, electricity and power.
Related titles: Online - full text ed.
Indexed: B02, B03, B15, B17, B18, G04, G06, G07, G08, I05, T03. **—CCC.**
Published by: Argus Media Ltd., Argus House, 175 St. John St, London, EC1V 4LW, United Kingdom. TEL 44-20-77804200, FAX 44-20-77804201, enquiries@argusmedia.com, http://www.argusmedia.com. Ed. Ian Bourne. Pub. Adrian Binks.

665.5 GBR ISSN 1368-7433
ARGUS GLOBAL MARKETS; oil price reporting, derivatives and analysis. Text in English. 1997. w. **Document type:** *Bulletin, Trade.* **Description:** Provides weekly analysis of the oil markets as well as expert commentary on key industry developments and market activity. Exclusive data includes fundamentals, derivatives and pricing in the global crude and products markets.
Supersedes in part (in 1997): Weekly Petroleum Argus (0268-7844); Which was formerly (until 1985): Europ-Oil Prices
Related titles: Online - full text ed.
Indexed: B02, B03, B15, B17, B18, G04, G06, G07, G08, I05, T03. **—CCC.**
Published by: Argus Media Ltd., Argus House, 175 St. John St, London, EC1V 4LW, United Kingdom. TEL 44-20-77804200, FAX 44-20-77804201, enquiries@argusmedia.com, http://www.argusmedia.com. Ed. Ian Bourne. Pub. Adrian Binks.

665.5 GBR ISSN 2046-2301
▼ **ARGUS L N G DAILY.** (Liquefied Natural Gas) Text in English. 2011. d. **Document type:** *Report, Trade.* **Description:** Provides daily information on the global market, demand and prices of LNG.
Media: Online - full text.
Published by: Argus Media Ltd., Argus House, 175 St. John St, London, EC1V 4LW, United Kingdom. TEL 44-20-77804200, FAX 44-20-77804201, london@argusmedia.com.

665.538 GBR ISSN 2047-1289
▼ **ARGUS MIDEAST GULF AND INDIAN OCEAN PRODUCTS.** Text in English. 2011. w. **Document type:** *Report, Trade.* **Description:** Provides price assessments, market news and in-depth analysis of refined oil products.
Published by: Argus Media Ltd., Argus House, 175 St. John St, London, EC1V 4LW, United Kingdom. TEL 44-20-77804200, FAX 44-20-77804201, london@argusmedia.com.

665.7 GBR ISSN 2152-7156
ARGUS NATURAL GAS AMERICAS. Text in English. 1995. d. back issues avail. **Document type:** *Newsletter, Trade.*
Media: Online - full text.
Published by: Argus Media Ltd., Argus House, 175 St. John St, London, EC1V 4LW, United Kingdom. TEL 44-20-77804200, FAX 44-20-77804201, london@argusmedia.com, http://www.argusmedia.com. Eds. Matthew Monteverde, Ian Bourne.

665.538 GBR
ARGUS RUSSIAN FUEL OIL. Text in English. 2006. d. **Document type:** *Newsletter, Trade.* **Description:** Designed to help fuel oil traders compare the profitability of exports and sales to the domestic market. Covers concluded deals in the Russian fuel oil market and market tendencies. Includes prices from all areas.
Published by: Argus Media Ltd., Argus House, 175 St. John St, London, EC1V 4LW, United Kingdom. TEL 44-20-77804200, FAX 44-20-77804201, enquiries@argusmedia.com.

665.5 USA ISSN 0570-9520
ARIZONA GEOLOGICAL SURVEY. OIL, GAS & HELIUM PRODUCTION. Text in English. 1958. irreg. stat. index. **Document type:** *Government.*
Media: Duplicated (not offset).
Indexed: SRI.
Published by: Arizona Geological Survey, 416 W Congress St, Ste 100, Tucson, AZ 85701. TEL 520-770-3500, FAX 520-770-3505. Ed. Larry D Fellows. R&P Rose Ellen McDonnell. Circ: 40.

557 622 USA
ARIZONA GEOLOGICAL SURVEY. OPEN-FILE REPORT. Text in English. irreg. **Document type:** *Government.*
Formerly: Arizona Geological Survey. Special Publication
Published by: Arizona Geological Survey, 416 W Congress St, Ste 100, Tucson, AZ 85701. TEL 520-770-3500, FAX 520-770-3505. Ed. Larry D Fellows. R&P Rose Ellen McDonnell.

665.7 USA
ARKANSAS PROPANE GAS NEWS. Text in English. 1972 (vol.24). bi-m. USD 2 (effective 2005). **Document type:** *Magazine, Trade.*
Formerly: Arkansas L P News (0044-8893)
Published by: Arkansas Propane Gas Association, Inc., PO Box 10, Lincoln, AR 72744-0010. TEL 479-824-4299, FAX 479-824-5251. Ed. Larry Snodgrass Jr. Circ: 800 (controlled).

665 USA
ARMSTRONG OIL DIRECTORIES: MINI BRIEFCASE EDITION; nation-wide coverage. (In 4 regional eds.) Text in English. a. **Document type:** *Directory, Trade.*
Published by: Armstrong Oil Directories, PO Box 52106, Amarillo, TX 79159. TEL 806-457-9300, FAX 806-457-9301, support@armstrongoil.com.

665.5 USA
ASHLAND SOURCE. Text in English. 1961. m. free. charts; illus.
Formerly: Ashland News
Indexed: EIA, EnvAb.
Published by: Ashland Oil, Inc., PO Box 391, Ashland, KY 41101. TEL 606-329-3214. Ed. Jeff Opperman. Circ: 32,000.

338.47 USA ISSN 1026-6461
ASIAN OIL AND GAS. Variant title: A O G. Text in English. 1980. m. free to qualified personnel (effective 2011). adv. **Document type:** *Magazine, Trade.* **Description:** Focuses on the oil industry.
Related titles: Online - full text ed.: free (effective 2011).
Indexed: GeoRef, SCOPUS.
Published by: Atlantic Communications, 1635 W Alabama, Houston, TX 77006. TEL 713-831-1768, FAX 713-523-2339. Circ: 15,041.

661.804 USA ISSN 1931-177X
ASIAN PETROCHEMICALSCAN. Text in English. 1987. w. USD 3,795 combined subscription (online & E-mail eds.) (effective 2008). back issues avail. **Document type:** *Newsletter, Trade.* **Description:** Provides weekly market updates, commentary and assessments ranging from naphtha feedstocks to aromatics, olefins and polymers in Southeast Asia, Korea, Taiwan and Japan.
Media: Online - full content. **Related titles:** E-mail ed.
Published by: Platts (Subsidiary of: McGraw-Hill Companies, Inc.), 1200 G St NW, Ste 1000, Washington, DC 20005. TEL 212-904-3070, 800-752-8878, FAX 202-383-2024, support@platts.com. Eds. Chuan Ong, Quintella Koh, Tom Enger.

ASPHALT EMULSION MANUFACTURERS ASSOCIATION. NEWSLETTER. *see* TRANSPORTATION—Roads And Traffic

662.63 FRA ISSN 1144-486X
ASSOCIATION FRANCAISE DES TECHNICIENS DU PETROLE. ANNUAIRE. Text in French. 1954. a.
Published by: Association Francaise des Techniciens et Professionnels du Petrole (A F T P), 45 Rue Louis Blanc, Courbevoie, 92400, France. TEL 33-1-47176732, FAX 33-1-47176744, secretariat@aftp.net, http://www.aftp.net. Circ: 4,000.

665.5 RUS ISSN 2073-9877
➤ **ASSOTSIATSIYA BUROVYH PODRYADCHIKOV. VESTNIK/ ASSOCIATION OF DRILLING CONTRACTORS. REPORTER.** Text in Russian. 2000. q. RUR 2,200 to institutions (effective 2010). abstr.; illus.; maps; charts; stat. **Document type:** *Bulletin, Academic/ Scholarly.* **Description:** Publishes scientific and technical articles in topical issues of technique and technology of construction of vertical, directional, horizontal, multi-branch and ultra-deep oil and gas wells; development of offshore oil and gas fields, industrial and environmental safety in the oil and gas industry.
Related titles: Online - full text ed.
Indexed: RefZh.
Published by: Assotsiatsiya Burovyh Podryadchikov/Association of Drilling Contractors, 65 Leninsky pr-kt, off 21029, Moscow, Russian Federation. TEL 7-499-1338770, FAX 7-495-3807230, abprus@mail.ru. Ed. Aleksandr Oganov. Pub. Boris Nikitin. Circ: 1,000.

665.5 CAN ISSN 1200-7676
ATLANTIC CANADA OIL WORKS MAGAZINE. Text in English. 1993. 4/yr. CAD 25; USD 30 in United States; USD 40 elsewhere. **Description:** Committed to providing political, legal and organizational insight into the development of the East Coast oil industry.
Published by: Publishing World Inc., 13 Signal Hill Rd, St. John's, NF A1A 1A8, Canada. TEL 709-722-5444, FAX 709-722-4555.

665.5 USA
THE ATLANTIC DEEPWATER REPORT. Text in English. m. USD 2,695 (effective 2007). **Document type:** *Newsletter, Trade.*
Published by: O D S - Petrodata, 3200 Wilcrest Dr, Ste 170, Houston, TX 77042. TEL 832-463-3000, FAX 832-463-3100, general@ods-petrodata.com, http://www.ods-petrodata.com. Pub. Thomas Marsh.

AUSTRALASIAN OIL & GAS EXPLORERS DIRECTORY. *see* BUSINESS AND ECONOMICS—Trade And Industrial Directories

665.5 AUS
AUSTRALIA. BUREAU OF RESOURCE SCIENCES. AUSTRALIAN PETROLEUM ACCUMULATIONS REPORT. Text in English. 1986. irreg. price varies.
Formerly: Australia. Bureau of Mineral Resources, Geology and Geophysics. Australian Petroleum Accumulations Report (0817-9263)
Indexed: AESIS, GeoRef, SpeleolAb.
—Linda Hall.
Published by: Bureau of Resource Sciences, Queen Victoria Terr., PO Box E 11, Parkes, ACT 2600, Australia. FAX 61-6-2724696.

661.804 994 338.47665 GBR ISSN 1749-2130
AUSTRALIA PETROCHEMICALS REPORT. Text in English. 2005. a. EUR 820, USD 1,030 combined subscription per issue (print & email eds.) (effective 2010). **Document type:** *Report, Trade.* **Description:** Provides industry professionals and strategists, sector analysts, trade associations and regulatory bodies with independent forecasts and competitive intelligence on the Australian petrochemicals industry.
Related titles: E-mail ed.
Indexed: A15, ABIn, B02, B15, B17, B18, G04, I05, P48, P51, P52, P56, PQC.
Published by: Business Monitor International Ltd., Senator House, 85 Queen Victoria St, London, EC4V 4AB, United Kingdom. TEL 44-20-72480468, FAX 44-20-72480467, subs@businessmonitor.com.

665.5 AUS ISSN 1324-6283
AUSTRALIAN GAS ASSOCIATION. RESEARCH PAPER. Text in English. 1995. irreg. **Document type:** *Report, Trade.*
Indexed: AESIS, GeoRef.
Published by: Australian Gas Association, 2 Park Way, PO Box 122, Braeside, VIC 3195, Australia. TEL 61-3-95804500, FAX 61-3-95805500, office@aga.asn.au, http://www.gas.asn.au.

696 AUS ISSN 0727-3541
THE AUSTRALIAN GAS INDUSTRY DIRECTORY. Text in English. a. free to members (effective 2008). **Document type:** *Directory, Trade.* **Description:** Lists members of the Australian Gas Association, Commonwealth and state government energy offices, overseas gas organizations, and suppliers to the gas industry.
Former titles (until 1977): Directory of the Australian Gas Industry (0727-3533); (until 1973): The Australian Gas Industry Directory and Utilities throughout Australia; Australian Gas Association. Directory
Published by: Australian Gas Association, 2 Park Way, PO Box 122, Braeside, VIC 3195, Australia. TEL 61-3-95804500, FAX 61-3-95805500, office@aga.asn.au, http://www.gas.asn.au.

553 AUS ISSN 0314-3171
AUSTRALIAN INSTITUTE OF PETROLEUM. ANNUAL REPORT. Text in English. 1977. a. free. **Document type:** *Corporate.*
Indexed: AESIS.
Published by: Australian Institute of Petroleum Ltd., GPO Box 279, Canberra, ACT 2601, Australia. TEL 61-2-6247-3044, FAX 61-2-6247-3844, http://www.aip.com.au. R&P E Grossman.

AUSTRALIAN MINING AND PETROLEUM LAW ASSOCIATION YEARBOOK. *see* MINES AND MINING INDUSTRY

665.5 AUS ISSN 1327-8312
AUSTRALIAN PETROLEUM COOPERATIVE RESEARCH CENTRE. ANNUAL REPORT. Text in English. 1992. a.
—BLDSC (1112.371500).
Published by: Australian Petroleum Cooperative Research Centre, Level 3, 24 Marcus Clarke St, P.O. Box 463, Canberra, ACT 2601, Australia. TEL 61-2-62003366, FAX 61-2-62300448, http://www.apcrc.com.au/index.htm.

AUSTRALIAN RESOURCES AND ENERGY LAW JOURNAL. *see* MINES AND MINING INDUSTRY

AUTOMOTIVE ENGINEER. *see* TRANSPORTATION—Automobiles

338.47 USA ISSN 0146-5236
HD9561
AUTOMOTIVE FUEL ECONOMY PROGRAM. ANNUAL REPORT TO THE CONGRESS. Text in English. 1977. a. **Document type:** *Government.*
Published by: U.S. Department of Transportation, National Highway and Traffic Safety Administration, National Center for Statistics and Analysis, 400 Seventh St, SW, Washington, DC 20590. TEL 202-366-4802, FAX 202-493-2739. Ed. Henrietta L Spinner. Circ: 200.

665.5 USA
AVERAGE CALENDAR DAY ALLOWABLE REPORT. Text in English. 19??. m. Included with subscr. to Drilling Completion and Plugging Summary. charts. **Document type:** *Report, Government.* **Description:** Shows the number of wells and allowables by district, with special production factors.
Published by: Railroad Commission, Oil and Gas Division, PO Box 12967, Austin, TX 78711. TEL 877-228-5740, publicassist@rrc.state.tx.us.

665.5 RUS ISSN 0132-2222
AVTOMATIZATSIYA, TELEMEKHANIZATSIYA I SVYAZ' V NEFTYANOI PROMYSHLENNOSTI; nauchno-tekhnicheskii zhurnal. Text in Russian. 1993. m. USD 270 in United States (effective 2004). **Document type:** *Journal, Trade.*
Indexed: RefZh.
—East View.
Published by: Vserossiiskii Nauchno-Issledovatel'skii Institut Organizatsii Upravleniya i Ekonomiki Neftegazovoi Promyshlennosti (VNIIOENG), Nametkina 14, korp B, Moscow, 117420, Russian Federation. TEL 7-095-3320022, FAX 7-095-3316877, vniioeng@mcn.ru, http://vniioeng.mcn.ru. Ed. L G Arusmakesyan. Circ: 300. **Dist. by:** East View Information Services, 10601 Wayzata Blvd, Minneapolis, MN 55305. TEL 952-252-1201, 800-477-1005, FAX 952-252-1202, info@eastview.com, http://www.eastview.com.

665.5 330 AZE ISSN 0365-8554
HD860 CODEN: AZNKAY
AZERBAIJAN NEFT TESERRUFATY. Text in Azerbaijani, Russian. m. USD 199 in the Americas (effective 2000).
Indexed: GeoRef, RASB, SpeleolAb.
—BLDSC (0005.400000), East View, INIST, Linda Hall. **CCC.**
Published by: State Oil Company, Ul. Aga Neimatully, 29, Baku, 370007, Azerbaijan. TEL 994-12-663931. Ed. A Kh. Mirzadzhanzade. **Dist. by:** East View Information Services, 10601 Wayzata Blvd, Minneapolis, MN 55305. TEL 952-252-1201, 800-477-1005, FAX 952-252-1202, info@eastview.com, http://www.eastview.com.

661.804 947.54 338.47665 GBR ISSN 1749-2149
AZERBAIJAN PETROCHEMICALS REPORT. Text in English. 2005. q. EUR 820, USD 1,030 combined subscription (print & email eds.) (effective 2010). **Document type:** *Report, Trade.* **Description:** Provides industry professionals and strategists, sector analysts, trade associations and regulatory bodies with independent forecasts and competitive intelligence on the Azerbaijani petrochemicals industry.
Related titles: E-mail ed.
Indexed: A15, ABIn, B02, B15, B17, B18, G04, I05, P48, P51, P52, P56, PQC.
Published by: Business Monitor International Ltd., Senator House, 85 Queen Victoria St, London, EC4V 4AB, United Kingdom. TEL 44-20-72480468, FAX 44-20-72480467, subs@businessmonitor.com.

665.5 ARG ISSN 1851-3972
B I P. (Boletin de Informaciones Petroleras) Text in Spanish. 2007. m.
Published by: Asociacion Argentina de Geologos y Geofisicos Petroleros, Maipu 645 1er Piso, Buenos Aires, C10006ACG, Argentina. TEL 54-11-43222820, FAX 54-11-43284078, http://www.aaggp.org.ar. Ed. Gustavo Carstens.

665.5 FRA ISSN 0300-4554
B I P. (Bulletin de l'Industrie Petroliere) Text in French. 1964. d. (250/yr.). EUR 2,451.80 (effective 2009). bk.rev. stat. **Document type:** *Bulletin, Trade.* **Description:** Daily news and comments on oil and gas in the world.
Indexed: ChemAb, PEBNI, SCOPUS.
—BLDSC (2862.090000), Linda Hall. **CCC.**
Published by: Groupe Moniteur, 17 rue d'Uzes, Paris, 75108, France. TEL 33-1-40133030, FAX 33-1-40135021, http://editionsdumoniteur.com. Ed. Jacques Marie. Circ: 1,000.

665.5 GBR
B P MAGAZINE. Text in English. 1924. q. free (effective 2009). charts; illus. back issues avail. **Document type:** *Magazine, Corporate.* **Description:** Covers business issues relating to activities of the BP group throughout the world.
Former titles (until 2000): Shield; (until 1995): B P Shield; (until 1985): B P Shield International (0045-1274)
Related titles: Online - full text ed.
Published by: B P plc., 1 St James's Sq, London, SW1Y 4PD, United Kingdom. TEL 44-20-74964000, FAX 44-20-74964630, careline@bp.com. Ed. Lisa Davison. **U.S. dist.:** BP America Inc.

665 HUN ISSN 0572-6034
TN860 CODEN: BKKFAC
➤ **BANYASZATI ES KOHASZATI LAPOK - KOOLAJ ES FOLDGAZ.** Text in Hungarian; Summaries in English. 1966. m. USD 50 (effective 2001). bk.rev. abstr.; charts; illus. 28 p./no.; **Document type:** *Journal, Academic/Scholarly.*
Formerly (until 1968): Koolaj es Foldgaz (0324-5357)
Indexed: CIN, ChemAb, ChemTitl, GeoRef, SpeleolAb.
—CASDDS, INIST, Linda Hall, PADDS.
Published by: Orszagos Magyar Banyaszati es Kohaszati Egyesulet, Fo utca 68, Budapest, 1027, Hungary. ombke@mtesz.hu, http://www.mtesz.hu/tagegy/ombke. Ed., Adv. contact E Dallos TEL 36-1-2150415. Circ: 600 (controlled).

➤ **BASIC OIL LAWS & CONCESSION CONTRACTS: ASIA & AUSTRALASIA.** *see* LAW—International Law

➤ **BASIC OIL LAWS & CONCESSION CONTRACTS: CENTRAL AMERICA & CARIBBEAN.** *see* LAW—International Law

➤ **BASIC OIL LAWS & CONCESSION CONTRACTS: EUROPE.** *see* LAW—International Law

661.804 338.47665 949.3 GBR ISSN 1749-2157
BELGIUM PETROCHEMICALS REPORT. Text in English. 2005. a. EUR 820, USD 1,030 combined subscription per issue (print & email eds.) (effective 2010). **Document type:** *Report, Trade.* **Description:** Provides industry professionals and strategists, sector analysts, trade associations and regulatory bodies with independent forecasts and competitive intelligence on the Belgian petrochemicals industry.
Related titles: E-mail ed.
Indexed: A15, ABIn, B02, B15, B17, B18, G04, I05, P48, P51, P52, P56, PQC.
Published by: Business Monitor International Ltd., Senator House, 85 Queen Victoria St, London, EC4V 4AB, United Kingdom. TEL 44-20-72480468, FAX 44-20-72480467, subs@businessmonitor.com.

629.286 FIN ISSN 0045-1738
BENSIINIUUTISET; Huoltamoiden erikoislehti. Text in Finnish, Swedish. 1958. 9/yr. membership. adv. **Document type:** *Newsletter, Trade.* **Description:** Discusses professional questions concerning oil products and automobile maintenance and automobile equipment.
Published by: Suomen Bensiinikauppiaitten Liitto S B L ry./Finnish Petrol Retailers Organization, Mannerheimintie 40 D 84, Helsinki, 00100, Finland. TEL 358-9-75195500, FAX 358-9-75195525. Eds. Paavo Karttunen, Sirpa Kekalainen. Adv. contact Pentti Ahonen TEL 358-14-3731434. B&W page EUR 1,600, color page EUR 2,800; 210 x 297. Circ: 3,000.

665.5 658.3 SGP ISSN 0005-9153
BERITA SHELL. Text in English, Malay. 1955. m. free to employees. bk.rev. **Document type:** *Magazine, Trade.*
Published by: Shell Eastern Petroleum Pty. Ltd., Singapore Land Tower, P.O. Box 643, Singapore, 048623, Singapore. TEL 65-384-8943. Ed. Wang Yean Sung. Circ: 3,800.

665.5384 330 USA ISSN 1935-7621
TP359.B46
BIODIESEL MAGAZINE. Text in English. 2004. bi-m. free (effective 2009). adv. back issues avail. **Document type:** *Magazine, Trade.* **Description:** Features business trends, production ideas and opportunities and a forum for communication for biodiesel industry workers.
Related titles: Online - full text ed.: ISSN 1949-1085.
Published by: B B I International Media, 308 2nd Ave N, Ste 304, Grand Forks, ND 58203. TEL 701-746-8385, 866-746-8385, FAX 701-746-5367. Ed. Ron Kotrba TEL 701-738-4942. Pub. Mike Bryan. Adv. contact Marla DeFoe. color page USD 3,242; bleed 9 x 11.375.

333.9539 628.53 GBR ISSN 1753-7576
BIOENERGY BUSINESS. Text in English. 2007 (Feb.). m. GBP 197 combined subscription in developing nations (print & online eds.); GBP 395 combined subscription elsewhere (print & online eds.) (effective 2009). adv. **Document type:** *Newsletter, Trade.* **Description:** Provides the latest news and analysis of major developments shaping the growing markets in biofuels and biomass.
Related titles: Online - full text ed.: ISSN 1753-7584.
Published by: Environmental Finance Publications, 22-24 Corsham St, London, N1 6DR, United Kingdom. TEL 44-20-72519151, FAX 44-20-72519161, info@environmental-finance.com, http://www.environmental-finance.com/. Ed. Vic Wyman. Adv. contact Matthew Colvan.

662.338 GBR ISSN 2046-2476
▼ **BIOENERGY INSIGHT.** Text in English. 2010. q. GBP 120, EUR 185, USD 240 (effective 2011). back issues avail. **Document type:** *Magazine, Trade.* **Description:** Contains details about companies producing biomass fuel in the form of pellets and briquettes, and those using biomass fuel to produce CHP, biogas, biopower, chemicals, heat and liquid biofuels.
Published by: Horseshoe Media Ltd., Marshall House, 124 Middleton Rd, Morden, Surrey SM4 6RW, United Kingdom. TEL 44-208-6487082, FAX 44-208-6874130, peter@horseshoemedia.com, http://www.horseshoemedia.com.

665.5 GBR ISSN 1932-104X
TP339 CODEN: BBBICH
➤ **BIOFUELS, BIOPRODUCTS AND BIOREFINING.** Text in English. 2007 (Jun.). bi-m. GBP 591 in United Kingdom to institutions; EUR 745 in Europe to institutions; USD 1,154 elsewhere to institutions (effective 2012). adv. back issues avail.; reprint service avail. from PSC. **Document type:** *Journal, Academic/Scholarly.* **Description:** Contains a balanced mixture of critical reviews, commentary, business news highlights, policy updates and patent intelligence.
Related titles: Online - full text ed.: ISSN 1932-1031. GBP 591 in United Kingdom to institutions; EUR 745 in Europe to institutions; USD 1,154 elsewhere to institutions (effective 2012).
Indexed: A28, A34, A35, A37, A38, APA, APIAb, AgBio, AgrForAb, B&BAb, B19, B26, BA, BP, BrCerAb, C&ISA, C25, C30, C33, CA/WCA, CABA, CIA, CPEI, CerAb, CivEngAb, CorrAb, CurCont, E&CAJ, E11, E12, EEA, EMA, ESPM, EnvEAb, F08, F11, F12, FCA, G11, GH, H15, H16, M&TEA, M09, MBF, METADEX, MaizeAb, N02, N04, P32, P40, PGegResA, PHN&I, PN&I, R11, R12, S12, S13, S16, SCI, SCOPUS, SSciA, SolStAb, SoyAb, T04, TAR, TriticAb, W07, W11, WAA.
—IE, Linda Hall. **CCC.**
Published by: (Society of Chemical Industry), John Wiley & Sons Ltd. (Subsidiary of: John Wiley & Sons, Inc.), The Atrium, Southern Gate, Chichester, West Sussex PO19 8SQ, United Kingdom. TEL 44-1243-779777, FAX 44-1243-775878, customer@wiley.co.uk. Ed. Bruce E Dale. Adv. contact Faith Pidduck TEL 44-1243-770254. **Subscr. to:** John Wiley & Sons, Inc., 350 Main St, Malden, MA 02148. TEL 781-388-8598, 800-835-6770, cs-journals@wiley.com, http://onlinelibrary.wiley.com/.

338.4366288098 GBR ISSN 1756-4883
BIOFUELS BRAZIL. Text in English. 2008. w. GBP 940 (effective 2009). **Document type:** *Newsletter, Trade.* **Description:** Offers a unique insiders view from this major producing and exporting country with news, data and comment on the Brazilian biofuels industry not available from other sources.
Related titles: Online - full text ed.: ISSN 1756-4891.
Published by: Agra Europe (London) Ltd. (Subsidiary of: Agra Informa Ltd.), 80 Calverley Rd, Tunbridge Wells, Kent TN1 2UN, United Kingdom. TEL 44-20-70177500, FAX 44-20-70177599, marketing@agra-net.com.

662.338 USA
BIOFUELS BUSINESS; the international magazine for the renewable fuels industry. Text in English. 2007. irreg. free to qualified personnel (print & online eds.) (effective 2009). adv. **Document type:** *Magazine, Trade.* **Description:** Provides indepth information, interviews with the biofuels industry leaders and country focus, that helps the readers to manage, operate and grow their business.
Related titles: Online - full text ed.
Published by: Sosland Publishing Company, 4800 Main St, Ste 100, Kansas, MO 64112. TEL 816-756-1000, 800-338-6201, FAX 816-756-2618, web@sosland.com, http://www.sosland.com. Ed. Susan Reidy. Pub. Nola Hector. adv.: page USD 3,320; trim 8 x 10.75.

338.47665 GBR ISSN 1754-2170
BIOFUELS INTERNATIONAL. Text in English. 2007. 10/yr. GBP 195, EUR 275, USD 370 (effective 2009). adv. back issues avail. **Document type:** *Magazine, Trade.* **Description:** Covers an array of topics including news and updates, features, country focus, interviews, technology, exhibitions & conferences.
—BLDSC (2072.146600). **CCC.**
Published by: Horseshoe Media Ltd., Marshall House, 124 Middleton Rd, Morden, Surrey SM4 6RW, United Kingdom. TEL 44-208-6487082, FAX 44-208-6874130, http://www.horseshoemedia.com. Adv. contact Pierre-Gomis Diallo TEL 44-208-6874126.

665.5 USA
BIOFUELS JOURNAL. Text in English. 2003. q. USD 25 domestic; USD 50 foreign; free to qualified personnel (effective 2011). adv. back issues avail.; reprints avail. **Document type:** *Journal, Trade.*
Related titles: Online - full text ed.: free (effective 2011).
Published by: Country Journal Publishing Company, 3065 Pershing Ct, Decatur, IL 62526. TEL 217-877-9660, 800-728-7511, FAX 217-877-6647. Ed. Jerry Perkins. Adv. contact Mark Avery.

BIOTECHNOLOGY FOR BIOFUELS. *see* BIOLOGY—Biotechnology

338.4766180409 GBR ISSN 1749-2165
BRAZIL PETROCHEMICALS REPORT. Text in English. 2005. q. EUR 820, USD 1,030 combined subscription (print & email eds.) (effective 2010). **Document type:** *Report, Trade.* **Description:** Provides industry professionals and strategists, sector analysts, trade associations and regulatory bodies with independent forecasts and competitive intelligence on the Brazilian petrochemicals industry.
Related titles: E-mail ed.
Indexed: A15, ABIn, B02, B15, B17, B18, G04, I05, P48, P51, P52, P56, PQC.
Published by: Business Monitor International Ltd., Senator House, 85 Queen Victoria St, London, EC4V 4AB, United Kingdom. TEL 44-20-72480468, FAX 44-20-72480467, subs@businessmonitor.com.

665.5 DEU ISSN 1864-8924
HD9553.1
BRENNSTOFFSPIEGEL UND MINERALOELRUNDSCHAU. Text in German. 2004. m. EUR 64.20 domestic; EUR 67 foreign; EUR 5.50 newsstand/cover (effective 2009). adv. **Document type:** *Magazine, Trade.*
Formed by the merger of (1975-2004): Brennstoffspiegel (0342-6580); Which was formerly (1962-1975): Der Brennstoffhandel (0342-6572); (1947-1962): Kohlen-Zeitung (0342-6599); (1956-2004): Mineraloel (0544-2524); Which incorporated (1972-1977): Mineraloelrundschau (0172-3308); Which was formerly (1953-1972): Uniti (0172-3316)
Indexed: RefZh.
Published by: Ceto Verlag GmbH, Industriestr 85-95, Leipzig, 04229, Germany. TEL 49-341-4924010, FAX 49-341-4924012. Ed., Pub. Hans-Henning Manz. Adv. contact Ricky Pasch. B&W page EUR 1,496; trim 210 x 297. Circ: 3,700 (paid).

BRITISH COLUMBIA. DEPARTMENT OF MINES AND PETROLEUM RESOURCES. BULLETIN. *see* EARTH SCIENCES—Geology

665.5 CAN
BRITISH COLUMBIA OIL AND GAS HANDBOOK. Text in English. 1991. irreg., latest 1999. looseleaf. price varies. back issues avail. **Document type:** *Government.* **Description:** Designed to assist the petroleum industry in planning and conducting operations in British Columbia and in adhering to its guiding principles. It consolidates a variety of legislative requirements, regulation, procedures and guidelines. It consists of a main looseleaf reference binder (Vol.1) and separate pull-out sections. A second binder (Vol.2) is available for the activity sections 4-9.
Published by: British Columbia, Ministry of Energy and Mines, c/o Communications Coordinator, Stn Prov Govt, PO Box 9324, Victoria, BC V8W 9N3, Canada. TEL 250-952-0525, http://www.ogc.gov.bc.ca.

661.804 338.47665 949.9 GBR ISSN 1749-2173
BULGARIA PETROCHEMICALS REPORT. Text in English. 2005. a. EUR 820, USD 1,030 combined subscription per issue (print & email eds.) (effective 2010). **Document type:** *Report, Trade.* **Description:** Provides industry professionals and strategists, sector analysts, trade associations and regulatory bodies with independent forecasts and competitive intelligence on the Bulgarian petrochemicals industry.
Related titles: E-mail ed.
Indexed: A15, ABIn, B02, B15, B17, B18, G04, I05, P48, P51, P52, P56, PQC.
Published by: Business Monitor International Ltd., Senator House, 85 Queen Victoria St, London, EC4V 4AB, United Kingdom. TEL 44-20-72480468, FAX 44-20-72480467, subs@businessmonitor.com.

665 553.28 622 CHE ISSN 1420-6846
TA703
BULLETIN FUER ANGEWANDTE GEOLOGIE/BULLETIN POUR LA GEOLOGIE APPLIQUEE. Text in English, French, German. 1934. s-a. CHF 30. adv. bk.rev. bibl.; charts; illus. cum.index. **Document type:** *Bulletin.*
Former titles (until 1996): Schweizerischer Vereinigung von Petroleum-Geologen und -Ingenieure. Bulletin (1421-2005); (until 1994): Vereinigung Schweizerischer Petroleum-Geologen und -Ingenieure. Bulletin (0366-4848)
Indexed: CABA, CPEI, E12, Englnd, F08, F11, GeoRef, S13, S16, SCOPUS, SpeleolAb, TAR.
—INIST.
Published by: Schweizerische Vereinigung von Petroleum-Geologen und -Ingenieuren, Speerstr 21, Richterswil, 8805, Switzerland. Ed. Peter Lehnert. Circ: 650.

THE BUNKER NEWS DIRECTORY OF INTERNATIONAL BUNKER SUPPLIERS, TRADERS & BROKERS. *see* BUSINESS AND ECONOMICS—International Commerce

665.5 338 GBR ISSN 1747-0536
BUNKERWORLD DIRECTORY. Text in English. 2005. s-a. **Document type:** *Directory, Trade.*
Published by: Petromedia Ltd., PO Box 17090, London, W4 4GW, United Kingdom. TEL 44-20-89945777, FAX 44-20-89942426, manager@petromedia.co.uk, http://www.petromedia.co.uk/.

665.5 DEU
BUSINESS NEWS. Text in German. 1932. 6/yr. adv. index. **Document type:** *Magazine, Trade.*
Former titles: Voran; Voran Aktuell
Published by: Aral AG, Wittener Str 45, Bochum, 44789, Germany. TEL 49-234-3150, FAX 49-234-3152679, info@aral.de, http://www.aral.de. Ed. Bernd Rodde. Pub. Sebastian Gruetz. adv.: B&W page EUR 1,227, color page EUR 2,045. Circ: 4,100 (controlled).

665.7 USA ISSN 0007-7259
TP761.B8
BUTANE - PROPANE NEWS. Text in English. 1939. m. USD 32 to qualified personnel (effective 2005). adv. charts; illus.; tr.lit. index. back issues avail.; reprints avail. **Document type:** *Magazine, Trade.*
Related titles: Microform ed.: (from PQC).
Indexed: ChemAb, F&EA.
—IE, Infotrieve, Linda Hall.
Published by: Butane - Propane News, Inc., PO Box 660698, Arcadia, CA 91006-0698. TEL 626-357-2168, FAX 626-303-2854. Ed. Ann Rey. Pub. Natalie Peal. Adv. contact Kurt Ruhl. B&W page USD 3,400, color page USD 5,000. Circ: 16,000 (controlled).

C E F I C PETROCHEMICALS ACTIVITY REVIEW. *see* ENGINEERING—Chemical Engineering

C I M MAGAZINE. *see* MINES AND MINING INDUSTRY

C O N C A W E REVIEW. (Conservation of Clean Air and Water in Europe) *see* ENVIRONMENTAL STUDIES

665.5 GBR
C O R G I DESIGN GUIDES. (Council for Registered Gas Installers) Text in English. 2003. s-a. **Document type:** *Handbook/Manual/Guide, Trade.*
Published by: Council for Registered Gas Installers (C O R G I), 1 Elmwood, Chineham Park, Crockford Ln, Basingstoke, Hants RG24 8WG, United Kingdom. TEL 44-870-402200, enquiries@corgi-gas.com, http://www.corgi-gas-safety.com/.

665.5 USA
TJ563 CODEN: JCTIDX
C T I JOURNAL. Text in English. 1980. s-a. free domestic; USD 30 foreign to individuals; USD 20 to institutions (effective 2010). adv. bk.rev. illus. back issues avail. **Document type:** *Journal, Academic/Scholarly.*
Formerly (until 1989): Cooling Tower Institute. Journal (0273-3250)
Related titles: Online - full text ed.: free (effective 2010).
Indexed: A28, APA, BrCerAb, C&ISA, CA/WCA, CIA, CerAb, CivEngAb, CorrAb, E&CAJ, E11, EEA, EMA, H15, ISMEC, M&TEA, M09, MBF, METADEX, SCOPUS, SolStAb, T04, WAA.
—IE, Ingenta, Linda Hall.
Published by: Cooling Technology Institute, PO Box 73383, Houston, TX 77273. TEL 281-583-4087, FAX 281-537-1721. Ed. Paul Lindhal. Adv. contact Virginia Manser.

665.5 USA
C T I NEWS (HOUSTON). Text in English. 19??. q. adv. back issues avail. **Document type:** *Newsletter, Trade.* **Description:** Contains news of CTI and its activities, items of general interest concerning cooling towers, a question and answer section and current literature references concerning cooling towers.
Related titles: Online - full text ed.: free (effective 2010).
Published by: Cooling Technology Institute, PO Box 73383, Houston, TX 77273. TEL 281-583-4087, FAX 281-537-1721. Ed. Terry Ogburn. Adv. contact Virginia Manser.

665.5 USA ISSN 0362-1243
TN872.C2 CODEN: CDOOAL
CALIFORNIA. DIVISION OF OIL, GAS AND GEOTHERMAL RESOURCES. ANNUAL REPORT OF THE STATE OIL AND GAS SUPERVISOR. Text in English. 1915. a. free. illus. **Document type:** *Government.*
Indexed: GeoRef, SpeleolAb.
Published by: Division of Oil, Gas, and Geothermal Resources, 801 K St, MS 20 20, Sacramento, CA 95814-3530. TEL 916-445-9686, FAX 916-323-0424. Ed. Susan Hodgson. Circ: 2,400.

665.5 USA
CALIFORNIA. ENERGY COMMISSION. QUARTERLY OIL REPORT. Text in English. 1987. q. free. **Document type:** *Government.*
Published by: Energy Commission, 1516 9th St., Sacramento, CA 95814-5512. TEL 916-324-3009.

665.5 GBR ISSN 2044-5814
▼ **CAMEROON OIL & GAS REPORT.** Text in English. 2010. q. USD 975 (effective 2011). **Document type:** *Report, Trade.*

P

Published by: Business Monitor International Ltd., Senator House, 85 Queen Victoria St, London, EC4V 4AB, United Kingdom. TEL 44-20-72480468, FAX 44-20-72480467, enquiry@businessmonitor.com.

CANADA A-Z; oil, gas, mining directory. *see* BUSINESS AND ECONOMICS—Trade And Industrial Directories

661.804 338.47665 971 GBR ISSN 1749-2181
CANADA PETROCHEMICALS REPORT. Cover title: Canada Petrochemicals & Chemicals Report. Text in English. 2005. a. EUR 820, USD 1,030 combined subscription per issue (print & email eds.) (effective 2010). **Document type:** *Report, Trade.* **Description:** Provides industry professionals and strategists, sector analysts, trade associations and regulatory bodies with independent forecasts and competitive intelligence on the Canadian petrochemicals industry.
Related titles: E-mail ed.
Indexed: A15, ABIn, B01, B02, B15, B17, B18, G04, I05, P48, P51, P52, P56, PQC.
Published by: Business Monitor International Ltd., Senator House, 85 Queen Victoria St, London, EC4V 4AB, United Kingdom. TEL 44-20-72480468, FAX 44-20-72480467, subs@businessmonitor.com.

CANADA. SHIP-SOURCE OIL POLLUTION FUND. ADMINISTRATOR'S ANNUAL REPORT. *see* ENVIRONMENTAL STUDIES—Pollution

CANADA. STATISTICS CANADA. PIPELINE TRANSPORTATION OF CRUDE OIL AND REFINED PETROLEUM PRODUCTS (ONLINE EDITION). *see* BUSINESS AND ECONOMICS—Abstracting, Bibliographies, Statistics

338.47665 CAN
CANADIAN ENERDATA LTD. WEEKLY PRICE UPDATE. Text in English. 1992. w. CAD 355 (effective 2003); Subscr. avail. to subscribers of the Canadian Natural Gas Market Report or Canadian Gas Price Reporter only. **Document type:** *Report, Trade.* **Description:** Contains daily, weekly and monthly Canadian natural gas prices from Enerdata's proprietary price survey.
Media: Online - full content. **Related titles:** Fax ed.: CAD 460 (effective 2003).
Published by: Canadian Enerdata Ltd., 100 Allstate Pkwy, Ste 304, Markham, ON L3R 6H3, Canada. TEL 905-479-9697, FAX 905-479-2515, publications@enerdata.com.

CANADIAN ENERGY NEWS. *see* ENERGY

665.5 CAN ISSN 0316-3547
HD9581.C3
CANADIAN GAS FACTS. Text in English. a. CAD 80 to non-members; CAD 40 to members. **Document type:** *Handbook/Manual/Guide, Trade.*
Published by: Canadian Gas Association, 243 Consumers Rd, Ste 1200, North York, ON M2J 5E3, Canada. TEL 416-498-1994, FAX 416-498-7465.

665.5 CAN ISSN 1483-0752
CANADIAN GAS PRICE REPORTER. Text in English. 1989. m. CAD 945 (effective 2003). **Document type:** *Magazine, Trade.*
Related titles: E-mail ed.; Online - full content ed.: ISSN 1498-8070. 1996. CAD 875 online or E-mail ed. (effective 2003); Online - full text ed.
Published by: Canadian Enerdata Ltd., 100 Allstate Pkwy, Ste 304, Markham, ON L3R 6H3, Canada. TEL 905-479-9697, FAX 905-479-2515, publications@enerdata.com.

CANADIAN NATIONAL ENERGY FORUM PROCEEDINGS. *see* ENERGY

333.8233097105 CAN ISSN 1196-0906
CANADIAN NATURAL GAS MARKET REPORT. Text in English. 1985. bi-w. CAD 620 (effective 2003).
Formerly (until 1992): Natural Gas Market Report (0827-6056)
Related titles: E-mail ed.; Online - full content ed.: ISSN 1498-8534. CAD 575 online or E-mail ed. (effective 2003).
—**CCC.**
Published by: Canadian Enerdata Ltd., 100 Allstate Pkwy, Ste 304, Markham, ON L3R 6H3, Canada. TEL 905-479-9697, FAX 905-479-2515, publications@enerdata.com.

340 665.5 CAN ISSN 0384-8965
KE0
CANADIAN OIL & GAS. Text in English. 1955. 10 base vols. plus a. updates. looseleaf. CAD 2,175 base vol(s). (effective 2010). **Document type:** *Handbook/Manual/Guide, Trade.* **Description:** Reproduces full text of statutes, regulations and case law for all 13 Canadian jurisdictions. Provides useful forms and precedents.
Published by: LexisNexis Canada Inc. (Subsidiary of: LexisNexis North America), 123 Commerce Valley Dr E, Ste 700, Markham, ON L3T 7W8, Canada. TEL 905-479-2665, 800-668-6481, FAX 905-479-3758, 800-461-3275, info@lexisnexis.ca, http://www.lexisnexis.ca. Eds. Bennett Jones, Nigel Bankes.

665 CAN ISSN 0068-9394
TN867
CANADIAN OIL REGISTER. Cover title: Nickle's Canadian Oil Register. Text in English. 1951. a. CAD 217 per issue domestic; USD 217 per issue foreign; CAD 395 combined subscription per issue print & online eds. (effective 2005). adv. 650 p./no.; **Document type:** *Directory, Trade.* **Description:** The recognized directory for information on the people, products and services available within Canada's oil and gas industry.
Formerly (until 1962): Canadian Oil and Gas Directory (0315-4866)
Related titles: Online - full text ed.
Published by: Nickle's Energy Group (Subsidiary of: Business Information Group), Ste 300, 999 8 St SW, Calgary, AB T2R 1N7, Canada. TEL 403-209-3500, 800-387-2446, FAX 403-245-8666, http://www.nickles.com/. Adv. contact Tony Poblete. Circ: 5,500.

338.47665 CAN ISSN 1204-2846
G1151.H8
CANADIAN OILFIELD GAS PLANT ATLAS. Text in English. 1995. biennial. maps.
Published by: June/Warren Publishing Ltd., #300, 5735 - 7 St. NE, Calgary, AB T3E 8V3, Canada. TEL 403-265-3700, FAX 403-265-3706. Pub. Bill Whitelaw.

553 CAN ISSN 0007-4802
TN873.C22 CODEN: BCPGAI
➤ **CANADIAN PETROLEUM GEOLOGY. BULLETIN.** Text in English. 1953 (vol.26). q. CAD 150 domestic to non-members; CAD 170 per issue in United States to non-members; CAD 200 per issue elsewhere to non-members; free to members (effective 2010). adv. bk.rev. charts; illus.; maps. Index. back issues avail.; reprints avail. **Document type:** *Journal, Academic/Scholarly.* **Description:** Contains scientific material of interest to the Canadian petroleum geoscience community including technical papers and notes, debates, and book reviews.
Former titles (until 1963): Alberta Society of Petroleum Geologists. Journal (0317-4107); (until 1955): A S P G News Bulletin (0317-4158)
Related titles: Online - full text ed.
Indexed: A22, AESIS, CPEI, ChemAb, CurCont, EnerRev, EngInd, GEOBASE, GSW, GeoRef, ISMEC, ISR, PetrolAb, SCI, SCOPUS, SpeleolAb, W07.
—BLDSC (2837.900000), IE, Infotrieve, Ingenta, INIST, Linda Hall, PADDS. **CCC.**
Published by: Canadian Society of Petroleum Geologists, 600, 640 8th Ave S W, Calgary, AB T2P 1G7, Canada. TEL 403-264-5610, FAX 403-264-5898. Ed. Denis Lavoie TEL 418-654-2571. Adv. contact Alyssa Middleton TEL 403-513-1229.

665.5029 USA
CANADIAN PETROLEUM INDUSTRY. Text in English. 19??. a. **Document type:** *Directory, Trade.* **Description:** Supplies company name, address, phone and fax numbers, names and titles of key personnel,division offices, and office location of petroleum companies in Canada.
Formerly: Oil Directory of Canada (0474-0114)
Media: Diskette.
Published by: Midwest Publishing Company, 2230 E 49th St, Ste E, Tulsa, OK 74105. TEL 800-829-2002, info@midwestpub.com, http://www.midwestpub.com/.

336.2 343.04 CAN ISSN 0838-0961
CANADIAN PETROLEUM TAX JOURNAL. Text in English. 1988. s-a. free membership (effective 2004). **Document type:** *Journal, Academic/Scholarly.*
Published by: Canadian Petroleum Tax Society, PO Box 2562, Sta. M, Calgary, AB T2P 3K8, Canada. http://www.cpts.ca/.

665.5 553 CAN ISSN 0703-1130
TN870.5 CODEN: MCPGD6
CANADIAN SOCIETY OF PETROLEUM GEOLOGISTS. MEMOIR. Text in English. 1980. irreg., latest vol.19, 2001. price varies. adv. bk.rev. charts; stat.
Indexed: A22, AESIS, GeoRef, SpeleolAb, Z01.
—IE, Ingenta. **CCC.**
Published by: Canadian Society of Petroleum Geologists, No 160, 540 Fifth Ave SW, Calgary, AB T2P 0M2, Canada. TEL 403-264-5610. Ed. Don Glass. Circ: 2,200.

665.5 USA
CANO ENERGY PIPELINE. Text in English. 2003. q. USD 39 (effective 2003). **Document type:** *Magazine, Trade.* **Description:** Covers the US oil and gas industry.
Published by: Cano Energy Corp., 309 W Seventh St Ste 1600, Fort Worth, TX 76102. TEL 817-698-0760, http://www.canoenergy.com/.

CARBON DIOXIDE EMISSIONS FROM FUEL COMBUSTION. *see* ENVIRONMENTAL STUDIES—Pollution

CARBUROL. *see* TRANSPORTATION—Automobiles

CARTA MINERA Y PANORAMA PETROLERO. *see* MINES AND MINING INDUSTRY

661.804 COL ISSN 1657-7205
CARTA PETROLERA. Text in Spanish. q.
Indexed: INIS AtomInd.
Published by: Ecopetrol, c/o Victor Eduardo Perez, Carrera 13 No. 36-24 piso 11, Bogota, Colombia. http://www.ecopetrol.com.co/.

CASPIAN INVESTOR. *see* BUSINESS AND ECONOMICS—Production Of Goods And Services

665.5 GBR
CAUCASUS ENERGY MONTHLY. Text in English. 200?. m. GBP 120 (effective 2009). back issues avail. **Document type:** *Newsletter, Trade.* **Description:** Features surveys of the oil, gas, coal and electricity industries of Azerbaijan, Georgia and Armenia.
Related titles: Online - full text ed.
Published by: Eastern Bloc Research Ltd., Tolsta Chaolais, Isle of Lewis, HS2 9DW, United Kingdom. TEL 44-1851-621315, mail@easternblocenergy.com.

665.5 CHN ISSN 1004-1338
TN871.35
CEJING JISHU/WELL LOGGING TECHNOLOGY. Text in Chinese; Abstracts in English. 1977. bi-m. USD 58.80 (effective 2009). adv. bk.rev. abstr.; bibl.; charts; illus.; mkt.; tr.lit. 80 p./no.; back issues avail. **Document type:** *Journal, Trade.* **Description:** Offers readers both of home and abroad the latest developments of China well logging technology. WLT's chief columns include petrophysical properties, logging methodology, logging equipment and log interpretation.
Formerly: Diqiu Wuli Cejing (1001-7135)
Related titles: E-mail ed.; Fax ed.; Online - full text ed.
Indexed: A22, GeoRef, PetrolAb, RefZh, SCOPUS.
—BLDSC (9294.177000), East View, IE, Ingenta, PADDS.
Published by: Xi'an Shiyou Kantan Yiqi Zongchang/Xi'an Petroleum Exploration Instrument Complex, 8 Hongzhuan Nan Lu, Xi'an, Shaanxi 710061, China. TEL 86-29-86583163. Ed. Hongshi Liu. R&P, Adv. contact Wang Huan TEL 86-29-5265999 ext 6110. B&W page USD 450, color page USD 800. Circ: 3,200 (paid); 1,800 (controlled). **Dist. overseas by:** China International Book Trading Corp, 35 Chegongzhuang Xilu, Haidian District, PO Box 399, Beijing 100044, China.

665.5 GBR
CENTRAL ASIA ENERGY MONTHLY. Text in English. 200?. m. GBP 120 (effective 2009). **Document type:** *Newsletter, Trade.* **Description:** Surveys the oil, gas, coal and electricity industries of Turkmenistan, Uzbekistan, Kyrgyzstan and Tajikistan.
Related titles: Online - full content ed.
Published by: Eastern Bloc Research Ltd., Tolsta Chaolais, Isle of Lewis, HS2 9DW, United Kingdom. TEL 44-1851-621315, mail@easternblocenergy.com.

338.4766180409 GBR ISSN 1752-4172
CENTRAL ASIA PETROCHEMICALS REPORT. Text in English. 2006. a. EUR 820, USD 1,030 combined subscription per issue (print & email eds.) (effective 2010). **Document type:** *Report, Trade.* **Description:** Provides industry professionals and strategists, sector analysts, trade associations and regulatory bodies with independent forecasts and competitive intelligence on the Kyrgyzstan, Kazakhstani, Tajikistani, Turkmen, Uzbekistani petrochemicals industry.
Related titles: E-mail ed.
Indexed: A15, ABIn, B02, B15, B17, B18, G04, I05, P48, P51, P52, P56, PQC.
Published by: Business Monitor International Ltd., Senator House, 85 Queen Victoria St, London, EC4V 4AB, United Kingdom. TEL 44-20-72480468, FAX 44-20-72480467, subs@businessmonitor.com.

665.5 CHN ISSN 2095-0411
CHANGZHOU DAXUE XUEBAO (ZIRAN KEXUE BAN)/CHANGZHOU UNIVERSITY. JOURNAL (NATURAL SCIENCE EDITION). Text in Chinese; Abstracts in Chinese, English. 1989. q. CNY 24, USD 24; CNY 6 per issue (effective 2011). **Document type:** *Journal, Academic/Scholarly.*
Former titles (until 2009): Jiangsu Gongye Xueyuan Xuebao/Jiangsu Polytechnic University. Journal (1673-9620); (until 2002): Jiangsu Shiyou Huagong Xueyuan Xuebao/Jiangsu Institute of Petrochemical Technology. Journal (1005-8893)
Related titles: Online - full text ed.
—IE, Ingenta.
Published by: Changzhou Daxue/Changzhou University, CZSET, Changzhou, 213164, China. FAX 86-519-86330175, http://www.cczu.edu.cn/. Ed. Yu-zhong Pu. Circ: 4,000. **Dist. by:** China International Book Trading Corp, 35 Chegongzhuang Xilu, Haidian District, PO Box 399, Beijing 100044, China. TEL 86-10-68412045, FAX 86-10-68412023, cibtc@mail.cibtc.com.cn, http://www.cibtc.com.cn.

"CHECK THE OIL!" MAGAZINE; the publication devoted exclusively to Petroliana. *see* HOBBIES

CHEMECA - AUSTRALASIAN CONFERENCE ON CHEMICAL ENGINEERING. PROCEEDINGS. *see* ENGINEERING—Chemical Engineering

CHEMICAL AND PETROLEUM ENGINEERING. *see* ENGINEERING—Chemical Engineering

665.5 668.4 GBR
CHEMICALS & POLYMERS NEWS. Text in English. 1981. m.
Formerly (until 1987): Petrochemicals and Plastics News
Published by: I C I Chemicals & Polymers Ltd., Weton, Middl., PO Box 54, Middlesbrough, Cleveland TS6 8JA, United Kingdom.

662 USA ISSN 0009-3092
TP315 CODEN: CTFOAK
➤ **CHEMISTRY AND TECHNOLOGY OF FUELS AND OILS.** Text in English. 1965. bi-m. EUR 5,074, USD 5,243 combined subscription to institutions (print & online eds.) (effective 2012). adv. back issues avail.; reprint service avail. from PSC. **Document type:** *Journal, Academic/Scholarly.* **Description:** Discusses improvements in the processing of petroleum and natural gas and cracking and refining techniques to produce high-quality fuels, lubricants, and specialty fluids.
Related titles: Microfilm ed.: (from PQC); Online - full text ed.: ISSN 1573-8310 (from IngentaConnect); ◆ Translation of: Khimiya i Tekhnologiya Topliv i Masel. ISSN 0023-1169.
Indexed: A01, A03, A08, A22, A26, APIAb, ASCA, Agr, BibLing, C33, CA, CCI, CEA, CPEI, Cadscan, ChemAb, ChemTitl, CurCont, E01, E14, EngInd, FR, I05, LeadAb, RefZh, SCI, SCOPUS, T02, TCEA, W07, Zincscan.
—BLDSC (0410.490000), East View, IE, Infotrieve, Ingenta, INIST, Linda Hall. **CCC.**
Published by: (Rossiiskaya Akademiya Nauk/Russian Academy of Sciences RUS), Springer New York LLC (Subsidiary of: Springer Science+Business Media), 233 Spring St, New York, NY 10013. TEL 212-460-1500, FAX 212-460-1575, service-ny@springer.com. Ed. Albert I Vladimirov.

665.5 CHN ISSN 1008-9446
CHENGDE SHIYOU GAODENG ZHUANKE XUEXIAO XUEBAO. Text in Chinese. 1999. q. CNY 5 newsstand/cover (effective 2006). **Document type:** *Journal, Academic/Scholarly.*
Related titles: Online - full text ed.
Published by: Chengde Shiyou Gaodeng Zhuanke Xuexiao, 9, Nanyuan Lu, Chengde, 067000, China. TEL 86-314-2157250 ext 6397, FAX 86-314-2157486.

665.5 CHN ISSN 1671-5152
CHENGSHI RANQI. Text in Chinese. m. CNY 10 per issue (effective 2010). **Document type:** *Journal, Academic/Scholarly.*
Former titles (until 2002): Chengshi Meiqi (1004-4485); (until 1988): Chengshi Meiqi Qingbao; Which was formed by the merger of (1975-1980): Chengshi Meiqi Jianxun; (1977-1979): Chengshi Meiqi Zhaiyi
Related titles: Online - full text ed.: (from WanFang Data Corp.).
Published by: Zhongguo Chengshi Ranqi Xiehui/China Gas Association, 22, Xizhimen Nanxiao Jie, Xicheng-qu, Beijing, 100035, China. TEL 86-10-66200018, FAX 86-10-66205544, cga@chinagas.org.cn.

661.804 338.47665983 GBR ISSN 1749-219X
CHILE PETROCHEMICALS REPORT. Text in English. 2005. a. EUR 820, USD 1,030 combined subscription per issue (print & email eds.) (effective 2010). **Document type:** *Report, Trade.* **Description:** Provides industry professionals and strategists, sector analysts, trade associations and regulatory bodies with independent forecasts and competitive intelligence on the Chilean petrochemicals industry.
Related titles: E-mail ed.
Indexed: A15, ABIn, B02, B15, B17, B18, G04, I05, P48, P51, P52, P56, PQC.
Published by: Business Monitor International Ltd., Senator House, 85 Queen Victoria St, London, EC4V 4AB, United Kingdom. TEL 44-20-72480468, FAX 44-20-72480467, subs@businessmonitor.com.

CHINA CHEMICALS REPORT. *see* BUSINESS AND ECONOMICS

665.5 CHN ISSN 1006-2696
TN876.C5
➤ **CHINA OIL AND GAS.** Text in Chinese. 1994. q. EUR 428, USD 478 to institutions (effective 2007). **Document type:** *Journal, Academic/ Scholarly.* **Description:** Provides a comprehensive overview of China's petroleum industry.
Related titles: Online - full text ed.
Indexed: A26, FR.
—INIST. **CCC.**
Published by: China National Offshore Oil Corporation, 22 East St, Gaobeidian, Hebei 074010, China. TEL 86-3235-212799, FAX 86-3235-212400. **Subscr. to:** Springer Distribution Center, Kundenservice Zeitschriften, Haberstr 7, Heidelberg 69126, Germany. TEL 49-6221-3454303, FAX 49-6221-3454229, subscriptions@springer.com.

661.804 338.47665951 GBR ISSN 1749-2203
CHINA PETROCHEMICALS REPORT. Text in English. 2005. q. EUR 820, USD 1,030 combined subscription (print & email eds.) (effective 2010). **Document type:** *Report, Trade.* **Description:** Provides industry professionals and strategists, sector analysts, trade associations and regulatory bodies with independent forecasts and competitive intelligence on the Chinese petrochemicals industry.
Related titles: E-mail ed.
Indexed: A15, ABIn, B02, B15, B17, B18, G04, I05, P48, P51, P52, P56, PQC.
Published by: Business Monitor International Ltd., Senator House, 85 Queen Victoria St, London, EC4V 4AB, United Kingdom. TEL 44-20-72480468, FAX 44-20-72480467, subs@businessmonitor.com.

665.5 CHN ISSN 1008-6234
CHINA PETROLEUM PROCESSING AND PETROCHEMICAL TECHNOLOGY. Text in English. 1999. q. CNY 20 newsstand/cover (effective 2005). **Document type:** *Journal, Academic/Scholarly.*
Related titles: Online - full text ed.
Indexed: APIAb, RefZh, SCI, SCOPUS, W07.
—BLDSC (3180.217600), IE, Ingenta.
Published by: SINOPEC, Research Institute of Petroleum Processing, 18, Yixueyuan Lu, PO Box 914, Beijing, 100083, China. TEL 86-10-62311582, FAX 86-10-62311290, 26@ripp-sinopec.com, http://www.ripp-sinopec.com/.

338.47665 USA ISSN 1931-1885
CHINAWIRE. Text in English. 1994. d. USD 6,995 combined subscription (online & E-mail eds.) (effective 2008). back issues avail. **Document type:** *Newsletter, Trade.* **Description:** Provides an insight into the world's fastest growing market with daily assessments and market commentary for the heavily traded fuel oil and gasoil markets, as well as gasoline assessments.
Media: Online - full content. **Related titles:** E-mail ed.; Fax ed.
Published by: Platts (Subsidiary of: McGraw-Hill Companies, Inc.), 1200 G St NW, Ste 1000, Washington, DC 20005. TEL 212-904-3070, 800-752-8878, FAX 202-383-2024, support@platts.com.

CHINESE MARKETS FOR PETROCHEMICALS. *see* BUSINESS AND ECONOMICS—Marketing And Purchasing

CHINESE MARKETS FOR PETROLEUM ADDITIVES. *see* BUSINESS AND ECONOMICS—Marketing And Purchasing

665.5 COL ISSN 0122-5383
TN860 CODEN: CCTFAC
➤ **CIENCIA TECNOLOGIA Y FUTURO.** Abbreviated title: C T & F. Text in Spanish. 1995. a. **Document type:** *Journal, Academic/Scholarly.* **Description:** Covers Ecopetrol's research and development scientific achievements, investigations in petroleum related areas, natural gas and alternative sources of energy.
Related titles: Online - full text ed.: free (effective 2011) (from SciELO).
Indexed: A28, A32, APA, APIAb, ASFA, BrCerAb, C&ISA, CA/WCA, CIA, CPEI, CerAb, CivEngAb, CorrAb, E&CAJ, E11, EEA, EMA, ESPM, EnvEAb, FLUIDEX, GEOBASE, GeoRef, H15, HPNRM, M&TEA, M09, MBF, METADEX, PetrolAb, PollutAb, SCI, SCOPUS, SSciA, SWRA, SolStAb, T04, W07, WAA.
—BLDSC (3490.452250), Ingenta, INIST, Linda Hall, PADDS.
Published by: Ecopetrol, c/o Victor Eduardo Perez, Carrera 13 No. 36-24 piso 11, Bogota, Colombia. vperez@ecopetrol.com.co, http://www.ecopetrol.com.co/. Ed. Gloria Esperanza Cobaleda Cobaleda. Circ: 500.

➤ **CLEAN TANKERWIRE.** *see* TRANSPORTATION—Ships And Shipping

665.53 USA ISSN 1946-0198
TA455.A63
▼ ➤ **COAL COMBUSTION AND GASIFICATION PRODUCTS.** Text in English. 2009 (Jul.). a. free (effective 2010). **Document type:** *Journal, Academic/Scholarly.* **Description:** Covers the science and technology of the production, sustainable utilization, and environmentally-sound handling of the byproducts of coal combustion and gasification.
Media: Online - full text.
Published by: University of Kentucky, Center for Applied Energy Research, 2540 Research Park Dr, Lexington, KY 40511. TEL 859-257-0305, FAX 859-257-0220, http://www.caer.uky.edu/. Ed. Dr. James Hower.

661.804 338.47665 986.1 GBR ISSN 1749-2211
COLOMBIA PETROCHEMICALS REPORT. Text in English. 2005. a. EUR 820, USD 1,030 combined subscription per issue (print & email eds.) (effective 2010). **Document type:** *Report, Trade.* **Description:** Provides industry professionals and strategists, sector analysts, trade associations and regulatory bodies with independent forecasts and competitive intelligence on the Colombian petrochemicals industry.
Related titles: E-mail ed.
Indexed: A15, ABIn, B02, B15, B17, B18, G04, I05, P48, P51, P52, PQC.
Published by: Business Monitor International Ltd., Senator House, 85 Queen Victoria St, London, EC4V 4AB, United Kingdom. TEL 44-20-72480468, FAX 44-20-72480467, subs@businessmonitor.com.

COMBUSTIBLES, CARBURANTS, CHAUFFAGE. *see* ENERGY

665.5029 USA
COMPOSITE CATALOG OF OIL FIELD EQUIPMENT & SERVICES. Text in English. 1929. biennial. tr.lit. index. reprints avail. **Document type:** *Catalog, Consumer.*
Formerly (until 1956): The Composite Catalog of Oil Field and Pipe Line Equipment
Related titles: CD-ROM ed.
Published by: Gulf Publishing Co., PO Box 2608, Houston, TX 77252. TEL 713-529-4301, FAX 713-520-4433, publications@gulfpub.com, http://www.gulfpub.com. Ed. Cheryl Willis. Pub. Rusty Meador. Adv. contact Lanie Finlayson. Circ: 18,000.

665.5 660 USA ISSN 1042-508X
COMPOUNDINGS. Text in English. 1949. m. free to members; USD 150 to non-members (effective 2005). adv. bk.rev. **Document type:** *Magazine, Trade.* **Description:** Features industry trends; marketing and manufacturing innovations; new plant operations, people in the industry, legislative and regulatory developments, meetings, news and employment and business opportunities.
Related titles: Online - full text ed.
Indexed: A15, ABIn, P48, P51, P52, P56, PQC.
Published by: Independent Lubricant Manufacturers Association, 651 S Washington St, Alexandria, VA 22314. TEL 703-684-5574, FAX 703-836-8503. Ed. Michael L Cannizzaro. Adv. contact Bruce Levine. Circ: 2,300.

665.7 USA
COMPRESSIONS. Text in English. 1982. m. looseleaf. membership. **Document type:** *Newsletter.* **Description:** Association newsletter for the compressed gas industry.
Published by: Compressed Gas Association, Inc., 4221 Walney Rd., # 5, Chantilly, VA 20151-2923. TEL 703-412-0900, FAX 703-412-0128. Ed. Andrew Tarpgaard. Circ: 1,700.

665.5 USA
COOLING TOWER INSTITUTE. BIBLIOGRAPHY OF TECHNICAL PAPERS. Text in English. m. price varies. back issues avail. **Document type:** *Monographic series, Bibliography.* **Description:** Lists available technical papers which were presented at meetings sponsored by the institute.
Published by: Cooling Technology Institute, PO Box 73383, Houston, TX 77273. TEL 281-583-4087, FAX 281-537-1721.

665.5 THA
COORDINATING COMMITTEE FOR GEOSCIENCE PROGRAMMES IN EAST AND SOUTHEAST ASIA. ANNUAL SESSION. PROCEEDINGS. PART II. Text in English. a. **Document type:** *Proceedings, Academic/Scholarly.* **Description:** Contains technical papers submitted for the Annual Session Meeting. Covers current geological research and development in the fields of oil and gas, mineral resources, coastal zone management and geohazards in East and Southeast Asian region.
Related titles: Online - full content ed.
Published by: Coordinating Committee for Geoscience Programmes in East and Southeast Asia, c/o CCOP Technical Secretariat, Thai CC Tower, 24th Fl., Ste. 244-245, 889 Sathorn Tai Rd., Sathorn, Bangkok, 10120, Thailand. TEL 662-6723080-1, FAX 662-6723082, ccopts@ccop.or.th.

665.5 333.79 USA ISSN 1931-1907
CRUDE OIL MARKET WIRE. Text in English. 19??. d. price varies. **Document type:** *Newsletter, Trade.* **Description:** Provides today's market information including crude oil price spreads, trading updates, OPEC and industry officials' commentary, market transactions and futures settlement prices.
Media: Online - full content.
—**CCC.**
Published by: Platts (Subsidiary of: McGraw-Hill Companies, Inc.), 1200 G St NW, Ste 1000, Washington, DC 20005. TEL 212-904-3070, 800-752-8878, FAX 202-383-2024, support@platts.com.

665.5 AUS ISSN 1834-6766
CURTIN UNIVERSITY OF TECHNOLOGY. SCHOOL OF ECONOMICS AND FINANCE. AREA OF RESEARCH EXCELLENCE IN OIL & GAS MANAGEMENT. WORKING PAPER SERIES. Text in English. 2007. irreg. **Document type:** *Monographic series, Academic/ Scholarly.*
Media: Online - full text.
Published by: (Curtin University of Technology, Curtin Business School), Curtin University of Technology, School of Economics and Finance, GPO Box U1987, Perth, W.A. 6845, Australia. TEL 61-8-9266-7147, FAX 61-8-9266-2378, hallsp@cbs.curtin.edu.au.

CZECH REPUBLIC CHEMICALS REPORT. *see* CHEMISTRY

661.804 338.47665 943.71 GBR ISSN 1749-222X
CZECH REPUBLIC PETROCHEMICALS REPORT. Text in English. 2005. q. EUR 820, USD 1,030 combined subscription (print & email eds.) (effective 2010). **Document type:** *Report, Trade.* **Description:** Provides industry professionals and strategists, sector analysts, trade associations and regulatory bodies with independent forecasts and competitive intelligence on the Czech petrochemicals industry.
Related titles: E-mail ed.
Indexed: A15, ABIn, B02, B15, B17, B18, G04, I05, P48, P51, P52, P56, PQC.
Published by: Business Monitor International Ltd., Senator House, 85 Queen Victoria St, London, EC4V 4AB, United Kingdom. TEL 44-20-72480468, FAX 44-20-72480467, subs@businessmonitor.com.

665.54 690 USA
D C A NEWS. Text in English. 1961. m. membership. adv. **Document type:** *Newsletter.*
Indexed: IDP.
Published by: Distribution Contractors Association, 101 W Renner Rd, Ste 250, Richardson, TX 75082. TEL 214-680-0261, FAX 214-680-0461. Ed., Adv. contact John P Churchill. R&P Dennis J Kennedy TEL 972-680-0261. Circ: 500.

665.5 DEU ISSN 1433-9013
CODEN: BWGTEK
D G M K TAGUNGSBERICHT. (Deutsche Gesellschaft fuer Mineraloelwissenschaft und Kohlechemie) Text in German. 198?. irreg. price varies. **Document type:** *Monographic series, Academic/ Scholarly.*
Formerly (until 1996): Deutsche Wissenschaftliche Gesellschaft fur Erdol, Erdgas und Kohle e.V. Tagungsbericht. Berichte (0938-068X)
Indexed: CIN, ChemAb, ChemTitl, GeoRef, SCOPUS, SpeleolAb.
—BLDSC (8598.433000), CASDDS, IE, Ingenta, Linda Hall. **CCC.**
Published by: Deutsche Wissenschaftliche Gesellschaft fuer Erdoel, Erdgas und Kohle e.V., Ueberseering 40, Hamburg, 22297, Germany. TEL 49-40-6390040, FAX 49-40-63900450, info@dgmk.de.

665.5 SRB ISSN 0352-0870
D I T; strucni casopis. (Drustvo Inzenjera i Tehnicara) Text in Serbo-Croatian. 1982. q. adv. bk.rev. back issues avail. **Document type:** *Journal, Trade.*
Published by: Drustvo Inzenjera i Tehnicara Naftagas, Sutjeska 1, Novi Sad, 21000. http://www.nis-naftagas.co.yu. Ed. Milan Mladenovic. Circ: 700.

665.5 CAN ISSN 1715-4944
DAILY CANADIAN OIL REPORT. Text in English. 2005. d. CAD 500 (effective 2006). **Document type:** *Newsletter, Trade.*
Media: Online - full text. **Related titles:** E-mail ed.
Published by: G L J Energy Publications Inc., 4100, 400 - 3 Ave. S.W., Calgary, AB T2P 4H2, Canada. TEL 403-270-0700, FAX 403-270-0716, glj@gljpublications.com, http://www.gljpublications.com/index.shtml.

665.5 USA ISSN 1559-2529
DAILY GAS BURN REPORT. Text in English. 2005. d. **Document type:** *Report, Trade.*
Media: Online - full text.
Published by: Genscape, Inc., 445 E Market St, Ste 200, Louisville, KY 40202. TEL 502-583-3435, FAX 502-583-3464, info@genscape.com, http://www.genscape.com/.

665.5 USA ISSN 0276-5934
DAILY MUNGER OILOGRAM. Text in English. 19??. bi-w. USD 900 (print or e-mail ed.) (effective 2011). stat. **Document type:** *Newsletter, Trade.* **Description:** Provides information on exploration wells, abandonment, map revisions, and developments affecting the industry, with a focus on California, Alaska, Arizona, Nevada, Oregon, and Washington.
Related titles: E-mail ed.
Published by: Munger Oil Information Service, Inc., HC1 Box 1205, Joshua Tree, CA 92252. TEL 760-366-4755, FAX 760-366-7625, service@mungeroilinfo.com.

665.5 DNK ISSN 1603-0885
DANISH OFFSHORE INDUSTRY. Cover title: Esbjerg Offshore Contacts. Text in English. 1983. a. adv. **Document type:** *Directory, Trade.* **Description:** Listing of the companies involved in the Danish offshore industry.
Formerly (until 2003): Esbjerg Offshore Contacts (0904-583X)
Related titles: Online - full content ed.
Published by: Forlaget Ole Camae, Lerbjergstien 8, Birkeroed, 3460, Denmark. TEL 45-48-176282, FAX 45-48-177880, info@camae.dk.

665.5 DNK ISSN 0907-2675
DANMARKS OLIE OG GASPRODUKTION, OG ANVENDELSE AF UNDERGRUNDEN. Text in Danish. 1987. a. back issues avail. **Document type:** *Government.*
Formerly (until 1992): Olie og Gas i Danmark (0903-2819)
Related titles: Online - full text ed.: ISSN 1398-4349; ◆ English ed.: Denmark's Oil and Gas Production, and Subsoil Use. ISSN 1904-0245.
Published by: Klima- og Energiministeriet, Energistyrelsen/Ministry of Climate and Energy, Danish Energy Agency, Amaliegade 44, Copenhagen K, 1256, Denmark. TEL 45-33-926700, FAX 45-33-114743, ens@ens.dk, http://www.ens.dk.

665.5 CHN ISSN 1000-1891
TN876.C5
DAQING SHIYOU XUEYUAN XUEBAO/DAQING PETROLEUM INSTITUTE. JOURNAL. Text in Chinese. 1977. q. USD 24.60 (effective 2009). **Document type:** *Academic/Scholarly.*
Related titles: Online - full text ed.
Indexed: A22, GeoRef, PetrolAb, RefZh, SpeleolAb.
—BLDSC (4732.669000), East View, IE, Ingenta, PADDS.
Published by: Daqing Shiyou Xueyuan/Daqing Petroleum Institute, Anda, Heilongjiang 1514000, China. TEL 86-459-4653714. **Dist. by:** China International Book Trading Corp, 35 Chegongzhuang Xilu, Haidian District, PO Box 399, Beijing 100044, China. TEL 86-10-68412045, FAX 86-10-68412023, cibtc@mail.cibtc.com.cn, http://www.cibtc.com.cn.

665.5 USA ISSN 0272-9539
TN863
DEEP DRILLING AND PRODUCTION SYMPOSIUM. PROCEEDINGS. Text in English. 19??. irreg. **Document type:** *Proceedings, Academic/Scholarly.*
Indexed: GeoRef.
—**CCC.**
Published by: Society of Petroleum Engineers, Inc., PO Box 833836, Richardson, TX 75083. TEL 972-952-9393, 800-456-6863, FAX 972-952-9435, spedal@spe.org, http://www.spe.org.

665.5 DNK ISSN 1904-0245
DENMARK'S OIL AND GAS PRODUCTION, AND SUBSOIL USE. Text in English. 1988. a. free. **Document type:** *Government.*
Former titles (until 2008): Oil and Gas Production in Denmark (0908-1704); (until 1992): Denmark. Energiministeriet. Oil and Gas in Denmark (0905-9733)
Related titles: Online - full text ed.: ISSN 1904-0253; ◆ Danish ed.: Danmarks Olie og Gasproduktion, og Anvendelse af Undergrunden. ISSN 0907-2675.
—BLDSC (3553.103150).
Published by: Klima- og Energiministeriet, Energistyrelsen/Ministry of Climate and Energy, Danish Energy Agency, Amaliegade 44, Copenhagen K, 1256, Denmark. TEL 45-33-926700, FAX 45-33-114743, ens@ens.dk, http://www.ens.dk. Ed. Mette Sondergaard.

665.5 DEU ISSN 0937-9762
DEUTSCHE WISSENSCHAFTLICHE GESELLSCHAFT FUER ERDOEL, ERDGAS UND KOHLE. FORSCHUNGSBERICHT. Text in German. 197?. irreg. price varies. **Document type:** *Monographic series, Academic/Scholarly.*
Formerly (until 1987): Deutsche Gesellschaft fuer Mineraloelwissenschaft und Kohlechemie. Berichte (0171-2187)
Indexed: GeoRef, SCOPUS.
—BLDSC (4011.171500), IE, Ingenta, Linda Hall.
Published by: Deutsche Wissenschaftliche Gesellschaft fuer Erdoel, Erdgas und Kohle e.V., Ueberseering 40, Hamburg, 22297, Germany. TEL 49-40-6390040, FAX 49-40-63900450, info@dgmk.de.

665.6 NLD ISSN 0376-7361
CODEN: DPSCDZ
➤ **DEVELOPMENTS IN PETROLEUM SCIENCE.** Text in English. 1976. irreg., latest vol.50, 2002. price varies. back issues avail. **Document type:** *Monographic series, Academic/Scholarly.* **Description:** Provides detailed information on all aspects of petroleum science.
Related titles: Online - full text ed.: ISSN 2212-0726.
Indexed: A22, CIN, ChemAb, ChemTitl, GeoRef, IMMAb, SCOPUS, SpeleolAb.
—BLDSC (3579.085800), CASDDS, IE, Ingenta, INIST. **CCC.**
Published by: Elsevier BV (Subsidiary of: Elsevier Science & Technology), Radarweg 29, PO Box 211, Amsterdam, 1000 AE, Netherlands. TEL 31-20-4853911, FAX 31-20-4852457, JournalsCustomerServiceEMEA@elsevier.com, http://www.elsevier.nl.

➤ **DIESEL FORECAST**; the leading source for diesel technology news. *see* ENERGY

➤ **DIESEL POWER.** *see* TRANSPORTATION—Automobiles

665.5 CHN ISSN 1004-8510
DIHUO. Text in Chinese. q. **Document type:** *Magazine, Trade.*
Related titles: Online - full text ed.
Published by: Dihuo Zazhishe, 112, Ande Rd, West Rm. 237, Beijing, 100011, China. TEL 86-10-62385123, FAX 86-10-62385121.

DIRECTORY OF ELECTRIC UTILITY INDUSTRY. *see* ENERGY—Electrical Energy

665.7 USA
DIRECTORY OF PUBLICLY OWNED NATURAL GAS SYSTEMS. Text in English. a. USD 25 (effective 2000). adv. **Document type:** *Directory.*
Formerly: Directory of Municipal Natural Gas Systems
Published by: American Public Gas Association, 201 Massachusetts Ave NE, Ste. C4, Washington, DC 20002-4988. TEL 703-352-3890. Ed. Kelly Bardzell. Circ: 750.

DIRTY TANKERWIRE. *see* TRANSPORTATION—Ships And Shipping

665.5 ITA
DISTRIBUZIONE CARBURANTI. Text in Italian. 8/yr. EUR 22 (effective 2009). adv. **Document type:** *Magazine, Trade.*
Published by: Reed Business Information Spa (Subsidiary of: Reed Business Information International), Viale Giulio Richard 1, Milan, 20143, Italy. TEL 39-02-818301, FAX 39-02-81830406, info@reedbusiness.it, http://www.reedbusiness.it. Circ: 18,000.

665 USA
DOMESTIC NATURAL GAS AND OIL INITIATIVE. Text in English. 1995. a.
Published by: U.S. Department of Energy, Office of Industrial Technologies, 1000 Independence Ave., S.W., CP-41, Washington, DC 20585.

DOW JONES CHINA ENERGY REPORT. *see* ENERGY—Electrical Energy

662.338 CAN ISSN 0228-5630
DRILLING ACTIVITY REPORT. Text in English. 1953. m. CAD 180 (effective 1999). **Document type:** *Government.* **Description:** Lists by production and disposition areas and classification the well licences issued, — wellls finished, drilling, well completions well abandonments etc.
Published by: Saskatchewan Energy & Mines, Petroleum Statistics Branch, 2101 Scarth St, Regina, SK S4P 3V7, Canada. TEL 306-787-2528, FAX 306-787-2527.

621.952029 USA
DRILLING & WELL SERVICING CONTRACTORS; drilling & well servicing contractors, equipment manufacturers & supply companies. Text in English. a. USD 150 domestic; USD 160 in Canada; USD 165 elsewhere (effective 2009). adv. **Document type:** *Directory, Trade.* **Description:** Lists drilling and well servicing companies both across North America and internationally as well as the support sectors in the industry.
Formerly: Directory of Oil Well Drilling Contractors (0415-9764)
Published by: Midwest Publishing Company, 2230 E 49th St, Ste E, Tulsa, OK 74105. TEL 918-582-2000, 800-829-2002, FAX 918-587-9349, info@midwestpub.com. adv.: B&W page USD 1,610, color page USD 1,710.

665.5 USA
DRILLING COMPLETION AND PLUGGING SUMMARY. Text in English. 19??. m. USD 5 (effective 2011). back issues avail. **Document type:** *Report, Government.* **Description:** Gives the number of drilling permits issued, oil and gas completions, dry holes, and other information, but does not include permits by individual company.
Related titles: Online - full text ed.: free (effective 2011).
Published by: Railroad Commission, Oil and Gas Division, PO Box 12967, Austin, TX 78711. TEL 877-228-5740, publicassist@rrc.state.tx.us.

622.338 USA ISSN 0046-0702
TN860
DRILLING CONTRACTOR. Text in English. 1944. bi-m. USD 70 domestic; USD 130 foreign; free to qualified personnel (effective 2007). adv. charts; illus.; stat.; tr.lit. back issues avail. **Document type:** *Magazine, Trade.* **Description:** Covers drilling, production operations, industry outlook. Contains association news, personalities, new equipment.
Indexed: A22, E&PHSE, F&EA, FR, GP&P, OffTech, PetrolAb, TM.
—IE, Ingenta, INIST, Linda Hall, PADDS. **CCC.**
Published by: (International Association of Drilling Contractors), Drilling Contractor Publications, Inc. (Subsidiary of: International Association of Drilling Contractors), PO Box 4287, Houston, TX 77210-4287. TEL 713-292-1945, FAX 713-292-1946, drilling.contractor@iadc.org, http://www.iadc.org. Ed. Mike Killalea. adv.: B&W page USD 5,350, color page USD 6,630. Circ: 28,239 (controlled).

665.5 USA
DRILLING PERMITS. Text in English. d. USD 325 (effective 2000). **Document type:** *Abstract/Index.* **Description:** Provides current information on new oil drilling permits filed with state and federal agencies for the Gulf of Mexico and Louisiana.
Published by: O D S - Petrodata, 3200 Wilcrest Dr, Ste 170, Houston, TX 77042. TEL 832-463-3000, FAX 832-463-3100, general@ods-petrodata.com, http://www.ods-petrodata.com.

665.5 CHN ISSN 1005-8907
➤ **DUANKUAI YOUQITIAN/FAULT-BLOCK OIL & GAS FIELD.** Text in Chinese; Abstracts in Chinese, English. 1994. bi-m. CNY 60; CNY 10 newsstand/cover (effective 2009). **Document type:** *Journal, Academic/Scholarly.* **Description:** Covers the latest developments of theoretical and applied research in the fields of petroleum and gas engineering.
Indexed: A28, APA, BrCerAb, C&ISA, CA/WCA, CIA, CerAb, CivEngAb, CorrAb, E&CAJ, E11, EEA, EMA, ESPM, EnvEAb, GeoRef, H15, M&TEA, M09, MBF, METADEX, PetrolAb, SolStAb, T04, WAA.
—PADDS.
Published by: Duankuai Youqitian Qikanshe, No 157, Zhongyuan Rd, Puyang, 457001, China. TEL 86-393-4820093, FAX 86-393-4824957, dkyqt@vip.163.com, http://www.zydzy.com. Ed. Shouping Wang. Circ: 2,000 (paid).

665.5 USA
HD9560.1 CODEN: EUJOE5
E & P. (Exploration and Production) Variant title: Hart's Euroil. Text in English. 1999. m. USD 149; free to qualified personnel (effective 2008). adv. bk.rev. charts; illus.; mkt.; maps; pat.; stat.; tr.lit. back issues avail.; reprints avail. **Document type:** *Magazine, Trade.* **Description:** Offers authoritative comment and analysis of new technology, industry trends, and the political-economic environment of all global exploration and production regions.
Formerly (until 2004): Hart's E & P (1527-4063); Which was formed by the merger of (1994-1999): Hart's Oil and Gas World (1075-5365); Hart's Petroleum Engineer International; Which was formerly (until 1994): Petroleum Engineer International (0164-8322); (until 1967): Petroleum Engineer (0031-6466); (1973-1999): Euroil (0802-9474); Which superseded in part (in 1990): Noroil (0332-544X); (1985-1999): Northeast Oil and Gas World (1070-4469); Which was formerly (until 1993): Northeast Oil World (0884-4771); (until 1985): Northeast Oil Reporter (0279-7798); (19??-1999): Gulf Coast Oil and Gas World (1070-4914); Which was formerly: Gulf Coast Oil World (0884-7967); (until 198?): Gulf Coast Oil Reporter (0744-9070)
Related titles: Microfiche ed.; Online - full text ed.: free to qualified personnel (effective 2008).
Indexed: A05, A12, A13, A22, ABIn, AS&TA, AS&TI, B02, B04, B15, B17, B18, BMT, BrGeoL, BrTechI, C10, CA, E11, E14, EIA, EnvAb, FR, G04, G06, G07, G08, GeoRef, I05, P26, P48, P51, P52, P53, P54, P56, PQC, PetrolAb, RASB, SCOPUS, SpeleolAb, T04, V03.
—IE, Infotrieve, Ingenta, INIST, Linda Hall, PADDS. **CCC.**
Published by: Hart Energy Publishing, LP (Subsidiary of: Chemical Week Associates), 1616 S Voss Rd, Ste 1000, Houston, TX 77057. TEL 713-260-6400, 800-874-2544, FAX 713-840-8585, custserv@hartenergy.com, http://www.hartenergy.com. Eds. Rhonda Duey, William Pike. Pub. Russell Laas TEL 713-260-6447. adv.: B&W page USD 9,335, color page USD 11,460; trim 8 x 10.5. Circ: 45,186 (paid).

665.5 USA ISSN 2152-2987
E & P FOCUS. (Exploration and Production) Text in English. 2005. q. free (effective 2010). back issues avail. **Document type:** *Newsletter, Trade.* **Description:** Promotes the widespread dissemination of research results among all types of oil and gas industry stakeholders: producers, researchers, educators, regulators, and policymakers.
Media: Online - full text.
Published by: National Energy Technology Laboratory, Office of Petroleum, 1450 Queen Ave, SW, Albany, OR 97321. TEL 541-967-5892, 800-553-7681.

E N I ANNUAL REPORT. (Ente Nazionale Idrocarburi) *see* ENERGY

EGYPT CHEMICALS REPORT. *see* CHEMISTRY

338.47665962 GBR ISSN 1749-2238
EGYPT PETROCHEMICALS REPORT. Text in English. 2005. q. EUR 820, USD 1,030 combined subscription (print & email eds.) (effective 2010). **Document type:** *Report, Trade.* **Description:** Provides industry professionals and strategists, sector analysts, trade associations and regulatory bodies with independent forecasts and competitive intelligence on the Egyptian petrochemicals industry.
Related titles: E-mail ed.
Indexed: A15, ABIn, B02, B15, B17, B18, G04, I05, P48, P51, P52, P56, PQC.
Published by: Business Monitor International Ltd., Senator House, 85 Queen Victoria St, London, EC4V 4AB, United Kingdom. TEL 44-20-72480468, FAX 44-20-72480467, subs@businessmonitor.com.

665.5 EGY
EGYPTIAN JOURNAL OF PETROLEUM. Text in English; Summaries in Arabic, English. 1992. 2/yr. EGP 50 domestic; USD 50 foreign (effective 2009). reprint service avail. from IRC. **Document type:** *Journal, Academic/Scholarly.*
—PADDS.
Published by: Egyptian Petroleum Research Institute, Seventh Region, 1 Ahmed El-Zomor St, Nasr City, Cairo, 11727, Egypt. TEL 202-2274-7847, FAX 202-2274-7433. Ed. Bahram M Mahmoud.

551 FRA ISSN 0181-0901
QE1
ELF-AQUITAINE. CENTRES DE RECHERCHES EXPLORATION-PRODUCTION. BULLETIN. MEMOIRE. Text in English, French. 1979.
Indexed: GeoRef, SpeleolAb.
—CCC.
Published by: Elf Edition Exploration, Avenue Larribau, Pau, Cedex 64018, France. TEL 33-5-59834242, FAX 33-5-59834242.

665.5 ESP
ENCICLOPEDIA NACIONAL DEL PETROLEO PETROLQUIMICA Y GAS. Text in Spanish. 1970. a. **Document type:** *Directory, Consumer.* **Description:** Spanish national encyclopedia on the petroleum, petrochemical and gas activities.
Published by: Sede Tecnica S.A., Avda Brasil, 17 planta 12, Madrid, 28020, Spain. TEL 34-91-5565004, FAX 34-91-5560962, editorial@sedetecnica.com, http://www.sedetecnica.com/. Ed. Carlos Martin. Circ: 6,000.

338.47665 CAN
ENER DATABOOK AND DATADISK. Text in English. s-a. CAD 1,095 combined subscription both print & disk eds. (effective 2003). **Document type:** *Handbook/Manual/Guide, Trade.* **Description:** Contains historical Enerdata natural gas price information.
Related titles: Diskette ed.; E-mail ed.; Online - full content ed.: CAD 980 online or E-mail ed. (effective 2003).
Published by: Canadian Enerdata Ltd., 100 Allstate Pkwy, Ste 304, Markham, ON L3R 6H3, Canada. TEL 905-479-9697, FAX 905-479-2515, publications@enerdata.com.

665.7 DEU
ENERGIE & LEBEN. Text in German. 198?. 5/yr. adv. **Document type:** *Magazine, Consumer.*
Published by: Energie & Medien Verlag GmbH, Gustav-Siegle-Str 16, Stuttgart, 70193, Germany. TEL 49-711-2535900, FAX 49-711-25359028, post@energie-medien-verlag.de, http://www.energie-medien-verlag.de. adv.: B&W page EUR 7,200, color page EUR 10,080. Circ: 340,000 (controlled).

ENERGIE - INFORMATIONSDIENST. *see* ENERGY

ENERGIEWIRTSCHAFTLICHE TAGESFRAGEN; Zeitschrift fuer Energie-Wirtschaft - Recht - Technik und Umwelt. *see* ENERGY

665.7 SWE ISSN 1653-5367
CODEN: GASNDU
ENERGIGAS. Text in Swedish. 1934. 4/yr. SEK 400 domestic; SEK 490 foreign; SEK 25 newsstand/cover (effective 2004). adv. bk.rev. charts; illus.; maps. index. **Document type:** *Magazine, Trade.*
Former titles (until 2005): Gasnytt (0039-6834); (until 1970): Svenska Gasfoereningens Maanadsblad (0370-9876)
Indexed: F&EA, GasAb.
—CASDDS.
Published by: Svenska Gasfoereningen, Sankt Eriksgatan 14, PO Box 49134, Stockholm, 10029, Sweden. TEL 46-8-6921840, FAX 46-8-6544615, info@gasforeningen.se. Ed. Lotta Brandt. Adv. contact Lennart Ekblom TEL 46-8-879700. Circ: 6,000 (controlled).

338.47 381.42282 DNK ISSN 1903-3028
ENERGINOTER & ENERGISTATISTIK. Text in Danish. 1979. a. free. illus.; stat. back issues avail. **Document type:** *Corporate.*
Fomer titles (until 2008): Olieberetning (0109-3916); (until 1980): Oliebranchens Faellesrepraesentation. Beretning
Related titles: Online - full text ed.: ISSN 1903-3036. 199?.
Published by: Energi- og Olieforum/Danish Petroleum Association, Landemaerket 10, 5, Copenhagen K, 1004, Denmark. eof@oliebranchen.dk, http://www.oliebranchen.dk. Ed. Per Folmer Hansen.

665.5 USA
ENERGY ALERT. Text in English. 1990. d. (or w.). free to qualified personnel (effective 2011). **Document type:** *Bulletin, Trade.* **Description:** Offers news briefs on share trends, mergers and acquisition activities, SEC filings, and corporate news in the North American energy and utilities industry.
Media: E-mail.
Published by: Energy Intelligence Group, Inc., 5 E 37th St, 5th Fl, New York, NY 10016. TEL 212-532-1112, FAX 212-532-4479, info@energyintel.com, http://www.energyintel.com.

ENERGY ANALECTS. *see* ENERGY

665.5 SGP
ENERGY ASIA; weekly newsletter on Asia's energy industry. Text in English. 1979. w. USD 150. back issues avail.
Published by: Petroleum News Publishing Pte. Ltd., 43 Middle Rd 04-00, Singapore, 188952, Singapore. TEL 3367128, FAX 3367919. Ed. Julie Bundy. Circ: 6,000.

665.5 USA ISSN 0962-9270
ENERGY COMPASS. Text in English. 1989. d. (or w.). back issues avail. **Document type:** *Newsletter, Trade.* **Description:** International executive briefing service focusing on worldwide political developments and their impact on the oil industry. Offers political risk analysis, trading intelligence and crude-product fundamentals.
Related titles: E-mail ed.; Fax ed.; Online - full text ed.
Indexed: A15, ABIn, P48, P51, P52, P56, PQC.
—CCC.
Published by: Energy Intelligence Group, Inc., 5 E 37th St, 5th Fl, New York, NY 10016. TEL 212-532-1112, FAX 212-532-4479. Eds. David Pike, Stephen MacSearraigh. Pub. Edward L Morse.

ENERGY DETENTE; monthly fuel price-tax series update. *see* PETROLEUM AND GAS—Abstracting, Bibliographies, Statistics

ENERGY IN JAPAN. *see* ENERGY

ENERGY INSTITUTE. JOURNAL. *see* ENERGY

665.5 USA ISSN 1931-8464
ENERGY PIPELINE NEWS. Text in English. 1999. d. USD 120 (effective 2011). back issues avail. **Document type:** *Newsletter, Trade.*
Related titles: Online - full text ed.: Energy Pipeline News. 1999. USD 30; USD 5 per month (effective 2011).
Published by: Anvil Publishers, PO Box 2694, Tucker, GA 30085. TEL 770-938-0289, 800-500-3524, FAX 770-493-7232, custserv@anvilpub.com, http://www.anvilpub.com. Ed. Noel Griese.

ENERGY POLICY. *see* ENERGY

ENERGY PROCESSING CANADA. *see* ENERGY

ENERGY REPORT; energy policy and technology news bulletin. *see* ENERGY

ENERGY SOURCES. PART A. RECOVERY, UTILIZATION, AND ENVIRONMENTAL EFFECTS. *see* ENERGY

ENERGY SOURCES. PART B. ECONOMICS, PLANNING, AND POLICY. *see* ENERGY

ENERGY TODAY. *see* ENERGY

ENERGY TRENDS. *see* ENERGY

ENERGY WORLD. *see* ENERGY

ENERSMART. *see* CONSERVATION

665 USA
ENGINE FLUIDS DATA BOOK. Text in English. 1975. biennial. looseleaf. USD 100 per issue (effective 2007). **Document type:** *Report, Trade.* **Description:** Contains oil data collected form oil suppliers from around the world.
Formerly: Lubricating Oils Data Book
Published by: Engine Manufacturers Association, 2 N La Salle St Ste 2200, Chicago, IL 60602-3801. TEL 312-827-8700, FAX 312-827-8737, ema@enginemanufacturers.org. Circ: 3,500 (paid).

665 338.2 AUT
ERDOEL. Text in German. 1969. 4/yr. free. index. **Document type:** *Bulletin.*
Supersedes: Shell Erdoel-Informationen (0037-3567)
—CCC.

Published by: Shell Austria AG, Rennweg 12, Vienna, W 1030, Austria. TEL 43-1-797972206, FAX 43-1-797972201, TELEX 133241-SHEL-A. Circ: 4,800.

665.5 DEU ISSN 0179-3187
TN860 CODEN: EEKOEY

ERDOEL - ERDGAS - KOHLE; Aufsuchung und Gewinnung, Verarbeitung und Anwendung, Petrochemie, chemische Kohlenveredlung. Summaries in English, German. 1884. m. EUR 298.21 domestic; EUR 311.20 in Europe (effective 2007). adv. bk.rev. abstr.; bibl.; charts; illus.; stat. index. 56 p./no. 3 cols./p.; **Document type:** *Journal, Trade.*
Incorporates (1970-1995): Erdoel und Kohle, Erdgas, Petrochemie vereinigt mit Brennstoff-Chemie (0367-0716); Which was formed by the merger of (1933-1970): Brennstoff-Chemie (0006-9620); Which superseded in part (in 1949): Oel und Kohle (0369-7177); Which was formed by the merger of (1920-1933): Brennstoff-Chemie (0724-2042); (1925-1933): Erdoel und Teer (0367-133X); (193?-1933): Bohrtechniker-Zeitung (0366-1814); Which was formed by the merger of (1883-193?): Allgemeine Oesterreichische Chemiker und Techniker-Zeitung (0365-5199); (1924-193?): Internationale Zeitschrift fuer Bohrtechnik, Erdoelbergbau und Geologie (0368-0843); (1905-1933): Petroleum (0369-9048); Which incorporated (1910-1919): Die Rohoelindustrie (0724-2077); (1948-1970): Erdoel und Kohle, Erdgas, Petrochemie (0014-0058); Which was formerly (until 1960): Erdoel und Kohle (0367-1305); Former titles (until 1986): Erdoel - Erdgas (0724-8555); (until 1983): Erdoel-Erdgas Zeitschrift (0014-004X); (until 1965): Erdoel-Zeitschrift fuer Bohr- und Foerdertechnik (0367-1542); (until 1955): Erdoel-Zeitung
Related titles: Online - full text ed.
Indexed: A22, APIAb, APICat, APIH&E, APIOC, APIPR, APIPS, APITS, ASCA, BrGeoL, C33, CBNB, CEA, CEABA, CIN, CISA, ChemAb, ChemTitl, E&PHSE, EIA, EngInd, F&EA, FR, G08, GP&P, GeoRef, IBR, IBZ, KES, OffTech, PetrolAb, RefZh, SCOPUS, SpeleolAb, TCEA, TM.
—BLDSC (3799.720000), CASDDS, IE, Infotrieve, Ingenta, INIST, Linda Hall, PADDS. **CCC.**
Published by: (German Scientific Society of Petroleum, Gas and Coal Chemistry), Urban-Verlag GmbH, Postfach 701606, Hamburg, 22016, Germany. TEL 49-40-6569450, FAX 49-40-65694550, info@oilgaspublisher.de. Eds. Hans Joerg Mager, T Vieth. Adv. contact Harald Jordan. B&W page EUR 2,250, color page EUR 3,300. Circ: 2,621 (controlled). **Co-sponsor:** Austrian Society of Petroleum Sciences.

665 MYS ISSN 0127-0710

ESSO IN MALAYSIA. Text in English, Malay. 1962. m. free. illus.
Formerly: Esso News (0014-102X)
Published by: Esso Malaysia Berhad, PO Box 10601, Kuala Lumpur, Malaysia. TEL 03-2428760, FAX 03-2422521. Ed. Chan Soon Ching. Circ: 3,900. **Co-sponsor:** Esso Production Malaysia Inc.

661.804 USA

ETHANOL RETAILER. Text in English. 2008. q. **Document type:** *Magazine, Trade.* **Description:** Covers the ethanol industry from the perspective of the fuel retailer.
Published by: (Ethanol Promotion and Information Council), ZimmComm New Media, LLC, 1600 Skyview Dr, Holts Summit, MO 65043. chuck@zimmcomm.biz, http://zimmcomm.biz. Pub. Robert White. Circ: 22,000 (controlled).

665.5 USA ISSN 1931-1796

EUROPE & AMERICAS PETROCHEMICAL SCAN. Variant title: Platts Europe & Americas Petrochemical Scan. Text in English. 2002. w. USD 3,715; USD 3,795 combined subscription (online & E-mail eds.) (effective 2008). back issues avail. **Document type:** *Newsletter, Trade.* **Description:** Provides weekly report on key product price ranges and market news in the spot markets of Europe and the Americas.
Media: Online - full content. **Related titles:** E-mail ed.
—CCC.
Published by: Platts (Subsidiary of: McGraw-Hill Companies, Inc.), 1200 G St NW, Ste 1000, Washington, DC 20005. TEL 212-904-3070, 800-752-8878, FAX 202-383-2024, support@platts.com. Ed. Jim Foster.

EUROPEAN DAILY CARBON MARKETS. *see* ENERGY

665.5 USA ISSN 1938-7644
HD9502.E8

EUROPEAN FUEL PRICE SERVICE. Text in English. 19??. q. **Document type:** *Report, Trade.* **Description:** Provides detailed fifteen-year forecasts and analyses of primary fuel prices, including gas, oil and coal for European nations.
Published by: I H S Global Insight (USA) Inc., 24 Hartwell Ave, Lexington, MA 02421. TEL 781-301-9100, FAX 781-301-9416, info@ihsglobalinsight.com.

665.5 USA ISSN 1943-8435
HD9502.G32

EUROPEAN FUEL PRICE SERVICE. GERMANY AND ITALY. Text in English. 2007. q. **Document type:** *Report, Trade.* **Description:** Provides detailed fifteen-year forecasts and analyses of primary fuel prices, including gas, oil and coal for Germany and Italy.
Published by: I H S Global Insight (USA) Inc., 24 Hartwell Ave, Lexington, MA 02421. TEL 781-301-9100, FAX 781-301-9416, info@ihsglobalinsight.com.

665.5 USA ISSN 1943-8443
HD9502.G7

EUROPEAN FUEL PRICE SERVICE. UNITED KINGDOM. Text in English. 2007. q. **Document type:** *Report, Trade.* **Description:** Provides detailed fifteen-year forecasts and analyses of primary fuel prices, including gas, oil and coal for the United Kingdom.
Published by: I H S Global Insight (USA) Inc., 24 Hartwell Ave, Lexington, MA 02421. TEL 781-301-9100, FAX 781-301-9416, info@ihsglobalinsight.com.

665.7 GBR ISSN 1466-8874

EUROPEAN GAS DAILY. Variant title: Gas Daily Europe. Text in English. 1999. d. USD 2,335 combined subscription (E-mail & Online eds.) (effective 2010). back issues avail.; reprints avail. **Document type:** *Newsletter, Trade.* **Description:** Provides briefings with news and analysis on the day's main market developments as well as key pricing data.
Media: E-mail. **Related titles:** Online - full text ed.
—CCC.
Published by: Platts (Subsidiary of: McGraw-Hill Companies, Inc.), 20 Canada Sq, 12th Fl, Canary Wharf, London, E14 5LH, United Kingdom. TEL 44-20-71766111, FAX 44-20-71766144, support@platts.com.

333.79 665.5 USA ISSN 0149-5836

EUROPEAN MARKETSCAN. Text in English. 1976. d. price varies. back issues avail. **Document type:** *Newsletter, Trade.* **Description:** Provides essential coverage of the refined products marketplace and features daily reporting of trading activity of the major refined products in Europe and price assessments for the north west European and Mediterranean cargo markets and the ARA barge market, including gasoil/diesel, gasoline, jet fuel, naphtha, fuel oil and feedstocks.
Formerly: Platt's Oilgram Marketscan. European Edition
—CCC.
Published by: Platts (Subsidiary of: McGraw-Hill Companies, Inc.), 1200 G St NW, Ste 1000, Washington, DC 20005. TEL 212-904-3070, 800-752-8878, FAX 202-383-2024, support@platts.com.

665.5 GBR ISSN 0332-5210

EUROPEAN OFFSHORE PETROLEUM NEWSLETTER. Text in English. 1992. w. GBP 775 (effective 2009). charts; maps; stat.; tr.lit. **Document type:** *Newsletter, Trade.* **Description:** Covers energy and petroleum, field development, seismic activity, subsea, licensing, decommissioning, pipelines, rig market, company news, for Europe, North Sea, Commonwealth of Independent States and West Africa.
Related titles: E-mail ed.; Online - full text ed.
Indexed: A15, ABIn, P48, P51, P56, PQC.
—CIS. **CCC.**
Published by: Ogilvie Publishing Ltd., Quatro House, Lyon Way, Frimley, Surrey GU16 7ER, United Kingdom. TEL 44-1276-804508, FAX 44-1276-804513, marketing@ogilviepub.com. Ed. Steven Hamlen.

665.5 DEU ISSN 1439-0124
HD9575.A1

EUROPEAN OIL AND GAS YEARBOOK. Text in English, French, German. 1963. a. EUR 111.20 (effective 2001). adv. maps; stat. 400 p./no.; **Document type:** *Yearbook, Trade.*
Formerly (until 1999): European Petroleum Yearbook (0342-6947); (until 1974): Jahrbuch der Europaeischen Erdoeindustrie (0066-1716)
Indexed: GeoRef, SpeleolAb.
—CCC.
Published by: Urban-Verlag GmbH, Postfach 701606, Hamburg, 22016, Germany. TEL 49-40-65694520, FAX 49-40-65694550, info@oilgaspublisher.de, http://www.oilgaspublisher.de. Ed. Thomas Vieth. Adv. contact Harald Jordan. Circ: 2,000.

665.5 GBR ISSN 1470-434X

EUROPETROLEUM. Text in English. 1989. bi-m. GBP 540 (effective 2009); includes with subscr. to Aberdeen Petroleum Report. adv. back issues avail. **Document type:** *Magazine, Trade.* **Description:** News and business intelligence about the petroleum industry.
Former titles (until 2000): Europetroleum Magazine; (until 1990): Aberdeen Petroleum Quarterly (0956-6333)
—CCC.
Published by: Aberdeen Petroleum Publishing Ltd., 37 Cochrane Park Ave, Newcastle upon Tyne, NE7 7JU, United Kingdom. TEL 44-870-4380001, FAX 44-870-4380002, info@aproil.co.uk, http://www.aproil.co.uk.

EUROPOORT KRINGEN. *see* TRANSPORTATION—Ships And Shipping

▼ **EXECUTIVE COMPLIANCE NEWS. INDEPENDENT NEWS FOR MINING & PETROLEUM.** *see* MINES AND MINING INDUSTRY

338.2728 GBR ISSN 1754-288X

EXPLORATION & PRODUCTION. THE OIL AND GAS REVIEW. Variant title: The Oil & Gas Review. Text in English. 2003. s-a. adv. back issues avail. **Document type:** *Journal, Trade.* **Description:** Focuses on the key areas of investment and technology that will be key in the continued growth and development of the upstream oil and gas sector.
Related titles: Online - full text ed.: ISSN 1754-2898.
Published by: Touch Briefings (Subsidiary of: Touch Group plc), Saffron House, 6-10 Kirby St, London, EC1N 8TS, United Kingdom. TEL 44-20-74525600, FAX 44-20-74525606, info@touchbriefings.com.

665.5 CAN ISSN 1910-0671

EXPORTATIONS DE GAZ NATUREL. Text in French. 1998. m. **Document type:** *Magazine, Trade.*
Media: Online - full text. **Related titles:** English ed.: Natural Gas Exports. ISSN 1910-0663.
Published by: National Energy Board/Office National de l'Energie, 444 Seventh Ave, S W, Calgary, AB T2P 0X8, Canada. TEL 403-299-3561, 800-899-1265, FAX 403-292-5576, publications@neb-one.gc.ca, orders@neb-one.gc.ca, http://www.neb-one.gc.ca.

662 USA ISSN 1066-503X
CODEN: FACTEQ

F A C T. (Fuel and Combustion Technologies) Text in English. 1987. irreg. back issues avail. **Document type:** *Monographic series.*
Indexed: A28, APA, BrCerAb, C&ISA, CA/WCA, CIA, CerAb, CivEngAb, CorrAb, E&CAJ, E11, EEA, EMA, EngInd, GeoRef, H15, M&TEA, M09, MBF, METADEX, SCOPUS, SolStAb, T04, WAA.
—BLDSC (1745.202540). **CCC.**
Published by: A S M E International, Three Park Ave, New York, NY 10016. TEL 800-843-2763, infocentral@asme.org, http://www.asme.org.

665.538 FRA ISSN 1962-9214

F F 3 C INFORMATIONS. Text in French. 2007. bi-m.
Published by: Federation Francaise des Combustibles Carburants et Chauffage, 114 avenue de Wagram, Paris, 75017, France. TEL 33-1-47634650, FAX 33-1-42271401, www.ff3c.org.

665.538 USA

F M A TODAY (SPRINGFIELD). Text in English. 1976. fortn. membership.
Published by: Fuel Merchants Association of New Jersey, 66 Morris Ave, Springfield, NJ 07081. TEL 201-467-1400, FAX 201-467-4066. Ed. Marjorie R Krampf. Circ: 900.

F S U ENERGY. (Former Soviet Union) *see* ENERGY

665.5 333.79 USA

FEDERAL TAXATION OF OIL AND GAS TRANSACTIONS. Text in English. 1959. latest 1987, 2 base vols. plus s-a. updates. looseleaf. USD 523 base vol(s). (effective 2008). **Document type:** *Handbook/Manual/Guide, Trade.* **Description:** Provides information about federal excise taxes on oil and gas, tax returns, audits and selected audit issues in the oil and gas industry.
Related titles: Online - full text ed.
Published by: Matthew Bender & Co., Inc. (Subsidiary of: LexisNexis North America), 1275 Broadway, Albany, NY 12204. TEL 518-487-3000, 800-424-4200, FAX 518-487-3083, international@bender.com, http://bender.lexisnexis.com. Eds. Cecil Smith, Robert Polevoi.

665.5 AUS ISSN 1325-9377

FIELDNOTES. Text in English. 1996. q. **Document type:** *Newsletter, Trade.*
Related titles: Online - full text ed.: ISSN 1834-2272. 2006.
Indexed: GeoRef.
Published by: Geological Survey of Western Australia, Mineral House, 100 Plain St, East Perth, W.A. 6004, Australia. TEL 61-8-92223222, FAX 61-8-92223369, publications@doir.wa.gov.au, http://www.doir.wa.gov.au/GSWA/.

697.9324 USA ISSN 1078-4136

FILTRATION NEWS. Text in English. 1982. bi-m. USD 19.80 domestic; USD 150 foreign (effective 2004). adv. **Document type:** *Magazine, Trade.* **Description:** Published for those who are interested in liquid & air filtration inside the industrial manufacturing plant.
Indexed: A28, APA, BrCerAb, C&ISA, CA/WCA, CIA, CerAb, CivEngAb, CorrAb, E&CAJ, E11, EEA, EMA, H15, M&TEA, M09, MBF, METADEX, SolStAb, T04, WAA.
—Linda Hall.
Published by: Eagle Publications, Inc., 42400 Grand River Ave, Ste 103, Novi, MI 48375-2572. TEL 248-347-3487, 800-783-3491, FAX 248-347-3492, sales@ameritooldie.com. Ed., R&P Carol Brown. Adv. contact Lori Rosario. Circ: 26,000 (controlled).

665.5 NLD ISSN 1872-2288

FLOW. Text in Dutch. 2005. s-a. free (effective 2009). **Document type:** *Magazine, Trade.*
Published by: Linde Gas Benelux, Postbus 78, Schiedam, 3100 AB, Netherlands. TEL 31-10-2461616, FAX 31-10-2461600, info@nl.lindegasbenelux.com, http://www.lindegasbenelux.com. Ed. Jurjen de Jong TEL 31-20-6413937.

FLUESSIGGAS. *see* ENERGY

FORECOURT TRADER. *see* BUSINESS AND ECONOMICS—Domestic Commerce

FORECOURT TRADER BUSINESS DIRECTORY. *see* BUSINESS AND ECONOMICS—Trade And Industrial Directories

665.7 USA ISSN 0095-1587
KF1870.A15

FOSTER NATURAL GAS REPORT. Text in English. 1956. w. USD 1,295 (effective 2000). index. **Document type:** *Newsletter, Trade.*
Related titles: E-mail ed.; Online - full text ed.
—CIS. **CCC.**
Published by: Foster Associates, 4550 Montgomery Ave, Ste 35ON, Bethesda, MD 20814-3341. TEL 202-408-7710, FAX 202-408-7723, www.foster-fa.com. Ed., R&P Edgar David Boshart TEL 301-664-7838. Circ: 800 (paid).

665.5 VEN

FRENTE NACIONAL PRO-DEFENSA DEL PETROLEO VENEZOLANO. ACTUACIONES. Text in Spanish. 1970. irreg. USD 5 per issue.
Published by: Frente Nacional Pro Defensa del Petroleo Venezolano, Apto. 50514, Caracas, 105, Venezuela. Circ: 3,000.

662.6 GBR ISSN 0016-2361
TP315 CODEN: FUELAC

➤ **FUEL**; the science and technology of fuel and energy. Text in English. 1922. 12/yr. EUR 3,537 in Europe to institutions; JPY 469,500 in Japan to institutions; USD 3,955 elsewhere to institutions (effective 2012). adv. bk.rev. illus.; abstr.; bibl.; charts. index, cum.index: 1922-1981. back issues avail.; reprints avail. **Document type:** *Journal, Academic/Scholarly.* **Description:** Studies the nature, conservation, preparation, use, physical and nuclear properties of gaseous, liquid and solid fuels.
Formerly (until 1948): Fuel in Science and Practice (0367-3367)
Related titles: Microfilm ed.: (from PQC); Online - full text ed.: ISSN 1873-7153 (from IngentaConnect, ScienceDirect).
Indexed: A01, A03, A08, A22, A26, A28, AESIS, APA, APIAb, APICat, APIH&E, APIOC, APIPR, APIPS, APITS, ASCA, ApMecR, B&BAb, B19, B21, BrCerAb, BrTechI, C&ISA, C24, C33, CA, CA/WCA, CCI, CEABA, CIA, CIN, CPEI, Cadscan, CerAb, ChemAb, ChemTitl, CivEngAb, CorrAb, CurCont, E&CAJ, E&PHSE, E11, E14, EEA, EIA, EMA, ESPM, EnerRev, EngInd, EnvAb, EnvEAb, EnvInd, GP&P, GeoRef, H15, I05, I10, ISMEC, ISR, LeadAb, M&TEA, M09, MBF, METADEX, MSB, OffTech, PetrolAb, PollutAb, RefZh, SCI, SCOPUS, SolStAb, SpeleolAb, T02, T04, TM, W07, WAA, Zincscan.
—BLDSC (4048.000000), CASDDS, IE, Infotrieve, Ingenta, INIST, Linda Hall, PADDS. **CCC.**
Published by: Elsevier Ltd (Subsidiary of: Elsevier Science & Technology), The Blvd, Langford Ln, Kidlington, Oxford, OX5 1GB, United Kingdom. TEL 44-1865-843000, FAX 44-1865-843010, journalscustomerserviceemea@elsevier.com. Eds. A Tomita, E Suuberg, John W Patrick. **Subscr. to:** Elsevier BV, Radarweg 29, PO Box 211, Amsterdam 1000 AE, Netherlands. http://www.elsevier.nl.

665.5 USA

FUEL ADVANTAGE; optimizing mpg and fuel choices. Text in English. 2006. q. free (effective 2008). adv. Supplement avail.; back issues avail. **Document type:** *Magazine, Trade.* **Description:** Aims to help fleet purchasers decide on the best fuel-saving strategies for their companies, and which products and technologies to invest in.
Related titles: Online - full text ed.: free (effective 2008).
Published by: Cygnus Business Media, Inc., 1233 Janesville Ave, PO Box 803, Fort Atkinson, WI 53538. TEL 920-563-6388, 800-547-7377, FAX 920-563-1702, http://www.cygnusb2b.com. Ed. Mark O'Connell TEL 920-563-1611. Pub. Larry M Greenberger TEL 847-454-2722. adv.: B&W page USD 2,815, color page USD 7,785; trim 7.875 x 10.75. Circ: 50,000.

665.5 USA

FUEL ETHANOL REPORT. Variant title: O P I S Fuel Ethanol Report. Text in English. w. **Document type:** *Newsletter, Trade.*
Media: E-mail.
Published by: Oil Price Information Service (Subsidiary of: United Communications Group), Two Washingtonian Center, 9737 Washingtonian Blvd, Ste 100, Gaithersburg, MD 20878. TEL 301-287-2700, 888-301-2645, FAX 301-287-2039, http://www.opisnet.com/.

P

388.324 665.538 GBR ISSN 1757-1057
FUEL OIL NEWS. Abbreviated title: F O N. Text in English. 1977. m. GBP 82 in UK & Republic of Ireland; GBP 100 elsewhere (effective 2009). adv. bk.rev. back issues avail. **Document type:** *Magazine, Trade.*
Description: Contains news, opinion, and information for the oil fuel distribution trade.
Former titles (until 2007): Fuel Oil News and Road Tanker Transport (1471-9460); (until 1979): National Fuel Oil Distributor
Related titles: Online - full text ed.: free (effective 2009).
Published by: Ashley and Dumville Ltd., Regent House, Bexton Ln, Knutsford, WA16 9AB, United Kingdom. TEL 44-1565-626750, mail@ashleyanddumville.co.uk, http://www.ashleyanddumville.co.uk. Ed. Jane Hughes. Adv. contact Jonathan Hibbert.

662.6 NLD ISSN 0378-3820
TP315 CODEN: FPTEDY
➤ **FUEL PROCESSING TECHNOLOGY.** Text in English. 1978. 12/yr. EUR 2,657 in Europe to institutions; JPY 353,000 in Japan to institutions; USD 2,987 elsewhere to institutions (effective 2012). illus. Index. back issues avail.; reprints avail. **Document type:** *Journal, Academic/Scholarly.* **Description:** Deals with the scientific and technological aspects of processing fuels to other fuels, chemicals and by-products.
Related titles: Microform ed.: (from PQC); Online - full text ed.: ISSN 1873-7188 (from IngentaConnect, ScienceDirect).
Indexed: A01, A03, A08, A22, A26, A28, AESIS, APA, APIAb, BrCerAb, C&ISA, C24, C33, CA, CA/WCA, CIA, CIN, CPEI, CerAb, ChemAb, ChemTitl, CivEngAb, CorrAb, CurCont, E&CAJ, E04, E05, E11, E14, EEA, EIA, EMA, ESPM, EnerInd, EnerRev, EngInd, EnvAb, EnvEAb, F&EA, GasAb, GeoRef, H15, I05, ISR, M&TEA, M09, MBF, METADEX, PetrolAb, RefZh, SCI, SCOPUS, SolStAb, SpeleolAb, T02, T04, W07, WAA.
—BLDSC (4052.760000), CASDDS, IE, Infotrieve, Ingenta, INIST, Linda Hall, PADDS. **CCC.**
Published by: Elsevier BV (Subsidiary of: Elsevier Science & Technology), Radarweg 29, PO Box 211, Amsterdam, 1000 AE, Netherlands. TEL 31-20-4853911, FAX 31-20-4852457, JournalsCustomerServiceEMEA@elsevier.com, http://www.elsevier.nl. Ed. A Boehman. **Subscr. to:** Elsevier, Subscription Customer Service, 6277 Sea Harbor Dr, Orlando, FL 32887-4800. TEL 407-345-4020, 877-839-7126, FAX 407-363-1354.

658.8 USA
FUELING INDIANA. Text in English. 1934. q. free to members (effective 2005). adv. bk.rev. charts; illus.; tr.lit. 40 p./no. 3 cols./p.; **Document type:** *Magazine, Trade.* **Description:** Covers subjects of interest to independent oil marketers, fuel oil dealers and operators for convenience stores and truck stops throughout Indiana.
Formerly: Hoosier Independent (0018-4764)
Published by: Indiana Petroleum Marketers and Convenience Store Association, 101 W Washington St, Ste 805E, Indianapolis, IN 46204. TEL 317-633-4662, FAX 317-630-1827, kbaber@ipca.org, http://www.ipca.org. Ed. Kara Baber. Adv. contact Aran Jackson. B&W page USD 430. Circ: 1,000 (controlled).

665.5 CHN ISSN 1674-4667
FUZA YOUQICANG/COMPLEX HYDROCARBON RESERVOIRS. Text in Chinese. 2008. q. **Document type:** *Journal, Academic/Scholarly.*
Former titles (until 2008): Xiaoxing youqicang/Small Hydrocarbon Reservoirs; (until 2001): Jiangsu Youqi
Published by: Zhongguo Shiyou Huagong Gufen Youxian Gongsi Jiangsu Youtian Fengongsi/S I N O P E C Jiangsu Oilfield Company, 1, Wenhui Xi Lu, Yangzhou, 225009, China. TEL 86-514-87762115.

665.7 FRA ISSN 1969-8860
▼ **G**; la revue des professionnels du gaz. Text in French. 2009. q. **Document type:** *Magazine.*
Published by: Adex Media and Communication, 12, Rue du Rocher, Paris, 75008, France.

665.5 FRA ISSN 1969-2587
G P L ACTUALITE (ENGLISH EDITION). (Gaz de Petrole Liquefie) Text in English. 1987. q. **Document type:** *Journal, Trade.*
Supersedes (until 2008): G P L Actualite (French Edition) (0985-200X)
Related titles: ◆ Supplement to: Petrole & Gaz Informations. ISSN 1622-1036.
Indexed: CBNB, FR, INIS AtomInd.
—BLDSC (4206.311200), IE, Infotrieve, INIST.
Published by: Editions Techniques pour l'Automobile et l'Industrie (E T A I), 20 rue de la Saussiere, Boulogne-Billancourt, 92641, France. TEL 33-1-46992424, FAX 33-1-48255692, http://www.groupe-etai.com.

665.5 ITA
G P L INFORMAZIONI. (Gas di Petrolio Liquefatti) Text in Italian. m. bk.rev.; software rev.; Website rev. mkt.; charts; stat. 8 p./no.; back issues avail. **Document type:** *Magazine, Trade.* **Description:** Reports on the production, consumption, and marketing of liquefied petroleum gas.
Related titles: Online - full text ed.
Published by: Rivista Italiana Petrolio Srl, Via Aventina 19, Rome, 00153, Italy. TEL 39-06-5741208, FAX 39-06-5754906, http://www.staffettaonline.com.

665.5 620 USA
G P S A ENGINEERING DATA BOOK. Text in English. 19??. irreg., latest 2004, 12th ed. USD 162 combined subscription to non-members (print & CD-ROM eds.); USD 72 combined subscription to members (print & CD-ROM eds.) (effective 2011). **Document type:** *Handbook/Manual/Guide, Trade.* **Description:** Compiles basic design information, current technical data, and approved procedures for use by gas processing personnel to determine operating and design parameters for hydrocarbon processing and related facilities.
Related titles: CD-ROM ed.
Published by: Gas Processors Suppliers Association, 6526 E 60th St, Tulsa, OK 74145. TEL 918-493-3872, FAX 918-493-3875.

665.7 628 CHE ISSN 1018-760X
TP700 CODEN: GWASA4
G W A. (Gas - Wasser - Abwasser) Text in English, French, German. 1921. m. CHF 215. adv. bk.rev. bibl.; charts; illus.; stat. index. back issues avail. **Document type:** *Magazine, Trade.*
Former titles: G W A - Gas Wasser Abwasser (0036-8008); Schweizerischer Verein von Gas und Wasserfachmaennern. Monatsbulletin
Indexed: A22, A32, CEABA, CIN, CISA, ChemAb, ChemTitl, FR, GeoRef, IBR, IBZ, SpeleolAb, TM.
—BLDSC (4085.900000), CASDDS, IE, Ingenta, INIST, Linda Hall.
Published by: Schweizerischer Verein des Gas- und Wasserfaches/Societe Suisse de l'Industrie du Gaz et des Eaux, Gruetlistr 44, Zuerich, 8027, Switzerland. TEL 41-1-2883333, FAX 41-1-2021633. Ed. C Nagel. Circ: 1,600.

665.7 628 338.2 DEU ISSN 0016-4909
TP700 CODEN: GWGEAQ
G W F - GAS - ERDGAS. Text in German. 1858. m. EUR 330; EUR 231 to members; EUR 37 newsstand/cover (effective 2011). adv. bk.rev. abstr.; charts; illus.; mkt.; tr.lit.; tr.mk. index. **Document type:** *Journal, Trade.* **Description:** Trade publication for the gas industry featuring gas production, distribution, installation and technology. Includes events, patents and positions available.
Formerly (until 1965): Gas- und Wasserfach. Gas (0341-2539); Which superseded in part (in 1944): Gas- und Wasserfach (0367-3839)
Indexed: A22, APIAb, APICat, APIH&E, APIOC, APIPR, APIPS, APITS, CIN, CISA, ChemAb, ChemTitl, F&EA, FLUIDEX, FR, GEOBASE, GeoRef, IBR, IBZ, SCOPUS, SpeleolAb, TM.
—BLDSC (4085.050000), CASDDS, IE, Infotrieve, Ingenta, INIST, Linda Hall. **CCC.**
Published by: (Deutsche Verein der Gas-und Wasserfaches Bundesverband der Deutscher Gas-und Wasserwirtschaft (DVGW)), Oldenbourg Industrieverlag GmbH (Subsidiary of: Oldenbourg Wissenschaftsverlag GmbH), Rosenheimer Str 145, Munich, 81671, Germany. TEL 49-89-450510, FAX 49-89-45051207, oiv-info@oldenbourg.de. Ed. Volker Trenkle. Adv. contact Eva Feil. Circ: 1,966 (paid and controlled).

665.7 628 697 AUT ISSN 1729-8725
CODEN: GAWWA6
G W W AKTUELL; das Magazin fuer Gas, Wasser und Waerme. (Gas, Wasser, Waerme) Text in German. 1907. bi-m. bk.rev. bibl.; charts; illus. **Document type:** *Magazine, Trade.*
Former titles (until 1999): Gas, Wasser, Waerme (0016-5018); (until 1946): Gas und Wasser (0367-3774); (until 1938): Oesterreichischer Verein von Gas- und Wasserfachmaennern. Zeitschrift (0372-9591)
Indexed: ChemAb, F&EA, GasAb, GeoRef, SpeleolAb.
—IE, Linda Hall. **CCC.**
Published by: Oesterreichische Vereinigung fuer das Gas- und Wasserfach, Schubertring 14, Vienna, 1010, Austria. TEL 43-1-51315880, FAX 43-1-513158825, office@ovgw.at, http://www.ovgw.at. Circ: 10,000. **Co-sponsor:** Fachverband der Gas- und Waermeversorgungsunternehmungen.

665.538 DEU ISSN 0343-2092
TN880.A1
GAS; Die Zeitschrift fuer Energieberatung und energiesparende Geraetetechnik. Text in German. 1950. 4/yr. EUR 37; EUR 18.50 to students; EUR 11 newsstand/cover (effective 2011). adv. bk.rev. **Document type:** *Magazine, Trade.* **Description:** Trade publication for the natural gas industry covering technology, air pollution control, energy savings, economics and international news.
Indexed: A22, KES.
—BLDSC (4073.100000), IE, Ingenta. **CCC.**
Published by: (Bundesverband der Energie- und Wasserwirtschaft), Oldenbourg Industrieverlag GmbH (Subsidiary of: Oldenbourg Wissenschaftsverlag GmbH), Rosenheimer Str 145, Munich, 81671, Germany. TEL 49-89-450510, FAX 49-89-45051207, oiv-info@oldenbourg.de. Ed. Martin Calovini. Adv. contact Eva Feil. Circ: 4,876 (paid and controlled). **Co-sponsors:** Deutscher Verein des Gas- und Wasserfaches; Bundesvereinigung der Firmen im Gas- und Wasserfach; Fachverband Heiz- und Kochgeraete Industrie.

THE GAS CARRIER REGISTER. *see* TRANSPORTATION—Ships And Shipping

665.7 USA ISSN 0885-5935
HD9581.A1
GAS DAILY. Text in English. 1984. d. USD 2,010 (effective 2008). charts; stat. back issues avail. **Document type:** *Newsletter, Trade.* **Description:** Provides detailed coverage of natural gas prices at interstate and intrastate pipeline and pooling points in major US markets.
Formerly (until 1985): Inside Gas Markets
Related titles: E-mail ed.: USD 1,810 (effective 2004); Fax ed.: USD 2,040 (effective 2004); Online - full text ed.: USD 2,195 combined subscription (online & E-mail eds.) (effective 2008).
Indexed: P48, P52, P56, PQC.
—CIS. **CCC.**
Published by: Platts (Subsidiary of: McGraw-Hill Companies, Inc.), 1200 G St NW, Ste 1000, Washington, DC 20005. TEL 212-904-3070, 800-752-8878, FAX 202-383-2024, support@platts.com. Ed. Stephanie Seay TEL 865-690-4319. Adv. contact Ann Forte TEL 720-548-5479. Circ: 1,400 (controlled and free).

665.5 USA ISSN 1524-0398
GAS DAILY'S GAS TRANSPORTATION & STORAGE WEEK. Variant title: Gas Transportation & Storage Week. Text in English. 1991. w. (50/yr.). USD 695 (effective 2001). charts; stat. **Document type:** *Newsletter, Trade.* **Description:** Monitors natural gas storage inventories, withdrawals and injections, open-access storage programs, federal and state regulatory actions, new business ventures, technological innovations and business trends.
Supersedes (in 1999): Gas Storage Report (1057-2279); Incorporates: Gas Transportation Report (1065-8661); Which was formerly: Natural Gas Marketing Report; Which superseded (1987-1992): Natural Gas Marketing Pipeline Guide
Related titles: Online - full text ed.
—**CCC.**
Published by: Platts (Subsidiary of: McGraw-Hill Companies, Inc.), 1200 G St NW, Ste 1000, Washington, DC 20005. TEL 212-904-3070, 800-752-8878, FAX 202-383-2024, support@platts.com, http://www.platts.com.

665.7 USA ISSN 1068-1299
HD9581.A1
GAS DAILY'S N G. (Natural Gas) Variant title: N G Magazine. Text in English. 1993. q. adv. illus. **Document type:** *Newsletter, Trade.* **Description:** For natural gas buyers and sellers focusing on the buying and selling of gas and features innovative companies and people.
—Linda Hall. **CCC.**
Published by: Financial Times Energy (Houston), Pasha Publications, 13111 Northwest Frwy, Ste 520, Houston, TX 77040. TEL 713-939-5803, FAX 713-460-9150. Ed. Daniel Macey. Adv. contact Michelle Murray. B&W page USD 2,750, color page USD 3,250; trim 10.88 x 8.38.

662 USA ISSN 0161-4851
TP700
GAS DIGEST; the magazine of gas operations. Text in English. 1975. q. free. adv. bk.rev.
Indexed: F&EA, PetrolAb.
—Linda Hall.
Published by: T-P Graphics, 5731 Arboles Dr, Houston, TX 77035. TEL 716-723-6736. Ed. Ken Kridner TEL 716-723-6736. Circ: 5,200.

665 USA ISSN 0361-4298
TP722
GAS FACTS; a statistical record of the gas industry. Text in English. 1946. a. USD 150 (print or online ed.) (effective 2010). **Document type:** *Journal, Trade.*
Former by the 1946 merger of: Annual Statistics of the Natural Gas Utility Industry; Annual Statistics of the Manufactured Gas Utility Industry
Related titles: Online - full text ed.: (from CIS).
Indexed: SRI.
Published by: (American Gas Association), Thomson Reuters (Subsidiary of: Thomson Reuters Corp.), 1500 Spring Garden, 4th Fl, Philadelphia, PA 19130. TEL 215-386-0100, FAX 215-386-2911, http://science.thomsonreuters.com/. Circ: 3,000.

665.5 RUS ISSN 2075-9371
GAS INDUSTRY OF RUSSIA. Text in English. 2006. q. RUR 2,900 domestic; EUR 74 foreign (effective 2010). abstr.; bibl.; charts; illus.; maps; stat. Index. back issues avail. **Document type:** *Magazine, Trade.* **Description:** Contains information relating to Russian gas and oil industry including science-intensive advanced technologies, offshore development, geology, economics, regulation and management, hydrocarbons processing, transportation and distribution, environmental challenges. Audience include chief executives and industry professionals from domestic and international oil and gas companies, as well as scientists and engineers, people whose business interests and industry operations are closely associated with oil and gas.
Related titles: E-mail ed.; Online - full text ed.; ◆ Translation of: Gazovaya Promyshlennost. ISSN 0016-5581.
Published by: GasOil Press LLC, pr-kt Vernadskogo, d 41, stroenie 1, Moscow, 119991, Russian Federation. TEL 7-495-4308740, FAX 7-495-4308739, office@gasoilpress.ru, http://www.gasoilpress.ru. Ed. Aleksandr Ananenkov. Pub. Grigory Shevchenko. R&P Denis Shevchenko. Circ: 600 (paid).

665.5 GBR ISSN 0964-6825
GAS INSTALLER. Text in English. 1992. q. **Document type:** *Magazine, Trade.*
—**CCC.**
Published by: Council for Registered Gas Installers (C O R G I), 1 Elmwood, Chineham Park, Crockford Ln, Basingstoke, Hants RG24 8WG, United Kingdom. TEL 44-870-402200, FAX 44-870-4012600, enquiries@corgi-gas.com, http://www.corgi-gas-safety.com/.

665.7 GBR ISSN 1755-5477
TP700 CODEN: GEMABL
➤ **GAS INTERNATIONAL**; engineering and management. Text in English. 1961. 10/yr. free to members (effective 2009). adv. bk.rev. bibl.; charts; illus.; stat. index. back issues avail.; reprints avail. **Document type:** *Journal, Academic/Scholarly.* **Description:** Features interesting news and important calender events.
Former titles (until 2007): International Gas Engineering and Management (1465-7058); (until 1998): Gas Engineering & Management (0306-6444); (until 1974): Institution of Gas Engineers. Journal (0020-3432)
Related titles: Microform ed.: (from PQC).
Indexed: A22, A28, APA, APICat, APIH&E, APIOC, APIPR, APIPS, APITS, ASCA, BrCerAb, BrTechI, C&ISA, CA/WCA, CIA, CISA, CerAb, CivEngAb, CorrAb, E&CAJ, E11, EEA, EMA, F&EA, FR, GasAb, H15, IBuildSA, M&TEA, M09, MBF, METADEX, R18, SCOPUS, SolStAb, T04, WAA.
—BLDSC (4077.985000), IE, Ingenta, INIST, Linda Hall.
Published by: Institution of Gas Engineers and Managers, IGEM House, High St, Kegworth, Derbyshire DE74 2DA, United Kingdom. TEL 44-844-3754436, FAX 44-1509-678198, general@igem.org.uk. Ed. Rebecca Bursnall TEL 44-1509-675157. Adv. contact Carol Baxter TEL 44-1509-678160. B&W page GBP 1,425, color page GBP 2,040; trim 210 x 297.

665.7 GBR ISSN 1746-823X
GAS MATTERS (ONLINE); reviewing international gas markets. Text in English. 1988. 10/yr. GBP 990 (effective 2010). adv. back issues avail. **Document type:** *Magazine, Trade.* **Description:** Provides regular information on gas market analysis.
Media: Online - full text.
Published by: Gas Strategies Group Ltd, 35 New Bridge St, London, EC4V 6BW, United Kingdom. TEL 44-20-73329981, FAX 44-20-73329901.

665.7 GBR ISSN 1746-8213
GAS MATTERS TODAY; the daily gas industry news bulletin. Text in English. 2000. d. GBP 550 (effective 2010). back issues avail. **Document type:** *Newsletter, Trade.*
Media: Online - full text.
Published by: Gas Strategies Group Ltd, 35 New Bridge St, London, EC4V 6BW, United Kingdom. TEL 44-20-73329981, FAX 44-20-73329901.

665.5 USA ISSN 1939-8344
TP751
GAS PROCESSES HANDBOOK. Text in English. 2004. biennial. USD 25 per issue (effective 2008). **Document type:** *Handbook/Manual/Guide, Trade.*
Media: CD-ROM.
Published by: Gulf Publishing Co., PO Box 2608, Houston, TX 77252. TEL 713-529-4301, FAX 713-520-4433, publications@gulfpub.com, http://www.gulfpub.com.

665.5 USA ISSN 0096-8870
TN880.A1 CODEN: PGPAAC
GAS PROCESSORS ASSOCIATION. ANNUAL CONVENTION. PROCEEDINGS. Text in English. 1921. a. back issues avail. **Document type:** *Proceedings, Trade.*

Former titles (until 1974): Natural Gas Processors Association. Annual Convention. Proceedings (0097-2363); (until 1962): Natural Gasoline Association of America. Technical Papers. Annual Convention. Proceedings (0099-4111); (until 1928): Association of Natural Gasoline Manufacturers. Annual Convention. Proceedings
Related titles: Online - full text ed.
Indexed: A22, APICat, APIH&E, APIOC, APIPR, APIPS, APITS, CIN, ChemAb, ChemTitl, EngInd, F&EA, GasAb, SCOPUS.
—CASDDS, Linda Hall.
Published by: Gas Processors Suppliers Association, 6526 E 60th St, Tulsa, OK 74145. TEL 918-493-3872, FAX 918-493-3875, http://gpsa.gpaglobal.org.

665.5 USA
GAS PROCESSORS ASSOCIATION. RESEARCH REPORTS. Text in English. 1971. irreg., latest vol.203. USD 500 per issue to non-members; USD 15 per issue to members (effective 2011). back issues avail. **Document type:** *Monographic series, Trade.*
Published by: Gas Processors Suppliers Association, 6526 E 60th St, Tulsa, OK 74145. TEL 918-493-3872, FAX 918-493-3875, http://gpsa.gpaglobal.org.

665.5 USA
GAS PROCESSORS ASSOCIATION. TECHNICAL PUBLICATIONS. Text in English. 19??. irreg., latest vol.30, 2007. price varies. back issues avail. **Document type:** *Monographic series, Trade.*
Related titles: Online - full text ed.
Published by: Gas Processors Suppliers Association, 6526 E 60th St, Tulsa, OK 74145. TEL 918-493-3872, FAX 918-493-3875, http://gpsa.gpaglobal.org.

665.5 USA ISSN 0740-5278
TP751
GAS PROCESSORS REPORT. Text in English. 1983. w. USD 1,245 (effective 2009). 8 p./no.; **Document type:** *Newsletter, Trade.* **Description:** Contains news and analysis of every North American processing region - projects, prices, strategic moves, financials, and more.
Related titles: Online - full text ed.
Indexed: A10, A15, ABIn, B01, B02, B03, B07, B11, B15, B17, B18, E14, G04, G06, G07, G08, I05, P48, P51, P52, P56, PQC, T02, V03.
—CCC.
Published by: Hart Energy Publishing, LP (Subsidiary of: Chemical Week Associates), 1616 S Voss Rd, Ste 1000, Houston, TX 77057. TEL 713-260-6400, 800-874-2544, FAX 713-840-8585, custserv@hartenergy.com. Pub. David Givens TEL 703-891-4811.

GAS REGULATION. *see* LAW—Corporate Law

665.5 333.8 AUS
GAS SUPPLY AND DEMAND STUDY. Text in English. 1985. irreg., latest 1997. free to members (effective 2008). charts; illus.; stat. back issues avail. **Document type:** *Report, Trade.* **Description:** Examines the market position of natural gas and the ability of Australia's gas reserves to meet expanding growth in future demand.
Published by: Australian Gas Association, 2 Park Way, PO Box 122, Braeside, VIC 3195, Australia. TEL 61-3-95804500, FAX 61-3-95805500, office@aga.asn.au, http://www.gas.asn.au.

662 USA
GAS TECHNOLOGY INSTITUTE. ANNUAL REPORT. Text in English. a. free. stat. **Document type:** *Corporate.*
Former titles (until 2000): Institute of Gas Technology. Annual Report; Institute of Gas Technology. Director's Report (0095-0734)
Published by: Gas Technology Institute, 1700 S Mt. Prospect Rd, Des Plaines, IL 60018. TEL 847-768-0500, FAX 847-768-0709.

665.5 DNK ISSN 0106-4355
GAS-TEKNIK. Text in Danish. 1911. bi-m. DKK 300 (effective 2008). adv. bk.rev. **Document type:** *Magazine, Trade.*
Formerly (until 1978): Gas-Teknikeren
Related titles: Online - full text ed.
—Linda Hall. **CCC.**
Published by: Dansk Gas Forening, c/oc Dansk Gasteknisk Center A/S, Dr. Neergaards Vej 5 A, Hoersholm, 2970, Denmark. TEL 45-20-169600, dgf@dgc.dk. Ed. Jens Utoft. Adv. contact Mogens Fogh. page DKK 6,900; 175 x 252. Circ: 1,925.

333.12 USA ISSN 1072-5113
GAS TRANSACTIONS REPORT. Text in English. 1993. bi-w. **Document type:** *Bulletin, Trade.*
Related titles: Online - full text ed.
Indexed: A15, ABIn, P48, P51, P52, P56, PQC.
—CCC.
Published by: Hart Energy Publishing, LP (Subsidiary of: Chemical Week Associates), 1616 S Voss Rd, Ste 1000, Houston, TX 77057. TEL 713-260-6400, 800-874-2544, FAX 713-840-8585, custserv@hartenergy.com, http://www.hartenergy.com.

GAS TURBINE WORLD. *see* ENERGY

GAS TURBINE WORLD HANDBOOK. *see* ENERGY

333.8233 USA
GAS UTILITY INDUSTRY. Text in English. 19??. a. USD 175 domestic; USD 185 in Canada; USD 190 elsewhere (effective 2009). adv. **Document type:** *Directory, Trade.* **Description:** Lists gas utility companies across North America and internationally as well as all the support sectors from worldwide engineers/contractors to local service and supply companies.
Formerly: Directory of Gas Utility Companies Worldwide
Published by: Midwest Publishing Company, 2230 E 49th St, Ste E, Tulsa, OK 74105. TEL 918-582-2000, 800-829-2002, FAX 918-587-9349, info@midwestpub.com. Adv. contact Jim Shelvy. B&W page USD 1,610, color page USD 1,710.

333.8233 USA ISSN 1074-3723
GAS UTILITY REPORT. Text in English. 1994. bi-w.
Related titles: Online - full text ed.
Indexed: A15, ABIn, P51, P52, P56, PQC.
—CCC.
Published by: McGraw-Hill Companies, Inc., 1221 Ave of the Americas, 43rd fl, New York, NY 10020. TEL 212-512-2000, FAX 212-426-7087, customer.service@mcgraw-hill.com, http://www.mcgraw-hill.com.

665.7 AUS ISSN 1444-9064
GAS WEEK (EMAIL). Text in English. 1996. w. (46/yr.). AUD 1,320 (effective 2008). **Document type:** *Newsletter, Trade.* **Description:** Focuses on oil and gas markets and on gas prices.
Incorporates (in 2007): Gas Week Brief (Email) (1833-5152); Formerly (until 2000): Australian Gas User Week (Print) (1328-4088)
Media: E-mail. **Related titles:** Online - full content ed.: AUD 5,648 domestic; EUR 5,040 foreign (effective 2008).
Published by: E W N Publishing Pty Ltd., PO Box 148, Balmain, NSW 2041, Australia. TEL 61-2-98188877, FAX 61-2-98188473, production@erisk.net, http://www.erisk.net. Ed. Laurel Fox-Allen.

665.5 USA
GASIFICATION NEWS. Text in English. 1998. m. USD 895 (effective 2009). **Document type:** *Newsletter, Trade.*
Formerly (until 200?): Gas-to-Liquids News (1522-4155)
Related titles: Online - full text ed.
Indexed: A09, A15, B02, B15, B17, B18, G04, G08, I05, P51, P56, V04.
—CCC.
Published by: Hart Energy Publishing, LP (Subsidiary of: Chemical Week Associates), 1616 S Voss Rd, Ste 1000, Houston, TX 77057. TEL 713-260-6400, 800-874-2544, FAX 713-840-8585, custserv@hartenergy.com. Ed. Suzanne McElligott TEL 703-891-4820. Pub. David Givens TEL 703-891-4811.

665.7 USA
GASLINES. Text in English. 1947. m. **Document type:** *Newsletter.*
Formerly: Gas Lines
Published by: Alabama Gas Corporation, 2101 Sixth Ave N, Birmingham, AL 35203. TEL 205-326-2750. Ed. Christopher Gagliano. Circ: 2,000.

665.7 NOR ISSN 1502-1645
GASSMAGASINET. Text in Norwegian. 1996. bi-m. NOK 490 (effective 2011). adv. **Document type:** *Magazine, Trade.*
Formerly (until 2000): Gassforum (0809-2761)
Related titles: Online - full text ed.
Published by: Skarland Press A-S, P O Box 2843, Toeyen, Oslo, 0608, Norway. TEL 47-22-708300, FAX 47-22-708301, firmapost@skarland.no, http://www.skarland.no. Ed. Per Oeyvind Nordberg. Adv. contact Helge Gravdal TEL 47-22-708313.

665.7 FRA ISSN 0016-5328
TP700 CODEN: GAZJAG
GAZ D'AUJOURD'HUI. Text in French. 1877. 10/yr. EUR 90 domestic to members; EUR 100 foreign to members; EUR 120 domestic to non-members; EUR 130 foreign to non-members (effective 2005). adv. bk.rev. abstr.; illus.; stat. index.
Formerly: Journal des Industries du Gaz
Indexed: CISA, FR, GasAb, INIS AtomInd.
—CASDDS, INIST, Linda Hall. **CCC.**
Published by: Association Technique de l'Industrie du Gaz en France, 62 rue de Courcelles, Paris, 75008, France. TEL 33-1-47543434, FAX 33-1-42274943, TELEX 642 621 F. Ed. Claude Bureau. Circ: 4,000.

662.6 RUS ISSN 0016-5581
TP700 CODEN: GZVPAJ
GAZOVAYA PROMYSHLENNOST/GAS INDUSTRY; ezhemesyachnyi nauchno-tekhnicheskii i proizvodstvennyi zhurnal. Text in Russian; Summaries in English. 1956. m. EUR 204 foreign (effective 2010). bibl.; charts; illus.; stat.; abstr.; maps. Index. back issues avail. **Document type:** *Journal, Trade.* **Description:** Delivers information relating to industry developments and science-intensive advanced technologies available for the gas industry, in particular: well drilling, production, gas processing and transmission, and gas distribution - together with environmental challenges.
Related titles: Online - full text ed.; ◆ English Translation: Gas Industry of Russia. ISSN 2075-9371.
Indexed: CIN, ChemAb, ChemTitl, F&EA, FR, GasAb, GeoRef, RASB, RefZh, SCOPUS, SpeleolAb.
—BLDSC (0047.020000), CASDDS, East View, INIST, Linda Hall. **CCC.**
Published by: GasOil Press LLC, pr-kt Vernadskogo, d 41, stroenie 1, Moscow, 119991, Russian Federation. TEL 7-495-4308740, FAX 7-495-4308739, info@gaspress.ru, http://www.gasoilpress.ru. Ed. Aleksandr Ananenkov. Pub. Grigory Shevchenko. Circ: 3,000.
Co-sponsor: Ministerstvo Gazovoi Promyshlennosti Rossiiskoi Federatsii.

665.5 JPN ISSN 0016-5069
GEKKAN GASORIN STUTANDO/MONTHLY GAS STATION. Text in Japanese. 1959. m. JPY 1,500. adv. bk.rev. abstr.; charts; illus.; stat.; tr.lit. index. **Document type:** *Journal, Trade.* **Description:** Covers gas stations in Japan.
Related titles: Microfiche ed.
Published by: Gekkan Gasorin Sutandosha, 3-2-3 Shinbashi, Minato-ku, Tokyo, 105-0004, Japan. TEL 81-3-3502-5941, FAX 81-3-3502-5940. Ed. Makoto Yoshitake. R&P, Adv. contact Shigeru Katsurada. Circ: 80,000.

665.5 BHR ISSN 1025-6059
TN876.N4
➤ **GEOARABIA.** Text in English. 1996. q. adv. 150 p./no. 1 cols./p.; back issues avail. **Document type:** *Journal, Academic/Scholarly.* **Description:** Focusing on the Petroleum Geosciences of the Middle East. It deals with all aspects of the petroleum geosciences, ranging from geology and geochemistry to geophysics and petrophysics.
Related titles: Supplement(s): GeoArabia Special Publication. ISSN 1819-169X. 2000.
Indexed: CurCont, GEOBASE, GeoRef, PetrolAb, SCI, SCOPUS, SpeleolAb, W07, Z01.
—BLDSC (4116.839000), IE, Ingenta, PADDS. **CCC.**
Published by: Gulf PetroLink, PO Box 20393, Manama, Bahrain. TEL 973-214881, FAX 973-214475, geoarabi@batelco.com.bh, http://www.gulfpetrolink.com.bh. Eds. David Grainger, Dr. Moujahed I Al-Husseini. Pub., R&P Dr. Moujahed I Al-Husseini. Adv. contact Anna Kelly TEL 973-214-881.

665.5 557 USA ISSN 0364-2984
CODEN: OGRADE
GEOLOGICAL SURVEY OF ALABAMA. OIL AND GAS REPORT. Text in English. 19??. irreg., latest vol.20, 2011. price varies. back issues avail. **Document type:** *Monographic series, Government.*
Indexed: GeoRef.
Published by: Geological Survey of Alabama, PO Box 869999, Tuscaloosa, AL 35486. TEL 205-349-2852, FAX 205-349-2861, info@ogb.state.al.us.

553.28 RUS ISSN 0016-7894
TN860 CODEN: GENGA9
GEOLOGIYA NEFTI I GAZA. Text in Russian; Contents page in English. 1957. m. USD 83 foreign (effective 2005). adv. bk.rev. abstr.; bibl.; charts; illus.; stat. index. **Document type:** *Journal, Trade.*
Indexed: CIN, ChemAb, ChemTitl, E&PHSE, GEOBASE, GP&P, GeoRef, OffTech, PetrolAb, RefZh, SCOPUS, SpeleolAb.
—CASDDS, East View, INIST, Linda Hall, PADDS. **CCC.**
Published by: Informatsionno-Izdatel'skii Tsentr po Geologii i Nedropol'zovaniu Geoinformmark, Goncharnaya 38, Moscow, 115172, Russian Federation. TEL 7-095-9156086, info@geoinform.ru, http://www.geoinform.ru. Ed. Olga Burdyanskaya. Circ: 5,000.

GEOPHYSICAL DIRECTORY. *see* EARTH SCIENCES—Geophysics

GEOPOLITICS OF ENERGY. *see* POLITICAL SCIENCE—International Relations

338.47665943 GBR ISSN 1749-2246
GERMANY PETROCHEMICALS REPORT. Text in English. 2005. q. EUR 820, USD 1,030 combined subscription (print & email eds.) (effective 2010). **Document type:** *Report, Trade.* **Description:** Provides industry professionals and strategists, sector analysts, trade associations and regulatory bodies with independent forecasts and competitive intelligence on the petrochemicals industry in Germany.
Related titles: E-mail ed.
Indexed: A15, ABIn, B02, B15, B17, B18, G04, I05, P48, P51, P52, P56, PQC.
Published by: Business Monitor International Ltd., Senator House, 85 Queen Victoria St, London, EC4V 4AB, United Kingdom. TEL 44-20-72480468, FAX 44-20-72480467, subs@businessmonitor.com.

661.804 USA ISSN 1937-1691
GLOBAL P E T REPORT. (Polyethylene Terephthalate) Text in English. 1999. w. USD 1,175 combined subscription (online & E-mail eds.) (effective 2008). back issues avail. **Document type:** *Newsletter, Trade.* **Description:** Covers bottle and film grade PET resin price assessments, plus feedstock assessments such as MEG, PTA, DMT and PX.
Former titles (until 2006): P E T Europe (1931-2164); (until 1998): P E T Wire Europe
Media: Online - full content. **Related titles:** E-mail ed.
Published by: Platts (Subsidiary of: McGraw-Hill Companies, Inc.), 1200 G St NW, Ste 1000, Washington, DC 20005. TEL 212-904-3070, 800-752-8878, FAX 202-383-2024, support@platts.com.

655.5 USA ISSN 1549-2931
HD9560.1
GLOBAL PETROLEUM MONTHLY. Text in English. 19??. m. **Document type:** *Report, Trade.*
Former titles (until 2003): Oil Market Outlook: Short Term Focus (1527-1730); (until 1994): Monthly Energy Price Outlook; (until 1992): Monthly Energy Outlook
Published by: I H S Global Insight (USA) Inc., 24 Hartwell Ave, Lexington, MA 02421. TEL 781-301-9100, FAX 781-301-9416, info@ihsglobalinsight.com, http://www.ihsglobalinsight.com/.

665.54 GBR ISSN 1756-2023
GLOBAL PIPELINE MONTHLY. Abbreviated title: G P M. Text in English. 2005. m. EUR 545 to individuals (effective 2010). back issues avail. **Document type:** *Magazine, Trade.* **Description:** Publishes technical articles and a summary of world pipeline-industry news.
Media: Online - full text.
Published by: Scientific Surveys Ltd., PO Box 21, Beaconsfield, Bucks HP9 1NS, United Kingdom. TEL 44-1494-675139, FAX 44-1494-670155, info@scientificsurveys.com, http://www.scientificsurveys.com/. Eds. John Tiratsoo TEL 44-1494-675139, Alexander Wostmann TEL 49-2662-948291. Adv. contact Yvonne Taylor TEL 44-1622-727088.

665.5 USA ISSN 1940-5162
TP315
GLOBAL REFINING & FUELS REPORT. Text in English. 1996. bi-w. USD 995 (effective 2009). **Document type:** *Newsletter, Consumer.* **Description:** Provides an ongoing analysis on the global refining industry for refiners and car manufacturers.
Incorporates (1997-2005): Hart's European Fuels News (1469-1078)
Related titles: Online - full text ed.: ISSN 1940-5170.
Indexed: A10, A15, ABIn, B01, B02, B07, B15, B17, B18, E14, G04, G08, I05, P34, P48, P51, P52, P56, PQC, T02, V03.
—CCC.
Published by: Hart Energy Publishing, LP (Subsidiary of: Chemical Week Associates), 1616 S Voss Rd, Ste 1000, Houston, TX 77057. TEL 713-993-9320, 800-874-2544, FAX 713-840-8585, custserv@hartenergy.com. Ed. Peter Haldis TEL 703-891-4823. Pub. David Givens TEL 703-891-4811.

338.74665 GBR ISSN 1750-6557
GLOBAL SUPPLY VESSEL FORECAST. Text in English. 2005. s-a. **Document type:** *Report, Trade.*
—CCC.
Published by: O D S - Petrodata Ltd., 2nd Fl, The Exchange No. 1, Market St, Aberdeen, AB11 5PJ, United Kingdom. TEL 44-1224-597800, FAX 44-1224-580320, general@ods-petrodata.com. Pub. David Bichard.

GOLOB'S OIL POLLUTION BULLETIN; the international newsletter on oil pollution prevention, control and cleanup. *see* ENVIRONMENTAL STUDIES—Pollution

GOSPODARKA PALIWAMI I ENERGIA/FUEL AND ENERGY MANAGEMENT. *see* ENERGY

665 USA
GOWER FEDERAL SERVICE - OIL AND GAS. Text in English. 1948. base vol. plus updates 5/yr. looseleaf. USD 215 base vol(s). (effective 2010). back issues avail. **Document type:** *Report, Government.* **Description:** Publishes decisions of the Department of the Interior, Interior Board of Land Appeals, and reports natural resources information from the Federal Register pertaining to onshore oil and gas issues.
Related titles: Online - full text ed.: 1948.
Published by: Rocky Mountain Mineral Law Foundation, 9191 Sheridan Blvd, Ste 203, Westminster, CO 80031. TEL 303-321-8100, FAX 303-321-7657, info@rmmlf.org, http://www.rmmlf.org.

622 USA
GOWER FEDERAL SERVICE - OUTER CONTINENTAL SHELF. Text in English. 1954. 4 base vols. plus updates 3/yr. looseleaf. USD 225 base vol(s). (effective 2010). back issues avail. **Document type:** *Report, Government.* **Description:** Publishes decisions of the Department of the Interior, Interior Board of Land Appeals, and reports natural resources information from the Federal register, pertaining to offshore oil and gas operations.
Related titles: Online - full text ed.: 1954.

P

Published by: Rocky Mountain Mineral Law Foundation, 9191 Sheridan Blvd, Ste 203, Westminster, CO 80031. TEL 303-321-8100, FAX 303-321-7657, info@rmmlf.org, http://www.rmmlf.org.

665.5 USA
GOWER FEDERAL SERVICE - ROYALTY VALUATION AND MANAGEMENT. Text in English. 1989. 39 base vols. plus updates 5/yr. looseleaf. USD 1,400 base vol(s). (effective 2010). cum.index. back issues avail. **Document type:** *Report, Government.* **Description:** Publishes decisions of the Department of the Interior, Minerals Management Service, on appeals relating to the collection of minerals royalty on federal lands.
Published by: Rocky Mountain Mineral Law Foundation, 9191 Sheridan Blvd, Ste 203, Westminster, CO 80031. TEL 303-321-8100, FAX 303-321-7657, info@rmmlf.org, http://www.rmmlf.org.

665.5 ITA
LA GUIDA ITALIANA DEL PETROLIO. Text in Italian. irreg. (approx. biennial) (in 7 vols.). price varies. charts; stat. **Document type:** *Directory, Trade.* **Description:** Describes in detail Italian laws dealing with liquid and gas petroleum; trends and figures for the production, refining, supply, and distribution of these hydrocarbons; foreign trade and transportation; and stocks and prices.
Related titles: CD-ROM ed.
Published by: Rivista Italiana Petrolio Srl, Via Aventina 19, Rome, 00153, Italy. TEL 39-06-5741208, FAX 39-06-5754906, http://www.staffettaonline.com.

665.7 GBR
GUIDE TO THE ECONOMIC REGULATION OF THE GAS INDUSTRY (ONLINE). Text in English. 1998. irreg. GBP 20 per vol. (effective 2010). **Document type:** *Handbook/Manual/Guide, Trade.* **Description:** Contains news on the UK gas market, including the introduction of competition and the evolving structure of BG plc.
Formerly (until 2004): Guide to the Economic Regulation of the Gas Industry (Print) (1463-1679)
Media: Online - full text.
—CCC.
Published by: O X E R A Consulting Ltd., Park Central, 40/41 Park End St, Oxford, OX1 1JD, United Kingdom. TEL 44-1865-253000, FAX 44-1865-251172, enquiries@oxera.com, http://www.oxera.com/.

GULF COAST OIL DIRECTORY. *see* BUSINESS AND ECONOMICS—Trade And Industrial Directories

665.538 USA ISSN 1058-5850
TN873.M64
GULF OF MEXICO DRILLING REPORT. Text in English. 1984. w. (m. version avail.). USD 1,525 (effective 2005). **Document type:** *Newsletter, Trade.* **Description:** Provides performance and statistical information on drilling activity in the U.S. Gulf of Mexico.
Formed by the merger of: Hunt Petro Information; Advance Drilling Data
Related titles: CD-ROM ed.; Diskette ed.: USD 1,750 (effective 2005); Online - full text ed.
—CCC.
Published by: O D S - Petrodata, 3200 Wilcrest Dr, Ste 170, Houston, TX 77042. TEL 832-463-3000, FAX 832-463-3100, general@ods-petrodata.com, http://www.ods-petrodata.com. Circ: 450.

665.5 USA
GULF OF MEXICO FIELD DEVELOPMENT LOCATOR. Text in English. 1986. m. USD 350 domestic; USD 400 foreign (effective 2000). **Document type:** *Magazine, Trade.* **Description:** Covers new oil and gas field development projects from the planning stages through final installation.
Related titles: Diskette ed.
Published by: O D S - Petrodata, 3200 Wilcrest Dr, Ste 170, Houston, TX 77042. TEL 832-463-3000, FAX 832-463-3100, general@ods-petrodata.com, http://www.ods-petrodata.com.

665.5 USA ISSN 1058-5885
GULF OF MEXICO NEWSLETTER. Text in English. 1986. w. USD 299 (effective 2007). 6 p./no. 2 cols./p.; back issues avail.; reprints avail. **Document type:** *Newsletter, Trade.* **Description:** Follows opportunities, projects, and companies in oil and gas exploration and development in the Gulf of Mexico.
Related titles: E-mail ed.; Online - full text ed.
Indexed: PEBNI, SCOPUS.
—Linda Hall. **CCC.**
Published by: O D S - Petrodata, 3200 Wilcrest Dr, Ste 170, Houston, TX 77042. TEL 832-463-3000, FAX 832-463-3100, general@ods-petrodata.com, http://www.ods-petrodata.com. Ed. Brad Baethe. Pub., R&P Thomas Marsh. Circ: 2,175.

665.5 338.2 USA
GULF OF MEXICO RIG LOCATOR. Text in English. 1986. w. USD 725 (effective 2007). **Document type:** *Newsletter, Trade.* **Description:** Provides location information and working status on all offshore rigs operating in the Gulf of Mexico.
Related titles: Diskette ed.
Published by: O D S - Petrodata, 3200 Wilcrest Dr, Ste 170, Houston, TX 77042. TEL 832-463-3000, FAX 832-463-3100, general@ods-petrodata.com, http://www.ods-petrodata.com. Pub. Tom Marsh. Circ: 525.

665.5 USA
GULF OF MEXICO RIG REPORT. Text in English. 1974. m. USD 1,815 (effective 2007). **Document type:** *Newsletter, Trade.* **Description:** Reports news and events affecting the international offshore drilling market.
Formerly (until 2004): Offshore Rig Newsletter (0147-1481)
—CCC.
Published by: O D S - Petrodata, 3200 Wilcrest Dr, Ste 170, Houston, TX 77042. TEL 832-463-3000, FAX 832-463-3100, general@ods-petrodata.com, http://www.ods-petrodata.com. Ed. Rina Samsudin. Pub. Tom Marsh. Circ: 825 (paid).

GUOWAI YOUQI KANTAN. *see* EARTH SCIENCES—Geology

665.5 CHN ISSN 1002-641X
GUOWAI YOUTIAN GONGCHENG/FOREIGN OIL FIELD ENGINEERING. Text in Chinese. 1985. m. CNY 240 (effective 2009). **Document type:** *Magazine, Trade.*
Related titles: Online - full text ed.
Published by: Daqing Youtian Gongcheng Youxian Gongsi/Daqing Oilfield Engineering Co. Ltd. (DOE), 42, Xikang Lu, Ranghulu-qu, Daqing, 163712, China. TEL 86-459-5902329, http://www.doe.com.cn/.

H C B TANK GUIDE. (Hazardous Cargo Bulletin) *see* TRANSPORTATION—Ships And Shipping

665.5 NLD ISSN 1567-8032
HANDBOOK OF PETROLEUM EXPLORATION AND PRODUCTION. Text in English. 2000 (Aug). irreg., latest vol.4, 2003. price varies. charts; illus.; stat. **Document type:** *Monographic series, Academic/Scholarly.* **Description:** Offers a comprehensive, detailed reference for information on all aspects of petroleum exploration and production.
Related titles: Online - full text ed.
Indexed: GeoRef, SCOPUS.
—BLDSC (4250.962470).
Published by: Elsevier BV (Subsidiary of: Elsevier Science & Technology), Radarweg 29, PO Box 211, Amsterdam, 1000 AE, Netherlands. TEL 31-20-4853911, FAX 31-20-4852457, JournalsCustomerServiceEMEA@elsevier.com, http://www.elsevier.nl. Ed. John Cubitt.

665.5 GBR ISSN 1469-106X
HART'S AFRICA OIL AND GAS; breaking news and analysis from Africa. Text in English. 1998. bi-w. GBP 645 (effective 2010). charts; mkt.; maps; stat.; tr.lit. back issues avail. **Document type:** *Newsletter, Trade.* **Description:** Provides analysis of political and environmental implications. Covers the entire African region.
Related titles: E-mail ed.; Online - full text ed.
Indexed: A15, ABIn, P48, P51, P52, P56, PQC.
—CCC.
Published by: Fraser Publications Ltd., PO Box 503, Winchester, SO23 3DG, United Kingdom. TEL 44-1962-711756, FAX 44-1962-713126. Ed. Mark Dixon.

665.5 USA ISSN 1092-2849
TP343
HART'S DIESEL FUEL NEWS. Variant title: Diesel Fuel News. Text in English. 1997. bi-m. USD 1,295 (effective 2009). **Document type:** *Newsletter, Trade.* **Description:** Provides world-wide intelligence on clean-diesel technology, vehicles, legislation, regulation, specifications, diesel and distillate fuels, engines, emissions controls, refining, alternative fuels, additives and markets.
Related titles: Online - full text ed.: ISSN 1940-5618.
Indexed: A10, A15, ABIn, B01, B02, B03, B07, B11, B15, B17, B18, E14, G04, G06, G07, G08, I05, P34, P48, P51, P52, P56, PQC, T02, T03, V03.
—CIS. **CCC.**
Published by: Hart Energy Publishing, LP (Subsidiary of: Chemical Week Associates), 1616 S Voss Rd, Ste 1000, Houston, TX 77057. TEL 713-260-6400, 800-874-2544, FAX 713-840-8585, custserv@hartenergy.com. Pub. David Givens TEL 703-891-4811. Circ: 400 (paid).

665.5 GBR
HART'S E & P DAILY (ONLINE). Text in English. 199?. d. GBP 975 (effective 2010). adv. back issues avail. **Document type:** *Bulletin, Trade.* **Description:** Provides daily news and information on the international oil and gas industry.
Former titles (until 200?): Hart's E & P Daily (Print) (1469-1108); (until 1999): Hart's Daily Petroleum Monitor
Media: Online - full text. **Related titles:** E-mail ed.; Fax ed.
Indexed: A15, ABIn, P48, P51, P52, P56, PQC.
—CIS. **CCC.**
Published by: Ogilvie Publishing Ltd., Quatro House, Lyon Way, Frimley, Surrey GU16 7ER, United Kingdom. TEL 44-1276-804508, FAX 44-1276-804513, marketing@ogilviepub.com, http://www.ogilviepub.com/.

HOUSTON BUSINESS JOURNAL; strictly Houston, strictly business. *see* BUSINESS AND ECONOMICS—Economic Situation And Conditions

665.5029 USA
HOUSTON PETROLEUM INDUSTRY. Text in English. a. **Document type:** *Directory, Trade.* **Description:** Supplies company name, address, phone and fax numbers, personnel information, producers, drilling and well service, pipelines, refineries, gas processing, petrochemical, engineering, equipment manufacturers and suppliers.
Formerly: Oil Directory of Houston, Texas (0471-3877)
Media: Diskette.
Published by: Midwest Publishing Company, 2230 E 49th St, Ste E, Tulsa, OK 74105. TEL 800-829-2002, info@midwestpub.com, http://www.midwestpub.com/. Ed., Pub. W L Hammack.

665.5029 USA ISSN 0739-3555
TN867
HOUSTON - TEXAS OIL DIRECTORY. Text in English. 1971. a. USD 99 per issue (effective 2011). adv. **Document type:** *Directory.* **Description:** Geared towards exploration and production of the oil and gas industry throughout the state of Texas.
Published by: Atlantic Communications, 1635 W Alabama, Houston, TX 77006. TEL 713-831-1768, FAX 713-523-2339. Pub. James W Self. Circ: 4,000.

HUADONG SHIFAN DAXUE XUEBAO (ZHEXUE SHEHUI KEXUE BAN)/EAST CHINA NORMAL UNIVERSITY. JOURNAL (PHILOSOPHY AND SOCIAL SCIENCES). *see* SOCIAL SCIENCES: COMPREHENSIVE WORKS

HUAGONG HUANBAO/ENVIRONMENTAL PROTECTION OF CHEMICAL INDUSTRY. *see* ENVIRONMENTAL STUDIES

HUAXUE YU NIANHE/CHEMISTRY AND ADHESION. *see* ENGINEERING—Chemical Engineering

HUNGARY CHEMICALS REPORT. *see* CHEMISTRY

338.4766180409 GBR ISSN 1749-2254
HUNGARY PETROCHEMICALS REPORT. Text in English. 2005. q. EUR 820, USD 1,030 combined subscription (print & email eds.) (effective 2010). **Document type:** *Report, Trade.* **Description:** Provides industry professionals and strategists, sector analysts, trade associations and regulatory bodies with independent forecasts and competitive intelligence on the petrochemicals industry in Hungary.
Related titles: E-mail ed.
Indexed: A15, ABIn, B02, B15, B17, B18, G04, I05, P48, P51, P52, P56, PQC.
Published by: Business Monitor International Ltd., Senator House, 85 Queen Victoria St, London, EC4V 4AB, United Kingdom. TEL 44-20-72480468, FAX 44-20-72480467, subs@businessmonitor.com.

665 GBR
HUNTING REVIEW. Text in English. 1951. s-a. free to qualified personnel (effective 2009). bk.rev. charts; illus. **Document type:** *Magazine, Corporate.* **Description:** Aims to provide information about Hunting's activities and interests.
Formerly (until 1995): Hunting Group Review (0018-7887)
Indexed: AESIS.
Published by: Hunting PLC, 3 Cockspur St, London, SW1Y 5BQ, United Kingdom. TEL 44-20-73210123, FAX 44-20-78392072, ceo@hunting.plc.uk.

552 CAN ISSN 0703-6655
TN873.C22
HYDROCARBON AND BYPRODUCT RESERVES IN BRITISH COLUMBIA. Text in English. a. USD 65. back issues avail. **Document type:** *Government.* **Description:** Contains tables of the reserves estimated by the division at the end of the year with an explanation of the definitions used throughout. A copy of the stratigraphic correlation chart and a map showing the location of the fields in the province is also included.
Formerly (until 1970): Oil, Natural Gas and Byproducts Reserves in British Columbia (0703-6663)
Indexed: GeoRef, SpeleolAb.
Published by: British Columbia, Ministry of Energy and Mines, c/o Communications Coordinator, Stn Prov Govt, PO Box 9324, Victoria, BC V8W 9N3, Canada. TEL 250-952-0525, http://www.ogc.gov.bc.ca. **Subscr. to:** Crown Publications Inc., 521 Fort St, Victoria, BC BC V8W 1E7, Canada. TEL 604-386-4636.

665.5 333.91 SGP ISSN 0217-1112
HYDROCARBON ASIA; refining, gas processing and petrochemical magazine. Text in English. 1991. 6/yr. USD 110 (effective 2004). adv. **Document type:** *Magazine, Trade.* **Description:** Covers the petroleum and gas industry news, technology, and other related information.
Indexed: APIAb, PEBNI, SCOPUS.
—BLDSC (4343.067000), IE, Ingenta.
Published by: Asia Pacific Energy Business Publications Pte. Ltd., 63 Robinson Rd, #02-10 Afro Asia Bldg, Singapore, 068894, Singapore. TEL 65-6-2223422, FAX 65-6-2225587, pansy@safan.com, http://www.safan.com. Ed. Jimmie Aung Khin. Adv. contact Eddie Raj. Circ: 5,000.

622.32 GBR ISSN 1812-7827
HYDROCARBON CHINA/GUOJI LIANYOU YU SHIHUA. Text in Chinese, English. 2004. q. free to qualified personnel (effective 2010). adv. **Document type:** *Magazine, Trade.* **Description:** Provides in-depth case studies on international developments of relevance to china's refining and petrochemical industries.
Related titles: ◆ Supplement to: Petroleum Technology Quarterly. ISSN 1362-363X.
—CCC.
Published by: Crambeth Allen Publishing, Hopesay, Craven Arms, SY7 8HD, United Kingdom. TEL 44-1588-660776, FAX 44-1588-660668, publisher@crambethallen.com, http://www.crambethallen.com. adv.: page USD 3,950, page EUR 2,835; trim 280 x 420. Circ: 8,000.

665.5 660 GBR ISSN 1468-9340
CODEN: IHYEF4
HYDROCARBON ENGINEERING. Text in English. 1996. m. GBP 110 domestic; GBP 125 foreign; GBP 30 per issue (effective 2010). adv. back issues avail. **Document type:** *Magazine, Trade.* **Description:** Contains technical, financial and analytical articles aimed at engineers and plant managers at hydrocarbon processing plants worldwide.
Formerly (until 1999): The International Journal of Hydrocarbon Engineering (1364-3177)
Related titles: ◆ Supplement(s): L N G Industry. ISSN 1747-1826.
Indexed: A28, APA, APIAb, BrCerAb, C&ISA, CA/WCA, CIA, CerAb, CivEngAb, CorrAb, E&CAJ, E11, EEA, EMA, ESPM, EngInd, EnvEAb, H15, M&TEA, M09, MBF, METADEX, SCOPUS, SolStAb, T04, WAA.
—BLDSC (4343.069000), CASDDS, IE, Ingenta, INIST, Linda Hall.
Published by: Palladian Publications Ltd., 15 South St, Farnham, Surrey GU9 7QU, United Kingdom. TEL 44-1252-718999, FAX 44-1252-821115, enquiries@energyglobal.com. adv.: page EUR 5,040, page USD 5,985; trim 210 x 297. Circ: 10,600.

665.5 USA ISSN 0887-0284
TP690.A1 CODEN: HYPRAX
HYDROCARBON PROCESSING. Text in English. 1922. m. USD 130 in US & Canada; USD 165 elsewhere (effective 2008). adv. bk.rev. charts; illus.; tr.lit. index. back issues avail.; reprints avail. **Document type:** *Magazine, Trade.*
Supersedes in part (in 1966): Hydrocarbon Processing & Petroleum Refiner (0096-2406); Which was formerly (until 1961): Petroleum Refiner (0096-6517); (until 1942): Refiner and Natural Gasoline Manufacturer (0096-0462)
Related titles: Microfilm ed.: (from PMC, PQC); Online - full text ed.; ◆ Partial Russian translation(s): Neftegazovye Tekhnologii; ◆ International ed.: Hydrocarbon Processing International Edition. ISSN 0018-8190.
Indexed: A22, AESIS, APICat, APIH&E, APIOC, APIPR, APIPS, APITS, ASCA, AcoustA, CEA, ChemAb, E&PHSE, EIA, EnerRev, F&EA, FPRD, GP&P, GasAb, HRIS, ISR, OffTech, PetrolAb, SCOPUS, TCEA.
—CIS, Linda Hall. **CCC.**
Published by: Gulf Publishing Co., PO Box 2608, Houston, TX 77252. TEL 713-529-4301, FAX 713-520-4433, publications@gulfpub.com, http://www.gulfpub.com. Ed. Laura Kane TEL 713-520-4449. Pub. Mark Peters. adv.: B&W page USD 6,170, color page USD 10,080; trim 8.125 x 10.875. Circ: 30,373.

665.5 USA ISSN 0018-8190
CODEN: IHPRBS
HYDROCARBON PROCESSING INTERNATIONAL EDITION. Text in English. 1922. m. USD 140 combined subscription in US & Canada; USD 195 combined subscription elsewhere (effective 2009). adv. bk.rev.; Website rev. illus.; charts. Index. back issues avail.; reprints avail. **Document type:** *Magazine, Trade.*
Supersedes in part (in 1966): Hydrocarbon Processing - Petroleum Refiner (0096-2406); Which was formerly (until 1961): Petroleum Refiner (0096-6517); (until 1942): Refiner and Natural Gasoline Manufacturer (0096-0462)
Related titles: Online - full text ed.; ◆ International ed. of: Hydrocarbon Processing. ISSN 0887-0284.

Indexed: A01, A02, A03, A05, A08, A09, A10, A15, A20, A22, A23, A24, A26, ABIn, APIAb, AS&TA, AS&TI, B03, B04, B10, B11, B13, BRD, C&ISA, C10, CA, CBNB, CEABA, CIN, ChemAb, ChemTitl, CurCont, E&CAJ, E04, E05, E08, EngInd, EnvAb, FR, G01, G06, G07, G08, GeoRef, I05, ISMEC, ISR, Inspec, P26, P34, P48, P51, P52, P54, P56, PQC, PetrolAb, R18, S&VD, S01, S04, S09, SCI, SolStAb, T02, TM, V03, V04, W03, W05, W07.
—BLDSC (4343.100000), CASDDS, IE, Infotrieve, Ingenta, INIST, Linda Hall, PADDS. **CCC.**
Published by: Gulf Publishing Co., PO Box 2608, Houston, TX 77252. TEL 713-529-4301, FAX 713-520-4433, publications@gulfpub.com, http://www.gulfpub.com. Ed. Les A Kane. Pub. Mark Peters. adv.: color page USD 9,410; trim 8.125 x 10.875. Circ: 30,323.

HYDROGEN FORECAST. *see* ENERGY

I E A OIL MARKET REPORT. (International Energy Agency) *see* ENERGY

665.6 HRV ISSN 1331-6095
HD9575.C87
I N A CASOPIS. (Industrija Nafte) Text in Croatian. 1997. bi-m. **Document type:** *Magazine, Trade.*
Published by: I N A - Industrija Nafte, Avenija Veceslava Holjevca 10, p.p. 555, Zagreb, 10002, Croatia. TEL 385-1-6451378, FAX 385-1-6452452, ina@ina.hr.

665.5 540 330 HRV ISSN 1331-9132
I N A GLASNIK. (Industrija Nafte) Text in Croatian. 1964. bi-w. free. **Document type:** *Newspaper, Trade.*
Former titles (until 1998): I N A (1331-9167); (until 1966): Vjesnik Industrije Nafte (1331-9159)
Related titles: Online - full content ed.
Published by: I N A - Industrija Nafte, Avenija Veceslava Holjevca 10, p.p. 555, Zagreb, 10002, Croatia. TEL 385-1-6451378, FAX 385-1-6452452, ina@ina.hr. Ed. Branko Franjic. Circ: 25,000.

I O G C C MEMBERS AND OIL AND GAS AGENCIES DIRECTORY. *see* BUSINESS AND ECONOMICS—Trade And Industrial Directories

665.5 NLD ISSN 1572-5324
THE I P L O C A YEARBOOK. Text in English. 2002. a. adv.
Published by: (International Pipe Line and Offshore Contractors Association), Pedemex, Mgr Schaepmanlaan 35, Dongen, 5103 BB, Netherlands. TEL 31-162-314181, FAX 31-162-319414, http://www.pedemex.nl. Pub. Pieter Schoonenberg. adv.: B&W page EUR 3,150, color page EUR 4,600; bleed 148 x 210.

665.5 USA ISSN 0199-5685
I U P I W VIEWS. Text in English. 1945. bi-m. USD 5. adv. **Document type:** *Newsletter.*
Published by: International Union of Petroleum & Industrial Workers, 8131 E Rosecrano Ave, Paramount, CA 90723. FAX 213-408-1073. Ed. Robert Davidson. Pub. George R Beltz. R&P Cathy Stimson TEL 562-630-6232. Circ: 9,000.

665.5 USA ISSN 0073-5108
TN872.I3 CODEN: ILGPA4
ILLINOIS PETROLEUM. Text in English. 1926. irreg., latest vol.159, 2003. abstr.; bibl.; charts; illus.; stat. back issues avail. **Document type:** *Monographic series, Government.*
Related titles: Online - full text ed.: free (effective 2011).
Indexed: AESIS, GeoRef, PetrolAb, SCOPUS, SpeleolAb.
—Ingenta, Linda Hall.
Published by: State Geological Survey, 615 E Peabody Dr, Champaign, IL 61820. TEL 217-333-4747, isgs@isgs.illinois.edu, http://www.isgs.illinois.edu/.

665.7 CAN ISSN 1910-0698
IMPORTATIONS DE GAZ NATUREL. Text in French. 1998. m. **Document type:** *Bulletin, Trade.*
Media: Online - full text. **Related titles:** English ed.: Natural Gas Imports. ISSN 1910-068X.
Published by: National Energy Board/Office National de l'Energie, 444 Seventh Ave, S W, Calgary, AB T2P 0X8, Canada. TEL 403-299-3561, 800-899-1265, FAX 403-292-5576, publications@neb-one.gc.ca.

665.5 310 USA
IMPORTS & EXPORTS OF CRUDE OIL AND PETROLEUM PRODUCTS. Text in English. 1977. m. USD 11,290 to non-members; USD 6,740 to members (effective 2008). back issues avail. **Document type:** *Report, Trade.* **Description:** Contains data on the imports of crude oil and petroleum products, including details such as importer of record, port of entry, country of origin, recipient, destination, quantity, and API gravity and sulphur content.
Formerly: Imported Crude Oil and Petroleum Products
Related titles: Magnetic Tape ed.; Online - full text ed.
Indexed: SRI.
Published by: American Petroleum Institute, Publications Section, 1220 L St, NW, Washington, DC 20005. TEL 202-682-8000, FAX 202-682-8408, apidata@api.org, http://www.api.org. Ed. Claudette Reid. Circ: 350.

665.5
INDEPENDENT GASOLINE MARKETING. Text in English. 1973. bi-m. membership. adv. **Document type:** *Magazine, Trade.* **Description:** Covers gasoline legislation and issues.
Former titles (until 1987): S I G M A Update; Capitol Digest
Published by: Society of Independent Gasoline Marketers of America, 11911 Freedom Dr, 590, Reston, VA 20190-5602. TEL 703-709-7000, FAX 703-709-7007. Ed. Angela M Angerosa. Pub., R&P Tom Osborne. Adv. contact Mary Alice Kutyn. B&W page USD 1,960, color page USD 2,485; 10.88 x 8.25. Circ: 5,500 (controlled).

665.5 USA
INDEPENDENT LIQUID TERMINALS ASSOCIATION. NEWSLETTER. Text in English. 1975. m. free to members. **Document type:** *Newsletter.* **Description:** Covers legislation and regulations affecting terminals, the tank farm industry and related industries.
Published by: Independent Liquid Terminals Association, 1444 I St NW, Ste 400, Washington, DC 20005-6538. TEL 202-842-9200, FAX 202-326-8660, info@ilta.org, http://www.ilta.org/. Circ: 1,200.

665.5 USA
INDIA OIL AND GAS NEWS. Text in English. w. USD 795 (effective 2002). back issues avail. **Description:** Designed for the oil, gas, pipeline, refinery, petrochemical, exploration, development and project finance sectors of India. Provides essential information on the most important events affecting your interests in this fast-growing market.
Media: E-mail.
Published by: Emerging Markets Online, 2476 Bolsover, Ste. 368, Houston, TX 77005. TEL 713-349-8281, FAX 713-349-8380, service@emerging-markets.com, http://www.emerging-markets.com/.

338.4766180409 GBR ISSN 1749-2262
INDIA PETROCHEMICALS REPORT. Text in English. 2005. q. EUR 820, USD 1,030 combined subscription (print & email eds.) (effective 2010). **Document type:** *Report, Trade.* **Description:** Provides industry professionals and strategists, sector analysts, trade associations and regulatory bodies with independent forecasts and competitive intelligence on the Indian petrochemicals industry.
Related titles: E-mail ed.
Indexed: A15, ABIn, B02, B15, B17, B18, G04, I05, P48, P51, P52, P56, PQC.
Published by: Business Monitor International Ltd., Senator House, 85 Queen Victoria St, London, EC4V 4AB, United Kingdom. TEL 44-20-72480468, FAX 44-20-72480467, subs@businessmonitor.com.

662.338 IND ISSN 0971-2542
TN876.I5
INDIAN JOURNAL OF PETROLEUM GEOLOGY. Text in English. 1992. s-a. adv. bk.rev. back issues avail. **Document type:** *Journal, Academic/Scholarly.* **Description:** Provides a forum for the exchange of scientific and technical information concerning petroleum exploration in Southeast Asian countries in particular and the world in general.
Indexed: AESIS, E&PHSE, GP&P, GeoRef, OffTech, PetrolAb, SCOPUS, SpeleolAb.
—BLDSC (4418.300000), IE, Ingenta, PADDS.
Published by: Indian Petroleum Publishers, 100/9 Nashvilla Rd, Dehra Dun, Uttar Pradesh 248 001, India. TEL 91-135-2654074, FAX 91-135-2652111, info@ippublishers.com. Ed. Kuldeep Chandra. **Subscr. to:** I N S I O Scientific Books & Periodicals.

665.5 305.897 CAN ISSN 1712-1221
INDIAN OIL AND GAS CANADA. ANNUAL REPORT (ONLINE). Text in English. 2002. a.
Media: Online - full text. **Related titles:** ◆ Print ed.: Indian Oil and Gas Canada. Annual Report (Print). ISSN 1706-3426; French ed.: ISSN 1712-123X.
Published by: Indian and Northern Affairs Canada/Affaires Indiennes et du Nord Canada, Terrasses de la Chaudiere, 10 Wellington St, N Tower, Rm 1210, Gatineau, PQ K1A 0H4, Canada. TEL 800-567-9604, FAX 866-817-3977, infopubs@ainc-inac.gc.ca, http://www.ainc-inac.gc.ca.

665.5 305.897 CAN ISSN 1706-3426
HD9574.C2
INDIAN OIL AND GAS CANADA. ANNUAL REPORT (PRINT). Text in English, French. 1994. a. **Document type:** *Report, Trade.*
Related titles: ◆ Online - full text ed.: Indian Oil and Gas Canada. Annual Report (Online). ISSN 1712-1221; French ed.: Petrole et Gaz des Indiens du Canada. Rapport Annuel. ISSN 1706-3434.
Published by: Indian and Northern Affairs Canada/Affaires Indiennes et du Nord Canada, Terrasses de la Chaudiere, 10 Wellington St, N Tower, Rm 1210, Gatineau, PQ K1A 0H4, Canada. TEL 800-567-9604, FAX 866-817-3977, infopubs@ainc-inac.gc.ca, http://www.ainc-inac.gc.ca.

665.5 IND
INDIAN PETROLEUM DIRECTORY. Text in English. 1996. biennial (in 2 vols., 1 no./vol.). INR 2,000 per issue domestic; USD 250 per issue foreign (effective 2011). adv. back issues avail. **Document type:** *Directory, Trade.* **Description:** Covers the petroleum industry in India and contains company details.
Published by: Indian Petroleum Publishers, 100/9 Nashvilla Rd, Dehra Dun, Uttar Pradesh 248 001, India. TEL 91-135-2654074, FAX 91-135-2652111, info@ippublishers.com.

338.4766180409 GBR ISSN 1749-2270
INDONESIA PETROCHEMICALS REPORT. Text in English. 2005. q. EUR 820, USD 1,030 combined subscription (print & email eds.) (effective 2010). **Document type:** *Report, Trade.* **Description:** Provides industry professionals and strategists, sector analysts, trade associations and regulatory bodies with independent forecasts and competitive intelligence on the Indonesian petrochemicals industry.
Related titles: E-mail ed.
Indexed: A15, ABIn, B02, B15, B17, B18, G04, I05, P48, P51, P52, P56, PQC.
Published by: Business Monitor International Ltd., Senator House, 85 Queen Victoria St, London, EC4V 4AB, United Kingdom. TEL 44-20-72480468, FAX 44-20-72480467, subs@businessmonitor.com.

665.7 662 USA ISSN 2160-4495
TP690.A1 CODEN: FOHCEU
INDOOR COMFORT MARKETING. Abbreviated title: I C M. Text in English. 1922. m. USD 48 domestic; USD 60 in Canada & Mexico; USD 135 elsewhere; free to qualified personnel (effective 2011). adv. illus.; stat. back issues avail.; reprints avail. **Document type:** *Journal, Trade.* **Description:** Covers all phases of fuel and oil heating.
Former titles (until 2011): Oilheating (1092-6003); (until 1997): Fueloil and Oil Heat with Air Conditioning (1060-9725); (until 1991): Fueloil and Oil Heat (1061-141X); (until 1990): Fueloil and Oil Heat Magazine (0888-0735); (until 1985): Fueloil and Oil Heat and Solar Systems (0148-9801); (until 1977): Fueloil and Oil Heat (0016-2418); Which was formed by the merger of (1938-1942): Air Conditioning & Oil Heat (0096-5308); (1929-1942): Fuel Oil Journal (0097-1995); Which was formerly (until 1929): Fuel Oil and Temperature Journal (0095-9413)
Related titles: Microform ed.: (from PQC); Online - full text ed.
Indexed: A22, A23, B01, B02, B04, B06, B07, B08, B09, B13, B15, B17, B18, BPI, BRD, BusI, C12, ChemAb, F&EA, G04, G06, G07, G08, I05, T&II, W01, W02, W03, W05.
—Ingenta, Linda Hall.
Published by: Industry Publications, Inc., 3621 Hill Rd, Parsippany, NJ 07054. TEL 973-331-9545, FAX 973-331-9547. Ed. Michael L SanGiovanni. Pub. Donald J Farrell.

INDUSTRI ENERGI. *see* LABOR UNIONS

665.5 MEX ISSN 0187-487X
HD9574.M6
INDUSTRIA PETROLERA EN MEXICO. Text in Spanish. 1979. irreg., latest 1988. MXN 2,500, USD 22.
Published by: Instituto Nacional de Estadistica, Geografia e Informatica, Secretaria de Programacion y Presupuesto, Prol. Heroe de Nacozari 2301 Sur, Puerta 11, Acceso, Aguascalientes, 20270, Mexico. TEL 52-4-918-1948, FAX 52-4-918-0739. Circ: 1,000.

338.0029 RUS
INFOTEK; neftegazovyi zhurnal. Text in Russian. 1993. m. USD 1,612 in North America (effective 2011). **Document type:** *Magazine, Trade.*
Published by: InfoTEK-Consult, Kitaiskii pr., 7, Moscow, 103074, Russian Federation. TEL 7-095-9273091, FAX 7-095-2204818, consult@citek.ru. **Dist. by:** East View Information Services, 10601 Wayzata Blvd, Minneapolis, MN 55305. TEL 952-252-1201, 800-477-1005, FAX 952-252-1202, info@eastview.com, http://www.eastview.com.

665.7 ESP ISSN 1134-3168
INGENIERIA DEL GAS. Short title: I D G. Text in Spanish. 1994. bi-m. free to qualified personnel (effective 2010). adv. **Document type:** *Magazine, Trade.* **Description:** Covers installation, equipment and gas engineering for domestic, commercial and industrial use of gas.
Published by: Sede Tecnica S.A., Avda Brasil, 17 planta 12, Madrid, 28020, Spain. TEL 34-91-5565004, FAX 34-91-5560962, editorial@sedetecnica.com, http://www.sedetecnica.com/. Ed. Julian Cid. Pub. Carlos Martin. Adv. contact Esther Navas. Circ: 6,500.

665.5 MEX ISSN 0185-3899
TN860 CODEN: INGPAI
INGENIERIA PETROLERA. Text in Spanish. 1958. m. MXN 40 (effective 1994). adv.
Related titles: Microfilm ed.
Indexed: C01, GeoRef, SpeleolAb.
Published by: Asociacion de Ingenieros Petroleros de Mexico A.C., Apdo. Postal 53-013, Mexico, DF CP-11490, Mexico. TEL 2-54-04-28, FAX 5-31-15-61. Ed. Javier Guirrion Garcia. Circ: 4,000.

665.5 USA ISSN 8756-3711
HD9581.U5
INSIDE F E R C'S GAS MARKET REPORT. Variant title: Gas Market Report. Text in English. 1985. bi-w. USD 2,175 (effective 2008). adv. reprints avail. **Document type:** *Newsletter, Trade.* **Description:** Features vital first-of-the-month gas prices for more than 40 pipeline locations and a number of key market centers.
Related titles: CD-ROM ed.; Online - full text ed.: USD 1,675 combined subscription (online & E-mail eds.) (effective 2008).
Indexed: A15, ABIn, P48, P51, P56, PQC.
—CIS. **CCC.**
Published by: (Federal Energy Regulatory Commission), Platts (Subsidiary of: McGraw-Hill Companies, Inc.), 1200 G St NW, Ste 1000, Washington, DC 20005. TEL 212-904-3070, 800-752-8878, FAX 202-383-2024, support@platts.com.

665.5 DZA ISSN 1112-3354
L'INSTITUT ALGERIEN DU PETROLE. REVUE. Text in French, English. 2001. s-a. **Document type:** *Journal, Trade.*
Related titles: French ed.: ISSN 1112-802X.
Published by: Institut Algerien du Petrole, Ave 1er Novembre, Boumerdes, 35000, Algeria. TEL 213-24-811860, FAX 213-24-818600.

665.5 FRA ISSN 0073-8360
TN860 CODEN: IPTCBP
INSTITUT FRANCAIS DU PETROLE. COLLECTION COLLOQUES ET SEMINAIRES. Text in French. 1964. irreg., latest vol.52, 1994. price varies. **Document type:** *Proceedings.*
Indexed: CIN, ChemAb, ChemTitl, GeoRef, GeophysAb, PetrolAb, SpeleolAb.
—CASDDS, INIST. **CCC.**
Published by: (Institut Francais du Petrole), Editions Technip, 27 rue Ginoux, Paris, Cedex 15 75737, France. TEL 33-1-45783380, FAX 33-1-45753711. Circ: 1,250.

665.5 FRA ISSN 0073-8379
INSTITUT FRANCAIS DU PETROLE. RAPPORT ANNUEL. Text in French, English. 195?. a. free. **Document type:** *Corporate.*
Related titles: Online - full text ed.; English ed.
Indexed: PetrolAb.
—INIST.
Published by: Institut Francais du Petrole (IFP), Direction de la Communication, 1 et 4 av. de Bois-Preau, Rueil Malmaison, Cedex 92852, France. TEL 33-1-47526000, FAX 33-1-47527096. Circ: 10,000.

665.5 GBR ISSN 0309-1880
INSTITUTE OF PETROLEUM. Text in English. 1914. irreg. price varies. **Document type:** *Monographic series, Trade.*
Former titles (until 1938): Institution of Petroleum Technologist. Journal (0368-2722); (until 1973): Institute of Petroleum. Journal (0020-3068)
Indexed: A23, A24, B13, GeoRef, SCOPUS.
—INIST. **CCC.**
Address: 61 New Cavendish St, London, W1G 7AR, United Kingdom. TEL 44-20-74677100, FAX 44-20-72551472, lis@petroleum.co.uk, http://www.petroleum.co.uk.

INSTITUTO DE CATALISIS Y PETROLEOQUIMICA. MEMORIA. *see* CHEMISTRY

665.5 622 553.28 POL ISSN 0209-0724
CODEN: PGNGDN
INSTYTUT GORNICTWA NAFTOWEGO I GAZOWNICTWA. PRACE. Text in Polish; Summaries in English, Russian. 1950. irreg. (5-7/yr.). price varies. charts; illus. **Document type:** *Academic/Scholarly.*
Formerly: Instytut Naftowy. Prace (0032-6232)
Indexed: B22, ChemAb, GeoRef, SpeleolAb.
—CASDDS.
Published by: Instytut Gornictwa Naftowego i Gazownictwa, ul Lubicz 25 A, Krakow, 31503, Poland. TEL 48-12-4210033, FAX 48-12-4210050, office@inig.pl. Circ: 1,000.

665.5 RUS
INTERFAX. RUSSIA & C I S ENERGY DAILY. Text in English. d. price varies. **Document type:** *Bulletin, Trade.* **Description:** Covers major events in the ex-USSR fuel and energy industries, covering the implementation progress of the major oil and gas projects.
Formerly: Interfax. Daily Petroleum Report (1523-2441)
Related titles: Online - full text ed.
Indexed: A15, P48, P51, P52, P56.

Published by: Interfax Ltd., 1-ya Tverskaya-Yamskaya, dom 2, stroenie 1, Moscow, 127006, Russian Federation. TEL 7-095-2509840, FAX 7-095-2509727, info@interfax.ru, http://www.interfax.ru. **Dist. elsewhere by:** Interfax America, Inc., 3025 S Parker Rd, Ste 737, Aurora, CO 80014. TEL 303-368-1421, FAX 303-368-1458, http://www.interfax.com; **Dist. in Germany, Austria and Switzerland by:** Interfax Deutschland GmbH, 54, Taunusstrasse, Frankfurt 61476, Germany. TEL 49-6171-695750, FAX 49-6171-989995; **Dist. in Western Europe by:** Interfax Europe Ltd., 2-3 Philpot Lane, 3rd Fl, London EC3M 8AQ, United Kingdom. TEL 44-20-76210595, FAX 44-20-79294263.

665.5 RUS
INTERFAX. RUSSIA & C I S OIL & GAS WEEKLY. (Commonwealth of Independent States) Text in English. 200?. w. price varies. **Document type:** *Bulletin, Trade.* **Description:** Highlights events in the oil and gas sectors in Russia and the former Soviet republics and provides experts' comments as well as reference information.
Formerly: Interfax. Petroleum Report (1072-267X)
Related titles: Online - full text ed.
Indexed: A15, E14, P48, P51, P52, P56, R01.
Published by: Interfax Ltd., 1-ya Tverskaya-Yamskaya, dom 2, stroenie 1, Moscow, 127006, Russian Federation. TEL 7-095-2509840, FAX 7-095-2509727, info@interfax.ru, http://www.interfax.ru. **Dist. elsewhere by:** Interfax America, Inc., 3025 S Parker Rd, Ste 737, Aurora, CO 80014. TEL 303-368-1421, FAX 303-368-1458, http://www.interfax.com; **Dist. in Germany Austria and Switzerland by:** Interfax Deutschland GmbH, 54, Taunusstrasse, Frankfurt 61476, Germany. TEL 49-6171-695750, FAX 49-6171-989995; **Dist. in Western Europe by:** Interfax Europe Ltd., 2-3 Philpot Lane, 3rd Fl, London EC3M 8AQ, United Kingdom. TEL 44-20-76210595, FAX 44-20-79294263.

665.5 USA ISSN 1931-1915
INTERMEDIATESWIRE. Text in English. 1996. w. USD 3,525; USD 3,595 combined subscription (online & E-mail eds.) (effective 2008). back issues avail. **Document type:** *Newsletter, Trade.* **Description:** Provides news, price assessments and transaction information on instrumental intermediates such as isobutanol, normal butanol, 2-ethyl hexanol and dioctyl phthalate.
Formerly (until 1996): Petrochemical Intermediateswire
Media: Online - full content. **Related titles:** E-mail ed.
Published by: Platts (Subsidiary of: McGraw-Hill Companies, Inc.), 1200 G St NW, Ste 1000, Washington, DC 20005. TEL 212-904-3070, 800-752-8878, FAX 202-383-2024, support@platts.com. Ed. Jim Foster.

THE INTERNATIONAL COMPARATIVE LEGAL GUIDE TO: GAS REGULATION (YEAR). *see* LAW

665.7 USA ISSN 0197-2782
CODEN: ICLNBT
INTERNATIONAL CONFERENCE ON LIQUEFIED NATURAL GAS. PAPERS. Text in English. 1968. triennial. **Document type:** *Proceedings, Trade.*
Formerly: International Conference on Liquefied Natural Gas. Proceedings (0538-611X)
Indexed: ChemAb, GasAb.
—CASDDS. **CCC.**
Published by: (Institut International du Froid/International Institute of Refrigeration FRA), Gas Technology Institute, 1700 S Mt. Prospect Rd, Des Plaines, IL 60018. TEL 847-768-0500, FAX 847-768-0709, http://www.gastechnology.org. **Co-sponsor:** International Gas Union.

338.2 665.5 GBR ISSN 1747-3268
INTERNATIONAL GAS REPORT (ONLINE). Text in English. 200?. bi-w. USD 1,995 combined subscription (Online & E-mail eds.) (effective 2010). adv. **Document type:** *Newsletter, Trade.*
Media: Online - full text. **Related titles:** E-mail ed.
Published by: Platts (Subsidiary of: McGraw-Hill Companies, Inc.), 20 Canada Sq, 12th Fl, Canary Wharf, London, E14 5LH, United Kingdom. TEL 44-20-71766111, FAX 44-20-71766144, support@platts.com. Ed. William Powell TEL 44-20-71766282.

338.39 CHE
INTERNATIONAL GAS UNION. PROCEEDINGS OF WORLD GAS CONFERENCES. Text in English, French. 1931. triennial. **Document type:** *Proceedings.*
Formerly: International Gas Union. Proceedings of Conferences (0074-6126)
Indexed: SpeleolAb.
Published by: International Gas Union/Union Internationale de l'Industrie du Gaz, Grutlistr 44, Case Postale 658, Zuerich, 8027, Switzerland. Ed. J P Lauper.

INTERNATIONAL JOURNAL OF MINING, RECLAMATION AND ENVIRONMENT. *see* MINES AND MINING INDUSTRY

INTERNATIONAL JOURNAL OF OFFSHORE AND POLAR ENGINEERING. *see* ENGINEERING—Mechanical Engineering

665.5 662.6 GBR ISSN 1753-3309
HD9560.1
➤ **INTERNATIONAL JOURNAL OF OIL, GAS AND COAL TECHNOLOGY.** Text in English. 2008. 4/yr. EUR 494 to institutions (print or online ed.); EUR 672 combined subscription to institutions (print & online eds.) (effective 2012). bk.rev. abstr.; bibl.; charts; illus. **Document type:** *Journal, Academic/Scholarly.* **Description:** Covers the exploration, production, processing and refining, storage and transportation, economical, managerial, business, environmental, safety and security issues related to oil, natural gas, coal and petrochemicals as well as manufacturing and refining of biofuels.
Related titles: Online - full text ed.: ISSN 1753-3317 (from IngentaConnect).
Indexed: A26, A28, APA, BrCerAb, C&ISA, CA/WCA, CIA, CerAb, CivEngAb, CorrAb, E&CAJ, E08, E11, EEA, EMA, ESPM, EnvEAb, H15, M&TEA, M09, MBF, METADEX, PollutAb, SCOPUS, SSciA, SolStAb, T04, WAA.
—BLDSC (4542.424350), INIST. **CCC.**
Published by: Inderscience Publishers, PO Box 735, Olney, Bucks MK46 5WB, United Kingdom. TEL 44-1234-240519, FAX 44-1234-240515, editorial@inderscience.com. Ed. M.-R. Riazi. **Subscr. to:** World Trade Centre Bldg, 29 Rte de Pre-Bois, Case Postale 856, Geneva 15 1215, Switzerland. FAX 41-22-7910885, subs@inderscience.com.

665.5 661 GBR ISSN 1754-8888
▼ ➤ **INTERNATIONAL JOURNAL OF PETROLEUM ENGINEERING.** Text in English. forthcoming 2011. 4/yr. EUR 494 to institutions (print or online ed.); EUR 672 combined subscription to institutions (print & online eds.) (effective 2011). **Document type:** *Journal, Academic/Scholarly.* **Description:** Fosters innovative solutions to design efficient petroleum operations.
Related titles: Online - full text ed.: ISSN 1754-8896. forthcoming.
—BLDSC (4542.452850). **CCC.**
Published by: Inderscience Publishers, PO Box 735, Olney, Bucks MK46 5WB, United Kingdom. TEL 44-1234-240519, FAX 44-1234-240515, editorial@inderscience.com. Ed. Brian Towler. **Subscr. to:** World Trade Centre Bldg, 29 Rte de Pre-Bois, Case Postale 856, Geneva 15 1215, Switzerland. FAX 41-22-7910885, subs@inderscience.com.

665.5 IND ISSN 0973-6328
➤ **INTERNATIONAL JOURNAL OF PETROLEUM SCIENCE AND TECHNOLOGY.** Abbreviated title: I J P S T. Text in English. 2007 (Mar.). s-a. INR 3,500 domestic to libraries; USD 320 foreign to libraries; USD 360 combined subscription foreign to libraries (print & online eds.) (effective 2011). back issues avail. **Document type:** *Journal, Academic/Scholarly.* **Description:** Covers the fields of petroleum geology, exploration, and technology.
Related titles: Online - full text ed.: ISSN 0974-4835. 2007. USD 300 to libraries (effective 2011).
Indexed: A01, A26, CA, E14, I05, T02.
Published by: Research India Publications, D1/71, Top Fl, Rohini Sec-16, New Delhi, 110 089, India. TEL 91-11-65394240, FAX 91-11-27297815, info@ripublication.com.

➤ **INTERNATIONAL OFFSHORE AND POLAR ENGINEERING CONFERENCE. PROCEEDINGS.** *see* ENGINEERING—Mechanical Engineering

338.7 USA ISSN 1059-7816
HD9560.3
INTERNATIONAL OFFSHORE OIL COMPANY DIRECTORY. Text in English. 1992. a. USD 399 (effective 2005). **Document type:** *Directory, Trade.* **Description:** Provides information on more than 300 companies, including national oil companies, with over 750 field office locations around the world.
Published by: O D S - Petrodata, 3200 Wilcrest Dr, Ste 170, Houston, TX 77042. TEL 832-463-3000, FAX 832-463-3100, general@ods-petrodata.com, http://www.ods-petrodata.com.

338.232 GBR ISSN 1364-9167
HD9560.1
INTERNATIONAL OIL & GAS FINANCE REVIEW (YEAR). Text in English. 1996. a. GBP 115, EUR 170, USD 195 per issue (effective 2005). **Document type:** *Yearbook, Trade.* **Description:** Serves as a guide for the oil and gas finance market. Includes a directory of 500 companies active in the market.
—**CCC.**
Published by: Euromoney Publications plc, Nestor House, Playhouse Yard, London, EC4V 5EX, United Kingdom. TEL 44-20-77798888, information@euromoneyplc.com, http://www.euromoneyplc.com.

333.13 USA ISSN 1540-8108
CODEN: IODNA4
INTERNATIONAL OIL DAILY. Text in English. 2002. d. USD 970 (effective 2009). adv. back issues avail. **Document type:** *Newsletter, Trade.* **Description:** Provides quick, accurate, and insightful coverage of the latest developments in the oil and gas business.
Media: Online - full content. **Related titles:** E-mail ed.: USD 1,020 (effective 2009).
—**CCC.**
Published by: Energy Intelligence Group, Inc., 5 E 37th St, 5th Fl, New York, NY 10016. TEL 212-532-1112, FAX 212-532-4479, info@energyintel.com. Ed. Jane Collin.

665 622 USA
INTERNATIONAL OIL NEWS. Text in English. 1953. w. USD 672.62 (effective 2006). illus.; mkt. 6 p./no. 2 cols./p.; back issues avail.; reprints avail. **Document type:** *Newsletter, Trade.* **Description:** Contains industry news for senior executives managing international oil and gas activities.
Formed by the 1993 merger of: International Oil News: Suppliers Edition; International Oil News: Management Edition; Which superseded (in 1986): International Oil News (0043-8855); Which was formerly (1954-1970): World Petroleum Report
Indexed: PEBNI, SpeleolAb.
Published by: Chase Energy Ventures, 359 Case School Rd., Madison, NC 27025-7509. TEL 336-427-2274, ioninfo@triad.rr.nc. Ed. James Price.

INTERNATIONAL OIL SCOUTS ASSOCIATION DIRECTORY. *see* BUSINESS AND ECONOMICS—Trade And Industrial Directories

665.5 USA ISSN 0148-0375
HD9560.1
INTERNATIONAL PETROLEUM ENCYCLOPEDIA. Text in English. 1968. a. USD 195 (print or CD-ROM ed.) (effective 2008). adv. **Document type:** *Directory, Trade.* **Description:** Provides plans, activities, statistics, technology and analysis in all segments of today's worldwide oil and gas businesses. Features new maps, updated country-by-country reports and brand new features on the most timely petroleum industry developments.
Related titles: CD-ROM ed.: ISSN 1521-4400.
Indexed: SRI.
—BLDSC (4544.914500). **CCC.**
Published by: PennWell Corporation, 1421 S Sheridan Rd, Tulsa, OK 74112. TEL 918-835-3161, 800-331-4463, FAX 918-831-9804, Headquarters@PennWell.com, http://www.pennwell.com. Ed. John C McCaslin.

665.5 332 USA ISSN 0193-9270
INTERNATIONAL PETROLEUM FINANCE; earnings, finances and management strategies in the petroleum industry. Abbreviated title: I P F. Text in English. 1978. m. USD 1,730 (effective 2009). stat. index. back issues avail. **Document type:** *Newsletter, Trade.* **Description:** Analyzes the management strategies, earnings, and finances of oil and gas companies worldwide. For financial officers and managers, portfolio managers, and energy bankers.
Related titles: E-mail ed.: USD 1,310 (effective 2009); Fax ed.; Online - full text ed.: USD 1,250 (effective 2009).
Indexed: B02, B15, B17, B18, G04, G06, G07, G08, I05, PEBNI, PQC.
—Linda Hall. **CCC.**
Published by: Energy Intelligence Group, Inc., 5 E 37th St, 5th Fl, New York, NY 10016. TEL 212-532-1112, FAX 212-532-4479, info@energyintel.com. Ed. James Bourne.

665.5029 USA
INTERNATIONAL PETROLEUM INDUSTRY. Text in English. a. **Document type:** *Directory, Trade.* **Description:** Supplies company name, address, phone and fax numbers, telex number, division offices, office locations and US office, if known.
Formerly: Oil Directory of Companies Outside the U.S. and Canada (0472-7711)
Published by: Midwest Publishing Company, 2230 E 49th St, Ste E, Tulsa, OK 74105. TEL 800-829-2002, info@midwestpub.com, http://www.midwestpub.com/.

665.5 GBR ISSN 1367-1359
INTERNATIONAL PETROLEUM INDUSTRY ENVIRONMENTAL CONSERVATION ASSOCIATION. REPORT SERIES. Text in English. 1991. irreg.
—BLDSC (4567.302500).
Published by: International Petroleum Industry Environmental Conservation Association, 209-215 Blackfriars Rd, 5th Fl, London, SE1 8NL, United Kingdom. TEL 44-20-76332388, FAX 44-20-76332389, info@ipieca.org, http://www.ipieca.org.

338.27 USA ISSN 1368-9118
INTERNATIONAL RIG REPORT. Text in English. 1993. m. **Document type:** *Newsletter, Trade.* **Description:** Provides monthly reviews and rolling twelve month forecasts of market trends in the floating and jackup rig markets.
Incorporates: International Rig Report; Which was formerly: Petrodata International Rig Report
Related titles: E-mail ed.; Online - full text ed.
Published by: O D S - Petrodata, 3200 Wilcrest Dr, Ste 170, Houston, TX 77042. TEL 832-463-3000, FAX 832-463-3100, general@ods-petrodata.com, http://www.ods-petrodata.com.

665 552 USA ISSN 0145-7594
INTERNATIONAL SCHOOL OF HYDROCARBON MEASUREMENT. PROCEEDINGS. Text in English. 19??. a. free to members (effective 2011). **Document type:** *Proceedings, Academic/Scholarly.* **Description:** Contains all class paper presented at the annual meeting.
Related titles: CD-ROM ed.: free (effective 2011).
Indexed: A22.
—BLDSC (4548.820000), IE, Ingenta.
Published by: International School of Hydrocarbon Measurement, 1700 Asp Ave, Norman, OK 73072. TEL 405-325-1217, FAX 405-325-1388, lcrowley@ou.edu.

665.5 332.6 CAN ISSN 1718-9799
IRADESSO QUARTERLY REPORT. Text in English. 2003. 3/yr. **Document type:** *Newsletter, Trade.* **Description:** Compares financial and operating results of junior oil and gas companies with production between 500 and 15,000 boe/d as well as conventional energy trusts.
Published by: Iradesso Communications, 400, 805 - 10th Ave SW, Calgary, AB T2R 0B4, Canada. TEL 403-503-0144, FAX 403-503-0174, contact@iradesso.com, http://www.iradesso.com/i/home.html.

665 IRN ISSN 0021-079X
IRAN OIL JOURNAL. Text in English. q. free.
Related titles: Persian, Modern ed.: Nameh Sanaat-e-Naft; French ed.: Iran Petrole.
Published by: Petroleum Ministry, Public Relations & Guidance Department, Central NIOC Bldg., Taleghani Ave., P O Box 1863, Teheran, Iran. TEL 021-6151, TELEX 212514. Ed. Yegandokht Mostofian.

665.5 IRN
IRAN OIL NEWS. Text in Persian, Modern. 1984. m. free. **Description:** Promotes a better understanding of the Petroleum Ministry of Iran and its policies, as well as providing analysis of the accomplishments within the industry. Addresses energy issues and international petroleum affairs.
Formerly: Petroleum Newsletter
Published by: Petroleum Ministry, Public Relations & Guidance Department, Central NIOC Bldg., Taleghani Ave., P O Box 1863, Teheran, Iran. TEL 561-997-7733.

338.47661955 GBR ISSN 1749-2289
IRAN PETROCHEMICALS REPORT. Text in English. 2005. q. EUR 820, USD 1,030 combined subscription (print & email eds.) (effective 2010). **Document type:** *Report, Trade.* **Description:** Provides industry professionals and strategists, sector analysts, trade associations and regulatory bodies with independent forecasts and competitive intelligence on the Iranian petrochemicals industry.
Related titles: E-mail ed.
Indexed: A15, ABIn, B02, B15, B17, B18, G04, I05, P48, P51, P52, P56, PQC.
Published by: Business Monitor International Ltd., Senator House, 85 Queen Victoria St, London, EC4V 4AB, United Kingdom. TEL 44-20-72480468, FAX 44-20-72480467, subs@businessmonitor.com.

338.95694 GBR ISSN 1749-2297
ISRAEL PETROCHEMICALS REPORT. Text in English. 2005. q. EUR 820, USD 1,030 combined subscription (print & email eds.) (effective 2010). **Document type:** *Report, Trade.* **Description:** Provides industry professionals and strategists, sector analysts, trade associations and regulatory bodies with independent forecasts and competitive intelligence on the Israeli petrochemicals industry.
Related titles: E-mail ed.
Indexed: A15, ABIn, B02, B15, B17, B18, G04, I05, P48, P51, P52, P56, PQC.
Published by: Business Monitor International Ltd., Senator House, 85 Queen Victoria St, London, EC4V 4AB, United Kingdom. TEL 44-20-72480468, FAX 44-20-72480467, subs@businessmonitor.com.

665.5 RUS
IZOBRETENIYA I RATSPREDLOZHENIYA V NEFTEGAZOVOI PROMYSHLENNOSTI. Text in Russian. q. **Document type:** *Journal.*
Published by: Vserossiiskii Nauchno-Issledovatel'skii Institut Organizatsii Upravleniya i Ekonomiki Neftegazovoi Promyshlennosti (VNIIOENG), Nametkina 14, korp B, Moscow, 117420, Russian Federation. TEL 7-095-3320022, FAX 7-095-3316877, vniioeng@mcn.ru, http://vniioeng.mcn.ru.

665.5 RUS ISSN 0445-0108
TN860 CODEN: IVUNA2
IZVESTIYA VYSSHIKH UCHEBNYKH ZAVEDENII. NEFT' I GAZ. Text in Russian. 1997. bi-m.
Indexed: GeoRef, Inspec, RefZh.
—Linda Hall, PADDS. **CCC.**
Published by: Tyumenskii Gosudarstvennyi Neftegazovyi Universitet, Volodarskogo, 38, Tyumen', 625000, Russian Federation. TEL 7-3452-251155. Ed. N. Karnaukhov.

665.5 USA ISSN 0149-2136
TN860 CODEN: JPTJAM
J P T. (Journal of Petroleum Technology) Text in English. 1949. m. USD 240 combined subscription domestic to non-members (print & online eds.); USD 300 combined subscription foreign to non-members (print & online eds.); free to members (effective 2009). adv. bk.rev. abstr.; bibl.; charts; illus. index, cum.index. back issues avail.; reprints avail. **Document type:** *Journal, Trade.* **Description:** Covers engineering and management of oil and gas drilling, exploration, and production. Includes issues facing the petroleum engineering profession, such as education, manpower, and professionalism.
Formerly (until 1979): Journal of Petroleum Technology (Print); Which was formed by the merger of (1938-1949): Petroleum Technology (0369-9013); (1919-1949): Mining and Metallurgy (0096-7289); Which was formerly (1905-1919): American Institute of Mining and Metallurgical Engineers. Bulletin (0376-1916)
Related titles: Microform ed.: (from PQC); Online - full text ed.: ISSN 1944-978X.
Indexed: A05, A20, A22, A23, A24, AESIS, APIAb, APICat, APIH&E, APIOC, APIPR, APIPS, APITS, AS&TA, AS&TI, ASCA, ASFA, ApMecR, B04, B10, B13, C&ISA, C10, CIN, CIS, CPEI, Cadscan, ChemAb, ChemTitl, E&CAJ, E&PHSE, E04, E05, E14, EIA, ESPM, EnerInd, EnerRev, EngInd, EnvAb, F&EA, FR, GP&P, GasAb, GeoRef, IMMAb, ISR, LeadAb, OceAb, OffTech, PetrolAb, PollutAb, RefZh, SCOPUS, SolStAb, SpeleolAb, Zincscan.
—CASDDS, IE, Infotrieve, Ingenta, INIST, Linda Hall, PADDS. **CCC.**
Published by: Society of Petroleum Engineers, Inc., 10777 Westheimer Rd, Ste 335, Houston, Dallas, TX 77042. TEL 713-779-9595, FAX 713-779-4216, spedal@spe.org. Ed. John Donnelly. Adv. contact Jim Klingele TEL 713-779-9595 ext 612. B&W page USD 6,045, color page USD 7,795; trim 206.375 x 276.225. Circ: 60,058 (paid and controlled).

665.5 USA ISSN 1098-5255
JACK STEVENSON'S TRANSACTIONS IN OIL & GAS. Text in English. 1997. m. USD 497 (effective 2000); includes 2 fax updates. adv. back issues avail. **Document type:** *Newsletter.* **Description:** Provides business information on transactions of the upstream, midstream and oilfield supply and service sectors of the oil and gas industry. Includes buying and selling of production, product lines, related companies, financing efforts for these companies, alliances and joint ventures.
Related titles: Diskette ed.
Published by: Tamarack Consulting Co., PO Box 571207, Houston, TX 77257. TEL 713-683-6688, FAX 713-683-9683. Ed., Pub. Jack Stevenson. Adv. contact J Stevenson. page USD 2,000.

665.7 628.1 DEU ISSN 1869-9731
JAHRBUCH GAS UND WASSER. BAND 1: ENERGIE- UND WASSERVERSORGUNGSUNTERNEHMEN, VERBAENDE UND VEREINE, ORGANISATIONEN. Text in German. 1954. biennial. EUR 220 base vol(s). (effective 2011). **Document type:** *Handbook/ Manual/Guide, Trade.*
Supersedes in part (in 2010): Jahrbuch Gas und Wasser (0342-8192); Which was formerly (until 1977): Taschenbuch fuer das Gas- und Wasserfach. 1. Teil: Jahrbuch Gas und Wasser (0342-846X)
—CCC.
Published by: Oldenbourg Industrieverlag GmbH (Subsidiary of: Oldenbourg Wissenschaftsverlag GmbH), Rosenheimer Str 145, Munich, 81671, Germany. TEL 49-89-450510, FAX 49-89-45051207, oiv-info@oldenbourg.de, http://www.oldenbourg-industrieverlag.de.

665.5 628.1 DEU ISSN 1869-974X
JAHRBUCH GAS UND WASSER. BAND 2: BRANCHENFUEHRER LEITUNGS- UND ANLAGENBAU. Text in German. 1954. biennial. EUR 220 base vol(s). (effective 2011). **Document type:** *Handbook/ Manual/Guide, Trade.*
Supersedes in part (in 2010): Jahrbuch Gas und Wasser (0342-8192); Which was formerly (until 1977): Taschenbuch fuer das Gas- und Wasserfach. 1. Teil: Jahrbuch Gas und Wasser (0342-846X)
—CCC.
Published by: Oldenbourg Industrieverlag GmbH (Subsidiary of: Oldenbourg Wissenschaftsverlag GmbH), Rosenheimer Str 145, Munich, 81671, Germany. TEL 49-89-450510, FAX 49-89-45051207, oiv-info@oldenbourg.de, http://www.oldenbourg-industrieverlag.de.

338.4766180409 GBR ISSN 1749-2300
JAPAN PETROCHEMICALS REPORT. Text in English. 2005. a. EUR 820, USD 1,030 combined subscription per issue (print & email eds.) (effective 2010). **Document type:** *Report, Trade.* **Description:** Provides industry professionals and strategists, sector analysts, trade associations and regulatory bodies with independent forecasts and competitive intelligence on the Japanese petrochemicals industry.
Related titles: E-mail ed.
Indexed: A15, ABIn, B02, B15, B17, B18, G04, I05, P48, P51, P52, P56, PQC.
Published by: Business Monitor International Ltd., Senator House, 85 Queen Victoria St, London, EC4V 4AB, United Kingdom. TEL 44-20-72480468, FAX 44-20-72480467, subs@businessmonitor.com.

665.5 JPN ISSN 0916-2623
JAPAN PETROLEUM AND ENERGY TRENDS. Text in English. 1966. m. looseleaf. JPY 180,000 (effective 2000). mkt.; stat. index. Supplement avail. **Document type:** *Newsletter, Trade.* **Description:** Covers petroleum and energy related news in Japan. Includes feature articles on energy supply and demand, as well as major government and corporate decisions which will impact Japan's overall energy market.
Former titles: Japan Petroleum and Energy Weekly; Japan Petroleum Weekly (0386-6165)
Published by: Japan Petroleum and Energy Consultants, Ltd./Nihon Sekiyu Konsarutanto K.K., P.O. Box 1185, Tokyo Central, Tokyo, 100-8693, Japan. TEL 81-42-570-0231, FAX 81-42-570-0232, kurokawa@japec.com, http://www.japec.com. Ed., Pub. Kurokawa Kiyotaka. Circ: 1,200.

665.5 JPN ISSN 1346-8804
TP690.A1 CODEN: JJPIAP
➤ **THE JAPAN PETROLEUM INSTITUTE. JOURNAL.** Text in English, Japanese. 1958. bi-m. free to members; complimentary copies to domestic and foreign universities, public research institute and the like. back issues avail. **Document type:** *Journal, Academic/Scholarly.* **Description:** Contains scientific and technical papers contributed by members, in either Japanese or English, and notes, and reports from various divisions of the Institute.
Formerly (until 2001): Sekiyu Gakkaishi (0582-4664)
Related titles: Online - full text ed.: ISSN 1349-273X. free (effective 2011).
Indexed: A22, A39, APIAb, C27, C29, C33, ChemAb, ChemTitl, CurCont, D03, D04, E13, FR, PetrolAb, R14, RefZh, S14, S15, S18, SCI, SCOPUS, W07.
—BLDSC (4805.700000), CASDDS, IE, Ingenta, INIST, Linda Hall, PADDS. **CCC.**
Published by: Japan Petroleum Institute/Sekiyu Gakkai, COSMO Hirakawa-cho Bldg, 1-3-14 Hirakawa-cho, Chiyoda-ku, Tokyo, 102-0093, Japan. TEL 81-3-32217301, FAX 81-3-32218175. Ed. Seitaro Namba. Circ: 1,350. **Subscr. to:** Maruzen Co., Ltd., 3-10 Nihonbashi, 2-Chome, Chuo-ku, Tokyo 103, Japan.

➤ **JET FUEL INTELLIGENCE.** *see* TRANSPORTATION—Air Transport

665.5 CHN ISSN 1009-301X
JIANGHAN SHIYOU ZHIGONG DAXUE XUEBAO/JIANGHAN PETROLEUM UNIVERSITY OF STAFF AND WORKERS. JOURNAL. Text in Chinese. 1988. bi-m. CNY 6 newsstand/cover (effective 2006). **Document type:** *Journal, Academic/Scholarly.*
Related titles: Online - full text ed.
Published by: Jianghan Shiyou Zhigong Daxue, Yi-cun, Qianjiang, 433121, China.

665.53 CHN ISSN 1003-9384
TP690.A1
JINGXI SHIYOU HUAGONG/SPECIALTY PETROCHEMICALS. Text in Chinese. 1984. bi-m. USD 24.60 (effective 2009). **Description:** Reports on new developments in research, advances of production and application, market trends relating to oil chemicals, daily necessary chemicals, dyeing and finishing auxiliaries, catalysts, adhesives, surfactants, detergent, and more.
Related titles: Online - full text ed.
Indexed: A28, APA, APIAb, BrCerAb, C&ISA, CA/WCA, CIA, CerAb, CivEngAb, CorrAb, E&CAJ, E11, EEA, EMA, ESPM, EnvEAb, FLUIDEX, H15, M&TEA, M09, MBF, METADEX, SCOPUS, SolStAb, T04, WAA.
—East View, Linda Hall.
Published by: Zhongguo Shiyou Huagong Zonggongsi/SINOPEC, Specialty Petrochemical S & T Information Center, Shanggulin Dagang-qu, Tianjin 300271, China. TEL 86-22-7356622. Ed. Qian Xu. **Dist. overseas by:** China International Book Trading Corp, 35 Chegongzhuang Xilu, Haidian District, PO Box 399, Beijing 100044, China.

665.5 CHN ISSN 1009-8348
JINGXI SHIYOU HUAGONG JINZHAN/ADVANCES IN FINE PETROCHEMICALS. Text in Chinese. 1986. m. **Document type:** *Journal, Academic/Scholarly.*
Formerly (until 2000): Jingxi Shiyou Huagong Wenzhai
Related titles: Online - full text ed.: (from WanFang Data Corp.).
—BLDSC (4669.038755), East View.
Published by: Zhongguo Shiyou Huagong Gufen Youxian Gongsi Jinling Fengongsi/Jinling Petrochemical Corporation, S I N O P E C, Ganjixiang, Qixia District, Nanjing, 210033, China. TEL 86-25-58985645, FAX 86-25-58985645.

665.5 CAN ISSN 0021-9487
TN860 CODEN: JCPMAM
JOURNAL OF CANADIAN PETROLEUM TECHNOLOGY. Text in English. 1962. 10/yr. CAD 140 domestic; USD 160 foreign (effective 2004). adv. bk.rev. abstr.; bibl.; charts; illus.; tr.lit. index. **Document type:** *Journal, Trade.* **Description:** Contains news and technical information of specific interest to the petroleum, oil and gas industries.
Related titles: CD-ROM ed.
Indexed: A22, AESIS, APIAb, APICat, APIH&E, APIOC, APIPR, APIPS, APITS, ASCA, CADCAM, CIN, CPEI, ChemAb, ChemTitl, CurCont, E&PHSE, E04, E05, EIA, EngInd, EnvAb, F&EA, FR, GP&P, GasAb, GeoRef, MSCI, OffTech, PetrolAb, SCI, SCOPUS, SpeleolAb, W07.
—BLDSC (4954.750000), CASDDS, IE, Infotrieve, Ingenta, INIST, Linda Hall, PADDS. **CCC.**
Published by: Canadian Institute of Mining, Metallurgy and Petroleum, 3400 de Maisonneuve Blvd W, Ste 1210, Montreal, PQ H3Z 3B8, Canada. TEL 514-939-2710, FAX 514-939-2714, cim@cim.org, http://www.cim.org. Ed., Adv. contact Catherine Buchanan. Circ: 5,800.

JOURNAL OF LIPID SCIENCE AND TECHNOLOGY. *see* CHEMISTRY—Organic Chemistry

665.7 547 USA ISSN 1003-9953
TP492.82.H93 CODEN: JGCHE8
JOURNAL OF NATURAL GAS CHEMISTRY. Abbreviated title: J N G C. Text in English. 1992. bi-m. EUR 410 in Europe to institutions; JPY 59,600 in Japan to institutions; USD 522 elsewhere to institutions (effective 2012). adv. back issues avail.; reprints avail. **Document type:** *Journal, Academic/Scholarly.* **Description:** Features as a medium for reporting research papers dealing with topics in the fields of natural gas chemistry, C1 chemistry, lower hydrocarbons chemistry as well as hydrogen energy sources.
Related titles: Online - full text ed.: (from ScienceDirect).
Indexed: A28, APA, APIAb, BrCerAb, C&ISA, C33, CA, CA/WCA, CCI, CIA, CIN, CPEI, CerAb, ChemAb, ChemTitl, CivEngAb, CorrAb, E&CAJ, E11, EEA, EMA, ESPM, EngInd, EnvEAb, GeoRef, H15, M&TEA, M09, MBF, METADEX, PetrolAb, RefZh, SCI, SCOPUS, SolStAb, T02, T04, W07, WAA.
—BLDSC (5021.196100), CASDDS, East View, IE, Ingenta, INIST, Linda Hall, PADDS. **CCC.**
Published by: (Chinese Academy of Sciences, Dalian Institute of Chemical Physics CHN), Elsevier Inc. (Subsidiary of: Elsevier Science & Technology), 1600 John F Kennedy Blvd, Philadelphia, PA 19103. TEL 215-239-3900, FAX 215-238-7883, JournalCustomerService-usa@elsevier.com, http://www.elsevier.com. Eds. Alexis T Bell, Xinhe Bao. Adv. contact Janine Castle TEL 44-1865-843844.

665.7 USA ISSN 1875-5100
TN880.A1
▼ **JOURNAL OF NATURAL GAS SCIENCE & ENGINEERING.** Text in English. 2009. bi-m. EUR 622 in Europe to institutions; JPY 79,900 in Japan to institutions; USD 698 elsewhere to institutions (effective 2012). adv. back issues avail.; reprints avail. **Document type:** *Journal, Academic/Scholarly.* **Description:** Covers fields of natural gas exploration, production, processing and transmission in its possible sense. Contains topics such as origin and accumulation of natural gas and natural gas geochemistry etc.
Related titles: Online - full text ed.: (from ScienceDirect).
Indexed: CPEI, SCOPUS, T02.
—IE, PADDS. **CCC.**
Published by: Elsevier Inc. (Subsidiary of: Elsevier Science & Technology), 1600 John F Kennedy Blvd, Philadelphia, PA 19103. TEL 215-239-3900, FAX 215-238-7883, JournalCustomerService-usa@elsevier.com. Ed. M J Economides TEL 713-647-0903. Adv. contact Janine Castle TEL 44-1865-843844.

665.5 NGA
➤ **JOURNAL OF PETROLEUM AND GAS ENGINEERING.** Text in English. m. free (effective 2010). adv. **Document type:** *Journal, Academic/Scholarly.*
Media: Online - full text.
Published by: Academic Journals, PO Box 73023, Victoria Island, Lagos, Nigeria. service@academicjournals.org. Eds. Dr. Amir H Jalili, Dr. Chuanbo Shen, Dr. Salima Baraka-Lokmane.

665.5 DEU ISSN 2190-0558
▼ ➤ **JOURNAL OF PETROLEUM EXPLORATION AND PRODUCTION TECHNOLOGY.** Text in English. 2011. q. free (effective 2011). **Document type:** *Journal, Academic/Scholarly.*
Related titles: Online - full text ed.: ISSN 2190-0566. 2011.
Published by: SpringerOpen (Subsidiary of: Springer Science+Business Media), Tiergartenstr 17, Heidelberg, 69121, Germany. info@springeropen.com, http://www.springeropen.com. Eds. Tariq Alkhalifah, Turgay Ertekin.

665.5 GBR ISSN 0141-6421
TN870.5 CODEN: JPEGD9
➤ **JOURNAL OF PETROLEUM GEOLOGY.** Abbreviated title: J P G. Text in English. 1978. q. GBP 400 combined subscription in United Kingdom to institutions (print & online eds.); EUR 508 combined subscription in Europe to institutions (print & online eds.); USD 745 combined subscription in the Americas to institutions (print & online eds.); USD 869 combined subscription elsewhere to institutions (print & online eds.) (effective 2012). adv. bk.rev. illus. Index. back issues avail.; reprint service avail. from PSC. **Document type:** *Journal, Academic/Scholarly.* **Description:** Presents papers on oilfield regions of the world outside North America and on topics of general application in petroleum exploration and development operations, including geochemical and geophysical studies, basin modelling and reservoir evaluation.
Related titles: CD-ROM ed.; Online - full text ed.: ISSN 1747-5457. GBP 350 in United Kingdom to institutions; EUR 446 in Europe to institutions; USD 669 in the Americas to institutions; USD 758 elsewhere to institutions (effective 2012) (from IngentaConnect).
Indexed: A01, A22, A26, AESIS, ASCA, ASFA, BrGeoL, CA, CIN, CPEI, ChemAb, ChemTitl, CurCont, E&PHSE, E01, E14, EngInd, GEOBASE, GP&P, GeoRef, I05, ISR, MinerAb, OceAb, OffTech, PetrolAb, RefZh, SCI, SCOPUS, SpeleolAb, T02, W07.
—BLDSC (5030.990000), CASDDS, IE, Infotrieve, Ingenta, Linda Hall, PADDS. **CCC.**
Published by: (Scientific Press Ltd.), Wiley-Blackwell Publishing Ltd. (Subsidiary of: John Wiley & Sons, Inc.), 9600 Garsington Rd, Oxford, OX4 2DQ, United Kingdom. TEL 44-1865-776868, FAX 44-1865-714591, customerservices@blackwellpublishing.com, http://www.wiley.com/. Ed. Christopher Tiratsoo TEL 44-1494-675139. Adv. contact Craig Pickett TEL 44-1865-476267.

665.5 NLD ISSN 0920-4105
TN860 CODEN: JPSEE6
➤ **JOURNAL OF PETROLEUM SCIENCE AND ENGINEERING.** Text in English. 1987. 20/yr. EUR 2,145 in Europe to institutions; JPY 284,600 in Japan to institutions; USD 2,398 elsewhere to institutions (effective 2012). adv. bk.rev. charts; illus.; stat.; abstr. back issues avail. **Document type:** *Journal, Academic/Scholarly.* **Description:** Covers the fields of petroleum geology, exploration and engineering.
Related titles: Microform ed.: (from PQC); Online - full text ed.: ISSN 1873-4715 (from IngentaConnect, ScienceDirect).
Indexed: A01, A03, A08, A22, A26, AESIS, APIAb, ASCA, C&ISA, C33, CA, CIN, CPEI, ChemAb, ChemTitl, CurCont, E&CAJ, E&PHSE, E14, EngInd, FLUIDEX, GEOBASE, GP&P, GeoRef, I05, ISMEC, ISR, OffTech, PetrolAb, RefZh, S01, SCI, SCOPUS, SolStAb, SpeleolAb, T02, W07.
—BLDSC (5030.998000), CASDDS, IE, Infotrieve, Ingenta, INIST, Linda Hall, PADDS. **CCC.**
Published by: Elsevier BV (Subsidiary of: Elsevier Science & Technology), Radarweg 29, PO Box 211, Amsterdam, 1000 AE, Netherlands. TEL 31-20-4853911, FAX 31-20-4852457, JournalsCustomerServiceEMEA@elsevier.com, http://www.elsevier.nl. Ed. B Dindoruk.

665.5 NGA
➤ **JOURNAL OF PETROLEUM TECHNOLOGY AND ALTERNATIVE FUELS.** Text in English. m. free (effective 2010). adv. **Document type:** *Journal, Academic/Scholarly.*
Media: Online - full text.
Published by: Academic Journals, PO Box 73023, Victoria Island, Lagos, Nigeria. service@academicjournals.org.

665.54 GBR ISSN 1753-2116
THE JOURNAL OF PIPELINE ENGINEERING. Text in English. 2002. q. USD 350 to non-members; USD 175 to members (effective 2010). back issues avail. **Document type:** *Journal, Academic/Scholarly.* **Description:** Covers all aspects of engineering for oil, gas, and products pipelines.
Formerly (until 2007): Journal of Pipeline Integrity (1475-4584)
Indexed: A28, APA, B01, B07, BrCerAb, C&ISA, CA, CA/WCA, CIA, CerAb, CivEngAb, CorrAb, E&CAJ, E11, E14, EEA, EMA, ESPM, EnvEAb, H15, M&TEA, M09, MBF, METADEX, PetrolAb, SolStAb, T02, T04, WAA.
—BLDSC (5040.329250), IE, PADDS. **CCC.**

P

Published by: Scientific Surveys Ltd., PO Box 21, Beaconsfield, Bucks HP9 1NS, United Kingdom. TEL 44-1494-675139, FAX 44-1494-670155, info@scientificsurveys.com, http://www.scientificsurveys.com/. Ed. John Tiratsoo TEL 44-1494-675139. **Co-publisher:** Clarion Technical Conferences.

665.538 USA ISSN 0742-4787
TJ1075.A2 CODEN: JOTRE9
➤ **JOURNAL OF TRIBOLOGY.** Text in English. 1880. q. USD 382 combined subscription in US & Canada to non-members (print & online eds.); USD 428 combined subscription elsewhere to non-members (print & online eds.); USD 50 combined subscription domestic to members (print & online eds.); USD 96 combined subscription foreign to members (print & online eds.) (effective 2011). bk.rev. charts; illus. index. back issues avail.; reprints avail. **Document type:** *Journal, Academic/Scholarly.* **Description:** Features a mix of experimental, numerical, and theoretical articles dealing with all aspects of the field, including friction and weather, fluid film lubrication, tribological systems, seals, bearing design and technology, gears, metalworking, lubricants and artificial joints.
Formerly (until 1984): Journal of Lubrication Technology (0022-2305); Which superseded in part (in 1967): American Society of Mechanical Engineers. Transactions (0097-6822); Which incorporated: Record and Index
Related titles: Online - full text ed.: ISSN 1528-8897. USD 43 to members (effective 2011).
Indexed: A05, A22, A23, A24, A26, A28, APA, APIAb, APICat, APIH&E, APIOC, APIPR, APIPS, APITS, AS&TA, AS&TI, ASCA, ApMecR, B13, BrCerAb, BrRB, C&ISA, C10, CA, CA/WCA, CIA, CMCI, CPEI, CerAb, ChemAb, CivEngAb, CorrAb, CurCont, E&CAJ, E08, E11, EEA, EMA, ESPM, EngInd, EnvEAb, FLUIDEX, G08, H15, I05, ISMEC, ISR, Inspec, M&TEA, M09, MBF, METADEX, MSCI, P30, RefZh, S&VD, S09, SCI, SCOPUS, SolStAb, T02, T04, TM, W07, WAA.
—BLDSC (8897.070000), AskIEEE, CASDDS, IE, Infotrieve, Ingenta, INIST, Linda Hall. **CCC.**
Published by: A S M E International, Three Park Ave, New York, NY 10016. TEL 973-882-1170, 800-843-2763, FAX 973-882-1717, infocentral@asme.org, http://www.asme.org. Ed. Michael D Bryant TEL 512-471-4870. **Subscr. to:** PO Box 2900, Fairfield, NJ 07007.

665.7 JPN ISSN 0914-496X
KANREICHI GIJUTSU KENKYU KAIHATSU SENTA HOKOKU/ RESEARCH CENTER FOR GAS INDUSTRY IN COLD DISTRICT. TECHNICAL REPORT. Text in Japanese. 1980. a.
Published by: (Kanreichi Gijutsu Kenkyu Kaihatsu Senta), Nihon Gasu Kyokai, Hokkaido Bukai/Japan Gas Association, Hokkaido Branch, Research Center for Gas Industry in Cold District, Higashi 5-chome, Kita 3-jo, Chuo-ku, Sapporo-shi, Hokkaido 060, Japan.

665.5 USA
KANSAS OIL MARKETER. Text in English. 1920. 6/yr. USD 35 to non-members.
Published by: Petroleum Market and Convenient Store Association of Kansas, P O Box 8479, Topeka, KS 66608-0479. TEL 913-233-9655, FAX 913-354-4374. Ed. Dennis Anderson. Circ: 700.

KARBO. *see* MINES AND MINING INDUSTRY

665.53 UKR
TP690.A1 CODEN: NEFNBY
KATALIZ I NEFTEKHIMIYA. Text in English, Russian, Ukrainian. 1965. s-a. USD 65.
Formerly: Neftepererabotka i Neftekhimiya (0548-1406)
Indexed: CIN, ChemAb, ChemTitl.
—CASDDS, INIST, Linda Hall. **CCC.**
Published by: Natsional'na Akademiya Nauk Ukrainy, Instytut Bioorhanichnoi Khimii i Naftokhimii, Ul Murmanskaya 1, Kiev, Ukraine. TEL 044-5732556. Ed. V T Sklyar. **Dist. by:** East View Information Services, 10601 Wayzata Blvd, Minneapolis, MN 55305. TEL 952-252-1201, 800-477-1005, FAX 952-252-1202, info@eastview.com, http://www.eastview.com.

665.5 GBR
KAZAKHSTAN ENERGY MONTHLY. Text in English. 200?. m. GBP 120 (effective 2009). **Document type:** *Newsletter, Trade.* **Description:** Features surveys the oil, gas, coal and electricity industries of Kazakhstan, with sections on Companies, Exploration, Production, Transportation, Refining, Trade, Consumption, Electricity, Engineering and Politics.
Related titles: Online - full content ed.
Published by: Eastern Bloc Research Ltd., Tolsta Chaolais, Isle of Lewis, HS2 9DW, United Kingdom. TEL 44-1851-621315, mail@easternblocenergy.com.

338.47665 658 GBR
KEY NOTE MARKET ASSESSMENT. FORECOURT RETAILING. Variant title: Forecourt Retailing Market Assessment. Text in English. 1997. irreg., latest 2010, Jan. GBP 899 per issue (effective 2010). **Document type:** *Report, Trade.* **Description:** Provides an in-depth strategic analysis across a broad range of industries and contains an examination on the scope, dynamics and shape of key UK markets in the consumer, financial, lifestyle and business to business sectors.
Formerly (until 2002): Key Note Market Report. Petrol Forecourt Retailing (1460-7557); Which superseded in part (in 2000): Key Note Market Report: C T Ns
Published by: Key Note Ltd. (Subsidiary of: Bonnier Business Information), Harlequin House, 5th Fl, 7 High St, Teddington, Richmond upon Thames, TW11 8EE, United Kingdom. TEL 44-845-5040452, FAX 44-845-5040453, info@keynote.co.uk.

KEY NOTE MARKET ASSESSMENT. THE EUROPEAN GAS INDUSTRY. *see* BUSINESS AND ECONOMICS—Production Of Goods And Services

KEY NOTE MARKET ASSESSMENT. THE EUROPEAN OIL AND GAS INDUSTRY. *see* BUSINESS AND ECONOMICS—Production Of Goods And Services

KEY NOTE MARKET REPORT: THE GAS INDUSTRY. *see* BUSINESS AND ECONOMICS—Production Of Goods And Services

665.5 GBR ISSN 1475-0457
KEY NOTE MARKET REPORT: THE OFFSHORE OIL & GAS INDUSTRY. Variant title: The Offshore Oil & Gas Industry. Text in English. 2000. irreg., latest 2009, Dec. GBP 460 per issue (effective 2010). **Document type:** *Report, Trade.* **Description:** Provides an overview of a specific UK market segment and includes executive summary, market definition, market size, industry background, competitor analysis, current issues, forecasts, company profiles, and more.
Supersedes in part (in 2001): Key Note Market Report: The Oil & Gas Industry (1471-941X)
Published by: Key Note Ltd. (Subsidiary of: Bonnier Business Information), Harlequin House, 5th Fl, 7 High St, Teddington, Richmond upon Thames, TW11 8EE, United Kingdom. TEL 44-845-5040452, FAX 44-845-5040453, info@keynote.co.uk.

KHIMICHESKOE I NEFTEGAZOVOE MASHINOSTROENIE/CHEMICAL AND OIL INDUSTRY. *see* ENGINEERING—Chemical Engineering

665.5 662 RUS ISSN 0023-1169
TP315 CODEN: KTPMAG
KHIMIYA I TEKHNOLOGIYA TOPLIV I MASEL. Text in Russian. 1956. bi-m. USD 298 foreign (effective 2005). bibl.; charts; illus. index. **Document type:** *Journal, Trade.* **Description:** Covers theoretical basis and methods of oil refining, economics, ecology, methods of analysis, related equipment.
Related titles: ◆ English Translation: Chemistry and Technology of Fuels and Oils. ISSN 0009-3092.
Indexed: A22, C&ISA, CEABA, ChemAb, ChemTitl, CorrAb, E&CAJ, FR, GeoRef, RefZh, SCOPUS, SolStAb, SpeleolAb, WAA.
—BLDSC (0394.000000), CASDDS, East View, IE, Infotrieve, INIST, Linda Hall. **CCC.**
Published by: Izdatel'stvo Neft' i Gaz, Leninskii pr-t 65, korp 2, etazh 7-I, Moscow, 117917, Russian Federation. TEL 7-095-1358406, FAX 7-095-1357416. Ed. V G Starikov. Circ: 3,270. **Dist. by:** East View Information Services, 10601 Wayzata Blvd, Minneapolis, MN 55305. TEL 952-252-1201, 800-477-1005, FAX 952-252-1202, info@eastview.com, http://www.eastview.com.

665.5 KWT ISSN 0304-7237
HD9576.K84
KUWAIT NATIONAL PETROLEUM COMPANY. ANNUAL REPORT. Text in English. 1963. a. **Document type:** *Corporate.*
Published by: Kuwait National Petroleum Company K.S.C., P O Box 70, Safat, 13001, Kuwait. TEL 965-2420121, FAX 965-2433839. Ed. Ahmad Abd Al Muhsin Al Mutair.

661.804 338.47665 953.67 GBR ISSN 1749-2319
KUWAIT PETROCHEMICALS REPORT. Text in English. 2005. q. EUR 820, USD 1,030 combined subscription (print & email eds.) (effective 2010). **Document type:** *Report, Trade.* **Description:** Provides industry professionals and strategists, sector analysts, trade associations and regulatory bodies with independent forecasts and competitive intelligence on the Kuwaiti petrochemicals industry.
Related titles: E-mail ed.
Indexed: A15, ABIn, B02, B15, B17, B18, G04, I05, P48, P51, P52, P56, PQC.
Published by: Business Monitor International Ltd., Senator House, 85 Queen Victoria St, London, EC4V 4AB, United Kingdom. TEL 44-20-72480468, FAX 44-20-72480467, subs@businessmonitor.com.

665.5 KWT ISSN 0023-5792
AL-KUWAITI. Text in Arabic. 1961. m. free. film rev.; play rev. illus.; tr.lit. **Document type:** *Trade.* **Description:** Articles on economics, energy, oil industry and science.
Published by: Kuwait Oil Company (K.S.C.), Supdt. Press Relations and Publications Division, P O Box 9758, Ahmadi, 61008, Kuwait. TEL 965-3989111, FAX 965-3983661, TELEX 44211 KUOCO. Ed. Ali H Murad. Circ: 6,500.

665.7 GBR ISSN 1759-233X
L N G BUSINESS REVIEW; global perspectives for LNG managers. (Liquified Natural Gas) Text in English. 2004. 10/yr. GBP 990 (effective 2010). adv. back issues avail. **Document type:** *Newsletter, Trade.* **Description:** Delivers the inside view on global LNG market trends and developments.
Formerly (until 2008): L N G Focus (1745-3372)
Related titles: Online - full text ed.: ISSN 1759-2348.
Published by: Gas Strategies Group Ltd, 35 New Bridge St, London, EC4V 6BW, United Kingdom. TEL 44-20-73329981, FAX 44-20-73329901.

665.7 USA ISSN 0276-5918
L N G DIGEST. (Liquefied Natural Gas) Text in English. m. USD 775 in US & Canada; USD 800 elsewhere (effective 2005).
—CCC.
Published by: Energy Research Associates, PO Box 1516, Wall Street Sta, New York, NY 10005. TEL 718-338-5384, FAX 718-951-0090, info@globalgastrade.com.

L N G INDUSTRY. (Liquified Natural Gas) *see* ENERGY

L N G JOURNAL. (Liquified Natural Gas) *see* ENERGY

L N G WORLD SHIPPING. (Liquefied Natural Gas) *see* TRANSPORTATION—Ships And Shipping

338.47665 GBR ISSN 1364-3711
L P G WORLD; news, prices and analysis. (Liquefied Petroleum Gas) Variant title: Argus L P G World. Text in English. 1995. s-m. **Document type:** *Newsletter, Trade.* **Description:** Provides in-depth analyses on the international LPG markets, including prices from all over the world, shipping, news and special supplements.
Related titles: Online - full text ed.
Indexed: A26, B02, B03, B15, B17, B18, G04, G06, G07, G08, I05, T03.
Published by: Argus Media Ltd., Argus House, 175 St. John St, London, EC1V 4LW, United Kingdom. TEL 44-20-77804200, FAX 44-20-77804201, enquiries@argusmedia.com, http://www.argusmedia.com. Ed. Ian Bourne. Pub. Adrian Binks.

L P G WORLD SHIPPING. (Liquid Petroleum Gas) *see* TRANSPORTATION—Ships And Shipping

665.7 USA ISSN 0024-7103
L P - GAS. Text in English. 1940. m. USD 33 domestic; USD 44 in Canada & Mexico; USD 110 elsewhere; free to qualified personnel (effective 2009). adv. illus.; stat.; tr.lit. Supplement avail.; back issues avail.; reprints avail. **Document type:** *Magazine, Trade.* **Description:** Covers propane retail industry with articles on gas production, storage, utilization and marketing.
Related titles: Microform ed.: (from PQC); Online - full text ed.
Indexed: A09, A10, A15, A22, ABIn, B01, B02, B03, B06, B07, B08, B09, B11, B15, B16, B17, B18, C12, E14, G04, G06, G07, G08, GasAb, I05, M01, M02, P10, P48, P51, P52, P53, P54, P56, PQC, T02, T03, V03, V04.
—IE, Infotrieve, Linda Hall. **CCC.**
Published by: Questex Media Group Inc., 600 Superior Ave E, Ste 1100, Cleveland, OH 44114. TEL 847-763-9594, FAX 847-763-9694, http://www.questex.com. Ed. Pat Hyland TEL 216-706-3724. Pub. Brian Kanaba TEL 216-706-3745. adv.: B&W page USD 4,600, color page USD 6,600; 7 x 8.25. Circ: 15,226 (paid and controlled).

665.5 USA ISSN 1937-9374
TP761.L5
L P-GAS CODE HANDBOOK. (Liquefied Petroleum-Gas Code Handbook) Text in English. 19??. irreg. **Document type:** *Handbook/ Manual/Guide, Trade.*
Published by: National Fire Protection Association, 1 Batterymarch Park, Quincy, MA 02169. TEL 617-770-3000, FAX 617-770-0700, http://www.nfpa.org.

665.5 USA ISSN 0023-7418
HD9560.1
THE LAMP. Text in English. 1918. q. free (effective 2009). adv. illus. cum.index every 3 yrs. back issues avail. **Document type:** *Corporate.*
Related titles: Online - full text ed.
Indexed: A22, ChemAb, EnvAb, GeoRef, IFP, P06, PAIS, SpeleolAb.
—BLDSC (5145.000000), Ingenta, Linda Hall.
Published by: Exxon - Mobil Corporation, 5959 Las Colinas Blvd, Irving, TX 75039. TEL 972-444-1000. Ed. Bob Davis.

665.5 USA ISSN 1043-7312
LAND RIG NEWSLETTER. Text in English. 1978. m. USD 250 (effective 2005); subscr. includes q. summary. **Document type:** *Newsletter, Trade.* **Description:** Provides market intelligence for the onshore drilling industry and includes business news on emerging onshore drilling markets, financial reports on acquisitions, rig sales, and company performance.
Published by: R J M Communications, PO Box 6645, Lubbock, TX 79493-6645. TEL 806-741-1531, FAX 806-741-1553. Ed., Pub. Richard Mason.

665.5 USA ISSN 0457-088X
HD9561
LANDMAN. Text in English. 1955. bi-m. free to members (effective 2005). adv. **Document type:** *Magazine, Trade.* **Description:** Covers oil and gas exploration, land management and local association news.
Indexed: GeoRef, SpeleolAb.
—Ingenta.
Published by: American Association of Professional Landmen, 4100 Fossil Creek Blvd, Fort Worth, TX 76137-2791. TEL 817-847-7700. Ed. Le'ann Pembroke Callihan. adv.: B&W page USD 520, color page USD 1,720. Circ: 10,000 (controlled).

665.5 CHN ISSN 1671-4067
LANZHOU SHIHUA ZHIYE JISHU XUEYUAN XUEBAO/LANZHOU PETROCHEMICAL COLLEGE OF TECHNOLOGY. JOURNAL. Text in Chinese. 1986. q. **Document type:** *Journal, Academic/Scholarly.*
Related titles: Online - full text ed.
Published by: Lanzhou Shihua Zhiye Jishu Xueyuan, Xigu-qu Shanzhoudan #1, Lanzhou, 730060, China. TEL 86-931-7941259, FAX 86-931-7556069.

LATAM ENERGY; news, prices and analysis from Latin America and the Caribbean. *see* ENERGY

LATIN AMERICAN POWER WATCH. *see* ENERGY—Electrical Energy

665.5 USA ISSN 1931-1923
LATIN AMERICAN WIRE. Text in English. 1995. d. USD 6,140; USD 6,295 combined subscription (online & E-mail eds.) (effective 2008). back issues avail. **Document type:** *Newsletter, Trade.* **Description:** Provides comprehensive coverage of the Latin crude and Caribbean markets with news, in-depth analyses and commentary on the Latin crude and products markets.
Media: Online - full content. **Related titles:** E-mail ed.
—CCC.
Published by: Platts (Subsidiary of: McGraw-Hill Companies, Inc.), 1200 G St NW, Ste 1000, Washington, DC 20005. TEL 212-904-3070, 800-752-8878, FAX 202-383-2024, support@platts.com.

665.5 VEN
LATINPETROLEUM MAGAZINE. Text in English. 199?. m. USD 99 to individuals (effective 2007). adv. **Document type:** *Magazine, Trade.*
Formerly (until 2005): LatAm Energy Journal
Media: Online - full content.
Published by: Editores Latin Petroleum, C.A., Avenida Mis Encantos, Edificio Victoria, CP 1060, Caracas, Venezuela. TEL 58-212-2675837, FAX 58-416-4038945, support@latinpetroleum.com.

665.7 USA ISSN 0887-6746
TP345.A1 CODEN: PLRCEX
LAURENCE REID GAS CONDITIONING CONFERENCE. PROCEEDINGS. Text in English. 195?. a. USD 50 (effective 2005).
Formerly (until 1985): University of Oklahoma. Gas Conditioning Conference. Proceedings (0474-067X)
—BLDSC (6847.250200), IE, Ingenta.
Published by: (Laurence Reid Gas Conditioning Conference), University of Oklahoma Outreach, c/o Betty Kettman, Engineering & Geosciences, 1610 Asp Ave, Rm 610, Norman, OK 73072-6400. TEL 405-325-3136, FAX 405-325-7329, bettyk@ou.edu.

665.5 USA
LAW OF FEDERAL OIL AND GAS LEASES. Text in English. 1963. 2 base vols. plus irreg. updates. looseleaf. USD 677 base vol(s). (effective 2008). **Document type:** *Handbook/Manual/Guide, Trade.* **Description:** Provides legal analysis and a practical approach to problems and questions concerning federal oil and gas leases.
Published by: (Rocky Mountain Mineral Law Foundation), Matthew Bender & Co., Inc. (Subsidiary of: LexisNexis North America), 1275 Broadway, Albany, NY 12204. TEL 518-487-3000, 800-424-4200, FAX 518-487-3083, international@bender.com, http://bender.lexisnexis.com. Ed. Linnea Mitchell Simons.

335 340 USA
THE LAW OF OIL AND GAS LEASES. Text in English. 1967. 2 base vols. plus a. updates. looseleaf. USD 435 base vol(s). (effective 2008). **Document type:** *Handbook/Manual/Guide, Trade.* **Description:** Provides information on assignment clauses, dry hole and lease extension clauses, entirety clauses, force majeure clauses, habendum clauses and warranty clauses.
Published by: Matthew Bender & Co., Inc. (Subsidiary of: LexisNexis North America), 1275 Broadway, Albany, NY 12204. TEL 518-487-3000, 800-424-4200, FAX 518-487-3083, international@bender.com, http://bender.lexisnexis.com. Ed. Earl Brown.

665.53 CHN ISSN 1002-106X
TP690.A1 CODEN: LISHEM
➤ **LIANYOU SHEJI/PETROLEUM REFINERY ENGINEERING.** Text in Chinese, English. 1971. m. USD 49.20 (effective 2009). adv. **Document type:** *Journal, Academic/Scholarly.* **Description:** Covers petroleum refining and the petrochemical industry, reporting on new technologies, new achievements in petroleum processing, and news from petrochemical companies.
Related titles: Online - full text ed.
Indexed: APIAb, CIN, ChemAb, ChemTitl, SCOPUS.
—BLDSC (6435.040000), CASDDS, East View, IE, Ingenta, Linda Hall.
Published by: (Luoyang Petrochemical Engineering Corporation), Lianyou Sheji Bianjibu, Qilihe, PO Box 063, Luoyang, Henan 471003, China. TEL 86-379-4887689, FAX 86-379-485-7177, TELEX 473009 LPEC CN. Ed. Zhang Lixin. R&P Guang Lin Zhang TEL 86-379-488-7689. Adv. contact Lin Yang. Circ: 5,000. **Dist. overseas by:** China International Book Trading Corp, 35 Chegongzhuang Xilu, Haidian District, PO Box 399, Beijing 100044, China.

665.5 CHN ISSN 1671-4962
LIANYOU YU HUAGONG/REFINING AND CHEMICALS. Text in Chinese. 1983. q. CNY 5 newsstand/cover (effective 2006). **Document type:** *Journal, Academic/Scholarly.*
Formerly (until 2002): Heilongjiang Shiyou Huagong/Heilongjiang Petrochemical Technology (1008-0201)
Related titles: Online - full text ed.
Published by: Daqing Shiyou Huagong Zongchang, Longfeng Dajie, Daqing, 163711, China. TEL 86-459-6756179, FAX 86-459-6757199.

665.5 CHN ISSN 1672-6952
LIAONING SHIYOU HUAGONG DAXUE XUEBAO/LIAONING UNIVERSITY OF PETROLEUM & CHEMICAL TECHNOLOGY. JOURNAL. Text in English. 1981. q. USD 20.80 (effective 2009). **Document type:** *Journal, Academic/Scholarly.*
Formerly (until 2002): Fushun Shiyou Xueyuan Xuebao/Fushun Petroleum Institute. Journal (1005-3883)
Related titles: Online - full content ed.; Online - full text ed.
Indexed: RefZh, SCOPUS.
—BLDSC (4812.248500), East View.
Published by: Liaoning Shiyou Huagong Daxue/Liaoning University of Petroleum & Chemical Technology, No. 1, West Dandong Road, Wanghua District, Fushun, Liaoning Province 113001, China. TEL 81-413-6650405, FAX 86-413-6650866, http://www.lnpu.edu.cn/. **Dist. by:** China International Book Trading Corp, 35 Chegongzhuang Xilu, Haidian District, PO Box 399, Beijing 100044, China. TEL 86-10-68412045, FAX 86-10-68412023, cibtc@mail.cibtc.com.cn, http://www.cibtc.com.cn.

665.773 JPN ISSN 0024-709X
LIQUEFIED PETROLEUM GAS/L P GASU. Text in Japanese. 1959. m. JPY 1,500 newsstand/cover. adv. charts; illus.
Published by: Sangyo Hodo Publications Inc., 4-7 Tsuki-Ji 3-chome, Chuo-ku, Tokyo, 104-0045, Japan.

665.5 GBR ISSN 1751-4703
▼ **LIQUIDS AND GAS HANDLING.** Abbreviated title: L G H. Text in English. 2009. q. free to qualified personnel (effective 2010). adv. back issues avail. **Document type:** *Magazine, Trade.* **Description:** Designed for managers and engineers who specify or purchase equipment or materials involved in the manufacture, process handling, storage or distribution of liquids or gases, or in the use of liquids and gases in other manufacturing processes or environments.
Address: Victoria House, 2 Mornington Rd, Sale, Cheshire M33 2DA, United Kingdom. TEL 44-161-3745615, FAX 44-161-3746436. Eds. Mark Simms TEL 44-1732-773268, George Bennett. Adv. contact Steve Beard TEL 44-1268-784843.

354.489 GRL ISSN 1399-5340
KDZ3371
LIST OF MINERAL AND PETROLEUM LICENSES IN GREENLAND. Text in English. 1972. 2/m. free. **Document type:** *Government.* **Description:** Provides information to potential applicants about current mineral exploration licenses.
Former titles (until 1998): Bi-Monthly List of Mineral and Petroleum Licenses in Greenland (1397-8039); (until 1996): Mineral and Hydrocarbon Licenses in Greenland (0908-7303); (until 1993): Specifications of Mineral and Hydrocarbon Licenses in Greenland (0907-5321); (until 1992): Specifications of Mineral Concessions and Licenses in Greenland (0107-430X); (until 1978): Specifications of Consessions and Prospecting Licenses grated by the Ministry of Greenland
Related titles: Online - full text ed.: List of Mineral and Petroleum Licenses in Greenland. ISSN 1399-1426. free.
Published by: Bureau of Minerals and Petroleum, PO Box 930, Nuuk, 3900, Greenland. TEL 299-346800, FAX 299-324302.

665 USA
TN867
LOUISIANA/GULF COAST REGIONAL DIRECTORY. Text in English. 19??. a. USD 80 per issue (effective 2011). **Document type:** *Directory, Trade.*
Former titles: Armstrong Oil Directories: Louisiana, Texas Gulf Coast, East Texas, Arkansas and Mississippi Edition (0273-4931); (until 1980): Hank Seale Oil Directory: Louisiana, Texas Gulf Coast, East Texas, Arkansas and Mississippi Edition
Published by: Armstrong Oil Directories, PO Box 52106, Amarillo, TX 79159. TEL 806-457-9300, FAX 806-457-9301, support@armstrongoil.com.

665.5 665 USA ISSN 1080-9449
CODEN: LUGRF9
LUBES 'N' GREASES; the magazine of industry in motion. Text in English. 1995. m. free in US & Canada to qualified personnel; USD 60 in Mexico; USD 95 elsewhere; USD 10 newsstand/cover (effective 2004). adv. charts; illus. back issues avail. **Document type:** *Magazine, Trade.* **Description:** Contains news and stories covering automotive and industrial lubricants, metalworking fluids, greases, base stocks, lube additives, packaging, biodegradable and synthetic products.
Related titles: Regional ed(s).: Lubes 'n' Greases (Europe - Middle East - Africa). ISSN 1935-8490. 2007 (Jun./Jul.). free to qualified personnel in Europe, the Middle East, and Africa; USD 90 elsewhere.
Indexed: APIAb, SCOPUS.
—BLDSC (5300.940000), Linda Hall.
Published by: LNG Publishing Company, Inc., 6105 G Arlington Blvd Ste G, Falls Church, VA 22044. TEL 703-536-0800, FAX 703-536-0803, nancy@LNGpublishing.com, http://www.LNGpublishing.com. Ed. Lisa Tocci. Pub. Nancy J Demarco. Adv. contact Gloria Steinberg Briskin. color page USD 4,915, B&W page USD 3,965; bleed 8.625 x 11.125. Circ: 16,500 (controlled).

665.538 USA ISSN 0024-7146
TJ1075.A2 CODEN: LUBRAD
LUBRICATION. Text in English. 1911. q.
Indexed: A22.
—CASDDS, Ingenta, INIST, Linda Hall.
Published by: Texaco Inc., 6001 Bollinger Canyon Rd, San Ramon, CA 94583. TEL 800-533-6571, lubetek@chevron.com, http://www.texaco.com.

620 GBR ISSN 0954-0075
CODEN: LUSCEN
➤ **LUBRICATION SCIENCE**; physics and chemistry of lubricants in tribological systems. Text in English. 1988. 10/yr. GBP 1,701 in United Kingdom to institutions; EUR 2,150 in Europe to institutions; USD 3,332 elsewhere to institutions; GBP 1,956 combined subscription in United Kingdom to institutions (print & online eds.); EUR 2,473 combined subscription in Europe to institutions (print & online eds.); USD 3,832 combined subscription elsewhere to institutions (print & online eds.) (effective 2012). bk.rev. back issues avail.; reprint service avail. from PSC. **Document type:** *Journal, Academic/Scholarly.* **Description:** Deals with the physics and chemistry of lubricants in tribological systems; and covers the design, formulation, testing, mechanisms and performance lubricants and additives, liquid and solid, in all types of tribological systems and appilcations.
Incorporates (1994-2009): Tribotest (1354-4063); (1984-2009): Journal of Synthetic Lubrication (0265-6582)
Related titles: Online - full text ed.: ISSN 1557-6833. GBP 1,701 in United Kingdom to institutions; EUR 2,150 in Europe to institutions; USD 3,332 elsewhere to institutions (effective 2012).
Indexed: A22, A28, APA, APIAb, BrCerAb, C&ISA, CA/WCA, CIA, CIN, CPEI, CerAb, ChemAb, ChemTitl, CivEngAb, CorrAb, CurCont, E&CAJ, E11, EEA, EMA, ESPM, EngInd, EnvEAb, FR, H15, M&TEA, M09, MBF, METADEX, SCI, SCOPUS, SolStAb, T04, TM, W07, WAA.
—CASDDS, IE, Infotrieve, Ingenta, Linda Hall. **CCC.**
Published by: John Wiley & Sons Ltd. (Subsidiary of: John Wiley & Sons, Inc.), 1-7 Oldlands Way, PO Box 808, Bognor Regis, West Sussex PO21 9FF, United Kingdom. TEL 44-1865-778315, FAX 44-1243-843232, cs-journals@wiley.com, http://eu.wiley.com/WileyCDA/. Ed. H A Spikes. **Subscr. to:** 1-7 Oldlands Way, PO Box 809, Bognor Regis, West Sussex PO21 9FG, United Kingdom. TEL 44-1865-778054, cs-agency@wiley.com.

665.5 SRB ISSN 1452-2012
LUKOIL - BEOPETROL; informativni list. Text in Serbo-Croatian. 1993. m.?. **Document type:** *Magazine, Trade.*
Formerly: Beopetrol
Published by: Beopetrol, Bulevar Mihaila Pupina 165/d, Novi Beograd, 11070. TEL 381-11-2220200, FAX 381-11-3132395, office@beopetrol.co.yu, http://www.beopetrol.co.yu. Ed. Svetozar Danchuo.

LUNDBERG LETTER. *see* PETROLEUM AND GAS—Abstracting, Bibliographies, Statistics

LUSTLINE. *see* ENVIRONMENTAL STUDIES

MADE IN HOLLAND. OIL & GAS. *see* BUSINESS AND ECONOMICS—International Commerce

665 HUN
MAGYAR OLAJIPARI MUZEUM. EVKONYV. Text in Hungarian. 1974. a. HUF 117 (effective 1997). illus.
Published by: Magyar Olajipari Muzeum/Hungarian Oil Museum, Wlassics Gyula utca 13, Zalaegerszeg, 8900, Hungary. TEL 36-92-313632, FAX 36-92-311081. Ed. Istvan Fulop. Circ: 2,000.

MAJOR CHEMICAL & PETROCHEMICAL COMPANIES OF THE WORLD (YEAR). *see* BUSINESS AND ECONOMICS—Trade And Industrial Directories

MALAYSIA CHEMICALS REPORT. *see* CHEMISTRY

661.801 338.47665 959.5 GBR ISSN 1749-2335
MALAYSIA PETROCHEMICALS REPORT. Text in English. 2005. a. EUR 820, USD 1,030 combined subscription per issue (print & email eds.) (effective 2010). **Document type:** *Report, Trade.* **Description:** Provides industry professionals and strategists, sector analysts, trade associations and regulatory bodies with independent forecasts and competitive intelligence on the Malaysian petrochemicals industry.
Related titles: E-mail ed.
Indexed: A15, ABIn, B02, B15, B17, B18, G04, I05, P48, P51, P52, P56, PQC.
Published by: Business Monitor International Ltd., Senator House, 85 Queen Victoria St, London, EC4V 4AB, United Kingdom. TEL 44-20-72480468, FAX 44-20-72480467, subs@businessmonitor.com.

662.338 USA
TN872
MARGINAL OIL AND GAS REPORT; fuel for economic growth. Text in English. 1951. a. USD 8 (effective 2003). **Document type:** *Journal, Trade.*
Former titles: Marginal Oil and Gas: Fuel for Economic Growth; Marginal Oil: Fuel for Economic Growth; National Stripper Well Survey (0470-3219)
—Linda Hall.
Published by: Interstate Oil and Gas Compact Commission, PO Box 53127, Oklahoma City, OK 73152-3127. TEL 405-525-3556, FAX 405-525-3592, iogcc@iogcc.state.ok.us, http://www.iogcc.state.ok.us.

MARINE AND PETROLEUM GEOLOGY. *see* EARTH SCIENCES—Geology

THE MARKETER (TOPEKA). *see* BUSINESS AND ECONOMICS—Marketing And Purchasing

338.2 665.5 USA
MARKETERS, PURCHASERS AND TRADING COMPANIES. Abbreviated title: M P & T. Text in English. 1945. a. USD 350 domestic; USD 360 in Canada; USD 365 elsewhere (effective 2009). adv. **Document type:** *Directory, Trade.* **Description:** Contains more listings of not only the marketers, purchasers and trading companies across the world, but also of all the support sectors in the industry, from the largest worldwide engineer/contractors to local service and supply companies in every area.
Former titles: Oil Marketing Industry; Directory of Oil Marketing and Wholesale Distributors (0070-5993)
Published by: Midwest Publishing Company, 2230 E 49th St, Ste E, Tulsa, OK 74105. TEL 918-582-2000, 800-829-2002, FAX 918-587-9349, info@midwestpub.com. Adv. contact Jim Shelvy. B&W page USD 1,610, color page USD 1,710.

665.5 QAT
AL-MASH'AL/TORCH. Text in Arabic, English. 1986. s-m. free.
Published by: Qatar General Petroleum Corporation, Public Relations Department, P O Box 3212, Doha, Qatar. TEL 974-491449, FAX 974-831995, TELEX 4343 PETCOR DH. Circ: 4,000.

MATERIALS AND COMPONENTS IN FOSSIL ENERGY APPLICATIONS. *see* ENERGY

665.5 340 USA
MAXWELL, MARTIN AND KRAMER'S THE LAW OF OIL AND GAS. Text in English. 19??. base vol. plus irreg. updates. USD 145 base vol(s). (effective 2010). **Document type:** *Journal, Trade.* **Description:** Covers major aspects of law governing oil and gas.
Related titles: ◆ Series of: University Casebook Series.
Published by: Thomson West (Subsidiary of: Thomson Reuters Corp.), 610 Opperman Dr, Eagan, MN 55123. TEL 651-687-7000, 800-344-5008, west.customer.service@thomson.com.

MEALEY'S LITIGATION REPORT: BENZENE. *see* LAW—Civil Law

388.476600972 GBR ISSN 1749-2068
MEXICO CHEMICALS REPORT. Text in English. 2005. a. USD 1,030 per issue (effective 2010). **Document type:** *Report, Trade.* **Description:** Provides industry professionals and strategists, sector analysts, trade associations and regulatory bodies with independent forecasts and competitive intelligence on the Mexican chemicals industry.
Indexed: A15, ABIn, B02, B15, B17, B18, G04, I05, P48, P51, P52, P56, PQC.
Published by: Business Monitor International Ltd., Senator House, 85 Queen Victoria St, London, EC4V 4AB, United Kingdom. TEL 44-20-72480468, FAX 44-20-72480467, subs@businessmonitor.com.

338.4766180409 GBR ISSN 1749-2343
MEXICO PETROCHEMICALS REPORT. Text in English. 2005. a. EUR 820, USD 1,030 combined subscription per issue (print & email eds.) (effective 2010). **Document type:** *Report, Trade.* **Description:** Provides industry professionals and strategists, sector analysts, trade associations and regulatory bodies with independent forecasts and competitive intelligence on the Mexican petrochemicals industry.
Related titles: E-mail ed.
Indexed: A15, ABIn, B02, B15, B17, B18, G04, I05, P48, P51, P52, P56, PQC.
Published by: Business Monitor International Ltd., Senator House, 85 Queen Victoria St, London, EC4V 4AB, United Kingdom. TEL 44-20-72480468, FAX 44-20-72480467, subs@businessmonitor.com.

665.5 USA
MICHIGAN OIL & GAS NEWS. Text in English. 1932. w. USD 150 (effective 2005). adv. **Document type:** *Magazine, Trade.*
Published by: The Michigan Oil And Gas Association, 124 W Allegan St, Ste 1610, Lansing, MI 48933. TEL 517-487-1092. Ed. Scott Bellinger. Circ: 700 (paid).

665.5029 USA
MIDCONTINENT PETROLEUM INDUSTRY. Text in English. 1945. a. **Document type:** *Directory, Trade.* **Description:** Supplies company name, address, phone and fax numbers, personnel, division offices, offshore operations, whether producer of oil or gas and if drilling contractor with rotary or cable tools for Oklahoma, Kansas, Missouri, Iowa, and Nebraska.
Formed by the 1992 merger of: Directory of Producers and Drilling Contractors: Kansas; Directory of Producers and Drilling Contractors: Oklahoma
Media: Diskette.
Published by: Midwest Publishing Company, 2230 E 49th St, Ste E, Tulsa, OK 74105. TEL 800-829-2002, info@midwestpub.com, http://www.midwestpub.com/.

338.47 CYP ISSN 0544-0424
HD9576.N36
MIDDLE EAST ECONOMIC SURVEY. Abbreviated title: M E E S. Text in English. 1957. w. USD 2,170 print or online eds. (effective 2005). bk.rev. charts; stat.; maps; mkt. index. **Document type:** *Newsletter, Trade.* **Description:** Reviews oil, finance, banking, and political developments in the Middle East and North Africa.
Related titles: E-mail ed.; Online - full text ed.
Indexed: KES, M10, PEBNI, SCOPUS.
—BLDSC (5761.373500), Linda Hall.
Published by: Middle East Petroleum and Economic Publications, PO Box 24940, Nicosia, 1355, Cyprus. TEL 357-22-665431, FAX 357-22-671988, info@mees.com. Ed. Gerlad Butt. Pub., R&P Basim W Itayim.

665.5 338.47665 NOR ISSN 1891-4551
MIDT-NORSK OLJE & GASS; informasjonsavisen for olje- og gassaktiviteter i Midt-Norge. Text in Norwegian. 1993. q. adv. **Document type:** *Trade.*
Formerly (until 2009): Midt-Norsk Oljeavis (0806-1130)
Related titles: Online - full text ed.: ISSN 1891-4624. 2006.

P

Published by: Midnor C N I AS, P O Box 3020, Lake, Trondheim, 7441, Norway. TEL 47-73-531550, FAX 47-73-531551, christian@midnor.no. Ed. John Borten. Circ: 8,000 (controlled and free).

662.6 DEU ISSN 0341-1893
CODEN: MTCKAZ

MINERALOELTECHNIK. Text in German. 1956. m. EUR 72.90; EUR 9.40 newsstand/cover (effective 2009). adv. bk.rev. index. back issues avail. **Document type:** *Magazine, Trade.* **Description:** Reports on mineral oil usage, research results on oil products, fuels, heating oils, and ubricants.
Indexed: A22, TM.
—BLDSC (5786.420000), CASDDS, IE, Infotrieve, Ingenta, Linda Hall. **CCC.**
Published by: Beratungsgesellschaft fuer Mineraloel-Anwendungstechnik mbH, Buchtstr 10, Hamburg, 22087, Germany. TEL 49-40-2270030, FAX 49-40-22700338, info@uniti.de, http://www.uniti.de. Ed., Adv. contact Wolfgang Schuetz. B&W page EUR 472.50, color page EUR 802.50; 108 x 168. Circ: 1,800 (paid and controlled).

MINERIA CHILENA. *see* MINES AND MINING INDUSTRY

MINING AND PETROLEUM LEGISLATION SERVICE. *see* LAW

MINING AND PETROLEUM LEGISLATION SERVICE (COMMONWEALTH). *see* MINES AND MINING INDUSTRY

MINING AND PETROLEUM LEGISLATION SERVICE (NEW SOUTH WALES / AUSTRALIAN CAPITAL TERRITORY). *see* PUBLIC ADMINISTRATION

MINING AND PETROLEUM LEGISLATION SERVICE (QUEENSLAND). *see* PUBLIC ADMINISTRATION

MINING AND PETROLEUM LEGISLATION SERVICE (SOUTH AUSTRALIA / NORTHERN TERRITORY). *see* PUBLIC ADMINISTRATION

MINING AND PETROLEUM LEGISLATION SERVICE (VICTORIA / TASMANIA). *see* PUBLIC ADMINISTRATION

MINING AND PETROLEUM LEGISLATION SERVICE (WESTERN AUSTRALIA MINING ONLY). *see* PUBLIC ADMINISTRATION

MINING AND PETROLEUM LEGISLATION SERVICE (WESTERN AUSTRALIA PETROLEUM ONLY). *see* PUBLIC ADMINISTRATION

MINING AND PETROLEUM LEGISLATION SERVICE (WESTERN AUSTRALIA). *see* PUBLIC ADMINISTRATION

THE MINING RECORD. *see* MINES AND MINING INDUSTRY

353.9 USA ISSN 0095-3024
HD9579.G5

MINNESOTA. DEPARTMENT OF REVENUE. PETROLEUM DIVISION. ANNUAL REPORT. Text in English. 1973. a. **Document type:** *Government.*
Published by: (Minnesota. Petroleum Division), Department of Revenue, MS 3333, St. Paul, MN 55146. TEL 612-296-0889.

338.2 USA ISSN 1079-557X
TN871.4

MOBILE RIG REGISTER. Text in English. 1994. biennial. **Document type:** *Directory, Trade.*
—CCC.
Published by: Offshore Data Services, Inc., 3200 Wilcrest Dr, Ste 170, Houston, TX 77042. TEL 832-463-3000, FAX 832-463-3100, general@ods-petrodata.com, http://www.ods-petrodata.com.

665.5 IDN

MONTHLY BULLETIN OF THE PETROLEUM AND NATURAL GAS INDUSTRY OF INDONESIA. Text in English. 1973. m. charts; stat.
Published by: Directorate General of Oil and Gas, Programming and Reporting Division/Direktorat Jenderal Minyak dan Gas Bumi, Gedung Plaza Centris, Jl. Rasuna Said Kav., B-5 Kuningan, Jakarta, 10110, Indonesia. TEL 62-21-351215, FAX 62-21-354987, TELEX 44363. Circ: 400.

665.5 USA

MONTHLY CRUDE OIL PRODUCTION. Text in English. 19??. m. USD 79 (effective 2011). **Document type:** *Report, Government.* **Description:** Contains preliminary information on allowables, production, number of wells flowing and pumping, number of delinquent leases, method of disposition, and other data listed by district and field. Also reviews some of the previous month's final data.
Former titles: Monthly Production of Crude Oil Allowable, Production and Removal from Leases in the State of Texas; Preliminary Statement of Crude Oil Allowable, Production and Removal from Leases in the State of Texas
Published by: Railroad Commission, Oil and Gas Division, PO Box 12967, Austin, TX 78711. TEL 877-228-5740, publicassist@rrc.state.tx.us.

665 JPN ISSN 0016-5964

MONTHLY JOURNAL OF GASOLINE SERVICE STATIONS/GEKKAN KYUYUSHO NIHON. Text in Japanese. 1965. m. JPY 6,000, USD 20 for 6 mos. adv. bk.rev. abstr.; bibl.; charts; illus.; pat.; stat.; tr.lit. index.
Published by: Yugyo Hochi Shinbunsha, 2-6-8 Shinkawa, Chuo-ku, Tokyo, 104-0033, Japan. Ed. Yoshio Takeda. Circ: 30,000.

665.5 USA
TN881.T4

MONTHLY SUMMARY OF TEXAS NATURAL GAS. Text in English. 1949. m. looseleaf. charts; stat. back issues avail. **Document type:** *Report, Government.* **Description:** Lists production of gas-well gas, casinghead gas, and natural gas liquids; indicates number of wells; contains some data on cycling, gasoline and pressure maintenance plant operations, and volumes exported and flared.
Related titles: Online - full text ed.: free (effective 2011).
Indexed: E14.
Published by: Railroad Commission, Oil and Gas Division, PO Box 12967, Austin, TX 78711. TEL 877-228-5740, publicassist@rrc.state.tx.us.

665.5 MAR

MOROCCO. MINISTERE DE L'ENERGIE ET DES MINES. ACTIVITE DU SECTEUR PETROLIER. Text in French. 1956. irreg. USD 10. stat.
Formerly: Morocco. Direction des Mines et de la Geologie. Activite du Secteur Petrolier
Published by: Direction des Mines et de la Geologie, Direction de l'Energie, Rabat, Morocco.

338.47 AUT

MOVE. Text in German. 1958. 10/yr. free (effective 2009). bk.rev. illus.; stat. **Document type:** *Magazine, Trade.* **Description:** Covers refineries, technological research, production, transportation, economics, events and industry of the entire Oe M V group.
Former titles (until 2004): O M V - Leben; (until 2001): O M V - Mix; (until 1987): Oe M V - Magazin; Oe M V - Zeitschrift (0029-7194); (until 1968): O M V - Werkzeitung
Indexed: SpeleolAb.
Published by: O M V Aktiengesellschaft, Trabrennstr 6-8, Vienna, W 1020, Austria. TEL 43-1-404400, FAX 43-1-4044027900, info@omv.com, http://www.omv.com. Circ: 17,000.

338.27285 USA ISSN 1532-1223

N G I'S DAILY GAS PRICE INDEX. Text in English. 1993. d. USD 990 (effective 2005). charts; illus.; mkt.; maps; stat.; tr.lit. back issues avail. **Document type:** *Newsletter, Trade.* **Description:** Provides natural gas industry news and prices.
Related titles: E-mail ed.; Fax ed.; Online - full text ed.: ISSN 1532-1231.
Published by: (Natural Gas Industry), Intelligence Press Inc., 22648 Glenn Dr, Ste 305, Sterling, VA 20164. TEL 703-318-8848, FAX 703-318-0597, http://www.intelligencepress.com. Ed. James Geanakos. Circ: 400 (paid).

665.7 USA ISSN 2158-8023

N G I'S SHALE DAILY. (Natural Gas Industry) Text in English. d. free (effective 2011). **Document type:** *Newspaper, Trade.*
Media: Online - full text.
Published by: Intelligence Press Inc., 22648 Glenn Dr, Ste 305, Sterling, VA 20164. TEL 703-318-8848, 800-427-5747, FAX 703-318-0597, info@intelligencepress.com, http://www.intelligencepress.com.

665.5 USA ISSN 1532-124X

N G I'S WEEKLY GAS PRICE INDEX. Text in English. 1987. w. USD 1,135 (effective 2005). charts; illus.; mkt.; maps; stat. back issues avail. **Document type:** *Newsletter, Trade.* **Description:** Reports on trading activity and pricing within the domestic spot natural gas market.
Related titles: E-mail ed.; Fax ed.; Online - full text ed.
—CCC.
Published by: (Natural Gas Industry), Intelligence Press Inc., 22648 Glenn Dr, Ste 305, Sterling, VA 20164. TEL 703-318-8848, FAX 703-318-0597. Ed. James Geanakos. Circ: 700 (paid).

665.538 USA ISSN 0027-6782
TJ1077.A1 CODEN: NLGIA4

N L G I SPOKESMAN. Text in English. 1937. m. USD 53 domestic; USD 65 in Canada; USD 85 elsewhere (effective 2005). adv. bk.rev. pat. index. reprints avail. **Document type:** *Magazine, Trade.* **Description:** Contains original articles on the manufacture of lubricating grease or new developments in application methods, as well as other items related to the industry.
Related titles: Microfilm ed.: (from PQC).
Indexed: A22, APIAb, APICat, APIH&E, APIOC, APIPR, APIPS, APITS, ApMecR, CIN, ChemAb, ChemTitl, EngInd, FLUIDEX, ISMEC, SCOPUS.
—BLDSC (6113.800000), CASDDS, IE, Infotrieve, Ingenta, INIST, Linda Hall. **CCC.**
Published by: National Lubricating Grease Institute, 4635 Wyandotte St, Kansas City, MO 64112. TEL 816-931-9480. Ed. Chuck Hitchcock. Circ: 2,600.

665.5 NGA ISSN 0189-0069

N N P C NEWS. Text in English. m. free. illus. **Document type:** *Bulletin.* **Description:** Covers corporate activities, community relations, profiles, technology, and special features.
Published by: Nigerian National Petroleum Corporation, PMB 12701, Lagos, Nigeria. TEL 234-1-269-0470. Ed. Thelma C Nwokedi Onyiuke.

665.7 USA ISSN 1040-0354

N P G A REPORTS. Text in English. 1982. fortn. USD 25. illus.; stat. **Description:** Covers industry trends for producers and marketers of liquified petroleum gas.
Formerly: N P L G A Reports (0744-4273)
Related titles: Online - full content ed.: ISSN 1549-1269.
Published by: National Propane Gas Association, 1600 Eisenhower Ln, Ste 100, Lisle, IL 60532. TEL 708-515-0600, FAX 708-515-8774. Ed. James K Burnham.

665.5 USA ISSN 0149-5267
HD9560.1

N P N MAGAZINE. (National Petroleum News) Abbreviated title: N P N. Text in English. 1909. m. USD 64 domestic; USD 74 in Canada & Mexico; USD 80 elsewhere; USD 74 combined subscription domestic (print & online eds.); USD 84 combined subscription in Canada & Mexico (print & online eds.); USD 90 combined subscription elsewhere (print & online eds.); free to qualified personnel (effective 2011). adv. bk.rev. charts; illus.; mkt.; stat.; tr.lit. s-a. cum.index. back issues avail.; reprints avail. **Document type:** *Magazine, Trade.* **Description:** Covers national and regional news, trends, analysis and statistics for petroleum and convenience store executives.
Related titles: Diskette ed.; Microfiche ed.: (from CIS); Microform ed.: (from PMC, PQC); Online - full text ed.: USD 10 (effective 2011).
Indexed: A09, A10, A12, A13, A14, A15, A17, A22, A23, A24, ABIn, APIAb, B01, B02, B03, B04, B06, B07, B08, B09, B11, B13, B15, B17, B18, BPI, BRD, C12, ChemAb, G04, G06, G07, G08, GeoRef, I05, M01, M02, P48, P51, P52, P53, P54, P56, PEBNI, PQC, RefZh, SCOPUS, SRI, SpeleolAb, T&II, T02, V02, V03, V04, W01, W02, W03, W05.
—BLDSC (6029.000000), IE, Infotrieve, Ingenta. **CCC.**
Published by: M2Media360, 1030 W Higgins Rd, Ste 230, Park Ridge, IL 60068. TEL 847-720-5600, FAX 847-720-5601, http://www.m2media360.com/. Ed. Keith Reid TEL 847-720-5615. Adv. contact Tom Butterick TEL 212-588-9200 ext 1329. Circ: 22,500.

665.53 661.804 USA

N P R A ANNUAL MEETING. CONFERENCE PAPERS. Text in English. a. back issues avail. **Document type:** *Proceedings, Academic/Scholarly.* **Description:** Publishes papers presented at the national conference on petrochemical plants and refineries.
Related titles: ◆ Cumulative ed(s).: N P R A Annual Meeting. Conference Papers. Multi-Year CD-ROM.
Published by: National Petrochemical & Refiners Association, 1667 K St, N W, Ste 700, Washington, DC 20006. TEL 202-457-0480, FAX 202-457-0486, info@npra.org, http://www.npradc.org.

665.53 661.804 USA

N P R A ANNUAL MEETING. CONFERENCE PAPERS. MULTI-YEAR CD-ROM. Text in English. 1999. a. **Description:** Presents a searchable database comprising all the papers presented at the NPRA annual conference on petrochemical plant and refinery operations and products.
Media: CD-ROM. **Related titles:** ◆ Cumulative ed. of: N P R A Annual Meeting. Conference Papers.
Published by: National Petrochemical & Refiners Association, 1667 K St, N W, Ste 700, Washington, DC 20006. TEL 202-457-0480, FAX 202-457-0486, info@npra.org, http://www.npradc.org.

665.53 USA

N P R A CRACKER SEMINAR TRANSCRIPTS. Variant title: Cat Cracker Seminar Transcripts. Text in English. biennial. back issues avail. **Document type:** *Proceedings, Trade.* **Description:** Publishes transcripts of the question-and-answer sessions and technical papers presented at the NPRA symposium held to address maintenance problems during the catalytic cracking process.
Published by: National Petrochemical & Refiners Association, 1667 K St, N W, Ste 700, Washington, DC 20006. TEL 202-457-0480, FAX 202-457-0486, info@npra.org, http://www.npradc.org.

665.53 661.804 628 USA

N P R A ENVIRONMENTAL CONFERENCE. PROCEEDINGS. Text in English. a. back issues avail. **Document type:** *Proceedings, Academic/Scholarly.* **Description:** Publishes papers presented on research conducted in environmental matters concerning petrochemical plants and refineries.
Published by: National Petrochemical & Refiners Association, 1667 K St, N W, Ste 700, Washington, DC 20006. TEL 202-457-0480, FAX 202-457-0486, info@npra.org, http://www.npradc.org.

665.5 USA

N P R A NATIONAL LUBRICANTS & WAXES MEETING. PROCEEDINGS. Text in English. a. back issues avail. **Document type:** *Proceedings, Academic/Scholarly.* **Description:** Publishes papers presented at the NPRA annual conference on lubricants and waxes.
Published by: National Petrochemical & Refiners Association, 1667 K St, N W, Ste 700, Washington, DC 20006. TEL 202-457-0480, FAX 202-457-0486, info@npra.org, http://www.npradc.org.

665.5 661.804 USA

N P R A NATIONAL SAFETY CONFERENCE. PROCEEDINGS. Text in English. a. back issues avail. **Document type:** *Proceedings, Academic/Scholarly.* **Description:** Presents research into petrochemical plant and refinery safety.
Published by: National Petrochemical & Refiners Association, 1667 K St, N W, Ste 700, Washington, DC 20006. TEL 202-457-0480, FAX 202-457-0486, info@npra.org, http://www.npradc.org.

665.53 661.804 USA
TP690.A1

N P R A QUESTION & ANSWER SESSION ON REFINING AND PETROCHEMICAL TECHNOLOGY TRANSCRIPTS (CD-ROM EDITION). Text in English. 19??. a., latest 2003. back issues avail. **Document type:** *Proceedings.* **Description:** Publishes transcripts of the question-and-answer session conducted during the NPRA annual meeting.
Former titles: N P R A Question & Answer Session on Refining and Petrochemical Technology Transcripts (Print Edition) (0162-0770); (until 1973): N P R A Question & Answer Session on Refining Technology. Transcripts (0162-0762)
Media: CD-ROM. **Related titles:** Cumulative ed(s).: N P R A Question & Answer Session on Refining and Petrochemical Technology Transcripts. 5-Year Volume.
Indexed: SCOPUS.
Published by: National Petrochemical & Refiners Association, 1667 K St, N W, Ste 700, Washington, DC 20006. TEL 202-457-0480, FAX 202-457-0486, info@npra.org, http://www.npradc.org.

665.53 661.804 USA

N P R A REFINERY AND PETROCHEMICAL PLANT MAINTENANCE CONFERENCE. Text in English. 197?. a. back issues avail. **Document type:** *Proceedings, Academic/Scholarly.* **Description:** Publishes research papers presented at the NPRA national conference on the maintenance of petrochemical plants and refineries.
Published by: National Petrochemical & Refiners Association, 1667 K St, N W, Ste 700, Washington, DC 20006. TEL 202-457-0480, FAX 202-457-0486, info@npra.org, http://www.npradc.org.

665.5 USA

N P R A REFINERY AND PETROCHEMICAL PLANT MAINTENANCE CONFERENCE. TECHNICAL TRANSCRIPTS. Variant title: Refinery and Petrochemical Plant Maintenance Conference. Technical Transcripts. Text in English. a., latest 1996. price varies. back issues avail. **Document type:** *Proceedings, Trade.* **Description:** Presents transcripts of discussions during the question-and-answer session conducted during the NPRA annual Plant Maintenance Conference, along with technical papers presented at the conference.
Published by: National Petrochemical & Refiners Association, 1667 K St, N W, Ste 700, Washington, DC 20006. TEL 202-457-0480, FAX 202-457-0486, info@npra.org, http://www.npradc.org.

665.5 AUS ISSN 1838-8345

N S W GAS NETWORKS PERFORMANCE REPORT. (New South Wales) Text in English. 2008. a. free (effective 2011). back issues avail. **Document type:** *Report, Government.*
Media: Online - full text.
Published by: Industry & Investment NSW, 161 Kite St, Locked Bag 21, Orange, NSW 2800, Australia. TEL 61-2-63913100, FAX 61-2-63913336, information-advisory@dpi.nsw.gov.au.

665 HRV ISSN 0027-755X
CODEN: NAFYA4

➤ **NAFTA.** Text mainly in English; Text occasionally in Croatian. 1950. m. EUR 50 domestic; USD 120 foreign (effective 2005). adv. bk.rev. charts; illus. index, cum.index. **Document type:** *Journal, Academic/Scholarly.* **Description:** Covers petroleum exploration, production, processing, petrochemistry, economy in petroleum industry.
Indexed: CIN, ChemAb, ChemTitl, FR, GeoRef, PetrolAb, SpeleolAb.
—CASDDS, IE, Infotrieve, INIST, PADDS. **CCC.**

Published by: Hrvatski Nacionalan Komitet Svjetskih Kongresa za Naftu/Croatian National Committee of the World Petroleum Congresses, Savska cesta 64-IV, Zagreb, 10000, Croatia. Ed., R&P, Adv. contact Stjepan Djurasek TEL 385-1-6001658. B&W page USD 1,250, color page USD 2,000; trim 272 x 205. Circ: 800 (paid); 100 (controlled).

665.5 POL ISSN 1428-6564
NAFTA & GAZ BIZNES. Text in Polish. 1997. m. EUR 56 foreign (effective 2005). **Document type:** *Magazine, Trade.*
Published by: USI Poland Sp. z o.o., ul Lubicz 25, Krakow, 31503, Poland. TEL 48-12-2943251, FAX 48-12-6197837. **Dist. by:** Ars Polona, Obroncow 25, Warsaw 03933, Poland. TEL 48-22-5098609, FAX 48-22-5098610, arspolona@arspolona.com.pl, http://www.arspolona.com.pl.

665 POL ISSN 0867-8871
TN860 CODEN: NGAZES
NAFTA - GAZ; miesiecznik poswiecony nauce i technice w przemysle naftowym i gazowniczym. Text in Polish; Summaries in English, Russian. 1945. m. EUR 194 foreign (effective 2005). adv. bk.rev. abstr.; bibl.; charts; illus.; stat. index. **Document type:** *Magazine, Trade.*
Formerly (until 1992): Nafta (0027-7541)
Indexed: AIA, B22, CEABA, CIN, ChemAb, ChemTitl, EIA, EnvAb, EnvInd, GeoRef, PetrolAb, SpeleolAb.
—BLDSC (6013.150000), CASDDS, INIST, Linda Hall, PADDS. **CCC.**
Published by: Instytut Gornictwa Naftowego i Gazownictwa, ul Lubicz 25 A, Krakow, 31503, Poland. TEL 48-12-4210033, FAX 48-12-4210050, office@inig.pl, http://www.igng.krakow.pl. Ed. Jozef Raczkowski. Circ: 1,460. **Dist. by:** Ars Polona, Obroncow 25, Warsaw 03933, Poland. TEL 48-22-5098609, FAX 48-22-5098610, arspolona@arspolona.com.pl, http://www.arspolona.com.pl.
Co-sponsor: Instytut Technologii Nafty.

665 UKR
NAFTOPRODUKTY. Text in Russian. w. UAK 78 per quarter domestic (effective 2004). **Document type:** *Newspaper, Trade.*
Formerly: Nefteprodukty
Published by: Psikhea, ul Nagornaya 25-27, ofis 58, Kiev, 04107, Ukraine. info@ukroil.com.ua. Ed. Oleg Kirnitskii.

NANKAI XUEBAO. ZHEXUE SHEHUI KEXUE BAN/NANKAI UNIVERSITY. JOURNAL. PHILOSOPHY AND SOCIAL SCIENCES EDITION. *see* SOCIAL SCIENCES: COMPREHENSIVE WORKS

665.5 338 NGA ISSN 0189-0050
NAPETCOR. Text in English. 1980. q. free to staff. illus. **Description:** Company magazine with news of the industry, human resource issues in the corporation, technology, safety and environmental issues, company activities and other features.
Published by: Nigerian National Petroleum Corporation, Group Public Affairs Division, 7 Kofo Abayomi St, Lagos, Victoria Island, Nigeria. TEL 234-1-269-4959. Ed. Edmund Ekajam.

NATIONAL DRILLER. *see* WATER RESOURCES

665.5 USA
NATIONAL PETROLEUM NEWS MARKET FACTS. Text in English. 19??. a. USD 315 per issue; USD 365 combined subscription (print & Online/CD-ROM eds.) (effective 2011). adv. back issues avail. **Document type:** *Report, Trade.* **Description:** Includes information on capital spending, domestic and international pricing, marketing management personnel, service station and C-store statistics, and the retail market share of the top petroleum C-store companies.
Related titles: CD-ROM ed.; Online - full text ed.: USD 315 per issue (effective 2011).
Published by: M2Media360, 1030 W Higgins Rd, Ste 230, Park Ridge, IL 60068. TEL 847-720-5600, FAX 847-720-5601, http://www.m2media360.com/. Ed. Keith Reid TEL 847-720-5615. Adv. contact Tom Butterick TEL 212-588-9200 ext 1329.

665.7 GBR ISSN 0140-3222
TN880.A1
NATURAL GAS; for industry and commerce. Text in English. 1928. bi-m. GBP 40; GBP 53 foreign. adv. bk.rev. illus.
Former titles: Industrial and Commercial Gas; Formed by the 1975 merger of: Natural Gas for Industry (0305-2028); Natural Gas for Commerce (0306-2414); Incorporates: Gas in Industry and Commerce (0016-4925)
Related titles: Microform ed.: (from PQC).
Indexed: BMT, WSCA.
Address: Oakfield House, 35 Perrymount Rd, Haywards Heath, W Sussex RH16 3DH, United Kingdom. TEL 0732-364422. Ed. Geoff Clarke. Circ: 29,270.

338.47 665.7 USA ISSN 1545-7893
HD9581.U49
NATURAL GAS & ELECTRICITY; the monthly journal for producers, marketers, pipelines, distributors and end users. Text in English. 1979. m. GBP 888 in United Kingdom to institutions; EUR 1,123 in Europe to institutions; USD 1,666 in United States to institutions; USD 1,738 elsewhere to institutions; GBP 1,022 combined subscription in United Kingdom to institutions (print & online eds.); EUR 1,293 combined subscription in Europe to institutions (print & online eds.); USD 1,916 combined subscription in United States to institutions (print & online eds.); USD 1,988 combined subscription elsewhere to institutions (print & online eds.) (effective 2012). adv. back issues avail.; reprint service avail. from PSC. **Document type:** *Magazine, Trade.* **Description:** Contains articles on financial and regulatory concerns: contracts pricing, purchasing, merging, acquisitions and financing. Examines federal and state regulation.
Former titles (until 2003): Natural Gas (0743-5665); (until 1984): Oil and Gas Analyst (0744-5725); (until 1983): Oil and Gas Regulation Analyst (0274-9033); (until 1980): Oil and Gas Price Regulation Analyst (0199-3410)
Related titles: Online - full text ed.: ISSN 1545-7907. GBP 851 in United Kingdom to institutions; EUR 1,077 in Europe to institutions; USD 1,666 elsewhere to institutions (effective 2012).
Indexed: A10, A12, A13, A22, ABIn, B01, B07, CA, E14, EIA, EnvAb, GeoRef, P48, P51, P52, P53, P54, P56, PQC, T02, V03.
—IE. **CCC.**
Published by: John Wiley & Sons, Inc., 111 River St, Hoboken, NJ 07030. TEL 201-748-6000, FAX 201-748-6088, info@wiley.com, http://www.wiley.com/WileyCDA/. **Subscr. to:** John Wiley & Sons Ltd.

NATURAL GAS FUELS. *see* TRANSPORTATION

665.7 FRA ISSN 1995-3933
HD9581.A1
NATURAL GAS INFORMATION. Variant title: I E A Natural Gas Information. Text in English. a., latest 2008. EUR 150 per issue (effective 2009); USD 150 per issue (effective 2003). **Document type:** *Journal, Trade.* **Description:** Provides a detailed reference work on gas supply and demand, covering not only the OECD countries but also the rest of the world.
Supersedes in part (in 1997): Oil and Gas Information (1016-5010); Which was formerly (until 1989): Annual Oil and Gas Statistics and Main Historical Series (1016-5002); (until 1983): Annual Oil and Gas Statistics (0256-3177); (until 1981): Oil Statistics (0259-8655)
Related titles: CD-ROM ed.: EUR 500 per issue (effective 2009); Online - full text ed.: ISSN 1683-4267. EUR 1,100, USD 1,430, GBP 880, JPY 160,400 (effective 2010) (from IngentaConnect).
Indexed: IIS.
—CCC.
Published by: Organisation for Economic Cooperation and Development (O E C D), International Energy Agency, 9 rue de la Federation, Paris, 75739 cedex 15, France. TEL 33-1-40576625, FAX 33-1-40576649, info@iea.org.

665.5 USA ISSN 0739-1811
NATURAL GAS INTELLIGENCE; weekly gas market newsletter. Text in English. 1981. w. USD 635 (effective 2005). charts; mkt.; stat.; tr.lit. back issues avail. **Document type:** *Newsletter, Trade.* **Description:** Provides the latest industry news for buyers and sellers of natural gas and power.
Related titles: E-mail ed.; Fax ed.; Online - full text ed.
—CCC.
Published by: Intelligence Press Inc., 22648 Glenn Dr, Ste 305, Sterling, VA 20164. TEL 703-318-8848, FAX 703-318-0597. Ed. James Geanakos. Circ: 700 (paid).

665.7 330.9 CAN ISSN 1491-2279
THE NATURAL GAS LOOKOUT. Text in English. 1994. m. CAD 695 (effective 2003). **Document type:** *Journal, Trade.*
Formerly (until 1996): Natural Gas Hedger (1202-3337)
Related titles: E-mail ed.; Online - full content ed.: ISSN 1498-8585. 1998. USD 650 online or E-mail ed. (effective 2003).
Published by: Canadian Enerdata Ltd., 100 Allstate Pkwy, Ste 304, Markham, ON L3R 6H3, Canada. TEL 905-479-9697, FAX 905-479-2515, publications@enerdata.com.

665.7 FRA ISSN 2106-6701
NATURAL GAS SURVEY, MIDDLE EAST & NORTH AFRICA. Text in English. 200?. a., latest 2010. EUR 810 combined subscription per issue (print & online eds.) (effective 2011).
Related titles: Online - full text ed.
Published by: Arab Petroleum Research Center, 7 avenue Ingres, Paris, Cedex 16 75781, France. TEL 33-01-45243310, FAX 33-01-45201685, aprc@arab-oil-gas.com.

665.54 338.47 CAN
TP714
NATURAL GAS UTILITY DIRECTORY. Text in English. 1955. a. CAD 80 to non-members; CAD 40 to members. **Document type:** *Directory.*
Former titles: Directory of Natural Gas Company Operations (1193-1345); Directory of Gas Distribution, Transmission and Production Companies (0840-9455); Canadian Gas Association Directory; Canadian Gas Utilities Directory (0576-5269); Directory of Gas Utilities (0315-8349)
Published by: (Economics and Statistics Department), Canadian Gas Association, 243 Consumers Rd, Ste 1200, North York, ON M2J 5E3, Canada. TEL 416-498-1994, FAX 416-498-7465.

665.5 USA ISSN 8756-3037
NATURAL GAS WEEK. Abbreviated title: N G W. Text in English. 1985. w. USD 4,100 (effective 2011). **Document type:** *Newsletter, Trade.* **Description:** Provides market reporting and analysis for the North American natural gas sector, including complete, up-to-date volume-weighted pricing and statistical data from wellhead to city gate.
Related titles: E-mail ed.; Fax ed.; Online - full text ed.: USD 3,100 (effective 2011).
Indexed: A15, ABIn, B02, B15, B17, B18, G04, G05, G06, G07, G08, GeoRef, I05, P48, P51, P52, P56, PQC, SpeleolAb.
—Ingenta, Linda Hall. **CCC.**
Published by: Energy Intelligence Group, Inc., 5 E 37th St, 5th Fl, New York, NY 10016. TEL 212-532-1112, FAX 212-532-4479. Ed. Tom Haywood.

NATURAL RESOURCES RESEARCH. *see* MINES AND MINING INDUSTRY

665.5 RUS ISSN 2221-2701
▼ ➤ **NAUKA I TEKHNOLOGII TRUBOPROVODNOGO TRANSPORTA NEFTI I NEFTEPRODUKTOV.** Text in Russian. 2011. q. RUR 1,800 domestic (effective 2011). bk.rev. bibl.; charts; illus.; stat. **Document type:** *Journal, Academic/Scholarly.* **Description:** Contains more than 20 subject areas which cover such categories as technology, science, design, construction, safety, innovations, current trends, education etc of pipeline transportation of oil and oil products. Designed for personnel working in the oil industry.
Related titles: Online - full text ed.
Published by: Nauchno-Isseldovatel'skii Institut Transporta, Nefti i Nefteproduktov, 2i Verhnii Mikhailovskii proezd 9, str. 5, Moscow, 115419, Russian Federation. TEL 7-495-9508295, FAX 7-495-9339647, http://www.niitnn.ru. Ed. A Y Soschenko. Circ: 4,000.

665.5 RUS ISSN 2070-6820
➤ **NAUKA I TEKHNIKA V GAZOVOI PROMYSHLENNOSTI/GAS AND TECHNOLOGY IN GAS INDUSTRY**; nauchno-tekhnicheskii zhurnal. Text in Russian; Summaries in English, Russian. 1999. q. RUR 4,248 (effective 2010). bk.rev. abstr.; bibl.; illus.; maps. back issues avail. **Document type:** *Journal, Academic/Scholarly.*
Indexed: RefZh.
Published by: Gazprom Expo LLC, ul Obrucheva 27/2, Moscow, 117630, Russian Federation. TEL 7-499-5804720, FAX 7-495-7193198. Ed. Artem Khegai. Pub. Sergey Kalityuk.

665.54 USA
NEBRASKA PETROLEUM AND CONVENIENCE STORE MARKETER. Text in English. 1917. m. adv. tr.lit. **Document type:** *Magazine, Trade.*
Former titles: Nebraska Petroleum Marketer; Nebraska Oil Jobber
Published by: Nebraska Petroleum Marketers and Convenience Store Association, Inc., 1320 Lincoln Mall, Lincoln, NE 68508. TEL 402-474-6691, FAX 402-474-2510. Ed., R&P Fred R Stone. Adv. contact Scott Pollard. B&W page USD 411; 8.5 x 11. Circ: 1,500.

330 665 RUS
NEFT', GAZ I BIZNES. Text in Russian. bi-m. **Document type:** *Journal.*
Address: Leninskii pr-t 65, Moscow, 117917, Russian Federation. TEL 7-095-1358406, 7-095-1358736. Ed. Igor Mishchenko. Circ: 3,000.

665 RUS ISSN 1607-5242
NEFT' PRIOB'YA. Text in Russian. w.
Published by: R I I TS Neft' Priobya, Ul Magistral'naya 19a, Surgut, 626400, Russian Federation. Ed. Lyudmila Stoyanova. Circ: 50,000.

665 USA ISSN 0968-6452
NEFTE COMPASS (PRINT). Text in English. 1992. w. **Document type:** *Newsletter, Trade.* **Description:** Focuses on the oil and gas industries in Russia, the newly independent republics and Eastern Europe.
Related titles: E-mail ed.; Online - full text ed.: Nefte Compass (Online). ISSN 1742-4372. 200?. USD 3,100 (effective 2011).
Indexed: A15, ABIn, B02, B15, B17, B18, G04, G06, G07, G08, I05, P48, P51, P52, P56, PQC.
—CCC.
Published by: Energy Intelligence Group, Inc., 5 E 37th St, 5th Fl, New York, NY 10016. TEL 212-532-1112, FAX 212-532-4479. Ed. Michael Ritchie.

665.5 RUS
NEFTEGAZONOSNYE I PERSPEKTIVNYE KOMPLEKSY TSENTRAL'NYKH I VOSTOCHNYKH OBLASTEI RUSSKOI PLATFORMY. Text in Russian. irreg. illus.
Published by: (Vsesoyuznyi Nauchno-Issledovatel'skii Geologorazvedochnyi Neftyanoi Institut), Izdatel'stvo Nedra, Tverskaya Zastava pl 3, Moscow, 125047, Russian Federation. TEL 7-095-2505255, FAX 7-095-2502772.

665 RUS
NEFTEGAZOVAYA VERTIKAL'. Text in Russian. m. USD 17.55 domestic; USD 193 foreign (effective 2002). **Document type:** *Journal.*
Address: Ul Marshala Timoshenko 30, et 10, Moscow, 121359, Russian Federation. TEL 7-095-1497245, 7-095-1492949. Ed. Nikolai Nikitin. Circ: 15,000.

665.5 RUS ISSN 1813-503X
HD9560.1
NEFTEGAZOVOE DELO. Text in Russian. 2001. w. free (effective 2011). **Document type:** *Journal, Academic/Scholarly.* **Description:** Designed for the specialists of the petroleum and gas industries, and also for teachers, students, post-graduate students and scientific employees.
Media: Online - full text. **Related titles:** English ed.: Oil and Gas Business Journal. free (effective 2011).
Published by: Ufimskii Gosudarstvennyi Negtyanoi Tekhnicheskii Universitet/Ufa State Petroleum Technological University, Zhurnal Neftegazovoe Delo, ul Kosmonavtov 1, Ufa, 450062, Russian Federation. TEL 7-3472-431910, info@ogbus.ru, http://www.ogbus.ru. Ed. R N Bakhtizin.

665.5 RUS
NEFTEGAZOVYE TEKHNOLOGII/OIL AND GAS TECHNOLOGIES; nauchno-tekhnicheskii zhurnal. Text in Russian; Summaries in English. 1979. bi-m. RUR 7,200 domestic; USD 599 foreign (effective 2008). **Document type:** *Journal, Trade.*
Formerly (until Mar. 1994): Neft', Gaz i Neftekhimiya za Rubezhom (0202-4578)
Related titles: ◆ Partial translation of: World Oil. ISSN 0043-8790; ◆ Partial translation of: Hydrocarbon Processing. ISSN 0887-0284.
Published by: Izdatel'stvo Toplivo i Energetika/Fuel & Energy Publishing Co., ul Skotoprogonnaya 29/1, Moscow, 109029, Russian Federation. TEL 7-495-1093368, catalog_publ@mtu-net.ru. Ed. H Gerikhanov. Pub. Vladimir U Krasik. Circ: 3,000. **Dist. by:** East View Information Services, 10601 Wayzata Blvd, Minneapolis, MN 55305. TEL 952-252-1201, 800-477-1005, FAX 952-252-1202, info@eastview.com, http://www.eastview.com.

665.5 547.8 RUS ISSN 0028-2421
TP690.A1 CODEN: NEFTAH
NEFTEKHIMIYA. Text in Russian. 1961. bi-m. RUR 930 for 6 mos. domestic (effective 2004). index. **Document type:** *Journal, Academic/Scholarly.* **Description:** Publishes research papers on the analysis, physical and chemical properties and behavior of individual petroleum constituents, as well as applications of petroleum chemistry in the manufacture of industrial products.
Related titles: Microfiche ed.: (from EVP); Online - full text ed.; ◆ English Translation: Petroleum Chemistry. ISSN 0965-5441.
Indexed: A22, APICat, APIH&E, APIOC, APIPR, APIPS, APITS, C33, CIN, ChemAb, ChemTitl, GeoRef, RefZh, SCOPUS, SpeleolAb.
—BLDSC (0124.280000), CASDDS, East View, IE, Infotrieve, INIST, Linda Hall. **CCC.**
Published by: (Rossiiskaya Akademiya Nauk/Russian Academy of Sciences), Izdatel'stvo Nauka, Profsoyuznaya ul 90, Moscow, 117864, Russian Federation. TEL 7-095-3347151, FAX 7-095-4202220, secret@naukaran.ru, http://www.naukaran.ru.

338.47665 GBR ISSN 1463-4295
NEFTEPANORAMA. Variant title: Argus Neftepanorama. Text in Russian. 1998. s-m. **Document type:** *Newsletter, Trade.* **Description:** Provides information and briefs on the international oil industry for Russian-speaking executives.
Published by: Argus Media Ltd., Argus House, 175 St. John St, London, EC1V 4LW, United Kingdom. TEL 44-20-7359-8792, FAX 44-20-7359-6661, editorial@argusmediagroup.com, http://www.argusmedia.com.

665.5 RUS ISSN 0233-5727
NEFTEPERERABOTKA I NEFTEKHIMIYA. NAUCHNO-TEKHNICHESKIE DOSTIZHENIYA I PEREDOVOI OPYT. Text in Russian. m. USD 189.95 in United States.
Indexed: ChemAb, RefZh.
—BLDSC (0124.240000), East View, INIST.
Address: Ul Bolotnaya 12, Moscow, 113035, Russian Federation. TEL 7-095-2311204, FAX 7-095-2332434. **Dist. by:** East View Information Services, 10601 Wayzata Blvd, Minneapolis, MN 55305. TEL 952-252-1201, 800-477-1005, FAX 952-252-1202, info@eastview.com, http://www.eastview.com.

P

665.5 RUS ISSN 0207-2351
NEFTEPROMYSLOVOE DELO/OILFIELD ENGINEERING; nauchno-tekhnicheskii zhurnal. Text in Russian. 1963. m. USD 299 in United States (effective 2004). **Document type:** *Journal.* **Description:** Covers activities in the area of new petroleum production.
Indexed: PetrolAb.
—BLDSC (0124.260000), INIST, Linda Hall, PADDS.
Published by: Vserossiiskii Nauchno-Issledovatel'skii Institut Organizatsii Upravleniya i Ekonomiki Neftegazovoi Promyshlennosti (VNIIOENG), Nametkina 14, korp B, Moscow, 117420, Russian Federation. TEL 7-095-3320022, FAX 7-095-3316877, vniioeng@mcn.ru, http://vniioeng.mcn.ru. **Dist. by:** East View Information Services, 10601 Wayzata Blvd, Minneapolis, MN 55305. TEL 952-252-1201, 800-477-1005, FAX 952-252-1202, info@eastview.com, http://www.eastview.com.

665.5 RUS
NEFTYANIK ORENBURZH'YA. Text in Russian. 1996. w. **Document type:** *Newspaper, Consumer.*
Address: Pr Br Korostelevykh 4, Orenburg, 460009, Russian Federation. TEL 7-3532-773304. Ed. V I Selezneva. Circ: 5,000.

665 622 RUS ISSN 0028-2448
TN860 CODEN: NEKHA6
NEFTYANOE KHOZYAISTVO/OIL INDUSTRY. Text in Russian, English; Summaries in English. 1920-1941; resumed 1946. m. USD 473 foreign (effective 2005). adv. bk.rev. bibl.; charts; illus. index. reprints avail. **Document type:** *Magazine, Trade.* **Description:** Covers well-drilling equipment and technology, field development, crude production and transmission, and environmental safety.
Indexed: ASCA, CIN, ChemAb, ChemTitl, FLUIDEX, FR, GeoRef, PetrolAb, RASB, RefZh, SCOPUS, SpeleolAb.
—CASDDS, East View, INIST, Linda Hall, PADDS. **CCC.**
Address: Sofiiskaya nab 26-1, Moscow, 115998, Russian Federation. TEL 7-095-7300717, FAX 7-095-9299610. Ed. L D Churilov. Adv. contact Helena Dorofeyeva. color page USD 3,000. Circ: 40,000. **Dist. by:** East View Information Services, 10601 Wayzata Blvd, Minneapolis, MN 55305. TEL 952-252-1201, 800-477-1005, FAX 952-252-1202, info@eastview.com, http://www.eastview.com.

665.5 382.029 NLD ISSN 1573-3033
NETHERLANDS OIL & GAS CATALOGUE. Text in English. 1981. a. adv.
Formerly (until 2004): Netherlands Offshore Catalogue (0922-3967)
Published by: (IRO - Association of Dutch Suppliers in the Oil & Gas Industry), Pedemex, Mgr Schaepmanlaan 53, Dongen, 5103 BB, Netherlands. TEL 31-162-314181, FAX 31-162-319414, http://www.pedemex.nl. Pub. Pieter Schoonenberg. adv.: B&W page EUR 1,600, color page EUR 1,900; 190 x 265.

338.47665 GBR ISSN 1749-2351
NETHERLANDS PETROCHEMICALS REPORT. Text in English. 2005. a. EUR 820, USD 1,030 combined subscription per issue (print & email eds.) (effective 2010). **Document type:** *Report, Trade.* **Description:** Provides industry professionals and strategists, sector analysts, trade associations and regulatory bodies with independent forecasts and competitive intelligence on the petrochemicals industry in the Netherlands.
Related titles: E-mail ed.
Indexed: A15, ABIn, B02, B15, B17, B18, G04, I05, P48, P51, P52, P56, PQC.
Published by: Business Monitor International Ltd., Senator House, 85 Queen Victoria St, London, EC4V 4AB, United Kingdom. TEL 44-20-72480468, FAX 44-20-72480467, subs@businessmonitor.com.

NEW WORLDWIDE TANKER NOMINAL FREIGHT SCALE; code name Worldscale. *see* TRANSPORTATION—Ships And Shipping

665.5 CAN ISSN 0709-681X
NICKLE'S DAILY OIL BULLETIN. Text in English. 1937. d. CAD 1,080 domestic; USD 1,180 foreign (effective 2005). back issues avail. **Document type:** *Bulletin, Trade.* **Description:** Covers the Canadian oil and gas industry, including news, analysis of oilpatch trends, activity snapshots, interviews with corporate leaders, reports on exploratory successes and failures, new well locations, feature stories on new technologies and more.
Related titles: Online - full content ed.: CAD 1,080 for 1 work-station; CAD 1,577 for 2 work-stations; CAD 2,041 for 3 work-stations; CAD 2,420 for 4-10 work-stations (effective 2005).
—CIS.
Published by: Nickle's Energy Group (Subsidiary of: Business Information Group), Ste 300, 999 8 St SW, Calgary, AB T2R 1N7, Canada. TEL 403-209-3500, 800-387-2446, FAX 403-245-8666, http://www.nickles.com/.

665.5 CAN
NICKLE'S DAILY WELL LICENCES. Text in English. d. CAD 225 for 1 workstation; CAD 365 for 2 workstations; CAD 465 for 3 workstations (effective 2005). **Document type:** *Newsletter, Trade.*
Media: Fax. **Related titles:** Online - full text ed.
Published by: Nickle's Energy Group (Subsidiary of: Business Information Group), Ste 300, 999 8 St SW, Calgary, AB T2R 1N7, Canada. TEL 403-209-3500, 800-387-2446, FAX 403-245-8666, http://www.nickles.com/.

665.5 CAN ISSN 1480-2147
NICKLE'S NEW TECHNOLOGY MAGAZINE. Variant title: New Technology Magazine. Text in English. 1937. 8/yr. CAD 89 for 1 workstation; CAD 69 2-10 workstations (effective 2005). adv. m. and a. index. back issues avail. **Document type:** *Magazine, Trade.* **Description:** Covers drilling and completions, information technology, pipelines, production, heavy oil and oilsands, seismic and geophysical technologies, and the environment.
Former titles (until 1997): Nickle's Technology Magazine (1484-4044); (until 1997): Nickle's Daily Oil Bulletin New Technology Magazine (1484-4036); Which superseded in part (in 1996): Nickle's Daily Oil Bulletin (0709-681X)
Related titles: Online - full text ed.: CAD 89 for 1 workstation; CAD 69 2-10 workstation (effective 2005).
Indexed: C03, CBCABus, P48, P52, P56, PQC, PetrolAb.
—PADDS.
Published by: Nickle's Energy Group (Subsidiary of: Business Information Group), Ste 300, 999 8 St SW, Calgary, AB T2R 1N7, Canada. TEL 403-209-3500, 800-387-2446, FAX 403-245-8666, http://www.nickles.com/. Ed. Maurice Smith. Pub. Stephen Marsters. Adv. contact Tony Poblete.

665.5 CAN ISSN 1204-2951
NICKLE'S PETROLEUM EXPLORER. Variant title: Petroleum Explorer. Text in English. 1995. bi-w. CAD 94 (effective 2005). **Document type:** *Newsletter, Trade.* **Description:** Informs about wildcat drilling results, company exploration targets, seismic surveys, hot exploration areas and land postings.
Related titles: Online - full text ed.
Indexed: C03, CBCABus, P52, P56, PQC.
Published by: Nickle's Energy Group (Subsidiary of: Business Information Group), Ste 300, 999 8 St SW, Calgary, AB T2R 1N7, Canada. TEL 403-209-3500, 800-387-2446, FAX 403-245-8666, http://www.nickles.com/.

665.5 CAN ISSN 1189-2927
NICKLE'S WEEKLY DRILLING REPORTS. Key Title: Nickle's Daily Oil Bulletin. Weekly Drilling Report. Text in English. 1937. w. CAD 415 for 1 workstation (effective 2005). **Document type:** *Report, Trade.* **Description:** Covers the drilling operations progress reported to the Daily Oil Bulletin each week.
Supersedes in part (in 1996): Nickle's Daily Oil Bulletin (0709-681X)
Related titles: Online - full content ed.: CAD 415 for 1 workstation (effective 2005).
Published by: Nickle's Energy Group (Subsidiary of: Business Information Group), Ste 300, 999 8 St SW, Calgary, AB T2R 1N7, Canada. TEL 403-209-3500, 800-387-2446, FAX 403-245-8666, http://www.nickles.com/. Adv. contact Tony Poblete.

665.7 DEU
NIEDERDRUCKANSCHLUSSVERORDNUNG - GASGRUNDVERSORGUNGSVERORDNUNG. Text in German. 1986. base vol. plus a. updates. looseleaf. EUR 60 base vol(s).; EUR 22 updates per issue (effective 2009). **Document type:** *Monographic series, Trade.*
Formerly (until 2009): Verordnung ueber Allgemeine Bedingungen fuer die Gasversorgung von Tarifkunden (0933-8993)
Published by: Erich Schmidt Verlag GmbH & Co. (Berlin), Genthiner Str 30 G, Berlin, 10785, Germany. TEL 49-30-2500850, FAX 49-30-250085305, vertrieb@esvmedien.de, http://www.erich-schmidt-verlag.de.

338.47665 GBR ISSN 1749-236X
NIGERIA PETROCHEMICALS REPORT. Text in English. 2005. a. EUR 820, USD 1,030 combined subscription per issue (print & email eds.) (effective 2010). **Document type:** *Report, Trade.* **Description:** Provides industry professionals and strategists, sector analysts, trade associations and regulatory bodies with independent forecasts and competitive intelligence on the Nigerian petrochemicals industry.
Related titles: E-mail ed.
Indexed: A15, ABIn, B02, B15, B17, B18, G04, I05, P48, P51, P52, P56, PQC.
Published by: Business Monitor International Ltd., Senator House, 85 Queen Victoria St, London, EC4V 4AB, United Kingdom. TEL 44-20-72480468, FAX 44-20-72480467, subs@businessmonitor.com.

338.2 NGA
HD9577.N5
NIGERIAN NATIONAL PETROLEUM CORPORATION. MONTHLY PETROLEUM INFORMATION. Text in English. m.
Formerly: Nigeria. Federal Department of Petroleum Resources. Monthly Petroleum Information (0549-2513)
Published by: Nigerian National Petroleum Corporation, PMB 12701, Lagos, Nigeria. Circ: 2,000.

665.7 JPN ISSN 0029-0211
TP700 CODEN: NIPGAM
NIHON GASU KYOKAISHI/JAPAN GAS ASSOCIATION. JOURNAL. Text in Japanese. 1948. m. JPY 4,200. adv.
Indexed: F&EA, GasAb, JTA.
—BLDSC (4805.000000), CASDDS, Linda Hall.
Published by: Nihon Gasu Kyokai/Japan Gas Association, 15-12 Toranomon 1-chome, Minato-ku, Tokyo, 105-0001, Japan. Ed. Kazutomo Mukoyama. Circ: 5,000.

665.5 JPN ISSN 1344-5871
NISSEKI MITSUBISHI REBYU/NISSEKI MITSUBISHI TECHNICAL REVIEW (YEAR). Text in Japanese. 1959. q. **Document type:** *Trade.*
Formerly: Nisseki Rebyu (0285-5275)
Published by: Nisseki Mitsubishi Kabushiki Gaisha/Nippon Mitsubishi Oil Corporation, 3-12, Nishi Shimbashi 1-Chome, Minato-ku, Tokyo, 105-8412, Japan. TEL 81-3-3502-9175, FAX 81-3-3502-9167, http://www.nmoc.co.jp/.

665.5 NOR ISSN 0964-4636
NOROIL CONTACTS - OFFSHORE DIRECTORY. Text in Norwegian. 1976. 3/yr. adv.
Formerly: Noroil Contacts
Published by: Hart Europe Ltd., Postboks 480, Stavanger, 4001, Norway. Circ: 5,292. **Subscr. to:** Richard Fry and Associates, Ste. 225, Surrey House, 34 Eden St, Kingston Upon Thames, Surrey KT1 1ER, United Kingdom. TEL 081-549-3444.

665.5 338.2 NOR
NOROIL NEWSWIRE. Text in English. 1978. s-w. USD 1,882, GBP 1,150.
Published by: Hart Europe Ltd., Postboks 480, Stavanger, 4001, Norway. Ed. Mark Scruton. **Subscr. to:** Richard Fry and Associates, Ste. 225, Surrey House, 34 Eden St, Kingston Upon Thames, Surrey KT1 1ER, United Kingdom. TEL 081-549-3444.

338.47665 NOR ISSN 1504-1468
NORSK SOKKEL; tidsskrift fra oljedirektoratet. Text in Norwegian. 2004. 3/yr. (2-3/yr). free. back issues avail. **Document type:** *Magazine, Government.*
Related titles: Online - full text ed.: ISSN 1890-4467; ◆ English ed.: Norwegian Continental Shelf. ISSN 1504-2065.
Published by: Oljedirektoratet/Norwegian Petroleum Directorate (Subsidiary of: Olje- og Energidepartementet/Ministry of Petroleum and Energy), Professor Olav Hanssens Vei 10, Stavanger, 4003, Norway. TEL 47-51-876000, FAX 47-51-551571, postbox@npd.no. Ed. Bjoern Rasen.

665.5 USA ISSN 1931-2210
NORTH AMERICAN CRUDE WIRE. Text in English. 2000. d. USD 875; USD 995 combined subscription (online & E-mail eds.) (effective 2008). back issues avail. **Document type:** *Newsletter, Trade.* **Description:** Focuses on the day's U.S. and Canadian crude oil market and price developments.
Formerly (until 2000): U.S. Crude Wire
Media: Online - full text. **Related titles:** E-mail ed.
—**CCC.**
Published by: Platts (Subsidiary of: McGraw-Hill Companies, Inc.), 1200 G St NW, Ste 1000, Washington, DC 20005. TEL 212-904-3070, 800-752-8878, FAX 202-383-2024, support@platts.com.

665.5 USA
NORTH AMERICAN EXPLORATION AND PRODUCTION INDUSTRY. Text in English. a. **Document type:** *Directory, Trade.* **Description:** Publishes for North American integrated oils companies and independent producers onshore and offshore.
Published by: Midwest Publishing Company, 2230 E 49th St, Ste E, Tulsa, OK 74105. TEL 918-582-2000, 800-829-2002, FAX 918-587-9349, info@midwestpub.com, http://www.midwestpub.com/.

665.54 USA ISSN 2150-9190
TN879.5
NORTH AMERICAN PIPELINES. Abbreviated title: N A P. Text in English. 2008. bi-m. USD 99 elsewhere; USD 10 per issue; free in US & Canada (effective 2009). adv. back issues avail. **Document type:** *Magazine, Trade.* **Description:** Covers the latest news on market developments that are shaping the industry, the most efficient methods of pipeline construction and maintenance, and managerial strategies that enhance every company's bottom line.
Published by: Benjamin Media, Inc., 1770 Main St, PO Box 190, Peninsula, OH 44264. TEL 330-467-7588, FAX 330-468-2289, info@benjaminmedia.com, http://www.benjaminmedia.com. Ed. James W Rush. Pub. Bernard P Kryzs. adv.: color page USD 3,310; 210 x 282. Circ: 12,500.

665.5 USA
NORTH AMERICAN SUPPLY, DISTRIBUTION, MANUFACTURING AND SERVICE. Text in English. a. **Document type:** *Directory, Trade.* **Description:** Lists some 44,000 supply companies and stores, distribution centers, equipment manufacturers, service, engineering and consulting companies, along with 33,000 key personnel.
Published by: Midwest Publishing Company, 2230 E 49th St, Ste E, Tulsa, OK 74105. TEL 918-582-2000, 800-829-2002, FAX 918-587-9349, info@midwestpub.com, http://www.midwestpub.com/.

665.7 USA
NORTH CAROLINA PROPANE GAS NEWS. Text in English. m. free to members. **Document type:** *Magazine, Trade.*
Formerly: Carolina L P Gas News
Published by: North Carolina Propane Gas Association, 5112 Bur Oak Circle, Raleigh, NC 27612-3101. TEL 919-787-8485, FAX 919-781-7481. Ed. Romaine Holt. Circ: 800.

665.5 GBR
NORTH SEA FACTS. Text in English. 19??. a. GBP 685, USD 1,233, EUR 857 per issue (effective 2009). adv. **Document type:** *Bulletin.*
Published by: Oilfield Publications Ltd., PO Box 11, Ledbury, Herefordshire HR8 1BN, United Kingdom. TEL 44-1531-634561, FAX 44-1531-634239, sales@crsl.com, http://www.oilpubs.com. Adv. contact Shaun Sturge.

338.27 USA ISSN 1369-1171
NORTH SEA RIG REPORT. Text in English. 1990. m. **Document type:** *Newsletter, Trade.* **Description:** Contains monthly commentary on the North Sea mobile rig market and provides a rolling 12 month forecast of semi-submersible and jackup demand, supply and utilization as well as reviewing chartering activity for the preceding month.
Superseded in part (in 199?): Petrodata North Sea Rig Report (0959-0986)
Related titles: E-mail ed.; Online - full text ed.
Published by: O D S - Petrodata, 3200 Wilcrest Dr, Ste 170, Houston, TX 77042. TEL 832-463-3000, FAX 832-463-3100, general@ods-petrodata.com, http://www.ods-petrodata.com.

338.47665 USA
NORTH SEA SUPPLY VESSEL FORECAST. Text in English. q. **Document type:** *Newsletter, Trade.*
Published by: O D S - Petrodata, 3200 Wilcrest Dr, Ste 170, Houston, TX 77042. TEL 832-463-3000, FAX 832-463-3100, general@ods-petrodata.com, http://www.ods-petrodata.com.

666.5029 USA
NORTHEAST STATES PETROLEUM INDUSTRY. Text in English. 1945. a. **Document type:** *Directory, Trade.* **Description:** Supplies company name, address, phone and fax number, personnel, division offices, offshore operations, producers of oil or gas and if drilling contractor with rotary or cable tools, pipelines, refineries, petrochemical, gas processing, manufacturers and suppliers, petroleum engineers, landmen.
Former titles: Northeast Petroleum Industry; Directory of Producers and Drilling Contractors Northeast: Michigan, Indiana, Illinois, Kentucky
Media: Diskette.
Published by: Midwest Publishing Company, 2230 E 49th St, Ste E, Tulsa, OK 74105. TEL 800-829-2002, info@midwestpub.com, http://midwestpub.com/.

338.272809481 GBR ISSN 1753-0474
NORWAY OIL & GAS REPORT. Text in English. 2006. q. EUR 820, USD 1,030 combined subscription (print & email eds.) (effective 2010). **Document type:** *Report, Trade.* **Description:** Provides professionals, consultancies, government departments, regulatory bodies and researchers with independent forecasts and competitive intelligence on the Norwegian oil and gas industry.
Related titles: E-mail ed.
Indexed: B02, B15, B17, B18, G04, I05.
Published by: Business Monitor International Ltd., Senator House, 85 Queen Victoria St, London, EC4V 4AB, United Kingdom. TEL 44-20-72480468, FAX 44-20-72480467, subs@businessmonitor.com.

338 665.5 NOR ISSN 1502-5446
NORWAY. OLJE- OG ENERGIDEPARTEMENTET. FACTS. Text in English. 1978. a. back issues avail. **Document type:** *Government.*
Former titles (until 2000): Norwegian Petroleum Activity (1501-6412); (until 1997): Royal Ministry of Industry and Energy. Fact Sheet (0804-3310); (until 1993): Royal Ministry of Petroleum and Energy. Fact Sheet (0800-7683)
Related titles: Online - full text ed.; ◆ Norwegian Bokmal ed.: Norway. Olje- og Energidepartementet. Fakta (Bokmaal). ISSN 1502-3133; ◆ Norwegian Nynorsk ed.: Norway. Olje- og Energidepartementet. Fakta (Nynorsk). ISSN 1504-3398.
Published by: Olje- og Energidepartementet/Ministry of Petroleum and Energy, PO Box 8148, Dep, Oslo, 0033, Norway. TEL 47-22-249090, FAX 47-22-249596, postmottak@oed.dep.no.

338 665.5 NOR ISSN 1502-3133
NORWAY. OLJE- OG ENERGIDEPARTEMENTET. FAKTA (BOKMAAL). Text in Norwegian Bokmal. 1993. a.
Former titles (until 2000): Norway. Norsk Petroleumsvirksomhet. Fakta (0809-1587); (until (1997): Norway. Naerings- og Energidepartementet. Faktaheftet (0804-306X)
Related titles: Online - full text ed.; ◆ English ed.: Norway. Olje- og Energidepartementet. Facts. ISSN 1502-5446; ◆ Norwegian Nynorsk ed.: Norway. Olje- og Energidepartementet. Fakta (Nynorsk). ISSN 1504-3398.
Published by: Olje- og Energidepartementet/Ministry of Petroleum and Energy, PO Box 8148, Dep, Oslo, 0033, Norway. TEL 47-22-249090, FAX 47-22-249596, postmottak@oed.dep.no.

665.5 338 NOR ISSN 1504-3398
NORWAY. OLJE- OG ENERGIDEPARTEMENTET. FAKTA (NYNORSK). Text in Norwegian Nynorsk. a. **Document type:** *Government.*
Related titles: Online - full text ed.; ◆ English ed.: Norway. Olje- og Energidepartementet. Facts. ISSN 1502-5446; ◆ Norwegian Bokmal ed.: Norway. Olje- og Energidepartementet. Fakta (Bokmaal). ISSN 1502-3133.
Published by: Olje- og Energidepartementet/Ministry of Petroleum and Energy, PO Box 8148, Dep, Oslo, 0033, Norway. TEL 47-22-249090, FAX 47-22-249596, postmottak@oed.dep.no.

338.47665 NOR ISSN 1504-2065
TN874.N8
NORWEGIAN CONTINENTAL SHELF. Text in English. 2004. 3/yr. (2-3/yr). free. back issues avail. **Document type:** *Magazine, Government.*
Related titles: Online - full text ed.: ISSN 1890-4475; ◆ Norwegian ed.: Norsk Sokkel. ISSN 1504-1468.
Published by: Oljedirektoratet/Norwegian Petroleum Directorate (Subsidiary of: Olje- og Energidepartementet/Ministry of Petroleum and Energy), Professor Olav Hanssens Vei 10, Stavanger, 4003, Norway. TEL 47-51-876000, FAX 47-51-551571, postbox@npd.no. Ed. Bjoern Rasen.

665.5 550 NLD ISSN 0928-8937
NORWEGIAN PETROLEUM SOCIETY. SPECIAL PUBLICATION. Variant title: Norwegian Petroleum Society. Annual Conference Proceedings. Text in English. 1992. irreg., latest vol.11, 2002. price varies. back issues avail. **Document type:** *Proceedings, Academic/ Scholarly.*
Related titles: Online - full text ed.: ISSN 2212-1390.
Indexed: GeoRef, SCOPUS.
—BLDSC (6152.298700). **CCC.**
Published by: (Norsk Petroleumsforening/Norwegian Petroleum Society NOR), Elsevier BV (Subsidiary of: Elsevier Science & Technology), Radarweg 29, PO Box 211, Amsterdam, 1000 AE, Netherlands. TEL 31-20-4853911, FAX 31-20-4852457, JournalsCustomerServiceEMEA@elsevier.com, http://www.elsevier.nl.

NOVOSTI ENERGETIKI. *see* ENERGY

NOZZLE. *see* TRANSPORTATION—Automobiles

338.47 KWT
O A P E C ENERGY RESOURCES MONITOR. Text in Arabic. 1981. q. free. **Description:** Coverage of Arab and world developments in petroleum exploration, drilling, production, field development and in alternative energy technology.
Published by: Organization of Arab Petroleum Exporting Countries, PO Box 20501, Safat, 13066, Kuwait. TEL 965-4959000, FAX 965-4959755, oapec@oapecorg.org, http://www.oapecorg.org. Circ: 250.

382.42 KWT ISSN 1018-595X
HD9578.A55
O A P E C MONTHLY BULLETIN. Text in English. 1975. m. USD 40 to individuals; USD 60 to institutions. adv. bk.rev. stat. **Document type:** *Bulletin, Trade.* **Description:** Covers O.A.P.E.C. library's new accessions plus contents of recent periodicals on energy, petroleum, economics and related subjects.
Formerly: O A P E C News Bulletin; Incorporating (after 1988): Organization of Arab Petroleum Exporting Countries. Current Awareness; Which was formerly: O A P E C Monthly Bulletin of Current Awareness
Related titles: Arabic ed.
Indexed: KES, MEA&I, RASB, WBA.
—BLDSC (6196.539000), Ingenta.
Published by: (Library & Information Department), Organization of Arab Petroleum Exporting Countries, PO Box 20501, Safat, 13066, Kuwait. TEL 965-4959000, FAX 965-4959755, oapec@oapecorg.org, http://www.oapecorg.org. Circ: 750.

665.5 USA ISSN 0192-009X
O AND A MARKETING NEWS. (Oil and Automotive) Text in English. 1966. 7/yr. USD 20 (effective 2007). adv. 40 p./no.; back issues avail. **Document type:** *Magazine, Trade.* **Description:** Covers the activities of the petroleum aftermarket in 13 western states, including the distribution, merchandising, installation and servicing of gasoline, oil, alternative fuel and automotive aftermarket products; convenience stores; quick lubes; and carwashes.
Published by: KAL Publications Inc., 559 S Harbor Blvd, #A, Anaheim, CA 92805-4525. TEL 714-563-9300, FAX 714-563-9310. Ed., Pub. Kathy Laderman. Adv. contact Stephanie Faris. B&W page USD 2,425, color page USD 3,425; 16.75 x 11.5. Circ: 2,000 (paid); 3,000 (controlled).

665.7 GBR
O I E S PAPERS. NATURAL GAS. Variant title: O I E S Papers. Gas. Text in English. 1994. irreg., latest vol.35, 2009. GBP 5 per issue (effective 2009). **Document type:** *Monographic series, Academic/Scholarly.*
Related titles: Online - full text ed.: free (effective 2009).
Published by: Oxford Institute for Energy Studies, 57 Woodstock Rd, Oxford, Oxfords OX2 6FA, United Kingdom. TEL 44-1865-311377, FAX 44-1865-310527, information@oxfordenergy.org.

665.5 GBR
O I E S PAPERS. WORLD PETROLEUM MARKET. Text in English. 19??. irreg., latest vol.38, 2009. GBP 5 per issue (effective 2009). **Document type:** *Monographic series, Academic/Scholarly.*
Related titles: Online - full text ed.: free (effective 2009).
Published by: Oxford Institute for Energy Studies, 57 Woodstock Rd, Oxford, Oxfords OX2 6FA, United Kingdom. TEL 44-1865-311377, FAX 44-1865-310527, information@oxfordenergy.org.

338.47 AUT
O M V ANNUAL REPORT (YEAR). (Oesterreichische Mineraloelverwaltung) Text in English, German. 1956. a. free. **Document type:** *Corporate.*
Published by: O M V Aktiengesellschaft, Trabrennstr 6-8, Vienna, W 1020, Austria. TEL 43-1-40440-0, FAX 43-1-40440-91. Ed. Brigitte Juen.

338.2 665.5 AUT ISSN 0257-1617
O P E C ANNUAL REPORT. (Organization of the Petroleum Exporting Countries) Text in English. 1967. a. **Document type:** *Report, Corporate.* **Description:** Contains news about world economic situations for oil-producing countries, developments in the energy market, and activities of the secretariat.
Formerly: Organization of the Petroleum Exporting Countries. Annual Review and Record (0474-6317)
Related titles: Microfiche ed.: (from CIS).
Indexed: IIS, SpeleolAb.
Published by: Organization of the Petroleum Exporting Countries (O P E C), Obere Donaustrasse 93, Vienna, W 1020, Austria. TEL 43-1-21112-0, FAX 43-1-2149827, prid@opec.org, http://www.opec.org. Ed. Ulunma Angela Agoawike.

665.5 AUT ISSN 0475-0608
O P E C ANNUAL STATISTICAL BULLETIN. (Organization of the Petroleum Exporting Countries) Text in English. a. USD 75 with a diskette (effective 2001). charts; illus. **Document type:** *Bulletin, Corporate.* **Description:** Contains nearly 150 pages of tables, charts and graphs detailing the world's oil and gas reserves, crude oil and product output, exports, refining, tankers, plus economic and other data.
Related titles: Online - full text ed.
Indexed: IIS.
Published by: Organization of the Petroleum Exporting Countries (O P E C), Obere Donaustrasse 93, Vienna, W 1020, Austria. TEL 43-1-21112-0, FAX 43-1-2149827, prid@opec.org, http://www.opec.org. Ed. Omar Farouk Ibrahim.

665.5 AUT ISSN 0474-6279
HD9560.1
O P E C BULLETIN. (Organization of the Petroleum Exporting Countries, PR and Information Department) Text in English. 1967. 12/yr. USD 70 (effective 2009). adv. bk.rev. charts; illus.; stat. index. **Document type:** *Magazine, Trade.* **Description:** Includes oil industry news, organization reports, market reviews, statistics, alternative energy news and surveys, OPEC publications and OPEC Fund for International Development news, new acquisitions in the OPEC library, and a calendar of industry events.
Related titles: Microfiche ed.: (from CIS); Online - full text ed.
Indexed: A22, APIAb, EIA, EnerRev, EnvAb, GeoRef, IIS, M10, PAIS, PEBNI, RASB, RefZh, SCOPUS, SpeleolAb.
—BLDSC (6265.940000), IE, Ingenta, Linda Hall. **CCC.**
Published by: Organization of the Petroleum Exporting Countries (O P E C), Obere Donaustrasse 93, Vienna, W 1020, Austria. TEL 43-1-22112-0, FAX 43-1-2149827, TELEX 134474, prid@opec.org, http://www.opec.org. Ed. Omar Farouk Ibrahim. adv.: B&W page USD 2,300, color page USD 2,700; 210 x 275. Circ: 20,000.

333.79 665.5 GBR ISSN 1753-0229
HD9560.1 CODEN: OPECDI
➤ **O P E C ENERGY REVIEW**; energy economics and related issues. Text in English. 1976. q. GBP 412 in United Kingdom to institutions; EUR 523 in Europe to institutions; USD 692 in the Americas to institutions; USD 807 elsewhere to institutions; GBP 474 combined subscription in United Kingdom to institutions (print & online eds.); EUR 602 combined subscription in Europe to institutions (print & online eds.); USD 795 combined subscription in the Americas to institutions (print & online eds.); USD 929 combined subscription elsewhere to institutions (print & online eds.) (effective 2012). adv. back issues avail.; reprint service avail. from PSC. **Document type:** *Journal, Academic/Scholarly.* **Description:** Publishes selected academic papers on energy, Third World development issues and related economic and policy matters.
Formerly (until 2008): O P E C Review (0277-0180)
Related titles: Microfiche ed.: (from CIS); Microfilm ed.: (from PQC); Online - full text ed.: ISSN 1753-0237. 1997. GBP 412 in United Kingdom to institutions; EUR 523 in Europe to institutions; USD 692 in the Americas to institutions; USD 807 elsewhere to institutions (effective 2012) (from IngentaConnect).
Indexed: A01, A03, A08, A12, A17, A22, A26, ABIn, AESIS, APEL, B01, B06, B07, B09, BibInd, CA, CREJ, E01, E04, E05, E14, EIA, ESPM, EconLit, EnvAb, FR, GeoRef, I05, IBR, IBSS, IBZ, IIS, JEL, KES, M10, P34, P48, P51, P52, P53, P54, P56, PAIS, PQC, PollutAb, RASB, RiskAb, SCOPUS, SSciA, SpeleolAb, T02, WBA.
—BLDSC (6265.940500), IE, Infotrieve, Ingenta, INIST. **CCC.**
Published by: (Organization of the Petroleum Exporting Countries AUT, Public Information Department AUS), Wiley-Blackwell Publishing Ltd. (Subsidiary of: John Wiley & Sons, Inc.), 9600 Garsington Rd, Oxford, OX4 2DQ, United Kingdom. TEL 44-1865-776868, FAX 44-1865-714591, customerservices@blackwellpublishing.com. Ed. Omar Farouk Ibrahim. Adv. contact Craig Pickett TEL 44-1865-476267.

665.5 AUT
O P E C MONTHLY OIL MARKET REPORT. (Organization of the Petroleum Exporting Countries) Text in English. m. USD 525 (effective 2001). adv. **Document type:** *Journal, Trade.* **Description:** Contains the Secretariat's analyses of oil and product price movements, futures markets, the energy supply and demand balance, stock movements and global economic trends.
Related titles: Online - full text ed.
Published by: Organization of the Petroleum Exporting Countries (O P E C), Obere Donaustrasse 93, Vienna, W 1020, Austria. FAX 43-1-22112-0, prid@opec.org, http://www.opec.org.

665.5 USA ISSN 2159-4457
O P I S ETHANOL & BIODIESEL INFORMATION SERVICE. Text in English. 200?. w. **Document type:** *Newsletter, Trade.*
Published by: Oil Price Information Service (Subsidiary of: United Communications Group), Two Washingtonian Ctr, 9737 Washingtonian Blvd, Ste 100, Gaithersburg, MD 20878. TEL 301-287-2645, 888-301-2645, FAX 301-287-2820, energycs@opisnet.com.

665.5 CAN ISSN 0835-1740
OCTANE. Text in English. 1987. 6/yr. CAD 36; CAD 8 newsstand/cover (effective 2005). adv. **Document type:** *Magazine, Trade.* **Description:** Provides national coverage of the downstream petroleum industry.
Related titles: Online - full text ed.
Indexed: C03, CBCABus, P48, P52, P56, PQC.
—PADDS. **CCC.**
Published by: June/Warren Publishing Ltd., #300, 5735 - 7 St. NE, Calgary, AB T3E 8V3, Canada. TEL 403-265-3700, 888-563-2946, FAX 403-265-3706, bwhitelaw@junewarren.com, http://www.junewarren.com. Ed. Gordon Jaremko. Pub. Tim Heath. Adv. contact Steve Henrich. B&W page CAD 2,985, color page CAD 4,235; trim 10.75 x 8. Circ: 7,557.

665.5 USA ISSN 1072-8740
OCTANE WEEK. Variant title: Hart's Octane Week. Text in English. 1986. w. USD 1,995 (effective 2008). **Document type:** *Newsletter, Trade.* **Description:** Covers topics of interest to refiners and gasoline marketers regarding the major transformations occurring in the areas of gasoline composition, grade mix, reformulated fuels, octane generation, refining and blending technologies and aromatics.
Related titles: Online - full text ed.
Indexed: A10, A15, ABIn, B01, B07, E14, I05, P34, P48, P51, P52, P56, PQC, PROMT, T02, V03.
—**CCC.**
Published by: Hart Energy Publishing, LP (Subsidiary of: Chemical Week Associates), 1616 S Voss Rd, Ste 1000, Houston, TX 77057. TEL 713-993-9320, FAX 713-840-8585. Ed. Carol Cole TEL 240-498-6311. Pub. David Givens TEL 703-891-4811.

621.3 USA ISSN 0160-3663
TC1505 CODEN: OSTCBA
OFF-SHORE TECHNOLOGY CONFERENCE. PROCEEDINGS. Text in English. 1969. a. price varies. back issues avail. **Document type:** *Proceedings, Trade.*
Formerly (until 1975): Offshore Technology Conference. Preprints (0160-8339)
Related titles: CD-ROM ed.
Indexed: EngInd, GeoRef, SCOPUS, SpeleolAb.
—Ingenta. **CCC.**
Published by: Offshore Technology Conference, PO Box 833868, Richardson, TX 75083-3868. TEL 972-952-9494, FAX 972-952-9435, TELEX 163245 SPEUT.

338.2 622 USA ISSN 0030-0608
CODEN: OFSHAU
OFFSHORE (TULSA). Variant title: Offshore Incorporating the Oilman. Text in English. 1954. m. USD 101 domestic (print or online ed.); USD 132 in Canada & Mexico; USD 167 elsewhere; free to qualified personnel (effective 2009). adv. charts; illus.; tr.lit. back issues avail.; reprints avail. **Document type:** *Magazine, Trade.* **Description:** Serves the worldwide petroleum industry in its marine operations, engineering and technology. Includes information pertaining to seismic services, exploration, drilling, production, process, transportation (pipeline, marine, and air), marine and underwater engineering and communications, naval architecture, design and construction, diving services, marine support facilities, and research in oceanography and meteorology.
Formerly (until 195?): Offshore Operations; Incorporates (1982-199?): Oilman (0264-0759); Which was formed by the merger of (1972-1982): Oilman (Tabloid Edition) (0143-6694); Which superseded in part (in 1979): Oilman (0305-2281); (1980-1982): Offshore Services and Technology (0952-6420); Which was formerly (1972-1980): Offshore Services (0306-2309); (1967-1972): Hydrospace (0018-8212)
Related titles: Microform ed.: (from PQC); Online - full text ed.: USD 92 (effective 2008); Regional ed(s).: Offshore (Euro-Asia Edition).
Indexed: A05, A09, A10, A15, A22, A23, A24, A28, ABIn, APA, AS&TA, AS&TI, B01, B02, B03, B04, B06, B07, B08, B09, B11, B13, B15, B17, B18, BMT, BrCerAb, BrTechI, C&ISA, C10, C12, CA/WCA, CIA, CerAb, CivEngAb, CorrAb, E&CAJ, E04, E05, E11, E14, EEA, EMA, ESPM, EnerRev, EnvEAb, FLUIDEX, FR, G01, G04, G06, G07, G08, GEOBASE, GeoRef, H15, I05, Inspec, JOF, KES, M&TEA, M01, M02, M09, MBF, METADEX, OceAb, P02, P26, P48, P51, P52, P54, P56, PQC, PetrolAb, R18, S01, SCOPUS, SRI, SolStAb, SpeleolAb, T&II, T02, T04, V02, V03, V04, WAA.
—BLDSC (6244.200000), CIS, IE, Infotrieve, Ingenta, INIST, Linda Hall, PADDS. **CCC.**
Published by: PennWell Corporation, 1421 S Sheridan Rd, Tulsa, OK 74112. TEL 918-835-3161, 800-331-4463, FAX 918-831-9804, Headquarters@PennWell.com, http://www.pennwell.com. Ed. Eldon R Ball. Adv. contact David Davis TEL 713-963-6206. color page USD 22,964; trim 9.5 x 15. Circ: 38,500 (paid and controlled).

665.5 UAE
OFFSHORE ARABIA. Text in English. m. free to qualified personnel. **Document type:** *Magazine, Trade.*
Published by: Reflex Publishing FZ LLC, Dubai Media City, PO Box 500643, Dubai, United Arab Emirates. TEL 971-4-3910830, FAX 971-4-3904570, info@reflexpublishingme.com, http://reflexpublishingme.com/.

OFFSHORE CENTRES REPORT. *see* BUSINESS AND ECONOMICS—International Commerce

665.5 620 SGP ISSN 0305-876X
TC1501
OFFSHORE ENGINEER. Text in English. 1975. m. GBP 60, EUR 86 (effective 2000). adv. charts; illus. back issues avail. **Document type:** *Journal, Trade.* **Description:** Covers engineering, technical and operational facets of offshore oil and gas exploration and production worldwide.
Incorporates: Northern Offshore (0332-5237)
Indexed: A22, AESIS, APA, ASFA, B21, BMT, BrGeoL, BrTechI, C&ISA, CorrAb, E&CAJ, EEA, ESPM, EnvEAb, F&EA, FLUIDEX, GEOBASE, GeoRef, H&SSA, KES, OceAb, PetrolAb, SCOPUS, SolStAb, SpeleolAb, WAA.
—BLDSC (6244.225000), IE, Infotrieve, Ingenta, INIST, Linda Hall, PADDS. **CCC.**
Published by: Emap Business Communications Asia Pte. Ltd. (Subsidiary of: Emap Business Communications Ltd.), 31 Tanjong Pagar Rd 02-01, Singapore, 088454, Singapore. TEL 65-220-9339, FAX 65-220-7610. Ed. David Morgan. Circ: 32,000 (controlled).

OFFSHORE ENGINEERING. *see* ENGINEERING—Civil Engineering

P

665.5 USA ISSN 8756-7539
TC1501
OFFSHORE FRONTIERS. Text in English. 1982. s-a. free. adv.
Document type: *Magazine, Trade.* **Description:** Published for employees, customers and other key audiences.
Formerly (until 1985): Subsea (8756-3843)
Published by: Transocean Inc., PO Box 2765, Houston, TX 77252-2765. TEL 713-232-7500, info@mail.deepwater.com. Circ: 280.

665.5 310 GBR ISSN 2044-9496
▼ **OFFSHORE INTELLIGENCE MONTHLY.** Text in English. 2011. m. GBP 825, USD 1,485, EUR 1,032 combined subscription in Europe (print & email eds.); GBP 855, USD 1,539, EUR 1,069 combined subscription elsewhere (print & email eds.) (effective 2011).
Document type: *Report, Trade.* **Description:** Provides information about the global offshore oil and gas industry.
Related titles: E-mail ed.: ISSN 2044-950X.
Published by: Clarkson Research Services Ltd., St Magnus House, 3 Lower Thames St, London, EC3R 6HE, United Kingdom. TEL 44-20-73343134, FAX 44-20-75220330, sales@crsl.com.

665.5 USA ISSN 1058-5842
THE OFFSHORE INTERNATIONAL NEWSLETTER. Text in English. 1974. w. USD 759 (effective 2007). charts; stat. 8 p./no.; back issues avail. **Document type:** *Newsletter, Trade.* **Description:** Follows offshore oil exploration and related concerns worldwide.
Formerly (until 1991): Ocean Construction Report (0147-152X); Which superseded in part (in 1975): Ocean Construction & Engineering Report
Related titles: E-mail ed.; Online - full text ed.: USD 650 (effective 2005).
Indexed: PetrolAb.
—CCC.
Published by: O D S - Petrodata, 3200 Wilcrest Dr, Ste 170, Houston, TX 77042. TEL 832-463-3000, FAX 832-463-3100, general@ods-petrodata.com, http://www.ods-petrodata.com. Ed. Brad Baethe.

OFFSHORE MARINE MONTHLY. *see* TRANSPORTATION—Ships And Shipping

338.476655 NOR ISSN 0803-3773
CODEN: OFFEES
OFFSHORE OG ENERGI. Variant title: Offshore & Energy. Text in English, Norwegian. 1982. q. NOK 480 domestic; NOK 600 foreign (effective 2005). adv. **Description:** Covers the entire oil and gas industry.
Former titles (until 1991): Offshore Norge (0801-0323); (until 1984): Offshore i Vest (0800-2460); Incorporates (1978-1990): North Sea Observer (0332-6144)
Indexed: INIS AtomInd, KES.
—CCC.
Published by: Offshore Media Group, Stortingsgata 12, Oslo, 0161, Norway. TEL 47-22-838368, FAX 47-22-833551, redaksjonen@offshore.no. adv.: B&W page NOK 22,000, B&W page EUR 2,590, B&W page USD 3,235; 180 x 240. Circ: 10,100.

665.5 USA
OFFSHORE PRODUCTION REPORT. Text in English. 19??. m. USD 29 (effective 2011). charts; stat. **Document type:** *Report, Government.* **Description:** Compiles data on oil and gas production by district and field from offshore state waters.
Published by: Railroad Commission, Oil and Gas Division, PO Box 12967, Austin, TX 78711. TEL 877-228-5740, publicassist@rrc.state.tx.us.

665.5 338.2 USA
OFFSHORE RIG LOCATOR. Text in English. 1974. m. USD 700 (effective 2005). **Document type:** *Newsletter, Trade.* **Description:** Provides location information and operating statistics on the activity of all offshore drilling rigs worldwide, with analyses of market conditions.
Formerly (until 1984): Offshore Rig Location Report (0733-0928)
Related titles: Diskette ed.: USD 950 (effective 2005); Online - full text ed.: USD 1,250 (effective 2005).
—CCC.
Published by: O D S - Petrodata, 3200 Wilcrest Dr, Ste 170, Houston, TX 77042. TEL 832-463-3000, FAX 832-463-3100, general@ods-petrodata.com, http://www.ods-petrodata.com. Eds. David Thomas, Rina Samsudin. Pub. Tom Marsh. Circ: 700.

665.5 USA
OFFSHORE RIG MONTHLY. Text in English. 197?. m. **Document type:** *Newsletter, Trade.* **Description:** Contains in-depth analysis and commentary focuses on a developing trend or an important industry issue.
Incorporates (1996-200?): Bassoe Offshore Monthly (0809-2168)
Published by: O D S - Petrodata, 3200 Wilcrest Dr, Ste 170, Houston, TX 77042. TEL 832-463-3000, FAX 832-463-3100, customerservice@ods-petrodata.com, http://www.ods-petrodata.com. Ed. Gavin Strachan. Pub. Thomas Marsh.

OFFSHORE SUPPORT JOURNAL. *see* TRANSPORTATION—Ships And Shipping

622.33819 GBR ISSN 0968-784X
CODEN: JOFTED
OFFSHORE TECHNOLOGY. Variant title: Journal of Offshore Technology. Text in English. 1993. q. adv. **Document type:** *Journal, Trade.* **Description:** Concentrates on in-depth coverage of the critical issues affecting the industry, offering a unique perspective on the international oil and gas market.
Indexed: A28, AESIS, APA, ASFA, BMT, BrCerAb, BrTechI, C&ISA, CA/WCA, CIA, CPEI, CerAb, CivEngAb, CorrAb, E&CAJ, E11, EEA, EMA, ESPM, EngInd, EnvEAb, GeoRef, H15, IBR, IBZ, M&TEA, M09, MBF, METADEX, PetrolAb, SCOPUS, SolStAb, T04, TM, WAA.
—BLDSC (6244.249500), IE, Ingenta, INIST, Linda Hall, PADDS. **CCC.**
Published by: Institute of Marine Engineering, Science and Technology, 80 Coleman St, London, EC2R 5BJ, United Kingdom. TEL 44-20-73822600, FAX 44-20-73822670, info@imarest.org. Ed. Bruce McMichael. Adv. contact Stephen Habermel TEL 44-20-73822633. color page GBP 2,345; trim 210 x 297.

665 NLD ISSN 0921-2477
OFFSHORE VISIE. Text in Dutch, English. 1984. s-m. EUR 30 domestic; EUR 35 in Europe; free to qualified personnel (effective 2009). adv. back issues avail. **Document type:** *Journal, Trade.* **Description:** Cover news and developments in the offshore petroleum industry.
—IE, Infotrieve.
Published by: Uitgeverij Tridens, Postbus 526, IJmuiden, 1970 AM, Netherlands. TEL 31-255-530577, FAX 31-255-536068, tridens@practica.nl. Ed. Han Heilig.

665.5 CAN ISSN 0848-2780
HD9574.C23
OIL ACTIVITY REVIEW. Text in English. 1982. a. free. charts; illus.; stat. **Document type:** *Government.* **Description:** Review of petroleum industry activity in Manitoba.
Published by: Manitoba Energy and Mines, Petroleum Branch, 360 1395 Ellice Ave, Winnipeg, MB R3G 3P2, Canada. TEL 204-945-6577, FAX 204-945-0586. Ed., Pub. Heather Tisdale. Circ: 700.

333.8 USA
OIL: AN INTEGRATED INDUSTRY. Text in English. 1991. a. **Description:** Analyzes historical and political events affecting the price, supply and demand, and bottom-line profits of the oil industry.
Published by: Dun & Bradstreet Information Services (Subsidiary of: Dun & Bradstreet, Inc.), 103 JFK Pkwy, Short Hills, NJ 07078. TEL 973-921-5500, 800-234-3867, SMSinfo@dnb.com, http://www.dnb.com.

665.5 KWT ISSN 0251-415X
OIL AND ARAB COOPERATION. Text in Arabic; Summaries in English. 1975. q. bk.rev. abstr. **Document type:** *Journal.* **Description:** Articles on petroleum sector and economic and social development in Arab countries.
Indexed: FR, GeoRef, MEA&I, RASB, SpeleolAb.
—INIST.
Published by: (Library & Information Department), Organization of Arab Petroleum Exporting Countries, PO Box 20501, Safat, 13066, Kuwait. TEL 965-4959000, FAX 965-4959755, oapec@oapecorg.org. Ed. Abdelaziz Al Abdulla Al Turki. Circ: 750.

665 USA
OIL & ENERGY. Text in English. 1955. m. USD 15 (effective 2007). adv. bk.rev.; Website rev. charts; mkt.; stat.; tr.lit. 48 p./no. 3 cols./p.; back issues avail. **Document type:** *Magazine, Trade.* **Description:** Serves retail/wholesale oilheat diesel fuel markets.
Formerly: Yankee Oilman (0044-0205)
Published by: Greystone Services, PO Box 4002, Beverly, MA 01915. TEL 978-535-9185, FAX 978-535-7826. Pub. Lee Yaffa. adv.: B&W page USD 1,280, color page USD 2,065; trim 7 x 10. Circ: 2,000 (paid); 6,700 (controlled).

OIL AND ENERGY TRENDS; a monthly publication of international energy statistics and analysis. *see* ENERGY

OIL AND ENERGY TRENDS: ANNUAL STATISTICAL REVIEW. *see* ENERGY—Abstracting, Bibliographies, Statistics

665.5 GBR ISSN 1742-7606
OIL & GAS (LONDON). Text in English. 2003. biennial. USD 200 per issue (effective 2011). **Document type:** *Journal, Trade.* **Description:** Aims to identify private practice lawyers with a proven track record in representing and advising major, independent and state oil and gas companies and financiers involved in the exploration, production, marketing and transportation of crude oil, natural gas and LNG.
Published by: (Who's Who Legal), Law Business Research Ltd., 87 Lancaster Rd, London, W11 1QQ, United Kingdom. TEL 44-20-79081188, FAX 44-20-72296910, http://www.lbresearch.com/. Eds. Tom Barnes TEL 44-20-79081180, Callum Campbell. Pub. Richard Davey.

665.5 557 USA
OIL AND GAS (ONLINE). Text in English. 1998. m. back issues avail. **Document type:** *Trade.*
Media: Online - full text.
Published by: State Geological Survey, 615 E Peabody Dr, Champaign, IL 61820. TEL 217-333-4747, isgs@isgs.illinois.edu.

665.5 531.64 USA
OIL AND GAS DEVELOPMENTS IN PENNSYLVANIA. Text in English. 1951. a. price varies. back issues avail.
Published by: (Pennsylvania Department of Conservation and Natural Resources, Bureau of Topographic and Geologic Survey, Department of Environmental Resources), Pennsylvania Geological Survey, Environmental Resources, 400 Waterfront Dr, Pittsburgh, PA 15222-4728. TEL 412-442-4235, FAX 412-442-4298. **Subscr. to:** State Book Store, PO Box 1365, Harrisburg, PA 17105.

338.0029 USA ISSN 0471-380X
OIL & GAS DIRECTORY. Text in English. 1970. irreg. USD 135 per issue domestic 38th ed. (effective 2008). adv. **Document type:** *Magazine, Trade.* **Description:** Lists oil companies, key personnel as well as service and supply companies in the drilling and producing industry.
Related titles: Diskette ed.
Indexed: SpeleolAb.
Published by: PennWell Corporation, 1421 S Sheridan Rd, Tulsa, OK 74112. TEL 918-835-3161, 800-331-4463, FAX 918-831-9804, Headquarters@PennWell.com, http://www.pennwell.com. Circ: 3,000.

665.5 RUS ISSN 1812-2086
OIL & GAS EURASIA. Text in Russian, English. 2000. m. **Document type:** *Journal, Trade.*
Indexed: RefZh.
—BLDSC (6249.840200).
Published by: Eurasia Press, Inc., PO box 92, Moscow, 125284, Russian Federation. Ed., Pub. Pat D Szymczak.

OIL & GAS EXECUTIVE. *see* BUSINESS AND ECONOMICS—Management

OIL AND GAS FIELD DESIGNATIONS. *see* EARTH SCIENCES—Geology

338.2328 USA ISSN 1555-4082
HD9560.1
OIL & GAS FINANCIAL JOURNAL. Text in English. 2004. m. USD 149; free to qualified personnel (effective 2009). adv. back issues avail. **Document type:** *Magazine, Trade.* **Description:** Provides petroleum industry managers, analysts and investors with information on important financial developments of oil exploration, oil and gas investing, international and regional oil and gas information, etc.
Related titles: Online - full text ed.: USD 149; free (effective 2009).
—CCC.
Published by: PennWell Corporation, 1421 S Sheridan Rd, Tulsa, OK 74112. TEL 918-835-3161, 800-331-4463, Headquarters@PennWell.com, http://www.pennwell.com. Ed. Don Stowers TEL 713-963-6235. Pub. Nicole Durham TEL 713-963-6234. Adv. contact Dana Griffin. color page USD 7,375, B&W page USD 6,375; trim 8 x 10.5. Circ: 12,523.

665.5 665.7 AUS ISSN 1038-1317
OIL & GAS GAZETTE. Text in English. 1990. m. AUD 148 domestic; AUD 200 foreign (effective 2008). adv. charts; illus.; stat.; tr.lit. index. back issues avail. **Document type:** *Magazine, Trade.* **Description:** Contains hard news stories relating to the Australian oil and gas industry, stock market news, latest in equipment and technology and some international coverage.
Related titles: Online - full text ed.
Indexed: ABIX, AESIS, GeoRef, SpeleolAb.
Published by: Resource Information Unit, PO Box 1533, Subiaco, W.A. 6904, Australia. TEL 61-8-93823955, FAX 61-8-93881025, riu@riu.com.au. Ed. Haydn Black. adv.: B&W page AUD 1,793, color page AUD 2,805.

665.5 USA ISSN 0744-5881
HD9561
OIL AND GAS INVESTOR. Text in English. 1981. m. USD 297; USD 997 combined subscription (print & online eds.) (effective 2008). adv. charts; illus. back issues avail. **Document type:** *Magazine, Trade.* **Description:** Covers the North American oil & gas exploration industry from an executive and financial standpoint.
Related titles: Online - full text ed.
Indexed: A10, A12, A13, A17, A22, ABIn, B01, B02, B03, B07, B11, B15, B17, B18, CA, E14, G04, G06, G07, G08, I05, P48, P51, P52, P53, P54, P56, PQC, T02, T03, V03.
—BLDSC (6249.958000), IE, Ingenta. **CCC.**
Published by: Hart Energy Publishing, LP (Subsidiary of: Chemical Week Associates), 1616 S Voss Rd, Ste 1000, Houston, TX 77057. TEL 713-260-6400, 800-874-2544, FAX 713-840-8585, custserv@hartenergy.com, http://www.hartenergy.com. Eds. Leslie Haines TEL 713-260-6428, Stephen Payne TEL 713-260-6431. Adv. contact Charlene Chase. color page USD 8,800, B&W page USD 7,300; trim 8.25 x 11.25. Circ: 7,725 (paid).

665.5 USA ISSN 1940-5189
HD9561
OIL AND GAS INVESTOR THIS WEEK. Variant title: Petroleum Finance Week. Text in English. 1993. w. USD 597 (effective 2009). **Document type:** *Newsletter, Trade.* **Description:** Contains news and analysis of breaking deals including new financings and M&A. It covers corporate strategy, stock performance, new E&P ventures and insider trading activity.
Former titles (until 200?): Oil and Gas Investor's Petroleum Finance Week (1077-5285); (until 1994): PetroMoney (1072-5105)
Related titles: Online - full text ed.: ISSN 1940-5197.
Indexed: A10, A15, ABIn, CA, I05, P48, P51, P52, P56, PQC, PROMT.
Published by: Hart Energy Publishing, LP (Subsidiary of: Chemical Week Associates), 1616 S Voss Rd, Ste 1000, Houston, TX 77057. TEL 713-993-9320, FAX 713-840-8585, custserv@hartenergy.com, http://www.hartenergy.com. Ed. Stephen Payne TEL 713-260-6431. Pub. David Givens TEL 703-891-4811.

665.5 USA ISSN 1940-8471
OIL AND GAS INVESTOR'S A & D WATCH. (Acquisitions & Divestitures) Variant title: A & D Watch. Text in English. 1986. m. USD 747 combined subscription (print & online eds.) (effective 2009). adv. 30 p./no.; reprints avail. **Document type:** *Newsletter, Trade.* **Description:** Provides business news about the domestic oil & gas industry, especially with regard to exploration and production companies. Includes acquisition, joint venture, bankruptcy and restructuring, financing, and merger information.
Formerly: Hart's Oil & Gas Interests (1073-0265)
Related titles: Microform ed.: (from PQC); Online - full text ed.: ISSN 1940-848X.
Indexed: A15, ABIn, P48, P51, P52, P56, PQC, PROMT.
—CCC.
Published by: Hart Energy Publishing, LP (Subsidiary of: Chemical Week Associates), 1616 S Voss Rd, Ste 1000, Houston, TX 77057. TEL 713-260-6400, FAX 713-840-8585, custserv@hartenergy.com. Ed. Steve Toon TEL 713-260-6431. Pub. David Givens TEL 703-891-4811.

665.5 USA ISSN 0030-1388
TN860 CODEN: OIGJAV
OIL & GAS JOURNAL. Abstracts and contents page in English; Text in English. 1902. w. USD 89 combined subscription domestic (print & online eds.); USD 94 combined subscription in Canada (print & online eds.); USD 139 combined subscription elsewhere (print & online eds.); free domestic to qualified personnel (effective 2009). adv. bk.rev. charts; illus.; mkt.; stat.; tr.lit. index. Supplement avail.; back issues avail.; reprints avail. **Document type:** *Magazine, Trade.* **Description:** Contains the latest international oil and gas news; analysis of issues and events; practical technology for design, operation and maintenance; and important statistics on international markets and activity.
Formerly (until 1910): Oil Investors' Journal
Related titles: E-mail ed.: USD 59 combined subscription (print & e-mail eds.) (effective 2008); Online - full text ed.: ISSN 1944-9151. USD 59 (effective 2008); Supplement(s): Oil & Gas Journal Petroleum Software & Technology Guide. ISSN 1544-4694; Oil & Gas Journal Data Book. ISSN 8756-7164. 1985.
Indexed: A05, A12, A13, A14, A15, A17, A20, A22, A23, A24, A25, A26, A33, ABIn, AESIS, APIAb, APICat, APIH&E, APIOC, APIPR, APIPS, APITS, AS&TA, AS&TI, ASFA, B02, B03, B04, B11, B13, B15, B16, B17, B18, BPI, BRD, BrGeoL, BusI, C&ISA, C13, CA, CADCAM, CBNB, CEA, CEABA, CISA, ChemAb, ChemTitl, CurCR, CurCont, DokArb, E&CAJ, E08, E14, EIA, EngInd, EnvAb, EnvInd, F&EA, FLUIDEX, FR, G04, G06, G07, G08, GEOBASE, GasAb, GeoRef, HRIS, I05, IMMAb, INIS AtomInd, ISMEC, KES, L09, MEA&I, OceAb, P02, P10, P13, P26, P34, P47, P48, P51, P52, P53, P54, P56, PEBNI, PQC, PetrolAb, R16, RASB, RefZh, S08, S09, SCI, SCOPUS, SRI, SolStAb, SpeleolAb, T&II, TCEA, TM, W01, W02, W03, W07.
—BLDSC (6250.000000), CASDDS, CIS, IE, Infotrieve, Ingenta, INIST, Linda Hall, PADDS. **CCC.**
Published by: PennWell Corporation, 1700 W Loop S, Ste 1000, Houston, TX 77027. TEL 713-963-6226, FAX 713-963-6228, patrickM@pennwell.com, http://www.pennwell.com. Ed. Bob Tippee TEL 713-963-6242. Pub. Bill Wageneck. adv.: B&W page USD 10,294, color page USD 12,803; trim 8 x 10.5. Circ: 101,695 (paid).

665.5 USA
OIL & GAS JOURNAL LATINOAMERICA. Text in Spanish. 19??. 6/yr. free to qualified personnel (effective 2009). adv. **Document type:** *Magazine, Trade.* **Description:** Aims to serve the management and engineering subscribers in the most important operating countries in Latin America that includes Argentina, Brazil, Colombia and Venezuela.
Related titles: Portuguese ed.
Indexed: PetrolAb, SCOPUS.
—PADDS.
Published by: PennWell Corporation, 1421 S Sheridan Rd, Tulsa, OK 74112. TEL 918-835-3161, 800-331-4463, FAX 918-831-9804, Headquarters@PennWell.com, http://www.pennwell.com. Ed. Bob Williams. adv.: B&W page USD 3,532.

343.077 665.5 665.7 USA
OIL AND GAS LAW. Text in English. 1959. 8 base vols. plus irreg. updates. looseleaf. USD 1,462 base vol(s). (effective 2008). **Document type:** *Handbook/Manual/Guide, Trade.* **Description:** Features information on the law relating to oil and gas and monitors changes to the law as well as new and developing areas.
Related titles: CD-ROM ed.: USD 1,492 (effective 2008).
Published by: Matthew Bender & Co., Inc. (Subsidiary of: LexisNexis North America), 1275 Broadway, Albany, NY 12204. TEL 518-487-3000, 800-424-4200, FAX 518-487-3083, international@bender.com, http://bender.lexisnexis.com. Eds. Charles Meyers, Howard Williams.

OIL AND GAS LEASE EQUIPMENT AND OPERATING COSTS. *see* BUSINESS AND ECONOMICS—Production Of Goods And Services

665.5 BHR ISSN 0217-6602
OIL AND GAS NEWS; the petroleum industry weekly for Asia - Pacific - Middle East. Text in English. 1983. w. USD 695 (effective 2001). adv. tr.lit. 20 p./no. 7 cols./p.; back issues avail. **Document type:** *Newspaper, Trade.* **Description:** Covers news of trends, products, events and other information for senior personnel in all sectors of the petroleum industry, including oil companies, exploration, supply, marine and offshore contractors, and government agencies.
Related titles: Online - full text ed.
Indexed: R01.
—CIS.
Published by: Al Hilal Publishing & Marketing Group, PO Box 224, Manama, Bahrain. TEL 973-293131, FAX 973-293400, info@tradearabia.net, hilalcirc@tradearabia.net. Ed. Mark Lazell. Adv. contact Geoffrey Milne. B&W page USD 2,800, color page USD 3,920; trim 290 x 420. Circ: 8,258.

OIL AND GAS POOL DESCRIPTIONS. *see* EARTH SCIENCES—Geology

665.5 CAN ISSN 0702-8202
HD9574.C23
OIL AND GAS PRODUCTION REPORT. Text in English. m. CAD 140. back issues avail. **Document type:** *Government.* **Description:** Includes a statistical summary of the drilling activity, well count, production and injection of all fluids on a pool basis, supply and disposition of gas plant and refinery operations.
Published by: British Columbia, Ministry of Energy and Mines, 7th Fl., 1810 Blanshard St, Victoria, BC BC V8W 9N3, Canada. TEL 604-356-2743, crown@pinc.com, http://www.ogc.gov.bc.ca/. Circ: 125. **Subscr. to:** Crown Publications Inc., 521 Fort St, Victoria, BC BC V8W 1E7, Canada. TEL 250-386-4636, FAX 250-386-0221, crown@pinc.com, http://www.crownpub.bc.ca.

665.5 AUS
OIL AND GAS RADAR. Text in English. 1969. w. AUD 2,465 (print or email or fax ed.) (effective 2009). Index. back issues avail. **Document type:** *Newsletter, Trade.* **Description:** Monitors oil and gas exploration and development in Australia, Papua New Guinea and New Zealand.
Formerly (until 2006): Lipscombe Report (0817-6191)
Related titles: E-mail ed.; Fax ed.
Published by: Pex Publications Pty. Ltd., Unit 5/1 Almondbury Rd, Mt Lawley, W.A. 6050, Australia. TEL 61-8-92726555, 800-739-855, FAX 61-8-92725556, oilinfo@pex.com.au. Ed. Paul Sullivan.

665.5 340 USA ISSN 0472-7630
OIL AND GAS REPORTER. Text in English. 1952. 2 base vols. plus m. updates. looseleaf. USD 2,108 base vol(s). (effective 2008). **Document type:** *Report, Trade.* **Description:** Covers timely report of cases and administrative rulings in the oil and gas law and taxation.
—**CCC.**
Published by: (Center For American and International Law), Matthew Bender & Co., Inc. (Subsidiary of: LexisNexis North America), 1275 Broadway, Albany, NY 12204. TEL 518-487-3000, 800-424-4200, FAX 518-487-3083, international@bender.com, http://bender.lexisnexis.com.

665 FRA ISSN 1294-4475
CODEN: RFPTBH
OIL & GAS SCIENCE & TECHNOLOGY; revue de l'Institut Francais du Petrole. Text in English, French; Summaries in English, French. 1946. bi-m. EUR 490 (effective 2009). bk.rev. bibl.; charts; illus. index, cum.index: 1946-1960, 1961-1965, 1966-1970, 1971-1975, 1976-1980, 1981-1985, 1986-1990. **Document type:** *Journal, Academic/Scholarly.* **Description:** Covers all disciplines and fields relevant to exploration, production, refining, petrochemicals, and the use and economics of petroleum, natural gas, and other sources of energy, in particular alternative energies with a view to sustainable development.
Former titles (until 1999): Institut Francais du Petrole. Revue (0020-2274); (until 1965): Institut Francais du Petrole. Revue et Annales des Liquides Combustibles (0370-5552); (until 1939): Office National des Combustibles Liquides. Annales (0365-1312)
Related titles: Online - full text ed.: free (effective 2011).
Indexed: A22, A28, APA, APIAb, APICat, APIH&E, APIOC, APIPR, APIPS, APITS, ASCA, ApMecR, BrCerAb, C&ISA, CA/WCA, CEA, CEABA, CIA, CISA, CPEI, CerAb, ChemAb, ChemTitl, CivEngAb, CorrAb, CurCont, E&CAJ, E11, EEA, EMA, ESPM, EngInd, EnvEAb, FLUIDEX, FR, GEOBASE, GeoRef, H15, IBR, IBZ, INIS AtomInd, ISMEC, ISR, M&TEA, M09, MBF, METADEX, PetrolAb, SCI, SCOPUS, SolStAb, SpeleolAb, T04, W07, WAA.
—BLDSC (6250.064500), CASDDS, IE, Infotrieve, Ingenta, INIST, Linda Hall, PADDS. **CCC.**
Published by: (Institut Francais du Petrole), Editions Technip, 27 rue Ginoux, Paris, Cedex 15 75737, France. TEL 33-1-45783380, FAX 33-1-45753711. Circ: 1,000.

665.5 IND ISSN 0970-1214
TN876.I5
OIL ASIA. Text in English. 1981. bi-m. INR 2,500 domestic; USD 300 foreign (effective 2011). **Document type:** *Journal, Trade.*
Published by: Oil Asia Publications Pvt. Ltd, 530, Laxmi Plz, Laxmi Industrial Estate, New Link Rd, Andheri (W), Mumbai, 400 053, India. TEL 91-22-40504900, FAX 91-22-26367676, oilasia@vsnl.com.

665 USA
THE OIL CAN. Text in English. 1926. q. USD 36 to non-members; free to members (effective 2005). adv. illus. 40 p./no. 3 cols./p.; back issues avail. **Document type:** *Magazine, Trade.* **Description:** Contains news about products and personnel in Illinois' petroleum industry.
Related titles: Online - full text ed.
Published by: Illinois Petroleum Marketers Association, Illinois Association of Convenience Stores, PO Box 12020, Springfield, IL 62791-2020. TEL 217-544-4609, FAX 217-789-0222, wjf@ipma-iacs.org, http://www.ipma-iacs.org. Ed. William J Fleischli. adv.: B&W page USD 400, color page USD 900; 8.5 x 11. Circ: 1,000 (paid).

665.5 338.2 USA ISSN 1529-4366
OIL DAILY (ONLINE). Text in English. 1951. d. USD 2,700 (effective 2011). stat. **Document type:** *Newsletter, Trade.*
Formerly (until 199?): The Oil Daily (Print) (0030-1434); Incorporates: Energy Alert
Media: Online - full text. **Related titles:** E-mail ed.; Fax ed.; Microform ed.: (from PQC).
Indexed: A15, A26, B02, B15, B17, B18, BusI, G04, G06, G07, G08, I05, M06, PEBNI, T&II.
—Linda Hall. **CCC.**
Published by: Energy Intelligence Group, Inc., 5 E 37th St, 5th Fl, New York, NY 10016. TEL 212-532-1112, FAX 212-532-4479. Ed. Andrew Kelly.

665.5 USA ISSN 0195-0576
OIL EXPRESS; inside report on trends in petroleum marketing without the influence of advertising. Text in English. 1967. w. (50/yr.). USD 557 (effective 2008); includes Fuel Oil Update; C-Store Digest; and U S Oil Week's Price Monitor. adv. Index. **Document type:** *Newsletter, Trade.* **Description:** Competitive coverage of profit opportunities and market trends for petroleum marketers across the country. Focuses on ways to thrive in a changing marketplace. Covers industry news; current and pending government regulations; underground tanks, insurance and environmental issues.
Formerly: U S Oil Week (0502-9767); Which incorporates (in 1989): C-Store Week (0887-4700)
Related titles: E-mail ed.; Online - full text ed.
Indexed: A26, B02, B15, B17, B18, G04, G06, G07, G08, I05, PEBNI, SCOPUS.
—Linda Hall. **CCC.**
Published by: Oil Price Information Service (Subsidiary of: United Communications Group), Two Washingtonian Center, 9737 Washingtonian Blvd, Ste 100, Gaithersburg, MD 20878. TEL 301-287-2700, 888-301-2645, FAX 301-287-2039, energycs@opisnet.com, http://www.opisnet.com/. Ed., Pub. Carole Donoghue TEL 703-280-1026.

OIL, GAS AND ENERGY LAW. *see* ENERGY

OIL, GAS AND ENERGY QUARTERLY. *see* BUSINESS AND ECONOMICS—Public Finance, Taxation

622 665 USA
TN871.5
OIL, GAS & PETROCHEM EQUIPMENT. Text in English. 1954. m. USD 53 domestic; USD 105 elsewhere; free to qualified personnel (effective 2008). adv. back issues avail. **Document type:** *Magazine, Trade.* **Description:** Provides information on what is new in oil and gas industry equipment, products, systems and services.
Formerly: Oil and Gas Equipment
Related titles: Online - full text ed.: USD 27; free to qualified personnel (effective 2008); Supplement(s): Literature Reviews; International Literature Review; Spanish Language Literature Review. suspended.
Indexed: PetrolAb.
—**CCC.**
Published by: PennWell Corporation, 1421 S Sheridan Rd, Tulsa, OK 74112. TEL 918-835-3161, 800-331-4463, FAX 918-831-9804, Headquarters@PennWell.com, http://www.pennwell.com. Pub. J B Avants TEL 918-832-9351. Adv. contacts Candice Doctor TEL 918-831-9884, Eric Freer TEL 713-963-6223. B&W page USD 8,566, color page USD 10,219. Circ: 30,000.

665.5 USA
OIL, GAS AND TECHNOLOGY. Text in Russian. bi-m. adv. **Document type:** *Journal, Trade.* **Description:** Covers technical articles for people in the gas and oil business throughout the former Soviet republics.
Formerly: Oil, Gas and Petrochemicals Abroad
Published by: Gulf Publishing Co., PO Box 2608, Houston, TX 77252. TEL 713-529-4301, FAX 713-520-4433, publications@gulfpub.com. Adv. contact Lanie Finlayson. B&W page USD 2,200, color page USD 3,000. Circ: 5,000.

665.5 DEU ISSN 0342-5622
TN860 CODEN: OGEMDJ
OIL GAS EUROPEAN MAGAZINE. Text in English. 1975. 4/yr. EUR 99.30 domestic; EUR 95.80 in Europe (effective 2009). adv. back issues avail. **Document type:** *Journal, Trade.* **Description:** Contains articles on topics of international importance for the oil and natural gas industry.
Formerly (until 1977): Erdoel - Erdgas - Zeitschrift. International Edition (0342-5584)
Indexed: A22, APIAb, ASCA, C33, CPEI, EngInd, FR, GasAb, GeoRef, INIS AtomInd, PetrolAb, RefZh, SCI, SCOPUS, SpeleolAb, TM, W07.
—BLDSC (6252.025000), IE, Infotrieve, Ingenta, INIST, Linda Hall, PADDS. **CCC.**
Published by: Urban-Verlag GmbH, Postfach 701606, Hamburg, 22016, Germany. TEL 49-40-65694520, FAX 49-40-65694550, info@oilgaspublisher.de. Ed. Hans Joerg Mager. Pub. Thomas Vieth. Adv. contact Harald Jordan. B&W page EUR 3,000, color page EUR 4,050. Circ: 5,980 (paid and controlled).

665.5 FRA ISSN 1029-4309
HD9560.1
OIL INFORMATION. Variant title: I E A Oil Information. Text in English. a., latest 2008. EUR 150 per issue (effective 2009). **Document type:** *Journal, Trade.* **Description:** Contains key data on world production, trade, prices and consumption of major oil product groups, with time series back to the early 1970s. Also provides a more detailed and comprehensive picture of oil supply, demand, trade, production and consumption by end-user for each OECD country individually and for the OECD regions.
Supersedes in part (in 1996): Oil and Gas Information (1016-5010); Which was formerly (until 1989): Annual Oil and Gas Statistics and Main Historical Series (1016-5002); (until 1983): Annual Oil and Gas Statistics (0256-3177); (until 1981): Oil Statistics (0259-8655)
Related titles: CD-ROM ed.: EUR 500 per issue (effective 2009); Online - full text ed.: ISSN 1683-4259. EUR 800, USD 1,040, GBP 640, JPY 115,300 (effective 2010) (from IngentaConnect).
Indexed: IIS.
—BLDSC (6252.087600).
Published by: Organisation for Economic Cooperation and Development (O E C D), International Energy Agency, 9 rue de la Federation, Paris, 75739 cedex 15, France. TEL 33-1-40576625, FAX 33-1-40576649, info@iea.org.

665.5 338.2 IRN ISSN 0030-1450
OIL NEWS. Text in Persian, Modern. fortn. free.
Indexed: F&EA.
Published by: Petroleum Ministry, Public Relations & Guidance Department, Central NIOC Bldg., Taleghani Ave., P O Box 1863, Teheran, Iran. TEL 021-6151.

665.5 RUS
OIL OF RUSSIA. Text in English. 1997. q. USD 100 (effective 2004). **Document type:** *Magazine, Trade.* **Description:** Provides coverage of oil and gas developments in Russia, the CIS and Eastern Europe.
Published by: Lukoil Inform, Sretenskii b-r 11, Moscow, 101000, Russian Federation. TEL 7-095-9271691, FAX 7-095-9271692, subscribe@oilru.com. Ed. Aleksandr Matveichuk. Pub. Anatolii Pecheikin.

665.5 USA ISSN 0279-6333
OIL PATCH HOTLINE. Text in English. 1978-1986; resumed 2006. bi-w. USD 1 per issue (effective 2007). adv. **Document type:** *Newsletter, Trade.* **Description:** Covers the oil and gas industry news, trends, government regulation, new well development, pipeline and production facilities in North Dakota, South Dakota, Montana and Wyoming.
Published by: Hotline Printing and Publishing, 4302 Second Ave, W, Williston, ND 58801. TEL 701-774-8757, FAX 701-774-0419, mail@hotlineprinting.com, http://www.hotlineprinting.com. Pub. Dennis Blank TEL 407-886-8782. adv.: B&W page USD 1,000; trim 8.5 x 11.

665.538 USA
OIL PRICE DAILY. Text in English. d. **Document type:** *Newsletter, Trade.* **Description:** Provides daily updated petroleum prices for kerosene, high and low sulfur diesel, no. 2, no. 4 and no. 6 oil, plus gasoline prices, a spot product price table and tank wagon delivery prices.
Media: E-mail. **Related titles:** Fax ed.
Published by: Journal of Commerce, Inc. (Subsidiary of: Commonwealth Business Media, Inc.), 2 Penn Plz E, Newark, NJ 07105. TEL 973-776-8660, 877-675-4761. Pub. Christine Oldenbrook TEL 973-776-7803.

338.47 USA ISSN 0279-7801
OIL PRICE INFORMATION SERVICE. Text in English. 1998. w. **Document type:** *Newsletter, Trade.* **Description:** Gives actual wholesale and spot gasoline, distillate and propane prices each week, plus trends, new sources, and new markets.
Related titles: Online - full text ed.
—Linda Hall. **CCC.**
Published by: United Communications Group, Two Washingtonian Ctr, 9737 Washingtonian Blvd, Ste 100, Gaithersburg, MD 20878. TEL 301-287-2700, FAX 301-287-2039, http://www.ucg.com.

665.5 USA
OIL PRICE INFORMATION SERVICE NEWSLETTER; independent refined products prices and comprehensive analysis for all us markets. Abbreviated title: O P I S Newsletter. Text in English. w. USD 1,275 (effective 2008). adv. **Document type:** *Newsletter, Trade.* **Description:** Contain critical information on benchmark prices used by the world to buy and sell U.S. gasoline, diesel, ethanol, biodiesel, LP-gas, jet fuel, crude, propane, feedstocks, resid and kerosene.
Published by: Oil Price Information Service (Subsidiary of: United Communications Group), 3349 Hwy 138, Bldg D, Ste D, Wall, NJ 07719. TEL 732-901-8800, FAX 732-280-0263, listings@opisnet.com. Adv. contact Greg Mosho TEL 732-730-2546.

665.5 USA ISSN 1096-3235
HD9563
OIL PRICE INFORMATION SERVICE'S PETROLEUM TERMINAL ENCYCLOPEDIA. Text in English. 1985. a. USD 645 domestic; USD 665 foreign; USD 1,795 combined subscription domestic (print & CD-ROM eds.); USD 1,815 combined subscription foreign (print & CD-ROM eds.) (effective 2009). **Document type:** *Directory, Trade.* **Description:** Lists bulk storage terminal facilities worldwide with product capacity, supply and outload detail.
Former titles (until 199?): Petroleum Terminal Encyclopedia (0897-2001); (until 1988): Stalsby's Petroleum Terminal Encyclopedia (0882-1747)
Related titles: CD-ROM ed.
Published by: Oil Price Information Service (Subsidiary of: United Communications Group), Two Washingtonian Center, 9737 Washingtonian Blvd, Ste 100, Gaithersburg, MD 20878. TEL 301-287-2700, 888-301-2645, FAX 301-287-2039, energycs@opisnet.com. Pub. Daine T Miller TEL 732-730-2530. Adv. contact Greg Mosho TEL 732-730-2546. **Subscr. to:** 11300 Rockville Pike, Ste 1100, Rockville, MD 20852. TEL 301-287-2525, FAX 301-816-8945.

P

665.7 USA
OIL PRICE INFORMATION SERVICE'S WHO'S WHO IN NATURAL GAS AND POWER. Text in English. 1988. a. USD 425 per issue domestic; USD 445 per issue foreign; USD 1,445 combined subscription per issue domestic (print & CD-ROM eds.); USD 1,465 combined subscription per issue foreign (print & CD-ROM eds.) (effective 2009). adv. **Document type:** *Directory, Trade.* **Description:** Designed to be a reference guide to locate alternate supply sources, find new business opportunities, identify financing partners and more.
Former titles (until 200?): Who's Who in Natural Gas; (until 199?): Oil Price Information Service's Who's Who in Natural Gas (1096-3219); Who's Who in Natural Gas Supply (0897-2028)
Related titles: CD-ROM ed.
Published by: Oil Price Information Service (Subsidiary of: United Communications Group), Two Washingtonian Center, 9737 Washingtonian Blvd, Ste 100, Gaithersburg, MD 20878. TEL 301-287-2700, 888-301-2645, FAX 301-287-2039, energycs@opisnet.com. Pub. Daine T Miller TEL 732-730-2530. Adv. contact Greg Mosho TEL 732-730-2546. **Subscr. to:** 11300 Rockville Pike, Ste 1100, Rockville, MD 20852. TEL 301-287-2525, FAX 301-816-8945.

OIL REGULATION. *see* LAW

338.476655096 GBR ISSN 1751-5513
OIL REVIEW AFRICA; covering oil, gas and hydrocarbon processing. Text in English. 2006. bi-m. GBP 63, USD 124, EUR 93 (effective 2010). adv. **Document type:** *Magazine, Trade.* **Description:** Contains industry news, country reports, sector surveys, technical feature articles, exhibition and conference reviews and news of the latest industry developments and product launches.
—CCC.
Published by: Alain Charles Publishing Ltd., University House, 11-13 Lower Grosvenor Pl, London, SW1W 0EX, United Kingdom. TEL 44-20-78347676, FAX 44-20-79730076, post@alaincharles.com. Circ: 8,000.

662.338 GBR ISSN 1464-9314
OIL REVIEW MIDDLE EAST; covering oil, gas and hydrocarbon processing. Text in English. 1997. 7/yr. GBP 63, USD 124, EUR 93 (effective 2010). adv. back issues avail. **Document type:** *Magazine, Trade.* **Description:** Contains industry news, country reports, sector surveys, technical feature articles, exhibition and conference previews and news of the latest industry developments and product launches.
Related titles: Online - full text ed.; ◆ Supplement(s): Technical Review Middle East. ISSN 0267-5307.
—CCC.
Published by: Alain Charles Publishing Ltd., University House, 11-13 Lower Grosvenor Pl, London, SW1W 0EX, United Kingdom. TEL 44-20-78347676, FAX 44-20-79730076, post@alaincharles.com. Ed. David Clancy. Circ: 11,000.

OIL SHALE/GORYUCHIE SLANTSY. *see* MINES AND MINING INDUSTRY

665.5 551 GBR ISSN 0923-1730
TN860 CODEN: OIREE7
➤ **OILFIELD REVIEW.** Text in English. 1989. q. USD 200 (effective 2009). bk.rev. illus. back issues avail. **Document type:** *Magazine, Trade.* **Description:** Provides a source of information on seismic surveying, drilling, MWD, well logging, well testing, reservoir stimulation and completion practices.
Formed by the 1990 merger of: Schlumberger Limited. Technical Review (0890-0221); Drilling and Pumping Journal
Related titles: Microform ed.: (from PQC); Online - full text ed.: ISSN 1878-6723.
Indexed: A22, ASCA, CIN, CPEI, ChemAb, ChemTitl, EngInd, GeoRef, PetrolAb, SCOPUS, SpeleolAb.
—BLDSC (6252.274680), CASDDS, IE, Infotrieve, Ingenta, INIST, PADDS. **CCC.**
Published by: Oilfield Review Services, Barbour Sq, High St, Tattenhall, Chester, CH3 9RF, United Kingdom. TEL 44-1829-770569, FAX 44-1829-771354.

665.5 ESP ISSN 0030-1493
OILGAS. Text in Spanish. 1967. m. USD 102 domestic; USD 195 in Europe; USD 265 elsewhere (effective 2010). **Document type:** *Trade.* **Description:** Discusses the petroleum, petrochemical and gas industries' activities.
Indexed: CBNB, FR, GasAb, GeoRef, IECT, SpeleolAb.
—CCC.
Published by: Sede Tecnica S.A., Avda Brasil, 17 planta 12, Madrid, 28020, Spain. TEL 34-91-5565004, FAX 34-91-5560962, editorial@sedetecnica.com, http://www.sedetecnica.com/. Ed. Carlos Martin Palomo. Circ: 6,500.

665.5 GBR
OILNEWS AND GAS INTERNATIONAL. Text in English. m. **Document type:** *Magazine, Trade.*
Published by: R A E - L I N Communications, PO Box 6, Haddington, E Lothian EH41 3NQ, United Kingdom. TEL 062-0822578, FAX 062-822758, TELEX 94026124-AREL-G. Ed. Richard Brown.

665.5 CAN ISSN 1912-5305
HD9574.A1
OILSANDS REVIEW. Text in English. 2006 (Jun). m. CAD 99 domestic; USD 198 foreign (effective 2007). **Description:** Focuses on the facts, the figures and the stories behind the business of unconventional oil.
Published by: June/Warren Publishing Ltd., #300, 5735 - 7 St. NE, Calgary, AB T3E 8V3, Canada. TEL 403-265-3700, FAX 403-265-3706, http://www.junewarren.com.

665.5 CAN ISSN 1207-7933
OILWEEK. Text in English. 1991. w.
Formerly (until 1995): Oilweek Pulse (1185-3794)
Related titles: Online - full text ed.
Indexed: A26, CPerI, E08, G06, G07, G08, I05, S09.
—CCC.
Published by: Maclean Hunter Ltd., Maclean Hunter Bldg, 777 Bay St, Ste 405, Toronto, ON M5W 1A7, Canada.

665.5 CAN ISSN 1200-9059
TN860 CODEN: OLWKAX
OILWEEK MAGAZINE. Text in English. 1948. m. CAD 99 domestic; USD 155 foreign; CAD 8 per issue (effective 2005). adv. bk.rev.; software rev. charts; maps; mkt.; stat.; tr.lit. back issues avail.; reprints avail. **Document type:** *Magazine, Trade.* **Description:** Serves the oil, gas and energy industries across Canada in all sectors from exploration, drilling, production, processing, refining, pipelines, transportation and marketing, to the environment and financing.
Former titles (until 1995): Oilweek (Calgary) (0030-1515); (until 1958): Myers' Oilweek (0318-0387); (until 1955): Myers' Oil Weekly (0380-1837)
Related titles: Microfiche ed.: (from MML); Microfilm ed.: (from MML); Microform ed.: (from MML, PQC); Online - full content ed.; Online - full text ed.
Indexed: A15, ABIn, APICat, APIH&E, APIOC, APIPR, APIPS, APITS, C03, CBCABus, CBPI, ChemAb, GeoRef, P48, P51, P52, P56, PQC, PetrolAb, SpeleolAb.
—BLDSC (6252.620000), IE, Ingenta. **CCC.**
Published by: June/Warren Publishing Ltd., #300, 5735 - 7 St. NE, Calgary, AB T3E 8V3, Canada. TEL 403-265-3700, 888-563-2946, FAX 403-265-3706, bwhitelaw@junewarren.com, http://www.junewarren.com. Pub. Tim Heath. Adv. contact Steve Henrich. B&W page CAD 3,092, color page CAD 4,392; trim 10.75 x 8. Circ: 10,088.

338.4762 USA ISSN 1469-378X
THE OMEGA REPORT: NORTH SEA SUPPLY VESSELS. Text in English. 1990. m. **Document type:** *Newsletter, Trade.* **Description:** Provides a detailed monthly review and rolling 12-month forecast of the North Sea supply vessel market.
Related titles: E-mail ed.; Online - full text ed.
Published by: O D S - Petrodata, 3200 Wilcrest Dr, Ste 170, Houston, TX 77042. TEL 832-463-3000, FAX 832-463-3100, general@ods-petrodata.com, http://www.ods-petrodata.com. Ed. Shaun Heywood. Pub. Tom Marsh.

622.338 DNK ISSN 1903-573X
ON/OFF NEWS; news on offshore business in Denmark. Text in English. 2003. irreg., latest vol.8, 2006. free. adv. back issues avail. **Document type:** *Newsletter, Trade.*
Formerly (until 2008): On/Off (1901-7782)
Related titles: Online - full text ed.: ISSN 1903-5748. 2003.
Published by: Offshore Center Danmark, Niels Bohrs Vej 6, Esbjerg, 6700, Denmark. TEL 45-36-973670, FAX 45-36-973679, info@offshorecenter.dk. Ed. Morten Holmager TEL 45-36-973672. Adv. contact Soeren Dybdahl TEL 45-28-582309. color page DKK 14,000; 180 x 260. Circ: 3,000.

622.338 DNK ISSN 1901-7774
ON/OFF YEARBOOK; offshore industry in Denmark. Text in English. 2006. a. back issues avail. **Document type:** *Yearbook, Trade.*
Related titles: Online - full text ed.: ISSN 1901-7804.
Published by: Offshore Center Danmark, Niels Bohrs Vej 6, Esbjerg, 6700, Denmark. TEL 45-36-973670, FAX 45-36-973679, info@offshorecenter.dk.

665.5 CAN ISSN 0078-5040
ONTARIO PETROLEUM INSTITUTE. ANNUAL CONFERENCE PROCEEDINGS. Text in English. 1962. a. CAD 40 (effective 2000). **Document type:** *Proceedings.*
Indexed: GeoRef, SpeleolAb.
—BLDSC (1082.317000). **CCC.**
Published by: Ontario Petroleum Institute, 555 Southdale Rd E, Ste 104, London, ON N6E 1A2, Canada. TEL 519-680-1620, FAX 519-680-1621. Circ: 100 (paid).

665.5 CAN ISSN 1480-2201
ONTARIO PETROLEUM INSTITUTE. NEWSLETTER. Text in English. bi-m. **Document type:** *Newsletter.*
Published by: Ontario Petroleum Institute, 555 Southdale Rd E, Ste 104, London, ON N6E 1A2, Canada. TEL 519-680-1620, FAX 519-680-1621. Circ: 400.

665.5 CAN
ONTARIO PETROLEUM INSTITUTE. TECHNICAL PAPERS. Text in English. a. CAD 40 (effective 2000). **Document type:** *Monographic series, Trade.*
Published by: Ontario Petroleum Institute, 555 Southdale Rd E, Ste 104, London, ON N6E 1A2, Canada. TEL 519-680-1620, FAX 519-680-1621.

665.5 CAN
ONTARIO PETROLEUM INSTITUTE. VOLUMES. Text in English. 1962. a. CAD 40 (effective 2000). **Document type:** *Proceedings.*
Published by: Ontario Petroleum Institute, 555 Southdale Rd E, Ste 104, London, ON N6E 1A2, Canada. TEL 519-680-1620, FAX 519-680-1621. Circ: 100.

665.5 NLD ISSN 1874-8341
TN860
➤ **THE OPEN PETROLEUM ENGINEERING JOURNAL.** Text in English. 2008. irreg. free (effective 2011). **Document type:** *Journal, Academic/Scholarly.*
Media: Online - full text.
Indexed: A39, C27, C29, CPEI, D03, D04, E04, E05, E13, R14, S14, S15, S18, SCOPUS.
Published by: Bentham Open (Subsidiary of: Bentham Science Publishers Ltd.), PO Box 294, Bussum, AG 1400, Netherlands. TEL 31-35-6923800, FAX 31-35-6980150, subscriptions@bentham.org. Ed. Goodarz Ahmadi.

553 USA ISSN 0078-5741
TN872.O7 CODEN: OGOGAE
OREGON. DEPARTMENT OF GEOLOGY AND MINERAL INDUSTRIES. OIL AND GAS INVESTIGATIONS. Text in English. 1963. irreg., latest vol.20. price varies. back issues avail. **Document type:** *Monographic series, Trade.*
Related titles: CD-ROM ed.: USD 25 per issue (effective 2010).
Indexed: GeoRef, SpeleolAb.
—Linda Hall.
Published by: Department of Geology and Mineral Industries, 800 NE Oregon St, #28, Ste 965, Portland, OR 97232. TEL 971-673-1555, FAX 971-673-1562, james.roddey@dogami.state.or.us, http://www.oregongeology.org.

341.7 KWT
ORGANIZATION OF ARAB PETROLEUM EXPORTING COUNTRIES. SECRETARY GENERAL'S ANNUAL REPORT. Text in English. 1974. a. free. charts; stat. **Document type:** *Corporate.* **Description:** Review of Arab and world economics and energy developments plus description of activities of OPEC and its sponsored ventures.
Related titles: Arabic ed.
Published by: Organization of Arab Petroleum Exporting Countries, PO Box 20501, Safat, 13066, Kuwait. TEL 965-4959000, FAX 965-4959755, oapec@oapecorg.org, http://www.oapecorg.org. Circ: 1,000.

665.5 338.47665 USA ISSN 1936-0355
TN860
THE P E I JOURNAL. Text in English. 2007. q. USD 49 to members; USD 129 to non-members (effective 2007). **Document type:** *Journal, Trade.* **Description:** Aims to be the leading authority and source of information for the petroleum handling equipment industry.
Related titles: Online - full text ed.: ISSN 1936-6892.
Published by: Petroleum Equipment Institute, PO Box 2380, Tulsa, OK 74101. TEL 918-494-9696, FAX 918-491-9895, http://www.pei.org. Ed. Robert N Renkes.

665.5 AUS ISSN 0729-4069
TN878
P E S A JOURNAL. Text in English. 1982. s-a. **Description:** Covers exploration industry's activities in the South East Asian and Australian oil and gas exploration sector.
Indexed: GeoRef, PetrolAb.
—PADDS.
Published by: (Petroleum Exploration Society of Australia), Oilfield Publications Pty Ltd, Ste 10, Level 1, Tower Plaza Business Centre, 7 Hector St W, Osborne Park, W.A. 6017, Australia. TEL 61-8-9446-3039, FAX 61-8-9244-3714, http://www.oilfield.com.au.

665.5 USA
P G W NEWSLINE. Text in English. 1928. m. free. **Description:** Magazine for PGW employees.
Formerly: P G W News
Published by: Philadelphia Gas Works, 800 W Montgomery Ave, Philadelphia, PA 19122. TEL 215-684-6564. Ed. Peter A Hussie. Circ: 4,500 (controlled).

P M A A JOURNAL. (Petroleum Marketers Association of America) *see* BUSINESS AND ECONOMICS—Marketing And Purchasing

665.5 CAN
P.O.S.T. REPORT. Text in English. w. CAD 1,010 (effective 2005). **Document type:** *Newsletter, Trade.* **Description:** Contains information on drilling, facility, pipeline and turnaround/maintenance projects.
Media: Fax.
Published by: Nickle's Energy Group (Subsidiary of: Business Information Group), Ste 300, 999 8 St SW, Calgary, AB T2R 1N7, Canada. TEL 403-209-3500, 800-387-2446, FAX 403-245-8666, http://www.nickles.com/.

661.804 USA ISSN 1931-2180
P P EUROPE. (Polypropylene) Text in English. 2000. w. USD 1,175 (online & E-mail eds.) (effective 2008). back issues avail. **Document type:** *Newsletter, Trade.* **Description:** Provides in-depth information for Copolymer and homo-injection polymer grades across Western Europe.
Media: Online - full content. **Related titles:** E-mail ed.
Published by: Platts (Subsidiary of: McGraw-Hill Companies, Inc.), 1200 G St NW, Ste 1000, Washington, DC 20005. TEL 212-904-3070, 800-752-8878, FAX 202-383-2024, support@platts.com.

665.5 USA ISSN 1098-1152
PACIFIC RUSSIA OIL AND GAS REPORT. Text in English. 1998. q. USD 495 domestic; USD 540 in Russian Federation (effective 2007). **Document type:** *Report, Trade.* **Description:** Covers current and future oil and gas projects of Sakhalin Island and other regions of the Russian Far East, of the Republic of Sakha and of Eastern Siberia.
Published by: Pacific Russia Information Group LLC, 300 Hermit St., Apt. 9, Juneau, AK 99801-1585. http://pacificrussia.com. Ed. Cheryl Frasca.

665 PAK ISSN 1017-0626
TP690.A1 CODEN: PJHREE
➤ **PAKISTAN JOURNAL OF HYDROCARBON RESEARCH.** Text in English. 1989. s-a. USD 10 (effective 2000). adv. **Document type:** *Journal, Academic/Scholarly.* **Description:** Publishes pure and applied research relating to Pakistan in the fields of oil and gas exploration, production, processing, utilization, economics, policy and planning.
Indexed: GeoRef, INIS AtomInd.
—BLDSC (6341.400000).
Published by: Hydrocarbon Development Institute of Pakistan, 230 Nizamuddin Rd., F 7-4, P O Box 1308, Islamabad, Pakistan. TEL 92-51-9203588, FAX 92-51-9204902. Ed., R&P Hilal A Raza. Adv. contact Muhammad Shafique. Circ: 500 (controlled).

665 PAK ISSN 0552-9115
PAKISTAN PETROLEUM LIMITED. ANNUAL REPORT. Text in English. 1952. a. **Document type:** *Corporate.* **Description:** Presents a complete picture of the company's finances and operations.
Published by: Pakistan Petroleum Ltd., 4th Fl., PIDC House, Dr. Ziauddin Ahmed Rd., P O Box 3942, Karachi, 75530, Pakistan. TEL 92-21-5651480, FAX 92-21-5680005, TELEX 29295 PPETK PK. Ed. Ahsan Halim. Circ: 2,250.

665.5 338 GBR ISSN 2044-5628
PAPUA NEW GUINEA OIL & GAS REPORT. Text in English. 200?. q. EUR 820, USD 1,150 combined subscription (print & email eds.) (effective 2010). **Document type:** *Report, Trade.* **Description:** Provides professionals, consultancies, government departments, regulatory bodies and researchers with independent forecasts and competitive intelligence on the Papuan oil and gas industry.
Related titles: E-mail ed.
Published by: Business Monitor International Ltd., Senator House, 85 Queen Victoria St, London, EC4V 4AB, United Kingdom. TEL 44-20-72480468, FAX 44-20-72480467, subs@businessmonitor.com.

665.5 CAN ISSN 1185-5444
PECTEN (ENGLISH EDITION). Text in English. irreg.
Formerly (until 1990): Sphere (English Edition) (0700-7434); Which superseded in part: Shell News (Toronto) (0227-5635)

Related titles: ◆ French ed.: Pecten (French Edition). ISSN 1185-5436. —CCC.
Published by: Shell Canada Ltd., 400 4th Ave S W, Calgary, AB T2P 0J4, Canada. questions@shell.com, http://www.shell.ca.

338.2 CAN ISSN 1185-5436
PECTEN (FRENCH EDITION). Text in French. 1970. bi-m. free to qualified personnel.
Formerly (until 1990): Sphere (French Edition) (0700-7426); Which superseded in part: Shell News (Toronto) (0227-5635)
Related titles: ◆ English ed.: Pecten (English Edition). ISSN 1185-5444.
Published by: Shell Canada Ltd., 400 4th Ave S W, Calgary, AB T2P 0J4, Canada. questions@shell.com, http://www.shell.ca. Ed. Lorna Visser Curnew. Circ: 11,700 (controlled).

665.5 GBR
PERFORMANCE. Text in English. 1990. q. **Document type:** *Newsletter.*
Published by: Phillips Petroleum Co. UK Ltd., 35 Guildford Rd, Woking, Surrey GU22 7QT, United Kingdom. TEL 01483-752657, FAX 01483-752607. Ed. Lynnda Robson. Circ: 5,000 (controlled).

665.5029 USA
PERMIAN BASIN PETROLEUM INDUSTRY. Text in English. 1991. irreg. **Document type:** *Directory, Trade.* **Description:** Lists integrated oil companies and independent producers in the Permian Basin region.
Media: Diskette.
Published by: Midwest Publishing Company, 2230 E 49th St, Ste E, Tulsa, OK 74105. TEL 800-829-2002, info@midwestpub.com, http://www.midwestpub.com/.

338.4766180409 GBR ISSN 1749-2378
PERU PETROCHEMICALS REPORT. Text in English. 2005. a. EUR 820, USD 1,030 combined subscription per issue (print & email eds.) (effective 2010). **Document type:** *Report, Trade.* **Description:** Provides industry professionals and strategists, sector analysts, trade associations and regulatory bodies with independent forecasts and competitive intelligence on the Peruvian petrochemicals industry.
Related titles: E-mail ed.
Indexed: A15, ABIn, B02, B15, B17, B18, G04, I05, P48, P51, P52, P56, PQC.
Published by: Business Monitor International Ltd., Senator House, 85 Queen Victoria St, London, EC4V 4AB, United Kingdom. TEL 44-20-72480468, FAX 44-20-72480467, subs@businessmonitor.com.

665.5 JPN ISSN 0386-2763
CODEN: PTRTD3
PETOROTEKKU/PETROTECH. Text in Japanese. 1978. m. free to members. **Document type:** *Journal, Academic/Scholarly.* **Description:** Contains reviews of the latest technical developments, both domestic and overseas, in oil exploration, development, refining, new fuels and chemicals, treatises on science and technologies of direct interest, commentaries, and current topics.
Indexed: RefZh, SCOPUS.
—Linda Hall.
Published by: Japan Petroleum Institute/Sekiyu Gakkai, COSMO Hirakawa-cho Bldg, 1-3-14 Hirakawa-cho, Chiyoda-ku, Tokyo, 102-0093, Japan. TEL 81-3-32217301, FAX 81-3-32218175, http://wwwsoc.nii.ac.jp/jpi/.

665.5 CAN ISSN 1719-3575
PETRO - CANADA STRATEGIC OVERVIEW REPORT. Text in English. 2004. a., latest 2005. **Document type:** *Report, Consumer.*
Supersedes in part: Petro - Canada Annual Report (0701-6727)
Published by: Petro - Canada, PO Box 2844, Calgary, AB T2P 3E3, Canada. TEL 403-296-8000, FAX 403-296-3030, custsvs@petro-canada.ca, http://www.petro-canada.ca.

665.5 330 GBR ISSN 1472-0590
PETRO INDUSTRY NEWS. Text in English. 2000. bi-m. free to qualified personnel (effective 2009). adv. back issues avail. **Document type:** *Newspaper, Trade.* **Description:** Covers products and technology for measurement and testing, flow, level and pressure instrumentation, analysis for the QA/QC and R&D laboratory, environmental compliance and safety for the Worldwide Chemical, Petrochemical and Oil/Gas industries.
Related titles: Online - full text ed.
Indexed: A01.
Published by: Environmental Technology (Publications) Limited, Oak Court Business Centre, Sandridge Park, Porters Wood, St. Albans, Hertfordshire AL3 6PH, United Kingdom. TEL 44-1727-858840, FAX 44-1727-840310, info@envirotech-online.com, http://www.envirotech-online.com. Pub. Marcus Pattison. Adv. contact Robert Parker TEL 44-1727-855 574. Circ: 33,133.

661 COL ISSN 2011-0529
PETROBRAS. ANNUAL REPORT. Text in English. 2007. a.
Published by: Petrobras, Carrera 7a No. 71-21, Torre B Piso 17, Bogota, Colombia. TEL 57-1-3135000, FAX 57-1-3135101, http://www.petrobras.com.

665.5 BRA ISSN 0102-9304
QE235 CODEN: BGPEEA
PETROBRAS. BOLETIM DE GEOCIENCIAS. Summaries in English, Portuguese, Spanish. 1987. s-a. free. **Document type:** *Bulletin.* **Description:** Covers original geoscientific studies concerning petroleum geology in Brazil.
Related titles: Online - full text ed.: ISSN 1806-2881.
Indexed: GEOBASE, GeoRef, PetrolAb, SCOPUS, SpeleolAb.
—INIST, Linda Hall, PADDS.
Published by: Petroleo Brasileiro (Petrobras), Av Republica do Chile 65, Rio de Janeiro, RJ 20035-900, Brazil. Circ: 1,200.

665 BRA ISSN 0006-6117
TN860 CODEN: BTPEAT
PETROBRAS. BOLETIM TECNICO. Summaries in English, Portuguese, Spanish. 1957. 4/yr. free to qualified personnel. abstr.; bibl.; charts; illus.; stat. index. **Document type:** *Bulletin, Trade.* **Description:** Covers all aspects of the petroleum industry worldwide with emphasis on Brazil.
Related titles: Online - full text ed.: ISSN 1676-6385. 1998; Ed.: Petrobras Technical Newsletter.
Indexed: APICat, APIH&E, APIOC, APIPR, APIPS, APITS, ASFA, B21, C01, CIN, ChemAb, ChemTitl, E&PHSE, ESPM, FR, GP&P, GeoRef, OffTech, PetrolAb, SpeleolAb.
—CASDDS, INIST, Linda Hall, PADDS. **CCC.**
Published by: Petroleo Brasileiro (Petrobras), Av Republica do Chile 65, Rio de Janeiro, RJ 20035-900, Brazil. http://www.petrobras.com.br. Circ: 800.

665.5 BRA
PETROBRAS. CONSOLIDATED REPORT. Text in English. a. charts; illus.; stat.
Published by: Petroleo Brasileiro (Petrobras), Av Republica do Chile 65, Rio de Janeiro, RJ 20035-900, Brazil. http://www.petrobras.com.br.

665.5 BRA
PETROBRAS MAGAZINE. Text in English. q. **Document type:** *Magazine, Corporate.*
Published by: Petroleo Brasileiro (Petrobras), Av Republica do Chile 65, Rio de Janeiro, RJ 20035-900, Brazil. http://www.petrobras.com.br.

665.5 BRA ISSN 0103-5266
PETROBRAS NEWS. Text in English. q. looseleaf. charts; illus.; stat. **Description:** Covers news in the petroleum and drilling field.
Indexed: EIA, EnvAb.
Published by: Petroleo Brasileiro (Petrobras), Av Republica do Chile 65, Rio de Janeiro, RJ 20035-900, Brazil. http://www.petrobras.com.br. Ed. Lanning Elwis.

665 NLD ISSN 1380-6386
PETROCHEM; managementblad voor de olie- en chemische industrie. Text in Dutch. 1989. m. (11/yr.). EUR 148.90 domestic; EUR 172.70 foreign; EUR 40 to students; EUR 18.45 newsstand/cover (effective 2010). adv. illus. **Document type:** *Journal, Trade.* **Description:** Covers all sectors of the petroleum, petrochemical and chemical industries.
Published by: Industrielinqs Pers en Platform, Postbus 12936, Amsterdam, 1100 AX, Netherlands. TEL 31-20-3122088, FAX 31-20-3122080, info@industrielinqs.nl, http://www.industrielinqs.nl. Eds. Mark Oosterveer TEL 31-20-3122793, Wim Raaijen. adv.: B&W page EUR 2,032, color page EUR 3,121; trim 210 x 297. Circ: 4,173.

PETROCHEMICAL EQUIPMENT. *see* ENGINEERING—Chemical Engineering

661.804029 USA
PETROCHEMICAL INDUSTRY; petrochemical plants, engineering, construction, equipment manufactures & supply companies. Text in English. 1991. a. USD 175 domestic; USD 185 in Canada; USD 190 elsewhere (effective 2009). adv. **Document type:** *Directory, Trade.* **Description:** Lists petrochemical companies across North America and internationally, and all support sectors from worldwide engineers/contractors to local service and supply companies.
Published by: Midwest Publishing Company, 2230 E 49th St, Ste E, Tulsa, OK 74105. TEL 918-582-2000, 800-829-2002, FAX 918-587-9349, info@midwestpub.com. adv.: B&W page USD 1,610, color page USD 1,710.

PETROCHEMICAL NEWS; a weekly news service in English devoted to the worldwide petrochemical industry. *see* ENGINEERING—Chemical Engineering

665.5 VEN ISSN 0798-1635
HD9574.V4
PETROGUIA. Text in Spanish. 1983. a. **Document type:** *Directory, Trade.*
Published by: Grupo Editorial Producto, Urb Sabana Grande, Av Venezuela, C C El Recreo, Torre Sur, piso 1, Caracas, DF 1050, Venezuela. TEL 58-212-7505011, FAX 58-212-7617744, gep@infoline.wtfe.com, http://www.gep.com.ve.

665.5 FRA ISSN 1622-1036
TN864 CODEN: PTIFEJ
PETROLE & GAZ INFORMATIONS. Text in French. 1968. bi-m. adv. illus.; tr.lit. **Document type:** *Journal, Trade.* **Description:** Comprehensive analysis of developments in the international oil and gas industries.
Incorporates (in 2004): Petrole et Techniques (0152-5425); Which was formerly (until 1977): Revue de l'Association Francaise des Techniciens du Petrole (0004-5470); (until 1965): l'Association Francaise des Techniciens du Petrole. Bulletin (0365-883X); Former titles (until 1999): Petrole Informations (0150-6463); (until 1969): Petrole Informations, la Revue Petroliere (0150-6471); Which was formed by the merger of (1959-1967): Petrole Informations (0031-6377); (1948-1967): La Revue Petroliere (0150-6838)
Related titles: ◆ Supplement(s): G P L Actualite (English Edition). ISSN 1969-2587.
Indexed: A22, APICat, APIH&E, APIOC, APIPR, APIPS, APITS, CBNB, FR, GeoRef, INIS AtomInd, PEBNI, PetrolAb, SCOPUS, SpeleolAb.
—BLDSC (6430.672000), CASDDS, IE, Infotrieve, Ingenta, INIST, Linda Hall, PADDS. **CCC.**
Published by: (Association Francaise des Techniciens et des Professionels du Petrole (A F T P)), Editions Techniques pour l'Automobile et l'Industrie (E T A I), 20 rue de la Saussiere, Boulogne-Billancourt, 92641, France. TEL 33-1-46992424, FAX 33-1-48255692, http://www.groupe-etai.com.

665.5 ESP ISSN 0213-8360
PETROLEO; actualidad nacional e internacional. Text in Spanish. 1973. w. EUR 299 domestic; EUR 435 foreign (effective 2010). **Document type:** *Magazine, Trade.* **Description:** Provides confidential information on international activities of the petroleum, petrochemical and gas markets.
Published by: Sede Tecnica S.A., Avda Brasil, 17 planta 12, Madrid, 28020, Spain. TEL 34-91-5565004, FAX 34-91-5560962, editorial@sedetecnica.com, http://www.sedetecnica.com/. Ed. Carlos Martin. Circ: 2,000.

665.5 USA ISSN 0093-7851
TN860 CODEN: PTRIB2
PETROLEO INTERNACIONAL. Text in Spanish, English. 1943. bi-m. free to qualified personnel (effective 2005). adv. bk.rev. charts; illus.; stat. **Document type:** *Magazine, Trade.*
Former titles: Petroleo y Petroquimica Internacional; Petroleo Interamericano (0031-6407)
Indexed: ChemAb, ChemTitl, GeoRef, PetrolAb, SpeleolAb.
—BLDSC (6430.780000), CASDDS, PADDS. **CCC.**
Published by: B2B Portales, Inc. (Subsidiary of: Carvajal International, Inc.), 901 Ponce de Leon, Ste. 901, Coral Gables, FL 33134. TEL 305-448-6875, FAX 305-448-9942, tbeirne@b2bportales.com, http://www.b2bportales.com. Ed. Santiago Algorta. Pub. Terry Beirne TEL 305-448-6875 ext 47311. adv.: B&W page USD 3,180, color page USD 4,240. Circ: 10,314 (controlled).

665.5 ECU
PETROLEO Y SOCIEDAD. Text in Spanish. q.?. USD 10 per issue.
Published by: Asociacion Sindical Petroecuador, General Salazar 945 y 12 de Octubre, Quito, Ecuador. TEL 593-2-566062, FAX 593-2-567260. Ed. Henry Llanes.

665.5 VEN ISSN 1316-4988
PETROLEUM. Text in Spanish. 1977. 6/yr. USD 80 domestic; USD 140 in Latin America; USD 180 in North America; USD 280 elsewhere (effective 1999). adv. bk.rev. **Document type:** *Trade.* **Description:** For professionals and technicians. Covers Latin American oil industry.
Formerly (until 1983): Petroleo y Tecnologia
—BLDSC (6431.100000).
Published by: Petroleum Editores, S.A., Calle 72, Av.19, Edf. Noel, Torre A, Piso 3, Ofc. F, Maracaibo, 4005, Venezuela. TEL 58-61-832424, FAX 58-61-513545, TELEX 64336 PEMIN UC. Ed., Pub., R&P Jorge Zajia. Adv. contact Gisela Vera. color page USD 2,400; trim 285 x 215. Circ: 5,647 (paid).

665.5 AUS
PETROLEUM; Australia's definitive energy review. Text in English. 2006. bi-m. AUD 59.40 domestic; AUD 78 foreign (effective 2008). adv. **Document type:** *Magazine, Trade.* **Description:** Provides definitive market intelligence of the upstream oil and gas sectors latest developments.
Published by: Aspermont Ltd., 613-619 Wellington St, Perth, W.A. 6000, Australia. TEL 61-8-62639100, FAX 61-8-62639148, corporate@aspermont.com, http://www.aspermont.com/. Ed. Steve Rotherham TEL 61-8-62639100. Adv. contact Scott Goodsell TEL 61-8-62639155. color page AUD 2,650, B&W page AUD 1,910; trim 210 x 297. Circ: 4,000.

338.47665 USA ISSN 1554-2904
HF5686.P3
PETROLEUM ACCOUNTING AND FINANCIAL MANAGEMENT JOURNAL. Text in English. 1982. 3/yr. USD 180 domestic; USD 220 foreign (effective 2011). back issues avail. **Document type:** *Journal, Academic/Scholarly.* **Description:** Covers both international and domestic issues confronting the oil and gas industry.
Former titles (until 1989): Journal of Petroleum Accounting (0890-8141); (until 1985): Journal of Extractive Industries Accounting (0885-3452)
Indexed: ATI, P26, P48, P52, P53, P54, P56, PQC.
—BLDSC (6431.305000), IE, Ingenta.
Published by: Institute of Petroleum Accounting, University of North Texas, 1155 Union Cir #305460, Denton, TX 76203. TEL 940-565-3170, FAX 940-369-8839, ipa@unt.edu.

P

665.5 USA ISSN 1930-5915
HD9561
THE PETROLEUM AGE. Text in English. 2004. q. **Document type:** *Newsletter, Consumer.*
Published by: American Oil & Gas Historical Society (A O G H S), 1201 15th St, NW, Ste 300, Washington, DC 20005. TEL 202-857-4785, FAX 202-857-4799.

PETROLEUM AND CHEMICAL INDUSTRY CONFERENCE. RECORD OF CONFERENCE PAPERS. *see* ENGINEERING—Chemical Engineering

665 SVK ISSN 1337-7027
TP690.A1 CODEN: ROUHAY
PETROLEUM AND COAL (ONLINE). Text in Czech, Slovak, English; Summaries in English, French, German, Russian. 1959. q. free (effective 2011). adv. bk.rev. abstr.; charts; pat.; stat. Index. **Document type:** *Journal, Academic/Scholarly.*
Former titles (until 2003): Petroleum and Coal (Print) (1335-3055); (until 1995): Ropa a Uhlie (1335-1141)
Media: Online - full text.
Indexed: A01, ChemAb, GasAb.
—CASDDS, IE, INIST.
Published by: (Vyskumny Ustav pre Ropu a Uhlovodikove Plyny/ Research Institute of Petroleum and Hydrocarbon Gases), Slovnaft VURUP a.s., Vlcie Hrdlo, PO Box 50, Bratislava, 820 03, Slovakia. TEL 420-7-248824, FAX 420-7-24676. Ed. Jozef Mikulec. **Co-sponsor:** Slovnaft, Slovak Society of Industrial Chemistry, Inc.

665.5 GBR ISSN 1469-4980
PETROLEUM AND OFFSHORE ENGINEERING BULLETIN. Text in English. 1975. m. **Document type:** *Bulletin, Trade.*
Former titles (until Dec. 1999): Offshore Engineering Information Bulletin (0961-8163); (until 1991): I O E Library Bulletin (0142-4793)
Related titles: Ed.
Published by: Offshore Engineering Information Service, Heriot-Watt University Library, Edinburgh, EH14 4AS, United Kingdom. TEL 44-131-451-3579, FAX 44-131-451-3164. Ed., Pub. Dr. Arnold Myers.

662.6 IND ISSN 0970-3098
TP690.2.A78
➤ **PETROLEUM ASIA JOURNAL.** Text in English. 1978. q. adv. **Document type:** *Journal, Academic/Scholarly.* **Description:** Covers articles related to Petroleum & Gas.
Indexed: SpeleolAb.
Published by: Himachal Times Group of publication, 57-B Rajpur Rd, Dehra Dun, Uttar Pradesh 248 001, India. TEL 91-135-2659684, FAX 91-135-2659684, devkpandhi@gmail.com, http://himachaltimesgroup.com.

661 RUS ISSN 0965-5441
TP690.A1 CODEN: PHEME4
➤ **PETROLEUM CHEMISTRY.** Text in English. 1962. bi-m. EUR 5,886, USD 7,055 combined subscription to institutions (print & online eds.) (effective 2012). adv. bk.rev. abstr.; bibl.; charts. back issues avail. **Document type:** *Journal, Academic/Scholarly.* **Description:** Publishes research papers on the analysis, physical and chemical properties and behavior of individual petroleum constituents, as well as applications of petroleum chemistry in the manufacture of industrial products.
Formerly (until 1992): Petroleum Chemistry U.S.S.R. (0031-6458)
Related titles: Online - full text ed.: ISSN 1555-6239; ◆ Translation of: Neftekhimiya. ISSN 0028-2421.
Indexed: A22, A26, APIAb, ASCA, B01, C24, CCI, CPEI, CurCont, E01, E14, EngInd, I05, ISR, R16, SCI, SCOPUS, T02, W07.
—BLDSC (0416.687000), East View, IE, Infotrieve, Ingenta, INIST, Linda Hall. **CCC.**

Published by: (Rossiiskaya Akademiya Nauk/Russian Academy of Sciences), M A I K Nauka - Interperiodica (Subsidiary of: Pleiades Publishing, Inc.), Profsoyuznaya ul 90, Moscow, 117997, Russian Federation. TEL 7-095-3347420, FAX 7-095-3360666, compmg@maik.ru, http://www.maik.ru. Ed. Salambek Khadzhiev. R&P Vladimir I Vasil'ev. Circ: 1,025. **Dist. in the Americas by:** Springer New York LLC, Journal Fulfillment, PO Box 2485, Secaucus, NJ 07096. TEL 212-460-1500, FAX 201-348-4505; **Dist. outside of the Americas by:** Springer, Haber Str 7, Heidelberg 69126, Germany. TEL 49-6221-3454303, FAX 49-6221-3454229.

665.5 330.9 USA ISSN 1548-808X
HD9560.4
THE PETROLEUM ECONOMICS MONTHLY. Text in English. m. USD 6,000 (effective 1998). charts. **Description:** Featuring in-depth articles on world petroleum market.
Formerly: Charles River Associates Petroleum Economics Monthly
Related titles: Online - full text ed.: ISSN 1548-8098.
Published by: P K Verleger LLC, 317 N. 4th St., Aspen, CO 81611-1205. TEL 978-287-5414, FAX 978-287-5414. Ed. Kim Pederson. R&P Philip K Jerleger.

665.5 GBR ISSN 0306-395X
HD9560.1 CODEN: PEECDK
PETROLEUM ECONOMIST; the international energy journal. Text in English. 1934. m. GBP 720 combined subscription domestic (print & online eds.); EUR 1,050 combined subscription in Europe (print & online eds.); USD 1,395 combined subscription elsewhere (print & online eds.) (effective 2010). bk.rev. charts; mkt.; stat.; illus. index. Supplement avail.; reprints avail. **Document type:** *Magazine, Trade.* **Description:** Informational articles, editorial commentary, news items, and statistical data pertaining to the marketing, exploratory, technological, and production aspects of the international oil, gas, and other energy-source industries. Includes company profiles.
Formerly: Petroleum Press Service (0031-6504); Incorporates (1996-2005): Power Economics (1367-1707); Which was formerly (until 2004): Power Economist (1365-4934)
Related titles: Microform ed.: (from PQC); Online - full text ed.: GBP 430, USD 795 (effective 2002); German ed.: Petroleum Economist (German Edition). ISSN 0306-4700; Spanish ed.: Petroleum Economist (Spanish Edition). ISSN 0306-4727; French ed.: Petroleum Economist (French Edition). ISSN 0306-4697. 1948; Japanese ed.: Petroleum Economist (Japanese Edition). ISSN 0306-4743; Arabic ed.: Petroleum Economist (Arabic Edition). ISSN 0306-4735.
Indexed: A12, A13, A15, A17, A22, A23, ABIn, AESIS, APEL, APIAb, B01, B02, B03, B04, B07, B13, B15, B17, B18, BMT, BPI, BRD, BrGeoL, BusI, E14, EIA, F&EA, FR, G04, G06, G07, G08, GasAb, GeoRef, I05, IBR, IBZ, IPARL, KES, P06, P48, P51, P52, P53, P54, P56, PAIS, PEBNI, PQC, PetrolAb, RASB, SCOPUS, SpeleolAb, T&II, T02, W01, W02, W03, W05.
—BLDSC (6431.680000), CIS, IE, Infotrieve, Ingenta, INIST, Linda Hall, PADDS. **CCC.**
Published by: Euromoney Institutional Investor Plc., Nestor House, Playhouse Yard, London, EC4V 5EX, United Kingdom. TEL 44-20-7779-8673, information@euromoneyplc.com, http://www.euromoneyplc.com/. Ed. Tom Nicholls. Circ: 4,400.

665 NLD ISSN 0955-0712
PETROLEUM ENGINEERING AND DEVELOPMENT STUDIES. Text in English. 1987. irreg., latest vol.4, 1993. price varies. **Document type:** *Monographic series, Academic/Scholarly.*
—BLDSC (6432.500000).
Published by: Springer Netherlands (Subsidiary of: Springer Science+Business Media), Van Godewijckstraat 30, Dordrecht, 3311 GX, Netherlands. TEL 31-78-6576050, FAX 31-78-6576474.

665.5 USA
PETROLEUM EQUIPMENT DIRECTORY. Text in English. 1955. a. USD 75 (effective 2001). adv. 264 p./no. 2 cols./p.; **Document type:** *Directory.*
Published by: Petroleum Equipment Institute, PO Box 2380, Tulsa, OK 74101. TEL 918-494-9696, FAX 918-491-9895, http://www.pei.org. Ed. Robert N Renkes. R&P Robert Renkes. Adv. contact Margaret Montgomery. color page USD 1,800; 7 x 10. Circ: 3,000.

665.5 NLD ISSN 1876-3804
PETROLEUM EXPLORATION AND DEVELOPMENT. Text in English. 2008. bi-m. **Document type:** *Journal, Academic/Scholarly.* **Description:** Covers all aspects of petroleum sciences, including petroleum geology, geophysics, geochemistry, exploration and development of oil and gas fields, reservoir engineering, reservoir protection and stimulation, oil storage and transportation, oil and gas chemistry, petroleum machinery, petroleum business administration and history of petroleum industry.
Media: Online - full text (from ScienceDirect). **Related titles:** ◆ Chinese ed.: Shiyou Kantan yu Kaifa. ISSN 1000-0747.
Indexed: CA, SCOPUS, T02.
—PADDS. **CCC.**
Published by: Elsevier BV (Subsidiary of: Elsevier Science & Technology), Radarweg 29, PO Box 211, Amsterdam, 1000 AE, Netherlands. TEL 31-20-4853911, FAX 31-20-4852457, JournalsCustomerServiceEMEA@elsevier.com.

665.5 USA ISSN 0740-1817
TN872
PETROLEUM FRONTIERS. Text in English. 1983. q. USD 390 combined subscription per issue (print & online eds.); USD 256 per issue (effective 2011). bibl.; charts; maps. back issues avail. **Document type:** *Magazine, Trade.* **Description:** Examines selected hydrocarbon provinces or horizons in the initial phases of discovery and development. Includes stratigraphic and structural analyses, mineralogy, drilling/discovery history, production/reservoir characteristics, leasing history and outlook, unique exploration and production problems and opportunities, etc.
Related titles: Online - full text ed.: USD 345 per issue (effective 2011).
Indexed: EngInd, GeoRef, PetrolAb, SCOPUS, SpeleolAb.
—BLDSC (6433.146000), IE, Ingenta, Linda Hall, PADDS.
Published by: I H S Inc. (Subsidiary of: I H S Energy Group), 321 Inverness Dr S, Bldg D, Englewood, CO 80112. TEL 303-790-0600, 800-525-7052, customer.support@ihs.com.

665.5 552 TWN ISSN 0553-8890
TN860 CODEN: PGTWAU
PETROLEUM GEOLOGY OF TAIWAN/T'AIWAN SHIH-YU TI-CHIH. Text in English. 1962. a. TWD 1,200 domestic; USD 54 foreign. **Document type:** *Bulletin.* **Description:** Publishes research papers on the geology of Taiwan.
Indexed: GeoRef, PetrolAb, SpeleolAb.
—CASDDS, Linda Hall, PADDS.
Published by: Chinese Petroleum Corporation, 83 Chung Hwa Rd, Sec1, Taipei, 100, Taiwan. TEL 886-2-361-0221, FAX 886-2-331-7473, TELEX 11215 CHINOL. Ed. Tai Hsuan Wu. Circ: 1,000.

665.5 551 CAN
PETROLEUM GEOLOGY SPECIAL PAPER SERIES. Text in English. 1990. a. price varies. **Document type:** *Government.*
Indexed: SpeleolAb.
Published by: British Columbia, Ministry of Energy and Mines, c/o Communications Coordinator, Stn Prov Govt, PO Box 9324, Victoria, BC V8W 9N3, Canada. TEL 250-952-0525, crown@pinc.com, http://www.ogc.gov.bc.ca. **Subscr. to:** Crown Publications Inc.

665.5 USA ISSN 0480-2160
HD9560.1
PETROLEUM INTELLIGENCE WEEKLY. Abbreviated title: P I W. Text in English. 1961. w. USD 3,000 (effective 2008). back issues avail. **Document type:** *Newsletter, Trade.* **Description:** Includes analysis and information on major developments, critical issues, and emerging trends in international oil and gas. For top-level executives.
Related titles: E-mail ed.: USD 2,770 (effective 2008); Fax ed.: USD 2,950; Online - full text ed.: USD 3,195 (effective 2008).
Indexed: B02, B15, B17, B18, F&EA, G04, G06, G07, G08, I05, PEBNI, SCOPUS.
—BLDSC (6433.630000), Linda Hall. **CCC.**
Published by: Energy Intelligence Group, Inc., 5 E 37th St, 5th Fl, New York, NY 10016. TEL 212-532-1112, FAX 212-532-4479, info@energyintel.com. Ed. Jim Washer. Adv. contact Mark Hoff TEL 212-532-1112 ext 1130.

665.5 GBR ISSN 0020-3076
TP690.A1 CODEN: PETRB2
PETROLEUM REVIEW. Text in English. 1914. m. GBP 250 domestic to non-members; GBP 420 foreign to non-members; GBP 42 to members (effective 2009). adv. bk.rev. illus.; stat.; tr.lit. index. back issues avail.; reprints avail. **Document type:** *Journal, Academic/Scholarly.* **Description:** Provides news, articles, and interviews relevant to the petroleum industry.
Formerly (until 1968): Institute of Petroleum Review (0367-9810)
Related titles: Microfilm ed.: (from PQC); Online - full text ed.; Supplement(s): UK Retail Marketin Survey.
Indexed: A22, A28, AESIS, APA, APIAb, APICat, APIH&E, APIOC, APIPR, APIPS, APITS, ASFA, B21, BMT, BrCerAb, BrGeoL, BrTechI, C&ISA, CA/WCA, CBNB, CIA, CPEI, CerAb, ChemAb, CivEngAb, CorrAb, E&CAJ, E11, EEA, EMA, ESPM, EnvEAb, F&EA, FR, GeoRef, H15, HRIS, IMMAb, ISMEC, Inspec, M&TEA, M09, MBF, METADEX, PetrolAb, RASB, SCOPUS, SolStAb, SpeleolAb, T04, WAA.
—BLDSC (6435.190000), IE, Infotrieve, Ingenta, INIST, Linda Hall, PADDS. **CCC.**
Published by: Energy Institute, 61 New Cavendish St, London, W1G 7AR, United Kingdom. TEL 44-20-74677100, FAX 44-20-72551472, info@energyinst.org.uk. Ed. Chris Skrebowski. Adv. contact Emma Parsons TEL 44-20-74677119. color page GBP 2,400; bleed 216 x 303.

665.5 CHN ISSN 1672-5107
TN860
PETROLEUM SCIENCE. Text in English. 1998. q. EUR 502, USD 672 combined subscription to institutions (print & online eds.) (effective 2012). **Document type:** *Journal, Academic/Scholarly.*
Related titles: Online - full text ed.: ISSN 1995-8226.
Indexed: A22, A26, E01, E08, ESPM, GeoRef, PetrolAb, PollutAb, RefZh, S09, SCI, SCOPUS, W07.
—BLDSC (6435.325000), IE, PADDS. **CCC.**
Published by: China University of Petroleum, 18 Fuxue Rd, Changpin, Beijing, 102249, China. TEL 86-10-89733266, waisb@cup.edu.cn, http://department1.cup.edu.cn/~waisb/about.htm. **Dist. outside of China by:** Springer, Haber Str 7, Heidelberg 69126, Germany. TEL 49-6221-3454303, FAX 49-6221-3454229. **Co-publisher:** Springer.

665.5 USA
HD9563
PETROLEUM SUPPLY AMERICAS. Text in English. 1978. s-a. USD 650 domestic; USD 688 foreign (effective 2009). adv. **Document type:** *Directory, Trade.* **Description:** Lists traders, marketers and suppliers of crude oil, refined products and natural gas liquids in North, Central and South America.
Former titles (until 1997): Oil Price Information Service's Petroleum Supply Americas (1096-3197); (until 199?): Stalsby - Wilson's Petroleum Supply America (1043-0369); (until 1989): Stalsby - Wilson's Who's Who in Petroleum Supply (1043-0148); (until 198?): Stalsby's Who's Who in Petroleum Supply (0735-0635); (until 19??): Stalsby's Directory of Petroleum Supply Personnel
Related titles: CD-ROM ed.: USD 2,095 domestic; USD 2,133 foreign (effective 2009); Online - full text ed.: USD 1,495 domestic; USD 1,533 foreign (effective 2009).
Published by: Oil Price Information Service (Subsidiary of: United Communications Group), Two Washingtonian Center, 9737 Washingtonian Blvd, Ste 100, Gaithersburg, MD 20878. TEL 301-287-2700, 888-301-2645, FAX 301-287-2039, energycs@opisnet.com. Adv. contact Greg Mosho TEL 732-730-2546.

665.5 USA
HD9575.A1
PETROLEUM SUPPLY EUROPE. Text in English. 1989. q. USD 425 domestic; USD 463 foreign; USD 1,445 combined subscription domestic (print & CD-ROM eds.); USD 1,483 combined subscription foreign (print & CD-ROM eds.) (effective 2009). adv. **Document type:** *Directory, Trade.* **Description:** Covers Asia, Africa, Australia, Europe and the Middle East, and provides reference guidance to locate alternate supply sources, find new business opportunities, identify financing partners and more.
Former titles (until 199?): Oil Price Information Service's Petroleum Supply Europe (1096-3200); Stalsby - Wilson's Petroleum Supply Europe (1043-0377)
Related titles: CD-ROM ed.
Published by: Oil Price Information Service (Subsidiary of: United Communications Group), Two Washingtonian Center, 9737 Washingtonian Blvd, Ste 100, Gaithersburg, MD 20878. TEL 301-287-2700, 888-301-2645, FAX 301-287-2039, energycs@opisnet.com. Pub. Daine T Miller TEL 732-730-2530. Adv. contact Greg Mosho TEL 732-730-2546. **Subscr. to:** 11300 Rockville Pike, Ste 1100, Rockville, MD 20852. TEL 301-287-2525, FAX 301-816-8945.

338.2 665 USA ISSN 0733-6241
K3911.2
PETROLEUM TAXATION & LEGISLATION REPORT. Abbreviated title: P T L R. Text in English. 19??. m. looseleaf. USD 4,500 base vol(s). (effective 2011). bk.rev. charts; mkt.; tr.lit. **Document type:** *Newsletter, Trade.* **Description:** Reviews changes in world oil and gas laws and tax regulations by country.
Formed by the merger of 1972: Petroleum Taxation Report (0031-6539); Petroleum Legislation Report
Published by: Barrows Co., Inc., 116 E 66th St, Ste 1B, New York, NY 10065. TEL 800-227-7697, gbarrows@barrowscompany.net.

665.5 GBR ISSN 1362-363X
TP690.A1
PETROLEUM TECHNOLOGY QUARTERLY; refining, gas processing and petrochemicals. Abbreviated title: P T Q. Text in English. 1996. q. free to qualified personnel (effective 2010). adv. back issues avail. **Document type:** *Magazine, Trade.* **Description:** Contains technical articles by engineers for engineers, highlighting case studies which demonstrate problem solving and cost effectiveness worldwide.
Related titles: Online - full text ed.; ◆ Supplement(s): Hydrocarbon China. ISSN 1812-7827; ◆ Biofuels Technology. ISSN 1757-6407.
Indexed: APIAb, SCOPUS.
—BLDSC (6435.960000), IE, Ingenta, INIST. **CCC.**
Published by: Crambeth Allen Publishing, Hopesay, Craven Arms, SY7 8HD, United Kingdom. TEL 44-1588-660776, FAX 44-1588-660668, publisher@crambethallen.com, http://www.crambethallen.com. Ed. Rene G Gonzalez TEL 44-844-5888773. adv.: page EUR 5,350; trim 297 x 420. Circ: 16,700.

665.5 SWE ISSN 0345-9314
PETROLEUMHANDELN. Text in Swedish. 1973. bi-m. SEK 390 (effective 2001). adv. **Document type:** *Magazine, Trade.*
Published by: Petroleumhandelns Riksforbund, Box 1763, Stockholm, 11187, Sweden. TEL 46-8-700-63-30, FAX 46-8-700-63-49. Ed., Adv. contact Angela Hampl. B&W page SEK 7,400, color page SEK 10,900; trim 184 x 260.

PETROLOGIYA. *see* EARTH SCIENCES—Geology

PETROLOGY. *see* EARTH SCIENCES—Geology

PETROLOGY AND STRUCTURAL GEOLOGY. *see* EARTH SCIENCES—Geology

665.5 531.64 SGP ISSN 0129-1122
HD9576.S652
PETROMIN. Text in English. 1974. 10/yr. USD 120 (effective 2007). adv. **Document type:** *Magazine, Trade.* **Description:** Covers the oil and gas industries in Asia, including issues such as technology, projects, and engineering.
Indexed: AESIS, APIAb, BAS, EnvAb, GeoRef, PEBNI, PetrolAb, SCOPUS, SpeleolAb.
—BLDSC (6436.489000), IE, Linda Hall, PADDS.
Published by: Asia Pacific Energy Business Publications Pte. Ltd., 63 Robinson Rd, #02-10 Afro Asia Bldg, Singapore, 068894, Singapore. TEL 65-6-2223422, FAX 65-6-2225587, pansy@safan.com, http://www.safan.com. Ed. Jimmie Aung Khin. Adv. contact Eddie Raj.

665 SGP
PETROMIN & HYDROCARBON ASIA OIL & GAS DIRECTORY. Text in English. a., latest 2001. USD 150 (effective 2004). **Document type:** *Directory, Trade.* **Description:** Covers oil & gas exploration, production, refining, petrochemical and gas processing plants, offshore engineering, fabrication & EPC management, pipeline construction and operation, rig owning/operation, oilfield services, equipment supplies and services, instrumentation & control.
Formerly: Petromin Oil & Gas Directory
Published by: Asia Pacific Energy Business Publications Pte. Ltd., 63 Robinson Rd, #02-10 Afro Asia Bldg, Singapore, 068894, Singapore. TEL 65-6-2223422, FAX 65-6-2225587, pansy@safan.com, http://www.safan.com.

665.5 SGP
PETROMIN & HYDROCARBON ASIA OIL AND GAS MAP. Text in English. a., latest vol.6. USD 150 (effective 2004). maps. **Document type:** *Journal, Trade.* **Description:** Provides the latest updates on concessions, pipelines, refineries, petrochemical and gas processing plants in South East Asia.
Formerly: Petromin Asia - Pacific Petroleum Map
Indexed: SpeleolAb.
Published by: Asia Pacific Energy Business Publications Pte. Ltd., 63 Robinson Rd, #02-10 Afro Asia Bldg, Singapore, 068894, Singapore. TEL 65-6-2223422, FAX 65-6-2225587, pansy@safan.com, http://www.safan.com.

665.54 SGP ISSN 1793-1851
PETROMIN PIPELINER. Text in English. q. USD 60 (effective 2007). **Document type:** *Magazine, Trade.* **Description:** Covers the latest news on construction, contracts, technology, government, companies and conferences. Includes interviews with industry figures, coverage of major pipeline projects, technical articles, analysis of issues facing the industry, and product and equipment reviews.
Indexed: PetrolAb.
—PADDS.
Published by: Asia Pacific Energy Business Publications Pte. Ltd., 63 Robinson Rd, #02-10 Afro Asia Bldg, Singapore, 068894, Singapore. TEL 65-6-2223422, FAX 65-6-2225587, http://www.safan.com.

338.34554 665.5 NOR ISSN 1891-7739
PETRONEWS. Text in English, Russian. 2004. 3/yr. adv. back issues avail. **Document type:** *Magazine, Trade.*
Formerly (until 2009): Oilinfo News (1504-4092)
Related titles: Online - full text ed.: ISSN 0809-8948. 2005.
Published by: Oil Information AS, PO Box 2144, Stavanger, 4095, Norway. TEL 47-51-884410, FAX 47-51-884419, post@oilinfo.no. Ed. Magnus Vaagen Birkenes TEL 45-51-885578. adv.: page NOK 10,000; 180 x 285. Circ: 12,000.

665.5 USA ISSN 1529-9074
TN871.35 CODEN: LGALAS
➤ **PETROPHYSICS.** Text in English. 1962. bi-m. free to members; USD 120 to non-members (effective 2009). adv. bk.rev. abstr.; bibl.; charts; illus. back issues avail. **Document type:** *Journal, Academic/Scholarly.* **Description:** Contains original contributions on theoretical and applied aspects of formation evaluation, including both open hole and cased hole well logging, core analysis and formation testing.
Formerly (until 2000): Log Analyst (0024-581X)
Indexed: A22, AESIS, CIS, CPEI, CurCont, E&PHSE, EngInd, GP&P, GeoRef, OffTech, PetrolAb, SCI, SCOPUS, SpeleolAb, W07.
—BLDSC (6436.595000), IE, Infotrieve, Ingenta, INIST, Linda Hall, PADDS.
Published by: Society of Petrophysicsts and Well Log Analysts (S P W L A), 8866 Gulf Fwy, Ste 320, Houston, TX 77017. TEL 713-947-8727, FAX 713-947-7181, http://www.spwla.org. Ed. James Howard TEL 918-661-9575. Circ: 3,000.

665.5 ARG ISSN 0031-6598
TN860
PETROTECNICA. Text in Spanish. 1960. bi-m. ARS 120 domestic; USD 150 foreign (effective 1999). adv. charts; illus. index. **Document type:** *Academic/Scholarly.*
Indexed: FR.
Published by: Instituto Argentino del Petroleo y del Gas, Maipu 645, 4th Fl, Buenos Aires, 1006, Argentina. TEL 54-11-4325800, FAX 54-11-43935494. Ed. Carlos Alberto Albano. Circ: 3,500.

338.47 GBR
PETROVIEW - GULF OF MEXICO. Text in English. 1997. q. maps. **Document type:** *Report, Trade.* **Description:** Provides integrated information on the upstream oil and gas business. Contains data on companies, licenses, wells, fields, platforms and pipelines. Query results can be viewed as a map, table or graph.
Media: Diskette. **Related titles:** CD-ROM ed.
Published by: The Petroleum Services Group at Deloitte (Subsidiary of: Deloitte Touche Tohmatsu International), 2 New St Sq, London, EC4A 3BZ, United Kingdom. TEL 44-20-70076074, FAX 44-20-75831198.

338.47 GBR
PETROVIEW - NORTH WEST EUROPE. Text in English. 1992. m. **Document type:** *Report, Trade.* **Description:** Provides data on licenses, new and existing wells, fields, platforms, and pipelines. Results of queries can be viewed as a map, table, or graph.
Formerly: PetroView
Media: Diskette. **Related titles:** CD-ROM ed.
Published by: The Petroleum Services Group at Deloitte (Subsidiary of: Deloitte Touche Tohmatsu International), 2 New St Sq, London, EC4A 3BZ, United Kingdom. TEL 44-20-70076074, FAX 44-20-75831198.

665.5 AUS
PEX MONTHLY. Text in English. 1972. 11/yr. AUD 340 (effective 2008). **Document type:** *Newsletter.* **Description:** Publishes news, views, comments and analysis.
Formerly: P E X: Australia's Petroleum Exploration Newsletter (0310-4184)
Indexed: AESIS, GeoRef.
Published by: Pex Publications Pty. Ltd., Unit 5/1 Almondbury Rd, Mt Lawley, W.A. 6050, Australia. TEL 61-8-92726555, 800-739-855, FAX 61-8-92725556, oilinfo@pex.com.au. Ed. Leith Nolan.

338.47665 GBR ISSN 1749-2386
PHILIPPINES PETROCHEMICALS REPORT. Text in English. 2005. q. EUR 820, USD 1,030 combined subscription (print & email eds.) (effective 2010). **Document type:** *Report, Trade.* **Description:** Provides industry professionals and strategists, sector analysts, trade associations and regulatory bodies with independent forecasts and competitive intelligence on the Philippine petrochemicals industry.
Related titles: E-mail ed.
Indexed: A15, ABIn, B02, B15, B17, B18, G04, I05, P48, P51, P52, P56, PQC.
Published by: Business Monitor International Ltd., Senator House, 85 Queen Victoria St, London, EC4V 4AB, United Kingdom. TEL 44-20-72480468, FAX 44-20-72480467, subs@businessmonitor.com.

665 USA
PHILNEWS. Text in English. 1937; N.S. 1976. m. free to qualified personnel. illus.
Published by: Phillips Petroleum Company, Corporate Communications, 16 A1 PB, Bartlesville, OK 74004. TEL 918-661-4974, FAX 918-662-2926. Ed. Bill Wertz. Circ: 34,000.

622 USA ISSN 0032-0188
TP757 CODEN: PLGJAT
PIPELINE & GAS JOURNAL; energy construction, transportation and distribution. Text in English. 1970. m. adv. charts; illus. back issues avail.; reprints avail. **Document type:** *Magazine, Trade.* **Description:** Serves pipeline industry. Covers design, operation, marketing and management of oil, natural gas, gas distribution and products with specialized departments on communications and corrosion as applied to the pipeline field.
Incorporates (1928-1990): Pipeline (Houston) (0148-4443); Which was formerly (until 1974): Pipe Line News (0032-0153); Formed by the merger of (19??-1970): Pipeline Engineer (0096-8293); Which was formerly (until 1956): Petroleum Engineer, Oil and Gas Pipelining Edition; (1859-1970): American Gas Journal (0096-4409); Which was formerly (until 1921): American Gas Engineering Journal (0096-4387); (until 1917): American Gas Light Journal (0096-4395)
Related titles: Microform ed.; Online - full text ed.; Series: Energy Management Report. ISSN 0013-7537.
Indexed: A05, A09, A10, A15, A22, A23, A24, A26, A28, ABIn, AESIS, APA, APIAb, APICat, APIOC, APIPR, APIPS, APITS, AS&TA, AS&TI, ASCA, B01, B02, B04, B06, B07, B08, B09, B10, B13, B15, B17, B18, BRD, BrCerAb, BusI, C&ISA, C10, C12, CA/WCA, CEA, CIA, CLT&T, CerAb, CivEngAb, CorrAb, E&CAJ, E04, E05, E08, E11, E14, EEA, EIA, EMA, ESPM, EnerInd, EnvAb, EnvEAb, F&EA, FR, G04, G06, G07, G08, GasAb, GeoRef, H15, HRIS, I05, M&TEA, M01, M02, M09, MBF, METADEX, P26, P34, P48, P51, P52, P54, P56, PQC, PetrolAb, S04, S09, S22, SCOPUS, SRI, SolStAb, SpeleolAb, T&II, T02, T04, V02, V03, V04, W03, W05, WAA.
—BLDSC (6502.060000), IE, Infotrieve, Ingenta, INIST, Linda Hall, PADDS. **CCC.**
Published by: Oildom Publishing Co. of Texas, Inc., PO Box 941669, Houston, TX 77094. TEL 281-558-6930, FAX 281-558-7029, maxine@oildompublishing.com, http://www.oildompublishing.com. Ed. Jeff Share TEL 281-558-6930, ext. 218. Pub. Oliver Klinger TEL 281-558-6930 ext 212. Circ: 28,938 (controlled).

665.54 USA ISSN 1540-3688
TJ930
PIPELINE AND GAS TECHNOLOGY. Abbreviated title: P G T. Text in English. 1954. m. (except Jan. & Dec.). free to qualified personnel (print & online eds.) (effective 2009). bk.rev. charts; illus. Index. reprints avail. **Document type:** *Magazine, Trade.* **Description:** Edited for personnel engaged in the design, operation, maintenance, construction and management of pipe lines and gas utilities worldwide. Includes gas transmission and distribution systems as well as pipe line systems for crude oil, products, water and slurries.
Former titles (until 2002): Pipe Line & Gas Industry (1079-8765); (until Jan.1995): Pipe Line Industry (0032-0145)
Related titles: Online - full text ed.
Indexed: A05, A10, A15, A22, A23, A24, A28, ABIn, APA, APICat, APIH&E, APIOC, APIPR, APIPS, APITS, AS&TA, AS&TI, B01, B02, B04, B06, B07, B08, B09, B13, B15, B17, B18, BrCerAb, C&ISA, C10, C12, CA/WCA, CIA, CerAb, CivEngAb, CorrAb, E&CAJ, E11, E14, EEA, EMA, ESPM, EnvEAb, F&EA, FR, G04, G06, G07, G08, GasAb, H15, I05, M&TEA, M01, M02, M09, MBF, METADEX, P48, P51, P52, P56, PQC, PetrolAb, SCOPUS, SolStAb, T02, T04, V02, V03, W04, WAA.
—IE, Infotrieve, Ingenta, INIST, Linda Hall, PADDS. **CCC.**
Published by: Hart Energy Publishing, LP (Subsidiary of: Chemical Week Associates), 1616 S Voss Rd, Ste 1000, Houston, TX 77057. TEL 713-260-6400, 800-874-2544, FAX 713-840-8585, custserv@hartenergy.com. Ed. Bruce Beaubouef TEL 713-260-6471. Pub. Ronnie Milam TEL 713-260-6420. Circ: 21,500.

621.8672 USA ISSN 1062-5801
TJ930
PIPELINE INDUSTRY (TULSA); transmission. Text in English. a. **Document type:** *Directory, Trade.* **Description:** Supplies company name, address, phone and fax numbers, personnel, division offices, size and length of pipes and type of lines, equipment manufacturers, suppliers, contractors, engineering and construction.
Formerly: Pipe Line and Pipe Line Contractors
Related titles: Online - full text ed.
Published by: Midwest Publishing Company, 2230 E 49th St, Ste E, Tulsa, OK 74105. TEL 800-829-2002, info@midwestpub.com, http://www.midwestpub.com/.

665.54 UAE
PIPELINE MAGAZINE. Text in English. m. USD 199 (effective 2006). **Document type:** *Magazine, Trade.*
Published by: Reflex Publishing FZ LLC, Dubai Media City, PO Box 500643, Dubai, United Arab Emirates. TEL 971-4-3910830, FAX 971-4-3904570, http://reflexpublishingme.com/.

665.54 USA
PIPELINE NEWS. Text in English. m. USD 65 domestic; USD 75 in Canada; USD 95 elsewhere (effective 2011). adv. **Document type:** *Magazine, Trade.*
Published by: Oildom Publishing Co. of Texas, P.O. Box 941669, Houston, TX 77094-8669. TEL 281-558-6930, FAX 281-558-7029, http://www.oildompublishing.com/. Ed. Rita Tubb. Pub. Oliver C Klinger III. Circ: 2,500 (paid).

665.5 GBR
PLATFORM OIL & GAS TECHNOLOGY REVIEW. Text in English. 1997. m. GBP 55, USD 110, EUR 84, NOK 750 (effective 2009). adv. software rev. illus.; maps; stat.; tr.lit. back issues avail. **Document type:** *Magazine, Trade.* **Description:** Contains information on new products and technologies within the oil and gas sector. It also covers people, contracts, international and local news and special articles.
Published by: Platform Media Limited, Woodburn Rd, Blackburn Industrial Est, Kinellar, Aberdeen AB21 0RX, United Kingdom. TEL 44-1224-791117, FAX 44-1224-791147, sales@platform-media.co.uk. Adv. contact Rick McTaggart. Circ: 7,000.

665.5 333.79 USA ISSN 1931-180X
PLATTS ASIA-PACIFIC/ARAB GULF MARKETSCAN (ONLINE). Text in English. 19??. d. price varies. **Document type:** *Newsletter, Trade.* **Description:** Contains reports on refined product assessments for FOB Singapore, C and F Japan and Cand F Arab Gulf markets and includes comprehensive market commentary detailing the players, price movements and the reasons behind them.
Formerly: Platts Asia-Pacific/Arab Gulf Marketscan (Print)
Media: Online - full content.
Published by: Platts (Subsidiary of: McGraw-Hill Companies, Inc.), 1200 G St NW, Ste 1000, Washington, DC 20005. TEL 212-904-3070, 800-752-8878, FAX 202-383-2024, support@platts.com.

333.79 665.5 USA ISSN 1931-2229
PLATT'S L P GASWIRE (ONLINE). Text in English. 1979. d. USD 4,995 combined subscription (online & E-mail eds.) (effective 2008). adv. back issues avail. **Document type:** *Newsletter, Trade.* **Description:** Details emerging market trends, pricing and market news for ethane, iso-butane, natural gasoline, normal butane and propane.
Formerly (until 19??): Platt's L P Gaswire (Print)
Media: Online - full content. **Related titles:** E-mail ed.
Published by: Platts (Subsidiary of: McGraw-Hill Companies, Inc.), 1200 G St NW, Ste 1000, Washington, DC 20005. TEL 212-904-3070, 800-752-8878, FAX 202-383-2024, support@platts.com.

665.5 USA ISSN 0163-1284
HD9561
PLATT'S OILGRAM NEWS. Text in English. 1923. w. USD 2,690 (effective 2007). back issues avail. **Document type:** *Newsletter, Trade.* **Description:** Provides report on supply and demand trends, corporate news, government actions, exploration and technology.
Former titles (until 19??): Platt's Oilgram News Service (0032-1427); Oilgram News Service
Related titles: E-mail ed.; Online - full text ed.: USD 2,995 combined subscription (online & E-mail eds.) (effective 2008).
Indexed: A15, ABIn, B02, B03, B11, B15, B17, B18, BusI, G04, G06, G07, G08, I05, P48, P51, P52, P56, PEBNI, PQC, RASB, T&II.
—CIS, Linda Hall. **CCC.**
Published by: Platts (Subsidiary of: McGraw-Hill Companies, Inc.), 1200 G St NW, Ste 1000, Washington, DC 20005. TEL 212-904-3070, 800-752-8878, FAX 202-383-2024, support@platts.com. Ed. Peter Zipf. Pub. H G Sachinis. Adv. contact Ann Forte TEL 720-548-5479.

665.5 USA
PLATT'S OILGRAM PRICE REPORT (ONLINE); an international daily oil-gas price and marketing letter. Variant title: Oilgram Price Report. Text in English. 1923. d. USD 3,245 in North America; USD 3,695 elsewhere (effective 2008). adv. **Document type:** *Newsletter, Trade.* **Description:** Covers market changes, market fundamentals and factors driving prices and also brings a vast array of international prices for crude and products, netback tables and market critical data.
Former titles (until 19??): Platt's Oilgram Price Report (Print) (0163-1292); (until 197?): Platt's Oilgram Price Service (0149-581X); Oilgram Price Service
Media: Online - full content. **Related titles:** Supplement(s): U.S. Futures Update. ISSN 1556-3200. 2003; O P R Extra. ISSN 1556-3219. 2003.
Indexed: A15, ABIn, P48, P51, P52, P56, PQC, RASB.
—CIS, Linda Hall. **CCC.**
Published by: Platts (Subsidiary of: McGraw-Hill Companies, Inc.), 1200 G St NW, Ste 1000, Washington, DC 20005. TEL 212-904-3070, 800-752-8878, FAX 202-383-2024, support@platts.com. Ed. Jeff Mower. Adv. contact Josie Parnell.

665.5 333.79 USA ISSN 1931-2202
PLATT'S OLEFINSCAN (ONLINE). Text in English. 19??. w. USD 3,595 combined subscription (online & E-mail eds.) (effective 2008). **Document type:** *Newsletter, Trade.* **Description:** Provides weekly analyses and pricing from key olefins markets around the world and in-depth market commentary on ethylene, propylene, butadiene and ethylene glycol markets.
Formerly: Platt's Olefinscan (Print)
Media: Online - full content. **Related titles:** E-mail ed.
Published by: Platts (Subsidiary of: McGraw-Hill Companies, Inc.), 1200 G St NW, Ste 1000, Washington, DC 20005. TEL 212-904-3070, 800-752-8878, FAX 202-383-2024, support@platts.com.

333.79 665.5 USA
PLATT'S PETROCHEMICALSCAN (ONLINE). Variant title: Europe and Americas Petrochemicalscan. Text in English. w. USD 3,715 (effective 2008). back issues avail. **Document type:** *Newsletter, Trade.* **Description:** Reports on key product price ranges and market news in the spot markets of Europe and the Americas.
Formerly: Platt's Petrochemicalscan (Print)
Media: Online - full content.
Published by: Platts (Subsidiary of: McGraw-Hill Companies, Inc.), 1200 G St NW, Ste 1000, Washington, DC 20005. TEL 212-904-3070, 800-752-8878, FAX 202-383-2024, info@platts.com, http://www.platts.com.

660 USA ISSN 1931-2199
PLATT'S POLYMERSCAN (ONLINE). Text in English. 19??. w. USD 3,995 combined subscription (online & E-mail eds.) (effective 2008). back issues avail. **Document type:** *Newsletter, Trade.* **Description:** Contains more than 130 price assessments, including export and domestic pricing, accompanied by in-depth market commentary.
Formerly: Platt's Polymerscan (Print)
Media: Online - full content. **Related titles:** E-mail ed.
Published by: Platts (Subsidiary of: McGraw-Hill Companies, Inc.), 1200 G St NW, Ste 1000, Washington, DC 20005. TEL 212-904-3070, 800-752-8878, FAX 202-383-2024, support@platts.com. Ed. Ilana Djelal.

665.5 531.64 USA ISSN 1931-2172
PLATT'S SOLVENTSWIRE (ONLINE). Text in English. 19??. w. USD 3,425 combined subscription (online & E-mail eds.) (effective 2008). **Document type:** *Newsletter, Trade.* **Description:** Provides weekly assessments, spot quotes, and market news on the European and US markets and covers products including solvent naphtha, IPA, MEK, MIBK hydrocarbons and oxygenated and chlorinated solvents.
Formerly: Platt's Solventswire (Print)
Media: Online - full content. **Related titles:** E-mail ed.
Published by: Platts (Subsidiary of: McGraw-Hill Companies, Inc.), 1200 G St NW, Ste 1000, Washington, DC 20005. TEL 212-904-3070, 800-752-8878, FAX 202-383-2024, support@platts.com. Eds. Ilana Djelal, Mike Davis, Shahrin Ismaiyatim.

333.79 665.5 USA
PLATT'S U S MARKETSCAN (ONLINE). Text in English. 1976. d. USD 6,845 combined subscription (online & E-mail eds.) (effective 2008). back issues avail. **Document type:** *Newsletter, Trade.* **Description:** Contains an overview of the major refined products in the United States and carries spot prices for all key products traded in the US market.
Former titles: Platt's U S Marketscan (Print); Platt's Oilgram Marketscan. U S Edition
Media: Online - full content. **Related titles:** E-mail ed.
Published by: Platts (Subsidiary of: McGraw-Hill Companies, Inc.), 1200 G St NW, Ste 1000, Washington, DC 20005. TEL 212-904-3070, 800-752-8878, FAX 202-383-2024, support@platts.com.

665.7 CZE ISSN 0032-1761
CODEN: PVZTAK
PLYN/GAS; manufacture, distribution and utilization of gas. Text in Czech; Summaries in English. 1950. m. (11/yr.). EUR 126 foreign (effective 2008). adv. bk.rev. abstr.; charts; illus.; stat. index. **Document type:** *Magazine, Trade.*
Formerly (until 1967): Paliva (0369-8262)
Related titles: Microform ed.
Indexed: CIN, CISA, ChemAb, ChemTitl, F&EA, FR, GasAb.
—CASDDS, INIST.
Published by: Cesky Plynarensky Svaz/Czech Gas Association, Novodvorska 803/82, Prague 4, 14200, Czech Republic. cpsvaz@cgoa.cz. Ed. Otto Smrcek. Circ: 3,000. **Dist. by:** Kubon & Sagner Buchexport - Import GmbH, Hessstr 39-41, Munich 80798, Germany. TEL 49-89-542180, FAX 49-89-54218218, postmaster@kubon-sagner.de, http://www.kubon-sagner.de.

338.47665 GBR ISSN 1749-2394
POLAND PETROCHEMICALS REPORT. Text in English. 2005. q. EUR 820, USD 1,030 combined subscription (print & email eds.) (effective 2010). **Document type:** *Report, Trade.* **Description:** Provides industry professionals and strategists, sector analysts, trade associations and regulatory bodies with independent forecasts and competitive intelligence on the petrochemicals industry in Poland.
Related titles: E-mail ed.
Indexed: A15, ABIn, B02, B15, B17, B18, G04, I05, P48, P51, P52, P56, PQC.

P

Published by: Business Monitor International Ltd., Senator House, 85 Queen Victoria St, London, EC4V 4AB, United Kingdom. TEL 44-20-72480468, FAX 44-20-72480467, subs@businessmonitor.com.

338.47665 658.8 NLD ISSN 0922-8896
POMPSHOP. Text in Dutch. 1985. m. EUR 59.80 domestic; EUR 77.30 foreign (effective 2010). adv. **Document type:** *Magazine, Trade.*
Supersedes in part (in 1988): Foodmarkt Extra (0922-8888)
Related titles: ◆ Supplement(s): TabakMag. ISSN 1876-7435.
Published by: Uitgeverij Lakerveld BV, Postbus 160, Wateringen, 2290 AD, Netherlands. TEL 31-174-315000, FAX 31-174-315001, uitgeverij@lakerveld.nl, http://www.lakerveld.nl. Ed. Jiri Hartog TEL 31-174-389697. Pub. Ad van Gaalen. Adv. contact Jos Tourne. B&W page EUR 1,595; trim 210 x 297. Circ: 2,177.

668.411 USA ISSN 1536-3937
PRACTICING OIL ANALYSIS; the magazine for the analysis and management of lubricants. Text in English. 1998. bi-m. USD 29; free to qualified personnel in the US, Canada & Europe (effective 2005). adv. **Document type:** *Magazine, Trade.*
Indexed: APIAb, FLUIDEX, SCOPUS.
Published by: Noria Corporation, 1328 E 43rd Court, Tulsa, OK 74105. TEL 800-597-5460, FAX 918-746-0925. Ed., Pub. James C Fitch. Adv. contact Brett O'Kelley. **Subscr. to:** Practicing Oil Analysis, 1209 Dundee Ave, Ste #8, Elgin, IL 60120. TEL 847-697-2111, 800-554-7470, FAX 847-697-8717.

665.5 USA ISSN 1085-4274
PRESTON PIPE & TUBE REPORT. Text in English. 1982. m. USD 2,995 (effective 2009). adv. charts; stat. **Document type:** *Report, Trade.* **Description:** Addresses the gross US and Canadian pipe and tube supply including the following commodities: oil country tubular goods, line pipe, standard pipe, mechanical tube, structural pipe and tube pressure pipe, and stainless pipe and tube.
Formerly: Preston Pipe Report
Related titles: Online - full text ed.: ISSN 1946-1623.
Published by: Preston Publishing Co., Inc., 14615 Manchester Rd, Ste 203, Ballwin, MO 63011. TEL 636-220-8170, FAX 636-220-8315, rpreckel@prestonpipe.com.

338.47665 CAN
PRICELINE. Text in English. d. CAD 1,300 (effective 2003).
Media: Online - full content. **Related titles:** Fax ed.: CAD 1,600 (effective 2003).
Published by: Canadian Enerdata Ltd., 100 Allstate Pkwy, Ste 304, Markham, ON L3R 6H3, Canada. TEL 905-479-9697, FAX 905-479-2515, publications@enerdata.com.

665.5 USA ISSN 2158-7868
PRIME SUPPLIER REPORT. Text in English. 199?. m. free (effective 2011). back issues avail. **Document type:** *Report, Trade.* **Description:** Measures primary petroleum product deliveries into the United States where they are locally marketed and consumed.
Media: Online - full text.
Published by: Energy Information Administration (Subsidiary of: U.S. Department of Energy, Office of Industrial Technologies), 1000 Independence Ave, SW, Washington, DC 20585. TEL 202-586-8800, infoctr@eia.doe.gov.

665.5 PAK ISSN 0033-0574
PROGRESS. Text in English. 1956. m. PKR 300 domestic; USD 30 foreign (effective 2000). bk.rev. charts; illus.; stat. **Document type:** *Newsletter.* **Description:** Provides news about the activities of the company in particular, and the Pakistani oil and gas industry in general. Includes activities and achievements of the company's employees.
Published by: Pakistan Petroleum Ltd., 4th Fl., PIDC House, Dr. Ziauddin Ahmed Rd., P O Box 3942, Karachi, 75530, Pakistan. TEL 92-21-5651480, FAX 92-21-5680005, TELEX 29295 PPETK PK. Ed. Nusrat Nasarullah. Circ: 4,750.

665.77 CAN ISSN 0033-1260
PROPANE - CANADA. Text in English. 1968. 6/yr. CAD 35 domestic; USD 37 in United States; USD 62 elsewhere (effective 2005). adv. abstr.; charts; stat.; tr.lit. **Document type:** *Journal, Trade.*
Media: Duplicated (not offset). **Related titles:** Online - full text ed.
Indexed: A15, ABIn, APIAb, C03, CBCABus, F&EA, GasAb, P48, P51, P52, P56, PQC, SCOPUS.
—CCC.
Published by: Northern Star Communications, 900 6th Ave S W, 5th Fl, Calgary, AB T2P 3K2, Canada. TEL 403-263-6881, FAX 403-263-6886, http://www.northernstar.ab.ca/channels/northernstar/home.htm. Ed. Alister Thomas. Pub. Scott Jeffrey. Adv. contact Pat McEachern. Circ: 5,106.

665.7 USA
PROPANE NEWS. Text in English. 1997. 5/yr. USD 49; includes Texas Propane. adv. **Description:** Covers new laws and regulations (both state and federal) affecting the industry, new technology and products, marketing opportunities, and safety issues.
Published by: Texas Propane Gas Association, PO Box 140735, Austin, TX 78714-0735. info@txpropane.com, http://www.txpropane.com. Adv. contact Ellen Terry. Circ: 1,193 (controlled).

PROPANE VEHICLE. *see* TRANSPORTATION

665.538 USA
PUMP PRICE REPORT. Text in English. bi-w. USD 107 (effective 1999). **Document type:** *Corporate.* **Description:** Offers an unbiased analysis of the latest gas price surveys published by the AAA, government agencies, the petroleum industry, and other price services.
Related titles: Fax ed.
Published by: William Berman, Ed. & Pub., PO Box 1062, Fairfax, VA 22030. TEL 800-734-0504, FAX 703-591-4188.

335.47665 GBR ISSN 1749-2408
QATAR PETROCHEMICALS REPORT. Text in English. 2005. q. EUR 820, USD 1,030 combined subscription (print & email eds.) (effective 2010). **Document type:** *Report, Trade.* **Description:** Provides industry professionals and strategists, sector analysts, trade associations and regulatory bodies with independent forecasts and competitive intelligence on the Qatar petrochemicals industry.
Related titles: E-mail ed.
Indexed: A15, ABIn, B02, B15, B17, B18, G04, I05, P48, P51, P52, P56, PQC.

Published by: Business Monitor International Ltd., Senator House, 85 Queen Victoria St, London, EC4V 4AB, United Kingdom. TEL 44-20-72480468, FAX 44-20-72480467, subs@businessmonitor.com.

665.5 GBR ISSN 2045-0834
▼ **QUARTERLY OIL DEMAND REPORT.** Abbreviated title: Q O D R. Text in English. 2010. q. GBP 850 (effective 2010). **Document type:** *Report, Trade.* **Description:** Features to analyse the key uncertainties surrounding the base-case oil price forecast.
Media: Online - full text.
Published by: Centre for Global Energy Studies, 17 Knightsbridge, London, SW1X 7LY, United Kingdom. TEL 44-20-72354334, FAX 44-20-72354338, marketing@cges.co.uk, http://www.cges.co.uk/.

622 HRV
RAFINERIJSKI LIST. Text in Croatian. 1974. fortn. free.
Published by: Rafinerija Nafte, Sisak, Sisak, Croatia. Ed. Bozidar Babic.

RANLIAO HUAXUE XUEBAO/JOURNAL OF FUEL CHEMISTRY AND TECHNOLOGY. *see* ENGINEERING—Chemical Engineering

665.5 540 IND
RECENT RESEARCH DEVELOPMENTS IN OIL CHEMISTRY. Text in English. 1997. a. **Document type:** *Monographic series, Academic/Scholarly.*
Published by: Transworld Research Network, T C 37-661 (2), Fort Post Office, Trivandrum, Kerala 695 023, India. TEL 91-471-2452918, FAX 91-471-2573051, ggcom@vsnl.com, http://www.trnres.com.

665.7 628 DEU
RECHT UND STEUERN IM GAS- UND WASSERFACH. Text in German. 1970. bi-m. EUR 56; EUR 11 newsstand/cover (effective 2011). **Document type:** *Journal, Trade.*
Related titles: ◆ Supplement to: G W F - Wasser, Abwasser. ISSN 0016-3651.
Published by: (Bundesverband der Deutschen Gas- und Wasserwirtschaft e.V.), Oldenbourg Industrieverlag GmbH (Subsidiary of: Oldenbourg Wissenschaftsverlag GmbH), Rosenheimer Str 145, Munich, 81671, Germany. TEL 49-89-450510, FAX 49-89-45051207, oiv-info@oldenbourg.de. Ed. Annett Heublein.

665.5 USA ISSN 1556-9357
REFINER. Text in English. d. USD 2,995 (effective 2008). **Document type:** *Newsletter, Trade.*
Formerly (until 200?): Feedstock Wire
Media: Online - full text.
Published by: Platts (Subsidiary of: McGraw-Hill Companies, Inc.), 2 Penn Plz, 25th Fl, New York, NY 10121. TEL 212-904-3070, 800-752-8878, FAX 212-904-4209, info@platts.com.

665.53 USA ISSN 1062-5658
REFINING & GAS PROCESSING INDUSTRY. Text in English. 19??. a. USD 175 domestic; USD 185 in Canada; USD 190 elsewhere (effective 2009). adv. **Document type:** *Directory, Trade.* **Description:** Lists refining and gas processing companies both across North America and internationally as well as the support sectors in the industry.
Former titles (until 1991): Refining, Construction, Petrochemical and Natural Gas Processing Plants (1054-951X); (until 1990): Directory of Oil Refineries (0889-597X)
Published by: Midwest Publishing Company, 2230 E 49th St, Ste E, Tulsa, OK 74105. TEL 918-582-2000, 800-829-2002, FAX 918-587-9349, info@midwestpub.com. adv.: B&W page USD 1,610, color page USD 1,710.

665.5 AUS ISSN 1441-5070
REGISTER OF AUSTRALASIAN PETROLEUM. Text in English. 1997. a. AUD 418 domestic; AUD 435 foreign; AUD 770 combined subscription domestic (print & CD-ROM eds.); AUD 755 combined subscription foreign (print & CD-ROM eds.) (effective 2008). adv. charts; illus.; stat.; tr.lit. index. back issues avail. **Document type:** *Report, Trade.* **Description:** Details of all Australian petroleum permits, projects, pipelines, and companies with interests in Australian, New Zealand and Papua New Guinea.
Formerly (until 1999): Register of Australian Petroleum (1328-0651)
Related titles: CD-ROM ed.: AUD 506 newsstand/cover domestic; AUD 490 newsstand/cover foreign (effective 2001).
Published by: Resource Information Unit, PO Box 1533, Subiaco, W.A. 6904, Australia. TEL 61-8-93823955, FAX 61-8-93881025, riu@riu.com.au. adv.: B&W page AUD 2,280, color page AUD 3,775.

665.7 346.066 USA
REGULATION OF THE GAS INDUSTRY. Text in English. 1981. 5 base vols. plus a. updates. looseleaf. USD 1,739 base vol(s). (effective 2008). **Document type:** *Journal, Trade.* **Description:** A vital work for gas industry officials, administrators, and attorneys, this treatise examines the evolution of the gas industry.
Published by: (American Gas Association), Matthew Bender & Co., Inc. (Subsidiary of: LexisNexis North America), 1275 Broadway, Albany, NY 12204. TEL 518-487-3000, 800-424-4200, FAX 518-487-3083, international@bender.com, http://bender.lexisnexis.com.

665.5 FRA ISSN 1779-2622
LES RENDEZ-VOUS DE L'INNOVATION. Text in French. 2006. s-a. free. back issues avail. **Document type:** *Newsletter, Trade.*
Related titles: Online - full text ed.
Published by: Institut Francais du Petrole, 1 et 4 av. de Bois-Preau, Rueil-Malmaison, 92852 Cedex, France. TEL 33-1-47527112, FAX 33-1-47527096.

665.5 553 CAN ISSN 1484-2238
RESERVOIR. Text in English. 1965. m.
Former titles (until 1997): C S P G Reservoir (0318-5788); (until 1974): C S P G Newsletter (0318-577X); (until 1973): A S P G Newsletter (0044-720X)
Indexed: GeoRef.
—PADDS. **CCC.**
Published by: Canadian Society of Petroleum Geologists, No 160, 540 Fifth Ave SW, Calgary, AB T2P 0M2, Canada. TEL 403-264-5610, FAX 403-264-5898, http://www.cspg.org.

RESOURCE WEEK. *see* BUSINESS AND ECONOMICS—Production Of Goods And Services

662 USA
RESOURCES (FORT WORTH). Text in English. 1975 (vol.22). 2/yr. free. charts; illus.
Formerly: Cycler
Published by: Union Pacific Resources Company, PO Box 7, Ft. Worth, TX 76101-0007. TEL 817-737-1000. Ed. James L Sailer. Circ: 12,000.

665.5 USA
RESULTS. Text in English. 1935. q. back issues avail. **Description:** Articles about various industrial concerns, Exxon products, and general technical interest items.
Formerly (until 1988): Oilways
Published by: Exxon Company USA, 800 Bell St, Box 2180, Houston, TX 77252-2180. TEL 713-656-8477, FAX 713-656-9742. Ed. Sue Berniard. Circ: 30,000.

665.5 USA
RETAIL FUEL WATCH; the oil and fleet market's benchmark for retail gasoline & diesel prices. Text in English. 19??. w. USD 645 (effective 2009). adv. **Document type:** *Newsletter, Trade.* **Description:** Offers insight into retail and wholesale fuel price trends from a national level down to a market-by-market look at each competitors profit performance.
Media: E-mail. **Related titles:** Online - full text ed.
Published by: Oil Price Information Service (Subsidiary of: United Communications Group), Two Washingtonian Center, 9737 Washingtonian Blvd, Ste 100, Gaithersburg, MD 20878. TEL 301-287-2700, 888-301-2645, FAX 301-287-2039, energycs@opisnet.com. Ed. Beth Heinsohn TEL 732-730-2564. Adv. contact Greg Mosho TEL 732-730-2546. **Subscr. to:** 11300 Rockville Pike, Ste 1100, Rockville, MD 20852. TEL 301-287-2525, FAX 301-816-8945.

665.5 MEX ISSN 0188-4107
REVISTA MEXICANA DEL PETROLEO. Text in English, Spanish. 1958. bi-m. USD 70. adv. charts; illus.; stat.; tr.lit. Supplement avail.; back issues avail. **Description:** Reports on the oil, gas and petrochemical industries throughout Mexico, Central and South America.
Indexed: C01, GasAb.
Published by: Ediciones y Publicaciones Petroleras, S.A. de C.V., Morelos 31 Desp. 303, Mexico City, DF 06040, Mexico. TEL 510-99-50, FAX 521-4630. Ed. Roberto Navarrete Espinosa. adv.: B&W page USD 1,800, color page USD 2,480; trim 11 x 8.25. Circ: 15,000.

338.47665 CAN ISSN 0848-8835
REVUE DE L'IMPERIALE. Text in French. 1955. q.
Former titles (until 1989): Compagnie Petroliere Imperiale. Revue (0700-5148); (until 1976): Revue Imperial Oil (0380-9048)
Related titles: ◆ English Translation: Imperial Oil Review. ISSN 0848-8843.
Indexed: A26, CPerI, I05.
—CCC.
Published by: Imperial Oil Ltd./Compagnie Petroliere Imperiale, 237 Fourth Ave SW, Calgary, AB T2P 3M9, Canada. TEL 403-237-3584, FAX 403-237-2838.

665.5 CAN ISSN 0711-0901
RIG LOCATOR. Text in English. 199?. w. CAD 395 domestic; USD 395 foreign (effective 2005). **Document type:** *Newsletter, Trade.* **Description:** Provides detailed information and reports on drilling in Canada.
Related titles: Fax ed.; Online - full text ed.
Published by: Nickle's Energy Group (Subsidiary of: Business Information Group), Ste 300, 999 8 St SW, Calgary, AB T2R 1N7, Canada. TEL 403-209-3500, 800-387-2446, FAX 403-245-8666.

665.5 ITA ISSN 1972-0122
TP315 CODEN: RICOAP
LA RIVISTA DEI COMBUSTIBILI E DELL'INDUSTRIA CHIMICA. Text in Italian. 1947. bi-m. free to qualified personnel. bk.rev. abstr.; illus.; stat. index. reprints avail. **Document type:** *Journal, Academic/Scholarly.*
Formerly (until 2001): La Rivista dei Combustibili (0370-5463)
Indexed: A22, APICat, APIH&E, APIOC, APIPR, APITS, CEA, CISA, ChemAb, ChemTitl, FR, GeoRef, INIS AtomInd, SCOPUS, TCEA.
—BLDSC (7984.000000), IE, Infotrieve, Ingenta, INIST.
Published by: Stazione Sperimentale per i Combustibili, Viale A. De Gasperi 3, San Donato Milanese, MI 20097, Italy. TEL 39-02-51604220, FAX 39-02-514286, redazione@ssc.it. Circ: 1,500.

662.6 USA ISSN 1074-6803
ROCKY MOUNTAIN OIL JOURNAL. Text in English. 1921. w. USD 119 domestic; USD 160 in Canada (effective 2005). adv. **Document type:** *Newspaper, Trade.*
Formerly (until 199?): Montana Oil Journal (0047-794X)
Related titles: Online - full content ed.: USD 79 (effective 2005).
Published by: Montana Oil Journal, Inc., 906 S Pearl St, Denver, CO 80209. TEL 303-778-8661, FAX 303-778-2351. Ed. Cody Huseby. Pub. Jerry Davis. Circ: 4,000.

665 USA
TN867
ROCKY MOUNTAIN REGIONAL DIRECTORY. Text in English. 19??. a. USD 80 per issue (effective 2011). **Document type:** *Directory, Trade.*
Former titles: Armstrong Oil Directories: Rocky Mountain - Central United States Edition (0273-5229); (until 1980): Hank Seale Oil Directory; Rocky Mountain and Central United States
Published by: Armstrong Oil Directories, PO Box 52106, Amarillo, TX 79159. TEL 806-457-9300, FAX 806-457-9301, support@armstrongoil.com.

665.5029 USA
ROCKY MOUNTAIN STATES PETROLEUM INDUSTRY. Text in English. 1945. a. **Document type:** *Directory, Trade.* **Description:** Supplies information on producing, drilling and well service, pipelines, refineries, gas processing, petrochemicals, engineering, equipment, manufacturers and suppliers, company names, addresses, phone and fax numbers, and personnel for CO, NM, UT, WY, MT, MN, ID, SD, ND.
Former titles: Rocky Mountain Petroleum Industry; Directory of Producers and Drilling Contractors: Rocky Mountain Region, Williston Basin, Four Corners New Mexico
Media: Diskette.
Published by: Midwest Publishing Company, 2230 E 49th St, Ste E, Tulsa, OK 74105. TEL 800-829-2002, info@midwestpub.com, http://www.midwestpub.com/.

338.47665 GBR ISSN 1749-2416
ROMANIA PETROCHEMICALS REPORT. Text in English. 2005. q. EUR 820, USD 1,030 combined subscription (print & email eds.) (effective 2010). **Document type:** *Report, Trade.* **Description:** Provides industry professionals and strategists, sector analysts, trade associations and regulatory bodies with independent forecasts and competitive intelligence on the Romanian petrochemicals industry.
Related titles: E-mail ed.
Indexed: A15, ABIn, B02, B15, B17, B18, G04, I05, P48, P51, P52, P56, PQC.
Published by: Business Monitor International Ltd., Senator House, 85 Queen Victoria St, London, EC4V 4AB, United Kingdom. TEL 44-20-72480468, FAX 44-20-72480467, subs@businessmonitor.com.

665.5 RUS
ROSSIISKII NEFTYANOI BYULLETEN'. Text in Russian. 24/yr. USD 1,200 in United States.
Address: Bumazhnyi pr 14, Moscow, 101462, Russian Federation. TEL 7-095-2573447, FAX 7-095-2504898. **Dist. by:** East View Information Services, 10601 Wayzata Blvd, Minneapolis, MN 55305. TEL 952-252-1201, 800-477-1005, FAX 952-252-1202, info@eastview.com, http://www.eastview.com.

665.5 GBR ISSN 1750-967X
ROUSTABOUT ENERGY INTERNATIONAL. Text in English. 1972. m. GBP 55 domestic; GBP 60 foreign (effective 2009). adv. back issues avail. **Document type:** *Magazine, Trade.* **Description:** Contains topics of interest for those in the oil industry as well as business news.
Formerly (until 2006): Roustabout Magazine
Related titles: Online - full text ed.: free (effective 2009).
Published by: Roustabout Publications Ltd., Ste 1, International Base, Greenwell Rd, E Tullos, Aberdeen, AB12 3AX, United Kingdom. TEL 44-1224-876582, FAX 44-1224-879757, info@energyinternat.com. Adv. contact Drew Hamilton. B&W page GBP 1,495, color page GBP 1,995; trim 205 x 275. Circ: 10,000.

338.4766180409 GBR ISSN 1749-2424
RUSSIA PETROCHEMICALS REPORT. Text in English. 2005. q. EUR 820, USD 1,030 combined subscription (print & email eds.) (effective 2010). **Document type:** *Report, Trade.* **Description:** Provides industry professionals and strategists, sector analysts, trade associations and regulatory bodies with independent forecasts and competitive intelligence on the Russian petrochemicals industry.
Related titles: E-mail ed.
Indexed: A15, ABIn, B02, B15, B17, B18, G04, I05, P48, P51, P52, P56, PQC.
Published by: Business Monitor International Ltd., Senator House, 85 Queen Victoria St, London, EC4V 4AB, United Kingdom. TEL 44-20-72480468, FAX 44-20-72480467, subs@businessmonitor.com.

665.5 GBR
RUSSIAN ENERGY MONTHLY. Text in English. 200?. m. GBP 320 (effective 2009). **Document type:** *Newsletter, Trade.* **Description:** Features surveys the oil, gas, coal and electricity industries of Russia, and also contains information on other CIS states and the countries of Eastern Europe.
Related titles: Online - full content ed.
Published by: Eastern Bloc Research Ltd., Tolsta Chaolais, Isle of Lewis, HS2 9DW, United Kingdom. TEL 44-1851-621315, mail@easternblocenergy.com.

RUSSIAN PETROLEUM INVESTOR. *see* BUSINESS AND ECONOMICS—Production Of Goods And Services

665.5 USA ISSN 1946-3952
TP343
➤ **S A E INTERNATIONAL JOURNAL OF FUELS AND LUBRICANTS.** (Society of Automotive Engineers) Text in English. 1906. a. USD 306 per issue to non-members; USD 244.80 per issue to members (effective 2009). back issues avail. **Document type:** *Journal, Academic/Scholarly.* **Description:** Provides an environment for academic and industrial researchers to report their findings and discuss new technologies in related areas.
Supersedes in part (in 2009): S A E Transactions (0096-736X); Which was formerly (until 1927): Society of Automotive Engineers. Transactions
Related titles: Online - full text ed.: ISSN 1946-3960. USD 367.09 per issue to non-members; USD 293.67 per issue to members (effective 2009).
Indexed: SCOPUS.
—BLDSC (8062.950000), IE, Linda Hall.
Published by: S A E Inc., 400 Commonwealth Dr, Warrendale, PA 15096. TEL 724-776-4970, 877-606-7323, FAX 724-776-0790, CustomerService@sae.org, http://www.sae.org.

665.5 USA
S D P M A PETROLEUM JOURNAL. Text in English. m. membership. **Document type:** *Journal, Trade.*
Former titles (until Jan. 1997): South Dakota Petroleum Marketers News; (until 1985): South Dakota Independent Oil Jobber
Published by: South Dakota Petroleum Marketer, PO Box 1058, Pierre, SD 57501-1058. TEL 605-224-8606. Ed. Dawna Leitzke Osborne. Circ: 500 (controlled).

S N L ENERGY DAILY GAS REPORT. (Savings and Loans) *see* BUSINESS AND ECONOMICS—Investments

665.5 USA ISSN 1559-7148
S N L ENERGY GAS UTILITY WEEK. (Savings and Loans) Variant title: Gas Utility Week. Text in English. 2006. w. USD 997 (effective 2008). adv. back issues avail. **Document type:** *Newsletter, Trade.* **Description:** Focuses on local distribution companies and all relevant issues inside the citygate or LDC territories.
Media: E-mail. **Related titles:** Online - full text ed.: ISSN 1559-7156.
Indexed: P52, P56.
Published by: S N L Financial LC, One SNL Plz, PO Box 2124, Charlottesville, VA 22902. TEL 434-977-1600, FAX 434-293-0407, salesdept@snl.com. Ed. Mark Hand TEL 703-373-0659. adv.: page USD 300; 7.5 x 10.

S P E. (Society of Petroleum Engineers) *see* ENGINEERING—Mechanical Engineering

665.5 USA ISSN 1064-6671
TN871.2 CODEN: SDCOE5
➤ **S P E DRILLING & COMPLETION.** Text in English. 1961. q. USD 210 combined subscription domestic to non-members (print & online eds.); USD 230 combined subscription foreign to non-members (print & online eds.); USD 70 to members (effective 2009). adv. index. back issues avail. **Document type:** *Journal, Academic/Scholarly.* **Description:** Features papers covering horizontal and directional drilling, drilling fluids, bit technology, sand control, perforating, cementing, well control, completions, and drilling operations.
Formerly (until 1993): S P E Drilling Engineering (0885-9744); Which supersedes in part (in 1986): Society of Petroleum Engineers. Journal (0197-7520)
Related titles: Online - full text ed.: ISSN 1930-0204. USD 135 to non-members; USD 45 to members (effective 2009).
Indexed: A05, A22, A28, AESIS, APA, AS&TA, AS&TI, ASCA, BrCerAb, C&ISA, C10, CA, CA/WCA, CIA, CPEI, CerAb, CivEngAb, CorrAb, CurCont, E&CAJ, E11, E14, EEA, EMA, EngInd, FLUIDEX, GEOBASE, GeoRef, H15, IMMAb, ISMEC, M&TEA, M09, MBF, METADEX, PetrolAb, SCI, SCOPUS, SolStAb, SpeleolAb, T02, T04, W07, WAA.
—BLDSC (8361.840900), CASDDS, IE, Infotrieve, Ingenta, INIST, Linda Hall, PADDS. **CCC.**
Published by: Society of Petroleum Engineers, Inc., PO Box 833836, Richardson, TX 75083. TEL 972-952-9393, 800-456-6863, FAX 972-952-9435, spedal@spe.org. Ed. Yannis C Yortsos. Adv. contact Jim Klingele TEL 713-779-9595 ext 612. B&W page USD 2,070, color page USD 3,275; trim 206.375 x 276.225.

▼ ➤ **S P E ECONOMICS & MANAGEMENT.** (Society of Petroleum Engineers) *see* ENGINEERING

665.5 USA ISSN 1086-055X
TN860 CODEN: SPJRFW
➤ **S P E JOURNAL.** Text in English. 1996. q. USD 315 combined subscription domestic to non-members (print & online eds.); USD 335 combined subscription foreign to non-members (print & online eds.); USD 105 to members (effective 2009). adv. back issues avail. **Document type:** *Journal, Academic/Scholarly.* **Description:** Covers research papers on all aspects of engineering for oil and gas exploration and production.
Related titles: Online - full text ed.: ISSN 1930-0220. USD 210 to non-members; USD 70 to members (effective 2009).
Indexed: A05, A23, A24, AESIS, AS&TA, AS&TI, B13, C10, CA, CPEI, CurCont, E14, EngInd, GeoRef, ISR, PetrolAb, RefZh, SCI, SCOPUS, T02, W07.
—BLDSC (8361.851000), IE, Ingenta, Linda Hall, PADDS. **CCC.**
Published by: Society of Petroleum Engineers, Inc., PO Box 833836, Richardson, TX 75083. TEL 972-952-9393, 800-456-6863, FAX 972-952-9435, spedal@spe.org. Ed. Yannis C Yortsos. Adv. contact Jim Klingele TEL 713-779-9595 ext 612. B&W page USD 2,070, color page USD 3,275.

665.5 USA ISSN 1930-1855
TN870 CODEN: SPEPCW
➤ **S P E PRODUCTION & OPERATIONS.** Text in English. 1961. q. USD 210 combined subscription domestic to non-members (print & online eds.); USD 230 combined subscription foreign to non-members (print & online eds.); USD 70 to members (effective 2009). adv. index. back issues avail. **Document type:** *Journal, Academic/Scholarly.* **Description:** Discusses the technical and professional aspects of oil production methods and facilities.
Former titles (until 2006): S P E Production & Facilities (Print) (1064-668X); (until 1993): S P E Production Engineering (0885-9221); Which superseded in part (in 1986): Society of Petroleum Engineers. Journal (0197-7520)
Related titles: Online - full text ed.: ISSN 1930-1863. USD 135 to non-members; USD 45 to members (effective 2009).
Indexed: A05, A22, AESIS, AS&TA, AS&TI, ASCA, C10, C33, CA, CIN, CPEI, ChemAb, ChemTitl, CurCont, E14, EngInd, FLUIDEX, GEOBASE, GeoRef, IMMAb, ISMEC, Inspec, PetrolAb, SCI, SCOPUS, SpeleolAb, T02, W07.
—CASDDS, IE, Infotrieve, Ingenta, INIST, Linda Hall, PADDS. **CCC.**
Published by: Society of Petroleum Engineers, Inc., PO Box 833836, Richardson, TX 75083. TEL 972-952-9393, 800-456-6863, FAX 972-952-9435, spedal@spe.org. Ed. Yannis C Yortsos. Adv. contact Jim Klingele TEL 713-779-9595 ext 612. B&W page USD 2,070, color page USD 3,275; trim 206.375 x 276.225.

665.5 USA ISSN 1942-2431
S P E PROJECTS, FACILITIES & CONSTRUCTION. Text in English. 2006. q. USD 150 to non-members; USD 50 to members (effective 2010). back issues avail. **Document type:** *Journal, Academic/Scholarly.*
Media: Online - full text.
—PADDS.
Published by: Society of Petroleum Engineers, Inc., 222 Palisades Creek Dr, Richardson, TX 75080. TEL 972-952-9393, 800-456-6863, FAX 972-952-9435, spedal@spe.org. Ed. Stephen A Holditch.

665.5 USA ISSN 1094-6470
TN871 CODEN: SREEFG
➤ **S P E RESERVOIR EVALUATION AND ENGINEERING.** Variant title: Reservoir Evaluation and Engineering. Text in English. 1998. bi-m. USD 315 combined subscription domestic to non-members (print & online eds.); USD 345 combined subscription foreign to non-members (print & online eds.); USD 105 to members (effective 2009). adv. index. back issues avail. **Document type:** *Journal, Academic/Scholarly.* **Description:** Provides informations about reservoir characterization, geology and geophysics, petrophysics, core analysis, well logging, well testing, geostatistics, reservoir management, EOR, PVT analysis, fluid mechanics, performance prediction, and reservoir simulation.
Formed by the 1997 merger of: S P E Formation Evaluation (0885-923X); S P E Reservoir Engineering (0885-9248); Both of which superseded in part (1961-1985): Society of Petroleum Engineers. Journal (0197-7520)
Related titles: Online - full text ed.: ISSN 1930-0212. USD 210 to non-members; USD 70 to members (effective 2009).
Indexed: A05, A22, A28, AESIS, APA, AS&TA, AS&TI, ASCA, BrCerAb, C&ISA, C10, C33, CA, CA/WCA, CIA, CIN, CPEI, CerAb, ChemAb, ChemTitl, CivEngAb, CorrAb, CurCont, E&CAJ, E11, E14, EEA, EMA, EngInd, FLUIDEX, GEOBASE, GeoRef, H15, IMMAb, ISMEC, ISR, Inspec, M&TEA, M09, MBF, METADEX, PetrolAb, SCI, SCOPUS, SolStAb, SpeleolAb, T02, T04, W07, WAA.
—BLDSC (8361.866500), CASDDS, IE, Infotrieve, Ingenta, INIST, Linda Hall, PADDS. **CCC.**
Published by: Society of Petroleum Engineers, Inc., PO Box 833836, Richardson, TX 75083. TEL 972-952-9393, 800-456-6863, FAX 972-952-9435, spedal@spe.org. Ed. Yannis C Yortsos. Adv. contact Jim Klingele TEL 713-779-9595 ext 612. B&W page USD 2,070, color page USD 3,275; trim 206.375 x 276.225.

665.5 GBR
S P E REVIEW. Text in English. 1989. m. membership. adv. back issues avail. **Document type:** *Newsletter.*
Published by: (Society of Petroleum Engineers), McQuillan Young Communications, 77 St John St, London, EC1M 4AN, United Kingdom. TEL 44-171-253-6450, FAX 44-171-253-6455. Ed. Tricia Young. R&P Patricia Young. Adv. contact Phillippa Low. page GBP 825; trim 184 x 264. Circ: 4,000 (controlled).

665.5 BRN
SALAM. Text in English, Malay. 1953. m. free to employees. **Document type:** *Magazine, Trade.*
Indexed: BAS, PerIslam.
Published by: Brunei Shell Petroleum Co Sdn Bhd, Seria, 7082, Brunei Darussalam. TEL 037-8624, FAX 037-4190. Ed. Molly McDaniel. Circ: 9,000.

SASKATCHEWAN ENERGY & MINES. ANNUAL REPORT. *see* MINES AND MINING INDUSTRY

SASKATCHEWAN ENERGY & MINES. MINERAL STATISTICS YEARBOOK. *see* MINES AND MINING INDUSTRY

665.5 CAN ISSN 0228-5622
HD9574.C23
SASKATCHEWAN ENERGY & MINES. MONTHLY OIL AND GAS PRODUCTION REPORT. Text in English. m. CAD 150. **Document type:** *Government.* **Description:** Lists by production and disposition areas the monthly production of oil, gas and water for units and pools.
Published by: Saskatchewan Energy & Mines, Petroleum Statistics Branch, 2101 Scarth St, Regina, SK S4P 3V7, Canada. TEL 306-787-2528, FAX 306-787-2527.

553 665 CAN ISSN 0707-2562
TN873.C22
SASKATCHEWAN ENERGY & MINES. RESERVOIR ANNUAL. Text in English. 1963. a. CAD 70 (effective 1999). **Document type:** *Government.* **Description:** Contains oil and gas reserves data, development and production data, information concerning enhanced recovery projects and related reservoir information.
Former titles: Saskatchewan Energy and Mines. Petroleum and Natural Gas Reservoir Annual (0704-5743); Saskatchewan Mineral Resources. Petroleum and Natural Gas Reservoir Annual; Saskatchewan. Department of Mineral Resources. Petroleum and Natural Gas Reservoir Annual
Indexed: GeoRef, SpeleolAb.
Published by: (Saskatchewan. Petroleum and Natural Gas Branch), Saskatchewan Energy & Mines, Petroleum Statistics Branch, 2101 Scarth St, Regina, SK S4P 3V7, Canada. TEL 306-787-2528, FAX 306-787-2527.

665 628.1 CAN ISSN 1182-9125
SASKATCHEWAN HORIZONTAL WELL SUMMARY. Text in English. 1990. m. CAD 150 (effective 1999). **Document type:** *Government.* **Description:** Lists all horizontal wells produced, abandoned, drilled, licensed and approved in Saskatchewan. Each well is listed by name, legal description, operator, approval date, spud date, finished drilling date, productive horizontal length, pool and first producing date.
Published by: Saskatchewan Energy & Mines, Petroleum Statistics Branch, 2101 Scarth St, Regina, SK S4P 3V7, Canada. TEL 306-787-2528, FAX 306-787-2527.

665.5 GBR ISSN 2045-6670
SAUDI ARABIA OIL & GAS. Text in English. 2007. bi-m. back issues avail. **Document type:** *Magazine, Trade.* **Description:** Covers field development expertise, technological programmes, technology applications and, from time to time, social developments.
Related titles: Online - full text ed.: ISSN 2045-6689. free (effective 2011).
Published by: EPRasheed, 11 Murray St, Camden, London, NW1 3RE, United Kingdom. TEL 44-20-71931602, adam.mehar@saudiarabiaoilandgas.com. Eds. Majid Rasheed, Mauro Martins.

338.4766180409 GBR ISSN 1749-2432
SAUDI ARABIA PETROCHEMICALS REPORT. Text in English. 2005. q. EUR 820, USD 1,030 combined subscription (print & email eds.) (effective 2010). **Document type:** *Report, Trade.* **Description:** Provides industry professionals and strategists, sector analysts, trade associations and regulatory bodies with independent forecasts and competitive intelligence on the Saudi petrochemicals industry.
Related titles: E-mail ed.
Indexed: A15, ABIn, B02, B15, B17, B18, G04, I05, P48, P51, P52, P56, PQC.
Published by: Business Monitor International Ltd., Senator House, 85 Queen Victoria St, London, EC4V 4AB, United Kingdom. TEL 44-20-72480468, FAX 44-20-72480467, subs@businessmonitor.com.

665.5 NOR ISSN 0332-5334
SCANDINAVIAN OIL - GAS MAGAZINE. Text in English. 1973. bi-m. NOK 720 in Scandinavia; NOK 920 in Europe; NOK 1,020 elsewhere; NOK 120 newsstand/cover (effective 2004). adv. bk.rev. **Document type:** *Magazine, Trade.* **Description:** Developments in the oil/gas industry in the Northern Seas.
Related titles: Online - full text ed.: ISSN 1500-709X.
Indexed: INIS AtomInd, PetrolAb, RefZh, SCOPUS.
—IE, PADDS. **CCC.**
Published by: Scandinavian Oil-Gas Publishing, PO Box 6865, St Olavs Plass, Oslo, 0130, Norway. TEL 47-22-447270, FAX 47-22-447287. Ed. Michael Rogers. Pub. Paal Gulbrandsen. Adv. contact Rolf Skoog. B&W page NOK 16,000, color page NOK 22,000; trim 178 x 252. Circ: 12,600.

665.5 622.338 627.75 JPN ISSN 1816-8957
QE39
SCIENTIFIC DRILLING. Text in English. 1975. s-a. **Document type:** *Journal, Academic/Scholarly.* **Description:** Provides reports on deep Earth sampling and monitoring from ocean drilling and continental drilling scientific research projects.

P

Formerly (until 2005): J O I D E S Journal (Joint Oceanographic Institutions for Deep Earth Sampling) (0734-5615)
Related titles: Online - full text ed.: ISSN 1816-3459. free (effective 2011).
Indexed: A01, A39, C27, C29, CPEI, D03, D04, E13, E14, GeoRef, M&GPA, OceAb, PetrolAb, R14, S14, S15, S18, SCOPUS, T02.
—BLDSC (8178.493000), IE, Ingenta, INIST, Linda Hall, PADDS.
Published by: (Integrated Ocean Drilling Program (I O D P) USA, International Continental Scientific Drilling Program DEU), Integrated Ocean Drilling Program Management International, IODP-MI, CRIS Building-Rm 05-101,, Hokkaido University, N21W10 Kita-ku,, Sapporo, Hokkaido,, 001-0021, Japan. TEL 81-11-738107, FAX 81-11-738352. Eds. Harms Harms, Hans Christian Larsen. **Co-publisher:** Integrated Ocean Drilling Program (I O D P).

665.5 USA
SEARCH & DISCOVERY. Text in English. 1998. d. **Document type:** *Journal, Trade.* **Description:** Features reviewed articles about the ideas and technology of exploring for oil and gas.
Media: Online - full text.
Published by: Datapages, Inc., 1743 E 71st St, Tulsa, OK 74136. TEL 918-496-7777, FAX 918-496-3756. Ed. Edward Beaumont.

SEDIMENTARY BASINS OF THE WORLD. *see* EARTH SCIENCES

550 665 NLD ISSN 0921-0911
➤ **SEDIMENTOLOGY AND PETROLEUM GEOLOGY.** Text in English. 1986. irreg., latest vol.4, 1987. price varies. **Document type:** *Monographic series, Academic/Scholarly.*
Indexed: Inspec.
Published by: Springer Netherlands (Subsidiary of: Springer Science+Business Media), Van Godewijckstraat 30, Dordrecht, 3311 GX, Netherlands. TEL 31-78-6576050, FAX 31-78-6576474.

665.5 JPN
SEKIYU GAKKAI SEISEI KOENKAI/J P I PETROLEUM REFINING CONFERENCE. Text in Japanese. irreg. **Document type:** *Proceedings, Academic/Scholarly.*
Published by: Japan Petroleum Institute/Sekiyu Gakkai, COSMO Hirakawa-cho Bldg, 1-3-14 Hirakawa-cho, Chiyoda-ku, Tokyo, 102-0093, Japan. TEL 81-3-32217301, FAX 81-3-32218175, http://wwwsoc.nii.ac.jp/jpi/.

665.5 JPN ISSN 0370-9868
CODEN: SGKYAO
SEKIYU GIJUTSU KYOKAISHI/JAPANESE ASSOCIATION FOR PETROLEUM TECHNOLOGY. JOURNAL. Text in Japanese. 1933. bi-m. JPY 7,000 membership (effective 2002). **Description:** Focuses on exploration, development, and production of petroleum and related technologies.
Indexed: FR, GeoRef, PetrolAb.
—BLDSC (4809.001000), INIST, Linda Hall, PADDS. **CCC.**
Published by: Sekiyu Gijutsu Kyokai/Japanese Association for Petroleum Technology, Keidanren-Kaikan Bldg, 9-4 Otemachi 1-chome, Chiyoda-ku, Tokyo, 100-0004, Japan. TEL 81-3-3279-5841, FAX 81-3-3279-5844, http://www.japt.org.

550 IND
SEMINAR ON PETROLIFEROUS BASINS OF INDIA. PROCEEDINGS. Text in English. a. adv. **Document type:** *Proceedings, Trade.*
Indexed: SpeleolAb.
Published by: (KDM Institute of Petroleum Exploration, Oil and Natural Gas Commission), Indian Petroleum Publishers, 100/9 Nashvilla Rd, Dehra Dun, Uttar Pradesh 248 001, India. TEL 91-135-2654074, FAX 91-135-2652111, info@ippublishers.com.

SHANXI DAXUE XUEBAO (SHEHUI KEXUE BAN)/SHANXI UNIVERSITY. JOURNAL (SOCIAL SCIENCE EDITION). *see* SOCIAL SCIENCES: COMPREHENSIVE WORKS

SHELL CHEMICALS MAGAZINE. *see* ENGINEERING—Chemical Engineering

665.5 NLD ISSN 1389-0859
SHELL-VENSTER. Text in Dutch. 1917. bi-m. free (effective 2010). bk.rev. charts; illus.; stat. index.
Formerly (until 1976): Olie (0030-2112)
Related titles: Online - full text ed.: ISSN 2211-9043.
—IE.
Published by: Shell Nederland B.V., Postbus 444, The Hague, 2501 CK, Netherlands. TEL 31-70-3778750, FAX 31-70-3778751, media-nl@shell.com, http://www.shell.nl.

665.5 660 CHN ISSN 1006-0235
TP692.3
SHI-HUA JISHU/PETROCHEMICAL INDUSTRY TECHNOLOGY. Text in Chinese. 1980. q. **Document type:** *Magazine, Trade.*
Related titles: Online - full text ed.
Published by: Zhongguo Shi-hua Gufen Youxian Changling Fengongsi, PO Box 10041, Beijing, 102500, China. TEL 86-10-69345106, FAX 86-10-69341930, petrochemtech@clpec.com.cn.

665.5 CHN ISSN 1009-0045
SHIHUA JISHU YU YINGYONG/PETROCHEMICAL TECHNOLOGY AND APPLICATION. Text in Chinese. 1983. bi-m. USD 31.20 (effective 2009). **Document type:** *Journal, Academic/Scholarly.*
Related titles: Online - full text ed.
Indexed: A28, APA, BrCerAb, C&ISA, CA/WCA, CIA, CerAb, CivEngAb, CorrAb, E&CAJ, E11, EEA, EMA, ESPM, EnvEAb, H15, M&TEA, M09, MBF, METADEX, RefZh, SolStAb, T04, WAA.
—BLDSC (6430.396200), East View, IE, Ingenta, Linda Hall.
Published by: Lanzhou Shihua Gongsi, Shiyou Huagong Yanjiuyuan/ Lanzhou Petrochemical Company Research Institute, 1, Xiguheshui Road North, Lanzhou, 730060, China. TEL 86-931-7314247, FAX 86-931-7981693, shjsyyy@public.lz.gs.cn, IZHM@chinajournal.net.cn.

SHIYOU DILI WULI KANTAN/OIL GEOPHYSICAL PROSPECTING. *see* EARTH SCIENCES—Geology

665.5 CHN ISSN 1673-8217
SHIYOU DIZHI YU GONGCHENG/PETROLEUM GEOLOGY AND ENGINEERING. Text in Chinese. 1987. bi-m. **Document type:** *Journal, Academic/Scholarly.*
Formerly (until 2006): Henan Shiyou (1006-4095)
Related titles: Online - full text ed.
Published by: (Zhongguo Shi-Hua Henan Youtian Fengongsi/S I N O P E C, Henan Oilfield Company, Henan Sheng Shiyou Xuehui/Henan Petroleum Society), Shiyou Dizhi yu Gongcheng Zazhishe, Youtain Zhongshan Lu, Nanyang, China. TEL 86-377-63830612, FAX 86-377-63838771.

665.5 CHN ISSN 1001-2206
TN860 CODEN: SGJIE9
SHIYOU GONGCHENG JIANSHE/PETROLEUM ENGINEERING CONSTRUCTION. Text in Chinese; Summaries in English. 1975. bi-m. USD 40.20 (effective 2009). adv. **Document type:** *Journal, Academic/Scholarly.* **Description:** Covers the engineering constructions and technical improvements of oil and gas fields, oil and gas pipelines, oil refineries, chemical plants, and petrochemical complexes.
Related titles: Online - full text ed.
Indexed: SCOPUS.
—BLDSC (8267.299130), East View.
Published by: Zhongguo Shiyou Tianranqi Zonggongsi, Gongcheng Jishu Yanjiusuo/China National Petroleum Corporation, Engineering Technology Research Institute, 40 Jin Tang Gonglu, Tanggu-qu, Tianjin, 300451, China. TEL 86-22-66310255, FAX 86-22-66310255. Ed. Yan Yiming. Adv. contact Yiming Yan. Circ: 6,000. **Dist. outside China by:** China International Book Trading Corp, 35 Chegongzhuang Xilu, Haidian District, PO Box 399, Beijing 100044, China.

665.5 CHN ISSN 1674-8980
SHIYOU HE HUAGONG SHEBEI/PETRO & CHEMICAL EQUIPMENT. Text in Chinese. 1998. m. **Document type:** *Magazine, Trade.*
Formerly: Huagong Shebei yu Fangfushi/Chemical Equipment and Anticorrosion (1009-6736)
Related titles: Online - full text ed.
Published by: Zhongguo Huagong Jixie Dongli Jishu Xiehui, 18, Anhuali Wu-qu, Chaoyang-qu, Beijing, 100011, China. TEL 86-10-64256689, FAX 86-10-64262500.

665.5 CHN ISSN 1000-8144
TP692.3 CODEN: SHHUE8
➤ **SHIYOU HUAGONG/PETROCHEMICAL TECHNOLOGY.** Text in Chinese; Abstracts in English. 1970. m. adv. bk.rev. abstr. 120 p./no.; **Document type:** *Journal, Academic/Scholarly.* **Description:** Contains original research & development papers, as well as review articles covering various fields of petrochemical industry and engineering.
Related titles: ◆ CD-ROM ed.: Chinese Academic Journals Full-Text Database. Science & Engineering, Series B. ISSN 1007-8029; Online - full text ed.
Indexed: A22, APIAb, C33, CIN, ChemAb, ChemTitl, EngInd, RefZh, SCOPUS.
—BLDSC (6430.395000), CASDDS, East View, IE, Ingenta.
Published by: Zhongguo Shiyou Huagong Gufeng Youxian Gongsi Beijing Huagong Yanjiuyuan/S I N O P E C Beijing Research Institute of Chemical Industry, 14, Beisanhuan Dong Lu, Chaoyang-qu, Beijing, 100013, China. TEL 86-10-64216131. Circ: 5,000. **Co-sponsor:** Chemical Industry & Engineering Society of China, Institute of Petrochemicals.

665.5 CHN ISSN 1673-8659
SHIYOU HUAGONG ANQUAN HUANBAO JISHU/PETROCHEMICAL SAFETY AND ENVIRONMENTAL PROTECTION TECHNOLOGY. Text in Chinese. 2007. bi-m.
Formed by the merger of (1986-2007): Shiyou Huagong Huanjing Baohu/Environment Protection in Petrochemical Industry (1005-7862); (1992-2007): Shiyou Huagong Anquan Jishu/Petrochemical Safety Technology (1006-3218)
Related titles: Online - full text ed.
Published by: Zhongguo Shi-hua Gongcheng Jianshe Gongsi/S I N O P E C Engineering Inc., 21 An Yuan, Anhui Bei Li, Chaoyang District, Beijing, 100101, China. TEL 86-10-84877006, FAX 86-10-84878856, http://www.sei.com.cn/.

SHIYOU HUAGONG FUSHI YU FANGHU/CORROSION & PROTECTION IN PETROCHEMICAL INDUSTRY. *see* PAINTS AND PROTECTIVE COATINGS

665.5 CHN ISSN 1006-396X
CODEN: SHGXEC
SHIYOU HUAGONG GAODENG XUEXIAO XUEBAO/JOURNAL OF PETROCHEMICAL UNIVERSITIES. Text in Chinese. 1988. q. abstr. 80 p./no.; **Document type:** *Journal, Academic/Scholarly.*
Related titles: ◆ CD-ROM ed.: Chinese Academic Journals Full-Text Database. Science & Engineering, Series B. ISSN 1007-8029; Online - full text ed.
Indexed: EngInd, RefZh, SCOPUS.
—BLDSC (5030.982100), IE, Ingenta.
Published by: Liaoning Shiyou Huagong Daxue/Liaoning University of Petroleum & Chemical Technology, No. 1, West Dandong Road, Wanghua District, Fushun, Liaoning Province 113001, China. TEL 81-413-6650405, FAX 86-413-6650866, http://www.lnpu.edu.cn/.

665.5 CHN ISSN 1006-8805
SHIYOU HUAGONG SHEBEI JISHU/PETRO-CHEMICAL EQUIPMENT TECHNOLOGY. Text in Chinese. 1980. bi-m. CNY 8 newsstand/cover (effective 2006). **Document type:** *Journal, Academic/Scholarly.*
Related titles: Online - full text ed.
Published by: Zhongguo Shi-hua Gongcheng Jianshe Gongsi/S I N O P E C Engineering Inc., 21 An Yuan, Anhui Bei Li, Chaoyang District, Beijing, 100101, China. TEL 86-10-84877582, FAX 86-10-84878856.

665.5 CHN ISSN 1007-7324
SHIYOU HUAGONG ZIDONGHUA/AUTOMATION IN PETRO-CHEMICAL INDUSTRY. Text in Chinese. 1964. bi-m. USD 24.60 (effective 2009). **Document type:** *Journal, Academic/Scholarly.*
Formerly (until 1998): Lianyou Huagong Zidonghua/Automation in Refined and Chemical Industry (1005-6572)
Related titles: Online - full text ed.
Indexed: A28, APA, BrCerAb, C&ISA, CA/WCA, CIA, CerAb, CivEngAb, CorrAb, E&CAJ, E11, EEA, EMA, ESPM, EnvEAb, H15, M&TEA, M09, MBF, METADEX, RefZh, SolStAb, T04, WAA.
—BLDSC (1831.446000), East View, Linda Hall.
Published by: Huaxue Gongyebu Zikong Sheji Jishu Zhongxinzhan/ Automatic Control Design Technology Center, 1, Fuli W. Rd., Lanzhou Design Institute, Xigu, Lanzhou 730060, China.

665.5 TWN ISSN 1022-9671
SHIYOU JIKAN/JOURNAL OF PETROLEUM. Text in English. 1963. q. **Document type:** *Journal, Academic/Scholarly.*
—BLDSC (5030.985500).
Published by: Zhongguo Shiyou Xuehui/Chinese Petroleum Institute, 9F, 7, Chung-Ching S. Road, Sec. 1, Taipei, 100, Taiwan. TEL 886-2-23812244, FAX 886-2-23314976.

665.5 CHN ISSN 1000-0747
TN870.5 CODEN: SKYKEG
➤ **SHIYOU KANTAN YU KAIFA.** Text in Chinese. 1974. bi-m. USD 66.60 (effective 2009). adv. bk.rev. 100 p./no.; **Document type:** *Journal, Academic/Scholarly.* **Description:** Covers new technologies and field practices in regional petroleum geology, structural geology, organic geochemistry, paleontology, seismogeology, well logging, mathematical geology and much more.
Related titles: Microfiche ed.; Online - full content ed.; Online - full text ed.; ◆ English ed.: Petroleum Exploration and Development. ISSN 1876-3804.
Indexed: A22, A28, APA, BrCerAb, C&ISA, CA/WCA, CIA, CPEI, CerAb, ChemAb, ChemTitl, CivEngAb, CorrAb, E&CAJ, E11, EEA, EMA, ESPM, EngInd, EnvEAb, GeoRef, H15, M&TEA, M09, MBF, METADEX, PetrolAb, RefZh, SCOPUS, SolStAb, SpeleolAb, T04, WAA.
—BLDSC (6433.130000), CASDDS, East View, IE, Ingenta, Linda Hall, PADDS.
Published by: (Zhongguo Shiyou Tianranqi Zonggongsi, Shiyou Kantan Kaifa Kexue Yanjiuyuan), Shiyou Kantan yu Kaifa, Haidian-qu, 20 Xueyuan Lu, Main building, 3rd Floor, Beijing, 100083, China. Ed., R&P Dakuang Han. Adv. contact Dongping Zou. **Dist. by:** China International Book Trading Corp, 35 Chegongzhuang Xilu, Haidian District, PO Box 399, Beijing 100044, China. TEL 86-10-68412045, FAX 86-10-68412023, cibtc@mail.cibtc.com.cn, http://www.cibtc.com.cn/.

➤ **SHIYOU KUANGCHANG JIXIE/OIL FIELD EQUIPMENT.** *see* MACHINERY

665.5 CHN ISSN 1005-2399
TP690.A1 CODEN: SLYHEE
➤ **SHIYOU LIANZHI YU HUAGONG/PETROLEUM PROCESSING AND PETROCHEMICALS.** Text in Chinese. 1957. m. USD 49.20 (effective 2009). adv. abstr.; charts; pat. 72 p./no.; back issues avail. **Document type:** *Journal, Academic/Scholarly.*
Formerly (until 1994): Shiyou Lianzhi (1001-4101)
Related titles: Online - full text ed.
Indexed: A22, APIAb, CIN, ChemAb, ChemTitl, RefZh, SCOPUS.
—BLDSC (6434.010000), CASDDS, IE, Ingenta, Linda Hall.
Published by: (Zhongguo Shiyou Huagong Jitungongsi/S I N O P E C, Shiyou Huagong Kexue Yanjiuyuan/Research Institute of Petroleum Processing (RIPP)), Shiyou Lianzhi yu Huagong Bianjibu/Editorial Office of Petroleum Processing & Petrochemicals, 18 Xueyuan Rd, Beijing, 100083, China. TEL 86-10-6231-1582, FAX 86-10-6231-1582. Ed. Zaiting Li. Pub., R&P Bingyue Wang. Adv. contact Yingchun Liu. Circ: 5,000. **Dist. overseas by:** China International Book Trading Corp, 35 Chegongzhuang Xilu, Haidian District, PO Box 399, Beijing 100044, China.

665.5 CHN ISSN 1674-0831
SHIYOU SHIHUA WUZI CAIGOU/PETROLEUM & PETROCHEMICAL MATERIAL PROCUREMENT. Text in Chinese. 1980. m. CNY 216; CNY 18 per issue (effective 2009).
Former titles (until 2007): Huagong Zhiliang/Quality for Chemical Industry (1009-3265); (until 1994): Huagong Zhiliang Guangli
Related titles: Online - full text ed.
Published by: (Zhongguo Shiyou he Huaxue Gongye Xiehui/China Petroleum and Chemical Industry Association), Shiyou Shihua Wuzi Caigou Jikanshe, 29, Nanmofang Lu, Xunjie Dasha 1107, Beijing, 100022, China. TEL 86-10-87798488, FAX 86-10-87799551. **Co-sponsor:** Zhongguo Shiyou Tianranqi Jituan Gongsi/China National Petroleum Corp.

553.282 CHN
TN860 CODEN: JSXUEW
SHIYOU TIANRANQI XUEBAO/JOURNAL OF OIL AND GAS TECHNOLOGY. Text in Chinese. 1978. bi-m. CNY 10 per issue. **Document type:** *Journal, Academic/Scholarly.*
Formerly (until 2003): Jianghan Shiyou Xueyuan Xuebao/Jianghan Petroleum Institute. Journal (1000-9752)
Related titles: Online - full text ed.: (from WanFang Data Corp.).
Indexed: GeoRef, PetrolAb, RefZh, SCOPUS.
—BLDSC (8267.299320), East View, PADDS.
Published by: Changjiang Daxue/Yangtze University, 1, Nanhuan Lu, Jingzhou, 434023, China. TEL 86-716-8060696. **Dist. by:** China International Book Trading Corp, 35 Chegongzhuang Xilu, Haidian District, PO Box 399, Beijing 100044, China. TEL 86-10-68412045, FAX 86-10-68412023, cibtc@mail.cibtc.com.cn, http://www.cibtc.com.cn/.

665.5 CHN ISSN 1000-1441
TN271.P4
SHIYOU WUTAN/GEOPHYSICAL PROSPECTING FOR PETROLEUM. Text in Chinese. 1979. q. USD 106.80 (effective 2009). adv. **Document type:** *Academic/Scholarly.* **Description:** Covers the technological developments and their applications in geophysical prospecting for petroleum.
Related titles: Online - full text ed.
Indexed: A22, GeoRef, PetrolAb, SpeleolAb.
—BLDSC (4156.100000), East View, IE, Ingenta, Linda Hall, PADDS.
Published by: Dizhi Kuangchan Bu, Shiyou Wutan Yanjiusuo, 21 Weigang, Nanjing, Jiangsu 210014, China. TEL 86-25-4432191, FAX 86-25-4432005. Ed. Zhu Xuan. Adv. contact Gao Lin. Circ: 2,500. **Dist. overseas by:** China International Book Trading Corp, 35 Chegongzhuang Xilu, Haidian District, PO Box 399, Beijing 100044, China.

665.5 CHN ISSN 0253-2697
TN860 CODEN: SYHPD9
SHIYOU XUEBAO/ACTA PETROLEI SINICA. Text in Chinese. 1980. bi-m. USD 74.40 (effective 2009). **Document type:** *Journal, Academic/Scholarly.*
Related titles: Online - full text ed.
Indexed: A22, A32, B&BAb, B19, B21, CPEI, ChemAb, ChemTitl, ESPM, EngInd, GeoRef, I10, OceAb, PetrolAb, RefZh, SCOPUS, SWRA, SpeleolAb.
—BLDSC (0644.500000), CASDDS, East View, IE, Ingenta, INIST, Linda Hall, PADDS.
Address: Xicheng-qu, 6, Liupukang jie, Beijing, 100724, China. TEL 86-10-62094537. **Dist. by:** China International Book Trading Corp, 35 Chegongzhuang Xilu, Haidian District, PO Box 399, Beijing 100044, China. TEL 86-10-68412045, FAX 86-10-68412023, cibtc@mail.cibtc.com.cn, http://www.cibtc.com.cn/.

665.5 CHN ISSN 1001-8719
CODEN: SXSHEY
SHIYOU XUEBAO. SHIYOU JIAGONG/ACTA PETROLEI SINICA. PETROLEUM PROCESSING SECTION. Text in Chinese. 1985. q. USD 37.20 (effective 2009).
Related titles: Online - full text ed.
Indexed: A22, APIAb, C33, CPEI, EngInd, RefZh, SCOPUS.
—BLDSC (0644.510000), East View, IE, Ingenta, Linda Hall.
Published by: Shiyou Xuebao, Xicheng-qu, 6, Liupukang jie, Beijing, 100724, China. TEL 86-10-62094537.

665.5 552 CHN ISSN 0253-9985
TN876.C5 CODEN: SYYCDL
➤ **SHIYOU YU TIANRANQI DIZHI/OIL AND GAS GEOLOGY.** Text in Chinese. 1980. bi-m. CNY 72; CNY 12 per issue (effective 2011). adv. 85 p./no.; **Document type:** *Journal, Academic/Scholarly.*
Description: Publishes the latest achievements in petroleum exploration, production, and scientific research in China.
Related titles: Online - full text ed.
Indexed: CIN, ChemAb, ChemTitl, GeoRef, PetrolAb, RefZh, SpeleolAb.
—BLDSC (6249.847000), East View, Linda Hall, PADDS.
Published by: Shiyou yu Tianranqi Dizhi Bianjibu, 31, Xueyuan Rd, Haidian District, Beijing, 100083, China. TEL 86-10-82312050, FAX 86-10-82312050. Ed. Liguo Cai. adv.: page USD 1,600. Circ: 2,000.
Dist. by: China International Book Trading Corp, 35 Chegongzhuang Xilu, Haidian District, PO Box 399, Beijing 100044, China.
Co-sponsors: Zhongguo Shiyou Huagong Jitungongsi Shiyou Kantan Kaifa Yanjiuyuan/S I N O P E C Exploration and Production Research Institute; Zhongguo Dizhi Xuehui Shiyou Dizhi Zhuanye Weiyuanhui/Geological Society of China, Petroleum Geological Committee.

665.5 CHN ISSN 1000-7393
TN871.3
SHIYOU ZUANCAI GONGYI/OIL DRILLING & PRODUCTION TECHNOLOGY. Text in Chinese. 1979. bi-m. USD 64.20 (effective 2009).
Related titles: Online - full text ed.
Indexed: A28, APA, BrCerAb, C&ISA, CA/WCA, CIA, CerAb, CivEngAb, CorrAb, E&CAJ, E11, EEA, EMA, ESPM, EnvEAb, H15, M&TEA, M09, MBF, METADEX, PetrolAb, RefZh, SCOPUS, SolStAb, T04, WAA.
—BLDSC (6250.880000), East View, Linda Hall, PADDS.
Published by: (Huabei Shiyou Guanliju/Huabei Oil Administration Bureau), Shiyou Zuancai Gongyi Bianjibu, Renqiu City, Hebei Province 062552, China. TEL 86-317-272-3370, FAX 86-317-272-4207. Ed. Qihan Huo. **Dist. overseas by:** China National Publications Import and Export Corporation, PO Box 88, Beijing 100020, China.

665.5 CHN ISSN 1001-0890
TN860
SHIYOU ZUANTAN JISHU/PETROLEUM DRILLING TECHNIQUES. Text in Chinese; Abstracts in English. 1973. bi-m. USD 37.20 (effective 2009). adv. bk.rev. 72 p./no.; **Document type:** *Journal, Trade.* **Description:** Covers the latest theories, scientific researches and technological developments in the field of petroleum drilling and production.
Related titles: Online - full text ed.
Indexed: A22, PetrolAb.
—BLDSC (6431.650000), East View, IE, Ingenta, PADDS.
Published by: (China National Star Petroleum Corp.), Shiyou Zuantan Jishu Bianjibu, 35 East Dongfeng Road, Dezhou, Shandong 253005, China. TEL 86-534-2670163, FAX 86-534-2622468. Ed. Huinian Chen. **Dist. overseas by:** China International Book Trading Corp, 35 Chegongzhuang Xilu, Haidian District, PO Box 399, Beijing 100044, China.

665.5 CHN ISSN 1008-2263
SHIYOUKU YU JIAYOUZHAN. Text in Chinese. 1995. bi-m. **Document type:** *Journal, Academic/Scholarly.*
Formerly (until 1998): Shiyouku Guanli yu Anquan (1007-1121)
Address: Jinganli 12-Lou, Beijing, 100028, China. TEL 86-10-64668601, FAX 86-10-64618538.

665.7 CAN ISSN 1714-5317
TN882.C3
SHORT-TERM CANADIAN NATURAL GAS DELIVERABILITY. Text in English. 2001. a. **Document type:** *Journal, Trade.*
Formerly (until 2006): Short Term Natural Gas Deliverability from the Western Canada Sedimentary Basin (1707-7915)
Related titles: Online - full text ed.: ISSN 1910-7773; ◆ French ed.: Productibilite a Court Terme de Gaz Naturel au Canada. ISSN 1714-5325.
Published by: National Energy Board/Office National de l'Energie, 444 Seventh Ave, S W, Calgary, AB T2P 0X8, Canada. TEL 403-299-3561, 800-899-1265, FAX 403-292-5576, publications@neb-one.gc.ca, http://www.neb-one.gc.ca.

SHUYOU SHIYAN DIZHI/PETROLEUM GEOLOGY & EXPERIMENT. *see* EARTH SCIENCES—Geology

338.4766180409 GBR ISSN 1749-2440
SINGAPORE PETROCHEMICALS REPORT. Text in English. 2005. a. EUR 820, USD 1,030 combined subscription per issue (print & email eds.) (effective 2010). **Document type:** *Report, Trade.* **Description:** Covers independent forecasts and competitive intelligence on the Singaporean petrochemicals industry.
Related titles: E-mail ed.
Indexed: A15, ABIn, B02, B15, B17, B18, G04, I05, P48, P51, P52, P56, PQC.
Published by: Business Monitor International Ltd., Senator House, 85 Queen Victoria St, London, EC4V 4AB, United Kingdom. TEL 44-20-72480468, FAX 44-20-72480467, subs@businessmonitor.com.

SITUATION & OUTLOOK REPORT. OIL CROPS YEARBOOK. *see* AGRICULTURE—Crop Production And Soil

338.4766180409 GBR ISSN 1749-2459
SLOVAKIA PETROCHEMICALS REPORT. Text in English. 2005. a. EUR 820, USD 1,030 combined subscription per issue (print & email eds.) (effective 2010). **Document type:** *Report, Trade.* **Description:** Covers independent forecasts and competitive intelligence on the Slovak petrochemicals industry.
Related titles: E-mail ed.
Indexed: A15, ABIn, B02, B15, B17, B18, G04, I05, P48, P51, P52, P56, PQC.
Published by: Business Monitor International Ltd., Senator House, 85 Queen Victoria St, London, EC4V 4AB, United Kingdom. TEL 44-20-72480468, FAX 44-20-72480467, subs@businessmonitor.com.

665.5 SVK ISSN 1335-3853
SLOVGAS. Text in Slovak. 1992. bi-m. CZK 264; CZK 44 newsstand/cover (effective 2006). **Document type:** *Magazine, Trade.*
Published by: Slovensky Plynarensky a Naftovy Zvaz, Mlynske Nivy 48, Bratislava 24, 821 09, Slovakia.

665 RUS
SLOVO NEFTYANNIKA. Text in Russian. w.
Published by: Izdatel'skii Dom Blagovest, Pr Mira 78a, Noyabrsk, Russian Federation. Ed. L Bondyreva. Circ: 8,469.

SOCIETY FOR MINING, METALLURGY, AND EXPLORATION. TRANSACTIONS. *see* MINES AND MINING INDUSTRY

665.5 622 USA ISSN 0891-0901
CODEN: SPESD8
SOCIETY OF PETROLEUM ENGINEERS. REPRINT SERIES. Text in English. 1958. irreg., latest vol.61, 2008. price varies. back issues avail. **Document type:** *Monographic series, Academic/Scholarly.*
Description: Anthologies of classic and important recent technical reports on broad oil and gas drilling, exploration and production.
Formerly (until 1967): Society of Petroleum Engineers of American Institute of Mining. Petroleum Transactions Reprint Series (0081-1688)
Related titles: CD-ROM ed.
Indexed: EngInd, GeoRef, SCOPUS, SpeleolAb.
—IE, Ingenta. **CCC.**
Published by: Society of Petroleum Engineers, Inc., PO Box 833836, Richardson, TX 75083. TEL 972-952-9393, 800-456-6863, FAX 972-952-9435, spedal@spe.org, http://www.spe.org.

622.338 USA ISSN 0081-1718
TN871.35 CODEN: SPWLA6
SOCIETY OF PROFESSIONAL WELL LOG ANALYSTS. S P W L A ANNUAL LOGGING SYMPOSIUM TRANSACTIONS. Text in English. 1960. a. price varies. charts; illus. **Document type:** *Proceedings, Trade.* **Description:** Includes technical papers presented at annual meeting.
Related titles: CD-ROM ed.
Indexed: EngInd, GeoRef, PetrolAb, SCOPUS, SpeleolAb.
Published by: Society of Petrophysicsts and Well Log Analysts (S P W L A), 8866 Gulf Fwy, Ste 320, Houston, TX 77017. TEL 713-947-8727, FAX 713-947-7181, http://www.spwla.org. R&P Vicki King. Circ: 2,500.

665.773 USA ISSN 0038-1500
SOONER L P G TIMES. Text in English. 1963. m. free. adv. bk.rev. charts; illus.; stat.
Media: Duplicated (not offset).
Published by: Oklahoma LP-Gas Association, 4200 N Lindsay, Oklahoma City, OK 73105. TEL 405-424-1775. Ed. Kurt S Winden. Circ: 1,450.

338.4766180409 GBR ISSN 1749-2467
SOUTH AFRICA PETROCHEMICALS REPORT. Text in English. 2005. q. EUR 820, USD 1,030 combined subscription (print & email eds.) (effective 2010). **Document type:** *Report, Trade.* **Description:** Provides industry professionals and strategists, sector analysts, trade associations and regulatory bodies with independent forecasts and competitive intelligence on the South African petrochemicals industry.
Related titles: E-mail ed.
Indexed: A15, ABIn, B02, B15, B17, B18, G04, I05, P48, P51, P52, P56, PQC.
Published by: Business Monitor International Ltd., Senator House, 85 Queen Victoria St, London, EC4V 4AB, United Kingdom. TEL 44-20-72480468, FAX 44-20-72480467, subs@businessmonitor.com.

665.5 USA
SOUTH DAKOTA PETROLEUM MARKETER. Text in English. m. **Document type:** *Newsletter.*
Address: PO Box 1058, Pierre, SD 57501-1058. TEL 605-224-8606. Ed., Pub. Dawna Leitzke Osborne. Circ: 500.

338.4766180409 GBR ISSN 1749-2475
SOUTH KOREA PETROCHEMICALS REPORT. Text in English. 2005. a. EUR 820, USD 1,030 combined subscription per issue (print & email eds.) (effective 2010). **Document type:** *Report, Trade.* **Description:** Provides industry professionals and strategists, sector analysts, trade associations and regulatory bodies with independent forecasts and competitive intelligence on the South Korean petrochemicals industry.
Related titles: E-mail ed.
Indexed: A15, ABIn, B02, B15, B17, B18, G04, I05, P48, P51, P52, P56, PQC.
Published by: Business Monitor International Ltd., Senator House, 85 Queen Victoria St, London, EC4V 4AB, United Kingdom. TEL 44-20-72480468, FAX 44-20-72480467, subs@businessmonitor.com.

665.538 USA
SOUTH LOUISIANA DRILLING REPORT. Text in English. 1984. w. (m. version avail.). USD 250 (effective 2005). **Document type:** *Newsletter, Trade.* **Description:** Covers drilling activity in Louisiana below the 31st parallel.
Formerly: South Louisiana Land Report
Related titles: CD-ROM ed.; Diskette ed.: USD 250 (effective 2005); Online - full text ed.
Published by: O D S - Petrodata, 3200 Wilcrest Dr, Ste 170, Houston, TX 77042. TEL 832-463-3000, FAX 832-463-3100, general@ods-petrodata.com, http://www.ods-petrodata.com. Pub., R&P Thomas Marsh.

665.5029 USA
SOUTHEAST STATES PETROLEUM INDUSTRY. Text in English. 1945. a. **Document type:** *Directory, Trade.* **Description:** Supplies company name, address, personnel, division offices, offshore operations, producer of oil or gas and if drilling contractor with rotary or cable tools, pipelines, refineries, petrochemical, gas processing, equipment manufacturers and suppliers, engineers.
Former titles: Southeast Petroleum Industry; Directory of Producers and Drilling Contractors Southeast: Louisiana, Arkansas, Florida, Georgia
Media: Diskette.
Published by: Midwest Publishing Company, 2230 E 49th St, Ste E, Tulsa, OK 74105. TEL 800-829-2002, info@midwestpub.com, http://www.midwestpub.com/.

665.5 USA
SOUTHEASTERN OIL REVIEW. Text in English. 1926. w. USD 30. adv.
Description: Covers oil and gas exploration and development, drilling and production activities in the Southeast states.
Published by: Oil Review Publishing Co., PO Box 145, Jackson, MS 39205. TEL 601-353-6213, FAX 601-353-0512. Ed. J Ishee. Adv. contact J. Ishee. Circ: 2,400.

665 ITA
STAFFETTA NEWS; English weekly on line. Text in English. w. EUR 475 (effective 2009). adv. bk.rev.; rec.rev.; Website rev. charts; stat. 20 p./no.; back issues avail. **Document type:** *Magazine, Trade.*
Description: Surveys what goes on in the Italian energy sector. Includes the latest energy statistics on consumption, prices and imports, as well as information on the company's activities in Italy and abroad.
Media: Online - full text. **Related titles:** Online - full text ed.
Published by: Rivista Italiana Petrolio Srl, Via Aventina 19, Rome, 00153, Italy. TEL 39-06-5741208, FAX 39-06-5754906, http://www.staffettaonline.com.

665.5 ITA
STAFFETTA PREZZI. Text in Italian. 1986. s-w. EUR 275 (effective 2009). charts; stat. cum.index 1986-1996, 1991-1997, 1997. **Document type:** *Bulletin, Trade.* **Description:** Reports the regional prices of the most important oil products for the wholesale trade.
Related titles: Fax ed.
Published by: Rivista Italiana Petrolio Srl, Via Aventina 19, Rome, 00153, Italy. TEL 39-06-5741208, FAX 39-06-5754906, http://www.staffettaonline.com.

665.5 ITA
STAFFETTA QUOTIDIANA. Text in Italian. 1933. d. EUR 1,101 combined subscription (print & online eds.) (effective 2009). adv. bk.rev.; software rev.; Website rev. mkt. 20 p./no.; back issues avail.
Document type: *Newspaper, Consumer.* **Description:** Lists energy sources; energy politics; oil, gas and other energy rates; companies and trade unions; congress events; calls for bids; and more.
Formerly: Staffetta Quotidiana Petrolifera
Related titles: CD-ROM ed.; Online - full text ed.
Published by: Rivista Italiana Petrolio Srl, Via Aventina 19, Rome, 00153, Italy. TEL 39-06-5741208, FAX 39-06-5754906.

STATION REPORTER; serving Atlantic Canada's automotive service industry. *see* TRANSPORTATION—Automobiles

665.5 NOR ISSN 0804-8266
STATOIL MAGASIN. Text in Norwegian. 1989. q.
Indexed: SCOPUS.
Published by: Statoil, Forusbeen 50, Stavanger, 4035, Norway. TEL 47-51-990000, FAX 47-51-990050, statoil@statoil.com, http://www.statoil.com.

665.5 DNK ISSN 1902-777X
STROEMNINGER. Text in Danish; Summaries in English. 1985. biennial. free (effective 2005). **Document type:** *Magazine, Trade.*
Former titles (until 2005): D O N G Magasinet (1399-4638); (until 1998): D - Magasinet (0902-445X)
Published by: Dansk Olie og Naturgas, Kraftvaerksvej 53, Fredericia, 7000, Denmark. TEL 45-99-551111, info@dongenergy.com, http://www.dongenergy.com.

665.5 RUS ISSN 0130-3872
STROITEL'STVO NEFTYANYKH I GAZOVYKH SKVAZHIN NA SUSHE I NA MORE/CONSTRUCTION OF OIL AND GAS WELLS ON DRY LAND AND OFFSHORE; nauchno-tekhnicheskii zhurnal. Text in Russian. 1993. m. USD 337 in United States (effective 2004).
Document type: *Journal.*
Indexed: PetrolAb, RefZh.
—BLDSC (0173.970000), East View, PADDS.
Published by: Vserossiiskii Nauchno-Issledovatel'skii Institut Organizatsii Upravleniya i Ekonomiki Neftegazovoi Promyshlennosti (VNIIOENG), Nametkina 14, korp B, Moscow, 117420, Russian Federation. TEL 7-095-3320022, FAX 7-095-3316877, vniioeng@mcn.ru, http://vniioeng.mcn.ru. Ed. Yu V Vedetskii. **Dist. by:** East View Information Services, 10601 Wayzata Blvd, Minneapolis, MN 55305. TEL 952-252-1201, 800-477-1005, FAX 952-252-1202, info@eastview.com, http://www.eastview.com.

665.5 GBR ISSN 0266-2205
SUBSEA ENGINEERING NEWS. Abbreviated title: S E N. Text in English. 1982. s-m. bk.rev. back issues avail. **Document type:** *Newsletter, Trade.* **Description:** Covers market information and technical details on subsea and underwater engineering, pipelines, floating production systems, offshore business news and government policy.
Formerly (until 1984): Oil and Gas Pipeline News (0262-7906)
Related titles: E-mail ed.: GBP 385 (effective 2010).
Indexed: PetrolAb.
Published by: Knighton Enterprises Ltd., PO Box 27, Cheltenham, GL53 0YH, United Kingdom. TEL 44-1242-574027, FAX 44-1242-574102.

665.5029 USA
SUPPLIER MEMBER DIRECTORY. Text in English. 1982. a. USD 30 per issue (effective 2006). index. **Document type:** *Directory.*
Description: Covers suppliers of equipment and services for terminal and tank farm industry.
Former titles: Independent Liquid Terminals Association. Directory of Bulk Liquid Terminal and Aboveground Storage Tank Equipment and Services: Suppliers of Equipment & Services; Independent Liquid Terminals Association. Directory of Suppliers of Goods and Services
Published by: Independent Liquid Terminals Association, 1444 I St NW, Ste 400, Washington, DC 20005-6538. TEL 202-842-9200, FAX 202-326-8660, info@ilta.org, http://www.ilta.org/. Circ: 900.

670.29 USA
SUPPLY, DISTRIBUTION, MANUFACTURING & SERVICE; supply and service companies & equipment manufacturers. Text in English. a. (2 vols.). **Document type:** *Directory.* **Description:** Supplies company name, address, phone and fax number, and personnel information.
Former titles: Supply and Distribution; Oil Well Supply Industry; Directory of Oil Well Supply Companies (0415-9772)
Media: Diskette.
Published by: Midwest Publishing Company, 2230 E 49th St, Ste E, Tulsa, OK 74105. TEL 800-829-2002, info@midwestpub.com, http://www.midwestpub.com/.

P

665.5 USA
SURFACE PRODUCTION OPERATIONS. Text in English. 1998. irreg. price varies. **Document type:** *Monographic series, Trade.*
Related titles: Online - full text ed.: ISSN 1874-8643.
Published by: Gulf Professional Publishing (Subsidiary of: Elsevier Science & Technology), 3251 Riverport Ln, Maryland Heights, MO 63043. TEL 314-453-7010, FAX 314-453-7095, http://www.elsevier.com.

T G A-FACHPLANER; das Magazin fuer die technische Gebaeudeausruestung. *see* HEATING, PLUMBING AND REFRIGERATION

665.5 658.8 NLD ISSN 1871-9414
T W S. (Tanken Wassen Shoppen) Text in Dutch. 200?. q. **Document type:** *Magazine, Trade.*
Published by: Belangenvereniging Tankstations BETA, Postbus 19128, Rotterdam, 3001 BC, Netherlands. TEL 31-10-4111180, FAX 31-10-4116661, info@beta-tankstations.nl, http://www.beta-tankstations.nl.

338.4766180409 GBR ISSN 1749-2483
TAIWAN PETROCHEMICALS REPORT. Text in English. 2005. a. EUR 820, USD 1,030 combined subscription per issue (print & email eds.) (effective 2010). **Document type:** *Report, Trade.* **Description:** Provides industry professionals and strategists, sector analysts, trade associations and regulatory bodies with independent forecasts and competitive intelligence on the Taiwanese petrochemicals industry.
Related titles: E-mail ed.
Indexed: A15, ABIn, B02, B15, B17, B18, G04, I05, P48, P51, P52, P56, PQC.
Published by: Business Monitor International Ltd., Senator House, 85 Queen Victoria St, London, EC4V 4AB, United Kingdom. TEL 44-20-72480468, FAX 44-20-72480467, subs@businessmonitor.com.

TAN JINGJI YUEKAN/CARBON ECONOMY MONTHLY. *see* BUSINESS AND ECONOMICS

665.5 UAE
AT-TAWZI'/DISTRIBUTION. Text in Arabic. 1984. m. free. **Description:** News of company activities.
Published by: Abu Dhabi National Oil Company, Distribution Division/ Sharikat Bitrul Abu Dhabi al-Wataniyyah lil-Tawzi', PO Box 4188, Abu Dhabi, United Arab Emirates. TEL 771300, TELEX 22358 FUDIST EM. Ed. Abdullah Majid Al Mansouri. Circ: 1,000.

TECHNICAL LITERATURE ABSTRACTS: CATALYSTS - ZEOLITES (ONLINE). *see* CHEMISTRY—Abstracting, Bibliographies, Statistics

TEK I STATISTIKA. *see* ENERGY

665.7 333.8 JPN
TENNEN GASU KANKEI SHIRYO/NATURAL GAS RESOURCES. Text in Japanese. a.
Published by: Sekiyu Kodan/Japan National Oil Corp., 2-2 Uchisaiwai-cho 2-chome, Chiyoda-ku, Tokyo, 100-0011, Japan.

665 UKR
TERMINAL (KIEV); neftyanoe obozrenie. Text in Russian. w. UAK 190 per month domestic (effective 2004). stat. 40 p./no.; **Document type:** *Magazine, Trade.* **Description:** Covers oil and petroleum markets throughout the world.
Related titles: E-mail ed.
Published by: Psikhea, ul Nagornaya 25-27, ofis 58, Kiev, 04107, Ukraine. info@ukroil.com.ua, http://ukroil.com.ua.

665.5029 USA
TERMINAL MEMBER DIRECTORY. Text in English. 1975. a. USD 100 per issue (effective 2006). index. **Document type:** *Directory.* **Description:** Locates 489 bulk liquid terminals and storage facilities, commodities handled and modes served.
Former titles: Independent Liquid Terminals Association. Directory of Bulk Liquid Terminal and Storage Facilities; Independent Liquid Terminals Association. Directory of Bulk Liquid Storage Facilities
Published by: Independent Liquid Terminals Association, 1444 I St NW, Ste 400, Washington, DC 20005-6538. TEL 202-842-9200, FAX 202-326-8660, info@ilta.org, http://www.ilta.org/. Circ: 900.

665 USA
TN867
TEXAS DIRECTORY. Text in English. 19??. a. USD 80 per issue (effective 2011). **Document type:** *Directory, Trade.*
Former titles: Armstrong Oil Directories: Texas and Southeastern New Mexico Edition (0277-2280); (until 1980): Texas Oil Directory
Published by: Armstrong Oil Directories, PO Box 52106, Amarillo, TX 79159. TEL 806-457-9300, FAX 806-457-9301, support@armstrongoil.com.

TEXAS LAW OF OIL AND GAS. *see* LAW

TEXAS NATURAL RESOURCES REPORTER. *see* WATER RESOURCES

662.338 381.147 USA ISSN 1087-9048
TEXAS PETROLEUM AND C-STORE JOURNAL. Text in English. 1951. q. adv. illus. **Document type:** *Journal, Trade.* **Description:** Directed to Texas petroleum marketers, and convenience store owners and operators.
Former titles (until 1996): Texas Oil Marketer (0896-8969); (until 1972): Texas Oil Jobber (0040-4527)
Indexed: B01, B07, E14.
Published by: (Texas Petroleum Marketers and Convenience Store Association), Naylor LLC, 5950 NW 1st Pl, Gainesville, FL 32607. TEL 800-369-6220, FAX 352-331-3525, http://www.naylor.com. Ed. Doug DuBois Jr. Pub. Kathleen Gardner. adv.: B&W page USD 1,450;. Circ: 1,487 (free).

665.5029 USA
TEXAS PETROLEUM INDUSTRY. Text in English. 1945. a. **Document type:** *Directory, Trade.* **Description:** Supplies company name, address, phone and fax numbers, personnel, division offices, offshore operations, whether producer of oil or gas and if drilling contractor with rotary or cable tools, pipelines, refineries, petrochemical, gas processing, equipment manufacturers and suppliers, engineers, landman.
Former titles: Directory of Producers and Drilling Contractors: Texas; Directory of Producers and Drilling Contractors: Texas
Media: Diskette.
Published by: Midwest Publishing Company, 2230 E 49th St, Ste E, Tulsa, OK 74105. TEL 800-829-2002, info@midwestpub.com, http://www.midwestpub.com/.

665.773 USA ISSN 1081-4051
TP359.L5
TEXAS PROPANE. Text in English. 1944. 7/yr. free. adv. illus. **Document type:** *Magazine, Trade.* **Description:** Covers new laws and regulations (both state and federal) affecting the industry, new technology and products, marketing opportunities, and safety issues.
Former titles (until 1992): Texas L P - Gas News (0040-4454); Texas Butane News
Related titles: Online - full content ed.
Published by: Texas Propane Gas Association, 8408 N Interregional Hwy 35, Austin, TX 78753-6438. TEL 512-836-8620, 800-325-7427, FAX 512-834-0758, info@txpropane.com. Adv. contact Lisa Grinstead. Circ: 1,200 (controlled).

665.538 USA
TEXAS. RAILROAD COMMISSION. OIL AND GAS DIVISION. ANNUAL REPORT. Text in English. 19??. a. charts; stat. back issues avail. **Document type:** *Report, Government.* **Description:** Includes oil and gas production, arranged by district and by field name. Lists county, discovery date, depth, and total wells for each field. Provides total production figures for gas and crude oil.
Related titles: Microfiche ed.
Indexed: SpeleolAb.
Published by: Railroad Commission, Oil and Gas Division, PO Box 12967, Austin, TX 78711. TEL 877-228-5740, publicassist@rrc.state.tx.us.

665.5 USA
TEXAS. RAILROAD COMMISSION. OIL AND GAS DIVISION. DRILLING PERMIT INDEX. Text in English. 19??. w. USD 239 (effective 2011). **Document type:** *Government.* **Description:** Lists all permits issued by district and by county, showing operator name and ID number, lease name, well number, API number, and permit date and number.
Media: Microfiche.
Published by: Railroad Commission, Oil and Gas Division, PO Box 12967, Austin, TX 78711. TEL 877-228-5740, publicassist@rrc.state.tx.us.

665.5 USA
TEXAS. RAILROAD COMMISSION. OIL AND GAS DIVISION. GAS LEASE INDEX. Text in English. 19??. m. USD 91 (effective 2011). **Document type:** *Government.* **Description:** Lists all leases on the gas proration schedule alphabetically within each district and gives field, operator, and gas well ID number.
Media: Microfiche.
Published by: Railroad Commission, Oil and Gas Division, PO Box 12967, Austin, TX 78711. TEL 877-228-5740, publicassist@rrc.state.tx.us.

665.5 USA
TEXAS. RAILROAD COMMISSION. OIL AND GAS DIVISION. GAS PRODUCTION LEDGER. (Avail. by RRC district) Text in English. 19??. m. USD 138 statewide (effective 2011). charts. **Document type:** *Government.* **Description:** Gives production, allowable, and production status by field, operator, and well.
Media: Microfiche.
Published by: Railroad Commission, Oil and Gas Division, PO Box 12967, Austin, TX 78711. TEL 877-228-5740, publicassist@rrc.state.tx.us.

665.538 USA
TEXAS. RAILROAD COMMISSION. OIL AND GAS DIVISION. GAS PRORATION SCHEDULE. Text in English. 19??. s-a. USD 779 statewide; USD 399 per issue statewide (effective 2011). **Document type:** *Government.* **Description:** Compiles monthly allowables by well and field.
Published by: Railroad Commission, Oil and Gas Division, PO Box 12967, Austin, TX 78711. TEL 877-228-5740, publicassist@rrc.state.tx.us.

665.5 USA
TEXAS. RAILROAD COMMISSION. OIL AND GAS DIVISION. GAS PURCHASER. Text in English. 19??. m. USD 101 (effective 2011). **Document type:** *Government.* **Description:** Lists gas purchasers alphabetically; for each operator, lists oil leases or gas wells in numerical sequence within district and field. Shows percentage of authorized take for each lease.
Media: Microfiche.
Published by: Railroad Commission, Oil and Gas Division, PO Box 12967, Austin, TX 78711. TEL 877-228-5740, publicassist@rrc.state.tx.us.

665.5 USA
TEXAS. RAILROAD COMMISSION. OIL AND GAS DIVISION. GATHERER STRIPOUT. Text in English. 19??. m. USD 99 (effective 2011). charts. **Document type:** *Government.* **Description:** Gives the proration schedule by gatherer; shows district, field name, operator name, lease or ID number, and monthly allowables.
Media: Microfiche.
Published by: Railroad Commission, Oil and Gas Division, PO Box 12967, Austin, TX 78711. TEL 877-228-5740, publicassist@rrc.state.tx.us.

665.5 USA
TEXAS. RAILROAD COMMISSION. OIL AND GAS DIVISION. NOTICES OF HEARINGS AND ORDERS. (Avail. by RRC district) Text in English. 19??. w. USD 1,298 statewide (effective 2011). **Document type:** *Government.* **Description:** Publishes all orders signed by the Railroad Commission and notices of hearings for all proceedings of the Oil and Gas Division.
Published by: Railroad Commission, Oil and Gas Division, PO Box 12967, Austin, TX 78711. TEL 877-228-5740, publicassist@rrc.state.tx.us.

665.5 USA
TEXAS. RAILROAD COMMISSION. OIL AND GAS DIVISION. OIL AND GAS FIELD NAMES. Text in English. 19??. m. USD 85 (effective 2011). **Document type:** *Government.* **Description:** Publishes all names on the Railroad Commission master field list, both active and inactive, showing district, field number, whether oil or gas, and county.
Media: Microfiche.
Published by: Railroad Commission, Oil and Gas Division, PO Box 12967, Austin, TX 78711. TEL 877-228-5740, publicassist@rrc.state.tx.us.

665.5 USA
TEXAS. RAILROAD COMMISSION. OIL AND GAS DIVISION. OIL AND GAS NOTICES AND FORMS. Text in English. 19??. m. USD 27 (effective 2011). **Document type:** *Government.* **Description:** Contains notices of procedure changes, requirements, new and revised forms, information on publications, and bulletins of forthcoming seminars of interest.
Published by: Railroad Commission, Oil and Gas Division, PO Box 12967, Austin, TX 78711. TEL 877-228-5740, publicassist@rrc.state.tx.us.

665.5 USA
TEXAS. RAILROAD COMMISSION. OIL AND GAS DIVISION. OIL LEASE INDEX. Text in English. 19??. m. USD 91 (effective 2011). **Document type:** *Government.* **Description:** Lists all leases on the oil proration schedule alphabetically within each district and gives field, operator, and lease number.
Media: Microfiche.
Published by: Railroad Commission, Oil and Gas Division, PO Box 12967, Austin, TX 78711. TEL 877-228-5740, publicassist@rrc.state.tx.us.

665.5 USA
TEXAS. RAILROAD COMMISSION. OIL AND GAS DIVISION. OIL LEASES AND GAS WELLS BY DISTRICT AND OPERATOR. Text in English. 19??. m. USD 97 (effective 2011). **Document type:** *Government.* **Description:** Lists operators within each district and shows their oil leases and gas wells, lease or gas ID number, field name and number, and county name and number.
Media: Microfiche.
Published by: Railroad Commission, Oil and Gas Division, PO Box 12967, Austin, TX 78711. TEL 877-228-5740, publicassist@rrc.state.tx.us.

665.5 USA
TEXAS. RAILROAD COMMISSION. OIL AND GAS DIVISION. OIL PRODUCTION LEDGER. (Avail. by RRC district) Text in English. 19??. m. USD 124 statewide (effective 2011). charts. **Document type:** *Government.* **Description:** Gives production status by field, operator, and lease.
Media: Microfiche.
Published by: Railroad Commission, Oil and Gas Division, PO Box 12967, Austin, TX 78711. TEL 877-228-5740, publicassist@rrc.state.tx.us.

665.538 USA
TEXAS. RAILROAD COMMISSION. OIL AND GAS DIVISION. OIL PRORATION SCHEDULE. Text in English. 19??. s-a. USD 790 statewide; USD 404 per issue statewide (effective 2011). **Document type:** *Government.* **Description:** Compiles monthly allowables listed by well and field.
Related titles: Microfiche ed.
Published by: Railroad Commission, Oil and Gas Division, PO Box 12967, Austin, TX 78711. TEL 877-228-5740, publicassist@rrc.state.tx.us.

665.5 USA
TEXAS. RAILROAD COMMISSION. OIL AND GAS DIVISION. OPERATOR STRIPOUT. Text in English. 19??. m. USD 120 (effective 2011). charts. **Document type:** *Government.* **Description:** Gives the proration schedule by operator; shows district, field name, operator name, lease or ID number, and monthly allowables.
Media: Microfiche.
Published by: Railroad Commission, Oil and Gas Division, PO Box 12967, Austin, TX 78711. TEL 877-228-5740, publicassist@rrc.state.tx.us.

665.5 USA
TEXAS. RAILROAD COMMISSION. OIL AND GAS DIVISION. P-5 ORGANIZATION DIRECTORY. Text in English. 19??. m. USD 144 (effective 2011). **Document type:** *Directory, Government.* **Description:** Lists all companies or individuals who have filed an organization report, including operator number, whether active or inactive, address, phone number, company officers, activity by district, and specialty codes.
Media: Microfiche.
Published by: Railroad Commission, Oil and Gas Division, PO Box 12967, Austin, TX 78711. TEL 877-228-5740, publicassist@rrc.state.tx.us.

665.538 USA
TEXAS. RAILROAD COMMISSION. OIL AND GAS DIVISION. PRORATED GAS FIELDS - MONTHLY SCHEDULE. Text in English. 19??. m. USD 184 statewide (effective 2011). **Document type:** *Government.* **Description:** Lists monthly allowables for gas fields produced under special field rules.
Formerly: Texas. Railroad Commission. Oil and Gas Division. Gas Monthly Proration Schedule
Published by: Railroad Commission, Oil and Gas Division, PO Box 12967, Austin, TX 78711. TEL 877-228-5740, publicassist@rrc.state.tx.us.

665.5 USA
TEXAS. RAILROAD COMMISSION. OIL AND GAS DIVISION. PURCHASER STRIPOUT. Text in English. 19??. m. USD 99 (effective 2011). charts. **Document type:** *Report, Government.* **Description:** Gives the proration schedule by purchaser; shows district, field name, purchaser name, purchaser systems, lease or ID number, system deliverability, and allowables.
Media: Microfiche.
Published by: Railroad Commission, Oil and Gas Division, PO Box 12967, Austin, TX 78711. TEL 877-228-5740, publicassist@rrc.state.tx.us.

665.54 CHN ISSN 1006-6535
TEZHONG YOUQICANG/SPECIAL OIL AND GAS RESERVOIRS. Text in Chinese. 1994. bi-m. USD 37.20 (effective 2009). **Document type:** *Journal, Academic/Scholarly.*
Related titles: Online - full text ed.
Indexed: B21, E17, ESPM, GeoRef, RefZh.
—East View, PADDS.
Published by: Zhongyou Liaohe Youtian Fenongsi, Kantan Kaifa Yanjiuyuan, Panjin, 124010, China. TEL 86-427-7823579.

338.4766180409 GBR ISSN 1749-2491
THAILAND PETROCHEMICALS REPORT. Text in English. 2005. q. EUR 820, USD 1,030 combined subscription (print & email eds.) (effective 2010). **Document type:** *Report, Trade.* **Description:** Provides industry professionals and strategists, sector analysts, trade associations and regulatory bodies with independent forecasts and competitive intelligence on the Thai petrochemicals industry.
Related titles: E-mail ed.
Indexed: A15, ABIn, B02, B15, B17, B18, G04, I05, P48, P51, P52, P56, PQC.
Published by: Business Monitor International Ltd., Senator House, 85 Queen Victoria St, London, EC4V 4AB, United Kingdom. TEL 44-20-72480468, FAX 44-20-72480467, subs@businessmonitor.com.

THUONGMAI/COMMERCIAL REVIEW. *see* BUSINESS AND ECONOMICS—International Commerce

665.7 CHN ISSN 1672-1926
TIANRANQI DIQIOU KEXUE/NATURAL GAS GEOSCIENCE. Text in Chinese; Abstracts in English. 1990. bi-m. USD 79.80 (effective 2009). Website rev.; bk.rev. 80 p./no.; **Document type:** *Journal, Academic/Scholarly.* **Description:** Reviews and reports the latest developments in gas geoscience research, new theories, and methods of natural gas exploration.
Related titles: Online - full text ed.
Indexed: GeoRef.
—East View.
Published by: Zhongguo Kexueyuan Ziyuan Huanjing Kexue Xinxi Zhongxin/Academia Sinica, Scientific Information Center for Resources and Environment, 342 Tianshui Rd, Lanzhou, Gansu 730000, China. TEL 86-931-8277790, FAX 86-931-8275743. Ed. Jinsing Dai. Adv. contact Junwei Zheng.

665.7 CHN ISSN 1000-0976
TN880.A1 CODEN: TIGOE3
➤ **TIANRANQI GONGYE/NATURAL GAS INDUSTRY.** Text in Chinese; Summaries in Chinese, English. 1981. bi-m. USD 133.20 (effective 2009). adv. bk.rev. charts; illus.; stat. index. back issues avail. **Document type:** *Academic/Scholarly.* **Description:** Contains articles on exploration and development, drilling-production technology and equipment, storage, transportation, engineering construction, gas processing and utilization, reforms and management in the industry.
Related titles: Diskette ed.; Online - full text ed.
Indexed: A22, APIAb, GeoRef, PetrolAb, SCOPUS, SpeleolAb.
—BLDSC (6037.315000), East View, IE, Ingenta, PADDS.
Published by: (Sichuan Shiyou Guanli-ju/Sichuan Petroleum Administration), Tianranqi Gongye Zazhishe/Natural Gas Industry Journal Agency, No3 Fuqing Lu Sec1, Chengdu, Sichuan 610051, China. TEL 86-28-6011178, FAX 86-28-3358727. Ed. Wang Xieqin. Pub. Yong Jie Wu. R&P Xieqin Wang TEL 86-28-6011178. Adv. contact Wang Xiegin Guanjie. Circ: 6,000. **Subscr. to:** China International Book Trading Corp, 35 Chegongzhuang Xilu, Haidian District, PO Box 399, Beijing 100044, China. TEL 86-10-68412045, FAX 86-10-68412023, cibtc@mail.cibtc.com.cn, http://www.cibtc.com.cn.

665.7 660 CHN ISSN 1001-9219
CODEN: THTKEF
TIANRANQI HUAGONG/NATURAL GAS CHEMICAL INDUSTRY; C I huaxue yu huagong. Text in Chinese; Summaries in Chinese, English. 1976. bi-m. USD 40.20 (effective 2009). adv. bk.rev. back issues avail. **Document type:** *Journal, Academic/Scholarly.* **Description:** Reports research, design, and production in natural gas chemical industry and CI chemistry and technology.
Related titles: Online - full text ed.
Indexed: ChemAb, ChemTitl.
—BLDSC (6037.308000), CASDDS, IE, Ingenta.
Published by: Xinan Huagong Yanjiu Shejiyuan/Southwest Research & Design Institute of Chemical Industry, Wainan Jichang Lu, Box 445, Chengdu, Sichuan 610225, China. TEL 81-28-85962641, FAX 81-28-85964046, http://www.swrchem.com/. adv.: color page USD 800. Circ: 3,000 (paid).

665.5 USA
TIPRO TARGET. Text in English. 1947. w. USD 275 domestic membership (effective 2005). adv. **Document type:** *Newsletter.*
Formerly (until 2004): The Tipro Tuesday Target Newsletter
Published by: Texas Independent Producers & Royalty Owners Assn., 515 Congress Ave., Ste. 1910, Austin, TX 78701. TEL 512-476-4452, FAX 512-476-8070. Eds. A. Scott Anderson, Martin Fleming. adv.: B&W page USD 895. Circ: 2,000 (controlled).

665.773 USA ISSN 1048-0935
TODAY'S REFINERY. Text in English. 1987. m. USD 25; free to qualified personnel. adv. **Document type:** *Magazine, Trade.* **Description:** Contains articles, column, abstracts and reviews of interest to petroleum refiners throughout the world.
Related titles: Online - full text ed.
Indexed: B02, B15, B17, B18, G04, G06, G07, G08, PEBNI, SCOPUS.
—CIS, Linda Hall. **CCC.**
Published by: Chemical Week Associates, 110 William St 11th Fl, New York, NY 10038. TEL 212-621-4900, FAX 212-621-4949, http://www.chemweek.com. Ed. Gregory D L Morris. Adv. contact Erin Ferriter TEL 212-621-4932. B&W page USD 3,325, color page USD 4,225; trim 10.88 x 8.13. Circ: 10,406 (controlled).

665 RUS
TOMSKAYA NEFT'. Text in Russian. w.
Address: Pr Neftyanikov 406/1, Strezhevoi, 636762, Russian Federation. Ed. V N Lykov. Circ: 4,070.

665.5 USA
TRADEQUIP INTERNATIONAL. Text in English. 1978. 36/yr. **Document type:** *Magazine, Trade.* **Description:** Covers all types of new and used energy equipment, related products and services.
Related titles: Online - full text ed.
Published by: T A P Publishing Co., PO Box 489, Crossville, TN 38557. TEL 931-484-5137, 800-251-6776, FAX 931-484-2532, 800-423-9030, http://www.tappublishing.com/.

665.5 385 RUS
➤ **TRANSPORT I KHRANENIE NEFTEPRODUKTOV/ TRANSPORTATION AND STORAGE OF PETROLEUM PRODUCTS;** nauchnyi informatsionnyi sbornik. Text in Russian. 1994. m. USD 256 foreign (effective 2007). **Document type:** *Journal, Academic/Scholarly.*
Indexed: RASB.
Published by: Tsentral'nyi Nauchno-Issledovatel'skii Institut Informatsii i Tekhniko-Ekonomicheskikh Issledovanii Neftepererabatyvayushchei i Neftekhimicheskoi Promyshlennosti, ul Bolotnaya 12, Moscow, 115998, Russian Federation. TEL 7-095-9530527, FAX 7-095-9532434, inforhimt@mtu-net.ru. Ed. S P Makarov. **Dist. by:** East View Information Services, 10601 Wayzata Blvd, Minneapolis, MN 55305. TEL 952-252-1201, 800-477-1005, FAX 952-252-1202, info@eastview.com, http://www.eastview.com.

➤ **TRANSPORTATION SAFETY REFLEXIONS. PIPELINE.** *see* TRANSPORTATION—Roads And Traffic

354 TTO
TRINIDAD AND TOBAGO. MINISTRY OF ENERGY. ANNUAL REPORT. Text in English. 1964. a., latest 1995. free. illus.; stat. 80 p./no.; **Document type:** *Government.*
Former titles: Trinidad and Tobago. Ministry of Energy and Natural Resources. Annual Report; Trinidad and Tobago. Ministry of Energy and Energy-Based Industries. Annual Report; Trinidad and Tobago. Ministry of Petroleum and Mines. Annual Report
Published by: Ministry of Energy, PO Box 96, Port-of-Spain, Trinidad, Trinidad & Tobago. Ed. Andrew Jupiter. Circ: 500.

622 338.2 TTO
TRINIDAD AND TOBAGO. MINISTRY OF ENERGY. MONTHLY BULLETIN. Text in English. 1964. m. free. charts; mkt. index, cum.index. 20 p./no.; **Document type:** *Bulletin, Government.*
Former titles: Trinidad and Tobago. Ministry of Energy and Natural Resources. Monthly Bulletin; Trinidad and Tobago. Ministry of Energy and Energy-Based Industries. Monthly Bulletin; Trinidad and Tobago. Ministry of Petroleum and Mines. Monthly Bulletin (0026-5322)
Published by: Ministry of Energy, PO Box 96, Port-of-Spain, Trinidad, Trinidad & Tobago. Ed. Rupert Mends. Circ: 570.

665.5 RUS ISSN 0869-8740
TRUBOPROVODNYI TRANSPORT NEFTI/OIL PIPELINE TRANSPORT; nauchno-tekhnicheskii zhurnal. Text in Russian. m. USD 399 in United States (effective 2004). **Document type:** *Journal.*
Indexed: RefZh.
—East View, Linda Hall.
Published by: Transneft', ul B Polyanka, 57, Moscow, 119180, Russian Federation. TEL 7-095-9508178, FAX 7-095-9508900, transneft@transneft.ru, http://www.transneft.ru. **Dist. by:** East View Information Services, 10601 Wayzata Blvd, Minneapolis, MN 55305. TEL 952-252-1201, 800-477-1005, FAX 952-252-1202, info@eastview.com, http://www.eastview.com.

665.5 USA ISSN 0193-9467
TULSALETTER. Text in English. 1976. s-m. free to members. **Document type:** *Newsletter.* **Description:** Focuses on industry and association news.
Media: E-mail.
Published by: Petroleum Equipment Institute, PO Box 2380, Tulsa, OK 74101. TEL 918-494-9696, FAX 918-491-9895.

TURAN-ENERGY. CONTRACTS. *see* LAW

658.8 AZE
TURAN INFORMATION AGENCY. ENERGY ANNUAL REPORT. Text in English. a. stat.
Published by: Turan Information Agency/Turna Informasiya Agentilyi, Khagani ul 33, Baku, 370000, Azerbaijan. TEL 994-12-935967, 994-12-984226, FAX 994-12-983817, root@turan.baku.az, http://www.turaninfo.com.

338.4766180409 GBR ISSN 1749-2505
TURKEY PETROCHEMICALS REPORT. Text in English. 2005. q. EUR 820, USD 1,030 combined subscription (print & email eds.) (effective 2010). **Document type:** *Report, Trade.* **Description:** Provides industry professionals and strategists, sector analysts, trade associations and regulatory bodies with independent forecasts and competitive intelligence on the Turkish petrochemicals industry.
Related titles: E-mail ed.; Online - full text ed.
Indexed: A15, ABIn, B02, B15, B17, B18, G04, I05, P48, P51, P52, P56, PQC.
Published by: Business Monitor International Ltd., Senator House, 85 Queen Victoria St, London, EC4V 4AB, United Kingdom. TEL 44-20-72480468, FAX 44-20-72480467, subs@businessmonitor.com.

665.5 551 TUR ISSN 1300-0942
TURKISH ASSOCIATION OF PETROLEUM GEOLOGISTS. BULLETIN. Text in English. 1988. s-a. **Document type:** *Bulletin, Academic/Scholarly.* **Description:** Focuses on developments in scientific concepts and technologies of the industry, business practices of general acceptance and global business perspectives.
Indexed: MinerAb.
Published by: Turkish Association of Petroleum Geologists, Izmir Caddesi II, No. 47/14, Kizilay, Ankara, Turkey. TEL 90-312-4198642, FAX 90-312-2855566, tpjd@tpjd.org.tr, http://www.tpjd.org.tr.

340 GBR
U K OIL & GAS LAW. (United Kingdom) Variant title: Daintith U K Oil & Gas Law. Text in English. 1984. 3 base vols. plus updates 3/yr. looseleaf. GBP 1,574 base vol(s). domestic; EUR 2,079 base vol(s). in Europe; USD 2,705 base vol(s). elsewhere (effective 2011). **Document type:** *Handbook/Manual/Guide, Trade.* **Description:** Provides a complete and authoritative account of the law relating to the exploration, production, offshore pipeline transportation and the sale of domestically produced oil and gas, with particular emphasis on offshore activities.
Published by: Sweet & Maxwell Ltd. (Subsidiary of: Thomson Reuters Corp.), 100 Avenue Rd, London, NW3 3PF, United Kingdom. TEL 44-20-73937000, FAX 44-20-74491144, sweetandmaxwell.customer.services@thomson.com. Eds. Geoff Hewitt, Terence C Daintith. **Subscr. to:** PO Box 1000, Andover SP10 9AF, United Kingdom. TEL 44-20-73938051, sweetandmaxwell.international.queries@thomson.com.

665.5 USA
U S CRUDE OIL, NATURAL GAS AND NATURAL GAS LIQUIDS RESERVES (YEAR) ANNUAL REPORT (ONLINE). Text in English. a., latest 2001. stat. **Document type:** *Government.*
Media: Online - full content.
Published by: U.S. Department of Energy, Energy Information Administration, Office of Oil and Gas, 1000 Independence Ave, SW, Washington, DC 20585. TEL 202-586-8800, InfoCtr@eia.doe.gov.

U.S. DEPARTMENT OF ENERGY. ENERGY INFORMATION ADMINISTRATION. INTERNATIONAL ENERGY OUTLOOK. *see* ENERGY

665.5 USA ISSN 1934-8509
U.S. DEPARTMENT OF ENERGY. ENERGY INFORMATION ADMINISTRATION. INTERNATIONAL PETROLEUM MONTHLY (ONLINE). Text in English. m. stat. back issues avail. **Document type:** *Government.*
Supersedes: International Petroleum Statistics Report (Online)
Media: Online - full text.
Published by: U.S. Department of Energy, Energy Information Administration, 1000 Independence Ave, SW, Washington, DC 20585. TEL 202-586-8800, infoctr@eia.gov.

665.7 USA
U.S. DEPARTMENT OF ENERGY. ENERGY INFORMATION ADMINISTRATION. NATURAL GAS ANNUAL (YEAR) (ONLINE EDITION). Text in English. a. stat. back issues avail. **Document type:** *Government.*
Media: Online - full content.
Published by: U.S. Department of Energy, Energy Information Administration, Office of Oil and Gas, 1000 Independence Ave, SW, Washington, DC 20585. TEL 202-586-8800, InfoCtr@eia.doe.gov, http://www.eia.doe.gov/.

665.7 USA
U.S. DEPARTMENT OF ENERGY. ENERGY INFORMATION ADMINISTRATION. NATURAL GAS MONTHLY (ONLINE). Text in English. 19??. m. free (effective 2011). stat. back issues avail. **Document type:** *Report, Government.*
Media: Online - full text.
Published by: U.S. Department of Energy, Energy Information Administration, 1000 Independence Ave, SW, Washington, DC 20585. TEL 202-586-8800, infoctr@eia.gov.

388 USA ISSN 1936-5454
U.S. DEPARTMENT OF ENERGY. ENERGY INFORMATION ADMINISTRATION. PETROLEUM MARKETING ANNUAL (YEAR). Text in English. 19??. a. free (effective 2011). charts; stat. back issues avail. **Document type:** *Report, Government.* **Description:** Reports U.S. petroleum marketing, crude oil and petroleum product prices and volumes data.
Media: Online - full text.
Indexed: EnvAb.
Published by: U.S. Department of Energy, Energy Information Administration, 1000 Independence Ave, SW, Washington, DC 20585. TEL 202-586-8800, infoctr@eia.gov.

P

665.5 USA ISSN 1936-5926
U.S. DEPARTMENT OF ENERGY. ENERGY INFORMATION ADMINISTRATION. PETROLEUM MARKETING MONTHLY (ONLINE). Text in English. 19??. m. free (effective 2011). stat. back issues avail. **Document type:** *Report, Government.*
Media: Online - full text.
Published by: U.S. Department of Energy, Energy Information Administration, 1000 Independence Ave, SW, Washington, DC 20585. TEL 202-586-8800, infoctr@eia.gov.

665.5 USA ISSN 1936-6922
U.S. DEPARTMENT OF ENERGY. ENERGY INFORMATION ADMINISTRATION. PETROLEUM SUPPLY ANNUAL (YEAR) (ONLINE). Text in English. 1981. a. (in 2 vols.). free (effective 2011). stat. back issues avail. **Document type:** *Report, Government.*
Media: Online - full text.
Published by: U.S. Department of Energy, Energy Information Administration, 1000 Independence Ave, SW, Washington, DC 20585. TEL 202-586-8800, infoctr@eia.gov.

665.5 USA ISSN 1936-6949
U.S. DEPARTMENT OF ENERGY. ENERGY INFORMATION ADMINISTRATION. PETROLEUM SUPPLY MONTHLY (ONLINE). Text in English. 1998. m. free (effective 2011). stat. back issues avail. **Document type:** *Report, Government.* **Description:** Covers supply and disposition of crude oil and petroleum products on a national and regional level.
Media: Online - full text.
Published by: U.S. Department of Energy, Energy Information Administration, 1000 Independence Ave, SW, Washington, DC 20585. TEL 202-586-8800, infoctr@eia.gov.

665.5 USA
U.S. DEPARTMENT OF ENERGY. ENERGY INFORMATION ADMINISTRATION. WEEKLY PETROLEUM STATUS REPORT (ONLINE). Text in English. w. stat. back issues avail. **Document type:** *Government.*
Media: Online - full text.
Published by: U.S. Department of Energy, Energy Information Administration, 1000 Independence Ave, SW, Washington, DC 20585. TEL 202-586-8800, infoctr@eia.gov.

665.5 USA ISSN 1089-3253
HD9563
U S OFFSHORE OIL COMPANY CONTACT LIST. Key Title: Oil Company Contact List. Text in English. 1988. a. USD 155 domestic; USD 180 foreign (effective 2000). **Document type:** *Directory, Trade.* **Description:** Lists operating personnel at 267 oil companies operating in the Gulf of Mexico.
Formerly (until 199?): Oil Company Contact List (1058-5877)
Related titles: Diskette ed.; E-mail ed.
Published by: O D S - Petrodata, 3200 Wilcrest Dr, Ste 170, Houston, TX 77042. TEL 832-463-3000, FAX 832-463-3100, general@ods-petrodata.com, http://www.ods-petrodata.com. Pub. Tom Marsh.

338.4766180409 661.804 GBR ISSN 1749-2513
UKRAINE PETROCHEMICALS REPORT. Text in English. 2005. q. EUR 820, USD 1,030 combined subscription (print & email eds.) (effective 2010). **Document type:** *Report, Trade.* **Description:** Covers independent forecasts and competitive intelligence on the Ukrainian petrochemicals industry.
Related titles: E-mail ed.; Online - full text ed.
Indexed: A15, ABIn, B02, B15, B17, B18, G04, I05, P48, P51, P52, P56, PQC.
Published by: Business Monitor International Ltd., Senator House, 85 Queen Victoria St, London, EC4V 4AB, United Kingdom. TEL 44-20-72480468, FAX 44-20-72480467, subs@businessmonitor.com.

665.7 USA ISSN 1938-2596
UNCONVENTIONAL NATURAL GAS REPORT. Text in English. 2001. m. **Document type:** *Newsletter, Trade.* **Description:** Contains the latest information, data and resources on the unconventional natural gas industry.
Formerly (until 2007): Coalbed Natural Gas Report (1551-6628)
Media: Online - full content.
Published by: Hart Energy Publishing, LP (Subsidiary of: Chemical Week Associates), 1616 S Voss Rd, Ste 1000, Houston, TX 77057. TEL 713-993-9320, 800-874-2544, FAX 713-840-1449, hartinfo@chemweek.com, http://www.hartenergy.com.

665.54 USA ISSN 1092-8634
TJ930
UNDERGROUND CONSTRUCTION. Text in English. 1945. m. free to qualified personnel (effective 2011). adv. bk.rev. tr.lit. back issues avail. **Document type:** *Magazine, Trade.* **Description:** Covers all aspects of underground systems construction as applied to pipelines and distribution systems: water, gas, cable, sewers, and storm drains. Also covers pipeline reconstruction.
Former titles (until 1997): Pipeline and Utilities Construction (0896-1069); (until 1985): Pipeline and Underground Utilities Construction (0032-0196)
Related titles: Online - full text ed.
Indexed: A09, A10, A28, A32, APA, B01, B02, B06, B07, B08, B09, B17, B18, BrCerAb, C&ISA, C12, CA/WCA, CIA, CerAb, CivEngAb, CorrAb, E&CAJ, E11, E14, EEA, EMA, ESPM, EnvEAb, F&EA, G04, G06, G07, G08, GeotechAb, H15, I05, M&TEA, M01, M02, M05, M06, M09, MBF, METADEX, P34, PetrolAb, S22, SRI, SolStAb, T02, T04, V02, V03, V04, WAA.
—IE, Infotrieve, Linda Hall, PADDS. **CCC.**
Published by: Oildom Publishing Co. of Texas, Inc., PO Box 941669, Houston, TX 77094. TEL 281-558-6930, http://www.oildompublishing.com. Ed. Robert Carpenter TEL 281-558-6930 ext 220. Pub. Oliver Klinger TEL 281-558-6930 ext 212. Adv. contact Rhonda Brown TEL 866-879-9144 ext 194. Circ: 38,000.

UNDERGROUND FOCUS; the magazine of below-ground damage prevention. *see* BUILDING AND CONSTRUCTION

665.5 USA
UNDERGROUND INJECTION CONTROL WELL INVENTORY. Text in English. 19??. m. USD 94 (effective 2011). **Document type:** *Report, Government.* **Description:** Lists all wells tacked by the Underground Injection Control Department; shows field name, well number, lease and ID number, status code, and control numbers.
Published by: Railroad Commission, Oil and Gas Division, PO Box 12967, Austin, TX 78711. TEL 877-228-5740, publicassist@rrc.state.tx.us.

338.4766180409 GBR ISSN 1749-2521
UNITED ARAB EMIRATES PETROCHEMICALS REPORT. Text in English. 2005. q. EUR 820, USD 1,030 combined subscription (print & email eds.) (effective 2010). **Document type:** *Report, Trade.* **Description:** Features independent forecasts and competitive intelligence on the UAE petrochemicals industry.
Related titles: E-mail ed.; Online - full text ed.
Indexed: A15, ABIn, B02, B15, B17, B18, G04, I05, P48, P51, P52, P56, PQC.
Published by: Business Monitor International Ltd., Senator House, 85 Queen Victoria St, London, EC4V 4AB, United Kingdom. TEL 44-20-72480468, FAX 44-20-72480467, subs@businessmonitor.com.

338.4766180409 GBR ISSN 1749-253X
UNITED KINGDOM PETROCHEMICALS REPORT. Text in English. 2005. q. EUR 820, USD 1,030 combined subscription (print & email eds.) (effective 2010). **Document type:** *Report, Trade.* **Description:** Features independent forecasts and competitive intelligence on the petrochemicals industry in UK.
Related titles: E-mail ed.; Online - full text ed.
Indexed: A15, ABIn, B02, B15, B17, B18, G04, I05, P48, P51, P52, P56, PQC.
Published by: Business Monitor International Ltd., Senator House, 85 Queen Victoria St, London, EC4V 4AB, United Kingdom. TEL 44-20-72480468, FAX 44-20-72480467, subs@businessmonitor.com.

338.4766180409 GBR ISSN 1749-2548
UNITED STATES PETROCHEMICALS REPORT. Text in English. 2005. q. EUR 820, USD 1,030 combined subscription (print & email eds.) (effective 2010). **Document type:** *Report, Trade.* **Description:** Covers independent forecasts and competitive intelligence on the petrochemicals industry in the US.
Related titles: E-mail ed.; Online - full text ed.
Indexed: B01.
Published by: Business Monitor International Ltd., Senator House, 85 Queen Victoria St, London, EC4V 4AB, United Kingdom. TEL 44-20-72480468, FAX 44-20-72480467, subs@businessmonitor.com.

UNIVERSITATEA PETROL - GAZE DIN PLOIESTI. SERIA STIINTE ECONOMICE. BULETINUL/PETROLEUM-GAS UNIVERSITY OF PLOIESTI BULLETIN, ECONOMIC SCIENCES SERIES. *see* BUSINESS AND ECONOMICS—Management

665.5 HUN ISSN 1417-5401
UNIVERSITY OF MISKOLC. PUBLICATIONS. SERIES A, MINING. PETROLEUM AND NATURAL GAS. Alternating issues in English, German, Hungarian. irreg.
Supersedes in part (in 1995): University of Miskolc. Publications. Series A, Mining (1219-008X); Which was formerly (until 1994): Technical University for Heavy Industry. Publications. Series A, Mining (0324-4628); Which superseded in part (in 1976): Nehezipari Muszaki Egyetem Idegennyelvu Kozlemenyei (0369-4852); Which was formerly (until 1960): Soproni Muszaki Egyetemi Karok Banyamernoki es Foldmernoki Karok Kozlemenyei (0371-1099); (until 1955): Banya- es Kohomernoki Osztaly Kozlemenyei (0367-6412); (until 1934): Soproni M Kir. Banyamernoki es Erdomernoki Foiskola Banyaszati es Kohaszati Osztalyanak Kozlemenyei (0324-4474)
Published by: Miskolci Egyetem/University of Miskolc, Miskolc, 3515, Hungary. TEL 36-46-565111, http://www.uni-miskolc.hu.

665.5 338.47665 NOR ISSN 0807-6472
UPSTREAM (OSLO); the essential reading for oil and gas professionals worldwide. Text in English. 1996. w. NOK 6,340, EUR 790, USD 830 combined subscription print & online (effective 2006). adv. **Document type:** *Newspaper, Trade.*
Related titles: Online - full text ed.: 1996.
—CCC.
Published by: Norges Handels og Sjoefartstidende/N H S T Media Group, Grev Wedels Plass 9, PO Box 1182, Sentrum, Oslo, 0107, Norway. TEL 47-22-001200, FAX 47-22-001210, http://www.nhst.no. Ed. Erik Means. adv.: B&W page USD 7,300, color page USD 11,163; 246 x 365. Circ: 5,692.

665.5 USA ISSN 2159-3035
UPSTREAM PUMPING SOLUTIONS; pumping and related technology for oil and gas. Text in English. 200?. q. USD 48 domestic; USD 125 foreign; free to qualified personnel (effective 2011). adv. back issues avail. **Document type:** *Magazine, Trade.* **Description:** Offers drilling contractors and completion professionals the practical, hands-on knowledge that readers in the oil and gas industry expect from pumps and systems.
Published by: Cahaba Media Group, 1900 28th Ave S, Ste 110, Birmingham, AL 35209. TEL 205-212-9402, 800-765-4603, FAX 205-212-9452, glake@pump-zone.com, http://www.cahabamedia.com. Ed. Michelle Segrest TEL 205-314-8279. Adv. contact Davis Leavelle TEL 205-561-2602. Circ: 12,000.

338.2 USA
UTAH GEOLOGICAL SURVEY. PETROLEUM NEWS. Text in English. 19??. irreg., latest 1997. **Document type:** *Government.*
Published by: Utah Geological Survey, 1594 W N Temple, PO Box 146100, Salt Lake City, UT 84114. TEL 801-537-3300, FAX 801-537-3400, rickallis@utah.gov, http://geology.utah.gov/.

665.5 UZB
UZBEKISTON NEFT VA GAZ ZHURNAL. Text in Russian, Uzbek. 1997. q. USD 165 in United States (effective 2000).
Published by: Uzbekneftegaz, Ul T Shevchenko 2, Tashkent, 700029, Uzbekistan. TEL 56-67-27. Ed. R Yakubovich. **Dist. by:** East View Information Services, 10601 Wayzata Blvd, Minneapolis, MN 55305. TEL 952-252-1201, 800-477-1005, FAX 952-252-1202, info@eastview.com, http://www.eastview.com.

V I M P REPORT. (Victorian Initiative for Minerals and Petroleum) *see* EARTH SCIENCES—Geology

VENEZUELA. MINISTERIO DE ENERGIA Y MINAS. INFORMATIONS. *see* MINES AND MINING INDUSTRY

VENEZUELA. MINISTERIO DE ENERGIA Y MINAS. MEMORIA Y CUENTA. *see* MINES AND MINING INDUSTRY

VENEZUELA. MINISTERIO DE ENERGIA Y MINAS. QUARTERLY BULLETIN. *see* MINES AND MINING INDUSTRY

338.4766180409 GBR ISSN 1749-2556
VENEZUELA PETROCHEMICALS REPORT. Text in English. 2005. a. EUR 820, USD 1,030 combined subscription per issue (print & email eds.) (effective 2010). **Document type:** *Report, Trade.* **Description:** Covers independent forecasts and competitive intelligence on the Venezuelan petrochemicals industry.
Related titles: E-mail ed.
Indexed: A15, ABIn, B02, B15, B17, B18, G04, I05, P48, P51, P52, P56, PQC.
Published by: Business Monitor International Ltd., Senator House, 85 Queen Victoria St, London, EC4V 4AB, United Kingdom. TEL 44-20-72480468, FAX 44-20-72480467, subs@businessmonitor.com.

338.4766180409 GBR ISSN 1749-2564
VIETNAM PETROCHEMICALS REPORT. Text in English. 2005. a. EUR 820, USD 1,030 combined subscription per issue (print & email eds.) (effective 2010). **Document type:** *Report, Trade.* **Description:** Covers independent forecasts and competitive intelligence on the Vietnamese petrochemicals industry.
Related titles: E-mail ed.; Online - full text ed.
Indexed: A15, ABIn, B02, B15, B17, B18, G04, I05, P48, P51, P52, P56, PQC.
Published by: Business Monitor International Ltd., Senator House, 85 Queen Victoria St, London, EC4V 4AB, United Kingdom. TEL 44-20-72480468, FAX 44-20-72480467, subs@businessmonitor.com.

665.5 VEN ISSN 1315-0855
CODEN: VITEFR
➤ **VISION TECNOLOGICA.** Text in Spanish. 1993. s-a. free. bk.rev. **Document type:** *Academic/Scholarly.* **Description:** Informs on scientific and technological innovations acheived by the Venezuelan oil industry personnel.
Formerly (until 1993): Revista Tecnica INTEVEP (0798-1643)
Related titles: Microform ed.: (from PQC).
Indexed: APIAb, ASCA, C01, CIN, CPEI, ChemAb, ChemTitl, CurCont, EngInd, FLUIDEX, GEOBASE, GeoRef, PetrolAb, SCOPUS, SpeleolAb.
—BLDSC (9240.951000), CASDDS, IE, Ingenta, Linda Hall, PADDS.
Published by: P D V S A - Intevep S.A., Centro de Informacion Tecnica, Apartado Postal 76343, Caracas, DF 1070-A, Venezuela. TEL 58-2-9087879, FAX 58-2-9087635, benitezmwy@pdusa.com. Ed. Alfredo Morales. R&P Maritza Benitez. Circ: 2,000 (controlled).

662 USA ISSN 1942-5961
TP358
VITAL (SIOUX FALLS). Text in English. 2008. q. USD 4.95 per issue (effective 2008). **Document type:** *Magazine, Trade.* **Description:** Focuses on the future of ethanol, community profiles, industry information and environmental advancements in the ethanol producing industry.
Published by: POET LLC, 4615 N Lewis Ave, Sioux Falls, SD 57104. TEL 605-965-2200, FAX 605-965-2203.

665.5 HRV
VJESNIK I N A - NAFTAPLIN. Text in Croatian. 1974. fortn.
Published by: I N A - Naftaplin, Subiceva 29, Zagreb, 41000, Croatia. TEL 418-011. Ed. Ivo Decak. Circ: 8,000.

338.467665 665.5 USA
WASHINGTON BULLETIN. Variant title: N P R A Washington Bulletin(National Petrochemical & Refiners Association). Text in English. w. back issues avail. **Document type:** *Newsletter, Trade.* **Description:** Summarizes important federal legislative developments affecting the petrochemical manufacturing and petroleum refining industries. Offers commentaries on activities in congress, federal agencies, and the courts.
Related titles: Online - full text ed.
Published by: National Petrochemical & Refiners Association, 1667 K St, N W, Ste 700, Washington, DC 20006. TEL 202-457-0480, FAX 202-457-0486, info@npra.org, http://www.npradc.org.

665.5 351 USA
WEEKLY LEGISLATIVE UPDATE. Variant title: N P R A Legislative Update(National Petrochemical & Refiners Association). Text in English. w. back issues avail. **Document type:** *Newsletter, Trade.* **Description:** Summarizes important US federal legislative developments and issues affecting the petroleum refining and petrochemical manufacturing industries.
Related titles: Online - full text ed.
Published by: National Petrochemical & Refiners Association, 1667 K St, N W, Ste 700, Washington, DC 20006. TEL 202-457-0480, FAX 202-457-0486, info@npra.org, http://www.npradc.org.

665.74 USA ISSN 2158-7841
WEEKLY NATURAL GAS STORAGE REPORT. Text in English. 2002. w. free (effective 2011). **Document type:** *Report, Trade.*
Media: Online - full text.
Published by: U.S. Energy Information Administration, 1000 Independence Ave, SW, Washington, DC 20585. TEL 202-586-8800, InfoCtr@eia.gov, http://www.eia.doe.gov/.

665.538 658.7 GBR ISSN 0268-7844
WEEKLY PETROLEUM ARGUS; energy, investment and politics. Text in English. 1969. w. looseleaf. bk.rev. index. back issues avail. **Document type:** *Report, Trade.* **Description:** Provides analyses of the oil markets and the news and events that affect them.
Formerly (until 1985): Europ-Oil Prices
Related titles: Online - full text ed.
Indexed: B02, B15, B17, B18, G04, G06, G07, G08, I05.
—CCC.
Published by: Argus Media Ltd., Argus House, 175 St. John St, London, EC1V 4LW, United Kingdom. TEL 44-20-77804200, FAX 44-20-77804201, enquiries@argusmedia.com, http://www.argusmedia.com. Ed. Ian Bourne. Pub. Adrian Binks.

665.7 USA ISSN 0193-4724
WEEKLY PROPANE NEWSLETTER. Text in English. 1971. w. USD 205 (effective 2005). 8 p./no.; **Document type:** *Newsletter.*
Related titles: E-mail ed.: USD 195 (effective 2004); Fax ed.: USD 555 (effective 2004).
Published by: Butane - Propane News, Inc., PO Box 660698, Arcadia, CA 91006-0698. TEL 800-214-4386, FAX 626-303-2854. Ed. Pete Ottman.

665.5 350 USA
WEEKLY REGULATORY UPDATE. Variant title: N P R A Weekly Regulatory Update(National Petrochemical & Refiners Association). Text in English. w. back issues avail. **Document type:** *Newsletter, Trade.* **Description:** Summarizes important regulatory developments and issues affecting the petrochemical manufacturing and petroleum refining industries.
Related titles: Online - full text ed.
Published by: National Petrochemical & Refiners Association, 1667 K St, N W, Ste 700, Washington, DC 20006. TEL 202-457-0480, FAX 202-457-0486, info@npra.org, http://www.npradc.org.

662.338 CAN ISSN 0709-3748
WEEKLY WELL ACTIVITY REPORT. Text in English. 1980. w. CAD 85 (effective 2000). **Document type:** *Government.* **Description:** Information on field activities in Manitoba: wells licensed, drilling information and well status.
Published by: Manitoba Energy and Mines, Petroleum Branch, 360 1395 Ellice Ave, Winnipeg, MB R3G 3P2, Canada. TEL 204-945-6577, FAX 204-945-0586. Ed. P Seymour. Circ: 25.

665.5 USA ISSN 1058-0646
THE WELL SERVICE MARKET REPORT. Text in English. 1991. m. USD 250 (effective 2000). **Document type:** *Newsletter.* **Description:** Provides market intelligence for the international well service industry, including well servicing and workover contractors. Includes business news on emerging markets, financial reports on acquisitions, company performance and surveys of rates and data.
Published by: R J M Communications, PO Box 6645, Lubbock, TX 79493-6645. TEL 806-741-1531, FAX 806-741-1533. Ed. Richard Mason.

622.338 USA ISSN 0043-2393
TN860
WELL SERVICING. Text in English. 1961. bi-m. free to qualified personnel (effective 2005). adv. bk.rev. charts; stat. 100 p./no.; back issues avail. **Document type:** *Magazine, Trade.*
Indexed: PetrolAb.
—BLDSC (9294.190000), IE, Ingenta, PADDS.
Published by: (Association of Energy Service Companies), Workover-Well Servicing Publications, Inc., 10200 Richmond Ave, Ste 275, Houston, TX 77042. TEL 713-781-0758, 800-692-0771, FAX 713 781-7542, pjordan@aesc.net. Ed. Polly Fisk. Pub., Adv. contact Patty Jordan. B&W page USD 2,270, color page USD 3,280. Circ: 10,000 (controlled).

665.5029 USA
WESTERN STATES PETROLEUM INDUSTRY. Text in English. 1945. a. **Document type:** *Directory, Trade.* **Description:** Supplies company name, address, phone and fax number, personnel, division offices, offshore operations, whether producer of oil or gas and if drilling contractor with rotary or cable tools, pipeline companies, refineries, gas processing, petrochemical and equipment manufacturers and suppliers.
Former titles: Western Petroleum Industry; Directory of Producers and Drilling Contractors: California
Media: Diskette.
Published by: Midwest Publishing Company, 2230 E 49th St, Ste E, Tulsa, OK 74105. TEL 800-829-2002, info@midwestpub.com, http://www.midwestpub.com/.

553.2 333.79 AUS ISSN 0159-1878
WHO'S DRILLING. Text in English. 1979. w. AUD 1,085 (print or email ed.) (effective 2008). **Document type:** *Newsletter, Trade.*
Description: National exploration newsletter analyzing all current and pending wells, rig and vessel movements, and seismic surveys.
Related titles: E-mail ed.; Fax ed.
Published by: Pex Publications Pty. Ltd., Unit 5/1 Almondbury Rd, Mt Lawley, W.A. 6050, Australia. TEL 61-8-92726555, 800-739-855, FAX 61-8-92725556, oilinfo@pex.com.au. Ed. Mark Armstrong.

665.5 POL ISSN 1507-0042
TN871.2 CODEN: WNGIBG
➤ **WIERNTNICTWO, NAFTA, GAZ/DRILLING, OIL, GAS.** Text in English, Polish; Summaries in English, Polish. 1985-1994; resumed 1997. a. PLZ 10.50 per issue (effective 2011). illus.; abstr.; bibl. 150 p./no. 1 cols./p.; **Document type:** *Journal, Academic/Scholarly.*
Description: Presents the vast range of issues related to the prospecting, development and management of liquid minerals, hydrocarbons in particular, management of deposits, rational use of the resources and environmental protecion.
Formerly (until 1997): Akademia Gorniczo-Hutnicza im. Stanislawa Staszica. Zeszyty Naukowe. Wiertnictwo - Nafta - Gas (0860-1860)
Indexed: A28, APA, B22, BrCerAb, C&ISA, CA/WCA, CIA, CerAb, CivEngAb, CorrAb, E&CAJ, E11, EEA, EMA, GeoRef, H15, M&TEA, M09, MBF, METADEX, SolStAb, T04, WAA.
—Ingenta.
Published by: (Akademia Gorniczo-Hutnicza im. Stanislawa Staszica/ University of Mining and Metallurgy), Wydawnictwo A G H, al Mickiewicza 30, Krakow, 30059, Poland. TEL 48-12-6173228, FAX 48-12-6364038, wydagh@uci.agh.edu.pl. Ed. Stanislaw Stryczek. Circ: 200 (paid).

665.5 GBR
WORLD EXPO. Text in English. 19??. s-a. GBP 5.95 per issue domestic; EUR 8 per issue in Europe; USD 8.95 per issue in United States; free to qualified personnel (effective 2010). back issues avail. **Document type:** *Magazine, Trade.* **Description:** Provides a clear overview of the latest industry thinking regarding the key stages of exploration and production.
Related titles: Online - full text ed.
Published by: S P G Media Ltd. (Subsidiary of: Sterling Publishing Group Plc.), Brunel House, 55-57 N Wharf Rd, London, W2 1LA, United Kingdom. TEL 44-20-79159660, FAX 44-20-77242089, info@spgmedia.com, http://www.spgmedia.com/. Eds. Lucy Schwerdtfeger TEL 44-20-79159714, John Lawrence. Pub. William Crocker.

665.5 GBR ISSN 0968-2996
WORLD EXPRO. Text in English. 1992. s-a. GBP 5.95, EUR 8, USD 8.95 per issue; free to qualified personnel (effective 2010). adv. back issues avail. **Document type:** *Journal, Trade.* **Description:** Focuses on contract allocation within the oil and gas industries.
Formerly (until 1993): Expro (0965-3368)
Related titles: Online - full text ed.
Published by: S P G Media Ltd. (Subsidiary of: Sterling Publishing Group Plc.), Brunel House, 55-57 N Wharf Rd, London, W2 1LA, United Kingdom. TEL 44-20-77534200, FAX 44-20-77242089, http:// www.spgmedia.com/. Eds. Lucy Schwerdtfeger TEL 44-20-79159714, John Lawrence. Pub. William Crocker.

665.7 USA ISSN 1052-8776
HD9581.A1
WORLD GAS INTELLIGENCE. Abbreviated title: W G I. Text in English. 1990. w. USD 2,440 (effective 2009). adv. back issues avail.
Document type: *Magazine, Trade.* **Description:** Provides coverage and analysis of developments in international natural gas markets, including coverage of LNG and gas pipeline developments.
Related titles: E-mail ed.: USD 2,320 (effective 2009); Fax ed.: USD 2,145 (effective 2004); Online - full text ed.: USD 2,100 (effective 2009).
Indexed: A15, ABIn, B02, B15, B17, B18, G04, G06, G07, G08, I05, P48, P51, P52, P56, PEBNI, PQC, SCOPUS.
—IE, Infotrieve, Linda Hall. **CCC.**
Published by: Energy Intelligence Group, Inc., 5 E 37th St, 5th Fl, New York, NY 10016. TEL 212-532-1112, FAX 212-532-4479, info@energyintel.com. Ed. Sarah Miller. Pub. Edward L Morse. R&P A J Conley.

665.5 USA ISSN 1053-9859
WORLD GEOPHYSICAL NEWS. Text in English. 1984. s-m. stat.
Document type: *Newsletter, Trade.* **Description:** Offers hundreds of detailed crew location reports including: international, domestic land, marine; working and available crews, seismic and nonseismic; contractor, client, crew name, and party chief; equipment used and number of channels, etc.
Related titles: Online - full text ed.
Indexed: GeoRef, SpeleolAb.
—Linda Hall.
Published by: I H S Inc. (Subsidiary of: I H S Energy Group), 321 Inverness Dr S, Bldg D, Englewood, CO 80112. TEL 303-736-3177, customer.support@ihs.com, http://www.ihs.com.

WORLD L N G - GAS CONTRACTS. *see* LAW—International Law

WORLD NATIONAL OIL COMPANY STATUTES. *see* LAW—International Law

665 338.2 USA ISSN 0043-8790
TN860 CODEN: WOOIAS
WORLD OIL. Text in English. 1916. m. USD 149 domestic (effective 2008). adv. bk.rev. charts; illus.; tr.lit. index. Supplement avail.; back issues avail.; reprints avail. **Document type:** *Magazine, Trade.*
Description: Contains information for personnel engaged in oil and gas exploration, drilling and production. Content is tailored to furnish engineering/operating ideas and interpretations of significant trends to industry decision makers-operating management, independent producers, drilling contractors, production engineers, drilling engineers and purchasing personnel.
Former titles (until 1947): The Oil Weekly; (until 1918): Gulf Coast Oil News
Related titles: Microfilm ed.: (from PQC); Online - full text ed.; ◆ Partial Russian translation(s): Neftegazovye Tekhnologii.
Indexed: A05, A09, A10, A15, A22, A23, A24, A33, ABIn, AESIS, APIAb, APIOC, AS&TA, AS&TI, ASCA, ASFA, B01, B02, B03, B04, B06, B07, B08, B09, B13, B15, B17, B18, BPI, BRD, BusI, C&ISA, C10, C12, CA, CIN, ChemAb, CurCont, E&CAJ, E04, E05, EIA, EnerRev, EngInd, F&EA, FR, G04, G06, G07, G08, GasAb, GeoRef, I05, ISMEC, Inspec, MEA&I, P26, P34, P48, P51, P52, P54, P56, PAIS, PEBNI, PQC, PetrolAb, RefZh, S04, SCOPUS, SPPI, SolStAb, SpeleolAb, T&II, T02, V03, V04, W01, W02, W03, W05.
—BLDSC (9356.950000), CASDDS, CIS, IE, Infotrieve, Ingenta, INIST, Linda Hall, PADDS. **CCC.**
Published by: Gulf Publishing Co., PO Box 2608, Houston, TX 77252. TEL 713-529-4301, FAX 713-520-4433, publications@gulfpub.com, http://www.gulfpub.com. Pub. Ron Higgins. Adv. contact Don DePugh TEL 713-520-4435. B&W page USD 8,600, color page USD 10,950; bleed 8.125 x 10.875. Circ: 35,393.

662.338 382 GBR ISSN 0950-1029
HD9560.1
WORLD OIL TRADE; an annual analysis and statistical review of international oil movements. Text in English. 1979. a. GBP 1,122 in United Kingdom to institutions; EUR 1,425 in Europe to institutions; USD 1,960 in the Americas to institutions; USD 2,198 elsewhere to institutions (effective 2012). back issues avail.; reprint service avail. from PSC. **Document type:** *Journal, Trade.* **Description:** Presents a view of world oil trading relationships.
Related titles: Online - full text ed.: ISSN 1467-9728.
—**CCC.**
Published by: (Blackwell Energy Research), Wiley-Blackwell Publishing Ltd. (Subsidiary of: John Wiley & Sons, Inc.), 9600 Garsington Rd, Oxford, OX4 2DQ, United Kingdom. TEL 44-1865-776868, FAX 44-1865-714591, customerservices@blackwellpublishing.com. Ed. Mark Hester TEL 44-1865-476218.

665.5 340 USA
WORLD PETROLEUM ARRANGEMENTS (YEAR). Abbreviated title: W P A. Text in English. 1980. biennial (in 4 vols.). USD 1,200 base vol(s). in Asia & Australasia; USD 6,550 base vol(s). elsewhere (effective 2011). **Document type:** *Monographic series, Trade.*
Description: Features summaries of oil and gas regulations by country, as well as discussion and valuation of production-sharing contracts versus risk contracts and concessions.
Formerly: World Petroleum Exploration and Exploitation Agreements
Related titles: Online - full text ed.
Published by: Barrows Co., Inc., 116 E 66th St, Ste 1B, New York, NY 10065. TEL 800-227-7697, gbarrows@barrowscompany.net.

665.5 GBR ISSN 0084-2176
WORLD PETROLEUM CONGRESS. PROCEEDINGS. Text in English. 1933. irreg., latest vol.18. back issues avail. **Document type:** *Proceedings, Trade.*
Related titles: Online - full text ed.; Optical Disk - DVD ed.: GBP 650 per issue (effective 2009).
Indexed: GeoRef, SCOPUS.
—**CCC.**
Published by: (World Petroleum Council), Energy Institute, 61 New Cavendish St, London, W1G 7AR, United Kingdom. TEL 44-20-74677100, FAX 44-20-72551472, info@energyinst.org.uk. **Subscr. to:** Portland Customer Services, Commerce Way, Colchester CO2 8HP, United Kingdom. TEL 44-1206-796351, FAX 44-1206-799331, sales@portland-services.com, http://www.portland-services.com.

665.5 GBR ISSN 0963-5807
WORLD PETROLEUM TRENDS. Text in English. a. GBP 750. **Document type:** *Journal, Trade.*
Published by: Petroconsultants (U.K.) Ltd., Europa House, 266 Upper Richmond Rd, London, SW15 6TQ, United Kingdom. TEL 44-181-780-2500, FAX 44-181-780-2036, TELEX 94018027-PUKL-G.

665.5 338.47665 USA ISSN 1942-3543
WORLD REFINING & FUELS TODAY. Text in English. 2006. d. USD 1,995 (effective 2008). **Document type:** *Newsletter, Trade.*
Description: Provides the latest intelligence about global refining and motor fuel use.
Media: Online - full content.
Indexed: A10, B02, B15, B17, B18, CA, G04, G06, G07, G08, I05, V03.
Published by: Hart Energy Publishing, LP (Subsidiary of: Chemical Week Associates), 1749 Old Meadow Rd, Ste 301, Mc Lean, VA 22102. TEL 703-891-4800, FAX 703-891-4880, http://www.hartenergy.com.

WORLD RIG FORECAST. *see* ENERGY

665.5 551 CHN ISSN 1671-0657
WU-TAN ZHUANGBEI/EQUIPMENT FOR GEOPHYSICAL PROSPECTING. Text in Chinese. 1991. q. CNY 12.50 newsstand/ cover (effective 2006). **Document type:** *Journal, Academic/Scholarly.*
Related titles: Online - full text ed.
Address: 11 Xinxiang, Zhuozhou, 072750, China. TEL 86-312-3820148, FAX 86-312-3820175.

665 550 USA ISSN 0160-2829
QE1 CODEN: WGGCAG
WYOMING GEOLOGICAL ASSOCIATION. GUIDEBOOK. Text in English. 1946. irreg., latest 2008. USD 55 per issue (effective 2010). back issues avail. **Document type:** *Guide, Consumer.* **Description:** Publishes papers on the geology of Wyoming to disseminate knowledge of it among geologists in industry and academia.
Indexed: GeoRef, SpeleolAb.
—BLDSC (4225.435000), Linda Hall.
Published by: Wyoming Geological Association, PO Box 545, Casper, WY 82602. TEL 307-237-0027, FAX 307-234-4048, info@wyogeo.org, http://www.wyogeo.org.

665 550 USA
WYOMING GEOLOGICAL ASSOCIATION. OIL & GAS FIELDS SYMPOSIUM. Text in English. 1989. irreg., latest 2000. looseleaf. price varies. back issues avail. **Document type:** *Monographic series, Academic/Scholarly.* **Description:** Provides technical data and structural maps of existing oil and gas fields in Wyoming.
Published by: Wyoming Geological Association, PO Box 545, Casper, WY 82602. TEL 307-237-0027, FAX 307-234-4048, info@wyogeo.org, http://www.wyogeo.org.

665.5 370 CHN ISSN 1008-9071
XINJIANG SHIYOU JIAOYU XUEYUAN XUEBAO/PETROLEUM EDUCATIONAL INSTITUTE OF XINJIANG. JOURNAL. Text in Chinese. 1987. bi-m. CNY 8 newsstand/cover (effective 2006).
Document type: *Journal, Academic/Scholarly.*
Related titles: Online - full text ed.
Published by: Xinjiang Shiyou Jiaoyu Xueyuan, 6, Xibei Lu, Karamay, 834000, China. TEL 86-990-6881941.

665.5 CHN ISSN 1673-2677
XINJIANG SHIYOU TIANRANQI/XINJIANG OIL & GAS. Text in Chinese. 1989. q. USD 26 (effective 2009). **Document type:** *Journal, Academic/Scholarly.*
Formerly: Xinjiang Shiyou Xueyuan Xuebao (1009-0207)
Related titles: Online - full text ed.
—East View.
Published by: Xinjiang Shiyou Xueyuan, 189, Youhao Nan Lu, Urumqi, 830000, China. TEL 86-991-7850854.

XUEXI YU TANSUO/STUDY & EXPLORATION. *see* SOCIAL SCIENCES: COMPREHENSIVE WORKS

550 CHN ISSN 1000-6524
CODEN: YKZAEN
YANSHI KUANGWUXUE ZAZHI/ACTA PETROLOGICA ET MINERALOGICA. Text in English. 1982. bi-m. USD 133.20 (effective 2009). **Document type:** *Journal, Academic/Scholarly.*
Related titles: Online - full content ed.; Online - full text ed.
Indexed: A28, APA, B21, BrCerAb, C&ISA, CA/WCA, CIA, CerAb, CivEngAb, CorrAb, E&CAJ, E11, EEA, EMA, ESPM, EnvEAb, GeoRef, H15, M&TEA, M09, MBF, METADEX, RefZh, SolStAb, T04, WAA.
—East View, Linda Hall.
Published by: Zhongguo Dizhi Kexueyuan/Chinese Academy of Geological Sciences, 26 Baiwanzhuang Dajie, Beijing, 100037, China. TEL 86-10-68328475, FAX 86-10-68997803, http:// www.cags.cn.net/.

661.804 CHN ISSN 1671-7120
YIXI GONGYE/ETHYLENE INDUSTRY. Text in Chinese. 1989. q. CNY 10 newsstand/cover (effective 2006). **Document type:** *Journal, Academic/Scholarly.*
Related titles: Online - full text ed.
Indexed: APIAb, SCOPUS.
—BLDSC (9418.496700).
Published by: Zhongguo Shi-hua Gongcheng Jianshe Gongsi/S I N O P E C Engineering Inc., 21 An Yuan, Anhui Bei Li, Chaoyang District, Beijing, 100101, China. TEL 86-10-84876209, FAX 86-10-84878856. Ed. Tieying Fu. **Co-publisher:** Zhongguo Shi-hua Gufen Gongsi, Qingdao Anquan Gongcheng Yanjiuyuan/S I N O P E C Qingdao Safety Engineering Institute.

P

665.5 388 CHN ISSN 1000-8241
CODEN: YOCHEP
➤ **YOUQI CHUYUN/OIL & GAS STORAGE AND TRANSPORTATION.** Text in Chinese; Abstracts in Chinese, English. 1977. m. CNY 216 (effective 2011). **Document type:** *Journal, Academic/Scholarly.*
Related titles: Online - full text ed.
Indexed: SCOPUS.
Published by: (Zhongguo Shiyou Guandao Gongsi), Youqi Chuyun Zazhishe, 51 Jinguang Rd., Langfang City, Hebei Province 065000, China. TEL 86-316-2170733, FAX 86-316-2170733. Ed. Zu-pei Yang.

665.5 551 CHN ISSN 1009-9603
YOUQI DIZHI YU CAISHOULU/PETROLEUM GEOLOGY AND RECOVERY EFFICIENCY. Text in Chinese. 1994. bi-m. USD 31.20 (effective 2009). **Document type:** *Journal, Academic/Scholarly.*
Formerly (until 2000): Youqi Caishoulu Jishu/Oil & Gas Recovery Technology (1007-2152)
Related titles: Online - full text ed.
Indexed: PetrolAb.
—East View, PADDS.
Address: 3, Liaocheng Lu, Dongying, 257015, China. TEL 86-546-8715240, FAX 86-546-8715261.

665.5 CHN ISSN 1004-4388
YOUQIJING CESHI/WELL TESTING. Text in Chinese. 1984. bi-m. USD 40.20 (effective 2009). **Document type:** *Journal, Academic/Scholarly.*
Related titles: Online - full text ed.
Indexed: EngInd, PetrolAb, RefZh, SCOPUS.
—East View, PADDS.
Published by: Huabei Shiyou Guanliju/Huabei Oil Administration Bureau, Wangzhuang 43 Xinxiang, Langfang, 065007, China. TEL 86-371-2551432.

662.338 CHN ISSN 1006-6896
YOUQITIAN DIMIAN GONGCHENG/OIL - GASFIELD SURFACE ENGINEERING. Text in Chinese. 1978. m. USD 120 (effective 2006). **Document type:** *Journal, Academic/Scholarly.*
Formerly (until 1995): Youtian Dimian Gongcheng/Oilfield Surface Engineering (1001-697X)
Related titles: Online - full text ed.
—BLDSC (6252.025500).
Published by: (Daqing Youtian Gongcheng Youxian Gongsi/Daqing Oilfield Engineering Co. Ltd. (DOE)), Youqitian Dimian Gongcheng Zazhishe, Rang-qu, 88, Xikang Lu, Daqing, 163712, China. TEL 86-459-6883159, FAX 86-459-5902347. **Co-sponsors:** Zhongguo Shiyou Tianranqi Jituan Gongsi/China National Petroleum Corp.; Daqing Youtian Youxian Zeren Gongsi/PetroChina Daqing Oilfield Co. Ltd.

YOUQITIAN HUANJING BAOHU/ENVIRONMENT PROTECTION OF OIL AND GAS FIELDS. *see* ENVIRONMENTAL STUDIES

622.18282 CHN ISSN 1000-4092
TN871
YOUTIAN HUAXUE/OILFIELD CHEMISTRY. Text in Chinese. 1983. q. USD 26 (effective 2009). **Document type:** *Journal, Academic/ Scholarly.* **Description:** Covers domestic oil & gas research, technology, chemistry, analysis, market and personnel.
Related titles: Online - full content ed.; Online - full text ed.
Indexed: APIAb, PetrolAb, SCOPUS.
—East View, Linda Hall, PADDS.
Published by: Gaofenzi Yanjiusuo, Chengdu Lianhe Daxue, Chengdu, 610065, China. TEL 86-28-85405414, FAX 86-28-85402465, ofchemythx@sina.com.cn.

YUKON OIL AND GAS, A NORTHERN INVESTMENT OPPORTUNITY. *see* BUSINESS AND ECONOMICS—Investments

665.5 RUS
ZASHCHITA OKRUZHAYUSHCHEI SREDY V NEFTEGAZOVOM KOMPLEKSE; nauchno-tekhnicheskii zhurnal. Text in Russian. 1993. m. **Document type:** *Journal.*
Indexed: C&ISA, CorrAb, E&CAJ, PetrolAb, SolStAb, WAA.

Published by: Vserossiiskii Nauchno-Issledovatel'skii Institut Organizatsii Upravleniya i Ekonomiki Neftegazovoi Promyshlennosti (VNIIOENG), Nametkina 14, korp B, Moscow, 117420, Russian Federation. TEL 7-095-3320022, FAX 7-095-3316877, vniioeng@mcn.ru, http://vniioeng.mcn.ru. Ed. F M Sharifullin.

665.5 USA ISSN 2158-3110
ZEUS GAS MONETIZATION REPORT. Text in English. 1997. m. USD 647; USD 946 combined subscription (print & online eds.) (effective 2010). adv. **Document type:** *Report, Trade.* **Description:** Covers gas development and stranded gas monetization within the world's most significant producing basins and export hubs.
Former titles (until 2008): Gas Leads for Suppliers of Products and Services to the World Gas Community (1930-0646); (until 2006): Remote Gas Strategies (1096-5424)
Related titles: Online - full text ed.: USD 597 (effective 2010).
—CCC.
Published by: Zeus Development Corporation, 2424 Wilcrest, Ste 100, Houston, TX 77042. TEL 713-952-9500, 888-478-3282, FAX 713-952-9526, consulting@zeuslibrary.com, http://www.zeuslibrary.com.

665.7 USA ISSN 1944-5881
ZEUS LIQUEFIED NATURAL GAS REPORT. Variant title: Zeus L N G Report. Text in English. 1990. s-m. USD 1,047 (effective 2011). back issues avail. **Document type:** *Report, Trade.* **Description:** Covers emerging trends in world liquefied natural gas markets.
Formerly (until 200?): L N G Express (1071-1198)
Related titles: Online - full text ed.: ISSN 2161-6523. USD 997 (effective 2011).
—CCC.
Published by: Zeus Development Corporation, 2424 Wilcrest, Ste 100, Houston, TX 77042. TEL 713-952-9500, 888-478-3282, FAX 713-952-9526, consulting@zeuslibrary.com.

665.5 CHN ISSN 1673-1506
ZHONGGUO HAISHANG YOUQI/CHINA OFFSHORE OIL AND GAS. Text in Chinese. 2004. bi-m. USD 31.20 (effective 2009). **Document type:** *Journal, Academic/Scholarly.*
Formed by the merger of (1989-2004): Zhongguo Haishang Youqi. Dizhi (1001-9308); (1989-2004): Zhongguo Haishang Youqi. Gongcheng (1001-7682)
Related titles: Online - full text ed.
—BLDSC (9512.735380), East View.
Published by: Zhongguo Haiyang Shiyou Zonggongsi/China National Offshore Oil Corp., No.25 Chaoyangmenbei Dajie, Dongcheng District, Beijing, 100010, China. TEL 86-10-84522635, FAX 86-10-64663695.

665.5 CHN ISSN 1001-4500
CODEN: ZHPNE2
➤ **ZHONGGUO HAIYANG PINGTAI/CHINA OFFSHORE PLATFORM.** Text in Chinese. 1986. bi-m. CNY 32, USD 25 (effective 2000 - 2001). adv. **Document type:** *Academic/Scholarly.* **Description:** Encompasses the aspects of technology, economy and management of offshore engineering. Backed up by 65 organizations of different sectors such as offshore oil and gas, communication, machine-building, geology and mine, the Navy, customs houses, high institutions and ship building.
Related titles: Online - full text ed.
Published by: (China National Offshore Oil Corporation), China Shipbuilding Industry, Shipbuilding Technology Research Institute, 851 Zhongshan Nan 2 Lu, PO Box 032 201, Shanghai, 200032, China. TEL 86-21-6439-9626, FAX 86-21-6439-0908. Ed. Xueguang Xu. Pub. Bin Hu. R&P Dixing Song. Adv. contact Zuyu Chen. Circ: 1,500 (paid).

665.5 CHN
ZHONGGUO HAIYANG SHIYOU BAO/CHINA OFFSHORE OIL PRESS. Text in Chinese. w. adv. **Document type:** *Newspaper, Trade.* **Description:** Covers the latest developments in China's offshore petroleum exploration, offshore engineering and environmental protection as well as relevant market news.
Published by: (Zhongguo Haiyang Shiyou Zonggongsi/China National Offshore Oil Corp.), Zhongguo Haiyang Shiyou Baoshe, Jingxin Dasha, Jia-2 Dongsanhuan Beilu, Chaoyang-qu, Beijing, 100027, China. TEL 86-10-4634690, FAX 86-10-4634690. **Dist. overseas by:** China International Book Trading Corp, 35 Chegongzhuang Xilu, Haidian District, PO Box 399, Beijing 100044, China.

ZHONGGUO LIANGYOU XUEBAO/CHINESE CEREALS AND OILS ASSOCIATION. JOURNAL. *see* AGRICULTURE—Feed, Flour And Grain

665.5 CHN
ZHONGGUO SHIYOU BAO/CHINESE PETROLEUM GAZETTE. Text in Chinese. d. (Mon.-Fri.). CNY 198 (effective 2004). **Document type:** *Newspaper, Trade.*
Published by: Zhongguo Shiyou Baoshe, 6, Liupukang Jie, Xicheng-qu, Zhongguo Shiyou Jietuan 323-shi, Beijing, 100724, China. TEL 86-10-62095052. **Dist. by:** China International Book Trading Corp, 35 Chegongzhuang Xilu, Haidian District, PO Box 399, Beijing 100044, China. TEL 86-10-68412045, FAX 86-10-68412023, cibtc@mail.cibtc.com.cn, http://www.cibtc.com.cn.

665.6 500 CHN ISSN 1673-5005
TN860 CODEN: SDXZE7
ZHONGGUO SHIYOU DAXUE XUEBAO (ZIRAN KEXUE BAN)/CHINA UNIVERSITY OF PETROLEUM. JOURNAL (NATURAL SCIENCE EDITION). Text in Chinese; Abstracts in English; Index in English. 1959. bi-m. USD 31.20 (effective 2009). abstr. **Document type:** *Journal, Academic/Scholarly.* **Description:** Includes petroleum-gas geology and exploration, petroleum-gas drilling and production engineering, mechanical engineering, petroleum refining and petrochemical engineering, computer sciences and application, electronics, environmental studies, chemistry, mathematics, physics, etc.
Former titles (until 2005): Shiyou Daxue Xuebao (Ziran Kexue Ban) (1000-5870); (until 1988): Huadong Shiyou Xueyuan Xuebao (1000-2316); (until 1977): Beijing Shiyou Xueyuan Xuebao
Related titles: Online - full text ed.
Indexed: A22, A28, APA, APIAb, BrCerAb, C&ISA, CA/WCA, CIA, CPEI, CerAb, ChemAb, ChemTitl, CivEngAb, CorrAb, E&CAJ, E11, EEA, EMA, ESPM, EnvEAb, GeoRef, H15, M&TEA, M09, MBF, METADEX, PetrolAb, RefZh, SCOPUS, SolStAb, SpeleolAb, T04, WAA.
—BLDSC (9512.799030), CASDDS, East View, IE, Ingenta, Linda Hall, PADDS.

Published by: Zhongguo Shiyou Daxue/China University of Petroleum, 271, Bei Er Lu, Dongying, Shandong 257061, China. TEL 86-546-8392495, FAX 86-546-8393341. Circ: 1,500 (controlled).

661.804 CHN ISSN 1008-1852
HD9579.C33
ZHONGGUO SHIYOU HE HUAGONG/CHINA PETROLEUM AND CHEMICAL INDUSTRY. Text in Chinese. 1994. m. USD 74.40 (effective 2009). **Document type:** *Journal, Academic/Scholarly.*
Formerly (until 1998): Zhongguo Huagong/China Chemical Industry (1005-4936)
Related titles: Online - full text ed.
—East View.
Address: 16 Bldg., Yayuncun Siqu,, Chaoyang-qu, Beijing, 100723, China. TEL 86-10-64952984, FAX 86-10-64963160, http://www.chinashh.com/. Ed. Kang Jiwu. **Dist. overseas by:** China International Book Trading Corp, 35 Chegongzhuang Xilu, Haidian District, PO Box 399, Beijing 100044, China.

665.5 CHN ISSN 1672-7703
ZHONGGUO SHIYOU KANTAN/CHINA PETROLEUM EXPLORATION. Text in Chinese. 2004. bi-m. CNY 20 newsstand/cover (effective 2006). **Document type:** *Journal, Academic/Scholarly.*
Related titles: Online - full text ed.
Indexed: GeoRef, PetrolAb.
—PADDS.
Published by: Shiyou Gongye Chubanshe/Petroleum Industry Press, Anhuali Er-qu, #1 Bldg., Beijing, 100011, China. http://www.petropub.com.cn/.

ZHONGGUO YOULIAO ZUOWU XUEBAO/CHINESE JOURNAL OF OIL CROP SCIENCES. *see* AGRICULTURE—Crop Production And Soil

665.5 CHN ISSN 1006-768X
ZUANCAI GONGYI/DRILLING AND PRODUCTION TECHNOLOGY. Text in Chinese. 1978 (Jul). bi-m. USD 40.20 (effective 2009). back issues avail. **Document type:** *Journal, Academic/Scholarly.*
Related titles: Online - full text ed.
Indexed: PetrolAb, SCOPUS.
—BLDSC (3627.000500), East View, IE, Ingenta, PADDS.
Published by: (Sichuan Sheng Shiyou Xuehui Zuancai Gongyi Ji Shebei Zhuanye Weiyuanhui), Zuancai Gongyi, Zhongshan Dadao Nan 2-Duan, Guanghan, 618300, China. **Co-sponsor:** Sichuan Shiyou Guanliju Zuancai Gongyi Yanjiusuo.

662.6 CHN ISSN 1001-5620
TN871.27
ZUANJING YE YU WANJING YE/DRILLING FLUID & COMPLETION FLUID. Text in Chinese. 1983. bi-m. USD 39 (effective 2009). adv. **Document type:** *Academic/Scholarly.* **Description:** Covers drilling fluid, well completion fluid and workover fluid.
Indexed: APIAb, ESPM, FLUIDEX, PetrolAb, SCOPUS, SWRA.
—BLDSC (3627.017000), PADDS.
Published by: North China Petroleum Administration, Drilling Technology Research Institute, P.O. Box 19, Renqiu, Hebei 062550, China. TEL 86-3426-72548, FAX 86-3426-724527. Ed. Zhang Xiaoyuan. Adv. contact Zhang Wanlong. Circ: 3,600.

PETROLEUM AND GAS—Abstracting, Bibliographies, Statistics

622 338.2 CAN
ALBERTA DRILLING PROGRESS WEEKLY REPORT. Text in English. 1950. w. CAD 325. **Description:** Summary of drilling activity in the province of Alberta.
Former titles: Alberta Drilling Progress and Pipeline Receipts. Weekly Report (0227-3357); Weekly Production and Drilling Statistics (0032-9827)
—CCC.
Published by: Energy and Utilities Board, 640 5th Ave, S W, Calgary, AB T2P 3G4, Canada. TEL 403-297-8311, FAX 403-297-7040.

665.5 338.2 USA
AMERICAN PETROLEUM INSTITUTE. DIVISION OF STATISTICS. WEEKLY STATISTICAL BULLETIN. Variant title: American Petroleum Institute. Weekly Statistical Bulletin and Monthly Statistical Report. Text in English. 1985. w. USD 250 (print or online ed.) (effective 2009). charts; stat. Supplement avail.; back issues avail. **Document type:** *Bulletin, Trade.* **Description:** Provides information for producers, users, traders, and analysts of petroleum. Reports total US and regional data relating to refinery operations and the production of the five major petroleum products: leaded and unleaded motor gasoline, naphtha and kerosene jet fuel, distilled and residual fuel oil.
Formerly: American Petroleum Institute. Division of Statistics and Economics. Weekly Statistical Bulletin (0003-0457)
Related titles: Microfiche ed.: (from CIS); Online - full text ed.
Indexed: SRI.
—CCC.
Published by: American Petroleum Institute, Publications Section, 1220 L St, NW, Washington, DC 20005. TEL 202-682-8000, FAX 202-682-8408, apidata@api.org, http://www.api.org. Circ: 2,500.

665.5 USA
AMERICAN PETROLEUM INSTITUTE. MONTHLY COMPLETION REPORT. Text in English. 1970. m. **Document type:** *Report, Trade.* **Description:** Provides data on the cumulative number of completions and related footage drilled, by month, for two prior years.
Former titles: Monthly Drilling Completion Report; Monthly Report on Drilling Activity in the U.S.
Related titles: Fax ed.; Online - full text ed.
Indexed: SRI.
Published by: American Petroleum Institute, Publications Section, 1220 L St, NW, Washington, DC 20005. TEL 202-682-8000, FAX 202-682-8408, http://www.api.org. Ed. Hazim Arafa. Circ: 500.

310 USA
AMERICAN PETROLEUM INSTITUTE. MONTHLY STATISTICAL REPORT. Abbreviated title: A P I Monthly Statistical Report. Text in English. 1977. m. looseleaf. USD 2,890 to non-members; USD 1,810 to members (effective 2008). charts; stat. back issues avail. **Document type:** *Report, Trade.* **Description:** Contains timely interpretation and analysis of recent developments for major products, production, imports, refinery operations and inventories.
Related titles: Fax ed.; Microfiche ed.: (from CIS).
Indexed: SRI.

Published by: American Petroleum Institute, Publications Section, 1220 L St, NW, Washington, DC 20005. TEL 202-682-8000, FAX 202-682-8408, apidata@api.org, http://www.api.org.

665.5 338.2 USA ISSN 0004-1874
ARKANSAS OIL AND GAS STATISTICAL BULLETIN. Text in English. 1942. m. looseleaf. free. **Document type:** *Government.*
Related titles: Microfiche ed.: (from CIS).
Indexed: SRI.
Published by: Oil and Gas Commission, PO Box 1472, El Dorado, AR 71731-1472. TEL 870-862-4965, FAX 870-862-8823. Circ: 350 (controlled).

662.338 CAN
B C WELL TAPE. Text in English. m. CAD 1,500. **Document type:** *Government.* **Description:** Lists every oil and gas well in BC and all drilling and analysis on these wells, such as cores, distance, and formation taps.
Media: Magnetic Tape.
Published by: British Columbia, Ministry of Energy and Mines, c/o Communications Coordinator, Stn Prov Govt, PO Box 9324, Victoria, BC V8W 9N3, Canada. TEL 250-952-0525, http://www.ogc.gov.bc.ca. **Subscr. to:** Crown Publications Inc., 521 Fort St, Victoria, BC BC V8W 1E7, Canada. TEL 250-386-4636, FAX 250-386-0221, crown@pinc.com, http://www.crownpub.bc.ca.

665.5 310 DEU ISSN 0341-8103
B G W GASSTATISTIK. Text in German. 1879. a. adv. **Document type:** *Journal, Trade.*
Former titles (until 1964): Gasstatistik fuer die Bundesrepublik Deutschland und Berlin, West; (until 1954): Zusammenstellung der Statistischen Angaben der Gasversorgungsunternehmen in der Bundesrepublik Deutschland und in Westberlin; (until 1936): Zusammenstellung der Betriebsergebnisse von Gaswerksverwaltungen; (until 1930): Statistische Zusammenstellung der Betriebsergebnisse von Gaswerksverwaltungen
Published by: Bundesverband der Energie- und Wasserwirtschaft, Reinhardtstr 32, Berlin, 10117, Germany. TEL 49-30-3001990, FAX 49-30-3001993900, info@bdew.de, http://www.bgw.de. Circ: (controlled).

338.2 GBR ISSN 1475-858X
HD9560.4
B P STATISTICAL REVIEW OF WORLD ENERGY (YEAR). (British Petroleum Statistical Review of World Energy) Text in English. 19??. a. free (effective 2009). back issues avail. **Document type:** *Journal, Trade.* **Description:** Consists of a compendium of energy statistics covering the previous 10 years.
Former titles (until 2001): B P Amoco Statistical Review of World Energy (1467-5692); (until 1999): B P Statistical Review of World Energy (0263-9815); (until 1982): Statistical Review of the World Oil Industry (0081-5039)
Related titles: Online - full text ed.
—BLDSC (2265.510000).
Published by: B P plc., 1 St James's Sq, London, SW1Y 4PD, United Kingdom. TEL 44-20-74964000, FAX 44-20-74964630, careline@bp.com. **Dist. in U.S. by:** BP America Inc.

665.5 USA ISSN 0730-5621
HD9564
BASIC PETROLEUM DATA BOOK. Text in English. 1974. 2/yr. USD 1,430 to non-members; USD 286 to members (effective 2008). back issues avail. **Document type:** *Handbook/Manual/Guide, Trade.* **Description:** Contains historical data on worldwide oil and natural gas reserves, exploration and drilling, production, refining, transportation, historical prices, product demand, imports, exports and environmental information.
Supersedes: Petroleum Facts and Figures; Incorporates: American Petroleum Institute. Division of Statistics and Economics. Annual Statistical Review (0569-6852)
Related titles: Microfiche ed.: (from CIS); Online - full text ed.: USD 5,295 to non-members; USD 2,720 to members (effective 2008).
Indexed: SRI.
—CCC.
Published by: American Petroleum Institute, Publications Section, 1220 L St, NW, Washington, DC 20005. TEL 202-682-8000, FAX 202-682-8408, apidata@api.org. Ed. Julie Scott.

665.5021 CAN ISSN 1912-6875
BULLETIN FLASH; produit interieur brut regional. Text in French. 2005. a. **Document type:** *Newsletter, Trade.*
Published by: Institut de la Statistique du Quebec, 200 chemin Ste Foy, Quebec, PQ G1R 5T4, Canada. TEL 418-691-2401, 800-463-4090, FAX 418-643-4129, direction@stat.gouv.qc.ca, http://www.stat.gouv.qc.ca.

665.5 UAE
AL-BUTRUL WAL-SINA'A FI ABU DHABI/PETROLEUM AND INDUSTRY IN ABU DHABI. Text in Arabic. 1970. a. per issue exchange basis. **Description:** Statistical review of petroleum and industrial activity in Abu Dhabi.
Published by: Ministry of Petroleum and Mineral Wealth, P O Box 59, Abu Dhabi, United Arab Emirates. TEL 651810, FAX 663414. Circ: 1,000.

665 USA ISSN 0749-730X
CODEN: CADMEB
C A SELECTS. DRILLING MUDS. Text in English. fortn. USD 385 to non-members; USD 115 to members; USD 575 combined subscription to individuals (print & online eds.) (effective 2011). **Document type:** *Abstract/Index.* **Description:** Covers formulation, properties, and performance of aqueous suspensions used in drilling of oil and gas wells.
Related titles: Online - full text ed.: USD 380 to non-members; USD 114 to members (effective 2011).
Published by: Chemical Abstracts Service (Subsidiary of: American Chemical Society), 2540 Olentangy River Rd, Columbus, OH 43210-0012. TEL 614-447-3600, FAX 614-447-3713, help@cas.com, http://caselects.cas.org. **Subscr. to:** PO Box 3012, Columbus, OH 43210. TEL 800-753-4227, FAX 614-447-3751.

C A SELECTS. FUEL & LUBRICANT ADDITIVES. *see* CHEMISTRY—Abstracting, Bibliographies, Statistics

665.7 CAN ISSN 1481-4218
CA1BS26C213
CANADA. STATISTICS CANADA. OIL AND GAS EXTRACTION. Text in English, French. 1926. a. CAD 29 domestic; USD 29 foreign (effective 1999). **Document type:** *Government.* **Description:** Presents data on the number of establishments, employment, payroll, production, disposition, exports and imports.
Formerly (until 1997): Canada. Statistics Canada. Crude Petroleum and Natural Gas Industry (0068-7103)
Related titles: Microform ed.: (from MML); ◆ Online - full text ed.: Canada. Statistics Canada. Oil and Gas Extraction. ISSN 1703-4930.
Published by: (Statistics Canada, Energy Section), Statistics Canada, Operations and Integration Division (Subsidiary of: Statistics Canada/Statistique Canada), Circulation Management, 120 Parkdale Ave, Ottawa, ON K1A 0T6, Canada. TEL 800-267-6677, FAX 613-951-1584, http://www.statcan.ca.

665.721 CAN ISSN 1703-4930
CANADA. STATISTICS CANADA. OIL AND GAS EXTRACTION. Text in English. 2000. a. **Document type:** *Report, Trade.*
Media: Online - full text. **Related titles:** Microform ed.: (from MML); ◆ Print ed.: Canada. Statistics Canada. Oil and Gas Extraction. ISSN 1481-4218; French ed.: Canada. Statistics Canada. Extraction de Petrole et de Gaz. ISSN 1911-4397. 2002.
Published by: (Statistics Canada, Energy Section), Statistics Canada, Operations and Integration Division (Subsidiary of: Statistics Canada/Statistique Canada), Circulation Management, 120 Parkdale Ave, Ottawa, ON K1A 0T6, Canada. TEL 800-267-6677, FAX 613-951-1584, infostats@statcan.ca, http://www.statcan.ca.

665.54 CAN ISSN 0380-4615
CANADA. STATISTICS CANADA. OIL PIPE LINE TRANSPORT. Text in English. 1951. m. CAD 100, USD 120 domestic; USD 140 foreign. **Description:** Receipts and deliveries by source and by movement of crude oil and refined petroleum products by gathering and trunk lines, by provinces; barrel-miles, operating revenues. Includes data analysis.
Published by: Statistics Canada, Operations and Integration Division (Subsidiary of: Statistics Canada/Statistique Canada), Circulation Management, 120 Parkdale Ave, Ottawa, ON K1A 0T6, Canada. TEL 613-951-7277, 800-267-6677, FAX 613-951-1584.

665.5 CAN ISSN 0835-0175
CANADA. STATISTICS CANADA. REFINED PETROLEUM AND COAL PRODUCTS INDUSTRIES/CANADA. STATISTIQUE CANADA. INDUSTRIES DES PRODUITS RAFFINES DU PETROLE ET DU CHARBON. Text in English, French. 1980. a. CAD 40 domestic; USD 40 foreign (effective 1999). **Document type:** *Government.*
Formerly (until 1985): Canada. Statistics Canada. Refined Petroleum and Coal Products (0319-9045); Which was formed by the merger of (1960-1981): Canada. Statistics Canada. Petroleum Refineries (0068-7162); (1970-1981): Canada. Statistics Canada. Miscellaneous Petroleum and Coal Products Industries (0384-4757); Which was formerly (until 1970): Canada. Statistics Canada. Other Petroleum and Coal Products Industries (0527-6004); (until 1960): Canada. Statistics Canada. Miscellaneous Products of Petroleum and Coal Industry (0384-4765); Petroleum Refineries was formerly (until 1960): Canada. Statistics Canada. Petroleum Products Industry (0700-0200); (until 1948): Canada. Statistics Canada. Petroleum Products Industry in Canada (0824-9342)
Related titles: Microform ed.: (from MML).
Published by: Statistics Canada, Operations and Integration Division (Subsidiary of: Statistics Canada/Statistique Canada), Circulation Management, 120 Parkdale Ave, Ottawa, ON K1A 0T6, Canada. TEL 613-951-7277, 800-267-6677, FAX 613-951-1584.

EMENTARIO DA LEGISLACAO DO PETROLEO. *see* LAW—Abstracting, Bibliographies, Statistics

665.5 016 USA
ENCOMPASSLIT. (Comprises 10 weekly and monthly bulletins: Automotive; Catalysts-Zeolites; Fuel Reformulation; Health & Environment; Natural Gas; Oilfield Chemicals; Petroleum Refining & Petrochemicals; Petroleum Substitutes; Transportation & Storage; Tribiology) Text in English. 19??. base vol. plus w. updates. **Document type:** *Database, Abstract/Index.* **Description:** Contains over 870,000 abstracts of technical literature, conference proceedings and trade and scientific journals from around the world.
Formerly: A P I Lit
Media: Online - full text.
Published by: Elsevier Engineering Information, Inc. (Subsidiary of: Elsevier Science & Technology), 360 Park Ave S, New York, NY 10010. TEL 314-447-8070, 800-221-1044, FAX 212-633-3680, eicustomersupport@elsevier.com, http://www.apiencompass.org.

665.021 USA
ENERGY DETENTE; monthly fuel price-tax series update. Text in English. 1980. s-m. looseleaf. USD 500 (effective 1999). back issues avail. **Document type:** *Newsletter.* **Description:** Provides petroleum statistics for the Western and Eastern hemispheres. Includes refining network pricing series, fuel price-tax series, and national petroleum end user prices in dollars worldwide.
Published by: Tele-Drop, Inc. (Subsidiary of: Lundberg Survey, Inc.), PO Box 6002, Camarillo, CA 93011-6002. TEL 805-383-2400, FAX 805-383-2424. Ed., Pub. Trilby Lundberg.

310.021 ESP ISSN 1137-277X
ESTADISTICA DE PROSPECCION Y PRODUCCION DE HIDROCARBUROS. Text in Spanish. 1974. a. **Document type:** *Government.*
Formerly (until 1992): Prospeccion y Produccion de Hidrocarburos. Estadisticas (1137-2761)
Published by: Ministerio de Industria, Paseo Castellana, 160, Madrid, 28046, Spain. FAX 259-84-80.

016 GBR ISSN 0140-6701
TP315 CODEN: FEABDN
FUEL AND ENERGY ABSTRACTS. Text in English. 1945. 6/yr. EUR 2,479 in Europe to institutions; JPY 329,200 in Japan to institutions; USD 2,775 elsewhere to institutions (effective 2012). back issues avail.; reprints avail. **Document type:** *Abstract/Index.* **Description:** A summary of world literature on all scientific, technical, commercial and environmental aspects of fuel and energy.
Former titles (until 1978): Fuel Abstracts and Current Titles (0016-2388); (until 1960): Fuel Abstracts (0367-3308)
Related titles: Microform ed.: (from PQC); Online - full text ed.: ISSN 1873-7161 (from IngentaConnect, ScienceDirect).
Indexed: A26, A33, E14, I05.
—Infotrieve, Ingenta, Linda Hall. **CCC.**
Published by: (Institute of Energy), Elsevier Ltd (Subsidiary of: Elsevier Science & Technology), The Blvd, Langford Ln, Kidlington, Oxford, OX5 1GB, United Kingdom. TEL 44-1865-843000, FAX 44-1865-843010, journalscustomerserviceemea@elsevier.com. Eds. E M Goodger, F J L Bindon. **Subscr. to:** Elsevier BV, Radarweg 29, PO Box 211, Amsterdam 1000 AE, Netherlands. TEL 31-20-4853757, FAX 31-20-4853432, http://www.elsevier.nl.

FUEL AND ENERGY CONSUMPTION IN THE CZECH REPUBLIC (YEAR). *see* ENERGY—Abstracting, Bibliographies, Statistics

665.7 333.8 AUS ISSN 1327-4627
GAS STATISTICS AUSTRALIA. Text in English. 1979. a. free to members (effective 2008). charts; stat. back issues avail. **Document type:** *Report, Trade.* **Description:** Provides statistical information on Australian gas industry including gas consumption, prices, customers, reserves, and pipelines.
Formed by the merger of (1980 -1995): Gas Industry Statistics (0157-731X); (1992 -199?): Gas Distribution Industry Performance Indicators (1039-8112)
Indexed: AESIS.
Published by: Australian Gas Association, 2 Park Way, PO Box 122, Braeside, VIC 3195, Australia. TEL 61-3-95804500, FAX 61-3-95805500, office@aga.asn.au, http://www.gas.asn.au.

INDEX AND ABSTRACTS OF A P I HEALTH-RELATED RESEARCH (YEARS). *see* PUBLIC HEALTH AND SAFETY—Abstracting, Bibliographies, Statistics

338.27 IDN
INDONESIA OIL STATISTICS/STATISTIK PERMINYAKAN INDONESIA. Text in English. 1971. q. (plus a. cumulation).
Published by: Directorate General of Oil and Gas, Programming and Reporting Division/Direktorat Jenderal Minyak dan Gas Bumi, Gedung Plaza Centris, Jl. Rasuna Said Kav., B-5 Kuningan, Jakarta, 10110, Indonesia. TEL 62-21-30541, FAX 62-21-354987. Circ: 400.

665.5 GBR
INSTITUTE OF PETROLEUM STATISTICS SERVICE. Text in English. 1989. irreg. looseleaf. GBP 140 per issue domestic (effective 2003). stat. **Description:** Contains statistical information, plus address lists, on the oil and gas industries in the UK and the rest of the world.
Related titles: Online - full text ed.: GBP 80 (effective 2003).
Published by: Institute of Petroleum, 61 New Cavendish St, London, W1G 7AR, United Kingdom. TEL 44-20-74677100, FAX 44-20-72551472, http://www.petroleum.co.uk. R&P Chris Baker.

665.773 USA
INVENTORIES OF NATURAL GAS LIQUIDS & LIQUIFIED REFINERY GASES. Text in English. 1956. m. USD 3,632 to non-members (effective 2008). **Document type:** *Report, Trade.* **Description:** Presents data on the inventory levels of ethane, propane, isobutane, normal butane and pentanes plus.
Formerly (until 1985): Liquified Petroleum Gas Report (0024-421X)
Related titles: Online - full text ed.
Published by: American Petroleum Institute, Publications Section, 1220 L St, NW, Washington, DC 20005. TEL 202-682-8000, FAX 202-682-8408, apidata@api.org, http://www.api.org. Circ: 150.

665.5 001.433 USA
JOINT ASSOCIATION SURVEY ON DRILLING COSTS. Text in English. 1953. a. USD 12,900 to non-members; USD 10,320 to members (effective 2008). back issues avail. **Document type:** *Report, Trade.* **Description:** Contains data on the number of oil and gas wells and dry holes drilled, their accompanying footage, and their estimated drilling costs for all active drilling areas - both onshore and off - in the U. S.
Former titles (until 1975): Joint Association Survey of the U.S. Oil and Gas Producing Industry; (until 1968): Joint Association Survey of Industry Drilling Costs
Related titles: Online - full text ed.
Indexed: SRI.
Published by: American Petroleum Institute, Publications Section, 1220 L St, NW, Washington, DC 20005. TEL 202-682-8000, FAX 202-682-8408, apidata@api.org, http://www.api.org. Circ: 1,600.

665.5 LBY ISSN 0075-9260
LIBYA. CENSUS AND STATISTICS DEPARTMENT. REPORT OF THE ANNUAL SURVEY OF PETROLEUM MINING INDUSTRY. Text in Arabic, English. 1965. a. free. **Document type:** *Government.*
Published by: Lybia. Secretariat of Planning, Census and Statistics Department, P O Box 600, Tripoli, Libya.

665.5 338.2 LBY
LIBYA. CENSUS AND STATISTICS DEPARTMENT. REPORT OF THE ANNUAL SURVEY OF UNITS PROVIDING TECHNICAL SERVICES TO THE PETROLEUM MINING INDUSTRY. Text in Arabic, English. 1965. a. free. **Document type:** *Government.*
Published by: Lybia. Secretariat of Planning, Census and Statistics Department, P O Box 600, Tripoli, Libya.

665.021 USA ISSN 0195-4563
LUNDBERG LETTER. Text in English. 1974. s-m. USD 950 (effective 1999). **Document type:** *Newsletter, Trade.* **Description:** Provides statistics and analysis of U.S. oil marketing primary data. Includes in depth single-subject profile of a development in the petroleum market in each issue. Discusses such topics as retail-wholesale (dealer tankwagon, branded racks, unbranded racks) pricing, market shares, and station characteristics nationwide and regionally.
Indexed: PEBNI.
Published by: Tele-Drop, Inc. (Subsidiary of: Lundberg Survey, Inc.), PO Box 6002, Camarillo, CA 93011-6002. TEL 805-383-2400, FAX 805-383-2424. Pub., R&P Trilby Lundberg.

665.7 USA ISSN 0085-3429
TN24.M5 CODEN: MGSDA3
MICHIGAN'S OIL AND GAS FIELDS: ANNUAL STATISTICAL SUMMARY. Text in English. 1964. a. price varies.
Indexed: GeoRef, SpeleolAb.
—Linda Hall.
Published by: Department of Environmental Quality, Geological Survey Division, Information Services Center, Box 30256 7756, Lansing, MI 48909. TEL 517-334-6907.

N P R A STATISTICAL REPORT. ANNUAL SURVEY OF OCCUPATIONAL INJURIES & INJURIES. *see* OCCUPATIONAL HEALTH AND SAFETY—Abstracting, Bibliographies, Statistics

665.5 338.47665 USA
N P R A STATISTICAL REPORT. LUBRICATING OIL AND WAX CAPACITY. Text in English. a. USD 25 per issue to non-members; free to members (effective 2009). back issues avail. **Document type:** *Report, Trade.* **Description:** Presents a statistical overview of lubricating oil and wax production in the US.
Published by: National Petrochemical & Refiners Association, 1667 K St, N W, Ste 700, Washington, DC 20006. TEL 202-457-0480, FAX 202-457-0486, info@npra.org.

338.47665 665.5 USA
N P R A STATISTICAL REPORT. U S LUBRICATING OIL & WAX SALES. Text in English. a. USD 300 per issue to non-members; USD 25 per issue to members (effective 2009). back issues avail. **Document type:** *Report, Trade.* **Description:** Provides a statistical overview of sales of lubricating oils in the US.
Formerly (until 2007): N P R A Statistical Report. U S Lubricating Oil Sales
Published by: National Petrochemical & Refiners Association, 1667 K St, N W, Ste 700, Washington, DC 20006. TEL 202-457-0480, FAX 202-457-0486, info@npra.org.

665.5 338.47665 USA
➤ **N P R A STATISTICAL REPORT. U S REFINING CAPACITY.** Text in English. a. USD 25 per issue (effective 2009). back issues avail. **Document type:** *Journal, Academic/Scholarly.* **Description:** Presents a statistical overview of refining capacity in the US.
Related titles: Online - full text ed.: free (effective 2009).
Published by: National Petrochemical & Refiners Association, 1667 K St, N W, Ste 700, Washington, DC 20006. TEL 202-457-0480, FAX 202-457-0486, info@npra.org.

665.5 CAN ISSN 1481-4234
CA1BS57C205
NATURAL GAS TRANSPORTATION AND DISTRIBUTION/CANADA. STATISTIQUE CANADA. SERVICES DE GAZ. Text in English, French. 1959. a. stat. **Document type:** *Government.* **Description:** Covers receipts and disposition of natural gas by month and province, pipeline distance, balance sheet, property account, income account, employees and earnings.
Formerly (until 1996): Canada. Statistics Canada. Gas Utilities (0527-5318)
Related titles: Microform ed.: (from MML); Online - full content ed.: ISSN 1492-3025. 1998; Online - full text ed.
Indexed: A10, B07, C05, CA, E14, V03.
—CCC.
Published by: Statistics Canada, Operations and Integration Division (Subsidiary of: Statistics Canada/Statistique Canada), Circulation Management, 120 Parkdale Ave, Ottawa, ON K1A 0T6, Canada. TEL 613-951-7277, 800-267-6677, FAX 613-951-1584.

665.5 RUS
NEFTYANIK (MOSCOW, 1974). Text in Russian. 1974. m. adv.
Formerly: Inzhener - Naftyanik
Published by: Izdatel'stvo Nedra, Tverskaya Zastava pl 3, Moscow, 125047, Russian Federation. TEL 7-095-2505255, FAX 7-095-2502772. Circ: 3,000.

662.338 CAN
NEW WELL AUTHORIZATIONS. Text in English. 3/w. USD 100 (effective 1999). back issues avail. **Document type:** *Government.* **Description:** Presents relevant data on wells authorized by the Oil and Gas Commision.
Formerly: Daily List of Well Authorizations
Published by: British Columbia, Ministry of Energy and Mines, c/o Communications Coordinator, Stn Prov Govt, PO Box 9324, Victoria, BC V8W 9N3, Canada. TEL 250-952-0525, http://www.ogc.gov.bc.ca. **Subscr. to:** Crown Publications Inc. TEL 250-386-4636, FAX 250-386-0221, crown@pinc.com, http://www.crownpub.bc.ca.

338.272021 NOR ISSN 0802-0477
HA1501
NORWAY. STATISTISK SENTRALBYRAA. OLJE- OG GASSVIRKSOMHET/STATISTICS NORWAY. OIL AND GAS ACTIVITY. Text in Norwegian. 1978. q. **Document type:** *Government.* **Description:** Gives a comprehensive, detailed statistical survey of the oil and gas activity on the Norwegian continental shelf.
Formerly (until 1986): Oljevirksomhet (0333-2101)
Related titles: Online - full text ed.: ISSN 1504-2111; ◆ Series of: Norges Offisielle Statistikk. ISSN 0300-5585.
Indexed: ASFA, B21, ESPM.
Published by: Statistisk Sentralbyraa/Statistics Norway, Kongensgate 6, P O Box 8131, Dep, Oslo, 0033, Norway. TEL 47-21-090000, FAX 47-21-094973, ssb@ssb.no.

338.4 NOR ISSN 0377-1806
TN867
NORWEGIAN OFFSHORE INDEX. Text in English. 1974. a. free (effective 2003). **Document type:** *Abstract/Index.*
Related titles: Online - full content ed.
—CCC.
Published by: (Export Council of Norway), Selvig Publishing A-S, Anthon Walles Vei 36, PO Box 384, Sandvika, 1301, Norway. TEL 47-67-808026, FAX 47-67-564762, adm@seadirectory.com, http://www.seadirectory.com. Circ: (controlled). **Co-sponsor:** Federation of Norwegian Industries.

665.7021 CAN
OIL AND GAS STATISTICS REPORT. Text in English. m. CAD 35; CAD 4 per issue (effective 2005). back issues avail. **Document type:** *Government.* **Description:** Provides a statistical summary of well licensing, wells drilled, meters drilled and well count, as well as the supply and disposition sections of the Oil and Gas Production Report.
Indexed: SpeleolAb.
Published by: British Columbia, Ministry of Energy and Mines, c/o Communications Coordinator, Stn Prov Govt, PO Box 9324, Victoria, BC V8W 9N3, Canada. TEL 250-952-0525, http://www.ogc.gov.bc.ca.

338.47 USA
HD9561
OIL & NATURAL GAS PRODUCING INDUSTRY IN YOUR STATE. Text in English. 1939. a. USD 75 (effective 2000). adv. charts; illus.; stat. **Document type:** *Journal, Trade.*
Former titles: Oil and Gas Producing Industry in Your State; (until 1984): Oil Producing Industry in Your State
Related titles: ◆ Supplement to: Petroleum Independent. ISSN 0747-2528.

P

Indexed: SRI.
Published by: (Independent Petroleum Association of America), Petroleum Independent Publishers, Inc., 1101 16th St, N W, Washington, DC 20036. TEL 202-857-4774, 800-433-2851, FAX 202-857-4799. Ed. Scott Espenshade. Circ: 7,000.

665.538 USA
OIL - ENERGY STATISTICS BULLETIN; and Canadian oil reports. Text in English. 1923. bi-w. USD 185 (effective 2000). adv. **Document type:** *Newsletter.*
Published by: Oil Statistics Company, Inc., 595 Plymouth St., Whitman, MA 02382-1632. TEL 781-447-6407, FAX 781-447-3977. Ed. John J McGilvray. R&P, Adv. contact Jennifer L McGilvray.

665.5 310 FRA ISSN 1025-9988
HD9560.1
OIL, GAS, COAL & ELECTRICITY QUARTERLY STATISTICS/O C D E STATISTIQUES TRIMESTRIELLES. ELECTRICITE, CHARBON, GAZ & PETROLE. Text in English, French. 1964. q. EUR 380, USD 510, GBP 303, JPY 55,800 combined subscription (print & online eds.) (effective 2012). stat. **Document type:** *Journal, Trade.* **Description:** Provides detailed data on production of crude oil, natural gas, and gas liquids, as well as refinery feedstocks, crude oil and product trades, refinery intake and output, final consumption; stock levels and changes.
Former titles: O E C D Quarterly Oil Statistics and Energy Balances (1013-9362); Organization for Economic Cooperation and Development. Quarterly Oil and Gas Statistics (0259-5478); Organization for Economic Cooperation and Development. Quarterly Oil Statistics (0378-6536)
Related titles: Online - full text ed.: ISSN 1609-753X. EUR 290, USD 381, GBP 235, JPY 44,600 (effective 2010) (from IngentaConnect).
Indexed: A22, B01, B06, B07, B09, CA, E01, E14, GeoRef, IIS, SpeleolAb.
—IE, Infotrieve, Ingenta, PADDS. **CCC.**
Published by: Organisation for Economic Cooperation and Development (O E C D)/Organisation de Cooperation et de Developpement Economiques (O C D E), 2 Rue Andre Pascal, Paris, 75775 Cedex 16, France. TEL 33-1-45248200, FAX 33-1-45248500, http://www.oecd.org. **Subscr. UK address:** O E C D Turpin North America, PO Box 194, Downingtown, PA 19335-0194. TEL 610-524-5361, 800-456-6323, FAX 610-524-5417, bookscustomer@turpinna.com.

666.5 338.2 USA ISSN 1089-1765
HD9560.1
OIL MARKET INTELLIGENCE. Abbreviated title: O M I. Text in English. 1996. m. USD 2,200 (effective 2009). charts; illus.; stat. back issues avail. **Document type:** *Magazine, Trade.* **Description:** Provides analyses of regional pricing, production figures, and key statistics on the oil market.
Formed by the merger of (1987-1996): Petroleum Market Intelligence (1047-630X); (1990-1996): Global Oil Stocks and Balances
Related titles: Diskette ed.; E-mail ed.: USD 1,860 (effective 2009); Fax ed.; Online - full text ed.: USD 1,660 (effective 2009).
—Linda Hall. **CCC.**
Published by: Energy Intelligence Group, Inc., 5 E 37th St, 5th Fl, New York, NY 10016. TEL 212-532-1112, FAX 212-532-4479, info@energyintel.com. Ed. David Knapp. Pub. Edward L Morse. R&P A J Conley.

665.5 MEX ISSN 0186-3401
PEMEX. BOLETIN BIBLIOGRAFICO. Text in English. 1986 (vol.31). m. free. **Document type:** *Abstract/Index.* **Description:** Contains abstracts from scientific and technical journals.
Formerly: Petroleos Mexicanos. Boletin Bibliografico
Published by: (Biblioteca Central), Petroleos Mexicanos, Unidad de Servicios Sociales y Culturales, Marina Nacional 329, Edif. A, Mezzanine, Mexico City, DF 11300, Mexico. Circ: 3,000.

665.5 016 USA ISSN 2153-1471
PETROLEUM ABSTRACTS (ONLINE). Text in English. 200?. w. free (effective 2010). **Document type:** *Bulletin, Abstract/Index.* **Description:** Contains abstracts from worldwide petroleum-related literature and patents dealing with exploration and production.
Media: Online - full text.
Published by: University of Tulsa, Information Services Division, 800 S Tucker Dr HH101, Tulsa, OK 74104. TEL 918- 631-2297, 800-247-8678, FAX 918-631-2100, news@utulsa.edu, http://www.utulsa.edu/.

665.5 CAN
PETROLEUM AND NATURAL GAS PRODUCTION TAPE. Text in English. m. CAD 1,500. **Document type:** *Government.* **Description:** Lists all oil and gas wells ever drilled in BC, historical production records for all wells from 1954, amounts produced and number of days productive.
Media: Magnetic Tape.
Published by: British Columbia, Ministry of Energy and Mines, c/o Communications Coordinator, Stn Prov Govt, PO Box 9324, Victoria, BC V8W 9N3, Canada. TEL 250-952-0525, http://www.ogc.gov.bc.ca. **Subscr. to:** Crown Publications Inc., 521 Fort St, Victoria, BC BC V8W 1E7, Canada. TEL 250-386-4636, FAX 250-386-0221, crown@pinc.com, http://www.crownpub.bc.ca.

665.5021 CZE
PETROLEUM, PETROLEUM PRODUCTS AND NATURAL GAS. Text in English. m. EUR 5 per issue (effective 2008). **Document type:** *Government.* **Description:** Contains balance statistics on primary petroleum processing, source parts of petroleum products and natural gas supply to the CR market in compliance with international methodology of the IEA.
Related titles: Online - full text ed.; ◆ Czech ed.: Ropa, Ropne Produkty a Zemni Plyn; ◆ Series: Cesky Statisticky Urad. Energetika.
Published by: Cesky Statisticky Urad, Na padesatem 81, Prague 10, 10082, Czech Republic. TEL 420-2-74051111, infoservis@czso.cz.

665.5 CAN
PETROLEUM TITLES DATA TAPE. Text in English. m. CAD 4,260 domestic; CAD 4,296 foreign; CAD 380 newsstand/cover domestic; CAD 383 newsstand/cover foreign (effective 1999). **Document type:** *Government.* **Description:** Contains information on each active provincial petroleum and natural gas tenure inclusive of term, tenure holder, location, rights conveyed, continuation and renewals.
Media: Magnetic Tape.
Published by: British Columbia, Ministry of Energy and Mines, c/o Communications Coordinator, Stn Prov Govt, PO Box 9324, Victoria, BC V8W 9N3, Canada. TEL 250-952-0525, http://www.ogc.gov.bc.ca. **Subscr. to:** Crown Publications Inc.

665.7 338.39 USA
PROPANE MARKET FACTS; statistical handbook of the LP-gas industry. Text in English. 1950. a. USD 8. index. **Description:** Presents market research information about the industry on a historical basis.
Former titles: Propane Industry Profile; L P - Gas Market Facts (0075-9759)
Media: Diskette.
Indexed: SRI.
Published by: National Propane Gas Association, 1600 Eisenhower Ln, Ste 100, Lisle, IL 60532. Ed. W H Butterbaugh.

665.5 CAN
PROVINCIAL CROWN OIL AND GAS ROYALTIES - PROVINCIAL FREEHOLD OIL AND GAS PRODUCTION TAXES - DRILLING INACTIVE PROGRAM. Text in English. 1982. irreg. free. **Document type:** *Government.* **Description:** Offers general overview of petroleum royalty-tax structure and incentive programs operating in Manitoba, Canada.
Former titles (until 2001): Provincial Crown Oil Royalties - Provincial Freehold Oil Production Taxes - Drilling Incentive Program; (until 1999): Manitoba Petroleum Incentive Programs and Petroleum Royalty - Tax Information; Manitoba Petroleum Royalty and Tax Information
Published by: Manitoba Energy and Mines, Petroleum Branch, 360 1395 Ellice Ave, Winnipeg, MB R3G 3P2, Canada. TEL 204-945-6577, FAX 204-945-0586. Ed. L R Dubreuil. Circ: 400.

REFERATIVNYI ZHURNAL. GORNOE I NEFTEPROMYSLOVOE MASHINOSTROENIE; otdel'nyi vypusk. *see* MINES AND MINING INDUSTRY—Abstracting, Bibliographies, Statistics

REFERATIVNYI ZHURNAL. KHIMIYA I PERERABOTKA GORYUCHIKH ISKOPAEMYKH I PRIRODNYKH GAZOV; vypusk svodnogo toma. *see* CHEMISTRY—Abstracting, Bibliographies, Statistics

016.6655 RUS ISSN 0202-9502
REFERATIVNYI ZHURNAL. RAZRABOTKA NEFTYANYKH I GAZOVYKH MESTOROZHDENII; vypusk svodnogo toma. Text in Russian. 1960. m. USD 584.40 foreign (effective 2011). **Document type:** *Journal, Abstract/Index.*
Related titles: CD-ROM ed.; Online - full text ed.
—East View.
Published by: VINITI RAN, ul Usievicha 20, Moscow, 125190, Russian Federation. TEL 7-499-1526113, FAX 7-499-9430060, dir@viniti.ru, http://www.viniti.ru. **Dist. by:** Informnauka Ltd., Ul Usievicha 20, Moscow 125190, Russian Federation. alfimov@viniti.ru.

665.5021 CZE
ROPA, ROPNE PRODUKTY A ZEMNI PLYN. Text in Czech. m. **Document type:** *Government.*
Formerly (until 2007): Ropa a Ropne Produkty
Related titles: Online - full text ed.; ◆ English ed.: Petroleum, Petroleum Products and Natural Gas; ◆ Series: Cesky Statisticky Urad. Energetika.
Published by: Cesky Statisticky Urad, Na padesatem 81, Prague 10, 10082, Czech Republic. TEL 420-2-74051111, infoservis@czso.cz.

665.5 USA ISSN 1937-9730
HD9581.2.L57
SALES OF NATURAL GAS LIQUIDS AND LIQUIFIED REFINERY GASES (YEAR). Text in English. 19??. a. USD 270 per issue (effective 2008). back issues avail. **Document type:** *Report, Trade.* **Description:** Provides information on the annual sales to consumers, and internal company use of ethane, propane, butane and pentane plus. Data are categorized by state and by type of use: residential and commercial, industrial, and chemical.
Indexed: SRI.
Published by: American Petroleum Institute, Publications Section, 1220 L St, NW, Washington, DC 20005. TEL 202-682-8000, FAX 202-682-8408, apidata@api.org, http://www.api.org.

SPOTREBA PALIV A ENERGIE V C R V ROCE (YEAR). (Ceska Republika) *see* ENERGY—Abstracting, Bibliographies, Statistics

665.5 CAN ISSN 1488-4771
SUPPLY AND DISPOSITION OF CRUDE OIL AND NATURAL GAS. Text in English. m. CAD 100, USD 120 domestic; USD 140 foreign. **Description:** Estimates the production and disposition of crude petroleum and natural gas, by province, monthly and cumulative.
Formerly (until 1999): Canada. Statistics Canada. Crude Petroleum and Natural Gas Production (0702-6846)
Published by: Statistics Canada, Operations and Integration Division (Subsidiary of: Statistics Canada/Statistique Canada), Circulation Management, 120 Parkdale Ave, Ottawa, ON K1A 0T6, Canada. TEL 613-951-7277, 800-267-6677, FAX 613-951-1584.

665.5 USA
CODEN: TOCHF5
TECHNICAL LITERATURE ABSTRACTS: OILFIELD CHEMICALS (ONLINE). Text in English. m. **Document type:** *Bulletin, Abstract/Index.* **Description:** Covers the manufacturing and use of chemicals in the oil and gas fields for drilling, well completion and stimulation, oil production, and enhanced recovery. Covers trade magazine articles and scientific journal papers published worldwide, as well as conference papers and patents.
Media: Online - full text.
Published by: Elsevier Engineering Information, Inc. (Subsidiary of: Elsevier Science & Technology), 360 Park Ave S, New York, NY 10010. TEL 314-447-8070, 800-221-1044, FAX 212-633-3680, eicustomersupport@elsevier.com.

665.5 011 USA
CODEN: TPRPF9
TECHNICAL LITERATURE ABSTRACTS: PETROLEUM REFINING & PETROCHEMICALS (ONLINE). Text in English. w. **Document type:** *Bulletin, Abstract/Index.* **Description:** Reports on petroleum and natural gas processing and catalysts; unit operations; primary and specialty products; chemical products processing and their catalysts; plant safety, refining and other topics.
Media: Online - full text.
Published by: Elsevier Engineering Information, Inc. (Subsidiary of: Elsevier Science & Technology), 360 Park Ave S, New York, NY 10010. TEL 314-447-8070, 800-221-1044, FAX 212-633-3680, eicustomersupport@elsevier.com.

665.5 USA
CODEN: TPSUFT
TECHNICAL LITERATURE ABSTRACTS: PETROLEUM SUBSTITUTES (ONLINE). Text in English. w. **Document type:** *Bulletin, Abstract/Index.* **Description:** Reports on oil shale, tar sand, coal gasification and liquefication; other synthetic liquid and gaseous fuels, and other energy sources.
Media: Online - full text.
Published by: Elsevier Engineering Information, Inc. (Subsidiary of: Elsevier Science & Technology), 360 Park Ave S, New York, NY 10010. TEL 314-447-8070, 800-221-1044, FAX 212-633-3680, eicustomersupport@elsevier.com.

665.5 310 USA
TEXAS PETROFACTS. Text in English. 198?. m. charts; stat. back issues avail. **Document type:** *Report, Government.* **Description:** Compiles monthly and annual statistical data on energy, energy prices, and the economy. Data are summarized by month and by year for Texas and the entire U.S.
Related titles: Online - full text ed.: free (effective 2011).
Published by: Railroad Commission, Oil and Gas Division, PO Box 12967, Austin, TX 78711. TEL 877-228-5740, publicassist@rrc.state.tx.us.

665.8 338.2 USA
TRANSPORTATION ACCIDENT BRIEFS. PIPELINE. Text in English. 19??. irreg. back issues avail. **Document type:** *Report, Government.*
Related titles: Microform ed.: (from NTI); ◆ Series of: Transportation Accident Briefs.
Published by: (U.S. Department of Transportation, National Transportation Safety Board), U.S. Department of Commerce, National Technical Information Service, 5301 Shawnee Rd, Alexandria, VA 22312. TEL 703-605-6000, info@ntis.gov.

665.8 338.2 USA
TRANSPORTATION ACCIDENT REPORTS. PIPELINE. Text in English. 19??. irreg. **Document type:** *Report, Government.*
Related titles: Microform ed.: (from NTI); ◆ Series of: Transportation Accident Reports.
Published by: (U.S. Department of Transportation, National Transportation Safety Board), U.S. Department of Commerce, National Technical Information Service, 5301 Shawnee Rd, Alexandria, VA 22312. TEL 703-605-6000, info@ntis.gov, http://www.ntis.gov.

665.5 USA
U.S. DEPARTMENT OF ENERGY. NATIONAL PETROLEUM TECHNOLOGY OFFICE. PUBLICATION LIST. Text in English. biennial. free. **Document type:** *Bibliography.* **Description:** Lists D.O.E. and D.O.E.-sponsored publications on oil recovery.
Related titles: Online - full content ed.
Published by: U.S. Department of Energy, National Petroleum Technology Office, 1 W. 3rd St., Tulsa, OK 74103-3532. TEL 918-699-2017, FAX 918-699-2005, htiedema@npto.doe.gov, http://www.npto.doe.gov.

665.538 310 USA ISSN 1936-5667
U.S. FEDERAL HIGHWAY ADMINISTRATION. MONTHLY MOTOR FUEL REPORTED BY STATES (ONLINE). Text in English. 19??. free (effective 2011). back issues avail. **Document type:** *Report, Government.*
Media: Online - full text.
Published by: U.S. Federal Highway Administration (Subsidiary of: U.S. Department of Transportation), 1200 New Jersey Ave, SE, Washington, DC 20590. TEL 202-366-4000, execsecretariat.fhwa@fhwa.dot.gov.

338.2 VEN
VENEZUELA. MINISTERIO DE ENERGIA Y MINAS. PETROLEO Y OTROS DATOS ESTADISTICOS. Text in Spanish. a. **Document type:** *Government.*
Formerly: Venezuela. Ministerio de Minas e Hidrocarburos. Oficina de Economia Petrolera. Petroleo y Otros Datos Estadisticos (0083-5390)
Related titles: ◆ English ed.: Venezuelan Petroleum Industry. Statistical Data.
Indexed: SpeleolAb.
Published by: (Venezuela. Direccion de Economia de Hidrocarburos), Ministerio de Energia y Minas, Torre Oeste, Parque Central Piso 9, Caracas, DF 1010, Venezuela. Ed. Gloria Mir.

338.2 VEN
VENEZUELAN PETROLEUM INDUSTRY. STATISTICAL DATA. Text in English. a.
Related titles: ◆ Spanish ed.: Venezuela. Ministerio de Energia y Minas. Petroleo y Otros Datos Estadisticos.
Published by: Ministerio de Energia y Minas, Torre Oeste, Parque Central Piso 9, Caracas, DF 1010, Venezuela.

665.5 USA
WEEKLY OXYGENATE REPORT. Text in English. w. USD 580; USD 750 by fax. **Document type:** *Report, Trade.* **Description:** Summarizes oxygenate production and inventories at the national level and at the PAD district level as well.
Related titles: Fax ed.
Published by: American Petroleum Institute, Publications Section, 1220 L St, NW, Washington, DC 20005. TEL 202-682-8000, FAX 202-682-8408, http://www.api.org.

PETROLEUM AND GAS—Computer Applications

665.5 USA
N P R A COMPUTER CONFERENCE. PROCEEDINGS. Text in English. a. back issues avail. **Document type:** *Proceedings, Academic/Scholarly.* **Description:** Publishes papers presented on research into computer applications in petrochemical plants and petroleum refineries.
Published by: National Petrochemical & Refiners Association, 1667 K St, N W, Ste 700, Washington, DC 20006. TEL 202-457-0480, FAX 202-457-0486, info@npra.org, http://www.npradc.org.

PETS

see also ANIMAL WELFARE

636.8 USA ISSN 0744-9631
A C F A BULLETIN. (American Cat Fanciers Association) Text in English. 1955. bi-m. free with membership. adv. **Document type:** *Bulletin.*
Description: Lists shows, judges and administrative personnel.
Media: Duplicated (not offset).
Published by: American Cat Fanciers Association, Inc., PO Box 1949, Nixa, MO 65714-1949. TEL 417-334-5430, FAX 417-334-5540. Ed., R&P Connie Vandre. adv.: B&W page USD 125; trim 10 x 7.5. Circ: 1,700 (paid).

636.8 AUS
A C I YEAR BOOK. (Australian Cat Federation) Text in English. 1978. a. adv. back issues avail. **Document type:** *Yearbook, Consumer.*
Former titles: A C F Journal; (until 1976): National Cat Journal (0311-2446)
Published by: Australian Cat Federation Inc., c/o Ms. J. Ruasack, 32 Tarrant St, Prospect, SA 5082, Australia. Circ: 1,000.

636.7 USA ISSN 1559-5072
A K C FAMILY DOG; all the best for your purebred pet. (American Kennel Club) Text in English. 2003. bi-m. USD 9.95 (effective 2011). adv. illus. **Document type:** *Magazine, Consumer.*
Published by: American Kennel Club, Inc., 260 Madison Ave, New York, NY 10016. TEL 212-696-8288, FAX 212-696-8299, ejm@akc.org. Adv. contact Bill Farmakis TEL 203-834-8832.

636 USA ISSN 1086-0940
SF421
A K C GAZETTE; the official journal for the sport of purebred dogs . (American Kennel Club) Text in English. 1918. m. adv. bk.rev.; software rev.; Website rev. bibl.; illus.; stat. Index. 96 p./no.; back issues avail.; reprints avail. **Document type:** *Magazine, Consumer.*
Former titles (until 1995): Pure-Bred Dogs, American Kennel Gazette (0033-4561); (until 1952): American Kennel Gazette, Pure-Bred Dogs (0737-8807); (until 1943): The American Kennel Gazette (0737-8793); Which superseded in part (in 1926): The American Kennel Gazette and Stud Book (0737-8785); Which was formed by the merger of (1888-1918): The American Kennel Gazette (0737-8777); (1887-1918): The American Kennel Club. Stud Book; Which was formerly (until 1887): American Kennel Stud Book; (until 1885): National American Kennel Club. Stud Book
Related titles: Microform ed.: (from PQC); Online - full text ed.: free (effective 2011).
Indexed: A22, G09, IAB, P10, P53, P54, PQC.
—Ingenta.
Published by: American Kennel Club, Inc., 260 Madison Ave, New York, NY 10016. TEL 212-696-8288, FAX 212-696-8299, ejm@akc.org. Ed. Erika Mansourian. Adv. contact Venus Rodriguez TEL 212-696-8260.

636 USA
A M C CENTERSCOPE. Text in English. 1977. 3/yr. donation. illus. **Document type:** *Newsletter.*
Published by: Animal Medical Center, 510 E 62nd St, New York, NY 10021. TEL 212-838-8100, FAX 212-832-9630. Circ: 15,000.

636.7 USA
A M S C O P E NEWSLETTER. Text in English. m. free to members (effective 2008). **Document type:** *Newsletter, Consumer.*
Published by: American Miniature Schnauzer Club, c/o Mary Ann Shandor, 2302 Cumberland Court, SW, Decatur, AL 35603-2617. publications@amsc.us, membership@amsc.us, http://amsc.us. Circ: 500.

599 AUS
ABYSSINIAN. Text in English. 1967. s-a. adv. bk.rev. **Document type:** *Newsletter.*
Published by: Abyssinian Cat Club of Australasia, PO Box 31, Branxton, NSW 2335, Australia. http://www.abyssinian.org.au. Ed., Adv. contact Diane Royal. R&P Diane Roayl. Circ: 100.

ACUARIO PRACTICO. *see* HOBBIES

636 796 AUS
THE ADVISER. Text in English. 1970. m. AUD 40 to non-members; AUD 30 to members (effective 2008). adv. bk.rev. **Document type:** *Magazine, Trade.*
Formerly (until 1999): Greyhound Adviser
Published by: Greyhound Racing Control Board (Victoria), 46-50 Chetwynd St, West Melbourne, VIC 3003, Australia. TEL 61-3-83291100, FAX 61-3-83291000, memberservices@grv.org.au. adv.: B&W page AUD 440, color page AUD 550; 210 x 275.
Co-sponsor: National Coursing Association of Victoria.

636.7 USA
ADVOCATE (OLD BROOKVILLE). Text in English. 1967. q. USD 10.
Published by: Owner Handler Association of America, c/o Mildred Mesh, Six Michaels Ln., Old Brookville, NY 11545. Circ: 2,000.

636.7 USA
AFGHAN HOUND CLUB OF AMERICA. BULLETIN. Text in English. 3/yr. membership only. **Document type:** *Bulletin.*
Published by: Afghan Hound Club of America, c/o Norma Cozzoni, Ed, 43 W 612 Tall Oaks Trail, Elburn, IL 60119. TEL 708-365-3647, helpafs@earthlink.net.

636.7 USA ISSN 8750-9776
SF429.A4
AFGHAN HOUND REVIEW. Text in English. 1974. bi-m. USD 44 domestic; USD 52 foreign (effective 2000). adv. bk.rev. **Document type:** *Magazine, Trade.* **Description:** Contains information and photographs of Afghan Hound showdogs.
Published by: Showdogs Publications, PO Box 30430, Santa Barbara, CA 93130-0430. TEL 805-692-2045, FAX 805-692-2055. Ed. Bo Bengtson. Pub. Paul Lepiane. R&P, Adv. contact Francine Reisman. B&W page USD 160, color page USD 500. Circ: 1,800.

636.7 SWE ISSN 0283-6971
AFGHANER. Text in Swedish. 1976. q. SEK 250 domestic to members; SEK 300 elsewhere to members (effective 2011). **Document type:** *Magazine, Consumer.*
Formerly (until 1985): Afghanen (0282-7786)
Published by: Sveriges Afghaner, c/o Louise Le Pluart, Lunnarp 6, Dalby, 24010, Sweden. TEL 46-46-201102.

636.7 JPN ISSN 1345-8841
AIKEN NO TOMO/FRIENDS OF DOG. Text in Japanese. 1952. m. JPY 12,840 (effective 2008). **Document type:** *Magazine, Consumer.*
Published by: Seibundo Shinkosha Inc., 3-3-11 Hongo, Bunkyoku, Tokyo, 164-0013, Japan. TEL 81-3-58005775, FAX 81-3-58005773, http://www.seibundo-shinkosha.net/. Circ: 65,000.

636.7 NLD ISSN 1875-2411
AIREDALE MAGAZINE. Text in Dutch. q. EUR 19.50 (effective 2008).
Formerly (until 2007): A T C N Clubblad (1571-4748)
Published by: Airedale Terrier Club Nederland, c/o Linda Stoppkotte-Linschoten, Reep 19, Schaijk, 5374 CX, Netherlands. TEL 31-486-463584, http://airedaleterrierclub.nl.

636.7 USA
AIREDALE TERRIER CLUB OF AMERICA. NEWSLETTER. Text in English. 1900. 5/yr. membership.
Published by: Airedale Terrier Club of America, c/o Aletta Moore, Epoch Farm, 14181 County Rd 40, Carver, MN 55315. Ed. Richard Schlicht. Circ: 700.

636.7 USA
AKITA DOG. Text in English. 1973. q. USD 40 (effective 2000). adv. **Document type:** *Newsletter.*
Formerly: Akita Magazine
Published by: Akita Club of America, c/o Lynn Morgan, Corresponding Sec, PO Box 154, Richmond, KY 40476. akitarescue@akitaclub.org, http://www.akitaclub.org. Adv. contact Nancy Lamm. Circ: 600.

636.7 USA ISSN 0745-1296
AKITA WORLD. Text in English. 1982. q. USD 54 domestic; USD 74 in Canada; USD 98 elsewhere; USD 15 per issue (effective 2011). adv. back issues avail. **Document type:** *Magazine, Consumer.*
Description: Contains breeder interviews, columns by people who know and love Akitas.
Published by: Hoflin Publishing, Inc., 4401 Zephyr St, Wheat Ridge, CO 80033. TEL 303-420-2222, FAX 720-207-0382, help@hoflin.com.

636.7 CHE ISSN 1663-2788
AKTEHUND. Text in German. 2006. 10/yr. CHF 59 in Switzerland & Liechtenstein; CHF 45 elsewhere (effective 2010). adv. **Document type:** *Magazine, Consumer.*
Address: Sonnengutstr 12, Bichelsee, 8363, Switzerland. TEL 41-71-9713444, FAX 41-71-9713444. Ed. Kitty Simione. adv.: page CHF 2,000; trim 208 x 290.

AKVARIEBLADET. *see* FISH AND FISHERIES

636.7 USA ISSN 0199-1310
ALASKAN MALAMUTE CLUB OF AMERICA. NEWSLETTER. Text in English. 19??. m. USD 42 domestic to non-members; USD 71 in Canada & Mexico to non-members; USD 74 elsewhere to non-members (effective 2003). adv. bk.rev. **Document type:** *Newsletter, Consumer.*
Published by: Alaskan Malamute Club of America, Inc., c/o Leneia Rogowski, 640 E 50 N, Hyrum, UT 84319. TEL 435-245-3634, info@alaskanmalamute.org, http://www.alaskanmalamute.org. Ed. Ruth Levesque. Circ: 800.

636 USA ISSN 1069-0743
ALERT (RENTON). Text in English. 1990. 4/yr. **Document type:** *Newsletter.* **Description:** Deals with service dogs and issues of interest to their owners, trainers, and persons with disabilities.
Media: Online - full text.
Published by: Delta Society, 875 124th Ave NE, Ste 101, Bellevue, WA 98055. TEL 425-226-7357, FAX 425-226-7357. Ed. Maureen Fredrickson. Circ: 2,500.

636.7 ZAF ISSN 1683-4224
ALL ABOUT DOGS IN SOUTH AFRICA. Text in English. 1999. bi-m. ZAR 83 domestic; ZAR 168 in neighboring countries (effective 2008). adv.
Formerly (until 2002): The South African Canine Chronicle (1606-9951)
Published by: Canine Chronicle cc, PO Box 650484, Benmore, 2010, South Africa. TEL 27-11-4625645, FAX 27-11-4625913. Ed. Cherry Foss TEL 27-12-2531636. Pub. Allan Swart. Adv. contact Yvonne Meintjes TEL 27-11-8054392.

636.7 ITA ISSN 1825-3202
ALLEVARE. IL CANILE MODERNO. Text in Italian. 1998. 9/yr. EUR 17 domestic; EUR 34 foreign (effective 2009). **Document type:** *Magazine, Trade.*
Formerly (until 2002): Il Canile Moderno (1825-3210)
Published by: Point Veterinaire Italie Srl (Subsidiary of: Wolters Kluwer N.V.), Via Medardo Rosso 11, Milan, 20159, Italy. TEL 39-02-6085231, FAX 39-02-6682866, info@pointvet.it, http://www.pointvet.it.

636.7 USA ISSN 0891-5555
ALPENHORN. Text in English. 1967. bi-m. USD 35 in North America; USD 45 elsewhere (effective 2000). adv. bk.rev. **Document type:** *Magazine, Consumer.* **Description:** Contains dog-related articles, club news and information.
Former titles: B M D C A; Bernese Mountain Dog Club of America. Newsletter
Published by: Bernese Mountain Dog Club of America, c/o Laurie Farley, 416 Maclor Forest Rd, Franklin, NC 28734. admin@bmdca.org, http://www.bmdca.org. Ed., Adv. contact Elizabeth Pearson. Circ: 1,500 (paid).

636.7537 USA ISSN 1539-7637
THE AMERICAN BEAGLER. Text in English. 2001. m. USD 12 (effective 2002). adv.
Published by: The American Beagler, P.O. Box 39327, Indianapolis, IN 46239. TEL 317-356-3303, FAX 317-356-3309. Ed., Pub. Beverly Saunders. Adv. contact Todd R. Bromley.

636.7 USA ISSN 0199-7297
SF429.B78
AMERICAN BRITTANY. Text in English. 194?. m. USD 25 to members (effective 1999). adv. bk.rev. **Document type:** *Bulletin.* **Description:** Covers all facets of dog ownership. Reports on field trials, shows, and hunting tests, and includes articles on training, health care, and breeding.
Published by: American Brittany Club, Inc., PO Box 616, Marshfield, MO 65706. TEL 417-468-6250, FAX 417-468-5860. Ed. Ronnie C Smith. Adv. contact April Turner Underwood. B&W page USD 125. Circ: 4,000 (paid).

636.7 USA
AMERICAN BRUSSELS GRIFFON ASSOCIATION. BULLETIN. Text in English. 1938. 3/yr. bk.rev. **Document type:** *Bulletin.*
Formerly: Brussels Griffon Quarterly
Published by: American Brussels Griffon Association, c/o Mrs Ann Catterson, Ed, 8004 Santa Rita St, Corona, CA 91719. FAX 818-444-3063. Circ: 120 (controlled).

636.7 USA
AMERICAN BULLMASTIFF ASSOCIATION. BULLETIN. Text in English. 3/yr. USD 36 to non-members. adv. bk.rev. **Document type:** *Bulletin.*
Published by: American Bullmastiff Association, Inc., 6283 Hellner Rd, Ann Arbor, MI 48105. TEL 313-741-7326, FAX 313-741-7332. Ed. Nicole Parker. Circ: 425.

636.9322 USA
AMERICAN CHECKERED GIANT RABBIT CLUB. NEWS BULLETIN. Text in English. bi-m. USD 15 (effective 2008).
Published by: American Checkered Giant Rabbit Club, c/o David Freeman, Sec., 1119 Klondyke Rd, Milford, OH 45150. http://www.acgrc.com.

636.7 USA
AMERICAN CHESAPEAKE CLUB. BULLETIN. Text in English. bi-m.
Address: PO Box 58082, Salt Lake City, UT 84158. http://www.amchessieclub.org. Ed. Mark Walsh.

636.7 USA
THE AMERICAN DOG MAGAZINE; your dog, your family, your lifestyle. Text in English. 200?. q. **Document type:** *Magazine, Consumer.*
Published by: The American Dog Magazine, 20269 E Smoky Hill Rd, Ste B-136, Centennial, CO 80015. TEL 303-840-6111. Ed., Pub. Jamie M Downey.

598 USA
AMERICAN DOVE ASSOCIATION NEWSLETTER. Text in English. 1955. bi-m. USD 10 to individuals; USD 7.50 to senior citizens. adv. bk.rev. illus.
Formerly: American Dove Association. Monthly Bulletin
Published by: American Dove Association, 7037 Haynes Rd., Georgetown, IN 47122-8610. Circ: 400.

636.935 658.048 USA
AMERICAN FANCY RAT AND MOUSE ASSOCIATION. DIRECTORY. Text in English. 1985. a. USD 8.50 per issue to non-members; USD 6.50 per issue to members (effective 2011). adv. 28 p./no.; **Document type:** *Directory, Consumer.* **Description:** Lists officers, champions, trophy winners and dates, veterinarian referrals, addresses of similar clubs, upcoming show and display dates, breeders directory, stud names, pet registry names.
Formerly (until 2001): American Fancy Rat and Mouse Association. Yearbook
Published by: American Fancy Rat and Mouse Association, 9230 64th St, Riverside, CA 92509. eastcoastmice@yahoo.com.

636.935 USA
AMERICAN FANCY RAT AND MOUSE ASSOCIATION. SHOW REGULATIONS AND STANDARDS BOOK. Text in English. 1997. biennial. USD 11.50 per issue to non-members; USD 6.50 per issue to members (effective 2011). illus. 40 p./no.; **Document type:** *Handbook/Manual/Guide, Consumer.* **Description:** Lists recognized rat and mouse standards, proposed new standards, show rules, helpful information on showing rats and mice, pictures of ideal markings.
Published by: American Fancy Rat and Mouse Association, 9230 64th St, Riverside, CA 92509. eastcoastmice@yahoo.com.

636.976 USA ISSN 1068-9451
SF459.F47
AMERICAN FERRET REPORT. Text in English. 1990. q. **Document type:** *Newsletter, Consumer.*
Published by: American Ferret Association, PMB 255, 626-C Admiral Dr, Annapolis, MD 21401. TEL 888-337-7381, FAX 516-908-5215, afa@ferret.org. Ed. Kevin Gifford.

636.7 USA
AMERICAN FOX TERRIER CLUB. NEWSLETTER. Text in English. bi-m. free to members (effective 2008). adv. **Document type:** *Newsletter, Consumer.*
Published by: American Fox Terrier Club, c/o Mrs James A Farrell, 2105 Chester Village W, Chester, CT 06412-1040. tls599@aol.com, http://www.aftc.org. Circ: 500.

636.7 USA ISSN 0888-627X
AMERICAN KENNEL CLUB AWARDS. Text in English. 1981. m. adv. **Document type:** *Journal, Trade.* **Description:** Provides new titles and results from shows, obedience trials, tracking tests, field trials, hunting tests and herding and lure coursing tests and trials.
Formerly (until 1986): The American Kennel Club Show, Obedience and Field Trial Awards (0272-4383)
Related titles: Microfilm ed.: (from PQC).
Published by: American Kennel Club, Inc., 260 Madison Ave, New York, NY 10016. TEL 212-696-8288, FAX 212-696-8345, http://www.akc.org.

636.7 USA
AMERICAN KENNEL CLUB PUPPIES. Text in English. a. **Description:** Contains information for new puppy owners.
Published by: American Kennel Club, Inc., 260 Madison Ave, New York, NY 10016. TEL 212-696-8288, FAX 212-696-8299, http://www.akc.org. Pub. George Berger TEL 212-696-8282. Adv. contact Gina Lash TEL 212-696-8260.

636.7 USA
AMERICAN SALUKI ASSOCIATION. NEWSLETTER. Text in English. 1963. q. membership only. **Document type:** *Newsletter.*
Address: c/o Sally Bell, 14118 228th St, S E, Snohomish, WA 98290. Circ: 600.

636.7 USA
AMERICAN SHETLAND SHEEPDOG ASSOCIATION. BULLETIN BOARD. Text in English. q. membership. **Document type:** *Bulletin, Newsletter, Corporate.*
Formerly: American Shetland Sheepdog Association. Bulletin
Published by: American Shetland Sheepdog Association, 18 Alberta St, Windsor, CT 06096. TEL 208-773-4256. Ed. Janet Leiper. Circ: 714.

636.7 USA
AMERICAN SPANIEL CLUB. BULLETIN. Text in English. 1951. q. membership. **Document type:** *Bulletin.*
Published by: American Spaniel Club, 35 Academy Rd., Hohokus, NJ 07423. FAX 706-860-0863. Ed. Debbie Pharr. Circ: 1,300.

636.9322 USA
AMERICAN STANDARD CHINCHILLA RABBIT ASSOCIATION. NEWSLETTER. Text in English. bi-m. **Document type:** *Newsletter.*
Published by: American Standard Chinchilla Rabbit Association, c/o Patricia Gest, 1607 Ninth St W, Palmetto, FL 34221. TEL 813-729-1184.

P

636 ITA ISSN 1591-0628
AMICI DI CASA. Text in Italian. 2000. bi-m. EUR 10.90 (effective 2009). charts; illus. **Document type:** *Magazine, Consumer.*
Published by: Sprea Editori Srl, Via Torino 51, Cernusco sul Naviglio, MI 20063, Italy. TEL 39-02-92432222, FAX 39-02-92432236, editori@sprea.it, http://www.sprea.it.

ANABANTOID ASSOCIATION OF GREAT BRITAIN. LABYRINTH. *see* BIOLOGY—Zoology

636.7 BRA ISSN 1413-5507
ANIMAIS E CIA. Text in Portuguese. 1996. m. BRL 5.90 newsstand/cover (effective 2006). adv. **Document type:** *Magazine, Consumer.*
Published by: Editora Escala Ltda., Av Prof Ida Kolb, 551, Casa Verde, Sao Paulo, 02518-000, Brazil. TEL 55-11-38552100, FAX 55-11-38579643, escala@escala.com.br, http://www.escala.com.br.

636 FRA ISSN 1959-173X
ANIMAL ATTITUDE; le guide des animaux et des maitres heureux. Text in French. 2007. q. EUR 12.50 (effective 2008). **Document type:** *Magazine, Consumer.*
Published by: Groupe J, BP 30, Rambouillet, Cedex 78511, France. TEL 33-1-34847060, FAX 33-1-34847055, contacts@groupej-sas.com.

636 FRA ISSN 0246-1854
ANIMAL DISTRIBUTION. Text in French. 1989. 13/yr. EUR 65 domestic; EUR 85 foreign (effective 2009). **Document type:** *Magazine, Trade.* **Description:** Gives the latest information on pet care. For veterinarians, groomers, pet product sellers etc.
Published by: Groupe J, BP 30, Rambouillet, Cedex 78511, France. TEL 33-1-34847060, FAX 33-1-34847055, contacts@groupej-sas.com, http://www.jardineries.com. Ed., R&P Valerie Langendorff. Adv. contact Francois Regis Arnoult. Circ: 7,000.

636 USA ISSN 1525-3309
SF415.45
ANIMAL FAIR; a lifestyle magazine for animal lovers. Text in English. 1999. q. USD 19.99 for 2 yrs. domestic; USD 37.99 for 2 yrs. in Canada; USD 45.99 for 2 yrs. elsewhere (effective 2008). bk.rev. illus. back issues avail. **Document type:** *Magazine, Consumer.* **Description:** Lifestyle magazine for pet owners and animal lovers. Presents new treatments, training techniques and chic fashion for pets.
Published by: Animal Fair Media, Inc., 545 8th Ave, Ste 401, New York, NY 10018. info@animalfair.com. Ed. Wendy Diamond. Adv. contact Beth Brandes. Circ: 200,000.

ANIMAL FINDERS' GUIDE. *see* AGRICULTURE—Poultry And Livestock

ANIMAL PEOPLE. *see* ANIMAL WELFARE

636 FRA ISSN 1957-1488
ANIMAL SANTE & BIEN-ETRE. Text in French. 2007. bi-m. EUR 35 for 18 mos. (effective 2009). **Document type:** *Magazine, Consumer.*
Published by: Editions Nebout, 6 Av. Jean-Baptiste Clement, Boulogne-Billancourt, 92100, France. TEL 33-1-46046321, FAX 33-1-46046317.

636 ZAF
ANIMAL TALK. (Includes Sport & Horse) Text in English. 1994. m. (11/yr.). ZAR 105 (effective 2000). adv.
Published by: Panorama Publications (Pty) Ltd., Private Bag X41, Bryanston, Johannesburg 2021, South Africa. TEL 27-11-4682090, FAX 27-11-4682091. Ed. Johann Theron. Pub. Urs Honegger. Adv. contact Carol Immeleman.

636.088 CAN ISSN 1710-1190
ANIMAL WELLNESS; for a long, healthy life!. Text in English. 1999. bi-m. CAD 24 domestic; USD 19 in United States; USD 80 elsewhere (effective 2010). adv. back issues avail. **Document type:** *Magazine, Consumer.*
Formerly (until 2001): Animal (1711-7305)
Related titles: Online - full text ed.
Published by: Redstone Media Group Inc., 164 Hunter St., West, Peterborough, ON K9H 2L2, Canada. TEL 888-466-5266, FAX 705-742-4596, submissions@animalanimal.com, http://redstonemediagroup.com/.

636 USA ISSN 0003-360X
ANIMALDOM. Text in English. 1930. m. (except Aug.). USD 2 to non-members. bk.rev. illus. **Document type:** *Newsletter.*
Published by: Pennsylvania S.P.C.A., 350 E Erie Ave, Philadelphia, PA 19134. TEL 215-426-6300. Ed. Charlene W Peters. Circ: 42,000 (controlled).

636 FRA ISSN 0296-6700
ANIMALERIE. Text in French. 1985. 9/yr. illus.
Published by: Bureau Europeen de Presse et de Publicite, 44 av. George V, Paris, 75008, France. Ed. Michel Chansiaux. Circ: 10,000.

636 ESP ISSN 0214-3151
ANIMALIA; revista especializada en animales de compania. Text in Spanish. m. (11/yr.). EUR 69.95 (effective 2010). adv. **Document type:** *Magazine, Trade.* **Description:** Dedicated to pets, including health care, medicines, diet, show activities and more.
Indexed: ASFA.
Published by: Reed Business Information SA (Subsidiary of: Reed Business Information International), Zancoeta 9, Bilbao, 48013, Spain. TEL 34-944-285600, FAX 34-944-425116, rbi@rbi.es. Ed. Nuria Martin. Circ: 6,600.

636 FRA ISSN 2108-372X
L'ANIMALIER. Text in French. 2008. bi-m. **Document type:** *Magazine, Trade.*
Published by: La Societe Nooe SARL, 23, Rue Pierre Brossolette, Chatillon, 92320, France. http://www.lanimalier.fr/index.php.

636 USA
ANIMALNEWS. Text in English. 1981. 3/yr. USD 25 membership (effective 2000). bk.rev. **Document type:** *Newsletter.* **Description:** Contains articles on foundation-sponsored animal health studies, and updates on awards and honors given by Morris Animal Foundation.
Formerly (until 1995): Companion Animal News
Published by: Morris Animal Foundation, 45 Inverness Dr E, Englewood, CO 80112. TEL 303-790-2345, 800-243-2345, FAX 303-790-4066, http://www.morrisanimalfoundation.org. Ed. Carissa Lester. Circ: 100,000.

ANIMALS AND YOU; for cool girls who love animals. *see* CHILDREN AND YOUTH—For

636 USA
ANIMALTOWN NEWS; news for animal lovers of all kinds. Text in English. 1994. m. USD 6. adv. bk.rev. illus. **Document type:** *Magazine, Consumer.* **Description:** Contains a wide variety of general-interest articles on animals and fish kept as pets, including detailed descriptions of specific breeds. Also publishes articles on pet health and how to deal with the loss of a pet.
Published by: Killian Graphics, PO Box 91, Chatham, NJ 07928. Ed. Judy Killian. Adv. contact Ron Christopher.

597 SGP
AQUARAMA MAGAZINE. Text in English. m. free in Asia to qualified personnel. **Document type:** *Magazine, Trade.*
Published by: C M P Asia Trade Fairs Ptd Ltd. (Subsidiary of: C M P Asia Ltd.), 111 Somerset Rd, #09-07, Singapore Power Bldg, Singapore, 238164, Singapore. Ed. John Dawes. Pub. Jean Oh.

AQUARISTIK; Aktuelle Suesswasserpraxis. *see* FISH AND FISHERIES

636 FRA ISSN 1278-060X
L'AQUARIUM A LA MAISON. Text in French. 1999. bi-m. EUR 31 domestic; EUR 36 foreign (effective 2010). back issues avail. **Document type:** *Magazine, Consumer.*
Published by: L R Presse, 12 Rue de Sablen, Auray, 56401 Cedex, France. TEL 33-2-97240165, FAX 33-2-97242830, http://www.lrpresse.fr.

636 USA ISSN 1942-5678
AQUARIUM FISH INTERNATIONAL. Text in English. 1988. m. USD 12.99 domestic; USD 24.99 foreign (effective 2011). adv. bk.rev. illus. reprints avail. **Document type:** *Magazine, Consumer.* **Description:** Covers freshwater and saltwater aquariums and ponds and pond fish. Provides information on the hobby for beginners and experienced hobbyists.
Incorporates (1978-2010): Freshwater and Marine Aquarium (0160-4317); Formerly (until 2007): Aquarium Fish Magazine (0899-045X)
Related titles: Online - full text ed.
—Ingenta.
Published by: BowTie, Inc., PO Box 6050, Mission Viejo, CA 92690. http://www.bowtieinc.com.

636 USA ISSN 1069-1871
AQUARIUM U S A; fishkeeping from a to z. Text in English. 199?. a. USD 7.50 newsstand/cover (effective 2006). adv. **Document type:** *Magazine, Consumer.* **Description:** Aims to help beginning to intermediate fishkeepers get started on the right foot. Encourages readers to study and research first and discourages running out to buy an aquarium setup that is more than he/she can handle.
Published by: BowTie, Inc., 2401 Beverly Blvd, PO Box 57900, Los Angeles, CA 90057. TEL 213-385-2222, FAX 213-385-8565, http://www.bowtieinc.com, http://www.animalnetwork.com/. Ed. Russ Cass. adv.: B&W page USD 2,980, color page USD 4,450; trim 8 x 10.875. Circ: 67,326.

636 BEL ISSN 1372-6501
AQUARIUMWERELD; maandblad voor aquarium-en terrariumkunde. Text in Dutch. 1948. m. EUR 22 domestic; EUR 27 in Netherlands (effective 2005). adv. bibl.; illus. back issues avail. **Document type:** *Consumer.* **Description:** Contains information about aquariums, terrariums and ponds.
Indexed: Z01.
Published by: Belgische Bond van Aquarium- en Terrariumhouders vzw, Kamerstraat 10, Buggenhout, 9255, Belgium. TEL 32-52334055, FAX 32-52334055, haerens.aqw@ven.be. Pub. Freddy Haerens. Adv. contact Hugo Bulte. Circ: 5,000.

636 ITA ISSN 1125-1115
ARGOS. Text in Italian. 1987. m. EUR 39.90; EUR 5.90 newsstand/cover (effective 2011). adv. **Document type:** *Magazine, Consumer.*
Published by: Sprea Editori Srl, Via Torino 51, Cernusco sul Naviglio, MI 20063, Italy. TEL 39-02-92432222, FAX 39-02-92432236, editori@sprea.it, http://www.sprea.it. Circ: 59,000.

636.7 ITA ISSN 1129-1761
ARGOS ANNUAL. Text in Italian. 1999. a. price varies. **Document type:** *Catalog, Consumer.*
Published by: Sprea Editori Srl, Via Torino 51, Cernusco sul Naviglio, MI 20063, Italy. TEL 39-02-92432222, FAX 39-02-92432236, editori@sprea.it, http://www.sprea.it.

636.7 USA
ARK (COLORADO SPRINGS). Text in English. 1974. bi-m. USD 30 domestic; USD 55 foreign (effective 2008).
Published by: American Rottweiler Club, c/o Marilyn E Plusz, 339 Co Hwy 106, Johnstown, NY 12095-3757. TEL 518-883-5806. Circ: 1,200.

636.7 179.3 POL ISSN 1231-6857
ASKO; dwumiesiecznik kynologiczny. Text in Polish. 1991. bi-m. adv. bk.rev. charts; illus.; tr.lit. back issues avail. **Document type:** *Magazine, Consumer.* **Description:** Concentrates on animal welfare, especially dogs. Provides description of dog races, short essays concerning dog shows.
Address: ul Kozielska 120 a, Raciborz, 47411, Poland. TEL 48-32-4157932. Ed. Elzbieta Boruch Priebe. adv.: page PLZ 800. Circ: 10,000.

ASSOCIATION DU REFUGE DES TORTUES. LA GAZETTE. *see* ANIMAL WELFARE

636.7 USA
ASSOCIATION OF OBEDIENCE CLUBS AND JUDGES. NEWSLETTER. Text in English. 1950. q. **Document type:** *Newsletter.*
Published by: Association of Obedience Clubs and Judges, c/o Patricia Scully, 328 Parkside Dr, Suffern, NY 10901. Circ: 500.

636.7 USA ISSN 2152-7989
THE ATOMIC DOGG; home of the bully breed magazine. Text in English. 2006. q. USD 29.99, CAD 39.99; USD 6.99, CAD 8.99 per issue (effective 2010). adv. back issues avail. **Document type:** *Magazine, Consumer.*
Published by: The Atomic Dogg Magazine, PO Box 811276, Los Angeles, CA 90081. TEL 562-253-6181. Ed. Eric Ptah Herbert. adv.: page USD 2,400; trim 8.25 x 10.875. Circ: 150,000 (paid).

636.8 FRA ISSN 0769-6027
ATOUT CHAT. Text in French. 1985. m. **Document type:** *Magazine, Consumer.*
Published by: Volta Sport, 109-111 Av. Gambetta, Paris, 75020, France. TEL 33-1-43152626, FAX 33-1-43664023, contact@volta-sports.com, http://www.volta-sports.com. Ed. Valerie Cochet. Circ: 32,000; 18,000 (controlled).

636.7 FRA ISSN 0298-2919
ATOUT CHIEN. Text in French. 1986. m. **Document type:** *Magazine, Consumer.*
Published by: Volta Sport, 109-111 Av. Gambetta, Paris, 75020, France. TEL 33-1-43152626, FAX 33-1-43664023, contact@volta-sports.com, http://www.volta-sports.com. Ed. Valerie Cochet. Circ: 80,000.

636 AUS ISSN 1030-8954
AUSTRALIAN BIRDKEEPER MAGAZINE. Text in English. 1987. bi-m. AUD 63 domestic; AUD 75 in New Zealand; AUD 85 elsewhere (effective 2008). adv. 62 p./no.; back issues avail. **Document type:** *Magazine, Consumer.* **Description:** Contains features and articles on all popular cage and aviary birds. Articles include veterinarian reports, tips on breeding, housing, nutrition and management.
Published by: A B K Publications, PO Box 6288, South Tweed Heads, NSW 2486, Australia. TEL 61-7-55907777, FAX 61-7-55907130. Ed., R&P Nigel Steele Boyce. Adv. contact Sheryll Steele-Boyce. Circ: 11,000 (paid).

636 636.0832 USA ISSN 2160-5254
BANFIELD JOURNAL; achieving success in pratice. Text in English. 2005. q. adv. back issues avail. **Document type:** *Journal, Academic/Scholarly.* **Description:** Aims to enrich the lives of general practitioners and veterinary students by providing additional resources to succeed in Pet practice.
Related titles: Online - full text ed.: free (effective 2011).
Published by: Banfield, The Pet Hospital, 8000 NE Tillamook, PO Box 13998, Portland, OR 97213. TEL 866-262-7387, 800-838-6929, careers@banfield.net. Pub. Kathleen J Baumgardner. Adv. contact Jill Taylor TEL 503-922-5462. Circ: 18,000.

636.7 USA ISSN 1535-1734
SF421
THE BARK; dog is my co-pilot. Text in English. 1997. bi-m. USD 15 domestic; USD 30 in Canada; USD 35 elsewhere (effective 2010). adv. bk.rev.; film rev.; Website rev. illus. 88 p./no.; back issues avail. **Document type:** *Magazine, Consumer.* **Description:** Magazine about life with dogs.
Published by: The Bark, Inc., 2810 8th St, Berkeley, CA 94710. TEL 510-704-0827, FAX 510-704-0933, editor@thebark.com. Ed. Claudia Kawczynska. Pub., Adv. contact Cameron Woo. B&W page USD 1,800, color page USD 3,000; trim 8.25 x 10.87. Circ: 100,000 (paid and controlled).

636.7 USA
BARKS. Text in English. 197?. q. USD 45 domestic; USD 57 in Canada & Mexico; USD 73 elsewhere (effective 2008). adv. **Document type:** *Magazine, Consumer.*
Published by: Bull Terrier Club of America, Victoria Corse, Managing Ed, P O Box 995, Marshfield, MA 02050-0995. TEL 781-834-0875, 617-596-1002, nwaynee@cox.net, corsairebt@comcast.net. adv.: page USD 60. Circ: 400.

636.7 USA ISSN 0094-9744
SF429.B15
BASENJI. Text in English. 1964. m. USD 24 (effective 2000). adv. bk.rev. illus.; stat. back issues avail. **Document type:** *Newsletter.* **Description:** Oriented to the needs & interests of Basenji fanciers and breeders.
Published by: Jon and Susan Coe, Eds. & Pubs., 789 Linton Hill Rd, Newtown, PA 18940-1207. TEL 215-860-8254. Circ: 1,500 (paid).

636.7 USA
BASENJI CLUB OF AMERICA. OFFICIAL BULLETIN. Text in English. 1942. bi-m.
Published by: Basenji Club of America, 2435 Hibiscus Dr, Hayward, CA 94545. Circ: 600.

636.7 SWE ISSN 0345-1321
BASSETBLADET. Text in Swedish. 1971. q. SEK 220 to members (effective 2004). **Document type:** *Consumer.*
Published by: Svenska Bassetklubben - SBK, c/o Susanne Lindquist, Backebo Laassa, Bro, 19791, Sweden. sbak@home.se, http://www.sbak.nu.

616.7 USA
BAY WOOF; news with bite for Bay area dog lovers. Text in English. 2007. m. USD 30 (effective 2009). adv. **Document type:** *Magazine, Consumer.* **Description:** Contains regular columns and special features covering a wide variety of topics, including dog training and health, dog-friendly travel, dog sports and all things canine.
Published by: Rocketgrrl Enterprises LLC, 3288 21st St, #249, San Francisco, CA 94110. TEL 415-525-4040. Ed. Mindy Toomay. Pub. M Rocket. Adv. contact Sandra Olson TEL 510-420-8624. B&W page USD 2,000. Circ: 35,000 (paid and free).

636.7 SWE ISSN 0283-4138
BEAGLE (TYRESOE). Text in Swedish. 1968. q. SEK 290 to members (effective 2004). **Document type:** *Consumer.*
Formerly (until 1978): Medlemskontakt
Published by: Svenska Beagleklubben, c/o Christer Nyberg, Balettvaegen 5, Bjaesta, 89331, Sweden. TEL 46-660220725, info@sblk.a.se, http://www.sblk.a.se.

636 USA ISSN 1946-1755
BEANTOWN TAILS; celebrating the relationship between pets and their people. Text in English. 2008. m. USD 36 (effective 2009). adv. **Document type:** *Magazine, Consumer.* **Description:** Lifestyle magazine for people with pets.
Related titles: Online - full text ed.: ISSN 1946-1763.
Published by: Tails Pet Media Group, Inc., 4527 N Ravenswood Ave, Chicago, IL 60640. TEL 773-561-4300, 866-803-8245, FAX 773-561-3030. Pub. Alan L Brown. Adv. contact Nikki Scheel.

636.7 USA ISSN 1077-9841
THE BELGIAN SHEEPDOG. Text in English. 1953. bi-m. USD 35 domestic to non-members; USD 55 foreign to non-members; free to members (effective 2008). adv. bk.rev. **Document type:** *Newsletter, Consumer.*
Formerly (until 199?): National Belgian Newsletter (1047-9112)
Published by: Belgian Sheepdog Club of America, c/o Kathy Lang, 1303 N 32nd St, Renton, WA 98056. TEL 425-793-1825, editorbsca@aol.com. Ed. Kathy Lang. Circ: 550.

636.8 USA ISSN 1947-752X
BENGALS ILLUSTRATED. Text in English. 200?. q. USD 35 domestic; USD 50 foreign (effective 2009). adv. back issues avail. **Document type:** *Magazine, Consumer.* **Description:** Includes "soul food", Bengal facts, information and photos of cats.
Related titles: CD-ROM ed.: ISSN 1947-7546. USD 30 domestic; USD 38 foreign (effective 2009); Online - full text ed.: ISSN 1947-7538. USD 25 (effective 2009).
Published by: The International Bengal Cat Connection, PO Box 6297, Oroville, CA 95966. info@bengalcatconnection.com, http://www.bengalcatconnection.com.

636 636.0832 USA ISSN 1949-0259
BEST FRIENDS (KANAB). Text in English. 19??. bi-m. donation. adv. illus. back issues avail. **Document type:** *Magazine, Consumer.*
Formerly (until 1992): Best Friends Magazine
Published by: Best Friends Animal Society, 5001 Angel Canyon Rd, Kanab, UT 84741. TEL 435-644-2001, FAX 435-644-2266, info@bestfriends.org. Ed. Carla Davis. Adv. contact Michelle Foster TEL 323-493-5277.

636.7 USA ISSN 0736-9743
BETTER BEAGLING. Text in English. 1977. m. USD 16 domestic; USD 34 in Canada; USD 50 elsewhere; USD 2.95 newsstand/cover (effective 2001). adv. bk.rev. **Document type:** *Magazine, Consumer.* **Description:** Covers breeding and care of beagle hunting hounds.
Formerly: Large Pack
Address: PO Box 8142, Essex, VT 05451. TEL 802-878-3616, FAX 802-878-0634. Ed. Pearl N Baker. adv.: B&W page USD 135; trim 11 x 8.5. Circ: 6,000.

636.7 USA ISSN 0199-8315
BICHON FRISE REPORTER. Text in English. 1979. q. USD 45 domestic; USD 60 in Canada & Mexico; USD 105 elsewhere; USD 15 per issue domestic; USD 20 per issue foreign (effective 2011). adv. bk.rev. 80 p./no.; back issues avail. **Document type:** *Magazine, Consumer.*
Published by: Reporter Publications, PO Box 6369, Los Osos, CA 93412. TEL 805-528-2007, FAX 805-528-8200.

179.3 USA
BIDE-A-WEE NEWS. Text in English. 1969. q. donation. adv. bk.rev. back issues avail. **Document type:** *Newsletter.* **Description:** Includes association news and activities, articles about adopting cats and dogs, caring for them, and pet health matters.
Published by: Bide-A-Wee Home Association, 410 E 38th St, New York, NY 10016. TEL 212-532-6358, FAX 212-532-4210. Ed., Pub., Adv. contact George Wirt. R&P Marguerite Howard. Circ: 40,000.

BIRD TALK; dedicated to better care for pet birds. *see* BIOLOGY—Ornithology

636 USA ISSN 1096-7923
BIRD TIMES; the magazine of the best about birds. Text in English. 1992. bi-m. USD 19.97 domestic; USD 25.97 in Canada; USD 31.97 elsewhere (effective 2006). adv. illus. back issues avail. **Document type:** *Magazine, Consumer.* **Description:** Contains articles about bird breed profiles, medical reports, training advice, bird puzzles and stories about special birds.
Formerly: Caged Bird Hobbyist (1062-7383)
Published by: Pet Publishing, Inc., 7-L Dundas Circle, Greensboro, NC 27407. TEL 336-292-4047, FAX 336-292-4272, editorial@petpublishing.com. Ed. Rita Davis. adv.: color page USD 1,965, B&W page USD 1,365; trim 8.125 x 11. Circ: 20,000.

636 USA ISSN 1041-1550
SF460
BIRDS U S A. Text in English. 1989. a. USD 7.50 newsstand/cover (effective 2006). adv. illus. **Document type:** *Magazine, Consumer.* **Description:** Contains articles on the basics of bird care for the pet bird owner.
Published by: BowTie, Inc., 2401 Beverly Blvd, PO Box 57900, Los Angeles, CA 90057. TEL 213-385-2222, FAX 213-385-8565, http://www.bowtieinc.com, http://www.animalnetwork.com/. Pub. Norman Ridker. adv.: B&W page USD 3,050, color page USD 4,470; trim 8 x 10.875. Circ: 97,591.

636.7 SWE ISSN 1101-1491
BJOERNHUNDEN. Text in Swedish. 1973. q. **Document type:** *Newsletter, Consumer.*
Published by: Svenska Bjoernhundsklubben, c/o Elmer Forsgren, Mossgatan 3, Skelleftea, 93170, Sweden. TEL 46-910-776959, elmer.forsgren@telia.com.

636.9322 DEU
DAS BLAUE JAHRBUCH; ein praktischer Wegweiser fuer den Kaninchenzuechter. Text in German. 1952. a. EUR 6 (effective 2010). adv. **Document type:** *Magazine, Consumer.*
Former titles (until 1988): Das Blaue Kaninchen-Jahrbuch; (until 1955): Taschenbuch fuer den Rassekaninchenzuechter
Published by: (Deutscher Kleintier Zuechter), Oertel & Spoerer Verlags GmbH und Co. KG, Beutterstr 10, Reutlingen, 72764, Germany. TEL 49-7121-302550, FAX 49-7121-302558, info@oertel-spoerer.de, http://www.oe-sp.de.

636.7 USA
BLOODHOUND BULLETIN. Text in English. 1958. 3/yr. adv.
Address: 7275 Jennings Rd, Whitmore Lake, MI 48189. Circ: 400.

636.7 USA ISSN 0890-8923
BLOODLINES. Text in English. 1905. 7/yr. USD 24 domestic; USD 34 foreign; USD 6 per issue (effective 2005). adv. bk.rev. 174 p./no.; back issues avail. **Document type:** *Magazine, Consumer.* **Description:** Devoted to dog sports and family dogs; covers obedience, breeding, tracking, agility, service dogs, therapy dogs, and herding dogs. Also covers obedience.
Formerly: Bloodlines Journal (0006-5013)
Related titles: Online - full text ed.
Published by: United Kennel Club, Inc., 100 E Kilgore Rd, Kalamazoo, MI 49002-5584. TEL 269-343-9020, FAX 269-343-7037, hounds@ukcdogs.com. Ed., R&P Vicki Rand. Circ: 4,500 (paid).

636.7 USA ISSN 1558-593X
BOCADOG MAGAZINE. Text in English. 2005. bi-m. USD 18 (effective 2007). **Document type:** *Magazine, Consumer.*
Address: P.O. Box 812485, Boca Raton, FL 33431. TEL 561-305-3351, info@bocadogmagazine.com, http://www.bocadogmagazine.com/index.html.

636.7 SWE ISSN 1100-0716
BORDERTERRIERBLADET. Text in Swedish. 1964. s-a. SEK 80 to members (effective 1990).
Published by: Borderterriersaellskapet (BTS), c/o I Bergman, Sund, Toretorpsvagen 27, Gastrike-hammarby, 81292, Sweden.

636.7 USA
BORZOI CONNECTION MAGAZINE. Text in English. 4/yr. USD 35 domestic membership; USD 40 in Canada membership (effective 2008). **Document type:** *Magazine, Consumer.*
Published by: Borzoi Club of America, Inc., c/o Joe E. Rogers, 6389 Tiger Trail, Fort Worth, TX 76126-5108. TEL 817-249-5558, FAX 817-249-8202, bcoa@borzoiclubofamerica.org, manager@borzoiconnection.com, http://www.borzoiclubofamerica.org. **Subscr. to:** Subscription Desk, P O Box 175, Elk Rapids, MI 49629. TEL 231-264-6667.

636.7 SWE ISSN 1653-5618
BORZOI-RINGEN. Text in Swedish. 1972. 4/yr. SEK 250 to members (effective 2006). **Document type:** *Magazine, Consumer.*
Formerly (until 2005): Borzoi (0281-3238)
Address: c/o Lars-Erik Jansson, Tubgatan 22, Hyltebruk, 31434, Sweden. TEL 46-345-71541, ordforande@borzoi-ringen.com, http://www.borzoi-ringen.com.

636.7 USA ISSN 0892-9742
THE BOSTON QUARTERLY. Text in English. 1987. q. USD 54 domestic; USD 74 in Canada; USD 98 elsewhere; USD 15 per issue (effective 2011). adv. back issues avail. **Document type:** *Magazine, Consumer.* **Description:** Contains breeder interviews, columns by people who know and love Boston.
Related titles: Microform ed.: (from PQC).
Published by: Hoflin Publishing, Inc., 4401 Zephyr St, Wheat Ridge, CO 80033. TEL 303-420-2222, FAX 720-207-0382, help@hoflin.com.

636.7 SWE ISSN 0346-9344
BOSTONTERRIERN; tidskrift foer Svenska bostonterrierklubben. Text in Swedish. 1958. 3/yr. SEK 200 domestic to members; SEK 250 foreign to members (effective 2005). adv. **Document type:** *Magazine, Consumer.*
Published by: Svenska Bostonterrierklubben, SBTK, c/o Svenska Kennelklubben, Spaanga, 16385, Sweden. TEL 46-8-7953000, FAX 46-8-7953040, http://www.bostonterrierklubben.nu. Ed. Marianne Eriksson TEL 46-18-365295. Pub. Taru Ylikylae. adv.: page SEK 300.

636.7 USA ISSN 1067-8875
BOXER REVIEW. Text in English. 1956. 10/yr. USD 40 domestic; USD 50 foreign (effective 2005). back issues avail. **Document type:** *Magazine, Consumer.* **Description:** Deals with the training of canine boxers, shows, and club activities.
Address: 8840 White Oak Ave., Northridge, CA 91325-3129. TEL 213-654-3147, FAX 213-654-8318. Ed., Pub. Kathy Cognate. Circ: 2,000 (paid).

636.7 SWE ISSN 0345-1690
BOXERBLADET. Text in Swedish. 1965. q. SEK 380 to members (effective 2004). adv. **Document type:** *Magazine, Consumer.*
Published by: Svenska Boxerklubben, c/o Maya Beike, Stenelidsvaegen 75, Skoevde, 76165, Sweden. Ed., Adv. contact Maya Beike.

636.7 SWE ISSN 1653-266X
BRA HUND. Text in Swedish. 2005. 10/yr. SEK 295 (effective 2005). **Document type:** *Magazine, Consumer.*
Published by: Peak Media AB, Skommarvaegen 3, Gustafs, 78300, Sweden. TEL 46-243-253900, FAX 46-243-240028. Ed. Jan Gyllensten. Pub. Robert Solin TEL 46-705-379630.

636 DEU ISSN 1430-7995
DAS BRANCHEN FORUM; das Fachhandels-Organ fuer Heimtierbedarf & Garten. Text in German. 1996. w. EUR 76.69 domestic; EUR 88.96 foreign (effective 2009). adv. **Document type:** *Magazine, Trade.*
Published by: Verlag Branchen Forum Zoo & Garten, Untere Lehmerhoefe 17, Lehmen, 56332, Germany. TEL 49-2607-963176, FAX 49-2607-963176, Schmidt.Branchenforum@T-online.de. Pub. Claudia Schmidt. adv.: B&W page EUR 1,800, color page EUR 3,150; trim 180 x 270.

636.7 USA ISSN 1084-0621
A BREED APART; greyhound ezine. Text in English. 1995. bi-m. free. illus. **Description:** Provides a vehicle for articles and information related to all aspects of greyhound ownership. Covers greyhounds as dogs, as pets, as friends or as retired racers. Topics include health, adoption, adapting to a new home, and helping hints.
Media: Online - full text.
Published by: Breed Apart Ed. Bruce Skinner.

798.8 DEU
BREEDER SPECIAL; Zuechterwissen kompakt und kompetent. Variant title: HundeWelt Breeder Special. Text in German. 2004. bi-m. EUR 14.40; EUR 2.70 newsstand/cover (effective 2010). adv. **Document type:** *Magazine, Consumer.*
Published by: Minerva Verlag GmbH, Hocksteiner Weg 38, Moenchengladbach, 41189, Germany. TEL 49-2166-621970, FAX 49-2166-6219710, info@minervaverlag.de, http://www.minervaverlag.de. adv.: B&W page EUR 912, color page EUR 1,550.40; trim 130 x 190. Circ: 10,500 (paid and controlled).

636.596 SWE ISSN 0280-7769
BREVDUVESPORT; Svenska Brevduvefoerbundets tidskrift. Text in Swedish. 1918. 10/yr. SEK 125 (effective 1991).
Address: c/o I Langkjaer, Tradgardsvagen 22, Bjarred, 23735, Sweden.

636.596 DEU
DIE BRIEFTAUBE. Text in German. 1990. w. EUR 45 domestic; EUR 60 foreign (effective 2007). adv. **Document type:** *Magazine, Consumer.*
Published by: Verband Deutscher Brieftaubenzuechter e.V., Katernberger Str 115, Essen, 45327, Germany. TEL 49-201-8722412, FAX 49-201-8722467, verband@brieftaube.de, http://www.brieftaube.de. Ed. Klaus Kuehntopp. Adv. contact Oliver Jaeschke. page EUR 2,204.80; trim 205 x 290. Circ: 31,944 (paid and controlled).

636.7 SWE ISSN 0345-1771
BRUKSHUNDEN. Text in Swedish. 1940. 8/yr. SEK 210 domestic; SEK 310 elsewhere (effective 2004). adv. 64 p./no. 4 cols./p.; **Document type:** *Magazine, Consumer.*
Published by: Svenska Brukshundklubben, Fryksdalsbacken 20, PO Box 2050, Farsta, 12329, Sweden. TEL 46-8-55681100, sbk@brukshundsklubben.se, http://www.sbk.nu. Ed. Gunnar Lundgren. Pub. Bjoern Bjuggren. Adv. contact Monica Wistedt. B&W page SEK 13,000, color page SEK 15,000; trim 185 x 265. Circ: 51,200.

636 GBR
BUDGERIGAR WORLD. Text in English. 1974. m. GBP 38 domestic; GBP 40 in Europe; GBP 50 elsewhere (effective 2009). adv. bk.rev. 48 p./no.; back issues avail. **Document type:** *Magazine, Consumer.*
Published by: Budgerigar World Ltd., County Press Buildings, Station Rd, Bala, Gwynedd LL23 7PG, United Kingdom. terry@budgerigarworld.com. Ed. Terry A Tuxford.

636.7 USA
BULLDOGGER. Text in English. 3/yr.
Published by: Bulldog Club of America, c/o Rita L Phethean, 133 Wild Oak Dr, Birmingham, AL 35210-2605. Circ: 1,600.

636.7 NLD ISSN 2210-8289
BULLMANIA. Text in Dutch. 2000. q. EUR 30 domestic; EUR 40 foreign (effective 2010). **Document type:** *Magazine, Consumer.*
Published by: Engelse Bulldog Club Nederland, Koningstraat 21, Afferden, 6654 AA, Netherlands. TEL 31-487-518778, secretariaatebcn@kpnmail.nl.

636.7 636.8 BRA ISSN 0103-278X
CAES E GATOS. Text in Portuguese. 1985. bi-m. USD 60 (effective 2000). adv. **Document type:** *Trade.*
Published by: Gessulli Editores Ltda., Praca Sergipe, 154, Caixa Postal 198, Porto Feliz, SP 18540-000, Brazil. TEL 55-152-623133, FAX 55-152-623919. Ed. Osvaldo Penha Gessulli. adv.: page USD 3,280.

CAGE & AVIARY BIRDS. *see* BIOLOGY—Ornithology

636.7 ROM ISSN 1453-701X
CAINELE MEU. Text in Romanian. 1998. m. adv. **Document type:** *Magazine, Consumer.*
Published by: Publimedia International, Str. Luterana nr. 11, bloc CINOR, et. 5, Bucharest, Romania. TEL 40-21-3033907, FAX 40-21-3033958.

636 CAN ISSN 0045-4052
CALQUARIUM. Text in English. 1959. m. CAD 24 to members. adv. bk.rev. **Description:** Articles and news on aquarium keeping. Subject matter is aimed at the average hobbyist.
Published by: Calgary Aquarium Society, P O Box 63180, Calgary, AB T2N 4S5, Canada. Ed. Laura Pylypow. Circ: 175.

636.7 ITA ISSN 1121-3000
CANI; una rivista di razza. Text in Italian. 1990. m. EUR 48 domestic (effective 2008). adv. 128 p./no.; back issues avail. **Document type:** *Magazine, Consumer.*
Published by: Gruppo Editoriale Olimpia SpA, Via E Fermi 24, Loc Osmannoro, Sesto Fiorentino, FI 50129, Italy. TEL 39-055-30321, FAX 39-055-3032280, http://www.edolimpia.it. Circ: 32,000. **Dist. by:** Parrini & C, Piazza Colonna 361, Rome, RM 00187, Italy. TEL 39-06-695141.

P

636.7 USA ISSN 0746-1410
CANINE CHRONICLE. Text in English. 1975. m. USD 80 (effective 2008). adv. **Document type:** *Magazine, Trade.* **Description:** Covers dog shows, breeders, judges, professional handlers and other topics of interest to pure-bred dog owners.
Address: 4727 NW 80th Ave, Ocala, FL 34482. TEL 352-369-1104, FAX 352-369-1108. Ed., Pub. Tom Grabe. Circ: 10,000.

636.7 AUS ISSN 1445-6435
CANINE COLLECTABLES COURIER. Text in English. 1999 (May). q. AUD 30 (effective 2009). **Document type:** *Magazine, Consumer.* **Description:** Features informative news articles, review of canine and dog themed collectibles from around the world and from all eras supported by illustrations and photos.
Related titles: Online - full text ed.: AUD 25 (effective 2009).
Published by: Erinrac Enterprises, PO Box 313, Upper Beaconsfield, VIC 3808, Australia. TEL 61-3-59443383, http://www.erinrac.com.

636.7 USA
CANINE CONNECTIONS. Text in English. m. free. adv. back issues avail. **Description:** Provides articles and information to help educate and expand the knowledge of all current and future dog owners, from the general pet owner to the experienced breeder.
Media: Online - full text.
Address: PO Box 1656, Leicester, NC 28748. TEL 828-683-5318. Ed. Carol Ross.

636.7 364.4 USA
CANINE COURIER. Text in English. 1979. q. USD 40 membership (effective 2004). adv. bk.rev. **Document type:** *Newspaper, Trade.*
Published by: United States Police Canine Association, Inc., c/o Russ Hess, PO Box 80, Springboro, OH 45066. TEL 800-531-1614, uspcadir@aol.com, http://www.uspcak9.com. Ed. Richard Rogers TEL 919-639-0490. Circ: 3,000 (controlled).

636.7 USA
CANINE IMAGES. Text in English. 2000. bi-m. USD 14.90; USD 4.95 newsstand/cover (effective 2001). adv. **Document type:** *Magazine, Consumer.*
Published by: Equine Images Ltd., 1003 Central Ave, Fort Dodge, IA 50501. TEL 515-955-1600, FAX 515-574-2213, canine@canineimages.com, http://www.canineimages.com. Pub. Amelia Presler.

CANINE LISTENER. *see* HANDICAPPED—Hearing Impaired

636.7 USA ISSN 1523-6625
CANINE TIMES. Text in English. bi-m. USD 70 (effective 1999). back issues avail. **Document type:** *Newsletter.* **Description:** Presents articles on breaking research, behavior, human-animal interactions, trends, events and major news of importance of dog owners.
Media: Online - full text.
Published by: C F N A, Inc., PO Box 955, Pullman, WA 99163-0955. Ed. Cynthia Freyer. Circ: 1,745.

636.7 FIN ISSN 1796-7201
CANIS; koiraharrastajan tietolehte. Text in Finnish. 2007. q. EUR 24 (effective 2007). adv. **Document type:** *Magazine, Consumer.*
Published by: Gemm Oy, Urheilukatu 24 a 16, Helsinki, 00250, Finland. TEL 358-50-4634408. adv.: page EUR 700; 210 x 145.

636 USA ISSN 1945-6638
CAPITAL TAILS; celebrating the relationship between pets and their people. Variant title: Tails. Text in English. 2000. m. USD 36; free to qualified personnel (effective 2008). adv. back issues avail. **Document type:** *Magazine, Consumer.*
Related titles: Online - full text ed.: ISSN 1945-6646. free.

Published by: Tails Pet Media Group, Inc., 4527 N Ravenswood Ave, Chicago, IL 60640. TEL 773-561-4300, 877-866-8245, FAX 773-561-3030, mail@tailsinc.org. Adv. contact Nikki Scheel. B&W page USD 2,100, color page USD 2,300; trim 10.5 x 10.5. Circ: 50,000 (controlled).

593 DEU ISSN 1863-2696
CARIDINA; Garnele, Krebs & Co. Text in German. 2006. 4/yr. EUR 22.80 domestic; EUR 25 foreign; EUR 5.95 newsstand/cover (effective 2011). adv. **Document type:** *Magazine, Consumer.*
Published by: Daehne Verlag GmbH, Am Erlengraben 8, Ettlingen, 76275, Germany. TEL 49-7243-5750, FAX 49-7243-575200, service@daehne.de, http://www.daehne.de. Pub. Karl-Heinz Daehne. Adv. contact Thomas Heinen. Circ: 8,386 (paid).

636.7 USA
CASSETTE. Text in English. 1970. q. USD 7. adv. bk.rev. **Description:** Articles, letters, and interviews pertaining to dog-breeding and showing, with show results. Focus is on Collies and Shetland sheepdogs.
Address: c/o Anne Lively, Ed, 2 Hemlock Cove Rd, R R 3, Falmouth, ME 04105. TEL 207-797-9635. Circ: 500.

636.8 179.3 GBR
THE CAT. Text in English. 1931. q. GBP 15 domestic to non-members; GBP 27 foreign to non-members; free to members (effective 2009). adv. bk.rev.; video rev. **Document type:** *Magazine, Consumer.* **Description:** Contains news, views and features on a range of issues affecting cats and their owners' lifestyles.
Former titles (until 200?): Cats Protection; (until 199?): Cat (0008-7599)
Published by: Cats' Protection League, National Cat Centre, Chelwood Gate, Haywards Heath, RH17 7TT, United Kingdom. TEL 800-917-2287, cp.contactsmanagement@cats.org.uk. Adv. contact Terry Lock TEL 44-1372-276233.

636.8 USA ISSN 0069-1003
CAT FANCIERS' ASSOCIATION. ANNUAL YEARBOOK. Text in English. 1958. a., latest vol.31. USD 36; USD 4.95 newsstand/cover domestic; USD 9.95 newsstand/cover in Canada & Mexico; USD 10.95 newsstand/cover in Europe; USD 11.95 newsstand/cover in Asia & Russia (effective 2003). adv. bk.rev.; film rev.; music rev.; rec.rev.; software rev.; video rev.; Website rev. bibl.; stat. **Document type:** *Yearbook, Consumer.* **Description:** Contains CFA Awards, as well as articles on cat breeds, health, art, and general care.
Published by: Cat Fanciers' Association, Inc., 1805 Atlantic Ave, Box 1005, Manasquan, NJ 08736-0805. TEL 732-528-9797, FAX 732-528-7391, cfa@cfainc.org, http://www.cfainc.org. Ed., R&P Carol A Krzanowski. Adv. contact Michael W Brim TEL 732-528-9797 ext. 33. Circ: 7,500 (controlled).

636.8 USA ISSN 0892-6514
SF441
CAT FANCY. Text in English. 1965. m. USD 13 domestic; USD 25 foreign (effective 2011). adv. bk.rev. illus. Index. reprints avail. **Document type:** *Magazine, Consumer.* **Description:** Provides information on how to better understand and care for cats. Covers medical problems, care technique, purebreds, personal and fictional stories. Includes questions and answers.
Supersedes (in 1986): International Cat Fancy (0199-0640)
Indexed: A22, BRI, IAB.
—Ingenta.
Published by: BowTie, Inc., PO Box 6050, Mission Viejo, CA 92690. http://www.bowtieinc.com.

636.8 USA ISSN 1095-9092
CAT WATCH. Text in English. 1997. m. USD 39 combined subscription in US & Canada (print & online eds.); USD 48 combined subscription elsewhere (print & online eds.) (effective 2010). back issues avail. **Document type:** *Newsletter, Consumer.* **Description:** Contains the latest news and advice on cat care.
Supersedes in part (in 1997): Animal Health Newsletter (0884-092X)
Related titles: Online - full text ed.
Indexed: G06, G07, G08, I05, I07.
Published by: (Cornell University, College of Veterinary Medicine), Belvoir Media Group, LLC, PO Box 5656, Norwalk, CT 06856. TEL 203-857-3100, 800-424-7887, FAX 203-857-3103, customer_service@belvoir.com, http://www.belvoir.com. Eds. Elizabeth Vesci, Fred W Scott. **Subscr. to:** Palm Coast Data, LLC, PO Box 420235, Palm Coast, FL 32142. TEL 800-829-8893, http://www.palmcoastdata.com.

636 USA ISSN 0163-1926
CAT WORLD. Text in English. 1973. bi-m. USD 23 (effective 2007). adv. bk.rev. Index. back issues avail. **Document type:** *Magazine, Consumer.*
Published by: Cat World International, 19219 N 109th Ave, Sun City, AZ 85015. TEL 602-995-1822, FAX 602-246-4840. Ed. Naomi Corn. Pub. Tom Corn. Circ: 8,000 (paid and controlled).

636.8 GBR ISSN 0952-2875
CAT WORLD. Text in English. 1981. m. GBP 33; GBP 3.95 per issue (effective 2009). adv. bk.rev. illus. back issues avail. **Document type:** *Magazine, Consumer.* **Description:** Features information and advice from cat care to breeding as well as lists breeders from around the UK.
Formerly (until 1982): Cat World Weekly
Related titles: Online - full text ed.: GBP 20 (effective 2009); Supplement(s): Paws. ISSN 0958-0484.
Published by: Ashdown Publishing Ltd., Ancient Lights, 19 River Rd, Arundel, W Sussex BN18 9EY, United Kingdom. TEL 44-1903-884988, FAX 44-1903-885514, info@ashdown.co.uk, http://www.ashdown.co.uk. Ed. Laura Quiggan. adv.: B&W page GBP 684, color page GBP 1,029; trim 210 x 297.

636.7 USA ISSN 1524-6310
CATAHOULA EZINE. Text in English. 1995. q. free. adv. illus. index. back issues avail. **Document type:** *Magazine, Consumer.* **Description:** For dog lovers of all ages, livestock producers, and hunters. Covers search and rescue teams, agility and other miscellaneous competitions.
Media: Online - full text.
Published by: McKay Productions, PO Box 1058, Canton, TX 75103. TEL 903-962-7445. Ed., Pub., R&P, Adv. contact Linda McKay.

CATCARE. *see* ANIMAL WELFARE

636.8 USA ISSN 1069-6687
CATNIP; the newsletter for caring cat owners. Text in English. 1993. m. USD 39 domestic; CAD 49 in Canada (effective 2008). illus. back issues avail. **Document type:** *Newsletter, Consumer.* **Description:** Gives cat owners practical ideas on how to best care for their felines.
Indexed: B04, BRD, R03, RGAb, RGPR, W03, W05.
—CCC.
Published by: Tufts University, Cummings School of Veterinary Medicine, Tufts Media, 196 Boston Ave, Ste 2100, Medford, MA 02155. TEL 800-829-5116, vetadmissions@tufts.edu. Eds. Arden Moore, John Berg. R&P Gloria Parkinson. Circ: 65,000.

636.8 JPN ISSN 1348-6667
CATS. Text in Japanese. m. JPY 8,500 (effective 2007). illus. **Document type:** *Magazine, Consumer.* **Description:** Provides general information for cat keepers.
Published by: Midori Shobo Co. Ltd. (Subsidiary of: Midori Group), JPR Crest Takebashi Bldg., 3-21 Kanda Nishikicho Chiyoda-ku, Tokyo, 101-0054, Japan. info@mgp.co.jp, http://www.mgp.co.jp/. Circ: 70,000.

636.8 USA ISSN 1079-8285
CATS & KITTENS. Text in English. 1995. bi-m. USD 19.97 domestic; USD 25.97 in Canada; USD 31.97 elsewhere (effective 2006). adv. illus. back issues avail. **Document type:** *Magazine, Consumer.* **Description:** Contains articles and features on cats at work and play, and the people who love them.
Related titles: Online - full text ed.
Published by: Pet Publishing, Inc., 7-L Dundas Circle, Greensboro, NC 27407. TEL 336-292-4047, FAX 336-292-4272, editorial@petpublishing.com. Ed. Rita Davis. adv.: B&W page USD 1,995, color page USD 2,895; trim 8.5 x 11.375. Circ: 50,000.

636.8 USA ISSN 1071-3999
CATS U S A; guide to buying and caring for purebred kittens. Text in English. 1992. a. USD 8.50 per issue (effective 2008). adv. illus. **Document type:** *Magazine, Consumer.* **Description:** Provides essential information on buying and caring for purebred kittens and introduces the reader to the world of pedigreed cats.
Published by: BowTie, Inc., 2401 Beverly Blvd, PO Box 57900, Los Angeles, CA 90057. TEL 213-385-2222, FAX 213-385-8565, adtraffic@bowtieinc.com, http://www.bowtieinc.com. Ed. Jackie Franza. Pub. Norman Ridker. adv.: B&W page USD 7,000, color page USD 10,320; trim 8 x 10.875. Circ: 87,790.

636.7 USA
CAVALIER KING CHARLES SPANIEL CLUB, U S A. BULLETIN. Text in English. 1964. q. USD 10. bk.rev.
Formerly: Cavalier King Charles Spaniel Club of America. Bulletin
Published by: Cavalier King Charles Spaniel Club, U S A, Inc., c/o Courtney Carter, Sec, 2 Brynwood Ln, Newtown, PA 18940. Ed. Jesse Cleveland. Circ: 750.

636.7 USA ISSN 1949-2790
SF425
▼ **CESAR'S WAY**; secrets from the dog whisperer. Text in English. 2009. bi-m. USD 14.99 (effective 2009). **Document type:** *Magazine, Consumer.* **Description:** Advice from dog trainer Cesar Millan.
Published by: I M G Worldwide, 304 Park Ave, 8th Fl, New York, NY 10010. TEL 646-871-2430, susank.lynch@imgworld.com, http://www.imgworld.com. Ed. Brandusa Niro.

636.8 FRA ISSN 1950-2192
LES CHATS. Text in French. 2006. irreg. back issues avail. **Document type:** *Monographic series, Consumer.*
Published by: Animalia Editions, B P 3, Mouleydier, 24520, France. TEL 33-5-53240760, FAX 33-5-53241224, information@animalia-editions.net.

636 USA ISSN 1535-3818
CHICAGOLAND TAILS; celebrating the relationship between pets and their people. Text in English. 2000. m. USD 36; free to qualified personnel (effective 2008). adv. back issues avail. **Document type:** *Magazine, Consumer.*
Related titles: Online - full text ed.: ISSN 1535-380X. free.
Published by: Tails Pet Media Group, Inc., 4527 N Ravenswood Ave, Chicago, IL 60640. TEL 773-561-4300, 877-866-8245, FAX 773-561-3030, mail@tailsinc.org. Adv. contact Nikki Scheel. B&W page USD 2,100, color page USD 2,300; trim 10.5 x 10.5. Circ: 138,000 (controlled).

799.2 636.7 FRA ISSN 1959-4135
CHIEN DE CHASSE MAGAZINE. Text in French. 2007. bi-m. EUR 35 (effective 2008). **Document type:** *Magazine, Consumer.*
Address: B P 10164, Rambouillet, Cedex 78515, France. **Dist. by:** Animal Otheque, Le Moulin de Luet, Beville le Comte 28700, France. TEL 33-1-34844869, monanimal@cophicom.com, http://www.animalotheque.com.

636.7 FRA ISSN 1776-1182
CHIEN MAG; le magazine des chiens de compagnie. Text in French. 200?. bi-m. **Document type:** *Magazine, Consumer.*
Formerly (until 2005): Chien Magazine (1769-3780)
Published by: Magbis, Complexe Industriel de la Huniere, Sonchamp, 78120, France.

636.7 CHE ISSN 1662-7202
LE CHIEN MAGAZINE. Text in French. 1935. 11/yr. CHF 60; CHF 7 newsstand/cover (effective 2011). adv. illus. **Document type:** *Magazine, Consumer.*
Formerly (until 1987): Chien (1662-7199)
Published by: Presses Centrales Lausanne SA, Ave de Longemalle 9, Case postale 137, Renens 1, 1020, Switzerland. TEL 41-21-3175151, FAX 41-21-3205950, pcl@worldcom.ch, http://www.pcl.ch.

636.7 FRA ISSN 1639-1586
LES CHIENS. Text in French. 2001. irreg. back issues avail. **Document type:** *Monographic series, Consumer.*
Published by: Animalia Editions, B P 3, Mouleydier, 24520, France. TEL 33-5-53240760, FAX 33-5-53241224, information@animalia-editions.net.

636 FRA ISSN 1963-2436
CHIENS CHATS & CO. Text in French. 2007. irreg. **Document type:** *Magazine, Consumer.*
Formerly (until 2007): Le Magazine Chiens et Chats (1956-2241)
Published by: E M I, 78 Av. Kleber, Paris, 75116, France. TEL 33-1-48123530, 33-1-48123531.

636 FRA ISSN 1287-0765
CHIENS SANS LAISSE; magazine de l'education et des sports canins. Text in French. 1978. bi-m. EUR 28 domestic; EUR 34 in Europe; EUR 36 DOM-TOM; EUR 37 in North America; EUR 35 in Africa; EUR 35 in the Middle East; EUR 40 elsewhere (effective 2009). adv. bk.rev. index. **Document type:** *Magazine, Consumer.* **Description:** Publishes articles on dog ownership as sport.
Former titles (until 1998): Sans Laisse (0768-8733); (until 1987): Berger Allemand (0183-3197)
Published by: Sans Laisse, 226 Av. du Vidourle, Lunel, 34400, France. TEL 33-4-67715569, FAX 33-4-67910089, message@sanslaisse.com. Ed. Alain Dupont. Circ: 18,000.

636 USA ISSN 0273-2335
LOS CHIHUAHUAS. Text in English. 1976. bi-m. USD 20 domestic; USD 40 foreign (effective 2007). adv. back issues avail. **Document type:** *Magazine, Consumer.*
Published by: Los Chihuahuas, 12860 Thonotosassa Rd, Dover, FL 33527. TEL 813-986-2943. Ed., Pub., R&P Myrle Hale. Adv. contact Charles Hale. Circ: 650.

636 CHN ISSN 1673-6702
CHONGWU SHIJIE/PET WORLD. (2 editions: Chongwu Shijie. Goumi/Pet World. Dog Fans; and Chongwu Shijie. Maomi/Pet World. Cat Fans.) Text in Chinese. 2000 (Sep.). m. CNY 240 for Dog Fans ed.; CNY 200 for Cat Fans ed.; CNY 20 per issue for Dog Fans ed.; CNY 16 per issue for Cat Fans ed. (effective 2011). **Document type:** *Magazine, Consumer.*
Former titles (until 2004): Chongwu - Shenghuo/Pets Life; (until 2003): Dongwu Shijie/Pets World (1009-7880)
Published by: Zhongguo Qinggongye Chubanshe/China Light Industry Press, 6, Chang'an Jie, Beijing, 100740, China. TEL 86-10-65259145, http://www.chlip.com.cn/. **Dist. by:** China International Book Trading Corp, 35 Chegongzhuang Xilu, Haidian District, PO Box 399, Beijing 100044, China. TEL 86-10-68412045, FAX 86-10-68412023, cibtc@mail.cibtc.com.cn, http://www.cibtc.com.cn.

636.7 179.3 AUS ISSN 1447-915X
CLUMBERS. Text in English. 1987. q. AUD 30 (effective 2009). bk.rev.; Website rev.; video rev. illus.; stat. 30 p./no.; back issues avail. **Document type:** *Magazine, Consumer.* **Description:** Contains information and news about the Clumber Spaniel from around the world supported by extraordinary photos and illustration.
Formerly (until 2003): Clumber Spaniel Correspondence (0819-5862)
Related titles: Online - full text ed.: AUD 25 (effective 2009).
Published by: Erinrac Enterprises, PO Box 313, Upper Beaconsfield, VIC 3808, Australia. TEL 61-3-59443383, http://www.erinrac.com.

636.7 USA ISSN 2154-2163
▼ **COAST TO COAST (JACKSON).** Text in English. 2010. q. **Document type:** *Newsletter, Consumer.* **Description:** Features articles, photos and information on terriers and affiliate clubs of the Boston Terrier Club of America.
Published by: Boston Terrier Club of America, W207 N295 Parkview Dr, Jackson, WI 53037. brook@gunthergraphics.com, http://www.bostonterrierclubofamerica.org/.

636.7 BRA ISSN 1808-5504
COLECAO GUIA DE RACAS. Text in Portuguese. 2005. irreg. BRL 5.90 newsstand/cover (effective 2006). **Document type:** *Magazine, Consumer.*
Published by: Editora Escala Ltda., Av Prof Ida Kolb, 551, Casa Verde, Sao Paulo, 02518-000, Brazil. TEL 55-11-38552100, FAX 55-11-38579643, escala@escala.com.br, http://www.escala.com.br.

636.7 USA
COLLIE CLUB OF AMERICA. BULLETIN. Text in English. bi-m. free to members (effective 2008). **Document type:** *Bulletin, Consumer.*
Published by: Collie Club of America, c/o Karen Murphy, Ed., 2088 Alabama Hwy 23, Springville, AL 35146. ccasec@tcelco.net. Ed. Ronald Dow. Circ: 3,500.

LA COLOMBOPHILIE BELGE. *see* SPORTS AND GAMES—Outdoor Life

636 USA
COLONIAL ROTTWEILER CLUB NEWSLETTER. Text in English. 1954. 6/yr. USD 25 to non-members (effective 2000). adv. back issues avail. **Document type:** *Newsletter.*
Published by: Colonial Rottweiler Club, 6535 Ellicott Rd, Portland, NY 14769. TEL 716-326-2370. Ed., R&P Norma Dikeman. Circ: 600.

COMPANION ANIMAL PRACTICE. *see* VETERINARY SCIENCE

636 NZL ISSN 1177-3766
THE COMPLETE PET TRAVEL GUIDE. Text in English. 1996. a. NZD 15 (effective 2008). **Document type:** *Handbook/Manual/Guide, Consumer.*
Published by: Pauline Wagner, Ed. & Pub., 114 Rahui Rd, Otaki, 5512, New Zealand.

COONHOUND BLOODLINES. *see* SPORTS AND GAMES—Outdoor Life

636.7 CAN ISSN 1926-299X
▼ **COTTAGE DOG**; for city dogs who love to get away. Text in English. 2010. 8/yr. CAD 26.99; free to qualified personnel (effective 2011). adv. back issues avail. **Document type:** *Magazine, Consumer.*
Related titles: Online - full text ed.: free (effective 2011).
Published by: Cottage Dog Publications, 1393 Brunel Rd, RR #2, Huntsville, ON P1H 2J3, Canada. TEL 705-789-9181, FAX 705-789-7952, storysubmissions@cottagedog.com. Ed. Bryan Dearsley. Pub. K L Brooks. Adv. contact Brenda Paterson TEL 705-640-1054.

636 CAN ISSN 0382-4497
COURRIER S P C A/S P C A COURIER. Text in English, French. 1974. q. USD 5.
Published by: Societe Canadienne de Protection des Animaux/Canadian Society for the Protection of Animals, 5215 Ouest, Rue Jean Talon, Montreal, PQ H4P 1X4, Canada. TEL 514-735-2711. Circ: 12,000.

599.3 USA ISSN 1093-9393
CRITTERS U S A. Text in English. 1996. a. USD 6.99 per issue (effective 2008). adv. illus. **Document type:** *Magazine, Consumer.* **Description:** Contains all the basics to educate beginners on the importance of proper care of a variety of small pets from hamsters and mice, to sugar gliders and hedgehogs.
Published by: BowTie, Inc., 2401 Beverly Blvd, PO Box 57900, Los Angeles, CA 90057. TEL 213-385-2222, FAX 213-385-8565, adtraffic@bowtieinc.com, http://www.bowtieinc.com.

636.753 DEU ISSN 0011-5231
DER DACHSHUND. Text in German. 1946. 10/yr. adv. bk.rev. **Document type:** *Magazine, Consumer.* **Description:** Highlights dog care and breeding.
Published by: Deutscher Teckelklub e.V., Prinzenstr 38, Duisburg, 47058, Germany. TEL 49-203-330005, FAX 49-203-330007, info@dtk1888.de, http://www.dtk1888.de. adv.: B&W page EUR 1,490, color page EUR 2,500; trim 210 x 297. Circ: 18,330 (controlled).

636 USA ISSN 1940-8544
DESERT DOG NEWS. Text in English. 2007. bi-m. USD 10; free newsstand/cover (effective 2008). adv. **Document type:** *Newspaper, Consumer.* **Description:** Focuses on issues, events and activities that support the companion animal community in the Tucson area. Features adoptable pets, training, activity and grooming information, community profiles and national news of interest to pet owners.
Published by: Sensible Press, 1933 E 10th St, Tucson, AZ 85719. TEL 520-903-4886. Ed. Gretel Hakanson. adv.: page USD 800; 10.25 x 15.75.

636.7 DEU
DEUTSCH-DRAHTHAAR BLAETTER. Text in German. m. adv. **Document type:** *Magazine, Trade.*
Published by: Verein Deutsch-Drahthaar e.V., Dorfstr 48, Wintzingerode, 37339, Germany. TEL 49-36074-63155, FAX 49-36074-63154, jan.schafberg@drahthaar.de, http://www.drahthaar.de. Ed. Jan Schafberg. adv.: B&W page EUR 426.30. Circ: 10,607 (controlled).

636.7 DEU ISSN 1435-649X
DAS DEUTSCHE HUNDE MAGAZIN. Text in German. 1998. m. EUR 28.95; EUR 2.80 newsstand/cover (effective 2011). adv. **Document type:** *Magazine, Consumer.* **Description:** Contains articles and features on all aspects of owning and caring for dogs.
Published by: Gong Verlag GmbH & Co. KG, Muenchener Str 101, Ismaning, 85737, Germany. TEL 49-89-272700, FAX 49-89-272707290, gonginfo@gongverlag.de, http://www.gong-verlag.de. Ed. Monika Binder. Adv. contact Sonja Haase. Circ: 50,000 (paid and controlled).

636.7 DEU
DER DEUTSCHE SPITZ. Text in German. 1952. q. adv. **Document type:** *Journal, Trade.*
Published by: Verein fuer Deutsche Spitze e.V., Angerstr 5, Augsburg, 86179, Germany. TEL 49-821-812943. Ed. Peter Machetanz. Circ: 3,000 (controlled).

636.75 DEU ISSN 0343-5474
DEUTSCHE WACHTELHUND-ZEITUNG. Text in German. 19??. m. adv. **Document type:** *Magazine, Trade.*
Published by: Verein fuer Deutsche Wachtelhunde e.V., Waldweg 10, Freudenberg, 57258, Germany. TEL 49-271-370661, FAX 49-271-7402609, ochs@wachtelhund.de, http://www-wid.fb5.uni-siegen.de/wachtelhund/framestart.htm. Ed. Conrad Henkens. adv.: B&W page EUR 243.60. Circ: 3,633 (controlled).

636 DEU
DEUTSCHER JAGDTERRIERCLUB. NACHRICHTENBLATT. Text in German. 1946. q. EUR 40 membership (effective 2009). adv. **Document type:** *Newsletter, Consumer.*
Published by: Deutscher Jagdterrier-Club e.V., Dietenhauser Str 1, Dietramszell-Lochen, 83623, Germany. TEL 49-8027-671, FAX 49-8027-904810, jenny-schroeder@t-online.de, http://www.djt-club.de. adv.: B&W page EUR 380, color page EUR 490. Circ: 4,000 (controlled).

636.7 USA
DEW CLAW. Text in English. 1928. bi-m. free to members (effective 2008). adv. bk.rev. **Document type:** *Magazine, Consumer.*
Published by: Briard Club of America, c/o Fran Ferrante, 5774 Victor Dr, Eldersburg, MD 21784. TEL 410-549-2354, webmaster@briardclubofamerica.org, bca_membership@verizon.net, http://www.briardclubofamerica.org. Ed. Diane McLeroth. Circ: 700.

636 NLD ISSN 1878-8432
DIBEVO VAKBLAD. Running title: Dibevo Vakblad dier tuin. Text in Dutch. 1947. m. (11/yr.). EUR 87.50 domestic to non-members; EUR 140 foreign to non-members (effective 2009). adv. bk.rev. charts; illus.; stat. **Document type:** *Journal, Trade.* **Description:** For pet shop owners, groomers, pet boarding houses, garden center owners, manufacturers, retail and wholesale traders, and importers-exporters of life stock.
Former titles (until 2008): Dier Tuin (1871-000X); (until 1999): Dibevo Vakblad (0921-5123); (until 1988): Dibevo (0012-2416)
Indexed: KES.
Published by: Landelijke Organisatie DIBEVO/Netherlands Organisation of Pet Retailers and Suppliers, Postbus 94, Amersfoort, 3800 AB, Netherlands. TEL 31-33-4550433, FAX 31-33-4552835, info@divevo.nl, http://www.dibevo.nl. Adv. contact Martijn Hagenaar. B&W page EUR 1,369, color page EUR 2,127; trim 210 x 297. Circ: 4,000 (controlled).

636 NLD ISSN 0166-5871
DIER EN VRIEND. Text in Dutch. 1977. q. EUR 8.25 domestic; EUR 9.25 in Belgium; EUR 18.50 elsewhere; EUR 3.25 newsstand/cover (effective 2010). adv. **Document type:** *Magazine, Consumer.*
Published by: Landelijke Organisatie DIBEVO/Netherlands Organisation of Pet Retailers and Suppliers, Postbus 94, Amersfoort, 3800 AB, Netherlands. TEL 31-33-4550433, FAX 31-33-4552835, info@divevo.nl. adv.: B&W page EUR 2,828, color page EUR 3,328; trim 210 x 297. Circ: 125,000.

636 NLD ISSN 1570-6370
DIER JOURNAAL. Text in Dutch. 2006. m. EUR 19.95 domestic; EUR 39.95 in Belgium; EUR 39.95 in Spain (effective 2010). adv. **Document type:** *Magazine, Consumer.*
Published by: Publi Force, Postbus 229, Alblasserdam, 2950 AE, Netherlands. TEL 31-78-6522700, FAX 31-78-6522701, info@publiforce.nl, http://www.publiforce.nl. adv.: page EUR 2,500; trim 230 x 297. Circ: 22,472.

DINGO SANCTUARY BARGO. NEWSLETTER. *see* CONSERVATION

636.7 RUS ISSN 1562-756X
DOBERMAN. Text in Russian, English. 1994. bi-m. USD 55 (effective 2001). adv. illus. 48 p./no.; back issues avail. **Document type:** *Magazine, Consumer.* **Description:** Contains articles on training, genetics, veterinary, feeding, history of the breed, famous kennels and people, show results, as well as news from all over the world.
Published by: Izdatel'skii Dom, Palikha ul 9-1-40, Moscow, 103055, Russian Federation. TEL 7-095-9730043, FAX 7-095-9730044. Ed. V Yu Belyakov. Pub., R&P, Adv. contact Tatiana Kulachenko. color page USD 300. **Dist. by:** East View Information Services, 10601 Wayzata Blvd, Minneapolis, MN 55305. TEL 952-252-1201, 800-477-1005, FAX 952-252-1202, info@eastview.com, http://www.eastview.com.

636.7 USA ISSN 0194-9756
DOG (MARSHALL). Text in English. 1979. fortn.
Published by: Ringside Publications, 4977 Midway Lane, Marshall, WI 53559.

636 AUS ISSN 1832-9446
DOG AND CAT MANAGEMENT BOARD OF SOUTH AUSTRALIA. ANNUAL REPORT. Text in English. 19??. a. free (effective 2009). back issues avail. **Document type:** *Government.* **Description:** Reports on the activities of the dog and cat management board as well as their plans, policies and financial performance.
Related titles: Online - full text ed.
Published by: Dog and Cat Management Board of South Australia, GPO Box 1047, Adelaide, SA 5001, Australia. TEL 61-8-81244975, FAX 61-8-91244856, dcmb@saugov.sa.gov.au.

636.7 USA ISSN 1079-8277
DOG & KENNEL. Text in English. 1997. bi-m. USD 19.97 domestic; USD 25.97 in Canada; USD 31.97 elsewhere (effective 2006). adv. illus. back issues avail. **Document type:** *Magazine, Consumer.* **Description:** Includes in-depth profiles of popular and not often seen breeds, chronicles of breeders, profiles of artists and celebrities, and Dogs in Service. A human-interest magazine for dog lovers.
Published by: Pet Publishing, Inc., 7-L Dundas Circle, Greensboro, NC 27407. TEL 336-292-4047, FAX 336-292-4272, editorial@petpublishing.com. Ed. Rita Davis. adv.: B&W page USD 2,695, color page USD 3,910; trim 8.125 x 11. Circ: 50,000.

636.7 USA ISSN 1542-5339
DOG DAYS OF DENVER. Text in English. 2002 (May/Jun.). bi-m. USD 18.95 (effective 2002). adv.
Published by: Dog Days Media Group, P. O. Box 24379, Denver, CO 80224-0379. TEL 303-757-3331, FAX 303-757-3374, kim@dogdaysdenver.com, http://www.dogdaysdenver.com. Ed., Pub. Kim Jackson. Adv. contact Jill Savino.

636.7 USA ISSN 0892-6522
SF421
DOG FANCY. Text in English. 1970. m. USD 13 domestic; USD 25 foreign (effective 2011). adv. bk.rev. illus. Index. back issues avail.; reprints avail. **Document type:** *Magazine, Consumer.* **Description:** Provides information for the dog lover - including professional breeders, show exhibitors and, especially, general pet owners. Covers information on canine diet, grooming, exotic and domestic breeds, medical news and tips for showing.
Former titles (until 1986): International Dog Fancy; (until 198?): Dog Fancy (0012-4834)
Indexed: BRI, IAB.
Published by: BowTie, Inc., PO Box 6050, Mission Viejo, CA 92690. http://www.bowtieinc.com.

THE DOG LOVER'S COMPANION TO BOSTON; the inside scoop on where to take your dog. *see* TRAVEL AND TOURISM

THE DOG LOVER'S COMPANION TO CALIFORNIA; the inside scoop on where to take your dog. *see* TRAVEL AND TOURISM

THE DOG LOVER'S COMPANION TO CHICAGO; the inside scoop on where to take your dog. *see* TRAVEL AND TOURISM

THE DOG LOVER'S COMPANION TO FLORIDA; the inside scoop on where to take your dog. *see* TRAVEL AND TOURISM

THE DOG LOVER'S COMPANION TO LOS ANGELES. *see* TRAVEL AND TOURISM

THE DOG LOVER'S COMPANION TO NEW ENGLAND; the inside scoop on where to take your dog. *see* TRAVEL AND TOURISM

THE DOG LOVER'S COMPANION TO NEW YORK CITY; the inside scoop on where to take your dog. *see* TRAVEL AND TOURISM

THE DOG LOVER'S COMPANION TO THE BAY AREA; the inside scoop on where to take your dog. *see* TRAVEL AND TOURISM

THE DOG LOVER'S COMPANION TO THE PACIFIC NORTHWEST. *see* TRAVEL AND TOURISM

THE DOG LOVER'S COMPANION TO WASHINGTON D.C. & BALTIMORE. *see* TRAVEL AND TOURISM

▼ **THE DOG LOVER'S GUIDE TO OREGON.** *see* TRAVEL AND TOURISM

636 USA ISSN 0886-2133
DOG NEWS. Text in English. 1984. w. (except last two weeks in Dec.). USD 150 domestic; USD 500 foreign (effective 2009). adv. back issues avail. **Document type:** *Newspaper, Consumer.* **Description:** Features the latest news concerning the purebred dog specifically and all dogs generally.
Published by: Harris Publications, Inc., 1115 Broadway, New York, NY 10010. TEL 212-807-7100, FAX 212-924-2352, subscriptions@harris-pub.com, http://www.harris-pub.com. Ed. Matt Stander. adv.: B&W page USD 250, color page USD 600.

636.7 AUS ISSN 1834-1837
DOG NEWS AUSTRALIA. Text in English. 2006. m. AUD 45 (effective 2007). adv. **Document type:** *Magazine, Consumer.*
Published by: Dog News Australia Pty Ltd, PO Box 3151, Austral, NSW 2179, Australia. TEL 61-2-9791-5332, http://www.dognewsaustralia.com.au/default.asp.

636.7 AUS ISSN 1837-2384
▼ **DOG SHOW SCENE.** Text in English. 2010. q. AUD 29.95 domestic; AUD 59.95 in Asia includes New Zealand; AUD 69.95 elsewhere; AUD 7.95 per issue (effective 2011). adv. **Document type:** *Magazine, Trade.* **Description:** Contains information for new dog owners including veterinary advice, training tips, tips on feeding, grooming and rearing etc.
Published by: Australian Canine Press Pty Ltd, PO Box 3151, Austral, NSW 2179, Australia. TEL 61-2-96062000, sales@dogshowscene.com.au. Eds. Celeste Bryson, Lauren Bryson, John Bryson.

636.7 790.1 USA ISSN 0279-4144
DOG SPORTS. Text in English. 1979. m. USD 44. adv. bk.rev. **Description:** Covers the world of the working dog. Includes canine search and rescue, dogs used for personal and industrial security and working dog sports.
Formerly (until 19??): Dog Sports Magazine (0194-6706)
Published by: D S M Publishing, Inc., 32 Cherokee Trail, Douglas, WY 82633-9232. TEL 707-745-6897, FAX 707-745-4581. Ed. Michael E McKown. Circ: 3,200.

636.7 GBR ISSN 0012-4885
DOG WORLD. Text in English. 1918. w. GBP 115 domestic; GBP 125 in Europe; GBP 170 elsewhere; GBP 1.80 per issue domestic; GBP 2.90 per issue in Europe; GBP 4.80 per issue elsewhere (effective 2009). adv. Supplement avail.; back issues avail.; reprints avail. **Document type:** *Newspaper, Consumer.* **Description:** Provides news and views from all aspects of the pedigree dog scene at home and overseas.
Formerly (until 1919): The Country World and Illustrated Kennel News
Related titles: Microform ed.: (from PQC); Online - full text ed.: GBP 50 (effective 2009); free for domestic subscribers; ◆ Supplement(s): Dog World Annual. ISSN 0070-7015.
—CCC.
Published by: The Dog World Ltd., Somerfield House, Wotton Rd, Ashford, Kent TN23 6LW, United Kingdom. FAX 44-1233-645669. Ed. Stuart Baillie. Adv. contact Lee Hutton.

636.7 USA ISSN 0012-4893
SF421
DOG WORLD; active dogs, active people. Text in English. 1916. m. USD 15 domestic; USD 27 foreign (effective 2011). adv. bk.rev. illus. Index. reprints avail. **Document type:** *Magazine, Consumer.* **Description:** Publication for breeders, exhibitors, hobbyists, professionals in kennel operations, and suppliers.
Related titles: Microform ed.: (from PQC); Online - full text ed.
Indexed: A11, A22, C05, G09, H20, IAB, M01, M02, MASUSE, P02, P10, P48, P53, P54, PQC, T02, U01.
—Ingenta. **CCC.**
Published by: BowTie, Inc., PO Box 6050, Mission Viejo, CA 92690. http://www.bowtieinc.com.

636.8 GBR ISSN 0070-7015
DOG WORLD ANNUAL. Text in English. 1929. a. GBP 5 per issue domestic; GBP 7.20 per issue in Europe; GBP 12.30 per issue elsewhere (effective 2009). adv. index. back issues avail. **Document type:** *Journal, Consumer.* **Description:** Features review of all the events that have affected the UK dog scene.
Related titles: Online - full text ed.: GBP 7 (effective 2009); ◆ Supplement to: Dog World. ISSN 0012-4885.
—CCC.
Published by: The Dog World Ltd., Somerfield House, Wotton Rd, Ashford, Kent TN23 6LW, United Kingdom. TEL 44-1233-621877, FAX 44-1233-645669. Adv. contact Lee Hutton. page GBP 295; 185 x 271.

DOGFRIENDLY.COM'S CAMPGROUND AND R V PARK GUIDE. (Recreational Vehicle) *see* TRAVEL AND TOURISM

636.7 NLD
DOGGENDAGEN. Text in Dutch. 2005. triennial. EUR 24.95 combined subscription per issue (effective 2009). illus.
Published by: BBPress, Broeksterweg 5, Pieterburen, 9968 TH, Netherlands. TEL 31-595-528429, basbosch@bbpress.nl, http://www.bbpress.nl.

636 USA
DOGGONE; the newsletter about fun places to go and cool stuff to do with your dog. Text in English. 1993. bi-m. USD 24 for 6 mos. domestic (effective 2001). bk.rev. 16 p./no. 3 cols./p.; back issues avail.
Address: 1846, Estes Park, CO 80517-1846. Pub. Wendy Ballard. Circ: 3,000.

636.7 DEU ISSN 1863-6330
DOGS. Text in German. 2006. bi-m. EUR 30; EUR 5 newsstand/cover (effective 2011). adv. **Document type:** *Magazine, Consumer.*
Published by: Gruner + Jahr AG & Co, Am Baumwall 11, Hamburg, 20459, Germany. TEL 49-40-37030, FAX 49-40-37035601, info@gujmedia.de, http://www.guj.de. Ed. Thomas Niederste-Werbeck. Adv. contact Heiko Hager.

636.7 DEU ISSN 1867-8726
▼ **DOG'S ELYSEE**; style - trend - shopping. Text in German. 2009. bi-m. EUR 19.20 domestic; EUR 25.20 in Europe; EUR 43.20 elsewhere; EUR 3.50 newsstand/cover (effective 2010). adv. **Document type:** *Magazine, Consumer.*
Published by: Minerva Verlag GmbH, Hocksteiner Weg 38, Moenchengladbach, 41189, Germany. TEL 49-2166-621970, FAX 49-2166-6219710, info@minervaverlag.de, http://www.minervaverlag.de. adv.: B&W page EUR 2,548, color page EUR 4,331.60; trim 192 x 260. Circ: 55,000 (paid).

636.7 CAN ISSN 0012-4915
DOGS IN CANADA; devoted to dogs and their Canadians. Text in English. 1889. m. CAD 39 domestic; USD 57 in United States; USD 92 elsewhere (effective 2008). adv. bk.rev. illus. **Document type:** *Magazine, Consumer.* **Description:** Serves the purebred dog breeder & exhibitor. Carries articles on health, training, behavior, shows & trials, genetics and various other aspects of the burebred dog.
Incorporates (1975-1976): Dogs Annual (0317-1485); Which was formerly (until 1974): Kennel Directory (0317-1477)
Indexed: C03, CBCARef, CBPI, P48, PQC.
Published by: Apex Publishing Ltd., 89 Skyway Ave, Ste 200, Etobicoke, ON M9W 6R4, Canada. TEL 416-798-9778, FAX 416-798-9671. Eds. Beth Marley, Kelly Caldwell. Pub. David Bell. R&P Patty Milton. Adv. contact Beverly Cantelon. B&W page CAD 2,285, color page CAD 3,199; trim 10.75 x 8.13. Circ: 41,390. **Dist. by:** Disticor, 695 Westney Rd S., Ste. 14, Ajax, ON L1S 6M9, Canada. TEL 905-619-6565, FAX 905-619-2903, http://www.disticor.com/.

636.7 CAN
DOGS IN CANADA ANNUAL. Text in English. 1974. a. CAD 9.50 per issue (effective 1999). adv. **Document type:** *Handbook/Manual/Guide, Consumer.* **Description:** Complete guide for pet owners and owners-to-be, from selection to training and health. Includes cross-Canada directory of dog breeders, with breed descriptions.

Published by: Apex Publishing Ltd., 89 Skyway Ave, Ste 200, Etobicoke, ON M9W 6R4, Canada. TEL 416-798-9778, FAX 416-798-9671. Ed. Allan Reznik. Pub. David Bell. R&P Patty Milton. Adv. contact Paul Doyle. B&W page CAD 6,644, color page CAD 7,689; trim 10.5 x 8.13. Circ: 101,000. **Dist. by:** Disticor, 695 Westney Rd S., Ste. 14, Ajax, ON L1S 6M9, Canada.

636.7 USA ISSN 1531-2380
DOGS IN REVIEW. Text in English. 1997. 11/yr. USD 48 domestic; USD 65 in Canada; USD 79 elsewhere (effective 2001). adv.
Published by: Show Dog Publications, PO Box 30430, Santa Barbara, CA 93130. TEL 805-692-2045, FAX 805-692-2055. Ed., Pub. Bo Bengtson. Adv. contact Christi McDonald TEL 972-227-3000. B&W page USD 250, color page USD 550.

636.7 AUS ISSN 1329-3583
DOG'S LIFE. Text in English. 1997. bi-m. AUD 65 in New Zealand; AUD 70 in Asia; AUD 95 elsewhere (effective 2008). adv. back issues avail. **Document type:** *Magazine, Consumer.* **Description:** Covers a wide range of topics that are paramount to being a responsible pet owner, such as canine nutrition, training tips and breed features.
Published by: Universal Magazines Pty. Ltd., Unit 5, 6-8 Byfield St, Private Bag 154, North Ryde, NSW 2113, Australia. TEL 61-2-98870300, FAX 61-2-98050714, info@universalmagazines.com.au, http://www.universalmagazines.com.au. Eds. Caroline Zambrano TEL 61-2-98870360, Tim Falk TEL 61-2-98870360. Adv. contact Adrienne Kotz TEL 61-2-94888661. page AUD 12,000.

636.7 USA ISSN 2151-092X
DOG'S LIFE. Text in English. 2007. q. USD 16.95; USD 4.95 per issue (effective 2009). adv. back issues avail. **Document type:** *Magazine, Consumer.* **Description:** Aims to provide best practices of modern and humane dog guardianship.
Published by: Dog's Life Magazine, 1223 Wilshire Blvd, 451, Santa Monica, CA 90403. TEL 877-224-8031, FAX 530-484-3227. Ed. Yvonne B Mejia.

636.7 CZE ISSN 1804-2619
▼ **DOGS MAGAZIN**; moderni cteni o psech. Text in Czech. 2010. bi-m. CZK 95 newsstand/cover (effective 2010). adv. **Document type:** *Magazine, Consumer.*
Published by: Polygraf Net, s.r.o., Jana Masaryka 26, Prague 2, 120 00, Czech Republic. TEL 420-222-522321, FAX 420-222-514677.

636.7 GBR ISSN 0266-7975
DOGS MONTHLY. Text in English. 1983. m. GBP 36.50 domestic; GBP 49.50 newsstand/cover foreign (effective 2009). adv. bk.rev. back issues avail. **Document type:** *Magazine, Consumer.*
—CCC.
Published by: A B M Publishing Ltd., 61 Great Whyte, Ramsey, Huntingdon, Cambridgeshire PE26 1HJ, United Kingdom. TEL 44-8707-662272, FAX 44-8707-662273, info@abmpublishing.co.uk, http://www.abmpublishing.co.uk/. Ed. Caroline Davis. Adv. contact Paula Turner TEL 44-1778-392445.

636 GBR ISSN 0959-891X
DOGS TODAY. Text in English. 1990. m. GBP 35 domestic; GBP 45 in Europe; GBP 61 elsewhere; GBP 3.75 newsstand/cover (effective 2011). adv. bk.rev. illus. back issues avail. **Document type:** *Magazine, Consumer.* **Description:** Contains advice on dog care, health and breeding, legal issues and news related to dogs, anecdotes about pet dogs, and an opinion section.
Incorporates: Perfect Pup
—CCC.
Published by: Pet Subjects Ltd., The Dog House, 4 Bonseys Ln, Chobham, Surrey GU24 8JJ, United Kingdom. TEL 44-1276-858880, FAX 44-1276-858860, enquiries@dogstodaymagazine.co.uk. Ed., Pub. Beverley Cuddy. Adv. contact Liz Dixon TEL 44-1276-858880. B&W page GBP 1,200, color page GBP 1,925; trim 297 x 210. **Dist. by:** MarketForce UK Ltd, The Blue Fin Bldg, 3rd Fl, 110 Southwark St, London SE1 0SU, United Kingdom.

636.7 DEU
DOGS TODAY; Hunde-Trend-Magazin. Text in German. 2008. bi-m. EUR 19.95 domestic; EUR 26.85 foreign; EUR 3.70 newsstand/cover (effective 2011). adv. **Document type:** *Magazine, Consumer.*
Published by: Gong Verlag GmbH & Co. KG, Muenchener Str 101, Ismaning, 85737, Germany. TEL 49-89-272700, FAX 49-89-272707290, gonginfo@gongverlag.de, http://www.gong-verlag.de. Eds. Rudolf Schroeck, Ursula Birr. Adv. contact Sonja Haase.

636.7 USA ISSN 0895-5581
DOGS U S A. Text in English. 1986. a. USD 8.99 per issue (effective 2008). adv. illus. **Document type:** *Magazine, Consumer.* **Description:** Focuses on breeding, keeping, caring for, and showing purebred dogs.
Published by: BowTie, Inc., 2401 Beverly Blvd, PO Box 57900, Los Angeles, CA 90057. TEL 213-385-2222, FAX 213-385-8565, adtraffic@bowtieinc.com, http://www.bowtieinc.com. Circ: 209,816.

636 AUS
DOGS VICTORIA. Text in English. 1936. m. free to members (effective 2008). adv. bk.rev. **Document type:** *Journal, Trade.* **Description:** Covers information about dogs.
Former titles (until 2007): VicDog; (until 1997): Dogs; (until 1962): K C C Kennel Gazette
Published by: Victorian Canine Association Inc., 655 Westernport Hwy, Skye, VIC 3977, Australia. TEL 61-3-97882500, FAX 61-3-97882599, office@vca.org.au, http://www.vca.org.au. Circ: 16,000.

636.8 RUS
DRUG: ZHURNAL DLYA LYUBITELEI KOSHEK. Text in Russian. bi-m. USD 85 in United States.
Published by: Izdatel'skii Dom Drug, Zubovskii bulv 17, Moscow, 119831, Russian Federation. TEL 7-095-2462546, FAX 7-095-2465636. **Dist. by:** East View Information Services, 10601 Wayzata Blvd, Minneapolis, MN 55305. TEL 952-252-1201, 800-477-1005, FAX 952-252-1202, info@eastview.com, http://www.eastview.com.

636.7 RUS ISSN 0868-6246
DRUG: ZHURNAL DLYA LYUBITELEI SOBAK. Text in Russian. bi-m. USD 99.95 in United States.
—East View.
Published by: Izdatel'skii Dom Drug, Zubovskii bulv 17, Moscow, 119831, Russian Federation. TEL 7-095-2462564, FAX 7-095-2465636. **Dist. by:** East View Information Services, 10601 Wayzata Blvd, Minneapolis, MN 55305. TEL 952-252-1201, 800-477-1005, FAX 952-252-1202, info@eastview.com, http://www.eastview.com.

630 DEU ISSN 0341-5759
DU UND DAS TIER. Text in German. 1971. 6/yr. free base vol(s). to members (effective 2011). adv. bk.rev. illus. index. **Document type:** *Magazine, Consumer.*
—CCC.
Published by: (Deutscher Tierschutzbund e.V.), Gong Verlag GmbH & Co. KG, Muenchener Str 101, Ismaning, 85737, Germany. TEL 49-89-272700, FAX 49-89-272707290, gonginfo@gongverlag.de, http://www.gong-verlag.de. Ed. Ursula Birr. Adv. contact Sonja Haase. Circ: 30,000 (paid and controlled).

636.0887 DNK ISSN 0902-3879
DYRENE & OS/PETS AND US. Text in Danish. 1985. bi-m. DKK 360 combined subscription inc. Dyrlaegemagasinet (effective 2009). adv. **Document type:** *Magazine, Consumer.* **Description:** Up to date veterinary information for the family.
Related titles: Online - full text ed.: ISSN 1903-9034; ◆ Issued with: Dyrlaegemagasinet for Praktiserende Dyrlaeger. ISSN 1603-8002.
Published by: Scanpublisher A/S, Emiliekildevej 35, Klampenborg, 2930, Denmark. TEL 45-39-908000, FAX 45-39-908280, info@scanpublisher.dk, http://www.scanpublisher.dk. Ed. Dr. Finn Boserup. Adv. contact Tina Lund Larsen. Circ: 3,400.

636.8 DEU ISSN 0013-0826
DIE EDELKATZE; illustrierte Fachzeitschrift fuer Rassekatzenzucht. Text in German. 1922. 4/yr. EUR 34 domestic; EUR 40 foreign (effective 2009). bk.rev.; Website rev. bibl. 46 p./no.; **Document type:** *Magazine, Consumer.* **Description:** Covers topics on animal welfare, pets and veterinary sciences.
Published by: Erster Deutscher Edelkatzenzuechter Verband e.V., Berliner Str 13, Asslar, 35614, Germany. TEL 49-6441-8479, FAX 49-6441-87413, office@dekzv.de, http://www.dekzv.de.

636 FIN ISSN 1459-6954
ELAINMAAILMA. Text in Finnish. 2000. 8/yr. EUR 4,150 (effective 2006). adv. **Document type:** *Magazine, Consumer.* **Description:** For school-aged children and adults. Articles vary from pets to wildlife and nature.
Formerly (until 2003): Lemmikit ja Elainmaailma (1457-8107); Which was formed by the merger of (1978-2000): Elainmaailma (0357-8747); (1993-2000): Koirat (1238-0326); Which was formerly (until 1995): Elainmaailma. Lemmikit (1236-7702)
Published by: Egmont Kustannus Oy, PO Box 317, Tampere, 33101, Finland. TEL 358-201-332222, FAX 358-201-332278, info@egmont-kustannus.fi, http://www.egmont-kustannus.fi. Ed. Virpi Kaivonen. Adv. contact Tommy Tenhunen TEL 358-201-332266. B&W page EUR 1,300, color page EUR 1,700; 210 x 297. Circ: 12,000.

636 DEU
EMILY; Das Tiermagazin. Text in German. m. adv. **Document type:** *Magazine, Consumer.*
Published by: Apotheken-Spiegel-Verlagsgesellschaft mbH, Edisonstr 3-5, Frankfurt am Main, 60388, Germany. TEL 49-6109-71200, FAX 49-6109-7120222, inbox@as-verlag.com, http://www.as-verlag.com.

636.7 USA
ENGLISH SETTER ASSOCIATION OF AMERICA. NEWSLETTER. Text in English. m. membership. **Document type:** *Newsletter.*
Published by: English Setter Association of America, c/o Dawn Ronyak, Sec, 114 Burlington Oval, Chardon, OH 44024-1452. FAX 216-729-8413. Circ: 1,000.

636.7 FRA ISSN 1959-0202
L'EPAGNEUL BRETON. Text in French. 198?. s-a.
Published by: Club de l'Epagneul Breton, Peillon Nord, Cidex 124, Belleville sur Saone, 69220, France. http://www.epagneul-breton.ws/fr/index.php.

636.7 DEU
EUROPEAN BORZOI. Text in English, German. q. EUR 50 domestic; EUR 55 in Europe; EUR 60 elsewhere (effective 2009). adv. **Document type:** *Magazine, Consumer.*
Address: Laagweg 9, Pattensen, 30982, Germany. TEL 49-5069-8048824, FAX 49-5069-8048829. Ed., Pub., Adv. contact Evelyn Kirsch. B&W page EUR 50, color page EUR 150.

FAAGLEHOBBY; medlemsblad foer Sveriges samarbetand burfaagelfoereningar. *see* BIOLOGY—Ornithology

636.8 USA
FANC-E-MEWS; an online magazine for cat owners & lovers. Text in English. bi-m. free. **Document type:** *Magazine, Consumer.* **Description:** Provides health and care information for cat, suggest a book or two, tell where to find a cat show in your area, point you in the direction of breed rescue groups, and advise where the pet legislation hotspots are across the country.
Media: Online - full text.
Published by: The Cat Fanciers' Association cfa@cfa.org.

636.7 NZL ISSN 1177-7869
FAST FRIENDS. Text in English. 2006. q. free. back issues avail. **Document type:** *Magazine, Consumer.*
Media: Online - full text. **Related titles:** Print ed.: NZD 20 (effective 2008).
Published by: Greyhounds As Pets, PO Box 257, Feilding, New Zealand. TEL 64-6-3293101, info@greyhoundsaspets.org.nz, http://www.greyhoundsaspets.org.nz. Ed. Jacqui Eyley TEL 64-4-5280460.

636 CZE ISSN 1211-538X
FAUNA. Text in Czech. 1990. fortn. CZK 720; CZK 35 newsstand/cover (effective 2010). adv. **Document type:** *Magazine, Consumer.*
Published by: Fauna Magazin, spol. s r.o., Veslarska 232/37, Brno, 637 00, Czech Republic. TEL 420-773-699995.

636.596 FRA ISSN 1637-5505
FEDERATION COLOMBOPHILE FRANCAISE. BULLETIN NATIONAL. Text in French. 1976. q. **Document type:** *Bulletin.*
Former titles (until 2002): L' Envol (1288-247X); (until 1998): Federation Colombophile Francaise. Bulletin National (1256-6500); (until 1994): Colombophilie (0398-1576)
Published by: Colombophilie, 54 Bd. Carnot, Lille, 59000, France. TEL 33-3-20068287, FAX 33-3-20150157, http://www.colombophiliefr.com. Ed. Marie L Lesecq.

636 330 GBR ISSN 1744-9294
FEED COMPOUNDER. PET FOOD SUPPLEMENT. Text in English. 2001. s-a. GBP 12, EUR 28 in Europe; GBP 14, USD 36 elsewhere; free to qualified personnel (effective 2009). adv. **Document type:** *Magazine, Trade.* **Description:** Covers pet food issues, it covers various aspects of nutrition, machinery, marketing, products news, and people.
Related titles: ◆ Supplement to: Feed Compounder. ISSN 0950-771X.
Indexed: O01, S12.
Published by: Pentlands Publishing Ltd., Station Rd, Great Longstone, Bakewell, Derbyshire DE45 1TS, United Kingdom. TEL 44-1629-640941, FAX 44-1629-640588, mail@pentlandspublishing.com. adv.: B&W page GBP 850, color page GBP 1,475; 210 x 297.

636.8 NLD ISSN 0166-2406
FELIKAT MAGAZINE. Text in Dutch. 1953. 5/yr. EUR 25 (effective 2009). adv. **Document type:** *Magazine, Consumer.* **Description:** Publishes articles on cat breeds and breeding, care and exhibition of cats, member activities and news.
Published by: Nederlandse Vereniging van Fokkers en Liefhebbers van Katten, Uitdammerdorpstraat 1, Uitdam, 1154 PR, Netherlands. TEL 31-20-4033661, info@felikat.com, http://www.felikat.org. adv.: B&W page EUR 210; trim 210 x 297. Circ: 2,500.

636 CAN ISSN 1918-3828
FELINE WELLNESS; hip, cool and healthy!. Text in English. 1999. q. USD 15 in US & Canada (effective 2010). illus. back issues avail. **Document type:** *Magazine, Consumer.*
Supersedes in part (in 2008): Animal Wellness (1710-1190); Which was formerly (until 2001): Animal (1711-7305)
Related titles: Online - full text ed.: USD 12 in US & Canada (effective 2010).
Published by: Redstone Media Group Inc., 164 Hunter St., West, Peterborough, ON K9H 2L2, Canada. TEL 888-466-5266, FAX 705-742-4596, submissions@animalanimal.com, http://redstonemediagroup.com/. Ed., R&P Dana Cox. Adv. contact Leslie Nicholson. Circ: 40,000.

636.8 FRA ISSN 1962-2406
FEMININ SPECIAL CHATS. Text in French. 2005. q. EUR 44 for 2 yrs. (effective 2008). **Document type:** *Magazine, Consumer.*
Published by: Lafont Presse, 53 Rue du Chemin Vert, Boulogne-Billancourt, 92100, France. http://www.lafontpresse.fr.

636.976 USA
FERRETS MAGAZINE. Text in English. 1997. m. free (effective 2011). **Document type:** *Magazine, Consumer.*
Formerly (until 2007): Ferrets (Print) (1528-9826)
Media: Online - full text.
Published by: BowTie, Inc., 3 Burroughs, Irvine, CA 92618-2804. TEL 949-855-8822, FAX 949-855-3045, http://www.bowtieinc.com.

636.976 USA ISSN 1093-9407
SF459.F47
FERRETS U S A. Text in English. 199?. a. USD 7.50 per issue (effective 2008). adv. **Document type:** *Magazine, Trade.* **Description:** Offers information and advice on buying and owning ferrets.
Related titles: Online - full text ed.
Published by: BowTie, Inc., 2401 Beverly Blvd, PO Box 57900, Los Angeles, CA 90057. TEL 213-385-2222, FAX 213-385-8565, adtraffic@bowtieinc.com, http://www.bowtieinc.com. Ed. Marylou Zarbock. Pub. Norman Ridker. Adv. contact Marc Fredman. B&W page USD 2,870, color page USD 4,190; trim 8 x 10.875. Circ: 51,841.

639 FRA ISSN 1772-2918
LA FEUILLE DE LOTUS. Text in French. q. back issues avail. **Document type:** *Newsletter.*
Published by: France Carpes Koi Club, FCKC, 16 Rue Charles Peguy, Aixe sur Vienne, 87700, France. afeytou@wanadoo.fr, http://www.francecarpekoi.com. Ed. Jacky Larivriere TEL 33-5-53044006.

FIDO FRIENDLY; the travel & lifestyle magazine for you & your dog. *see* TRAVEL AND TOURISM

636.7 USA
FIELD ADVISORY NEWS. Text in English. 1971. bi-m. USD 30. adv. bk.rev. **Document type:** *Bulletin.*
Published by: American Sighthound Field Association, Inc., c/o Vicky Clarke, Ed, Box 399, Alpaugh, CA 93201-0399. Circ: 650.

636 USA
FIELD TRIAL MAGAZINE. Text in English. 1997. q. **Description:** Covers field trials for pointing dogs.
Published by: Androscoggin Publishing, Inc., Box 98, Milan, NH 03588-0098. TEL 617-449-6767, FAX 603-449-2462, birddog@ncia.net, http://www.fielddog.com/ftm. Ed. Craig Doherty. Circ: 6,000 (paid and controlled).

636 USA
FIRST COAST PET. Text in English. 2005. q. USD 12 (effective 2007). adv. **Document type:** *Magazine, Consumer.* **Description:** Published for the Northeast Florida area covering Duval, St. Johns, Clay and Nassau counties. Discusses different topics that help pet owners learn more about caring for their animals.
Published by: J K Harris Publications, LLC, 12276 San Jose Blvd, Ste 212, Jacksonville, FL 32223. TEL 888-708-5700, FAX 904-346-3337. Ed. Dee Emery. Pub. Dina Kessler. adv.: color page USD 1,050; trim 5.375 x 8.375. Circ: 25,000.

636.7374 636.7 GBR ISSN 1361-5580
FREEDOM OF SPIRIT. Abbreviated title: F O S. Text in English. 1994. bi-m. GBP 17 domestic; GBP 19 in Europe; GBP 22 elsewhere (effective 2009). bk.rev. 24 p./no. 4 cols./p.; back issues avail. **Document type:** *Magazine, Consumer.* **Description:** Contains regular features, information on the different disciplines, training and behaviour, letters and news updates, gardening, and countryside issues.
Related titles: E-mail ed.; Fax ed.; Online - full text ed.
Published by: Mainline Border Collies Centre, Golcar Farm, Spring Ln, Eldwick, Bingley, W Yorks BD16 3AU, United Kingdom. TEL 44-1274-564163, info@bordercollies.co.uk.

636 179.3 DEU
FRESSNAPF JOURNAL. Text in German. 2000. m. free (effective 2010). adv. **Document type:** *Magazine, Consumer.* **Description:** Contains information and advice on caring for a wide variety of pets.
Formerly (until 2002): Fressnapf Zeitung
Published by: Fressnapf Tiernahrungs GmbH, WestpreuBenstr 32-38, Krefeld, 47809, Germany. TEL 49-1801-990990.

636.7 USA ISSN 1073-7537
FRONT AND FINISH: THE DOG TRAINER'S NEWS. Text in English. 1970. m. USD 32 (effective 1997). adv. bk.rev. index. **Document type:** *Newspaper.*
Published by: H and S Publications, Inc., PO Box 333, Galesburg, IL 61402. Ed. Robert T Self. Pub. Robert Taylor Self. Adv. contact Robert Thomas Self. Circ: 7,500.

FUND FOR ANIMALS NEWSLETTER. *see* CONSERVATION

636.7 USA
G S P C A SHORTHAIR. Text in English. 1954. m. USD 25. bk.rev.
Description: Reports on breed activities in show, field trial, hunt test and obedience. Covers training, dog care, nutrition, new products, industry news, dog rescue, and health and welfare.
Formerly (until 1986): G S P C A Newsletter
Published by: German Shorthaired Pointer Club of America, 18151 Harrison St, Omaha, NE 68136. TEL 402-895-4843, FAX 402-731-2874. Ed. Jean Armbrust. adv.: B&W page USD 125, color page USD 400; 10.13 x 7.5. Circ: 3,140.

GAITED HORSE INTERNATIONAL MAGAZINE. *see* SPORTS AND GAMES—Horses And Horsemanship

636.8 ITA ISSN 1594-5782
GATTO MAGAZINE. Text in Italian. 2002. bi-m. EUR 14.90 (effective 2009). **Document type:** *Magazine, Consumer.*
Published by: Sprea Editori Srl, Via Torino 51, Cernusco sul Naviglio, MI 20063, Italy. TEL 39-02-92432222, FAX 39-02-92432236, editori@sprea.it, http://www.sprea.it.

636 DEU ISSN 0016-5824
GEFLUEGEL-BOERSE. Text in German. 1879. s-m. EUR 78 domestic; EUR 84 foreign (effective 2011). adv. bk.rev. **Document type:** *Magazine, Trade.*
Published by: (Bund Deutscher Rassegefluegelzuechter e.V), Verlag Juergens GmbH, Postfach 140 220, Muenchen, 80452, Germany. TEL 49-89-20959181, FAX 49-89-20028115. Ed. M von Luettwitz. Pub. D Juergens. adv.: B&W page EUR 1,508, color page EUR 2,150. Circ: 25,000 (paid and controlled).

636.8 DEU ISSN 0946-6215
GELIEBTE KATZE; Europas groesstes Katzenmagazin. Text in German. 1993. m. EUR 28.95; EUR 2.80 newsstand/cover (effective 2011). adv. **Document type:** *Magazine, Consumer.*
Published by: Gong Verlag GmbH & Co. KG, Muenchener Str 101, Ismaning, 85737, Germany. TEL 49-89-272700, FAX 49-89-272707290, gonginfo@gongverlag.de, http://www.gong-verlag.de. Ed. Ursula Birr. Adv. contact Sonja Haase. Circ: 40,182 (paid and controlled).

636.7 USA ISSN 0046-5852
SF429.S6
GERMAN SHEPHERD DOG REVIEW. Text in English. 1922. m. USD 55; USD 10 newsstand/cover (effective 2000). adv. bk.rev.; video rev. stat. 90 p./no. 2 cols./p.; back issues avail. **Document type:** *Magazine, Consumer.* **Description:** Provides information concerning the breeding, raising, training, and showing of German Shepherd dogs.
Published by: German Shepherd Dog Club of America, 1902C N Abrego, Green Valley, AZ 85614. TEL 520-625-9528, FAX 520-625-4789. Ed. Gail Sprock. adv.: B&W page USD 125, color page USD 425; trim 8.5 x 11. Circ: 3,500.

636.7 USA ISSN 0745-1849
THE GERMAN SHEPHERD QUARTERLY. Text in English. 1982. q. USD 54 domestic; USD 74 in Canada; USD 98 elsewhere; USD 15 per issue (effective 2011). adv. back issues avail. **Document type:** *Magazine, Consumer.* **Description:** Contains breeder interviews, columns by people who know and love German Shepherds.
Published by: Hoflin Publishing, Inc., 4401 Zephyr St, Wheat Ridge, CO 80033. TEL 303-420-2222, FAX 720-207-0382, help@hoflin.com.

636.7 USA ISSN 1065-0830
GERMAN SHORTHAIRED POINTER NEWS. Text in English. 1954. m. USD 20. adv. bk.rev. stat. back issues avail. **Description:** Focuses on breeding, puppies, competition; includes articles on training.
Published by: Shirley L. Carlson, Ed. & Pub., 86 N Heck Hill Rd, Box 850, Saint Paris, OH 43072. TEL 513-663-4773. Circ: 1,500.

636 DEU
GESUNDE TIERLIEBE. Text in German. q. adv. **Document type:** *Magazine, Consumer.*
Published by: Gong Verlag GmbH & Co. KG, Muenchener Str 101, Ismaning, 85737, Germany. TEL 49-89-272700, FAX 49-89-272707290, gonginfo@gongverlag.de, http://www.gong-verlag.de. Ed. Ursula Birr. Adv. contact Sonja Haase. Circ: 55,000 (controlled).

636.5 USA ISSN 2155-0867
GOOD BIRD MAGAZINE. Text in English. 2005. q. USD 19 (print or online ed.); USD 6 per issue (print or online ed.) (effective 2010). back issues avail. **Document type:** *Magazine, Consumer.* **Description:** Provides information about parrot and it's behaviour.
Related titles: Online - full text ed.
Published by: Good Bird Inc., PO Box 150604, Austin, TX 78715. TEL 512-423-7734, Info@goodbirdinc.com.

636.7 USA
GORDON SETTER NEWS. Text in English. 1947. m. membership. adv. bk.rev. **Document type:** *Newsletter.*
Published by: Gordon Setter Club of America, Inc., 47 Taylor Blair Rd, West Jefferson, OH 43162. Eds. Crystal Todor, William Todor. R&P, Adv. contact Crystal Todor. Circ: 1,100.

636.7 USA
GREAT DANE CLUB OF AMERICA. MONTHLY BULLETIN. Text in English. m.
Published by: Great Dane Club of America, c/o Pattie Glanz, Gage Rd, RR 5, Brewster, NY 10509. Circ: 2,000.

636.7 USA ISSN 0889-7727
GREAT DANE REPORTER. Text in English. 1976. bi-m. USD 48 domestic; USD 58 in Canada & Mexico; USD 68 elsewhere. adv. bk.rev. **Description:** For Great Dane owners, breeders, lovers. contains articles about showing, caring for, and training Great Danes.
Published by: Tomar Publications, PO Box 150, Riverside, CA 92502-0150. TEL 909-784-5437, FAX 909-369-7056. Ed., Pub., R&P, Adv. contact Sally Silva. Circ: 2,000.

636 USA ISSN 1945-6654
GREATER PHILLY TAILS; celebrating the relationship between pets and their people. Text in English. 2000. m. USD 36; free (effective 2008). adv. back issues avail. **Document type:** *Magazine, Consumer.*
Related titles: Online - full text ed.: ISSN 1945-6662. free (effective 2007).
Published by: Tails Pet Media Group, Inc., 4527 N Ravenswood Ave, Chicago, IL 60640. TEL 773-561-4300, 877-866-8245, FAX 773-561-3030, mail@tailsinc.org. Adv. contact Nikki Scheel. B&W page USD 2,100, color page USD 2,300; trim 10.5 x 10.5. Circ: 50,000 (controlled).

636.7 GBR ISSN 0017-4165
GREYHOUND OWNER & BREEDER. Text in English. 1946. w. GBP 6.50 for 6 mos. adv. stat. cum.index.
Published by: Greyhound Owner Ltd., 8 Greenford Ave, London, W7 3QP, United Kingdom. Ed. Jim Shepherd. Circ: 9,800.

636 976 AUS ISSN 1320-9507
THE GREYHOUND RECORDER. Text in English. 1935. w. AUD 266 domestic; AUD 380 in New Zealand; AUD 607 elsewhere (effective 2008). adv. back issues avail. **Document type:** *Newspaper, Consumer.*
Published by: Greyhound Publications Pty. Ltd., Locked Bag 1700, Lidcombe, NSW 1825, Australia. TEL 61-2-96465855, FAX 61-2-96465433. Adv. contact Gary Clark.

636.7 GBR ISSN 0955-047X
GREYHOUND STAR. Text in English. 1983. m. GBP 17 domestic; GBP 22 in Europe; GBP 34 elsewhere; GBP 1.50 newsstand/cover. **Document type:** *Newspaper, Consumer.* **Description:** Features articles of interest to greyhound dog owners or racing enthusiasts.
Address: Greyhound Star, PO Box 49, Letchworth, Herts SG6 2XB, United Kingdom. TEL 44-1462-679439. Ed. Floyd Amphlett.

636.0833 USA
GROOMER TO GROOMER. Text in English. bi-m.
Published by: Barkleigh Publications, Inc., 6 State Rd, Ste 113, Mechanicsburg, PA 17055.

636.7 USA
GROOMER'S VOICE. Text in English. 1969. q. membership. adv.
Published by: National Dog Groomer's Association of America, c/o Jeffrey L Reynolds, Box 101, Clark, PA 16113. TEL 412-962-2711, FAX 724-962-1919. Circ: 2,500.

636.596 DEU ISSN 0935-5405
DAS GRUENE JAHRBUCH; ein praktischer Wegweiser fuer den Gefluegel- und Taubenzuechter. Text in German. 1953. a. EUR 6 (effective 2010). adv. **Document type:** *Consumer.*
Formerly (until 1988): Das Gruene Gefluegel-Jahrbuch (0344-2438)
Published by: (Deutscher Kleintier Zuechter), Oertel & Spoerer Verlags GmbH und Co. KG, Beutterstr 10, Reutlingen, 72764, Germany. TEL 49-7121-302550, FAX 49-7121-302558, info@oertel-spoerer.de, http://www.oe-sp.de. Circ: 7,500.

636.7 362.41 USA
GUIDE LINES (YORKTOWN HEIGHTS). Text in English. 1954. q. free. **Document type:** *Newsletter.*
Published by: Guiding Eyes for the Blind, 611 Granite Springs Rd, Yorktown Heights, NY 10598-3499. Ed. Karen McClure.

636 GBR ISSN 2044-4400
▼ **GUINEA PIG MAGAZINE.** Text in English. 2011. bi-m. GBP 30 domestic; GBP 35.40 in Europe; GBP 41.10 elsewhere; GBP 3.95 per issue (effective 2011). adv. back issues avail. **Document type:** *Magazine, Consumer.* **Description:** Aims to provide accurate, unbiased and up to date information on all aspects of guinea pig health, happiness, care and welfare.
Published by: Alison Byford, Ed. & Pub., PO Box 1, Plymouth, PL1 9AT, United Kingdom. TEL 44-7580-189194, alison@guineapigmagazine.com.

GUN DOG; upland bird and waterfowl dogs. *see* SPORTS AND GAMES—Outdoor Life

636.7 USA
GUN DOGS ONLINE.COM. Text in English. m. free (effective 2005). **Description:** Dedicated to promoting the grace, elegance, and natural hunting ability of all sporting breeds. Features articles on a wide range of topics and provides readers with educational and entertaining insight into gundogs from some of the industry's leading outdoor writers, breeders and trainers.
Media: Online - full text.
Published by: Gundogs Online.Com, P.O. Box 444, Southbury, CT 06488-0444. FAX 203-881-9985, support@gundogsonline.com.

636.7 SWE
HAERLIGA HUND. Text in Swedish. 2005. m. SEK 429 (effective 2006). adv. **Document type:** *Magazine, Consumer.*
Published by: L R F Media AB, Gaevlegatan 22, Stockholm, 11392, Sweden. TEL 46-8-58836600, FAX 46-8-58836989, lrfmedia@lrfmedia.lrf.se. Eds. Karl Zetterberg, Ebba Svanholm TEL 46-8-58836853. adv.: page SEK 18,900; 200 x 275. Circ: 38,400.

636 ZAF ISSN 1996-7438
HAPPY TAILS. Text in English. 2007. q.
Published by: (The Emma Animal Rescue Society), Red Ink Media, 156 Main Rd, Muizenberg, 7945, South Africa. TEL 27-21-7885698, FAX 27-21-7884506, http://www.redinkmedia.co.za.

HART VOOR DIEREN. *see* ANIMAL WELFARE

636 DEU
HAUSTIER ANZEIGER. Text in German. 1995. m. EUR 30.80 domestic; EUR 63.60 foreign; EUR 2.80 newsstand/cover (effective 2011). adv. **Document type:** *Magazine, Consumer.*
Published by: Der Heisse Draht Verlag GmbH und Co., Drostestr 14, Hannover, 30161, Germany. TEL 49-511-390910, FAX 49-511-39091196, zentrale@dhd.de, http://www.dhd.de. Adv. contact Lars Schnatmann.

636.7 USA ISSN 1949-856X
▼ **HAUTEDOG: WET NOSE CULTURE: AUSTIN.** Text in English. 2009. q. USD 18 (effective 2009). **Document type:** *Magazine, Consumer.* **Description:** Features information for dog-owners in Austin, Texas.
Published by: Bluedogg Innovation Marketing, LLC, 4701 W Gate Blvd, Ste D-402, Austin, TX 78745. TEL 512-891-6232, susan@bluedogginnovation.com, http://bluedogginnovation.com.

636.7 USA ISSN 1949-8578
▼ **HAUTEDOG: WET NOSE CULTURE: CINCINNATI.** Text in English. forthcoming 2011. q. USD 18 (effective 2009). **Document type:** *Magazine, Consumer.* **Description:** Features information for dog owners in Cincinnati, Ohio.
Published by: Bluedogg Innovation Marketing, LLC, 4701 W Gate Blvd, Ste D-402, Austin, TX 78745. TEL 512-891-6232, susan@bluedogginnovation.com, http://bluedogginnovation.com.

636.7 USA ISSN 1949-8543
▼ **HAUTEDOG: WET NOSE CULTURE: DALLAS.** Text in English. forthcoming 2011. q. USD 18 (effective 2009). **Document type:** *Magazine, Consumer.* **Description:** Features information for dog owners in Dallas, Texas.
Published by: Bluedogg Innovation Marketing, LLC, 4701 W Gate Blvd, Ste D-402, Austin, TX 78745. TEL 512-891-6232, susan@bluedogginnovation.com, http://bluedogginnovation.com.

636.7 USA ISSN 1949-8551
▼ **HAUTEDOG: WET NOSE CULTURE: LOUISVILLE.** Text in English. forthcoming 2011. q. USD 18 (effective 2009). **Document type:** *Magazine, Consumer.* **Description:** Features information for dog owners in Louisville, Kentucky.
Published by: Bluedogg Innovation Marketing, LLC, 4701 W Gate Blvd, Ste D-402, Austin, TX 78745. TEL 512-891-6232, susan@bluedogginnovation.com, http://bluedogginnovation.com.

636 USA
HEALTHY PET MAGAZINE. Text in English. 2000. q. adv. back issues avail. **Document type:** *Magazine, Consumer.* **Description:** Promotes educated, responsible pet ownership. It provides readers with a balanced mix of general and seasonal veterinary topics as well as heart-warming stories of the human-animal bond and features on celebrities and their pets.
Published by: Zoasis Corp., 1500 Olympic Blvd., Santa Monica, CA 90404. TEL 310-314-5250, FAX 310-314-5205. Adv. contact Jim Escobar. color page USD 112,000; trim 8 x 10.5. Circ: 3,410,129 (paid).

636 USA ISSN 0193-1997
HEART OF AMERICA AQUARIUM SOCIETY NEWS. Text in English. 1979 (vol.24). m. (11/yr.). USD 12 to members. adv. **Description:** Provides current news and information on all species of fish; tropical and native.
Published by: Heart of America Aquarium Society, 2029 W. 84th Terr., Leawood, KS 66206. Ed. Betty Ryne. Circ: 300.

636.7 NLD ISSN 1878-4585
DE HEIDEWACHTEL. Text in Dutch. bi-m. EUR 30 membership (effective 2011). **Document type:** *Magazine, Consumer.*
Published by: Nederlandse Vereniging van Heidewachtelliefhebbers, Sullivanlijn 48, Zoetermeer, 2728 BP, Netherlands. TEL 31-79-3421737, heidewachtel@reeskamp-bnlok.nl, http://www.heidewachtelvereniging.nl.

HENSTON SMALL ANIMAL VETERINARY VADE MECUM (PETERBOROUGH, 2005). *see* VETERINARY SCIENCE

636 DEU ISSN 0935-0217
EIN HERZ FUER TIERE; Das Magazin fuer alle, die Tiere und Natur leiben. Text in German. 1982. m. EUR 28.95; EUR 2.80 newsstand/cover (effective 2011). adv. **Document type:** *Magazine, Consumer.*
Published by: Gong Verlag GmbH & Co. KG, Muenchener Str 101, Ismaning, 85737, Germany. TEL 49-89-272700, FAX 49-911-5325309, 49-911-5325493, 49-89-272707290, gonginfo@gongverlag.de, http://www.gong-verlag.de. Ed. Ursula Birr. Adv. contact Sonja Haase. Circ: 100,000 (paid and controlled).
Subscr. to: dsb Abo-Betreuung GmbH, Konrad-Zuse-Str 16, Neckarsulm 74172, Germany. TEL 49-1805-959500, FAX 49-1805-959511, gongverlag.abo@dsb.net, http://www.dsb.net.

636.7 USA
HOLLYWOOD DOG. Text in English. 2005 (Oct.). bi-m. USD 4.99 newsstand/cover (effective 2005). **Document type:** *Magazine, Consumer.*
Published by: Gatsby Publishing, Inc., The SoHo Building, 110 Greene St, Ste 405, New York, NY 10012. TEL 212-226-3955, FAX 212-226-5707, editorial@thenydog.com, http://www.thenydog.com. Circ: 50,000.

636.7 NLD ISSN 1874-9860
HONDENLEVEN. Text in Dutch. 2007. m. EUR 39.95; EUR 3.95 newsstand/cover (effective 2010). adv. **Document type:** *Magazine, Consumer.*
Published by: Uitgeverij De Fontein - Tirion, Julianalaan 11, Baarn, 3743 JG, Netherlands. TEL 31-35-5486600, FAX 31-35-5486615, info@tirionuitgevers.nl, http://www.defonteintirion.nl. adv.: B&W page EUR 910, color page EUR 1,060; trim 210 x 297. Circ: 17,000.

636.7 NLD ISSN 1569-9129
HONDENMANIEREN. Text in Dutch. 199?. m. (11/yr.). EUR 41.50 domestic; EUR 46.50 in Belgium; EUR 67 foreign (effective 2008). **Document type:** *Magazine, Consumer.*
Published by: Compasso Media bv, Postbus 111, Deurne, 5750 AC, Netherlands. TEL 31-493-328600, FAX 31-493-328601, http://www.compassomedia.nl. Ed. Hanneke Reitsma.

636.7 798.8 799.2 NLD ISSN 1389-1960
HONDENSPORT & SPORTHONDEN; het tijdschrift voor liefhebbers van hondensport en africhting. Text in Dutch. 1998. bi-m. EUR 26.95 domestic; EUR 30 in Belgium; EUR 35 in Europe; EUR 50 elsewhere (effective 2009). adv. bk.rev. illus.; stat. back issues avail. **Document type:** *Magazine, Consumer.* **Description:** Reports on all dog sports and sports dogs in the Netherlands, Belgium, and Luxembourg.
Published by: Topaaz Consultancy, Kamplaan 2, Gasselte, 9462 TS, Netherlands. TEL 31-599-563980, FAX 31-599-563858, topaaz@wxs.nl, http://www.topaaz.com.

636.7 NLD ISSN 0018-4527
HONDENWERELD. Text in Dutch. 1946. m. (11/yr.). EUR 38.50; EUR 3.95 newsstand/cover (effective 2008). adv. bk.rev. abstr.; illus. index.
Published by: (Stichting de Hondenwereld), Compasso Media bv, Postbus 111, Deurne, 5750 AC, Netherlands. TEL 31-493-328600, FAX 31-493-328601, http://www.compassomedia.nl. Circ: 9,000.

636.7 USA ISSN 0018-6384
SF421
HOUNDS AND HUNTING. Text in English. 1903. m. USD 18 domestic; USD 3 newsstand/cover (effective 2007). adv. bk.rev. illus. **Document type:** *Magazine, Consumer.* **Description:** Covers the breeding, raising, training and handling of Beagle Hounds.
Published by: Hounds and Hunting Publishing Co., 554 Derrick Rd, Bradford, PA 16701. TEL 814-368-6154, FAX 814-368-3522. Ed., R&P Robert F Slike. Adv. contact Linda Slike. B&W page USD 491; trim 8.15 x 10.75. Circ: 8,000 (paid).

636.7 NLD ISSN 1871-4552
HOVAWARTAAL. Text in Dutch. 5/yr.

P

Published by: Hovawart Club Nederland, Opsterland 1, Emmeloord, 8302 LJ, Netherlands. TEL 31-527-623392, secretariaat@hovawartclub.nl, http://www.hovawartclub.nl.

636.7 DEU ISSN 0323-4924
DER HUND. Text in German. 187?. m. EUR 35 domestic; EUR 52 foreign; EUR 3 newsstand/cover (effective 2011). adv. **Document type:** *Magazine, Consumer.*
Incorporates (1987-2007): Hunde Revue (0936-1154); (1995-2004): Mein Hund (0947-1294)
Related titles: Online - full text ed.
Published by: Deutscher Bauernverlag GmbH, Wilhelmsaue 37, Berlin, 10713, Germany. TEL 49-30-464060, FAX 49-30-46406205, info@bauernverlag.de, http://www.bauernverlag.de. Ed. Susanne Kerl. Adv. contact Jana Schuschke. Circ: 33,728 (paid and controlled).

636 AUT
HUND, KATZ UND CO. Text in German. 2004. 4/yr. free. adv. **Document type:** *Magazine, Consumer.*
Published by: N.J. Schmid Verlag, Leberstr 122, Vienna, 1110, Austria. TEL 43-1-74032735, FAX 43-1-74032750, g.milletich@schmid-verlag.at, http://www.schmid-verlag.at. Ed. Helmut Widmann. Adv. contact Thomas Pichler. color page EUR 4,000; trim 193 x 262. Circ: 60,000 (controlled).

636.7 CHE ISSN 0259-4072
HUNDE HALTUNG ZUCHT SPORT. Text in German. 1920. fortn. CHF 71 domestic; CHF 106 foreign; CHF 6 newsstand/cover (effective 2003). adv. charts; illus. **Document type:** *Magazine, Consumer.*
Former titles (until 1986): Hundesport (0259-3122); (until 1981): Schweizer Hundesport (0036-7354); (until 1926): Schweizer Hundesport und Jagd (1421-1807); Which was formed by the merger of (1884-1920): Centralblatt fuer Jagd- und Hunde-Liebhaber (1421-1785); (1898-1920): Schweizerische Tier-Boerse (1421-1793)
—CCC.
Published by: (Schweizerischen Kynologischen Gesellschaft), Paul Haupt AG, Falkenplatz 14, Bern, 3001, Switzerland. TEL 41-31-3012434, FAX 41-31-3015469, druckerei@haupt.ch, http://www.haupt.ch.de/druck/fdruck.htm. Ed. Hans Raeber. Circ: 25,000.

636.7 DNK ISSN 1601-5819
HUNDE-JOURNALEN - KATTE-JOURNALEN; bladet for dyrevenner. Variant title: Katte-Journalen. Text in Danish. 1945. 6/yr. DKK 175 (effective 2009). adv. bk.rev. **Document type:** *Magazine, Consumer.*
Formerly (until 2000): Hunde-Journalen (0108-6839)
Related titles: Online - full text ed.
Published by: Dyrefondet, Ericaparken 23, Gentofte, 2820, Denmark. TEL 45-39-563000, FAX 45-39-563360, post@dyrefondet.dk. Eds. Jan Nielsen, Aase Reinhard. Adv. contact Jan Nielsen. page DKK 5,700; 172 x 253. Circ: 8,800.

636.7 DNK ISSN 0018-7674
HUNDEN. Text in Danish. 1891. 10/yr. DKK 395 to individual members (effective 2008). adv. **Document type:** *Magazine, Consumer.*
Published by: (Dansk Kennel Klub), Mediehuset Wiegaarden, Blaakildevej 15, PO Box 315, Hobro, 9500, Denmark. TEL 45-98-512066, FAX 45-98-512006, mediahuset@wiegaarden.dk, http://www.wiegaarden.dk. Ed. Joergen Hindse. Adv. contact Joergen Bak Rasmussen. color page DKK 12,850; 210 x 280. Circ: 33,000.

636.7 NOR ISSN 0332-8813
HUNDESPORT. Text in Norwegian. 1900. 10/yr. adv. **Document type:** *Consumer.* **Description:** Carries material of interest to dog enthusiasts: breeding, shows, work dogs, hunting dogs, etc.
Formerly (until 1955): Norsk Kennel Klubs Tidsskrift (0332-9445)
Related titles: Online - full text ed.
Published by: Norsk Kennel Klub, PO Box 163, Bryn, Oslo, 0611, Norway. TEL 47-21-600900, FAX 47-21-600901, info@nkk.no. Ed. Stepaka Horakova. Adv. contact Frode Frantzen TEL 47-62-946971. Circ: 75,000.

636.7 DEU ISSN 0018-7682
HUNDEWELT; Deutschlands Top-Magazin rund um den Hund. Text in Czech, German. 1928. m. EUR 28.80; EUR 2.70 newsstand/cover (effective 2010). adv. **Document type:** *Magazine, Consumer.*
Related titles: Online - full text ed.
Published by: Minerva Verlag GmbH, Hocksteiner Weg 38, Moenchengladbach, 41189, Germany. TEL 49-2166-621970, FAX 49-2166-6219710, info@minervaverlag.de, http://www.minervaverlag.de. adv.: B&W page EUR 2,548, color page EUR 4,331.60; trim 192 x 260. Circ: 80,000 (paid).

636.7 DEU ISSN 1862-1023
HUNDEWELT SPORT. Text in German. 1996. bi-m. EUR 24 domestic; EUR 30 in Europe; EUR 48 elsewhere; EUR 4.50 newsstand/cover (effective 2010). adv. **Document type:** *Magazine, Consumer.* **Description:** Provides information and coverage of dog agility and obstacle course competitions.
Former titles (until 2006): Agility Welt & More (1862-1015); (until 2004): Agility Welt (0949-3719)
Related titles: Online - full text ed.
Published by: Minerva Verlag GmbH, Hocksteiner Weg 38, Moenchengladbach, 41189, Germany. TEL 49-2166-621970, FAX 49-2166-6219710, info@minervaverlag.de, http://www.minervaverlag.de. adv.: B&W page EUR 1,456, color page EUR 2,475.20; trim 192 x 260. Circ: 12,000 (paid).

636.7 SWE ISSN 0018-7690
HUNDSPORT. Text in Swedish. 1887. 10/yr. SEK 340 domestic to members; SEK 440 foreign to members (effective 2004). adv. bk.rev. **Document type:** *Magazine, Consumer.*
Former titles (until 1955): Hundar och Hundsport; (until 1933): Svenska Kennelklubbens Tidskrift; (until 1893): Tidning foer Idrott; Which supersedes (in 1890): Hunden
Related titles: Online - full text ed.
Published by: Svenska Kennelklubben/Swedish Kennel Club, Rinkebysvaengen 70, Spaanga, 16385, Sweden. TEL 46-8-7953000, FAX 46-8-7953040, vd@skk.se, http://www.skk.se. Ed., R&P Torsten Widholm TEL 46-8-808565. Adv. contact Lars Goeran Fransson TEL 46-8-6423720. B&W page SEK 22,900, color page SEK 27,900; trim 185 x 265. Circ: 89,700.

636.7 USA ISSN 8750-6629
HUNTING RETRIEVER. Text in English. 1984. bi-m. USD 25 to members. adv. bk.rev. **Document type:** *Magazine, Consumer.* **Description:** Official organ of the Hunting Retriever Club, an organization devoted to retriever performance testing.
Published by: United Kennel Club, Inc., 100 E Kilgore Rd, Kalamazoo, MI 49002-5584. hounds@ukcdogs.com, http://www.ukcdogs.com. Ed. Vicki Rand. Adv. contact Andrea Wood. Circ: 3,000.

636.8 USA ISSN 0899-9570
I LOVE CATS. Text in English. 1988. bi-m. USD 36 domestic; USD 46 in Canada; USD 56 elsewhere (effective 2008). adv. illus. **Document type:** *Magazine, Consumer.* **Description:** Features information necessary for cat owners to help their cats live healthier and happier lives. Includes proper nutrition, veterinarian advice, dental care and stories about cat lovers and their adventures with cats.
Related titles: Online - full text ed.
Published by: I Love Cats Publishing Company, 900 Oaktree Ave, Ste C, South Plainfield, NJ 07080. TEL 908-222-1811. Eds. Lisa Allmendinger, Marcia Cavan. Circ: 15,000.

636 GBR ISSN 2044-4737
I LOVE PONIES & PETS. Text in English. 2007. 10/yr. GBP 32; GBP 2.99 per issue (effective 2011). **Document type:** *Magazine, Consumer.* **Description:** Contains colorful posters of pets and ponies, plus stories, puzzles and games.
Formerly (until 2010): I Love Ponies Official Magazine (1752-3575)
Published by: Signature Publishing Ltd., Headley House, Headley Rd, Grayshott, Surrey GU26 6TU, United Kingdom. TEL 44-1428-601020, FAX 44-1428-601030, email@signaturepl.co.uk.

636.96 NLD ISSN 1877-5624
I R F NIEUWSBRIEF. Text in Dutch. 199?. bi-m. **Document type:** *Newsletter, Consumer.*
Formerly (until 2008): Ratatouille (1567-7087)
Published by: Internationale Ratten Fokkers/Fanclub, Leembruggenstraat 21, Hillegom, 2182 KM, Netherlands. http://www.irf-rattenclub.nl. Ed. Marja Rijsdijk.

636.7 USA
ICELANDIC SHEEPDOG INTERNATIONAL MAGAZINE. Text in English. q. USD 25 domestic; USD 35 in Canada; USD 45 elsewhere (effective 2001). adv. **Description:** Specializes in all breeds of sheepdogs, providing information that addresses education, self-help, culture, and entertainment.
Address: 507 N Sullivan Rd Ste A-3, Veradle, WA 99037-8531. TEL 509-232-2664, FAX 509-232-2665. adv.: B&W page USD 135, color page USD 595; bleed 8.75 x 11.75.

636.7 NLD ISSN 1879-6990
IERDIE. Text in Dutch. 5/yr. EUR 35 domestic; EUR 45 foreign (effective 2010). **Document type:** *Magazine, Consumer.*
Published by: Nederlandse Vereniging voor de Ierse Wolfshond Ierdie, Barchman Wuytierslaan 54, Amersfoort, 3818 NL, Netherlands. TEL 31-334-618018, FAX 31-334-655938, secretaris.ierdie@gmail.com, http://www.ierdie.net. Eds. Ilonka Lourenz, Ria de Jager.

636 USA ISSN 1945-6670
INDY TAILS; celebrating the relationship between pets and their people. Text in English. 2000. m. USD 36; free to qualified personnel (effective 2008). adv. back issues avail. **Document type:** *Magazine, Consumer.*
Related titles: Online - full text ed.: ISSN 1945-6689.
Published by: Tails Pet Media Group, Inc., 4527 N Ravenswood Ave, Chicago, IL 60640. TEL 773-561-4300, 877-866-8245, FAX 773-561-3030, mail@tailsinc.org. Adv. contact Nikki Scheel. B&W page USD 1,300, color page USD 1,800; trim 10.5 x 10.5. Circ: 30,000 (controlled).

636.7 CHE ISSN 2234-9448
INFO CHIENS. CYNOLOGIE ROMANDE. Text in French. 1935. bi-m. CHF 47 domestic; CHF 57 foreign (effective 2011). adv. **Document type:** *Magazine, Trade.*
Formerly (until 2011): Cynologie Romande (1662-789X); Which superseded in part (in 1987): Le Chien (1662-7199)
Published by: Federation Romande de Cynologie, c/o Madeleine Vallotton, R de Catogne 6, Martigny, 1920, Switzerland. TEL 41-27-7223692, FAX 41-27-7223692, secretaire@cynofrc.ch.

636 USA
INTERACTIONS (BELLEVUE). Text in English. 1983. 2/yr. USD 50 membership (effective 2007). 32 p./no. 2 cols./p.; **Document type:** *Magazine, Consumer.* **Description:** Provides "how-to" information for health care professionals and volunteers involved in programs of animal-assisted activities and therapy.
(until 1991): People, Animals, Environment (8755-5875)
Related titles: Online - full text ed.
—CCC.
Published by: Delta Society, 875 124th Ave NE, Ste 101, Bellevue, WA 98055. TEL 425-679-5500, FAX 425-679-5539, info@deltasociety.org, http://www.deltasociety.org. Ed. Michelle Cobey. Circ: 10,000 (paid and controlled).

636.974 USA
INTERNATIONAL FERRET REVIEW. Text in English. 1985. q. USD 20 domestic; USD 30 foreign (effective 2000). adv. bk.rev.; video rev. back issues avail. **Document type:** *Newsletter.* **Description:** News and information on ferrets, including breeding, care, legislation, products and exhibitions.
Published by: Ferret Fanciers Club, 2916 Perrysville Ave, Pittsburgh, PA 15214. TEL 412-322-1161. Ed., Pub., R&P, Adv. contact Mary Field. page USD 195; trim 11 x 8.5. Circ: 7,300.

636 USA ISSN 1074-780X
INTERNATIONAL PET INDUSTRY NEWS. Text in English. 1993. m. USD 295 (effective 2000). **Document type:** *Newsletter.* **Description:** For executives in the pet products industry. Covers marketing, new products and promotions for pet food and pet products around the world.
Published by: Good Communications, Inc., PO Box 7076, Huntington Wd, MI 48070-7076. TEL 512-454-6090, 800-968-1738, FAX 512-454-3420. Ed. Ross Becker. Adv. contact Kathy Seiden.

636.7 USA
IRISH TERRIER CLUB OF AMERICA. NEWSLETTER. Text in English. 1970. 6/yr. membership. bk.rev. **Document type:** *Newsletter, Consumer.*
Published by: Irish Terrier Club of America, 5494 Oak Trail, Norton, MA 02766. TEL 508-285-9655, http://www.itca.info. Circ: 350.

636.7 USA
IRISH WATER SPANIEL CLUB OF AMERICA. NEWSLETTER. Text in English. m. **Document type:** *Newsletter, Consumer.*
Published by: Irish Water Spaniel Club of America, c/o Kim Kezer, 86 High St, Amesbury, MA 01913. cavaniws@linkline.com, http://clubs.akc.org/iwsc/index.htm. Ed. Jennifer Waever.

636.7 USA ISSN 0164-8675
THE IRISH WOLFHOUND QUARTERLY. Text in English. 1978. q. USD 54 domestic; USD 74 in Canada; USD 98 elsewhere; USD 15 per issue (effective 2011). adv. back issues avail. **Document type:** *Magazine, Consumer.* **Description:** Contains breeder interviews, columns by people who know and love Irish Wolfhounds.
Published by: Hoflin Publishing, Inc., 4401 Zephyr St, Wheat Ridge, CO 80033. TEL 303-420-2222, FAX 720-207-0382, help@hoflin.com.

636.752 DEU ISSN 0021-3950
DER JAGDSPANIEL. Text in German. 1907. 6/yr. adv. charts; illus.; stat.; tr.lit. **Document type:** *Magazine, Consumer.*
Published by: Jagdspaniel-Klub e.V., Kleine Lange Hecke 5, Kaarst, 41564, Germany. http://www.jagdspaniel-klub.de. Ed. Hermine Bonin. adv.: B&W page EUR 100. Circ: 2,600 (controlled).

JAGTHUNDEN. *see* SPORTS AND GAMES—Outdoor Life

636 USA ISSN 1945-6697
JERSEY TAILS; celebrating the relationship between pets and their people. Text in English. 2000. m. USD 36; free to qualified personnel (effective 2008). adv. back issues avail. **Document type:** *Magazine, Consumer.*
Related titles: Online - full text ed.: ISSN 1945-6700. free.
Published by: Tails Pet Media Group, Inc., 4527 N Ravenswood Ave, Chicago, IL 60640. TEL 773-561-4300, 877-866-8245, FAX 773-561-3030, mail@tailsinc.org. Adv. contact Nikki Scheel. B&W page USD 2,100, color page USD 2,300; trim 10.5 x 10.5. Circ: 40,000 (controlled).

636.7 USA ISSN 1534-0341
SF429.L3
JUST LABS; a celebration of the labrador retriever. Text in English. 2001. bi-m. USD 23.95 domestic; USD 35.95 in Canada; USD 42.95 elsewhere (effective 2011). adv. illus. **Document type:** *Magazine, Trade.* **Description:** Provides information about dogs.
Published by: Village Press, Inc., 2779 Aero Park Dr, PO Box 968, Traverse City, MI 49685. TEL 231-946-3712, 800-327-7377, FAX 231-946-3289, info@villagepress.com, http://www.villagepress.com. Ed. Jason Smith. Adv. contact John Roddy.

636 AUT ISSN 0022-8117
KAMERAD TIER. Text in German. 1965. irreg. (4-6/yr.). looseleaf. membership. adv. bk.rev. illus.
Published by: Tierschutzaktion "der Blaue Kreis", Goldschlagstrasse 15, Vienna, W 1150, Austria. TEL 0222-9218573. Ed. Kurt Kolar.

636.8 NLD ISSN 2210-979X
KATTENMANIEREN. Text in Dutch. 1999. bi-m. EUR 19.95; EUR 3.95 newsstand/cover (effective 2008). adv. **Document type:** *Magazine, Consumer.*
Published by: Compasso Media bv, Postbus 111, Deurne, 5750 AC, Netherlands. TEL 31-493-328600, FAX 31-493-328601, administratie@compassomedia.nl, http://www.compassomedia.nl. Circ: 10,000.

636.8 NLD ISSN 1383-7451
KATTENWERELD. Text in Dutch. 1967. q. EUR 25.50 (effective 2009); includes Jaarboek.
Related titles: ◆ Supplement(s): Nederlandse Kattenfokkers Vereniging. Jaarboek. ISSN 1383-746X.
Published by: Nederlandse Kattenfokkers Vereniging, Zandsteenlaan 16, Groningen, Netherlands. TEL 31-6-22283632, FAX 31-84-8316186, http://www.nkfv.nl.

636.8 DEU ISSN 0176-4853
KATZEN EXTRA. Text in German. 1979. m. EUR 35; EUR 3.50 newsstand/cover (effective 2011). adv. back issues avail. **Document type:** *Magazine, Consumer.*
Published by: Gong Verlag GmbH & Co. KG, Muenchener Str 101, Ismaning, 85737, Germany. TEL 49-89-272700, FAX 49-89-272707290, gonginfo@gongverlag.de, http://www.gong-verlag.de. Ed. Monika Binder. Adv. contact Sonja Haase. Circ: 33,000 (paid and controlled).

599.722 CHE ISSN 1423-6869
KATZEN MAGAZIN. Text in German. 1979. bi-m. CHF 40.95; CHF 7.70 newsstand/cover (effective 2008). adv. **Document type:** *Magazine, Consumer.*
Formerly (until 1980): Katzen Extra (1423-6877)
Published by: Roro-Press Verlag AG, Erlenweg, Dietlikon, 8305, Switzerland. TEL 41-44-8357735, FAX 41-44-8357705. Ed. Claudia Kasper. Pub. Rolf Boffa. Adv. contact Chantal Jueni.

636.7 USA
KEEZETTE. Text in English. 1976. bi-m. USD 10. adv.
Address: c/o Carol Cash, Ed & Pub, 15646 Creekwood Ln, Strongsville, OH 44136.

636 GBR
KENNEL AND CATTERY MANAGEMENT. Text in English. 1983. bi-m. GBP 20 domestic; GBP 24 in Europe; GBP 28 elsewhere (effective 2009). adv. bk.rev. back issues avail. **Document type:** *Magazine, Trade.* **Description:** Covers nutrition, hygiene, veterinary advice, breeding, and management.
Published by: Albatross Publications, PO Box 523, Horsham, W Sussex RH12 4WL, United Kingdom. TEL 44-1293-871201, FAX 44-1293-871301.

636.7 GBR ISSN 0305-442X
KENNEL CLUB YEARBOOK. Text in English. a. free to members. **Document type:** *Bulletin.*
—BLDSC (5089.540000).
Published by: Kennel Club, 1-5 Clarges St, Piccadilly, London, W1J 8AB, United Kingdom. TEL 44-870-606-6750, FAX 44-20-7518-1058. Ed. Charles Colborn. Circ: 3,000.

636.7 GBR ISSN 0022-9962
KENNEL GAZETTE. Text in English. 1880. m. GBP 20 domestic; GBP 27 in Europe; GBP 32 elsewhere; GBP 2.25 per issue (effective 2009). adv. bk.rev. illus. **Document type:** *Magazine, Trade.* **Description:** Covers information about the developments about the canine world.
Published by: Kennel Club, 1-5 Clarges St, Piccadilly, London, W1J 8AB, United Kingdom. TEL 44-844-4633980, FAX 44-20-75181058. Ed. Daniela Tranquada TEL 44-20-75181038. Adv. contact Tricia McDougall TEL 44-1536-747333. B&W page GBP 465, color page GBP 880; trim 210 x 297. Circ: 8,250.

636.7 USA
KERRY BLUEPRINTS. Text in English. q. USD 15; USD 18 foreign. adv.
Published by: United States Kerry Blue Terrier Club, 602 W Fernwood Dr, Toronto, OH 43964. Ed. Joann Custer. Circ: 400.

KEY NOTE MARKET ASSESSMENT. THE PET MARKET. *see* BUSINESS AND ECONOMICS—Production Of Goods And Services

636 USA ISSN 1930-0689
KINDNESS SPEAKS ALL LANGUAGES. Text in English. 2005. m. **Document type:** *Newsletter, Consumer.*
Related titles: Online - full text ed.: ISSN 1930-0697.
Published by: Anupo Joy, 991 Lomas Sante Fe Ave, Solana Beach, CA 92075. TEL 760-840-0973, contactus@uniquebliss.com, http://www.anupojoy.com/index.html. Pub. Anupo Joy.

636.8 FIN ISSN 1236-4525
KISSAFANI. Text in Finnish. 1992. bi-m. EUR 31 (effective 2007). adv. **Document type:** *Magazine, Consumer.*
Published by: Karprint Oy, Vanha Turunrie 371, Huhmari, 03150, Finland. TEL 358-9-41397300, FAX 358-9-41397405, http://www.karprint.fi. Ed. Reetta Ahola. Adv. contact Arja Blom. page EUR 1,534. Circ: 16,500.

636.8 USA ISSN 1093-9415
KITTENS U S A. Text in English. 1997. a. USD 7.50 per issue (effective 2008). adv. **Document type:** *Magazine, Trade.* **Description:** A guide to adopting and caring for your new kitten. Includes information about how to find a kitten, get your home ready and basic care and nutrition tips. It is geared to owners of mixed breed and purebred kittens.
Published by: BowTie, Inc., 2401 Beverly Blvd, PO Box 57900, Los Angeles, CA 90057. TEL 213-385-2222, FAX 213-385-8565, adtraffic@bowtieinc.com, http://www.bowtieinc.com. Ed. Jackie Franza. adv.: B&W page USD 4,310, color page USD 8,440; trim 8 x 10.875. Circ: 76,842.

639.37483 USA ISSN 1093-9423
KOI WORLD AND WATER GARDENS. Text in English. 1998. a. USD 6.99 per issue (effective 2008). adv. **Document type:** *Magazine, Trade.* **Description:** Provides basic koi care information and emerging koi-keeping practices. It also enlightens and entertains readers by exploring topics like koi shows, koi art and public koi ponds.
Published by: BowTie, Inc., 2401 Beverly Blvd, PO Box 57900, Los Angeles, CA 90057. TEL 213-385-2222, FAX 213-385-8565, adtraffic@bowtieinc.com, http://www.bowtieinc.com. Ed. Tom Barthel. Pub. Norman Ridker. Adv. contact Marc Fredman. B&W page USD 2,850, color page USD 2,050; trim 8 x 10.875. Circ: 31,426.

636.7 FIN ISSN 0355-7235
KOIRAMME/VAARA HUNDAR. Text in Finnish. 1935. 10/yr. adv. **Document type:** *Magazine, Consumer.*
Formerly (until 1959): S K L; Suomen Kennel-liitton Julkaisu
Published by: Suomen Kennelliitto/Finnish Kennel Club, Kamreerintie 8, Espoo, 02770, Finland. TEL 358-9-887300, FAX 358-9-88730331, info@kennelliitto.fi, http://www.kennelliitto.fi. Ed. Tapio Eerola. adv.: B&W page EUR 1,780, color page EUR 3,549; 210 x 297. Circ: 102,000.

636.7 USA
KOMONDOR KOMMENTS. Text in English. 1971. q. USD 30 (effective 1999). adv. bk.rev. **Document type:** *Newsletter.* **Description:** Contains news about the Kommodor breed of dogs and other things of interest to the members of the Kommodor Club of America.
Published by: (Komondor Club of America), Wynne S. Vaught, Ed. & Pub., 151 Grace Lane, Liberty, SC 29657. TEL 864-306-0110. R&P, Adv. contact Wynne S Vaught. Circ: 300.

636 USA ISSN 1940-5677
L.A. TAILS. (Los Angeles) Text in English. 2007 (Dec.). m. USD 36; free to qualified personnel (effective 2008). adv. back issues avail. **Document type:** *Magazine, Consumer.* **Description:** Features the latest in animal news, information on health and wellness, celebrity interviews, inspirational stories, local happenings in the pet community, cool products and more.
Related titles: Online - full text ed.: ISSN 1940-5685. free.
Published by: Tails Pet Media Group, Inc., 4527 N Ravenswood Ave, Chicago, IL 60640. TEL 773-561-4300, 877-866-8245, FAX 773-561-3030, mail@tailsinc.org. Adv. contact Nikki Scheel. B&W page USD 1,640, color page USD 1,955; trim 10.5 x 10.5.

636.7 NLD ISSN 1571-4098
LABRADOR POST. Text in Dutch. bi-m. EUR 27.50 domestic; EUR 43.50 foreign (effective 2009).
Published by: Nederlandse Labrador Vereniging, c/o Anke ter Riet, Rozensteinweg 61, Laag Soeren, 6957 BK, Netherlands. nlv-leden@planet.nl, http://www.nederlandselabradorvereniging.nl.

636.7 USA ISSN 8750-3557
THE LABRADOR QUARTERLY. Text in English. 1984. q. USD 58 domestic; USD 91 in Canada; USD 112 elsewhere; USD 15 per issue (effective 2011). adv. back issues avail. **Document type:** *Magazine, Consumer.* **Description:** Contains breeder interviews, columns by people who know and love Labs.
Published by: Hoflin Publishing, Inc., 4401 Zephyr St, Wheat Ridge, CO 80033. TEL 303-420-2222, FAX 720-207-0382, help@hoflin.com.

636.73 GBR ISSN 0260-5627
LABRADOR RETRIEVER CLUB OF WALES. YEARBOOK. Text in English. 1980. a. GBP 2. adv. bk.rev. illus.
Published by: Labrador Retriever Club of Wales, c/o M. Williams, 6 Dan-y-Felin, Llantrisant, Pontyclun, Mid Glam CF7 8EH, United Kingdom. Circ: 500.

636 USA ISSN 1047-9252
LAJOIE. Text in English. 1990. q. USD 4.50 newsstand/cover. **Document type:** *Magazine, Consumer.*
Address: PO Box 145, Batesville, VA 22924. TEL 540-456-6204. Ed. Rita Reynolds.

636.7 USA
LAKELANDER. Text in English. bi-m. USD 10.
Published by: United States Lakeland Terrier Club, 4259 Bear Hollow Trail, Haymarket, VA 22069. Circ: 200.

636.752 DNK ISSN 0107-8585
LANGHAARS-NYT. Text in Danish. 1979. bi-m. illus. **Document type:** *Bulletin, Consumer.*
Published by: Klubben for den Langhaarede Hoensehund, c/o Bent Hansen, Fyrrevaenget 9, Jaegerspris, 3630, Denmark. info@langhaarsklubben.org, http://www.langhaarsklubben.org.

636.7 SWE ISSN 0283-8958
LAPPHUNDEN. Variant title: Tidningen Lapphunden. Text in Swedish. 1963. 5/yr. SEK 200 domestic to members; SEK 240 foreign to members (effective 2004). **Document type:** *Consumer.*
Published by: Svenska Lapphundklubben, c/o Ann-Christin Wanhatalo, Liljevaegen 15, Kvissleby, 86234, Sweden. TEL 46-60-560030, FAX 46-60-6614001, cs@slk.nu, http://www.slk.nu.

636 USA
LEARNFREE LIVING. Text in English. bi-w.
Media: Online - full text.
Published by: LearnFree Inc, PO Box 163895, Austin, TX 78716-3895. FAX 877-675-3276. Ed. Whitney Temple.

636.8 FRA ISSN 1959-7320
LEGENDES DE CHATS. Text in French. 2007. q. **Document type:** *Magazine, Consumer.*
Published by: Societe Francaise de Revues, 60 rue Greneta, Paris, 75002, France. TEL 33-1-44769831.

636.7 FIN ISSN 0787-6424
LEMMIKKI. Text in Finnish. 1990. m. EUR 35 (effective 2005). adv. **Document type:** *Magazine, Consumer.* **Description:** Reports on animals and how to care for them, as well as items that animal owners buy for their pets.
Published by: Yhtyneet Kuvalehdet Oy/United Magazines Ltd., Maistraatinportti 1, Helsinki, 00015, Finland. TEL 358-9-15661, FAX 358-9-145650, http://www.kuvalehdet.fi. Ed. Sirkku Kuusava. Circ: 19,856.

636.7 USA ISSN 0273-8333
THE LHASA APSO REPORTER. Text in English. 1973. bi-m. USD 40 domestic; USD 45 in Canada; USD 90 elsewhere (effective 1999). adv. bk.rev. **Description:** Articles on the Lhasa Apso breed, health care and grooming topics, and other information of interest.
Published by: Lhasa Apso Reporter, PO Box 327, Romeo, MI 48065. TEL 810-752-5674, FAX 810-752-4142. Ed. Denise Olejniczak. Circ: 1,000.

636.7 USA
LHASA BULLETIN. Text in English. bi-m. USD 7.50 to non-members.
Address: c/o Susan S Giles, Ed, 2372 Wheatland Dr, Manakin Sabot, VA 23103. Circ: 750.

636 RUS ISSN 1726-0868
LIZA. MOI LIUBIMYE ZHIVOTNYE. Text in Russian. 2002. m. RUR 16 newsstand/cover (effective 2003). adv. **Document type:** *Magazine, Consumer.* **Description:** Contains a wide range of useful and interesting articles and veterinarians' tips on pets.
Published by: Izdatel'skii Dom Burda, ul Pravdy 8, Moscow, 125040, Russian Federation. TEL 7-095-7979849, FAX 7-095-2571196, vertrieb@burda.ru, http://www.burda.ru. adv.: page USD 2,500. Circ: 50,000 (paid and controlled).

636.7 SVN ISSN 1408-4295
LORD. Text in Slovenian. 1997. m. adv. **Document type:** *Magazine, Consumer.*
Published by: Delo Revije d.o.o., Dunajska 5, Ljubljana, 1509, Slovenia. TEL 386-1-4737000, FAX 386-1-4737352, narocnine@delo-revije.si, http://www.delo-revije.si.

636.7 USA
LUCKY DOG. Text in English. 2006 (Jan./Feb.). bi-m. **Document type:** *Magazine, Consumer.*
Address: 2620 Regatta Dr., Ste. 102, Las Vegas, NV 89128. TEL 702-925-8288, FAX 702-925-8375. Ed., Pub. Michelle Danks.

636 CAN ISSN 1495-222X
MAGAZINE ANIMAL; pour l'amour des animaux. Text in French. 1998. m. CAD 24.99 (effective 2007). **Document type:** *Magazine, Consumer.*
Formerly (until 2000): Animal Hebdo (1488-9560)
Address: 7 Ch. Bates, Outremont, PQ H2V 4V7, Canada. TEL 514-848-7164.

636.7 USA ISSN 8750-5487
MALTESE MAGAZINE. Text in English. 1980. q. USD 44 domestic; USD 50 in Canada & Mexico; USD 105 elsewhere; USD 15 per issue domestic; USD 20 per issue in Canada & Mexico; USD 30 per issue elsewhere (effective 2011). adv. illus. 40 p./no.; back issues avail. **Document type:** *Magazine, Consumer.* **Description:** News and information of interest to Maltese owners.
Formerly (until 198?): Maltese Tails (0274-7022)
Published by: Reporter Publications, PO Box 6369, Los Osos, CA 93412. TEL 805-528-2007, FAX 805-528-8200.

636.822 USA
THE MANX LINE. Text in English. 2001. bi-m. USD 24; USD 4 newsstand/cover (effective 2001). **Document type:** *Magazine, Consumer.* **Description:** Contains information about the Manx breed & breeder listings.
Published by: The Manx Line, 19324 2nd Ave NW, Seattle, WA 98177. Eds. Joanne Stone, Lisa Franklin.

636 USA ISSN 1523-5106
QL620.45
MARINE FISH & REEF U S A; you guide to saltwater habitats. Text in English. 1999. a. USD 6.99 per issue (effective 2008). adv. **Document type:** *Magazine, Trade.* **Description:** Provides a guide to maintaining saltwater habitats and fish.
Published by: BowTie, Inc., 2401 Beverly Blvd, PO Box 57900, Los Angeles, CA 90057. TEL 213-385-2222, FAX 213-385-8565, adtraffic@bowtieinc.com, http://www.bowtieinc.com. Ed. Russ Case. adv.: B&W page USD 2,810, color page USD 2,040; trim 8 x 10.875. Circ: 53,037.

636.7 USA
MASTIFF CLUB OF AMERICA. JOURNAL. Text in English. 1970. q. USD 21 domestic; USD 28 in Canada; USD 39 in Australia, New Zealand & Japan; USD 37 elsewhere (effective 2008). adv. bk.rev. **Document type:** *Magazine, Consumer.*
Formerly: Mastiff Journal
Published by: (Mastiff Club of America), Kentucky Pre-Press, 157-B Trade St, Lexington, KY 40511. Ed. Linda Cain. Circ: 600. **Subscr. to:** Mastiff Club of America, c/o Sherry White, 7529 Curtis Creek Rd, Junction City, KS 66441. TEL 785-238-8929, FAX 785-238-1892, Sarabella1@earthlink.net.

636.7 USA
MATCH SHOW BULLETIN. Text in English. 1969. m. USD 29 (effective 2005). adv. back issues avail. **Document type:** *Bulletin, Consumer.* **Description:** Lists locations and details of dog match shows, seminars, and training classes.
Published by: Myrna Lieber, Ed.& Pub., PO Box 214, Massapequa, NY 11758. TEL 516-541-3442, FAX 516-541-3442. Ed. Myrna Lieber. adv.: B&W page USD 360; trim 10.88 x 8.38. Circ: 6,700 (paid and controlled).

636.7 NLD ISSN 2211-3991
▼ **ME & MY DOG.** Variant title: M & M D Magazine. Text in Dutch. 2010. bi-m. EUR 25; EUR 4.95 newsstand/cover (effective 2011). adv. **Document type:** *Magazine, Consumer.*
Published by: M & M D, Bernhardstraat 13, Mill, 5451 BN, Netherlands. Adv. contact Darek Ostrowski TEL 31-485-470142. Circ: 25,000.

636.7 DEU ISSN 1860-7071
MEIN FREUND, DER RASSEHUND. Text in German. 2005. q. EUR 15 membership (effective 2006). **Document type:** *Magazine, Trade.*
Published by: Rassehunde-Zuchtverband Deutschland e.V., Gravestr 23, Gnarrenburg, 27442, Germany. TEL 49-4285-925896, FAX 49-4285-9249093, info@rassehunde-zuchtverband.de, http://www.rassehunde-zuchtverband.de.

179.3 AUT
MENSCH UND TIER. Text in German. 1910. q. membership. bk.rev. **Document type:** *Newsletter.*
Published by: Liga gegen Tierquaelerei und Missbrauch der Tierversuche, Blindengasse 38, Vienna, W 1080, Austria. Ed. Albert Schwarz. Circ: 16,000.

636 USA ISSN 1945-6719
MICHIGAN TAILS; celebrating the relationship between pets and their people. Text in English. 2000. m. USD 36; free to qualified personnel (effective 2008). adv. back issues avail. **Document type:** *Magazine, Consumer.*
Related titles: Online - full text ed.: ISSN 1945-6727. free.
Published by: Tails Pet Media Group, Inc., 4527 N Ravenswood Ave, Chicago, IL 60640. TEL 773-561-4300, 877-866-8245, FAX 773-561-3030, mail@tailsinc.org. Adv. contact Nikki Scheel. B&W page USD 2,100, color page USD 2,300; trim 10.5 x 10.5. Circ: 130,000 (controlled).

636.7 AUS ISSN 1833-0541
MINI FOXIE NEWSLETTER. Text in English. 19??. q. **Document type:** *Newspaper, Consumer.*
Formerly (until 1992): Miniature (Fox) Terrier Club of Australia. Newsletter
Published by: Mini Foxie Club of Australia Inc., 51 Bingham Ln, Tallong, NSW 2579, Australia. admin@minifoxie.org, http://www.minifoxie.org.

636 FRA ISSN 1950-8786
MINIZOO; le magazine des petits mammiferes de compagnie. Text in French. 2006. bi-m. EUR 28 (effective 2009). back issues avail. **Document type:** *Magazine, Consumer.*
Published by: Edizoo, 4 square Lamartine, Paris, 75116, France. contact@minizoo.fr, redaction@minizoo.fr.

636 ITA ISSN 1127-3526
IL MIO ACQUARIO. Text in Italian. 1998. m. EUR 45 (effective 2009). **Document type:** *Magazine, Consumer.*
Published by: Sprea Editori Srl, Via Torino 51, Cernusco sul Naviglio, MI 20063, Italy. TEL 39-02-92432222, FAX 39-02-92432236, editori@sprea.it, http://www.sprea.it.

636.7 ITA ISSN 1123-4202
IL MIO CANE. Text in Italian. 1994. m. EUR 35.90 (effective 2009). **Document type:** *Magazine, Consumer.*
Published by: Sprea Editori Srl, Via Torino 51, Cernusco sul Naviglio, MI 20063, Italy. TEL 39-02-92432222, FAX 39-02-92432236, editori@sprea.it, http://www.sprea.it.

636.7 CAN ISSN 1703-812X
MODERN DOG; the lifestyle magazine for modern dogs and their companions. Text in English. 2002. q. CAD 18 domestic; USD 15 in United States; USD 45 elsewhere (effective 2008). adv. illus. **Document type:** *Magazine, Consumer.* **Description:** Contains expert advice, travel destinations, full fashion spreads, the latest accessories and information on what's new in the world of dogs.
Address: 343 Railway St, Ste 202, Vancouver, BC V6A 1A4, Canada. TEL 604-734-3131, FAX 604-734-3031, connie@moderndog.ca. Ed., Pub. Connie Wilson. adv.: page CAD 2,180; trim 10.875 x 8. Circ: 240,000.

636.7 POL ISSN 2081-5905
MOJ KOCHANY PIES. Text in Polish. m. PLZ 2.99 newsstand/cover (effective 2010). adv. **Document type:** *Magazine, Consumer.*
Published by: Hubert Burda Media, ul Warecka 11a, Warsaw, 00034, Poland. TEL 48-22-4488000, FAX 48-22-4488001, kontakt@burdamedia.pl. Ed. Malgorzata Janicka-Gruca. Adv. contact Katarzyna Kolakowska-Frackowiak TEL 48-22-4488384.

636.7 SVN ISSN 1318-296X
MOJ PES. Text in Slovenian. 1992. m. EUR 17.53 (effective 2007). **Document type:** *Magazine, Consumer.*
Related titles: Online - full text ed.: ISSN 1581-1425. 2000.
Published by: Dedal d.o.o., Podutiska 148, Ljubljana, 1000, Slovenia. TEL 386-1-5190513, FAX 386-1-5190756.

636.7 POL ISSN 0867-2822
MOJ PIES. Text in Polish. 1991. m. PLZ 139.01 (effective 2004). adv. **Document type:** *Magazine, Consumer.*
Published by: Agencja Wydawniczo-Reklamowa "Wprost" sp. z o.o., Reform Plaza, Al. Jerozolimskie 123, Warszawa, 02017, Poland. TEL 48-22-5291100, FAX 48-22-8529016, http://www.wprost.pl. Ed. Malgorzata Nowotny. Adv. contact Olga Bak.

636.7 ITA ISSN 1591-0261
MOLOSSI. Text in Italian. 2000. bi-m. EUR 19.90 (effective 2009). **Document type:** *Magazine, Consumer.*
Published by: Sprea Editori Srl, Via Torino 51, Cernusco sul Naviglio, MI 20063, Italy. TEL 39-02-92432222, FAX 39-02-92432236, editori@sprea.it, http://www.sprea.it.

636.7 ITA ISSN 1593-9804
MOLOSSI & GUARDIANI. Variant title: Guardiani & Molossi. Text in Italian. 2001. a. price varies. **Document type:** *Magazine, Consumer.*
Published by: Sprea Editori Srl, Via Torino 51, Cernusco sul Naviglio, MI 20063, Italy. TEL 39-02-92432222, FAX 39-02-92432236, editori@sprea.it, http://www.sprea.it.

P

636.8 USA
MORRIS REPORT. Text in English. 1987. q. USD 7.50. adv. bk.rev.
Published by: 9-Lives Cat Food - Hogan Communications, 150 E Olive Ave, Ste 208, Burbank, CA 91502. FAX 818-848-4995.

636.7 CZE ISSN 1804-3399
▼ **MUJ PES**; miluj sveho psa. Text in Czech. 2010. m. CZK 179; CZK 19.90 newsstand/cover (effective 2010). adv. **Document type:** *Magazine, Consumer.*
Published by: Burda Praha spol. s.r.o., Premyslovska 2845/43, Prague 2, 13000, Czech Republic. TEL 420-2-21589111, FAX 420-2-21589368, burda@burda.cz, http://www.burda.cz. **Subscr. to:** Mediaservis s.r.o., Pacericka 2773/1, Prague 9 193 00, Czech Republic. TEL 420-2-71199100, FAX 420-2-72700025, info@mediaservis.cz, http://www.mediaservis.cz.

636.8 ESP ISSN 1133-0007
EL MUNDO DEL GATO. Text in Spanish. 1993. bi-m. adv. **Document type:** *Magazine, Academic/Scholarly.* **Description:** Includes news, shows, advertisement, educational activities and veterinarian issues on cats.
Published by: Editorial America Iberica, C. Miguel Yuste 33bis, Madrid, 28037, Spain. TEL 34-91-3277950, FAX 34-91-3044746, editorial@eai.es, http://www.eai.es/. Ed. Nati Sierra. Circ: 13,000.

363.7 ESP ISSN 0212-4947
MUNDO DEL PERRO. Text in Spanish. 1980. m. adv. **Document type:** *Magazine, Consumer.* **Description:** Includes news, advertisement, educational activities and veterinarian issues on dogs.
Published by: Editorial America Iberica, C. Miguel Yuste 33bis, Madrid, 28037, Spain. TEL 34-91-3277950, FAX 34-91-3044746, editorial@eai.es, http://www.eai.es/. Ed. Antonio Lopez. adv.: page EUR 900; trim 230 x 297. Circ: 30,000 (controlled).

636.7 USA
MUSTARD AND PEPPER. Text in English. 1973. q. USD 24. adv.
Published by: Dandie Dinmont Terrier Club of America, 12109 Piney Glen Ln, Potomac, MD 20854. TEL 301-299-2330, FAX 301-299-3107. Ed. Cathy Nelson. Circ: 300.

179.3 USA ISSN 1090-3992
N A C A NEWS. Text in English. 1978. bi-m. USD 25 domestic; USD 35 foreign (effective 2006). adv. bk.rev.; film rev. charts; stat.; tr.lit. 44 p./no.; **Document type:** *Magazine, Trade.* **Description:** Contains articles addressing issues of interest to its members and others concerned with the ongoing Animal/Human relationship problem.
Published by: National Animal Control Association, PO Box 480851, Kansas City, MO 64148-0851. TEL 913-768-1319, FAX 913-768-1378. Ed., Pub., R&P, Adv. contact John Mays. Circ: 4,500.

636 NZL
N Z DOG WORLD. (New Zealand) Text in English. m. NZD 50 domestic; NZD 125 foreign (effective 2008). **Document type:** *Magazine, Consumer.*
Formerly (until Nov.2008): New Zealand Kennel Gazette (1175-2750)
Published by: New Zealand Kennel Club, Private Bag 50903, Porirua, 6220, New Zealand. TEL 64-4-2374489, FAX 64-4-2370721, nzkc@nzkc.org.nz.

636.7 USA
NAPLES DOG; shopping, stories and doggone fun. Text in English. 2006. q. USD 20 domestic; USD 34 in Canada; USD 34 elsewhere (effective 2007). adv. **Document type:** *Magazine, Consumer.* **Description:** Offers an entertaining, informative resource for dog-loving residents and tourists in southwest Florida who want to share the good life with their dogs.
Published by: Naples Dog Magazine, PO Box 111205, Naples, FL 34108. TEL 239-293-1552, FAX 239-236-4364. Pub. Ericka Basile. Adv. contact Amy Farrell. color page USD 1,800; trim 8.5 x 11. Circ: 10,000 (paid and controlled).

636.8 AUS ISSN 1035-6398
NATIONAL CAT. Text in English. 1991. bi-m. adv. **Description:** Covers show reports, cat world news and activities (local, overseas), veterinary advice and research reports, domestic pet care.
Published by: Retail Media Pty Ltd., Parramatta Business Centre, PO Box 6104, Parramatta, NSW 2150, Australia. TEL 61-2-98901199, FAX 61-2-98901877, subscriptions@retailmedia.com, http://www.retailmedia.com.au. adv.: B&W page AUD 800, color page AUD 1,390. Circ: 15,000 (paid).

636.7 AUS ISSN 0728-8727
NATIONAL DOG. Text in English. 1947. m. AUD 84 domestic; AUD 125 in New Zealand; AUD 140 in US & Canada includes Asia; AUD 155 elsewhere; AUD 71 to senior citizens; AUD 6.50 newsstand/cover (effective 2009). adv. back issues avail. **Document type:** *Magazine, Consumer.* **Description:** Covers regular breed features, show results, dog world news (local, overseas), veterinary advice and research reports, canine issues.
Former titles (until 1982): National Dog Newspaper (0811-4021); (until 1969): Australasian Kennel Review and Dog News; Which was formed by the merger of (1939-1960): Australasian Kennel Review; (1947-1960): Australian Dog News
Published by: RingLeader Way, 51 Taber Street, Menangle Park, NSW 2563, Australia. TEL 61-2-46338055, FAX 61-2-46338057, ringleader@ringleader.com.au. adv.: B&W page AUD 270, color page AUD 580; 265 x 330.

636 USA ISSN 0028-0267
NATIONAL STOCK DOG. Text in English. 1954. bi-m. USD 18. adv. abstr.; illus. **Description:** For the preservation and advancement of the livestock working breeds of America and the world.
Published by: National Stock Dog Registry, PO Box 402, Butler, IN 46721-0402. TEL 219-868-2670. Ed. J R Russell. Circ: 5,000.

636.8 USA ISSN 1523-5092
NATURAL CAT; your complete guide to holistic cat care. Text in English. 1999. a. adv. **Document type:** *Magazine, Consumer.*
Published by: BowTie, Inc., 2401 Beverly Blvd, PO Box 57900, Los Angeles, CA 90057. TEL 213-385-2222, FAX 213-385-8565, adtraffic@bowtieinc.com, http://www.bowtieinc.com. Ed. Lisa Hanks. Pub. Beth Landrigan.

636.7 USA ISSN 1523-5084
NATURAL DOG. Text in English. 1998. a. adv. **Document type:** *Guide, Consumer.* **Description:** Complete guide to holistic dog care.
Published by: BowTie, Inc., 3 Burroughs, Irvine, CA 92618-2804. TEL 949-855-8822, FAX 949-855-3045, http://www.bowtieinc.com. adv.: color page USD 4,980; trim 8 x 10.875. Circ: 52,120 (paid).

636 USA ISSN 1933-9291
NATURAL LIVING FOR ANIMALS. Text in English. 2006. q. USD 30 (effective 2006). **Document type:** *Magazine, Consumer.* **Description:** Explores a natural approach to animal health and well-being, including natural foods and medicines, and addresses alternative methods of communicating with and training animals.
Related titles: Online - full text ed.: Natural Animal Connections. ISSN 1559-095X.
Published by: Natural Animal Publishing, PO Box 484, Keene Valley, NY 12943. kinna@natanimal.com, http://www.natanimal.com. Ed. Kinna Ohman.

636 USA ISSN 1559-9175
NATURE'S CORNER. Text in English. 2005. q. USD 23.95 domestic; USD 25.95 in Canada & Mexico; USD 34.50 elsewhere; USD 7.50 per issue (effective 2007). **Document type:** *Magazine, Consumer.*
Published by: Equatorial Group, Ltd., 13835 N Tatum Blvd, Ste 9-609, Phoenix, AZ 85032. TEL 212-888-1784, maggie@naturescornermagazine.com. Pub. Margaret Wright.

636.8 NLD ISSN 1383-746X
NEDERLANDSE KATTENFOKKERS VERENIGING. JAARBOEK. Text in Dutch. 1980. a.
Related titles: ◆ Supplement to: Kattenwereld. ISSN 1383-7451.
Published by: Nederlandse Kattenfokkers Vereniging, Zandsteenlaan 16, Groningen, Netherlands. TEL 31-6-22283632, FAX 31-84-8316186, http://www.nkfv.nl.

636.7 USA
NEW PUPPY HANDBOOK. Text in English. 1993. q. free to members (effective 2011). **Document type:** *Handbook/Manual/Guide, Trade.* **Description:** Focuses on healthcare training, nutrition, behavior and other information of interest to new dog owners.
Published by: American Kennel Club, Inc., 260 Madison Ave, New York, NY 10016. TEL 212-696-8288, FAX 212-696-8345.

636 USA ISSN 1940-5650
NEW YORK CITY TAILS. Text in English. 2007 (Dec.). m. USD 36; free to qualified personnel (effective 2008). adv. back issues avail. **Document type:** *Magazine, Consumer.* **Description:** Features the latest in animal news, information on health and wellness, celebrity interviews, inspirational stories, local happenings in the pet community, cool products and more.
Related titles: Online - full text ed.: ISSN 1940-5669. free.
Published by: Tails Pet Media Group, Inc., 4527 N Ravenswood Ave, Chicago, IL 60640. TEL 773-561-4300, 877-866-8245, FAX 773-561-3030, mail@tailsinc.org. Adv. contact Nikki Scheel. B&W page USD 1,640, color page USD 1,955; trim 10.5 x 10.5.

636 USA ISSN 1544-8789
NEW YORK TAILS; a magazine for the people and pets of New York. Text in English. 2002 (Win.). q. USD 10 (effective 2003). adv.
Address: P. O. Box 287414, New York, NY 10128-0024. TEL 212-214-0653. Ed., Pub. Diane West.

636.7 NZL ISSN 1177-2557
NEW ZEALAND KENNEL CLUB. YEAR BOOK. Text in English. a. **Document type:** *Yearbook, Consumer.*
Supersedes in part (in 2005): New Zealand Kennel Club. Annual Report and Year Book
Published by: New Zealand Kennel Club, Private Bag 50903, Porirua, 6220, New Zealand. TEL 64-4-2374489, FAX 64-4-2370721, nzkc@nzkc.org.nz, http://www.nzkc.org.nz.

636.7 USA ISSN 0194-7206
NEWF-TIDE. Text in English. 196?. q. USD 55 domestic to non-members; USD 110 foreign to non-members; free to members (effective 2008). adv. bk.rev. **Document type:** *Magazine, Consumer.*
Published by: Newfoundland Club of America, PO Box 335, Washington, ME 04574. Eds. Allan Saeger, Peggy Saeger. Circ: 3,200.

636.7 USA
NORSK ELGHUND QUARTERLY. Text in English. 1979. q. USD 20. adv. **Description:** Articles on Norwegian Elkhounds.
Address: 31 Peck St, Rehoboth, MA 02769. Circ: 400.

636.7 179.3 USA ISSN 1041-1496
NORTHEAST CANINE COMPANION. Text in English. 1986. m. USD 20 (effective 1998). adv. bk.rev. back issues avail. **Document type:** *Magazine, Consumer.* **Description:** For dog fanciers, especially owners of show dogs.
Published by: Companion Publishing Co., PO Box 377, Sudbury, MA 01776-0377. TEL 978-443-8387, FAX 978-443-0183. Ed. Christine Harris. Pub., R&P, Adv. contact Alan Alford. B&W page USD 150; trim 11 x 8.5. Circ: 12,000.

636.7 USA
▼ **NORTHERN VIRGINIA DOG MAGAZINE**; the ultimate guide to canine-inspired living in the DC metro area. Text in English. 2009. q. USD 19 (effective 2010). adv. **Document type:** *Magazine, Consumer.* **Description:** Celebrates the canine-human bond with informative and insightful articles on a broad range of topics important to every dog owner.
Published by: 2hounds Productions, LLC, PO Box 30072, Alexandria, VA 22310. TEL 709-850-6963, FAX 419-858-6963. Pub. Janelle Welch. Adv. contact Angela Meyers TEL 703-887-8387. color page USD 1,900; trim 8.375 x 10.875. Circ: 30,000.

636.7 USA
NORWEGIAN ELKHOUND NEWS. Text in English. 197?. bi-m. USD 25 membership (effective 2008). **Document type:** *Newsletter.*
Related titles: Online - full content ed.
Published by: Norwegian Elkhound Association of America, c/o Karen Elvin, Secretary, 14465 St Croix Trail N, Marine on St. Croix, MN 55047. Ed. Robin L Anderson. Circ: 600.

636.7 USA
NORWICH & NORFOLK NEWS. Text in English. 1962. s-a. USD 15 domestic; USD 20 foreign (effective 2001). bk.rev. illus. 60 p./no.; back issues avail. **Document type:** *Newsletter.* **Description:** Contains articles on canine health (Norwich and Norfolk terriers), rescue, national specialties (dog shows), and working terrier events for Norwich and Norfolk terrier owners.
Published by: Norwich and Norfolk Terrier Club, c/o Alison G Freehling, 3500 Huntertown Rd, Versailles, KY 40383-9198. FAX 859-879-0734, nntcnews@hotmail.com, http://clubs.akc.org/nntc. Ed., R&P Alison G Freehling. Circ: 725 (paid).

636 ITA ISSN 1592-9345
I NOSTRI AMICI ANIMALI. Text in Italian. 2001. m. EUR 24.90 (effective 2009). **Document type:** *Magazine, Consumer.*
Published by: Sprea Editori Srl, Via Torino 51, Cernusco sul Naviglio, MI 20063, Italy. TEL 39-02-92432222, FAX 39-02-92432236, editori@sprea.it, http://www.sprea.it.

636 ITA ISSN 0029-3784
I NOSTRI CANI. Text in Italian. 1955. m. (11/yr.). free to members (effective 2009). adv. **Document type:** *Magazine, Consumer.*
Published by: Ente Nazionale della Cinofilia Italiana, Viale Corsica 20, Milan, MI 20137, Italy. TEL 39-02-7002031, FAX 39-02-70020323, enci@enci.it. Circ: 75,700.

636.7 USA ISSN 1089-0793
SF431
OFFLEAD. Text in English. 1972-1999; resumed. bi-m. USD 24.95 (effective 2003). adv. bk.rev. illus.; stat. index. back issues avail.; reprints avail. **Document type:** *Journal, Consumer.* **Description:** Communication among professional and amateur dog trainers, animal behaviourists, pet owners, and veterinarians. Presents techniques, events, equipment, seminars and other educational material.
Former titles (until 199?): Off-Lead Dog Training (1079-5537); Off-Lead (Canastota) (0094-0186)
Published by: Barkleigh Productions, Inc., 6 State Rd #113, Mechanicsburg, PA 17050 . TEL 717-691-3388, FAX 717-691-3381, barkleigh@aol.com, http://www.barkleigh.com/. Ed. Therese Backowski. Pub. Sally Liddick. Circ: 5,000 (paid).

636 USA ISSN 1945-6735
OHIO VALLEY TAILS; celebrating the relationship between pets and their people. Text in English. 2000. m. USD 36; free to qualified personnel (effective 2008). adv. back issues avail. **Document type:** *Magazine, Consumer.*
Related titles: Online - full text ed.: ISSN 1945-6743. free.
Published by: Tails Pet Media Group, Inc., 4527 N Ravenswood Ave, Chicago, IL 60640. TEL 773-561-4300, 877-866-8245, FAX 773-561-3030, mail@tailsinc.org. Adv. contact Nikki Scheel. B&W page USD 1,500, color page USD 2,000; trim 10.5 x 10.5. Circ: 30,000 (controlled).

636.7 USA
OLD ENGLISH TIMES. Text in English. 1972. bi-m. USD 20. adv. bk.rev.
Published by: Old English Sheepdog Club of America, Inc., c/o Kathryn Bunnell, Corresponding Sec, 14219 E 79th St S, Derby, KS 67037. Ed. Sam Middleton. Circ: 1,000.

636.7 NLD ISSN 2211-4106
ONS HOENDERBLAD. Text in Dutch. 197?. q. EUR 15 membership (effective 2011). **Document type:** *Newsletter, Consumer.*
Published by: Nederlandsche Hoenderclub, c/o W Bleijenberg, Sec., Vossestaart 5, Wilnis, 3648 HP, Netherlands. TEL 31-297-281896, ned.hoenderclub@kpnmail.nl, http://www.nederlandsehoenderclub.eu. Eds. L Hans, P A Kroon, W Bleijenberg.

636.7 NLD ISSN 1384-7406
ONZE BOSTONS. Text in Dutch. q. EUR 20 (effective 2008). adv. bk.rev.
Published by: Boston Terrier Club Nederland, c/o Marcel Bergen, Hoogte Kadijk 176, Amsterdam, 1018 BW, Netherlands. TEL 31-20-4286638, btcn@noob.nl, http://www.boston-terrier.nl. Circ: 250. **Subscr. to:** A.M. Geerlings, Schoolberg 34, Beesel 5954 AR, Netherlands.

636.7 NLD ISSN 0165-327X
ONZE HOND. Text in Dutch. 1976. m. EUR 42.50; EUR 4.50 newsstand/cover (effective 2009). adv. **Document type:** *Magazine, Trade.*
Published by: BCM Publishing, Postbus 1392, Eindhoven, 5602 BJ, Netherlands. TEL 31-40-8447644, FAX 31-40-8447655, bcm@bcm.nl, http://www.bcm.nl. Ed. Marlies Strik. Adv. contact Sandra Saris-Jongen. B&W page EUR 1,092, color page EUR 1,285; 215 x 285. Circ: 30,000.

636 DNK ISSN 0900-5226
OPDRAETTERVEJVISEREN. Text in Danish. 1959. a. free. illus. **Document type:** *Catalog, Consumer.*
Former titles (until 1982): Dansk Kennel Klub's Opdraetter-Vejviser (0900-517X); (until 1980): Den Nye Opdraettervejviser (0106-6714); (until 1976): Opdraettervejviseren (0900-5234)
Related titles: Online - full text ed.
Published by: Dansk Kennel Klub, Parkvej 1, Solroed Strand, 2680, Denmark. TEL 45-56-188100, FAX 45-56-188191, post@dansk-kennel-klub.dk, http://www.dansk-kennel-klub.dk.

636 USA
ORIGINAL FLYING MACHINE. Text in English. 2000. bi-m. USD 24; USD 4.50 newsstand/cover (effective 2001). adv. **Document type:** *Magazine, Consumer.*
Published by: Original Flying Machine, LLC, 10645 N Tatum Blvd, Ste 200, Phoenix, AZ 85028. TEL 877-636-2473, http://www.originalflyingmachine.com. Ed., Pub. Elizabeth Gurklys.

636.7 USA ISSN 1084-1822
OUR AFGHANS. Text in English. 1968. m. USD 30 domestic; USD 37 foreign (effective 2007). adv. bk.rev. 16 p./no.; back issues avail. **Document type:** *Magazine, Consumer.* **Description:** Provides news and advice for Afghan hound owners.
Published by: Weddle Publications, 22235 Parthenia St., West Hills, CA 91304-1348. Ed., Pub., R&P, Adv. contact Ruth Weddle. B&W page USD 125. Circ: 750 (paid).

636.8 GBR ISSN 1468-5787
OUR CATS. Text in English. 1981. fortn. adv. bk.rev.; Website rev. illus. 48 p./no.; back issues avail. **Document type:** *Newspaper, Consumer.* **Description:** Contains articles and features of interest to all types of cat enthusiasts.
Formerly (until 1999): Cats (0260-3837)
Related titles: Online - full text ed.: free to members (effective 2009).
Published by: Our Dogs Publishing Co. Ltd., 1 Lund St, Trafford Park, Manchester, M16 9EJ, United Kingdom. TEL 44-844-5049001, 44-844-5049013, sales@ourdogs.co.uk, http://www.ourdogs.co.uk. Ed. Alison Smith. Pub. Mr. David Cavill.

636.8 DEU ISSN 0944-6192
OUR CATS; Deutschlands modernes Katzenmagazin. Text in German. 1992. m. EUR 28.80 domestic; EUR 34.80 in Europe; EUR 52.20 elsewhere; EUR 2.70 newsstand/cover (effective 2010). adv. **Document type:** *Magazine, Consumer.*
Related titles: Online - full text ed.

Published by: Minerva Verlag GmbH, Hocksteiner Weg 38, Moenchengladbach, 41189, Germany. TEL 49-2166-621970, FAX 49-2166-6219710, info@minervaverlag.de, http://www.minervaverlag.de. adv.: B&W page EUR 2,028, color page EUR 3,447.60; trim 192 x 260. Circ: 50,000 (paid).

636.7 GBR ISSN 0955-9469
OUR DOGS. Text in English. 1895. w. GBP 100 domestic; GBP 102 in Europe; GBP 165 elsewhere; GBP 115 combined subscription domestic (print & online eds.); GBP 117 combined subscription in Europe (print & online eds.); GBP 180 combined subscription elsewhere (print & online eds.) (effective 2009). adv. bk.rev.; video rev.; Website rev. tr.lit. 88 p./no. 6 cols./p.; back issues avail. **Document type:** *Newspaper, Consumer.*
Related titles: Online - full text ed.: GBP 59.95 (effective 2009).
Published by: Our Dogs Publishing Co. Ltd., 1 Lund St, Trafford Park, Manchester, M16 9EJ, United Kingdom. TEL 44-844-5049001, 44-844-5049013, sales@ourdogs.co.uk. Ed. Alison Smith. Pub. Mr. David Cavill. Adv. contact Mr. John Holden TEL 44-0844-5049006. color page GBP 795, B&W page GBP 576; 265 x 365. Circ: 22,000.

636.7 USA ISSN 1934-5666
OUR HAVANESE. Text in English. 2006. bi-m. **Document type:** *Magazine, Consumer.*
Published by: K B Publications, PO Box 3044, Great Falls, MT 59403. TEL 800-995-1555.

P B W NEWS. (Pet Business World) *see* BUSINESS AND ECONOMICS—Small Business

636.68 DEU ISSN 0934-327X
PAPAGEIEN. Text in German. 1988. m. EUR 70.80 domestic; EUR 77.80 foreign (effective 2008). adv. **Document type:** *Magazine, Consumer.* **Description:** Provides content and information for parrot owners and breeders.
Published by: Arndt-Verlag, Brueckenfeldstr 28, Bretten, 75015, Germany. TEL 49-7252-957970, FAX 49-7252-78224, info@vogelbuch.com.

636.0832 USA
PARADE OF ROYALTY (YEAR). Text in English. 1980. a. USD 25 (effective 2001). adv. back issues avail. **Description:** Publishes year-end awards, articles of interest to cat fanciers.
Published by: American Cat Fanciers Association, Inc., PO Box 1949, Nixa, MO 65714-1949. TEL 417-334-5430, FAX 427-334-5540. R&P Connie Vandre. adv.: B&W page USD 200, color page USD 450. Circ: 1,200.

636.6865 USA
PARROT CHRONICLES.COM; the online magazine for parrot lovers. Text in English. bi-m. free. **Document type:** *Magazine, Consumer.*
Media: Online - full text.

636.7 DEU ISSN 0946-6223
PARTNER HUND. Text in German. 1993. m. EUR 28.95 (effective 2011). adv. **Document type:** *Magazine, Consumer.*
Published by: Gong Verlag GmbH & Co. KG, Muenchener Str 101, Ismaning, 85737, Germany. TEL 49-89-272700, FAX 49-89-272707290, gonginfo@gongverlag.de, http://www.gong-verlag.de. Ed. Ursula Birr. Adv. contact Sonja Haase. Circ: 55,390 (paid and controlled).

PARTNERS (SYLMAR). *see* SOCIAL SERVICES AND WELFARE

636.7 362.41 USA
PAW TRACKS. Text in English. 1969. q. **Document type:** *Newsletter, Consumer.*
Related titles: Braille ed.: 1969.
Published by: Guide Dog Users, Inc., 14311 Astrodome Dr, Silver Spring, MD 20906-2245. TEL 888-858-1008, info@gdui.org, http://www.gdua.org. Circ: 400.

636.7 USA
PEKINGESE CLUB OF AMERICA. BULLETIN. Text in English. q.
Published by: Pekingese Club of America, Inc., 3 Carolyn ter., Southboro, MA 01772. Ed. Hetty Orringer. Circ: 225.

636.7 USA ISSN 1069-0425
PEMBROKE WELSH CORGI CLUB OF AMERICA. NEWSLETTER. Text in English. 1967. q. USD 10. adv. bk.rev. **Document type:** *Newsletter.*
Published by: Pembroke Welsh Corgi Club of America, c/o Mrs. Anne H. Bowes, P.O. Box 2141, Duxbury, MA 02331-2141. TEL 781-934-0110, FAX 781-934-6597. Circ: 850.

636.7 USA
PEPPER'N SALT. Text in English. 196?. 3/yr. USD 20 to members. adv. illus. **Document type:** *Newsletter.* **Description:** Contains pictures, lists of breeders, dog show results, articles, and other club publications pertaining to the Standard Schnauzer dog.
Published by: Standard Schnauzer Club of America, 1884 W Lake Storey Rd, Galesburg, IL 61401. TEL 309-344-1140. Ed. John Pazereskis. Pub., R&P, Adv. contact Dorothy Pazereskis. Circ: 600 (controlled).

636.7 ESP ISSN 1989-9629
▼ **EL PERRO DE AGUA.** Text in Spanish. 2010. q. back issues avail. **Document type:** *Magazine, Consumer.*
Media: Online - full text.
Published by: Asociacion Mergablum, Canil de la Frontera s-n, Cadiz, 43907, Spain. TEL 34-902-886496, FAX 34-902-889078, info@mergablu.org, http://www.mergablum.org/.

636.7 ESP
PERROS & COMPANIA. Text in Spanish. m. EUR 2.60 newsstand/cover (effective 2009). adv. **Document type:** *Magazine, Consumer.*
Published by: Grupo V, C Valportillo Primera, 11, Alcobendas, Madrid, 28108, Spain. TEL 34-91-6622137, FAX 34-91-6622654, secretaria@grupov.es, http://www.grupov.es/. Ed. Paloma Lazaro. Adv. contact Amador Moreno. page EUR 1,750; trim 19.5 x 26.5. Circ: 21,116.

636.7 MEX ISSN 0188-1469
LOS PERROS DEL MUNDO; la revista de la canofilia Mexicana. Text in Spanish. 1985. m. adv. back issues avail. **Document type:** *Magazine, Trade.*
Formerly (until 1989): Xolo (0186-3851)
Published by: Publitecnic S.A., Calle 4, no. 188, Apdo. Postal 74-290, Mexico City, DF 09070, Mexico. TEL 52-6852819, FAX 52-6706318. Ed. Fernando Ulacia Esteve. Circ: 10,000 (controlled).

636 SVK ISSN 1335-7778
PES A MACKA. Text in Slovak. 2001. 10/yr. EUR 15 (effective 2009). adv. **Document type:** *Magazine, Consumer.*
Published by: Samosato, spol. s.r.o., Placheho 53, Bratislava 42, 840 02, Slovakia. TEL 421-02-64533541, FAX 421-02-64533542. Ed. Miron Sramka. Adv. contact Eva Pastuchova.

636.7 CZE ISSN 0231-5424
PES PRITEL CLOVEKA. Text in Czech. 1956. m. CZK 540 (effective 2011). adv. **Document type:** *Magazine, Consumer.*
Published by: Prazska Vydavatelska Spolecnost, s.r.o., Olsanska 3, Prague 3, 13000, Czech Republic. TEL 420-222-317812, info@pvsp.cz, http://www.pvsp.cz. Ed. Stanislava Jansova. Adv. contact Jana Lukasova.

599.75 DEU ISSN 0175-2936
PET; Fachmagazin fuer die Heimtierbranche. Text in German. 1979. 11/yr. EUR 92 domestic; EUR 100 foreign (effective 2011). adv. **Document type:** *Magazine, Trade.*
Former titles (until 1983): Pet-Zoo-Report (0173-9743); (until 1980): Zoo-Report (0172-844X)
—IE.
Published by: Daehne Verlag GmbH, Am Erlengraben 8, Ettlingen, 76275, Germany. TEL 49-7243-5750, FAX 49-7243-575200, service@daehne.de, http://www.daehne.de. Ed. Ralf Majer-Abele. Pub. Karl-Heinz Daehne. Adv. contact Thomas Heinen. Circ: 6,320 (paid and controlled).

636 NZL ISSN 1177-7737
PET. Text in English. 1997. q. NZD 20; NZD 7.20 newsstand/cover (effective 2008). **Document type:** *Magazine, Consumer.*
Formerly (until 2005): Pet New Zealand (1174-3581)
Published by: Fusion Group, PO Box 37 356, Parnell, Auckland, 1151, New Zealand. TEL 64-9-3361188, FAX 64-9-3361189. Circ: 14,625.

636 USA ISSN 0098-5406
SF414.7
PET AGE. Text in English. 1971. m. USD 50 domestic; USD 100 foreign; free to qualified personnel (effective 2007). adv. charts; illus.; stat. index. 100 p./no. 3 cols./p.; back issues avail. **Document type:** *Magazine, Trade.*
Published by: H.H. Backer Associates, Inc., 200 S Michigan Ave, Ste 840, Chicago, IL 60604-2455. TEL 312-663-4040, FAX 312-663-5676, hhbacker@hhbacker.com, http://www.hhbacker.com. Ed., R&P, Adv. contact Karen Long MacLeod TEL 312-663-4040. Pub. Patty Backer. B&W page USD 1,895, color page USD 2,795; trim 8.25 x 10.88. Circ: 23,545 (controlled).

636 CAN ISSN 1714-4892
PET BIZ. Text in English. 2004. bi-m. **Document type:** *Magazine, Trade.* **Description:** Focuses on providing pet specialty retailers across the country with the information they need to succeed in today's competitive retail marketplace.
Published by: Kenilworth Media Inc., 15 Wertheim Ct, Ste 710, Richmond Hill, ON L4B 3H7, Canada. TEL 905-771-7333, 800-409-8688, FAX 905-771-7336, production@kenilworth.com, http://www.kenilworth.com.

636 658 USA ISSN 0191-4766
PET BUSINESS. Text in English. 1973. m. free to qualified personnel (effective 2009). bk.rev. tr.lit. back issues avail. **Document type:** *Magazine, Trade.* **Description:** Provides a source of information about the dynamics of the pet industry and pet product retailing.
Formerly (until 1978): Aquarium Industry
Published by: Macfadden Communications Group, LLC, 333 Seventh Ave, 11th Fl, New York, NY 10001. TEL 212-979-4800, FAX 646-674-0102, http://www.macfad.com. Ed. Mark Kalaygian TEL 212-979-4907. Pub. Craig M Rexford TEL 212-979-4828.

636 GBR ISSN 1475-892X
PET BUSINESS NEWS. Text in English. 2001. 11/yr. GBP 60 (effective 2009). **Document type:** *Magazine, Trade.* **Description:** Features extensive news coverage to keep readers up-to-date with recent events, promotions and company news from the pet industry.
Published by: Datateam Publishing Ltd, 15a London Rd, Maidstone, Kent ME16 8LY, United Kingdom. TEL 44-1622-687031, FAX 44-1622-757646, info@datateam.co.uk, http://www.datateam.co.uk.

599.75 DEU ISSN 1863-5032
PET BUYERS' GUIDE INTERNATIONAL. Text in German. 1984. a. EUR 32 (effective 2011). adv. **Document type:** *Magazine, Trade.*
Formerly (until 2005): Pet - Einkaufsfuehrer fuer Heimtierbedarf (0177-770X)
Published by: Daehne Verlag GmbH, Am Erlengraben 8, Ettlingen, 76275, Germany. TEL 49-7243-5750, FAX 49-7243-575200, service@daehne.de, http://www.daehne.de. Pub. Karl-Heinz Daehne.

636 CAN ISSN 1490-7488
PET COMMERCE. Text in English. 1998. q. CAD 40 (effective 2005). **Document type:** *Magazine, Trade.* **Description:** Dedicated to the Canadian retail pet and pet supply industry.
Published by: Kenilworth Media Inc., 15 Wertheim Ct, Ste 710, Richmond Hill, ON L4B 3H7, Canada. TEL 905-771-7333, 800-409-8688, FAX 416-771-7336, 905-771-7336, production@kenilworth.com. Circ: 8,400 (controlled).

636 AUS
THE PET DIRECTORY (Q L D - N T - W A EDITION); the who's who of the pet industry. (Queensland - Northern Territory - Western Australia) Text in English. 2003. a. AUD 25 per issue (effective 2009). adv. **Document type:** *Directory, Consumer.* **Description:** Lists gorgeous animal photos with pet friendly accommodation, agricultural show dates, and dog, cat, horse etc. show and event dates.
Supersedes in part (in 2007): The Pet Directory (1449-597X)
Related titles: Online - full text ed.; Regional ed(s).: The Pet Directory (V I C - S A - T A S Edition); Pet Directory (N S W - A C T Edition). 2005.
Published by: GoldOnLine, Unit 2, 3 Fermont Rd, Underwood, QLD 4119, Australia. TEL 61-7-56304013, FAX 61-7-35039066. Ed., Pub. Kim Cooney. adv.: color page AUD 2,900; bleed 215 x 302.

636 GBR ISSN 2046-7303
PET GAZETTE. Text in English. 200?. m. free to qualified personnel (effective 2011). adv. back issues avail. **Document type:** *Magazine, Trade.* **Description:** Provides latest news and articles relevant to those involved in pet trade.
Related titles: Online - full text ed.: free (effective 2011).
Published by: Mulberry Publications Ltd, Wellington House, Butt Rd, Colchester, CO3 3DA, United Kingdom. TEL 44-1206-767797, FAX 44-1206-767532, http://www.mulberrypublications.co.uk. Ed. Sam Guiry. Adv. contact Kelly Smith.

636 IRL ISSN 1649-5101
PET LIFE. Text in English. 2004. q. adv. **Document type:** *Magazine, Consumer.*
Published by: B E S & R Media, 51 Allen Park Rd, Stillorgan, Co. Dublin, Ireland. TEL 353-1-2056895, FAX 353-1-2100884. adv.: page EUR 1,800; 210 x 295. Circ: 10,000.

636 AUS ISSN 1834-9633
PET LIFESTYLE. Text in English. 2007. q. AUD 4.95 newsstand/cover to non-members; free to members (effective 2011). adv. back issues avail. **Document type:** *Magazine, Consumer.* **Description:** Covers the issues that are important to pet owners, including pet care, veterinary care and accessories.
Related titles: Online - full text ed.: free (effective 2011).
Published by: Nuance Multimedia Australia Pty Ltd., Ste 2, Level 1, 10 Queens Rd, Melbourne, VIC 3004, Australia. TEL 61-3-98604500, FAX 61-3-98604508, info@nuancemultimedia.com, http://www.nuancemultimedia.com. Ed. Robert Drane. Adv. contact Scott Elmslie TEL 61-3-98604505. Circ: 24,163.

636 GBR ISSN 0262-5849
PET PRODUCT MARKETING. Text in English. 1954. m. free to qualified personnel (effective 2009). adv. bk.rev. illus.; mkt.; pat. back issues avail. **Document type:** *Magazine, Trade.* **Description:** Provides new products, market news, business advice and analysis, as well as features written by leading experts in the pet trade.
Former titles (until 1980): Pet Product Marketing and Garden Supplies - The Pet Trade Journal (0031-6202); Pet Trade Journal
—CCC.
Published by: H. Bauer Publishing Ltd. (Subsidiary of: Bauer Media Group), Bushfield House, Orton Centre, Peterborough, PE2 5UW, United Kingdom. TEL 44-1733-237111, http://www.bauer.co.uk. Ed. Matt Clarke TEL 44-1733-395084. Adv. contact Jayne Phillips.

636 USA ISSN 1935-6323
SF411
PET PRODUCT NEWS INTERNATIONAL. Abbreviated title: P P N. Text in English. 1993. m. USD 42 domestic; USD 70 in Canada; USD 105 elsewhere; free to qualified personnel (effective 2008); l. adv. illus. reprints avail. **Document type:** *Magazine, Trade.* **Description:** Covers industry news, including trade shows, legal issues, corporate takeovers and personnel changes, with emphasis on new products.
Former titles (until 2006): Pet Product News (1076-5573); (until 199?): Pet Product News & P S M (1068-5979); Which was formed by the merger of (1946-1993): Pet Supplies Marketing (0162-8666); Which was formerly (until 1976): Pet Mass Marketing (0095-6627); (until 1972): P S M (0031-6180); (until 196?): Pet Shop Management; (1988-1993): Pet Product News (0899-2177)
Related titles: Online - full text ed.; Supplement(s): Pet Industry Directory and Buying Guide. ISSN 1941-997X; Pet Product News Buyer's Guide.
Indexed: B02, B03, B15, B17, B18, G04, G06, G07, G08, I05.
Published by: BowTie, Inc., 2401 Beverly Blvd, PO Box 57900, Los Angeles, CA 90057. adtraffic@bowtieinc.com, http://www.bowtieinc.com. Ed. Carol Boker. Pub. Desiree Lynch.

P

636 338 USA
PET SERVICES JOURNAL. Text in English. 1977. bi-m. membership. adv. bk.rev. 30 p./no.; **Document type:** *Journal, Trade.* **Description:** Covers the pet care industry as it concerns the business person.
Formerly (until 1992): Borderline Magazine
Published by: American Boarding Kennels Association, 1702 E Pikes Peak Ave, Colorado Springs, CO 80909. TEL 719-667-1600, FAX 719-667-0116, info@aol.com. Ed., R&P, Adv. contact Tracy Sellars. Circ: 2,100 (controlled).

636 USA ISSN 1932-9237
PET STYLE NEWS. Text in English. 2006. bi-m. USD 28 domestic; USD 33.25 in Canada; USD 42 elsewhere; free to qualified personnel (effective 2008). adv. **Document type:** *Magazine, Trade.* **Description:** Features the latest products to keep pets and their owners in style.
Related titles: Online - full text ed.
Published by: BowTie, Inc., PO Box 6040, Mission Viejo, CA 92690-6040. adtraffic@bowtieinc.com, http://www.bowtieinc.com. Ed. Carol Boker. adv.: page USD 2,800; trim 10.875 x 14.75. Circ: 1,779 (controlled).

636 DEU ISSN 1868-2707
PET WORLDWIDE; specialist magazine for the international pet market. Text in English. 2002. bi-m. EUR 62 (effective 2011). adv. **Document type:** *Magazine, Consumer.*
Formerly (until 2008): Pet in Europe (1613-0014)
Published by: Daehne Verlag GmbH, Am Erlengraben 8, Ettlingen, 76275, Germany. TEL 49-7243-5750, FAX 49-7243-575200, service@daehne.de, http://www.daehne.de. Ed. Ralf Majer-Abele. Pub. Karl-Heinz Daehne. Adv. contact Thomas Heinen. Circ: 11,295 (paid and controlled).

PETFOOD INDUSTRY. *see* FOOD AND FOOD INDUSTRIES

PETFOOD MAGAZINE. *see* FOOD AND FOOD INDUSTRIES

058.7 SWE ISSN 1651-8381
PETS. Variant title: Djurtidningen Pets. Text in Swedish. 2003. 9/yr. SEK 259 (effective 2009). adv. **Document type:** *Magazine, Consumer.*
Published by: Egmont Seriefoerlaget AB, Stora Varvsgatan 19A, Malmo, 20507, Sweden. TEL 46-40-385200, FAX 46-40-385396, tord.joensson@egmont.se, http://www.egmont.se. adv.: page SEK 14,400; trim 210 x 275. Circ: 20,000 (controlled).

636 NLD
PETS INTERNATIONAL BUYERS GUIDE. Text in English; Summaries in Dutch, French, German, Italian, Spanish. 1992. a. EUR 35; EUR 45 combined subscription (print & online eds.) (effective 2009). adv. illus.; tr.lit. back issues avail. **Document type:** *Directory, Trade.*
Related titles: Online - full text ed.: EUR 50 (effective 2009); ◆ Supplement to: Pets International Magazine. ISSN 1388-4638.
Published by: InterMedium Publishers BV, PO Box 2008, Amersfoort, 3800 CA, Netherlands. TEL 31-33-4225833, FAX 31-33-4225838, info@pets.nl. Ed., Pub., R&P Reinder Sterenborg. Adv. contact Corine van Winden. B&W page EUR 1,785, color page EUR 3,095; trim 210 x 297.

636 NLD ISSN 1388-4638
PETS INTERNATIONAL MAGAZINE. Text in English. 1900. 6/yr. EUR 89 in Europe; EUR 139 elsewhere; EUR 105 combined subscription in Europe (print & online eds.); EUR 155 combined subscription elsewhere (print & online eds.) (effective 2009). adv. bk.rev.; Website rev. illus.; tr.lit. 80 p./no.; back issues avail. **Document type:** *Magazine, Trade.* **Description:** Covers marketing issues in the pet and garden industries.
Formed by the 1998 merger of: Pets Europe (English Edition - Deutsche Ausgabe) (0928-6241); Pets Europe (Edition Francaise - Nederlandse Editie) (0928-625X); Both of which superseded (in 1989): Pets Europe (0928-5091); I P T O Bulletin (International Pet Trade Organization)
Related titles: Online - full text ed.: EUR 89 (effective 2009); ◆ Supplement(s): Pets International Buyers Guide.
Published by: InterMedium Publishers BV, PO Box 2008, Amersfoort, 3800 CA, Netherlands. TEL 31-33-4225833, FAX 31-33-4225838, info@pets.nl. Ed., Pub., R&P Reinder Sterenborg. Adv. contact Corine van Winden. color page EUR 3,220; trim 210 x 297. Circ: 10,500.

636 CAN ISSN 0831-2621
PETS MAGAZINE; exploring the human-animal bond. Text in English. 1983. bi-m. CAD 24 domestic; USD 30 in United States (effective 2008). adv. bk.rev. illus. back issues avail. **Document type:** *Magazine, Consumer.* **Description:** For the concerned and caring pet owner.
Former titles (until 1985): Pets (0715-8947); (until 1983): Pets Magazine (0822-8892)
Related titles: Online - full text ed.
Indexed: C03, CBCARef, CBPI, CPerI, G08, P48, PQC.
Published by: Simmons Publishing Ltd., 32 Foster Crescent, Whitby, ON L1R 1W1, Canada. TEL 905-665-9669, FAX 905-665-9249. Ed. John Simmons. Circ: 34,500.

PETS WELCOME; animal lovers' holiday guide. *see* TRAVEL AND TOURISM

636 USA
PETTPOURI. Text in English. q. adv. **Document type:** *Newsletter.*
Published by: Andrea Pett, Ed. & Pub., 5907 Cahill Ave, Tarzana, CA 91356-1207. TEL 818-343-1249. R&P, Adv. contact Andrea Pett. Circ: 2,500.

636.4 USA ISSN 1054-5123
PIG TALE TIMES. Text in English. 1989. bi-m. USD 18; USD 20 in Canada; USD 22 elsewhere. adv. bk.rev. illus. back issues avail. **Document type:** *Newsletter, Trade.* **Description:** Provides news and information for pot belly pig owners and enthusiasts.
Published by: (International Gold Star Pot Belly Pig Register), Kiyoko and Company, PO Box 1478, Pacifica, CA 94044. TEL 415-738-8659, FAX 415-359-8768. Ed. Kiyoko Hancock. Circ: 2,500.

PIPELINE (FRAMINGHAM). *see* CLUBS

636.8 NLD ISSN 0166-1345
DE POEZENKRANT. Text in Dutch. 1974. 3/yr. EUR 10 for 3 nos. (effective 2010). bk.rev. illus. back issues avail. **Description:** Includes news, photos, artwork, and advertisements related to cats.
Published by: Poezenkrant, PO Box 70053, Amsterdam, 1007 KB, Netherlands. TEL 31-20-6266724, info@depoezenkrant.nl. Ed. Piet Schreuders. Circ: 3,000.

636.7 USA
POINTER POINTS. Text in English. q. USD 35 domestic membership; USD 55 foreign membership (effective 2008). adv.
Published by: American Pointer Club, Inc., c/o Kathy Parks, 266 Parkway Dr, Pittsburgh, PA 15228. http://www.americanpointerclub.org. Ed. Tina McDonnell. adv.: page USD 75; 8.5 x 11. Circ: 200.

636.7 USA ISSN 0744-8546
POMERANIAN REVIEW. Text in English. bi-m. USD 45 domestic; USD 55 in Canada & Mexico; USD 100 elsewhere (effective 2008). adv.
Published by: American Pomeranian Club, c/o Annette Davis, Membership Sec., 391 N Mink Creek Rd, Pocatello, ID 83204. TEL 208-234-0932, FAX 208-234-0792. Ed. Brenda Segelken TEL 217-347-5731. Adv. contact Joan Behrend TEL 631-366-2330. B&W page USD 100, color page USD 275; 8.5 x 11.

636.7 USA ISSN 0477-5449
SF429.P85
POODLE REVIEW. Text in English. 1955. 5/yr. USD 55 domestic; USD 83 in Canada; USD 111 elsewhere; USD 12 per issue (effective 2011). adv. bk.rev. illus. 212 p./no. 2 cols./p.; back issues avail. **Document type:** *Magazine, Consumer.* **Description:** Contains breeder interviews, columns by people who know and love Poodles.
Published by: Hoflin Publishing, Inc., 4401 Zephyr St, Wheat Ridge, CO 80033. TEL 303-420-2222, FAX 720-207-0382, help@hoflin.com.

636.7 USA ISSN 0882-2816
POODLE VARIETY. Text in English. 1977. 5/yr. USD 44 domestic; USD 52 foreign (effective 2000). adv. bk.rev. **Document type:** *Magazine, Trade.* **Description:** Information and photographs of poodle showdogs.
Published by: Showdogs Publications, PO Box 30430, Santa Barbara, CA 93130-0430. TEL 805-692-2045, FAX 805-692-2055. Ed. Bo Bengtson. Pub. Paul Lepiane. Adv. contact Francine Reisman. B&W page USD 160, color page USD 500. Circ: 2,000.

636 USA ISSN 1559-4890
SF459.R63
POPULAR PETS SERIES. Text in English. 2004. irreg. USD 9.99 per issue (effective 2006).
Published by: BowTie, Inc., 2401 Beverly Blvd, PO Box 57900, Los Angeles, CA 90057. TEL 213-385-2222, FAX 213-385-8565, adtraffic@bowtieinc.com, http://www.bowtieinc.com.

636 USA ISSN 1946-1739
PORTLAND TAILS; celebrating the relationship between pets and their people. Text in English. 2008 (Apr.). m. USD 36 (effective 2009). adv. **Document type:** *Magazine, Consumer.* **Description:** Lifestyle magazine for people with pets.
Related titles: Online - full text ed.: ISSN 1946-1747.
Published by: Tails Pet Media Group, Inc., 4527 N Ravenswood Ave, Chicago, IL 60640. TEL 773-561-4300, 866-803-8245, FAX 773-561-3030, mail@tailsinc.org. Pubs. Alan L Brown, Cheryl Sullivan TEL 781-799-6610.

636.7 USA
PORTUGUESE WATER DOG CLUB OF AMERICA. NEWSLETTER. Text in English. bi-m. **Document type:** *Newsletter.*
Published by: Portuguese Water Dog Club of America, c/o Diana H Metcalf, 243 Cheswold Ln, Haverford, PA 19041.

636 USA
POT-BELLIED PIGS; a journal for breeders & pet owners. Text in English. 1990. bi-m. USD 30. adv. illus. **Document type:** *Journal, Consumer.*
Published by: Sarnan Publications, PO Box 768, Pleasant Grove, CA 95668. Eds. Robert Clark, Ruth Blaney. R&P Robert Clark.

636.7 CZE
PSI KUSY. Text in Czech. m. CZK 386 domestic (effective 2008). **Document type:** *Magazine, Consumer.*
Published by: Casopisy pro Volny Cas s.r.o., Saldova 7, Prague 8, 186 00, Czech Republic. TEL 420-2-26517911, FAX 420-2-26517938, casopisy@provolnycas.cz. Ed. Dusan Stuchlik.

636.7 CZE ISSN 1802-1867
PSI SPORTY. Text in Czech. 2007. bi-m. CZK 186 (effective 2008). **Document type:** *Magazine, Consumer.*
Published by: Czech Press Group a.s., Klisska 1432-18, Usti nad Labem, 400 01, Czech Republic. TEL 420-47-5211088, FAX 420-47-5216182, inzerce@koktejl.cz, http://www.czech-press.cz.

636 DEU
DER PUDEL SPIEGEL. Text in German. 1952. q. EUR 23 (effective 2006). adv. **Document type:** *Magazine, Consumer.*
Published by: Verband der Pudelfreunde Deutschland e.V., Dorfstr 27, Wohltorf, 21521, Germany. TEL 49-4104-2095, FAX 49-4104-961570, pudelfreunde@t-online.de, http://www.verband-der-pudelfreunde.de. Ed. Barbara Schweigert. Circ: 2,400.

636.7 USA
PUG DOG CLUB OF AMERICA. BULLETIN. Text in English. 1966. q. USD 10.
Published by: Pug Dog Club of America, c/o Polly J Lamarine, 61 Fairfax Ave, Meriden, CT 06450. Ed. Alice Faye Sproul. Circ: 410.

636.7 USA
PULI NEWS. Text in English. bi-m.
Published by: Puli Club of America, c/o Laurel Colton, 655 Amesbury Dr, Dixon, CA 95620.

636.7 USA ISSN 1093-9377
PUPPIES U S A. Text in English. 1997. a. USD 8.50 per issue (effective 2008). adv. **Document type:** *Magazine, Consumer.* **Description:** Guide to adopting and caring for your new puppy and includes care, nutrition, grooming and training information about purebred and mixed-breed puppies and dogs—whether adopted, found, purchased or rescued.
Published by: BowTie, Inc., 2401 Beverly Blvd, PO Box 57900, Los Angeles, CA 90057. TEL 213-385-2222, FAX 213-385-8565, adtraffic@bowtieinc.com. Ed. Jackie Franza. Pub. Norman Ridker.

636.7 CAN ISSN 1719-5713
PUPPY & DOG BASICS. Text in English. 2005. 3/yr. **Document type:** *Magazine, Consumer.*
Formerly (until 2006): Puppy Basics (1716-5970)
Published by: Family Communications, Inc., 65 The East Mall, Etobicoke, ON M8Z 5W3, Canada. TEL 416-537-2604, FAX 416-538-1794.

636 ITA ISSN 0394-5898
QUATTRO ZAMPE. Text in Italian. 1987. m. (10/yr.). adv. **Document type:** *Magazine, Consumer.*
Published by: Fabbri Editori (Subsidiary of: R C S Libri), Via Mecenate 91, Milan, 20138, Italy.

636.7 AUS
QUEENSLAND DOG WORLD. Text in English. 1954. m. free to members (effective 2008). stat. back issues avail. **Document type:** *Magazine, Consumer.* **Description:** Publishes articles, show schedules and results for pure bred dog fanciers in Queensland.
Formerly: Canine Chronicle
Related titles: Supplement(s): Canine Control Council. Annual Report Incorporating Annual General Meeting Notice and Agenda.
Published by: Canine Control Council (Queensland), 5-9 Costin St, PO Box 495, Fortitude Valley, QLD 4006, Australia. TEL 61-7-32522661, FAX 61-7-32523864, dogsqld@powerup.com.au, http://www.cccq.org.au/.

RABBIT GAZETTE. *see* AGRICULTURE—Poultry And Livestock

636.9322 USA ISSN 1093-9458
RABBITS U S A. Text in English. 1996. a. USD 7.50 per issue (effective 2008). adv. **Document type:** *Magazine, Trade.* **Description:** Provides a guide to buying and caring for pet rabbits.
Published by: BowTie, Inc., 2401 Beverly Blvd, PO Box 57900, Los Angeles, CA 90057. TEL 213-385-2222, FAX 213-385-8565, adtraffic@bowtieinc.com, http://www.bowtieinc.com. Pub. Norman Ridker. Adv. contact Marc Fredman. B&W page USD 2,780, color page USD 4,050; trim 8 x 10.875. Circ: 71,685.

636 USA ISSN 1048-986X
SF105.27
RARE BREEDS JOURNAL; the digest of the world of alternative livestock, wildlife, animals and pets. Text in English. 1987. bi-m. USD 30 domestic; USD 40 in Canada & Mexico; USD 50 elsewhere (effective 2008). adv. bk.rev. illus. reprints avail. **Document type:** *Magazine, Trade.* **Description:** Covers the raising and care of minor breeds of domesticated livestock, exotic animals, unique and rare pets, small mammals, ornamental birds and fowl.
Incorporates (in 2003): Animals Exotic and Small (1526-7857); Incorporates in part: The Jumping Pouch
Address: PO Box 66, Crawford, NE 69339. TEL 308-665-1431, FAX 308-665-1931, http://www.ckcusa.com/webads/exotics/rarebre.htm. Ed., R&P, Adv. contact Maureen Neidhardt. Pub. Marlin Neidhardt. Circ: 4,000 (paid).

636 GBR ISSN 2044-2327
RAT & MOUSE MAGAZINE. Text in English. 2008. q. GBP 29.99 domestic; GBP 34.99 in Europe; GBP 40.65 elsewhere; GBP 7.95 per issue domestic; GBP 9.20 per issue in Europe; GBP 11.70 per issue elsewhere (effective 2010). adv. back issues avail. **Document type:** *Magazine, Consumer.* **Description:** Brings out regular sections on nutrition and health, expert topics, make and do, and product reviews as well as articles, a health and nutrition column written by resident specialist vet.
Related titles: Online - full text ed.: ISSN 2044-2335. GBP 15; GBP 4.50 per issue (effective 2010).
Published by: Solaris Publishing, 7 Deyley Way, Ashford, Kent TN23 5HX, United Kingdom. TEL 44-1233-884908, distribution@solarispublishing.com, http://www.solarispublishing.com.

636.935 USA ISSN 1078-2311
RAT AND MOUSE TALES. Text in English. 1984. q. free to members (effective 2011). back issues avail. **Document type:** *Newsletter, Consumer.* **Description:** Club newsletter with technical, informative, helpful as well as human interest stories, and articles about rats and mice.
Related titles: Online - full text ed.
Published by: American Fancy Rat and Mouse Association, 9230 64th St, Riverside, CA 92509. eastcoastmice@yahoo.com.

636.7 USA
RAT TALES. Text in English. 1961. 3/yr. membership. adv. **Document type:** *Newsletter.*
Address: c/o Muriel S Henkel, Ed, 4961 N E 193rd St, Seattle, WA 98155-2942. TEL 206-365-0445. Ed. Muriel S Henkel. Circ: 21.

597.9 FRA ISSN 1620-9540
REPTIL MAG. Text in French. 2000. q. EUR 21 domestic; EUR 27 foreign (effective 2008). **Document type:** *Magazine, Consumer.*
Related titles: Online - full text ed.: ISSN 1951-6924.
Published by: Animalia Editions, B P 3, Mouleydier, 24520, France. TEL 33-5-53240760, FAX 33-5-53241224, information@animalia-editions.net.

597.9 USA ISSN 1525-4712
REPTILE & AMPHIBIAN HOBBYIST. Text in English. 1989. bi-m. USD 28 in United States (effective 2002); USD 39 in Canada & Mexico; USD 48 elsewhere (effective 1998). adv. bk.rev. illus. **Document type:** *Magazine, Consumer.* **Description:** For amateur reptile keepers.
Formerly: Reptile & Amphibian Magazine (1059-0668)
Published by: T.F.H. Publications, Inc., One TFH Plaza, Third and Union Aves, Neptune, NJ 07753. TEL 732-988-8400, 800-631-2188, FAX 732-988-9635, info@tfh.com, http://www.tfh.com. Ed. Tom Mazorlig. Adv. contacts Nancy S Rivadeneira, Chris O'Brien. B&W page USD 500, color page USD 850; trim 8.5 x 5.5. Circ: 14,500 (paid).

597.9 636 USA ISSN 1093-944X
REPTILES U S A. Text in English. 1996. a. USD 7.50 per issue (effective 2008). adv. illus. **Document type:** *Magazine, Trade.* **Description:** Offers pet owners practical advice on caring for their reptilian pets.
Published by: BowTie, Inc., 2401 Beverly Blvd, PO Box 57900, Los Angeles, CA 90057. TEL 213-385-2222, FAX 213-385-8565, adtraffic@bowtieinc.com, http://www.bowtieinc.com. Eds. Jackie Franza, Russ Case. Pub. Norman Ridker. Adv. contact Sandy Quinn. B&W page USD 2,670, color page USD 3,880; trim 8 x 10.875. Circ: 70,137 (paid).

636.7 DEU
DER RETRIEVER. Text in German. 1980. bi-m. adv. **Document type:** *Magazine, Consumer.*
Published by: (Deutscher Retriever Club e.V.), C. Kohlmann Druck & Verlag GmbH, Hauptstr 36-38, Bad Lauterberg, 37431, Germany. TEL 49-5524-85000, FAX 49-5524-850039. adv.: B&W page EUR 550, color page EUR 754. Circ: 10,000 (controlled).

636.7 USA ISSN 0279-9693
RETRIEVER FIELD TRIAL NEWS. Text in English. 1964. 11/yr. USD 46 domestic; USD 55 in Canada & Mexico; USD 135 elsewhere (effective 2007). adv. bk.rev.; video rev. 66 p./no. 4 cols./p.; back issues avail. **Document type:** *Magazine, Trade.* **Description:** Provides results of trials, tests and other matters of interest to the owners, breeders and trainers of retrievers.
Related titles: Online - full text ed.
Published by: Retriever Field Trial News, Inc., 4379 S Howell Ave, Ste 17, Milwaukee, WI 53207. TEL 414-481-2760, FAX 414-481-2743. Adv. contact Jan Nelson. color page USD 690. Circ: 5,000 (paid).
Co-sponsors: National Amateur Retriever Club; National Retriever Club.

636.7 FRA ISSN 0397-6866
REVUE CHIEN 2000. Text in French. 1976. 11/yr. EUR 39 (effective 2009). **Document type:** *Magazine, Consumer.*
Formerly: Revue du Chien
Published by: Revue Chiens 2000, 48 Rue de Provence, Paris, 75009, France. Ed. Gwen Seznec. Circ: 69,000. **Subscr. to:** Groupe A T C, 23 Rue Dupont des Loges, Metz 57000, France. TEL 33-3-87691818, FAX 33-3-87691814.

636.7 USA
RIDGEBACK. Text in English. q. USD 50 in US & Canada; USD 75 elsewhere (effective 2008). adv.
Published by: Rhodesian Ridgeback Club of the United States, c/o Ross Jones, 2008 Dorothy St NE, Albuquerque, NM 87112. TEL 505-296-3611, http://www.rrcus.org. Ed. Carol Munsch. Adv. contact Cheryl Fraser. B&W page USD 100, color page USD 265.

636 USA ISSN 1945-6751
RIVER CITY TAILS. Text in English. 2007. m. USD 36; free to qualified personnel (effective 2008). adv. back issues avail. **Document type:** *Magazine, Consumer.* **Description:** Features the latest in animal news, information on health and wellness, celebrity interviews, inspirational stories, local happenings in the pet community.
Related titles: Online - full text ed.: ISSN 1945-676X. free.
Published by: Tails Pet Media Group, Inc., 4527 N Ravenswood Ave, Chicago, IL 60640. TEL 773-561-4300, 877-866-8245, FAX 773-561-3030, mail@tailsinc.org. Adv. contact Nikki Scheel. B&W page USD 1,640, color page USD 1,955; trim 10.5 x 10.5. Circ: 20,000.

636 USA ISSN 1945-6778
ROCKY MOUNTAIN TAILS. Text in English. 2007. m. USD 36; free to qualified personnel (effective 2008). adv. back issues avail. **Document type:** *Magazine, Consumer.* **Description:** Features the latest in animal news, information on health and wellness, celebrity interviews, inspirational stories, local happenings in the pet community.
Related titles: Online - full text ed.: ISSN 1945-6786. free.
Published by: Tails Pet Media Group, Inc., 4527 N Ravenswood Ave, Chicago, IL 60640. TEL 773-561-4300, 877-866-8245, FAX 773-561-3030, mail@tailsinc.org. Adv. contact Nikki Scheel. B&W page USD 1,640, color page USD 1,955; trim 10.5 x 10.5. Circ: 20,000.

636.7 USA ISSN 1040-8037
THE ROTTWEILER QUARTERLY. Text mainly in English; Text occasionally in German; Text in English. 1987. q. USD 40 domestic; USD 55 foreign (effective 2005). adv. **Document type:** *Magazine, Consumer.* **Description:** Covers training, showing, breeding, health issues, statistics and humor for Rottweiler owners.
Published by: G R Q Publications, 1405 Villa Real, Gilroy, CA 95020. TEL 408-848-1313, FAX 408-842-0451. Ed., R&P, Adv. contact Robin Stark. Pubs. Robin Stark, Tomi Edmiston. Circ: 3,260 (controlled and free).

636.7 USA ISSN 1938-629X
THE ROYAL DISPATCH. Text in English. 2004. q. USD 40 domestic; USD 65 foreign (effective 2008). adv. **Document type:** *Magazine, Consumer.*
Published by: American Cavalier King Charles Spaniel Club, 17912 NE 232nd Ave, Brush Prairie, WA 98606. http://www.ackcsc.org. Ed. Carol Williams.

636.7 USA ISSN 1096-0759
THE ROYAL SPANIELS. Text in English. 1995. q. USD 45 (effective 2001). adv. illus. 48 p./no. 3 cols./p.; back issues avail.
Published by: American Cocker Magazine, Inc., 14531 Jefferson St, Midway City, CA 92655. TEL 714-893-0053, FAX 714-893-5085. Ed., Pub., R&P Michael Allen. Circ: 2,500.

636.7 USA
SAINT FANCIER. Text in English. 1888. bi-m. USD 45 to members (effective 2000). adv. **Description:** Focuses on pure-bred St. Bernard dogs, i.e.: dog shows, health care, advances in science and medicine related to dogs, etc.
Published by: Saint Bernard Club of America, c/o Joanne Alstede, Ed, 1734 Rocky Ford Rd, Kittrell, NC 27544-9581. TEL 252-431-1609, folklore@ncol.com. Circ: 800.

636.7 USA
SALUKI CLUB OF AMERICA. NEWSLETTER. Text in English. q. **Document type:** *Newsletter.*
Published by: Saluki Club of America, 3816 E Waterloo Rd, Akron, OH 44312. Circ: 108.

636.7 DNK ISSN 0108-2736
SAMOJEDEN. Text in Danish. 1981. 5/yr. DKK 330 membership (effective 2009). adv. bk.rev. illus. **Document type:** *Magazine, Consumer.*
Published by: Samojedhundeklubben i Danmark/Samoyed Club of Denmark, c/o Eva Nielsen, Holloesegade 42, Vejle, 3210, Denmark. TEL 45-48-702408, formand@samojed.dk, http://www.samojed.dk. Ed., Adv. contact Rikke Stengade. color page DKK 600.

636.7 USA ISSN 0161-0651
SF429.S35
THE SAMOYED QUARTERLY. Text in English. 1976. q. USD 54 domestic; USD 74 in Canada; USD 98 elsewhere; USD 15 per issue (effective 2011). adv. back issues avail. **Document type:** *Magazine, Consumer.* **Description:** Contains breeder interviews, columns by people who know and love Sams.
Published by: Hoflin Publishing, Inc., 4401 Zephyr St, Wheat Ridge, CO 80033. TEL 303-420-2222, FAX 720-207-0382, help@hoflin.com.

636 USA
SAN DIEGO PETS MAGAZINE. Text in English. 2006. bi-m. free (effective 2011). adv. back issues avail. **Document type:** *Magazine, Consumer.* **Description:** Lifestyle magazine for pet lovers.
Related titles: Online - full text ed.
Published by: San Diego Community Newspaper Group, PO Box 601081, San Diego, CA 92160. TEL 619-573-5615, http://www.sdnews.com. Pub., Adv. contact Casey Dean.

636.9322 USA
SATIN NEWS. Text in English. q.
Published by: American Satin Rabbit Breeders Association, c/o Clarence Linsey, Sec./Treas., 316 S Mahaffie, Olathe, KS 66061. TEL 913-764-1531. Ed. Chris Fauser.

636.7 NLD ISSN 1574-6674
SCANDIA. Text in Dutch. q. EUR 25 membership (effective 2009).
Published by: Scandia - Vereniging van Liefhebbers en Fokkers van Scandinavische Spitshondenrassen, Mariapolder 15a, Strijensas, 3292 LC, Netherlands. FAX 31-78-6746040, http://www.scandia-rasvereniging.nl.

636.7 USA
SCHIPPERKE CLUB OF AMERICA. BULLETIN. Text in English. q. USD 40 domestic; USD 55 in Europe; USD 60 in Australia & New Zealand (effective 2008). adv.
Published by: Schipperke Club of America, PO Box 2760, Elizabeth, CO 80107. TEL 303-646-5961. Ed. Joie Chandler. adv.: page USD 50. Circ: 350.

636.7 USA ISSN 0276-1521
SF429.S37
SCHNAUZER SHORTS. Text in English. 1960. 7/yr. USD 30 domestic; USD 42 foreign (effective 2000). adv. **Document type:** *Journal, Trade.* **Description:** For miniature Schnauzer enthusiasts and breeders.
Published by: Dan Kiedrowski Company, P.O. Drawer A, Lahonda, CA 94020. TEL 415-747-0549, FAX 415-747-0549. Ed. Dan Kiedrowski. Pub. Daniel Kiedrowski. adv.: B&W page USD 120. Circ: 980.

599.742 CHE ISSN 1423-6834
SCHWEIZER HUNDE MAGAZIN. Text in German. 1989. 9/yr. CHF 57.95; CHF 7.70 newsstand/cover (effective 2008). adv. **Document type:** *Magazine, Consumer.*
Formed by the merger of (1977-1989): Hundemagazin (1423-6842); (1985-1989): Schweizer Hunde Revue (1423-6850)
Published by: Roro-Press Verlag AG, Erlenweg, Dietlikon, 8305, Switzerland. TEL 41-44-8357735, FAX 41-44-8357705. Ed. Jolanda Giger-Merki. Pub. Rolf Boffa. Adv. contact Chantal Jueni.

636.7 USA ISSN 1947-7449
SEARCH DOG NEWS; rescue and recovery. Text in English. 2008. bi-m. USD 36; USD 8 per issue (effective 2009). adv. back issues avail. **Document type:** *Journal, Trade.* **Description:** Focuses on working dogs that locate missing people around the world.
Published by: Hi-Flow Graphics, 14512 Filmore St, Arleta, CA 91331. TEL 818-896-1106, FAX 818-899-0758, customerservice@sarshop.com.

636.7 USA ISSN 0886-3997
SETTERS, INCORPORATED. Text in English. 1975. bi-m. USD 24. adv. bk.rev.
Formerly: Setters
Address: 12 Bay Path Ct, Huntington, NY 11743. Ed. Marilyn Sturz. Circ: 1,000.

636.7 USA ISSN 0745-2012
SHELTIE INTERNATIONAL. Text in English. 1982. q. adv. illus. 90 p./no.; back issues avail. **Document type:** *Magazine, Consumer.* **Description:** News and information of interest to Sheltie owners.
Published by: Reporter Publications, PO Box 6369, Los Osos, CA 93412. TEL 805-528-2007, FAX 805-528-8200.

636.7 USA ISSN 0744-6608
CODEN: SEWSEM
SHELTIE PACESETTER. Text in English. 1977. bi-m. USD 61.95 domestic; USD 77.70 in Canada & Mexico; USD 82.95 elsewhere (effective 2007). adv. bk.rev. illus. back issues avail. **Document type:** *Magazine, Consumer.* **Description:** Contains informative articles and photos on the Shetland sheepdog.
Related titles: E-mail ed.: CAD 450 (effective 1999); Fax ed.
Address: 9428 Blue Mound Dr, Fort Wayne, IN 46804. Ed., Pub., R&P, Adv. contact Nancy Lee Cathcart. B&W page USD 174, color page USD 439; trim 11 x 8.5. Circ: 3,000.

636 USA
SHIH TZU BULLETIN. Text in English. 1951. q. USD 50 domestic; USD 55 in Canada & Mexico; USD 75 elsewhere (effective 2008). adv. illus. **Document type:** *Bulletin.*
Published by: American Shih Tzu Club, Inc., 279 Sun Valley Ct, Ripon, CA 95366. Ed. Bobbi Walton. Circ: 850.

636.7 USA ISSN 1040-5801
THE SHIH TZU REPORTER. Text in English. 1975. q. USD 45 domestic; USD 55 in Canada & Mexico; USD 105 elsewhere; USD 15 per issue domestic; USD 20 per issue in Canada & Mexico; USD 30 per issue elsewhere (effective 2011). adv. 40 p./no.; back issues avail. **Document type:** *Magazine, Consumer.*
Published by: Reporter Publications, PO Box 6369, Los Osos, CA 93412. TEL 805-528-2007, FAX 805-528-8200.

636.8 USA
SIAMESE NEWS QUARTERLY. Text in English. 1936. q. USD 15 domestic; USD 18 in Canada; USD 20 elsewhere. adv. bk.rev. **Document type:** *Newsletter.* **Description:** Provides owners and breeders of Siamese cats with the latest information on breeding, genetics, general care, and health problems.
Published by: Siamese Cat Society of America, Inc., PO Box 1149, Green Valley, AZ 85622. TEL 602-967-4459. Ed., Pub., R&P, Adv. contact Shirley Johnson. Circ: 600 (paid). **Subscr. to:** Z. Kozaczka, 917B S Acapulco, Tempe, AZ 85281.

636.7 NLD ISSN 1872-146X
SIBERIAN NIEUWS. Text in Dutch. 5/yr. EUR 22.50 (effective 2010).
Published by: Siberian Husky Klub voor Nederland, Buitenweg 18, Oudehorne, 8413 NX, Netherlands. TEL 31-513-541331, http://www.shkn.nl. Ed. Gudrun van den Broek.

636.7 USA ISSN 8750-1953
SIGHTHOUND REVIEW. Text in English. 1984. bi-m. USD 43; USD 54 foreign (effective 1999). adv. bk.rev. **Document type:** *Magazine, Consumer.* **Description:** Contains information and photographs of the sighthound-greyhound breeds.
Address: 10177 Blue River Hills Rd, Manhattan, KS 66503. TEL 785-485-2992, FAX 785-485-2096. Ed., Pub., R&P, Adv. contact James Gaidos. B&W page USD 145, color page USD 425. Circ: 1,600.

636 USA ISSN 1945-6794
SILICON VALLEY TAILS. Text in English. 2007. m. USD 36; free to qualified personnel (effective 2008). adv. back issues avail. **Document type:** *Magazine, Consumer.* **Description:** Features the latest in animal news, information on health and wellness, celebrity interviews, inspirational stories, local happenings in the pet community.
Related titles: Online - full text ed.: ISSN 1945-6808. free.
Published by: Tails Pet Media Group, Inc., 4527 N Ravenswood Ave, Chicago, IL 60640. TEL 773-561-4300, 877-866-8245, FAX 773-561-3030, mail@tailsinc.org. Adv. contact Nikki Scheel. B&W page USD 1,640, color page USD 1,955; trim 10.5 x 10.5. Circ: 50,000.

636 USA ISSN 0037-539X
SIMIAN. Text in English. 1958. 8/yr. adv. bk.rev.; film rev. bibl.; illus. index. **Document type:** *Magazine, Consumer.*
Formerly: Monkey Business
Published by: Simian Society of America, Inc., c/o Mel Orr, Secretary, 6 Stephens St., Dillsburg, PA 17019. chairman@simiansociety.com. Ed. Barbara E O'Brien. Circ: 3,000.

636.7 SWE ISSN 1652-4780
SKOCKEN. Text in Swedish. 1972. q. SEK 250 domestic membership; SEK 300 foreign membership (effective 2006). **Document type:** *Magazine, Consumer.*
Published by: Specialklubben foer Bearded Collie, c/o Kjell Nielsen, Grinneroedslycken 185, Svenshoejen, 44497, Sweden. TEL 46-303775581. Ed. Marie Kindstedt TEL 46-13-120144.

636.7 USA ISSN 1072-8899
SKYE TERRIER CLUB OF AMERICA. BULLETIN. Text in English. 1938. q. USD 20 domestic to non-members; USD 30 foreign to non-members (effective 2003). adv. **Document type:** *Bulletin, Consumer.* **Description:** Provides exclusive coverage of the Skye terrier. Features include specialty show results, health care, breeding, histories of famous Skye terrier kennels, and exhibitions.
Published by: Skye Terrier Club of America, c/o Elaine Hersey, 46 Moulton Rd, Hampton, NH 03842. TEL 603-926-6915, seamistskyes@comcast.net, http://clubs.akc.org/skye/index.html. Ed., R&P Michael J Pesare. adv.: page USD 60. Circ: 275 (paid); 200 (controlled).

636 USA ISSN 1945-6816
SONORAN TAILS; celebrating the relationship between pets and their people. Text in English. 2000. m. USD 36 (effective 2008). adv. back issues avail. **Document type:** *Magazine, Consumer.*
Related titles: Online - full text ed.: ISSN 1945-6824.
Published by: Tails Pet Media Group, Inc., 4527 N Ravenswood Ave, Chicago, IL 60640. TEL 773-561-4300, 877-866-8245, FAX 773-561-3030, mail@tailsinc.org. Adv. contact Nikki Scheel. B&W page USD 2,100, color page USD 2,300; trim 10.5 x 10.5. Circ: 50,000 (controlled).

636.7 USA ISSN 1043-5034
SPANIELS IN THE FIELD. Text in English. 1980. q. USD 39 domestic; USD 41 in Canada; USD 56 elsewhere (effective 2000). adv. bk.rev. back issues avail. **Document type:** *Magazine, Trade.* **Description:** Dedicated to the advancement and promotion of all flushing spaniels.
Former titles: On the Line (Cincinnati); Springers on the Line
Related titles: Online - full text ed.
Published by: Chiridion Wild Wings, Inc., 5312 Wolf Knoll, Orr, MN 55771-8337. TEL 218-343-6253, FAX 218-343-6258. Ed. Sandy Henriques. Pub., R&P, Adv. contact Harry Henriques. B&W page USD 125, color page USD 280; 11 x 8.5. Circ: 1,700 (paid).

636.7 FRA ISSN 1959-0970
SPECIAL CHIENS. Text in French. 2007. q. EUR 44 for 2 yrs. (effective 2010). **Document type:** *Magazine, Consumer.*
Published by: Lafont Presse, 53 Rue du Chemin Vert, Boulogne-Billancourt, 92100, France. TEL 33-1-46102121, FAX 33-1-45792211.

636.8 ITA ISSN 1721-3444
SPECIALE GATTO MAGAZINE. Text in Italian. 2002. a. **Document type:** *Catalog, Consumer.*
Published by: Sprea Editori Srl, Via Torino 51, Cernusco sul Naviglio, MI 20063, Italy. TEL 39-02-92432222, FAX 39-02-92432236, editori@sprea.it, http://www.sprea.it.

636.7 ITA ISSN 1720-1772
SPECIALE MOLOSSI. Text in Italian. 2002. a. **Document type:** *Catalog, Consumer.*
Published by: Sprea Editori Srl, Via Torino 51, Cernusco sul Naviglio, MI 20063, Italy. TEL 39-02-92432222, FAX 39-02-92432236, editori@sprea.it, http://www.sprea.it.

636 MEX
SPLASH MAGAZINE; acuarismo de vanguardia. Text in Spanish. 1993. bi-m. MXN 90 domestic; USD 12 in United States; MXN 15 newsstand/cover. adv. bk.rev. illus. index. back issues avail. **Document type:** *Magazine, Consumer.* **Description:** Contains general pet information for owners of dogs, cats, birds, fish, and reptiles.
Published by: Grupo Editorial Ocean, CIRCUNVALACION PONIENTE 32 K, Ciudad Satelite, Mexico City, MEX 53100, Mexico. TEL 52-5-393-4244, FAX 52-5-393-1495. Ed. Jose Luis Oliver Aguillon. Adv. contact Gabriela Rodriguez. page USD 535; trim 290 x 225. Circ: 30,000 (paid). **Dist. by:** Lago Erie, c/o Lago Erie, 44 Col Tacuba, Mexico City, DF 11410, Mexico. TEL 52-5-399-3554, FAX 52-5-527-4244.

636.7 USA
SPOTTER. Text in English. 1971. q. USD 49 domestic; USD 54 in Canada; USD 65 elsewhere; USD 13 per issue domestic (effective 2008). adv. bk.rev. back issues avail. **Document type:** *Magazine, Consumer.*
Published by: Dalmatian Club of America, PO Box 450, Maple Valley, WA 98038. Questions@thedca.org, http://www.thedca.org. Ed., Adv. contact Paula M Olcott. Circ: 1,000.

636 USA ISSN 1945-6832
ST. LOUIE TAILS; celebrating the relationship between pets and their people. Text in English. 2000. m. USD 36; free to qualified personnel (effective 2008). adv. back issues avail. **Document type:** *Magazine, Consumer.*
Related titles: Online - full text ed.: ISSN 1945-6840. free.
Published by: Tails Pet Media Group, Inc., 4527 N Ravenswood Ave, Chicago, IL 60640. TEL 773-561-4300, 877-866-8245, FAX 773-561-3030, mail@tailsinc.org. Adv. contact Nikki Scheel. B&W page USD 1,500, color page USD 2,000; trim 10.5 x 10.5. Circ: 30,000 (controlled).

636.7 USA
STAFF STATUS. Text in English. 3/yr. USD 45 in US & Canada (effective 2008). adv. **Document type:** *Magazine, Consumer.*
Formerly: Staffordshire Bull Terrier Club of America. Newsletter
Published by: Staffordshire Bull Terrier Club of America, c/o Dana Merrit, 6253 Hinman Dr., Clinton, WA 98236. dfmerrit@aol.com, http://www.sbtca.com/site01/index.php.

636.7 GBR ISSN 2047-0657
▼ **SURREY DOG LIFE.** Text in English. 2011. q. GBP 12.50; GBP 2.50 per issue (effective 2011). adv. **Document type:** *Magazine, Trade.* **Description:** Dedicated to dog lovers and their companions in Surrey.
Published by: Surrey Dog Life Magazine, The Dog House, 163 Saunders Ln, Woking, Surrey GU22 0NT, United Kingdom. TEL 44-1483-755505.

636.7 SWE ISSN 1404-6555
SVENSKA BLODHUNDEN. Variant title: Blodhunden. Text in Swedish. 1980. q. SEK 175. adv. **Document type:** *Bulletin, Consumer.*
Formerly (until 1999): Blodhundskamraten (0284-0863)
Published by: Svenska Blodhundskamraterna, c/o Marie Edman, Olstorpsv 64, Graabo, 44370, Sweden. TEL 46-302-44004. Ed. Marie Edman. Pub. Gerd Andersson. Adv. contact Kjell Axelsson. B&W page SEK 600. Circ: 150.

636.7 HRV ISSN 1331-8993
SVIJET PASA I KUCNIH LJUBIMACA. Text in Croatian. 1997. bi-m. **Document type:** *Magazine, Consumer.*
Formerly (until 1998): Svijet Pasa (1331-2707)
Address: Selska Cesta 125-I, Zagreb, 10000, Croatia. TEL 385-1-217917. Ed. Laszlo Molnar.

636.7 USA
TALKABOUT. Text in English. 1959. q. USD 15 domestic to non-members; USD 20 foreign to non-members (effective 2008). adv. **Document type:** *Newsletter, Consumer.* **Description:** Contains original and reprinted articles, essays, and stories about Australian Terriers plus related topics on purebred dogs, national club news, upcoming regional Australian Terrier club events and more.
Formerly: Australian Terrier Club of America Newsletter
Media: Duplicated (not offset).
Published by: Australian Terrier Club of America, c/o Darlene Evans, 42742 Lemonwood St, Fremont, CA 94538-4026. info@australianterrier.org. Ed. Mae Roo. Circ: 250.

636.7 USA
TALLY-HO. Text in English. bi-m. free to members (effective 2008). **Document type:** *Newsletter, Consumer.* **Description:** Contains informative articles on a wide variety of subjects pertaining to the basset hound.

P

Published by: Basset Hound Club of America, c/o Carol Ann Hunt, Ed, 3107 Nichol Ave, Anderson, IN 46011-3175. hounds@qvtc.com. Ed. Sherry Neiberger. Circ: 800.

636.7 USA
TASSELS AND TAILS. Text in English. 3/yr. USD 10.
Published by: Bedlington Terrier Club of America, 12 Irma Pl, Oceanport, NJ 07757. Circ: 330.

641.5 636.7 USA ISSN 1947-4636
▼ **TASTY TREATS**; that will bow wow your canine pals. Text in English. 2009 (Oct.). biennial. USD 12 per issue (effective 2009). **Document type:** *Consumer.* **Description:** A collection of recipes for dogs from agility clubs.
Published by: Paul Abramson, Ed. & Pub., 16 Pierce Pl, Surfside, SC 29575. TEL 843-450-7417, agilityisfun@msn.com.

636.596 DEU ISSN 1862-9504
TAUBENMARKT, DIE SPORTAUBE. Text in German. 1994. m. EUR 24 (effective 2008). **Document type:** *Magazine, Consumer.*
Formed by the merger of (19??-1994): Taubenmarkt; (1956-1994): Sporttaube (0490-5687); Which superseded in part (1954-1956): Sport und Technik. Ausgabe E: Sportschiessen, Sporttauben, Reit- und Hundesport (0232-6841); Which superseded in part (1952-1954): Sport und Technik (0490-5105)
Published by: B I W Kreuzfeldt GmbH, Hungenbach 6-8, Kuerten, 51515, Germany. TEL 49-2268-1591, FAX 49-2268-3054, info@taubenmarkt-kassel.de, http://www.taubenmarkt-kassel.de.

636.7 796 USA
TEAM AND TRAIL; the musher's monthly news. Text in English. 1963. m. USD 25 domestic; USD 31 in Canada; USD 32 elsewhere. adv. bk.rev. back issues avail. **Document type:** *Newsletter.* **Description:** Provides worldwide sled dog racing news and information on other related events.
Published by: Team & Trail Publishers, PO Box 128, Center Harbor, NH 03226-0128. TEL 603-253-6265, FAX 603-253-9513. Ed., Pub., R&P, Adv. contact Cynthia J Molburg. Circ: 1,200.

636.7 DEU
DER TERRIER. Text in German. 1894. m. adv. **Document type:** *Magazine, Consumer.*
Published by: Klub fuer Terrier e.V., Schoene Aussicht 9, Kelsterbach, 65451, Germany. TEL 49-6107-75790, FAX 49-6107-757928, info@kft-online.de, http://www.kft-online.de. adv.: B&W page EUR 375, color page EUR 780. Circ: 9,400 (controlled).

636.7 NLD ISSN 1871-1847
THE TERRIER TIMES. Text in Dutch. 2005. q. EUR 20 (effective 2010). **Document type:** *Magazine, Consumer.*
Published by: Stichting de Werkende Terrier, Kladseweg 46, Lepelstraat, 4664 RE, Netherlands. TEL 31-84-7546212, http://www.terrierclub.nl.

636.7 USA ISSN 0199-6495
TERRIER TYPE. Text in English. 1961. 11/yr. USD 40 domestic; USD 50 foreign (effective 2000). adv. **Document type:** *Magazine, Trade.* **Description:** For show dog enthusiasts and breeders of terriers.
Published by: Dan Kiedrowski Company, P.O. Drawer A, Lahonda, CA 94020. TEL 415-747-0549, FAX 415-747-0549. Ed., R&P Dan Kiedrowski. Pub. Daniel Kiedrowski. Adv. contact Denis Shaw. B&W page USD 120. Circ: 1,700.

TIDSSKRIFT FOR KANINAVL. *see* AGRICULTURE—Poultry And Livestock

636 DEU ISSN 1864-3531
TIER - A B C. Text in German. 1985. m. EUR 24; EUR 2 newsstand/cover (effective 2007). adv. **Document type:** *Magazine, Consumer.*
Formerly (until 2007): Tierschuetzer (0932-769X)
Published by: Thilo Raiskup Verlag, Nebeniusstr 26, Karlsruhe, 7613, Germany. TEL 49-721-22820, FAX 49-721-29686. Ed., Pub. Thilo Raiskup. adv.: B&W page EUR 960, color page EUR 1,200. Circ: 28,000 (paid and controlled).

TIERE - FREUNDE FUERS LEBEN. *see* BIOLOGY—Zoology

636.7 ESP ISSN 1134-7252
TODO PERROS. Text in Spanish. 1994. m. EUR 36 domestic (effective 2009). **Document type:** *Magazine, Consumer.*
Related titles: Supplement(s): Todo Perros. Extra. ISSN 2173-5697. 2009.
Published by: M C Ediciones, Paseo de Sant Gervasi 16-20, Barcelona, 08022, Spain. TEL 34-93-2541250, FAX 34-93-2541262, http://www.mcediciones.net.

TOTAL TIERLIEB!; Dein suesses Tiermagazin. *see* CHILDREN AND YOUTH—For

TRAVELLING WITH YOUR PET. *see* TRAVEL AND TOURISM

THE TRUMPETER (WESTBROOK). *see* THEATER

636.7 DEU
UNSER RASSEHUND. Text in German. 1949. m. EUR 33; EUR 3.20 newsstand/cover (effective 2006). adv. **Document type:** *Magazine, Trade.*
Published by: Verband fuer das Deutsche Hundewesen e.V., Westfalendamm 174, Dortmund, 44141, Germany. TEL 49-231-565000, FAX 49-231-592440, info@vdh.de, http://www.vdh.de. adv.: B&W page EUR 1,500, color page EUR 3,000. Circ: 28,000 (paid and controlled).

636.7 AUT
UNSERE HUNDE; kynologische Zeitschrift. Text in German. m. adv. **Document type:** *Magazine, Consumer.*
Published by: Oesterreichischer Kynologenverband, Siegfried Marcus Str 7, Biedermannsdorf, W 2362, Austria. TEL 43-2236-710667, FAX 43-2236-71066730, office@oekv.at, http://www.oekv.at. Ed. Hans Meyer.

636.7 DEU
UNSERE WINDHUNDE. Text in German. 1965. m. EUR 33 domestic; EUR 39 foreign (effective 2009). illus. **Document type:** *Magazine, Consumer.*
Published by: Deutscher Windhundzucht- und Rennverbands e.V., Hildesheimer Str 26, Soehlde, 31185, Germany. TEL 49-5129-8919, FAX 49-5129-8810, dwzrv@dwzrv.com, http://www.dwzrv.com. Ed. Angelika Heydrich. Adv. contact Evelyn Kirsch TEL 49-5069-96420. Circ: 4,000.

636 AUS ISSN 1832-1542
URBAN ANIMAL; connecting you with your inner (city) animal. Text in English. 2004. q. AUD 20; free in city (effective 2009). adv. 36 p./no.; back issues avail. **Document type:** *Magazine, Consumer.* **Description:** A lifestyle magazine for animal lovers, celebrating pets and the relationships with them.
Related titles: Online - full text ed.
Published by: Immedia, 20 Hordern St, Newtown, NSW 2042, Australia. TEL 61-2-95577766, FAX 61-2-95577788, info@immedia.com.au, http://www.immedia.com.au. Ed. Lisa Treen. Pub., Adv. contact Phil Tripp. color page AUD 2,750; 28 x 39.5.

636 CAN
V.I.PETS; the magazine for your dogs and cats. Text in English. 6/yr. CAD 15.95 (effective 2000). **Document type:** *Magazine, Consumer.*
Address: 185-911 Yates St, Ste 339, Victoria, BC V8V 4Y9, Canada. TEL 250-361-1431, VIPets@coolcom.com.

636.7 SWE ISSN 0042-269X
VAARA HUNDAR. Text in Swedish. 1923. 6/yr. SEK 130 to members (effective 1995). adv. bk.rev. **Description:** Publishes articles on club matters, reports on dog shows and obedience competitions, as well as articles on the caring and training of dogs.
Published by: Svenska Hundklubben, Arkeologgatan 18, Torshalla, 64435, Sweden. TEL 46-16-35-59-78, FAX 46-18-52-37-10. Ed. Erik Skye. Pub. Thomnas Staeav. adv.: B&W page SEK 500. **Subscr. to:** Norbyvaegen 57 D, Uppsala 75239, Sweden. TEL 18-52-37-10.

636.8 SWE ISSN 1404-3181
VAARA KATTER; medlemstidning. Text in Swedish. 1950. 6/yr. SEK 300 domestic; SEK 400 foreign (effective 2011). adv. back issues avail. **Document type:** *Magazine, Consumer.*
Former titles (until 1999): Kattjournalen (1102-8440); (until 1991): Vaara Katter (0346-4741); (until 1969): Felix
Published by: Sveriges Kattklubbars Riksfoerbund, Aasbogatan 33, Boras, 50456, Sweden. TEL 46-33-101565, FAX 46-33-100899, sverak@sverak.se, http://www.sverak.se. Ed. Ulf Lindstroem.

636 CAN ISSN 1715-1066
VANCOUVER ISLAND PETS. Text in English. 2005. bi-m. CAD 12 (effective 2006). **Document type:** *Magazine, Consumer.*
Published by: Muse Communications, 25-850 Parklands Dr., Victoria, BC V9A 7L9, Canada. TEL 250-381-7386, FAX 250-853-3348. Ed. Janet Peto.

636.7 SWE ISSN 0282-7662
VARGHUNDEN. Text in Swedish. 1976. 3/yr. SEK 150 membership (effective 2004).
Published by: Svenska Irlaendsk Varghund Klub, c/o Matias Bener, Bellevuegatan 1, Joenkoeping, 46-36, Sweden. TEL 46-36-129980, m.bener@telia.com, http://www.svivk.com.

636.7 DEU ISSN 1610-8612
VEREIN FUER POINTER UND SETTER. NEWS. Text in German. 19??. bi-m. adv. **Document type:** *Newsletter, Consumer.*
Former titles (until 2002): Verein fuer Pointer und Setter. Nachrichtenheft (0949-5452); (until 1994): Pointer und Setter Nachrichten (0551-1968)
Published by: Verein fuer Pointer und Setter e.V., Marquardsholz C22, Hilpoltstein, 91161, Germany. TEL 49-9174-1525, FAX 49-9174-48453, geschaeftsstelle@pointer-und-setter.de, http://www.pointer-und-setter.de. Ed. Thomas Possehl. adv.: B&W page EUR 217. Circ: 1,650 (controlled).

636 613.2 FRA
➤ **VETERINARY FOCUS**; the worlwide journal for the companion animal veterinarian. Text in English. 1991. q. **Document type:** *Journal, Trade.*
Former titles (until 199?): Waltham Focus (English Edition) (1354-0157); (until 1994): Waltham International Focus (0964-7082)
Related titles: ◆ Japanese ed.: Waltham Focus (Japanese Edition). ISSN 1355-5413; Greek ed.: Waltham International Focus (Greek Edition). ISSN 0965-4542. 1991; German ed.: Waltham International Focus (German Edition). ISSN 0965-4593. 1991; Italian ed.: Waltham International Focus (Italian Edition). ISSN 0965-4569. 1991; Spanish ed.: Waltham International Focus (Spanish Edition). ISSN 0965-4577. 1991; French ed.: Waltham International Focus (French Edition). ISSN 0965-4585. 1991; English ed.: Waltham Focus (American Edition). ISSN 1353-5684. 1991; Dutch ed.: Veterinary Focus (Dutch Edition). 1986.
Indexed: A34, CABA, H17, N04, P33, R08.
Published by: Buena Media Plus, 85 Av. Pierre Grenier, Boulogne Billancourt, 92100, France. TEL 33-1-72446200, FAX 33-1-73446202, contact@equus-international.com, http://www.equus-international.com.

➤ **VETSTREAM CANIS.** *see* VETERINARY SCIENCE

➤ **VETSTREAM FELIS.** *see* VETERINARY SCIENCE

➤ **VETSTREAM LAPIS.** *see* VETERINARY SCIENCE

636.7 NOR
VI MED HUND. Text in Norwegian. 10/yr. NOK 398 (effective 2009). **Document type:** *Magazine, Consumer.*
Published by: Aller Forlag AS, Stenersgaten 2, Sentrum, Oslo, 0189, Norway. TEL 47-21-301000, FAX 47-21-301205, allerforlag@aller.no, http://www.aller.no.

636.7 DNK ISSN 1901-2691
VI MED HUND. Text in Danish. 2006. m. DKK 594 (effective 2010). adv. **Document type:** *Magazine, Consumer.*
Related titles: Online - full text ed.: ISSN 1902-4932.
Published by: J S L Publications A/S, Dortheavej 59, Copenhagen NV, 2400, Denmark. TEL 45-32-711200, FAX 45-32-711212, info@jslpublications.dk, http://www.jslp.dk. Ed. Anette Hvidkjaer. Adv. contact Steen Ingmann.

636.7 AUS
VICTORIAN CANINE ASSOCIATION JOURNAL. Variant title: V C A Journal. Text in English. 1957. m. free to members (effective 2008). adv. bk.rev. illus.; stat. **Document type:** *Journal, Trade.* **Description:** Covers information about Victorian canine association.
Formerly: R A S Kennel Control Journal (0033-6777)
Published by: Victorian Canine Association Inc., 655 Westernport Hwy, Skye, VIC 3977, Australia. TEL 61-3-97882500, FAX 61-3-97882599, office@vca.org.au, http://www.vca.org.au. Circ: 16,000.

636.7 USA ISSN 0747-4636
VIZSLA NEWS. Text in English. 1953. m. free to members (effective 2006).
Published by: Vizsla Club of America, c/o Patricia Perkins 8808 N Central Ave, Ste 278, Phoenix, AZ 85020. http://clubs.akc.org/vizsla/index.htm.

DER VOGELFREUND. *see* BIOLOGY—Ornithology

636.7 FRA ISSN 0766-3889
VOS CHIENS; la revue de reference en Europe. Text in French. m. EUR 51 domestic (effective 2009). **Document type:** *Magazine, Consumer.*
Published by: Editions d' Anglon, 735 Route de Jarcieu, Lapeyrouse, 26210, France. TEL 33-4-75319639, FAX 33-4-75318095.

636 USA ISSN 2153-6368
▼ **VTARC COMPANION.** Text in English. 2009. q. USD 12 (effective 2010). adv. **Document type:** *Magazine, Trade.* **Description:** Focuses on a variety of topics that may vary from issue to issue, including: helping homeless pets, updates on new breakthroughs in animal care.
Related titles: Online - full text ed.: ISSN 2153-6384.
Published by: The Phoenix VT Group, LLC, PO Box 278, Auburn, KS 66402. Ed. Carlene A Decker. Adv. contact Dennis Lively TEL 605-484-2215.

636.737 AUS
W K C NEWS BULLETIN. (Working Kelpie Council) Text in English. 1965. m. free to members (effective 2009). illus. back issues avail. **Document type:** *Bulletin, Trade.* **Description:** Presents informative and educational articles for breeders and owners of Kelpie sheepdogs used in the pastoral industries.
Formerly (until 1987): Working Kelpie Council. News Bulletin
Related titles: Online - full text ed.
Published by: The Working Kelpie Council of Australia, PO Box 306, Castle Hill, NSW 1765, Australia. TEL 61-2-98999224, FAX 61-2-98942140, johnnloyis@bigpond.com.

636 USA
WAG MAGAZINE. Text in English. 2005. q. USD 9.99 (effective 2005). adv. **Document type:** *Magazine, Consumer.* **Description:** Covers dog fashion and accessories.
Address: PO Box 85, Modesto, CA 95353. TEL 888-949-0700, FAX 209-575-2160. adv.: page USD 1,487.50. Circ: 50,000.

636 613.2 GBR ISSN 1355-5413
WALTHAM FOCUS (JAPANESE EDITION). Text in Japanese. 1991. q. **Document type:** *Journal, Consumer.*
Formerly (until 1994): Waltham International Focus (Japanese Edition) (0965-4534)
Related titles: ◆ English ed.: Veterinary Focus; Greek ed.: Waltham International Focus (Greek Edition). ISSN 0965-4542. 1991; German ed.: Waltham International Focus (German Edition). ISSN 0965-4593. 1991; Italian ed.: Waltham International Focus (Italian Edition). ISSN 0965-4569. 1991; Spanish ed.: Waltham International Focus (Spanish Edition). ISSN 0965-4577. 1991; French ed.: Waltham International Focus (French Edition). ISSN 0965-4585. 1991; English ed.: Waltham Focus (American Edition). ISSN 1353-5684. 1991; Dutch ed.: Veterinary Focus (Dutch Edition). 1986.
Published by: Waltham Centre for Pet Nutrition, Waltham-on-the-Wolds, Melton Mowbray, Leics LE14 4RT, United Kingdom. TEL 44-1664-415400, FAX 44-1664-415440, waltham.foundation@waltham.com, http://www.waltham.com/.

636.7 JPN
WAN. Text in Japanese. m. JPY 9,000 (effective 2007). illus. **Document type:** *Magazine, Consumer.* **Description:** Provides general information for dog keepers.
Published by: Midori Shobo Co. Ltd. (Subsidiary of: Midori Group), JPR Crest Takebashi Bldg., 3-21 Kanda Nishikicho Chiyoda-ku, Tokyo, 101-0054, Japan. info@mgp.co.jp, http://www.mgp.co.jp/. Circ: 85,000.

636.7 USA ISSN 0162-315X
WEIMARANER MAGAZINE. Text in English. 1949. m. USD 27 to non-members (effective 1999). adv. bk.rev.; film rev. illus. **Description:** Includes event reports, articles of interest on the wide variety of activities open to Weimaraners, and lists of top competitors.
Formerly: Weimaraner
Published by: Weimaraner Club of America, c/o Dorothy Derr, Ed, Box 2907, Muskogee, OK 74402-2907. TEL 918-686-6027. Circ: 1,800.

636.7 NLD ISSN 1383-3960
DE WELSH SPRINGER. Text in Dutch. 1976. bi-m. EUR 26.50 domestic; EUR 36.50 foreign (effective 2010). adv. bk.rev. **Document type:** *Bulletin.*
Published by: Welsh Springer Spaniel Club Nederland, c/o Hanneke Wiss, Eekhoormakker 20, Houten, 3994 EW, Netherlands. TEL 31-30-6374720, secretaris@wssc.nl, http://www.wssc.nl.

636.7 USA
WESTIE IMPRINT. Text in English. 1985. q. USD 35 (effective 2001). adv. bk.rev. back issues avail. **Document type:** *Magazine, Consumer.* **Description:** Provides fanciers of the West Highland White Terrier Club with information on the breed. Contains educational and entertaining articles on the breed and specific dogs.
Formerly (until 1985): West Highland White Terrier Club of America. Bulletin
Published by: West Highland White Terrier Club of America, 1826 Manakin Rd, Manakin-Sabot, VA 23103. TEL 804-288-7424, FAX 804-288-7424, http://www.westiec/vbamerica.com/whwtca/imprint.html. Ed., R&P, Adv. contact Daphne Gentry TEL 804-784-3215. B&W page USD 75; trim 5.5 x 8.5. Circ: 1,300.

636.7 USA
WHIPPET NEWS. Text in English. m. USD 25 (effective 2000). adv. **Document type:** *Newsletter.*
Published by: American Whippet Club, 130 34th E, Seattle, WA 98112. TEL 206-322-5872, FAX 206-323-8314. Ed., Pub., R&P, Adv. contact Christine Hopperstad. Circ: 850.

636.7 USA
WHIPPET NEWSLETTER. Text in English. m. USD 8. **Document type:** *Newsletter.*
Address: 1462 Granger Rd, Medina, OH 44256.

636.7 USA ISSN 1097-5322
WHOLE DOG JOURNAL; a monthly guide to natural dog care and training. Text in English. 1998. m. USD 39 combined subscription in US & Canada (print & online eds.); USD 48 combined subscription elsewhere (print & online eds.) (effective 2010). illus. back issues avail. **Document type:** *Journal, Consumer.* **Description:** Contains well-researched, in-depth articles about all aspects of dog care and training.

Related titles: Online - full text ed.: Whole-Dog-Journal.com. USD 16 (effective 2004).
Indexed: A26, G06, G07, G08, I05.
Published by: Belvoir Media Group, LLC, PO Box 5656, Norwalk, CT 06856. TEL 203-857-3100, 800-424-7887, FAX 203-857-3103, customer_service@belvoir.com, http://www.belvoir.com. Ed. Nancy Kerns. **Subscr. to:** Palm Coast Data, LLC, PO Box 420234, Palm Coast, FL 32142. TEL 800-829-9165, http://www.palmcoastdata.com.

636.0887 CAN ISSN 1926-3074
WILD LIFE. Text in English. 1969. q. CAD 4.95 per issue (effective 2011). back issues avail. **Document type:** *Magazine, Consumer.*
Former titles (until 2011): What's New at the Zoo (1204-1297); (until 1994): Dinny's Digest (1204-1270); (until 1982): Dinny's Calgary Digest (0046-029X)
Related titles: Online - full text ed.: free (effective 2011).
Published by: Calgary Zoological Society, Botanical Garden & Prehistoric Park, 1300 Zoo Rd NE, Calgary, AB T2E 7V6, Canada. TEL 403-232-9300, 800-588-9993, FAX 403-237-7582, lostandfound@calgaryzoo.ab.ca.

636.7 USA ISSN 1059-6267
THE WORKING BORDER COLLIE. Text in English. 1988. bi-m. USD 25; USD 35 foreign (effective 1995). adv. bk.rev. illus. **Document type:** *Magazine, Trade.* **Description:** Helps farmers and ranchers to train stock dogs. From beginners to top handlers.
Published by: Bruce Fogt, Pub., 14933 Kirkwood Rd, Sidney, OH 45365. TEL 513-492-2215. Circ: 2,000.

636.7 NLD ISSN 2211-2049
▼ **THE WORLD OF BULLDOGS.** Text in English. 2010. biennial. EUR 57.50 per vol. (effective 2011).
Published by: BBPress, Broeksterweg 5, Pieterburen, 9968 TH, Netherlands. TEL 31-595-528429, FAX 31-595-528659, sales@bbpress.nl, http://www.bbpress.nl. Pubs. Bas Bosch, Janneke Leunissen-Rooseboom.

636.7 NLD ISSN 1874-8716
THE WORLD OF BULLMASTIFFS (YEARS). Text in English. 2005. biennial. price varies. illus.
Published by: BBPress, Broeksterweg 5, Pieterburen, 9968 TH, Netherlands. TEL 31-595-528429, basbosch@bbpress.nl, http://www.bbpress.nl.

636.7 NLD ISSN 1876-7036
THE WORLD OF CAVALIERS (YEARS). Text in English. 2008. triennial. EUR 52.50 per issue (effective 2009). illus.
Published by: BBPress, Broeksterweg 5, Pieterburen, 9968 TH, Netherlands. TEL 31-595-528429, basbosch@bbpress.nl, http://www.bbpress.nl.

636.7 NLD ISSN 1871-6474
THE WORLD OF CHOWS (YEARS). Text in English. 2001. biennial. EUR 59.50 per issue (effective 2009). adv.
Published by: BBPress, Broeksterweg 5, Pieterburen, 9968 TH, Netherlands. TEL 31-595-528429, basbosch@bbpress.nl, http://www.bbpress.nl. Pubs. Bas Bosch, Janneke Leunissen-Rooseboom.

636.7 NLD
THE WORLD OF DOGUES DE BORDEAUX (YEARS). Text in English. 2006. biennial. price varies. illus.
Published by: BBPress, Broeksterweg 5, Pieterburen, 9968 TH, Netherlands. TEL 31-595-528429, basbosch@bbpress.nl, http://www.bbpress.nl.

636.7 NLD ISSN 1879-5757
▼ **THE WORLD OF FRENCHIES (YEARS).** Text in English. 2009. biennial. EUR 59.50 (effective 2010).
Published by: BBPress, Broeksterweg 5, Pieterburen, 9968 TH, Netherlands. TEL 31-595-528429, rooseboom@bbpress.nl, basbosch@bbpress.nl, http://www.bbpress.nl. Pubs. Bas Bosch, Janneke Leunissen-Rooseboom.

636.7 NLD
THE WORLD OF NEWFOUNDLANDS (YEARS). Text in English. 2006. biennial. price varies. illus.
Published by: BBPress, Broeksterweg 5, Pieterburen, 9968 TH, Netherlands. TEL 31-595-528429, basbosch@bbpress.nl, http://www.bbpress.nl.

636.68 DEU ISSN 0947-3092
WP-MAGAZIN. Variant title: Wellensittich-Papageien Magazin. Text in German. 1995. bi-m. EUR 22 domestic; EUR 29 foreign (effective 2008). adv. **Document type:** *Magazine, Consumer.* **Description:** Covers all aspects of the care and nurturing of house birds.
Published by: Arndt-Verlag, Brueckenfeldstr 28, Bretten, 75015, Germany. TEL 49-7252-957970, FAX 49-7252-78224, info@vogelbuch.com.

636.7 AUT ISSN 1605-5276
WUFF; Das Hundemagazin. Text in German. 10/yr. EUR 29.90; EUR 3.30 newsstand/cover (effective 2007). adv. **Document type:** *Magazine, Consumer.*
Published by: Petmedia Verlagsgesellschaft mbH, Grossrassberg 11, Maria Anzbach, 3034, Austria. TEL 43-2772-558110, FAX 43-2772-558114, info@petmedia.at. adv.: color page EUR 2,980. Circ: 34,000 (paid).

636.7 USA
YORKIE EXPRESS. Text in English. 1951. bi-m. membership. **Document type:** *Newsletter, Consumer.*
Published by: Yorkshire Terrier Club of America, PO Box 265, Saint Peters, PA 19470-0265. http://www.ytca.org/. Circ: 500.

636.8 GBR ISSN 1353-260X
YOUR CAT; Britain's best selling cat magazine. Text in English. 1994. m. GBP 37.20 domestic; GBP 52.80 in Europe; GBP 63.80 elsewhere (effective 2010). adv. illus. back issues avail. **Document type:** *Magazine, Consumer.* **Description:** Covers all aspects of caring for and pampering cats.
Related titles: Online - full text ed.: free (effective 2010).
—CCC.
Published by: Bourne Publishing Group Ltd. (B P G), Roebuck House, 33 Broad St, Stamford, Lincs PE9 1RB, United Kingdom. TEL 44-1780-766199, FAX 44-1780-754774, info@bournepublishinggroup.co.uk, http://www.bournepublishinggroup.com/. Ed. Sue Parslow. Adv. contact Becky Kane TEL 44-1780-754900.

636.7 GBR ISSN 1355-7386
YOUR DOG; Britain's best selling dog magazine. Text in English. 1994. m. GBP 40.80 domestic; GBP 55.20 in Europe; GBP 69.30 elsewhere (effective 2010). adv. illus. back issues avail. **Document type:** *Magazine, Consumer.*
Related titles: Online - full text ed.: free (effective 2010).
—CCC.
Published by: Bourne Publishing Group Ltd. (B P G), Roebuck House, 33 Broad St, Stamford, Lincs PE9 1RB, United Kingdom. TEL 44-1780-766199, FAX 44-1780-754774, info@bournepublishinggroup.co.uk, http://www.bournepublishinggroup.com/. Ed. Sarah Wright. Pub. Alson Queenborough. Adv. contact Becky Kane TEL 44-1780-754900. Circ: 31,299.

636.7 USA ISSN 1078-0343
YOUR DOG; the newsletter for caring dog owners. Text in English. 1994. m. USD 39 domestic; USD 72 foreign (effective 2008). illus. **Document type:** *Newsletter, Consumer.* **Description:** Offers practical advice for dog owners.
Indexed: BRD, R03, RGAb, RGPR, W03, W05.
—CCC.
Published by: Tufts University, Cummings School of Veterinary Medicine, Tufts Media, 196 Boston Ave, Ste 2100, Medford, MA 02155. vetadmissions@tufts.edu. Eds. Betty Liddick, John Berg. Circ: 65,000.

636.8 GBR ISSN 2046-6730
▼ **YOUR FIRST KITTEN.** Text in English. 2011. s-a. GBP 5.99 per issue (effective 2011). **Document type:** *Handbook/Manual/Guide, Trade.*
Published by: Bourne Publishing Group Ltd. (B P G), Roebuck House, 33 Broad St, Stamford, Lincs PE9 1RB, United Kingdom. TEL 44-1780-766199, FAX 44-1780-754774, info@bournepublishinggroup.co.uk, http://www.bournepublishinggroup.com/. Adv. contact Becky Kane TEL 44-1780-754900.

636.7 GBR ISSN 2046-6722
▼ **YOUR FIRST PUPPY.** Text in English. 2011. a. GBP 5.99 per issue (effective 2011). **Document type:** *Handbook/Manual/Guide, Trade.*
Published by: Bourne Publishing Group Ltd. (B P G), Roebuck House, 33 Broad St, Stamford, Lincs PE9 1RB, United Kingdom. TEL 44-1780-766199, FAX 44-1780-754774, info@bournepublishinggroup.co.uk, http://www.bournepublishinggroup.com/. Adv. contact Becky Kane TEL 44-1780-754900.

639.34 FRA ISSN 1957-2840
ZEBRASO'MAG; l'aquarium marin et recifal pour tous. Variant title: ZebrasOmag. Text in French. 2007. q. EUR 21 domestic; EUR 27 foreign (effective 2008). **Document type:** *Magazine, Consumer.*
Published by: Animalia Editions, B P 3, Mouleydier, 24520, France. TEL 33-5-53240760, FAX 33-5-53241224, information@animalia-editions.net, http://www.animalia-editions.net/.

636 RUS ISSN 1563-390X
ZHIVOTNYE STRASTI. Text in Russian. m. USD 125 in United States (effective 2001).
Published by: Izdatel'sko-Proizvodsvennoe Ob'edinenie Pisatelei, Tsvetnoi bulv 30, Moscow, 103051, Russian Federation. TEL 7-095-2002323, FAX 7-095-2002323, plife@postman.ru, http://www.privatelife.ru. Ed. V I Shvarts.

636 DEU ISSN 1864-8215
ZOOFACH-TREND; das Magazin fuer den Zoofachhandel. Text in German. 2007. bi-m. free to qualified personnel (effective 2010). adv. **Document type:** *Magazine, Trade.*
Published by: Minerva Verlag GmbH, Hocksteiner Weg 38, Moenchengladbach, 41189, Germany. TEL 49-2166-621970, FAX 49-2166-6219710, info@minervaverlag.de, http://www.minervaverlag.de. Ed. Holger Crynen. Adv. contact Petra Sklebeny. B&W page EUR 1,400, color page EUR 2,700; trim 215 x 280. Circ: 8,500 (controlled).

636 DEU
ZUCHTBUCH FUER DEUTSCHE SCHAEFERHUNDE. Text in German. 1901. a. EUR 29 (effective 2006). **Document type:** *Catalog.*
Related titles: CD-ROM ed.
Published by: Verein fuer Deutsche Schaeferhunde, Steinerne Furt 71-71a, Augsburg, 86167, Germany. TEL 49-821-740020, FAX 49-821-74002903, info@schaeferhunde.de, http://www.schaeferhunde.de. Circ: 2,450.

636 FRA ISSN 0984-4708
30 MILLIONS D'AMIS. Text in French. 1987. m. EUR 33 (effective 2009). illus. back issues avail. **Document type:** *Magazine, Consumer.*
Formerly (until 1987): Vie des Betes
Indexed: PdeR.
Published by: Fondation 30 Millions d'Amis, 40 Cours Albert 1er, Paris, 75008, France. TEL 33-1-56590444. Circ: 107,657.

PHARMACY AND PHARMACOLOGY

see also DRUG ABUSE AND ALCOHOLISM ; MEDICAL SCIENCES

615 378 USA
A A C P NEWS. Text in English. 1972. m. adv. bibl.; illus. **Document type:** *Newsletter.* **Description:** Provides current information on issues/ events and employment opportunities available in pharmaceutical education.
Published by: American Association of Colleges of Pharmacy, 1727 King St, Alexandria, VA 22314. TEL 703-739-2330, FAX 703-836-8982, mail@aacp.org, http://www.aacp.org/.

615 USA ISSN 1550-7416
RS199.5
➤ **THE A A P S JOURNAL.** Text in English. 1998. irreg. EUR 373, USD 501 to institutions (effective 2012). **Document type:** *Journal, Academic/Scholarly.* **Description:** The journal covers all areas of pharmaceutical research, including drug discovery, development, and therapy.
Formerly (until 2004): A A P S PharmSci (1522-1059)
Media: Online - full text.
Indexed: A22, A26, B19, E01, E08, EMBASE, ExcerpMed, I12, MEDLINE, P30, R10, Reac, S09, SCI, SCOPUS, W07.
—BLDSC (0537.513440), IE. **CCC.**
Published by: (American Association of Pharmaceutical Scientists), Springer New York LLC (Subsidiary of: Springer Science+Business Media), 233 Spring St, New York, NY 10013. TEL 212-460-1500, FAX 212-460-1575. Ed. Ho-Leung Fung.

615 USA ISSN 1099-3606
A A P S NEWSMAGAZINE. Text in English. 1986. m. free to members (effective 2010). adv. back issues avail. **Document type:** *Newsletter, Trade.* **Description:** Contains pharmaceutical science research information for AAPS members and the research community.
Former titles (until 2000): A A P S Newsletter; (until 1998): A A P S News
Related titles: Online - full text ed.: ISSN 2155-7985.
Published by: American Association of Pharmaceutical Scientists, 2107 Wilson Blvd, Ste 700, Arlington, VA 22201. TEL 703-243-2800, FAX 703-243-7650, aaps@aaps.org. Circ: 12,000 (paid and controlled).

615.1 USA ISSN 1530-9932
RS200 CODEN: AAPHFZ
A A P S PHARMSCITECH. (American Association of Pharmaceutical Scientists) Text in English. 2000. q. EUR 376, USD 507 to institutions (effective 2012). **Document type:** *Journal, Academic/Scholarly.* **Description:** Aims to disseminate scientific and technical information on drug product design, development, evaluation and processing to the global pharmaceutical research community, taking full advantage of web-based publishing by presenting innovative text with 3D graphics, interactive figures and databases, video and audio files.
Media: Online - full text.
Indexed: A22, A26, B19, E01, E08, EMBASE, ExcerpMed, I12, MEDLINE, P30, R10, Reac, S09, SCI, SCOPUS, W07.
—BLDSC (0537.513490), IE. **CCC.**
Published by: (American Association of Pharmaceutical Scientists), Springer New York LLC (Subsidiary of: Springer Science+Business Media), 233 Spring St, New York, NY 10013. TEL 212-460-1500, FAX 212-460-1575, journals@springer-ny.com. Ed. Lee Kirsch.

615 POL ISSN 1642-445X
A B C APTEKI; miesiecznik dla pacjentow aptek. Text in Polish. 2001. m. free (effective 2006). **Document type:** *Magazine, Consumer.*
Published by: Wydawnictwo Apteka, ul Szewska 3a, Wroclaw, Poland. TEL 48-71-3699330, FAX 48-71-3699331, info@wydawnictwoapteka.pl, http://www.otcindeks.pl.

A B C PRZEZIEBIENIA. *see* MEDICAL SCIENCES—Communicable Diseases

615.1 GBR ISSN 0001-0561
A B P I NEWS. Text in English. 1962. 6/yr. free to members. bk.rev. charts; illus.; pat.; stat. **Document type:** *Newsletter, Trade.*
Formerly: A B P I Action
—BLDSC (0549.746000).
Published by: Association of the British Pharmaceutical Industry, 12 Whitehall, London, SW1A 2DY, United Kingdom. TEL 44-870-8904333, FAX 44-20-77471414, http://www.abpi.org.uk/. Circ: 17,000.

615.1 CAN ISSN 1497-715X
A C P NEWS. Text in English. 1958. bi-m.
Former titles (until 2000): Alberta College of Pharmacists. Communications (1495-771X); Alberta Pharmaceutical Association. A. Ph. A. Communications (0382-4292); (until 1972): Alberta Pharmaceutical Association. A. Ph. A. Bulletin (0044-717X)
Published by: Alberta College of Pharmacists, Suite 1200, 10303 Jasper Ave NW, Edmonton, AB T5J 3N6, Canada. TEL 780-990-0321, 877-227-3838, FAX 780-990-0328, acpinfo@pharmacists.ab.ca.

▼ **A C S MEDICINAL CHEMISTRY LETTERS.** *see* MEDICAL SCIENCES

615 USA ISSN 1063-8792
RS131.2 CODEN: ADINE4
➤ **A H F S DRUG INFORMATION.** Abbreviated title: A H F S D I. Text in English. 1959. base vol. plus updates 3/yr. USD 299 to non-members; USD 265 to members (effective 2011). 3720 p./no.; reprints avail. **Document type:** *Journal, Academic/Scholarly.* **Description:** Contains detailed monographs on virtually every drug entity available in the US. Includes information on uses, cautions, drug interactions, chemistry, stability, pharmacology, pharmaco-kinetics, toxicity, dosage and administration.
Former titles (until 1989): American Hospital Formulary Service Drug Information (8756-6028); (until 1984): American Hospital Formulary Service
Related titles: CD-ROM ed.: Drug Information Fulltext. ISSN 1077-2782. 1996; Online - full text ed.: 1984. free (effective 2009).
—CCC.
Published by: American Society of Health-System Pharmacists, 7272 Wisconsin Ave, Bethesda, MD 20814. TEL 301-664-8860, 301-657-3000, 866-279-0681, FAX 301-664-8700, custserv@ashp.org, http://www.ashp.org.

615 USA
A H F S DRUG INFORMATION ESSENTIALS; a resource for healthcare professionals. Text in English. 2005. a. **Document type:** *Guide, Trade.* **Description:** Provides a resource that focuses on the essential, evidence-based information that will allow pharmacists, nurses, physicians, and other health-care providers to access quickly, in a straight-forward fashion, the specific guidance needed to safely and effectively prescribe and monitor drug therapy.
Formerly (until 2008): A H F S Drug Information Essentials (Print) (1556-4517)
Media: Online - full text.
Published by: American Society of Health-System Pharmacists, 7272 Wisconsin Ave, Bethesda, MD 20814. TEL 301-664-8860, 866-279-0681, custserv@ashp.org, http://www.ashp.org.

615.19 USA
A I H P NOTES. Text in English. N.S. 1965-1957; resumed 1955. q. free to members (effective 2009). back issues avail. **Document type:** *Newsletter.* **Description:** News and information on the history of pharmacy and about activities of the institute.
Published by: American Institute of the History of Pharmacy, Pharmacy Bldg, 777 Highland Ave, Madison, WI 53705. TEL 608-262-5378, aihp@aihp.org, http://www.pharmacy.wisc.edu/aihp/. Ed. Gregory J Higby.

615 IND ISSN 0975-9581
▼ **A N U JOURNAL OF PHARMACEUTICAL TECHNOLOGY AND RESEARCH.** Text in English. 2009. s-a. **Document type:** *Journal, Academic/Scholarly.*

P

Published by: Acharya Nagarjuna University, Nagarjuna Nagar, Guntur, Andhra Pradesh 522 510, India. TEL 91-863-2293007, FAX 91-863-2293378, http://www.nagarjunauniversity.ac.in.

615 IND ISSN 0973-1288
A P T I BULLETIN. Text in English. 1999. bi-m. free (effective 2011). back issues avail. **Document type:** *Bulletin, Academic/Scholarly.*
Related titles: Online - full text ed.: free (effective 2011).
Published by: Association of Pharmaceutical Teachers of India, Al-Ameen College of Pharmacy, Opposite Lalbagh Main Gate, Hosur Main Rd, Bangalore, 560 027, India. TEL 91-80-22234619, FAX 91-80-22225834, aptienquiry@gmail.com. Ed. B G Shivananda.

615 DEU
A P V NEWS. (Arbeitsgemeinschaft fuer Pharmazeutische Verfahrenstechnik) Text in German. q. adv. **Document type:** *Journal, Trade.*
Published by: Arbeitsgemeinschaft fuer Pharmazeutische Verfahrenstechnik e. V., Kurfuerstenstr 59, Mainz, 55118, Germany. TEL 49-6131-97690, FAX 49-6131-976969, apv@apv-mainz.de. Ed. Frank Stieneker. adv.: B&W page EUR 3,250, color page EUR 4,810; trim 216 x 303. Circ: 20,613 (controlled). **Co-publisher:** Editio Cantor Verlag.

615 USA ISSN 1050-5725
A S C P UPDATE. Text in English. 1969. m. looseleaf. free to members (effective 2010). bk.rev. 8 p./no. 3 cols./p.; back issues avail. **Document type:** *Newsletter, Trade.* **Description:** Covers news on issues and legislation relevant to members of the American Society of Consultant Pharmacists.
Related titles: Online - full text ed.
Published by: American Society of Consultant Pharmacists, 1321 Duke St, Alexandria, VA 22314. TEL 703-739-1300, 800-355-2727, FAX 703-739-1321, 800-220-1321, info@ascp.com. Ed. Diana Duvall.

615 USA ISSN 1557-0606
A S H P MIDYEAR CLINICAL MEETING SYMPOSIUM HIGHLIGHTS. Text in English. a.
—CCC.
Published by: American Society of Health-System Pharmacists, 7272 Wisconsin Ave, Bethesda, MD 20814. TEL 301-664-8601, FAX 301-634-5701, pdiso@ashp.org, http://www.ashp.org.

615.1 USA ISSN 0001-2483
A S H P NEWSLETTER. Text in English. 1968. m. illus. **Document type:** *Newsletter, Trade.* **Description:** Contains articles on pharmacy and member news.
—CCC.
Published by: American Society of Health-System Pharmacists, 7272 Wisconsin Ave, Bethesda, MD 20814. TEL 301-664-8700, 866-279-0681, custserv@ashp.org, http://www.ashp.org.

A T S D R'S TOXICOLOGICAL PROFILES ON CD-ROM. (Agency for Toxic Substances and Disease Registry) *see* ENVIRONMENTAL STUDIES—Toxicology And Environmental Safety

330 DEU ISSN 0935-0829
A W A - AKTUELLER WIRTSCHAFTSDIENST FUER APOTHEKER. Text in German. 1986. 2/m. EUR 82; EUR 6 newsstand/cover (effective 2012). adv. **Document type:** *Magazine, Trade.*
Published by: Deutscher Apotheker Verlag, Postfach 101061, Stuttgart, 70009, Germany. TEL 49-711-25820, FAX 49-711-2582290, service@deutscher-apotheker-verlag.de, http://www.deutscher-apotheker-verlag.de. Ed. Claudia Mittmeyer. Adv. contact Thomas Christ. Circ: 7,462 (controlled).

615.19 ARG ISSN 1851-0612
ACADEMIA NACIONAL DE FARMACIA Y BIOQUIMICA. Text in Spanish. 2007. s-a.
Address: Juan 956, Buenos Aires, PB1113, Argentina. TEL 54-11-49648213, acad@ffyb.uba.ar, http://www.ffyb.uba.ar/academia/historia.htm.

615 AUS ISSN 1449-3535
THE ACCREDITED PHARMACIST. Text in English. 2004. bi-m. **Document type:** *Magazine, Trade.*
Published by: Australian Association of Consultant Pharmacy, PO Box 7071, Canberra Business Centre, ACT 2610, Australia. TEL 61-2-61202800, FAX 61-2-62738160, aacp@aacp.com.au, https://www.aacp.com.au.

615.1 370.58 USA
ACCREDITED PROFESSIONAL PROGRAMS OF COLLEGES AND SCHOOLS OF PHARMACY. Variant title: American Council on Pharmaceutical Education Annual Directory (Year). Text in English. 1940. a. free. **Document type:** *Directory, Consumer.*
Formerly: Accredited Colleges of Pharmacy (0065-7980)
Published by: American Council on Pharmaceutical Education, 20 N. Clark St., Ste. 2500, Chicago, IL 60602-5109. TEL 312-664-3575, FAX 312-664-4652. Ed. Dr. Peter H Vlasses. Circ: 10,000.

615.1 HRV ISSN 1330-0075
RS1 CODEN: ACPHEE
➤ **ACTA PHARMACEUTICA.** Text in English. 1951. q. adv. bk.rev. charts; illus. cum.index. 70 p./no.; reprints avail. **Document type:** *Journal, Academic/Scholarly.* **Description:** Publishes review articles, original papers and preliminary communications dealing with pharmacy and related fields.
Formerly (until 1992): Acta Pharmaceutica Iugoslavica (0001-6667)
Related titles: Online - full text ed.: ISSN 1846-9558. free (effective 2011).
Indexed: A36, ASCA, AgrForAb, B25, BIOSIS Prev, BP, C25, C30, C33, CABA, CIN, ChemAb, ChemTitl, DBA, E12, EMBASE, ExcerpMed, F08, F11, F12, FR, GH, H16, H17, I12, ISR, MEDLINE, MOS, MycolAb, N02, N03, NPU, P30, P32, P33, P39, P40, PGegResA, R10, R13, RA&MP, RM&VM, Reac, RefZh, SCI, SCOPUS, SoyAb, T05, TAR, W07.
—BLDSC (0645.650000), CASDDS, GNLM, IE, Ingenta, INIST, Linda Hall.
Published by: Hrvatsko Farmaceutsko Drustvo/Croatian Pharmaceutical Society, Masarykova 2, Zagreb, 10000, Croatia. TEL 385-1-4872849, FAX 385-1-4872853, hfd-fg-ap@zg.tch.hr. Ed. Svjetlana Luterotti. adv.: B&W page USD 440; 165 x 240. Circ: 600.

615.1 HUN ISSN 0001-6659
CODEN: APHGAO
ACTA PHARMACEUTICA HUNGARICA. Text mainly in Hungarian; Summaries in English. 1925. bi-m. adv. bk.rev. charts; illus. back issues avail.; reprint service avail. from IRC. **Document type:** *Journal, Academic/Scholarly.*
Related titles: Online - full text ed.
Indexed: A22, B&BAb, B21, CIN, ChemAb, ChemTitl, DBA, DentInd, EMBASE, ExcerpMed, I12, IndMed, MEDLINE, NPU, P30, R10, Reac, SCOPUS, ToxAb.
—BLDSC (0645.000000), CASDDS, GNLM, IE, Infotrieve, Ingenta, INIST, Linda Hall.
Published by: Magyar Gyogyszereszttudomanyi Tarsasag/Hungarian Pharmaceutical Association, Gyulai Pal u 16, Budapest, 1085, Hungary. TEL 36-1-4314620, FAX 36-1-2605604, titkarsag@mgyt.hu, http://www.mgyt.hu. Ed., R&P Sandor Gorog. Pub. Z Vincze. Adv. contact Zoltan Hanko. Circ: 2,900. **Subscr. to:** Kultura, PO Box 149, Budapest 1389, Hungary.

615.19 TUR ISSN 1307-2080
CODEN: APTUES
➤ **ACTA PHARMACEUTICA SCIENCIA;** a trimesterly international publication of pharmaceutical, chemical, phytochemical, botanical cosmetic, medical, biomedical and envirnmental sciences. Text in English, French, German; Summaries in English, Turkish. 1954. q. USD 10 domestic; USD 30 foreign (effective 2010). bk.rev. abstr. back issues avail. **Document type:** *Proceedings, Academic/Scholarly.* **Description:** Publishes original research and reviews concerning pharmacy, pharmacology, cosmetics, medicine, chemistry, environment, microbiology, biology and biotechnology.
Former titles: Acta Pharmaceutica Turcica (1300-638X); (until 1984): Eczacilik Bulteni (0367-0236)
Related titles: Online - full text ed.
Indexed: CIN, ChemAb, ChemTitl, EMBASE, ExcerpMed, FS&TA, I12, NPU, SCOPUS.
—BLDSC (0646.619000), CASDDS, GNLM, IE, Ingenta.
Published by: Istanbul University, Faculty of Pharmacy, Department of Pharmaceutical Technology, Istanbul, 34116, Turkey. TEL 90-222-2360051, FAX 90-222-3350127, info@actapharmasciencia.org, http://www.istanbul.edu.tr/eczacilik. Eds. Erdal Cevher, Kasim Cemal Guven. Circ: 1,125; 1,125 (controlled).

615 USA ISSN 1671-4083
CODEN: APSCG5
ACTA PHARMACOLOGICA SINICA. Abbreviated title: A P S. Text in English. 1980. m. EUR 1,223 in Europe to institutions; JPY 209,100 in Japan to institutions; USD 1,499 in the Americas to institutions; GBP 789 to institutions in the UK & elsewhere (effective 2011). adv. back issues avail.; reprints avail. **Document type:** *Journal, Academic/Scholarly.* **Description:** Covers current original research on all aspects of life sciences, both experimental and clinical.
Formerly (until 2000): Zhongguo Yaoli Xuebao (0253-9756)
Related titles: Online - full text ed.: ISSN 1745-7254 (from IngentaConnect).
Indexed: A20, A22, A26, A29, A34, A35, A36, A38, AgBio, AgrForAb, B&BAb, B19, B20, B21, B25, BIOSIS Prev, BP, BioEngAb, C24, C30, C33, CA, CABA, CTA, ChemoAb, CurCont, D01, DBA, E01, E12, EMBASE, ESPM, ExcerpMed, F08, F11, F12, FS&TA, GH, H12, H16, I10, ISR, IndMed, IndVet, Inpharma, M&PBA, MEDLINE, MycolAb, N02, N03, N05, NSA, P20, P22, P30, P32, P33, P35, P37, P39, P40, P48, P54, PGegResA, PGrRegA, PQC, R07, R08, R10, R12, R13, RA&MP, RM&VM, Reac, RefZh, S02, S03, S12, SCI, SCOPUS, SoyAb, T02, T05, VS, VirolAbstr, W07, W10, W11.
—BLDSC (0648.100000), East View, IE, Ingenta, INIST, Linda Hall. **CCC.**
Published by: (Chinese Academy Of Sciences, Shanghai Institute of Materia Medica CHN), Nature Publishing Group (Subsidiary of: Macmillan Publishers Ltd.), 75 Varick St, 9th Fl, New York, NY 10013. TEL 212-726-9200, FAX 212-696-9006, subscriptions@nature.com. Eds. Juan Huang, Qian-Rong Zhu, Jian Ding TEL 86-21-50806600. **Co-sponsor:** Chinese Pharmacological Society.

ACTA PHYSIOLOGICA ET PHARMACOLOGICA BULGARICA. *see* BIOLOGY—Physiology

ACTA PHYSIOLOGICA HUNGARICA. *see* BIOLOGY—Physiology

ACTA PHYSIOLOGICA PHARMACOLOGICA ET THERAPEUTICA LATINOAMERICANA; fisiologia, farmacologia, bioquimica y ciencias afines. *see* BIOLOGY—Physiology

615.1 POL ISSN 0001-6837
RS1 CODEN: APPHAX
➤ **ACTA POLONIAE PHARMACEUTICA**; drug research. Text and summaries in English. 1937. bi-m. EUR 163 foreign (effective 2006). charts; illus. index. **Document type:** *Journal, Academic/Scholarly.* **Description:** Publishes scientific papers on pharmaceutical analysis, natural drugs, pharmacology, and drug synthesis.
Indexed: A22, ASCA, C24, CIN, ChemAb, ChemTitl, DBA, EMBASE, ExcerpMed, I12, ISR, IndMed, MEDLINE, MOS, NPU, P30, R10, Reac, RefZh, SCI, SCOPUS, W07.
—BLDSC (0659.000000), CASDDS, GNLM, IE, Ingenta, INIST, Linda Hall.
Published by: Polskie Towarzystwo Farmaceutyczne/Polish Pharmaceutical Society, ul Dluga 16, Warsaw, 00238, Poland. wydawnictwa@ptfarm.pl, http://www.ptfarm.pl. Ed. Aleksander P Mazurek. **Dist. by:** Ars Polona, Obroncow 25, Warsaw 03933, Poland. TEL 48-22-5098609, FAX 48-22-5098610, arspolona@arspolona.com.pl, http://www.arspolona.com.pl.

615.9 POL ISSN 1731-6383
RA1190
ACTA TOXICOLOGICA. Text in Polish, English. 1993. s-a. USD 11 to individuals; USD 13 to institutions (effective 2006). **Document type:** *Journal, Academic/Scholarly.* **Description:** Published articles on clinical and experimental toxicology, pharmacology, biochemistry and medical chemistry, experimental medicine and pathomorphology.
Formerly (until 2003): Acta Poloniae Toxicologica (1230-6967)
Indexed: A01, AgrAg, AgrLib, CA, EMBASE, ExcerpMed, R10, Reac, SCOPUS, T02.
—BLDSC (0665.465000).
Published by: (Polskie Towarzystwo Toksykologiczne/Polish Society of Toxicology), Instytut Medycyny Pracy im. Jerzego Nofera/Nofer Institute of Occupational Medicine, ul Sw Teresy 8, PO Box 199, Lodz, 90950, Poland. TEL 48-42-6314718, FAX 48-42-6314719, redakcja@imp.lodz.pl. Circ: 500.

615 CHL ISSN 0716-9663
ACTUALIDAD FARMACEUTICA. Text in Spanish. 1933. bi-m. **Document type:** *Journal, Academic/Scholarly.*
Former titles (until 1991): Colegio Quimico - Farmaceutico (0366-7855); (until 1959): Colegio Farmaceutico (0366-7618); (until 1951): Revista Quimico Farmaceutica (0370-6915); (until 1935): Asociacion Chilena de Quimica y Farmacia (0716-5005)
Published by: Colegio Quimico Farmaceutico de Chile, Merced 50, Santiago, Chile. TEL 56-2-6392505, FAX 56-2-6399780, http://www.colegiofarmaceutico.cl.

615.1 CAN ISSN 1195-2857
L'ACTUALITE PHARMACEUTIQUE. Text in French. 1929. m. free domestic to qualified personnel; CAD 75.20 domestic; CAD 110 foreign (effective 2007). adv. illus. **Document type:** *Magazine, Trade.* **Description:** For French-speaking pharmacists in retail and hospital locations.
Formerly: Pharmacien (0031-692X)
Related titles: Microfiche ed.: (from MML); Microform ed.: (from MML); Online - full text ed.; ◆ English ed.: Pharmacist News. ISSN 1195-2849.
Indexed: C03, CBCARef, P24, PQC.
—CCC.
Published by: Rogers Publishing Ltd./Les Editions Rogers Limitee, Rogers Healthcare & Financial Services Group, 1200, ave McGill College, bureau 800, Montreal, PQ H3B 4G7, Canada. TEL 514-845-5141, FAX 514-843-2180, http://www.rogerspublishing.ca. Ed. Caroline Baril TEL 514-843-2573. Circ: 4,109.

615 FRA ISSN 0515-3700
ACTUALITES PHARMACEUTIQUES. Text in French. 1961. 11/yr. EUR 280 in Europe to institutions; EUR 221.35 in France to institutions; JPY 29,900 in Japan to institutions; USD 364 elsewhere to institutions (effective 2012). adv. **Document type:** *Journal, Academic/Scholarly.* **Description:** Provides practical and scientific information. Offers clarifications on categories of medicines or illnesses and articles on pharmaceutical and socio-professional news. Summarizes all the medicines put on the market in the preceding year as well as less recent medicines that may have undergone modifications.
Supersedes: Officine et Techniques Pharmaceutiques
Related titles: Online - full text ed.: (from ScienceDirect).
Indexed: A22, ChemAb, EMBASE, ExcerpMed, FR, P30, R10, Reac, SCOPUS, T02.
—BLDSC (0677.324000), GNLM, IE, Ingenta, INIST. **CCC.**
Published by: Elsevier Masson (Subsidiary of: Elsevier Health Sciences), 62 Rue Camille Desmoulins, Issy les Moulineaux, Cedex 92442, France. TEL 33-1-71165500, FAX 33-1-71165600, infos@elsevier-masson.fr.

615 FRA ISSN 1769-7344
ACTUALITES PHARMACEUTIQUES HOSPITALIERES. Text in French. 2005. q. EUR 96 in Europe to institutions; EUR 85.21 in France to institutions; JPY 11,200 in Japan to institutions; USD 106 elsewhere to institutions (effective 2012). **Document type:** *Journal, Academic/Scholarly.*
Related titles: Online - full text ed.: (from ScienceDirect).
Indexed: CA, EMBASE, ExcerpMed, R10, Reac, SCOPUS, T02.
—BLDSC (0677.324050), IE. **CCC.**
Published by: Elsevier Masson (Subsidiary of: Elsevier Health Sciences), 62 Rue Camille Desmoulins, Issy les Moulineaux, Cedex 92442, France. TEL 33-1-71165500, FAX 33-1-71165600, infos@elsevier-masson.fr.

615 FRA ISSN 1764-1837
ACTULABO. Text in French. 2003. bi-w. **Document type:** *Trade.*
Related titles: ◆ Supplement(s): Actulabo. Le Magazine. ISSN 2108-2030.
Published by: Editions Asklepios, BP 92031, Tours, 37000, France. http://www.actulabo.com.

615 FRA ISSN 2108-2030
ACTULABO. LE MAGAZINE. Text in French. 200?. irreg. **Document type:** *Trade.*
Related titles: ◆ Supplement to: Actulabo. ISSN 1764-1837.
Published by: Editions Asklepios, BP 92031, Tours, 37000, France. http://www.actulabo.com.

616.8005 GBR ISSN 1752-5713
ADELPHI LIFECYCLE SOLUTIONS. Text in English. 2005. m. **Document type:** *Magazine, Trade.*
Related titles: Online - full text ed.: ISSN 1752-5721.
Published by: Adelphi Group, Adelphi Mill, Grimshaw Ln, Bollington, Cheshire, SK10 5JB, United Kingdom. TEL 44-1625-577233, FAX 44-1625-575853, http://www.adelphigroup.com/.

615.19 NLD ISSN 0169-409X
RS199.5 CODEN: ADDREP
➤ **ADVANCED DRUG DELIVERY REVIEWS.** Text in English. 1987. 15/yr. EUR 5,779 in Europe to institutions; JPY 767,200 in Japan to institutions; USD 6,465 elsewhere to institutions (effective 2012). adv. bk.rev. index. back issues avail.; reprints avail. **Document type:** *Journal, Academic/Scholarly.* **Description:** Publishes critical review articles on current and emerging aspects of research into the design and development of advanced drug delivery systems and their application to experimental and clinical therapeutics.
Related titles: Microform ed.: (from PQC); Online - full text ed.: ISSN 1872-8294 (from IngentaConnect, ScienceDirect).
Indexed: A01, A03, A08, A22, A26, A28, A29, APA, ASCA, B&BAb, B19, B20, B21, BIOBASE, BIOSIS Prev, BioEngAb, BrCerAb, C&ISA, C33, CA, CA/WCA, CIA, CIN, CPEI, CerAb, ChemAb, ChemTitl, CivEngAb, CorrAb, CurCont, DBA, E&CAJ, E11, EEA, EMA, EMBASE, ESPM, EngInd, EnvEAb, ExcerpMed, H15, I05, I12, IABS, ISR, IndMed, Inpharma, M&PBA, M&TEA, M09, MBF, MEDLINE, METADEX, MycolAb, P30, R10, Reac, SCI, SCOPUS, SolStAb, T02, T04, VirolAbstr, W07, WAA.
—BLDSC (0696.845000), CASDDS, GNLM, IE, Infotrieve, Ingenta, INIST. **CCC.**
Published by: Elsevier BV (Subsidiary of: Elsevier Science & Technology), Radarweg 29, PO Box 211, Amsterdam, 1000 AE, Netherlands. TEL 31-20-4853911, FAX 31-20-4852457, JournalsCustomerServiceEMEA@elsevier.com, http://www.elsevier.nl. Ed. V H L Lee.

615 USA ISSN 1558-0342
ADVANCED STUDIES IN PHARMACY. Text in English. 2004 (Nov.). irreg. USD 150 per issue domestic; USD 200 per issue foreign (effective 2010). **Document type:** *Journal, Academic/Scholarly.*
Related titles: Online - full text ed.: ISSN 1558-0350.
Indexed: A01.
Published by: (University of Tennessee, College of Pharmacy), Galen Publishing, LLC, 166 W Main St, PO Box 340, Somerville, NJ 08876. TEL 908-253-9001, FAX 908-253-9002, info@asimcme.com, http://www.galenpublishing.com.

615.19 USA ISSN 1075-8593
RM411 CODEN: AADDEU
ADVANCES IN ANTIVIRAL DRUG DESIGN. Text in English. 1993. irreg., latest vol.5, 2007. price varies. back issues avail. **Document type:** *Monographic series, Academic/Scholarly.* **Description:** Provides a comprehensive account on the inception of antiviral drugs, their design, synthesis, and demonstration of therapeutic potential.
Related titles: Online - full text ed.
Indexed: CIN, ChemAb, ChemTitl, EMBASE, ExcerpMed, SCOPUS.
—BLDSC (0698.920000), CASDDS, GNLM. **CCC.**
Published by: J A I Press Inc. (Subsidiary of: Elsevier Science & Technology), 360 Park Ave S, New York, NY 10010. TEL 212-989-5800, FAX 212-633-3990, usinfo-f@elsevier.com. Ed. Erik De Clercq.

615 CHE
➤ **ADVANCES IN PHARMACOLOGICAL SCIENCES.** Text in English. 1990. irreg. price varies. **Document type:** *Monographic series, Academic/Scholarly.*
Published by: Birkhaeuser Verlag AG (Subsidiary of: Springer Science+Business Media), Viaduktstr 42, Postfach 133, Basel, 4051, Switzerland. TEL 41-61-2050707, FAX 41-61-2050799, birkhauser@springer.de, http://www.birkhauser.ch.

615 USA ISSN 1687-6334
➤ **ADVANCES IN PHARMACOLOGICAL SCIENCES.** Text in English. 2007. irreg. USD 495 (effective 2011). **Document type:** *Journal, Academic/Scholarly.* **Description:** Publishes research on all aspects of experimental and clinical pharmacology.
Related titles: Online - full text ed.: ISSN 1687-6342. free (effective 2011).
Indexed: A01, A26, B21, CA, EMBASE, ExcerpMed, NSA, P30, SCOPUS, T02.
—IE.
Published by: Hindawi Publishing Corporation, 410 Park Ave, 15th Fl, PMB 287, New York, NY 10022. FAX 215-893-4392, 866-446-3294, hindawi@hindawi.com. Ed. Steven Hollady.

615.1 USA ISSN 1054-3589
RM30 CODEN: ADPHEL
➤ **ADVANCES IN PHARMACOLOGY.** Text in English. 1962. irreg., latest vol.57, 2009. USD 234 per issue (effective 2010). index. back issues avail.; reprints avail. **Document type:** *Monographic series, Academic/Scholarly.* **Description:** Emphasizes on the molecular bases of drug action, both applied and experimental.
Formerly (until 1990): Advances in Pharmacology and Chemotherapy (0065-3144); Which was formed by the merger of (1962-1969): Advances in Pharmacology (0568-0123); (1964-1969): Advances in Chemotherapy (0567-9877)
Related titles: Online - full text ed.: ISSN 1557-8925.
Indexed: A22, CIN, ChemAb, ChemTitl, DBA, EMBASE, ExcerpMed, ISR, IndMed, MEDLINE, P30, R10, Reac, SCOPUS.
—BLDSC (0709.760000), CASDDS, GNLM, IE, Ingenta, INIST, Linda Hall. **CCC.**
Published by: Academic Press (Subsidiary of: Elsevier Science & Technology), 3251 Riverport Ln, Maryland Heights, MO 63043. TEL 314-447-8010, FAX 314-447-8030, JournalCustomerService-usa@elsevier.com, http://www.elsevierdirect.com/imprint.jsp?iid=5. Eds. Ferid Murad, J August.

615 NLD ISSN 1572-557X
RM666.H33 CODEN: APDHB8
ADVANCES IN PHYTOMEDICINE. Text in English. 2002. irreg., latest vol.3, 2006. price varies. **Document type:** *Monographic series, Academic/Scholarly.*
Indexed: SCOPUS.
—**CCC.**
Published by: Elsevier BV (Subsidiary of: Elsevier Science & Technology), Radarweg 29, PO Box 211, Amsterdam, 1000 AE, Netherlands. TEL 31-20-4853911, FAX 31-20-4852457, JournalsCustomerServiceEMEA@elsevier.com, http://www.elsevier.com. Ed. Maurice Iwu.

615.1 615 USA ISSN 0044-6394
RM300 CODEN: ADRBBA
ADVERSE DRUG REACTION BULLETIN. Text in English. 1966. bi-m. looseleaf. USD 212 domestic to institutions; USD 227 foreign to institutions (effective 2011). adv. Index. back issues avail.; reprints avail. **Document type:** *Journal, Academic/Scholarly.* **Description:** Provides comprehensive coverage on adverse drug reactions.
Related titles: Online - full text ed.; ◆ Italian ed.: Adverse Drug Reaction Bulletin (Italian Edition). ISSN 0393-9499.
Indexed: A22, B&BAb, B19, B21, B25, BIOSIS Prev, CA, EMBASE, ESPM, ExcerpMed, H&SSA, I12, IDIS, IndMed, Inpharma, MycolAb, NSA, P30, P35, R10, Reac, RiskAb, SCOPUS, T02, ToxAb.
—BLDSC (0712.232000), GNLM, IE, Infotrieve, Ingenta, INIST. **CCC.**
Published by: Lippincott Williams & Wilkins (Subsidiary of: Wolters Kluwer N.V.), 530 Walnut St, Philadelphia, PA 19106. TEL 215-521-8300, FAX 215-521-8902, customerservice@lww.com, http://www.lww.com. Ed. Robin E Ferner. Pub. Phil Daly.

615 ITA ISSN 0393-9499
ADVERSE DRUG REACTION BULLETIN (ITALIAN EDITION). Text in Italian. 1978. bi-m. EUR 23.90 (effective 2009). **Document type:** *Magazine, Trade.*
Related titles: Online - full text ed.: ISSN 1973-8048. 2000; ◆ English ed.: Adverse Drug Reaction Bulletin. ISSN 0044-6394.
—**CCC.**
Published by: C I S Editore S.r.l., Via San Siro 1, Milan, 20149, Italy. TEL 39-02-4694542, FAX 39-02-48193584, http://www.ciseditore.it.

615 USA ISSN 1550-5332
ADVERSE EVENT REPORTING NEWS. Text in English. 2004. bi-m. USD 1,084 (effective 2011). **Document type:** *Newsletter, Trade.*
Media: Online - full text.
Indexed: A26, H12, I05.
Published by: Washington Information Source Co., 19-B Wirt St, SW, Leesburg, VA 20175. TEL 703-779-8777, FAX 703-779-2508, service@fdainfo.com, http://www.fdainfo.com/wisindex.html.

615 USA ISSN 2152-7822
▼ ➤ **AFRICAN JOURNAL OF PHARMACEUTICAL SCIENCES AND PHARMACY.** Text in English. 2010 (Mar.). bi-m. USD 200 (effective 2011). **Document type:** *Journal, Academic/Scholarly.* **Description:** Provides a forum for pharmaceutical science research and pharmacy practice in Africa and around the world.
Related titles: Online - full text ed.: ISSN 2152-7849. 2010 (Mar.). free.
Published by: Pyramid Pharmaceutical Group, P.O Box 7817, Aurora, IL 60507. TEL 630-801-0801, FAX 630-801-1777, gudeani@msn.com, http://www.pyramidpharmaceutical.com. Ed. M Adikwu.

615 NGA ISSN 1996-0816
RS1
AFRICAN JOURNAL OF PHARMACY AND PHARMACOLOGY. Variant title: A J P P. Text in English. 2007. m. free (effective 2011). **Document type:** *Journal, Academic/Scholarly.*
Media: Online - full text.
Indexed: A34, A35, A36, A37, A38, AgrForAb, BP, C25, C30, CABA, D01, E12, EMBASE, ExcerpMed, F08, F11, F12, FCA, GH, H16, H17, IndVet, LT, MaizeAb, N02, N03, N04, P32, P33, P37, P38, P39, P40, PGegResA, PGrRegA, PHN&I, R07, R08, R12, R13, RA&MP, RM&VM, RRTA, S12, S13, S16, S17, SCI, SCOPUS, SoyAb, T05, TAR, VS, W07, W10, W11.
Published by: Academic Journals, PO Box 73023, Victoria Island, Lagos, Nigeria. service@academicjournals.org. Ed. John M Haigh.

AGENCE CANADIENNE DES MEDICAMENTS ET DES TECHNOLOGIES DE LA SANTE. RAPPORT TECHNOLOGIQUE. *see* MEDICAL SCIENCES

615.1 GBR ISSN 1465-3745
THE AGRICULTURAL AND VETERINARY PHARMACIST. Text in English. 1998. q. **Document type:** *Newsletter, Trade.* **Description:** Provides a means of promoting agricultural and veterinary pharmacy.
—**CCC.**
Published by: Royal Pharmaceutical Society of Great Britain, Agricultural and Veterinary Pharmacists Group, 1 Lambeth High St, London, SE1 7JN, United Kingdom. TEL 44-20-7735-9141, FAX 44-20-7582-7327, editor@pharmj.org.uk, http://www.rpsgb.org.uk. Ed. Steven Kayne.

AKTUELLT. *see* DRUG ABUSE AND ALCOHOLISM

615.1 EGY ISSN 1110-1792
ALEXANDRIA JOURNAL OF PHARMACEUTICAL SCIENCES. Text in English. 1987. 3/yr. **Document type:** *Journal, Academic/Scholarly.*
—BLDSC (0786.941000), IE, Ingenta.
Published by: Alexandria University, Faculty of Pharmacy, Al-Khartoum Square, Azareta, P O Box 21521, Alexandria, Egypt. TEL 20-3-4831351, FAX 20-3-4833273. Ed. Dr. Husain A El-Sherbini.

615 610 GBR ISSN 1759-4227
ALGERIA PHARMACEUTICALS & HEALTHCARE REPORT. Text in English. 200?. q. EUR 820, USD 1,150 combined subscription (print & email eds.) (effective 2010). **Document type:** *Report, Trade.* **Description:** Provides industry professionals, market investors and corporate and financial services analysts with independent forecasts and competitive intelligence on the Algerian pharmaceutical and healthcare industry.
Related titles: E-mail ed.
Published by: Business Monitor International Ltd., Senator House, 85 Queen Victoria St, London, EC4V 4AB, United Kingdom. TEL 44-20-72480468, FAX 44-20-72480467, subs@businessmonitor.com.

THE ALKALOIDS: CHEMISTRY AND BIOLOGY. *see* CHEMISTRY—Organic Chemistry

615 USA
AMERICAN ASSOCIATION OF COLLEGES OF PHARMACY. (YEAR) PROFILE OF PHARMACY FACULTY. Text in English. 1980. a. USD 25 per issue (effective 2006). **Description:** Offers information on the faculty members of the AACP.
Formerly: American Association of Colleges of Pharmacy. Annual Survey of Faculty Salaries
Published by: American Association of Colleges of Pharmacy, Office of Academic Affairs, 1426 Prince St, Alexandria, VA 22314-2815. TEL 703-739-2330, FAX 703-836-8982, mail@aacp.org. Ed. Susan M Meyer. R&P Richard Penna. Circ: 2,500.

AMERICAN HEALTH & DRUG BENEFITS; the peer-reviewed forum for evidence in benefit design. *see* INSURANCE

AMERICAN HERB ASSOCIATION NEWSLETTER. *see* GARDENING AND HORTICULTURE

615.1 USA ISSN 0270-0611
AMERICAN INSTITUTE OF THE HISTORY OF PHARMACY. PUBLICATIONS. Text in English. 1972. irreg. **Document type:** *Monographic series.*
Indexed: EMBASE, ExcerpMed, MEDLINE, P30, SCOPUS.
Published by: American Institute of the History of Pharmacy, Pharmacy Bldg, 777 Highland Ave, Madison, WI 53705. TEL 608-262-5378, 608-262-5635, aihp@aihp.org, http://www.pharmacy.wisc.edu/aihp/.

AMERICAN JOURNAL OF CARDIOVASCULAR DRUGS. *see* MEDICAL SCIENCES—Cardiovascular Diseases

615 USA ISSN 2150-427X
▼ ➤ **AMERICAN JOURNAL OF DRUG DISCOVERY AND DEVELOPMENT.** Text in English. 2010. q. **Document type:** *Journal, Academic/Scholarly.* **Description:** Scholarly research on all aspects of drug discovery and development.
Related titles: Online - full text ed.: ISSN 2150-4296. 2010.
Published by: Academic Journals Inc., 224, 5th Ave, No 2218, New York, NY 10001. TEL 845-863-0090, FAX 845-591-0669, academicjournals@gmail.com.

615.547 USA ISSN 1543-5946
➤ **THE AMERICAN JOURNAL OF GERIATRIC PHARMACOTHERAPY;** the peer-reviewed journal of geriatric drug therapy. Abbreviated title: A J G P. Text in English. 2003. bi-m. USD 360 elsewhere to institutions (effective 2012). adv. Supplement avail.; back issues avail.; reprints avail. **Document type:** *Journal, Academic/Scholarly.* **Description:** Provides rapid publication of original reports of recent developments in drug therapy, pharmacoepidemiology, clinical pharmacology, health services research related to drug therapy and pharmaceutical outcomes research in older patients, as well as in-depth review articles on special topics related to drugs and the elderly.
Related titles: Online - full text ed.: ISSN 1876-7761. free (effective 2009) (from IngentaConnect, ScienceDirect).
Indexed: A26, B21, C06, C07, CA, CTA, CurCont, EMBASE, ExcerpMed, I05, I12, IDIS, Inpharma, MEDLINE, NSA, P03, P30, P35, PsycInfo, PsycholAb, R10, Reac, SCI, SCOPUS, T02, W07.
—BLDSC (0824.656000), IE, Ingenta. **CCC.**
Published by: Excerpta Medica, Inc. (Subsidiary of: Elsevier Health Sciences), 685 US-202, Bridgewater, NJ 08807. TEL 908-547-2100, FAX 908-547-2200, excerptamedica@elsevier.com, http://www.excerptamedica.com/. Eds. Joseph T Hanlon, Dr. Kenneth E Schmader. Pub. Jo-Ann E West TEL 908-547-2082. adv.: B&W page USD 3,380, color page USD 4,895; bleed 8.25 x 11. Circ: 5,100.

615.1 USA ISSN 1079-2082
RS1 CODEN: AHSPEK
➤ **AMERICAN JOURNAL OF HEALTH-SYSTEM PHARMACY.** Abbreviated title: A J H P. Text in English. 1943. s-m. USD 278 to non-members; free to members (effective 2009). adv. bk.rev.; software rev.; video rev. abstr.; bibl.; charts; illus.; tr.lit. Index. 96 p./no.; Supplement avail.; back issues avail.; reprints avail. **Document type:** *Journal, Academic/Scholarly.* **Description:** Covers all facets of pharmacy in components of health systems. Provides current information on the clinical use of new drugs - current thinking on drug therapy in selected diseases and clinical trials evaluating drug effects and adverse drug reactions.
Former titles (until 1995): American Journal of Hospital Pharmacy (0002-9289); Which incorporated (1982-1993): Clinical Pharmacy (0278-2677); (until 1958): American Society of Hospital Pharmacists.Bulletin (0099-7501)
Related titles: CD-ROM ed.; Microform ed.: (from PQC); Online - full text ed.: ISSN 1535-2900. 1999; Spanish Translation: ISSN 1695-0674.
Indexed: A01, A02, A03, A08, A20, A22, A26, A34, A35, A36, AHCMS, AIDS Ab, ASCA, AgBio, B20, B21, BP, C06, C07, C08, C11, CA, CABA, CIN, CINAHL, CTA, ChemAb, ChemTitl, ChemoAb, CurCont, D01, DBA, DentInd, E12, EMBASE, ESPM, ExcerpMed, FR, GH, H04, H12, HospLI, I05, I12, IDIS, INI, ISR, IndMed, IndVet, Inpharma, Kidney, MCR, MEDLINE, MS&D, N02, N03, NSA, P30, P33, P34, P35, P37, R10, R12, RA&MP, RM&VM, Reac, S01, S02, S03, S12, SCI, SCOPUS, T02, T05, VS, W07.
—BLDSC (0824.770000), CASDDS, GNLM, IE, Infotrieve, Ingenta, INIST. **CCC.**
Published by: American Society of Health-System Pharmacists, 7272 Wisconsin Ave, Bethesda, MD 20814. TEL 301-657-3000, 866-279-0681, FAX 301-664-8700, custserv@ashp.org, http://www.ashp.org. Ed. C Richard Talley. Adv. contact Nasrine L Sabi. B&W page USD 4,155, color page USD 6,570; bleed 8.5 x 11.25. Circ: 38,000.
Subscr. to: PO Box 17693, Baltimore, MD 21297.

615.10711 USA ISSN 0002-9459
RS110 CODEN: AJPDAD
➤ **AMERICAN JOURNAL OF PHARMACEUTICAL EDUCATION.** Abbreviated title: A J P E. Text in English. 1937. a. USD 150 per issue to non-members; free to members (effective 2009). bk.rev. bibl.; charts; illus. index, cum.index every 10 yrs. back issues avail. **Document type:** *Journal, Academic/Scholarly.* **Description:** Aims to document and advance pharmaceutical education in the United States and Internationally.
Related titles: Microfilm ed.: (from PMC, PQC); Online - full text ed.: ISSN 1553-6467. free (effective 2011).
Indexed: A01, A20, A22, A26, ASCA, CA, CPE, ChemAb, CurCont, E03, EMBASE, ERI, ExcerpMed, H12, HECAB, HospLI, I05, I12, ISR, Inpharma, L09, MEDLINE, P10, P16, P20, P22, P24, P30, P48, P53, P54, PQC, R10, Reac, SCI, SCOPUS, T02, W07.
—BLDSC (0830.000000), CASDDS, GNLM, IE, Infotrieve, Ingenta, INIST, Linda Hall. **CCC.**
Published by: American Association of Colleges of Pharmacy, 715 Sumter St, Columbia, SC 29208. TEL 803-777-3096, FAX 803-777-3097, mail@aacp.org, http://www.aacp.org/. Ed. Joseph T DiPiro TEL 706-721-4915.

615 USA ISSN 1557-4962
➤ **AMERICAN JOURNAL OF PHARMACOLOGY AND TOXICOLOGY.** Text in English. 2006. q. USD 1,600 (effective 2009). **Document type:** *Journal, Academic/Scholarly.*
Related titles: Online - full text ed.: ISSN 1557-4970.
Indexed: A01, A26, A34, A35, A36, A37, A38, AgBio, AgrForAb, BP, C30, CA, CABA, D01, E12, EMBASE, ExcerpMed, F08, F11, F12, G05, G06, G07, G08, GH, H16, H17, I05, IndVet, N02, N03, P30, P32, P33, P39, PGegResA, PN&I, R08, RA&MP, S12, S13, S16, SCOPUS, T02, T05, TAR, VS.
—BLDSC (0830.550000), IE.
Published by: Science Publications, 244, 5th Ave, Ste 207, New York, NY 10001. TEL 845-510-3028, FAX 866-250-7082, support@scipub.org, http://www.thescipub.com.

615 USA ISSN 1945-4481
▼ **THE AMERICAN JOURNAL OF PHARMACY BENEFITS.** Abbreviated title: A J P B. Text in English. 2009. bi-m. free to qualified personnel (effective 2010). **Document type:** *Journal, Trade.* **Description:** Presents case studies, research, and evidence-based tools to help decision makers develop clinical strategies to manage pharmacy benefits for large populations.
Indexed: EMBASE, P30, SCOPUS.
—**CCC.**
Published by: Managed Care & Healthcare Communications LLC., 666 Plainsboro Rd, Ste 300, Plainsboro, NJ 08536. TEL 609-716-7777, FAX 609-716-4747, info@ajpblive.com.

AMERICAN JOURNAL OF THERAPEUTICS. *see* MEDICAL SCIENCES

615 USA ISSN 1099-8012
RS192 CODEN: APHRFS
AMERICAN PHARMACEUTICAL REVIEW. Text in English. q. free in US & Canada to qualified personnel; USD 120 elsewhere (effective 2004). **Document type:** *Magazine, Trade.* **Description:** Reviews the latest technology and techniques that impact all aspects of pharmaceutical manufacturing from drug discovery to the final product.
Related titles: Online - full text ed.: ISSN 1938-2669.
Indexed: EMBASE, ExcerpMed, R10, Reac, SCOPUS.
—BLDSC (0850.575500), IE, Ingenta. **CCC.**
Published by: Russell Publishing LLC, 9225 Priority Way West Dr, Ste 120, Indianapolis, IN 46240. TEL 317-816-8787, FAX 317-816-8788, info@russpub.com, http://www.russpub.com. Ed. Nicole Mawbey. Pub. Nigel Russell.

P

615.1 USA ISSN 1544-3191
RS1 CODEN: AMPHDF
➤ **AMERICAN PHARMACISTS ASSOCIATION. JOURNAL.** Text in English. 1912. bi-m. USD 495 combined subscription to institutions (print & online eds.); free to members (effective 2009). adv. bk.rev. charts; illus. Index. back issues avail.; reprints avail. **Document type:** *Journal, Academic/Scholarly.* **Description:** Provides information on pharmaceutical care, drug therapy, diseases and other health issues, trends in pharmacy practice and therapeutics, informed opinion, and original research.
Incorporates: Abstracts. Symposia Papers Presented Before the APhA Academy of Pharmaceutical Sciences at the Annual Meeting of the American Pharmaceutical Association (0098-6437); Former titles (until 2003): American Pharmaceutical Association. Journal (1086-5802); (until 1996): American Pharmacy (0160-3450); (until 1978): American Pharmaceutical Association. Journal (0003-0465); (until 1961): American Pharmaceutical Association. Journal. Practical Pharmacy Edition (0095-9561); Which superseded in part (in 1940): American Pharmaceutical Association. Journal (0898-140X); Which was formerly (1906-1912): American Pharmaceutical Association. Bulletin (0096-6789)
Related titles: Microform ed.: (from PMC, PQC); Online - full text ed.: ISSN 1544-3450.
Indexed: A20, A22, C06, C07, CA, ChemAb, CurCont, EMBASE, ExcerpMed, I12, IDIS, INI, IndMed, MCR, MEDLINE, MEDSOC, P30, R10, Reac, SCI, SCOPUS, T02, W07.
—BLDSC (4662.587000), CASDDS, GNLM, IE, Ingenta, INIST, Linda Hall. **CCC.**
Published by: American Pharmacists Association, 2215 Constitution Ave, NW, Washington, DC 20037. TEL 202-628-4410, FAX 202-783-2351, InfoCenter@aphanet.org, http://www.japha.org. Ed. Michael L Posey. Adv. contact Kristin Hodges TEL 202-429-7583. B&W page USD 3,640, color page USD 5,360; trim 7.75 x 10.5. Circ: 16,989. **Subscr. to:** PO Box 11806, Birmingham, AL 35202. TEL 800-633-4931, FAX 205-995-1588, japha@subscriptionoffice.com.

338.4761091812 GBR ISSN 1750-757X
HD9670.A1
AMERICAS PHARMA & HEALTHCARE INSIGHT. Text in English. 2006. m. USD 1,010 combined subscription (print & online eds.) (effective 2010). adv. **Document type:** *Report, Trade.* **Description:** Provides analysis, forecasts and company profiles on a country-by-country basis, covering the key trends impacting pharma and healthcare markets across the Americas.
Related titles: Online - full text ed.
Indexed: A15, ABIn, P21, P48, P51, PQC.
Published by: Business Monitor International Ltd., Senator House, 85 Queen Victoria St, London, EC4V 4AB, United Kingdom. TEL 44-20-72480468, FAX 44-20-72480467, subs@businessmonitor.com, http://www.businessmonitor.com. Adv. contact Leila Scott TEL 44-207-2465131.

615.1 USA ISSN 1093-5401
HD9666.1
AMERICA'S PHARMACIST. Text in English. 1902. m. free to members (effective 2009). adv. charts; illus.; tr.lit. **Document type:** *Magazine, Trade.* **Description:** Features articles on activities of independent pharmacists and issues to which they relate: legislative, regulatory, clinical, and marketing.
Former titles (until 1997): N A R D Journal (0027-5972); (until 1915): National Association of Retail Druggists. Journal (0276-2595); (until 1913): N.A.R.D. Notes (0270-8582)
Indexed: I12, Search.
—Ingenta, Linda Hall.
Published by: National Community Pharmacists Association, 100 Daingerfield Rd, Alexandria, VA 22314. TEL 703-683-8200, 800-544-7447, FAX 703-683-3619, info@ncpanet.org, http://www.ncpanet.org/. Pub. Mike Conlan TEL 703-838-2688. Adv. contact Nina Dadgar TEL 703-838-2673. B&W page USD 5,260, color page USD 7,510; bleed 8.375 x 11.125. Circ: 24,669.

ANDREWS LITIGATION REPORTER: DRUG RECALL. *see* LAW

ANDREWS LITIGATION REPORTER: PHARMACEUTICAL. *see* LAW—Civil Law

615 USA ISSN 1531-6416
QP106.6
ANGIOGENESIS WEEKLY. Text in English. 1998. w. USD 2,295 in US & Canada; USD 2,495 elsewhere; USD 2,525 combined subscription in US & Canada (print & online eds.); USD 2,755 combined subscription elsewhere (print & online eds.) (effective 2008). back issues avail. **Document type:** *Newsletter, Trade.*
Related titles: E-mail ed.; Online - full text ed.: ISSN 1531-6904. 1998. USD 2,295 combined subscription (online & email eds.); single user (effective 2008).
Indexed: A26, CWI, G08, H11, H12, H13, I05, P10, P19, P20, P48, P53, P54, PQC.
—CIS.
Published by: NewsRx, 2727 Paces Ferry Rd SE, Ste 2-440, Atlanta, GA 30339. TEL 770-435-8286, 800-726-4550, FAX 770-435-6800, pressrelease@newsrx.com, http://www.newsrx.com. Pub. Susan Hasty TEL 770-507-7777.

615 610 CHN ISSN 1009-6469
ANHUI YIYAO/ANHUI MEDICAL AND PHARMACEUTICAL JOURNAL. Text in English. 1997. m. **Document type:** *Journal, Academic/Scholarly.*
Related titles: Online - full text ed.
Published by: Anhui Sheng Yaoxuehui/Anhui Pharmaceutical Association, 96, Wangjiang Dong Lu, Zhongtiesiju Zhaodaisuo Beiyilou, Hefei, 230023, China. TEL 86-551-4672615, FAX 86-551-3677697. **Co-sponsor:** Anhui Sheng Shipin Yaopin Jiandu Guanliju/Ahui Food & Drug Administration.

615.7 USA
ANIMAL DRUGS. Text in English. 1989. m. free (effective 2011). **Document type:** *Directory, Government.*
Formerly (until 2008): F D A Approved Animal Drug Products (1064-0258)
Related titles: Online - full text ed.
Published by: U.S. Department of Health and Human Services, Food and Drug Administration, 10903 New Hampshire Ave, Silver Spring, MD 20993. TEL 301-796-8240, 888-463-6332, druginfo@fda.hhs.gov, http://www.fda.gov.

615 TUR ISSN 1015-3918
ANKARA UNIVERSITESI. ECZACILIK FAKULTESI. DERGISI/ANKARA UNIVERSITY. FACULTY OF PHARMACY. JOURNAL. Text in Multiple languages. 1971. s-a. **Document type:** *Journal, Academic/Scholarly.* **Description:** Publishes original research report, short communications and reviews on relevant developments in all fields of pharmaceutical sciences.
Formerly (until 1993): Ankara Universitesi. Eczacilik Fakultesi Mecmuasi (0377-9734)
Indexed: EMBASE, ExcerpMed, R10, Reac, SCOPUS.
—BLDSC (0905.250150).
Published by: Ankara Universitesi, Eczacilik Fakultesi/Ankara University Faculty of Pharmacy, Dogol Caddesi, Tandogan, Ankara, 06100, Turkey. TEL 90-4-3122126040, FAX 90-4-3122126049, onur@pharmacy.ankara.edu.tr, http://www.ankara.edu.tr. Ed. Feyyaz Onur.

615.1 BEL ISSN 0365-5474
ANNALES PHARMACEUTIQUES BELGES. Text in French. 1942. m. adv. bk.rev. index. **Document type:** *Journal, Academic/Scholarly.* **Description:** For Belgian community pharmacists.
Former titles (until 1949): Pharmaceutica (0370-1433); (until 1944): Ordre des Pharmaciens. Bulletin (0366-4562)
Related titles: Dutch ed.: Het Apothekerblad. ISSN 0003-6579. 1942.
Indexed: I12.
—INIST.
Published by: Algemene Pharmaceutische Bond/Association Pharmaceutique Belge, Archimedesstraat 11, Brussels, 1000, Belgium. TEL 32-2-2854200, FAX 32-2-2854285, http://www.apb.be. Ed. D Broeckx. Circ: 4,500.

615.1 FRA ISSN 0003-4509
RS1 CODEN: APFRAD
ANNALES PHARMACEUTIQUES FRANCAISES. Text in French; Summaries in English. 1943. 6/yr. EUR 514 in Europe to institutions; EUR 422.14 in France to institutions; JPY 79,500 in Japan to institutions; USD 668 elsewhere to institutions (effective 2012). adv. bk.rev. bibl.; illus. index. reprints avail. **Document type:** *Journal, Academic/Scholarly.* **Description:** Publishes original articles, technical notes of interest to practitioners, and meeting reports of the Academy.
Related titles: Online - full text ed.: (from ScienceDirect).
Indexed: A22, ApicAb, B25, BIOSIS Prev, C24, C33, CIN, CISA, ChemAb, ChemTitl, DBA, EMBASE, ExcerpMed, FR, I12, IBR, IBZ, ISR, IndMed, MEDLINE, MOS, MycolAb, NPU, P30, R10, Reac, SCOPUS.
—BLDSC (0992.000000), CASDDS, GNLM, IE, Infotrieve, Ingenta, INIST, Linda Hall. **CCC.**
Published by: (Academie Nationale de Pharmacie), Elsevier Masson (Subsidiary of: Elsevier Health Sciences), 62 Rue Camille Desmoulins, Issy les Moulineaux, Cedex 92442, France. TEL 33-1-71165500, infos@elsevier-masson.fr. Ed. Alain Astier. Circ: 1,500.

615.1 POL ISSN 0867-0609
RS1 CODEN: MSCGDJ
➤ **ANNALES UNIVERSITATIS MARIAE CURIE-SKLODOWSKA. SECTIO DDD. PHARMACIA.** Text in English, Polish; Summaries in English. 1988. a. price varies. **Document type:** *Journal, Academic/Scholarly.*
Indexed: A34, A36, BP, C25, C30, CABA, EMBASE, FCA, GH, H17, IndVet, N02, N03, N04, P33, PGrRegA, PHN&I, R13, RA&MP, SCOPUS, VS, W10.
Published by: (Uniwersytet Marii Curie-Sklodowskiej w Lublinie), Wydawnictwo Uniwersytetu Marii Curie-Sklodowskiej w Lublinie, Pl Marii Curie-Sklodowskiej 5, Lublin, 20031, Poland. TEL 48-81-5375304, press@ramzes.umcs.lublin.pl, http://www.press.umcs.lublin.pl. Ed. Romuald Langwinski. Circ: 600.

615.1 USA ISSN 1060-0280
RM300 CODEN: APHRER
➤ **THE ANNALS OF PHARMACOTHERAPY.** Text in English; Summaries in French, Spanish. 1967. m. (July-Aug. combined). USD 188 in North America to individuals; USD 235 elsewhere to individuals; USD 536 in North America to institutions; USD 570 elsewhere to institutions; USD 193 combined subscription in North America to individuals (print & online eds.); USD 241 combined subscription elsewhere to individuals (print & online eds.); USD 558 combined subscription in North America to institutions (print & online eds.); USD 594 combined subscription elsewhere to institutions (print & online eds.) (effective 2009). adv. bk.rev.; software rev. abstr.; bibl.; charts; illus. index. 178 p./no. 2 cols./p.; back issues avail.; reprints avail. **Document type:** *Journal, Academic/Scholarly.* **Description:** Aimed at health care professionals involved in drug therapy. Provides an interdisciplinary approach to the study of pharmacotherapy.
Former titles (until 1992): D I C P - The Annals of Pharmacotherapy (1042-9611); (until 1989): Drug Intelligence and Clinical Pharmacy (0012-6578); (until 1969): Drug Intelligence (1044-6192)
Related titles: Microform ed.: (from PQC); Online - full text ed.: ISSN 1542-6270. 1998. USD 182 to individuals; USD 536 to institutions; USD 95 to students (effective 2009); ◆ Spanish ed.: Annals of Pharmacotherapy (Spanish Edition). ISSN 1133-178X.
Indexed: A20, A22, A29, A34, A36, A38, AHCMS, AIDS Ab, AgrForAb, B&BAb, B19, B20, B21, B25, BIOSIS Prev, C06, C07, C08, CABA, CIN, CINAHL, CTA, ChemAb, ChemTitl, ChemoAb, CurCont, D01, DBA, DentInd, E12, EMBASE, ESPM, ExcerpMed, F08, F11, F12, FR, GH, H16, H17, HospLI, I10, I12, IDIS, INI, ISR, IndMed, Inpharma, Kidney, MEDLINE, MycolAb, N02, N03, NSA, OR, P30, P33, P35, P39, PHN&I, PN&I, R10, R12, R13, RA&MP, RM&VM, Reac, RefZh, SCI, SCOPUS, SoyAb, T05, TAR, THA, VS, VirolAbstr, W07, W10, W11.
—BLDSC (1043.417500), CASDDS, GNLM, IE, Infotrieve, Ingenta, INIST, Linda Hall. **CCC.**
Published by: Harvey Whitney Books Company, PO Box 42696, Cincinnati, OH 45242. TEL 513-793-3555, FAX 513-793-3600, http://www.hwbooks.com. Ed. Milap C Nahata. Pub. Harvey A K Whitney.

615.1 ESP ISSN 1988-8147
ANNALS OF PHARMACOTHERAPY (ONLINE SPANISH EDITION). Text in Spanish. 2008. 3/yr. EUR 63.05 to individuals; EUR 42.02 to institutions (effective 2008). back issues avail. **Document type:** *Journal, Academic/Scholarly.*
Media: Online - full text. **Related titles:** ◆ Print ed.: Annals of Pharmacotherapy (Spanish Edition). ISSN 1133-178X.
Published by: Grupo Ars XXI de Comunicacion, SA, Muntaner 262 Atico 2a., Barcelona, 08021, Spain. TEL 34-90-2195484, FAX 34-93-2722902, info@arsxxi.com, http://www.stmeditores.com, http://www.arsxxi.com.

615 FRA ISSN 1285-7599
ANNUAIRE DES PHARMACIENS. Text in French. 1932. a. EUR 175 per issue (effective 2009). adv. **Document type:** *Directory, Trade.*
Formerly (until 1997): Annuaire General de la Pharmacie Francaise (0066-3158)
Published by: (Association Generale des Syndicats Pharmaceutiques), Rosenwald, 137 rue d'Aguesseau, Boulogne Billancourt Cedex, 92641, France. TEL 33-1-49098761, FAX 33-1-49098762.

ANNUAL IN THERAPEUTIC RECREATION. *see* MEDICAL SCIENCES

615.19 GBR ISSN 2042-1745
ANNUAL REGISTER OF PHARMACISTS. Text in English. 1869. a. free to members (effective 2010). index. **Document type:** *Directory.* **Description:** Contains an alphabetical list of names and addresses of all registered pharmacists; corporate bodies operating retail pharmacy businesses with the names of their superintendents; and the business titles and addresses of all registered retail pharmacies in country, county and town order.
Former titles (until 2008): Annual Register of Pharmaceutical Chemists (0260-955X); (until 1956): Register of Pharmaceutical Chemists
Related titles: Online - full text ed.
—**CCC.**
Published by: Royal Pharmaceutical Society of Great Britain, 1 Lambeth High St, London, SE1 7JN, United Kingdom. TEL 44-20-77359141, FAX 44-20-77357629, enquiries@rpsgb.org, http://www.rpsgb.org.uk/. Circ: 1,000.

615.1 USA ISSN 0065-7743
RS402 CODEN: ARMCBI
➤ **ANNUAL REPORTS IN MEDICINAL CHEMISTRY.** Text in English. 1966. irreg., latest vol.44, 2009. USD 156 per vol. (effective 2010). back issues avail.; reprints avail. **Document type:** *Monographic series, Academic/Scholarly.* **Description:** Provides reviews of important topics in medicinal chemistry together with an emphasis on emerging topics in the biological sciences, which are expected to provide the basis for entirely new future therapies.
Related titles: Online - full text ed.: ISSN 1557-8437.
Indexed: A22, ASCA, BIOSIS Prev, C33, CIN, ChemAb, ChemTitl, ISR, MycolAb, P30, SCI, SCOPUS, W07.
—BLDSC (1513.050000), CASDDS, GNLM, IE, Infotrieve, Ingenta, INIST, Linda Hall. **CCC.**
Published by: Academic Press (Subsidiary of: Elsevier Science & Technology), 3251 Riverport Ln, Maryland Heights, MO 63043. TEL 314-447-8010, FAX 314-447-8030, JournalCustomerService-usa@elsevier.com, http://www.elsevierdirect.com/imprint.jsp?iid=5.

615.1 USA ISSN 0362-1642
RM16 CODEN: ARPTDI
➤ **ANNUAL REVIEW OF PHARMACOLOGY AND TOXICOLOGY.** Text in English. 1961. a. USD 272 combined subscription per issue to institutions (print & online eds.); USD 227 per issue to institutions (print or online ed.) (effective 2012). bibl.; charts; abstr. index, cum.index. back issues avail.; reprint service avail. from PSC. **Document type:** *Journal, Academic/Scholarly.* **Description:** Reviews, filters and synthesizes primary research to identify the principal contributions in the fields of pharmacology and toxicology.
Formerly (until 1976): Annual Review of Pharmacology (0066-4251)
Related titles: Microfilm ed.: (from PQC); Online - full text ed.: ISSN 1545-4304.
Indexed: A01, A03, A08, A22, A36, ASCA, ASFA, Agr, B21, BIOBASE, BIOSIS Prev, C13, C33, CA, CABA, CIN, CTA, ChemAb, ChemTitl, CurCont, DBA, E-psyche, E04, E05, E12, EMBASE, ESPM, ExcerpMed, F08, GH, GenetAb, I12, IABS, IBR, IBZ, ISR, IndMed, Inpharma, MEDLINE, MRD, MycolAb, N02, N03, NSA, P03, P15, P20, P22, P24, P25, P26, P30, P33, P39, P48, P52, P54, P56, PQC, PsycholAb, R07, R10, RA&MP, Reac, S01, SCI, SCOPUS, T02, THA, ToxAb, VirolAbstr, W07.
—BLDSC (1525.880000), CASDDS, GNLM, IE, Infotrieve, Ingenta, INIST, Linda Hall. **CCC.**
Published by: Annual Reviews, PO Box 10139, Palo Alto, CA 94303. TEL 650-493-4400, FAX 650-424-0910, 800-523-8635, service@annualreviews.org. Eds. Paul A Insel TEL 858-534-2295, Samuel Gubins.

615.19 NLD ISSN 2210-268X
▼ **ANTI-ANGIOGENESIS DRUG DISCOVERY AND DEVELOPMENT.** Text in English. 2011. irreg. **Document type:** *Monographic series, Academic/Scholarly.*
Media: Online - full text.
Published by: Bentham Science Publishers Ltd., PO Box 294, Bussum, 1400 AG, Netherlands. TEL 31-35-6923800, FAX 31-35-6980150, sales@bentham.org, http://www.bentham.org.

615 NLD
RM265 CODEN: AAMCC2
➤ **ANTI-INFECTIVE AGENTS.** Text in English. 2002 (Jan). s-a. USD 400 to institutions (print or online ed.) (effective 2012). adv. back issues avail.; reprints avail. **Document type:** *Journal, Academic/Scholarly.* **Description:** Aims to cover all the latest and outstanding developments in medicinal chemistry and rational drug design for the discovery of new anti-infective agents.
Former titles (until 2011): Anti-Infective Agents in Medicinal Chemistry (Print) (1871-5214); (until 2006): Current Medicinal Chemistry. Anti-Infective Agents (1568-0126)
Related titles: Online - full text ed.: (from IngentaConnect).
Indexed: A01, A03, A08, A29, B&BAb, B19, B20, B21, BIOSIS Prev, C33, CA, ChemAb, EMBASE, ESPM, ExcerpMed, MycolAb, R10, Reac, SCOPUS, T02, VirolAbstr.
—BLDSC (1546.715600), IE, Infotrieve, Ingenta. **CCC.**
Published by: Bentham Science Publishers Ltd., PO Box 294, Bussum, 1400 AG, Netherlands. TEL 31-35-6923800, FAX 31-35-6980150, sales@bentham.org. Eds. Roberto Manfredi, Sanjay Batra. **Subscr. to:** Bentham Science Publishers Ltd., c/o Richard E Morrissy, PO Box 446, Oak Park, IL 60301. TEL 312-413-5867, FAX 312-996-7107, subscriptions@bentham.org.

615.329 NZL ISSN 1174-5924
RM265
ANTI-INFECTIVES TODAY. Text in English. 1999. m. USD 315 to individuals; USD 1,345 to institutions (effective 2008). back issues avail. **Document type:** *Newsletter, Academic/Scholarly.* **Description:** Rapid alerts service on all aspects of drug therapy and disease management of infections.
Indexed: A01, Inpharma, P34.
—CCC.
Published by: Adis International Ltd. (Subsidiary of: Wolters Kluwer N.V.), 41 Centorian Dr, Mairangi Bay, Private Bag 65901, Auckland, 1311, New Zealand. TEL 64-9-4770700, FAX 64-9-4770764, queries@adisonline.com, http://www.adisonline.info/. Ed. Suzanne Sullivan. **Americas subscr. to:** Adis International Inc., Subscriptions Dept, Ste F 10, 940 Town Center Dr, Langhorne, PA 19047. TEL 877-872-2347.

615 NLD ISSN 1871-5230
RS400 CODEN: AAAMC6
➤ **ANTI-INFLAMMATORY & ANTI-ALLERGY AGENTS IN MEDICINAL CHEMISTRY.** Variant title: Anti-Inflammatory & Anti-Allergy Agents. Text in English. 2002 (Mar.). bi-m. USD 770 to institutions (print or online ed.) (effective 2012). adv. back issues avail.; reprints avail. **Document type:** *Journal, Academic/Scholarly.* **Description:** Covers developments in medicinal chemistry and rational drug design for the discovery of new anti-inflammatory and anti-allergy agents.
Formerly (until 2006): Current Medicinal Chemistry. Anti-Inflammatory & Anti-Allergy Agents (1568-0142)
Related titles: Online - full text ed.: ISSN 1875-614X (from IngentaConnect).
Indexed: A01, A03, A08, B&BAb, B19, B21, BIOSIS Prev, C33, CA, ChemAb, EMBASE, ExcerpMed, ImmunAb, MycolAb, P30, R10, Reac, SCOPUS, T02.
—BLDSC (1547.536800), IE, Infotrieve, Ingenta. **CCC.**
Published by: Bentham Science Publishers Ltd., PO Box 294, Bussum, 1400 AG, Netherlands. TEL 31-35-6923800, FAX 31-35-6980150, sales@bentham.org. Eds. Bahar Tunctan, Domenico Capone. **Subscr. addr. in the US:** Bentham Science Publishers Ltd., c/o Richard E Morrissy, PO Box 446, Oak Park, IL 60301. TEL 312-413-5867, FAX 312-996-7107, subscriptions@bentham.org.

615.329 CHE ISSN 2079-6382
▼ ➤ **ANTIBIOTICS.** Text in English. forthcoming 2011. q. free (effective 2011). **Document type:** *Journal, Academic/Scholarly.*
Media: Online - full text.
Published by: M D P I AG, Postfach, Basel, 4005, Switzerland. TEL 41-61-6837734, FAX 41-61-3028918, http://www.mdpi.org/.

615.1 CHE ISSN 0066-4758
RM260 CODEN: ANBCB3
➤ **ANTIBIOTICS AND CHEMOTHERAPY.** Text in English. 1954. irreg., latest vol.50, 2000. price varies. reprints avail. **Document type:** *Monographic series, Academic/Scholarly.* **Description:** Provides thorough coverage of a specific problem undergoing investigation in the field of anti-infective and cytostatic chemotherapy.
Formerly (until 1971): Antibiotica et Chemotherapia (0376-0227)
Related titles: Online - full text ed.; Print ed.: ISSN 1662-2863.
Indexed: A22, CIN, ChemAb, ChemTitl, EMBASE, ExcerpMed, IndMed, P30, R10, Reac, SCOPUS.
—BLDSC (1546.980000), CASDDS, GNLM, IE, Infotrieve, Ingenta, INIST. **CCC.**
Published by: S. Karger AG, Allschwilerstr 10, Basel, 4055, Switzerland. TEL 41-61-3061111, FAX 41-61-3061234, karger@karger.ch, http://www.karger.ch. Eds. A Dalhoff, H Schoenfeld.

615.329 RUS ISSN 0235-2990
CODEN: ANKHEW
ANTIBIOTIKI I KHIMIOTERAPIYA/ANTIBIOTICS AND CHEMOTHERAPY. Text in Russian. 1956. m. USD 430 in North America (effective 2010). adv. **Document type:** *Journal, Academic/Scholarly.* **Description:** Covers research and chemical transformation of antibiotics, relation between structure and function, experimental and clinical antibiotic therapy, molecular mechanisms of action of antimicrobial antibiotics, antibiotic resistance mechanisms, antitumour, and more.
Former titles: Antibiotiki i Meditsinskaya Biotekhnologiya (0233-7525); Antibiotiki (0003-5637)
Indexed: B25, BIOSIS Prev, C33, CBTA, CIN, ChemAb, ChemTitl, DBA, EMBASE, ExcerpMed, FR, ISR, IndMed, MEDLINE, MycolAb, NPU, P30, R10, Reac, RefZh, SCOPUS.
—CASDDS, East View, GNLM, Infotrieve, INIST. **CCC.**
Published by: Gosudarstvennyi Nauchnyi Tsentr po Antibiotikam, Nagatinskaya ul, 3a, Moscow, 117105, Russian Federation. TEL 7-095-6112077, FAX 7-095-6114238, fgup_gnca@mail.ru, http://www.gntca.ru. Ed. Aleksei Egorov. **Dist. by:** East View Information Services, 10601 Wayzata Blvd, Minneapolis, MN 55305. TEL 952-252-1201, 800-477-1005, FAX 952-252-1202, info@eastview.com, http://www.eastview.com.

ANTIVIRAL CHEMISTRY AND CHEMOTHERAPY (ONLINE). *see* BIOLOGY—Biochemistry

549 DEU ISSN 1432-4091
APO-ONLINE NEWS. Text in German. 1996. q. EUR 27.10, USD 48 to institutions (effective 2010). adv. **Document type:** *Magazine, Trade.*
Indexed: A26.
—CCC.
Published by: Urban und Vogel Medien und Medizin Verlagsgesellschaft mbH (Subsidiary of: Springer Science+Business Media), Neumarkter Str 43, Munich, 81673, Germany. TEL 49-89-4372-1411, FAX 49-89-4372-1410, verlag@urban-vogel.de, http://www.urban-vogel.de. Ed. Markus Seidl. Adv. contact Peter Urban. B&W page EUR 2,600, color page EUR 4,000; trim 184 x 252. Circ: 23,500 (paid and controlled).

615.1 NOR ISSN 0809-635X
APOTEK OG LEGEMIDLER; bransjestatistik om apotekenes virksomhet og rammevilkaar. Text in Norwegian. 2005. a. charts; illus.; stat. **Document type:** *Trade.* **Description:** Contains basic facts and figures on Norwegian pharmacies, sales of medicines, regulation of pharmacies, the Norwegian reimbursement system, etc.
Related titles: Online - full text ed.
Published by: Norges Apotekerforening/Norwegian Association of Pharmacists, PO Box 5070, Majorstuen, Oslo, 0301, Norway. TEL 47-21-620200, FAX 47-22-608173, apotekerforeningen@apotek.no.

615 SWE ISSN 0349-2516
APOTEKET; tidning foer apotekens kunder. Text in Swedish. 1980. q. free. back issues avail. **Document type:** *Magazine, Consumer.*
Related titles: Audio cassette/tape ed.; Online - full text ed.
Published by: Apoteket AB, Fabrikoervaegen 4, Stockholm, 13188, Sweden. TEL 46-8-4661000, FAX 46-8-4661515. Ed. Lena Boija. Circ: 525,000.

615 AUT
DIE APOTHEKE. Text in German. bi-m. adv. **Document type:** *Magazine, Consumer.*
Published by: Oesterreichische Apotheker-Verlagsgesellschaft mbH, Spitalgasse 31, Vienna, W 1094, Austria. TEL 43-1-4023588, FAX 43-1-4085355, direktion@apoverlag.at. Ed. Monika Heinrich. Adv. contact Margit Moser. Circ: 100,000 (controlled).

615 DEU
APOTHEKE AKTUELL. Text in German. bi-m. **Document type:** *Magazine, Trade.* **Description:** Contains information and advice for pharmacists and their clients.
Published by: (Bundesverband Deutscher Apotheker e.V.), BurdaYukom Publishing GmbH (Subsidiary of: Hubert Burda Media Holding GmbH & Co. KG), Konrad-Zuse-Platz 11, Munich, 81829, Germany. TEL 49-89-306200, FAX 49-89-30620100, info@burdayukom.de, http://www.yukom.de. Circ: 10,000 (controlled).

615.5 DEU ISSN 0942-3982
APOTHEKE & MARKETING. Text in German. 1992. m. EUR 50; EUR 7 newsstand/cover (effective 2010). adv. **Document type:** *Magazine, Trade.*
Published by: Springer Gesundheits- und Pharmazieverlag GmbH (Subsidiary of: Springer Science+Business Media), Am Forsthaus Gravenbruch 5, Neu-Isenburg, 63263, Germany. TEL 49-6102-882700, FAX 49-6102-8827082, kontakt@springer-gup.de. Adv. contact Jochen Malzburg. Circ: 22,300 (paid and controlled).

APOTHEKE HEUTE; Schaufenster - Werbung - Einrichtung - Marketing. *see* ADVERTISING AND PUBLIC RELATIONS

615 DEU ISSN 0948-8588
APOTHEKEN-DEPESCHE. Text in German. 1995. 10/yr. EUR 30 (effective 2010). adv. **Document type:** *Magazine, Trade.*
Published by: Gesellschaft fuer Medizinische Information, Paul-Wassermann-Str 15, Munich, 81829, Germany. TEL 49-89-4366300, FAX 49-89-436630210, info@gfi.online.de. Ed. Monika Walter.

615 DEU
DER APOTHEKEN-FAX-BRIEF. Text in German. 9/yr. **Document type:** *Magazine, Trade.*
Published by: Sommer-Verlag GmbH, Waidplatzstr 5, Teningen, 79331, Germany. TEL 49-7663-94510, FAX 49-7663-945135, info@sommer-verlag.de, http://www.sommer-verlag.de. Circ: 22,000 (controlled).

615.19 DEU ISSN 1435-8018
APOTHEKEN JOURNAL REISE UND PHARMAZIE. Text in German. 1979. bi-m. EUR 6.50 newsstand/cover (effective 2007). adv. bk.rev. **Document type:** *Magazine, Trade.*
Formerly (until 1997): Apotheker Journal (0720-1028)
—GNLM. **CCC.**
Published by: Otto Hoffmanns Verlag GmbH, Arnulfstr 10, Munich, 80335, Germany. TEL 49-89-5458450, FAX 49-89-54584530, 49-89-54584520, info@ohv-online.de. Ed. Dr. Helmut Becker. Adv. contact Edeltraud Koller. B&W page EUR 2,510, color page EUR 4,250; trim 185 x 257. Circ: 13,000 (paid and controlled).

615.19 DEU
APOTHEKEN KURIER. Text in German. 1985. m. adv. **Document type:** *Magazine, Trade.*
Published by: Gotha Druck und Verpackung GmbH & Co. KG, Gutenbergstr 3, Wechmar, 99869, Germany. TEL 49-36256-2800, FAX 49-36256-280132, info@gothadruck.de. adv.: B&W page EUR 7,160, color page EUR 9,995; trim 210 x 280. Circ: 213,119 (controlled).

615 DEU ISSN 0724-9950
APOTHEKEN-MAGAZIN. Text in German. 1983. 10/yr. adv. **Document type:** *Magazine, Trade.*
Published by: Gebr. Storck GmbH & Co. Verlags-oHG, Duisburger Str 375, Oberhausen, 46049, Germany. TEL 49-208-8480211, FAX 49-208-8480238, kalender@storckverlag.de. Adv. contact Birgit Voelkel.

615.1 DEU ISSN 0721-8370
APOTHEKEN-PRAXIS; Zeitschrift fuer Marketing - Management - Kommunikation. Text in German. 1979. 6/yr. **Document type:** *Journal, Trade.*
Published by: Deutscher Apotheker Verlag, Postfach 101061, Stuttgart, 70009, Germany. TEL 49-711-25820, FAX 49-711-2582290, daz@deutscher-apotheker-verlag.de, http://www.deutscher-apotheker-verlag.de. Ed. Peter Ditzel.

APOTHEKEN RAETSEL MAGAZIN. *see* SPORTS AND GAMES

APOTHEKEN-RAETSEL SPEZIAL. *see* SPORTS AND GAMES

340 DEU
APOTHEKENRECHT. Text in German. 1998. bi-m. EUR 198 (effective 2009). adv. reprint service avail. from SCH. **Document type:** *Magazine, Trade.*
Formerly (until 2007): Apotheke und Recht (1434-7970)
Published by: P M I Verlag AG, Oberfeldstr 29, Frankfurt Am Main, 60439, Germany. TEL 49-69-5480000, FAX 49-69-54800066, pmiverlag@t-online.de, http://www.pmi-verlag.de. adv.: B&W page EUR 1,600, color page EUR 2,725. Circ: 550 (paid and controlled).

615 DEU ISSN 0720-549X
DER APOTHEKER-BERATER. Text in German. 1980. m. EUR 94.50 for 6 mos. (effective 2010). **Document type:** *Journal, Trade.*
Related titles: Online - full text ed.
Published by: (I W W - Institut fuer Wirtschaftspublizistik), Vogel Business Media GmbH & Co.KG, Max-Planck-Str 7-9, Wuerzburg, 97064, Germany. TEL 49-931-4180, FAX 49-931-4182750, info@vogel.de, http://www.vogel-media.de. Ed. Franziska David. **Subscr. to:** DataM-Services GmbH, Fichtestr 9, Wuerzburg 97074, Germany. TEL 49-931-417001, FAX 49-931-4170499, http://www.datam-services.de.

615.1 DEU ISSN 0066-5347
APOTHEKER - JAHRBUCH. Text in German. 1915. a. EUR 64 per issue (effective 2010). adv. index, cum.index. **Document type:** *Yearbook, Trade.* **Description:** Focuses on new pharmaceutical laws and decrees, jurisdiction, statistical data and important addresses.
—GNLM, Linda Hall.
Published by: Wissenschaftliche Verlagsgesellschaft mbH, Postfach 101061, Stuttgart, 70009, Germany. TEL 49-711-25820, FAX 49-711-2582290, service@wissenschaftliche-verlagsgesellschaft.de, http://www.wissenschaftliche-verlagsgesellschaft.de. Eds. Gert Schorn, Peter Ditzel.

615.1 DEU ISSN 0178-4862
APOTHEKER-ZEITUNG; Politik, Wirtschaft, Management, Recht. Text in German. 1985. w. adv. **Document type:** *Newspaper, Trade.*
Related titles: ◆ Supplement to: Deutsche Apotheker Zeitung. ISSN 0011-9857.
—Linda Hall. **CCC.**
Published by: Deutscher Apotheker Verlag, Postfach 101061, Stuttgart, 70009, Germany. TEL 49-711-25820, FAX 49-711-2582290, service@deutscher-apotheker-verlag.de, http://www.deutscher-apotheker-verlag.de. Eds. Dr. Klaus Brauer, Peter Ditzel. Circ: 29,530 (controlled).

615 DEU
APOTHEKERKAMMER NACHRICHTEN. Text in German. 1947. m. adv. **Document type:** *Magazine, Trade.*
Formerly: Apothekerkammer Niedersachsen. Mitteilungsblatt
Published by: Apothekerkammer Niedersachsen, An der Markuskirche 4, Hannover, 30163, Germany. TEL 49-511-390990, FAX 49-511-3909936, info@apothekerkammer-nds.de, http://www.apothekerkammer-niedersachsen.de. adv.: B&W page EUR 610, color page EUR 976. Circ: 5,900 (controlled).

615.9 USA
APPROVED BIOEQUIVALENCY CODES. Abbreviated title: A B C. Text in English. 1992. m. looseleaf. USD 255 base vol(s). (effective 2008). **Document type:** *Journal, Trade.* **Description:** Features the most current FDA bioequivalency evaluations, as well as new information on OTC drug products, orphan drug designations and patent exclusivity data.
Published by: Facts and Comparisons (Subsidiary of: Wolters Kluwer N.V.), 77 West Port Plz, Ste 450, St. Louis, MO 63146. TEL 314-216-2100, 800-223-0554, FAX 317-735-5390.

615.7 USA ISSN 1048-5996
RM301.45 .A66
APPROVED DRUG PRODUCTS WITH THERAPEUTIC EQUIVALENCE EVALUATIONS. Variant title: Orange Book. Text in English. 1979. base vol. plus m. updates. looseleaf. Index. **Document type:** *Government.* **Description:** Contains information required to identify a particular drug product. Includes N.D.A. and A.N.D.A. number for each entry.
Former titles (until 1985): Approved Prescription Drug Products with Therapeutic Equivalence Evaluations (0733-4036); (until 1980): Approved Rx Drug Products
Related titles: Online - full text ed.: 1997. free (effective 2011).
Published by: U.S. Department of Health and Human Services, Food and Drug Administration, 10903 New Hampshire Ave, Silver Spring, MD 20993. TEL 301-796-8240, 888-463-6332, druginfo@fda.hhs.gov.

615.10715 USA
APPROVED PROVIDERS OF CONTINUING PHARMACEUTICAL EDUCATION. Text in English. a. free. **Document type:** *Directory.*
Published by: American Council on Pharmaceutical Education, 20 N. Clark St., Ste. 2500, Chicago, IL 60602-5109. TEL 312-664-3575, FAX 312-664-4652. Ed. Dr. Peter H Vlasses.

615 UKR
APTEKA. Text in Ukrainian. 1995. w. **Document type:** *Newspaper, Trade.* **Description:** Carries information on availability of medicines, news of medicine and pharmaceutics, and regulatory documents.
Related titles: Online - full content ed.
Published by: Morion LLC, pr-kt M Bazhana, 10A, Kyiv, 02140, Ukraine. public@morion.kiev.ua, http://www.morion.kiev.ua.

615.12 344.041 POL
APTEKA PLUS. PRAWO I ZARZADZANIE. Text in Polish. 2003. 2 base vols. plus m. updates. PLZ 198.45 base vol(s). (effective 2011). 1800 p./no.; **Document type:** *Journal, Trade.*
Former titles (until 2008): Apteka Plus Prawo (1732-9876); (until 2004): Apteka Plus (1733-2001)
Published by: Dr. Josef Raabe Spolka Wydawnicza z o.o., ul Kurpinskiego 55a, Warsaw, 02-733, Poland. TEL 48-22-8430660, FAX 48-22-8433317, raabe@raabe.com.pl.

615 RUS
APTEKAR'. Text in Russian. 2006. m. USD 118 foreign (effective 2007). **Document type:** *Magazine, Trade.*
Published by: Izdatel'skii Dom Bionika, ul Profsoyuznaya 57, ofis 249, Moscow, Russian Federation. TEL 7-495-3342557, FAX 7-495-3342255, info@idbionika.ru, http://idbionika.ru. Circ: 20,000. **Dist. by:** East View Information Services, 10601 Wayzata Blvd, Minneapolis, MN 55305. TEL 952-252-1201, 800-477-1005, FAX 952-252-1202, info@eastview.com, http://www.eastview.com.

615.1 DEU ISSN 0365-6233
RS1 CODEN: ARPMAS
➤ **ARCHIV DER PHARMAZIE.** Text in English. 1924. m. GBP 1,048 in United Kingdom to institutions; EUR 1,600 in Europe to institutions; USD 2,053 elsewhere to institutions; GBP 1,206 combined subscription in United Kingdom to institutions (print & online eds.); EUR 1,840 combined subscription in Europe to institutions (print & online eds.); USD 2,362 combined subscription elsewhere to institutions (print & online eds.) (effective 2012). bk.rev. charts; illus. index. reprint service avail. from PSC. **Document type:** *Journal, Academic/Scholarly.* **Description:** Devoted to research and development in all fields of pharmaceutical chemistry.
Formerly (until 1972): Archiv der Pharmazie und Berichte der Deutschen Pharmazeutischen Gesellschaft (0376-0367); Which was formed by the merger of (1839-1924): Archiv der Pharmazie (0342-9385); Which incorporated (1903-1923): Vierteljahresschrift fuer Praktische Pharmazie (0372-6630); (1891-1924): Deutsche Pharmazeutische Gesellschaft. Berichte (0365-9925); Which was formerly (until 1899): Pharmaceutische Gesellschaft. Berichte (0342-9377)

P

Related titles: Microfiche ed.: (from BHP); Online - full text ed.: ISSN 1521-4184. GBP 1,048 in United Kingdom to institutions; EUR 1,600 in Europe to institutions; USD 2,053 elsewhere to institutions (effective 2012).
Indexed: A22, A29, A34, A36, A38, ASCA, B20, B21, B25, BIOSIS Prev, BP, C24, C31, C33, CABA, CCI, CIN, ChemAb, ChemTitl, CurCR, CurCont, DBA, EMBASE, ESPM, ExcerpMed, F08, F12, GH, H17, I10, I12, ISR, IndChem, IndMed, IndVet, Inpharma, MEDLINE, MOS, MSB, MycolAb, N02, N03, NPU, NSA, P30, P33, P39, R08, R10, R13, R16, RA&MP, RM&VM, Reac, RefZh, S12, SCI, SCOPUS, SoyAb, T05, VS, VirolAbstr, W07.
—BLDSC (1622.800000), CASDDS, GNLM, IE, Infotrieve, Ingenta, INIST, Linda Hall. **CCC.**
Published by: (Deutsche Pharmazeutische Gesellschaft), Wiley - V C H Verlag GmbH & Co. KGaA (Subsidiary of: John Wiley & Sons, Inc.), Postfach 101161, Weinheim, 69451, Germany. TEL 49-6201-606400, FAX 49-6201-606184, subservice@wiley-vch.de, http://www.wiley-vch.de. Ed. Holger Stark. R&P Claudia Rutz. Circ: 800. **Subscr. in the Americas to:** John Wiley & Sons, Inc., 111 River St, Hoboken, NJ 07030. TEL 201-748-6645, FAX 201-748-6088, subinfo@wiley.com; **Subscr. outside Germany, Austria & Switzerland to:** John Wiley & Sons Ltd., The Atrium, Southern Gate, Chichester, West Sussex PO19 8SQ, United Kingdom. TEL 44-1243-779777, FAX 44-1243-775878.

615.7 USA ISSN 1753-5174
RM300
➤ **ARCHIVES OF DRUG INFORMATION.** Abbreviated title: A D I. Text in English. 2007. q. free (effective 2010). back issues avail.; reprint service avail. from PSC. **Document type:** *Journal, Academic/Scholarly.* **Description:** Dedicated to publishing the results of drug trials and clinical studies and making them easily accessible to drug development scientists and the public.
Media: Online - full text.
Indexed: A22, B21, E01, EMBASE, ESPM, ExcerpMed, H&SSA, Inpharma, P30, SCOPUS.
—CCC.
Published by: Wiley-Blackwell Publishing, Inc. (Subsidiary of: Wiley-Blackwell Publishing Ltd.), 111 River St, Hoboken, NJ 07030. TEL 201-748-6000, FAX 201-748-6088, info@wiley.com, http://www.wiley.com/. Ed. C Michael Stein.

615 KOR ISSN 0253-6269
RM1 CODEN: APHRDQ
➤ **ARCHIVES OF PHARMACAL RESEARCH.** Text in English. 1978. m. EUR 1,313, USD 1,758 combined subscription to institutions (print & online eds.) (effective 2012). adv. back issues avail.; reprint service avail. from PSC. **Document type:** *Journal, Academic/Scholarly.* **Description:** Publishes original research reports that aim to develop new drugs in the fields of medicinal chemistry and pharmacology/ pharmacy.
Related titles: Online - full text ed.: ISSN 1976-3786.
Indexed: A22, A26, A34, A35, A36, A37, ASCA, AgBio, AgrForAb, B&BAb, B21, B23, B25, B27, BIOSIS Prev, BP, BioEngAb, C25, C30, C33, CABA, CIN, ChemAb, ChemTitl, CurCont, D01, DBA, E01, E08, E12, EMBASE, ExcerpMed, F08, F11, F12, G11, GH, H16, H17, I12, IndMed, IndVet, Inpharma, M&PBA, MEDLINE, MycolAb, N02, N03, N04, N05, O01, OR, P30, P32, P33, P35, P39, P40, PGegResA, PGrRegA, PHN&I, R07, R08, R10, R13, RA&MP, RM&VM, Reac, S09, S12, S13, S16, S17, SCI, SCOPUS, SoyAb, T05, TAR, VS, W07, W10.
—BLDSC (1638.975000), CASDDS, GNLM, IE, Infotrieve, Ingenta, INIST. **CCC.**
Published by: Pharmaceutical Society of Korea, 1489-3 Suhcho-3-Dong, Suhcho-Ku, Seoul, 137-073, Korea, S. TEL 86-2-5833257, FAX 86-2-5211781, pskor@korea.com, http://www.psk.or.kr. Ed. Kyu-Won Kim. Circ: 1,500. **Co-publisher:** Springer Netherlands.

615 GBR ISSN 2045-080X
▼ ➤ **ARCHIVES OF PHARMACY PRACTICE.** Text in English. 2010 (Oct.). s-a. free (effective 2011). back issues avail. **Document type:** *Journal, Academic/Scholarly.*
Media: Online - full text.
Indexed: A01, CABA, E12, F08, GH, H12, H16, I05, N02, N03, P33, R08, T05.
Address: c/o School of Health & Related Research, University of Sheffield, Regent Court, 30 Regent St., Sheffield, S1 4DA, United Kingdom. editorampp@gmail.com. Ed. Tahir Mehmood Khan.

615.9 SRB ISSN 0354-3854
➤ **ARCHIVES OF TOXICOLOGY, KINETICS AND XENOBIOTIC METABOLISM**; official journal of the Toxicology Section of the Serbian Medical Society. Text in English; Summaries in English, Serbian. 1993. q. bk.rev.; software rev. back issues avail. **Document type:** *Journal, Academic/Scholarly.* **Description:** Devoted to the evaluation of data, methods and opinions in the areas of toxicology, pharmacology, clinical pharmacology and xenobiotic metabolism.
Related titles: E-mail ed.
—BLDSC (1643.512000).
Published by: Srpsko Lekarsko Drustvo, Toksikoloska Sekcija/Serbian Medical Society, Toxicology Section, c/o Dr Zoran Segrt, Centr za Kontrolu Trovanja VMA, Crnotravska 17, Belgrade, 11000. sld@bvcom.net, http://www.sld.org.yu. Ed. Bogdan Boskovic. R&P, Adv. contact Matej Maksimovic TEL 381-11-543690. Circ: 200.

615.1 SRB ISSN 0004-1963
CODEN: ARFMAC
ARHIV ZA FARMACIJU. Text in Serbo-Croatian; Summaries in English, French, German, Russian. 1951. 6/yr. CSD 1,200 domestic (effective 2007). adv. bk.rev. abstr.; bibl.; charts; illus. index. **Document type:** *Journal, Academic/Scholarly.*
Related titles: Online - full text ed.: 1951.
Indexed: CIN, ChemAb, ChemTitl, EMBASE, P30, SCOPUS.
—BLDSC (1665.500000), CASDDS.
Published by: Farmaceutsko Drustvo Srbije/Serbian Pharmaceutical Society, Bulevar Vojvode Misica 25, PO Box 664, Belgrade, 11000. TEL 381-11-2648385, FAX 381-11-2648386, fds@farmacija.org. Ed. Dubravka Urosev.

615.1 USA ISSN 1949-0941
RS100.35.A6
ARIZONA JOURNAL OF PHARMACY. Text in English. 1921. q. USD 40 to non-members; free to members (effective 2009). illus. 36 p./no.; back issues avail. **Document type:** *Journal, Trade.* **Description:** Covers issues relevant to pharmacists and others working in that field. Includes new products, continuing education, alternative therapies, and patient care.
Former titles (until 2009): Arizona Pharmacist; New Arizona Pharmacist; Arizona Pharmacist (0004-1602)
Related titles: Supplement(s): Pharmacy Post (Tempe).
Published by: Arizona Pharmaceutical Association, 1845 E Southern Ave, Tempe, AZ 85282. TEL 480-838-3385, FAX 480-838-3557, azpa@azpharmacy.org.

615.1 ESP ISSN 0004-2927
CODEN: APHRAN
ARS PHARMACEUTICA. Text in Spanish; Summaries in English. 1960. 4/yr. EUR 60 to individuals; EUR 120 to institutions (effective 2010). adv. bk.rev. bibl.; charts; illus. index. back issues avail. **Document type:** *Journal, Academic/Scholarly.*
Related titles: Online - full text ed.
Indexed: B21, CIN, ChemAb, ChemTitl, EMBASE, ExcerpMed, FR, IBR, IBZ, IECT, IME, R10, Reac, SCOPUS, VirolAbstr.
—BLDSC (1697.700000), CASDDS, GNLM, INIST. **CCC.**
Published by: (Universidad de Granada, Facultad de Farmacia), Universidad de Granada, Editorial, Antiguo Colegio Maximo, Campus de Cartuja, Granada, 18071, Spain. TEL 34-958-246220, FAX 34-958-243931, comunicacion@editorialugr.com, http://www.editorialugr.com. Ed. Jesus Cabo Torres. Circ: 1,000.

ARTERE. *see* HEALTH FACILITIES AND ADMINISTRATION

615 DEU ISSN 0066-8192
ARZNEI-TELEGRAMM. Text in German. 1970. m. EUR 48 to individuals; EUR 96 to institutions; EUR 33 to students (effective 2008). bk.rev. **Document type:** *Journal, Academic/Scholarly.*
Related titles: Online - full text ed.
Indexed: A22.
—GNLM, IE, Infotrieve.
Published by: Arzneimittel Information Berlin GmbH (A.T.I.), Bergstr 38A, Berlin, 12169, Germany. TEL 49-30-79490220, FAX 49-30-79490218, vertrieb@arznei-telegramm.de. Ed. Wolfgang Becker-Brueser. Circ: 29,000.

615.1 DEU ISSN 0004-4172
RM301.25 CODEN: ARZNAD
➤ **ARZNEIMITTEL-FORSCHUNG/DRUG RESEARCH.** Text in English, German. 1951. m. EUR 394 combined subscription (print & online eds.); EUR 38 newsstand/cover (effective 2011). adv. bk.rev. charts; illus.; tr.lit. index. reprint service avail. from IRC. **Document type:** *Journal, Academic/Scholarly.* **Description:** Presents the results of research in novel drug molecules and the evaluation of new drugs in development.
Related titles: Online - full text ed.: ISSN 1616-7066.
Indexed: A22, A34, A35, A36, A38, ASCA, AgBio, AgrForAb, ApicAb, B&BAb, B19, B21, B23, B25, BIOBASE, BIOSIS Prev, BP, C24, C31, C33, CA, CABA, CBTA, CEABA, CIS, ChemAb, CurCR, CurCont, D01, DBA, E12, EMBASE, ESPM, ExcerpMed, F08, F11, F12, GH, H16, H17, I10, I12, IABS, INI, ISR, IndChem, IndMed, Inpharma, MEDLINE, MycolAb, N02, N03, N04, OR, P30, P32, P33, P35, P39, P40, R08, R10, R12, R13, R16, RA&MP, RM&VM, Reac, RefZh, S02, S03, S12, SCI, SCOPUS, SoyAb, T02, T05, ToxAb, VS, W07, W10.
—BLDSC (1738.000000), CASDDS, GNLM, IE, Infotrieve, Ingenta, INIST, Linda Hall. **CCC.**
Published by: Editio Cantor Verlag, Baendelstockweg 20, Aulendorf, 88326, Germany. TEL 49-7525-9400, FAX 49-7525-940180, info@ecv.de. Eds. Hans G Classen, V Schramm. Adv. contact Judith Scheller. B&W page EUR 850, color page EUR 1,750; trim 216 x 303. Circ: 1,178 (paid).

615.19 DEU ISSN 0933-1859
ARZNEIMITTEL, REZEPTPRUEFUNG, BERATUNG UND REGRESS. Text in German. 1978. 2 base vols. plus updates 6/yr. looseleaf. EUR 96 base vol(s).; EUR 37.60 updates per issue (effective 2009). **Document type:** *Monographic series, Trade.*
Published by: Erich Schmidt Verlag GmbH & Co. (Berlin), Genthiner Str 30 G, Berlin, 10785, Germany. TEL 49-30-2500850, FAX 49-30-250085305, vertrieb@esvmedien.de, http://www.erich-schmidt-verlag.de.

615.19 DEU ISSN 1860-5338
ARZNEIMITTEL UND RECHT; Zeitschrift fuer Arzneimittelrecht und Arzneimittelpolitik. Text in German. 2005. bi-m. EUR 239; EUR 42 newsstand/cover (effective 2012). adv. **Document type:** *Magazine, Trade.*
Published by: Wissenschaftliche Verlagsgesellschaft mbH, Postfach 101061, Stuttgart, 70009, Germany. TEL 49-711-25820, FAX 49-711-2582290, service@wissenschaftliche-verlagsgesellschaft.de, http://www.wissenschaftliche-verlagsgesellschaft.de. Eds. Peter Wigge, Ulrich Lau. Circ: 1,000 (controlled).

615.19 DEU ISSN 0935-2767
ARZNEIMITTEL ZEITUNG. Text in German. 1988. fortn. EUR 50 (effective 2008). adv. bk.rev. **Document type:** *Newspaper, Trade.* **Description:** Information for employers in the pharmaceutical industry.
Related titles: Online - full text ed.
—IE, Infotrieve.
Published by: Aerzte Zeitung Verlagsgesellschaft mbH (Subsidiary of: Springer Science+Business Media), Am Forsthaus Gravenbruch 5, Neu-Isenburg, 63263, Germany. TEL 49-6102-506157, FAX 49-6102-506123. Ed. Dieter Eschenbach. Pub. Gerald Kosaris. Adv. contact Ute Krille. B&W page EUR 4,750, color page EUR 5,650; trim 291 x 408. Circ: 3,313 (paid and controlled).

615 DEU ISSN 1611-2733
DER ARZNEIMITTELBRIEF; unabhaengiges Informationsblatt fuer den Arzt. Text in German. 1967. m. EUR 48 to individuals; EUR 140 to institutions; EUR 30 to students (effective 2010). **Document type:** *Magazine, Academic/Scholarly.*
Related titles: Online - full text ed.
Published by: Westkreuz Verlag GmbH Berlin-Bonn, Potsdamerstr 17, Berlin, 12205, Germany. TEL 49-30-84314361, FAX 49-30-84314362, verlag@westkreuz.de, http://www.westkreuz.de. Eds. D von Herrath, W Thimme.

615.19 DEU ISSN 0723-6913
CODEN: TEPAEC
➤ **ARZNEIMITTELTHERAPIE**; Unabhaengige Informationen zur Pharmakotherapie. Abbreviated title: A M T. Text in German. 1983. m. EUR 78; EUR 51 to students; EUR 11 newsstand/cover (effective 2012). adv. bk.rev. **Document type:** *Journal, Academic/Scholarly.*
Indexed: A22, ChemAb, EMBASE, ExcerpMed, IBR, IBZ, RefZh, SCOPUS.
—BLDSC (1738.120000), GNLM, IE, Infotrieve, Ingenta. **CCC.**
Published by: Wissenschaftliche Verlagsgesellschaft mbH, Postfach 101061, Stuttgart, 70009, Germany. TEL 49-711-25820, FAX 49-711-2582290, service@wissenschaftliche-verlagsgesellschaft.de, http://www.wissenschaftliche-verlagsgesellschaft.de. Ed. Heike Oberpichler-Schwenk. Adv. contact Kornelia Wind TEL 49-711-2582245. Circ: 17,143 (paid and controlled).

615.19 SGP ISSN 0217-9687
CODEN: APJPEV
➤ **ASIA PACIFIC JOURNAL OF PHARMACOLOGY.** Text in English. 1986. q. **Document type:** *Journal, Academic/Scholarly.* **Description:** Covers all aspects of experimental and clinical research on synthetic and natural drugs.
Indexed: A20, A22, ASCA, CIN, ChemAb, ChemTitl, Inpharma, MycolAb, PsycholAb, SCOPUS.
—CASDDS, GNLM, IE, Ingenta, INIST.
Published by: N U S Press Pte Ltd, National University of Singapore, 3 Arts Link, Singapore, 117569, Singapore. TEL 65-67761148, FAX 65-67740652, orders.nuspress@nus.edu.sg, http://www.nus.edu.sg/sup/cij. Ed. K Hashimoto.

615 IND ISSN 2231-2218
▼ ➤ **ASIAN JOURNAL OF PHARMACEUTICAL AND BIOLOGICAL RESEARCH.** Abbreviated title: A J P B R. Text and summaries in English. 2011 (Mar.). q. free (effective 2011). adv. bk.rev. abstr. Index. back issues avail.; reprints avail. **Document type:** *Journal, Academic/Scholarly.* **Description:** Publishes articles in the field of pharmaceutical, biological, biochemical and health related research.
Media: Online - full text. **Related titles:** E-mail ed.
Published by: Young Pharmaceutical and Biological Scientist Group, 8/569, Peachi Amman Nagar, Kalpathy, Palakkad, Kerala 679 325, India. TEL 91-9656111659, karthikeyanpgt@gmail.com, http://www.scopemed.org/journal.php?jid=13. Ed., Pub., R&P, Adv. contact Karthikeyan M.

615 IND ISSN 0974-2441
RS122
ASIAN JOURNAL OF PHARMACEUTICAL AND CLINICAL RESEARCH. Text in English. 2008. q. INR 500 domestic to individuals; USD 30 foreign to individuals; INR 1,000 domestic to institutions; USD 50 foreign to institutions (effective 2011). back issues avail. **Document type:** *Journal, Trade.* **Description:** Aims to cover all the fields of research which have any correlation and impact on the pharmaceutical science.
Related titles: Online - full text ed.: free (effective 2011).
Indexed: A01, EMBASE, SCOPUS, T02.
Address: c/o Shubham Hospital, Behind Dashpur Kunj, Mandsaur, 458 001, India. http://www.ajpcr.com. Ed. Dr. Sharad Jain.

615 IND ISSN 2231-2331
▼ ➤ **ASIAN JOURNAL OF PHARMACEUTICAL AND HEALTH SCIENCES.** Abbreviated title: A J P H S. Text and summaries in English. 2011 (Mar.). q. INR 1,500 domestic (effective 2011). reprints avail. **Document type:** *Journal, Academic/Scholarly.* **Description:** Aims to contribute, propagate and disseminate innovative ideas in the field of pharmaceutical and biological research.
Related titles: Online - full text ed.: ISSN 2231-234X. free (effective 2011).
Published by: Pharmaceutical and Biological Society, No.47, Ayodhya Nagar, Pallippuram Post, Palakkad, Kerala 678 006, India. TEL 91-9447005783, editorajphs@gmail.com. Ed., Pub. Dr. Sankar C.

615.405 HKG ISSN 1818-0876
➤ **ASIAN JOURNAL OF PHARMACEUTICAL SCIENCES.** Text in English. 2006. bi-m. HKD 360; HKD 60 newsstand/cover (effective 2009). **Document type:** *Journal, Academic/Scholarly.* **Description:** Devoted to the dissemination of scientific knowledge relating to all aspects of pharmaceutics.
Indexed: SCOPUS.
Published by: Hong Kong Asiamed Publish House, 5/F, Chinamed Century Tower, 178 Gloucester Rd, Wanchai, Hong Kong. TEL 852-3427-8708, FAX 852-3428-5636, asiamed@chinamed.com.hk, http://www.chinamed.com.hk. Eds. Fude Cui, Paul Heng, Yoshiaki Kawashima.

615 IND ISSN 0973-8398
➤ **ASIAN JOURNAL OF PHARMACEUTICS.** Text in English. 2006. q. INR 1,000 domestic to individuals; USD 100 foreign to individuals; INR 2,000 domestic to institutions; USD 200 foreign to institutions; INR 1,200 combined subscription domestic to individuals; USD 120 combined subscription foreign to individuals; INR 2,400 combined subscription domestic to institutions; USD 240 combined subscription foreign to institutions (effective 2011). **Document type:** *Journal, Academic/Scholarly.*
Related titles: Online - full text ed.: ISSN 1998-409X. INR 800 domestic to individuals; USD 80 foreign to individuals; INR 1,600 domestic to institutions; USD 160 foreign to institutions (effective 2011).
Indexed: A01, A26, CA, E08, EMBASE, ExcerpMed, H12, I05, P10, P48, P53, P54, PQC, S09, SCOPUS, T02.
—CCC.
Published by: (B.R. Nahata Smriti Sansthan), Medknow Publications and Media Pvt. Ltd., B-9, Kanara Business Ctr, Off Link Rd, Ghatkopar (E), Mumbai, Maharastra 400 075, India. TEL 91-22-66491816, FAX 91-22-66491817, http://www.medknow.com.

615 HKG
ASIAN JOURNAL OF PHARMACODYNAMICS AND PHARMACOKINETICS. Text in English. 2000. q. **Document type:** *Journal, Academic/Scholarly.*
Formerly (until 2007): Asian Journal of Drug Metabolism and Pharmacokinetics (1608-2281)
—BLDSC (1742.482500).
Published by: Hong Kong Medical Publisher, 24/F Yuen Long Trading Center, 99-109, Castle Peak Rd, Hong Kong, Hong Kong. TEL 852-24750383, FAX 852-24751168. Ed. Chang-Xiao Liu.

615.14 HKG
ASIAN JOURNAL OF SOCIAL PHARMACY. Text in English. 2006. 4/yr. **Document type:** *Journal, Academic/Scholarly.*
Published by: Hong Kong Asiamed Publish House, 5/F, Chinamed Century Tower, 178 Gloucester Rd, Wanchai, Hong Kong. TEL 852-3427-8708, FAX 852-3428-5636, asiamed@chinamed.com.hk.

615.1 URY ISSN 0797-9150
ASOCIACION DE QUIMICA Y FARMACIA DEL URUGUAY. REVISTA. Text in Spanish. 1991. 3/yr.
Indexed: INIS AtomInd.
Published by: Asociacion de Quimica y Farmacia del Uruguay/ Association of Chemistry and Pharmacy of Uruguay, Ejido 1589, Montevideo, 11100, Uruguay. info@aqfu.org.uy, http://www.aqfu.org.uy/.

615 USA ISSN 1540-658X
RM301.25 CODEN: ADDTAR
➤ **ASSAY AND DRUG DEVELOPMENT TECHNOLOGIES.** Text in English. 2002 (Fall). bi-m. USD 1,147 domestic to institutions; USD 1,390 foreign to institutions; USD 1,317 combined subscription domestic to institutions (print & online eds.); USD 1,622 combined subscription foreign to institutions (print & online eds.) (effective 2012). adv. reprint service avail. from PSC. **Document type:** *Journal, Academic/Scholarly.* **Description:** Provides early-stage screening techniques and tools that enable to optimize and identify novel leads and targets for new drug development.
Related titles: Online - full text ed.: ISSN 1557-8127. USD 1,149 to institutions (effective 2012).
Indexed: A22, A26, B&BAb, B19, B21, B25, B27, BIOSIS Prev, BioEngAb, C33, CA, ChemAb, E01, E07, EMBASE, ExcerpMed, H12, I05, M&PBA, MEDLINE, MycolAb, P30, R10, Reac, SCI, SCOPUS, T02, W07.
—BLDSC (1746.404500), IE, Ingenta. **CCC.**
Published by: Mary Ann Liebert, Inc. Publishers, 140 Huguenot St, 3rd Fl, New Rochelle, NY 10801. TEL 914-740-2100, FAX 914-740-2101, 800-654-3237, info@liebertpub.com. Ed. Jim Inglese. Adv. contact Harriet I Matysko TEL 914-740-2182.

615 IRL
THE ASSISTANT. Text in English. q. adv. **Document type:** *Bulletin, Trade.* **Description:** Contains information aimed at the counter and pharmacy assistant, including topics such as cosmetics, over-the-counter medicines, everyday ailments, alternative health and customer care.
Published by: Eireann Healthcare Publications, 25-26 Windsor Pl., Dublin, 2, Ireland. TEL 353-1-4753300, FAX 353-1-4753311, mhenderson@eireannpublications.ie. Ed. Tim Ilsley. Pub. Graham Cooke. adv.: B&W page EUR 1,555, color page EUR 1,778; trim 210 x 297. Circ: 2,500 (controlled).

615.1 CAN ISSN 0066-9555
ASSOCIATION OF FACULTIES OF PHARMACY OF CANADA. PROCEEDINGS. Text in English. 1970. a. membership. **Document type:** *Proceedings.*
Formerly (until vol.26, 1969): Canadian Conference of Pharmaceutical Faculties. Proceedings
Published by: Association of Faculties of Pharmacy, c/o J. Blackburn, 2609 Eastview, Saskatoon, SK S7J 3G7, Canada. FAX 604-822-4451. Ed. J Blackburn. Circ: 200.

615 GBR ISSN 1460-034X
THE ASSOCIATION OF THE BRITISH PHARMACEUTICAL INDUSTRY. ANNUAL REVIEW. Text in English. 19??. a. free (effective 2009).
Former titles (until 198?): The Association of the British Pharmaceutical Industry. Annual Report (0571-6179); (until 1970): The Association of the British Pharmaceutical Industry. Annual Report and Year Book (0571-673X)
Related titles: Online - full text ed.
Published by: The Association of the British Pharmaceutical Industry, 12 Whitehall, London, SW1A 2DY, United Kingdom. TEL 44-870-8904333, FAX 44-20-77471414, abpi@abpi.org.uk, http://www.apbi.org.uk.

615 ESP ISSN 1139-7357
CODEN: FACLE2
ATENCION FARMACEUTICA; European journal of clinical pharmacy/ revista europea de farmacia clinica. Text in English, Spanish. 1983. bi-m. EUR 77.39 in Europe; EUR 281.50 elsewhere (effective 2010). back issues avail. **Document type:** *Journal, Academic/Scholarly.*
Formerly (until 1999): Farmacia Clinica (0212-6583)
Indexed: A22, B25, BIOSIS Prev, CIN, ChemAb, ChemTitl, EMBASE, ExcerpMed, I12, IECT, Inpharma, MycolAb, P30, R10, Reac, SCI, SCOPUS, W07.
—BLDSC (1765.858350), CASDDS, GNLM, IE, Ingenta. **CCC.**
Published by: Rasgo Editorial S.A., Llanca, 16, Ent. 4a, Barcelona, 08015, Spain. TEL 34-93-2239982, FAX 34-93-2117561, revista@farmclin.com. Ed. Manuela Velazquez.

615 340 DEU ISSN 1863-6969
AUGSBURGER SCHRIFTEN ZUM ARZNEIMITTEL- UND MEDIZINPRODUKTERECHT. Text in German. 2006. irreg., latest vol.10, 2010. price varies. **Document type:** *Monographic series, Academic/Scholarly.*
Published by: Shaker Verlag GmbH, Kaiserstr 100, Herzogenrath, 52134, Germany. TEL 49-2407-95960, FAX 49-2407-95969, info@shaker.de. Ed. Dr. Ulrich Gassner.

615.1 ESP ISSN 1697-543X
AULA DE LA FARMACIA. Text in Spanish. 2004. m. EUR 50 domestic to individuals; EUR 75 domestic to institutions; EUR 40 domestic to qualified personnel; EUR 110 in the European Union; EUR 136 elsewhere. back issues avail. **Document type:** *Magazine, Trade.*
Formerly (until 2004): Aula Farmaceutica (1697-2287)
Related titles: Online - full text ed.; Supplement(s): Aula de la Farmacia. Suplemento. ISSN 1699-7638. 2004.
Published by: Grupo Saned, Capitan Haya 60, 1o, Madrid, 28028, Spain. TEL 34-91-7499500, FAX 34-91-7499501, saned@medynet.com, http://www.gruposaned.com. Ed. Alejandro Eguilleor. Circ: 20,000.

615 AUS ISSN 0812-3837
RM302.5
AUSTRALIAN ADVERSE DRUG REACTIONS BULLETIN. Text in English. 1982. bi-m. free (effective 2008). Index. back issues avail. **Document type:** *Bulletin, Government.*
Related titles: Online - full text ed.: ISSN 1325-8540.
Indexed: IDIS, Inpharma, P35.
Published by: Australian Government. Department of Health and Ageing. Therapeutic Goods Administration, PO Box 100, Woden, ACT 2606, Australia. TEL 61-2-62328610, FAX 61-2-62328605, info@health.gov.au.

615.1 AUS ISSN 0311-8002
THE AUSTRALIAN JOURNAL OF PHARMACY. Text in English. 1886. m. AUD 93.50 domestic to non-members; AUD 140 foreign to non-members; AUD 84 to members; AUD 38.50 to students (effective 2008). adv. bk.rev. illus.; mkt. Index. back issues avail. **Document type:** *Magazine, Trade.* **Description:** Aims to support both the professional and business interests of Australian community pharmacists by publishing valuable information and education resources every month.
Former titles (until 1971): Australasian Journal of Pharmacy (0004-8399); The Chemist & Druggist and Pharmacist of Australasia
Related titles: Online - full text ed.: AUD 44 domestic; AUD 40 foreign (effective 2008); Supplement(s): Australian Journal of Pharmaceutical Sciences. ISSN 0310-7116. 1921.
Indexed: A11, A22, ASI, ChemAb, EMBASE, ExcerpMed, I12, Inpharma, P30, SCOPUS.
—BLDSC (1810.850000), GNLM, IE, Ingenta, INIST, Linda Hall. **CCC.**
Published by: Australian Pharmaceutical Publishing Company Pty Ltd., Level 5, 8 Thomas St, Chatswood, NSW 2067, Australia. TEL 61-2-81179500, FAX 61-2-81179511. Ed. Matthew Eton TEL 61-2-81179542. Adv. contact Sarah Stanbridge TEL 61-2-81179520. page AUD 4,580; trim 235 x 275. Circ: 16,500.

615 AUS ISSN 0728-4632
AUSTRALIAN PHARMACIST. Text in English. 1982. m. AUD 170 domestic to non-members; AUD 230 foreign to non-members; free to members (effective 2008). adv. bk.rev. Supplement avail.; back issues avail. **Document type:** *Journal, Trade.* **Description:** Contains continuing education material, news and information, research papers, therapeutic management reviews.
Indexed: R10, Reac, SD.
—BLDSC (1817.685000), IE, Ingenta. **CCC.**
Published by: Pharmaceutical Society of Australia, PO Box 21, Curtin, ACT 2605, Australia. TEL 61-2-62884777, FAX 61-2-62852869, psa.nat@psa.org.au, http://www.psa.org.au. Ed., R&P Julie Wissmann. Adv. contact Jonathan Tremain. page AUD 4,320; trim 210 x 275. Circ: 10,029.

AUSTRALIAN PHYSIOLOGICAL SOCIETY. PROCEEDINGS. *see* BIOLOGY—Physiology

615 AUS ISSN 0312-8008
RS1 CODEN: AUPRFZ
➤ **AUSTRALIAN PRESCRIBER.** Text in English. 1975. bi-m. free to qualified personnel (effective 2009). adv. bk.rev.; Website rev. abstr.; illus. Index. back issues avail. **Document type:** *Journal, Academic/ Scholarly.* **Description:** Provides an independent review of drugs and therapeutics.
Formerly (until 1975): Prescriber's Journal (0085-5103)
Related titles: Online - full text ed.: free (effective 2011).
Indexed: A01, A22, AusPAIS, CA, EMBASE, ExcerpMed, IDIS, Inpharma, P35, R10, Reac, SCI, SCOPUS, T02, W07.
—BLDSC (1818.260000), GNLM, IE, Ingenta.
Published by: National Prescribing Service Ltd., Ste 3, 2 Phipps Close, Deakin, ACT 2600, Australia. TEL 61-2-62023100, FAX 61-2-92117578, info@nps.org.au, http://www.nps.org.au. Ed. Dr. John S Dowden. Circ: 60,000 (controlled).

615.7 AUS ISSN 1321-9758
RS153
AUSTRALIAN PRESCRIPTION PRODUCTS GUIDE. Variant title: Australian Prescription Products Guide. Text in English. 1959. a. **Document type:** *Monographic series, Trade.* **Description:** Provides reference material such as Australian approved food additive numbers, medicines in pregnancy, patient support organizations and a pharmacological and therapeutic index.
Former titles (until 1993): Prescription Products Guide (0818-4445); (until 1986): Prescription Proprietaries Guide (0729-2333)
Related titles: CD-ROM ed.: E A P P Guide. AUD 319 (effective 2008); Online - full text ed.: A P P Guide. AUD 200 (effective 2008).
—CCC.
Published by: C M P Medica Australia Pty Ltd (Subsidiary of: United Business Media Limited), Level 2, 1 Chandos St, St Leonards, NSW 2065, Australia. TEL 61-2-99027700, FAX 61-2-99027701, http://www.au.cmpmedica.com/. Circ: 5,000.

615 GBR ISSN 1474-8665
RM323 CODEN: AAPUC3
➤ **AUTONOMIC & AUTACOID PHARMACOLOGY.** Text in English. 1980. q. GBP 791 in United Kingdom to institutions; EUR 1,004 in Europe to institutions; USD 1,461 in the Americas to institutions; USD 1,704 elsewhere to institutions; GBP 910 combined subscription in United Kingdom to institutions (print & online eds.); EUR 1,155 combined subscription in Europe to institutions (print & online eds.); USD 1,681 combined subscription in the Americas to institutions (print & online eds.); USD 1,960 combined subscription elsewhere to institutions (print & online eds.) (effective 2011). adv. abstr.; bibl.; illus. index. back issues avail.; reprint service avail. from PSC. **Document type:** *Journal, Academic/Scholarly.* **Description:** Contains the effects of drugs acting on the autonomic nervous system and its effector organs in humans.
Formerly (until 2002): Journal of Autonomic Pharmacology (Print) (0144-1795)
Related titles: Microform ed.: (from PQC); ◆ Online - full text ed.: Autonomic & Autacoid Pharmacology Online. ISSN 1474-8673.
Indexed: A01, A02, A03, A08, A22, A26, A29, ASCA, ApicAb, B20, B21, B25, BIOBASE, BIOSIS Prev, C11, C33, CA, CIN, ChemAb, ChemTitl, DBA, E01, EMBASE, ESPM, ExcerpMed, H04, H12, I10, IABS, ISR, IndMed, Inpharma, MEDLINE, MycolAb, NSA, P30, R10, Reac, S01, SCOPUS, T02, VirolAbstr.
—BLDSC (1835.051000), CASDDS, GNLM, IE, Ingenta, INIST. **CCC.**
Published by: Wiley-Blackwell Publishing Ltd. (Subsidiary of: John Wiley & Sons, Inc.), 9600 Garsington Rd, Oxford, OX4 2DQ, United Kingdom. TEL 44-1865-776868, FAX 44-1865-714591, customerservices@blackwellpublishing.com. Eds. Kenneth J Broadley TEL 44-2920-874000 ext 5832, William R Ford. Circ: 200.

615 GBR ISSN 1474-8673
➤ **AUTONOMIC & AUTACOID PHARMACOLOGY ONLINE.** Text in English. 1999. q. GBP 791 in United Kingdom to institutions; EUR 1,004 in Europe to institutions; USD 1,461 in the Americas to institutions; USD 1,704 elsewhere to institutions; GBP 910 combined subscription in United Kingdom to institutions (print & online eds.); EUR 1,155 combined subscription in Europe to institutions (print & online eds.); USD 1,681 combined subscription in the Americas to institutions (print & online eds.); USD 1,960 combined subscription elsewhere to institutions (print & online eds.); GBP 839 in United Kingdom to institutions; EUR 1,065 in Europe to institutions; USD 1,549 in the Americas to institutions; USD 1,807 elsewhere to institutions (effective 2012). adv. back issues avail.; reprints avail. **Document type:** *Journal, Academic/Scholarly.* **Description:** Contains the effects of drugs acting on the autonomic nervous system and its effector organs in humans.
Formerly (until 2002): Journal of Autonomic Pharmacology (Online) (1365-2680)
Media: Online - full text (from IngentaConnect). **Related titles:** Microform ed.: (from PQC); ◆ Print ed.: Autonomic & Autacoid Pharmacology. ISSN 1474-8665.
—CCC.
Published by: Wiley-Blackwell Publishing Ltd. (Subsidiary of: John Wiley & Sons, Inc.), 9600 Garsington Rd, Oxford, OX4 2DQ, United Kingdom. TEL 44-1865-776868, FAX 44-1865-714591, customerservices@blackwellpublishing.com, http://www.wiley.com/. Eds. Kenneth J Broadley TEL 44-2920-874000 ext 5832, William R Ford.

615.19 EGY ISSN 1110-1644
AL AZHAR JOURNAL OF PHARMACEUTICAL SCIENCES. Text in English. 1982. s-a. **Document type:** *Journal, Academic/Scholarly.*
—BLDSC (0786.277000).
Published by: Al-Azhar University, Faculty of Pharmacy, Al-Mukhayam El-Daem Str., 6th District, Nassr City, Cairo, Egypt. TEL 20-2-2632252, FAX 20-2-2611404. Ed. Dr. Muhammed Hussain El-Zahabi.

B B E CHEF-TELEGRAMM. APOTHEKEN SPEZIAL. *see* BUSINESS AND ECONOMICS—Management

615.9 CAN ISSN 1203-214X
B C PHARMACY. Text in English. 1987. q. adv.
Formerly (until 1992): B C Pharmacist (0843-168X)
Published by: Canada Wide Media Ltd., 4180 Lougheed Hwy, 4th Fl, Burnaby, BC V5C 6A7, Canada. TEL 604-299-7311, FAX 604-299-9188. Pub. Peter Legge. Circ: 2,703.

615.2 ESP ISSN 1138-1043
B I T - BOLETIN DE INFORMACION FARMACOTERAPEUTICA DE NAVARRA. Text in Spanish. 1992. q. **Document type:** *Journal, Trade.*
Published by: Servicio Navarro de Salud, Plaza de la Paz, s/n, Pamplona, 31002, Spain. TEL 34-948-848429047, FAX 34-948-848429010, farmacia.atprimaria@cfnavarra.es, http://www.navarra.es/home_es/Gobierno+de+Navarra/Organigrama/Los+departamentos/Salud/.

615.19 BRA ISSN 1984-8250
RS1 CODEN: RBCFFM
➤ **B J P S BRAZILIAN JOURNAL OF PHARMACEUTICAL SCIENCES.** Abbreviated title: R B C F. Text in Portuguese. 1963. q. bk.rev. back issues avail. **Document type:** *Journal, Academic/Scholarly.*
Former titles (until 2009): Revista Brasileira de Ciencias Farmaceuticas (1516-9332); (until 1999): Universidade de Sao Paulo. Revista de Farmacia e Bioquimica (0370-4726); (until 1970): Universidade de Sao Paulo. Faculdade de Farmacia e Bioquimica. Revista (0014-6676); Which superseded in part (1939-1963): Universidade de Sao Paulo. Faculdade de Farmacia. Anais (0365-2181)
Related titles: Online - full text ed.: ISSN 2175-9790. free (effective 2011).
Indexed: A34, A36, A37, AgrForAb, B25, BIOSIS Prev, BP, C01, C25, C30, CABA, ChemAb, ChemTitl, D01, DBA, E12, EMBASE, ExcerpMed, F08, F11, F12, GH, H16, I12, MycolAb, N02, N03, P30, P32, P33, P40, PGegResA, PHN&I, PN&I, R10, R12, RA&MP, Reac, SCI, SCOPUS, SoyAb, T05, TAR, TriticAb, VS, W07, W11.
—BLDSC (2277.419530), CASDDS, GNLM, INIST.
Published by: Universidade de Sao Paulo, Faculdade de Ciencias Farmaceuticas, Divisao de Bibliotecas e Documentacao, Caixa Postal 66083, Sao Paulo, SP 05315-970, Brazil. TEL 55-11-30913804, FAX 55-11-30978627, rbcf@edu.usp.br, http://www.rbcf.fcf.ucp.br. Circ: 1,000.

615.1 GBR ISSN 1472-6904
RM1 CODEN: BCPMC4
➤ **B M C CLINICAL PHARMACOLOGY.** (BioMed Central) Text in English. 2000. irreg. free (effective 2011). adv. back issues avail.; reprints avail. **Document type:** *Journal, Academic/Scholarly.* **Description:** Features original research articles in all aspects of clinical pharmacology.
Media: Online - full text.
Indexed: A26, A36, C06, C07, CA, CABA, E12, EMBASE, ExcerpMed, F08, F11, F12, GH, I05, MEDLINE, N02, N03, P30, P33, P39, R10, R12, RA&MP, RM&VM, Reac, SCOPUS, SoyAb, T02, T05.
—Infotrieve. **CCC.**
Published by: BioMed Central Ltd. (Subsidiary of: Springer Science+Business Media), 236 Gray's Inn Rd, London, WC1X 8HB, United Kingdom. TEL 44-20-31922000, FAX 44-20-31922010, info@biomedcentral.com. Ed. Dr. Melissa Norton. Adv. contact Natasha Bailey TEL 44-20-31922231.

615.19 GBR ISSN 1471-2210
RM300 CODEN: BPMHBU
➤ **B M C PHARMACOLOGY.** (BioMed Central) Text in English. 2000. irreg. free (effective 2011). adv. back issues avail. **Document type:** *Journal, Academic/Scholarly.* **Description:** Publishes original research articles in all aspects of the design, uses, effects, and modes of action of therapeutic agents.
Media: Online - full text.
Indexed: A26, A34, A35, A36, A38, AgBio, AnBeAb, B19, B25, BIOSIS Prev, BioEngAb, C25, CA, CABA, EMBASE, ExcerpMed, GH, H16, I05, IndVet, M&PBA, MEDLINE, MycolAb, N02, N03, N05, P30, P32, P33, P40, PGegResA, PGrRegA, PN&I, R07, R08, R10, RA&MP, Reac, SCOPUS, SoyAb, T02, VS, W10.
—Infotrieve. **CCC.**

P

Published by: BioMed Central Ltd. (Subsidiary of: Springer Science+Business Media), 236 Gray's Inn Rd, London, WC1X 8HB, United Kingdom. TEL 44-20-31922000, FAX 44-20-31922010, info@biomedcentral.com. Ed. Dr. Melissa Norton. Adv. contact Natasha Bailey TEL 44-20-31922231.

615 DEU
B P I GESCHAEFTSBERICHT. Text in German. 1953. a. **Document type:** *Magazine, Corporate.*
Former titles (until 2001): B P I Jahresbericht; (until 1993): Pharma-Jahresbericht; (until 1970): Bundesverband der Pharmazeutischen Industrie. Bericht
Published by: Bundesverband der Pharmazeutischen Industrie e.V., Friedrichstr 148, Berlin, 10117, Germany. TEL 49-30-27909131, FAX 49-30-27909331, presse@bpi.de, http://www.bpi.de.

615 BGD ISSN 1991-007X
RS1
➤ **BANGLADESH JOURNAL OF PHARMACOLOGY.** Text in English. 2008. s-a. **Document type:** *Journal, Academic/Scholarly.* **Description:** Seeks to promote research, exchange of scientific information, consideration of regulatory mechanisms that affect drug development and utilization and medical education.
Related titles: Online - full text ed.: free (effective 2011).
Indexed: A01, A34, A35, A36, A38, AgrForAb, B25, BIOSIS Prev, BP, C30, CA, CABA, E12, EMBASE, ExcerpMed, F08, F11, F12, GH, H16, MycolAb, N02, N03, N04, P32, P33, P39, P40, PGegResA, PHN&I, R07, R08, R12, R13, RA&MP, RM&VM, S13, S16, SCI, SCOPUS, SoyAb, T02, T05, TAR, VS, W07.
Published by: Bangladesh Pharmacological Society, Department of Pharmacology, Bangabandhu Shheikh Mujib Medical University, Shahbag, Dhaka, 1000, Bangladesh. TEL 880-2-8615316.

615 BGD ISSN 0301-4606
CODEN: BPJLAQ
BANGLADESH PHARMACEUTICAL JOURNAL. Text in English. 1972. q. **Document type:** *Journal, Academic/Scholarly.*
Related titles: Online - full text ed.
Indexed: ChemAb.
—CASDDS, Linda Hall.
Published by: Bangladesh Pharmaceutical Society, 22 Dhanmondi Rd, Dhaka, 1205, Bangladesh. TEL 880-2-8611370, FAX 880-2-8613588, bps@agni.com.

615 USA ISSN 0891-2033
RM300
BASIC AND CLINICAL PHARMACOLOGY. Text in English. 1982. irreg., latest 2009, 11th ed. USD 64.95 per vol. (effective 2010). back issues avail. **Document type:** *Monographic series, Trade.* **Description:** Covers all the important concepts students need to know about the science of pharmacology and its application to clinical practice.
Formerly (until 1980): Review of Medical Pharmacology (0557-7519)
—CCC.
Published by: McGraw-Hill Education (Subsidiary of: McGraw-Hill Companies, Inc.), 148 Princeton-Hightstown Rd, Hightstown, NJ 08520. TEL 609-426-5793, FAX 609-426-7917, customer.service@mcgraw-hill.com, http://www.mheducation.com/. Ed. Bertram G Katzung.

615.902 GBR ISSN 1742-7835
QP901 CODEN: BCPTBO
➤ **BASIC & CLINICAL PHARMACOLOGY & TOXICOLOGY.** Abbreviated title: B C P T(Basic & Clinical Pharmacology & Toxicology). Text in English. 1944. 12/yr. (2 combined). GBP 598 in United Kingdom to institutions; EUR 761 in Europe to institutions; USD 1,004 in the Americas to institutions; USD 1,171 elsewhere to institutions; GBP 688 combined subscription in United Kingdom to institutions (print & online eds.); EUR 875 combined subscription in Europe to institutions (print & online eds.); USD 1,156 combined subscription in the Americas to institutions (print & online eds.); USD 1,347 combined subscription elsewhere to institutions (print & online eds.) (effective 2012). adv. bibl.; charts; illus. index. reprint service avail. from PSC. **Document type:** *Journal, Academic/Scholarly.* **Description:** Contains experimental animal pharmacology and toxicology and molecular, biochemical and cellular pharmacology and toxicology.
Former titles (until 2004): Pharmacology & Toxicology (Print) (0901-9928); (until 1987): Acta Pharmacologica et Toxicologica (0001-6683)
Related titles: Microfilm ed.: (from PMC); ◆ Online - full text ed.: Basic & Clinical Pharmacology & Toxicology Online. ISSN 1742-7843; ◆ Supplement(s): Basic & Clinical Pharmacology & Toxicology. Supplement (Print). ISSN 1742-7851.
Indexed: A01, A03, A08, A22, A26, A34, A35, A36, ASCA, AgBio, AgrForAb, B21, B25, BA, BIOBASE, BIOSIS Prev, BP, C24, C30, C33, CA, CABA, CISA, CTA, ChemAb, CurCont, D01, DBA, DentInd, E01, E04, E05, E12, EMBASE, ESPM, ExcerpMed, F08, F11, F12, GH, H12, H16, H17, IABS, ISR, IndMed, IndVet, Inpharma, MEDLINE, MycolAb, N02, N03, N04, NRN, NSA, P30, P32, P33, P35, P37, P39, P40, PN&I, PsycholAb, R07, R08, R10, R13, RA&MP, RM&VM, Reac, S01, S12, SCI, SCOPUS, SoyAb, T02, T05, TAR, THA, ToxAb, VS, W07, W10.
—BLDSC (1863.914250), CASDDS, GNLM, IE, Infotrieve, Ingenta, INIST, Linda Hall. **CCC.**
Published by: (Nordic Pharmacological Society DNK, Panum Institute DNK), Wiley-Blackwell Publishing Ltd. (Subsidiary of: John Wiley & Sons, Inc.), 9600 Garsington Rd, Oxford, OX4 2DQ, United Kingdom. TEL 44-1865-776868, FAX 44-1865-714591, customerservices@blackwellpublishing.com. Ed. Kim Broesen. Adv. contact Katrina Erskine. Circ: 400.

615.902 GBR ISSN 1742-7843
➤ **BASIC & CLINICAL PHARMACOLOGY & TOXICOLOGY ONLINE.** Text in English. 1987. m. GBP 598 in United Kingdom to institutions; EUR 761 in Europe to institutions; USD 1,004 in the Americas to institutions; USD 1,171 elsewhere to institutions (effective 2012). adv. back issues avail.; reprints avail. **Document type:** *Journal, Academic/Scholarly.* **Description:** Contains experimental animal pharmacology and toxicology and molecular, biochemical and cellular pharmacology and toxicology.
Formerly (until 2004): Pharmacology & Toxicology (Online) (1600-0773)
Media: Online - full text (from IngentaConnect). **Related titles:** Microfilm ed.: (from PMC); ◆ Print ed.: Basic & Clinical Pharmacology & Toxicology. ISSN 1742-7835.
—BLDSC (1863.914250), Linda Hall. **CCC.**
Published by: (Nordic Pharmacological Society DNK), Wiley-Blackwell Publishing Ltd. (Subsidiary of: John Wiley & Sons, Inc.), 9600 Garsington Rd, Oxford, OX4 2DQ, United Kingdom. TEL 44-1865-776868, FAX 44-1865-714591, customerservices@blackwellpublishing.com, http://www.wiley.com/. Ed. Kim Broesen. Adv. contact Katrina Erskine.

615.1 GBR ISSN 1742-786X
BASIC & CLINICAL PHARMACOLOGY & TOXICOLOGY. SUPPLEMENT (ONLINE). Text in English. 2003. irreg. includes with subscr. to Basic & Clinical Pharmacology & Toxicology. **Document type:** *Monographic series, Academic/Scholarly.*
Formerly (until 2004): Pharmacology & Toxicology. Supplement (Online) (1600-5570)
Media: Online - full text. **Related titles:** ◆ Print ed.: Basic & Clinical Pharmacology & Toxicology. Supplement (Print). ISSN 1742-7851.
—IE.
Published by: Wiley-Blackwell Publishing Ltd. (Subsidiary of: John Wiley & Sons, Inc.), 9600 Garsington Rd, Oxford, OX4 2DQ, United Kingdom. TEL 44-1865-776868, FAX 44-1865-714591, customerservices@blackwellpublishing.com, http://www.wiley.com/.

615.1 GBR ISSN 1742-7851
QP901 CODEN: PTSUEC
➤ **BASIC & CLINICAL PHARMACOLOGY & TOXICOLOGY. SUPPLEMENT (PRINT).** Text in English. 1947. irreg., latest vol.89, 2001. includes with subscr. to Basic & Clinical Pharmacology & Toxicology. reprints avail. **Document type:** *Monographic series, Academic/Scholarly.*
Former titles (until 2004): Pharmacology & Toxicology. Supplement (Print) (0901-9936); (until 1987): Acta Pharmacologica et Toxicologica. Supplementum (0065-1508)
Related titles: ◆ Online - full text ed.: Basic & Clinical Pharmacology & Toxicology. Supplement (Online). ISSN 1742-786X; ◆ Supplement to: Basic & Clinical Pharmacology & Toxicology. ISSN 1742-7835.
Indexed: A22, ChemAb, IndMed, SCOPUS.
—CASDDS, IE, Infotrieve, INIST, Linda Hall. **CCC.**
Published by: Wiley-Blackwell Publishing Ltd. (Subsidiary of: John Wiley & Sons, Inc.), 9600 Garsington Rd, Oxford, OX4 2DQ, United Kingdom. TEL 44-1865-776868, FAX 44-1865-714591, customerservices@blackwellpublishing.com, http://www.wiley.com/.

615 USA
BAYER ALKALIZER. Text in English. 1936. q. free (effective 2007). back issues avail. **Description:** Employee news of research-based healthcare products manufacturer.
Former titles: Miles Alkalizer; (until 1989): Alkalizer
Published by: Bayer Corp., 100 Bayer Rd, Pittsburgh, PA 15205-9741. TEL 412-777-2000, 800-422-9374, http://www.bayerus.com. Ed. Catherine Wells Bentz. Circ: 6,500 (controlled).

615 540 DEU ISSN 1437-8175
BAYER REPORT. Text in German. 1958. 2/yr. abstr.; bibl.; charts; illus.; stat. back issues avail. **Document type:** *Magazine, Corporate.*
Formerly: Bayer Berichte (0005-6960)
Related titles: French ed.: ISSN 1438-0056; Italian ed.: ISSN 1437-8191; English ed.: ISSN 0343-1630; Portuguese ed.; Spanish ed.: ISSN 1437-8183; Japanese ed.
Indexed: IBR, IBZ, R18.
Published by: Bayer AG, Corporate Communications, Gebaeude W11, Leverkusen, 51368, Germany. TEL 49-217-383617, 49-214-3057681, FAX 49-214-30571985, 49-214-3071985, serviceline@bayer-ag.de. Ed. Heiner Springer. Circ: 350,000.

615.19 DEU
BAYER SCHERING PHARMA. ANNUAL REPORT (YEAR). Text in English. a. **Document type:** *Yearbook, Trade.*
Formerly (until 2006): Schering Annual Report (Year)
Related titles: German ed.
Published by: Bayer Schering Pharma AG, Muellerstr 178, Berlin, 13353, Germany. TEL 49-30-4681111, FAX 49-30-46815305, https://www.bayerscheringpharma.de.

615 150 USA ISSN 0955-8810
RM1 CODEN: BPHAEL
➤ **BEHAVIOURAL PHARMACOLOGY.** Text in English. 1989. 7/yr. USD 1,588 domestic to institutions; USD 1,700 foreign to institutions (effective 2011). adv. index. back issues avail.; reprints avail. **Document type:** *Journal, Academic/Scholarly.* **Description:** Brings out research reports in diverse areas, ranging from ethopharmacology to the pharmacology of schedule-controlled operant behaviour.
Related titles: CD-ROM ed.; Online - full text ed.: ISSN 1473-5849. 2001. USD 955.50 domestic for academic site license; USD 955.50 foreign for academic site license; USD 1,065.75 domestic for corporate site license; USD 1,065.75 foreign for corporate site license (effective 2002).
Indexed: A22, ASCA, B21, B25, BIOBASE, BIOSIS Prev, BibInd, CIN, ChemTitl, CurCont, E-psyche, E01, EMBASE, ExcerpMed, FoP, IABS, ISR, IndMed, Inpharma, MEDLINE, MycolAb, NSA, NSCI, P03, P30, P35, PsycInfo, PsycholAb, R10, Reac, SCI, SCOPUS, W07.
—BLDSC (1877.630000), CASDDS, GNLM, IE, Infotrieve, Ingenta, INIST. **CCC.**
Published by: (European Behavioural Pharmacology Society GBR), Lippincott Williams & Wilkins (Subsidiary of: Wolters Kluwer N.V.), 530 Walnut St, Philadelphia, PA 19106. TEL 215-521-8300, FAX 215-521-8902, customerservice@lww.com, http://www.lww.com. Ed. Paul Willner TEL 44-1792-295844. Pub. Phil Daly. Circ: 143.

615 MNG ISSN 1672-8351
BEIFANG YAOXUE. Text in Chinese. 2004. bi-m. CNY 72 (effective 2009). **Document type:** *Journal, Academic/Scholarly.*
Published by: Neimenggu Zizhiqu Yaopin Xuehui, 77, Wulanchabu Dong Jie, Hohhot, 010010, Mongolia. TEL 86-471-4914963, FAX 86-471-4914949.

615 338.476 GBR ISSN 2040-5030
▼ **BELARUS PHARMACEUTICALS & HEALTHCARE REPORT.** Text in English. 2009. q. USD 975, EUR 695 combined subscription (print & email eds.) (effective 2011). back issues avail. **Document type:** *Report, Trade.* **Description:** Provides industry professionals, market investors and corporate and financial services analysts with independent forecasts and competitive intelligence on the Belarusian pharmaceutical and healthcare industry.
Related titles: E-mail ed.
Published by: Business Monitor International Ltd., Senator House, 85 Queen Victoria St, London, EC4V 4AB, United Kingdom. TEL 44-20-72480468, FAX 44-20-72480467, subs@businessmonitor.com.

615.1 DEU ISSN 1611-0536
BERLINER BEITRAEGE ZUR PHARMAZIE. Text in German. 2002. irreg., latest vol.6, 2006. price varies. **Document type:** *Monographic series, Academic/Scholarly.*
Published by: Weissensee Verlag e.K., Simplonstr 59, Berlin, 10245, Germany. TEL 49-30-29049192, FAX 49-30-27574315, mail@weissensee-verlag.de.

615.1 USA ISSN 1555-8975
RA975.5.P5
BEST PRACTICES FOR HOSPITAL & HEALTH-SYSTEM PHARMACY; position and guidance documents of ASHP. Text in English. 1983. a. USD 75 per issue to non-members; USD 60 per issue to members (effective 2009). back issues avail. **Document type:** *Directory, Academic/Scholarly.* **Description:** Contains ASHP statements, guidelines, technical assistance bulletins, technician training program accreditation regulations and standards, residency accreditation regulations and standards, therapeutic positions statements, and therapeutic guidelines.
Former titles (until 2005): Best Practices for Health-System Pharmacy (1533-9572); (until 1999): American Society of Hospital Pharmacists. Practice Standards (0898-6738)
Indexed: C06, C07.
—CCC.
Published by: American Society of Health-System Pharmacists, 7272 Wisconsin Ave, Bethesda, MD 20814. TEL 301-657-3000, 866-279-0681, FAX 301-664-8700, custserv@ashp.org.

▼ **BIOANALYSIS.** *see* BIOLOGY—Biochemistry

615.1 USA ISSN 0006-2952
QP901 CODEN: BCPCA6
➤ **BIOCHEMICAL PHARMACOLOGY.** Text in English. 1958. 24/yr. EUR 7,828 in Europe to institutions; JPY 1,039,900 in Japan to institutions; USD 8,758 elsewhere to institutions (effective 2012). adv. bk.rev. charts; illus.; abstr. index. back issues avail.; reprints avail. **Document type:** *Journal, Academic/Scholarly.* **Description:** Publishes research findings in biochemical pharmacology, with particular emphasis on molecular and structural biology and genetics.
Related titles: Microfilm ed.: (from PQC); Online - full text ed.: ISSN 1873-2968 (from IngentaConnect, ScienceDirect).
Indexed: A01, A03, A08, A22, A26, A34, A35, A36, A38, AIDS Ab, AIIM, ASCA, AgBio, AgrForAb, ApicAb, B&BAb, B19, B21, B23, B25, B26, B27, BIOBASE, BIOSIS Prev, BP, C24, C30, C33, CA, CABA, CIN, CISA, CTA, ChemAb, ChemTitl, ChemoAb, CurCont, D01, DBA, DentInd, E12, EMBASE, ESPM, ExcerpMed, F08, F11, F12, GH, H16, H17, I05, IABS, IBR, IBZ, ISR, IndMed, IndVet, Inpharma, LT, M&PBA, MEDLINE, MaizeAb, MycolAb, N02, N03, N04, N05, NSA, OR, P30, P32, P33, P35, P37, P39, P40, PGegResA, PGrRegA, PN&I, PsycholAb, R07, R08, R10, R11, R13, RA&MP, RM&VM, Reac, RefZh, S13, S16, S17, SCI, SCOPUS, SoyAb, T02, T05, ToxAb, VITIS, VS, W07, W10.
—BLDSC (2067.700000), CASDDS, GNLM, IE, Infotrieve, Ingenta, INIST, Linda Hall. **CCC.**
Published by: Elsevier Inc. (Subsidiary of: Elsevier Science & Technology), 1600 John F Kennedy Blvd, Philadelphia, PA 19103. TEL 215-239-3900, FAX 215-238-7883, JournalCustomerService-usa@elsevier.com. Eds. G Z Feuerstein, J G Piette, S J Enna.

➤ **BIOCOMMERCE DATA'S BIOTECHNOLOGY COMPANY COMPENDIUM. EUROPE.** *see* BIOLOGY—Biotechnology

615.3705 NZL ISSN 1173-8804
RM301.4 CODEN: BIDRF4
➤ **BIODRUGS;** biotechnology and clinical innovation. Text in English. 1994. bi-m. price varies based on the number of users. back issues avail.; reprints avail. **Document type:** *Journal, Academic/Scholarly.* **Description:** Covers clinical aspects of immunopharmacology, immune disorder treatments, clinical use of immunomodulating agents and cytokines.
Formerly (until 1997): Clinical Immunotherapeutics (1172-7039)
Related titles: Online - full text ed.: ISSN 1179-190X (from IngentaConnect).
Indexed: A01, A03, A08, A22, A26, A34, A36, ASCA, B&BAb, B19, B21, BIOSIS Prev, CA, CABA, CurCont, D01, E01, E08, E12, EMBASE, ExcerpMed, F08, F12, FoMM, GH, H12, I05, I12, ISR, ImmunAb, IndVet, Inpharma, MEDLINE, MycolAb, N02, N03, P20, P22, P30, P33, P35, P39, P52, P54, P56, PQC, R10, R12, Reac, S09, SCI, SCOPUS, T02, T05, VS, W07, W10.
—BLDSC (2071.900000), CASDDS, GNLM, IE, Infotrieve, Ingenta. **CCC.**
Published by: Adis International Ltd. (Subsidiary of: Wolters Kluwer N.V.), 41 Centorian Dr, Mairangi Bay, Private Bag 65901, Auckland, 1311, New Zealand. TEL 64-9-4770700, FAX 64-9-4770764, journals@adis.com, http://www.adisonline.info/. Ed. Anne Bardsley-Elliot.

➤ **BIOFARBO.** *see* BIOLOGY—Biochemistry

▼ ➤ **BIOIMPACTS.** *see* BIOLOGY

615.1 JPN ISSN 0918-6158
QP501 CODEN: BPBLEO
➤ **BIOLOGICAL & PHARMACEUTICAL BULLETIN.** Text in English. 1978. m. USD 125 combined subscription incls. Chemical & Pharmaceutical Bulletin (effective 2004). adv. charts; stat. Index. 130 p./no.; **Document type:** *Journal, Academic/Scholarly.* **Description:** Covers analytical biochemistry, biochemistry, molecular and cell biology, microbiology, pharmacology, medicinal chemistry, pharmacognosy and bio-/clinical-pharmacy, including all fields of life sciences such as genomics, proteomics, bioinformatics, structural biology, chemical biology and so on.
Formerly (until 1993): Journal of Pharmacobio-Dynamics (0386-846X)
Related titles: Online - full text ed.: ISSN 1347-5215. 2001.
Indexed: A22, A34, A35, A36, A38, ASCA, AgBio, AgrForAb, B21, B25, BA, BIOSIS Prev, BP, C24, C25, C30, C33, CABA, CIN, CTA, ChemAb, ChemTitl, ChemoAb, CurCont, D01, DBA, DentInd, E12, EMBASE, ESPM, ExcerpMed, F08, F11, F12, FR, GH, H16, H17, INIS AtomInd, ISR, IndMed, IndVet, Inpharma, MEDLINE, MaizeAb, MycolAb, N02, N03, N04, N05, NPU, NSA, P30, P32, P33, P35, P37, P39, P40, PGegResA, PGrRegA, PHN&I, PN&I, R07, R08, R10, R11, R12, R13, RA&MP, RM&VM, Reac, RefZh, S12, S13, S16, S17, SCI, SCOPUS, SoyAb, T05, TAR, ToxAb, TriticAb, VS, VirolAbstr, W07, W10.

—BLDSC (2074.650000), CASDDS, GNLM, IE, Infotrieve, Ingenta, INIST, Linda Hall. **CCC.**
Published by: Pharmaceutical Society of Japan/Nihon Yakugakkai, 2-12-15, Shibuya, Shibuya-ku, Tokyo, 150-0002, Japan. TEL 81-3-34063321, FAX 81-3-34981835. Ed. Yasuyuki Nomura. Circ: 3,650. **Dist. by:** Japan Publications Trading Co., Ltd., Book Export II Dept, PO Box 5030, Tokyo International, Tokyo 101-3191, Japan. TEL 81-3-32923753, FAX 81-3-32920410, infoserials@jptco.co.jp, http://www.jptco.co.jp.

615 GBR ISSN 1177-5491
➤ **BIOLOGICS (ONLINE).** Text in English. 2007. irreg. free (effective 2011). back issues avail. **Document type:** *Journal, Academic/Scholarly.* **Description:** Covers patho-physiological rationale for and clinical application of biologic agents in the management of autoimmune diseases, cancers or other pathologies where a molecular target can be identified.
Media: Online - full text.
—CCC.
Published by: Dove Medical Press Ltd., Beechfield House, Winterton Way, Macclesfield, SK11 0JL, United Kingdom. TEL 44-1625-509130, FAX 44-1625-617933. Ed. Doris Mangiaracina Benbrook.

▼ ➤ **BIOLOGY AND CHEMISTRY OF BETA GLUCAN.** *see* BIOLOGY—Biotechnology

➤ **BIOLOGY OF SPORT**; a quarterly journal of sport and exercise sciences. *see* MEDICAL SCIENCES—Sports Medicine

615 610 NZL ISSN 1177-2719
R853.B54
➤ **BIOMARKER INSIGHTS.** Text in English. 2006. irreg. free (effective 2011). **Document type:** *Journal, Academic/Scholarly.* **Description:** Covers the latest advances in the application of biomarkers toward the discovery of new knowledge, and toward the clinical translation of that knowledge to increase the efficacy of practicing clinicians.
Media: Online - full text.
Indexed: A01, A39, C27, C29, CA, D03, D04, E13, EMBASE, ExcerpMed, P30, R14, S14, S15, S18, SCOPUS, T02.
—CCC.
Published by: Libertas Academica Ltd., PO Box 302-624, North Harbour, Auckland, 1330, New Zealand. TEL 64-21-662617, FAX 64-21-740006. Ed. Stephen F Kingsmore.

➤ **BIOMEDICAL AND ENVIRONMENTAL SCIENCES/BIOMEDICAL AND ENVIRONMENTAL SCIENCES.** *see* MEDICAL SCIENCES

➤ **BIOMEDICINE & PHARMACOTHERAPY.** *see* MEDICAL SCIENCES

615 KOR ISSN 1976-9148
BIOMOLECULES & THERAPEUTICS. Text in English. 1993. q. **Document type:** *Journal, Academic/Scholarly.* **Description:** Reports on new information about drug action, toxicity and biologically active substances in biological systems.
Formerly (until 2008): Eung'yong Yagmul Haghoeji/Journal of Applied Pharmacology (1225-6110)
Related titles: Online - full text ed.
Indexed: B25, BIOSIS Prev, EMBASE, ExcerpMed, MycolAb, P30, SCI, SCOPUS, W07.
—BLDSC (2089.263000), IE, Ingenta.
Published by: Korean Society of Applied Pharmacology/Han'gug Eung'yong Yagmul Haghoe, Yeoksam-Dong, 635-4 Kangnam-Ku, KSTC Main Bldg. Room 805, Seoul, 135-703, Korea, S. TEL 82-2-5652167, FAX 82-2-5545378, ksap1992@hanmail.net.

615 USA ISSN 1542-166X
CODEN: BPRME5
BIOPHARM INTERNATIONAL; the applied technologies of biopharmaceutical development. Text in English. 1987. m. USD 79 domestic; USD 107 in Canada & Mexico; USD 152 elsewhere; USD 14 newsstand/cover domestic; USD 15 newsstand/cover in Canada & Mexico; USD 17 newsstand/cover elsewhere (effective 2011). adv. back issues avail.; reprints avail. **Document type:** *Magazine, Trade.* **Description:** Focuses on the science and industry of developing biotechnology-derived pharmaceutical products and biotherapeutic methods. Covers scientific and technical applications as well as issues, regulatory affairs, and business matters for scientists, engineers, managers, technicians, and corporate management.
Former titles (until 2002): BioPharm (1040-8304); (until 1988): Biopharm Manufacturing (1040-8045)
Related titles: Online - full text ed.: ISSN 1939-1862. USD 115 (effective 2011).
Indexed: A10, A15, A22, A26, ABIn, AIDS&CR, Agr, B&BAb, B02, B03, B07, B11, B15, B17, B18, B21, B26, BioEngAb, CA, CWI, DBA, EMBASE, ESPM, ExcerpMed, G04, G06, G07, G08, I05, I10, M&PBA, P10, P24, P26, P34, P48, P51, P52, P53, P54, P56, PQC, R10, Reac, S10, SCI, SCOPUS, T02, Telegen, ToxAb, V03, ViroIAbstr, W07.
—BLDSC (2089.353900), CASDDS, GNLM, IE, Ingenta, INIST. **CCC.**
Published by: Advanstar Communications, Inc., 6200 Canoga Ave, 2nd Fl, Woodland Hills, CA 91367. TEL 818-593-5000, FAX 818-593-5020, info@advanstar.com, http://www.advanstar.com. Ed. Laura Bush TEL 732-346-3020. Pub. Mike Tessalone TEL 732-346-3016.

BIOPHARMA (FRENCH EDITION). *see* BIOLOGY—Genetics

615 GBR ISSN 0142-2782
RM301.4 CODEN: BDDID8
➤ **BIOPHARMACEUTICS & DRUG DISPOSITION.** Text in English. 1980. 9/yr. GBP 1,817 in United Kingdom to institutions; EUR 2,298 in Europe to institutions; USD 3,562 elsewhere to institutions; GBP 2,091 combined subscription in United Kingdom to institutions (print & online eds.); EUR 2,643 combined subscription in Europe to institutions (print & online eds.); USD 4,096 combined subscription elsewhere to institutions (print & online eds.) (effective 2012). adv. back issues avail.; reprint service avail. from PSC. **Document type:** *Journal, Academic/Scholarly.* **Description:** Presents original reports of studies in biopharmaceutics, drug disposition and pharmacokinetics, especially those which have a direct relation to the therapeutic use of drugs.
Related titles: Microform ed.: (from PQC); Online - full text ed.: ISSN 1099-081X. GBP 1,817 in United Kingdom to institutions; EUR 2,298 in Europe to institutions; USD 3,562 elsewhere to institutions (effective 2012).
Indexed: A22, ASCA, ASFA, B&BAb, B19, B21, B25, B27, BIOSIS Prev, BioEngAb, C33, CIN, CTA, ChemAb, ChemTitl, ChemoAb, CurCont, DBA, EMBASE, ESPM, ExcerpMed, I12, IDIS, ISR, IndMed, Inpharma, MEDLINE, MycolAb, NSA, P30, P35, R10, Reac, RefZh, SCI, SCOPUS, ToxAb, ViroIAbstr, W07.
—CASDDS, GNLM, IE, Infotrieve, Ingenta, INIST. **CCC.**
Published by: John Wiley & Sons Ltd. (Subsidiary of: John Wiley & Sons, Inc.), 1-7 Oldlands Way, PO Box 808, Bognor Regis, West Sussex PO21 9FF, United Kingdom. TEL 44-1865-778315, FAX 44-1243-843232, cs-journals@wiley.com, http://eu.wiley.com/WileyCDA/. **Subscr. in the Americas to:** John Wiley & Sons, Inc., 111 River St, Hoboken, NJ 07030. TEL 201-748-6645, subinfo@wiley.com; **Subscr. to:** 1-7 Oldlands Way, PO Box 809, Bognor Regis, West Sussex PO21 9FG, United Kingdom. TEL 44-1865-778054, cs-agency@wiley.com.

660 USA ISSN 1090-2759
BIOQUALITY. Text in English. 1996. m. USD 435 (effective 2004). back issues avail. **Document type:** *Newsletter, Trade.* **Description:** Covers quality, regulatory, and technical issues for biopharmaceuticals.
Related titles: Online - full content ed.
Published by: i2i Corp., PO Box 1137, Idyllwild, CA 92549. TEL 909-659-1187, FAX 909-659-3233, info@i2icorp.com.

615 ITA ISSN 2038-1522
▼ **BIOSIMILARI.** Text in Italian. 2010. q. **Document type:** *Journal, Trade.*
Related titles: Online - full text ed.
Published by: Editoriale Fernando Folini, Il Battaglino, Casalnoceto, AL 15052, Italy. http://www.edifolini.com.

615 GBR ISSN 2230-245X
▼ ➤ **BIOSIMILARS.** Text in English. 2011. irreg. free (effective 2011). **Document type:** *Journal, Academic/Scholarly.* **Description:** Focuses on the manufacture, development and medicinal use of biopharmaceutical compounds considered similar to an innovator agent.
Media: Online - full text.
—CCC.
Published by: Dove Medical Press Ltd., Beechfield House, Winterton Way, Macclesfield, SK11 0JL, United Kingdom. TEL 44-1625-509130, FAX 44-1625-617933. Ed. Dr. Ajay Singh.

➤ **BIOSPECTRUM ASIA**; the business of life sciences. *see* BIOLOGY—Biotechnology

▼ ➤ **BIOSUPPLY TRENDS QUARTERLY.** *see* BUSINESS AND ECONOMICS

➤ **BIOTECH BUSINESS WEEK.** *see* BIOLOGY—Biotechnology

615 USA ISSN 1931-9010
BIOWORLD PHASE III REPORT. Text in English. 1995. q. USD 599 domestic; USD 699 foreign (effective 2010). reprints avail. **Document type:** *Newsletter, Trade.* **Description:** Features source for tracking the progress of biotech products in advanced clinical trials.
Indexed: H01, H02.
Published by: A H C Media LLC (Subsidiary of: Thomson Corporation, Healthcare Information Group), 3525 Piedmont Rd, NE, Bldg 6, Ste 400, Atlanta, GA 30305. TEL 404-262-7436, 800-688-2421, FAX 404-262-7837, 800-284-3291, customerservice@ahcmedia.com, http://www.ahcmedia.com/. **Subscr. to:** PO Box 105109, Atlanta, GA 30348. TEL 404-262-5476, FAX 404-262-5560.

615.328 JPN ISSN 0006-386X
QP771 CODEN: BTMNA7
BITAMIN/VITAMINS. Text in Japanese; Summaries in English. 1948. m. free to members. **Document type:** *Journal, Academic/Scholarly.*
Related titles: Online - full text ed.
Indexed: B25, BIOSIS Prev, C33, ChemAb, FS&TA, JPI, MycolAb, RefZh.
—BLDSC (9243.500000), CASDDS, INIST, Linda Hall. **CCC.**
Published by: Nippon Bitamin Gakkai/Vitamin Society of Japan, Kyodai Kaikan 2nd Fl., 15-9 Kawaramachi, Yoshida, Sakyo-ku, Kyoto, 606-8305, Japan. TEL 81-75-7510314, FAX 81-75-7512870, vsojkn@mbox.kyoto-inet.or.jp, http://web.kyoto-inet.or.jp/people/vsojkn/.

615.328 JPN
BITAMIN E KENKYU NO SHINPO/ADVANCES IN VITAMIN E RESEARCH. Text in English, Japanese. 1990. a. membership. **Document type:** *Journal, Academic/Scholarly.*
—BLDSC (2095.650000).
Published by: Bitamin E Kenkyukai, 2-15-6 Ohtsuka, Bunkyo-ku, Tokyo, 112-0012, Japan. TEL 86-3-59402623, FAX 86-3-39426396, vitamin-e@sunpla-mcv.com, http://www.sunpla-mcv.com/vitaminE/.

615.1 USA ISSN 0006-503X
BLUE AND GOLD TRIANGLE OF LAMBDA KAPPA SIGMA. Text in English. 1926. irreg. (4 nos. every 2 yrs.). free to members. adv. bk.rev. illus. **Document type:** *Newsletter.*
Published by: Lambda Kappa Sigma International Pharmaceutical Fraternity, W179 S6769 Muskego Dr, Muskego, WI 53150. TEL 800-LKS-1913, FAX 262-679-4558, lks@lks.org, http://www.lks.org. Ed. Nancy Horst. Circ: 12,000.

615.2 ESP ISSN 1575-8087
BOLETIN DE INFORMACION TERAPEUTICA. Text in Spanish. 1993. q. **Document type:** *Journal, Trade.*
—CCC.
Published by: Servicio Aragones de Salud, Via Universitas 34, Zaragoza, 50017, Spain. TEL 34-976-765800, infosalud@aragon.es, http://portal.aragon.es/portal/page/portal/SAS.

615 ESP ISSN 0212-9450
BOLETIN TERAPEUTICO ANDALUZ. Text in Spanish. 1984. bi-m. free (effective 2008). back issues avail. **Document type:** *Bulletin, Consumer.*
Related titles: Print ed.: Alerta de Farmacovigilancia. ISSN 1130-9180. 1991.
Published by: Junta de Andalucia, Centro Andaluz de Documentacion e Informacion de Medicamentos, Campus Universitario de Cartuja, Apdo Postal 2070, Granada, Andalucia 18080, Spain. TEL 34-958-027400, FAX 34-958-027503, cadime@casp.es, http://www.easp.es/web/cadime/index.asp?idSub=303&idSec=303&idCab=303.

615.778 GBR ISSN 1754-7318
➤ **THE BOTULINUM JOURNAL.** Text in English. 2008 (Jun.). 4/yr. EUR 494 to institutions (print or online ed.); EUR 672 combined subscription to institutions (print & online eds.) (effective 2012). bk.rev. abstr.; bibl.; illus.; charts; stat. back issues avail. **Document type:** *Journal, Academic/Scholarly.* **Description:** Provides a forum to exchange scholarly ideas relevant to health, science, application, and regulatory issues related to the botulinum neurotoxin and Clostridium botulinum.
Related titles: Online - full text ed.: ISSN 1754-7326 (from IngentaConnect).
Indexed: A26, A28, APA, B&BAb, B19, B20, B21, BrCerAb, C&ISA, CA/WCA, CIA, CerAb, CivEngAb, CorrAb, E&CAJ, E08, E11, EEA, EMA, ESPM, EnvEAb, H15, I10, M&TEA, M09, MBF, METADEX, SolStAb, T04, ToxAb, WAA.
—BLDSC (2264.029000), IE. **CCC.**
Published by: Inderscience Publishers, PO Box 735, Olney, Bucks MK46 5WB, United Kingdom. TEL 44-1234-240519, FAX 44-1234-240515, editorial@inderscience.com. Ed. Bal Ram Singh. **Subscr. to:** World Trade Centre Bldg, 29 Rte de Pre-Bois, Case Postale 856, Geneva 15 1215, Switzerland. FAX 41-22-7910885, subs@inderscience.com.

615 DEU ISSN 0722-7159
BRAUNSCHWEIGER VEROEFFENTLICHUNGEN ZUR GESCHICHTE DER PHARMAZIE UND NATURWISSENSCHAFTEN. Text in German. 1957. irreg., latest vol.46, 2008. price varies. **Document type:** *Monographic series, Academic/Scholarly.*
Former titles (until 1982): Technische Universitaet Braunschweig. Pharmaziegeschichtlichen Seminar. Veroeffentlichungen (0068-0729); (until 1970): Technische Hochschule Braunschweig. Pharmaziegeschichtlichen Seminar. Veroeffentlichungen (0521-2855)
Indexed: P30.
Published by: (Technische Universitaet Braunschweig, Presse- und Oeffentlichkeitsarbeit), Deutscher Apotheker Verlag, Postfach 101061, Stuttgart, 70009, Germany. TEL 49-711-25820, FAX 49-711-2582290, service@deutscher-apotheker-verlag.de, http://www.deutscher-apotheker-verlag.de. Ed. Erika Hickel.

BRIGGS UPDATE: DRUGS IN PREGNANCY AND LACTATION. *see* MEDICAL SCIENCES—Obstetrics And Gynecology

615 USA
BRISTOL-MYERS SQUIBB COMPANY. ANNUAL REPORT. Text in English. a., latest 2002.
Related titles: Online - full content ed.
Published by: Bristol-Myers Squibb Company, 345 Park Ave, New York, NY 10154-0037. TEL 212-546-4000, http://www.bms.com.

617.96 GBR ISSN 0306-5251
RM1 CODEN: BCPHBM
➤ **BRITISH JOURNAL OF CLINICAL PHARMACOLOGY.** Abbreviated title: B J C P. Text in English. 1974. m. (in 2 vols., 6 nos./vol.). GBP 1,407 in United Kingdom to institutions; EUR 1,787 in Europe to institutions; USD 2,599 in the Americas to institutions; USD 3,032 elsewhere to institutions; GBP 1,619 combined subscription in United Kingdom to institutions (print & online eds.); EUR 2,055 combined subscription in Europe to institutions (print & online eds.); USD 2,989 combined subscription in the Americas to institutions (print & online eds.); USD 3,487 combined subscription elsewhere to institutions (print & online eds.) (effective 2012). adv. bk.rev. abstr.; bibl.; charts; illus. index. Supplement avail.; back issues avail.; reprint service avail. from PSC. **Document type:** *Journal, Academic/Scholarly.* **Description:** Contains papers and reports on all aspects of drug action in humans.
Related titles: Microform ed.: (from PQC); Online - full text ed.: ISSN 1365-2125. 1997. GBP 1,407 in United Kingdom to institutions; EUR 1,787 in Europe to institutions; USD 2,599 in the Americas to institutions; USD 3,032 elsewhere to institutions (effective 2012) (from IngentaConnect); ◆ Supplement(s): British Journal of Clinical Pharmacology. Supplement. ISSN 0264-3774.
Indexed: A01, A02, A03, A08, A22, A26, A36, AIIM, ASCA, B&BAb, B19, B21, B25, BIOBASE, BIOSIS Prev, BP, C11, CA, CABA, CIN, ChemAb, ChemTitl, CurCont, D01, DBA, DentInd, E01, E12, EMBASE, ESPM, ExcerpMed, F08, F11, F12, FR, GH, H04, H12, H16, H17, I12, IABS, IDIS, INI, ISR, IndMed, Inpharma, Kidney, LT, MEDLINE, MS&D, MycolAb, N02, N03, NSA, OR, P30, P33, P35, P39, R08, R10, R12, RA&MP, RM&VM, RRTA, Reac, RefZh, S01, SCI, SCOPUS, T02, T05, THA, ToxAb, VS, ViroIAbstr, W07.
—BLDSC (2307.180000), CASDDS, GNLM, IE, Infotrieve, Ingenta, INIST. **CCC.**
Published by: (British Pharmacological Society), Wiley-Blackwell Publishing Ltd. (Subsidiary of: John Wiley & Sons, Inc.), 9600 Garsington Rd, Oxford, OX4 2DQ, United Kingdom. TEL 44-1865-776868, FAX 44-1865-714591, customerservices@blackwellpublishing.com, http://www.wiley.com/. Eds. E J Begg, J M Ritter, M S Lennard. Pub. Elizabeth Whelan. R&P Sophie Savage. Adv. contact Jenny Applin. Circ: 1,570.

617.96 GBR ISSN 0264-3774
BRITISH JOURNAL OF CLINICAL PHARMACOLOGY. SUPPLEMENT. Text in English. 1976. irreg. includes with subscr. to British Journal of Clinical Pharmacology. **Document type:** *Journal, Academic/Scholarly.*
Related titles: ◆ Supplement to: British Journal of Clinical Pharmacology. ISSN 0306-5251.
Indexed: SCOPUS.
—Infotrieve, INIST. **CCC.**
Published by: Wiley-Blackwell Publishing Ltd. (Subsidiary of: John Wiley & Sons, Inc.), 9600 Garsington Rd, Oxford, OX4 2DQ, United Kingdom. TEL 44-1865-776868, FAX 44-1865-714591, customerservices@blackwellpublishing.com, http://www.wiley.com/.

615 GBR ISSN 0007-1188
RM1 CODEN: BJPCBM
➤ **BRITISH JOURNAL OF PHARMACOLOGY.** Abbreviated title: B J P. Text in English. 1946. 24/yr. GBP 2,233 in United Kingdom to institutions; EUR 3,461 in Europe to institutions; USD 4,019 in the Americas to institutions; USD 4,375 elsewhere to institutions; GBP 2,568 combined subscription in United Kingdom to institutions (print & online eds.); EUR 3,980 combined subscription in Europe to institutions (print & online eds.); USD 4,622 combined subscription in the Americas to institutions (print & online eds.); USD 5,032 combined subscription elsewhere to institutions (print & online eds.) (effective 2012). adv. charts; illus.; stat. index. back issues avail.; reprint service avail. from PSC. **Document type:** *Journal, Academic/Scholarly.* **Description:** Presents original papers in experimental pharmacology.
Formerly (until 1968): British Journal of Pharmacology and Chemotherapy (0366-0826)
Related titles: Online - full text ed.: ISSN 1476-5381. 1997. GBP 2,233 in United Kingdom to institutions; EUR 3,461 in Europe to institutions; USD 4,019 in the Americas to institutions; USD 4,375 elsewhere to institutions (effective 2012) (from IngentaConnect); Supplement(s): British Journal of Pharmacology. Proceedings Supplement. ISSN 1359-5075.

P

Indexed: A01, A02, A03, A08, A22, A34, A35, A36, A38, ASCA, AgBio, AgrForAb, B21, B25, B27, BIOBASE, BIOSIS Prev, BP, C06, C07, C08, C11, C13, C24, C30, C33, CA, CABA, CIN, CINAHL, CISA, CTA, ChemAb, ChemTitl, CurCR, CurCont, D01, DBA, DentInd, E01, E12, EMBASE, ESPM, ExcerpMed, F08, F11, F12, GH, H04, H16, H17, IABS, ISR, IndChem, IndMed, IndVet, Inpharma, JW-P, LT, MEDLINE, MycolAb, N02, N03, N04, N05, NSA, P20, P22, P24, P30, P32, P33, P35, P37, P39, P48, P54, PGegResA, PGrRegA, PHN&I, PN&I, PQC, R07, R08, R10, R11, R13, R16, RA&MP, RM&VM, RRTA, Reac, S12, S13, S16, SCI, SCOPUS, SoyAb, T02, T05, THA, ToxAb, VS, W07, W10.
—BLDSC (2314.700000), CASDDS, GNLM, IE, Infotrieve, Ingenta, INIST, Linda Hall. **CCC.**
Published by: (British Pharmacological Society), John Wiley & Sons Ltd. (Subsidiary of: John Wiley & Sons, Inc.), The Atrium, Southern Gate, Chichester, West Sussex PO19 8SQ, United Kingdom. TEL 44-1243-779777, FAX 44-1243-775878, customer@wiley.co.uk. Ed. J C McGrath. Pub. Kim Thompkins TEL 201-748-6921. Adv. contact Neil Chesher TEL 44-1865-476383. **Subscr. to:** John Wiley & Sons, Inc., 350 Main St, Malden, MA 02148. TEL 781-388-8598, 800-835-6770, cs-journals@wiley.com, http://onlinelibrary.wiley.com/.

615 GBR ISSN 2044-2459
▼ **BRITISH JOURNAL OF PHARMACOLOGY AND TOXICOLOGY.** Text in English. 2010. bi-m. reprints avail. **Document type:** *Journal, Academic/Scholarly.* **Description:** Features informative articles on pharmacology and toxicology.
Related titles: Online - full text ed.: ISSN 2044-2467.
Indexed: A34, D01, E12, F08, H16, N03, N04, P33, S13, T05.
Published by: Maxwell Science Publications, 74 Kenelm Rd, Birmingham, B10 9AJ, United Kingdom. admin@maxwellsci.com. Ed. Saber Mohamed Abd-Allah.

615.1 GBR ISSN 0260-535X
RS125
BRITISH NATIONAL FORMULARY. Text in English. 1981. s-a. GBP 55 (effective 2011). adv. index. **Document type:** *Journal, Trade.* **Description:** Provides prescribers in the National Health Service and other health care professionals with information about drugs and medicines available on prescriptions in the UK.
Related titles: CD-ROM ed.: GBP 70 (effective 2004); Single user only; other prices on application; Online - full text ed.: USD 145; free to qualified personnel (effective 2010); subscr. includes BNF for Children, Nurse Prescriber's Formulary.
—BLDSC (2331.060000). **CCC.**
Published by: (Royal Pharmaceutical Society of Great Britain), Pharmaceutical Press (Subsidiary of: Royal Pharmaceutical Society of Great Britain), 1 Lambeth High St, London, SE1 7JN, United Kingdom. TEL 44-20-75722665, FAX 44-20-75722509, pharmpress@macmillansolutions.com, http://www.pharmpress.com/. Pub. Lindsey Fountain TEL 44-20-75722655. **Co-sponsor:** British Medical Association.

615.58083 GBR ISSN 1747-5503
RJ560
BRITISH NATIONAL FORMULARY FOR CHILDREN. Abbreviated title: B N F C. Text in English. 2005. a. free to members (effective 2009). **Document type:** *Journal, Trade.* **Description:** Contains practical information for all healthcare professionals involved in the prescribing, dispensing, monitoring, and administration of medicines to children.
Related titles: CD-ROM ed.: ISSN 1747-5511. 2005; Online - full content ed.: ISSN 1747-552X. 2005. free to members (effective 2009).
Published by: (Royal Pharmaceutical Society of Great Britain), B M J Group, BMA House, Tavistock Sq, London, WC1H 9JR, United Kingdom. TEL 44-20-73836373, FAX 44-20-73836668, http://group.bmj.com.

615.11941 GBR ISSN 1354-6643
BRITISH PHARMACOPOEIA. Key Title: British Pharmacopoeia and British Pharmacopoeia (Veterinary). Text in English. 1864. irreg., latest 2005, Aug. GBP 830 combined subscription (print, online & CD-ROM eds.) (effective 2010). 3500 p./no.; **Document type:** *Government.* **Description:** Collection of standards for UK medicinal substances and an essential reference point for everyone involved in their research, development and manufacture.
Incorporates (1977-1994): British Pharmacopoeia: Veterinary Edition
Related titles: CD-ROM ed.; Online - full text ed.
—CCC.
Published by: (British Pharmacopoeia Commission), The Stationery Office, St Crispins, Duke St, Norwich, NR3 1PD, United Kingdom. TEL 44-1603-622211, FAX 44-870-6005533, customer.services@tso.co.uk, http://www.tso.co.uk. **Subscr. to:** PO Box 29, Norwich NR3 1GN, United Kingdom. TEL 44-870-6005522.

615.9 615.19 POL ISSN 0365-9445
RA1258 CODEN: BCTKAG
➤ **BROMATOLOGIA I CHEMIA TOKSYKOLOGICZNA.** Text in Polish; Summaries in English. q. EUR 85 foreign (effective 2006). **Document type:** *Journal, Academic/Scholarly.* **Description:** Deals with bromatology and toxicological chemistry. Contains scientific papers.
Indexed: A22, ASFA, AgrAg, AgrLib, ApicAb, B21, B25, BIOSIS Prev, CIN, ChemAb, ChemTitl, ESPM, FS&TA, MycolAb, ToxAb, Z01.
—BLDSC (2349.500000), CASDDS, GNLM, IE, Ingenta, INIST, Linda Hall.
Published by: Polskie Towarzystwo Farmaceutyczne/Polish Pharmaceutical Society, ul Dluga 16, Warsaw, 00238, Poland. wydawnictwa@ptfarm.pl. **Dist. by:** Ars Polona, Obroncow 25, Warsaw 03933, Poland. TEL 48-22-5098609, FAX 48-22-5098610, arspolona@arspolona.com.pl, http://www.arspolona.com.pl.

➤ **BROOKERS PHARMACY LAW HANDBOOK.** *see* LAW—Corporate Law

➤ **THE BROWN UNIVERSITY GERIATRIC PSYCHOPHARMACOLOGY UPDATE.** *see* GERONTOLOGY AND GERIATRICS

615 EGY ISSN 1110-0052
CODEN: BPAUEC
➤ **BULLETIN OF PHARMACEUTICAL SCIENCES/NASHRAT AL-'LUM AL-SAYDALIYYAT GAMI'T ASIUT.** Text in English; Summaries in Arabic. 1978. s-a. bk.rev. abstr.; charts; bibl.; illus. back issues avail.; reprints avail. **Document type:** *Journal, Academic/Scholarly.*
Indexed: I12, SCI, W07.
—BLDSC (2882.697000), IE, Ingenta.
Published by: Assiut University, Faculty of Pharmacy, c/o Dr. Samya M. El-Sayed, Assiut, Egypt. TEL 20-88-331711, FAX 20-88-332776, http://www.acc.aun.edu.eg. Ed. Gamal A Saleh.

614.27 DEU ISSN 0521-7598
BUNDES-APOTHEKEN-REGISTER. Text in German. 1953. base vol. plus updates 3/yr. **Document type:** *Trade.*
Published by: Deutscher Apotheker Verlag, Postfach 101061, Stuttgart, 70009, Germany. TEL 49-711-25820, FAX 49-711-2582290, service@deutscher-apotheker-verlag.de, http://www.deutscher-apotheker-verlag.de.

789.56 658.8 GBR ISSN 1474-0869
BUSINESS RATIO REPORT. PHARMACEUTICAL MANUFACTURERS AND DEVELOPERS. Text in English. 1973. a. GBP 365 per issue (effective 2010). charts; stat. back issues avail. **Document type:** *Report, Trade.* **Description:** Covers companies active as pharmaceutical manufacturers and developers.
Former titles (until 2001): Business Ratio. Pharmaceutical Manufacturers & Developers (1470-7012); (until 1999): Business Ratio Plus: Pharmaceutical Manufacturers and Developers (1358-8435); (until 1995): Business Ratio Plus. Pharmaceutical Manufacturers; (until 1992): Business Ratio Report. Pharmaceutical Manufacturers (0261-9350)
Published by: Key Note Ltd. (Subsidiary of: Bonnier Business Information), Harlequin House, 5th Fl, 7 High St, Teddington, Richmond upon Thames, TW11 8EE, United Kingdom. TEL 44-845-5040452, FAX 44-845-5040453, sales@keynote.co.uk.

615 658.8 GBR ISSN 1474-9947
BUSINESS RATIO REPORT. RETAIL AND WHOLESALE CHEMISTS. Text in English. 1981. a. GBP 365 per issue (effective 2010). charts; stat. back issues avail. **Document type:** *Report, Trade.* **Description:** Covers companies active as retail and wholesale chemists.
Former titles (until 2001): Business Ratio. Retail and Wholesale Chemists (1467-8926); (until 1999): Business Ratio Plus: Retail & Wholesale Chemists (1356-6067); (until 1994): Business Ratio Report. Retail and Wholesale Chemists (0261-9482)
Published by: Key Note Ltd. (Subsidiary of: Bonnier Business Information), Harlequin House, 5th Fl, 7 High St, Teddington, Richmond upon Thames, TW11 8EE, United Kingdom. TEL 44-845-5040452, FAX 44-845-5040453, sales@keynote.co.uk.

615.1 ESP ISSN 0214-1930
BUTLLETI GROC. Text in Spanish. 1984. bi-m. **Document type:** *Bulletin, Consumer.*
Formerly (until 1987): Notificacion Voluntaria de Reacciones Adversas a Medicamentos. Tarjeta Amarilla. Boletin Informativo (0214-1914)
—CCC.
Published by: Fundacio Institut Catala de Farmacologia, Pg. Vall d'Hebron, 119-129, Barcelona, 08023, Spain. TEL 34-93-4283029, FAX 34-93-4894109, ficf@cf.uab.es. Ed. Joan Ramon Laporte.

615.1 ESP ISSN 0214-1922
BUTLLETI GROC (CATALAN EDITION). Text in Catalan. 1984. bi-m. back issues avail. **Document type:** *Bulletin, Consumer.*
Formerly (until 1987): Notificacio Voluntaria de Reaccions Adverses a Medicaments. Targeta Groga. Butlleti Informatiu (0214-1906)
Published by: Fundacio Institut Catala de Farmacologia, Pg. Vall d'Hebron, 119-129, Barcelona, 08023, Spain. TEL 34-93-4283029, FAX 34-93-4894109, ficf@cf.uab.es. Ed. Joan Ramon Laporte.

C A SELECTS. ALKOXYLATED OLEOCHEMICALS. *see* PHARMACY AND PHARMACOLOGY—Abstracting, Bibliographies, Statistics

C A SELECTS. DRUG ANALYSIS BIOLOGICAL FLUIDS & TISSUES. *see* PHARMACY AND PHARMACOLOGY—Abstracting, Bibliographies, Statistics

615 USA
C H P A EXECUTIVE NEWSLETTER. Text in English. fortn. **Document type:** *Newsletter.*
Published by: Consumer Healthcare Products Association, 900 19th St, NW, Ste 700, Washington, DC 20006. TEL 202-429-9260, FAX 202-223-6835, eassey@chpa-info.org, http://www.chpa-info.org.

C H P PACKER INTERNATIONAL. (Cosmetics, Healthcare, Pharmaceuticals) *see* PACKAGING

615.19 GBR
C M R INTERNATIONAL (YEAR) PHARMACEUTICAL R & D FACTBOOK. (Centre for Medicines Research, Research & Development) Text in English. 1996. a. **Document type:** *Directory, Trade.* **Description:** Provides insight into the state of the pharmaceutical industry and a source of emerging trends in worldwide pharmaceutical R&D.
Former titles (19??): Pharmaceutical R & D Compendium (1369-0027); (until 1997): Trends in Pharmaceutical R & D C M R Fact Book (1367-8051)
Related titles: Online - full text ed.: USD 3,990 (effective 2009).
Published by: (Centre for Medicines Research), C M R International (Subsidiary of: Thomson Reuters), The Johnson Bldg, 77, 2nd Fl, Hatton Garden, London, EC1N8JS, United Kingdom. TEL 44-207-4334299, FAX 44-207-4334310, cmr@thomsonreuters.com.

615 GBR ISSN 1462-656X
C N S DRUG NEWS. (Central Nervous System) Text in English. 1998. fortn. GBP 590, USD 1,120, EUR 885; GBP 45, USD 85, EUR 70 per issue (effective 2009). back issues avail. **Document type:** *Newsletter, Trade.* **Description:** Designed for the pharmaceutical company executives, researchers and commercial managers.
Related titles: E-mail ed.; Online - full text ed.: ISSN 1473-1576.
Published by: Espicom Business Intelligence, Lincoln House, City Fields Business Park, City Fields Way, Chichester, W Sussex PO20 2FS, United Kingdom. TEL 44-1243-533322, FAX 44-1243-533418, Annette_Bulbeck@espicom.com, http://www.espicom.com. Ed. Lucy Vann.

615.1 616.8 NZL ISSN 1172-7047
RM315 CODEN: CNDREF
➤ **C N S DRUGS.** (Central Nervous System) Text in English. 1994. m. price varies based on the number of users. bk.rev. back issues avail.; reprints avail. **Document type:** *Journal, Academic/Scholarly.* **Description:** Covers clinical aspects of psychiatric and neurological pharmacology.
Related titles: Online - full text ed.: ISSN 1179-1934 (from IngentaConnect).
Indexed: A01, A03, A08, A22, A26, ASCA, B21, BIOSIS Prev, C06, C07, CA, CIN, CTA, ChemAb, ChemTitl, CurCont, E-psyche, E01, E08, EMBASE, ESPM, ExcerpMed, FoP, H&SSA, H12, I05, I12, ISR, Inpharma, MEDLINE, MycolAb, NSA, NSCI, P03, P20, P22, P25, P30, P35, P43, P54, PQC, PsycInfo, PsycholAb, R09, R10, Reac, S09, SCI, SCOPUS, SD, T02, W07.
—BLDSC (3287.314345), CASDDS, GNLM, IE, Infotrieve, Ingenta, INIST. **CCC.**
Published by: Adis International Ltd. (Subsidiary of: Wolters Kluwer N.V.), 41 Centorian Dr, Mairangi Bay, Private Bag 65901, Auckland, 1311, New Zealand. TEL 64-9-4770700, FAX 64-9-4779764, journals@adis.com, http://www.adisonline.info/. Ed. Katharine Palmer.

615.1 GBR ISSN 1755-5930
RM315 CODEN: CDREFB
➤ **C N S NEUROSCIENCE & THERAPEUTICS.** Text in English. 1995. q. GBP 379 in United Kingdom to institutions; EUR 480 in Europe to institutions; USD 551 in the Americas to institutions; USD 740 elsewhere to institutions; GBP 436 combined subscription in United Kingdom to institutions (print & online eds.); EUR 552 combined subscription in Europe to institutions (print & online eds.); USD 633 combined subscription in the Americas to institutions (print & online eds.); USD 852 combined subscription elsewhere to institutions (print & online eds.) (effective 2012). index. back issues avail.; reprint service avail. from PSC. **Document type:** *Journal, Academic/Scholarly.* **Description:** Reviews of pharmacology, toxicology, pharmacokinetics, clinical trials with new drugs affecting the central nervous system, and reports on current scientific meetings.
Formerly (until 2008): C N S Drug Reviews (1080-563X)
Related titles: Online - full text ed.: C N S Neuroscience & Therapeutics (Online). ISSN 1755-5949. GBP 379 in United Kingdom to institutions; EUR 480 in Europe to institutions; USD 551 in the Americas to institutions; USD 740 elsewhere to institutions (effective 2012) (from IngentaConnect).
Indexed: A01, A22, A26, B&BAb, B21, BIOSIS Prev, CA, CIN, ChemAb, ChemTitl, CurCont, E-psyche, E01, EMBASE, ExcerpMed, FoP, H12, I12, Inpharma, MEDLINE, MycolAb, NSA, NSCI, P03, P30, PsycInfo, PsycholAb, R10, Reac, SCI, SCOPUS, T02, W07.
—BLDSC (9830.140000), CASDDS, GNLM, IE, Infotrieve, Ingenta. **CCC.**
Published by: Wiley-Blackwell Publishing Ltd. (Subsidiary of: John Wiley & Sons, Inc.), 9600 Garsington Rd, Oxford, OX4 2DQ, United Kingdom. TEL 44-1865-776868, FAX 44-1865-714591, customer@wiley.co.uk, http://www.wiley.com/. Eds. Roger Bullock, Dr. Mark H Pollack.

615.1 USA
C P F I NEWSLETTER. Text in English. 1984. q. free. bk.rev. back issues avail. **Document type:** *Newsletter.* **Description:** Communication link and network of Christian pharmacists around the world.
Published by: Christian Pharmacists Fellowship International, University of Maryland, School of Pharmacy, 20 North Pine St, Baltimore, MD 21201. http://www.pharmacy.umaryland.edu/studentorg/cpfi/. Ed. James E Thompson. Circ: 2,000.

615 NLD ISSN 1879-6540
C2W MEDICINES. (Chemisch2Weekblad) Text in Dutch. 1994. bi-m. EUR 42.75; EUR 9.50 newsstand/cover (effective 2010). adv. **Document type:** *Magazine, Trade.*
Formerly (until 2009): Conceptuur (1381-4613); Which was formed by the merger of (1990-1994): N V F W Nieuwsbrief (0929-2888); (1998-1994): Nederlandse Stichting ter Bevordering van Medisch-Farmaceutische Research. Nieuwsbrief (0929-2942)
Published by: (Federatie voor Innovatief Geneesmiddel Onderzoek Nederland), Beta Publishers, Postbus 19949, The Hague, 2500 CX, Netherlands. TEL 31-70-2629100, info@betapublishers.nl, http://www.betapublishers.nl.

615 EGY ISSN 1110-0931
CAIRO UNIVERSITY. FACULTY OF PHARMACY. BULLETIN. Text in English. 1962. a. **Document type:** *Bulletin, Academic/Scholarly.*
—BLDSC (2508.700000).
Published by: Cairo University, Faculty of Pharmacy, Qassr, el-Aini St, Cairo, 11562, Egypt. TEL 20-2-5311260, FAX 20-2-3628426. Ed. Dr. Nadya M Mursi.

615.19 USA ISSN 1097-6337
CALIFORNIA JOURNAL OF HEALTH - SYSTEM PHARMACY. Text in English. 1989. m. USD 125 membership (effective 2005). adv. back issues avail. **Document type:** *Journal, Trade.* **Description:** Reports news and legislature updates.
Formerly: California Journal of Hospital Pharmacy (1072-7809)
Indexed: I12.
—GNLM.
Published by: California Society of Health - System Pharmacists, 725 30th St, Ste 208, Sacramento, CA 95816-3842. TEL 916-447-1033, FAX 916-447-2396. Ed. Teresa Ann Miller. R&P Susan Trembly. Adv. contact Diana Granger. Circ: 3,800.

615.1 USA ISSN 0739-0483
CALIFORNIA PHARMACIST. Text in English. 1954. q. USD 50 to non-members; free to members (effective 2005). adv. bk.rev. charts; illus.; stat. index. **Document type:** *Magazine, Trade.* **Description:** Contains infomation for pharmacists to enable them to serve the public health and welfare. Includes continuing education articles. Readers California pharmacists, professors of pharmacy and pharmacy students.
Formerly: California Pharmacy (0008-1388)
Indexed: I12.
—BLDSC (3015.180000), IE, Ingenta.
Published by: California Pharmacists Association, 4030 Lennane Dr, Sacramento, CA 95834. TEL 916-779-1400, FAX 916-779-1401, cpha@cpha.com, http://www.cpha.com. R&P, Adv. contact Jamie Kesweder. B&W page USD 1,070, color page USD 1,800; trim 8.5 x 11. Circ: 6,000 (controlled).

CANADA. PATENTED MEDICINE PRICES REVIEW BOARD. ANNUAL REPORT. *see* PUBLIC ADMINISTRATION

615.1 CAN ISSN 1499-9447
CANADIAN ADVERSE REACTION NEWSLETTER. Text in English. q.
Related titles: Online - full text ed.: ISSN 1499-9455.
Indexed: C06, C07, Inpharma, P35, R10, Reac.
Published by: Health Canada/Sante Canada, Address Locator 0900C2, Ottawa, ON K1A OK9, Canada. TEL 613-954-8842, FAX 613-990-7097, http://www.hc-sc.gc.ca.

CANADIAN AGENCY FOR DRUGS AND TECHNOLOGIES IN HEALTH. TECHNOLOGY REPORT. *see* MEDICAL SCIENCES

615 CAN ISSN 1198-581X
RM301.28 CODEN: CJCPFB
CANADIAN JOURNAL OF CLINICAL PHARMACOLOGY/JOURNAL CANADIEN DE PHARMACOLOGIE CLINIQUE. Text in English. 1994. q. CAD 80 domestic to individuals; USD 80 in United States to individuals; USD 95 elsewhere to individuals; CAD 105 domestic to institutions; USD 105 in United States to institutions; USD 115 elsewhere to institutions (effective 2005). adv. **Document type:** *Journal, Academic/Scholarly.*
Related titles: Online - full text ed.: ISSN 1710-6222. free to individuals.
Indexed: EMBASE, ExcerpMed, IndMed, MEDLINE, P30, R10, Reac, SCOPUS.
—GNLM, IE, Infotrieve, Ingenta. **CCC.**
Published by: (Canadian Society for Clinical Pharmacology), Pulsus Group Inc., 2902 S Sheridan Way, Oakville, ON L6J 7L6, Canada. TEL 905-829-4770, FAX 905-829-4799, pulsus@pulsus.com, http://www.pulsus.com. Ed. Dr. Mitchell Levine TEL 905-522-1155 ext 4276. Pub. Robert B Kalina. adv.: B&W page CAD 1,530, color page CAD 2,840; trim 10.88 x 8.13. Circ: 7,000.

CANADIAN JOURNAL OF HERBALISM. *see* ALTERNATIVE MEDICINE

615.1 CAN ISSN 0008-4123
CODEN: CJHPAV
➤ **CANADIAN JOURNAL OF HOSPITAL PHARMACY.** Text in English, French. 1948. bi-m. CAD 100 domestic; CAD 125 in United States; CAD 165 elsewhere (effective 2008). adv. bk.rev. abstr.; charts; illus.; pat.; tr.lit. index. back issues avail.; reprints avail. **Document type:** *Journal, Academic/Scholarly.* **Description:** Publishes original research, clinical reviews, case reports, and topical discussions on pharmacy practice that are of use and interest to pharmacists engaged in institutional practice.
Formerly: Hospital Pharmacist
Related titles: Microform ed.: (from PQC); Online - full text ed.
Indexed: A22, C06, ChemAb, DBA, EMBASE, ExcerpMed, HospLI, I12, IDIS, Inpharma, P30, P35, R10, Reac, SCOPUS.
—BLDSC (3031.700000), GNLM, IE, Infotrieve, Ingenta. **CCC.**
Published by: Canadian Society of Hospital Pharmacists, 30 Concourse Gate, Unit 3, Ottawa, ON K2E 7V7, Canada. TEL 613-736-9733, FAX 613-736-5660. Ed. Scott Walker. Adv. contact Marnie Boggs Reach. Circ: 3,300.

➤ **CANADIAN JOURNAL OF PHYSIOLOGY AND PHARMACOLOGY/ JOURNAL CANADIEN DE PHYSIOLOGIE ET PHARMACOLOGIE.** *see* BIOLOGY—Physiology

615.1 CAN ISSN 1182-2902
CANADIAN PHARMACEUTICAL MARKETING. Text in English. 1988. q. USD 35 (effective 2005). back issues avail. **Document type:** *Journal, Trade.* **Description:** Features news about industry trends and developments, as well as special feature articles on pharmaceutical firms and advertising agencies.
Related titles: Online - full text ed.
Published by: S T A Communications Inc., 955 Blvd St Jean, Ste 306, Pointe Claire, PQ H9R 5K3, Canada. TEL 514-695-7623, FAX 514-695-8554. Ed. Paul F Brand. Pub. Robert Passaretti.

615.1 CAN ISSN 1715-1635
CODEN: CPJOAC
CANADIAN PHARMACISTS JOURNAL/REVUE PHARMACEUTIQUE CANADIENNE. Short title: C P J - R P C. Text in English. 1868. 10/yr. CAD 77 domestic to individuals; USD 117.75 foreign to individuals; CAD 110 domestic to institutions; USD 146 foreign to institutions (effective 2006). adv. bk.rev. **Document type:** *Journal, Trade.*
Formerly (until Jun. 2005): C P J - Canadian Pharmaceutical Journal (0828-6914); Which superseded in part (in 1984): Canadian Pharmaceutical Journal (0317-199X)
Related titles: Microfiche ed.: (from MML); Microform ed.: (from MML); Online - full text ed.
Indexed: A22, C03, C06, CBCARef, CBPI, DBA, EMBASE, ExcerpMed, I12, IDIS, Inpharma, P24, P30, P48, PQC, R10, Reac, SCOPUS, T02.
—BLDSC (3043.805000), CIS, GNLM, IE, Infotrieve, Ingenta, INIST, Linda Hall. **CCC.**
Published by: Canadian Pharmaceutical Association, 1785 Alta Vista Dr, Ottawa, ON K1G 3Y6, Canada. TEL 613-523-7877, 800-917-9489, FAX 613-523-0445, info@pharmacists.ca. Circ: 20,000.

CANCER BIOTHERAPY & RADIOPHARMACEUTICALS. *see* MEDICAL SCIENCES—Oncology

CANCER CHEMOTHERAPY AND PHARMACOLOGY. *see* MEDICAL SCIENCES—Oncology

CANCER CHEMOTHERAPY AND PHARMACOLOGY. SUPPLEMENT. *see* MEDICAL SCIENCES—Oncology

CARDIOVASCULAR DRUGS AND THERAPY. *see* MEDICAL SCIENCES—Cardiovascular Diseases

615 GBR ISSN 1755-5914
RM345 CODEN: CDREEA
➤ **CARDIOVASCULAR THERAPEUTICS.** Text in English. 1983. q. GBP 377 in United Kingdom to institutions; EUR 477 in Europe to institutions; USD 547 in the Americas to institutions; USD 737 elsewhere to institutions; GBP 434 combined subscription in United Kingdom to institutions (print & online eds.); EUR 550 combined subscription in Europe to institutions (print & online eds.); USD 630 combined subscription in the Americas to institutions (print & online eds.); USD 848 combined subscription elsewhere to institutions (print & online eds.) (effective 2012). adv. back issues avail.; reprint service avail. from PSC. **Document type:** *Journal, Academic/Scholarly.* **Description:** Reviews of pharmacology, pharmacokinetics, toxicology, clinical trials of new cardiovascular drugs, and reports on current scientific meetings.
Former titles (until 2008): Cardiovascular Drug Reviews (0897-5957); (until 1988): New Cardiovascular Drugs (0891-3692); (until 1985): New Drugs Annual, Cardiovascular Drugs (0742-387X)
Related titles: Online - full text ed.: Cardiovascular Therapeutics (Online). ISSN 1755-5922. GBP 377 in United Kingdom to institutions; EUR 477 in Europe to institutions; USD 547 in the Americas to institutions; USD 737 elsewhere to institutions (effective 2012) (from IngentaConnect).
Indexed: A01, A22, A26, ASCA, B25, BIOSIS Prev, CA, CIN, ChemAb, ChemTitl, CurCont, E01, EMBASE, ExcerpMed, H12, I12, ISR, Inpharma, MEDLINE, MycolAb, P30, R10, Reac, SCI, SCOPUS, T02, W07.
—BLDSC (3051.520500), CASDDS, GNLM, IE, Infotrieve, Ingenta, INIST. **CCC.**
Published by: Wiley-Blackwell Publishing Ltd. (Subsidiary of: John Wiley & Sons, Inc.), 9600 Garsington Rd, Oxford, OX4 2DQ, United Kingdom. TEL 44-1865-776868, FAX 44-1865-714591, customer@wiley.co.uk. Eds. Chim C Lang, Henry Krum, Jane E Freedman. adv.: B&W page USD 500; trim 8.25 x 10.875. Circ: 143 (paid).

615.19 USA ISSN 1545-6471
THE CATHOLIC PHARMACIST. Text in English. 1968. q. USD 20 to members (effective 2000). adv. bk.rev. 8 p./no.; back issues avail. **Document type:** *Newsletter, Trade.* **Description:** Acquaints members with the latest developments in their church affecting their profession, as well as feature articles and membership news.
Published by: National Catholic Pharmacists Guild of the United States, 1012 Surrey Hills Dr., St. Louis, MO 63117-1438. TEL 314-645-0085. Ed., R&P, Adv. contact John Paul Winkelmann. Circ: 375.

615 610 GBR ISSN 2044-3536
▼ **CENTRAL AMERICA PHARMACEUTICALS & HEALTHCARE REPORT.** Text in English. 2010. q. EUR 820, USD 1,150 combined subscription (print & email eds.) (effective 2010). **Document type:** *Report, Trade.* **Description:** Provides industry professionals, market investors and corporate and financial services analysts with independent forecasts and competitive intelligence on the Central American pharmaceutical and healthcare industry.
Related titles: E-mail ed.
Published by: Business Monitor International Ltd., Senator House, 85 Queen Victoria St, London, EC4V 4AB, United Kingdom. TEL 44-20-72480468, FAX 44-20-72480467, subs@businessmonitor.com.

615 NLD
➤ **CENTRE FOR MEDICINES RESEARCH WORKSHOP.** Variant title: C M R Workshop. Text in English. irreg., latest 1998. price varies. **Document type:** *Proceedings, Academic/Scholarly.*
Published by: (Centre for Medicines Research GBR), Springer Netherlands (Subsidiary of: Springer Science+Business Media), Van Godewijckstraat 30, Dordrecht, 3311 GX, Netherlands. TEL 31-78-6576050, FAX 31-78-6576474.

615 CZE ISSN 1210-7816
RS1 CODEN: CSLFEK
➤ **CESKA A SLOVENSKA FARMACIE/CZECH AND SLOVAK PHARMACY.** Text in Czech, Slovak; Summaries in Czech, English. 1952. 6/yr. CZK 900, EUR 39.60 (effective 2010). adv. bk.rev. index. **Document type:** *Journal, Academic/Scholarly.* **Description:** Publishes original papers, reviews and short communications form the field of pharmacy and allied disciplines. Provides information on research dealing with synthetic and natural drugs, pharmacokinetics, technology of new drug forms, cultivation of medicinal plants, pharmaceutical care, dispensing, etc.
Formerly (until 1994): Ceskoslovenska Farmacie (0009-0530)
Related titles: Online - full text ed.
Indexed: A22, C33, CIN, CISA, ChemAb, ChemTitl, DBA, EMBASE, ExcerpMed, I12, IndMed, MEDLINE, P30, R10, Reac, SCOPUS.
—BLDSC (3120.258380), CASDDS, GNLM, IE, Infotrieve, Ingenta, INIST, Linda Hall. **CCC.**
Published by: (Ceska Lekarska Spolecnost J.E. Purkyne/Czech Medical Association), Nakladatelske Stredisko C L S J.E. Purkyne, Sokolska 31, Prague, 12026, Czech Republic. nts@cls.cz. Ed. Pavel Komarek. adv.: B&W page CZK 29,300, color page CZK 41,000; 246 x 180. Circ: 900.

➤ **CHEMANAGER EUROPE.** *see* CHEMISTRY

➤ **CHEMICAL & PHARMACEUTICAL BULLETIN.** *see* CHEMISTRY

➤ **CHEMICAL RESEARCH IN TOXICOLOGY.** *see* ENVIRONMENTAL STUDIES—Toxicology And Environmental Safety

➤ **CHEMISCHE RUNDSCHAU**; Magazin fuer Chemie, Lebensmitteltechnologie, Pharmazie und Biotechnologie. *see* CHEMISTRY

615.1 GBR ISSN 0009-3033
RS1.C54 CODEN: CHDRA3
CHEMIST & DRUGGIST; for retailer, wholesaler, manufacturer. Text in English. 1859. w. GBP 190 domestic without price list; GBP 305 foreign without price list; GBP 290 domestic includes price list; GBP 355 foreign includes price list (effective 2009). adv. bk.rev. charts; illus.; mkt.; pat.; tr.mk. s-a. index. **Document type:** *Magazine, Trade.*
Incorporates: Retail Chemist (0034-6020)
Related titles: Microform ed.: (from PQC); Online - full text ed.; ◆ Supplement(s): Chemist & Druggist Monthly Price List. ISSN 1369-3980; ◆ Over the Counter. ISSN 0957-7831; Chemist & Druggist Generics. ISSN 0266-3031. 1984.
Indexed: A15, A26, ABIn, B01, B02, B03, B07, B11, B15, B17, B18, CWI, ChemAb, E08, G04, G06, G07, G08, I05, M06, P16, P24, P30, P48, P51, P53, P54, PQC, S09.
—CASDDS, CIS, IE, Infotrieve, Ingenta, Linda Hall. **CCC.**
Published by: (Pharmaceutical Society of Northern Ireland), C M P Medica Ltd. (Subsidiary of: United Business Media Limited), Ludgate House, 245 Blackfriars Rd, London, SE1 9UY, United Kingdom. TEL 44-20-79215000, FAX 44-20-79218312, info@cmpmedica.com, http://www.cmpmedica.com/. Ed. Fiona Salvage TEL 44-1732-377435. Adv. contact Dan Spruytenburg TEL 44-20-89218126. page GBP 4,301; trim 210 x 297.

615.10294 GBR ISSN 1369-3980
CHEMIST & DRUGGIST MONTHLY PRICE LIST. Variant title: C + D Price List. Text in English. 1960. m. GBP 240 (effective 2009); includes subscr. to Chemist + Druggist. adv. **Document type:** *Report, Trade.* **Description:** Includes details of more than 1,000 manufacturers and distributors, new and deleted products, pack sizes, trade prices and retail prices.
Former titles (until 1988): Chemist & Druggist Price List (0266-3023); (until 1973): Chemist & Druggist Quarterly Price List
Related titles: ◆ Supplement to: Chemist & Druggist. ISSN 0009-3033.
—**CCC.**
Published by: C M P Medica Ltd. (Subsidiary of: United Business Media Limited), Riverbank House, Angel Ln, Tonbridge, Kent TN9 1SE, United Kingdom. TEL 44-1732-377612, FAX 44-1732-367065, info@cmpmedica.com. Circ: 15,413.

CHEMISTRY & INDUSTRY. *see* CHEMISTRY

615.1 PAK ISSN 0009-3149
CHEMISTS REVIEW. Text in English, Urdu. 1957. m. PKR 250. adv. bk.rev. charts; illus. **Document type:** *Journal, Academic/Scholarly.*
Address: P O Box 376, Karachi, Pakistan. Ed. M Y Ansari. Circ: 5,000.

615.19 DEU ISSN 1860-7179
RS400 CODEN: CHEMGX
CHEMMEDCHEM; chemistry enabling drug discovery. Text in German. 2006. m. GBP 1,493 in United Kingdom to institutions; EUR 2,278 in Europe to institutions; USD 2,925 elsewhere to institutions (effective 2012). reprint service avail. from PSC. **Document type:** *Journal, Academic/Scholarly.* **Description:** Aims to integrate the wide and flourishing field of medicinal and pharmaceutical sciences, ranging from drug design and discovery to drug development and delivery.
Related titles: Online - full text ed.: ISSN 1860-7187. GBP 1,493 in United Kingdom to institutions; EUR 2,278 in Europe to institutions; USD 2,925 elsewhere to institutions (effective 2012).
Indexed: B25, BIOSIS Prev, C33, CurCont, EMBASE, ExcerpMed, MEDLINE, MycolAb, P30, R10, Reac, SCI, SCOPUS, W07.
—BLDSC (3172.254000), IE, Ingenta, INIST, Linda Hall. **CCC.**
Published by: Wiley - V C H Verlag GmbH & Co. KGaA (Subsidiary of: John Wiley & Sons, Inc.), Postfach 101161, Weinheim, 69451, Germany. TEL 49-6201-606400, FAX 49-6201-606184, info@wiley-vch.de, http://www.wiley-vch.de. Ed. Rainer Metternich.

615.1 CHE ISSN 0009-3157
RM260 CODEN: CHTHBK
➤ **CHEMOTHERAPY**; international journal of experimental and clinical chemotherapy. Text in English. 1960. bi-m. CHF 2,268, EUR 1,813, USD 2,222.50 to institutions; CHF 2,490, EUR 1,990, USD 2,438.50 combined subscription to institutions (print & online eds.) (effective 2012). adv. bk.rev. bibl.; charts; illus. back issues avail. **Document type:** *Journal, Academic/Scholarly.* **Description:** Publishes the results of investigations into the mode of action and pharmacologic properties of antibacterial, antiviral and antitumor substances.
Formerly (until 1967): Chemotherapia (0366-7170)
Related titles: Microfilm ed.; Online - full text ed.: ISSN 1421-9794. CHF 2,217, EUR 1,774, USD 2,152 to institutions (effective 2012).
Indexed: A01, A03, A08, A22, A34, A35, A36, ASCA, AgBio, AgrForAb, B25, BIOSIS Prev, BP, BioDAb, C33, CA, CABA, CIN, ChemAb, ChemTitl, CurCont, DBA, E01, E12, EMBASE, ExcerpMed, F08, F11, F12, GH, H13, H16, IBR, IBZ, IDIS, ISR, IndMed, IndVet, Inpharma, MEDLINE, MycolAb, N02, N03, P02, P10, P20, P22, P30, P32, P33, P35, P39, P48, P53, P54, PQC, R08, R10, R12, RA&MP, RM&VM, Reac, SCI, SCOPUS, T02, T05, VS, W07, W10.
—BLDSC (3172.304000), CASDDS, GNLM, IE, Infotrieve, Ingenta, INIST. **CCC.**
Published by: S. Karger AG, Allschwilerstr 10, Basel, 4055, Switzerland. TEL 41-61-3061111, FAX 41-61-3061234, karger@karger.ch, http://www.karger.ch. Ed. F. Soergel. adv.: page CHF 1,730; trim 177 x 252. Circ: 800.

P

615.9 JPN
CHIBA DAIGAKU. DAIGAKUIN. YAKUGAKUBU KENKYU GYOSEKI MOKUROKU/CHIBA UNIVERSITY. GRADUATE SCHOOL OF PHARMACEUTICAL SCIENCES. RECORD OF RESEARCH ACTIVITIES. Text in Japanese. 1984. biennial. **Document type:** *Academic/Scholarly.*
Formerly (until 1999): Chiba Daigaku Yakugakubu Kenkyu Gyoseki Mokuroku/Chiba University. Faculty of Pharmaceutical Sciences. List of Research Activities
Published by: Chiba Daigaku, Yakugakubu/Chiba University, Faculty of Pharmaceutical Sciences, 1-33 Yayoi-cho, Inage-ku, Chiba-shi, 263-0022, Japan. TEL 81-43-290-2981, FAX 81-43-290-2974. Circ: 300.

615.9 617.6 JPN ISSN 0300-029X
CHIKEN ISHIYAKU JOHO/INVESTIGATIONAL DRUG INFORMATION. MEDICAL AND DENTAL. Text in Japanese. 1970. a. **Document type:** *Journal, Academic/Scholarly.*
Related titles: ◆ Supplement to: Shinryo to Shinyaku. ISSN 0037-380X.
Published by: Iji Shuppansha, 1-2-8 Shinkawa, Chuo-ku, Tokyo, 104-0033, Japan. TEL 81-3-35550815, FAX 81-3-35551150, http://www.iji.co.jp/.

CHILD AND ADOLESCENT PSYCHOPHARMACOLOGY NEWS. *see* MEDICAL SCIENCES—Psychiatry And Neurology

CHIMICA OGGI/CHEMISTRY TODAY. *see* CHEMISTRY

CHINESE MEDICAL SCIENCES JOURNAL. *see* MEDICAL SCIENCES

615 IND ISSN 0975-9212
R21
▼ ➤ **CHRONICLES OF YOUNG SCIENTISTS.** Text in English. 2010. irreg. free (effective 2011). abstr. back issues avail. **Document type:** *Journal, Academic/Scholarly.* **Description:** Provides a platform to young scientists and students for the publication of their short communications and general reviews on all interdisciplinary aspects of pharmaceutical sciences, medicinal chemistry, pharmacology, biotechnology, phytomedicine, biomedical and other bioallied sciences.
Media: Online - full text.
Indexed: A26, H11, H12, I05, I07.
—**CCC.**
Published by: Open Publications, 21 Jaina Bldg., Roshanara Rd., Delhi, 110007, India. http://www.opubs.com. Ed. Roop K. Khar. Pub., R&P, Adv. contact Himanshu Gupta.

▼ ➤ **CHRONOPHYSIOLOGY AND THERAPY.** *see* MEDICAL SCIENCES—Physical Medicine And Rehabilitation

➤ **CHUDOKU KENKYU/JAPANESE JOURNAL OF TOXICOLOGY.** *see* ENVIRONMENTAL STUDIES—Toxicology And Environmental Safety

615.1 PER ISSN 1561-0861
CIENCIA E INVESTIGACION. Text in Spanish. 1998. s-a.
Related titles: Online - full text ed.: ISSN 1609-9044.
Published by: Universidad Nacional Mayor de San Marcos, Facultad de Farmacia y Bioquimica, Ciudad Universitaria, Ave Venezuela Cdra 34, Lima, 1, Peru. TEL 51-1-3284743, FAX 51-1-3281560, http://www.unmsm.edu.pe/farmacia/farmacia.htm.

CLINICAL AND EXPERIMENTAL PHARMACOLOGY & PHYSIOLOGY. *see* BIOLOGY—Physiology

615.9 USA
CLINICAL CONSULT. Text in English. 1982. m. back issues avail.; reprints avail. **Document type:** *Newsletter, Consumer.* **Description:** Focuses on geriatric drug therapy and, or clinical illness and offers guidance to readers on drug therapy monitoring criteria.
Related titles: Online - full text ed.
Published by: American Society of Consultant Pharmacists, 1321 Duke St, Alexandria, VA 22314. TEL 703-739-1300, 800-355-2727, FAX 703-739-1321, 800-220-1321, info@ascp.com, http://www.ascp.com.

615 NZL ISSN 1173-2563
CODEN: CDINFR
➤ **CLINICAL DRUG INVESTIGATION.** Text in English. 1989. m. price varies based on the number of users. back issues avail.; reprints avail. **Document type:** *Journal, Academic/Scholarly.* **Description:** Brings out research covering all phases of clinical drug development and therapeutic use of drugs.
Formerly (until 1995): Drug Investigation (0114-2402)
Related titles: Online - full text ed.: ISSN 1179-1918 (from IngentaConnect).
Indexed: A01, A03, A08, A22, A26, A36, ASCA, B25, BIOBASE, BIOSIS Prev, CA, CABA, CIN, ChemAb, ChemTitl, CurCont, D01, DBA, E01, E08, EMBASE, ExcerpMed, F08, F11, F12, GH, H12, I05, I12, IABS, ISR, IndMed, Inpharma, MEDLINE, MycolAb, N02, N03, P20, P22, P30, P33, P35, P54, PQC, R09, R10, R11, RA&MP, RM&VM, Reac, S09, SCI, SCOPUS, SD, T02, T05, W07.
—BLDSC (3286.273600), CASDDS, GNLM, IE, Infotrieve, Ingenta, INIST, Linda Hall. **CCC.**
Published by: Adis International Ltd. (Subsidiary of: Wolters Kluwer N.V.), 41 Centorian Dr, Mairangi Bay, Private Bag 65901, Auckland, 1311, New Zealand. TEL 64-9-4770700, FAX 64-9-4770764, journals@adis.com, http://www.adisonline.info/. Ed. Jasbir Singh. **Americas subscr. to:** Adis International Inc.

615 USA ISSN 1208-6495
RM315
CLINICAL HANDBOOK OF PSYCHOTROPIC DRUGS. Text in English. 1988. irreg., latest 2009, 18th ed. USD 79 per issue domestic; CAD 86 per issue in Canada; EUR 57 per issue in Europe (effective 2009). 348 p./no.; **Document type:** *Handbook/Manual/Guide, Trade.* **Description:** Designed for psychiatrists, psychologists, physicians, nurses, pharmacists, and all categories of mental health professionals. Contains a summary of information about psychotropic drugs.
Published by: Hogrefe Publishing Corp., 875 Massachusetts Ave, 7th Fl, Cambridge, MA 02139. TEL 866-823-4726, FAX 617-354-6875, customservices@hogrefe-publishing.com, http://www.hogrefe.com. Eds. J Joel Jeffries, Kalyna Bezchlibnyk-Butler.

570 615 USA ISSN 1068-1191
CLINICAL INVESTIGATOR NEWS. Text in English. 1993. m. USD 857 in US & Canada; USD 897 elsewhere (effective 2011). bibl.; pat.; stat.; tr.lit. back issues avail.; reprints avail. **Document type:** *Newsletter, Trade.* **Description:** Covers new drug study opportunities, which companies are targeting, what compounds, when they plan to begin trials, and where they stand in their research.
Incorporates (in 2003): Clinical Trials Monitor
Related titles: Online - full text ed.
Indexed: Inpharma.
—CCC.
Published by: C T B International Publishing Inc., PO Box 218, Maplewood, NJ 07040. TEL 973-966-0997, FAX 973-966-0242, info@ctbintl.com.

615 NZL ISSN 1179-2558
▼ ➤ **CLINICAL MEDICINE REVIEWS IN THERAPEUTICS.** Text in English. 2009. irreg. free (effective 2011). **Document type:** *Journal, Academic/Scholarly.* **Description:** Focuses on the role of therapeutics in human clinical medicine.
Media: Online - full text.
—CCC.
Published by: Libertas Academica Ltd., PO Box 300-874, Mairangi Bay, Auckland, 0751, New Zealand. TEL 64-9-4763930, FAX 64-9-3531397, editorial@la-press.com. Ed. Garry Walsh.

615 USA ISSN 0362-5664
RM315 CODEN: CLNEDB
➤ **CLINICAL NEUROPHARMACOLOGY.** Text in English. 1976. bi-m. USD 897 domestic to institutions; USD 1,061 foreign to institutions (effective 2011). adv. charts; illus. index. back issues avail.; reprints avail. **Document type:** *Journal, Academic/Scholarly.* **Description:** Covers all aspects of mechanisms of action, structure-activity relationships, and drug metabolism and pharmacokinetics, to practical clinical problems such as drug interactions, drug toxicity, and therapy for specific syndromes and symptoms.
Related titles: Online - full text ed.: ISSN 1537-162X. USD 598 domestic for academic site license; USD 683 foreign for academic site license; USD 667 domestic for corporate site license; USD 752 foreign for corporate site license (effective 2002).
Indexed: A22, ASCA, B21, B25, BIOBASE, BIOSIS Prev, CIN, ChemAb, ChemTitl, CurCont, DBA, E-psyche, EMBASE, ESPM, ExcerpMed, FoP, IABS, ISR, IndMed, Inpharma, MEDLINE, MLA-IB, MycolAb, NSA, NSCI, P03, P30, P35, PsycInfo, PsycholAb, R10, Reac, SCI, SCOPUS, ToxAb, W07.
—BLDSC (3286.310600), CASDDS, GNLM, IE, Infotrieve, Ingenta, INIST. **CCC.**
Published by: Lippincott Williams & Wilkins (Subsidiary of: Wolters Kluwer N.V.), 530 Walnut St, Philadelphia, PA 19106. TEL 215-521-8300, FAX 215-521-8902, customerservice@lww.com, http://www.lww.com. Ed. Peter A LeWitt TEL 248-355-2452. Pub. Harry Dean. Adv. contact Michelle Smith TEL 646-674-6537. Circ: 205.

615 GBR ISSN 1758-9061
CLINICAL PHARMACIST. Text in English. 1994. 11/yr. GBP 227 domestic (effective 2010); EUR 310 in Europe (effective 2009); USD 450 in United States; GBP 286 elsewhere; free to qualified personnel (effective 2010). adv. back issues avail. **Document type:** *Journal, Trade.* **Description:** Provides coverage of material devoted to hospital pharmacists.
Formerly (until 2009): The Hospital Pharmacist (1352-7967)
Related titles: Online - full text ed.
Indexed: EMBASE, ExcerpMed, I12, R10, Reac, SCOPUS.
—BLDSC (3286.326650), IE, Ingenta. **CCC.**
Published by: (Royal Pharmaceutical Society of Great Britain), Pharmaceutical Press (Subsidiary of: Royal Pharmaceutical Society of Great Britain), 1 Lambeth High St, London, SE1 7JN, United Kingdom. TEL 44-20-77359141, FAX 44-20-75722509, enquiries@rpsgb.org, http://www.pharmpress.com/. Ed. Gareth Malson. Pub., R&P Charles Fry TEL 44-20-75722274. Adv. contact Jack Richmond. Circ: 6,500. **Dist. by:** Turpin Distribution Services Ltd., Pegasus Dr, Stratton Business Park, Biggleswade, Bedfordshire SG18 8QB, United Kingdom. TEL 44-1767-604800, FAX 44-1767-601640, custserv@turpin-distribution.com, http://www.turpin-distribution.com/.

615 NZL ISSN 0312-5963
RM1 CODEN: CPKNDH
➤ **CLINICAL PHARMACOKINETICS.** Text in English. 1976. m. price varies based on the number of users. back issues avail.; reprints avail. **Document type:** *Journal, Academic/Scholarly.* **Description:** Provides clinically relevant pharmacokinetic knowledge to aid in the delivery of rational drug therapy.
Related titles: Online - full text ed.: ISSN 1179-1926 (from IngentaConnect).
Indexed: A01, A03, A08, A22, A26, A34, A36, ASCA, BIOSIS Prev, BP, C06, C07, CA, CABA, CIN, ChemAb, ChemTitl, CurCont, D01, DBA, DentInd, E01, E08, E12, EMBASE, ExcerpMed, F08, GH, H12, I05, I12, IBR, IBZ, ISR, IndMed, Inpharma, Kidney, MEDLINE, MycolAb, N02, N03, P20, P22, P30, P33, P35, P39, P54, PQC, R10, RA&MP, RM&VM, Reac, S01, S09, SCI, SCOPUS, T02, T05, THA, W07.
—BLDSC (3286.327000), CASDDS, GNLM, IE, Infotrieve, Ingenta, INIST. **CCC.**
Published by: Adis International Ltd. (Subsidiary of: Wolters Kluwer N.V.), 41 Centorian Dr, Mairangi Bay, Private Bag 65901, Auckland, 1311, New Zealand. TEL 64-9-4770700, FAX 64-9-4770764, journals@adis.com, http://www.adisonline.info/. Ed. Amitabh Prakash. **Americas subscr. to:** Adis International Inc.

▼ ➤ **CLINICAL PHARMACOLOGY**; advances and applications. *see* MEDICAL SCIENCES—Experimental Medicine, Laboratory Technique

615 USA ISSN 0009-9236
RM1 CODEN: CLPTAT
➤ **CLINICAL PHARMACOLOGY AND THERAPEUTICS.** Abbreviated title: C P T. Text in English. 1960. m. EUR 717 in Europe to institutions; USD 824 in the Americas to institutions; JPY 123,900 in Japan to institutions; GBP 486 to institutions in the UK & elsewhere (effective 2011). adv. charts; illus. s-a. index. back issues avail.; reprints avail. **Document type:** *Journal, Academic/Scholarly.* **Description:** Devoted to the study of the nature, action, disposition, efficacy and total evaluation of drugs as they are used in man.
Related titles: CD-ROM ed.: ISSN 1085-8733. 199?; Microform ed.: (from PQC); Online - full text ed.: ISSN 1532-6535.
Indexed: A22, A26, A34, A36, AIIM, AIM, ASCA, B&BAb, B19, B21, B25, BIOSIS Prev, C06, C07, C08, C13, C24, C30, CA, CABA, CIN, CINAHL, CIS, CTA, ChemAb, ChemTitl, CurCont, D01, DBA, DentInd, E01, E12, EMBASE, ESPM, ExcerpMed, FR, GH, H12, I05, I12, IDIS, ISR, IndMed, IndVet, Inpharma, JW-D, JW-P, Kidney, MEDLINE, MS&D, MycolAb, N02, N03, NRN, P30, P33, P35, P37, P39, PN&I, R10, R12, RA&MP, RM&VM, Reac, RefZh, SCI, SCOPUS, T02, T05, THA, VS, W07, W11.
—BLDSC (3286.330000), CASDDS, GNLM, IE, Infotrieve, Ingenta, INIST. **CCC.**
Published by: (American Society for Clinical Pharmacology and Therapeutics), Nature Publishing Group (Subsidiary of: Macmillan Publishers Ltd.), 75 Varick St, 9th Fl, New York, NY 10013. TEL 212-726-9200, FAX 212-696-9006, subscriptions@nature.com. Ed. Scott Waldman. Adv. contact Ben Harkinson TEL 212-726-9360. **Subscr. to:** Nature Publishing Group, Brunel Rd, Houndmills, Basingstoke, Hamps RG21 6XS, United Kingdom. TEL 44-1256-329242, FAX 44-1256-812358, subscriptions@nature.com. **Co-sponsor:** American Society for Pharmacology and Experimental Therapeutics.

➤ **CLINICAL PSYCHOPHARMACOLOGY AND NEUROSCIENCE.** *see* MEDICAL SCIENCES—Psychiatry And Neurology

➤ **CLINICAL RESEARCH MANUAL.** *see* MEDICAL SCIENCES

➤ **CLINICAL RESEARCH & CONTRACT MANUFACTURING.** *see* BUSINESS AND ECONOMICS

615.1072 GBR ISSN 1060-1333
RS122 CODEN: CRRAES
➤ **CLINICAL RESEARCH AND REGULATORY AFFAIRS.** Text in English. 1983. q. GBP 845, EUR 1,115, USD 1,395 combined subscription to institutions (print & online eds.); GBP 1,720, EUR 2,270, USD 2,840 combined subscription to corporations (print & online eds.) (effective 2010). bk.rev. illus.; charts; stat. index. back issues avail.; reprint service avail. from PSC. **Document type:** *Journal, Academic/Scholarly.* **Description:** Aims to the dissemination of knowledge about the issues and challenges of clinical research with a special emphasis on the design, conduct, analysis, synthesis, history, ethics, regulation, and clinical and policy aspects of drug development.
Formerly (until 1992): Clinical Research Practices and Drug Regulatory Affairs (0735-7915)
Related titles: Microform ed.: (from RPI); Online - full text ed.: ISSN 1532-2521.
Indexed: A01, A03, A08, A20, A22, ASCA, B07, B20, B21, CA, E01, EMBASE, ESPM, ExcerpMed, FR, H&SSA, I12, P30, R10, Reac, RefZh, SCOPUS, T02.
—BLDSC (3286.372100), GNLM, IE, Infotrieve, Ingenta, INIST. **CCC.**
Published by: Informa Healthcare (Subsidiary of: T & F Informa plc), Telephone House, 69-77 Paul St, London, EC2A 4LQ, United Kingdom. TEL 44-20-70175000, FAX 44-20-70176792, healthcare.enquiries@informa.com. Eds. Uday B Kompella, Dr. Sandy B Weinberg. **Subscr. in N. America to:** Taylor & Francis Inc., Customer Services Dept, 325 Chestnut St, 8th Fl, Philadelphia, PA 19106. TEL 215-625-8900, 800-354-1420, FAX 215-625-8914, customerservice@taylorandfrancis.com; **Subscr. outside N. America to:** Taylor & Francis Ltd., Journals Customer Service, Sheepen Pl, Colchester, Essex CO3 3LP, United Kingdom. TEL 44-20-70175544, FAX 44-20-70175198, tf.enquiries@tfinforma.com.

615 USA ISSN 0149-2918
RM260 CODEN: CLTHDG
➤ **CLINICAL THERAPEUTICS**; the international peer-reviewed journal of drug therapy. Text in English. 1977. m. USD 670 elsewhere to institutions (effective 2012). charts; illus. index. Supplement avail.; back issues avail.; reprints avail. **Document type:** *Journal, Academic/Scholarly.* **Description:** Publishes review articles and results of original clinical and pharmacoeconomic research in the broad field of medical and pharmaceutical therapy and related areas, with a specialty section on pediatric research.
Related titles: Online - full text ed.: ISSN 1879-114X (from IngentaConnect, ScienceDirect).
Indexed: A01, A03, A08, A22, A26, A34, A36, ASCA, AgrForAb, B25, BIOSIS Prev, BP, C06, C07, C08, CA, CABA, CINAHL, ChemAb, CurCont, D01, DBA, E-psyche, E12, EMBASE, ExcerpMed, F08, F11, F12, FR, GH, H12, I05, I12, IDIS, ISR, IndMed, Inpharma, MEDLINE, MS&D, MycolAb, N02, N03, P03, P30, P32, P33, P35, P39, PsycholAb, R10, R12, RA&MP, RM&VM, Reac, SCI, SCOPUS, T02, T05, VS, W07, W11.
—BLDSC (3286.399450), CASDDS, GNLM, IE, Infotrieve, Ingenta, INIST. **CCC.**
Published by: Excerpta Medica, Inc. (Subsidiary of: Elsevier Health Sciences), 685 US-202, Bridgewater, NJ 08807. TEL 908-547-2100, FAX 908-547-2200, excerptamedica@elsevier.com, http://www.excerptamedica.com/. Ed. Dr. Philip D Walson. Pub. Jo-Ann E West TEL 908-547-2082.

615 USA ISSN 1556-3650
RA1190 CODEN: JTCTDW
➤ **CLINICAL TOXICOLOGY.** Text in English. 1968. 10/yr. GBP 2,995, EUR 3,955, USD 4,940 combined subscription to institutions (print & online eds.); GBP 6,095, EUR 8,050, USD 10,065 combined subscription to corporations (print & online eds.) (effective 2010). adv. back issues avail.; reprint service avail. from PSC. **Document type:** *Journal, Academic/Scholarly.* **Description:** Correlates the various disciplines that deal directly with and contribute to the practical aspects of poisoning.
Formerly (until 2005): Journal of Toxicology. Clinical Toxicology (0731-3810); Which superseded (in 1982): Clinical Toxicology (0009-9309)
Related titles: Microform ed.: (from RPI); Online - full text ed.: ISSN 1556-9519 (from IngentaConnect).
Indexed: A01, A02, A03, A08, A20, A22, A26, A34, A36, A37, A38, AIM, ASCA, Agr, AgrForAb, B21, B23, B25, BIOBASE, BIOSIS Prev, BP, C11, C25, CA, CABA, CIN, CISA, CTA, ChemAb, ChemTitl, CurCont, D01, DBA, DentInd, E01, E04, E05, E08, E12, EMBASE, ESPM, EnerRev, EnvAb, EnvInd, ExcerpMed, F08, F11, F12, FCA, G06, G07, G08, G11, GH, H&SSA, H04, H11, H12, H16, I05, IABS, IDIS, INIS AtomInd, ISR, IndMed, IndVet, Inpharma, JW-EM, LT, MEDLINE, MedAb, MycolAb, N02, N03, N05, NRN, NSA, P30, P32, P33, P35, P37, P39, P40, PGegResA, PHN&I, PN&I, R07, R08, R10, R11, R12, R13, RA&MP, RM&VM, RRTA, Reac, RefZh, S09, S12, SCI, SCOPUS, T02, T05, TAR, THA, ToxAb, TriticAb, VS, W07, W10, WildRev.
—CASDDS, GNLM, IE, Infotrieve, Ingenta, INIST, Linda Hall. **CCC.**
Published by: (American Academy of Clinical Toxicology), Informa Healthcare (Subsidiary of: T & F Informa plc), 52 Vanderbilt Ave, New York, NY 10017. TEL 212-262-8230, FAX 212-262-8234, healthcare.enquiries@informa.com, http://www.informahealthcare.com. Ed. Nicholas Bateman. Adv. contact Daniel Wallen. **Subscr. outside N. America to:** Taylor & Francis Ltd. **Co-sponsor:** European Association of Poison Centres and Clinical Toxicologists.

➤ **CLINICAL TRIALS.** *see* MEDICAL SCIENCES—Experimental Medicine, Laboratory Technique

615 ARG ISSN 1667-9172
COLECCION TRABAJOS DISTINGUIDOS. SERIE MEDICINA FARMACEUTICA. Text in Spanish. 2003. 6/yr. back issues avail. **Document type:** *Journal, Academic/Scholarly.*
Media: Online - full text.
Published by: Sociedad Iberoamericana de Informacion Cientifica (S I I C), Ave Belgrano 430, Buenos Aires, C1092AAR, Argentina. TEL 54-11-43424901, FAX 54-11-43313305, atencionallector@siicsalud.com, http://www.siicsalud.com. Ed. Rafael Bernal Castro.

615.1 ESP ISSN 0009-7314
CODEN: CFPBE5
COLEGIO OFICIAL DE FARMACEUTICO. CIRCULAR FARMACEUTICA. Text in Spanish. 1943. 4/yr. adv. charts; illus. **Document type:** *Bulletin, Consumer.*
Related titles: Online - full text ed.: 1943; ◆ Supplement(s): I CoFB. ISSN 2013-4398.
Indexed: I12, IECT, P30, R10, Reac, SCOPUS.
—CASDDS, INIST. **CCC.**
Published by: Colegio Oficial de Farmaceuticos de la Provincia de Barcelona, Girona, 64-66, Barcelona, Cataluna 08009, Spain. TEL 34-93-2440710, cofb@cofb.net, http://www.farmaceuticonline.com.

615 GBR ISSN 2045-838X
▼ **COLLEGE OF MENTAL HEALTH PHARMACY. BULLETIN.** Text in English. 2010. q. free to members (effective 2010). back issues avail. **Document type:** *Bulletin, Trade.* **Description:** Designed for psychiatric pharmacists to help and support them in improving pharmaceutical care for people with mental health needs.
Related titles: Online - full text ed.: free (effective 2010).
Published by: (College of Mental Health Pharmacy), The Pharmacy Publishing Company, 4 Clark's Courtyard, 145 Granville St, Birmingham, B1 1SB, United Kingdom. TEL 44-121-6334691, FAX 44-121-6330055, info@pharmacypublishing.co.uk, http://www.clinicalpharmacy.org.uk/. Ed. Justine Raynsford.

615.1 USA
COLORADO PHARMACISTS SOCIETY JOURNAL. Text in English. q. free to members. adv. **Document type:** *Journal, Trade.* **Description:** Provides articles of professional interest, national pharmacy organization news and recaps of pharmacy events in Colorado.
Published by: Colorado Pharmacists Society, 6825 E Tennessee Ave, #440, Denver, CO 80224. TEL 303-756-3069, FAX 303-756-3649, val@copharm.org, http://www.copharm.org/. adv.: B&W page USD 425; trim 7.5 x 10.

615 USA ISSN 2161-3923
KF1297.D7
COLUMNS. DRUGS & MEDICAL DEVICES. Text in English. 2002. m. USD 950 combined subscription (print & online eds.) (effective 2011). **Document type:** *Report, Trade.*
Formerly (until 200?): HarrisMartin Columns. Drugs & Supplements (1547-6367)
Related titles: Online - full text ed.
Published by: HarrisMartin Publishing, 900 W Sproul Rd, Ste 101, Springfield, PA 19064. TEL 800-496-4319, FAX 610-647-5164, service@harrismartin.com, http://www.harrismartin.com.

615.1 USA ISSN 1096-9179
COMMUNITY PHARMACIST; meeting the professional and educational needs of today's practitioner. Text in English. 1996. bi-m. USD 12 (effective 2006). adv. bk.rev. 40 p./no.; back issues avail.; reprints avail. **Document type:** *Magazine, Trade.* **Description:** Addresses the professional and business needs, concerns, and continuing education of retail pharmacists.
Formed by the merger of (1979-1996): Southern Pharmacy Journal (0192-5792); Which was formerly (1975-1979): Southeastern Drug - Southern Pharmaceutical Journal (0193-9971); Which was formed by the merger of (1973-1975): Southeastern Drug - Southern Pharmaceutical Journal (0095-2354); Which was formerly (1908-1973): Southern Pharmaceutical Journal (0038-4410); (1973-1975): Southeastern Drug - Southern Pharmaceutical Journal. Southeastern Drug Edition (0092-5608); Which was formerly (1926-1973): Southeastern Drug Journal (0038-3651); (1976-1996): Pharmacy West (0191-6394); Which was formerly: West Coast - Rocky Mountain Druggist; Which was formed by the merger of: West Coast Druggist (0043-3101); Rocky Mountain Druggist (0035-757X)
Indexed: I12.
Published by: E L F Publications, 5285 W Louisiana Ave, Ste 112, Lakewood, CO 80232-5976. TEL 303-975-0075, 800-922-8513, FAX 303-975-0132, mcasey@elfpublications.com, http://www.elfpublications.com. Pub., R&P Judith D Lane. Adv. contact Jerry Lester. B&W page USD 4,900; trim 8.375 x 10.825. Circ: 34,000 (controlled).

COMPARATIVE BIOCHEMISTRY AND PHYSIOLOGY. PART C: TOXICOLOGY & PHARMACOLOGY. *see* BIOLOGY—Biochemistry

615 CAN ISSN 0069-7966
COMPENDIUM OF PHARMACEUTICALS AND SPECIALTIES. Text in English, French. 1960. a. price varies. bk.rev. **Document type:** *Catalog, Trade.* **Description:** Serves those who need a convenient source of the important therapeutic equivalence information and selected federal requirements that affect the prescribing and dispensing of prescription drugs and controlled substances.
Related titles: CD-ROM ed.; French ed.: Compendium des Produits et Specialites Pharmaceutiques. ISSN 0317-2813; English ed.
—BLDSC (3363.971000). **CCC.**
Published by: Canadian Pharmacists Association, 1785 Alta Vista Dr, Ottawa, ON K1G 3Y6, Canada. TEL 613-523-7877, FAX 613-523-0445, info@pharmacists.ca, http://www.pharmacists.ca. Pub. Leesa Bruce. Circ: 100,000.

615.1 CAN ISSN 1703-2563
COMPENDIUM OF SELF-CARE PRODUCTS. Text in English. 1991. a. USD 59 per issue to non-members; USD 49 per issue to members (effective 2005). **Document type:** *Journal, Consumer.* **Description:** Covers nonprescription products, including comparative product tables, production information, patient information, and a directory.
Former titles (until 2001): Compendium of Nonprescription Products (1202-9114); (until 1993): Self-Medication, Product Information (1188-9284)
Published by: Canadian Pharmacists Association, 1785 Alta Vista Dr, Ottawa, ON K1G 3Y6, Canada. TEL 613-523-7877, FAX 613-523-0445, info@pharmacists.ca, http://www.pharmacists.ca.

615 SWE ISSN 0282-7484
COMPREHENSIVE SUMMARIES OF UPPSALA DISSERTATIONS FROM THE FACULTY OF PHARMACY. Text in English. 1975. irreg., latest vol.254, 2001. price varies. back issues avail. **Document type:** *Abstract/Index.*
Formerly (until 1985): Abstracts of Uppsala Dissertations from the Faculty of Pharmacy (0346-6353)
Related titles: ◆ Series of: Acta Universitatis Upsaliensis. ISSN 0346-5462.
—IE, Ingenta.
Published by: Uppsala Universitet, Acta Universitatis Upsaliensis/ University Publications from Uppsala, PO Box 256, Uppsala, 75105, Sweden. TEL 46-18-4716804, FAX 46-18-4716804, acta@ub.uu.se, http://www.ub.uu.se/upu/auu/index.html. Ed. Bengt Landgren. **Dist. by:** Almqvist & Wiksell International.

615.9 ESP ISSN 1578-8601
CONDUCTAS ADICTIVAS. Text in Spanish. 2001. q. **Document type:** *Journal, Academic/Scholarly.*
Media: Online - full text.
Published by: Sociedad Espanola de Toxicomanias, Juan Llorens 20-4, Valencia, 46008, Spain. TEL 34-96-3130027, FAX 34-96-3130120, editorial@conductasadictivas.org, http://www.conductasadictivas.org/.

615 RUS
CONSILIUM PROVISORUM; zhurnal poslediplomnogo obrazovaniya dlya provizorov. Text in Russian. 10/yr. **Document type:** *Journal, Trade.*
Published by: Izdatel'stvo Media Medica, ul 1-ya Brestskaya, 15, Moscow, 125047, Russian Federation. media@consilium-medicum.com.

615.328 USA ISSN 0888-5109
RM301.28
➤ **THE CONSULTANT PHARMACIST.** Text in English. 1986. m. USD 395 combined subscription to institutions (print & online eds.); free to members (effective 2010). adv. Website rev. index. back issues avail.; reprints avail. **Document type:** *Journal, Academic/Scholarly.* **Description:** Dedicated exclusively to the medication needs of the elderly in all settings, including adult day care, ambulatory care, assisted living, community, hospice, and nursing facilities.
Related titles: Online - full text ed.: USD 295 to institutions (effective 2010).
Indexed: A22, C06, C07, EMBASE, ExcerpMed, I12, MEDLINE, P30, R10, Reac, SCOPUS.
—BLDSC (3423.763000), GNLM, IE, Ingenta.
Published by: American Society of Consultant Pharmacists, 1321 Duke St, Alexandria, VA 22314. TEL 703-739-1300, 800-355-2727, FAX 703-739-1321, 800-220-1321, info@ascp.com. Ed. H Edward Davidson. Adv. contact Rick Lyons TEL 267-893-5676. Circ: 8,000.

615 640.73 USA ISSN 1543-754X
RS51
CONSUMER DRUG REFERENCE. Variant title: Consumer Reports Consumer Drug Reference. Text in English. 1987. a. USD 65 per issue to non-members; USD 52 per issue to members (effective 2009). **Document type:** *Report, Consumer.* **Description:** Contains information about drug companies.
Former titles (until 2002): The Complete Drug Reference (1063-6498); (until 1991): United States Pharmacopeia Drug Information for the Consumer
Published by: Consumers Union of the United States, Inc., 101 Truman Ave, Yonkers, NY 10703. TEL 914-378-2000, 800-234-1645, FAX 914-378-2900, http://www.consumersunion.org.

615.9 USA ISSN 0738-0615
CONSUMER PHARMACIST; drug information newsletter. Text in English. 1982. bi-m. USD 48 (effective 2001). adv. bk.rev. **Document type:** *Newsletter, Consumer.*
Published by: Elba Medical Foundation, 4924 Folse Dr., Box 1403, Metairie, LA 70004-1403. TEL 504-833-3600. Ed. John F Dimaggio. Circ: 6,000.

615 USA ISSN 1944-6357
▼ **CONSUMER REPORTS HEALTH: BEST BUY DRUGS FOR LESS.** Short title: Best Buy Drugs for Less. Text in English. 2009. a. USD 5.95 per issue (effective 2009). **Document type:** *Magazine, Consumer.* **Description:** Provides unbiased information about prescription medicines to help consumers make wise choices.
Published by: Consumers Union of the United States, Inc., 101 Truman Ave, Yonkers, NY 10703. TEL 914-378-2000, FAX 914-378-2900.

615 NGA ISSN 2141-4149
➤ **CONTINENTAL JOURNAL OF PHARMACEUTICAL SCIENCES.** Text in English. 2007. s-a. NGN 2,500 domestic to individuals; USD 120 foreign to individuals; NGN 5,000 domestic to institutions; USD 200 foreign to institutions (effective 2010). Index. back issues avail.; reprints avail. **Document type:** *Journal, Academic/Scholarly.* **Description:** Covers pharmaceutics, industrial pharmacy, pharmacology, ethnopharmacology, pharmacognosy, medicinal plants, toxicology, medicinal chemistry, novel analytical methods for drug characterization, computational and modeling approaches to drug design, bio-medical experience, clinical investigation, rational drug prescribing, pharmacoeconomics, biotechnology, biopharmaceutics and physical pharmacy.
Related titles: Online - full text ed.
Indexed: A26, H12, I05.
Published by: Wilolud Journals, 2 Church Ave, Oke Eri qrt, Oba Ile, Ondo State 340001, Nigeria. TEL 234-803-4458674, managingeditor.olawale71@gmail.com. Ed. Peter A. Akah.

615 NGA ISSN 2141-4238
CONTINENTAL JOURNAL OF PHARMACOLOGY AND TOXICOLOGY RESEARCH. Text in English. 2007. a. NGN 2,500 domestic to individuals; USD 120 foreign to individuals; NGN 5,000 domestic to institutions; USD 200 foreign to institutions (effective 2010). Index. back issues avail.; reprints avail. **Document type:** *Academic/Scholarly.* **Description:** Publishes full-length papers, short communications and rapid communications on the mechanisms of action of chemical substances affecting biological systems.
Related titles: Online - full text ed.
Published by: Wilolud Journals, 2 Church Ave, Oke Eri qrt, Oba Ile, Ondo State 340001, Nigeria. TEL 234-803-4458674, managingeditor.olawale71@gmail.com. Ed. Amole O.O.

615 USA
CONTRACT PHARMA. Text in English. 1999. m. (except Feb./Aug./Dec.). USD 100; free to qualified personnel (effective 2008). adv. back issues avail. **Document type:** *Magazine, Trade.* **Description:** Provides a mix of industry news, technical features, and association event coverage for the pharmaceutical and biopharmaceutical industries.
Related titles: Online - full text ed.: free to qualified personnel (effective 2008).
Indexed: H01.
Published by: Rodman Publishing, Corp., 70 Hilltop Rd, 3rd Fl, Ramsey, NJ 07446. TEL 201-825-2552, FAX 201-825-0553, info@rodpub.com, http://www.rodmanpublishing .com. Ed. Gil Roth TEL 201-880-2240. Pubs. Gary Durr TEL 201-880-2229, Matthew Montgomery TEL 201-825-2552 ext 355. adv.: B&W page USD 5,450, color page USD 6,700; trim 8 x 10.75. Circ: 20,077.

CONTROLLED RELEASE SOCIETY. TRANSACTIONS. *see* CHEMISTRY—Organic Chemistry

615 ESP ISSN 1695-002X
CORREO FARMACEUTICO. Text in Spanish. 2001. w. **Document type:** *Magazine, Trade.* **Description:** Delivered every Monday to all pharmacists and related professionals in the pharmaceutical industry in Spain.
Indexed: P20.
Published by: Unidad Editorial, Ave de San Luis, 25-27, Madrid, 28033, Spain. TEL 34-91-4435000, http://www.unidadeditorial.com. Ed. Francisco J. Fernandez.

615.19 USA ISSN 0743-4863
RS201.V43 CODEN: CRTSEO
➤ **CRITICAL REVIEWS IN THERAPEUTIC DRUG CARRIER SYSTEMS.** Text in English. 1984. bi-m. USD 1,150 to institutions; USD 230 per issue (effective 2010). adv. back issues avail.; reprints avail. **Document type:** *Journal, Academic/Scholarly.* **Description:** Brings out review papers encompassing the basic biological, medical, pharmaceutical, and physical sciences with emphasis on clinical applications.
Related titles: Online - full text ed.
Indexed: A22, ASCA, B&BAb, B19, BIOSIS Prev, CIN, ChemAb, ChemTitl, CurCont, EMBASE, ExcerpMed, I12, ISR, IndMed, Inpharma, MEDLINE, MycolAb, P30, R10, Reac, SCI, SCOPUS, W07.
—BLDSC (3487.483700), CASDDS, GNLM, IE, Infotrieve, Ingenta, INIST, Linda Hall. **CCC.**
Published by: Begell House Inc., 50 Cross Hwy, Redding, CT 06896. TEL 203-938-1300, FAX 203-938-1304, orders@begellhouse.com. Ed. Mandip Sachdeva.

➤ **CRITICAL REVIEWS IN TOXICOLOGY.** *see* ENVIRONMENTAL STUDIES—Toxicology And Environmental Safety

615.1 ITA ISSN 0011-1783
CODEN: CRFMAY
CRONACHE FARMACEUTICHE. Text in English, French, Italian. 1958. bi-m. adv. bk.rev. abstr.; bibl.; illus. index. back issues avail. **Document type:** *Journal, Trade.*
Indexed: ChemAb, I12.
—CASDDS, GNLM, INIST.
Published by: Societa Italiana di Scienze Farmaceutiche (S I S F), Viale Abruzzi 32, Milan, 20131, Italy. TEL 39-02-29513303, FAX 39-02-29520179, info@sisf.it, http://www.milanopharma.it. Ed. Piero Sensi.

CURRENT BIOACTIVE COMPOUNDS. *see* CHEMISTRY

CURRENT CANCER THERAPY REVIEWS. *see* MEDICAL SCIENCES—Oncology

CURRENT CARDIOVASCULAR DRUGS. *see* MEDICAL SCIENCES—Cardiovascular Diseases

615.1 NLD ISSN 1574-8847
➤ **CURRENT CLINICAL PHARMACOLOGY.** Text in English. 2006. q. USD 650 per issue to institutions (print or online ed.) (effective 2012). adv. back issues avail.; reprints avail. **Document type:** *Journal, Academic/Scholarly.*
Related titles: Online - full text ed.: (from IngentaConnect).
Indexed: A01, B&BAb, B19, B21, CA, EMBASE, ExcerpMed, GenetAb, ImmunAb, MEDLINE, P30, R10, Reac, SCOPUS, T02.
—IE, Ingenta. **CCC.**
Published by: Bentham Science Publishers Ltd., PO Box 294, Bussum, 1400 AG, Netherlands. TEL 31-35-6923800, FAX 31-35-6980150, sales@bentham.org. Ed. Jos H Beijnen. **Subscr. to:** Bentham Science Publishers Ltd., c/o Richard E Morrissy, PO Box 446, Oak Park, IL 60301. TEL 312-413-5867, FAX 312-996-7107, subscriptions@bentham.org.

615 NLD ISSN 1567-2018
CODEN: CDDUBJ
➤ **CURRENT DRUG DELIVERY.** Text in English. 2004. bi-m. USD 850 to institutions (print or online ed.) (effective 2012). adv. back issues avail.; reprints avail. **Document type:** *Journal, Academic/Scholarly.* **Description:** Covers the latest outstanding developments in drug and vaccine delivery employing physical, physico-chemical and chemical methods.
Related titles: Online - full text ed.: ISSN 1875-5704 (from IngentaConnect).
Indexed: A01, A03, A08, B&BAb, B19, B21, B25, BIOSIS Prev, BioEngAb, C33, CA, EMBASE, ExcerpMed, M&PBA, MEDLINE, MycolAb, P30, R10, Reac, SCI, SCOPUS, T02, W07.
—BLDSC (3496.385000), IE, Ingenta. **CCC.**
Published by: Bentham Science Publishers Ltd., PO Box 294, Bussum, 1400 AG, Netherlands. TEL 31-35-6923800, FAX 31-35-6980150, sales@bentham.org. Ed. Istvan Toth TEL 61-7-33651386. **Subscr. to:** Bentham Science Publishers Ltd., c/o Richard E Morrissy, PO Box 446, Oak Park, IL 60301. TEL 312-413-5867, FAX 312-996-7107, subscriptions@bentham.org.

615 NLD ISSN 1570-1638
RS410 CODEN: CDDTAF
➤ **CURRENT DRUG DISCOVERY TECHNOLOGIES.** Text in English. 2004. q. USD 610 to institutions (print or online ed.) (effective 2012). adv. back issues avail.; reprints avail. **Document type:** *Journal, Academic/Scholarly.* **Description:** Provides comprehensive overviews of all the major modern techniques and technologies used in drug design and discovery.
Related titles: Online - full text ed.: ISSN 1875-6220 (from IngentaConnect).
Indexed: A01, A03, A08, B&BAb, B19, B21, BioEngAb, C33, CA, EMBASE, ExcerpMed, M&PBA, MEDLINE, P30, R10, Reac, SCOPUS, T02.
—BLDSC (3496.395000), IE, Ingenta. **CCC.**
Published by: Bentham Science Publishers Ltd., PO Box 294, Bussum, 1400 AG, Netherlands. TEL 31-35-6923800, FAX 31-35-6980150, sales@bentham.org. Ed. Vladimir P Torchilin. **Subscr. to:** Bentham Science Publishers Ltd., c/o Richard E Morrissy, PO Box 446, Oak Park, IL 60301. TEL 312-413-5867, FAX 312-996-7107, subscriptions@bentham.org.

615 NLD ISSN 1389-2002
CODEN: CDMUBU
➤ **CURRENT DRUG METABOLISM.** Text in English. 2000 (Jun.). 10/yr. USD 2,070 to institutions (print or online ed.) (effective 2012). adv. **Document type:** *Journal, Academic/Scholarly.* **Description:** Features reviews in drug metabolism, disposition and related areas.
Related titles: Online - full text ed.: ISSN 1875-5453 (from IngentaConnect).
Indexed: A01, A03, A08, B&BAb, B19, B21, B27, BIOSIS Prev, BioEngAb, C33, CA, CTA, ChemAb, EMBASE, ESPM, ExcerpMed, M&PBA, MEDLINE, MycolAb, NSA, P30, R10, Reac, SCI, SCOPUS, T02, ToxAb, W07.
—BLDSC (3496.400200), IE, Infotrieve, Ingenta, INIST. **CCC.**
Published by: Bentham Science Publishers Ltd., PO Box 294, Bussum, 1400 AG, Netherlands. TEL 31-35-6923800, FAX 31-35-6980150, sales@bentham.org. Ed. Chandra Prakash. **Subscr. addr. in the US:** Bentham Science Publishers Ltd., c/o Richard E Morrissy, PO Box 446, Oak Park, IL 60301. TEL 312-413-5867, FAX 312-996-7107, subscriptions@bentham.org.

615 NLD ISSN 1574-8863
➤ **CURRENT DRUG SAFETY.** Text in English. 2006. 5/yr. USD 780 to institutions (print or online ed.) (effective 2012). adv. back issues avail.; reprints avail. **Document type:** *Journal, Academic/Scholarly.* **Description:** Publishes frontier reviews on all the latest advances on drug safety. Topics covered include: adverse effects of individual drugs and drug classes, management of adverse effects, pharmacovigilance and pharmacoepidemiology of new and existing drugs, post-marketing surveillance.
Related titles: Online - full text ed.: (from IngentaConnect).
Indexed: A01, B&BAb, B19, B21, CA, EMBASE, ESPM, ExcerpMed, H&SSA, ImmunAb, MEDLINE, P30, R10, Reac, RiskAb, SCOPUS, T02, ToxAb.
—IE, Ingenta. **CCC.**
Published by: Bentham Science Publishers Ltd., PO Box 294, Bussum, 1400 AG, Netherlands. TEL 31-35-6923800, FAX 31-35-6980150, sales@bentham.org. Ed. Seetal Dodd. **Subscr. to:** Bentham Science Publishers Ltd., c/o Richard E Morrissy, PO Box 446, Oak Park, IL 60301. TEL 312-413-5867, FAX 312-996-7107, subscriptions@bentham.org.

P

615 NLD ISSN 1389-4501
RS199.5 CODEN: CDTUAU
➤ **CURRENT DRUG TARGETS.** Text in English. 2000 (Jun.). 14/yr. USD 2,860 to institutions (print or online ed.) (effective 2012). adv. back issues avail.; reprints avail. **Document type:** *Journal, Academic/Scholarly.* **Description:** Features reviews on the discovery, characterization, and validation of novel human drug targets for drug discovery.
Related titles: Online - full text ed.: ISSN 1873-5592 (from IngentaConnect).
Indexed: A01, A03, A08, A29, B&BAb, B19, B20, B21, B27, BIOSIS Prev, BioEngAb, C33, CA, ChemAb, EMBASE, ESPM, ExcerpMed, M&PBA, MEDLINE, MycolAb, NSA, NucAcAb, P30, R10, Reac, SCI, SCOPUS, T02, ViroIAbstr, W07.
—BLDSC (3496.400300), IE, Infotrieve, Ingenta. **CCC.**
Published by: Bentham Science Publishers Ltd., PO Box 294, Bussum, 1400 AG, Netherlands. TEL 31-35-6923800, FAX 31-35-6980150, sales@bentham.org. Ed. Francis J Castellino TEL 574-631-9152. **Subscr. addr. in the US:** Bentham Science Publishers Ltd., c/o Richard E Morrissy, PO Box 446, Oak Park, IL 60301. TEL 312-413-5867, FAX 312-996-7107, subscriptions@bentham.org.

615 NLD ISSN 1574-8855
➤ **CURRENT DRUG THERAPY.** Text in English. 2006. q. USD 650 to institutions (print or online ed.) (effective 2012). adv. back issues avail.; reprints avail. **Document type:** *Journal, Academic/Scholarly.* **Description:** Publishes frontier reviews on all the latest advances in drug therapy. Topics covered include: new and existing drugs, therapies and medical devices.
Related titles: Online - full text ed.: (from IngentaConnect).
Indexed: A01, B&BAb, B19, CA, EMBASE, ExcerpMed, P30, SCOPUS, T02.
—BLDSC (3496.400800), IE, Ingenta. **CCC.**
Published by: Bentham Science Publishers Ltd., PO Box 294, Bussum, 1400 AG, Netherlands. TEL 31-35-6923800, FAX 31-35-6980150, sales@bentham.org. Ed. Joachim F Wernicke. **Subscr. to:** Bentham Science Publishers Ltd., c/o Richard E Morrissy, PO Box 446, Oak Park, IL 60301. TEL 312-413-5867, FAX 312-996-7107, subscriptions@bentham.org.

615 NLD ISSN 1573-4080
CURRENT ENZYME INHIBITION. Text in English. 2005 (Jan.). s-a. USD 240 to institutions (print or online ed.) (effective 2012). adv. back issues avail.; reprints avail. **Document type:** *Journal, Academic/Scholarly.* **Description:** Aims to publish all the latest and outstanding developments in enzyme inhibition studies with regards to the mechanisms of inhibitory processes of enzymes, recognition of active sites, and the discovery of agonists and antagonists, leading to the design and development of new drugs of significant therapeutic value.
Related titles: Online - full text ed.: ISSN 1875-6662 (from IngentaConnect).
Indexed: A01, B&BAb, B19, CA, EMBASE, ExcerpMed, R10, Reac, SCOPUS, T02.
—IE, Ingenta. **CCC.**
Published by: Bentham Science Publishers Ltd., PO Box 294, Bussum, 1400 AG, Netherlands. TEL 31-35-6923800, FAX 31-35-6980150, sales@bentham.org, http://www.bentham.org. Ed. Dimitra Hadjipavlou-Litina. **Subscr. to:** Bentham Science Publishers Ltd., c/o Richard E Morrissy, PO Box 446, Oak Park, IL 60301. TEL 312-413-5867, FAX 312-996-7107, subscriptions@bentham.org.

615.7 NLD ISSN 1874-4672
CODEN: CMPUB6
➤ **CURRENT MOLECULAR PHARMACOLOGY.** Text in English. 2008. 3/yr. USD 580 to institutions (print or online ed.) (effective 2012). adv. back issues avail.; reprints avail. **Document type:** *Journal, Academic/Scholarly.* **Description:** Aims to publish the latest developments in cellular and molecular pharmacology with a major emphasis on the mechanism of action of novel drugs under development, innovative pharmacological technologies, cell signaling, transduction pathway analysis, genomics, proteomics, and metabonomics applications to drug action.
Related titles: Online - full text ed.: ISSN 1874-4702. 2008.
Indexed: A01, C33, CA, EMBASE, ExcerpMed, MEDLINE, P30, T02.
—BLDSC (3500.458000), IE. **CCC.**
Published by: Bentham Science Publishers Ltd., PO Box 294, Bussum, 1400 AG, Netherlands. TEL 31-35-6923800, FAX 31-35-6980150, sales@bentham.org. Ed. Nouri Neamati TEL 323-442-2341. **Subscr. to:** Bentham Science Publishers Ltd., c/o Richard E Morrissy, PO Box 446, Oak Park, IL 60301. TEL 312-413-5867, FAX 312-996-7107, subscriptions@bentham.org.

➤ **CURRENT NANOSCIENCE.** *see* ENGINEERING

616.8 USA ISSN 1083-9429
RM315.
CURRENT NEUROLOGIC DRUGS. Text in English. 1995. irreg., latest 2000. reprints avail. **Document type:** *Monographic series.*
Published by: Current Medicine Group LLC (Subsidiary of: Springer Science+Business Media), 400 Market St, Ste 700, Philadelphia, PA 19106. TEL 215-574-2266, 800-427-1796, FAX 215-574-2225, info_phl@currentmedicinegroup.com. Ed. Lewis P Rowland. **Co-publisher:** Lippincott Williams & Wilkins.

CURRENT NEUROPHARMACOLOGY. *see* MEDICAL SCIENCES—Psychiatry And Neurology

615.19 GBR ISSN 2040-3437
CURRENT OPINION IN DRUG DISCOVERY & DEVELOPMENT (ONLINE). Text in English. 1998. irreg. GBP 2,648, USD 5,039, EUR 3,838 to institutions (corporate), 1-500 users; GBP 193, USD 350, EUR 288 to institutions (academic), 1-20 users (effective 2010). **Document type:** *Bulletin, Trade.* **Description:** Covers all of the chemical aspects involved in the drug discovery and development process.
Media: Online - full text.
Published by: Current Drugs Ltd. (Subsidiary of: Thomson Reuters Corp.), 1 Chapel Quarter, Mount St, Nottingham, NG1 6HQ, United Kingdom. TEL 44-207-5424300, general.info@thomsonreuters.com, http://science.thomsonreuters.com/.

615 GBR ISSN 2040-3429
CURRENT OPINION IN INVESTIGATIONAL DRUGS (ONLINE). Text in English. 2000. m. GBP 2,648, USD 5,039, EUR 3,838 to institutions (corporate), 1-500 users; GBP 193, USD 350, EUR 288 to institutions (academic), 1-20 users (effective 2010). **Document type:** *Bulletin, Trade.* **Description:** Provides comprehensive coverage of all therapeutic areas, including a general section containing patent and paper alerts, individual therapeutic chapters provide short, focused overviews, reviews and evaluations on the latest drug developments.
Media: Online - full text.
—CCC.
Published by: Current Drugs Ltd. (Subsidiary of: Thomson Reuters Corp.), 1 Chapel Quarter, Mount St, Nottingham, NG1 6HQ, United Kingdom. TEL 44-207-5424300, general.info@thomsonreuters.com, http://science.thomsonreuters.com/.

615.7 GBR ISSN 2040-3445
CURRENT OPINION IN MOLECULAR THERAPEUTICS (ONLINE). Text in English. 1999. bi-m. GBP 2,648, USD 5,039, EUR 3,838 to institutions (corporate), 1-500 users; GBP 193, USD 350, EUR 288 to institutions (academic), 1-20 users (effective 2010). **Document type:** *Journal, Trade.* **Description:** Covers all aspects of molecular medicine research while focusing on clinical developments in gene transfer therapeutics and the utilization of recombinant technologies.
Media: Online - full text.
—CCC.
Published by: Current Drugs Ltd. (Subsidiary of: Thomson Reuters Corp.), 1 Chapel Quarter, Mount St, Nottingham, NG1 6HQ, United Kingdom. TEL 44-207-5424300, general.info@thomsonreuters.com, http://science.thomsonreuters.com/.

615 GBR ISSN 1471-4892
RM1 CODEN: COPUBK
CURRENT OPINION IN PHARMACOLOGY. Text in English. 2001. bi-m. EUR 1,785 in Europe to institutions; JPY 247,400 in Japan to institutions; USD 1,994 elsewhere to institutions (effective 2012). adv. back issues avail.; reprints avail. **Document type:** *Journal, Academic/Scholarly.* **Description:** Presents over 90 reviews a year from leading international contributors in the field of pharmacology.
Related titles: Online - full text ed.: ISSN 1471-4973 (from IngentaConnect, ScienceDirect).
Indexed: A01, A03, A08, A22, A26, A35, A36, AgBio, B&BAb, B19, B21, BIOSIS Prev, BP, BioEngAb, C33, CA, CABA, CTA, ChemAb, ChemoAb, E12, EMBASE, ESPM, ExcerpMed, GH, GenetAb, I05, M&PBA, MEDLINE, MycolAb, N02, N03, NSA, NucAcAb, P30, P33, P39, R10, RA&MP, RM&VM, Reac, S01, SCI, SCOPUS, SoyAb, T02, T05, ToxAb, VS, W07.
—BLDSC (3500.776920), IE, Infotrieve, Ingenta. **CCC.**
Published by: Elsevier Ltd., Current Opinion Journals (Subsidiary of: Elsevier Science & Technology), 84 Theobald's Rd, London, WC1X 8RR, United Kingdom. TEL 44-20-76114000, FAX 44-20-76114485, JournalsCustomerServiceEMEA@elsevier.com. Eds. N G Bowery, T P Kenakin.

615 IND ISSN 2230-7834
▼ ➤ **CURRENT PHARMA RESEARCH.** Text and summaries in English. 2010. q. INR 1,000 domestic to individuals; USD 100 foreign to individuals; INR 1,500 domestic to institutions; USD 150 foreign to institutions (effective 2011). **Document type:** *Journal, Academic/Scholarly.* **Description:** Publishes original research in the field of pharmaceutical sciences.
Related titles: Online - full text ed.: ISSN 2230-7842.
Indexed: A34, A36, C30, D01, E12, F08, H16, N03, P33, S13, T05.
Published by: Unicorn Publications, India, P-1, Sangam Nagar, Satara, Maharastra 415 003, India. TEL 91-7709366816, 91-9423262115, 91-2162-247675, editor@cpronline.in, amit9590@gmail.com. Ed., Pub., R&P Amit J Kasabe.

615 NLD ISSN 1573-4129
➤ **CURRENT PHARMACEUTICAL ANALYSIS.** Text in English. 2005 (Jan.). q. USD 480 to institutions (print or online ed.) (effective 2012). adv. back issues avail.; reprints avail. **Document type:** *Journal, Academic/Scholarly.* **Description:** Publishes authoritative reviews, written by experts in the field on all the most recent advances in pharmaceutical and biomedical analysis. All aspects of the field are represented including drug analysis, analytical methodology and instrumentation.
Related titles: Online - full text ed.: ISSN 1875-676X (from IngentaConnect).
Indexed: A01, B&BAb, B19, B27, CA, EMBASE, ExcerpMed, R10, Reac, SCI, SCOPUS, T02, W07.
—BLDSC (3501.280445), IE, Ingenta. **CCC.**
Published by: Bentham Science Publishers Ltd., PO Box 294, Bussum, 1400 AG, Netherlands. TEL 31-35-6923800, FAX 31-35-6980150, sales@bentham.org, http://www.bentham.org. Ed. Atta-ur Rahman TEL 92-21-34824924. **Subscr. to:** Bentham Science Publishers Ltd., c/o Richard E Morrissy, PO Box 446, Oak Park, IL 60301. TEL 312-413-5867, FAX 312-996-7107, subscriptions@bentham.org.

➤ **CURRENT PHARMACEUTICAL BIOTECHNOLOGY.** *see* BIOLOGY—Biotechnology

615 NLD ISSN 1381-6128
RS420 CODEN: CPDEFP
➤ **CURRENT PHARMACEUTICAL DESIGN.** Text in English. 1995. 38/yr. USD 7,410 to institutions (print or online ed.) (effective 2012). adv. back issues avail.; reprints avail. **Document type:** *Journal, Academic/Scholarly.* **Description:** Features reviews from pharmaceutical researchers in the field, covering all aspects of current research in rational drug design.
Related titles: Online - full text ed.: ISSN 1873-4286 (from IngentaConnect).
Indexed: A01, A03, A08, A22, A29, A34, A36, AgrForAb, B&BAb, B19, B20, B21, B27, BIOSIS Prev, BP, BioEngAb, C30, C33, CA, CABA, CIN, ChemAb, ChemTitl, CurCont, D01, E12, EMBASE, ESPM, ExcerpMed, F08, GH, H16, H17, I10, ISR, IndMed, IndVet, Inpharma, M&PBA, MEDLINE, MycolAb, N02, N03, N04, N05, NSA, P20, P22, P30, P32, P33, P37, P39, P40, P48, P54, PGegResA, PHN&I, PQC, R08, R10, R13, RA&MP, RM&VM, Reac, S13, S16, SCI, SCOPUS, SoyAb, T02, T05, VS, ViroIAbstr, W07, W11.
—BLDSC (3501.280460), CASDDS, GNLM, IE, Infotrieve, Ingenta, INIST. **CCC.**
Published by: Bentham Science Publishers Ltd., PO Box 294, Bussum, 1400 AG, Netherlands. TEL 31-35-6923800, FAX 31-35-6980150, sales@bentham.org. Ed. William A Banks. **Subscr. addr. in the US:** Bentham Science Publishers Ltd., c/o Richard E Morrissy, PO Box 446, Oak Park, IL 60301. TEL 312-413-5867, FAX 312-996-7107, subscriptions@bentham.org.

615.1 576.5 NLD ISSN 1875-6921
CODEN: CPPMC4
➤ **CURRENT PHARMACOGENOMICS AND PERSONALIZED MEDICINE**; the international journal for expert reviews in pharmacogenomics. Abbreviated title: C P P M. Text in English. 2003 (Mar.). q. USD 820 to institutions (print or online ed.) (effective 2012). adv. back issues avail.; reprints avail. **Document type:** *Journal, Academic/Scholarly.* **Description:** Established to provide comprehensive overviews of all current researches on pharmacogenomics and pharmacogenetics.
Formerly (until 2008): Current Pharmacogenomics (1570-1603)
Related titles: Online - full text ed.: ISSN 1875-6913 (from IngentaConnect).
Indexed: A01, A03, A08, B&BAb, B19, B21, BIOSIS Prev, C33, CA, EMBASE, ExcerpMed, GenetAb, M&PBA, MycolAb, P30, R10, Reac, SCOPUS, T02.
—BLDSC (3501.280467), IE, Ingenta. **CCC.**
Published by: Bentham Science Publishers Ltd., PO Box 294, Bussum, 1400 AG, Netherlands. TEL 31-35-6923800, FAX 31-35-6980150, sales@bentham.org. Ed. Vural Ozdemir. **Subscr. to:** Bentham Science Publishers Ltd., c/o Richard E Morrissy, PO Box 446, Oak Park, IL 60301. TEL 312-413-5867, FAX 312-996-7107, subscriptions@bentham.org.

615 USA ISSN 1934-8282
RM301.25
CURRENT PROTOCOLS IN PHARMACOLOGY. Text in English. 1998. 3 base vols. plus q. updates. USD 725 to individuals base vols. & updates (effective 2010). adv. back issues avail.; reprints avail. **Document type:** *Journal, Academic/Scholarly.* **Description:** Covers the full range of molecular, cellular, physiological, and chemical techniques used for the discovery and development of novel therapeutics.
Related titles: CD-ROM ed.: USD 595 combined subscription to institutions for base vol. & updates; USD 350 renewals to institutions (effective 2006); Online - full text ed.: ISSN 1934-8290.
Indexed: EMBASE, ExcerpMed, P30, SCOPUS.
—BLDSC (3501.544500).
Published by: John Wiley & Sons, Inc., 111 River St, Hoboken, NJ 07030. TEL 201-748-6000, FAX 201-748-6088, info@wiley.com, http://www.wiley.com/WileyCDA/. **Subscr. outside the Amesricas to:** John Wiley & Sons Ltd.

615.1 616.8 NLD ISSN 2211-5560
▼ ➤ **CURRENT PSYCHOPHARMACOLOGY.** Text in English. forthcoming 2012. q. USD 720 to institutions (print or online ed.) (effective 2012). adv. **Document type:** *Journal, Academic/Scholarly.* **Description:** Covers all aspects of preclinical and clinical research in psychopharmacology.
Related titles: Online - full text ed.: ISSN 2211-5579. forthcoming.
Published by: Bentham Science Publishers Ltd., PO Box 294, Bussum, 1400 AG, Netherlands. TEL 31-35-6923800, FAX 31-35-6980150, sales@bentham.org, http://www.bentham.org. Ed. Silvio Bellino. **Subscr. to:** Bentham Science Publishers Ltd., c/o Richard E Morrissy, PO Box 446, Oak Park, IL 60301. TEL 312-413-5867, FAX 312-996-7107, subscriptions@bentham.org.

615.19 NLD ISSN 1874-4710
CODEN: CRUAC7
➤ **CURRENT RADIOPHARMACEUTICALS.** Text in English. 2008. 3/yr. USD 730 to institutions (print or online ed.) (effective 2012). adv. back issues avail.; reprints avail. **Document type:** *Journal, Academic/Scholarly.* **Description:** Publishes original research articles, letters and reviews on all aspects of research and development of radiolabelled compound preparations.
Related titles: Online - full text ed.: ISSN 1874-4729. 2008.
Indexed: A01, C33, CA, EMBASE, ExcerpMed, P30, SCOPUS, T02.
—CCC.
Published by: Bentham Science Publishers Ltd., PO Box 294, Bussum, 1400 AG, Netherlands. TEL 31-35-6923800, FAX 31-35-6980150, sales@bentham.org. Eds. Luigi Mansi, Sean L Kitson TEL 44-28-38332200. **Subscr. to:** Bentham Science Publishers Ltd., c/o Richard E Morrissy, PO Box 446, Oak Park, IL 60301. TEL 312-413-5867, FAX 312-996-7107, subscriptions@bentham.org.

615 USA ISSN 0011-393X
RM111 CODEN: CTCEA9
➤ **CURRENT THERAPEUTIC RESEARCH**; clinical and experimental. Text in English. 1959. bi-m. USD 360 elsewhere to institutions (effective 2012). Supplement avail.; back issues avail.; reprints avail. **Document type:** *Journal, Academic/Scholarly.* **Description:** Publishes results of original research in the broad field of medical and pharmaceutical therapy and related areas, including specialty sections such as "Trials in Special Populations" and "Trials in Resource-Limited Settings".
Related titles: Online - full text ed.: ISSN 1879-0313 (from IngentaConnect, ScienceDirect).
Indexed: A01, A03, A08, A22, A26, A36, ASCA, B25, BIOBASE, BIOSIS Prev, C06, C07, C08, CA, CABA, CIN, CINAHL, ChemAb, ChemTitl, CurCont, DBA, E-psyche, E12, EMBASE, ExcerpMed, F08, F11, F12, GH, H12, H16, I05, I12, IABS, IDIS, INI, ISR, Inpharma, MycolAb, N02, N03, P03, P30, P33, P35, P39, PsycholAb, R07, R10, R11, R12, RA&MP, Reac, S12, SCI, SCOPUS, SoyAb, T02, T05, VS, W07.
—BLDSC (3504.600000), CASDDS, GNLM, IE, Infotrieve, Ingenta, INIST. **CCC.**
Published by: Excerpta Medica, Inc. (Subsidiary of: Elsevier Health Sciences), 685 US-202, Bridgewater, NJ 08807. TEL 908-547-2100, FAX 908-547-2200, excerptamedica@elsevier.com, http://www.excerptamedica.com/. Ed. Dr. Judd Walson. Pub. Jo-Ann E West TEL 908-547-2082.

615 IND ISSN 0972-4559
➤ **CURRENT TOPICS IN PHARMACOLOGY.** Text in English. 1992. s-a. INR 6,854 domestic; JPY 17,582 in Japan; EUR 134.10 in Europe; USD 149 elsewhere (effective 2010). bk.rev. abstr.; bibl.; charts; illus.; maps; stat. back issues avail. **Document type:** *Journal, Academic/Scholarly.* **Description:** Covers research in basic and clinical pharmacology and related fields, including: Biochemical pharmacology, molecular pharmacology, immunopharmacology, pharmacogenetics, analytical toxicology, neuropsychopharmacology, drug metabolism, pharmacokinetics and clinical pharmacology.
Related titles: Online - full text ed.
Indexed: B&BAb, B19, B21, CTA, EMBASE, ESPM, I12, NSA, SCOPUS.
Published by: Research Trends (P) Ltd., T.C. 17 / 250 (3), Chadiyara Rd, Poojapura, Trivandrum, Kerala 695 012, India. TEL 91-471-2344424, FAX 91-471-2344423, info@researchtrends.net. Circ: 1,000.

615.19 IND ISSN 0973-0532
➤ **CURRENT TRENDS IN MEDICINAL CHEMISTRY.** Text in English. 1993. a. INR 6,854 domestic; EUR 134.10 in Europe; JPY 17,582 in Japan; USD 149 elsewhere (effective 2010). adv. bk.rev. abstr.; bibl.; charts; illus.; maps; stat. back issues avail.; reprints avail. **Document type:** *Journal, Academic/Scholarly.* **Description:** Provides an international forum for the publication of review articles and original research papers on all aspects of medicinal chemistry research.
Formerly: Current Topics in Medicinal Chemistry
Related titles: CD-ROM ed.
Indexed: A29, B20, B21, ESPM, I10.
Published by: Research Trends (P) Ltd., T.C. 17 / 250 (3), Chadiyara Rd, Poojapura, Trivandrum, Kerala 695 012, India. TEL 91-471-2344424, FAX 91-471-2344423, info@researchtrends.net. Circ: 1,000.

➤ **CURRENT VASCULAR PHARMACOLOGY.** *see* MEDICAL SCIENCES—Cardiovascular Diseases

615.1 USA ISSN 1877-1297
▼ ➤ **CURRENTS IN PHARMACY TEACHING AND LEARNING.** Text in English. 2009. q. USD 441 in North America to institutions; USD 551 elsewhere to institutions (effective 2012).
Related titles: Online - full text ed.: ISSN 1877-1300 (from ScienceDirect).
Indexed: E03, EMBASE, SCOPUS, T02.
—CCC.
Published by: Elsevier Inc. (Subsidiary of: Elsevier Science & Technology), 360 Park Ave S, New York, NY 10010. TEL 212-633-3100, 888-437-4636, FAX 212-633-3140, usinfo-f@elsevier.com. Ed. Robin M Zavod.

615.9 USA ISSN 1556-9527
RL803 CODEN: JTOTDO
➤ **CUTANEOUS AND OCULAR TOXICOLOGY.** Text in English. 1982. q. GBP 1,190, EUR 1,570, USD 1,965 combined subscription to institutions (print & online eds.); GBP 2,415, EUR 3,185, USD 3,985 combined subscription to corporations (print & online eds.) (effective 2010). adv. back issues avail.; reprint service avail. from PSC. **Document type:** *Journal, Academic/Scholarly.* **Description:** Explores the phenomena of cutaneous and ocular irritation, sensitization, phototoxicity and photoallergenicity of cosmetics, etc. Contains in vitro and in vivo research as well as the clinical description, diagnosis, and treatment of such effects.
Formerly (until 2005): Journal of Toxicology. Cutaneous and Ocular Toxicology (0731-3829)
Related titles: Microform ed.: (from RPI); Online - full text ed.: ISSN 1556-9535 (from IngentaConnect).
Indexed: A01, A03, A08, A22, A34, A35, A36, ASCA, ASFA, AgBio, B21, B25, BIOBASE, BIOSIS Prev, BP, CA, CABA, CIN, ChemAb, ChemTitl, E01, E04, E05, E12, EMBASE, ESPM, EnerRev, EnvAb, ExcerpMed, F08, GH, H&SSA, IABS, ISR, IndVet, Inpharma, MEDLINE, MycolAb, P30, P33, PHN&I, PN&I, R07, R08, R10, R12, RA&MP, Reac, SCI, SCOPUS, T02, T05, ToxAb, VS, W07, W10.
—CASDDS, GNLM, IE, Infotrieve, Ingenta, INIST. **CCC.**
Published by: Informa Healthcare (Subsidiary of: T & F Informa plc), 52 Vanderbilt Ave, New York, NY 10017. TEL 212-262-8230, FAX 212-262-8234, healthcare.enquiries@informa.com, http://www.informahealthcare.com. Ed. Dr. A Wallace Hayes. Adv. contact Daniel Wallen. **Subscr. outside N. America to:** Taylor & Francis Ltd.

615 658.8 NLD ISSN 1871-384X
D A LEVE JE LIJF BLAD. (Drogisten Associatie) Cover title: Live je Lijf. Text in Dutch. 1999. q.
Former titles (until 2005): Vie (1573-6458); (until 2004): Drogisten Associatie Magazine (1389-2762)
Published by: DA Retailgroep B.V., Postbus 450, Leusden, 3830 AM, Netherlands. TEL 31-33-4346800, FAX 31-33-4346850, info@da.nl, http://www.da.nl.

615 USA ISSN 1944-1991
▼ **D I A GLOBAL FORUM.** Text in English. 2009 (Feb.). bi-m. free to members. **Description:** Provides a multi-disciplinary, neutral forum for communicating information related to drug development and lifecycle management on a global basis.
Related titles: Online - full text ed.
—CCC.
Published by: Drug Information Association, 800 Enterprise Rd, Ste 200, Horsham, PA 19044. TEL 215-442-6100, FAX 215-442-6199, dia@diahome.org, http://www.diahome.org. Ed. Lisa Zoks.

615 PER ISSN 1990-6528
D I G E M I D. BOLETIN INFORMATIVO. (Direccion General de Medicamentos Insumos y Drogas) Text in Spanish. 2006. q. **Document type:** *Bulletin, Government.*
Media: Online - full text.
Published by: Ministerio de Salud, Direccion General de Medicamentos Insumos y Drogas (D I G E M I D), Calle Coronel Odriozola 111, Altura Av Arequipa Cuadra 32, San Isidro, Peru. http://www.digimid.minsa.gob.pe.

615.1 CHE ISSN 1662-338X
D-INSIDE. Text in German. 2007. 10/yr. adv. **Document type:** *Magazine, Trade.*
Formed by the merger of (2002-2007): Inside (French Edition) (1660-9360); (2002-2007): Inside (German Edition) (1660-9352); Which was formed by the merger of (1994-2002): Drogissima (1660-928X); (1999-2002): Schweizerische Drogisten-Zeitschrift (1423-8713); Which was formerly (1991-1999): S D Z (1422-3791); (1982-1991): Drogisten-Zeitung (0255-6723); (1960-1982): Schweizerische Drogistenzeitung (0036-7567); (1951-1960): Journal Suisse des Droguistes (0376-5105); (1901-1951): Schweizerische Drogisten-Zeitung (0376-5113)
Indexed: P30.
Published by: Schweizerischer Drogistenverband, Nidaugasse 15, Biel, 2502, Switzerland. TEL 41-32-3285030, FAX 41-32-3285031, info@drogistenverband.ch. adv.: page CHF 5,800; trim 210 x 297.

658.834 USA
D T C PERSPECTIVES. (Direct-to-Customer) Text in English. 2001. q. USD 72 domestic; USD 96 foreign; free to qualified personnel (effective 2003). adv. **Document type:** *Journal, Trade.* **Description:** Source for direct-to-consumer pharmaceutical marketing leaders.
Related titles: Online - full content ed.
Published by: D T C Perspectives, Inc., 477 Route 10 East, Ste 201, Randolph, NJ 07869. TEL 973-328-9997, FAX 973-328-9998. Ed. Jason Youner. adv.: color page USD 2,500; trim 8.5 x 10.875. Circ: 7,193.

615.1 NLD ISSN 0165-6112
D W: DROGISTEN WEEKBLAD; onafhankelijk vakblad voor drogisterij, parfumerie, reformzaak. Text in Dutch. 1968. w. (Thu.). EUR 95 (effective 2009). adv. bk.rev.; film rev. abstr.; charts; illus.; mkt.; pat.; stat. **Document type:** *Newspaper, Trade.*
Former titles: Drogisten Weekblad; (until 1975): Drogistenblad de Vergulde Gaper (0012-6349)
Related titles: ◆ Supplement(s): D W Dossier. ISSN 1878-3244.
Indexed: KES.
Published by: Van der Weij Periodieken B.V., Franciscusweg 351, Postbus 285, Hilversum, 1200 AG, Netherlands. TEL 31-35-6249741, FAX 31-35-6214354. Eds. Janneke Swart, Suzanne Ruigrok. adv.: B&W page EUR 3,001, color page EUR 4,272; 303 x 405.

615.19 DEU
D W Z - D D Z. (Drogerie Waren Zeitung - Deutsche Drogisten Zeitung) Short title: D D Z. Text in German. 2007. m. EUR 50 domestic; EUR 60 foreign (effective 2010). adv. **Document type:** *Magazine, Trade.*
Formed by the merger of (19??-2007): Drogerie Waren Zeitung; (1970-2007): D D Z - Deutsche Drogisten Zeitung (0174-0164); Which was formerly (until 1970): Deutsche Drogisten Zeitung (0012-0049); (1946-1947): Sueddeutsche Drogisten Zeitung (0174-0172)
Indexed: P30.
Published by: (Verband Deutscher Drogisten e.V.), Wintherburg Medienagentur, Bergsonstr 29a, Munich, 81246, Germany. TEL 49-89-12768801, FAX 49-89-12768803, info@wintherburg.de, http://www.wintherburg.de. Ed. Aleksander Schwaab. adv.: B&W page EUR 2,600, color page EUR 4,400; trim 175 x 264. Circ: 11,553 (paid and controlled).

615 SWE ISSN 2000-3455
▼ **DAGENS APOTEK.** Text in Swedish. 2009. 15/yr. SEK 495 (effective 2010). adv. **Document type:** *Newspaper, Consumer.*
Related titles: Online - full text ed.
Published by: Dagens Medicin Sverige AB, PO Box 4612, Stockholm, 11390, Sweden. TEL 46-8-54512300, redaktionen@dagensmedicin.se. Ed. Lina Oesterberg TEL 46-8-56624140. Adv. contact Stefan Hjaerpe TEL 46-8-56624104. Circ: 9,000 (controlled and free).

615.1 DNK ISSN 1399-5200
DANSKE LAEGEMIDDELSTANDARDER (ONLINE). Text in Danish. 2005. 3/yr. back issues avail. **Document type:** *Government.*
Media: Online - full text.
Published by: Laegemiddelstyrelsen/Danish Medicines Agency, Axel Heides Gade 1, Copenhagen S, 2300, Denmark. TEL 45-44-889595, FAX 45-44-889599, dkma@dkma.dk, http://www.dkma.dk.

615 IRN ISSN 1560-8115
RM1
➤ **DARU/DRUGS.** Text in English. 1972. 4/yr. adv. bk.rev. **Document type:** *Journal, Academic/Scholarly.* **Description:** Publishes original research articles in pharmaceutical sciences.
Formerly: University of Teheran. School of Pharmacy. Journal
Related titles: Online - full text ed.. **Related titles:** 2002. free (effective 2011).
Indexed: A01, A34, A35, A36, A38, AgBio, AgrForAb, B&BAb, B19, B25, BIOSIS Prev, BP, CA, CABA, CIN, ChemAb, ChemTitl, E12, EMBASE, ExcerpMed, F08, F11, F12, GH, H16, I12, MycolAb, N02, N03, P10, P20, P22, P32, P33, P39, P40, P48, P53, P54, PQC, R08, R10, R12, R13, RA&MP, RM&VM, Reac, S12, S17, SCI, SCOPUS, SoyAb, T02, T05, VS, W07.
—BLDSC (3533.846250).
Published by: Tehran University of Medical Sciences Publications, Central Library & Documents Center, Poursina St, Tehran, 14174, Iran. TEL 98-21-6112743, FAX 98-21-6404377, http://diglib.tums.ac.ir/pub/journals.asp. Ed. Ali Khalaj.

615 FRA ISSN 1293-8890
DECISION SANTE. LE PHARMACIEN HOPITAL. Text in French. 1995. m. **Document type:** *Magazine, Trade.*
Published by: Decision et Strategie Sante - P G P, 21 Rue Camille Desmoulins, Issy Les Moulineaux, 92789 Cedex 9, France. TEL 33-1-73281610, FAX 33-1-73281611, http://www.decision-sante.com.

DELMAR NURSE'S DRUG HANDBOOK. *see* MEDICAL SCIENCES—Nurses And Nursing

DEMENTIA AND GERIATRIC COGNITIVE DISORDERS. *see* MEDICAL SCIENCES—Psychiatry And Neurology

615 CAN ISSN 1910-0957
DEPENSES EN MEDICAMENTS AU CANADA. Text in French. a. **Document type:** *Government.*
Media: Online - full text. **Related titles:** Print ed.: ISSN 1910-4766; English ed.: Drug Expenditures in Canada. ISSN 1910-0949.
Published by: Canadian Institute for Health Information/Institut Canadien d'Information sur la Sante, 377 Dalhousie St, Ste 200, Ottawa, ON K1N 9N8, Canada. TEL 613-241-7860, FAX 613-241-8120, http://www.cihi.ca.

615.1 DEU ISSN 0366-8622
CODEN: DAPOAG
DER DEUTSCHE APOTHEKER; die aktuelle Zeitschrift fuer pharmazeutische Berufe. Text in German. 1949. m. EUR 184.60 (effective 2011). adv. bk.rev. bibl.; charts; illus. index. **Document type:** *Magazine, Trade.*
Formerly (until 1953): Der Deutsche Apotheker in Hessen (0173-7589)
Related titles: Online - full text ed.
Indexed: ChemAb, I12, IPackAb, P30.
—CCC.
Published by: Deutscher Apotheker Verlag, Postfach 101061, Stuttgart, 70009, Germany. TEL 49-711-25820, FAX 49-711-2582290, http://www.deutscher-apotheker-verlag.de. Ed. Peter Ditzel. Circ: 18,000.

615.1 DEU ISSN 0011-9857
CODEN: DAZEA2
DEUTSCHE APOTHEKER ZEITUNG; vereinigt mit Sueddeutsche Apotheker-Zeitung. Unabhaengige pharmazeutische Zeitschrift fuer Wissenschaft und Praxis. Abbreviated title: D A Z. Text in German. 1861. w. EUR 199; EUR 123 to students; EUR 10 newsstand/cover (effective 2012). adv. bk.rev. charts; illus. index. **Document type:** *Newspaper, Trade.*
Related titles: CD-ROM ed.: EUR 129.48 plus postage (effective 2003); Online - full text ed.; ◆ Supplement(s): P K A Aktiv. ISSN 1860-8736; ◆ Geschichte der Pharmazie. ISSN 0939-334X; ◆ Neue Arzneimittel. ISSN 0724-567X; ◆ Apotheke Heute. ISSN 0173-1882; ◆ Pharmazie Heute. ISSN 0369-979X; ◆ Student und Praktikant. ISSN 0721-8672; ◆ Apotheker-Zeitung. ISSN 0178-4862; Deutsche Apotheker Zeitung. Das Jahr. ISSN 1616-9018. 1997.
Indexed: CIN, ChemAb, ChemTitl, DBA, EMBASE, ExcerpMed, P30, R10, Reac, SCOPUS, VITIS.
—BLDSC (3563.000000), CASDDS, GNLM, IE, Infotrieve, Ingenta, INIST, Linda Hall. **CCC.**
Published by: Deutscher Apotheker Verlag, Postfach 101061, Stuttgart, 70009, Germany. TEL 49-711-25820, FAX 49-711-2582290. Eds. Dr. Klaus Brauer, Peter Ditzel. Adv. contact Klaus Graef TEL 49-711-2582245. Circ: 30,245 (paid).

615.1 DEU
CODEN: ISHPAO
DEUTSCHE GESELLSCHAFT FUER GESCHICHTE DER PHARMAZIE. VEROEFFENTLICHUNGEN ZUR PHARMAZIEGESCHICHTE. Text in German. 1953; N.S. irreg., latest vol.7, 2008. price varies. **Document type:** *Monographic series, Academic/Scholarly.*
Formerly (until 2001): Internationale Gesellschaft fuer Geschichte der Pharmazie. Veroeffentlichungen. Neue Folge (0074-9729)
Indexed: P30, SCOPUS.
—CASDDS, GNLM.
Published by: (Deutsche Gesellschaft fuer Geschichte der Pharmazie), Deutscher Apotheker Verlag, Postfach 101061, Stuttgart, 70009, Germany. TEL 49-711-25820, FAX 49-711-2582290, service@deutscher-apotheker-verlag.de, http://www.deutscher-apotheker-verlag.de.

P

615.01 DEU ISSN 0932-2841
DEUTSCHES ARZNEIBUCH. Text in German. 1951. a. EUR 25 (effective 2008). **Document type:** *Trade.*
Published by: Deutscher Apotheker Verlag, Postfach 101061, Stuttgart, 70009, Germany. TEL 49-711-25820, FAX 49-711-2582290, service@deutscher-apotheker-verlag.de, http://www.deutscher-apotheker-verlag.de.

615 NLD ISSN 0167-6431
CODEN: DEPHDQ
DEVELOPMENTS IN PHARMACOLOGY. Text in English. 1980. irreg., latest vol.3, 1983. price varies. **Document type:** *Monographic series, Academic/Scholarly.*
—CASDDS, INIST. **CCC.**
Published by: Springer Netherlands (Subsidiary of: Springer Science+Business Media), Van Godewijckstraat 30, Dordrecht, 3311 GX, Netherlands. TEL 31-78-6576050, FAX 31-78-6576474.

615 RUS
DIABET. OBRAZ ZHIZNI. Text in Russian. 1994. q. USD 190 foreign (effective 2007). **Document type:** *Magazine, Consumer.* **Description:** Educates patients about diabetes mellitus.
Published by: Mezhdunarodnaya Programma Diabet, Chasovaya ul 20, Moscow, 125315, Russian Federation. TEL 7-095-4900394, FAX 7-095-1521982. Ed. A S Ametov. **Dist. by:** East View Information Services, 10601 Wayzata Blvd, Minneapolis, MN 55305. TEL 952-252-1201, 800-477-1005, FAX 952-252-1202, info@eastview.com, http://www.eastview.com.

615.19 610 USA ISSN 1054-9609
CODEN: DIINF5
DIAGNOSTICS INTELLIGENCE. Text in English. 1989. m. USD 721 in US & Canada; USD 772 elsewhere (effective 2011). illus. back issues avail. **Document type:** *Newsletter, Trade.* **Description:** For executives in the medical in vitro diagnostics business. Covers the latest in research, new markets, new product launches, regulatory affairs, litigation, business opportunities, finance and patents.
Related titles: Supplement(s): In Vitro Diagnostics Industry Directory; Commercial Opportunities in Pharmacogenomics; Commercial Opportunities in Cardiovascular Diagnosis; Emerging Infectious Disease Test Markets.
Indexed: CBNB, CIN, ChemAb, ChemTitl.
—CASDDS. **CCC.**
Published by: C T B International Publishing Inc., PO Box 218, Maplewood, NJ 07040. TEL 973-966-0997, FAX 973-966-0242, info@ctbintl.com.

615 MEX
DICCIONARIO DE ESPECIALIDADES FARMACEUTICAS. Text in Spanish. 1944. a. adv. **Document type:** *Directory, Trade.*
Published by: Thomson PLM, SA, Av Barranca del Muerto 8, Col Credito Constructor, Mexico City, 03940, Mexico. TEL 52-55-54807800, FAX 52-55-56628746.

615 610.28 USA ISSN 1073-4414
DICKINSON'S F D A REVIEW; human & animal drugs - biologics - medical devices. (Food and Drug Administration) Text in English. 1994. m. USD 865 in North America; USD 915 elsewhere (effective 2005). bk.rev. charts; bibl. Supplement avail.; back issues avail. **Document type:** *Newsletter, Trade.* **Description:** Reviews F.D.A. policy, litigation issues, and enforcement of regulations of drugs, biologics, medical devices and veterinary medicines.

Formed by the merger of (1985-1994): Dickinson's F D A (0885-159X); (1992-1994): Dickinson's F D A Inspection (1063-2433)
—CCC.
Published by: Ferdic Inc., PO Box 28, Camp Hill, PA 17011. TEL 717-731-1426, FAX 717-731-1427, info@fdaweb.com, http://www.fdaweb.com. Ed., Pub., R&P James G Dickinson TEL 520-684-3112.

547.7 GBR ISSN 0966-2146
DICTIONARY OF NATURAL PRODUCTS ON CD-ROM. Text in English. 199?. s-a. USD 22,000 (effective 2010). **Document type:** *Directory, Trade.* **Description:** Provides fast access to chemical, physical and biological data on over 203,000 compounds contained in nearly 62,000 entries.
Media: CD-ROM. **Related titles:** Online - full text ed.
Published by: Chapman & Hall/C R C (Subsidiary of: C R C Press, LLC), 24 Blades Ct, Deodar Rd, London, SW15 2NU, United Kingdom. TEL 44-20-70176000, FAX 44-20-70176747, http://www.crcpress.co.uk/.

615 FRA ISSN 0419-1153
LE DICTIONNAIRE VIDAL. Text in French. 1914. a. (plus updates 2/yr.), latest 2010. EUR 170 domestic; EUR 174 in Europe; EUR 213 elsewhere (effective 2010). **Document type:** *Trade.* **Description:** Directory to ethical pharmaceuticals, diagnostic products and OTC products.
Supersedes: Dictionnaire des Specialites Pharmaceutiques
Related titles: CD-ROM ed.: 1914.
—CCC.
Published by: Vidal S.A., 21 rue Camille Desmoulins, Issy les Moulineaux Cedex 9, 92789, France. TEL 33-1-73281100. Circ: 185,000.

615.1 USA ISSN 1529-2460
THE DIETARY SUPPLEMENT. Text in English. 2000. q. **Description:** Provides information on the use of vitamins,minerals, botanicals, and other related supplements.
Indexed: C06, C07, C08, CINAHL.
Published by: Dietary Supplement Llc, 11905 Bristol Manor Court, Rockville, MD 20852-5802. http://www.nal.usda.gov/fnic/pubs/bibs/gen/dietsupp.html.

615.19 USA ISSN 1521-298X
CODEN: DITEFX
DISSOLUTION TECHNOLOGIES. Text in English. 1994. q.
Indexed: EMBASE, I12, SCI, SCOPUS, W07.
—BLDSC (3602.503800), IE, Ingenta.
Published by: Dissolution Technologies, Inc., PO Box 26626, Shawnee Mission, KS 66225-6626. TEL 913-529-5050, FAX 913-491-4899, distech@solve.net.

DOJIN NYUSU/DOJIN NEWS. *see* CHEMISTRY—Analytical Chemistry

615.1 ARG ISSN 0327-2818
DOMINGUEZIA. Text in Spanish. 1978. s-a. ARS 15 newsstand/cover. back issues avail. **Document type:** *Journal, Academic/Scholarly.*
Related titles: Online - full text ed.
Published by: Universidad de Buenos Aires, Museo de Farmabotanica "Juan Jose A. Dominguez", Junin 956 Piso 1, Buenos Aires, 1113, Argentina. Ed. Jose L Amorin. Circ: 500.

DONJINDO NEWSLETTER. *see* CHEMISTRY—Analytical Chemistry

615.7 RUS ISSN 1812-948X
RC1230
➤ **DOPING JOURNAL.** Text in English. 2004. irreg. free (effective 2012). adv. **Document type:** *Journal, Academic/Scholarly.* **Description:** Provides online-only peer-reviewed publication of the results and conclusions of original research on doping with a particular emphasis on novel findings in chemistry and biology of doping chemicals, nonchemical agents, nutritional supplements, and healthy natural alternatives for the doping usage.
Media: Online - full content. Ed., Pub. Aleksey R Koudinov.

➤ **DOSE-RESPONSE**; assessing the nature, mechanisms, and implications of dose-response relationships. *see* MEDICAL SCIENCES

615.1 FIN ISSN 0783-4233
DOSIS. Text in Finnish; Summaries in English. 1985. q. EUR 60 (effective 2005). adv. **Document type:** *Journal, Academic/Scholarly.* **Description:** Publishes scientific articles and reports in pharmacology.
Published by: Suomen Farmasialiitto/Finish Pharmacists' Association, Iso Roobertinkatu 7A, Helsinki, 00120, Finland. FAX 358-9-605112. Ed. Jouni Hirvonen. Circ: 7,000.

615 616.8 FRA ISSN 1962-4263
DOULEUR & SANTE MENTALE. Text in French. 2007. q. free. **Document type:** *Newsletter, Trade.*
Related titles: Online - full text ed.
Published by: Institut UPSA de la Douleur, 3 rue Joseph Monier, B P 325, Rueil Malmaison Cedex, 92506, France. TEL 33-1-58838994, FAX 33-1-58838901, institut.upsa@bms.com.

DR. MED. MABUSE; Zeitschrift fuer Gesundheitswesen. *see* MEDICAL SCIENCES

615.1 AUT
DROGERIE JOURNAL. Text in German. 1947. 10/yr. EUR 2 newsstand/cover (effective 2008). **Document type:** *Magazine, Trade.*
Former titles: Oesterreichische Drogen Zeitung (0253-536X); (until 1979): Oe D Z - Oesterreichische Drogisten Zeitung (0253-5351); (until 197?): Oesterreichische Drogisten Zeitung (0253-5343)
Published by: Oesterreichischer Drogistenverband, Krugerstr 3, Vienna, 1010, Austria. TEL 43-1-5126229, FAX 43-1-512680875, drogistenverband@aon.at, http://www.drogistenverband.at. Circ: 2,400.

615 CHE
DROGISTENSTERN. Text in German. 10/yr. free (effective 2007). adv. **Document type:** *Magazine, Trade.*
Published by: Schweizerischer Drogistenverband, Nidaugasse 15, Biel, 2502, Switzerland. TEL 41-32-3285030, FAX 41-32-3285031, info@drogistenverband.ch, http://www.drogistenverband.ch. adv.: page CHF 17,800; trim 210 x 297. Circ: 300,452 (controlled).

DROIT & DISPOSITIFS MEDICAUX ACTUALITES. *see* MEDICAL SCIENCES—Experimental Medicine, Laboratory Technique

615 FRA ISSN 1165-5372
DROIT & PHARMACIE ACTUALITES. Text in French. 1993. 48/yr. EUR 3,811.22 (effective 2001). **Document type:** *Journal, Trade.* **Description:** Contains in-depth analyses of the latest French and European regulatory news on drugs and other healthcare products.
Incorporates (in 2004): Bulletin International d'Informations - Droit et Pharmacie (0153-288X)
Related titles: CD-ROM ed.: ISSN 1778-400X.
Published by: Droit & Pharmacie, 12 rue de Lorraine, Levallois-Perret Cedex, 92309, France. TEL 33-1-55-46-91-00, FAX 33-1-55-46-91-01, info@droit-et-pharmacie.fr, http://www.droit-et-pharmacie.fr.

615.1 USA ISSN 0148-0545
RA1190 CODEN: DCTODJ
➤ **DRUG AND CHEMICAL TOXICOLOGY**; an international journal for rapid communication. Text in English. 1978. q. GBP 1,165, EUR 1,540, USD 1,925 combined subscription to institutions (print & online eds.); GBP 2,380, EUR 3,140, USD 3,920 combined subscription to corporations (print & online eds.) (effective 2010). adv. back issues avail.; reprint service avail. from PSC. **Document type:** *Journal, Academic/Scholarly.* **Description:** Features full-length research papers, review articles, and short notes. Presents findings on a broad range of topics related to the safety evaluation of drugs, chemicals, and medical products.
Related titles: Microform ed.: (from RPI); Online - full text ed.: ISSN 1525-6014.
Indexed: A01, A03, A08, A22, A34, A35, A36, ASCA, AgBio, AgrForAb, B21, B25, B27, BIOBASE, BIOSIS Prev, BP, C25, C30, C33, CA, CABA, CIN, ChemAb, ChemTitl, CurCont, D01, DBA, E01, E04, E05, E12, EMBASE, ESPM, EnvAb, ExcerpMed, F08, F11, F12, GH, H16, I12, IABS, ISR, IndMed, Inpharma, MEDLINE, MycolAb, N02, N03, N05, NSA, O01, P30, P32, P33, P37, P40, PGegResA, R07, R10, R13, RA&MP, RM&VM, Reac, RefZh, S02, S03, S12, S13, S16, SCI, SCOPUS, T02, T05, ToxAb, VS, W07, W10.
—BLDSC (3627.985000), CASDDS, GNLM, IE, Infotrieve, Ingenta, INIST, Linda Hall. **CCC.**
Published by: Informa Healthcare (Subsidiary of: T & F Informa plc), 52 Vanderbilt Ave, New York, NY 10017. TEL 212-262-8230, FAX 212-262-8234, healthcare.enquiries@informa.com, http://www.informahealthcare.com. Ed. Gerald L Kennedy Jr. Adv. contact Daniel Wallen. **Subscr. outside N. America to:** Taylor & Francis Ltd.

615.5 GBR ISSN 0012-6543
RM1
DRUG AND THERAPEUTICS BULLETIN; the independent review of medical treatment. Abbreviated title: D T B. Text in English. 1962. m. GBP 1,969 combined subscription domestic small FTE (print & online eds.); GBP 1,268 combined subscription foreign small FTE (print & online eds.) (effective 2011). cum.index. back issues avail.; reprints avail. **Document type:** *Bulletin, Trade.* **Description:** Provides impartial and expert information for doctors and pharmacists on the clinical use of drugs.
Formerly (until 1963): Medical Letter on Drugs & Therapeutics (British Edition) (0543-2766)
Related titles: CD-ROM ed.; Online - full text ed.: ISSN 1755-5248; ◆ Italian ed.: Drug and Therapeutics Bulletin (Italian Edition). ISSN 1972-9227; German Translation: Medikament und Therapie. ISSN 0761-361X.
Indexed: A22, B28, C06, C07, C08, CINAHL, DentInd, DiabCont, EMBASE, ExcerpMed, FAMLI, I12, IDIS, IndMed, Inpharma, MEDLINE, P30, P35, R10, Reac, SCOPUS.
—BLDSC (3629.100000), GNLM, IE, Infotrieve, Ingenta, INIST. **CCC.**
Published by: (Consumers' Association), B M J Group, BMA House, Tavistock Sq, London, WC1H 9JR, United Kingdom. TEL 44-20-73836373, FAX 44-20-73836668, http://group.bmj.com. Ed. Ike Iheanacho. Pub. Allison Lang TEL 44-20-73836212.

615 ITA ISSN 1972-9227
DRUG AND THERAPEUTICS BULLETIN (ITALIAN EDITION). Text in Italian. 1992. m. **Document type:** *Magazine, Trade.*
Related titles: ◆ English ed.: Drug and Therapeutics Bulletin. ISSN 0012-6543.
Published by: Farmacie Comunali Riunite di Reggio Emilia, Servizio Informazione e Documentazione Scientifica, Via Doberdo 9, Reggio Emilia, 42100, Italy. TEL 39-0522-5431, http://www.fcr.re.it.

615 JPN ISSN 0289-9922
KNX3091.A27
DRUG APPROVAL AND LICENSING PROCEDURES IN JAPAN. Text in English. 1973. a., latest 2005. JPY 92,400 (effective 2007). **Document type:** *Handbook/Manual/Guide, Trade.* **Description:** Explains Japanese pharmaceutical approval procedures.
Related titles: ◆ Japanese ed.: Iyakuhin Seizo Hanbai Shishin.
Published by: Jiho, Inc., Hitotsubashi Bldg. 5F, Hitotsubashi 2-6-3, Chiyoda-ku, Tokyo, 101-8421, Japan. TEL 81-3-32657751, FAX 81-3-32657769, pj@jiho.co.jp, http://www.jiho.co.jp/.

615 USA ISSN 1080-5826
CODEN: DBTRFN
DRUG BENEFIT TRENDS; for pharmacy managers and managed health care professionals. Abbreviated title: D B T. Text in English. 1989. m. USD 100 domestic; USD 110 foreign; USD 45 to students; USD 10 per issue domestic; USD 15 per issue foreign; free to qualified personnel (effective 2009). adv. charts; illus. Index. back issues avail. **Document type:** *Magazine, Trade.* **Description:** Provides practical information to improve management of the drug benefit.
Related titles: Online - full text ed.
Indexed: A26, EMBASE, ExcerpMed, G08, H11, H12, I05, I12, P03, PsycholAb, R10, Reac, SCOPUS, T02.
—BLDSC (3629.103100), IE, Ingenta. **CCC.**
Published by: C M P Medica LLC (Subsidiary of: United Business Media Limited), 535 Connecticut Ave, Ste 300, Norwalk, CT 06854. TEL 203-523-7000, FAX 203-662-6420, http://www.cmpmedica.com. Ed. Russell Steele. Pub. R Dublin.

615.1 330 USA ISSN 1530-3438
DRUG COST MANAGEMENT REPORT. Text in English. 2000. m. USD 76 (effective 2005). **Document type:** *Newsletter.* **Description:** Includes data and information gathered from HMOs and PBMs, coupled with information on what's working in efforts to control drug costs.
Related titles: Online - full text ed.
Indexed: A26, G08, H11, H12, I05.
—CCC.
Published by: Atlantic Information Services, Inc., 1100 17th St, NW, Ste 300, Washington, DC 20036. TEL 202-775-9008, 800-521-4323, FAX 202-331-9542, customerserv@aispub.com, http://www.aishealth.com. Ed. Susan Namovicz-Peat. Pub. Richard Biehl.

615 ESP ISSN 1579-1793
DRUG DATA REPORT. Text in English. 1971. m. adv. back issues avail. **Document type:** *Journal, Trade.* **Description:** Contains essential drug information in a condensed monograph form. Publishes about 10,000 new compounds each year.
Formerly (until 1984): Annual Drug Data Report (0379-4121)
Related titles: Online - full text ed.
Indexed: Inpharma.
—GNLM, INIST, Linda Hall. **CCC.**
Published by: Prous Science (Subsidiary of: Thomson Reuters), Provenza 388, Barcelona, 08025, Spain. TEL 34-93-4592220, FAX 34-93-4581535, service@prous.com, http://www.prous.com.

615.19 USA ISSN 1071-7544
RS199.5 CODEN: DDELEB
➤ **DRUG DELIVERY**; journal of delivery and targeting of therapeutic agents. Text in English. 1992. 8/yr. GBP 835, EUR 1,105, USD 1,375 combined subscription to institutions (print & online eds.); GBP 1,720, EUR 2,270, USD 2,835 combined subscription to corporations (print & online eds.) (effective 2010). adv. index. back issues avail.; reprint service avail. from PSC. **Document type:** *Journal, Academic/Scholarly.* **Description:** Focuses on drug delivery technology at the theoretical as well as practical level. Includes basic research, development, and application principles on the molecular, cellular, and higher levels of targeting sites, as well as physical, chemical and immunokinetic modes of delivery.
Formerly (until 1993): Drug Targeting and Delivery (1058-241X)
Related titles: Online - full text ed.: ISSN 1521-0464 (from IngentaConnect).
Indexed: A01, A03, A08, A22, B&BAb, B19, B21, B27, BioEngAb, C33, CA, ChemAb, E01, EMBASE, ESPM, ExcerpMed, I12, IndMed, Inpharma, M&PBA, MEDLINE, P30, R10, Reac, SCI, SCOPUS, T02, ToxAb, W07.
—BLDSC (3629.417000), CASDDS, GNLM, IE, Infotrieve, Ingenta. **CCC.**
Published by: Informa Healthcare (Subsidiary of: T & F Informa plc), 52 Vanderbilt Ave, New York, NY 10017. TEL 212-262-8230, FAX 212-262-8234, healthcare.enquiries@informa.com, http://www.informahealthcare.com. Eds. Alfred Stracher, Vladimir Torchilin. **Subscr. outside N. America to:** Taylor & Francis Ltd.

615.1 DEU ISSN 2190-393X
▼ ➤ **DRUG DELIVERY AND TRANSLATIONAL RESEARCH.** Text in English. forthcoming 2011 (Feb.). bi-m. EUR 384, USD 472 combined subscription to institutions (print & online eds.) (effective 2012). **Document type:** *Journal, Academic/Scholarly.* **Description:** Focuses on translational aspects of drug delivery.
Related titles: Online - full text ed.: ISSN 2190-3948. forthcoming 2011 (Feb.) (from IngentaConnect).
Indexed: P30, SCOPUS.
—IE. **CCC.**
Published by: (Controlled Release Society, Inc. USA), Springer (Subsidiary of: Springer Science+Business Media), Tiergartenstr 17, Heidelberg, 69121, Germany. Ed. Dr. Vinod Labhasetwar.

615 NLD ISSN 2210-3031
▼ **DRUG DELIVERY LETTERS.** Text in English. 2011. s-a. USD 370 to institutions (print or online ed.) (effective 2012). adv. **Document type:** *Journal, Academic/Scholarly.* **Description:** Covers all basic and applied research in drug delivery and targeting at molecular and cellular levels and novel delivery systems.
Related titles: Online - full text ed.: ISSN 2210-304X.
—CCC.
Published by: Bentham Science Publishers Ltd., PO Box 294, Bussum, 1400 AG, Netherlands. TEL 31-35-6923800, FAX 31-35-6980150, sales@bentham.org. Eds. Istvan Toth TEL 61-7-33651386, Marc Schneider. **Subscr. to:** Bentham Science Publishers Ltd., c/o Richard E Morrissy, PO Box 446, Oak Park, IL 60301. TEL 312-413-5867, FAX 312-996-7107, subscriptions@bentham.org.

615 JPN ISSN 0913-5006
RS199.5 CODEN: DDSYEI
DRUG DELIVERY SYSTEM. Short title: D D S. Text in Japanese; Summaries in English. 1986. bi-m. JPY 8,000 membership (effective 2007). **Document type:** *Journal, Academic/Scholarly.*
Related titles: Online - full text ed.: ISSN 1881-2732. 2006.
Indexed: B&BAb, B19, CIN, ChemAb, ChemTitl, EMBASE, SCOPUS.
—BLDSC (3629.104800), CASDDS, IE, Ingenta. **CCC.**
Published by: Nihon D D S Gakkai/Japan Society of Drug Delivery System, c/o Marianna University School of Medicine, Institute of Medical Science, 2-16-1 Sugao Miyamae-ku, Kawasaki, Kanagawa 216-8512, Japan. js-dds@umin.ac.jp, http://square.umin.ac.jp/js-dds/.

615.605 GBR ISSN 1472-4715
CODEN: DDSSAU
➤ **DRUG DELIVERY SYSTEMS AND SCIENCES.** Abbreviated title: D D S S. Text in English. 2001. q. bk.rev. back issues avail.; reprints avail. **Document type:** *Journal, Academic/Scholarly.* **Description:** Contains primarily original work resulting from research and technological developments in the drug delivery field.
—BLDSC (3629.104870), IE, Ingenta. **CCC.**
Published by: (United Kingdom & Ireland Controlled Release Society), Euromed Scientific Ltd., Ste 9, The Heybridge Ctr, Maldon, Essex CM9 4NN, United Kingdom. TEL 44-1621-851007.

➤ **DRUG DESIGN, DEVELOPMENT AND THERAPY.** *see* MEDICAL SCIENCES

615 GBR ISSN 2045-8894
▼ **DRUG DEVELOPMENT.** Text in English. 2009. a. EUR 180, USD 225 to institutions (effective 2011). adv. illus. back issues avail.; reprints avail. **Document type:** *Journal, Trade.* **Description:** Serves the information needs of the pharmaceutical research community. It provides valuable insight into the latest developments and issues shaping this field. Driven by the expertise and guidance of eminent industry bodies, this series comprises the views of strategic decision makers, providing unparalleled analysis and comment.
Formerly (until 2010): Drug - Discovery, Development, Delivery (2042-5163); Which was formed by the merger of (2007-2009): Drug Delivery (1755-1161); (2006-2009): Drug Discovery (1756-1892); (200?-2009): Drug Development (1754-6125)
Related titles: Online - full text ed.: ISSN 2045-8908.

Published by: Touch Briefings (Subsidiary of: Touch Group plc), Saffron House, 6-10 Kirby St, London, EC1N 8TS, United Kingdom. TEL 44-20-74525600, FAX 44-20-74525606, info@touchbriefings.com. Ed. Jonathan McKenna. Pub., Adv. contact Fergus Brunning.

615.19 USA
RS199.5 CODEN: DDTRAW
DRUG DEVELOPMENT & DELIVERY. Text in English. 2001 (Oct.). 8/yr. adv. **Document type:** *Magazine, Trade.* **Description:** Contains technical articles that describe practical solutions to drug delivery challenges.
Formerly: Drug Delivery Technology (1537-2898)
Related titles: Online - full text ed.: free (effective 2011).
Indexed: EMBASE, ExcerpMed, SCOPUS.
—BLDSC (3629.115455), IE, Ingenta.
Address: 219 Changebridge Rd, Montville, NJ 07045. TEL 973-299-1200, FAX 973-299-7937. Ed. Cindy Dubin. Pub. Ralph Vitaro. Adv. contact Warren DeGraff. B&W page USD 4,875, color page USD 6,210; trim 8.125 x 10.875. Circ: 20,000 (paid and controlled).

615 USA ISSN 0363-9045
RS402 CODEN: DDIPD8
➤ **DRUG DEVELOPMENT AND INDUSTRIAL PHARMACY.** Text in English. 1975. m. GBP 2,430, EUR 3,205, USD 4,010 combined subscription to institutions (print & online eds.); GBP 4,995, EUR 6,595, USD 8,240 combined subscription to corporations (print & online eds.) (effective 2010). adv. back issues avail.; reprint service avail. from PSC. **Document type:** *Journal, Academic/Scholarly.* **Description:** Covers aspects of the development, production, and evaluation of drugs and pharmaceutical products.
Formerly (until 1977): Drug Development Communications (0095-5183)
Related titles: Microform ed.: (from RPI); Online - full text ed.: ISSN 1520-5762 (from IngentaConnect).
Indexed: A22, A34, A36, ASCA, AgrForAb, B&BAb, B01, B06, B07, B09, B19, B21, BP, BioEngAb, C25, C33, CA, CABA, CIN, ChemAb, ChemTitl, CurCont, D01, DBA, E01, E12, EMBASE, ExcerpMed, F08, F11, F12, FCA, GH, H01, H16, H17, I12, ISR, IndMed, IndVet, Inpharma, MEDLINE, MaizeAb, N02, N03, N04, P30, P33, P35, P39, PN&I, R08, R10, R12, RA&MP, RM&VM, Reac, RefZh, S12, SCI, SCOPUS, SoyAb, T02, T05, TAR, VS, W07.
—CASDDS, GNLM, IE, Infotrieve, Ingenta, INIST. **CCC.**
Published by: Informa Healthcare (Subsidiary of: T & F Informa plc), 52 Vanderbilt Ave, New York, NY 10017. TEL 212-262-8230, FAX 212-262-8234, healthcare.enquiries@informa.com, http://www.informahealthcare.com. Ed. Robert O Williams III. Adv. contact Daniel Wallen. **Subscr. outside N. America to:** Taylor & Francis Ltd.

615.1 USA ISSN 1088-5447
DRUG DEVELOPMENT PIPELINE. Text in English. 1996. m. USD 279 in US & Canada; USD 309 elsewhere (effective 2011). back issues avail. **Document type:** *Newsletter, Trade.* **Description:** Summarizes changes in the drug development plans of U.S. and Canadian pharmaceutical companies.
—**CCC.**
Published by: C T B International Publishing Inc., PO Box 218, Maplewood, NJ 07040. TEL 973-966-0997, FAX 973-966-0242, info@ctbintl.com.

615.19 USA ISSN 0272-4391
RM301.25 CODEN: DDREDK
➤ **DRUG DEVELOPMENT RESEARCH.** Text in English. 1981. 8/yr. GBP 3,719 in United Kingdom to institutions; EUR 4,703 in Europe to institutions; USD 7,121 in United States to institutions; USD 7,233 in Canada & Mexico to institutions; USD 7,289 elsewhere to institutions; GBP 4,278 combined subscription in United Kingdom to institutions (print & online eds.); EUR 5,410 combined subscription in Europe to institutions (print & online eds.); USD 8,189 combined subscription in United States to institutions (print & online eds.); USD 8,301 combined subscription in Canada & Mexico to institutions (print & online eds.); USD 8,357 combined subscription elsewhere to institutions (print & online eds.) (effective 2012). adv. bibl.; charts; illus. index. back issues avail.; reprint service avail. from PSC. **Document type:** *Journal, Academic/Scholarly.* **Description:** Brings out research articles on medicinal chemistry, pharmacology, biotechnology and biopharmaceuticals, toxicology, and drug delivery, formulation, and pharmacokinetics.
Related titles: Microform ed.: (from PQC); Online - full text ed.: ISSN 1098-2299. GBP 3,633 in United Kingdom to institutions; EUR 4,595 in Europe to institutions; USD 7,121 elsewhere to institutions (effective 2012).
Indexed: A20, A22, A34, A35, A36, ASCA, AgBio, B&BAb, B19, B21, B25, BIOSIS Prev, BP, BioEngAb, C30, C33, CABA, CIN, CTA, ChemAb, ChemTitl, ChemoAb, CurCont, DBA, EMBASE, ESPM, ExcerpMed, F08, F11, F12, FR, GH, H16, H17, I12, ISR, Inpharma, M&PBA, MycolAb, N02, N03, NSA, P30, P33, P35, P39, R10, R12, RA&MP, Reac, RefZh, SCI, T05, ToxAb, VS, W07.
—BLDSC (3629.119000), CASDDS, GNLM, IE, Infotrieve, Ingenta, INIST. **CCC.**
Published by: John Wiley & Sons, Inc., 111 River St, Hoboken, NJ 07030. TEL 201-748-6000, FAX 201-748-6088, info@wiley.com, http://www.wiley.com/WileyCDA/. Ed. Michael Williams. Pub., Adv. contact Kim Thompkins TEL 212-850-6921. **Subscr. outside the Americas to:** John Wiley & Sons Ltd., The Atrium, Southern Gate, Chichester, West Sussex PO19 8SQ, United Kingdom. TEL 44-1243-779777, 800-243407, FAX 44-1243-775878, cs-journals@wiley.com.

615 JPN ISSN 1881-7831
➤ **DRUG DISCOVERIES & THERAPEUTICS.** Text in English. 2007. bi-m. back issues avail. **Document type:** *Journal, Academic/ Scholarly.* **Description:** Publishes original articles, brief reports, reviews, policy forum articles, case reports, news, and letters on all aspects of the field of pharmaceutical research, Including medicinal chemistry, pharmacology, pharmaceutical analysis, pharmaceutics, pharmaceutical administration, and experimental and clinical studies of effects, mechanisms, or uses of various treatments. Also covers studies in drug-related fields such as biology, biochemistry, physiology, microbiology, and immunology.
Related titles: Online - full text ed.: ISSN 1881-784X. free.
Published by: (International Research and Cooperation Association for Bio & Socio-Sciences Advancement), International Advancement Center for Medicine & Health Research Co., Ltd., Pearl City Koishikawa 603, 2-4-5 Kasuga, Bunkyo-ku, Tokyo, 112-0003, Japan. TEL 81-3-58409697, FAX 81-3-58409698, office@iacmhr.com, http://www.iacmhr.com/. Ed. Kazuhisa Sekimizu.

615.1 USA ISSN 1524-783X
RS1 CODEN: DDDEFK
DRUG DISCOVERY & DEVELOPMENT. Text in English. 1999. m. USD 109 domestic; USD 157 in Canada; USD 151 in Mexico; USD 250 elsewhere; USD 15 per issue domestic; USD 20 per issue foreign; free to qualified personnel (effective 2008). adv. illus.; tr.lit. back issues avail.; reprints avail. **Document type:** *Magazine, Trade.* **Description:** Provides information on technologies, tools and business/regulatory strategies that help scientists and executives accelerate the pace and productivity of drug research and development.
Related titles: Online - full text ed.: ISSN 1558-6022. free to qualified personnel (effective 2008).
Indexed: A01, A03, A08, A09, A10, A15, ABIn, B01, B02, B03, B06, B07, B09, B11, B15, B17, B18, CA, G04, I05, P21, P24, P26, P48, P51, P54, PQC, T02, V03, V04, W01, W02.
—BLDSC (3629.120200). **CCC.**
Published by: Advantage Business Media, 100 Enterprise Dr, Ste 600, PO Box 912, Rockaway, NJ 07886. TEL 973-920-7000, FAX 973-920-7531, AdvantageCommunications@advantagemedia.com, http://www.advantagebusinessmedia.com. Eds. James Netterwald TEL 973-920-7033, Michelle Hoffman TEL 973-920-7034, Rita C Peters TEL 973-920-7034. Pub. Sofia Goller TEL 973-920-7051. adv.: B&W page USD 6,250; trim 10.5 x 7.88. Circ: 35,541 (paid).

615 USA ISSN 1944-6713
DRUG DISCOVERY NEWS. Text in English. 2005. m. free to qualified personnel (effective 2009). adv. back issues avail.; reprints avail. **Document type:** *Newspaper, Trade.* **Description:** Focuses on covering issues, trends and product news that impacts decision makers in the pharmaceutical drug development and discovery arena.
Related titles: Online - full text ed.
Published by: Old River Publications, LLC, 19035 Old Detroit Rd, Rocky River, OH 44116. TEL 440-331-6600, FAX 440-331-7563. Eds. Jeffrey Bouley, Amy Swinderman. adv.: page USD 5,840; trim 8.125 x 10.625. Circ: 30,131.

615 USA
DRUG DISCOVERY SERIES. Text in English. 2005. irreg., latest 2009. price varies. back issues avail. **Document type:** *Monographic series, Academic/Scholarly.* **Description:** Covers information about Pharmacoeconomics.
Published by: Taylor & Francis Inc. (Subsidiary of: Taylor & Francis Group), 325 Chestnut St, Ste 800, Philadelphia, PA 19106. TEL 215-625-2940, 800-354-1420, orders@taylorandfrancis.com. Ed. Andrew Carmen.

615.1 660.6 GBR ISSN 1359-6446
RS420 CODEN: DDTOFS
➤ **DRUG DISCOVERY TODAY.** Abbreviated title: D D T. Text in English. 1996. 24/yr. EUR 3,323 in Europe to institutions; JPY 462,500 in Japan to institutions; USD 3,719 elsewhere to institutions (effective 2012). adv. back issues avail.; reprints avail. **Document type:** *Journal, Academic/Scholarly.* **Description:** Offers pharmacists and physicians news in pharmacologic research.
Incorporates (2003-2005): Drug Discovery Today: Targets (1741-8372); Which was formerly (2002-2003): Targets (1477-3627); (1998-2001): Pharmaceutical Science and Technology Today (1461-5347)
Related titles: Online - full text ed.: ISSN 1878-5832 (from IngentaConnect, ScienceDirect).
Indexed: A01, A03, A08, A22, A26, A28, A29, APA, B&BAb, B19, B20, B21, B27, BIOSIS Prev, BioEngAb, BrCerAb, C&ISA, CA, CA/WCA, CIA, CIN, CerAb, ChemAb, ChemTitl, CivEngAb, CorrAb, CurCont, E&CAJ, E11, EEA, EMA, EMBASE, ESPM, EnvEAb, ExcerpMed, H15, I05, I10, I12, ISR, Inpharma, M&PBA, M&TEA, M09, MBF, MEDLINE, METADEX, MycolAb, NSA, P30, R10, Reac, S01, SCI, SCOPUS, SolStAb, T02, T04, ViroIAbstr, W07, WAA.
—BLDSC (3629.120500), CASDDS, GNLM, IE, Infotrieve, Ingenta, INIST. **CCC.**
Published by: Elsevier Ltd., Trends Journals (Subsidiary of: Elsevier Science & Technology), 32 Jamestown Rd, London, NW1 7BY, United Kingdom. TEL 44-20-74244200, FAX 44-20-74832293, JournalsCustomerServiceEMEA@elsevier.com, http://www.elsevier.com. Ed. Steve L Carney TEL 44-20-74244314. Adv. contact Kevin Partridge TEL 44-1865-843717. page GBP 1,540; trim 216 x 280.

615 GBR ISSN 1741-8364
➤ **DRUG DISCOVERY TODAY: BIOSILICO;** information technology for drug discovery. Text in English. 2003. bi-m. free to qualified personnel (effective 2010). adv. back issues avail.; reprints avail. **Document type:** *Journal, Academic/Scholarly.*
Formerly (until 2004): Biosilico (1478-5382)
Related titles: Online - full text ed.
Indexed: A01, A03, A08, CA, MycolAb, P30, S01, SCOPUS.
—IE, Ingenta. **CCC.**
Published by: Elsevier Ltd., Trends Journals (Subsidiary of: Elsevier Science & Technology), The Blvd, Langford Ln, Kidlington, OX5 1GB, United Kingdom. TEL 44-1865-843434, FAX 44-1865-843970, JournalsCustomerServiceEMEA@elsevier.com. Ed. C Watson.

615.1 GBR ISSN 1740-6765
RM301.25
➤ **DRUG DISCOVERY TODAY: DISEASE MECHANISMS.** Text in English. 2005. q. EUR 2,208 in Europe to institutions; JPY 293,300 in Japan to institutions; USD 2,483 elsewhere to institutions (effective 2011). back issues avail. **Document type:** *Journal, Academic/ Scholarly.* **Description:** Covers the essential elements of molecular medicine and drug discovery, in a manner that has relevance to those actually working on the discovery and development of new drugs.
Media: Online - full text (from ScienceDirect).
Indexed: CA, EMBASE, ExcerpMed, P30, R10, Reac, SCOPUS, T02.
—BLDSC (3629.120625), IE, Ingenta. **CCC.**
Published by: Elsevier Ltd., Trends Journals (Subsidiary of: Elsevier Science & Technology), 84 Theobald's Rd, London, WC1X 8RR, United Kingdom. TEL 44-20-76114000, FAX 44-20-76114485, JournalsCustomerServiceEMEA@elsevier.com. Eds. Charles Lowenstein, Toren Finkel.

615.1 GBR ISSN 1740-6757
RM301.25
➤ **DRUG DISCOVERY TODAY: DISEASE MODELS.** Text in English. 2005. q. EUR 2,229 in Europe to institutions; JPY 296,000 in Japan to institutions; USD 2,506 elsewhere to institutions (effective 2011). back issues avail. **Document type:** *Journal, Academic/Scholarly.* **Description:** Provides critical analysis and evaluation of which models can genuinely inform the research community about the direct process of human disease, those which may have value in basic toxicology, and those which are simply designed for effective expression and raw characterization.
Media: Online - full text (from ScienceDirect).
Indexed: CA, EMBASE, ExcerpMed, P30, R10, Reac, SCOPUS, T02.
—IE, Ingenta. **CCC.**
Published by: Elsevier Ltd., Trends Journals (Subsidiary of: Elsevier Science & Technology), 84 Theobald's Rd, London, WC1X 8RR, United Kingdom. TEL 44-20-76114000, FAX 44-20-76114485, JournalsCustomerServiceEMEA@elsevier.com. Eds. Andrew McCulloch, Jan Tornell.

615.1 GBR ISSN 1740-6749
RM301.25
➤ **DRUG DISCOVERY TODAY: TECHNOLOGIES.** Text in English. 2005. q. EUR 2,353 in Europe to institutions; JPY 312,600 in Japan to institutions; USD 2,646 elsewhere to institutions (effective 2011). back issues avail. **Document type:** *Journal, Academic/Scholarly.*
Media: Online - full text (from ScienceDirect).
Indexed: CA, EMBASE, ExcerpMed, P30, R10, Reac, SCOPUS, T02.
—IE, Ingenta. **CCC.**
Published by: Elsevier Ltd., Trends Journals (Subsidiary of: Elsevier Science & Technology), 84 Theobald's Rd, London, WC1X 8RR, United Kingdom. TEL 44-20-76114000, FAX 44-20-76114485, JournalsCustomerServiceEMEA@elsevier.com. Eds. Henk Timmerman, Kelvin Lam.

615.1 GBR ISSN 1740-6773
HD9665.1
➤ **DRUG DISCOVERY TODAY: THERAPEUTIC STRATEGIES.** Text in English. 2005. q. EUR 2,336 in Europe to institutions; JPY 310,200 in Japan to institutions; USD 2,627 elsewhere to institutions (effective 2011). back issues avail. **Document type:** *Journal, Academic/ Scholarly.* **Description:** Discusses the biotechnical challenges in ensuring drug action, especially with regard to biopharmaceuticals.
Media: Online - full text (from ScienceDirect).
Indexed: CA, EMBASE, ExcerpMed, P30, R10, Reac, SCOPUS, T02.
—IE, Ingenta. **CCC.**
Published by: Elsevier Ltd., Trends Journals (Subsidiary of: Elsevier Science & Technology), 84 Theobald's Rd, London, WC1X 8RR, United Kingdom. TEL 44-20-76114000, FAX 44-20-76114485, JournalsCustomerServiceEMEA@elsevier.com. Eds. Eliot Ohlstein, Raymond Baker.

P

615 GBR ISSN 1469-4344
DRUG DISCOVERY WORLD; the quarterly business review of drug discovery & development. Abbreviated title: D D W(Drug Discovery World). Text in English. 2000. q. GBP 89 in Europe; USD 175 in US & Canada; GBP 99 elsewhere; free to qualified personnel (effective 2009). adv. back issues avail. **Document type:** *Journal, Trade.* **Description:** Aims to help the industry survive for all those involved in the drug discovery & development arena.
Related titles: Online - full text ed.: free (effective 2009).
Indexed: EMBASE, ExcerpMed, R10, Reac, SCOPUS.
—BLDSC (3535.923650), IE, Ingenta. **CCC.**
Published by: R J Communications & Media World Ltd., 39 Vineyard Path, Mortlake, London, SW14 8ET, United Kingdom. TEL 44-20-84875656, FAX 44-20-84875666, info@rjcoms.com. Ed., Pub. Robert Jordan. adv.: page GBP 4,350; trim 210 x 297. Circ: 15,000.

615.1 USA ISSN 0277-9714
RM300
DRUG FACTS AND COMPARISONS. Text in English. 1947. m. looseleaf. USD 494 base vol(s). (effective 2009). index. reprints avail. **Document type:** *Directory, Trade.* **Description:** Provides comprehensive and timely drug information, which includes over 22,000 Rx and 6,000 OTC products, including generic and trade names and more than 3,000 unique charts and tables.
Formerly (until 19??): Facts and Comparisons (0162-1491)
Related titles: Online - full text ed.: USD 359.95 (effective 2002); Alternate Frequency ed(s).: a. USD 179.95 (effective 2002).
Indexed: Inpharma.
—BLDSC (3629.126000).
Published by: Facts and Comparisons (Subsidiary of: Wolters Kluwer N.V.), 77 West Port Plz, Ste 450, St. Louis, MO 63146. TEL 314-216-2100, 800-223-0554, FAX 317-735-5390. Ed. Bernie R Olin.

615.7 USA ISSN 1548-2790
DRUG FORMULARY REVIEW. Text in English. 1985. m. USD 499 combined subscription (print & online eds.); USD 83 per issue (effective 2010). back issues avail.; reprints avail. **Document type:** *Newsletter, Trade.*
Formerly (until 2004): Drug Utilization Review (0884-8521)
Related titles: Online - full text ed.
Indexed: A26, B02, B15, B17, B18, C06, C07, E08, G04, G06, G07, G08, H11, H12, I05, P20, P24, P48, P54, PQC, S09.
—BLDSC (4333.189940). **CCC.**
Published by: A H C Media LLC (Subsidiary of: Thomson Corporation, Healthcare Information Group), 3525 Piedmont Rd, NE, Bldg 6, Ste 400, Atlanta, GA 30305. TEL 404-262-7436, 800-688-2421, FAX 404-262-7837, 800-284-3291, customerservice@ahcmedia.com, http://www.ahcmedia.com/. Pub. Brenda L Mooney TEL 404-262-5403. **Subscr. to:** PO Box 105109, Atlanta, GA 30348. TEL 404-262-5476, FAX 404-262-5560.

615 614.4 USA ISSN 1061-2335
DRUG G M P REPORT. (Good Manufacturing Practices) Text in English. 1992. m. looseleaf. USD 939 (print or online ed.); USD 1,502 combined subscription (print & online eds.) (effective 2009). 8 p./no.; back issues avail. **Document type:** *Newsletter, Trade.* **Description:** Reports on good manufacturing practices as they relate to the pharmaceutical industry.
Related titles: Online - full text ed.: USD 789 (effective 2005).
—IE. **CCC.**
Published by: Washington Business Information, Inc., 300 N Washington St, Ste 200, Falls Church, VA 22046. customerservice@fdanews.com. Ed. Christopher Hollis TEL 703-538-7650. Pub. Matt Salt TEL 703-538-7642.

615.06 NLD ISSN 0921-2582
CODEN: DRDIER

➤ **DRUG INDUCED DISORDERS.** Text in Dutch. 1985. irreg., latest vol.5, 1992. price varies. back issues avail. **Document type:** *Monographic series, Academic/Scholarly.* **Description:** Discusses disorders caused by the side-effects of drugs.
Indexed: CIN, ChemAb, ChemTitl.
—CASDDS.
Published by: Elsevier BV (Subsidiary of: Elsevier Science & Technology), Radarweg 29, PO Box 211, Amsterdam, 1000 AE, Netherlands. TEL 31-20-4853911, FAX 31-20-4852457, JournalsCustomerServiceEMEA@elsevier.com, http://www.elsevier.nl.

615 USA ISSN 1541-6607
DRUG INDUSTRY DAILY. Text in English. 2002 (Sept.). d. (Mon.-Fri.). USD 1,895 (effective 2009). back issues avail. **Document type:** *Newsletter, Trade.* **Description:** Delivers coverage of what is happening on capitol hill and at the FDA, FTC, HHS, NIH and other key agencies and decision making bodies that affect the pharmaceutical industry.
Incorporates (1975-2003): Regulatory Watchdog Service (0275-0902)
Media: Online - full content.
Published by: Washington Business Information, Inc., 300 N Washington St, Ste 200, Falls Church, VA 22046. customerservice@fdanews.com.

615.13 USA ISSN 1533-4511
RM301.12
DRUG INFORMATION HANDBOOK. Text in English. 1994. a. USD 66.95 per issue (effective 2011). back issues avail. **Document type:** *Handbook/Manual/Guide, Trade.*
Published by: (American Pharmacists Association), Lexi-Comp, Inc., 1100 Terex Rd, Hudson, OH 44236. TEL 330-650-6506, 800-837-5394, FAX 330-656-4307, http://www.lexi.com.

615.1 USA ISSN 1551-4765
RM301.12
DRUG INFORMATION HANDBOOK FOR NURSING. Text in English. 1998. a. USD 46.95 per issue (effective 2011). back issues avail. **Document type:** *Handbook/Manual/Guide, Trade.*
Published by: Lexi-Comp, Inc., 1100 Terex Rd, Hudson, OH 44236. TEL 330-650-6506, 800-837-5394, FAX 330-656-4307, http://www.lexi.com. Eds. Beatrice B Turkoski, Brenda R Lance, Elizabeth A Tomsik.

615.13 USA ISSN 1533-4341
RM315
DRUG INFORMATION HANDBOOK FOR PSYCHIATRY. Text in English. 2000. a. USD 51.95 per issue (effective 2011). **Document type:** *Handbook/Manual/Guide, Trade.*
Published by: Lexi-Comp, Inc., 1100 Terex Rd, Hudson, OH 44236. TEL 330-650-6506, 800-837-5394, FAX 330-656-4307, http://www.lexi.com. Eds. Martha Sajatovic, Matthew A Fuller.

615.1 USA ISSN 0092-8615
RM1 CODEN: DGIJB9
➤ **DRUG INFORMATION JOURNAL.** Abbreviated title: D I J. Text in English. 1966. bi-m. USD 25 per issue domestic; USD 30 per issue foreign; free to members (effective 2009). adv. index. back issues avail. **Document type:** *Journal, Academic/Scholarly.* **Description:** Aims to disseminate information on manual and automated drug research, development, and information system.
Formerly (until 1972): Drug Information Bulletin (0012-656X)
Related titles: CD-ROM ed.; Microfilm ed.: (from PQC); Online - full text ed.: free (effective 2009).
Indexed: A22, B21, CA, CIS, ChemAb, EMBASE, ESPM, ExcerpMed, FR, H&SSA, H13, I12, IBR, IBZ, Inpharma, L04, LISTA, P10, P20, P24, P26, P30, P48, P53, P54, PQC, R10, Reac, RiskAb, SCI, SCOPUS, T02, ToxAb, W07.
—BLDSC (3629.160000), CASDDS, GNLM, IE, Infotrieve, Ingenta, INIST, Linda Hall. **CCC.**
Published by: Drug Information Association, 800 Enterprise Rd, Ste 200, Horsham, PA 19044. TEL 215-442-6100, FAX 215-442-6199, dia@diahome.org, http://www.diahome.org. Ed. Michael R Hamrell. Adv. contact Steve Everly TEL 267-893-5686. B&W page USD 3,095, color page USD 4,695; bleed 8.25 x 11.125. Circ: 18,000.

615.1 USA
DRUG INFORMATION TODAY. Text in English. 19??. d.
Published by: Drug Information Association, 800 Enterprise Rd, Ste 200, Horsham, PA 19044. TEL 215-442-6100, FAX 215-442-6199, dia@diahome.org, http://www.diahome.org.

615.7 USA ISSN 0899-4951
RM302
DRUG INTERACTION FACTS. Text in English. 1988. q. looseleaf. USD 270 base vol(s). (effective 2009). Supplement avail.; reprints avail. **Document type:** *Directory, Trade.* **Description:** Reference for drug and food interactions of clinical significance, suspected but unsubstantiated interactions, with concise synopsis of onset, severity and documentation.
Related titles: CD-ROM ed.: USD 179.95 (effective 2002); Online - full text ed.; Alternate Frequency ed(s).: a. USD 79.97 (effective 2002).
Published by: Facts and Comparisons (Subsidiary of: Wolters Kluwer N.V.), 77 West Port Plz, Ste 450, St. Louis, MO 63146. TEL 314-216-2100, 800-223-0554, FAX 317-735-5390.

615 IND ISSN 0975-7619
RM301.25
▼ ➤ **DRUG INVENTION TODAY.** Text in English. 2009. m. free (effective 2011). **Document type:** *Journal, Academic/Scholarly.*
Media: Online - full text.
Indexed: A01, T02.
Published by: Association of Pharmaceutical Innovators, Santosh Stone Wale Ka Makan, Near Kumawat Dharamsala, Nursinghpura Rd, Ramtekari, Mandsaur, Madhya Pradesh 458 001, India. admin@ditonline.info. Ed. Varaprasad Bobbarala.

615 344.041 USA ISSN 1551-532X
DRUG LAW WEEKLY. Text in English. 2004. w. USD 2,295 in US & Canada; USD 2,495 elsewhere; USD 2,525 combined subscription in US & Canada (print & online eds.); USD 2,755 combined subscription elsewhere (print & online eds.) (effective 2008). back issues avail. **Document type:** *Newsletter, Trade.*
Related titles: E-mail ed.; Online - full text ed.: ISSN 1551-5311. USD 2,295 combined subscription (online & email eds.); single user (effective 2008).
Indexed: L10, P10, P21, P48, P53, P54, PQC.
Published by: NewsRx, 2727 Paces Ferry Rd SE, Ste 2-440, Atlanta, GA 30339. TEL 770-435-8286, 800-726-4550, FAX 770-435-6800, pressrelease@newsrx.com, http://www.newsrx.com. Pub. Susan Hasty TEL 770-507-7777.

615 JPN ISSN 0389-746X
DRUG MAGAZINE/DORAGGU MAGAJIN. Text in Japanese. 1958. m. JPY 20,370 (effective 2007). **Document type:** *Journal, Academic/Scholarly.*
Published by: Doraggu Magajin/Drugmagazine Co., Ltd., 2-3-15 Nihonbashihoncho, Chuo-ku, Tokyo, 103-0023, Japan. TEL 81-3-32414661, FAX 81-3-32414594.

615 USA ISSN 0090-9556
RM301 CODEN: DMDSAI
➤ **DRUG METABOLISM AND DISPOSITION**; the biological fate of chemicals. Abbreviated title: D M D. Text in English. 1973. m. USD 137 to members; USD 436 combined subscription domestic to institutions (print & online eds.); USD 515 combined subscription foreign to institutions (print & online eds.); USD 40 per issue (effective 2010). adv. bk.rev. illus. index. back issues avail.; reprints avail. **Document type:** *Journal, Academic/Scholarly.* **Description:** Covers metabolism of pharmacological agents or drugs and environmental chemicals, reactants and preservatives for pharmacologists, toxicologists and medical chemists.
Related titles: Online - full text ed.: ISSN 1521-009X. USD 392 to institutions (effective 2010).
Indexed: A22, ASCA, Agr, B21, B25, B27, BIOBASE, BIOSIS Prev, C33, CIN, ChemAb, ChemTitl, CurCont, DBA, EMBASE, ESPM, ExcerpMed, I12, IABS, IDIS, ISR, IndMed, Inpharma, MEDLINE, MSB, MycolAb, NSA, P30, P35, RefZh, SCI, SCOPUS, ToxAb, W07.
—BLDSC (3629.325000), CASDDS, GNLM, IE, Infotrieve, Ingenta, INIST, Linda Hall. **CCC.**
Published by: American Society for Pharmacology and Experimental Therapeutics, 9650 Rockville Pike, Bethesda, MD 20814. TEL 301-634-7060, FAX 301-634-7061, info@aspet.org, http://www.aspet.org. Ed. Eric F Johnson. adv.: B&W page USD 615, color page USD 1,095; trim 8.125 x 10.875. Circ: 500.

615.19 DEU ISSN 0792-5077
RM302 CODEN: DMDIEQ
➤ **DRUG METABOLISM AND DRUG INTERACTIONS.** Text in English. 1972. q. EUR 364, USD 546 to institutions; EUR 419, USD 629 combined subscription to institutions (print & online eds.) (effective 2012). adv. bk.rev. index. back issues avail. **Document type:** *Journal, Academic/Scholarly.* **Description:** Devoted to the mechanisms by which drugs and other foreign compounds are metabolised, the mechanisms by which drugs may interact with each other as well as with biological systems, and the pharmacological and toxicological consequences of such metabolism and interactions.
Former titles (until 1988): Reviews on Drug Metabolism and Drug Interactions (0334-2190); (until vol. 3, 1978): Reviews on Drug Interactions (0048-7546)
Related titles: Online - full text ed.: ISSN 2191-0162. EUR 364, USD 546 to institutions (effective 2012).
Indexed: A22, A34, A35, A36, AgBio, B25, BIOSIS Prev, C25, C30, C33, CABA, CIN, ChemAb, ChemTitl, DBA, E12, EMBASE, ExcerpMed, GH, IBR, IBZ, IndMed, MEDLINE, MycolAb, N02, N03, N04, P30, P32, P33, P40, R07, R08, R10, R11, RA&MP, Reac, SCOPUS.
—BLDSC (3629.326000), CASDDS, GNLM, IE, Infotrieve, Ingenta, INIST.
Published by: Walter de Gruyter GmbH & Co. KG, Genthiner Str 13, Berlin, 10785, Germany. TEL 49-30-260050, FAX 49-30-26005251, info@degruyter.com, http://www.degruyter.de.

615 612.39 NLD ISSN 1872-3128
CODEN: DMLRBM
➤ **DRUG METABOLISM LETTERS.** Text in English. 2007. q. USD 450 combined subscription to institutions (print or online ed.) (effective 2012). adv. back issues avail.; reprints avail. **Document type:** *Journal, Academic/Scholarly.* **Description:** Publishes short papers on major advances in all areas of drug metabolism and disposition.
Related titles: Online - full text ed.: (from IngentaConnect).
Indexed: A01, B&BAb, B19, C33, CA, EMBASE, ExcerpMed, MEDLINE, P30, R10, Reac, SCOPUS, T02.
—BLDSC (3629.329000), IE, Ingenta. **CCC.**
Published by: Bentham Science Publishers Ltd., PO Box 294, Bussum, 1400 AG, Netherlands. TEL 31-35-6923800, FAX 31-35-6980150, sales@bentham.org. Ed. Chandra Prakash. **Subscr. to:** Bentham Science Publishers Ltd., c/o Richard E Morrissy, PO Box 446, Oak Park, IL 60301. TEL 312-413-5867, FAX 312-996-7107, subscriptions@bentham.org.

➤ **DRUG METABOLISM REVIEWS.** *see* MEDICAL SCIENCES

615.19 ESP ISSN 0214-0934
RS1 CODEN: DNPEED
DRUG NEWS & PERSPECTIVES; the international drug newsmagazine. Text in English. 1988. 10/yr. adv. bk.rev. back issues avail. **Document type:** *Journal, Trade.* **Description:** For scientists and managers in pharmaceutical research and development.
Related titles: Online - full text ed.: ISSN 2013-0139; Supplement(s): Novedades y Perspectivas Terapeuticas. ISSN 1134-8577. 1989.
Indexed: A20, A22, B27, EMBASE, ExcerpMed, I12, Inpharma, MEDLINE, P30, PROMT, R10, Reac, SCI, SCOPUS, W07.
—CASDDS, GNLM, IE, Infotrieve. **CCC.**
Published by: Prous Science (Subsidiary of: Thomson Reuters), Provenza 388, Barcelona, 08025, Spain. TEL 34-93-4592220, FAX 34-93-4581535, service@prous.com, http://www.prous.com.

DRUG PRODUCT LIABILITY. *see* LAW

DRUG RESISTANCE UPDATES; reviews and commentaries in antimicrobial and anticancer chemotherapy. *see* MEDICAL SCIENCES

615 NZL ISSN 0114-5916
RM302.5 CODEN: DRSAEA
➤ **DRUG SAFETY.** Text in English. 1986. m. price varies based on the number of users. bk.rev. back issues avail.; reprints avail. **Document type:** *Journal, Academic/Scholarly.* **Description:** Provides evaluations of adverse drug experience and risk-benefit. Contains articles which are designed to assist in the safe utilization of today's drugs.
Former titles (until 1990): Medical Toxicology and Adverse Drug Experience (0113-5244); (until 1987): Medical Toxicology (0112-5966)
Related titles: Online - full text ed.: ISSN 1179-1942 (from IngentaConnect).
Indexed: A01, A03, A08, A22, A26, B21, BIOBASE, BIOSIS Prev, C06, C07, CA, CIN, ChemAb, ChemTitl, CurCont, DBA, E01, E04, E05, EMBASE, ESPM, ExcerpMed, H&SSA, H12, I05, I12, IABS, ISR, IndMed, Inpharma, MEDLINE, MS&D, MycolAb, NRN, NSA, P20, P22, P24, P30, P35, P54, PQC, R10, Reac, RiskAb, S02, S03, SCI, SCOPUS, T02, ToxAb, W07.
—BLDSC (3629.395000), CASDDS, GNLM, IE, Infotrieve, Ingenta, INIST. **CCC.**
Published by: (International Society of Pharmacovigilance GBR), Adis International Ltd. (Subsidiary of: Wolters Kluwer N.V.), 41 Centorian Dr, Mairangi Bay, Private Bag 65901, Auckland, 1311, New Zealand. TEL 64-9-4770700, FAX 64-9-4770764, journals@adis.com, http://www.adisonline.info/. Ed. Rosie Stather. **Subscr. in the Americas to:** Adis International Inc.

615.1 614 USA ISSN 1557-3532
DRUG SAFETY ADVISOR. Text in English. 2005 (May). m. USD 649 domestic; USD 664 foreign (effective 2006). **Document type:** *Newsletter, Trade.* **Description:** Covers the latest drug safety developments on the national and global scale.
Related titles: Online - full text ed.: ISSN 1557-3540. USD 649 (effective 2005).
Published by: Washington Business Information, Inc., 300 N Washington St, Ste 200, Falls Church, VA 22046. customerservice@fdanews.com, http://www.fdanews.com.

614.3 GBR
DRUG SAFETY UPDATE. Text in English. 1975. q. free (effective 2009). 16 p./no. 2 cols./p.; back issues avail. **Document type:** *Bulletin, Government.* **Description:** Covers information and clinical advice from the MHRA and the Commission on Human Medicines, its independent advisor, about the safe use of medicines.
Supersedes (in 2007): Current Problems in Pharmacovigilance; Which was formerly (until 19??): Current Problems
Related titles: Online - full text ed.
Indexed: Inpharma.
Published by: The Medicines and Healthcare Products Regulatory Agency, Department of Health, 10-2 Market Towers, 1 Nine Elms Ln, London, SW8 5NQ, United Kingdom. TEL 44-20-70842000, FAX 44-20-70842353, info@mhra.gsi.gov.uk, http://www.mhra.gov.uk. Ed. Claire Tilstone. **Co-sponsor:** Committee on Safety of Medicines.

615.5 381.456151 USA ISSN 1527-5981
DRUG STORE NEWS. CONTINUING EDUCATION QUARTERLY. Text in English. 1986. q. illus. **Document type:** *Journal, Trade.*
Former titles (until 1999): Drug Store News. Chain Pharmacy (1524-5276); (until 1997): Drug Store News for the Pharmacist (1055-2952); (until 1991): Drug Store News, Inside Pharmacy (0891-9828)
Indexed: A22.
—**CCC.**
Published by: Lebhar-Friedman, Inc., 425 Park Ave, New York, NY 10022. TEL 212-756-5000, FAX 212-756-5250, info@lf.com, http://www.lf.com.

615 NZL ISSN 1177-3928
RM301.63
➤ **DRUG TARGET INSIGHTS.** Text in English. 2006. a. free (effective 2011). **Document type:** *Journal, Academic/Scholarly.* **Description:** Covers current developments in all areas of the field of clinical therapeutics.
Media: Online - full text.
Indexed: A01, CA, EMBASE, ExcerpMed, R10, Reac, SCOPUS, T02.
—**CCC.**
Published by: Libertas Academica Ltd., PO Box 302-624, North Harbour, Auckland, 1330, New Zealand. TEL 64-21-662617, FAX 64-21-740006, editorial@la-press.com. Ed. MonicaTowia Milani.

615 GBR ISSN 1942-7603
RS189 CODEN: DTARBG
▼ **DRUG TESTING AND ANALYSIS.** Text in English. 2009 (Jan.). m. GBP 321 in United Kingdom to institutions; EUR 328 in Europe to institutions; USD 508 elsewhere to institutions; GBP 369 combined subscription in United Kingdom to institutions (print & online eds.); EUR 378 combined subscription in Europe to institutions (print & online eds.); USD 585 combined subscription elsewhere to institutions (print & online eds.) (effective 2012). adv. back issues avail.; reprints avail. **Document type:** *Journal, Academic/Scholarly.* **Description:** Provides a critical evaluation of the methods used in the characterization of established and newly outlawed compounds.
Related titles: Online - full text ed.: ISSN 1942-7611. GBP 321 in United Kingdom to institutions; EUR 328 in Europe to institutions; USD 508 elsewhere to institutions (effective 2012).
Indexed: C33, EMBASE, ExcerpMed, FoSS&M, MEDLINE, P30, SCI, SCOPUS, W07.
—IE. **CCC.**
Published by: John Wiley & Sons Ltd. (Subsidiary of: John Wiley & Sons, Inc.), The Atrium, Southern Gate, Chichester, West Sussex PO19 8SQ, United Kingdom. TEL 44-1243-779777, FAX 44-1243-775878, customer@wiley.co.uk. Ed. Mario Thevis. Pub. Kim Thompkins TEL 201-748-6921. Adv. contact Wayne Frost TEL 44-1243-770350.

615 JPN
DRUG TOPICS/DORAGGU TOPIKKUSU. Text in Japanese. 1970. w. (Mon.). JPY 19,656 (effective 2007). **Document type:** *Newspaper, Trade.*
Published by: Doraggu Magajin/Drugmagazine Co., Ltd., 2-3-15 Nihonbashihoncho, Chuo-ku, Tokyo, 103-0023, Japan. TEL 81-3-32414661, FAX 81-3-32414594.

615.1 USA ISSN 0012-6616
RS1 CODEN: DGTNA7
DRUG TOPICS. Text in English. 1883. m. USD 61 domestic; USD 109 foreign; USD 17 newsstand/cover domestic; USD 21 newsstand/cover foreign (effective 2011). adv. bk.rev. charts; illus.; mkt.; pat.; tr.lit. back issues avail. **Document type:** *Magazine, Trade.* **Description:** Publishes current trends and developments affecting the pharmacy field. Includes merchandising, government affairs, management, professional and clinical news, and continuing education.
Incorporates (1907-1940): Druggist Circular; Which was formerly (until 1907): Druggists' Circular and Chemical Gazette
Related titles: Microform ed.: (from PQC, RPI); Online - full text ed.: ISSN 1937-8157.

Indexed: A12, A13, A14, A15, A17, A22, A23, A26, ABIn, B01, B02, B03, B04, B06, B07, B08, B09, B13, B15, B17, B18, BPI, BRD, BusI, CA, E07, EMBASE, ExcerpMed, G04, G06, G07, G08, H01, H11, H12, H13, HlthInd, I05, I12, M06, P07, P10, P16, P20, P30, P34, P48, P51, P53, P54, PQC, R10, Reac, S02, S03, SCOPUS, T&II, W01, W02, W03, W05.
—BLDSC (3629.450000), GNLM, IE, Infotrieve, Ingenta, INIST. **CCC.**
Published by: Advanstar Medical Economics Healthcare Communications (Subsidiary of: Advanstar Communications, Inc.), 6200 Canoga Ave, 2nd Fl, Woodland Hills, CA 91367. TEL 818-593-5000, FAX 818-593-5020, info@advanstar.com, http://web.advanstar.com. Ed. Julia Talsma TEL 440-891-2792. Pub. Jim Granato TEL 732-346-3071. Circ: 158,150.

615.1 USA
DRUG WAR CHRONICLE. Text in English. w. free. **Document type:** *Newsletter.* **Description:** Covers the drug war and the growing global reform movement, includes news from around the world and expert commentary from leading reform voices. Dedicated to raising awareness of the consequences of drug prohibition.
Formerly (until Aug.2003): The Week Online
Media: Online - full text.
Published by: Drug Reform Coordination Network (DRCNet), PO Box 18402, Washington, DC 20036. TEL 202-293-8340, FAX 202-293-8344. Ed. Phillip S Smith.

615 USA ISSN 1531-6440
RM1
DRUG WEEK. Text in English. 2000. w. USD 2,295 in US & Canada; USD 2,495 elsewhere; USD 2,525 combined subscription in US & Canada (print & online eds.) (effective 2008); USD 2,755 combined subscription elsewhere (print & online eds.) (effective 2007). 900 p./no.; back issues avail. **Document type:** *Newsletter, Trade.* **Description:** Covers the latest front line drug developments and therapies including clinical trials, global partnerships and programs, industry news, research findings, conference proceedings, and much more.
Related titles: E-mail ed.; Online - full text ed.: ISSN 1532-4575. USD 2,295 combined subscription (online & email eds.); single user (effective 2008).
Indexed: A26, CWI, G08, H11, H12, I05, P19, P20, P48, P54, PQC.
—CIS.
Published by: NewsRx, 2727 Paces Ferry Rd SE, Ste 2-440, Atlanta, GA 30339. TEL 770-435-8286, 800-726-4550, FAX 770-435-6800, pressrelease@newsrx.com, http://www.newsrx.com. Pub. Susan Hasty TEL 770-507-7777.

615.7 USA ISSN 1089-5590
DRUGLINK. Text in English. 1982. m. **Document type:** *Newsletter, Trade.* **Description:** Summarizes new findings and recent developments in drug therapy. Information on investigational drugs, OTCs, actions, reactions and interactions and more.
Formerly (until 1997): Drug Newsletter (0731-5163)
Indexed: E-psyche.
Published by: Facts and Comparisons (Subsidiary of: Wolters Kluwer N.V.), 77 West Port Plz, Ste 450, St. Louis, MO 63146. TEL 800-223-0554, FAX 317-735-5390, http://www.factsandcomparisons.com.

615.1 NZL ISSN 0012-6667
RM1 CODEN: DRUGAY
➤ **DRUGS.** Text in English. 1971. 18/yr. price varies based on the number of users. abstr.; bibl.; charts; illus. back issues avail.; reprints avail. **Document type:** *Journal, Academic/Scholarly.* **Description:** Features comprehensive drug evaluations on new and established drugs, review articles on all aspects of drugs and drug therapy and disease management articles.
Related titles: Online - full text ed.: ISSN 1179-1950 (from IngentaConnect).
Indexed: A01, A03, A08, A22, A26, A36, AddicA, B21, BIOBASE, BIOSIS Prev, C06, C07, C08, CA, CABA, CIN, CINAHL, ChemAb, ChemTitl, CurCont, DBA, DentInd, E01, E08, E12, EMBASE, ESPM, ExcerpMed, F08, F11, F12, FamI, GH, H&SSA, H12, I05, I12, IABS, IBR, IBZ, ISR, IndMed, Inpharma, MEDLINE, MS&D, MycolAb, N02, N03, NSA, P20, P22, P24, P30, P33, P35, P39, P54, PQC, R08, R09, R10, R13, RA&MP, RM&VM, Reac, RiskAb, S01, S02, S03, S09, S12, SCI, SCOPUS, SD, T02, T05, ToxAb, VirolAbstr, W07, W11.
—BLDSC (3629.600000), CASDDS, GNLM, IE, Infotrieve, Ingenta, INIST, Linda Hall. **CCC.**
Published by: Adis International Ltd. (Subsidiary of: Wolters Kluwer N.V.), 41 Centorian Dr, Mairangi Bay, Private Bag 65901, Auckland, 1311, New Zealand. TEL 64-9-4770700, FAX 64-9-4770764, journals@adis.com, http://www.adisonline.info/. Ed. Dene C Peters. **Americas subscr. to:** Adis International Inc.

615.58 NZL ISSN 1170-229X
RC953.7 CODEN: DRAGE6
➤ **DRUGS & AGING.** Text in English. 1991. m. price varies based on the number of users. back issues avail.; reprints avail. **Document type:** *Journal, Academic/Scholarly.* **Description:** Promotes rational pharmacotherapy for elderly population.
Related titles: Online - full text ed.: ISSN 1179-1969 (from IngentaConnect).
Indexed: A01, A03, A08, A22, A26, A34, A36, ASCA, ASG, BIOBASE, BIOSIS Prev, C06, C07, C08, CA, CABA, CIN, CINAHL, ChemAb, ChemTitl, CurCont, DBA, E01, E08, E12, EMBASE, ExcerpMed, F08, GH, H12, H16, I05, I12, IABS, INI, ISR, IndMed, IndVet, Inpharma, MEDLINE, MycolAb, N02, N03, P03, P20, P22, P24, P30, P33, P35, P54, PQC, PsycInfo, R08, R10, R12, RA&MP, RM&VM, Reac, S09, SCI, SCOPUS, SoyAb, T02, T05, VS, W07, W11.
—BLDSC (3629.612000), CASDDS, GNLM, IE, Infotrieve, Ingenta, INIST. **CCC.**
Published by: Adis International Ltd. (Subsidiary of: Wolters Kluwer N.V.), 41 Centorian Dr, Mairangi Bay, Private Bag 65901, Auckland, 1311, New Zealand. TEL 64-9-4770700, FAX 64-9-4770764, journals@adis.com, http://www.adisonline.info/. Ed. David Williamson. **Americas subscr. to:** Adis International Inc.

615.7 USA ISSN 0360-2583
CODEN: DPHSDS
DRUGS AND THE PHARMACEUTICAL SCIENCES. Text in English. 1975. irreg., latest vol.138, 2004. price varies. **Document type:** *Monographic series.*
Related titles: Online - full text ed.: ISSN 2154-5219.
Indexed: A22, CIN, ChemAb, ChemTitl, FR.
—BLDSC (3629.630000), CASDDS, IE, Ingenta, INIST. **CCC.**
Published by: C R C Press, LLC (Subsidiary of: Taylor & Francis Group), 6000 Broken Sound Pky, NW, Ste 300, Boca Raton, FL 33487. TEL 800-272-7737, FAX 800-374-3401, orders@crcpress.com.

615 NZL ISSN 1172-0360
RM260 CODEN: DTHPEE
➤ **DRUGS & THERAPY PERSPECTIVES.** Text in English. 1993. m. price varies based on the number of users. back issues avail. **Document type:** *Journal, Academic/Scholarly.* **Description:** Provides reviews of new drugs, disease treatment algorithms, brief economic evaluations of new drugs.
Related titles: Online - full text ed.: ISSN 1179-1977 (from IngentaConnect).
Indexed: A01, A03, A22, A26, C06, C07, C08, CA, CINAHL, E01, EMBASE, ExcerpMed, H12, I05, Inpharma, P20, P24, P35, P54, PQC, R10, Reac, SCOPUS, T02.
—BLDSC (3629.665000), GNLM, IE, Infotrieve, Ingenta. **CCC.**
Published by: Adis International Ltd. (Subsidiary of: Wolters Kluwer N.V.), 41 Centorian Dr, Mairangi Bay, Private Bag 65901, Auckland, 1311, New Zealand. TEL 64-9-4770700, FAX 64-9-4770764, journals@adis.com, http://www.adisonline.info/. Ed. Katherine Lyseng-Williamson. **Subscr. in the Americas to:** Adis International Inc.

615.9 JPN
DRUGS IN JAPAN; ethical drugs. Text in Japanese. 1974. a. JPY 23,500 (effective 2001).
Related titles: CD-ROM ed.: Drugs in Japan D B. JPY 35,000 (effective 2000).
Published by: Japan Pharmaceutical Information Center/Nihon Iyaku Joho Senta, 3rd Fl Nagai-Kinenkan, 2-12-15 Shibuya, Shibuya-ku, Tokyo, 150-0002, Japan. TEL 81-3-5466-1812, FAX 81-3-5466-1814.

344.042 USA ISSN 1088-9469
KF1297.D7
DRUGS IN LITIGATION: DAMAGE AWARDS INVOLVING PRESCRIPTION AND NONPRESCRIPTION DRUGS. Text in English. a. USD 148 per vol. (effective 2005). **Description:** Summarizes hundreds of trial and appellate decisions involving drugs and medicines.
Published by: Michie Company (Subsidiary of: LexisNexis North America), 701 E Water St, Charlottesville, VA 22902. TEL 434-972-7600, 800-446-3410, FAX 434-972-7677, customer.support@lexisnexis.com, http://www.michie.com.

615 NZL ISSN 1174-5886
RM300 CODEN: DRDDFD
DRUGS IN R & D. (Research & Development) Text in English. 1999. bi-m. USD 300 combined subscription to individuals (print & online eds.); USD 960 combined subscription to institutions (print & online eds.) (effective 2008). back issues avail. **Document type:** *Journal, Academic/Scholarly.* **Description:** Provides information on emerging drug classes and new treatments for specific disorders, allowing healthcare decision-makers to keep up to date with clinically applicable knowledge about the likely place in therapy of new drugs.
Related titles: Online - full text ed.: USD 295 to individuals; USD 950 to institutions (effective 2008) (from IngentaConnect).
Indexed: A01, A03, A08, A22, A26, B&BAb, CA, E01, E08, H12, I05, I12, IndMed, Inpharma, MEDLINE, P20, P22, P30, P54, PQC, SCOPUS, T02.
—BLDSC (3630.101700), CASDDS, IE, Infotrieve, Ingenta. **CCC.**
Published by: Adis International Ltd. (Subsidiary of: Wolters Kluwer N.V.), 41 Centorian Dr, Mairangi Bay, Private Bag 65901, Auckland, 1311, New Zealand. TEL 64-9-4770700, FAX 64-9-4770764, queries@adisonline.com, http://www.adisonline.info/. Ed. Jasbir Singh. **Subscr. in the Americas to:** Adis International Inc., Subscriptions Dept, Ste F 10, 940 Town Center Dr, Langhorne, PA 19047. TEL 877-872-2347.

615 ESP ISSN 0377-8282
RM1 CODEN: DRFUD4
DRUGS OF THE FUTURE. Text in English. 1976. m. adv. **Document type:** *Journal, Trade.* **Description:** Offers comprehensive drug monographs on new compounds, including their synthesis, pharmacological action, pharmacokinetics and metabolism, toxicity, and clinical studies.
Related titles: Online - full text ed.
Indexed: A22, B25, BIOSIS Prev, ChemAb, CurCont, EMBASE, ExcerpMed, I12, Inpharma, MycolAb, P30, P35, R10, Reac, SCI, SCOPUS, W07.
—CASDDS, GNLM, IE, Infotrieve, INIST. **CCC.**
Published by: Prous Science (Subsidiary of: Thomson Reuters), Provenza 388, Barcelona, 08025, Spain. TEL 34-93-4592220, FAX 34-93-4581535, service@prous.com, http://www.prous.com. R&P Pat Leeson. Circ: 3,000.

615.1 ESP ISSN 1699-3993
CODEN: MDACAP
DRUGS OF TODAY. Text in English. 1965. 10/yr. adv. bk.rev. back issues avail. **Document type:** *Journal, Trade.* **Description:** Provides physicians and other healthcare professionals with practical, up-to-date monographs on recently approved and launched drugs.
Formerly (until 1999): Medicamentos de Actualidad (0025-7656)
Related titles: Online - full text ed.: ISSN 1699-4019. 1998.
Indexed: A22, B25, BIOSIS Prev, C06, C07, CIN, ChemAb, ChemTitl, CurCont, I12, Inpharma, MEDLINE, MycolAb, P30, R10, Reac, SCI, SCOPUS, W07.
—CASDDS, GNLM, IE, Infotrieve, Ingenta, INIST. **CCC.**
Published by: Prous Science (Subsidiary of: Thomson Reuters), Provenza 388, Barcelona, 08025, Spain. TEL 34-93-4592220, FAX 34-93-4581535, service@prous.com, http://www.prous.com. Circ: 3,000.

615 CHE ISSN 0378-6501
CODEN: DECRDP
➤ **DRUGS UNDER EXPERIMENTAL AND CLINICAL RESEARCH.** Short title: Drugs under Research. Text in English. 1977. bi-m. CHF 450 (effective 2003). reprints avail. **Document type:** *Journal, Academic/Scholarly.* **Description:** Devoted to the study of compounds and molecules which may have possible therapeutic application. Covers animal and clinical pharmacology, medicinal chemistry, toxicology, teratology, mutagenesis, drug metabolism, pharmacokinetics, and clinical trials.
Related titles: Microform ed.: (from PQC).
Indexed: A22, ASCA, B&BAb, B21, BIOSIS Prev, BioEngAb, CIN, ChemAb, ChemTitl, DBA, I12, IBR, IBZ, ISR, IndMed, Inpharma, MycolAb, P30, R10, Reac, SCOPUS, ToxAb, VITIS.
—CASDDS, GNLM, IE, Infotrieve, Ingenta, INIST. **CCC.**
Published by: Bioscience Ediprint Inc., Rue Alexandre Gavard 16, Carouge, 1227, Switzerland. TEL 41-22-3003383, FAX 41-22-3002489, TELEX 423355-BIOS-CH, bioscience.smey@gkb.com. Ed. A Bertelli.

➤ **DRUGSTORE MANAGEMENT**; the annual drug store state of the industry. *see* BUSINESS AND ECONOMICS—Management

615 DEU ISSN 1867-075X
▼ **DUESSELDORFER SCHRIFTEN ZUR PHARMAZIE- UND NATURWISSENSCHAFTSGESCHICHTE.** Text in German. 2009. irreg. price varies. **Document type:** *Monographic series, Academic/Scholarly.*
Published by: Peter Lang GmbH (Subsidiary of: Peter Lang Publishing Group), Eschborner Landstr 42-50, Frankfurt Am Main, 60489, Germany. TEL 49-69-7807050, FAX 49-69-78070550, zentrale.frankfurt@peterlang.com. Ed. Frank Leimkugel.

615 ESP ISSN 1886-2322
E-FARMACEUTICO COMUNITARIO. Text in Spanish. 2006. q. 36 p./no.; **Document type:** *Journal, Trade.*
Published by: Ediciones Mayo S.A., Calle Aribau 185-187, 2a Planta, Barcelona, 08021, Spain. TEL 34-93-2090255, FAX 34-93-2020643, edmayo@ediciones.mayo.es, http://www.edicionesmayo.es. Circ: 4,800.

615 BEL ISSN 1781-9989
E J H P PRACTICE. (European Journal of Hospital Pharmacy) Text in English. 1995. bi-m. EUR 25 membership (effective 2006). **Document type:** *Journal, Trade.*
Supersedes in part (in Mar. 2005): E J H P (European Journal of Hospital Pharmacy) (English Edition) (1378-1510); (2002-Mar. 2005): E J H P (French Edition) (1378-1529); (2002-Mar. 2005): E J H P (German Edition) (1378-1537); All 3 of which superseded in part (in 2001): E H P (European Hospital Pharmacy) (1381-4060)
Related titles: ◆ German ed.: E J H P (German Edition). ISSN 1378-1537; ◆ French ed.: E J H P (French Edition). ISSN 1378-1529.
Indexed: EMBASE, I12, SCI, SCOPUS, W07.
—BLDSC (3668.425800), GNLM, IE, Ingenta. **CCC.**
Published by: (European Association of Hospital Pharmacists FRA), Pharma Publishing & Media Europe, Postbus 10001, Mol, B-2400, Belgium. TEL 32-474-989572, editorial@ejop.eu, http://www.ejhp.eu.

615 BEL ISSN 1781-7595
E J H P SCIENCE. (European Journal of Hospital Pharmacy) Text in English. 1995. bi-m. EUR 20 membership (effective 2006). **Document type:** *Journal, Trade.*
Supersedes in part (in 2005): E J H P (European Journal of Hospital Pharmacy) (English Edition) (1378-1510); Which superseded in part (in 2002): E H P (European Hospital Pharmacy) (1381-4060)
Indexed: I12.
—BLDSC (3668.426000), IE, Ingenta. **CCC.**
Published by: (European Association of Hospital Pharmacists FRA), Pharma Publishing & Media Europe, Postbus 10001, Mol, B-2400, Belgium. TEL 32-474-989572, editorial@ejop.eu, http://www.ejhp.eu.

▼ **E M S POCKET DRUG GUIDE.** (Emergency Medical Services) *see* MEDICAL SCIENCES

615 KEN ISSN 1026-552X
EAST AND CENTRAL AFRICAN JOURNAL OF PHARMACEUTICAL SCIENCES. Text in English. 1998. 3/yr. back issues avail. **Document type:** *Journal, Academic/Scholarly.*
Related titles: Online - full text ed.
Indexed: A36, AgrForAb, BP, C25, CABA, D01, E12, F08, F11, F12, G11, GH, H16, H17, N02, P32, P33, P39, PGegResA, PHN&I, R07, R12, RA&MP, RM&VM, T05, TAR, VS, W10.
Published by: University of Nairobi, Faculty of Pharmacy, PO Box 19676-00202, Nairobi, Kenya. daru@swiftkenya.com. Ed. Charles K Maitai.

615 ITA ISSN 1970-0474
ECONOMIA & POLITICA DEL FARMACO. Text in Italian. 2004. q. **Document type:** *Journal, Academic/Scholarly.*
Published by: Economia Sanitaria, Via Giuba 7, Milan, Italy. http://www.economiasanitaria.com/home.asp.

615 NZL ISSN 1176-9009
THE EDGE. Text in English. 1990. m. free membership. **Document type:** *Newsletter.*
Formerly (until 2004): Pharmacy Interactions (1174-0639); Which was formed by the 1996 merger of: Pharmaceutical Society of New Zealand. Inform (1173-1109); (1990-1996): Inform-ed (1170-1919)
Published by: Pharmaceutical Society of New Zealand, 124 Dixon St, Wellington, New Zealand. TEL 64-4-8020030, FAX 64-4-3829297, p.society@psnz.org.nz, http://www.psnz.org.nz.

615.1 EGY ISSN 0301-5068
RS1 CODEN: EJPSBZ
➤ **EGYPTIAN JOURNAL OF PHARMACEUTICAL SCIENCES/AL-MAGALLAT AL-MISRIYYA LIL-'ULUM AL SAYDALIYYAT.** Text in English; Summaries in Arabic, English. 1960. bi-m. USD 112 (effective 2002). charts; illus. reprint service avail. from IRC. **Document type:** *Journal, Academic/Scholarly.*
Former titles (until 1972): United Arab Republic Journal of Pharmaceutical Sciences (0301-5076); (until 1969): Journal of Pharmaceutical Sciences of the United Arab Republic (0022-3557)
Related titles: CD-ROM ed.; Online - full text ed.
Indexed: A22, A34, A36, AgrForAb, B25, BIOSIS Prev, BP, C25, CABA, CIN, ChemAb, ChemTitl, D01, E12, ExtraMED, F08, F11, F12, FS&TA, G11, GH, H16, H17, MycolAb, N02, N03, P33, P39, RA&MP, S12, SoyAb, T05, VS, W10.
—BLDSC (3664.410000), CASDDS, GNLM, IE, Ingenta, INIST, Linda Hall.
Published by: (Pharmaceutical Society of Egypt, Research Department), National Information and Documentation Centre (NIDOC), Tahrir St., Dokki, Awqaf P.O., Giza, Egypt. TEL 20-2-3371696, FAX 20-2-3371746. Ed. Dr. A A Abdel-Rahman. Circ: 1,750.

615 EGY ISSN 1110-7510
EGYPTIAN SOCIETY OF PHARMACOLOGY AND EXPERIMENTAL THERAPEUTICS. JOURNAL/MAGALLAT AL-GAMI'IAT AL-MISRIYYAT LIL-ADWIYYAT WA-AL-'ILAG AL-TAGRIBI. Text in English. 1982. a. **Document type:** *Journal, Academic/Scholarly.*
Published by: Egyptian Society of Pharmacology and Experimental Therapeutics, Manoura University, Faculty of Pharmacy, Mansoura, Egypt. Ed. Dr. Mahmoud Hamdy Aly.

P

615.9 RUS ISSN 0869-2092
RS1 CODEN: EKFAE9
EKSPERIMENTAL'NAYA I KLINICHESKAYA FARMAKOLOGIYA. Text in Russian; Summaries in English. 1938. bi-m. USD 120 foreign (effective 2004). adv. index. **Document type:** *Journal, Academic/Scholarly.* **Description:** Publishes articles devoted to the pharmacological study of medicinal preparations and of the effects produced by various poisons on animals and man.
Formerly (until 1992): Farmakologiya i Toksikologiya (0014-8318)
Indexed: A22, B25, BIOSIS Prev, C33, ChemAb, DBA, DentInd, E-psyche, EMBASE, ExcerpMed, ISR, IndMed, MEDLINE, MycolAb, P30, PsycholAb, R10, Reac, RefZh, SCOPUS.
—BLDSC (0397.988500), CASDDS, East View, GNLM, IE, Infotrieve, Ingenta, INIST, Linda Hall. **CCC.**
Published by: (Akademiya Meditsinskikh Nauk Rossii/Russian Academy of Medical Sciences), Izdatel'stvo Folium, Dmitrovskoe shosse 58, Moscow, 127238, Russian Federation. TEL 7-095-4825544, 7-095-4825590, info@folium.ru. Ed. D A Kharkevich. Adv. contact V F Strizhova. Circ: 80,000. **Dist. by:** M K - Periodica, ul Gilyarovskogo 39, Moscow 129110, Russian Federation. TEL 7-095-2845008, FAX 7-095-2813798, info@periodicals.ru, http://www.mkniga.ru. **Co-sponsor:** Nauchnoe Obshchestvo Farmakologov.

615.7 USA ISSN 2155-1510
▼ **ELECTRONIC PAIN JOURNAL.** Text in English. forthcoming 2011. q. USD 8 per issue (effective 2010). **Document type:** *Journal, Trade.* **Description:** Presents research articles, reviews, and working code on the subject of opioid pharmacokinetics, pharmacodynamics, and pharmacogenomics.
Media: Online - full text.
Published by: S A A M, Inc., 13872 Lake Dr, Monroe, MI 48161. TEL 734-637-7997, oalinaresmd@gmail.com.

615.1 SWE ISSN 1401-5374
ELIXIR; apotekarsocietetens medlemsblad. Text in Swedish. 1995. 6/yr.
Related titles: Online - full content ed.; ◆ Issued with: Laekemedelsvaerlden. ISSN 1402-1927.
Published by: Apotekarsocieteten/Swedish Academy of Pharmaceutical Sciences, PO Box 1136, Stockholm, 11881, Sweden. TEL 46-8-7235000, FAX 46-8-7235011, apotekarsocieteten@swepharm.se.

615.3 DEU ISSN 0177-6967
DIE ELLIPSE. Text in German. 1984. q. **Document type:** *Magazine, Trade.* **Description:** Contains information on a variety of pharmaceutical and medical products produced by Baxter Deutschland GmbH.
—BLDSC (3732.155000).
Published by: Baxter Deutschland GmbH, Im Breitspiel 13, Heidelberg, 69126, Germany. TEL 49-6221-397163, FAX 49-6221-397180, presse_de@baxter.com. Eds. Dr. Anke Taeubert, Dr. Norbert Dum, Dr. Rudolf Schosser. Circ: 6,000 (controlled).

615.7 AUS ISSN 1034-8719
ENCAPSULATOR. Text in English. 1989. q. back issues avail. **Document type:** *Bulletin.*
Formed by the merger of (1979-1985): Prince Henry's Hospital. Pharmacy Bulletin; Queen Victoria Medical Centre. Pharmacy Bulletin
Published by: (Pharmacy Department), Monash Medical Centre, Southern Health, 246 Clayton Rd, Clayton, VIC 3168, Australia. TEL 61-3-95946666, FAX 61-3-95946727, publicaffairs@southernhealth.org.au, http://www.southernhealth.org.au/.

ENVIRONMENTAL TOXICOLOGY AND PHARMACOLOGY. *see* ENVIRONMENTAL STUDIES—Toxicology And Environmental Safety

EOS; rivista di immunologia ed immunofarmacologia. *see* MEDICAL SCIENCES—Allergology And Immunology

EPILEPSY CURRENTS (ENGLISH EDITION). *see* MEDICAL SCIENCES—Psychiatry And Neurology

EPILEPSY RESEARCH. *see* MEDICAL SCIENCES—Psychiatry And Neurology

▼ **EPILEPSY RESEARCH AND TREATMENT.** *see* MEDICAL SCIENCES—Psychiatry And Neurology

615.1 GRC ISSN 1011-6583
CODEN: EKIEE
EPITHEORESE KLINIKES FARMAKOLOGIAS KAI FARMAKOKINETIKES (INTERNATIONAL EDITION)/REVIEW OF CLINICAL PHARMACOLOGY AND PHARMACOKINETICS (INTERNATIONAL EDITION). Text in English. 1987. 3/yr. **Document type:** *Journal, Academic/Scholarly.*
Related titles: ◆ Greek ed.: Epitheorese Klinikes Farmakologias kai Farmakokinetikas (Ellenike Ekdosis). ISSN 1011-6575; ◆ International ed.: Epitheorese Klinikes Farmakologias kai Farmakokinetikas (Ellenike Ekdosis). ISSN 1011-6575.
Indexed: CIN, ChemAb, ChemTitl, EMBASE, ExcerpMed, R10, Reac, SCOPUS.
—BLDSC (7788.985000), CASDDS, GNLM, IE, Ingenta, INIST.
Published by: Pharmakon Press, 20 Daskalaki St, Athens, 115 26, Greece. TEL 30-1-7778-101.

615.321 635.7 ITA ISSN 1121-2896
L'ERBORISTA. Text in Italian. 1986. m. (9/yr.). EUR 40 domestic; EUR 80 in Europe; EUR 100 elsewhere (effective 2011). adv. **Document type:** *Magazine, Trade.*
Related titles: Online - full text ed.
Published by: Tecniche Nuove SpA, Via Eritrea 21, Milan, MI 201, Italy. TEL 39-02-390901, FAX 39-02-7570364, info@tecnichenuove.com. Ed. Raffaella Bergaglio. Circ: 5,000.

ERKE YAOXUE ZAZHI/JOURNAL OF PEDIATRIC PHARMACY. *see* MEDICAL SCIENCES—Pediatrics

615 CHE ISSN 1015-0919
RS1
ESSENTIAL DRUGS MONITOR. Text in English, French, Russian, Spanish, Chinese. 1986. s-a. free. back issues avail. **Document type:** *Bulletin, Trade.* **Description:** Contains regular features on national drug policies, rational drug use, supply, operational research and public education.
Related titles: Online - full text ed.: ISSN 1564-121X. 199?.
Indexed: B07, C06, C07, P30, T02.
—BLDSC (3811.792510). **CCC.**
Published by: World Health Organization, Department of Essential Drugs & Medicines Policy, Geneva 27, 1211, Switzerland. FAX 41-22-7914167, darec@who.ch. Ed., R&P R. Laing. Circ: 200,000.

615.1 USA
ETHICAL SPECTACLE. Text in English. 1995. m.
Media: Online - full content.
Address: 41 Schermerhorn St No 121, Brooklyn, NY 11201. Ed. Jonathan Wallace.

615 ETH ISSN 1029-5933
RS1
➤ **ETHIOPIAN PHARMACEUTICAL JOURNAL.** Text in English. 1983. s-a. ETB 15 domestic; USD 5 foreign (effective 2007). **Document type:** *Journal, Academic/Scholarly.* **Description:** Devoted to research concerning all aspects of pharmaceutical sciences.
Related titles: Online - full text ed.
Indexed: EMBASE, ExcerpMed, SCOPUS.
Published by: Ethiopian Pharmaceutical Association, c/o Kaleab Asres, Editor, Addis Ababa University, Dept of Pharmacognosy, Addis Ababa, Ethiopia. kasres@gmail.com. Ed. Kaleab Asres TEL 251-11-1564770.

➤ **ETHNOBOTANY**; international journal of the Society of Ethonobotanists. *see* BIOLOGY—Botany

615 USA ISSN 1944-8228
ETHNOPHARMACOGNOSY SERIES. Text in English. 2008. irreg. USD 13 per issue (effective 2011). **Document type:** *Monographic series, Academic/Scholarly.*
Published by: Windward Community College, 45-720 Keaahala Rd, Kaneohe, HI 96744. TEL 808-235-7400, FAX 808-247-5362, http://www.windward.hawaii.edu/.

EURO PHARMA. *see* BUSINESS AND ECONOMICS—Trade And Industrial Directories

615 DEU ISSN 0721-3514
EUROPAEISCHE HOCHSCHULSCHRIFTEN. REIHE 7: MEDIZIN. ABTEILUNG A: PHARMAKOLOGIE. Text in German. 1970. irreg., latest vol.3, 1980. price varies. **Document type:** *Monographic series, Academic/Scholarly.*
Published by: Peter Lang GmbH (Subsidiary of: Peter Lang Publishing Group), Eschborner Landstr 42-50, Frankfurt Am Main, 60489, Germany. TEL 49-69-7807050, FAX 49-69-78070550, zentrale.frankfurt@peterlang.com, http://www.peterlang.com.

EUROPAEISCHE HOCHSCHULSCHRIFTEN. REIHE 8: CHEMIE. ABTEILUNG A: PHARMAZIE. *see* CHEMISTRY

615.19 GBR ISSN 1369-0663
EUROPEAN BIOPHARMACEUTICAL REVIEW. Abbreviated title: E B R. Text in English. 1997. q. GBP 125 domestic; USD 230 foreign; free to qualified personnel (effective 2010). adv. back issues avail. **Document type:** *Journal, Trade.* **Description:** Provides a unique platform of communication and information for the market across Europe, North America and the rest of the developed world.
Related titles: Online - full text ed.
Indexed: SCOPUS.
—BLDSC (3829.489290). **CCC.**
Published by: Samedan Ltd, 16 Hampden Gurney Rd, London, W1H 5AL, United Kingdom. TEL 44-20-77243456, FAX 44-20-77242632, info@samedanltd.com. Ed. Dr. Helen Tayton-Martin. Adv. contact Neil Clarke. page GBP 2,850; trim 210 x 297.

615.1 DEU ISSN 0031-6970
RM1 CODEN: EJCPAS
➤ **EUROPEAN JOURNAL OF CLINICAL PHARMACOLOGY.** Text in English. 1968. m. EUR 3,383, USD 4,072 combined subscription to institutions (print & online eds.) (effective 2012). adv. bk.rev. illus. reprint service avail. from PSC. **Document type:** *Journal, Academic/Scholarly.* **Description:** Publishes original papers, short communications, and letters to the editor on all aspects of clinical pharmacology and drug therapy in man. Focuses on clinical pharmacology and pharmacokinetics.
Related titles: Microform ed.: (from PQC); Online - full text ed.: ISSN 1432-1041 (from IngentaConnect).
Indexed: A01, A03, A08, A22, A26, A36, AIIM, ASCA, Agr, B21, B25, BIOBASE, BIOSIS Prev, BP, C06, C07, C24, C30, CA, CABA, CIN, CISA, ChemAb, ChemTitl, CurCont, D01, DBA, DentInd, E01, E12, EMBASE, ESPM, ExcerpMed, F08, F11, F12, FR, GH, H12, H17, IABS, IDIS, INI, ISR, IndMed, Inpharma, Kidney, MEDLINE, MS&D, MycolAb, N02, N03, NSA, P20, P22, P24, P30, P32, P33, P35, P39, P48, P54, PQC, R08, R10, R12, RA&MP, RM&VM, Reac, SCI, SCOPUS, T02, T05, THA, ToxAb, VS, VirolAbstr, W07, W10.
—BLDSC (3829.728100), CASDDS, GNLM, IE, Infotrieve, Ingenta, INIST. **CCC.**
Published by: (European Association for Clinical Pharmacology and Therapeutics), Springer (Subsidiary of: Springer Science+Business Media), Tiergartenstr 17, Heidelberg, 69121, Germany. TEL 49-6221-4870, FAX 49-6221-345229. Ed. R Dahlqvist. **Subscr. in the Americas to:** Springer New York LLC, Journal Fulfillment, PO Box 2485, Secaucus, NJ 07096. TEL 800-777-4643, 201-348-4033, FAX 201-348-4505, journals-ny@springer.com, http://www.springer.com; **Subscr. to:** Springer Distribution Center, Kundenservice Zeitschriften, Haberstr 7, Heidelberg 69126, Germany. TEL 49-6221-3454303, FAX 49-6221-3454229, subscriptions@springer.com.

615.7 FRA ISSN 0378-7966
RM301 CODEN: EJDPD2
➤ **EUROPEAN JOURNAL OF DRUG METABOLISM AND PHARMACOKINETICS.** Text in English, French. 1976. q. EUR 262, USD 356 combined subscription to institutions (print & online eds.) (effective 2012). **Document type:** *Journal, Academic/Scholarly.*
Related titles: Online - full text ed.: ISSN 2107-0180 (from IngentaConnect).
Indexed: A22, A36, ASCA, B25, BIOBASE, BIOSIS Prev, C30, C33, CABA, CIN, ChemAb, ChemTitl, D01, DBA, DentInd, EMBASE, ExcerpMed, F08, F11, F12, GH, H16, IABS, ISR, IndMed, Inpharma, MycolAb, N02, N03, P30, P32, P33, P37, P39, PGegResA, RA&MP, RM&VM, SCI, SCOPUS, T05, VS, W07.
—BLDSC (3829.728300), CASDDS, GNLM, IE, Infotrieve, Ingenta, INIST. **CCC.**
Published by: Springer France (Subsidiary of: Springer Science+Business Media), 22 Rue de Palestro, Paris, 75002, France. TEL 33-1-53009860, FAX 33-1-53009861, sylvie.kamara@springer.com.

615 GBR ISSN 1352-4755
CODEN: EJHMAA
➤ **EUROPEAN JOURNAL OF HERBAL MEDICINE.** Text in English. 1994. 3/yr. free to members (effective 2009). bk.rev. **Document type:** *Journal, Academic/Scholarly.* **Description:** Articles concerning theory, research and practice in herbal medicine.
Indexed: AMED, EMBASE, ExcerpMed, IDIS, R10, Reac, SCOPUS.
—BLDSC (3829.729870), IE, Ingenta.
Published by: National Institute of Medical Herbalists, Elm House, 54 Mary Arches St, Exeter, EX4 3BA, United Kingdom. TEL 44-1392-426022, FAX 44-1392-498963, info@nimh.org.uk, http://www.nimh.org.uk.

➤ **EUROPEAN JOURNAL OF MEDICINAL CHEMISTRY.** *see* BIOLOGY—Biochemistry

➤ **EUROPEAN JOURNAL OF ONCOLOGY PHARMACY.** *see* MEDICAL SCIENCES—Oncology

615.19 GBR ISSN 1740-6277
➤ **EUROPEAN JOURNAL OF PARENTERAL & PHARMACEUTICAL SCIENCES.** Abbreviated title: E J P P S. Text in English. 1992. q. GBP 110 to institutions; GBP 55 to non-members; free to members (effective 2009). adv. bk.rev. index. back issues avail. **Document type:** *Journal, Academic/Scholarly.* **Description:** Provides European forum for publishing original papers, editorials, and reviews on subjects that cover all aspects of the parenteral sciences, both practical and scientific.
Formerly (until 2003): European Journal of Parenteral Sciences (0964-4679)
Indexed: EMBASE, I12, SCOPUS.
—BLDSC (3829.733410), IE, Ingenta. **CCC.**
Published by: (European Sterile Products Confederation, The Pharmaceutical and Healthcare Sciences Society), Euromed Communications Ltd., Passfield Business Ctr, Lynchborough Rd, Passfield, Liphook, Hampshire GU30 7SB, United Kingdom. TEL 44-1428-752222, FAX 44-1428-752223, info@euromed.uk.com. Ed. Gordon Farquharson.

615.1 NLD ISSN 0928-0987
RM301.25 CODEN: EPSCED
➤ **EUROPEAN JOURNAL OF PHARMACEUTICAL SCIENCES.** Text and summaries in English. 1992. 15/yr. EUR 1,218 in Europe to institutions; JPY 161,700 in Japan to institutions; USD 1,360 elsewhere to institutions (effective 2012). adv. index. **Document type:** *Journal, Academic/Scholarly.* **Description:** Publishes original multidisciplinary research, short communications and reviews in the pharmaceutical sciences, from both academia and industry, including topics such as drug bioanalysis, medicinal chemistry and drug delivery, biomedical drug research and drug targeting, pharmacokinetics, pharmacodynamics, drug metabolism and toxicology, as well as pharmaceutical biotechnology.
Incorporates (1926-2000): Pharmaceutica Acta Helvetiae (0031-6865); Formed by the merger of (1977-1992): Acta Pharmaceutica Fennica (0356-3456); Which was formerly (1892-1976): Farmaseuttinen Aikakauslehti (0367-259X); (1988-1992): Acta Pharmaceutica Nordica (1100-1801); Which was formed by the merger of (1964-1988): Acta Pharmaceutica Suecica (0001-6675); (1982-1988): Norwegica Pharmaceutica Acta (0800-2606); Which was formerly (1939-1982): Norsk Farmaceutisk Selskap. Meddelelser (0029-1927); (1927-1939): Norsk Farmaceutisk Selskap. Arbok (0802-6793); (1987-1988): Farmaci. Scientific Edition (0904-0897); Which was formerly (1973-1987): Archiv for Pharmaci og Chemi. Scientific Edition (0302-248X); (1926-1972): Dansk Tidsskrift for Farmaci (0011-6513)
Related titles: Microform ed.: (from PQC); Online - full text ed.: ISSN 1879-0720 (from IngentaConnect, ScienceDirect).
Indexed: A01, A03, A08, A22, A26, A34, A35, A36, ASCA, AgBio, B&BAb, B21, B25, BIOSIS Prev, BP, BioEngAb, C30, C33, CA, CABA, CIN, ChemAb, ChemTitl, CurCR, CurCont, D01, DBA, E12, EMBASE, ExcerpMed, F08, F11, F12, GH, H16, H17, I05, I12, IBR, IBZ, ISR, IndChem, IndMed, IndVet, Inpharma, MEDLINE, MOS, MycolAb, N02, N03, NPU, P30, P32, P33, P35, P39, PN&I, R08, R10, R16, RA&MP, RM&VM, Reac, S01, S12, SCI, SCOPUS, SoyAb, T02, VS, W07.
—BLDSC (3829.733850), CASDDS, GNLM, IE, Infotrieve, Ingenta, INIST, Linda Hall. **CCC.**
Published by: (European Federation for Pharmaceutical Sciences), Elsevier BV (Subsidiary of: Elsevier Science & Technology), Radarweg 29, PO Box 211, Amsterdam, 1000 AE, Netherlands. TEL 31-20-4853911, FAX 31-20-4852457, JournalsCustomerServiceEMEA@elsevier.com, http://www.elsevier.nl. Ed. A Urtti.

615 NLD ISSN 0939-6411
RM301.4 CODEN: EJPBEL
➤ **EUROPEAN JOURNAL OF PHARMACEUTICS AND BIOPHARMACEUTICS.** Text in English, French, German. 1955. 9/yr. EUR 1,016 in Europe to institutions; JPY 135,000 in Japan to institutions; USD 1,141 elsewhere to institutions (effective 2012). abstr. back issues avail. **Document type:** *Journal, Academic/Scholarly.* **Description:** Provides a medium for publication of research from areas of pharmaceutical technology, drug delivery systems, controlled release systems, drug targeting, physical pharmacy, and pharmacodynamics and pharmacokinetics.
Formerly (until 1991): Acta Pharmaceutica Technologica (0340-3157)
Related titles: Online - full text ed.: ISSN 1873-3441 (from IngentaConnect, ScienceDirect).
Indexed: A01, A03, A08, A22, A26, A29, A34, A35, A36, ASCA, AgBio, AgrForAb, B&BAb, B19, B20, B21, B25, B27, BIOSIS Prev, BP, C25, C30, CA, CABA, CIN, CTA, ChemAb, ChemTitl, CurCont, D01, DBA, EMBASE, ESPM, ExcerpMed, F08, F11, F12, GH, GenetAb, H16, H17, I05, I10, I12, IBR, IBZ, ISR, ImmunAb, IndMed, IndVet, Inpharma, MEDLINE, MaizeAb, MycolAb, N02, N03, NSA, P30, P33, P39, PHN&I, PN&I, R10, RA&MP, RM&VM, Reac, S01, S12, SCI, SCOPUS, SoyAb, T02, T05, ToxAb, TriticAb, VS, VirolAbstr, W07, W10.
—BLDSC (3829.733900), CASDDS, GNLM, IE, Infotrieve, Ingenta, INIST, Linda Hall. **CCC.**
Published by: (Arbeitsgemeinschaft fuer Pharmazeutische Verfahrenstechnik e.V. DEU), Elsevier BV (Subsidiary of: Elsevier Science & Technology), Radarweg 29, PO Box 211, Amsterdam, 1000 AE, Netherlands. TEL 31-20-4853911, FAX 31-20-4852457, JournalsCustomerServiceEMEA@elsevier.com, http://www.elsevier.nl. Ed. R Gurny.

615.1 NLD ISSN 0014-2999
RS1 CODEN: EJPHAZ

➤ **EUROPEAN JOURNAL OF PHARMACOLOGY.** Text in Dutch. 1967. 72/yr. EUR 11,363 in Europe to institutions; JPY 1,510,400 in Japan to institutions; USD 12,710 elsewhere to institutions (effective 2012). adv. charts; illus.; abstr. back issues avail.; reprints avail. **Document type:** *Journal, Academic/Scholarly.* **Description:** Publishes full length papers as well as short and rapid communications on the mechanisms of action of chemical substances affecting biological systems.
Incorporates (1989-1997): European Journal of Pharmacology. Molecular Pharmacology Section (0922-4106)
Related titles: Microform ed.: (from PQC); Online - full text ed.: ISSN 1879-0712 (from IngentaConnect, ScienceDirect).
Indexed: A01, A03, A08, A22, A26, A29, A34, A35, A36, A38, ASCA, ASFA, AgBio, AgrForAb, ApicAb, B&BAb, B19, B20, B21, B25, B27, BIOBASE, BIOSIS Prev, BP, C13, C24, C30, C33, CA, CABA, CIN, ChemAb, ChemTitl, CurCont, D01, DBA, DentInd, E12, EMBASE, ESPM, ExcerpMed, F08, F11, F12, FR, GH, GenetAb, H16, H17, I05, I10, IABS, ISR, IndMed, IndVet, Inpharma, MEDLINE, MaizeAb, MycolAb, N02, N03, N04, NSA, NucAcAb, P30, P32, P33, P35, P37, P39, PGegResA, PGrRegA, PHN&I, PN&I, PsycholAb, R07, R08, R10, R12, R13, RA&MP, RM&VM, Reac, RefZh, S01, S12, S17, SCI, SCOPUS, SoyAb, T02, T05, TAR, THA, ToxAb, VITIS, VS, VirolAbstr, W07, W10, WildRev.
—BLDSC (3829.734000), CASDDS, GNLM, IE, Infotrieve, Ingenta, INIST, Linda Hall. **CCC.**
Published by: Elsevier BV (Subsidiary of: Elsevier Science & Technology), Radarweg 29, PO Box 211, Amsterdam, 1000 AE, Netherlands. TEL 31-20-4853911, FAX 31-20-4852457, JournalsCustomerServiceEMEA@elsevier.com, http://www.elsevier.nl. Eds. F P Nijkamp, W H Gispen.

▼ ➤ **EUROPEAN MEDICAL, HEALTH AND PHARMACEUTICAL JOURNAL.** *see* MEDICAL SCIENCES

➤ **EUROPEAN NEUROPSYCHOPHARMACOLOGY.** *see* MEDICAL SCIENCES—Psychiatry And Neurology

615 GBR ISSN 1364-369X
CODEN: EPCUCJ

EUROPEAN PHARMACEUTICAL CONTRACTOR. Abbreviated title: E P C. Text in English. 1996. q. GBP 125 domestic; USD 230 foreign; free to qualified personnel (effective 2010). adv. software rev.; Website rev.; bk.rev. pat.; stat.; tr.lit. back issues avail. **Document type:** *Magazine, Trade.* **Description:** Covers contract research and development, clinical trials and outsourcing plus promotion of specific topics.
Related titles: Online - full text ed.
Indexed: EMBASE, ExcerpMed, R10, Reac, SCOPUS.
—BLDSC (3829.776600). **CCC.**
Published by: Samedan Ltd, 16 Hampden Gurney Rd, London, W1H 5AL, United Kingdom. TEL 44-20-77243456, FAX 44-20-77242632, info@samedanltd.com. Ed. Dr. Graham Hughes. Adv. contact Jonathan Smith. page GBP 2,850; trim 210 x 297.

615 GBR ISSN 1360-8606

EUROPEAN PHARMACEUTICAL REVIEW. Text in English. 1996. bi-m. GBP 90 combined subscription (print & online eds.) (effective 2009). adv. 100 p./no.; back issues avail. **Document type:** *Magazine, Trade.* **Description:** Addresses the new technologies and developments in the European pharmaceutical industry.
Related titles: Online - full text ed.
Indexed: EMBASE, ExcerpMed, SCOPUS.
—BLDSC (3829.776700), IE, Ingenta. **CCC.**
Published by: Russell Publishing Ltd., Court Lodge, Hogtrough Hill, Brasted, Kent TN16 1NU, United Kingdom. TEL 44-1959-563311, FAX 44-1959-563123, info@russellpublishing.com, http://www.russellpublishing.com/. Adv. contact Jason Vencatasen TEL 44-1959-563311. page GBP 5,184; trim 210 x 297.

EUROPEAN REVIEW FOR MEDICAL AND PHARMACOLOGICAL SCIENCES. *see* MEDICAL SCIENCES

615.19 USA ISSN 0090-6654
RM302

EVALUATIONS OF DRUG INTERACTIONS. Text in English. 1973. base vol. plus bi-m. updates. looseleaf. USD 229 base vol(s). with 6 updates (effective 2005). adv. **Document type:** *Directory.* **Description:** Comprehensive reference source for prescription and OTC drug conflicts.
Related titles: Online - full text ed.
—CCC.
Published by: (American Pharmacists Association), First DataBank, Inc., 1111 Bayhill Dr, San Bruno, CA 94066. TEL 650-588-5454, 800-633-3453, FAX 650-588-4003, rick_zucchero@firstdatabank.com. Eds. Fredric J Zucchero, Mark J Hogan. R&P Pat Bremerkamp. Adv. contact Christine D Schultz.

EXPERIMENTAL AND CLINICAL PSYCHOPHARMACOLOGY. *see* PSYCHOLOGY

EXPERIMENTAL AND TOXICOLOGIC PATHOLOGY. *see* MEDICAL SCIENCES

615 GBR ISSN 1742-5247

➤ **EXPERT OPINION ON DRUG DELIVERY.** Text in English. 2004 (Nov.). m. GBP 1,665, EUR 2,200, USD 3,325 combined subscription to institutions (print & online eds.); GBP 3,205, EUR 4,230, USD 6,410 combined subscription to corporations (print & online eds.) (effective 2010). adv. back issues avail.; reprint service avail. from PSC. **Document type:** *Journal, Academic/Scholarly.* **Description:** Provides a forum for commentary and analysis relating to current and emerging drug delivery technologies, from initial concept to potential therapeutic application and final relevance in clinical use.
Related titles: Online - full text ed.: ISSN 1744-7593 (from IngentaConnect).
Indexed: B&BAb, B19, B21, BIOBASE, CTA, CurCont, EMBASE, ExcerpMed, GenetAb, IABS, ImmunAb, MEDLINE, NSA, NucAcAb, P30, R10, Reac, SCI, SCOPUS, W07.
—BLDSC (3842.002941), IE, Ingenta. **CCC.**
Published by: Informa Healthcare (Subsidiary of: T & F Informa plc), Telephone House, 69-77 Paul St, London, EC2A 4LQ, United Kingdom. TEL 44-20-70175000, FAX 44-20-70176792, healthcare.enquiries@informa.com. Adv. contact Per Sonnerfeldt. **Subscr. to:** Taylor & Francis Inc., Customer Services Dept, 325 Chestnut St, 8th Fl, Philadelphia, PA 19106. TEL 215-625-8900, 800-354-1420, FAX 215-625-8914, customerservice@taylorandfrancis.com; Taylor & Francis Ltd., Journals Customer Service, Sheepen Pl, Colchester, Essex CO3 3LP, United Kingdom. TEL 44-20-70175544, FAX 44-20-70175198, subscriptions@tandf.co.uk.

615 GBR ISSN 1746-0441

➤ **EXPERT OPINION ON DRUG DISCOVERY.** Text in English. 2006 (June). m. GBP 2,635, EUR 3,485, USD 5,275 combined subscription to institutions (print & online eds.); GBP 5,080, EUR 6,705, USD 10,160 combined subscription to corporations (print & online eds.) (effective 2010). adv. back issues avail.; reprint service avail. from PSC. **Document type:** *Journal, Academic/Scholarly.* **Description:** Provides a forum for the commentary and analysis of drug discovery in the post-genomic era, with emphasis placed on the current and emerging disciplines involved, and strategic planning.
Related titles: Online - full text ed.: ISSN 1746-045X (from IngentaConnect).
Indexed: B&BAb, B19, B21, CTA, EMBASE, ExcerpMed, GenetAb, ImmunAb, NSA, NucAcAb, P30, SCI, SCOPUS, W07.
—BLDSC (3842.002942), IE, Ingenta. **CCC.**
Published by: Informa Healthcare (Subsidiary of: T & F Informa plc), Telephone House, 69-77 Paul St, London, EC2A 4LQ, United Kingdom. healthcare.enquiries@informa.com. Adv. contact Per Sonnerfeldt. **Subscr. to:** Taylor & Francis Inc., Customer Services Dept, 325 Chestnut St, 8th Fl, Philadelphia, PA 19106. TEL 215-625-8900, 800-354-1420, FAX 215-625-8914, customerservice@taylorandfrancis.com; Taylor & Francis Ltd., Journals Customer Service, Sheepen Pl, Colchester, Essex CO3 3LP, United Kingdom. TEL 44-20-70175544, FAX 44-20-70175198, tf.enquiries@tfinforma.com.

615.9 572.4 615.739 GBR ISSN 1742-5255

➤ **EXPERT OPINION ON DRUG METABOLISM & TOXICOLOGY.** Text in English. 2005 (June). m. GBP 1,160, EUR 1,535, USD 2,320 combined subscription to institutions (print & online eds.); GBP 2,320, EUR 3,070, USD 4,645 combined subscription to corporations (print & online eds.) (effective 2010). adv. back issues avail.; reprint service avail. from PSC. **Document type:** *Journal, Academic/Scholarly.* **Description:** Provides a forum for the commentary and analysis of current and emerging research approaches in the ADME-Tox arena, as well as metabolic, pharmacokinetic and toxicological issues relating to specific drugs or drug classes.
Related titles: Online - full text ed.: ISSN 1744-7607 (from IngentaConnect).
Indexed: B&BAb, B19, B21, B27, EMBASE, ESPM, ExcerpMed, H&SSA, MEDLINE, NSA, P30, R10, Reac, SCI, SCOPUS, ToxAb, W07.
—BLDSC (3842.002943), IE, Ingenta. **CCC.**
Published by: Informa Healthcare (Subsidiary of: T & F Informa plc), Telephone House, 69-77 Paul St, London, EC2A 4LQ, United Kingdom. TEL 44-20-70175000, FAX 44-20-70177667, healthcare.enquiries@informa.com, http://www.expertopin.com/action/showJournals. Pub. Phil Garner. **Subscr. to:** Taylor & Francis Inc., Customer Services Dept, 325 Chestnut St, 8th Fl, Philadelphia, PA 19106. TEL 215-625-8900, 800-354-1420, FAX 215-625-8914, customerservice@taylorandfrancis.com; Taylor & Francis Ltd., Journals Customer Service, Sheepen Pl, Colchester, Essex CO3 3LP, United Kingdom. TEL 44-20-70175544, FAX 44-20-70175198.

615 GBR ISSN 1474-0338
CODEN: EODSA9

➤ **EXPERT OPINION ON DRUG SAFETY.** Text in English. 2002 (May). bi-m. GBP 1,135, EUR 1,500, USD 2,275 combined subscription to institutions (print & online eds.); GBP 2,195, EUR 2,895, USD 4,385 combined subscription to corporations (print & online eds.) (effective 2010). adv. abstr.; bibl. Index. back issues avail.; reprint service avail. from PSC. **Document type:** *Journal, Academic/Scholarly.* **Description:** Contains expert reviews on clinical tests and drug safety.
Related titles: Online - full text ed.: ISSN 1744-764X (from IngentaConnect).
Indexed: B21, EMBASE, ESPM, ExcerpMed, H&SSA, MEDLINE, P30, R10, Reac, SCI, SCOPUS, W07.
—BLDSC (3842.002945), IE, Ingenta. **CCC.**
Published by: Informa Healthcare (Subsidiary of: T & F Informa plc), Telephone House, 69-77 Paul St, London, EC2A 4LQ, United Kingdom. TEL 44-20-70175000, FAX 44-20-70177667, healthcare.enquiries@informa.com. Adv. contact Per Sonnerfeldt. **Subscr. to:** Taylor & Francis Inc., Customer Services Dept, 325 Chestnut St, 8th Fl, Philadelphia, PA 19106. TEL 215-625-8900, 800-354-1420, FAX 215-625-8914, customerservice@taylorandfrancis.com; Taylor & Francis Ltd., Journals Customer Service, Sheepen Pl, Colchester, Essex CO3 3LP, United Kingdom. TEL 44-20-70175544, FAX 44-20-70175198.

615.1 GBR ISSN 1472-8214
CODEN: EMDRFV

➤ **EXPERT OPINION ON EMERGING DRUGS.** Text in English. 1996. q. GBP 1,050, EUR 1,385, USD 2,095 combined subscription to institutions (print & online eds.); GBP 2,050, EUR 2,710, USD 4,100 combined subscription to corporations (print & online eds.) (effective 2010). adv. abstr.; bibl. 2 cols./p.; back issues avail.; reprint service avail. from PSC. **Document type:** *Journal, Academic/Scholarly.* **Description:** Contains structured reviews on drugs/drug classes emerging onto the market across all therapy areas, providing expert opinion on their potential impact on the current management of specific diseases.
Formerly (until 2001): Emerging Drugs (1361-9195)
Related titles: Online - full text ed.: ISSN 1744-7623 (from IngentaConnect).
Indexed: A29, B&BAb, B19, B20, B21, CTA, CurCont, DBA, EMBASE, ESPM, ExcerpMed, H&SSA, ImmunAb, MEDLINE, NSA, P30, R10, Reac, SCI, SCOPUS, VirolAbstr, W07.
—BLDSC (3842.002950), IE, Ingenta, INIST. **CCC.**
Published by: Informa Healthcare (Subsidiary of: T & F Informa plc), Telephone House, 69-77 Paul St, London, EC2A 4LQ, United Kingdom. TEL 44-20-70175000, FAX 44-20-70177667, healthcare.enquiries@informa.com. **Subscr. to:** Taylor & Francis Inc., Customer Services Dept, 325 Chestnut St, 8th Fl, Philadelphia, PA 19106. TEL 215-625-8900, 800-354-1420, FAX 215-625-8914; Taylor & Francis Ltd., Journals Customer Service, Sheepen Pl, Colchester, Essex CO3 3LP, United Kingdom. TEL 44-20-70175544, FAX 44-20-70175198.

615.1 GBR ISSN 1354-3784
CODEN: EOIDER

➤ **EXPERT OPINION ON INVESTIGATIONAL DRUGS;** authoritative analysis of R&D trends. Abbreviated title: E O I D. Text in English. 1992. m. GBP 2,815, EUR 3,715, USD 5,630 combined subscription to institutions (print & online eds.); GBP 5,530, EUR 7,295, USD 11,055 combined subscription to corporations (print & online eds.) (effective 2010). adv. abstr.; illus.; bibl. 2 cols./p.; back issues avail.; reprint service avail. from PSC. **Document type:** *Journal, Academic/Scholarly.* **Description:** Brings out review articles and papers on drugs in preclinical and early stage clinical development, providing expert opinion on the scope for future development.
Formerly (until 1994): Current Opinion in Investigational Drugs (0967-8298)
Related titles: Online - full text ed.: ISSN 1744-7658 (from IngentaConnect).
Indexed: A29, B&BAb, B19, B20, B21, C33, CTA, ChemAb, CurCont, EMBASE, ESPM, ExcerpMed, I10, ImmunAb, IndMed, Inpharma, MEDLINE, NSA, P30, P35, R10, Reac, SCI, SCOPUS, VirolAbstr, W07.
—BLDSC (3842.002953), CASDDS, GNLM, IE, Infotrieve, Ingenta, INIST. **CCC.**
Published by: Informa Healthcare (Subsidiary of: T & F Informa plc), Telephone House, 69-77 Paul St, London, EC2A 4LQ, United Kingdom. TEL 44-20-70175000, FAX 44-20-70176792, healthcare.enquiries@informa.com. Ed. Dimitri Mikhalidis. Adv. contact Per Sonnerfeldt. **Subscr. to:** Taylor & Francis Inc., Customer Services Dept, 325 Chestnut St, 8th Fl, Philadelphia, PA 19106. TEL 215-625-8900, 800-354-1420, FAX 215-625-8914, customerservice@taylorandfrancis.com; Taylor & Francis Ltd., Journals Customer Service, Sheepen Pl, Colchester, Essex CO3 3LP, United Kingdom. TEL 44-20-70175544, FAX 44-20-70175198.

615.5805 GBR ISSN 1465-6566

➤ **EXPERT OPINION ON PHARMACOTHERAPY.** Text in English. 1999. 18/yr. GBP 2,540, EUR 3,355, USD 5,080 combined subscription to institutions (print & online eds.); GBP 4,895, EUR 6,465, USD 9,795 combined subscription to corporations (print & online eds.) (effective 2010). adv. abstr.; bibl. 2 cols./p.; back issues avail.; reprint service avail. from PSC. **Document type:** *Journal, Academic/Scholarly.* **Description:** Brings out review articles and papers on newly approved/near to launch compounds, providing expert opinion on the likely impact of these new agents on existing pharmacotherapy of specific diseases.
Related titles: Online - full text ed.: ISSN 1744-7666 (from IngentaConnect).
Indexed: B21, CurCont, EMBASE, ExcerpMed, Inpharma, MEDLINE, NSA, P30, P35, R10, Reac, SCI, SCOPUS, W07.
—BLDSC (3842.002956), IE, Infotrieve, Ingenta. **CCC.**
Published by: Informa Healthcare (Subsidiary of: T & F Informa plc), Telephone House, 69-77 Paul St, London, EC2A 4LQ, United Kingdom. TEL 44-20-70175000, FAX 44-20-70177667, healthcare.enquiries@informa.com. Ed. Dimitri Mikhalidis. Adv. contact Per Sonnerfeldt. **Subscr. to:** Taylor & Francis Inc., Customer Services Dept, 325 Chestnut St, 8th Fl, Philadelphia, PA 19106. TEL 215-625-8900, 800-354-1420, FAX 215-625-8914, customerservice@taylorandfrancis.com; Taylor & Francis Ltd., Journals Customer Service, Sheepen Pl, Colchester, Essex CO3 3LP, United Kingdom. TEL 44-20-70175544, FAX 44-20-70175198.

615.1 GBR ISSN 1354-3776
CODEN: EOTPEG

➤ **EXPERT OPINION ON THERAPEUTIC PATENTS.** Text in English. 1991. m. GBP 3,400, EUR 4,490, USD 6,795 combined subscription to institutions (print & online eds.); GBP 6,670, EUR 8,805, USD 13,340 combined subscription to corporations (print & online eds.) (effective 2010). adv. pat.; abstr.; bibl. 170 p./no.; back issues avail.; reprint service avail. from PSC. **Document type:** *Journal, Academic/Scholarly.* **Description:** Brings out articles on recent pharmaceutical patent claims, providing expert opinion the scope for future development, in the context of the scientific literature.
Formerly (until Feb.1994): Current Opinion on Therapeutic Patents (0962-2594); Which was formed by the merger of (1988-1991): Current Antimicrobial Patents (0954-8041); (1988-1991): Current Cardiovascular Patents (0954-8033); (19??-1991): Current C N S Patents (0958-1685)
Related titles: Online - full text ed.: ISSN 1744-7674 (from IngentaConnect).
Indexed: B&BAb, B21, C33, ChemAb, CurCont, EMBASE, ExcerpMed, ImmunAb, Inpharma, MEDLINE, NSA, P30, SCI, SCOPUS, W07.
—BLDSC (3842.002960), CASDDS, GNLM, IE, Infotrieve, Ingenta, INIST. **CCC.**
Published by: Informa Healthcare (Subsidiary of: T & F Informa plc), Telephone House, 69-77 Paul St, London, EC2A 4LQ, United Kingdom. healthcare.enquiries@informa.com. Ed. Sultana Ara. Pub. Phil Garner. **Subscr. to:** Taylor & Francis Inc., Customer Services Dept, 325 Chestnut St, 8th Fl, Philadelphia, PA 19106. TEL 215-625-8900, 800-354-1420, FAX 215-625-8914, customerservice@taylorandfrancis.com; Taylor & Francis Ltd., Journals Customer Service, Sheepen Pl, Colchester, Essex CO3 3LP, United Kingdom. TEL 44-20-70175544, FAX 44-20-70175198.

615 GBR ISSN 1472-8222
CODEN: EOTTAO

➤ **EXPERT OPINION ON THERAPEUTIC TARGETS.** Text in English. 1997. m. GBP 1,970, EUR 2,605, USD 3,945 combined subscription to institutions (print & online eds.); GBP 3,775, EUR 4,985, USD 7,550 combined subscription to corporations (print & online eds.) (effective 2010). adv. abstr. 150 p./no. 2 cols./p.; back issues avail.; reprint service avail. from PSC. **Document type:** *Journal, Academic/Scholarly.* **Description:** Contains structured profiles of research projects for which the originators are seeking support from an industrial partner. Includes details of therapeutic target, mechanism of action, indications, advantages of approach, current research goals and type of collaborative research envisaged.

P

Formerly (until Jun.2001): Emerging Therapeutic Targets (1460-0412)
Related titles: Online - full text ed.: ISSN 1744-7631 (from IngentaConnect).
Indexed: B&BAb, B21, EMBASE, ExcerpMed, ImmunAb, MEDLINE, NSA, P30, R10, Reac, SCI, SCOPUS, W07.
—BLDSC (3842.002965), IE, Infotrieve, Ingenta. **CCC.**
Published by: Informa Healthcare (Subsidiary of: T & F Informa plc), Telephone House, 69-77 Paul St, London, EC2A 4LQ, United Kingdom. healthcare.enquiries@informa.com. Adv. contact Per Sonnerfeldt. **Subscr. to:** Taylor & Francis Inc., Customer Services Dept, 325 Chestnut St, 8th Fl, Philadelphia, PA 19106. TEL 215-625-8900, 800-354-1420, FAX 215-625-8914, customerservice@taylorandfrancis.com; Taylor & Francis Ltd., Journals Customer Service, Sheepen Pl, Colchester, Essex CO3 3LP, United Kingdom. TEL 44-20-70175544, FAX 44-20-70175198.

615.1 616.992 GBR ISSN 1473-7140
CODEN: ERATBJ

➤ **EXPERT REVIEW OF ANTICANCER THERAPY.** Text in English. 2001. m. GBP 1,095 combined subscription domestic (print & online eds.); USD 1,915 combined subscription in North America (print & online eds.); JPY 203,500 combined subscription in Japan (print & online eds.); EUR 1,530 combined subscription elsewhere (print & online eds.) (effective 2011). adv. bibl.; abstr. back issues avail.; reprints avail. **Document type:** *Journal, Academic/Scholarly.* **Description:** Provides expert appraisal and commentary on the major trends in cancer care and highlights the performance of new therapeutics and diagnostic approaches.
Related titles: Online - full text ed.: ISSN 1744-8328. GBP 985 domestic to institutions; USD 1,730 in North America to institutions; JPY 185,000 in Japan to institutions; EUR 1,385 elsewhere to institutions (effective 2011) (from IngentaConnect).
Indexed: A26, C06, C07, CA, CurCont, E08, EMBASE, ExcerpMed, H11, H12, I05, MEDLINE, P20, P22, P30, P48, P50, P54, PQC, R10, Reac, SCI, SCOPUS, W07.
—BLDSC (3842.002982), IE, Infotrieve, Ingenta, INIST. **CCC.**
Published by: Expert Reviews Ltd. (Subsidiary of: Future Science Ltd.), Unitec House, 2 Albert Pl, London, N3 1QB, United Kingdom. TEL 44-20-83716080, FAX 44-20-83716099, info@expert-reviews.com. Ed. Elisa Manzotti TEL 44-20-83716090. Pub. David Hughes. Adv. contact Simon Boisseau. Circ: 850.

615.1 GBR ISSN 1751-2433

➤ **EXPERT REVIEW OF CLINICAL PHARMACOLOGY.** Text in English. 2008. bi-m. GBP 695 combined subscription domestic (print & online eds.); USD 1,220 combined subscription in North America (print & online eds.); JPY 129,000 combined subscription in Japan (print & online eds.); EUR 975 combined subscription elsewhere (print & online eds.) (effective 2011). adv. back issues avail.; reprints avail. **Document type:** *Journal, Academic/Scholarly.* **Description:** Provides an essential role in integrating the expertise of all of the specialists and players who are active in meeting such challenges in modern biomedical practice.
Related titles: Online - full text ed.: ISSN 1751-2441. GBP 615 domestic to institutions; USD 1,080 in North America to institutions; JPY 115,500 in Japan to institutions; EUR 865 elsewhere to institutions (effective 2011) (from IngentaConnect).
Indexed: A26, E08, EMBASE, ExcerpMed, H12, I05, P20, P30, P48, P54, PQC, SCOPUS, T02.
—BLDSC (9830.068000), IE. **CCC.**
Published by: Expert Reviews Ltd. (Subsidiary of: Future Science Ltd.), Unitec House, 2 Albert Pl, London, N3 1QB, United Kingdom. TEL 44-20-83716080, FAX 44-20-83716099, info@expert-reviews.com. Ed. Elisa Manzotti TEL 44-20-83716090. Pub. David Hughes. Adv. contact Simon Boisseau. Circ: 410.

615.1 GBR ISSN 1473-7159
CODEN: ERMDCW

➤ **EXPERT REVIEW OF MOLECULAR DIAGNOSTICS.** Text in English. 2001. 8/yr. GBP 855 combined subscription domestic (print & online eds.); USD 1,500 combined subscription in North America (print & online eds.); JPY 159,500 combined subscription in Japan (print & online eds.); EUR 1,200 combined subscription elsewhere (print & online eds.) (effective 2011). adv. abstr.; bibl. back issues avail.; reprints avail. **Document type:** *Journal, Academic/Scholarly.* **Description:** Provides a resource for commentary and debate that will help to shape decision-making in patient care.
Related titles: Online - full text ed.: ISSN 1744-8352. GBP 770 domestic to institutions; USD 1,350 in North America to institutions; JPY 145,000 in Japan to institutions; EUR 1,080 elsewhere to institutions (effective 2011) (from IngentaConnect).
Indexed: A26, B26, BIOBASE, CA, CurCont, E08, EMBASE, ExcerpMed, H12, I05, IABS, MEDLINE, P20, P22, P30, P48, P54, PQC, R10, Reac, SCI, SCOPUS, W07.
—BLDSC (3842.002987), IE, Infotrieve, Ingenta. **CCC.**
Published by: Expert Reviews Ltd. (Subsidiary of: Future Science Ltd.), Unitec House, 2 Albert Pl, London, N3 1QB, United Kingdom. TEL 44-20-83716080, FAX 44-20-83716099, info@expert-reviews.com. Ed. Elisa Manzotti TEL 44-20-83716090. Pub. David Hughes. Adv. contact Simon Boisseau. Circ: 720.

615 616.8 GBR ISSN 1473-7175
CODEN: ERNXAR

➤ **EXPERT REVIEW OF NEUROTHERAPEUTICS.** Text in English. 2001. m. GBP 1,095 combined subscription domestic (print & online eds.); USD 1,915 combined subscription in North America (print & online eds.); JPY 203,500 combined subscription in Japan (print & online eds.); EUR 1,530 combined subscription elsewhere (print & online eds.) (effective 2011). adv. abstr.; bibl. back issues avail.; reprints avail. **Document type:** *Journal, Academic/Scholarly.* **Description:** Provides expert appraisal and commentary on the major therapeutic and diagnostic advances in neurology and neuropsychiatry.
Related titles: Online - full text ed.: ISSN 1744-8360. GBP 985 domestic to institutions; USD 1,730 in North America to institutions; JPY 185,000 in Japan to institutions; EUR 1,385 elsewhere to institutions (effective 2011) (from IngentaConnect); Polish Translation: ISSN 1734-8803.
Indexed: A26, B&BAb, B19, B21, BIOBASE, CA, CurCont, E08, EMBASE, ExcerpMed, H11, H12, I05, IABS, MEDLINE, NSA, P03, P20, P22, P30, P48, P54, PQC, PsycInfo, R10, Reac, SCI, SCOPUS, W07.
—BLDSC (3842.002995), IE, Ingenta. **CCC.**
Published by: Expert Reviews Ltd. (Subsidiary of: Future Science Ltd.), Unitec House, 2 Albert Pl, London, N3 1QB, United Kingdom. TEL 44-20-83716080, FAX 44-20-83716099, info@expert-reviews.com. Ed. Elisa Manzotti TEL 44-20-83716090. Pub. David Hughes. Adv. contact Simon Boisseau. Circ: 850.

615 GBR ISSN 1473-7167
CODEN: ERPOBB

➤ **EXPERT REVIEW OF PHARMACOECONOMICS & OUTCOMES RESEARCH.** Text in English. 2001. bi-m. GBP 695 combined subscription domestic to institutions (print & online eds.); USD 1,220 combined subscription in North America to institutions (print & online eds.); JPY 129,000 combined subscription in Japan to institutions (print & online eds.); EUR 975 combined subscription elsewhere to institutions (print & online eds.) (effective 2011). adv. abstr.; bibl. back issues avail.; reprints avail. **Document type:** *Journal, Academic/Scholarly.* **Description:** Features commentary and analysis on the growing relationship between economic factors and clinical prescribing decisions that provide a practical background to informed prescribing decisions and allocation of healthcare resources.
Related titles: Online - full text ed.: ISSN 1744-8379. GBP 615 domestic to institutions; USD 1,080 in North America to institutions; JPY 115,500 in Japan to institutions; EUR 865 elsewhere to institutions (effective 2011) (from IngentaConnect).
Indexed: A12, A26, ABIn, C06, C07, CA, E08, EMBASE, EconLit, ExcerpMed, H12, I05, JEL, MEDLINE, P20, P22, P24, P30, P48, P51, P53, P54, PQC, SCOPUS.
—BLDSC (3842.002996), IE, Ingenta. **CCC.**
Published by: Expert Reviews Ltd. (Subsidiary of: Future Science Ltd.), Unitec House, 2 Albert Pl, London, N3 1QB, United Kingdom. TEL 44-20-83716080, FAX 44-20-83716099, info@expert-reviews.com. Ed. Elisa Manzotti TEL 44-20-83716090. Pub. David Hughes. Adv. contact Simon Boisseau. Circ: 600.

615.1 TUR ISSN 1300-4182

F A B A D FARMASOTIK BILIMLER DERGISI/F A B A D JOURNAL OF PHARMACEUTICAL SCIENCES. Text in Turkish. 1981. q. **Document type:** *Journal, Academic/Scholarly.*
Indexed: EMBASE, ExcerpMed, I12, NPU, P10, P20, P48, P53, P54, PQC, R10, Reac, SCOPUS.
Published by: Hacettepe Universitesi, Faculty of Pharmacy, Sihhiye, Ankara, 06100, Turkey. TEL 90-312-3052342, FAX 90-312-3101524, eczdekan@hacettepe.edu.tr, info@hacettepe.edu.tr, http://www.farma.hacettepe.edu.tr, http://www.hun.edu.tr/. Ed. Sema Calis. Pub. Dr. Filiz Oener.

615 SWE ISSN 1400-6588

F A S S - LAEKEMEDEL I SVERIGE. (Farmacevtiska Specialiteter i Sverige) Key Title: F A S S. Text in Swedish. 1966. a. SEK 669 (effective 2001). adv. **Document type:** *Catalog.*
Formerly (until 1995): F A S S - Farmacevtiska Specialiteter i Sverige (0430-1080)
Published by: LINFO - Laekemedelsinformation AB, Fack 17608, Stockholm, 11892, Sweden. TEL 46-8-462-37-00, FAX 46-8-462-02-88. Ed. Anna Greta Hedstrand. R&P, Adv. contact Maia Sundberg TEL 46-8-462-37-74.

636.089 SWE ISSN 0347-1136

F A S S VET; laekemedel foer veterinaermedicinsk bruk. (Farmacevtiska Specialiteter i Sverige) Text in Swedish. 1973. a. SEK 366 (effective 2001). adv. **Document type:** *Catalog.*
Published by: LINFO - Laekemedelsinformation AB, Fack 17608, Stockholm, 11892, Sweden. TEL 46-8-462-37-00, FAX 46-8-462-02-88. Ed. Anna Greta Hedstrand. R&P, Adv. contact Maia Sundberg TEL 46-8-462-37-74.

F D A COMPLIANCE POLICY GUIDANCE. MANUAL. (Food and Drug Administration) *see* FOOD AND FOOD INDUSTRIES

F D A ENFORCEMENT MANUAL. (Food and Drug Administration) *see* PUBLIC HEALTH AND SAFETY

F D A LAW WEEKLY. *see* LAW

615 614 USA

F D A NEWS DRUG DAILY BULLETIN. (Federal Drug Administration) Variant title: Drug Daily Bulletin. Text in English. 2004. d. (Mon.-Fri.). free (effective 2009). back issues avail. **Document type:** *Newsletter, Trade.* **Description:** Provides FDA regulatory, legislative and business news briefs in the pharmaceutical and biologics industries.
Media: Online - full text.
Published by: Washington Business Information, Inc., 300 N Washington St, Ste 200, Falls Church, Arlington, VA 22046. TEL 703-538-7600, 888-838-5578, FAX 703-538-7676, customerservice@fdanews.com. Pub. Matt Salt TEL 703-538-7642. Adv. contact Andrew McSherry TEL 703-538-7643.

615 USA ISSN 1554-0049

F D A NEWS NUTRACEUTICAL WEEKLY BULLETIN. (Federal Drug Administration) Variant title: Nutraceutical Weekly Bulletin. Text in English. 2004 (Sept.). w. **Document type:** *Newsletter, Trade.*
Media: E-mail. **Related titles:** Online - full text ed.
—CIS.
Published by: Washington Business Information, Inc., 300 N Washington St, Ste 200, Falls Church, VA 22046. customerservice@fdanews.com, http://www.fdanews.com.

F D A WEEK. (Food and Drug Administration) *see* CONSUMER EDUCATION AND PROTECTION

F D C CONTROL NEWSLETTER (ONLINE). (Food, Drug, Cosmetics) *see* FOOD AND FOOD INDUSTRIES

615.1 ESP ISSN 2172-8771

▼ **FARMA FLASHES.** Text in Spanish. 2010. s-a. **Document type:** *Magazine, Trade.*
Published by: Colegio Oficial de Farmaceuticos de Ciudad Real, Ronda de la Mata, 13, Ciudad Real, 13004, Spain. TEL 34-926-222300, FAX 34-926-222315, cofciudadreal@redfarma.org, http://www.cofciudadreal.com/.

615.1 BGR ISSN 1311-5162

FARMA NEWS. Text in English, Bulgarian. q. BGL 14 domestic; USD 40 foreign (effective 2005). **Document type:** *Journal, Academic/Scholarly.* **Description:** Presents news on the field of pharmacology, clinical pharmacy, technology of medicine forms, analyses of medicines, herbalism.
Published by: Meditsinski Universitet - Sofia, Tsentralna Meditsinska Biblioteka, Tsentur za Informatsiia po Meditsina/Medical University - Sofia, Central Medical Library, Medical Information Center, 1 Sv Georgi Sofiiski ul, Sofia, 1431, Bulgaria. TEL 359-2-9522342, FAX 359-2-9522393, pslavova@medun.acad.bg, http://www.medun.acad.bg/cmb_htm/cmb1_home_bg.htm. R&P, Adv. contact Lydia Tacheva.

615.1 SVK ISSN 0014-8172
CODEN: FAOBAS

FARMACEUTICKY OBZOR. Text in Czech, Slovak; Summaries in English, German, Russian. 1931. m. EUR 60 (effective 2009). adv. bk.rev. stat.; abstr.; charts; illus. index. **Document type:** *Journal, Academic/Scholarly.*
Related titles: Online - full text ed.
Indexed: A22, CIN, ChemAb, ChemTitl, EMBASE, ExcerpMed, I12, INIS AtomInd, P30, R10, Reac, SCOPUS.
—BLDSC (3881.850000), CASDDS, GNLM, Ingenta, INIST, Linda Hall.
Published by: (Slovenska Zdravotnicka Univerzita), Vydavatelstvo Herba, Svabinsheho 4-a, Bratislava, 85101, Slovakia. TEL 421-2-54776683, FAX 421-1-54774992, herbapress@stonline.sk. Circ: 2,500. **Dist. by:** Slovart G.T.G. s.r.o., Krupinska 4, PO Box 152, Bratislava 85299, Slovakia. TEL 421-2-63839472, FAX 421-2-63839485, http://www.slovart-gtg.sk.

615 ESP ISSN 0213-7283

EL FARMACEUTICO; profesion y cultura. Text in Spanish. 1984. bi-w. EUR 77 domestic; EUR 123 foreign (effective 2009). adv. bk.rev. **Document type:** *Journal, Trade.* **Description:** Addressed to all pharmacists, pharmaceutical industry, and pharmacy services in hospitals.
Related titles: ◆ Supplement(s): Informativo Farmaceutico.
Indexed: I12.
Published by: Ediciones Mayo S.A., Calle Aribau 185-187, 2a Planta, Barcelona, 08021, Spain. TEL 34-93-2090255, FAX 34-93-2020643, edmayo@ediciones.mayo.es, http://www.edicionesmayo.es. Circ: 20,000.

615 ESP ISSN 0214-4697

EL FARMACEUTICO HOSPITALES. Text in Spanish. 1988. bi-m. EUR 31 domestic; EUR 71.50 foreign (effective 2009). adv. **Document type:** *Journal, Trade.* **Description:** Contains interviews with prominent pharmacists, original articles about therapeutics and pharmacology, and reviews of international medical journals.
Related titles: Online - full text ed.; Supplement(s): Area Terapeutica. ISSN 1885-947X. 2005.
Indexed: A01, EMBASE, ExcerpMed, I12, P02, P20, P48, P54, PQC, SCOPUS.
—GNLM. **CCC.**
Published by: Ediciones Mayo S.A., Calle Aribau 185-187, 2a Planta, Barcelona, 08021, Spain. TEL 34-93-2090255, FAX 34-93-2020643, http://www.edicionesmayo.es. Circ: 2,800.

615.1 BEL ISSN 0771-2367

FARMACEUTISCH TIJDSCHRIFT VOOR BELGIE. Text in Flemish. 1923. bi-m. **Document type:** *Journal, Trade.*
Formerly (until 1971): Pharmaceutisch Tijdschrift voor Belgie (0369-9714)
Indexed: A22, EMBASE, ExcerpMed, I12, R10, Reac, SCOPUS.
—BLDSC (3881.990000), IE, Ingenta, Linda Hall. **CCC.**
Published by: Algemene Pharmaceutische Bond/Association Pharmaceutique Belge, Archimedesstraat 11, Brussels, 1000, Belgium. TEL 32-2-2854200, FAX 32-2-2854285, info@mail.apb.be, http://www.apb.be.

615.1 HRV ISSN 0014-8202
CODEN: FAGLAI

➤ **FARMACEUTSKI GLASNIK.** Text in Croatian; Summaries in English. 1907. m. USD 80 (effective 2002). adv. bk.rev. abstr.; bibl.; charts; illus.; stat. index. 40 p./no.; reprints avail. **Document type:** *Journal, Academic/Scholarly.*
Formerly (until 1944): Farmaceutski Vjesnik
Related titles: Online - full text ed.
Indexed: A22, CIN, ChemAb, ChemTitl, DBA, EMBASE, ExcerpMed, I12, P30, R10, Reac, SCOPUS.
—BLDSC (3884.000000), CASDDS, IE, Ingenta, INIST, Linda Hall.
Published by: Hrvatsko Farmaceutsko Drustvo/Croatian Pharmaceutical Society, Masarykova 2, Zagreb, 10000, Croatia. TEL 385-1-4872849, FAX 385-1-4872853, hfd-fg-ap@zg.tch.hr. Ed. Maja Jaksevac Miksa. Adv. contact Marina Carevic. B&W page USD 200, color page USD 300; 165 x 240. Circ: 2,300.

615.1 SVN ISSN 0014-8229
RS1 CODEN: FMVTAV

FARMACEVTSKI VESTNIK; strokovno glasilo slovenske farmacije. Text in Serbo-Croatian, Slovenian. 1950. q. adv. bk.rev. charts; illus.; tr.lit. index. reprints avail. **Document type:** *Journal, Academic/Scholarly.*
Related titles: Online - full text ed.
Indexed: CIN, ChemAb, ChemTitl, DBA, EMBASE, ExcerpMed, I12, P30, R10, Reac, SCOPUS.
—CASDDS, GNLM, INIST, Linda Hall.
Published by: Slovensko Farmacevtsko Drustvo, Dunajska 184 A, Box 311, Ljubljana, 1000, Slovenia. Ed. Ales Krbavcic. Circ: 1,900.

615.1 DNK ISSN 0903-9198
CODEN: APCEAR

FARMACI. Text in Danish. 1844. m. DKK 640 (effective 2008). adv. bk.rev. abstr.; charts; illus. index. back issues avail. **Document type:** *Journal, Trade.* **Description:** Features articles relating to Danish pharmacists, political and economic developments in the Danish pharmacy sector and abroad, Danish national health politics and scholarly articles relating to pharmacy.
Former titles (until 1988): Archiv for Pharmaci og Chemi (0003-8938); (until 1894): Archiv for Pharmacie og Technisk Chemie med deres Grundvidenskaber
Related titles: Online - full text ed.
Indexed: ChemAb, P30.
—CASDDS, GNLM, INIST. **CCC.**
Published by: Danmarks Apotekerforening/Danish Pharmaceutical Association, Bredgade 54, PO Box 2181, Copenhagen K, 1017, Denmark. TEL 45-33-767600, FAX 45-33-767699, apotekerforeningen@apotekerforeningen.dk. Ed. Birger Lenvig. adv.: color page DKK 15,900; 179 x 265. Circ: 1,600 (controlled).

615 ITA ISSN 1724-5893

FARMACI, SALUTE & SOCIETA; comunicare la scienza. Text in Italian. 2003. bi-m. **Document type:** *Journal, Academic/Scholarly.*

Media: Online - full text.
Published by: Universita degli Studi di Milano, Istituto di Farmacologia, Via Luigi Vanvitelli, 32, Milan, MI 20129, Italy.

615 MEX
FARMACIA ACTUAL. Text in Spanish. m. MXN 380 (effective 2007). back issues avail. **Document type:** *Magazine, Consumer.*
Related titles: Online - full text ed.
Published by: Ediciones Franco (Subsidiary of: Grupo Galo), Alfonso Esparza Oteo, No. 153, Col. Guadalupe Inn, Mexico, D.F., 01020, Mexico. TEL 52-55-30004600, FAX 52-55-30004612, editorial@grupogalo.com, http://www.grupogalo.com/index.php?option=com_content&task=view&id=30&Itemid=48. Ed. Rosalina Rocha Manzano. Circ: 10,000.

615.1 ESP ISSN 1698-4358
FARMACIA DE ATENCION PRIMARIA. Text in Spanish. 2003. q. free to qualified personnel; EUR 28 domestic (effective 2008). 32 p./no.; **Document type:** *Journal, Trade.*
Related titles: Online - full text ed.
Published by: Ediciones Mayo S.A., Calle Aribau 185-187, 2a Planta, Barcelona, 08021, Spain. TEL 34-93-2090255, FAX 34-93-2020643, edmayo@ediciones.mayo.es, http://www.edicionesmayo.es. Circ: 1,000.

615.1 PRT ISSN 0873-5301
FARMACIA DISTRIBUICAO. Cover title: Revista Profissional dos Sectores da Saude Higiene e Beleza. Text in Portuguese. 1991. m. EUR 60 domestic; EUR 71.40 in Spain; EUR 76.50 in Europe; EUR 91 rest of world (effective 2005). index. **Document type:** *Trade.* **Description:** Presents business news in the pharmacy and drugstore industry.
Published by: A J E Sociedade Editorial Lda., Rua Barao de Sabrosa, 165-A, Lisbon, 1900-088, Portugal. TEL 351-21-8110100, FAX 351-21-8140044, aje@aje.pt. Ed. Carina Machado. Pub. A J Esteves. Adv. contact Paulo Silva. Circ: 6,000 (paid).

615 PRT ISSN 1646-4818
FARMACIA HOSPITALAR. Text in Portuguese. 2006. q. **Document type:** *Magazine, Trade.*
Published by: Associacao Nacional das Farmacias (A N F), Rua Marechal Saldanha 1, Lisbon, 1249-069, Portugal.

615 658 ESP ISSN 1130-6343
CODEN: FAHOE
➤ **FARMACIA HOSPITALARIA.** Text in Spanish. 1977. bi-m. EUR 94.33 combined subscription to individuals print & online eds.; EUR 238.80 to institutions print & online eds. (effective 2009). adv. back issues avail.; reprints avail. **Document type:** *Journal, Academic/Scholarly.*
Former titles (until 1990): Sociedad Espanola de Farmacia Hospitalaria. Revista (0214-753X); (until 1989): Asociacion Espanola de Farmaceuticas de Hospitales. Revista (0210-6329)
Related titles: Online - full text ed.: ISSN 2171-8695. 199?. EUR 78.58 (effective 2009).
Indexed: A22, A36, C06, C07, CABA, CIN, ChemAb, ChemTitl, E12, EMBASE, ExcerpMed, GH, I12, IECT, IME, Inpharma, MEDLINE, N02, N03, P30, P33, R10, RA&MP, RM&VM, Reac, SCOPUS, T05.
—BLDSC (3886.200000), CASDDS, GNLM, IE, Infotrieve, Ingenta. **CCC.**
Published by: (Sociedad Espanola de Farmacia Hospitalaria), Elsevier Doyma (Subsidiary of: Elsevier Health Sciences), Traversa de Gracia 17-21, Barcelona, 08021, Spain. TEL 34-932-418800, FAX 34-932-419020, editorial@elsevier.com. Ed. Bernando Santos. Circ: 3,000.

615 ITA ISSN 1590-3699
FARMACIA NEWS. Text in Italian. 1983. m. (11/yr.). EUR 45 domestic; EUR 90 in Europe; EUR 110 elsewhere (effective 2010). adv. **Document type:** *Magazine, Trade.* **Description:** Covers phytotherapy, homeopathy and nutrition.
Former titles (until 1999): Farmacia Naturale (1121-1350); (until 1990): Natom (0394-8196); (until 1985): Naturopatia Omeopatia (0394-8188)
Related titles: Online - full text ed.
Published by: Tecniche Nuove SpA, Via Eritrea 21, Milan, MI 201, Italy. TEL 39-02-390901, FAX 39-02-7570364, info@tecnichenuove.com. Ed. Chiara Cominoli.

615 PRT ISSN 0870-0230
FARMACIA PORTUGUESA. Text in Portuguese. 1940. bi-m. **Document type:** *Magazine, Trade.*
Indexed: I12.
Published by: Associacao Nacional das Farmacias (A N F), Rua Marechal Saldanha 1, Lisbon, 1249-069, Portugal. TEL 351-21-3400600, FAX 351-21-3472994, http://www.anf.pt.

615 PRT ISSN 1646-7949
FARMACIA PRACTICA. Text in Portuguese. 2005. bi-m. **Document type:** *Magazine, Trade.*
Formerly (until 2007): Farmacia Tecnica (1646-7639)
Published by: Associacao Nacional das Farmacias (A N F), Rua Marechal Saldanha 1, Lisbon, 1249-069, Portugal. TEL 351-21-3400600, FAX 351-21-3472994, http://www.anf.pt.

615 ESP ISSN 0213-9324
FARMACIA PROFESIONAL. Text in Spanish. 1987. 11/yr. **Document type:** *Journal, Trade.*
Related titles: Online - full text ed.: ISSN 1578-9543. 1995; Supplement(s): Farmacia Profesional. Monografias. ISSN 1699-082X. 2005.
Published by: Elsevier Doyma (Subsidiary of: Elsevier Health Sciences), Traversa de Gracia 17-21, Barcelona, 08021, Spain. TEL 34-932-418800, FAX 34-932-419020, editorial@elsevier.com, http://www.elsevier.es/. Circ: 8,500.

615.19 SWE ISSN 1102-8033
FARMACIFACKET. Text in Swedish. 1931. 10/yr. SEK 408 (effective 2003). adv. **Document type:** *Magazine, Trade.*
Former titles (until 1991): Apotekstjaenstemannen (0281-6040); (until 1983): Apoteksteknikern (0345-0945); (until 1956): Tekniska Apotekspersonalens Tidskrift; (until vol.4, 1932): Meddelande fraan Sveriges Tekniska Apotekspersonals Foerbundscentralstyrelse
Published by: Farmaciforbundet, Vastmannagatan 66, Stockholm, 11325, Sweden. TEL 46-8-31-64-10, FAX 46-8-34-08-08, http://www.farmaciforbundet.se. Ed. Anna Calissendorff. adv.: B&W page SEK 9,500, color page SEK 17,600; trim 181 x 260. Circ: 7,000.

615 ROM ISSN 1584-6539
FARMACIST.RO. Text in Romanian. 1996. m. ROL 90 (effective 2011). adv. **Document type:** *Magazine, Trade.*
Formerly (until 2004): Lumea Farmaceutica (1224-368X)
Related titles: Online - full text ed.: ISSN 1841-3145.
Published by: Versa Puls Media, s.r.l., Calea Rahovei 266-268, corp 1, etaj 2, Bucharest, 050912, Romania. TEL 40-31-4254040, FAX 40-31-4254041, office@pulsmedia.ro. Ed. Madalina Mihaltianu. Adv. contact George Pavel.

615.1 POL ISSN 0014-8261
RS1 CODEN: FAPOA4
➤ **FARMACJA POLSKA.** Text in Polish; Summaries in English, Russian. 1945. bi-w. EUR 185 foreign (effective 2006). adv. bk.rev. charts; illus.; tr.lit. index. 48 p./no. 2 cols./p.; back issues avail. **Document type:** *Journal, Academic/Scholarly.* **Description:** Devoted to scientific and social and professional problems of pharmacy.
Related titles: Online - full text ed.
Indexed: A22, ChemAb, DBA, I12, P30.
—BLDSC (3887.000000), CASDDS, GNLM, IE, Ingenta, INIST, Linda Hall.
Published by: Polskie Towarzystwo Farmaceutyczne/Polish Pharmaceutical Society, ul Dluga 16, Warsaw, 00238, Poland. wydawnictwa@ptfarm.pl. Ed. Jerzy Lazowski. Circ: 4,000. **Dist. by:** Ars Polona, Obroncow 25, Warsaw 03933, Poland. TEL 48-22-5098609, FAX 48-22-5098610, arspolona@arspolona.com.pl, http://www.arspolona.com.pl.

615 ITA ISSN 1126-4705
FARMACOECONOMIA NEWS. Text in Italian. 1997. q. free to qualified personnel. adv. **Document type:** *Newspaper, Trade.*
Published by: C I C Edizioni Internazionali, Corso Trieste 42, Rome, 00198, Italy. TEL 39-06-8412673, FAX 39-06-8412688, info@gruppocic.it, http://www.gruppocic.it.

615 NLD ISSN 1878-4577
▼ **FARMACOTHERAPIE BIJ KINDEREN.** Text in Dutch. 2009. q. EUR 99.50 (effective 2010). **Document type:** *Journal, Trade.*
Related titles: Online - full text ed.: ISSN 1878-7215.
Published by: Prelum Uitgevers, Postbus 545, Houten, 3990 GH, Netherlands. TEL 31-30-6355060, FAX 31-30-6355069, info@prelum.nl, http://www.prelum.nl.

615 NLD ISSN 1574-3802
FARMACOTHERAPIE VOOR DE HUISARTS. Text in Dutch. 200?. a. EUR 31.10 (effective 2008).
Published by: (Nederlands Huisartsengenootschap), Bohn Stafleu van Loghum B.V. (Subsidiary of: Springer Science+Business Media), Postbus 246, Houten, 3990 GA, Netherlands. TEL 31-30-6383838, FAX 31-30-6383839, boekhandels@bsl.nl.

615 ITA
FARMAECONOMIA E PERCORSI TERAPEUTICI. Text in Italian. 200?. q. EUR 100 to institutions (effective 2010). **Document type:** *Journal, Academic/Scholarly.*
Related titles: Online - full text ed.
Published by: Seed Edizioni Scientifiche, Piazza Carlo Emanuele II, 19, Turin, 10123, Italy. TEL 39-011-5660258, FAX 39-011-5186892, http://www.edizioniseed.it.

615 UKR
FARMAKOLOHICHNYI VISNYK. Text in English, Russian, Ukrainian. 1996. bi-m. UAK 10 per issue domestic; USD 1.45 per issue foreign (effective 2001). adv. bk.rev. **Document type:** *Journal, Academic/Scholarly.*
Published by: Farmakolohichnyi Komitet Ministerstva Okhorony Zdorov'ya Ukrainy, Ul Grushevs'kogo 7, Kiev, Ukraine. TEL 380-44-2935439, FAX 380-44-2935439, journal@pharma.viaduk.net. Ed. Vladimir S Danilenko. **Dist. by:** East View Information Services, 10601 Wayzata Blvd, Minneapolis, MN 55305. TEL 952-252-1201, 800-477-1005, FAX 952-252-1202, info@eastview.com, http://www.eastview.com.

FARMAKOTERAPIA W PSYCHIATRII I NEUROLOGII. *see* MEDICAL SCIENCES—Psychiatry And Neurology

615 ESP ISSN 1888-5535
FARMANOTAS. Text in Spanish. 2007. m. **Document type:** *Bulletin, Government.*
Related titles: Online - full text ed.: ISSN 1988-8082. 2007.
Published by: Gobierno de Cantabria, Consejeia de Sanidad. Hospital Comarcal de Laredo, Ave de los Derechos Humanos, s-n, Laredo, Cantabria, 39770, Spain. TEL 34-942-638500, FAX 34-942-607876, http://www.scsalud.es/atencion_especializada/ficha_hospital.php?Id3=3.

615 FIN ISSN 1796-6116
FARMASIA. Text in Finnish; Summaries in Swedish. 1917. m. adv. bk.rev. **Document type:** *Newspaper, Trade.*
Formerly (until 2007): Semina (0049-0164)
Indexed: ChemAb, FS&TA.
—BLDSC (8239.000000).
Published by: Suomen Farmasialiitto/Finish Pharmacists' Association, Iso Roobertinkatu 7A, Helsinki, 00120, Finland. FAX 358-9-605112. Ed. Annemari Backman. Adv. contact Marketta Harinen. Circ: 7,800.

FARMASILIV. *see* LABOR UNIONS

615 RUS
FARMATEKA. Text in Russian. 1994. 20/yr. USD 325 in United States (effective 2008). **Document type:** *Journal, Academic/Scholarly.* **Description:** Introduces readers to the latest achievements of the medical science, the new in the world of pharmaceutics and pharmacology.
—BLDSC (0389.037000).
Published by: Izdatel'skii Dom Bionika, ul Profsoyuznaya 57, ofis 249, Moscow, Russian Federation. TEL 7-495-3342557, FAX 7-495-3342255, info@idbionika.ru, http://idbionika.ru. Ed. V M Polonskii. Circ: 25,350. **Dist. by:** East View Information Services, 10601 Wayzata Blvd, Minneapolis, MN 55305. TEL 952-252-1201, 800-477-1005, FAX 952-252-1202, info@eastview.com, http://www.eastview.com.

615.1 BGR
FARMATSEVTICHEN MONITOR. Text in Bulgarian. q. USD 48 foreign (effective 2002). **Description:** Contains information surveys for pharmacologists.
Published by: Meditsinski Universitet - Sofia, Tsentralna Meditsinska Biblioteka, Tsentur za Informatsiia po Meditsina/Medical University - Sofia, Central Medical Library, Medical Information Center, 1 Sv Georgi Sofiiski ul, Sofia, 1431, Bulgaria. TEL 359-2-9522342, FAX 359-2-9522393, http://www.medun.acad.bg/cmb_htm/cmb1_home_bg.htm. **Dist. by:** Sofia Books, ul Silivria 16, Sofia 1404, Bulgaria. TEL 359-2-9586257, info@sofiabooks-bg.com, http://www.sofiabooks-bg.com.

615 RUS
FARMATSEVTICHESKII VESTNIK. Text in Russian. 1994. 42/yr. USD 327 foreign (effective 2007). **Document type:** *Newspaper, Trade.*
Published by: Izdatel'skii Dom Bionika, ul Profsoyuznaya 57, ofis 249, Moscow, Russian Federation. TEL 7-495-3342557, FAX 7-495-3342255, info@idbionika.ru, http://idbionika.ru. Ed. M V Zenin. **Dist. by:** East View Information Services, 10601 Wayzata Blvd, Minneapolis, MN 55305. TEL 952-252-1201, 800-477-1005, FAX 952-252-1202, info@eastview.com, http://www.eastview.com.

615.1 UKR ISSN 0367-3057
RS1 CODEN: FRZKAP
FARMATSEVTYCHNYI ZHURNAL. Text in Ukrainian. 1928-1942; resumed 1958. bi-m. USD 117 foreign (effective 2004). charts; illus. index. **Document type:** *Journal, Academic/Scholarly.* **Description:** Consults Ukrainian pharmacists on questions of science, practical activities and legislation regulating the activities of research and pharmaceutical establishments of various specialization, productions, firms and other organizations.
Indexed: ApicAb, ChemAb, DBA, INIS AtomInd, IndMed, RefZh, VITIS.
—BLDSC (0389.100000), CASDDS, East View, GNLM, INIST, Linda Hall. **CCC.**
Published by: Vydavnytstvo Zdorov'ya, vul Kominterna 16, Kyiv, Ukraine. TEL 380-44-2442892. Circ: 7,900. **Dist. by:** East View Information Services, 10601 Wayzata Blvd, Minneapolis, MN 55305. TEL 952-252-1201, 800-477-1005, FAX 952-252-1202, info@eastview.com, http://www.eastview.com.

615 BGR ISSN 0428-0296
CODEN: FMTYA2
➤ **FARMATSIA.** Text and summaries in Bulgarian, English. 1951. q. adv. bk.rev. abstr. index. 48 p./no. 2 cols./p.; back issues avail. **Document type:** *Journal, Academic/Scholarly.* **Description:** Presents original articles and reviews of a range of pharmacy research topics.
Indexed: ABSML, ChemAb, EMBASE, ExcerpMed, IndMed, P30, R10, Reac, RefZh.
—CASDDS, GNLM, INIST.
Published by: Meditsinski Universitet - Sofia, Tsentralna Meditsinska Biblioteka, Tsentur za Informatsiia po Meditsina/Medical University - Sofia, Central Medical Library, Medical Information Center, 1 Sv Georgi Sofiiski ul, Sofia, 1431, Bulgaria. TEL 359-2-9522342, FAX 359-2-9522393, pslavova@medun.acad.bg, http://www.medun.acad.bg/cmb_htm/cmb1_home_bg.htm. Ed. Ivan Assenov. R&P Lydia Tacheva. Adv. contact St Nikolov TEL 359-2-9879874. B&W page USD 50, color page USD 125. Circ: 300.

615.19 RUS ISSN 0367-3014
CODEN: FRMTAL
➤ **FARMATSIYA/PHARMACY.** Text in Russian; Summaries in English. 1938. bi-m. USD 154 in United States (effective 2004). adv. bibl. **Document type:** *Journal, Academic/Scholarly.* **Description:** Publishes actual pharmaceutical information, scientific articles, problem-oriented publications and reviews, latest achievements in pharmaceutical science and practice, materials on both domestic and foreign pharmaceutical companies. Regularly includes the columns: Branch Strategy, Investigation, Experiment, Current Events, History of Pharmacy, etc. Also includes reviews, criticism, a discussion section, and news on conferences.
Former titles (until 1966): Aptechnoe Delo (0430-0947); (until 1947): Farmatsiya (0367-1674)
Related titles: Online - full text ed.
Indexed: A22, ApicAb, B25, BIOSIS Prev, CIN, ChemAb, ChemTitl, DBA, MycolAb, P30, RefZh, SCOPUS.
—BLDSC (0389.180000), CASDDS, East View, GNLM, IE, Ingenta, INIST, Linda Hall. **CCC.**
Published by: (Rossiiskii Tsentr Farmatsevticheskoi i Mediko-Tekhnicheskoi Informatsii), Izdatel'skii Dom Russkii Vrach, ul Bol'shaya Pirogovskaya, dom 2, str. 3, Moscow, Russian Federation. rvrach@mmascience.ru, http://www.rusvrach.ru. Ed. I A Samylina. adv.: color page USD 1,200. Circ: 6,000. **Dist. by:** East View Information Services, 10601 Wayzata Blvd, Minneapolis, MN 55305. TEL 952-252-1201, 800-477-1005, FAX 952-252-1202, info@eastview.com, http://www.eastview.com.

615.1 SWE ISSN 0014-8520
FARMIS-REPTILEN. Variant title: Reptilen. Text occasionally in English; Text in Swedish. 1964. 7/yr. adv. bk.rev. **Document type:** *Bulletin, Consumer.*
Formerly (until vol.3, 1964): Reptilen
Published by: Farmacevtiska Studentkaaren/Swedish National Association of Pharmaceutical Students, Dag Hammerskjoeld Vaeg 16, PO Box 957, Uppsala, 75109, Sweden. TEL 46-18-527833, FAX 46-18-504323, http://www.student.uu.se/farmis. Circ: 1,200 (controlled).

615.1 JPN ISSN 0014-8601
CODEN: FARUAW
➤ **FARUMASHIA.** Text in Japanese. 1965. m. USD 120 (effective 2004). adv. bk.rev. abstr.; bibl.; charts; mkt.; stat. index. 170 p./no.; **Document type:** *Journal, Academic/Scholarly.* **Description:** Covers all aspects of pharmaceutical sciences.
Indexed: CIN, ChemAb, ChemTitl.
—BLDSC (3896.500000), CASDDS, Linda Hall. **CCC.**
Published by: Pharmaceutical Society of Japan/Nihon Yakugakkai, 2-12-15, Shibuya, Shibuya-ku, Tokyo, 150-0002, Japan. TEL 81-3-34063321, FAX 81-3-34981835, http://www.pharm.or.jp/. Ed. Masakatsu Shbasaki. Circ: 22,000 (controlled).

615 USA
FDANEWS DRUG DRUG PIPELINE ALERT. Variant title: Drug Pipeline Alert. Text in English. 2003. d. (Mon.-Fri.). **Document type:** *Newsletter, Trade.* **Description:** Covers intelligence on the research and development of new drugs in high-cost therapeutic areas such as oncology/hematology, cardiovascular, pediatrics, respiratory and others.
Media: Online - full text.

P

Published by: Washington Business Information, Inc., 300 N Washington St, Ste 200, Falls Church, Arlington, VA 22046. TEL 703-538-7600, 888-838-5578, FAX 703-538-7676, customerservice@fdanews.com.

FINANCIAL SURVEY REPORT. THE PHARMACEUTICAL INDUSTRY. *see* BUSINESS AND ECONOMICS—Trade And Industrial Directories

FITOTERAPIA. *see* BIOLOGY—Botany

615.1 USA ISSN 0897-4616
FLORIDA PHARMACY TODAY. Text in English. 1937. m. USD 145 membership (effective 2005). adv. bk.rev. illus. **Document type:** *Magazine, Trade.*
Former titles: Florida Pharmacy Journal (0161-746X); Florida Pharmaceutical Journal (0015-4202); Florida Pharmacist
Indexed: I12.
Published by: Florida Pharmacy Association, 610 N Adams St, Tallahassee, FL 32301. TEL 850-222-2400, FAX 850-561-6758, fpa@pharmview.com. Ed., R&P Julia Hanway TEL 850-926-2405. Adv. contacts Julia Hanway TEL 850-926-2405, Paul Payne. B&W page USD 600, color page USD 1,100; trim 8 x 11. Circ: 3,200 (controlled).

615.5 GBR ISSN 1465-3753
R733
➤ **FOCUS ON ALTERNATIVE AND COMPLEMENTARY THERAPIES**; an evidence based approach. Cover title: F A C T. Text in English. 1996. q. GBP 234 in United Kingdom to institutions; EUR 324 in Europe to institutions; USD 461 elsewhere to institutions; GBP 269 combined subscription in United Kingdom to institutions (print & online eds.); EUR 373 combined subscription in Europe to institutions (print & online eds.); USD 530 combined subscription elsewhere to institutions (print & online eds.) (effective 2012). adv. bk.rev. back issues avail. **Document type:** *Journal, Academic/Scholarly.*
Description: Systematically considers both the mainstream medical and pharmaceutical literature along with complementary medicine related journals. The most importantant papers from all journals are then summarized and commented on in FACT.
Related titles: Online - full text ed.: ISSN 2042-7166. GBP 234 in United Kingdom to institutions; EUR 324 in Europe to institutions; USD 461 elsewhere to institutions (effective 2012).
Indexed: A22, A26, AMED, BP, C06, C07, C08, CABA, CINAHL, EMBASE, ExcerpMed, GH, H12, OR, R10, Reac, SCOPUS, T02.
—BLDSC (3964.203750), IE, Ingenta. **CCC.**
Published by: John Wiley & Sons Ltd. (Subsidiary of: John Wiley & Sons, Inc.), 1-7 Oldlands Way, PO Box 808, Bognor Regis, West Sussex PO21 9FF, United Kingdom. FAX 44-1243-843232, customer@wiley.co.uk, http://onlinelibrary.wiley.com/.

615 CZE ISSN 1210-9495
➤ **FOLIA PHARMACEUTICA UNIVERSITATIS CAROLINAE.** Text in English, German, Czech. 1977. irreg., latest vol.33, 2005. **Document type:** *Journal, Academic/Scholarly.*
Formerly (until 1988): Folia Pharmaceutica (0139-939X)
Related titles: Online - full text ed.: ISSN 1212-5121.
Indexed: I12.
—BLDSC (3973.200000).
Published by: Univerzita Karlova v Praze, Farmaceuticka Fakulta v Hradci Kralove, Heyrovskeho 1203, Hradec Kralove, 50005, Czech Republic. TEL 420-49-5067307, FAX 420-49-5210002.

615 JPN ISSN 0015-5691
RS1 CODEN: NYKZAU
➤ **FOLIA PHARMACOLOGICA JAPONICA (KYOTO, 1944)/NIPPON YAKURIGAKU ZASSHI.** Text in Japanese. 1925. m. JPY 12,000 domestic (effective 2005). bk.rev. Index. 126 p./no.; Supplement avail.; back issues avail.; reprints avail. **Document type:** *Journal, Academic/Scholarly.* **Description:** Publishes original research and review articles on pharmacology and related fields.
Former titles (until 1943): Nihon Yakubutsugaku Zasshi (0369-4461); Folia Japonica Pharmacologica (Kyoto, 1925)
Related titles: Microform ed.: (from PQC); Online - full text ed.: ISSN 1347-8397.
Indexed: A22, B25, BIOSIS Prev, ChemAb, DBA, DentInd, EMBASE, ExcerpMed, INIS AtomInd, ISR, IndMed, MEDLINE, MycolAb, P30, R10, Reac, SCOPUS.
—CASDDS, GNLM, IE, Infotrieve, INIST, Linda Hall. **CCC.**
Published by: Nihon Yakuri Gakkai Henshuubu/Japanese Pharmacological Society, Kantohya Bldg, Gokomachi-Ebisugawa, Nakagyo-ku, Kyoto-shi, 604-0982, Japan. TEL 81-75-2524641, FAX 81-75-2524618, journal@pharmacol.or.jp, http://www.pharmacol.or.jp. Ed. Toshitaka Nabeshima. Pubs. Yoko Ashida, Ms. Yoko Takezaki. R&P Yoko Ashida. Circ: 6,200. **Institutions subscr. to:** Maruzen Co., Ltd., 3-10 Nihonbashi 2-chome, Chuo-ku, Tokyo 103-0027, Japan. TEL 81-3-3272-0521, FAX 81-3-3272-0693, http://www.maruzen.co.jp.

615 664 GBR ISSN 1944-0049
TX553.A3 CODEN: FACPAA
➤ **FOOD ADDITIVES & CONTAMINANTS: PART A - CHEMISTRY, ANALYSIS, CONTROL, EXPOSURE & RISK ASSESSMENT.** Text in English. 1984. m. GBP 2,467, EUR 3,260, USD 4,094 combined subscription to institutions (print & online eds.) (effective 2009). adv. bk.rev. illus. back issues avail.; reprint service avail. from PSC. **Document type:** *Journal, Academic/Scholarly.* **Description:** Contains original research and review articles relating to the detection, determination, occurrence, persistence, safety evaluation and control of naturally occurring and man-made additives and contaminants in the food chain.
Supersedes in part (in 2008): Food Additives and Contaminants (0265-203X)
Related titles: Online - full text ed.: ISSN 1944-0057. GBP 2,344, EUR 3,097, USD 3,889 to institutions (effective 2009) (from IngentaConnect).
Indexed: A22, A34, A35, A36, A37, A38, ABIPC, ASCA, AgrForAb, B21, B23, B25, BIOSIS Prev, BibAg, BioDAb, C25, C30, C33, CA, CABA, CIN, ChemAb, ChemTitl, ChemoAb, CorrAb, CurCont, D01, E01, E12, EMBASE, ESPM, EnvAb, ExcerpMed, F08, FCA, FS&TA, GH, H&SSA, H16, IPackAb, ISR, IndMed, MEDLINE, MaizeAb, MycolAb, N02, N03, N04, NRN, P30, P32, P33, P50, P52, PST, R07, R08, S13, SCI, SCOPUS, SoyAb, T05, TAR, VITIS, W07, W10, W11, WAA.
—CASDDS, GNLM, IE, Infotrieve, Ingenta, INIST, Linda Hall. **CCC.**
Published by: (International Society for Mycotoxicology ITA), Taylor & Francis Ltd. (Subsidiary of: Taylor & Francis Group), 4 Park Sq, Milton Park, Abingdon, Oxfordshire OX14 4RN, United Kingdom. TEL 44-20-70176000, FAX 44-20-70176336, subscriptions@tandf.co.uk, http://www.taylorandfrancis.com. Ed. J Gilbert. Adv. contact Linda Hann. **Subscr. in N. America to:** Taylor & Francis Inc., Customer Services Dept, 325 Chestnut St, 8th Fl, Philadelphia, PA 19106. TEL 215-625-8900, 800-354-1420, FAX 215-625-2940, customerservice@taylorandfrancis.com; **Subscr. to:** Journals Customer Service, Sheepen Pl, Colchester, Essex CO3 3LP, United Kingdom. TEL 44-20-70175544, FAX 44-20-70175198, tf.enquiries@tfinforma.com.

615 664 GBR ISSN 1939-3210
TX553.A3 CODEN: FACPBB
➤ **FOOD ADDITIVES & CONTAMINANTS. PART B. SURVEILLANCE COMMUNICATIONS.** Text in English. 1984. s-a. GBP 2,467, EUR 3,260, USD 4,094 combined subscription to institutions (effective 2009). adv. back issues avail.; reprint service avail. from PSC. **Document type:** *Journal, Academic/Scholarly.* **Description:** Publishes surveillance data indicating the presence and levels of occurrence of designated food additives, residues and contaminants in foods and animal feed.
Supersedes in part (in 2008): Food Additives and Contaminants (0265-203X)
Related titles: Online - full text ed.: ISSN 1939-3229. GBP 2,344, EUR 3,097, USD 3,889 to institutions (effective 2009) (from IngentaConnect).
Indexed: A22, A34, A36, Agr, AgrForAb, B25, BIOSIS Prev, C25, C33, CA, CABA, CurCont, D01, E01, E12, EMBASE, ExcerpMed, F08, F10, FS&TA, GH, H16, IndVet, MEDLINE, MaizeAb, MycolAb, N02, N03, N04, OR, P33, P37, P38, P39, P50, P52, PHN&I, PN&I, R07, R08, R11, R13, RA&MP, RM&VM, S12, SCI, SCOPUS, SoyAb, T02, T05, TAR, TriticAb, VS, W07, W10.
—IE, INIST, Linda Hall. **CCC.**
Published by: (International Society for Mycotoxicology ITA), Taylor & Francis Ltd. (Subsidiary of: Taylor & Francis Group), 4 Park Sq, Milton Park, Abingdon, Oxfordshire OX14 4RN, United Kingdom. TEL 44-20-70176000, FAX 44-20-70176336, subscriptions@tandf.co.uk, http://www.taylorandfrancis.com. Ed. J Gilbert. Adv. contact Linda Hann. **Subscr. to:** Journals Customer Service, Sheepen Pl, Colchester, Essex CO3 3LP, United Kingdom. TEL 44-20-70175544, FAX 44-20-70175198, tf.enquiries@tfinforma.com.

➤ **FOOD AND DRUG ADMINISTRATION.** *see* LAW

615 664 USA ISSN 1086-024X
FOOD & DRUG INSPECTION MONITOR. Text in English. 1996. m. USD 799 (effective 2011). 10 p./no. 2 cols./p.; back issues avail.; reprints avail. **Document type:** *Newsletter, Trade.* **Description:** Contains strategic information you need about FDA inspections, including what FDA inspectors are really looking for, how companies are responding to 483 and EIR citations, which companies are targeted for enforcement proceedings and who's making FOIA requests for FDA 483s and EIRs.
Related titles: Online - full text ed.
—IE. **CCC.**
Published by: Washington Information Source Co., 19-B Wirt St, SW, Leesburg, VA 20175. TEL 703-779-8777, FAX 703-779-2508, service@fdainfo.com, http://www.fdainfo.com/wisindex.html.

FOOD AND DRUG LAW JOURNAL. *see* LAW

344.04232 USA ISSN 1551-5397
FOOD & DRUG LAW WEEKLY. Text in English. 2004. w. USD 2,295 in US & Canada; USD 2,495 elsewhere; USD 2,525 combined subscription in US & Canada (print & online eds.); USD 2,755 combined subscription elsewhere (print & online eds.) (effective 2008). back issues avail. **Document type:** *Newsletter, Trade.*
Related titles: E-mail ed.; Online - full text ed.: ISSN 1551-5400. USD 2,295 combined subscription (online & email eds.); single user (effective 2008).
Indexed: L10, P10, P11, P20, P48, P51, P52, P53, P54, P56, PQC.
Published by: NewsRx, 2727 Paces Ferry Rd SE, Ste 2-440, Atlanta, GA 30339. TEL 770-435-8286, 800-726-4550, FAX 770-435-6800, http://www.newsrx.com. Pub. Susan Hasty TEL 770-507-7777.

614 USA ISSN 0362-6466
HD9009.9.U5
THE FOOD & DRUG LETTER. Abbreviated title: F D L. Text in English. 1976. bi-w. looseleaf. USD 1,245 (print or online ed.); USD 1,992 combined subscription (print & online eds.) (effective 2009). bk.rev. charts. 12 p./no.; Supplement avail.; back issues avail. **Document type:** *Newsletter, Trade.* **Description:** Focuses on major regulatory issues of foods, drugs and cosmetics.
Incorporates: Nutrition Intelligence
Related titles: E-mail ed.; Online - full text ed.
—CCC.
Published by: Washington Business Information, Inc., 300 N Washington St, Ste 200, Falls Church, VA 22046. customerservice@fdanews.com. Ed. Lauren Lentini TEL 703-538-7663. Pub. Matt Salt TEL 703-538-7642.

615 340 USA ISSN 0162-1122
FOOD, DRUG, AND COSMETIC LAW REPORTER (RX EDITION). Text in English. 1938. base vol. plus w. updates. USD 3,289 base vol(s). print or online eds. (effective 2005). **Description:** Covering federal and state laws and regulations and court decisions that govern the safety, effectiveness, purity, packaging and labeling of food, drugs and cosmetics.
Related titles: CD-ROM ed.: USD 2,939 (effective 2003); Online - full text ed.
—CCC.
Published by: C C H Inc. (Subsidiary of: Wolters Kluwer N.V.), 2700 Lake Cook Rd, Riverwoods, IL 60015. TEL 847-267-7000, 800-449-6439, cust_serv@cch.com, http://www.cch.com. Pub. Catherine Wolfe.

615.1 USA ISSN 1082-801X
RA975.5.P5 CODEN: FORMF9
➤ **FORMULARY**; a peer-reviewed drug management journal for managed care and hospital decision makers. Text in English. 1966. m. USD 67 domestic; USD 96 in Canada & Mexico; USD 132 elsewhere; USD 14 newsstand/cover domestic; USD 15 newsstand/cover in Canada & Mexico; USD 23 newsstand/cover elsewhere (effective 2011). adv. abstr.; bibl.; charts. index. 85 p./no.; back issues avail.; reprints avail. **Document type:** *Journal, Academic/Scholarly.*
Description: Provides information on newly approved drugs, pharmaceutical comparisons for managing disease states, formulary management issues, rational prescribing approaches, and insights into effective formulary committee structure and function.
Former titles (until 1995): Hospital Formulary (0098-6909); (until 1975): Hospital Formulary Management (0018-5655)
Related titles: Microform ed.: (from PQC); Online - full text ed.: ISSN 1938-1166.
Indexed: A15, A22, A26, ABIn, ASCA, B01, B03, B06, B07, B09, B11, C06, C07, C08, C11, CA, CINAHL, ChemAb, CurCont, DBA, E08, EMBASE, ExcerpMed, G08, H01, H02, H04, H11, H12, H13, HospLI, I05, I12, IDIS, Inpharma, M01, M02, P10, P20, P21, P24, P30, P34, P35, P48, P51, P53, P54, PQC, R10, Reac, S09, SCI, SCOPUS, T02, W07.
—BLDSC (4008.805800), CASDDS, CIS, GNLM, IE, Infotrieve, Ingenta, INIST. **CCC.**
Published by: Advanstar Communications, Inc., 6200 Canoga Ave, 2nd Fl, Woodland Hills, CA 91367. TEL 818-593-5000, FAX 818-593-5020, info@advanstar.com, http://www.advanstar.com. Ed. Julia Talsma TEL 440-891-2792. Pub. James Granato TEL 732-346-3071. Circ: 33,726 (controlled).

615.1 CHE ISSN 0071-786X
RS122 CODEN: FAZMAE
➤ **FORTSCHRITTE DER ARZNEIMITTELFORSCHUNG/PROGRES DES RECHERCHES PHARMACEUTIQUES/PROGRESS IN DRUG RESEARCH.** Text in English. 1959. irreg., latest vol.61, 2003. price varies. **Document type:** *Monographic series, Academic/Scholarly.*
Description: Contains articles and reviews on highly topical areas in current pharmaceutical and pharmacological research.
Related titles: Online - full text ed.
Indexed: A22, CIN, ChemAb, ChemTitl, DBA, EMBASE, ExcerpMed, FR, IndMed, MEDLINE, P30, R10, Reac, SCOPUS.
—BLDSC (6868.200000), CASDDS, GNLM, IE, Infotrieve, Ingenta, INIST, Linda Hall. **CCC.**
Published by: Birkhauser Verlag AG (Subsidiary of: Springer Science+Business Media), Viaduktstr 42, Postfach 133, Basel, 4051, Switzerland. TEL 41-61-2050707, FAX 41-61-2050792, birkhauser@springer.de, http://www.birkhauser.ch. Ed. Ernst Jucker.

615.1 DEU
➤ **FORUM KLINISCHE PHARMAZIE.** Text in German. 2001. irreg., latest vol.1, 2001. price varies. **Document type:** *Monographic series, Academic/Scholarly.*
Published by: W. Zuckschwerdt Verlag GmbH, Industriestr 1, Germering, 82110, Germany. TEL 49-89-8943490, FAX 49-89-89434950, post@zuckschwerdtverlag.de, http://www.zuckschwerdtverlag.de.

➤ **FOURNI LABO.** *see* BUSINESS AND ECONOMICS—Trade And Industrial Directories

615 ZAF ISSN 1607-9620
FRONT SHOP. Text in English. 1994. m. ZAR 250 domestic; ZAR 336 foreign (effective 2003).
Published by: Primedia Publishing, 366 Pretoria Ave, Ferndale, Randburg, Transvaal 2194, South Africa. TEL 27-11-787-5725, FAX 27-11-787-5776, http://www.primediapublishing.co.za/.

615 616.994 NLD ISSN 1879-6656
▼ **FRONTIERS IN ANTI-CANCER DRUG DISCOVERY.** Text in English. 2010. irreg. **Document type:** *Monographic series, Academic/Scholarly.*
Media: Online - full text.
Published by: Bentham Science Publishers Ltd., PO Box 294, Bussum, 1400 AG, Netherlands. TEL 31-35-6923800, FAX 31-35-6980150, sales@bentham.org, http://www.bentham.org. Eds. Atta-ur Rahman TEL 92-21-34824924, M Iqbal Choudhary.

615.19 NLD ISSN 1574-0889
FRONTIERS IN DRUG DESIGN AND DISCOVERY. Text in English. 2005. a. USD 190 per vol. (effective 2009). **Document type:** *Monographic series, Academic/Scholarly.* **Description:** Publishes the latest and most important advances in drug design and discovery.
Related titles: CD-ROM ed.; Online - full text ed.: ISSN 2212-1064 (from IngentaConnect).
Indexed: SCOPUS.
—BLDSC (4042.003200), Ingenta. **CCC.**
Published by: Bentham Science Publishers Ltd., PO Box 294, Bussum, 1400 AG, Netherlands. TEL 31-35-6923800, FAX 31-35-6980150, sales@bentham.org. Eds. Atta-ur Rahman TEL 92-21-34824924, Gary W Caldwell, Zhengyin Yan. **Subscr. to:** Bentham Science Publishers Ltd., c/o Richard E Morrissy, PO Box 446, Oak Park, IL 60301. TEL 312-413-5867, FAX 312-996-7107, subscriptions@bentham.org, morrissy@bentham.org.

FRONTIERS IN MEDICINAL CHEMISTRY. *see* MEDICAL SCIENCES

615 CHE ISSN 1663-9812
RS1
▼ **FRONTIERS IN PHARMACOLOGY.** Text in English. 2010. irreg. free (effective 2011). **Document type:** *Journal, Academic/Scholarly.*
Media: Online - full text.
Published by: Frontiers Research Foundation, Science Park PSE-A, Lausanne, 1015, Switzerland. TEL 41-21-6939202, FAX 41-21-6939201, info@frontiersin.org, http://frontiersin.org. Ed. Theophile Godfraind.

615 NLD ISSN 1568-5071
FTO-ONLINE. Text in Dutch. 2001. free to qualified personnel (effective 2011).
Media: Online - full text.
Published by: E-WISE Nederland b.v., Janssoniuslaan 38-40, Utrecht, 3528 AJ, Netherlands. TEL 31-30-2644100, FAX 31-30-2644199, informatie@e-wise.nl, http://www.e-wise.nl. Ed. Anneta Bits. Circ: 5,600.

615.6 610.5 CHN ISSN 1002-2600
R97.7.C5
FUJIAN YIYAO ZAZHI/FUJIAN MEDICAL JOURNAL. Text in Chinese. 1979. bi-m. USD 31.20 (effective 2009). adv. **Document type:** *Journal, Academic/Scholarly.* **Description:** Presents research results and developments in pharmacology and the medical sciences.
Related titles: Online - full text ed.
—East View.
Published by: Zhonghua Yixuehui, Fujian Fenhui, 7, 54-Lu, Fuzhou, 350001, China. **Dist. by:** China International Book Trading Corp, 35 Chegongzhuang Xilu, Haidian District, PO Box 399, Beijing 100044, China. TEL 86-10-68412045, FAX 86-10-68412023, cibtc@mail.cibtc.com.cn, http://www.cibtc.com.cn.

615 JPN ISSN 0913-1736
CODEN: FDYKES
FUKUOKA DAIGAKU YAKUGAKU KIYO/FUKUOKA UNIVERSITY. PHARMACEUTICAL BULLETIN. Text in English, Japanese; Summaries in English. 1963. a.
Indexed: ChemAb.
—CCC.
Published by: Fukuoka Daigaku, Sogo Kenkyusho/Fukuoka University, Central Research Institute, 19-1 Nanakuma 8-chome, Jonan-ku, Fukuoka-shi, 814-0133, Japan. TEL 81-92-8716631, FAX 81-92-8662308.

615 JPN
FUKUOKA-KEN BYOIN YAKUZAISHIKAI. IYAKUHIN JOHO/FUKUOKA SOCIETY OF HOSPITAL PHARMACIST. DRUG INFORMATION NEWS. Text in Japanese. 1965. q. membership. **Document type:** *Trade.*
Related titles: Online - full text ed.
Published by: Fukuoka-ken Byoin Yakuzaishikai/Fukuoka Society of Hospital Pharmacist, 2-20-15, Sumiyosi, Hakata-ku,, Fukuoka, 812-0018, Japan. TEL 81-92-2711585, FAX 81-92-2814104, info@fshp.jp, http://www.fshp.jp/.

615 JPN ISSN 0288-724X
FUKUYAMA DAIGAKU YAKUGAKUBU KENKYU NENPO/FUKUYAMA UNIVERSITY. FACULTY OF PHARMACY & PHARMACEUTICAL SCIENCES. ANNUAL REPORT. Text in English, Japanese; Summaries in English. 1982. a. **Document type:** *Report, Academic/Scholarly.*
Published by: Fukuyaka Daigaku, Yakugakubu/Fukuyama University, Faculty of Pharmacy and Pharmaceutical Sciences, 1 Gakuen-cho, Fukuyama, Hiroshima 729-0292, Japan. http://www.fukuyama-u.ac.jp/pharm/.

615.19 GBR ISSN 0767-3981
RM1 CODEN: FCPHEZ
➤ **FUNDAMENTAL AND CLINICAL PHARMACOLOGY.** Text in English. 1970. bi-m. GBP 674 in United Kingdom to institutions; EUR 857 in Europe to institutions; USD 1,243 in the Americas to institutions; USD 1,450 elsewhere to institutions; GBP 775 combined subscription in United Kingdom to institutions (print & online eds.); EUR 986 combined subscription in Europe to institutions (print & online eds.); USD 1,429 combined subscription in the Americas to institutions (print & online eds.); USD 1,668 combined subscription elsewhere to institutions (print & online eds.) (effective 2012). adv. bk.rev. index. back issues avail.; reprint service avail. from PSC. **Document type:** *Journal, Academic/Scholarly.* **Description:** Provides reports describing important and novel developments in fundamental as well as clinical research relevant to drug therapy.
Incorporates (in 1997): Archives Internationales de Pharmacodynamie et de Therapie (0003-9780); Which was formerly (1898 -1899): Archives Internationales de Pharmacodynamie (0301-4533); (until 1898): Archives de Pharmacodynamie (0770-1071)
Related titles: Microform ed.: (from PQC); Online - full text ed.: ISSN 1472-8206. GBP 674 in United Kingdom to institutions; EUR 857 in Europe to institutions; USD 1,243 in the Americas to institutions; USD 1,450 elsewhere to institutions (effective 2012) (from IngentaConnect); Supplement(s): Fundamental & Clinical Pharmacology. Supplement. ISSN 1744-3377.
Indexed: A01, A03, A08, A20, A22, A26, A29, A34, A36, ASCA, AnBeAb, B&BAb, B19, B20, B21, B25, BIOBASE, BIOSIS Prev, BP, C30, C33, CA, CABA, CIN, CIS, ChemAb, ChemTitl, CurCR, CurCont, D01, DBA, E01, E12, EMBASE, ESPM, ExcerpMed, F08, F11, F12, FR, GH, H12, H16, I10, IABS, ISR, IndChem, IndMed, Inpharma, MEDLINE, MycolAb, N02, N03, NSA, P30, P33, P35, P39, R08, R10, R12, R16, RA&MP, RM&VM, Reac, S01, SCI, SCOPUS, SoyAb, T02, T05, ToxAb, VS, VirolAbstr, W07.
—BLDSC (4056.033000), CASDDS, GNLM, IE, Infotrieve, Ingenta, INIST, Linda Hall. **CCC.**
Published by: (Societe Francaise de Pharmacologie et de Therapeutique FRA, Federation of European Pharmacological Societies FIN), Wiley-Blackwell Publishing Ltd. (Subsidiary of: John Wiley & Sons, Inc.), 9600 Garsington Rd, Oxford, OX4 2DQ, United Kingdom. TEL 44-1865-776868, FAX 44-1865-714591, customerservices@blackwellpublishing.com. Eds. Faiez Zannad TEL 33-3-83656620, Pascal Bousquet TEL 33-3-90243397.

▼➤ **FUTURE MEDICINAL CHEMISTRY.** *see* BIOLOGY—Biochemistry

615 GBR ISSN 1468-9871
FUTURE PRESCRIBER. Text in English. 1999. q. GBP 61 in United Kingdom to institutions; EUR 92 in Europe to institutions; USD 167 elsewhere to institutions; GBP 70 combined subscription in United Kingdom to institutions (print & online eds.); EUR 105 combined subscription in Europe to institutions (print & online eds.); USD 192 combined subscription elsewhere to institutions (print & online eds.) (effective 2012). **Document type:** *Magazine, Trade.*
Related titles: Online - full text ed.: ISSN 1931-2261. GBP 61 in United Kingdom to institutions; EUR 92 in Europe to institutions; USD 167 elsewhere to institutions (effective 2012); ◆ Supplement to: Prescriber. ISSN 0959-6682.
—IE. **CCC.**
Published by: John Wiley & Sons Ltd. (Subsidiary of: John Wiley & Sons, Inc.), The Atrium, Southern Gate, Chichester, West Sussex PO19 8SQ, United Kingdom. TEL 44-1243-779777, FAX 44-1243-775878, customer@wiley.co.uk, http://eu.wiley.com/WileyCDA/.

615 340 JPN
G M P REGULATIONS OF JAPAN. Text in English, Japanese. irreg., latest 2001. price varies. **Document type:** *Handbook/Manual/Guide, Trade.* **Description:** Covers G.M.P. provisions on drugs, sterile drug preparations, bulk pharmaceutical chemicals, medical devices, cosmetics and more.
Published by: (Japan. Ministry of Health and Welfare, Pharmaceutical Affairs Bureau, Inspection and Guidance Division), Yakuji Nippo Ltd., Kanda-Izumi-cho, Chiyoda-ku, Tokyo, 101-0024, Japan. TEL 81-3-3862-2141, FAX 81-3-5821-8757, shuppan@yakuji.co.jp, http://www.yakuji.co.jp/.

615 GBR ISSN 1476-4547
G M P REVIEW; analysing international pharmaceutical regulations. (Good Medical Practice) Text in English. 2002. q. GBP 175, EUR 315, USD 280 (effective 2009). back issues avail. **Document type:** *Journal, Trade.* **Description:** Dedicated to helping you understand and keep up with the often complex and jargon-riddled regulations what are introduced all the time from Brussels, the FDA and other agencies.
Indexed: I12.
—CCC.
Published by: Euromed Communications Ltd., Passfield Business Ctr, Lynchborough Rd, Passfield, Liphook, Hampshire GU30 7SB, United Kingdom. TEL 44-1428-752222, FAX 44-1428-752223, info@euromed.uk.com. Ed. Kate McCormick. Pub. Joe Ridge.

G M P TRENDS. (Good Manufacturing Practice) *see* BUSINESS AND ECONOMICS—Production Of Goods And Services

GAN YAKURI/JAPANESE JOURNAL OF OCULAR PHARMACOLOGY. *see* MEDICAL SCIENCES—Ophthalmology And Optometry

615.1 POL ISSN 1230-9923
GAZETA FARMACEUTYCZNA. Text in Polish. 1992. m. EUR 127 foreign (effective 2006). **Document type:** *Magazine, Trade.*
Published by: Wydawnictwo Kwadryga, ul Chelmska 19/21, Warsaw, 00724, Poland. TEL 48-22-8516668, FAX 48-22-5593565, gfarm@kwadryga.pl, http://www.kwadryga.pl. **Dist. by:** Ars Polona, Obroncow 25, Warsaw 03933, Poland. TEL 48-22-5098609, FAX 48-22-5098610, arspolona@arspolona.com.pl, http://www.arspolona.com.pl.

615 TUR ISSN 1015-9592
CODEN: GUEDE
➤ **GAZI UNIVERSITESI ECZACILIK FAKULTESI DERGISI/GAZI UNIVERSITY. FACULTY OF PHARMACY. JOURNAL.** Abbreviated title: G U E D E - J. Fac. Pharm. Gazi. Text in Turkish. 1984. s-a. USD 100. Index. **Document type:** *Journal, Academic/Scholarly.*
Indexed: B25, BIOSIS Prev, DBA, EMBASE, ExcerpMed, MycolAb, R10, Reac, SCOPUS.
—CASDDS, GNLM, IE, Ingenta.
Published by: Gazi Universitesi, Eczacilik Fakultesi/Gazi University, Faculty of Pharmacy, University Campus, Etiler - Ankara, 06330, Turkey. TEL 90-312-2023000, FAX 90-312-2235018, http://www.gazi.edu.tr/, http://www.pharmacy.gazi.edu.tr/. Ed. Dr. M. Fethi Sahin. Pub. Dr. Riza Ayhan.

615.1 JPN ISSN 0016-5980
CODEN: YAKUD5
GEKKAN YAKUJI/PHARMACEUTICALS MONTHLY. Text in Japanese. 1959. m. JPY 22,680 (effective 2005). adv. bk.rev. abstr. index. **Description:** Developments in medical treatment.
Related titles: Online - full text ed.
Indexed: CIN, ChemAb, ChemTitl.
—BLDSC (6444.390000), CASDDS.
Published by: (Yakugyo Jihosha/Pharmaceutical Research Association), Jiho, Inc., Hitotsubashi Bldg. 5F, Hitotsubashi 2-6-3, Chiyoda-ku, Tokyo, 101-8421, Japan. TEL 81-3-32657751, FAX 81-3-32657769, pj@jiho.co.jp. Circ: 14,400. **Subscr. to:** ORIOX Japan, Ltd., 3-4-25, Shimomeguro, Meguro-ku, Tokyo 153-0064, Japan. TEL 81-3-3792-5600, FAX 81-3-3792-7500, orioxj@gol.com.

615 DEU ISSN 1616-198X
GELBE LISTE IDENTA. Text in German. 1979. a. **Document type:** *Directory, Trade.*
Formerly (until 1998): Pharmazeutika-Bestimmungsliste (0171-6255)
Published by: Medizinische Medien Informations GmbH, Am Forsthaus Gravenbruch 7, Neu-Isenburg, 63263, Germany. TEL 49-6102-5020, FAX 49-6102-502243, info@mmi.de, http://www.mmi.de.

615.19 DEU ISSN 0942-2951
GELBE LISTE PHARMINDEX. Text in German. 1971. q. EUR 32 newsstand/cover (effective 2007). adv. **Document type:** *Directory, Trade.*
Formerly (until 1992): Liste Pharmindex (0344-015X)
—GNLM.
Published by: Medizinische Medien Informations GmbH, Am Forsthaus Gravenbruch 7, Neu-Isenburg, 63263, Germany. TEL 49-6102-5020, FAX 49-6102-502243, http://www.mmi.de. adv.: B&W page EUR 8,200, color page EUR 10,480; trim 148 x 225. Circ: 43,000 (paid and controlled).

615.26 DEU ISSN 0942-3117
GELBE LISTE PHARMINDEX. DERMATOLOGEN. Text in German. 1985. s-a. adv. **Document type:** *Magazine, Trade.*
Former titles (until 1992): Die Liste Pharmindex. Dermatologen-Ausgabe (0933-727X); (until 198?): Die Liste Pharmindex. Dermatologika (0177-2341)
Published by: Medizinische Medien Informations GmbH, Am Forsthaus Gravenbruch 7, Neu-Isenburg, 63263, Germany. TEL 49-6102-5020, FAX 49-6102-502243, info@mmi.de, http://www.mmi.de. adv.: B&W page EUR 5,400, color page EUR 6,690.

615.25 DEU ISSN 0942-3125
GELBE LISTE PHARMINDEX. GYNAEKOLOGEN. Text in German. 1983. a. adv. **Document type:** *Magazine, Trade.*
Former titles (until 1992): Die Liste Pharmindex. Gynaekologen-Ausgabe (0936-2312); (until 1989): Die Liste Pharmindex. Gynaekologika (0724-3480)
Published by: Medizinische Medien Informations GmbH, Am Forsthaus Gravenbruch 7, Neu-Isenburg, 63263, Germany. TEL 49-6102-5020, FAX 49-6102-502243, info@mmi.de, http://www.mmi.de. adv.: B&W page EUR 6,100, color page EUR 7,390. Circ: 9,000 (controlled).

615.23 DEU ISSN 0942-3133
GELBE LISTE PHARMINDEX. H N O-AERZTE. (Hals-Nasen-Ohren) Text in German. 1985. a. adv. **Document type:** *Directory, Trade.*
Formerly (until 1992): Die Liste Pharmindex. H N O Ausgabe (0177-2333)
Published by: Medizinische Medien Informations GmbH, Am Forsthaus Gravenbruch 7, Neu-Isenburg, 63263, Germany. TEL 49-6102-5020, FAX 49-6102-502243, info@mmi.de, http://www.mmi.de. adv.: B&W page EUR 5,400, color page EUR 6,690. Circ: 3,600 (paid and controlled).

615 DEU ISSN 1431-6072
GELBE LISTE PHARMINDEX. INTERNISTEN. Text in German. 199?. a. **Document type:** *Directory, Trade.*
Published by: Medizinische Medien Informations GmbH, Am Forsthaus Gravenbruch 7, Neu-Isenburg, 63263, Germany. TEL 49-6102-5020, FAX 49-6102-502243, info@mmi.de, http://www.mmi.de.

615.214 DEU ISSN 0942-3141
GELBE LISTE PHARMINDEX. NEUROLOGEN, PSYCHIATER. Text in German. 1984. 2/yr. adv. **Document type:** *Directory, Trade.*
Former titles (until 1992): Die Liste Pharmindex. Neurologen-, Psychiater-Ausgabe (0940-1261); (until 1991): Die Liste Pharmindex. Neurologen-Ausgabe (0936-2320); (until 1989): Die Liste Pharmindex. Neurologika (0175-5722)
Published by: Medizinische Medien Informations GmbH, Am Forsthaus Gravenbruch 7, Neu-Isenburg, 63263, Germany. TEL 49-6102-5020, FAX 49-6102-502243, info@mmi.de, http://www.mmi.de. adv.: B&W page EUR 5,500, color page EUR 6,790. Circ: 4,200 (paid and controlled).

615.457 DEU ISSN 0942-3168
GELBE LISTE PHARMINDEX. OPHTHALMOLOGEN. Text in German. 197?. a. EUR 13 (effective 2007). adv. **Document type:** *Directory, Trade.*
Former titles (until 1992): Die Liste Pharmindex. Ophthalmologen-Ausgabe (0936-2339); (until 1990): Die Liste Pharmindex. Ophthalmica (0171-0729)
Published by: Medizinische Medien Informations GmbH, Am Forsthaus Gravenbruch 7, Neu-Isenburg, 63263, Germany. TEL 49-6102-5020, FAX 49-6102-502243, info@mmi.de, http://www.mmi.de. adv.: B&W page EUR 5,500, color page EUR 6,790. Circ: 5,800 (paid and controlled).

615 DEU ISSN 0942-3176
GELBE LISTE PHARMINDEX. ORTHOPAEDEN. Text in German. 1984. a. EUR 15 (effective 2007). adv. **Document type:** *Directory, Trade.*
Former titles (until 1992): Die Liste Pharmindex. Orthopaeden-Ausgabe (0936-2347); (until 1989): Die Liste Pharmindex. Orthopaedika (0176-7372)
Published by: Medizinische Medien Informations GmbH, Am Forsthaus Gravenbruch 7, Neu-Isenburg, 63263, Germany. TEL 49-6102-5020, FAX 49-6102-502243, info@mmi.de, http://www.mmi.de. adv.: B&W page EUR 5,500, color page EUR 6,790. Circ: 5,000 (controlled).

615.2 DEU ISSN 0942-3184
GELBE LISTE PHARMINDEX. PAEDIATER. Text in German. 1984. a. EUR 15 (effective 2007). adv. **Document type:** *Directory, Trade.*
Formerly (until 1992): Die Liste Pharmindex. Paediater-Ausgabe (0176-7380)
Published by: Medizinische Medien Informations GmbH, Am Forsthaus Gravenbruch 7, Neu-Isenburg, 63263, Germany. TEL 49-6102-5020, FAX 49-6102-502243, info@mmi.de, http://www.mmi.de. adv.: B&W page EUR 5,500, color page EUR 6,790. Circ: 6,000 (paid and controlled).

615 DEU ISSN 0942-3192
GELBE LISTE PHARMINDEX. PHYTOPHARMAKA UND HOMOEOPATHIKA. Text in German. 1990. a. adv. **Document type:** *Journal, Trade.*
Formerly (until 1992): Die Liste Pharmindex. Phytopharmaka und Pflanzliche Kombinationspraeparate (0938-9725)
Published by: Medizinische Medien Informations GmbH, Am Forsthaus Gravenbruch 7, Neu-Isenburg, 63263, Germany. TEL 49-6102-5020, FAX 49-6102-502243, info@mmi.de. adv.: B&W page EUR 6,100, color page EUR 7,390. Circ: 15,000 (controlled).

P

615 DEU ISSN 0942-315X
GELBE LISTE PHARMINDEX. UROLOGEN. Text in German. 1985. a. EUR 15 (effective 2005). adv. **Document type:** *Directory, Trade.*
Former titles (until 1992): Die Liste Pharmindex. Urologen-Ausgabe (0936-2355); (until 1990): Die Liste Pharmindex. Urologika (0177-2325)
Published by: Medizinische Medien Informations GmbH, Am Forsthaus Gravenbruch 7, Neu-Isenburg, 63263, Germany. TEL 49-6102-5020, FAX 49-6102-502243, info@mmi.de, http://www.mmi.de. adv.: B&W page EUR 5,400, color page EUR 6,690. Circ: 2,700 (paid and controlled).

615 DEU ISSN 1436-1906
GELBE LISTE VADEMECUM. Text in German. 1997. a. EUR 13 (effective 2007). adv. **Document type:** *Directory, Trade.*
Published by: Medizinische Medien Informations GmbH, Am Forsthaus Gravenbruch 7, Neu-Isenburg, 63263, Germany. TEL 49-6102-5020, FAX 49-6102-502243, info@mmi.de, http://www.mmi.de. adv.: B&W page EUR 5,500, color page EUR 6,790. Circ: 5,600 (controlled).

GENDER MEDICINE. *see* MEDICAL SCIENCES

615 618.2 613.04244 NLD ISSN 1871-0239
GENEESMIDDELEN, ZWANGERSCHAP EN BORSTVOEDING. Text in Dutch. 2000. irreg., latest vol.4, 2007. EUR 30 per issue (effective 2010).
Published by: (Netherlands. Rijksinstituut voor Volksgezondheid en Milieu), Stichting Health Base, De Molen 43, Houten, 3994 DA, Netherlands. TEL 31-30-6355150, FAX 31-30-6355155, info@healthbase.nl, http://www.healthbase.nl.

615 NLD ISSN 0304-4629
CODEN: GNMBA
➤ **GENEESMIDDELENBULLETIN.** Text in Dutch. 1967. m. free to qualified personnel (effective 2010). 10-year index. 12 p./no. 2 cols./p.; back issues avail. **Document type:** *Journal, Academic/Scholarly.*
Related titles: Online - full text ed.; ◆ Supplement to: Medisch Contact. ISSN 0025-8245.
Indexed: A22, EMBASE, ExcerpMed, R10, Reac, SCOPUS.
—BLDSC (4096.468000), GNLM, IE, Infotrieve, Ingenta.
Published by: Stichting Geneesmiddelenbulletin, College voor Zorgverzekeringen, Postbus 320, Diemen, 1110 AH, Netherlands. TEL 31-20-7978555, FAX 31-20-7978500.

615 NLD ISSN 2210-9536
GENEESMIDDELENWET. Text in Dutch. 2006. a. EUR 46.23 (effective 2010).
Published by: Sdu Uitgevers bv, Postbus 20025, The Hague, 2500 EA, Netherlands. TEL 31-70-3789911, FAX 31-70-3854321, sdu@sdu.nl, http://www.sdu.nl/.

615 GBR ISSN 1746-7829
GENERIC COMPANIES ANALYSIS. Abbreviated title: G C A. Text in English. 2005. q. GBP 1,025, USD 1,950, EUR 1,540; GBP 995, USD 1,995, EUR 1,695 combined subscription (print & online eds.) (effective 2009). **Document type:** *Journal, Trade.* **Description:** Contains facts, figures and statistics, providing thorough ongoing monitoring of the important generic companies.
Media: Online - full text. **Related titles:** Print ed.: ISSN 1746-7810.
Published by: Espicom Business Intelligence, Lincoln House, City Fields Business Park, City Fields Way, Chichester, W Sussex PO20 2FS, United Kingdom. TEL 44-1243-533322, FAX 44-1243-533418, Annette_Bulbeck@espicom.com, http://www.espicom.com. **Subscr. in the US to:** Espicom USA Inc.

615.1 332.6 USA ISSN 1076-884X
GENERIC LINE. Text in English. 1984. bi-w. USD 897 (print or online ed.); USD 1,435 combined subscription (print & online eds.) (effective 2009). 8 p./no.; back issues avail. **Document type:** *Newsletter, Trade.* **Description:** Aims at business leaders in the generic drug industry. Covers business, FDA and Congressional actions.
Related titles: Online - full text ed.: USD 747 (effective 2005).
—CCC.
Published by: Washington Business Information, Inc., 300 N Washington St, Ste 200, Falls Church, VA 22046. customerservice@fdanews.com. Ed. Elizabeth Jones TEL 703-538-7661. Pub. Matt Salt TEL 703-538-7642.

615.1 USA
GENERIC RX PRODUCT REPORT. Text in English. 200?. q. free with subscr. to Pharmacy Times.
Related titles: ◆ Supplement to: Pharmacy Times. ISSN 0003-0627.
Published by: Ascend Media (Subsidiary of: B N P Media), 7015 College Blvd, Ste 600, Overland Park, KS 66211. TEL 913-469-1110, FAX 913-469-0806, info@ascendmedia.com, http://www.ascendmedia.com.

615 GBR ISSN 1742-0784
GENERICS BULLETIN; the business newsletter for the generic medicines industry. Text in English. 2003 (Nov.). 20/yr. GBP 495 in Europe; GBP 525 elsewhere; GBP 50 per issue (effective 2010); includes News@Genericsbulletin. **Document type:** *Bulletin, Trade.* **Description:** Provides a single source of accurate, regular and reliable commercial and regulatory information for the global generics industry.
Related titles: Supplement(s): News@Genericsbulletin.
Indexed: EMBASE, ExcerpMed.
—CCC.
Published by: Bulletin Publishing Group (Subsidiary of: O T C Publications Ltd.), 54 Creynolds Ln, Solihull, W Mids B90 4ER, United Kingdom. TEL 44-1564-777550, FAX 44-1564-777524.

615.1 DEU ISSN 0939-334X
GESCHICHTE DER PHARMAZIE. Text in German. 1948. q. EUR 36; EUR 16 newsstand/cover (effective 2012); free with subscr. to Deutsche Apotheker Zeitung. bk.rev. illus. index. **Document type:** *Journal, Trade.*
Former titles: Beitraege zur Geschichte der Pharmazie (0341-0099); Zur Geschichte der Pharmazie (0044-5509)
Related titles: ◆ Supplement to: Deutsche Apotheker Zeitung. ISSN 0011-9857.
Indexed: IBR, IBZ.
—BLDSC (4162.518000), GNLM.
Published by: (Deutsche Gesellschaft fuer Geschichte der Pharmazie), Deutscher Apotheker Verlag, Postfach 101061, Stuttgart, 70009, Germany. TEL 49-711-25820, FAX 49-711-2582290, http://www.deutscher-apotheker-verlag.de. Ed. Wolf-Dieter Mueller-Jahncke.

615 JPN ISSN 0285-1458
GINKAI. Text in Japanese. 1964. m. JPY 500 per issue. adv. **Document type:** *Consumer.*
Published by: Senju Seiyaku K.K./Senju Pharmaceutical Co., Ltd., 2-5-8, Hirano-machi, Chuo-ku, Osaka-shi, 541-0046, Japan. TEL 81-6-62012512, FAX 81-6-62260406, http://www.senju.co.jp/.

615.19 ITA ISSN 0393-8476
IL GIORNALE DEL FARMACISTA. Abbreviated title: G d F. Text in Italian. 1986. fortn. EUR 57 per issue (effective 2009). **Document type:** *Magazine, Trade.*
Indexed: SCOPUS.
Published by: Elsevier Masson (Subsidiary of: Elsevier Health Sciences), Via Paleocapa 7, Milan, 20121, Italy. TEL 39-02-881841, FAX 39-02-88184302, info@masson.it, http://www.masson.it. Circ: 15,000.

GIORNALE DI NEUROPSICOFARMACOLOGIA. *see* MEDICAL SCIENCES—Psychiatry And Neurology

615 ITA ISSN 1120-3749
GIORNALE ITALIANO DI FARMACIA CLINICA; epidemiologia - informazione - ricerca. Text in Italian; Summaries in English. 1987. 4/yr. EUR 130 domestic to institutions; EUR 200 foreign to institutions (effective 2009). bk.rev. bibl. 64 p./no.; **Document type:** *Journal, Academic/Scholarly.*
Indexed: EMBASE, ExcerpMed, I12, R10, Reac, SCOPUS.
—BLDSC (4178.215500), GNLM, IE, Ingenta.
Published by: (Societa Italiana di Farmacia Ospedaliera), Il Pensiero Scientifico Editore, Via Bradano 3-C, Rome, 00199, Italy. TEL 39-06-862821, FAX 39-06-86282250, pensiero@pensiero.it, http://www.pensiero.it.

615 ITA ISSN 1974-4633
GIORNALE ITALIANO DI FARMACOECONOMIA E FARMACOUTILIZZAZIONE. Text in Multiple languages. 2008. 3/yr. **Document type:** *Journal, Academic/Scholarly.*
Published by: Elsevier Masson (Subsidiary of: Elsevier Health Sciences), Via Paleocapa 7, Milan, 20121, Italy. TEL 39-02-881841, FAX 39-02-88184302, info@masson.it, http://www.masson.it.

GLOBAL COSMETIC INDUSTRY. *see* BEAUTY CULTURE—Perfumes And Cosmetics

615.9 616.1 BRA ISSN 1414-0330
GLOSSARIUM CARDIOLOGIA. Text in Portuguese. 1993. a. adv. back issues avail. **Document type:** *Magazine, Trade.* **Description:** Provides dosing and administration information, along with indications and contraindications for heart medications.
Published by: Elea Ciencia Editorial Ltda., Rua Barao de Uba 48, Rio de Janeiro, RJ 20260-050, Brazil. TEL 55-21-2932112, FAX 55-21-2937818. Ed. Luiz Augusto Rodrigues. Adv. contact Alexandre Augusto Rodrigues. Circ: 6,000.

615.9 616.5 BRA ISSN 1414-0349
GLOSSARIUM DERMATOLOGIA. Text in Portuguese. 1995. a. adv. back issues avail. **Document type:** *Trade.* **Description:** Compiles dosing and administration information, along with indications and contraindications for skin-treatment medications.
Published by: Elea Ciencia Editorial Ltda., Rua Barao de Uba 48, Rio de Janeiro, RJ 20260-050, Brazil. TEL 55-21-2932112, FAX 55-21-2937818. Ed. Luiz Augusto Rodrigues. Adv. contact Alexandre Augusto Rodrigues. Circ: 4,500.

615.9 616.99 BRA ISSN 1414-0284
GLOSSARIUM ONCOLOGIA. Text in Portuguese. 1995. a. adv. back issues avail. **Document type:** *Magazine, Trade.* **Description:** Supplies dosing and administration, along with indications and contraindications for cancer medications.
Published by: Elea Ciencia Editorial Ltda., Rua Barao de Uba 48, Rio de Janeiro, RJ 20260-050, Brazil. TEL 55-21-2932112, FAX 55-21-2937818. Ed. Luiz Augusto Rodrigues. Adv. contact Alexandre Augusto Rodrigues.

615 USA ISSN 1530-6194
CODEN: QUCRB6
THE GOLD SHEET; pharmaceutical & biotechnology quality control. Text in English. 1967. m. looseleaf. USD 1,000 in United States to institutions; USD 1,000 elsewhere to institutions (effective 2012). adv. back issues avail.; reprints avail. **Document type:** *Journal, Trade.* **Description:** Focuses on important changes in the FDA's policies for regulating good manufacturing practices for pharmaceutical companies and their suppliers.
Formerly (until 1999): Quality Control Reports: The Gold Sheet (0163-2418)
Related titles: Diskette ed.; Online - full text ed.
Indexed: P48, P53, P54, PNI, PQC.
—BLDSC (3901.327000). **CCC.**
Published by: Elsevier Business Intelligence (Subsidiary of: Elsevier Health Sciences), 5635 Fishers Ln, Ste 6000, Rockville, MD 20852. TEL 800-332-2181, FAX 240-221-4400, http://www.fdcreports.com. Eds. William Paulson, Michael McCaughan. R&P Laura Desimio.

GREAT BRITAIN. LABORATORY OF THE GOVERNMENT CHEMIST. REPORT AND ACCOUNTS. *see* BUSINESS AND ECONOMICS—Accounting

615.1 USA ISSN 1530-6208
CODEN: WPHRAR
THE GREEN SHEET (CHEVY CHASE). Text in English. 1951. 51/yr. looseleaf. USD 225 to institutions (effective 2010). back issues avail.; reprints avail. **Document type:** *Journal, Trade.* **Description:** Presents news and information on the pharmacy profession and the pharmaceutical distribution system. Covers professional policy, pharmacy association activities, reimbursement issues, new drug introductions and pharmaceutical pricing and deals.
Former titles (until 2000): Weekly Pharmacy Reports: The Green Sheet (0043-1893); Which incorporated (in 1968): Drug News Weekly; (until 1957): F D C Drug Letter
Related titles: Online - full text ed.
Indexed: P48, P53, P54, PNI, PQC.
—CCC.
Published by: Elsevier Business Intelligence (Subsidiary of: Elsevier Health Sciences), 5550 Friendship Blvd, Ste One, Chevy Chase, MD 20815-7278. TEL 301-657-9830, 800-332-2181, FAX 301-656-3094, http://www.fdcreports.com. Ed. Scott Steinke. R&P Michael Keville. Adv. contact Ken May.

615 DEU
DIE GROSSE REISEAPOTHEKE. Text in German. a. EUR 2.50 per issue (effective 2006). adv. **Document type:** *Magazine, Consumer.*
Published by: Media Dialog Verlag, Am Bahndamm 2, Ortenberg, 63683, Germany. TEL 49-6041-823390, FAX 49-6041-8233920, info@media-dialog.com, http://www.media-dialog.com. adv.: page EUR 9,800.

615 CHN ISSN 1006-8783
GUANGDONG YAOXUEYUAN XUEBAO/ACADEMIC JOURNAL OF GUANGDONG COLLEGE OF PHARMACY. Text in Chinese. 1985. bi-m. USD 24.60 (effective 2009). **Document type:** *Journal, Academic/Scholarly.*
Formerly (until 1994): Guangdong Yiyao Xueyuan Xuebao/Academic Journal of Guangdong Medical and Pharmaceutical College (1005-2607)
Related titles: Online - full text ed.
—BLDSC (0570.511591), East View.
Published by: Guangdong Yaoxueyuan/Guangdong College of Pharmacy, 40, Guanghanzhi Jie, Haizhu-qu, Guangzhou, 510240, China. TEL 86-20-39352063, FAX 86-20-39352065. **Dist. by:** China International Book Trading Corp, 35 Chegongzhuang Xilu, Haidian District, PO Box 399, Beijing 100044, China. TEL 86-10-68412045, FAX 86-10-68412023, cibtc@mail.cibtc.com.cn, http://www.cibtc.com.cn.

615 CHN ISSN 1000-8535
R97.7.C5
GUANGZHOU YIYAO/GUANGZHOU MEDICAL JOURNAL. Text in Chinese. 1970. bi-m. CNY 36 (effective 2009). **Document type:** *Journal, Academic/Scholarly.*
Formerly (until 1981): Xin Yiyao Tongxun
Related titles: Online - full text ed.
—BLDSC (4223.859780).
Published by: Guangzhou Weisheng Jishu Jianding he Pinggu Zhongxin, Xihua Lu 534, 536, Guangzhou, 510170, China. TEL 86-20-81088143. Ed. Shufeng Yan. **Dist. by:** China International Book Trading Corp, 35 Chegongzhuang Xilu, Haidian District, PO Box 399, Beijing 100044, China. TEL 86-10-68412045, FAX 86-10-68412023, cibtc@mail.cibtc.com.cn, http://www.cibtc.com.cn.

615 ESP ISSN 1576-1533
GUIA PUNTEX. ANUARIO ESPANOL DE E F P Y PARAFARMACIA. (Especialidades Farmaceuticas y Publicitarias) Text in Spanish. 1984. a. EUR 110 domestic; EUR 139 in Europe; EUR 171 elsewhere (effective 2007). adv. back issues avail. **Document type:** *Directory, Trade.*
Former titles (until 1997): Guia Puntex. Vademecum Espanol de E F P y Para-Farmarcia (1576-2858); (until 1996): Guia Puntex. Anuario Espanol de Especialidades Farmaceuticas Publicitarias y Para-Farmacia (1576-284X); (until 1994): Guia Puntex. Vedemecum Espanol de Especialidades Farmaceuticas Publicitarias y Para-Farmacia (1576-2823); (until 1992): Guia Puntex. Anuario Espanol de Especialidades Farmaceuticas Publicitarias y Para-Farmacia (1576-1525); (until 1987): Guia Puntex. Anuario Espanol de Para-Farmacia (1576-1517)
Published by: Publicaciones Nacionales Tecnicas y Extranjeras (PUNTEX), Padilla 323, Barcelona, 08025, Spain. TEL 34-934-462820, FAX 34-934-462064, puntex@puntex.es, http://www.puntex.es. Ed. Martin Yolanda. adv.: color page EUR 2,770; 170 x 240. Circ: 20,000.

GUIDE TO FEDERAL PHARMACY LAW. *see* LAW—Corporate Law

615 USA ISSN 1098-0539
RM301.27
➤ **GUINEA PIG ZERO**; a journal for human research subjects. Abbreviated title: G P Z. Text in English. 1996. irreg., latest vol.8. USD 14.95 newsstand/cover (effective 2011). bk.rev.; film rev.; play rev.; tel.rev.; video rev. illus.; maps; tr.mk. back issues avail. **Document type:** *Journal, Academic/Scholarly.* **Description:** Serves as an occupational jobzine for people who are used as medical or pharmaceutical research subjects. Various sections are devoted to bioethics, historical facts, current news and research, evaluations of particular research facilities by volunteers, and true stories of guinea pig adventures.
Address: PO Box 42531, Philadelphia, PA 19101. Ed. Robert Helms.

615 CHN ISSN 1674-0440
GUOJI YAOXUE YANJIU ZAZHI/INTERNATIONAL JOURNAL OF PHARMACEUTICAL RESEARCH. Text in Chinese. 1958. bi-m. USD 31.20 (effective 2009). **Document type:** *Journal, Academic/Scholarly.*
Formerly: Guowai Yixue (Yaoxue Fence)/Foreign Medical Sciences (Pharmacy) (1001-0971)
Related titles: Online - full text ed.
Indexed: A35, A36, AgBio, B&BAb, B20, B21, CABA, D01, E12, ESPM, F08, F11, F12, GH, H16, ImmunAb, N02, N03, P32, P33, RA&MP, RM&VM, S12, SCOPUS.
—BLDSC (3987.039920), East View, IE.
Published by: Junshi Yixue Kexueyuan, Duwu Yaowu Jianjiusuo/Military Academy of Medical Sciences, Institute of Poisonous and Medical Substances, 27 Taiping Lu, Beijing, 100850, China. TEL 86-10-66931618. **Dist. by:** China International Book Trading Corp, 35 Chegongzhuang Xilu, Haidian District, PO Box 399, Beijing 100044, China. TEL 86-10-68412045, FAX 86-10-68412023, cibtc@mail.cibtc.com.cn, http://www.cibtc.com.cn.

615.329 CHN ISSN 1001-8751
GUOWAI YIYAO (KANGSHENGSU FENCE)/WORLD NOTES ON ANTIBIOTICS. Text in Chinese. 1980. bi-m. USD 24.60 (effective 2009). bk.rev. 48 p./no.; **Document type:** *Journal, Academic/Scholarly.*
Related titles: Online - full text ed.
Indexed: B20, B21, ESPM, ImmunAb.
—BLDSC (9356.825000), East View.
Published by: Sichuan Kangjunsu Gongye Yanjiusuo/Sichuan Industrial Institute of Antibiotics, 20, Shanbanqiao Lu, Chengdu, Sichuan 610051, China. TEL 86-28-84363651, FAX 86-28-84363651. **Dist. by:** China International Book Trading Corp, 35 Chegongzhuang Xilu, Haidian District, PO Box 399, Beijing 100044, China. TEL 86-10-68412045, FAX 86-10-68412023, cibtc@mail.cibtc.com.cn, http://www.cibtc.com.cn.

615 615.5 CHN ISSN 1002-1078
GUOYI LUNTAN/FORUM ON TRADITIONAL CHINESE MEDICINE. Text in Chinese. 1986. bi-m. USD 14.40 (effective 2009). **Document type:** *Journal, Academic/Scholarly.*
Related titles: Online - full text ed.
—BLDSC (4232.148700), East View.
Published by: Henan Sheng Nanyang Zhongyao Xuexiao, 1439, Wolong Lu, Nanyang, 473061, China. TEL 86-377-3529058, FAX 86-377-3529580. **Dist. by:** China International Book Trading Corp, 35 Chegongzhuang Xilu, Haidian District, PO Box 399, Beijing 100044, China. TEL 86-10-68412045, FAX 86-10-68412023, cibtc@mail.cibtc.com.cn, http://www.cibtc.com.cn.

615.7 DEU ISSN 1861-6046
GUTE PILLEN - SCHLECHTE PILLEN; unabhaengige Informationen zu Ihrer Gesundheit. Text in German. 2005. bi-m. EUR 15 to individuals; EUR 30 to institutions (effective 2010). **Document type:** *Magazine, Trade.* **Description:** Reports on the effects and efficacy of various drugs and pharmacological agents.
Address: August-Bebel-Str 62, Bielefeld, 33602, Germany. FAX 49-521-63789, GPSP@bukopharma.de. Ed. Christian Wagner. **Subscr. to:** Westkreuz Verlag GmbH Berlin-Bonn, Toepchiner Weg 198-200, Berlin 12309, Germany. TEL 49-30-7452047, FAX 49-30-7453066.

615 HUN ISSN 1787-1204
GYOGYSZEREINK, O G Y I KOZLEMENYEK. Text in Hungarian. 2005. m. **Document type:** *Journal, Academic/Scholarly.*
Formed by the merger of (1976-2004): O G Y I Kozlemenyek (0231-4398); (1950-2004): Gyszereink (0434-9784)
Indexed: P30.
Published by: Orszagos Gyogyszereszeti Intezet/National Institute of Pharmacy, Zrinyi u 3, Budapest, 1051, Hungary. http://www.ogyi.hu.

615.1 HUN ISSN 0017-6036
CODEN: GYOGAI
GYOGYSZERESZET. Text in Hungarian; Summaries in English, German, Russian. 1957. m. USD 130 foreign (effective 2008). adv. bk.rev. abstr. index.
Related titles: Online - full text ed.: 1957.
Indexed: A22, CIN, ChemAb, ChemTitl, IndMed, P30, SCOPUS.
—BLDSC (4233.900000), CASDDS, GNLM, IE, Ingenta, INIST, Linda Hall.
Published by: Magyar Gyogyszereszetudomanyi Tarsasag/Hungarian Pharmaceutical Association, Gyulai Pal u 16, Budapest, 1085, Hungary. TEL 36-1-4831466, titkarsag@mgyt.hu, http://www.mgyt.hu. Circ: 2,330.

H M E BUSINESS. *see* MEDICAL SCIENCES

615 JPN ISSN 0917-1681
H O P NYUSU/HOKKAIDO HOSPITAL PHARMACISTS' NEWSLETTER. Text in Japanese. 1990. s-a. JPY 11,500 membership (effective 2007). **Document type:** *Newsletter, Academic/Scholarly.*
Published by: Hokkaido Byoin Yakuzaishikai/Hokkaido Society of Hospital Pharmacists, Sapporo Medical University Hospital, Department of Pharmacy, 291 Nishi 16-chome, Minami 1-jo, Chuo-ku, Sapporo, Hokkaido 060-8543, Japan. TEL 81-11-6112111 ext 3598, 5599, FAX 81-11-6152524, hokubyo@doyaku.or.jp, http://www.doyaku.or.jp/hokubyo/index.html.

615 TUR ISSN 1300-0608
HACETTEPE UNIVERSITESI. ECZACILIK FAKULTESI. DERGISI/ HACETTEPE UNIVERSITTY. FACULTY OF PHARMACY. JOURNAL. Text in Turkish. 1986. s-a. **Document type:** *Journal, Academic/Scholarly.*
Related titles: English ed.
Indexed: EMBASE, ExcerpMed, SCOPUS.
—BLDSC (4237.437900), IE.
Published by: Hacettepe Universitesi, Eczacilik Fakultesi, c/o A. Ahmet Basaran, Hacettepe Universitesi Hastaneleri Basimevi, Sihhiye - Ankara, 06100, Turkey. TEL 90-312-3109790, eczder@hacettepe.edu.tr, basimevi@hacettepe.edu.tr. Pub. Dr. A Ahmet Basaran.

615 CHN ISSN 1001-8131
HA'ERBIN YIYAO/HA'ERBIN MEDICAL JOURNAL. Text in Chinese. 1960. bi-m. **Document type:** *Journal, Academic/Scholarly.*
Formerly (until 1978): Ha'erbin Xinyiyao
Related titles: Online - full text ed.
—BLDSC (4238.096600).
Published by: Harbin Shi Yixuehui/Harbin Medical Association, 12, Minan Jie, Daoli-qu, Ha'erbin, 150067, China. TEL 86-451-83080757. **Dist. by:** China International Book Trading Corp, 35 Chegongzhuang Xilu, Haidian District, PO Box 399, Beijing 100044, China. TEL 86-10-68412045, FAX 86-10-68412023, cibtc@mail.cibtc.com.cn, http://www.cibtc.com.cn.

615 CHN ISSN 1006-3765
HAIXIA YAOXUE/STRAIT PHARMACEUTICAL JOURNAL. Text in Chinese. 1988. m. CNY 8 newsstand/cover (effective 2008). **Document type:** *Journal, Academic/Scholarly.*
Related titles: Online - full text ed.
—BLDSC (4238.306550).
Published by: Zhongguo Yaoxuehui, Fujian, 330 Tonghu Rd, Fuzhou, 350001, China. TEL 86-591-87663829, FAX 86-591-87663714.

615.19 USA ISSN 0171-2004
QP905 CODEN: HEPHD2
HANDBOOK OF EXPERIMENTAL PHARMACOLOGY. Text in English. 1950. irreg., latest vol.199, 2010. price varies. back issues avail.; reprints avail. **Document type:** *Monographic series, Academic/ Scholarly.* **Description:** Provides discussions of the significant areas of pharmacological research, written by international authorities.
Formerly (until 1978): Handbuch der Experimentellen Pharmakologie (0073-0033)
Related titles: Online - full text ed.
Indexed: A22, CIN, ChemAb, ChemTitl, EMBASE, ExcerpMed, MEDLINE, P30, R10, Reac, SCOPUS.
—BLDSC (4250.460000), CASDDS, IE, Ingenta, INIST. **CCC.**
Published by: Springer New York LLC (Subsidiary of: Springer Science+Business Media), 233 Spring St, New York, NY 10013. TEL 212-460-1500, FAX 212-460-1575, service-ny@springer.com. Ed. Franz B Hofmann.

615 CAN ISSN 1912-3531
HANDBOOK OF LIMITED USE DRUG PRODUCTS. Text in English. 2003. irreg. **Document type:** *Handbook/Manual/Guide, Trade.*
Published by: Ontario, Ministry of Health and Long-Term Care, Ste M1-57, Macdonald Block, 900 Bay St, Toronto, ON M7A 1N3, Canada. TEL 800-268-1154, FAX 416-314-8721.

615 USA ISSN 0889-7816
RS250
HANDBOOK OF NON-PRESCRIPTION DRUGS. Text in English. 1967. irreg., latest 16th ed. USD 159.95 per issue to non-members; USD 144 per issue to members (effective 2009). back issues avail. **Document type:** *Monographic series, Trade.* **Description:** Contains information on nonprescription drug pharmacotherapy, nutritional supplements, medical foods, non-drug and preventive measures, and complementary and alternative therapies.
—CCC.
Published by: American Pharmacists Association, 2215 Constitution Ave, NW, Washington, DC 20037. TEL 202-628-4410, FAX 202-783-2351, InfoCenter@aphanet.org, http://www.japha.org. Ed. Rosemary R Berardi.

614 ISR ISSN 0793-7407
HANDBOOK OF PHARMACEUTICAL GENERIC DEVELOPMENT. Text in English. 1997. a., latest 2008, 8th ed. **Document type:** *Directory, Trade.*
—CCC.
Published by: Locum International Publishers, Locum International House, PO Box 874, Kochav Yair, 44864, Israel. TEL 972-9-7494965, FAX 972-9-7494532, info@locumusa.com, http://www.locum.co.il/.

615.9 USA ISSN 1544-1059
RM143
HANDBOOK ON INJECTABLE DRUGS. Text in English. 1976. base vol. plus biennial updates. USD 263 per issue to non-members; USD 210 per issue to members; USD 325 combined subscription per issue to non-members (print & CD-ROM eds); USD 260 combined subscription per issue to members (print & CD-ROM eds) (effective 2009). 1430 p./no.; Supplement avail.; back issues avail. **Document type:** *Journal, Academic/Scholarly.* **Description:** Covers of injectable drugs used in admixtures including investigational drugs.
Related titles: CD-ROM ed.: USD 263 per issue to non-members; USD 210 per issue to members (effective 2009); Online - full text ed.: ISSN 1938-9582.
Published by: (Product Development Office), American Society of Health-System Pharmacists, 7272 Wisconsin Ave, Bethesda, MD 20814. TEL 866-279-0681, FAX 301-664-8700, custserv@ashp.org. Ed. Lawrence A Trissel.

615.7 USA ISSN 1092-048X
HANSTEN AND HORN'S DRUG INTERACTIONS ANALYSIS AND MANAGEMENT. Abbreviated title: D I A M. Text in English. 1981. base vol. plus q. updates. looseleaf. adv. back issues avail. **Document type:** *Newsletter, Trade.* **Description:** Concise and authoritative guide to drug interactions. Includes a comprehensive index.
Supersedes: Drug Interactions and Updates; Former titles: Drug Interactions; (until vol.8, no.11, 1989): Drug Interactions Newsletter (0271-8707); Incorporates (in 1989): Drug Interactions
Indexed: Inpharma.
—BLDSC (4262.337500), GNLM, INIST.
Published by: Facts and Comparisons (Subsidiary of: Wolters Kluwer N.V.), 77 West Port Plz, Ste 450, St. Louis, MO 63146. TEL 314-216-2100, 800-223-0554, FAX 317-735-5390, http://www.factsandcomparisons.com.

615.1 USA ISSN 1096-9160
HD9666.1
HEALTHCARE DISTRIBUTOR; the industry's multi-market information resource. Text in English. 1948. bi-m. USD 29.95 domestic; USD 80 foreign (effective 2006). adv. charts; illus.; tr.lit.; stat. back issues avail.; reprints avail. **Document type:** *Journal, Trade.* **Description:** Covers news as it affects the wholesale drug, chain drug industries, home-health care. Distributed nationwide as well as in Canada and abroad.
Formerly (until 1997): Wholesale Drugs Magazine (0743-3778)
Indexed: I12.
Published by: E L F Publications, 5285 W Louisiana Ave, Ste 112, Lakewood, CO 80232-5976. TEL 303-975-0075, 800-922-8513, FAX 303-975-0132, mcasey@elfpublications.com, http://www.elfpublications.com. Ed. Chuck Austin. Pub. Judith D Lane. Adv. contact Jerry Lester. B&W page USD 2,475; trim 8.38 x 10.88. Circ: 12,000 (controlled).

HEALTHCARE PACKAGING. *see* PACKAGING

615 CHN ISSN 1002-7386
HEBEI YIYAO/HEBEI MEDICAL JOURNAL. Text in Chinese. 1973. bi-m. USD 86.40 (effective 2009). **Document type:** *Journal, Academic/ Scholarly.*
Related titles: Online - full text ed.
—East View.
Published by: Hebei Yixue Kexueyuan/Hebei Academy of Medical Sciences, 241, Qingyuan Jie, Shijiazhuang, Hebei 050021, China. TEL 86-311-5882942, FAX 86-311-5812687. Ed. Wang Rongjie. **Dist. by:** China International Book Trading Corp, 35 Chegongzhuang Xilu, Haidian District, PO Box 399, Beijing 100044, China. TEL 86-10-68412045, FAX 86-10-68412023, cibtc@mail.cibtc.com.cn, http://www.cibtc.com.cn.

615.1 DEU
HEIDELBERGER SCHRIFTEN ZUR PHARMAZIE- UND NATURWISSENSCHAFTSGESCHICHTE. Text in German. irreg., latest vol.20, 2007. price varies. **Document type:** *Monographic series, Academic/Scholarly.*
Published by: Wissenschaftliche Verlagsgesellschaft mbH, Postfach 101061, Stuttgart, 70009, Germany. TEL 49-711-25820, FAX 49-711-2582290, service@wissenschaftliche-verlagsgesellschaft.de, http://www.wissenschaftliche-verlagsgesellschaft.de.

HEILONGJIANG YIYAO KEXUE/HEILONGJIANG MEDICINE AND PHARMACY. *see* MEDICAL SCIENCES

HERBAL MEDICINES. *see* ALTERNATIVE MEDICINE

HERBALGRAM; the journal of the American Botanical Council & the Herb Research Foundation. *see* BIOLOGY—Botany

615 JPN ISSN 0388-2616
CODEN: HBYNDA
HIROSHIMAKEN BYOIN YAKUZAISHIKAI GAKUJUTSU NENPO/ HIROSHIMA SOCIETY OF HOSPITAL PHARMACISTS. ANNUAL RESEARCH REPORT. Text in Japanese. 1975. a. **Document type:** *Academic/Scholarly.*
Indexed: CIN, ChemAb, ChemTitl.
—CASDDS.
Published by: Hiroshimaken Byoin Yakuzaishikai/Hiroshimaken Hospital Pharmacists Association, Hiroshima University School of Medicine, 1-2-3 Kasumi, Minami-ku, Hiroshima-shi, 734-0037, Japan. TEL 81-82-2575572, FAX 81-82-2575598, http://www.nissy.jp/hshp/.

615 JPN ISSN 0389-4061
HIROSHIMAKEN HOSPITAL PHARMACISTS ASSOCIATION. DRUG INFORMATION NEWS. Text in Japanese. 1973. q. **Document type:** *Newsletter, Academic/Scholarly.*
Published by: Hiroshimaken Byoin Yakuzaishikai/Hiroshimaken Hospital Pharmacists Association, Hiroshima University School of Medicine, 1-2-3 Kasumi, Minami-ku, Hiroshima-shi, 734-0037, Japan. TEL 81-82-2575572, FAX 81-82-2575598, http://www.nissy.jp/hshp/.

HIV & AIDS SERVICES WORLDWIDE. (Human Immunodeficiency Virus) *see* MEDICAL SCIENCES—Communicable Diseases

615 GBR ISSN 2045-9327
▼ **HIV PHARMACY ASSOCIATION BULLETIN.** Text in English. 2011. 3/yr. back issues avail. **Document type:** *Newsletter, Trade.*
Published by: HIV Pharmacy Association, c/o Health Sector Publishing, 4 Clark's Courtyard, 145 Granville St, Birmingham, B1 1SB, United Kingdom. TEL 44-121-6334691, FAX 44-121-6330055, info@hivpa.org, http://www.hivpa.org/.

HIV SERVICES IN THE U K. (Human Immunodeficiency Virus) *see* MEDICAL SCIENCES—Communicable Diseases

HIV TRANSMISSION & TESTING. (Human Immunodeficiency Virus) *see* MEDICAL SCIENCES—Communicable Diseases

HIV TREATMENT UPDATE. *see* MEDICAL SCIENCES—Communicable Diseases

HIV TREATMENTS DIRECTORY. (Human Immunodeficiency Virus) *see* MEDICAL SCIENCES—Communicable Diseases

615 JPN ISSN 0917-0936
HOKKAIDO BYOIN YAKUZAISHIKAISHI/HOKKAIDO SOCIETY OF HOSPITAL PHARMACISTS. JOURNAL. Text in Japanese. 1960. s-a. JPY 11,500 membership (effective 2007). **Document type:** *Journal, Academic/Scholarly.*
Published by: Hokkaido Byoin Yakuzaishikai/Hokkaido Society of Hospital Pharmacists, Sapporo Medical University Hospital, Department of Pharmacy, 291 Nishi 16-chome, Minami 1-jo, Chuo-ku, Sapporo, Hokkaido 060-8543, Japan. TEL 81-11-6112111 ext 3598, 5599, FAX 81-11-6152524, hokubyo@doyaku.or.jp, http://www.doyaku.or.jp/hokubyo/index.html.

615 HKG ISSN 1727-2874
HONG KONG PHARMACEUTICAL JOURNAL. Text in English. 1992. q. **Document type:** *Journal, Academic/Scholarly.*
Address: GPO Box 3274, Hong Kong, Hong Kong. **Co-sponsors:** Pharmaceutical Society of Hong Kong; Society of Hospital Pharmacists of Hong Kong; Practising Pharmacists Association of Hong Kong.

615 JPN ISSN 0441-2559
CODEN: HYDKAK
HOSHI YAKKA DAIGAKU KIYO/HOSHI COLLEGE OF PHARMACY. ANNUAL REPORT. Text in English, Japanese; Summaries in English. 1951. a.
Indexed: B25, BIOSIS Prev, ChemAb, MycolAb.
Published by: Hoshi Yakka Daigaku, 4-41 Ebara 2-chome, Shinagawa-ku, Tokyo, 142-8501, Japan.

615.1 USA ISSN 0018-5787
RA975.5.P5 CODEN: HOPHAZ
HOSPITAL PHARMACY. Text in English. 1966. m. USD 229 combined subscription to individuals (print & online eds.); USD 357 combined subscription to institutions (print & online eds.); free to qualified personnel (effective 2010). adv. illus. Index. 3 cols./p.; back issues avail.; reprints avail. **Document type:** *Journal, Academic/Scholarly.* **Description:** Features clinical information applicable to pharmacists in hospitals and organized health systems, managed care practice, nursing homes, pharmacy schools, long term care, and other settings where state-of-the-art practice information is required.
Related titles: Microform ed.: (from PQC); Online - full text ed.: ISSN 1945-1253. 1966. USD 179 to individuals; USD 309 to institutions (effective 2010).
Indexed: A01, A22, AHCMS, C06, C07, CA, EMBASE, ExcerpMed, HospLI, I12, IDIS, P30, R10, Reac, SCOPUS, T02.
—BLDSC (4333.207200), GNLM, IE, Infotrieve, Ingenta, INIST, Linda Hall. **CCC.**
Published by: Thomas Land Publishers, Inc., 255 Jefferson Rd, St Louis, MO 63119. TEL 314-963-7445, FAX 314-963-9345, publisher@thomasland.com, http://www.thomasland.com/. Ed. Joyce A Generali. Adv. contact Steve West TEL 856-432-1555.

615.409405 GBR ISSN 1477-1896
HOSPITAL PHARMACY EUROPE. Abbreviated title: H P E. Text in English. 2001. bi-m. free to qualified personnel (effective 2010). adv. back issues avail. **Document type:** *Magazine, Trade.* **Description:** Contains up-to-date information critical to the practice of today's pharmacists and prescribing clinicians.
Formerly (until 2002): Hospital Prescriber Europe (1474-1970)
Related titles: Online - full text ed.: free (effective 2010).
—CCC.
Published by: Campden Publishing Ltd., 1 St John's Sq, London, EC1M 4PN, United Kingdom. TEL 44-20-72140500, FAX 44-20-72140501, enquiries@campden.com, http://www.campden.com. Ed. Stephen Taylor TEL 44-20-72140573. Adv. contact Neil Morris.

615 CHN ISSN 1006-0103
CODEN: HYZAE2
HUAXI YAOXUE ZAZHI/WEST CHINA JOURNAL OF PHARMACEUTICAL SCIENCES. Text in Chinese. 1985. bi-m. USD 31.20 (effective 2009). **Document type:** *Journal, Academic/Scholarly.*
Related titles: Online - full text ed.
Indexed: CIN, ChemAb, ChemTitl.
—BLDSC (9298.863200), CASDDS, East View, IE, Ingenta.
Published by: Zhongguo Yaoxuehui, Sichuan Fenhui, 17, Renmin Nanlu, 3-duan, Chengdu, 610041, China. **Dist. by:** China International Book Trading Corp, 35 Chegongzhuang Xilu, Haidian District, PO Box 399, Beijing 100044, China. TEL 86-10-68412045, FAX 86-10-68412023, cibtc@mail.cibtc.com.cn, http://www.cibtc.com.cn.

HUMAN & EXPERIMENTAL TOXICOLOGY. *see* ENVIRONMENTAL STUDIES—Toxicology And Environmental Safety

HUMAN GENOMICS (ONLINE). *see* BIOLOGY—Genetics

HUMAN PSYCHOPHARMACOLOGY: CLINICAL AND EXPERIMENTAL. *see* MEDICAL SCIENCES—Psychiatry And Neurology

HUMAN REPRODUCTION. *see* MEDICAL SCIENCES—Obstetrics And Gynecology

615.372 USA ISSN 1554-8600
QR189
➤ **HUMAN VACCINES.** Text in English. 2005 (Jan./Feb.). m. USD 1,900 combined subscription in US & Canada to institutions (print & online eds.); USD 1,900 combined subscription elsewhere to institutions (print & online eds.) (effective 2009). **Document type:** *Journal, Academic/Scholarly.* **Description:** Covers the increasing prominence of vaccines in medical profession. Includes coverage of discovery, research, enabling technologies, product development, clinical studies, policy, safety and commercial utilization.
Related titles: Online - full text ed.: ISSN 1554-8619. USD 1,500 to institutions (effective 2009).
Indexed: B25, B26, BIOSIS Prev, EMBASE, ExcerpMed, MEDLINE, P30, R10, Reac, SCI, SCOPUS, W07.
—BLDSC (4336.468650), IE, Ingenta. **CCC.**
Published by: Landes Bioscience, 1002 W Ave, Austin, TX 78701. TEL 512-637-6050, info@landesbioscience.com. Ed. Ronald W Ellis.

615 IND ISSN 0975-6221
▼ **HYGEIA**; journal for drugs and medicines. Text in English. 2009 (May). 2/yr. INR 1,500 domestic to individuals; USD 100 foreign to individuals; INR 2,500 domestic to institutions; USD 500 foreign to institutions (effective 2010). adv. a. index. back issues avail.; reprints avail. **Document type:** *Journal, Academic/Scholarly.* **Description:** Publishes papers concerning pharmaceutical sciences like medicinal chemistry, formulation technologies, pharmacognosy, medicinal natural products, pharmacology, clinical pharmacy, bio-technology, biopharmaceutics, pharmacy practice and other related fields.
Related titles: Online - full text ed.: ISSN 2229-3590. free (effective 2011).

P

Published by: Hygeia Club, c/o C Dremedies, 36 A-1, Gandhi Nagar, Ganapathy, Coimbatore, Tamil Nadu 641 006, India. TEL 91-422-2539477, madhu.divakar@gmail.com. Ed., Pub. Dr. Madhu C Divakar. **Dist. by:** Syosys, Thalassery, Kannur, Kerala, India. TEL 91-490-2322232, sales@syosys.com, http://www.syosys.com.

615 JPN ISSN 0916-7587
HYOGOKEN YAKUZAISHIKAISHI/HYOGO PHARMACEUTICAL SOCIETY. JOURNAL. Text in Japanese. 1951. m. JPY 28,200 per issue membership; JPY 48,100 per issue membership to pharmacy managers (effective 2007). **Document type:** *Journal, Academic/ Scholarly.*
Formerly (until 1991): Hyoyakukai/Pharmaceutical Society of Hyogo. Journal (0367-6501)
Published by: Hyogoken Yakuzaishikai/Pharmaceutical Society of Hyogo, 6-4-3,Shimoyamate-dori,Chuo-ku, Kobe, Hyogo 650-0011, Japan. TEL 81-78-3417585, FAX 81-78-3417113, info@hps.or.jp, http://www.hyoyaku.org/.

615.1 JPN
I C H E5 HANDBOOK (YEAR). Text in English. a. USD 60 (effective 2001).
Related titles: Japanese ed.
Published by: Yakuji Nippo Ltd., Kanda-Izumi-cho, Chiyoda-ku, Tokyo, 101-0024, Japan. TEL 81-3-3862-2141, FAX 81-3-3866-8495, shuppan@yakuji.co.jp, http://www.yakuji.co.jp/.

615.1 ESP ISSN 2013-4398
I COFB. (In formatiu Col.legi de Farmaceutics de la Provincia de Barcelona) Text in Catalan. 1969. m. **Document type:** *Bulletin, Trade.*
Former titles (until 2009): Informatiu - Col.legi de Farmaceutics de la Provincia de Barcelona (0214-0470); (until 1986): Butlleti Informatiu de Circular Farmaceutica (0212-0674); (until 1977): Boletin Informativo de Circular Farmaceutica (0366-0362)
Related titles: ◆ Supplement to: Colegio Oficial de Farmaceutico. Circular Farmaceutica. ISSN 0009-7314.
—CCC.
Published by: Col.legi de Farmaceutics de la Provincia de Barcelona, C Girona, 64, Barcelona, 08009, Spain. TEL 34-93-2440710, http://www.famaceuticonline.com/.

615.1 IND
I D M A ANNUAL PUBLICATION. Text in English. 1963. a. adv. **Document type:** *Journal, Trade.* **Description:** Contains a wealth of information and data on the Indian pharmaceutical industry.
Published by: Indian Drug Manufacturers' Association, 102-B, Poonam Chambers, Dr. A B Rd, Worli, Mumbai, Maharashtra 400 018, India. TEL 91-22-24944624, FAX 91-22-24950723, idma1@idmaindia.com.

615.1 IND ISSN 0970-6054
I D M A BULLETIN. Text in English. 1970. w. adv. **Document type:** *Bulletin, Trade.* **Description:** Discusses topics of interest to professionals in the Indian pharmaceutical manufacturing industry.
Indexed: SCOPUS.
—BLDSC (4362.490500).
Published by: Indian Drug Manufacturers' Association, 102-B, Poonam Chambers, Dr. A B Rd, Worli, Mumbai, Maharashtra 400 018, India. TEL 91-22-24944624, FAX 91-22-24950723, idma1@idmaindia.com.

615.19005 GBR ISSN 1369-7056
I DRUGS: THE INVESTIGATIONAL DRUGS JOURNAL. Variant title: IDrugs. Text in English. 1997. m. print prices upon request. **Document type:** *Journal, Academic/Scholarly.* **Description:** Presents information disclosed at scientific meetings as well as a selection of expert evaluations of investigational drugs and reviews highlighting important issues in drug research and analysis.
Related titles: Online - full text ed.: ISSN 2040-3410. GBP 2,648, USD 5,039, EUR 3,838 to institutions (corporate), 1-500 users; GBP 193, USD 350, EUR 288 to institutions (academic), 1-20 users) (effective 2010); Subscr. price varies per number of users. Please contact publisher.
Indexed: A34, A35, A36, AgBio, CABA, E12, EMBASE, ExcerpMed, GH, H16, MEDLINE, P30, P32, P33, P39, P40, R08, R10, RA&MP, RM&VM, Reac, SCI, SCOPUS, T05, VS, W07.
—BLDSC (4362.565750), IE, Ingenta. **CCC.**
Published by: Current Drugs Ltd. (Subsidiary of: Thomson Reuters Corp.), 1 Chapel Quarter, Mount St, Nottingham, NG1 6HQ, United Kingdom. TEL 44-207-5424300, general.info@thomsonreuters.com, http://science.thomsonreuters.com/.

615.7 USA ISSN 1949-4548
I G LIVING. (Immune Globulin) Text in English. 2006. bi-m. free (effective 2009). adv. back issues avail. **Document type:** *Magazine, Consumer.* **Description:** Features include such topics as product and manufacturer news, resources for healthy living, immune globulin treatment options, reimbursement and clinical trials.
Related titles: Online - full text ed.
Published by: F F F Enterprises, 41093 County Center Dr, Temecula, CA 92591. TEL 951-296-2500, 800-843-7477, FAX 800-418-4333, sperez@fffenterprises.com, http://www.fffenterprises.com/. Ed., Adv. contact Cheryl Brooks. color page USD 7,000; trim 8.375 x 10.5.

I H E RAPPORT. *see* BUSINESS AND ECONOMICS—Production Of Goods And Services

615 330 GBR
I M S COMPANY PROFILES. (Intelligence Marketing Services) Text in English. 1991. m. **Document type:** *Journal, Trade.* **Description:** Contains information on company strategy, financial performance, R and D pipeline, licensing and collaboration, products, and key events.
Formerly: Pharmaceutical Company Profiles
Related titles: CD-ROM ed.; Online - full text ed.
Published by: I M S Health Inc., 7 Harewood Ave, London, NW1 6JB, United Kingdom. TEL 44-20-30755000, FAX 44-20-30755888, http://www.imshealth.com/.

615 USA
I M S RETAIL DRUG MONITOR. Text in English. m. **Document type:** *Newsletter, Trade.* **Description:** Tracks monthly sales of medicinal products by retail pharmacy outlets in 13 key markets worldwide.
Published by: I M S Health, 1499 Post Rd, 2nd Fl, Fairfield, CT 06824. TEL 203-319-4700.

658 GBR
I P M FOCUS. (Institute of Pharmacy Management) Text in English. 19??. q. GBP 40 to non-members; free to members (effective 2009). bk.rev. **Document type:** *Journal, Trade.* **Description:** Covers management issues in pharmacy.
Former titles (until 2006): Institute of Pharmacy Management International. Institute News (1369-8540); (until 1978): Journal of Management and Communication (0958-482X)
—CCC.
Published by: (Institute of Pharmacy Management International Ltd.), Communications International Group, 207 Linen Hall, 162-168 Regent St, London, W1B 5TB, United Kingdom. TEL 44-20-74341530, FAX 44-20-75347208. Circ: 1,000.

615.1 613 613.081 NLD ISSN 1024-0268
I P S F NEWS BULLETIN. Text in English, French, German, Spanish. 1960. 2/yr. free to members (effective 2009). adv. charts; illus. index. 30 p./no. 2 cols./p.; **Document type:** *Bulletin, Trade.* **Description:** Contains articles, news, information and a calendar of worldwide pharmaceutical events of interest to pharmaceutical students.
Related titles: Online - full content ed.: 2000. free.
Published by: International Pharmaceutical Students Federation, PO Box 84200, The Hague, 2508 AE, Netherlands. TEL 31-70-3021992, FAX 31-70-3021999, ipsf@ipsf.org.

615 IRL ISSN 0332-2130
I P U REVIEW. Text in English. 1976. 11/yr. adv. bk.rev. **Document type:** *Journal, Trade.* **Description:** Primary objectives are to reflect the authentic views of the pharmaceutical profession, to acquaint pharmacists of Union policy and information, and to ensure that developments in pharmacy are published and commented on as they occur.
Related titles: Online - full text ed.: free.
Published by: Irish Pharmaceutical Union, Butterfield House, Butterfield Ave, Rathfarnham, Dublin, 14, Ireland. TEL 353-1-4936401, FAX 353-1-4936407, info@ipu.ie. Ed. Majella Lane. Adv. contacts Janice Burke, Wendy McGlashan. B&W page EUR 800, color page EUR 11,000; trim 210 x 297.

615.1 USA ISSN 1520-8281
I S M P MEDICATION SAFETY ALERT! (ACUTE CARE EDITION). Text in English. 199?. bi-w. USD 160 (effective 2010). **Document type:** *Newsletter, Academic/Scholarly.* **Description:** Provides vital and potentially life-saving information about medication and device errors and adverse drug reactions.
Related titles: E-mail ed.: ISSN 1550-6312.
Published by: Institute for Safe Medication Practices, 200 Lakeside Dr, Ste 200, Horsham, PA 19044. TEL 215-947-7797, FAX 215-914-1492. Ed. Judy Smetzer.

615 USA ISSN 1550-6290
I S M P MEDICATION SAFETY ALERT! (COMMUNITY - AMBULATORY CARE EDITION). Text in English. 2002. m. USD 52 (effective 2010). **Document type:** *Newsletter, Trade.* **Description:** Covers medication-related errors, adverse drug reactions, as well as recommendations to reduce the risk of medication errors and other adverse drug events in community practice site.
Media: E-mail.
Published by: Institute for Safe Medication Practices, 200 Lakeside Dr, Ste 200, Horsham, PA 19044. TEL 215-947-7797, FAX 215-914-1492. Ed. Judy Smetzer.

615 USA ISSN 1538-5108
I S P O R CONNECTIONS. (International Society for Pharmaeconomics and Outcomes Research) Text in English. bi-m. adv.
Formerly (until 2002): I S P O R News (1531-7404)
Published by: International Society of Pharmaeconomics and Outcomes Research, 3100 Princeton Pike Bldg. 3, Ste. D, Lawrenceville, NJ 08648. TEL 609-219-0773, FAX 609-219-0774, http://www.ispor.org. Ed. Steven E. Marx. Adv. contact Nadia Naaman.

615.1 USA ISSN 2090-6145
▼ ➤ **I S R N PHARMACEUTICS.** (International Scholarly Research Network) Text in English. 2011. **Document type:** *Journal, Academic/ Scholarly.* **Description:** Publishes original research articles, review articles, and clinical studies in all areas of pharmaceutics.
Related titles: Online - full text ed.: ISSN 2090-6153. 2011. free (effective 2011).
Published by: Hindawi Publishing Corporation, 410 Park Ave, 15th Fl, PMB 287, New York, NY 10022. FAX 215-893-4392, 866-446-3294, info@hindawi.com.

615.1 USA ISSN 2090-5165
▼ ➤ **I S R N PHARMACOLOGY.** (International Scholarly Research Network) Text in English. 2011. **Document type:** *Journal, Academic/ Scholarly.* **Description:** Publishes original research articles as well as review articles in all areas of pharmacology.
Related titles: Online - full text ed.: ISSN 2090-5173. 2011. free (effective 2011).
Published by: Hindawi Publishing Corporation, 410 Park Ave, 15th Fl, PMB 287, New York, NY 10022. FAX 215-893-4392, 866-446-3294, info@hindawi.com.

➤ **I V S.** (Index of Veterinary Specialists) *see* VETERINARY SCIENCE

➤ **I V S DESK REFERENCE.** (Index of Veterinary Specialists) *see* VETERINARY SCIENCE

615.1 USA ISSN 0019-1221
IDAHO PHARMACIST. Text in English. 1964. s-a. free membership. adv. stat. **Document type:** *Newsletter, Trade.* **Description:** For registered pharmacists, pharmacies, hospitals, wholesale drug houses, colleges of pharmacy faculty members and students, drug travelers, nursing associations.
Published by: Idaho State Pharmacy Association, Inc., PO Box 191345, Boise, ID 83719-1345. TEL 208-424-1107, webmaster@idahopharmacy.org, http://www.idahopharmacy.org/. Ed., R&P, Adv. contact Jo An Condie. page USD 275; trim 9.75 x 7.5. Circ: 500.

615 JPN ISSN 0389-3898
CODEN: IGYAEI
IGAKU TO YAKUGAKU/JOURNAL OF MEDICINE AND PHARMACEUTICAL SCIENCE. Text in Japanese. 1975. m. JPY 24,000 (effective 2007). **Document type:** *Journal, Academic/ Scholarly.*
Indexed: CIN, ChemAb, ChemTitl, Inpharma.
—CASDDS, GNLM.
Published by: Shizen Kagakusha Co. Ltd., 2-1-4 Iida-Bashi, Chiyoda-ku, Tokyo, 102-0072, Japan. TEL 81-3-32344121, FAX 81-3-32344127, http://www.shizenkagaku.com/.

615.1 USA ISSN 0195-2099
ILLINOIS PHARMACIST. Text in English. 1977. bi-m. USD 36 (effective 2005). adv. tr.lit. back issues avail.; reprints avail. **Document type:** *Magazine, Trade.* **Description:** Covers a broad range of pharmacy topics including regulatory, legal and pharmacy practice issues.
Formerly (until 1979): Illinois Journal of Pharmacy (0147-8222); Which was formed by the merger of (1963-1977): Illinois Pharmacist (0019-2163); (1904-1977): C R D A News (0007-9030)
Related titles: Microform ed.: (from PQC).
—Linda Hall.
Published by: Illinois Pharmacists Association, 204 W Cook St, Springfield, IL 62704. TEL 217-522-7300, FAX 217-522-7349, ipha@ipha.org. Ed. J. Michael Patton. adv.: B&W page USD 525, color page USD 1,125; trim 8.5 x 11. Circ: 2,000.

615 616.9 USA ISSN 1559-4599
IMMUNOFACTS VACCINES & IMMUNOLOGIC DRUGS. Text in English. 1993. a. looseleaf. USD 87 per issue (effective 2009). Supplement avail. **Document type:** *Handbook/Manual/Guide, Trade.* **Description:** Provides unbiased, comparative information on immunologic agents.
Formerly (until 2002): ImmunoFacts
Published by: Facts and Comparisons (Subsidiary of: Wolters Kluwer N.V.), 77 West Port Plz, Ste 450, St. Louis, MO 63146. TEL 314-216-2100, 800-223-0554, FAX 317-735-5390.

615 USA ISSN 0892-3973
RM370 CODEN: IITOEF
➤ **IMMUNOPHARMACOLOGY AND IMMUNOTOXICOLOGY.** Text in English. 1979. q. GBP 1,075, EUR 1,420, USD 1,775 combined subscription to institutions (print & online eds.); GBP 2,150, EUR 2,840, USD 3,545 combined subscription to corporations (print & online eds.) (effective 2009). adv. back issues avail.; reprint service avail. from PSC. **Document type:** *Journal, Academic/Scholarly.* **Description:** Offers readers an interdisciplinary approach to subjects integrating pharmacology and toxicology with immunology.
Former titles: Journal of Pharmacology and Immunotoxicology; Journal of Immunopharmacology (0163-0571)
Related titles: Microform ed.: (from RPI); Online - full text ed.: ISSN 1532-2513 (from IngentaConnect).
Indexed: A01, A03, A08, A22, A34, A35, A36, A38, AIDS&CR, ASCA, ASFA, AgBio, AgrForAb, B21, B25, BIOBASE, BIOSIS Prev, BP, C30, CA, CABA, CIN, ChemAb, ChemTitl, CurCont, D01, DBA, E01, E12, EMBASE, ESPM, ExcerpMed, F08, F11, F12, G11, GH, H16, H17, IABS, ISR, ImmunAb, IndMed, IndVet, Inpharma, MEDLINE, MycolAb, N02, N03, N04, P30, P32, P33, P35, P37, P39, P40, PGegResA, PGrRegA, PN&I, R07, R08, R10, RA&MP, RM&VM, Reac, RefZh, SCI, SCOPUS, SoyAb, T02, T05, ToxAb, VS, W07, W10, W11.
—BLDSC (4369.760200), CASDDS, GNLM, IE, Infotrieve, Ingenta, INIST. **CCC.**
Published by: Informa Healthcare (Subsidiary of: T & F Informa plc), 52 Vanderbilt Ave, New York, NY 10017. TEL 212-262-8230, FAX 212-262-8234, healthcare.enquiries@informa.com, http://www.informahealthcare.com. Adv. contact Daniel Wallen. **Subscr. outside N. America to:** Taylor & Francis Ltd.

➤ **IMMUNOPHARMACOLOGY REVIEWS.** *see* MEDICAL SCIENCES—Allergology And Immunology

615 NLD ISSN 1873-9822
IMMUNOTOXICOLOGY OF DRUGS AND CHEMICALS. Text in English. 2004. irreg. **Document type:** *Monographic series, Academic/ Scholarly.*
Related titles: Online - full text ed.: ISSN 2212-2079.
Indexed: SCOPUS.
—CCC.
Published by: Elsevier BV (Subsidiary of: Elsevier Science & Technology), Radarweg 29, PO Box 211, Amsterdam, 1000 AE, Netherlands. TEL 31-20-4853911, FAX 31-20-4852457, JournalsCustomerServiceEMEA@elsevier.com, http://www.elsevier.com.

615 KOR ISSN 1225-5467
RM301.28
➤ **IMSANG YAGRI HAGHOEJI/KOREAN SOCIETY FOR CLINICAL PHARMACOLOGY AND THERAPEUTICS. JOURNAL.** Text in Korean. 1993. s-a. membership (effective 2008). adv. **Document type:** *Journal, Academic/Scholarly.* **Description:** Publishes articles dealing with the effects of drugs, including pharmacodynamics, clinical trials, pharmacoepidemiology, pharmacogenetics and other studies of drugs.
Indexed: EMBASE, ExcerpMed, R10, Reac, SCOPUS.
—Ingenta.
Published by: Daehan Imsang Yagri Haghoe/Korean Society for Clinical Pharmacology and Therapeutics, Inha University Hospital, 7-206, 3-Ga, Sinheung-dong, Jung-gu, Incheon, 405-760, Korea, S. TEL 82-32-8902131, 82-32-8902132, kscpt@gilhospital.com, http://www.kscpt.org/.

615 POL ISSN 1642-4441
INDEKS O T C. Text in Polish. 2000. a. **Document type:** *Magazine, Consumer.*
Published by: Wydawnictwo Apteka, ul Szewska 3a, Wroclaw, Poland. TEL 48-71-3699330, FAX 48-71-3699331, info@wydawnictwoapteka.pl, http://www.otcindeks.pl.

615 GBR ISSN 0963-0759
THE INDEPENDENT COMMUNITY PHARMACIST. Text in English. 1990. m. GBP 66 domestic; GBP 115 foreign; GBP 3.25 newsstand/cover (effective 2009). adv. bk.rev. back issues avail. **Document type:** *Magazine, Trade.* **Description:** Designed for the independent retail pharmacists.
Related titles: Online - full text ed.: free (effective 2009).
—CCC.
Published by: (Independent Pharmacy Federation), Independent Community Pharmacist, Linen Hall, 162-168 Regent St, London, W1B 5TB, United Kingdom. TEL 44-207-4341530, FAX 44-207-4370915, icp@1530.com. Ed. Douglas Simpson. Adv. contact Julian de Bruxelles TEL 44-207-5347233. Circ: 6,506.

615 DEU
INDEX NOMINUM; international drug directory. Text in English, French, German. 1956. irreg. (in 2 vols.), latest 2011. EUR 298 per vol. (effective 2011). **Document type:** *Monographic series, Academic/ Scholarly.* **Description:** Provides reference information on active substances, their synonyms, chemical structures and formulas, the medications prepared from them, and their manufacturers.
Related titles: CD-ROM ed.
Published by: Deutscher Apotheker Verlag, Postfach 101061, Stuttgart, 70009, Germany. TEL 49-711-25820, FAX 49-711-2582290, service@deutscher-apotheker-verlag.de, http://www.deutscher-apotheker-verlag.de.

615 IND ISSN 0971-8125
RS131.68
INDIAN DRUG REVIEW. Variant title: I D R. Text in English. 1995. m. **Document type:** *Journal, Academic/Scholarly.*
Published by: C M P Medica (Subsidiary of: C M P Medica Ltd.), Sagar Tech Plz A 615-617, 6th Fl, Andheri Kurla Rd, Saki Naka Jct, Andheri E, Mumbai, 400 072, India. TEL 91-22-66122600, FAX 91-22-66122626, info.india@ubm.com, http://www.ubmindia.in/cmp-medica.asp.

615.1 IND ISSN 0019-462X
HD9672.I5 CODEN: INDRBA
INDIAN DRUGS. Text in English. 1963. m. adv. bk.rev. charts; tr.lit. **Document type:** *Journal, Trade.* **Description:** Readership: Pharmaceutical Industry & Pharmacy Educational & Research Institutions.
Indexed: A22, CIN, ChemAb, ChemTitl, EMBASE, ExcerpMed, I12, R10, Reac, SCOPUS.
—BLDSC (4396.180000), CASDDS, GNLM, IE, Ingenta, INIST.
Published by: Indian Drug Manufacturers' Association, 102-B, Poonam Chambers, Dr. A B Rd, Worli, Mumbai, Maharashtra 400 018, India. TEL 91-22-24944624, FAX 91-22-24950723, idma1@idmaindia.com.

615.1 IND ISSN 0019-526X
RA975.5.P5 CODEN: IJHPBU
➤ **INDIAN JOURNAL OF HOSPITAL PHARMACY.** Abbreviated title: I J H P. Text in English. 1964. bi-m. bk.rev. charts; illus.; stat. index. **Document type:** *Journal, Academic/Scholarly.* **Description:** Aims to develop advanced technology for the manufacture of several vital drugs ranging from antiasthmatics and cardiovascular medicines to antibacterials, antiarthritics, antiparasitics and medical aerosols.
Related titles: Online - full text ed.
Indexed: CIN, ChemAb, ChemTitl, P30.
—CASDDS, GNLM.
Published by: (Indian Hospital Pharmacists' Association), Manipal University, Madhava Nagar, Manipal, 576 104, India. TEL 91-820-2922482, FAX 91-820-2571998, info.mcops@manipal.edu. Ed. N Udupa.

615 IND ISSN 0975-5500
▼ **INDIAN JOURNAL OF NOVEL DRUG DELIVERY.** Text in English. 2009. q. INR 2,000 to individuals; INR 3,000 to institutions (effective 2011). **Document type:** *Journal, Academic/Scholarly.* **Description:** Publishes innovative papers, reviews, mini-reviews, rapid communications and notes dealing with physical, chemical, biological, microbiological and engineering studies related to the conception, design, production, characterization and evaluation of drug delivery systems in vitro and in vivo.
Indexed: A36, F08, H16, P33.
Published by: Karnataka Education and Scientific Society, D-408, Shantiniketan, Bhairidevarkoppa, Hubli, 580 025, India. TEL 91-98-45463472, secretary.kess@gmail.com, http://kess.cfsites.org/custom.php?pageid=33494. Ed. V G Jamakandi. Pub., R&P J S Mulla.

615.1 IND
RS119.I5 CODEN: IJPEB3
➤ **INDIAN JOURNAL OF PHARMACEUTICAL EDUCATION & RESEARCH.** Abbreviated title: I J P E R. Text in English. 1967. q. INR 3,000 domestic; USD 300 foreign (effective 2011). adv. bk.rev. abstracted in international pharma abstract. 44 p./no. 2 cols./p.; back issues avail. **Document type:** *Journal, Academic/Scholarly.*
Formerly (until 2005): Indian Journal of Pharmaceutical Education (0019-5464)
Related titles: CD-ROM ed.; Online - full content ed.
Indexed: ChemAb, EMBASE, ExcerpMed, SCI, SCOPUS, W07.
—BLDSC (4418.720000), CASDDS, IE, Ingenta.
Published by: Association of Pharmaceutical Teachers of India, Al-Ameen College of Pharmacy, Opposite Lalbagh Main Gate, Hosur Main Rd, Bangalore, 560 027, India. TEL 91-80-22234619, FAX 91-80-22225834, aptienquiry@gmail.com, http://www.aptiindia.org. Ed. P N Sanjay Pai.

615.1 IND ISSN 0250-474X
RS1 CODEN: IJSIDW
➤ **INDIAN JOURNAL OF PHARMACEUTICAL SCIENCES.** Text in English. 1939. bi-m. bk.rev. reprints avail. **Document type:** *Journal, Academic/Scholarly.* **Description:** Devoted to the science and practice of pharmacy in all its branches.
Formerly (until 1978): Indian Journal of Pharmacy (0019-5472)
Related titles: CD-ROM ed.; Microfilm ed.: (from PQC); Online - full text ed.: ISSN 1998-3743. free (effective 2011).
Indexed: A01, A22, A26, A34, A35, A36, A37, AgBio, AgrForAb, B25, BIOSIS Prev, BP, C25, C30, CA, CABA, CIN, ChemAb, ChemTitl, D01, DBA, E12, EMBASE, ExcerpMed, ExtraMED, F08, F11, F12, FCA, GH, H11, H12, H16, H17, I05, I12, IndVet, MycolAb, N02, N03, P10, P30, P32, P33, P39, P40, P48, P53, P54, PGegResA, PGrRegA, PHN&I, PQC, R07, R08, R10, R11, R12, R13, RA&MP, RM&VM, Reac, S12, S13, S16, S17, SCI, SCOPUS, SoyAb, T02, T05, TAR, TriticAb, VS, W07, W10.
—BLDSC (4418.750000), CASDDS, GNLM, IE, Infotrieve, Ingenta, INIST, Linda Hall. **CCC.**
Published by: (Indian Pharmaceutical Association), Medknow Publications and Media Pvt. Ltd., B-9, Kanara Business Ctr, Off Link Rd, Ghatkopar (E), Mumbai, Maharastra 400 075, India. TEL 91-22-66491816, FAX 91-22-66491817, http://www.medknow.com. Ed. Dr. M L Schroff.

615 IND ISSN 0253-7613
CODEN: INJPD2
➤ **INDIAN JOURNAL OF PHARMACOLOGY.** Text in English. 1969. bi-m. INR 3,500 domestic to institutions; USD 250 foreign to institutions; USD 4,200 combined subscription domestic to institutions (print & online eds.); USD 300 combined subscription foreign to institutions (print & online eds.) (effective 2011). adv. bk.rev. **Document type:** *Journal, Academic/Scholarly.* **Description:** Contains original research articles, and reviews on pharmacology, clinical pharmacology, chemotherapy, ethnopharmacology and molecular biology related to drug action.
Related titles: CD-ROM ed.; Online - full text ed.: ISSN 1998-3751. free (effective 2011).
Indexed: A01, A26, A34, A35, A36, A38, AgBio, AgrForAb, B23, B25, BIOSIS Prev, BP, C30, CA, CABA, CIN, ChemAb, ChemTitl, D01, E08, E12, EMBASE, ExcerpMed, ExtraMED, F08, F11, F12, G08, GH, H16, H17, I05, IndVet, MycolAb, N02, N03, N04, OR, P10, P20, P30, P32, P33, P37, P39, P48, P53, P54, PGegResA, PQC, R07, R08, R10, R12, R13, RA&MP, RM&VM, Reac, S09, S12, SCI, SCOPUS, T02, T05, TriticAb, VS, W07, W10.
—BLDSC (4418.900000), CASDDS, GNLM, IE, Ingenta, INIST. **CCC.**
Published by: (Indian Pharmacological Society), Medknow Publications and Media Pvt. Ltd., B-9, Kanara Business Ctr, Off Link Rd, Ghatkopar (E), Mumbai, Maharastra 400 075, India. TEL 91-22-66491818, 91-22-66491816, publishing@medknow.com, http://www.medknow.com. Ed. R K Dikshit. adv.: page USD 100. Circ: 3,000.

➤ **INDIAN JOURNAL OF PHYSIOLOGY AND PHARMACOLOGY.** *see* BIOLOGY—Physiology

615.1 IND ISSN 0073-6635
INDIAN PHARMACEUTICAL GUIDE. Text in English. 1963. a. USD 80 (effective 2009). adv. **Document type:** *Directory.* **Description:** Contains various information on drugs and pharmaceuticals produced in India for local consumption and exports.
Published by: Pamposh Publications, 507 Ashok Bhawan, 93 Nehru Place, New Delhi, 110 019, India. TEL 91-11-6433315, 91-11-6432797, FAX 91-11-6225885. Ed. Mohan C Bazaz. Adv. contact Kong Posh. Circ: 5,000. **Subscr. to:** I N S I O Scientific Books & Periodicals, PO Box 7234, Indraprastha HPO, New Delhi 110 002, India. iihm@ap.nic.in, http://iihm.ap.nic.in/.

615 IND ISSN 0972-7914
THE INDIAN PHARMACIST. Text in English. 2002. m. INR 765 (effective 2011). **Document type:** *Journal, Academic/Scholarly.*
—BLDSC (4426.080000), INIST.
Published by: Bazaz Publications, 507 Ashok Bhawan, 93 Nehru Place, New Delhi, 110 019, India. TEL 91-11-26443169, FAX 91-11-26443169, info@indianpharmacist.com.

615 USA ISSN 1083-4974
INDIANA PHARMACIST. Text in English. 1882. q. USD 15 (effective 2005). adv. **Document type:** *Magazine, Trade.* **Description:** Departments include pharmaceutical dynamics (new products, research developments carried as an extension service from the Purdue University School of Pharmacy and Pharmaceutical Sciences), biology, chemistry, pharmacy, including technical material from the Butler University College of Pharmacy.
Published by: Indiana Pharmacists Alliance, 729 N Pennsylvania St, Indianapolis, IN 46204-1171. TEL 317-634-4968, FAX 317-632-1219, http://www.indianapharmacists.org/. Ed. Lawrence Sage. adv.: page USD 500. Circ: 1,700 (controlled).

615 IND ISSN 2249-1023
▼ **INDO GLOBAL JOURNAL OF PHARMACEUTICAL SCIENCES.** Text in English. 2011. bi-m. free (effective 2011). **Document type:** *Journal, Academic/Scholarly.*
Media: Online - full text.
Published by: Rajeev K Singla, Ed.& Pub., Rajeev K Singla, Assistant Professor, Department of Pharmaceutical Chemistry, Jaipur National University, Jaipur, 302025, India. Ed. Rajeev K Singla.

615.19 ESP ISSN 0213-5574
INDUSTRIA FARMACEUTICA; investigacion y tecnologia. Text in Spanish. 1986. 6/yr. EUR 109.62 domestic; EUR 132.79 in Europe; USD 143.08 elsewhere (effective 2009). adv. bk.rev. illus. index. **Document type:** *Magazine, Trade.*
Related titles: Online - full text ed.
Indexed: IECT.
Published by: Reed Business Information SA (Subsidiary of: Reed Business Information International), C Albarracin 34, Madrid, 28037, Spain. TEL 34-91-4402920, FAX 34-91-4402931, info@mad@rbi.es, http://www.alcion.es/. Ed. Mar Canas Asanza. Circ: 2,000.

615 579 GBR ISSN 1740-4975
INDUSTRIAL PHARMACEUTICAL MICROBIOLOGY; standards & controls. Text in English. 2003. a. looseleaf. GBP 325 per issue (effective 2009). back issues avail. **Document type:** *Journal, Academic/Scholarly.* **Description:** Provides expert insights into translating new advances in quality assurance, safety, validation and sterility into good laboratory practices and successful drugs.
Related titles: Supplement(s):.
—CCC.
Published by: Euromed Communications Ltd., Passfield Business Ctr, Lynchborough Rd, Passfield, Liphook, Hampshire GU30 7SB, United Kingdom. TEL 44-1428-752222, FAX 44-1428-752223, info@euromed.uk.com. Eds. Geoff Hanlon, Norman Hodges.

615 GBR ISSN 1741-4911
INDUSTRIAL PHARMACY. Text in English. 1997. q. GBP 58 (effective 2009). adv. back issues avail. **Document type:** *Journal, Trade.* **Description:** Covers a variety of topics of interest to those working in the worldwide pharma industry.
Formerly (until 2004): Industrial Pharmacist (1369-6831)
Related titles: Online - full text ed.: free to members (effective 2009).
—CCC.
Published by: (International Pharmaceutical Federation, Industrial Pharmacy Section NLD), Euromed Communications Ltd., Passfield Business Ctr, Lynchborough Rd, Passfield, Liphook, Hampshire GU30 7SB, United Kingdom. TEL 44-1428-752222, FAX 44-1428-752223, info@euromed.uk.com. Ed. Joe Ridge.

615 FRA ISSN 1766-8719
INDUSTRIE PHARMA MAGAZINE. Text in French. 2003. 6/yr. EUR 188 domestic; EUR 204 in Europe; EUR 245 elsewhere (effective 2009). **Document type:** *Magazine, Trade.*
Formerly (until 2004): Info Pharma Magazine (1638-8348)
Published by: Societe d'Expansion Technique et Economique S.A., 4 rue de Seze, Paris, 75009, France. TEL 33-1-44945060, FAX 33-1-44945075, http://www.infochimie.presse.fr.

615 BRA ISSN 0104-0219
INFARMA; informativo profissional do Conselho Federal de Farmacia. Text in Portuguese. 1992. q. free. bk.rev. illus. **Document type:** *Magazine, Trade.*
Formerly (until 1991): Brazil. Conselho Federal de Farmacia. Relatorio
Published by: Conselho Federal de Farmacia, SBS Quadra 01, Bloco K, Brasilia, DF 70093900, Brazil. TEL 55-61-224-68-49, FAX 55-61-224-68-25.

615 NLD ISSN 0923-9405
CODEN: IDTSEQ
➤ **INFLAMMATION AND DRUG THERAPY SERIES.** Text in English. 1987. irreg., latest vol.5, 1992. price varies. **Document type:** *Monographic series, Academic/Scholarly.*
Indexed: CIN, ChemAb, ChemTitl.
—CASDDS. **CCC.**
Published by: Springer Netherlands (Subsidiary of: Springer Science+Business Media), Van Godewijckstraat 30, Dordrecht, 3311 GX, Netherlands. TEL 31-78-6576050, FAX 31-78-6576474.

615 CHE ISSN 1023-3830
RM1 CODEN: INREFB
➤ **INFLAMMATION RESEARCH.** Text in English. 1969. m. EUR 2,499, USD 2,903 combined subscription to institutions (print & online eds.) (effective 2012). index. back issues avail.; reprint service avail. from PSC. **Document type:** *Journal, Academic/Scholarly.* **Description:** Contains original research papers, short communications, reviews, commentaries, selected reviewed society proceedings and meeting reports on all aspects of inflammation and related fields.
Formerly (until 1995): Agents and Actions (0065-4299)
Related titles: Online - full text ed.: ISSN 1420-908X (from IngentaConnect).
Indexed: A01, A03, A08, A22, A26, A29, A34, A35, A36, AIDS&CR, ASCA, AgBio, Agr, AgrForAb, ApicAb, B20, B21, B25, BIOBASE, BIOSIS Prev, C24, C30, C33, CA, CABA, CIN, ChemAb, ChemTitl, CurCont, D01, DBA, DentInd, E01, E08, E12, EMBASE, ESPM, ExcerpMed, F08, F11, F12, GH, H16, H17, I10, IABS, ISR, ImmunAb, IndMed, IndVet, Inpharma, MEDLINE, MycolAb, N02, N03, N04, P20, P22, P30, P33, P35, P37, P39, P48, P54, PHN&I, PN&I, PQC, R07, R08, R10, R11, R13, RA&MP, RM&VM, Reac, S09, S12, S17, SCI, SCOPUS, SoyAb, T02, T05, VS, VirolAbstr, W07.
—BLDSC (4478.845300), CASDDS, GNLM, IE, Infotrieve, Ingenta, INIST, Linda Hall. **CCC.**
Published by: (European Histamine Research Society), Birkhaeuser Verlag AG (Subsidiary of: Springer Science+Business Media), Viaduktstr 42, Postfach 133, Basel, 4051, Switzerland. TEL 41-61-2050707, FAX 41-61-2050799, info@birkhauser.ch, http://www.birkhauser.ch/journals. Circ: 900. **Subscr. in the Americas to:** Springer New York LLC, Journal Fulfillment, PO Box 2485, Secaucus, NJ 07096. TEL 201-348-4033, 800-777-4643, FAX 201-348-4505, journals@birkhauser.com; **Subscr. to:** Springer Distribution Center, Kundenservice Zeitschriften, Haberstr 7, Heidelberg 69126, Germany. TEL 49-6221-3454303, FAX 49-6221-3454229, birkhauser@springer.de. **Co-sponsors:** European Workshop on Inflammation; British Inflammation Research Association; American Inflammation Research Association.

P

616.047 CHE ISSN 0925-4692
RM405 CODEN: IAOAES
➤ **INFLAMMOPHARMACOLOGY**; experimental and clinical studies. Text in English. 1991. bi-m. EUR 981, USD 1,208 combined subscription to institutions (print & online eds.) (effective 2012). back issues avail.; reprint service avail. from PSC. **Document type:** *Journal, Academic/Scholarly.* **Description:** Publishes papers on all aspects of inflammation and its pharmacological control.
Related titles: Online - full text ed.: ISSN 1568-5608 (from IngentaConnect).
Indexed: A01, A03, A08, A22, A26, B21, B25, BIOBASE, BIOSIS Prev, CA, CIN, ChemAb, ChemTitl, E01, EMBASE, ExcerpMed, H12, IABS, ImmunAb, Inpharma, MEDLINE, MycolAb, P30, R10, Reac, S01, SCOPUS, T02.
—BLDSC (4478.845700), CASDDS, GNLM, IE, Infotrieve, Ingenta. **CCC.**
Published by: Birkhaeuser Verlag AG (Subsidiary of: Springer Science+Business Media), Viaduktstr 42, Postfach 133, Basel, 4051, Switzerland. TEL 41-61-2050707, FAX 41-61-2050799, info@birkhauser.ch, http://www.birkhauser.ch. Ed. Kim Rainsford. **Dist. by:** Turpin Distribution Services Ltd., Pegasus Dr, Stratton Business Park, Biggleswade, Bedfordshire SG18 8QB, United Kingdom. TEL 44-1767-604800, FAX 44-1767-601640, custserv@turpin-distribution.com, http://www.turpin-distribution.com/.

615.1 CAN ISSN 1924-228X
INFO-PHARM. Text in English. 1983. q. **Document type:** *Trade.* **Description:** Covers drug/pharmacotherapy topics that are pertinent to hospital practice("pharmacotherapy" section).
Formerly (until 2010): Clinical Drug Administration Notes (1914-461X)
Published by: Ottawa Hospital, Drug Information Services, 1967 Riverside Dr, Ottawa, ON K1H 7W9, Canada. TEL 613-722-7000.

615 ESP ISSN 1130-8427
INFORMACION TERAPEUTICA DEL SISTEMA NACIONAL DE SALUD. Text in Spanish. 1977. m. free.
Formerly (until 1990): Informacion Terapeutica de la Seguridad Social (0210-9417)
Related titles: Online - full text ed.: ISSN 2174-0089. 1997.
Indexed: IECT.
Published by: Ministerio de Sanidad, Politica Social e Igualdad, Paseo del Prado 18-20, P.B. Esq con Lope de Vega, Madrid, 28014, Spain. TEL 34-91-5964175, FAX 34-91-5964488, publicaciones@mpsi.es.

615 SWE ISSN 1101-7104
INFORMATION FRAAN LAEKEMEDELSVERKET. Text in Swedish. 1976. bi-m. free. **Document type:** *Bulletin, Trade.*
Formerly (until 1990): Information fraan Socialstyrelsens Laekemedelsavdeling (0347-5107)
Related titles: Online - full text ed.
Published by: Laekemedelsverket/Medical Products Agency, PO Box 26, Uppsala, 75103, Sweden. TEL 46-18-174600, FAX 46-18-548566, http://www.lakemedelserket.se. Ed. Gunnar Alvan. R&P Bjoern Beermann.

INFORMATIONS PHARMACEUTIQUES O M S. (Organisation Mondiale de la Sante) *see* PUBLIC HEALTH AND SAFETY

615 ESP
INFORMATIVO FARMACEUTICO. Text in Spanish. 1987. 12/yr.
Document type: *Newspaper, Consumer.*
Former title (until 1994): Farmaceutico Informativo (1130-0949); (until 1988): Farmaceutico. Suplemento (0213-7291)
Related titles: ◆ Supplement to: El Farmaceutico. ISSN 0213-7283.
Published by: Ediciones Mayo S.A., Calle Aribau 185-187, 2a Planta, Barcelona, 08021, Spain. TEL 34-93-2090255, FAX 34-93-2020643, edmayo@ediciones.mayo.es, http://www.edicionesmayo.es. Ed. Josep M Ferrando. Circ: 19,000.

615 ITA ISSN 0392-3010
RS141.46
L'INFORMATORE FARMACEUTICO; annuario italiano dei medicinali e dei laboratori. Text in Italian. 1940. a. EUR 262.50 (effective 2009).
Document type: *Directory, Trade.*
Former titles (until 1967): Informatore Farmaceutico Italiano (0443-1839); (until 1949): Informatore Farmaceutico (0073-7984)
—GNLM, IE. **CCC.**
Published by: Elsevier Masson (Subsidiary of: Elsevier Health Sciences), Via Paleocapa 7, Milan, 20121, Italy. TEL 39-02-881841, FAX 39-02-88184302, info@masson.it, http://www.masson.it.

615.1 ITA
L'INFORMATORE FARMACEUTICO. EDIMED; il prontuario dei medicinali. Text in Italian. a. **Document type:** *Directory, Trade.*
Formerly (until 2001): Notiziario Medico Farmaceutico (0029-439X)
Indexed: A22.
Published by: Elsevier Masson (Subsidiary of: Elsevier Health Sciences), Via Paleocapa 7, Milan, 20121, Italy. TEL 39-02-881841, FAX 39-02-88184302, info@masson.it, http://www.masson.it.

615 ITA ISSN 1121-1644
INFORMAZIONI SUI FARMACI. Text in Italian. 1977. bi-m. EUR 80 domestic to institutions; EUR 95 foreign (effective 2009). bk.rev. charts; stat. index. back issues avail. **Document type:** *Bulletin, Trade.* **Description:** Contains information on individual drugs, selection of drugs, adverse drug reactions or interactions, drug treatment of diseases, patient information. Includes articles on selected topics.
Related titles: Online - full text ed.: ISSN 1973-8064.
Published by: Farmacie Comunali Riunite di Reggio Emilia, Servizio Informazione e Documentazione Scientifica, Via Doberdo 9, Reggio Emilia, 42100, Italy. TEL 39-0522-5431, http://www.fcr.re.it. Circ: 4,800.

615 USA ISSN 1937-0717
INHALATION. Text in English. 2007 (Oct.). bi-m. free to qualified personnel (effective 2009). adv. **Document type:** *Magazine, Trade.*
Description: Features a variety of articles designed to help readers make informed decisions when selecting and using equipment, excipients, and other materials.
Related titles: Online - full text ed.: ISSN 1940-414X.
Published by: C S C Publishing, Inc., 1155 Northland Dr, Saint Paul, MN 55120. TEL 651-287-5600, FAX 651-287-5650, rpbe@csc.com. Ed. Beth Ellen Roberts. adv.: color page USD 2,200; trim 8.125 x 10.875. Circ: 3,268 (controlled).

INHALATION TOXICOLOGY. *see* ENVIRONMENTAL STUDIES—Toxicology And Environmental Safety

615 GBR ISSN 1471-7204
INNOVATIONS IN PHARMACEUTICAL TECHNOLOGY. Abbreviated title: I P T. Text in English. 1997. q. GBP 125 domestic; USD 230 foreign; free to qualified personnel (effective 2010). back issues avail.
Document type: *Journal, Trade.* **Description:** Features articles dedicated to the analysis and discovery of new ideas, developments and innovations affecting the research and production of finished pharmaceuticals.
Related titles: Online - full text ed.: USD 200 (effective 2007); Supplement(s): Innovations in Clinical Trials. ISSN 1747-1397. 2003.
Indexed: EMBASE, ExcerpMed, SCOPUS.
—**CCC.**
Published by: Samedan Ltd, 16 Hampden Gurney Rd, London, W1H 5AL, United Kingdom. TEL 44-20-77243456, FAX 44-20-77242632, info@samedanltd.com, http://www.samedanltd.com/. Ed. Pam Barnacal. Adv. contact Keith Martinez.

615 USA ISSN 2155-0417
RS1
INNOVATIONS IN PHARMACY. Text in English. q. free (effective 2010).
Document type: *Journal, Trade.* **Description:** Features case studies, clinical experiences, original research, review articles, and student projects that focus on improving, modernizing, and advancing pharmacy practice, education, and policy.
Media: Online - full text.
Published by: University of Minnesota, Department of Pharmaceutical Care & Health Systems, 308 Harvard St SE, Minneapolis, MN 55455. TEL 612-624-1900, schom010@umn.edu.

615 NZL ISSN 1179-7401
INPHARMATION. Text in English. 19??. 3/yr. free (effective 2010). back issues avail. **Document type:** *Newsletter, Trade.*
Media: Online - full text.
Published by: Pharmaceutical Management Agency, Level 9, 40 Mercer St, PO Box 10-254, Wellington, 6143, New Zealand. TEL 64-4-4604990, 800-660-050, FAX 64-4-4604995, receptionist@pharmac.govt.nz.

615 USA ISSN 1932-2410
RA975.5.P5
INSTITUTIONAL PHARMACY PRACTICE. HANDBOOK. Text in English. 1979. irreg., latest 2006. **Document type:** *Handbook/Manual/Guide, Trade.*
Published by: (American Society of Health-System Pharmacists), American Society of Hospital Pharmacists, 7272 Wisconsin Ave., Bethesda, MD 20814. TEL 301-657-3000, 866-279-0681, FAX 301-657-1251, http://www.ashp.org/s_ashp/index.asp.

615 330 HKG
INTERFAX. CHINA PHARMACEUTICALS & HEALTH TECHNOLOGIES WEEKLY. Text in English. w. price varies. **Document type:** *Bulletin, Trade.* **Description:** Provides information on China's pharmaceutical and health industries. Describes relevant policies, regulations, operations and market activities of Chinese and foreign companies as well as joint ventures.
Related titles: Online - full text ed.
Indexed: P48, P51, P54.
Published by: Interfax China, Ste 1601, Wilson House 19-27, Wyndham St Central, Hong Kong, Hong Kong. TEL 852-25372262, FAX 852-25372264. **Dist. by:** Interfax America, Inc., 3025 S Parker Rd, Ste 737, Aurora, CO 80014. TEL 303-368-1421, FAX 303-368-1458, america@interfax-news.com, http://www.interfax.com.

615 330 RUS
INTERFAX. HEALTH & PHARMACEUTICALS. Text in English. 200?. w. price varies. **Document type:** *Bulletin, Trade.* **Description:** Contains materials on the state and prospects of the pharmaceutical industry in Russia and CIS countries as well as tenders for supplies of medicine and medical equipment, customs regulations and legislation.
Related titles: Online - full text ed.
Indexed: P51.
Published by: Interfax Ltd., 1-ya Tverskaya-Yamskaya, dom 2, stroenie 1, Moscow, 127006, Russian Federation. TEL 7-095-2509840, FAX 7-095-2509727, info@interfax.ru, http://www.interfax.ru.

INTERLABOR-PARAMETER. *see* FOOD AND FOOD INDUSTRIES

INTERNATIONAL CLINICAL PSYCHOPHARMACOLOGY. *see* PSYCHOLOGY

615.507 GBR ISSN 1750-2330
INTERNATIONAL CLINICAL TRIALS. Abbreviated title: I C T. Text in English. 2006. q. GBP 125 domestic; USD 230 foreign; free to qualified personnel (effective 2010). **Document type:** *Journal, Academic/Scholarly.* **Description:** Designed to provide global coverage of key topics pertinent to the clinical trials sector.
Related titles: Online - full text ed.
—**CCC.**
Published by: Samedan Ltd, 16 Hampden Gurney Rd, London, W1H 5AL, United Kingdom. TEL 44-20-77243456, FAX 44-20-77242632, info@samedanltd.com. Ed. Dr. Graham Hughes. Adv. contact David Hirsh.

615 659 344.04 GBR ISSN 1743-3363
THE INTERNATIONAL COMPARATIVE LEGAL GUIDE TO: PHARMACEUTICAL ADVERTISING (YEAR). Text in English. 2004. a. **Document type:** *Handbook/Manual/Guide, Trade.*
Related titles: Online - full text ed.: free (effective 2009).
Published by: Global Legal Group Ltd., 59 Tanner St, London, SE1 3PL, United Kingdom. TEL 44-207-3670720, FAX 44-207-4075255, http://www.glgroup.co.uk. Pub. Richard Firth TEL 44-207-3670722.

THE INTERNATIONAL DIRECTORY OF DRUGS AND PHARMACEUTICALS IMPORTERS. *see* BUSINESS AND ECONOMICS—Trade And Industrial Directories

615 USA ISSN 2150-4792
INTERNATIONAL DRUG DISCOVERY. Text in English. 2006 (Jun.). bi-m. USD 135 (effective 2010). **Document type:** *Journal, Trade.*
Description: Covers the process of pharmaceutical manufacturing: drug delivery, information technology, research and development, analytical development and control, equipment and facility manufacturing and regulatory affairs.
Formerly (until 2009): American Drug Discovery (1558-4461)
Related titles: Online - full text ed.: ISSN 2150-4806.
—BLDSC (0812.870000), IE. **CCC.**
Published by: Russell Publishing LLC, 9225 Priority Way West Dr, Ste 120, Indianapolis, IN 46240. TEL 317-816-8787, FAX 317-816-8788, info@russpub.com, http://www.russpub.com. Ed. Adam Young. Pub. Nigel Russell.

615 616.97 GBR ISSN 1567-5769
RM370 CODEN: IINMBA
➤ **INTERNATIONAL IMMUNOPHARMACOLOGY.** Text in English. 2001. 14/yr. EUR 2,782 in Europe to institutions; JPY 369,200 in Japan to institutions; USD 3,111 elsewhere to institutions (effective 2012). adv. back issues avail.; reprints avail. **Document type:** *Journal, Academic/Scholarly.* **Description:** Features contributions of clinical relevance which integrate pharmacology and immunology.
Formed by the merger of (1979-2000): International Journal of Immunopharmacology (0192-0561); (1978-2000): Immunopharmacology (0162-3109)
Related titles: Microfilm ed.: (from PQC); Online - full text ed.: ISSN 1878-1705 (from IngentaConnect, ScienceDirect).
Indexed: A01, A03, A08, A22, A26, A29, A34, A35, A36, A38, AIDS&CR, ASCA, AgBio, AgrForAb, B&BAb, B19, B20, B21, B25, BIOBASE, BIOSIS Prev, BP, C25, C30, C33, CA, CABA, CIN, ChemAb, ChemTitl, CurCont, D01, DBA, E12, EMBASE, ESPM, ExcerpMed, F08, F11, F12, FCA, GH, H16, H17, I05, I10, IABS, ISR, ImmunAb, IndMed, IndVet, Inpharma, MEDLINE, MycolAb, N02, N03, N04, P30, P32, P33, P35, P37, P39, PGegResA, PGrRegA, PN&I, R07, R08, R10, R11, R12, R13, RA&MP, RM&VM, Reac, S01, S12, S17, SCI, SCOPUS, SoyAb, T02, T05, ToxAb, TriticAb, VS, VirolAbstr, W07, W10.
—BLDSC (4541.038960), CASDDS, GNLM, IE, Infotrieve, Ingenta, INIST. **CCC.**
Published by: Elsevier Ltd (Subsidiary of: Elsevier Science & Technology), The Blvd, Langford Ln, Kidlington, Oxford, OX5 1GB, United Kingdom. TEL 44-1865-843000, FAX 44-1865-843010, journalscustomerserviceemea@elsevier.com. Eds. Dr. J E Talmadge TEL 402-559-5639, Dr. T. E. Hugli. Circ: 1,250. **Subscr. to:** Elsevier BV, Radarweg 29, PO Box 211, Amsterdam 1000 AE, Netherlands. TEL 31-20-4853757, FAX 31-20-4853432, http://www.elsevier.nl.

613.2 CHE ISSN 0300-9831
QP771 CODEN: IJVNAP
➤ **INTERNATIONAL JOURNAL FOR VITAMIN AND NUTRITION RESEARCH.** Text in English. 1930. bi-m. CHF 658 domestic to institutions; EUR 439 in Europe to institutions; USD 609 elsewhere to institutions (effective 2011). adv. bk.rev. abstr.; illus. Index. reprints avail. **Document type:** *Journal, Academic/Scholarly.* **Description:** Provides a scientific international forum for work on the two vast and closely connected research fields of vitaminology and nutrition.
Former titles (until 1971): Internationale Zeitschrift fuer Vitaminforschung (0020-9406); (until 1947): Zeitschrift fuer Vitaminforschung (0373-0239)
Related titles: Online - full text ed.: ISSN 1664-2821; Supplement(s): International Journal for Vitamin and Nutrition Research. Supplement. ISSN 0373-0883. 1940.
Indexed: A22, A34, A35, A36, A37, A38, ASCA, AgBio, Agr, B25, BIOBASE, BIOSIS Prev, C25, C33, CABA, CIN, ChemAb, ChemTitl, CurCont, D01, DBA, E12, EMBASE, ExcerpMed, F05, F06, F07, F08, F09, FS&TA, GH, H16, IABS, IBR, IBZ, ISR, IndMed, Inpharma, LT, MEDLINE, MaizeAb, MycolAb, N02, N03, N04, NRN, P30, P33, P37, P38, P39, PN&I, R08, R10, R11, R12, RA&MP, RRTA, Reac, S12, SCI, SCOPUS, SoyAb, T05, TAR, TOSA, TriticAb, VITIS, VS, W07, W11, WildRev.
—BLDSC (4542.698000), CASDDS, GNLM, IE, Infotrieve, Ingenta, INIST, Linda Hall. **CCC.**
Published by: Verlag Hans Huber AG (Subsidiary of: Hogrefe Verlag GmbH & Co. KG), Laenggassstr 76, Bern 9, 3000, Switzerland. TEL 41-31-3004500, FAX 41-31-3004590, verlag@hanshuber.com, http://www.hanshuber.com. Ed. Richard Hurrell. Circ: 500 (controlled).

615 IND ISSN 2230-7583
▼ ➤ **INTERNATIONAL JOURNAL OD ADVANCES IN PHARMACEUTICAL RESEARCH.** Text in English. 2010. m. free (effective 2011). **Document type:** *Journal, Academic/Scholarly.*
Media: Online - full text.
Published by: KMR Pharma Welfare Association http://www.pharmaadvice.org. Ed. William Carey.

615 IND ISSN 0976-1055
▼ **INTERNATIONAL JOURNAL OF ADVANCES IN PHARMACEUTICAL SCIENCES.** Text in English. 2010. q. free (effective 2011). **Document type:** *Journal, Academic/Scholarly.*
Media: Online - full text.
Indexed: A01, T02.
Published by: Advanced Research Journals Eds. Fatma Ulku Afifi, Talaj Ahmad Aburjai.

▼ **INTERNATIONAL JOURNAL OF APPLIED BIOLOGY AND PHARMACEUTICAL TECHNOLOGY.** *see* BIOLOGY

615 IND ISSN 0975-7058
▼ **INTERNATIONAL JOURNAL OF APPLIED PHARMACEUTICS.** Abbreviated title: I J A P. Text in English. 2009. q. **Document type:** *Journal, Academic/Scholarly.* **Description:** Publishes original research work that contributes significantly to further the scientific knowledge in pharmaceutical sciences.
Media: Online - full text.
Address: c/o Avijeet Jain, 6/1 Sanjeevani Medical Stores, Shastri Chowk, Sadar Bazar, Sagar, Madhya Pradesh, India. Ed. Abhilasha Jain.

INTERNATIONAL JOURNAL OF BIOMEDICAL AND PHARMACEUTICAL SCIENCES. *see* MEDICAL SCIENCES

615.1 DEU ISSN 0946-1965
RM1 CODEN: ICTHEK
➤ **INTERNATIONAL JOURNAL OF CLINICAL PHARMACOLOGY AND THERAPEUTICS.** Text in English. 1967. m. USD 305 to institutions; USD 330 combined subscription to institutions (print & online eds.) (effective 2011). adv. bibl.; charts; illus.; abstr. back issues avail.; reprints avail. **Document type:** *Journal, Academic/Scholarly.*
Description: Presents articles and features on all aspects of clinical pharmacology including clinical trials, pharmacoepidemiology, pharmacodynamics, drug disposition and pharmacokinetics, quality assurance, pharmacogenetics, and biotechnological drugs such as cytokines and recombinant antibiotics.
Former titles (until 1994): International Journal of Clinical Pharmacology, Therapy and Toxicology (0174-4879); (until 1980): International Journal of Clinical Pharmacology and Biopharmacy (0340-0026); (until 1975): International Journal of Clinical Pharmacology, Therapy and Toxicology (0300-9718); (until 1972): Internationale Zeitschrift fuer Klinische Pharmakologie, Therapie und Toxikologie (0020-9392)
Related titles: Online - full text ed.: USD 305 to institutions (effective 2011); Supplement(s): Advances in Clinical Pharmacology. ISSN 0303-2671. 1969.
Indexed: A22, A34, A35, A36, ASCA, AgBio, B25, BIOBASE, BIOSIS Prev, BP, CA, CABA, CIN, CIS, CMCI, ChemAb, ChemTitl, CurCont, D01, DBA, DentInd, E12, EMBASE, ExcerpMed, F08, F11, F12, FR, GH, H16, H17, I12, IABS, IBR, IBZ, IDIS, ISR, IndMed, Inpharma, LT, MEDLINE, MycolAb, N02, N03, P30, P33, P35, P39, PN&I, PsycholAb, R08, R10, R12, R13, RA&MP, RM&VM, RRTA, Reac, SCI, SCOPUS, T02, T05, TAR, VS, W07.
—BLDSC (4542.170700), CASDDS, GNLM, IE, Infotrieve, Ingenta, INIST, Linda Hall. **CCC.**
Published by: Dustri-Verlag Dr. Karl Feistle, Bajuwarenring 4, Oberhaching, 82041, Germany. TEL 49-89-6138610, FAX 49-89-6135412, info@dustri.de, http://www.dustri.de. Ed. B Woodcock. Circ: 1,200.

615.19 CHE ISSN 0251-1649
CODEN: CPHRDE
➤ **INTERNATIONAL JOURNAL OF CLINICAL PHARMACOLOGY RESEARCH.** Short title: Clinical Pharmacology Research. Text in English. 1981. q. CHF 400 (effective 2003). reprints avail. **Document type:** *Journal, Academic/Scholarly.*
Indexed: A22, ASCA, BIOSIS Prev, CIN, ChemAb, ChemTitl, DBA, EMBASE, ExcerpMed, FR, ISR, IndMed, Inpharma, Kidney, MEDLINE, MycolAb, P30, R10, Reac, SCOPUS, ToxAb.
—CASDDS, GNLM, IE, Infotrieve, Ingenta, INIST. **CCC.**
Published by: Bioscience Ediprint Inc., Rue Alexandre Gavard 16, Carouge, 1227, Switzerland. TEL 41-22-3003383, FAX 41-22-3002489, bioscience.smey@gkb.com. Ed. A Bertell.

615 NLD ISSN 2210-7703
CODEN: PWSCED
➤ **INTERNATIONAL JOURNAL OF CLINICAL PHARMACY.** Text in English. 1979. bi-m. EUR 333, USD 338 combined subscription to institutions (print & online eds.) (effective 2012). adv. bk.rev. reprint service avail. from PSC. **Document type:** *Journal, Academic/Scholarly.* **Description:** Provides a medium for the publication of articles on clinical pharmacy and related practice-oriented subjects in the pharmaceutical sciences. The scope of the journal is clinical pharmacy, its research and its application in e.g. pharmaceutical care.
Former titles (until 2011): Pharmacy World and Science (0928-1231); (until 1992): Pharmaceutisch Weekblad. Scientific Edition (0167-6555)
Related titles: Online - full text ed.: ISSN 2210-7711 (from IngentaConnect).

Indexed: A20, A22, A26, A36, ASCA, Agr, B21, BibLing, C06, C07, CA, CABA, CIN, ChemAb, ChemTitl, CurCont, DBA, E01, EMBASE, ESPM, ExcerpMed, GH, H&SSA, H17, I12, IDIS, INI, ISR, IndMed, Inpharma, MEDLINE, N02, N03, P20, P22, P24, P30, P33, P35, P48, P54, PHN&I, PQC, R10, R12, RA&MP, Reac, RefZh, RiskAb, SCI, SCOPUS, T02, T05, W07, W11.
—BLDSC (6447.541000), CASDDS, GNLM, IE, Infotrieve, Ingenta, INIST, Linda Hall. **CCC.**
Published by: (Koninklijke Nederlandse Maatschappij ter Bevordering der Pharmacie/Royal Netherlands Pharmaceutical Society), Springer Netherlands (Subsidiary of: Springer Science+Business Media), Van Godewijckstraat 30, Dordrecht, 3311 GX, Netherlands. TEL 31-78-6576050, FAX 31-78-6576474, http://www.springer.com. Ed. J W F van Mil. **Co-sponsor:** European Society of Clinical Pharmacy.

➤ **INTERNATIONAL JOURNAL OF COMPUTATIONAL BIOLOGY AND DRUG DESIGN.** *see* BIOLOGY

615 IND ISSN 0975-0215
RS199.5
▼ **INTERNATIONAL JOURNAL OF DRUG DELIVERY.** Text in English. 2009. irreg. free (effective 2011). **Document type:** *Journal, Academic/Scholarly.*
Media: Online - full text.
Indexed: A01, T02.
Published by: Advanced Research Journals http://www.arjournals.org. Ed. Vladimir P Torchilin.

615 IND ISSN 0975-4423
▼ ➤ **INTERNATIONAL JOURNAL OF DRUG DISCOVERY.** Text in English. 2009. s-a. USD 425 (effective 2011). **Document type:** *Journal, Academic/Scholarly.* **Description:** Aims to publish all the latest and outstanding research articles, reviews and letters in all areas of modern drug discovery by the pharmaceutical industry, current drug discovery technologies, rational drug design and discovery including medicinal chemistry, in-silico drug design, combinatorial chemistry, high-throughput screening, drug targets, and structure-activity relationships.
Related titles: Online - full text ed.: ISSN 0975-914X. free (effective 2011).
Indexed: A01, T02.
Published by: Bioinfo Publications, 49/F-72, Vighnahar Complex, Front of Overseas Bank, Sector 12, Kharghar, Navi Mumbai, 410 210, India. TEL 91-22-27743967, FAX 91-22-66736413, editor@bioinfo.in. Ed. Marc Poirot.

615 IND ISSN 2229-5054
▼ ➤ **INTERNATIONAL JOURNAL OF DRUG FORMULATION AND RESEARCH.** Text in English. 2010. bi-m. free (effective 2011). **Document type:** *Journal, Academic/Scholarly.*
Media: Online - full text.
Address: editor@ordonearresearchlibrary.org. Ed. Manoj Sharma.

➤ **INTERNATIONAL JOURNAL OF DRUG POLICY.** *see* DRUG ABUSE AND ALCOHOLISM

615 ISR ISSN 0793-694X
INTERNATIONAL JOURNAL OF GENERIC DRUGS. Text in English. 1996. q. EUR 999, USD 1,499 to individuals; EUR 1,199, USD 1,699 to institutions; EUR 1,399, USD 1,999 combined subscription to institutions print & online eds. (effective 2008). **Document type:** *Journal, Academic/Scholarly.* **Description:** Publishes articles reviews and papers on all aspects of Generic and Innovative Drug Development from pre-formulation to aspects of regulatory strategy.
Related titles: Online - full text ed.
—CCC.
Published by: Locum International Publishers, Locum International House, PO Box 874, Kochav Yair, 44864, Israel. TEL 972-9-7494965, FAX 972-9-7494532, info@locumusa.com, http://www.locum.co.il/.

615 IND ISSN 0973-8258
INTERNATIONAL JOURNAL OF GREEN PHARMACY. Abbreviated title: I J G P. Text in English. 2006. q. INR 1,500 domestic to individuals; USD 100 foreign to individuals; INR 2,500 domestic to institutions; USD 200 foreign to institutions; INR 1,800 combined subscription domestic to individuals (print & online eds.); USD 120 combined subscription foreign to individuals (print & online eds.); INR 3,000 combined subscription domestic to institutions (print & online eds.); USD 240 combined subscription foreign to institutions (print & online eds.) (effective 2011). adv. **Document type:** *Journal, Academic/Scholarly.*
Related titles: Online - full text ed.: ISSN 1998-4103. INR 1,200 domestic to individuals; USD 80 foreign to individuals; INR 2,000 domestic to institutions; USD 160 foreign to institutions (effective 2011).
Indexed: A01, A26, A34, A35, A36, A38, AgBio, AgrForAb, B23, BA, BP, C04, C25, C30, CA, CABA, D01, E12, EMBASE, ExcerpMed, F08, F11, F12, FCA, GH, H12, H16, H17, I05, I11, IndVet, MaizeAb, N02, N03, N05, O01, P05, P10, P32, P33, P39, P40, P48, P53, P54, PGegResA, PHN&I, PQC, R07, R12, R13, RA&MP, RM&VM, S12, S13, S16, S17, SCOPUS, SoyAb, T02, T05, TAR, VS, W10, W11.
—BLDSC (4542.268900), IE. **CCC.**
Published by: (B R Nahata College of Pharmacy), Medknow Publications and Media Pvt. Ltd., B-9, Kanara Business Ctr, Off Link Rd, Ghatkopar (E), Mumbai, Maharastra 400 075, India. TEL 91-22-66491816, FAX 91-22-66491817, http://www.medknow.com.

▼ **INTERNATIONAL JOURNAL OF HIGH THROUGHPUT SCREENING.** *see* CHEMISTRY

INTERNATIONAL JOURNAL OF IMMUNOPATHOLOGY AND PHARMACOLOGY. *see* MEDICAL SCIENCES—Allergology And Immunology

615 610 IND ISSN 2231-2188
▼ ➤ **INTERNATIONAL JOURNAL OF MEDICAL AND PHARMACEUTICAL SCIENCES.** Abbreviated title: I J M P S. Text in English. 2011 (Feb.). m. INR 4,500 domestic to individuals; USD 120 foreign to individuals; INR 5,500 domestic to institutions; USD 150 foreign to institutions (effective 2011). a. index. back issues avail.; reprints avail. **Document type:** *Journal, Academic/Scholarly.* **Description:** Contains research and review articles in all fields of medical and pharmaceutical sciences.
Related titles: Online - full text ed.
Published by: Radiance Multipurpose Society, Radiance Bahu-uddeshiya Sanstha, 242/8, Snehgandha Apt, Near Shikshak Sahkari Bank, New Nandanwan, Nagpur, Maharastra 440 009, India. TEL 91-9890099611, ijmps@gmail.com. Ed., Pub. Sushant P. Circ: 500.

➤ **INTERNATIONAL JOURNAL OF MEDICAL TOXICOLOGY AND LEGAL MEDICINE.** *see* ENVIRONMENTAL STUDIES—Toxicology And Environmental Safety

▼ ➤ **INTERNATIONAL JOURNAL OF MEDICINE AND PUBLIC HEALTH.** *see* PUBLIC HEALTH AND SAFETY

610 GBR ISSN 1178-2013
➤ **INTERNATIONAL JOURNAL OF NANOMEDICINE (ONLINE).** Text in English. irreg. free (effective 2011). back issues avail. **Document type:** *Journal, Academic/Scholarly.* **Description:** Covers the application of nanotechnology in diagnostics, therapeutics, and drug delivery systems throughout the biomedical field.
Media: Online - full text.
—CCC.
Published by: Dove Medical Press Ltd., Beechfield House, Winterton Way, Macclesfield, SK11 0JL, United Kingdom. TEL 44-1625-509130, FAX 44-1625-617933. Ed. Thomas J Webster.

615 615.5 MYS ISSN 1985-0735
▼ ➤ **INTERNATIONAL JOURNAL OF NATURAL PRODUCTS AND PHARMACEUTICAL SCIENCES.** Text in English. 2009. bi-m. free (effective 2010). **Document type:** *Journal, Academic/Scholarly.* **Description:** Publishes research reports in the form of original articles or short communications, reviews or mini-reviews on all aspects of the natural product as well as pharmaceutical sciences, with strong prominence on innovation and scientific excellence.
Media: Online - full content.
Published by: Science Beacon Journals

615.1 616.89 GBR ISSN 1461-1457
RM315 CODEN: IJNUFB
➤ **INTERNATIONAL JOURNAL OF NEUROPSYCHOPHARMACOLOGY.** Text in English. 1998. 10/yr. GBP 615, USD 1,075 to institutions; GBP 680, USD 1,190 combined subscription to institutions (print & online eds.) (effective 2012). adv. Supplement avail.; back issues avail.; reprint service avail. from PSC. **Document type:** *Journal, Academic/Scholarly.* **Description:** Publishes original research in basic pharmacology, human psychopharmacological research, and related areas.
Related titles: Online - full text ed.: ISSN 1469-5111. 1998. GBP 425, USD 745 to institutions (effective 2012).
Indexed: A20, A22, AddicA, B21, B25, BIOBASE, BIOSIS Prev, CA, CurCont, E-psyche, E01, EMBASE, ExcerpMed, FoP, IABS, ISR, Inpharma, MEDLINE, MycolAb, NSA, NSCI, P03, P20, P22, P25, P30, P35, P48, P54, PQC, PsycInfo, PsycholAb, R10, Reac, RefZh, SCI, SCOPUS, T02, W07.
—BLDSC (4542.383000), IE, Infotrieve, Ingenta, INIST. **CCC.**
Published by: (Collegium Internationale Neuro-Psychopharmacologicum), Cambridge University Press, The Edinburgh Bldg, Shaftesbury Rd, Cambridge, CB2 8RU, United Kingdom. TEL 44-1223-312393, FAX 44-1223-315052, journals@cambridge.org, http://www.cambridge.org/uk. Ed. Alan Frazer. R&P Linda Nicol TEL 44-1223-325702. Adv. contact Rebecca Roberts TEL 44-1223-325083. **Subscr. to:** Cambridge University Press, 32 Ave of the Americas, New York, NY 10013. TEL 212-337-5000, FAX 212-691-3239, journals_subscriptions@cup.org.

615 570 IND ISSN 0975-6299
▼ ➤ **INTERNATIONAL JOURNAL OF PHARMA AND BIO SCIENCES.** Text in English. 2010. q. free (effective 2011). back issues avail. **Document type:** *Journal, Academic/Scholarly.* **Description:** Covers pharmaceutics, novel drug delivery system, pharmacognosy, pharmacology, microbiology, cytology, biotechnology, chemistry, biophysics, and pharmaceutical analysis.
Media: Online - full text.
Indexed: A01, A34, A35, A36, AgBio, AgrForAb, C25, C30, CABA, E12, F08, FCA, GH, H16, I11, N02, N03, N04, O01, P32, P33, P40, R12, R13, RA&MP, RM&VM, S13, S16, T05, TAR.
Published by: P. Muthuprasanna Pub. & Ed., 4-17-91/18A,Velangini Nagar, Amaravathi Rd., Guntur, Andrapradesh 522002, India. Ed., Pub. P. Muthuprasanna.

615 IND ISSN 0976-6723
▼ **INTERNATIONAL JOURNAL OF PHARMA PROFESSIONAL'S RESEARCH.** Abbreviated title: I J P P R. Text in English. 2010. q. **Document type:** *Journal, Academic/Scholarly.* **Description:** Publishes innovative research articles on pharmaceutical research.
Media: Online - full text.
Address: c/o Akhil Sharma, Managing Ed., 741/21, Kailash Colony, Jail Rd, Rohtak, Haryana 124 001, India. TEL 91-9458422699. Ed. KK Jha.

615 570 IND ISSN 0976-3333
▼ **INTERNATIONAL JOURNAL OF PHARMACEUTICAL AND BIOLOGICAL ARCHIVES.** Text in English. 2010. bi-m. free (effective 2011). **Document type:** *Journal, Academic/Scholarly.*
Media: Online - full text.
Published by: Mandsaur Institute of Pharmacy, Rewas-Dewda Rd, Near MIT Campus, Mandsaur, Madhia Pradesh 458 001, India. Ed. M A Naidu.

615 570 IND ISSN 0976-285X
▼ ➤ **INTERNATIONAL JOURNAL OF PHARMACEUTICAL AND BIOLOGICAL RESEARCH.** Text in English. 2010. bi-m. free (effective 2011). bk.rev. **Document type:** *Journal, Academic/Scholarly.* **Description:** Publishes research and review articles in pharmaceutics, pharmaceutical nanotechnology, pharmaceutical analysis, pharmaceutical chemistry, medicinal chemistry, industrial pharmacy, biopharmaceutics,pharmacokinetics, physical pharmacy, pharmacognosy, phytochemistry, pharmacology, ethnopharmacology, toxicology, pharmacy practice, clinical and hospital pharmacy, genomics and proteomics, bioinformatics and biotechnology, pharmacogenomics and pharmacoeconomics, bioengineering, bioethics, biomedical engineering, biotechnology, medical informatics, medicine, medical sciences, pharmacy, psychology and all areas of allied health sciences, management, technology, law and public health and bioentrepreneurship & biomarketing, geosciences, atmospheric sciences, and remote sensing; biometrics and forensics.
Media: Online - full text.
Indexed: A34, A35, A36, A38, AgrForAb, CABA, E12, F08, GH, H16, P33, T05.
Published by: K E J A Publications, 4/122, Perumal Naicker Complex, 2nd Fl, G.S.T. Rd, Otteri, Vandalur Post, Chennai, Tamil Nadu 600 048, India. TEL 91-904-3687764. Ed., Pub., R&P S Selvi.

615 IND ISSN 0976-0350
RM300
▼ ➤ **INTERNATIONAL JOURNAL OF PHARMACEUTICAL AND BIOMEDICAL RESEARCH.** Text in English. 2010. q. free (effective 2011). **Document type:** *Journal, Academic/Scholarly.*
Media: Online - full text.
Published by: PharmSciDirect Publications

➤ **INTERNATIONAL JOURNAL OF PHARMACEUTICAL AND HEALTHCARE MARKETING.** *see* BUSINESS AND ECONOMICS—Marketing And Purchasing

615 IND ISSN 2249-6084
▼ ➤ **INTERNATIONAL JOURNAL OF PHARMACEUTICAL AND PHYTOPHARMACOLOGICAL RESEARCH.** Abbreviated title: I J P P R. Text in English. 2011. bi-m. adv. back issues avail. **Document type:** *Journal, Academic/Scholarly.* **Description:** Publishes research papers, review articles and short communications dealing with pharmaceuticals. It promotes communication between educators, researchers, industry and government personnel involved in pharmaceutical research and developments.
Media: Online - full text.
Address: c/o Mrs. Anjali Harshal Pawar, EIC, C/O-613-E, Matru-Ami Apt, Behind New High school, Joshi Baug, Kalyan West, Maharastra 421 301, India. TEL 91-8097148638, editor@eijppr.com, submit@eijppr.com. Ed., Pub., R&P Anjali Pawar.

615 USA ISSN 1092-4221
RS200
➤ **INTERNATIONAL JOURNAL OF PHARMACEUTICAL COMPOUNDING.** Abbreviated title: I J P C. Text in English. 1997. bi-m. USD 175 in US & Canada to individuals; USD 225 elsewhere to individuals; USD 200 in US & Canada to institutions; USD 250 elsewhere to institutions (effective 2011). adv. cum. index: 1997-1999. back issues avail. **Document type:** *Journal, Academic/Scholarly.* **Description:** Provides information about contemporary pharmaceutical compounding.
Related titles: Online - full text ed.: ISSN 1943-5223. USD 175 to individuals; USD 200 to institutions (effective 2011); Portuguese ed.
Indexed: C06, C07, C08, CINAHL, EMBASE, ExcerpMed, I12, IDIS, P24, P48, PQC, R10, Reac, SCOPUS.
—BLDSC (4542.452930), IE, Ingenta. **CCC.**
Address: 122 N Bryant Ave, Edmond, OK 73034. TEL 405-330-0094, 800-757-4572, FAX 405-330-5622, 877-757-4575, subs@ijpc.com. Ed. Loyd V Allen Jr. TEL 405-330-0094 ext 2. Adv. contact Lauren Bernick TEL 405-513-4236.

615 IND ISSN 0975-2366
▼ **INTERNATIONAL JOURNAL OF PHARMACEUTICAL RESEARCH.** Abbreviated title: I J P R. Text and summaries in English. 2009 (Jan.). q. INR 1,800 domestic to individuals; USD 100 foreign to individuals; INR 2,000 domestic to institutions; USD 150 foreign to institutions (effective 2011). adv. **Document type:** *Journal, Academic/Scholarly.* **Description:** Publishes innovative papers, reviews, and rapid communication, in pharmaceutics, biopharmaceutics, pharmaceutical chemistry, pharmacognosy, pharmacology, pharmaceutical analysis, pharmacy practice, clinical and hospital pharmacy.
Media: Online - full text. **Related titles:** CD-ROM ed.
Published by: Association of Indian Pharmacist, B/302, Green Ave - I, O/P Shivalik Western, L. P. Savani School Rd, Adajan, Surat, 395 009, India. TEL 91-261-2739527, info@ijpronline.com. Ed., R&P Dr. Vineet C Jain. Adv. contact Dr. Dhiren P Shah. Circ: 80 (paid); 20 (controlled).

615 IND ISSN 0974-9446
RM300
▼ **INTERNATIONAL JOURNAL OF PHARMACEUTICAL RESEARCH AND DEVELOPMENT.** Added title page title: I J P R D. Text in English. 2009. m. free (effective 2011). **Document type:** *Journal, Academic/Scholarly.*
Media: Online - full text.
Published by: International Journal of Pharmaceutical Research and Development (I J P R D) Ed. Kishor Jaysingh Nagargoje.

615 GBR ISSN 2046-5114
▼ **INTERNATIONAL JOURNAL OF PHARMACEUTICAL RESEARCH AND INNOVATION.** Abbreviated title: I J P R I. Text in English. 2010. q. free (effective 2011). **Document type:** *Journal, Academic/Scholarly.* **Description:** Publishes high-quality solicited and unsolicited articles, in English, in all areas of pharmaceutical sciences related to formulation and development.
Media: Online - full text.
Published by: Whites Science International, Editorial Office, 32, City Garden, Grangetown, Cardiff, CF11 8HD, United Kingdom. TEL 44-29-20666174, info@whitesscience.com. Ed. Alfred Kim.

615 660.6 IND ISSN 2229-3604
▼ **INTERNATIONAL JOURNAL OF PHARMACEUTICAL SCIENCE AND BIOTECHNOLOGY.** Text in English. 2010. m. **Document type:** *Journal, Academic/Scholarly.*
Media: Online - full text.
Address: 14, Sudama Colony 2, Sudama Nagar, Ramtakari, Madsaur 458110, India. Ed. C P Jain.

615 IND ISSN 0975-4725
▼ **INTERNATIONAL JOURNAL OF PHARMACEUTICAL SCIENCES.** Text in English. 2009. 3/yr. free (effective 2011). **Document type:** *Journal, Academic/Scholarly.*
Media: Online - full text.
Published by: RR College of Pharmacy, 67 RR Layout, Chikkabanavara, Bangalore, India.

615 IND ISSN 0975-248X
▼ ➤ **INTERNATIONAL JOURNAL OF PHARMACEUTICAL SCIENCES AND DRUG RESEARCH.** Text in English. 2009. q. free (effective 2011).
Media: Online - full text.
Address: c/o Kalpesh Gaur, 238 Gali Buchi Ram, Ratiya Bazar, Raya, Mathura, Uttar Pradesh 281 204, India. TEL 91-5663-274765. Ed. Kalpesh Gaur.

P

615 IND ISSN 0975-8232
▼➤ **INTERNATIONAL JOURNAL OF PHARMACEUTICAL SCIENCES AND RESEARCH.** Text in English. 2010. m. free (effective 2010). adv. abstr. **Document type:** *Journal, Academic/Scholarly.* **Description:** Contains research papers, reviews, mini-reviews, short communications and notes dealing with pharmaceutical sciences, including: Pharmaceutical technology, pharmaceutics, biopharmaceutics, pharmacokinetics, pharmaceutical/medicinal chemistry, computational chemistry and molecular drug design, pharmacognosy and phytochemistry, pharmacology, pharmaceutical analysis, pharmacy practice, clinical and hospital pharmacy, cell biology, genomics and proteomics, pharmacogenomics, bioinformatics and biotechnology of pharmaceutical interest.
Media: Online - full text.
Indexed: A34, A35, A36, A37, A38, AgrForAb, C25, C30, CABA, E12, F08, GH, H16, N02, N03, P32, P33, R07, R08, S13, T05.
Published by: Shashi Alok Ed. & Pub., A-14, Bundelkhand University, BU Campus, Jhansi, Uttar Pradesh 284128, India. TEL 91-945-0036362.

615 IND ISSN 0976-044X
RM300
▼➤ **INTERNATIONAL JOURNAL OF PHARMACEUTICAL SCIENCES REVIEW AND RESEARCH.** Text in English. 2010. bi-m. free (effective 2011). Index. back issues avail. **Document type:** *Journal, Academic/Scholarly.* **Description:** Publishes review and research articles on pharmaceutical sciences.
Media: Online - full text.
Indexed: A01, P20, P48, P54, PQC, T02.
Published by: Global Research Online, Plot No: 6, R. K. Lake View, Hebbagudi, Anekal Taluk, Bangalore, India. Ed., Pub., R&P, Adv. contact N. Santosh Kumar.

615 IND ISSN 0975-3079
INTERNATIONAL JOURNAL OF PHARMACEUTICALS ANALYSIS. Text in English. s-a. USD 425 (effective 2011). **Document type:** *Journal, Academic/Scholarly.* **Description:** Publishes all the latest research articles, reviews and letters in all areas of major importance to pharmaceutical, biochemical and clinical analysis, clinical research, modern drug design, medicinal chemistry, pharmacology, drug targets and disease mechanism, pharmaceutical drug targets involved in diseases e.g. disease specific proteins, receptors, enzymes, genes, biochemistry, biophysics.
Related titles: Online - full text ed.: ISSN 0975-9190. free (effective 2011).
Indexed: A01.
Published by: Bioinfo Publications, 49/F-72, Vighnahar Complex, Front of Overseas Bank, Sector 12, Kharghar, Navi Mumbai, 410 210, India. TEL 91-22-27743967, FAX 91-22-66736413, editor@bioinfo.in, subscription@bioinfo.in. Eds. Benny Abraham Kaipparettu, Dr. Feng Liang, Dr. Virendra S Gomase.

615 NLD ISSN 0378-5173
RS1 CODEN: IJPHDE
➤ **INTERNATIONAL JOURNAL OF PHARMACEUTICS.** Text in English. 1978. 38/yr. EUR 9,189 in Europe to institutions; JPY 1,220,500 in Japan to institutions; USD 10,280 elsewhere to institutions (effective 2012). adv. abstr. back issues avail.; reprints avail. **Document type:** *Journal, Academic/Scholarly.* **Description:** Publishes research results dealing with all aspects of pharmaceutics including physical, chemical, analytical, biological and engineering studies related to drug delivery.
Related titles: Microform ed.: (from PQC); Online - full text ed.: ISSN 1873-3476 (from IngentaConnect, ScienceDirect).
Indexed: A01, A03, A08, A22, A26, A34, A35, A36, ASCA, ASFA, AgBio, AgrForAb, B&BAb, B19, B21, B25, BIOSIS Prev, BP, BioDAb, BioEngAb, C25, C33, CA, CABA, CIN, CTA, ChemAb, ChemTitl, CurCont, D01, DBA, E12, EMBASE, ESPM, ExcerpMed, F08, F11, F12, GH, GenetAb, GeoRef, H&SSA, H16, H17, I05, I10, I12, ISR, IndMed, IndVet, Inpharma, M&PBA, MEDLINE, MycolAb, N02, N03, N04, NSA, O01, P30, P32, P33, P35, P38, P39, P40, PHN&I, PN&I, R07, R08, R10, RA&MP, RM&VM, Reac, RefZh, S01, S12, SCI, SCOPUS, SoyAb, T02, T05, ToxAb, VS, W07, W10.
—BLDSC (4542.454000), CASDDS, GNLM, IE, Infotrieve, Ingenta, INIST, Linda Hall. **CCC.**
Published by: Elsevier BV (Subsidiary of: Elsevier Science & Technology), Radarweg 29, PO Box 211, Amsterdam, 1000 AE, Netherlands. TEL 31-20-4853911, FAX 31-20-4852457, JournalsCustomerServiceEMEA@elsevier.com, http://www.elsevier.nl. Ed. A T Florence.

615 PAK ISSN 1811-7775
➤ **INTERNATIONAL JOURNAL OF PHARMACOLOGY.** Text in English. 2005. q. **Document type:** *Journal, Academic/Scholarly.* **Description:** Provides broad coverage of all aspects of the interactions of chemicals with biological systems, including autonomic, behavioral, cardiovascular, cellular, clinical, developmental, gastrointestinal, immuno-, neuro-, pulmonary, and renal pharmacology, as well as analgesics, drug abuse, metabolism and disposition, chemotherapy, and toxicology.
Related titles: Online - full text ed.: ISSN 1812-5700. free (effective 2011).
Indexed: A01, A34, A35, A36, A38, AgBio, AgrForAb, B&BAb, B19, B21, B25, BIOSIS Prev, BP, BioEngAb, C25, C30, CA, CABA, D01, E12, EMBASE, ESPM, ExcerpMed, F08, F11, F12, GH, H16, H17, IndVet, LT, M&PBA, MycolAb, N02, N03, N04, N05, P32, P33, P37, P39, P40, PGegResA, PGrRegA, PHN&I, PN&I, R07, R08, R10, R13, RA&MP, RM&VM, RRTA, Reac, S12, S13, S16, SCI, SCOPUS, SoyAb, T02, T05, TAR, VS, W07, W10.
—BLDSC (4542.454250), IE, Ingenta.
Published by: A N S I Network, 308 Lasani Town, Sargodha Rd, Faisalabad, 38090, Pakistan. TEL 92-41-2001145, FAX 92-41-731433, http://www.ansijournals.com.

615 IND ISSN 2249-1848
▼➤ **INTERNATIONAL JOURNAL OF PHARMACY.** Abbreviated title: I J P. Text and summaries in English. 2011. q. free (effective 2011). adv. back issues avail. **Document type:** *Journal, Academic/Scholarly.* **Description:** Promotes the latest advancements in research, publishes the latest research findings in pharmacy. It publishes original articles, review articles and short communications in various streams of pharmacy, chemistry and allied health sciences.
Media: Online - full text.
Published by: Pharma Scholars Library, Plot no. 877, Vasanth Nagar, Hyderabad, Andhra Pradesh 500 085, India. TEL 91-9866418484, editor@pharmascholars.com. Ed. Dr. Sridhar S. Pub. S Anji Raju. R&P Madhusudhana Reddy Induri.

615 IND ISSN 0975-1491
RM300
▼ **INTERNATIONAL JOURNAL OF PHARMACY AND PHARMACEUTICAL SCIENCES.** Text in English. 2009. q. free (effective 2011). back issues avail. **Document type:** *Journal, Academic/Scholarly.*
Media: Online - full text.
Indexed: A01, EMBASE, SCOPUS, T02.
Address: c/o Avijeet Jain, 6/1 Sanjeevani Medical Stores, Shastri Chowk, Sadar Bazar, Sagar, Madhya Pradesh 470 001, India. Ed. M S Bhatia.

615 IND ISSN 0975-766X
RS1
▼ **INTERNATIONAL JOURNAL OF PHARMACY AND TECHNOLOGY.** Text in English. 2009. q. free (effective 2011). **Document type:** *Journal, Academic/Scholarly.* **Description:** Publishes original research paper or short communication on pharmacy and technology related to: Pharmaceutical chemistry, pharmaceutical technology, pharmacognosy, natural product research, pharmaceutics, novel drug delivery, biopharmaceutics, pharmacokinetics, pharmaceutical/medicinal chemistry, computational chemistry and molecular drug design, pharmacology, pharmaceutical analysis, pharmacy practice, clinical and hospital pharmacy, cell biology, genomics and proteomics, pharmacogenomics, bioinformatics and biotechnology of pharmaceutical interest.
Media: Online - full text.
Indexed: A34, A35, A36, A37, AgrForAb, C30, CABA, E12, F08, F11, GH, H16, N02, N03, P32, P33, R13, S13, SoyAb, T05.
Published by: B. Anil Reddy, Ed. & Pub. TEL 91-99-5904-2280, info@ijptonline.com. Ed., Pub. Dr. Reddy Anil B.

615 USA ISSN 1557-1017
RS101
➤ **INTERNATIONAL JOURNAL OF PHARMACY EDUCATION.** Abbreviated title: I J P E. Text in English. 2003. irreg. free (effective 2011). back issues avail. **Document type:** *Journal, Academic/Scholarly.* **Description:** Emphasizes scholarly publication and communication among pharmacists, researchers, students and other health care professionals.
Media: Online - full text.
Indexed: A01, CA, I12, T02.
Published by: Samford University, McWhorter School of Pharmacy, 800 Lakeshore Dr, Birmingham, AL 35229. TEL 205-726-2011, wanunnel@samford.edu, http://pharmacy.samford.edu/. Ed. Danielle Cruthirds.

615 GBR ISSN 0961-7671
CODEN: IJPPF6
➤ **INTERNATIONAL JOURNAL OF PHARMACY PRACTICE.** Text in English. 1991. bi-m. (q. until 2008). GBP 313 in United Kingdom to institutions; EUR 432 in Europe to institutions; USD 625 elsewhere to institutions; GBP 361 combined subscription in United Kingdom to institutions (print & online eds.); EUR 498 combined subscription in Europe to institutions (print & online eds.); USD 719 combined subscription elsewhere to institutions (print & online eds.) (effective 2012). bk.rev. 2 cols./p.; back issues avail. **Document type:** *Journal, Academic/Scholarly.* **Description:** Publishes peer-reviewed papers describing research into all aspects of the practice of pharmacy and related fields.
Related titles: Online - full text ed.: ISSN 2042-7174. GBP 313 in United Kingdom to institutions; EUR 432 in Europe to institutions; USD 625 elsewhere to institutions (effective 2012).
Indexed: A22, A36, B28, BP, CABA, E01, EMBASE, ExcerpMed, GH, H01, I12, Inpharma, MEDLINE, P30, P33, P39, R10, R12, Reac, SCOPUS, T02, T05, TAR.
—BLDSC (4542.454300), GNLM, IE, Ingenta. **CCC.**
Published by: John Wiley & Sons Ltd. (Subsidiary of: John Wiley & Sons, Inc.), 1-7 Oldlands Way, PO Box 808, Bognor Regis, West Sussex PO21 9FF, United Kingdom. FAX 44-1243-843232, customer@wiley.co.uk, http://onlinelibrary.wiley.com/. Circ: 800.

615 IND ISSN 0975-9492
RM300
▼➤ **INTERNATIONAL JOURNAL OF PHARMASCIENCES AND RESEARCH.** Abbreviated title: I J P S R. Text in English. 2010. m. free (effective 2011). **Document type:** *Journal, Academic/Scholarly.*
Media: Online - full text.
Published by: K E J A Publications, 4/122, Perumal Naicker Complex, 2nd Fl, G.S.T. Rd, Otteri, Vandalur Post, Chennai, Tamil Nadu 600 048, India. TEL 91-904-3687764. Ed., Pub., R&P S Selvi.

▼➤ **INTERNATIONAL JOURNAL OF PHYSIOLOGY, PATHOPHYSIOLOGY AND PHARMACOLOGY.** *see* MEDICAL SCIENCES

➤ **INTERNATIONAL JOURNAL OF PSYCHOPATHOLOGY, PSYCHOPHARMACOLOGY, AND PSYCHOTHERAPY.** *see* PSYCHOLOGY

▼➤ **INTERNATIONAL JOURNAL OF RESEARCH IN AYURVEDA AND PHARMACY.** *see* ALTERNATIVE MEDICINE

615 IND ISSN 0975-7538
RM300
▼➤ **INTERNATIONAL JOURNAL OF RESEARCH IN PHARMACEUTICAL SCIENCES.** Text in English. 2010. q. free (effective 2011). abstr. Index. back issues avail. **Document type:** *Journal, Academic/Scholarly.* **Description:** Contains original research papers and reviews on current topics of special interest and relevance on pharmaceutical sciences and related disciplines including biotechnology, cell and molecular biology, drug utilization including adverse drug events, medical and other life sciences. Also provides an international forum for the communication and evaluation of data, methods and findings in pharmaceutical sciences and related disciplines.
Media: Online - full text.
Indexed: SCOPUS.
Published by: J K Welfare & Pharmascope Foundation, No. 95, PTR Nagar, Jawaharpuram West, Madurai, Tamil Nadu 625 007, India. http://www.pharmascope.org. Ed. T Velpandian. Pub., R&P K. Gnanaprakash.

➤ **INTERNATIONAL JOURNAL OF TOXICOLOGY.** *see* ENVIRONMENTAL STUDIES—Toxicology And Environmental Safety

615 USA ISSN 0257-3717
HV5800
INTERNATIONAL NARCOTICS CONTROL BOARD. REPORT FOR (YEAR). Text in English. 1968. a. USD 30 (effective 2008). back issues avail. **Document type:** *Report, Consumer.* **Description:** Focuses on the operation of the international drug control system, with an analysis of the world drug situation.
Former titles (until 1967): Report to the Economic and Social Council on Statistics of Narcotic Drugs (1013-400X); United Nations. International Narcotics Control Board. Annual Report; United Nations. Permanent Central Opium Board. Report of the Permanent Central Opium Board on Its Work; United Nations. Permanent Central Opium Board. Report to the Economic and Social Council on the Work of the Permanent Central Narcotics (Opium) Board (0082-8343)
Related titles: Online - full text ed.: free (effective 2008); Chinese ed.: Guoji Mazuipin Guanzhiju (Year) Baogao. ISSN 0257-3741; Arabic ed.: Al Hay'a al-Duwaliyyatt li-Muraqaba al-Muhaddirat li'Am (Year). Taqrir. ISSN 0257-375X; Russian ed.: Mezdunarodnyi Komitet po Kontrolu nad Narkotikami. Doklad za (God). ISSN 0257-3768; French ed.: L' Organe International de Controle des Stupefiants pour (Year). Rapport. ISSN 0257-3725. 1968; Spanish ed.: Informe de la Junta Internacional de Fiscalizacion de Estupefacientes Correspondiente a (Year).
Indexed: IIS.
—CCC.
Published by: (International Narcotics Control Board AUT), United Nations Publications, 2 United Nations Plaza, Rm DC2-853, New York, NY 10017. TEL 212-963-8302, 800-253-9646, FAX 212-963-3489, publications@un.org, https://unp.un.org.

615 USA ISSN 1937-6898
RS189
INTERNATIONAL PHARMACEUTICAL QUALITY. Text in English. 2007. bi-m. USD 400 (effective 2008). adv. **Document type:** *Journal, Trade.*
Related titles: Online - full text ed.: ISSN 1937-6901.
—CCC.
Address: PO Box 30510, Bethesda, MD 20824. TEL 301-656-5900. Ed. Bill Paulson.

615 NLD ISSN 1010-0423
CODEN: IPHJEN
INTERNATIONAL PHARMACY JOURNAL. Text in English; Summaries in French, German, Spanish. 1912. s-a. free to members (effective 2009). back issues avail. **Document type:** *Journal, Academic/Scholarly.* **Description:** Publishes review and original articles on pharmacy practice, and up-to-date information on new drugs and drug reactions and interactions.
Former titles (until 1986): Pharmacy International (0167-3157); (until 1980): Journal Mondial de Pharmacie (0449-2099); Bulletin del la F I P
Related titles: Microform ed.
Indexed: A20, A22, ChemAb, DBA, I12, IBR, IBZ, Inpharma, SCOPUS.
—CASDDS, GNLM, IE, INIST. **CCC.**
Published by: International Pharmaceutical Federation/Federation Internationale Pharmaceutique, PO Box 84200, The Hague, 2508 AE, Netherlands. TEL 31-70-3021970, FAX 31-70-3021999, fip@fip.org, http://www.fip.org. Eds. Lowell Anderson, Myriah Lesko.

615 IND ISSN 2230-8407
▼➤ **INTERNATIONAL RESEARCH JOURNAL OF PHARMACY.** Text and summaries in English. 2010. m. free (effective 2011). abstr.; bibl. Index. back issues avail. **Document type:** *Journal, Academic/Scholarly.* **Description:** Publishes original research work that felicitates scientific knowledge in pharmaceutical sciences. It contains original research articles, review articles, short notes, abstracts and letter to the editor in various disciples of pharmaceutical sciences.
Media: Online - full text.
Address: C/o Dr. Saurabh Sharma, Shiv Ganga Hospital, Lakser Rd, Kankhal, Haridwar, Uttaranchal 249408, India. TEL 91-9341666852, irjponline@gmail.com. Ed., Pub. Richa Sharma.

615.1 USA ISSN 1531-2976
RM1
➤ **THE INTERNET JOURNAL OF PHARMACOLOGY.** Text in English. 2001. s-a. free (effective 2011). adv. **Document type:** *Journal, Academic/Scholarly.*
Media: Online - full text.
Indexed: A01, A02, A03, A08, A26, C06, C07, CA, EMBASE, G08, H11, H12, I05, SCOPUS, T02.
Published by: Internet Scientific Publications, Llc., 23 Rippling Creek Dr, Sugar Land, TX 77479. TEL 832-443-1193, FAX 281-240-1533, wenker@ispub.com. Ed. Sam T Mathew.

615.9 USA ISSN 1559-3916
➤ **THE INTERNET JOURNAL OF TOXICOLOGY.** Text in English. 2004. s-a. free (effective 2011). **Document type:** *Journal, Academic/Scholarly.*
Media: Online - full text.
Indexed: A01, A26, C06, C07, CA, EMBASE, G08, H11, H12, I05, S06, SCOPUS, T02.
Published by: Internet Scientific Publications, Llc., 23 Rippling Creek Dr, Sugar Land, TX 77479. TEL 832-443-1193, FAX 281-240-1533, wenker@ispub.com. Ed. Dr. Francisco Leyva.

615 USA ISSN 1066-7474
RS3
INTERPHEX U S A. PROCEEDINGS OF THE TECHNICAL PROGRAM. Text in English. 19??. a. **Document type:** *Proceedings, Trade.*
Formerly (until 198?): Interphex U S A. Proceedings (1066-7482)
—CCC.
Published by: Reed Exhibitions, 383 Main Ave, Norwalk, CT 06851. TEL 203-840-4820, 888-267-3796, FAX 203-840-5580, inquiry@reedexpo.com, http://www.reedexpo.com/.

615.6 USA ISSN 1556-7443
RM170
INTRAVENOUS MEDICATIONS; a handbook for nurses and other health professionals. Text in English. 1973. a. price varies. back issues avail. **Document type:** *Monographic series.*
Published by: Mosby, Inc. (Subsidiary of: Elsevier Health Sciences), 1600 John F. Kennedy Blvd, Ste 1800, Philadelphia, PA 19103. TEL 215-239-3900, 800-523-1649, FAX 215-239-3990, elspcs@elsevier.com, http://www.us.elsevierhealth.com.

INVENTI IMPACT CLINICAL RESEARCH. *see* MEDICAL SCIENCES

615 668.5 IND ISSN 0976-7517
➤ **INVENTI IMPACT COSMECEUTICALS.** Text and summaries in English. q. INR 2,000 domestic to individuals; USD 50 foreign to individuals; INR 3,000 domestic to institutions; USD 60 foreign to institutions (effective 2011). adv. a. index. back issues avail.; reprints avail. **Document type:** *Journal, Academic/Scholarly.* **Description:** Publishes research reports, review articles and scientific commentaries on cosmeceuticals.
Media: Online - full text. **Related titles:** Print ed.: ISSN 2229-4228.
Published by: Inventi Journals Pvt. Ltd., SDX 33, Minal Residency, JK Rd, Bhopal, Madhya Pradesh 462 023, India. TEL 91-9425536487, FAX 91-11-66173705, info@inventi.in, editor@inventi.in, http://www.inventi.in. Ed. Dr. Ozgen Ozar. Pub., R&P V B Gupta. Circ: 50.

615 IND ISSN 0976-7568
➤ **INVENTI IMPACT ETHNOPHARMACOLOGY.** Text and summaries in English. q. INR 2,000 domestic to individuals; USD 50 foreign to individuals; INR 3,000 domestic to institutions; USD 60 foreign to institutions (effective 2011). adv. a. index. back issues avail.; reprints avail. **Document type:** *Journal, Academic/Scholarly.* **Description:** Publishes research reports, review articles and scientific commentaries on ethnopharmacology.
Media: Online - full text. **Related titles:** Print ed.: ISSN 2229-4155.
Published by: Inventi Journals Pvt. Ltd., SDX 33, Minal Residency, JK Rd, Bhopal, Madhya Pradesh 462 023, India. TEL 91-9425536487, FAX 91-11-66173705, info@inventi.in, editor@inventi.in, http://www.inventi.in. Ed. Dr. Rozangela Curi Pedrosa. Pub., R&P V B Gupta. Circ: 50.

615 616.027 IND ISSN 0976-7541
➤ **INVENTI IMPACT MEDCHEM.** Text and summaries in English. q. INR 2,000 domestic to individuals; USD 50 foreign to individuals; INR 3,000 domestic to institutions; USD 60 foreign to institutions (effective 2011). adv. a. index. back issues avail.; reprints avail. **Document type:** *Journal, Academic/Scholarly.* **Description:** Publishes research reports, review articles and scientific commentaries on medicinal chemistry.
Media: Online - full text. **Related titles:** Print ed.: ISSN 2229-421X.
Published by: Inventi Journals Pvt. Ltd., SDX 33, Minal Residency, JK Rd, Bhopal, Madhya Pradesh 462 023, India. TEL 91-9425536487, FAX 91-11-66173705, info@inventi.in, editor@inventi.in, http://www.inventi.in. Ed. Dr. El Ashry. Pub., R&P V B Gupta. Circ: 50.

615 IND ISSN 0976-7509
▼ ➤ **INVENTI IMPACT MOLECULAR PHARMACOLOGY.** Text and summaries in English. 2010. q. INR 2,000 domestic to individuals; USD 50 foreign to individuals; INR 3,000 domestic to institutions; USD 60 foreign to institutions (effective 2011). adv. a. index. back issues avail.; reprints avail. **Document type:** *Journal, Academic/Scholarly.* **Description:** Publishes research reports, review articles and scientific commentaries on molecular pharmacology.
Media: Online - full text. **Related titles:** Print ed.: ISSN 2229-4171.
Published by: Inventi Journals Pvt. Ltd., SDX 33, Minal Residency, JK Rd, Bhopal, Madhya Pradesh 462 023, India. TEL 91-9425536487, FAX 91-11-66173705, info@inventi.in, editor@inventi.in, http://www.inventi.in. Ed. Dr. Patricia Dias. Pub., R&P V B Gupta. Circ: 50.

615 IND ISSN 0976-7584
▼ ➤ **INVENTI IMPACT N D D S.** (Novel Drug Delivery System) Text and summaries in English. 2010. q. INR 2,000 domestic to individuals; USD 50 foreign to individuals; INR 3,000 domestic to institutions; USD 60 foreign to institutions (effective 2011). adv. a. index. back issues avail.; reprints avail. **Document type:** *Journal, Academic/Scholarly.* **Description:** Publishes research reports, review articles and scientific commentaries on drug delivery system.
Media: Online - full text. **Related titles:** Print ed.: ISSN 2229-4147.
Published by: Inventi Journals Pvt. Ltd., SDX 33, Minal Residency, JK Rd, Bhopal, Madhya Pradesh 462 023, India. TEL 91-9425536487, FAX 91-11-66173705, info@inventi.in, editor@inventi.in, http://www.inventi.in. Ed. Dr. Rosario Pignatello. Pub., R&P V B Gupta. Circ: 50.

615 613.2 IND ISSN 0976-7495
▼ ➤ **INVENTI IMPACT NUTRACEUTICALS.** Text and summaries in English. 2010. q. INR 2,000 domestic to individuals; USD 50 foreign to individuals; INR 3,000 domestic to institutions; USD 60 foreign to institutions (effective 2011). adv. a. index. back issues avail. **Document type:** *Journal, Academic/Scholarly.* **Description:** Publishes research reports, review articles and scientific commentaries on nutraceuticals.
Media: Online - full text. **Related titles:** Print ed.: ISSN 2229-418X.
Published by: Inventi Journals Pvt. Ltd., SDX 33, Minal Residency, JK Rd, Bhopal, Madhya Pradesh 462 023, India. TEL 91-9425536487, FAX 91-11-66173705, info@inventi.in, editor@inventi.in, http://www.inventi.in. Ed. Dr. Glen Stephen Patten. Pub., R&P V B Gupta. Circ: 50.

615 IND ISSN 0976-755X
▼ ➤ **INVENTI IMPACT PHARM ANALYSIS & QUALITY ASSURANCE.** Text and summaries in English. 2010. q. INR 2,000 domestic to individuals; USD 50 foreign to individuals; INR 3,000, INR 60 domestic to institutions (effective 2011). adv. a. index. back issues avail.; reprints avail. **Document type:** *Journal, Academic/Scholarly.* **Description:** Publishes research reports, review articles and scientific commentaries on pharmaceutical analysis & quality assurance.
Media: Online - full text. **Related titles:** Print ed.: ISSN 2229-4198.
Published by: Inventi Journals Pvt. Ltd., SDX 33, Minal Residency, JK Rd, Bhopal, Madhya Pradesh 462 023, India. TEL 91-9425536487, FAX 91-11-66173705, info@inventi.in, editor@inventi.in, http://www.inventi.in. Ed. Dr. Luiz Alberto Lira Soares. Pub., R&P V B Gupta. Circ: 50.

615 IND ISSN 0976-7576
▼ ➤ **INVENTI IMPACT PHARM TECH.** Text and summaries in English. 2010. q. INR 2,000 domestic to individuals; USD 50 foreign to individuals; INR 3,000 domestic to institutions; USD 60 foreign to institutions (effective 2011). a. index. back issues avail. **Document type:** *Journal, Academic/Scholarly.* **Description:** Publishes research reports, review articles and scientific commentaries on pharmaceutical technology.
Media: Online - full text. **Related titles:** Print ed.: ISSN 2229-4139.
Published by: Inventi Journals Pvt. Ltd., SDX 33, Minal Residency, JK Rd, Bhopal, Madhya Pradesh 462 023, India. TEL 91-9425536487, FAX 91-11-66173705, info@inventi.in, editor@inventi.in, http://www.inventi.in. Ed. Dr. A Nokhodchi. Pub., R&P V B Gupta. Circ: 50.

615 IND ISSN 0976-7525
▼ ➤ **INVENTI IMPACT PHARMACY PRACTICE.** Text and summaries in English. 2010. q. INR 2,000 domestic to individuals; USD 50 foreign to individuals; INR 3,000 domestic to institutions; USD 60 foreign to institutions (effective 2011). a. index. back issues avail.; reprints avail. **Document type:** *Journal, Academic/Scholarly.* **Description:** Publishes research reports, review articles and scientific commentaries on pharmacy practice.
Media: Online - full text. **Related titles:** Print ed.: ISSN 2229-4201.
Published by: Inventi Journals Pvt. Ltd., SDX 33, Minal Residency, JK Rd, Bhopal, Madhya Pradesh 462 023, India. TEL 91-9425536487, FAX 91-11-66173705, info@inventi.in, editor@inventi.in, http://www.inventi.in. Ed. Dr. Ravi Iyer. Pub., R&P V B Gupta. Circ: 50.

615.1 668.5 IND ISSN 0976-3864
▼ **INVENTI RAPID COSMECEUTICALS.** Text and summaries in English. 2010. q. INR 1,000 domestic; USD 20 foreign (effective 2011). a. index. back issues avail.; reprints avail. **Document type:** *Journal, Academic/Scholarly.* **Description:** Publishes research reports, review articles and scientific commentaries on pharmaceutical sciences.
Media: Online - full text.
Published by: Inventi Journals Pvt. Ltd., SDX 33, Minal Residency, JK Rd, Bhopal, Madhya Pradesh 462 023, India. TEL 91-9425536487, FAX 91-11-66173705, info@inventi.in, http://www.inventi.in. Ed. Dr. Ozgen Ozar. Pub., R&P V B Gupta. Circ: 50.

615.19 IND ISSN 0976-3805
▼ ➤ **INVENTI RAPID ETHNOPHARMACOLOGY.** Text and summaries in English. 2010. q. INR 1,000 domestic; USD 50 foreign (effective 2011). a. index. back issues avail.; reprints avail. **Document type:** *Journal, Academic/Scholarly.* **Description:** Contains research reports, review articles and scientific commentaries on ethnopharmacology.
Media: Online - full text.
Published by: Inventi Journals Pvt. Ltd., SDX 33, Minal Residency, JK Rd, Bhopal, Madhya Pradesh 462 023, India. TEL 91-9425536487, FAX 91-11-66173705, info@inventi.in, editor@inventi.in, http://www.inventi.in. Ed. Dr. Rozangela Curi Pedrosa. Pub., R&P V B Gupta. Circ: 50.

610 616.027 IND ISSN 0976-3821
▼ ➤ **INVENTI RAPID MEDCHEM.** Text and summaries in English. 2010. q. INR 1,000 domestic; USD 20 foreign (effective 2011). a. index. back issues avail. **Document type:** *Journal, Academic/Scholarly.* **Description:** Contains research reports, review articles and scientific commentaries on medicinal chemistry.
Media: Online - full text.
Published by: Inventi Journals Pvt. Ltd., SDX 33, Minal Residency, JK Rd, Bhopal, Madhya Pradesh 462 023, India. TEL 91-9425536487, FAX 91-11-66173705, info@inventi.in, editor@inventi.in, http://www.inventi.in. Ed. Dr. El Ashry. Pub., R&P V B Gupta.

615 IND ISSN 0976-3856
▼ ➤ **INVENTI RAPID MOLECULAR PHARMACOLOGY.** Text and summaries in English. 2010. q. INR 1,000 domestic; USD 20 foreign (effective 2011). a. index. back issues avail.; reprints avail. **Document type:** *Journal, Academic/Scholarly.* **Description:** Publishes research reports, review articles and scientific commentaries on molecular pharmacology.
Media: Online - full text.
Published by: Inventi Journals Pvt. Ltd., SDX 33, Minal Residency, JK Rd, Bhopal, Madhya Pradesh 462 023, India. TEL 91-9425536487, FAX 91-11-66173705, info@inventi.in, editor@inventi.in, http://www.inventi.in. Ed. Dr. Patricia Dias. Pub., R&P V B Gupta. Circ: 50.

615 IND ISSN 0976-3791
▼ ➤ **INVENTI RAPID N D D S.** (Novel Drug Delivery System) Text and summaries in English. 2010. q. INR 1,000 domestic; USD 20 foreign (effective 2011). a. index. back issues avail.; reprints avail. **Document type:** *Journal, Academic/Scholarly.* **Description:** Publishes research reports, review articles and scientific commentaries on drug delivery system.
Media: Online - full text.
Published by: Inventi Journals Pvt. Ltd., SDX 33, Minal Residency, JK Rd, Bhopal, Madhya Pradesh 462 023, India. TEL 91-9425536487, FAX 91-11-66173705, info@inventi.in, editor@inventi.in, http://www.inventi.in. Ed. Dr. Rosario Pignatello. Pub., R&P V B Gupta. Circ: 50.

615.1 613.5 IND ISSN 0976-3872
▼ ➤ **INVENTI RAPID NUTRACEUTICALS.** Text in English. 2010. q. INR 1,000 domestic; USD 20 foreign (effective 2011). adv. a. index. back issues avail.; reprints avail. **Document type:** *Journal, Academic/Scholarly.* **Description:** Publishes research reports, review articles and scientific commentaries on nutraceuticals.
Media: Online - full text.
Published by: Inventi Journals Pvt. Ltd., SDX 33, Minal Residency, JK Rd, Bhopal, Madhya Pradesh 462 023, India. TEL 91-9425536487, FAX 91-11-66173705, info@inventi.in, editor@inventi.in, http://www.inventi.in. Ed. Dr. Glen Stephen Patten. Pub., R&P V B Gupta. Circ: 50.

615 IND ISSN 0976-3813
▼ ➤ **INVENTI RAPID PHARM ANALYSIS & QUALITY ASSURANCE.** Text and summaries in English. 2010. q. INR 1,000 domestic; USD 20 foreign (effective 2011). adv. a. index. back issues avail.; reprints avail. **Document type:** *Journal, Academic/Scholarly.* **Description:** Publishes research reports, review articles and scientific commentaries on pharmaceutical analysis & quality assurance.
Media: Online - full text.
Published by: Inventi Journals Pvt. Ltd., SDX 33, Minal Residency, JK Rd, Bhopal, Madhya Pradesh 462 023, India. TEL 91-9425536487, FAX 91-11-66173705, info@inventi.in, editor@inventi.in, http://www.inventi.in. Ed. Dr. Luiz Alberto Lira Soares. Pub., R&P V B Gupta. Circ: 50.

615 IND ISSN 0976-3783
▼ ➤ **INVENTI RAPID PHARM TECH.** Text and summaries in English. 2010. q. INR 1,000 domestic; USD 20 foreign (effective 2011). adv. a. index. back issues avail.; reprints avail. **Document type:** *Journal, Academic/Scholarly.* **Description:** Publishes research reports, review articles and scientific commentaries on pharmaceutical technology.
Media: Online - full text.
Published by: Inventi Journals Pvt. Ltd., SDX 33, Minal Residency, JK Rd, Bhopal, Madhya Pradesh 462 023, India. TEL 91-9425536487, FAX 91-11-66173705, info@inventi.in, editor@inventi.in, http://www.inventi.in. Ed. Dr. A Nokhodchi. Pub., R&P V B Gupta. Circ: 50.

615 IND ISSN 0976-3848
➤ **INVENTI RAPID PHARMACY PRACTICE.** Text and summaries in English. q. INR 1,000 domestic; USD 20 foreign (effective 2011). adv. a. index. back issues avail.; reprints avail. **Document type:** *Journal, Academic/Scholarly.* **Description:** Publishes research reports, review articles and scientific commentaries on pharmacy practice.
Media: Online - full text.
Published by: Inventi Journals Pvt. Ltd., SDX 33, Minal Residency, JK Rd, Bhopal, Madhya Pradesh 462 023, India. TEL 91-9425536487, FAX 91-11-66173705, info@inventi.in, editor@inventi.in, http://www.inventi.in. Ed. Dr. Ravi Iyer. Pub., R&P V B Gupta. Circ: 50.

615.7 ESP ISSN 1131-8910
INVESTIGACION CLINICA Y BIOETICA. Text in Spanish. 1991. q. **Document type:** *Journal, Academic/Scholarly.*
Related titles: Online - full text ed.: I C B Digital. free (effective 2009).
—CCC.
Published by: Sociedad Espanola de Farmacologia Clinica, Paseo Vall d'Hebron 119-129, Barcelona, 08035, Spain. TEL 34-93-4283029, FAX 34-93-4894109.

INVESTIGACION CLINICA Y FARMACEUTICA. *see* MEDICAL SCIENCES

615 USA ISSN 0167-6997
RC271.C5 CODEN: INNDDK
➤ **INVESTIGATIONAL NEW DRUGS;** the journal of new anti-cancer agents. Text in English. 1983. bi-m. EUR 960, USD 1,013 combined subscription to institutions (print & online eds.) (effective 2012). adv. bk.rev. back issues avail.; reprint service avail. from PSC. **Document type:** *Journal, Academic/Scholarly.* **Description:** Provides a forum for the dissemination of information on new anticancer agents.
Related titles: Microform ed.: (from PQC); Online - full text ed.: ISSN 1573-0646 (from IngentaConnect).
Indexed: A22, A26, ASCA, B&BAb, B19, B25, BIOBASE, BIOSIS Prev, BibLing, C06, C07, CA, CIN, ChemAb, ChemTitl, CurCont, DBA, E01, E08, EMBASE, ExcerpMed, G08, H11, I05, IABS, ISR, IndMed, Inpharma, MEDLINE, MycolAb, P20, P22, P24, P30, P35, P48, P54, PQC, RefZh, S09, SCI, SCOPUS, T02, Telegen, W07.
—BLDSC (4559.885000), CASDDS, GNLM, IE, Infotrieve, Ingenta, INIST. **CCC.**
Published by: Springer New York LLC (Subsidiary of: Springer Science+Business Media), 233 Spring St, New York, NY 10013. TEL 212-460-1500, FAX 212-460-1575, service-ny@springer.com. Ed. Eric K Rowinsky.

615 USA ISSN 1525-7894
IOWA PHARMACY ASSOCIATION. JOURNAL. Text in English. 1946. bi-m. free domestic to members; USD 60 domestic to non-members (effective 2006). **Document type:** *Magazine, Trade.*
Formerly (until 1999): Iowa Pharmacist (0889-7735)
Indexed: I12.
Published by: Iowa Pharmacy Association, 8515 Douglas, Ste. 16, Des Moines, IA 50322. TEL 515-270-0713. Ed. Jenny Erlmeier. Circ: 2,000 (paid and controlled).

615.1 IRN ISSN 1735-0328
IRANIAN JOURNAL OF PHARMACEUTICAL RESEARCH. Text in English. 2002. q. back issues avail. **Document type:** *Journal, Academic/Scholarly.* **Description:** Publishes articles relevant to the Middle East region. Includes, but are not limited to: pharmaceutics, industrial pharmacy, pharmacology, ethnopharmacology, pharmacognosy, medicinal plants, toxicology, medicinal chemistry, novel analytical methods for drug characterization, computational and modeling approaches to drug design, bio-medical experience, clinical investigation, rational drug prescribing, pharmacoeconomics, biotechnology, biopharmaceutics and physical pharmacy.
Related titles: CD-ROM ed.: ISSN 1726-6882. 2002; Online - full text ed.: ISSN 1726-6890. 2002. free (effective 2011).
Indexed: A01, A34, A35, A36, AgBio, AgrForAb, B25, BIOSIS Prev, BP, C25, C30, CABA, D01, E12, EMBASE, ExcerpMed, F08, F11, F12, GH, H16, I12, MaizeAb, MycolAb, N02, N03, P32, P33, P39, PGegResA, PGrRegA, PHN&I, R07, R08, R12, R13, RA&MP, RM&VM, S12, S17, SCI, SCOPUS, SoyAb, T02, T05, TAR, VS, W07.
Published by: Shaheed Beheshti Medical University, School of Pharmacy, No. 10 Shams Alley, Vali-e Asr St, Tehran, Iran. TEL 98-21-8773521, FAX 98-21-8795008, editorial@ijpr-online.com.

615.1 IRN ISSN 1735-2657
➤ **IRANIAN JOURNAL OF PHARMACOLOGY AND THERAPEUTICS.** Text in English. 2002. q. free (effective 2011). back issues avail. **Document type:** *Journal, Academic/Scholarly.* **Description:** Publishes regular research papers, reviews, mini-reviews and case reports which deal with all aspects of experimental and clinical pharmacology.
Media: Online - full text.
Indexed: A01, CA, EMBASE, ExcerpMed, R10, Reac, SCOPUS, T02.
Published by: Iran University of Medical Sciences, Razi Institute for Drug Research, PO Box 15785-6171, Tehran, Iran. TEL 98-21-8052941, FAX 98-21-8052191, ijpt@iums.ac.ir, http://www.iums.ac.ir. Ed. Massoud Mahmoudian.

615.1 IRL ISSN 1649-9298
IRISH MEDICINES FORMULARY. Text in English. 2007. s-a. EUR 40 per issue (effective 2007). **Description:** Provides access to information on product-authorized pharmaceuticals currently marketed in Ireland.
Published by: Meridian Ireland, 49 Castlerosse View, Baldoyle, Dublin, 13, Ireland. TEL 353-1-8390073, info@meridianireland.com.

615.1 IRL
THE IRISH O T C DIRECTORY. (Over the Counter) Text in English. a. EUR 15 per issue (effective 2005). adv. **Document type:** *Directory, Trade.* **Description:** Contains complete information on over-the-counter pharmaceutical products available in Ireland.
Published by: Eireann Healthcare Publications, 25-26 Windsor Pl., Dublin, 2, Ireland. TEL 353-1-4753300, FAX 353-1-4753311, mhenderson@eireannpublications.ie, http://www.eireannpublications.ie. Ed. Ann-Marie Hardiman. Pub. Graham Cooke. Adv. contact Clodagh Lenehan. B&W 1/2 page EUR 950; trim 148.5 x 210. Circ: 5,431 (paid and controlled).

615 IRL ISSN 1649-4563
IRISH PHARMACIST. Text in English. 1999. m. EUR 76 (effective 2005). adv. **Document type:** *Magazine, Trade.* **Description:** Contains news stories and features covering developments in the clinical, business and financial sides of pharmacy.

P

Published by: Eireann Healthcare Publications, 25-26 Windsor Pl., Dublin, 2, Ireland. TEL 353-1-4753300, FAX 353-1-4753311, mhenderson@eireannpublications.ie, http://www.eireannpublications.ie. Ed. Stephen Meyler. Pub. Graham Cooke. Adv. contact Patrick Daly. B&W page EUR 1,672; trim 245 x 340. Circ: 2,085 (paid and controlled).

615.1 IRL ISSN 0332-0707
IRISH PHARMACY JOURNAL. Text in English. 1923. m. adv. bk.rev. illus.; tr.lit. **Document type:** *Journal, Trade.*
Formerly (until 1972): Irish Chemist and Druggist (0021-1109)
Indexed: I12.
—BLDSC (4574.640000), IE, Ingenta.
Published by: (Pharmaceutical Society of Ireland), Irish Marine Press, 2 Lower Glenageary Rd., Dun Laoghaire, Dublin, 4, Ireland. TEL 353-1-2846161, FAX 353-1-2846192, info@afloat.ie. Ed., R&P Val J Harte. Adv. contact Angela J Fealy TEL 353-1-2020374. B&W page EUR 850, color page EUR 1,100; trim 210 x 296. Circ: 2,950.

615.9 JPN ISSN 1346-342X
CODEN: BYYADW
IRYO YAKUGAKU/JAPANESE JOURNAL OF PHARMACEUTICAL HEALTH CARE AND SCIENCES. Text in English, Japanese; Summaries in English. 1975. bi-m. JPY 9,500 per issue membership (effective 2004); subscr. incld. with membership. **Document type:** *Journal, Academic/Scholarly.*
Formerly (until 2000): Byoin Yakugaku/Japanese Journal of Hospital Pharmacy (0389-9098)
Indexed: CIN, ChemAb, ChemTitl, I12.
—BLDSC (4656.975000), CASDDS, GNLM. **CCC.**
Published by: Nihon Byoin Yakuzaishikai/Japanese Society of Hospital Pharmacists, Nagai Kinenkan 8F, 2-12-15 Shibuya, Shibuya-ku, Tokyo, 150-0002, Japan. TEL 81-3-34060485, FAX 81-3-37975303, http://www.jsphcs.jp/.

615 JPN ISSN 1348-0863
IRYOU YAKUGAKU FORAMU KOUEN YOUSHISHUU/CLINICAL PHARMACY SYMPOSIUM. Text in Japanese. 1985. a.
Formerly (until 2001): Kurinikaru Famashi Shinpojumu Koen Yoshishu/ Symposium on Clinical Pharmacy (0919-2107)
Published by: Nihon Yakugakkai, Iryou Yakkagaku Bukai/Pharmaceutical Society of Japan, Division of Clinical Pharmaceutical Sciences, Hiroshima University, Laboratory of Clinical Pharmaceutics, 1-2-3 Minami-ku, Hiroshima, 734-8553, Japan. TEL 81-82-2575316, FAX 81-82-2575319, ryumoto@hiroshima-u.ac.jp, http://bukai.pharm.or.jp/ bukai_iryo/clinicalH.htm.

ISHI SHIKAISHI YAKUZAISHI CHOSA/SURVEY ON PHYSICIANS, DENTISTS AND PHARMACEUTISTS. *see* MEDICAL SCIENCES

615.19 TUR ISSN 0367-7524
CODEN: IEFMA9
ISTANBUL UNIVERSITESI ECZACILIK FAKULTESI MECMUASI. Text in Turkish. 1965. s-a. **Document type:** *Journal, Academic/Scholarly.*
Related titles: English ed.: Istanbul University. Faculty of Pharmacy. Journal.
Indexed: EMBASE, ExcerpMed, R10, Reac, SCOPUS.
—BLDSC (4585.500000).
Published by: Istanbul University, Faculty of Pharmacy, Department of Pharmaceutical Technology, Istanbul, 34116, Turkey. TEL 90-212-4400250, FAX 91-212-4400252, info@actapharmasciencia.org, http://www.istanbul.edu.tr/eczacilik, http://www.istanbul.edu.tr/ english/socrates/includes/f7_1.htm. Ed. Neriman Ozhatay.

615 338.476 GBR ISSN 1748-8826
ITALY PHARMACEUTICALS & HEALTHCARE REPORT. Text in English. 2005. q. EUR 820, USD 1,030 combined subscription (print & email eds.) (effective 2010). **Document type:** *Report, Trade.* **Description:** Provides industry professionals, market investors and corporate and financial services analysts with independent forecasts and competitive intelligence on the Italian pharmaceutical and healthcare industry.
Related titles: E-mail ed.
Indexed: A15, ABIn, B02, B15, B17, B18, G04, I05, P21, P48, P51, PQC.
Published by: Business Monitor International Ltd., Senator House, 85 Queen Victoria St, London, EC4V 4AB, United Kingdom. TEL 44-20-72480468, FAX 44-20-72480467, subs@businessmonitor.com.

615 JPN ISSN 0287-4741
IYAKU JOURNAL/MEDICINE AND DRUG JOURNAL. Text in Japanese. 1965. m. JPY 35,385; JPY 2,625 newsstand/cover (effective 2005). adv. **Document type:** *Journal, Academic/Scholarly.*
—BLDSC (5534.005700).
Published by: Iyaku Journal-sha/Medicine & Drug Journal Co., Ltd., Highness Awajimachi Bldg. 21/F, 3-1-5 Awajimachih, Chuo-Ku, Osaka, 541-0047, Japan. TEL 81-6-62027280, FAX 81-6-62025295, ij-main@iyaku-j.com, http://www.iyaku-j.com/. Ed. Minoru Numata. R&P, Adv. contact Kiriko Numata.

615.19 JPN ISSN 1341-4607
IYAKU KANREN JOHO/J A P I C MONTHLY BULLETIN. Text in Japanese. 1973. m. JPY 100,000 to members (effective 2001). bk.rev. cum.index. **Document type:** *Bulletin.*
Former titles (until 1995): Nihon Iyaku Joho Senta. Joho (0915-163X); Japan Pharmaceutical Information Center. Information
Published by: Japan Pharmaceutical Information Center/Nihon Iyaku Joho Senta, 3rd Fl Nagai-Kinenkan, 2-12-15 Shibuya, Shibuya-ku, Tokyo, 150-0002, Japan. TEL 81-3-5466-1812, FAX 81-3-5466-1814. Ed. H Miyake. Circ: 600.

615 JPN ISSN 0579-2762
IYAKU NO MON/GATEWAY TO MEDICINE. Text in Japanese. 1961. bi-m. **Document type:** *Journal, Academic/Scholarly.*
Published by: Torii Yakuhin K.K., 3-4-1 Honcho, Nihonbashi, Chuo-ku, Tokyo, 103-8439, Japan. TEL 81-3-32316811, FAX 81-3-52037333, http://www.torii.co.jp/.

615.9 JPN ISSN 1342-2049
IYAKUHIN FUKUSAYO BUNKEN JOHOSHU. YAKKOBETSU FUKUSAYO ICHIRAN-HEN/ADVERSE REACTIONS TO DRUGS INFORMATION COMPENDIUM FOR EXPERTS. PRODUCT - ADVERSE REACTION INFORMATION. Text in Japanese. 1975. s-a. JPY 50,000 includes Iyakuhin Fukusayo Bunken Johoshu. Shorokushu-Hen (effective 2001). **Document type:** *Academic/ Scholarly.*
Supersedes in part (in 1995): Kokunai Iyakuhin Fukusayo Ichiran (0912-2133)
Published by: Japan Pharmaceutical Information Center/Nihon Iyaku Joho Senta, 3rd Fl Nagai-Kinenkan, 2-12-15 Shibuya, Shibuya-ku, Tokyo, 150-0002, Japan. TEL 81-3-5466-1812, FAX 81-3-5466-1814. Ed. H Miyake. Circ: 3,000.

615 JPN ISSN 0286-6153
➤ **IYAKUHIN FUKUSAYO JOHO/INFORMATION ON SIDE EFFECTS OF DRUGS.** Text in Japanese. 1977. irreg. price varies. **Document type:** *Monographic series, Academic/Scholarly.*
Published by: Yakuma Kohosha, 4-28-3-203 Kouenjiminami, Suginami-ku, Tokyo, 166-0003, Japan. TEL 81-3-33153821, FAX 81-3-53777275, info@yakumukohosha.co.jp, http://www.yakumukohosha.co.jp/.

615 JPN
IYAKUHIN SEIZO HANBAI SHISHIN. Text in Japanese. 1962. a. JPY 9,450 (effective 2007).
Formerly (until 2004): Iyakuhin Seizo Shishin (0911-9329)
Related titles: ◆ English ed.: Drug Approval and Licensing Procedures in Japan. ISSN 0289-9922.
Published by: Jiho, Inc., Hitotsubashi Bldg. 5F, Hitotsubashi 2-6-3, Chiyoda-ku, Tokyo, 101-8421, Japan. TEL 81-3-32657751, FAX 81-3-32657769, pj@jiho.co.jp, http://www.jiho.co.jp/.

615.9 JPN ISSN 0385-5015
CODEN: ISSKEY
IYAKUHIN SOGO SAYO KENKYU/RESEARCH ON DRUG ACTIONS AND INTERACTIONS. Text in Japanese. 1975. q. JPY 3,000. bk.rev. **Document type:** *Journal, Academic/Scholarly.*
Indexed: CIN, ChemAb, ChemTitl.
—CASDDS.
Published by: Iyakuhin Sogo Sayo Kenkyukai/Research Society of Drug Actions and Interactions, Yamagata University Hospital Pharmacy, 2-2-2 Iida, Nishi, Yamagata 990-9585, Japan. TEL 81-236-355121, FAX 81-236-285828. Circ: 1,200.

JAPANESE JOURNAL OF ANTIBIOTICS. *see* MEDICAL SCIENCES

615 JPN
THE JAPANESE PHARMACOPOEIA. Text in Japanese, English. irreg., latest 2001, 14th Ed. JPY 53,000, USD 600 (effective 2001). **Document type:** *Government.* **Description:** Contains general notices, general rules for preparation, general tests, processes and apparatus, and monographs.
Formerly: Pharmacopoeia of Japan
Related titles: CD-ROM ed.: USD 12,000 (effective 2001); Supplement(s): The Japanese Pharmacopoeia. Supplement II. JPY 8,600, USD 100 (effective 2001); The Japanese Pharmacopoeia. Supplement I. USD 85 (effective 2001).
Published by: (Pharmaceutical and Medical Device Regulatory Science Society of Japan), Yakuji Nippo Ltd., Kanda-Izumi-cho, Chiyoda-ku, Tokyo, 101-0024, Japan. TEL 81-3-3862-2141, FAX 81-3-3866-8495, shuppan@yakuji.co.jp, http://www.yakuji.co.jp/.

344.04233 JPN
JAPAN'S AND I C H GUIDELINES FOR NEW DRUG REGISTRATION (YEAR). Text in English. irreg., latest 1999. JPY 13,000 (effective 2011). **Document type:** *Monographic series, Trade.*
Related titles: Supplement(s): JPY 7,350, USD 95 newsstand/cover (effective 2001).
Published by: Yakuji Nippo Ltd., Kanda-Izumi-cho, Chiyoda-ku, Tokyo, 101-0024, Japan. TEL 81-3-3862-2141, FAX 81-3-3866-8495, shuppan@yakuji.co.jp, http://www.yakuji.co.jp/.

615.371 AUT ISSN 1561-5251
JATROS VACCINES. Text in German. 1996. 3/yr. EUR 18 (effective 2007). adv. **Document type:** *Journal, Academic/Scholarly.*
Related titles: Online - full text ed.: ISSN 1991-9212. 1999.
Published by: Universimed Verlags- und Service GmbH, Markgraf-Ruediger-Str 8, Vienna, 1150, Austria. TEL 43-1-87679560, FAX 43-1-876795620, office@universimed.com, http://www.universimed.com. Ed. Friederike Hoerandl. Adv. contact Wolfgang Chlud. Circ: 11,000 (controlled).

615 CHN ISSN 1674-4640
JIATING YAOSHI/PHARMACIST. Text in Chinese. 2008. m. **Document type:** *Magazine, Trade.*
Published by: Zhongguo Jiating Yisheng Zazhishe/China Family Doctors Magazine Press, 77, Tiyu Xi Lu Guangli Lu, Dongzhou Dasha B23-26, Tianhe-qu, Guangzhou, China. http://www.jtys.cn/.

615 CHN ISSN 1008-9926
JIEFANGJUN YAOXUE XUEBAO/PHARMACEUTICAL JOURNAL OF CHINESE PEOPLE'S LIBERATION ARMY. Text in Chinese. 1998. bi-m. **Document type:** *Journal, Academic/Scholarly.*
Formed by the merger of (1985-1998): Jiefangjun Yiyaoxue Zhuankan/ Special Journal of Pharmacy, People's Military Surgeon; Jundui Yaoshi
Related titles: Online - full text ed.
—BLDSC (4668.903000), East View.
Published by: Zhongguo Renmin Jiefangjun Zonghouqinbu Weishengbu Yaopin Yiqi Jianyansuo/Health Department of the General Logistics Department of P L A, 17, Fengtai Xi Lu, Beijing, 100071, China. TEL 86-10-66949020, FAX 86-10-63858411.

JILIN ZHONGYIYAO/JILIN JOURNAL OF TRADITIONAL CHINESE MEDICINE. *see* ALTERNATIVE MEDICINE

615 CHN ISSN 1674-229X
JINRI YAOXUE/PHARMACY TODAY. Text in Chinese. 1991. bi-m. **Document type:** *Journal, Academic/Scholarly.*
Former titles (until 2008): Xiandai Shipin yu Yaopin Zazhi/Journal of Modern Food and Pharmaceuticals (1673-4610); Guangdong Yaoxue/Guangdong Pharmaceutical Journal (1007-9939)
Related titles: Online - full text ed.
—BLDSC (4223.858380), East View.
Published by: Guangdong Sheng Yaoxuehui, 753-2, Dongfeng Dong Lu, 10F, Guangzhou, 510080, China. TEL 86-20-37886320, FAX 86-20-37886330, gdsyxh45@tom.com. **Dist. by:** China International Book Trading Corp, 35 Chegongzhuang Xilu, Haidian District, PO Box 399, Beijing 100044, China. TEL 86-10-68412045, FAX 86-10-68412023, cibtc@mail.cibtc.com.cn, http://www.cibtc.com.cn.

615 USA ISSN 1528-6002
JOBWATCH. Text in English. 1997. d. free (effective 2009). adv. **Document type:** *Bulletin, Consumer.* **Description:** Lists job and career opportunities in all areas of the pharmaceutical industry, including management, research, and informaton systems.
Related titles: Online - full text ed.: free to members (effective 2009).
Indexed: A26, G08, H12, I05.
Published by: CenterWatch (Subsidiary of: Jobson Medical Information LLC.), 100 N Washington St, Ste 301, Boston, MA 02114. TEL 617-948-5100, 866-219-3440, FAX 617-948-5101, customerservice@centerwatch.com, http://www.centerwatch.com.

615 BRA ISSN 1677-5848
JORNAL BRASILEIRO DE FITOTERAPIA. Abbreviated title: J B F. Text in Portuguese. 2002. q. **Document type:** *Journal, Academic/ Scholarly.*
—BLDSC (4674.635000).
Published by: Apsen Farmaceutica, Rua La Paz 37-67, Santo Amarao, Sao Paulo, 04755-020, Brazil. apsen@apsen.com.br, http://www.apsen.com.br.

615 344.041 NLD ISSN 1574-6755
JOURNAAL FARMARECHT. Variant title: J F R. Text in Dutch. 2006. bi-m. EUR 183.96 (effective 2009). **Document type:** *Magazine, Trade.*
—IE.
Published by: Sdu Uitgevers bv, Postbus 20025, The Hague, 2500 EA, Netherlands. TEL 31-70-3789911, FAX 31-70-3854321, sdu@sdu.nl.

615.19 FRA ISSN 0291-1981
CODEN: JPCLDE
JOURNAL DE PHARMACIE CLINIQUE. Text in French. 1982. q. EUR 364 combined subscription domestic to institutions (print & online eds.); EUR 384 combined subscription in the European Union to institutions (print & online eds.); EUR 388 combined subscription elsewhere to institutions (print & online eds.) (effective 2011). **Document type:** *Journal, Academic/Scholarly.* **Description:** Papers on all aspects of pharmaceutical sciences applied to human use.
Related titles: Online - full text ed.: ISSN 1952-4064. FRF 670 to individuals; FRF 1,120 to institutions (effective 2001).
Indexed: A22, B25, BIOSIS Prev, CIN, ChemAb, ChemTitl, DBA, EMBASE, ExcerpMed, FR, I12, IBR, IBZ, Inpharma, MycolAb, R10, Reac, SCOPUS.
—BLDSC (5032.050000), CASDDS, GNLM, IE, Ingenta, INIST. **CCC.**
Published by: John Libbey Eurotext, 127 Av. de la Republique, Montrouge, 92120, France. TEL 33-1-46730660, FAX 33-1-40840999, contact@jle.com, http://www.john-libbey-eurotext.fr. Ed. Francoise Brion. Circ: 1,300.

615 BEL ISSN 0047-2166
CODEN: JPBEAJ
JOURNAL DE PHARMACIE DE BELGIQUE. Text in French. 1919; N.S. 1945. 6/yr. adv. illus. Supplement avail.; reprints avail. **Document type:** *Journal, Academic/Scholarly.* **Description:** Contains original papers and reviews covering the entire field of pharmaceutical sciences: pharmacology, pharmakokinetics, pharmaceutical chemistry, galenics and phytotherapy.
Indexed: A22, C33, CIN, ChemAb, ChemTitl, DBA, EMBASE, ExcerpMed, FR, I12, ISR, IndMed, MEDLINE, P30, R10, Reac, SCOPUS.
—BLDSC (5032.000000), CASDDS, GNLM, IE, Infotrieve, Ingenta, INIST, Linda Hall. **CCC.**
Published by: Algemene Pharmaceutische Bond/Association Pharmaceutique Belge, Archimedesstraat 11, Brussels, 1000, Belgium. TEL 32-2-2854200, FAX 32-2-2854285, http://www.apb.be.

615.329 FRA ISSN 2210-6545
CODEN: ANTBFQ
JOURNAL DES ANTI-INFECTIEUX. Text in French. 1999. q. EUR 312 in Europe to institutions; EUR 258.57 in France to institutions; JPY 52,500 in Japan to institutions; USD 421 elsewhere to institutions (effective 2012). **Document type:** *Journal, Academic/Scholarly.* **Description:** Provides information on the universe of anti-infection agents including up to date knowledge of non conventional therapies.
Formerly (until 2011): Antibiotiques (1294-5501)
Related titles: Online - full text ed.
Indexed: B25, BIOSIS Prev, EMBASE, ExcerpMed, MycolAb, R10, Reac, SCI, SCOPUS, W07.
—BLDSC (1547.242000), INIST. **CCC.**
Published by: Elsevier Masson (Subsidiary of: Elsevier Health Sciences), 62 Rue Camille Desmoulins, Issy les Moulineaux, Cedex 92442, France. TEL 33-1-71165500, infos@elsevier-masson.fr. Ed. Bruno Fantin.

615.1 DEU ISSN 1432-4334
JOURNAL FUER PHARMAKOLOGIE UND THERAPIE/JOURNAL OF PHARMACOLOGY AND THERAPY. Text in English, German. 1992. bi-m. adv. **Document type:** *Journal, Academic/Scholarly.*
Indexed: A22, EMBASE, ExcerpMed, SCOPUS.
—BLDSC (5034.040000), IE, Ingenta. **CCC.**
Published by: Verlag Perfusion GmbH, Regensburger Str 44-46, Nuernberg, 90478, Germany. TEL 49-911-49108, FAX 49-911-493579. Ed. Brigitte Soellner. Adv. contact Sibylle Michna.

615 IND ISSN 2229-3787
▼ ➤ **JOURNAL OF ADVANCED PHARMACEUTICAL RESEARCH.** Abbreviated title: J A P R. Text in English. 2010. q. free (effective 2011). cum. index. back issues avail.; reprints avail. **Document type:** *Journal, Academic/Scholarly.*
Media: Online - full text.
Published by: Pharmaceutical Research Foundation, c/o Debashisha Panda, Utkala Ashram Rd, Ganjam District, Berhampur, Orissa 760 001, India. TEL 91-9437617602, editor.japr@gmail.com. Ed. Subrata Mallik. Pub., Adv. contact Debashisha Panda.

615 IND ISSN 0976-4984
▼ ➤ **JOURNAL OF ADVANCED PHARMACEUTICAL STUDIES.** Text in English. 2010 (June). m. **Document type:** *Journal, Academic/ Scholarly.* **Description:** Publishes articles from all pharmaceutical disciplines.
Media: Online - full text.
Address: http://www.pharmawebsite.com/journal/. Ed. Akondi B Raju.

615 IND ISSN 2231-4040

▼ ➤ **JOURNAL OF ADVANCED PHARMACEUTICAL TECHNOLOGY AND RESEARCH.** Abbreviated title: J A P T R. Text in English. 2010. q. Index. back issues avail. **Document type:** *Journal, Academic/Scholarly.* **Description:** Publishes original research work, reviews, and short communications that contributes significantly to further the scientific knowledge in pharmaceutical sciences, pharmaceutics, pharmacology, pharmacognosy, pharmaceutical analysis, pharmaceutical technology, natural products, novel drug delivery, biopharmaceutics, pharmacokinetics, pharmaceutical/medicinal chemistry, computational chemistry, drug design, pharmacy practice, clinical and hospital pharmacy, bioinformatics and biotechnology of pharmaceuticals, pharmacogenomics, allied health, biosciences, chemistry, engineering & technology, food sciences & technology, mathematics and statistics, medicine, toxicology.

Related titles: Online - full text ed.: ISSN 0976-2094. free (effective 2011).

Indexed: A01, E12, F08, F11, F12, H16, P33, P39, R13, T02, T05.

Published by: (Society of Pharmaceutical Education and Research), Medknow Publications and Media Pvt. Ltd., B-9, Kanara Business Ctr, Off Link Rd, Ghatkopar (E), Mumbai, Maharastra 400 075, India. TEL 91-22-66491818, FAX 91-22-66491817, journals@medknow.com, http://www.medknow.com. Ed., Pub., R&P Upendra Nagaich.

615 IND ISSN 2249-3379

▼ ➤ **JOURNAL OF ADVANCED PHARMACY EDUCATION & RESEARCH.** Abbreviated title: J A P E R. Text and summaries in English. 2011. m. adv. back issues avail. **Document type:** *Journal, Academic/Scholarly.* **Description:** Contains original research work, reviews, short communications, case report, ethics forum, education forum and letter to editor in the field of pharmacy. It inclues articles related to pharmaceutics, pharmacology, pharmacognosy, pharmaceutical chemistry.

Media: Online - full text.

Published by: Society of Pharmaceutical Education and Research, 22-C, Jawahar Colony, Gwalior, Madhya Pradesh 474 001, India. TEL 91-957-5065454. Ed. Eric Jones. Pub. J Pandey.

615 IND ISSN 2230-861X

▼ **JOURNAL OF ADVANCES IN DRUG RESEARCH.** Text in English. 2010. s-a. **Document type:** *Journal, Academic/Scholarly.*

Related titles: Online - full text ed.: ISSN 2230-7761.

Address: c/o Dr D Sujatha, 7-6-251/B, Mitta St, Tirupathi, Andhra Pradesh 51701, India. TEL 91-877-2220477. Ed. D Sujatha.

JOURNAL OF ANAESTHESIOLOGY - CLINICAL PHARMACOLOGY. *see* MEDICAL SCIENCES—Anaesthesiology

JOURNAL OF ANALYTICAL TOXICOLOGY. *see* ENVIRONMENTAL STUDIES—Toxicology And Environmental Safety

THE JOURNAL OF ANTIBIOTICS; an international journal devoted to research on bioactive microbial products. *see* MEDICAL SCIENCES

615 USA ISSN 1948-5964

▼ ➤ **JOURNAL OF ANTIVIRALS AND ANTIRETROVIRALS.** Text in English. 2009. bi-m. free (effective 2011). **Document type:** *Journal, Academic/Scholarly.* **Description:** Features new research and development of antiviral and antiretroviral drugs for diseases such as AIDS, the flu, and hepatitis.

Media: Online - full text.

Indexed: A01, P30, SCOPUS, T02.

Published by: Omics Publishing Group, 5716 Corse Ave, Ste 110, Westlake, Los Angeles, CA 91362. TEL 650-268-9744, info@omicsonline.com, http://www.omicsonline.com.

615 CAN ISSN 1920-4159

➤ **JOURNAL OF APPLIED PHARMACY.** Text in English. q. free. Index. back issues avail. **Document type:** *Journal, Academic/Scholarly.* **Description:** Aims to provide a forum for pharmacists to exchange information, promote better health management and encourage research attitude all over the world.

Media: Online - full text.

Published by: Intellectual Consortium of Drug Discovery & Technology Development Incorporation, 34-115 V N., Saskatoon, SK S7L3E4, Canada. TEL 306-261-9809, http://icdtd.wordpress.com/. Ed. Khalid Ahmad Sheikh. R&P Taha Nazir.

615 GBR ISSN 1029-2659
CODEN: JATRFE

JOURNAL OF APPLIED THERAPEUTIC RESEARCH. Abbreviated title: J A T R. Text in English. 1997. q. GBP 75 to individuals; GBP 150 to institutions (effective 2009). back issues avail.; reprints avail. **Document type:** *Journal, Academic/Scholarly.* **Description:** Focuses on the efficacy, safety and rational use of drugs following approval.

Formerly (until 1998): Journal of Applied Therapeutics (1072-1754)

Related titles: CD-ROM ed.; Online - full text ed.

Indexed: DBA, I12, Inpharma, SCOPUS.

—BLDSC (4947.121000), IE, Ingenta. **CCC.**

Published by: Euromed Communications Ltd., Passfield Business Ctr, Lynchborough Rd, Passfield, Liphook, Hampshire GU30 7SB, United Kingdom. TEL 44-1428-752222, FAX 44-1428-752223, info@euromed.uk.com. Ed. David Luscombe TEL 44-1222-874783.

JOURNAL OF APPLIED TOXICOLOGY. *see* ENVIRONMENTAL STUDIES—Toxicology And Environmental Safety

615 IND ISSN 0976-0105

➤ **JOURNAL OF BASIC AND CLINICAL PHARMACY.** Text in English. q. adv. abstr.; bibl.; illus.; pat.; stat. Index. back issues avail.; reprints avail. **Document type:** *Journal, Academic/Scholarly.* **Description:** Covers basic pharmacy concepts, recent developments in pharmacy in general, and clinical pharmacy including pharmaceutical research, with an aim of promoting research and development, post-graduate training, and further enhancements in the field of pharmacy.

Related titles: Online - full text ed.: ISSN 0976-0113. free (effective 2011).

Indexed: A01, A34, A35, A36, AgrForAb, CABA, D01, E12, F08, GH, H16, N02, N03, P33, R07, R08, T02, T05.

Published by: Global Scientific Research Forum, Mylareshwara Palace, No, 56, 1st Main Rd., Palace Guttahalli, Bangalore, Karnataka 560003, India. TEL 91-80-23568229. Ed., Pub. Sree Harsha.

615.328 DEU ISSN 0792-6855
CODEN: RCBPEJ

➤ **JOURNAL OF BASIC AND CLINICAL PHYSIOLOGY AND PHARMACOLOGY.** Text in English. 1980. q. EUR 375 to institutions; EUR 431 combined subscription to institutions (print & online eds.) (effective 2012). adv. bk.rev. illus. back issues avail. **Document type:** *Journal, Academic/Scholarly.*

Former titles (until 1987): Reviews in Clinical and Basic Pharmacology (0334-1534); (until 1985): Reviews in Pure and Applied Pharmacological Sciences (0197-2839)

Related titles: Online - full text ed.: ISSN 2191-0286.

Indexed: B25, BIOSIS Prev, CIN, ChemAb, ChemTitl, DBA, EMBASE, ExcerpMed, IBR, IBZ, IndMed, MEDLINE, MycolAb, P30, R10, Reac, SCOPUS.

—BLDSC (4951.117000), CASDDS, GNLM, IE, Infotrieve, Ingenta, Linda Hall.

Published by: (Israel Physiological and Pharmacological Society ISR), Walter de Gruyter GmbH & Co. KG, Genthiner Str 13, Berlin, 10785, Germany. TEL 49-30-26005220, FAX 49-30-26005251, info@degruyter.com, http://www.degruyter.de.

615 616.1 USA ISSN 0160-2446
RM345 CODEN: JCPCDT

➤ **JOURNAL OF CARDIOVASCULAR PHARMACOLOGY.** Text in English. 1979. m. USD 2,094 domestic to institutions; USD 2,756 foreign to institutions (effective 2011). adv. bk.rev. index. back issues avail.; reprints avail. **Document type:** *Journal, Academic/Scholarly.* **Description:** Brings out articles and pertinent review articles on basic and clinical aspects of cardiovascular pharmacology.

Related titles: Online - full text ed.: ISSN 1533-4023.

Indexed: A22, A29, A34, A35, A36, A38, ASCA, AgBio, AgrForAb, B20, B21, B25, BIOBASE, BIOSIS Prev, C24, C33, CABA, CIN, CTA, ChemAb, ChemTitl, CurCont, DBA, E12, EMBASE, ESPM, ExcerpMed, F08, F11, F12, GH, H16, I10, I12, IABS, IDIS, ISR, IndMed, IndVet, Inpharma, Kidney, MEDLINE, MycolAb, N02, N03, P30, P32, P33, P35, P39, PN&I, R08, R10, RA&MP, Reac, S17, SCI, SCOPUS, T05, THA, VITIS, VS, VirolAbstr, W07.

—BLDSC (4954.868000), CASDDS, GNLM, IE, Infotrieve, Ingenta, INIST. **CCC.**

Published by: Lippincott Williams & Wilkins (Subsidiary of: Wolters Kluwer N.V.), Two Commerce Sq, 2001 Market St, Philadelphia, PA 19103. TEL 215-521-8300, FAX 215-521-8902, customerservice@lww.com, http://www.lww.com. Ed. Dr. Michael R Rosen. Pub. Kim Jansen.

615 616.1 USA ISSN 1074-2484
CODEN: JCPTFE

JOURNAL OF CARDIOVASCULAR PHARMACOLOGY AND THERAPEUTICS. Text in English. 1996. q. USD 826, GBP 485 combined subscription to institutions (print & online eds.); USD 809, GBP 475 to institutions (effective 2011). adv. reprint service avail. from PSC. **Document type:** *Journal, Academic/Scholarly.*

Related titles: Online - full text ed.: ISSN 1940-4034. USD 743, GBP 437 to institutions (effective 2011).

Indexed: A22, A26, B25, BIOSIS Prev, C06, C07, CA, CIN, ChemAb, ChemTitl, CurCont, E01, E08, EMBASE, ExcerpMed, G08, H11, H12, I05, IndMed, Inpharma, MEDLINE, MycolAb, P30, P35, R10, Reac, S09, SCI, SCOPUS, T02, W07.

—BLDSC (4954.868500), CASDDS, GNLM, IE, Infotrieve, Ingenta, INIST. **CCC.**

Published by: Sage Publications, Inc., 2455 Teller Rd, Thousand Oaks, CA 91320. TEL 805-499-9774, FAX 805-499-0871, info@sagepub.com, http://www.sagepub.com/. Ed. Dr. Robert A Kloner. adv.: B&W page USD 1,225, color page USD 2,425; 8.25 x 11. Circ: 1,000 (paid).

▼ **JOURNAL OF CHEMICAL AND PHARMACEUTICAL RESEARCH.** *see* CHEMISTRY

JOURNAL OF CHEMOTHERAPY. *see* MEDICAL SCIENCES—Oncology

JOURNAL OF CHILD AND ADOLESCENT PSYCHOPHARMACOLOGY. *see* MEDICAL SCIENCES—Psychiatry And Neurology

615.19 CHN ISSN 1003-1057
CODEN: JCHSE4

➤ **JOURNAL OF CHINESE PHARMACEUTICAL SCIENCES.** Text in English. 1992. q. USD 90 (effective 2011). adv. **Document type:** *Journal, Academic/Scholarly.* **Description:** Covers all areas of pharmaceutical researches including medicinal chemistry, pharmacognosy, natural products, pharmaceutical analysis, pharmaceutics, biological drugs, pharmacology, drug administration and clinical pharmacy. It publishes original research articles, reviews, notes, and introductions of new drugs.

Related titles: Online - full text ed.

Indexed: CIN, ChemAb, ChemTitl.

—BLDSC (4958.128000), CASDDS, GNLM, IE, Ingenta.

Published by: Beijing Daxue Yaoxueyuan/Peking University, School of Pharmaceutical Sciences, Haidian District, 38, Xueyuan Road, Room 208, Beijing, 100083, China. TEL 86-10-82801713, FAX 86-10-82805496, http://sps.bjmu.edu.cn/. Ed. Li-He Zhang. adv.: page USD 200. Circ: 1,000. **Dist. by:** China International Book Trading Corp, 35 Chegongzhuang Xilu, Haidian District, PO Box 399, Beijing 100044, China. TEL 86-10-68412045, FAX 86-10-68412023, cibtc@mail.cibtc.com.cn, http://www.cibtc.com.cn. **Co-sponsor:** Chinese Pharmaceutical Association/Zhongguo Yaoxuehui.

➤ **JOURNAL OF CLINICAL ONCOLOGY.** *see* MEDICAL SCIENCES—Oncology

615.1 USA ISSN 0091-2700
RM300.A2 CODEN: JCPCBR

➤ **THE JOURNAL OF CLINICAL PHARMACOLOGY.** Text in English. 1960. m. USD 876, GBP 515 combined subscription to institutions (print & online eds.); USD 858, GBP 505 to institutions (effective 2011). adv. bk.rev. charts; illus. index. 100 p./no. 2 cols./p.; back issues avail.; reprint service avail. from PSC. **Document type:** *Journal, Academic/Scholarly.* **Description:** Geared toward clinical pharmacologists and physicians concerned with and responsible for the appropriate selection, investigation and prescribing of drugs.

Former titles (until 1973): Journal of Clinical Pharmacology and New Drugs (0021-9754); (until 1970): Journal of Clinical Pharmacology and the Journal of New Drugs (0095-9863); (until 1966): Journal of New Drugs (0096-0284)

Related titles: Microform ed.: (from PQC); Online - full text ed.: ISSN 1552-4604. USD 788, GBP 464 to institutions (effective 2011); Supplement(s): Clinical Consequences of Marijuana. 2002 (Nov.).

Indexed: A01, A03, A08, A22, A26, A34, A36, ASCA, B&BAb, B07, B19, B21, B25, BIOSIS Prev, CIN, C06, C07, C08, C24, CA, CABA, CIN, CINAHL, CTA, ChemAb, ChemTitl, ChemoAb, CurCont, D01, DBA, DentInd, E01, E08, E12, EMBASE, ESPM, ExcerpMed, F08, F11, F12, FR, G08, GH, GenetAb, H&SSA, H04, H11, H12, H16, I05, I12, IDIS, ISR, IndMed, Inpharma, Kidney, MEDLINE, MS&D, MycolAb, N02, N03, NSA, P20, P24, P30, P33, P35, P39, P48, P54, PN&I, PQC, PsycholAb, R10, RA&MP, RM&VM, Reac, S09, SCI, SCOPUS, T02, T05, ToxAb, V02, W07.

—BLDSC (4958.680000), CASDDS, GNLM, IE, Infotrieve, Ingenta, INIST. **CCC.**

Published by: (American College of Clinical Pharmacology), Sage Publications, Inc., 2455 Teller Rd, Thousand Oaks, CA 91320. TEL 805-499-9774, 800-818-7243, FAX 805-499-0871, 800-583-2665, info@sagepub.com. Ed. Daniel S Sitar. adv.: B&W page USD 850, color page USD 1,725; bleed 8.375 x 11.25. Circ: 1,764 (paid). **Subscr. outside the Americas to:** Sage Publications Ltd., 1 Oliver's Yard, 55 City Rd, London EC1Y 1SP, United Kingdom. TEL 44-20-73248701, FAX 44-20-73248733, subscription@sagepub.co.uk.

615 GBR ISSN 0269-4727
RM301.28 CODEN: JCPTED

➤ **JOURNAL OF CLINICAL PHARMACY AND THERAPEUTICS.** Text in English. 1976. bi-m. GBP 969 in United Kingdom to institutions; EUR 1,231 in Europe to institutions; USD 1,791 in the Americas to institutions; USD 2,089 elsewhere to institutions; GBP 1,116 combined subscription in United Kingdom to institutions (print & online eds.); EUR 1,417 combined subscription in Europe to institutions (print & online eds.); USD 2,060 combined subscription in the Americas to institutions (print & online eds.); USD 2,402 combined subscription elsewhere to institutions (print & online eds.) (effective 2012). adv. bk.rev. abstr.; bibl. index. back issues avail.; reprint service avail. from PSC. **Document type:** *Journal, Academic/Scholarly.* **Description:** Provides a forum for clinicians, pharmacists and other health-care professionals to explore and report on issues of common interest.

Former titles (until 1987): Journal of Clinical and Hospital Pharmacy (0143-3180); (until 1980): Journal of Clinical Pharmacy (0308-6593)

Related titles: Microform ed.: (from PQC); Online - full text ed.: ISSN 1365-2710. 1999. GBP 969 in United Kingdom to institutions; EUR 1,231 in Europe to institutions; USD 1,791 in the Americas to institutions; USD 2,089 elsewhere to institutions (effective 2012) (from IngentaConnect).

Indexed: A01, A02, A03, A08, A22, A26, A36, ASCA, B21, B25, BIOSIS Prev, BP, C06, C07, C08, C11, CA, CABA, CIN, CINAHL, ChemAb, ChemTitl, CurCont, D01, DBA, E01, E12, EMBASE, ESPM, ExcerpMed, F08, F11, F12, FR, GH, H&SSA, H04, H12, H16, H17, I12, IDIS, INI, ISR, IndMed, Inpharma, MEDLINE, MS&D, MycolAb, N02, N03, O01, P03, P30, P33, P35, P39, PsycInfo, R10, R12, RA&MP, RM&VM, Reac, RiskAb, SCI, SCOPUS, T02, T05, TAR, VITIS, W07.

—BLDSC (4958.685000), CASDDS, GNLM, IE, Infotrieve, Ingenta, INIST. **CCC.**

Published by: Wiley-Blackwell Publishing Ltd. (Subsidiary of: John Wiley & Sons, Inc.), 9600 Garsington Rd, Oxford, OX4 2DQ, United Kingdom. TEL 44-1865-776868, FAX 44-1865-714591, customerservices@blackwellpublishing.com. Eds. Alain Li Wan Po TEL 44-1159-285979, Gregory Peterson, M J Kendall. Adv. contact Joanna Baker TEL 44-1865-476271.

615.19 USA ISSN 0271-0749
CODEN: JCPYDR

➤ **JOURNAL OF CLINICAL PSYCHOPHARMACOLOGY.** Text in English. 1981. bi-m. USD 966 domestic to institutions; USD 1,068 foreign to institutions (effective 2011). adv. bk.rev. back issues avail.; reprints avail. **Document type:** *Journal, Academic/Scholarly.* **Description:** Provides articles reporting on clinical trials and studies, side effects, drug interactions, overdose management, pharmacogenetics, pharmacokinetics, and psychiatric effects of non-psychiatric drugs.

Related titles: CD-ROM ed.; Online - full text ed.: ISSN 1533-712X.

Indexed: A22, A34, A35, A36, AD&D, AMHA, ASCA, AddicA, AgBio, B21, B25, BIOSIS Prev, CABA, CIN, ChPerI, ChemAb, ChemTitl, CurCont, D01, DBA, DentInd, E-psyche, E12, EMBASE, ExcerpMed, F08, F11, F12, FR, FoP, GH, I12, IDIS, INI, ISR, IndMed, Inpharma, JW-P, MEDLINE, MycolAb, N02, N03, N04, NSA, NSCI, P03, P30, P35, PsycInfo, PsycholAb, R10, RA&MP, Reac, S02, S03, SCI, SCOPUS, THA, VS, W07.

—BLDSC (4958.691000), CASDDS, GNLM, IE, Infotrieve, Ingenta, INIST. **CCC.**

Published by: Lippincott Williams & Wilkins (Subsidiary of: Wolters Kluwer N.V.), 530 Walnut St, Philadelphia, PA 19106. TEL 215-521-8300, FAX 215-521-8902, customerservice@lww.com, http://www.lww.com. Eds. Dr. David J Greenblatt, Dr. Richard I Shader TEL 617-636-2178. Pub. Terry Materese. Circ: 744.

615 GBR ISSN 1369-5207

➤ **JOURNAL OF CLINICAL RESEARCH.** Abbreviated title: J C R. Text in English. 1997. irreg., latest vol.5, 2002. adv. abstr. 2 cols./p.; Supplement avail.; back issues avail.; reprints avail. **Document type:** *Journal, Academic/Scholarly.* **Description:** Brings out studies determining the efficacy of new clinical interventions, from phase I to post-marketing investigations.

Formed by the merger of (1990-1998): British Journal of Clinical Research (0961-1053); (1991-1998): European Journal of Clinical Research (0961-3692)

Indexed: C06, C07, EMBASE, ExcerpMed, I12, R10, Reac, SCOPUS.

—IE. **CCC.**

Published by: Informa Healthcare (Subsidiary of: T & F Informa plc), Telephone House, 69-77 Paul St, London, EC2A 4LQ, United Kingdom. TEL 44-20-70175000, FAX 44-20-70176792, healthcare.enquiries@informa.com, http://informahealthcare.com/. Adv. contact Per Sonnerfeldt. **Subscr. to:** Taylor & Francis Inc., Customer Services Dept, 325 Chestnut St, 8th Fl, Philadelphia, PA 19106. TEL 215-625-8900, 800-354-1420, FAX 215-625-8914, customerservice@taylorandfrancis.com; Taylor & Francis Ltd., Journals Customer Service, Sheepen Pl, Colchester, Essex CO3 3LP, United Kingdom. TEL 44-20-70175544, FAX 44-20-70175198.

P

615.1 NLD ISSN 0168-3659
RS201.C64 CODEN: JCREEC
➤ **JOURNAL OF CONTROLLED RELEASE.** Text and summaries in English. 1984. 24/yr. EUR 3,894 in Europe to institutions; JPY 516,400 in Japan to institutions; USD 4,356 elsewhere to institutions (effective 2012). adv. bk.rev. abstr.; bibl.; illus.; pat. index. back issues avail.; reprints avail. **Document type:** *Journal, Academic/Scholarly.* **Description:** Publishes research and reviews on the science and technology of all types of controlled release of active agents, including applications in pharmacology, agricultural sciences, and relevant work in toxicology.
Related titles: Microform ed.: (from PQC); Online - full text ed.: ISSN 1873-4995 (from IngentaConnect, ScienceDirect).
Indexed: A01, A03, A08, A22, A26, A34, A35, A36, A37, A38, ASCA, AgBio, B&BAb, B19, B21, B23, B25, BIOSIS Prev, BioEngAb, C24, C25, C33, CA, CABA, CIN, CPEI, ChemAb, ChemTitl, CurCont, D01, DBA, E12, EMBASE, EngInd, ExcerpMed, F08, F11, F12, FCA, GH, GenetAb, H17, I05, I11, I12, ISR, IndMed, IndVet, Inpharma, M&PBA, MEDLINE, MycolAb, N02, N03, OR, P30, P33, P39, PN&I, R07, R08, R10, R11, R13, RA&MP, RM&VM, Reac, S01, S12, S13, S16, SCI, SCOPUS, SoyAb, T02, T05, VS, W07, W10.
—BLDSC (4965.260000), CASDDS, GNLM, IE, Infotrieve, Ingenta, INIST, Linda Hall. **CCC.**
Published by: (Controlled Release Society), Elsevier BV (Subsidiary of: Elsevier Science & Technology), Radarweg 29, PO Box 211, Amsterdam, 1000 AE, Netherlands. TEL 31-20-4853911, FAX 31-20-4852457, JournalsCustomerServiceEMEA@elsevier.com, http://www.elsevier.nl. Ed. K Park.

615 IND ISSN 0976-3171
RM1
▼ **JOURNAL OF CURRENT PHARMACEUTICAL RESEARCH.** Text in English. 2010. q. free (effective 2011). abstr. back issues avail. **Document type:** *Journal, Academic/Scholarly.* **Description:** Contains mini-reviews, short communication, original research articles and review articles in all fields of experimental or theoretical pharmaceutical sciences.
Media: Online - full text.
Published by: Medipoeia Publication, Dawa Bazar, Hujrat Pul, Dawa Bazar, Huzrat Bridge, Gwalior, 474001, India. Ed. Asgar Ali. Pub., R&P Paras Sharma.

615.1 USA ISSN 1939-0211
➤ **JOURNAL OF DIETARY SUPPLEMENTS.** Abbreviated title: J N F M F. Text in English. 2008. q. GBP 155, EUR 205, USD 285 combined subscription to institutions (print & online eds.); GBP 330, EUR 435, USD 590 combined subscription to corporations (print & online eds.) (effective 2010). adv. 120 p./no. 1 cols./p.; back issues avail.; reprint service avail. from PSC. **Document type:** *Journal, Academic/Scholarly.* **Description:** Offers a forum to explore the many product, business and policy issues that surround the technology allowing for the development of "superfoods.".
Formed by the merger of (1997-2008): Journal of Nutraceuticals, Functional & Medical Foods (1089-4179); (2001-2008): Journal of Herbal Pharmacotherapy (1522-8940)
Related titles: Microform ed.; Online - full text ed.: ISSN 1939-022X.
Indexed: A22, A34, A35, A36, AMED, ASFA, Agr, AgrForAb, B&BAb, B19, B21, B25, BIOSIS Prev, BP, BiolDig, C06, C07, C08, C25, CA, CABA, CINAHL, D01, E01, E12, ESPM, F05, F06, F07, F08, F10, F11, F12, FS&TA, GH, H&SSA, H16, I10, I12, IBR, IBZ, LT, M02, MycolAb, N02, N03, N04, NSA, P30, P32, P33, P40, R07, R10, R11, R12, RA&MP, RM&VM, RRTA, Reac, RefZh, SCOPUS, T02, T05, TAR, VS, W11.
—BLDSC (4969.463000), IE, Infotrieve, Ingenta, INIST. **CCC.**
Published by: Informa Healthcare (Subsidiary of: T & F Informa plc), 52 Vanderbilt Ave, New York, NY 10017. TEL 212-262-8230, FAX 212-262-8234, healthcare.enquiries@informa.com, http://www.informahealthcare.com. Ed. Catherine E Ulbricht. adv.: B&W page USD 315, color page USD 550; trim 4.375 x 7.125. Circ: 321 (paid).

615 GBR ISSN 2155-6660
▼ ➤ **JOURNAL OF DRUG ASSESSMENT (LONDON).** Text in English. 2010 (Sep.). irreg. free (effective 2010). **Document type:** *Journal, Trade.* **Description:** Features articles on null/negative/inconclusive/incomplete/discontinued results from Phase I-Phase IV drug trials and other studies.
Media: Online - full text.
Published by: Informa U K Ltd. (Subsidiary of: T & F Informa plc), 30-32 Mortimer St, London, W1W 7RE, United Kingdom. TEL 44-20-70175532, FAX 44-20-70174781, enquiries@informa.com, http://www.informa.com.

615 USA ISSN 2090-3014
▼ ➤ **JOURNAL OF DRUG DELIVERY.** Text in English. 2011. USD 195 (effective 2011). **Document type:** *Journal, Academic/Scholarly.* **Description:** Publishes original research articles and review articles related to all aspects of drug delivery.
Related titles: Online - full text ed.: ISSN 2090-3022. 2011. free (effective 2011).
Indexed: A01.
Published by: Hindawi Publishing Corporation, 410 Park Ave, 15th Fl, PMB 287, New York, NY 10022. FAX 215-893-4392, 866-446-3294, info@hindawi.com.

615.1 FRA ISSN 1773-2247
CODEN: STSSE5
➤ **JOURNAL OF DRUG DELIVERY SCIENCE AND TECHNOLOGY.** Variant title: J D D S T. Text in French; Summaries in English. 1985. 6/yr. EUR 449 domestic; EUR 479 foreign (effective 2009). bk.rev. charts; illus. index. **Document type:** *Journal, Academic/Scholarly.*
Formerly (until 2003): S T P Pharma Sciences (1157-1489); Which superseded in part (in 1991): S T P Pharma (0758-6922); Which was formed by the merger of (1972-1985): Sciences et Techniques Pharmaceutiques (0373-1219); (1965-1985): Labo - Pharma Problemes et Techniques (0458-5747); Which was formed by the merger of (1953-1965): Labo-Pharma (0023-6470); (1951-1965): Problemes et Techniques (0478-3611)
Indexed: ASCA, B&BAb, B19, B21, BioEngAb, CIN, ChemAb, ChemTitl, CurCont, EMBASE, ExcerpMed, I12, ISR, Inpharma, M&PBA, P30, R10, Reac, RefZh, SCI, SCOPUS, W07.
—BLDSC (4970.525200), CASDDS, GNLM, IE, Infotrieve, Ingenta, INIST, Linda Hall. **CCC.**
Published by: Editions de Sante, 49 Rue Galilee, Paris, 75116, France. TEL 33-1-40701615, FAX 33-1-40701614, editions.de.sante@wanadoo.fr. Ed. Dominique Dupont. Circ: 2,000.

615.7 615.9 IND
▼ ➤ **JOURNAL OF DRUG METABOLISM AND TOXICOLOGY.** Text in English. 2010. s-a. USD 425 (effective 2011). **Document type:** *Journal, Academic/Scholarly.* **Description:** Publishes all the latest research articles, reviews and letters in all areas of drug metabolism & toxicology.
Related titles: Online - full text ed.: free (effective 2011).
Published by: Bioinfo Publications, 49/F-72, Vighnahar Complex, Front of Overseas Bank, Sector 12, Kharghar, Navi Mumbai, 410 210, India. TEL 91-22-27743967, FAX 91-22-66736413, editor@bioinfo.in, subscription@bioinfo.in. Eds. Dr. Somnath Tagore, Dr. Virendra S Gomase.

615 GBR ISSN 1061-186X
RS199.5 CODEN: JDTAEH
➤ **JOURNAL OF DRUG TARGETING.** Text in English. 1993. 10/yr. GBP 1,395, EUR 1,755, USD 2,195 combined subscription to institutions (print & online eds.); GBP 2,845, EUR 3,590, USD 4,490 combined subscription to corporations (print & online eds.) (effective 2010). adv. back issues avail.; reprint service avail. from PSC. **Document type:** *Journal, Academic/Scholarly.* **Description:** Covers on all aspects of drug delivery and targeting for molecular and macromolecular drugs including the design and characterization of carrier systems (whether colloidal, protein or polymeric) for both vitro and/or in vivo applications of these drugs.
Related titles: CD-ROM ed.: ISSN 1026-7158. 1995; Microform ed.; Online - full text ed.: ISSN 1029-2330 (from IngentaConnect).
Indexed: A01, A03, A08, A22, ASCA, B&BAb, B19, B21, B25, BIOBASE, BIOSIS Prev, BioEngAb, C33, CA, ChemAb, CurCont, DBA, E01, EMBASE, ESPM, ExcerpMed, I12, IABS, ISR, IndMed, Inpharma, M&PBA, MEDLINE, MycolAb, NSA, P30, R10, Reac, SCI, SCOPUS, T02, ToxAb, W07.
—GNLM, IE, Infotrieve, Ingenta, INIST. **CCC.**
Published by: Informa Healthcare (Subsidiary of: T & F Informa plc), Telephone House, 69-77 Paul St, London, EC2A 4LQ, United Kingdom. TEL 44-20-70175000, healthcare.enquiries@informa.com, http://www.tandf.co.uk/journals/. Ed. Saghir Akhtar. Adv. contact Per Sonnerfeldt. **Subscr. in N. America to:** Taylor & Francis Inc., Customer Services Dept, 325 Chestnut St, 8th Fl, Philadelphia, PA 19106. TEL 215-625-8900, 800-354-1420, FAX 215-625-2940, customerservice@taylorandfrancis.com; **Subscr. outside N. America to:** Taylor & Francis Ltd., Journals Customer Service, Sheepen Pl, Colchester, Essex CO3 3LP, United Kingdom. TEL 44-20-70175544, FAX 44-20-70175198, tf.enquiries@tfinforma.com.

615 USA ISSN 2161-4865
▼ ➤ **JOURNAL OF ENCAPSULATION AND ADSORPTION SCIENCES.** Abbreviated title: J E A S. Text in English. 2011. q. USD 156 (effective 2011). **Document type:** *Journal, Academic/Scholarly.* **Description:** Covers original contributions concerning with the processes and technology adsorption and also encapsulation.
Related titles: Online - full text ed.: ISSN 2161-4873. free (effective 2011).
Published by: Scientific Research Publishing, Inc., PO Box 54821, Irvine, CA 92619. service@scirp.org. Ed. Bouzid Menaa.

615 571 NLD ISSN 1875-0443
QP88.4
➤ **JOURNAL OF EPITHELIAL BIOLOGY & PHARMACOLOGY.** Text in English. irreg. free (effective 2011). **Document type:** *Journal, Academic/Scholarly.* **Description:** Publishes research work on the interaction of drugs and molecules with epithelial systems.
Media: Online - full text.
Indexed: A39, C27, C29, CTA, D03, D04, E13, EMBASE, ExcerpMed, P30, R14, S14, S15, S18, SCOPUS.
Published by: Bentham Open (Subsidiary of: Bentham Science Publishers Ltd.), PO Box 294, Bussum, AG 1400, Netherlands. TEL 31-35-6923800, FAX 31-35-6980150, subscriptions@bentham.org. Ed. Xiangdong Wang.

615.19 IRL ISSN 0378-8741
RS1 CODEN: JOETD7
➤ **JOURNAL OF ETHNOPHARMACOLOGY.** Text in English. 1979. 18/yr. EUR 2,946 in Europe to institutions; JPY 390,700 in Japan to institutions; USD 3,294 elsewhere to institutions (effective 2012). bk.rev. abstr. 2 cols./p.; back issues avail.; reprints avail. **Document type:** *Journal, Academic/Scholarly.* **Description:** Dedicated to the exchange of information and understandings about people's use of plants, fungi, animals, microorganisms and minerals and their biological and pharmacological effects based on the principles established through international conventions.
Related titles: Microform ed.: (from PQC); Online - full text ed.: ISSN 1872-7573 (from IngentaConnect, ScienceDirect).
Indexed: A01, A03, A08, A20, A22, A26, A34, A35, A36, A37, A38, ASCA, ASFA, AbAn, AgBio, Agr, AgrForAb, B21, B23, B25, B27, BA, BIOBASE, BIOSIS Prev, BNNA, BP, BibAg, C06, C07, C25, C30, CA, CABA, CIN, CTA, CTFA, ChemAb, ChemTitl, ChemoAb, Chicano, CurCont, D01, E12, EMBASE, ESPM, ExcerpMed, F08, F11, F12, FR, G11, GH, H&SSA, H16, H17, I05, I10, I11, I12, IABS, IDIS, ISR, IndMed, IndVet, Inpharma, LT, MEDLINE, MaizeAb, MycolAb, N02, N03, N04, NSA, OR, P30, P32, P33, P37, P38, P39, P40, PGegResA, PGrRegA, PHN&I, PN&I, R07, R08, R10, R11, R12, R13, RA&MP, RM&VM, RRTA, Reac, RiskAb, S12, S13, S16, S17, SCI, SCOPUS, SoyAb, T02, T05, TAR, TOSA, TriticAb, VS, W07, W10, W11.
—BLDSC (4979.602400), CASDDS, GNLM, IE, Infotrieve, Ingenta, INIST. **CCC.**
Published by: Elsevier Ireland Ltd (Subsidiary of: Elsevier Science & Technology), Elsevier House, Brookvale Plaza, E. Park, Shannon, Co. Clare, Ireland. TEL 353-61-709600, FAX 353-61-709100, nlinfo@elsevier.nl. Ed. R Verpoorte. **Subscr. to:** Elsevier BV, Radarweg 29, PO Box 211, Amsterdam 1000 AE, Netherlands. TEL 31-20-4853757, FAX 31-20-4853432, http://www.elsevier.nl.

615.1 MLT ISSN 1023-3857
➤ **JOURNAL OF EUROMED PHARMACY.** Text in English. 1994. irreg. **Document type:** *Journal, Academic/Scholarly.* **Description:** Promotes pharmacy in the Mediterranean region. Includes research work by local and foreign pharmacy graduates and other papers relating to pharmacy.
Published by: University of Malta, Department of Pharmacy, Msida, Malta. TEL 356-21343764, FAX 356-21340427, http://home.um.edu.mt/phcy. Ed. Anthony Serracino Inglott. Pub. Bhabkar Sharma. Circ: 1,500.

615 658.8 USA ISSN 2150-2668
RS201.E87
▼ ➤ **JOURNAL OF EXCIPIENTS AND FOOD CHEMICALS.** Text in English. 2010. q. free (effective 2011). bk.rev. illus. back issues avail. **Document type:** *Journal, Academic/Scholarly.* **Description:** Offers forum for the discussion and communication of research, reviews or commentary related exclusively to these materials. The Journal publishes research papers, reviews, technical notes, commentary and communications related to the effect of excipients on drug formulation development, drug delivery, bioavailability, efficacy, stability, ability to manufacture, safety, and toxicity. Excipients or Food Chemicals may be small molecule, macromolecules, proteins, polymers, lipidic or polymeric self assembled nanocarriers or nanostructured dispersions, adjuvants or of genetic origin. Areas of particular interest include, but are not limited to: novel excipients and their physical chemistry; new or improved analytical methods to characterize excipients; co-processed excipients and/or performance modifying excipients; drug-excipient interactions and compatibility; and excipient and food chemical regulatory and compendial issues, including excipient harmonization.
Media: Online - full text.
Indexed: A01, CABA, F10, GH, H16, N02, N03, T02.
Published by: International Pharmaceutical Excipients Council, Americas, 1655 N Fort Myer Dr, Ste 700, Arlington, VA 22209. TEL 703-875-2127, info@ipecamericas.org, http://www.ipecamericas.org. Ed. Shireesh Apte. Pub. David Schoneker.

615.1 GBR ISSN 1179-1454
▼ ➤ **JOURNAL OF EXPERIMENTAL PHARMACOLOGY.** Text in English. 2009. a. free (effective 2011). back issues avail. **Document type:** *Journal, Academic/Scholarly.* **Description:** Brings out research, reports, reviews and commentaries on all areas of laboratory and experimental pharmacology.
Media: Online - full text.
Indexed: P30.
—CCC.
Published by: Dove Medical Press Ltd., Beechfield House, Winterton Way, Macclesfield, SK11 0JL, United Kingdom. TEL 44-1625-509130, FAX 44-1625-617933.

➤ **JOURNAL OF FOOD AND DRUG ANALYSIS/YAOWU SHIPIN FENXI.** see FOOD AND FOOD INDUSTRIES

615 IND ISSN 0974-0031
JOURNAL OF G M P & INDUSTRIAL PHARMACY. (Good Manufacturing Practice) Text in English. 2007. q. INR 600 domestic; USD 60 foreign (effective 2011). adv. **Document type:** *Journal, Academic/Scholarly.*
Published by: Lords, Center for GMP & Pharmaceutical Technology, India, c/o Lords Research & life science Laboratory Pvt Ltd, Plot No BH-1/52-53, N-2, Thakare Nagar, CIDCO, Aurangabad, Maharashtra 431 006, India. TEL 91-240-2480237, contact@lordsgreen.com, pamec_lords@rediffmail.com, www.lordsgreen.com.

615.1 GBR ISSN 1741-1343
RS55.2
➤ **JOURNAL OF GENERIC MEDICINES.** Abbreviated title: J G M. Text in English. 2003 (Oct.). q. USD 673 in North America to institutions; GBP 376 elsewhere to institutions (effective 2011). adv. back issues avail.; reprint service avail. from PSC. **Document type:** *Journal, Academic/Scholarly.* **Description:** Publishes referenced articles on the latest developments and ideas in the field, and illustrates how these impact on the practice and research of those working in, and with, generic medicines.
Related titles: Online - full text ed.: ISSN 1741-7090 (from IngentaConnect).
Indexed: A01, A22, A26, CA, E01, E08, EMBASE, ExcerpMed, H12, I05, P02, P19, P20, P48, P54, PQC, R10, Reac, S09, SCOPUS, T02.
—BLDSC (4989.500000), IE, Ingenta. **CCC.**
Published by: (European Generic Medicines Association BEL), Sage Publications Ltd. (Subsidiary of: Sage Publications, Inc.), 1 Oliver's Yard, 55 City Rd, London, EC1Y 1SP, United Kingdom. TEL 44-20-73248500, FAX 44-20-73248600, info@sagepub.co.uk, http://www.uk.sagepub.com/home.nav. Pub. Neil Henderson TEL 44-1256-302959 ext 3116. Circ: 600. **Subscr. to:** Palgrave Macmillan Ltd., Subscription Department, Brunel Rd, Houndmills, Basingstoke, Hants RG21 2XS, United Kingdom. TEL 44-1256-357893, FAX 44-1256-328339, orders@palgrave.com, subscriptions@palgrave.com, http://www.palgrave.com.

615 KOR ISSN 1226-8453
CODEN: KINHEK
JOURNAL OF GINSENG RESEARCH. Text in Korean. 1976. q. membership. **Document type:** *Journal, Academic/Scholarly.* **Description:** Publishes research papers on original work, either experimental or theoretical, that advance our understanding of ginseng science, including questions on the cultivation, biology, chemistry, pharmacology and biochemistry of ginseng.
Formerly (until 1997): Goryeo Insam Haghoeji /Korean Journal of Ginseng Science (1016-2615)
Related titles: Online - full text ed.
Indexed: A22, B25, BIOSIS Prev, FS&TA, P30, SCI, W07.
—BLDSC (4995.600000), CASDDS, IE, Ingenta.
Published by: Korean Society of Ginseng/Go'ryeo Insam Haghoe, c/o Chang Ho Lee, PhD, General Secretary, Rm #804 Seocho World Officetel, 1355-3 Seocho-dong, Seocho-Ku, Seoul, 137-862, Korea, S. TEL 82-2-34738772, FAX 82-2-34742330, ginsengsociety@hanmail.net, http://www.ginsengsociety.org/.

615 IND ISSN 0975-8542
RM1
▼ **JOURNAL OF GLOBAL PHARMA TECHNOLOGY.** Text in English. 2009. m. free (effective 2011). **Document type:** *Journal, Academic/Scholarly.* **Description:** Aims to promote pharmaceutical research, technology and science and the profession of pharmacy in general.
Media: Online - full text.
Address: 23 Rajiv Nagar, Near Police Line, Neemuch, MP 458441, India. Pub. Shweta Chundawat.

615 IND ISSN 2230-7346
▼ **JOURNAL OF GLOBAL TRENDS IN PHARMACEUTICAL SCIENCES.** Text in English. 2010. q. free (effective 2011). **Document type:** *Journal, Academic/Scholarly.*
Media: Online - full text.
Published by: Annamacharya College of Pharmacy, New Boyanapalli, Rajampet, Kadapa, Andhra Pradesh, India. http://www.ancpap.org.

JOURNAL OF HEALTH SCIENCE/EISEI KAGAKU. *see* ENVIRONMENTAL STUDIES—Toxicology And Environmental Safety

615.1 610 JPN ISSN 1341-321X
RM260 CODEN: JICHFN
➤ **JOURNAL OF INFECTION AND CHEMOTHERAPY.** Text in English. 1995. bi-m. EUR 370, USD 421 combined subscription to institutions (print & online eds.) (effective 2012). 70 p./no.; reprint service avail. from PSC. **Document type:** *Journal, Academic/Scholarly.* **Description:** Covers the combined area of infection and chemotherapy, including the pathogenesis, diagnosis, treatment and control of infectious diseases.
Related titles: Online - full text ed.: ISSN 1437-7780 (from IngentaConnect).
Indexed: A01, A03, A08, A22, A26, A29, A34, A36, B20, B21, B25, BIOSIS Prev, CA, CABA, CIN, ChemAb, ChemTitl, CurCont, D01, E01, E12, EMBASE, ESPM, ExcerpMed, GH, H17, I10, IndVet, MEDLINE, MycolAb, N02, N03, OR, P30, P33, P39, R07, R08, R10, R12, R13, RM&VM, Reac, S13, SCI, SCOPUS, T02, T05, VS, VirolAbstr, W07.
—BLDSC (5006.691000), CASDDS, IE, Infotrieve, Ingenta, INIST. **CCC.**
Published by: (Japan Society of Chemotherapy), Springer Japan KK (Subsidiary of: Springer Science+Business Media), No 2 Funato Bldg, 1-11-11 Kudan-kita, Chiyoda-ku, Tokyo, 102-0073, Japan. TEL 81-3-68317000, FAX 81-3-68317001, http://www.springer.jp. Ed. Yoshio Kobayashi. Circ: 1,500 (paid). **Subscr. in the Americas to:** Springer New York LLC, Journal Fulfillment, PO Box 2485, Secaucus, NJ 07096. TEL 800-777-4643, 201-348-4033, FAX 201-348-4505, journals-ny@springer.com, http://www.springer.com; **Subscr. to:** Springer Distribution Center, Kundenservice Zeitschriften, Haberstr 7, Heidelberg 69126, Germany. TEL 49-6221-3454303, FAX 49-6221-3454229, subscriptions@springer.com.

➤ **JOURNAL OF INFLAMMATION.** *see* MEDICAL SCIENCES—Surgery

615 IND ISSN 0975-8593
RM1
▼ ➤ **JOURNAL OF INNOVATIVE TRENDS IN PHARAMACEUTICAL SCIENCES.** Text in English. 2010. m. free (effective 2011). abstr.; bibl. Index. back issues avail. **Document type:** *Journal, Academic/Scholarly.* **Description:** Publishes original research articles, research Articles and Short Communications, in pharmaceutical fields (pharmaceutics, pharmaceutical technology, pharmaceutical analysis, biopharmaceutics, pharmacokinetics, pharmacology, toxicology, genomics and proteomics, pharmacognosy and phytochemistry).
Media: Online - full text.
Published by: Trendz Publications, ABRA-368(B), Annor, Tirumala, Trivandrum 695006, India. TEL 91-471-2355642, FAX 91-471-2355642. Ed., R&P Rahul Nair. Pub. M. K. Nair.

615 USA ISSN 0194-5106
JOURNAL OF KANSAS PHARMACY. Text in English. 1964. q. USD 63 to non-members (effective 2005). adv. illus.; stat.; tr.lit. **Document type:** *Magazine, Trade.* **Description:** Statewide pharmacy news; association news, reports, health-system pharmacy news; original articles; and president's editorials.
Published by: Kansas Pharmacists Association, 1020 SW Fairlawn Rd, Topeka, KS 66604. info@kansaspharmacy.org, http://www.kansaspharmacy.org. Ed., R&P, Adv. contact Jenith Hoover TEL 785-232-0439. B&W page USD 500, color page USD 832; trim 11 x 8.5. Circ: 1,300 (controlled).

615.19 USA ISSN 0898-2104
RS201.L55 CODEN: JLREE7
➤ **JOURNAL OF LIPOSOME RESEARCH.** Text in English. 1991. q. GBP 1,080, EUR 1,425, USD 1,785 combined subscription to institutions (print & online eds.); GBP 2,220, EUR 2,930, USD 3,660 combined subscription to corporations (print & online eds.) (effective 2010). adv. back issues avail.; reprint service avail. from PSC. **Document type:** *Journal, Academic/Scholarly.* **Description:** Presents high quality liposome research. Subjects are broad, ranging from biophysical analysis of liposome membranes to clinical applications of liposome-encapsulated drugs.
Related titles: Microform ed.: (from RPI); Online - full text ed.: ISSN 1532-2394 (from IngentaConnect).
Indexed: A01, A03, A08, A22, A29, ASCA, B&BAb, B19, B20, B21, B25, B27, BIOBASE, BIOSIS Prev, BioEngAb, CA, ChemAb, ChemTitl, CurCont, DBA, E01, EMBASE, ESPM, ExcerpMed, I10, IABS, Inpharma, M&PBA, MEDLINE, MycolAb, NSA, P30, R10, Reac, RefZh, S01, SCI, SCOPUS, T02, Telegen, VirolAbstr, W07.
—BLDSC (5010.505000), CASDDS, GNLM, IE, Infotrieve, Ingenta. **CCC.**
Published by: Informa Healthcare (Subsidiary of: T & F Informa plc), 52 Vanderbilt Ave, New York, NY 10017. TEL 212-262-8230, FAX 212-262-8234, healthcare.enquiries@informa.com, http://www.informahealthcare.com. Ed. Yvonne Perrie. Adv. contact Daniel Wallen. **Subscr. outside N. America to:** Taylor & Francis Ltd.

615 368.382 USA ISSN 1083-4087
RS100.3
➤ **JOURNAL OF MANAGED CARE PHARMACY.** Abbreviated title: J M C P. Text in English. 1995. bi-m. USD 90 domestic; USD 120 foreign; USD 15 per issue (effective 2010). back issues avail. **Document type:** *Journal, Academic/Scholarly.* **Description:** Presents scholarly, peer-reviewed articles in the areas of managed care pharmacy practice, pharmacotherapy, research, education, economics, and other pertinent areas of pharmacy practice.
Related titles: Online - full text ed.: ISSN 1944-706X. free (effective 2010).
Indexed: C06, C07, CurCont, EMBASE, ExcerpMed, I12, IDIS, Inpharma, MEDLINE, P30, P35, R10, Reac, SCI, SCOPUS, W07.
—BLDSC (5011.080000), IE, Ingenta. **CCC.**
Published by: Academy of Managed Care Pharmacy, 100 N Pitt St, 400, Alexandria, VA 22314. TEL 703-683-8416, 800-827-2627, FAX 703-683-8417, ccampbell@mitchellpeterson.org. Pub. Judith A Cahill. R&P Tricia Rudis TEL 717-560-2001. Adv. contact Bob Heiman TEL 856-673-4000. Circ: 19,000.

➤ **JOURNAL OF MEDICAL AND PHARMACEUTICAL MARKETING.** *see* BUSINESS AND ECONOMICS—Marketing And Purchasing

615 658.8 GBR ISSN 1745-7904
HD9994.A1 CODEN: JRAAAG
➤ **JOURNAL OF MEDICAL MARKETING**; device, diagnostic and pharmaceutical marketing. Abbreviated title: J M M. Text in English. 2000. q. USD 741 in North America to institutions; GBP 399 elsewhere to institutions (effective 2011). adv. abstr. 96 p./no. 2 cols./p.; back issues avail.; reprint service avail. from PSC. **Document type:** *Journal, Academic/Scholarly.* **Description:** Aims to facilitate excellence in medical marketing by providing a source of marketing expertise that is tailored specifically to pharmaceutical, medical device and diagnostic markets.
Formerly (until 2005): International Journal of Medical Marketing (1469-7025)
Related titles: Online - full text ed.: ISSN 1745-7912 (from IngentaConnect).
Indexed: A12, A17, A22, A26, ABIn, B01, B06, B07, B09, CA, E01, E08, H01, H12, I05, P21, P48, P51, P53, P54, PQC, S09, SCOPUS, T02.
—BLDSC (5017.078700), IE, Ingenta. **CCC.**
Published by: Sage Publications Ltd. (Subsidiary of: Sage Publications, Inc.), 1 Oliver's Yard, 55 City Rd, London, EC1Y 1SP, United Kingdom. TEL 44-20-73248500, FAX 44-20-73248600, info@sagepub.co.uk, http://www.uk.sagepub.com/home.nav. Circ: 550.

615.9 USA ISSN 1556-9039
RA1190
➤ **JOURNAL OF MEDICAL TOXICOLOGY**; official journal of the American College of Medical Toxicology. Text in English. 2005 (Dec.). q. EUR 206, USD 279 combined subscription to institutions (print & online eds.) (effective 2012). reprint service avail. from PSC. **Document type:** *Journal, Academic/Scholarly.* **Description:** Focuses on the diagnosis, management and prevention of poisoning/toxicity and other adverse effects resulting from medications, chemicals, occupational and environmental substances, and biological hazards.
Related titles: Online - full text ed.: ISSN 1937-6995.
Indexed: A01, A22, A26, CA, E01, E08, EMBASE, ExcerpMed, H12, I05, MEDLINE, P10, P20, P22, P30, P48, P53, P54, PHN&I, PQC, R10, R13, Reac, S09, SCOPUS, T02.
—BLDSC (5017.090200), IE. **CCC.**
Published by: (American College of Medical Toxicology), Springer New York LLC (Subsidiary of: Springer Science+Business Media), 233 Spring St, New York, NY 10013. TEL 212-460-1500, FAX 212-460-1575, journals-ny@springer.com. Ed. Christian A Tomaszewski.

615.19 610 USA ISSN 0022-2623
RS402 CODEN: JMCMAR
➤ **JOURNAL OF MEDICINAL CHEMISTRY.** Text in English. 1958. 24/yr. USD 2,562 in North America to institutions; USD 2,814 elsewhere to institutions (effective 2011). adv. bk.rev. charts. index. back issues avail.; reprints avail. **Document type:** *Journal, Academic/Scholarly.* **Description:** Focuses on the relationship of chemistry to biological activity. Provides valuable research findings and comprehensive book reviews on medicinal chemistry and related areas.
Formerly (until 1963): Journal of Medicinal and Pharmaceutical Chemistry (0095-9065)
Related titles: Microfiche ed.: USD 1,419 in North America to institutions; USD 1,458 elsewhere to institutions (effective 2002); Microfilm ed.: USD 1,419 in North America to institutions; USD 1,439 elsewhere to institutions (effective 2002); Online - full text ed.: ISSN 1520-4804.
Indexed: A01, A03, A08, A22, A29, A34, A35, A36, AIDS Ab, ASCA, AgBio, AgrForAb, B&BAb, B19, B20, B21, B23, B25, B27, BIOSIS Prev, BP, BioEngAb, C&CR, C13, C24, C30, C31, C33, CA, CABA, CCI, CIN, CIS, CTA, ChemAb, ChemTitl, CurCR, CurCont, DBA, DentInd, E12, EMBASE, ESPM, ExcerpMed, F08, F11, F12, GH, GenetAb, H16, H17, HGA, INIS AtomInd, ISR, IndChem, IndMed, IndVet, Inpharma, MEDLINE, MOS, MycolAb, N02, N03, N04, N05, NPU, NSA, NucAcAb, OR, P30, P33, P35, P37, P39, PGrRegA, PN&I, R08, R10, R13, R16, RA&MP, RM&VM, Reac, RefZh, S12, SCI, SCOPUS, SoyAb, T02, T05, VS, VirolAbstr, W07, W10.
—BLDSC (5017.200000), CASDDS, GNLM, IE, Infotrieve, Ingenta, INIST, Linda Hall. **CCC.**
Published by: American Chemical Society, 1155 16th St, NW, Washington, DC 20036. TEL 202-872-4600, 800-227-5558, FAX 202-776-8264. Ed. Dr. Philip S Portoghese TEL 612-624-6184. **Subscr. to:** PO Box 3337, Columbus, OH 43210. TEL 614-447-3674, 888-338-0012, FAX 614-447-5475, liblink@acs.org.

615.19 610 IND ISSN 2230-9314
▼ ➤ **JOURNAL OF MEDICINAL CHEMISTRY LETTERS.** Text in English. 2010. s-a. USD 425 (effective 2011). **Document type:** *Journal, Academic/Scholarly.* **Description:** Publishes all the latest research articles, reviews and letters in all areas of medicinal chemistry.
Related titles: Online - full text ed.: ISSN 2230-9322. free (effective 2011).
Published by: Bioinfo Publications, 49/F-72, Vighnahar Complex, Front of Overseas Bank, Sector 12, Kharghar, Navi Mumbai, 410 210, India. TEL 91-22-27743967, FAX 91-22-66736413, editor@bioinfo.in, subscription@bioinfo.in. Eds. Dr. Ravi Kant, Dr. Virendra S Gomase.

616.01 GBR ISSN 0265-2048
RS201.C3 CODEN: JOMIEF
➤ **JOURNAL OF MICROENCAPSULATION.** Text in English. 1984. 8/yr. GBP 1,075, EUR 1,470, USD 1,840 combined subscription to institutions (print & online eds.); GBP 2,060, EUR 2,820, USD 3,520 combined subscription to corporations (print & online eds.) (effective 2010). adv. back issues avail.; reprint service avail. from PSC. **Document type:** *Journal, Academic/Scholarly.* **Description:** Brings out the preparation, properties and uses of individually encapsulated small particles. Its scope extends beyond microcapsules to all other small-particle dosage forms involving preparative manipulating.
Related titles: Online - full text ed.: ISSN 1464-5246 (from IngentaConnect).
Indexed: A01, A02, A03, A08, A22, A34, A36, A37, ASCA, AgrForAb, B&BAb, B19, B21, B23, B25, BIOSIS Prev, BioEngAb, C11, C33, CA, CABA, ChemAb, ChemTitl, CurCont, D01, DBA, E01, E12, EMBASE, ExcerpMed, F08, F11, F12, FS&TA, GH, H04, H16, ISR, IndMed, Inpharma, MEDLINE, MycolAb, N02, N03, N04, P30, P33, PHN&I, R07, R08, R10, R13, R16, RA&MP, RM&VM, Reac, S12, S13, S16, SCI, SCOPUS, SoyAb, T02, TAR, W07.
—CASDDS, GNLM, IE, Infotrieve, Ingenta, INIST, Linda Hall. **CCC.**
Published by: Informa Healthcare (Subsidiary of: T & F Informa plc), Telephone House, 69-77 Paul St, London, EC2A 4LQ, United Kingdom. TEL 44-20-70175000, FAX 44-20-70176792, healthcare.enquiries@informa.com. Ed. Oya Alpar. Adv. contact Per Sonnerfeldt. **Subscr. in N. America to:** Taylor & Francis Inc., Customer Services Dept, 325 Chestnut St, 8th Fl, Philadelphia, PA 19106. TEL 215-625-8900, 800-354-1420, FAX 215-625-8914, customerservice@taylorandfrancis.com; **Subscr. outside N. America to:** Taylor & Francis Ltd., Journals Customer Service, Sheepen Pl, Colchester, Essex CO3 3LP, United Kingdom. TEL 44-20-70175544, FAX 44-20-70175198, tf.enquiries@tfinforma.com.

615 ZAF ISSN 1683-6707
JOURNAL OF MODERN PHARMACY; up-to-the-minute practical pharmacy. Cover title: Modern Pharmacy. Text in English. 1994. m. ZAR 253 (effective 2006). adv. illus. **Document type:** *Magazine, Trade.* **Description:** For pharmacists in community, hospital and health clinic pharmacies.
Indexed: ISAP.
Published by: National Publishing (Pty) Ltd., PO Box 2271, Clareinch, 7740, South Africa. info@natpub.co.za, http://www.natpub.co.za/.

615.1 JPN
RS160 CODEN: NMEDEO
JOURNAL OF NATURAL MEDICINES. Text in English, Japanese; Summaries in English. 1947. q. EUR 326, USD 407 combined subscription to institutions (print & online eds.) (effective 2012). adv. bk.rev. charts; illus. cum.index. reprint service avail. from PSC. **Document type:** *Journal, Academic/Scholarly.* **Description:** Presents research on naturally occurring medicines and their related foods and cosmetics.
Former titles (until 2005): Natural Medicines (1340-3443); (until 1994): Shoyakugaku Zasshi/Japanese Journal of Pharmacognosy (0037-4377); (until 1952): Yakuyo Shokubutsu to Shoyaku (0372-7831)
Related titles: Online - full text ed.: (from IngentaConnect).
Indexed: A22, A26, A34, A35, A36, AgBio, Agr, AgrForAb, B25, BA, BIOSIS Prev, BP, C25, C30, CABA, CIN, ChemAb, ChemTitl, E01, E12, EMBASE, ExcerpMed, F08, F11, G11, GH, H16, H17, MEDLINE, MycolAb, N02, N03, N05, P30, P32, P33, P39, P40, PGegResA, PGrRegA, PHN&I, R07, R08, R10, R11, R13, RA&MP, RM&VM, Reac, S12, S13, S16, S17, SCI, SCOPUS, SoyAb, T05, TAR, VITIS, VS, W07, W11.
—BLDSC (6040.735550), CASDDS, GNLM, IE, Ingenta, Linda Hall. **CCC.**
Published by: (Japanese Society of Pharmacognosy/Nihon Shoyaku Gakkai), Springer Japan KK (Subsidiary of: Springer Science+Business Media), No 2 Funato Bldg, 1-11-11 Kudan-kita, Chiyoda-ku, Tokyo, 102-0073, Japan. TEL 81-3-68317000, FAX 81-3-68317001, orders@springer.jp, http://www.springer.jp. Ed. Hiromitsu Takayama. Circ: 700.

P

547.7 USA ISSN 0163-3864
QH1 CODEN: JNPRDF
➤ **JOURNAL OF NATURAL PRODUCTS.** Text in English. 1900. m. USD 1,064 in North America to institutions; USD 1,190 elsewhere to institutions (effective 2011). adv. bk.rev. charts; illus.; stat. index. back issues avail.; reprints avail. **Document type:** *Journal, Academic/Scholarly.* **Description:** Covers natural products research - chemistry, biochemistry and biology of naturally occurring compounds.
Former titles (until 1979): Lloydia (0024-5461); (until 1938): Lloyd Library of Botany, Pharmacy and Materia Medica. Bulletin (0893-1453)
Related titles: Online - full text ed.: ISSN 1520-6025.
Indexed: A22, A29, A34, A35, A36, A38, AEBA, AMED, ASCA, ASFA, AgBio, Agr, AgrForAb, B&AI, B&BAb, B04, B10, B19, B21, B23, B27, BA, BIOBASE, BP, BibAg, C&CR, C06, C07, C13, C24, C25, C30, C33, CA, CABA, CBTA, CCI, CEABA, ChemAb, ChemTitl, ChemoAb, CurCR, CurCont, D01, DBA, E12, EMBASE, ESPM, ExcerpMed, F08, F11, F12, FCA, FS&TA, G11, GH, GeoRef, H16, H17, I10, I12, IABS, ISR, IndChem, IndMed, IndVet, Inpharma, M&PBA, MEDLINE, MOS, MSB, MaizeAb, N02, N03, N04, N05, NPU, OR, P30, P32, P33, P37, P38, P39, P40, PGegResA, PGrRegA, PHN&I, PN&I, R07, R08, R10, R11, R12, R13, R16, RA&MP, RM&VM, Reac, RefZh, S12, S13, S16, S17, SCI, SCOPUS, SPPI, SoyAb, T02, T05, TAR, TriticAb, VITIS, VS, W07, W10, W11, Z01.
—BLDSC (5021.225000), CASDDS, GNLM, IE, Infotrieve, Ingenta, INIST, Linda Hall. **CCC.**
Published by: American Chemical Society, 1155 16th St, NW, Washington, DC 20036. TEL 202-872-4600, 800-227-5558, FAX 202-776-8264. Ed. A Douglas Kinghorn TEL 614-247-8101. **Subscr. to:** PO Box 3337, Columbus, OH 43210. TEL 614-447-3674, 888-338-0012, FAX 614-447-5475, liblink@acs.org. **Co-publisher:** American Society of Pharmacognosy.

615.1 USA ISSN 1557-1890
RM315
JOURNAL OF NEUROIMMUNE PHARMACOLOGY. Abbreviated title: J N I P. Text in English. 2006. q. EUR 658, USD 801 combined subscription to institutions (print & online eds.) (effective 2012). back issues avail.; reprint service avail. from PSC. **Document type:** *Journal, Academic/Scholarly.* **Description:** Expresses the disciplines of immunology, pharmacology and experimental neuroscience by acting as a platform for research discoveries into the pathogenesis and pharmacology of brain disorders affecting the immune system.
Related titles: Online - full text ed.: ISSN 1557-1904. 2006 (from IngentaConnect).
Indexed: A22, A26, Agr, B21, B25, BIOSIS Prev, E01, EMBASE, ExcerpMed, I05, ImmunAb, MEDLINE, MycolAb, NSA, NSCI, P30, R10, Reac, SCI, SCOPUS, W07.
—BLDSC (5021.549000), IE, Ingenta. **CCC.**
Published by: (Society of Neuroimmune Pharmacology), Springer New York LLC (Subsidiary of: Springer Science+Business Media), 233 Spring St, New York, NY 10013. TEL 212-460-1500, FAX 212-460-1575, service-ny@springer.com, http://www.springer.com/. Ed. Howard E Gendelman.

JOURNAL OF OCULAR PHARMACOLOGY AND THERAPEUTICS. *see* MEDICAL SCIENCES—Ophthalmology And Optometry

615 616.99 GBR ISSN 1078-1552
RC271.C5 CODEN: JOPPFI
➤ **JOURNAL OF ONCOLOGY PHARMACY PRACTICE.** Text in English. 1995. q. USD 1,302, GBP 704 combined subscription to institutions (print & online eds.); USD 1,276, GBP 690 to institutions (effective 2011). adv. abstr.; bibl.; charts; illus.; stat. back issues avail.; reprint service avail. from PSC. **Document type:** *Journal, Academic/Scholarly.* **Description:** Provides education and practice-related issues as well as original research, new therapies, patient management, and pharmacoeconomic evaluations for this emerging pharmacy specialty.
Related titles: Online - full text ed.: ISSN 1477-092X. USD 1,172, GBP 634 to institutions (effective 2011).
Indexed: A01, A03, A08, A22, BIOBASE, C06, C07, CA, CIN, ChemAb, ChemTitl, E01, EMBASE, ExcerpMed, H13, I12, IABS, IDIS, MEDLINE, P10, P20, P22, P24, P30, P48, P53, P54, PQC, R10, Reac, SCOPUS, T02.
—BLDSC (5026.314560), CASDDS, GNLM, IE, Infotrieve, Ingenta. **CCC.**
Published by: (International Society for Oncology Pharmacy Practitioners USA), Sage Publications Ltd. (Subsidiary of: Sage Publications, Inc.), 1 Oliver's Yard, 55 City Rd, London, EC1Y 1SP, United Kingdom. TEL 44-20-73248500, FAX 44-20-73248600, info@sagepub.co.uk, http://www.uk.sagepub.com/home.nav. Ed. Barry R Goldspiel. adv.: B&W page GBP 450; trim 180 x 250.

615 USA ISSN 1536-0288
RB127 CODEN: JPPSEX
➤ **JOURNAL OF PAIN & PALLIATIVE CARE PHARMACOTHERAPY.** Text in English. 1993. q. GBP 400, EUR 525, USD 705 combined subscription to institutions (print & online eds.); GBP 795, EUR 1,045, USD 1,410 combined subscription to corporations (print & online eds.) (effective 2010). adv. bk.rev. illus. 120 p./no. 2 cols./p.; back issues avail.; reprint service avail. from PSC. **Document type:** *Journal, Academic/Scholarly.*
Formerly (until 2002): Journal of Pharmaceutical Care in Pain & Symptom Control (1056-4950); Incorporates (1985-2002): The Hospice Journal (0742-969X)
Related titles: Microfiche ed.: (from PQC); Microform ed.; Online - full text ed.: ISSN 1536-0539.
Indexed: A01, A03, A22, AMED, BiolDig, C06, C07, C08, CA, CINAHL, E-psyche, E01, EMBASE, ExcerpMed, FamI, H04, I12, Inpharma, MEDLINE, P03, P30, P34, PerIslam, PsycInfo, PsycholAb, R10, Reac, SCOPUS, T02, ToxAb.
—BLDSC (5027.787000), GNLM, IE, Ingenta. **CCC.**
Published by: Informa Healthcare (Subsidiary of: T & F Informa plc), 52 Vanderbilt Ave, New York, NY 10017. TEL 212-262-8230, FAX 212-262-8234, healthcare.enquiries@informa.com, http://www.informahealthcare.com. Ed. Arthur G Lipman. adv.: B&W page USD 315, color page USD 550; trim 4.375 x 7.125. Circ: 529 (paid).

➤ **JOURNAL OF PEDIATRIC PHARMACOLOGY AND THERAPEUTICS.** *see* MEDICAL SCIENCES—Pediatrics

615 NGA ISSN 1596-8499
➤ **JOURNAL OF PHARMACEUTICAL AND ALLIED SCIENCES.** Text in English. s-a. NGN 1,000 domestic; USD 35 foreign (effective 2007). **Document type:** *Journal, Academic/Scholarly.* **Description:** Publishes original scientific and technical research works on drugs and drug-related products, within and outside Nigeria in the fields of pharmacy, medical sciences and veterinary medicine.
Published by: University of Nigeria, Department of Pharmaceutics, c/o Dr EC Ibezim, Editor, Nsukka, Enugu State, Nigeria. TEL 234-804-3180627, FAX 234-42-770644, ecibezim@yahoo.com. Ed. E C Ibezim.

615.19 NLD ISSN 0731-7085
RS400 CODEN: JPBADA
➤ **JOURNAL OF PHARMACEUTICAL AND BIOMEDICAL ANALYSIS.** Text in English. 1983. 15/yr. EUR 3,634 in Europe to institutions; JPY 482,500 in Japan to institutions; USD 4,067 elsewhere to institutions (effective 2012). back issues avail. **Document type:** *Journal, Academic/Scholarly.* **Description:** Publishes research reports and reviews on pharmaceutical and biomedical analysis.
Related titles: Microfilm ed.: (from PQC); Online - full text ed.: ISSN 1873-264X (from IngentaConnect, ScienceDirect).
Indexed: A01, A03, A08, A22, A26, A34, A35, A36, A40, ASCA, AgBio, AgrForAb, B&BAb, B19, B21, B25, B27, BA, BIOBASE, BIOSIS Prev, BP, C24, C25, C30, C33, CA, CABA, CIN, CIS, ChemAb, ChemTitl, ChromAb, CurCont, D01, DBA, E12, EMBASE, ESPM, ExcerpMed, F08, F11, F12, FCA, GH, H16, H17, I05, I11, I12, IABS, ISR, IndMed, IndVet, Inpharma, LT, MEDLINE, MSB, MycolAb, N02, N03, N04, P30, P32, P33, P37, P39, P40, PGegResA, PGrRegA, PHN&I, PN&I, R07, R08, R10, R11, R12, R13, RA&MP, RM&VM, RRTA, Reac, RefZh, S12, S13, S16, S17, SCI, SCOPUS, SoyAb, T02, T05, TAR, ToxAb, VS, W07, W10.
—BLDSC (5031.600000), CASDDS, GNLM, IE, Infotrieve, Ingenta, INIST. **CCC.**
Published by: Elsevier BV (Subsidiary of: Elsevier Science & Technology), Radarweg 29, PO Box 211, Amsterdam, 1000 AE, Netherlands. TEL 31-20-4853911, FAX 31-20-4852457, JournalsCustomerServiceEMEA@elsevier.com, http://www.elsevier.nl. Eds. Bezhan Chankvetadze, Jun Haginaka, Sergio Pinzauti.

615 IND ISSN 2230-7885
▼ ➤ **JOURNAL OF PHARMACEUTICAL AND BIOMEDICAL SCIENCES.** Abbreviated title: J P B M S. Text in English. 2010. m. free (effective 2011). cum. index. back issues avail.; reprints avail. **Document type:** *Journal, Academic/Scholarly.*
Media: Online - full text.
Address: c/o Meenakshi Gusain, Kundan Singh Digari, A-3 /B/2, Lawerence Rd, New Delhi, 110 035, India. Ed., Pub. Meenakshi Gusain.

615 IND ISSN 0976-8173
▼ ➤ **JOURNAL OF PHARMACEUTICAL EDUCATION AND RESEARCH.** Abbreviated title: J P E R. Text in English. 2010 (Jun.). s-a. INR 1,000 (effective 2011). **Document type:** *Journal, Academic/Scholarly.*
Related titles: Online - full text ed.: ISSN 0976-8238. free (effective 2011).
Indexed: A01, A34, A36, F08, N03, N04, P02, P10, P18, P33, P48, P53, P54, PQC.
Published by: Punjab College of Technical Education (PCTE) Group of Institutes, Ferozepur Road, Near Baddowal Cantt., Ludhiana, Punjab 142 021, India. TEL 91-161-2888500, FAX 91-161-2888505, http://www.pcte.edu.in/index.asp. Ed. Dr. B. S. Sekhon. Pub. Dr. K N S Kang.

615 GBR ISSN 1759-8885
▼ ➤ **JOURNAL OF PHARMACEUTICAL HEALTH SERVICES RESEARCH**; connecting pharmaceutical economics, policy, outcomes and quality studies. Text in English. 2010 (Feb.). q. GBP 259 in United Kingdom to institutions; EUR 304 in Europe to institutions; USD 405 elsewhere to institutions (effective 2012). adv. **Document type:** *Journal, Academic/Scholarly.* **Description:** Covers all aspects of research within the field of health services research that relate to pharmaceuticals.
Related titles: Online - full text ed.: ISSN 1759-8893. GBP 259 in United Kingdom to institutions; EUR 304 in Europe to institutions; USD 405 elsewhere to institutions (effective 2012).
Indexed: A22, E01.
—**CCC.**
Published by: Pharmaceutical Press (Subsidiary of: Royal Pharmaceutical Society of Great Britain), 1 Lambeth High St, London, SE1 7JN, United Kingdom. TEL 44-20-77359141, FAX 44-20-75722509, enquiries@rpsgb.org. Ed. Albert Wertheimer.

615 USA ISSN 1872-5120
HD9665.5
➤ **JOURNAL OF PHARMACEUTICAL INNOVATION.** Text in English. 2006. q. EUR 399, USD 534 combined subscription to institutions (print & online eds.) (effective 2012). adv. back issues avail.; reprint service avail. from PSC. **Document type:** *Journal, Academic/Scholarly.* **Description:** Brings out papers emphasizing innovative research and applied technologies within the pharmaceutical and biotechnology industries.
Related titles: Online - full text ed.: ISSN 1939-8042 (from IngentaConnect).
Indexed: A22, A26, E01, E08, EMBASE, ExcerpMed, H12, P30, S09, SCOPUS.
—BLDSC (5031.875000), IE. **CCC.**
Published by: (International Society for Pharmaceutical Engineering, Inc.), Springer New York LLC (Subsidiary of: Springer Science+Business Media), 233 Spring St, New York, NY 10013. TEL 212-460-1500, FAX 212-460-1575, journals@springer-ny.com, http://www.springer.com. Ed. James K Drennen.

615 KOR ISSN 2093-5552
➤ **JOURNAL OF PHARMACEUTICAL INVESTIGATION.** Text in English. 1970. bi-m. EUR 825, USD 1,095 combined subscription to institutions (print & online eds.) (effective 2012). **Document type:** *Journal, Academic/Scholarly.* **Description:** Publishes research articles, notes, information and reviews on topics such as: Engineering, regulatory, physico-chemical, biological, and microbiological studies related to the conception, design, production, characterization and evaluation of pharmaceutical products and drug delivery system.
Formerly (until 2010): Journal of Korean Pharmaceutical Sciences (0259-2347)
Related titles: Online - full text ed.: ISSN 2093-6214.
—BLDSC (5031.875500), IE, Ingenta.
Published by: Korean Society of Pharmaceutical Sciences and Technology, Rm 805, Korea Science & Technology Center, 635-4, Yeogsam-dong, Kangnam-ku, Seoul, 135-703, Korea, S. TEL 82-2-5644019, FAX 82-2-5545378, kspst@kspst.or.kr, http://www.kspst.or.kr/. Ed. Dae-Duk Kim. Pub. Hoo Kyun Choi.

615 IND ISSN 0975-5772
RS1
▼ ➤ **JOURNAL OF PHARMACEUTICAL SCIENCE AND TECHNOLOGY.** Text in English. 2009. m. free (effective 2011). **Document type:** *Journal, Academic/Scholarly.*
Media: Online - full text.
Published by: PharmTech Publications

615.1 USA ISSN 0022-3549
RS1 CODEN: JPMSAE
➤ **JOURNAL OF PHARMACEUTICAL SCIENCES.** Text in English. 1961 (vol.50). m. GBP 1,007 in United Kingdom to institutions; EUR 1,273 in Europe to institutions; USD 1,859 in United States to institutions; USD 1,916 elsewhere to institutions; GBP 1,155 combined subscription in United Kingdom to institutions (print & online eds.); EUR 1,460 combined subscription in Europe to institutions (print & online eds.); USD 2,139 combined subscription in United States to institutions (print & online eds.); USD 2,196 combined subscription elsewhere to institutions (print & online eds.) (effective 2012). adv. bk.rev. bibl.; charts; illus. index. back issues avail.; reprint service avail. from PSC. **Document type:** *Journal, Academic/Scholarly.* **Description:** Primary research in pharmaceutical science; graduate level and above.
Formed by the merger of (1951-1961): Drug Standards (0096-0225); Which was formerly (until 1951): National Formulary Committee. Bulletin (0097-0506); (1940-1961): American Pharmaceutical Association. Journal (Scientific Edition) (0095-9553); Which superseded in part (in 1940): American Pharmaceutical Association. Journal (0898-140X); Which was formerly (until 1912): American Pharmaceutical Association. Bulletin (0096-6789)
Related titles: Online - full text ed.: ISSN 1520-6017. GBP 978 in United Kingdom to institutions; EUR 1,236 in Europe to institutions; USD 1,859 elsewhere to institutions (effective 2012).
Indexed: A01, A22, A34, A35, A36, A38, AIDS Ab, ASCA, AgBio, B&BAb, B19, B21, B25, BIOSIS Prev, BP, C13, C24, C33, CA, CABA, CIN, CMCI, CTA, ChemAb, ChemTitl, ChemoAb, ChromAb, CurCR, CurCont, D01, DBA, DentInd, E12, EMBASE, ESPM, ExcerpMed, GH, GenetAb, H&SSA, H16, H17, I12, IBR, IBZ, IDIS, ISR, IndChem, IndMed, IndVet, Inpharma, MEDLINE, MycolAb, N02, N03, N04, NSA, P30, P33, P39, PN&I, R08, R10, R16, RA&MP, RM&VM, Reac, RefZh, S12, SCI, SCOPUS, SoyAb, T02, T05, VS, W07, W10, W11.
—BLDSC (5031.900000), CASDDS, GNLM, IE, Infotrieve, Ingenta, INIST, Linda Hall. **CCC.**
Published by: (American Pharmacists Association), John Wiley & Sons, Inc., 111 River St, Hoboken, NJ 07030. FAX 201-748-6088, info@wiley.com, http://www.wiley.com/WileyCDA/. Ed. Ronald T Borchardt TEL 785-864-5919. Pub., Adv. contact Kim Thompkins TEL 212-850-6921. **Subscr. outside the Americas to:** John Wiley & Sons Ltd.

615 IND ISSN 0975-1459
▼ ➤ **JOURNAL OF PHARMACEUTICAL SCIENCES AND RESEARCH.** Text in English. 2009 (Mar.). q. free (effective 2011). **Document type:** *Journal, Academic/Scholarly.*
Media: Online - full text.
Indexed: A01, EMBASE, P20, P48, P54, PQC, SCOPUS, T02.
Published by: Pharmainfo Publications, c/o R.Pushpalatha, 8/8, Thirumalai Nagar, Subbarayalu Nagar, Cuddalore, Tamil Nadu 607002, India. TEL 91-984-3675681, http://www.pharmainfo.in. Ed., Pub. R. Pushpalatha.

615 IND ISSN 0975-3648
RM1
▼ ➤ **JOURNAL OF PHARMACEUTIOCAL RESEARCH AND HEALTH CARE**; international open access pharmaceutical journal. Text in English. 2009. q. free (effective 2011). back issues avail. **Document type:** *Journal, Academic/Scholarly.* **Description:** Contains original research, short papers, reviews, correspondence and case reports that covers interdisciplinary research in pharmaceutical sciences.
Media: Online - full text.
Indexed: A01, EMBASE, SCOPUS, T02.
Published by: Journal of Pharmaceutical Research and Health Care, 202, B-Block, Vuda Apartments, Seethammadhara, Visakhapatnam, Andhra Pradesh 530013, India. Ed. A. Annapurna. Pub., R&P Raju B. Akondi.

▼ ➤ **JOURNAL OF PHARMACOGENOMICS & PHARMACOPROTEOMICS.** *see* BIOLOGY—Genetics

615 IND ISSN 0976-884X
▼ ➤ **JOURNAL OF PHARMACOGNOSY.** Text in English. 2010. s-a. USD 425 (effective 2011). **Document type:** *Journal, Academic/Scholarly.* **Description:** Publishes all the latest research articles, reviews and letters in all areas of pharmacognosy.
Related titles: Online - full text ed.: ISSN 0976-8858. free (effective 2011).
Published by: Bioinfo Publications, 49/F-72, Vighnahar Complex, Front of Overseas Bank, Sector 12, Kharghar, Navi Mumbai, 410 210, India. TEL 91-22-27743967, FAX 91-22-66736413, editor@bioinfo.in, subscription@bioinfo.in. Ed. Dr. Virendra S Gomase.

615 NGA
▼ ➤ **JOURNAL OF PHARMACOGNOSY AND PHYTOTHERAPY.** Text in English. 2010. m. free (effective 2010). adv. **Document type:** *Journal, Academic/Scholarly.*
Media: Online - full text.
Published by: Academic Journals, PO Box 73023, Victoria Island, Lagos, Nigeria. service@academicjournals.org. Eds. Dr. Bhaskar C Behera, Dr. Muzamil Ahmad, Talal Ahmad Aburjai.

615 USA ISSN 1567-567X
RM1 CODEN: JPPOAH
➤ **JOURNAL OF PHARMACOKINETICS AND PHARMACODYNAMICS.** Text in English. 1973. bi-m. EUR 995, USD 1,033 combined subscription to institutions (print & online eds.) (effective 2012). adv. index. back issues avail.; reprint service avail. from PSC. **Document type:** *Journal, Academic/Scholarly.* **Description:** Emphasizes the importance of pharmacokinetics, pharmacodynamics, and pharmacometrics in the understanding of drug action, therapy, design, development, and evaluation.
Formerly (until 2001): Journal of Pharmacokinetics and Biopharmaceutics (0090-466X)
Related titles: Microfilm ed.: (from PQC); Online - full text ed.: ISSN 1573-8744 (from IngentaConnect).
Indexed: A22, A26, A29, ASCA, B20, B21, B25, B27, BIOBASE, BIOSIS Prev, BibLing, C24, CA, CIN, CMCI, ChemAb, ChemTitl, CurCont, DBA, E01, EMBASE, ESPM, ExcerpMed, GenetAb, I10, I12, IABS, IDIS, ISR, IndMed, Inpharma, MEDLINE, MycolAb, P20, P22, P30, P35, P48, P54, PQC, R10, Reac, RefZh, SCI, SCOPUS, T02, VirolAbstr, W07.
—BLDSC (5032.610000), CASDDS, GNLM, IE, Infotrieve, Ingenta, INIST, Linda Hall. **CCC.**
Published by: Springer New York LLC (Subsidiary of: Springer Science+Business Media), 233 Spring St, New York, NY 10013. TEL 212-460-1500, FAX 212-460-1575, service-ny@springer.com, http://www.springer.com/. Ed. William J Jusko.

➤ **JOURNAL OF PHARMACOLOGICAL AND TOXICOLOGICAL METHODS.** *see* ENVIRONMENTAL STUDIES—Toxicology And Environmental Safety

615 JPN ISSN 1347-8648
JOURNAL OF PHARMACOLOGICAL SCIENCES (ONLINE). Text in English. 1998. m. free (effective 2011). **Document type:** *Journal, Academic/Scholarly.*
Formerly (until 2002): The Japanese Journal of Pharmacology (Online) (1347-3506)
Media: Online - full text. **Related titles:** Microform ed.: (from PQC); ◆ Print ed.: Journal of Pharmacological Sciences (Print Edition). ISSN 1347-8613.
Indexed: SCOPUS.
—**CCC.**
Published by: Nihon Yakuri Gakkai Henshuubu/Japanese Pharmacological Society, Kantohya Bldg, Gokomachi-Ebisugawa, Nakagyo-ku, Kyoto-shi, 604-0982, Japan. TEL 81-75-2524641, FAX 81-75-2524618, journal@pharmacol.or.jp, http://www.pharmacol.or.jp.

615.1 JPN ISSN 1347-8613
QP901 CODEN: JPSTGJ
➤ **JOURNAL OF PHARMACOLOGICAL SCIENCES (PRINT EDITION).** Text in English. 1951. m. JPY 20,000 domestic; USD 277 foreign (effective 2005). Index. 110 p./no.; Supplement avail.; back issues avail.; reprints avail. **Document type:** *Journal, Academic/Scholarly.* **Description:** Publishes original research and review articles on pharmacology and related fields.
Formerly (until 2002): The Japanese Journal of Pharmacology (Print Edition) (0021-5198)
Related titles: Microform ed.: (from PQC); ◆ Online - full text ed.: Journal of Pharmacological Sciences (Online). ISSN 1347-8648.

Indexed: A22, A34, A35, A36, ASCA, AgBio, AgrForAb, B21, B25, BIOBASE, BIOSIS Prev, C30, C33, CABA, CIN, CTA, ChemAb, ChemTitl, CurCont, D01, DBA, DentInd, E12, EMBASE, ExcerpMed, F08, F11, F12, GH, H16, H17, IABS, IBR, IBZ, ISR, ImmunAb, IndMed, Inpharma, JTA, MEDLINE, MycolAb, N02, N03, N04, NSA, P30, P33, P35, P37, P39, PGrRegA, PHN&I, PN&I, PsycholAb, R07, R08, R10, R11, RA&MP, RM&VM, Reac, S12, SCI, SCOPUS, SoyAb, T05, TAR, THA, VS, W07.
—BLDSC (5032.750000), CASDDS, GNLM, IE, Ingenta, INIST, Linda Hall. **CCC.**
Published by: Nihon Yakuri Gakkai Henshuubu/Japanese Pharmacological Society, Kantohya Bldg, Gokomachi-Ebisugawa, Nakagyo-ku, Kyoto-shi, 604-0982, Japan. TEL 81-75-2524641, FAX 81-75-2524618, journal@pharmacol.or.jp, http://www.pharmacol.or.jp. Ed. Toshitaka Nabeshima. Circ: 1,650.

615.1 USA ISSN 0022-3565
RS1 CODEN: JPETAB
➤ **THE JOURNAL OF PHARMACOLOGY AND EXPERIMENTAL THERAPEUTICS.** Abbreviated title: J P E T. Text in English. 1909. m. (4 vols./yr.). USD 975 combined subscription domestic to institutions (print & online eds.); USD 1,140 combined subscription foreign to institutions (print & online eds.); USD 220 to members; USD 85 per issue (effective 2010). adv. bibl.; charts; illus. Index. back issues avail.; reprints avail. **Document type:** *Journal, Academic/Scholarly.* **Description:** Provides pharmacologists, toxicologists and biochemists with documents on interactions of chemicals with biological systems.
Related titles: Online - full text ed.: ISSN 1521-0103. USD 878 to institutions (effective 2010).
Indexed: A22, A29, A34, A35, A36, AIDS Ab, ASCA, ASFA, AddicA, AgBio, ApicAb, B20, B21, B25, B27, BIOBASE, BIOSIS Prev, BP, C13, C24, C30, C33, CABA, CIN, CTA, ChemAb, ChemTitl, CurCont, D01, DBA, DentInd, E-psyche, E12, EMBASE, ESPM, ExcerpMed, F08, F11, F12, GH, GenetAb, H16, H17, I10, IABS, ISR, IndMed, IndVet, Inpharma, Kidney, MEDLINE, MS&D, MycolAb, N02, N03, N04, NSA, P03, P30, P32, P33, P35, P39, P40, PsycInfo, PsycholAb, R07, R08, R10, R13, RA&MP, RM&VM, Reac, RefZh, S12, S17, SCI, SCOPUS, SoyAb, T05, THA, VS, VirolAbstr, W07, W10.
—BLDSC (5033.000000), CASDDS, GNLM, IE, Infotrieve, Ingenta, INIST, Linda Hall. **CCC.**
Published by: American Society for Pharmacology and Experimental Therapeutics, 9650 Rockville Pike, Bethesda, MD 20814. TEL 301-634-7060, FAX 301-634-7061, info@aspet.org, http://www.aspet.org. Ed. Rick G Schnellmann. adv.: B&W page USD 775, color page USD 1,095; trim 8.125 x 10.875. Circ: 950.

615 IND ISSN 0976-500X
▼ **JOURNAL OF PHARMACOLOGY AND PHARMACOTHERAPEUTICS.** Text in English. 2010. q. **Document type:** *Journal, Academic/Scholarly.*
Related titles: Online - full text ed.: free (effective 2010).
Published by: Medknow Publications and Media Pvt. Ltd., B-9, Kanara Business Ctr, Off Link Rd, Ghatkopar (E), Mumbai, Maharastra 400 075, India. TEL 91-22-66491818, FAX 91-22-66491817, journals@medknow.com, http://www.medknow.com.

615.9 USA ISSN 1816-496X
RM1
➤ **JOURNAL OF PHARMACOLOGY AND TOXICOLOGY.** Text in English. 2005. 8/yr. **Document type:** *Journal, Academic/Scholarly.* **Description:** Includes all aspects of clinical pharmacology: pharmacokinetics, pharmacodynamics, therapeutic drug monitoring, drug interactions, pharmacogenetics, pharmacoepidemiology, pharmacovigilance, pharmacoeconomics, randomized controlled clinical trials and rational pharmacotherapy.
Related titles: Online - full text ed.: ISSN 2152-100X. free (effective 2010).
Indexed: A01, A34, A35, A36, A37, AgBio, AgrForAb, B&BAb, B19, B21, BP, C25, C30, CA, CABA, E12, EMBASE, ESPM, ExcerpMed, F08, F11, F12, GH, H16, H17, ImmunAb, IndVet, N02, N03, N04, NSA, P32, P33, P37, P39, P40, PGegResA, PHN&I, R07, R08, R12, R13, RA&MP, RM&VM, S12, SCOPUS, T02, T05, TAR, ToxAb, VS, W10.
—BLDSC (5033.105000), IE.
Published by: Academic Journals Inc., 224, 5th Ave, No 2218, New York, NY 10001. FAX 888-777-8532, support@scialert.com, http://www.academicjournalsinc.com/.

615.19 IND ISSN 0976-7134
▼ ➤ **JOURNAL OF PHARMACOLOGY RESEARCH.** Text in English. 2010. s-a. USD 425 (effective 2011). **Document type:** *Journal, Academic/Scholarly.* **Description:** Publishes all the latest research articles, reviews and letters in all areas of pharmacology research.
Related titles: Online - full text ed.: ISSN 0976-7142. free (effective 2011).
Published by: Bioinfo Publications, 49/F-72, Vighnahar Complex, Front of Overseas Bank, Sector 12, Kharghar, Navi Mumbai, 410 210, India. TEL 91-22-27743967, FAX 91-22-66736413, editor@bioinfo.in, subscription@bioinfo.in.

615 IND ISSN 0975-7406
RS1
▼ ➤ **JOURNAL OF PHARMACY AND BIOALLIED SCIENCES.** Text in English. 2009. irreg. free (effective 2011). Index. back issues avail. **Document type:** *Journal, Academic/Scholarly.* **Description:** publishes papers, reviews, mini-reviews, rapid communications and notes which cover all branches of pharmaceutical sciences, medicinal/analytical chemistry, biotechnology and bioallied sciences related to the conception, design, production, characterization and evaluation of drugs and their delivery systems in vitro and in vivo. Topics include: pharmaceutics, pharmacy practice, drug regulatory affairs, pharmacology, synthesis of novel medicinal compound, analytical sciences, phytomedicine, nanotechnology, physical pharmacy, polymer chemistry and microbiology as applied to pharmaceutical, medical and health sciences.
Media: Online - full text.
Indexed: A26, H12, I05.
—CCC.
Published by: Medknow Publications and Media Pvt. Ltd., B-9, Kanara Business Ctr, Off Link Rd, Ghatkopar (E), Mumbai, Maharastra 400 075, India. TEL 91-22-66491816, 91-22-66491818, publishing@medknow.com, http://www.medknow.com. Ed. Roop K. Khar. Pub., R&P, Adv. contact Himanshu Gupta.

615 NGA ISSN 0189-8442
➤ **JOURNAL OF PHARMACY AND BIORESOURCES.** Text in English. s-a. NGN 950 domestic to individuals; NGN 1,900 domestic to institutions (effective 2007). **Document type:** *Journal, Academic/Scholarly.* **Description:** Publishes scientific work in all areas of pharmaceutical and life sciences.
Indexed: A34, A36, A37, AgrForAb, BA, BP, C25, CABA, D01, E12, F08, F11, F12, GH, H16, MaizeAb, N02, N03, N04, O01, P32, P33, P37, P39, PGegResA, PHN&I, PN&I, R07, R08, R12, R13, RA&MP, RM&VM, T05, VS, W11.
—BLDSC (5033.600000).
Published by: University of Jos, Faculty of Pharmaceutical Sciences, c/o Prof E N Sokomba, Editor, Jos, Nigeria. TEL 234-803-7006372. Ed. Dr. E N Sokomba.

615.19 IND ISSN 0973-9874
CODEN: JPCOCM
JOURNAL OF PHARMACY AND CHEMISTRY. Text in English. 2007. s-a. **Document type:** *Journal, Academic/Scholarly.* **Description:** Publishes original research work that contributes significantly to further the scientific knowledge in pharmaceutical sciences.
Indexed: C33.
Published by: Science Tech Foundation, Plot No.22, Vidhyut Nagar, Anantapur, Andhra Pradesh 515 001, India. TEL 91-8554-274677, jpcanantapur@gmail.com. Ed. Jayaveera K N.

615 PAK
JOURNAL OF PHARMACY AND CLINICAL SCIENCES. Abbreviated title: J P C S. Text in English. q. **Document type:** *Journal, Academic/Scholarly.* **Description:** Provides the forum for reporting innovations, technologies, initiatives and the application of scientific knowledge to all aspects of pharmacy and health sciences. It publishes original research work, review, mini reviews, short communications, case reports, case series, letters to editors etc.
Related titles: Online - full text ed.
Published by: Academic Research Publishing Agency, Flat No.2, Block No.22, CAT-III, Sector G-10/2, Islamabad, 44000, Pakistan. TEL 92-300-5156970, arpapress@gmail.com, editor@arpapress.com, publisher@arpapress.com. Ed. Karthikeyan M. Pub. Jawad Ahmed.

JOURNAL OF PHARMACY & LAW. *see* LAW

615 CAN ISSN 1482-1826
RS1
➤ **JOURNAL OF PHARMACY AND PHARMACEUTICAL SCIENCES.** Text in English. 1998. q. free (effective 2011). bk.rev. **Document type:** *Journal, Academic/Scholarly.* **Description:** Features original research articles, reviews, news and views on pharmaceutical sciences.
Media: Online - full text.
Indexed: A34, A35, A36, AgBio, BP, C06, C07, CABA, CurCont, D01, E12, EMBASE, ExcerpMed, F08, F12, GH, H16, H17, IndMed, Inpharma, MEDLINE, N02, N03, N04, P30, P32, P33, P35, P38, P39, P40, PHN&I, PN&I, R10, R12, RA&MP, RM&VM, Reac, SCI, SCOPUS, T05, TAR, VS, W07, W11.
—CCC.
Published by: Canadian Society for Pharmaceutical Sciences, 3118 Dentistry/Pharmacy Centre, Univ of Alberta Campus, Edmonton, AB T6G 2N8, Canada. TEL 780-492-0950, FAX 780-492-0951, sandra.hutt@ualberta.ca. Ed. Fakhreddin Jamali.

615.1 GBR ISSN 0022-3573
RS187 CODEN: JPPMAB
➤ **JOURNAL OF PHARMACY AND PHARMACOLOGY;** an international journal of pharmaceutical science. Text in English. 1870. m. GBP 1,088 in United Kingdom to institutions; EUR 1,489 in Europe to institutions; USD 2,061 elsewhere to institutions; GBP 1,251 combined subscription in United Kingdom to institutions (print & online eds.); EUR 1,712 combined subscription in Europe to institutions (print & online eds.); USD 2,371 combined subscription elsewhere to institutions (print & online eds.) (effective 2012). adv. bibl.; charts; illus. Index. back issues avail.; reprint service avail. from PSC. **Document type:** *Journal, Academic/Scholarly.* **Description:** Publishes original research papers and reviews articles about the development and evaluation of medicinal substances.
Incorporates (1995-2000): Pharmacy and Pharmacology Communications (1460-8081); Former titles (until 1948): Quarterly Journal of Pharmacy and Pharmacology (0370-2979); (until 1928): Quarterly Journal of Pharmacy and Allied Sciences (0370-2960); (until 1927): Yearbook of Pharmacy (0372-7688)
Related titles: Microfilm ed.; Online - full text ed.: ISSN 2042-7158. GBP 1,088 in United Kingdom to institutions; EUR 1,489 in Europe to institutions; USD 2,061 elsewhere to institutions (effective 2012); Supplement(s): Journal of Pharmacy and Pharmacology. Supplement. ISSN 0373-1022.
Indexed: A01, A03, A08, A20, A22, A29, A34, A35, A36, A37, A38, ASCA, ASFA, AgrForAb, ApicAb, B&BAb, B19, B20, B21, B23, B25, BIOBASE, BIOSIS Prev, BP, C25, C30, C33, CA, CABA, CIN, CTA, ChemAb, ChemTitl, CurCR, CurCont, D01, DBA, DentInd, E01, E12, EMBASE, ESPM, ExcerpMed, F08, F11, F12, FCA, GH, GenetAb, H16, H17, I12, IABS, IDIS, ISR, IndChem, IndMed, IndVet, Inpharma, MEDLINE, MS&D, MaizeAb, MycolAb, N02, N03, N04, NPU, NSA, P30, P32, P33, P35, P39, PGegResA, PGrRegA, PN&I, R07, R08, R10, R12, R13, R16, RA&MP, RM&VM, Reac, RefZh, S12, S17, SCI, SCOPUS, SoyAb, T02, T05, TAR, THA, ToxAb, VITIS, VS, VirolAbstr, W07, W11.
—BLDSC (5034.000000), CASDDS, GNLM, IE, Infotrieve, Ingenta, INIST, Linda Hall. **CCC.**
Published by: John Wiley & Sons Ltd. (Subsidiary of: John Wiley & Sons, Inc.), 1-7 Oldlands Way, PO Box 808, Bognor Regis, West Sussex PO21 9FF, United Kingdom. TEL 44-1865-778315, FAX 44-1243-843232, cs-journals@wiley.com, http://onlinelibrary.wiley.com/. Circ: 1,000.

615 USA ISSN 0897-1900
RS1 CODEN: JPPREU
JOURNAL OF PHARMACY PRACTICE. Text in English. 1988. bi-m. USD 1,405, GBP 826 combined subscription to institutions (print & online eds.); USD 1,377, GBP 809 to institutions (effective 2011). adv. back issues avail.; reprint service avail. from PSC. **Document type:** *Journal, Academic/Scholarly.* **Description:** Covers current information on new drugs, pharmocokinetics, drug administration, and adverse drug reactions. Also considers legal issues, economic concerns, and new problems rising from managed care.
Related titles: E-mail ed.; Online - full text ed.: ISSN 1531-1937. USD 1,265, GBP 743 to institutions (effective 2011).
Indexed: A01, A03, A08, A22, A26, B21, C06, C07, CA, E01, E08, EMBASE, ESPM, ExcerpMed, G08, H&SSA, H11, H12, I05, I12, MEDLINE, P03, PsycInfo, R10, Reac, RiskAb, S09, SCOPUS, T02.
—BLDSC (5034.020000), GNLM, IE, Infotrieve, Ingenta. **CCC.**
Published by: Sage Publications, Inc., 2455 Teller Rd, Thousand Oaks, CA 91320. TEL 805-499-9774, FAX 805-499-0871, info@sagepub.com. Ed. Henry Cohen. adv.: color page USD 675, B&W page USD 385; 7 x 10. Circ: 285 (paid). **Subscr. overseas to:** Sage Publications Ltd., 1 Oliver's Yard, 55 City Rd, London EC1Y 1SP, United Kingdom. TEL 44-207-3248701, FAX 44-207-3248733, subscription@sagepub.co.uk.

615 AUS ISSN 1445-937X
RS1 CODEN: AUHPAI
➤ **JOURNAL OF PHARMACY PRACTICE AND RESEARCH.** Abbreviated title: J P P R. Text in English. 1966. q. AUD 120 domestic; AUD 170 foreign (effective 2009). adv. bk.rev. abstr.; illus.; stat. back issues avail. **Document type:** *Journal, Academic/Scholarly.* **Description:** Aims to assist in the development of the practice of hospital pharmacy in Australia.
Supersedes in part (in 2002): Australian Journal of Hospital Pharmacy (0310-6810)
Related titles: Online - full text ed.
Indexed: A22, B25, BIOSIS Prev, C06, C07, CA, CIN, ChemAb, ChemTitl, DBA, EMBASE, ExcerpMed, IDIS, Inpharma, MycolAb, R10, Reac, SCOPUS, T02.
—BLDSC (5034.021000), CASDDS, GNLM, IE, Ingenta. **CCC.**
Published by: Society of Hospital Pharmacists of Australia, Ste 3, 65 Oxford St, PO Box 1774, Collingwood, VIC 3066, Australia. TEL 61-3-94860177, FAX 61-3-94860311, shpa@shpa.org.au. Ed. Jo-anne E Brien. Adv. contact Terry Maunsell TEL 61-2-95158259. B&W page AUD 2,795; trim 210 x 297. Circ: 2,100.

615 IND ISSN 0974-6943
JOURNAL OF PHARMACY RESEARCH. Text in English. 2008. q. free (effective 2011). **Document type:** *Journal, Academic/Scholarly.*
Media: Online - full text.
Indexed: A01, A37, A38, Agr, B23, CA, D01, F12, H17, O01, P40, R11, R13, S12, S13, S16, T02.
Published by: Association of Pharmaceutical Innovators, Santosh Stone Wale Ka Makan, Near Kumawat Dharamsala, Nursinghpura Rd, Ramtekari, Mandsaur, Madhya Pradesh 458 001, India. TEL 91-9424532372, admin@ditonline.info, http://ditonline.info. Ed. Swapnadeep Parial.

P

615.329 USA ISSN 8755-1225
CODEN: JPTEEB
➤ **JOURNAL OF PHARMACY TECHNOLOGY.** Abbreviated title: J P T. Text in English. 1985. bi-m. USD 68 in North America to individuals; USD 93 elsewhere to individuals; USD 181 in North America to institutions; USD 206 elsewhere to institutions; USD 40 in North America to students; USD 65 elsewhere to students; USD 16 per issue (effective 2009). adv. bk.rev.; software rev. abstr.; bibl.; charts; illus. index. back issues avail.; reprints avail. **Document type:** *Journal, Academic/Scholarly.* **Description:** Covers new drugs, products, and equipment; therapeutic trends; organizational, legal, and educational activities; drug distribution and administration; and includes continuing education articles.
Related titles: Microform ed.: (from PQC); Online - full text ed.: ISSN 1549-4810.
Indexed: A22, AHCMS, B25, BIOSIS Prev, C06, C07, C08, CIN, CINAHL, ChemAb, ChemTitl, EMBASE, ExcerpMed, I12, IDIS, Inpharma, MycolAb, P30, P35, R10, Reac, SCOPUS.
—BLDSC (5034.030000), CASDDS, GNLM, IE, Infotrieve, Ingenta, INIST. **CCC.**
Published by: Harvey Whitney Books Company, PO Box 42696, Cincinnati, OH 45242. TEL 513-793-3555, FAX 513-793-3600, http://www.hwbooks.com. Ed., Pub. Harvey A K Whitney.

➤ **JOURNAL OF PHYSIOLOGY AND PHARMACOLOGY.** *see* BIOLOGY—Physiology

615 NGA
JOURNAL OF PHYTOMEDICINE AND THERAPEUTICS. Text in English. 1996. s-a. **Document type:** *Journal, Academic/Scholarly.*
Formerly (until 1999): Journal of Pharmaceutical Research and Development (1118-1028)
Indexed: EMBASE, ExcerpMed, R10, Reac, SCOPUS.
Published by: National Institute for Pharmaceutical Research and Development, Idu, P.M.B. 21, Abuja, Nigeria.

JOURNAL OF PLANAR CHROMATOGRAPHY - MODERN TLC. (Thin Layer Chromatography) *see* CHEMISTRY—Analytical Chemistry

▼ **JOURNAL OF POSTGENOMICS;** drug & biomarker development. *see* BIOLOGY—Genetics

JOURNAL OF PSYCHOACTIVE DRUGS; a multidisciplinary forum. *see* DRUG ABUSE AND ALCOHOLISM

615.7 616.8 GBR ISSN 0269-8811
CODEN: JOPSEQ
➤ **JOURNAL OF PSYCHOPHARMACOLOGY.** Text in English. 1987. 8/yr. USD 1,827, GBP 988 combined subscription to institutions (print & online eds.); USD 1,790, GBP 968 to institutions (effective 2011). adv. bk.rev. back issues avail.; reprint service avail. from PSC. **Document type:** *Journal, Academic/Scholarly.* **Description:** Presents original research and review articles on both preclinical and clinical aspects of psychopharmacology.
Formerly: British Association for Psychopharmacology. Journal
Related titles: Online - full text ed.: ISSN 1461-7285. USD 1,644, GBP 889 to institutions (effective 2011); Supplement(s): Journal of Psychopharmacology. Supplement. ISSN 1359-7868.
Indexed: A01, A03, A08, A20, A22, A26, A36, ASCA, AddicA, B07, B21, B25, BIOBASE, BIOSIS Prev, C06, C07, CA, CABA, CIN, ChemAb, ChemTitl, CurCont, D01, DBA, E-psyche, E01, E08, E12, EMBASE, ESPM, ExcerpMed, F08, F11, F12, FoP, G08, GH, H04, H16, I05, I12, IABS, ISR, IndMed, Inpharma, MEDLINE, MycolAb, N02, N03, NSA, NSCI, P03, P10, P12, P25, P30, P35, P48, P53, P54, PQC, PsycInfo, PsycholAb, R10, RA&MP, Reac, S09, SCI, SCOPUS, T02, T05, ToxAb, V02, VITIS, VS, W07.
—BLDSC (5043.450000), CASDDS, GNLM, IE, Infotrieve, Ingenta, INIST. **CCC.**

Published by: (British Association for Psychopharmacology), Sage Publications Ltd. (Subsidiary of: Sage Publications, Inc.), 1 Oliver's Yard, 55 City Rd, London, EC1Y 1SP, United Kingdom. TEL 44-20-73248500, FAX 44-20-73248600, info@sagepub.co.uk, http://www.uk.sagepub.com/home.nav. Eds. David Nutt, Pierre Blier. **Subscr. in the Americas to:** Sage Publications, Inc., 2455 Teller Rd, Thousand Oaks, CA 91320. TEL 805-499-9774, FAX 805-499-0871, journals@sagepub.com.

▼ ➤ **JOURNAL OF SCIENTIFIC SPECULATIONS AND RESEARCH.** *see* MEDICAL SCIENCES

➤ **JOURNAL OF TEXTURE STUDIES**; an international journal of texture, rheology, and the physical and sensory testing of foods and consumer goods. *see* FOOD AND FOOD INDUSTRIES

➤ **JOURNAL OF TOXICOLOGIC PATHOLOGY.** *see* ENVIRONMENTAL STUDIES—Toxicology And Environmental Safety

➤ **JOURNAL OF TOXICOLOGICAL SCIENCES.** *see* ENVIRONMENTAL STUDIES—Toxicology And Environmental Safety

➤ **JOURNAL OF TOXICOLOGY AND ENVIRONMENTAL HEALTH. PART A: CURRENT ISSUES.** *see* ENVIRONMENTAL STUDIES—Toxicology And Environmental Safety

➤ **JOURNAL OF TOXICOLOGY AND ENVIRONMENTAL HEALTH. PART B: CRITICAL REVIEWS.** *see* ENVIRONMENTAL STUDIES—Toxicology And Environmental Safety

615.9 571.95 IND ISSN 0976-8769
▼ ➤ **JOURNAL OF TOXICOLOGY RESEARCH.** Text in English. 2010. s-a. USD 425 (effective 2011). **Document type:** *Journal, Academic/Scholarly.* **Description:** Publishes all the latest research articles, reviews and letters in all areas of toxicology.
Related titles: Online - full text ed.: ISSN 0976-8777. free (effective 2011).
Published by: Bioinfo Publications, 49/F-72, Vighnahar Complex, Front of Overseas Bank, Sector 12, Kharghar, Navi Mumbai, 410 210, India. TEL 91-22-27743967, FAX 91-22-66736413, editor@bioinfo.in, subscription@bioinfo.in. Ed. Dr. Abdel Nasser El Moghazy.

➤ **JOURNAL OF TRADITIONAL CHINESE MEDICINE.** *see* ALTERNATIVE MEDICINE

615 JPN ISSN 1880-1447
CODEN: WIGAES
➤ **JOURNAL OF TRADITIONAL MEDICINES.** Text in English, Japanese; Abstracts in English. 1967. 4/yr. JPY 10,000 membership (effective 2007). adv. back issues avail. **Document type:** *Journal, Academic/Scholarly.* **Description:** Contains chemical, pharmaceutical, pharmacological and clinical studies on Sino-Japanese traditional medicines.
Former titles (until 2003): Wakan Iyakugaku Zasshi/Journal of Traditional Medicines (1340-6302); (until 1994): Wakan Iyaku Gakkaishi/Journal of Medical and Pharmaceutical Society for Wakan-yaku (0289-730X); (until 1984): Wakan-Yaku Shinpojumu/Symposium on Wakan-yaku. Proceedings (0388-7413)
Related titles: Online - full text ed.
Indexed: A22, A34, A35, A36, AgBio, AgrForAb, BP, C30, CABA, E12, F08, F11, F12, GH, H16, N02, N03, P32, P33, P39, P40, PGegResA, R07, R08, R11, R12, R13, RA&MP, RM&VM, SoyAb, T05, TAR, VS, W10, W11.
—BLDSC (5069.745300), CASDDS, IE, Ingenta. **CCC.**
Published by: Wakan Iyaku Gakkai/Medical and Pharmaceutical Society for Wakan-Yaku, 2630 Sugitani, Toyama Medical & Pharmaceutical University, Institute of Natural Medicine, Toyama, 930-0194, Japan. TEL 81-76-4347635, FAX 81-76-4345062, info@wakan-iyaku.gr.jp. Circ: 1,300.

615.49 GBR ISSN 2044-0324
▼ ➤ **JOURNAL OF VENOM RESEARCH.** Text in English. 2010. irreg. free (effective 2011). **Document type:** *Journal, Academic/Scholarly.*
Media: Online - full text.
Published by: Library Publishing Media inquiries@libpubmedia.co.uk, http://www.libpubmedia.co.uk/index.htm. Ed. Edward G Rowan.

➤ **JOURNAL OF VENOMOUS ANIMALS AND TOXINS INCLUDING TROPICAL DISEASES.** *see* BIOLOGY—Zoology

615 636.089 GBR ISSN 0140-7783
SF915 CODEN: JVPTD9
➤ **JOURNAL OF VETERINARY PHARMACOLOGY AND THERAPEUTICS.** Text in English. 1978. bi-m. GBP 953 in United Kingdom to institutions; EUR 1,211 in Europe to institutions; USD 1,760 in the Americas to institutions; USD 2,056 elsewhere to institutions; GBP 1,097 combined subscription in United Kingdom to institutions (print & online eds.); EUR 1,393 combined subscription in Europe to institutions (print & online eds.); USD 2,024 combined subscription in the Americas to institutions (print & online eds.); USD 2,364 combined subscription elsewhere to institutions (print & online eds.) (effective 2012). adv. bk.rev. bibl. back issues avail.; reprint service avail. from PSC. **Document type:** *Journal, Academic/Scholarly.* **Description:** Devoted to the publication of scientific papers in the basic and clinical aspects of veterinary pharmacology and toxicology.
Related titles: Microform ed.: (from PQC); ◆ Online - full text ed.: Journal of Veterinary Pharmacology and Therapeutics Online. ISSN 1365-2885; Supplement(s): Journal of Veterinary Pharmacology and Therapeutics. Supplement. ISSN 1368-440X.
Indexed: A01, A02, A03, A08, A22, A26, A34, A35, A36, A37, A38, ASCA, AgBio, Agr, B21, B25, BIOSIS Prev, C11, CA, CABA, CIN, CTA, ChemAb, ChemTitl, CurCont, D01, DBA, E01, E12, EMBASE, ESPM, ExcerpMed, F08, FoVS&M, G11, GH, H04, H12, H16, H17, I10, ISR, IndMed, IndVet, LT, MEDLINE, MaizeAb, MycolAb, N02, N03, N04, P30, P33, P37, P39, PN&I, R08, R13, RA&MP, RM&VM, RRTA, S12, S13, S16, SAA, SCI, SCOPUS, SoyAb, T02, T05, TAR, VS, W07, W10, W11, WildRev.
—BLDSC (5072.420000), CASDDS, GNLM, IE, Infotrieve, Ingenta, INIST. **CCC.**
Published by: (Association for Veterinary Clinical Pharmacology & Therapeutics), Wiley-Blackwell Publishing Ltd. (Subsidiary of: John Wiley & Sons, Inc.), 9600 Garsington Rd, Oxford, OX4 2DQ, United Kingdom. TEL 44-1865-776868, FAX 44-1865-714591, customerservices@blackwellpublishing.com. Eds. Jim E Riviere TEL 919-513-6305, Johanna Fink-Gremmels TEL 31-30-2535453. Adv. contact Mia Scott-Ruddock TEL 44-1865-476354. **Co-sponsors:** European Association for Veterinary Pharmacology and Toxicology, American College of Veterinary Clinical Pharmacology; American Academy of Veterinary Pharmacology and Therapeutics.

615 636.089 GBR ISSN 1365-2885
➤ **JOURNAL OF VETERINARY PHARMACOLOGY AND THERAPEUTICS ONLINE.** Text in English. 1999. bi-m. GBP 953 in United Kingdom to institutions; EUR 1,211 in Europe to institutions; USD 1,760 in the Americas to institutions; USD 2,056 elsewhere to institutions (effective 2012). adv. back issues avail. **Document type:** *Journal, Academic/Scholarly.*
Media: Online - full text (from IngentaConnect). **Related titles:** Microform ed.: (from PQC); ◆ Print ed.: Journal of Veterinary Pharmacology and Therapeutics. ISSN 0140-7783.
—CCC.
Published by: (Association for Veterinary Clinical Pharmacology & Therapeutics), Wiley-Blackwell Publishing Ltd. (Subsidiary of: John Wiley & Sons, Inc.), 9600 Garsington Rd, Oxford, OX4 2DQ, United Kingdom. TEL 44-1865-776868, FAX 44-1865-714591, customerservices@blackwellpublishing.com, http://www.wiley.com/. Eds. Jim E Riviere TEL 919-513-6305, Johanna Fink-Gremmels TEL 31-30-2535453. Adv. contact Mia Scott-Ruddock TEL 44-1865-476354. **Co-sponsor:** American Academy of Veterinary Pharmacology and Therapeutics.

615 ITA ISSN 2039-4713
▼ ➤ **JOURNAL OF XENOBIOTICS.** Text in English. 2010. irreg. **Document type:** *Journal, Academic/Scholarly.*
Media: Online - full text.
Published by: Pagepress, Via Giuseppe Belli 4, Pavia, 27100, Italy. TEL 39-0382-1751762, FAX 39-0382-1750481, http://www.pagepress.org. Ed. Francois Gagne.

615 IND ISSN 0975-1483
▼ **JOURNAL OF YOUNG PHARMACISTS.** Abbreviated title: J Y P. Text in English. 2009. q. INR 2,000 domestic; USD 350 foreign; INR 2,400 combined subscription domestic (print & online eds.); USD 420 combined subscription foreign (print & online eds.) (effective 2011). adv. **Document type:** *Journal, Academic/Scholarly.* **Description:** Provides comprehensive coverage of issues affecting pharmaceutical education and career.
Related titles: Online - full text ed.: ISSN 0975-1505. INR 1,600 domestic; USD 280 foreign (effective 2011).
Indexed: A01, P10, P30, P48, P53, P54, PQC, SCOPUS, T02.
—CCC.
Published by: (InPharm Association), Medknow Publications and Media Pvt. Ltd., B-9, Kanara Business Ctr, Off Link Rd, Ghatkopar (E), Mumbai, Maharastra 400 075, India. TEL 91-22-66491816, http://www.medknow.com.

615 JPN
JOUSAI DAIGAKU YAKUGAKUBU KYOUIKU KENKYUU GYOUSEKISHUU/JOSAI UNIVERSITY. PHARMACEUTICAL BULLETIN. Text in English, Japanese; Summaries in English. 1979. a. **Document type:** *Journal, Academic/Scholarly.*
Former titles (until 2005): Jousai Daigaku Yakugakubu Kiyou (1348-4931); (until 2000): Josai Daigaku Yakugakubu Kenkyu Gyosekishu (0913-5340); (until 1985): Josai Daigaku Yakugakubu Kiyo (0387-6950)
Published by: Josai Daigaku, Yakugakubu/Josai University, Department of Pharmaceutical Science, 1-1 Keyakidai, Sakado, Saitama 350-0295, Japan. http://www.josai.ac.jp/~pharm/index.htm.

615 IRN ISSN 1735-7780
JUNDISHAPUR JOURNAL OF NATURAL PHARMACEUTICAL PRODUCTS. Text in English. 2006. q. **Document type:** *Journal, Academic/Scholarly.*
Related titles: Print ed.: free (effective 2011).
Published by: Ahvaz Jundishapur University of Medical Sciences, PO Box 61357-33184, Ahvaz, Iran. TEL 98-611-3330074, FAX 98-611-3332036, jjm@ajums.ac.ir, http://jjm.ajums.ac.ir. Ed. Heibatullah Kalantari.

JURISPRUDENTIE GENEESMIDDELENRECHT. *see* LAW

JURISPRUDENTIE GENEESMIDDELENRECHT PLUS. *see* LAW

615 JPN ISSN 0285-4775
CODEN: KKBYDO
KANAGAWAKEN BYOIN YAKUZAISHIKAI KAISHI/KANAGAWA HOSPITAL PHARMACISTS ASSOCIATION. JOURNAL. Text in Japanese. 1968. 3/yr. **Document type:** *Journal, Academic/Scholarly.*
—CASDDS.
Published by: Kanagawaken Byoin Yakuzaishikai/Kanagawaken Hospital Pharmacists Association, 14-11 Nishimachi Isogo-Ku, 406 Kanagawa Prefecture Medical and Health Center, Yokohama, Kanagawa 235-0007, Japan. TEL 81-45-7613345, FAX 81-45-7613347, http://www003.upp.so-net.ne.jp/kshp-jp/.

615 CHN ISSN 1672-7878
KANGGANRAN YAOXUE/ANTI-INFECTION PHARMACY. Text in Chinese. 2004. q. CNY 8 newsstand/cover (effective 2006). **Document type:** *Journal, Academic/Scholarly.*
Related titles: Online - full text ed.
Published by: Jiangsu Sheng Suzhou Shi Di-5 Renmin Yiyuan/The Fifth People's Hospital of Suzhou, Jiangsu, China, 2, Nanmen Xi Er-Lu, Suzhou, 215007, China.

KAOHSIUNG JOURNAL OF MEDICAL SCIENCES. *see* MEDICAL SCIENCES

615.9 JPN ISSN 0287-2358
KAPUSERU/CAPSULE. Text in Japanese. 1982. 3/yr. **Document type:** *Magazine, Trade.*
Published by: Nihon Seiyaku Kogyo Kyokai/Japan Pharmaceutical Manufacturers Association, Torii Nihonbashi Bldg., 3-4-1 Nihonbashi-Honcho, Chuo-Ku, Tokyo, 103-0023, Japan. TEL 81-3-32410326, FAX 81-3-32421767.

615 JPN ISSN 0289-4750
KATEIYAKU KENKYU/RESEARCH ON HOME MEDICINES. Text in Japanese. 1982. a.
Published by: Toyamaken Kateiyaku Kaihatsu Kenkyukai/Toyama Research Society for Home Medicine, 1-7 Shinsokawa, Toyama-shi, 930-0006, Japan.

615 FIN ISSN 0355-1075
RF1
KAYTANNON LAAKARI. Text in Finnish. 1958. q. **Document type:** *Journal, Trade.* **Description:** Publishes concise summaries on medication recommendations for the treatment of significant widespread diseases.
Related titles: Online - full content ed.
Published by: Oy Leiras Finland Ab, Paciuksenkatu 21, PO Box 1406, Helsinki, FIN-00101, Finland. TEL 358-20-7465090, Info@leirasfinland.fi.

615 USA ISSN 0194-567X
THE KENTUCKY PHARMACIST. Text in English. 1878. m. (10/yr.). USD 99 domestic to non-members; free to members (effective 2008). adv. bk.rev. **Document type:** *Magazine, Trade.*
—Linda Hall.
Published by: (Kentucky Pharmacists Association, Inc.), Newsletters Ink, Corp., 473 W 4800 S, Salt Lake Cty, Murray, UT 84123. TEL 801-288-2434, 800-639-0465, info@newslettersink.com, http://www.newslettersink.com. Ed. Mike Mayes. Pub. Kate Olson. adv.: B&W page USD 429; trim 7.5 x 10. Circ: 1,800 (paid).

KEY NOTE MARKET ASSESSMENT. NUTRACEUTICALS. *see* BUSINESS AND ECONOMICS—Production Of Goods And Services

KEY NOTE MARKET ASSESSMENT. VITAMINS & SUPPLEMENTS. *see* BUSINESS AND ECONOMICS—Production Of Goods And Services

KEY NOTE MARKET REPORT: LABORATORY EQUIPMENT. *see* BUSINESS AND ECONOMICS—Production Of Goods And Services

KEY NOTE MARKET REPORT: O T C PHARMACEUTICALS. (Over The Counter) *see* BUSINESS AND ECONOMICS—Production Of Goods And Services

615 GBR
KEY NOTE MARKET REPORT: RETAIL CHEMISTS & DRUGSTORES. Variant title: Retail Chemists & Drugstores Market Report. Text in English. 1993. irreg., latest 2008, Jul. GBP 460 per issue (effective 2010). **Document type:** *Report, Trade.* **Description:** Provides an overview of a specific UK market segment and includes executive summary, market definition, market size, industry background, competitor analysis, current issues, forecasts, company profiles, and more.
Formerly (until 1996): Key Note Report: Retail Chemists and Drugstores (1352-6979)
Related titles: CD-ROM ed.; Online - full text ed.
Published by: Key Note Ltd. (Subsidiary of: Bonnier Business Information), Harlequin House, 5th Fl, 7 High St, Teddington, Richmond upon Thames, TW11 8EE, United Kingdom. TEL 44-845-5040452, FAX 44-845-5040453, info@keynote.co.uk.

615 658.8 GBR
KEY NOTE MARKET REVIEW: THE PHARMACEUTICAL INDUSTRY. Variant title: The Pharmaceutical Industry Market Review. Text in English. 19??. irreg., latest 2008, Mar. GBP 750 per issue (effective 2010). **Document type:** *Report, Trade.* **Description:** Designed to keep you up to date with the developments and opportunities across entire industry sectors. They provide a comprehensive analysis of the industry by drawing together key related market segments under one cover.
Formerly (until 2002): Key Note Market Review: U K Pharmaceutical Industry; Incorporates (1997-199?): Key Note Market Report: Prescribed Pharmaceuticals (1460-2032); Which was formerly (until 1997): Key Note Report: Prescribed Pharmaceuticals (1352-7134)
Related titles: CD-ROM ed.; Online - full text ed.
Published by: Key Note Ltd. (Subsidiary of: Bonnier Business Information), Harlequin House, 5th Fl, 7 High St, Teddington, Richmond upon Thames, TW11 8EE, United Kingdom. TEL 44-845-5040452, FAX 44-845-5040453, info@keynote.co.uk.

615 GBR
KEY PHARMA NEWS. Text in English. 2000. irreg. GBP 560, USD 1,065, EUR 840 (effective 2009). **Document type:** *Journal, Trade.* **Description:** Provides latest news and developments involving pharmaceutical companies worldwide.
Formerly (until 2009): Pharma Company Insight (1473-1533)
Media: Online - full content.
Published by: Espicom Business Intelligence, Lincoln House, City Fields Business Park, City Fields Way, Chichester, W Sussex PO20 2FS, United Kingdom. TEL 44-1243-533322, FAX 44-1243-533418, Annette_Bulbeck@espicom.com, sales_desk@espicom.com.

615 DEU
KEY SALE; Fachmagazin fuer Drogeriemaerkte - Parfuemerien - Kauf- und Warenhaeuser - Apotheken. Text in German. 2007. m. EUR 53.55 (effective 2009). adv. **Document type:** *Magazine, Trade.*
Published by: Bergmann Verlag GmbH, Gotthardstr 105, Munich, 80689, Germany. TEL 49-89-58909890, FAX 49-89-58909919, info@bergmann-verlag.de. Pub. Thomas Bergmann. adv.: B&W page EUR 2,800, color page EUR 4,400. Circ: 10,000 (controlled).

615.1 RUS ISSN 0023-1134
RS402 CODEN: KHFZAN
KHIMIKO-FARMATSEVTICHESKII ZHURNAL/JOURNAL OF PHARMACEUTICAL CHEMISTRY. Text in Russian. 1967. m. USD 234 foreign (effective 2004). bk.rev.; play rev. bibl.; charts; illus. index. **Document type:** *Journal, Academic/Scholarly.* **Description:** Publishes articles on scientific-technical and production activities of chemo-pharmaceutic enterprises.
Related titles: Online - full text ed.; ◆ English Translation: Pharmaceutical Chemistry Journal. ISSN 0091-150X.
Indexed: C31, CTFA, ChemAb, ChemTitl, DBA, I12, ISR, MycolAb, RefZh.
—BLDSC (0391.922000), CASDDS, East View, GNLM, INIST, Linda Hall. **CCC.**
Published by: (Tsentr Khimii i Lekarstvennykh Sredstv), Izdatel'stvo Folium, Dmitrovskoe shosse 58, Moscow, 127238, Russian Federation. TEL 7-095-4825544, 7-095-4825590, info@folium.ru. Ed. R G Glushkov. **Dist. by:** M K - Periodica, ul Gilyarovskogo 39, Moscow 129110, Russian Federation. TEL 7-095-2845008, FAX 7-095-2813798, info@periodicals.ru, http://www.mkniga.ru.

615 USA ISSN 1533-3671
RS201.P37
KING GUIDE TO PARENTAL ADMIXTURES FOR WINDOWS (CD-ROM EDITION). Text in English. 1998 (Aug.). q. USD 299 (effective 2006). **Document type:** *Journal, Academic/Scholarly.*
Media: CD-ROM. **Related titles:** Online - full text ed.; ◆ Print ed.: King Guide to Parenteral Admixtures (Print Edition).
Published by: King Guide Publications, Inc., PO Box 10317, Napa, CA 94581. TEL 707-257-7573, 888-546-4484, FAX 707-257-7566. Eds. James C King, Patrick N. Catania. Pub., R&P, Adv. contact Misha Hudnell.

615.1 USA
KING GUIDE TO PARENTERAL ADMIXTURES (PRINT EDITION). Text in English. 1971. q. looseleaf. USD 215 (effective 2006). **Document type:** *Journal, Trade.* **Description:** Contains injectable drug compatibility and stability information on over 400 drugs in 12,000 combinations in 12 fluids.
Related titles: ◆ CD-ROM ed.: King Guide to Parental Admixtures for Windows (CD-ROM Edition). ISSN 1533-3671; Online - full text ed.
Published by: King Guide Publications, Inc., PO Box 10317, Napa, CA 94581. TEL 707-257-7573, 888-546-4484, FAX 707-257-7566. Eds. James C King, Patrick N. Catania. Pub., R&P, Adv. contact Misha Hudnell. Circ: 4,000 (paid).

615 JPN ISSN 0914-5079
KITASATO DAIGAKU DAIGAKUIN YAKUGAKU KENKYUKA RINSHO YAKUGAKU TOKURON KIYO/KITASATO UNIVERSITY. CLINICAL PHARMACY BULLETIN. Text in Japanese. 1982. a.
Published by: Kitasato Daigaku, Yakugakubu/Kitasato University, School of Pharmacy, 5-9-1 Shirokane, Minato-ku, Tokyo, 108-8641, Japan. Fnyuushi@pharm.kitasato-u.ac.jp, http://www.pharm.kitasato-u.ac.jp/.

615.1 NLD ISSN 2210-6405
▼ **DE KLEINE GIDS IN DE APOTHEEK.** Text in Dutch. 2010. a. EUR 12.16 (effective 2010).
Published by: Kluwer B.V. (Subsidiary of: Wolters Kluwer N.V.), Postbus 23, Deventer, 7400 GA, Netherlands. TEL 31-570-673449, FAX 31-570-691555, info@kluwer.nl, http://www.kluwer.nl.

615 RUS ISSN 0869-5490
KLINICHESKAYA FARMAKOLOGIYA I TERAPIYA/CLINICAL PHARMACOLOQY AND THERAPY. Text in Russian. 1992. q. USD 122 foreign (effective 2007). **Document type:** *Journal, Academic/ Scholarly.*
—East View.
Published by: Klinika Terapii i Profzabolevenii, ul Rossolimo 11-a, Moscow, 119021, Russian Federation. TEL 7-095-2482544. **Dist. by:** East View Information Services, 10601 Wayzata Blvd, Minneapolis, MN 55305. TEL 952-252-1201, 800-477-1005, FAX 952-252-1202, info@eastview.com, http://www.eastview.com.

615 UKR ISSN 1562-725X
KLINICHNA FARMATSIYA. Text in Ukrainian. q. **Document type:** *Journal, Academic/Scholarly.*
Indexed: RefZh.
Published by: Natsional'nyi Farmatsevtychnyi Universytet/National University of Pharmacy, Vul Pushkins'ka 53, Kharkiv, 310002, Ukraine. TEL 380-572-142289, zupanets@ukrfa.kharkov.ua, http://www.ukrfa.kharkov.ua. Ed. Igor Zupanets' TEL 380-572-431980. **Co-sponsor:** Ministerstvo Okhorony Zdorov'ya Ukrainy, Derzhavnyi Farmakologichnyi Tsentr.

615 CZE ISSN 1212-7973
➤ **KLINICKA FARMAKOLOGIE A FARMACIE.** Text in Czech. 1995. q. CZK 320; CZK 80 per issue (effective 2010). **Document type:** *Journal, Academic/Scholarly.*
Formerly (until 1999): Zpravodaj Klinicke Farmakologie a Farmacie (1211-166X)
Related titles: Online - full text ed.: ISSN 1803-5353.
Indexed: EMBASE, ExcerpMed, R10, Reac, SCOPUS.
—BLDSC (5099.284793), IE.
Published by: Solen s.r.o., Lazecka 297/51, Olomouc 51, 779 00, Czech Republic. TEL 420-582-396038, FAX 420-582-396099, solen@solen.cz, http://www.solen.cz. Ed. Dr. Karel Urbanek. Circ: 2,000. **Co-sponsor:** Slovenska Spolocnost Klinickej Farmakologie.

615.1 IRL ISSN 1649-1254
KNOW YOUR MEDICINE. Text in English. 2001. biennial. **Document type:** *Directory, Consumer.* **Description:** Provides a consumer guide to over the counter medicines and pharmaceutical products.
Published by: Eireann Healthcare Publications, 25-26 Windsor Pl., Dublin, 2, Ireland. TEL 353-1-4753300, FAX 353-1-4753311, mhenderson@eireannpublications.ie. Ed. Ann-Marie Hardiman. Pub. Graham Cooke. Circ: 40,000.

615 JPN ISSN 0911-9191
KOBE GAKUIN DAIGAKU YAKUGAKKAISHI/KOBE GAKUIN UNIVERSITY. PHARMACEUTICAL SOCIETY. ANNUAL BULLETIN. Text in English, Japanese. 1977. a. free. **Document type:** *Journal, Academic/Scholarly.*
Published by: Kobe Gakuin Daigaku, Yakugakkai/Pharmaceutical Society of Kobe Gakuin University, 518 Arise, Ikawadani-cho, Nishi-ku, Kobe, Hyogo 651-2180, Japan. FAX 81-78-9745912, yakugaku@pharm.kobegakuin.ac.jp, http://www.yaku-kgu.com/index.html.

615 JPN ISSN 0911-9183
KOBE GAKUIN DAIGAKU YAKUGAKUBU KIYO/KOBE GAKUIN UNIVERSITY. FACULTY OF PHARMACEUTICAL SCIENCES. MEMOIRS. Text in English, Japanese. 1978. every 5 yrs., latest 2002. **Document type:** *Monographic series, Academic/Scholarly.*
Published by: Kobe Gakuin Daigaku, Yakugakubu/Kobe Gakuin University, Faculty of Pharmaceutical Sciences, 518 Arise, Ikawadani-cho, Nishi-ku, Kobe, 651-2180, Japan. dean@pharm.kobegakuin.ac.jp, http://www.kobegakuin.ac.jp/~pharm/.

615 JPN ISSN 0388-211X
KOKUSAI IYAKUHIN JOHO/INTERNATIONAL PHARMACEUTICAL INTELLIGENCE. Text in Japanese. 1972. 2/m. JPY 106,000 (effective 2007). **Document type:** *Newsletter, Trade.*
Published by: Kokusai Shogyo Shuppan K.K./Kokusai Shogyo Publishing Corp., 6-14-5 Ginza, Chuo-ku, Tokyo, 104-0061, Japan. TEL 81-3-35431771, FAX 81-3-35453919.

615 JPN
KONNICHI NO CHIRYOYAKU. Text in Japanese. 1977. a. JPY 4,830 newsstand/cover (effective 2007). **Document type:** *Monographic series, Academic/Scholarly.*
Published by: Nankodo Co. Ltd., 3-42-6 Hongo, Bunkyo-ku, Tokyo, 113-8410, Japan. TEL 81-3-38117140, FAX 81-3-38117265, http://www.nankodo.co.jp/.

615 KOR ISSN 1226-4512
CODEN: KJPPFS
➤ **KOREAN JOURNAL OF PHYSIOLOGY AND PHARMACOLOGY.** Text and summaries in English. 1997. bi-m. free to members (effective 2008). back issues avail. **Document type:** *Journal, Academic/ Scholarly.* **Description:** Provides original research papers on physiological and pharmacological sciences.
Formed by the merger of (1965-1997): Daiham Yangrihag Jabji/Korean Journal of Pharmacology (0377-9459); (1967-1997): Daeham Saengri Haghoeji/Korean Journal of Physiology (0300-4015)
Related titles: Fax ed.; Online - full text ed.
Indexed: A01, B25, BIOSIS Prev, CIN, ChemAb, ChemTitl, EMBASE, ExcerpMed, MycolAb, P30, R10, Reac, SCI, SCOPUS, W07.
—BLDSC (5113.573350), CASDDS, GNLM, IE, Ingenta.
Published by: Korean Society of Pharmacology, Mapo-gu, Seogyo-dong 448-13, Medicinal Studies Bldg 1st Fl, Seoul, 121-841, Korea, S. TEL 82-02-3260370, FAX 82-02-3260371, head@kosphar.org, http://www.kosphar.or.kr. Circ: 1,400. **Co-sponsor:** Korean Physiological Society.

615 DEU ISSN 0176-7186
KRANKENHAUSAPOTHEKEN-REGISTER; Verzeichnis der Krankenhausapotheken und Krankenhausapotheker in der Bundesrepublik Deutschland. Text in German. 19??. irreg., latest 2008. **Document type:** *Directory, Trade.*
Published by: Deutscher Apotheker Verlag, Postfach 101061, Stuttgart, 70009, Germany. TEL 49-711-25820, FAX 49-711-2582290, service@deutscher-apotheker-verlag.de, http://www.deutscher-apotheker-verlag.de.

615 DEU ISSN 0173-7597
CODEN: KRANDZ
KRANKENHAUSPHARMAZIE; Zeitschrift des Bundesverbandes Deutscher Krankenhausapotheker. Text in German; Summaries in English, German. 1950. m. EUR 284; EUR 25 newsstand/cover (effective 2012). adv. **Document type:** *Journal, Trade.*
Formerly (until 1980): Krankenhaus-Apotheke (0075-7071)
Indexed: A22, ChemAb, DBA, EMBASE, ExcerpMed, IBR, IBZ, Inpharma, R10, Reac, SCOPUS.
—BLDSC (5118.146200), CASDDS, GNLM, IE, Infotrieve, Ingenta, INIST. **CCC.**
Published by: (Arbeitsgemeinschaft Deutscher Krankenhausapotheker), Deutscher Apotheker Verlag, Postfach 101061, Stuttgart, 70009, Germany. TEL 49-711-25820, FAX 49-711-2582290, service@deutscher-apotheker-verlag.de, http://www.deutscher-apotheker-verlag.de. Ed. Heike Oberpichler-Schwenk. Adv. contact Klaus Graef TEL 49-711-2582245. Circ: 3,000 (paid).

615 JPN
KUSURI HAKUBUTSUKAN DAYORI/NAITO MUSEUM. SEMI-ANNUAL REPORT. Text in Japanese. 1978. s-a. free. adv. **Document type:** *Corporate.*
Published by: Naito Kinen Kursuri Hakubutsukan/Naito Museum of Pharmaceutical Science and Industry, 1, Takehaya, Kawashima-cho, Hashima-gun, Gifu 501-6195, Japan. TEL 81-586-892101, FAX 81-586-892197, http://www.eisai.co.jp/museum/.

KWALITEITSINDICATOREN APOTHEKEN. *see* BUSINESS AND ECONOMICS—Management

615 JPN ISSN 1880-5116
KYOURITSU YAKKA DAIGAKU ZASSHI/KYORITSU UNIVERSITY OF PHARMACY. JOURNAL. Text in Japanese. 2006. a. **Document type:** *Journal, Academic/Scholarly.*
Related titles: Online - full text ed.
—BLDSC (5134.918000).
Published by: Kyouritsu Yakka Daigaku/Kyoritsu University of Pharmacy, 1-5-30, Shibakoen, Minato-ku, Tokyo, 105-8512, Japan. TEL 81-3-34346241, http://www.pha.keio.ac.jp/.

615 JPN ISSN 0368-7279
CODEN: KYYKBN
KYUSHU YAKUGAKKAI KAIHO/KYUSHU PHARMACEUTICAL SOCIETY. JOURNAL. Text in Japanese; Summaries in English. 1927. a.
Indexed: CIN, ChemAb, ChemTitl.
—CASDDS.
Published by: Kyushu Yamaguchi Yakugakkai, c/o Kyushu Daigaku Igakubu Fuzoku Byoin Yakuzaibu, 1-1 Maidashi 3-chome, Higashi-ku, Fukuoka-shi, 812-0054, Japan.

615.1 NOR ISSN 1892-1213
▼ **L M IS FORSKNINGS- OG UTVIKLINGSUNDERSOEKELSE.** (Legemiddelindustriforeningen) Text in Norwegian. 2010. a. **Document type:** *Report, Trade.*
Related titles: Online - full text ed.
Published by: Legemiddelindustriforeningen/Norwegian Association of Pharmaceutical Manufacturers, PO Box 5094, Majorstuen, Oslo, 0301, Norway. TEL 47-23-161500, FAX 47-23-161501, lmi@lmi.no.

615.1 ESP ISSN 1137-6619
LABORATORIO Y CLINICA. Text in Spanish. 1986. q. **Document type:** *Journal, Academic/Scholarly.*
Formerly (until 1995): Cuadernos de Formacion Continuada (0214-8978)
Published by: Asociacion Espanola de Farmaceuticos Analistas (A E F A), Calle Modesto Lafuente 3, Madrid, 28010, Spain. http://www.aefa.es.

615 354.489 DNK ISSN 1902-8377
LAEGEMIDDELSTYRELSEN. BERETNING. Text in Danish. 1982. a. free. back issues avail. **Document type:** *Government.*
Former titles (until 2006): Laegemiddelstyrelsen. Aarsberetning (1399-7785); (until 1998): Denmark. Sundhedsstyrelsen. Laegemiddelafdelingen. Aarsberetning (1396-9323); (until 1995): Laegemiddelafdelingens Aarsberetning (0109-9930)
Related titles: Online - full text ed.; English ed.: Danish Medicines Agency. Report. ISSN 1902-8369. 200?.
Published by: Laegemiddelstyrelsen/Danish Medicines Agency, Axel Heides Gade 1, Copenhagen S, 2300, Denmark. TEL 45-44-889595, FAX 45-44-889599, dkma@dkma.dk, http://www.dkma.dk.

615.5 SWE ISSN 0347-8343
LAEKEMEDELSBOKEN. Text in Swedish. 1977. biennial. SEK 300 (effective 2001). **Document type:** *Trade.*
Published by: Apoteket AB, Fabrikoervaegen 4, Stockholm, 13188, Sweden. TEL 46-8-466-10-00, FAX 46-8-466-15-15. Ed. Signe Bogentoft.

615.1 SWE ISSN 1402-1927
CODEN: SFTIAE
LAEKEMEDELSVAERLDEN. Text in Swedish. 1897. 10/yr. SEK 447 domestic; SEK 178 to students (effective 2004); SEK 670 elsewhere (effective 2003). adv. bk.rev. illus.; stat. Index. 64 p./no.; **Document type:** *Magazine, Trade.*
Formerly (until 1996): Svensk Farmacevtisk Tidskrift (0039-6524)
Related titles: Microfilm ed.: (from PQC); Online - full text ed.; ◆ Includes: Elixir. ISSN 1401-5374.
Indexed: ChemAb, IndMed, P30.
—CASDDS, INIST, Linda Hall.
Published by: Apotekarsocieteten/Swedish Academy of Pharmaceutical Sciences, PO Box 1136, Stockholm, 11881, Sweden. TEL 46-8-7235000, FAX 46-8-7235011, apotekarsocieteten@swepharm.se, http://www.swepharm.se. Ed. Fredrik Hed TEL 46-8-7235024. Adv. contact Paer Berghstroem TEL 46-8-4445213. B&W page SEK 24,000, color page SEK 32,000; trim 398 x 255. Circ: 11,200.

615.1 USA ISSN 1542-6866
RM1
LANGE SMART CHARTS: PHARMACOLOGY. Text in English. 2003. triennial. USD 42.95 per issue (effective 2008). **Document type:** *Report, Trade.* **Description:** Provides comparison and clarifies relationships among drugs in terms of interactions, pharmacokinetics, uses and side effects.
Published by: McGraw-Hill Companies, Inc., 1221 Ave of the Americas, 43rd fl, New York, NY 10020. TEL 212-512-2000, FAX 212-426-7087, customer.service@mcgraw-hill.com, http://www.mcgraw-hill.com.

615 ARG
CODEN: AFBODJ
LATIN AMERICAN JOURNAL OF PHARMACY. Text in Multiple languages. 1982. 3/yr. ARS 33 domestic; ARS 66 in South America; ARS 80 elsewhere (effective 2002).
Former titles (until 2006): Acta Farmaceutica Bonaerense (0326-2383); Colegio de Farmaceuticos de la Provincia de Buenos Aires. Revista
Indexed: A22, B25, BIOSIS Prev, C01, EMBASE, ExcerpMed, I12, IBR, IBZ, MycolAb, R10, Reac, RefZh, SCI, SCOPUS, W07.
—IE, Ingenta.
Published by: Colegio de Farmaceuticos de la Provincia de Buenos Aires, Calle 5 No 966, La Plata, 1900, Argentina. http://www.colfarma.com.ar. Ed. Nestor O Caffini. Circ: 1,000.

LAW & MORTAR. *see* LAW

615 BRA ISSN 0104-0987
LECTA. Text in Portuguese. 1993. s-a. **Document type:** *Journal, Academic/Scholarly.*
Related titles: Online - full text ed.
Indexed: C01, I12.
Published by: Universidade Sao Francisco, Editora, Ave Sao Francisco de Assis, 218, Jardim Sao Jose, Braganca Paulista, SP 12916-900, Brazil. TEL 55-11-40348448, FAX 55-11-40341825, edusf@saofrancisco.edu.br. Ed. Heloisa Helena de Aradujo Ferreira.

615.1 NOR ISSN 1890-6192
LEGEMIDLER OG HELSETJENESTE. Text in Norwegian. 2005. a. stat. back issues avail. **Document type:** *Report, Consumer.*
Formerly (until 2007): Tall og Fakta. Kortversjon (1504-372X)
Related titles: Online - full text ed.
Published by: Legemiddelindustriforeningen/Norwegian Association of Pharmaceutical Manufacturers, PO Box 5094, Majorstuen, Oslo, 0301, Norway. TEL 47-23-161500, FAX 47-23-161501, lmi@lmi.no.

LEGISLATION PROFESSIONNELLE. INDUSTRIE DU MEDICAMENT. *see* LAW

LEGISLATION PROFESSIONNELLE. PHARMACIE HOSPITALIERE. *see* LAW

615 POL ISSN 1231-028X
➤ **LEK W POLSCE.** Text in Polish. 1991. m. EUR 109 foreign (effective 2011). **Document type:** *Journal, Academic/Scholarly.*
Published by: Medyk Spolka z o.o., ul Czluchowska 66, Warsaw, 01360, Poland. TEL 48-22-6664332, FAX 48-22-6640451, poczta@medyk.com.pl. Ed. Wojciech Luszczyna. **Dist. by:** Ars Polona, Obroncow 25, Warsaw 03933, Poland. TEL 48-22-5098609, FAX 48-22-5098610, arspolona@arspolona.com.pl, http://www.arspolona.com.pl.

➤ **LEKARSKY OBZOR.** *see* MEDICAL SCIENCES

615 NLD ISSN 1570-1808
RS420
LETTERS IN DRUG DESIGN & DISCOVERY. Text in English. 2004. 10/yr. USD 1,120 combined subscription to institutions (print & online eds.) (effective 2012). adv. **Document type:** *Journal, Academic/ Scholarly.* **Description:** Publishes original letters on all areas of rational drug design and drug discovery including medicinal chemistry, in-silico drug design, combinatorial chemistry, high-throughput screening, drug targets, and structure-activity relationships.
Related titles: Online - full text ed.: ISSN 1875-628X (from IngentaConnect).
Indexed: A01, A02, A03, A08, B&BAb, B21, BioEngAb, CA, CCI, EMBASE, ExcerpMed, M&PBA, P30, R10, Reac, SCI, SCOPUS, T02, W07.
—IE, Ingenta. **CCC.**
Published by: Bentham Science Publishers Ltd., PO Box 294, Bussum, 1400 AG, Netherlands. TEL 31-35-6923800, FAX 31-35-6980150, sales@bentham.org, http://www.bentham.org. Ed. Atta-ur Rahman TEL 92-21-34824924. **Subscr. to:** Bentham Science Publishers Ltd., c/o Richard E Morrissy, PO Box 446, Oak Park, IL 60301. TEL 312-413-5867, FAX 312-996-7107, subscriptions@bentham.org, morrissy@bentham.org.

LETTRE DE LA PHARMACOVIGILANCE VETERINAIRE. *see* VETERINARY SCIENCE

615.1 FRA ISSN 0984-452X
CODEN: LPEHAV
➤ **LA LETTRE DU PHARMACOLOGUE.** Text in French. 1987. m. EUR 75 in Europe to individuals; EUR 75 DOM-TOM to individuals; EUR 75 in Africa to individuals; EUR 87 elsewhere to individuals; EUR 96 in Europe to institutions; EUR 96 DOM-TOM to institutions; EUR 96 in Africa to institutions; EUR 108 elsewhere to institutions (effective 2009). **Document type:** *Academic/Scholarly.*
Related titles: ◆ Supplement(s): La Lettre du Pharmacologue. Supplement. ISSN 1245-4893.

P

—BLDSC (5185.215200), GNLM, INIST. **CCC.**
Published by: Edimark S.A.S., 2 Rue Sainte-Marie, Courbevoie, Cedex 92418, France. TEL 33-1-41458000, FAX 33-1-41458025, contact@edimark.fr. Ed. P Jaillon. Pub. Claudie Damour-Terrasson.

615.1 FRA ISSN 1245-4893
LA LETTRE DU PHARMACOLOGUE. SUPPLEMENT. Text in French. 1987. irreg. price varies. **Document type:** *Academic/Scholarly.*
Related titles: ◆ Supplement to: La Lettre du Pharmacologue. ISSN 0984-452X.
—INIST.
Published by: Edimark S.A.S., 2 Rue Sainte-Marie, Courbevoie, Cedex 92418, France. TEL 33-1-41458000, FAX 33-1-41458025, contact@edimark.fr, http://www.edimark.fr. Ed. P Jaillon. Pub. C Damour Terrasson.

LIAONING ZHONGYI ZAZHI/LIAONING JOURNAL OF TRADITIONAL CHINESE MEDICINE. *see* ALTERNATIVE MEDICINE

LIFE SCIENCE LAW REVIEW. *see* LAW

615 NLD ISSN 1381-3145
LIJFBLAD. Text in Dutch. 1995. 10/yr. EUR 49.90; free to qualified personnel (effective 2009). adv. **Document type:** *Trade.* **Description:** Covers drug store products and educational matters for salespersons in drug stores and pharmacies.
Published by: H & B Publishing B.V., Postbus 68, Almere Haven, 1300 AB, Netherlands. TEL 31-36-5486333, FAX 31-36-5486330. Ed. Berry de Nijs. Pub. Ruud Vester. Circ: 10,000 (controlled).

615 610.73 USA ISSN 1081-857X
RM301.12
LIPPINCOTT'S NURSING DRUG GUIDE. Variant title: Nursing Drug Guide. Text in English. 1996. a. USD 39.95 per issue (effective 2010). adv. 1472 p./no.; back issues avail.; reprints avail. **Document type:** *Monographic series, Trade.* **Description:** Covers more than 800 complete drug monographs, including generic and trade names; pronunciations; pregnancy risk category; controlled substance schedule if appropriate; drug class; therapeutic actions; indications, including unlabeled indications; contraindications and cautions; available forms; dosage information; pharmacokinetics; IV facts section; adverse effects; interactions; assessment; intervention; and teaching points.
Related titles: CD-ROM ed.; Online - full text ed.; Regional ed(s).: Lippincott's Nursing Drug Guide (Canadian Version).
Published by: Lippincott Williams & Wilkins (Subsidiary of: Wolters Kluwer N.V.), 530 Walnut St, Philadelphia, PA 19106. TEL 215-521-8300, customerservice@lww.com.

615 USA ISSN 0192-3838
RS1
LOUISIANA PHARMACIST. Text in English. 1943. q. USD 25 (effective 2005). adv. illus. **Document type:** *Magazine, Trade.*
Published by: Louisiana Pharmacists Association, 234 St Joseph St, Baton Rouge, LA 70802. TEL 225-408-2730, FAX 225-381-7424. Ed. Linda Foreman. Circ: 1,500 (paid).

615 GBR
M C A GUIDANCE NOTE. (Medicines Control Agency) Text in English. 1997. irreg. free (effective 2009). back issues avail. **Document type:** *Bulletin, Trade.*
Related titles: Online - full text ed.: free (effective 2009).
Published by: Medicines and Healthcare Products Regulatory Agency, 10-2 Market Towers, 1 Nine Elms Ln, London, SW8 5NQ, United Kingdom. TEL 44-20-70842000, FAX 44-20-70842353, info@mhra.gsi.gov.uk.

615.1 FIN ISSN 0024-8045
M D S. (Misce, Da, Signa) Variant title: Misca, Da, Signa. Text in Finnish; Summaries in English, Swedish. 1901. q. looseleaf. EUR 18 (effective 2005). adv. bk.rev. charts; illus.; pat.; stat.; tr.lit. **Document type:** *Magazine, Trade.*
Published by: Yliopiston Farmasiakunta r.y./University Pharmaceutical Association, Biokeskus 1 B, Viikinkaari 5, PO Box 56, Helsingin Yliopisto, 00014, Finland. TEL 358-9-37452273, FAX 358-9-22431877. Ed. Petteri Heljo. adv.: page EUR 298. Circ: 700.

M H R A BUSINESS PLAN. (Medicines and Healthcare Products Regulatory Agency) *see* MEDICAL SCIENCES

615 GBR ISSN 0957-9095
M I M S. (Monthly Index of Medical Specialties) Text in English. 1959. m. GBP 165; free to qualified personnel (effective 2009). adv. back issues avail. **Document type:** *Journal, Trade.* **Description:** Provides doctors and pharmacists in the UK with reviews of new products, news of important licensing changes and prescribing notes.
Indexed: Inpharma, P35.
—BLDSC (5775.410000), GNLM, IE. **CCC.**
Published by: Haymarket Medical Publications Ltd. (Subsidiary of: Haymarket Media Group), 174 Hammersmith Rd, London, W6 7JP, United Kingdom. TEL 44-20-82675000, healthcare.republic@haymarket.com, http://www.healthcarerepublic.com. Ed. Jenny Gowans TEL 44-20-82674614. Adv. contact Rob Nuzzaci TEL 44-20-82674884. Circ: 41,488. **Subscr. to:** 12-13 Cranleigh Gardens Industrial Estate, Southall UB1 2DB, United Kingdom. TEL 44-8451-557355, FAX 44-8451-948840, subscriptions@haymarket.com, http://www.haymarketbusinesssubs.com.

615.19 AUS ISSN 0725-4709
RS153 CODEN: IJSMDA
M I M S ANNUAL. (Monthly Index of Medical Specialties) Text in English. 1977. a. AUD 195 (effective 2008). adv. charts. **Document type:** *Directory, Trade.* **Description:** Provides information on all pharmaceuticals available for prescription in Australia.
Incorporates (1966-1978): Australian Drug Compendium (0313-6191)
Related titles: CD-ROM ed.
—IE.
Published by: M I M S Australia (Subsidiary of: C M P Medica Australia Pty Ltd), PO Box 3000, St Leonards, NSW 1590, Australia. TEL 61-2-99027700, FAX 61-2-99027701, info@mims.com.au. Ed. Amanda Caswell. Pub. Chris Wills. Adv. contact Sue McElroyy. Circ: 24,000.

615.19 AUS ISSN 1035-5723
M I M S BI-MONTHLY. (Monthly Index of Medical Specialties) Text in English. 1963. bi-m. AUD 164 (effective 2008). **Document type:** *Directory, Trade.* **Description:** Contains abbreviated information on all prescription and many non-prescription medicines, including over-the-counter complementary medicines.
Related titles: CD-ROM ed.
Indexed: Inpharma.
—IE.
Published by: M I M S Australia (Subsidiary of: C M P Medica Australia Pty Ltd), PO Box 3000, St Leonards, NSW 1590, Australia. TEL 61-2-99027700, FAX 61-2-99027701, info@mims.com.au. Ed. Amanda Caswell. Pub. Chris Wills. Adv. contact Sue McElroy. Circ: 28,000.

615 ZAF ISSN 0076-8847
M I M S DESK REFERENCE. (Monthly Index of Medical Specialties) Text in English. 1965. a. ZAR 350 domestic; ZAR 516 in United States; ZAR 528 in Europe; ZAR 547 in Australia & New Zealand (effective 2000). adv. index. **Description:** Contains full product information on human medicines, tablet and capsule identification chart, and a reference section.
Formerly: M I M S Reference Manual
Published by: M I M S (Subsidiary of: Johnnic Communications Ltd.), 83 Hendrik Verwoerd Dr, Gauteng, 2194, South Africa. TEL 27-12-3485010, FAX 27-12-3617716. Ed. Jacques Snyman. Adv. contact Peter McGonigle. Circ: 6,800.

615.1 NZL ISSN 1176-5844
M I M S NEW ETHICALS. (Monthly Index of Medical Specialties) Text in English. 1966. 2/yr. NZD 310 domestic; NZD 350 foreign (effective 2008). adv. **Document type:** *Journal, Academic/Scholarly.* **Description:** Provides basic details of brand name pharmaceutical products available in New Zealand.
Former titles (until 2004): New Ethicals Catalogue (0110-9510); (until 1975): Catalogue of Drugs; Incorporates (1998-200?): New Ethicals Journal (1174-4502); Which was formed by the merger of (1972-1998): New Zealand Patient Management (1172-630X); Which was formerly (until 1985): Patient Management (0110-4578); (1964-1998): New Ethicals (0111-0020); Which was formerly (until 1976): New Ethicals and Medical Progress (0548-4545); (until 1967): New Ethicals
Related titles: ◆ Supplement to: New Ethicals Journal. ISSN 1174-4502.
—GNLM. **CCC.**
Published by: CMPMedica New Zealand Ltd. (Subsidiary of: United Business Media Limited), 3 Shea Terrace, Takapuna, Auckland, New Zealand. TEL 64-9-4884278, FAX 64-9-4886240, http://www.cmpmedica.co.nz. Adv. contact Rhonda Jackson TEL 64-9-4884274. page NZD 4,880; trim 133 x 197. Circ: 6,000.

615 USA
M P R (HEMATOLOGY/ONCOLOGY EDITION). (Monthly Prescribing Reference) Text in English. 2008 (Feb.). q. USD 32 domestic; USD 56 foreign; USD 16 per issue domestic; USD 21 per issue foreign (effective 2008). adv. **Document type:** *Handbook/Manual/Guide, Trade.* **Description:** Consists of all hematologic and oncologic agents used at the point of chemotherapeutic intervention and for supportive therapy, including anti-emetics, pain medications, anti-infectives, NSAIDs, laxatives etc.
Published by: Prescribing Reference, Inc. (Subsidiary of: Haymarket Group Ltd.), 114 W 26th St, 4th Fl, New York, NY 10001. TEL 646-638-6000, FAX 646-638-6117. Adv. contact Don Bruccoleri TEL 646-638-6007. B&W page USD 6,920, color page USD 9,870; trim 5.25 x 8.25. Circ: 20,974 (controlled).

615 USA ISSN 1938-9531
RM301.12
M P R (LONG TERM CARE EDITION). (Monthly Prescribing Reference) Text in English. 2006. q. USD 32 domestic; USD 56 foreign; USD 16 per issue domestic; USD 21 per issue foreign (effective 2008). adv. back issues avail.; reprints avail. **Document type:** *Magazine, Trade.* **Description:** Provides prescribing information to Physicians specializing in long-term care, Medical Directors, Geriatric Psychiatrists, Geriatric PAs & NPs, Consultant Pharmacists, and Directors of Nursing.
Related titles: Online - full text ed.
Indexed: A01.
—CCC.
Published by: Prescribing Reference, Inc. (Subsidiary of: Haymarket Group Ltd.), 114 W 26th St, 4th Fl, New York, NY 10001. TEL 646-638-6000, FAX 646-638-6117, Online@PrescribingRef.com. Eds. Anissa Lee, Diana Ernst. Pub. James Pantaleo TEL 646-638-6137. Adv. contact Don Bruccoleri TEL 646-638-6007. Circ: 43,057 (paid).

615 618.1 USA
M P R (OBSTETRICIAN & GYNECOLOGIST EDITION). (Monthly Prescribing Reference) Variant title: Prescribing Reference for Obstetricians and Gynecologists. Text in English. 1991. q. USD 32 domestic; USD 56 foreign; USD 16 per issue domestic; USD 21 per issue foreign (effective 2008). adv. back issues avail.; reprints avail. **Document type:** *Magazine, Trade.* **Description:** Provides prescribing information to Physicians and Residents specializing in obstetrics and gynecology.
Formerly: Prescribing Reference for Obstetricians and Gynecologists (1051-4171)
Related titles: Online - full text ed.
Indexed: A01, A26, E08, H11, H12, I05, S09.
—CCC.
Published by: Prescribing Reference, Inc. (Subsidiary of: Haymarket Group Ltd.), 114 W 26th St, 4th Fl, New York, NY 10001. TEL 646-638-6000, FAX 646-638-6117, Online@PrescribingRef.com. Eds. Anissa Lee, Diana Ernst. Pub. James Pantaleo TEL 646-638-6137. Adv. contact Don Bruccoleri TEL 646-638-6007. Circ: 36,862 (paid).

615 USA
M P R (PEDIATRICIANS' EDITION). (Monthly Prescribing Reference) Text in English. 1990. s-a. USD 28 domestic; USD 44 foreign; USD 16 per issue domestic; USD 21 per issue foreign (effective 2008). adv. back issues avail.; reprints avail. **Document type:** *Magazine, Trade.* **Description:** Provides prescribing information to Physicians and Residents specializing in pediatrics.
Formerly: Prescribing Reference for Pediatricians (1051-3280)
Related titles: Online - full text ed.
Indexed: A01, A26, H11, H12, I05.
—CCC.
Published by: Prescribing Reference, Inc. (Subsidiary of: Haymarket Group Ltd.), 114 W 26th St, 4th Fl, New York, NY 10001. TEL 646-638-6000, FAX 646-638-6117, Online@PrescribingRef.com. Eds. Anissa Lee, Diana Ernst. Pub. James Pantaleo TEL 646-638-6137. Adv. contact Don Bruccoleri TEL 646-638-6007. Circ: 45,078 (paid).

615 USA ISSN 1938-9523
RM301.12
M P R (PHARMACISTS' EDITION). (Monthly Prescribing Reference) Text in English. 2007. quinquennial. USD 32 domestic; USD 56 foreign; USD 16 per issue domestic; USD 21 per issue foreign (effective 2008). adv. **Document type:** *Handbook/Manual/Guide, Trade.* **Description:** Concise drug reference designed to help community pharmacists to make appropriate drug therapy decisions in their daily practice.
Indexed: A01, A26, E08, H12, I05, S09.
—CCC.
Published by: Prescribing Reference, Inc. (Subsidiary of: Haymarket Group Ltd.), 114 W 26th St, 4th Fl, New York, NY 10001. TEL 646-638-6000, FAX 646-638-6117. Pub. James Pantaleo TEL 646-638-6137. Adv. contact Don Bruccoleri TEL 646-638-6007. B&W page USD 9,250; trim 5.25 x 8.25. Circ: 57,445 (controlled).

615 USA
RS125
M P R (RESIDENTS' EDITION). (Monthly Prescribing Reference) Text in English. 1992. s-a. USD 28 domestic; USD 44 foreign; USD 16 per issue domestic; USD 24 per issue foreign (effective 2008). adv. **Document type:** *Magazine, Trade.* **Description:** Provides prescribing information to primary care Residents and Interns.
Formerly: Residents' Prescribing Reference (1061-6632)
Indexed: A01, A26, H11, H12, I05.
—CCC.
Published by: Prescribing Reference, Inc. (Subsidiary of: Haymarket Group Ltd.), 114 W 26th St, 4th Fl, New York, NY 10001. TEL 646-638-6000, FAX 646-638-6117. Pub. James Pantaleo TEL 646-638-6137. Adv. contact Don Bruccoleri TEL 646-638-6007. B&W page USD 6,070; trim 5.25 x 8.25. Circ: 15,000 (controlled).

615 616.6 USA ISSN 1938-9515
RM375
M P R (UROLOGISTS EDITION). (Monthly Prescribing Reference) Text in English. 2004. q. USD 28 domestic; USD 44 foreign; USD 16 per issue domestic; USD 21 per issue foreign (effective 2008). adv. back issues avail.; reprints avail. **Document type:** *Magazine, Trade.* **Description:** Provides prescribing information to Physicians and Residents specializing in urology.
Related titles: Online - full text ed.
Indexed: A01, A26, E08, H12, I05, S09.
—CCC.
Published by: Prescribing Reference, Inc. (Subsidiary of: Haymarket Group Ltd.), 114 W 26th St, 4th Fl, New York, NY 10001. TEL 646-638-6000, FAX 646-638-6117, Online@PrescribingRef.com. Eds. Anissa Lee, Diana Ernst. Pub. James Pantaleo TEL 646-638-6137. Adv. contact Don Bruccoleri TEL 646-638-6007. Circ: 8,590 (paid).

615 GBR
MACROVIEW. Text in English. 2004. 10/m. **Document type:** *Newsletter, Trade.* **Description:** Contains news and information on the macro forces in politics, economics, technology and demographics that are affecting the pharmaceutical marketplace.
Media: Online - full content.
Published by: Wood Mackenzie, Kintore House, 74-77 Queen St, Edinburgh, EH2 4NS, United Kingdom. TEL 44-131-2434400, FAX 44-131-2434495, info@woodmac.com.

MAGNESIUM RESEARCH (ONLINE). *see* MEDICAL SCIENCES

MAJOR PHARMACEUTICAL AND BIOTECHNOLOGY COMPANIES OF THE WORLD (YEAR). *see* BUSINESS AND ECONOMICS—Trade And Industrial Directories

615 MKD ISSN 1409-8695
MAKEDONSKO FARMACEVTSKI BILTEN. Text in Macedonian, English. 2001. s-a. **Document type:** *Bulletin.*
—BLDSC (0098.520000).
Published by: Makedonsko Farmacevtsko Drustvo/Macedonian Pharmaceutical Association, c/o Svetlana Kulevanova, Faculty of pharmacy, Vodnjanska 17, Skopje, 1000, Macedonia. svku@baba.ff.ukim.edu.mk. Ed. Svetlana Kulevanova. Circ: 500.

615 MYS ISSN 1675-7319
MALAYSIAN JOURNAL OF PHARMACEUTICAL SCIENCES. Text in English. 2003. a. **Document type:** *Journal, Academic/Scholarly.*
Related titles: Online - full text ed.: ISSN 1985-8396. free (effective 2011).
Indexed: A34, A35, AgrForAb, CABA, E12, F08, GH, H16, N02, N03, T05, W10.
Published by: (Universiti Sains Malaysia, School of Pharmaceutical Sciences), Penerbit Universiti Sains Malaysia/Universiti Sains Malaysia Press, Pulau Pinang, Pinang 11800, Malaysia. TEL 60-4-6537788 ext 4425, 4421, FAX 60-4-6575714, penerbit@notes.usm.my, http://www.penerbit.usm.my. Ed. Ab Fatah Ab Rahman.

615 USA ISSN 2152-2138
▼ **MALOY GROUP NEWSLETTER.** Text in English. 2009. m. free to qualified personnel (effective 2010). back issues avail. **Document type:** *Newsletter, Trade.* **Description:** Contains information on topics and events of interest to the various stakeholders in the healthcare products industry.
Media: Online - full text.
Published by: The Maloy Group, Llc, 13718 Queensgate Rd, Midlothian, VA 23114. TEL 804-615-6791.

615 USA ISSN 1540-2355
MANAGED CARE PHARMACY UPDATE. Text in English. 2002 (June). irreg.
Indexed: SCOPUS.
—CCC.
Published by: Excerpta Medica, Inc. (Subsidiary of: Elsevier Health Sciences), 685 US-202, Bridgewater, NJ 08807. TEL 908-547-2100, FAX 908-547-2200, excerptamedica@elsevier.com, http://www.excerptamedica.com/.

615 USA ISSN 1931-146X
RM302
MANAGING CLINICALLY IMPORTANT DRUG INTERACTIONS. Text in English. 2002. a., latest 2007. USD 94.95 per issue (effective 2007).
Document type: *Handbook/Manual/Guide, Trade.*
Published by: (Hansten and Horn), Facts and Comparisons (Subsidiary of: Wolters Kluwer N.V.), 77 West Port Plz, Ste 450, St. Louis, MO 63146. TEL 800-223-0554, FAX 317-735-5390, http://www.factsandcomparisons.com. Eds. Dr. John R Horn, Dr. Philip D Hansten.

615.19 CHE ISSN 1660-3397
RS160.7 CODEN: MDARE6
➤ **MARINE DRUGS.** Text in English. 2003. q. free (effective 2011).
Document type: *Journal, Academic/Scholarly.* **Description:** Contains information on the research, development and production of drugs from the sea, including marine natural product chemistry.
Media: Online - full text.
Indexed: A34, A35, A36, ASFA, AgBio, B21, B23, B25, B27, BIOSIS Prev, BP, C25, C30, CABA, E04, E05, E12, EMBASE, ExcerpMed, F08, F12, FCA, GH, H16, H17, I11, IndVet, LT, MEDLINE, MycolAb, N02, N03, N04, P30, P32, P33, P39, P40, PGegResA, R07, R08, R13, RA&MP, RM&VM, RRTA, S12, S13, S16, SCI, SCOPUS, SoyAb, T02, T05, TAR, VS, W07, W10.
Published by: M D P I AG, Postfach, Basel, 4005, Switzerland. TEL 41-61-6837734, FAX 41-61-3028918. Pub. Shu-Kun Lin.

615.1 658 NLD ISSN 0929-8444
MARKETING RESULTS; vakblad voor verkopers van drogisterijartikelen. Text in Dutch. 1988. 20/yr. EUR 78.50 (effective 2010). adv. illus.
Document type: *Journal, Trade.* **Description:** Covers the retail market for personal health care products.
Published by: Mons Media bv, Postbus 45, Ravenstein, 5370 AA, Netherlands. TEL 31-486-417277, FAX 31-486-417279, info@monsmedia.nl. Ed. Franca van Dalen. Pubs. Frans Akkermans, Ryan Hoogenboom. adv.: B&W page EUR 3,695; trim 210 x 297. Circ: 8,100.

615 GBR
MARTINDALE: THE COMPLETE DRUG REFERENCE. Text in English. 1883. triennial. GBP 399.99 per issue; GBP 499.99 combined subscription per issue (print & online eds.) (effective 2011). adv. index. **Document type:** *Journal, Academic/Scholarly.* **Description:** Provides a concise summary of the properties, actions and uses of drugs and medicines for the practising pharmacists and medical practitioners.
Formerly (until 2001): Martindale: the Extra Pharmacopoeia (0263-5364); Incorporates: Squires Companion
Related titles: CD-ROM ed.; Online - full text ed.: GBP 239 (effective 2011).
—CCC.
Published by: (Royal Pharmaceutical Society of Great Britain), Pharmaceutical Press (Subsidiary of: Royal Pharmaceutical Society of Great Britain), 1 Lambeth High St, London, SE1 7JN, United Kingdom. TEL 44-20-75722665, FAX 44-20-75722509, pharmpress@macmillansolutions.com. Ed. Sean C Sweetman. Pub. Lindsey Fountain TEL 44-20-75722655. **Dist. in U.S. by:** Rittenhouse Book Distributors, 61565, Kng Of Prussa, PA 19406-0965. customerservice@rittenhouse.com.

615.1 USA ISSN 0025-4347
MARYLAND PHARMACIST. Text in English. 1925. q. USD 30 (effective 2005). adv. bk.rev. charts; illus. **Document type:** *Magazine, Trade.*
Indexed: ChemAb.
—Linda Hall.
Published by: Maryland Pharmacists Association, 650 W Lombard St, Baltimore, MD 21201. TEL 410-727-0746, FAX 410-727-2253, hschiff@marylandpharmacist.org, http://www.marylandpharmacist.org. Ed. Howard Schiff. R&P, Adv. contact Elsie Prince. page USD 450; trim 11 x 8.5. Circ: 1,000 (controlled).

615.1 378 USA ISSN 0025-4789
MASSACHUSETTS COLLEGE OF PHARMACY. BULLETIN. Text in English. 1911. s-a. free to qualified personnel. illus. **Document type:** *Bulletin.* **Description:** Contains organization news.
Related titles: Online - full text ed.: free.
Published by: Massachusetts College of Pharmacy and Allied Health Sciences, 179 Longwood Ave, Boston, MA 02115. TEL 617-732-2800, FAX 617-732-2801. Ed. George E Humphrey. Circ: 9,500 (controlled).

615 USA ISSN 1931-5481
RS105
MASTER THE P C A T. (Pharmacy College Admission Test) Text in English. irreg. (9th ed.), latest 2006. USD 18.99 per issue (effective 2007). **Document type:** *Guide, Academic/Scholarly.*
Former titles (until 2005): P C A T Success (1551-4099); P C A T
Published by: Peterson's A R C O (Subsidiary of: Thomson Reuters Corp.), PO Box 67005, Lawrenceville, NJ 08648. TEL 1-609-896-1800, http://www.petersons.com.

MEALEY'S DIET DRUGS REPORT. *see* LAW

MEALEY'S LITIGATION REPORT: ANTIDEPRESSANT DRUGS. *see* LAW

MEALEY'S LITIGATION REPORT: ARTHRITIS DRUGS. *see* LAW—Civil Law

344.04233 615.35 USA ISSN 1097-5497
KF1297.D7
MEALEY'S LITIGATION REPORT: FEN-PHEN - REDUX. Text in English. 1997 (Nov.). m. looseleaf. USD 1,065 (effective 2008). adv. index. back issues avail. **Document type:** *Newsletter, Trade.* **Description:** Provides detailed coverage of the litigation surrounding fen-phen, Redux and other diet drugs.
Related titles: Diskette ed.; Online - full text ed.: USD 930 (effective 2002).
—CCC.
Published by: Mealey Publications & Conferences Group (Subsidiary of: LexisNexis North America), 1018 W 9th Ave, 3rd Fl, King of Prussia, PA 19406. TEL 610-768-7800, 800-632-5397, FAX 610-962-4991, info@mealeys.com, http://www.mealeys.com. Ed. Michael Lefkowitz. Pub. Tom Hagy. R&Ps Scott M. Jacobs, Tom Hagy.

MEALEY'S LITIGATION REPORT: HEART DRUGS & DEVICES. *see* LAW

615 USA ISSN 1541-2814
KF1297.D7
MEALEY'S LITIGATION REPORT: THIMEROSAL & VACCINES. Text in English. 2002 (July). m. USD 1,129 (effective 2011). **Document type:** *Report, Trade.* **Description:** Tracks the litigation surrounding vaccines, including thimerosal, a mercury-containing preservative. Other vaccine-related litigation in state and federal courts will be covered, as well as the National Childhood Vaccine Injury Program.
Related titles: Online - full text ed.: ISSN 2158-5792.
—CCC.
Published by: LexisNexis (Subsidiary of: Reed Elsevier Group plc), 1016 W Ninth Ave, 1st Fl, King of Prussia, PA 19406. TEL 215 564-1788, 800 448-1515, customer.support@lexisnexis.com. Ed. Michael Lefkowitz.

MED AD NEWS. *see* BUSINESS AND ECONOMICS—Marketing And Purchasing

▼ **MEDCHEMCOMM.** *see* BIOLOGY—Biochemistry

615 GBR ISSN 1474-9610
MEDICAL DEVICE DEVELOPMENTS. Text in English. 1997. s-a. GBP 5.95 per issue domestic; EUR 8 per issue in Europe; USD 8.95 per issue in United States; free to qualified personnel (effective 2010).
Document type: *Journal, Trade.* **Description:** Contains technical articles and case histories on leading edge developments, new products and applications, drawing on the expertise of leading engineers and designers from around the globe.
Formerly (until 2001): Medical Manufacturing International (1365-8786)
Related titles: Online - full text ed.
Published by: S P G Media Ltd. (Subsidiary of: Sterling Publishing Group Plc.), Brunel House, 55-57 N Wharf Rd, London, W2 1LA, United Kingdom. TEL 44-20-79159660, FAX 44-20-77242089, info@spgmedia.com, http://www.spgmedia.com/. Eds. Andrew Tunniccliffe, John Lawrence. Pub. William Crocker.

615 USA ISSN 0897-5418
➤ **THE MEDICAL LETTER HANDBOOK OF ADVERSE DRUG INTERACTION.** Text in English. 1983. irreg. **Document type:** *Monographic series, Academic/Scholarly.*
Formerly (until 1985): Medical Letter Handbook of Drug Interactions
Published by: Medical Letter, Inc., 145 Huguenot St, Ste 312, New Rochelle, NY 10801. TEL 914-235-0500, 800-211-2769, FAX 914-632-1733, custserv@medicalletter.org, http://secure.medicalletter.org/. Eds. Jean-Marie Pflomm, Dr. Mark Abramowicz.

615 USA ISSN 0025-732X
RM1
➤ **THE MEDICAL LETTER ON DRUGS AND THERAPEUTICS (ENGLISH EDITION).** Text in English. 1959. 26/yr. looseleaf. USD 98 combined subscription to individuals (print & online eds.) (effective 2009). illus.; mkt.; charts. cum.index every 5 yrs. back issues avail.; reprints avail. **Document type:** *Journal, Academic/Scholarly.*
Description: Provides critical evaluations of drugs for physicians and other members of the health professions.
Related titles: Online - full text ed.: ISSN 1523-2859.
Indexed: A22, AIM, ASCA, C06, C07, C08, CINAHL, DentInd, EMBASE, ExcerpMed, FAMLI, H13, I12, IDIS, ISR, IndMed, Inpharma, MEDLINE, P02, P10, P13, P20, P30, P35, P48, P53, P54, PQC, R10, Reac, SCI, SCOPUS, W07.
—BLDSC (5529.700000), GNLM, IE, Infotrieve, Ingenta, INIST. **CCC.**
Published by: Medical Letter, Inc., 145 Huguenot St, Ste 312, New Rochelle, NY 10801. TEL 914-235-0500, 800-211-2769, FAX 914-632-1733, custserv@medicalletter.org. Eds. Jean-Marie Pflomm, Dr. Mark Abramowicz.

615 CHE ISSN 0253-8512
THE MEDICAL LETTER ON DRUGS AND THERAPEUTICS (FRENCH EDITION). Text in French. 1978. 26/yr. CHF 88, EUR 57.14 domestic; CHF 90, EUR 58.44 foreign (effective 2002). **Document type:** *Journal, Academic/Scholarly.*
—INIST.
Published by: Editions Medecine et Hygiene, Chemin de la Mousse 46, CP 475, Chene-Bourg 4, 1225, Switzerland. TEL 41-22-7029311, FAX 41-22-7029355, abonnements@medhyg.ch, http://www.medhyg.ch.

615 ITA ISSN 0393-9391
THE MEDICAL LETTER ON DRUGS AND THERAPEUTICS (ITALIAN EDITION). Abbreviated title: The Medical Letter. Text in Italian. 1972. bi-w. EUR 60 (effective 2009). **Document type:** *Journal, Trade.*
Published by: C I S Editore S.r.l., Via San Siro 1, Milan, 20149, Italy. TEL 39-02-4694542, FAX 39-02-48193584, http://www.ciseditore.it.

613 USA ISSN 0214-3178
THE MEDICAL LETTER ON DRUGS AND THERAPEUTICS (SPANISH EDITION). Text in Spanish. 1979. bi-w. looseleaf. USD 55 (effective 2011). index. back issues avail. **Document type:** *Journal, Academic/Scholarly.*
—CCC.
Published by: Medical Letter, Inc., 145 Huguenot St, Ste 312, New Rochelle, NY 10801. TEL 914-235-0500, 800-211-2769, FAX 914-632-1733, custserv@medicalletter.org.

610 658.8 USA ISSN 0025-7354
HD9665.1 CODEN: MMKMBX
MEDICAL MARKETING & MEDIA. Abbreviated title: M M & M. Text in English. 1966. m. USD 148 domestic; USD 178 in Canada; USD 248 elsewhere (effective 2009). adv. bk.rev. charts; illus.; stat. index. back issues avail.; reprints avail. **Document type:** *Magazine, Trade.*
Description: Contains a mix of industry news and in-depth feature articles on marketing and promotion.
Formerly (until 1969): Pharmaceutical Marketing and Media
Related titles: Microfilm ed.: (from PQC); Online - full text ed.; Supplement(s): M M & M Healthcare Advertising Goldbook.
Indexed: A12, A13, A15, A17, A22, A26, ABIn, B01, B03, B06, B07, B08, B09, B11, BPIA, C06, C07, C08, CA, CINAHL, CWI, G06, G07, G08, H01, H12, H13, I05, P10, P20, P21, P24, P30, P34, P48, P51, P53, P54, PQC, T02, T03.
—BLDSC (5529.950000), GNLM, IE, Infotrieve, Ingenta. **CCC.**
Published by: Haymarket Media Inc. (Subsidiary of: Haymarket Group Ltd.), 114 W 26th St, 4th Fl, New York, NY 10001. TEL 646-638-6000, FAX 646-638-6117, custserv@haymarketmedia.com, http://www.haymarket.com. Eds. Matthew Arnold, James Chase. Pub. Scott Dattoli. adv.: B&W page USD 5,444, color page USD 7,647; trim 8.25 x 10.875. Circ: 4,000 (paid and controlled).

615.1 JPN ISSN 0025-7427
MEDICAL PHARMACY. Text in Japanese. 1967. bi-m. adv. Index.
Document type: *Journal, Academic/Scholarly.*
Indexed: ChemAb.
Published by: Daiichi Seiyaku Co. Ltd./Daiichi Pharmaceutical Co., Ltd., 14-10, Nihonbashi 3-chome, Chuo-ku, Tokyo, 103-8234, Japan. TEL 81-3-32720611, http://www.daiichipharm.co.jp/. Circ: 6,500.

615 PRT ISSN 1647-3787
▼ **MEDICAL TAPING CONCEPT BULLETIN.** Text in Portuguese. 2009. irreg. **Document type:** *Bulletin, Trade.*
Related titles: ◆ Portuguese ed.: Noticias de Bandas Neuromusculares. ISSN 1647-3795; ◆ Spanish ed.: Noticias de Vendaje Neuromuscolar. ISSN 1647-2012.
Published by: ANEID, Productos Farmaceuticos, Rua Jose Florindo - Quinta da Pedra 44 D, Cascais, 2750-401, Portugal. TEL 351-21-4849620, info@aneid.pt, http://www.aneid.pt.

THE MEDICAL TECHNOLOGY ACQUISITION RECORD. *see* BUSINESS AND ECONOMICS—Banking And Finance

615 PRT ISSN 0872-2331
MEDICAMENTO, HISTORIA E SOCIEDADE. Text in Portuguese. 1989. 3/yr. **Document type:** *Journal, Academic/Scholarly.*
Indexed: P30.
Published by: Associacao Nacional das Farmacias (A N F), Rua Marechal Saldanha 1, Lisbon, 1249-069, Portugal. TEL 351-21-3400600, FAX 351-21-3472994, http://www.anf.pt.

615 USA ISSN 1934-2187
RJ216
MEDICATIONS AND MOTHERS' MILK. Text in English. 1992. biennial.
Published by: Pharmasoft Medical Publishing, 1712 N Forest St, Amarillo, TX 79106-7017. TEL 806-376-9900, FAX 806-376-9901.

615 DNK ISSN 1603-4783
MEDICIN OG MENING; information og nyheder fra medicinalindustrien i Danmark. Text in Danish. 2003. s-a. free. back issues avail.
Document type: *Newsletter, Consumer.*
Related titles: Online - full text ed.
Published by: Laegemiddelindustriforeningen/Association of Danish Pharmaceutical Industry, Stroedamvej 50 A, Copenhagen Oe, 2100, Denmark. TEL 45-39-276060, FAX 45-39-276070, info@tifdk.dk, http://www.tifdk.dk. Circ: 167,000 (controlled and free).

615.1 DNK ISSN 1902-1453
MEDICIN.DK. Text in Danish. 1964. a. DKK 940 print ed.; DKK 456 online ed. (effective 2009). **Document type:** *Catalog, Trade.* **Description:** Descriptions of currently marketed medications.
Former titles (until 2006): Laegemiddelkataloget (0105-287X); (until 1976): M E F A Katalog
Related titles: Online - full text ed.: ISSN 1902-147X. 200?.
—CCC.
Published by: Infomatum A/S, Stroedamsvej 50 A, Copenhagen OE, 2100, Denmark. TEL 45-39-150950, kontakt@infomatum.dk, http://www.infomatum.dk. Ed. Court Pedersen.

615.1 DNK ISSN 1902-1461
RS153
MEDICIN.DK, KITTELBOGEN. Text in Danish. 1963. a. DKK 575 per issue (effective 2009). **Document type:** *Catalog, Trade.*
Formerly (until 2006): Laegeforeningens Medicinfortegnelse (0106-1275)
Published by: Infomatum A/S, Stroedamsvej 50 A, Copenhagen OE, 2100, Denmark. TEL 45-39-150950, kontakt@infomatum.dk, http://www.infomatum.dk. Ed. Court Pedersen.

615.1 ESP ISSN 1134-248X
CODEN: MPALF5
➤ **MEDICINA PALIATIVA.** Text in Spanish; Abstracts in Spanish, English. 1994. q. EUR 59 to qualified personnel; EUR 100 to institutions; EUR 44 to students (effective 2007). adv. abstr.; bibl.; illus.; stat. back issues avail. **Document type:** *Journal, Academic/Scholarly.*
Related titles: Online - full text ed.
Indexed: B21, CTA, EMBASE, ExcerpMed, R10, Reac, SCI, SCOPUS, W07.
—BLDSC (5533.637000), INIST. **CCC.**
Published by: (Sociedad Espanola de Cuidados Paliativos/Spanish Society of Palliative Medicine), Aran Ediciones, Castello 128, 1o, Madrid, 28006, Spain. TEL 34-91-7820030, FAX 34-91-5615787, edita@grupoaran.com, http://www.grupoaran.com. Ed. Maria Nabal Vicuna. Pub. Jose Jimenez Marquez. R&P Maria Dolores Linares TEL 34-91-7820035.

615.19 IND
MEDICINAL CHEMISTRY; an Indian journal. Text in English. 4/yr.
Document type: *Journal, Academic/Scholarly.* **Description:** Publishes fundamental research papers on all phases of medicinal chemistry.
Related titles: Online - full text ed.
Published by: Trade Science, Inc., 126, Prasheel Park, SanjayRaj Farm House, Nr. Saurashtra University, Rajkot, Gujarat 360 005, India. tsijournals@tsijournals.com.

MEDICINAL CHEMISTRY. *see* MEDICAL SCIENCES

▼ **MEDICINAL PLANTS.** *see* BIOLOGY—Botany

615.19 USA ISSN 0198-6325
RM300 CODEN: MRREDD
➤ **MEDICINAL RESEARCH REVIEWS.** Text in English. 1981. bi-m. GBP 1,415 in United Kingdom to institutions; EUR 1,789 in Europe to institutions; USD 2,647 in United States to institutions; USD 2,731 in Canada & Mexico to institutions; USD 2,773 elsewhere to institutions; GBP 1,628 combined subscription in United Kingdom to institutions (print & online eds.); EUR 2,058 combined subscription in Europe to institutions (print & online eds.); USD 3,045 combined subscription in United States to institutions (print & online eds.); USD 3,129 combined subscription in Canada & Mexico to institutions (print & online eds.); USD 3,171 combined subscription elsewhere to institutions (print & online eds.) (effective 2012). adv. back issues avail.; reprint service avail. from PSC. **Document type:** *Journal, Academic/Scholarly.* **Description:** Embraces all aspects of research addressing the study of disease and the consequent development of therapeutic agents.
Related titles: Microform ed.: (from PQC); Online - full text ed.: ISSN 1098-1128. 1996. GBP 1,351 in United Kingdom to institutions; EUR 1,708 in Europe to institutions; USD 2,647 elsewhere to institutions (effective 2012).

P

Indexed: A22, ASCA, B21, BIOBASE, BIOSIS Prev, C31, ChemAb, ChemTitl, CurCR, CurCont, DBA, EMBASE, ESPM, ExcerpMed, I10, IABS, ISR, ImmunAb, IndMed, Inpharma, MEDLINE, MycolAb, NSA, P30, R10, R16, Reac, RefZh, SCI, SCOPUS, T02, VirolAbstr, W07.
—BLDSC (5533.992000), CASDDS, GNLM, IE, Infotrieve, Ingenta, INIST, Linda Hall. **CCC.**
Published by: John Wiley & Sons, Inc., 111 River St, Hoboken, NJ 07030. TEL 201-748-6000, FAX 201-748-6088, info@wiley.com, http://www.wiley.com/WileyCDA/. Ed. Binghe Wang. Pub., Adv. contact Kim Thompkins TEL 212-850-6921. **Subscr. outside the Americas to:** John Wiley & Sons Ltd., The Atrium, Southern Gate, Chichester, West Sussex PO19 8SQ, United Kingdom. TEL 44-1243-779777, FAX 44-1243-775878, cs-journals@wiley.com.

615.1742 340 GBR ISSN 1465-6663
MEDICINE, ETHICS AND PRACTICE. Text in English. 1988. s-a. **Document type:** *Journal, Trade.* **Description:** Designed to be a practical guide to the legal restrictions on the sale or supply of medicinal products and poisons.
Formerly (until 1989): Medicine and Ethics (0955-4254)
Related titles: Online - full text ed.
Indexed: P30.
—CCC.
Published by: Royal Pharmaceutical Society of Great Britain, 1 Lambeth High St, London, SE1 7JN, United Kingdom. TEL 44-20-77359141, FAX 44-20-77357327, enquiries@rpsgb.org.

615 DNK ISSN 1602-8910
MEDICINPRISER. Text in Danish. 193?. bi-w. DKK 1,373 Print Edition (effective 2009). **Document type:** *Government.*
Formerly (until 2003): Specialitetstakst (0909-9905)
Related titles: Online - full text ed.
Published by: Laegemiddelstyrelsen/Danish Medicines Agency, Axel Heides Gade 1, Copenhagen S, 2300, Denmark. TEL 45-44-889595, FAX 45-44-889599, dkma@dkma.dk, http://www.dkma.dk.

▼ **MEDICOLEGAL AND BIOETHICS.** *see* LAW

615.19 610 NGA ISSN 0331-4782
MEDIPHARM. Text in English. 1969. a. USD 130 (effective 2000). **Document type:** *Abstract/Index.* **Description:** Covers pharmaceutical specialties in Nigeria.
—GNLM.
Published by: Literamed Publications Nigeria Ltd, PMB 21068, Ikeja, Oregun Village, Lagos, Nigeria. TEL 234-64-962512, FAX 234-64-961037. Ed. L A Aladesuyi. Pub. O M Lawar Solarin. Circ: 10,000.

615.1 NLD ISSN 0168-7670
MEDISCH - FARMACEUTISCHE MEDELINGEN. Text in Dutch. 1963. 10/yr. EUR 104, USD 156 combined subscription to institutions (print & online eds.) (effective 2009). **Document type:** *Journal, Academic/Scholarly.* **Description:** Reports on pharmaceutical research.
Related titles: Online - full text ed.: ISSN 1876-5971.
Indexed: A22, E01.
Published by: Bohn Stafleu van Loghum B.V. (Subsidiary of: Springer Science+Business Media), Postbus 246, Houten, 3990 GA, Netherlands. TEL 31-30-6383872, FAX 31-30-6383991, boekhandels@bsl.nl, http://www.bsl.nl. Ed. J M A Sitsen.

MEDITSINSKII BIZNES. *see* INSTRUMENTS

615 DEU ISSN 0939-6292
MEDIZIN OHNE NEBENWIRKUNGEN. Text in German. q. EUR 55.14 domestic; EUR 74.14 foreign; EUR 42.06 domestic to students; EUR 61.06 foreign to students; EUR 14.02 per issue (effective 2003). **Document type:** *Journal, Academic/Scholarly.*
—GNLM. **CCC.**
Published by: Urban und Vogel Medien und Medizin Verlagsgesellschaft mbH (Subsidiary of: Springer Science+Business Media), Neumarkter Str 43, Munich, 81673, Germany. TEL 49-89-43721411, FAX 49-89-43721410, verlag@urban-vogel.de. Ed. Dr. Dirk Einecke. Adv. contact Barbara Kanters. **Subscr. to:** Springer Distribution Center, Kundenservice Zeitschriften, Haberstr 7, Heidelberg 69126, Germany. TEL 49-6221-345-0, FAX 49-6221-345-4229, subscriptions@springer.com.

615.2 DEU ISSN 0934-9170
CODEN: MEKOEK
MEDIZINISCH-PHARMAKOLOGISCHES KOMPENDIUM. Text in German. 1985. irreg., latest vol.19, 2008. price varies. **Document type:** *Monographic series, Academic/Scholarly.*
Published by: Wissenschaftliche Verlagsgesellschaft mbH, Postfach 101061, Stuttgart, 70009, Germany. TEL 49-711-25820, FAX 49-711-2582290, service@wissenschaftliche-verlagsgesellschaft.de, http://www.wissenschaftliche-verlagsgesellschaft.de.

615 JPN ISSN 0543-3975
CODEN: MYDKA7
MEIJI YAKKA DAIGAKU KENKYU KIYO/MEIJI PHARMACEUTICAL UNIVERSITY. BULLETIN. Text in English, Japanese; Summaries in English. 1962. a.
Indexed: ChemAb.
Published by: Meiji Yakka Daigaku/Meiji Pharmaceutical University, 2-522-1, Noshio, Kiyose, Tokyo, 204-8588, Japan.

615 DEU
MEINE APOTHEKE. Text in German. 1987. m. adv. **Document type:** *Magazine, Consumer.*
Published by: Gebr. Storck GmbH & Co. Verlags-oHG, Duisburger Str 375, Oberhausen, 46049, Germany. TEL 49-208-8480211, FAX 49-208-8480238, kalender@storckverlag.de, http://www.storckverlag.de.

MEINE GESUNDHEIT. *see* TRAVEL AND TOURISM

615 FRA ISSN 2109-0939
▼ **MES RECAPS.** Text in French. 2009. bi-m. **Document type:** *Trade.*
Published by: O C P Repartition, 2 Rue Galien, Saint-Ouen Cedex, 93587, France. TEL 33-1-49187575, http://www.point.ocp.fr/OCP/public/text/index.html.

METAL-BASED DRUGS. *see* CHEMISTRY—Analytical Chemistry

615.19 ESP ISSN 0379-0355
RM1 CODEN: MFEPDX
➤ **METHODS AND FINDINGS IN EXPERIMENTAL AND CLINICAL PHARMACOLOGY.** Text in English. 1979. 10/yr. adv. bk.rev. back issues avail. **Document type:** *Journal, Academic/Scholarly.* **Description:** Forum for papers dealing with the methodology employed and the results obtained in the scientific assessment of drugs in animals and humans.
Related titles: Online - full text ed.: ISSN 2013-0155.
Indexed: A22, ASCA, B25, BIOBASE, BIOSIS Prev, ChemAb, ChemTitl, CurCont, DBA, DentInd, EMBASE, ExcerpMed, IABS, IME, ISR, IndMed, Inpharma, MEDLINE, MycolAb, P30, P35, R10, Reac, RefZh, SCI, SCOPUS, W07.
—CASDDS, GNLM, IE, Infotrieve, Ingenta, INIST. **CCC.**
Published by: Prous Science (Subsidiary of: Thomson Reuters), Provenza 388, Barcelona, 08025, Spain. TEL 34-93-4592220, FAX 34-93-4581535, service@prous.com, http://www.prous.com. Ed. L Revel.

615.1 USA ISSN 1557-2153
➤ **METHODS IN PHARMACOLOGY AND TOXICOLOGY.** Text in English. 2001. irreg., latest 2008. price varies. illus. back issues avail.; reprints avail. **Document type:** *Monographic series, Academic/Scholarly.* **Description:** Covers all aspects of pharmacology, including toxicology, physiology, and molecular and cell biology.
Related titles: Online - full text ed.: ISSN 1940-6053.
Indexed: EMBASE, ExcerpMed, GenetAb, SCOPUS, ToxAb, VirolAbstr.
—CCC.
Published by: Humana Press, Inc. (Subsidiary of: Springer Science+Business Media), 233 Spring St, New York, NY 10013. TEL 212-460-1500, FAX 212-460-1575, service-ny@springer.com. Ed. Y James Kang.

615.7 NLD ISSN 0376-7396
RM302.5 CODEN: MSEFDQ
MEYLER'S SIDE EFFECTS OF DRUGS; the encyclopedia of adverse reactions. Text in English. 1956. irreg. (approx. every 4 yrs.), latest vol.15, 2006. price varies. charts; illus. **Document type:** *Monographic series, Trade.* **Description:** Lists the side effects of every type of prescription drug.
Formerly (until 1975): Side Effects of Drugs (0583-1881)
Related titles: CD-ROM ed.; Online - full text ed.; ◆ Supplement(s): Side Effects of Drugs Annual. ISSN 0378-6080.
—BLDSC (5751.800000), CASDDS. **CCC.**
Published by: Elsevier BV (Subsidiary of: Elsevier Science & Technology), Radarweg 29, PO Box 211, Amsterdam, 1000 AE, Netherlands. TEL 31-20-4853911, FAX 31-20-4852457, JournalsCustomerServiceEMEA@elsevier.com, http://www.elsevier.nl. Eds. Jeffrey K Aronson, M N G Dukes.

615.1 USA ISSN 1081-6089
MICHIGAN PHARMACIST. Text in English. 1963. bi-m. USD 40; USD 5 newsstand/cover (effective 2005). adv. bk.rev. charts; illus.; stat. **Document type:** *Magazine, Trade.*
Formerly (until 1995): Journal Michigan Pharmacist (1045-6481)
Related titles: Microform ed.: (from PQC).
Indexed: A22, MCR, MMI.
Published by: Michigan Pharmacists Association, 815 N Washington Ave, Lansing, MI 48906. Ed. Larry D Wagenknecht. adv.: B&W page USD 630, color page USD 1,230; trim 8.5 x 11. Circ: 3,835 (controlled).

MICROBIAL DRUG RESISTANCE; mechanism, epidemiology, and disease. *see* MEDICAL SCIENCES

615.7 GBR ISSN 1461-1732
➤ **MICROSPHERES, MICROCAPSULES & LIPOSOMES.** Text in English. 1999. irreg., latest vol.8. price varies. adv. abstr.; bibl.; charts; illus.; pat.; stat. back issues avail. **Document type:** *Monographic series, Academic/Scholarly.* **Description:** Contains fundamental and state of the art information on microspheres, microcapsules and liposomes, their preparation, properties and applications in chemical and life sciences, medicine, biotechnology and related industries.
Related titles: Diskette ed.
—BLDSC (5879.795100), IE, Ingenta. **CCC.**
Published by: Citus Books, 56B Nutcroft Rd, London, SE15 1AF, United Kingdom. TEL 44-20-76393305, FAX 44-20-76393305, books@citus.globalnet.co.uk, http://www.magneticmicrosphere.com/citus/. Ed., R&P, Adv. contact Reza Arshady.

615.1 USA ISSN 0026-5616
MINNESOTA PHARMACIST. Text in English. 1946. bi-m. adv. charts; illus. **Document type:** *Journal, Trade.*
Indexed: ChemAb, P30.
—Infotrieve.
Published by: Minnesota Pharmacists Association, 1935 County Rd B2 W., Ste. 165, Saint Paul, MN 55113-2795. TEL 800-451-8349, mpha@mpha.org, http://www.mpha.org/. adv.: B&W page USD 640; trim 8.5 x 11. Circ: 5,200 (paid).

616.97 JPN ISSN 0388-4783
MINOPHAGEN MEDICAL REVIEW. Text in Japanese. 1956. bi-m. **Document type:** *Journal, Academic/Scholarly.*
—BLDSC (5810.550000).
Published by: Minofagen Seiyaku Honpo/Minophagen Pharmaceutical Co., 8-10-22 Akasaka, Minato-ku, Tokyo, 107-0052, Japan. TEL 81-3-34026201, FAX 81-3-34026397, http://www.minophagen.co.jp/index_j.html.

615 USA ISSN 0161-3189
MISSISSIPPI PHARMACIST. Text in English. 1975. q. USD 12 (effective 2005). adv. **Document type:** *Magazine, Trade.*
Published by: Mississippi Pharmacists Association, 341 Edgewood Terrace Dr, Jackson, MS 39206-6299. TEL 601-981-0416, FAX 601-981-0451, http://www.mspharm.org. Ed. Bo Balton. Adv. contact Brenda Bland. B&W page USD 360. Circ: 1,750 (controlled).

615.1 USA ISSN 0026-6663
MISSOURI PHARMACIST. Text in English. 1926. q. free membership. adv. bk.rev. **Document type:** *Magazine, Trade.* **Description:** Includes news items, continuing education articles and professional articles of interest to Missouri pharmacists.
Published by: Missouri Pharmaceutical Association, 211 East Capitol Ave, Jefferson City, MO 65101. TEL 573-636-7522, FAX 573-636-7485. Ed., R&P Misty Adolphson. Circ: 1,500 (controlled).

615 ISL ISSN 1021-0075
MIXTURA; blad lyfjafraedinema. Text in Icelandic. 1987. a. free. illus. back issues avail. **Document type:** *Academic/Scholarly.*
Published by: Haskoli Islands, Lyfjafraedinema/University of Iceland. Department of Pharmacy, Hagi, Hofsvallagata 53, Reykjavik, 107, Iceland. TEL 354-525-4353, FAX 354-525-4071, lyf@hi.is, http://www.hi.is/page/fac_Pharmacy.

615 JPN ISSN 0913-2147
MIYAGI-KEN YAKUJI JOHO/MIYAGI PREFECTURE DRUG INFORMATION. Text in Japanese. 1982. s-a. **Document type:** *Academic/Scholarly.*
Incorporates (1990-1996): Miyagiken Yakuji Joho Yakkyoku Yakuten'yo (0917-6209)
Published by: Miyagi-ken Yakuzaishikai/Miyagi Prefecture Pharmaceutical Association, 2-15-26, Ochiai, Aoba-ku, Sendai, Miyagi 989-3126, Japan. TEL 81-22-3911180, FAX 81-22-3916640, http://www.mypha.or.jp/.

615.19 USA ISSN 1940-9257
RS122
➤ **MODERN PHARMACEUTICAL RESEARCH.** Abbreviated title: M P R. Text in English. 2008. m. back issues avail. **Document type:** *Journal, Academic/Scholarly.* **Description:** Covers recent advances and trends in drug discovery, clinical trials, and business strategies in pharmaceutical research.
Published by: Taney Academy of Sciences Inc., 306 Buttry Rd, Gaithersburg, MD 20877. TEL 301-792-8576, mpr@tausa.org.

➤ **MODERN TRENDS IN PHARMACOPSYCHIATRY.** *see* MEDICAL SCIENCES—Psychiatry And Neurology

615 610 GBR ISSN 2040-4085
MOLDOVA PHARMACEUTICALS & HEALTHCARE REPORT. Text in English. 200?. q. EUR 820, USD 1,150 combined subscription (print & email eds.) (effective 2010). **Document type:** *Report, Trade.* **Description:** Provides industry professionals, market investors and corporate and financial services analysts with independent forecasts and competitive intelligence on the Moldovan pharmaceutical & healthcare industry.
Related titles: E-mail ed.
Published by: Business Monitor International Ltd., Senator House, 85 Queen Victoria St, London, EC4V 4AB, United Kingdom. TEL 44-20-72480468, FAX 44-20-72480467, subs@businessmonitor.com.

615 572.8 USA ISSN 1938-1247
RM301.65
▼ ➤ **MOLECULAR AND CELLULAR PHARMACOLOGY.** Text in English. 2009. irreg. free (effective 2011). **Document type:** *Journal, Academic/Scholarly.* **Description:** Publishes research articles, reviews and PharmSights in all aspects of pharmacological sciences.
Media: Online - full text.
Indexed: A36, CABA, EMBASE, GH, N02, N03, P30, P32, P33, P39, R08, R13, RA&MP, SCOPUS, SoyAb.
Published by: LumiText Publishing, PO Box 774, Ellicot City, MD 21041.

615.19 DEU ISSN 1868-1743
RM301.42
➤ **MOLECULAR INFORMATICS.** Text in English. 1982. 12/yr. GBP 1,223 in United Kingdom to institutions; EUR 1,886 in Europe to institutions; USD 2,396 elsewhere to institutions; GBP 1,406 combined subscription in United Kingdom to institutions (print & online eds.); EUR 2,169 combined subscription in Europe to institutions (print & online eds.); USD 2,756 combined subscription elsewhere to institutions (print & online eds.) (effective 2012). adv. reprint service avail. from PSC. **Document type:** *Journal, Academic/Scholarly.* **Description:** Interdisciplinary forum for contributions on molecular modelling, computer graphics and other computer-assisted methods helpful in the design and development of biologically active compounds as applied to medicinal, agricultural and environmental chemistry.
Former titles (until 2010): Q S A R & Combinatorial Science (1611-020X); (until 2003): Quantitative Structure-Activity Relationships (0931-8771); (until 1986): Quantitative Structure-Activity Relationships in Pharmacology, Chemistry and Biology (0722-3676)
Related titles: Online - full text ed.: ISSN 1868-1751. GBP 1,223 in United Kingdom to institutions; EUR 1,886 in Europe to institutions; USD 2,396 elsewhere to institutions (effective 2012).
Indexed: A22, ASCA, B25, BIOBASE, BIOSIS Prev, C31, CA, CCI, ChemAb, ChemTitl, CurCont, DBA, EMBASE, ExcerpMed, IABS, ISR, Inpharma, MycolAb, P30, R10, Reac, SCI, SCOPUS, T02, W07.
—BLDSC (7163.869500), CASDDS, GNLM, IE, Infotrieve, Ingenta, INIST. **CCC.**
Published by: Wiley - V C H Verlag GmbH & Co. KGaA (Subsidiary of: John Wiley & Sons, Inc.), Postfach 101161, Weinheim, 69451, Germany. TEL 49-6201-606400, FAX 49-6201-606184, info@wiley-vch.de, http://www.wiley-vch.de. Eds. Gerhard Ecker, Dr. Gisbert Schneider, Jordi Mestres, Knut Baumann TEL 49-531-3912751. Pub. Carina S Kniep. adv.: page EUR 990; trim 210 x 280. Circ: 930. **Subscr. in the Americas to:** John Wiley & Sons, Inc., 111 River St, Hoboken, NJ 07030. TEL 201-748-6645, subinfo@wiley.com; **Subscr. outside Germany, Austria & Switzerland to:** John Wiley & Sons Ltd., The Atrium, Southern Gate, Chichester, West Sussex PO19 8SQ, United Kingdom. TEL 44-1243-779777, FAX 44-1243-775878.

615.7 USA ISSN 1534-0384
RM300 CODEN: MIONAR
MOLECULAR INTERVENTIONS; pharmacological perspectives from biology, chemistry and genomics. Abbreviated title: M I. Text in English. 2001 (Apr.). 6/yr. USD 60 combined subscription domestic to non-members (print & online eds.); USD 70 combined subscription foreign to non-members (print & online eds.); USD 298 combined subscription domestic to institutions (print & online eds.); USD 322 combined subscription foreign to institutions (print & online eds.); USD 54 per issue; free to members (effective 2010). adv. back issues avail.; reprints avail. **Document type:** *Journal, Academic/Scholarly.* **Description:** Features articles on the interplay between science and society, interviews with leaders in pharmacology, information about relevant web sites, reviews of pharmacology and science in the media, and a comprehensive meetings calendar.
Related titles: Online - full text ed.: ISSN 1543-2548. USD 54 to individuals; USD 268 to institutions (effective 2010).
Indexed: B21, B27, EMBASE, ESPM, ExcerpMed, GenetAb, MEDLINE, P30, R10, Reac, SCI, SCOPUS, ToxAb, W07.
—BLDSC (5900.817820), IE. **CCC.**
Published by: American Society for Pharmacology and Experimental Therapeutics, 9650 Rockville Pike, Bethesda, MD 20814. TEL 301-634-7060, FAX 301-634-7061, info@aspet.org, http://www.aspet.org. Ed. Harry B Smith. adv.: B&W page USD 1,380, color page USD 2,475; trim 8.375 x 10.875. Circ: 4,300.

616.4 USA ISSN 1076-1551
CODEN: MOMEF3
➤ **MOLECULAR MEDICINE.** Text in English. 1994. bi-m. USD 99 domestic to individuals; USD 110 in Canada & Mexico to individuals; USD 120 elsewhere to individuals; USD 250 domestic to institutions; USD 275 in Canada & Mexico to institutions; USD 290 elsewhere to institutions (effective 2011). adv. back issues avail. **Document type:** *Journal, Academic/Scholarly.* **Description:** Focused on understanding the molecules that are key to the normal functioning of the body and those related to the fundamental mechanisms of disease.
Related titles: Online - full text ed.: ISSN 1528-3658. free (effective 2011).
Indexed: A01, A03, A08, A22, A34, A35, A36, AgBio, B25, B27, BIOBASE, BIOSIS Prev, C33, CA, CABA, CIN, ChemAb, ChemTitl, CurCont, E01, E12, EMBASE, ExcerpMed, FoMM, GH, H16, IABS, ISR, IndMed, IndVet, Inpharma, MEDLINE, MycolAb, N02, N03, P30, P33, P35, P39, R08, R10, RA&MP, RM&VM, Reac, SCI, SCOPUS, T02, T05, VS, W07.
—BLDSC (5900.817920), CASDDS, GNLM, IE, Infotrieve, Ingenta, INIST. **CCC.**
Published by: (Molecular Medicine Society), The Feinstein Institute for Medical Research, 350 Community Dr, Manhasset, NY 11030. TEL 516-562-2114, FAX 516-562-1022, http://www.feinsteininstitute.org. Eds. Anthony Cerami, Kevin J Tracey.

615.7 USA ISSN 0026-895X
QP901 CODEN: MOPMA3
➤ **MOLECULAR PHARMACOLOGY.** Text in English. 1965. m. USD 180 to members; USD 707 combined subscription domestic to institutions (print & online eds.); USD 799 combined subscription foreign to institutions (print & online eds.); USD 63 per issue (effective 2010). adv. index. back issues avail. **Document type:** *Journal, Academic/ Scholarly.* **Description:** Covers research on drug action and selective toxicity at the molecular level, for pharmacologists and biochemists.
Related titles: Online - full text ed.: ISSN 1521-0111. USD 617 to institutions (effective 2010).
Indexed: A22, A34, A35, A36, ASCA, AgrForAb, B&BAb, B19, B21, B25, B27, BIOBASE, BIOSIS Prev, BP, BioEngAb, C24, C25, C30, C33, CABA, CIN, CTA, ChemAb, ChemTitl, CurCont, DBA, DentInd, E12, EMBASE, ESPM, ExcerpMed, F08, F11, F12, GH, GenetAb, H16, H17, HGA, IABS, INIS AtomInd, ISR, IndMed, Inpharma, MEDLINE, MycolAb, N02, N03, N05, NSA, NucAcAb, P30, P32, P33, P39, PGegResA, R07, R08, R10, RA&MP, Reac, SCI, SCOPUS, SoyAb, T05, THA, ToxAb, VS, W07, W10.
—BLDSC (5900.818000), CASDDS, GNLM, IE, Infotrieve, Ingenta, INIST, Linda Hall. **CCC.**
Published by: American Society for Pharmacology and Experimental Therapeutics, 9650 Rockville Pike, Bethesda, MD 20814. TEL 301-634-7060, FAX 301-634-7061, info@aspet.org, http://www.aspet.org. Ed. Jeffrey P Conn. adv.: B&W page USD 645, color page USD 1,095; trim 8.375 x 10.875. Circ: 600.

615.1 FRA ISSN 1956-9831
LE MONITEUR DES PHARMACIES. Text in French. 1946. w. adv. illus. **Document type:** *Directory, Trade.*
Formerly (until 2007): Moniteur des Pharmacies et des Laboratoires (0026-9689)
Indexed: FR, P30.
—IE, Infotrieve, INIST.
Published by: Wolters Kluwer - Pharma (Subsidiary of: Wolters Kluwer France), 1 Rue Eugene et Armand Peugeot, Rueil-Malmaison, Cedex 92856, France. TEL 33-1-76734809, FAX 33-1-76733040, contact@wk-pharma.fr. Circ: 30,000.

615 USA ISSN 1088-2111
THE MONITOR. Text in English. 198?. bi-m. **Document type:** *Magazine, Trade.*
—CCC.
Published by: Association of Clinical Research Professionals, 500 Montgomery St, Ste 800, Alexandria, VA 22314. TEL 703-254-8100, FAX 703-254-8101, office@acrpnet.org. Ed. A Veronica Precup.

615 NLD ISSN 1871-0956
MONITOR HULPMIDDELEN. Text in Dutch. 2000. a.
Published by: (Projectgroep Monitor Hulpmiddelen), College voor Zorgverzekeringen, Postbus 320, Diemen, 1110 AH, Netherlands. TEL 31-20-7978555, FAX 31-20-7978500, info@cvz.nl, http://www.cvz.nl.

615 USA ISSN 0883-0266
MONTHLY PRESCRIBING REFERENCE. Abbreviated title: M P R. Text in English. 1985. m. USD 79 domestic; USD 159 foreign; USD 16 per issue domestic; USD 21 per issue foreign (effective 2008). adv. back issues avail.; reprints avail. **Document type:** *Magazine, Trade.* **Description:** Provides up-to-date information to prescribing physicians including the latest Federal Drug Administration drug approvals.
Related titles: Online - full text ed.
Indexed: A01, A26, G08, H11, H12, I05, Inpharma, P20, P48, P54, PQC.
—CCC.
Published by: Prescribing Reference, Inc. (Subsidiary of: Haymarket Group Ltd.), 114 W 26th St, 4th Fl, New York, NY 10001. TEL 646-638-6000, FAX 646-638-6117, Online@PrescribingRef.com. Eds. Anissa Lee, Diana Ernst. Pub. James Pantaleo TEL 646-638-6137. Adv. contact Don Bruccoleri TEL 646-638-6007. Circ: 150,013 (paid).

MOSBY'S NURSING DRUG REFERENCE. *see* MEDICAL SCIENCES—Nurses And Nursing

615 PRT ISSN 1647-2683
MUNDO FARMACEUTICO. Text in Portuguese. 2002. bi-m. **Document type:** *Magazine, Trade.*
Published by: JAS Farma, Edificio Lisboa Oriente, Avenida Infante D Henrique 333, Lisbon, 1800-282, Portugal. TEL 351-21-8504000, FAX 351-21-8504009, http://www.jasfarma.pt.

615.1 USA ISSN 8756-4483
N A B P NEWSLETTER. Text in English. 1936. 10/yr. USD 35 to non-members; free to members (effective 2010). abstr.; charts; illus.; stat. index. back issues avail. **Document type:** *Newsletter, Trade.* **Description:** Brings the objectives and programs of the Association and its 67 member boards of pharmacy to the professionals and the public.
Former titles (until 1971): N A B P Quarterly (0027-5700); (until 1967): N A B P Bulletin
Related titles: Online - full text ed.
Published by: National Association of Boards of Pharmacy, 1600 Feehanville Dr, Mount Prospect, IL 60056. TEL 847-391-4406, FAX 847-391-4502, custserv@nabp.net.

615 340 USA
N A B P STATE BOARD NEWSLETTERS. (National Association of Boards of Pharmacy) Variant title: Bureau of Voluntary Compliance Newsletters. (Avail. in 35 state editions each with a national news section.) Text in English. 1979. q. USD 100 (effective 2011). **Document type:** *Newsletter, Trade.* **Description:** Provides pharmacists in 34 states with vital information about their state's pharmacy laws and board of pharmacy regulations.
Related titles: Online - full text ed.
Published by: National Association of Boards of Pharmacy, 1600 Feehanville Dr, Mount Prospect, IL 60056. TEL 847-391-4406, FAX 847-391-4502, custserv@nabp.net. Circ: 145,000.

615.328 USA ISSN 1092-4272
N A C D S CHAIN PHARMACIST PRACTICE MEMO. Text in English. 1997. m. **Document type:** *Newsletter, Trade.* **Description:** Includes practice related information for the chain pharmacist.
Related titles: Online - full text ed.
Published by: National Association of Chain Drug Stores, PO Box 1417-D49, Alexandria, VA 22313. jcovert@nacds.org, http://www.nacds.org. Ed. Nancy J Olins.

615 USA
N A C D S SOURCEBOOK (ONLINE). Text in English. 19??. w. free (effective 2011). **Document type:** *Handbook/Manual/Guide, Trade.* **Description:** Contains listings of boards of pharmacy and publications serving the chain drug store industry.
Media: Online - full text.
Published by: National Association of Chain Drug Stores, 413 N Lee St, Alexandria, VA 22314. TEL 703-549-3001.

615 570 660 USA
N A P R A L E R T. (Natural Products Alert) Text in English. 1974. irreg. **Document type:** *Directory, Trade.* **Description:** Comprehensive resource on the medicinal aspects of biological species. Covers marine and terrestrial organisms, their chemical constituents, biological and pharmacological activities, and their ethnomedical uses. Aimed at medicinal chemists and other drug researchers, pharmacologists and bioscientists with a related research interest.
Formerly: Napralert on CD-ROM (1360-3019)
Media: Online - full text.
Published by: University of Illinois at Chicago, College of Pharmacy, Program for Collaborative Research in the Pharmaceutical Sciences, 833 S Wood St, Chicago, IL 60612. TEL 312-996-7253, FAX 312-996-7107, PCRPS@uic.edu, http://www.uic.edu/pharmacy/centers/collaborative_research/.

615.19 ITA ISSN 0393-3733
N C F. NOTIZIARIO CHIMICO E FARMACEUTICO. Text in Italian. 1961. m. (10/yr.). EUR 45 domestic; EUR 90 in Europe; EUR 110 elsewhere (effective 2011). adv. bk.rev. bibl. **Document type:** *Magazine, Trade.* **Description:** Aims to present a global and current view of the technical and commercial evolution of this field.
Formerly (until 1983): Notiziario Chimico e Farmaceutico (0550-1156)
Related titles: Online - full text ed.
Indexed: A22.
—BLDSC (6174.278000), IE, INIST, Linda Hall.
Published by: Tecniche Nuove SpA, Via Eritrea 21, Milan, MI 201, Italy. TEL 39-02-390901, FAX 39-02-7570364, info@tecnichenuove.com. Ed. Cristiana Bernini. Circ: 6,000.

615.1 USA
HD9666.1
N C P A NEWSLETTER. Text in English. 1970. s-m. **Document type:** *Newsletter.*
Formerly (until 1997): N A R D Newsletter (0162-1602); Which superseded in part (in 1977): N A R D Journal (0027-5972); Which was formerly (until 1915): National Association of Retail Druggists. Journal (0276-2595); (until 1913): N.A.R.D. Notes (0270-8582)
Related titles: Fax ed.
—Linda Hall.
Published by: National Community Pharmacists Association, 100 Daingerfield Rd, Alexandria, VA 22314. TEL 703-683-8200, 800-544-7447, FAX 703-683-3619, info@ncpanet.org, http://www.ncpanet.org/.

615 GBR
N P A SUPPLEMENT. Text in English. 1921. m. looseleaf. membership. index. **Document type:** *Newsletter.*
Formerly: N P U Supplement
Published by: National Pharmaceutical Association, Mallinson House, 38-42 St. Peter's St, St. Albans, Herts AL1 3NP, United Kingdom. TEL 44-1727-832161, FAX 44-1727-840858, npa@npa.co.uk, http://www.npa.co.uk. Ed. Veronica Wray. Circ: 10,500.

615.1 AUS ISSN 1832-3596
➤ **N P S R A D A R.** (National Prescribing Service Rational Assessment of Drugs and Research) Variant title: N P S Rational Assessment of Drugs and Research. Text in English. 2004. 3/yr. free (print or online ed.) (effective 2009). adv. back issues avail. **Document type:** *Journal, Academic/Scholarly.* **Description:** Presents independent, evidence-based assessment of new drugs, new PBS listings and research for health professionals.
Related titles: Online - full text ed.: ISSN 1832-3588.
Published by: National Prescribing Service Ltd., Ste 3, 2 Phipps Close, Deakin, ACT 2600, Australia. TEL 61-2-82178700, FAX 61-2-92117578, info@nps.org.au.

615.1 POL ISSN 1426-0514
NACZELNA IZBA APTEKARSKA. BIULETYN. Text in Polish. q.
—BLDSC (2102.729000).
Published by: Naczelna Izba Aptekarska, ul. Dluga 16, Warszawa, 00-238, Poland. TEL 48-22-7815102, FAX 48-227815102.

615.1 USA
THE NATIONAL DRUG CODE DIRECTORY (ONLINE). Text in English. irreg. free (effective 2011). **Document type:** *Directory, Government.* **Description:** Covers prescription drugs and insulin products that have been manufactured, prepared, propagated, compounded, or processed by registered establishments for commercial distribution.
Media: Online - full text.
Published by: U.S. Department of Health and Human Services, Food and Drug Administration, 10903 New Hampshire Ave, Silver Spring, MD 20993. TEL 301-796-8240, 888-463-6332, druginfo@fda.hhs.gov.

615 GHA ISSN 0855-6059
➤ **NATIONAL DRUG INFORMATION JOURNAL.** Text in English. 2003. s-a. free to qualified personnel. back issues avail. **Document type:** *Journal, Academic/Scholarly.* **Description:** Covers drug information news and activities, update news, research publications, medicine alerts, and other information to address medicines information needs among health professionals as well as the general public.
Published by: National Drug Information Resource Centre, Pharmacy Council Bldg., Adjabeng Yard, PO Box AN 10344, Accra North, Ghana. TEL 233-21-678559, FAX 233-21-678557, ghanadruginfo@yahoo.com, pw_anum@yahoo.com, http://www.ghanadruginfo.org/. Ed. Philip Anum. Circ: 1,500.

615 571 IND
▼ ➤ **NATIONAL JOURNAL OF PHYSIOLOGY, PHARMACY AND PHARMACOLOGY.** Abbreviated title: N J P P. Text and summaries in English. 2011 (Mar.). s-a. free (effective 2011). bk.rev. abstr.; bibl.; charts; illus.; maps; stat. a. index. back issues avail. **Document type:** *Journal, Academic/Scholarly.* **Description:** Contains original articles, review articles, short communications, letters, education forum, guest editorials, books reviews from the field of clinical physiology, experimental physiology, medical education in physiology, pharmacy practices, social pharmacy, experimental pharmacy, pharmacy education, pharmaceutical marketing, clinical pharmacology, experimental pharmacology, clinical trials, medical education in pharmacology etc.
Media: Online - full text.
Published by: Association of Physiologist, Pharmcists and Pharmacologists, B- 2, AP Qtr, GMC, Surat, Gujarat 395 001, India. TEL 91-9825219196, drjaykaran@yahoo.co.in. Ed., R&P Jaykaran Dr. Pub. Deepika Charan.

615.4 KOR ISSN 1226-3907
NATURAL PRODUCT SCIENCES. Text in English. q. USD 30 domestic to members; USD 40 foreign to non-members (effective 2008). **Document type:** *Journal, Academic/Scholarly.*
Indexed: A34, A35, AgBio, AgrForAb, B23, BP, C25, C30, C33, CABA, CIN, ChemAb, ChemTitl, E12, EMBASE, ExcerpMed, F08, F11, F12, FCA, GH, H16, N02, N03, NPU, P32, P33, P40, PGegResA, PHN&I, PN&I, R07, R10, R11, R13, RA&MP, RM&VM, Reac, S12, S17, SCOPUS, SoyAb, T05, TAR, VS, W10.
—BLDSC (6040.738200), IE, Ingenta.
Published by: Han'gug Saeng'yag Haghoe/Korean Society of Pharmacognosy, Sahmyook University, 26-21, Gongneung 2-dong Nowon-gu, Seoul, 139-742, Korea, S. TEL 82-2-33991604. Ed. Hee-Juhn Park.

P

NATURAL PRODUCTS. *see* CHEMISTRY—Organic Chemistry

NATURAL PRODUCTS MARKETPLACE. *see* NUTRITION AND DIETETICS

615 GBR ISSN 1474-1776
CODEN: NRDDAG
NATURE REVIEWS. DRUG DISCOVERY. Text in English. 2002. m. EUR 3,214 in Europe academic institutions; USD 4,048 in the Americas academic institutions; GBP 2,077 academic institutions; in the UK & elsewhere; EUR 4,011 in Europe to corporations; USD 4,658 in the Americas to corporations; GBP 2,250 to corporations in the UK & elsewhere (effective 2011). adv. back issues avail. **Document type:** *Journal, Academic/Scholarly.* **Description:** Contains reviews and perspectives highlighting the most important developments across the entire field, from chemistry to disease mechanisms and novel therapeutic approaches.
Related titles: Online - full text ed.; ISSN 1474-1784.
Indexed: A01, A02, A03, A08, A22, A26, B26, BIOSIS Prev, BioEngAb, C33, CA, ChemAb, CurCont, EMBASE, ExcerpMed, H12, I05, ISR, Inpharma, M&PBA, MEDLINE, P20, P22, P30, P34, P48, P54, PQC, SCI, SCOPUS, T02, W07.
—BLDSC (6047.224000), IE, Infotrieve, Ingenta, Linda Hall. **CCC.**
Published by: Nature Publishing Group (Subsidiary of: Macmillan Publishers Ltd.), The MacMillan Bldg, 4 Crinan St, London, N1 9XW, United Kingdom. TEL 44-20-78334000, FAX 44-20-78334640, NatureReviews@nature.com. Eds. Peter Kirkpatrick, Dr. Philip Campbell. Adv. contact Andy Douglas TEL 44-22-78434975. **Subscr. elsewhere to:** Brunel Rd, Houndmills, Basingstoke, Hamps RG21 6XS, United Kingdom. TEL 44-1256-329242, FAX 44-1256-812358, subscriptions@nature.com; **Subscr. in Japan, China & Korea to:** Nature Japan KK; **Subscr. in N. & S. America to:** Nature Publishing Group.

615.1 DEU ISSN 0028-1298
RM1 CODEN: NSAPCC
➤ **NAUNYN-SCHMIEDEBERG'S ARCHIVES OF PHARMACOLOGY.** Text in German. 1873. m. EUR 2,871, USD 3,515 combined subscription to institutions (print & online eds.) (effective 2012). adv. charts; illus. back issues avail.; reprint service avail. from PSC. **Document type:** *Journal, Academic/Scholarly.* **Description:** Original papers, ranging from reports on the molecular effects of drugs within the cell to observations of their effects on the whole organism. Focuses on pharmacology and toxicology.
Former titles (until 1972): Naunyn-Schmiedebergs Archiv fuer Pharmakologie (0340-5249); (until 1969): Naunyn-Schmiedebergs Archiv fuer Pharmakologie und Experimentelle Pathologie (0365-5423); (until 1966): Naunyn-Schmiedebergs Archiv fuer Experimentelle Pathologie und Pharmakologie (0365-2009); (until 1925): Archiv fuer Experimentelle Pathologie und Pharmakologie (0365-2041)
Related titles: Microform ed.: (from PMC, PQC); Online - full text ed.: ISSN 1432-1912 (from IngentaConnect).
Indexed: A22, A26, ASCA, B&BAb, B19, B21, B25, BIOBASE, BIOSIS Prev, C24, C33, CA, CABA, CIN, CTA, ChemAb, ChemTitl, CurCR, CurCont, DBA, DentInd, E01, EMBASE, ESPM, ExcerpMed, GH, H12, H16, IABS, ISR, IndChem, IndMed, Inpharma, M&PBA, MEDLINE, MycolAb, N02, N03, NSA, P30, P33, P35, P39, R10, R16, RA&MP, Reac, SCI, SCOPUS, T02, THA, ToxAb, W07.
—BLDSC (6060.200000), CASDDS, GNLM, IE, Infotrieve, Ingenta, INIST, Linda Hall. **CCC.**

Published by: (Deutsche Gesellschaft fuer Experimentelle und Klinische Pharmakologie und Toxikologie), Springer (Subsidiary of: Springer Science+Business Media), Tiergartenstr 17, Heidelberg, 69121, Germany. TEL 49-6221-4870, FAX 49-6221-345229. Adv. contact Stephan Kroeck TEL 49-30-827875739. **Subscr. in the Americas to:** Springer New York LLC, Journal Fulfillment, PO Box 2485, Secaucus, NJ 07096. TEL 800-777-4643, 201-348-4033, FAX 201-348-4505, journals-ny@springer.com, http://www.springer.com; **Subscr. to:** Springer Distribution Center, Kundenservice Zeitschriften, Haberstr 7, Heidelberg 69126, Germany. TEL 49-6221-3454303, FAX 49-6221-3454229, subscriptions@springer.com.

615.1 USA ISSN 0028-1891
NEBRASKA MORTAR AND PESTLE. Text in English. 1937. bi-m. USD 30 (effective 2005). adv. charts; illus. back issues avail. **Document type:** *Magazine, Trade.* **Description:** Articles that relate to store operation, layout and management.
Indexed: I12.
Published by: Nebraska Pharmacists Association, Inc., 6221 S 58th St, Ste A, Lincoln, NE 68516-3687. TEL 402-420-1500, FAX 402-420-1406, http://www.npharm.org/. Ed., Adv. contact Darlene K Lowe. B&W page USD 365, color page USD 965; trim 8.5 x 11. Circ: 1,809 (paid).

615 NLD ISSN 2210-4518
▼ **NEDERLANDSE GALENUSPRIJS.** Variant title: Galenus Geneesmiddelenprijs. Text in Dutch. 2010. a.
Published by: (Stichting Galenusprijs Nederland), Van Zuiden Communications B.V., Postbus 2122, Alphen aan den Rijn, 2400 CC, Netherlands. TEL 31-172-476191, FAX 31-172-471882, zuiden@zuidencomm.nl, http://www.zuidencomm.nl. Circ: 20,000.

615.19 NPL ISSN 0253-8261
CODEN: JONPD6
NEPAL PHARMACEUTICAL ASSOCIATION. JOURNAL. Text in English, Nepali. 1974. s-a. NPR 20, USD 5. adv. bk.rev. **Document type:** *Journal, Academic/Scholarly.* **Description:** Research articles on pharmacy, pharmaceuticals, medicinal plants and allied sciences.
Indexed: ChemAb.
—CASDDS.
Published by: Nepal Pharmaceutical Association, Minbhawon, Baneshwor, P O Box 5061, Kathmandu, Nepal. TEL 977-1-5522278, 977-1-4254955, dhyan@wlink.com.np, http://www.nepalpharma.org. Ed. R R Prasad. Circ: 500.

▼ **NETHERLANDS. INSPECTIE VOOR DE GEZONDHEIDSZORG. HET RESULTAAT TEIT OPENBARE APOTHEKEN.** *see* FOOD AND FOOD INDUSTRIES—Grocery Trade

615 DEU ISSN 0047-9381
NEUE APOTHEKEN ILLUSTRIERTE. Text in German. 1950. fortn. adv. bk.rev. **Document type:** *Magazine, Consumer.*
Incorporates (1977-1997): Gesundheit (0942-2129); Which was formerly (until 1991): Wegweiser aus der Apotheke (0721-9938); Der Wegweiser in Gesunden und Kranken Tagen - Der Bote aus der Apotheke (0721-992X); Which was formed by the merger of (1956-1977): Der Bote aus der Apotheke (0006-8217); (19??-1977): Der Wegweiser in Gesunden und Kranken Tagen (0721-9911)
Published by: (Arbeitsgemeinschaft der Berufsvertretungen Deutscher Apotheker), Govi Verlag Pharmazeutischer Verlag GmbH, Carl Mannich Str 26, Eschborn, 65760, Germany. TEL 49-6196-928262, FAX 49-6196-928203, service@govi.de, http://www.govi.de. Ed. Jutta Petersen-Lehmann. Adv. contact Elke Ebeling.

615.1 DEU ISSN 1862-8907
DER NEUE APOTHEKER; Das Fachmagazin fuer alle Apotheker. Text in German. 2006. 10/yr. EUR 50 (effective 2008). adv. **Document type:** *Magazine, Trade.*
Published by: Apotheken-Spiegel-Verlagsgesellschaft mbH, Edisonstr 3-5, Frankfurt am Main, 60388, Germany. TEL 49-6109-71200, FAX 49-6109-7120222, inbox@as-verlag.com. Ed. Heinz Egon Schmitt. Adv. contact Christoph Wigand. B&W page EUR 3,000, color page EUR 4,500; trim 182 x 262. Circ: 12,000 (paid and controlled).

615 DEU ISSN 0724-567X
NEUE ARZNEIMITTEL. Text in German. 1953. m. EUR 39; EUR 5 newsstand/cover (effective 2012); free with subscr. to Deutsche Apotheker Zeitung. **Document type:** *Journal, Trade.*
Formerly: Neue Arzneimittel und Spezialitaeten (0548-2674)
Related titles: ◆ Supplement to: Deutsche Apotheker Zeitung. ISSN 0011-9857.
Indexed: A22, ChemAb.
—BLDSC (6077.237900), GNLM. **CCC.**
Published by: Deutscher Apotheker Verlag, Postfach 101061, Stuttgart, 70009, Germany. TEL 49-711-25820, FAX 49-711-2582290, daz@deutscher-apotheker-verlag.de, http://www.deutscher-apotheker-verlag.de. Ed. Bettina Hellwig.

NEUROMOLECULAR MEDICINE. *see* MEDICAL SCIENCES—Psychiatry And Neurology

615.1 GBR ISSN 0028-3908
RM315 CODEN: NEPHBW
➤ **NEUROPHARMACOLOGY.** Text in English. 1962. 16/yr. EUR 4,246 in Europe to institutions; JPY 462,100 in Japan to institutions; USD 4,749 elsewhere to institutions (effective 2012). adv. bk.rev. bibl.; charts; illus. index. back issues avail.; reprints avail. **Document type:** *Journal, Academic/Scholarly.* **Description:** Features the understanding of the mechanisms of drug actions on the nervous system.
Formerly (until 1970): International Journal of Neuropharmacology (0375-9458)
Related titles: Microfilm ed.: (from PQC); Online - full text ed.: ISSN 1873-7064 (from IngentaConnect, ScienceDirect).
Indexed: A01, A03, A08, A22, A26, ASCA, B&BAb, B19, B21, B25, B27, BIOBASE, BIOSIS Prev, C33, CA, CIN, ChemAb, ChemTitl, ChemoAb, CurCont, DBA, DentInd, E-psyche, EMBASE, ESPM, ExcerpMed, GenetAb, I05, IABS, ISR, IndMed, Inpharma, MEDLINE, MycolAb, NSA, NSCI, P03, P30, P35, PsycInfo, PsycholAb, R10, Reac, SCI, SCOPUS, T02, THA, ToxAb, W07.
—BLDSC (6081.517500), CASDDS, GNLM, IE, Infotrieve, Ingenta, INIST, Linda Hall. **CCC.**

Published by: Pergamon (Subsidiary of: Elsevier Science & Technology), The Blvd, Langford Ln, East Park, Kidlington, Oxford OX5 1GB, United Kingdom. TEL 44-1865-843000, FAX 44-1865-843010, JournalsCustomerServiceEMEA@elsevier.com. Ed. Graham L. Collingridge. **Subscr. to:** Elsevier BV, Radarweg 29, PO Box 211, Amsterdam 1000 AE, Netherlands. TEL 31-20-4853757, FAX 31-20-4853432, http://www.elsevier.nl.

➤ **NEUROPSYCHOBIOLOGY**; international journal of experimental and clinical research in biological psychiatry, pharmacopsychiatry, biological psychology, pharmacopsychology and pharmacoelectroencephalography. *see* MEDICAL SCIENCES—Psychiatry And Neurology

➤ **NEUROPSYCHOPHARMACOLOGY.** *see* MEDICAL SCIENCES—Psychiatry And Neurology

615.1 DEU
NEW DRUGS. Text in English. 2001. bi-m. EUR 120 (effective 2006). adv. **Document type:** *Magazine, Trade.* **Description:** Provides news and information of interest to international pharmaceutical research concerns.
Published by: Vogel Business Media GmbH & Co.KG, Max-Planck-Str 7-9, Wuerzburg, 97064, Germany. TEL 49-931-4180, FAX 49-931-4182750, http://www.vogel-media.de. adv.: B&W page EUR 4,410, color page EUR 5,515. Circ: 15,000 (controlled).

615.1 USA ISSN 0028-5773
RS1
NEW JERSEY JOURNAL OF PHARMACY. Text in English. 1927. q. USD 40 domestic to non-members; USD 100 foreign to non-members; free to members (effective 2011). adv. bk.rev. illus. back issues avail.; reprints avail. **Document type:** *Journal, Academic/Scholarly.* **Description:** Contains articles pertaining to the practice of pharmacy, both scientific and economic. Covers proceedings of the annual meetings of the New Jersey Pharmaceutical Association.
Related titles: Microform ed.: (from PQC).
Indexed: P30.
—Linda Hall.
Published by: New Jersey Pharmacists Association, 760 Alexander Rd, PO Box 1, Princeton, NJ 08543. TEL 609-275-4246, FAX 609-275-4066. Ed. Richard Meadows.

615 GBR
NEW PRODUCT FOCUS. Variant title: I M S Lifecycle New Product Focus. I M S New Product Focus. Text in English. 1976. m. **Document type:** *Magazine, Trade.* **Description:** Provides comprehensive worldwide tracking of historical pharmaceutical product launches internationally.
Former titles: New Product Launch Letter; (until 1990): New Product Card Index
Related titles: CD-ROM ed.; Online - full text ed.
Published by: I M S Health Inc., 7 Harewood Ave, London, NW1 6JB, United Kingdom. TEL 44-20-30755000, FAX 44-20-30755888.

615.329 USA ISSN 0739-7062
NEW YORK STATE PHARMACIST - CENTURY II. Text in English. 1927. bi-m. USD 40 to non-members; free to members (effective 2007). adv. **Document type:** *Journal, Trade.* **Description:** Covers many stories of interest to the pharmacy professional, including Society news. Offers at home continuing education, convention registration forms, discounts and specials from advertisers.
Former titles (until 1982): N Y State Pharmacist (0163-1586); (until 1977): New York State Pharmacist (0028-7660); (until 1935): The New York Pharmacist (0271-4752)
Indexed: P30.
Published by: Pharmacists Society of the State of New York, 201 Washington Ave Extension, Ste 101, Albany, NY 12203-5221. TEL 518-869-6595, 800-632-8822, FAX 518-464-0618, staff@pssny.org. Ed. Craig Burridge. Adv. contact Mary Prediger. Circ: 2,000.

NEW ZEALAND GAZETTE TRADE LISTS. REGISTER OF PHARMACIES. *see* BUSINESS AND ECONOMICS—Trade And Industrial Directories

615.1 NZL ISSN 0111-431X
NEW ZEALAND PHARMACY JOURNAL. Text in English. 1981. m. NZD 75 domestic; NZD 100 in Australia; NZD 200 elsewhere (effective 2008). adv. bk.rev. **Document type:** *Journal, Trade.* **Description:** Provides information for pharmacists and the pharmaceutical iindustry.
Formed by the merger of (1977-1981): Pharmacy Digest (0110-8832); (1910-1981): Pharmaceutical Journal of New Zealand (0031-6881)
Related titles: Online - full text ed.
Indexed: ABIX, ChemAb, I12, INZP, Inpharma.
—BLDSC (6096.495000), GNLM, IE, Ingenta. **CCC.**
Published by: (Pharmaceutical Society of New Zealand), 3 Media Group, Wellesley St, PO Box 5544, Auckland, 1141, New Zealand. TEL 64-9-9098400, FAX 64-9-9098401, http://www.admedia.co.nz. Ed. Brent Leslie TEL 64-9-9098428. adv.: color page NZD 2,900; 240 x 340. Circ: 3,200.

615 660.6 USA ISSN 1944-2572
NEWSRX HEALTH. Text in English. 2008. w. USD 2,295 in US & Canada; USD 2,495 elsewhere; USD 2,525 combined subscription in US & Canada (print & online eds.); USD 2,755 combined subscription elsewhere (print & online eds.) (effective 2011). adv. back issues avail. **Document type:** *Newsletter, Trade.* **Description:** Covers the most significant drug and biotechnology studies includes the research reports from US teaching hospitals and universities.
Related titles: E-mail ed.; Online - full text ed.: ISSN 1944-2580. USD 2,295 combined subscription (online & e-mail eds.) (effective 2011).
Indexed: H11, I05, P20, P26, P48, P54, PQC.
Published by: NewsRx, 2727 Paces Ferry Rd SE, Ste 2-440, Atlanta, GA 30339. TEL 770-435-8286, 800-726-4550, FAX 770-435-6800, pressrelease@newsrx.com, http://www.newsrx.com. Pub., Adv. contact Susan Hasty TEL 770-507-7777.

615 GBR
NICHOLAS HALL'S INSIGHT ASIA. Text in English. 1994. m. GBP 2,300 (effective 2009). 2 cols./p.; back issues avail. **Document type:** *Magazine, Trade.* **Description:** Provides data and analysis on Asian markets.
Formerly (until 19??): Far East Focus (1354-5299)
Related titles: CD-ROM ed.; Online - full text ed.: GBP 5,000 (effective 2010).
Indexed: B03.
—CIS. **CCC.**

Published by: Nicholas Hall & Company, 35 Alexandra St, Southend-on-Sea, Essex SS1 1BW, United Kingdom. TEL 44-1702-220200, FAX 44-1702-430787, info@nicholashall.com, http://www.nicholashall.com. Ed. Nicola Jay.

615 GBR
NICHOLAS HALL'S INSIGHT CENTRAL & EASTERN EUROPE. Text in English. bi-m. GBP 2,300 (effective 2010). **Document type:** *Report, Trade.* **Description:** Contains data and analysis of the European markets.
Related titles: Online - full text ed.: GBP 5,000 (effective 2010).
Published by: Nicholas Hall & Company, 35 Alexandra St, Southend-on-Sea, Essex SS1 1BW, United Kingdom. TEL 44-1702-220200, FAX 44-1702-430787, info@nicholashall.com, http://www.nicholashall.com.

615 GBR
NICHOLAS HALL'S INSIGHT LATIN AMERICA. Text in English. 1995. bi-m. GBP 2,300 (effective 2010). 2 cols./p.; back issues avail. **Document type:** *Magazine, Trade.* **Description:** Provides data and analysis on Latin American markets.
Formerly (until 19??): O T C LatinA (1360-4619)
Related titles: CD-ROM ed.; Online - full text ed.: GBP 5,000 (effective 2010).
Indexed: B03.
—CIS. **CCC.**
Published by: Nicholas Hall & Company, 35 Alexandra St, Southend-on-Sea, Essex SS1 1BW, United Kingdom. TEL 44-1702-220200, FAX 44-1702-430787, info@nicholashall.com, http://www.nicholashall.com. Ed. Mary Brooks.

615 GBR
NICHOLAS HALL'S INSIGHT NORTH AMERICA. Text in English. 1990. m. GBP 2,300 (effective 2010). 2 cols./p.; back issues avail. **Document type:** *Magazine, Trade.* **Description:** Contains data and analysis on North American markets.
Formerly (until 19??): O T C Update
Related titles: Online - full text ed.: GBP 5,000 (effective 2010).
Published by: Nicholas Hall & Company, 35 Alexandra St, Southend-on-Sea, Essex SS1 1BW, United Kingdom. TEL 44-1702-220200, FAX 44-1702-430787, info@nicholashall.com, http://www.nicholashall.com. Ed. Samantha Carter.

615 GBR
NICHOLAS HALL'S INSIGHT WESTERN EUROPE. Text in English. 1988. m. GBP 2,300 (effective 2010). adv. back issues avail. **Document type:** *Magazine, Trade.* **Description:** Contains data and analysis of the European markets.
Formerly (until 19??): O T C News and Market Report (0956-2559)
Related titles: CD-ROM ed.; Online - full text ed.: GBP 5,000 (effective 2010).
Indexed: B03, B11.
—IE, Infotrieve. **CCC.**
Published by: Nicholas Hall & Company, 35 Alexandra St, Southend-on-Sea, Essex SS1 1BW, United Kingdom. TEL 44-1702-220200, FAX 44-1702-430787, info@nicholashall.com, http://www.nicholashall.com. Ed. David Redford.

615.1 NLD ISSN 0927-0574
NIEUWE DROGIST. Text in Dutch. 1902. 10/yr. EUR 85 (effective 2010). adv. bk.rev. illus. **Document type:** *Journal, Trade.* **Description:** Covers all aspects of the retail drug industry.
Formerly (until 1991): Drogist (0012-6330); Incorporates (1994-1997): InPharmatie (1380-7102)
Indexed: KES.
Published by: Mons Media bv, Postbus 45, Ravenstein, 5370 AA, Netherlands. TEL 31-486-417277, FAX 31-486-417279, info@monsmedia.nl. Ed. Franca van Dalen. Pubs. Frans Akkermans, Ryan Hoogenboom. adv.: B&W page EUR 3,550; trim 240 x 340. Circ: 6,100 (paid and controlled).

615 NGA ISSN 1118-6267
RS160
NIGERIAN JOURNAL OF NATURAL PRODUCTS AND MEDICINE. Text in English, French. 1982. a. NGN 500 domestic to individuals; USD 50 foreign to individuals; NGN 1,000 domestic to institutions; USD 100 foreign to institutions (effective 2005). back issues avail. **Document type:** *Journal, Academic/Scholarly.* **Description:** Publishes articles covering phytomedicine, natural product chemistry and biochemistry, pharmacognosy and traditional medicine.
Related titles: Online - full text ed.
Indexed: F12, P30.
—BLDSC (6112.126910).
Published by: Nigerian Society of Pharmacognosy, OAU Campus Branch, Ile-Ife, Nigeria. TEL 234-36-232595, FAX 234-36-231733, sadesanya@aouife.edu.ng. Ed. S. Adesanya.

615 JPN ISSN 1341-8815
NIHON BYOIN YAKUZAISHIKAI ZASSHI/JAPANESE SOCIETY OF HOSPITAL PHARMACISTS. JOURNAL. Text in Japanese. 1965. m. membership. **Document type:** *Journal, Academic/Scholarly.*
Former titles (until 1995): Nippon Byoin Yakuzaishikai Zasshi/Journal of Japanese Society of Hospital Pharmacists (0914-0697); (until 1982): Japan Hospital Pharmacists Association. Journal (0914-0689); (until 1981): Nippon Hospital Pharmacists Association. Journal (0914-0670); (until 1969): Nippon Byoin Yakuzaishikai Kaishi
Indexed: I12.
—BLDSC (4809.452000). **CCC.**
Published by: Nihon Byoin Yakuzaishikai/Japanese Society of Hospital Pharmacists, Nagai Kinenkan 8F, 2-12-15 Shibuya, Shibuya-ku, Tokyo, 150-0002, Japan. TEL 81-3-34060485, FAX 81-3-37975303, info@jshp.or.jp, http://www.jsphcs.jp/.

NIHON GAN YAKURI GAKKAI PUROGURAMU KOEN YOSHISHU/ JAPANESE SOCIETY FOR OCULAR PHARMACOLOGY. PROGRAM AND ABSTRACTS OF THE MEETING. *see* MEDICAL SCIENCES—Abstracting, Bibliographies, Statistics

616.89 JPN ISSN 1340-7007
CODEN: NKRZE5
➤ **NIHON KAGAKU RYOHO GAKKAI ZASSHI/JAPANESE JOURNAL OF CHEMOTHERAPY.** Text in English, Japanese. 1953. m. membership. adv. abstr. Index. **Document type:** *Journal, Academic/ Scholarly.*
Formerly (until 1994, vol.42): Nihon Kagaku Ryoho Gakkai Zasshi/ Chemotherapy (0009-3165)
Indexed: ChemAb, DBA, EMBASE, ExcerpMed, ISR, IndMed, Inpharma, R10, Reac, SCOPUS.

—BLDSC (4651.320000), CASDDS, GNLM, INIST, Linda Hall.
Published by: Nihon Kagaku Ryoho Gakkai/Japan Society of Chemotherapy, 2-20-8 Kami-Osaki, Shinagawa-ku, Tokyo, 141-0021, Japan. TEL 81-3-34937129, FAX 81-3-54340843, karyo@jc4.so-net.ne.jp, http://www.chemotherapy.or.jp/. Ed. Kohya Shiba. Circ: 4,000.

615 JPN ISSN 1344-4891
RS192
NIHON P D A GAKUJUTSUSHI GMP TO BARIDESHON. (Personal Digital Assistant) Text in Japanese. 1999. s-a. JPY 5,250 per issue (effective 2004). **Document type:** *Journal, Academic/Scholarly.*
—BLDSC (6413.644200).
Published by: Nihon P D A/000Japan P D A, Flora Bldg, 4-2-8 Hongo, Bunkyo-ku, Tokyo, 113-0033, Japan. TEL 81-3-38151681, FAX 81-3-38151691, hharada@bcasj.or.jp.

NIHON SHINKEI SEISHIN YAKURIGAKU ZASSHI/JAPANESE JOURNAL OF PSYCHOPHARMACOLOGY. *see* MEDICAL SCIENCES—Psychiatry And Neurology

615 JPN ISSN 1342-6753
NIHON SHONI RINSHO YAKURI GAKKAI ZASSHI/JAPANESE JOURNAL OF DEVELOPMENTAL AND THERAPEUTIC PHARMACOLOGY. Text in Japanese; Summaries in English. 1988. a. **Document type:** *Journal, Academic/Scholarly.*
Formerly (until 1995): Hattatsu Yakuri Yakubutsu Chiryo Kenkyukai Zasshi (0914-9864)
—BLDSC (4651.630000).
Published by: Nihon Shoni Rinsho Yakuri Gakkai, Henshushitsu/Japan Society of Developmental Pharmacology and Therapeutics, Kagawa University, Faculty of Medicine, 1750-1 Ikenobe, Miki-cho, Kita-gun, Kagawa 761-0793, Japan. TEL 81-87-8912171, FAX 81-87-8912172.

615 JPN ISSN 1344-6541
NIHON YAKKYOKUHO FORAMU/JAPANESE PHARMACOPOEIAL FORUM. Text in English, Japanese. 1992. q. USD 260 (effective 2011). **Document type:** *Monographic series, Academic/Scholarly.*
—BLDSC (4660.250000). **CCC.**
Published by: Pharmaceutical and Medical Device Regulatory Science Society of Japan, 2-12-15, Shibuya, Shibuya-ku, Tokyo, 150-0002, Japan. TEL 81-3-34005634, FAX 81-3-34003158. **Subscr. to:** Yakuji Nippo Ltd., Kanda-Izumi-cho, Chiyoda-ku, Tokyo 101-0024, Japan. TEL 81-3-3862-2141, FAX 81-3-3866-8495, shuppan@yakuji.co.jp, http://www.yakuji.co.jp/.

615 JPN ISSN 0285-3663
CODEN: NYDHDC
NIIGATA YAKKA DAIGAKU KENKYU HOKOKU/NIIGATA COLLEGE OF PHARMACY AND APPLIED LIFE SCIENCES. BULLETIN. Text in Japanese. 1981. a. **Document type:** *Journal, Academic/Scholarly.*
Published by: Niigata Yakka Daigaku/Niigata College of Pharmacy and Applied Life Sciences, 5-13-2 Kamishinei-cho, Niigata, 950-2081, Japan. TEL 86-25-2693170, FAX 86-25-2681230, http://www.niigatayakudai.jp/.

615 JPN
NIKKEI DRUG INFORMATION. Text in Japanese. 1998. m. JPY 9,600. adv. **Document type:** *Consumer.* **Description:** Contains the latest information on pharmaceutical products provided by manufacturers. Includes information useful to pharmacists and drug store management.
Published by: Nikkei Business Publications Inc. (Subsidiary of: Nihon Keizai Shimbun, Inc.), 2-7-6 Hirakawa-cho, Chiyoda-ku, Tokyo, 102-8622, Japan. TEL 81-3-5210-8311, FAX 81-3-5210-8530, info@nikkeibp-america.com. Ed. Katsuniro Sekimoto. Pub. Hitoshi Sawai. Adv. contact Kenji Tameishi. B&W page JPY 440,000, color page JPY 640,000; trim 210 x 280. Circ: 40,589. **Dist. in America by:** Nikkei Business Publications America Inc., 575 Fifth Ave, 20th Fl, New York, NY 10017.

615.19 JPN
NIPPON KAYAKU. ANNUAL REPORT. Text in Japanese. a. **Document type:** *Corporate.*
Published by: Nippon Kayaku Co., Tokyo Fujimi Bldg., 11-2, Fujimi 1-chome, Tokyo, 102-8172, Japan. TEL 81-3-32375046.

615 JPN
NIPPON KAYAKU SOGO KENKYUJO NENPO/NIPPON KAYAKU RESEARCH LABORATORIES. ANNUAL REPORT. Text in English, Japanese. 1984. a. **Document type:** *Corporate.*
Published by: Nippon Kayaku K.K., Iryo Jigyo Honbu Sogo Kenkyujo/Nippon Kayaku Co., Ltd., Pharmaceuticals Group, Research Laboratories, 31-12, Shimo 3 chome, Kita-ku,, Tokyo, 115-8588, Japan. TEL 81-3-35985204.

615 JPN ISSN 0369-674X
CODEN: NYZZA3
NIPPON YAKUZAISHIKAI ZASSHI/JAPAN PHARMACEUTICAL ASSOCIATION. JOURNAL. Text in Japanese. 1949. m. **Document type:** *Journal, Academic/Scholarly.*
—BLDSC (4805.740000), Linda Hall.
Published by: Nippon Yakuzaishikai/Japan Pharmaceutical Association, Nagai House 4F, 2-12-15 Shibuya, Shibuya-ku, Tokyo, 150-8389, Japan. TEL 81-3-34061171, FAX 81-3-34061499, jpa@nichiyaku.or.jp, http://www.nichiyaku.or.jp/index.html.

615.78 JPN ISSN 1343-4144
CODEN: NNOKFZ
NO NO KAGAKU/BRAIN SCIENCE. Text in Japanese. 1979. m. JPY 2,100 newsstand/cover (effective 2007). **Document type:** *Journal, Academic/Scholarly.*
Formerly (until 1997): Shinkei Seishin Yakuri/Japanese Journal of Neuropsychopharmacology (0388-7588)
Indexed: FoP, SCOPUS.
Published by: Seiwa Shoten Co. Ltd., 2-5 Kamitakaido, 1-chome, Suginami-ku, Tokyo, 168-0074, Japan. TEL 81-3-33290031, FAX 81-3-53747186, http://www.seiwa-pb.co.jp.

615.328 CAN
NON-PRESCRIPTION DRUG REFERENCE FOR HEALTHCARE PROFESSIONALS. Text in English. quadrennial. CAD 120 to non-members; CAD 95 to members (effective 2000). **Document type:** *Directory.*
Former titles: Self-Medication; Canadian Self-Medication
Published by: Canadian Pharmacists Association, 1785 Alta Vista Dr, Ottawa, ON K1G 3Y6, Canada. TEL 613-523-7877, FAX 613-523-0445, info@pharmacists.ca, http://www.pharmacists.ca.

615 USA ISSN 1940-2449
RM671.A1
NONPRESCRIPTION DRUG THERAPY; guiding patient self-care. Text in English. 1999. a. USD 84.95 per issue (effective 2007).
Formerly (until 2002): Nonprescription Drug Therapy
Published by: Facts and Comparisons (Subsidiary of: Wolters Kluwer N.V.), 77 West Port Plz, Ste 450, St. Louis, MO 63146. TEL 314-216-2100, 800-223-0554, FAX 314-216-2280, salessupport@wolterskluwer.com, http://www.factsandcomparisons.com.

615 NOR ISSN 0802-8400
NORGES APOTEKERFORENINGS TIDSSKRIFT. Variant title: N A T. Text in Norwegian. 1893. q. adv. bk.rev. charts; illus. index. 24 p./no.; back issues avail. **Document type:** *Magazine, Trade.*
Formerly (until 1902): Tidsskrift for Apothekvaesen (0332-9259)
Related titles: Online - full text ed.
Indexed: ChemAb.
Published by: Norges Apotekerforening/Norwegian Association of Pharmacists, PO Box 5070, Majorstuen, Oslo, 0301, Norway. TEL 47-21-620200, FAX 47-22-608173, apotekerforeningen@apotek.no. Eds. Unni Eriksen, Trygve Fjeldstad.

615.1 NOR ISSN 0029-1935
CODEN: NFTDAC
NORSK FARMACEUTISK TIDSSKRIFT. Text in Norwegian. 1893. m. NOK 885 in Nordic Region; NOK 1,265 elsewhere; NOK 95 per issue (effective 2007). adv. bk.rev. abstr.; charts; illus.; tr.lit. index. **Document type:** *Magazine, Trade.*
Formerly (until 1915): Farmaceutisk Tidende (0808-1956)
Published by: Norges Farmaceutiske Forening, Tollbugten 35, Oslo, 0157, Norway. TEL 47-21-023354, FAX 47-21-023350, nff@farmaceutene.no. Ed. Hanne Nessing. Adv. contact Magne Egil Rendalen. B&W page NOK 8,150, color page NOK 14,400; 185 x 240. Circ: 3,042 (controlled).

615 USA ISSN 1529-918X
NORTH CAROLINA PHARMACIST. Text in English. 1915. q. adv. back issues avail. **Document type:** *Journal, Trade.* **Description:** Covers issues related to pharmacy practice with emphasis on North Carolina pharmacy.
Formerly (until 1999): Carolina Journal of Pharmacy (0528-1725)
Indexed: P30.
—Linda Hall.
Published by: North Carolina Association of Pharmacists, 109 Church St., Chapel Hill, NC 27516. TEL 919-967-2237, FAX 919-968-9430. Ed. Fred Eckel. R&P, Adv. contact Brent Spodek. Circ: 3,000.

LA NOTICE D'ANTIDOTE. *see* MEDICAL SCIENCES—Experimental Medicine, Laboratory Technique

615 PRT ISSN 1647-3795
▼ **NOTICIAS DE BANDAS NEUROMUSCOLARES.** Text in Portuguese. 2009. irreg. **Document type:** *Bulletin, Trade.*
Related titles: ◆ Spanish ed.: Noticias de Vendaje Neuromuscolar. ISSN 1647-2012; ◆ Portuguese ed.: Medical Taping Concept Bulletin. ISSN 1647-3787.
Published by: ANEID, Productos Farmaceuticos, Rua Jose Florindo - Quinta da Pedra 44 D, Cascais, 2750-401, Portugal. TEL 351-21-4849620, info@aneid.pt, http://www.aneid.pt.

615 PRT ISSN 1647-2012
NOTICIAS DE VENDAJE NEUROMUSCOLAR. Text in Spanish. 2007. irreg. **Document type:** *Magazine, Trade.*
Related titles: ◆ Portuguese ed.: Noticias de Bandas Neuromusculares. ISSN 1647-3795; ◆ Portuguese ed.: Medical Taping Concept Bulletin. ISSN 1647-3787.
Published by: ANEID, Productos Farmaceuticos, Rua Jose Florindo - Quinta da Pedra 44 D, Cascais, 2750-401, Portugal. TEL 351-21-4849620, info@aneid.pt, http://www.aneid.pt.

615.7 ITA
NUOVO COLLEGAMENTO. Text in Italian. 1957. m. (10/yr.). free (effective 2009). **Document type:** *Magazine, Trade.*
Formerly: Collegamento (0390-8739)
Related titles: Online - full text ed.
Published by: Unione Tecnica Italiana Farmacisti, Via Caccianino 3, Milan, 20131, Italy. TEL 39-02-70608367, FAX 39-02-70600297, utifar@utifar.it, http://www.utifar.it. Circ: 16,000.

615 USA ISSN 1074-3871
NURSE PRACTITIONERS' PRESCRIBING REFERENCE. Abbreviated title: N P P R. Text in English. 1994. q. USD 32 domestic; USD 56 foreign; USD 16 per issue domestic; USD 21 per issue foreign (effective 2008). adv. back issues avail.; reprints avail. **Document type:** *Magazine, Trade.* **Description:** Provides prescribing information to Nurse Practitioners and other related healthcare professionals.
Related titles: Online - full text ed.
Indexed: A26, C06, C07, C08, CINAHL, H11, H12, I05.
—CCC.
Published by: Prescribing Reference, Inc. (Subsidiary of: Haymarket Group Ltd.), 114 W 26th St, 4th Fl, New York, NY 10001. TEL 646-638-6000, FAX 646-638-6117, Online@PrescribingRef.com. Eds. Anissa Lee, Diana Ernst. Pub. James Pantaleo TEL 646-638-6137. Circ: 58,541 (paid).

615 USA ISSN 1550-2554
NURSE'S POCKET DRUG GUIDE (YEAR). Text in English. 2004. a., latest 2009. USD 12.95 per issue (effective 2009). back issues avail. **Document type:** *Yearbook, Trade.*
Published by: McGraw-Hill Professional (Subsidiary of: McGraw-Hill Companies, Inc.), 1221 Ave of the Americas, New York, NY 10020. TEL 212-904-2000, FAX 212-512-2000, customer.service@mcgraw-hill.com, http://www.mhprofessional.com/index.php. Eds. Dr. Judith Barberio, Dr. Leonard G Gomella. Pub. Martin J Wonsiewicz.

NURSING (YEAR) DRUG HANDBOOK. *see* MEDICAL SCIENCES—Nurses And Nursing

615 USA ISSN 1941-739X
NURSING (YEAR) STUDENT DRUG HANDBOOK. Text in English. 1997. a. USD 39.95 per issue (effective 2010). adv. back issues avail.; reprints avail. **Document type:** *Handbook/Manual/Guide, Academic/Scholarly.* **Description:** Provides comprehensive, student-focused information on over 750 generic and over 3,500 trade-name drugs in an easy-to-use A-to-Z format, including recently-approved drugs and indications.
Formerly (until 2009): Springhouse Nurse's Drug Guide (1088-8063)
Published by: Lippincott Williams & Wilkins (Subsidiary of: Wolters Kluwer N.V.), 530 Walnut St, Philadelphia, PA 19106. TEL 215-521-8300, FAX 215-521-8902, customerservice@lww.com.

615 610.73 USA ISSN 1550-0543
RM301.12
NURSING SPECTRUM DRUG HANDBOOK. Text in English. 2005. a. USD 29.95 per issue (effective 2011). **Document type:** *Journal, Academic/Scholarly.*
Related titles: Online - full text ed.
Published by: Nursing Spectrum (Subsidiary of: Gannett Company, Inc.), c/o Gannett Healthcare Group, 1721 Moon Lake Blvd, Ste 540, Hoffman Estates, IL 60169. TEL 800-279-0014, OnlineSupport@GannettHG.com, http://www.nurse.com.

NUTRACEUTICAL SCIENCE AND TECHNOLOGY. *see* NUTRITION AND DIETETICS

615 613.2 FRA ISSN 1772-7553
NUTRIFORM' MAGAZINE. Text in French. 2003. bi-m. (9/yr). EUR 350 (effective 2009). **Document type:** *Magazine, Trade.*
Related titles: ◆ Supplement(s): Vitaform'. ISSN 2101-8308.
Published by: Editions Business Group Media, 12 rue Frederic Soddy, ZAC Des Coteaux Sarrazins, Creteil, 94044 Cedex, France. TEL 33-1-56711840, FAX 33-1-43396709.

615.328 658.8 GBR ISSN 1179-1489
▼ ➤ **NUTRITION AND DIETARY SUPPLEMENTS.** Text in English. 2009. a. free (effective 2011). back issues avail. **Document type:** *Journal, Academic/Scholarly.* **Description:** Focuses on research into nutritional requirements in health and disease, impact on metabolism and the identification and optimal use of dietary strategies and supplements necessary for normal growth and development.
Media: Online - full text.
Indexed: A36, F08, N03, SCOPUS.
—CCC.
Published by: Dove Medical Press Ltd., Beechfield House, Winterton Way, Macclesfield, SK11 0JL, United Kingdom. TEL 44-1625-509130, FAX 44-1625-617933. Ed. Chandrika J Piyathilake.

615 330.9 GBR ISSN 1350-1097
O T C BULLETIN; the business newsletter for Europe's consumer healthcare industry. (Over the Counter) Text in English. 1993. 20/yr. GBP 595 in Europe; GBP 625 elsewhere; GBP 50 per issue (effective 2010); includes News@OTCbulletin. adv. Website rev.; bk.rev. 3 cols./p.; back issues avail. **Document type:** *Newsletter, Trade.* **Description:** Contains news and information covering Europe's nonprescription medicine market.
Related titles: Supplement(s): News@OTCbulletin. ISSN 1740-2646. 2002.
Indexed: EMBASE, ExcerpMed.
—CCC.
Published by: O T C Publications Ltd., 54 Creynolds Ln, Shirley, Solihull, W Midlands B90 4ER, United Kingdom. TEL 44-1564-777550, FAX 44-1564-777524. Adv. contact Val Davis. B&W page GBP 940, color page GBP 1,460; trim 297 x 210.

338.476 GBR ISSN 1366-0284
O T C YEARBOOK. (Over the Counter) Variant title: Nicholas Hall's O T C YearBook. Text in English. 1996. a. GBP 850 per issue (effective 2009). **Document type:** *Directory, Trade.* **Description:** Contains comprehensive market data through December 2008 drawn from a database of 60 countries.Covers the facts and figures needed together with unique insight into the major issues facing OTC marketers around the globe.
Related titles: Online - full text ed.
—CCC.
Published by: Nicholas Hall & Company, 35 Alexandra St, Southend-on-Sea, Essex SS1 1BW, United Kingdom. TEL 44-1702-220200, FAX 44-1702-430787, info@nicholashall.com.

615 FRA ISSN 2107-7053
▼ **L'OBSERVANCE.** Text in French. 2009. m. **Document type:** *Bulletin.*
Published by: Federation Nationale des Syndicats d'Internes en Pharmacie http://www.fnsip.fr.

615.1 AUT ISSN 0029-8859
CODEN: OAZEAL
OESTERREICHISCHE APOTHEKER-ZEITUNG. Text in German. 1946. fortn. EUR 108.13; EUR 5.06 newsstand/cover (effective 2007). adv. bk.rev. abstr. index. **Document type:** *Newspaper, Trade.* **Description:** Information and networking for Austrian pharmacists.
Indexed: ChemAb, I12, P30.
—CASDDS, GNLM, INIST. **CCC.**
Published by: Oesterreichische Apotheker-Verlagsgesellschaft mbH, Spitalgasse 31, Vienna, W 1094, Austria. TEL 43-1-4023588, FAX 43-1-4085355, direktion@apoverlag.at, http://www.apoverlag.at. Ed. Monika Heinrich. Adv. contact Margit Moser. Circ: 4,500 (paid and controlled).

615 ESP ISSN 0212-047X
OFFARM. Text in Spanish. 1982. 11/yr. EUR 101.79 combined subscription to individuals print & online eds.; EUR 265.76 to institutions print & online eds. (effective 2009). back issues avail. **Document type:** *Journal, Trade.*
Related titles: Online - full text ed.: ISSN 1578-1569. 1998. EUR 69.84 (effective 2009).
Published by: Elsevier Doyma (Subsidiary of: Elsevier Health Sciences), Traversa de Gracia 17-21, Barcelona, 08021, Spain. TEL 34-932-418800, FAX 34-932-419020, editorial@elsevier.com, http://www.elsevier.es/. Ed. Juan Esteva de Sagrera. Circ: 18,000.

615 USA
THE OFFICIAL INTERNATIONAL PHARMACY DIRECTORY. Text in English. irreg., latest vol.4. USD 49.95 newsstand/cover (effective 2002). **Document type:** *Directory, Consumer.* **Description:** Contains listing of international pharmacies and mail order information to obtain some medications without prescriptions; compiled by an ex-steroid smuggler.
Published by: Anabolicstore.com, Inc., 1155 S Havana, Ste 11-392, Aurora, CO 80012. TEL 303-750-8844, 888-577-4464, FAX 303-752-0719, http://www.anabolicstore.com/. Ed. Andy Beck.

615.1 USA ISSN 1072-2424
OHIO PHARMACIST. Text in English. 1952. m. USD 30; free membership (effective 2005). adv. illus. **Document type:** *Magazine, Trade.*
Published by: Ohio Pharmacists Association, 2155 Riverside Dr, Columbus, OH 44321. TEL 614-586-1497, FAX 614-586-1545. Ed. Amy Bennett. Circ: 4,000 (paid).

615.1 616.992 USA ISSN 1944-9607
THE ONCOLOGY PHARMACIST. Text in English. 2008. 5/yr. free to qualified personnel. adv. **Document type:** *Newspaper, Trade.* **Description:** Provides timely and relevant information to oncology pharmacists on the front line of patient care.
Related titles: Online - full text ed.: ISSN 1944-9593.
Published by: Greenhill Healthcare Communications, 241 Forsgate Dr, Ste 205D, Monroe Township, NJ 08831. TEL 732-656-7935, FAX 732-656-7938, editorial@greenhillhc.com, http://www.greenhillhc.com. Ed. Karen Rosenberg. adv.: B&W page USD 3,570; trim 10.875 x 13.875. Circ: 10,928.

ONKOLOGIYA. *see* MEDICAL SCIENCES—Oncology

615.19 AUS ISSN 1443-2285
➤ **ONLINE JOURNAL OF PHARMACOKINETICS.** Abbreviated title: O J P K. Text in English. 1996. a. USD 80 per issue to institutions (effective 2009). **Document type:** *Journal, Academic/Scholarly.* **Description:** Encourages submissions dealing with interactive pharmacokinetic profiles.
Media: Online - full content.
Published by: Pestsearch International Pty. Ltd., 173 Chatswood Rd, Daisy Hill, QLD 4127, Australia. TEL 61-7-33882588, onlinejournals@comcen.com.au. Ed. Vincent H Guerrini.

➤ **THE OPEN BIOMARKERS JOURNAL.** *see* BIOLOGY

615 NLD ISSN 1874-1266
RS199.5
➤ **THE OPEN DRUG DELIVERY JOURNAL.** Text in English. 2007. irreg. free (effective 2011). **Document type:** *Journal, Academic/Scholarly.* **Description:** Publishes research articles and letters in all areas of drug delivery, including drug targeting.
Media: Online - full text.
Indexed: A01, B19, CA, EMBASE, ExcerpMed, NSA, SCOPUS, T02. —CCC.
Published by: Bentham Open (Subsidiary of: Bentham Science Publishers Ltd.), PO Box 294, Bussum, AG 1400, Netherlands. TEL 31-35-6923800, FAX 31-35-6980150, subscriptions@bentham.org.

615 NLD ISSN 1877-3818
▼ **THE OPEN DRUG DISCOVERY JOURNAL.** Text in English. 2010. irreg. free (effective 2011). **Document type:** *Journal, Academic/Scholarly.*
Media: Online - full text.
Published by: Bentham Open (Subsidiary of: Bentham Science Publishers Ltd.), PO Box 294, Bussum, AG 1400, Netherlands. TEL 31-35-6923800, FAX 31-35-6980150, subscriptions@bentham.org. Ed. Narender R Gavva.

615 NLD ISSN 1874-0731
RM301.55
➤ **THE OPEN DRUG METABOLISM JOURNAL.** Text in English. 2008. irreg. free (effective 2011). **Document type:** *Journal, Academic/Scholarly.*
Media: Online - full text.
Indexed: A01, EMBASE, ExcerpMed, NSA, SCOPUS.
Published by: Bentham Open (Subsidiary of: Bentham Science Publishers Ltd.), PO Box 294, Bussum, AG 1400, Netherlands. TEL 31-35-6923800, FAX 31-35-6980150, subscriptions@bentham.org. Ed. Bruce D Hammock.

615.7 NLD ISSN 1876-5211
QR177
➤ **THE OPEN DRUG RESISTANCE JOURNAL.** Text in English. 2008. irreg. free (effective 2009). **Document type:** *Journal, Academic/Scholarly.*
Media: Online - full text.
Published by: Bentham Open (Subsidiary of: Bentham Science Publishers Ltd.), PO Box 294, Bussum, AG 1400, Netherlands. TEL 31-35-6923800, FAX 31-35-6980150, subscriptions@bentham.org.

615 614 NLD ISSN 1876-8180
▼ ➤ **THE OPEN DRUG SAFETY JOURNAL.** Text in English. 2010. a. free (effective 2011). **Document type:** *Journal, Trade.* **Description:** Covers advances in the field of drug safety, including adverse effects of individual drugs and drug classes, management of adverse effects, pharmacovigilance and pharmacoepidemiology of new and existing drugs, and post-marketing surveillance.
Media: Online - full text.
Published by: Bentham Open (Subsidiary of: Bentham Science Publishers Ltd.), PO Box 294, Bussum, AG 1400, Netherlands. TEL 31-35-6923800, FAX 31-35-6980150, subscriptions@bentham.org, http://www.bentham.org. Ed. Roberto Manfredi.

615 NLD ISSN 1874-1045
QD415.A1
➤ **THE OPEN MEDICINAL CHEMISTRY JOURNAL.** Text in English. 2007. irreg. free (effective 2011). **Document type:** *Journal, Academic/Scholarly.* **Description:** Covers all areas of medicinal chemistry and rational drug design.
Media: Online - full text.
Indexed: A01, CA, EMBASE, ExcerpMed, NSA, P30, SCOPUS, T02.
Published by: Bentham Open (Subsidiary of: Bentham Science Publishers Ltd.), PO Box 294, Bussum, AG 1400, Netherlands. TEL 31-35-6923800, FAX 31-35-6980150, subscriptions@bentham.org, http://www.bentham.org. Ed. Jonathan F Head.

➤ **THE OPEN NUTRACEUTICALS JOURNAL.** *see* NUTRITION AND DIETETICS

615 NLD ISSN 1874-1436
➤ **THE OPEN PHARMACOLOGY JOURNAL.** Text in English. 2007. irreg. free (effective 2011). **Document type:** *Journal, Academic/Scholarly.* **Description:** Covers all areas of pharmacology.
Media: Online - full text.
Indexed: A01, AnBeAb, CA, EMBASE, ExcerpMed, NSA, P30, R10, Reac, SCOPUS, T02.
Published by: Bentham Open (Subsidiary of: Bentham Science Publishers Ltd.), PO Box 294, Bussum, AG 1400, Netherlands. TEL 31-35-6923800, FAX 31-35-6980150, subscriptions@bentham.org. Ed. Geoffrey Burnstock.

615.9 NLD ISSN 1874-3404
RA1190
➤ **THE OPEN TOXICOLOGY JOURNAL.** Text in English. 2007. irreg. free (effective 2011). **Document type:** *Journal, Academic/Scholarly.*
Media: Online - full text.
Indexed: A01, EMBASE, ESPM, ExcerpMed, SCOPUS, ToxAb. —Linda Hall.
Published by: Bentham Open (Subsidiary of: Bentham Science Publishers Ltd.), PO Box 294, Bussum, AG 1400, Netherlands. TEL 31-35-6923800, FAX 31-35-6980150, subscriptions@bentham.org. Ed. Jacques Descotes.

615.95 NLD ISSN 1875-4147
QP631
➤ **THE OPEN TOXINOLOGY JOURNAL.** Text in English. 2008. irreg. free (effective 2011). **Document type:** *Journal, Academic/Scholarly.* **Description:** Covers all areas on toxins derived from plants, animals and microbes.
Media: Online - full text.
Indexed: E04, E05.
Published by: Bentham Open (Subsidiary of: Bentham Science Publishers Ltd.), PO Box 294, Bussum, AG 1400, Netherlands. TEL 31-35-6923800, FAX 31-35-6980150, subscriptions@bentham.org. Ed. Holger Barth.

615 NLD ISSN 1875-0354
QR189
➤ **THE OPEN VACCINE JOURNAL.** Text in English. 2008. irreg. free (effective 2011). **Document type:** *Journal, Academic/Scholarly.*
Media: Online - full text.
Indexed: A01, EMBASE, ExcerpMed, P30, SCOPUS.
Published by: Bentham Open (Subsidiary of: Bentham Science Publishers Ltd.), PO Box 294, Bussum, AG 1400, Netherlands. TEL 31-35-6923800, FAX 31-35-6980150, subscriptions@bentham.org. Ed. Dr. Marc H V Van Regenmortel.

➤ **OPHTHALMIC DRUG FACTS.** *see* MEDICAL SCIENCES—Ophthalmology And Optometry

615 PRT ISSN 0872-7554
ORDEM DOS FARMACEUTICOS. REVISTA. Text in Portuguese. 1983. bi-m. adv. bk.rev. back issues avail. **Document type:** *Magazine, Trade.* **Description:** Presents current information on the society's activities and short articles of interest to the average pharmacist.
Formerly (until 1994): Ordem dos Farmaceuticos. Boletim Informativo (0872-7767)
Related titles: Online - full text ed.
Published by: Ordem dos Farmaceuticos, Rua da Sociedade Farmaceutica, 18, Lisbon, Lisboa 1169-075, Portugal. TEL 351-213-191370, FAX 351-213-191399, secretariogeral@ordemfarmaceuticos.pt, http://www.ordemfarmaceuticos.pt. Ed. Jose Aranda da Silv. R&P Ivana Silva. Adv. contact Antonio Viveiros. Circ: 9,500.

610.951 NLD ISSN 1598-2386
➤ **ORIENTAL PHARMACY & EXPERIMENTAL MEDICINE.** Text in English. 2000. 4/yr. EUR 434, USD 535 combined subscription to institutions (print & online eds.) (effective 2012). **Document type:** *Journal, Academic/Scholarly.*
Formerly (until 2001): International Journal of Oriental Medical (1229-7763)
Related titles: Online - full text ed.: ISSN 2211-1069.
Published by: Springer Netherlands (Subsidiary of: Springer Science+Business Media), Van Godewijckstraat 30, Dordrecht, 3311 GX, Netherlands. TEL 31-78-6576050, FAX 31-78-6576474, http://www.springer.com.

641.2 NLD ISSN 1382-7529
ORTHO; orthomoleculair magazine. Text in Dutch. 1983. bi-m. EUR 79.85 (effective 2010). adv. **Document type:** *Magazine, Trade.*
Formerly (until 1994): Orthomoleculair (0168-1087)
Published by: Ortho Communications & Science b.v., Anholtseweg 36, Gendringen, 7081 CM, Netherlands. TEL 31-315-695211, FAX 31-315-695215, ortho@orthoeurope.com. Eds. J van Dongen, Dr. G E Schuitemaker. adv.: page EUR 1,810; 210 x 280. Circ: 6,500.

615.1 JPN ISSN 0030-669X
OTSUKA YAKUHO/OTSUKA PHARMACEUTICAL FACTORY. JOURNAL. Text in Japanese. 1950. 11/yr. illus. **Document type:** *Journal, Academic/Scholarly.*
Published by: Otsuka Seiyaku Kojo/Otsuka Pharmaceutical Factory, 115 Tateiwa, Muya-cho, Naruto, Tokushima 772-8601, Japan. TEL 81-88-6851151, FAX 81-88-6857667, http://www.otsukakj.jp/. Ed. M Ohsaka. Circ: 61,500.

615 GBR ISSN 0957-7831
RS1
OVER THE COUNTER. Abbreviated title: O T C. Text in English. 1989. m. includes subscr. with Chemist+Druggist. adv. **Document type:** *Magazine, Trade.*
Related titles: ◆ Supplement to: Chemist & Druggist. ISSN 0009-3033. —BLDSC (6314.899800). **CCC.**
Published by: U B M Medica Ltd, Ludgate House, 245 Blackfriars Rd, London, SE1 9UY, United Kingdom. TEL 44-20-79215000, FAX 44-20-79218312, http://www.ubmmedica.com. Adv. contact Dan Spruytenburg TEL 44-20-79218126. page GBP 4,430; trim 165 x 297.

615 JPN ISSN 0300-8533
CODEN: OYYAA2
➤ **OYO YAKURI/PHARMACOMETRICS.** Text in English, Japanese. 1967. m. JPY 10,000, USD 120 (effective 2000). adv. bk.rev. index. back issues avail. **Document type:** *Journal, Academic/Scholarly.* **Description:** Applied pharmacology, pharmacodynamics, pharmacokinetics and toxicity studies of new drugs.
Indexed: A22, B25, BIOSIS Prev, C33, ChemAb, ChemTitl, EMBASE, ExcerpMed, Inpharma, MycolAb, R10, Reac, SCOPUS. —BLDSC (6447.085000), CASDDS, GNLM, IE, Infotrieve, Ingenta, INIST. **CCC.**
Published by: Oyo Yakuri Kenkyukai/Japanese Society of Pharmacometrics, C.P.O. Box 180, Sendai, 980-8691, Japan. TEL 81-22-267-3810, FAX 81-22-222-0515. Ed. Dr. Hikaru Ozawa. Adv. contact Oyo Yakuri Kenkyukai. Circ: 1,200.

615 USA ISSN 1052-1372
CODEN: PPTTEK
➤ **P & T;** journal for formulary management. (Pharmacy and Therapeutics) Variant title: Pharmacy and Therapeutics Journal. Text in English. 1976. m. USD 85 domestic; USD 120 foreign; USD 12 per issue domestic; USD 22 per issue foreign; free to qualified personnel (effective 2010). adv. back issues avail.; reprints avail. **Document type:** *Journal, Academic/Scholarly.*
Former titles (until 1990): Hospital Therapy (8750-6831); (until 1985): Drug Therapy. Clinical Therapeutics in the Hospital (0887-4433); (until 1982): Drug Therapy Hospital (0887-4441); (until 1980): Drug Therapy (0160-9459)
Related titles: Online - full text ed.: free (effective 2010).
Indexed: A22, C06, C07, EMBASE, ExcerpMed, I12, Inpharma, P30, P35, R10, Reac, SCOPUS. —BLDSC (6327.163000), GNLM, IE, Ingenta. **CCC.**
Published by: MediMedia USA, Inc. (Subsidiary of: United Business Media Limited), 780 Township Line Rd, Yardley, PA 19067. TEL 267-685-2300, FAX 267-685-2966, info@medimedia.com, http://www.medimedia.com. Ed. Sonja Sherritze TEL 267-685-2779. Pub. Timothy P Search TEL 267-685-2781.

615.1 USA ISSN 1079-7440
CODEN: JPHTEU
➤ **P D A JOURNAL OF PHARMACEUTICAL SCIENCE AND TECHNOLOGY.** (Parenteral Drug Association) Text in English. 1946. bi-m. free to members (effective 2009). bk.rev. charts; illus. index. 80 p./no.; back issues avail.; reprints avail. **Document type:** *Journal, Academic/Scholarly.* **Description:** Technical articles in the field of pharmaceutical science and technology.
Former titles (until vol.48, no.5, 1994): Journal of Pharmaceutical Science and Technology (1076-397X); (until vol.48, no.1, 1994): Journal of Parenteral Science and Technology (0279-7976); (until 1981): Parenteral Drug Association. Journal (0161-1933); (until vol.32, 1978): Parenteral Drug Association. Bulletin (0048-2986)
Related titles: CD-ROM ed.; Online - full text ed.: ISSN 1948-2124. free (effective 2009); ◆ Supplement(s): P D A Technical Reports.
Indexed: A22, ASCA, B&BAb, ChemAb, ChemTitl, DBA, EMBASE, ExcerpMed, F09, I12, IDIS, IndMed, MEDLINE, P30, R10, Reac, SCOPUS. —BLDSC (6413.644300), CASDDS, GNLM, IE, Ingenta, INIST, Linda Hall. **CCC.**
Published by: Parenteral Drug Association, Bethesda Towers, 4350 EW Hwy, Ste 150, Bethesda, MD 20814. TEL 301-656-5900, FAX 301-986-1093, info@pda.org, http://www.pda.org. Circ: 10,000.

615.19 USA
P D A LETTER; science, technology, quality, regulatory, community. Text in English. 1964. 10/yr. free to members (effective 2010). 48 p./no.; back issues avail. **Document type:** *Newsletter, Consumer.* **Description:** Covers pharmaceutical science and technology news, PDA activities and events, member news, international regulatory updates and commentary, as well as services and publications of the PDA.
Related titles: Online - full text ed.
Published by: Parenteral Drug Association, Bethesda Towers, 4350 EW Hwy, Ste 150, Bethesda, MD 20814. TEL 301-656-5900, FAX 301-986-1093, info@pda.org.

615.19 USA
P D A TECHNICAL REPORTS. Text in English. 1978. irreg., latest vol.50, 2010. price varies. back issues avail. **Document type:** *Monographic series, Academic/Scholarly.* **Description:** Provides guidance and opinions on a variety of important scientific and regulatory topics pertaining to pharmaceutical and biopharmaceutical production.
Former titles (until 19??): Parenteral Drug Association. Technical Report (0277-3406); (until 1981): Parenteral Drug Association. Technical Monograph (0196-3619)
Related titles: Online - full text ed.; ◆ Supplement to: P D A Journal of Pharmaceutical Science and Technology. ISSN 1079-7440. —INIST, Linda Hall.
Published by: Parenteral Drug Association, Bethesda Towers, 4350 EW Hwy, Ste 150, Bethesda, MD 20814. TEL 301-656-5900, FAX 301-986-1093, info@pda.org.

P D R DRUG GUIDE FOR MENTAL HEALTH PROFESSIONALS. (Physicians' Desk Reference) *see* MEDICAL SCIENCES—Psychiatry And Neurology

615 USA ISSN 1523-9411
RM301.15
P D R FAMILY GUIDE TO PRESCRIPTION DRUGS. (Physicians' Desk Reference) Variant title: Family Guide to Prescription Drugs. Text in English. 1993. irreg. **Document type:** *Monographic series, Trade.*
Related titles: Online - full text ed.
Published by: Thomson P D R, Five Paragon Dr, Montvale, NJ 07645. TEL 888-227-6469, FAX 201-722-2680, TH.customerservice@thomson.com, http://www.pdr.net.

P D R FOR HERBAL MEDICINES. (Physicians' Desk Reference) *see* ALTERNATIVE MEDICINE

P D R FOR NONPRESCRIPTION DRUGS, DIETARY SUPPLEMENTS, AND HERBS. (Physicians' Desk Reference) *see* MEDICAL SCIENCES

615 USA ISSN 1540-6156
P D R GUIDE TO BIOLOGICAL AND CHEMICAL WARFARE RESPONSE. (Physicians' Desk Reference) Variant title: Guide to Biological and Chemical Warfare Response. Text in English. 2002. s-a. USD 39.95 newsstand/cover (effective 2005). **Document type:** *Journal, Academic/Scholarly.* **Description:** Contains all the basics required for safe, effective emergency action when confronted with a biological or chemical attack.
Published by: Thomson P D R, Five Paragon Dr, Montvale, NJ 07645. TEL 888-227-6469, FAX 201-722-2680, TH.customerservice@thomson.com, http://www.pdr.net.

P D R GUIDE TO DRUG INTERACTIONS, SIDE EFFECTS, AND INDICATIONS. (Physicians' Desk Reference) *see* MEDICAL SCIENCES

P D R PHARMACOPOEIA POCKET DOSING GUIDE. (Physician's Desk Reference) *see* MEDICAL SCIENCES

615 USA ISSN 1542-1945
P F ONLINE. Text in English. 1975. bi-m. USD 685 (effective 2011). **Document type:** *Directory, Trade.* **Description:** Presents proposed U.S.P. National Formulary revisions for public comment.
Media: Online - full text.
Published by: United States Pharmacopeial Convention, Inc., 12601 Twinbrook Pkwy, Rockville, MD 20852. TEL 301-881-0666, 301-881-0666, 800-877-7633, 800-877-6733, 800-227-8772, 800-227-8772, FAX 301-816-8148, 802-864-7626, 301-816-8148, custsvc@usp.org.

615 DEU ISSN 0945-7704
P H B - PHARMAZIEHISTORISCHE BIBLIOGRAPHIE. Text in German. 1955. a. EUR 16.30 (effective 2010). **Document type:** *Journal, Trade.*
Formerly (until 1993): Pharmaziegeschichtliche Rundschau (0936-7322)
Indexed: P30.

Published by: Govi Verlag Pharmazeutischer Verlag GmbH, Carl Mannich Str 26, Eschborn, 65760, Germany. TEL 49-6196-928262, FAX 49-6196-928203, service@govi.de, http://www.govi.de.

615 DEU ISSN 1860-8736 CODEN: AMCHDI
P K A AKTIV; Forum fuer die Pharmazeutisch-kaufmaennische Angestellte. (Pharmazeutisch Kaufmaennische Angestellte) Text in German. 1952. 3/yr. EUR 12; EUR 8 newsstand/cover (effective 2012); free with subscr. to Deutsche Apotheker Zeitung. **Document type:** *Journal, Trade.* **Description:** Aimed at enlightening pharmaceutical assistants.
Former titles (until 2005): P K A Aktuell (0944-7032); (until 1993): Apothekenhelferin Heute (0939-3331); Apothekenhelferin (0570-4723)
Related titles: ◆ Supplement to: Deutsche Apotheker Zeitung. ISSN 0011-9857.
—CASDDS, GNLM, INIST.
Published by: Deutscher Apotheker Verlag, Postfach 101061, Stuttgart, 70009, Germany. TEL 49-711-25820, FAX 49-711-2582290, http://www.deutscher-apotheker-verlag.de.

615 USA ISSN 1555-0087
P L JOURNAL CLUB. (Prescriber's Letter) Text in English. 2004 (Dec.). m. USD 197 combined subscription (print & online eds.) (effective 2011). **Document type:** *Journal, Trade.*
Related titles: Online - full text ed.: ISSN 1555-0095.
Published by: Therapeutic Research Center, 3120 W March Ln, PO Box 8190, Stockton, CA 95208. TEL 209-472-2240, FAX 209-472-2249, http://www.therapeuticresearch.com.

P M 360; the full spectrum of product management. (Product Management) *see* BUSINESS AND ECONOMICS—Marketing And Purchasing

615.1 USA ISSN 1941-9481
P.R.N. Text in English. 2007. m. USD 48 (effective 2008). **Document type:** *Newsletter, Trade.*
Published by: P R N Publishing, 68-37 Yellowstone Blvd, Ste C-22, Forest Hills, NY 11375. TEL 718-263-4632, askprn@gmail.com. Ed. James Murphy.

615 DEU
P T A DIALOG. (Pharmazeutisch - Technische Assistentin) Text in German. 1987. q. back issues avail. **Document type:** *Trade.*
Published by: (Beiersdorf AG), Industrie-Contact GmbH, Bahrenfelder Marktplatz 7, Hamburg, 22761, Germany. TEL 49-40-8996660, FAX 49-49-8902641, pr@ic-gruppe.com. Ed. Juergen Klimke.

615 DEU
P T A FORUM. (Pharmazeutisch Technische Assistentin) Text in German. 1993. m. EUR 25.80; EUR 3.50 newsstand/cover (effective 2010). adv. **Document type:** *Magazine, Trade.*
Published by: Govi Verlag Pharmazeutischer Verlag GmbH, Carl Mannich Str 26, Eschborn, 65760, Germany. TEL 49-6196-928262, FAX 49-6196-928203, service@govi.de, http://www.govi.de. Circ: 36,686 (controlled).

615 DEU ISSN 0302-167X CODEN: PTAHAF
P T A HEUTE; Zeitschrift der DAZ fuer die Pharmazeutisch-technische Assistentin. (Pharmazeutisch Technische Assistentin) Text in German. 1954. 2/m. EUR 52; EUR 6 newsstand/cover (effective 2012). adv. bk.rev. **Document type:** *Journal, Trade.*
Former titles (until 1974): Apothekerpraktikant und Pharmazeutisch-Technische Assistent (0303-6219); (until 1971): Praktikantenbriefe (0554-9957)
Indexed: A22, ChemAb.
—GNLM, IE, Infotrieve. **CCC.**
Published by: Deutscher Apotheker Verlag, Postfach 101061, Stuttgart, 70009, Germany. TEL 49-711-25820, FAX 49-711-2582290, service@deutscher-apotheker-verlag.de, http://www.deutscher-apotheker-verlag.de. Ed. Reinhild Berger. Adv. contact Thomas Christ. Circ: 50,903 (paid).

615 DEU ISSN 0722-1029 CODEN: PTAED9
DIE P T A IN DER APOTHEKE; Fachzeitschrift fuer pharmazeutisch-technische Assistenten. (Pharmazeutisch Technische Assistenten) Text in German. 1972. m. EUR 60; EUR 48 to students (effective 2010). adv. **Document type:** *Magazine, Trade.*
Former titles (until 1981): P T A in der Praktischen Pharmazie (0344-3760); (until 1978): P T A in Apotheke und Industrie (0342-8389)
Related titles: ◆ Supplement(s): P T A - Repetitorium. ISSN 0342-8397.
—CASDDS. **CCC.**
Published by: Umschau Zeitschriftenverlag Breidenstein GmbH, Otto-Volger-Str 15, Sulzbach, 65843, Germany. TEL 49-6196-76670, FAX 49-6196-7667269, TELEX 411964, info@uzv.de.

615 DEU ISSN 1864-2756
DAS P T A MAGAZIN. (Pharmazeutisch Technischen Assistentin) Text in German. 2007. m. EUR 49; EUR 39 to students; EUR 7 newsstand/cover (effective 2010). adv. **Document type:** *Magazine, Trade.*
Published by: Springer Gesundheits- und Pharmazieverlag GmbH (Subsidiary of: Springer Science+Business Media), Am Forsthaus Gravenbruch 5, Neu-Isenburg, 63263, Germany. TEL 49-6102-882700, FAX 49-6102-8827082, kontakt@springer-gup.de. Adv. contact Jochen Malzburg.

615 DEU ISSN 0342-8397 CODEN: PTARDE
P T A - REPETITORIUM. Text in German. 1972. m.
Related titles: ◆ Supplement to: Die P T A in der Apotheke. ISSN 0722-1029.
Published by: Umschau Zeitschriftenverlag Breidenstein GmbH, Otto-Volger-Str 15, Sulzbach, 65843, Germany. TEL 49-69-2600621, FAX 49-69-2600609.

615 DEU ISSN 0945-5566 CODEN: PZPREU
P Z PRISMA. (Pharmazeutische Zeitung) Text in German. 1983. q. EUR 50; EUR 15 newsstand/cover (effective 2010). adv. **Document type:** *Journal, Academic/Scholarly.*
Former titles (until 1994): P Z Wissenschaft (0935-5901); (until 1988): Pharmazeutische Zeitung. Scientific Edition (0724-6315)
Indexed: A22, CIN, ChemAb, ChemTitl, P30, SCOPUS.
—BLDSC (7163.530500), CASDDS, GNLM, IE, Infotrieve, Ingenta. **CCC.**
Published by: (Bundesvereinigung Deutscher Apothekerverbaende), Govi Verlag Pharmazeutischer Verlag GmbH, Carl Mannich Str 26, Eschborn, 65760, Germany. TEL 49-6196-928262, FAX 49-6196-928203, service@govi.de, http://www.govi.de.

615.1 DEU ISSN 0936-658X
P Z SCHRIFTENREIHE. (Pharmazeutische Zeitung) Text in German. 1989. irreg., latest vol.15, 2005. price varies. **Document type:** *Monographic series, Academic/Scholarly.*
—CCC.
Published by: Govi Verlag Pharmazeutischer Verlag GmbH, Carl Mannich Str 26, Eschborn, 65760, Germany. TEL 49-6196-928262, FAX 49-6196-928203, service@govi.de.

615 GBR
P3; pharmacy from a new perspective. Text in English. 1992. m. adv. **Document type:** *Magazine, Trade.*
Formerly (until 2006): Pharmacy Products Review
Related titles: Online - full text ed.
Published by: Communications International Group, 207 Linen Hall, 162-168 Regent St, London, W1B 5TB, United Kingdom. TEL 44-20-74341530, FAX 44-20-75347208, cosint@1530.com.

615 ITA ISSN 1972-3245
PACCHETTI INFORMATIVI SUI FARMACI. Text in Multiple languages. 2001. q. **Document type:** *Trade.*
Formerly (until 2005): Pacchetto Informativo (1972-3261)
Related titles: Online - full text ed.: ISSN 1972-3210.
Published by: Centro per la Valutazione dell'Efficacia dell'Assistenza Sanitaria, Viale L A Muratori 201, Modena, Italy. TEL 39-059-435200, FAX 39-059-435222.

615 618.92 NZL ISSN 1174-5878 CODEN: PTDGFW
➤ **PAEDIATRIC DRUGS.** Variant title: Pediatric Drugs. Text in English. 1999. bi-m. price varies based on the number of users. back issues avail.; reprints avail. **Document type:** *Journal, Academic/Scholarly.* **Description:** Provides practical advice and reviews on the safe and effective use of drugs in children.
Related titles: Online - full text ed.: ISSN 1179-2019 (from IngentaConnect).
Indexed: A01, A03, A08, A22, A26, CA, CurCont, E01, E08, EMBASE, ExcerpMed, H12, I05, I12, IndMed, Inpharma, MEDLINE, P20, P22, P30, P35, P54, PQC, R10, Reac, S02, S03, S09, SCI, SCOPUS, T02, W07.
—BLDSC (6333.399732), IE, Infotrieve, Ingenta. **CCC.**
Published by: Adis International Ltd. (Subsidiary of: Wolters Kluwer N.V.), 41 Centorian Dr, Mairangi Bay, Private Bag 65901, Auckland, 1311, New Zealand. TEL 64-9-4770700, FAX 64-9-4770764, journals@adis.com, http://www.adisonline.info/. Ed. Michelle I Wilde. **Americas subscr. to:** Adis International Inc.

615.19 PAK ISSN 1011-601X CODEN: PJPSEN
➤ **PAKISTAN JOURNAL OF PHARMACEUTICAL SCIENCES.** Text in English. s-a. PKR 150, USD 25. **Document type:** *Journal, Academic/Scholarly.* **Description:** Publishes short research papers and reviews in pharmaceutical chemistry, pharmaceutics, pharmacognosy, pharmacology, and related studies in toxicology.
Related titles: CD-ROM ed.
Indexed: A34, A35, A36, A37, AgBio, AgrForAb, BP, C25, C30, CA, CABA, ChemAb, ChemTitl, D01, E12, EMBASE, ExcerpMed, ExtraMED, F08, F11, F12, FS&TA, GH, H16, H17, IndVet, LT, MEDLINE, N02, N03, N04, P30, P32, P33, P37, P39, P40, PGegResA, PGrRegA, PHN&I, R07, R08, R10, R11, R12, R13, RA&MP, RM&VM, RRTA, Reac, S12, S13, S16, SCI, SCOPUS, SoyAb, T02, T05, TAR, TriticAb, VS, W07, W10.
—CASDDS.
Address: University of Karachi, Faculty of Pharmacy, Karachi, 75270, Pakistan. Ed. Dr. Anwar Ejaz Beg.

615 PAK ISSN 0255-7088 CODEN: PJPHEO
PAKISTAN JOURNAL OF PHARMACOLOGY. Text in English. 1983. s-a. USD 50. **Document type:** *Journal, Academic/Scholarly.*
Indexed: CIN, ChemAb, ChemTitl.
—CASDDS.
Published by: University of Karachi, Department of Pharmacology, Karachi, 75270, Pakistan. TEL 479001. Ed. S.I. Ahmad.

615 USA
PALMETTO PHARMACIST. Text in English. 1966. bi-m. free to members. adv. **Document type:** *Journal, Academic/Scholarly.*
Published by: South Carolina Pharmacy Association, 1350 Browning Rd, Columbia, SC 29210. TEL 803-354-9977, 800-532-4033, FAX 803-354-9207, http://www.scrx.org. Circ: 1,500.

PARTICULATE SCIENCE AND TECHNOLOGY; an international journal. *see* ENGINEERING—Chemical Engineering

615.10272 GBR ISSN 1462-2394
PATENT FAST-ALERT. Text in English. 199?. w. **Document type:** *Handbook/Manual/Guide, Trade.* **Description:** Provides a therapeutic patent monitoring service which includes clues to research trends and represents a vital competitive intelligence tool for research and development groups.
Formerly (until 1998): Investigational Drug Patent Fast-Alert (1357-7026)
Media: Online - full text.
—CCC.
Published by: Current Drugs Ltd. (Subsidiary of: Thomson Reuters Corp.), 1 Chapel Quarter, Mount St, Nottingham, NG1 6HQ, United Kingdom. TEL 44-207-5424300, general.info@thomsonreuters.com, http://science.thomsonreuters.com/.

615 USA
PATIENT'S DIGEST. Text in English. 2006 (Jan.). bi-m. **Document type:** *Magazine, Trade.* **Description:** Aims to help physicians and their staff provide their patients with clear and practical information on how to analyze prescription coverage options and to provide patients with all the information they need to successfully navigate the Medicare Part D process.
Published by: Brandofino Communications, LLC, 12 Spruce Park, Syosset, NY 11791. TEL 516-364-2575, http://brandofinocommunications.com/. Ed. Paula S Katz. Pub. Jeanette Brandofino.

615.13 USA ISSN 1533-578X
RJ560
PEDIATRIC DOSAGE HANDBOOK. Text in English. 1992. a. USD 59.95 per issue (effective 2011). back issues avail. **Document type:** *Handbook/Manual/Guide, Trade.*
Published by: Lexi-Comp, Inc., 1100 Terex Rd, Hudson, OH 44236. TEL 330-650-6506, 800-837-5394, FAX 330-656-4307, http://www.lexi.com.

PEDIATRIC PHARMACOTHERAPY; a monthly review for health care professionals. *see* MEDICAL SCIENCES—Pediatrics

615.1 USA ISSN 0031-4633
THE PENNSYLVANIA PHARMACIST. Text in English. 1926. bi-m. USD 100 to non-members (effective 2005); includes Pharmacy News and Review. adv. bk.rev. illus.; tr.lit. cum.index. 32 p./no. 3 cols./p.; **Document type:** *Journal, Trade.* **Description:** Provides information on issues and concerns of interest to pharmacists.
Indexed: P30.
—BLDSC (6421.748800), IE, Ingenta, Linda Hall. **CCC.**
Published by: Pennsylvania Pharmacists Association, 508 N Third St, Harrisburg, PA 17101-1199. TEL 717-234-6151, FAX 717-236-1618, ppa@papharmacists.com, http://www.papharmacists.com. Ed. Pat Peppie. Adv. contact Tammy A Linn. B&W page USD 429; trim 7.5 x 10. Circ: 1,500 (paid).

615 NZL ISSN 1177-391X
RS400
➤ **PERSPECTIVES IN MEDICINAL CHEMISTRY.** Text in English. 2007. irreg. free (effective 2011). **Document type:** *Journal, Academic/Scholarly.*
Media: Online - full text.
Indexed: A01, P30, T02.
—CCC.
Published by: Libertas Academica Ltd., PO Box 302-624, North Harbour, Auckland, 1330, New Zealand. TEL 64-21-662617, FAX 64-21-740006, editorial@la-press.com, http://www.la-press.com. Ed. Yitzhak Tor.

615 ESP ISSN 1888-2528
PHARM. Text in Spanish. 2007. m. **Document type:** *Magazine, Trade.*
Published by: Editores Medicos, S.A., Alsasua 16, Madrid, 28013, Spain. TEL 34-91-3768140, FAX 34-91-3769907, edimsa@edimsa.es, http://www.edimsa.es.

615 ISR
THE PHARMA. Text in Hebrew. 2007. irreg., latest no.11, 2010. **Document type:** *Academic/Scholarly.*
Media: Online - full text.
Published by: The Medical esther@themedical.co.il.

615 DNK ISSN 1902-7966
PHARMA; medlemsblad for pharmadanmark. Text in Danish; Summaries in English. 1890. m. DKK 900 (effective 2008). adv. bk.rev. abstr.; bibl.; charts; illus.; stat. index, cum.index. back issues avail. **Document type:** *Magazine, Trade.*
Former titles (until 2007): Farmaceuten (0904-6542); (until 1989): Farmaceutisk Tidende (0367-1720); (until 1895): Blad for Pharmaceutisk Medhjaelperforening (0301-8792)
Related titles: Online - full text ed.: ISSN 1902-7974. 2002.
Indexed: ChemAb, P30.
—GNLM.
Published by: Pharmadanmark/Danish Pharmacists' Association, Rygaards Alle 1, Hellerup, 2900, Denmark. TEL 45-39-463600, FAX 45-39-463639, df@pharmadanmark.dk. Ed. Christian K Thorsted TEL 45-39-463614. Adv. contact Carsten Ploughmann. Circ: 5,500.

616 DEU ISSN 1617-8645
PHARMA AKTUELL; Europaeisches Journal fuer Medizin, Pharmazie und Finanzen. Text in German. 2000. bi-m. EUR 41; EUR 7 newsstand/cover (effective 2008). adv. **Document type:** *Magazine, Trade.*
Published by: Pharma Aktuell Verlagsgruppe GmbH, Lehmweg 11, Varel, 26316, Germany. TEL 49-4451-950395, FAX 49-4451-950390. Ed. Maria Gerigk. Adv. contact Barbara Bepler. B&W page EUR 4,550, color page EUR 5,502. Circ: 57,873 (paid and controlled).

615 USA ISSN 1556-3677
PHARMA & BIO INGREDIENTS. Text in English. 2004 (Dec.). bi-m. free to qualified personnel (effective 2009). adv. back issues avail. **Document type:** *Magazine, Trade.* **Description:** Designed for the formulation needs of the pharmaceutical and biopharmaceutical chemist.
Related titles: Online - full text ed.
Published by: Rodman Publishing, Corp., 70 Hilltop Rd, 3rd Fl, Ramsey, NJ 07446. TEL 201-825-2552, FAX 201-825-0553, info@rodpub.com, http://www.rodmanpublishing .com. Pub. Tom Branna. Circ: 20,000 (free).

PHARMA, BIOPHARMA & NUTRACEUTICALS CANADA DIRECTORY, INDUSTRY & SUPPLIERS GUIDE. *see* BUSINESS AND ECONOMICS—Trade And Industrial Directories

615 USA
PHARMA BUSINESS WEEK (CD-ROM). Text in English. 2003. w. USD 2,295 (effective 2009). back issues avail. **Document type:** *Newsletter, Trade.* **Description:** Contains reports from the pharmaceutical industry, including new drug development, clinical trials and research findings, with an emphasis on business trends and analysis.
Formerly: Pharma Business Week (Print) (1543-6675)
Media: CD-ROM.
Indexed: A26, B02, B15, B17, B18, E08, G04, G08, H11, H12, I05, S09.
—CIS.
Published by: NewsRx, 2727 Paces Ferry Rd SE, Ste 2-440, Atlanta, GA 30339. TEL 770-435-8286, 800-726-4550, FAX 770-435-6800, pressrelease@newsrx.com. Ed. Carol Kohn. Pub. Susan Hasty TEL 770-507-7777.

615 DEU
PHARMA DATEN. Text in German. 1972. a. **Document type:** *Journal, Trade.*
Related titles: English ed.
Published by: Bundesverband der Pharmazeutischen Industrie e.V., Friedrichstr 148, Berlin, 10117, Germany. TEL 49-30-27909131, FAX 49-30-27909331, presse@bpi.de, http://www.bpi.de. Ed. Thomas Postina.

P

615 CHE ISSN 0378-7958
PHARMA-FLASH. Text in French. 1972. 6/yr. CHF 49 to individuals; CHF 56 to institutions; CHF 26 to students (effective 2007). **Document type:** *Journal, Trade.*
—**CCC.**
Published by: Editions Medecine et Hygiene, Chemin de la Mousse 46, CP 475, Chene-Bourg 4, 1225, Switzerland. TEL 41-22-7029311, FAX 41-22-7029343, abonnements@medhyg.ch.

615.1 DEU ISSN 1863-6845
PHARMA FOKUS GYNAEKOLOGIE. Text in German. 2006. a. adv. **Document type:** *Magazine, Academic/Scholarly.*
—BLDSC (6441.879500).
Published by: Georg Thieme Verlag, Ruedigerstr 14, Stuttgart, 70469, Germany. TEL 49-711-8931421, FAX 49-711-8931410, leser.service@thieme.de, http://www.thieme.de. adv.: color page EUR 3,350.

615 CHE ISSN 0301-1348
HD9665.1 CODEN: PHAID5
PHARMA INTERNATIONAL. Text in Multiple languages. 1973. bi-m. CHF 202 domestic; CHF 214 foreign; CHF 29 newsstand/cover (effective 2011). adv. **Document type:** *Magazine, Trade.*
Formed by the merger of (1968-1973): Pharma International. Deutsche Sprache Ausgabe (0340-2533); (19??-1973): Pharma International. English Edition (0301-1356); (19??-1973): Pharma International. Edition en Francais (0340-2630)
Indexed: RefZh.
—BLDSC (6441.880500), CASDDS, GNLM, IE, Ingenta, INIST, Linda Hall. **CCC.**
Published by: Rek & Thomas Medien AG, Schmiedgasse 5, St Gallen, 9001, Switzerland. TEL 41-71-2282011, FAX 41-71-2282014. Ed., Adv. contact Michael Richardt. Circ: 7,900 (controlled).

615 332.6 USA ISSN 1551-5540
PHARMA INVESTMENTS, VENTURES AND LAW WEEKLY. Text in English. 2004. w. USD 2,295 in US & Canada; USD 2,495 elsewhere; USD 2,525 combined subscription in US & Canada (print & online eds.); USD 2,755 combined subscription elsewhere (print & online eds.) (effective 2008). back issues avail. **Document type:** *Newsletter, Trade.*
Related titles: E-mail ed.; Online - full text ed.: ISSN 1551-5532. USD 2,295 combined subscription (online & email eds.); single user (effective 2008).
Indexed: L10, P10, P21, P48, P53, P54, PQC.
Published by: NewsRx, 2727 Paces Ferry Rd SE, Ste 2-440, Atlanta, GA 30339. TEL 770-435-8286, 800-726-4550, FAX 770-435-6800, pressrelease@newsrx.com, http://www.newsrx.com. Pub. Susan Hasty TEL 770-507-7777.

615 JPN
CODEN: PHAREX
PHARMA JAPAN; Japan drug industry news. Text in English. 1960. w. JPY 180,000 (effective 2007). pat.; stat. **Document type:** *Newsletter, Trade.* **Description:** Focuses on matters of importance in the Japanese pharmaceutical and medical industries.
Former titles: Pharma (0285-4937); (until 1975): Pharmaceutical Daily News
Related titles: Online - full text ed.
Indexed: B03, CBNB, CEABA, CWI, ChemAb, ChemTitl, P53, P54, PNI, PQC.
—BLDSC (6441.881000), CASDDS, IE, Ingenta.
Published by: Jiho, Inc., Hitotsubashi Bldg. 5F, Hitotsubashi 2-6-3, Chiyoda-ku, Tokyo, 101-8421, Japan. TEL 81-3-32657751, FAX 81-3-32657769, pj@jiho.co.jp, http://www.jiho.co.jp/. **Dist. in N. America by:** ORIOX Japan, Ltd., 3-4-25, Shimomeguro, Meguro-ku, Tokyo 153-0064, Japan. TEL 81-3-3792-5600, FAX 81-3-3792-7500, orioxj@gol.com.

615 JPN
PHARMA JAPAN YEARBOOK. Text in English. a., latest 2003. JPY 16,000 per issue (effective 2007). **Document type:** *Yearbook, Trade.* **Description:** Explains trends in Japanese pharmaceutical and medical fields.
Former titles: Japan Drug Industry Review; (until 1976): Handbook of the Japan Drug Industry
Published by: Jiho, Inc., Hitotsubashi Bldg. 5F, Hitotsubashi 2-6-3, Chiyoda-ku, Tokyo, 101-8421, Japan. TEL 81-3-32657751, FAX 81-3-32657769, pj@jiho.co.jp, http://www.jiho.co.jp/.

615 DEU ISSN 1612-7676
PHARMA KODEX. BAND 1: ARZNEIMITTELSICHERHEIT. Text in German. 197?. a. EUR 58.50 (effective 2009). **Document type:** *Directory, Trade.*
Supersedes in part (in 2000): Pharma Kodex (0948-7182)
Published by: Bundesverband der Pharmazeutischen Industrie e.V., Friedrichstr 148, Berlin, 10117, Germany. TEL 49-30-27909131, FAX 49-30-27909331, presse@bpi.de, http://www.bpi.de.

615 DEU ISSN 1612-7684
PHARMA KODEX. BAND 2: ARZNEIMITTELMARKT, WERBUNG UND INFORMATION. Text in German. 197?. a. EUR 58.50 (effective 2009). **Document type:** *Directory, Trade.*
Supersedes in part (in 2000): Pharma Kodex (0948-7182)
Published by: Bundesverband der Pharmazeutischen Industrie e.V., Friedrichstr 148, Berlin, 10117, Germany. TEL 49-30-27909131, FAX 49-30-27909331, presse@bpi.de, http://www.bpi.de.

615 DEU ISSN 1612-7692
PHARMA KODEX. BAND 3: EUROPA. Text in German. 197?. a. EUR 58.50 (effective 2009). **Document type:** *Directory, Trade.*
Supersedes in part (in 2000): Pharma Kodex (0948-7182)
Published by: Bundesverband der Pharmazeutischen Industrie e.V., Friedrichstr 148, Berlin, 10117, Germany. TEL 49-30-27909131, FAX 49-30-27909331, presse@bpi.de, http://www.bpi.de.

615 CHE ISSN 1010-5409
CODEN: PHKRFG
PHARMA KRITIK. Text in German. 1979. 11/yr. CHF 40, EUR 28; CHF 20, EUR 14 to students (effective 2005). **Document type:** *Newsletter, Trade.*
Indexed: EMBASE, ExcerpMed, R10, Reac, SCOPUS.
—BLDSC (6441.881700), GNLM.
Published by: Infomed-Verlags AG, Postfach 528, Wil, 9501, Switzerland. TEL 41-71-9100866, FAX 41-71-9100877, infomed@infomed.org. Circ: 5,500.

615 344.041 USA ISSN 1551-563X
PHARMA LAW WEEKLY. Text in English. 2004. w. USD 2,295 in US & Canada; USD 2,495 elsewhere; USD 2,525 combined subscription in US & Canada (print & online eds.); USD 2,755 combined subscription elsewhere (print & online eds.) (effective 2008). back issues avail. **Document type:** *Newsletter, Trade.*
Related titles: E-mail ed.; Online - full text ed.: ISSN 1551-5648. USD 2,295 combined subscription (online & email eds.); single user (effective 2008).
Published by: NewsRx, 2727 Paces Ferry Rd SE, Ste 2-440, Atlanta, GA 30339. TEL 770-435-8286, 800-726-4550, FAX 770-435-6800, pressrelease@newsrx.com, http://www.newsrx.com. Pub. Susan Hasty TEL 770-507-7777.

615.1 ESP ISSN 1886-161X
PHARMA MARKET. Text in Spanish. 2006. 6/yr. EUR 40 (effective 2009). **Document type:** *Magazine, Consumer.*
Published by: Ediciones y Publicaciones Alimentarias S.A., C Santa Engracia, 90 4a. Planta, Madrid, 28010, Spain. TEL 34-91-4469659, FAX 34-91-5933744, informacion@eypasa.com, http://www.eypasa.com/.

615 USA ISSN 1547-9994
PHARMA MARKET RESEARCH REPORT. Abbreviated title: P M R 2. Text in English. 2003 (Jun./Jul.). bi-m. USD 399 to institutions (effective 2011). back issues avail. **Document type:** *Newsletter, Trade.*
Published by: R F L Communications, Inc., PO Box 4514, Skokie, IL 60076. TEL 847-673-6284, FAX 847-673-6286, info@rflonline.com, http://www.rflonline.com. Ed., Pub. Robert Lederer.

PHARMA-MARKETING JOURNAL. *see* BUSINESS AND ECONOMICS—Marketing And Purchasing

615 JPN ISSN 0289-5803
CODEN: PMEDEC
PHARMA MEDICA. Text in Japanese. 1983. m. JPY 20,568 per issue (effective 2005). **Document type:** *Journal, Academic/Scholarly.*
Indexed: CIN, ChemAb, ChemTitl.
—BLDSC (6441.883000), CASDDS.
Published by: Medikaru Rebyusha/Medical Review Co., Ltd., 1-7-3 Hirano-Machi, Chuo-ku, Yoshida Bldg., Osaka-shi, 541-0046, Japan. TEL 81-6-62231468, FAX 81-6-62231245.

PHARMA POLAND NEWS. *see* BUSINESS AND ECONOMICS—Marketing And Purchasing

615 GBR ISSN 1741-5756
PHARMA PRICING & REIMBURSEMENT. Variant title: I M S Pharma Pricing & Reimbursement. Text in English. 1996. m. **Document type:** *Magazine, Trade.* **Description:** Designed to keep readers up to date with critical global developments in the arena of drug pricing and reimbursement.
Formerly (until 2002): Pharma Pricing Review (1360-0079)
Related titles: Online - full text ed.
—IE.
Published by: I M S Health Inc., 7 Harewood Ave, London, NW1 6JB, United Kingdom. TEL 44-20-30755000, FAX 44-20-30755888, http://www.imshealth.com/.

615.105 GBR ISSN 2040-2791
PHARMA PROJECTS (CD-ROM). Text in English. 2003. m. **Document type:** *Journal, Trade.*
Media: CD-ROM. **Related titles:** Online - full text ed.
Published by: Informa Healthcare (Subsidiary of: T & F Informa plc), Telephone House, 69-77 Paul St, London, EC2A 4LQ, United Kingdom. TEL 44-20-70175000, FAX 44-20-70176792, healthcare.enquiries@informa.com, http://informahealthcare.com/. Ed. Jo Woodcock TEL 44-20-70176881.

344.0416 DEU ISSN 0172-6617
PHARMA RECHT; Fachzeitschrift fuer das gesamte Arzneimittelrecht. Abbreviated title: PharmR. Text in German. 1979. m. EUR 420; EUR 41 newsstand/cover (effective 2011). adv. bk.rev. back issues avail.; reprint service avail. from SCH. **Document type:** *Magazine, Trade.* **Description:** Publishes current acts and court rulings concerning the production, distribution and marketing of pharmaceuticals, cosmetics, and dietary supplements.
Incorporates (1998-2001): Food and Drug Austria (1436-6266); (1980-1999): P P I - Pro Pharma Inform (0940-0508); Which was formerly (until 1988): Pharma (0175-3800); (until 1983): Pro Pharma Inform (0173-220X)
Indexed: DIP, IBR, IBZ.
—GNLM, IE, Infotrieve. **CCC.**
Published by: Verlag C.H. Beck oHG, Wilhelmstr 9, Munich, 80801, Germany. TEL 49-89-381890, FAX 49-89-38189398, bestellung@beck.de, http://www.beck.de. Circ: 800 (paid).

615 DEU ISSN 1618-4629
PHARMA RELATIONS. Text in German. 2001. m. EUR 120; EUR 60 to students (effective 2009). adv. **Document type:** *Magazine, Trade.*
Published by: eRelation AG, Koelnstr 119, Bonn, 53111, Germany. TEL 49-228-9692270, FAX 49-228-9692299. Ed., Pub. Peter Stegmaier. Adv. contact Anke Heiser. color page EUR 2,650; trim 210 x 297. Circ: 3,112 (paid and controlled).

615 IND ISSN 0975-8216
▼ ➤ **THE PHARMA RESEARCH.** Text in English. 2009. s-a. free (effective 2011). abstr.; bibl. back issues avail. **Document type:** *Journal, Academic/Scholarly.* **Description:** Emphasizes scholarly publication and communication among pharmacists, researchers, students and other health care professionals. The focus is multi-dimensional: pharmacy issues, pharmacy practice and education, clinical practice, pharmaceutical sciences, drug information, commentaries and editorials. Publishes original research work that contributes significantly to further the scientific knowledge in pharmaceutical sciences, pharmaceutical technology, pharmaceutics, biopharmaceutics, pharmacokinetics, pharmaceutical/medicinal chemistry, computational chemistry and molecular drug design, pharmacognosy and phytochemistry, pharmacology, pharmaceutical analysis, pharmacy practice, clinical and hospital pharmacy, cell biology, genomics and proteomics, pharmacogenomics, bioinformatics and biotechnology of pharmaceutical interest.
Media: Online - full text.
Indexed: A01, T02.
Published by: Sudarshan Institute of Technical & Education Publication P. Ltd., 1455, Krishan Ganj, Gandhi Ashram, Pilkhuwa, Ghaziabad 245304, India. TEL 91-991-7053824, http://www.sudarshanonline.co.in/index1.html. Ed. Dr. Sayeed Ahmad. Pub., R&P Mr. Anuj Mittal. Adv. contact Amit Kumar.

615 IND ISSN 0973-399X
➤ **THE PHARMA REVIEW.** Text and summaries in English. 2002. bi-m. INR 1,000 domestic; USD 125 foreign (effective 2011). adv. bk.rev. abstr.; charts; bibl.; tr.lit. back issues avail. **Document type:** *Journal, Academic/Scholarly.* **Description:** Contains original research articles and review articles on all aspects of pharmaceutics. It publishes articles from all the pharma and allied medical and paramedical healthcare professionals.
Related titles: CD-ROM ed.
Published by: Kongposh Publications, ICS House, C-19, 2nd Fl, Commercial Complex, S.D.A., New Delhi, 110 016, India. TEL 91-9811195411, 91-11-26855839, FAX 91-11-26855876, info@kppub.com, kongposhpub@gmail.com. Ed. Raman Sehgal. Pub., R&P Kongposh Bazaz. Circ: 4,000 (paid); 5,000 (controlled).

615 IND ISSN 0976-9242
▼ ➤ **PHARMA SCIENCE MONITOR.** Text in English. 2010. q. free. Index. back issues avail. **Document type:** *Journal, Academic/Scholarly.* **Description:** Publishes original research work either as a full research paper or as a short communication and review articles on a current topic in pharmaceutical sciences.
Related titles: Online - full text ed.: ISSN 0976-7908. free (effective 2011).
Indexed: AgrForAb, C30, CABA, F08, GH, H16, N02, P33, T05.
Address: 201, Satyam Appartment, Nr. Kinjal Classes, Station Rd., Bardoli, Surat, Gujarat 394601, India. TEL 91-997-8262799. Eds. Dr. Bhavesh S. Nayak, Mr. Biren N. Shah, Dr. A. K. Seth.

615 NLD ISSN 0169-6882
PHARMA SELECTA. Text in Dutch, English; Summaries in English. 1985. bi-w. EUR 95; free to qualified personnel (effective 2010). adv. back issues avail. **Document type:** *Newsletter, Trade.* **Description:** Provides pharmacotherapy and drug information for hospital and community pharmacists.
Related titles: CD-ROM ed.: EUR 95 (effective 2010); Online - full text ed.
Published by: Stichting Pharma Selecta, Voorstraat 13, Buitenpost, 9285 NM, Netherlands. FAX 31-511-543660, postmaster@pharmaselecta.nl.

615.014 DEU ISSN 0931-9700
CODEN: PTJOEH
PHARMA TECHNOLOGIE JOURNAL. Text in German. 1984. 2/yr. EUR 64 per issue (effective 2009). adv. **Document type:** *Journal, Trade.* **Description:** Deals with special technological aspects of pharmaceutical processing.
Indexed: A22.
—BLDSC (6441.887000), IE, Infotrieve, Ingenta.
Published by: (Concept Heidelberg), Editio Cantor Verlag, Baendelstockweg 20, Aulendorf, 88326, Germany. TEL 49-7525-9400, FAX 49-7525-940180, info@ecv.de, http://www.ecv.de. Adv. contact Judith Scheller.

615 GBR ISSN 0963-6366
PHARMA TIMES. Variant title: Pharmaceutical Times. Text in English. 1988. m. free to qualified personnel (effective 2009). adv. bk.rev. back issues avail. **Document type:** *Magazine, Trade.* **Description:** Provides information about pharmaceutical, biotechnology and healthcare industries.
Related titles: Online - full text ed.
Indexed: CBNB, Inpharma.
—BLDSC (6441.890100), IE, Infotrieve, Ingenta. **CCC.**
Published by: Pharmaceutical Times, The Coach House, 173 Sheen Ln, East Sheen, London, SW14 8NA, United Kingdom. TEL 44-20-88788566, FAX 44-20-88768834. Ed. Claire Bowie. Adv. contact Tracy Ventriglia TEL 44-20-84879111. page GBP 3,500; 220 x 307. Circ: 10,299.

615.1 IND ISSN 0973-452X
CODEN: PHTIDW
PHARMA TIMES. Text in English. 1969. m. INR 1,500 domestic; USD 150 foreign; INR 150 per issue domestic; USD 15 per issue foreign (effective 2011). adv. bk.rev. pat. **Document type:** *Magazine, Trade.* **Description:** Features general articles of professional interest, proceedings of the Central Executive Council of IPA, the annual report and accounts of the association, reports on branch activities, proceedings of IPA Convention, notifications of IPA and other information such as articles, advertisements, announcements etc.
Related titles: Online - full text ed.
—CASDDS, GNLM, Infotrieve. **CCC.**
Published by: (Indian Pharmaceutical Association), Medknow Publications and Media Pvt. Ltd., B-9, Kanara Business Ctr, Off Link Rd, Ghatkopar (E), Mumbai, Maharastra 400 075, India. TEL 91-22-66491816, 91-22-66491818, journals@medknow.com, http://www.medknow.com.

615.328 613.2 DEU ISSN 1434-8942
PHARMA UND FOOD; Hygiene - Produktion - Ausruestung. Text in German. 1998. 7/yr. EUR 79 domestic; EUR 84 foreign; EUR 12.50 newsstand/cover (effective 2010). adv. **Document type:** *Magazine, Trade.*
Indexed: FS&TA, TM.
Published by: Huethig GmbH & Co. KG, Postfach 102869, Heidelberg, 69018, Germany. TEL 49-6221-4890, FAX 49-6221-489279, aboservice@huethig.de, http://www.huethig.de. Ed. Armin Scheuermann.

615.1 HRV ISSN 0031-6857
CODEN: PHAMBF
PHARMACA; casopis za farmakoterpiju. Text in Croatian; Summaries in English. 1963. q. EUR 10 foreign (effective 2005). bk.rev. **Document type:** *Journal, Academic/Scholarly.*
Formerly (until 1965): Lijekovi (1331-6273)
Indexed: ChemAb, ChemTitl, EMBASE, ExcerpMed, R10, Reac, SCOPUS.
—CASDDS, GNLM, Linda Hall.
Published by: Hrvatsko Drustvo za Klinicku Farmakologiju i Terapiju/ Croatian Society of Clinical Pharmacology and Therapy, Subiceva 9, Zagreb, 10000, Croatia. bvrhovac@zkf.hr. Ed. Bozidar Vrhovac. Circ: 3,500.

615 USA ISSN 2153-2435
▼ ➤ **PHARMACEUTICA ANALYTICA ACTA.** Text in English. 2010 (Oct.). m. free (effective 2011). **Document type:** *Journal, Academic/Scholarly.* **Description:** Aims to encourage research in drug discovery and development by creating awareness about the chemistry of substances.
Media: Online - full text.
Published by: Omics Publishing Group, 5716 Corse Ave, Ste 110, Westlake, Los Angeles, CA 91362. TEL 650-268-9744, 800-216-6499, contact.omics@omicsonline.org.

615 340 JPN
PHARMACEUTICAL ADMINISTRATION IN JAPAN. Text in English, Japanese. irreg., latest 10th Ed. JPY 16,800 domestic; USD 180 foreign (effective 2001). **Document type:** *Government.* **Description:** Gives a broad description of the Japanese Government's recent steps in the pharmaceutical administration.
Published by: (Japan. Ministry of Health and Welfare, Pharmaceutical Affairs Bureau), Yakuji Nippo Ltd., Kanda-Izumi-cho, Chiyoda-ku, Tokyo, 101-0024, Japan. TEL 81-3-3862-2141, FAX 81-3-3866-8495, shuppan@yakuji.co.jp, http://www.yakuji.co.jp/.

PHARMACEUTICAL & COSMETIC REVIEW; devoted to the manufacture & marketing of medicines, toiletries, soaps, detergents in South Africa. *see* BEAUTY CULTURE—Perfumes And Cosmetics

PHARMACEUTICAL AND HEALTHCARE INDUSTRY REMUNERATION REVIEW. *see* BUSINESS AND ECONOMICS—Personnel Management

PHARMACEUTICAL & MEDICAL PACKAGING NEWS. *see* PACKAGING

615 USA ISSN 1530-6232
PHARMACEUTICAL APPROVALS MONTHLY. Text in English. 1996. m. USD 1,000 in United States to institutions; USD 1,000 elsewhere to institutions (effective 2012). adv. back issues avail.; reprints avail. **Document type:** *Journal, Trade.* **Description:** Provides an in-depth look at the process of FDA review and approval for drugs in the US.
Formerly (until 2000): F-D-C Reports. Pharmaceutical Approvals Monthly (1086-2218)
Related titles: Online - full text ed.
Indexed: Inpharma, P48, P53, P54, PNI, PQC.
—CCC.
Published by: Elsevier Business Intelligence (Subsidiary of: Elsevier Health Sciences), 5635 Fishers Ln, Ste 6000, Rockville, MD 20852. TEL 800-332-2181, FAX 240-221-4400, http://www.fdcreports.com. Eds. Bridget Silverman, Michael McCaughan.

615 GBR ISSN 1388-0209
RS160 CODEN: PHBIFC
➤ **PHARMACEUTICAL BIOLOGY.** Text in English. 1961; N.S. 1975. m. GBP 1,720, EUR 2,400, USD 3,000 combined subscription to institutions (print & online eds.); GBP 3,455, EUR 4,820, USD 6,025 combined subscription to corporations (print & online eds.) (effective 2010). adv. bk.rev. charts; illus. Supplement avail.; back issues avail.; reprint service avail. from PSC. **Document type:** *Journal, Academic/Scholarly.* **Description:** Covers all aspects of contemporary pharmacognosy, including the biological evaluation of natural products, and issues relating to the understanding of the efficacy or safety of natural product drugs.
Former titles (until 1998): International Journal of Pharmacognosy (0925-1618); (until 1991): International Journal of Crude Drug Research (0167-7314); (until 1982): Quarterly Journal of Crude Drug Research (0033-5525)
Related titles: Microform ed.: N.S. (from SWZ); Online - full text ed.: ISSN 1744-5116. N.S. (from IngentaConnect).
Indexed: A01, A03, A04, A08, A22, A29, A34, A35, A36, A37, A38, ASCA, AgBio, Agr, AgrForAb, B&BAb, B19, B20, B21, B23, B25, B27, BIOBASE, BIOSIS Prev, BP, BibAg, BioEngAb, C11, C25, C30, CA, CABA, CIN, ChemAb, ChemTitl, D01, DBA, E01, E12, EMBASE, ESPM, ExcerpMed, F08, F11, F12, FCA, FR, GH, H16, H17, I10, I12, IABS, IndVet, M&PBA, MEDLINE, MaizeAb, MycolAb, N02, N03, N04, N05, NPU, NSA, OR, P30, P32, P33, P37, P38, P39, P40, PGegResA, PGrRegA, PHN&I, PN&I, R07, R08, R11, R12, R13, RA&MP, RM&VM, RefZh, S01, S12, S13, S16, S17, SCI, SCOPUS, SoyAb, T02, T05, TAR, TriticAb, VITIS, VS, VirolAbstr, W07, W10, W11.
—CASDDS, GNLM, IE, Infotrieve, Ingenta, INIST, Linda Hall. **CCC.**
Published by: Informa Healthcare (Subsidiary of: T & F Informa plc), Telephone House, 69-77 Paul St, London, EC2A 4LQ, United Kingdom. TEL 44-20-70175000, FAX 44-20-70176792, healthcare.enquiries@informa.com. Ed. John M Pezzuto. Adv. contact Per Sonnerfeldt. **Subscr. to:** Taylor & Francis Inc., Customer Services Dept, 325 Chestnut St, 8th Fl, Philadelphia, PA 19106. TEL 215-625-8900, 800-354-1420, FAX 215-625-8914, customerservice@taylorandfrancis.com; Taylor & Francis Ltd., Journals Customer Service, Sheepen Pl, Colchester, Essex CO3 3LP, United Kingdom. TEL 44-20-70175544, FAX 44-20-70175198, tf.enquiries@tfinforma.com.

➤ **PHARMACEUTICAL BIOTECHNOLOGY.** *see* BIOLOGY—Biotechnology

615 CAN ISSN 1499-1977
PHARMACEUTICAL CANADA. Text in English. 2000. q. free domestic; USD 250 in US & Mexico; USD 350 elsewhere (effective 2005). **Document type:** *Magazine, Trade.*
—BLDSC (6443.260000). **CCC.**
Address: 200 Consumers Rd, Ste 610, North York, ON, Canada. TEL 416-410-7486, FAX 416-491-3428. Ed. Ronald Turton.

615 ESP ISSN 1139-6202
CODEN: PCEACX
PHARMACEUTICAL CARE ESPANA. Text in Spanish. 1999. bi-m. EUR 80 (effective 2009). back issues avail. **Document type:** *Magazine, Academic/Scholarly.*
Indexed: EMBASE, ExcerpMed, R10, Reac, SCOPUS.
—BLDSC (6443.300000), IE, Ingenta. **CCC.**
Published by: Fundacion Pharmaceutical Care Espana, C Rosellon 331-333, Entlo 2a., Barcelona, 08037, Spain. secretaria@pharmaceutical-care.org.

615.19 USA ISSN 0091-150X
RS402 CODEN: PCJOAU
➤ **PHARMACEUTICAL CHEMISTRY JOURNAL.** Text in English. 1967. m. EUR 4,730, USD 4,929 combined subscription to institutions (print & online eds.) (effective 2012). adv. back issues avail.; reprint service avail. from PSC. **Document type:** *Journal, Academic/Scholarly.* **Description:** Addresses scientific and technical research on the creation of new drugs and the improvement of manufacturing technology of drugs and intermediates.
Related titles: Microfilm ed.: (from PQC); Online - full text ed.: ISSN 1573-9031 (from IngentaConnect); ◆ Translation of: Khimiko-Farmatsevticheskii Zhurnal. ISSN 0023-1134.
Indexed: A01, A03, A08, A22, A26, Agr, B&BAb, B19, B21, B25, BIOSIS Prev, BibLing, C33, CA, CCI, ChemAb, ChemTitl, E01, EMBASE, ESPM, ExcerpMed, I10, MycolAb, R10, Reac, RefZh, SCI, SCOPUS, T02, W07.
—BLDSC (0416.770000), East View, GNLM, IE, Infotrieve, Ingenta, INIST. **CCC.**
Published by: Springer New York LLC (Subsidiary of: Springer Science+Business Media), 233 Spring St, New York, NY 10013. TEL 212-460-1500, FAX 212-460-1575, service-ny@springer.com, http://www.springer.com. Ed. R G Glushkov.

615 GBR ISSN 0952-2220
PHARMACEUTICAL COMPANY LEAGUE TABLES. Text in English. 1982. a., latest 2009. includes subscr. with Scrip. charts; stat. back issues avail. **Document type:** *Yearbook, Trade.* **Description:** Guide to performance in the pharmaceutical marketplace. Containing the 200 top players in the pharmaceutical industry ranked in terms of sales, R&D, profitability, ROI, ROCE, EPS, geophysical sales, etc.
Formerly (until 198?): Scrip's Pharmaceutical Company League Tables
Related titles: Online - full text ed.
—IE, Ingenta. **CCC.**
Published by: Informa Healthcare (Subsidiary of: T & F Informa plc), Telephone House, 69-77 Paul St, London, EC2A 4LQ, United Kingdom. TEL 44-20-70175000, FAX 44-20-70176792, healthcare.enquiries@informa.com, http://informahealthcare.com/. Pub. Phil Jarvis.

▼ **PHARMACEUTICAL CROPS.** *see* AGRICULTURE—Crop Production And Soil

615.1 USA ISSN 1083-7450
RS199.5 CODEN: PDTEFS
➤ **PHARMACEUTICAL DEVELOPMENT AND TECHNOLOGY.** Text in English. 1996. bi-m. GBP 730, EUR 960, USD 1,200 combined subscription to institutions (print & online eds.); GBP 1,495, EUR 1,970, USD 2,465 combined subscription to corporations (print & online eds.) (effective 2010). adv. bk.rev. back issues avail.; reprint service avail. from PSC. **Document type:** *Journal, Academic/Scholarly.* **Description:** Publishes articles exploring the research, design, development, manufacture and evaluation of traditional and novel drug delivery, with an emphasis on practical solutions and applications to theoretical and research-based problems.
Related titles: Online - full text ed.: ISSN 1097-9867 (from IngentaConnect).
Indexed: A22, B&BAb, B01, B06, B07, B09, B19, B21, BioEngAb, C33, CA, ChemAb, ChemTitl, DBA, E01, EMBASE, ExcerpMed, H01, I12, IndMed, M&PBA, MEDLINE, P30, R10, Reac, RefZh, SCI, SCOPUS, T02, W07.
—BLDSC (6443.625000), CASDDS, IE, Infotrieve, Ingenta, INIST. **CCC.**
Published by: (American Association of Pharmaceutical Scientists), Informa Healthcare (Subsidiary of: T & F Informa plc), 52 Vanderbilt Ave, New York, NY 10017. TEL 212-262-8230, FAX 212-262-8234, healthcare.enquiries@informa.com, http://www.informahealthcare.com. Ed. Michael J Akers. Adv. contact Daniel Wallen. **Subscr. outside N. America to:** Taylor & Francis Ltd.

➤ **PHARMACEUTICAL ENGINEERING.** *see* ENGINEERING

615 USA ISSN 0279-6570
RS1 CODEN: PHEXD2
PHARMACEUTICAL EXECUTIVE; for global business and marketing leaders. Text in English. 1981. m. USD 70 domestic; USD 90 in Canada & Mexico; USD 135 elsewhere; USD 17 newsstand/cover domestic; USD 19 newsstand/cover in Canada & Mexico; USD 22 newsstand/cover elsewhere (effective 2011). adv. illus. back issues avail.; reprints avail. **Document type:** *Magazine, Trade.* **Description:** Designed to meet the management and marketing needs of professionals in the pharmaceutical industry.
Related titles: Online - full text ed.: ISSN 2150-735X. USD 50 (effective 2011); Supplement(s): e-Health.
Indexed: A12, A13, A15, A17, A22, ABIn, Agr, B01, B02, B03, B04, B06, B07, B08, B09, B11, B17, B18, BPI, BPIA, BRD, C12, CWI, CurPA, G04, H01, H13, I05, I12, P10, P20, P21, P24, P34, P48, P51, P53, P54, PQC, PROMT, T02, Telegen, W01, W02, W03, W05.
—BLDSC (6443.680000), IE, Infotrieve, Ingenta. **CCC.**
Published by: Advanstar Communications, Inc., 6200 Canoga Ave, 2nd Fl, Woodland Hills, CA 91367. TEL 818-593-5000, FAX 818-593-5020, info@advanstar.com, http://www.advanstar.com. Ed. William Looney. adv.: B&W page USD 6,020, color page USD 8,245; trim 7.75 x 10.5.

615.1 GBR
PHARMACEUTICAL EXECUTIVE EUROPE (ONLINE). Text in English. w. free (effective 2011). **Document type:** *Magazine, Trade.*
Media: Online - full text.
Published by: Advanstar Communications (UK) Ltd. (Subsidiary of: Advanstar Communications, Inc.), Advanstar House, Park West, Sealand Rd, Chester, CH1 4RN, United Kingdom. TEL 44-1244-378888, info@advanstar.com, http://www.advanstar.com. Ed. Julian Upton TEL 44-208-9562660. Pub. Andy Davies TEL 44-1244-393408.

615.19 USA ISSN 1531-2135
PHARMACEUTICAL FORMULATION & QUALITY; for product development and quality professionals. Abbreviated title: P F Q. Text in English. 1996. bi-m. GBP 74 in United Kingdom to institutions; EUR 92 in Europe to institutions; USD 143 elsewhere to institutions (effective 2012). adv. reprint service avail. from PSC. **Document type:** *Magazine, Trade.* **Description:** Covers the latest technologies, techniques and regulations affecting product development, formulation, quality assurance and quality control in the pharmaceutical industry.
Formerly (until 19??): Pharmaceutical & Cosmetic Quality (1092-7522)
Related titles: Online - full text ed.: ISSN 1936-3435.
Indexed: EMBASE, SCOPUS.
—BLDSC (6443.682000). **CCC.**
Published by: John Wiley & Sons, Inc., 111 River St, Hoboken, NJ 07030. TEL 201-748-6000, FAX 201-748-6088, info@wiley.com, http://www.wiley.com/WileyCDA/. Ed. Patrick McGee TEL 201-748-8811. Adv. contact ken Potuznik TEL 480-419-1851.

615 668.5 USA
PHARMACEUTICAL FORMULATION & QUALITY BUYERS' GUIDE. Text in English. a. **Document type:** *Directory, Trade.* **Description:** Lists products and services for the pharmaceutical and cosmetics industries.
Related titles: Online - full text ed.
Published by: Carpe Diem Communications, Inc., 208 Floral Vale Blvd, Yardley, PA 19067. TEL 215-860-7800, FAX 215-860-7900, staff@carpediemcomm.com.

615.1 GBR ISSN 0079-1393
RS61
PHARMACEUTICAL HISTORIAN. Text in English. 1967. q. GBP 20 membership (effective 2009). **Document type:** *Newsletter, Academic/Scholarly.*
Indexed: EMBASE, ExcerpMed, I12, MEDLINE, P30, SCOPUS.
—BLDSC (6443.700000).
Published by: British Society for the History of Pharmacy, 840 Melton Rd, Thurmaston, Leics LE4 8BN, United Kingdom. TEL 44-116-2640083, FAX 44-116-2640141, http://www.bshp.org/.

615.1 GBR ISSN 0031-6873
CODEN: PHJOAV
PHARMACEUTICAL JOURNAL. Text in English. 1841. w. (51/yr.). GBP 390 domestic to institutions; EUR 540 in Europe to institutions; USD 780 in the Americas to institutions; GBP 507 elsewhere to institutions; GBP 550 combined subscription domestic to institutions (print & online eds.); EUR 750 combined subscription in Europe to institutions (print & online eds.); USD 1,100 combined subscription in the Americas to institutions (print & online eds.); GBP 667 combined subscription elsewhere to institutions (print & online eds.) (effective 2010). adv. bk.rev. charts; tr.lit. index. back issues avail. **Document type:** *Journal, Academic/Scholarly.* **Description:** Provides comprehensive news coverage of all aspects of pharmacy in Great Britain and abroad.
Former titles (until 1933): Pharmaceutical Journal and Pharmacist (0301-5432); (until 1908): Pharmaceutical Journal (0958-8450); (until 1895): Pharmaceutical Journal and Transactions (0301-5440)
Related titles: Microform ed.; Online - full text ed.: P J Online. EUR 620 in Europe to institutions; USD 900 in the Americas to institutions; GBP 450 elsewhere to institutions (effective 2010).
Indexed: A22, AHCMS, AMED, ChemAb, DBA, EMBASE, ExcerpMed, HECAB, I12, Inpharma, P30, P35, R10, Reac, SCOPUS.
—BLDSC (6444.000000), CASDDS, GNLM, IE, Infotrieve, Ingenta, INIST. **CCC.**
Published by: (Royal Pharmaceutical Society of Great Britain), Pharmaceutical Press (Subsidiary of: Royal Pharmaceutical Society of Great Britain), 1 Lambeth High St, London, SE1 7JN, United Kingdom. TEL 44-20-77359141, FAX 44-20-75722509, enquiries@rpsgb.org, http://www.pharmpress.com/. Ed. Olivia Timbs. Pub., R&P Charles Fry TEL 44-20-75722274. Circ: 47,351. **Dist. & subscr.addr.:** Turpin Distribution Services Ltd., Pegasus Dr, Stratton Business Park, Biggleswade, Bedfordshire SG18 8QB, United Kingdom. TEL 44-1767-604800, FAX 44-1767-601640, custserv@turpin-distribution.com, http://www.turpin-distribution.com/.

615 ZWE
PHARMACEUTICAL JOURNAL OF ZIMBABWE. Variant title: Zimbabwe Pharmaceutical Journal. Text in English. 19??. bi-m. ZWD 250 membership. adv. **Document type:** *Journal, Academic/Scholarly.*
Published by: Pharmaceutical Society of Zimbabwe, PO Box 1476, Harare, Zimbabwe. TEL 263-14-706967, FAX 263-14-706967. Ed. Rtee Mithal. adv.: B&W page ZWD 1,200. Circ: 350.

615 340 USA ISSN 1542-9547
KF2915.P4
PHARMACEUTICAL LAW & INDUSTRY REPORT. Text in English. 2003 (Jan.). w. USD 2,072 (effective 2010 - 2011). back issues avail. **Document type:** *Report, Trade.* **Description:** Covers federal and state legal, regulatory and legislative developments affecting the pharmaceutical and biotechnology industries.
Formerly (until 2003): Pharmaceutical Law & Policy Report (1536-1128)
Related titles: Online - full text ed.: ISSN 1542-9555. USD 2,094 (effective 2010 - 2011).
—CCC.
Published by: The Bureau of National Affairs, Inc., 1801 S Bell St, Arlington, VA 22202. TEL 703-341-3000, 800-372-1033, FAX 703-341-4634, bnaplus@bna.com.

615 GBR ISSN 1747-4981
PHARMACEUTICAL LAW INSIGHT. Text in English. 2005 (June). m. (10/yr). GBP 875 combined subscription (print & online eds.) (effective 2010). **Document type:** *Newsletter, Trade.* **Description:** Provides the latest cases and related developments in pharmaceutical law.
Related titles: Online - full text ed.: ISSN 1747-499X.
—CCC.
Published by: Informa Professional (Subsidiary of: T & F Informa plc), Telephone House, 69-77 Paul St, London, EC2A 4LQ, United Kingdom. TEL 44-20-70175532, FAX 44-20-70175274, professional.enquiries@informa.com.

615 ESP ISSN 1575-3611
➤ **THE PHARMACEUTICAL LETTER.** Text in Spanish. fortn. looseleaf. EUR 100.88 (effective 2010). illus.; bibl.; charts. cum.index:1999-2010. back issues avail. **Document type:** *Newsletter, Academic/Scholarly.* **Description:** Provides information on pharmacotherapy and news about the medical protocols of treatment for doctors and pharmacist.
Related titles: Online - full text ed.
Published by: D I C A F, s.l., c/ Rabassa, 41 Bxs. 2o, Barcelona, 08024, Spain. TEL 34-932-113093, FAX 34-932-123811, dicaf@dicaf.es, http://www.dicaf.es/. Ed., R&P Alex Bonal.

➤ **PHARMACEUTICAL MANUFACTURERS OF JAPAN.** *see* BUSINESS AND ECONOMICS—Trade And Industrial Directories

615 USA ISSN 1550-6509
RS192
PHARMACEUTICAL MANUFACTURING. Text in English. 2002. m. USD 68 in US & Canada; USD 200 elsewhere; free to qualified personnel (effective 2008). adv. back issues avail.; reprints avail. **Document type:** *Magazine, Trade.* **Description:** Dedicated to serving the information needs of the engineering and operations professionals whose job it is to design, build and run the pharmaceutical industry's manufacturing assets.
Related titles: Online - full text ed.: free (effective 2008).
—CCC.
Published by: Putman Media, 555 W Pierce Rd, Ste 301, Itasca, IL 60143. TEL 630-467-1300, FAX 630-467-1124, ckappel@putman.net, http://www.putman.net. Ed. Agnes Shanley TEL 630-467-1300 ext 410. Pub. Becker Tonia TEL 630-467-1300 ext 455. adv.: color page USD 5,900, B&W page USD 5,605; trim 7.875 x 10.5. Circ: 25,082 (paid).

615 688.8 GBR ISSN 1463-1245
PHARMACEUTICAL MANUFACTURING & PACKING SOURCER. Text in English. 1998. q. GBP 125 domestic; USD 230 foreign; free to qualified personnel (effective 2010). adv. Website rev.; bk.rev. 128 p./no. 2 cols./p.; back issues avail. **Document type:** *Journal, Trade.* **Description:** Covers all aspects of pharmaceutical manufacturing from initial formulation development, drug delivery systems, pilot and bulk production through to packaging.
Related titles: Online - full text ed.
Indexed: EMBASE, ExcerpMed, SCOPUS.
—CCC.
Published by: (Technomark Consulting Services), Samedan Ltd, 16 Hampden Gurney Rd, London, W1H 5AL, United Kingdom. TEL 44-20-77243456, FAX 44-20-77242632, info@samedanltd.com. Adv. contact Lee Atkinson. page GBP 2,850; trim 210 x 297.

615 USA ISSN 0149-0885
HD9666.3
PHARMACEUTICAL MARKETERS DIRECTORY. Abbreviated title: P M D. Text in English. 1977. a. USD 295 per issue (effective 2009). adv. 900 p./no.; **Document type:** *Directory, Trade.* **Description:** Covers the entire healthcare field including names, titles, addresses, phone, fax, e-mail and Internet addresses for over 1,500 pharmaceutical and healthcare manufacturers, 300 advertising agencies, over 800 healthcare journals, as well as alternative media. Includes suppliers to the health care industry.
Incorporates: Medical Products Marketers Directory
Published by: Haymarket Media Inc. (Subsidiary of: Haymarket Group Ltd.), 551 SE 8th St, Ste 503, Delray Beach, FL 33483. TEL 561-665-6000, FAX 561-665-6058, custserv@haymarketmedia.com, http://www.haymarket.com. Pub., Adv. contact Suzanne Besse TEL 561-237-6122. B&W page USD 2,815, color page USD 4,965; trim 8.25 x 10.875. Circ: 2,500 (paid).

615 GBR ISSN 0969-3963
PHARMACEUTICAL MARKETING. Text in English. 1989. m. GBP 120 domestic; GBP 180 in Europe; GBP 210 elsewhere (effective 2009). adv. **Document type:** *Magazine, Trade.*
Related titles: ◆ Supplement(s): Pharmaceutical Marketing. Practical Guide Series. ISSN 0969-3971.
Indexed: Inpharma.
—BLDSC (6444.038000), IE, Ingenta. **CCC.**
Published by: P M Group, Vincent House, Vincent Ln, Dorking, Surrey RH4 3JD, United Kingdom. TEL 44-1306-740777, FAX 44-1306-741069, info@pmlive.com, http://www.pmgrouplive.com. Ed. Natalie Uhlarz. Adv. contact Paul Waddingham. Circ: 7,800.

615.10688 GBR ISSN 1740-5084
PHARMACEUTICAL MARKETING EUROPE. Text in English. 2003. bi-m. GBP 96 domestic; GBP 96 in Europe; GBP 120 elsewhere (effective 2009). adv. **Document type:** *Magazine, Trade.* **Description:** Contains information of interest to pharmaceutical marketing decision-makers in Europe.
—BLDSC (6444.050950). **CCC.**
Published by: P M Group, Vincent House, Vincent Ln, Dorking, Surrey RH4 3JD, United Kingdom. TEL 44-1306-740777, FAX 44-1306-741069, info@pmlive.com. Ed. Kerry Holmes. Adv. contact Chonell Roy.

615 GBR ISSN 0969-3971
PHARMACEUTICAL MARKETING. PRACTICAL GUIDE SERIES. Text in English. 1992. irreg. **Document type:** *Monographic series, Trade.*
Related titles: ◆ Supplement to: Pharmaceutical Marketing. ISSN 0969-3963.
—BLDSC (6444.038100). **CCC.**
Published by: P M Group, Vincent House, Vincent Ln, Dorking, Surrey RH4 3JD, United Kingdom. TEL 44-1306-740777, FAX 44-1306-741069, info@pmlive.com, http://www.pmgrouplive.com. Ed. Andy Rice.

615 610 NZL ISSN 1178-2595
RM300 CODEN: IJPMFV
➤ **PHARMACEUTICAL MEDICINE.** Text in English. 1997. bi-m. price varies based on the number of users. bk.rev. back issues avail.; reprints avail. **Document type:** *Journal, Academic/Scholarly.* **Description:** Provides assesses for new and old methods used to test drugs for clinical use.
Formerly (until 2008): International Journal of Pharmaceutical Medicine (1364-9027); Which was formed by the merger of (1984-1997): Pharmaceutical Medicine (0265-0673); (1991-1997): Journal of Pharmaceutical Medicine (0958-0581)
Related titles: CD-ROM ed.; Microform ed.: (from PQC); Online - full text ed.: ISSN 1179-1993 (from IngentaConnect).
Indexed: A01, A22, A26, A36, B&BAb, BIOBASE, CA, CABA, DBA, E01, E08, EMBASE, ExcerpMed, FR, GH, H12, I05, I12, IABS, Inpharma, N02, N03, P20, P30, P32, P35, P54, PGegResA, PQC, R10, R12, RA&MP, Reac, S09, SCOPUS, T02, T05, TAR.
—BLDSC (6444.055000), CASDDS, GNLM, IE, Infotrieve, Ingenta, INIST. **CCC.**
Published by: (International Federation of Associations of Pharmaceutical Physicians USA, Society of Pharmaceutical Medicine GBR), Adis International Ltd. (Subsidiary of: Wolters Kluwer N.V.), 41 Centorian Dr, Mairangi Bay, Private Bag 65901, Auckland, 1311, New Zealand. TEL 64-9-4770700, FAX 64-9-4770764, journals@adis.com, http://www.adisonline.info/. Ed. Susan Pochon.

615.1 USA ISSN 1522-6735
PHARMACEUTICAL NEWS DAILY. Text in English. 1996. d. USD 359 (effective 2011). back issues avail. **Document type:** *Newsletter, Trade.* **Description:** Includes summaries of 8 to 12 business and product development stories.
Media: E-mail. **Related titles:** Fax ed.
Published by: C T B International Publishing Inc., PO Box 218, Maplewood, NJ 07040. TEL 973-966-0997, FAX 973-966-0242, info@ctbintl.com.

615 USA ISSN 1945-3337
CODEN: APOMCB
PHARMACEUTICAL OUTSOURCING. Text in English. 2001. bi-m. USD 120 combined subscription print & online eds.; free to qualified personnel (effective 2005). **Document type:** *Newsletter, Trade.*
Formerly (until 2008): American Pharmaceutical Outsourcing (1529-6318)
Related titles: Online - full text ed.: ISSN 1945-3345. USD 75 foreign (effective 2005).
Indexed: R10, Reac, SCOPUS.
—BLDSC (0850.575250). **CCC.**
Published by: Russell Publishing LLC, 9225 Priority Way West Dr, Ste 120, Indianapolis, IN 46240. TEL 317-816-8787, FAX 317-816-8788, http://www.russpub.com. Ed. Nicole Mawbey. Pub. Nigel Russell.

615 658.405 GBR
PHARMACEUTICAL OUTSOURCING DECISIONS. Text in English. 200?. s-a. **Document type:** *Magazine, Trade.* **Description:** Aims to encourage action among readers looking to align with organisations that will enable them to fulfil their strategic objectives.
Related titles: ◆ Supplement to: World Pharmaceutical Frontiers.
Published by: S P G Media Ltd. (Subsidiary of: Sterling Publishing Group Plc.), Brunel House, 55-57 N Wharf Rd, London, W2 1LA, United Kingdom. TEL 44-20-79159660, FAX 44-20-77242089, info@spgmedia.com, http://www.spgmedia.com/. Eds. Andrew Tunnicliffe, John Lawrence. Pub. William Crocker.

615.19 USA ISSN 1049-9156
CODEN: PLPREY
PHARMACEUTICAL PROCESSING. Abbreviated title: P R. Text in English. 1984. m. USD 69 domestic; USD 74 in Canada & Mexico; USD 100 elsewhere; USD 10 per issue domestic; USD 15 per issue foreign; free domestic to qualified personnel (effective 2008). adv. tr.lit. back issues avail. **Document type:** *Magazine, Trade.* **Description:** Contains articles on pharmaceutical development and manufacturing and includes topics such as regulatory affairs, contract services, drug delivery systems, processing, packaging, validation, instrumentation and IT.
Formerly (until 198?): Pharmaceutical and Cosmetic Equipment (0895-2795)
Related titles: Online - full text ed.: free to qualified personnel (effective 2008); Supplement(s): Pharmaceutical Processing Annual Buyers Guide.
Indexed: B01, B02, B03, B07, B15, B17, B18, EMBASE, ExcerpMed, G04, G06, G07, G08, I05, SCOPUS.
—CCC.
Published by: Advantage Business Media, 100 Enterprise Dr, Ste 600, PO Box 912, Rockaway, NJ 07886. TEL 973-920-7000, FAX 973-920-7531, AdvantageCommunications@advantagemedia.com, http://www.advantagebusinessmedia.com. Ed. Mike Auerbach TEL 973-920-7055. Pubs. Michael Kelly TEL 630-971-9739, Tim Canny TEL 973-920-7122. adv.: B&W page USD 8,715, color page USD 10,440; trim 9 x 10.875. Circ: 31,045 (paid).

615 USA ISSN 0891-9461
PHARMACEUTICAL PRODUCTION TECHSOURCE. Text in English. 1986. m.
Indexed: P48, PQC.
Published by: Medical Manufacturing TechSource, Inc, Box 1145, Ann Arbor, MI 48106-1145. TEL 313-487-5989, FAX 313-487-8181.

615 005.1 GBR ISSN 1757-0921
PHARMACEUTICAL PROGRAMMING. Text in English. 2008. s-a. GBP 291 combined subscription to institutions (print & online eds.); USD 580 combined subscription in United States to institutions (print & online eds.) (effective 2012). reprint service avail. from PSC. **Document type:** *Journal, Academic/Scholarly.* **Description:** Focus on programming in the regulated environment of the pharmaceutical and life sciences industry.
Related titles: Online - full text ed.: ISSN 1757-093X. GBP 262 to institutions; USD 522 in United States to institutions (effective 2012) (from IngentaConnect).
Indexed: A01, B&BAb, B19, CA, T02.
—CCC.
Published by: (Pharmaceutical Users Software Exchange), Maney Publishing, Ste 1C, Joseph's Well, Hanover Walk, Leeds, W Yorks LS3 1AB, United Kingdom. TEL 44-113-2432800, FAX 44-113-3868178, maney@maney.co.uk, http://www.maney.co.uk. Ed. Dirk Spruck. **Subscr. in N. America to:** Maney Publishing, 875 Massachusetts Ave, 7th Fl, Cambridge, MA 02139. TEL 866-297-5154, FAX 617-354-6875, maney@maneyusa.com.

615 AUS ISSN 1834-500X
PHARMACEUTICAL REFORMS. Text in English. 2006. m. **Document type:** *Newsletter, Trade.*
Media: Online - full text.
Published by: South Australia, Department of Health, Citi Centre Bldg, 11 Hindmarsh Sq, Rundle Mall, PO Box 287, Adelaide, SA 5000, Australia. TEL 61-8-82266000, FAX 61-8-82266899, health.library@health.sa.gov.au, http://www.health.sa.gov.au.

615 USA ISSN 0161-8415
PHARMACEUTICAL REPRESENTATIVE. Text in English. 1971. m. USD 52.95 domestic; USD 67.95 in Canada & Mexico; USD 139.95 elsewhere; USD 14 newsstand/cover domestic; USD 16 newsstand/cover foreign (effective 2011). adv. bk.rev. abstr.; charts; illus.; stat.; tr.lit. back issues avail. **Document type:** *Magazine, Trade.* **Description:** Features new products, industry and research news, and market trends.
Formerly (until 1978): Pharmaceutical Salesman (0048-3621)
Related titles: Microform ed.: (from PQC); Online - full text ed.: ISSN 2150-7368. USD 40.95 (effective 2011).
Indexed: A01, A03, A08, B02, B15, B17, B18, CA, G04, H01, H12, I05, P16, P34, P48, P53, P54, PQC, S01, T02.
—CCC.
Published by: Advanstar Communications, Inc., 6200 Canoga Ave, 2nd Fl, Woodland Hills, CA 91367. TEL 818-593-5000, FAX 818-593-5020, info@advanstar.com, http://www.advanstar.com. Ed. Reid Paul TEL 212-951-6730. Pub. Jay Berfas TEL 212-951-6614. Adv. contact Angela Gibbs TEL 815-772-7871.

615.19 USA ISSN 0724-8741
CODEN: PHREEB
➤ **PHARMACEUTICAL RESEARCH.** Text in English. 1983. m. EUR 2,167, USD 2,235 combined subscription to institutions (print & online eds.) (effective 2012). adv. bk.rev. back issues avail.; reprint service avail. from PSC. **Document type:** *Journal, Academic/Scholarly.* **Description:** Presents papers which describe innovative research spanning the entire spectrum of drug discovery, development, evaluation, and regulatory approval.
Related titles: Microfilm ed.: (from PQC); Online - full text ed.: ISSN 1573-904X (from IngentaConnect).
Indexed: A01, A03, A08, A22, A26, A34, A35, A36, ASCA, AgBio, Agr, B21, B25, BIOSIS Prev, BibLing, C24, C30, C33, CA, CABA, ChemAb, ChemTitl, CurCont, D01, DBA, E01, E12, EMBASE, ExcerpMed, F08, F11, F12, FR, GH, H16, H17, I12, ISR, IndMed, IndVet, Inpharma, MEDLINE, MycolAb, N02, N03, NSA, P20, P22, P24, P30, P32, P33, P35, P39, P48, P54, PHN&I, PN&I, PQC, R08, R10, R13, RA&MP, RM&VM, Reac, RefZh, S12, SCI, SCOPUS, SoyAb, T02, VS, W07.
—BLDSC (6444.080000), CASDDS, GNLM, IE, Infotrieve, Ingenta, INIST, Linda Hall. **CCC.**
Published by: (American Association of Pharmaceutical Scientists), Springer New York LLC (Subsidiary of: Springer Science+Business Media), 233 Spring St, New York, NY 10013. TEL 212-460-1500, FAX 212-460-1575, service-ny@springer.com, http://www.springer.com/. Ed. Peter W Swaan.

615 USA ISSN 1934-8231
PHARMACEUTICAL RESEARCH AND MANUFACTURERS OF AMERICA. INDUSTRY PROFILE. Text in English. a. **Document type:** *Report, Trade.*
Formerly (until 1996): P M A Annual Survey Report
Published by: Pharmaceutical Research and Manufacturers of America, 950 F Street, NW, Ste 300, Washington, DC 20004. TEL 202-835-3400, FAX 202-835-3414, http://www.phrma.org.

615 CAN ISSN 1918-5561
RS1
PHARMACEUTICAL REVIEWS. Text in English. 2003. irreg. free (effective 2011). **Document type:** *Journal, Academic/Scholarly.*
Media: Online - full text.
Indexed: EMBASE, ExcerpMed, SCOPUS.
Published by: Pharmainfo.net

PHARMACEUTICAL SOLUTIONS; the nation's marketplace serving buyers and sellers of pharmaceutical, processing, chemical, packaging, equipment, services and supplies. *see* PACKAGING

615 001.422 GBR ISSN 1539-1604
RS57
➤ **PHARMACEUTICAL STATISTICS**; the journal of applied statistics in the pharmaceutical industry. Text in English. 2002 (Jun.). q. GBP 372 in United Kingdom to institutions; EUR 470 in Europe to institutions; USD 727 elsewhere to institutions; GBP 428 combined subscription in United Kingdom to institutions (print & online eds.); EUR 542 combined subscription in Europe to institutions (print & online eds.); USD 836 combined subscription elsewhere to institutions (print & online eds.) (effective 2012). adv. back issues avail.; reprint service avail. from PSC. **Document type:** *Journal, Academic/Scholarly.* **Description:** Covers all aspects of pharmaceutical statistical applications from discovery, through pre-clinical development, clinical development, post-marketing surveillance, consumer health, production, epidemiology, and health economics.
Related titles: Online - full text ed.: ISSN 1539-1612. GBP 372 in United Kingdom to institutions; EUR 470 in Europe to institutions; USD 727 elsewhere to institutions (effective 2012).
Indexed: CMCI, CurCont, EMBASE, ExcerpMed, I12, MEDLINE, P30, R10, Reac, SCI, SCOPUS, W07.
—IE, Ingenta. **CCC.**
Published by: (Statisticians in the Pharmaceutical Industry), John Wiley & Sons Ltd. (Subsidiary of: John Wiley & Sons, Inc.), 1-7 Oldlands Way, PO Box 808, Bognor Regis, West Sussex PO21 9FF, United Kingdom. TEL 44-1865-778315, FAX 44-1243-843232, cs-journals@wiley.com, http://eu.wiley.com/WileyCDA/. Eds. Mike K Smith, Scott Patterson, Sue Jane Wang. **Subscr. to:** 1-7 Oldlands Way, PO Box 809, Bognor Regis, West Sussex PO21 9FG, United Kingdom. TEL 44-1865-778054, cs-agency@wiley.com.

615 USA ISSN 1543-2521
RS1 CODEN: PTHEC9
PHARMACEUTICAL TECHNOLOGY. Text in English. 1977. m. USD 76 domestic; USD 99 in Canada & Mexico; USD 141 elsewhere; USD 14 newsstand/cover domestic; USD 15 newsstand/cover in Canada & Mexico; USD 18 newsstand/cover elsewhere (effective 2011). adv. abstr.; charts; illus.; pat.; stat.; tr.lit. cum.index. back issues avail.; reprints avail. **Document type:** *Magazine, Trade.* **Description:** Offers practical hands-on information about the manufacture of pharmaceutical products, focusing on applied technology.
Former titles (until 2003): Pharmaceutical Technology North America (1534-2131); (until 2001): Pharmaceutical Technology (0147-8087)
Related titles: Online - full text ed.: ISSN 2150-7376. USD 70 (effective 2011).
Indexed: A10, A12, A13, A15, A17, A22, A26, ABIn, Agr, B01, B02, B03, B06, B07, B09, B11, B15, B17, B18, CIN, CPEI, ChemAb, ChemTitl, CurPA, DBA, E08, EMBASE, EngInd, ExcerpMed, FR, G04, G06, G07, G08, H01, H12, I05, P10, P16, P24, P26, P48, P51, P53, P54, PNI, PQC, R10, Reac, S09, SCOPUS, T02, Telegen, V03.
—BLDSC (6444.130000), CASDDS, GNLM, IE, Ingenta, INIST, Linda Hall. **CCC.**
Published by: Advanstar Communications, Inc., 6200 Canoga Ave, 2nd Fl, Woodland Hills, CA 91367. TEL 818-593-5000, FAX 818-593-5020, info@advanstar.com, http://www.advanstar.com. Ed. Michelle Hoffman. Adv. contact Kathy Tarnowski TEL 218-740-6339. color page USD 9,955, B&W page USD 8,105; trim 8 x 10.75. Circ: 34,000 (controlled).

615.1905 HKG ISSN 1753-9013
PHARMACEUTICAL TECHNOLOGY ASIA PACIFIC. Text in English. 2006. q. free to qualified personnel (effective 2008). back issues avail. **Document type:** *Magazine, Trade.* **Description:** Provides news and updates on all aspects of pharmaceutical development and manufacturing, enabling pharmaceutical manufacturers to advance and optimize their development and production processes.
Formerly (until 2007): Pharmaceutical Technology Asia (1933-9194)
Related titles: Online - full text ed.
Indexed: A10, A26, B06, B09, G08, H12, V03.
—BLDSC (6444.145000), IE. **CCC.**
Published by: Advanstar Asia Ltd. (Subsidiary of: Advanstar Communications, Inc.), 2501-2, 25/F, Pacific Plaza, 401 Des Voeux Rd W, Hong Kong, Hong Kong. TEL 852-2559-2772, FAX 852-2559-7002, customer_service@telecomasia.net, http://www.telecomasia.net/telecomasia/. R&P Emily Fu.

615 GBR ISSN 1753-7967
CODEN: PTEUFB
➤ **PHARMACEUTICAL TECHNOLOGY EUROPE.** Abbreviated title: P T E. Text in English. 1978; N.S. 1989. m. GBP 140 in United States; GBP 100 elsewhere; GBP 20 newsstand/cover (effective 2011). adv. abstr.; bibl.; charts; illus.; stat.; tr.lit. back issues avail.; reprints avail. **Document type:** *Journal, Academic/Scholarly.* **Description:** Targets the pharmaceutical industry in Europe; contains peer-reviewed technical articles on the manufacturing of pharmaceuticals and biopharmaceuticals.
Formerly (until 1993): Pharmaceutical Technology International (0164-6826)
Related titles: Online - full text ed.
Indexed: A10, A15, A26, ABIn, B01, B03, B06, B07, B09, B11, CEABA, E08, EMBASE, ExcerpMed, G08, H01, H12, I05, P24, P48, P51, PQC, R10, Reac, S09, SCOPUS, T02, V03.
—BLDSC (6444.155000), CASDDS, GNLM, IE, Ingenta. **CCC.**
Published by: Advanstar Communications (UK) Ltd. (Subsidiary of: Advanstar Communications, Inc.), Advanstar House, Park West, Sealand Rd, Chester, CH1 4RN, United Kingdom. TEL 44-1244-378888, FAX 44-1244-370011, info@advanstar.com, http://www.advanstar.com. Ed. Fedra Pavlou TEL 44-1244-393121. Pub. Andrew Davies TEL 44-1244-393408. Adv. contact Richard Hodson TEL 44-1244-393419. color page GBP 7,261; trim 197 x 267. Circ: 18,000 (paid and controlled).

615.19 CHE ISSN 1424-8247
RS400
➤ **PHARMACEUTICALS.** Text in English. irreg. free (effective 2011). **Document type:** *Journal, Academic/Scholarly.* **Description:** Presents comprehensive reviews of molecules that are drugs or active pharmaceutical ingredients and research papers on molecular medicine.
Media: Online - full text.
Indexed: A01, A35, A36, ASFA, B&BAb, B21, CABA, D01, E12, EMBASE, ExcerpMed, F08, GH, H16, N02, N03, P30, P33, P39, R08, R10, R13, Reac, SCOPUS, T05.
Published by: M D P I AG, Postfach, Basel, 4005, Switzerland. TEL 41-61-6837734, FAX 41-61-3028918. Ed. Derek J McPhee.

615.1 NLD ISSN 1389-2827
RA401.E85
➤ **PHARMACEUTICALS POLICY AND LAW.** Text in English. 1999. 4/yr. (in 6 vols., 1 no./vol.). USD 531 combined subscription in North America (print & online eds.); EUR 380 combined subscription elsewhere (print & online eds.) (effective 2012). adv. back issues avail. **Document type:** *Journal, Academic/Scholarly.* **Description:** Studies and evaluates the legal status of medicinal products in the EU, along with implications for markets in the US, Japan, and developing nations.
Related titles: Online - full text ed.: ISSN 2210-495X.
Indexed: A01, A03, A08, A22, B01, B06, B07, B09, B21, CA, E01, EMBASE, ESPM, H&SSA, H05, Inspec, L03, P34, RiskAb, SCOPUS, T02.
—BLDSC (6444.450000), IE. **CCC.**
Published by: I O S Press, Nieuwe Hemweg 6B, Amsterdam, 1013 BG, Netherlands. TEL 31-20-6883355, FAX 31-20-6870019, info@iospress.nl. Ed. Jose Luis Valverde TEL 34-958-243898. **Subscr. to:** I O S Press, Inc, 4502 Rachael Manor Dr, Fairfax, VA 22032-3631. sales@iospress.com; Globe Publication Pvt. Ltd., C-62 Inderpuri, New Delhi 100 012, India. TEL 91-11-579-3211, 91-11-579-3212, FAX 91-11-579-8876, custserve@globepub.com, http://www.globepub.com; Kinokuniya Co Ltd., Shinjuku 3-chome, Shinjuku-ku, Tokyo 160-0022, Japan. FAX 81-3-3439-1094, journal@kinokuniya.co.jp, http://www.kinokuniya.co.jp.

615 CHE ISSN 1999-4923
▼ **PHARMACEUTICS.** Text in English. 2009. q. free (effective 2011). **Document type:** *Journal, Academic/Scholarly.* **Description:** Publishes reviews, regular research papers, communications, and short notes on pharmacokinetics, toxicokinetics, pharmacodynamics, pharmacogenetics and pharmacogenomics, and pharmaceutical formulation.
Media: Online - full text.
Indexed: A01, P30.
Published by: M D P I AG, Postfach, Basel, 4005, Switzerland. TEL 41-61-6837734, FAX 41-61-3028918, http://www.mdpi.org/. Ed. Yvonne Perrie TEL 44-121-2043991.

615 FRA ISSN 1240-0866
PHARMACEUTIQUES; sante - medicament & industrie. Text in French. 1992. 10/yr. EUR 150 domestic; EUR 170 foreign (effective 2009).
Indexed: A22, FR.
—IE, Infotrieve. **CCC.**
Published by: P R Editions, 22, av. d'Eylau, Paris, 75116, France. TEL 33-1-4405-8300, FAX 33-1-4727-1522, n.meynaud@groupepr.com, http://www.groupepr.com/pr_ed.html. Ed. Pascal Vayssette. Circ: 20,000.

615.1 NLD ISSN 0031-6911
RS1.P53 CODEN: PHWEAW
➤ **PHARMACEUTISCH WEEKBLAD.** Text in Dutch. 1864. w. adv. bk.rev. abstr.; charts; illus.; mkt. index. **Document type:** *Journal, Academic/Scholarly.* **Description:** Practice oriented journal aimed at improving the scientific and professional practice by community, hospital, industrial and other pharmacists.
Indexed: A22, ChemAb, ChemTitl, DBA, EMBASE, ExcerpMed, I12, IndMed, KES, P30, R10, Reac, SCOPUS.
—BLDSC (6446.000000), CASDDS, GNLM, IE, Infotrieve, Ingenta, INIST.
Published by: Koninklijke Nederlandse Maatschappij ter Bevordering der Pharmacie/Royal Netherlands Pharmaceutical Society, Alexanderstraat 11, The Hague, 2514 JL, Netherlands. TEL 31-70-3737373, FAX 31-70-3106530, communicatie@knmp.nl, http://www.knmp.nl.

615 NLD ISSN 1873-8982
PHARMACEUTISCHE WEEKBLAD WETENSCHAPPELIJK PLATFORM. Key Title: P W Wetenschappelijk Platform. Text in Dutch. 2007. bi-m.
Indexed: EMBASE, ExcerpMed, SCOPUS.
Published by: Koninklijke Nederlandse Maatschappij ter Bevordering der Pharmacie/Royal Netherlands Pharmaceutical Society, Alexanderstraat 11, The Hague, 2514 JL, Netherlands. TEL 31-70-3737373, FAX 31-70-3106530, communicatie@knmp.nl, http://www.knmp.nl.

615 540 ITA ISSN 1720-4003
➤ **PHARMACHEM.** Text and summaries in English. 2002 (Jan.). m. adv. abstr.; mkt.; tr.lit.; pat.; tr.mk. Index. back issues avail.; reprints avail. **Document type:** *Journal, Academic/Scholarly.* **Description:** Provides information on fine, specialty and performance chemicals, custom manufacturing, soap and detergents, surfactants, biocides, biotechnology, flame retardants and other topics.
Related titles: Online - full text ed.
Indexed: A34, A36, BA, C25, C30, CABA, D01, E12, F08, F11, F12, FCA, GH, H16, IndVet, N02, N03, P32, R07, R13, RA&MP, VS, W10.
Published by: B5 S.r.l., Via Cesare da Sesto 10, Milano, 20123, Italy. TEL 39-02-83241119, FAX 39-02-8376457, http://www.b5srl.com. Ed. Mr. Franca Leone Mori. R&P, Adv. contact Ms. Micky Carmagnola TEL 39-02-83241358. B&W page EUR 2,110, color page EUR 2,815; trim 205 x 292. Circ: 30 (paid); 6,000.

615 IND ISSN 0975-5071
▼ ➤ **DER PHARMACIA LETTRE.** Text in English. 2009 (Sep.). q. free (effective 2011). abstr. Index. back issues avail. **Document type:** *Journal, Academic/Scholarly.* **Description:** Publishes research papers, short communications, reviews and notes dealing with entire aspects of pharmaceutical sciences.
Media: Online - full text.
Indexed: A01, A34, A35, A36, A37, AgBio, AgrForAb, B&BAb, B19, B21, C25, C30, CABA, D01, E12, F08, F11, F12, GH, H16, H17, ImmunAb, N02, N03, NSA, O01, P32, P33, P39, P40, R07, R08, R12, R13, S12, T02, T05, TAR, W11.
Published by: Scholars Research Library, 20, Kumbha Nagar, Sector4, Udaipur, Rajasthan, India. TEL 91-982-8173650, editor@scholarsresearchlibrary.com, http://www.scholarsresearchlibrary.com/.

615 IND ISSN 0976-8688
CODEN: PSHIBD
▼ ➤ **DER PHARMACIA SINICA.** Text in English. 2010 (Aug.). bi-m. free (effective 2011). back issues avail. **Document type:** *Journal, Academic/Scholarly.* **Description:** Publishes research and review articles, rapid and short communication covering: Drug discovery, over drug delivery to drug development. More specifically, the journal publishes reports in chemistry, medicinal chemistry, pharmacology, pharmaceutics, pharmacognosy, drug absorption and metabolism, pharmacokinetics and pharmacodynamics, pharmaceutical and biomedical analysis, drug delivery including gene delivery, drug targeting, pharmaceutical technology, pharmaceutical biotechnology and clinical drug evaluation.
Media: Online - full text.
Indexed: A01, C33.
Published by: Pelagia Research Library, 20, Kumbha Nagar, Udaipur, India. TEL 91-982-8173650, info@pelagiaresearchlibrary.com. Ed. H P Singh. Pub., R&P C S Sharma.

615 ZAF
PHARMACIAE. Text in Afrikaans, English. 1985. q. illus. **Document type:** *Magazine, Trade.*
Formerly (until 1993): South African Pharmacy Council. Report
Indexed: I12.
Published by: South African Pharmacy Council/Suid-Afrikaanse Aptekersraad, Posbus 40040, Arcadia, Pretoria 0007, South Africa. TEL 27-12-3198500, FAX 27-12-3211492, assistants@pharmcouncil.co.za. Ed. J S Du Toit. R&P Riana Steyn. Circ: 11,000.

615 FRA ISSN 1957-0953
LA PHARMACIE. Text in French. 1896. q. **Document type:** *Journal, Trade.*
Formerly (until 1996): La Pharmacie Laborieuse (1279-9688)
Published by: Federation Nationale de la Pharmacie, Force Ouvriere, 7 Passage Tenaille, Paris, 75014, France. TEL 33-1-40528560, FAX 33-1-40528561, fopharma@wanadoo.fr.

615 IND ISSN 0976-8157
▼ ➤ **PHARMACIE GLOBALE: INTERNATIONAL JOURNAL OF COMPREHENSIVE PHARMACY.** Abbreviated title: I J C P. Text and summaries in English. 2010 (Aug.). m. free (effective 2011). adv. abstr.; bibl.; charts; illus.; stat. cum. index. back issues avail. **Document type:** *Journal, Academic/Scholarly.* **Description:** Publishes scholarly articles and communication among pharmacists, researchers, students and other health care professionals.
Media: Online - full text.
Indexed: A01.
Published by: Pharmacie Globale, D-238, Shubhas Nagar, Roorkee, Haridwar, Uttarkhand 247 667, India. TEL 91-9993104370, support@pharmacie-globale.info, editor@pharmacie-globale.info. Ed., Pub. Meenakshi Gusain.

615 BEL
LE PHARMACIEN. Text in French. fortn. adv. **Document type:** *Journal, Trade.*
Related titles: Dutch ed.: De Apotheker.
Published by: Roularta Media Group, Meiboomlaan 33, Roeselare, 8800, Belgium. TEL 32-51-266111, FAX 32-51-266866, info@roularta.be, http://www.roularta.be. Pub. Eric Mertens. Adv. contact Nathalie Roels. page EUR 3,550. Circ: 9,000 (controlled).

615.1 FRA ISSN 0031-6938
PHARMACIEN DE FRANCE; organe d'informations scientifiques et professionnelles. Text in French. 1925. 20/yr. EUR 90 domestic; EUR 154 foreign (effective 2009). **Document type:** *Magazine, Trade.*
Related titles: Online - full text ed.
Indexed: ChemAb, FR, P30.
—Linda Hall.
Published by: Federation des Syndicats Pharmaceutiques de France, 13 Rue Ballu, Paris, 75311, France. TEL 33-1-42811596, FAX 33-1-42819661, http://www.fspf.fr. Ed. Laurent Gainza.

615.8 658 FRA ISSN 0768-9179
LE PHARMACIEN HOSPITALIER; la revue des pharmaciens des etablissements de sante et des collectivites. Text in French. 1966. q. EUR 149 in Europe to institutions; EUR 145.94 in France to institutions; JPY 17,900 in Japan to institutions; USD 194 elsewhere to institutions (effective 2012). adv. **Document type:** *Magazine, Trade.*
Related titles: Online - full text ed.: ISSN 1953-8359 (from ScienceDirect).
Indexed: EMBASE, ExcerpMed, FR, R10, Reac, SCOPUS.
—BLDSC (6446.180000), INIST. **CCC.**
Published by: (Office Francais des Relations Exterieures), Elsevier Masson (Subsidiary of: Elsevier Health Sciences), 62 Rue Camille Desmoulins, Issy les Moulineaux, Cedex 92442, France. TEL 33-1-71165500, infos@elsevier-masson.fr. Ed. Bruno Edouard. Circ: 1,600.

615 FRA ISSN 1624-8953
PHARMACIEN MANAGER. Text in French. 2000. m. **Document type:** *Magazine, Trade.*
Published by: Wolters Kluwer - Pharma (Subsidiary of: Wolters Kluwer France), 1 Rue Eugene et Armand Peugeot, Rueil-Malmaison, Cedex 92856, France. TEL 33-1-76734809, FAX 33-1-76733040, contact@wk-pharma.fr.

615.1 CAN ISSN 1195-2849
PHARMACIST NEWS. Text in English. 14/yr. CAD 38. adv. illus. **Document type:** *Newspaper, Trade.* **Description:** News about retail pharmacy and hospital and clinic-based pharmacists.
Formerly (until 1993): Drug Merchandising (0012-6586)
Related titles: Microfiche ed.: (from MML); Microform ed.: (from MML, PQC); Online - full text ed.; ◆ French ed.: L' Actualite Pharmaceutique. ISSN 1195-2857.
Indexed: C03, CBCABus, CBPI, P30, PQC.
Published by: Healthcare and Financial Publishing (Subsidiary of: Rogers Publishing Ltd./Les Editions Rogers Limitee), 777 Bay Street, 5th Fl, Toronto, ON M5W 1A7, Canada. TEL 416-596-5950. Ed. Polly Thompson. Circ: 16,600.

615 USA ISSN 1935-9373
PHARMACIST'S DIGEST. Text in English. 2007 (Mar.). q. USD 40 domestic; USD 80 foreign; USD 12 per issue (effective 2011). **Document type:** *Journal, Trade.* **Description:** Designed to provide independent and chain pharmacists with relevant and application information on industry developments, continuing education and career development.
Related titles: Online - full text ed.: USD 18 (effective 2011).
Published by: Brandofino Communications, LLC, 12 Spruce Park, Syosset, NY 11791. TEL 516-364-2575, http://brandofinocommunications.com/. Ed. Paula S Katz. Pub. Jeanette Brandofino.

615 USA ISSN 0883-0371
PHARMACIST'S LETTER. Text in English. 1985. m. looseleaf. USD 85 combined subscription (print & online eds.) (effective 2011). index. back issues avail. **Document type:** *Newsletter, Trade.* **Description:** Advises pharmacists on current drug therapy, including drug interactions, proper drug use, trends in therapy, new research findings, and new drugs.
Related titles: Online - full text ed.
Published by: Therapeutic Research Center, 3120 W March Ln, PO Box 8190, Stockton, CA 95208. TEL 209-472-2240, FAX 209-472-2249, http://www.therapeuticresearch.com.

615.1 NLD ISSN 0165-7208
CODEN: PHLIDQ
➤ **PHARMACOCHEMISTRY LIBRARY.** Text in English. 1977. irreg., latest vol.32, 2002. price varies. back issues avail. **Document type:** *Monographic series, Academic/Scholarly.* **Description:** Examines developments in the field of quantitative structure-activity relationships (QSARs).
Related titles: Online - full text ed.: ISSN 2212-0637.
Indexed: A22, ChemAb, ChemTitl, SCOPUS.
—BLDSC (6446.245000), CASDDS, IE, Ingenta, INIST. **CCC.**
Published by: Elsevier BV (Subsidiary of: Elsevier Science & Technology), Radarweg 29, PO Box 211, Amsterdam, 1000 AE, Netherlands. TEL 31-20-4853911, FAX 31-20-4852457, JournalsCustomerServiceEMEA@elsevier.com, http://www.elsevier.nl. Ed. H Timmerman.

615 338 NZL ISSN 1170-7690
RM260 CODEN: PARMEK
➤ **PHARMACOECONOMICS.** Text in English. 1992. m. price varies based on the number of users. back issues avail.; reprints avail. **Document type:** *Journal, Academic/Scholarly.* **Description:** Promotes the development and study of health economics as applied to rational drug therapy.
Related titles: Online - full text ed.: ISSN 1179-2027 (from IngentaConnect); ◆ Supplement(s): PharmacoEconomics. Italian Research Articles. ISSN 1590-9158.
Indexed: A01, A03, A08, A12, A13, A17, A22, A26, ABIn, ASCA, B01, B06, B07, B08, B09, C06, C07, CA, ChemAb, ChemTitl, CurCont, E01, E08, EMBASE, EconLit, ExcerpMed, H01, H05, H12, I05, I12, ISR, Inpharma, JEL, MEDLINE, P03, P20, P21, P22, P30, P34, P35, P50, P51, P53, P54, PQC, PsycInfo, R10, Reac, S09, SCI, SCOPUS, SSCI, T02, W07.
—BLDSC (6446.246500), CASDDS, GNLM, IE, Infotrieve, Ingenta, INIST. **CCC.**
Published by: Adis International Ltd. (Subsidiary of: Wolters Kluwer N.V.), 41 Centorian Dr, Mairangi Bay, Private Bag 65901, Auckland, 1311, New Zealand. TEL 64-9-4770700, FAX 64-9-4770764, journals@adis.com, http://www.adisonline.info/. Ed. Christopher I Carswell. **Subscr. in the Americas to:** Adis International Inc.

615 338 ITA ISSN 1590-9158
PHARMACOECONOMICS. ITALIAN RESEARCH ARTICLES. Text in English; Abstracts in Italian. 1999. s-a. **Document type:** *Journal, Academic/Scholarly.*
Related titles: Online - full text ed.: ISSN 2035-6137; ◆ Supplement to: PharmacoEconomics. ISSN 1170-7690.
Indexed: A22, EMBASE, ExcerpMed, Inpharma, P35, R10, Reac, SCOPUS.
—BLDSC (6446.246550), IE, Ingenta, INIST. **CCC.**

P

Published by: Wolters Kluwer Health Italy (Subsidiary of: Wolters Kluwer N.V.), Via B Lanino 5, Milan, 20144, Italy. http://www.wkhealth.it.

615 GBR ISSN 1053-8569
RM302.5 CODEN: PDSAEA

➤ **PHARMACOEPIDEMIOLOGY AND DRUG SAFETY**; an international journal. Text in English. 1992. m. GBP 1,058 in United Kingdom to institutions; EUR 1,338 in Europe to institutions; USD 2,073 elsewhere to institutions; GBP 1,217 combined subscription in United Kingdom to institutions (print & online eds.); EUR 1,540 combined subscription in Europe to institutions (print & online eds.); USD 2,384 combined subscription elsewhere to institutions (print & online eds.) (effective 2012). adv. back issues avail.; reprint service avail. from PSC. **Document type:** *Journal, Academic/Scholarly.* **Description:** Provides an international forum for the communication and evaluation of data, methods and opinion in the emerging discipline of pharmacoepidemiology.

Incorporates (1986-1993): Post Marketing Surveillance (0269-2333)

Related titles: Microform ed.: (from PQC); Online - full text ed.: ISSN 1099-1557. 1997. GBP 1,058 in United Kingdom to institutions; EUR 1,338 in Europe to institutions; USD 2,073 elsewhere to institutions (effective 2012).

Indexed: A22, B21, B25, BIOBASE, BIOSIS Prev, CIN, CIS, ChemAb, ChemTitl, CurCont, E04, E05, EMBASE, ESPM, ExcerpMed, H&SSA, I12, IABS, IDIS, ISR, Inpharma, MEDLINE, MycolAb, NSA, P30, P35, R10, Reac, SCI, SCOPUS, ST&MA, ToxAb, W07.

—CASDDS, GNLM, IE, Infotrieve, Ingenta, INIST. **CCC.**

Published by: (International Society for Pharmacoepidemiology USA), John Wiley & Sons Ltd. (Subsidiary of: John Wiley & Sons, Inc.), 1-7 Oldlands Way, PO Box 808, Bognor Regis, West Sussex PO21 9FF, United Kingdom. TEL 44-1865-778315, FAX 44-1243-843232, cs-journals@wiley.com, http://eu.wiley.com/WileyCDA/. Ed. Ronald D Mann. **Subscr. in the Americas to:** John Wiley & Sons, Inc., 111 River St, Hoboken, NJ 07030. TEL 201-748-6645, subinfo@wiley.com; **Subscr. to:** 1-7 Oldlands Way, PO Box 809, Bognor Regis, West Sussex PO21 9FG, United Kingdom. TEL 44-1865-778054, cs-agency@wiley.com.

➤ **PHARMACOGENETICS AND GENOMICS.** *see* BIOLOGY—Genetics

615 GBR ISSN 1462-2416

➤ **PHARMACOGENOMICS.** Text in English. 2000. m. included with subscr. to Personalized Medicine. adv. Website rev. abstr.; bibl.; illus.; pat. 150 p./no.; back issues avail.; reprints avail. **Document type:** *Journal, Academic/Scholarly.* **Description:** Addresses major initiatives in genomics which are impacting on drug discovery and creating opportunities in molecular diagnostics.

Related titles: Online - full text ed.: ISSN 1744-8042 (from IngentaConnect).

Indexed: A26, B21, B26, CA, CurCont, E08, EMBASE, ExcerpMed, H12, I05, ImmunAb, Inpharma, MEDLINE, NSA, NucAcAb, P20, P22, P30, P35, P48, P54, PQC, R10, Reac, SCI, SCOPUS, W07.

—BLDSC (6446.249700), IE, Infotrieve, Ingenta. **CCC.**

Published by: Future Medicine Ltd. (Subsidiary of: Future Science Ltd.), Unitec House, 2 Albert Pl, London, N3 1QB, United Kingdom. TEL 44-20-83716080, FAX 44-20-83716099, info@futuremedicine.com. Ed. Elisa Manzotti TEL 44-20-83716090. Pub. David Hughes. Adv. contact Simon Boisseau TEL 44-208-3716083. Circ: 750.

615 GBR ISSN 1178-7066

➤ **PHARMACOGENOMICS AND PERSONALIZED MEDICINE.** Text in English. 2008. irreg. free (effective 2011). **Document type:** *Journal, Academic/Scholarly.*

Media: Online - full text.

Indexed: EMBASE, P30, SCOPUS.

—CCC.

Published by: Dove Medical Press Ltd., Beechfield House, Winterton Way, Macclesfield, SK11 0JL, United Kingdom. TEL 44-1625-509130, FAX 44-1625-617933. Ed. Martin H Bluth.

615.7 GBR ISSN 1470-269X
RM301.3.G45 CODEN: PJHOAZ

➤ **THE PHARMACOGENOMICS JOURNAL.** Abbreviated title: T P J. Text in English. 2001. bi-m. EUR 1,754 in Europe to institutions; USD 2,206 in the Americas to institutions; JPY 299,900 in Japan to institutions; GBP 1,132 to institutions in the UK & elsewhere (effective 2011). adv. back issues avail.; reprints avail. **Document type:** *Journal, Academic/Scholarly.* **Description:** Aims to provide the caliber of coverage concerning the effects of genetic variablity on drug toxicity and efficacy, and the identification of novel genomic targets for drug development.

Related titles: Online - full text ed.: ISSN 1473-1150.

Indexed: A01, A02, A03, A08, A22, A26, A36, B&BAb, B19, B21, B25, B26, BIOSIS Prev, BioEngAb, C33, CA, CTA, CurCont, E01, EMBASE, ExcerpMed, GH, GenetAb, H12, I05, Inpharma, MEDLINE, MycolAb, NSA, P20, P22, P30, P35, P48, P54, PQC, R10, Reac, S01, SCI, SCOPUS, T02, W07.

—BLDSC (6446.249600), IE, Infotrieve, Ingenta, INIST. **CCC.**

Published by: Nature Publishing Group (Subsidiary of: Macmillan Publishers Ltd.), The MacMillan Bldg, 4 Crinan St, London, N1 9XW, United Kingdom. TEL 44-20-78334000, FAX 44-20-78334640. Ed. Dr. Julio Licinio TEL 61-2-61252550. Adv. contact Ben Harkinson TEL 617-475-9222. **Subscr. to:** Brunel Rd, Houndmills, Basingstoke, Hamps RG21 6XS, United Kingdom. TEL 44-1256-329242, FAX 44-1256-812358, subscriptions@nature.com.

615 IND ISSN 0975-3575

▼ ➤ **PHARMACOGNOSY JOURNAL.** Text in English. 2009 (Jun.). irreg. free (effective 2011). abstr. back issues avail. **Document type:** *Journal, Academic/Scholarly.* **Description:** Contains original articles, basic research, critical reviews, commentaries, special articles, editorials, and others.

Media: Online - full text.

Indexed: A01, EMBASE, SCOPUS, T02.

Published by: Pharmacognosy Network Worldwide, Al-Ameen College of Pharmacy, Hosur Rd, Bangalore, Karnataka 560 027, India. TEL 91-80-22234619, FAX 91-80-22225834, info@phcog.net, http://www.phcog.net. Ed. Srisailam Keshetti.

615 IND ISSN 0973-1296

➤ **PHARMACOGNOSY MAGAZINE.** Abbreviated title: P M. Text in English. 2005. q. INR 2,000 domestic; USD 350 foreign; INR 2,400 combined subscription domestic (print & online eds.); USD 420 combined subscription foreign (print & online eds.) (effective 2011). adv. abstr. Index. back issues avail.; reprints avail. **Document type:** *Journal, Academic/Scholarly.* **Description:** Serves the needs of scientists and others involved in medicinal plant research and development. Each issue covers different topics in natural product drug discovery, and also publishes manuscripts that describe investigations, clinical reports, methods, techniques and applications of all forms of medicinal plant research and that are of immediate interest to users in industry, academia, and government.

Related titles: Online - full text ed.: ISSN 0976-4062. INR 1,600 domestic; USD 280 foreign (effective 2011); ◆ Supplement(s): Pharmacognosy Research. ISSN 0976-4836.

Indexed: A01, A26, A34, A35, A36, A37, AgBio, AgrForAb, B&BAb, B19, B21, B23, BP, C25, C30, CA, CABA, D01, E12, EMBASE, ExcerpMed, F08, F11, F12, FCA, GH, H12, H16, H17, I05, M&PBA, MaizeAb, N02, N03, N04, O01, OR, P10, P30, P32, P33, P37, P39, P40, P48, P53, P54, PGegResA, PGrRegA, PHN&I, PQC, R07, R08, R11, R12, R13, RA&MP, RM&VM, S12, S13, S17, SCI, SCOPUS, SoyAb, T02, T05, TAR, TriticAb, VS, W07, W10, W11.

—BLDSC (6446.249700), IE. **CCC.**

Published by: Pharmacognosy Network Worldwide, Al-Ameen College of Pharmacy, Hosur Rd, Bangalore, Karnataka 560 027, India. TEL 91-80-22234619, FAX 91-80-22225834, info@phcog.net, http://www.phcog.net. Eds. Arun Kumar, G B Shivananda.

615 580 GBR

PHARMACOGNOSY, PHYTOCHEMISTRY, MEDICINAL PLANTS. Text in English. irreg., latest 2nd Ed. price varies. stat.; illus. **Document type:** *Monographic series, Academic/Scholarly.* **Description:** Contains more than 1300 literature references & the most recent statistics. Four dozen botanical families are classified alphabetically with over 350 plant species including plant monographs and numerous illustrations.

Published by: Intercept Ltd, PO Box 716, Andover, Hants SP10 1YG, United Kingdom. TEL 44-1264-334748, FAX 44-1264-334058, intercept@andover.co.uk, http://www.intercept.co.uk.

615 615.535 IND ISSN 0976-4836

▼ ➤ **PHARMACOGNOSY RESEARCH.** Text in English. 2009. bi-m. INR 2,000, USD 200; INR 400, USD 200 per issue (effective 2009). abstr. Index. back issues avail. **Document type:** *Journal, Academic/Scholarly.* **Description:** Contains original research articles from the field of natural products.

Related titles: Online - full text ed.: ISSN 0974-8490. free (effective 2011); ◆ Supplement to: Pharmacognosy Magazine. ISSN 0973-1296.

Indexed: A26, H12, I05, T02.

—CCC.

Published by: Medknow Publications and Media Pvt. Ltd., B-9, Kanara Business Ctr, Off Link Rd, Ghatkopar (E), Mumbai, Maharastra 400 075, India. TEL 91-22-66491816, 91-22-66491818, journals@medknow.com, http://www.medknow.com.

615 IND ISSN 0973-7847

➤ **PHARMACOGNOSY REVIEWS.** Text in English. 2007. s-a. INR 2,000 domestic; USD 400 foreign; INR 2,400 combined subscription domestic (print & online eds.); USD 480 combined subscription foreign (print & online eds.) (effective 2011). abstr. Index. back issues avail. **Document type:** *Journal, Academic/Scholarly.*

Related titles: Online - full text ed.: ISSN 0976-2787. INR 1,600 domestic; USD 320 foreign (effective 2011).

Indexed: A01, A26, A34, A35, A36, AgBio, AgrForAb, BA, BP, CABA, E08, E12, EMBASE, ExcerpMed, F08, F11, F12, G11, GH, H12, H16, H17, I05, N02, N03, O01, P10, P32, P33, P39, P40, P48, P53, P54, PGegResA, PGrRegA, PHN&I, PQC, R07, R08, R12, R13, RA&MP, RM&VM, S12, SCOPUS, SoyAb, T05, TAR, VS, W10, W11.

Published by: Pharmacognosy Network Worldwide, Al-Ameen College of Pharmacy, Hosur Rd, Bangalore, Karnataka 560 027, India. TEL 91-80-22234619, FAX 91-80-22225834, info@phcog.net, http://www.phcog.net. Eds. Arun Kumar, G B Shivananda.

615.1 GBR ISSN 2044-4648

▼ **PHARMACOLOGIA**; a science magazine. Text in English. 2010. m. free to qualified personnel (effective 2011). back issues avail. **Document type:** *Magazine, Trade.* **Description:** Features research in the field of clinical and experimental pharmacology.

Related titles: Online - full text ed.: ISSN 2044-4656.

Published by: Science Reuters, 26 York St, London, W1U 6PZ, United Kingdom. FAX 44-20-70234830, http://www.sciencereuters.com.

615.1 POL ISSN 1734-1140
RM1 CODEN: PJPAE3

➤ **PHARMACOLOGICAL REPORTS.** Text and summaries in English. 1949. bi-m. PLZ 180 domestic; USD 150 foreign to individuals; USD 210 foreign to institutions (effective 2005). bk.rev. charts; illus. index. **Document type:** *Journal, Academic/Scholarly.* **Description:** Covers original experimental studies in the field of pharmacology in its broadest sense.

Former titles (until 2004): Polish Journal of Pharmacology (1230-6002); (until 1992): Polish Journal of Pharmacology and Pharmacy (0301-0244); (until 1973): Dissertationes Pharmaceuticae et Pharmacologicae (0012-3870)

Related titles: Online - full text ed.: free (effective 2011).

Indexed: A22, B21, B25, B27, BIOSIS Prev, ChemAb, ChemTitl, DBA, EMBASE, ExcerpMed, IBR, IBZ, IndMed, MEDLINE, MycolAb, NPU, P30, R10, Reac, SCI, SCOPUS, ViroIAbstr, W07.

—BLDSC (6446.545000), CASDDS, GNLM, IE, Infotrieve, Ingenta, INIST, Linda Hall.

Published by: Polska Akademia Nauk, Instytut Farmakologii/Polish Academy of Sciences, Institute of Pharmacology, ul Smetna 12, Krakow, 31343, Poland. TEL 48-12-6374022, FAX 48-12-6374500, ifpan@if-pan.krakow.pl. Ed. Wladyslaw Lason. Circ: 725.

615.1 GBR ISSN 1043-6618
RS122 CODEN: PHMREP

➤ **PHARMACOLOGICAL RESEARCH.** Text in English. 19??. m. EUR 1,622 in Europe to institutions; JPY 175,300 in Japan to institutions; USD 1,441 elsewhere to institutions (effective 2012). adv. back issues avail.; reprint service avail. from PSC. **Document type:** *Journal, Academic/Scholarly.* **Description:** Presents papers on basic and applied pharmacological research in both animals and man for the specialist whose fields of study vary widely within the discipline of pharmacology.

Former titles (until 1989): Pharmacological Research Communications (0031-6989); (until 1969): Archivio Italiano di Farmacologia

Related titles: Online - full text ed.: ISSN 1096-1186. USD 1,283 to institutions (effective 2009) (from IngentaConnect, ScienceDirect).

Indexed: A01, A03, A08, A22, A26, A34, A35, A36, ASCA, ASFA, AgBio, AgrForAb, B&BAb, B19, B21, B25, BIOBASE, BIOSIS Prev, C25, C30, CA, CABA, CTA, ChemAb, ChemTitl, ChemoAb, CurCont, D01, DBA, E01, E12, EMBASE, ESPM, ExcerpMed, F08, F11, F12, GH, H16, I05, IABS, ISR, IndMed, IndVet, Inpharma, LT, M&PBA, MEDLINE, MaizeAb, MycolAb, N02, N03, NSA, P30, P32, P33, P35, P37, P39, P40, PGegResA, PGrRegA, R07, R08, R10, RA&MP, RRTA, Reac, S12, SCI, SCOPUS, SoyAb, T02, T05, TAR, THA, ToxAb, VITIS, VS, W07.

—BLDSC (6446.550000), CASDDS, GNLM, IE, Infotrieve, Ingenta, INIST, Linda Hall. **CCC.**

Published by: (Italian Pharmacological Society ITA), Academic Press (Subsidiary of: Elsevier Science & Technology), 32 Jamestown Rd, Camden, London, NW1 7BY, United Kingdom. TEL 44-20-74244200, FAX 44-20-74832293, corporatesales@elsevier.com. Ed. Francesco Visioli. R&P Catherine John. Adv. contact Nik Screen.

615.1 USA ISSN 0031-6997
RS1 CODEN: PAREAQ

➤ **PHARMACOLOGICAL REVIEWS.** Text in English. 1909. q. USD 89 to members; USD 277 combined subscription domestic to institutions (print & online eds.); USD 324 combined subscription foreign to institutions (print & online eds.); USD 77 per issue (effective 2010). adv. bibl.; charts. back issues avail. **Document type:** *Journal, Academic/Scholarly.* **Description:** Contains review articles on topics of interest to pharmacologists, toxicologists and biochemists.

Supersedes in part (in 1949): The Journal of Pharmacology and Experimental Therapeutics (0022-3565)

Related titles: Online - full text ed.: ISSN 1521-0081. USD 249 to institutions (effective 2010).

Indexed: A22, A36, ASCA, B21, BIOBASE, BIOSIS Prev, CABA, CTA, ChemAb, ChemTitl, CurCont, DBA, DentInd, EMBASE, ESPM, ExcerpMed, GH, GenetAb, IABS, IDIS, ISR, IndMed, Inpharma, MEDLINE, MycolAb, N02, N03, NSA, NucAcAb, P30, R10, RA&MP, Reac, SCI, SCOPUS, T05, THA, ToxAb, W07.

—BLDSC (6447.000000), CASDDS, GNLM, IE, Infotrieve, Ingenta, INIST, Linda Hall. **CCC.**

Published by: American Society for Pharmacology and Experimental Therapeutics, 9650 Rockville Pike, Bethesda, MD 20814. TEL 301-634-7060, FAX 301-634-7061, info@aspet.org, http://www.aspet.org. Ed. Ross Feldman. adv.: B&W page USD 685, color page USD 1,095; trim 8.375 x 10.875. Circ: 850.

615.1 USA ISSN 0031-7004
RM1 CODEN: PHMCAA

PHARMACOLOGIST. Text in English. 1959. q. USD 45 domestic to non-members; USD 70 foreign to non-members; USD 20 to members (effective 2009). abstr.; charts; illus. index. back issues avail.; reprints avail. **Document type:** *Journal, Trade.* **Description:** Designed to serve as a means of communication among members of ASPET about regional and national meetings of the society including ASPET colloquia and ASPET-Ray Fuller symposia; news from ASPET divisions, chapters, and interest groups; news about ASPET members; guidelines for ASPET programs including summer undergraduate research fellowships; graduate student, SURF fellow, and young scientist travel awards.

Related titles: Microform ed.: (from PQC); Online - full text ed.: free (effective 2009).

Indexed: A22, ChemAb, DBA, Inpharma.

—BLDSC (6447.050000), GNLM, IE, Infotrieve, Ingenta, INIST, Linda Hall. **CCC.**

Published by: American Society for Pharmacology and Experimental Therapeutics, 9650 Rockville Pike, Bethesda, MD 20814. TEL 301-634-7060, FAX 301-634-7061, info@aspet.org. Ed. Suzie Thompson.

615.1 CHE ISSN 0031-7012
RM1 CODEN: PHMGBN

➤ **PHARMACOLOGY**; international journal of experimental and clinical pharmacology. Text in English. 1959. 12/yr. CHF 3,472, EUR 2,774, USD 3,413 to institutions; CHF 3,810, EUR 3,044, USD 3,741 combined subscription to institutions (print & online eds.) (effective 2012). adv. abstr.; bibl.; charts; illus. index. back issues avail. **Document type:** *Journal, Academic/Scholarly.* **Description:** Communicates basic and clinical research in general pharmacology and related fields. Covers biochemical pharmacology, molecular pharmacology, immunopharamacology, drug metabolism, pharmacogenetics, analytical toxicology, neuropsychopharmacology, pharmacokinetics, and clinical pharmacology.

Supersedes in part (in 1967): Medicina et Pharmacologia Experimentalis (0543-3002); Which was formerly (until 1964): Medicina Experimentalis (0258-2589)

Related titles: Microfilm ed.; Online - full text ed.: ISSN 1423-0313. 1999. CHF 3,370, EUR 2,696, USD 3,272 to institutions (effective 2012).

Indexed: A01, A03, A08, A22, A36, ASCA, ASFA, AgrForAb, B21, B25, BIOSIS Prev, BP, C33, CA, CABA, ChemAb, ChemTitl, CurCont, DBA, DentInd, E01, E12, EMBASE, ESPM, ExcerpMed, F08, F11, F12, GH, H16, ISR, IndMed, Inpharma, MEDLINE, MycolAb, N02, N03, NSA, P30, P33, P35, P39, PN&I, R10, R13, RA&MP, RM&VM, Reac, SCI, SCOPUS, SoyAb, T02, T05, THA, ToxAb, VS, W07.

—BLDSC (6447.060000), CASDDS, GNLM, IE, Infotrieve, Ingenta, INIST, Linda Hall. **CCC.**

Published by: S. Karger AG, Allschwilerstr 10, Basel, 4055, Switzerland. TEL 41-61-3061111, FAX 41-61-3061234, karger@karger.ch, http://www.karger.ch. Eds. J Donnerer, M L Billingsley. adv.: page CHF 1,730; trim 210 x 280. Circ: 800.

615 USA ISSN 2157-9423
▼ **PHARMACOLOGY AND PHARMACY.** Text in English. 2010. q. back issues avail. **Document type:** *Journal, Academic/Scholarly.*
Description: Aims to keep a record of the state-of-the-art research and to promote study, research and improvement within its various specialties.
Related titles: Online - full text ed.: ISSN 2157-9431. free (effective 2011).
Indexed: CABA, E12, F08, GH, P33, T05, W11.
Published by: Scientific Research Publishing, Inc., PO Box 54821, Irvine, CA 92619. TEL 408-329-4591, service@scirp.org. Ed. George Perry.

615.1 USA ISSN 0163-7258
RM1 CODEN: PHTHDT
➤ **PHARMACOLOGY & THERAPEUTICS.** Text in English. 1979. m. EUR 5,531 in Europe to institutions; JPY 734,300 in Japan to institutions; USD 6,188 elsewhere to institutions (effective 2012). adv. bk.rev. charts; illus.; stat. index. back issues avail.; reprints avail. **Document type:** *Journal, Academic/Scholarly.* **Description:** Presents reviews of important topics in pharmacology.
Formed by the merger of (1976-1979): Pharmacology and Therapeutics. Part A. Chemotherapy, Toxicology and Metabolic Inhibitors (0362-5478); (1975-1979): Pharmacology and Therapeutics. Part B. General and Systematic Pharmacology (0306-039X); (1976-1979): Pharmacology and Therapeutics. Part C. Clinical Pharmacology and Therapeutics (0362-5486)
Related titles: Microfilm ed.: (from PQC); Online - full text ed.: ISSN 1879-016X (from IngentaConnect, ScienceDirect).
Indexed: A01, A03, A08, A22, A26, A34, A35, A36, ASCA, B21, BIOBASE, BIOSIS Prev, C33, CA, CABA, CIN, CTA, ChemAb, ChemTitl, CurCont, DBA, DentInd, E12, EMBASE, ESPM, ExcerpMed, F08, GH, GenetAb, H16, I05, I12, IABS, ISR, IndMed, Inpharma, MEDLINE, MS&D, MycolAb, N02, N03, NSA, NucAcAb, P30, P32, P33, P35, P39, PGegResA, R08, R10, RA&MP, Reac, S01, S12, SCI, SCOPUS, T02, T05, THA, ToxAb, VS, W07.
—BLDSC (6447.061800), CASDDS, GNLM, IE, Infotrieve, Ingenta, INIST. **CCC.**
Published by: Elsevier Inc. (Subsidiary of: Elsevier Science & Technology), 1600 John F Kennedy Blvd, Philadelphia, PA 19103. TEL 215-239-3900, FAX 215-238-7883, JournalCustomerService-usa@elsevier.com. Ed. S J Enna.

615.1 USA ISSN 0091-3057
QP901 CODEN: PBBHAU
➤ **PHARMACOLOGY, BIOCHEMISTRY AND BEHAVIOR.** Text in English. 1973. m. EUR 4,595 in Europe to institutions; JPY 610,700 in Japan to institutions; USD 5,142 elsewhere to institutions (effective 2012). adv. illus. index. back issues avail.; reprints avail. **Document type:** *Journal, Academic/Scholarly.* **Description:** Brings out reports in the areas of pharmacology, biochemistry, and toxicology, in which the primary emphasis and theoretical context are behavioral.
Related titles: E-mail ed.; Microfilm ed.: (from PQC); Online - full text ed.: ISSN 1873-5177 (from IngentaConnect, ScienceDirect).
Indexed: A01, A03, A08, A22, A26, A34, A35, A36, A38, ASCA, AddicA, AgBio, AgrForAb, AnBeAb, B21, B25, B27, BIOBASE, BIOSIS Prev, C25, C30, C33, CA, CABA, ChemAb, ChemTitl, ChemoAb, CurCont, D01, DBA, DentInd, E-psyche, E12, EMBASE, ESPM, ExcerpMed, F08, F11, F12, FoP, GH, GenetAb, H16, H17, I05, IABS, IPsyAb, ISR, IndMed, IndVet, Inpharma, MEDLINE, MaizeAb, MycolAb, N02, N03, N04, N05, NSA, NSCI, NucAcAb, P03, P30, P32, P33, P35, P37, P40, PGrRegA, PsycInfo, PsycholAb, R07, R08, R10, R11, RA&MP, Reac, S01, S02, S03, S12, S13, SCI, SCOPUS, SoyAb, T02, T05, THA, ToxAb, VS, W07, W10, WildRev.
—BLDSC (6447.078000), CASDDS, GNLM, IE, Infotrieve, Ingenta, INIST. **CCC.**
Published by: Elsevier Inc. (Subsidiary of: Elsevier Science & Technology), 1600 John F Kennedy Blvd, Philadelphia, PA 19103. TEL 215-239-3900, FAX 215-238-7883, JournalCustomerService-usa@elsevier.com. Ed. G F Koob. Adv. contact Janine Castle TEL 44-1865-843844.

615 AUT ISSN 1437-6873
➤ **PHARMACOLOGY FAST.** Text in German. 1999. irreg. price varies. **Document type:** *Monographic series, Academic/Scholarly.*
Published by: Springer Wien (Subsidiary of: Springer Science+Business Media), Sachsenplatz 4-6, Vienna, W 1201, Austria. TEL 43-1-3302415-0, FAX 43-1-330242665, books@springer.at, http://www.springer.at. R&P Angela Foessl TEL 43-1-3302415517. **Subscr. to:** Springer New York LLC, 233 Spring St, New York, NY 10013. TEL 800-777-4643, FAX 201-348-4505.

615.105 GBR ISSN 1757-8175
PHARMACOLOGY MATTERS. Abbreviated title: P M. Text in English. 2003. 3/yr. free to members (effective 2009). adv. back issues avail. **Document type:** *Magazine, Trade.* **Description:** Contains articles from across the pharmacology spectrum, including contributions from an honorary member of the BPS.
Formerly (until 2008): P A 2 (1741-1149)
Related titles: Online - full text ed.: ISSN 1757-8183. free (effective 2009).
—CCC.
Published by: British Pharmacological Society, 16 Angel Gate, City Rd, London, EC1V 2PT, United Kingdom. TEL 44-20-74170110, FAX 44-20-74170114, cmj@bps.ac.uk. Ed. Kate Baillie TEL 44-20-74170113. Adv. contact Hazel O'Mullan TEL 44-20-72390180. page GBP 500.

615 ITA ISSN 1827-8620
PHARMACOLOGYONLINE. Text in English. 2005. 3/yr. free (effective 2011). **Document type:** *Journal, Academic/Scholarly.*
Media: Online - full text.
Indexed: EMBASE, SCOPUS.
Published by: Universita degli Studi di Salerno, Via Ponte Don Melillo, Salerno, 84084, Italy. http://www.unisa.it. Ed. Anna Capasso.

615 IND ISSN 2229-5402
▼ ➤ **PHARMACOPHORE.** Text in English. 2010. bi-m. **Document type:** *Journal, Academic/Scholarly.* **Description:** Devoted to the promotion of research, the current health needs of the world, in the pharmaceutical and medical science or related disciplines.
Media: Online - full text.
Published by: Jadoun Science Publishing Group, Kanchanpur, Dholpur District, Bari, Rajasthan 328 041, India. TEL 91-9468692746, editorpharmacophore@gmail.com. Eds. Ram B S Jadoun, R K Godwaara. Pub., R&P Ram B S Jadoun.

615 CHN
PHARMACOPOEIA OF THE PEOPLE'S REPUBLIC OF CHINA. Text in English. a. **Document type:** *Monographic series, Academic/Scholarly.*
Related titles: Chinese ed.
Published by: People's Medical Publishing House, Fengtai-qu, Fangzhuang, Fangqunyuan 3-qu, no.3 Bldg., Beijing, 100078, China. TEL 86-10-67616688, FAX 86-10-67617314, pmph@pmph.com, http://www.pmph.com/. **Dist. by:** China Pharmaceutical Books Company, Rm. 1001-4 Champion Bldg, 287-291 Des Voeus Rd, Central, Hong Kong, Hong Kong.

PHARMACOPSYCHIATRY; clinical pharmacology, psychiatry, psychology, neurophysiology, neurobiology, gerontopsychiatry. *see* MEDICAL SCIENCES—Psychiatry And Neurology

PHARMACOPSYCHIATRY. SUPPLEMENT. *see* MEDICAL SCIENCES—Psychiatry And Neurology

615.19 USA ISSN 0277-0008
CODEN: PHPYDQ
➤ **PHARMACOTHERAPY**; the journal of human pharmacology and drug therapy. Text in English. 1981. m. USD 495 combined subscription in North America (print & online eds.); EUR 360 combined subscription elsewhere (print & online eds.) (effective 2012). adv. bk.rev. charts; illus. index. 130 p./no. 2 cols./p.; back issues avail.; reprints avail. **Document type:** *Journal, Academic/Scholarly.* **Description:** Publishes original articles of interest to physicians, pharmacists, and other health professionals with major interests in drug therapy or clinical drug research.
Related titles: CD-ROM ed.; Microfilm ed.: (from PQC); Online - full content ed.; Online - full text ed.: ISSN 1875-9114.
Indexed: A01, A03, A08, A22, A34, A36, ASCA, B&BAb, B19, B21, B25, BIOBASE, BIOSIS Prev, BioEngAb, CA, CABA, CTA, ChemAb, CurCont, D01, DBA, DentInd, E12, EMBASE, ESPM, ExcerpMed, F08, F11, F12, FR, GH, H&SSA, I12, IABS, IBR, IBZ, IDIS, INI, ISR, IndMed, IndVet, Inpharma, Kidney, MEDLINE, MycolAb, N02, N03, NSA, P30, P33, P35, P37, P39, R08, R10, R13, RA&MP, RM&VM, Reac, RefZh, SCI, SCOPUS, T02, T05, THA, ToxAb, VS, W07.
—BLDSC (6447.089000), CASDDS, GNLM, IE, Infotrieve, Ingenta, INIST. **CCC.**
Published by: (American College of Clinical Pharmacy), Pharmacotherapy Publications, Inc., 750 Washington St, Box 806, Boston, MA 02111. TEL 617-636-5390, FAX 617-636-5318. Ed., Pub. Richard Scheife. adv.: B&W page USD 1,540, color page USD 1,530. Circ: 10,000 (paid and free). **Dist. by:** I O S Press, Nieuwe Hemweg 6B, Amsterdam 1013 BG, Netherlands. TEL 31-20-6883355, FAX 31-20-6203419.

615.19 CAN ISSN 0834-065X
➤ **PHARMACTUEL**; la revue de la pratique pharmaceutique en etablissement de sante au Quebec. Text in French. 1967. bi-m. CAD 50 in North America to non-members; CAD 150 foreign to non-members (effective 2005). adv. bk.rev.; Website rev. abstr.; charts; illus. index. back issues avail. **Document type:** *Journal, Academic/Scholarly.* **Description:** Presents articles regarding the pharmaceutical field, written by pharmacists, for members of the Association of Pharmacists of the Health Estabishments of Quebec (A. P. E. S.), subscribers and manufacturers.
Indexed: I12.
—CCC.
Published by: Association des Pharmaciens des Etablissements de Sante du Quebec, 1470 rue Peel, Tour B, Bureau 900, Montreal, PQ H3A 1T1, Canada. TEL 514-286-0776, FAX 514-286-1081, apes@globetrotter.net. Ed. France Boulet. adv.: B&W page USD 1,000, color page USD 1,600; trim 10.88 x 8.13. Circ: 1,300 (controlled).

615.1 NLD ISSN 1477-2701
▼ ➤ **PHARMACY EDUCATION (ONLINE).** Text in English. 2009. q. free (effective 2010). back issues avail.; reprints avail. **Document type:** *Journal, Academic/Scholarly.* **Description:** Provides a forum for communication between academic teachers and practitioners, with an emphasis on new and established teaching and learning methods; new curriculum and syllabus directions; guidance on structuring courses and assessing achievement as well as the dissemination of new ideas.
Media: Online - full text (from IngentaConnect).
Indexed: S21.
—CCC.
Published by: International Pharmaceutical Federation/Federation Internationale Pharmaceutique, PO Box 84200, The Hague, 2508 AE, Netherlands. TEL 31-70-3021970, FAX 31-70-3021999, fip@fip.org, http://www.fip.org. Eds. Sarah Carter, Sarah Whitmarsh, Ian Bates.

615.9 CAN
PHARMACY ELECTRONIC COMMUNICATIONS STANDARD. Text in English. biennial. CAD 35 (effective 2000). **Document type:** *Handbook/Manual/Guide, Trade.*
Former titles (until 1998): Pharmacy Claim Standard; Electronic Claim Standard
Published by: Canadian Pharmacists Association, 1785 Alta Vista Dr, Ottawa, ON K1G 3Y6, Canada. TEL 613-523-7877, FAX 613-523-0445, info@pharmacists.ca, http://www.pharmacists.ca.

615.19 AUS ISSN 1032-3279
PHARMACY GUILD OF AUSTRALIA. ANNUAL REPORT. Text in English. 1975. a. **Document type:** *Journal, Trade.*
Formerly (until 1982): Pharmacy Guild of Australia. National Report
Published by: The Pharmacy Guild of Australia, PO Box 7036, Canberra, ACT 2610, Australia. TEL 61-2-62701888, FAX 61-2-62701800, guild.nat@guild.org.au, http://www.guild.org.au. Circ: 5,500.

615.19 AUS ISSN 0155-8595
PHARMACY GUILD OF AUSTRALIA. NATIONAL NEWSLETTER. Text in English. 1976. irreg. free to members. back issues avail. **Document type:** *Newsletter, Trade.*
Published by: The Pharmacy Guild of Australia, PO Box 7036, Canberra, ACT 2610, Australia. TEL 61-2-62701888, FAX 61-2-62701800, guild.nat@guild.org.au, http://www.guild.org.au. Circ: 5,300.

615.1 USA ISSN 0031-7047
RS61 CODEN: PHHIB4
➤ **PHARMACY IN HISTORY.** Text in English. 1955. q. free to members (effective 2009). adv. bk.rev. bibl.; charts; illus. index every 3 yrs. reprints avail. **Document type:** *Journal, Academic/Scholarly.* **Description:** Provides essays on the history of pharmaceutical practice, science, and industry, including the history of drugs and therapeutics and facets of the related medical sciences.
Formerly (until 1959): A I H P Notes
Related titles: Microfilm ed.: (from PQC); Online - full text ed.
Indexed: A22, AmH&L, CA, EMBASE, ExcerpMed, FR, HistAb, I12, MEDLINE, MLA-IB, P30, SCOPUS, T02.
—BLDSC (6447.350000), IE, Infotrieve, Ingenta, INIST, Linda Hall.
Published by: American Institute of the History of Pharmacy, Pharmacy Bldg, 777 Highland Ave, Madison, WI 53705. TEL 608-262-5378, aihp@aihp.org, http://www.pharmacy.wisc.edu/aihp/. Ed. Gregory J Higby.

615 USA ISSN 2160-441X
▼ ➤ **PHARMACY INFORMATION.** Abstracts in English; Text in Chinese. forthcoming 2011. q. **Document type:** *Journal, Academic/Scholarly.*
Related titles: Online - full text ed.: ISSN 2160-4452. forthcoming. free.
Published by: Hansi Chubanshe/Hans Publishers, 40 E. Main St., Box 275, Newark, DE 19711. TEL 926408-329-4591.

615 USA ISSN 1931-6119
PHARMACY INSIDER; the professional's guide to products and career opportunities. Text in English. 2006 (May). a., latest 2007. adv. back issues avail. **Document type:** *Handbook/Manual/Guide, Trade.* **Description:** Designed to meet the information needs of hospital pharmacists, whose increasing role in patient safety, clinical outcomes, and reducing health care costs makes them valuable and influential members of a hospital's patient care team.
Related titles: Online - full text ed.: ISSN 1931-6127.
Published by: Lippincott Williams & Wilkins (Subsidiary of: Wolters Kluwer N.V.), 323 Norristown Rd, Ste 200, Ambler, PA 19002. TEL 215-646-8700, FAX 215-654-1328, customerservice@lww.com, http://www.lww.com.

615.329 USA
PHARMACY JOURNAL OF NEW ENGLAND. Text in English. 1943. q. USD 40 (effective 2007). adv. **Document type:** *Journal, Trade.*
Formerly: Connecticut Pharmacist
Published by: Connecticut Pharmacists Association, 35 Cold Spring Rd, Ste 121, Rocky Hill, CT 06067-3167. TEL 860-563-4619, FAX 860-257-8241, http://www.ctpharmacists.org. Ed., Adv. contact Marc S McQuaid. B&W page USD 450, color page USD 650; trim 11 x 8.5. Circ: 1,500.

P

615.19 340 USA ISSN 0149-1717
KF2915.P4
PHARMACY LAW DIGEST. Text in English. 1965. irreg., latest 40th ed. looseleaf. USD 62.95 40th ed. (effective 2008). **Document type:** *Monographic series, Trade.* **Description:** Addresses federal laws regulating controlled substances, constitutional considerations in dealing with governmental inspections, regulation of pharmaceuticals, civil liability and business law.
Published by: Facts and Comparisons (Subsidiary of: Wolters Kluwer N.V.), 77 West Port Plz, Ste 450, St. Louis, MO 63146. TEL 314-216-2100, 800-223-0554, FAX 317-735-5390.

615 GBR
PHARMACY MAGAZINE; first in professional & business development. Text in English. 1995. m. GBP 80 (effective 2009). back issues avail. **Document type:** *Magazine, Trade.* **Description:** Provides trade information for pharmacists.
Published by: Communications International Group, 207 Linen Hall, 162-168 Regent St, London, W1B 5TB, United Kingdom. TEL 44-20-74341530, FAX 44-20-75347208. Ed. Richard Thomas. Circ: 19,468.

615.1 GBR ISSN 1755-6619
PHARMACY.ME. Text in English. 1993. bi-m. GBP 40 (effective 2010). adv. **Document type:** *Journal, Trade.* **Description:** Focuses on topics that enable pharmacists to consider the impact of changes in the region's healthcare systems, and to review case study profiles and treatments.
Formerly (until 2007): Middle East Pharmacy (1368-5945)
—CCC.
Published by: Pharmedia International, 6 Tobin Close, Epsom, Surrey KT19 8AE, United Kingdom. TEL 44-1372-742347, FAX 44-1372-745187, info@pharmedia.co.uk. adv.: page GBP 2,500; trim 210 x 297. Circ: 8,040.

615 AUS ISSN 1448-207X
PHARMACY NEWS. Text in English. 1967. fortn. AUD 200 domestic; AUD 210 in New Zealand; AUD 220 elsewhere; free to qualified personnel (effective 2008). adv. **Document type:** *Magazine, Trade.* **Description:** Provides industry news to clinical reviews and new product developments for pharmacists.
Former titles (until 2002): Australian Pharmacy Trade (1444-3376); (until 2000): Pharmacy Trade with Contact; (until 1994): Pharmacy Trade (1325-8605)
Related titles: Online - full text ed.
Indexed: A15, ABIn, B02, B15, B17, B18, C06, C07, G04, G08, I05, P48, P51, PQC, SCOPUS, T02.
—CCC.
Published by: Reed Business Information Pty Ltd. (Subsidiary of: Reed Business Information International), Tower 2, 475 Victoria Ave, Locked Bag 2999, Chatswood, NSW 2067, Australia. TEL 61-2-94222999, FAX 61-2-94222922, customerservice@reedbusiness.com.au, http://www.reedbusiness.com.au. Ed. Graham Smith TEL 61-2-94222825. Adv. contact Annya Azzopardi TEL 61-2-94222550. color page AUD 5,135; trim 248 x 345. Circ: 7,080.

615 USA ISSN 8750-4790
PHARMACY NEWS AND REVIEW. Text in English. 6/yr. USD 100 to non-members; USD 50 to members (effective 2000). 8 p./no.; **Document type:** *Newsletter, Trade.* **Description:** Covers current legal, administrative and medical issues affecting pharmacists.
Published by: Pennsylvania Pharmacists Association, 508 N Third St, Harrisburg, PA 17101-1199. TEL 717-234-6151, FAX 717-236-1618, ppa@papharmacists.com, http://www.papharmacists.com. Ed. Pat Peppie. Adv. contact Tammy A Linn.

615 USA
PHARMACY NOW. Text in English. 2001. m. USD 5 per issue (effective 2004). adv. **Document type:** *Magazine, Trade.*
Published by: Now Publishing, 1026 Chestnut St, West Bend, WI 53095. TEL 262-334-4112. adv.: B&W page USD 3,595; trim 8.25 x 10.75. Circ: 21,290 (controlled).

615.1 GBR ISSN 1471-5252
➤ **PHARMACY ON-LINE**; the international journal of pharmacy. Text in English. 1997. m. free (effective 2009). bk.rev.; software rev.; video rev. illus. **Document type:** *Journal, Academic/Scholarly.*
Description: Covers pharmacy, pharmaceuticals and pharmacology.
Media: Online - full text.
Published by: Priory Lodge Education Ltd., 2 Cornflower Way, Moreton, Wirral CH46 1SV, United Kingdom. Ed. Dr. Ben Green.

615 CAN ISSN 1199-2131
PHARMACY POST; your news, business and otc market report. Text in English. 1993. m. CAD 71.69 domestic; CAD 108 foreign (effective 2007). adv. **Document type:** *Magazine, Trade.* **Description:** Complete resource for news, OTC drug information, and business management for Canada's 16,000 community pharmacists as well as 2,000 buyers and frontshop managers.
Related titles: Online - full text ed.
Indexed: A15, ABIn, C03, CBCABus, H13, P10, P20, P24, P53, P54, PQC.
Published by: Rogers Publishing Ltd./Les Editions Rogers Limitee, One Mount Pleasant Rd, 11th Fl, Toronto, ON M4Y 2Y5, Canada. TEL 416-764-2000, FAX 416-764-1740, http://www.rogerspublishing.ca. Ed. Vicki Wood TEL 416-764-3923. Circ: 12,636.

615.1 CAN ISSN 0829-2809
CODEN: PHRPEA
PHARMACY PRACTICE. Text in English. 1985. 12/yr. CAD 71.69 domestic; CAD 108 foreign (effective 2007). adv. **Document type:** *Magazine, Trade.* **Description:** Provides readers with information on the new and significant developments that affect the profession of pharmacy.
Related titles: Online - full text ed.
Indexed: A15, ABIn, C03, CBCARef, I12, P10, P24, P53, P54, PQC.
—CCC.
Published by: Rogers Publishing Ltd./Les Editions Rogers Limitee, One Mount Pleasant Rd, 11th Fl, Toronto, ON M4Y 2Y5, Canada. TEL 416-764-2000, FAX 416-764-3941, http://www.rogerspublishing.ca. Ed. Rosalind Stefanac TEL 416-764-3926. adv.: B&W page CAD 2,620. Circ: 20,100.

615 ESP ISSN 1886-3655
RS1
➤ **PHARMACY PRACTICE (ONLINE).** Text in English. 2006. q. free (effective 2011). Index. back issues avail. **Document type:** *Journal, Academic/Scholarly.* **Description:** Covers pharmacy practice and pharmaceutical care.
Media: Online - full text.
Indexed: C06, C07, CA, EMBASE, ExcerpMed, T02.
—CCC.
Published by: Centro de Investigaciones y Publicaciones Farmaceuticas, Rua das Regateiras, 55, Redondela, 36800, Spain. FAX 34-986-401889, sft@cipf-es.org, http://www.cipf-es.org. Ed. Dr. Fernando Fernandez-Llimos.

615 USA ISSN 0886-988X
PHARMACY PRACTICE NEWS. Text in English. 1974. m. USD 70 domestic; USD 90 foreign; USD 7 newsstand/cover domestic; USD 10 newsstand/cover foreign; free to qualified personnel (effective 2010); Free to qualified subscribers. adv. illus. back issues avail. **Document type:** *Newspaper, Trade.* **Description:** Provides health-system pharmacists with information that improves their clinical practice, such as continuing education lessons, new FDA drug approvals and educational reviews.
Former titles (until 1985): Intravenous Therapy News (8750-3182); (until 1984): American Journal of Intravenous Therapy and Clinical Nutrition (0195-0282); (until 1979): American Journal of Intravenous Therapy (0161-3065); (until 1977): American Journal of I.V. Therapy (0095-4012)
Related titles: Online - full text ed.; Special ed(s).
Indexed: C06, C07, C08, CINAHL, I12, SCOPUS.
—GNLM. **CCC.**
Published by: McMahon Group, 545 W 45th St, 8th Fl, New York, NY 10036. TEL 212-957-5300, FAX 212-957-7230, info@mcmahongroup.com, http://www.mcmahongroup.com. Ed. David Bronstein TEL 212-957-5300 ext 212. Pub. Raymond E McMahon. Circ: 43,718.

615.1 GBR ISSN 2042-4493
▼ **PHARMACY PROFESSIONAL.** Text in English. 2009. m. free to members (effective 2010). **Document type:** *Magazine, Trade.*
Published by: Royal Pharmaceutical Society of Great Britain, 1 Lambeth High St, London, SE1 7JN, United Kingdom. TEL 44-20-77359141, FAX 44-20-77357629, enquiries@rpsgb.org, http://www.rpsgb.org.uk/. Ed. J Mills.

615 USA ISSN 1549-635X
PHARMACY PURCHASING & PRODUCTS. Text in English. 2004. 10/yr. free to qualified personnel (effective 2007). **Document type:** *Magazine, Trade.*
Published by: Ridgewood Medical Media LLC, 211 1st St, Ho Ho Kus, NJ 07423. TEL 201-670-1356, FAX 201-670-1780, http://ridgewoodmedia.com. Pub. R M Halvorsen.

615.1 NZL ISSN 1178-6175
PHARMACY RESEARCH REVIEW. Text in English. 2007. bi-m. free to qualified personnel (effective 2009). back issues avail. **Document type:** *Journal, Academic/Scholarly.*
Media: Online - full text.
Published by: Research Review Ltd., N Shore Mail Centre, PO Box 100116, Auckland, New Zealand. TEL 64-9-4102277, info@researchreview.co.nz.

615.19 AUS ISSN 0314-6316
PHARMACY REVIEW. Text in English. 1976. q. **Description:** Informs members about decisions relating to pharmacy in Australia.
Indexed: I12.
—CCC.
Published by: The Pharmacy Guild of Australia, PO Box 7036, Canberra, ACT 2610, Australia. TEL 61-2-62701888, FAX 61-2-62701800, guild.nat@guild.org.au, http://www.guild.org.au. Circ: 5,200.

615.1071 USA ISSN 0149-1113
RS110
PHARMACY SCHOOL ADMISSION REQUIREMENTS. Text in English. 1974. a. USD 28 (effective 2007). **Description:** Informs students interested in getting into Pharmacy schools.
Published by: American Association of Colleges of Pharmacy, Office of Academic Affairs, 1426 Prince St, Alexandria, VA 22314-2815. TEL 703-739-2330, FAX 703-836-8982, mail@aacp.org, http://www.aacp.org.

615.1 USA ISSN 1098-1853
PHARMACY SOCIETY OF WISCONSIN. JOURNAL. Abbreviated title: J P S W. Text in English. 1930 (vol.40). bi-m. USD 60 domestic; USD 120 foreign (effective 2009). adv. back issues avail. **Document type:** *Journal, Trade.*
Formerly (until 1997): Wisconsin Pharmacist (0043-6585)
Indexed: ChemAb, I12.
—BLDSC (4840.130000), IE.
Published by: Pharmacy Society of Wisconsin, 701 Heartland Trail, Madison, WI 53717-1916. TEL 608-827-9200, FAX 608-827-9292. Ed. Curtis A Johnson. adv.: B&W page USD 440, color page USD 1,040. Circ: 2,200 (controlled).

615 USA ISSN 1946-035X
PHARMACY TECHNICIAN'S LETTER. Text in English. 2007. m. USD 77 combined subscription (print & online eds.) (effective 2011). **Document type:** *Newsletter, Trade.*
Related titles: Online - full text ed.: ISSN 1946-0414.
Published by: Therapeutic Research Center, 3120 W March Ln, PO Box 8190, Stockton, CA 95208. TEL 209-472-2240, FAX 209-472-2249, http://www.therapeuticresearch.com. Ed. Jeff M Jellin.

615.1 USA ISSN 0003-0627
RS1
PHARMACY TIMES; practical information for today's pharmacist. Text in English. 1897. m. USD 65 domestic to individuals; USD 115 domestic to institutions; USD 39 domestic to senior citizens; USD 120 in Canada; free to qualified personnel (effective 2009). adv. bk.rev. abstr.; illus. index. back issues avail.; reprints avail. **Document type:** *Magazine, Trade.* **Description:** Deals with pharmaceutical news, pharmacy economics and prescription practice.
Formerly (until 1969): American Professional Pharmacist (0096-0349); Which superseded (in 1935): Practical Druggist and Spatula; Which was formerly (until 1925): Practical Druggist and Pharmaceutical Review of Reviews
Related titles: Microform ed.: (from PQC); Online - full text ed.; ◆ Supplement(s): Generic Rx Product Report; Pharmacy Careers. ISSN 1543-9607.
Indexed: A01, A22, A26, ChemAb, EMBASE, ExcerpMed, H12, I05, I12, P30, P34, R10, Reac, SCOPUS.
—BLDSC (6447.530000), IE, Infotrieve, Ingenta, INIST. **CCC.**
Published by: Intellisphere, LLC (Subsidiary of: MultiMedia Healthcare Inc.), Office Center at Princeton Meadows, 666 Plainsboro Rd, Bldg 300, Plainsboro, NJ 08536. TEL 609-716-7777, FAX 609-716-4747, info@mdnetguide.com, http://www.hcplive.com. Ed. Fred Eckel. adv.: color page USD 7,085, B&W page USD 6,235. Circ: 180,666 (paid and controlled).

615 USA ISSN 1042-0991
PHARMACY TODAY. Text in English. 1962. m. USD 200 domestic to non-members; USD 250 foreign to non-members; free to qualified personnel (effective 2009). adv. bibl.; illus. back issues avail.; reprints avail. **Document type:** *Magazine, Academic/Scholarly.* **Description:** Reports on current news and opinions, including pharmacotherapeutic, legislative and socioeconomic news.
Former titles (until 1995): Pharmacy Weekly; (until 1985): A-Ph-Armacy Weekly (0098-2814); (until 1975): A Ph A Newsletter (0567-4069)
Related titles: Online - full text ed.
Indexed: B07, I12, T02.
—CCC.
Published by: American Pharmacists Association, 2215 Constitution Ave, NW, Washington, DC 20037. TEL 202-628-4410, FAX 202-783-2351, InfoCenter@aphanet.org, http://www.japha.org. Ed. Michael L Posey. Pub. Frank Bennicasa. adv.: B&W page USD 8,310, color page USD 10,390; trim 7.75 x 10.5. Circ: 139,566. **Subscr. to:** PO Box 11806, Birmingham, AL 35202. TEL 800-633-4931, FAX 205-995-1588, japha@subscriptionoffice.com.

615.4 NZL ISSN 1170-1927
PHARMACY TODAY (AUCKLAND). Text in English. m. NZD 160 domestic; NZD 288 in Australia; NZD 340 in US & Canada; NZD 406 elsewhere (effective 2008). adv. **Document type:** *Magazine, Trade.* **Description:** Resource on news, current issues and business management, plus in-depth articles on clinical pharmacy practice.
Related titles: Online - full text ed.
Published by: CMPMedica New Zealand Ltd. (Subsidiary of: United Business Media Limited), 3 Shea Terrace, Takapuna, Auckland, New Zealand. TEL 64-9-488-4290, FAX 64-9-489-6240. Ed. Andrea Svendsen TEL 64-9-4884269. Adv. contact Vivienne Fraser TEL 64-9-4884295.

615.1 USA
PHARMACY UPDATE. Text in English. bi-m. back issues avail. **Document type:** *Bulletin, Trade.*
Related titles: Online - full text ed.
Published by: (Pharmacy Department), U.S. National Institutes of Health, Clinical Center, 10 Center Dr, Room 1N257, Bethesda, MD 20892-1196. TEL 301-496-4363, http://www.cc.nih.gov/phar/updates/. Ed. Karim Anton Calis.

615 USA ISSN 1075-2552
PHARMACY WEEK. Text in English. 1992. w. free to qualified personnel (effective 2007). adv. **Document type:** *Newsletter, Trade.* **Description:** For hospital and home health care pharmacists. Covers management and employment issues.
Related titles: Online - full text ed.
Address: 7780 Elmwood Ave, Ste 210, Middleton, WI 53562-5407. TEL 608-828-4400, FAX 608-828-4401. Adv. contacts Bill Koenen, Tracy Oswald. B&W page USD 2,500, color page USD 4,500; trim 8.5 x 11. Circ: 12,000 (controlled).

615.19 USA ISSN 1557-3516
PHARMADEVICE I T REPORT. Text in English. 2001. bi-w. USD 525 (print or online ed.); USD 840 combined subscription (print & online eds.) (effective 2009). 4 p./no.; back issues avail. **Document type:** *Newsletter, Trade.* **Description:** Provides case studies, expert interviews and practical advice on how to comply with 21 CFR Part 11 requirements and other technology initiatives at the FDA and in the industry.
Formerly (until 2005): Part 11 Compliance Report (1538-3091)
Related titles: Online - full text ed.: ISSN 1557-3524. USD 799 (effective 2005); ◆ Supplement to: The G M P Letter. ISSN 0196-626X.
Published by: Washington Business Information, Inc., 300 N Washington St, Ste 200, Falls Church, VA 22046. customerservice@fdanews.com. Pub. Matt Salt TEL 703-538-7642.

615 GBR ISSN 1465-5403
PHARMAFOCUS. Text in English. 1999. m. GBP 115 domestic; GBP 145 in Europe; GBP 185 elsewhere; free to qualified personnel (effective 2010). adv. **Document type:** *Newspaper, Trade.* **Description:** Provides quality pharmaceutical intelligence for the UK and European markets.
Related titles: Online - full text ed.: free (effective 2010).
—CCC.
Published by: InPharm (Subsidiary of: John Wiley & Sons Ltd.), First House, Park St, Guildford, Surrey GU1 4XB, United Kingdom. sales@Pharmafile.com. Ed. Andrew McConaghie. Adv. contact Wayne Elliot. Circ: 9,000.

615.1 CHE ISSN 1661-8785
CODEN: SAZTA8
PHARMAJOURNAL/GIORNALE SVIZZERO DI FARMACIA/JOURNAL SUISSE DE PHARMACIE. Text in German. 1863. s-m. CHF 248, EUR 180 (effective 2011). adv. bk.rev. **Document type:** *Newspaper, Trade.*
Former titles (until 2006): Schweizer Apothekerzeitung (1420-4932); (until 1994): Schweizerische Apotheker-Zeitung (0036-7508)
Indexed: A22, ChemAb, P30, SCOPUS.
—BLDSC (6441.881600), CASDDS, GNLM, IE, Infotrieve, Ingenta, INIST, Linda Hall.
Published by: (Schweizerischer Apothekerverband), Verlag Hans Huber AG (Subsidiary of: Hogrefe Verlag GmbH & Co. KG), Laenggassstr 76, Bern 9, 3000, Switzerland. TEL 41-31-3004500, FAX 41-31-3004590, verlag@hanshuber.com. Ed. Markus Kamber. Circ: 6,000 (controlled).

615 ROM
PHARMAKON. Text in Romanian. m. **Document type:** *Magazine, Trade.*
Published by: Crier Media Group S.R.L. (Subsidiary of: Crier Media Group Ltd.), Piata Alba Iulia nr. 6, bl. i5, sc. 3, ap. 75, sector 3, Bucharest, Romania. TEL 40-21-3217631, FAX 40-21-3235055, office@crier.ro, http://www.crier.ro.

615 USA ISSN 2155-2630
▼ **PHARMALOGIC REPORT.** Text in English. forthcoming 2010 (July). m. **Document type:** *Bulletin, Trade.* **Description:** Provides updates on the clinically-based pharma and biotech financial sectors.
Related titles: Online - full text ed.: ISSN 2155-2649. forthcoming 2010 (July).
Published by: PharmaLogic, LLC, 2410 Shorecrest Dr, Rockwall, TX 75807. TEL 972-345-5296, pharmalogicinfo@yahoo.com, http://www.pharmalogicllc.com/.

615.19 DEU ISSN 2191-1177
▼ **PHARMAPRODUKTION**; das Fachmagazin fuer die GMP-gerechte Produktion. Text in German. 2010. 4/yr. EUR 21.20 (effective 2011). adv. **Document type:** *Magazine, Trade.*
Published by: Konradin Verlag Robert Kohlhammer GmbH, Ernst Mey Str 8, Leinfelden-Echterdingen, 70771, Germany. TEL 49-711-75940, FAX 49-711-7594390, info@konradin.de, http://www.konradin.de. Ed. Guenter Eckhardt. Adv. contact Manuela Bumler. Circ: 11,000 (paid).

615.19 DEU ISSN 1863-0766
PHARMAREPORT. Text in German. 1986. bi-m. EUR 8.70 (effective 2010). **Document type:** *Newsletter, Trade.*
Formerly (until 2005): Pharma und Wir (0933-0909)
Related titles: Online - full text ed.
Published by: (Bundesverband der Pharmazeutischen Industrie e.V.), Dr. Curt Haefner Verlag GmbH (Subsidiary of: Konradin Verlag Robert Kohlhammer GmbH), Dischingerstr 8, Heidelberg, 69123, Germany. TEL 49-6221-64460, FAX 49-6221-644640, info@haefner-verlag.de, http://www.haefner-verlag.de. Ed. Dieter Neumann. Circ: 5,200 (paid).

615.1 DEU
RS1 CODEN: PHMRAL
PHARMARUNDSCHAU. Text in German. 1968. m. EUR 108 domestic; EUR 128 foreign; EUR 8.50 newsstand/cover (effective 2008). adv. bk.rev. **Document type:** *Journal, Trade.* **Description:** Contains pharmaceutical news and cover issues important to professional in the industy.
Formerly: Pharmazeutische Rundschau (0031-7128)
Indexed: P30.
—INIST. **CCC.**
Published by: P. Keppler Verlag GmbH und Co. KG, Industriestr 2, Heusenstamm, 63150, Germany. TEL 49-6104-6060, FAX 49-6104-606333, info@kepplermediengruppe.de, http://www.kepplermediengruppe.de. Ed. Silvia Schmidtke. Adv. contact Margitta Mueller. B&W page EUR 3,480, color page EUR 4,620; trim 185 x 263. Circ: 23,275 (paid and controlled).

615.1 NGA ISSN 1597-4030
PHARMASCOPE. Text in English. 2004. bi-m. NGN 200 newsstand/cover (effective 2007). **Document type:** *Magazine, Consumer.* **Description:** Presents a global perspective on issues of health and diseases as they may affect local consumers.
Published by: Global Village Limited, 11, Rev Onilaja Close, off Ramat Cresent Ogudu GRA, Lagos, Nigeria. TEL 234-1-8130956. Ed., Pub. Chuba Keshi.

615 USA ISSN 1875-7774
PHARMASIA NEWS. Text in English. 2008. d. USD 1,660 (effective 2011). adv.
Media: Online - full text.
Published by: Elsevier Business Intelligence (Subsidiary of: Elsevier Health Sciences), 685 Route 202/206, Bridgewater, NJ 08807. TEL 908-547-2159, 800-332-2181, http://www.elsevierbi.com.

PHARMAVET. *see* VETERINARY SCIENCE

615 USA ISSN 1932-961X
PHARMAVOICE. Text in English. 2001. 10/yr. adv. **Document type:** *Magazine, Trade.* **Description:** Provides a forum for the views and opinions of pharmaceutical industry executives on key issues and trends.
Published by: PharmaLinx LLC, PO Box 327, Titusville, NJ 08650. TEL 609-730-0196, FAX 609-730-0197. Ed. Taren Grom. Pub. Lisa Banket. adv.: B&W page USD 3,425, color page USD 4,825; trim 9.5 x 11.5. Circ: 10,000 (controlled).

615 USA
PHARMAWEEK. Text in English. w. **Document type:** *Newsletter, Trade.*
Media: E-mail.
Published by: Cambridge Healthtech Institute, 1037 Chestnut St., Newton Upper Falls, MA 02464. TEL 617-630-1300, FAX 617-630-1325, chi@healthtech.com, http://www.healthtech.com/.

615 DEU ISSN 0480-2624
CODEN: PHBEDW
DER PHARMAZEUTISCHE BETRIEB. Text in German, English. 1955. irreg. price varies. **Document type:** *Monographic series, Trade.*
Published by: Editio Cantor Verlag, Baendelstockweg 20, Aulendorf, 88326, Germany. TEL 49-7525-9400, FAX 49-7525-940180, info@ecv.de, http://www.ecv.de.

615.1 DEU ISSN 0031-711X
CODEN: PHINAN
DIE PHARMAZEUTISCHE INDUSTRIE. Variant title: Pharmind. Text in English, German. 1939. m. EUR 258 combined subscription (print & online eds.); EUR 28 newsstand/cover (effective 2011). adv. bk.rev. abstr.; bibl.; charts; illus.; mkt.; pat.; tr.lit. index. reprint service avail. from IRC. **Document type:** *Journal, Trade.* **Description:** Provides a forum for the pharmaceutical industry covering pharmaceutics, health care and social politics as well as public health affairs affecting the market members.
Related titles: Online - full text ed.: ISSN 1616-7074.
Indexed: A22, ASCA, B03, CBNB, CEABA, ChemAb, ChemTitl, DBA, EMBASE, ExcerpMed, FR, I12, IPackAb, KES, P30, R10, Reac, RefZh, SCI, SCOPUS, W07.
—BLDSC (6447.650000), CASDDS, GNLM, IE, Infotrieve, Ingenta, INIST, Linda Hall. **CCC.**
Published by: Editio Cantor Verlag, Baendelstockweg 20, Aulendorf, 88326, Germany. TEL 49-7525-9400, FAX 49-7525-940180, info@ecv.de. Eds. Claudius Arndt, Viktor Schramm. Adv. contact Judith Scheller. B&W page EUR 1,560, color page EUR 2,550; trim 216 x 303. Circ: 4,023 (paid and controlled).

615.1 DEU ISSN 0031-7136
RS1 CODEN: PHZIAP
PHARMAZEUTISCHE ZEITUNG. Abbreviated title: P Z. Text in German. 1953. w. EUR 2.10 newsstand/cover (effective 2008). adv. bk.rev. bibl.; charts; illus. index. **Document type:** *Newspaper, Trade.*
Incorporates (1986-1990): Mitteilungen aus dem Deutschen Apotheken-Museum im Heidelberger Schloss (0931-0673); Formed by the merger of (1951-1953): Pharmazeutische Zeitung-Nachrichten (0369-9803); (1934-1953): Apotheker-Zeitung (0174-1675); Which was formerly (until 1949): Deutsche Apotheker-Zeitung (0370-9280); Which was formed by the merger of (1886-1934): Apotheker-Zeitung (0365-5830); (1932-1934): Die Deutsche Apotheke (0933-2472)
Indexed: A22, ChemAb, ChemTitl, DBA, EMBASE, ExcerpMed, I12, P30, R10, Reac, SCOPUS.
—BLDSC (6447.693000), CASDDS, GNLM, IE, Infotrieve, Ingenta, INIST. **CCC.**
Published by: (Bundesvereinigung Deutscher Apothekerverbaende), Govi Verlag Pharmazeutischer Verlag GmbH, Carl Mannich Str 26, Eschborn, 65760, Germany. TEL 49-6196-928262, FAX 49-6196-928203, service@govi.de, http://www.govi.de. Ed. Dr. Hartmut Morck. Adv. contact Hans Juergen Renn. page EUR 5,580. Circ: 37,495 (paid and controlled).

615.1 DEU ISSN 0031-7144
RS1 CODEN: PHARAT
➤ **DIE PHARMAZIE**; an international journal of pharmaceutical sciences. Text in English, German. 1946. m. EUR 216; EUR 18 per issue (effective 2009). adv. bk.rev. abstr.; bibl.; charts; illus. index. **Document type:** *Journal, Academic/Scholarly.*
Related titles: Online - full text ed.: (from IngentaConnect).
Indexed: A20, A22, A34, A35, A36, A37, A40, ASCA, AgBio, AgrForAb, B23, B25, BIOSIS Prev, BP, C24, C25, C30, C31, C33, CABA, CEABA, ChemAb, ChemTitl, CurCR, CurCont, D01, DBA, DentInd, E12, EMBASE, ExcerpMed, F08, F11, F12, FCA, FR, G11, GH, H16, H17, I12, ISR, IndChem, IndMed, IndVet, Inpharma, MEDLINE, MOS, MSB, MaizeAb, MycolAb, N02, N03, NPU, O01, OR, P30, P32, P33, P35, P39, P40, PGegResA, PGrRegA, PHN&I, PN&I, R07, R08, R10, R13, R16, RA&MP, RM&VM, Reac, RefZh, S12, S13, S16, S17, SCI, SCOPUS, SoyAb, T05, TAR, VS, W07, W10.
—BLDSC (6448.000000), CASDDS, GNLM, IE, Infotrieve, Ingenta, INIST, Linda Hall. **CCC.**
Published by: Govi Verlag Pharmazeutischer Verlag GmbH, Carl Mannich Str 26, Eschborn, 65760, Germany. TEL 49-6196-928262, FAX 49-6196-928203, service@govi.de. Eds. Dr. Peter Pflegel, Dr. Theodor Dingermann. adv.: B&W page EUR 456, color page EUR 931. Circ: 800 (paid and controlled).

615.19 DEU ISSN 0369-979X
CODEN: PHZHAM
PHARMAZIE HEUTE; Beilage der Deutschen Apotheker Zeitung zur Fortbildung. Text in German. 1971. irreg., latest vol.118, 2011. **Document type:** *Journal, Trade.*
Related titles: ◆ Supplement to: Deutsche Apotheker Zeitung. ISSN 0011-9857.
Indexed: CIN, ChemAb, ChemTitl.
—CASDDS, GNLM. **CCC.**
Published by: Deutscher Apotheker Verlag, Postfach 101061, Stuttgart, 70009, Germany. TEL 49-711-25820, FAX 49-711-2582290, daz@deutscher-apotheker-verlag.de, http://www.deutscher-apotheker-verlag.de. Ed. Ernst Mutschler.

615 DEU ISSN 0048-3664
RS1 CODEN: PHUZBI
➤ **PHARMAZIE IN UNSERER ZEIT.** Text in German. 1924. bi-m. GBP 151 in United Kingdom to institutions; EUR 266 in Europe to institutions; USD 294 elsewhere to institutions; GBP 174 combined subscription in United Kingdom to institutions (print & online eds.); EUR 306 combined subscription in Europe to institutions (print & online eds.); USD 338 combined subscription elsewhere to institutions (print & online eds.) (effective 2012). adv. bk.rev. charts; illus. reprint service avail. from PSC. **Document type:** *Journal, Academic/Scholarly.* **Description:** Presents review articles pertinent to all areas of drug research.
Formerly (until 1972): Deutsche Pharmazeutische Gesellschaft. Mitteilungen (0012-0561)
Related titles: Online - full text ed.: ISSN 1615-1003. GBP 151 in United Kingdom to institutions; EUR 266 in Europe to institutions; USD 294 elsewhere to institutions (effective 2012).
Indexed: A22, C31, ChemAb, ChemTitl, DBA, EMBASE, ExcerpMed, IndMed, MEDLINE, P30, R10, Reac, SCOPUS.
—BLDSC (6448.600000), CASDDS, GNLM, IE, Infotrieve, Ingenta, INIST, Linda Hall. **CCC.**
Published by: (Deutsche Pharmazeutische Gesellschaft), Wiley - V C H Verlag GmbH & Co. KGaA (Subsidiary of: John Wiley & Sons, Inc.), Postfach 101161, Weinheim, 69451, Germany. TEL 49-6201-606400, FAX 49-6201-606184, subservice@wiley-vch.de, info@wiley-vch.de. Ed. Theodor Dingermann. R&P Claudia Rutz. Adv. contact Marion Schulz TEL 49-6201-606565. B&W page EUR 2,950, color page EUR 4,300; trim 185 x 260. Circ: 9,945 (paid and controlled).

615 DEU ISSN 0946-4158
PHARMAZIEHISTORISCHE FORSCHUNGEN. Text in German. 1996. irreg., latest vol.5, 2004. price varies. **Document type:** *Monographic series, Academic/Scholarly.*
Indexed: P30.
Published by: Peter Lang GmbH (Subsidiary of: Peter Lang Publishing Group), Eschborner Landstr 42-50, Frankfurt Am Main, 60489, Germany. TEL 49-69-7807050, FAX 49-69-78070550, zentrale.frankfurt@peterlang.com, http://www.peterlang.com. Ed. Peter Dilg.

615.1 FRA ISSN 1013-5294
PHARMEUROPA. Text in French. 1988. q. EUR 89 (effective 2009). **Document type:** *Journal, Trade.*
Related titles: Online - full text ed.: ISSN 1816-9279. 2005; English ed.: ISSN 1013-5308. 1988.
—IE. **CCC.**
Published by: Council of Europe/Conseil de l'Europe, Avenue de l'Europe, Strasbourg, 67075, France. TEL 33-3-88412033, FAX 33-3-88412745, publishing@coe.int, http://www.coe.int.

615 FRA ISSN 2075-2164
▼ **PHARMEUROPA BIO & SCIENTIFIC NOTES.** Text in English. 2009. s-a. **Document type:** *Journal, Academic/Scholarly.*
Formed by the merger of (1999-2009): Pharmeuropa Bio (1684-7075); (2005-2009): Pharmeuropa Scientific Notes (1814-2435)
Related titles: Online - full text ed.: ISSN 1816-8523. 2003.
Indexed: EMBASE, ExcerpMed, MEDLINE, P30, R10, Reac, SCOPUS.
—BLDSC (6448.683000), IE. **CCC.**
Published by: Council of Europe/Conseil de l'Europe, Avenue de l'Europe, Strasbourg, 67075, France. TEL 33-3-88412033, FAX 33-3-88412745, publishing@coe.int.

615 AUT
PHARMIG INFO. Text in German. 10/yr. adv. **Document type:** *Magazine, Trade.*
Address: Zieglergasse 5, Vienna, 1072, Austria. TEL 43-1-5232956, FAX 43-1-52329519, office@pharmig.at, http://www.pharmig.at. Ed. Ruth Mayrhofer. R&P, Adv. contact Karin Vallaszkovits. Circ: 4,000.

615.1 NLD
➤ **PHUTURE SUPPLEMENT.** Text in English. 1998. a. illus. 1 cols./p.; **Document type:** *Journal, Academic/Scholarly.* **Description:** Contains review and research articles and information on relevant topics in pharmaceutical science.
Published by: International Pharmaceutical Students Federation, PO Box 84200, The Hague, 2508 AE, Netherlands. TEL 31-70-3021992, FAX 31-70-3021999, ipsf@ipsf.org, http://www.ipsf.org.

615 USA ISSN 1074-388X
PHYSICIAN ASSISTANTS' PRESCRIBING REFERENCE. Abbreviated title: P A P R. Text in English. 1994. q. USD 32 domestic; USD 56 foreign; USD 16 per issue domestic; USD 21 per issue foreign (effective 2008). adv. back issues avail. **Document type:** *Magazine, Trade.*
Related titles: Online - full text ed.
Indexed: A26, C06, C07, H11, H12, I05.
—**CCC.**
Published by: Prescribing Reference, Inc. (Subsidiary of: Haymarket Group Ltd.), 114 W 26th St, 4th Fl, New York, NY 10001. TEL 646-638-6000, FAX 646-638-6117, Online@PrescribingRef.com. Eds. Anissa Lee, Diana Ernst. Pub. James Pantaleo TEL 646-638-6137. Circ: 47,897 (paid).

615.1 GBR ISSN 2046-1194
▼ **PHYTOPHARMACOLOGY.** Text in English. 2010. q. back issues avail. **Document type:** *Journal, Academic/Scholarly.* **Description:** Full length research articles, short communications and reviews on pharmacology, toxicology and clinical studies of bioactive natural products.
Media: Online - full text.
Published by: Inforesights Publishing editorial@inforesights.com, http://inforesights.com. Ed. P Johnson.

615.19 FRA ISSN 1628-6847
LA PHYTOTHERAPIE EUROPEENNE; de la prescription a la dispensation. Text in French. 2001. bi-m. **Document type:** *Journal, Trade.*
Indexed: EMBASE, ExcerpMed, SCOPUS, T02.
—INIST.
Published by: Meditions Carline (Subsidiary of: Groupe Meditions), 1-3 rue du Depart, Paris, 75014, France. TEL 33-1-40640075, FAX 33-1-43222699, carline@groupemeditions.com.

PICTORIAL DIRECTORY OF SPOKANE PHYSICIANS. *see* MEDICAL SCIENCES

615 USA ISSN 1530-6240
CODEN: FRPBEK
THE PINK SHEET; prescription pharmaceuticals and biotechnology. Text in English. 1939. w. looseleaf. USD 730 in United States to institutions; USD 730 elsewhere to institutions (effective 2012). adv. charts; illus.; stat.; tr.lit. back issues avail.; reprints avail. **Document type:** *Journal, Trade.* **Description:** Provides in-depth news and analysis about developments affecting prescription medicines.
Formerly (until 1998): F D C Reports. Prescription Pharmaceuticals and Biotechnology: The Pink Sheet (1068-5324); Which superseded in part (in 1993): F D C Reports. Prescription and O T C Pharmaceuticals: The Pink Sheet (0734-6514); Which was formerly (until 1982): F D C Reports. Ethical and O T C Pharmaceuticals (0272-913X)
Related titles: Online - full text ed.
Indexed: Inpharma, P48, P53, P54, PNI, PQC.
—CASDDS. **CCC.**
Published by: Elsevier Business Intelligence (Subsidiary of: Elsevier Health Sciences), 5635 Fishers Ln, Ste 6000, Rockville, MD 20852. TEL 800-332-2181, FAX 240-221-4400, http://www.fdcreports.com. Eds. W Paulson, Michael McCaughan. Adv. contacts Nicole Deschamps TEL 301-664-7208, Pat Hampton TEL 212-633-3181. B&W page USD 4,850, color page USD 6,500; trim 8.5 x 11. Circ: 5,300 (paid).

615 USA
THE PINK SHEET DAILY. Text in English. d. USD 2,700 to institutions (effective 2011). **Document type:** *Trade.* **Description:** Comprehensive, up-to-the-minute news service for and about the pharmaceutical industry and provides the latest coverage of new drug approvals, generic drug launches, biotechnology, FDA regulatory actions, CMS reimbursement policies, business developments, legislation and and other events shaping the landscape of the pharmaceutical industry.
Published by: Elsevier Business Intelligence (Subsidiary of: Elsevier Health Sciences), 5550 Friendship Blvd, Ste One, Chevy Chase, MD 20815-7278. TEL 301-657-9830, 800-332-2181, FAX 301-656-3094, http://www.fdcreports.com.

615.7 AUT ISSN 1608-5523
CODEN: PLACCE
➤ **PLACEBO.** Text in English. 2000. q. USD 75 domestic; USD 115 foreign; USD 35 newsstand/cover (effective 2001). adv. back issues avail. **Document type:** *Journal, Academic/Scholarly.* **Description:** Publishes articles, case reports, reviews, and letters that improve communication in the understanding of placebo research.
Related titles: Online - full text ed.
Published by: V I C E R Publishing, PO Box 14, Vienna, A-1097, Austria. TEL 43-676-9568085, FAX 43-676-9568086, vicer@vicer.org, http://www.vicer.org. Ed., R&P Roland Hofbauer. adv.: B&W page USD 1,700, color page USD 2,200. Circ: 1,000 (paid and controlled).

P

615 DEU ISSN 0032-0943
RS164 CODEN: PLMEAA
➤ **PLANTA MEDICA**; natural products and medicinal plant research. Text in English. 1935. 18/yr. EUR 1,319 to institutions (print & online eds.); EUR 94 newsstand/cover (effective 2011). adv. bk.rev. charts; illus.; tr.lit. index. **Document type:** *Journal, Academic/Scholarly.*
Related titles: Microfiche ed.; Online - full text ed.: ISSN 1439-0221. EUR 1,319 to institutions (effective 2011).
Indexed: A01, A03, A08, A20, A22, A26, A34, A35, A36, A37, A38, AMED, ASCA, AgBio, Agr, AgrForAb, ApicAb, B23, B25, B27, BIOBASE, BIOSIS Prev, BP, BibAg, C06, C07, C08, C24, C25, C30, C33, CA, CABA, CBTA, CEABA, CIN, CINAHL, ChemAb, ChemTitl, CurCont, D01, DBA, E12, EMBASE, ExcerpMed, F08, F11, F12, FCA, FR, FS&TA, G11, GH, H16, H17, I11, I12, IABS, IBR, IBZ, ISR, IndMed, MEDLINE, MSB, MycolAb, N02, N03, NPU, OR, P30, P32, P33, P37, P38, P39, P40, PGegResA, PGrRegA, PHN&I, PN&I, R07, R08, R11, R12, R13, RA&MP, RM&VM, S12, S13, S16, S17, SCI, SCOPUS, SoyAb, T02, T05, TAR, TriticAb, VITIS, VS, W07, W10, W11.
—BLDSC (6524.100000), CASDDS, GNLM, IE, Infotrieve, Ingenta, INIST, Linda Hall. **CCC.**
Published by: (Gesellschaft fuer Arzneipflanzenforschung), Georg Thieme Verlag, Ruedigerstr 14, Stuttgart, 70469, Germany. TEL 49-711-8931421, FAX 49-711-8931410, leser.service@thieme.de. Ed. Dr. Adolf Nahrstedt. R&P Alessandra Kreibaum. Adv. contact Ulrike Bradler. B&W page EUR 920, color page EUR 2,045. Circ: 1,250 (paid and controlled). **Subscr. to:** Thieme Medical Publishers, 333 Seventh Ave, New York, NY 10001. custserv@thieme.com, http://www.thieme.com/journals.

615.83 NLD ISSN 0929-5380
PODOSOPHIA. Text in Dutch. 1980. bi-m. EUR 49, USD 74 to institutions (effective 2009). adv. **Document type:** *Magazine, Trade.*
Formerly (until 1993): Nederlands Tijdschrift voor Podotherapeuten (0928-2823)
Published by: (Nederlandse Vereniging van Podotherapeuten), Bohn Stafleu van Loghum B.V. (Subsidiary of: Springer Science+Business Media), Postbus 246, Houten, 3990 GA, Netherlands. TEL 31-30-6383872, FAX 31-30-6383991, boekhandels@bsl.nl, http://www.bsl.nl. adv.: B&W page EUR 852, color page EUR 1,103; trim 215 x 285.

615 FRA ISSN 1264-3688
PORPHYRE (COLLECTION). Variant title: Collection Porphyre. Text in French. 1994. irreg. **Document type:** *Monographic series, Trade.*
Published by: Wolters Kluwer France (Subsidiary of: Wolters Kluwer N.V.), 1 Rue Eugene et Armand Peugeot, Rueil-Malmaison, Cedex 92856, France. TEL 33-1-76734809, FAX 33-1-76733040, www.wkf.fr.

615 FRA ISSN 0181-1169
LE PORPHYRE (REVUE); revue professionnelle des preparatrices, preparateurs en pharmacie, collaborateurs de l'officine et candidats aux examens. Text in French. 1949. m. adv. bk.rev. **Document type:** *Magazine, Trade.*
Published by: Wolters Kluwer - Pharma (Subsidiary of: Wolters Kluwer France), 1 Rue Eugene et Armand Peugeot, Rueil-Malmaison, Cedex 92856, France. TEL 33-1-76734809, FAX 33-1-76733040, contact@wk-pharma.fr. Circ: 14,641.

615.610 GBR ISSN 2042-4213
▼ **PORTUGAL PHARMACEUTICALS & HEALTHCARE REPORT.** Text in English. 2010. q. EUR 820, USD 1,150 combined subscription (print & email eds.) (effective 2010). **Document type:** *Report, Trade.* **Description:** Provides industry professionals, market investors and corporate and financial services analysts with independent forecasts and competitive intelligence on the Portuguese pharmaceutical & healthcare industry.
Related titles: E-mail ed.
Published by: Business Monitor International Ltd., Senator House, 85 Queen Victoria St, London, EC4V 4AB, United Kingdom. TEL 44-20-72480468, FAX 44-20-72480467, subs@businessmonitor.com.

615.7 AUS ISSN 0156-0433
POST SCRIPT. Abbreviated title: P S. Text in English. 1976. 10/yr. AUD 55; free to qualified personnel (effective 2008). adv. back issues avail. **Document type:** *Magazine, Trade.* **Description:** Provide information for pharmacy assistants.
Published by: Australian Pharmaceutical Publishing Company Pty Ltd., Level 5, 8 Thomas St, Chatswood, NSW 2067, Australia. TEL 61-2-81179500, FAX 61-2-81179511, http://www.appco.com.au. Ed. Louise Goldsbury TEL 61-2-81179547. adv.: color page AUD 4,580; trim 206 x 270. Circ: 16,553. **Subscr. to:** 40 Burwood Rd, PO Box 777, Hawthorn, VIC 3122, Australia. TEL 61-3-98109900, subs@appco.com.au.

615.537 POL ISSN 1509-8699
POSTEPY FITOTERAPII. Text in Polish. 2000. q. PLZ 48 domestic (effective 2008). **Document type:** *Journal, Academic/Scholarly.*
Related titles: Online - full content ed.: ISSN 1731-2477.
Indexed: A34, A35, A36, A38, AgrForAb, BP, CABA, D01, E12, F08, F11, F12, GH, H16, IndVet, MaizeAb, N02, N03, N04, P32, P33, PGegResA, PGrRegA, PHN&I, R07, R08, R13, RA&MP, RM&VM, S12, S17, SoyAb, T05, VS, W11.
Published by: (Polskie Towarzystwo Lekarskie), Wydawnictwo Medyczne Borgis, ul Walbrzyska 3/5, Warsaw, 02739, Poland. wydawnictwo@borgis.pl, http://www.borgis.pl. Ed. Anna Nowakowska. Circ: 3,000.

615.1 JPN ISSN 0044-0035
PRACTICAL PHARMACY/YAKKYOKU. Variant title: Journal of Practical Pharmacy. Text in Japanese. 1950. m. JPY 28,980 (effective 2000). adv. **Document type:** *Academic/Scholarly.*
Indexed: ChemAb, SpeleolAb.
Published by: Nanzando Co. Ltd., 4-1-11 Yushima, Bunkyo-ku, Tokyo, 113-0034, Japan. TEL 81-3-5689-7868, FAX 81-3-5689-7869. Ed., Adv. contact Hisao Nakamura. Pub., R&P Hajime Suzuki. Circ: 15,500.

615.014 CZE ISSN 1801-2434
➤ **PRAKTICKE LEKARENSTVI.** Text in Czech. 2005. bi-m. CZK 480; CZK 80 per issue (effective 2010). **Document type:** *Journal, Academic/Scholarly.*
Related titles: Online - full text ed.: ISSN 1803-5329.
Published by: Solen s.r.o., Lazecka 297/51, Olomouc 51, 779 00, Czech Republic. TEL 420-582-396038, FAX 420-582-396099, solen@solen.cz, http://www.solen.cz. Circ: 3,000.

615 GBR ISSN 0959-6682
➤ **PRESCRIBER.** Text in English. 1990. s-m. GBP 269 in United Kingdom to institutions; EUR 343 in Europe to institutions; USD 530 elsewhere to institutions; GBP 309 combined subscription in United Kingdom to institutions (print & online eds.); EUR 395 combined subscription in Europe to institutions (print & online eds.); USD 610 combined subscription elsewhere to institutions (print & online eds.) (effective 2012). adv. back issues avail.; reprints avail. **Document type:** *Journal, Academic/Scholarly.* **Description:** Covers therapeutics and issues around prescribing.
Related titles: Online - full text ed.: ISSN 1931-2253. GBP 269 in United Kingdom to institutions; EUR 343 in Europe to institutions; USD 530 elsewhere to institutions (effective 2012); ◆ Supplement(s): Future Prescriber. ISSN 1468-9871.
Indexed: C06, Inpharma.
—BLDSC (6609.700100), IE, Ingenta. **CCC.**
Published by: A & M Publishing Ltd. (Subsidiary of: John Wiley & Sons Ltd.), The Atrium, Southern Gate, Chichester, PO19 8SQ, United Kingdom. http://www.escriber.com/. Adv. contact Steve Ripsher TEL 44-1243-770159. Circ: 21,000.

➤ **PRESCRIBER UPDATE.** *see* PUBLIC HEALTH AND SAFETY

615 USA ISSN 1073-7219
RM1
PRESCRIBER'S LETTER. Text in English. 1994. m. USD 197 combined subscription (print & online eds.) (effective 2011). index. back issues avail. **Document type:** *Newsletter, Trade.* **Description:** Advises prescribing physicians on current drug therapy, including drug interactions, proper drug use, trends in therapy, new research findings, and new drugs.
Related titles: Online - full text ed.
Published by: Therapeutic Research Center, 3120 W March Ln, PO Box 8190, Stockton, CA 95208. TEL 209-472-2240, FAX 209-472-2249, http://www.therapeuticresearch.com.

615 FRA ISSN 1167-7422
CODEN: PRINFU
PRESCRIRE INTERNATIONAL. Text in English. 1992. bi-m. EUR 112 domestic to individuals; EUR 283 domestic to institutions (effective 2005). **Document type:** *Bulletin, Trade.* **Description:** For health professionals concerned with therapeutics and medical evaluation.
Related titles: ◆ International ed.: La Revue Prescrire. ISSN 0247-7750.
Indexed: EMBASE, ExcerpMed, I12, Inpharma, MEDLINE, P30, P35, R10, Reac, SCOPUS.
—BLDSC (6609.709200), GNLM, IE, Infotrieve, Ingenta, INIST. **CCC.**
Published by: Association Mieux Prescrire, BP 459, Paris, 75527 Cedex 11, France. TEL 33-1-49237280, FAX 33-1-48078732, international@prescrire.org. Ed. Christophe Kopp. R&P E Hoen. Circ: 500.

615.7 USA ISSN 1559-565X
PRIMARY CARE DRUG ALERTS. Text in English. 1992. m. looseleaf. USD 89 domestic to individuals; USD 97.50 in Canada to individuals; USD 107.50 elsewhere to individuals; USD 141 to institutions (effective 2010). Index. 8 p./no.; back issues avail. **Document type:** *Newsletter, Academic/Scholarly.* **Description:** Contains abstracts of journal articles regarding pharmacology and pharmacotherpy in a primary care setting.
Incorporates (1988-1998): Cardiovascular Drug Alerts (0897-3830); Formerly (until Oct.1998): Primary Care Medicine Drug Alerts (1061-0359); Which was formed by the merger of (1995-1992): Women's Medicine Alerts (1078-0459); (1980-1992): Physicians Drug Alert (0277-4194); (1988-1992): Drug Alerts for Internal Medicine (1040-4589)
Related titles: Online - full content ed.: ISSN 1559-5668.
Indexed: C06, CINAHL.
Published by: M.J. Powers & Co. Publishers, 65 Madison Ave, Morristown, NJ 07960. TEL 973-898-1200, FAX 973-898-1201.

615.19 DEU
PROCESS PHARMATEC. Text in German. 1994. 4/yr. EUR 88 (effective 2010). adv. **Document type:** *Magazine, Trade.* **Description:** Specifically intended for pharmaceutical industry, it targets engineers, technicians and specialists. Informs readers about the innovative procedures, components, production processes and management topics.
Published by: Vogel Business Media GmbH & Co.KG, Max-Planck-Str 7-9, Wuerzburg, 97064, Germany. TEL 49-931-4180, FAX 49-931-4182750, info@vogel.de, http://www.vogel-media.de. adv.: color page EUR 5,780, B&W page EUR 4,640; trim 210 x 297. Circ: 12,023 (paid and controlled).

PRODUCT MANAGEMENT TODAY. *see* BUSINESS AND ECONOMICS—Marketing And Purchasing

615 FRA ISSN 1771-2874
PROFESSION PHARMACIEN. Text in French. 2004. bi-m. **Document type:** *Journal, Trade.*
Published by: J C M Sante (Subsidiary of: E D P Sciences), 42 Rue Carves, Montrouge, 92120, France. TEL 33-1-42532105, FAX 33-1-42532156, jcm-sante@wanadoo.fr.

615.4 DEU ISSN 1869-375X
PROFILE. Text in German. 1930. 7/yr. EUR 42 (effective 2011). adv. **Document type:** *Magazine, Trade.*
Former titles (until 2009): Drogerie und Parfuemerie (0945-4500); (until 1993): Deutsche Drogerie (0722-9518); Which incorporated (in 1991): D D F - Journal (0720-633X); Which was formerly (until 1981): D D F. Drogeriewaren - Fachenmagazin (0720-6348); (1965-1977): D D F - Das Drogisten Fachblatt (0011-4804)
Published by: Marken Verlag GmbH, Hansaring 97, Cologne, 50670, Germany. TEL 49-221-9574270, FAX 49-221-95742777, marken-info@markenverlag.de, http://www.markenverlag.de. Circ: 7,500 (paid and controlled).

615.19 USA ISSN 1871-5125
RS189 CODEN: APDSB7
➤ **PROFILES OF DRUG SUBSTANCES, EXCIPIENTS AND RELATED METHODOLOGY.** Text in English. 1972. irreg., latest vol.35, 2010. USD 224 per vol. (effective 2010). back issues avail.; reprints avail. **Document type:** *Monographic series, Academic/Scholarly.* **Description:** The official compendia define a drug substance as to identity, purity, strength, and quality, they normally do not provide other physical or chemical data, nor do they list methods of synthesis or pathways of physical or biological degradation and metabolism. Such information is scattered throughout the scientific literature and the files of pharmaceutical laboratories. Analytical Profiles of Drug Substances and Excipients, brings the latest information together in one source.
Former titles (until 2003): Analytical Profiles of Drug Substances and Excipients (1075-6280); (until 1992): Analytical Profiles of Drug Substances (0099-5428)
Related titles: Online - full text ed.
Indexed: ChemAb, EMBASE, ExcerpMed, SCOPUS.
—CASDDS, GNLM, IE, Ingenta, INIST. **CCC.**
Published by: Academic Press (Subsidiary of: Elsevier Science & Technology), 3251 Riverport Ln, Maryland Heights, MO 63043. TEL 314-447-8010, FAX 314-447-8030, JournalCustomerService-usa@elsevier.com, http://www.elsevierdirect.com/imprint.jsp?iid=5. Ed. Harry Brittain.

615 ITA ISSN 1827-9856
PROFILI IN FARMAECONOMIA. Text in Italian. 2006. q. EUR 20 per issue (effective 2011). **Document type:** *Monographic series, Academic/Scholarly.*
Published by: Seed Edizioni Scientifiche, Piazza Carlo Emanuele II, 19, Turin, 10123, Italy. TEL 39-011-5660258, FAX 39-011-5186892, http://www.edizioniseed.it.

615.7 CHE ISSN 1011-0267
RM30 CODEN: PBCPET
➤ **PROGRESS IN BASIC AND CLINICAL PHARMACOLOGY.** Text in English. 1988. irreg., latest vol.11, 2004. price varies. **Document type:** *Monographic series, Academic/Scholarly.* **Description:** Designed to promote a rational approach to drug treatment.
Related titles: Online - full text ed.: ISSN 1662-3908.
Indexed: A22, CIN, ChemAb, ChemTitl.
—CASDDS, IE, INIST. **CCC.**
Published by: S. Karger AG, Allschwilerstr 10, Basel, 4055, Switzerland. TEL 41-61-3061111, FAX 41-61-3061234, karger@karger.ch, http://www.karger.ch. Eds. C. Scarpignato, E. S. Vesell.

615 USA ISSN 0278-5846
RM315 CODEN: PNPPD7
➤ **PROGRESS IN NEURO-PSYCHOPHARMACOLOGY & BIOLOGICAL PSYCHIATRY.** Text in English. 1977. 8/yr. EUR 2,328 in Europe to institutions; JPY 309,300 in Japan to institutions; USD 2,604 elsewhere to institutions (effective 2012). adv. bk.rev. abstr. index. back issues avail.; reprints avail. **Document type:** *Journal, Academic/Scholarly.* **Description:** Aims to assure publication of reviews and research papers dealing with experimental and clinical aspects of neuro-psychopharmacology and biological psychiatry.
Formerly (until 1982): Progress in Neuro-Psychopharmacology (0364-7722)
Related titles: Microfilm ed.: (from PQC); Online - full text ed.: ISSN 1878-4216 (from IngentaConnect, ScienceDirect).
Indexed: A01, A03, A08, A22, A26, A29, A34, A36, ASCA, AddicA, AgrForAb, AnBeAb, B20, B21, B25, BIOBASE, BIOSIS Prev, CA, CABA, ChemAb, ChemTitl, CurCont, D01, DBA, DentInd, E-psyche, E12, EMBASE, ESPM, ExcerpMed, F08, F11, F12, FR, FoP, GH, H17, I05, I10, IABS, IPsyAb, ISR, IndMed, IndVet, Inpharma, MEDLINE, MycolAb, N02, N03, N04, NSA, NSCI, P03, P30, P32, P33, P35, P40, PGegResA, PGrRegA, PsycInfo, PsycholAb, R08, R10, R12, RA&MP, Reac, S12, SCI, SCOPUS, SoyAb, T02, T05, THA, VS, VirolAbstr, W07.
—BLDSC (6870.380000), CASDDS, GNLM, IE, Infotrieve, Ingenta, INIST. **CCC.**
Published by: (C H U L Research Centre (CHUQ) CAN), Elsevier Inc. (Subsidiary of: Elsevier Science & Technology), 1600 John F Kennedy Blvd, Philadelphia, PA 19103. TEL 215-239-3900, FAX 215-238-7883, JournalCustomerService-usa@elsevier.com. Ed. Guy Drolet. Adv. contact Janine Castle TEL 44-1865-843844.

➤ **PROGRESS IN NEUROTHERAPEUTICS AND NEUROPSYCHOPHARMACOLOGY.** *see* MEDICAL SCIENCES—Psychiatry And Neurology

615.1 GBR ISSN 1464-3456
PROGRESS IN PHARMACEUTICAL AND BIOMEDICAL ANALYSIS. Text in English. 1994. irreg., latest vol.6, 2005. price varies. back issues avail.; reprints avail. **Document type:** *Monographic series, Academic/Scholarly.*
Indexed: SCOPUS.
—CCC.
Published by: Elsevier Ltd (Subsidiary of: Elsevier Science & Technology), The Blvd, Langford Ln, Kidlington, Oxford, OX5 1GB, United Kingdom. TEL 44-1865-843434, FAX 44-1865-843970, journalscustomerserviceemea@elsevier.com.

615 ESP ISSN 1888-1327
PROTOCOLOS DE MEDICAMENTOS FUERA DE INDICACION. Text in Spanish. 2007. s-a.
Published by: Comunidad de Madrid, Servicio de Publicaciones, Gran Via, 3, Madrid, 28013, Spain. TEL 34-91-7200952, FAX 34-91-7200831, http://www3.madrid.org/edupubli/.

615.9 CAN
PROVINCIAL DRUG BENEFIT PROGRAMS. Text in English. s-a. CAD 275 to non-members; CAD 220 to members. **Document type:** *Journal, Trade.*
Published by: Canadian Pharmacists Association, 1785 Alta Vista Dr, Ottawa, ON K1G 3Y6, Canada. TEL 613-523-7877, FAX 613-523-0445, info@pharmacists.ca, http://www.pharmacists.ca.

615 UKR
PROVIZOR. Text in Russian, Ukrainian. s-m. UAK 10 newsstand/cover (effective 2003). adv. pat.; charts; stat.; illus.; mkt. Index. back issues avail. **Document type:** *Journal, Academic/Scholarly.* **Description:** Covers different issues in pharmaceutical sciency and industry.
Related titles: Online - full content ed.
Published by: Megapolis, Pr-t Lenina 40, Off 249, Khar'kov, 61166, Ukraine. TEL 380-572-321210, FAX 380-572-321210, megapolis@mega.kharkiv.com, http://www.mega.kharkiv.com/. Ed. Elena Shuvanova. adv.: color page USD 2,250. **Dist. by:** East View Information Services, 10601 Wayzata Blvd, Minneapolis, MN 55305. TEL 952-252-1201, 800-477-1005, FAX 952-252-1202, info@eastview.com, http://www.eastview.com.

615.1 ARG ISSN 1666-6690
PSICOFARMACOLOGIA. Text in Spanish. 1999. bi-m. back issues avail. **Document type:** *Journal, Academic/Scholarly.*
Related titles: Online - full text ed.: ISSN 1851-8710. 2003.
Published by: Sciens Editorial, Scalabrini Ortiz 3183 2o. A, Buenos Aires, Argentina. TEL 54-11-48028775, 54-11-48028775, info@sciens.com.ar. Ed. Fernando Martin Gomez.

615 RUS ISSN 1606-8181
➤ **PSIHOFARMAKOLOGIA I BIOLOGICESKAA NARKOLOGIA/ PSYCHOPHARMACOLOGY AND BIOLOGICAL NARCOLOGY.** Text in Russian; Summaries in English, Russian. 2000. q. RUR 990 to individuals; RUR 1,980 to institutions; free to qualified personnel (effective 2008). back issues avail. **Document type:** *Journal, Academic/Scholarly.*
Indexed: EMBASE, SCOPUS.
Published by: J S C, Universitetsky pr 2/18, St Petersburg, 198504, Russian Federation. TEL 7-921-9530867, FAX 7-812-5424397, ebase@rambler.ru. Ed. Petr D Shabanov. Pub. Marina V Burova.

615 USA ISSN 0894-4873
PSYCHIATRY DRUG ALERTS. Text in English. 1986. m. looseleaf. USD 89 domestic to individuals; USD 97.50 in Canada to individuals; USD 107.50 elsewhere to individuals; USD 141 to institutions (effective 2010). 8 p./no.; back issues avail. **Document type:** *Newsletter, Trade.* **Description:** Provides efficacy and safety of psychiatric drugs.
Indexed: E-psyche, T02.
Published by: M.J. Powers & Co. Publishers, 65 Madison Ave, Morristown, NJ 07960. TEL 973-898-1200, FAX 973-898-1201.

PSYCHOPHARM REVIEW. *see* MEDICAL SCIENCES—Psychiatry And Neurology

615.1 ITA ISSN 1973-302X
PSYCHOPHARMA. Text in Italian. 2007. q. **Document type:** *Journal, Academic/Scholarly.*
Published by: C I C Edizioni Internazionali, Corso Trieste 42, Rome, 00198, Italy. TEL 39-6-8412673, FAX 39-6-44242033, info@gruppocic.it, http://www.gruppocic.it.

615.1 DEU ISSN 0033-3158
RM315 CODEN: PSCHDL
➤ **PSYCHOPHARMACOLOGY.** Text mainly in English. 1959. s-m. EUR 7,278, USD 8,847 combined subscription to institutions (print & online eds.) (effective 2012). adv. charts; illus. back issues avail.; reprint service avail. from PSC. **Document type:** *Journal, Academic/Scholarly.* **Description:** Original research into the effects of drugs on behavior.
Formerly (until vol.47, 1976): Psychopharmacologia
Related titles: Microform ed.: (from PQC); Online - full text ed.: ISSN 1432-2072 (from IngentaConnect).
Indexed: A01, A03, A08, A20, A22, A26, A35, A36, A37, AgBio, AnBeAb, B21, B25, BIOSIS Prev, C33, CA, CABA, ChemAb, ChemTitl, ChemoAb, CurCont, DBA, E-psyche, E01, E12, EMBASE, ESPM, ExcerpMed, F08, F11, F12, FoP, GH, H12, H16, IBR, IBZ, ISR, IndMed, Inpharma, JW-P, LT, MEDLINE, MycolAb, N02, N03, NSA, NSCI, P03, P20, P22, P24, P25, P30, P32, P33, P35, P43, P48, P54, PQC, PsycInfo, PsycholAb, R07, R09, R10, RA&MP, RM&VM, Reac, S02, S03, S12, SCI, SCOPUS, SD, T02, T05, THA, ToxAb, VS, W07.
—BLDSC (6946.546500), CASDDS, GNLM, IE, Infotrieve, Ingenta, INIST, Linda Hall. **CCC.**

Published by: Springer (Subsidiary of: Springer Science+Business Media), Tiergartenstr 17, Heidelberg, 69121, Germany. TEL 49-6221-4870, FAX 49-6221-345229. Eds. H de Wit, P J Cowen. adv.: B&W page EUR 830, color page EUR 1,870. Circ: 630 (paid). **Subscr. in the Americas to:** Springer New York LLC, Journal Fulfillment, PO Box 2485, Secaucus, NJ 07096. TEL 800-777-4643, 201-348-4033, FAX 201-348-4505, journals-ny@springer.com, http://www.springer.com; **Subscr. to:** Springer Distribution Center, Kundenservice Zeitschriften, Haberstr 7, Heidelberg 69126, Germany. TEL 49-6221-3454303, FAX 49-6221-3454229, subscriptions@springer.com.

615.1 150 USA ISSN 0048-5764
RM1 CODEN: PSYBB9

PSYCHOPHARMACOLOGY BULLETIN. Text in English. 19??. q. USD 250 domestic to individuals; USD 325 domestic to institutions; USD 450 foreign to institutions (effective 2010). cum.index: 1969-1975. back issues avail.; reprints avail. **Document type:** *Bulletin, Trade.* **Description:** Provides up-to-date and otherwise inaccessible information on ongoing psychopharmacological research and alerts readers to places and proceedings of national and international meetings.
Former titles (until 1966): Psychopharmacology Service Center Bulletin (0376-0162); (until 1961): Psycho-Pharmacology Service Center Reports
Related titles: Microform ed.: (from PQC); Online - full text ed.
Indexed: A22, ASCA, ASD, AddicA, BibInd, C13, CIN, ChemAb, ChemTitl, CurCont, DBA, E-psyche, EMBASE, ExcerpMed, FoP, IPsyAb, ISR, IUSGP, IndMed, Inpharma, JW-P, MEDLINE, MEDOC, P20, P22, P30, P48, P54, PQC, PsycholAb, R10, Reac, SCI, SCOPUS, THA, W07.
—BLDSC (6946.549000), CASDDS, GNLM, IE, Infotrieve, Ingenta, INIST, Linda Hall. **CCC.**
Published by: MedWorks Media LLC, 1756 2nd St., Manhattan Beach, CA 90266 . TEL 310-374-1300, FAX 310-374-1336. Ed. Michael E Thase. Pub. James M La Rossa.

615.7 USA ISSN 1553-8907

PSYCHOPHARMACOLOGY EDUCATIONAL UPDATE. Text in English. 2005. m. free (effective 2011). back issues avail. **Document type:** *Newsletter, Consumer.* **Description:** Provides readers with information from the psychopharmacologist's perspective and serves as a resource in the dynamic climate of psychopharmacology. Offers a perspective of current developments and controversies in psychopharmacology.
Related titles: Online - full text ed.: ISSN 1553-8915.
Indexed: A26, G08, H11, H12, I05.
Published by: N E I Press, 1930 Palomar Pt Way, Ste 101, Carlsbad, CA 92008. TEL 760-931-8857, 888-535-5600, FAX 760-931-8713, customerservice@neiglobal.com, http://www.neiglobal.com.

615.1 USA ISSN 1068-5308

➤ **PSYCHOPHARMACOLOGY UPDATE.** Variant title: The Brown University Psychopharmacology Update. Text in English. 1990. m. GBP 801 in United Kingdom to institutions; EUR 1,012 in Europe to institutions; USD 1,500 in United States to institutions; USD 1,548 in Canada & Mexico to institutions; USD 1,566 elsewhere to institutions; GBP 922 combined subscription in United Kingdom to institutions (print & online eds.); EUR 1,165 combined subscription in Europe to institutions (print & online eds.); USD 1,727 combined subscription in United States to institutions (print & online eds.); USD 1,775 combined subscription in Canada & Mexico to institutions (print & online eds.); USD 1,793 combined subscription elsewhere to institutions (print & online eds.) (effective 2012). adv. 8 p./no. 3 cols./p.; back issues avail.; reprint service avail. from PSC. **Document type:** *Journal, Academic/Scholarly.* **Description:** Advises mental health professionals on treating behavioral disorders with pharmacological agents.
Related titles: E-mail ed.; Online - full text ed.: ISSN 1556-7532. GBP 767 in United Kingdom to institutions; EUR 969 in Europe to institutions; USD 1,500 elsewhere to institutions (effective 2012).
Indexed: A01, A02, A03, A08, A26, C06, C07, C08, C12, CA, CINAHL, E-psyche, E07, E08, G08, H01, H11, H12, I05, M01, M02, S09, T02.
—BLDSC (2352.376000), IE. **CCC.**
Published by: John Wiley & Sons, Inc., 111 River St, Hoboken, NJ 07030. TEL 201-748-6000, FAX 201-748-6088, info@wiley.com, http://www.wiley.com/WileyCDA/. Ed. Lawrence H Price. Pub. Sue Lewis.

615 DEU ISSN 0944-6877

➤ **PSYCHOPHARMAKOTHERAPIE**; Arzneimitteltherapie psychischer und neurologischer Erkrankungen. Abbreviated title: P P T. Text and summaries in German; Summaries in English. 1994. bi-m. EUR 94.80; EUR 21 newsstand/cover (effective 2011). adv. **Document type:** *Journal, Academic/Scholarly.*
Related titles: Supplement(s): Psychopharmakotherapie. Supplement. ISSN 0946-5146. 1994.
Indexed: A22, EMBASE, ExcerpMed, FoP, NSCI, R10, Reac, SCI, SCOPUS, W07.
—BLDSC (6946.550600), GNLM, IE, Ingenta. **CCC.**
Published by: Wissenschaftliche Verlagsgesellschaft mbH, Postfach 101061, Stuttgart, 70009, Germany. TEL 49-711-25820, FAX 49-711-2582290, sheinzl@wissenschaftliche-verlagsgesellschaft.de, http://www.wissenschaftliche-verlagsgesellschaft.de. Ed. Heike Oberpichler-Schwenk. Adv. contact Kornelia Wind TEL 49-711-2582245. Circ: 10,529 (paid).

➤ **PSYFAR**; praktische nascholing over psychofarmacologie. *see* MEDICAL SCIENCES—Psychiatry And Neurology

➤ **PULMONARY PHARMACOLOGY AND THERAPEUTICS.** *see* MEDICAL SCIENCES—Respiratory Diseases

615.1 USA ISSN 0033-4529

PURDUE PHARMACIST. Text in English. 1924. s-a. (until 2010: 3/yr). free. adv. cum.index: 1924-1935. **Description:** Alumni news from the Purdue University School of Pharmacy.
Indexed: P30.
—Linda Hall.
Published by: Purdue University, College of Pharmacy, Helne Pharmacy Bldg Rm 104, 575 Stadium Mall Dr, W. Lafayette, IN 47907. TEL 765-494-1361, FAX 765-494-7880. Circ: 6,000.

615 CHN ISSN 1672-7738

QILU YAOSHI/QILU PHARMACEUTICAL AFFAIRS. Text in Chinese. 1975. m. **Document type:** *Journal, Academic/Scholarly.*
Formerly (until 2003): Shandong Yiyao Gongye (1003-1693)
Related titles: Online - full text ed.: (from WanFang Data Corp.).
—BLDSC (7163.619515).
Published by: Shandong Sheng Yaopin Jianyansuo/Shandong Institute for Drug Control, 2749, Xinluo Dajie, High-tech Industrial Development Zone, Ji'nan, 250101, China. TEL 86-531-81216586, FAX 86-531-81216586, http://www.shdidc.org.cn/. **Co-sponsor:** Shandong Sheng Yiyao Gongye Yanjiusuo/Shandong Institute of Pharmaceutical Industry.

THE QUALITY ASSURANCE JOURNAL. *see* MEDICAL SCIENCES

615 CAN ISSN 0826-9874

QUEBEC PHARMACIE. Text in English. 1953. m. free to qualified personnel; CAD 53.50 domestic; CAD 90.87 foreign (effective 2007). adv. bk.rev. **Document type:** *Magazine, Trade.*
Indexed: I12.
—**CCC.**
Published by: Rogers Publishing Ltd./Les Editions Rogers Limitee, One Mount Pleasant Rd, 11th Fl, Toronto, ON M4Y 2Y5, Canada. TEL 416-764-2000, 800-268-9119, FAX 416-764-1740, http://www.rogerspublishing.ca. Circ: 5,590.

615.1 DEU ISSN 0085-5367

QUELLEN UND STUDIEN ZUR GESCHICHTE DER PHARMAZIE. Text in German. 1960. irreg., latest vol.89, 2008. price varies. **Document type:** *Monographic series, Academic/Scholarly.*
Indexed: P30.
Published by: Wissenschaftliche Verlagsgesellschaft mbH, Postfach 101061, Stuttgart, 70009, Germany. TEL 49-711-25820, FAX 49-711-2582290, service@wissenschaftliche-verlagsgesellschaft.de, http://www.wissenschaftliche-verlagsgesellschaft.de.

615 FRA ISSN 0764-5104

LE QUOTIDIEN DU PHARMACIEN. Text in French. 1985. 100/yr. EUR 102.80 (effective 2009). **Document type:** *Newspaper, Trade.*
Published by: Federation Nationale de la Presse d'Information Specialisee (F N P S), 21 Rue Camille Desmoulins, Issy les Moulineaux, 92789, France. http://www.fnps.fr.

615 USA ISSN 1079-9397

R & D DIRECTIONS. (Research and Development) Text in English. 1995. 10/yr. USD 175 (effective 2008). adv. **Document type:** *Magazine, Trade.* **Description:** Covers the latest areas of drug research and development.
Related titles: Online - full text ed.: ISSN 1945-0052.
Indexed: A15, ABIn, B02, B03, B11, B15, B17, B18, CWI, G04, G06, G07, G08, I05, Inpharma, P24, P48, P51, PQC.
—BLDSC (7218.331000), IE, Ingenta. **CCC.**
Published by: Canon Communications Pharmaceutical Media Group, 828 A Newtown-Yardley Rd, Newtown, PA 18940. TEL 215-867-0044, FAX 215-867-0053. Ed. Christiane Truelove. Adv. contact Bob Aberman. B&W page USD 3,710, color page USD 5,310; trim 8.25 x 10.875. Circ: 12,700 (controlled).

615 GBR

R & D FOCUS. (Research and Development) Variant title: I M S Lifecycle R & D Focus. Text in English. 1978. w. **Document type:** *Newsletter, Trade.* **Description:** Examines R&D strategy against market size and growth of leading companies and drugs.
Formerly: Drug License Opportunities
Media: CD-ROM. **Related titles:** Online - full text ed.
Published by: I M S Health Inc., 7 Harewood Ave, London, NW1 6JB, United Kingdom. TEL 44-20-30755000, FAX 44-20-30755888.

615 USA

R P M REPORT. (Regulation, Policy and Market Access) Text in English. 2008. m. USD 1,650 combined subscription (print & online eds.) (effective 2008). **Document type:** *Newsletter, Trade.*
Related titles: Online - full text ed.
Published by: Windhover Information, Inc. (Subsidiary of: Elsevier Inc.), 5635 Fishers Ln, Rockville, MD 20852. TEL 800-332-2181, FAX 240-221-4400, fdcwindhover.custcare@elsevier.com, http://www.windhover.com. Ed. Cole Werble.

615.19 GBR ISSN 2041-3203

▼ **R S C DRUG DISCOVERY SERIES.** Text in English. 2010. irreg., latest vol.14, 2011. price varies. **Document type:** *Monographic series, Academic/Scholarly.*
Related titles: Online - full text ed.: ISSN 2041-3211. 2010.
—**CCC.**
Published by: Royal Society of Chemistry, Thomas Graham House, Science Park, Milton Rd, Cambridge, CB4 0WF, United Kingdom. TEL 44-1223-420066, FAX 44-1223-423623, sales@rsc.rg.

615 DNK ISSN 1600-2555

RATIONEL FARMAKOTERAPI. Text in Danish. 2000. m. **Document type:** *Government.*
Related titles: Online - full text ed.
Published by: Laegemiddelstyrelsen, Institut for Rationel Farmakoterapi, Axel Heides Gade 1, Coprenhagen S, 2300, Denmark. TEL 45-44-889121, FAX 45-44-889122, irf@dkma.dk. Ed. Jens Peter Kampmann.

615 ESP ISSN 1134-749X

REAL ACADEMIA DE FARMACIA DE CATALUNYA. REVISTA. Text in Spanish, Catalan. 1957. a. **Document type:** *Magazine, Academic/Scholarly.*
Former titles (until 1993): Revista de la Reial Academia de Farmacia de Barcelona (1134-7503); (until 1992): Revista de la Real Academia de Farmacia de Barcelona (0375-9709)
Indexed: IECT.
—INIST.
Published by: Real Academia de Farmacia de Catalunya, Carrer Hospital, 56, Barcelona, Cataluna 08001, Spain. TEL 34-93-4430088, FAX 34-93-3248157, rafc@retemail.es, http://www.rafc.es/.

615.1 ESP ISSN 1697-4271
CODEN: ARAFAY

➤ **REAL ACADEMIA NACIONAL DE FARMACIA. ANALES.** Text in English, French, Spanish; Summaries in English, French. 1933. q. EUR 60.11. bk.rev. bibl. index. back issues avail. **Document type:** *Monographic series, Academic/Scholarly.*
Former titles (until 2002): Real Academia de Farmacia. Anales (0034-0618); (until 1936): Academia Nacional de Farmacia. Anales (0365-4796)
Related titles: Print ed.: ISSN 1697-428X. 2000.
Indexed: A22, B25, BIOSIS Prev, CIN, ChemAb, ChemTitl, DBA, GeoRef, IECT, IndMed, MycolAb, P30, RefZh, SCI, SCOPUS, SpeleolAb, W07.
—BLDSC (0882.110000), CASDDS, GNLM, IE, Ingenta, INIST. **CCC.**
Published by: Real Academia Nacional de Farmacia, Farmacia 9 y 11, Madrid, 28004, Spain. TEL 34 915-223147, FAX 34-915-310306, edicion.raf@insde.es, http://www.ranf.com/. Ed. Antonio Portoles Alonso. Circ: 1,500.

➤ **RECENT PATENTS ON ANTI-INFECTIVE DRUG DISCOVERY.** *see* MEDICAL SCIENCES—Allergology And Immunology

615 NLD ISSN 2210-3090

▼ **RECENT PATENTS ON BIOMARKERS.** Text in English. 2011. 3/yr. USD 840 to institutions (print or online ed.) (effective 2012). adv. **Document type:** *Journal, Academic/Scholarly.* **Description:** Publishes review articles on important recent patents on biomarkers.
Related titles: Online - full text ed.: ISSN 2210-3104.
—**CCC.**
Published by: Bentham Science Publishers Ltd., PO Box 294, Bussum, 1400 AG, Netherlands. TEL 31-35-6923800, FAX 31-35-6980150, sales@bentham.org. **Subscr. to:** Bentham Science Publishers Ltd., c/o Richard E Morrissy, PO Box 446, Oak Park, IL 60301. TEL 312-413-5867, FAX 312-996-7107, subscriptions@bentham.org.

RECENT PATENTS ON C N S DRUG DISCOVERY. (Central Nervous System) *see* MEDICAL SCIENCES—Psychiatry And Neurology

RECENT PATENTS ON CARDIOVASCULAR DRUG DISCOVERY. *see* MEDICAL SCIENCES—Cardiovascular Diseases

610 NLD ISSN 1872-2113
RS199.5 CODEN: RPODBY

➤ **RECENT PATENTS ON DRUG DELIVERY & FORMULATION.** Text in English. 2007. 3/yr. USD 930 to institutions (print or online ed.) (effective 2012). adv. back issues avail.; reprints avail. **Document type:** *Journal, Academic/Scholarly.* **Description:** Publishes review articles by experts on recent patents on drug delivery and formulation. Includes a selection of important and recent annotated patents on drug delivery and formulation.
Related titles: Online - full text ed.: (from IngentaConnect).
Indexed: A01, A28, A34, A35, A36, A38, APA, AgBio, B&BAb, B19, BrCerAb, C&ISA, C33, CA, CA/WCA, CABA, CIA, CerAb, CivEngAb, CorrAb, E&CAJ, E11, EEA, EMA, EMBASE, ESPM, EnvEAb, ExcerpMed, GH, H15, IndVet, M&TEA, M09, MBF, MEDLINE, METADEX, P30, P33, RM&VM, SCOPUS, SolStAb, T02, T04, VS, WAA.
—IE, Ingenta, Linda Hall. **CCC.**
Published by: Bentham Science Publishers Ltd., PO Box 294, Bussum, 1400 AG, Netherlands. TEL 31-35-6923800, FAX 31-35-6980150, sales@bentham.org. Ed. Mark A Babizhayev. **Subscr. to:** Bentham Science Publishers Ltd., c/o Richard E Morrissy, PO Box 446, Oak Park, IL 60301. TEL 312-413-5867, FAX 312-996-7107, subscriptions@bentham.org.

615.19 IND

RECENT RESEARCH DEVELOPMENTS IN MEDICINAL CHEMISTRY. Text in English. 2001. a. **Document type:** *Monographic series, Academic/Scholarly.*
Published by: Transworld Research Network, T C 37-661 (2), Fort Post Office, Trivandrum, Kerala 695 023, India. TEL 91-471-2452918, FAX 91-471-2573051, ggcom@vsnl.com, http://www.trnres.com.

THE RECEPTORS. *see* MEDICAL SCIENCES—Psychiatry And Neurology

615 GBR ISSN 1743-2928

➤ **REDOX REPORT (ONLINE).** Text in English. 1999. bi-m. GBP 593 to institutions; USD 960 in United States to institutions (effective 2012). adv. **Document type:** *Journal, Academic/Scholarly.* **Description:** Publishes reviews, research articles, hypotheses, debates, and correspondence on the role of free radicals, oxidative stress, activated oxygen, peroxidative, and redox processes, primarily in human biology and pathology.
Media: Online - full text (from IngentaConnect).
—**CCC.**
Published by: (Society for Free Radical Research AUS), Maney Publishing, Ste 1C, Joseph's Well, Hanover Walk, Leeds, W Yorks LS3 1AB, United Kingdom. TEL 44-113-2432800, FAX 44-113-3868178, maney@maney.co.uk, http://www.maney.co.uk. Ed. Nicholas Hunt. Adv. contact Kirsty Bailey. B&W page GBP 180; 165 x 230. Circ: 150. **Subscr. in N. America to:** Maney Publishing, 875 Massachusetts Ave, 7th Fl, Cambridge, MA 02139. TEL 866-297-5154, FAX 617-354-6875, maney@maneyusa.com.

615.83 NLD ISSN 1380-3174

REFLEXZONE. Text in Dutch. 1994. bi-m. EUR 34, USD 51 to institutions (effective 2009). adv. **Document type:** *Magazine, Trade.*
Published by: Bohn Stafleu van Loghum B.V. (Subsidiary of: Springer Science+Business Media), Postbus 246, Houten, 3990 GA, Netherlands. TEL 31-30-6383872, FAX 31-30-6383991, boekhandels@bsl.nl, http://www.bsl.nl. adv.: color page EUR 1,050; trim 215 x 285. Circ: 1,852.

615 GBR ISSN 0969-4129

➤ **REGULATORY AFFAIRS JOURNAL. DEVICES.** Abbreviated title: R A J Devices. Text in English. 1993. bi-m. GBP 1,265, EUR 1,950, USD 2,530 combined subscription (print & online eds.) (effective 2010). adv. back issues avail.; reprints avail. **Document type:** *Journal, Trade.* **Description:** Provides comprehensive coverage of regulations affecting medical devices for governments and the medical device industry worldwide.
Related titles: CD-ROM ed.; Online - full text ed.
—BLDSC (7349.620500), IE. **CCC.**
Published by: Informa Healthcare (Subsidiary of: T & F Informa plc), Telephone House, 69-77 Paul St, London, EC2A 4LQ, United Kingdom. TEL 44-20-70175000, FAX 44-20-70176792, healthcare.enquiries@informa.com, http://informahealthcare.com/. Ed. Maureen Kenny. Pub. Phil Solomon. **Subscr. to:** Taylor & Francis Inc., Customer Services Dept, 325 Chestnut St, 8th Fl, Philadelphia, PA 19106. TEL 215-625-8900, 800-354-1420, FAX 215-625-8914, customerservice@taylorandfrancis.com; Taylor & Francis Ltd., Journals Customer Service, Sheepen Pl, Colchester, Essex CO3 3LP, United Kingdom. TEL 44-20-70175544, FAX 44-20-70175198.

P

615 GBR ISSN 1740-1240
THE REGULATORY AFFAIRS JOURNAL. PHARMA. Abbreviated title: R A J Pharma. Text in English. 1990. m. GBP 2,695, EUR 4,250, USD 5,450 combined subscription (print & online eds.) (effective 2010). adv. back issues avail.; reprints avail. **Document type:** *Journal, Trade.* **Description:** Provides comprehensive coverage of licensing of pharmaceuticals for governments and the pharmaceutical industry worldwide.
Formerly (until 2003): Regulatory Affairs Journal (0960-7889); Which incorporated: EURALex; Which incorporated (2005-2006): The Healthcare Lobbyist (1747-4159); Which was formerly (until 2005): E R A News (1462-3129); (until Jan.1998): G P L C Update
Related titles: CD-ROM ed.; Online - full text ed.
Indexed: P30.
—BLDSC (7349.625250), GNLM, IE, Infotrieve, Ingenta. **CCC.**
Published by: Informa Healthcare (Subsidiary of: T & F Informa plc), Telephone House, 69-77 Paul St, London, EC2A 4LQ, United Kingdom. TEL 44-20-70175000, FAX 44-20-70176792, healthcare.enquiries@informa.com, http://informahealthcare.com/. Ed. Maureen Kenny. Pub. Phil Solomon. Adv. contact Per Sonnerfeldt.

615.9 USA ISSN 1933-8791
REGULATORY RESEARCH PERSPECTIVES. Text in English. 2001. irreg. **Document type:** *Monographic series, Trade.*
Media: Online - full text.
Published by: U.S. Food and Drug Administration, National Center for Toxicological Research, 900 NCTR Road, Jefferson, Arkansas 72079, Jefferson, AR 72079. TEL 870-543-7000, http://www.fda.gov/nctr/index.html.

REGULATORY TOXICOLOGY AND PHARMACOLOGY. *see* ENVIRONMENTAL STUDIES—Toxicology And Environmental Safety

615 IND
▼ ➤ **RESEACH JOURNAL OF PHARMACEUTICAL DOSAGE FORMS AND TECHNOLOGY.** Abbreviated title: R J P D F T. Text in English. 2009. bi-m. INR 1,200 domestic; USD 220 foreign (effective 2011). **Document type:** *Journal, Academic/Scholarly.* **Description:** Publishes original research articles, short communications, review articles in all areas of pharmaceutics, pharmacokinetics and pharmaceutical technology.
Formerly: International Journal of Pharmaceutical Dosage Forms and Technology (Print) (0975-234X)
Related titles: Online - full text ed.: INR 500 domestic; USD 100 foreign (effective 2011).
Published by: A & V Publications, E-282 Saikripa Sector-4, Pt. Deendayal Upadhya Nagar, Raipur, Chattisgarh 492 010, India. TEL 91-9406051618, avpublications@gmail.com. Ed. Daharwal S Monika.

615.19 DEU ISSN 0179-8618
RESEARCH (GERMAN EDITION). Text in German. 1986. a. free (effective 2010). back issues avail. **Document type:** *Magazine, Trade.* **Description:** Contains articles on popular scientific topics concerning all aspects of research at Bayer.
Related titles: ◆ Spanish ed.: Research (Spanish Edition). ISSN 1438-6747; English ed.: Research (English Edition). ISSN 0932-8394. 1986.
—CCC.
Published by: Bayer AG, Corporate Communications, Gebaeude W11, Leverkusen, 51368, Germany. TEL 49-214-3057681, FAX 49-214-3071985, serviceline@bayer-ag.de. Ed. Ute Bode. Circ: 350,000 (controlled).

615.19 DEU ISSN 1438-6747
RESEARCH (SPANISH EDITION). Text in Spanish. 1988. a. free (effective 2010). **Document type:** *Magazine, Trade.*
Related titles: ◆ German ed.: Research (German Edition). ISSN 0179-8618; English ed.: Research (English Edition). ISSN 0932-8394. 1986.
—CCC.
Published by: Bayer AG, Corporate Communications, Gebaeude W11, Leverkusen, 51368, Germany. TEL 49-214-3057681, FAX 49-214-3071985, serviceline@bayer-ag.de, http://www.bayer.com.

RESEARCH COMMUNICATIONS IN MOLECULAR PATHOLOGY AND PHARMACOLOGY. *see* MEDICAL SCIENCES

615.19 660.6 NGA
➤ **RESEARCH IN PHARMACEUTICAL BIOTECHNOLOGY.** Text in English. m. free (effective 2010). adv. **Document type:** *Journal, Academic/Scholarly.*
Media: Online - full text.
Published by: Academic Journals, PO Box 73023, Victoria Island, Lagos, Nigeria. service@academicjournals.org. Eds. Dr. Claude Kirimuhuzya, Jian W Wang, Teresa A Akenga.

615 USA ISSN 1551-7411
RS100
RESEARCH IN SOCIAL AND ADMINISTRATIVE PHARMACY. Abbreviated title: R S A P. Text in English. 2005 (Mar.). q. USD 235 in United States to institutions; USD 309 elsewhere to institutions (effective 2012). adv. back issues avail.; reprints avail. **Document type:** *Journal, Academic/Scholarly.* **Description:** Features articles and reports on such topics as outcomes research, patient education, program evaluation, direct-to-consumer advertising of prescription medications, medication adherence, health systems reform and health profession workforce issues.
Related titles: Online - full text ed.: ISSN 1934-8150 (from ScienceDirect).
Indexed: A20, A26, C06, C07, CA, CurCont, EMBASE, ExcerpMed, I05, I12, MEDLINE, P03, P30, PsycInfo, R10, Reac, SCOPUS, SSCI, T02, W07.
—IE, Ingenta. **CCC.**
Published by: Elsevier Inc. (Subsidiary of: Elsevier Science & Technology), 1600 John F Kennedy Blvd, Philadelphia, PA 19103. TEL 215-239-3900, FAX 215-238-7883, JournalCustomerService-usa@elsevier.com, http://www.elsevier.com. Ed. Shane P Desselle. Adv. contact Janine Castle TEL 44-1865-843844.

615 570 IND ISSN 0975-8585
RM1
▼ **RESEARCH JOURNAL OF PHARMACEUTICAL, BIOLOGICAL AND CHEMICAL SCIENCES.** Text in English. 2010. irreg. free (effective 2011).
Media: Online - full text.
Indexed: A34, A35, A37, AgrForAb, B23, C25, C30, CABA, E12, F08, FCA, GH, H16, N02, N03, N04, P32, P33, P39, P40, R07, R08, R12, R13, S13, S16, SoyAb, T05, W10. Ed. G Girish.

615 572 IND ISSN 0975-2331
▼ ➤ **RESEARCH JOURNAL OF PHARMACOGNOSY AND PHYTOCHEMISTRY.** Abbreviated title: R J P P. Text in English. 2009. bi-m. INR 1,200 domestic; USD 220 foreign (effective 2011). **Document type:** *Journal, Academic/Scholarly.* **Description:** Publishes original research articles, short communications, review articles in all areas of pharmacognosy and phytochemistry.
Related titles: Online - full text ed.: ISSN 0975-4385. INR 500 domestic; USD 100 foreign (effective 2011).
Published by: A & V Publications, E-282 Saikripa Sector-4, Pt. Deendayal Upadhya Nagar, Raipur, Chattisgarh 492 010, India. TEL 91-9406051618, avpublications@gmail.com. Ed. Daharwal S Monika.

615.1 PAK ISSN 1815-9362
RESEARCH JOURNAL OF PHARMACOLOGY. Text in English. 2007. 4/yr. EUR 900 to individuals; EUR 1,200 to institutions; EUR 150 newsstand/cover (effective 2007). **Document type:** *Journal, Academic/Scholarly.*
Related titles: Online - full text ed.: ISSN 1993-6109. free (effective 2007).
Indexed: EMBASE, ExcerpMed, SCOPUS.
Published by: Medwell Journals, ANSInet Bldg, 308-Lasani Town, Sargodha Rd, Faisalabad, 38090, Pakistan. TEL 92-41-5010004, 92-41-5004000, FAX 92-21-5206789, medwellonline@gmail.com, http://www.medwellonline.net.

615.1 IND ISSN 0975-4407
▼ ➤ **RESEARCH JOURNAL OF PHARMACOLOGY AND PHARMACODYNAMICS.** Abbreviated title: R J P P D. Text in English. 2009. bi-m. INR 1,200 domestic; USD 220 foreign (effective 2011). **Document type:** *Journal, Academic/Scholarly.* **Description:** Publishes original research articles, short communications, review articles in all areas of pharmacology, pharmacokinetics and human physiology.
Related titles: Online - full text ed.: INR 500 domestic; USD 100 foreign (effective 2011).
Published by: A & V Publications, E-282 Saikripa Sector-4, Pt. Deendayal Upadhya Nagar, Raipur, Chattisgarh 492 010, India. TEL 91-9406051618, avpublications@gmail.com. Ed. Daharwal S Monika.

615 IND ISSN 0974-3618
➤ **RESEARCH JOURNAL OF PHARMACY AND TECHNOLOGY.** Abbreviated title: R J P T. Text in English. 2008. m. INR 2,000 domestic; USD 400 foreign (effective 2011). adv. **Document type:** *Journal, Academic/Scholarly.* **Description:** Publishes original research articles, short communications, review articles in all areas of pharmaceutical sciences from the discovery of a drug up to clinical evaluation.
Related titles: Online - full text ed.: ISSN 0974-360X. INR 1,000 domestic; USD 200 foreign (effective 2011).
Indexed: A34, A36, AgrForAb, B23, CABA, E12, F08, GH, H16, N02, N03, N04, P33, R07, S13, T05.
Published by: A & V Publications, E-282 Saikripa Sector-4, Pt. Deendayal Upadhya Nagar, Raipur, Chattisgarh 492 010, India. TEL 91-9406051618, avpublications@gmail.com. Ed. R Saudagar. Pub. Daharwal S Monika.

615 616.2 CHE
➤ **RESPIRATORY PHARMACOLOGY AND PHARMACOTHERAPY.** Text in English. 1994. irreg. price varies. **Document type:** *Monographic series, Academic/Scholarly.*
Published by: Birkhaeuser Verlag AG (Subsidiary of: Springer Science+Business Media), Viaduktstr 42, Postfach 133, Basel, 4051, Switzerland. TEL 41-61-2050707, FAX 41-61-2050792, birkhauser@springer.de, http://www.birkhauser.ch. Eds. D Raeburn, M Giembycz. **Subscr. in the Americas to:** Springer New York LLC; **Subscr. to:** Springer Distribution Center, Kundenservice Zeitschriften. birkhauser@springer.de.

➤ **RESTORATIVE NEUROLOGY AND NEUROSCIENCE.** *see* MEDICAL SCIENCES—Psychiatry And Neurology

615 AUS
RETAIL PHARMACY. Abbreviated title: R P. Text in English. 1992. m. (except Jan.). AUD 137.50 (print & online eds.) (effective 2009). adv. back issues avail. **Document type:** *Magazine, Trade.* **Description:** Provides general and industry news, and research material that relates to pharmacists and pharmaceutical industry. Includes case success stories of pharmacists and industry analyses.
Related titles: Online - full text ed.
Published by: Retail Media Pty Ltd., Parramatta Business Centre, PO Box 6104, Parramatta, NSW 2150, Australia. TEL 61-2-98901199, FAX 61-2-98901877, subscriptions@retailmedia.com, http://www.retailmedia.com.au. Ed. Amy Looker TEL 61-2-96830117. Pub. Barry Flanagan. Adv. contact Janet Robertson TEL 61-2-96830132. page AUD 4,890; trim 340 x 240. Circ: 7,413 (controlled).

615.19 USA ISSN 1089-5302
RS160 CODEN: LRNSEP
THE REVIEW OF NATURAL PRODUCTS. Text in English. 1980. m. looseleaf. USD 203 base vol(s). (effective 2008). Supplement avail. **Document type:** *Journal, Trade.* **Description:** Provides up-to-date, objective assessment of the latest medical and scientific studies on natural products, including medically active foods (nutraceuticals).
Formerly (until 1996): The Lawrence Review of Natural Products (0734-4961)
Published by: Facts and Comparisons (Subsidiary of: Wolters Kluwer N.V.), 77 West Port Plz, Ste 450, St. Louis, MO 63146. TEL 314-216-2100, 800-223-0554, FAX 317-735-5390.

REVIEWS OF PHYSIOLOGY, BIOCHEMISTRY AND PHARMACOLOGY. *see* BIOLOGY—Physiology

REVIEWS ON RECENT CLINICAL TRIALS. *see* MEDICAL SCIENCES

615 COL ISSN 0121-9073
REVISTA A S O C O L D R O. (Asociacion Colombiana de Droguistas Detallistas) Text in Spanish. 1989. s-w. **Document type:** *Magazine, Trade.*
Published by: Asociacion Colombiana de Droguistas Detallistas (ASOCOLDRO), Cra 27A, 53A-33, Bogota, Colombia. asocoldro@hotmail.com.

615.1 BRA ISSN 0370-372X
CODEN: RBFAAH
REVISTA BRASILEIRA DE FARMACIA. Text in Portuguese; Summaries in English, Portuguese. 1920. q. adv. charts; illus.; stat. **Document type:** *Journal, Academic/Scholarly.* **Description:** Contains original papers in pharmacology and chemistry.
Former titles (until 1942): Associacao Brasileira de Farmaceuticos. Revista (0370-3126); (until 1937): Associacao Brasileira de Farmaceuticos. Boletim (0366-158X)
Indexed: ChemAb, ChemTitl, P30, SCOPUS.
—CASDDS, GNLM.
Published by: (Associacao Brasileira de Farmaceuticos), Nuno Alvares Pereira Ed.& Pub., Rua dos Andradas, 96-Andar 10, Centro, Rio De Janeiro, RJ 20051-000, Brazil. FAX 55-21-2333672.

615 BRA ISSN 0102-695X
REVISTA BRASILEIRA DE FARMACOGNOSIA. Text in Portuguese, English. 1986. s-a. **Document type:** *Journal, Academic/Scholarly.*
Related titles: Online - full text ed.: ISSN 1981-528X. free (effective 2011).
Indexed: A34, A35, A36, A37, A38, AgBio, AgrForAb, B23, B25, BIOSIS Prev, BP, C25, C30, CABA, D01, E12, EMBASE, ExcerpMed, F08, F11, F12, G11, GH, H16, H17, I11, I12, MycolAb, N02, N03, N04, NPU, O01, P32, P33, P39, P40, PGegResA, PGrRegA, PHN&I, PN&I, R07, R08, R12, R13, RA&MP, RM&VM, S12, S13, S16, S17, SCI, SCOPUS, SoyAb, T05, TAR, VS, W07, W10, W11.
—BLDSC (7844.755000), IE.
Published by: Sociedade Brasileira de Farmacognosia, c/o Prof Jose Maria Barbosa Filho, Universidade Federal de Paraiba, Laboratorio de Tecnologia Farmaceutica, Joao Pessoa, PB 58051-970, Brazil. rbgnosia@ltf.ufpb.br. Ed. Jose Maria Barbosa Filho.

REVISTA BRASILEIRA DE TOXICOLOGIA. *see* ENVIRONMENTAL STUDIES—Toxicology And Environmental Safety

615.1 COL ISSN 0034-7418
RS402 CODEN: RCQFAQ
REVISTA COLOMBIANA DE CIENCIAS QUIMICO FARMACEUTICAS. Text in Spanish; Summaries in English. 1969. 2/yr. free. illus. **Document type:** *Journal, Academic/Scholarly.*
Related titles: Online - full text ed.
Indexed: C01, CIN, ChemAb, ChemTitl.
—CASDDS.
Published by: Universidad Nacional de Colombia, Departamento de Farmacia, Apartado Aereo 14490, Bogota, Colombia. TEL 57-1-3165045, FAX 57-1-3165060. Ed. Jaime Humberto Rojas Bermudez.

615.1 CUB ISSN 0034-7515
RS1 CODEN: RCUFAC
REVISTA CUBANA DE FARMACIA. Text in Spanish; Summaries in English, Spanish. 1967. 3/yr. USD 28 in North America; USD 30 in South America; USD 32 elsewhere (effective 2005). abstr.; bibl.; charts; illus. index. back issues avail. **Document type:** *Journal, Academic/Scholarly.* **Description:** Covers the fields of pharmacy, pharmacology and the drug industry.
Related titles: Online - full text ed.: ISSN 1561-2988. 1995. free (effective 2011).
Indexed: A01, C01, CA, ChemAb, ChemTitl, EMBASE, ExcerpMed, IBR, IBZ, IndMed, SCOPUS, T02.
—CASDDS, GNLM.
Published by: (Centro Nacional de Informacion de Ciencias Medicas (C N I C M), Cuba. Ministerio de Salud Publica), Editorial Ciencias Medicas, Linea Esq 1, 10o, Vedado, Havana, 10400, Cuba. TEL 53-7-8323863, ecimed@infomed.sld.cu. Ed. Ana Dolores del Campo. Circ: 1,300. **Co-sponsors:** Industria Medico-Farmaceutica de Cuba; Sociedad Cubana de Farmacia.

615.321 CUB ISSN 1028-4796
REVISTA CUBANA DE PLANTAS MEDICINALES. Text in Spanish. 1996. q. free (effective 2011). back issues avail. **Document type:** *Journal, Academic/Scholarly.*
Media: Online - full text.
Indexed: A34, A35, AgBio, AgrForAb, B23, BP, C30, CABA, D01, E12, F08, F11, F12, G11, GH, H16, I11, N02, OR, P32, P33, P40, PGegResA, PHN&I, R07, R08, R12, R13, RA&MP, RM&VM, S12, S13, S16, S17, SCOPUS, T05, TAR, VS, W10, W11.
Published by: (Centro Nacional de Informacion de Ciencias Medicas (C N I C M)), Editorial Ciencias Medicas, Linea Esq 1, 10o, Vedado, Havana, 10400, Cuba. TEL 53-7-8323863, ecimed@infomed.sld.cu. Ed. Dania Silva Hernandez.

615.1 BRA ISSN 1808-4532
CODEN: RCIFDN
➤ **REVISTA DE CIENCIAS FARMACEUTICAS BASICA E APLICADA.** Text in Portuguese, Spanish, English. 1967. q. BRL 45 domestic to individuals; USD 30 foreign to individuals; BRL 90 domestic to institutions; USD 60 foreign to institutions (effective 2006). charts; stat.; abstr.; bibl. back issues avail. **Document type:** *Journal, Academic/Scholarly.* **Description:** Contains original articles, notes and technical reviews on clinical cases in all areas of pharmacology.
Former titles (until 2005): Revista de Ciencias Farmaceuticas (0101-3793); (until 1978): Faculdade de Farmacia e Odontologia de Araraquara. Revista
Related titles: Online - full text ed.: ISSN 2179-443X. free (effective 2011).
Indexed: A29, B20, B21, B25, BIOSIS Prev, C01, CIN, ChemAb, ChemTitl, EMBASE, ESPM, ExcerpMed, I10, I12, MycolAb, NSA, R10, Reac, RefZh, SCOPUS, ToxAb, VirolAbstr.
—CASDDS, GNLM, INIST.
Published by: (Universidade Estadual Paulista "Julio de Mesquita Filho", Faculdade de Ciencias Farmaceuticas), Universidade Estadual Paulista, Fundacao Editora U N E S P, Praca da Se 108, Sao Paulo, SP 01001-900, Brazil. TEL 55-11-32427171, cgb@marilia.unesp.br, http://www.unesp.br. Ed. Cleopatra da Silva Planeta. Circ: (controlled).

615.19 PER ISSN 0377-4708
RS1
REVISTA DE FARMACIA Y BIOQUIMICA. Variant title: Facultad de Farmacia y Bioquimica. Revista. Text in Spanish. 1939. s-a. charts; illus.; stat. **Document type:** *Journal, Academic/Scholarly.*
Formerly (until 1969): Universidad Nacional Mayor de San Marcos. Facultad de Farmacia y Bioquimica. Revista

Published by: Universidad Nacional Mayor de San Marcos, Facultad de Farmacia y Bioquimica, Jr Pruno, Apartado 1760, Lima, Peru. TEL 51-1-3284737, FAX 51-1-3284741, http://www.unmsm.edu.pe/farmacia/farmacia.htm.

615 ESP ISSN 1576-0952
REVISTA DE FITOTERAPIA. Text in Multiple languages. 2000. s-a. EUR 90 (effective 2008). back issues avail. **Document type:** *Magazine, Trade.*
Related titles: Online - full text ed.: ISSN 1988-5806. 2000.
Indexed: EMBASE, ExcerpMed, SCOPUS.
—CCC.
Published by: C I T A Publicaciones y Documentacion, Na Jordana 11, Carlet, Valencia 46240, Spain. TEL 34-96-2993239.

615.1 BRA ISSN 1808-0804
REVISTA ELECTRONICA DE FARMACIA. Text in Spanish. 2004. q. free (effective 2011). back issues avail. **Document type:** *Journal, Academic/Scholarly.*
Media: Online - full text.
Published by: Universidade Federal de Goias, Faculdade de Farmacia, Ave Universitaria com 1a. Ave s-n, Setor Universitario, Goias, 74605-220, Brazil. TEL 55-62-32096044, FAX 55-62-32096037, ref@farmacia.ufg.br, http://www.farmacia.ufg.br/page.php. Ed. Ricardo Menegatti.

615.1 ARG ISSN 0034-9496
RS1 CODEN: RFABAN
REVISTA FARMACEUTICA. Text in Spanish. 1858. 12/yr. (in 6 double issues). adv. bk.rev. bibl.; charts; illus. **Document type:** *Journal, Academic/Scholarly.*
Related titles: Online - full text ed.
Indexed: C01, ChemAb, IBR, IBZ.
—CASDDS.
Published by: Academia Argentina de Farmacia y Bioquimica, Junin 956, Buenos Aires, 1113, Argentina. Ed. Alfredo Jose Bandoni.

615 PRT ISSN 1646-9275
REVISTA FARMACIAS PORTUGUESAS. Text in Portuguese. 2008. s-a. **Document type:** *Magazine, Consumer.*
Published by: Farmacias Portuguesas, Travessa de Santa Caterina 8, Lisbon, 1200-403, Portugal. TEL 351-707-273273, geral@farmaciasportuguesas.pt, http://www.farmaciasportuguesas.pt.

615 MEX ISSN 1027-3956
REVISTA MEXICANA DE CIENCIAS FARMACEUTICAS. Text in Spanish, English. 1971. bi-m. free to members. **Document type:** *Journal, Academic/Scholarly.*
Related titles: Online - full text ed.: ISSN 1870-0195.
Indexed: C01, EMBASE, ExcerpMed, I12, R10, Reac, SCOPUS.
—BLDSC (7866.240000).
Published by: Asociacion Farmaceutica Mexicana, Calle Nicolas San Juan 1511, Col Del Valle, Mexico City, 03100, Mexico. TEL 52-55-91832060, FAX 52-55-56882069, info@afmac.org.mx. Ed. Emma D. Perez. Adv. contact Mario Trias TEL 669-1214. Circ: 3,500.

615 PRT ISSN 0484-811X
CODEN: RPTFAU
REVISTA PORTUGUESA DE FARMACIA. Text in Portuguese; Summaries in English. 1835. q. bk.rev. bibl.; charts; stat. cum.index. back issues avail. **Document type:** *Academic/Scholarly.* **Description:** Presents original papers in pharmacy and pharmacology research.
Former titles (until 1951): Jornal dos Farmaceuticos (0368-2129); (until 1941): Sindicato Nacional dos Farmaceuticos. Jornal (0870-1261); (until 1933): Sociedade Farmaceutica Lusiana. Jornal (0870-1679); (until 1837): Sociedad Farmaceutica de Lisboa. Jornal (0870-1113)
Related titles: Online - full text ed.
Indexed: A22, ApicAb, CIN, ChemAb, ChemTitl, EMBASE, ExcerpMed, FS&TA, I12, IBR, IBZ, P30, R10, Reac, SCOPUS.
—CASDDS, GNLM, Ingenta, Linda Hall.
Published by: Ordem dos Farmaceuticos, Rua da Sociedade Farmaceutica, 18, Lisbon, Lisboa 1169-075, Portugal. TEL 351-213-191370, FAX 351-213-191399, secretariogeral@ordemfarmaceuticos.pt, http://www.ordemfarmaceuticos.pt. Ed. Jose Guimaraes Morais. R&P Ivana Silva. Circ: 1,500.

615 PRT ISSN 1647-354X
▼ **REVISTA PORTUGUESA DE FARMACOTERAPIA.** Text in Portuguese. 2009. q. **Document type:** *Magazine, Trade.*
Published by: Formifarma, Rua Luiz marques Lote 8, Alto dos Gaios, Estoril, 2765-448, Portugal. TEL 351-21-4659087, FAX 351-21-4659090, http://www.formifarma.com, formifarma@formifarma.com.

615.1 FRA ISSN 0035-2349
REVUE D'HISTOIRE DE LA PHARMACIE. Text in French. 1913. q. EUR 45 domestic to members; EUR 70 foreign to members (effective 2009). adv. bk.rev. abstr.; illus.; bibl. index, cum.index: 1913-1963, 1964-1983. **Document type:** *Academic/Scholarly.*
Formerly (until 1930): La Societe d'Histoire de la Pharmacie. Bulletin (0995-838X)
Indexed: EMBASE, ExcerpMed, FR, IBR, IBZ, MEDLINE, P30, RILM, SCOPUS.
—GNLM, INIST.
Published by: Societe d'Histoire de la Pharmacie, 4 av. de l' Observatoire, Paris, Cedex 6 75270, France. Ed. Thierry Lefebvre. Circ: 1,400.

615 610 FRA ISSN 0247-7750
LA REVUE PRESCRIRE. Text in French. 1980. m. (11/yr). EUR 220 to individuals; EUR 490 to institutions (effective 2005). **Document type:** *Bulletin.*
Related titles: Online - full text ed.: ISSN 1961-909X; ◆ International ed. of: Prescrire International. ISSN 1167-7422.
Indexed: A22, FR.
—BLDSC (7943.440000), IE, INIST. **CCC.**
Published by: Association Mieux Prescrire, BP 459, Paris, 75527 Cedex 11, France. TEL 33-1-49237280, 33-1-49237265, FAX 33-1-49237648, revue@prescrire.org. Ed. Gilles Bardelay. Pub. Philippe Schilliger.

615.1 USA
THE RHODE ISLAND PHARMACIST. Text in English. q. **Document type:** *Journal, Trade.*
Published by: (Rhode Island Pharmacists Association), Newsletters Ink, Corp., 473 W 4800 S, Salt Lake Cty, Murray, UT 84123. TEL 801-288-2434, 800-639-0465, info@newslettersink.com, http://www.newslettersink.com.

615.1 JPN ISSN 0388-1601
CODEN: RIYADS
RINSHO YAKURI. Variant title: Japanese Journal of Clinical Pharmacology and Therapeutics. Text in Japanese, English. 1970. q. free to members (effective 2005). **Document type:** *Journal, Academic/Scholarly.*
Indexed: A22, EMBASE, ExcerpMed, R10, Reac, SCOPUS.
—BLDSC (4651.410000), IE, Ingenta, INIST.
Published by: Nihon Rinsho Yakuri Gakkai/Japanese Society of Clinical Pharmacology and Therapeutics, Gakkai Center Bldg, 2-4-16 Yayoi, Bunkyo-ku, Tokyo, 113-0032, Japan. TEL 81-3-38151761, FAX 81-3-38151762, clinphar@jade.dti.ne.jp.

615 DEU
ROTE LISTE. Text in German. 1935. a. EUR 78 (effective 2009). **Document type:** *Directory, Trade.* **Description:** Provides a comprehensive survey on drugs made in Germany from a pharmacological-therapeutic view as well as regarding the preparations, package sizes and prices.
Related titles: CD-ROM ed.: EUR 54 (effective 2009).
Published by: (Verbaende der Pharmazeutischen Industrie in Deutschland), Rote Liste Service GmbH, Mainzer Landstr 55, Frankfurt am Main, 60329, Germany. TEL 800-7683835, FAX 800-7683329. Circ: 280,000.

615 GBR ISSN 1755-1056
RULES AND GUIDANCE FOR PHARMACEUTICAL MANUFACTURERS AND DISTRIBUTORS. Text in English. 2007. a., latest 2007, Feb. USD 160 per issue (effective 2010). adv. **Document type:** *Handbook/Manual/Guide, Trade.* **Description:** Collates European and UK guidance documents and information on legislation relating to the manufacture and distribution of medicines for human use.
Media: Online - full text. **Related titles:** CD-ROM ed.; Print ed.: USD 75 per issue (print or CD-ROM ed.); USD 115 combined subscription per issue (print & CD-ROM eds.) (effective 2010).
Published by: Pharmaceutical Press (Subsidiary of: Royal Pharmaceutical Society of Great Britain), 1 Lambeth High St, London, SE1 7JN, United Kingdom. TEL 44-20-75722665, FAX 44-20-75722509, pharmpress@macmillansolutions.com. Pub. Lindsey Fountain TEL 44-20-75722655.

615 AUS ISSN 1833-0827
RURAL PHARMACY NEWSLETTER. Text in English. 2002. s-a. free (effective 2009). back issues avail. **Document type:** *Newsletter, Government.* **Description:** Information, news and networking for Australia's rural and remote pharmacists.
Related titles: Online - full text ed.
Published by: Pharmacy Guild of Australia, The Rural and Remote Pharmacy Workforce Development Program, PO Box 7036, Canberra BC, ACT 2610, Australia. TEL 61-2-62701888, FAX 61-2-62701800, guild.nat@guild.org.au, http://beta.guild.org.au/Rural.

615 USA ISSN 1066-7741
THE RX CONSULTANT. Text in English. 1991. m. USD 79 domestic; USD 89 in Canada; USD 104 elsewhere; USD 6.75 newsstand/cover (effective 2008). **Document type:** *Journal, Trade.* **Description:** Contains practical updates and reviews covering all the top-selling drugs and common health conditions.
Published by: The Rx Consultant, PO Box 1516, Martinez, CA 94553. TEL 925-229-5440, 800-798-3353, FAX 925-229-5442.

615 USA ISSN 1939-8328
CODEN: TXPDAE
➤ **RX.PERTS.** Text in English. 2007. q. bk.rev. index. 40 p./no.; **Document type:** *Magazine, Trade.* **Description:** Contains news of interest to pharmacists and offers practice and management tips, trends in pharmacy, legislative issues coverage, profiles of outstanding practitioners, disease state information and new products information.
Formed by the merger of (1959-2007): Texas Pharmacy (0362-7926); (197?-2007): T P A Speedletter (1096-9268); Which was formerly (until 1959): Texas Druggist
Published by: Texas Pharmacy Association, 12007 Research Blvd, Ste 201, Austin, TX 78759. TEL 512-836-8350, FAX 512-836-0308.

615 JPN ISSN 1348-2688
S A F E - D I WEEKLY. Text in Japanese. 1988. w. **Document type:** *Magazine, Trade.*
Formerly (until 2003): Fine D I Weekly (0919-9128)
Published by: S A F E Gakujutsubu/S A F E Co., Ltd., 1-12-1, Uchikanda, Chiyoda-ku, Tokyo, 101-0047, Japan. TEL 81-3-52172300, http://www.kk-safe.co.jp/index.html.

615 ZAF
S A PHARMACEUTICAL JOURNAL. (South Africa) Variant title: South African Pharmaceutical Journal. Text in English. 1980. 10/yr. ZAR 75, USD 80 (effective 1995). adv. 64 p./no. 3 cols./p.; back issues avail. **Document type:** *Journal, Trade.* **Description:** Contains management and clinical articles written by South African specialists.
Formerly (until 2000): Pharmacy Management (1015-1362)
—GNLM.
Published by: Medical and Pharmaceutical Publications (Pty) Ltd., PO Box 14804, Lyttleton, 0157, South Africa. http://www.medpharm.co.za. Ed. Lorraine Osman. Pub., R&P Rene F Smulders. Adv. contact Sandy Barnardt. Circ: 6,500.

615.1 ZAF ISSN 2221-5875
➤ **S A PHARMACEUTICAL JOURNAL INCORPORATING PHARMACY MANAGEMENT/S A TYDSKRIF VIR APTEEKWESE WAARBY INGELYF PHARMACY MANAGEMENT.** (South African) Text in Afrikaans, English. 1934. 10/yr. ZAR 310; ZAR 31 per issue (effective 2011). adv. bk.rev. charts; illus. back issues avail. **Document type:** *Journal, Academic/Scholarly.* **Description:** Contains clinical reviews on symptomatic therapy, information on prescription medication, and medical referrals.
Formerly (until 2000): South African Pharmaceutical Journal/Suid-Afrikaanse Vir Apteekwese (0257-8719); Which incorporated (1984-2000): Pharmacy Management (1015-1362)
Related titles: Online - full text ed.: ISSN 2220-1017. 1934; ◆ Supplement(s): Medifile. ISSN 1021-6987.
Indexed: ISAP, P30.
—BLDSC (8344.000000), IE.
Published by: (Pharmaceutical Society of South Africa/ Aptekersvereniging van Suid-Afrika), Medpharm Publications (Pty) Ltd, PO Box 14804, Lyttelton, 0140, South Africa. TEL 27-12-6647460, FAX 27-12-6646276, reception@medpharm.co.za, http://www.medpharm.co.za. Ed. Lorraine Osman. Adv. contact Sandy Laranja.

615 ZAF ISSN 1608-9634
➤ **S A PHARMACIST'S ASSISTANT.** (South African) Variant title: S A P A. Text in English. 2001. q. **Document type:** *Magazine, Trade.*
Related titles: Online - full text ed.: ISSN 2220-1068. 2009.
Indexed: ISAP.
Published by: Medpharm Publications (Pty) Ltd, PO Box 14804, Lyttelton, 0140, South Africa. TEL 27-12-6647460, FAX 27-12-6646276, reception@medpharm.co.za, http://www.medpharm.co.za.

615.1 NLD ISSN 1871-6016
S B A MAGAZINE. (Stichting Bedrijfsfonds Apotheken) Text in Dutch. 1995. 10/yr. **Document type:** *Magazine, Trade.*
Formerly (until 2005): S B A Berichten (1388-9443)
Published by: Stichting Bedrijfsfonds Apotheken, Postbus 219, Nieuwegein, 3430 AE, Netherlands. TEL 31-30-6008520, FAX 31-30-6008530, sba@sbaweb.nl, http://www.sbaweb.nl. Ed. Liesbeth Kuipers. Circ: 25,000.

S I A R NEWS; giornale della Societa Italiana Attivita Regolatorie. (Societa Italiana Attivita Regolatorie) *see* MEDICAL SCIENCES

615 FRA ISSN 1157-1497
CODEN: SPPRER
S T P PHARMA PRATIQUES. (Sciences Techniques Pratiques) Text in French; Summaries in English. 1953. 6/yr. EUR 470 domestic; EUR 500 foreign (effective 2009). adv. **Document type:** *Journal, Trade.* **Description:** Covers reports, symposiums proceedings, industrial, commercial and technical information, regulatory affairs articles.
Supersedes in part (in 1991): S T P Pharma (0758-6922)
Indexed: A22, A36, A37, B&BAb, B21, CABA, DBA, E12, EMBASE, ExcerpMed, FR, GH, P33, R07, R10, R13, RA&MP, RM&VM, Reac, RefZh, S13, S16, SCOPUS.
—BLDSC (8467.293000), CASDDS, GNLM, IE, Infotrieve, Ingenta, INIST, Linda Hall. **CCC.**
Published by: Editions de Sante, 49 Rue Galilee, Paris, 75116, France. TEL 33-1-40701615, FAX 33-1-40701614, editions.de.sante@wanadoo.fr. Circ: 2,000.

P

615 JPN
SAIKIN NO SHINYAKU/NEW DRUGS IN JAPAN. Text in Japanese. 1950. a., latest vol.48. JPY 4,515 (effective 2001). adv. back issues avail. **Document type:** *Government.* **Description:** Description of old and new drugs marketed in Japan.
Published by: Yakuji Nippo Ltd., Kanda-Izumi-cho, Chiyoda-ku, Tokyo, 101-0024, Japan. TEL 81-3-3862-2141, FAX 81-3-3866-8495, shuppan@yakuji.co.jp, http://www.yakuji.co.jp/. Circ: 20,000.

615.19 JPN ISSN 1341-741X
CODEN: SKKNAJ
SANKYO RESEARCH LABORATORIES. ANNUAL REPORT. Text in English. 1946. a. free. abstr. reprints avail. **Document type:** *Corporate.*
Former titles (until 1991): Sankyo Kenkyusho Nempo (0080-6064); (until 1963): Takamine Kenkyujo Nenpo (0371-8670)
Indexed: A22, ChemAb.
—CASDDS, IE, Ingenta, INIST.
Published by: Sankyo Co. Ltd., Research Institute/Sankyo K.K. Sogo Kenkyujo, 1-2-58 Hiro-Machi, Shinagawa-ku, Tokyo, 140-0005, Japan. TEL 81-3-3492-3131, FAX 81-3-5436-7066. Ed., R&P Tetsuo Hiraoka.

SASKATCHEWAN DRUG PLAN AND EXTENDED BENEFITS BRANCH. ANNUAL STATISTICAL REPORT. *see* PHARMACY AND PHARMACOLOGY—Abstracting, Bibliographies, Statistics

615 CAN ISSN 1923-0761
SASKATCHEWAN FORMULARY BULLETIN. Text in English. 197?. q. free (effective 2010). back issues avail. **Document type:** *Bulletin, Government.*
Formerly (until 2009): Saskatchewan Formulary Committee. Bulletin (0708-3246)
Published by: Saskatchewan Ministry of Health, Drug Plan & Extended Benefits Branch, Second Fl, 3475 Albert St, Regina, SK S4S 6X6, Canada. TEL 306-787-3420, FAX 306-787-8679.

615 SAU ISSN 1319-0164
RS1
➤ **SAUDI PHARMACEUTICAL JOURNAL.** Text in English. 1993. s-a. **Document type:** *Journal, Academic/Scholarly.* **Description:** Contains original research articles, review articles, short communications, case studies, and letters to the editor.
Media: Online - full content. **Related titles:** Online - full text ed.: (from ScienceDirect).
Indexed: A35, A36, AgBio, AgrForAb, BP, CABA, D01, E12, EMBASE, ExcerpMed, F08, F11, F12, GH, H16, H17, I12, IDIS, N02, N03, P32, P33, P39, P40, R07, R08, R10, R12, R13, RA&MP, RM&VM, Reac, S12, SCI, SCOPUS, T02, T05, TAR, VS, W07.
—BLDSC (8076.978600), IE, Ingenta. **CCC.**
Published by: Saudi Pharmaceutical Society spj@ksu.edu.sa. Ed. Farid J Al-Muhtadi.

615.1071 USA
SCHOOLS IN THE UNITED STATES AND CANADA OFFERING GRADUATE EDUCATION IN PHARMACOLOGY (ONLINE). Text in English. 1963. biennial. free. **Document type:** *Directory.*
Formerly (until 199?): Schools in the United States and Canada Offering Graduate Education in Pharmacology (Print)
Media: Online - full text.
Published by: American Society for Pharmacology and Experimental Therapeutics, 9650 Rockville Pike, Bethesda, MD 20814. TEL 301-634-7060, FAX 301-634-7061, info@aspet.org, http://www.aspet.org.

615 CHE ISSN 0255-7681
SCHWEIZER HAUSAPOTHEKE. Text in German. 1930. 9/yr. adv. **Document type:** *Magazine, Trade.*
Published by: Perpress Medien AG, Industriestr 5, Boesingen, 3178, Switzerland. TEL 41-31-7409700, FAX 41-31-7409728. Ed. Silvia Felber. Adv. contact Christoph Tshang. B&W page CHF 13,770, color page CHF 16,799. Circ: 325,000.

615 CHE ISSN 0255-6693
SCHWEIZERISCHE GESELLSCHAFT FUER GESCHICHTE DER PHARMAZIE. VEROEFFENTLICHUNGEN. Text in German. 1982. irreg., latest vol.27, 2005. price varies. **Document type:** *Monographic series, Academic/Scholarly.*
Published by: Schweizerische Gesellschaft fuer Geschichte der Pharmazie, Stationsstr 12, Bern, 3097, Switzerland. ursula.streit@sphin.ch, http://www.histpharm.ch.

615.1 AUT ISSN 0036-8709
CODEN: SCPHA4
➤ **SCIENTIA PHARMACEUTICA.** Text in German, English. 1930. q. EUR 140; EUR 35 newsstand/cover (effective 2011). bk.rev. index. **Document type:** *Journal, Academic/Scholarly.* **Description:** Covers all scientific aspects of pharmacy and related disciplines.
Incorporates (1920-1938): Pharmazeutische Monatshefte (0369-9609); (1930-1933): Pharmazeutische Presse - Wissenschaftlich-Praktische Hefte (0370-1387)
Related titles: Online - full text ed.: ISSN 2218-0532. free (effective 2011).
Indexed: A01, A22, A34, A35, A36, AgBio, AgrForAb, BP, C24, C25, C30, C31, C33, CABA, CIN, ChemAb, ChemTitl, DBA, EMBASE, ExcerpMed, F08, F11, F12, GH, H16, I12, MOS, N02, N03, NPU, P20, P30, P32, P33, P39, P40, P48, P54, PGegResA, PGrRegA, PN&I, PQC, R10, R12, R13, RA&MP, RM&VM, Reac, RefZh, S12, S17, SCOPUS, SoyAb, T02, T05, TriticAb, VS, W10.
—BLDSC (8173.000000), CASDDS, GNLM, IE, Infotrieve, Ingenta, INIST, Linda Hall. **CCC.**
Published by: (Oesterreichische Apothekerkammer), Oesterreichische Apotheker-Verlagsgesellschaft mbH, Spitalgasse 31, Vienna, W 1094, Austria. TEL 43-1-4023588, FAX 43-1-4085355, direktion@apoverlag.at, http://www.apoverlag.at. Ed. Dr. Wolfgang Kubelka. Circ: 250.

➤ **SCOTT'S CANADIAN PHARMACISTS DIRECTORY.** *see* BUSINESS AND ECONOMICS—Trade And Industrial Directories

615.19 DEU ISSN 1616-5888
SCREENING; trends in drug discovery. Text in English. 2000. q. EUR 49; EUR 14 newsstand/cover (effective 2009). adv. **Document type:** *Magazine, Trade.* **Description:** Focuses on the latest trends and developments in the field of drug discovery.
—BLDSC (8211.815572), IE.
Published by: G I T Verlag GmbH (Subsidiary of: Wiley - V C H Verlag GmbH & Co. KGaA), Roesslerstr 90, Darmstadt, 64293, Germany. TEL 49-6151-8090, FAX 49-6151-8090146, info@gitverlag.com. Ed. Dr. Martin Friedrich. Adv. contact Nicole Schaefer. B&W page EUR 3,250, color page EUR 4,730; 210 x 297. Circ: 10,000 (controlled).

615 GBR ISSN 0143-7690
CODEN: SCRIDK
SCRIP; world pharmaceutical news. Text in English. 1972. w. GBP 2,195 domestic (print or online ed.); EUR 3,400 in Europe (print or online ed.); USD 4,390 elsewhere (print or online ed.) (effective 2010). adv. bk.rev. 2 cols./p.; back issues avail.; reprints avail. **Document type:** *Newsletter, Trade.* **Description:** Covers company news, product developments politics, market data and regulatory affairs on the international pharmaceutical industry.
Incorporates: Pharmaceutical Business News (0956-0661)
Related titles: Online - full text ed.; ◆ Supplement(s): Scrip's Bio-Pharma Partnering.
Indexed: A22, ABC, Agr, G08, H11, H12, I05, Inpharma, P35, P48, P53, P54, PNI, PQC, R10, Reac.
—BLDSC (8211.859000), CASDDS, GNLM, IE, Infotrieve. **CCC.**
Published by: Informa Healthcare (Subsidiary of: T & F Informa plc), Telephone House, 69-77 Paul St, London, EC2A 4LQ, United Kingdom. TEL 44-20-70175000, FAX 44-20-70176792, healthcare.enquiries@informa.com, http://informahealthcare.com/. Ed. Alexandra Shimmings. Pub. Phil Jarvis. Adv. contact Jennifer Cheng TEL 44-20-70174099. Circ: 4,210. **Subscr. to:** Taylor & Francis Inc., Customer Services Dept, 325 Chestnut St, 8th Fl, Philadelphia, PA 19106. TEL 215-625-8900, 800-354-1420, FAX 215-625-8914, customerservice@taylorandfrancis.com; Taylor & Francis Ltd., Journals Customer Service, Sheepen Pl, Colchester, Essex CO3 3LP, United Kingdom. TEL 44-20-70175544, FAX 44-20-70175198, tf.enquiries@tfinforma.com.

615 GBR
RS1 CODEN: SMAGEY
SCRIP SUPPLEMENT. Text in English. 1992. m. adv. 4 cols./p.; back issues avail.; reprints avail. **Document type:** *Magazine, Trade.* **Description:** Features commentary, trends and analysis on the pharmaceutical industry.
Formerly (until 2006): Scrip Magazine (1353-6303)
Indexed: A22, Inpharma.
—BLDSC (8211.859355), IE, Ingenta. **CCC.**
Published by: Informa Healthcare (Subsidiary of: T & F Informa plc), Telephone House, 69-77 Paul St, London, EC2A 4LQ, United Kingdom. TEL 44-20-70175000, FAX 44-20-70176792, healthcare.enquiries@informa.com, http://informahealthcare.com/. Pub. Phil Jarvis.

615 GBR ISSN 0959-1796
SCRIP'S YEARBOOK (YEAR). Text in English. 1984. a., latest vol.2, 2007, 24th ed. EUR 1,232, USD 1,670, JPY 190,800, GBP 795 per issue (effective 2010). charts; mkt.; stat.; tr.lit. back issues avail. **Document type:** *Yearbook, Trade.* **Description:** Contains company profiles, information on drugs in R&D, market data, background information and essential statistics on a wide range of diseases, and data on country markets.
Related titles: Online - full text ed.: GBP 895, EUR 1,387, USD 1,880, JPY 214,800 per issue (effective 2010).
—**CCC.**
Published by: Informa Healthcare (Subsidiary of: T & F Informa plc), Telephone House, 69-77 Paul St, London, EC2A 4LQ, United Kingdom. TEL 44-20-70175000, FAX 44-20-70176792, healthcare.enquiries@informa.com, http://informahealthcare.com/. Pub. Phil Jarvis. **Subscr. to:** Taylor & Francis Inc., Customer Services Dept, 325 Chestnut St, 8th Fl, Philadelphia, PA 19106. TEL 215-625-8900, 800-354-1420, FAX 215-625-8914, customerservice@taylorandfrancis.com; Taylor & Francis Ltd., Journals Customer Service, Sheepen Pl, Colchester, Essex CO3 3LP, United Kingdom. TEL 44-20-70175544, FAX 44-20-70175198, tf.enquiries@tfinforma.com.

615 USA ISSN 1441-1202
SCRIPTNEWS. Text in English. 1997. q. **Document type:** *Newsletter, Trade.* **Description:** Offers "relationship marketing" through newsletters for the community pharmacy.
Former titles (until 1998): Australian Script Centre. Newsletter (1324-9193); (until 1993): Salamanca National Script Centre. Newsletter; (until 1990): Salamanca Script Resource Centre. Newsletter
Published by: Newsletters Ink, Corp., 473 W 4800 S, Salt Lake Cty, Murray, UT 84123. info@newslettersink.com, http://www.newslettersink.com.

SEMINARS IN HEMATOLOGY. *see* MEDICAL SCIENCES—Hematology

SEMINARS IN ONCOLOGY NURSING. *see* MEDICAL SCIENCES—Nurses And Nursing

615.4 KOR ISSN 0253-3073
RS160 CODEN: SYHJAM
➤ **SENGYAKHAK-HOEJI/KOREAN JOURNAL OF PHARMACOGNOSY.** Text in English, Korean; Summaries in English. 1970. q. membership. adv. bk.rev. 100 p./no.; back issues avail. **Document type:** *Journal, Academic/Scholarly.*
Indexed: A22, A34, AgrForAb, BP, CABA, ChemAb, E12, EMBASE, ExcerpMed, F08, F11, F12, FS&TA, GH, H16, MaizeAb, N02, NPU, P32, PGrRegA, PHN&I, R07, R10, R12, RA&MP, Reac, S12, S17, SCOPUS, SoyAb, TAR, VS.
—BLDSC (5113.572000), CASDDS, GNLM, IE, Ingenta.
Published by: Han'gug Saeng'yag Haghoe/Korean Society of Pharmacognosy, Sahmyook University, 26-21, Gongneung 2-dong Nowon-gu, Seoul, 139-742, Korea, S. TEL 82-2-33991604, sskang@plaza.snu.ac.kr. Ed. Yeong Shik Kim. Circ: 800.

615 USA ISSN 2153-148X
▼ **SENTINEL MAGAZINE**; ISI's communicatiom forum for pharmaceutical regulatory professionals. Text in English. 2009. q. **Document type:** *Magazine, Trade.* **Description:** Covers issues for the life sciences industry and global regulators.
Related titles: Online - full text ed.: ISSN 2153-1501. free (effective 2010).
Published by: I S I Inc., 100 S Jefferson Rd, Whippany, NJ 07981. TEL 973-560-0404, FAX 973-560-0240, info@imagesolutions.com, http://www.imagesolutions.com. Ed. Kim Ribbink. Pub. Lisa Meyer.

615 338.476 GBR ISSN 2046-2468
▼ **SERBIA PHARMACEUTICALS & HEALTHCARE REPORT.** Text in English. 2010. q. USD 975, EUR 695 combined subscription (print & email eds.) (effective 2011). **Document type:** *Report, Trade.* **Description:** Provides industry professionals, market investors and corporate and financial services analysts with independent forecasts and competitive intelligence on the Serbian pharmaceutical & healthcare industry.
Related titles: E-mail ed.
Published by: Business Monitor International Ltd., Senator House, 85 Queen Victoria St, London, EC4V 4AB, United Kingdom. TEL 44-20-72480468, FAX 44-20-72480467, subs@businessmonitor.com.

SHAANXI ZHONGYI XUEYUAN XUEBAO/SHAANXI INSTITUTE OF TRADITIONAL CHINESE MEDICINE. JOURNAL. *see* MEDICAL SCIENCES

SHANGHAI YIYAO/SHANGHAI MEDICAL & PHARMACEUTICAL JOURNAL. *see* MEDICAL SCIENCES

SHANGHAI ZHONGYIYAO ZAZHI/REVISTA DE MEDICINA TRADICIONAL CHINA DE SHANGHAI/REVUE DE MEDECINE TRADITIONNELLE CHINOISE/SHANGHAI JOURNAL OF TRADITIONAL CHINESE MEDICINE. *see* ALTERNATIVE MEDICINE

615 CHN ISSN 0253-9926
R97.7.C5 CODEN: SIYCDB
➤ **SHANXI YIYAO ZAZHI/SHANXI MEDICAL JOURNAL.** Text in Chinese; Summaries in English. 1957. bi-m. USD 72 (effective 2009). adv. abstr.; bibl.; charts; maps; stat. back issues avail. **Document type:** *Journal, Academic/Scholarly.* **Description:** Offers reports, reviews, and columns, along with editorials, original articles, experimental studies, and clinical studies on quickening the blood and transforming stasis, diagnostic imaging, medical eletrophysiology, pharmaceutical reports, elementary knowledge forum, and clinical nursing cases reporting.
Related titles: CD-ROM ed.; Fax ed.; Online - full text ed.
—BLDSC (8254.601590), CASDDS, East View.
Published by: Zhonghua Yixuehui, Shanxi Fenhui/Chinese Medical Association, Shanxi Branch, 23 Donghuamen, Taiyuan, Shanxi 030013, China. TEL 86-351-3580183, FAX 86-351-3173607. Ed., R&P, Adv. contact Haiyuan Dong TEL 86-351-3071551 ext 2153. Circ: 8,500 (paid); 200 (controlled). **Dist. by:** China International Book Trading Corp, 35 Chegongzhuang Xilu, Haidian District, PO Box 399, Beijing 100044, China. TEL 86-10-68412045, FAX 86-10-68412023, cibtc@mail.cibtc.com.cn, http://www.cibtc.com.cn.

615 CHN ISSN 1006-2858
CODEN: SYXUE3
➤ **SHENYANG YAOKE DAXUE XUEBAO/SHENYANG PHARMACEUTICAL UNIVERSITY. JOURNAL.** Text in Chinese. 1957. bi-m. USD 49.20 (effective 2009). adv. abstr. 80 p./no.; **Document type:** *Journal, Academic/Scholarly.* **Description:** Contains research reports on pharmaceutics, pharmaceutical analysis, pharmaceutical chemistry, pharmacology, traditional Chinese medicine and synthesis of drugs.
Formerly (until 1995): Shenyang Yaoxueyuan Xuebao/ Shenyang College of Pharmacy. Journal (1000-1727)
Related titles: Online - full text ed.
Indexed: ChemAb, ChemTitl.
—BLDSC (4874.937000), CASDDS, East View, GNLM.
Published by: Shenyang Yaoke Daxue, 103 Wenhua Rd, Shenyang, Liaoning 110016, China. adv.: page USD 1,200; trim 208 x 297. Circ: 2,200. **Dist. by:** China International Book Trading Corp, 35 Chegongzhuang Xilu, Haidian District, PO Box 399, Beijing 100044, China. TEL 86-10-68412045, FAX 86-10-68412023, cibtc@mail.cibtc.com.cn, http://www.cibtc.com.cn.

615 CHN ISSN 1672-9188
SHIJIE LINCHUANG YAOWU/WORLD CLINICAL DRUGS. Text in Chinese. 1980. m. USD 138 (effective 2009). **Document type:** *Journal, Academic/Scholarly.*
Former titles: Guowai Yiyao (Hechengyao, Shenghuayao, Zhiji Fence) (1001-8247); (until 1989): Guowai Yaoxue (Hechengyao Shenghuayao Zhiji Fence) (1000-8233)
Related titles: Online - full text ed.
—BLDSC (8256.502500), East View.
Published by: Shanghai Yiyao Gongye Yanjiuyuan/Shanghai Institute of Pharmaceutical Industry, 1320 Beijing Xilu, Shanghai, 200040, China. TEL 86-21-62894305, FAX 86-21-62890581. **Dist. by:** China International Book Trading Corp, 35 Chegongzhuang Xilu, Haidian District, PO Box 399, Beijing 100044, China. TEL 86-10-68412045, FAX 86-10-68412023, cibtc@mail.cibtc.com.cn, http://www.cibtc.com.cn.

615.7 JPN ISSN 0288-1012
CODEN: SYRYEJ
SHIKA YAKUBUTSU RYOHO/ORAL THERAPEUTICS AND PHARMACOLOGY. Text in Japanese. 1982. s-a. JPY 7,000 membership (effective 2006). **Document type:** *Journal, Academic/Scholarly.*
Indexed: A22, ChemAb, ChemTitl, EMBASE, ExcerpMed, R10, Reac, SCOPUS.
—BLDSC (6277.802000), CASDDS, GNLM, IE, Ingenta.
Published by: Shika Yakubutsu Ryoho Kenkyukai/Japanese Society of Oral Therapeutics and Pharmacology, c/o Hitotsubashi Printing Co., Ltd., 2-4-11 Fukagawa Kotoku, Tokyo, 135-0033, Japan. TEL 81-3-56201953, FAX 81-3-56201960, http://www.jsotp.org/.

SHINRYO NAIKA/PSYCHOSOMATIC MEDICINE. *see* MEDICAL SCIENCES—Psychiatry And Neurology

SHIPIN YU YAOPIN/FOOD AND DRUG. *see* FOOD AND FOOD INDUSTRIES

615.328 615.5 CHN ISSN 1008-0805
SHIZHEN GUOYI GUOYAO/LISHIZHEN MEDICINE AND MATERIA MEDICA RESEARCH. Text in Chinese; Abstracts in Chinese, English. 1990. m. USD 80.40 (effective 2009). adv. **Document type:** *Journal, Academic/Scholarly.* **Description:** Researches Li Shizhen, the reknowned ancient Chinese physician. Covers the pharmacology of traditional Chinese medicine and its clinical applications. Also examines the preparation of and recipes for traditional herbal medicines, along with modern medical research.
Formerly (until 1998): Shizhen Guoyao Yanjiu/Shizhen Journal of Traditional Chinese Medicine Research (1004-0919)
Related titles: Online - full text ed.
—BLDSC (8267.370230), East View.
Published by: Hubei Sheng Huangshi Shi Weishengju, 874, Huangshi Dadao, Huangshi, 435000, China. Ed. Xiao Peigen. Pub. Zhu Baohua. R&P, Adv. contact Baohua Zhu. page USD 4,000. Circ: 10,000 (paid); 3,000 (controlled). **Dist. by:** China International Book Trading Corp, 35 Chegongzhuang Xilu, Haidian District, PO Box 399, Beijing 100044, China. TEL 86-10-68412045, FAX 86-10-68412023, cibtc@mail.cibtc.com.cn, http://www.cibtc.com.cn.

615 510 CHN ISSN 1004-4337
SHULI YIYAOXUE ZAZHI/JOURNAL OF MATHEMATICAL PHARMACY. Text in Chinese. 1988. bi-m. USD 31.20 (effective 2009). **Document type:** *Journal, Academic/Scholarly.*
Related titles: Online - full text ed.
—East View.
Published by: Wuhan Daxue Yixueyuan, 115, Donghu Lu, Wuhan, 430071, China. TEL 86-27-87331117, FAX 86-27-87640256. **Dist. by:** China International Book Trading Corp, 35 Chegongzhuang Xilu, Haidian District, PO Box 399, Beijing 100044, China. TEL 86-10-68412045, FAX 86-10-68412023, cibtc@mail.cibtc.com.cn, http://www.cibtc.com.cn.

615.1 340 DEU ISSN 0947-269X
SICHERHEITSVORSCHRIFTEN FUER MEDIZINPRODUKTE. Text in German. 1994. base vol. plus a. updates. EUR 76 base vol(s).; EUR 56.80 updates per issue (effective 2009). **Document type:** *Monographic series, Trade.*
Published by: Erich Schmidt Verlag GmbH & Co. (Berlin), Genthiner Str 30 G, Berlin, 10785, Germany. TEL 49-30-2500850, FAX 49-30-250085305, esv@esvmedien.de, http://www.erich-schmidt-verlag.de.

SICHUAN DAXUE XUEBAO (YIXUE BAN)/SICHUAN UNIVERSITY. JOURNAL (MEDICAL SCIENCE EDITION). *see* MEDICAL SCIENCES

615.7 NLD ISSN 0378-6080
RM302.5 CODEN: SEDAD8
➤ **SIDE EFFECTS OF DRUGS ANNUAL**; a yearly critical survey of the world's literature on adverse reactions to drugs. Text in Dutch. 1972. a., latest vol.30, 2008. price varies. **Document type:** *Monographic series, Academic/Scholarly.*
Related titles: CD-ROM ed.; Online - full text ed.; ◆ Supplement to: Meyler's Side Effects of Drugs. ISSN 0376-7396.
Indexed: A22, SCOPUS.
—CASDDS, GNLM, IE, Ingenta, INIST. **CCC.**
Published by: Elsevier BV (Subsidiary of: Elsevier Science & Technology), Radarweg 29, PO Box 211, Amsterdam, 1000 AE, Netherlands. TEL 31-20-4853911, FAX 31-20-4852457, JournalsCustomerServiceEMEA@elsevier.com, http://www.elsevier.nl. Ed. Jeffrey K Aronson.

615.7 CHE ISSN 1660-5527
RL801 CODEN: SPPKE6
➤ **SKIN PHARMACOLOGY AND PHYSIOLOGY**; journal of pharmacological and biophysical research. Text in English. 1988. bi-m. CHF 1,596, EUR 1,275, USD 1,570.50 to institutions; CHF 1,751, EUR 1,399, USD 1,720.50 combined subscription to institutions (print & online eds.) (effective 2012). adv. bk.rev. charts; illus. index. back issues avail. **Document type:** *Journal, Academic/Scholarly.* **Description:** Includes articles on skin pharmacology, immunosuppressive topicals, and new strategies in the therapy of malignant melanoma and wound healing.
Former titles (until 2004): Skin Pharmacology and Applied Skin Physiology (1422-2868); (until 1998): Skin Pharmacology (1011-0283); Which incorporated (1985-1990): Bioengineering and the Skin (0266-3082)
Related titles: Microform ed.: (from PQC); Online - full text ed.: ISSN 1660-5535. CHF 1,545, EUR 1,236, USD 1,500 to institutions (effective 2012).
Indexed: A01, A03, A08, A22, ASCA, B25, BIOSIS Prev, C24, CA, ChemAb, ChemTitl, CurCont, DBA, E01, EMBASE, ExcerpMed, ISR, IndMed, Inpharma, MEDLINE, MS&D, MycolAb, P20, P22, P30, P35, P48, P54, PQC, R10, Reac, SCI, SCOPUS, T02, W07.

—BLDSC (8295.938500), CASDDS, GNLM, IE, Infotrieve, Ingenta, INIST. **CCC.**
Published by: (Skin Pharmacology Society), S. Karger AG, Allschwilerstr 10, Basel, 4055, Switzerland. TEL 41-61-3061111, FAX 41-61-3061234, karger@karger.ch, http://www.karger.ch. Ed. J. Lademann. R&P Tatjana Sepin. adv.: page CHF 1,815; trim 210 x 280. Circ: 800 (controlled).

615.19 616.89 USA
SMART LIFE NEWS. Text in English. 1992. 10/yr. USD 119 72 issues (vol.1, no.1 through vol.8 no.2) (effective 2007). bk.rev. illus. **Document type:** *Newsletter, Consumer.* **Description:** Provides information on improving mental performance, increasing energy and alleviating symptoms of aging. It also includes special sections dealing with Alzheimer's, Down's Syndrome and Parkinson's Disease.
Formerly: Smart Drug News (1060-8427)
Related titles: Online - full text ed.: USD 49 36 issues (effective 2007).
Indexed: E-psyche.
Published by: Cognitive Enhancement Research Institute, PO Box 4029, Menlo Park, CA 94026. TEL 650-321-2374, FAX 650-323-3864, http://www.ceri.com. Ed. Steven W Fowkes.

615.9 658 ESP ISSN 1130-8230
SOCIEDAD ESPANOLA DE FARMACIA HOSPITALARIA. BOLETIN INFORMATIVO. Cover title: Boletin Informativo - S E F H. Text in Spanish. q. **Document type:** *Bulletin, Trade.*
Formerly (until 1989): Asociacion Espanola de Farmaceuticos de Hospitales. Boletin Informativo (1130-8222)
Related titles: Online - full text ed.
Published by: Sociedad Espanola de Farmacia Hospitalaria, General Orgaz 23, 1o A, Madrid, 28020, Spain. TEL 34-91-5714487, FAX 34-91-5714586, sefh@sefh.es.

615 BRA ISSN 1808-4540
SOCIEDADE BRASILEIRA DE FARMACIA HOSPITALAR. REVISTA. Text in Portuguese. 2003. s-m. **Document type:** *Magazine, Trade.*
Published by: Sociedade Brasileira de Farmacia Hospitalar (S B R A F H), Rua Vergueiro 1855, 12o Andar, VI. Mariana, Sao Paulo, SP 04101-000, Brazil. TEL 55-11-50834297.

615.1 ITA ISSN 0037-8798
RS1 CODEN: BSFOB3
SOCIETA ITALIANA DI FARMACIA OSPEDALIERA. BOLLETTINO. Text in Italian. 1955. bi-m. EUR 130 domestic to institutions; EUR 200 foreign to institutions (effective 2009). adv. bk.rev. charts; illus.; stat. 64 p./no.; reprints avail. **Document type:** *Journal, Academic/Scholarly.*
Related titles: Online - full text ed.: ISSN 2038-1786 (from PQC).
Indexed: A22, ChemAb, DBA, I12.
—BLDSC (2231.200000), CASDDS, GNLM, IE, Ingenta, INIST. **CCC.**
Published by: (Societa Italiana di Farmacia Ospedaliera), Il Pensiero Scientifico Editore, Via Bradano 3-C, Rome, 00199, Italy. TEL 39-06-862821, FAX 39-06-86282250, pensiero@pensiero.it, http://www.pensiero.it.

615 NLD ISSN 1566-7685
SOLVAY PHARMACEUTICALS CONFERENCES. Text in English. 2000. a. price varies. **Document type:** *Monographic series, Academic/Scholarly.*
Related titles: Online - full text ed.: ISSN 1879-8306.
—BLDSC (8327.805700), IE.
Published by: I O S Press, Nieuwe Hemweg 6B, Amsterdam, 1013 BG, Netherlands. TEL 31-20-6883355, FAX 31-20-6870039, info@iospress.nl. **Dist. by:** Ohmsha Ltd, 3-1 Kanda Nishiki-cho, Chiyoda-ku, Tokyo 101-8460, Japan. TEL 86-3-32330643, FAX 86-3-32936224.

615 NZL ISSN 1174-2704
RS122
➤ **SOUTHERN MED REVIEW.** Text in English. 2008. s-a. free (effective 2011). Index. back issues avail. **Document type:** *Journal, Academic/Scholarly.* **Description:** Provides a platform for researchers to disseminate commentary and empirical research findings, with a view to improving the rational use of and access to essential medicines.
Media: Online - full text. **Related titles:** E-mail ed.
Indexed: A01, A26, A36, CA, CABA, E12, GH, H12, I05, N02, P33, PHN&I, R08, R12, RA&MP, SCOPUS, T02, T05, TAR, W11.
Published by: Zaheer Babar, Ed. & Pub., c/o Dr Zaheer Babar, School of Pharmacy, University of Auckland, Private Bag 92019, Auckland, 1142, New Zealand. TEL 64-9-3737599 ext 88436, FAX 64-9-3677192. Ed., Pub., R&P Zaheer Babar.

615 USA ISSN 1555-6727
HD9666.1
SPECIALTY PHARMA; strategies for business development. Text in English. 2005. bi-m. free domestic to qualified personnel; USD 99 in Canada & Mexico; USD 153 elsewhere; USD 20 per issue (effective 2006). adv. **Document type:** *Magazine, Trade.*
Related titles: Online - full text ed.: ISSN 1555-6735.
Address: 219 Changebridge Rd, Montvale, NJ 07045. TEL 973-299-1200, FAX 973-299-7937, rvitaro@specialtypharma.com. Ed. Cindy Dubin TEL 248-618-8404. Pub. Ralph Vitaro. Adv. contact Victoria Geis TEL 703-212-7735. B&W page USD 3,555, color page USD 4,890; trim 8.125 x 10.875. Circ: 12,000 (controlled).

615 USA ISSN 1937-6685
SPECIALTY PHARMACY NEWS; news and strategies for managing high-cost biotech and injectable products. Abbreviated title: S P N. Text in English. 2004. m. USD 495 combined subscription (print & email eds.) (effective 2008). adv. **Document type:** *Newsletter, Trade.* **Description:** Designed to help health plans, PBMs, providers and employers manage costs more aggressively and deliver biotechs and injectables more effectively.
Related titles: E-mail ed.; Online - full text ed.: ISSN 1937-6723.
Published by: Atlantic Information Services, Inc., 1100 17th St, NW, Ste 300, Washington, DC 20036. TEL 202-775-9008, 800-521-4323, FAX 202-331-9542, customerserv@aispub.com. Adv. contact Bailey Sterrett.

615 DEU
SPEKTRUM. Text in German. bi-m. EUR 30; EUR 5 newsstand/cover (effective 2006). adv. **Document type:** *Magazine, Trade.*
Published by: (Landesapothekerverband Niedersachsen e.V.), Signum-Kom Agentur fuer Kommunikation GmbH, Richard-Wagner-Str 18, Cologne, 50674, Germany. TEL 49-221-9255512, FAX 49-221-9255513, kontakt@signum-kom.de, http://www.signum-kom.de. Ed. Tina Gerstenkorn. Adv. contact Monika Gloecklhofer. color page EUR 1,990; trim 210 x 297. Circ: 3,500 (paid and controlled).

615.1 NLD ISSN 2210-2035
SPREEKUUR FARMACIE. Text in Dutch. 2000. q. free to qualified personnel (effective 2010). adv. **Document type:** *Journal, Trade.*
Formerly (until 2010): Apothekers Vademecum (1566-7480)
Published by: Bohn Stafleu van Loghum B.V. (Subsidiary of: Springer Science+Business Media), Postbus 246, Houten, 3990 GA, Netherlands. TEL 31-30-6383872, FAX 31-30-6383991, boekhandels@bsl.nl, http://www.bsl.nl. adv.: color page EUR 3,268; trim 210 x 297. Circ: 1,352.

615 BGD ISSN 1999-7108
STAMFORD JOURNAL OF PHARMACEUTICAL SCIENCES. Text in English. 2008. s-a. free (effective 2011). **Document type:** *Journal, Academic/Scholarly.*
Media: Online - full text.
Published by: Stamford University, Department of Pharmacy, 51 Siddeswari Road, Dhaka, 1217, Bangladesh. Ed. Abdul Ghani.

STANDARDS FOR THE PRACTICE OF THERAPEUTIC RECREATION. *see* MEDICAL SCIENCES

615.1 USA ISSN 1946-6315
▼ **STATISTICS IN BIOPHARMACEUTICAL RESEARCH.** Abbreviated title: S B R. Text in English. 2009. q. GBP 86 in United Kingdom to institutions; EUR 114, USD 142 to institutions (effective 2012). back issues avail. **Document type:** *Journal, Academic/Scholarly.* **Description:** Publishes articles that focus on the needs of researchers and applied statisticians in biopharmaceutical industries.
Media: Online - full content.
Indexed: P30.
—**CCC.**
Published by: American Statistical Association, 732 N Washington St, Alexandria, VA 22314. TEL 703-684-1221, 888-231-3473, FAX 703-684-2037, asainfo@amstat.org, http://www.amstat.org. Ed. Joseph F Heyse.

LES STATISTIQUES PROFESSIONNELLES PHARMACIE (YEAR). *see* BUSINESS AND ECONOMICS—Production Of Goods And Services

615.3 GBR
STOCKLEY'S DRUG INTERACTIONS. Text in English. 1981. a. GBP 145 per issue (print or CD-ROM ed.); GBP 205 combined subscription per issue (print & CD-ROM eds.) (effective 2011). adv. **Document type:** *Directory, Trade.* **Description:** Provides a series of detailed yet concise monographs containing a summary, details of the interaction under discussion, its probable mechanism, clinical importance and management.
Related titles: CD-ROM ed.; Online - full text ed.: ISSN 1752-3605. USD 325 per issue (effective 2010).
Published by: Pharmaceutical Press (Subsidiary of: Royal Pharmaceutical Society of Great Britain), 1 Lambeth High St, London, SE1 7JN, United Kingdom. TEL 44-20-75722665, FAX 44-20-75722509, pharmpress@macmillansolutions.com. Pub. Lindsey Fountain TEL 44-20-75722655.

615.10711 USA ISSN 1559-7210
STUDENT PHARMACIST; newsmagazine of the nation's student pharmacists. Text in English. 1976 (vol.7). bi-m. free to members (effective 2009). adv. back issues avail.; reprints avail. **Document type:** *Magazine, Academic/Scholarly.* **Description:** Designed to help the PharmD candidates regarding their pharmacy career planning.
Former titles (until 2005): Pharmacy Student (0279-5272); (until vol.8,1978): S A Ph A News
Related titles: Online - full text ed.
—**CCC.**
Published by: American Pharmacists Association, 2215 Constitution Ave, NW, Washington, DC 20037. TEL 202-628-4410, FAX 202-783-2351, InfoCenter@aphanet.org, http://www.japha.org. Pub. Frank Bennicasa. Adv. contact Kristin Hodges TEL 202-429-7583. B&W page USD 3,050, color page USD 4,640; trim 7.75 x 10.5. Circ: 21,832. **Subscr. to:** PO Box 11806, Birmingham, AL 35202. TEL 800-633-4931, FAX 205-995-1588, japha@subscriptionoffice.com.

615.1071 DEU ISSN 0721-8672
STUDENT UND PRAKTIKANT; Forum fuer die Pharmazeutische Ausbildung. Text in German. 1982. irreg. adv. bk.rev. **Document type:** *Journal, Trade.*
Related titles: ◆ Supplement to: Deutsche Apotheker Zeitung. ISSN 0011-9857.
—BLDSC (8480.100000), GNLM.
Published by: Deutscher Apotheker Verlag, Postfach 101061, Stuttgart, 70009, Germany. TEL 49-711-25820, FAX 49-711-2582290, http://www.deutscher-apotheker-verlag.de. Ed. Wolfgang Caesar.

615.9 UKR ISSN 1609-0446
➤ **SUCHASNI PROBLEMY TOKSYKOLOHII/SOVREMENNYE PROBLEMY TOKSIKOLOGII.** Text in Ukrainian, Russian. 1998. q. **Document type:** *Journal, Academic/Scholarly.*
Related titles: Online - full text ed.: ISSN 1609-0470.
Indexed: RefZh.
—East View.
Published by: (Instytut Ekohihieny i Toksykolohii, Akademiya Medychnykh Nauk Ukrainy, Instytut Farmakolohii i Toksykolohii/ Academy of Medical Sciences of Ukraine, Institute of Pharmacology and Toxicology, Tovarystvo Toksykolohiv Ukrainy), Vydavnytsvo Medytsyna Ukrainy, vul Popudrenka, 34, Kyiv, Ukraine. TEL 380-44-5740756, FAX 380-44-5529502. Ed. E I Levyts'kyi.

615.9 340 USA ISSN 1559-4262
KF2915.P4
SURVEY OF PHARMACY LAW (CD-ROM). Text in English. 1950. a. USD 195 per issue (effective 2010). stat.; charts. back issues avail. **Document type:** *Report, Trade.*
Formerly (until 2004): Survey of Pharmacy Law (Print) (0098-714X)
Media: CD-ROM.
Published by: National Association of Boards of Pharmacy, 1600 Feehanville Dr, Mount Prospect, IL 60056. TEL 847-391-4406, FAX 847-391-4502, custserv@nabp.net.

615.1 SWE
SVENSK FARMACI. Text in Swedish. 1902. 6/yr. SEK 500 (effective 2011). adv. bk.rev. **Document type:** *Magazine, Trade.*
Formerly (until 2011): Farmacevtisk Revy (0014-8210)
Related titles: Online - full text ed.
Indexed: ChemAb, P30.
—GNLM, Linda Hall.
Published by: Sveriges Farmacevtfoerbund/Swedish Pharmaceutical Association, Vasagatan 48, Box 3215, Stockholm, 10364, Sweden. TEL 46-8-50799900, FAX 46-8-50799999, post@farmacevtforbundet.se, http://www.farmacevtforbundet.se. Ed. Nils Bergeaa-Nygren TEL 46-8-50799913. Adv. contact Ingrid Bilkenroth TEL 46-8-50799902. Circ: 6,250 (controlled).

615 610 GBR ISSN 2044-5660
SWEDEN PHARMACEUTICALS & HEALTHCARE REPORT. Text in English. 200?. q. EUR 820, USD 1,150 combined subscription (print & email eds.) (effective 2010). **Document type:** *Report, Trade.* **Description:** Provides industry professionals, market investors and corporate and financial services analysts with independent forecasts and competitive intelligence on the Swedish pharmaceutical and healthcare industry.
Related titles: E-mail ed.
Published by: Business Monitor International Ltd., Senator House, 85 Queen Victoria St, London, EC4V 4AB, United Kingdom. TEL 44-20-72480468, FAX 44-20-72480467, subs@businessmonitor.com.

615 POL ISSN 1734-4506
SWIAT FARMACJI. Text in Polish. 2004. a. **Document type:** *Magazine, Trade.*
Published by: Wydawnictwo Apteka, ul Szewska 3a, Wroclaw, Poland. TEL 48-71-3699330, FAX 48-71-3699331, info@wydawnictwoapteka.pl, http://www.otcindeks.pl.

615.1 POL ISSN 1508-1850
SWIAT MEDYCYNY I FARMACJI; medyczny miesiecznik specjalistyczny dla lekarzy i farmaceutow. Text in Polish. 1999. m. PLZ 72 domestic (effective 2006). **Document type:** *Magazine, Trade.*
Published by: Agencja Reklamowa Lion-Art, ul Staromiejska 2/13, Katowice, 40013, Poland. TEL 48-32-2016016, info@lion-art.com.pl.

615 CHE ISSN 0251-1673
SWISS PHARMA; Schweizerische Zeitschrift fuer die pharmazeutische industrie. Text in German, English. 1979. 10/yr. CHF 180 domestic; CHF 200 in Europe; CHF 340 elsewhere; CHF 50 newsstand/cover elsewhere (effective 2005). adv. back issues avail. **Document type:** *Journal, Trade.* **Description:** Publishes original selected papers and interviews with top leaders in pharmaceutical production in Switzerland.
Indexed: A22.
—GNLM, IE, INIST. **CCC.**
Published by: Verlag Dr. Felix Wuest AG, Kuesnachterstr 36, Postfach 161, Zumikon, 8126, Switzerland. TEL 41-1-9198060, FAX 41-1-9198069. Ed., Pub., Adv. contact Dr. Felix Wuest. B&W page CHF 1,750, color page CHF 3,460; trim 185 x 265. Circ: 1,000 (paid).

SWISSMEDIC JOURNAL/OFFICE INTERCANTONAL DE CONTROLE DE MEDICAMENTS. BULLETIN MENSUEL/UFFICIO INTERCANTONALE DI CONTROLLO DEI MEDICAMENTI. BOLLETTINO MENSILE. *see* MEDICAL SCIENCES

610 CHE ISSN 0082-0504
SWITZERLAND. BUNDESAMT FUER SOZIALVERSICHERUNG. SPEZIALITAETENLISTE - LISTE DES SPECIALITES - ELENCO DELLE SPECIALITA. Text in French, German, Italian. 1955. a. CHF 34 (effective 2000). **Document type:** *Catalog, Government.* **Description:** List of drugs being reimbursed by Swiss sickness insurers.
Related titles: CD-ROM ed.
Published by: Bundesamt fuer Sozialversicherung, Effingerstr 20, Bern, 3003, Switzerland. TEL 41-31-3229011, FAX 41-31-3227880, info@bsv.admin.ch. Ed. Reinhard Kampf. Circ: 24,000. **Dist. by:** Bundesamt fur Bauten und Logistik, Effingerstr 33, Bern 3003, Switzerland. TEL 41-31-3223908, FAX 41-31-9920023.

615 IND ISSN 0975-8453
▼ **SYSTEMATIC REVIEWS IN PHARMACY.** Text in English. 2009. s-a. INR 3,500 domestic; USD 500 foreign (effective 2010). bk.rev. abstr. **Document type:** *Journal, Academic/Scholarly.*
Related titles: Online - full text ed.: ISSN 0976-2779.
Indexed: A01, P10, P48, P53, P54, PQC, T02.
—**CCC.**
Published by: Medknow Publications and Media Pvt. Ltd., B-9, Kanara Business Ctr, Off Link Rd, Ghatkopar (E), Mumbai, Maharastra 400 075, India. TEL 91-22-66491816, 91-22-66491818, publishing@medknow.com, http://www.medknow.com. Ed. Mueen Ahmed KK. Pub. Dr. D K Sahu. Adv. contact Kaushik Shah. Circ: 500.

615 JPN ISSN 0911-1026
T D M KENKYU/JAPANESE JOURNAL OF THERAPEUTIC DRUG MONITORING. (Therapeutic Drug Monitoring) Text in Japanese. 1984. s-a. **Document type:** *Journal, Academic/Scholarly.*
—BLDSC (4658.866500).
Published by: Nihon TDM Gakkai/Japan Society for Therapeutic Drug Monitoring, Kobe University Graduate School of Medicine, Department of Pharmacy, 7-5-1 Kusunoki-cho, Chuo-ku, Kobe, 650-0017, Japan. TEL 81-78-3825111ext 6668, FAX 81-78-3826678.

615 AUS ISSN 1325-8559
T G A NEWS. Text in English. 1995. 3/yr. free (effective 2008). back issues avail. **Document type:** *Newsletter, Government.*
Incorporates (1995-2001): Australian Therapeutic Device Bulletin (Online) (1325-8567)
Media: Online - full content. **Related titles:** ◆ Print ed.: T G A News (Print Edition). ISSN 1327-6662.
Published by: Australian Government. Department of Health and Ageing. Therapeutic Goods Administration, PO Box 100, Woden, ACT 2606, Australia. TEL 61-2-62328610, FAX 61-2-62328605, info@health.gov.au.

615 AUS ISSN 1327-6662
T G A NEWS (PRINT EDITION). (Therapeutic Goods Administration) Text in English. 1995. 3/yr. **Document type:** *Newsletter, Trade.*
Incorporates (1987-2001): Australian Therapeutic Device Bulletin (Print) (1031-8542); Which was formerly (1987-1987): Therapeutic Device Bulletin (1030-1933)
Related titles: ◆ Online - full content ed.: T G A News. ISSN 1325-8559.

P

Published by: Australian Government. Department of Health and Ageing. Therapeutic Goods Administration, PO Box 100, Woden, ACT 2606, Australia. TEL 61-2-62328610, 61-2-62328444, FAX 61-2-62328605, info@health.gov.au.

615 DEU
T V APOTHEKE. Text in German. 1994. m. adv. **Document type:** *Magazine, Consumer.*
Published by: Intermed Verlagsgesellschaft mbH, Woerth Str 3, Fulda, 36037, Germany. TEL 49-661-94960, FAX 49-661-949630, info@intermedverlag.de. adv.: B&W page EUR 12,271, color page EUR 14,801. Circ: 269,000 (paid and controlled).

615 USA ISSN 1549-9928
TABLETS AND CAPSULES. Text in English. 2004. bi-m. free to qualified personnel (effective 2010). adv. back issues avail. **Document type:** *Magazine, Trade.* **Description:** Devoted exclusively to readers in the tablet and capsule processing industries.
Related titles: Online - full text ed.: ISSN 1938-9159. free to qualified personnel (effective 2010).
Published by: C S C Publishing, Inc., 1155 Northland Dr, Saint Paul, MN 55120. TEL 651-287-5600, FAX 651-287-5650, info@cscpub.com, http://cscpublishinginc.com. Eds. Emily Nystrom, Matthew Knopp. Pub. Richard R Cress TEL 651-287-5601.

615 615.1021 DNK ISSN 0107-1181
TAL OG DATA, MEDICIN OG SUNDHEDSVAESEN/FACTS, MEDICINE AND HEALTH CARE, DENMARK. Text in Danish, English. 1976. irreg. free. illus. **Document type:** *Journal, Consumer.*
Formerly (until 1978): Tal og Data om Medicin (0900-3444)
Related titles: Online - full content ed.: ISSN 1398-5574. 1997.
Published by: Laegemiddelindustriforeningen/Association of Danish Pharmaceutical Industry, Stroedamvej 50 A, Copenhagen Oe, 2100, Denmark. TEL 45-39-276060, FAX 45-39-276070, info@tifdk.dk, http://www.tifdk.dk.

615.1 NOR ISSN 1503-352X
TALL OG FAKTA/FIGURES AND FACTS. DRUGS AND HEALTH CARE; legemidler og helsevesen. Text in English, Norwegian. 1990. a. stat. **Document type:** *Report, Consumer.*
Formerly (until 2000): Legemidler og Helsevesen (1501-8059)
Related titles: Online - full text ed.: ISSN 1503-8149.
Published by: Legemiddelindustriforeningen/Norwegian Association of Pharmaceutical Manufacturers, PO Box 5094, Majorstuen, Oslo, 0301, Norway. TEL 47-23-161500, FAX 47-23-161501, lmi@lmi.no.

615 USA ISSN 1530-1206
THE TAN SHEET; nonprescription pharmaceuticals and nutritionals. Text in English. 1939. w. USD 1,795 in United States to institutions; USD 1,795 elsewhere to institutions (effective 2012). charts; illus.; stat.; tr.lit. back issues avail.; reprints avail. **Document type:** *Newsletter, Trade.* **Description:** Provides in-depth coverage of nonprescription pharmaceuticals and dietary supplement-nutritionals.
Formerly (until 2000): F D C Reports. Nonprescription Pharmaceuticals and Nutritionals: The Tan Sheet (1068-5316); Which superseded in part (in 1993): F D C Reports. Prescription and O T C Pharmaceuticals: The Pink Sheet (0734-6514); Which was formerly (until 1982): F D C Reports. Ethical and O T C Pharmaceuticals (0272-913X)
Related titles: Online - full text ed.
—CCC.
Published by: Elsevier Business Intelligence (Subsidiary of: Elsevier Health Sciences), 5635 Fishers Ln, Ste 6000, Rockville, MD 20852. TEL 800-332-2181, FAX 240-221-4400, http://www.fdcreports.com. Ed. Michael McCaughan.

615.9 FRA ISSN 1764-092X
TAREX. Text in French. 1969. a., latest 2009 plus q. updates. looseleaf. EUR 107.64 domestic; EUR 109 in Europe; EUR 115 elsewhere (effective 2010). adv. bk.rev. **Document type:** *Trade.*
Related titles: Microfiche ed.; Optical Disk - DVD ed.: ISSN 1773-1348. 199?.
Published by: Vidal S.A., 21 rue Camille Desmoulins, Issy les Moulineaux Cedex 9, 92789, France. TEL 33-1-73281100, 33-8-20901345, http://www.vidal.fr.

TARGET ORGAN TOXICOLOGY SERIES. *see* ENVIRONMENTAL STUDIES—Toxicology And Environmental Safety

615 ITA ISSN 1827-3718
TEMA FARMACIA; rivista di formazione e aggiornamento professionale. Text in Italian. 1983. 11/yr. EUR 45 domestic; EUR 90 in Europe; EUR 110 elsewhere (effective 2011). adv. **Document type:** *Magazine, Trade.*
Related titles: Online - full text ed.
Published by: Tecniche Nuove SpA, Via Eritrea 21, Milan, MI 20121, Italy. TEL 39-02-390901, FAX 39-02-7570364, info@tecnichenuove.com. Ed. Mercedes Bradaschia. Circ: 163,100.

615.19 USA ISSN 1047-0166
RS1
TENNESSEE PHARMACIST. Text in English. 1965. q. free to members. adv. bk.rev. **Document type:** *Newsletter, Trade.*
Published by: Tennessee Pharmacists Association, 500 Church St., Ste 650, Nashville, TN 37219. TEL 615-256-3023, FAX 615-255-3528, tpa@tnpharm.org, http://www.tnpharm.org. Ed. Baeteena Black. Adv. contact Marcia Williams. Circ: 2,500.

TEXAS PHARMACY LAWS AND REGULATIONS. *see* LAW

615 FRA ISSN 1638-2110
THERA. Text in French. 1984. a., latest vol.21, 2009. EUR 59 per issue domestic; EUR 79.92 per issue in Europe; EUR 93.92 per issue elsewhere (effective 2010). **Document type:** *Trade.*
Supersedes (1944-1979): Formulaire Thera (0071-7622)
Published by: Vidal S.A., 21 rue Camille Desmoulins, Issy les Moulineaux Cedex 9, 92789, France. TEL 33-1-73281100. Circ: 24,400.

615 GBR ISSN 2042-0986
RM302.5
▼ ➤ **THERAPEUTIC ADVANCES IN DRUG SAFETY.** Text in English. 2010. bi-m. (2 issues in 2010). **Document type:** *Journal, Academic/Scholarly.*
Related titles: Online - full text ed.: ISSN 2042-0994.
Indexed: A22.
—CCC.
Published by: Sage Publications Ltd. (Subsidiary of: Sage Publications, Inc.), 1 Oliver's Yard, 55 City Rd, London, EC1Y 1SP, United Kingdom. TEL 44-20-73248500, FAX 44-20-73248600, info@sagepub.co.uk, http://www.uk.sagepub.com/home.nav. Ed. Arduino Mangoni.

➤ **THERAPEUTIC ADVANCES IN GASTROENTEROLOGY.** *see* MEDICAL SCIENCES—Gastroenterology

615 616.8 GBR ISSN 2045-1253
▼ ➤ **THERAPEUTIC ADVANCES IN PSYCHOPHARMACOLOGY.** Text in English. forthcoming 2011. 6/yr. **Document type:** *Journal, Academic/Scholarly.*
Related titles: Online - full text ed.: ISSN 2045-1261. forthcoming.
Published by: (British Association of Psychopharmacology), Sage Publications Ltd. (Subsidiary of: Sage Publications, Inc.), 1 Oliver's Yard, 55 City Rd, London, EC1Y 1SP, United Kingdom. TEL 44-20-73248500, FAX 44-20-73248600, info@sagepub.co.uk, http://www.uk.sagepub.com/home.nav.

▼ ➤ **THERAPEUTIC DELIVERY.** *see* BIOLOGY—Biochemistry

615 USA ISSN 0163-4356
RM301.5 CODEN: TDMODV
➤ **THERAPEUTIC DRUG MONITORING.** Abbreviated title: T D M. Text in English. 1979. bi-m. USD 1,342 domestic to institutions; USD 1,474 foreign to institutions (effective 2011). adv. bk.rev. illus. Index. back issues avail.; reprints avail. **Document type:** *Journal, Academic/Scholarly.* **Description:** Features include review articles on specific classes of drugs, original articles, case reports, technical notes, and continuing education articles.
Related titles: Online - full text ed.: ISSN 1536-3694.
Indexed: A22, A34, A36, A40, ASCA, B25, BIOBASE, BIOSIS Prev, BP, CABA, ChemAb, ChemTitl, CurCont, D01, DBA, DentInd, E-psyche, E12, EMBASE, ExcerpMed, F08, GH, H13, H16, H17, I12, IABS, IDIS, ISR, IndMed, Inpharma, Kidney, LT, MEDLINE, MycolAb, N02, N03, N04, P10, P20, P30, P33, P35, P39, P48, P53, P54, PHN&I, PQC, R07, R10, R13, RA&MP, RM&VM, RRTA, Reac, SCI, SCOPUS, T05, THA, VS, W07.
—BLDSC (8814.643000), CASDDS, GNLM, IE, Infotrieve, Ingenta, INIST. **CCC.**
Published by: (International Association of Therapeutic Drug Monitoring and Clinical Toxicology CAN), Lippincott Williams & Wilkins (Subsidiary of: Wolters Kluwer N.V.), Two Commerce Sq, 2001 Market St, Philadelphia, PA 19103. TEL 215-521-8300, FAX 215-521-8902, customerservice@lww.com, http://www.lww.com. Eds. Dr. Gideon Koren TEL 416-813-5781, Dr. Michael Oellerich TEL 49-551-39-8561. Pub. Jason Pointe. Circ: 438.

615 GBR ISSN 1178-203X
➤ **THERAPEUTICS AND CLINICAL RISK MANAGEMENT (ONLINE).** Text in English. irreg. free (effective 2011). back issues avail. **Document type:** *Journal, Academic/Scholarly.* **Description:** Covers all therapeutic areas, outcomes, safety, and programs for the effective, safe, and sustained use of medicines.
Media: Online - full text.
—CCC.
Published by: Dove Medical Press Ltd., Beechfield House, Winterton Way, Macclesfield, SK11 0JL, United Kingdom. TEL 44-1625-509130, FAX 44-1625-617933. Ed. Garry Walsh.

610.9 DNK ISSN 0082-4003
THERIACA; samlinger til farmaciens og medicinens historie. Text in Danish; Summaries in English. 1956. irreg., latest vol.37, 2008. price varies. back issues avail. **Document type:** *Monographic series, Academic/Scholarly.*
Indexed: EMBASE, ExcerpMed, MEDLINE, P30, SCOPUS.
Published by: Dansk Farmacihistorisk Selskab/Danish Society of the History of Pharmacy, Loekketoften 39, Vallensbaek, 2625, Denmark. pk@dfhf.dk.

615.1 USA
THIRD PARTY RX. Text in English. 1989. m. free to members. **Document type:** *Magazine, Trade.*
Published by: National Community Pharmacists Association, 100 Daingerfield Rd, Alexandria, VA 22314. TEL 703-683-8200, FAX 703-683-3619, info@ncpanet.org, http://www.ncpanet.org/. Circ: 3,000.

615 CHN ISSN 1006-5687
TIANJIN YAOXUE/TIANJIN PHARMACY. Text in Chinese. bi-m. USD 31.20 (effective 2009). **Document type:** *Journal, Academic/Scholarly.*
Related titles: Online - full text ed.
—East View.
Address: Room 420, no.237, Hongqi Nanlu, Tianjin, 300191, China. **Dist. by:** China International Book Trading Corp, 35 Chegongzhuang Xilu, Haidian District, PO Box 399, Beijing 100044, China. TEL 86-10-68412045, FAX 86-10-68412023, cibtc@mail.cibtc.com.cn, http://www.cibtc.com.cn.

615 CHN ISSN 0253-9896
R97.7.C5 CODEN: TIYADG
➤ **TIANJIN YIYAO/TIANJIN MEDICAL JOURNAL.** Text in Chinese. 1959. m. CNY 96; CNY 8 per issue (effective 2009). **Document type:** *Journal, Academic/Scholarly.*
Related titles: Online - full text ed.
Indexed: A22, ChemAb, ChemTitl, P30.
—BLDSC (8820.510000), CASDDS, East View, IE, Infotrieve, Ingenta.
Published by: Tianjin Yixue Keji Qingbao Yanjiusuo/Tianjin Medical Science and Technology Information Institute, 96-D, Guizhou Lu, Heping-qu, Tianjin, 300070, China. TEL 86-22-23337519, http://www.tjmic.ac.cn/. **Dist. by:** China International Book Trading Corp, 35 Chegongzhuang Xilu, Haidian District, PO Box 399, Beijing 100044, China. TEL 86-10-68412045, FAX 86-10-68412023, cibtc@mail.cibtc.com.cn, http://www.cibtc.com.cn.

615 ARG ISSN 1852-4362
▼ **TIEMPO TEMIS.** Text in Spanish. 2009. bi-m. **Document type:** *Magazine, Consumer.*
Published by: Laboratorios Temis Lostalo, S.A., Zepita 3178, Buenos Aires, C1285ABF, Argentina. TEL 54-11-63441300, FAX 54-11-63441390, info@temislostalo.com.ar, http://www.temislostalo.com.ar/.

615 GBR ISSN 1470-5761
TOMORROW'S PHARMACIST. Text in English. 1999. a. free to qualified personnel (effective 2009). **Document type:** *Journal, Trade.*
—CCC.
Published by: Royal Pharmaceutical Society of Great Britain, 1 Lambeth High St, London, SE1 7JN, United Kingdom. TEL 44-20-77359141, library@rpsgb.org, http://www.rpsgb.org.uk/. Ed. Gemma Cleveland.

TOXICOLOGICAL AND ENVIRONMENTAL CHEMISTRY. *see* ENVIRONMENTAL STUDIES—Toxicology And Environmental Safety

TOXICOLOGICAL SCIENCES. *see* ENVIRONMENTAL STUDIES—Toxicology And Environmental Safety

TOXICOLOGY. *see* ENVIRONMENTAL STUDIES—Toxicology And Environmental Safety

TOXICOLOGY AND APPLIED PHARMACOLOGY. *see* ENVIRONMENTAL STUDIES—Toxicology And Environmental Safety

TOXICOLOGY AND INDUSTRIAL HEALTH; an international journal. *see* ENVIRONMENTAL STUDIES—Toxicology And Environmental Safety

TOXICOLOGY IN VITRO. *see* ENVIRONMENTAL STUDIES—Toxicology And Environmental Safety

TOXICOLOGY LETTERS. *see* ENVIRONMENTAL STUDIES—Toxicology And Environmental Safety

TOXICOLOGY MECHANISMS AND METHODS. *see* ENVIRONMENTAL STUDIES—Toxicology And Environmental Safety

615.9 GBR ISSN 0041-0101
QP631 CODEN: TOXIA6
➤ **TOXICON.** Text in English, French, German, Spanish. 1962. 16/yr. EUR 2,988 in Europe to institutions; JPY 396,600 in Japan to institutions; USD 3,341 elsewhere to institutions (effective 2012). adv. bk.rev.; software rev. abstr.; charts; illus. index. back issues avail.; reprints avail. **Document type:** *Journal, Academic/Scholarly.* **Description:** Features original research on the chemical, pharmacological, zootoxicological and immunological properties of naturally occurring poisons, including clinical and therapeutic observations.
Related titles: Microfilm ed.: (from PQC); Online - full text ed.: ISSN 1879-3150 (from IngentaConnect, ScienceDirect); Supplement(s): Toxicon. Supplement. ISSN 0190-5368.
Indexed: A01, A03, A08, A22, A26, A28, A34, A35, A36, A37, A38, APA, ASCA, ASFA, AgBio, Agr, AgrForAb, ApicAb, B21, B23, B25, BA, BIOBASE, BIOSIS Prev, BP, BibAg, BrCerAb, C&ISA, C25, C30, C33, CA, CA/WCA, CABA, CIA, CIN, CerAb, ChemAb, CivEngAb, CorrAb, CurCont, D01, E&CAJ, E04, E05, E11, E12, EEA, EMA, EMBASE, ESPM, EntAb, EnvEAb, ExcerpMed, F08, F11, F12, FCA, G11, GH, GeoRef, H&SSA, H15, H16, H17, I05, I11, IABS, ISR, IndMed, IndVet, Inpharma, LT, M&TEA, M09, MBF, MEDLINE, METADEX, MaizeAb, MycolAb, N02, N03, N04, N05, NSA, O01, OR, OceAb, P30, P32, P33, P37, P38, P39, P40, PGegResA, PGrRegA, PHN&I, PN&I, PollutAb, R07, R08, R10, R11, R12, R13, RA&MP, RM&VM, RRTA, Reac, RefZh, S01, S12, S13, S16, SAA, SCI, SCOPUS, SolStAb, SoyAb, T02, T04, T05, TAR, ToxAb, TriticAb, VS, W07, W08, W10, W11, WAA, WildRev, Z01.
—BLDSC (8873.050000), CASDDS, GNLM, IE, Infotrieve, Ingenta, INIST, Linda Hall. **CCC.**
Published by: (International Society on Toxinology), Pergamon (Subsidiary of: Elsevier Science & Technology), The Blvd, Langford Ln, East Park, Kidlington, Oxford OX5 1GB, United Kingdom. TEL 44-1865-843000, FAX 44-1865-843010. Ed. Alan L Harvey. **Subscr. to:** Elsevier BV, Radarweg 29, PO Box 211, Amsterdam 1000 AE, Netherlands. TEL 31-20-4853757, FAX 31-20-4853432, JournalsCustomerServiceEMEA@elsevier.com, http://www.elsevier.nl.

615.9 USA ISSN 1556-9543
RA1190 CODEN: JTTRD9
➤ **TOXIN REVIEWS.** Text in English. 1982. q. GBP 1,145, EUR 1,515, USD 1,890 combined subscription to institutions (print & online eds.); GBP 2,355, EUR 3,105, USD 3,880 combined subscription to corporations (print & online eds.) (effective 2010). adv. reprint service avail. from PSC. **Document type:** *Journal, Academic/Scholarly.* **Description:** Brings information on toxins (their characteristics, activities and mechanisms of action) from the full range of clinical and scientific disciplines in which toxins impinge.
Formerly (until 2005): Journal of Toxicology. Toxin Reviews (0731-3837)
Related titles: Microform ed.: (from RPI); Online - full text ed.: ISSN 1556-9551 (from IngentaConnect).
Indexed: A01, A03, A08, A22, A34, A35, A36, ASCA, ASFA, AgBio, AgrForAb, B21, B23, B25, BA, BIOSIS Prev, BP, C25, C30, CA, CABA, CIN, ChemAb, ChemTitl, CurCont, D01, E01, E04, E05, E12, EMBASE, ESPM, EntAb, EnvAb, EnvInd, ExcerpMed, F08, FCA, G11, GH, H&SSA, H16, ISR, IndVet, Inpharma, MaizeAb, MycolAb, N02, N03, N04, NRN, NSA, OR, P32, P33, P39, P40, PGrRegA, PHN&I, PN&I, PollutAb, R07, R08, R10, R11, R12, R13, RA&MP, RM&VM, Reac, S13, S16, S17, SCI, SCOPUS, T02, T05, TAR, ToxAb, TriticAb, VS, W07, W10, W11, WildRev.
—BLDSC (8873.059000), CASDDS, GNLM, IE, Infotrieve, Ingenta, INIST. **CCC.**
Published by: Informa Healthcare (Subsidiary of: T & F Informa plc), 52 Vanderbilt Ave, New York, NY 10017. TEL 212-262-8230, FAX 212-262-8234, healthcare.enquiries@informa.com, http://www.informahealthcare.com. Eds. Anthony T Tu, Dr. W Thomas Shier. **Subscr. outside N. America to:** Taylor & Francis Ltd.

615 USA ISSN 1948-3600
▼ **TRANSDERMAL**; exclusively for the delivery of pharmaceuticals through the skin. Text in English. 2009. bi-m. free to qualified personnel (effective 2009). **Document type:** *Magazine, Trade.* **Description:** Includes information for doctors and the pharmaceutical industry on new pharmaceuticals delivered through the skin.
Related titles: Online - full text ed.: ISSN 1948-5824. 2009.
Published by: C S C Publishing, Inc., 1155 Northland Dr, Saint Paul, MN 55120. TEL 651-287-5600, FAX 651-287-5650, rpbe@csc.com.

TRANSMITTER. *see* BUSINESS AND ECONOMICS—Marketing And Purchasing

TRANSPLANTATION PROCEEDINGS. *see* MEDICAL SCIENCES—Surgery

615 ITA ISSN 1722-3407
TREATMENT GUIDELINES (ITALIAN EDITION). Text in Italian. 2003. m. EUR 93 (effective 2009). **Document type:** *Magazine, Trade.*
Published by: C I S Editore S.r.l., Via San Siro 1, Milan, 20149, Italy. TEL 39-02-4694542, FAX 39-02-48193584, http://www.ciseditore.it.

615 ISSN 1594-2848
➤ **TRENDS IN MEDICINE.** Text in Italian. 3/yr. EUR 58 (effective 2009). **Document type:** *Journal, Academic/Scholarly.*

Indexed: EMBASE, ExcerpMed, R10, Reac, SCOPUS.
—BLDSC (9049.661050).
Published by: Pharma Project Group srl, Viale Rimembranze 43/A, Saronno, 21047, Italy. TEL 39-0296-702708, FAX 39-0296-702677, http://www.ppgedizioni.it.

615.1 GBR ISSN 0165-6147
RM300 CODEN: TPHSDY
➤ **TRENDS IN PHARMACOLOGICAL SCIENCES.** Text in English. 1979. m. EUR 1,826 in Europe to institutions; JPY 253,300 in Japan to institutions; USD 2,042 elsewhere to institutions (effective 2012). adv. bk.rev. bibl.; illus.; abstr. index. back issues avail.; reprints avail. **Document type:** *Journal, Academic/Scholarly.* **Description:** Covers the sciences of pharmacology and toxicology.
Related titles: Microform ed.: (from PQC); Online - full text ed.: ISSN 1873-3735. 199? (from IngentaConnect, ScienceDirect); Supplement(s): Receptor and Ion Channel Nomenclature Supplement. ISSN 1357-485X.
Indexed: A01, A02, A03, A08, A20, A22, A26, A29, A34, A36, ASCA, B&BAb, B19, B20, B21, BIOBASE, BIOSIS Prev, BP, BioEngAb, C33, CA, CABA, CIN, CTA, ChemAb, ChemTitl, CurCont, D01, DBA, E08, E12, EMBASE, ESPM, ExcerpMed, F08, F11, F12, FR, G08, GH, GeoRef, H11, H12, H17, I05, I10, IABS, ISR, IndMed, Inpharma, MEDLINE, MycolAb, N02, N03, NSA, OR, P30, P33, P37, P39, R07, R08, R10, R13, RA&MP, Reac, RefZh, S09, SCI, SCOPUS, T02, T05, Telegen, VS, VirolAbstr, W07, W10.
—BLDSC (9049.675000), CASDDS, GNLM, IE, Infotrieve, Ingenta, INIST. **CCC.**
Published by: Elsevier Ltd., Trends Journals (Subsidiary of: Elsevier Science & Technology), 84 Theobald's Rd, London, WC1X 8RR, United Kingdom. TEL 44-20-76114000, FAX 44-20-76114485, JournalsCustomerServiceEMEA@elsevier.com, http://www.elsevier.com. Ed. Lekshmy Balakrishnan. Adv. contact James Kenney TEL 44-20-74244216. **Co-sponsors:** International Union of Toxicology; International Union of Pharmacology.

615.1 NGA
➤ **TROPICAL JOURNAL OF PHARMACEUTICAL RESEARCH.** Text in English. 2002. s-a. USD 30 in developing nations to individuals; USD 60 rest of world to individuals; USD 80 in developing nations to institutions; USD 150 rest of world to institutions (effective 2004). back issues avail. **Document type:** *Journal, Academic/Scholarly.* **Description:** Devoted to the promotion of pharmaceutical sciences and related disciplines; including biotechnology, cell and molecular biology, medical and other life sciences, and related engineering fields.
Related titles: Online - full text ed.: ISSN 1596-5996. free (effective 2011).
Published by: Pharmacotherapy Group, c/o Faculty of Pharmacy, University of Benin, Benin City, Nigeria. TEL 234-802-3360318, erah@uniben.edu. Ed. Augustine Okhamafe.

615 USA ISSN 1535-2374
TUFTS CENTER FOR THE STUDY OF DRUG DEVELOPMENT. IMPACT REPORT. Text in English. 1999. bi-m. **Document type:** *Report, Consumer.*
—**CCC.**
Published by: Tufts Center for the Study of Drug Development, Tufts University, 192 South Street, Ste 550, Boston, MA 02111, MA 02111. TEL 617-636-2170, FAX 617-636-2425, csdd@tufts.edu, http://csdd.tufts.edu.

615 TUR ISSN 1304-530X
➤ **TURKISH JOURNAL OF PHARMACEUTICAL SCIENCES.** Text in English; Summaries in English, Turkish. 2004. 3/yr. back issues avail. **Document type:** *Journal, Academic/Scholarly.* **Description:** Publishes research articles, short communications, reviews, technical notes on all aspects of pharmaceutical sciences.
Related titles: Online - full text ed.: free.
Indexed: A01, A40, EMBASE, SCOPUS.
Published by: Turkish Pharmacists' Association, Academy of Pharmacy, Willy Brandt Sok., No.9, Cankaya, Ankara, 06690, Turkey. TEL 90-312-4098136, FAX 90-312-4098132, http://www.teb.org.tr. Ed., R&P Dr. Feyyaz Onur. Circ: 1,300.

615.1 POL ISSN 1508-9746
TWOJ MAGAZYN MEDYCZNY. Text in Polish. 1997. m. **Document type:** *Journal.*
Formerly (until 1999): Magazyn Farmaceutyczny (1427-9762)
Published by: Agencja Wydawniczo-Reklamowa, ul Wadowicka 8a, Krakow, 30415, Poland. medicus@medicus.com.pl, http://www.medicus.com.pl.

615 POL ISSN 1233-5266
TWOJA APTEKA; poradnik medyczny. Text in Polish. 1994. bi-m. **Document type:** *Magazine, Consumer.*
Published by: Wydawnictwo Kwadryga, ul Chelmska 19/21, Warsaw, 00724, Poland. TEL 48-22-8516668, FAX 48-22-5593565, gfarm@kwadryga.pl, http://www.kwadryga.pl.

615.1 NLD ISSN 2211-0941
▼ **U A.** (Uitsluitens Apothekersassistenten) Text in Dutch. 2011. bi-m. EUR 30; EUR 6 newsstand/cover (effective 2011). adv. **Document type:** *Magazine, Trade.*
Published by: H & B Publishing B.V., Postbus 68, Almere Haven, 1300 AB, Netherlands. TEL 31-36-5486333, FAX 31-36-5486330, info@hbpublishing.nl, http://www.hbpublishing.nl. Eds. Margot van Gils, Winifred Hazelhoff Roelfzema. Pub. Ruud Vester. Circ: 11,000.

615.1 USA
U G A - R X. Text in English. q. back issues avail. **Document type:** *Journal, Academic/Scholarly.*
Formerly: Georgia Pharmacist Quarterly
Related titles: Online - full text ed.: free (effective 2010).
Published by: University of Georgia, College of Pharmacy, RC Wilson Pharmacy Bldg, Athens, GA 30602. TEL 706-542-1911, FAX 706-542-5269, robertson@rx.uga.edu. Ed. Sheila Roberson.

U N M C DISCOVER. *see* MEDICAL SCIENCES

U.S. DEPARTMENT OF HEALTH AND HUMAN SERVICES. FOOD AND DRUG ADMINISTRATION. PRESCRIPTION DRUG USER FEE ACT. FINANCIAL REPORT TO CONGRESS. *see* PUBLIC ADMINISTRATION

U.S. DEPARTMENT OF HEALTH AND HUMAN SERVICES. FOOD AND DRUG ADMINISTRATION. PRESCRIPTION DRUG USER FEE ACT. PERFORMANCE REPORT TO CONGRESS. *see* PUBLIC ADMINISTRATION

615 USA
U.S. FEDERAL TRADE COMMISSION. BUREAU OF COMPETITION. SUMMARY OF AGREEMENTS FILED IN F Y (YEAR). Text in English. 200?. a. free. **Document type:** *Government.* **Description:** Provides information about the agreements filed with the FTC & DoJ as required by the Medicare Prescription Drug, Improvement, and Modernization Act of 2003.
Media: Online - full content.
Published by: U.S. Federal Trade Commission, Bureau of Competition, Office of Policy & Coordination, Rm 383, 600 Pennsylvania Avenue, NW, Washington, DC 20580. TEL 202-326-3300, antitrust@ftc.gov.

615 USA ISSN 0740-6916
RM300 CODEN: USPIE9
U S P - D I. VOL. 2. ADVICE FOR THE PATIENT; drug information in lay language. (United States Pharmacopeia) Text in English. 1980. a. (plus m. update). USD 93 (effective 2007); includes Update. **Document type:** *Handbook/Manual/Guide, Trade.* **Description:** Contains information to educate and counsel patients on drug use, available dosage forms, side effects, and contraindications.
Supersedes in part (in 1983): United States Pharmacopeia Dispensing Information (0276-5373)
Related titles: CD-ROM ed.; Online - full text ed.
—GNLM. **CCC.**
Published by: Micromedex, 6200 South Syracuse Way, Suite 300, Greenwood Village, CO 80111-4740. TEL 303-486-6400, 800-525-9083, FAX 303-486-6464, mdx.info@thomson.com.

615 340 USA ISSN 1045-8298
RS131.2
U S P - D I. VOL. 3. APPROVED DRUG PRODUCTS AND LEGAL REQUIREMENTS. (United States Pharmacopeia) Text in English. 1989. a. USD 145 (effective 2004). **Document type:** *Handbook/Manual/Guide, Trade.* **Description:** Contains important therapeutic equivalence information, as well as selected federal and state requirements that affect the prescribing and dispensing of prescription drugs and controlled substances.
Supersedes in part (in 1981): United States Pharmacopeia Dispensing Information (0276-5373)
—IE.
Published by: Micromedex, 6200 South Syracuse Way, Suite 300, Greenwood Village, CO 80111-4740. TEL 303-486-6400, 800-525-9083, FAX 303-486-6464, mdx.info@thomson.com.

615 USA ISSN 1076-4275
RS55 CODEN: USDIEH
U S P DICTIONARY OF U S A N AND INTERNATIONAL DRUG NAMES. (United States Pharmacopeial Convention and the United States Adopted Names) Text in English. 1963. a. USD 348 per issue (print or online ed.) (effective 2011). **Document type:** *Database, Trade.* **Description:** Lists more than 8,100 nonproprietary drug entries from the U.S., the U.K., and Japan.
Former titles (until 1995): U S A N and the U S P Dictionary of Drug Names (0090-6816); (until 1971): United States Adopted Names
Related titles: Online - full text ed.
—CASDDS. **CCC.**
Published by: United States Pharmacopeial Convention, Inc., 12601 Twinbrook Pkwy, Rockville, MD 20852. TEL 301-881-0666, 800-227-8772, FAX 301-816-8148, custsvc@usp.org.

615.11 USA
U S P - N F. SUPPLEMENT. (United States Pharmacopeia National Formulary) Text in English. 19??. a. **Document type:** *Newsletter, Trade.*
Formerly (until 1980): United States Pharmacopeia - National Formulary. Supplement (0190-5384)
Related titles: ◆ Supplement to: United States Pharmacopeia. National Formulary. ISSN 0195-7996.
—**CCC.**
Published by: United States Pharmacopeial Convention, Inc., 12601 Twinbrook Pkwy, Rockville, MD 20852. TEL 301-881-0666, 800-227-8772, FAX 301-816-8148, custsvc@usp.org, http://www.usp.org/.

615 USA ISSN 1930-2908
RS141.2
U S P PHARMACISTS' PHARMACOPEIA. (United States Pharmacopeial) Text in English. 2005. a. USD 250 per issue (effective 2011). **Document type:** *Journal, Trade.*
Related titles: Online - full text ed.: ISSN 1930-2916.
Published by: United States Pharmacopeial Convention, Inc., 12601 Twinbrook Pkwy, Rockville, MD 20852. TEL 301-881-0666, 800-227-8772, FAX 301-816-8148, custsvc@usp.org.

615 USA
U S P QUALITY REVIEW. (United States Pharmacopeia) Text in English. 1988. 10/yr. free to members (effective 2010). **Document type:** *Journal, Academic/Scholarly.* **Description:** Presents information and advisories relating to the reported information gathered through the network.
Related titles: Online - full text ed.: free (effective 2010).
Published by: U.S. Pharmacopoeial Practitioners' Reporting Network, 12601 Twinbrook Pky, Rockville, MD 20852. TEL 301-881-0666, 800-227-8772, FAX 301-816-8148, custsvc@usp.org.

615.105 USA ISSN 0148-4818
RS1
➤ **U S PHARMACIST**; the journal for pharmacists' education. Text in English. 1976. m. USD 58 domestic; USD 81 in Canada; USD 157 elsewhere; USD 6 per issue; free to qualified personnel (effective 2009). adv. index. back issues avail. **Document type:** *Journal, Academic/Scholarly.* **Description:** Provides significant articles on intellectual property law.
Related titles: Online - full text ed.: 1996. free (effective 2011).
Indexed: A22, A26, EMBASE, ExcerpMed, I12, P30, SCOPUS.
—BLDSC (9124.762000), GNLM, IE, Infotrieve, Ingenta. **CCC.**
Published by: Jobson Medical Group (Subsidiary of: Jobson Publishing LLC), 160 Chubb Ave, Ste 306, Lyndhurst, NJ 07071. TEL 201-623-0999, FAX 201-623-0991, http://www.jmihealth.com. Ed., Pub. Harold E Cohen TEL 201-623-0982. Circ: 127,619. **Subscr. to:** US Pharmacist.

➤ **U.S. PHARMACY STAFF COMPENSATION SURVEY.** *see* BUSINESS AND ECONOMICS—Labor And Industrial Relations

615 DNK ISSN 1602-4532
RS67.D4
UNDERSOEGELSE OVER APOTEKERNES DRIFTSFORHOLD (ONLINE); regnskabsresultater fra apoteker. Text in Danish. 1936. a. **Document type:** *Government.*
Formerly (until 2002): Undersoegelse over Apotekernes Driftsforhold (Print) (0108-948X)
Media: Online - full content.
Published by: Laegemiddelstyrelsen/Danish Medicines Agency, Axel Heides Gade 1, Copenhagen S, 2300, Denmark. TEL 45-44-889595, FAX 45-44-889599, dkma@dkma.dk, http://www.dkma.dk.

615.11 USA ISSN 0195-7996
RS141.2 CODEN: USPFDX
UNITED STATES PHARMACOPEIA. NATIONAL FORMULARY. Abbreviated title: U S P N F. Text in English. 1820. a. USD 820 per issue (effective 2011). **Document type:** *Handbook/Manual/Guide, Trade.* **Description:** Compiles all the legally enforceable standards of strength, purity, packaging, labeling, and storage for drugs and excipients.
Formed by the 1979 merger of: National Formulary (0084-6414); Pharmacopeia of the United States of America (0079-1407)
Related titles: CD-ROM ed.: USD 1,210 per issue (effective 2011); Online - full text ed.: U S P - N F. ISSN 1930-2932. USD 890 (effective 2008); Spanish ed.: ISSN 1930-2924; ◆ Supplement(s): U S P - N F. Supplement.
Indexed: A22.
—BLDSC (9100.172000), CASDDS, IE, Ingenta. **CCC.**
Published by: United States Pharmacopeial Convention, Inc., 12601 Twinbrook Pkwy, Rockville, MD 20852. TEL 301-881-0666, 800-227-8772, FAX 301-816-8148, custsvc@usp.org.

615.1 VEN ISSN 0041-8307
RM101 CODEN: RFFVA6
➤ **UNIVERSIDAD CENTRAL DE VENEZUELA. FACULTAD DE FARMACIA. REVISTA.** Text in English, Spanish; Summaries in English. 1958. s-a. per issue exchange basis. bk.rev. abstr.; bibl.; charts; illus.; stat. index. back issues avail. **Document type:** *Journal, Academic/Scholarly.*
Related titles: Fax ed.
Indexed: C01, P30.
—CASDDS, Linda Hall.
Published by: Universidad Central de Venezuela, Facultad de Farmacia, Av Los Ilustres, Ciudad Universitaria, Edif Facultad de Farmacia, Los Chaguaramos, Caracas, 1051, Venezuela. http://www.ucv.ve/Farmacia/. Ed. Fanny C Padilla. Pub. Miguel Garcia.

615 ITA ISSN 0430-3210
UNIVERSITA DI FERRARA. ANNALI. SEZIONE 11: FARMACOLOGIA E TERAPIA. Text in Italian. 1936. a. price varies. **Document type:** *Journal, Academic/Scholarly.*
Supersedes in part (in 1951): Universita di Ferrara. Annali (0365-7833)
—Linda Hall.
Published by: Universita degli Studi di Ferrara, Via Savonarola 9, Ferrara, 44100, Italy. TEL 39-0532-293111, FAX 39-0532-293031, http://www.unife.it.

615.1 SVK ISSN 0301-5467
UNIVERSITAS COMENIANA. ACTA FACULTATIS PHARMACEUTICAE. Text in English, German, Russian. 1958. irreg., latest 2005. price varies. charts; illus. index. **Document type:** *Journal, Academic/Scholarly.*
Formerly: Acta Facultatis Pharmaceuticae Bohemoslovenicae
Indexed: ChemAb.
Published by: Univerzita Komenskeho, Farmaceuticka Fakulta/Comenius University, Faculty of Pharmacy, Odbojarov 10, Bratislava, 83232, Slovakia. TEL 421-2-50117101, FAX 421-2-50117111, sd@fpharm.uniba.sk. Ed. Milan Chalabala. Circ: 500.

615.1 USA ISSN 1524-8348
UNIVERSITY OF THE SCIENCES IN PHILADELPHIA. BULLETIN. Text in English. 1865. q. free to alumni (effective 2011). illus. reprints avail. **Document type:** *Bulletin, Academic/Scholarly.* **Description:** Information pertaining to the University and its alumni.
Former titles (until 1999): Philadelphia College of Pharmacy and Science Bulletin (0031-725X); (until 1920): Philadelphia College of Pharmacy. Bulletin and Alumni Report (0747-8089)
Published by: University of the Sciences in Philadelphia, 600 S 43rd St, Philadelphia, PA 19104. TEL 215-596-8800, admit@usip.edu, http://www.usciences.edu/.

UPDATE (WASHINGTON, D.C., 1982); food and drug law, regulation, and education. *see* LAW

615.1 USA ISSN 1948-1136
UPDATES IN THERAPEUTICS. Text in English. 2000. a. USD 210 per issue to non-members; USD 145 per issue to members (effective 2009). back issues avail. **Document type:** *Journal, Trade.* **Description:** Provides a comprehensive review of the knowledge domains covered in the pharmacotherapy specialty certification examination.
Related titles: CD-ROM ed.: USD 315 per issue to non-members; USD 210 per issue to members (effective 2009); Online - full text ed.: USD 200 to non-members; USD 135 to members (effective 2009).
Published by: American College of Clinical Pharmacy, 13000 W 87th St Pky, Lenexa, KS 66215. TEL 913-492-3311, FAX 913-492-0088, accp@accp.com.

615 USA ISSN 2158-1436
▼ **US-CHINA PHARMA & BIOTECH FORUM.** Text in English. 2010. s-a. free (effective 2010). **Document type:** *Newsletter, Trade.* **Description:** Provides information about technologies and applications in drug discovery and development.
Media: Online - full text.
Published by: American-Chinese Biotech-Pharma Association, PO Box 5459, Vernon Hills, IL 60061. info@acbpa.org. Eds. Gui-Dong Zhu, Yupeng He.

615.1 USA
THE UTAH PHARMACIST. Text in English. bi-m. adv. **Document type:** *Journal, Trade.*
Published by: (Utah Pharmacists Association, Utah Society of Health-System Pharmacists), Newsletters Ink, Corp., 450 N Prince St, P O Box 4008, Lancaster, PA 17604. TEL 717-393-1000, 800-379-5585, FAX 717-393-4702, info@newslettersink.com, http://www.newslettersink.com. adv.: B&W page USD 429; trim 7.5 x 10. Circ: 1,050.

P

615.1 NLD ISSN 1574-6089
UW EIGEN DROGIST. Variant title: Beter Beslist Gezondheidsmagazine. Text in Dutch. 1999. q. adv. **Document type:** *Magazine, Consumer.*
Published by: Brocacef, Straatweg 2, Postbus 75, Maarssen, 3600 AA, Netherlands. TEL 31-30-2452911, FAX 31-30-2452222, info@brocacef.nl, http://www.brocacef.nl. Circ: 360,000.

615 610 GBR ISSN 2040-3089
▼ **UZBEKISTAN PHARMACEUTICALS & HEALTHCARE REPORT.** Text in English. 2009. q. EUR 820, USD 1,150 combined subscription (print & email eds.) (effective 2010). **Document type:** *Report, Trade.* **Description:** Provides industry professionals, market investors and corporate and financial services analysts with independent forecasts and competitive intelligence on the Uzbekistani pharmaceutical and healthcare industry.
Related titles: E-mail ed.
Published by: Business Monitor International Ltd., Senator House, 85 Queen Victoria St, London, EC4V 4AB, United Kingdom. TEL 44-20-72480468, FAX 44-20-72480467, subs@businessmonitor.com.

VACCINATIEGRAAD RIJKSVACCINATIEPROGRAMMA NEDERLAND. *see* MEDICAL SCIENCES—Allergology And Immunology

616.6 615.372 USA ISSN 1074-2921
QR189
VACCINE WEEKLY. Text in English. 1988. w. (43/yr.). USD 2,295 in US & Canada; USD 2,495 elsewhere; USD 2,525 combined subscription in US & Canada (print & online eds.); USD 2,755 combined subscription elsewhere (print & online eds.) (effective 2008). back issues avail. **Document type:** *Newsletter, Trade.* **Description:** Brings together relevant news and breakthroughs from interrelated topics ranging from therapeutic vaccines for AIDS, cancer, and other diseases, efficacy and safety trials, FDA regulations and approvals, and prevention.
Related titles: E-mail ed.; Online - full text ed.: ISSN 1532-4702. USD 2,295 combined subscription (online & email eds.); single user (effective 2008).
Indexed: A26, B03, E08, G08, H11, H12, H13, I05, P10, P19, P20, P30, P48, P50, P53, P54, PQC, PROMT, S09, SCOPUS.
—CCC.
Published by: NewsRx, 2727 Paces Ferry Rd SE, Ste 2-440, Atlanta, GA 30339. TEL 770-435-8286, 800-726-4550, FAX 770-435-6800, pressrelease@newsrx.com. Pub. Susan Hasty TEL 770-507-7777.

▼ **VACCINES.** *see* MEDICAL SCIENCES—Allergology And Immunology

615 USA ISSN 1525-5255
VALIDATION TIMES. Text in English. 1998. m. USD 1,711 combined subscription (print & online eds.) (effective 2011). 20 p./no.; back issues avail. **Document type:** *Newsletter, Trade.*
Incorporates (1992-2001): Medical Device Approval Letter with G M P - Design Controls Reviews (1060-8338); Former titles (until 1999): Drug, Evaluation and Compliance Report (1094-9321); Validation Timer
Related titles: E-mail ed.; Online - full text ed.
Indexed: B02, B15, B17, B18, G04, G06, G07, G08, I05.
—CCC.
Published by: Washington Information Source Co., 19-B Wirt St, SW, Leesburg, VA 20175. TEL 703-779-8777, FAX 703-779-2508, service@fdainfo.com, http://www.fdainfo.com/wisindex.html.

615.1 USA ISSN 1098-3015
CODEN: VIHLFM
➤ **VALUE IN HEALTH.** Text in English. 1998. 8/yr. USD 535 elsewhere to institutions (effective 2012). adv. back issues avail.; reprints avail. **Document type:** *Journal, Academic/Scholarly.* **Description:** Evaluates medical technologies, including pharmaceutical, biologics, devices, procedures, and other medical interventions.
Related titles: Online - full text ed.: ISSN 1524-4733. GBP 318 in United Kingdom to institutions; EUR 404 in Europe to institutions; USD 406 in the Americas to institutions; USD 624 elsewhere to institutions (effective 2010) (from IngentaConnect, ScienceDirect).
Indexed: A01, A03, A08, A20, A22, A26, ASSIA, C06, C07, C08, CA, CINAHL, CurCont, E01, EMBASE, ExcerpMed, H05, H12, I12, Inpharma, MEDLINE, P03, P30, P34, P35, PsycInfo, PsycholAb, R10, Reac, SCI, SCOPUS, SSCI, T02, W07.
—BLDSC (9142.093500), IE, Infotrieve, Ingenta, INIST. **CCC.**
Published by: (International Society for Pharmacoeconomics and Outcomes Research), Wiley-Blackwell Publishing, Inc. (Subsidiary of: Wiley-Blackwell Publishing Ltd.), 111 River St, Hoboken, NJ 07030. TEL 201-748-6000, FAX 201-748-6088, info@wiley.com. Eds. C Daniel Mullins, Michael Drummond.

615.1 USA ISSN 1537-1891
RM1 CODEN: VPAHAJ
➤ **VASCULAR PHARMACOLOGY.** Text in English. 1970. m. EUR 3,456 in Europe to institutions; JPY 458,800 in Japan to institutions; USD 3,865 elsewhere to institutions (effective 2012). adv. bk.rev. abstr.; charts; illus.; stat. index. back issues avail.; reprints avail. **Document type:** *Journal, Academic/Scholarly.* **Description:** Covers all aspects of pharmacology of the vascular system.
Former titles (until 2002): General Pharmacology (0306-3623); (until 1975): Comparative and General Pharmacology (0010-4035)
Related titles: Microfilm ed.: (from PQC); Online - full text ed.: ISSN 1879-3649 (from IngentaConnect, ScienceDirect).
Indexed: A01, A03, A08, A22, A26, A29, A34, A35, A36, ASCA, AgBio, AgrForAb, B20, B21, B25, BIOBASE, BIOSIS Prev, C30, C33, CA, CABA, CIN, ChemAb, ChemTitl, CurCont, D01, DBA, DentInd, E12, EMBASE, ESPM, ExcerpMed, F08, F11, F12, GH, H16, H17, I05, I10, IABS, ISR, IndMed, Inpharma, MEDLINE, MycolAb, N02, N03, NSA, P30, P32, P33, P35, PGrRegA, PN&I, R08, R10, R12, RA&MP, Reac, S01, SCI, SCOPUS, SoyAb, T02, T05, THA, VS, VirolAbstr, W07, W10, W11.
—BLDSC (9148.875000), CASDDS, GNLM, IE, Ingenta, INIST, Linda Hall. **CCC.**
Published by: Elsevier Inc. (Subsidiary of: Elsevier Science & Technology), 1600 John F Kennedy Blvd, Philadelphia, PA 19103. TEL 215-239-3900, FAX 215-238-7883, JournalCustomerService-usa@elsevier.com. Ed. Dr. John D. Catravas TEL 706-721-1660. Adv. contact Janine Castle TEL 44-1865-843844.

615 NOR ISSN 0042-3351
VENEFICUS; farmasistudentenes tidsskrift. Text in Norwegian. 1935. bi-m. bk.rev. charts; illus. index. **Document type:** *Bulletin, Consumer.* **Description:** Forum for pharmacy students' activities, with reviews of social events, articles on sports and scientific discussions.
Indexed: ChemAb.
Address: c/o Farmasoeytisk Institutt, PO Box 1068, Blindern, Oslo, 0316, Norway. TEL 47-22-85578, veneficus-foreningen@farmasi.uio.no, http://www.veneficus.no.

615.1 NLD ISSN 2210-9013
VERMINDERDE NIERFUNCTIE. Text in Dutch. 2007. a.
Published by: Koninklijke Nederlandse Maatschappij ter Bevordering der Pharmacie/Royal Netherlands Pharmaceutical Society, Alexanderstraat 11, The Hague, 2514 JL, Netherlands. TEL 31-70-3737373, FAX 31-70-3106530, communicatie@knmp.nl, http://www.knmp.nl.

VIGILANCES. *see* MEDICAL SCIENCES

615.1 USA ISSN 0042-6717
RS1
THE VIRGINIA PHARMACIST. Text in English. 1882. m. USD 50 domestic to non-members; USD 100 elsewhere to non-members (effective 2007). adv. bk.rev. charts; illus.; mkt.; pat.; tr.lit. back issues avail. **Document type:** *Magazine, Trade.* **Description:** Publishes articles of interest concerning the pharmaceutical industry for an audience of pharmacists and practitioners of related industries.
—Linda Hall.
Published by: Virginia Pharmacists Association, 5501 Patterson Ave, Ste 200, Richmond, VA 23226. TEL 800-527-8742, FAX 804-285-4227, info@vapharmacy.org. Ed. Rebecca P Snead. adv.: B&W page USD 525; trim 7.5 x 10. Circ: 2,000 (paid).

615 BRA ISSN 1518-5192
RS1
➤ **VISAO ACADEMICA.** Text in Portuguese; Summaries in Portuguese, English. 2000. s-a. bk.rev. abstr.; bibl.; charts; illus.; stat.; tr.lit. **Document type:** *Magazine, Academic/Scholarly.*
Related titles: Online - full content ed.
Indexed: C01.
Published by: Universidade Federal do Parana, N I P C F, Curso de Farmacia UFPR, Lothario Meissner 3400, Jardim Botanico, Curitiba, PR 80270-170, Brazil. TEL 55-041-3604107, FAX 55-041-3604101, nipcif@subsede.ufpr.br, http://zerbini.subsede.ufpr.br. Ed., R&P Marilis Dallarmi Miguel. Pub. Maria Madalena Gabriel.

615 362 FRA ISSN 1258-4711
VISITE ACTUELLE. Text in French. 1994. 10/yr. EUR 93.05 to individuals; EUR 46.53 to students (effective 2010). back issues avail. **Document type:** *Magazine, Trade.*
Address: 84 Av. du General Leclerc, Boulogne, 92100, France. TEL 33-1-46040066, FAX 33-1-46040214. Circ: 20,000.

615 FRA
VISITE ACTUELLE "MEDECINE, HOPITAL, PHARMACIE". Text in French. 2007. m. EUR 80.71 to individuals; EUR 40.35 to students (effective 2007). 64 p./no.; back issues avail. **Document type:** *Magazine, Trade.*
Formerly (until 2010): Visite Pharma (1954-1988)
Published by: Visite Actuelle, 84 Av. du General Leclerc, Boulogne, 92100, France. TEL 33-1-46040066, FAX 33-1-46040214.

615 UKR ISSN 1562-7241
VISNYK FARMATSII. Text in Ukrainian. 1993. q. **Document type:** *Journal, Academic/Scholarly.*
Indexed: RefZh.
—East View.
Published by: Natsional'nyi Farmatsevtychnyi Universytet/National University of Pharmacy, Vul Pushkins'ka 53, Kharkiv, 310002, Ukraine. TEL 380-572-142289, FAX 380-572-470164, rector@ukrfa.kharkov.ua, http://www.ukrfa.kharkov.ua. Ed. Valentin Chernykh.

615.1 COL ISSN 0121-4004
VITAE; revista de la Facultad de Quimica Farmaceutica. Text in Spanish. 1991. s-a. back issues avail. **Document type:** *Journal, Academic/Scholarly.* **Description:** Publishes original research in pharmaceutical chemistry, cosmetic and food sciences and technology.
Related titles: Online - full text ed.: free (effective 2011).
Indexed: EMBASE, ExcerpMed, SCI, SCOPUS, W07.
Published by: Universidad de Antioquia, Facultad de Quimica Farmaceutica, Apartado Postal 1226, Medellin, Colombia. TEL 57-4-210-5475, FAX 57-4-210-5456, vitae@muiscas.udea.edu.co.

615.328 USA
VITAMIN RETAILER; the dietary supplement industry's leading magazine. Text in English. m. USD 60 domestic; USD 100 in Canada & Mexico; USD 175 elsewhere (effective 2004). adv. **Document type:** *Magazine, Trade.* **Description:** Includes information about vitamins, minerals, herbs, specialty supplements, sports nutrition, natural remedies and HBA products.
Published by: Vitamin Retailer Magazine, Inc. 431 Cranbury Rd, East Brunswick, NJ 08816. TEL 732-432-9600, FAX 732-432-9288, info@vitaminretailer.com. Ed. Paul Bubny TEL 732-432-9600 ext 105. Pub. Daniel McSweeney TEL 805-646-2921. Adv. contact Russ Fields TEL 732-432-9600 ext 102.

615.328 612.405 USA ISSN 0083-6729
QP801.V5 CODEN: VIHOAQ
➤ **VITAMINS AND HORMONES.** Text in English. 1943. irreg., latest vol.84, 2010. USD 192 combined subscription per issue (print & online eds.) (effective 2011). index, cum.index: vols.1-5 (1943-1947), vols.6-10 (1948-1952), vols.11-15 (1953-1957). back issues avail.; reprints avail. **Document type:** *Monographic series, Academic/Scholarly.*
Related titles: Online - full text ed.: ISSN 2162-2620.
Indexed: A22, ASCA, Agr, BIOSIS Prev, C06, C07, C13, ChemAb, DBA, EMBASE, ExcerpMed, ISR, IndMed, MEDLINE, MycolAb, P30, R10, Reac, SCI, SCOPUS, W07.
—BLDSC (9244.000000), CASDDS, GNLM, IE, Infotrieve, Ingenta, INIST, Linda Hall. **CCC.**
Published by: Academic Press (Subsidiary of: Elsevier Science & Technology), 3251 Riverport Ln, Maryland Heights, MO 63043. TEL 314-447-8010, FAX 314-447-8030, JournalCustomerService-usa@elsevier.com, http://www.elsevierdirect.com/imprint.jsp?iid=5. Ed. Gerald Litwack.

615.9 USA ISSN 0507-2379
VOICE OF THE PHARMACIST. Text in English. 1946. q. looseleaf. USD 65 (effective 2007). **Document type:** *Newsletter.*
Related titles: Online - full text ed.: USD 40 (effective 2007).
Published by: American College of Apothecaries, 2830 Summer Oaks Drive, Bartlett, TN 38134-3811. TEL 901-383-8119, FAX 901-383-8882, aca@acainfo.org, http://www.acainfo.org. Ed. D C Huffman Jr. Circ: 1,000.

VOJNOSANITETSKI PREGLED/MILITARY MEDICAL AND PHARMACEUTICAL; casopis lekara i farmaceuta Srbije i Crne Gore. *see* MILITARY

VOPROSY BIOLOGICHESKOI, MEDITSINSKOI, I FARMATSEVTICHESKOI KHIMII/PROBLEMS OF BIOLOGICAL, MEDICAL AND PHARMACOLOGICAL. *see* BIOLOGY

W H O DRUG INFORMATION. *see* PUBLIC HEALTH AND SAFETY

615 CHE ISSN 1564-1120
W H O PHARMACEUTICALS NEWSLETTER. Text in English. 199?. 6/yr. free (effective 2007). **Document type:** *Newsletter, Trade.* **Description:** Disseminates information on the safety and efficacy of pharmaceutical products.
Media: Online - full text.
—CCC.
Published by: World Health Organization/Organisation Mondiale de la Sante, Avenue Appia 20, Geneva 27, 1211, Switzerland. TEL 41-22-7912111, FAX 41-22-7913111, publications@who.int.

615 JPN ISSN 0509-5832
WAKSMAN FOUNDATION OF JAPAN. REPORT. Text in English. 1962. a. per issue exchange basis.
—Linda Hall.
Published by: Waksman Foundation of Japan/Nihon Wakkusuman Zaidan, 30-8 Daikyo-cho, Shinjuku-ku, Tokyo, 160-0015, Japan. TEL 81-3-53633741, FAX 81-3-33514827, http://www.waksman.or.jp/.

WARNING LETTER BULLETIN. *see* MEDICAL SCIENCES

616 USA ISSN 0194-1291
KF3885.A15
WASHINGTON DRUG LETTER (WASHINGTON, 1979). Text in English. 1969. w. (50/yr.). looseleaf. USD 1,247 (print or online ed.); USD 1,995 combined subscription (print & online eds.) (effective 2009). adv. bk.rev. 8 p./no.; Supplement avail.; back issues avail. **Document type:** *Newsletter, Trade.* **Description:** Provides concise summaries of FDA regulatory changes and key legislation that affects prescription and OTC drugs.
Incorporates (in 2002): Drug Marketing (1527-1498); (2000-2002): Genomics Newswire (1528-963X); (1998-2002): Strategic Outsourcing Report (1521-2467); Former titles (until 1979): Washington Drug and Device Letter (0162-2994); Washington Drug Letter; Incorporates (in 1994): Pharmaceutical and Biotech Daily (1074-8636); Which was formed by the merger of (1993-1994): Pharmaceutical Daily (1071-5096); (1992-1994): Biotech Daily (1067-1196); Which superseded (1981-1992): Genetic Engineering Letter (0276-1882)
Related titles: Online - full text ed.: USD 1,097 (effective 2005).
Indexed: A22, Agr, B02, B15, B17, B18, G04, G06, G07, G08, I05, P30, Telegen.
—CCC.
Published by: Washington Business Information, Inc., 300 N Washington St, Ste 200, Falls Church, Arlington, VA 22046. TEL 703-538-7600, 888-838-5578, FAX 703-538-7676, customerservice@fdanews.com. Eds. Annette Licitra, Elizabeth Tilley-Hinkle. Pub. Matt Salt TEL 703-538-7642. Adv. contact Andrew McSherry TEL 703-538-7643.

615 USA ISSN 0745-7413
THE WASHINGTON PHARMACIST. Text in English. 1959. 4/yr. membership. adv. bk.rev. **Document type:** *Magazine, Trade.* **Description:** Focuses on current issues and challenges of the profession. Appeals to a broad spectrum of pharmacy professionals with articles about new products.
Formerly: Washington - Alaska Pharmacist
Published by: Washington State Pharmacists Association, 1501 Taylor Ave, S W, Renton, WA 98055-3139. TEL 425-228-7171, FAX 425-277-3897. Ed. Rod Shafer. R&P Sheri Ray. Adv. contact Sheri L Ray. Circ: 2,000.

WEHRMEDIZIN UND WEHRPHARMAZIE. *see* MEDICAL SCIENCES

615.1 CAN ISSN 1701-9583
WELCOME TO THE C I H R - RX & D PROGRESS REPORT (YEAR)/ RAPPORT D'ETAPE D'I R S C/RX & D. (Canadian Institutes of Health Research) Text in English, French. 2001. a.
Published by: Canadian Institutes of Health Research (C I H R)/Instituts de Recherche en Sante au Canada (I R S C), 160 Elgin St, 9th Fl, Ottawa, ON K1A 0W9, Canada. TEL 613-941-2672, 888-603-4178, FAX 613-954-1800, info@cihr-irsc.gc.ca, http://www.cihr-irsc.gc.ca.

615 GBR
▼ **WELLARDS ANNUAL REVIEW (YEAR).** Text in English. 2009. a. GBP 24.95 per issue (effective 2011). **Document type:** *Trade.*
Incorporates (2007-2009): Wellard's N H S Guide (Year)
—BLDSC (9294.197550).
Published by: J M H Publishing, The Oast, Great Danegate, Eridge, E Sussex TN3 9HU, United Kingdom. TEL 44-1892-752407, FAX 44-1892-752404, sales@wellards.co.uk. Ed. Peter Merry.

615.19 DEU ISSN 1618-9795
WER UND WAS - PHARMAZEUTISCHE INDUSTRIE. Text in German. 1978. biennial. EUR 169.50 (effective 2009). adv. **Document type:** *Directory, Trade.*
Formerly (until 2001): Wer und Was in der Deutschen Pharmazeutischen - Industrie (0171-4449)
—GNLM.
Published by: B. Behr's Verlag GmbH & Co. KG, Averhoffstr 10, Hamburg, 22085, Germany. TEL 49-40-2270080, FAX 49-40-2201091, info@behrs.de, http://www.behrs.de. adv.: B&W page EUR 2,240, color page EUR 3,620; trim 210 x 297. Circ: 2,200 (paid and controlled).

615.19 NGA ISSN 0303-691X
CODEN: WAJPAS
➤ **WEST AFRICAN JOURNAL OF PHARMACOLOGY AND DRUG RESEARCH.** Text in English. 1974. biennial. GBP 60, USD 100 (effective 2004). back issues avail. **Document type:** *Journal, Academic/Scholarly.* **Description:** Publishes papers on all aspects of drug action and related topics including chemotherapy and toxicology.
Related titles: Online - full text ed.
Indexed: A34, A36, AgrForAb, BP, CABA, ChemAb, E12, F08, F11, F12, GH, H16, IndMed, N02, N03, P30, P33, P39, R08, R12, RA&MP, RM&VM, S12, T05, VS.
—CASDDS, GNLM.

Published by: (West African Society for Pharmacology), Literamed Publications Nigeria Ltd, PMB 21068, Ikeja, Oregun Village, Lagos, Nigeria. TEL 234-64-962512, FAX 234-64-961037. Pub. O M Lawal Solarin.

615.1 CAN ISSN 0043-3829
WESTERN HORIZONS; a quarterly magazine for Western Canadian pharmacists. Text in English. 1966. q. free. adv. **Document type:** *Magazine, Trade.*
Published by: National Drug & Chemical Co. of Canada Ltd., P O Box 758, Winnipeg, MB, Canada. TEL 204-774-4511. Ed. T H Glenwright. Circ: 3,200.

615.1 USA ISSN 0083-8969
RM30 CODEN: PWPSA8
➤ **WESTERN PHARMACOLOGY SOCIETY. PROCEEDINGS.** Text in English. 1958. a. back issues avail.; reprints avail. **Document type:** *Proceedings, Academic/Scholarly.*
Related titles: Microform ed.: (from PQC).
Indexed: A22, B21, CIN, ChemAb, ChemTitl, EMBASE, ExcerpMed, IndMed, MEDLINE, P30, R10, Reac, SCOPUS, VirolAbstr.
—BLDSC (6834.200000), CASDDS, GNLM, IE, Infotrieve, Ingenta, INIST, Linda Hall. **CCC.**
Published by: Western Pharmacology Society, Inc., c/o Linda Hedley, Ricerca Biosciences, 22011 30th Dr SE, Bothell, WA 98021. TEL 650-619-8971, linda.hedley@ricerca.com. Ed. Iain L O Buxton.

▼ ➤ **WORLD JOURNAL OF GASTROINTESTINAL PHARMACOLOGY AND THERAPEUTICS.** *see* MEDICAL SCIENCES—Gastroenterology

615 USA ISSN 2160-5815
▼ ➤ **WORLD JOURNAL OF VACCINES.** Abbreviated title: W J V. Text in English. 2011. q. USD 156 (effective 2011). **Document type:** *Journal, Academic/Scholarly.* **Description:** Provides a platform for researchers and academics all over the world to promote, share, and discuss various new issues and developments in vaccine related problems.
Related titles: Online - full text ed.: ISSN 2160-5823. free (effective 2011).
Published by: Scientific Research Publishing, Inc., PO Box 54821, Irvine, CA 92619. service@scirp.org. Ed. Andrew W Heath.

615 338 658 GBR
THE WORLD MARKET FOR O T C HEALTHCARE. (Over the Counter) Text in English. 1999. irreg. GBP 5,075, EUR 7,613, USD 10,150 per issue (effective 2010). **Document type:** *Directory, Trade.* **Description:** Features global investigation into the worldwide OTC healthcare products industry. Includes in-depth sales, share and distribution analysis.
Related titles: Online - full text ed.
Published by: Euromonitor International Plc., 60-61 Britton St, London, EC1M 5UX, United Kingdom. TEL 44-20-72518024, FAX 44-20-76083149, info@euromonitor.com.

615 USA ISSN 1935-7753
HD9675.D532
WORLD NUTRACEUTICALS. Text in English. 1998. irreg. USD 5,100 per issue (print or online ed.) (effective 2011). back issues avail. **Document type:** *Monographic series, Trade.*
Related titles: Online - full text ed.
Published by: The Freedonia Group, Inc., 767 Beta Dr, Cleveland, OH 44143. TEL 440-684-9600, 800-927-5900, FAX 440-646-0484, info@freedoniagroup.com.

615 USA ISSN 1529-4331
WORLD OF DRUG INFORMATION. Text in English. 19??. q. free (effective 2010). **Document type:** *Journal, Academic/Scholarly.* **Description:** Contains articles and information on clinical drugs and therapies.
Related titles: Online - full text ed.: ISSN 1559-6451.
Indexed: IDIS.
Published by: University of Iowa, Division of Drug Information Service, University of Iowa Research Park, 2500 Crosspark Rd, Rm W145, Coralville, IA 52241. TEL 319-335-4800, 800-525-4347, FAX 319-335-4440, idis@uiowa.edu. Ed. Kevin Moores.

615 GBR
WORLD PHARMACEUTICAL FRONTIERS; providing a global perspective on th pharmaceutical industry. Text in English. 200?. s-a. GBP 5.95 per issue domestic; EUR 8 per issue in Europe; USD 8.95 per issue in United States; free to qualified personnel (effective 2010). back issues avail.; reprints avail. **Document type:** *Magazine, Trade.* **Description:** Provides pharmaceutical companies, with reliable and accurate intelligence on emerging trends and breakthrough technologies to help them make critical business decisions.
Related titles: Online - full text ed.; ◆ Supplement(s): Pharmaceutical Outsourcing Decisions.
—BLDSC (9358.055250).
Published by: S P G Media Ltd. (Subsidiary of: Sterling Publishing Group Plc.), Brunel House, 55-57 N Wharf Rd, London, W2 1LA, United Kingdom. TEL 44-20-79159660, FAX 44-20-77242089, info@spgmedia.com, http://www.spgmedia.com/. Eds. Andrew Tunnicliffe, John Lawrence. Pub. William Crocker.

WORLDWIDE BIOTECH. *see* BIOLOGY—Biotechnology

615 CHN ISSN 1674-5515
XIANDAI YAOWU YU LINCHUANG/DRUGS & CLINIC. Text in Chinese. 1980. bi-m. CNY 90 (effective 2010). **Document type:** *Journal, Academic/Scholarly.*
Formerly (until 2009): Guowai Yiyao (Zhiwuyao Fence)/World Phytomedicines (1001-6856)
Related titles: Online - full text ed.
Indexed: A34, A35, C30, E12, F08, H16, N03, P32, P33, R08.
—BLDSC (4232.145252), East View.
Published by: (Tianjin Yaowu Yanjiusuo), Tainjin Zhongcaoyao Zazhishe, 308, An-shan Xi Dao, Tianjin, 300193, China. TEL 86-22-23006823, FAX 86-22-27381305, tjipr_office@126.com, http://www.tjipr.com/netbook.asp. Ed. Hong-zhu Li. **Dist. by:** China International Book Trading Corp, 35 Chegongzhuang Xilu, Haidian District, PO Box 399, Beijing 100044, China. TEL 86-10-68412045, FAX 86-10-68412023, cibtc@mail.cibtc.com.cn, http://www.cibtc.com.cn.

615 CHN ISSN 1004-2407
XIBEI YAOXUE ZAZHI/NORTHWEST PHARMACEUTICAL JOURNAL. Text in Chinese. 1986. bi-m. USD 21.60 (effective 2009). **Document type:** *Journal, Academic/Scholarly.*
Related titles: Online - full text ed.
—BLDSC (9367.041850).
Published by: Xi'an Jiaotong Daxue, Yixuejiao-qu, Nanjiao, 205, Zhuqiao Dajie, Xi'an, 710061, China. **Dist. by:** China International Book Trading Corp, 35 Chegongzhuang Xilu, Haidian District, PO Box 399, Beijing 100044, China. TEL 86-10-68412045, FAX 86-10-68412023, cibtc@mail.cibtc.com.cn, http://www.cibtc.com.cn.

XINZHONGYI/NEW JOURNAL OF TRADITIONAL CHINESE MEDICINE. *see* ALTERNATIVE MEDICINE

615 KOR ISSN 0377-9556
CODEN: YAHOA3
➤ **YAKHAK HOEJI/PHARMACEUTICAL SOCIETY OF KOREA. JOURNAL.** Text in Korean; Summaries in English. 1948. bi-m. adv. bk.rev. back issues avail. **Document type:** *Journal, Academic/Scholarly.*
Indexed: A22, B25, BIOSIS Prev, C33, CIN, ChemAb, IndMed, MycolAb.
—BLDSC (9369.430000), GNLM, Ingenta.
Published by: Pharmaceutical Society of Korea, 1489-3 Suhcho-3-Dong, Suhcho-Ku, Seoul, 137-073, Korea, S. TEL 82-2-5843257, FAX 82-2-5211781, pskor@chollian.net, pskor@korea.com, http://www.pharmbiomed.org, http://www.apr.psk.or.kr. Ed. Uhtaek Oh. Pub. Chang Jong Kim. R&P, Adv. contact Young Choong Kim. Circ: 1,500.

➤ **YAKUGAKU TOSHOKAN/PHARMACEUTICAL LIBRARY BULLETIN.** *see* LIBRARY AND INFORMATION SCIENCES

615.1 JPN ISSN 0031-6903
RS1 CODEN: YKKZAJ
➤ **YAKUGAKU ZASSHI/PHARMACEUTICAL JOURNAL.** Variant title: Pharmaceutical Society of Japan. Journal. Text in English, Japanese; Abstracts and contents page in English. 1881. m. USD 95 (effective 2004). adv. tr.lit.; tr.mk.; bibl. 90 p./no.; back issues avail. **Document type:** *Journal, Academic/Scholarly.* **Description:** Covers all pharmaceutical sciences.
Related titles: Microform ed.: (from PMC); Online - full text ed.: ISSN 1347-5231. free (effective 2011).
Indexed: A22, A34, A35, A36, ASCA, AgBio, AgrForAb, B25, BIOSIS Prev, BP, C25, C30, C31, C33, CABA, CIN, ChemAb, ChemTitl, CurCR, CurCont, D01, DBA, E12, EMBASE, ExcerpMed, F08, F11, F12, FCA, FS&TA, GH, H16, H17, I12, INIS AtomInd, ISR, IndChem, IndMed, IndVet, Inpharma, MEDLINE, MycolAb, N02, N03, P30, P32, P33, P35, P39, P40, PGegResA, PGrRegA, PHN&I, R07, R08, R10, R13, R16, RA&MP, RM&VM, Reac, S12, S13, S16, S17, SCI, SCOPUS, SoyAb, T05, TAR, VS, W07, W10, W11.
—BLDSC (4840.000000), CASDDS, GNLM, IE, Infotrieve, Ingenta, INIST, Linda Hall. **CCC.**
Published by: Pharmaceutical Society of Japan/Nihon Yakugakkai, 2-12-15, Shibuya, Shibuya-ku, Tokyo, 150-0002, Japan. TEL 81-3-34063321, FAX 81-3-34981835. Ed. Hiroshi Hara. Circ: 2,400.

615 JPN
YAKUJI NYUSU/PHARMACEUTICAL AFFAIRS NEWS. Text in Japanese. w. JPY 12,233 (effective 2007). **Document type:** *Newspaper, Academic/Scholarly.*
Published by: Yakuji Nyususha/YakujiNews Co., Ltd., 3-2-8 Fushimi-tyo,Tyuo-ku, Osaka, 541-0045, Japan. TEL 81-6-62317328, FAX 81-6-62317856.

615 JPN ISSN 0386-3603
CODEN: YACHDS
YAKURI TO CHIRYO/JAPANESE PHARMACOLOGY AND THERAPEUTICS. Text in Japanese; Summaries in English. 1973. m. JPY 16,500; JPY 1,500 newsstand/cover (effective 2004). **Document type:** *Journal, Academic/Scholarly.* **Description:** Contains articles on non-clinical and clinical trials of newly developed drugs under development, reviews based on data from new drugs under development, case studies, short reports, proceedings of symposia and round-table discussions.
Related titles: Online - full text ed.
Indexed: A22, CIN, ChemAb, EMBASE, ExcerpMed, Inpharma, R10, Reac, SCOPUS.
—BLDSC (4660.200000), CASDDS, GNLM, IE, Ingenta, INIST.
Published by: Raifu Saiensu Shuppan K.K./Life Science Publishing Co. Ltd., Daisen Bldg, 11-7 Nihonbashikobuna-cho, Chuo-ku, Tokyo, 103-0024, Japan. TEL 81-3-36647917, info@lifescience.co.jp. Ed. Tamio Teramoto.

615 JPN ISSN 0917-3994
YAKURI TO RINSHO/CLINICAL PHARMACOLOGY. Text in Japanese. 1991. bi-m. JPY 20,160 (effective 2005). **Document type:** *Journal, Academic/Scholarly.*
—BLDSC (9369.884500).
Published by: Iyakushuppan Co., 1-15, Kanda-Awajicyo, Chiyoda-Ku, Tokyo, 101-0063, Japan. TEL 81-3-32532995, FAX 81-120-570583.

615.1 JPN ISSN 0372-7629
CODEN: YAKUA2
YAKUZAIGAKU/ARCHIVES OF PRACTICAL PHARMACY. Text in English, Japanese; Summaries in English. 1934. q. free to members. **Document type:** *Journal, Academic/Scholarly.*
Formerly (until 1955): Yakuzai-Buchokai-Nempo/Archives of Practical Pharmacy
Indexed: A22, B25, BIOSIS Prev, CIN, ChemAb, ChemTitl, I12, MycolAb.
—BLDSC (5031.890000), CASDDS, GNLM, IE, Ingenta, Linda Hall. **CCC.**
Published by: Academy of Pharmaceutical Science and Technology, 52-1 Yada, University of Shizuoka, College of Pharmacy, Shizuoka, 422-8526, Japan. sonobe@u-shizuoka-ken.ac.jp, http://wwwsoc.nii.ac.jp/apstj/. Circ: 1,200.

615 CHN ISSN 1672-2809
YAOPIN PINGJIA/DRUG EVALUATION. Text in Chinese. 2004. bi-m. USD 62.40 (effective 2009). **Document type:** *Journal, Academic/Scholarly.*
Related titles: Online - full text ed.
—East View.
Published by: Jiangxi Sheng Yaxuehui, 104, Beijing Xilu, Nanchang, 330046, China. TEL 86-791-6285219, FAX 86-791-6279953. **Dist. by:** China International Book Trading Corp, 35 Chegongzhuang Xilu, Haidian District, PO Box 399, Beijing 100044, China. TEL 86-10-68412045, FAX 86-10-68412023, cibtc@mail.cibtc.com.cn, http://www.cibtc.com.cn.

615 CHN ISSN 1008-5734
YAOWU BULIANG FANYING ZAZHI/ADVERSE DRUG REACTIONS JOURNAL. Text in Chinese. 1999. bi-m. USD 30.60 (effective 2009). **Document type:** *Journal, Academic/Scholarly.*
Related titles: Online - full text ed.
Indexed: I12.
—BLDSC (9371.576380), East View.
Published by: Beijing Ditan Yiyuan, 13, Ditan Gongyuan, Beijing, 100011, China. TEL 86-10-64266618, FAX 86-10-64289612.

615 CHN ISSN 0254-1793
RS189 CODEN: YFZADL
➤ **YAOWU FENXI ZAZHI/CHINESE JOURNAL OF PHARMACEUTICAL ANALYSIS.** Text in Chinese. 1981. m. USD 106.80 (effective 2009). adv. **Document type:** *Journal, Academic/Scholarly.*
Related titles: Online - full text ed.
Indexed: A22, A40, CIN, ChemAb, ChemTitl, I12.
—BLDSC (3180.473000), CASDDS, East View, IE, Ingenta, Linda Hall.
Published by: Chinese Pharmaceutical Association/Zhongguo Yaoxuehui, 2, Tianting Xili, Beijing, 100050, China. TEL 86-10-67058427, FAX 86-10-67012819. **Dist. by:** China International Book Trading Corp, 35 Chegongzhuang Xilu, Haidian District, PO Box 399, Beijing 100044, China. TEL 86-10-68412045, FAX 86-10-68412023, cibtc@mail.cibtc.com.cn, http://www.cibtc.com.cn.

615 CHN ISSN 1674-6376
YAOWU PINGJIA YANJIU/DRUG EVALUATION RESEARCH. Text in Chinese. 1977. bi-m. CNY 210; CNY 30 per issue (effective 2010). Index. back issues avail. **Document type:** *Journal, Academic/Scholarly.*
Formerly (until 2009): Zhongwen Keji Ziliao Mulu (Zhongcaoyao Fence)
Published by: Tainjin Zhongcaoyao Zazhishe, 308, An-shan Xi Dao, Tianjin, 300193, China. TEL 86-22-23006822, FAX 86-22-23006822, tjipr_office@126.com, http://www.tjipr.com/netbook.asp.

615 660.6 CHN ISSN 1005-8915
YAOWU SHENGWU JISHU/PHARMACEUTICAL BIOTECHNOLOGY. Text in Chinese. 1994. bi-m. USD 40.20 (effective 2009). **Document type:** *Journal, Academic/Scholarly.*
Related titles: Online - full text ed.
Indexed: A22, B&BAb, B19, B21, BIOBASE, BioEngAb, EMBASE, ExcerpMed, IABS, M&PBA, RefZh.
—BLDSC (6442.768000), East View, IE, Ingenta.
Published by: China Pharmaceutical University/Zhongguo Yaoke Daxue, 24, Tong Jia Xiang, 75 Xinxiang, Beijing, 210009, China.

615 CHN ISSN 1671-2838
YAOXUE FUWU YU YANJIU/PHARMACEUTICAL CARE AND RESEARCH. Text in Chinese. 2001. q. USD 31.20 (effective 2009).
Related titles: Online - full text ed.
Indexed: A22, EMBASE, ExcerpMed, I12, R10, Reac, SCOPUS.
—BLDSC (6443.270000), East View, IE, Ingenta.
Published by: Di-2 Junyi Daxue Changhai Yiyuan/Changhai Hospital of Second Military Medical University, 174, Changhai Lu, Yangpu-qu, Shanghai, 200433, China. TEL 86-21-65519829, FAX 86-21-25074639. **Dist. by:** China International Book Trading Corp, 35 Chegongzhuang Xilu, Haidian District, PO Box 399, Beijing 100044, China. TEL 86-10-68412045, FAX 86-10-68412023, cibtc@mail.cibtc.com.cn, http://www.cibtc.com.cn.

615 CHN ISSN 1001-5094
YAOXUE JINZHAN/PROGRESS IN PHARMACEUTICAL SCIENCES. Text in Chinese. 1959. m. USD 49.20 (effective 2009). **Document type:** *Journal, Academic/Scholarly.*
—BLDSC (9371.576740), East View.
Published by: China Pharmaceutical University/Zhongguo Yaoke Daxue, 24, Tong Jia Xiang, 75 Xinxiang, Beijing, 210009, China. TEL 86-25-83271475, FAX 86-25-83271156.

615 CHN ISSN 1006-0111
YAOXUE SHIJIAN ZAZHI/FISHING MAGAZINE. Text in Chinese. 1983. bi-m. **Document type:** *Journal, Academic/Scholarly.*
Related titles: Online - full text ed.
Address: 325, Guohe Lu, Shanghai, 200433, China. TEL 86-21-25074468 ext 19, FAX 86-21-25074468 ext 18.

615.19 CHN ISSN 0513-4870
RS1 CODEN: YHHPAL
YAOXUE XUEBAO/ACTA PHARMACEUTICA SINICA. Text in Chinese. 1936. m. USD 106.80 (effective 2009). **Document type:** *Journal, Academic/Scholarly.*
Formerly (until 1952): Chung-Kuo Yao Hsueh Tsa Chih (0366-6689)
Related titles: Online - full text ed.
Indexed: A22, A34, A35, A36, A37, A38, AgBio, AgrForAb, B25, BA, BIOSIS Prev, BP, C25, C30, CABA, CIN, ChemAb, ChemTitl, D01, E12, EMBASE, ExcerpMed, F08, F11, F12, FCA, GH, H16, H17, I12, IndMed, IndVet, MEDLINE, MaizeAb, MycolAb, N02, N03, N05, P30, P32, P33, P39, P40, PGegResA, PGrRegA, PHN&I, PN&I, R07, R08, R10, R13, RA&MP, RM&VM, Reac, RefZh, S12, S13, S16, S17, SCOPUS, SoyAb, T05, TAR, VS, W10.
—BLDSC (0646.500000), CASDDS, East View, GNLM, IE, Infotrieve, Ingenta, INIST, Linda Hall.
Address: Nongtan Jie, 1, Beijing, 100050, China. TEL 86-10-63035116, FAX 86-10-63026192. **Dist. by:** China International Book Trading Corp, 35 Chegongzhuang Xilu, Haidian District, PO Box 399, Beijing 100044, China. TEL 86-10-68412045, FAX 86-10-68412023, cibtc@mail.cibtc.com.cn, http://www.cibtc.com.cn.

615 GBR ISSN 1745-848X
THE YEAR IN THERAPEUTICS. Text in English. 2005 (Jan.). a. USD 139.95 per issue in US & Canada; GBP 75 per issue elsewhere (effective 2009). 384 p./no.; **Document type:** *Journal, Academic/Scholarly.* **Description:** Contains medical literature review and three distinguished clinical pharmacologists.
Related titles: Online - full text ed.
Indexed: P20, P22, P48, P54, PQC.
—**CCC.**
Published by: Clinical Publishing (Subsidiary of: Atlas Medical Publishing Ltd), Oxford Centre for Innovation, Mill St, Oxford, OX2 OJX, United Kingdom. TEL 44-1865-811116, FAX 44-1865-251550, info@clinicalpublishing.co.uk. Eds. D J Webb, David Flockhart, K R Paterson. **Dist. by:** Marston Book Services Ltd., Unit 160, Milton Park, Abingdon, Oxfordshire OX14 4SD, United Kingdom. TEL 44-1235-465500, FAX 44-1235-465555, trade.orders@marston.co.uk, http://www.marston.co.uk/.

(YEAR) ONCOLOGY NURSING DRUG HANDBOOK. *see* MEDICAL SCIENCES—Nurses And Nursing

615 CHN ISSN 1008-455X
YIYAO GONGCHENG SHEJI/PHARMACEUTICAL & ENGINEERING DESIGN. Text in Chinese. 1980. bi-m. CNY 7 newsstand/cover (effective 2006). **Document type:** *Journal, Academic/Scholarly.*
Related titles: Online - full content ed.; Online - full text ed.

P

Published by: Zhongguo Shi-hua Jituan Shanghai Gongcheng Youxiang Gongsi, Yanan Xilu 376 Alley, no.22, 11/F, Yongxingshangwu Dalou, Shanghai, 200040, China. TEL 86-21-32140428, FAX 86-21-62489867.

YOKOHAMA MEDICAL JOURNAL. *see* MEDICAL SCIENCES

YUNNAN ZHONGYI ZHONGYAO ZAZHI/YUNNAN JOURNAL OF TRADITIONAL CHINESE MEDICINE AND MATERIA MEDICA. *see* ALTERNATIVE MEDICINE

615 EGY ISSN 1110-5089
CODEN: ZJPSEV
ZAGAZIG JOURNAL OF PHARMACEUTICAL SCIENCES. Text in Arabic, English. 1990. s-a. USD 150 (effective 1998). **Document type:** *Journal, Academic/Scholarly.*
Indexed: CIN, ChemTitl.
—CASDDS.
Published by: Zagazig University, Faculty of Pharmacy, Campus, Zagazig, Egypt. TEL 20-55-2363635 Ext 13026. Ed. Dr. Muhammad Abdel al-Muhammad Ibrahim.

615.1 DEU ISSN 1431-9292
ZEITSCHRIFT FUER ARZNEI- UND GEWUERZPFLANZEN. Text in German. 1997. q. EUR 122.40 domestic; EUR 123.80 foreign; EUR 32.80 newsstand/cover (effective 2008). adv. **Document type:** *Journal, Academic/Scholarly.*
Indexed: A22, A34, A35, A36, A37, AMED, AgBio, AgrForAb, BA, BP, C25, C30, CABA, E12, F08, F11, F12, FCA, FS&TA, G11, GH, H16, I11, IndVet, LT, N02, N03, N04, N05, OR, P32, P33, P40, PGegResA, PGrRegA, PHN&I, R07, R12, R13, RA&MP, RM&VM, RRTA, S12, S13, S16, S17, SCI, SCOPUS, T05, TAR, VS, W07, W10, W11.
—BLDSC (9452.270000), GNLM, IE, Ingenta. **CCC.**
Published by: Agrimedia GmbH, Spithal 4, Bergen-Dumme, 29468, Germany. TEL 49-5845-988110, FAX 49-5845-988111, mail@agrimedia.com, http://www.agrimedia.com. Ed. Peter Erling. Adv. contact Karin Monneweg. B&W page EUR 790, color page EUR 1,560. Circ: 1,000 (paid and controlled).

615 NLD ISSN 1879-9051
ZELFREGULERING FARMACIE. Variant title: Teksten Zelfregulering Farmacie. Text in Dutch. 200?. biennial. EUR 40.09 per issue (effective 2010).
Published by: Sdu Uitgevers bv, Postbus 20025, The Hague, 2500 EA, Netherlands. TEL 31-70-3789911, FAX 31-70-3854321, sdu@sdu.nl, http://www.sdu.nl/.

▼ **ZELFZORG ZAKEN.** *see* PUBLIC HEALTH AND SAFETY

ZHEJIANG ZHONGYI ZAZHI/ZHEJIANG JOURNAL OF TRADITIONAL CHINESE MEDICINE. *see* ALTERNATIVE MEDICINE

ZHEJIANG ZHONGYIYAO DAXUE XUEBAO/ZHEJIANG COLLEGE OF TRADITIONAL CHINESE MEDICINE. JOURNAL. *see* MEDICAL SCIENCES

615 CHN ISSN 1001-1528
➤ **ZHONGCHENYAO/CHINESE TRADITIONAL PATENT MEDICINE.** Text in Chinese; Abstracts occasionally in English. 1978. m. USD 133.20 (effective 2009). adv. bk.rev. **Document type:** *Journal, Academic/Scholarly.* **Description:** Reports the recent research achievements in industry of Chinese patent medicine and introduces new products, dosage formulations, processes and new equipment used in this industry.
Related titles: Online - full text ed.
—BLDSC (3181.122320), East View.
Published by: Guojia Yiyao Guanliju, Zhongchengyao Qingbao Zhongxinzhan/Information Center of State Food and Drug Administration, Chinese Patent Medicine Information Station, Room 129-131, 239 Hankou Road, Shanghai, 200-002, China. TEL 86-21-63213275, FAX 86-21-63213363. Ed. Lizhong Zhu. Circ: 10,000. **Dist. outside China by:** China International Book Trading Corp, 35 Chegongzhuang Xilu, Haidian District, PO Box 399, Beijing 100044, China. TEL 86-10-68412045, FAX 86-10-68412023, cibtc@mail.cibtc.com.cn, http://www.cibtc.com.cn.

578.77 CHN ISSN 1002-3461
ZHONGGUO HAIYANG YAOWU ZAZHI/CHINESE JOURNAL OF MARINE DRUGS. Text in Chinese. 1982. bi-m. USD 23.40 (effective 2009). **Document type:** *Journal, Academic/Scholarly.*
Formerly: Haiyang Yaowu Zazhi
Related titles: Online - full text ed.
Indexed: A22, ASFA, B21, ESPM.
—BLDSC (3180.369500), East View, IE, Ingenta.
Published by: Shandong Sheng Haiyang Yaowu Kexue Yanjiuso, 2, Laiwu Lu, Qingdao, 266003, China. TEL 86-532-2795939. **Dist. by:** China International Book Trading Corp, 35 Chegongzhuang Xilu, Haidian District, PO Box 399, Beijing 100044, China. TEL 86-10-68412045, FAX 86-10-68412023, cibtc@mail.cibtc.com.cn, http://www.cibtc.com.cn.

ZHONGGUO JICENG YIYAO/CHINESE JOURNAL OF PRIMARY MEDICINE AND PHARMACY. *see* MEDICAL SCIENCES

615.329 CHN ISSN 1001-8689
CODEN: ZKZAEY
ZHONGGUO KANGSHENGSU ZAZHI/CHINESE JOURNAL OF ANTIBIOTICS. Text in Chinese, English. 1976. m. USD 56.40 (effective 2009). 80 p./no.; **Document type:** *Journal, Academic/Scholarly.*
Former titles (until 1988): Kang Shengsu; (until 1978): Kang Junsu
Related titles: Online - full text ed.
Indexed: A22, B25, BIOSIS Prev, CIN, ChemAb, ChemTitl, EMBASE, ExcerpMed, I12, MycolAb, R10, Reac, SCOPUS.
—BLDSC (3180.293500), CASDDS, GNLM, IE, Ingenta.
Address: 9, Shabanqiao Lu, Chengdu, 610051, China. **Dist. by:** China International Book Trading Corp, 35 Chegongzhuang Xilu, Haidian District, PO Box 399, Beijing 100044, China. TEL 86-10-68412045, FAX 86-10-68412023, cibtc@mail.cibtc.com.cn, http://www.cibtc.com.cn.

615 CHN ISSN 1009-2501
ZHONGGUO LINCHUANG YAOLIXUE YU ZHILIAOXUE/CHINESE JOURNAL OF CLINICAL PHARMACOLOGY AND THERAPEUTICS. Text in Chinese. 1996. m. CNY 144 domestic; USD 216 foreign (effective 2005). **Document type:** *Journal, Academic/Scholarly.*
Related titles: Online - full text ed.
—BLDSC (9512.774700).
Published by: Anhui Sheng Yaowu Linchuang Pingjia Zhongxin/Anhui Provincial Center for Drug Clinical Evaluation, Yijishan Hospital, Wuhu, 241001, China. TEL 86-553-5738350, FAX 86-553-5739333. **Dist. overseas by:** China National Publications Import & Export Corp., 16 Gongti Dong Lu, Chaoyang-qu, PO Box 88, Beijing 100020, China. **Co-sponsor:** Zhongguo Yaoli Xuehui/Chinese Society of Pharmacology.

615 CHN ISSN 1001-6821
ZHONGGUO LINCHUANG YAOLIXUE ZAZHI/CHINESE JOURNAL OF CLINICAL PHARMACOLOGY. Text in Chinese. 1985. bi-m. USD 37.20 (effective 2009). **Document type:** *Journal, Academic/Scholarly.*
Related titles: Online - full text ed.
Indexed: B&BAb, B21, ESPM, ImmunAb, NSA.
—BLDSC (3180.303000), IE, Ingenta.
Address: 38 Xueyuan Lu, Haidian-qu, Beijing, 100083, China. TEL 86-10-82802540, FAX 86-10-62072817.

615 CHN ISSN 1007-4406
ZHONGGUO LINCHUANG YAOXUE ZAZHI/CHINESE JOURNAL OF CLINICAL PHARMACY. Text in Chinese. 1992. bi-m. USD 24.60 (effective 2009). **Document type:** *Journal, Academic/Scholarly.*
Related titles: Online - full text ed.
Indexed: I12.
—BLDSC (3180.302900), East View.
Published by: Chinese Pharmaceutical Association/Zhongguo Yaoxuehui, 138, Yixueyuan Lu, 290 Xinxiang, Shanghai, 200032, China. TEL 86-21-54237256, FAX 86-21-64176498.

615 CHN ISSN 1005-1678
ZHONGGUO SHENGHUA YAOWU ZAZHI. Text in Chinese; Abstracts in English. 1992. bi-m. USD 37.20 (effective 2009). bk.rev. illus. Index. 54 p./no.; **Document type:** *Journal, Academic/Scholarly.*
Formerly: Shenghua Yaowu Zazhi
Related titles: Online - full text ed.
Indexed: A29, A34, A35, A36, A38, AgBio, AgrForAb, B&BAb, B19, B20, B21, C25, C30, CABA, D01, E12, ESPM, F08, F11, F12, FCA, GH, H16, N02, N03, N04, N05, O01, P32, P33, P39, R08, R11, R13, RA&MP, RM&VM, S13, SoyAb, T05, TAR, VS, W10.
—BLDSC (3180.295550), East View, IE, Ingenta.
Published by: (Zhongguo Shenghua Zhiyao Gongye Xiehui/Chinese Association of the Pharmaceutical Industry, Nanjing Shenghua Zhiyao Yanjiusuo/Nanjing Institute of Biochemical Pharmaceutics), Quanguo Shenghua Zhiyao Qingbao Zhongxinzhan/National Information Center of Biochemical Pharmaceutics, 18 Jiangdong Lu, Nanjing, 210011, China. TEL 86-25-6222179, FAX 86-25-8808442, shyw@jloline.com. **Dist. outside of China by:** China International Book Trading Corp, 35 Chegongzhuang Xilu, Haidian District, PO Box 399, Beijing 100044, China. TEL 86-10-68412045, FAX 86-10-68412023, cibtc@mail.cibtc.com.cn, http://www.cibtc.com.cn/.

615 CHN ISSN 1005-9903
ZHONGGUO SHIYAN FANGJIXUE ZAZHI/CHINESE JOURNAL OF EXPERIMENTAL TRADITIONAL MEDICAL FORMULAE. Text in Chinese. 1995. bi-m. USD 62.40 (effective 2009). **Document type:** *Academic/Scholarly.*
Related titles: Online - full text ed.
—East View.
Published by: Zhongguo Zhongyi Yanjiuyuan, Zhongyi Yanjiusuo, 18 Bei Xincang, Beijing, 100700, China. **Dist. by:** China International Book Trading Corp, 35 Chegongzhuang Xilu, Haidian District, PO Box 399, Beijing 100044, China. TEL 86-10-68412045, FAX 86-10-68412023, cibtc@mail.cibtc.com.cn, http://www.cibtc.com.cn.

615 CHN ISSN 1007-7693
ZHONGGUO XIANDAI YINGYONG YAOXUE/CHINESE JOURNAL OF MODERN APPLIED PHARMACY. Text in Chinese. 1984. bi-m. USD 40.20 (effective 2009). **Document type:** *Abstract/Index.*
Related titles: Online - full content ed.; Online - full text ed.
Indexed: I12.
—East View.
Published by: Chinese Pharmaceutical Association/Zhongguo Yaoxuehui, Muganshan Lu, 27, Wenbei Hang, Hangzhou, China. TEL 86-571-8822697, 86-571-8843848. Ed. Shu-Chun Liu. **Dist. by:** China International Book Trading Corp, 35 Chegongzhuang Xilu, Haidian District, PO Box 399, Beijing 100044, China. TEL 86-10-68412045, FAX 86-10-68412023, cibtc@mail.cibtc.com.cn, http://www.cibtc.com.cn.

615 CHN ISSN 1007-7669
RM300 CODEN: XYLIEU
➤ **ZHONGGUO XINYAO YU LINCHUANG ZAZHI/CHINESE JOURNAL OF NEW DRUGS AND CLINICAL REMEDIES.** Text in Chinese; Abstracts in English. 1982. m. (bi-m until 2002). USD 62.40 (effective 2009). adv. **Document type:** *Journal, Academic/Scholarly.* **Description:** Covers the clinical research on new drugs (including new indications of old drugs), clinical trials, clinical verifications, pharmacology, adverse reactions, retional prescriptions, drug interactions, drug evaluation and other related news.
Formerly: Xinyao yu Linchuang - New Drugs and Clinical Remedies (1000-3843)
Related titles: Online - full content ed.; Online - full text ed.
Indexed: A22, B25, BIOSIS Prev, I12, MycolAb.
—BLDSC (3180.436600), CASDDS, IE, Ingenta.
Published by: Shanghai Yaopin Jiandu Guanliju, Keji Qingbaosuo/Scientific and Technic Information Institute of Shanghai Municipal Drug Administration, No. 50 Lane 532, Yuyuan Road, Shanghai, 200040, China. Ed. Guangsheng Ding. R&P Yao Song Yu. Adv. contact Yaosong Yu. page USD 2,000. Circ: 20,000. **Subscr. to:** China International Book Trading Corp, 35 Chegongzhuang Xilu, Haidian District, PO Box 399, Beijing 100044, China. TEL 86-10-68412045, FAX 86-10-68412023, cibtc@mail.cibtc.com.cn, http://www.cibtc.com.cn. **Co-sponsor:** Chinese Pharmaceutical Association/Zhongguo Yaoxuehui.

615 CHN ISSN 1003-3734
ZHONGGUO XINYAO ZAZHI/CHINESE NEW DRUGS JOURNAL. Text in Chinese. 1992. m. (10/yr.). USD 148.80 (effective 2009). **Document type:** *Journal, Academic/Scholarly.*
Related titles: Online - full content ed.; Online - full text ed.
Indexed: A22, EMBASE, ExcerpMed, I12, R10, Reac, SCOPUS.
—BLDSC (3181.030300), East View, GNLM, IE, Ingenta.
Address: 12, Yongwai Sanyuan Xikong Jia, Chongwen-qu, Beijing, 100077, China. TEL 86-10-87274021, FAX 86-10-87240527. **Dist. by:** China International Book Trading Corp, 35 Chegongzhuang Xilu, Haidian District, PO Box 399, Beijing 100044, China. TEL 86-10-68412045, FAX 86-10-68412023, cibtc@mail.cibtc.com.cn, http://www.cibtc.com.cn.

615 CHN ISSN 1001-0408
RS1
➤ **ZHONGGUO YAOFANG/CHINA PHARMACY.** Text in Chinese. 1990. w. (48/yr.). CNY 480; CNY 10 per issue (effective 2010). **Document type:** *Journal, Academic/Scholarly.*
Related titles: Online - full text ed.
Indexed: A29, B&BAb, B19, B20, B21, ESPM, I12, ImmunAb, NSA, OGFA, RefZh, ToxAb.
—BLDSC (3180.217750), East View.
Published by: (Zhongguo Yiyuan Xiehui/Chinese Hospital Association), Zhongguo Yaofang Zazhishe, 129, Dapingzheng Jie, Chongqing, 400042, China. TEL 86-23-68586827, FAX 86-23-68586827. **Dist. by:** China International Book Trading Corp, 35 Chegongzhuang Xilu, Haidian District, PO Box 399, Beijing 100044, China. TEL 86-10-68412045, FAX 86-10-68412023, cibtc@mail.cibtc.com.cn, http://www.cibtc.com.cn.

615 CHN ISSN 1000-5048
ZHONGGUO YAOKE DAXUE XUEBAO/CHINESE PHARMACEUTICAL UNIVERSITY. JOURNAL. Text in Chinese; Abstracts in English. 1956. bi-m. USD 53.40 (effective 2009). **Document type:** *Journal, Academic/Scholarly.* **Description:** Focuses on original research articles of synthesis, pharmaceutical analysis, pharmacology, pharmacokinetics and pharmacognosy.
Related titles: Online - full content ed.; Online - full text ed.
Indexed: A22, A34, A35, A36, AgBio, AgrForAb, B&BAb, B19, B21, BP, C30, CABA, CTA, D01, E12, EMBASE, ExcerpMed, F08, F11, F12, GH, H16, I12, N02, N03, NSA, P32, P33, P37, P40, PGegResA, PGrRegA, PHN&I, R07, R08, R10, RA&MP, RM&VM, Reac, SCOPUS, SoyAb, TAR, VS, W10.
—BLDSC (4729.218950), IE, Ingenta.
Published by: China Pharmaceutical University/Zhongguo Yaoke Daxue, 24, Tong Jia Xiang, 75 Xinxiang, Beijing, 210009, China. TEL 86-25-83271566, FAX 86-25-83271279. Ed. Si-Xun Peng. **Dist. by:** China International Book Trading Corp, 35 Chegongzhuang Xilu, Haidian District, PO Box 399, Beijing 100044, China. TEL 86-10-68412045, FAX 86-10-68412023, cibtc@mail.cibtc.com.cn, http://www.cibtc.com.cn.

615 CHN ISSN 1001-1978
CODEN: ZYTOE
ZHONGGUO YAOLIXUE TONGBAO/CHINESE PHARMACOLOGICAL BULLETIN. Text in Chinese. 1985. m. USD 106.80 (effective 2009). adv. bk.rev. **Document type:** *Bulletin, Trade.* **Description:** Includes original articles, reviews, and new test methods.
Related titles: Online - full text ed.
Indexed: A22, B25, BIOSIS Prev, CIN, ChemAb, ChemTitl, EMBASE, ExcerpMed, MycolAb, NPU, SCOPUS.
—BLDSC (3181.046600), East View, IE, Ingenta.
Published by: Zhongguo Yaoli Xuehui/Chinese Society of Pharmacology, c/o Anhui Medical University, 81 Meishen Lu, Hefei, Anhui 230032, China. huanghs@mail.hf.ah.cn.

ZHONGGUO YAOLIXUE YU DULIXUE ZAZHI/CHINESE JOURNAL OF PHARMACOLOGY AND TOXICOLOGY. *see* ENVIRONMENTAL STUDIES—Toxicology And Environmental Safety

615 CHN ISSN 1002-7777
ZHONGGUO YAOSHI (BEIJING)/CHINESE PHARMACEUTICAL AFFAIRS. Text in Chinese. 1987. bi-m. USD 62.40 (effective 2009). **Document type:** *Academic/Scholarly.*
Related titles: Online - full content ed.; Online - full text ed.
—BLDSC (3181.044000), East View, IE, Ingenta.
Published by: Zhongguo Yaopin Shengwu Zhipin Jiandingsuo, 2,Tiantan Xili, Beijing, 100050, China. TEL 86-1-67033529. Ed. Guo-Wei Sang. **Dist. by:** China International Book Trading Corp, 35 Chegongzhuang Xilu, Haidian District, PO Box 399, Beijing 100044, China. TEL 86-10-68412045, FAX 86-10-68412023, cibtc@mail.cibtc.com.cn, http://www.cibtc.com.cn.

615 CHN ISSN 1008-049X
ZHONGGUO YAOSHI (WUYI)/CHINA PHARMACIST. Text in Chinese. bi-m. USD 74.40 (effective 2009). **Document type:** *Academic/Scholarly.*
Related titles: Online - full content ed.; Online - full text ed.
Indexed: I12.
—BLDSC (3180.217720), East View.
Published by: Yaowu Liuxingbingxue Zazhishe, 2, Lanling Lu, Wuyi, Hubei 430014, China. TEL 86-27-82835077, FAX 86-27-82778580, acjpe077@public.wh.hb.cn. Ed. Shi-Bin Zhu. **Dist. by:** China International Book Trading Corp, 35 Chegongzhuang Xilu, Haidian District, PO Box 399, Beijing 100044, China. TEL 86-10-68412045, FAX 86-10-68412023, cibtc@mail.cibtc.com.cn, http://www.cibtc.com.cn.

615 330 CHN ISSN 1673-5846
ZHONGGUO YAOWU JINGJIXUE/CHINA JOURNAL OF PHARMACEUTICAL ECONOMICS. Text in Chinese. 2006. bi-m. **Document type:** *Journal, Academic/Scholarly.*
Related titles: Online - full text ed.
Published by: (Zhongguo Zhongyiyao Yanjiu Cujinhui), Zhongguo Yaowu Jingjixue Zazhishe, 55, Andingmen Wai Dajie, Dongcheng-qu, Beijing, 100011, China. TEL 86-10-84113228, FAX 86-10-84113228.

615 CHN ISSN 1672-8157
ZHONGGUO YAOWU YINGYONG YU JIANCE/CHINESE JOURNAL OF DRUG APPLICATION AND MONITORING. Text in Chinese. bi-m. CNY 9 newsstand/cover (effective 2006). **Document type:** *Journal, Academic/Scholarly.*
Formerly (until 2003): Yaowu yu Linchuang
Related titles: Online - full text ed.
Published by: Jiefangjun Zongyiyuan/China P L A General Hospital, 28, Fuxing Lu, Beijing, 100853, China.

615.19 CHN ISSN 1005-0108
CODEN: ZYHZEF
ZHONGGUO YAOWUHUAXUE ZAZHI/CHINESE JOURNAL OF MEDICINAL CHEMISTRY. Text in Chinese; Abstracts in English. 1990. bi-m. USD 24.60 (effective 2009). adv. abstr. 64 p./no.; back issues avail. **Document type:** *Journal, Academic/Scholarly.* **Description:** Contains original articles, research notes, and reviews relating to pharmaceutical chemistry.
Related titles: Online - full content ed.; Online - full text ed.
Indexed: RefZh.
—BLDSC (3180.428500), CASDDS, East View, IE, Ingenta.
Address: 103 Wenhua Rd, Shenyang, Liaoning 110016, China. TEL 86-24-23994540, FAX 86-24-23994540. Eds. Li-he Zhang, Shou-fang Zhang. Adv. contact Ren-yong Liu. page USD 300. Circ: 2,500. **Dist. by:** China International Book Trading Corp, 35 Chegongzhuang Xilu, Haidian District, PO Box 399, Beijing 100044, China. TEL 86-10-68412045, FAX 86-10-68412023, cibtc@mail.cibtc.com.cn, http://www.cibtc.com.cn.

615.19 CHN ISSN 1001-2494
RS1 CODEN: ZYZAEU
ZHONGGUO YAOXUE ZAZHI/CHINESE PHARMACEUTICAL JOURNAL. Text in Chinese; Abstracts in English. 1953. m. USD 148.80 (effective 2009). **Document type:** *Journal, Academic/Scholarly.*
Formerly: Yaoxue Tongbao - Chinese Pharmaceutical Bulletin (0512-7343)
Related titles: CD-ROM ed.; Online - full text ed.
Indexed: A22, ApicAb, CIN, ChemAb, ChemTitl, EMBASE, ExcerpMed, ExtraMED, I12, NPU, P30, R10, Reac, SCOPUS.
—BLDSC (3181.046000), CASDDS, East View, GNLM, IE, Infotrieve, Ingenta, Linda Hall.
Published by: Chinese Pharmaceutical Association/Zhongguo Yaoxuehui, 42 Dongsixi Dajie, Beijing, 100710, China. TEL 86-10-65229531, FAX 86-10-65597969. **Dist. outside of China by:** China International Book Trading Corp, 35 Chegongzhuang Xilu, Haidian District, PO Box 399, Beijing 100044, China.

615 CHN ISSN 1001-8255
HD9672.C5 CODEN: ZYGZEA
ZHONGGUO YIYAO GONGYE ZAZHI/CHINESE JOURNAL OF PHARMACEUTICALS. Text in Chinese. 1970. m. USD 74.40 (effective 2009). adv. bk.rev. **Document type:** *Journal, Academic/Scholarly.*
Formerly (until 1989): Yiyao Gongye/Pharmaceutical industry (0255-7223)
Related titles: Online - full text ed.
Indexed: A22, B25, BIOSIS Prev, CIN, ChemAb, ChemTitl, I12, MycolAb.
—BLDSC (3180.473500), CASDDS, East View, GNLM, IE, Ingenta.
Published by: Shanghai Yiyao Gongye Yanjiuyuan/Shanghai Institute of Pharmaceutical Industry, 1320 Beijing Xilu, Shanghai, 200040, China. TEL 86-21-62793151, FAX 86-21-62890581. Ed. Yixin Li. Pub. Houquan Shi. Adv. contact Peijun Shi. Circ: 8,000. **Dist. by:** China International Book Trading Corp, 35 Chegongzhuang Xilu, Haidian District, PO Box 399, Beijing 100044, China. TEL 86-10-68412045, FAX 86-10-68412023, cibtc@mail.cibtc.com.cn, http://www.cibtc.com.cn.

615 CHN ISSN 1001-5213
CODEN: ZYYAEP
ZHONGGUO YIYUAN YAOXUE ZAZHI/CHINESE JOURNAL OF HOSPITAL PHARMACY. Text in Chinese. 1981. m. USD 98.40 (effective 2009). **Document type:** *Academic/Scholarly.*
Related titles: Online - full content ed.; Online - full text ed.
Indexed: CIN, ChemAb, ChemTitl, I12.
—BLDSC (3180.352000), CASDDS, East View, IE, Ingenta.
Published by: Zhongguo Yaoxuehui (Hankou)/Chinese Pharmaceutical Association, Hankou Branch, 177 Shengli St, Hankou, Hubei 430014, China. TEL 86-27-82836596, pharmacy@public.wh.hb.cn. **Dist. overseas by:** China International Book Trading Corp, 35 Chegongzhuang Xilu, Haidian District, PO Box 399, Beijing 100044, China. TEL 86-10-68412045, FAX 86-10-68412023, cibtc@mail.cibtc.com.cn, http://www.cibtc.com.cn.

615 CHN ISSN 1672-5433
ZHONGGUO ZHIYE YAOSHI/CHINA LICENSED PHARMACIST. Text in Chinese; Abstracts in Chinese, English. 2003. m. CNY 96, USD 96; CNY 8 per issue (effective 2011 & 2012). back issues avail. **Document type:** *Journal, Academic/Scholarly.*
Related titles: Online - full text ed.
Published by: Zhongguo Zhiye Yaoshi Xiehui/China Licensed Pharmacist Association, Xicheng-qu, 9, Chegongzhuang Dajie, Wudong Dalou B1-1001, Beijing, 100044, China. TEL 86-10-88312157, FAX 86-10-88312155, http://www.clponline.cn/. Circ: 20,000.

615.328 615.5 CHN ISSN 1001-5302
CODEN: ZZZAE3
➤ **ZHONGGUO ZHONGYAO ZAZHI/CHINA JOURNAL OF CHINESE MATERIA MEDICA.** Text in Chinese. 1955. s-m. USD 160.80 (effective 2009). bk.rev. 64 p./no.; **Document type:** *Academic/Scholarly.* **Description:** Contains researches on herbs, resources, production, and pharmacology of Chinese medicine.
Formerly (until 1989): Zhongyao Tongbao/Bulletin of Chinese Meteria Medica (0254-0029)
Related titles: Online - full text ed.
Indexed: A22, A34, A35, A36, A37, AgBio, AgrForAb, B23, B25, BIOSIS Prev, C25, C30, CABA, CIN, ChemAb, ChemTitl, E12, EMBASE, ExcerpMed, F08, F11, F12, FCA, GH, H16, I11, I12, IndMed, MEDLINE, MaizeAb, MycolAb, N02, N03, O01, P30, P32, P33, P37, P40, PGegResA, PGrRegA, PHN&I, R07, R08, R10, R11, R12, R13, RA&MP, RM&VM, Reac, S12, S13, S16, S17, SCOPUS, SoyAb, T05, TAR, VITIS, VS, W10, W11.
—BLDSC (3180.180500), CASDDS, East View, GNLM, IE, Infotrieve, Ingenta, INIST.
Published by: (Chinese Pharmaceutical Association/Zhongguo Yaoxuehui), Zhongguo Zhongyao Zazhishe, Dongzhimen-Nei, 16, Nanxiaojie, Beijing, 100700, China. TEL 86-10-64045830, FAX 86-10-84038684. **Dist. overseas by:** China International Book Trading Corp, 35 Chegongzhuang Xilu, Haidian District, PO Box 399, Beijing 100044, China. TEL 86-10-68412045, FAX 86-10-68412023, cibtc@mail.cibtc.com.cn, http://www.cibtc.com.cn.

➤ **ZHONGHUA FENGSHIBINGXUE ZAZHI/CHINESE JOURNAL OF RHEUMATOLOGY.** *see* MEDICAL SCIENCES—Rheumatology

615.19 TWN ISSN 1016-1015
ZHONGHUA YAOXUE ZAZHI (TAIPEI)/CHINESE PHARMACEUTICAL JOURNAL (TAIBEI). Text in Chinese. 1988. bi-m.
Indexed: ASFA, B21, B25, BIOSIS Prev, EMBASE, ESPM, ExcerpMed, I12, MycolAb, R10, Reac, SCOPUS.
—BLDSC (3181.046300), IE, Ingenta, INIST, Linda Hall.
Published by: Zhongguo Yaoxuehui, 1 Jen-ai Rd, 1st section, Taipei, Taiwan. TEL 886-2-3416347, FAX 886-2-3919098.

615 CHN ISSN 1673-1727
R97.7.C5
ZHONGHUA ZHONGYIYAO ZAZHI/CHINA JOURNAL OF TRADITIONAL CHINESE MEDICINE AND PHARMACY. Text in Chinese; Abstracts in English. 1986. bi-m. USD 80.40 (effective 2009). **Document type:** *Journal, Academic/Scholarly.* **Description:** Covers the new developments and clinical applications of traditional Chinese medicine and pharmacy.
Formerly: Zhongguo Yiyao Xuebao/Acta Medica Sinica (1000-4971)
Related titles: Online - full text ed.
Indexed: A34, A35, A36, AgBio, AgrForAb, B21, BP, C25, C30, CABA, CTA, D01, E12, F08, F11, F12, FCA, GH, H16, ImmunAb, LT, N02, N03, NSA, OGFA, P32, P33, P40, PGegResA, PHN&I, PN&I, R07, R08, R12, R13, RA&MP, RM&VM, RRTA, S12, S13, S16, S17, SoyAb, T05, TAR, VS, W10, W11.
—BLDSC (9512.844074), East View.
Published by: Zhonghua Zhongyiyao Xuehui, No A4, E. St, Yinghuayuan, Chaoyang District, Beijing, 100029, China. TEL 86-10-64216650, FAX 86-10-64216650. Ed. Zhi-an Yan. **Dist. overseas by:** China International Book Trading Corp, 35 Chegongzhuang Xilu, Haidian District, PO Box 399, Beijing 100044, China. TEL 86-10-68412045, FAX 86-10-68412023, cibtc@mail.cibtc.com.cn, http://www.cibtc.com.cn.

615 CHN ISSN 1672-2981
ZHONGNAN YAOXUE/CENTRAL SOUTH PHARMACY. Text in Chinese. 2003. bi-m. CNY 10 newsstand/cover (effective 2006). **Document type:** *Journal, Academic/Scholarly.*
Related titles: Online - full text ed.
Indexed: B&BAb, B19, B20, B21, CTA, ESPM, NSA, ToxAb.
Address: Zhongnan Daxue, Xiangya Er Yiyuan, 139, Renmin Zhong Lu, Changsha, 410011, China. TEL 86-731-4895602, FAX 86-731-2258487.

615 CHN ISSN 1003-9783
ZHONGYAO XINYAO YU LINGCHUANG YAOLI/TRADITIONAL CHINESE DRUG RESEARCH & CLINICAL PHARMACOLOGY. Text in Chinese. 1990. bi-m. USD 31.20 (effective 2009). **Document type:** *Journal, Academic/Scholarly.* **Description:** Covers the latest development in traditional Chinese drug research and clinical pharmacology in China.
Related titles: Online - full text ed.
—BLDSC (8881.070820), East View.
Published by: Guangzhou Zhongyiyao Daxue/Guangzhou University of Traditional Chinese Medicine, 12, Jichang Lu, Guangzhou, Guangdong 510405, China. **Dist. by:** China International Book Trading Corp, 35 Chegongzhuang Xilu, Haidian District, PO Box 399, Beijing 100044, China. TEL 86-10-68412045, FAX 86-10-68412023, cibtc@mail.cibtc.com.cn, http://www.cibtc.com.cn.

615 CHN ISSN 1001-859X
ZHONGYAO YAOLI YU LINCHUANG/PHARMACOLOGY AND CLINICS OF CHINESE MATERIA MEDICA. Text in Chinese. 1985. bi-m. CNY 8 newsstand/cover (effective 2007). **Document type:** *Bulletin, Academic/Scholarly.*
Related titles: Online - full text ed.
—BLDSC (6447.060750), IE, Ingenta.
Published by: Sichuan Sheng Zhongyao Yanjiusuo/Sichuan Institute of Chinese Materia Medica, Renmin N. Rd., Sec. 4, no.51, Chengdu, Sichuan 610041, China.

615 CHN ISSN 1674-926X
▼ **ZHONGYAO YU LINCHUANG/PHARMACY AND CLINICS OF CHINESE MATERIA MEDICA.** Text in Chinese. 2010. bi-m. **Document type:** *Journal, Academic/Scholarly.*
Related titles: Online - full text ed.
Published by: Chengdu Zhongyiyao Daxue/Chengdu University of T C M (Traditional Chinese Medicine), 19, Xiawangjiaguai Jie, Chengdu, 610041, China. TEL 86-28-86137393.

ZHONGYI ZAZHI. *see* ALTERNATIVE MEDICINE

ZHONGYIYAO DAOBAO/GUIDING JOURNAL OF TRADITIONAL CHINESE MEDICINE AND PHARMACOLOGY. *see* MEDICAL SCIENCES

ZHONGYIYAO XUEBAO/ACTA CHINESE MEDICINE AND PHARMACOLOGY. *see* MEDICAL SCIENCES

615 547 UKR
CODEN: ZOFKAM
ZHURNAL ORHANICHNOI TA FARMATSEVTYCHNOI KHIMII/ JOURNAL OF ORGANIC AND PHARMACEUTICAL CHEMISTRY; naukovyi zhurnal. Text in Russian, Ukrainian. 1966. s-a. USD 95 foreign (effective 2005).
Formerly (until 2003): Fiziologicheski Aktivnye Veshchestva (0533-1153)
Indexed: C33, CIN, ChemAb, ChemTitl, RefZh.
—BLDSC (0064.325000), CASDDS, East View, INIST, Linda Hall. **CCC.**
Published by: (Natsional'na Akademiya Nauk Ukrainy, Instytut Organichnoyi Khimii), Natsional'nyi Farmatsevtychnyi Universytet/ National University of Pharmacy, Vul Pushkins'ka 53, Kharkiv, 310002, Ukraine. TEL 380-572-142289, FAX 380-572-470164, help@ukrfa.kharkov.ua, http://www.ukrfa.kharkov.ua. Ed. Myron Lozyns'kyi. **Dist. by:** East View Information Services, 10601 Wayzata Blvd, Minneapolis, MN 55305. TEL 952-252-1201, 800-477-1005, FAX 952-252-1202, info@eastview.com, http://www.eastview.com. **Co-sponsor:** Ministerstvo Okhorony Zdorov'ya Ukrainy.

615 NLD ISSN 1879-4270
ZORGSPECIAAL. Text in Dutch. 199?. q. free (effective 2010). adv. **Document type:** *Magazine, Consumer.* **Description:** Designed for medical specialty store customers.
Formerly (until 2009): Zorgkundig Nieuws (1572-3011)
Published by: (Hoogland Medical), Axioma Communicatie BV/Axioma Communications BV (Subsidiary of: Springer Science+Business Media), Lt Gen Van Heutszlaan 4, Postbus 176, Baarn, 3740 AD, Netherlands. TEL 31-35-5488140, FAX 31-35-5425820, informatie@axioma.nl, http://www.axioma.nl. Circ: 7,500.

615 330.9 GBR
4D PHARMA; pipeline - products - performance - potential. Text in English. 1995. m. GBP 595, USD 1,130, EUR 895 (effective 2009). adv. back issues avail. **Document type:** *Monographic series, Trade.* **Description:** Contains reports the latest pharmaceutical business, product and company news.
Formerly (until 2008): Pharmaceutical Companies Analysis (1359-625X)
Related titles: CD-ROM ed.: GBP 1,075; E-mail ed.; Online - full text ed.
Published by: Espicom Business Intelligence, Lincoln House, City Fields Business Park, City Fields Way, Chichester, W Sussex PO20 2FS, United Kingdom. TEL 44-1243-533322, FAX 44-1243-533418, Annette_Bulbeck@espicom.com, http://www.espicom.com.

PHARMACY AND PHARMACOLOGY— Abstracting, Bibliographies, Statistics

016.6151 USA ISSN 1551-1081
THE A A P S JOURNAL. ANNUAL MEETING ABSTRACTS. Text in English. 1998. a. back issues avail. **Document type:** *Journal, Academic/Scholarly.*
Formerly (until 2004): A A P S PharmSci. Supplement (1522-0893)
Media: CD-ROM. **Related titles:** Online - full text ed.
—CCC.
Published by: American Association of Pharmaceutical Scientists, 2107 Wilson Blvd, Ste 700, Arlington, VA 22201. TEL 703-243-2800, FAX 703-243-7650, aaps@aaps.org, http://www.aaps.org.

016.6151 USA ISSN 0065-8111
RS355
AMERICAN DRUG INDEX. Abbreviated title: A D I. Text in English. 1950. a. USD 87 per issue (effective 2009). **Document type:** *Abstract/Index.* **Description:** Designed to be the source for identification, explanation and correlation of thousands of pharmaceuticals.
Related titles: CD-ROM ed.: USD 64.95 (effective 2002); Series: Quarterly Drug Index. ISSN 1092-7654. USD 59.95 (effective 2001).
Indexed: Inpharma.
—GNLM.
Published by: Facts and Comparisons (Subsidiary of: Wolters Kluwer N.V.), 77 West Port Plz, Ste 450, St. Louis, MO 63146. TEL 314-216-2100, 800-223-0554, FAX 317-735-5390. Ed. Norman F Billups.

016.615 USA ISSN 1051-3884
CODEN: CAAOE2
C A SELECTS. ALKOXYLATED OLEOCHEMICALS. Text in English. 1990. s-w. USD 385 to non-members; USD 115 to members; USD 575 combined subscription to individuals (print & online eds.) (effective 2011). **Document type:** *Abstract/Index.* **Description:** Covers analysis, preparation, properties, reactions, and uses of ethoxylated and - or propoxylated alcohols.
Related titles: Online - full text ed.: USD 380 to non-members; USD 114 to members (effective 2011).
Published by: Chemical Abstracts Service (Subsidiary of: American Chemical Society), 2540 Olentangy River Rd, Columbus, OH 43210-0012. TEL 614-447-3600, FAX 614-447-3713, help@cas.com, http://caselects.cas.org. **Subscr. to:** PO Box 3012, Columbus, OH 43210. TEL 800-753-4227, FAX 614-447-3751.

350 USA ISSN 0148-2459
CODEN: CSBADM
C A SELECTS. BETA-LACTAM ANTIBIOTICS. Text in English. s-w. USD 385 to non-members; USD 115 to members; USD 575 combined subscription to individuals (print & online eds.) (effective 2011). **Document type:** *Abstract/Index.* **Description:** Covers synthesis, biosynthesis, chemical reactivity, antimicrobial activity, pharmacodynamics, metabolism, toxicology, analysis, and formulation.
Related titles: Online - full text ed.: USD 380 to non-members; USD 114 to members (effective 2011).
Published by: Chemical Abstracts Service (Subsidiary of: American Chemical Society), 2540 Olentangy River Rd, Columbus, OH 43210-0012. TEL 614-447-3600, FAX 614-447-3713, help@cas.com, http://caselects.cas.org. **Subscr. to:** PO Box 3012, Columbus, OH 43210. TEL 800-753-4227, FAX 614-447-3751.

016.615 USA ISSN 1045-8530
CODEN: CSDTEM
C A SELECTS. DRUG ANALYSIS BIOLOGICAL FLUIDS & TISSUES. Text in English. s-w. USD 385 to non-members; USD 115 to members; USD 575 combined subscription to individuals (print & online eds.) (effective 2011). **Document type:** *Abstract/Index.* **Description:** Covers newly developed methods (gas chromatography, HPLC, mass spectrometry, immunoassay) for the analysis of drugs in biological fluids (blood, urine, saliva) and tissues (liver, lungs, kidneys).
Related titles: Online - full text ed.: USD 380 to non-members; USD 114 to members (effective 2011).
Published by: Chemical Abstracts Service (Subsidiary of: American Chemical Society), 2540 Olentangy River Rd, Columbus, OH 43210-0012. TEL 614-447-3600, FAX 614-447-3713, help@cas.com, http://caselects.cas.org. **Subscr. to:** PO Box 3012, Columbus, OH 43210. TEL 800-753-4227, FAX 614-447-3751.

615.9 USA ISSN 0162-7775
CODEN: CSDTDL
C A SELECTS. DRUG & COSMETIC TOXICITY. Text in English. s-w. USD 385 to non-members; USD 114 to members; USD 575 combined subscription to individuals (print & online eds.) (effective 2011). **Document type:** *Abstract/Index.* **Description:** Covers toxic manifestations of drugs, cosmetics, and ingredients of drug and cosmetic preparations, e.g., mutagenicity, teratogenicity, carcinogenicity, allergic potential; health hazards, side effects, and safety of drugs.
Related titles: Online - full text ed.: USD 380 to non-members; USD 114 to members (effective 2011).
Published by: Chemical Abstracts Service (Subsidiary of: American Chemical Society), 2540 Olentangy River Rd, Columbus, OH 43210-0012. TEL 614-447-3600, FAX 614-447-3713, help@cas.com, http://caselects.cas.org. **Subscr. to:** PO Box 3012, Columbus, OH 43210. TEL 800-753-4227, FAX 614-447-3751.

C A SELECTS. FOOD, DRUGS, & COSMETICS - LEGISLATIVE & REGULATORY ASPECTS. *see* FOOD AND FOOD INDUSTRIES—Abstracting, Bibliographies, Statistics

P

615 USA ISSN 0895-5875
CODEN: CSNAEF

C A SELECTS. NEW ANTIBIOTICS. Text in English. 1988. s-w. USD 385 to non-members; USD 115 to members; USD 575 combined subscription to individuals (print & online eds.) (effective 2011). **Document type:** *Abstract/Index.* **Description:** Covers production, isolation, characterization, structure determination, and antimicrobial activity of antibiotics, both natural and synthetic.
Related titles: Online - full text ed.: USD 380 to non-members; USD 114 to members (effective 2011).
Published by: Chemical Abstracts Service (Subsidiary of: American Chemical Society), 2540 Olentangy River Rd, Columbus, OH 43210-0012. TEL 614-447-3600, FAX 614-447-3713, help@cas.com, http://caselects.cas.org. **Subscr. to:** PO Box 3012, Columbus, OH 43210. TEL 800-753-4227, FAX 614-447-3751.

615.19 USA ISSN 0890-1910
CODEN: CAPCE7

C A SELECTS. PHARMACEUTICAL CHEMISTRY (JOURNALS). Text in English. 1987. s-w. USD 385 to non-members; USD 115 to members; USD 575 combined subscription to individuals (print & online eds.) (effective 2011). **Document type:** *Abstract/Index.* **Description:** Covers all aspects of pharmaceutical chemistry: drug standards, pharmacopeia, formulations, prosthetic materials, surgical goods, and properties of pharmaceuticals.
Related titles: Online - full text ed.: USD 380 to non-members; USD 114 to members (effective 2011).
Published by: Chemical Abstracts Service (Subsidiary of: American Chemical Society), 2540 Olentangy River Rd, Columbus, OH 43210-0012. TEL 614-447-3600, FAX 614-447-3713, help@cas.com, http://caselects.cas.org. **Subscr. to:** PO Box 3012, Columbus, OH 43210. TEL 800-753-4227, FAX 614-447-3751.

615.19 USA ISSN 0890-1929
CODEN: CPCPEI

C A SELECTS. PHARMACEUTICAL CHEMISTRY (PATENTS). Text in English. 1987. s-w. USD 385 to non-members; USD 115 to members; USD 575 combined subscription to individuals (print & online eds.) (effective 2011). **Document type:** *Abstract/Index.* **Description:** Covers formulations, prosthetic materials, and surgical goods.
Related titles: Online - full text ed.: USD 380 to non-members; USD 114 to members (effective 2011).
Published by: Chemical Abstracts Service (Subsidiary of: American Chemical Society), 2540 Olentangy River Rd, Columbus, OH 43210-0012. TEL 614-447-3600, FAX 614-447-3713, help@cas.com, http://caselects.cas.org. **Subscr. to:** PO Box 3012, Columbus, OH 43210. TEL 800-753-4227, FAX 614-447-3751.

350 USA ISSN 1084-2349
CODEN: CSDFFF

C A SELECTS PLUS. DRUG DELIVERY SYSTEMS & DOSAGE FORMS. Text in English. 1989. s-w. USD 385 domestic to non-members; USD 115 to members; USD 575 combined subscription (print & online eds.) (effective 2011). **Document type:** *Abstract/Index.* **Description:** Covers pharmaceutical dosage forms, such as tablets, capsules, ointments; newer delivery systems and forms such as controlled-release devices, transdermal systems, ocular inserts. osmotic devices, antibody conjugates. and liposomes; properties, formulation bioavailability, and pharmacokinetic studies of drugs from the delivery systems and dosage forms.
Formerly: C A Selects. Drug Delivery Systems and Dosage Forms (1040-7162)
Related titles: Online - full text ed.: USD 380 to non-members; USD 114 to members (effective 2011).
Published by: Chemical Abstracts Service (Subsidiary of: American Chemical Society), 2540 Olentangy River Rd, Columbus, OH 43210-0012. TEL 614-447-3600, FAX 614-447-3713, help@cas.com, http://caselects.cas.org. **Subscr. to:** PO Box 3012, Columbus, OH 43210. TEL 800-753-4227, FAX 614-447-3751.

615.19 USA ISSN 1084-239X
CODEN: CPPAF5

C A SELECTS PLUS. PHARMACEUTICAL ANALYSIS. Text in English. 1987. s-w. USD 385 to non-members; USD 115 to members; USD 575 combined subscription to members (print & online eds.) (effective 2011). **Document type:** *Abstract/Index.* **Description:** Covers analysis of drugs in pure form or in pharmaceutical preparations.
Formerly: C A Selects. Pharmaceutical Analysis (0890-1902)
Related titles: Online - full text ed.: USD 380 to non-members; USD 114 to members (effective 2011).
Published by: Chemical Abstracts Service (Subsidiary of: American Chemical Society), 2540 Olentangy River Rd, Columbus, OH 43210-0012. TEL 614-447-3600, FAX 614-447-3713, help@cas.com, http://caselects.cas.org. **Subscr. to:** PO Box 3012, Columbus, OH 43210. TEL 800-753-4227, FAX 614-447-3751.

C A SELECTS. STEROIDS (CHEMICAL ASPECTS). *see* CHEMISTRY—Abstracting, Bibliographies, Statistics

016.615 USA ISSN 0069-4770

CLIN-ALERT. Text in English. 1962. s-m. looseleaf. USD 1,111, GBP 653 combined subscription to institutions (print & online eds.); USD 1,089, GBP 640 to institutions (effective 2011). q. cum.index. back issues avail.; reprint service avail. from PSC. **Document type:** *Newsletter, Consumer.* **Description:** Provides pharmacists, physicians, and other health care professionals with comprehensive summaries of adverse drug reactions, drug interactions, and market withdrawals from over 100 key medical and research journals from around the world.
Related titles: E-mail ed.; Online - full text ed.: ISSN 1530-812X. USD 1,000, GBP 588 to institutions (effective 2011).
Indexed: A22, A26, E01, E08, EMBASE, ExcerpMed, G08, H11, H12, I05, S09.
—IE, Ingenta. **CCC.**
Published by: Sage Publications, Inc., 2455 Teller Rd, Thousand Oaks, CA 91320. TEL 805-499-9774, 800-818-7243, FAX 805-499-0871, 800-583-2665, info@sagepub.com, http://www.sagepub.com/. Ed. Joyce Generali. Circ: 350 (paid). **Subscr. outside the Americas to:** Sage Publications Ltd., 1 Oliver's Yard, 55 City Rd, London EC1Y 1SP, United Kingdom. TEL 44-20-73248701, FAX 44-20-73248733, subscription@sagepub.co.uk.

COMPREHENSIVE SUMMARIES OF UPPSALA DISSERTATIONS FROM THE FACULTY OF PHARMACY. *see* PHARMACY AND PHARMACOLOGY

615 JPN ISSN 0385-6747

CONTENTS. Text in Japanese. 1971. w. JPY 100,000 (effective 2001). **Document type:** *Bibliography.* **Description:** Lists titles of medical and pharmaceutical journals.
Published by: Japan Pharmaceutical Information Center/Nihon Iyaku Joho Senta, 3rd Fl Nagai-Kinenkan, 2-12-15 Shibuya, Shibuya-ku, Tokyo, 150-0002, Japan. TEL 81-3-5466-1812, FAX 81-3-5466-18184. Ed. H Miyake. Circ: 900.

DRUG FILE UPDATE; a current awareness index to publications on drugs and doping in sport. *see* SPORTS AND GAMES—Abstracting, Bibliographies, Statistics

016.6151 NLD ISSN 1573-000X

EMBASE. DRUGS & PHARMACOLOGY. Text in English. 199?. q. **Document type:** *Abstract/Index.* **Description:** Contains more than 1,560,000 abstracts and citations, providing comprehensive coverage of drug and pharmacology literature.
Media: CD-ROM.
Published by: Excerpta Medica (Subsidiary of: Elsevier Health Sciences), Radarweg 29, Amsterdam, 1043 NX, Netherlands. TEL 31-20-4853975, FAX 31-20-4853188, excerptamedica@elsevier.com, http://www.excerptamedica.com.

016.6151 NLD ISSN 0927-2798

EXCERPTA MEDICA. SECTION 30: CLINICAL AND EXPERIMENTAL PHARMACOLOGY. Text in English. 1948. 32/yr. EUR 10,930 in Europe to institutions; JPY 1,450,500 in Japan to institutions; USD 12,190 elsewhere to institutions (effective 2012). adv. abstr. index, cum.index. **Document type:** *Journal, Abstract/Index.* **Description:** Provides a comprehensive current-awareness service of clinical and academic articles covering all aspects of experimental and clinical pharmacology, including pharmacokinetics, pharmacodynamics, methodology, mathematical models, and experimental studies on human organs, tissues, and cells and on the mechanisms of action of exogenous substances.
Formerly (until 1992): Excerpta Medica. Section 30: Pharmacology (0167-9643); Which superseded in part (in 1983): Excerpta Medica. Section 30: Pharmacology and Toxicology (0014-4347); Which was formerly (until 1968): Excerpta Medica. Section 2C: Pharmacology and Toxicology (0367-1100); Which superseded in part (in 1965): Excerpta Medica. Section 2: Physiology, Biochemistry and Pharmacology (0014-4061)
Related titles: CD-ROM ed.; Online - full text ed.
—GNLM. **CCC.**
Published by: Excerpta Medica (Subsidiary of: Elsevier Health Sciences), Radarweg 29, Amsterdam, 1043 NX, Netherlands. TEL 31-20-4853975, FAX 31-20-4853188, excerptamedica@elsevier.com, http://www.excerptamedica.com. **Subscr. to:** Elsevier BV, Radarweg 29, PO Box 211, Amsterdam 1000 AE, Netherlands. TEL 31-20-4853757, FAX 31-20-4853432, JournalsCustomerServiceEMEA@elsevier.com, http://www.elsevier.nl.

016.615 NLD ISSN 0167-9090
CODEN: ADRTA

EXCERPTA MEDICA. SECTION 38: ADVERSE REACTIONS TITLES. Text in English. 1966. 12/yr. EUR 25,990 in Europe to institutions; JPY 3,439,300 in Japan to institutions; USD 28,980 elsewhere to institutions (effective 2012). adv. index, cum.index. **Document type:** *Journal, Abstract/Index.* **Description:** Offers a comprehensive awareness service for articles and other academic and professional writings dealing with pharmacological adverse reactions.
Formerly (until 1966): Adverse Reactions Titles (0001-8848)
Related titles: CD-ROM ed.
—CCC.
Published by: Excerpta Medica (Subsidiary of: Elsevier Health Sciences), Radarweg 29, Amsterdam, 1043 NX, Netherlands. TEL 31-20-4853975, FAX 31-20-4853188, excerptamedica@elsevier.com, http://www.excerptamedica.com. **Subscr. to:** Elsevier BV, Radarweg 29, PO Box 211, Amsterdam 1000 AE, Netherlands. TEL 31-20-4853757, FAX 31-20-4853432, JournalsCustomerServiceEMEA@elsevier.com, http://www.elsevier.nl.

EXCERPTA MEDICA. SECTION 52: TOXICOLOGY. *see* ENVIRONMENTAL STUDIES—Abstracting, Bibliographies, Statistics

615.19 AUS ISSN 0155-9885

GUILD DIGEST (YEAR). Key Title: Pharmacy Guild Digest. Text in English. 1972. a. index. back issues avail. **Document type:** *Newsletter, Trade.* **Description:** Compares interfirm survey statistics on financial performance of pharmacies and some detail of drug usage and cost.
Former titles: Community Pharmacy in Australia; Guild Digest
Published by: The Pharmacy Guild of Australia, PO Box 7036, Canberra, ACT 2610, Australia. TEL 61-2-62701888, FAX 61-2-62701800, guild.nat@guild.org.au, http://www.guild.org.au. Ed. Vasken Demirian. Circ: 5,500.

016.6151 USA ISSN 0891-8511

IDIS. (Iowa Drug Information Service) Text in English. 1966. base vol. plus m. updates. price varies based on number of users. **Document type:** *Database, Trade.* **Description:** Contains indexed bibliographic records, including abstracts and full-text articles related to drugs and drug therapy in humans from over 200 leading medical and pharmaceutical journals.
Media: Online - full text. **Related titles:** CD-ROM ed.; Microfiche ed.
Published by: University of Iowa, Division of Drug Information Service, University of Iowa Research Park, 2500 Crosspark Rd, Rm W145, Coralville, IA 52241. TEL 319-335-4800, 800-525-4347, FAX 319-335-4440, idis@uiowa.edu.

614.021 USA ISSN 1564-8753

INTERNATIONAL NARCOTICS CONTROL BOARD. PSYCHOTROPIC SUBSTANCES; assessments of medical and scientific requirements. Text in English, French, Spanish. 1977. a.
Formerly (until 1989): International Narcotics Control Board. Statistics on Psychotropic Substances Furnished by Governments in Accordance with the Convention of 1971 on Psychotropic Substances (0253-9403)
Related titles: Microfiche ed.: (from CIS); Online - full content ed.: free.
Indexed: IIS.
Published by: (International Narcotics Control Board AUT), United Nations Publications, 2 United Nations Plaza, Rm DC2-853, New York, NY 10017. TEL 212-963-8302, 800-253-9646, FAX 212-963-3489, publications@un.org, https://unp.un.org.

615 016 USA ISSN 0020-8264
RS1 CODEN: IPMAAH

INTERNATIONAL PHARMACEUTICAL ABSTRACTS (PRINT); key to the world's literature of pharmacy. Text in English. 1964. s-m. index. back issues avail.; reprints avail. **Document type:** *Abstract/Index.* **Description:** Covers approximately 600 worldwide pharmaceutical, cosmetics, medical and health care publications.
Related titles: CD-ROM ed.: ISSN 1077-3770. 1970; Microform ed.: (from PQC); Online - full text ed.: International Pharmaceutical Abstracts.
Indexed: Inpharma.
—BLDSC (4544.924000), GNLM, Linda Hall. **CCC.**
Published by: Thomson Reuters (Subsidiary of: Thomson Reuters Corp.), 1500 Spring Garden, 4th Fl, Philadelphia, PA 19130. TEL 215-386-0100, 800-336-4474, FAX 215-386-2911, general.info@thomson.com, http://science.thomsonreuters.com/.

016.615 JPN ISSN 1342-2030

IYAKUHIN FUKUSAYO BUNKEN JOHOSHU. SHOROKUSHU-HEN/ ADVERSE REACTION TO DRUGS INFORMATION COMPENDIUM FOR EXPERTS. ABSTRACTS. Text in Japanese. 1975. s-a. JPY 50,000 includes Iyakuhin Fukusayo Bunken Johoshu. Yakkobeetsu Fukusayo Ichiran-hen (effective 2000).
Supersedes in part (in 1995): Kokunai Iyakuhin Fukusayo Ichiran
Published by: Japan Pharmaceutical Information Center/Nihon Iyaku Joho Senta, 3rd Fl Nagai-Kinenkan, 2-12-15 Shibuya, Shibuya-ku, Tokyo, 150-0002, Japan. TEL 81-3-5466-1812, FAX 81-3-5466-1814.

615 310 USA ISSN 1054-3406
RS57 CODEN: JBSTEL

➤ **JOURNAL OF BIOPHARMACEUTICAL STATISTICS.** Text in English. 1991. bi-m. GBP 1,256 combined subscription in United Kingdom to institutions (print & online eds.); EUR 1,661, USD 2,086 combined subscription to institutions (print & online eds.) (effective 2012). adv. reprint service avail. from PSC. **Document type:** *Journal, Academic/Scholarly.* **Description:** Discusses quality applications of statistics in biopharmaceutical research and development.
Related titles: Online - full text ed.: ISSN 1520-5711. GBP 1,130 in United Kingdom to institutions; EUR 1,494, USD 1,877 to institutions (effective 2012) (from IngentaConnect).
Indexed: A01, A03, A08, A22, B&BAb, B01, B06, B07, B09, B19, CA, CCMJ, CIS, E-psyche, E01, EMBASE, ExcerpMed, H01, IndMed, MEDLINE, MSN, MathR, P30, P50, R10, Reac, S01, SCI, SCOPUS, ST&MA, T02, W07, Z02.
—BLDSC (4953.910000), GNLM, IE, Infotrieve, Ingenta, Linda Hall. **CCC.**
Published by: Taylor & Francis Inc. (Subsidiary of: Taylor & Francis Group), 325 Chestnut St, Ste 800, Philadelphia, PA 19106. TEL 215-625-2940, 800-354-1420, orders@taylorandfrancis.com, http://www.taylorandfrancis.com. Ed. Shein-Chung Chow. Adv. contact Linda Hann TEL 44-1344-779945.

615.1021 NOR ISSN 1890-9647

LEGEMIDDELSTATISTIKK/DRUG CONSUMPTION IN NORGE. Text in English, Norwegian. 2008. s-a. **Document type:** *Government.*
Incorporates (1977-2008): Legemiddelforbruket i Norge (0332-6535)
Related titles: Online - full text ed.
Published by: Nasjonalt Folkehelseinstitutt/Norwegian Institute of Public Health, PO Box 4404, Nydalen, Oslo, 0403, Norway. TEL 47-21-077000, FAX 47-22-353605, folkehelseinstituttet@fhi.no.

M I M S MEDICAL SPECIALITIES. (Monthly Index of Medical Specialties) *see* MEDICAL SCIENCES—Abstracting, Bibliographies, Statistics

615 JPN

MEDICAL COMPANIES GUIDE TO JAPAN. Text in English. 1987. irreg. JPY 26,250 (effective 2005). **Document type:** *Directory.* **Description:** Lists pharmaceutical companies and those dealing with diagnostic agents and medical apparatuses with up-to-date information including company name, address, turnover, features, and main products.
Formerly (until 1992): Japan Medical and Pharmaceutical Directory
Published by: Chemical Daily Co. Ltd., 16-8, Nihonbashi-Hamacho 3-Chome, Chuo-ku, Tokyo, 103-8485, Japan. TEL 81-3-36637932, FAX 81-3-36637275, info@jcw-online.com, http://www.chemicaldaily.co.jp/.

MEDITSINSKI PREGLED. *see* MEDICAL SCIENCES—Abstracting, Bibliographies, Statistics

615 USA ISSN 0076-6518

THE MERCK INDEX: AN ENCYCLOPEDIA OF CHEMICALS AND DRUGS. Variant title: The Merck Index : An Encyclopedia of Chemicals, Drugs and Biologicals. Text in English. 1889. irreg., latest vol.14, 2006. USD 125 per issue (effective 2011). **Document type:** *Handbook/Manual/Guide, Trade.*
Related titles: CD-ROM ed.: CAD 236.99 per issue (effective 2011); Online - full text ed.
Published by: Merck Publishing Group, 126 E Lincoln Ave, PO Box 2000, Rahway, NJ 07065. TEL 732-594-4600, FAX 732-388-9778. Ed. Maryadele J O'Neil.

300 614.35 USA ISSN 1013-3453
HV5800

NARCOTIC DRUGS: ESTIMATED WORLD REQUIREMENTS FOR (YEAR). Text in English, French, Spanish. 1989. a. USD 45 per issue (effective 2008). back issues avail. **Document type:** *Report, Consumer.* **Description:** Provides analysis of recent trends and statistics for estimated requirements and actual movements of narcotic drugs.
Formed by the 1989 merger of: United Nations. International Narcotics Control Board. Statistics on Narcotics Drugs for (Year) (1014-8817); Which was formerly: United Nations. International Narcotics Control Board. Statistics on Narcotic Drugs Furnished by Governments in Accordance with the International Treaties; United Nations. International Narcotics Control Board. Comparative Statement of Estimates and Statistics on Narcotic Drugs for (Year) (0255-9374); Which was formerly: United Nations. International Narcotics Control Board. Comparative Statement of Estimates and Statistics on Narcotics Drugs Furnished by Governments in Accordance with the International Treaties; Estimated World Requirements of Narcotic Drugs (0082-8335); United Nations. International Narcotics Control Board. Statistics on Narcotic Drugs Furnished by Governments in Accordance with the International Treaties; Which was formerly (until 1984): United Nations. International Narcotics Control Board. Statistics on Narcotic Drugs Furnished by Governments in Accordance with the International Treaties and Maximum Level of Opium Stocks (0566-7658)

Related titles: Online - full text ed.: USD 36 per issue (effective 2008).
Indexed: IIS, RASB.
—CCC.
Published by: (International Narcotics Control Board AUT, Vienna International Center AUT), United Nations Publications, 2 United Nations Plaza, Rm DC2-853, New York, NY 10017. TEL 212-963-8302, 800-253-9646, FAX 212-963-3489, publications@un.org, https://unp.un.org.

016.615 JPN ISSN 0915-1621
NIHON IYAKU BUNKEN SHOROKUSHU/JAPAN PHARMACEUTICAL ABSTRACTS. Text in Japanese. 1972. bi-m. JPY 300,000 to members (effective 2001). **Document type:** *Abstract/Index.*
Published by: Japan Pharmaceutical Information Center/Nihon Iyaku Joho Senta, 3rd Fl Nagai-Kinenkan, 2-12-15 Shibuya, Shibuya-ku, Tokyo, 150-0002, Japan. TEL 81-3-5466-1811, FAX 81-3-5466-1814. Circ: 1,100 (controlled).

016.615 USA
PHARMACEUTICAL NEWS INDEX. Abbreviated title: P N I. Text in English. 1974. base vol. plus d. updates. **Document type:** *Database, Abstract/Index.* **Description:** Contains bibliographic information and indexing for 22 key U.S. and international pharmaceutical, healthcare, biotechnology, medical device, and cosmetic industry newsletters.
Media: Online - full text. **Related titles:** Magnetic Tape ed.
Published by: ProQuest (Subsidiary of: Cambridge Information Group), 789 E Eisenhower Pky, PO Box 1346, Ann Arbor, MI 48106. TEL 734-761-4700, 800-521-0600, FAX 734-997-4040, 888-241-5612, info@proquest.com.

016.615 NZL ISSN 1173-5503
PHARMACOECONOMICS AND OUTCOMES NEWS (PRINT). Text in English. 1994. 25/yr. price varies based on the number of users. back issues avail.; reprints avail. **Document type:** *Newsletter, Consumer.* **Description:** Provides summaries of current pharmacoeconomic and outcomes research from the world biomedical literature.
Formerly (until 1996): PharmacoResources (1172-8299)
Related titles: CD-ROM ed.; Online - full text ed.: (from IngentaConnect).
Indexed: A01, A03, A26, E08, H05, H12, I05, Inpharma, P20, P34, P35, P54, PQC, R10, Reac, S09, T02.
—IE, Infotrieve, Ingenta. **CCC.**
Published by: Adis International Ltd. (Subsidiary of: Wolters Kluwer N.V.), 41 Centorian Dr, Mairangi Bay, Private Bag 65901, Auckland, 1311, New Zealand. TEL 64-9-4770700, FAX 64-9-4770764, journals@adis.com, http://www.adisonline.info/. Ed. Suzanne Berresford. **Subscr. in Americas to:** Adis International Inc.

PHILIPPINES INDEX OF MEDICAL SPECIALITIES. *see* MEDICAL SCIENCES—Abstracting, Bibliographies, Statistics

615 USA
PHRMA ANNUAL REPORT. Text in English. a. free. stat. **Description:** Provides annual and historical statistical information on pharmaceutical industry sales and research.
Formerly: Pharmaceutical Manufacturers Association. Annual Survey Report
Related titles: Online - full content ed.
Indexed: SRI.
Published by: Pharmaceutical Research and Manufacturers of America, 950 F Street, NW, Ste 300, Washington, DC 20004. TEL 202-835-3400, FAX 202-835-3414.

016.61578 USA
PSYCSCAN: PSYCHOPHARMACOLOGY. (Subset of PsycINFO) Text in English. 200?. base vol. plus m. updates. USD 75 to non-members (effective 2008). **Document type:** *Database, Abstract/Index.* **Description:** Provides abstracts from subscriber-selected journals covering clinical and experimental psychopharmacology.
Media: Online - full text.
Published by: American Psychological Association, 750 First St, NE, Washington, DC 20002. TEL 800-374-2721.

016.615 NZL ISSN 0114-9954
RM302.5
REACTIONS WEEKLY (PRINT). Text in English. 1979. 50/yr. price varies based on the number of users. bk.rev. q. cum.index. back issues avail.; reprints avail. **Document type:** *Newsletter, Consumer.* **Description:** Provides alerts to adverse drug experiences reported in international medical journals.
Formerly (until 1990): Reactions (0157-7271)
Related titles: CD-ROM ed.; Online - full text ed.: Reactions Weekly. ISSN 1179-2051 (from IngentaConnect).
Indexed: A01, A03, A26, E08, H12, I05, Inpharma, P20, P34, P35, P54, PQC, S09, T02.
—IE, Infotrieve, Ingenta. **CCC.**
Published by: Adis International Ltd. (Subsidiary of: Wolters Kluwer N.V.), 41 Centorian Dr, Mairangi Bay, Private Bag 65901, Auckland, 1311, New Zealand. TEL 64-9-4770700, FAX 64-9-4770764, journals@adis.com, http://www.adisonline.info/. Ed. Suzanne Berresford. **US subscr. to:** Adis International Inc.

615 RUS
▼ **REFERATIVNYI ZHURNAL. FARMAKOLOGIIA OBSHCHAIA. KHIMIOTERAPEVTITCHESKIE SREDSTVA**; vypusk razdela-toma. Text in Russian. 2009. m. USD 666 foreign (effective 2011). **Document type:** *Journal, Abstract/Index.*
Formed by the merger of (1958-2009): Referativnyi Zhurnal. Farmakologiya Effektornykh Sistem. Khimioterapevticheskie Sredstva (0202-5132); (1958-2009): Referativnyi Zhurnal. Farmakologiya Obshchaya. Farmakologiya Nervnoi Sistemy (0134-580X)
Related titles: CD-ROM ed.; Online - full text ed.
Published by: VINITI RAN, ul Usievicha 20, Moscow, 125190, Russian Federation. TEL 7-499-1526113, FAX 7-499-9430060, http://www.viniti.ru. **Dist. by:** Informnauka Ltd., Ul Usievicha 20, Moscow 125190, Russian Federation. alfimov@viniti.ru.

016.615 RUS ISSN 0869-4109
REFERATIVNYI ZHURNAL. FARMAKOLOGIYA. TOKSIKOLOGIYA; razdel-tom. Text in Russian. 1987. m. USD 2,254.80 foreign (effective 2011). **Document type:** *Journal, Abstract/Index.*
Related titles: CD-ROM ed.; Online - full text ed.
—East View.
Published by: VINITI RAN, ul Usievicha 20, Moscow, 125190, Russian Federation. TEL 7-499-1526113, FAX 7-499-9430060, dir@viniti.ru, http://www.viniti.ru. **Dist. by:** Informnauka Ltd., Ul Usievicha 20, Moscow 125190, Russian Federation. alfimov@viniti.ru; East View Information Services, 10601 Wayzata Blvd, Minneapolis, MN 55305. TEL 952-252-1201, 800-477-1005, FAX 952-252-1202, info@eastview.com, http://www.eastview.com.

016.615 RUS ISSN 0202-9162
REFERATIVNYI ZHURNAL. KLINICHESKAYA FARMAKOLOGIYA; vypusk razdela-toma. Text in Russian. 1979. m. USD 870 foreign (effective 2011). **Document type:** *Journal, Abstract/Index.*
Related titles: CD-ROM ed.; Online - full text ed.
Published by: VINITI RAN, ul Usievicha 20, Moscow, 125190, Russian Federation. TEL 7-499-1526113, FAX 7-499-9430060, dir@viniti.ru, http://www.viniti.ru. **Dist. by:** Informnauka Ltd., Ul Usievicha 20, Moscow 125190, Russian Federation. alfimov@viniti.ru.

REFERATIVNYI ZHURNAL. TEKHNOLOGIYA ORGANICHESKIKH LEKARSTVENNYKH VESHCHESTV, VETERINARNYKH PREPARATOV I PESTITSIDOV; vypusk svodnogo toma. *see* CHEMISTRY—Abstracting, Bibliographies, Statistics

016.6159 RUS ISSN 0202-9219
RA1190 CODEN: RZTODS
REFERATIVNYI ZHURNAL. TOKSIKOLOGIYA; vypusk razdela-toma. Text in Russian. 1958. m. USD 678 foreign (effective 2011). **Document type:** *Journal, Abstract/Index.*
Related titles: CD-ROM ed.; Online - full text ed.
Indexed: ChemAb.
—CASDDS, Linda Hall.
Published by: VINITI RAN, ul Usievicha 20, Moscow, 125190, Russian Federation. TEL 7-499-1526113, FAX 7-499-9430060, dir@viniti.ru, http://www.viniti.ru. **Dist. by:** Informnauka Ltd., Ul Usievicha 20, Moscow 125190, Russian Federation. alfimov@viniti.ru.

615.1021 CAN ISSN 1487-198X
SASKATCHEWAN DRUG PLAN AND EXTENDED BENEFITS BRANCH. ANNUAL STATISTICAL REPORT. Text in English. 1976. a. **Document type:** *Government.*
Former titles (1991-1996): Saskatchewan Health. Prescription Drug Services Branch. Annual Statistical Report (1187-8991); (1989-1990): Saskatchewan Health. Statistical Supplement to the Annual Report (1182-218X); (1976-1988): Saskatchewan. Prescription Drug Plan. Annual Report (0707-0152)
Published by: Saskatchewan Health, T C Douglas Bldg, 3475 Albert St, Regina, SK S4S 6X6, Canada. TEL 306-787-3317, FAX 306-787-8679. Circ: 700.

615.9 016 RUS ISSN 0233-6588
SIGNAL'NAYA INFORMATSIYA. TOKSIKOLOGIYA LEKARSTVENNAYA. Text in Russian. m. **Document type:** *Abstract/Index.*
Formerly: Signal'naya Informatsiya. Toksikologiya (0202-8514)
Published by: VINITI RAN, ul Usievicha 20, Moscow, 125190, Russian Federation. **Dist. by:** M K - Periodica, ul Gilyarovskogo 39, Moscow 129110, Russian Federation. TEL 7-095-2845008, FAX 7-095-2813798, info@periodicals.ru, http://www.mkniga.ru.

TAL OG DATA, MEDICIN OG SUNDHEDSVAESEN/FACTS, MEDICINE AND HEALTH CARE, DENMARK. *see* PHARMACY AND PHARMACOLOGY

016.6151 CHN ISSN 1003-3521
ZHONGGUO YAOXUE WENZHAI/CHINESE PHARMACEUTICAL ABSTRACTS. Text in Chinese. 1982. m. USD 211.20 (effective 2009). adv. **Document type:** *Abstract/Index.* **Description:** Published on the basis of the Traditional Chinese Medicines (TCMs) Contemporary Literature Database, as well as abstracts in modern drugs in China. Covers 420 current domestic medical journals.
Related titles: Online - full content ed.
Published by: Guojia Shipin Yaopin Jiandu Guanliju, 38, Beilishi Lu, Beijing, 100810, China. TEL 86-10-62214665, http://www.cpi.gov.cn/. **Dist. in the US by:** Cypress Book Co., Inc., 3450 Third Street, Unit 4B, San Francisco, CA 94124. TEL 415-821-3582, FAX 415-821-3523, http://www.cypressbook.com/.

PHARMACY AND PHARMACOLOGY— Computer Applications

610.285 USA
COMPUTERTALK; for contemporary pharmacy management. Text in English. 1981. bi-m. USD 50 domestic; USD 75 foreign (effective 2001). adv. back issues avail. **Document type:** *Magazine, Trade.* **Description:** Offers practical advice to familiarize pharmacists with computers and computer applications. Short articles cover a broad range of topics.
Formerly: ComputerTalk for the Pharmacist (0736-3893)
Indexed: I12.
—Ingenta.
Published by: ComputerTalk Associates, Inc., 492 Norristown Rd, 160, Blue Bell, PA 19422-2355. TEL 610-825-7686, FAX 610-825-7641. Ed. Margaret L Lockwood. Pub., Adv. contact William A Lockwood Jr. B&W page USD 4,820, color page USD 6,115; trim 10.75 x 8. Circ: 36,000.

610.285 USA
COMPUTERTALK PHARMACY SYSTEMS BUYERS GUIDE. Text in English. 1982. a. USD 25 (effective 2001). adv. 85 p./no.; **Document type:** *Magazine, Trade.* **Description:** A guide to available computer systems and services designed for pharmacy use. Information contained within product profiles written by vendors. Articles cover a range of topics on computers and applications.
Formerly: ComputerTalk Directory of Pharmacy Systems (0736-3877)
Published by: ComputerTalk Associates, Inc., 492 Norristown Rd, 160, Blue Bell, PA 19422-2355. TEL 610-825-7686, FAX 610-825-7641. Ed. Margaret L Lockwood. Pub., Adv. contact William A Lockwood Jr. B&W page USD 4,900, color page USD 5,500; trim 8 x 10.75. Circ: 38,000.

PHILATELY

see also HOBBIES

769.56 GBR ISSN 1353-6869
A B P S NEWS. (Association of British Philatelic Societies) Text in English. 1946. m. adv. bk.rev. **Document type:** *Newsletter, Trade.* **Description:** Covers update news about Association of British Philatelic Societies.
Former titles (until 1994): New Stamp Mail (1353-1662); (until 1993): Stamp Mail (0953-5241); (until 1988): Stamp World (0951-5119); (until 1987): Stamp News (0265-8216); (until 1983): Stamp and Postal History News (0261-1899); Stamp World incorporated (1946-1981): Philately (0031-739X); Stamp News incorporated (1913-1984): Stamp Collecting (0038-9269); (1916-198?): Philatelic Magazine (0031-7357)
Indexed: SJI.
Published by: The Association of British Philatelic Societies, Freeling House, Phoenix Pl, London, WC1X 0DL, United Kingdom. TEL 44-20-72392571, abpssec@ukphilately.org.uk. Circ: 2,200.

769.569 DNK ISSN 0901-7003
A F A DANMARK, FAEROEERNE, GROENLAND, DANSK VESTINDIEN FRIMAERKEKATALOG. Cover title: A F A Danmark Frimaerkekatalog. Text in Danish. 1973. a. DKK 225; DKK 195 CD-ROM (effective 2008). illus. **Document type:** *Catalog, Consumer.*
Former titles (until 1976): A F A Danmark, Groenland, Faeroeerne, Dansk Vestindien Frimaerkekatalog (0906-6810); (until 1975): A F A Danmark, Groenland, Faeroeerne Frimaerkekatalog (0906-6829); (until 1975): A F A Danmark, Groenland, Thule Frimaerkekatalog (0906-6802)
Related titles: CD-ROM ed.: ISSN 1398-9898. 1998. DKK 268 (effective 2002).
Published by: A F A - Forlaget (Subsidiary of: Nordfrim A/S), Kvindevadet 42, Otterup, 5450, Denmark. TEL 45-64-821256, FAX 45-64-821056, http://www.afa.dk. **Dist. by:** Nordfrim A/S, Kvindevadet 42, Otterup 5450, Denmark. mail@nordfrim.dk, http://www.nordfrim.dk.

769.569 DNK ISSN 0901-6996
A F A DANMARK FIREBLOKKE. Text in Danish. 1974. a. DKK 95 (effective 2008). illus. **Document type:** *Catalog, Consumer.* **Description:** Covers Denmark, the Faroe Islands, and Greenland.
Published by: A F A - Forlaget (Subsidiary of: Nordfrim A/S), Kvindevadet 42, Otterup, 5450, Denmark. TEL 45-64-821256, FAX 45-64-821056, afa@afa.dk, http://www.afa.dk. **Dist. by:** Nordfrim A/S, Kvindevadet 42, Otterup 5450, Denmark. mail@nordfrim.dk, http://www.nordfrim.dk.

P

769.5694 DNK ISSN 0901-6643
A F A OESTEUROPA FRIMAERKEKATALOG. Variant title: Oesteuropa Frimaerkekatalog. Text in Danish. 1959. a. (in 2 vols.). DKK 790 Vol. 1-2 (effective 2008). illus. **Document type:** *Catalog, Consumer.* **Description:** Covers Eastern Europe.
Supersedes in part (in 1974): A F A Europa Frimaerkekatalog
Published by: A F A - Forlaget (Subsidiary of: Nordfrim A/S), Kvindevadet 42, Otterup, 5450, Denmark. TEL 45-64-821256, FAX 45-64-821056, afa@afa.dk, http://www.afa.dk. **Dist. by:** Nordfrim A/S, Kvindevadet 42, Otterup 5450, Denmark. mail@nordfrim.dk, http://www.nordfrim.dk.

769.569 DNK ISSN 0901-6635
A F A SKANDINAVIEN FRIMAERKEKATALOG. Text in Danish. 1948. a. DKK 225 (effective 2008). illus. **Document type:** *Catalog, Consumer.* **Description:** Descriptions of stamps from the Scandinavian and Baltic countries.
Published by: A F A - Forlaget (Subsidiary of: Nordfrim A/S), Kvindevadet 42, Otterup, 5450, Denmark. TEL 45-64-821256, FAX 45-64-821056, afa@afa.dk, http://www.afa.dk. **Dist. by:** Nordfrim A/S, Kvindevadet 42, Otterup 5450, Denmark. mail@nordfrim.dk, http://www.nordfrim.dk.

769.56 DNK ISSN 1395-0320
A F A SPECIALKATALOG; Danmark, Faeroeerne, Groenland, Dansk Vestindien og Slesvig. Text in Danish. 1966. a. DKK 595 (effective 2008). illus. **Document type:** *Catalog, Consumer.* **Description:** Color illustrations of all stamps from Denmark, Faero Islands, Greenland, Danish West Indies and Slesvig.
Former titles (until 1994): A F A Danmark, Faeroeerne, Groenland, Dansk Vestindien, Slesvig-Holsten Specialkatalog (0901-7011); (until 1987): A F A Danmark, Faeroeerne, Groenland, Dqansk Vestindien Specialkatalog (1395-0312)
Published by: A F A - Forlaget (Subsidiary of: Nordfrim A/S), Kvindevadet 42, Otterup, 5450, Denmark. TEL 45-64-821256, FAX 45-64-821056, afa@afa.dk, http://www.afa.dk. **Dist. by:** Nordfrim A/S, Kvindevadet 42, Otterup 5450, Denmark. mail@nordfrim.dk, http://www.nordfrim.dk.

769.569 DNK ISSN 0901-702X
A F A VESTEUROPA FRIMAERKEKATALOG. Variant title: Vesteuropa Frimaerkekatalog. Text in Danish. 1959. a. (in 2 vols.). DKK 850 Vol. 1-2 (effective 2008). illus. **Document type:** *Catalog, Consumer.* **Description:** Covers Western Europe.
Supersedes in part (in 1974): A F A Europa Frimaerkekatalog
Published by: A F A - Forlaget (Subsidiary of: Nordfrim A/S), Kvindevadet 42, Otterup, 5450, Denmark. TEL 45-64-821256, FAX 45-64-821056, afa@afa.dk, http://www.afa.dk. **Dist. by:** Nordfrim A/S, Kvindevadet 42, Otterup 5450, Denmark. mail@nordfrim.dk, http://www.nordfrim.dk.

769.56 ARG ISSN 0001-1193
A F R A BOLETIN INFORMATIVO. Text in Spanish. 1939. bi-w. membership. adv. bk.rev.
Former titles (until 1970): A F R A Boletin; Asociacion Filatelica de la Republica Argentina. Revista
Published by: Asociacion Filatelica de la Republica Argentina, Tucuman 672, Piso 1, Depto. 2, Buenos Aires, 1049, Argentina. **Subscr. to:** Casilla de Correo 1992, Buenos Aires 1000, Argentina.

769.56 DEU
A P H V MAGAZIN. Text in German. m. adv. **Document type:** *Magazine, Trade.*
Published by: Allgemeiner Postwertzeichen Haendler Verband e.V., Barbarossaplatz 2, Cologne, 50674, Germany. TEL 49-221-407900, FAX 49-221-409597, bundesverband@aphv.de, http://www.aphv.de. adv.: B&W page EUR 220. Circ: 700 (controlled).

769.56 USA
A S D A NEWSLETTER. Text in English. 1914. m. membership. adv. bk.rev. tr.lit. 16 p./no.; **Document type:** *Newsletter.*
Formerly: A.S.D.A. Bulletin

Published by: American Stamp Dealers' Association, 3 School St, Ste 205, Glen Cove, NY 11542. TEL 516-759-7000. Ed. John A Scott. Circ: 2,500.

796.56 DEU ISSN 0933-1409
A T M; der aktuelle Informationsdienst zum Thema Briefmarken-Automation. Text in German. 1984. bi-w. looseleaf. EUR 30 (effective 2001). adv. bk.rev. back issues avail. **Document type:** *Newsletter, Consumer.*
Published by: Kulleraugen Verlag, Laaseweg 4, Schellerten, 31174, Germany. TEL 49-5123-4330, FAX 49-5123-2015, redaktion.kulleraugen@epost.de, http://www.kulleraugen-verlag.de. Ed. Hans-Juergen Tast. Circ: 250 (paid).

769.56 FIN ISSN 0355-7650
ABOPHIL. Text in Finnish. 1964. irreg.
Published by: Turun postimerkkikerho, Joesse Sakonkatu 8 A 73, Turku, 20610, Finland.

769.56 USA
AERONAUTICA AND AIR LABEL COLLECTOR. Text in English. 1943. q. adv. bk.rev. **Document type:** *Catalog, Trade.* **Description:** Air transport catalog of the world.
Published by: Aeronautica & Air Label Collectors Club, PO Box 1239, Elgin, IL 60121. bsburrell@hotmail.com, http://www.americanairmailsociety.org. Circ: (controlled).

769.56 USA ISSN 0739-0939
HE6187
AIRPOST JOURNAL. Text in English. 1929. m. USD 3 per issue (effective 2010). adv. bk.rev. illus. Index. 48 p./no. 1 cols./p.; back issues avail. **Document type:** *Journal, Academic/Scholarly.* **Description:** Tells the history of air mail through stamps and covers.
Indexed: SJI.
Published by: American Air Mail Society, PO Box 110, Mineola, NY 11501. Ed., Adv. contact Wayne Youngblood.

ALAN SHAWN FEINSTEIN INSIDERS REPORT. *see* BUSINESS AND ECONOMICS—Investments

769.56 USA
ALBUM PAGE. Text in English. 1960. 10/yr. free to members. adv. **Document type:** *Newsletter.* **Description:** Contains club news, Library additions, upcoming philatelic events in the Northwest, and feature articles by experienced philatelists.
Published by: Oregon Stamp Society, PO Box 18165, Portland, OR 97218-0165. http://www.oregonstampsociety.org. Ed. Dr. Vance Terrall. Circ: 400.

769.56 USA ISSN 0003-0473
HE6187
AMERICAN PHILATELIST. Text in English. 1887. m. USD 48 domestic; USD 50 in Canada; USD 58 elsewhere; USD 4.95 per issue (effective 2009). adv. bk.rev.; Website rev. illus. index, cum.index: 1887-1986. 100 p./no.; back issues avail.; reprints avail. **Document type:** *Magazine, Consumer.*
Indexed: ABS&EES, BRI, CBRI, MLA-IB, P30.
—Ingenta.
Published by: American Philatelic Society, Inc., 100 Match Factory Pl, Bellefonte, PA 16823. TEL 814-933-3803, FAX 814-933-6128, flsente@stamps.org, http://www.philately.com/philately/aps.htm. Ed. Barbara Boal. Circ: 39,500 (paid).

769.56 USA ISSN 0163-1608
HJ5321.Z7
AMERICAN REVENUER. Text in English. 1947. bi-m. USD 21 to members (effective 2004 & 2005). adv. bk.rev. illus. index, cum.index. back issues avail. **Document type:** *Magazine, Trade.* **Description:** Articles about and catalogue listings of tax stamps of the US and the world.
Indexed: SJI.
—Ingenta.
Published by: American Revenue Association, PO Box 56, Rockford, IA 50468-0056. TEL 641-756-3542. Ed., R&P Kenneth Trettin. adv.: B&W page USD 120. Circ: 1,189 (paid).

769.56 USA
AMERICAN SOCIETY FOR NETHERLANDS PHILATELY. NEWSLETTER. Text in English. 1975. q. USD 16 domestic; USD 21 foreign (effective 1999); includes the Journal. **Document type:** *Newsletter.*
Published by: American Society for Netherlands Philately, W6428 Riverview Dr, Onalaska, WI 54650. TEL 608-781-8612. Ed. Jan Enthowen. Circ: 400.

769.56 USA ISSN 1055-8616
AMERICAN SOCIETY FOR PHILATELIC PAGES AND PANELS. PAGE & PANEL JOURNAL. Text in English. 1984. q. USD 15 in North America to members; USD 21 elsewhere to members (effective 2004). adv. charts; illus. index. back issues avail. **Document type:** *Newsletter.* **Description:** Gathers and distributes information on all philatelic pages and panels, especially on U.S. souvenir pages and commemorative panels.
Formerly: U.S. Souvenir Page Society Bulletin
Published by: American Society for Philatelic Pages and Panels, P O Box 475, Crosby, TX 77532. asppp134@aol.com, ronw@asppp.org. Ed. Ron Walenciak. adv.: B&W page USD 40. Circ: 800.

769.56 USA
AMERICANA PHILATELIC NEWS. Text in English. 1951. q. USD 6. bk.rev. **Document type:** *Newsletter.* **Description:** News of stamps worldwide that have some relationship to the U.S. Official journal of Americana Unit.
Published by: American Topical Association, Inc., Americana Unit, c/o David Kent, Box 127, New Britain, CT 06050. Ed. Melvin Morris. Circ: 150 (paid).

769.56 USA
ANCHORAGE PHILATELIST. Text in English. 1953. m. USD 10 (effective 1998). **Document type:** *Newsletter.*
Published by: Anchorage Philatelic Society, Inc., PO Box 10 2214, Anchorage, AK 99510. Ed. Eric Knapp. Circ: 150.

789.56 GBR ISSN 0269-9249
THE ANGLO-BOER WAR PHILATELIST. Text in English. 1958. q. GBP 15 (effective 2009). adv. bk.rev. **Document type:** *Journal, Consumer.*
Published by: Anglo-Boer War Philatelic Society, c/o Mr Nick Harris, 3 Mermaid Way, Maldon, Essex CM9 5LA, United Kingdom. TEL 44-1631-858933, mmphboer@aol.com, http://www.boerwarsociety.org. Ed. Alan Harley TEL 44-1743-361785.

THE APPRAISERS STANDARD; published solely for collectors, auctioneers, dealers, etc. *see* ART

769.56 DEU
ARBEITSGEMEINSCHAFT DEUTSCHE OSTGEBIETE. RUNDSCHREIBEN. Text in German. 1959. q. EUR 30; EUR 8 newsstand/cover (effective 2008). bk.rev. **Document type:** *Bulletin, Consumer.*
Published by: Arbeitsgemeinschaft Deutsche Ostgebiete e.V., Sudetenstr 11, Uttenreuth, 91080, Germany. TEL 49-9131-58489, http://arge-ost.de. Ed. Hans Georg Klemm.

769.56 DEU
ARBEITSGEMEINSCHAFT MALTA. RUNDBRIEFE. Text in German. 1974. 3/yr. bk.rev. back issues avail. **Document type:** *Newsletter, Consumer.* **Description:** Reports and studies on the postal history of Malta for advanced philatelists.
Former titles: A G M - Magazin; G M Z
Published by: Arbeitsgemeinschaft Malta im Bund Deutscher Philatelisten e.V., Lagerstr 47, Homburg, 66424, Germany. TEL 49-6841-64363, FAX 49-7131-772601, c.juncker@surfeu.de, http://www.arge-malta.de. Ed., R&P Peter C Hansen. Circ: 100.

794 USA
ARIZONA PHILATELIST. Text in English. 1958. q. free to members (effective 2008). adv. bk.rev. **Document type:** *Newsletter, Consumer.*
Related titles: Online - full text ed.
Published by: Arizona Federation of Stamp Clubs, Inc., 8930 N. Spinel Pl, Tucson, AZ 85742. TEL 520-794-3921, 520-572-8980, mman3@comcast.net. Ed., R&P, Adv. contact Edward Leahy. Circ: 500 (controlled).

ARTISTAMP NEWS. *see* ART

769.56 USA
ASTROFAX. Text in English. 1972. q. USD 6 domestic; USD 10 foreign (effective 2000). **Document type:** *Newsletter.* **Description:** Focuses on astronomy, astronomers, astrology and related subjects appearing on stamps and covers.
Published by: Astronomy Study Unit, c/o George Young, Box 632, Tewksbury, MA 01876. TEL 978-851-8283.

769.56 SWE
ATALAYA. Text in Swedish. 1974. 2/yr. USD 3. adv. bk.rev.
Published by: Christer Brunstrom Ed. & Pub., Kungsgatan 23, Halmstad, 30245, Sweden.

759.56 FRA ISSN 1277-2054
ATOUT TIMBRES; le journal des affranchis. Text in French. 1996. m. adv. charts; illus.; mkt. back issues avail. **Document type:** *Magazine, Consumer.* **Description:** Discusses the history and meaning of stamps, along with issues in collecting stamps and other aspects of philately.
Published by: Echo de la Timbrologie, 37 rue des Jacobins, Amiens, Cedex 1 80036, France. TEL 33-3-22717180, FAX 33-3-22717189.

769.56 AUS ISSN 0155-8498
AUSTRALASIAN STAMP CATALOGUE. Abbreviated title: A S C. Text in English. 1960. irreg., latest vol.2, 2007, 30th ed. AUD 38.50 per issue (effective 2009). illus.; mkt. 3 cols./p.; back issues avail. **Document type:** *Catalog, Consumer.* **Description:** Contains illustrated and priced catalog of all Australian commonwealth stamps and postal stationery.
Supersedes in part (in 1968): Australian Stamp Catalogue (0155-851X)
Published by: Seven Seas Stamps Pty. Ltd., 5/7 Clearview Pl, PO Box 321, Brookvale, NSW 2100, Australia. TEL 61-2-99053255, FAX 61-2-99057922, stamps@sevenseas.com.au.

760 AUS ISSN 1833-1564
AUSTRALIAN STAMP BULLETIN. Text in English. 1979. bi-m. free (effective 2008). bk.rev. illus. back issues avail. **Document type:** *Magazine, Consumer.* **Description:** Covers information about new Australian stamps and stamp collecting.
Former titles (until 1988): Stamp Bulletin Australia (1833-1556); (until 1985): Australian Stamp Bulletin (1833-1548); Which was formed by the 1979 merger of: Stamp Preview (1833-1521); (1953-1978): Philatelic Bulletin (1833-153X)
Related titles: Online - full text ed.
Published by: Australia Post, Philatelic Group, GPO Box 1777, Melbourne, VIC 3001, Australia. FAX 61-3-92047777, mailorder@auspost.com.au, http://www.auspost.com.au/stamps. Ed. Noel Leahy. Circ: 380,000.

769.56 AUS
AUSTRALIAN STAMP EXPLORER. Text in English. 1977. q. free (effective 2008). **Document type:** *Bulletin, Consumer.* **Description:** Provides stamp collecting tips, jokes, competitions and puzzles for children.
Formerly (until 1985): Junior Stamp Preview
Related titles: Online - full text ed.
Published by: Australia Post, Philatelic Group, GPO Box 1777, Melbourne, VIC 3001, Australia. FAX 61-3-92047777, mailorder@auspost.com.au, http://www.auspost.com.au/stamps. Ed. Carol Daniels. Circ: 340,000.

769.56 GBR ISSN 0142-9760
HE6185.A92
AUSTRIA & HUNGARY STAMP CATALOGUE. Text in English. 1979. irreg., latest 2009, 6th ed. GBP 34.95 per issue (effective 2010). **Document type:** *Catalog, Trade.* **Description:** Covers the stamp issues of both Austria and Hungary.
Published by: Stanley Gibbons Publications Ltd., 399 Strand, London, WC2R 0LX, United Kingdom. TEL 44-207-8368444, FAX 44-207-8367342, kfinney@stanleygibbons.co.uk.

769.56 AUT ISSN 0005-0512
AUSTRIA-PHILATELIST; Oesterreichische Briefmarken-Zeitung. Text in German. 1945. q. adv. bk.rev. **Document type:** *Newspaper, Consumer.*
Published by: Verlag Adolf Kosel KG, Hebragasse 7-9, Vienna, 1095, Austria. TEL 43-1-40643030, FAX 43-1-406430333, info@kosel.at, http://www.kosel.com. Ed. Leopold Sander. Circ: 5,000.

769.56 CAN ISSN 1203-4657
B N A PORTRAITS. (British North America) Text in English. 1993. q. USD 18 (effective 2000). adv. **Document type:** *Newsletter.* **Description:** Publishes the society's activities.
Published by: British North America Philatelic Society Ltd., 5295 Mongton St, Richmond, BC V7E 3B2, Canada. TEL 604-272-5090, beaver@telus.net. Ed. Everett Parker. Adv. contact Henry Narbonne. Circ: 1,500.

769.56 CAN ISSN 0045-3129
HE6187
B N A TOPICS. (British North America) Text in English. 1943. 4/yr. USD 18 (effective 2000). adv. bk.rev. **Document type:** *Journal, Academic/Scholarly.* **Description:** Specialist philatelic journal featuring articles on stamps, postal history and related subjects of Canada and the provinces of Canada before their confederation.
Indexed: SJI.
Published by: British North America Philatelic Society Ltd., 5295 Mongton St, Richmond, BC V7E 3B2, Canada. TEL 604-272-5090, beaver@telus.net. Ed. David Handelman. Pub. K Wayne Smith. Adv. contact Henry Narbonne. Circ: 1,500.

769.56 GBR ISSN 0953-8720
B W I STUDY CIRCLE BULLETIN. (British West Indies) Text in English. 1954. q. free to members (effective 2009). bk.rev. back issues avail. **Document type:** *Bulletin, Trade.*
Related titles: Online - full text ed.
Indexed: SJI.
Published by: British West Indies Study Circle, c o Ray Stanton, The Old Rectory, Salmonby, Horncastle, LN9 6PX, United Kingdom. TEL 44-1507-533742, info@bwisc.org.

769.56 USA
BADGER POSTAL HISTORY. Text in English. 1947. q. USD 12 membership (effective 2003). adv. **Document type:** *Newsletter.* **Description:** Contains feature articles, news about membership activities, and other items of general interest to the Wisconsin postal historian.
Published by: Wisconsin Postal History Society, N95 W32259 County Line Rd, Hartland, WI 53029. TEL 920-499-3877. Ed. William B Robinson. R&P, Adv. contact Frank Moertl TEL 262-966-7096. B&W page USD 30; trim 11 x 8.5. Circ: 203 (paid).

769.56 GBR ISSN 0142-9779
BALKANS STAMP CATALOGUE. Text in English. 1980. irreg., latest 2009, 5th ed. GBP 42.50 per issue (effective 2010). **Document type:** *Catalog, Consumer.* **Description:** Covers stamps from countries such as Albania, Bosnia and Herzegovina, Bulgaria, Croatia, Greece, Macedonia, Montenegro, Romania, Serbia, Slovenia and Yugoslavia.
Supersedes in part (in 1980): Stanley Gibbons Foreign Stamp Catalogue. Europe (0305-8085)
Published by: Stanley Gibbons Publications Ltd., 399 Strand, London, WC2R 0LX, United Kingdom. TEL 44-207-8368444, FAX 44-207-8367342, info@stanleygibbons.co.uk.

769.56 USA ISSN 0951-9955
BATON. Text in English. 1968. 3/yr. USD 15 (effective 1999). back issues avail. **Document type:** *Bulletin.* **Description:** Provides information on music, fine art stamps and stamp auctions.
Published by: Philatelic Music Circle, PO Box 1781, Sequim, WA 98382. TEL 360-683-6373. Ed. Alena Pascual.

769.55 USA ISSN 8756-5153
BAY PHIL. Text in English. 1971. bi-m. USD 15 domestic membership; USD 17 in Canada membership; USD 23 elsewhere membership (effective 2005). bk.rev. tr.lit. 16 p./no.; **Document type:** *Newsletter, Consumer.*
Indexed: H20, T02.
Published by: Friends of the Western Philatelic Library, Inc., PO Box 2219, Sunnyvale, CA 94087. dmcnamee@aol.com. Ed. Harold A Short. Circ: 400 (paid).

769.56 GBR ISSN 0269-2759
BELGAPOST. Text in English. 19??. q. free to members (effective 2011). back issues avail. **Document type:** *Journal, Academic/Scholarly.* **Description:** Contains a mixture of articles on Belgian postal history and philately.
Formerly (until 1981): Belgian Study Circle. Newsletter
Published by: Belgian Philatelic Study Circle, c/o C R Howe, 14 Sandringham Gardens, Fishtoft, Boston, Lincolnshire PE21 9QA, United Kingdom. enquiries@belgianphilatelicstudycircle.org.uk. Ed. R T Harrison.

759.56 USA
BELGIOPHILE. Text in English. 1983. q. looseleaf. USD 7.50 domestic membership; USD 8.50 in Canada & Mexico membership; USD 12.50 elsewhere membership (effective 2000). adv. bk.rev. cum.index: 1983-1993. back issues avail. **Document type:** *Bulletin.* **Description:** Covers philatelic matters of interest to persons from beginning to very advanced level.
Published by: American-Belgian Philatelic Society, 1123 Cheyenne Drive, Indian Harbour Beach, FL 32937. Ed. Donald J Landis. Pub. William V Miller. R&P, Adv. contact Ralph Yorio TEL 321-773-1487. Circ: 145. **Subscr. to:** 621 Virginius Dr, Virginia Beach, VA 23452-4417.

769.56 USA
BELIZE COLLECTOR. Text in English. 1987. q. **Description:** Focuses on all aspects of British Honduran and Belizean philately.
Published by: Belize Philatelic Society Circle, c/o Charles R Gambill, 730 Collingswood, Corpus Christi, TX 78412.

769.56 GBR ISSN 0142-9787
HE6185.B43
BENELUX STAMP CATALOGUE. Text in English. 1979. irreg., latest 2010, 6th ed. GBP 39.95 per issue (effective 2010). back issues avail. **Document type:** *Catalog, Consumer.* **Description:** Contains list of all the stamps from the earliest issues of Belgium, the Netherlands, Netherland Antilles, Luxembourg and Aruba, including all the major varieties, notably perforation, watermark and shade variations, overprint types and major errors.
Supersedes in part (in 1979): Stanley Gibbons Foreign Stamp Catalogue. Europe (0305-8085)
Published by: Stanley Gibbons Publications Ltd., 399 Strand, London, WC2R 0LX, United Kingdom. TEL 44-207-8368444, FAX 44-207-8367342, kfinney@stanleygibbons.co.uk.

769.56 CHE ISSN 0005-9404
BERNER BRIEFMARKEN-ZEITUNG/JOURNAL PHILATELIQUE DE BERNE. Text in French, German. 1908. 10/yr. (including two double nos.). CHF 37; CHF 48 foreign (effective 1998). bk.rev. illus. **Document type:** *Consumer.* **Description:** Stamp collectors magazine covering all countries of the world. Includes news, values, special issues, history, events and exhibitions, list of special collections, and list of new catalogs.
Related titles: CD-ROM ed.

Published by: Zumstein und Cie, Postfach 1079, Bern 7, 3000, Switzerland. TEL 41-31-3120055, FAX 41-31-3122326. Ed., Pub. Max Hertsch. Circ: 10,000.

789.56 ZWE
BORDER POST. Text in English. bi-m. **Document type:** *Bulletin.*
Published by: Manicaland Philatelic Society, PO Box 684, Mutare, Zimbabwe.

769.56 AUT ISSN 0007-0033
BRIEFMARKE. Text in German. 1952. m. adv. bk.rev. charts; illus.; mkt. **Document type:** *Newsletter, Consumer.*
Published by: Verband Oesterreichischer Philatelisten-Vereine, Getreidemarkt 1, Vienna, W 1010, Austria. TEL 43-1-5876469, FAX 43-1-5877026, office@voeph.at, http://www.voeph.at. Ed. Richard Zimmerl TEL 43-1-8692395. Circ: 7,000.

383.2 LIE
BRIEFMARKEN-AUSGABE. Text in English, French, German. 1980. q. **Document type:** *Bulletin, Consumer.*
Former titles (until 2007): Briefmarken aus dem Fuerstentum Liechtenstein; (until 1994): Die Briefmarkenausgabe
Published by: Liechtensteinische Post AG, Kundendienst, Alte Zollstr 11, Schaan, 9494, Liechtenstein. TEL 423-399-4444, FAX 423-399-4499, info@post.li, http://www.post.li/liechtensteinische-post-ag/. Circ: 25,000.

789.56 DEU ISSN 0007-005X
BRIEFMARKEN POST. Text in German. 1958. m. adv. **Document type:** *Magazine, Consumer.*
Published by: Philapress Verlag der Goettinger Tageblatt GmbH, Benzstr 1c, Goettingen, 37083, Germany. TEL 49-551-499050, FAX 49-551-4990530, info@philapress.de, http://www.philapress.de. Ed. Gerd Aschoff. Adv. contact Irmgard Kessler Winkelbach. B&W page EUR 670, color page EUR 1,019; trim 122 x 176. Circ: 16,800 (controlled).

769.56 DEU ISSN 0007-0041
BRIEFMARKEN-SPIEGEL; internationale Philatelie. Text in German. 1961. m. EUR 33.60 domestic; EUR 48 foreign; EUR 3.30 newsstand/cover (effective 2006). adv. bk.rev. **Document type:** *Magazine, Consumer.*
Published by: Philapress Verlag der Goettinger Tageblatt GmbH, Benzstr 1c, Goettingen, 37083, Germany. TEL 49-551-499050, FAX 49-551-4990530, info@philapress.de, http://www.philapress.de. Ed. Gerd Aschoff. Adv. contact Irmgard Kessler Winkelbach. B&W page EUR 1,333, color page EUR 2,001; trim 185 x 261. Circ: 35,651 (paid and controlled).

769.56 USA ISSN 0045-2890
HE6187
BRITISH CARIBBEAN PHILATELIC JOURNAL. Text in English. 1961. q. free to members (effective 2010). adv. bk.rev. charts; illus. index. back issues avail. **Document type:** *Journal, Academic/Scholarly.* **Description:** Publishes research and information about the stamps and postal history of the British West Indies, British Honduras (Belize), British Guiana (Guyana) and Bermuda.
Related titles: Online - full text ed.: free (effective 2010).
Indexed: SJI.
Published by: British Caribbean Philatelic Study Group, c/o Bob Stewart, 7 W Dune Ln, Beach Haven, NJ 08008. TEL 609-492-4379, stewart99@comcast.net, http://www.bcpsg.com. Ed. Everett L Parker TEL 207-695-3163. Adv. contact Robert Fashingbauer TEL 773-994-5148.

769.56 CAN ISSN 1926-5654
BRITISH COLUMBIA PHILATELIC SOCIETY. NEWSLETTER. Text in English. 1974. 3/yr. free to members (effective 2011). **Document type:** *Newsletter, Trade.*
Formerly (until 1990): British Columbia Philatelic Society. Bulletin (1926-5662)
Related titles: Online - full text ed.: free (effective 2011).
Published by: British Columbia Philatelic Society, The Grosvenor Bldg, 1040 W Georgia St, PO Box 40, Vancouver, BC V6E 4H1, Canada. edm@telus.net, http://www.bcphilatelic.org. Ed. Mulberry Sang TEL 604-808-5889.

769.56 GBR ISSN 0953-8119
BRITISH PHILATELIC BULLETIN. Text in English. 1963. m. GBP 12.95 in Europe; GBP 17.95 elsewhere (effective 2009). bk.rev. charts; illus.; stat. index. back issues avail. **Document type:** *Magazine, Consumer.* **Description:** Covers a wide range of philatelic topics pertaining to the British post.
Formerly (until 1983): Philatelic Bulletin
Indexed: ChLitAb.
Published by: British Post Office, Royal Mail, PO Box 740, Barnsley, S73 0ZJ, United Kingdom. TEL 44-8457740740, customercare@postoffice.co.uk. Ed. John Holman TEL 44-20-7847-3321.

789.56 GBR ISSN 0955-923X
BRITISH POSTMARK BULLETIN. Text in English. 1971. fortn. GBP 12.25 in Europe; GBP 24.95 elsewhere (effective 2009). bk.rev. illus. **Document type:** *Bulletin, Consumer.* **Description:** Provides details of forthcoming postmarks and background articles on postmarks of the past.
Formerly (until 1983): Postmark Bulletin
Published by: British Post Office, Royal Mail, PO Box 740, Barnsley, S73 0ZJ, United Kingdom. TEL 44-8457740740, customercare@postoffice.co.uk.

769.56 GBR ISSN 1753-0717
BRITISH POSTMARK SOCIETY. JOURNAL. Text in English. 1958. q. looseleaf. free to members (effective 2009). bk.rev. illus. back issues avail. **Document type:** *Journal, Consumer.* **Description:** Covers UK postal history, especially from the twentieth and twenty-first centuries.
Formerly (until 2007): British Postmark Society. Quarterly Bulletin (1470-2711)
Published by: British Postmark Society, c o John Strachan, 12 Dunavon Park, Strathaven, ML10 6LP, United Kingdom. johlen@straciml10.freeserve.co.uk.

769.56 FRA ISSN 1167-4024
BULLETIN MENSUEL DE THEODORE CHAMPION. Text in French. 1902. m. **Document type:** *Bulletin, Consumer.*
Former titles (until 1991): Bulletin Mensuel de l'Ancienne Maison Theodore Champion (1153-2564); (until 1955): Bulletin Mensuel de la Maison Theodore Champion et Cie (1153-2556)
Published by: Theodore Champion, 8, Rue des Messageries, Paris, F-75010, France. TEL 33-1-42-46-70-38, FAX 33-1-48-24-08-27, 33-1-42-46-73-49.

769.56 DEU
BUNDESARBEITSGEMEINSCHAFT SAAR FUER PHILATELIE UND POSTGESCHICHTE. MITTEILUNGSBLATT. Text in German. 1969. q. membership. **Document type:** *Newsletter, Trade.*
Formerly (until 2005): Arge-Saar. Mitteilungsblatt
Published by: Bundesarbeitsgemeinschaft Saar fuer Philatelie und Postgeschichte e.V., Donnersbergstr 15c, Schiffweiler, 66578, Germany. TEL 49-6821-65186, FAX 49-6821-634952, info@arge-saar.de, http://www.arge-saar.de.

769.56 CAN
C A F I P BULLETIN. Text in English. bi-m. CAD 35 (effective 2006). bk.rev. abstr.; bibl.; illus. back issues avail. **Document type:** *Bulletin.*
Published by: Canadian Association for Israel Philately, 33-260 Adelaide St E, Toronto, ON M5A 1N1, Canada. TEL 416-635-1749. Ed. Joseph Berkovits. Circ: 60.

769.56 USA ISSN 0746-2433
C O R O S CHRONICLE. Text in English. 1945. q. USD 22 domestic; USD 24 foreign (effective 2007). adv. bk.rev. 36 p./no. 2 cols./p.; back issues avail. **Document type:** *Journal, Consumer.*
Published by: Collectors of Religion on Stamps, c/o Verna Shackleton, 425 N. Linwood Ave Apt. 110, Appleton, WI 54914. TEL 920-734-2417, corosec@powernetonline.com, http://www.powernetonline.com/~corosec/corosl.htm. Ed., Adv. contact Fr. Augustine Serafini TEL 920-233-5633. page USD 60. Circ: 350; 300 (paid).

769.56 NZL ISSN 1172-0166
CAMPBELL PATERSON NEWSLETTER; for collectors of New Zealand Stamps. Text in English. 1948. m. bk.rev. **Document type:** *Newsletter, Consumer.*
Former titles (until 1992): C.P. Newsletter Monthly (0112-8388); Campbell Paterson Newsletter
—CCC.
Published by: Campbell Paterson Ltd., Level 3, General Building, Corner O'Connell and Shortland Streets, PO Box 5555, Auckland, 1141, New Zealand. TEL 64-9-3793086, FAX 64-9-3793087. Ed. Warwick R Paterson. Circ: 2,000.

769.56 NZL
CAMPBELL PATERSON'S LOOSE-LEAF COLOUR CATALOGUE OF NEW ZEALAND STAMPS (SPECIALISED). Text in English. 1950. a. NZD 215 (effective 2008). **Document type:** *Catalog.* **Description:** Guide for collectors of New Zealand stamps from 1854 to the present day.
Published by: Campbell Paterson Ltd., Level 3, General Building, Corner O'Connell and Shortland Streets, PO Box 5555, Auckland, 1141, New Zealand. TEL 64-9-3793086, FAX 64-9-3793087. Ed. Campbell Paterson.

769.56 CAN ISSN 1195-0064
THE CANADIAN CONNECTION. Text in English. 1987. q. looseleaf. CAD 10 domestic; USD 10 in United States (effective 2002). illus. 30 p./no.; back issues avail. **Document type:** *Newsletter, Consumer.* **Description:** Presents thematic stamps and journals for collectors of world wide stamps and other philatelic items.
Published by: Canadiana Study Unit, c/o John G Peebles, Ed, P O Box 3262, Sta A, London, ON N6A 4K3, Canada. R&P John G Peebles TEL 519-672-0885. Circ: 125 (paid).

769.56 CAN ISSN 1922-4508
▼ **THE CANADIAN DEAD LETTER OFFICE.** Text in English. 2009. irreg., latest 2010. USD 20 per issue in US & Canada (effective 2010). back issues avail. **Document type:** *Newsletter, Trade.*
Related titles: Online - full text ed.
Published by: Dead Letter Office Study Group, c/o Brian Plain, Chairman, Unit 4 132 Michigan St, Victoria, BC V8V 1R1, Canada. TEL 250-380-2820, bcplain@shaw.ca. Ed. Gary Steele TEL 902-864-3976.

769.56 CAN ISSN 0045-5253
CANADIAN PHILATELIST/PHILATELISTE CANADIEN. Text in English, French. 1950. bi-m. free to members; CAD 30 to non-members (effective 2011). adv. bk.rev. illus. index. back issues avail.; reprints avail. **Document type:** *Journal, Academic/Scholarly.* **Description:** Contains philatelic articles, philatelic news, auction and events calendars, meeting notices and Society reports.
Related titles: Microfiche ed.: (from MML); Microform ed.: (from MML).
Indexed: C03, CBCARef, CBPI, H20, PQC, SJI, T02.
Published by: (Royal Philatelic Society of Canada), Philaprint Ltd., 10 Summerhill Ave, Toronto, ON M4T 1AB, Canada. TEL 416-361-2348. Ed. Tony Shaman. Circ: 2,300 (controlled).

769.56 CAN ISSN 0702-3154
HE6187
CANADIAN STAMP NEWS. Text in English. 1976. 26/yr. CAD 37.40 domestic; USD 37.40 in United States; CAD 149 elsewhere (effective 2004). adv. bk.rev. illus.; stat. **Document type:** *Magazine, Consumer.*
Related titles: Microfilm ed.: (from MML); Microform ed.: (from MML).
Indexed: C03, CBCARef, CBPI, P48, PQC.
Published by: Trajan Publishing Corp., 103 Lakeshore Rd, Ste 202, St Catharines, ON L2N 2T6, Canada. TEL 905-646-7744, FAX 905-646-0995, office@trajan.com, http://www.trajan.com. Ed. John Sarko. adv.: B&W page USD 859. Circ: 7,625.

769.56 USA ISSN 0746-004X
HE6185.C24
CANAL ZONE PHILATELIST. Text in English. 1952. q. USD 8 membership (effective 2008). adv. bk.rev.
Indexed: SJI.
Published by: Canal Zone Study Group, c/o Richard F. Murphy, 1489 Oakhurst Dr, Mt Pleasant, SC 29466. http://www.canalzonestudygroup.com/index.html. Circ: 1,000.

769.56 FRA
CATALOGUE YVERT ET TELLIER TIMBRES DU MONDE. NOUVAUTES DE L'ANNEE (YEAR). Text in French. a. illus.; mkt. **Document type:** *Catalog, Consumer.* **Description:** Gives stamp collectors and other persons interested in philately news and information on stamps issued during the preceding year.
Published by: Echo de la Timbrologie, 37 rue des Jacobins, Amiens, Cedex 1 80036, France. TEL 33-3-22717180, FAX 33-3-22717189.

769.56 794.1 USA
CHESSTAMP REVIEW. Text in English. 1978. q. USD 17 in North America; USD 24 elsewhere (effective 2008). back issues avail. **Document type:** *Magazine, Consumer.* **Description:** Includes check lists alternatively covering stamps, postal stationery and EFO (Errors, Freaks and Oddities on chess stamps).
Published by: Chess on Stamps Study Unit, c/o Anne N. Kasonic, Secretary-Treasurer, 7625 County Rd 153, Interlaken, NY 14847. chessstuff911459@aol.com, akasonic@capital.net, cwouscg@aol.com. Ed. Russ Ott. Circ: 175.

769.56 CHL
CHILE FILATELICO. Text in Spanish. 1929. q. USD 5 per issue (effective 2001). tr.lit. back issues avail. **Document type:** *Magazine.*
Published by: Sociedad Filatelica de Chile, Casilla 13245, Almirante Simpson, 75, Santiago, Chile. TEL 56-2-2228036. Ed. Manuel de la Lastra B. Circ: 750 (paid).

769.56 USA ISSN 0885-9779
CHINA CLIPPER. Text in English. 1936. bi-m. free to members (effective 2010). adv. bk.rev. back issues avail. **Document type:** *Magazine, Trade.* **Description:** Consists of discussions of Chinese philately and articles of interest, brief reports of new findings, inquiries and response, and data concerning new issues.
Indexed: SJI.
Published by: China Stamp Society, Inc., PO Box 20711, Columbus, OH 43220. pgault@columbus.rr.com. Eds. Ralph Weil TEL 513-521-1536, Tom Shea. Pub. Ralph Weil TEL 513-521-1536.

769.56 GBR ISSN 0142-9892
CHINA STAMP CATALOGUE. Text in English. 1979. irreg., latest 2006, 7th ed. GBP 34.95 per issue (effective 2010). **Document type:** *Catalog, Consumer.* **Description:** Lists the stamps of China as well as those of treaty Port Municipal posts, the foreign post offices in China, Japanese occupation issues, the colonial issues of Hong Kong and Macao (as well as the stamps of the Chinese special regions), Taiwan and Tibet.
Supersedes in part (in 1979): Stanley Gibbons Foreign Stamp Ccatalogue. Overseas (0305-8093)
Published by: Stanley Gibbons Publications Ltd., 399 Strand, London, WC2R 0LX, United Kingdom. TEL 44-207-8368444, FAX 44-207-8367342, kfinney@stanleygibbons.co.uk.

769.56 USA
CHINA TRADER NEWSLETTER. Text in English. 1980. q. USD 7.50. adv. **Document type:** *Newsletter.*
Formerly: China
Published by: China Trader Supply, PO Box 630, Millbrook, NY 12545. Ed. Gene Klein. Circ: 200.

769.56 USA ISSN 0009-6008
HE6187
CHRONICLE OF U S CLASSIC POSTAL ISSUES. Text in English. 19??. q. free to members (effective 2010). bk.rev. illus.; tr.lit. **Document type:** *Journal, Academic/Scholarly.*
Formerly (until 1964): Chronicle of the U S Classic Issues
Indexed: SJI.
Published by: U S Philatelic Classics Society, Inc., c/o Mark D Rogers, Box 80708, Austin, TX 78708. http://www.uspcs.org.

769.56 GBR
CIVIL CENSORSHIP STUDY GROUP. BULLETIN. Text in English. 1973. q. GBP 10, USD 20 to non-members; free to members (effective 2009). adv. bk.rev. 32 p./no.; back issues avail. **Document type:** *Bulletin, Academic/Scholarly.* **Description:** Contains articles that cover a wide range of censorship subjects from all time periods.
Related titles: Online - full text ed.
Published by: Civil Censorship Study Group, c o Robert Johnson, 65 Manor Park, Redland, Bristol, BS6 7HW, United Kingdom. robert@johnson83.wanadoo.co.uk. Ed. Graham Mark.

769.56 VEN
CLUB FILATELICO DE CARACAS. GACETA MENSUAL. Text in Spanish. 1978-1981; resumed 1986. m. per issue exchange basis. adv. bk.rev.
Formerly (until no.80, 1981): Fila Nova; Supersedes (1961-1978): Club Filatelico de Caracas. Revista (0529-9853)
Published by: Club Filatelico de Caracas, Apartado 61.197, Caracas, 1060-A, Venezuela. FAX 782-17-31. Circ: 500.

769.56 PRT ISSN 0009-9651
CLUBE FILATELICO DE PORTUGAL. BOLETIM. Text in Portuguese. 1943. 4/yr. USD 15 (effective 2000). adv. bk.rev. illus. **Document type:** *Bulletin.*
Published by: Clube Filatelico de Portugal, Avenida Almirante Reis, 70, 5 Dto., Lisbon, 1100, Portugal. TEL 351-1-8123936, FAX 351-1-8123936. Ed. Lage Cardoso. Adv. contact J Dias Ferreira. Circ: 5,000.

769.56 USA ISSN 0896-3533
CODEX FILATELICA. Text in English. 1974. bi-m. USD 8 domestic; USD 9 in Canada & Mexico; USD 16 elsewhere (effective 2001). bk.rev. **Document type:** *Newsletter.* **Description:** Newsletter for collectors of worldwide stamps that illustrate or relate to Pre-Columbian archeology and New World peoples.
Published by: Meso American Archeology Study Unit, PO Box 1442, Riverside, CA 92502. Ed. Larry L Crain. Circ: 95 (paid).

769.56 FRA ISSN 2102-7714
COLFRA. BULLETIN. Variant title: Bulletin de la Colfra. Text in French. 1977. q. bk.rev. **Document type:** *Bulletin.* **Description:** Postal and philatelic history of former French colonies and territories; study and research.
Published by: L' Association Col.Fra, COL.FRA, B.P. 628, Paris, Cedex 8 75367, France. clubcolfra@aol.com, http://www.colfra.com. Circ: 160.

769.56 GBR ISSN 0264-679X
COLLECT BIRDS ON STAMPS. Text in English. 1983. irreg., latest 2003, 5th ed. GBP 29.95 per issue (effective 2010). **Document type:** *Catalog.* **Description:** Contains listings for more than 10,000 stamps illustrated country wise with detailed thematic descriptions.
Published by: Stanley Gibbons Publications Ltd., 399 Strand, London, WC2R 0LX, United Kingdom. TEL 44-207-8368444, FAX 44-207-8367342, kfinney@stanleygibbons.co.uk.

P

769.56 GBR ISSN 0069-5262
COLLECT BRITISH STAMPS. Text in English. 1967. irreg., latest 2003, 5th ed. GBP 29.95 per issue (effective 2010). adv. **Document type:** *Catalog, Consumer.* **Description:** Covers all the basics of stamp collecting (what to collect, how to obtain stamps, how to store them, what special equipment is available) and how to understand the Sg numbering system.
Published by: Stanley Gibbons Publications Ltd., 399 Strand, London, WC2R 0LX, United Kingdom. TEL 44-207-8368444, FAX 44-207-8367342, kfinney@stanleygibbons.co.uk.

769.56 GBR
COLLECT RAILWAYS ON STAMPS. Text in English. 1986. irreg., latest 1999, 3rd ed. GBP 19.95 per issue (effective 2010). **Document type:** *Catalog, Consumer.*
Published by: Stanley Gibbons Publications Ltd., 399 Strand, London, WC2R 0LX, United Kingdom. TEL 44-207-8368444, FAX 44-207-8367342, kfinney@stanleygibbons.co.uk, http://www.stanleygibbons.com.

769.56 GBR
COLLECT SHIPS ON STAMPS. Text in English. 1989. irreg., latest 2001, 3rd ed. GBP 22.95 per issue (effective 2010). **Document type:** *Catalog, Consumer.* **Description:** Lists over 14,250 stamps and over 3,550 named ships.
Published by: Stanley Gibbons Publications Ltd., 399 Strand, London, WC2R 0LX, United Kingdom. TEL 44-207-8368444, FAX 44-207-8367342, kfinney@stanleygibbons.co.uk, http://www.stanleygibbons.com.

769.56 CAN ISSN 1482-1230
HE6185 C22 S62
COLLECTION CANADA. Text in Multiple languages. 1995. a.
Formerly (until 1995): Canada. The Collection of .. Stamps (1482-1222)
Published by: Canada Post Corporation, 4567 Dixie Rd, Mississauga, ON L4W 1S2, Canada. http://www.canadapost.ca/.

769.56 990 AUS ISSN 0727-4211
COLLECTION OF AUSTRALIAN STAMPS. Text in English. 1981. a. AUD 99.95 (effective 2008). illus. back issues avail. **Document type:** *Catalog, Consumer.* **Description:** Features all the gummed stamp issues and miniature sheets from 2008. Containing $94.95 worth of stamps, this will make a wonderful gift for collecting enthusiasts.
Published by: Australia Post, Philatelic Group, GPO Box 1777, Melbourne, VIC 3001, Australia. TEL 800-000-242, FAX 61-3-92047777, mailorder@auspost.com.au, http://www.auspost.com.au/stamps.

769.56 USA ISSN 0010-0838
HE6187
➤ **COLLECTORS CLUB PHILATELIST.** Text in English. 1922. bi-m. USD 42 (effective 2005). adv. bk.rev. abstr.; illus. index, cum.index. **Document type:** *Journal, Academic/Scholarly.* **Description:** Contains scholarly articles by members, as well as details of regular meetings and discussions of business matters.
Indexed: SJI.
Published by: Collectors Club, Inc., 22 E 35th St, New York, NY 10016. TEL 212-683-0559, FAX 212-481-1269, collectorsclub@nac.net, http://www.collectorsclub.org. Ed. Joseph E Foley. R&P Thomas Mazza. Adv. contact Richard Pounder. page USD 300; 7 x 10. Circ: 1,500.

769.56 USA
COLLECTOR'S MARKETPLACE; buy, trade, sell. Text in English. 1981. q. USD 8.95 (effective 1999). adv. bk.rev. **Document type:** *Magazine, Consumer.*
Formerly (until 1986): Stamp Exchange
Address: PO Box 25, Stewartsville, NJ 08886. TEL 908-479-4614, FAX 908-479-6158. Ed. Dorothy J Graf.

769.56 ITA ISSN 1123-5985
HE6187
IL COLLEZIONISTA. FRANCOBOLLI. Text in Italian. 1984. m. adv. bk.rev. illus. index. **Document type:** *Magazine, Consumer.*
Formed by the merger of (1951-1984): Collezionista - Italia Filatelica (0010-1265); Which was formed by the merger of (1945-1951): Il Collezionista (1123-5969); Which was formerly (until 1950): La Settimana del Collezionista (1123-5950); (until 1949): La Settimana Filatelica (1123-5942); (1945-1951): Italia Filatelica (1125-8128); (1966-1984): Francobolli (1125-8101); Which was formerly (until 1974): Rivista dei Francobolli (1125-8152); (until 1970): Francobolli (0532-5803)
Published by: (Societa Culturale Opere Tipografiche), Giulio Bolaffi Editore SpA, Via Cavour 17-F, Turin, TO 10123, Italy. TEL 39-011-5625556, FAX 39-011-5620456, http://www.bolaffi.it. Circ: 20,300.

769.56 USA
COLUMBIAN (COLUMBUS). Text in English. 1925. m. USD 10 to members. adv. bk.rev. **Document type:** *Newsletter.* **Description:** News, announcements, and articles of interest to the activities and members of the club, with lists of auction items.
Published by: Columbus Philatelic Club, Inc., PO Box 20582, Columbus, OH 43220-0582. FAX 614-457-5205. Ed. Gary Saum. Pub. Walton Beauvals. Circ: 145 (paid).

769.56 USA
COMMONWEALTH PHILATELY. Text in English. 1980. bi-m. USD 7. adv.
Indexed: SJI.
Published by: Commonwealth International Philatelic Society, c/o Bill Scheuermann, Box 195, Minetto, NY 13115. TEL 315-343-5372. Ed. Ryan G Lorenz. Circ: 125.

769.55 AUS
COMPACT AUSTRALIAN STAMP CATALOGUE. Text in English. 1970. irreg., latest 2005, 2006th ed. AUD 14.50 per issue (effective 2009); includes thematic (topical) index cross-referenced to stamps by catalogue number. illus.; mkt. 320 p./no. 1 cols./p.; back issues avail. **Document type:** *Catalog, Consumer.* **Description:** Provides simplified catalog of Australian commonwealth and Australian antarctic territory stamps issued from 1913 to the present.
Former titles (until 1997): Pocket Australian Stamp Catalogue (1034-6449); (until 1989): Australian Stamp Handbook (1033-0968); (until 1988): Pocket Australian Stamp Catalogue (0155-6215)
Published by: Seven Seas Stamps Pty. Ltd., 5/7 Clearview Pl, PO Box 321, Brookvale, NSW 2100, Australia. TEL 61-2-99053255, FAX 61-2-99057922, stamps@sevenseas.com.au, http://www.sevenseas.com.au.

769.56 USA
THE COMPULATELIST. Text in English. q. 20 p./no.; **Document type:** *Newsletter.* **Description:** Contains reviews and descriptions of computer-based resources for the stamp collector.
Published by: Philatelic Computing Study Group, c/o Robert de Violini, P.O. Box 5025, Oxnard, CA 93031-5025. http://www.pcsg.org/pcsg.htm.

769.56 ITA ISSN 0393-1307
CRONACA FILATELICA; mensile di filatelia, storia postale, annulli e interi. Text in Italian. 1970. m. (11/yr.). EUR 42 (effective 2008). bk.rev. **Document type:** *Magazine, Consumer.*
Published by: Gruppo Editoriale Olimpia SpA, Via E Fermi 24, Loc Osmannoro, Sesto Fiorentino, FI 50129, Italy. TEL 39-055-30321, FAX 39-055-3032280, info@edolimpia.it, http://www.edolimpia.it. Circ: 22,500.

769.56 GBR ISSN 0268-4349
HE6931
CROSS POST. Text in English. 1985. GBP 15 domestic to members; GBP 20 foreign to members (effective 2010). **Document type:** *Magazine, Consumer.* **Description:** Contains features on all aspects of postal history.
—BLDSC (3488.875000).
Published by: The Friends of the British Postal Museum & Archive, Freeling House, Phoenix Place, London, WC1X 0DL, United Kingdom. TEL 44-20-72392570, FAX 44-20-72392576, info@postalheritage.org.uk, http://postalheritage.org.uk/support/friends.

769.56 GBR
CZECHOSLOVAK PHILATELIC SOCIETY OF GREAT BRITAIN. MONOGRAPH. Text in English. 19??. irreg., latest vol.18, 2005. price varies. back issues avail. **Document type:** *Monographic series, Academic/Scholarly.* **Description:** Covers topics of interest regarding stamps from the Czech and Slovak republics.
Published by: Czechoslovak Philatelic Society of Great Britain, c/o Rex Dixon, 39 Braybank, Bray, Maidenhead, SL6 2BH, United Kingdom. TEL 44-1628-628628, http://www.cpsgb.org.uk. Ed. Colin W Spong. Pub. Richard Beith. R&P Rex Dixon.

769.56 USA ISSN 0526-5843
THE CZECHOSLOVAK SPECIALIST. Text in English. 1939. bi-m. free to members (effective 2010). bk.rev. charts; illus. cum.index: 1939-1994. 44 p./no.; back issues avail. **Document type:** *Journal, Academic/Scholarly.* **Description:** Focuses on philatelic issues, particularly on Czech and Slovakian stamps. Also contains sales circuit updates and opinion.
Indexed: SJI.
Published by: Society for Czechoslovak Philately, Inc., c/o Phil Rhoade, 905 E Oakside St, S Bend, IN 46614.

769.56 GBR ISSN 0142-9795
HE6185.C952
CZECHOSLOVAKIA & POLAND STAMP CATALOGUE. Text in English. 1980. irreg., latest 2002, 6th ed. GBP 24.95 per issue (effective 2010). **Document type:** *Catalog, Consumer.* **Description:** Covers stamps of Czechoslovakia, East Silesia, Bohemia and Moravia, The Czech Republic, Slovakia, Poland, Poli sh Military Post and Polish Post Offices Abroad.
Supersedes in part (in 1980): Stanley Gibbons Foreign Stamp Catalogue. Europe (0305-8085)
Published by: Stanley Gibbons Publications Ltd., 399 Strand, London, WC2R 0LX, United Kingdom. TEL 44-207-8368444, FAX 44-207-8367342, kfinney@stanleygibbons.co.uk.

769.56 GBR ISSN 0142-3525
CZECHOUT. Text in English. 1975. q. GBP 14 domestic membership; GBP 17 foreign membership (effective 2009). bk.rev. **Document type:** *Journal, Consumer.* **Description:** Disseminates and exchanges information on the philately of the Czech Republic and Slovakia.
Formerly (until 1978): Czechoslovak Philatelic Society of Great Britain. Bulletin (0142-2944)
Published by: Czechoslovak Philatelic Society of Great Britain, c/o Colin W. Spong, Ed, 70 Westlake Gardens, Worthing, W Sussex BN13 1LF, United Kingdom. TEL 44-1903-267803. Pub. Rex Dixon. R&P Colin Spong. Circ: 300. **Orders to:** Rex Dixon, Honorary Secretary, 39 Braybank, Bray, Maidenhead, Berks SL6 2BH, United Kingdom.

769.56 DEU ISSN 1438-2830
D B Z - S E. (Deutsche Briefmarken Zeitung - Sammler Express) Text in German. 1992. fortn. EUR 85.80 (effective 2011). adv. index. back issues avail. **Document type:** *Magazine, Consumer.*
Formed by the merger of (1947-1992): S E - Sammler Express (1438-2822); Which was formerly (until 1990): Sammler Express (0036-3820); (1925-1992): D B Z - Deutsche Briefmarken Zeitung (0931-4393); Which was formerly (until 1985): D B Z - Deutsche Zeitung fuer Briefmarkenkunde (0011-4790)
Published by: Verlag M. und H. Schaper GmbH, Bischofsholer Damm 24, Hannover, 30173, Germany. TEL 49-511-8503050, FAX 49-511-85030510, info@schaper-verlag.de, http://www.schaper-verlag.de. adv.: B&W page EUR 1,360, color page EUR 2,176; trim 189 x 269. Circ: 36,900 (controlled).

769.56 USA ISSN 0882-0236
D O S S U JOURNAL. (Dogs on Stamps Study Unit) Text in English. 1979. q. USD 5 domestic; USD 10 foreign (effective 2001). adv. **Document type:** *Newsletter.* **Description:** For philatelists interested in the collection and study of postal materials depicting dogs.
Published by: American Topical Association, Dogs on Stamps Study Unit, 202A Newport Rd, Monroe TWP, NJ 08831-3920. TEL 609-655-7411. Ed. Morris Raskin. Circ: 275.

769.56 USA
DAKOTA COLLECTOR. Text in English. 1983. q. membership. adv. bk.rev. back issues avail. **Description:** Publishes articles on various cancels and postal history of North and South Dakota.
Published by: Dakota Postal History Society, c/o Gary Anderson, PO Box 600039, St. Paul, MN 55106. adv.: B&W page USD 20; trim 11 x 8.5. Circ: 70 (paid).

769.36 DNK ISSN 0903-2444
DANSK FILATELISTISK TIDSSKRIFT. Text in Danish. 1934. 7/yr. DKK 300 (effective 2008). adv. bk.rev. illus. **Document type:** *Magazine, Consumer.*
Formerly (until 1985): Dansk Filatelist Tidsskrift (0109-3738); Incorporates (1946-1986): Den Unge Frimaerkesamlers Blad (0902-5790)
Published by: Danmarks Filatelist Forbund/Danish Philatelic Federation, Jagtvej 74, 1, Copenhagen N, 2200, Denmark. TEL 45-32-501886, FAX 45-32-501887, danfil@danfil.dk. Ed. Ib Krarup Rasmussen TEL 45-45-813478.

769.56 USA
DAYTON STAMP CLUB. NEWSLETTER. Text in English. 1982 (vol.8). m. **Document type:** *Newsletter.*
Published by: Dayton Stamp Club, Inc., PO Box 1574, Dayton, OH 45401. Ed. Martin Richardson.

737 769 DEU ISSN 0930-858X
DEUTSCHE BRIEFMARKEN - REVUE. Text in German. 1949. m. EUR 31 domestic; EUR 42 foreign; EUR 2.80 newsstand/cover (effective 2006). adv. bk.rev. illus. back issues avail. **Document type:** *Magazine, Consumer.*
Published by: (Fachblatt fuer Philatelie), P S B N - Verlagsgesellschaft mbH, Eisenhuettenstr 4, Ratingen, 40882, Germany. TEL 49-2102-2046830, FAX 49-2102-895825. Ed. Dieter Stein. R&P, Adv. contact Hannelore Thiele. B&W page EUR 750, color page EUR 1,400; trim 188 x 263. Circ: 21,000 (paid and controlled).

769.56 FRA ISSN 0992-8588
DILIGENCE D'ALSACE. Text in French. 1969. s-a. EUR 6.90 newsstand/cover (effective 2008). back issues avail. **Document type:** *Journal.*
Published by: Amis de l'Histoire des PTT d'Alsace, 5 Rue des Clarisses, Strasbourg, 67000, France. TEL 33-3-88529899, FAX 33-3-88521811, contact@shpta.com.

769.56 USA
THE DISPATCHER (ROCHESTER, 1950). Text in English. 1950. bi-m. USD 10 domestic; USD 12 in Canada & Mexico; USD 15 elsewhere (effective 2009). adv. bk.rev. illus. **Document type:** *Newsletter, Trade.* **Description:** News and announcements pertaining to railroad-stamp collecting, with lists of recent and special issues.
Formerly: American Topical Association. Casey Jones Railroad Unit. Newsletter
Related titles: Microfilm ed.: (from LIB).
Published by: American Topical Association, Casey Jones Railroad Unit, PO Box 18615, Rochester, NY 14618-8615. normaned@rochester.rr.com. Ed. Norman E Wright. Circ: 500.

769.56 FRA ISSN 1141-1341
DOCUMENTS PHILATELIQUES. Text in French. 1959. q. EUR 25 (effective 2008). bk.rev. illus. **Document type:** *Bulletin.*
Published by: Academie de Philatelie de Paris, 8 rue des Fosses, 7 avenue de la Tranquilite, Pont-a-Mousson, 54700, France. Ed. Brigitte Abensur. Circ: 500.

769.56 NLD ISSN 0167-9376
DRUK DOENDE. Text in Dutch. 1981. 3/yr. EUR 20 membership; EUR 2.50 newsstand/cover (effective 2009). adv. bk.rev. bibl.; illus. back issues avail. **Document type:** *Bulletin, Consumer.* **Description:** Covers stamp collecting, focusing on printing and paper.
Published by: Filatelistische Motiefgroep "Papier & Druk" Nederland, Florastr 34 A, Blokker, 1695 BK, Netherlands. Ed., Pub., Adv. contact A J Cornet. Circ: 135 (paid).

769.56 USA
E F O COLLECTOR. (Errors, Freaks & Oddities) Text in English. 1978. 6/yr. USD 16; USD 30 foreign (effective 1999). adv. bk.rev. back issues avail. **Document type:** *Newsletter, Trade.*
Published by: E F O Collectors Club, 138 Lake lamont Dr E, Kingsland, GA 31548-8921. TEL 912-729-1579, 800-236-2128, FAX 912-729-1585, cwouscg@aol.com. Ed. Cwo Jim McDevitt. Circ: 350.

769.56 305.89 USA
E S P E R NEWSLETTER. Text in English. bi-m. USD 15 to members. illus. **Document type:** *Newsletter.* **Description:** Promotes the commemoration of notable African Americans on US postage stamps and the collection of such stamps, to raise public awareness of the achievements of these individuals.
Related titles: Online - full text ed.
Published by: Ebony Society of Philatelic Events and Reflections, c/o A A W W S P, Box 1864, Midland, MI 48641-1864. FAX 517-839-5942. Ed., Pub. Sanford L Byrd.

769.56 942 GBR ISSN 1470-2037
EASTERN ANGLE. Text in English. 1966. q. GBP 10 (effective 2010). adv. bk.rev. 1 cols./p.; back issues avail. **Document type:** *Bulletin, Academic/Scholarly.* **Description:** Official bulletin of the study circle. Covers the complete postal history of the counties of Cambridgeshire, Essex, Huntingdonshire, Lincolnshire, Norfolk, Suffolk, and Hertfordshire.
Formerly (until 1999): East Anglia Postal History Study Circle. Bulletin
Published by: East Anglia Postal History Study Circle, c/o Barry R. Reynolds, Ed., 74 Edgecomb Rd, Stowmarket, IP14 2DW, United Kingdom. TEL 44-1449-613319, barry.reynolds@tiscali.co.uk, http://www.freewebs.com/eaphsc. Ed., Pub., R&P Mr. Barry R Reynolds. Adv. contact J U Redgewell TEL 44-1787-460364. Circ: 100.

769.56 FRA ISSN 1269-5017
L'ECHO DE LA TIMBROLOGIE; la tribune des philatelistes. Text in French. 1887. m. adv. bk.rev. bibl.; illus.; mkt. index. **Document type:** *Magazine, Consumer.* **Description:** Discusses issues and themes related or reflected in the world of stamp collecting.
Published by: Echo de la Timbrologie, 37 rue des Jacobins, Amiens, Cedex 1 80036, France. TEL 33-3-22717180, FAX 33-3-22717189. Ed., Adv. contact Benoit Gervais.

769.56 737 ESP ISSN 2173-1055
EL ECO FILATELICO Y NUMISMATICO. Text in Spanish. 1945. m. adv. bk.rev. back issues avail. **Document type:** *Magazine, Trade.*
Formerly (until 1969): El Eco Filatelico (2173-1233)
Related titles: Online - full text ed.
Published by: Jaia Publicaciones, Paseo Sarasate, 36 5o, Pamplona, Navarra 31001, Spain. TEL 34-948-220073.

769.56 CAN ISSN 0046-1318
EDMONTON STAMP CLUB BULLETIN. Text in English. 1965. m. CAD 15. adv. bk.rev. **Document type:** *Newsletter.*
Published by: Edmonton Stamp Club, P O Box 399, Edmonton, AB T5J 2J6, Canada. TEL 780-492-0473, FAX 780-492-7196. Ed., R&P Keith R Spencer TEL 780-437-1787. Adv. contact Alan Meech. Circ: 300.

769.56 USA
EESTI FILATELIST/ESTONIAN PHILATELIST. Text in English, Estonian, German, Swedish. 1955. a. back issues avail. **Document type:** *Magazine, Consumer.*

Published by: Estonian Philatelic Society, c/o Eo Vaher, 39 Clafford Ln, Melville, NY 11747. esto4@aol.com, http://www.eestipost.com. Circ: 700.

769.56 USA
EMERT'S STAMP QUARTERLY. Text in English. q. USD 2.
Address: 1135 Foxridge Dr., Earlysville, VA 22936.

769.56 USA
EMPIRE STATE POSTAL HISTORY SOCIETY. BULLETIN. Text in English. 1969. 4/yr. membership. adv. **Document type:** *Bulletin, Consumer.*
Published by: Empire State Postal History Society, c/o George McGowen, PO Box 482, East Schodack, NY 12063-0482. Ed. Glenn Estus. Circ: 200.

769.56 DEU
ERINNOPHILIE INTERNATIONAL. Text in German. 1965. irreg. back issues avail. **Document type:** *Magazine, Consumer.*
Published by: Erinnophilie International im Bund Deutscher Philatelisten e.V., c/o Alfred Kruse, Graubuendener Str 45, Bremen, 28325, Germany. TEL 49-421-424405, FAX 49-421-424405, krusebremen@t-online.de.

769.56 USA
ESTONIAN PHILATELIC SOCIETY IN U.S.A. Text in English. 1971. a. looseleaf. USD 10 to members (effective 2002). bk.rev. back issues avail. **Document type:** *Bulletin.*
Formerly: N Y Eesti Pilatelistide Seltsi Bulletaan
Address: 29 Clifford Ave, Pelham, NY 10803. TEL 831-335-0734. Ed. Rudolf Hamar. Circ: 200.

789.56 737 LUX
EUROPHIL NEWS. Text in Dutch, English, French, German. 1986. m. EUR 15 (effective 2005). **Document type:** *Newsletter, Consumer.*
Published by: Europhil, 19 rue du Golf, Senningerberg, 1638, Luxembourg. FAX 352-340469. Pub. Oege Weijs. Circ: 1,000 (paid).

769.56 USA
F A P JOURNAL. (Fine Arts Philatelists) Text in English. 1955. q. looseleaf. USD 20 in United States; USD 25 elsewhere (effective 2001). bibl.; illus. back issues avail.
Published by: Fine Arts Philatelists, c/o H. Ruth Richards, 10393 Derby Drive, Laurel, MD 20723. Circ: 600.

769.56 BEL ISSN 1437-4382
F G G B RUNDBRIEFE. Text in German. 1970. q. bk.rev. **Document type:** *Magazine, Consumer.*
Published by: Forschungsgemeinschaft Grossbritannien, Lichtenbuscher Str 340 C, Raeren-Lichtenbusch, 4731, Belgium. fggb@fggb.de, http://www.fggb.de. Circ: 250.

769.56 DEU
F I A S - REPORT; Mitteilungsblatt der Forschungsgemeinschaft Internationale Antwortscheine, Bundesarbeitsgemeinschaft im Bund Deutscher Philatelisten. Text in German. 1972. s-a. adv. bk.rev. back issues avail. **Document type:** *Bulletin, Consumer.*
Published by: Forschungsgemeinschaft Internationale Antwortscheine, c/o Juergen Debus, Lahnstr 82, Bremen, 28199, Germany. Circ: 100.

769.56 USA
EL FARO. Text in English. 1975. q. USD 22 (effective 2000). adv. **Document type:** *Newsletter.* **Description:** Dedicated to the study of the stamps and postal history of El Salvador.
Formerly (until 1978): A C E S
Media: Duplicated (not offset).
Indexed: SJI.
Published by: Associated Collectors of El Salvador, c/o Jeff Brasor, Ed., P O Box 173, Coconut Creek, FL 33097. Pub. Bob Fisher. Circ: 100 (controlled).

769.56 DEU
FEUERMELDER RUNDBRIEF. Text in German. 1975. s-a. EUR 4 (effective 2006). **Document type:** *Newsletter.*
Published by: Motiv-Arbeitsgemeinschaft Feuerwehr e.V., c/o Stefan Wernz, Kapellenstr 15, Mainz, 55124, Germany. Circ: 125.

769.56 FRA ISSN 0755-8945
LES FEUILLES MARCOPHILES. Text in French. 1927. q. 40 p./no.
Published by: Union Marcophile et de la Societe des Collectionneurs d'Estampilles et d'Obliterations Reunies, c/o M. Jean-Louis Narjoux, 21 rue Alphonse Daudet, Paris, 75014, France.

769.56 BGR ISSN 0204-8752
FILATELEN PREGLED. Text in Bulgarian; Summaries in French, German, Russian. 1959. m. USD 58 foreign (effective 2002).
Published by: Komitet za Informatsiiat i Suobshteniiata/Committee for Telecommunications, Foreign Trade Co "Hemus", 1-B Raiko Daskalov ul, Sofia, 1000, Bulgaria. TEL 359-2-871686, FAX 395-2-9803319. Ed. I Kostov. Circ: 6,016. **Dist. by:** Sofia Books, ul Silivria 16, Sofia 1404, Bulgaria. TEL 359-2-9586257, info@sofiabooks-bg.com, http://www.sofiabooks-bg.com.
Co-sponsor: Suiuz na Bulgarski Filatelisti.

769.56 ROM ISSN 1220-6679
FILATELIA. Text in Romanian; Summaries in English, French, German, Russian. 1958. m. USD 46. adv. bk.rev. bibl.; illus.
Published by: Federatia Filatelica Romana/Romanian Philatelic Federation, Str. Boteanu 6, Bucharest, Romania. Ed. Aurelian Darnu. Circ: 12,000.

769.56 CUB ISSN 0138-631X
FILATELIA CUBANA. Text in Spanish; Summaries in English, French. 3/yr. USD 10 in the Americas; USD 12 in Europe. illus. **Description:** Contains articles on stamp history; critical studies of Cuban stamps; and information on the activities carried out by the Federation and stamp clubs in Cuba and abroad; for collectors of stamps and first-day issues.
Published by: (Federacion Filatelica Cubano), Ediciones Cubanas, Obispo 527, Havana, Cuba.

769.56 HUN ISSN 0133-168X
HE6187
FILATELIAI SZEMLE. Text in Hungarian. m. USD 22.50.
Address: PF 4, Budapest, 1387, Hungary. Ed. Bela Milassin. **Subscr. to:** Kultura, PF 149, Budapest 1389, Hungary.

769.56 DOM
EL FILATELICO. Text in Spanish. 1977. bi-m. DOP 200 domestic; USD 20 foreign (effective 2000). adv. bk.rev. back issues avail. **Document type:** *Bulletin.*
Published by: (Sociedad Filatelica Dominicana), Jose M. Frometa C. por A., Apartado 1930, Santo Domingo, Dominican Republic. TEL 809-565-2990. Ed. Danilo A Mueses. R&P, Adv. contact Gustavo More. Circ: 425.

769.56 CZE ISSN 0015-0959
HE6187
FILATELIE. Text in Czech, Slovak; Summaries in English, German. 1951. m. CZK 398 domestic; EUR 39 in Europe; USD 80 elsewhere (effective 2009). adv. bk.rev. 52 p./no.; **Document type:** *Journal.*
Indexed: RASB.
Published by: Dum Filatelie, Klimentska 6, Prague 1, 110 00, Czech Republic. TEL 420-2-24810210, FAX 420-2-24810900, stamps@stamps.cz, http://www.stamps.cz. Ed., Pub. Frantisek Benes. adv.: page CZK 10,000. Circ: 5,500.

769.56 SWE ISSN 1100-0198
HE6187
FILATELISTEN; svensk filatelistisk tidskrift. Key Title: Filatelisten (Skara). Text in Swedish. 1900. 8/yr. SEK 200 (effective 2011). adv. bk.rev. index. **Document type:** *Magazine, Consumer.* **Description:** Contains articles and information for philatelists, stamp collectors and dealers in the Scandinavian countries.
Formerly (until 1988): Svensk Filatelistisk Tidskrift (0039-6532); Incorporates (1981-1983): Frimaerksledaren (0281-322X)
Published by: Sveriges Filatelist Foerbund, P O Box 91, Skillingaryd, 56822, Sweden. info@sff.nu, http://www.sff.nu. Ed. Ulf Nilsson. Circ: 9,700 (paid and controlled).

769.56 FIN ISSN 0786-9363
FILATELISTI; stamp journal. Text in Finnish, Swedish. 1951. 10/yr. EUR 34 in Nordic countries; EUR 47 elsewhere (effective 2005). adv. bk.rev. illus. cum.index. **Document type:** *Magazine, Consumer.*
Formerly (until 1989): Philatelia Fennica (0355-502X)
Published by: Oy Finlandia 88 AB (Subsidiary of: Philatelic Federation of Finland), Mannerheiminaukio 1 E, Helsinki, 00101, Finland. TEL 358-9-58400190, FAX 358-9-58400192, sfff@sci.fi, http://www.sci.fi/~sfff/. Eds. Lauri Poropudas, Risto-Matti Kauhanen. Adv. contact Tarja Pohjolainen. Circ: 6,000.

769.56 RUS ISSN 0869-4478
HE6187
FILATELIYA. Text in Russian. 1966. m. USD 87 foreign (effective 2003). illus. index.
Formerly: Filateliya S.S.S.R. (0015-0983)
—East View.
Published by: (Rossiiskoe Obshchestvo Filatelistov/Russian Philatelic Society), Torgovyi Tsentr "Marka"/"Marka" Publishing and Trading Centre, Khlebnyi per 8, Moscow, 121069, Russian Federation. Ed. J G Bekhterev. Circ: 70,000. **Dist. by:** M K - Periodica, ul Gilyarovskogo 39, Moscow 129110, Russian Federation. TEL 7-095-2845008, FAX 7-095-2813798, info@periodicals.ru, http://www.mkniga.ru; East View Information Services, 10601 Wayzata Blvd, Minneapolis, MN 55305. TEL 952-252-1201, 800-477-1005, FAX 952-252-1202, info@eastview.com, http://www.eastview.com.

769.56 NLD ISSN 2211-5048
FILITALIA. Variant title: Verslag Bijeenkomst Filitalia. Text in Dutch. 1998. bi-m. EUR 15 domestic; EUR 20 foreign (effective 2011). **Document type:** *Magazine, Consumer.*
Address: c/o Leo van den Brun, Sec., Van Kinsbergenstraat 33, The Hague, 2518 GV, Netherlands. TEL 31-6-51140411, secretaris@filitalia.nl. Ed. Vincent Prange TEL 31-20-6269793.

769.56 USA ISSN 0428-4836
HE6230
FIRST DAYS. Text in English. 1956. 8/yr. USD 25 domestic; USD 21 foreign (effective 2005). adv. bk.rev. illus. index. **Document type:** *Magazine, Consumer.*
Indexed: SJI.
Published by: American First Day Cover Society, 65960, Tucson, AZ 85728-5960. TEL 520-321-0880, FAX 520-321-0879. Ed. Peter Martin. adv.: B&W page USD 148; trim 8 x 4.75. Circ: 2,900 (paid).

769.56 USA ISSN 1547-2299
FIRST ISSUES. Text in English. 1990. q. looseleaf. USD 6; USD 10 foreign (effective 1999). bk.rev. charts; illus.; mkt.; stat.; tr.lit. back issues avail. **Document type:** *Newsletter.* **Description:** Covers the collection of the first post issues of the nations of the world.
Published by: First Issues Collections Club, 13 Idlewood Place, River Ridge, LA 70123. Ed., Pub., R&P Robert K Sylvester. Circ: 100 (paid).

769.56 DEU
FLUGPOST KURIER. Text in German. 1952. a. looseleaf. free (effective 2010). adv. bk.rev. illus. **Document type:** *Magazine, Consumer.*
Formerly: Ballon Kurier (0005-4364)
Published by: Freunde der Kinderdorf Flugpost, Sonnhalde 6, Stockach, 78333, Germany. TEL 49-7771-8003230, FAX 49-7771-929707, info@kinderdorf-flugpost.de, http://www.kinderdorf-flugpost.de. Ed. Hermann Johannes Scheer.

769.56 GBR ISSN 0951-7561
FORCES POSTAL HISTORY SOCIETY. NEWSLETTER. Text in English. 1952. q. free to members (effective 2009). adv. bk.rev. back issues avail. **Document type:** *Newsletter, Trade.* **Description:** Presents items on the postal history of naval, military and air forces of all countries and periods.
Published by: Forces Postal History Society, c/o Martin Hopkinson, Membership Secretary, Trewinney Barton, Mevagissey, St Austell, Cornwall PL26 6TD, United Kingdom. TEL 44-1726-843887, martinhopkinson@hotmail.co.uk, http://www.postalcensorship.com/fphs/index.html. Ed. Colin Tabeart TEL 44-1489-572974.

789.56 USA ISSN 1076-2612
FORERUNNERS. Text in English. 1987. 3/yr. free to members (effective 2010). bk.rev. back issues avail. **Document type:** *Journal, Trade.* **Description:** Publishes scholarly articles, reviews, research efforts relating to stamps issued by past and present countries of greater southern Africa, and questions and answers.
Published by: Philatelic Society for Greater Southern Africa, c/o Bill Brooks, 2854 W Calle Vista Dr, Rialto, CA 92377. billpatti99@sbcglobal.net.

769.56 GBR ISSN 0269-5006
FRANCE & COLONIES PHILATELIC SOCIETY OF GREAT BRITAIN. JOURNAL. Text in English. 1951. q. free to members (effective 2009). adv. bk.rev. back issues avail. **Document type:** *Journal, Trade.* **Description:** Contains articles on all aspects of philately, postal history and related topics concerning France and her former Colonies.
Former titles: France and Colonies Philatelic Society. Bulletin; France and Colonies Philatelic Society. Newsletter; France and Colonies Philatelic Society. Journal
Published by: France & Colonies Philatelic Society, c/o P R A Kelly, Secretary, Malmsy House, Church Rd, Leigh Woods, Bristol, BS8 3PG, United Kingdom. secretary@fcps.org.uk. Ed. M S Tyler.

769.56 GBR ISSN 0142-9809
FRANCE STAMP CATALOGUE. Text in English. 1979. irreg., latest 2010, 7th ed. GBP 44.95 per issue (effective 2010). **Document type:** *Catalog, Consumer.* **Description:** Contains detailed and up to date listings of all current stamp issuing countries (France, French Polynesia, Mayotte, New Caledonia, St. Pierre and Miquelon, Wallis and Futuna, Monaco, Spanish Andorra and French Andorra) as well as many other areas of interest including French Colonies Vichy issues and all French Colonies.
Supersedes in part (in 1979): Stanley Gibbons Foreign Stamp Catalogue. Europe (0305-8085)
Published by: Stanley Gibbons Publications Ltd., 399 Strand, London, WC2R 0LX, United Kingdom. TEL 44-207-8368444, FAX 44-207-8367342, kfinney@stanleygibbons.co.uk.

769.56 DNK ISSN 0108-4089
FRIMAERKERNES VERDEN. Text in Danish. 1982. 6/yr. DKK 95 (effective 2009). adv. bk.rev. illus. **Document type:** *Magazine, Consumer.*
Published by: Nordfrim A/S, Kvindevadet 42, Otterup, 5450, Denmark. TEL 45-64-821256, FAX 45-64-821056, mail@nordfrim.dk, http://www.nordfrim.dk.

769.56 DNK ISSN 0016-1438
FRIMAERKESAMLEREN; the Danish stamp collector. Text in Danish. 1942. 6/yr. DKK 250 (effective 2009). adv. bk.rev. **Document type:** *Magazine, Consumer.*
Published by: Frederiksberg Frimaerke Forening, c/o Flemming Petersen, Poppel Alle 35, Hareskov, Vaerloese, 3500, Denmark. TEL 45-44-443412, fp@fpstamps.dk, http://www.3fff.dk. Ed. Johnny Speich TEL 45-33-310848.

769.56 NOR ISSN 0333-080X
FRIMERKE FORUM. Text in Norwegian. 1970. q. **Document type:** *Magazine, Consumer.*
Published by: Frimerke-Ringen Posthorn, PO Box 5165, Sentrum, Oslo, 0105, Norway.

769.56 737 NOR ISSN 0801-1869
FRIMERKER OG MYNTER. Text in Norwegian. 1984. 3/yr. NOK 50.
Published by: Alva Trading A-S, Postboks 889, Sentrum, Oslo, 0104, Norway.

769.56 USA ISSN 0732-5517
HE6187
FROM THE DRAGON'S DEN. Text in English. 1969. 4/yr. membership. adv. bk.rev. charts; illus.; stat. back issues avail.
Indexed: SJI.
Published by: Ryukyu Philatelic Specialist Society, PO Box 172, Great Falls, VA 22066. Ed. Russ W Carter. Circ: 350.

769.56 GBR ISSN 0430-8913
G B JOURNAL. (Great Britain) Abbreviated title: G B J. Text in English. 1955. bi-m. GBP 3.50 per issue. adv. bk.rev. illus. index. **Document type:** *Journal, Academic/Scholarly.*
Published by: Great Britain Philatelic Society, c/o Debbie Harman, Greylands, Melton, Woodbridge, Suffolk IP12 1QE, United Kingdom. gbpsmemsec@aol.com, gbps@mjpublications.com, http://www.gbps.org.uk/index.htm. Circ: 900.

769.56 USA
G I P S. Text in English. bi-m. membership.
Published by: Government Imprinted Penalty Stationery Society, 10926 Annette Ave, Tampa, FL 33612.

769.56 USA ISSN 0016-8823
HE6187
GERMAN POSTAL SPECIALIST. Text in English. 1950. m. free to members (effective 2010). bk.rev. charts; illus.; maps. index, cum.index: vols.1-30. 48 p./no. 1 cols./p.; back issues avail. **Document type:** *Magazine, Consumer.* **Description:** Covers philately and postal history.
Indexed: SJI.
Published by: Germany Philatelic Society, Inc., PO Box 779, Arnold, MD 21012-4779. info@germanyphilatelicsocietyusa.org, http://www.germanyphilatelicsocietyusa.org.

769.56 GBR ISSN 0142-9817
HE6185.G3
GERMANY STAMP CATALOGUE. Text in English. 1979. irreg., latest 2007, 8th ed. GBP 29.95 per issue (effective 2010). **Document type:** *Catalog, Consumer.* **Description:** Features stamps issued during the German occupation of the Channel Islands, as well as revisions in the Germany design index.
Supersedes in part (in 1979): Stanley Gibbons Foreign Stamp catalogue. Europe (0305-8085)
Published by: Stanley Gibbons Publications Ltd., 399 Strand, London, WC2R 0LX, United Kingdom. TEL 44-207-8368444, FAX 44-207-8367342, kfinney@stanleygibbons.co.uk.

769.56 GBR ISSN 0954-8084
GIBBONS STAMP MONTHLY. Text in English. 1890. m. GBP 42 domestic; GBP 67.20 foreign (effective 2011). adv. bk.rev. illus.; mkt. index. reprints avail. **Document type:** *Magazine, Consumer.*
Formerly (until 1977): Stamp Monthly (0016-9676)
Related titles: Online - full text ed.: GBP 9.95 (effective 2005); Supplement(s): Philatelic Discoveries.
Indexed: SJI.
—CCC.
Published by: Stanley Gibbons Publications Ltd., 5 Parkside, Christchurch Rd, Ringwood, Hampshire BH24 3SH, United Kingdom. TEL 44-1425-472363, FAX 44-1425-470247, info@stanleygibbons.co.uk. Ed., R&P Hugh Jefferies. Adv. contact Lucy Pearce. Circ: 25,000 (paid). **Dist. by:** Comag, Tavistock Rd, W Drayton, Middlesex UB7 7QE, United Kingdom. TEL 44-1895-444055, FAX 44-1895-433602.

769.56 USA ISSN 1060-0361
GLOBAL STAMP NEWS. Text in English. 1990. m. USD 10.95 (effective 2009). adv. bk.rev. illus. reprints avail. **Document type:** *Magazine, Consumer.* **Description:** Covers worldwide stamp markets and collecting interests.

P

Published by: Brandewie Inc., 110 N Ohio Ave, Box 97, Sidney, OH 45365. TEL 937-492-3183, FAX 937-492-6514. Ed. Jan Brandewie. Circ: 33,000 (controlled).

769.56 USA
GREAT BRITAIN COLLECTORS CLUB. QUARTERLY NEWSLETTER. Text in English. 1979. q. USD 15; USD 22 foreign (effective 1998). adv. bk.rev. **Document type:** *Newsletter.* **Description:** News, articles, and announcements pertaining to this stamp collection association.
Formerly: Great Britain Correspondence Club. Quarterly Newsletter (0887-6819)
Published by: (Great Britain Collectors Club), Frank J. Koch, Ed. & Pub., PO Box 309, Batavia, OH 45103-0309. TEL 513-634-4264. Circ: 415.

769.56 GBR
GREAT BRITAIN CONCISE STAMP CATALOGUE. Text in English. 1986. a., latest 2009. GBP 27.95 per issue (effective 2010). adv. **Document type:** *Catalog, Consumer.* **Description:** Provides information for the semi-advanced stamp collector.
Published by: Stanley Gibbons Publications Ltd., 399 Strand, London, WC2R 0LX, United Kingdom. TEL 44-207-8368444, FAX 44-207-8367342, kfinney@stanleygibbons.co.uk.

769.56 GBR ISSN 0072-7229
GREAT BRITAIN SPECIALISED STAMP CATALOGUE. Text in English. 1963. irreg., latest vol.2, 2009, 13th ed. GBP 39.95 per issue (effective 2010). adv. index. back issues avail. **Document type:** *Catalog, Consumer.* **Description:** Designed to be a reference work for specialist collectors of popular "Four Kings" period of British Philately, from 1902-1952.
Published by: Stanley Gibbons Publications Ltd., 399 Strand, London, WC2R 0LX, United Kingdom. TEL 44-207-8368444, FAX 44-207-8367342.

769.56 NLD ISSN 2211-0925
GRUNOPOST. Text in Dutch. bi-m. EUR 35 membership (effective 2011). **Document type:** *Magazine, Consumer.*
Published by: Philatelisten Vereniging Groningen, Emmastraat 5, Groningen, 9722 EW, Netherlands. TEL 31-50-5259610, info@philatelist.nl, http://www.philatelist.nl. Eds. C A E Volckmann, J P A Tolsma.

769.56 GTM ISSN 0046-6549
HE6187
GUATEMALA FILATELICA. Text in Spanish. 1932. a. USD 6 to members. adv. bk.rev. charts; illus.; stat.
Published by: Asociacion Filatelica de Guatemala, Apartado Postal 39, Guatemala City, 01901, Guatemala. Ed. Col Romeo J Routhier. Circ: 500.

769.56 USA
HAITI PHILATELY. Text in English. 1975. q. USD 12; USD 15 foreign.
Indexed: SJI.
Published by: Haitian Philatelic Society, c/o Dr Gerald L Boarino, 834 Pierce St, Port Townsend, WA 98363. Circ: 100.

769.56 GBR ISSN 0950-3102
HELLENIC PHILATELIC SOCIETY OF GREAT BRITAIN. BULLETIN. Text in English. s-a. GBP 3 per issue (effective 2001). adv. bk.rev. **Document type:** *Bulletin.*
Supersedes (in 1968): Hellenic Philatelic Society of Great Britain. Newsletter
Indexed: SJI.
Published by: Hellenic Philatelic Society of Great Britain, Flat 20, Merlynn, 5-7 Devonshire Pl, Eastbourne, E Sussex BN21 4AQ, United Kingdom. TEL 44-1323-639160. Ed. C Ruffley. Circ: 170.

789.56 USA
HIGGINS & GAGE WORLD POSTAL STATIONERY CATALOG. Text in English. 1965. irreg. looseleaf. USD 280 per issue (effective 2005). **Document type:** *Catalog.* **Description:** Lists alphabetically by country, governmental postal issues of postal stationery.
Published by: Classic Philatelics, PO Box 5637, Huntington Beach, CA 92615. TEL 714-968-1717, FAX 714-968-6704, patmel@att.net. Ed., R&P Mel Feiner. Circ: 1,500.

769.56 USA
HOLLYWOOD PHILATELIST. Text in English. 1968. m. membership. bk.rev. **Document type:** *Newsletter.*
Published by: Hollywood Stamp Club, 4380 Casper Ct, Hollywood, FL 33021. Ed. Ben Wishnietsky. Circ: 500.

383 769.56 ISR ISSN 0333-6875
HOLY LAND POSTAL HISTORY. Text in English. 1979. q. USD 18 (effective 2001). adv. bk.rev. index. back issues avail. **Document type:** *Bulletin.*
Published by: Society of the Postal History of Eretz-Israel, P O Box 10175, Jerusalem, 91101, Israel. TEL 972-2-6711719. Eds. E Glassman, Z Shimony. Circ: 250.

769.56 USA
EL HONDURENO. Text in English. 1996. q. USD 16 (effective 2001). **Document type:** *Newsletter.* **Description:** Focuses on the study of stamps and postal history of Honduras.
Published by: Honduras Collectors Club, PO Box 173, Coconut Creek, FL 33097. FAX 954-753-5742. Ed., Pub. Jeff Brasor. Circ: 100.

769.56 USA ISSN 2153-8131
HUNTSVILLE PHILATELIC CLUB. NEWSLETTER. Text in English. 1967. q. free to members (effective 2010). back issues avail. **Document type:** *Newsletter, Trade.*
Related titles: Online - full text ed.: ISSN 2153-814X. free (effective 2010).
Published by: Huntsville Philatelic Club, PO Box 4384, Huntsville, AL 35815. hpc-stamps@att.net, http://www.stampclubs.com/huntsville.

769.56 USA ISSN 0019-1051
ICE CAP NEWS. Abbreviated title: I C N. Text in English. 1956. q. USD 22 in US & Canada; USD 30 elsewhere (effective 2011). adv. bk.rev. illus. index, cum.index: vols.1-39 (CD-ROM). 32 p./no. 2 cols./p.; back issues avail. **Document type:** *Magazine, Trade.* **Description:** Articles and columns about the Arctic, Antarctic and related areas and their postal history.
Indexed: A33, GeoRef.
Published by: American Society of Polar Philatelists, c/o Alan Warren, Ed., PO Box 39, Exton, PA 19341. Ed. Alan Warren.

769.56 GBR ISSN 0952-7729
➤ **INDIA POST.** Text in English. 1950. 3/yr. free to members (effective 2009). software rev. charts; illus. cum.index every 3 yrs. 40 p./no. 2 cols./p.; back issues avail. **Document type:** *Journal, Academic/Scholarly.* **Description:** Philatelic study and research of the stamps both postal & revenue, and postal history of the South Asian Subcontinent.
Formerly (until 1967): India Study Circle Bulletin
Indexed: SJI.
Published by: India Study Circle for Philately, c/o Brian Allcock, Secretary, 9 Golspie Croft, Hodge Lea, Milton Keynes, MK12 6JU, United Kingdom. TEL 44-1908-222695. Ed. Peter Leevers.

769.56 USA ISSN 0884-8254
INFORMER. Text in English. 1947. q. USD 17 in US & Canada membership; USD 24 elsewhere membership (effective 2007). adv. bk.rev. **Document type:** *Newsletter.* **Description:** Publishes original articles pertaining to Australasian postal history and stamp issues.
Published by: Society of Australasian Specialists - Oceania, Inc., 7442 Spring Village Dr, No PV 107, Springfield, VA 22150-4446. TEL 703-573-0317, stulev@ix.netcom.com. Ed., Pub., R&P Hugh Wynn TEL 703-573-0317. Adv. contact Joel L Bromberg. Circ: 285 (paid). **Subscr. to:** Stuart Levin, PO Box 24764, San Jose, CA 95154-4764.

769.56 USA ISSN 0892-9793
INTERLEAF. Text in English. 1983. q. USD 10; USD 15 foreign. adv. bk.rev. **Document type:** *Newsletter.* **Description:** Devoted to the study of worldwide booklets and booklet collecting, with emphasis on United States booklets.
Published by: Booklet Collectors Club, 3307 Concord Dr., Cinnaminson, NJ 08077-4015. Ed. Gerhard G Korn. Circ: 300.

INTERNATIONAL ART POST. *see* ART

769.56 DEU ISSN 0074-1701
INTERNATIONAL ASSOCIATION OF PHILATELIC JOURNALISTS. BULLETIN. Variant title: Association Internationale des Journalistes Philateliques. Bulletin. Text in English, French, German. 1962. s-a. free to members (effective 2008).
Published by: International Association of Philatelic Journalists/ Association Internationale des Journalistes Philateliques, c/o Schwaneberger Verlag, Herrn Jochen Stenzke, Ohmstr 1, Unterschleissheim, 85716, Germany. TEL 49-89-3232402, http://www.aijp.org.

INTERNATIONAL FLIER. *see* MACHINERY

769.56 CHE ISSN 0074-7343
INTERNATIONAL PHILATELIC FEDERATION. GENERAL ASSEMBLY. PROCES-VERBAL. Text in English. 1973. a. free to members. **Document type:** *Proceedings.*
Published by: International Philatelic Federation/Federation Internationale de Philatelie, Zollikerstr 128, Zuerich, 8008, Switzerland. FAX 01-3831446. Ed. Ms. M L Heiri. Circ: 180.

769.56 USA
INTERNATIONAL PHILATELIC PRESS CLUB. REPORT TO MEMBERS. Text in English. 1964. m. looseleaf. membership. bk.rev. **Document type:** *Newsletter.*
Published by: International Philatelic Press Club, Inc., PO Box 114, Jamaica, NY 11419. Ed. Dennis Dengel. Circ: 250.

769.56 GBR
IRAN PHILATELIC STUDY CIRCLE BULLETIN. Text in English. 1966. 5/yr. looseleaf. GBP 8, USD 15 (effective 2001). adv. bk.rev.; Website rev. **Document type:** *Bulletin.*
Formerly: Persian Study Circle Bulletin
Published by: Iran Philatelic Study Circle, Flat 10, One Grand Ave, Hove, E Sussex BN3 2LA, United Kingdom. TEL 44-1273-777623. Ed. P A Greenway. Circ: 150. **Subscr. to:** B. Lucas, Secretary, 99 Moseley Wood Dr, Leeds LS16 7HD, United Kingdom; **US subscr. to:** Behruz Nassre, PMB 173, 1819 Polk St, San Francisco, CA 94109.

769.56 USA ISSN 0161-0074
HE6187
ISRAEL PHILATELIST. Text in English. 1948. m. USD 14 to members. adv. bk.rev.
Indexed: J01, SJI.
Published by: Society of Israel Philatelists, 24355 Tunbridge Ln, Beachwood, OH 44122. TEL 216-292-3843. Ed. Oscar Stadtler. Circ: 2,700.

769.56 GBR ISSN 0142-9825
HE6185.I7
ITALY & SWITZERLAND STAMP CATALOGUE. Text in English. 1980. irreg., latest 2009, 7th ed. price varies. **Document type:** *Catalog, Consumer.* **Description:** Designed to aid the collector in researching and finding stamps and new design indexes for Liechtenstein and San Marino.
Supersedes in part (in 1980): Stanley Gibbons Foreign Stamp Catalogue. Europe (0305-8085)
Published by: Stanley Gibbons Publications Ltd., 399 Strand, London, WC2R 0LX, United Kingdom. TEL 44-207-8368444, FAX 44-207-8367342.

769.56 NLD ISSN 1872-0420
JAARBOEK NEDERLANDSE POSTZEGELS. Text in Dutch. 2003. a. EUR 62.50 (effective 2008).
Published by: (TNT Post), Uitgeverij Davo, Postbus 411, Deventer, 7400 AK, Netherlands. TEL 31-570-502700, FAX 31-570-502705, info@davo.nl, http://www.davo.nl.

769.56 USA
THE JACK KNIGHT AIR LOG. Abbreviated title: J K A L. Text in English. 1943. q. free to members (effective 2010). adv. bk.rev. bibl.; charts; illus.; stat. 100 p./no.; back issues avail. **Document type:** *Journal, Consumer.* **Description:** For persons interested in aero, astro and specialized philately.
Formerly: Jack Knight Air Log and A F A News; Which was formed by the 1995 merger of: A F A News; Jack Knight Air Log
Published by: American Air Mail Society, PO Box 110, Mineola, NY 11501.

789.56 JAM
JAMAICA PHILATELIC SOCIETY. NEWSLETTER. Text in English. 1977. m. USD 60 (effective 2000). **Document type:** *Newsletter.*
Published by: Jamaica Philatelic Society, c/o D.O. Uhlman, Treas., PO Box 201, Constant Spring P.O., Kingston, 8, Jamaica. TEL 876-905-1654. Ed. Ewan Cameron. Circ: 50.

769.56 GBR ISSN 0142-9906
HE6185.J32
JAPAN & KOREA STAMP CATALOGUE. Text in English. 1980. irreg., latest 2008, 5th ed. GBP 34.95 per issue (effective 2010). **Document type:** *Catalog, Consumer.* **Description:** Contains a full listing of the Japanese Prefecture issues from 1989 to date.
Supersedes in part (in 1980): Stanley Gibbons Foreign Stamp Catalogue. Overseas (0305-8093)
Published by: Stanley Gibbons Publications Ltd., 399 Strand, London, WC2R 0LX, United Kingdom. TEL 44-207-8368444, FAX 44-207-8367342, kfinney@stanleygibbons.co.uk.

769.56 USA ISSN 0146-0994
HE6187
JAPANESE PHILATELY. Text in English. 1946. bi-m. free to members (effective 2011). bk.rev. charts; illus. index, cum.index. back issues avail. **Document type:** *Magazine, Trade.* **Description:** Covers various aspects of the postal system and postal history of Japan.
Related titles: Microfilm ed.
Indexed: BAS, SJI.
Published by: International Society for Japanese Philately, Inc., c/o William Eisenhauer, PO Box 230462, Tigard, OR 97281. secretary@isjp.org.

769.56 CHN ISSN 0529-0325
JIYOU/PHILATELY MAGAZINE. Text in Chinese. 1955. m. USD 49.20 (effective 2009). illus. **Document type:** *Magazine, Consumer.*
Related titles: English ed.: Chinese Philatelic Magazine.
—East View.
Published by: Renmin Youdian Chubanshe/People's Posts and Telecommunications Publishing House, 14 A Xizhaosi Street, Chongwen District, Beijing, 100061, China. TEL 86-10-67132756, FAX 86-10-67129931, abc@ptpress.com.cn, http://www.ptpress.com.cn/.

769.56 GBR ISSN 0951-8878
JOURNAL OF CHINESE PHILATELY. Text in English. 1954. bi-m. GBP 2 to non-members; free to members (effective 2009). adv. illus. **Document type:** *Journal, Consumer.* **Description:** Medium through which members can publish articles on any facet of Chinese philately or write in with their queries or items of interest.
Formerly (until 1957): China Section Bulletin
Published by: China Philatelic Society of London, c/o David Sibley, Secretary CPSL, 63 Colcester Rd, Coggeshall, Colchester, Essex CO6 1RR, United Kingdom. dws123@tiscali.co.uk. Ed. John Barefoot. adv.: page GBP 50.

769.56 USA ISSN 0447-953X
HE6187
JOURNAL OF SPORTS PHILATELY. Text in English. 1962. q. USD 20 domestic; USD 30 foreign (effective 2005). bk.rev. illus.; stat. index. 40 p./no. 2 cols./p.; **Document type:** *Journal, Trade.* **Description:** Presents variety of news on Olympic and sports philately.
Indexed: SD, SportS.
Published by: Sports Philatelists International, PO Box 98, Orlando Park, IL 60462. TEL 708-590-6257. Ed. Mark Maestrone. Pub. John La Porta. Circ: 450 (paid).

769.56 DNK ISSN 1604-5599
JULEMAERKER NORDEN. Variant title: Nordic Christmas Seal Catalogue. Text in Danish. 2005. biennial. DKK 265 (effective 2008). **Document type:** *Catalog, Consumer.*
Published by: A F A - Forlaget (Subsidiary of: Nordfrim A/S), Kvindevadet 42, Otterup, 5450, Denmark. TEL 45-64-821256, FAX 45-64-821056, afa@afa.dk, http://www.afa.dk. **Dist. by:** Nordfrim A/S, Kvindevadet 42, Otterup 5450, Denmark. mail@nordfrim.dk, http://www.nordfrim.dk.

769.56 DEU ISSN 0022-6343
JUNGE SAMMLER; Zeitschrift fuer junge Briefmarkenfreunde. Text in German. 1955. q. EUR 10 domestic; EUR 13 in Europe; EUR 20 elsewhere; EUR 2.50 newsstand/cover (effective 2009). adv. bk.rev. illus. **Document type:** *Magazine, Consumer.*
Formerly (until 1961): Der Jungsammler
Published by: Deutsche Philatelisten Jugend e.V., Postfach 1353, Geilenkirchen, 52503, Germany. info@dphj.de. Ed., Adv. contact Guenter Latz. B&W page EUR 398, color page EUR 695. Circ: 12,000 (paid and controlled).

769.56 KEN
KENYA STAMP BUREAU. PHILATELIC BULLETIN. Variant title: Philatelic Bulletin. Text in English. 1977; N.S. 1979. q. free. illus. **Document type:** *Bulletin.* **Description:** Announces the issue and availability of special commemorative stamps from Kenya and provides ordering information.
Published by: Kenya Posts and Telecommunications Corporation, Kenya Stamp Bureau, PO Box 30368, Nairobi, Kenya. TEL 254-2-227401, FAX 254-2-333704, TELEX 22245 IJIR POSTS. Circ: 3,000.

769.56 FIN ISSN 1235-645X
KERAILYUUTISET. Text in Finnish. 1990. irreg.
Published by: Kerailyuutiset-yhtio, Krootilankatu 6, Kokemaki, 32800, Finland.

769.56 CAN ISSN 1922-0618
KINGSTON STAMP CLUB. Variant title: Kingston Stamp Club Newsletter. Text in English. 2006. q. free to members (effective 2010). **Document type:** *Newsletter, Trade.*
Address: c/o Richard Weigand, President, 218 Richmond St, RR1, Bath, ON K0H 1G0, Canada.

769.56 JPN
KITTE SHUMI. Text in Japanese. 1980 (vol.91). 12/yr. JPY 42, USD 20.
Published by: Kitte Shumi-sha, 3-12-28 Mejiro, Toshima-ku, Tokyo, 171-0031, Japan.

769.56 GBR ISSN 0964-7821
THE KIWI. Text in English. 1952. bi-m. free to members (effective 2009). bk.rev. index. 24 p./no. 1 cols./p.; back issues avail. **Document type:** *Journal, Trade.* **Description:** Covers the philately and postal history of New Zealand.
Published by: New Zealand Society of Great Britain, 9 Ashley Dr, Walton on Thames, Surrey KT12 1JL, United Kingdom. Ed. Andrew Dove.

769.56 BEL ISSN 0779-8830
KOERIER; 't postzegelblad voor iedereen. Text in Dutch. 1945. m. EUR 25 (effective 2005). adv. bk.rev. bibl.; illus.
Formerly: Postiljon

Published by: Pax Christi Vlaanderen, Italielei 98a, Antwerp, 2000, Belgium. TEL 32-3-2251000, FAX 32-3-2250799, http://www.paxchristi.be. Circ: 800.

KOLEKCJONER LOMZYNSKI. *see* ANTIQUES

769.56 USA ISSN 1087-5107
HE6187
KOREAN PHILATELY. Text in English. 1952. q. USD 25 to members (effective 2000). adv. bk.rev. **Document type:** *Newsletter, Consumer.*
Indexed: SJI.
Published by: Korea Stamp Society, Inc., PO Box 8142, St. Paul, MN 55108. TEL 651-646-2391, FAX 651-646-2391. Ed. Gary N McLean. Circ: 130.

769.56 USA
LAMBDA PHILATELIC JOURNAL. Text in English. q. **Description:** Promotes, studies and collects worldwide philatelic material depicting gay history and awareness.
Published by: Gay - Lesbian History Stamp Club, PO Box 230940, Hartford, CT 06123-0940.

769.56 USA
LATVIAN COLLECTOR. Text in English. 1974. 3/yr. USD 8.50. back issues avail.
Address: PO Box 5403, San Mateo, CA 94402. Ed. Maris Tirums. Circ: 200.

769.56 USA
LIBERIAN PHILATELIC SOCIETY JOURNAL. Text in English. 1979. q. USD 15 domestic; USD 18 foreign (effective 2000). adv. back issues avail. **Description:** Notes and articles on the activities and issues of interest to members of this stamp collector's association.
Formerly (until Fall 1988): Liberian Philatelic Society Newsletter
Published by: (Liberian Philatelic Society), Roy P. Mackal, Ed. & Pub., 9027 S Oakley Ave, Chicago, IL 60620-6131. TEL 773-238-6516, FAX 773-238-6516. R&P Roy P Mackal. Circ: 102 (paid).

769.56 USA
LILAC HINGE. Text in English. m. membership.
Published by: Inland Empire Philatelic Society, N 10710 Nelson Rd, Spokane, WA 99218. Ed. Maude P Wilson.

769.56 USA ISSN 0161-6234
HE6187
LINN'S STAMP NEWS. Text in English. 1928. w. USD 59.99 domestic; USD 104.99 in Canada; USD 134.99 elsewhere (effective 2011). adv. bk.rev. charts; illus.; stat. **Document type:** *Magazine, Consumer.* **Description:** Weekly news magazine for the philatelist and stamp dealer.
Formerly: Linn's Weekly Stamp News (0024-4104)
Related titles: Microform ed.: (from PQC); Online - full text ed.: ISSN 1541-9533.
Indexed: A22, SJI.
Published by: Amos Publishing, Hobby (Subsidiary of: Amos Publishing), PO Box 29, Sidney, OH 45365-0029. http://www.amospress.com. Ed. Michael Baadke. adv.: B&W page USD 1,904, color page USD 2,154; trim 8.625 x 10.75. Circ: 40,678 (paid).

769.56 GBR ISSN 0024-6131
LONDON PHILATELIST. Text in English. 1892. 10/yr. free to members (effective 2009). bk.rev. bibl.; illus. index, cum.index: vols.1-77. back issues avail. **Document type:** *Journal, Academic/Scholarly.* **Description:** Covers the whole world's philately and postal history, and tries to publish articles, often the work of a member who has given a display to the society.
Indexed: SJI.
Published by: The Royal Philatelic Society London, 41 Devonshire Pl, London, W1G 6JY, United Kingdom. TEL 44-20-74861044, FAX 44-20-74860803, secretary@rpsl.org.uk. Ed. Frank L Walton.

769.56 GBR ISSN 0969-8701
LONDON POSTAL HISTORY GROUP NOTEBOOK. Text in English. 1971. 5/yr. free to members (effective 2009). bk.rev. illus. index. back issues avail. **Document type:** *Newsletter, Trade.*
Published by: London Postal History Group, 64 Gordon Rd, Carshalton Beeches, Surrey SM5 3RE, United Kingdom. lphgat64@aol.com, http://www.londonpostalhistorygroup.com.

769.56 USA
LUNDY COLLECTORS CLUB PHILATELIC QUARTERLY. Text in English. 1979. q. USD 12.50 (effective 1994). bk.rev. **Description:** Disseminates information pertaining to the collecting and study of Lundy stamps, covers and postal history.
Published by: Lundy Collectors Club, c/o Rosemoor Stamp & Coin, 208 Centre St, Park Forest, IL 60466-2063. TEL 708-747-9000. Ed. Roger S Cichorz. Circ: 220.

769.56 USA
M C S C C ON COVER. Text in English. 1957. m. membership. adv. illus.; maps. **Document type:** *Newsletter.*
Published by: Motor City Stamp and Cover Club, 22608 Poplar Ct, Hazel Park, MI 48030. TEL 248-546-0038. Ed., Pub. Robert Quintero. Circ: 150.

769.56 USA
MACHINE CANCEL FORUM. Text in English. 1974. q. USD 15 in United States; USD 22 in Canada; USD 35 in Europe; USD 42 in Japan (effective 2008). bk.rev. 40 p./no.; back issues avail. **Document type:** *Magazine, Consumer.*
Published by: Machine Cancel Society, 7 Hillside Rd, No D, Greenbelt, MD 20770-1754. Eds. John R McGee, John Koontz. Circ: 300.

769.56 NZL ISSN 0542-0997
THE MAIL COACH. Text in English. 1964. bi-m. free to members. adv. bk.rev. **Document type:** *Magazine, Consumer.* **Description:** Covers postal history of New Zealand and South Pacific.
—CCC.
Published by: Postal History Society of New Zealand, Inc., PO Box 99 673, Newmarket, Auckland, New Zealand. TEL 64-9-5220311, http://www.nzpf.org.nz/societies/northern/historynz/index.html. Ed. J Campbell. Circ: 500.

769.56 GBR ISSN 0951-5283
HE6187
MAPLE LEAVES. Text in English. 1946. q. free to members (effective 2009). bk.rev. **Document type:** *Journal, Academic/Scholarly.* **Description:** Contains articles concerning philately and the postal history of British North America.
Published by: Canadian Philatelic Society of Great Britain, c/o John Wright, Secretary, 12 Milchester House, Staveley Rd, Meads, Eastbourne, BN20 7JX, United Kingdom. **Subsc. in US & Canada to:** c/o Mike Street, 73 Hatton Dr, Ancaster, ON L9G 2H5, Canada.

769.56 USA
MASSACHUSETTS SPY. Text in English. 1975. bi-m. looseleaf. USD 7. adv. bk.rev. charts; illus.; stat. cum.index: 1975-1991. back issues avail. **Description:** Postal history research of Massachusetts.
Published by: Massachusetts Postal Research Society, PO Box 202, North Abington, MA 02351. TEL 617-878-4446. Ed. Robert S Borden. Circ: 90.

769.56 USA ISSN 1095-0443
HE6187
MEKEEL'S AND STAMPS MAGAZINE. Text in English. 1995. w. USD 47.50 (effective 2009). adv. bk.rev. illus.; mkt. back issues avail. **Document type:** *Magazine, Consumer.* **Description:** Contains news and features for active stamp collectors.
Formed by the merger of (1891-1995): Mekeel's Stamp News (0025-8857); Stamp Auction News (0273-7078)
Related titles: Online - full text ed.: USD 15 (effective 2009).
Indexed: H20, M02, T02.
Published by: Philatelic Communications Corp., PO Box 5050, White Plains, NY 10602. TEL 800-635-3351, stampnews@mindspring.com. Ed. John L Leszak. Pub., R&P, Adv. contact John F Dunn. Circ: 8,000.

789.56 USA ISSN 1075-2226
MENELIK'S JOURNAL. Text in English. 1985. q. USD 7.50 in US & Canada; USD 8.50 elsewhere. **Description:** Focuses upon any and all philatelic matters related to Ethiopia.
Published by: Ethiopian Philatelic Society, c/o Floyd Heiser, 5710 S.E. Gamet Way, Milwaukie, OR 97267.

769.56 USA
MERCHANTVILLE STAMP CLUB. MONTHLY BULLETIN. Text in English. 1932. m. USD 5. adv. bk.rev.
Published by: Merchantville Stamp Club, PO Box 2913, Cherry Hill, NJ 08034. Ed. Paul Schumacher. Circ: 130.

769.56 DEU ISSN 0076-7727
MICHEL-BRIEFMARKEN-KATALOGE. Text in German. 1910. irreg. price varies. adv. **Document type:** *Catalog, Consumer.*
Published by: Schwaneberger Verlag GmbH, Ohmstr 1, Unterschleissheim, 85716, Germany. TEL 49-89-32393333, FAX 49-89-32392402, vertrieb@michel.de, http://www.michel.de. Ed., R&P Jochen Stenzke. Adv. contact Hans Hohenester TEL 49-89-32393309.

769.56 DEU ISSN 0026-198X
MICHEL-RUNDSCHAU. Text in German. 1957. 12/yr. adv. bk.rev. **Document type:** *Magazine, Consumer.*
—CCC.
Published by: Schwaneberger Verlag GmbH, Ohmstr 1, Unterschleissheim, 85716, Germany. TEL 49-89-3239302, FAX 49-89-32393248, vertrieb@michel.de. Ed., R&P Jochen Stenzke. Adv. contact Hans Hohenester TEL 49-89-32393309. B&W page EUR 870, color page EUR 1,230. Circ: 24,500 (controlled).

789.56 USA ISSN 1075-5640
HE6184.C65
MILITARY POSTAL HISTORY SOCIETY BULLETIN. Text in English. 1937. q. USD 10 membership.
Published by: Military Postal History Society, c/o John Azarkevich, 1400 Altamore Ave, Ste 111, Schenectady, NY 12303.

N J P H. *see* COMMUNICATIONS—Postal Affairs

769.56 DEU
NAVICULA. Text in German. 1959. bi-m. adv. bk.rev. back issues avail. **Document type:** *Newsletter.*
Published by: S M S Navicula e.V., c/o Ingo Maahz, Almerweeg 5, Suedbrookmerland, 26624, Germany. TEL 49-4942-912544, webmaster@navicula.de, http://www.navicula.de.

796.56 DEU
NEDERLAND ONDER DE LOEP. Text in German. 19??. irreg. (2-3/yr.). EUR 20 membership (effective 2009). back issues avail. **Document type:** *Newsletter, Consumer.* **Description:** Covers all aspects of Dutch philately.
Formerly (until 1974): Bund Deutscher Philatelisten. Arbeitsgemeinschaft Niederlande. Rundbrief
Published by: Bund Deutscher Philatelisten e.V., Arbeitsgemeinschaft Niederlande e.V., Tiefengasse 33, Oestrich-Winkel, 65375, Germany. TEL 49-6723-7366, webmaster@arge-niederlande.de, http://www.arge-niederlande.de. Ed. Peter Heck. Circ: 150 (controlled).

769.56 USA
NETHERLANDS PHILATELY JOURNAL. Text in English. 1975. q. USD 16 domestic; USD 21 foreign (effective 1999); includes Newsletter. adv. bk.rev. **Document type:** *Newsletter.*
Indexed: SJI.
Published by: American Society for Netherlands Philately, W6428 Riverview Dr, Onalaska, WI 54650. TEL 608-781-8612. Ed. Hans Kremer. Pub. J Enthoven. Adv. contact J. Enthoven. Circ: 400.

769.56 USA ISSN 1930-2053
HE6183.M3
THE NEW CARTOPHILATELIST. Text in English. 1955-1995 (Dec., vol.40, no.3-4); resumed 2003 (Apr.). q. free to members (effective 2006). adv. bk.rev. **Description:** News and articles on the science and art of map making and their depiction on postage stamps.
Formerly (until Apr. 2003): Carto-Philatelist (0891-0758)
Published by: CartoPhilatelic Society, c/o Alf Jordan, 156 W Elm St, Yarmouth, ME 04096. http://www.mapsonstamps.com/index.html. Eds. Dan Nelson, Mark D Larkin. Circ: 210.

789.56 USA ISSN 1073-0222
NEW STAMPS GAZETTE. Text in English. 1992. biennial. **Document type:** *Catalog.* **Description:** Lists stamp collections available to collectors; contains some editorial material.
Published by: Shield Stamp Company, PO BOX 2977, GRAND CENTRAL STA, New York, NY 10163. TEL 212-629-7979, FAX 212-629-3350. Ed. Daniel Keren. Circ: 15,000 (controlled).

769.56 NZL ISSN 1177-2271
NEW ZEALAND COLLECTION. Text in English. 1984. a. NZD 89 (effective 2009). **Document type:** *Directory, Consumer.* **Description:** Features a selection of the year's stamps, accompanied by captivating photographs and fascinating in-depth commentary from some of New Zealand's best-known personalities.
Formerly (until 2005): New Zealand Stamp Collection (0114-3468)
Published by: New Zealand Post, Stamps and Collectables Business, 60 Ridgway, Private Bag 3001, Wanganui, 5020, New Zealand. TEL 64-6-3491234, FAX 64-6-3457120.

769.56 NZL ISSN 0112-5443
NEW ZEALAND STAMP COLLECTOR. Text in English. 1919. q. NZD 60 domestic membership; NZD 70 in Australia membership; NZD 72 elsewhere membership (effective 2009). adv. bk.rev. back issues avail. **Document type:** *Journal, Consumer.*
—CCC.
Published by: Royal Philatelic Society of New Zealand, PO Box 1269, Wellington, 6140, New Zealand. TEL 64-4-4722590, FAX 64-4-4725426, rpsnz@orcon.net.nz. Circ: 500.

769.56 USA
NEWS OF HUNGARIAN PHILATELY. Text in English. 1970. q. USD 15 domestic membership; USD 20 foreign membership (effective 2000). bk.rev. **Document type:** *Newsletter.*
Indexed: SJI.
Published by: Society for Hungarian Philately, 2201 Roscomare Rd., Samp Mortar Sta, Los Angeles, CA 90077-2222. Ed. Csaba Kohalmi. Circ: 250.

769.56 NLD ISSN 2211-7717
NIEUWS OVER ONS VERZAMELGEBIED. Text in Dutch. 2003. s-a. EUR 15 membership (effective 2011).
Published by: Vereniging voor Tsjechoslowakije Filatelie, Postbus 136, Rijen, 5120 AC, Netherlands. TEL 31-161-226507, cs-filatelie@home.nl, http://www.cs-filatelie.nl.

769.56 SWE ISSN 1603-2985
NIPPON KITTE NYT. Text in Danish, Norwegian, Swedish. 1979. bi-m. adv. bk.rev. illus. back issues avail. **Document type:** *Consumer.*
Former titles (until 2003): ScaJaCo Nyt (1602-4494); (until 1990): Nippon Nyt (0107-752X)
Published by: Skandinavisk Japan Samlerforening/Scandinavian Society for Japanese Philately, c/o Anker Nielsen, Hestra Ringvaeg 9, Boraas, 50479, Sweden. info@ssjp.dk. Ed. Boerge Tilt. Circ: 200.

769.56 737 SWE ISSN 0029-134X
NORDISK FILATELI. Text in Swedish. 1937. 9/yr. SEK 289 domestic (effective 2011). adv. bk.rev. **Document type:** *Magazine, Consumer.*
Incorporates (1985-1989): Skandinaviska Myntmagasinet (0283-6769)
Published by: Nordisk Filateli AB, PO Box 90, Kivik, 27721, Sweden. nordisk@fialteli.se, http://www.filateli.se. Ed. Morten Persson.

769.56 DNK ISSN 0903-3440
NORDISK FILATELISTISK TIDSSKRIFT. Variant title: N F T. Text in Danish. 1894. 4/yr. DKK 290 domestic membership; DKK 380 elsewhere membership (effective 2009). adv. bk.rev. cum index: 1894-1930. **Document type:** *Magazine, Consumer.*
Published by: Kjoebenhavns Philatelist Klub, Lygten 37, Copenhagen NV, 2400, Denmark. kpk@kpk.dk. Ed. Rene Kejlskov Joergensen TEL 45-36-774087. Circ: 1,050.

769.56 NOR ISSN 0332-8848
NORSK FILATELISTISK TIDSSKRIFT. Variant title: N F T. Text in Norwegian. 1942. 8/yr. NOK 250 domestic membership; NOK 300 in Europe membership; NOK 350 elsewhere membership (effective 2005). adv. bk.rev. illus.; stat. index. 3 cols./p.; **Document type:** *Magazine, Consumer.*
Published by: Norsk Filatelistforbund/Federation of Norwegian Philatelists, PO Box 875, Sentrum, Oslo, 0104, Norway. TEL 47-22-208053, FAX 47-22-208054, nf@filatelist.no. Ed. Marius Brinch Gabrielsen.

769.56 ZAF ISSN 1016-6734
O F S PHILATELIC MAGAZINE. Text in English. 1951. m. ZAR 60 to members. adv. bk.rev. **Document type:** *Newsletter.*
Published by: Orange Free State Philatelic Society, The Secretary, PO Box 702, Bloemfontein, 9300, South Africa. FAX 27-51-4306550. Ed. J A van Beukering. Circ: 150 (paid).

769.56 GBR ISSN 0267-8071
➤ **O P A L JOURNAL.** Text in English. 1949. 3/yr. free to members (effective 2009). bk.rev.; Website rev. back issues avail. **Document type:** *Journal, Academic/Scholarly.* **Description:** Contains Papers, informational articles, exchange listings, and historical sketches pertaining to stamp collectors of philately of the Ottoman Empire.
Related titles: E-mail ed.; Supplement(s): O P A L Supplement.
Published by: Oriental Philatelic Association of London, c/o Jeff Ertughrul, Ed, 62 Leopold Rd, London, N2 8BG, United Kingdom. http://www.mclstamps.co.uk/opal/opalhome.html. Ed. Kemal Giray. **Subscr. to:** c/o Michael Fulford, Ruth Cottage, Main St, E Langston LE16 7TW, United Kingdom.

769.56 USA ISSN 0737-0954
HE6185.C67
THE OXCART. Text in English. 1960. q. looseleaf. USD 12 domestic; USD 15 foreign (effective 2002). bk.rev. 32 p./no.; back issues avail. **Document type:** *Newsletter, Consumer.* **Description:** Offers a study of postage and revenue stamps and related materials of Costa Rica.
Indexed: SJI.
Published by: Society for Costa Rica Collectors, PO Box 14831, Baton Rouge, LA 70808. hrmena7@cox.net, http://www.socorico.org/. Ed. William E Critzer. R&P H R Mena. Circ: 200. **Dist. by:** Raul Hernandez, 4204 Haring Road, Metaire, LA 70006. rherman3870@aol.com.

769.56 USA ISSN 1072-8732
P H S G NEWSLETTER. Text in English. 1987. q. USD 14 domestic membership; USD 16 in Canada membership; USD 18 elsewhere membership (effective 2000). adv. bk.rev. cum.index: 1987-1993. **Document type:** *Newsletter.* **Description:** Covers all aspects of cover collecting with regard to the 1941 attack on Pearl Harbor, including WWII in the Pacific arena, aviation and shipping history, airmail covers of the Pacific PAA flights, history of Hawaii philately, wartime censorship of the mails, and more.
Published by: Pearl Harbor Study Group, 6155 Main St, Springfield, OR 97479-5403. TEL 651-741-2400, phil@jb.com. Ed., Pub., R&P, Adv. contact Larry R Wendell Jr. Circ: 73 (paid).

769.56 USA ISSN 1041-4894
HE6187
P M C C BULLETIN. Text in English. 1947. m. (11/yr.). USD 16.50 (effective 1999). adv. illus. **Document type:** *Bulletin.* **Description:** Articles on the hobby of postmark collecting. Covers current developments and historical information to aid collectors.

P

Published by: Post Mark Collectors Club, c/o David H Proulx, 7629 Homestead Dr, Baldwinsville, NY 13027. TEL 315-638-0532. Ed. Kevin M Tanzillo. Circ: 950.

796.56 USA
P M C C MEMBERSHIP ROSTER. Text in English. 1947. triennial. membership. **Document type:** *Directory.* **Description:** Provides historic information on the club and its services. Lists names and addresses of members.
Published by: Post Mark Collectors Club, c/o David H Proulx, 7629 Homestead Dr, Baldwinsville, NY 13027. TEL 315-638-0532. Circ: 1,500.

769.56 GBR
P T S NEWS. (Philatelic Traders Society) Text in English. 1947. m. free to members (effective 2009). bk.rev. bibl. **Document type:** *Newsletter, Trade.* **Description:** Contain news, views, pictures and information beneficial to the membership.
Formerly: P T S Journal (0048-3729)
Published by: Philatelic Traders Society Ltd., Fleet, PO Box 371, Hampshire, GU52 6ZX, United Kingdom. TEL 44-1252-628006, 44-1252-684674, office.pts@btinternet.com, http://www.philatelic-traders-society.co.uk.

769.56 GBR ISSN 0306-0896
PACIFICA. Text in English. 1962. 4/yr. free to members (effective 2009). adv. bk.rev. back issues avail. **Document type:** *Newsletter, Trade.* **Description:** Contains book reviews, new issue information, auction realizations, study circle news, as well as member articles on a wide range of topics.
Indexed: ABS&EES, GSS&RPL, SJI.
Published by: Pacific Islands Study Circle, c/o John Ray, 24 Woodvale Ave, London, SE25 4AE, United Kingdom. info@pisc.org.uk. Ed. Bryan Jones.

769.56 USA
PASTE-UP. Text in English. 1981 (vol.33). m. USD 5 membership (effective 2000). **Description:** Club meeting notices.
Published by: Cedar Rapids Stamp Club, PO Box 2554, Cedar, IA 52406. Ed., Pub., R&P, Adv. contact Dennis Lynch. Circ: 50 (controlled).

769.56 MYS ISSN 0126-6497
PEMUNGUT SETEM MALAYSIA/MALAYSIAN PHILATELIST. Text in English. 1970. 3/yr. MYR 40, USD 15 domestic members only; MYR 50, USD 20 foreign members only (effective 2000). adv. bk.rev. **Document type:** *Bulletin.* **Description:** Contains special reference to Malayan/Malaysian philately, news from the world of philately, articles on philatelic guidelines and collecting interest, news of new stamp issues from around the world, features on how to collect stamps, how to exhibit, how to arrange and write-up, etc.
Published by: Philatelic Society of Malaysia, PO Box 10588 GPO, Kuala Lumpur, 50718, Malaysia. Ed. C. Nagarajah. R&P C Nagarajah. Circ: 1,100.

769.56 USA
PENINSULAR PHILATELIST. Text in English. 1951. q. USD 5 (effective 1994). adv. bk.rev. illus. **Description:** Provides data on the collecting scene in Michigan. Acts as a clearinghouse for stamp exhibition dates.
Published by: Peninsular State Philatelic Society, PO Box 80946, Lansing, MI 48908. Ed. William C Allen. Circ: 175.

769.56 USA
PHILA-QUAD. Text in English. m. **Document type:** *Newsletter, Consumer.*
Published by: Quad-City Stamp Club, PO Box 1301, Moline, IL 61266-9301. pmats5@aol.com, http://qcstampclub.com.

769.56 USA
PHILAGEMS INTERNATIONAL. Text in English. 1976. q. USD 10 domestic; USD 15 foreign (effective 2000). **Document type:** *Newsletter.* **Description:** Focuses on gems, minerals, jewelry, fossils, mining and coins.
Published by: Gems, Minerals & Jewelry Study Unit, c/o George Young, Box 632, Tewksbury, MA 01876. TEL 978-851-8283.

769.56 USA
PHILAMATH; a journal of mathematical philately. Text in English. 1979. q. looseleaf. back issues avail. **Document type:** *Newsletter, Academic/Scholarly.* **Description:** Articles about mathematics and computers on postage stamps.
Address: c/o Estelle A. Buccino, 5615 Glenwood Rd, Bethesda, MD 20817.

769.56 AUS ISSN 0725-2323
PHILAS NEWS. Text in English. 1972. q. AUD 5 domestic; AUD 15 foreign (effective 2008). bk.rev. **Document type:** *Newsletter.*
Published by: Philatelic Association of New South Wales Inc., PO Box 220, Darlinghurst, NSW 1300, Australia. TEL 61-2-92648406, FAX 61-2-92674741.

769.56 USA ISSN 0739-6198
HE6184.D4
PHILATELI-GRAPHICS. Text in English. 1976. q. looseleaf. USD 10 domestic; USD 15 foreign (effective 2001). bk.rev. illus. index, cum.index: 1976-1982 in no.24. back issues avail. **Document type:** *Newsletter.* **Description:** For people interested in printing and graphic arts of and on postage stamps and other philatelic items of the world.
Published by: Graphics Philately Association, PO Box 1513, Thousand Oaks, CA 91358. Circ: 130 (paid).

769.56 USA ISSN 1041-2999
HE6183.C413
PHILATELIA CHIMICA ET PHYSICA. Text in English. 1979. q. USD 16; USD 18 foreign (effective 2001). bk.rev. index. 72 p./no.; back issues avail. **Document type:** *Journal, Academic/Scholarly.*
Formerly: Philatelia Chimica
Published by: (Chemistry and Physics on Stamps Study Unit), C P O S S U, 13 Roxbury Dr, Athens, OH 45701. TEL 614-593-3729. Ed. Foil Miller. Circ: 260.

769.56 USA ISSN 0896-4173
PHILATELIC COMMUNICATOR. Text in English. 1968. q. USD 15 domestic; USD 17.50 in Canada & Mexico; USD 20 elsewhere (effective 2008). adv. bk.rev. **Document type:** *Newsletter.*
Formerly (until 1987): A.P.S. Writers Unit Number Thirty News Bulletin (0147-3646)
Published by: American Philatelic Society, Writers Unit No. 30, c/o George B Griffenhagen, Sec./Treas., 2501 Drecel St, Vienna, VA 22180. Ed. Albert W Starkweather. Circ: 850.

769.56 658.048 USA ISSN 0892-032X
PHILATELIC EXHIBITOR. Text in English. 1986. q. USD 15 to members. adv. bk.rev. back issues avail. **Description:** A forum for debate and information on philatelic exhibiting, judging, and exhibition administration. Offers encouragement to novices.
Published by: American Association of Philatelic Exhibitors, c/o Russell V Skavaril, Exec Sec, 222 E Torrence Rd, Columbus, OH 43214. Ed. John M Hotchner. Circ: 1,300.

769.56 GBR ISSN 0031-7381
THE PHILATELIC EXPORTER; the World stamp trade journal. Text in English. 1945. m. GBP 29 domestic; GBP 36 foreign (effective 2009). adv. bk.rev. bibl.; charts; illus.; stat.; tr.lit. back issues avail. **Document type:** *Journal, Trade.* **Description:** Designed for the international postage stamp trade.
Incorporates: Coin and Note Dealer; Philatelic Trader; Wholesale Philatelic Post
Published by: Philatelic Exporter, 7 Parkside, Christchurch Rd, Ringwood, Hampshire, BH24 3SH, United Kingdom. TEL 44-1425-472363, FAX 44-1425-470247. Ed. Graham Phillips TEL 44-1473-311266. Adv. contact Brian Case TEL 44-1425-481054.

796.56 USA ISSN 0196-5034
PHILATELIC FOUNDATION QUARTERLY. Text in English. 1983. q. USD 50; per issue contribution. adv. bk.rev. charts; illus. back issues avail. **Document type:** *Newsletter.* **Description:** Presents articles and opinions about the foundation's Expert Committee, its reference collections, research library, the educational programs, and its publications.
Formerly: Philatelic Foundation Bulletin
Published by: Philatelic Foundation, 501 Fifth Ave, 1901, New York, NY 10017-6103. TEL 212-867-3699, FAX 212-867-3984. Ed. Harlan F Stone. Circ: 1,700 (controlled).

789.56 366 USA
THE PHILATELIC FREEMASON. Text in English. 1977. bi-m. USD 8 in North America; USD 14 elsewhere (effective 2000). cum.index: vols.1-17. back issues avail. **Document type:** *Newsletter.* **Description:** Publishes articles concerning stamps and Masons, and information pertaining to Masonic stamp collections.
Published by: (Masonic Study Unit), R A D Publishing Co., 59 Greenwood Rd, Andover, MA 01810. TEL 978-470-0583. Ed., Pub., R&P Robert A Domingue. Circ: 280.

769.56 GBR ISSN 1746-5990
PHILATELIC LECTURERS & DISPLAYS. Text in English. 2000. a. free to members (effective 2011). **Document type:** *Handbook/Manual/ Guide, Trade.*
Published by: The Association of British Philatelic Societies, Greystones, Green Ln, Crowborough, East Sussex TN6 2BX, United Kingdom. chair@abps.org.uk.

769.56 USA ISSN 0270-1707
PHILATELIC LITERATURE REVIEW. Text in English. 1942. q. free to members (effective 2010). adv. bk.rev. illus. cum.index: 1942-1970. reprints avail. **Document type:** *Bulletin, Consumer.* **Description:** Contains indexes and bibliographies, reviews of current philatelic literature, market and price information, news from the APRL, and "The Clearinghouse," a forum where subscribers list literature they want to buy or sell.
Indexed: A26, B14, BRI, CBRI, E08, G08, I05, S09.
Published by: American Philatelic Research Library, 100 Match Factory Pl, Bellefonte, PA 16823. TEL 814-933-3803, FAX 814-933-6128, plr@stamps.org. Ed. Barbara Boal TEL 814-933-3803 ext.221. Adv. contact Helen Bruno TEL 814-933-3803 ext.224.

769.56 USA
PHILATELIC PROSPECTOR. Text in English. m. USD 15 to members. bk.rev. **Document type:** *Newsletter.*
Published by: Sacramento Philatelic Society, PO Box 13284, Sacramento, CA 95813. TEL 916-972-0263, http://www.softcom.net/users/johnpava, http://web.interx.com/pavalask/index.html. Ed. John J Pavalasky. Pub. Bob Short. R&P John Pavalasky. Circ: 240.

769.56 TTO
PHILATELIC SOCIETY OF T & T BULLETIN. Text in English. 1946. q. USD 10 (effective 1999). adv. bk.rev. **Document type:** *Newsletter.*
Formerly: Trinidad Philatelic Society Bulletin
Media: Duplicated (not offset).
Published by: Philatelic Society of Trinidad & Tobago, PO Box 596, Port-of-Spain, Trinidad, Trinidad & Tobago. TEL 868-622-1673, FAX 868-632-2759. Ed. John Chay. Circ: 250.

769.56 DEU ISSN 1619-5892
PHILATELIE. Text in German. 1949. 10/yr. membership. adv. bk.rev. **Document type:** *Magazine, Consumer.*
Formerly: Philatelie Bundesnachrichten
Published by: (Bund Deutscher Philatelisten e.V.), Phila-Promotion GmbH, Postfach 1240, Forchheim, 91294, Germany. TEL 49-9545-443562, FAX 49-9545-443562, mich.adler@t-online.de, http://www.phila-promotion.de. Ed. Wolfgang Maassen. Adv. contact Claire van de Flierdt. B&W page EUR 1,495, color page EUR 1,885; trim 210 x 285. Circ: 66,000 (paid and controlled).

769.56 NLD ISSN 0166-3437
PHILATELIE; Nederlandsch maandblad voor philatelie. Variant title: Filatelie. Text in Dutch. 1922. 11/yr. EUR 28.75 domestic; EUR 29.80 in Belgium; EUR 47.05 in Europe; EUR 71.05 elsewhere (effective 2010). adv. bk.rev. illus. index. **Document type:** *Magazine, Consumer.* **Description:** Covers philately and postage stamps from all over the world for the Dutch speaking regions.
Formerly (until 1973): Nederlandsch Maandblad voor Philatelie (0028-2081)
Published by: Stichting Nederlandsch Maandblad voor Philatelie, c/o SWD Veenstra, Roelofsstraat 31, The Hague, 2596 VK, Netherlands. TEL 31-70-3280342. Ed. Aad Knikman TEL 31-35-5254391. Circ: 33,000.

769.56 FRA ISSN 0183-3634
LA PHILATELIE FRANCAISE; organe officiel de la Federation Francaise des Associations Philateliques. Text in French. 1952. bi-m. EUR 20 domestic; EUR 30 foreign (effective 2009). adv. bk.rev. charts; illus. index. **Document type:** *Journal, Trade.*
Published by: Federation Francaise des Associations Philateliques, 47 rue de Maubeuge, Paris, 75009, France. TEL 33-1-42855025, FAX 33-1-44630139, ffap.philatelie@laposte.net. Circ: 14,000.

769.56 CAN ISSN 0381-7547
PHILATELIE QUEBEC. Key Title: Philatelie au Quebec. Text in French. 1969. bi-m. CAD 25 domestic to individuals; CAD 35 domestic to institutions; CAD 35 in United States; CAD 50 elsewhere (effective 2000). adv. illus. **Document type:** *Bulletin.*
Indexed: PdeR.
Published by: (Federation Quebecoise de Philatelie), Editions Phibec Inc., 4545 ave Pierre de Coubertin, C P 1000, Succ M, Montreal, PQ H1V 3R2, Canada. TEL 514-252-3035, FAX 514-251-8038. Ed., Adv. contact Yvan Latulippe. R&P Pierre Lavigne TEL 450-676-2776. B&W page CAD 350, color page CAD 850. Circ: 1,500.

769.56 AUS ISSN 0031-7403
PHILATELY FROM AUSTRALIA. Text in English. 1949. q. bk.rev. charts; illus. index, cum.index: 1949-1958, 1959-1968, 1969-1978. **Document type:** *Journal, Trade.*
Indexed: SJI.
Published by: Royal Philatelic Society of Victoria, PO Box 2071, Melbourne, VIC 3001, Australia.

769.56 JPN
PHILATELY IN JAPAN. Text in English. 1977. q. JPY 2,000 (effective 2000). **Document type:** *Bulletin.*
Published by: Japan Philatelic Society Foundation, PO Box 96, Toshima, Tokyo-to 170-8668, Japan.

769.56 USA
PHILATEX. Text in English. 1982 (vol.86). bi-m. free. **Document type:** *Newsletter.*
Published by: San Antonio Philatelic Association, 2903 Nacogdoches Rd, San Antonio, TX 78217. LTC519@satx.rr.com. Circ: 220.

769.56 GRC ISSN 0031-8264
PHILOTELIA. Text in English, Greek. 1924. bi-m. adv. bk.rev.; Website rev. abstr.; bibl.; charts; illus.; stat. index, cum.index: 1924-1953; 1954-1973; 1974-1983; 1984-1993. 64 p./no.; back issues avail. **Document type:** *Magazine, Consumer.* **Description:** Covers Hellenic philately and postal history.
Related titles: Microfiche ed.; Online - full text ed.
Published by: Hellenic Philotelic Society, 57 Akadimias St, Athens, 106 79, Greece. TEL 301-210-3621125, FAX 301-210-9422157, hps@hps.gr, http://www.hps.gr. Ed. Anthony Virvilis. Circ: 1,000.

769.56 USA ISSN 0888-675X
THE PITCAIRN LOG. Text in English. 1973. q. free to members (effective 2010). adv. bk.rev. **Document type:** *Journal, Academic/Scholarly.* **Description:** Contains articles and regular columns that will be of interest to all Pitcairn enthusiasts.
Indexed: SJI.
Published by: (Pitcairn Islands Study Group), Everett L. Parker, Ed. & Pub., 249 NW Live Oak Pl, Lake City, FL 32055. eparker@hughes.net.

769.56 DNK ISSN 0032-4418
POPULAER FILATELI. Text in Danish. 1939. 10/yr. DKK 295 (effective 2008). adv. bk.rev. illus.; mkt. back issues avail. **Document type:** *Magazine, Consumer.*
Published by: A F A - Forlaget (Subsidiary of: Nordfrim A/S), Kvindevadet 42, Otterup, 5450, Denmark. TEL 45-64-821256, FAX 45-64-821056, afa@afa.dk, http://www.afa.dk. Ed. Vivi Larsen. adv.: color page DKK 2,650; 148 x 210. Circ: 4,000. **Dist. by:** Nordfrim A/S, Kvindevadet 42, Otterup 5450, Denmark. mail@nordfrim.dk, http://www.nordfrim.dk.

794 USA ISSN 0892-5178
PORTU-INFO. Text in English. 1961. q. USD 15; USD 20 foreign. adv. bk.rev. illus.; tr.lit. index. **Description:** Examines stamps and postal history of Portugal and ex-colonies.
Indexed: SJI.
Published by: International Society for Portuguese Philately, 39565 Westview Dr, Box 43146, Oakhurst, CA 93644. TEL 209-683-3274. Ed. John K Cross. Pub. Nelson Press. R&P John Cross. Adv. contact John Liles. Circ: 450.

769.56 GBR ISSN 0142-9833
PORTUGAL & SPAIN STAMP CATALOGUE. Text in English. 1980. irreg., latest 2004, 5th ed. GBP 29.95 per issue (effective 2010). **Document type:** *Catalog, Consumer.* **Description:** Lists stamps from Spain and Portugal as well as covers shades, booklets, paper changes, set prices, missing colours and errors and footnotes on forgeries.
Supersedes in part (in 1980): Stanley Gibbons Foreign Stamp Catalogue. Europe (0305-8085)
Published by: Stanley Gibbons Publications Ltd., 399 Strand, London, WC2R 0LX, United Kingdom. TEL 44-207-8368444, FAX 44-207-8367342.

769.56 USA ISSN 0164-6184
HE6204.U5
POSSESSIONS. Text in English. 1978. q. USD 10. adv. bk.rev.
Indexed: SJI.
Published by: United States Possessions Philatelic Society, c/o W T Zuehlke, Sec -Treas, 8100 Willow Steam Dr, Sandy, UT 84093. Ed. Gilbert N Plass. Circ: 600.

LA POSTA; a journal of American postal history. *see* COMMUNICATIONS—Postal Affairs

769.56 USA
POSTAL ORDER NEWS. Text in English. 1985. q. USD 10 (effective 1999). **Document type:** *Newsletter.*
Published by: Postal Order Society, c/o Jack Harwood, Dir, Box 32015, Midtown Sta, Sarasota, FL 34239. TEL 941-364-5172. Ed. Mal Tedds. R&P Jack Harwood. Circ: 75.

383.2 USA
POSTAL SERVICE GUIDE TO U S STAMPS. Text in English. 1927. a. illus. 575 p./no.; **Document type:** *Guide, Consumer.*
Former titles: United States Postage Stamps; (until 1970): Postage Stamps of the United States (0079-4244)
Published by: U.S. Postal Service, 475 L'Enfant Plz, SW, Rm 5300, Washington, DC 20260. https://www.usps.com/.

769.56 BOL
POSTALES DE BOLIVIA. Text in Spanish. 1971. q. free. **Document type:** *Bulletin.*
Published by: Federacion Filatelica Boliviana, PO Box 4247, La Paz, Bolivia. Ed. Eugenio von Boeck. Circ: 950.

769.56 DEU ISSN 1430-8533
POSTFRISCH; Das Philatelie-Journal. Text in German. bi-m. **Document type:** *Magazine, Consumer.*

Published by: Deutsche Post AG, Charles-de-Gaulle-Str 20, Bonn, 53113, Germany. info@deutschepost.de, 49-228-1820, http://www.deutschepost.de.

769.56 USA ISSN 0551-6897
➤ **POSTHORN.** Text in English. 1943. q. bk.rev. illus. 48 p./no.; back issues avail. **Document type:** *Journal, Academic/Scholarly.*
Indexed: SJI.
Published by: Scandinavian Collectors Club, PO Box 13196, El Cajon, CA 92020. dbrent47@sprynet.com. **Subscr. to:** SCC.

769.56 DEU
POSTILLON. Text in German. 1954. 3/yr. EUR 20 membership (effective 2009). adv. bk.rev. **Document type:** *Magazine, Consumer.* **Description:** Covers philately of France, its French colonies and its offices abroad.
Published by: Bund Deutscher Philatelisten e.V., Arbeitsgemeinschaft Frankreich e.V., Tucholskyweg 5, Mainz, 55127, Germany. TEL 49-6131-71727, rainervonscharpen@t-online.de, http://www.argefrankreich.de. Ed. Rainer von Scharpen. Circ: 500.

789.56 BEL
DE POSTZEGEL. Text in Dutch. 1938. m. (11/yr). EUR 15 domestic; EUR 15 in Netherlands; EUR 17.50 in Europe; EUR 20 elsewhere (effective 2005). bk.rev.; Website rev. illus. 48 p./no.; **Document type:** *Newsletter, Consumer.* **Description:** Reports philatelic news from Belgium, the Netherlands, and other countries.
Published by: Koninklijke Vlaamse Bond van Postzegelverzamelaars vzw, Werfplein 6, Bruges, 8000, Belgium. Ed., Adv. contact Emile Schepens. Pub., R&P Joseph Ysenbrandt. Circ: 8,000.

769.56 USA ISSN 0273-5415
HE6187
PRECANCEL FORUM. Text in English. 1940. m. USD 15 membership (effective 2005). adv. bk.rev. charts; illus. **Document type:** *Newsletter, Consumer.* **Description:** Covers activities of the society and its branch clubs. Includes articles on precancelled stamps and their collection.
Indexed: SJI.
Published by: Precancel Stamp Society Inc., c/o Jim Hirstein, PO Box 4072, Missoula, MT 51806-4072. wcummings@woh.rr.com, http://www.precancels.com/PSS/pssinfo.htm. Ed., Pub. William Cummings. Circ: 1,200 (paid).

769.56 USA
PRECANCEL STAMP COLLECTOR. Text in English. 1951. m. USD 15. adv. bk.rev. **Document type:** *Newsletter.* **Description:** Contains information on precanceled stamps.
Published by: National Association of Precancel Collectors, Inc., 84 W National Dr, Newark, OH 43055-5358. Ed., R&P Glenn W Dye. Circ: 7,710 (paid). **Co-sponsor:** New Jersey Precancel Society.

769.56 USA ISSN 0162-7902
HE6185.G9
EL QUETZAL. Text in English. 1949. q. USD 15 to members. adv. bk.rev. **Document type:** *Newsletter.* **Description:** Concerned with the philatelic history of Guatemala and other portions of Central America.
Published by: International Society of Guatemala Collectors, c/o Michael Barie, Box 1445, Detroit, MI 48231. TEL 313-538-3865. Ed. Cecile Gruson. Circ: 300.

769.56 GBR
RAILWAY PHILATELIC GROUP. NEWSLETTER. Text in English. 1982. free to members. **Document type:** *Newsletter, Consumer.*
Published by: Railway Philatelic Group, c/o F W Taylor, Membership Secretary, 5 Garth Ln, Widdrington, Morpeth, Northumb NE61 5EN, United Kingdom. f.will.taylor@btinternet.com, http://railwayphilatelicgroup.com/.

769.56 GBR ISSN 0951-886X
RAILWAY PHILATELY. Text in English. 1966. q. free to members (effective 2009). bk.rev. illus. 52 p./no.; back issues avail. **Document type:** *Journal, Trade.*
Related titles: Supplement(s): Postal Auction.
Published by: Railway Philatelic Group, c/o F W Taylor, Membership Secretary, 5 Garth Ln, Widdrington, Morpeth, Northumb NE61 5EN, United Kingdom. TEL 44-1670-760252, f.will.taylor@btinternet.com. Ed. Fred W Taylor.

RALPH'S REVIEW. *see* LITERATURE—Science Fiction, Fantasy, Horror

769.56 629.4 USA
RAPID NOTICE NEWS SERVICE. Text in English. 1977. bi-m. looseleaf. USD 10. back issues avail.
Published by: Space Philatelist International Society, PO Box 771, West Nyack, NY 10994. TEL 914-623-8149, FAX 914-591-6683. Ed. Scott Michaels. Circ: 250.

769.56 USA ISSN 0484-6125
REVEALER. Text in English. 1951. q. USD 15 membership (effective 2008). **Document type:** *Magazine, Consumer.*
Indexed: SJI.
Published by: Eire Philatelic Association, PO Box 704, Bernardsville, NJ 07924. brennan704@aol.com. Ed. Patrick Ryan.

769.56 ZWE
RHODESIA STAMP CATALOGUE. Text in English. 1971. a. ZWD 9.75. illus.
Published by: Zimbabwe Stamp Co. (Pvt.) Ltd., PO Box 200, Harare, Zimbabwe. Ed. D G Pollard. Circ: 7,000.

789.56 GBR ISSN 0269-1574
RHODESIAN STUDY CIRCLE JOURNAL. Text in English. 1948. q. GBP 4 to non-members; free to members (effective 2009). bk.rev. back issues avail. **Document type:** *Journal, Academic/Scholarly.*
Published by: Rhodesian Study Circle, c/o Richard Barnett, 2 Cox Ley, Hatfield Heath, Bishop's Stortford, Herts CM22 7ER, United Kingdom. richdiane@uwclub.net. Ed. Derek Lambert.

769.56 USA ISSN 0035-8363
HE6187
➤ **ROSSICA SOCIETY OF RUSSIAN PHILATELY JOURNAL.** Text in English. 1929. s-a. free to members (effective 2010). bk.rev. charts; illus.; maps; bibl. index. back issues avail. **Document type:** *Journal, Academic/Scholarly.* **Description:** Includes articles an short notes on Russian philately and postal history.
Indexed: NumL, SJI.
Published by: Rossica Society of Russian Philately, Inc., c/o David Skipton, 50-D Ridge Rd, Greenbelt, MD 20770. david.skipton@rossica.org. Ed. William Moskoff.

769.56 NZL
ROYAL PHILATELIC SOCIETY OF NEW ZEALAND. ANNUAL REPORT. Text in English. a. adv. **Document type:** *Report, Consumer.*
Published by: Royal Philatelic Society of New Zealand, PO Box 1269, Wellington, 6140, New Zealand. TEL 64-4-4722590, FAX 64-4-4725426, rpsnz@orcon.net.nz, http://www.rpsnz.org.nz/. Ed. Wayne Kitching.

769.56 NZL ISSN 1176-693X
ROYAL PHILATELIC SOCIETY OF NEW ZEALAND. MONOGRAPH HANDBOOK. Text in English. 1953. irreg. price varies. **Document type:** *Monographic series.*
Formerly (until no.13, 2004): Royal Philatelic Society of New Zealand. Monograph Series (0112-2053)
Published by: Royal Philatelic Society of New Zealand, PO Box 1269, Wellington, 6140, New Zealand. TEL 64-4-4722590, FAX 64-4-4725426, rpsnz@orcon.net.nz, http://www.rpsnz.org.nz/.

769.56 NLD ISSN 2211-7237
RUIMTEVAART FILATELIE CLUB NEDERLAND. NIEUWSBRIEF. Text in Dutch. q. EUR 20 domestic membership; EUR 25 foreign membership (effective 2011). **Document type:** *Newsletter, Consumer.*
Published by: Ruimtevaart Filatelie Club Nederland, Lupine 30, Noordwijkerhout, 2211 MJ, Netherlands. http://www.nedvision.nl/thematische-filatelie/rfc. Ed. A P H M Jacobs.

769.56 GBR ISSN 0142-9841
HE6185.S652
RUSSIA STAMP CATALOGUE. Text in English. 1981. irreg., latest 2008, 6th ed. GBP 34.95 per issue (effective 2010). **Document type:** *Catalog, Consumer.* **Description:** Lists stamps from Russia, the former Soviet Republics, Russian Post Offices overseas, wartime occupation issues as well as the stamps of Mongolia.
Supersedes in part (in 1981): Stanley Gibbons Foreign Stamp Catalogue. Europe (0305-8085)
Published by: Stanley Gibbons Publications Ltd., 399 Strand, London, WC2R 0LX, United Kingdom. TEL 44-207-8368444, FAX 44-207-8367342.

769.56 369.46 USA ISSN 1066-6028
HE6187
S O S S I JOURNAL. Text in English. 1951. 6/yr. looseleaf. USD 15 in North America; USD 18 elsewhere (effective 2006). adv. bk.rev. illus. 28 p./no. 2 cols./p.; **Document type:** *Magazine, Consumer.* **Description:** Presents a forum for those interested in collecting stamps and other philatelic material related to the Boy Scouts, Girl Scouts and girl guides of the world.
Published by: Scouts on Stamps Society International, c/o Lawrence E Clay, PO Box 6228, Kennewick, WA 99336. TEL 509-735-3731, FAX 509-735-2789, lclay3731@charter.net. Ed. Patrick R Rourk TEL 315-353-8892. Circ: 1,000.

769.56 USA
S O S SIGNAL. Text in English. 1959. q. USD 8 in North America; USD 11 elsewhere. **Document type:** *Newsletter.* **Description:** Focuses on stamp reproductions, from actual pictures of former stamps to simulations of stamps.
Published by: Stamps on Stamps Centenary Unit, 1360 Trinity Dr, Menlo Park, CA 94025. TEL 716-773-5141. Ed. William E Critzer. Circ: 100.

769.56 USA
ST. HELENA AND DEPENDENCIES PHILATELIC SOCIETY NEWSLETTER. Text in English. 1977. q. USD 10. adv. bk.rev.
Indexed: SJI.
Published by: St. Helena and Dependencies Philatelic Society, 222 E Torrence Rd, Columbus, OH 43214. TEL 614-262-3046. Ed. Russell V Skavaril. Circ: 250.

769.56 GBR ISSN 0261-7226
SARAWAK JOURNAL. Text in English. 1947. q. free domestic to members (effective 2009). adv. bk.rev. back issues avail. **Document type:** *Journal, Consumer.* **Description:** Contains much original research material as well as society news.
Formerly (until 1948): Sarawak News Sheet
Indexed: SJI.
Published by: Sarawak Specialists' Society, c/o Claire Scott, FRPSL, Tumblins, Winterbourne Stickland, England DT11 0ED, United Kingdom. TEL 44-1258-880841, http://www.britborneostamps.org.uk/. Ed. Claire Scott. **Subscr. to:** David Brown.

769.56 610.9 USA ISSN 0048-9255
SCALPEL AND TONGS; medical philately. Text in English. 1955. q. USD 15 domestic; USD 18 foreign (effective 2011). adv. bk.rev. **Document type:** *Journal, Academic/Scholarly.* **Description:** Deals with all aspects of philately related to medicine and allied subjects, such as nursing and blood transfusion. Covers the history of medicine as well.
Related titles: Microform ed.: (from PQC).
Indexed: P30, SCOPUS.
Published by: American Topical Association, Inc., Medical Subjects Unit, c/o Frederick Skvara, PO Box 6228, Bridgewater, NJ 08807. fcskvara@optonline.net.

769.56 GBR ISSN 0142-985X
SCANDINAVIA STAMP CATALOGUE. Text in English. 1980. irreg., latest 2008, 6th ed. GBP 34.95 per issue (effective 2010). **Document type:** *Catalog, Consumer.* **Description:** Features stamps from countries such as Denmark, Finland, Iceland, Norway and Sweden as well as the Aland Islands, Danish West Indies, the Faroes and Greenland.
Supersedes in part (in 1980): Stanley Gibbons Foreign Stamp Catalogue. Europe (0305-8085)
Published by: Stanley Gibbons Publications Ltd., 399 Strand, London, WC2R 0LX, United Kingdom. TEL 44-207-8368444, FAX 44-207-8367342, kfinney@stanleygibbons.co.uk.

769.56 USA
SCANDINAVIAN PHILATELIC FOUNDATION. NEWSLETTER. Text in English. 1980. s-a. USD 10 (effective 2000). **Document type:** *Newsletter.* **Description:** Focuses on informing members of current projects in the field of translating Scandinavian area philatelic articles into English.
Published by: Scandinavian Philatelic Foundation, PO Box 6716, Thousand Oaks, CA 91359. Ed. George B Koplowitz. Circ: 150 (paid).

769.56 CHE
SCHWEIZER BRIEFMARKEN-ZEITUNG. Text in German. 1889. 9/yr. CHF 42 (effective 2008). adv. **Document type:** *Magazine, Consumer.*
Published by: Verband Schweizerischer Philatelistenvereine, Biberlinstr 6, Zurich, 8032, Switzerland. TEL 41-44-3122877, FAX 41-44-3122877, sekretariat@vsphv.ch. Ed. Hans Schwarz. Adv. contact Susanne Minder. Circ: 23,000.

769.56 USA ISSN 0737-0741
HE6187
SCOTT STAMP MONTHLY. Text in English. 1920. m. USD 31.97 domestic; USD 46.97 in Canada; USD 61.97 elsewhere (effective 2008). adv. bk.rev. illus.; tr.lit. Index. back issues avail.; reprints avail. **Document type:** *Magazine, Consumer.* **Description:** Aims to entertain and educate readers on the hobby of stamp collecting through well illustrated, informative features and how-to articles.
Supersedes in part (until 1982): Scott's Monthly Stamp Journal; Which was formerly: Scott's Monthly Journal (0036-9454)
Related titles: Online - full text ed.: ISSN 1543-9348.
Indexed: G06, G07, G08, I05.
—Ingenta.
Published by: Scott Publishing Company (Subsidiary of: Amos Publishing), 911 Vandemark Rd, PO Box 828, Sidney, OH 45365. TEL 937-498-0802, 800-572-6885, FAX 937-498-0807, http://www.scottonline.com. Ed. Donna Houseman. Adv. contact Patty Wheeler. B&W page USD 1,353, color page USD 1,628; trim 7.75 x 10.5. Circ: 24,183 (paid).

769.56 USA ISSN 0161-5084
HE6226
SCOTT STANDARD POSTAGE CATALOGUE. Text in English. a. USD 57.99 domestic; USD 68.98 in Canada (effective 2007).
Related titles: CD-ROM ed.: ISSN 1555-1776.
Published by: Scott Publishing Company (Subsidiary of: Amos Publishing), 911 Vandemark Rd, PO Box 828, Sidney, OH 45365. TEL 937-498-0802, 800-572-6885, FAX 937-498-0807, http://www.scottonline.com.

769 GBR
SCOTTISH STAMP NEWS. Text in English. 1970. m. GBP 3.50. adv. bk.rev. illus. index.
Published by: Stanley K. Hunter Ed. & Pub., 34 Gray St, Glasgow, G3 7TY, United Kingdom. Circ: 120.

769.56 USA
SCOTT'S SPECIALIZED CATALOGUE OF U.S. STAMPS. Text in English. 1923. a. USD 57.99 domestic; USD 68.98 in Canada (effective 2007). adv. **Document type:** *Catalog.*
Published by: Scott Publishing Company (Subsidiary of: Amos Publishing), 911 Vandemark Rd, PO Box 828, Sidney, OH 45365. TEL 937-498-0802, 800-572-6885, FAX 937-498-0807, http://www.scottonline.com. Ed. James Kloetzel. Pub., R&P Stuart Morrissey. Adv. contact Angela Nolte.

769.56 USA
SCOTT'S STANDARD POSTAGE STAMP CATALOGUE. Text in English. 1867. a. (in 5 vols.). USD 57.99 per vol. domestic; USD 68.98 per vol. in Canada (effective 2007). adv. **Document type:** *Catalog.*
Published by: Scott Publishing Company (Subsidiary of: Amos Publishing), 911 Vandemark Rd, PO Box 828, Sidney, OH 45365. TEL 937-498-0802, 800-572-6885, FAX 937-498-0807, http://www.scottonline.com. Ed. James Kloetzel. Pub., R&P Stuart Morrissey. Adv. contact Angela Nolte.

769.56 USA
SEAL NEWS. Text in English. 1946. q. USD 10 domestic membership; USD 12 in Canada & Mexico membership; USD 17 elsewhere membership (effective 2000). adv. bk.rev. illus. index. **Document type:** *Newsletter.* **Description:** Researches worldwide charity seal producing organizations to help members identify seals for their collections.
Media: Duplicated (not offset).
Published by: Christmas Seal & Charity Stamp Society, c/o Florence H Wright, Sec y Treas, Box 18615, Rochester, NY 14618-8615. Ed., Adv. contact Joseph D Ward Jr. Circ: 400 (paid).

769.56 USA ISSN 0048-9891
HE6187
SEAPOSTER. Text in English. 1939. bi-m. looseleaf. USD 10 domestic membership; USD 15 foreign membership (effective 2004). bk.rev. 18 p./no.; back issues avail. **Document type:** *Newsletter, Consumer.* **Description:** Aims to encourage the study and collecting of all merchant marine markings and postmarks.
Published by: Maritime Postmark Society, PO Box 497, Wadsworth, OH 44282. postcard@judnick.com, http://www.judnick.com/Judnick/MaritimePostmarkSociety.htm. Ed. Tom Hirschinger. Circ: 175 (paid).

SEMPRE PRONTO; mensario escotista. *see* EDUCATION

769.56 CHN ISSN 1004-6321
SHANGHAI JIYOU/SHANGHAI PHILATELY. Text in Chinese. 1982. m. USD 28.80 (effective 2009). **Document type:** *Journal, Academic/Scholarly.*
Related titles: Online - full text ed.
—East View.
Published by: Shanghai Shi Jiyou Xiehui/Shanghai Association of Philately, 698, Nanjing Xilu, 7/F, Shanghai, 200041, China. TEL 86-21-62725902.

769.56 ZAF
SOUTH AFRICA. PHILATELIC SERVICES AND INTERSAPA. PHILATELIC BULLETIN. Text in Afrikaans, English. 1947. 44/yr. free. **Document type:** *Bulletin.* **Description:** News of forthcoming stamp issues, with technical and historical notes.
Formerly: South Africa. Philatelic Services. Philatelic Bulletin
Published by: Philatelic Services and Intersapa, Private Bag X505, Pretoria, 0001, South Africa. FAX 286025. Circ: 67,000.

769.56 ZAF ISSN 0038-2566
SOUTH AFRICAN PHILATELIST. Text mainly in English; Text occasionally in Afrikaans. 1923. bi-m. ZAR 140, USD 23 (effective 2000). adv. bk.rev. bibl.; charts; illus.; mkt.; stat. index. 36 p./no.; **Document type:** *Magazine, Consumer.* **Description:** Concerns the philately of southern Africa.
Indexed: ISAP, SJI.
Published by: Philatelic Federation of Southern Africa, PO Box 2789, Cape Town, 8000, South Africa. TEL 27-21-238763, grutter@dieburger.com. Ed., R&P Andries van der Walt. Adv. contact Jonas Michelson. Circ: 3,000 (controlled).

P

769.56 CAN ISSN 1922-7299
STAMP AND COIN AUCTION. Text in English. 1977. bi-m. back issues avail. **Document type:** *Trade.* **Description:** Provides information about auction and private treaty offers, specials, etc.
Former titles (until 2009): Coin & Stamp Sale (1922-7280); (until 2008): Stamp and Coin Sale (1919-8752); (until 2002): Stamp and Coin Auction (1919-8744); (until 2001): Coin & Stamp Auction (1919-8736); (until 1987): Stamp Auction (1919-8728); (until 1977): Summer Auction (1919-871X)
Published by: John H. Talman Auctions, Adelaide St, PO Box 70, Toronto, ON M5C 2H8, Canada. TEL 416-363-9997, 877-375-5229, FAX 416-863-0850, 877-753-7338, jtalman@interlog.com.

769.56 USA
STAMP AND COIN DIGEST. Text in English. 1980. q. USD 1.50 per issue.
Published by: M & H Publications, 38 S Madison Ave, Spring Valley, NY 10977. Ed. Martin R Schranz.

STAMP & COIN MART. *see* HOBBIES

769.56 USA
STAMP EXCHANGERS ANNUAL DIRECTORY. Text in English. 1963. a. USD 22 (effective 2001). adv. bk.rev. charts; illus. **Document type:** *Directory.*
Published by: Levine Publications, PO Box 9090, Trenton, NJ 08650. Ed. L Jan Olssen. Circ: 963.

769.56 GBR ISSN 0038-9277
STAMP LOVER. Text in English. 1908. bi-m. GBP 17 to non-members; GBP 2.50 per issue to non-members; free to members (effective 2009). adv. bk.rev. illus. index, cum.index approx. every 10 yrs. back issues avail. **Document type:** *Magazine, Trade.* **Description:** Contains a selection of articles on various aspects of the hobby, news about the Society's activities, reports on recent philatelic auctions and details about forthcoming philatelic exhibitions at home and abroad.
Indexed: SJI.
Published by: National Philatelic Society, c/o The British Postal Museum & Archive, Freeling House, Phoenix Pl, London, WC1X 0DL, United Kingdom. TEL 44-20-72392571, nps@ukphilately.org.uk. Ed. Michael L Goodman TEL 44-20-85682433.

769.56 GBR ISSN 0307-6679
STAMP MAGAZINE. Text in English. 1934. m. GBP 29.99 domestic; USD 141.30 in US & Canada; EUR 74 in Europe; GBP 71 elsewhere; GBP 3.45 newsstand/cover (effective 2009). adv. bk.rev. illus. back issues avail.; reprints avail. **Document type:** *Magazine, Consumer.* **Description:** Provides information and news, technical guidance, a list of expositions, and a market catalog for the serious and avocational philatelist in the UK.
Incorporates (1938-1940): World Stamp Digest (0038-9307); (1967-19??): Stamp Weekly
Related titles: Online - full text ed.
Indexed: SJI.
Published by: I P C Country & Leisure Media Ltd. (Subsidiary of: I P C Media Ltd.), Leon House, 233 High St, Croydon, CR9 1HZ, United Kingdom. TEL 44-20-87268000, http://www.ipcmedia.com. Ed. Guy Thomas TEL 44-20-87268243. Pub. Clive Birch TEL 44-20-87268235. Adv. contact Jay Jones TEL 44-20-87268229. color page GBP 980, B&W page GBP 715; 181 x 265. **Subscr. to:** Rockwood House, Perrymount Rd, Haywards Heath RH16 3DH, United Kingdom. TEL 44-1444-475675, FAX 44-1444-445599, IPCsubs@quadrantsubs.com, http://www.magazinesdirect.co.uk. **Dist. by:** MarketForce UK Ltd, The Blue Fin Bldg, 3rd Fl, 110 Southwark St, London SE1 0SU, United Kingdom. TEL 44-20-31483300, FAX 44-20-31488105, salesinnovation@marketforce.co.uk, http://www.marketforce.co.uk/.

769.56 AUS ISSN 1448-1014
STAMP NEWS AUSTRALASIA; incorporating the australian stamp monthly. Text in English. 1954. m. AUD 89.50 domestic; AUD 8.95 newsstand/cover domestic; NZD 9.50 newsstand/cover in New Zealand; CAD 11 newsstand/cover in Canada; USD 9 newsstand/cover in United States; GBP 5.50 newsstand/cover in United Kingdom; EUR 7 newsstand/cover in Europe (effective 2009). adv. bk.rev. back issues avail. **Document type:** *Magazine, Consumer.*
Former titles (until 2003): Stamp News (1324-5201); Which incorporated (1930-1991): Australian Stamp Monthly (0005-0296); (until 1991): Stamp News Australasia; (until 1989): Stamp News (0038-9293)
Published by: Stamp News Pty Ltd., PO Box 1290, Upwey, VIC 3158, Australia. TEL 61-3-97522677, FAX 61-3-97582488, info@stampnews.com.au. Ed., Adv. contact Kevin Morgan. color page AUD 995; trim 210 x 297. Circ: 15,000.

769.56 USA ISSN 0038-9358
HE6187
STAMPS; the weekly magazine of philately. Text in English. 1932. w. USD 23.50. adv. bk.rev. illus.; mkt. q. index. reprints avail. **Document type:** *Newspaper, Consumer.*
Related titles: Microform ed.: (from PQC); Online - full text ed.
Indexed: A22, G05, G06, G07, G08, G09, MagInd, P02, P10, P48, P53, P54, PQC, SJI.
Published by: American Publishing Company of New York (Subsidiary of: H.L. Lindquist Publications), 85 Canisteo St, Hornell, NY 14843. TEL 607-324-2212, FAX 607-324-1753. Ed. Denise M Axtell. adv.: B&W page USD 780, color page USD 1,030; trim 14 x 11.25. Circ: 18,500.

769.56 USA
STAMPS.NET; the Internet magazine for stamp collectors. Text in English. 1998. irreg. **Document type:** *Magazine, Consumer.*
Media: Online - full content.
Published by: Champion Stamp Company Inc., 432 W 54th St, New York, NY 10019. http://www.stamps.net. Ed. Randy L Neil.

769.56 IND ISSN 0972-3587
STAMPS OF INDIA. Text in English. 2000. w. free (effective 2011). back issues avail. **Document type:** *Magazine, Trade.*
Media: Online - full text. **Related titles:** E-mail ed.
Address: 18 School Ln, 1st Fl, New Delhi, 110 001, India. TEL 91-11-3320052, FAX 91-11-3356828.

769.56 GBR ISSN 2044-902X
▼ **STAMPS OF PAULOVIA.** Text in English. 2010. a. GBP 3, EUR 3.54 per issue (effective 2011). **Document type:** *Trade.*
Published by: Paulovia Philatelic Bureau, c/o 6 Norton Ave, Canvey Island, Essex SS8 8LQ, United Kingdom. TEL 44-7531-825570, FAX 44-7531-825570, stamps@store.paulovia.org.

769.56 GBR ISSN 0953-6027
STANLEY GIBBONS COLLECT CHANNEL ISLANDS AND ISLE OF MAN STAMPS. Text in English. 1972. a. GBP 24.95 per issue (effective 2010). adv. **Document type:** *Catalog, Consumer.* **Description:** Covers all the stamps (complete sets) of the Independent Postal Administrations of Guernsey, Isle of Man and Jersey including detailed information, listing first day covers, presentation packs, stamp cards and gutter pairs.
Formerly (until 1987): Collect Channel Islands and Isle of Man Stamps (0265-5608); Which was formed by the merger of (1976-1984): Collect Isle of Man Stamps (0307-7098); (1972-1984): Collect Channel Islands Stamps (0306-5103)
Published by: Stanley Gibbons Publications Ltd., 399 Strand, London, WC2R 0LX, United Kingdom. TEL 44-207-8368444, FAX 44-207-8367342, kfinney@stanleygibbons.co.uk.

769.56 GBR ISSN 0081-4210
STANLEY GIBBONS SIMPLIFIED CATALOGUE. STAMPS OF THE WORLD. Text in English. 1934; N.S. 1989. irreg. (in 5 vols.), latest 2009. GBP 175 per issue (effective 2010). adv. illus. **Document type:** *Catalog, Consumer.* **Description:** Provides general and thematic stamp collector with collection of over 260,000 stamps with 60,000 illustrations.
Formerly (until 1970): Stanley Gibbons Simplified Stamp Catalogue
Published by: Stanley Gibbons Publications Ltd., 399 Strand, London, WC2R 0LX, United Kingdom. TEL 44-207-8368444, FAX 44-207-8367342, kfinney@stanleygibbons.co.uk.

769.569171241 GBR ISSN 1751-1380
STANLEY GIBBONS STAMP CATALOGUE. COMMONWEALTH & BRITISH EMPIRE STAMPS, 1840-1970. Text in English. 189?. a. GBP 72.50 per issue (effective 2010). back issues avail. **Document type:** *Catalog, Consumer.* **Description:** Features stamp issues of the Commonwealth and British Empire 1840-1970 from Queen Victoria to George VI.
Former titles (until 2002): Stanley Gibbons Stamp Catalogue. Part 1. British Commonwealth (0142-9752); (until 1979): Stanley Gibbons British Commonwealth Stamp Catalogue (0068-1903)
Published by: Stanley Gibbons Ltd., 391 Strand, London, WC2R 0LX, United Kingdom. TEL 44-207-8368444, FAX 44-207-8367342, info@stanleygibbons.co.uk, http://www.stanleygibbons.com/.

769.56 USA ISSN 1542-0523
HJ5321.Z7
STATE REVENUE NEWS. Text in English. 1957. q. bk.rev. illus. cum.index: 1957-1976. 32 p./no. 3 cols./p.; back issues avail. **Document type:** *Journal, Academic/Scholarly.* **Description:** Provides research articles, current news, information on stamps and licenses used by states that show payment of various taxes.
Formerly (until 19??): State Revenue Newsletter (0883-6760)
Published by: State Revenue Society, PO Box 270184, Oklahoma City, OK 73137. ivesters@swbell.net. Ed. Scott Troutman.

769.56 USA ISSN 1529-4552
SYNCOPATED PERFS. Text in English. 1967. bi-m. USD 4 membership (effective 2005). adv. 6 p./no.; **Document type:** *Newsletter, Consumer.* **Description:** Covers philately issues in the Greater Cincinnati, OH region.
Published by: Greater Cincinnati Philatelic Society, 6508 Craigland Ct, Cincinnati, OH 45230-2821. TEL 513-231-4208, FAX 513-231-9430, rmaifeld@fuse.net. Ed., R&P Ronald Maifeld. Circ: 157 (controlled).

769.56 796.352 USA
TEE TIME. Text in English. 1987. q. USD 10. adv. **Description:** Focuses on all aspects of the game on stamps, including singles, errors, proofs, blocks, covers, and postal stationery.
Published by: International Philatelic Golf Society, c/o Kevin Hadlock, 447 Skyline Dr, Orange, CT 06477. Ed. Stuart MacKenzie. Circ: 250.

769.56 USA
TELL (WILLIAMSBURG). Text in English. bi-m. adv. bk.rev.
Formed by the merger of: Helvetia Alphorn; Helvetia Herald
Published by: American Helvetia Philatelic Society, c/o Richard T Hall, PO Box 15053, Asheville, NC 28813-0053. http://www.swiss-stamps.org. Ed. George Struble. Circ: 550.

769.56 USA ISSN 0893-2670
HE6204.T4
THE TEXAS PHILATELIST. Text in English. 1963. bi-m. USD 12 to members (effective 2000). adv. bk.rev. **Document type:** *Newsletter.* **Description:** Provides members with articles on stamp collecting and association news and bulletins.
Published by: Texas Philatelic Association, Inc., 10325 Little Sugar Creek, Converse, TX 78109-2409. TEL 210-566-1436. Ed., R&P, Adv. contact Jane King Fohn. Circ: 400 (paid).

769.56 USA ISSN 0198-7992
HE6185.T45
THAI PHILATELY. Text in English. 1978. 3/yr. bk.rev. index. back issues avail. **Document type:** *Journal, Academic/Scholarly.* **Description:** Covers all aspects of the postage stamp and postal history of Thailand.
Related titles: Online - full text ed.
Indexed: SJI.
Published by: Society for Thai Philately, PO Box 44142, Oklahoma City, OK 73144.

769.56 CHN
TIANJIN JIYOU/TIANJIN PHILATELY. Text in Chinese. 1983. q. CNY 1.10 per issue. adv.
Published by: Tianjin Jiyou Xiehui/Tianjin Philately Association, 89 Jiefang Beilu, Tianjin 300041, China. TEL 314613. Ed. Jia Yingdong. Circ: 20,000.

769.56 FRA ISSN 1620-252X
TIMBRES MAGAZINE. Text in French. 2000. m. (11/yr). EUR 50 (effective 2008). **Document type:** *Magazine, Consumer.*
Published by: Timbropresse, 6 Rue du Sentier, Paris, Cedex 02 75080, France. TEL 33-1-55349255.

769.56 USA ISSN 0049-4135
TOPICAL STAMP HANDBOOKS. Text in English. 1951. irreg., latest vol.130, 1996. price varies.
Published by: American Topical Association, Inc., PO Box 8, Carterville, IL 62918. TEL 618-985-5131, americantopical@msn.com, http://www.americantopicalassn.org. Ed. George Griffenhagen. R&P Paul Tyler.

769.56 USA ISSN 0040-9332
HE6187
TOPICAL TIME. Text in English. 1949. bi-m. USD 25 domestic; USD 33 foreign (effective 2011). adv. bk.rev. charts; illus.; mkt. cum.index: 1949-1959, then every 5 yrs. 96 p./no. 2 cols./p.; back issues avail.; reprints avail. **Document type:** *Magazine, Consumer.* **Description:** Includes articles, columns, checklists and topical information.
Indexed: SJI.
Published by: American Topical Association, Inc., PO Box 8, Carterville, IL 62918. TEL 618-985-5131, americantopical@msn.com. Ed. Wayne L Youngblood. Circ: 3,500 (paid).

796.56 USA
TOPICAL WOMAN. Text in English. 1979. q. looseleaf. USD 8 domestic; USD 12 foreign (effective 2000). adv. bibl. index. 12 p./no. 2 cols./p.; back issues avail. **Document type:** *Newsletter.* **Description:** Features biographies of women on stamps, women stamp designers and engravers, collecting and exhibiting tips, and lists of new issues and information on new bio materials recently published - (Bibliography).
Published by: Women on Stamps Study Unit, 515 Ocean Ave, No 608S, Santa Monica, CA 90402. FAX 310-899-3927. Ed., Pub., R&P, Adv. contact Davida Kristy TEL 310-394-5587. Circ: 100.

769.56 USA ISSN 0041-1175
HE6185.U5
TRANSIT POSTMARK COLLECTOR. Text in English. 194?. bi-m. looseleaf. free to members (effective 2011). bk.rev. illus. 24 p./no.; back issues avail. **Document type:** *Journal, Academic/Scholarly.* **Description:** Publishes articles on postal history of mail postmarked in transit on trains, street cars, busses, boats, RFD wagons, etc. Also includes society news.
Formerly (until 1966): H P O Notes
Published by: Mobile Post Office Society, c/o Douglas N Clark, PO Box 427, Marston Mills, MA 02648. TEL 508-428-9132, dnc@math.uga.edu, http://www.eskimo.com/~rkunz/mposhome.html.

789.56 GBR ISSN 0267-789X
THE TRANSVAAL PHILATELIST. Text in English. 1966. q. GBP 5 per issue to non-members; free to members (effective 2009). back issues avail. **Document type:** *Journal, Academic/Scholarly.* **Description:** Contains information on philatelic research.
Published by: Transvaal Study Circle, c/o Jeff Woolgar, Treasurer, PO Box 379, Gravesend, DA12 9EW, United Kingdom.

769.56 737 USA ISSN 0882-1674
HE6185.U45
TRIDENT - VISNYK. Text in English. 1952. bi-m. free to members (effective 2010). bk.rev. back issues avail. **Document type:** *Newsletter, Trade.* **Description:** Ukrainian philatelic and numismatic news and events.
Formerly: Visnyk
Published by: Ukrainian Philatelic and Numismatic Society, PO Box 303, Southfields, NY 10975. yurko@frontiernet.net.

769.56 USA ISSN 0148-673X
TRUMPETER. Text in English. 1972. q. USD 22 (effective 2000). adv. bk.rev.; music rev.; rec.rev. illus.; tr.lit. index. 36 p./no. 1 cols./p.; back issues avail.; reprints avail. **Document type:** *Newsletter.*
Media: Duplicated (not offset).
Indexed: Perlslam, SJI.
Published by: Croatian Philatelic Society, PO Box 696, Fritch, TX 79036-0696. TEL 806-857-0129, http://www.dalmatia.net/cps/. Ed., R&P Eck Spahich. adv.: B&W page USD 50; trim 11 x 8.5. Circ: 700.

769.56 USA ISSN 0279-6139
HE6188
U S C S LOG. Text in English. 1932. m. USD 16 domestic; USD 21 foreign (effective 1999). adv. bk.rev. **Document type:** *Newsletter, Consumer.* **Description:** Dedicated to the collection and study of naval and maritime postal history.
Published by: Universal Ship Cancellation Society, PO Box 981, Healdsburg, CA 95448. TEL 904-672-2112. Ed. Richard D Jones. R&P, Adv. contact Robert D Rawlins. Circ: 1,400 (paid).

769.56 USA ISSN 1082-9423
HE6187
U. S. STAMP NEWS. Text in English. 1995. m. USD 26.95 for 2 yrs. (effective 2007). **Document type:** *Magazine, Consumer.*
Related titles: Online - full text ed.
Indexed: H20, M02, T02.
Published by: Philatelic Communications Corp., PO Box 5050, White Plains, NY 10602. TEL 800-635-3351, stampnews@mindspring.com. Pub., R&P, Adv. contact John F Dunn.

769.56 USA
U S TAX-STAMP REVIEW. Text in English. 1978. bi-m. USD 10 to members. adv. bk.rev. illus. **Document type:** *Newsletter.* **Description:** Covers revenue and Cinderella stamps issued by the United States and its possessions. Promotes issuance of catalogs and listings.
Formerly (until 1995): I C A R Newsletter
Published by: Interstate Cinderellans and Revenuers Educational Club, PO Box 9128, San Jose, CA 95157-9128. TEL 408-296-4171. Ed. Elbert S A Hubbard. Circ: 100.

760 USA ISSN 0198-6252
HE6185.U45
UKRAINIAN PHILATELIST. Text in English, Ukrainian. 1951. s-a. free to members (effective 2010). bk.rev. back issues avail.; reprints avail. **Document type:** *Journal, Trade.* **Description:** Contains articles and studies on Ukrainian philately and numismatics.
Formerly (until 1975): Ukrayins'kyi Filatelist
Published by: Ukrainian Philatelic and Numismatic Society, PO Box 303, Southfields, NY 10975. yurko@frontiernet.net.

760 USA
UNITED NATIONS POSTAL ADMINISTRATION PHILATELIC BULLETIN. Text in English. 1993. 9/yr. **Document type:** *Bulletin.*
Published by: United Nations Postal Administration, PO BOX 5900, GRAND CENTRAL STA, New York, NY 10163-9992.

794 USA ISSN 0164-923X
HE6187
THE UNITED STATES SPECIALIST. Text in English. 1930. m. bk.rev. illus. **Document type:** *Journal, Academic/Scholarly.* **Description:** Promotes the study of United States stamps.
Formerly (until 19??): Bureau Specialist

Published by: United States Stamp Society, c/o Larry Ballantyne, PO Box 6634, Katy, TX 77491.

769.56 URY ISSN 0042-1189
URUGUAY FILATELICO. Text in Spanish. 1928. 4/yr. USD 5. illus.
Published by: Club Filatelico del Uruguay, Box 518, Montevideo, Uruguay. Ed. Elias Casal Gari.

789.56 ITA ISSN 1120-6934
VACCARI MAGAZINE; rivista di informazione filatelica e storico postale. Text in Italian; Text occasionally in English. 1989. s-a. EUR 35 domestic (effective 2009). adv. bk.rev. 112 p./no.; back issues avail. **Document type:** *Magazine, Consumer.*
Related titles: Online - full content ed.
Published by: Vaccari Srl, Via M Buonarroti 46, Vignola, MO 41058, Italy. TEL 39-059-764106, FAX 39-059-760157, http://www.vaccari.it. Ed. Mr. Paolo Vaccari. R&P, Adv. contact Mrs. Valeria Vaccari.

769.56 PRT ISSN 1647-1970
▼ **VALE DO NEIVA FILATELICO.** Text in Portuguese. 2009. s-a. **Document type:** *Magazine, Consumer.*
Published by: Associacao de Filatelia e Coleccionismo do Vale do Neiva, Rua dos Passionistas, Barroselas, Viana do Castelo 4905-394, Portugal. TEL 351-914-201352, FAX 351-696-072614, http://www.filaneiva.com.

769.56 USA ISSN 1945-1504
HE6185.V3
VATICAN NOTES. Text in English. 1953. bi-m. USD 9. adv. bk.rev.
Related titles: Online - full text ed.: ISSN 1945-1512.
Published by: Vatican Philatelic Society, 3348 Clubhouse Rd, Virginia Beach, VA 23452. TEL 804-486-3614. Ed. Daniel A Piazza. Circ: 600.

769.56 NLD ISSN 1574-7271
VERENIGING VOOR KINDERPOSTZEGELS EN MAXIMAFILIE. BULLETIN. Text in Dutch. 3/yr.
Formerly (until 1999): Kontaktgroep voor het Kind en Maximafilie. Bulletin (1380-0000)
Published by: Vereniging voor Kinderpostzegels en Maximafilie, Gaard 3, Beuningen, 6641 WN, Netherlands. TEL 31-24-6771262, p.klaassen5@hetnet.nl.

769.56 USA ISSN 1053-9204
HE6185.U7
VERMONT PHILATELIST. Text in English. 1956. q. free to members. adv. bk.rev. cum.index: nos.1-60. **Document type:** *Magazine, Consumer.*
Published by: Vermont Philatelic Society, c/o Bill Lizotte, 98 Brooklyn Heights #5, PO Box 451, Morrisville, VT 05661-5907. http://www.vermontps.org/. Circ: (controlled).

765.56 CAN ISSN 1074-5890
WATERCRAFT PHILATELY. Text in English. 1954. bi-m. looseleaf. USD 15 in North America; USD 22 elsewhere (effective 2006). adv. bk.rev. 14 p./no.; back issues avail. **Document type:** *Newsletter.* **Description:** Features histories of watercraft depicted on stamps.
Formerly: Ships on Stamps Newsletter
Published by: (Robert P. Stuckert USA), American Topical Association, Ships on Stamps Unit, 367 McAnolly St, Trail, BC VIR 3R3, Canada. TEL 817-274-1181, FAX 817-274-1184. Ed., Pub. Dan Rodlie. Circ: 250 (paid and controlled).

769.56 DEU ISSN 0948-6097
WELTRAUM-PHILATELIE. Text in German; Summaries in English. 1976. q. EUR 25 membership (effective 2010). adv. back issues avail. **Document type:** *Magazine, Consumer.*
Published by: Weltraum Philatelie e.V., c/o Florian Noller, Postfach 1249, Weil der Stadt, 71256, Germany. TEL 49-151-23507761, Florian@spaceflori.com. Ed. P Wilhelm. Circ: 300.

769.56 USA ISSN 1529-6377
WORLD POSTAL STATIONERY - NEW ISSUE REPORT. Text in English. 1961. 3/yr. USD 12 domestic; USD 16 foreign (effective 2005). **Document type:** *Newsletter.* **Description:** Lists of new postal stationery philatelic releases by governments of the world, with pricing in mint, first day of issue condition.
Former titles: New Issue Report; (until 1983): Entire Truth
Published by: Classic Philatelics, PO Box 5637, Huntington Beach, CA 92615. TEL 714-968-1717, FAX 714-968-6704. Ed. Pat Feiner. R&P Mel Feiner. Circ: 250.

769.56 USA
YUBA - SUTTER PHILATELIC SOCIETY. NEWSLETTER. Text in English. 1980 (vol.4). m. **Document type:** *Newsletter.*
Published by: Yuba - Sutter Philatelic Society, 11222 Loma Rica Rd, Marysville, CA 95901.

769.56 USA ISSN 0843-7394
HE6187
YULE LOG. Text in English. 1969. bi-m. USD 15 domestic membership; USD 22 foreign membership (effective 2003). adv. bk.rev. illus. **Document type:** *Newsletter, Consumer.* **Description:** Features articles on Christmas philately for collectors. Includes cancel and new issue reports and a 100 lot auction.
Published by: Christmas Philatelic Club, 312 Northwood Dr, Lexington, KY 40505-2104. cpc@hwcn.org. Ed., R&P Linda Lawrence. Circ: 420.

769.56 JPN
YUSHU; philatelic magazine. Text in Japanese. m. JPY 8,800 (effective 2000).
Indexed: ChemAb.
Published by: Japan Philatelic Society Foundation, PO Box 96, Toshima, Tokyo-to 170-8668, Japan.

769.56 CHN ISSN 1002-6789
ZHONGGUO JIYOU/CHINA PHILATELY. Text in Chinese. 1982. m. USD 20.40; USD 1.70 newsstand/cover (effective 2001). adv. back issues avail. **Document type:** *Consumer.* **Description:** News of Chinese stamps, philatelic findings, trends in China and abroad, philatelic activities, and latest market values.
Published by: China Philately, 14 Xizhaosi St, Chongwen District, Beijing, 100061, China. FAX 86-10-6713-2749. Ed. Wang Anjun. Adv. contact Huang Yami. B&W page USD 500, color page USD 1,500. Circ: 30,000. **Dist. by:** China International Book Trading Corp, 35 Chegongzhuang Xilu, Haidian District, PO Box 399, Beijing 100044, China. TEL 86-10-68412045, FAX 86-10-68412023, cibtc@mail.cibtc.com.cn, http://www.cibtc.com.cn.

769.56 CHN
ZHONGGUO JIYOU BAO/CHINA PHILATELY NEWS. Text in Chinese. 2/w. CNY 36 (effective 2009). **Document type:** *Newspaper, Consumer.*
Published by: Zhongha Quanguo Jiyou Lianhehui, 11, Anyuan Lu, 3/F, Youdian Xinwen Dasha, Beijing, 100029, China. TEL 86-10-64963010, FAX 86-10-64982815. **Dist. by:** China International Book Trading Corp, 35 Chegongzhuang Xilu, Haidian District, PO Box 399, Beijing 100044, China. TEL 86-10-68412045, FAX 86-10-68412023, cibtc@mail.cibtc.com.cn, http://www.cibtc.com.cn.

769.56 TWN
ZHONGGUO YOUKAN/CHINA PHILATELIC MAGAZINE. Text in Chinese. 1954. s-a. **Document type:** *Magazine, Consumer.*
Published by: Zhongguo Jiyou Xiehui/Chinese Taipei Philatelic Society, PO Box 18, Taipei, 231, Taiwan. Ed. Wang Yun Chiu.

769.56 ZWE
ZIMBABWE STAMP CATALOGUE. Text in English. a. **Document type:** *Catalog.*
Published by: Zimbabwe Stamp Co. (Pvt.) Ltd., PO Box 200, Harare, Zimbabwe. Ed. D G Pollard.

769.56 USA
ZIP ME NEWS. Text in English. m. USD 5.
Published by: Zippy Collectors Club, Inc., 2021 W 9th, Emporia, KS 66801.

769.56 NLD ISSN 1874-4117
ZUIDHOLLANDSE VERENIGING VAN POSTZEGELVERZAMELAARS. MEDEDELINGENBLAD. Text in Dutch. 5/yr.
Formerly (until 2003): ZuidHollandse Vereniging van Postzegelverzamelaars. Maandblad (1384-7295)
Published by: ZuidHollandse Vereniging van Postzegelverzamelaars, Beijerland 40, Zoetermeer, 2716 CN, Netherlands. TEL 31-79-3515336, http://www.zhpv.nl. Ed. Max Molenaar.

769.56 USA ISSN 0363-6542
HE6185.U5
1869 TIMES. Text in English. 1975. q. membership. adv. bk.rev.
Published by: U S 1869 Pictorial Research Associates, Inc., c/o Jonathan Rose, Ed, 30 Golf Rd, Pleasanton, CA 94566. Circ: 300.

PHILATELY—Abstracting, Bibliographies, Statistics

769.56 NZL ISSN 1174-3921
ROYAL PHILATELIC SOCIETY OF NEW ZEALAND. BIBLIOGRAPHIC SERIES. Text in English. irreg. NZD 15 per issue to members; NZD 20 per issue to non-members (effective 2009). **Document type:** *Monographic series, Consumer.*
Published by: Royal Philatelic Society of New Zealand, PO Box 1269, Wellington, 6140, New Zealand. TEL 64-4-4722590, FAX 64-4-4725426, rpsnz@orcon.net.nz, http://www.rpsnz.org.nz/.

PHILOSOPHY

see also RELIGIONS AND THEOLOGY

111.85 CAN
A E: CANADIAN AESTHETICS JOURNAL - REVUE CANADIENNE D'ESTHETIQUE. Text in English, French. q. **Document type:** *Journal, Academic/Scholarly.*
Media: Online - full content.
Published by: Canadian Society for Aesthetics - Societe Canadienne d'Esthetique, Dept de Philosophie, Universite du Quebec a Trois-Rivieres, C.P. 500, Trois-Rivieres, PQ G9A 5H7, Canada. Ed. Claude Therien.

100 200 USA
A F S NEWSLETTER. Text in English. 1992. m. USD 15 domestic; USD 20 in Canada; USD 25 elsewhere (effective 2000). adv. bk.rev. **Document type:** *Newsletter.* **Description:** Aims to educate the public about freethinkers, non-theists and church-state separation.
Published by: Atlanta Freethought Society, PO Box 813392, Smyrna, GA 30081-3392. TEL 770-641-2903. Ed. Steve Yothment. R&P, Adv. contact Ed Buckner TEL 770-432-3049. Circ: 225 (paid); 300 (controlled).

100 AUS ISSN 1838-5869
▼ **THE A I D C BULLETIN.** (Australian International Disputes Centre) Text in English. 2010. q. free (effective 2011). **Document type:** *Bulletin, Trade.*
Media: Online - full text.
Published by: Australian International Disputes Centre, Level 16, 1 Castlereagh St, Sydney, NSW 2000, Australia. TEL 61-2-92390700, FAX 61-2-92237053, LynneRichards@disputescentre.com.au.

▼ **A J O B NEUROSCIENCE.** (American Journal of Bioethics) *see* MEDICAL SCIENCES—Psychiatry And Neurology

▼ **A J O B PRIMARY RESEARCH.** *see* MEDICAL SCIENCES

A L T E X. ALTERNATIVES TO ANIMAL EXPERIMENTATION. *see* MEDICAL SCIENCES—Experimental Medicine, Laboratory Technique

182.2 BRA ISSN 0103-4898
A LAMPADA. Text in English, Portuguese, Spanish. 1931. q. free. bk.rev. abstr.; bibl. **Document type:** *Journal, Academic/Scholarly.*
Published by: Instituto Neo Pitagorico, CP 1047, Curitiba, Parana 80011-970, Brazil. neo@pitagorico.org.br, http://www.pitagorico.org.br. Circ: 500.

100 USA ISSN 2155-9708
A P A NEWSLETTERS (ONLINE). Text in English. s-a. free (effective 2010). adv. bk.rev. **Document type:** *Newsletter, Academic/Scholarly.* **Description:** Contains articles, course outlines and announcements in eight separate newsletters: Black Experience; Computers; Feminism; Law; Medicine; Teaching; International Cooperation; and Lesbian, Gay, Bisexual & Transgender Issues.
Former titles (until 2004): A P A Newsletters (Print); (until 1998): A P A Newsletters on the Black Experience, Computer Use, Feminism, Law, Medicine, Teaching (1067-9464); (until 1992): Newsletters on the Black Experience, Computer Use, Feminism, Law, Medicine, Teaching (1067-9456); (until 1991): A P A Newsletters on Computer Use, Feminism, Law, Medicine, Teaching (1049-8788); (until 1989): A P A Newsletters on Feminism, Law, Medicine, Teaching (1049-7870); Which was formed by the 1988 merger of: A P A Newsletter on Philosophy and the Black Experience; A P A Newsletter on Philosophy and Medicine; A P A Newsletter on Philosophy and Law; A P A Newsletter on Teaching Philosophy; A P A Newsletter on Feminism and Philosophy; A P A Newsletter on Computer Use in Philosophy
Media: Online - full text.
Indexed: CA, MLA-IB, PhilInd, T02, W09.
Published by: American Philosophical Association, c/o University of Delaware, 31 Amstel Ave, Newark, DE 19716. TEL 302-831-1112, FAX 302-831-8690, http://www.udel.edu/apa. adv.: page USD 150. Circ: 2,000.

111.85 USA ISSN 1946-1879
BH39
➤ **A S A G E.** (American Society for Aesthetics Graduate Ejournal) Text in English. 2008. s-a. free (effective 2011). back issues avail. **Document type:** *Journal, Academic/Scholarly.* **Description:** Provides a theoretical and interdisciplinary approach to the arts and matters of aesthetic interest.
Media: Online - full text.
Indexed: T02.
Published by: American Society for Aesthetics, c/o Editor, Philosophy Department, 1 University Station, University of Texas at Austin, Austin, TX 78713. asa@aesthetics-online.org, http://www.aesthetics-online.org. Ed. Jenn Neilson.

➤ **A S A NEWSLETTER.** *see* ART

100 NLD
A S C A YEARBOOK. (Amsterdam School for Cultural Analysis) Variant title: Profanations. Text in English. 1996. a. price varies. **Document type:** *Yearbook, Academic/Scholarly.* **Description:** Publishes studies on issues in cultural analysis.
Published by: Universiteit van Amsterdam, Amsterdam School for Cultural Analysis (A S C A), Spuistraat 210, Rm 113, Amsterdam, 1012, Netherlands. TEL 31-20-5253874, FAX 31-20-5254773, asca-fgw@uva.nl, http://www.hum.uva.nl/asca/.

A S E B L JOURNAL. (Association for the Study of Ethical Behavior in Literature) *see* LITERATURE

100 BRA ISSN 1807-9792
BD143
ABSTRACTA; linguagem, mente e acao. Text in English, Portuguese. 2004. s-a. free (effective 2011). **Document type:** *Journal, Academic/Scholarly.*
Media: Online - full text. Eds. Andre Abath, Carlos Eduardo Batista de Sousa, Leonardo de Mello Ribeiro.

170 320 BRA ISSN 1413-9871
ACADEMIA BRASILEIRA DE CIENCIAS MORAIS E POLITICAS. REVISTA. Text in Portuguese. 1995. irreg.
Published by: Academia Brasileira de Ciencias Morais e Politicas, Rua Vaz de Toledo 144, Grupo 108, Engenho Novo, Rio de Janeiro, 20780-150, Brazil. TEL 55-21-5012364, FAX 55-21-5012364.

100 340 MDA
ACADEMIA DE STIINTE A REPUBLICII MOLDOVA. REVISTA FILOSOFIE SI DREPT/AKADEMIYA NAUK RESPUBLIKI MOLDOVA. VOPROSY FILOSOFII I PRAVA. Text in Romanian, Russian. 1951. 3/yr. bk.rev. **Document type:** *Academic/Scholarly.* **Description:** Devoted to socio-philosophical, spiritual and political-legal problems.
Formerly: Academia de Stiinte a R.S.S. Moldova. Buletinul. Filosofie, Drept, Studiul Artelor, Arhelogie (0236-3062); Supersedes in part (in 1990): Akademiya Nauk Moldavskoi S.S.R. Izvestiya. Seriya Obshchestvennykh Nauk (0321-1681)
Indexed: RASB.
—East View. **CCC.**
Published by: Academia de Stiinte a Moldovej, Biblioteca Stiintifica Centrala, Bd Stefan cel Mare 1, Chisinau, 2001, Moldova. http://www.asm.md/altstruc/library. Circ: 610. **Dist. by:** M K - Periodica, ul Gilyarovskogo 39, Moscow 129110, Russian Federation. TEL 7-095-2845008, FAX 7-095-2813798, info@periodicals.ru, http://www.mkniga.ru.

100 ARG ISSN 1667-5061
ACADEMIA LUVENTICUS REPORTES/LUVENTICUS ACADEMY REPORTS. Text in Spanish. 2003. s-a. **Document type:** *Journal, Academic/Scholarly.*
Related titles: Online - full text ed.: ISSN 1667-5088. 2003.
Indexed: A26, I04, I05.
Published by: Academia de Ciencias Luventicus/Luventicus Academy of Sciences, Pasaje Monroe 2766, Rosario, 2000, Argentina. TEL 54-341-4487316, contact@luventicus.org, http://luventicus.org/. Ed. A Luetich.

100 PRT ISSN 1647-6875
ACADEMICA. Text in Portuguese. 2006. irreg. **Document type:** *Monographic series, Academic/Scholarly.*
Published by: Universidade de Lisboa, Faculdade de Letras, Centro de Filosofia, Alameda da Universidade, Lisbon1600-214, Portugal. http://www.centrofilosofia.org.

ACME; annali della Facolta di Lettere e Filosofia dell'Universita degli Studi di Milano. *see* LITERATURE

100 NLD ISSN 0353-5150
B808.5.A1
ACTA ANALYTICA. Text in English. 1986. q. EUR 267, USD 358 combined subscription to institutions (print & online eds.) (effective 2012). adv. reprint service avail. from PSC. **Document type:** *Journal, Academic/Scholarly.*
Related titles: Online - full text ed.: ISSN 1874-6349 (from IngentaConnect).
Indexed: A01, A20, A22, A26, ArtHuCI, CA, DIP, E01, E08, IBR, IBZ, IPB, PhilInd, S09, SCOPUS, T02, W07.
—BLDSC (0593.900000), IE. **CCC.**
Published by: Springer Netherlands (Subsidiary of: Springer Science+Business Media), Van Godewijckstraat 30, Dordrecht, 3311 GX, Netherlands. TEL 31-78-6576050, FAX 31-78-6576474. Ed. Danilo Suster.

110 NLD ISSN 1567-8512
ACTA LAUNIANA. Text in Dutch. 2000. irreg., latest vol.5, 2008. price varies. **Document type:** *Monographic series, Academic/Scholarly.*

P

Published by: (Rudolf van Laun Instituut), Deventer Universitaire Pers, Sandrasteeg 8, Deventer, 7411 KS, Netherlands. TEL 31-570-613663, info@deventeruniversitairepers.nl.

174.2 610 BEL ISSN 0775-9053
ACTA MEDICA CATHOLICA. Text in Dutch, French, English, German. 1922. q. EUR 25; EUR 20 to students (effective 2005). adv. bk.rev. **Description:** Provides articles about spirituality, medical ethics, and medical rights.
Formerly (until 1988): Saint-Luc Medical (0036-3057)
Indexed: P30.
—**CCC.**
Published by: Societe Medicale Belge de Saint-Luc/Belgische Geneesherenvereniging Sint-Lucas, C/o Abbaye des Norbertins, Kerkplein 1, Grimbergen, 1850, Belgium. http://www.smslgv.be. Circ: 1,000.

100 ITA ISSN 1121-2179
ACTA PHILOSOPHICA; rivista internazionale di filosofia. Text in Italian. 1992. s-a. EUR 54 combined subscription domestic to institutions (print & online eds.); EUR 74 combined subscription foreign to institutions (print & online eds.) (effective 2009). **Document type:** *Journal, Academic/Scholarly.*
Related titles: Online - full text ed.: ISSN 1825-6562. 2004.
Indexed: ArtHuCI, CurCont, DIP, IBR, IBZ, IPB, PhilInd, W07.
Published by: (Pontificia Universita della Santa Croce), Fabrizio Serra Editore (Subsidiary of: Accademia Editoriale), c/o Accademia Editoriale, Via Santa Bibbiana 28, Pisa, 56127, Italy. TEL 39-050-542332, FAX 39-050-574888, accademiaeditoriale@accademiaeditoriale.it, http://www.libraweb.net. Ed. Juan Jose Sanguineti.

100 FIN ISSN 0355-1792
B28.F5 CODEN: APFEDB
➤ **ACTA PHILOSOPHICA FENNICA.** Text mainly in English. 1935. irreg., latest vol.63, 1998. price varies. back issues avail.; reprint service avail. from SCH. **Document type:** *Monographic series, Academic/Scholarly.*
Indexed: A22, DIP, IBR, IBZ, IPB, MathR, PCI, PhilInd, Z02.
—BLDSC (0648.300000), IE, Ingenta. **CCC.**
Published by: Suomen Filosofinen Yhdistys/Philosophical Society of Finland, c/o Dept of Philosophy, University of Helsinki, PO Box 9, Helsinki, 00014, Finland. TEL 358-9-1911, FAX 358-9-1917627. Ed. Ilkka Niiniluoto.

100 SWE ISSN 0283-2380
ACTA PHILOSOPHICA GOTHOBURGENSIA. Text in English. 1986. irreg., latest vol.14, 2002. price varies. **Document type:** *Monographic series, Academic/Scholarly.*
Published by: Acta Universitatis Gothoburgensis, Renstroemsgatan 4, P O Box 222, Goeteborg, 40530, Sweden. TEL 46-31-773-17-33, FAX 46-31-163-797. Eds. Mats Furberg, Per Lindstroem.

370.1 POL ISSN 0208-6107
B1
ACTA UNIVERSITATIS LODZIENSIS: FOLIA PHILOSOPHICA. Text in Polish; Summaries in Multiple languages. 1955-1974; N.S. 1981. irreg., latest vol.23, 2010. price varies. **Document type:** *Monographic series, Academic/Scholarly.* **Description:** Contains work from the members of the philosophical faculty and papers presented at symposiums and conferences organized by the faculty on the history of philosophy during the 19th and 20th centuries. Covers philosophical anthropology, the ethics of ecology and aesthetics.
Supersedes in part: Uniwersytet Lodzki. Zeszyty Naukowe. Seria 1: Nauki Humanistyczno-Spoleczne (0076-0358)
Indexed: BibLing, CCMJ, MSN, MathR, RASB.
Published by: Wydawnictwo Uniwersytetu Lodzkiego/Lodz University Press, ul Lindleya 8, Lodz, 90-131, Poland. TEL 48-42-6655861, FAX 48-42-6655861, wdwul@uni.lodz.pl, http://www.wydawnictwo.uni.lodz.pl.

100 POL
ACTA UNIVERSITATIS WRATISLAVIENSIS. FILOZOFIA. Text in English, German, Polish; Summaries in English, German. 1992. irreg., latest vol.44, 2006. price varies. **Document type:** *Monographic series, Academic/Scholarly.*
Published by: (Uniwersytet Wroclawski), Wydawnictwo Uniwersytetu Wroclawskiego Sp. z o.o., pl Uniwersytecki 15, Wroclaw, 50137, Poland. TEL 48-71-3752809, FAX 48-71-3752735, marketing@wuwr.com.pl, http://www.wuwr.com.pl. Eds. Anna Olejarczyk, Janusz Jaskula. Circ: 300.

160 POL
ACTA UNIVERSITATIS WRATISLAVIENSIS. LOGIKA. Text in Polish; Summaries in English, German. 1993. irreg., latest vol.24, 2009. price varies. **Document type:** *Monographic series, Academic/Scholarly.*
Published by: (Uniwersytet Wroclawski), Wydawnictwo Uniwersytetu Wroclawskiego Sp. z o.o., pl Uniwersytecki 15, Wroclaw, 50137, Poland. TEL 48-71-3752809, FAX 48-71-3752735, marketing@wuwr.com.pl, http://www.wuwr.com.pl. Ed. Marek Magdziak. Circ: 300.

ACTUALIDAD BIBLIOGRAFICA DE FILOSOFIA Y TEOLOGIA; selecciones de libros. *see* RELIGIONS AND THEOLOGY—Abstracting, Bibliographies, Statistics

100 DEU ISSN 1613-947X
AD FONTES (FRANKFURT AM MAIN). Text in German. 2006. irreg., latest vol.6, 2009. price varies. **Document type:** *Monographic series, Academic/Scholarly.*
Published by: Peter Lang GmbH (Subsidiary of: Peter Lang Publishing Group), Eschborner Landstr 42-50, Frankfurt Am Main, 60489, Germany. TEL 49-69-7807050, FAX 49-69-78070550, zentrale.frankfurt@peterlang.com. Ed. Tadeusz Guz.

THE ADAM SMITH REVIEW. *see* LITERATURE

174.957 GBR ISSN 1479-3709
ADVANCES IN BIOETHICS. Text in English. 1996. irreg., latest vol.11, 2008. price varies. back issues avail. **Document type:** *Monographic series, Academic/Scholarly.*
Related titles: Online - full text ed.
Indexed: SCOPUS.
—**CCC.**
Published by: Emerald Group Publishing Ltd., Howard House, Wagon Ln, Bingley, W Yorks BD16 1WA, United Kingdom. TEL 44-1274-777700, FAX 44-1274-785201, emerald@emeraldinsight.com. Ed. Robert Baker. **Dist. by:** Turpin Distribution Services Ltd., Pegasus Dr, Stratton Business Park, Biggleswade, Bedfordshire SG18 8QB, United Kingdom. TEL 44-1767-604951, FAX 44-1767-601640, custserv@turpin-distribution.com, http://www.turpin-distribution.com/.

THE ADVENT. *see* RELIGIONS AND THEOLOGY—Hindu

299.984 IND ISSN 0972-1878
ADYAR NEWSLETTER. Text in English. 1960. q. INR 25 to non-members; free to members (effective 2011). **Document type:** *Newsletter, Trade.* **Description:** Provides news about the international headquarters of the Theosophical Society.
Published by: Theosophical Publishing House, Adyar, Chennai, Tamil Nadu 600 020, India. TEL 91-44-24912474, intl.hq@ts-adyar.org.

111.85 700 ITA ISSN 0393-8522
AESTHETICA PREPRINT. Text in Italian. 1983. 3/yr. **Document type:** *Journal, Academic/Scholarly.*
Indexed: IBR, IBZ, IPB.
Published by: Centro Internazionale Studi di Estetica, Viale delle Scienze, Palermo, PA 90128, Italy. Circ: 1,000.

111.85 JPN ISSN 0289-0895
AESTHETICS. Text in English, French, German. 1983. biennial.
Indexed: PhilInd, RILM.
Published by: Bigaku-kai/Japanese Society of Aesthetics, University of Tokyo, Faculty of Letters, 7-3-1 Hongo, Bunkyo-ku, Tokyo, 113-0033, Japan. http://wwwsoc.nii.ac.jp/bigaku/index-e.htm.

100 DEU
AESTHETIK - MEDIEN - BILDUNG. Text in German. 2000. irreg., latest vol.11, 2008. price varies. **Document type:** *Monographic series, Academic/Scholarly.*
Published by: KoPaed Verlag, Pfaelzer-Wald-Str 64, Munich, 81539, Germany. TEL 49-89-68890098, FAX 49-89-6891912, info@kopaed.de, http://www.kopaed.de.

100 306.4 AUT ISSN 1430-5321
➤ **AESTHETIK UND NATURWISSENSCHAFTEN.** Text in German. 1996. irreg., latest 2002. price varies. **Document type:** *Monographic series, Academic/Scholarly.*
Indexed: MathR.
Published by: Springer Wien (Subsidiary of: Springer Science+Business Media), Sachsenplatz 4-6, Vienna, W 1201, Austria. TEL 43-1-3302415-0, FAX 43-1-330242665, books@springer.at, http://www.springer.at. Ed. B Brock. R&P Angela Foessl TEL 43-1-3302415517. **Subscr. in N. America to:** Springer New York LLC, 233 Spring St, New York, NY 10013. TEL 800-777-4643, FAX 201-348-4505.

100 KEN ISSN 0251-043X
AFRICA THOUGHT AND PRACTICE. Text in English. 1974. s-a. **Document type:** *Journal, Academic/Scholarly.*
Related titles: Online - full text ed.: Thought and Practice. ISSN 2076-7714. free (effective 2011).
Published by: Philosophical Association of Kenya, PO Box 30197-00100, Nairobi, Kenya. Ed. Reginald MJ Oduor.

AFRICAN AMERICAN HISTORY MONTH. *see* RELIGIONS AND THEOLOGY—Roman Catholic

109 305.896 NLD
AFRICAN AMERICAN PHILOSOPHY. Abbreviated title: A F A M. Text in English. 1999. irreg. price varies. bibl.; illus. back issues avail. **Document type:** *Monographic series, Academic/Scholarly.* **Description:** Publishes research into the philosophy of such African American thinkers as WEB DuBois, Alain Locke, Angela Davis, Joyce Mitchell Cook, Roy D Morrison, Martin Luther King Jr, and William R Jones.
Related titles: ◆ Series of: Value Inquiry Book Series. ISSN 0929-8436.
Published by: Editions Rodopi B.V., Tijnmuiden 7, Amsterdam, 1046 AK, Netherlands. TEL 31-20-6114821, FAX 31-20-4472979, info@rodopi.nl. Ed. J Everet Green. **Dist in France by:** Nordeal, 30 rue de Verlinghem, BP 139, Lambersart 59832, France. TEL 33-3-20099060, FAX 33-3-20929495; **Dist in N America by:** Rodopi - USA, 606 Newark Ave, 2nd fl, Kenilworth, NJ 07033. TEL 908-497-9031, 800-225-3998, FAX 908-497-9035.

100 COD
AFRIQUE ET PHILOSOPHIE. Text in French. 1976. a. XAF 350. adv. bk.rev.
Published by: (Cercle Philosophique de Kinshasa COG), Faculte Catholique de Kinshasa, BP 1534, Kinshasa-Limite, Congo, Dem. Republic. Ed. Ngwey Ngond'a Ndende. Circ: 100.

THE AG BIOETHICS FORUM. *see* AGRICULTURE

111.85 ITA ISSN 1723-0284
AGALMA; rivista di studi culturali e di estetica. Text in Italian. 2000. s-a. **Document type:** *Journal, Academic/Scholarly.*
Published by: Universita degli Studi di Roma "Tor Vergata", Dipartimento di Ricerche Filosofiche, Via Columbia 1, Rome, 00133, Italy. FAX 39-06-72595051. Ed. Mario Perniola.

100 FRA ISSN 1278-3862
L'AGE DES LUMIERES. Text in French. 1997. irreg., latest vol.2, 1997. **Document type:** *Monographic series, Academic/Scholarly.*
Published by: Honore Champion, 3 Rue Corneille, Paris, 75006, France. TEL 33-1-46340729, FAX 33-1-46346406, champion@honorechampion.com, http://www.honorechampion.com. Eds. Antony McKenna, Raymond Trousson.

110 NOR ISSN 0800-7136
B8.N67
AGORA; journal for metafysisk spekulasjon. Text in Norwegian. 1983. q. NOK 240 to individuals; NOK 430 to institutions (effective 2007). bk.rev. back issues avail. **Document type:** *Magazine, Academic/Scholarly.*
Published by: Aschehoug & Co. (W. Nygaard) AS, P O Box 363, Sentrum, Oslo, 0102, Norway. TEL 47-22-400400, FAX 47-22-206395, kundeservice@aschehoug.no, epost@aschehoug.no, http://www.aschehoug.no.

190 DNK ISSN 1603-3280
➤ **AGORA**; tidsskrift for forskning, udvikling og ideudveksling. Text in Danish. 2003. s-a. free (effective 2005). bk.rev. back issues avail. **Document type:** *Monographic series, Academic/Scholarly.*
Media: Online - full content.
Published by: C V U Storkoebenhavn/Centre for Higher Education, Copenhagen, Ejbyvej 35, Skovlunde, 2740, Denmark. TEL 45-70-202840, FAX 45-44-516199, cvustork@cvustork.dk. Ed. Joergen Thorslund.

100 ESP ISSN 0211-6642
B5
➤ **AGORA (SANTIAGO DE COMPOSTELA)**; papeles de filosofia. Text in Spanish, Gallegan; Summaries in Spanish, English, 1981. s-a. back issues avail. **Document type:** *Journal, Academic/Scholarly.*
Indexed: F04, FR, P09, PCI, PhilInd, T02.
—INIST.
Published by: Universidade de Santiago de Compostela, Servizo de Publicacions e Intercambio Cientifico, Campus Universitario Sur, Santiago de Compostela, 15782, Spain. TEL 34-981-593500, FAX 34-981-593963, spublic@usc.es, http://www.usc.es/spubl. Eds. Luis Garcia Soto, Marcelino Agis Villaverde.

170 ARG ISSN 1515-3142
AGORA PHILOSOPHICA. Text in Spanish. 2000. s-a. **Document type:** *Journal, Academic/Scholarly.*
Indexed: PhilInd.
Published by: Asociacion Argentina de Investigaciones Eticas, Coronel Dias 2277 - 11 F, Buenos Aires, Argentina. TEL 55-15-55090436, info@etica.org.ar, http://www.etica.org.ar/. Ed. Graciela Fernandez.

100 NLD ISSN 1871-0751
AGORA REEKS. Text in Dutch. 1986. irreg., latest 2009. price varies. **Document type:** *Monographic series.*
Formerly (until 2005): Agora Editie (1871-0743)
Published by: Uitgeverij Ten Have, Postbus 5018, Kampen, 8260 GA, Netherlands. TEL 31-38-3392500, http://www.uitgeverijtenhave.nl.

174.95 COL ISSN 1657-8031
AS82.A1
EL AGORA U S B. (Universidad de San Buenaventura) Variant title: Revista El Agora U S B. Text in Spanish. 2001. s-a. **Document type:** *Journal, Academic/Scholarly.*
Related titles: Online - full text ed.: free (effective 2011).
Indexed: A01, C01, CA, F03, F04, T02.
Published by: Universidad de San Buenaventura, Medellin, Departamento de Formacion Humana y Bioetica, San Benito (Centro), Carrera 56C Nro. 51-90, Medellin, Colombia. TEL 57-4-5762600 ext 216, formacion.humana@usbmed.edu.co, http://www.usbmed.edu.co/formacion/index.htm. Ed. Carlos Maria Cardona Ramirez.

AGRICULTURE AND HUMAN VALUES. *see* AGRICULTURE

111.85 ITA ISSN 2035-8466
AISTHESIS. Text in Multiple languages. 2008. s-a. **Document type:** *Journal, Academic/Scholarly.*
Media: Online - full text.
Published by: Associazione Culturale Seminario Permanente di Estetica (S P E S), c/o Massimo Baldi, Via Monfalcone 13, Pistoia, 51100, Italy. http://www.seminariodiestetica.it.

100 FIN ISSN 0355-1725
B31
AJATUS. Text in Finnish. 1926. a. price varies. back issues avail. **Document type:** *Yearbook.*
Indexed: PCI, PhilInd.
Published by: Suomen Filosofinen Yhdistys/Philosophical Society of Finland, c/o Dept of Philosophy, University of Helsinki, PO Box 9, Helsinki, 00014, Finland. TEL 358-9-635177, FAX 358-9-635017, http://www.helsinki.fi/filosofia/sfy.htm. Ed. Sami Pihlstroem.

100 340 TJK ISSN 1026-3306
AKADEMIAI ILMHOI CUMHURII TOCIKISTON. SILSILAI FALSAFA VA HUKUKSINOSI. AHBORI. Text in Tajik, Russian. 1986. q.
Former titles (until 1993): Akademiya Nauk Tajikistana. Seriya: Filosofiya i Pravovedenie; (until 1992): Akademiya Nauk Tadzhikskoi S.S.R. Seriaya: Filosofiya, Ekonomika, Pravovedenie (0235-005X)
Indexed: AICP, RASB.
Published by: Akademiai Ilmhoi Cumhurii Tocikiston/Academy of Sciences of the Republic of Tajikistan, 33 Rudaki Ave, Dushanbe, 734025, Tajikistan. TEL 992-372-215083, FAX 992-372-214911, ulmas@tajik.net.

100 900 DEU ISSN 0930-4304
➤ **AKADEMIE DER WISSENSCHAFTEN ZU GOETTINGEN. ABHANDLUNGEN. PHILOLOGISCH-HISTORISCHE KLASSE.** Text in German. 1942-2007 (vol.279); N.S. 2008. irreg., latest vol.10, 2011. price varies. **Document type:** *Monographic series, Academic/Scholarly.*
Published by: Walter de Gruyter GmbH & Co. KG, Genthiner Str 13, Berlin, 10785, Germany. TEL 49-30-260050, FAX 49-30-26005251, info@degruyter.com, http://www.degruyter.de.

111.85 DEU ISSN 0177-4700
AKTEN INTERNATIONALER KONGRESSE AUF DEN GEBIETEN DER AESTHETIK UND DER LITERATURWISSENSCHAFT. Text in German. 1986. irreg., latest vol.7, 1991. price varies. **Document type:** *Monographic series, Academic/Scholarly.*
Published by: Peter Lang GmbH (Subsidiary of: Peter Lang Publishing Group), Eschborner Landstr 42-50, Frankfurt Am Main, 60489, Germany. TEL 49-69-78070550, FAX 49-69-78070550, zentrale.frankfurt@peterlang.com.

101 PAK ISSN 1993-3789
➤ **AL-HIKMAT.** Text in English, Urdu. 1967. a. PKR 200 domestic; USD 20 foreign (effective 2007). **Document type:** *Journal, Academic/Scholarly.*
Related titles: Online - full text ed.: ISSN 1993-7695. 2006.
Published by: University of the Punjab, Department of Philosophy, New Campus, Lahore, 54590, Pakistan. TEL 92-42-9230884, info@phil.pu.edu.pk, http://www.pu.edu.pk/departments/default.asp?deptid=13. Ed., Adv. contact Sajid Ali. Circ: 500 (paid and controlled).

100 DEU
ALBER-REIHE PRAKTISCHE PHILOSOPHIE. Text in German. 1975. irreg., latest vol.83, 2009. price varies. **Document type:** *Monographic series, Academic/Scholarly.*
Formerly (until 1988): Praktische Philosophie
Published by: Verlag Karl Alber, Hermann-Herder-Str 4, Freiburg, 79104, Germany. TEL 49-761-2717436, FAX 49-761-2717212, info@verlag-alber.de.

100 DEU
ALBER THESEN PHILOSOPHIE. Text in German. 1999. irreg., latest vol.38, 2009. price varies. **Document type:** *Monographic series, Academic/Scholarly.*
Published by: Verlag Karl Alber, Hermann-Herder-Str 4, Freiburg, 79104, Germany. TEL 49-761-2717436, FAX 49-761-2717212, info@verlag-alber.de.

100 ITA ISSN 1126-9588
NA1123.A5
ALBERTIANA. Text in Italian. 1998. a., latest vol.8, 2005. EUR 85 combined subscription foreign to institutions (print & online eds.) (effective 2012). **Document type:** *Journal, Academic/Scholarly.*
Related titles: Online - full text ed.: ISSN 2035-6307.
Indexed: B24, MLA-IB, SpeleolAb.
Published by: (Istituto Italiano per gli Studi Filosofici (I I S F)), Casa Editrice Leo S. Olschki, Viuzzo del Pozzetto 8, Florence, 50126, Italy. TEL 39-055-6530684, FAX 39-055-6530214, celso@olschki.it, http://www.olschki.it. Ed. Francesco Furlan. **Dist. by:** Editions de la Maison des Sciences de l'Homme, 54 Blvd Raspail, Paris Cedex 6 75270, France. TEL 33-1-49542000, FAX 33-1-49542133, http://www.msh-paris.fr. **Co-sponsor:** Societe Internationale Leon Battista Alberti.

ALBO ALBO; inspiracje Jungowskie - problemy psychologii i kultury. *see* PSYCHOLOGY

100 CHL ISSN 0718-316X
ALCANCES. Text in Spanish. 2006. a. **Document type:** *Monographic series, Academic/Scholarly.*
Published by: LOM Ediciones, Concha y Toro 23, Santiago, Chile. TEL 56-2-6885273, FAX 56-2-6966388, lom@lom.cl, http://www.lom.cl/.

128 ITA ISSN 1825-1536
L'ALDILA. Text in Italian. 1995. s-a. **Document type:** *Journal, Academic/Scholarly.*
Published by: Istituto Storico Lucchese, Cortile Francesco Carrara 12, Lucca, 55100, Italy. isl@istitutostoricolucchese.org, http://istitutostoricolucchese.org.

100 ESP ISSN 1576-4494
ALEA; revista internacional de fenomenologia y hermeneutica. Text in Multiple languages. 1999. a. price varies. **Document type:** *Journal, Academic/Scholarly.*
Published by: Universitat de Barcelona, Servei de Publicacions, Gran Via Corts Catalanes 585, Barcelona, 08007, Spain. TEL 34-93-4021100, http://www.publicacions.ub.es.

100 CHE ISSN 0149-2004
B1
ALETHEIA; an international yearbook of philosophy. Text in English, German. 1977. irreg., latest vol.7, 2003. price varies. **Document type:** *Monographic series, Academic/Scholarly.*
Indexed: DIP, IBR, IBZ, PCI, PhilInd.
Published by: (Internationale Akademie fuer Philosophie LIE), Peter Lang AG (Subsidiary of: Peter Lang Publishing Group), Hochfeldstr 32, Postfach 746, Bern 9, 3000, Switzerland. TEL 41-31-3061717, FAX 41-31-3061727, info@peterlang.com, http://www.peterlang.com. Ed. Josef Seifert.

100 ESP ISSN 1137-8360
ALFA; revista de la asociacion andaluza de filosofia. Text in Spanish. 1987. s-a. back issues avail. **Document type:** *Journal, Abstract/Index.*
Related titles: Online - full text ed.
Published by: Asociacion Andaluza de Filosofia, Paseo de la Estacion 44, Jaen, 23008, Spain. http://aafi.filosofia.net.

150 NLD ISSN 0002-5275
B8.D8
➤ **ALGEMEEN NEDERLANDS TIJDSCHRIFT VOOR WIJSBEGEERTE.** Text in Dutch; Summaries in English. 1907. 4/yr. EUR 58 domestic to individuals; EUR 75.80 domestic to institutions; EUR 46.25 domestic to students; EUR 77 foreign to individuals; EUR 94 foreign to institutions; EUR 62.70 foreign to students (effective 2008). adv. bk.rev. bibl. cum.index: vols.1-50 (1907-1958). **Document type:** *Journal, Academic/Scholarly.*
Formerly (until 1970): Algemeen Nederlands Tijdschrift voor Wijsbegeerte en Psychologie
Indexed: DIP, FR, IBR, IBZ, IPB, L&LBA, PCI, PhilInd, RILM, SCOPUS, SOPODA, SociolAb.
—INIST.
Published by: Koninklijke Van Gorcum BV/Royal Van Gorcum BV, PO Box 43, Assen, 9400 AA, Netherlands. TEL 31-592-379555, FAX 31-592-372064, info@vangorcum.nl. adv.: B&W page EUR 300, color page EUR 1,050; 120 x 200. Circ: 600.

100 DEU ISSN 0340-7969
B3
➤ **ALLGEMEINE ZEITSCHRIFT FUER PHILOSOPHIE.** Text in German. 1976. 3/yr. EUR 57; EUR 34 to students; EUR 30 newsstand/cover (effective 2010). adv. bk.rev. 90 p./no. 1 cols./p.; back issues avail. **Document type:** *Journal, Academic/Scholarly.*
Indexed: A20, A22, ArtHuCI, BibLing, DIP, IBR, IBZ, IPB, PCI, PhilInd, RASB, W07.
—IE, Infotrieve.
Published by: (Deutsche Gesellschaft fuer Philosophie e.V.), Frommann-Holzboog Verlag e.K., Koenig-Karl-Str 27, Stuttgart, 70372, Germany. TEL 49-711-9559690, FAX 49-711-9559691, info@frommann-holzboog.de. Ed. Tilman Borsche. Adv. contact Sybille Wittmann. page EUR 300; 112 x 180. Circ: 700 (paid).

149 DNK ISSN 0905-4545
ALMEN SEMIOTIK. Text in Danish; Summaries in English. 1978. irreg., latest vol.16, 2002. price varies. back issues avail. **Document type:** *Monographic series, Academic/Scholarly.*
Former titles (until 1987): Semiotek (0107-2935); (until 1980): Sprog, subject, ideologi (0105-9300)
Published by: (Aarhus Universitet, Nordisk Institut/University of Aarhus, Nordic Institute), Aarhus Universitetsforlag/Aarhus University Press, Langelandsgade 177, Aarhus N, 8200, Denmark. TEL 45-89-425370, FAX 45-89-425380, unipress@au.dk, http://www.unipress.dk.

ALPHA OMEGA; rivista di filosofia e teologia dell'Ateneo Pontificio Regina Apostolorum. *see* RELIGIONS AND THEOLOGY—Roman Catholic

100 ITA ISSN 2036-5020
ALVEARIUM. Text in Multiple languages. 2008. irreg. **Document type:** *Monographic series, Academic/Scholarly.*
Media: Online - full text.
Published by: Universita degli Studi del Salento, Edificio "Studium 2000", Via di Valesio, Lecce, 73100, Italy.

149 USA ISSN 1072-2548
BL2747.3
AMERICAN ATHEIST NEWSLETTER. Text in English. 1959. m. (except Jun. & Dec.). USD 35 (effective 2005). bk.rev. **Document type:** *Newsletter, Consumer.* **Description:** Keeps the atheist community abreast of state-church separation violations and the latest religious financial schemes and reports news of general interest to atheists.
Former titles (until 1965): American Atheist Insiders' Newsletter; Poor Richard's Newsletter
Related titles: Online - full text ed.
Indexed: G05, G06, G07, G08, I05, I07, R05, RASB.
Published by: (Charles E Stevens American Atheist Library & Archives), American Atheist Press, Inc., PO Box 5733, Parsippany, NJ 07054-6733. TEL 908-276-7300, FAX 908-276-7402, info@atheists.org, http://www.atheists.org. R&P Frank Zindler TEL 614-299-1036. Circ: 5,000 (paid and free).

215 282.06 USA ISSN 0065-7638
B11
➤ **AMERICAN CATHOLIC PHILOSOPHICAL ASSOCIATION. PROCEEDINGS.** Text in English. 1926. a. USD 46 per issue to institutions; USD 248 combined subscription per issue to institutions (print & online eds.); free to members (effective 2009). adv. cum.index: vols.1-63 (1926-1989). back issues avail.; reprint service avail. from PSC. **Document type:** *Proceedings, Academic/Scholarly.* **Description:** Contains revised papers orignially presented at the annual conference of the American Catholic Philosophical Association.
Formerly (until 1935): Annual Meeting of the American Catholic Philosophical Association. Proceedings
Related titles: Microfilm ed.: (from PQC); Online - full text ed.: ISSN 2153-7925. USD 230 per issue to institutions (effective 2009); ◆ Supplement to: American Catholic Philosophical Quarterly. ISSN 1051-3558.
Indexed: A01, A03, A08, A26, AmHI, CA, CPL, DIP, E08, G08, H07, I05, IBR, IBZ, IPB, MLA-IB, P30, PCI, PhilInd, R05, RASB, S09, T02.
—CCC.
Published by: (American Catholic Philosophical Association), Philosophy Documentation Center, PO Box 7147, Charlottesville, VA 22906. TEL 434-220-3300, FAX 434-220-3301, order@pdcnet.org, http://www.pdcnet.org. Ed. Thomas Osborne. R&P George Leaman. Adv. contact Greg Swope.

149.2 USA ISSN 1051-3558
B1
➤ **AMERICAN CATHOLIC PHILOSOPHICAL QUARTERLY.** Abbreviated title: A C P Q. Text in English. 1927. q. USD 80 to institutions; USD 277 combined subscription to institutions (print & online eds.); USD 25 per issue; free to members (effective 2010). adv. bk.rev. tr.lit. cum.index: vols.1-65 (1927-1991). back issues avail.; reprint service avail. from PSC. **Document type:** *Journal, Academic/Scholarly.* **Description:** Features scholarly articles, topical discussions, and book reviews dealing with all philosophical areas and approaches.
Formerly (until 1990): New Scholasticism (0028-6621)
Related titles: Microform ed.: (from PQC); Online - full text ed.: ISSN 2153-8441. USD 231 to institutions (effective 2010); ◆ Supplement(s): American Catholic Philosophical Association. Proceedings. ISSN 0065-7638.
Indexed: A01, A03, A08, A20, A22, A26, ASCA, AmHI, ArtHuCI, B04, BRD, CA, CERDIC, CPL, CurCont, DIP, E08, FR, G08, H07, H08, HAb, HumInd, I05, IBR, IBZ, IPB, MEA&I, MLA-IB, P30, PCI, PhilInd, PsycholAb, R&TA, R05, RASB, S09, T02, W03, W07.
—IE, Ingenta, INIST. **CCC.**
Published by: (American Catholic Philosophical Association), Philosophy Documentation Center, PO Box 7147, Charlottesville, VA 22906. TEL 434-220-3300, FAX 434-220-3301, order@pdcnet.org, http://www.pdcnet.org. Ed. David Clemenson. Adv. contact Greg Swope.

➤ **THE AMERICAN JOURNAL OF BIOETHICS.** *see* BIOLOGY—Genetics

➤ **AMERICAN JOURNAL OF THEOLOGY & PHILOSOPHY.** *see* RELIGIONS AND THEOLOGY

➤ **AMERICAN LIVING PRESS.** *see* ART

106 USA ISSN 0065-972X
B11
AMERICAN PHILOSOPHICAL ASSOCIATION. PROCEEDINGS AND ADDRESSES. Text in English. 1901. 5/yr. USD 75 to non-members; free to members (effective 2011). adv. reprints avail. **Document type:** *Proceedings, Academic/Scholarly.*
Supersedes (in 1927): American Philosophical Association. Annual Meeting. Proceedings
Related titles: Microfilm ed.: (from PQC); Online - full text ed.
Indexed: A22, FR, IPB, MLA-IB, PCI, PhilInd, RASB.
—INIST.
Published by: American Philosophical Association, c/o University of Delaware, 31 Amstel Ave, Newark, DE 19716. TEL 302-831-1112, FAX 302-831-8690, apaonline@udel.edu. Adv. contact Erin Shepherd TEL 302-831-2895.

100 USA ISSN 0003-0481
➤ **AMERICAN PHILOSOPHICAL QUARTERLY.** Abbreviated title: A P Q. Text in English. 1964. q. USD 55 to individuals; USD 297 to institutions (print or online ed.); USD 331 combined subscription to institutions (print & online eds.) (effective 2011). adv. illus. Index. back issues avail.; reprints avail. **Document type:** *Journal, Academic/Scholarly.* **Description:** Contains scholarly work in philosophy.
Media: Large Type. **Related titles:** Online - full text ed.: ISSN 2152-1123.
Indexed: A01, A02, A03, A08, A20, A21, A22, A26, ASCA, AmHI, ArtHuCI, B04, BRD, CA, CurCont, DIP, E08, FR, G08, H07, H08, H09, H10, H14, HAb, HumInd, I05, IBR, IBSS, IBZ, IPB, P02, P10, P30, P48, P53, P54, PCI, PQC, PhilInd, R05, RASB, RI-1, S09, SCOPUS, T02, W03, W07.
—BLDSC (0850.590000), IE, Infotrieve, Ingenta, INIST. **CCC.**
Published by: University of Illinois Press, 1325 S Oak St, Champaign, IL 61820. TEL 217-333-0950, 866-244-0626, FAX 217-244-8082, journals@uillinois.edu. Ed. Paul Moser. Adv. contact Jeff McArdle TEL 217-244-0381.

211 USA ISSN 0003-0708
BL2700
AMERICAN RATIONALIST. Text in English. 1956. bi-m. USD 13 in North America; USD 21 elsewhere (effective 2001). adv. bk.rev. back issues avail. **Document type:** *Magazine, Consumer.* **Description:** Concerns free thought, philosophy, critique of religion and theology, and the history of unbelief.
Related titles: Microform ed.: (from PQC).
Indexed: A22, PCI.
Published by: Rationalist Association, Inc., 1806 Allen Ave, St Louis, MO 63188. Ed. Dr. Kaz Dziamka. Circ: 1,500.

100 NLD
AMERICAN UNIVERSITY PUBLICATIONS IN PHILOSOPHY. Text in English. irreg., latest vol.4, 1987. price varies. **Document type:** *Monographic series, Academic/Scholarly.*
Published by: (American University), Springer Netherlands (Subsidiary of: Springer Science+Business Media), Van Godewijckstraat 30, Dordrecht, 3311 GX, Netherlands. TEL 31-78-6576050, FAX 31-78-6576474, http://www.springer.com.

100 USA ISSN 0739-6392
AMERICAN UNIVERSITY STUDIES. SERIES 5. PHILOSOPHY. Text in English. 1983. irreg., latest vol.205, 2009. price varies. back issues avail. **Document type:** *Monographic series, Academic/Scholarly.* **Description:** Explores issues in all areas of philosophy.
Indexed: CCMJ.
Published by: Peter Lang Publishing, Inc. (Subsidiary of: Peter Lang Publishing Group), 29 Broadway, New York, NY 10006. TEL 212-647-7706, 212-647-7700, 800-770-5264, FAX 212-647-7707, customerservice@plang.com.

AMOSINTERNATIONAL; Internationale Zeitschrift fuer christliche Sozialethik. *see* RELIGIONS AND THEOLOGY

AMSTERDAM CLASSICAL MONOGRAPHS. *see* CLASSICAL STUDIES

100 CAN ISSN 1918-7351
▼ ➤ **ANALECTA HERMENEUTICA.** Text in English. 2009. a.
Related titles: Online - full text ed.: free (effective 2011).
Published by: International Institute for Hermeneutics/Institut International d'Hermeneutique, 85 Thorncliffe Park Dr, Toronto, ON M4H 1L6, Canada. TEL 416-429-8944, FAX 928-244-7275, iihweb@chass.utoronto.ca, http://groups.chass.utoronto.ca. Ed. S J McGrath.

100 NLD ISSN 0167-7276
➤ **ANALECTA HUSSERLIANA**; the yearbook of phenomenological research. Text in English. 1971. irreg., latest vol.103, 2009. price varies. back issues avail. **Document type:** *Monographic series, Academic/Scholarly.*
Indexed: DIP, FR, IBR, IBZ, MLA-IB, PCI, RASB.
—BLDSC (0869.154000), IE, Ingenta, INIST. **CCC.**
Published by: Springer Netherlands (Subsidiary of: Springer Science+Business Media), Van Godewijckstraat 30, Dordrecht, 3311 GX, Netherlands. TEL 31-78-6576050, FAX 31-78-6576474. Ed. A T Tymieniecka.

100 ARG ISSN 0326-1301
B808.5
ANALISIS FILOSOFICO. Text in Spanish. 1981. s-a. **Document type:** *Journal, Academic/Scholarly.*
Related titles: Online - full text ed.: ISSN 1851-9636 (from SciELO).
Indexed: P09, PCI, PhilInd.
Published by: Sociedad Argentina de Analisis Filosofico, Bulnes, 642, Buenos Aires, 1176, Argentina. info@sadaf.org.ar, http://www.sadaf.org.ar/. Ed. Marcelo Alegre.

100 MEX ISSN 0188-896X
B2
ANALOGIA. Text in Spanish. 1988. s-a.
Indexed: FR, PhilInd.
—INIST.
Published by: Universidad Nacional Autonoma de Mexico, Instituto de Investigaciones Filologicas, Circuito Mario de la Cueva, Zona Cultural, Ciudad Universitaria, Mexico City, DF 04510, Mexico. TEL 52-5-622-3909, FAX 52-5-616-0653, http://www.astroscu.unam.mx/rmaa.html.

100 GBR ISSN 0003-2638
B1
➤ **ANALYSIS.** Text in English. 1933-1940; N.S. 1947. q. GBP 107 in United Kingdom to institutions; EUR 160 in Europe to institutions; USD 212 in US & Canada to institutions; GBP 107 elsewhere to institutions; GBP 116 combined subscription in United Kingdom to institutions (print & online eds.); EUR 174 combined subscription in Europe to institutions (print & online eds.); USD 232 combined subscription in US & Canada to institutions (print & online eds.); GBP 116 combined subscription elsewhere to institutions (print & online eds.) (effective 2012). illus. index. back issues avail.; reprint service avail. from PSC. **Document type:** *Journal, Academic/Scholarly.* **Description:** Include Analysis reviews, a new section which will be devoted to reviewing recent work in analytic philosophy.
Related titles: Microform ed.: N.S.; Online - full text ed.: ISSN 1467-8284. N.S. GBP 97 in United Kingdom to institutions; EUR 145 in Europe to institutions; USD 193 in US & Canada to institutions; GBP 97 elsewhere to institutions (effective 2012) (from IngentaConnect).
Indexed: A01, A03, A08, A20, A22, A26, AmHI, ArtHuCI, CA, CCMJ, CurCont, DIP, E01, FR, H07, IBR, IBZ, IPB, MLA-IB, MSN, MathR, P30, PCI, PhilInd, RASB, SCOPUS, SOPODA, T02, W07, Z02.
—BLDSC (0892.100000), IE, Infotrieve, Ingenta, INIST. **CCC.**
Published by: (The Analysis Trust), Oxford University Press, Great Clarendon St, Oxford, OX2 6DP, United Kingdom. TEL 44-1865-556767, FAX 44-1865-556646, enquiry@oup.co.uk. Ed. Michael Clark. Adv. contact Linda Hann TEL 44-1344-779945. Circ: 1,350.

100 USA ISSN 1584-8574
➤ **ANALYSIS AND METAPHYSICS.** Text in English. 2002. a. USD 15 per issue to individuals; USD 20 per issue to institutions (effective 2010). bk.rev. tr.lit. back issues avail.; reprints avail. **Document type:** *Journal, Academic/Scholarly.* **Description:** Publishes contributions fitting within various philosophical traditions, but manifests a preference of the analytic tradition in the broad sense of commitment to clarity and responsibility.
Related titles: Online - full text ed.
Indexed: P02, P10, P28, P48, P53, P54, PQC.

P

Published by: Addleton Academic Publishers, 30-18 50th St, Woodside, NY 11377. TEL 718-626-6017, sales@addletonacademicpublishers.com. Ed. George Lazaroiu. Pub. Adrian Constantinescu. R&P Theodor Damian. Circ: 300.

➤ **ANALYTIC PHILOSOPHY.** *see* PHILOSOPHY—Abstracting, Bibliographies, Statistics

100 RUS ISSN 2222-5331
ANALYTICA. Text in Russian, English. 2007. a. free. bk.rev. **Document type:** *Journal, Academic/Scholarly.* **Description:** Aims to lead to the realization of the possibility of research into the history of the analytic philosophy as well as its main problems.
Media: Online - full text. Eds. Dmitry Ankin, Lev Lamberov. Pub. Maksim Lebedev.

ANARCHIST YELLOW PAGES. *see* POLITICAL SCIENCE

100 BEL
ANCIENT AND MEDIEVAL PHILOSOPHY. SERIES 1, PUBLICATIONS OF DE WULF-MANSION CENTRE. Text in English. 1978. irreg., latest vol.27, 2000. price varies. back issues avail. **Document type:** *Monographic series, Academic/Scholarly.* **Description:** Discusses research and ideas in ancient and medieval philosophy.
Published by: Leuven University Press, Blijde Inkomststraat 5, Leuven, 3000, Belgium. TEL 32-16-325345, FAX 32-16-325352, university.press@upers.kuleuven.ac.be, http://www.kuleuven.ac.be/upers. Ed. C Steel.

100 BEL
ANCIENT AND MEDIEVAL PHILOSOPHY. SERIES 2, HENRICI DE GANDAVO OPERA OMNIA. Text in English. 1979. irreg., latest vol.29, 1999. price varies. back issues avail. **Document type:** *Monographic series, Academic/Scholarly.*
Formerly: Ancient and Medieval Philosophy. Series 2, Henrici de Gandavo Opera
Published by: Leuven University Press, Blijde Inkomststraat 5, Leuven, 3000, Belgium. TEL 32-16-325345, FAX 32-16-325352, university.press@upers.kuleuven.ac.be, http://www.kuleuven.ac.be/upers. Ed. R Macken.

141 956 NLD ISSN 1871-188X
ANCIENT MEDITERRANEAN AND MEDIEVAL TEXTS AND CONTEXTS; studies in platonism, neoplatonism and the platonic tradition. Text in English. 2005. irreg., latest vol.7, 2008. price varies. **Document type:** *Monographic series, Academic/Scholarly.*
Indexed: IZBG.
Published by: Brill, PO Box 9000, Leiden, 2300 PA, Netherlands. TEL 31-71-5353500, FAX 31-71-5317532, cs@brill.nl, http://www.brill.nl. Eds. John F Finamore, Robert M Berchman.

180 215 USA ISSN 0740-2007
B111
➤ **ANCIENT PHILOSOPHY**; semi-annual journal devoted to original research in ancient Greek and Roman philosophy and science. Text in English. 1980. s-a. USD 32 to individuals; USD 70 to institutions; USD 25 to students (effective 2010). bk.rev. illus. 250 p./no.; back issues avail.; reprint service avail. from PSC. **Document type:** *Journal, Academic/Scholarly.* **Description:** Contains articles and reviews about classical philosophy and science.
Related titles: Online - full text ed.: ISSN 2154-4689.
Indexed: A21, A22, A26, AmHI, B04, BRD, CA, DIP, E08, G08, H07, H08, HAb, HumInd, I05, IBR, IBZ, IPB, PCI, PhilInd, R05, RASB, RI-1, RI-2, S09, T02, W03.
—BLDSC (0900.325400), IE, Infotrieve, Ingenta.
Published by: Duquesne University, Department of Philosophy, 600 Forbes Ave, Pittsburgh, PA 15282. TEL 412-396-6500, FAX 412 396 5353, http://www.sites.duq.edu/philosophy/. Ed. Dr. Ronald Polansky.

➤ **ANFORA**; revista cuatrimestral de literatura y filosofia. *see* LITERATURE

➤ **ANGELAKI**; journal of the theoretical humanities. *see* HUMANITIES: COMPREHENSIVE WORKS

➤ **ANGELICUM**; periodicum trimestre pontificae studiorum universitatis a Santo Thoma Aquinate in Urbe. *see* RELIGIONS AND THEOLOGY—Roman Catholic

170 DEU
ANGEWANDTE ETHIK. Text in English. 2006. irreg., latest vol.11, 2009. price varies. **Document type:** *Monographic series, Academic/Scholarly.*
Published by: Verlag Karl Alber, Hermann-Herder-Str 4, Freiburg, 79104, Germany. TEL 49-761-2717436, FAX 49-761-2717212, info@verlag-alber.de.

190 CAN ISSN 1209-0689
B1
➤ **ANIMUS**; a philosophical journal for our time. Text in English. 1996. a. free (effective 2011). bk.rev. **Document type:** *Journal, Academic/Scholarly.* **Description:** Covers the works of Western civilization and contemporary views of these works.
Media: Online - full text.
Indexed: C03, CBCARef, P48, PQC, PhilInd.
—CCC.
Published by: Memorial University of Newfoundland, Department of Philosophy, c/o Floy E. Andrews, Ed, Memorial University of Newfoundland, St Johns, NF A1C 5S7, Canada. TEL 709-737-8336. Ed., R&P Floy E Andrews. Circ: 600.

107.1 POL ISSN 1644-793X
ANNALES ACADEMIAE PAEDAGOGICAE CRACOVIENSIS. STUDIA PHILOSOPHICA. Text in Polish. 1972. irreg., latest vol.60, 2008. price varies. **Document type:** *Monographic series, Academic/Scholarly.*
Formerly (until 2002): Wyzsza Szkola Pedagogiczna im. Komisji Edukacji Narodowej w Krakowie. Rocznik Naukowo-Dydaktyczny. Prace Filozoficzne (0239-2348)
Published by: (Uniwersytet Pedagogiczny im. Komisji Edukacji Narodowej w Krakowie), Wydawnictwo Naukowe Uniwersytetu Pedagogicznego im. Komisji Edukacji Narodowej w Krakowie, ul Podchorazych 2, Krakow, 30084, Poland. TEL 48-12-6626383, redakcja@wydawnictwoup.pl, http://www.wydawnictwoap.pl. Eds. Miroslaw Zabierowski, Teresa Grabinska. **Co-sponsor:** Ministerstwo Edukacji Narodowej.

100 ROM ISSN 2067-3159
▼ **ANNALES PHILOSOPHICI**; University of Oradea's annals of philosophy. Text in English. 2010. s-a. free. **Document type:** *Journal, Academic/Scholarly.*
Related titles: Online - full text ed.: free (effective 2011).
Published by: (University of Oradea, Faculty of Social and Humanistic Sciences, Philosophy Department/Universitatea din Oradea. Facultatea de Stiinte Socio-Umane. Catedra de Filosofie), Editura Universitatii din Oradea/University of Oradea Publishing House, Str Universitatii 1, Geotermal Bldg., 2nd Fl., Oradea, Jud.Bihor 410087, Romania. TEL 40-259-408642, editura@uoradea.ro, http://webhost.uoradea.ro/editura/. Ed. Dan Patroc.

301.01 POL ISSN 0137-2025
➤ **ANNALES UNIVERSITATIS MARIAE CURIE-SKLODOWSKA. SECTIO I. PHILOSOPHIA - SOCIOLOGIA.** Text in English, Polish; Summaries in English, French, German. 1976. a. price varies. **Document type:** *Journal, Academic/Scholarly.*
Indexed: IPB, PhilInd, RASB.
Published by: (Uniwersytet Marii Curie-Sklodowskiej w Lublinie, Wydzial Filozofii i Socjologii), Wydawnictwo Uniwersytetu Marii Curie-Sklodowskiej w Lublinie, Pl Marii Curie-Sklodowskiej 5, Lublin, 20031, Poland. TEL 48-81-5375304, press@ramzes.umcs.lublin.pl, http://www.press.umcs.lublin.pl. Ed. Zdzislaw J Czarnecki. Circ: 500.

100 DEU ISSN 0563-1483
ANNALES UNIVERSITATIS SARAVIENSIS. REIHE PHILOSOPHISCHE FAKULTAET. Text in German. 1952. irreg., latest vol.19, 2002. price varies. **Document type:** *Monographic series, Academic/Scholarly.*
Formerly (until 1964): Annales Universitatis Saraviensis. Philosophie, Lettres (0563-1467)
Indexed: MLA-IB.
Published by: Roehrig Universitaetsverlag, Postfach 1806, St Ingbert, 66368, Germany. TEL 49-6894-87957, FAX 49-6894-870330, info@roehrig-verlag.de, http://www.roehrig-verlag.de.

174.2 GBR ISSN 1567-2468
ANNALS OF BIOETHICS; a forum of foundational, clinical and emerging topics. Text in English. 2003. irreg., latest 2008. price varies. 150 p./no.; back issues avail. **Document type:** *Monographic series, Trade.* **Description:** Covers through foundational philosophical, religious, and cultural perspectives, clinical case studies, and legal analysis, the Annals of Bioethics documents, reviews, and explores emerging bioethical viewpoints as well as the state-of-the-art of this global endeavor.
Related titles: Online - full text ed.: 2005.
Published by: Routledge (Subsidiary of: Taylor & Francis Group), 4 Park Sq, Milton Park, Abingdon, Oxon OX14 4RN, United Kingdom. TEL 44-20-70176000, FAX 44-20-70176336, http://www.tandf.co.uk/journals.

ANNALS OF PURE AND APPLIED LOGIC. *see* MATHEMATICS

ANTHROPOLOGY & PHILOSPPHY. *see* ANTHROPOLOGY

ANNUAL EDITIONS: BUSINESS ETHICS. *see* BUSINESS AND ECONOMICS

100 ITA ISSN 0394-1809
B4
ANNUARIO FILOSOFICO (YEAR). Text in Italian. 1985. irreg. price varies. bk.rev. **Document type:** *Directory, Academic/Scholarly.*
Indexed: IPB.
Published by: Ugo Mursia Editore, Via Melchiorre Gioia 45, Milan, 20124, Italy. TEL 39-02-67378500, FAX 39-02-67378605, info@mursia.com, http://www.mursia.com.

159 DEU ISSN 1437-9376
ANSCHAULICHE WISSENSCHAFT. Text in German. 1999. irreg., latest vol.3, 1999. price varies. **Document type:** *Monographic series, Academic/Scholarly.*
Published by: Shaker Verlag GmbH, Kaiserstr 100, Herzogenrath, 52134, Germany. TEL 49-2407-95960, FAX 49-2407-95969, info@shaker.de.

ANTHROPOETICS; the journal of generative anthropolgy. *see* ANTHROPOLOGY

100 ITA ISSN 1973-5030
B1
ANTIQUORUM PHILOSOPHIA. Text in Multiple languages. 2007. a. **Document type:** *Journal, Academic/Scholarly.*
Related titles: Online - full text ed.: ISSN 1974-4501.
Published by: Fabrizio Serra Editore (Subsidiary of: Accademia Editoriale), c/o Accademia Editoriale, Via Santa Bibbiana 28, Pisa, 56127, Italy. TEL 39-050-542332, FAX 39-050-574888, accademiaeditoriale@accademiaeditoriale.it, http://www.libraweb.net.

100 158 301 ESP ISSN 1139-8132
B1
ANUARIO FILOSOFIA, PSICOLOGIA Y SOCIOLOGIA. Variant title: Filosofia, Psicologia y Sociologia. Text in Multiple languages. 1999. a. EUR 18 per issue (effective 2009). **Document type:** *Journal, Academic/Scholarly.*
Published by: Universidad de las Palmas de Gran Canaria, Departamento de Psicologia y Sociologia, Edif. de Humanidades Campus Universitario del Obelisco, C. Perez del Toro, 1, Las Palmas de Gran Canaria, 35003, Spain. TEL 34-928-451774, FAX 34-928-452880, thdez@dps.ulpgc.es, http://www.ulpgc.es/.

100 ESP ISSN 0066-5215
B25 CODEN: ANFIEA
➤ **ANUARIO FILOSOFICO.** Text in Spanish. 1968. 3/yr. EUR 38 in the European Union; EUR 43 elsewhere (effective 2009). bk.rev. back issues avail. **Document type:** *Journal, Academic/Scholarly.*
Related titles: Online - full text ed.; ◆ Supplement(s): Cuadernos de Anuario Filosofico. Serie Universitaria. ISSN 1137-2176.
Indexed: A01, A02, A03, A08, A20, A26, AmHI, ArtHuCI, BibInd, CA, CurCont, F03, F04, FR, H07, I04, I05, IBR, IBZ, IPB, P09, PCI, PhilInd, SCOPUS, SOPODA, SociolAb, T02, W07.
—INIST.
Published by: (Universidad de Navarra, Facultad de Filosofia y Letras), Universidad de Navarra, Servicio de Publicaciones, Campus Universitario, Pamplona, 31009, Spain.

100 DEU ISSN 0003-6390
B171
➤ **APEIRON**; a journal of ancient philosophy and science. Text in English. 1966. q. EUR 165, USD 248 to institutions; EUR 190, USD 285 combined subscription to institutions (print & online eds.) (effective 2012). adv. bk.rev. **Document type:** *Journal, Academic/Scholarly.*
Related titles: Online - full text ed.: ISSN 2156-7093. EUR 165, USD 248 to institutions (effective 2012).
Indexed: A21, A22, CCMJ, DIP, E08, FR, I05, IBR, IBZ, IPB, Inspec, MSN, MathR, PCI, PhilInd, RASB, RI-1, RI-2, S09, Z02.
—BLDSC (1567.867200), IE, Infotrieve, Ingenta, INIST. **CCC.**
Published by: (University of Texas at Austin, Department of Philosophy USA), Walter de Gruyter GmbH & Co. KG, Genthiner Str 13, Berlin, 10785, Germany. TEL 49-30-260050, FAX 49-30-26005251, info@degruyter.com. Ed. James Hankinson. Circ: 375.

109 USA
APORIA; a student journal of philosophy. Text in English. 19??. s-a. free (effective 2010). back issues avail. **Document type:** *Journal, Academic/Scholarly.* **Description:** Contains a selection of exemplary philosophical studies done at the undergraduate level.
Related titles: Online - full text ed.
Indexed: IPB.
Published by: Brigham Young University, Philosophy Department, 4086 JFSB, Brigham Young University, Provo, UT 84602. phil_dept@byu.edu, http://philosophy.byu.edu.

101 GBR ISSN 1358-3336
B1
APPRAISAL. Text in English. 1996. s-a. GBP 12 domestic to individuals; GBP 15 in Europe to individuals; GBP 18 elsewhere to individuals; GBP 20 domestic to institutions; GBP 24 in Europe to institutions; GBP 26 elsewhere to institutions (effective 2009). back issues avail. **Description:** Covers all aspects of philosophy and the application of philosophical ideas to other areas of thought and practice.
Related titles: CD-ROM ed.; Online - full text ed.: GBP 5 (effective 2009).
Indexed: A26, AmHI, BrHumI, CA, E08, H07, I05, PhilInd, S09, T02.
Published by: Society for Post-Critical and Personalist Studies, c/o Dr R T Allen, 20 Ulverscroft Rd, Loughborough, Leics LE11 3PU, United Kingdom. TEL 44-1509-215438, FAX 44-1509-215438, rt.allen@ntlworld.com.

▼ **APUNTES DE BIOETICA.** *see* MEDICAL SCIENCES

100 VEN ISSN 1316-7553
APUNTES DE FILOSOFIA. Text in Spanish. 1992. s-a. back issues avail. **Document type:** *Journal, Academic/Scholarly.*
Related titles: Online - full text ed.
Indexed: MLA-IB, PhilInd.
Published by: Universidad Central de Venezuela, Escuela de Filosofia, Apdo Postal 47209, Caracas, 1041-A, Venezuela. TEL 58-212-6052863, apuntesfilosoficos@platino.gov.ve. Ed. Omar Astorga. Circ: 1,000.

100 VAT ISSN 0003-7362
B765.T54
AQUINAS; rivista internazionale di filosofia. Text in Italian. 1958. 3/yr. USD 78. bk.rev.
Indexed: A21, DIP, FR, IBR, IBZ, IPB, MLA, MLA-IB, PCI, PhilInd, RI-1, RI-2.
—BLDSC (1583.150000), IE, Ingenta, INIST.
Published by: Pontificia Universita Lateranense/Pontificia Universitas Lateranensis, Piazza S. Giovanni in Laterano 4, Vatican City, 00120, Vatican City. Ed. Sanchez Sorondo.

100 USA ISSN 0066-5614
AQUINAS LECTURE SERIES. Text in English. 1937. a. USD 15 per issue (effective 2009). back issues avail. **Document type:** *Monographic series, Academic/Scholarly.* **Description:** Documents annual lecture originating at Marquette University.
Published by: (Aristotelean Society), Marquette University, Memorial Library, Rm 164, P O Box 3141, Milwaukee, WI 53201. TEL 414-288-1564, FAX 414-288-7813. **Subscr. to:** Book Masters, Standing Order Dept, 1444 U S Rt 2, Mansfield, OH 44903.

ARABIC SCIENCES AND PHILOSOPHY; a historical journal. *see* HISTORY

ARCHITECTURAL THEORY REVIEW. *see* ARCHITECTURE

100 DEU ISSN 0003-8946
B49
ARCHIV FUER BEGRIFFSGESCHICHTE. Text in German. 1955. a. EUR 106 (effective 2010). bk.rev. reprint service avail. from SCH. **Document type:** *Yearbook, Academic/Scholarly.*
Related titles: Supplement(s): Archiv fuer Begriffsgeschichte. Sonderheft. ISSN 1617-4399. 2000; Archiv fuer Begriffsgeschichte. Supplementheft. ISSN 0343-7035. 1976.
Indexed: A22, BibInd, DIP, FR, IBR, IBZ, IPB, MLA-IB, PCI, PhilInd, RASB.
—IE, INIST.
Published by: Felix Meiner Verlag GmbH, Richardstr 47, Hamburg, 22081, Germany. TEL 49-40-2987560, FAX 49-40-29875620, info@meiner.de. R&P, Adv. contact Johannes Kambylis. Circ: 600.

109 DEU ISSN 0003-9101
B3
➤ **ARCHIV FUER GESCHICHTE DER PHILOSOPHIE.** Text in German, English, Italian, French. 1976 (vol.58). 3/yr. EUR 206, USD 309 to institutions; EUR 238, USD 357 combined subscription to institutions (print & online eds.) (effective 2012). adv. bk.rev. illus. index. reprint service avail. from SCH. **Document type:** *Journal, Academic/Scholarly.*
Related titles: Online - full text ed.: ISSN 1613-0650. EUR 206, USD 309 to institutions (effective 2012).
Indexed: A20, A22, A26, ASCA, AmHI, ArtHuCI, BibInd, CurCont, DIP, E01, FR, H07, I05, IBR, IBRH, IBZ, IPB, MLA, MLA-IB, PCI, PhilInd, RASB, SCOPUS, T02, W07.
—BLDSC (1612.060000), IE, Infotrieve, Ingenta, INIST. **CCC.**
Published by: Walter de Gruyter GmbH & Co. KG, Genthiner Str 13, Berlin, 10785, Germany. TEL 49-30-260050, FAX 49-30-26005251, info@degruyter.com. Eds. Christoph Horn, Wolfgang Bartuschat. Adv. contact Dietlind Makswitat TEL 49-30-260050. page EUR 550; trim 108 x 176. Circ: 650 (paid).

170 340 300 100 DEU ISSN 0001-2343
➤ **ARCHIV FUER RECHTS- UND SOZIALPHILOSOPHIE/ARCHIVES DE PHILOSOPHIE DU DROIT ET DE PHILOSOPHIE SOCIALE/ ARCHIVES FOR PHILOSOPHY OF LAW AND SOCIAL PHILOSOPHY.** Short title: A R S P. Text in English, French, German, Spanish. 1907. q. EUR 259.80; EUR 62 newsstand/cover (effective 2012). adv. bk.rev. cum.index. back issues avail.; reprint service avail. from SCH. **Document type:** *Journal, Academic/Scholarly.*
Former titles (until 1964): Archiv fuer Rechts- und Sozialphilosophie (0177-1094); (until 1933): Archiv fuer Rechts- und Wirtschaftsphilosophie (0177-1108)

Related titles: Online - full text ed.: (from IngentaConnect); ◆ Supplement(s): Archiv fuer Rechts und Sozialphilosophie. Supplementa. ISSN 0722-5679; ◆ Archiv fuer Rechts- und Sozialphilosophie. Beihefte. ISSN 0341-079X.
Indexed: A22, DIP, FLP, FR, I13, IBR, IBSS, IBZ, IPB, PCI, PhilInd, RASB.
—IE, Infotrieve, Ingenta, INIST. **CCC.**
Published by: (Internationale Vereinigung fuer Rechts- und Sozialphilosophie), Franz Steiner Verlag GmbH, Birkenwaldstr 44, Stuttgart, 70191, Germany. TEL 49-711-25820, FAX 49-711-2582290, service@steiner-verlag.de. R&P Sabine Koerner. Adv. contact Susanne Szoradi. Circ: 900 (paid).

340 100 300 DEU ISSN 0341-079X
ARCHIV FUER RECHTS- UND SOZIALPHILOSOPHIE. BEIHEFTE. Text in English, French, German. 1964. irreg., latest vol.126, 2011. price varies. reprints avail. **Document type:** *Monographic series, Academic/Scholarly.*
Related titles: ◆ Supplement to: Archiv fuer Rechts- und Sozialphilosophie. ISSN 0001-2343.
Indexed: A22.
—BLDSC (1731.750050), IE, Ingenta.
Published by: (Internationale Vereinigung fuer Rechts- und Sozialphilosophie), Franz Steiner Verlag GmbH, Birkenwaldstr 44, Stuttgart, 70191, Germany. TEL 49-711-25820, FAX 49-711-2582290, service@steiner-verlag.de, http://www.steiner-verlag.de.

340 300 100 DEU ISSN 0722-5679
ARCHIV FUER RECHTS UND SOZIALPHILOSOPHIE. SUPPLEMENTA. Text in German. 1934. irreg., latest vol.120, 2010. price varies. **Document type:** *Monographic series, Academic/Scholarly.*
Related titles: ◆ Supplement to: Archiv fuer Rechts- und Sozialphilosophie. ISSN 0001-2343.
Indexed: RASB.
Published by: (Internationale Vereinigung fuer Rechts- und Sozialphilosophie), Franz Steiner Verlag GmbH, Birkenwaldstr 44, Stuttgart, 70191, Germany. TEL 49-711-25820, FAX 49-711-2582290, service@steiner-verlag.de, http://www.steiner-verlag.de.

100 FRA ISSN 0003-9632
B1
ARCHIVES DE PHILOSOPHIE; recherches et documentation. Text in French; Summaries in English, French. 1923. 4/yr. adv. bk.rev. abstr.; charts.
Indexed: A20, A21, A22, ASCA, ArtHuCI, BibInd, CurCont, DIP, FR, I13, IBR, IBSS, IBZ, IPB, MLA-IB, P30, PCI, PhilInd, RASB, RI-1, RI-2, RILM, SCOPUS, W07.
—IE, Infotrieve, INIST.
Published by: Association Centre Sevres, Faculte Jesuites de Paris, 35 bis rue de Sevres, Paris, 75006, France. Circ: 800.

180 FRA ISSN 0373-5478
B720
ARCHIVES D'HISTOIRE DOCTRINALE ET LITTERAIRE DU MOYEN AGE. Text in English, French, German, Latin. 1926. a., latest vol.76, 2009. price varies. index. back issues avail. **Document type:** *Journal, Academic/Scholarly.*
Related titles: Microfiche ed.: (from IDC).
Indexed: A22, BibInd, FR, IBR, IBZ, IPB, MLA, MLA-IB, P30, PCI, PhilInd, RASB.
—IE, INIST.
Published by: Librairie Philosophique J. Vrin, 6 place de la Sorbonne, Paris, F-75005, France. TEL 33-1-43540347, FAX 33-1-43544818, contact@vrin.fr, http://www.vrin.fr. Ed. F Hudry. R&P Mr. Paulhac. Circ: 750.

100 NLD ISSN 0066-6610
B20.6
➤ **ARCHIVES INTERNATIONALES D'HISTOIRE DES IDEES/ INTERNATIONAL ARCHIVES OF THE HISTORY OF IDEAS.** Text in English, French. 1963. irreg., latest vol.199, 2009. price varies. back issues avail. **Document type:** *Monographic series, Academic/ Scholarly.* **Description:** Covers the history of philosophy, science, political and religious thought, and other areas of intellectual history.
Indexed: A22, FR, P30, RASB.
—BLDSC (4536.110000), IE, Infotrieve, Ingenta, INIST. **CCC.**
Published by: Springer Netherlands (Subsidiary of: Springer Science+Business Media), Van Godewijckstraat 30, Dordrecht, 3311 GX, Netherlands. TEL 31-78-6576050, FAX 31-78-6576474, http://www.springer.com. Ed. Sarah Hutton.

100 ITA ISSN 0004-0088
B4
ARCHIVIO DI FILOSOFIA/ARCHIVES OF PHILOSOPHY. Text in English, French, German, Italian. 1931. 3/yr. EUR 425 combined subscription domestic to institutions (print & online eds.); EUR 495 combined subscription foreign to institutions (print & online eds.) (effective 2009). **Document type:** *Journal, Academic/Scholarly.* **Description:** Publishes on themes of current international interest.
Related titles: Online - full text ed.: ISSN 1970-0792. 2005.
Indexed: A21, A22, BibInd, CERDIC, DIP, IBR, IBZ, IPB, MLA-IB, PhilInd, RASB, RI-1, RI-2.
—IE, Infotrieve.
Published by: (Universita degli Studi di Roma "La Sapienza", Istituto di Studi Filosofici), Fabrizio Serra Editore (Subsidiary of: Accademia Editoriale), c/o Accademia Editoriale, Via Santa Bibbiana 28, Pisa, 56127, Italy. TEL 39-050-542332, FAX 39-050-574888, accademiaeditoriale@accademiaeditoriale.it, http:// www.libraweb.net.

109 POL ISSN 0066-6874
B6
ARCHIWUM HISTORII FILOZOFII I MYSLI SPOLECZNEJ. Text in Polish; Summaries in English, German. 1957. a., latest vol.45, 2000. price varies. **Document type:** *Academic/Scholarly.* **Description:** Studies the history of philosophy in Poland and throughout the world.
Indexed: FR, IBR, IBZ, MLA-IB, RASB.
Published by: Polska Akademia Nauk, Instytut Filozofii i Socjologii, Nowy Swiat 72, Warsaw, 00330, Poland. TEL 48-22-8267181, FAX 48-22-8267823, secretar@ifispan.waw.pl, http://www.ifispan.waw.pl. Ed. Zbigniew Ogonowski.

DAS ARGUMENT; Zeitschrift fuer Philosophie und Sozialwissenschaften. *see* SOCIAL SCIENCES: COMPREHENSIVE WORKS

100 NLD ISSN 0920-427X
BC1 CODEN: ARGMEL
➤ **ARGUMENTATION**; an international journal on reasoning. Text in English. 1987. q. EUR 565, USD 602 combined subscription to institutions (print & online eds.) (effective 2012). adv. bk.rev. illus.; bibl. back issues avail.; reprint service avail. from PSC. **Document type:** *Journal, Academic/Scholarly.* **Description:** Covers all aspects of rhetoric and argumentation, ranging from literary rhetoric to linguistics, from theological arguments to legal reasoning.
Related titles: Microform ed.: (from PQC); Online - full text ed.: ISSN 1572-8374 (from IngentaConnect).
Indexed: A22, A26, AmHI, BEL&L, BibInd, BibLing, CA, CMM, CommAb, DIP, E01, H07, IBR, IBZ, IPB, L&LBA, MLA-IB, P10, P27, P48, P53, P54, PQC, PhilInd, RASB, S11, SCOPUS, SOPODA, SociolAb, T02.
—BLDSC (1664.356100), IE, Infotrieve, Ingenta. **CCC.**
Published by: (European Centre for the Study of Argumentation), Springer Netherlands (Subsidiary of: Springer Science+Business Media), Van Godewijckstraat 30, Dordrecht, 3311 GX, Netherlands. TEL 31-78-6576050, FAX 31-78-6576474, http://www.springer.com. Eds. Erik C W Krabbe, John Woods, Scott Jacobs, Frans H van Eemeren.

100 ESP ISSN 1139-3327
ARGUMENTOS DE RAZON TECNICA. Text in Spanish. 1998. a., latest vol.3, 2000. **Document type:** *Journal, Academic/Scholarly.*
Related titles: Online - full text ed.
Indexed: PhilInd.
Published by: Universidad de Sevilla, Secretariado de Publicaciones, Calle Porvenir 27, Sevilla, 41013, Spain. TEL 34-95-4487444, FAX 34-95-4487443, secpub10@us.es, http://www.us.es/publius/ inicio.html.

100 GBR
ARGUMENTS OF THE PHILOSOPHERS. Text in English. 197?. irreg., latest 1999. price varies. **Document type:** *Monographic series, Academic/Scholarly.* **Description:** Provides a contemporary assessment and history of the entire course of philosophical thought. Each book constitutes a detailed critical introduction to the work of a philosopher of major influence and significance.
Published by: Routledge (Subsidiary of: Taylor & Francis Group), 2 Park Sq, Milton Park, Abingdon, Oxon OX14 4RN, United Kingdom. TEL 44-20-70176000, FAX 44-20-70176699, info@routledge.co.uk, http://www.routledge.com.

184 BEL
➤ **ARISTOTE**; traductions et etudes. Text in French. 1945. irreg., latest vol.9. price varies. bk.rev. back issues avail. **Document type:** *Monographic series, Academic/Scholarly.*
Published by: (Universite Catholique de Louvain, Departement d'Etudes Greques, Latines et Orientales), Peeters Publishers, Bondgenotenlaan 153, Leuven, 3000, Belgium. TEL 32-16-235170, FAX 32-16-228500, http://www.peeters-leuven.be.

141 NLD ISSN 0927-4103
ARISTOTELES SEMITICO-LATINUS. Text in English. 1975. irreg., latest vol.21, 2010. price varies. **Document type:** *Monographic series, Academic/Scholarly.*
Indexed: IZBG.
Published by: Brill, PO Box 9000, Leiden, 2300 PA, Netherlands. TEL 31-71-5353500, FAX 31-71-5317532, cs@brill.nl.

100 GBR
ARISTOTELIAN SOCIETY. PROCEEDINGS (HARDBACK EDITION). Text in English. 1888. a. GBP 83 domestic to institutions; EUR 105 in Europe to institutions; USD 147 in the Americas to institutions; USD 188 elsewhere to institutions; GBP 91 combined subscription domestic to institutions (print & online eds.); EUR 116 combined subscription in Europe to institutions (print & online eds.); USD 162 combined subscription in the Americas to institutions (print & online eds.); USD 207 combined subscription elsewhere to institutions (print & online eds.) (effective 2009). adv. back issues avail.; reprints avail. **Document type:** *Proceedings, Academic/Scholarly.* **Description:** Contains the papers read at the Society's fortnightly meetings in London throughout the academic year, and short discussion notes on these papers.
Related titles: ◆ Online - full text ed.: Aristotelian Society. Proceedings (Online). ISSN 1467-9264; ◆ Alternate Frequency ed(s).: Aristotelian Society. Proceedings (Paper Back Edition). ISSN 0066-7374. a.
—CCC.
Published by: Aristotelian Society, c/o Rachel Carter, Rm 281 Stewart House, Russell Square, London, WC1B 5DN, United Kingdom. TEL 44-20-78628685, mail@aristoteliansociety.org.uk, http:// www.aristoteliansociety.org.uk. Ed. Dr. Mark Eli Kalderon. **Subscr. to:** Wiley-Blackwell Publishing Ltd., Journal Customer Services, 9600 Garsington Rd, PO Box 1354, Oxford OX4 2XG, United Kingdom. TEL 44-1865-778315, FAX 44-1865-471775.

100 GBR ISSN 1467-9264
ARISTOTELIAN SOCIETY. PROCEEDINGS (ONLINE). Text in English. 3/yr. GBP 100 in United Kingdom to institutions; EUR 127 in Europe to institutions; USD 176 in the Americas to institutions; USD 225 elsewhere to institutions (effective 2012). **Document type:** *Journal, Academic/Scholarly.*
Media: Online - full text (from IngentaConnect). **Related titles:** ◆ Print ed.: Aristotelian Society. Proceedings (Hardback Edition); ◆ Aristotelian Society. Proceedings (Paper Back Edition). ISSN 0066-7374.
—CCC.
Published by: Aristotelian Society, c/o Georgia Testa, Rm 260, Senate House, Malet St, London, WC1E 7HU, United Kingdom. mail@aristoteliansociety.org.uk, http://www.sas.ac.uk/ aristotelian_society/.

100 GBR ISSN 0066-7374
B11 CODEN: PRASE4
ARISTOTELIAN SOCIETY. PROCEEDINGS (PAPER BACK EDITION). Text in English. 1888. a. GBP 100 in United Kingdom to institutions; EUR 127 in Europe to institutions; USD 176 in the Americas to institutions; USD 225 elsewhere to institutions; GBP 116 combined subscription in United Kingdom to institutions (print & online eds.); EUR 146 combined subscription in Europe to institutions (print & online eds.); USD 203 combined subscription in the Americas to institutions (print & online eds.); USD 259 combined subscription elsewhere to institutions (print & online eds.) (effective 2012). adv. back issues avail.; reprint service avail. from PSC. **Document type:** *Proceedings, Academic/Scholarly.* **Description:** Contains the papers read at the Society's fortnightly meetings in London throughout the academic year, and short discussion notes on these papers.
Related titles: ◆ Online - full text ed.: Aristotelian Society. Proceedings (Online). ISSN 1467-9264; ◆ Alternate Frequency ed(s).: Aristotelian Society. Proceedings (Hardback Edition). a.; ◆ Supplement(s): Aristotelian Society. Proceedings. Supplementary Volume. ISSN 0309-7013.
Indexed: A01, A03, A08, A22, A26, CA, E01, FR, IPB, PCI, PhilInd, RASB, SCOPUS, SOPODA, SociolAb, T02.
—BLDSC (6648.800000), IE, Infotrieve, Ingenta, INIST. **CCC.**
Published by: Aristotelian Society, c/o Rachel Carter, Rm 281 Stewart House, Russell Square, London, WC1B 5DN, United Kingdom. TEL 44-20-78628685, mail@aristoteliansociety.org.uk, http:// www.aristoteliansociety.org.uk. Ed. Dr. Mark Eli Kalderon. **Subscr. to:** Wiley-Blackwell Publishing Ltd., Journal Customer Services, 9600 Garsington Rd, PO Box 1354, Oxford OX4 2XG, United Kingdom. TEL 44-1865-778315, FAX 44-1865-471775.

100 GBR ISSN 0309-7013
B11
➤ **ARISTOTELIAN SOCIETY. PROCEEDINGS. SUPPLEMENTARY VOLUME.** Text in English. 1887. a. GBP 100 in United Kingdom to institutions; EUR 127 in Europe to institutions; USD 176 in the Americas to institutions; USD 225 elsewhere to institutions; GBP 116 combined subscription in United Kingdom to institutions (print & online eds.); EUR 146 combined subscription in Europe to institutions (print & online eds.); USD 203 combined subscription in the Americas to institutions (print & online eds.); USD 259 combined subscription elsewhere to institutions (print & online eds.) (effective 2012). adv. illus. back issues avail.; reprint service avail. from PSC. **Document type:** *Proceedings, Academic/Scholarly.* **Description:** Contains the Symposia to be read at the Annual Joint Session of the Aristotelian Society and the Mind Association.
Related titles: Online - full text ed.: ISSN 1467-8349. GBP 100 in United Kingdom to institutions; EUR 127 in Europe to institutions; USD 176 in the Americas to institutions; USD 225 elsewhere to institutions (effective 2012) (from IngentaConnect); ◆ Supplement to: Aristotelian Society. Proceedings (Paper Back Edition). ISSN 0066-7374.
Indexed: A01, A03, A08, A22, A26, CA, E01, PCI, PhilInd, RASB, T02.
—BLDSC (8547.400000), IE, Infotrieve, Ingenta. **CCC.**
Published by: Aristotelian Society, c/o Rachel Carter, Rm 281 Stewart House, Russell Square, London, WC1B 5DN, United Kingdom. TEL 44-20-78628685, mail@aristoteliansociety.org.uk, http:// www.aristoteliansociety.org.uk. Ed. Dr. Mark Eli Kalderon. **Subscr. to:** Wiley-Blackwell Publishing Ltd., Journal Customer Services, 9600 Garsington Rd, PO Box 1354, Oxford OX4 2XG, United Kingdom. TEL 44-1865-778315, FAX 44-1865-471775.

100 ITA ISSN 1974-1499
ARKETE. Text in Multiple languages. 2005. s-a. **Document type:** *Journal, Academic/Scholarly.*
Published by: Universita degli Studi di Siena, Dipartimento di Studi Storico - Sociali e Filosofici, Via Banchi di Sotto 55, Siena, 53100, Italy. http://www.unisi.it.

ARQUITECTONICS; mind, land and society. *see* ARCHITECTURE

109 901 NOR ISSN 0802-7005
ARR; idehistorisk tidsskrift. Text in Norwegian. 1989. q. NOK 220 (effective 2006). back issues avail. **Document type:** *Journal, Academic/Scholarly.*
Incorporates (1984-1992): Profil (0800-7128); Which was formerly (1983-1984): Nordisk Profil (0800-3602); (1959-1983): Profil (Oslo, 1995) (0800-0573); (1938-1959): Fiiilogen (0800-1596)
Indexed: RILM.
Address: Huitfeldt Gate 15, Oslo, 0254, Norway. Ed. Ellen Krefting. Circ: 1,500.

215 200 NLD ISSN 1566-5399
BL51
➤ **ARS DISPUTANDI**; the online journal for philosophy of religion. Text and summaries in English. 2000. irreg. free (effective 2011). bk.rev. bibl. Index. back issues avail. **Document type:** *Journal, Academic/ Scholarly.* **Description:** Publishes articles, literature surveys and discussion notes on philosophy of religion.
Media: Online - full content. **Related titles:** Online - full text ed.
Indexed: A21, AmHI, CA, H07, PhilInd, RI-1, T02.
Published by: Igitur, Utrecht Publishing & Archiving Services, Postbus 80124, Utrecht, 3508 TC, Netherlands. TEL 31-30-2536635, FAX 31-30-2536959, info@igitur.uu.nl, http://www.igitur.uu.nl. Eds. Maarten Wisse, Marcel Sarot, Michael Scott. Pub. Saskia Franken.

100 610 DEU ISSN 2190-7463
▼ **ARS MORIENDI NOVA.** Text in German. 2010. irreg. price varies. **Document type:** *Monographic series, Academic/Scholarly.*
Published by: Franz Steiner Verlag GmbH, Birkenwaldstr 44, Stuttgart, 70191, Germany. TEL 49-711-25820, FAX 49-711-2582290, service@steiner-verlag.de, http://www.steiner-verlag.de. Eds. Andreas Frewer, Christof Mueller-Busch, Daniel Schaefer.

ASIAN BIOETHICS REVIEW. *see* BIOLOGY

100 TWN
ASIAN JOURNAL OF PHILOSOPHY. Text in English. 1988. s-a. USD 10 to individuals; USD 12 to institutions; USD 5 to students (effective 2000). bk.rev. **Document type:** *Monographic series, Academic/ Scholarly.*
Indexed: PerIslam.
Published by: Asian Association of Catholic Philosophers, National Taiwan University, Dept. of Philosophy, Roosevelt Rd, Sec 4, Taipei, 10764, Taiwan. TEL 886-35-2317216. Ed., R&P Tran Van Doan TEL 886-2-2364-0261.

P

100 950 GBR ISSN 0955-2367
B5000

➤ **ASIAN PHILOSOPHY**; an international journal of Indian, Chinese, Japanese, Buddhist, Persian and Islamic philosophical traditions. Text in English. 1991. 3/yr. GBP 762 combined subscription in United Kingdom to institutions (print & online eds.); EUR 1,006, USD 1,263 combined subscription to institutions (print & online eds.) (effective 2012). adv. bk.rev. illus. index. back issues avail.; reprint service avail. from PSC. **Document type:** *Journal, Academic/Scholarly.*
Description: Focuses on Indian, Chinese, Japanese, Buddhist, Persian, and Islamic philosophical traditions.
Related titles: Microfiche ed.; Online - full text ed.: ISSN 1469-2961. GBP 686 in United Kingdom to institutions; EUR 905, USD 1,137 to institutions (effective 2012) (from IngentaConnect).
Indexed: A01, A02, A03, A08, A20, A22, A25, A26, AmHI, ArtHuCI, BAS, BRD, BibLing, BrHumI, CA, CurCont, DIP, E01, E08, G08, H07, H08, H14, HAb, HumInd, I05, I08, IBR, IBZ, P02, P10, P13, P28, P48, P53, P54, PCI, PQC, PerIslam, PhilInd, R05, RASB, S08, S09, S21, S23, SCOPUS, T02, W03, W07.
—IE, Infotrieve, Ingenta. **CCC.**
Published by: Routledge (Subsidiary of: Taylor & Francis Group), 4 Park Sq, Milton Park, Abingdon, Oxon OX14 4RN, United Kingdom. TEL 44-20-70176000, FAX 44-20-70176336, subscriptions@tandf.co.uk, http://www.routledge.com. Eds. Dr. Brian Carr, Indira Mahalingam Carr. Adv. contact Linda Hann TEL 44-1344-779945. **Subscr. to:** Taylor & Francis Ltd., Journals Customer Service, Sheepen Pl, Colchester, Essex CO3 3LP, United Kingdom. TEL 44-20-70175544, FAX 44-20-70175198.

179.7 ESP ISSN 2171-5947
ASOCIACION FEDERAL DERECHO A MORIR DIGNAMENTE. BOLETIN. Text in Spanish. 1984. a. **Document type:** *Bulletin, Consumer.*
Published by: Asociacion Federal Derecho a Morir Dignamente, Puerta del Sol No. 6 3o Iaq., Madrid, 28013, Spain. TEL 34-91-3691746, informacion@eutanasia.ws, http://www.eutanasia.es/. Ed. Fernando Pedros.

ASPEKTE DER MEDIZINPHILOSOPHIE. *see* MEDICAL SCIENCES

ASSOCIATION OF BRITISH THEOLOGICAL AND PHILOSOPHICAL LIBRARIES. BULLETIN. *see* LIBRARY AND INFORMATION SCIENCES

100 FRA ISSN 1762-6110
B1

➤ **ASTERION**; philosophie, histoire des idees. pensee politique. Text in French. 2003. irreg. free (effective 2011). **Document type:** *Journal, Academic/Scholarly.* **Description:** As the subtitle explains, it focuses on philosophy, the history of ideas and political thought.
Media: Online - full text.
Indexed: A39, C27, C29, D03, D04, E13, R14, S14, S15, S18.
—CCC.
Published by: Ecole Normale Superieure de Lyon, Lettres et Sciences Humaines, 15 Parvis Rene Descartes, Lyon, 69364, France. TEL 33-4-72728000, FAX 33-4-72728080, http://www.ens-lsh.fr. Ed. Marie Gaille-Nikodimov.

100 ESP ISSN 1699-7549
ASTROLABIO. Text in Spanish, Catalan, English. 2005. s-a. free (effective 2011). **Document type:** *Journal, Academic/Scholarly.*
Media: Online - full text.
Published by: Universitat de Barcelona, Facultat de Filosofia, Avda. Jose Antonio 585, Barcelona 7, Spain. Ed. Jose Manuel Bermudo Avila.

170 CAN ISSN 1718-9977
JA79

➤ **LES ATELIERS DE L'ETHIQUE.** Text in English, French. 2006. irreg. free (effective 2011). **Document type:** *Journal, Academic/Scholarly.*
Media: Online - full text.
Indexed: A39, C27, C29, D03, D04, E13, PhilInd, R14, S14, S15, S18.
Published by: Universite de Montreal, P O Box 6128, Montreal, PQ H3C 3J7, Canada. TEL 514-343-6044.

➤ **ATLANTIDE.** *see* NEW AGE PUBLICATIONS

111.85 701.17 320.5 USA
ATOPIA: PHILOSOPHY, POLITICAL THEORY, AESTHETICS. Text in English. 2000. irreg., latest 2004. price varies. back issues avail. **Document type:** *Monographic series, Academic/Scholarly.* **Description:** Questions the foundation that lead to provocative new ways of imagining and re-imagining the shared disciplines of philosophical reflection, political thought, and aesthetics.
Published by: Stanford University Press (Subsidiary of: Stanford University), 1450 Page Mill Rd, Palo Alto, CA 94304. TEL 650-723-9434, FAX 650-725-3457, info@www.sup.org. Eds. Frederick M Dolan, Judith Butler. **In Europe:** Cambridge University Press, The Edinburgh Bldg, Shaftesbury Rd, Cambridge CB2 8RU, United Kingdom. TEL 44-1223-312393, FAX 44-1223-315052, information@cambridge.org, http://www.cambridge.org/uk; **In the Americas:** Cambridge University Press Distribution Center, 100 Brookhill Dr, West Nyack, NY 10994. TEL 845-353-7500, FAX 845-353-4141, http://www.cambridge.org.

100 150.19 ITA ISSN 1120-9364
RC437.5
ATQUE; materiali tra filosofia e psicoterapia. Text in Italian. 1990. s-a. EUR 18 domestic; EUR 52 foreign (effective 2009). **Document type:** *Magazine, Consumer.* **Description:** Covers relational studies between philosophy and psychotherapy.
Indexed: E-psyche.
Published by: Moretti e Vitali Editori, Via Sergentini 6a, Bergamo, BG 24128, Italy. TEL 39-035-251300, FAX 39-035-4329409, http://www.morettievitali.it.

100 800 780 DEU ISSN 1613-5709
AUFGANG; Jahrbuch fuer Denken, Dichten, Musik. Text in German. 2004. a. EUR 35 (effective 2011). **Document type:** *Journal, Academic/Scholarly.*
Published by: W. Kohlhammer GmbH, Hessbruehlstr 69, Stuttgart, 70565, Germany. TEL 49-711-78630, FAX 49-711-78638204, kohlhammerkontakt@kohlhammer.de, http://www.kohlhammer.de.

189 261.51 USA ISSN 0094-5323
BR65.A9

➤ **AUGUSTINIAN STUDIES.** Text mainly in English. 1970. s-a. USD 35 to individuals; USD 60 to institutions; USD 82 combined subscription to individuals (print & online eds.); USD 216 combined subscription to institutions (print & online eds.) (effective 2009). bk.rev. back issues avail.; reprint service avail. from PSC. **Document type:** *Journal, Academic/Scholarly.* **Description:** Designed to the study of the life, teachings, and influence of Augustine of Hippo.
Related titles: Online - full text ed.: ISSN 2153-7917. USD 50 to individuals; USD 180 to institutions (effective 2009).
Indexed: A01, A03, A08, A22, A26, CA, CPL, DIP, E08, G08, I05, IBR, IBZ, IPB, PCI, PhilInd, S09, T02.
—IE, Infotrieve.
Published by: Philosophy Documentation Center, PO Box 7147, Charlottesville, VA 22906. TEL 434-220-3300, FAX 434-220-3301, order@pdcnet.org, http://www.pdcnet.org. Ed. Allan Fitzgerald. R&P George Leaman. Adv. contact Greg Swope.

100 ESP ISSN 1575-5045
PQ6647.A514
AURORA; papeles del Seminario Maria Zambrano. Text in Spanish. 1999. irreg. **Document type:** *Journal, Academic/Scholarly.* **Description:** Covers the life and works of the Spanish philosopher Maria Zambrano (1904-1991).
Indexed: PhilInd.
Published by: (Universitat de Barcelona, Departamento de Historia de la Filosofia Estetica), Universitat de Barcelona, Servei de Publicacions, Gran Via Corts Catalanes 585, Barcelona, 08007, Spain. TEL 34-93-4021100, http://www.publicacions.ub.es.

100 USA ISSN 0733-4311
B1
AUSLEGUNG; a journal of philosophy. Text in English. 1973. s-a. USD 12 to individuals; USD 15 to institutions; USD 10 to students (effective 2008). adv. bk.rev. charts. back issues avail.; reprints avail. **Document type:** *Journal, Academic/Scholarly.*
Indexed: A20, FR, PhilInd.
—BLDSC (1792.939000), IE, Ingenta, INIST.
Published by: (Graduate Association of Students in Philosophy), University of Kansas, Department of Philosophy, 1445 Jayhawk Blvd, Rm 3090, Wescoe Hall, Lawrence, KS 66045. TEL 913-864-2700. Ed. Tamela Ice.

160 AUS ISSN 1448-5052

➤ **THE AUSTRALASIAN JOURNAL OF LOGIC.** Abbreviated title: The A J L. Text in English. 2003. a. free (effective 2011). back issues avail. **Document type:** *Journal, Academic/Scholarly.* **Description:** Covers all areas of pure and applied logic.
Media: Online - full text.
Indexed: A39, C27, C29, CCMJ, D03, D04, E13, MSN, MathR, PhilInd, R14, S14, S15, S18, Z02.
Published by: Australasian Association for Logic, c/o The University of Melbourne, School of Philosophy, Carlton, VIC 3010, Australia. TEL 61-3-83445142, FAX 61-3-83444280, office@philosophy.unimelb.edu.au. Ed. Martin Bunder.

100 GBR ISSN 0004-8402
B1

➤ **AUSTRALASIAN JOURNAL OF PHILOSOPHY.** Abbreviated title: A J P. Text in English. 1923. q. GBP 151 combined subscription in United Kingdom to institutions (print & online eds.); EUR 200, AUD 288, USD 252 combined subscription to institutions (print & online eds.) (effective 2012). bk.rev. abstr.; bibl.; illus. index, cum.index every 10 yrs. 156 p./no.; back issues avail.; reprint service avail. from PSC. **Document type:** *Journal, Academic/Scholarly.* **Description:** Contains original articles and discussion notes of high quality in any area of philosophy.
Formerly (until 1947): Australasian Journal of Psychology and Philosophy (1832-8660)
Related titles: Microform ed.: (from MIM); Online - full text ed.: ISSN 1471-6828. GBP 133 in United Kingdom to institutions; EUR 176, AUD 259, USD 222 to institutions (effective 2012) (from IngentaConnect).
Indexed: A11, A20, A22, ASCA, AmHI, ArtHuCI, AusPAIS, BrHumI, CA, CurCont, E01, FR, H07, H14, IBR, IBRH, IBZ, IPB, MLA-IB, P10, P28, P30, P48, P53, P54, PCI, PQC, PhilInd, RASB, SCOPUS, SOPODA, T02, W07.
—IE, Infotrieve, Ingenta. **CCC.**
Published by: (Australasian Association of Philosophy AUS), Routledge (Subsidiary of: Taylor & Francis Group), 4 Park Sq, Milton Park, Abingdon, Oxon OX14 4RN, United Kingdom. TEL 44-20-70176000, FAX 44-20-70176336, journals@routledge.com, http://www.routledge.com. Ed. Stewart Candlish TEL 61-8-64882357. Adv. contact Linda Hann TEL 44-1344-779945.

170.5 AUS ISSN 1328-4576

➤ **AUSTRALIAN JOURNAL OF PROFESSIONAL AND APPLIED ETHICS.** Text in English. 1999. s-a. AUD 50 domestic to individuals; AUD 75 foreign to individuals; AUD 90 domestic to institutions; AUD 110 foreign to institutions (effective 2010). **Document type:** *Journal, Academic/Scholarly.*
Indexed: P30, PhilInd.
—BLDSC (1811.260000), IE.
Published by: (Australian Association for Professional and Applied Ethics), Charles Sturt University, Centre for Applied Philosophy and Public Ethics, LPO Box 8260, ANU, Canberra, ACT 2601, Australia. cappe@csu.edu.au, http://www.cappe.edu.au/.

211 AUS ISSN 1036-8191
AUSTRALIAN RATIONALIST. Text in English. 1969. q. free to members (effective 2009). adv. bk.rev.; film rev. illus. back issues avail. **Document type:** *Journal, Trade.*
Incorporates (1986-1990): News and Views; Formed by the merger of: Rationalist (0034-0065); Australian Rationalist (0005-0113)
Related titles: Online - full text ed.
Indexed: A11, AEI, AmHI, H07.
—Ingenta.
Published by: Rationalist Society of Australia, PO Box 1219, Fitzroy North, VIC 3068, Australia. TEL 61-3-95302954, rationalist@bigpond.com. Ed. Kevin Childs.

517.1 DEU
AUSTRIAN LUDWIG WITTGENSTEIN SOCIETY. PUBLICATIONS. Text in English. 1976; N.S. 2005. irreg., latest vol.2, 2006. price varies. **Document type:** *Monographic series, Academic/Scholarly.*
Formerly (until 2005): Wittgenstein Gesellschaft. Schriftenreihe (1026-9347)
—IE, Ingenta.
Published by: (The Austrian Ludwig Wittgenstein Society AUT), Ontos Verlag, Frankfurter Str 39, Heusenstamm, 63150, Germany. TEL 49-6104-665733, FAX 49-6104-665734, info@ontosverlag.de, http://www.ontosverlag.de.

100 ITA ISSN 0005-0601
B4
AUT AUT; rivista di filosofia e di cultura. Text in Italian. 1951. bi-m. EUR 60 domestic (effective 2009). adv. index. **Document type:** *Journal, Trade.*
Indexed: A20, ASCA, ArtHuCI, BibInd, CurCont, DIP, FR, IBR, IBZ, IPB, MLA, MLA-IB, PCI, SCOPUS, W07.
—INIST.
Published by: Gruppo Editoriale Il Saggiatore, Via Melzo 9, Milan, 20129, Italy. TEL 39-02-29513061, http://www.saggiatore.it/home_saggiatore.php?. Circ: 3,000.

100 MEX ISSN 1665-1103
P306.A1
AVATARES. Text in Spanish. 2000. s-a. **Document type:** *Journal, Academic/Scholarly.*
Indexed: A01, CA, F03, F04, T02.
Published by: Universidad Intercontinental, Escuela de Filosofia, Insurgentes Sur 4303, Col. Sta Ursula Xitla, De. Tlalpan, Mexico, D.F., 14420, Mexico. TEL 52-22-54871430, FAX 52-22-54871337, http://www.uic.edu.mx. Ed. Jesus Ayaquica Martinez. Circ: 200.

100 GBR ISSN 0955-9582
AVEBURY SERIES IN PHILOSOPHY. Text in English. 1986. irreg., latest 2000. price varies. back issues avail. **Document type:** *Monographic series, Academic/Scholarly.*
Published by: Ashgate Publishing Ltd (Subsidiary of: Gower Publishing Co. Ltd.), Gower House, Croft Rd, Aldershot, Hants GU11 3HR, United Kingdom. TEL 44-1252-331551, FAX 44-1252-344405, info@ashgate.com. **Dist. by:** Ashgate Publishing Co, PO Box 2225, Williston, VT 05495. TEL 800-535-9544, FAX 802-864-7626, orders@ashgate.com

109 BEL

➤ **AVERROES LATINUS.** Text in French, Latin. irreg., latest vol.12, 1996. price varies. back issues avail. **Document type:** *Monographic series, Academic/Scholarly.* **Description:** Translates the works of Averroes and offers scholarly critique.
Published by: (Academie Royale de Belgique), Peeters Publishers, Bondgenotenlaan 153, Leuven, 3000, Belgium. TEL 32-16-235170, FAX 32-16-228500, http://www.peeters-leuven.be.

109 BEL

➤ **AVICENNA LATINUS.** Text in French, Latin. 1968. irreg., latest vol.9, 1994. price varies. back issues avail. **Document type:** *Monographic series, Academic/Scholarly.* **Description:** Translates the writings of Avicenna and provides scholarly commentary.
Published by: (Academie Royale des Sciences, des Lettres et des Beaux-Arts de Belgique/Koninklijke Vlaamse Academie van Belgie voor Wetenschappen en Kunsten), Peeters Publishers, Bondgenotenlaan 153, Leuven, 3000, Belgium. TEL 32-16-235170, FAX 32-16-228500, http://www.peeters-leuven.be.

181.45 294.54 USA ISSN 1941-823X
BL1238.56.K86
THE AWAKENING. Text in English. 1995. q. USD 12 domestic; USD 15 in Canada; USD 25 elsewhere; USD 5 newsstand/cover (effective 2005). adv. **Document type:** *Magazine, Consumer.* **Description:** Dedicated to bring about awareness about the knowledge and science of Kundalini Mahayoga or Shaktipat and the Shaktipat lineage of Swami Shivom Tirth.
Published by: Swami Shivom Tirth Ashram Inc., 124 Rock Harbor Ln, Foster City, CA 94404. TEL 415-806-1007, FAX 650-506-5439, drathi@yahoo.com, http://www.shivomtirthashram.org. Ed., R&P, Adv. contact Dinesh H Rathi. B&W page USD 50. Circ: 100 (paid).

100 NLD ISSN 1572-8390

➤ **AXIOMATHES (ONLINE)**; an international journal in ontology and cognitive systems. Text in English. q. EUR 457, USD 473 to institutions (effective 2012). reprint service avail. from PSC. **Document type:** *Journal, Academic/Scholarly.*
Media: Online - full text (from IngentaConnect).
Indexed: A22, A26, E01, P03, PsycholAb.
—CCC.
Published by: Springer Netherlands (Subsidiary of: Springer Science+Business Media), Van Godewijckstraat 30, Dordrecht, 3311 GX, Netherlands. TEL 31-78-6576050, FAX 31-78-6576474, http://www.springer.com. Ed. Roberto Poli.

➤ **AYAANGWAAMIZIN.** *see* ETHNIC INTERESTS

100 ESP ISSN 0213-3563
B4561

➤ **AZAFEA**; estudios de historia de la filosofia hispanica. Text in Spanish. 1985. a., latest vol.11, 2009. EUR 21 per issue (effective 2011). **Document type:** *Journal, Academic/Scholarly.*
Related titles: Supplement(s): Cuadernos Azafea. ISSN 1137-0602.
Published by: (Universidad de Salamanca, Facultad de Filosofia), Universidad de Salamanca, Ediciones, Apartado 325, Salamanca, 37080, Spain. TEL 34-923-294598, FAX 34-923-262579, pedidos@universitas.usal.es, http://www.eusal.es/. Ed. Miguel Cirilo Florez.

➤ **B E A R S**; in moral and political philosophy. (Brown Electronic Article Review Service) *see* POLITICAL SCIENCE

144 GBR
B H A NEWS. Text in English. 1965. bi-m. looseleaf. free to members (effective 2009). adv. bk.rev. illus. **Document type:** *Newsletter, Trade.* **Description:** Examines moral issues from a nonreligious viewpoint.
Former titles: Humanist News; (until 19??): Humanity; (until 1997): Humanist News (0953-1327); (until 1983): Humanist Newsletter; Humanist News (0018-7410)
Published by: British Humanist Association, 1 Gower St, London, WC1E 6HD, United Kingdom. TEL 44-20-70793580, FAX 44-20-70793588, bob@humanism.org.uk. Ed. Pepper Harow. Circ: 4,000 (paid).

B M C MEDICAL ETHICS. (BioMed Central) *see* MEDICAL SCIENCES

BACK TO GODHEAD; magazine of the Hare Krishna movement. *see* RELIGIONS AND THEOLOGY—Hindu

100 USA
BALANCE (BRANFORD). Text in English. 1985. bi-m. USD 18.
Description: Promotes holistic health.
Published by: Balance Center, 359 Walden Green, Branford, CT 06405. TEL 203-481-6331. Ed. Donna Sommers. adv.: B&W page USD 900, color page USD 2,000. Circ: 10,000.

146 USA ISSN 1944-3676
B808.5.A1
THE BALTIC INTERNATIONAL YEARBOOK OF COGNITION, LOGIC AND COMMUNICATION (ONLINE). Text in English. 2005. a. free (effective 2011). **Document type:** *Journal, Academic/Scholarly.* **Description:** Publishes in the field of philosophy and connected disciplines such a psychology, computer sciences and linguistics.
Formerly (until 2007): The Baltic International Yearbook of Cognition, Logic and Communication (Print)
Media: Online - full text.
Published by: New Prairie Press, 201 Dickens Hall, Manhattan, KS 66506. http://newprairiepress.org. Ed. Jurgis Skilters.

100 FRA ISSN 1622-6909
BANC D'ESSAIS. Text in French. 2000. irreg. **Document type:** *Monographic series.*
Related titles: Online - full text ed.: ISSN 2105-2743. 2008.
Published by: Editions Agone, BP 70072, Marseille, 13192, France. info@agone.org.

BASILEUS; an international and interdisciplinary journal for the philosophy of the law. *see* LAW

100 DEU ISSN 0941-9918
BASLER STUDIEN ZUR PHILOSOPHIE. Text in German. 1992. irreg., latest vol.16, 2010. price varies. **Document type:** *Monographic series, Academic/Scholarly.*
Published by: A. Francke Verlag GmbH, Dischinger Weg 5, Tuebingen, 72070, Germany. TEL 49-7071-97970, FAX 49-7071-979711, info@francke.de, http://www.francke.de.

THE BEACON (MIAMI). *see* NEW AGE PUBLICATIONS

100 USA ISSN 0005-7339
THE BEACON (NEW YORK, 1922). Text in English. 1922. q. USD 18.50, GBP 11; USD 5, GBP 2.80 newsstand/cover (effective 2007). bk.rev. back issues avail. **Document type:** *Magazine, Consumer.* **Description:** A forum for esotericists to contribute their visions, to share their experiences, and to develop their ideas about the evolution of humanity and the unfolding Plan for our world.
Published by: (Lucis Trust), Lucis Publishing Co., 120 Wall St, Fl 24, New York, NY 10005-4001. TEL 212-292-0707, FAX 212-292-0808, newyork@lucistrust.org. **European and British Commonwealth countries, except Canada, subscr. to:** Lucis Press Ltd.

190 DNK ISSN 1601-3395
BEGREBSHISTORISKE STUDIER. Text in Danish. 1996. irreg., latest vol.3, 2000.
Published by: Aarhus Universitet, Center for Kulturforskning/University of Aarhus. Centre for Cultural Research, Jens Chr. Skous Vej 3, Aarhus C, 8000, Denmark. TEL 45-89-426900, FAX 45-89-426919, cfk@au.dk, http://www.hum.au.dk/ckulturf.

BEIHEFTE ZU EDITIO. *see* LITERATURE

107.1 DEU ISSN 0005-8157
BEITRAEGE PAEDAGOGISCHER ARBEIT. Text in German. 1956. q. membership. bk.rev. bibl. **Document type:** *Academic/Scholarly.*
Published by: Gemeinschaft Evangelischer Erzieher in Baden, Blumenstr 1, Karlsruhe, 76133, Germany. TEL 49-721-9175410. Ed. Hans Maas. Circ: 4,000.

141 CHE ISSN 1661-1012
BEITRAEGE ZU FRIEDRICH NIETZSCHE. Text in German. 1999. irreg., latest vol.14, 2009. price varies. **Document type:** *Monographic series, Academic/Scholarly.*
Published by: Schwabe und Co. AG, Steinentorstr 13, Basel, 4010, Switzerland. TEL 41-61-2789565, FAX 41-61-2789566, verlag@schwabe.ch, http://www.schwabe.ch.

100 200 DEU ISSN 0067-5024
B720 B4
BEITRAEGE ZUR GESCHICHTE DER PHILOSOPHIE UND THEOLOGIE DES MITTELALTERS. NEUE FOLGE. Text in German. 1894; N.S. 1970. irreg., latest vol.73, 2010. price varies. **Document type:** *Monographic series, Academic/Scholarly.*
Formerly (until 1928): Beitraege zur Geschichte der Philosophie des Mittelalters (0934-2664)
—CCC.
Published by: Aschendorff Verlag GmbH & Co. KG, Soester Str 13, Muenster, 48135, Germany. TEL 49-251-6900, FAX 49-251-6904570, buchverlag@aschendorff.de, http://www.aschendorff-buchverlag.de.

BEITRAEGE ZUR GESCHICHTE, THEORIE UND ETHIK DER MEDIZIN. *see* MEDICAL SCIENCES

100 DEU
BEITRAEGE ZUR PHILOSOPHIE. Text in German. 1912-1938; N.S. 1993. irreg., latest 2009. price varies. **Document type:** *Monographic series, Academic/Scholarly.*
Published by: Universitaetsverlag Winter GmbH, Dossenheimer Landstr 13, Heidelberg, 69121, Germany. TEL 49-6221-770260, FAX 49-6221-770269, info@winter-verlag-hd.de, http://www.winter-verlag-hd.de.

100 CHE ISSN 1421-4903
BERNER REIHE PHILOSOPHISCHER STUDIEN. Text in German. 1982. irreg., latest vol.41, 2010. price varies. **Document type:** *Monographic series, Academic/Scholarly.*
Published by: Peter Lang AG (Subsidiary of: Peter Lang Publishing Group), Hochfeldstr 32, Postfach 746, Bern 9, 3000, Switzerland. TEL 41-31-3061717, FAX 41-31-3061727, info@peterlang.com. Ed. Andreas Graeser.

100 USA
THE BERTRAND RUSSELL RESEARCH CENTRE. NEWSLETTER. Abbreviated title: B R R C Newsletter. Text in English. 2002. a. free to members (effective 2010). **Document type:** *Newsletter, Trade.* **Description:** Features the Russell world on work on the collected papers of Bertrand Russell.
Published by: Bertrand Russell Society, Inc., Carman Hall, Rm 360, Lehman College-CUNY, 250 Bedford Park Blvd W, Bronx, NY 10468. rosalind.carey@lehman.cuny.edu, http://users.drew.edu/~jlenz/brs.html.

100 USA ISSN 1547-0334
B1649.R94
➤ **THE BERTRAND RUSSELL SOCIETY QUARTERLY.** Text in English. 1974. q. looseleaf. USD 20 to non-members; USD 5 per issue to non-members; free to members (effective 2010). bk.rev. cum.index: 1974-1990. back issues avail. **Document type:** *Journal, Academic/Scholarly.* **Description:** Brings out society news and proceedings, essays and discussions on all aspects of Bertrand Russell's life and works, and reviews of recent work on Russell.
Former titles (until 2001): Russell Society News; (until 2000): The Bertrand Russell Society Quarterly; (until 1995): Russell Society News (1052-7729); (until 1978): Bertrand Russell Society. Newsletter
Indexed: PhilInd.
Published by: Bertrand Russell Society, Inc., Carman Hall, Rm 360, Lehman College-CUNY, 250 Bedford Park Blvd W, Bronx, NY 10468. http://users.drew.edu/~jlenz/brs.html. Eds. John Ongley, Rosalind Carey.

170 590 USA
➤ **BETWEEN THE SPECIES (ONLINE)**; an online journal for the study of philosophy and animals. Text in English. 1984. a. free (effective 2011). illus. back issues avail. **Document type:** *Journal, Academic/Scholarly.* **Description:** Journal of moral philosophy. Welcomes contributions from animal rights activists and the scientific community.
Formerly (until 2002): Between the Species (Print)
Media: Online - full text.
Published by: San Francisco Bay Institute, Schweitzer Center, PO Box 8496, Berkeley, CA 94707. Ed. Joseph Lynch.

181.4 IND ISSN 0006-0496
BHARATHA DARSHANA. Text in Kannada. 1957. m. free to members (effective 2011). **Document type:** *Magazine, Consumer.*
Published by: Bharatha Darshana Prakashana, II Block, Thyagarajanagar, 163 Manjunatha Rd., Bangalore, Karnataka 560 028, India. TEL 91-80-22278231.

100 011 DEU ISSN 0173-1831
BIBLIOGRAPHIEN ZUR PHILOSOPHIE. Text in English, German. 1979. irreg., latest vol.18, 2006. price varies. back issues avail. **Document type:** *Monographic series, Academic/Scholarly.*
Published by: Edition Gemini, Juelichstr 7, Huerth, 50354, Germany. TEL 49-2233-63550, FAX 49-2233-65866. Ed. Gernot U Gabel. Pub. Gisela Gabel. Circ: 200.

110 ITA ISSN 1721-9094
BIBLIOTECA DEL GIORNALE DI METAFISICA. Text in Multiple languages. 1947. irreg. **Document type:** *Monographic series, Academic/Scholarly.*
Published by: Tilgher Genova, Via Assarotti 31-15, Genoa, GE 16122, Italy. TEL 39-010-8391140, FAX 39-010-870653, tilgher@tilgher.it, http://www.tilgher.it.

BIBLIOTECA DI ARCHEOLOGIA DI FILOSOFIA. *see* ARCHAEOLOGY

100 ITA ISSN 1828-0889
BIBLIOTECA DI STUDI KANTIANI. Text in Italian. 1994. irreg. price varies. **Document type:** *Monographic series, Academic/Scholarly.*
Published by: Fabrizio Serra Editore (Subsidiary of: Accademia Editoriale), c/o Accademia Editoriale, Via Santa Bibbiana 28, Pisa, 56127, Italy. TEL 39-050-542332, FAX 39-050-574888, accademiaeditoriale@accademiaeditoriale.it, http://www.libraweb.net.

100 ITA ISSN 1973-977X
BIBLIOTECA FILOSOFICA DI QUAESTIO. Text in Italian. 2004. irreg. price varies. **Document type:** *Monographic series, Academic/Scholarly.*
Published by: Edizioni di Pagina, Via dei Mille 205, Bari, 70126, Italy. info@paginasc.it, http://www.paginasc.it.

100 ITA ISSN 1972-022X
BIBLIOTECA. LAOCOONTE. Text in Italian. 1990. irreg. **Document type:** *Monographic series, Academic/Scholarly.*
Published by: Liguori Editore, Via Posillipo 394, Naples, 80123, Italy. TEL 39-081-7206111, FAX 39-081-7206244, liguori@liguori.it, http://www.liguori.it.

100 DEU
BIBLIOTHEK DIALEKTISCHER GRUNDBEGRIFFE. Text in German. 1998-2001; resumed 2002. irreg., latest vol.16, 2005. price varies. **Document type:** *Monographic series, Academic/Scholarly.*
Published by: Transcript, Muehlenstr 47, Bielefeld, 33607, Germany. TEL 49-521-63454, FAX 49-521-61040, live@transcript-verlag.de.

109 BEL ISSN 0067-8430
➤ **BIBLIOTHEQUE PHILOSOPHIQUE DE LOUVAIN.** Text in French. 1947. irreg., latest vol.53, 2000. price varies. back issues avail. **Document type:** *Monographic series, Academic/Scholarly.* **Description:** Discusses Western philosophy throughout the ages.
Published by: (Universite Catholique de Louvain, Institut Superieur de Philosophie), Peeters Publishers, Bondgenotenlaan 153, Leuven, 3000, Belgium. TEL 32-16-235170, FAX 32-16-228500, http://www.peeters-leuven.be.

111.85 JPN ISSN 0520-0962
BH8.J3
BIGAKU. Text in Japanese. 1950. q.
Indexed: PhilInd, RILM.
Published by: Bigaku-kai/Japanese Society of Aesthetics, University of Tokyo, Faculty of Letters, 7-3-1 Hongo, Bunkyo-ku, Tokyo, 113-0033, Japan. http://wwwsoc.nii.ac.jp/bigaku/index-e.htm.

210 BEL ISSN 0006-2278
➤ **BIJDRAGEN**; international journal for philosophy and theology. Text in Dutch, English, German, French. 1936. q. EUR 82 combined subscription (print & online eds.) (effective 2011). adv. bk.rev. back issues avail. **Document type:** *Journal, Academic/Scholarly.* **Description:** Examines topics and themes in philosophy and theology.
Formerly (until 1945): Philosophische en Theologische Faculteiten der Nederlandsche Jezuieten. Bijdragen (0923-7984)
Related titles: Online - full text ed.: ISSN 1783-1377.
Indexed: A21, A22, FR, IBR, IBZ, IPB, IZBG, MLA-IB, OTA, P30, PhilInd, R&TA, RI-1.
—BLDSC (2057.400000), IE, Infotrieve, Ingenta, INIST.
Published by: (Universite Catholique de Louvain, Universiteit Utrecht NLD), Peeters Publishers, Bondgenotenlaan 153, Leuven, 3000, Belgium. TEL 32-16-235170, FAX 32-16-228500, peeters@peeters-leuven.be, http://www.peeters-leuven.be. Eds. T W M Rikhof, W Van Herck. **Co-sponsor:** Universiteit van Tilburg.

➤ **BINDU**; magazine on yoga, tantra and meditation. *see* NEW AGE PUBLICATIONS

➤ **BIO - ETHOS.** *see* BIOLOGY

174.95 DNK ISSN 1603-8444
BIO-ETIK I PRAKSIS. Text in Danish. 2000. irreg. (4-6/yr). free. **Document type:** *Newsletter, Trade.*
Formerly (until 2004): Gen-Etik i Praksis (1600-9711)
Related titles: Online - full text ed.: ISSN 1604-3561. 2000.
Published by: Center for Bioteknik og Risikovurdering/Danish Centre for Bioethics and Risk Assessment, Rolighedsvej 25, Frederiksberg C, 1958, Denmark. TEL 45-35-333010, FAX 45-35-336801, bioethicks@kvl.dk. Eds. Geir Tveit, Peter Sandoe.

101 CHE ISSN 1662-6001
➤ **BIOETHICA FORUM**; Schweizer Zeitschrift fuer Biomedizinische Ethik. Text in German. 2008. 2/yr. CHF 50 to individuals; CHF 100 to institutions (effective 2009). **Document type:** *Journal, Academic/Scholarly.* **Description:** Focuses on contributions to ethics in the domains of health care, research, biotechnologies, and public health.
Former titles (until Jun.2008): S G B E Bulletin (1662-6079); (until Mar.2008): Bioethica Forum (1422-5840)
Related titles: Online - full text ed.: ISSN 1662-601X. 2008.
Published by: (Schweizerische Gesellschaft fuer Biomedizinische Ethik/Societe Suisse d'Ethique Biomedicale - Societa Svizzera di Etica Biomedica), Schwabe und Co. AG, Steinentorstr 13, Basel, 4010, Switzerland. TEL 41-61-2789565, FAX 41-61-2789566, verlag@schwabe.ch, http://www.schwabe.ch. Ed. Dr. Samia Hurst.

174.957 GBR ISSN 0269-9702
QH332
➤ **BIOETHICS.** Text in English. 1987. 9/yr. GBP 852 domestic to institutions; EUR 852 in Europe to institutions; USD 1,474 in the Americas to institutions; USD 1,719 elsewhere to institutions; GBP 739 combined subscription domestic to institutions (print & online eds.); EUR 938 combined subscription in Europe to institutions (print & online eds.); USD 1,622 combined subscription in the Americas to institutions (print & online eds.); USD 1,891 combined subscription elsewhere to institutions (print & online eds.) (effective 2009). adv. bk.rev. illus. back issues avail.; reprint service avail. from PSC. **Document type:** *Journal, Academic/Scholarly.* **Description:** Provides a forum for well-argued articles on the ethical questions raised by current issues such as international collaborative clinical research in developing countries, organ transplants and xenotransplantation, ageing and the human lifespan, AIDS, genomics, and stem cell research.
Related titles: Online - full text ed.: ISSN 1467-8519. GBP 671 domestic to institutions; EUR 852 in Europe to institutions; USD 1,474 in the Americas to institutions; USD 1,719 elsewhere to institutions (effective 2009) (from IngentaConnect); ◆ Supplement(s): Developing World Bioethics. ISSN 1471-8731.
Indexed: A01, A02, A03, A08, A20, A21, A22, A26, ASCA, ASSIA, B04, BRD, C06, C07, C08, C11, CA, CINAHL, CurCont, DIP, E01, E08, EMBASE, ESPM, ExcerpMed, FamI, G03, G08, GSA, GSI, H01, H04, H05, H11, H12, H13, H14, I05, IBR, IBSS, IBZ, MEDLINE, P02, P03, P10, P20, P30, P34, P42, P48, P52, P53, P54, P56, PAIS, PCI, PQC, PSA, PhilInd, PsycInfo, PsycholAb, R05, R10, RASB, RI-1, RI-2, Reac, RefZh, RiskAb, S02, S03, S09, S10, S21, SCI, SCOPUS, SOPODA, SSA, SSAI, SSAb, SSCI, SSI, SociolAb, T02, W03, W07, W09.
—BLDSC (2072.119500), GNLM, IE, Infotrieve, Ingenta. **CCC.**
Published by: (The/International Association of Bioethics PHL), Wiley-Blackwell Publishing Ltd. (Subsidiary of: John Wiley & Sons, Inc.), 9600 Garsington Rd, Oxford, OX4 2DQ, United Kingdom. TEL 44-1865-776868, FAX 44-1865-714591, customerservices@blackwellpublishing.com. Eds. Ruth Chadwick, Udo Schueklenk.

➤ **BIOETHICS BULLETIN.** *see* LAW

174.95 AUS ISSN 1037-6410
BIOETHICS OUTLOOK. Text in English. 1990. q. bk.rev. back issues avail. **Document type:** *Newsletter.* **Description:** Contains articles on current issues in bioethics (euthanasia, informed consent, resource allocation).
—BLDSC (2072.121800).
Published by: Plunkett Centre for Ethics, St. Vincents Hospital, Darlinghurst, NSW 2010, Australia. plunkett@plunkett.edu.au. Circ: 400.

174.95 AUS ISSN 1033-6206
BIOETHICS RESEARCH NOTES. Text in English. 1989. q. AUD 38.50 domestic; GBP 25, USD 40 foreign (effective 2009). **Document type:** *Journal, Academic/Scholarly.* **Description:** Provides abstracts of articles relevant to bioethics.
Related titles: Online - full text ed.: AUD 27.50 domestic; GBP 12.50, USD 20 foreign (effective 2009).
Indexed: P30.
Published by: Southern Cross Bioethics Institute, 1E/336 Marion Rd, North Plympton, SA 5037, Australia. TEL 61-8-82970022, FAX 61-8-82975738, scbi@bioethics.org.au.

BIOETICA. *see* BIOLOGY

BIOETICA & SOCIETA. *see* BIOLOGY

170 ITA ISSN 1827-2606
BIOETICA E VALORI. Text in Italian. 1998. irreg. price varies. **Document type:** *Monographic series, Academic/Scholarly.*
Published by: Edizioni Scientifiche Italiane SpA, Via Chiatamone 7, Naples, NA 80121, Italy. TEL 39-081-7645443, FAX 39-081-7646477, info@edizioniesi.it, http://www.edizioniesi.it.

BIOLOGY AND PHILOSOPHY. *see* BIOLOGY

BIOPOLITICS. *see* ENVIRONMENTAL STUDIES

BIOPOLITICS - THE BIO ENVIRONMENT. SYMPOSIUM PROCEEDINGS. *see* ENVIRONMENTAL STUDIES

100 GBR
BLACKWELL PHILOSOPHY GUIDES. Text in English. 199?. irreg., latest 2006. price varies. **Document type:** *Handbook/Manual/Guide, Academic/Scholarly.*
Published by: Wiley-Blackwell Publishing Ltd. (Subsidiary of: John Wiley & Sons, Inc.), 9600 Garsington Rd, Oxford, OX4 2DQ, United Kingdom. TEL 44-1865-776868, FAX 44-1865-714591, customerservices@blackwellpublishing.com, http://www.wiley.com/. Ed. Steven M Cahn.

P

100 DEU ISSN 0947-6563
B3
➤ **DER BLAUE REITER**; Journal fuer Philosophie. Text in German. 1995. 2/yr. EUR 24.10; EUR 15.10 newsstand/cover (effective 2003). 116 p./no.; **Document type:** *Journal, Academic/Scholarly.* **Description:** Presents essays and articles on all aspects of philosophy.
Indexed: DIP, IBR, IBZ.
Published by: Omega Verlag Siegfried Reusch, Cheruskerstr 9, Stuttgart, 70435, Germany. TEL 49-711-8790746, FAX 49-711-8790744, omegaverlagreusch@t-online.de. Ed., R&P Siegfried Reusch. Adv. contact Frank Augustin.

141 NLD ISSN 2211-176X
▼ **BLIK OP HET NIEUWS.** Variant title: Lilaiesche Blik op het Nieuws. Text in Dutch. 2009. a. EUR 14.95 (effective 2010).
Published by: Stichting Elektoor, Rijksweg-Zuid 57, Rucphen, 4715 TA, Netherlands. TEL 31-165-343251, FAX 31-165-341641, http://www.elektoor.com.

BLOCH-ALMANACH. *see* LITERARY AND POLITICAL REVIEWS

180 NLD ISSN 1384-6663
B173
➤ **BOCHUMER PHILOSOPHISCHES JAHRBUCH FUER ANTIKE UND MITTELALTER.** Text in German; Summaries in English. 1996. a. EUR 146 combined subscription (print & online eds.) (effective 2012). bk.rev. 300 p./no.; back issues avail. **Document type:** *Journal, Academic/Scholarly.* **Description:** Concentrates on research documenting the connections between ancient and medieval philosophy, including Arabic, Judaic, Byzantine and Latin philosophical traditions.
Related titles: Online - full text ed.: ISSN 1569-9684. EUR 142 (effective 2012) (from IngentaConnect).
Indexed: A01, A03, A08, A22, CA, DIP, HistAb, IBR, IBZ, MLA-IB, PhilInd, T02.
—IE, Ingenta. **CCC.**
Published by: John Benjamins Publishing Co., PO Box 36224, Amsterdam, 1020 ME, Netherlands. TEL 31-20-6304747, FAX 31-20-6739773, subscription@benjamins.nl, http://www.benjamins.com. Eds. Burkhard Mojsisch, Manuel Baumbach.

100 NLD ISSN 1384-668X
BOCHUMER STUDIEN ZUR PHILOSOPHIE. Text in Dutch. 1982. irreg., latest vol.52, 2011. price varies. **Document type:** *Monographic series, Academic/Scholarly.*
Published by: John Benjamins Publishing Co., PO Box 36224, Amsterdam, 1020 ME, Netherlands. TEL 31-20-6304747, FAX 31-20-6739773, customer.services@benjamins.nl. Eds. Burkhard Mojsisch, Kurt Flasch, Ruedi Imbach.

100 800 DEU
BOEHME-STUDIEN; Beitraege zu Philosophie und Philologie. Text in German. 2007. irreg., latest vol.2, 2008. price varies. **Document type:** *Monographic series, Academic/Scholarly.*
Published by: Weissensee Verlag e.K., Simplonstr 59, Berlin, 10245, Germany. TEL 49-30-29049192, FAX 49-30-27574315, mail@weissensee-verlag.de.

100 DEU ISSN 1435-6597
BOETHIANA; Forschungsergebnisse zur Philosophie. Text in German. 1991. irreg., latest vol.90, 2010. price varies. **Document type:** *Monographic series, Academic/Scholarly.*
Published by: Verlag Dr. Kovac, Leverkusenstr 13, Hamburg, 22761, Germany. TEL 49-40-3988800, FAX 49-40-39888055, info@verlagdrkovac.de.

BOHAI DAXUE XUEBAO (ZHEXUE SHEHUI KEXUE BAN)/BOHAI UNIVERSITY. JOURNAL (PHILOSOPHY AND SOCIAL SCIENCE EDITION). *see* SOCIAL SCIENCES: COMPREHENSIVE WORKS

100 ARG
BOLETIN DE INFORMACIONES. Text in Spanish. 1998 (no. 19). irreg. back issues avail.
Media: Online - full text.
Published by: Universidad de Buenos Aires, Facultad de Filosofia y Letras, Puan 470, Buenos Aires, 1406, Argentina. TEL 54-11-44320606, info@filo.uba.ar.

142.7 ITA ISSN 1970-7983
BOLLETTINO DI STUDI SARTRIANI. Text in Italian. 2005. a. **Document type:** *Journal, Academic/Scholarly.*
Media: Online - full text.
Published by: Biblink Editori, Viale XXI Aprile 63, Rome, 00162, Italy. http://www.biblink.it.

100 200 USA
BOLLINGEN SERIES. Text in English. 1941. irreg., latest 2006. price varies. back issues avail. **Document type:** *Monographic series, Academic/Scholarly.*
Published by: (Bollingen Foundation), Princeton University Press, 41 William St, Princeton, NJ 08540. TEL 609-258-4900, 800-777-4726, FAX 609-258-6305, cpriday@pupress.co.uk. **Subscr. addr.:** California - Princeton Fulfillment Services, Inc., 1445 Lower Ferry Rd, Ewing, NJ 08618. TEL 609-883-1759, 800-777-4726, FAX 609-883-7413, 800-999-1958, orders@cpfsinc.com. **Dist. addr. in Canada:** University Press Group.; **Dist. addr. in UK:** John Wiley & Sons Ltd.

180 NLD ISSN 1059-986X
B171
BOSTON AREA COLLOQUIUM IN ANCIENT PHILOSOPHY. PROCEEDINGS. Text in English. 1985. a. price varies. **Document type:** *Proceedings, Academic/Scholarly.*
Indexed: IZBG, PhilInd.
—BLDSC (6842.611500), IE. **CCC.**
Published by: (Boston Area Colloquium in Ancient Philosophy USA), Brill, PO Box 9000, Leiden, 2300 PA, Netherlands. TEL 31-71-5353500, FAX 31-71-5317532, cs@brill.nl, http://www.brill.nl. Eds. Gary Gurtler, John J. Cleary. **Dist. in N. America by:** Brill, PO Box 605, Herndon, VA 20172-0605. TEL 703-661-1585, 800-337-9255, FAX 703-661-1501, cs@brillusa.com; **Dist. by:** Turpin Distribution Services Ltd., Pegasus Dr, Stratton Business Park, Biggleswade, Bedfordshire SG18 8QB, United Kingdom. TEL 44-1767-604954, FAX 44-1767-601640, custserv@turpin-distribution.com, http://www.turpin-distribution.com/.

BOSTON STUDIES IN THE PHILOSOPHY OF SCIENCE; Boston colloquium for the philosophy of science. *see* SCIENCES: COMPREHENSIVE WORKS

170 DEU ISSN 1864-077X
BRAUNSCHWEIGER BEITRAEGE ZUR SOZIALETHIK. Text in German. 2007. irreg., latest vol.2, 2010. price varies. **Document type:** *Monographic series, Academic/Scholarly.*
Published by: Peter Lang GmbH (Subsidiary of: Peter Lang Publishing Group), Eschborner Landstr 42-50, Frankfurt Am Main, 60489, Germany. TEL 49-69-7807050, FAX 49-69-78070550, zentrale.frankfurt@peterlang.com. Ed. Hans-Georg Babke.

BREATH SERIES; a progression of pranayama practices. *see* NEW AGE PUBLICATIONS

BREATHE (NEW YORK). *see* NEW AGE PUBLICATIONS

100 DEU ISSN 0935-7009
B3212.Z7
BRENTANO STUDIEN. Text in English, German. 1988. irreg., latest vol.12, 2009. price varies. **Document type:** *Monographic series, Academic/Scholarly.*
Indexed: IBR, IBZ, IPB, PhilInd.
—**CCC.**
Published by: J.H. Roell, Wuerzburgerstr 16, Dettelbach, 97337, Germany. TEL 49-9324-99770, FAX 49-9324-99771, info@roell-verlag.de.

121 USA ISSN 1937-7002
AS30
➤ **BRIDGES (CONWAY)**; an interdisciplinary journal in celebration of inquiry. Text in English. 2007. a. free (effective 2010). back issues avail. **Document type:** *Journal, Academic/Scholarly.* **Description:** Seeks to enhance the academic community by bringing together a wide range of intellectual perspectives in the arts, sciences, business, education and humanities in discussion around a common philosphical theme.
Media: Online - full text.
Published by: Coastal Carolina University, PO Box 261954, Conway, SC 29528. TEL 843-347-3161, yoav@coastal.edu. Ed. Scott Pleasant.

100 GBR ISSN 0960-8788
B1
➤ **BRITISH JOURNAL FOR THE HISTORY OF PHILOSOPHY.** Abbreviated title: B J H P. Text in English. 1993. 5/yr. GBP 555 combined subscription in United Kingdom to institutions (print & online eds.); EUR 735, USD 919 combined subscription to institutions (print & online eds.) (effective 2012). adv. bk.rev. illus. Index. back issues avail.; reprint service avail. from PSC. **Document type:** *Journal, Academic/Scholarly.* **Description:** Includes articles and reviews on the history of philosophy and related intellectual history from the ancient world through to the early decades of the twentieth century.
Related titles: Online - full text ed.: ISSN 1469-3526. GBP 500 in United Kingdom to institutions; EUR 661, USD 828 to institutions (effective 2012) (from IngentaConnect).
Indexed: A01, A02, A03, A08, A20, A22, AmH&L, AmHI, ArtHuCI, B04, BRD, BrHumI, CA, CurCont, E01, FR, H07, H08, HAb, HistAb, HumInd, I14, IPB, P30, PCI, PhilInd, SCOPUS, T02, W03, W07.
—IE, Infotrieve, Ingenta, INIST. **CCC.**
Published by: (British Society for the History of Philosophy), Routledge (Subsidiary of: Taylor & Francis Group), 4 Park Square, Milton Park, Abingdon, Oxon OX14 4RN, United Kingdom. subscriptions@tandf.co.uk, http://www.routledge.com. Ed. G A J Rogers. Adv. contact Linda Hann TEL 44-1344-779945. Circ: 400. **Subscr. in US & Canada to:** Taylor & Francis Inc., Customer Services Dept, 325 Chestnut St, 8th Fl, Philadelphia, PA 19106. TEL 800-354-1420, FAX 215-625-2940; **Subscr. to:** Taylor & Francis Ltd., Journals Customer Service, Sheepen Pl, Colchester, Essex CO3 3LP, United Kingdom. TEL 44-20-70175544, FAX 44-20-70175198, tf.enquiries@tfinforma.com.

➤ **THE BRITISH JOURNAL FOR THE PHILOSOPHY OF SCIENCE.** *see* SCIENCES: COMPREHENSIVE WORKS

111.85 GBR ISSN 0007-0904
BH1
➤ **BRITISH JOURNAL OF AESTHETICS.** Text in English. 1960. q. GBP 175 in United Kingdom to institutions; EUR 262 in Europe to institutions; USD 349 in US & Canada to institutions; GBP 175 elsewhere to institutions; GBP 191 combined subscription in United Kingdom to institutions (print & online eds.); EUR 286 combined subscription in Europe to institutions (print & online eds.); USD 380 combined subscription in US & Canada to institutions (print & online eds.); GBP 191 combined subscription elsewhere to institutions (print & online eds.) (effective 2012). adv. bk.rev. illus. Index. 132 p./no.; back issues avail.; reprint service avail. from PSC. **Document type:** *Journal, Academic/Scholarly.* **Description:** Discusses general philosophical aesthetics and articles on the principles of appraisal.
Related titles: Microform ed.: (from PQC); Online - full text ed.: ISSN 1468-2842. GBP 159 in United Kingdom to institutions; EUR 238 in Europe to institutions; USD 317 in US & Canada to institutions; GBP 159 elsewhere to institutions (effective 2012) (from IngentaConnect).
Indexed: A01, A02, A03, A06, A07, A08, A20, A22, A26, A27, A30, A31, AA, ABCT, ABM, AES, ASCA, AmHI, ArtHuCI, ArtInd, B04, B24, BEL&L, BRD, BrHumI, CA, CurCont, DIP, E01, E08, FR, G08, H07, H08, H09, H10, H14, HAb, HumInd, I05, IBR, IBRH, IBZ, IDP, IPB, MLA, MLA-IB, MusicInd, P02, P10, P48, P53, P54, PCI, PQC, PhilInd, RASB, RILM, S09, SCOPUS, SOPODA, SociolAb, T02, W03, W07.
—BLDSC (2303.890000), IE, Infotrieve, Ingenta, INIST. **CCC.**
Published by: (British Society of Aesthetics), Oxford University Press, Great Clarendon St, Oxford, OX2 6DP, United Kingdom. TEL 44-1865-556767, FAX 44-1865-556646, enquiry@oup.co.uk, http://www.oxfordjournals.org. Ed. John Hyman. Pub. Nina Curtis. Adv. contact Linda Hann TEL 44-1344-779945. B&W page GBP 295, B&W page USD 490; 115 x 190. Circ: 1,750.

142.7 GBR ISSN 0007-1773
B829.5
➤ **BRITISH SOCIETY FOR PHENOMENOLOGY. JOURNAL.** Abbreviated title: J B S P. Text in English. 1970. 3/yr. GBP 40 to individuals in UK & Ireland; GBP 45 elsewhere to individuals; GBP 50 to institutions; free to members (effective 2009). adv. bk.rev. bibl. reprints avail. **Document type:** *Journal, Academic/Scholarly.* **Description:** Features papers on phenomenology and existential philosophy as well as contributions from other fields of philosophy.
Related titles: Online - full text ed.: (from IngentaConnect).
Indexed: A20, A21, A22, AES, ASCA, ArtHuCI, CurCont, FR, IBR, IBRH, IBZ, IPB, PCI, PhilInd, RASB, RI-1, RI-2, SCOPUS, W07.
—BLDSC (4719.223000), IE, Infotrieve, Ingenta, INIST.
Published by: (British Society for Phenomenology), Jackson Publishing and Distribution, Heaton Moor, 3 Gibsons Rd, Stockport, Ches SK4 4JX, United Kingdom. TEL 44-161-9479669, FAX 44-161-9479669, jacksonpub@aol.com, http://jacksonpub.co.uk. Ed. Ullrich Haase TEL 44-161-2473452.

100 509 ITA ISSN 1125-3819
B783.Z7
BRUNIANA & CAMPANELLIANA. Text in English, French, German, Italian, Spanish. 1995. 2/yr. EUR 425 combined subscription domestic to institutions (print & online eds.); EUR 495 combined subscription foreign to institutions (print & online eds.) (effective 2009). **Document type:** *Journal, Academic/Scholarly.* **Description:** Publishes contributions, editions of texts and archival material intended to clarify and document aspects of the culture of the High and Late Renaissance and Early Baroque era, with particular emphasis on the development, activity and fortunes of Giordano Bruno and Tommaso Campanella.
Related titles: Online - full text ed.
Indexed: ArtHuCI, BibInd, CurCont, PhilInd, W07.
Published by: Fabrizio Serra Editore (Subsidiary of: Accademia Editoriale), c/o Accademia Editoriale, Via Santa Bibbiana 28, Pisa, 56127, Italy. TEL 39-050-542332, FAX 39-050-574888, accademiaeditoriale@accademiaeditoriale.it, http://www.libraweb.net. Eds. Eugenio Canone, Germana Ernst.

BUDDHA WORLD. *see* RELIGIONS AND THEOLOGY—Buddhist

100 BEL ISSN 1782-2041
B829.5
BULLETIN D'ANALYSE PHENOMENOLOGIQUE. Text in French. 2005. irreg. free (effective 2011). **Document type:** *Journal, Academic/Scholarly.*
Media: Online - full text.
Indexed: A39, C27, C29, D03, D04, E13, R14, S14, S15, S18.
Published by: Universite de Liege, Faculte de Philosophie et Lettres, Place du Vingt Aout 7, Liege, 4000, Belgium. TEL 32-4-3663286, FAX 32-4-3665184.

180 BEL ISSN 0068-4023
B721
BULLETIN DE PHILOSOPHIE MEDIEVALE. Text occasionally in English, German, Italian, Spanish; Text mainly in French. 1959. a., latest vol.38, 1996. EUR 119 combined subscription (print & online eds.) (effective 2012). adv. back issues avail. **Document type:** *Journal, Academic/Scholarly.* **Description:** Publishes articles and material of interest to those concentrating on the history of medieval philosophy.
Formerly (until 1963): Societe Internationale pour l'Etude de la Philosophie Medievale. Bulletin
Related titles: Online - full text ed.
Indexed: FR, I14, IPB, P30, PCI.
—IE, INIST.
Published by: (Societe Internationale pour l'Etude de la Philosophie Medievale), Brepols Publishers, Begijnhof 67, Turnhout, 2300, Belgium. TEL 32-14-448020, FAX 32-14-428919, periodicals@brepols.net, http://www.brepols.net. Ed. J Hamesse. Circ: 1,000.

174 330 USA ISSN 0277-2027
HF5387
➤ **BUSINESS & PROFESSIONAL ETHICS JOURNAL.** Abbreviated title: B J E J. Text in English. 1981. q. USD 95 to institutions; USD 380 combined subscription to institutions (print & online eds.) (effective 2010). adv. bk.rev. illus. Index. 112 p./no. 1 cols./p.; back issues avail.; reprint service avail. from PSC. **Document type:** *Journal, Academic/Scholarly.* **Description:** Provides an interdisciplinary approach to the study and analysis of ethical issues that arise at the interface of business and the professions.
Incorporates (1992-2003): Professional Ethics (1063-6579)
Related titles: Online - full text ed.: ISSN 2153-7828.
Indexed: A22, A25, A26, B01, B06, B07, B09, B16, BPI, BRD, CA, E08, G08, I05, P02, P10, P12, P13, P30, P34, P48, P53, P54, PAIS, PCI, PQC, PhilInd, RI-1, RI-2, S08, S09, SCOPUS, SSAI, SSAb, SSI, T02, W01, W02, W03.
—BLDSC (2933.219000), IE, Infotrieve, Ingenta. **CCC.**
Published by: (University of Florida, Center for Applied Philosophy and Ethics in the Professions), Philosophy Documentation Center, PO Box 7147, Charlottesville, VA 22906. TEL 434-220-3300, FAX 434-220-3301. Ed. Robert Baum TEL 352-392-2084 ext.302.

174.4 USA ISSN 1052-150X
HF5387
➤ **BUSINESS ETHICS QUARTERLY.** Abbreviated title: B E Q. Text in English. 1991. q. USD 185 to institutions; USD 590 combined subscription to institutions (print & online eds.); USD 25 per issue to individuals; USD 50 per issue to institutions; free to members (effective 2010); subscr. includes Journal of Business Ethics Education. back issues avail.; reprint service avail. from PSC. **Document type:** *Journal, Academic/Scholarly.* **Description:** Contains scholarly articles from a wide variety of disciplinary orientations on the general subject of the application of ethics to the business community.
Related titles: CD-ROM ed.: Business Ethics Quarterly on CD-ROM. USD 60 to individuals; USD 135 to institutions (effective 2002); Microform ed.: (from PQC); Online - full text ed.: ISSN 2153-3326. USD 470 to institutions (effective 2010).
Indexed: A12, A13, A17, A20, A21, A22, A26, ABIn, ABS&EES, B01, B02, B04, B06, B07, B08, B09, B15, B16, B17, B18, BPI, BRD, C12, CA, CurCont, DIP, E08, Emerald, G04, G08, I05, IBR, IBSS, IBZ, N06, P02, P10, P27, P30, P34, P48, P51, P53, P54, PAIS, PCI, PQC, PhilInd, RI-1, RI-2, S02, S03, S09, SCOPUS, SSAI, SSAb, SSCI, SSI, T02, W01, W02, W03, W05, W07.
—BLDSC (2933.637000), IE, Infotrieve, Ingenta. **CCC.**
Published by: (Society for Business Ethics CAN), Philosophy Documentation Center, PO Box 7147, Charlottesville, VA 22906. TEL 434-220-3300, 800-444-2419, FAX 434-220-3301, order@pdcnet.org, http://www.pdcnet.org. Ed. Gary R Weaver TEL 302-831-4568.

➤ **BUSINESS SPIRITUALITEIT MAGAZINE NYENRODE.** *see* BUSINESS AND ECONOMICS—Personnel Management

➤ **BUSINESS STRATEGY FOR THE BIO-ENVIRONMENT.** *see* ENVIRONMENTAL STUDIES

➤ **C A P E S - AGREGATION. PHILOSOPHIE.** (Certificat d'Aptitude au Professorat de l'Enseignement du Second Degre) *see* EDUCATION—Higher Education

100 ESP ISSN 2173-2558
C D L DE CASTILLA - LA MANCHA. BOLETIN. (Colegio de Doctores y Licenciados) Text in Spanish. 1987. s-a. **Document type:** *Bulletin, Academic/Scholarly.*
Former titles (until 1995): Boletin del C D L (2173-2701); (until 1992): Boletin del C D L en Filosofia y Letras y en Ciencias de Castilla - La Mancha (2173-2582)
Published by: Colegio Oficial de Doctores y Licenciados en Filosofia y Letras y en Ciencias de Castilla-La Mancha, C Instituto, 25, Toledo, Spain. TEL 34-925-212166, FAX 34-925-220416, cdl-clm@cdlclm.es, http://www.cdlclm.es/.

130 BRA ISSN 1519-9681
C L E E-PRINTS. (Centro de Logica, Epistemiologia) Text in Portuguese, English. 2001. irreg. free (effective 2006). back issues avail. **Document type:** *Journal, Academic/Scholarly.*
Media: Online - full text.
Published by: Universidade Estadual de Campinas, Centro de Logica Epistemologia e Historia da Ciencia/State University of Campinas, Center for Logic, Epistemology and History of Science, Cidade Universitaria, Caixa Postal 6133, Campinas, SP 13083-970, Brazil. TEL 55-19-37886518, FAX 55-19-32893269, logica@cle.unicamp.br. Ed. Walter Carnielli.

100 FRA ISSN 1248-5284
C N R S PHILOSOPHIE. (Centre Nationale de la Recherche Scientifique) Text in French. 1993. irreg. price varies. **Document type:** *Monographic series, Academic/Scholarly.*
Published by: Centre National de la Recherche Scientifique, Campus Gerard-Megie, 3 Rue Michel-Ange, Paris, 75794, France. TEL 33-1-44964000, FAX 33-1-44965390, http://www.cnrseditions.fr.

100 USA ISSN 1049-9245
C P 2: COMMENTARIES - PHYSICAL AND PHILOSOPHIC. Text in English. 1990. q. USD 25; USD 30 foreign.
Published by: Cri-de-Coeur Press, 5070 Avenida del Sol, Laguna Hills, CA 92653-1876. Ed. A S Iberall. Pub. A.S. Iberall.

100 500 DNK ISSN 1904-3740
▼ **C P S. WORKING PAPERS.** (Centre for Philosophy and Science Studies) Text in Danish, Norwegian, Swedish. 2010. irreg. **Document type:** *Monographic series, Academic/Scholarly.*
Media: Online - full text.
Published by: Aalborg Universitet, Danish Centre for Philosophy and Science Studies, Fibigerstraede 2, Aalborg E, 9220, Denmark. TEL 45-99-408397.

CADERNOS DE HISTORIA E FILOSOFIA DA CIENCIA. *see* SCIENCES: COMPREHENSIVE WORKS

170 320 FRA ISSN 1624-2165
CAHIER DES SCIENCES MORALES ET POLITIQUES. Text in French. 2000. irreg. **Document type:** *Monographic series, Academic/Scholarly.*
Published by: (Academie des Sciences Morales et Politiques), Presses Universitaires de France, 6 Avenue Reille, Paris, 75685, France. TEL 33-1-58103161, FAX 33-1-45897530, revues@puf.com, http://www.puf.com.

144 360 FRA ISSN 0153-6087
CAHIERS ALBERT SCHWEITZER. Text in French. 1955. q. bk.rev. bibl.; illus.
Formerly (until 1976): Association Francaise des Amis d'Albert Schweitzer. Cahiers (0153-6133)
Published by: Association Francaise des Amis d'Albert Schweitzer, 1 quai Saint Thomas, Strasbourg, Cedex 67081, France. TEL 33-3-88259099, http://www.schweitzer.org. Ed. Jean Christian. Circ: 2,750.

174 FRA ISSN 1773-3170
LES CAHIERS DE L'ETHIQUE. Text in French. 2005. irreg.
Published by: Ethique Editions, Cercle d'Ethique des Affaires, 19 Bd de Sebastopol, Paris, 75001, France. TEL 33-1-46662465, FAX 33-1-46660156, cercle-ethique@cercle-ethique.net.

100 FRA ISSN 1285-3321
CAHIERS DE PHILOSOPHIE DU LANGAGE. Text in French. 1994. irreg. price varies. **Document type:** *Monographic series, Academic/Scholarly.*
Formerly (until 1997): Universite de Paris XII - Val - de - Marne. Serie Philosophie et Langage. Cahiers de Philosophie Ancienne et du Langage. (1263-9125)
Published by: L' Harmattan, 5 Rue de l'Ecole Polytechnique, Paris, 75005, France. TEL 33-1-43257651, FAX 33-1-43258203, http://www.editions-harmattan.fr.

100 FRA ISSN 1779-8213
LES CAHIERS D'HISTOIRE DE LA PHILOSOPHIE. Text in French. 2006. irreg. **Document type:** *Monographic series, Consumer.*
Published by: Editions du Cerf, 29 Boulevard La Tour Maubourg, Paris, 75340 Cedex 07, France.

100 054 FRA ISSN 1163-0183
LES CAHIERS DU SENS. Text in French. 1991. 3/yr. EUR 18 per issue (effective 2009). **Document type:** *Consumer.*
Published by: Nouvel Athanor, 50 rue du Disque, Paris, Cedex 13 75645, France. TEL 45-70-83-84, FAX 45-43-73-91. Circ: 250.

100 BEL ISSN 0008-0284
BF458
CAHIERS INTERNATIONAUX DE SYMBOLISME. Text in French. 1962. irreg. (approx. 3/yr.). EUR 16 domestic to individuals; EUR 23 foreign to individuals; EUR 30 domestic to institutions; EUR 38 foreign to institutions (effective 2002). bk.rev. **Document type:** *Academic/Scholarly.*
Indexed: FR, IPB, MLA, MLA-IB, PCI.
—IE, INIST.
Published by: Universite de Mons - Hainaut, Centre Interdisciplinaire d'Etudes Philosophiques, Pl du Parc 20, Mons, 7000, Belgium. TEL 32-65-335084, FAX 32-65-373054. Ed. Claire Lejeune. Circ: 1,200.

CAHIERS PARISIENS/PARISIAN NOTEBOOKS. *see* LITERATURE

100 FRA ISSN 0241-2799
CAHIERS PHILOSOPHIQUES. Text in French. 1979. 4/yr. EUR 22.61 domestic to individuals; EUR 27.62 foreign to individuals; EUR 26.60 domestic to institutions; EUR 32.50 foreign to institutions (effective 2008). bk.rev. **Document type:** *Journal, Academic/Scholarly.* **Description:** Articles and essays on all aspects of philosophical research and thought.
Indexed: FR.
—INIST.
Published by: Centre National de Documentation Pedagogique, 4 Av du Futuroscope, Teleport 1, B P 80158, Futuroscope, Cedex 86961, France. TEL 33-1-46349000, FAX 33-1-46345544, http://www.cndp.fr. Ed. Jean Louis Poirier. **Subscr. to:** CNDP - Abonnement, B.P. 750, Sainte Genevieve Cedex 60732, France. FAX 33-3-44033013.

100 COD ISSN 0379-4105
CAHIERS PHILOSOPHIQUES AFRICAINS/AFRICAN PHILOSOPHICAL JOURNAL. Text in French. 1972. irreg. bk.rev.
Indexed: CERDIC.
Published by: (Universite de Lubumbashi), Presses Universitaires de Lubumbashi, BP 1825, Lubumbashi, Congo, Dem. Republic.

LES CAHIERS RATIONALISTES. *see* SCIENCES: COMPREHENSIVE WORKS

100 FRA ISSN 0181-1126
B2430.W474
CAHIERS SIMONE WEIL. Text in French. 1974. q. EUR 35 domestic; EUR 40 in Asia and America; EUR 36.50 elsewhere (effective 2004).
Former titles (until 1978): Association pour l'Etude de la Pensee de Simone Weil. Bulletin de Liaison (0184-9735); (until 1977): Association pour l'Etude de le Pensee de Simone Weil. Bulletin (0181-1118)
Indexed: FR, MLA-IB, PhilInd, RILM.
—INIST.
Published by: Association pour l'Etude de la Pensee de Simone Weil, c/o M Robert Chenavier, 87, ave. des Grandes Platieres, Passy-Marlioz, 74190, France. TEL 33-4-50781610.

135 FRA ISSN 1635-141X
LES CAILLOUX BLANCS. Text in French. 2002. irreg. back issues avail. **Document type:** *Monographic series, Consumer.*
Published by: Editions Cheminements, 1 Chemin des Pieces - Bron, Le Coudray-Macouard, 49260, France. TEL 33-2-41677454, FAX 33-2-41677406, jgiard@cheminements.fr.

101 GBR ISSN 0950-6306
CAMBRIDGE STUDIES IN PHILOSOPHY. Text in English. 1979. irreg. price varies. adv. back issues avail.; reprints avail. **Document type:** *Monographic series, Academic/Scholarly.* **Description:** Serves as a forum for a broad scope of monographs and collections of essays on the cutting edge of epistemology, the philosophy of language and mind, ethics and metaphysics.
Indexed: CCMJ.
Published by: Cambridge University Press, The Edinburgh Bldg, Shaftesbury Rd, Cambridge, CB2 8RU, United Kingdom. TEL 44-1223-312393, FAX 44-1223-315052, journals@cambridge.org, http://www.cambridge.org/uk. Eds. Gilbert Harman, John Haldane, Jonathan Dancy. R&P Linda Nicol TEL 44-1223-325702.

174.957 CAN ISSN 1488-2426
QH332
CANADIAN BIOETHICS REPORT. Text in English. q. free (effective 2003). **Document type:** *Report, Academic/Scholarly.*
Media: Online - full text. **Related titles:** Online - full text ed.
—CCC.
Published by: Canadian Medical Association/Association Medicale Canadienne, 1867 Alta Vista Dr, Ottawa, ON K1G 3Y6, Canada. TEL 613-731-8610, FAX 613-236-8864. R&P Janis Murrey.

100 CAN ISSN 0045-5091
➤ **CANADIAN JOURNAL OF PHILOSOPHY.** Abbreviated title: C J P. Text in English, French. 1971. q. CAD 30 domestic to individuals; USD 30 foreign to individuals; CAD 80 domestic to institutions; USD 130 foreign to institutions; CAD 15 domestic to students; USD 15 foreign to students; CAD 9 per issue domestic; USD 9 per issue foreign (effective 2011). bk.rev. illus. index. back issues avail.; reprints avail. **Document type:** *Journal, Academic/Scholarly.* **Description:** Publishes works in all areas of philosophy.
Related titles: Microfiche ed.: (from MML); Microform ed.: (from MML); Online - full text ed.: ISSN 1911-0820; ◆ Supplement(s): Canadian Journal of Philosophy. Supplementary Volume Series. ISSN 0229-7051.
Indexed: A01, A02, A03, A08, A20, A21, A22, A25, A26, ASCA, AmHI, ArtHuCI, B04, BRD, C03, CA, CBCARef, CBPI, CPerI, CWPI, CurCont, DIP, E01, E08, FR, G08, H07, H08, H14, HAb, HumInd, I05, IBR, IBSS, IBZ, IPB, M01, M02, MLA, MLA-IB, MSN, P02, P10, P28, P30, P48, P53, P54, PCI, PQC, PhilInd, R05, RASB, RI-1, RI-2, S08, S09, SCOPUS, T02, W03, W07.
—BLDSC (3033.900000), IE, Infotrieve, Ingenta, INIST. **CCC.**
Published by: University of Calgary Press, 2500 University Dr NW, Calgary, AB T2N 1N4, Canada. TEL 403-220-7578, FAX 403-282-0085, ucpmail@ucalgary.ca, http://www.uofcpress.com.

100 CAN ISSN 0229-7051
CANADIAN JOURNAL OF PHILOSOPHY. SUPPLEMENTARY VOLUME SERIES. Text in English. 1970. irreg., latest vol.32, 2006. price varies. bk.rev. 150 p./no.; back issues avail. **Document type:** *Monographic series, Academic/Scholarly.* **Description:** Publishes philosophical work of high quality in any field of philosophy.
Related titles: Online - full text ed.; ◆ Supplement to: Canadian Journal of Philosophy. ISSN 0045-5091.
Indexed: DIP, FR, IBR, IBZ, PCI, PhilInd.
—BLDSC (3033.910000), Ingenta, INIST. **CCC.**
Published by: University of Calgary Press, 2500 University Dr NW, Calgary, AB T2N 1N4, Canada. TEL 403-220-7578, FAX 403-282-0085, ucpmail@ucalgary.ca, http://www.uofcpress.com.

212.5 CAN ISSN 0045-544X
BP500
CANADIAN THEOSOPHIST. Text in English. 1920. bi-m. CAD 12 domestic; CAD 16 foreign (effective 1999). bk.rev. index. back issues avail. **Document type:** *Bulletin.*
Published by: Theosophical Society in Canada, R.R. No.3, Burk's Falls, ON P0A 1C0, Canada. TEL 705-382-6012. Ed. S L Treloar. R&P S.L. Treloar. Circ: 250.

100 301.1 CAN ISSN 1499-7487
CANADIAN UNDERGRADUATE JOURNAL OF COGNITIVE SCIENCE. Text in English. 2002. a. **Document type:** *Journal, Academic/Scholarly.*
Media: Online - full content.
Published by: Simon Fraser University, Cognitive Science Program (Subsidiary of: Simon Fraser University), 8888 University Dr, Burnaby, BC V5A 1S6, Canada. Ed. Chris Mathieson.

100 CAN ISSN 0317-073X
➤ **THE CARLETON UNIVERSITY STUDENT JOURNAL OF PHILOSOPHY.** Text in English. 1973. 3/yr. back issues avail. **Document type:** *Journal, Academic/Scholarly.* **Description:** Contains articles written on a wide variety of philosophical topics by graduate and undergraduate students.
Media: Online - full text. **Related titles:** Online - full text ed.
Published by: Carleton University, Department of Philosophy, 1125 Colonel By Dr., Ottawa, ON K1S 5B6, Canada. TEL 613-520-6613, ddubrule@ccs.carleton.ca.

189 USA ISSN 1075-4407
B659.Z7
➤ **CARMINA PHILOSOPHIAE.** Variant title: International Boethius Society. Journal. Text in English. 1992. a., latest 2006. bk.rev. back issues avail. **Document type:** *Journal, Academic/Scholarly.* **Description:** Devoted to the study of Boethius, his age, and his influence.
Indexed: MLA-IB, PhilInd.
Published by: International Boethius Society, c/o Dr Noel Harold Kaylor, Department of English, Troy University, Troy, AL 36082. FAX 334-670-3519, nkaylor@troy.edu, http://www.mtsu.edu/english/Journals/boethius/index.shtml.

➤ **CARNEGIE COUNCIL NEWSLETTER.** *see* POLITICAL SCIENCE—International Relations

100 FRA ISSN 1960-7431
LES CARNETS DE LA PHILOSOPHIE. Text in French. 2007. q. EUR 96 for 2 yrs. (effective 2008).
Published by: Lafont Presse, 53 Rue du Chemin Vert, Boulogne-Billancourt, 92100, France. FAX 33-1-45792211, http://www.lafontpresse.fr.

121 DEU
CASSIRER-FORSCHUNGEN. Text in German. 1995. irreg., latest vol.14, 2010. price varies. **Document type:** *Monographic series, Academic/Scholarly.*
Published by: Felix Meiner Verlag GmbH, Richardstr 47, Hamburg, 22081, Germany. TEL 49-40-2987560, FAX 49-40-29875620, info@meiner.de. R&P, Adv. contact Johannes Kambylis.

100 ITA ISSN 2035-3960
CASSIRER STUDIES. Text in Multiple languages. 2008. a. **Document type:** *Journal, Academic/Scholarly.* **Description:** Studies about Ernst Cassirer, German philosopher of the 20th Century .
Related titles: Online - full text ed.: ISSN 2038-6575.
Published by: (Universita degli Studi di Napoli "L'Orientale"), Bibliopolis, Via Vincenzo Arangio Ruiz 83, Naples, NA 80122, Italy. TEL 39-081-664606, FAX 39-081-7616273, info@bibliopolis.it, http://www.bibliopolis.it.

100 860 ESP ISSN 0210-749X
B4568.U54
CATEDRA MIGUEL DE UNAMUNO. CUADERNOS. Text in Spanish. 1948. irreg., latest vol.41, 2006. EUR 18 (effective 2009). **Document type:** *Monographic series, Academic/Scholarly.* **Description:** Presents studies on the life and work of Miguel de Unamuno.
Indexed: A26, FR, I04, I05, MLA-IB, P09, PCI.
—INIST. **CCC.**
Published by: Universidad de Salamanca, Ediciones, Apartado 325, Salamanca, 37080, Spain. TEL 34-923-294598, FAX 34-923-262579, pedidos@universitas.usal.es, http://www.eusal.es/. Ed. Ricardo Senabre.

THE CATHOLIC NEW WORLD. *see* RELIGIONS AND THEOLOGY—Roman Catholic

CATHOLIC THOUGHT FROM LUBLIN. *see* RELIGIONS AND THEOLOGY—Roman Catholic

100 320 ESP ISSN 1579-3974
EL CATOBLEPAS; revista critica del presente. Text in Spanish. 2002. m. free (effective 2011). back issues avail. **Document type:** *Journal, Academic/Scholarly.*
Media: Online - full text.
—CCC.
Published by: Asociacion Nodulo Materialista Ed. Maria Santillana Acosta.

CAVEAT LECTOR. *see* LITERATURE—Poetry

100 ESP ISSN 1577-0567
B5
LA CAVERNA DE PLATON. Text in Spanish. 1997. q. **Document type:** *Journal, Consumer.*
Media: Online - full text. **Related titles:** CD-ROM ed.: ISSN 1577-0346.
Published by: La Caverna de Platon

100 HRV ISSN 1330-7193
B6
CEMU; casopis studenata filozofije. Text in Croatian. 1994. m. **Document type:** *Journal.*
Related titles: Online - full content ed.: ISSN 1334-6857. 2003.
Indexed: A26, RILM.
Published by: Sveuciliste u Zagrebu, Filozofski Fakultet, Udruzenje Studenata Filozofije, Ivana Lucica 3, Zagreb, 10000, Croatia.

100 NLD
CENTRAL-EUROPEAN VALUE STUDIES. Text in English. irreg. price varies. **Document type:** *Monographic series, Academic/Scholarly.*
Related titles: ◆ Series of: Value Inquiry Book Series. ISSN 0929-8436.
Published by: Editions Rodopi B.V., Tijnmuiden 7, Amsterdam, 1046 AK, Netherlands. TEL 31-20-6114821, FAX 31-20-4472979, info@rodopi.nl. Ed. Emil Visnovsky. **Dist. by:** Rodopi - USA, 606 Newark Ave, 2nd fl, Kenilworth, NJ 07033. TEL 908-497-9031, FAX 908-497-9035.

174.280 600 610 DNK ISSN 1395-5470
R724
CENTRALE VIDENSKABSETISKE KOMITE. AARSBERETNING/CENTRAL SCIENTIFIC - ETHICAL COMMITTEE OF DENMARK. REPORT. Text in Danish. 1982. a. free. **Document type:** *Yearbook.*
Formerly (until 1994): Centrale Videnskabsetiske Komite. Beretning (0107-9786)
Related titles: Online - full text ed.: ISSN 1901-3973. 1996.
Published by: Den Centrale Videnskabsetiske Komite/Danish National Committee on Biomedical Research Ethics, Slotsholmsgade 12, Copenhagen K, 1216, Denmark. TEL 45-72-269370, FAX 45-72-269380, cvk@sum.dk. Circ: 2,000.

P

160 CHE ISSN 1013-8765
CENTRE DE RECHERCHES SEMIOLOGIQUES. TRAVAUX. Text in French. 1970. irreg. **Document type:** *Monographic series, Academic/Scholarly.*
Indexed: FR.
—INIST.
Published by: Universite de Neuchatel, Institut de Logique. Centre de Recherches Semiologiques, Espace Louis Agassiz 1, Neuchatel, 2000, Switzerland. TEL 41-32-7181858, FAX 41-32-7181701.

141 GRC ISSN 1015-2563
CENTRE INTERNATIONAL D'ETUDES PLATONICIENNES ET ARISTOTELICIENNES. SERIE RECHERCHES. Text in French. 1986. a. **Document type:** *Monographic series.* **Description:** Studies the philosophical legacies of Plato, Aristotle, and the Neoplatonists.
Published by: (Hellenic Society for Philosophical Studies/Societe Hellenique d'Etudes Philosophiques), Evanghelos A. Moutsopoulos Ed. & Pub., 40 Hypsilantou St, Athens, 115 21, Greece. TEL 30-10-725-1212, FAX 30-10-722-7322. R&P Evanghelos A Moutsopoulos.

CENTRE PROTESTANT D'ETUDES DE GENEVE. BULLETIN. *see* RELIGIONS AND THEOLOGY—Protestant

100 ITA ISSN 0392-7334
B3583
CENTRO DI STUDI VICHIANI. BOLLETTINO. Text in Italian. 1971. a. price varies. **Document type:** *Journal, Academic/Scholarly.* **Description:** Focuses on Gian Battista Vico's life and works and all the studies pertinent to the Neapolitan philosopher.
Related titles: Online - full text ed.: ISSN 2035-2727. 2007.
Indexed: BibInd, CA, FR, IPB, MLA, MLA-IB, PhilInd, SOPODA, SociolAb.
—INIST.
Published by: (Centro di Studi Vichiani), Rubbettino Editore, Viale Rosario Rubbettino 10, Soveria Mannelli, CZ 88049, Italy. TEL 39-0968-662034, FAX 39-0968-662055, segreteria@rubbettino.it, http://www.rubbettino.it.

CENTRO ITALIANO DI STUDI SULL'ALTO MEDIOEVO. BIBLIOTECA. *see* HISTORY—History Of Europe

CENTRO ITALIANO DI STUDI SULL'ALTO MEDIOEVO. QUADERNI. *see* HISTORY—History Of Europe

140 028.5 NLD ISSN 1871-0050
CENTRUM VOOR KINDERFILOSOFIE. NIEUWSBRIEF. Text in Dutch. 1990. q. EUR 12.50 domestic; EUR 16 in Belgium (effective 2008).
Formerly (until 2003): Filosoferen met Kinderen (1385-5808)
Published by: Hogeschool InHolland, Centrum voor Kinderfilosofie, Dirklangendwarsstr 40, Delft, 2611 JA, Netherlands. TEL 31-72-5183584.

100 LKA ISSN 0577-4772
CEYLON RATIONALIST AMBASSADOR. Text in English. 196?. a. LKR 5, USD 1. back issues avail.
Published by: Ceylon Rationalist Association, 89 Pamankada Ln., Colombo, 6, Sri Lanka. Ed. Abraham T Kovoor. Circ: 3,000.

CHALCEDON REPORT. *see* RELIGIONS AND THEOLOGY

160 USA ISSN 0009-1774
B945.P44
➤ **CHARLES S. PEIRCE SOCIETY. TRANSACTIONS**; a quarterly journal in American philosophy. Text in English. 1965. q. USD 109.50 combined subscription to institutions (print & online eds.) (effective 2012). adv. bk.rev. back issues avail.; reprint service avail. from PSC. **Document type:** *Journal, Academic/Scholarly.* **Description:** Features essays, and every significant book published in the field of American Philosophy is discussed in a review essay.
Related titles: Online - full text ed.: ISSN 1558-9587. USD 72.50 to institutions (effective 2012).
Indexed: A01, A03, A08, A20, A21, A22, A26, ASCA, AmH&L, AmHI, ArtHuCI, B04, BRD, CA, CurCont, DIP, E01, E08, FR, G08, H07, H08, H14, HAb, HumInd, I05, IBR, IBRH, IBZ, IPB, MLA-IB, MSN, P10, P28, P48, P53, P54, PCI, PQC, PhilInd, RI-1, RI-2, S09, SCOPUS, T02, W03, W05, W07.
—BLDSC (8912.377000), IE, Ingenta, INIST. **CCC.**
Published by: (Charles S. Peirce Society), Indiana University Press, 601 N Morton St, Bloomington, IN 47404. TEL 812-855-8817, 800-842-6796, FAX 812-855-7931, journals@indiana.edu, http://iupress.indiana.edu. Eds. Cornelis de Waal, Scott Pratt, Douglas R Anderson. Circ: 600.

➤ **CHELSEA SCHOOL RESEARCH CENTRE EDITION.** *see* EDUCATION

➤ **THE CHESTERTON REVIEW.** *see* LITERATURE

100 300 MNG ISSN 1673-3231
CHIFENG XUEYUAN XUEBAO (MENGWEN ZHEXUE SHEHUI KEXUE BAN)/CHIFENG COLLEGE. JOURNAL. (PHILOSOPHY AND SOCIAL SCIENCE MONGOLIAN EDITION). Text in Mongol. 1981. bi-m. **Document type:** *Journal, Academic/Scholarly.*
Published by: Chifeng Xueyuan, 1, Jichang Lu, Hongshan-qu, Chifeng, 024000, Mongolia. TEL 86-476-2205717, http://www.cfxy.cn/.

100 300 MNG ISSN 1673-2596
CHIFENG XUEYUAN XUEBAO (ZHEXUE SHEHUI KEXUE BAN)/ CHIFENG UNIMERSITY. JOURNAL (PHILOSOPHY AND SOCIAL SCIENCE CHINESE EDITION). Text in Chinese. 1984. m.
Formerly: Zhaowuda Mengzu Shi-Zhuan Xuebao (Hanwen Zhexue Shehui Kexue Ban)/Zhaowuda Mongolian Teachers College. Journal (1001-0467)
Published by: Chifeng Xueyuan, 1, Jichang Lu, Hongshan-qu, Chifeng, 024000, Mongolia. TEL 86-476-2205717, http://www.cfxy.cn/.

100 370 BRA ISSN 1984-5987
CHILDHOOD & PHILOSOPHY. Text in Multiple languages. 2005. s-a. free (effective 2011). **Document type:** *Journal, Academic/Scholarly.*
Media: Online - full text.
Published by: Universidade do Estado do Rio de Janeiro, Programa de Pos-Graduacao em Educacao, c/o Walter Omar Kohan, R Sao Francisco Xavier 524, Sala 12037 F, Maracana, Rio de Janeiro, 20559-900, Brazil. Eds. Walter Knowles Kennedy, Walter Omar Kohan.

THE CHILDREN'S FRIEND. *see* RELIGIONS AND THEOLOGY

CHINMAYA MANAGEMENT REVIEW. *see* BUSINESS AND ECONOMICS—Management

100 ITA ISSN 1974-1979
CHORA; laboratorio di attualita, scrittura e cultura filosofica. Text in Italian. 2001. q. free (effective 2010). **Document type:** *Journal, Consumer.*
Published by: Associazione Culturale AlboVersorio, Via Torino 11B, Senago, MI 20030, Italy. TEL 39-340-9247340, http://www.alboversorio.it. Ed. Massimiliano Cappuccio.

CHRISTIAN BIOETHICS; non-ecumenical studies in medical morality. *see* MEDICAL SCIENCES

100 DEU
CHRISTIAN WOLFF, WERKE. ABTEILUNG III: MATERIALIEN UND DOKUMENTE. Text in German, French. 1973. irreg., latest vol.120, 2010. price varies. **Document type:** *Monographic series, Academic/Scholarly.*
Published by: Georg Olms Verlag, Hagentorwall 7, Hildesheim, 31134, Germany. TEL 49-5121-15010, FAX 49-5121-150150, info@olms.de.

111.85 700 GRC ISSN 1105-0462
NX1.A1
➤ **CHRONIKA AISTHETIKES/ANNALES D'ESTHETIQUE/ANNALS FOR AESTHETICS.** Text in English, French, German, Greek, Italian. 1962. a., latest vol.43, 2005. EUR 27 per vol. in Europe; EUR 30 per vol. elsewhere; EUR 15 per vol. to students (effective 2007). bk.rev. back issues avail. **Document type:** *Journal, Academic/Scholarly.* **Description:** Promotes the postgraduate-level study of aesthetics.
Indexed: MLA-IB.
Published by: (Hellenike Hetaireia Aisthetikes/Hellenic Society for Aesthetics - Societe Hellenique d'Esthetique), P. and E. Michelis Foundation, 79 Vassilissis Sophias, Athens, 115 21, Greece. TEL 30-210-7258245, FAX 30-210-7218626. Eds. G Anagnostopoulos, G Apostolopoulou, T Valala. R&P Caterina Basba. Circ: 1,000.

122 GBR ISSN 0953-0053
CHRONOLOGY AND CATASTROPHISM REVIEW. Abbreviated title: C & C R. Text in English. 1976. a. free to members (effective 2009). bk.rev. illus. back issues avail.; reprints avail. **Document type:** *Journal, Academic/Scholarly.* **Description:** Features scholarly articles on a wide variety of scientific topics from a multidisciplinary perspective.
Incorporates (in 1996): Chronology and Catastrophism Workshop (0951-5984); Which superseded (1978-1985): S I S Workshop (0260-2806); Formerly (until 1986): S I S Review (0308-3276)
Published by: Society for Interdisciplinary Studies, 10 Witley Green, Darley Heights, Stopsley, Beds LU2 8TR, United Kingdom.

CHUMIR ETHICS FORUM; sheldon chumir foundation for ethics in leadership. *see* POLITICAL SCIENCE

CHUNG-KUO FO CHIAO. *see* RELIGIONS AND THEOLOGY—Buddhist

CINCINNATI JOURNAL OF MAGIC. *see* PARAPSYCHOLOGY AND OCCULTISM

▼ **CINEMA: JOURNAL OF PHILOSOPHY AND THE MOVING IMAGE.** *see* MOTION PICTURES

121 CHL ISSN 0717-554X
BD175
➤ **CINTA DE MOEBIO**; revista electronica de epistemologia de ciencias sociales. Text in Spanish; Abstracts in English. 1997. every 3 yrs. free (effective 2011). back issues avail. **Document type:** *Journal, Academic/Scholarly.* **Description:** The aim of the electronic publication is to discuss and argue in Spanish about the social science epistemology.
Media: Online - full text.
Indexed: A26, CA, F04, I04, I05, T02.
Published by: Universidad de Chile, Facultad de Ciencias Sociales, Ave. Ignacio Carrera Pinto, 1045, Santiago de Chile, Chile. TEL 56-2-678-7757, FAX 56-2-678-7756, fosorio@uchile.cl, http://www.facso.uchile.cl/. Ed., Pub. Francisco Osorio.

100 320 FRA ISSN 1299-5495
B2
➤ **CITES.** Text in French. 2000. s-a. EUR 80 domestic to institutions (effective 2012). reprint service avail. from SCH. **Document type:** *Journal, Academic/Scholarly.*
Related titles: Online - full text ed.: ISSN 1969-6876.
Indexed: IBSS, MLA-IB.
Published by: Presses Universitaires de France, 6 Avenue Reille, Paris, 75685, France. TEL 33-1-58103161, FAX 33-1-45897530, revues@puf.com, http://www.puf.com. Ed. Yves Charles Zarka.

160 USA ISSN 2042-9991
CLARENDON LIBRARY OF LOGIC AND PHILOSOPHY. Text in English. 1973. irreg., latest 2002. price varies. illus. back issues avail. **Document type:** *Monographic series, Academic/Scholarly.*
Published by: Oxford University Press (Subsidiary of: Oxford University Press), 2001 Evans Rd, Cary, NC 27513. TEL 919-677-0977, FAX 919-677-1303, orders.us@oup.com, http://www.us.oup.com.

CLINICAL MEDICAL ETHICS. *see* MEDICAL SCIENCES

CLIO (FT. WAYNE); a journal of literature, history, and the history of philosophy. *see* HISTORY

100 378 AUS ISSN 1833-2005
➤ **COGITO.** Text in English. 1966. q. adv. back issues avail. **Document type:** *Journal, Academic/Scholarly.* **Description:** Contains articles, essays and papers relevant to philosophy.
Published by: University of New South Wales, Socratic Society, c/o School of History and Philosophy, Level 3, Morven Brown Bldg, Faculty of Arts and Social Sciences, Sydney, NSW 2052, Australia. TEL 61-2-93851000, thesocraticsociety@gmail.com.

➤ **COGNITION, TECHNOLOGY AND WORK.** *see* PSYCHOLOGY

100 ESP ISSN 0069-5076
COLECCION FILOSOFICA. Text in Spanish. 1963. irreg., latest vol.66, 1990. price varies. back issues avail. **Document type:** *Monographic series, Academic/Scholarly.*
Published by: (Universidad de Navarra, Facultad de Filosofia y Letras), Universidad de Navarra, Servicio de Publicaciones, Campus Universitario, Pamplona, 31009, Spain. http://www.unav.es/publicaciones/.

100 MEX ISSN 2007-056X
COLECCION PAEDIA. Text in Spanish. 2000. a. **Document type:** *Monographic series, Academic/Scholarly.*
Published by: Universidad Nacional Autonoma de Mexico, Facultad de Filosofia y Letras, Cicuito Interior, Ciudad Universitaria, Mexico, D.F., 04510, Mexico. TEL 52-55-56221833, ffyl@filos.unam.mx, http://www.filos.unam.mx/.

181.45 USA ISSN 0164-1522
COLLABORATION; journal of the Integral Yoga of Sri Aurobindo and the Mother. Text in English. 1974. 3/yr. USD 20 domestic; USD 32 foreign (effective 2002). bk.rev. bibl.; illus. **Document type:** *Newsletter.* **Description:** Explores various yoga techniques and philosophies of Integral Yoga by Sri Aurobindo and the Mother, as well as the role of Integral Yoga in the world, especially in the US.
Incorporates (1970-1995): Nexus (Berkeley)
Related titles: Online - full text ed.
Published by: Sri Aurobindo Association, PO Box 163237, Sacramento, CA 95816. TEL 209-339-3710, FAX 916-451-9039. Ed. Lynda Lester. R&P David Hutchinson. Circ: 250 (paid and controlled).

THE COLLECTED WORKS OF JACQUES MARITAIN. *see* POLITICAL SCIENCE

100 FRA ISSN 1159-6007
COLLECTION CURSUS. PHILOSOPHIE. Variant title: Cursus. Philosophie. Text in French. 1992. irreg. price varies. **Document type:** *Monographic series, Academic/Scholarly.*
Published by: Armand Colin, 21 Rue du Montparnasse, Paris, 75283 Cedex 06, France. TEL 33-1-44395447, FAX 33-1-44394343, infos@armand-colin.fr.

100 FRA ISSN 1770-7374
COLLECTION CURSUS. SERIE COMPRENDRE. Text in French. 2004. irreg. price varies. **Document type:** *Monographic series, Academic/Scholarly.*
Published by: Armand Colin, 21 Rue du Montparnasse, Paris, 75283 Cedex 06, France. TEL 33-1-44395447, FAX 33-1-44394343, infos@armand-colin.fr, http://www.armand-colin.com.

100 FRA ISSN 1952-2487
COLLECTION PHILOSOPHICA. Variant title: Philosophica. Text in French. 2006. irreg., latest 2009. back issues avail. **Document type:** *Monographic series, Academic/Scholarly.*
Published by: Presses Universitaires de Rennes, Campus de la Harpe, 2 Rue du Doyen Denis-Leroy, Rennes, Cedex 35044, France. TEL 33-2-99141401, FAX 33-2-99141407, pur@univ-rennes2.fr.

COLLECTION THEATRE ET CONNAISSANCES. *see* THEATER

100 FRA ISSN 1142-3072
LE COLLEGE DE PHILOSOPHIE. Text in French. 1990. irreg. back issues avail. **Document type:** *Monographic series, Consumer.*
Published by: Editions Grasset & Fasquelle, 61 Rue des Saints-Peres, Paris, 75006, France. TEL 33-1-44392200, FAX 33-1-42226418, editorial@grasset.fr, http://www.grasset.fr.

184 DEU
COLLEGIUM HERMENEUTICUM. Text in German. 1999. irreg., latest vol.13, 2011. price varies. **Document type:** *Monographic series, Academic/Scholarly.*
Published by: Boehlau Verlag GmbH & Cie, Ursulaplatz 1, Cologne, 50668, Germany. TEL 49-221-913900, FAX 49-221-9139011, vertrieb@boehlau.de, http://www.boehlau.de.

100 DEU ISSN 2191-6683
▼ **COLLEGIUM METAPHYSICUM.** Text in German. 2011. irreg., latest vol.2, 2011. price varies. **Document type:** *Monographic series, Academic/Scholarly.*
Media: Large Type.
Published by: Mohr Siebeck GmbH & Co. KG, Wilhelmstr 18, Tuebingen, 72074, Germany. TEL 49-7071-9230, FAX 49-7071-51104, info@mohr.de.

100 GBR ISSN 1744-9413
B1618.C74
➤ **COLLINGWOOD AND BRITISH IDEALISM STUDIES.** Text in English. 1994. s-a. GBP 63 combined subscription domestic to institutions (print & online eds.); USD 126 combined subscription foreign to institutions (print & online eds.) (effective 2009). back issues avail. **Document type:** *Journal, Academic/Scholarly.*
Incorporates (1995-2005): Bradley Studies (1362-0916); Formerly (until 2000): Collingwood Studies (1356-0670)
Related titles: Online - full text ed.: (from IngentaConnect).
Indexed: DIP, I13, IBR, IBZ, MLA-IB, PhilInd.
—Ingenta.
Published by: (The Collingwood and British Idealism Centre (The Collingwood Society)), Imprint Academic, PO Box 200, Exeter, Devon EXS 5YX, United Kingdom. TEL 44-1392-851550, FAX 44-1392-851178.

100 POL ISSN 0239-6815
COLLOQUIA COMMUNIA. Text in Polish. 1979. s-a. (in 2 vols.). EUR 47 foreign (effective 2011). **Document type:** *Journal, Academic/Scholarly.*
Published by: Wydawnictwo Adam Marszalek, ul Lubicka 44, Torun, 87100, Poland. TEL 48-56-6485070, FAX 48-56-6608160, info@marszalek.com.pl, http://www.marszalek.com.pl. **Dist. by:** Ars Polona, Obroncow 25, Warsaw 03933, Poland. TEL 48-22-5098609, FAX 48-22-5098610, arspolona@arspolona.com.pl, http://www.arspolona.com.pl.

100 ITA ISSN 1126-9170
COLLOQUIUM PHILOSOPHICUM. Text in Italian. 1996. a., latest vol.8, 2002. EUR 40 domestic; EUR 44 foreign (effective 2007). **Document type:** *Monographic series, Academic/Scholarly.*
Published by: (Universita degli Studi di Roma Tre, Dipartimento di Filosofia), Casa Editrice Leo S. Olschki, Viuzzo del Pozzetto 8, Florence, 50126, Italy. TEL 39-055-6530684, FAX 39-055-6530214, celso@olschki.it, http://www.olschki.it. Ed. Franco Bianco.

COLLOQUY (ONLINE). *see* LITERATURE

170 FRA ISSN 1260-8599
➤ **COMITE CONSULTATIF NATIONAL D'ETHIQUE POUR LES SCIENCES DE LA VIE ET DE LA SANTE. LES CAHIERS.** Text in French. 1985. q. EUR 40 domestic; EUR 45 foreign (effective 2008). bk.rev. 50 p./no.; **Document type:** *Journal, Academic/Scholarly.*
Former titles (until 1993): Comite Consultatif National d'Ethique pour les Sciences de la Vie et de la Sante. Lettre (1169-1476); (until 1991): Comite Consultatif National d'Ethique pour les Sciences de la Vie et de la Sante. Lettre d'Information (0296-4074)
Related titles: Microfiche ed.
Indexed: FR.
—INIST.

Published by: Comite Consultatif National d'Ethique pour les Sciences de la Vie et de la Sante, 7 Rue Saint-Georges, Paris, 75009, France. TEL 33-1-53861149, FAX 33-1-53861140. Pub. Didier Sicard. R&P Anne Bernard. Circ: 1,000 (paid). **Subscr. to:** Mazarine Image, 2 Square Villaret de Joyeuse, Paris 75017, France. TEL 33-1-58054925, FAX 33-1-58054904.

➤ **COMMENTS & CRITICISMS.** *see* PSYCHOLOGY

100 809 USA ISSN 0961-754X
AS121
➤ **COMMON KNOWLEDGE.** Text in English. 1992. 3/yr. USD 27 to individuals; USD 140 to institutions; USD 147 combined subscription to institutions (print & online eds.); USD 47 per issue to institutions (effective 2012). adv. bk.rev. back issues avail.; reprint service avail. from PSC. **Document type:** *Journal, Academic/Scholarly.* **Description:** Addresses restructuring of traditional debates within intellectual communities.
Related titles: Online - full text ed.: ISSN 1538-4578. USD 122 to institutions (effective 2012).
Indexed: A01, A03, A08, A20, A22, ABS&EES, AmHI, ArtHuCI, B24, CA, CCME, E01, H07, I14, MLA-IB, P42, PCI, S02, S03, SociolAb, T02, W07.
—BLDSC (3339.239000), IE, Infotrieve, Ingenta. **CCC.**
Published by: Duke University Press, 905 W Main St, Ste 18 B, Durham, NC 27701. TEL 919-688-5134, 888-651-0122, FAX 919-688-2615, 888-651-0124, subscriptions@dukeupress.edu, http://www.dukeupress.edu. Ed. Jeffrey M Perl.

100 GBR ISSN 0264-5211
COMMUNIQUE. Text in English. 1988. 3/yr. GBP 4.50.
Published by: Sundial House Publications, Sundial House, Sundial House, The Midway, Nevill Court, Tunbridge Wells, Kent TN4 8NJ, United Kingdom.

174.2 610.9 360 GBR
➤ **COMMUNITY, CULTURE AND CHANGE.** Text in English. 1998. irreg., latest 2006. price varies. back issues avail. **Document type:** *Monographic series, Academic/Scholarly.* **Description:** Encompasses a wide range of ideas and theoretical models related to communities and cultures as a whole, embracing key Therapeutic Community concepts such as collective responsibility, citizenship and empowerment, as well as multidisciplinary ways of working and the social origins of distress.
Formerly (until 2004): Therapeutic Communities
—BLDSC (3363.608650).
Published by: Jessica Kingsley Publishers, 116 Pentonville Rd, London, N1 9JB, United Kingdom. TEL 44-20-78332307, FAX 44-20-78372917, post@jkp.com. Eds. Jan Lees, Rex Haigh.

199 GBR ISSN 1757-0638
▼ ➤ **COMPARATIVE AND CONTINENTAL PHILOSOPHY.** Abbreviated title: C C P. Text in English. 2009 (May). s-a. USD 220 combined subscription in North America to institutions (print & online eds.); GBP 135 combined subscription elsewhere to institutions (print & online eds.) (effective 2012). adv. back issues avail.; reprints avail. **Document type:** *Journal, Academic/Scholarly.* **Description:** Features academic journal accessible to readers of various disciplines such as philosophy, religion, art history, critical theory, phenomenological psychology, and cultural theory.
Related titles: Online - full text ed.: ISSN 1757-0646. USD 176 in North America to institutions; GBP 108 elsewhere to institutions (effective 2012).
Indexed: PhilInd.
—IE. **CCC.**
Published by: Equinox Publishing Ltd., Unit S3, Kelham House, 3 Lancaster St, Sheffield, S6 3AF, United Kingdom. TEL 44-114-2725957, FAX 44-560-3459046, journals@equinoxpub.com, http://www.equinoxpub.com/. Ed. David Jones. Adv. contact Val Hall.

100 USA ISSN 2151-6014
B1
▼ **COMPARATIVE PHILOSOPHY.** Text in English. 2010. irreg. free (effective 2011). **Document type:** *Journal, Academic/Scholarly.*
Media: Online - full text.
Published by: San Jose State University, One Washington Sq, San Jose, CA 95192. TEL 408-924-1000, FAX 408-924-3282. Ed. Bo Mou.

170 IND ISSN 0973-9483
THE COMPASS. Text in English. 2007. s-a. **Document type:** *Magazine, Academic/Scholarly.*
Published by: Baha'i Academy, Shivaji Nagar, Mahabaleshwar, Satara, Panchgani, Maharashtra 412 805, India. TEL 91-2168-240100, FAX 91-2168-240661, director@bahaiacademy.org. Eds. Dr. H T D Rost, L Azadi.

100 ITA ISSN 1128-9082
B4
COMUNICAZIONE FILOSOFICA; rivista tematica di ricerca e didattica filosofica. Text in Italian. 1997. 3/yr. free (effective 2011). **Document type:** *Journal, Academic/Scholarly.*
Media: Online - full text.
Published by: Societa Filosofica Italiana (S F I), Dipartimento di Studi Filosofici, Universita degli Studi di Roma "La Sapienza", Via Nomentana 118, Rome, 00161, Italy. sfi@getnet.it.

140 190 ITA ISSN 1121-8444
B4
CON-TRATTO; rivista di filosofia tomista e di filosofia contemporanea. Text in Italian. 1992. a. price varies. **Document type:** *Monographic series, Academic/Scholarly.*
Published by: Istituto Filosofico di Studi Tomistici, Via San Cataldo 97, Modena, Italy. http://www.istitutotomistico.it.

CONCEPTS IN SOCIAL THOUGHT SERIES. *see* POLITICAL SCIENCE

100 DEU ISSN 0010-5155
CONCEPTUS; Zeitschrift fuer Philosophie. Text in German; Summaries in English, German. 1967. s-a. EUR 25; EUR 18.50 to students (effective 2008). adv. bk.rev. abstr.; bibl.; charts. index, cum.index. back issues avail.; reprints avail. **Document type:** *Journal, Academic/Scholarly.*
Indexed: CCMJ, DIP, FR, IBR, IBZ, IPB, MSN, MathR, PCI, PhilInd.
—INIST.
Published by: (Johannes Kepler Universitaet Linz, Institut fuer Paedagogik und Psychologie AUT, Institut fuer Philosophie AUT), Academia Verlag GmbH, Bahnstr 7, Sankt Augustin, 53757, Germany. TEL 49-2241-345210, FAX 49-2241-345316, kontakt@academia-verlag.de. Circ: 500.

100 AUT ISSN 0259-0670
CONCEPTUS - STUDIEN. Text in German. 1984. irreg., latest vol.8, 1991. price varies. **Document type:** *Monographic series.*
Published by: Johannes Kepler Universitaet Linz, Institut fuer Philosophie, Linz-Auhof, A-4040, Austria. Ed. Rainer Born.

100 USA ISSN 1940-1914
B20
CONFERENCE ADDRESSES OF THE LONG ISLAND PHILOSOPHICAL SOCIETY ONLINE. Abbreviated title: C A L I P S O. Text in English. 2007. s-a. back issues avail. **Document type:** *Journal, Academic/Scholarly.* **Description:** Features work from a wide range of philosophical viewpoints based upon Long Island Philosophical Society meetings.
Media: Online - full text.
Published by: Long Island Philosophical Society, Long Island University, Brooklyn Campus, 1 University Plz, Brooklyn, NY 11201. TEL 718-488-1485, FAX 718-488-1439, admissions@brooklyn.liu.edu. Eds. Anton Alterman, Margaret Cuonzo.

170 351 CAN ISSN 1717-7626
CONFLICT OF INTEREST AND POST-EMPLOYMENT CODE FOR PUBLIC OFFICE HOLDERS. Text in English. 2003. a. **Document type:** *Monographic series, Trade.*
Published by: Canada, Office of the Ethics Commissioner, Parliament of Canada, Centre Block, PO Box 16, Ottawa, ON K1A 0A6, Canada. TEL 613-995-0721, FAX 613-995-7308, oec-bce@parl.gc.ca.

100 370 BRA ISSN 0103-1457
➤ **CONJECTURA: FILOSOFIA E EDUCACAO.** Text in Portuguese. 1988. 3/yr. **Document type:** *Journal, Academic/Scholarly.*
Related titles: Online - full text ed.: ISSN 2178-4612. free (effective 2011).
Indexed: PhilInd.
Published by: Universidade de Caxias do Sul, Editora, Rua Francisco Getulio Vargas, 1130, Caxias do Sul, 95070-560, Brazil. TEL 55-54-32182100, FAX 55-54-32182197, educs@ucs.br. Ed. Everaldo Cescon.

100 DEU ISSN 0589-4069
CONSCIENTIA. Text in German. 1968. irreg., latest vol.19, 1992. price varies. **Document type:** *Monographic series, Academic/Scholarly.*
Published by: Bouvier Verlag, Fuerstenstr 3, Bonn, 53111, Germany. TEL 49-228-3918210, FAX 49-228-3918221, info@bouvier-verlag.de, http://www.bouvier-verlag.de. Ed. Gerhard Funke.

CONSTELLATIONS; an international journal of critical and democratic theory. *see* POLITICAL SCIENCE

100 DEU ISSN 1619-9219
CONSTRUCTIVIANA; interdisziplinaere und interkulturelle Wissenschaftstheorie. Text in German. 2002. irreg., latest vol.5, 2006. price varies. **Document type:** *Monographic series, Academic/Scholarly.*
Published by: Verlag Dr. Kovac, Leverkusenstr 13, Hamburg, 22761, Germany. TEL 49-40-3988800, FAX 49-40-39888055, info@verlagdrkovac.de. Ed. Fritz Wallner.

100 BRA ISSN 1809-1911
CONTEMPLACAO. Text in Portuguese. 2005. s-a. back issues avail. **Document type:** *Journal, Academic/Scholarly.*
Media: Online - full text.
Published by: Faculdade de Joao Paulo II, Rua Olavo Bilac, 554, Jardim America, Marilia, SP 17506-270, Brazil. TEL 55-14-34141965.

111.85 USA ISSN 1932-8478
BH1
➤ **CONTEMPORARY AESTHETICS.** Abbreviated title: C A. Text in English. 2003. a. free (effective 2011). back issues avail. **Document type:** *Journal, Academic/Scholarly.* **Description:** Encourages aesthetic inquiry on current interests, in particular constructive approaches to aesthetic issues that enrich and widen our aesthetic horizon, whether of subject matter or cultural traditions.
Media: Online - full text.
Indexed: A07, A30, A31, A39, AA, ArtInd, C27, C29, CA, D03, D04, E13, PhilInd, R14, S14, S15, S18, T02, W03, W05.
Address: PO Box 52, Castine, ME 04421. Ed. Arnold Berleant.

100 USA ISSN 1097-1467
B1
➤ **CONTEMPORARY CHINESE THOUGHT**; a journal of translations. Abbreviated title: C S P. Text in English. 1967. q. USD 1,040 combined subscription domestic to institutions (print & online eds.); USD 1,124 combined subscription foreign to institutions (print & online eds.) (effective 2012). adv. index. back issues avail.; reprint service avail. from PSC. **Document type:** *Journal, Academic/Scholarly.* **Description:** Translates current writings on all aspects of philosophy, including theoretical essays on systems, studies of China's cultural and religious development, interpretations of Chinese classics, and exegeses on Marxist thought.
Formerly (until 1997): Chinese Studies in Philosophy (0023-8627); Which superseded in part (in 1969): Chinese Studies in History and Philosophy
Related titles: Online - full text ed.: ISSN 1558-0997. USD 953 to institutions (effective 2012).
Indexed: A20, A22, ASCA, AmHI, ArtHuCI, BAS, CA, CurCont, DIP, E01, H07, IBR, IBZ, MLA-IB, PCI, PhilInd, RASB, RI-1, RI-2, SCOPUS, T02, W07.
—BLDSC (3425.177320), IE, Infotrieve, Ingenta. **CCC.**
Published by: M.E. Sharpe, Inc., 80 Business Park Dr, Armonk, NY 10504. TEL 914-273-1800, 800-541-6563, FAX 914-273-2106, custserv@mesharpe.com. Ed. Carine Defoort. Adv. contact Barbara Ladd TEL 914-273-1800.

100 USA ISSN 0732-4944
B1
CONTEMPORARY PHILOSOPHY. Text in English. 1966. 3/yr. USD 37 domestic to individuals; USD 56 foreign to individuals (effective 2008). adv. bk.rev. **Document type:** *Magazine, Consumer.* **Description:** Contains papers from academic and professionally trained persons from many fields and diciplines. Issues may focus on specific subjects or be general in nature.
Formerly: Philosophic Research and Analysis (0048-3907)
Indexed: A22, P30, PhilInd.
—IE, Infotrieve, Ingenta.
Published by: (Institute for Advanced Philosophic Research), Realia, 181 Main St, #444, Presque isle, ME 04769. TEL 207-762-3800.

190 NLD
➤ **CONTEMPORARY PHILOSOPHY**; a new survey. Text in English, French. 1981. irreg., latest vol.9, 2007. price varies. back issues avail. **Document type:** *Monographic series, Academic/Scholarly.* **Description:** Publishes philosophical research in various world cultures.
Published by: (Institut International de Philosophie FRA), Springer Netherlands (Subsidiary of: Springer Science+Business Media), Van Godewijckstraat 30, Dordrecht, 3311 GX, Netherlands. TEL 31-78-6576050, FAX 31-78-6576474. Ed. G Floistad.

➤ **CONTEMPORARY POLITICAL THEORY.** *see* POLITICAL SCIENCE

144.3 NLD ISSN 1572-3429
B832
➤ **CONTEMPORARY PRAGMATISM.** Text in English. 2004 (June). s-a. EUR 38, USD 47.50 combined subscription to individuals (print & online eds.); EUR 90, USD 112.50 combined subscription to libraries (print & online eds.) (effective 2008). **Document type:** *Journal, Academic/Scholarly.* **Description:** Contains discussions of applying pragmatism, broadly understood, to today's issues.
Related titles: Online - full text ed.: ISSN 1875-8185 (from IngentaConnect).
Indexed: AmHI, H07, IBR, IBZ, PhilInd, T02.
—BLDSC (3425.210500), IE, Ingenta. **CCC.**
Published by: Editions Rodopi B.V., Tijnmuiden 7, Amsterdam, 1046 AK, Netherlands. TEL 31-20-6114821, FAX 31-20-4472979, info@rodopi.nl, http://www.rodopi.nl. Eds. John R Shook TEL 405-744-9231, Paulo Ghiraldelli Jr. **Dist. in the US by:** Rodopi - USA, 295 North Michigan Avenue, Suite 1B, Kenilworth, NJ 07033. TEL 908-298-9071, 800-225-3998, FAX 908-298-9075.

➤ **CONTEMPORARY PSYCHOANALYTIC STUDIES.** *see* PSYCHOLOGY

199 NLD
CONTEMPORARY RUSSIAN PHILOSOPHY. Text in English. irreg. price varies. **Document type:** *Monographic series, Academic/Scholarly.* **Description:** Explores a variety of perspectives in and on philosophy as it is currently practiced in Russia.
Related titles: ◆ Series of: Value Inquiry Book Series. ISSN 0929-8436.
Published by: Editions Rodopi B.V., Tijnmuiden 7, Amsterdam, 1046 AK, Netherlands. TEL 31-20-6114821, FAX 31-20-4472979, info@rodopi.nl. Ed. Dr. William C Gay. **Dist. by:** Rodopi - USA, 606 Newark Ave, 2nd fl, Kenilworth, NJ 07033. TEL 908-497-9031, FAX 908-497-9035.

CONTEXTOS. *see* LINGUISTICS

100 USA ISSN 1050-3412
CONTINENTAL PHILOSOPHY. Text in English. 1988. irreg., latest 2002. price varies. back issues avail. **Document type:** *Monographic series, Academic/Scholarly.*
—BLDSC (3425.610000). **CCC.**
Published by: Routledge (Subsidiary of: Taylor & Francis Group), 325 Chestnut St, Ste 800, Philadelphia, PA 19106. TEL 800-354-1420, FAX 215-625-2940, journals@routledge.com.

P

100 NLD ISSN 1387-2842
B1
➤ **CONTINENTAL PHILOSOPHY REVIEW.** Text in English, French, German. 1968. q. EUR 560, USD 581 combined subscription to institutions (print & online eds.) (effective 2012). bk.rev. bibl. index. reprint service avail. from PSC. **Document type:** *Journal, Academic/Scholarly.* **Description:** Provides a forum for dialogue on philosophical issues and fundamental philosophical problems, including both theoretical topics, practical problems, and philosophical concerns relating to the arts, science and religion.
Formerly (until 1998): Man and World (0025-1534)
Related titles: Microform ed.: (from PQC); Online - full text ed.: ISSN 1573-0611 (from IngentaConnect).
Indexed: A20, A22, A26, ASCA, AmHI, ArtHuCI, BRD, BibLing, CA, CurCont, E01, FR, H07, H08, HAb, HumInd, I13, IPB, MLA-IB, P28, P42, P48, P53, P54, PCI, PQC, PhilInd, RASB, SCOPUS, T02, W03, W05, W07.
—BLDSC (3425.615000), IE, Infotrieve, Ingenta, INIST. **CCC.**
Published by: Springer Netherlands (Subsidiary of: Springer Science+Business Media), Van Godewijckstraat 30, Dordrecht, 3311 GX, Netherlands. TEL 31-78-6576050, FAX 31-78-6576474, http://www.springer.com. Ed. Anthony J Steinbock.

100 ESP ISSN 1136-4076
CONTRASTES; revista interdisciplinar de filosofia. Text in Spanish. 1988. a. **Document type:** *Journal, Academic/Scholarly.*
Formerly (until 1996): Philosophica Malacitana (0214-6207)
Related titles: Online - full text ed.; ◆ Supplement(s): Contrastes. Suplemento. ISSN 1136-9922.
Indexed: IPB, P09, PCI, PhilInd.
—INIST.
Published by: Universidad de Malaga, Facultad de Filosofia y Letras, Campus de Teatinos, Malaga, 29071, Spain. candrade@uma.es.

100 ESP ISSN 1136-9922
CONTRASTES. SUPLEMENTO. Text in Spanish. 1993. a. **Document type:** *Monographic series, Academic/Scholarly.*
Formerly (until 1996): Philosophica Malacitana. Suplemento (1136-2898)
Related titles: ◆ Supplement to: Contrastes. ISSN 1136-4076.
Indexed: P09, PCI, PhilInd.
—INIST.
Published by: Universidad de Malaga, Facultad de Filosofia y Letras, Campus de Teatinos, Malaga, 29071, Spain. candrade@uma.es.

100 AUS ISSN 1443-7619
B1
➤ **CONTRETEMPS**; an online journal of philosophy. Text in English. 2000. irreg., latest vol.6, 2006. free. back issues avail. **Document type:** *Journal, Academic/Scholarly.* **Description:** Aims to enact philosophical engagement with social and political events.
Media: Online - full content.
Published by: University of Sydney, Department of Philosophy, c/o School of Philosophical and Historical Inquiry, Quadrangle A14, Sydney, NSW 2006, Australia. TEL 61-2-93512862, FAX 61-2-93513918, sophi.enquiries@arts.usyd.edu.au, http://www.arts.usyd.edu.au/departs/philos/. Ed. John Dalton.

100 ITA ISSN 1825-7755
CONTRIBUTI CARTESIANI. Text in Multiple languages. 2005. a. **Document type:** *Journal, Academic/Scholarly.*
Media: Online - full text.

Published by: Conte Editore, Via Luigi Carluccio 3, Lecce, 73100, Italy. TEL 39-0832-228827, FAX 39-0832-220280, casaeditrice@conteeditore.it, http://www.conteeditore.it.

▼ **CONTRIBUTIONES BONNENSES. REIHE 2: THEOLOGIE, PHILOSOPHIE.** *see* RELIGIONS AND THEOLOGY

100 USA ISSN 0084-926X
CONTRIBUTIONS IN PHILOSOPHY. Text in English. 1968. irreg., latest vol.89, 2004. price varies. back issues avail. **Document type:** *Monographic series, Academic/Scholarly.*
—BLDSC (3461.110000), IE, Ingenta. **CCC.**
Published by: Greenwood Publishing Group Inc. (Subsidiary of: A B C - C L I O), 88 Post Rd W, PO Box 5007, Westport, CT 06881. TEL 203-226-3571, 800-225-5800, FAX 877-231-6980, sales@greenwood.com, http://www.greenwood.com.

140 NLD ISSN 0923-9545
➤ **CONTRIBUTIONS TO PHENOMENOLOGY.** Text in English. 1989. irreg., latest vol.58, 2009. price varies. **Document type:** *Monographic series, Academic/Scholarly.* **Description:** Fosters the development of phenomenological philosophy through creative research.
—BLDSC (3461.108000), IE, Ingenta.
Published by: Springer Netherlands (Subsidiary of: Springer Science+Business Media), Van Godewijckstraat 30, Dordrecht, 3311 GX, Netherlands. TEL 31-78-6576050, FAX 31-78-6576474. Eds. Dermot Moran, Nicolas de Warren.

100 DEU ISSN 1433-643X
CONTRIBUTIONS TO PHILOSOPHICAL THEOLOGY. Text in English. 1999. irreg., latest vol.12, 2009. price varies. **Document type:** *Monographic series, Academic/Scholarly.*
Published by: Peter Lang GmbH (Subsidiary of: Peter Lang Publishing Group), Eschborner Landstr 42-50, Frankfurt Am Main, 60489, Germany. TEL 49-69-7807050, FAX 49-69-78070550, zentrale.frankfurt@peterlang.com.

100 ITA ISSN 0391-2418
AS221
IL CONTRIBUTO. Text in Italian. 1976. 3/yr. EUR 30 (effective 2010). bk.rev. **Document type:** *Journal, Academic/Scholarly.*
Related titles: Online - full text ed.: ISSN 1974-482X.
Published by: Centro per la Filosofia Italiana, Via Annibaldeschi 2, Monte Compatri, RM 00040, Italy. TEL 39-06-94288758, FAX 39-06-94789077, http://www.filosofia-italiana.org. Ed. Teresa Serra.

100 ITA ISSN 1973-8757
CONVERSAZIONI FILOSOFICHE. Text in Italian. 1995. irreg. **Document type:** *Journal, Academic/Scholarly.*
Published by: Edizioni Scientifiche Italiane SpA, Via Chiatamone 7, Naples, NA 80121, Italy. TEL 39-081-7645443, FAX 39-081-7646477, info@edizioniesi.it, http://www.edizioniesi.it.

100 ESP ISSN 0010-8235
B5
CONVIVIUM; revista de filosofia. Text in Spanish. 1956. 3/yr. bk.rev. abstr. **Document type:** *Journal, Academic/Scholarly.*
Related titles: Online - full text ed.: free (effective 2011).
Indexed: A20, ArtHuCI, E-psyche, MLA, MLA-IB, P09, PCI, PhilInd, W07.
—**CCC.**
Published by: (Universitat de Barcelona, Facultat de Filosofia), Universitat de Barcelona, Servei de Publicacions, Gran Via Corts Catalanes 585, Barcelona, 08007, Spain.

LE COQ HERON. *see* MEDICAL SCIENCES—Psychiatry And Neurology

CORONA. *see* LITERATURE

CORPORATE RESPONSIBILITY MAGAZINE. *see* BUSINESS AND ECONOMICS

CORPUS DEI PAPIRI FILOSOFICI GRECI E LATINI. *see* CLASSICAL STUDIES

182 BEL
CORPUS LATINUM COMMENTARIORUM IN ARISTOTELEM GRAECORUM. Text in Dutch, English, French. 1987. irreg. price varies. **Document type:** *Monographic series, Academic/Scholarly.*
Published by: Leuven University Press, Blijde Inkomststraat 5, Leuven, 3000, Belgium. TEL 32-16-325345, FAX 32-16-325352, university.press@upers.kuleuven.ac.be, http://www.kuleuven.ac.be/upers.

100 840 FRA ISSN 1965-1244
LE CORRESPONDANCIER DU COLLEGE DE PATAPHYSIQUE. Text in French. 1949. q. illus.
Former titles (until 2007): College de 'Pataphysique. Carnets Trimestriels (1625-2721); (until 2000): Monitoires du Cymbalum Pataphysicum (0982-0191); (until 1986): Organographes du Cymbalum Pataphysicum (0339-7203); (until 1975): Subsidia Pataphysica (0039-4386); College de Pataphysique. Dossiers
Indexed: FR.
—INIST.
Published by: College de Pataphysique, Courtaumont par Sermiers, Rilly La Montagne, 51500, France. college.pataphysique@free.fr, http://www.college-de-pataphysique.fr. Ed. Paul Gayot.

100 AUS ISSN 1832-9101
B1
➤ **COSMOS AND HISTORY**; the journal of natural and social philosophy. Text in English. 2005. a. free (effective 2009). bk.rev. back issues avail. **Document type:** *Journal, Academic/Scholarly.* **Description:** Aims at those who see philosophy's vocation in questioning and challenging prevailing assumptions about ourselves and our place in the world, developing new ways of thinking about physical existence, life, humanity and society, so helping to create the future insofar as thought affects the issue.
Media: Online - full text.
Indexed: A26, A39, AmHI, C27, C29, CA, D03, D04, E13, H07, I05, L06, MLA-IB, PhilInd, R14, S14, S15, S18, T02.
Published by: Cosmos Publishing Cooperative, c/o Arran Gare, Philosophy & Cultural Inquiry, Swinburne University, PO Box 218, Hawthorn, VIC 3122, Australia. Eds. Arran Gare, Paul Ashton.

➤ **CREATION.** *see* RELIGIONS AND THEOLOGY

345 USA ISSN 0731-129X
HV7231
➤ **CRIMINAL JUSTICE ETHICS.** Text in English. 1982. 3/yr. GBP 133 combined subscription in United Kingdom to institutions (print & online eds.); EUR 212, USD 266 combined subscription to institutions (print & online eds.) (effective 2012). bk.rev. illus. back issues avail.; reprint service avail. from PSC. **Document type:** *Journal, Academic/Scholarly.* **Description:** Focus on ethical issues in criminal justice by philosophers, criminal justice professionals, lawyers and judges, and the general public.
Related titles: Microform ed.: (from PQC); Online - full text ed.: ISSN 1937-5948. GBP 120 in United Kingdom to institutions; EUR 191, USD 239 to institutions (effective 2012).
Indexed: A01, A02, A03, A08, A22, A25, A26, AC&P, B04, B07, BRD, C12, CA, CJA, CJPI, CLI, E08, G05, G06, G07, G08, I02, I05, IBR, IBZ, L03, LRI, M01, M02, M06, P02, P10, P27, P30, P48, P53, P54, PCI, PQC, PhilInd, R02, R05, RI-1, RI-2, S02, S03, S08, S09, S11, S23, SCOPUS, SSAI, SSAb, SSI, T02, W01, W02, W03, W05.
—BLDSC (3487.350100), IE, Infotrieve, Ingenta. **CCC.**
Published by: (Institute for Criminal Justice Ethics), Routledge (Subsidiary of: Taylor & Francis Group), 325 Chestnut St, Ste 800, Philadelphia, PA 19106. TEL 215-625-8900, FAX 215-625-8914, journals@routledge.com, http://www.routledge.com. Eds. Elizabeth Yukins, John Kleinig, William C Heffernan.

100 MEX ISSN 0011-1503
B1
➤ **CRITICA**; revista Hispanoamericana de filosofia. Text in English, Spanish. 1967. q. MXN 150, USD 30 elsewhere to individuals; MXN 200, USD 36 elsewhere to institutions; MXN 70 per issue elsewhere to individuals; USD 12 per issue elsewhere to institutions (effective 2003). adv. bk.rev. abstr. cum. index 1967-2001. back issues avail. **Document type:** *Journal, Academic/Scholarly.* **Description:** Publishes essays, discussions, critical studies, states of the art and critical book reviews.
Related titles: Online - full text ed.: ISSN 1870-4905.
Indexed: A01, A02, A03, A08, A20, A22, A26, AmHI, ArtHuCI, C01, CA, CurCont, F03, F04, FR, H07, H14, H21, I04, I05, IBR, IBZ, L05, L06, M08, P08, P09, P10, P30, P53, P54, PCI, PQC, PhilInd, RASB, SCOPUS, T02, W07.
—BLDSC (3487.394700), IE, Infotrieve, Ingenta, INIST.
Published by: Universidad Nacional Autonoma de Mexico, Instituto de Investigaciones Filologicas, Apdo. Postal 70-447, Mexico City, DF, Mexico. TEL 52-55-56227434, FAX 52-55-56654991. Ed. Carlos Pereda. Pub., R&P Carolina Celorio. Adv. contact Juan Carlos Hernandez TEL 52-55-56249109. Circ: 800 (controlled).

100 PRT ISSN 0870-970X
CRITICA; revista do pensamento contemporaneo. Text in Portuguese. 1987. s-a.
Published by: Nucleo de Estudos Pragmaticos, c/o Joao Saagua, Dpto. de Filosofia Univ. Nova de Lisboa, Avenida de Berna, 26-C, Lisbon, 1000, Portugal. Ed. Manuel Maria Carrilho.

CRITICAL HORIZONS. *see* SOCIOLOGY

144 NLD ISSN 1872-0943
▼ **CRITICAL POSTHUMANISMS.** Text in English. 2009. irreg. **Document type:** *Monographic series, Academic/Scholarly.* **Description:** Focuses on the rise of posthumanism and its probable directions.
Indexed: AmHI, H07, T02.
Published by: Editions Rodopi B.V., Tijnmuiden 7, Amsterdam, 1046 AK, Netherlands. TEL 31-20-6114821, FAX 31-20-4472979, info@rodopi.nl. Eds. Dr. Ivan Callus, Dr. Stefan Herbrechter. **Dist. by:** Rodopi - USA, 606 Newark Ave, 2nd fl, Kenilworth, NJ 07033. TEL 908-497-9031, FAX 908-497-9035.

CRITICAL REVIEW OF INTERNATIONAL SOCIAL AND POLITICAL PHILOSOPHY. *see* POLITICAL SCIENCE—International Relations

141 NLD ISSN 1878-9986
▼ **CRITICAL STUDIES IN GERMAN IDEALISM.** Text in English. 2010. irreg., latest vol.3, 2010. price varies. **Document type:** *Monographic series, Academic/Scholarly.*
Related titles: Online - full text ed.: ISSN 1878-9994.
Published by: Brill, PO Box 9000, Leiden, 2300 PA, Netherlands. TEL 31-71-5353500, FAX 31-71-5317532, cs@brill.nl. Ed. Paul G Cobben.

100 HRV ISSN 1333-1108
➤ **CROATIAN JOURNAL OF PHILOSOPHY.** Text in English. 2001. 3/yr. EUR 75 in Europe; USD 100 elsewhere (effective 2011). bk.rev. **Document type:** *Journal, Academic/Scholarly.* **Description:** Publishes original scientific papers in the field of philosophy.
Related titles: Online - full text ed.
Indexed: A20, ArtHuCI, FR, IBR, IBZ, PhilInd, W07.
—BLDSC (3487.498150), INIST.
Published by: Kruzak d. o. o., Zastavnice 29, Zagreb, 10251, Croatia. TEL 385-1-6590417, kruzak@kruzak.hr. Ed. Nenad Miscevic.

➤ **CROSSROADS**; an interdisciplinary journal for the study of history, philosophy, religion and classics. *see* HISTORY

100 ESP ISSN 1137-2176
CUADERNOS DE ANUARIO FILOSOFICO. SERIE UNIVERSITARIA. Text in Spanish. 1995. irreg., latest vol.39. price varies. back issues avail. **Document type:** *Monographic series, Academic/Scholarly.* **Description:** Examines themes in philosophy.
Related titles: ◆ Supplement to: Anuario Filosofico. ISSN 0066-5215.
Published by: (Universidad de Navarra, Facultad de Filosofia y Letras), Universidad de Navarra, Servicio de Publicaciones, Campus Universitario, Pamplona, 31009, Spain. http://www.unav.es/publicaciones/.

100 ESP ISSN 1133-293X
CUADERNOS DE ESPIRITU. Text in Spanish. 1992. a. **Document type:** *Monographic series, Academic/Scholarly.*
Related titles: ◆ Supplement to: Espiritu. ISSN 0014-0716.
—INIST.
Published by: (Instituto Filosofico de Balmesiana), Editorial Balmes S.A., Duran I Bas, 9, Apartado 1382, Barcelona, 08002, Spain. TEL 34-93-3026840, FAX 34-93-3170498, info@balmesiana.org, http://www.balsmesiana.org/. Ed. Juan Pegueroles.

170 ARG ISSN 0326-9523
CUADERNOS DE ETICA. Text in Spanish. 1986. s-a. USD 20 domestic; USD 27 foreign (effective 2006). back issues avail. **Document type:** *Monographic series, Academic/Scholarly.*
Indexed: P09, PCI, PhilInd.
Published by: Asociacion Argentina de Investigaciones Eticas, Coronel Dias 2277 - 11 F, Buenos Aires, Argentina. TEL 55-15-55090436, info@etica.org.ar, http://www.etica.org.ar/.

100 COL ISSN 0120-8462
B1001
CUADERNOS DE FILOSOFIA LATINOAMERICANA. Text in Spanish. 1980. q. COP 2,500 domestic; USD 30 in Latin America; USD 10 in United States; USD 40 elsewhere (effective 2000). adv. bk.rev. **Document type:** *Academic/Scholarly.*
Indexed: A01, C01, CA, F03, F04, MLA-IB, PhilInd, T02.
Published by: Universidad Santo Tomas, Cr. 9 no. 51-23, Bogota, CUND, Colombia. compublica@usta.edu.co, http://www.usta.edu.co. Ed., Adv. contact Juan Jose Sanz Adrados.

100 ESP ISSN 1576-2270
CUADERNOS DE ONTOLOGIA/ONTOLOGY STUDIES. Text in Multiple languages. 2000. s-a. **Document type:** *Journal, Academic/Scholarly.*
Related titles: Online - full text ed.: free (effective 2011).
Published by: Universidad del Pais Vasco, Departamento de Filosofia, Avenida de Tolosa 70, San Sebastian, 20018, Spain. Ed. Victor Gomez Pin.

100 ESP ISSN 0214-0284
CUADERNOS DE PENSAMIENTO. Text in Spanish. 1987. s-a. **Document type:** *Journal, Academic/Scholarly.*
Published by: Fundacion Universitaria Espanola, Alcala, 93, Madrid, 28009, Spain. TEL 34-91-4311122, FAX 34-91-5767352, fuesp@fuesp.com, http://www.fuesp.com/.

CUADERNOS ELECTRONICOS DE FILOSOFIA DEL DERECHO. *see* LAW

100 ARG ISSN 1850-3667
CUADERNOS FILOSOFICOS. Text in Spanish. 2006. a. **Document type:** *Monographic series, Academic/Scholarly.*
Published by: Universidad Nacional de Rosario, Escuela de Filosofia, Sarmiento, 825, Rosario, Santa Fe, S2000CMJ, Argentina. TEL 34-341-4406892, FAX 34-341-4253852, editorial@homosapiens.com.ar, http://www.fhumyar.unr.edu.ar/index.php?id=escuelas/esc2&cod_esc=2. Circ: 500.

100 ESP ISSN 0210-4857
B5
CUADERNOS SALMANTINOS DE FILOSOFIA. Text in Spanish. 1974. a. **Document type:** *Journal, Academic/Scholarly.*
Indexed: DIP, IBR, IBZ, IPB, P09, PCI, PhilInd.
Published by: Universidad Pontificia de Salamanca, Servicio de Publicaciones, Calle Compania 5, Salamanca, 37002, Spain. TEL 34-923-277100.

100 ESP ISSN 1130-7498
B3580.A1
➤ **CUADERNOS SOBRE VICO.** Text in Spanish; Summaries in English, Spanish. 1991. a. adv. bk.rev. abstr.; bibl.; illus. cum.index 1991-1998. back issues avail. **Document type:** *Journal, Academic/Scholarly.* **Description:** Presents studies that focus on the philosphical thought of Giambattista Vico.
Related titles: Online - full text ed.
Indexed: IPB, P09, PCI, PhilInd, RILM.
Published by: (Centro de Investigaciones sobre Vico), Universidad de Sevilla, Secretariado de Publicaciones, Calle Porvenir 27, Sevilla, 41013, Spain. TEL 34-95-4487444, FAX 34-95-4487443, secpub10@us.es, http://www.us.es/publius/inicio.html.

100 ROM ISSN 2065-5002
CULTURA; international journal of philosophy of culture and axiology. Text in Multiple languages. 2005. s-a. free (effective 2010). **Document type:** *Journal, Academic/Scholarly.*
Related titles: Online - full text ed.: ISSN 1584-1057. free (effective 2011).
Indexed: A20, ArtHuCI.
Published by: Universitatea "Alexandru Ioan Cuza" din Iasi/"Alexandru Ioan Cuza" University of Iasi, Carol I Boulevard, Iasi, 6600, Romania. TEL 40-032-201000, FAX 40-032-201201, sysadmin@uaic.ro, http://www.uaic.ro. Ed. Nicolae Rambu.

CULTURA, HISTORIA E FILOSOFIA. *see* HISTORY—History Of Europe

306 GBR ISSN 0921-3740
GN357 CODEN: CUDYEH
➤ **CULTURAL DYNAMICS.** Text in English. 1988-1992; resumed 1994. 3/yr. USD 1,056, GBP 571 combined subscription to institutions (print & online eds.); USD 1,035, GBP 560 to institutions (effective 2011). adv. bk.rev. back issues avail.; reprint service avail. from PSC. **Document type:** *Journal, Academic/Scholarly.* **Description:** Committed to a relational and dynamic account of socio-cultural phenomena, moving beyond cultural and social anthropology to include work from sociology, psychology, philosophy, and any other areas that can shed light on culture and society.
Related titles: Online - full text ed.: ISSN 1461-7048. USD 950, GBP 514 to institutions (effective 2011).
Indexed: A01, A03, A08, A22, AICP, B07, BibInd, CA, E01, FamI, GEOBASE, H04, I14, IBR, IBSS, IBZ, P34, P42, PCI, PRA, PSA, PerIslam, RASB, S02, S03, SCOPUS, SOPODA, SSA, SociolAb, T02, V02.
—BLDSC (3491.662500), IE, Infotrieve, Ingenta. **CCC.**
Published by: Sage Publications Ltd. (Subsidiary of: Sage Publications, Inc.), 1 Oliver's Yard, 55 City Rd, London, EC1Y 1SP, United Kingdom. TEL 44-20-73248500, FAX 44-20-73248600, info@sagepub.co.uk, http://www.uk.sagepub.com/home.nav. **Subscr. in the Americas to:** Sage Publications, Inc., 2455 Teller Rd, Thousand Oaks, CA 91320. TEL 805-499-9774, FAX 805-499-0871, journals@sagepub.com.

➤ **CULTURAL GEOGRAPHIES**; a journal of cultural geographies. *see* ENVIRONMENTAL STUDIES

➤ **CULTURAL MEMORY IN THE PRESENT.** *see* ANTHROPOLOGY

100 USA ISSN 1934-1474
B1
CULTURE AND PHILOSOPHY; a journal of phenomenological inquiry. Text in English. 2008 (Jan.). a., latest 2008. **Document type:** *Journal, Academic/Scholarly.*
Related titles: Online - full text ed.: ISSN 1934-1555.
Published by: Council for Research in Values and Philosophy, Gibbons Hall, B-12, 620 Michigan Ave, NE, Washington, DC 20064. TEL 202-319-6089, FAX 202-319-6089, cua-rvp@cua.edu, http://www.crvp.org.

CURRENT PERSPECTIVES IN PSYCHOLOGICAL, LEGAL AND ETHICAL ISSUES. *see* PSYCHOLOGY

128 USA ISSN 2152-1859
QP360
CURRENTS (NORTHAMPTON). Text in English. 199?. a. USD 15 per issue institutional non-members; USD 20 per issue to individual members; USD 10 per issue to institutional members (effective 2010). adv. back issues avail. **Document type:** *Journal, Consumer.*
Description: Reflects the depth and breadth of the body-mind centering work and includes articles and case studies about working with infants, children and adults.
Formerly (until 1998): B M C A Newsletter
Published by: The Body-Mind Centering Association, Inc., 16 Center St, Ste 530, Northampton, MA 01060. TEL 413-594-1273, admin@bmcassoc.org. adv.: page USD 200; 6.75 x 9.

CUSANUS-JAHRBUCH. *see* RELIGIONS AND THEOLOGY—Roman Catholic

111 NLD ISSN 1570-3193
CUSANUS STUDIEN CENTRUMS. VEROEFFENTLICHUNGEN/ CUSANUS STUDY CENTRE. PUBLICATIONS/ETUDES CUSANIENNES. PUBLICATIONS. Text in Dutch, English, French. 2001. irreg., latest vol.5, 2005. price varies. **Document type:** *Monographic series, Academic/Scholarly.*
Published by: (Cusanus Studie Centrum), Shaker Publishing BV, Postbus 3167, Maastricht, 6202 ND, Netherlands. TEL 31-43-3500424, FAX 31-43-3255090, info@shaker.nl, http://www.shaker.nl/.

100 ARG ISSN 1514-9935
CUYO; anuario de filosofia argentina y americana. Text in Spanish. 1965. a. back issues avail. **Document type:** *Monographic series, Academic/Scholarly.*
Formerly (until 1984): Cuyo Anuario de Historia del Pensamiento Argentino (0590-4595)
Related titles: Online - full text ed.: ISSN 1853-3175. 2008.
Published by: Universidad Nacional de Cuyo, Instituto de Filosofia, Facultad de Filosofia y Letras, Parque General San Martin, Mendoza, 5500, Argentina. TEL 54-261-4205335, FAX 54-261-4380150, http://ffyl.uncu.edu.ar/. Ed. Clara Alicia Jalif de Bertranou. Circ: 300.

CYBERNETICS & HUMAN KNOWING; a journal of second order cybernetics, autopoiesis and cyber-semiotics. *see* COMPUTERS—Cybernetics

D N W E SCHRIFTENREIHE. *see* BUSINESS AND ECONOMICS—Labor And Industrial Relations

174.95 DEU
D R Z E NEWSLETTER. Text in German. 2007. q. free (effective 2008). **Document type:** *Newsletter, Trade.*
Media: E-mail.
Published by: Deutsches Referenzzentrum fuer Ethik in den Biowissenschaften, Bonner Talweg 57, Bonn, 53113, Germany. TEL 49-228-33641930, webmaster@drze.de.

D W D NEWSLETTER. *see* GERONTOLOGY AND GERIATRICS

DA'AT; Jewish philosophy and Kabbalah. *see* RELIGIONS AND THEOLOGY—Judaic

193 DEU ISSN 0938-9547
DAEDALUS; Europaeisches Denken in deutscher Philosophie. Text in German. 1991. irreg., latest vol.18, 2008. price varies. **Document type:** *Monographic series, Academic/Scholarly.*
—**CCC.**
Published by: Peter Lang GmbH (Subsidiary of: Peter Lang Publishing Group), Eschborner Landstr 42-50, Frankfurt Am Main, 60489, Germany. TEL 49-69-7807050, FAX 49-69-78070550, zentrale.frankfurt@peterlang.com.

170 MEX ISSN 1870-557X
HF5387
DAENA; international journal of good conscience. Text in Spanish. 2006. irreg. free (effective 2011). **Document type:** *Journal, Academic/ Scholarly.*
Media: Online - full text.
Indexed: AmHI, CA, F04, H07, T02.
Published by: Spenta University Mexico, Plaza Comercial los Pinos, Avenida Conchello 2083, Of 2, Monterrey, Nuevo Leon 64550, Mexico. TEL 52-81-11603413, spentamex@yahoo.com, http://www.spentamexico.org.

100 ESP ISSN 1130-0507
B5
➤ **DAIMON;** revista de filosofia. Text in English, French, Spanish. 1955-1986; resumed 1989. 3/yr. EUR 30 (effective 2010). back issues avail. **Document type:** *Monographic series, Academic/Scholarly.*
Description: One issue is monographic, the other publishes about 15 papers, 4 discussions, 6 critical notes and 15 reviews.
Formerly (until 1989): Universidad de Murcia. Anales de Filosofia (0212-9698); Supersedes in part (in 1983): Universidad de Murcia. Anales. Filosofia y Letras (0463-9863)
Related titles: Online - full text ed.: ISSN 1989-4651.
Indexed: DIP, FR, IBR, IBZ, IPB, MLA-IB, P09, PCI, PhilInd.
—INIST.
Published by: Universidad de Murcia, Servicio de Publicaciones, Edificio Saavedra Fajardo, C/ Actor Isidoro Maiquez 9, Murcia, 30007, Spain. TEL 34-968-363887, FAX 34-968-363414, http://www.um.es/publicaciones/. Ed. Antonio Campillo.

100 NLD
DAISAKU IKEDA STUDIES. Text in English. irreg. price varies. **Document type:** *Monographic series, Academic/Scholarly.*
Description: Investigates the philosophical thought of Daisaku Ikeda.
Related titles: ◆ Series of: Value Inquiry Book Series. ISSN 0929-8436.
Published by: Editions Rodopi B.V., Tijnmuiden 7, Amsterdam, 1046 AK, Netherlands. TEL 31-20-6114821, FAX 31-20-4472979, info@rodopi.nl. Ed. George David Miller. **Dist. by:** Rodopi - USA, 606 Newark Ave, 2nd fl, Kenilworth, NJ 07033. TEL 908-497-9031, FAX 908-497-9035.

THE DALHOUSIE REVIEW; a Canadian journal of literature and opinion. *see* LITERARY AND POLITICAL REVIEWS

DANISH CENTRE FOR STUDIES IN RESEARCH AND RESEARCH POLICY. WORKING PAPERS. *see* STATISTICS

190 DNK ISSN 1395-0983
DANISH COMMITTEE ON SCIENTIFIC DISHONESTY. ANNUAL REPORT. Text in English. 1994. a. **Document type:** *Government.*
Related titles: Online - full text ed.: ISSN 1901-1113. 200?; ◆ Danish ed.: Udvalgene Vedroerende Videnskabelige Uredelighed. Aarsberetning. ISSN 1604-5203.
Published by: Forsknings- og Innovationsstyrelsen, Udvalgene Vedroerende Videnskabelige Uredelighed/Danish Agency for Science, Technology and Innovation, Danish Committee on Scientific Dishonesty, c/o Frej Sorento Dichmann, Bredgade 40, Copenhagen K, 1260, Denmark. TEL 45-35-446200, 45-35-446279, FAX 45-35-446201, fi@fi.dk, fdi@fi.dk, http://www.uvvu.dk.

DANISH COUNCILS FOR INDEPENDENT RESEARCH. ACTION PLAN. *see* HUMANITIES: COMPREHENSIVE WORKS

100 DNK ISSN 0070-2749
B1
➤ **DANISH YEARBOOK OF PHILOSOPHY.** Text in English. 1964. a. DKK 225 per vol. (effective 2011). index. back issues avail.; reprints avail. **Document type:** *Journal, Academic/Scholarly.* **Description:** Articles by Danish philosophers on Danish or foreign philosophy. Often special issues or contributions from symposia.
Related titles: CD-ROM ed.
Indexed: DIP, FR, IBR, IBZ, MLA-IB, PCI, PhilInd, RASB, RILM.
—BLDSC (3519.900000), INIST. **CCC.**
Published by: Museum Tusculanum Press, c/o University of Copenhagen, Njalsgade 126, Copenhagen S, 2300, Denmark. TEL 45-35-329109, FAX 45-35-329113, info@mtp.dk, http://www.mtp.dk. Ed. Finn Collin. Circ: 400. **Dist. in France by:** Editions Picard, Editions Picard, Paris 75006, France. TEL 33-1-43269778, FAX 33-1-43264264; **Dist. in UK by:** Gazelle Book Services Ltd., White Cross Mills, Hightown, Lancaster LA1 4UU, United Kingdom. TEL 44-1524-68765, FAX 44-1524-63232, sales@gazellebooks.co.uk, http://www.gazellebookservices.co.uk/; **Dist. in US & Canada by:** International Specialized Book Services Inc.

181 NLD ISSN 1540-3009
B1
➤ **DAO;** a journal of comparative philosophy. Text in English. 2001. q. EUR 364, USD 450 combined subscription to institutions (print & online eds.) (effective 2012). reprint service avail. from PSC. **Document type:** *Journal, Academic/Scholarly.*
Related titles: Online - full text ed.: ISSN 1569-7274 (from IngentaConnect).
Indexed: A20, A21, A22, A26, AmHI, ArtHuCI, BRD, CA, CurCont, E01, E08, H07, H08, HAb, HumInd, MLA-IB, P10, P48, P53, P54, PQC, PhilInd, RI-1, S09, SCOPUS, T02, W03, W05, W07.
—BLDSC (3533.185500), IE. **CCC.**
Published by: Springer Netherlands (Subsidiary of: Springer Science+Business Media), Van Godewijckstraat 30, Dordrecht, 3311 GX, Netherlands. TEL 31-78-6576050, FAX 31-78-6576474, http://www.springer.com. Ed. Yong Huang.

181 NLD ISSN 2211-0275
▼ **DAO COMPANIONS TO CHINESE PHILOSOPHY.** Text in English. 2010. irreg. EUR 169.95 per vol. (effective 2011). **Document type:** *Monographic series, Academic/Scholarly.*
Published by: Springer Netherlands (Subsidiary of: Springer Science+Business Media), Van Godewijckstraat 30, Dordrecht, 3311 GX, Netherlands. TEL 31-78-6576050, FAX 31-78-6576474. Ed. Yong Huang.

▼ **DARMSTAEDTER ARBEITEN ZUR LITERATURWISSENSCHAFT UND PHILOSOPHIE.** *see* LITERATURE

100 FRA ISSN 0418-4459
DE PETRARQUE A DESCARTES. Text in French. 1957. irreg. back issues avail. **Document type:** *Monographic series, Academic/ Scholarly.*
Indexed: A22.
—BLDSC (3535.948100), IE, Ingenta. **CCC.**
Published by: Librairie Philosophique J. Vrin, 6 place de la Sorbonne, Paris, F-75005, France. TEL 33-1-43540347, FAX 33-1-43544818, contact@vrin.fr, http://www.vrin.fr.

100 FRA ISSN 1298-8510
DEBATS PHILOSOPHIQUES. Text in French. 1999. irreg., latest 2009. back issues avail. **Document type:** *Monographic series, Academic/ Scholarly.*
Published by: Presses Universitaires de France, 6 Avenue Reille, Paris, 75685, France. TEL 33-1-58103161, FAX 33-1-45897530. Ed. Yves Charles Zarka.

DEGRES; revue de synthese a orientation semiologique. *see* LINGUISTICS

108 GBR ISSN 1754-2065
DELEUZE CONNECTIONS. Text in English. 2000. irreg. price varies. back issues avail. **Document type:** *Monographic series, Academic/ Scholarly.* **Description:** Coves studies of Deleuze's thought in connection with feminist theory, music, space, geography, queer theory, performance, postcolonial studies, and contemporary art.
Published by: Edinburgh University Press, 22 George Sq, Edinburgh, Scotland EH8 9LF, United Kingdom. TEL 44-131-6504218, FAX 44-131-6620053, journals@eup.ed.ac.uk. Ed. Ian Buchanan.

DELEUZE STUDIES. *see* LITERATURE

170 370.1524 USA ISSN 1529-6547
DELIBERATIONS (DURHAM). Text in English. 2000 (Spring). a.
Published by: Duke University, Kenan Institute of Ethics, 102 W. Duke Bldg., Box 90432, Durham, NC 27708. TEL 919-660-3033, FAX 919-660-3049, kie@duke.edu, http://kenan.ethics.duke.edu.

DEMOKRATICHESKI PREGLED. *see* POLITICAL SCIENCE

100 COL ISSN 2011-4583
DEMOSOPHIA. Text in Spanish. 2008. s-a. **Document type:** *Journal, Academic/Scholarly.*
Published by: Universidad de San Buenaventura, Cartagena, Barrio Ternera Calle Real Dg. 32 No. 30-966, Cartagena de Indias, Colombia. TEL 57-5-6539594, FAX 57-5-6539590, usabuctg@usbctg.edu.co, http://www.usbctg.edu.co.

128 DEU
DENKWEGE; philosophische Aufsaetze. Text in German. irreg., latest vol.3, 2004. price varies. **Document type:** *Monographic series, Academic/Scholarly.*
Published by: Attempto Verlag, Dischingerweg 5, Tuebingen, 72070, Germany. TEL 49-7071-97970, FAX 49-7071-979711, info@attempto-verlag.de, http://www.narr.de.

DESIGN PHILOSOPHY PAPERS. *see* ARCHITECTURE

100 MEX ISSN 0187-8522
DESLINDE. Text in Spanish. 1982. q.
Indexed: MLA-IB.
Published by: Universidad Autonoma de Nuevo Leon, Facultad de Filosofia y Letras, Ciudad Universitaria, Monterrey, Nuevo Leon, 64000, Mexico. http://www.filosofia.uanl.mx/.

▼ **DEUTSCH-JUEDISCHE AUTOREN DES 19. JAHRHUNDERTS.** *see* RELIGIONS AND THEOLOGY—Judaic

100 DEU ISSN 0012-1045
B3
➤ **DEUTSCHE ZEITSCHRIFT FUER PHILOSOPHIE.** Text in German. 1953. bi-m. EUR 99 combined subscription to individuals (print & online eds.); EUR 188 combined subscription to institutions (print & online eds.); EUR 69 combined subscription to students (print & online eds.); EUR 29.90 newsstand/cover (effective 2011). adv. bk.rev. bibl. index. reprints avail. **Document type:** *Journal, Academic/ Scholarly.* **Description:** Promotes an open philosophical discourse and includes interdisciplinary aspects of philosophy. Contains specialised essays, interviews, and symposia, as well as commentaries, reports, archive materials and reviews.
Related titles: Microform ed.: (from SWZ); Online - full text ed.: EUR 99 to individuals; EUR 178 to institutions; EUR 69 to students (effective 2011).
Indexed: A20, A22, ASCA, ArtHuCI, BibInd, CurCont, DIP, FR, IBR, IBT&D, IBZ, IPB, MLA-IB, P30, PCI, PRA, PhilInd, RASB, SCOPUS, SOPODA, SociolAb, W07.
—BLDSC (3575.840000), IE, Infotrieve, Ingenta, INIST.
Published by: Akademie Verlag GmbH (Subsidiary of: Oldenbourg Wissenschaftsverlag GmbH), Markgrafenstr 12-14, Berlin, 10969, Germany. TEL 49-30-4220060, FAX 49-30-42200657, info@akademie-verlag.de, http://www.akademie-verlag.de. Ed. Mischka Dammaschke. Adv. contact Christina Gericke. Circ: 1,300 (paid and controlled).

100 DEU
DEUTSCHES JAHRBUCH PHILOSOPHIE. Text in German. 2008. a. EUR 128 (effective 2011). **Document type:** *Journal, Academic/ Scholarly.*
Published by: (Deutsche Gesellschaft fuer Philosophie e.V.), Felix Meiner Verlag GmbH, Richardstr 47, Hamburg, 22081, Germany. TEL 49-40-2987560, FAX 49-40-29875620, info@meiner.de. Ed. Peter Janich.

174.957 GBR ISSN 1471-8731
QH332 CODEN: DWBEA2
DEVELOPING WORLD BIOETHICS. Text in English. 2001. 3/yr. includes with subscr. to Bioethics. adv. back issues avail.; reprint service avail. from PSC. **Document type:** *Journal, Academic/Scholarly.*
Description: Provides long needed case studies, teaching materials, news in brief, and legal backgrounds to bioethics scholars and students in developing and developed countries alike.
Related titles: Online - full text ed.: ISSN 1471-8847 (from IngentaConnect); ◆ Supplement to: Bioethics. ISSN 0269-9702.
Indexed: A01, A03, A08, A22, A26, C06, C07, CA, CurCont, E01, EMBASE, ESPM, ExcerpMed, H05, H12, IBSS, MEDLINE, P03, P30, P34, P42, PAIS, PSA, PhilInd, PsycInfo, PsycholAb, R10, Reac, RiskAb, S02, S03, S21, SCI, SCOPUS, SSCI, SociolAb, T02, W07.
—BLDSC (3578.580500), IE, Ingenta. **CCC.**
Published by: Wiley-Blackwell Publishing Ltd. (Subsidiary of: John Wiley & Sons, Inc.), 9600 Garsington Rd, Oxford, OX4 2DQ, United Kingdom. TEL 44-1865-776868, FAX 44-1865-714591, customerservices@blackwellpublishing.com. Ed. Udo Schueklenk. Adv. contact Craig Pickett TEL 44-1865-476267. B&W page GBP 445, B&W page USD 823; 190 x 112. Circ: 1,000.

DHARMA; a quarterly devoted to universal religion, righteousness & culture. *see* RELIGIONS AND THEOLOGY

100 300 DEU ISSN 1619-005X
➤ **DIA-LOGOS;** Schriften zu Philosophie und Sozialwissenschaften. Text in German. 2002. irreg., latest vol.11, 2009. price varies. **Document type:** *Monographic series, Academic/Scholarly.*
Published by: Peter Lang GmbH (Subsidiary of: Peter Lang Publishing Group), Eschborner Landstr 42-50, Frankfurt Am Main, 60489, Germany. TEL 49-69-7807050, FAX 49-69-78070550, zentrale.frankfurt@peterlang.com. Eds. Piotr Juchacz, Tadeusz Buksinski.

➤ **DIACRITICA.** *see* LITERATURE

100 CHL ISSN 0717-4292
DIADOKHE; revista de estudios de filosofia platonica y cristiana. Text in Spanish. 1998. a. **Document type:** *Journal, Academic/Scholarly.*
Published by: Pontificia Universidad Catolica de Chile, Instituto de Filosofia, Avda Bernardo O'Higgins 340, Santiago, Chile.

100 AUS ISSN 0084-9804
DIALECTIC. Text in English. 1967. irreg. price varies. **Document type:** *Monographic series, Academic/Scholarly.* **Description:** Contains articles written by senior academis and, occasionally, postgraduate students, as well as by philosophers who work in other disciplines.
Published by: Newcastle University Philosophy Club, c/o Department of Philosophy, Callaghan, NSW 2308, Australia. TEL 61-2-49215186, FAX 61-2-49216928.

120 USA ISSN 0012-2017
B1
➤ **DIALECTICA.** Text in English, French, German. 1947. q. GBP 252 in United Kingdom to institutions; EUR 321 in Europe to institutions; USD 465 in the Americas to institutions; USD 541 elsewhere to institutions; GBP 290 combined subscription in United Kingdom to institutions (print & online eds.); EUR 369 combined subscription in Europe to institutions (print & online eds.); USD 535 combined subscription in the Americas to institutions (print & online eds.); USD 623 combined subscription elsewhere to institutions (print & online eds.) (effective 2012). adv. bk.rev. index. back issues avail.; reprint service avail. from PSC. **Document type:** *Journal, Academic/ Scholarly.*
Related titles: Online - full text ed.: ISSN 1746-8361. GBP 252 in United Kingdom to institutions; EUR 321 in Europe to institutions; USD 465 in the Americas to institutions; USD 541 elsewhere to institutions (effective 2012) (from IngentaConnect).
Indexed: A20, A22, A26, AmHI, ArtHuCI, CA, CCMJ, CurCont, DIP, E01, FR, H07, IBR, IBZ, IPB, L&LBA, MSN, MathR, PCI, PhilInd, RASB, SCOPUS, SOPODA, SociolAb, T02, W07, Z02.
—BLDSC (3579.700000), IE, Infotrieve, Ingenta, INIST. **CCC.**

P

Published by: (Dialectica CHE, European Society for Analytic Philosophy CHE), Wiley-Blackwell Publishing, Inc. (Subsidiary of: Wiley-Blackwell Publishing Ltd.), 111 River St, Hoboken, NJ 07030. TEL 201-748-6000, FAX 201-748-6088, info@wiley.com. Ed. Pascal Engel.

100 ITA ISSN 1128-5478
DIALEGESTHAI; rivista telematica di filosofia. Text in Italian; Summaries in English. 1999. irreg. free. bk.rev. **Document type:** *Journal, Academic/Scholarly.* **Description:** Devoted to philosophy and anthropology, with special attention to intercultural issues and dialogue.
Media: Online - full text.
Published by: Universita degli Studi di Roma "La Sapienza", Facolta di Filosofia, Via Carlo Fea 2, Rome, RM 00161, Italy. TEL 39-06-49917297, http://www.filosofia.uniroma1.it. Ed. Emilio Baccarini.

100 ARG
DIALEKTICA; produccion intelectual estudiantil. Text in Spanish. 1992. s-a. **Document type:** *Journal, Academic/Scholarly.*
Indexed: ASCA.
Published by: Instituto de Filosofia, 25 de Mayo 217, 2o piso, Buenos Aires, Argentina.

160 ITA
LA DIALETTICA. Text in Italian. irreg., latest vol.5. price varies. **Document type:** *Monographic series, Academic/Scholarly.*
Published by: Edizioni Studium, Via Cassiodoro 14, Rome, 00193, Italy. TEL 39-06-6865846, FAX 39-06-6875456, info@edizionistudium.it, http://www.edizionistudium.it.

100 POL ISSN 1505-4594
DIALOGIKON. Text in Polish. 1995. irreg., latest vol.15, 2010. price varies. **Document type:** *Monographic series, Academic/Scholarly.*
Published by: (Uniwersytet Jagiellonski, Instytut Filozofii/Jagiellonian University, Institute of Philosophy), Wydawnictwo Uniwersytetu Jagiellonskiego/Jagiellonian University Press, ul Grodzka 26, Krakow, 31044, Poland. TEL 48-12-4312364, FAX 48-12-4301995, wydaw@if.uj.edu.pl. Ed. Wojciech Suchonia.

100 ESP ISSN 0213-1196
DIALOGO FILOSOFICO. Text in Spanish. 1985. 3/yr. EUR 27 domestic; EUR 34 foreign (effective 2009). back issues avail. **Document type:** *Journal, Academic/Scholarly.*
Indexed: FR, IPB, PhilInd.
—INIST.
Address: Apdo. Postal 121, Colmenar Viejo, Madrid, 28770, Spain. TEL 34-961-0707473, FAX 34-91-8462973, dialfilo@telefonica.net.

100 PRI ISSN 0012-2122
B5
➤ **DIALOGOS.** Text in English, Spanish. 1964. s-a. USD 12 to individuals; USD 16 to institutions. adv. bk.rev. bibl. **Document type:** *Journal, Academic/Scholarly.* **Description:** Publishes philosophical articles.
Indexed: BibInd, C01, FR, H21, IBR, IBZ, IPB, P08, P09, PCI, PhilInd.
—Ingenta, INIST.
Published by: Universidad de Puerto Rico, Departamento de Filosofia, PO Box 21572, San Juan, 00931, Puerto Rico. TEL 787-764-0000 ext. 2072, FAX 787-764-5899. Ed. Raul Iturrino Montes. R&P Raul Iturrino-Montes. Circ: 800. **Subscr. to:** EDUPR, P O Box 23322, San Juan 00931-3322, Puerto Rico. TEL 787-250-0615.

100 COL ISSN 0124-0021
DIALOGOS DE SABERES. Text in Spanish. 1998. s-a. **Document type:** *Bulletin, Academic/Scholarly.*
Published by: Universidad Libre de Colombia, Calle 8 No. 5-80, Bogota, Colombia. TEL 57-1-3821000, http://www.unilibre.edu.co/.

100 GBR ISSN 0012-2173
B1
➤ **DIALOGUE**; Canadian philosophical review/revue Canadienne de philosophie. Text in English, French. 1962. q. GBP 91, USD 180 combined subscription to institutions (print & online eds.) (effective 2012). adv. bk.rev. illus. cum.index: vols. 1-10. back issues avail.; reprints avail. **Document type:** *Journal, Academic/Scholarly.* **Description:** Covers the history of philosophy, metaphysics, epistemology, logic, philosophy of science, political philosophy, ethics, and the philosophy of religion.
Related titles: Online - full text ed.: ISSN 1759-0949. GBP 72, USD 144 to institutions (effective 2012).
Indexed: A20, A21, A22, A26, AmHI, ArtHuCI, B04, B14, BRD, BRI, C03, CA, CBCARef, CBRI, CCMJ, CPerI, CurCont, E08, FR, G08, H07, H08, HAb, HumInd, I05, IPB, L&LBA, MLA, MLA-IB, MSN, MathR, P30, P48, PCI, PQC, PhilInd, R05, RASB, RI-1, RI-2, RILM, S02, S03, S09, SCOPUS, SOPODA, SociolAb, T02, W03, W07, Z02.
—BLDSC (3579.755000), IE, Infotrieve, Ingenta, INIST. **CCC.**
Published by: (Canadian Philosophical Association CAN), Cambridge University Press, The Edinburgh Bldg, Shaftesbury Rd, Cambridge, CB2 8RU, United Kingdom. TEL 44-1223-326070, FAX 44-1223-325150, journals@cambridge.org, http://journals.cambridge.org. Eds. Eric Dayton, Mathieu Marion. Circ: 1,200 (paid).

100 USA ISSN 0012-2246
B1
DIALOGUE (MILWAUKEE). Text in English. 1956; N.S. 3/yr. USD 25 membership (effective 2005). adv. bk.rev. bibl. index. **Document type:** *Newsletter, Consumer.*
Indexed: A20, AmHI, DIP, FR, H07, IBR, IBZ, PhilInd.
—BLDSC (3579.758000), IE, Ingenta, INIST.
Published by: Phi Sigma Tau, Dept of Philosophy, Marquette University, Milwaukee, WI 53233. TEL 414-288-6857. Ed. Daniel T Primozic. Circ: 1,500.

100 POL ISSN 1234-5792
B1
➤ **DIALOGUE AND UNIVERSALISM**; toward synergy of civilizations. Text in English. 1973. q. USD 50 foreign to individuals; USD 80 foreign to institutions (effective 2006). bibl. reprints avail. **Document type:** *Journal, Academic/Scholarly.*
Former titles (until 1995): Dialogue and Humanism (0867-504X); (until 1991): Dialectics and Humanism (0324-8275)
Related titles: Online - full text ed.
Indexed: A01, A03, A08, A21, CA, DIP, FR, IBR, IBZ, IPB, MEA&I, P30, P34, PhilInd, RASB, RI-1, RI-2, S02, S03, T02.
—Ingenta, INIST.
Published by: Uniwersytet Warszawski, Instytut Filozofii/Warsaw University, Institute of Philosophy, Krakowskie Przedmiescie 3, Warsaw, 00047, Poland. TEL 48-22-5523705, FAX 48-22-8265734. Ed. Janusz Kuczynski.

100 USA ISSN 2160-4339
▼ **DIALOGUE AND UNIVERSALISME.** Text in English. 2010. q. free (effective 2011). back issues avail. **Document type:** *Journal, Academic/Scholarly.*
Media: Online - full text.
Published by: Emporia State University, Division of Social Sciences, 1200 Commercial St, 411 Plumb Hall, Campus Box 4032, Emporia, KS 66801. TEL 316-341-5461, http://www.emporia.edu/socsci/divis.htm, FAX 316-341-5143, dgerish@emporia.edu. Ed. Janusz Kuczynski.

100 616.8 ITA ISSN 2035-0031
DIALOGUES IN PHIULOSOPHY, MENTAL AND NEURO SCIENCES. Text in English. 2008. s-a. **Document type:** *Journal, Academic/Scholarly.*
Media: Online - full text.
Indexed: A01.
Published by: Associazione Crossing Dialogues, Via Trapani 20, Rome, 00161, Italy. Ed. Massimiliano Aragona.

100 POL ISSN 1733-5566
➤ **DIAMETROS**; internetowe czasopismo filozoficzne. Text in Polish, English. 2004. q. free (effective 2011). **Document type:** *Journal, Academic/Scholarly.*
Media: Online - full text.
Indexed: AmHI, CA, H07, PhilInd, T02.
Published by: Uniwersytet Jagiellonski, Instytut Filozofii/Jagiellonian University, Institute of Philosophy, ul Grodzka 52, Krakow, 31-041, Poland. TEL 48-12-4227111, FAX 48-12-4224916, infoiph@iphils.uj.edu.pl, http://www.iphils.uj.edu.pl. Ed. Wlodzimierz Galewicz.

100 MEX ISSN 0185-2450
➤ **DIANOIA.** Text in Spanish. 1955. s-a. MXN 264 domestic to institutions; USD 24 foreign to institutions (effective 2009). bk.rev. cum. index 1955-2001. back issues avail. **Document type:** *Journal, Academic/Scholarly.* **Description:** Publishes essays, discussions, critical studies and critical book reviews.
Related titles: Online - full text ed.
Indexed: A01, A26, C01, CA, F03, F04, H21, I04, I05, P08, P09, PCI, PhilInd, T02.
Published by: Universidad Nacional Autonoma de Mexico, Instituto de Investigaciones Filologicas, Apdo. Postal 70-447, Mexico City, DF, Mexico. TEL 52-55-56227434, FAX 52-55-56654991. Ed. Ricardo Salles. R&P Manola Rius.

100 ITA ISSN 2036-5217
▼ **DIAPSALMATA**; rivista di filosofia. Text in Multiple languages. 2009. q. **Document type:** *Journal, Academic/Scholarly.*
Media: Online - full text.
Published by: (Societa Italiana per gli Studi Kierkegaardiani (S I S K)), Universita degli Studi di Venezia (Ca' Foscari), Facolta di Lettere e Filosofia, San Sebastiano, Dorsoduro 1686, Venice, 30123, Italy. http://www.unive.it.

141 NLD ISSN 1873-8338
DICTIONARY OF GNOSIS & WESTERN ESOTERICISM. Text in English. EUR 140, USD 190 (effective 2010). **Document type:** *Academic/Scholarly.*
Media: Online - full text.
Published by: Brill, PO Box 9000, Leiden, 2300 PA, Netherlands. TEL 31-71-5353500, FAX 31-71-5317532, cs@brill.nl.

DICTIONNAIRE PERMANENT: BIOETHIQUE ET BIOTECHNOLOGIES. *see* BIOLOGY—Biotechnology

100 CHE ISSN 0070-4806
PQ1979
DIDEROT STUDIES. Text in English, French. 1949. irreg., latest vol.29, 2003. price varies. bk.rev. **Document type:** *Monographic series, Academic/Scholarly.*
Indexed: DIP, FR, IBR, IBZ, LIFT, MLA, MLA-IB, PCI, RASB, RILM, SCOPUS.
—INIST. **CCC.**
Published by: Librairie Droz S.A., 11 rue Firmin-Massot, Geneva 12, 1211, Switzerland. TEL 41-22-3466666, FAX 41-22-3472391, droz@droz.org, http://www.droz.org. Ed. Diana Guiragossian Carr.

100 DEU ISSN 1868-257X
▼ **DIES ACADEMICUS**; Heiligenkreuzer Schriftenreihe. Text in German. 2010. irreg. price varies. **Document type:** *Monographic series, Academic/Scholarly.*
Published by: Peter Lang GmbH (Subsidiary of: Peter Lang Publishing Group), Eschborner Landstr 42-50, Frankfurt Am Main, 60489, Germany. TEL 49-69-7807050, FAX 49-69-78070550, zentrale.frankfurt@peterlang.com. Eds. Marian Gruber, Wolfgang Wehrmann.

DIETRICH'S INDEX PHILOSOPHICUS. *see* RELIGIONS AND THEOLOGY—Abstracting, Bibliographies, Statistics

DIJALEKTIKA/DIALECTICS; casopis za metodolosko filozofske probleme matematickih, prirodnih i tehnickih nauka. *see* SCIENCES: COMPREHENSIVE WORKS

100 ESP ISSN 1138-4050
DILEMA; revista de filosofia. Text in Spanish. 1997. s-a. **Document type:** *Journal, Academic/Scholarly.*
Related titles: Online - full text ed.
Indexed: PhilInd.
Published by: Universitat de Valencia, A.D.R. de la Facultad de Filosofia y Ciencias de la Educacion, Ave. Blasco Ibanez, 30, Valencia, 46010, Spain. dilema.adrfp@uv.es, http://www.uv.es/adrfp/dilema/.

100 ESP ISSN 1989-7022
▼ **DILEMATA**; revista internacional de eticas aplicadas/international journal of applied ethics. Text in Spanish, English. 2009. 3/yr. free (effective 2011). **Document type:** *Journal, Academic/Scholarly.*
Media: Online - full text.
Address: c/o Instituto de Filosofia, Calle Albasanz 26-28, Madrid, 28037, Spain. Ed. Txetxu Ausin.

100 DEU ISSN 0175-0135
➤ **DILTHEY-JAHRBUCH**; fuer Philosophie und Geschichte der Geisteswissenschaften. Text in English, German; Summaries in German. 1983. a. EUR 52; EUR 38 to students (effective 2010). back issues avail. **Document type:** *Yearbook, Academic/Scholarly.* **Description:** Provides an annual international forum for the study of the works of Wilhelm Dilthey, areas of inquiry associated with his thought (i.e., philosophy and the human sciences), and relevant historical figures (i.e., his predecessors, contemporaries, and interpreters).
Indexed: DIP, IBR, IBZ, IPB, PCI, PhilInd, RASB.
—**CCC.**
Published by: Frommann-Holzboog Verlag e.K., Koenig-Karl-Str 27, Stuttgart, 70372, Germany. TEL 49-711-9559690, FAX 49-711-9559691, info@frommann-holzboog.de, http://www.frommann-holzboog.de. Eds. Hans-Ulrich Lessing, Riccardo Pozzo, Rudolf Makkreel. Circ: 800.

100 FRA ISSN 0419-1633
AS4
➤ **DIOGENE.** Text in French; Abstracts in English. 1952. q. EUR 65 to institutions (effective 2012).
Related titles: Online - full text ed.: ISSN 2077-5253; ◆ English ed.: Diogenes (English Edition). ISSN 0392-1921; Japanese ed.: Diogenesu. ISSN 0911-5404; Portuguese ed.: Diogenes (Brazilian Edition). ISSN 0102-6984; Spanish ed.: Diogenes (Spanish Edition). ISSN 0012-3048; Chinese ed.: Di'ougenni. ISSN 1000-6575; Arabic ed.; Hindi ed.
Indexed: FR, I13, IBR, IBSS, IBZ, PCI, RILM.
—INIST.
Published by: Presses Universitaires de France, 6 Avenue Reille, Paris, 75685, France. TEL 33-1-58103161, FAX 33-1-45897530, revues@puf.com, http://www.puf.com. Ed. Luca Maria Scarantino.

100 ITA ISSN 1826-4778
B804
DIOGENE FILOSOFAREOGGI. Text in Italian. 2005. q. EUR 15 domestic (effective 2009); EUR 28 foreign (effective 2008). **Document type:** *Magazine, Consumer.*
Related titles: Online - full text ed.
Published by: (Associazione Diogene), Ibis Edizioni, Via Crispi 8, Como, 22100, Italy. TEL 39-031-337367, FAX 39-031-306829, http://www.ibisedizioni.it.

105 930 GRC ISSN 1010-7363
B1
➤ **DIOTIMA**; epitheoresis philosophikes erevnes - revue de recherche philosophique - review of philosophical research. Text in English, French. 1973. a., latest vol.31, 2003. EUR 60 (effective 2003). adv. bk.rev. bibl. index. 200 p./no.; back issues avail. **Document type:** *Journal, Academic/Scholarly.* **Description:** Discusses the philosophy and history of art and values and the philosophy of history.
Indexed: FR, IPB, P30, PhilInd.
—INIST.
Published by: (Hellenic Society for Philosophical Studies/Societe Hellenique d'Etudes Philosophiques), Evanghelos A. Moutsopoulos Ed. & Pub., 40 Hypsilantou St, Athens, 115 21, Greece. TEL 30-10-725-1212, FAX 30-10-722-7322. Ed., R&P, Adv. contact Evanghelos A Moutsopoulos. page USD 20; 1075 x 1830. Circ: 240.

100 FRA ISSN 1953-8197
➤ **DIOTIME L'AGORA**; revue internationale de didactique de la philosophie. Text in French. 1999. q. **Document type:** *Journal, Academic/Scholarly.*
Media: Online - full text.
Published by: Editions Alcofribas Nasier, 2 Passage Flourens, Paris, 75017, France. TEL 33-1-30760624, FAX 33-1-39960420. Ed. Michel Tozzi.

100 USA ISSN 0070-508X
B935
DIRECTORY OF AMERICAN PHILOSOPHERS. Text in English. 1962. biennial, latest 2009, 24th ed. USD 190 per issue (effective 2009). **Document type:** *Directory, Trade.* **Description:** Provides a comprehensive listing of philosophy faculty and the colleges and universities where philosophy is taught, with information on graduate programs, philosophy journals, publishers, centers, institutes and societies.
Related titles: Online - full text ed.
Published by: Philosophy Documentation Center, PO Box 7147, Charlottesville, VA 22906. TEL 434-220-3300, FAX 434-220-3301, order@pdcnet.org. R&P George Leaman. Adv. contact Greg Swope.

DISCOURSE (HESLINGTON); learning and teaching in philosophical and religious studies. *see* RELIGIONS AND THEOLOGY

100 ARG ISSN 0327-2214
DISCURSO Y REALIDAD. Text in Spanish. 1985. 2/yr. ARS 250,000, USD 25. bk.rev.
Address: Block C Piso 10-B, 25 De Mayo, 950, San Miguel De Tucuman, Tucuman 4000, Argentina. Ed. Rolo Maris.

100 COL ISSN 0124-6127
➤ **DISCUSIONES FILOSOFICAS.** Text in English, Portuguese, Spanish; Summaries in English, Spanish. 2000. s-a. COP 20,000 domestic to individuals; USD 15 foreign to individuals; COP 30,000 domestic to institutions; USD 20 foreign to institutions; COP 15,000 per issue domestic; USD 10 per issue foreign (effective 2011). bk.rev. Index. back issues avail. **Document type:** *Journal, Academic/Scholarly.* **Description:** Publishes original contributions such as research papers, reviews, translations, and articles on the topics that include philosophy on all fields and philosophy of literature.
Related titles: Online - full text ed.: (from SciELO).
Indexed: PhilInd.
Published by: Universidad de Caldas, Departamento de Filosofia, Calle 65 No 26-10, Edificio Central, Manizales, Caldas 275, Colombia. TEL 57-6-8781500 ext 12442, FAX 57-6-8781500 ext 12622. Ed., R&P Carlos E. Garcia. Circ: 300.

100 BRA
DISCUTINDO FILOSOFIA. Text in Portuguese. bi-m. BRL 47.40 (effective 2006). **Document type:** *Journal, Academic/Scholarly.*
Published by: Editora Escala Ltda., Av Prof Ida Kolb, 551, Casa Verde, Sao Paulo, 02518-000, Brazil. TEL 55-11-38552100, FAX 55-11-38579643, escala@escala.com.br, http://www.escala.com.br.

160 401 PRT ISSN 0873-626X
DISPUTATIO; revista semestral de filosofia analitica. Text in Portuguese. 1996. s-a. free (effective 2011). **Document type:** *Journal, Academic/Scholarly.*
Media: Online - full content.
Indexed: AmHI, CA, H07, PhilInd, T02.
Published by: Sociedade Portuguesa de Filosofia, Av. da Republica, 37, Piso 4, Lisboa, 1050, Portugal. TEL 351-795-2348, FAX 351-795-2349.

100 BRA ISSN 1413-9448
DISSERTATIO; revista de filosofia. Text in Multiple languages. 1995. s-a. **Document type:** *Journal, Academic/Scholarly.*
Related titles: Online - full text ed.: ISSN 1983-8891. free (effective 2011).
Indexed: C01.
Published by: Universidade Federal de Pelotas, Departamento de Filosofia, Caixa Postal 354, Pelotas, RS 96001-970, Brazil. TEL 55-53-32845543. Ed. Joao Hobuss.

DISSERTATIONEN. PHILOSOPHISCHE REIHE. *see* RELIGIONS AND THEOLOGY—Roman Catholic

DISTANT DRUMS. *see* RELIGIONS AND THEOLOGY

DIVRE HA-AKADEMIA HA-LE'UMIT HA-YISR'ELIT LE-MADDA'IM. *see* HUMANITIES: COMPREHENSIVE WORKS

DIVUS THOMAS. *see* RELIGIONS AND THEOLOGY

100 900 ITA ISSN 2035-7362
B721
DOCTOR VIRTUALIS. Text in Italian, English. 2002. a. free (effective 2011). **Document type:** *Journal, Academic/Scholarly.*
Media: Online - full text.
Published by: Universita degli Studi di Milano, Facolta di Lettere e Filosofia, Via Festa del Perdono 7, Milan, 20122, Italy. TEL 39-02-58352720, http://www.lettere.unimi.it.

180 ITA ISSN 1122-5750
B721
DOCUMENTI E STUDI SULLA TRADIZIONE FILOSOFICA MEDIEVALE. Text in Italian. 1990. a. price varies. **Document type:** *Monographic series, Academic/Scholarly.*
Indexed: I14, IPB, PhilInd.
Published by: Fondazione Centro Italiano di Studi sull'Alto Medioevo (C I S A M), Palazzo Ancaiani, Piazza della Liberta 12, Spoleto, PG 06049, Italy. TEL 39-0743-225630, FAX 39-0743-49902, cisam@cisam.org, http://www.cisam.org. **Dist. by:** Brepols Publishers, Begijnhof 67, Turnhout 2300, Belgium.

100 BRA ISSN 1807-3883
DOISPONTOS. Text in Portuguese, English, Spanish. 2004. irreg. free (effective 2011). **Document type:** *Journal, Academic/Scholarly.*
Media: Online - full text.
Indexed: C01, PhilInd.
Published by: Universidade Federal do Parana, Editora, Rua Joao Negrao 280, Curitiba, Parana 80060-200, Brazil. TEL 55-41-33605000. Ed. Vinicius B de Figuereido.

100 ESP ISSN 1889-0202
DOKOS; revista de filosofia. Text in Spanish. 2008. 3/yr. back issues avail. **Document type:** *Journal, Academic/Scholarly.*
Related titles: Online - full text ed.: ISSN 1989-2020. 2008.
Published by: Editorial Plaza y Valdes, Calle de las Eras 30 B, Villaviciosade Odon, Madrid, 28670, Spain. madrid@plazayvaldes.com, http://www.plazayvaldes.com/. Ed. Jesus Padilla Galvez.

DONGBEI SHI-DAXUEBAO (ZHEXUE SHEHUI KEXUE BAN)/ NORTHEAST NORMAL UNIVERSITY. JOURNAL (PHILOSOPHY, SOCIAL SCIENCES EDITION). *see* SOCIAL SCIENCES: COMPREHENSIVE WORKS

DONGNAN DAXUE XUEBAO (ZHEXUE SHEHUI KEXUE BAN)/ SOUTHEAST UNIVERSITY. JOURNAL (PHILOSOPHY AND SOCIAL SCIENCE). *see* SOCIAL SCIENCES: COMPREHENSIVE WORKS

128.5 200 NLD
DOODGEWOON (ONLINE); tijdschrift over de dood. Text in Dutch. 1994. q. free (effective 2005). adv. bk.rev. illus. back issues avail. **Description:** Publishes historical, philosophical and anthropological articles relating to death, grieving and funerary customs.
Formerly (until 2001): Doodgewoon (Print) (1381-0324)
Published by: Stichting Eindelijk, C.J.K. van Aalststraat 7, Amsterdam, 1019 JZ, Netherlands. TEL 31-20-6869349, FAX 31-20-4191923. Ed., Pub. Anja Krabben.

DORTMUNDER POLITISCH-PHILOSOPHISCHE DISKURSE. *see* POLITICAL SCIENCE

100 ITA ISSN 1973-2821
DOTTORATO DI RICERCA IN STORIA DELLA FILOSOFIA E STORIA DELLE IDEE. QUADERNI. Text in Multiple languages. 2005. a. **Document type:** *Monographic series, Academic/Scholarly.*
Published by: Universita degli Studi di Roma "La Sapienza", Facolta di Filosofia, Via Carlo Fea 2, Rome, RM 00161, Italy. TEL 39-06-49917297, http://www.filosofia.uniroma1.it.

100.7 CHL ISSN 0717-5701
DOXA; la verdad como aventura. Text in Spanish. 2000. q. free (effective 2006). back issues avail. **Document type:** *Journal, Academic/Scholarly.*
Media: Online - full text.
Published by: Universidad Metropolitana de Ciencias de la Educacion, Facultad de Filosofia y Educacion, Ave Jose Pedro Alessandri, 774, Santiago, Chile. TEL 56-2-2412733, http://www.umce.cl/. Ed. Jose Luis Reyes.

DOXA; cuadernos de filosofia y derecho. *see* LAW

100 600 DEU ISSN 1861-423X
DRESDEN PHILOSOPHY OF TECHNOLOGY STUDIES/DRESDNER STUDIEN ZUR PHILOSOPHIE DER TECHNOLOGIE. Text in English, German. 2006. irreg., latest vol.2, 2007. price varies. **Document type:** *Monographic series, Academic/Scholarly.*
Published by: Peter Lang GmbH (Subsidiary of: Peter Lang Publishing Group), Eschborner Landstr 42-50, Frankfurt Am Main, 60489, Germany. TEL 49-69-7807050, FAX 49-69-78070550, zentrale.frankfurt@peterlang.com.

DROIT ET SOCIETE. SERIE ETHIQUE. *see* LAW

100 USA ISSN 1547-8556
B1
THE DUALIST. Text in English. 1994. a. back issues avail. **Document type:** *Journal, Academic/Scholarly.*
Media: Online - full text.
Published by: Stanford University, Department of Philosophy, Stanford, CA 94305. Ed. Nikola Milanovic.

301.01 DEU
DUISBURGER STUDIEN; Geistes- und Gesellschaftswissenschaften. Text in German. 1979. s-a. adv. bk.rev. **Document type:** *Academic/Scholarly.*
Published by: Gilles & Francke Verlag, Blumenstr 67-69, Duisburg, 47057, Germany. TEL 49-203-362787, FAX 49-203-355520. Ed., Pub. Werner Francke. R&P Barbara Francke. Adv. contact Sigrid Krenz.

181.4 NOR ISSN 0332-5792
DL401
DYADE. Text in Norwegian. 1968. q. NOK 220 (effective 2006). back issues avail. **Document type:** *Magazine, Consumer.* **Description:** Publishes articles on art and culture in their broadest sense, psychology related to Acem-meditation and various philosophical issues.
Related titles: Online - full text ed.: ISSN 0807-2736. 1996.
Published by: (Acem International School of Meditation), Dyade Forlag, PO Box 2559, Solli, Oslo, 0202, Norway. TEL 47-22-118708, FAX 47-22-831831. Eds. Halvor Eifring, Ole Nygaard.

168 ARG ISSN 1852-0278
E + E. (E Mas E) Text in Spanish. 2008. a. **Document type:** *Journal, Academic/Scholarly.*
Published by: Universidad Nacional de Cordoba, Facultad de Filosofia y Humanidades, Pabellon Residencial, Ciudad Universitaria, Cordoba, 5000, Argentina. TEL 54-351-4334107, FAX 54-351-4334056, http://www.ffyh.unc.edu.ar/index2.php.

150 100 AUT ISSN 1813-7784
BF1
E-JOURNAL PHILOSOPHIE DER PSYCHOLOGIE. Text in German. 2005. 4/yr. free (effective 2011). **Document type:** *Journal, Academic/Scholarly.* **Description:** Approaches the research and study of psychology from various philosophical viewpoints.
Media: Online - full content.
Published by: Forschungsinitiative Philosophie der Psychologie, Siegelgasse 1/4/6, Vienna, 1030, Austria. charlotte.annerl@univie.ac.at. Ed., Pub. Charlotte Annerl.

140 NLD ISSN 1873-8230
E-LEVINAS. Text in English. 2005. a. free (effective 2011). **Document type:** *Database, Academic/Scholarly.*
Media: Online - full text.
Published by: Levinas Studiekring, Postbus 797, Utrecht, 3500 AT, Netherlands. TEL 31-30-2390114, FAX 31-30-2340738, levinas@uvh.nl. Eds. Coby von Pagee, Joachim Duyndam.

100 CZE ISSN 1211-0442
➤ **E-LOGOS**; electronic journal for philosophy. Text in Czech. 1994. irreg. free. **Document type:** *Journal, Academic/Scholarly.* **Description:** Covers the fields of epistemology, history of philosophy, logic, and the philosophy of language, mind, and science.
Media: Online - full content.
Published by: Vysoka Skola Ekonomicka v Praze, Narodohospodarska Fakulta, Katedra Filosofie, Nam. W. Churchilla 4, Prague 3, 13067, Czech Republic. Ed. Jan Pavlik.

100 ARG ISSN 0327-7089
E T C. (Ensayo Teoria Critica) Variant title: Etc. Text in Spanish. 1990. s-a.
Published by: Universidad Nacional de Cordoba, Facultad de Filosofia y Humanidades, Pabellon Residencial, Ciudad Universitaria, Cordoba, 5000, Argentina.

E-TOPIA; revista electronica de estudos sobre a utopia. *see* LITERATURE

E Z W - TEXTE; Informationen - Impulse - Arbeitstexte. *see* RELIGIONS AND THEOLOGY

EARTHHUMAN. *see* GENERAL INTEREST PERIODICALS—United States

ECCLESIA; revista de cultura catolica. *see* RELIGIONS AND THEOLOGY—Roman Catholic

EDGE. *see* LITERARY AND POLITICAL REVIEWS

100 GBR
THE EDINBURGH EDITION OF THOMAS REID. Text in English. irreg. price varies. back issues avail. **Document type:** *Monographic series, Academic/Scholarly.* **Description:** Covers the philosophical treatises of Thomas Reid as the great critic of David Hume, including previously unpublished manuscript materials.
Published by: Edinburgh University Press, 22 George Sq, Edinburgh, Scotland EH8 9LF, United Kingdom. TEL 44-131-6504218, FAX 44-131-6503286, journals@eup.ed.ac.uk.

100 GBR
EDINBURGH PHILOSOPHICAL GUIDES. Text in English. irreg. price varies. back issues avail. **Document type:** *Monographic series, Academic/Scholarly.*
Published by: Edinburgh University Press, 22 George Sq, Edinburgh, Scotland EH8 9LF, United Kingdom. TEL 44-131-6504218, FAX 44-131-6503286, journals@eup.ed.ac.uk. Ed. Douglas Burnham.

170 GBR
EDINBURGH STUDIES IN WORLD ETHICS. Text in English. irreg. price varies. back issues avail. **Document type:** *Monographic series, Academic/Scholarly.* **Description:** Covers the ethical issues concerning international relations between states and institutions and global relations between individuals.
Published by: Edinburgh University Press, 22 George Sq, Edinburgh, Scotland EH8 9LF, United Kingdom. TEL 44-131-6504218, FAX 44-131-6503286, journals@eup.ed.ac.uk. Ed. Nigel Dower.

EDITIO; Internationales Jahrbuch fuer Editionswissenschaft. *see* LITERATURE

EDUCACAO E FILOSOFIA. *see* EDUCATION

100 302 ITA ISSN 2037-7355
L'EDUCAZIONE SENTIMENTALE. Text in Italian. 2003. s-a. **Document type:** *Journal, Academic/Scholarly.*
Related titles: Online - full text ed.: ISSN 2037-7649.
Published by: Franco Angeli Edizioni, Viale Monza 106, Milan, 20127, Italy. TEL 39-02-2837141, FAX 39-02-26144793, redazioni@francoangeli.it, http://www.francoangeli.it.

100 GBR ISSN 0142-3371
B8.W45
EFRYDIAU ATHRONYDDOL. Text in Welsh. 1938. a. GBP 25 (effective 2006). bk.rev. **Document type:** *Journal, Academic/Scholarly.*
Related titles: Online - full text ed.: (from IngentaConnect).
Indexed: MLA-IB, PCI.
—Ingenta.
Published by: University of Wales Press, 10 Columbus Walk, Brigantine Pl, Cardiff, CF10 4UP, United Kingdom. TEL 44-29-20496899, FAX 44-29-20496108. Eds. John Daniel, W L Gealey. Circ: 350 (paid).

100 CAN ISSN 0707-2287
B1E5
➤ **EIDOS**; the Canadian graduate journal of philosophy. Text in English, French. 1978. s-a. CAD 18 to individuals; CAD 35 to institutions; CAD 9 to students. adv. bk.rev. back issues avail. **Document type:** *Journal, Academic/Scholarly.* **Description:** Provides a forum for academic discussion on philosophical themes to graduate students and recent Ph.D.s in Canada and abroad.
Indexed: PhilInd.
Published by: University of Waterloo, Philosophy Graduate Student Association, Dept of Philosophy, Waterloo, ON N2L 3G1, Canada. TEL 519-888-4567, FAX 519-746-3097. Eds. Anne Marie Power, Irene Switankowsky. R&P Anne-Marie Power. Adv. contact Christine Freeman. Circ: 160.

100 COL ISSN 1692-8857
B5
➤ **EIDOS**; revista de filosofia de la Universidad del Norte. Text in Spanish. 2003. s-a. **Document type:** *Journal, Academic/Scholarly.*
Related titles: Online - full text ed.: ISSN 2011-7477. 2006. free (effective 2011) (from SciELO).
Indexed: A01, CA, F03, F04, I04, I05, PhilInd, T02.
Published by: Universidad del Norte, Ediciones Uninorte, Km 5 Via a Puerto Colombia, Barranquilla, Colombia. TEL 57-5-3509218, FAX 57-5-3509489, ediciones@uninorte.edu.co, http://www.uninorte.edu.co. Ed. Jose Joaquin Andrade Alvarez. Circ: 150.

➤ **THE EIGHTEENTH CENTURY CURRENT BIBLIOGRAPHY.** *see* BIBLIOGRAPHIES

100 USA ISSN 1545-0449
CB411
➤ **EIGHTEENTH-CENTURY THOUGHT.** Text in English. 2003. a. USD 137.50 per issue (effective 2009). back issues avail.; reprints avail. **Document type:** *Journal, Academic/Scholarly.* **Description:** Provides study of early modern thought by publishing research pertinent to the fields of philosophy, natural philosophy, medicine, law, historiography, political theory, religion, economics, and the human sciences.
Indexed: MLA-IB, PhilInd.
Published by: A M S Press, Inc., Brooklyn Navy Yard, 63 Flushing Ave, Bldg 292, Unit #221, Brooklyn, NY 11205. FAX 718-875-3800, queries@amspressinc.com. Ed. James G. Buickerood.

100 USA ISSN 1071-5800
B808.5
➤ **ELECTRONIC JOURNAL OF ANALYTIC PHILOSOPHY.** Abbreviated title: E J A P. Text in English. 1993-1998; N.S. 2001. a. free (effective 2010). illus. reprints avail. **Document type:** *Journal, Academic/Scholarly.* **Description:** Focuses on the philosophy of Gilbert Ryle.
Media: Online - full text.
Published by: The University of Louisiana at Lafayette, Edith Garland Dupre Library, 400 E Saint Mary Blvd, PO Box 40199, Lafayette, LA 70504. TEL 337-482-6030, reference@louisiana.edu, http://library.louisiana.edu/. Ed., Pub. Istvan S N Berkeley.

➤ **ELECTRONIC JOURNAL OF BUSINESS ETHICS AND ORGANIZATION STUDIES.** *see* BUSINESS AND ECONOMICS

100 NLD
ELEMENTA (AMSTERDAM, 1975); Schriften zur Philosophie und ihrer Problemgeschichte. Text in English, German. 1975. irreg., latest vol.79, 2006. price varies. back issues avail. **Document type:** *Monographic series, Academic/Scholarly.*
Published by: Editions Rodopi B.V., Tijnmuiden 7, Amsterdam, 1046 AK, Netherlands. TEL 31-20-6114821, FAX 31-20-4472979, info@rodopi.nl. Ed. Wiebke Schrader. **Dist in France by:** Nordeal, 30 rue de Verlinghem, BP 139, Lambersart 59832, France. TEL 33-3-20099060, FAX 33-3-20929495; **Dist in N America by:** Rodopi - USA, 606 Newark Ave, 2nd fl, Kenilworth, NJ 07033. TEL 908-497-9031, 800-225-3998, FAX 908-497-9035.

100 ITA ISSN 0392-7342
B175.I7
ELENCHOS; rivista di studi sul pensiero antico. Text in Italian. 1980. s-a. EUR 26 domestic; EUR 30 foreign (effective 2008). **Document type:** *Journal, Academic/Scholarly.* **Description:** Devoted exclusively to ancient philosophy.
Indexed: IPB, PCI.
Published by: (Centro di Studi sul Pensiero Antico), Bibliopolis, Via Vincenzo Arangio Ruiz 83, Naples, NA 80122, Italy. TEL 39-081-664606, FAX 39-081-7616273, info@bibliopolis.it, http://www.bibliopolis.it.

180 DEU ISSN 1439-7536
ELEUSIS; Geisteswissenschaftliche Abhandlungen. Text in German. 2000. irreg., latest vol.15, 2005. price varies. **Document type:** *Monographic series, Academic/Scholarly.*
Published by: Verlag Dr. Kovac, Leverkusenstr 13, Hamburg, 22761, Germany. TEL 49-40-3988800, FAX 49-40-39888055, info@verlagdrkovac.de. Ed. Joerg Villwock.

100 GTM ISSN 1990-2433
ELEUTHERIA. Text in Spanish. 2004. q. free (effective 2011). back issues avail. **Document type:** *Journal, Academic/Scholarly.*
Media: Online - full text.
Published by: Universidad Francisco Marroquin, Centro Henry Hazlitt, Edif. Academico, D-409, 6 Calle Final, Zona 10, Guatemala City, Guatemala. TEL 502-2338-7720, chh@ufm.edu.gt, http://www.chh.ufm.edu.gt/. Ed. Jose Antonio Romero.

P

100 AUS ISSN 1837-5871
EMERGENT AUSTRALIAN PHILOSOPHERS. Text in English. 2008. s-a. free (effective 2011). **Document type:** *Journal, Academic/Scholarly.*
Description: Conceived to provide an arena for final year and honours philosophy students to publish articles in an academic journal format.
Media: Online - full text.
Published by: Dean Goorden and Matthew Paul, Ed. & Pub. editor@eap.philosophy-australia.com.

EMERGING. *see* NEW AGE PUBLICATIONS

100 USA ISSN 0883-6000
EMORY VICO STUDIES. Text in English. 1987. irreg., latest vol.8, 2001. price varies. **Document type:** *Monographic series, Academic/Scholarly.*
Published by: Peter Lang Publishing, Inc. (Subsidiary of: Peter Lang Publishing Group), 29 Broadway, New York, NY 10006. TEL 212-647-7706, 212-647-7700, 800-770-5264, FAX 212-647-7707, customerservice@plang.com. Ed. Donald Verene.

100 GBR ISSN 1757-1952
▼ ➤ **EMPEDOCLES**; European journal for the philosophy of communication. Text in English. 2009 (Feb.). s-a. GBP 36, USD 68 to individuals; GBP 180, USD 290 to institutions (effective 2012). adv. back issues avail. **Document type:** *Journal, Academic/Scholarly.*
Description: Aims to provide a publication and discussion platform for those working at the interface of philosophy and the study of communication, in all its aspects.
Related titles: Online - full text ed.: ISSN 1757-1960. GBP 147, USD 220 (effective 2012).
Indexed: CA, CMM, CommAb, L&LBA, T02.
Published by: Intellect Ltd., The Mill, Parnall Rd, Fishponds, Bristol, BS16 3JG, United Kingdom. TEL 44-117-9589910, FAX 44-117-9589911, info@intellectbooks.com. Ed. Dr. Johan Seibers. Pub. Masoud Yazdani. **Subscr. to:** Turpin Distribution Services Ltd., Pegasus Dr, Stratton Business Park, Biggleswade, Bedfordshire SG18 8QB, United Kingdom. TEL 44-1767-604951, FAX 44-1767-601640, custserv@turpin-distribution.com, http://www.turpin-distribution.com/.

➤ **EMSHOCK LETTER.** *see* NEW AGE PUBLICATIONS

100 ESP ISSN 1133-5351
ENDOXA. Text in Spanish. 1993. s-a. **Document type:** *Journal, Academic/Scholarly.*
Indexed: F04, IPB, PhilInd.
Published by: Universidad Nacional de Educacion a Distancia, Bravo Murillo 38, Madrid, Spain. TEL 34-91-3986000, FAX 34-91-3986600, infouned@adm.uned.es, http://www.uned.es/.

100 GBR ISSN 1472-5819
B1
ENDS AND MEANS. Text in English. 1996. s-a. back issues avail. **Document type:** *Journal, Academic/Scholarly.* **Description:** Includes short articles on any topic in the area of philosophy.
Related titles: Online - full text ed.: ISSN 1472-5827. free (effective 2009).
Published by: University of Aberdeen, Department of Philosophy, Old Brewery, High St, Aberdeen, Aberdeenshire AB24 3UB, United Kingdom. TEL 44-1224-272366, FAX 44-1224-273750, philosophy@abdn.ac.uk. Ed. Jonathan Friday.

100 ARG ISSN 1666-5732
HB72
ENERGEIA; revista internacional de filosofia y epistemologia de las ciencias. Text in Spanish. 2002. s-a. back issues avail. **Document type:** *Journal, Academic/Scholarly.*
Indexed: EconLit, JEL.
Published by: Universidad de Ciencias Empresariales y Sociales, Paraguay 1338 7to.Piso, Buenos Aires, 1057, Argentina. TEL 54-11-48153290, FAX 54-11-48135635, energeia@uces.edu.ar, http://www.uces.edu.ar/publicaciones/index.php. Ed. Eduardo R. Scarano. Circ: 600.

100 GBR ISSN 2045-0567
▼ **ENGAGE NEWCASTLE.** Text in English. 2010. s-a. **Document type:** *Journal, Academic/Scholarly.* **Description:** Features scholarly work which is intended solely for educational and academic uses.
Related titles: Online - full text ed.
Published by: Newcastle Philosophy Society Publishing, 5 Falconar House, Falconar Ct, Grainger Town, Newcastle Upon Tyne, NE1 5PY, United Kingdom. information@newphilsoc.org.uk. Ed. Patrick Jemmer.

100 ESP ISSN 0211-402X
B5
➤ **ENRAHONAR**; quaderns de filosofia. Text in Catalan, Spanish, French. 1981. s-a. EUR 12 per issue (effective 2008). bk.rev. abstr. back issues avail.; reprints avail. **Document type:** *Journal, Academic/Scholarly.* **Description:** Publishes research into philosophy and reviews books on philosophy.
Related titles: Online - full text ed.: free (effective 2011).
Indexed: IPB, P09, PCI, PhilInd.
Published by: Universitat Autonoma de Barcelona, Servei de Publicacions, Edifici A, Bellaterra, Cardanyola del Valles, Barcelona, 08193, Spain. TEL 34-93-5811022, FAX 34-93-5813239, sp@uab.es, http://www.uab.es/publicacions/. Circ: 500.

107.1 FRA ISSN 0986-1653
L'ENSEIGNEMENT PHILOSOPHIQUE. Text in French. 1950. 6/yr. EUR 24.10 to individual members; EUR 48 to institutions (effective 2008). bk.rev. bibl.; charts; stat. cum.index 1950-1988. **Document type:** *Journal, Academic/Scholarly.*
Formerly: Revue de l'Enseignement Philosophique (0035-1393)
Indexed: A22, FR, IPB, P30, RILM.
—BLDSC (3776.301100), IE, Ingenta, INIST.
Published by: Association des Professeurs de Philosophie de l'Enseignement Public, c/o Gerard Schmitt, 22 Rue Edgard Quinet, Saint-Max, 54130, France. Ed. Gerard Schmitt.

179.1 USA ISSN 0163-4275
GF80 CODEN: ENETDD
➤ **ENVIRONMENTAL ETHICS**; an interdisciplinary journal dedicated to the philosophical aspects of environmental problems. Text in English. 1979. q. USD 36 per vol. (effective 2010). adv. bk.rev. illus. cum.index: 1979-1998 in vol.20. 112 p./no.; back issues avail.; reprints avail. **Document type:** *Journal, Academic/Scholarly.*
Description: Provides a forum for diverse interests and attitudes. Seeks to bring together the nonprofessional environmental philosophy tradition with the newly emerging professional interest in the subject.
Related titles: Microform ed.: (from PQC); Online - full text ed.: ISSN 2153-7895.
Indexed: A01, A02, A03, A08, A20, A21, A22, A25, A26, ASCA, ASFA, Agr, AmHI, B04, B21, B25, BIOSIS Prev, BRD, CA, CTA, CurCont, DIP, E04, E05, E08, E11, ESPM, EnerRev, EnvAb, EnvInd, FR, G02, G03, G08, GSA, GSI, H07, H08, H09, H10, HAb, HPNRM, HumInd, I05, IBR, IBZ, IPB, MLA-IB, MycolAb, P02, P10, P13, P26, P30, P34, P48, P52, P53, P54, P56, PCI, PQC, PerIslam, PhilInd, R&TA, RI-1, RI-2, RefZh, S02, S03, S08, S09, S10, SCOPUS, SOPODA, SSCI, SSciA, SWRA, SociolAb, T02, T04, ToxAb, W03, W07, W08, WLR, WildRev, Z01.
—BLDSC (3791.465000), IE, Infotrieve, Ingenta. **CCC.**
Published by: Environmental Philosophy, Inc., 1155 Union Cir, 310980, University of North Texas, Denton, TX 76203. TEL 940-565-2727, FAX 940-565-4439, cep@unt.edu. Ed. Eugene C Hargrove.

➤ **ENVIRONMENTAL VALUES.** *see* ENVIRONMENTAL STUDIES

➤ **EPIMELIA.** *see* RELIGIONS AND THEOLOGY

100 DEU ISSN 1434-1492
EPISTEMATA. REIHE PHILOSOPHIE. Text in German. 1979. irreg., latest vol.139, 2010. price varies. **Document type:** *Monographic series, Academic/Scholarly.*
Published by: Verlag Koenigshausen und Neumann GmbH, Leistenstr 7, Wuerzburg, 97082, Germany. TEL 49-931-3298700, FAX 49-931-83620, info@koenigshausen-neumann.de, http://koenigshausen-neumann.gebhardt-riegel.de.

100 GBR ISSN 1742-3600
➤ **EPISTEME**; a journal of social epistemology. Text in English. 2004 (Jun). 3/yr. GBP 190, USD 325 combined subscription to institutions (print & online eds.) (effective 2012). adv. back issues avail.; reprints avail. **Document type:** *Journal, Academic/Scholarly.* **Description:** Addresses issues in epistemology integral to the philosophy of science, the philosophy of social science and metaphysics.
Related titles: Online - full text ed.: ISSN 1750-0117.
Indexed: A22, AmHI, CA, E01, H07, MLA-IB, P30, S02, S03, T02.
—BLDSC (3793.848000), IE. **CCC.**
Published by: (Episteme Trust), Edinburgh University Press, 22 George Sq, Edinburgh, Scotland EH8 9LF, United Kingdom. TEL 44-131-6504218, FAX 44-131-6503286, journals@eup.ed.ac.uk. Ed. Alvin Goldman. Adv. contact Ruth Allison TEL 44-131-6504220.

100 BRA ISSN 1413-5736
Q174
EPISTEME; uma revista brasileira de filosofia e historia das ciencias. Text in Portuguese. 1996. s-a. BRL 30 (effective 2006). back issues avail. **Document type:** *Journal, Academic/Scholarly.*
Related titles: Online - full text ed.
Indexed: ASFA, B21, PhilInd, SociolAb.
Published by: Universidade Federal do Rio Grande do Sul, Grupo Interdisciplinari em Filosofia e Historia das Ciencias, Ave Bento Goncalves, 9500, Campus do Vale Sala 104 Predio 43322, Porto Alegre, RS 91509-900, Brazil. TEL 55-51-3166941, FAX 55-51-2272295, gifhc@ilea.ufrgs.br.

100 USA ISSN 1542-7072
EPISTEME; undergraduate journal of philosophy. Text in English. 1990. a. **Document type:** *Journal, Academic/Scholarly.* **Description:** Aims to recognize and encourage excellence in undergraduate philosophy by providing examples of some of the best work currently being done in undergraduate philosophy programs.
Published by: Denison University, Department of Philosophy, Knapp Hall 205, Denison University, Granville, OH 43023. TEL 740-587-6387, FAX 740-587-8544, philosophy@denison.edu.

100 PRT ISSN 0874-0437
EPISTEME; revista multidisciplinar. Text in Portuguese. 1997. s-a. **Document type:** *Journal, Academic/Scholarly.*
Published by: Universidade Tecnica de Lisboa, Centro de Estudios de Epistemologia e Historia das Ciencias e das Tecnicas, Alameda St. Antonio das Capuchos 1, Lison, 1169-047, Portugal. TEL 351-21-8811920, FAX 351-21-8811991, http://www.utl.pt/. Ed. Adelino Torres.

EPISTEME (ONLINE); an international journal of science, history and philosophy. *see* SCIENCES: COMPREHENSIVE WORKS

100 900 VEN ISSN 0798-4324
B5
➤ **EPISTEME N S**; revista del Instituto de Filosofia. Text in Spanish, French, Italian, English; Summaries in English, Spanish. 1957. s-a. VEB 26 domestic; USD 25 foreign (effective 2010). bk.rev. abstr. Index. back issues avail. **Document type:** *Journal, Academic/Scholarly.* **Description:** Contains articles on general philosophy, history of philosophy, philosophy of natural and social sciences, philosophy of language, ethics and political philosophy.
Formerly (until 1969): Episteme. Anuario
Related titles: Online - full text ed.
Indexed: PhilInd.
Published by: (Universidad Central de Venezuela, Instituto de Filosofia), Universidad Central de Venezuela, Facultad de Humanidades y Educacion, Edificio Trasbordo, Planta Baja, Calle Minerva, Urb los Chaguaramos, Caracas, 1051, Venezuela. http://www.ucv.ve/humanidades/FHE2005/index.htm. Ed. Nancy Nunez de Morillo.

121 501 ITA ISSN 0392-9760
Q174
➤ **EPISTEMOLOGIA**; rivista italiana di filosofia della scienza. Text in English, Italian; Text occasionally in French. 1978. s-a. EUR 76 combined subscription domestic (print & online eds.); EUR 93 combined subscription in Europe (print & online eds.); EUR 101.50 combined subscription elsewhere (print & online eds.) (effective 2011). bk.rev. index. Supplement avail. **Document type:** *Journal, Academic/Scholarly.*
Related titles: Microform ed.; Online - full text ed.: ISSN 1825-652X.
Indexed: A20, A22, AmHI, ArtHuCI, CA, DIP, H07, IBR, IBZ, IPB, PCI, PhilInd, SCI, SCOPUS, T02, W07, Z02.
—IE, Infotrieve, Linda Hall.
Published by: Tilgher Genova, Via Assarotti 31-15, Genoa, GE 16122, Italy. TEL 39-010-8391140, FAX 39-010-870653, tilgher@tilgher.it. Ed. Evandro Agazzi. R&P Lucio Bozzi.

100 BRA ISSN 1517-7823
EPISTEMOLOGIQUES. Text in Portuguese, French. 2000. q. **Document type:** *Journal, Academic/Scholarly.*
Related titles: Online - full text ed.
Published by: (Universite de Paris VII (Denis Diderot) FRA), Universidade de Sao Paulo, Faculdade de Filosofia, Letras e Ciencias Humanas, Av Professor Luciano Gualberto 315, Butanta, Sao Paulo, SP 05508-010, Brazil. http://www.fflch.usp.br.

109 USA ISSN 1085-1968
B1
➤ **EPOCHE**; a journal for the history of philosophy. Text in English. 1993. s-a. USD 35 to individuals; USD 80 to institutions; USD 20 to students; USD 82 combined subscription to individuals (print & online eds.); USD 288 combined subscription to institutions (print & online eds.) (effective 2009). back issues avail. **Document type:** *Journal, Academic/Scholarly.* **Description:** Contains articles that offer a continental or hermeneutic approach, but is committed to a pluralist orientation and dedicated to an exchange of diverse ideas and approaches.
Related titles: Online - full text ed.: ISSN 2153-8603. USD 56 to individuals; USD 240 to institutions (effective 2009).
Indexed: A01, A03, A08, A26, AmHI, CA, DIP, E08, FR, G08, H07, I05, IBR, IBZ, IPB, MLA-IB, PhilInd, R05, S09, T02.
—BLDSC (3794.343800), IE, Ingenta, INIST. **CCC.**
Published by: Philosophy Documentation Center, PO Box 7147, Charlottesville, VA 22906. TEL 434-220-3300, FAX 434-220-3301, order@pdcnet.org, http://www.pdcnet.org. Ed. Walter Brogan TEL 610-519-4712. R&P George Leaman. Adv. contact Greg Swope.

➤ **ERASMUS JOURNAL FOR PHILOSOPHY AND ECONOMICS.** *see* BUSINESS AND ECONOMICS

200 NLD ISSN 0276-2854
B785.E64
➤ **ERASMUS OF ROTTERDAM SOCIETY YEARBOOK.** Text in English. 1980. a. EUR 74, USD 102 to institutions; EUR 80, USD 112 combined subscription to institutions (print & online eds.) (effective 2012). bk.rev. reprint service avail. from PSC. **Document type:** *Journal, Academic/Scholarly.* **Description:** Contains articles on Erasmus, a scholar and humanist of Renaissance and Reformation, his contemporaries, and his intellectual milieu.
Related titles: Online - full text ed.: ISSN 1874-9275. EUR 67, USD 93 to institutions (effective 2012) (from IngentaConnect).
Indexed: A22, AmHI, CA, E01, H07, IZBG, MLA-IB, SCOPUS, T02.
—IE. **CCC.**
Published by: (Erasmus of Rotterdam Society USA), Brill, PO Box 9000, Leiden, 2300 PA, Netherlands. TEL 31-71-5353500, FAX 31-71-5317532. Ed. Kathy Eden. Circ: 600.

100 DEU ISSN 0425-1806
ERFAHRUNG UND DENKEN. Text in German. 1959. irreg., latest vol.101, 2010. price varies. **Document type:** *Monographic series, Academic/Scholarly.*
Published by: Duncker und Humblot GmbH, Carl-Heinrich-Becker-Weg 9, Berlin, 12165, Germany. TEL 49-30-7900060, FAX 49-30-79000631, info@duncker-humblot.de.

100 DEU ISSN 0179-163X
BJ1388
ERINNYEN; Zeitschrift fuer materialistische Ethik. Text in German. 1985. a. EUR 5 (effective 2004). adv. bk.rev. back issues avail. **Document type:** *Journal, Academic/Scholarly.* **Description:** Examines materialistic-dialectic ethics and socialistic morals.
Published by: Verein zur Foerderung des Dialektischen Denkens e.V., Hertzstr 39, Garbsen, 30827, Germany. TEL 49-5131-1623, FAX 49-5131-443970, vorstand@vereindialektik.de, http://www.vereindialektik.de. Ed. Bodo Gassmann. Circ: 700.

146 NLD ISSN 0165-0106
B1 CODEN: ERKEDQ
➤ **ERKENNTNIS**; an international journal of analytic philosophy. Text in English. 1930. bi-m. (in 2 vols., 3 nos./vol.). EUR 1,106, USD 1,158 combined subscription to institutions (print & online eds.) (effective 2012). adv. bk.rev. illus. Index. reprint service avail. from PSC. **Document type:** *Journal, Academic/Scholarly.* **Description:** Publishes papers in philosophical disciplines associated with analytic philosophy, including epistemology, logic, philosophy of language, philosophy of science, practical philosophy and ethics.
Related titles: Microform ed.: (from PQC); Online - full text ed.: ISSN 1572-8420 (from IngentaConnect).
Indexed: A20, A22, A26, AmHI, ArtHuCI, BibLing, CA, CCMJ, CurCont, DIP, E01, FR, H07, H14, IBR, IBRH, IBZ, IPB, MSN, MathR, P10, P48, P53, P54, PCI, PQC, PhilInd, SCOPUS, SOPODA, SociolAb, T02, W07, Z02.
—IE, Infotrieve, Ingenta, INIST, Linda Hall. **CCC.**
Published by: Springer Netherlands (Subsidiary of: Springer Science+Business Media), Van Godewijckstraat 30, Dordrecht, 3311 GX, Netherlands. TEL 31-78-6576050, FAX 31-78-6576474, http://www.springer.com. Ed. Hans Rott.

➤ **ESCRITOS.** *see* LITERATURE

100 ESP ISSN 1885-5687
PN53
➤ **ESCRITURA E IMAGEN.** Text in Spanish. 2005. a., latest vol.6, 2010. EUR 15 domestic; EUR 20 in Europe; EUR 24 elsewhere (effective 2011). **Document type:** *Journal, Academic/Scholarly.*
Related titles: Online - full text ed.: ISSN 1988-2416. free.
Indexed: H21, MLA-IB, P08, P28, P48, P53, P54, PQC.
—INIST.
Published by: (Universidad Complutense de Madrid, Facultad de Filosofia), Universidad Complutense de Madrid, Servicio de Publicaciones, C/ Obispo Trejo 2, Ciudad Universitaria, Madrid, 28040, Spain. TEL 34-91-3941127, FAX 34-91-3941126, servicio.publicaciones@rect.ucm.es, http://www.ucm.es/publicaciones. Ed. Ana Maria Leyra Soriano.

100 ITA ISSN 1970-0164
B4
ESERCIZI FILOSOFICI (ONLINE). Text in Italian, English, French. 1992. s-a. free (effective 2011). **Document type:** *Journal, Academic/Scholarly.*
Formerly (until 2009): Esercizi Filosofici (Print) (1124-8599)

Media: Online - full text.
Published by: Universita degli Studi di Trieste, Dipartimento di Filosofia, Androna Campo Marzio 10, Trieste, 34123, Italy. TEL 39-040-5584314, FAX 39-040-311796, http://www.univ.trieste.it/~dipfilo/vari.html.

100 FRA ISSN 1777-5477
➤ **ESPACESTEMPS.NET.** Text in Multiple languages. 2002. d. free (effective 2011). **Document type:** *Journal, Academic/Scholarly.*
Media: Online - full text.
Published by: Revues.org, 3 Place Victor Hugo, Case no 86, Marseille, 13331, France. http://www.revues.org.

100 ARG ISSN 1851-5541
ESPACIO PENSAMIENTO Y VERDAD. Text in Spanish. 2007. m.
Media: Online - full text.
Published by: Ediciones Pensamiento y Verdad, Madres de Plaza de Mayo 1317, Junin, Buenos Aires, 6000, Argentina. TEL 54-2362-455196, FAX 54-2362-150509.

100 ECU
ESPACIOS; aportes al pensamiento critico contemporaneo. Text in Spanish. 1993. q. ECS 35,000; USD 30 in Latin America; USD 40 in United States.
Indexed: AIAP.
Published by: Centro de Investigaciones para el Desarrollo, Apdo 17 10 7169, Quito, Pichincha, Ecuador.

160 ARG ISSN 0326-7946
ESPACIOS DE CRITICA Y PRODUCCION. Text in Spanish. 1984. s-a.
Published by: Secretaria de Bienestar Estudiantil y Extension Universitaria, Facultad de Filosofia y Letra (UBA), Marcelo T. de Alvear 2230, 1 Piso, Buenos Aires, Argentina.

100 ESP ISSN 0014-0716
B5
ESPIRITU. Text in Spanish. 1952. s-a. EUR 20 domestic; EUR 40 foreign (effective 2009). bk.rev. cum.index: 1952-1977. **Document type:** *Magazine, Consumer.*
Related titles: ◆ Supplement(s): Cuadernos de Espiritu. ISSN 1133-293X.
Indexed: FR, PhilInd.
—INIST.
Published by: (Instituto Filosofico de Balmesiana), Editorial Balmes S.A., Duran I Bas, 9, Apartado 1382, Barcelona, 08002, Spain. TEL 34-93-3026840, FAX 34-93-3170498, info@balmesiana.org, http://www.balmesiana.org/. Ed. Juan Pegueroles. Circ: 300.

L'ESPLUMEOIR. *see* LITERATURE

L'ESPRIT DU TEMPS; revue de culture humaine inspiree de l'enseignement de Rudolf Steiner. *see* EDUCATION

100 BEL ISSN 0071-1349
➤ **ESSAIS PHILOSOPHIQUES.** Text in French. 1950. irreg., latest 1992. price varies. back issues avail. **Document type:** *Monographic series, Academic/Scholarly.* **Description:** Monographs on different topics in philosophy by scholars of the institute.
Published by: (Institut Superieur de Philosophie), Peeters Publishers, Bondgenotenlaan 153, Leuven, 3000, Belgium. TEL 32-16-235170, FAX 32-16-228500, http://www.peeters-leuven.be.

100 USA ISSN 1526-0569
B1
➤ **ESSAYS IN PHILOSOPHY.** Text in English. 2000. s-a. free (effective 2011). **Document type:** *Journal, Academic/Scholarly.* **Description:** Publishes philosophical papers and contributions to the literature on a certain topic.
Media: Online - full text.
Indexed: AmHI, H07, MLA-IB, PhilInd, T02.
Published by: Pacific University, 2043 College Way, Forest Grove, OR 97116. silkroad.pacific@gmail.com. Ed. David Boersema.

100 USA ISSN 1522-7340
B821.A1
➤ **ESSAYS IN THE PHILOSOPHY OF HUMANISM.** Text in English. 1997. s-a. USD 25 to non-members; USD 20 to members (effective 2010). back issues avail. **Document type:** *Journal, Academic/Scholarly.* **Description:** Deals with the philosophical, historical or theoretical aspects of Humanism, as well as with the application of its principles to problems of everyday life.
Indexed: MLA-IB, PhilInd.
—BLDSC (3811.747000). **CCC.**
Published by: American Humanist Association, 1777 T St, NW, Washington, DC 20009. TEL 202-238-9088, 800-837-3792, FAX 202-238-9003, aha@americanhumanist.org, http://www.americanhumanist.org/index.html.

➤ **ESTETIKA/AESTHETICS**; the central european journal of aesthetics. *see* ART

111.85 320 FRA ISSN 1150-3696
ESTHETIQUE & POLITIQUE. Text in French. 1986. irreg. price varies. **Document type:** *Monographic series, Academic/Scholarly.*
Published by: Centre National de la Recherche Scientifique, Campus Gerard-Megie, 3 Rue Michel-Ange, Paris, 75794, France. TEL 33-1-44964000, FAX 33-1-44965390, http://www.cnrseditions.fr.

100 ARG ISSN 0325-4933
B5
ESTUDIOS DE FILOSOFIA. Text in Spanish. 1978. s-a. back issues avail. **Document type:** *Journal, Academic/Scholarly.*
Indexed: P09, PCI, PhilInd.
Published by: Academia Nacional de Ciencias, Centro de Estudios Filosoficos, Ave. Alvear, 1711 3o Piso, Buenos Aires, 1014, Argentina. TEL 54-11-48113066, FAX 54-11-48111657, http://www.ciencias.org.ar/.

100 COL ISSN 0121-3628
➤ **ESTUDIOS DE FILOSOFIA.** Text in Spanish; Summaries in English. 1990. s-a. COP 27,000 domestic; USD 25 foreign (effective 2010). adv. bk.rev. back issues avail. **Document type:** *Journal, Academic/Scholarly.* **Description:** Promotes philosophical research.
Related titles: Cumulative ed(s).: (from SciELO).
Indexed: AmHI, C01, DIP, F04, H07, IBR, IBZ, PhilInd, T02.
—INIST.
Published by: Universidad de Antioquia, Instituto de Filosofia, Apdo. Aereo 1226, Medellin, Colombia. TEL 57-4-2105680, FAX 57-4-2105681, estufilo@quimbaya.udea.edu.co, http://institutodefilosofia.udea.edu.co. Ed. Jorge A Mejia. Circ: 700.

100 ARG ISSN 1515-7180
ESTUDIOS DE FILOSOFIA PRACTICA E HISTORIA DE LAS IDEAS. Text in Spanish. 2000. a. **Document type:** *Journal, Academic/Scholarly.*
Related titles: Online - full text ed.: ISSN 1851-9490. free (effective 2011) (from SciELO).
Published by: (Consejo Nacional de Investigaciones Cientificas y Tecnicas (C O N I C E T), Instituto de Investigaciones Geohistoricas), Instituto de Ciencias Humanas, Sociales y Ambientales, CC 131, Mendoza, 5500, Argentina. TEL 54-261-4288797, FAX 54-261-4202196.

100 300 ESP ISSN 0210-6086
B5
ESTUDIOS FILOSOFICOS; revista de investigacion y critica. Text in Spanish. 1952. 3/yr. EUR 50 domestic; EUR 62 in Europe; EUR 66 elsewhere (effective 2009). adv. bk.rev. abstr.; bibl. index. 210 p./no.; back issues avail.; reprints avail. **Document type:** *Journal, Academic/Scholarly.*
Indexed: A22, CA, F04, FR, IPB, P09, P42, PCI, PhilInd, S02, S03, SCOPUS, SOPODA, SociolAb, T02.
—IE, Infotrieve, INIST.
Published by: (Instituto Superior de Filosofia), Editorial San Esteban, Plaza Concilio de Trento s-n, Apartado 17, Salamanca, 37001, Spain. TEL 34-923-264781, FAX 34-923-265480, info@sanestebaneditorial.com, http://www.sanestebaneditorial.com/. Ed. Sixto J Castro. Circ: 900.

100 ESP ISSN 1578-6676
ESTUDIOS NIETZSCHE; revista internacional de filosofia. Text in Spanish. 2001. a. EUR 20 domestic (effective 2009). **Document type:** *Journal, Academic/Scholarly.*
Indexed: FR, PhilInd.
—INIST.
Published by: (Sociedad Espanola de Estudios sobre F. Nietzsche), Universidad de Malaga, Facultad de Filosofia y Letras, Campus de Teatinos, Malaga, 29071, Spain. candrade@uma.es, http://www.uma.es.

100 CHL ISSN 0717-4667
ET CETERA. Text in Spanish. 1985. a. back issues avail. **Document type:** *Monographic series, Academic/Scholarly.*
Formerly (until 1999): Faro (0717-0475)
Published by: Universidad de Playa Ancha de Ciencias de la Educacion, Avenida Playa Ancha 850, Valparaiso, Chile. TEL 56-32-281758, FAX 56-32-285041.

100 BRA ISSN 1413-8093
➤ **ETHICA.** Text in Portuguese; Text occasionally in English, French. 1996. s-a. **Document type:** *Journal, Academic/Scholarly.* **Description:** Specializes in three lines of philosophy research: ethics and society; ethics and practical reason; contemporary French philosophy.
Related titles: Online - full text ed.
Indexed: PhilInd.
Published by: Universidade Gama Filho, Rua Manoel Vitorino 625, Piedade, Rio de Janeiro, RJ 20748-900, Brazil. TEL 55-21-32137735, FAX 55-21-32137731, http://www.ugf.br.

170 DEU
ETHICA. Text in German. 2000. irreg., latest vol.6, 2003. price varies. **Document type:** *Monographic series, Academic/Scholarly.*
Published by: Mentis Verlag GmbH, Schulze-Delitzsch-Str 19, Paderborn, 33100, Germany. TEL 49-5251-687902, FAX 49-5251-687905, webmaster@mentis.de, http://www.mentis.de.

170 BRA ISSN 1677-2954
BJ5
ETHIC@; an international journal for moral philosophy. Text in English, Portuguese. 2002. irreg. free (effective 2011). **Document type:** *Journal, Academic/Scholarly.*
Media: Online - full text.
Published by: Universidade Federal de Santa Catarina, Departamento de Filosofia, Caixa Postal 476, Florianopolis, SC 88010-970, Brazil. ethic@cfh.ufsc.br.

170 USA ISSN 2156-244X
ETHICAL CONNECTION. Text in English. 200?. bi-w. USD 20 to non-members; free to members (effective 2010). back issues avail. **Document type:** *Newsletter, Trade.*
Formerly (until 2008): Ethical Weekly
Related titles: Online - full text ed.: ISSN 2156-2466. free (effective 2010).
Published by: The Ethical Society of St. Louis, 9001 Clayton Rd, St. Louis, MO 63117. TEL 314-991-0955, FAX 314-991-3875, office@ethicalstl.org. Ed. Cathy Spalding TEL 314-991-0955 ext 242.

ETHICAL CONSUMER. *see* CONSUMER EDUCATION AND PROTECTION

170 BEL ISSN 1370-0049
BJ1
➤ **ETHICAL PERSPECTIVES**; journal of the European Ethics Network. Text in English. 1994. q. EUR 60 combined subscription (print & online eds.) (effective 2011). Index. 75 p./no.; **Document type:** *Journal, Academic/Scholarly.* **Description:** Aims to promote dialogue between fundamental and applied ethics at an international level.
Related titles: Online - full text ed.: ISSN 1783-1431; ◆ Dutch ed.: Ethische Perspectieven. ISSN 0778-6069.
Indexed: A21, AmHI, CA, FR, H07, P30, P42, PSA, PhilInd, R&TA, RI-1, RI-2, S02, S03, SCOPUS, SociolAb, T02.
—IE, INIST.
Published by: (Universite Catholique de Louvain, Overlegcentrum Ethiek/Katholieke Universiteit Leuven), Peeters Publishers, Bondgenotenlaan 153, Leuven, 3000, Belgium. TEL 32-16-235170, FAX 32-16-228500, peeters@peeters-leuven.be, http://www.peeters-leuven.be. Ed. Bart Pattyn.

170 BEL
➤ **ETHICAL PERSPECTIVES MONOGRAPH SERIES.** Text in English. 2000. irreg., latest 2007. price varies. back issues avail. **Document type:** *Monographic series, Academic/Scholarly.* **Description:** Discusses issues in ethics as they relate to contemporary events and issues.
Published by: Peeters Publishers, Bondgenotenlaan 153, Leuven, 3000, Belgium. TEL 32-16-235170, FAX 32-16-228500, http://www.peeters-leuven.be.

200 GBR ISSN 0014-1690
ETHICAL RECORD. Text in English. 1895. 11/yr. GBP 18 (effective 2010). bk.rev. reprints avail. **Document type:** *Journal, Academic/Scholarly.* **Description:** Contains lectures given at the Sunday meetings of the Society. The lectures cover such subjects as philosophy, science, the arts, history and current affairs.
Formerly (until 1965): South Place Ethical Society. Monthly Record
Related titles: Microform ed.: (from PQC).
Indexed: PhilInd.
—BLDSC (3814.645000). **CCC.**
Published by: South Place Ethical Society, The Hon. Registrar, Conway Hall Humanist Centre, 25 Red Lion Sq, London, WC1R 4RL, United Kingdom. library@ethicalsoc.org.uk.

ETHICAL SPACE; the international journal of communication ethics. *see* COMMUNICATIONS

170 NLD ISSN 1386-2820
BJ1 CODEN: ETMPFH
➤ **ETHICAL THEORY AND MORAL PRACTICE**; an international forum. Text in English, French, German. 1998. 5/yr. EUR 461, USD 477 combined subscription to institutions (print & online eds.) (effective 2012). adv. illus. reprint service avail. from PSC. **Document type:** *Journal, Academic/Scholarly.* **Description:** Covers plurality of philosophical traditions from mainstream to less well known philosophical tradition and cultures; subjects include analytic philosophy, phenomenology, neo-Kantian, neo-Hegelian and neo-Aristotelian traditions.
Related titles: Online - full text ed.: ISSN 1572-8447 (from IngentaConnect).
Indexed: A01, A02, A03, A08, A20, A22, A26, AmHI, ArtHuCI, BRD, BibLing, CA, CurCont, E01, E08, FR, H07, H08, HAb, HumInd, I05, IBSS, IPB, P10, P27, P28, P30, P46, P48, P53, P54, PQC, PhilInd, S02, S03, S09, SCOPUS, SociolAb, T02, W03, W05, W07.
—BLDSC (3814.646000), IE, Infotrieve, Ingenta, INIST. **CCC.**
Published by: Springer Netherlands (Subsidiary of: Springer Science+Business Media), Van Godewijckstraat 30, Dordrecht, 3311 GX, Netherlands. TEL 31-78-6576050, FAX 31-78-6576474, http://www.springer.com. Eds. Albert W Musschenga, F R Heeger.

➤ **ETHICOMP.** *see* COMPUTERS

170 USA ISSN 0014-1704
BJ1
➤ **ETHICS**; an international journal of social, political, and legal philosophy. Text in English. 1888. q. USD 241 combined subscription to institutions (print & online eds.) (effective 2012). adv. bk.rev. bibl.; illus. cum.index: vols.1-75. 240 p./no.; back issues avail.; reprint service avail. from PSC. **Document type:** *Journal, Academic/Scholarly.* **Description:** Takes an interdisciplinary approach to the study of the ideas and principles forming the basis for individual and collective action.
Former titles (until 1938): International Journal of Ethics (1526-422X); (until 1890): The Ethical Record (1947-0592)
Related titles: Microform ed.: (from MIM, PMC, PQC); Online - full text ed.: ISSN 1539-297X. USD 205 to institutions (effective 2012).
Indexed: A01, A02, A03, A08, A20, A21, A22, A25, A26, ABCPolSci, ABRCLP, AC&P, AmHI, ArtHuCI, B04, B05, B07, B14, BRD, BRI, CA, CBRI, CERDIC, CLI, ChPerI, CurCont, DIP, E08, FR, FamI, G05, G06, G07, G08, G10, GSS&RPL, H07, H08, H09, H10, H14, HAb, HumInd, I05, I07, I13, IBR, IBRH, IBSS, IBZ, IPB, L03, LRI, M06, MLA-IB, P02, P06, P10, P13, P21, P27, P28, P30, P42, P43, P45, P48, P53, P54, PCI, PQC, PRA, PSA, PhilInd, R04, R05, R10, RI-1, RI-2, Reac, S02, S03, S05, S08, S09, S23, SCOPUS, SOPODA, SSA, SSAI, SSAb, SSCI, SSI, SociolAb, T02, W01, W02, W03, W07, W09.
—BLDSC (3814.650000), IE, Infotrieve, Ingenta, INIST. **CCC.**
Published by: University of Chicago Press, 1427 E 60th St, Chicago, IL 60637. TEL 773-702-7600, FAX 773-702-0694, subscriptions@press.uchicago.edu. Ed. Henry S Richardson. Adv. contact Cheryl Jones TEL 773-702-7361. **Subscr. to:** PO Box 370050, Chicago, IL 60637. TEL 773-753-3347, 877-705-1878, FAX 773-753-0811, 877-705-1879.

100 170 USA ISSN 1547-5425
BJ1
➤ **ETHICS AND CRITICAL THINKING JOURNAL.** Text in English. 1987. q. USD 285 domestic; USD 320 foreign; USD 80 per issue domestic; USD 92 per issue foreign (effective 2010). bk.rev. back issues avail. **Document type:** *Journal, Academic/Scholarly.*
Indexed: T02.
Published by: Franklin Publishing Company, 2723 Steamboat Cir, Arlington, TX 76006. TEL 817-548-1124, FAX 817-369-2689. Pub. Dr. Ludwig Otto.

➤ **ETHICS AND INFORMATION TECHNOLOGY.** *see* LIBRARY AND INFORMATION SCIENCES

➤ **ETHICS AND JUSTICE**; an interdisciplinary public affairs journal. *see* LAW

179.1 USA ISSN 1085-6633
GE42 CODEN: EENVF3
➤ **ETHICS & THE ENVIRONMENT.** Text in English. 1996. s-a. USD 146.75 combined subscription to institutions (print & online eds.) (effective 2012). adv. abstr. 150 p./no.; back issues avail.; reprint service avail. from PSC. **Document type:** *Journal, Academic/Scholarly.* **Description:** Provides a forum for theoretical and practical articles, discussions, reviews, and book reviews in the field of environmental ethics, including conceptual approaches in ethical theory and ecological philosophy.
Related titles: Online - full text ed.: ISSN 1535-5306. USD 97.50 to institutions (effective 2012) (from IngentaConnect).
Indexed: A01, A03, A08, A22, A26, ASFA, B04, BRD, C04, CA, E01, E04, E05, E08, ESPM, FR, G02, G08, H01, H14, HPNRM, I05, LeftInd, P02, P05, P10, P21, P27, P34, P48, P51, P52, P53, P54, P56, PAIS, PQC, PhilInd, PollutAb, S02, S03, S06, S09, S10, SOPODA, SSAI, SSAb, SSI, SSciA, SWRA, SociolAb, T02, W03, W05.
—BLDSC (3814.656100), IE, Ingenta, INIST. **CCC.**
Published by: Indiana University Press, 601 N Morton St, Bloomington, IN 47404. TEL 812-855-8817, 800-842-6796, FAX 812-855-7931, journals@indiana.edu, http://iupress.indiana.edu. Ed. Victoria Davion. Adv. contact Linda Bannister TEL 812-855-9449. Circ: 200.

▼ ➤ **ETHICS IN BIOLOGY, ENGINEERING AND MEDICINE.** *see* SCIENCES: COMPREHENSIVE WORKS

➤ **ETHICS IN GOVERNMENT REPORTER.** *see* PUBLIC ADMINISTRATION

P

➤ **ETHICS IN SCIENCE AND ENVIRONMENTAL POLITICS.** *see* ENVIRONMENTAL STUDIES

➤ **ETHICS OF SCIENCE AND TECHNOLOGY ASSESSMENT.** *see* SCIENCES: COMPREHENSIVE WORKS

179 GBR ISSN 2155-0085
GE42
➤ **ETHICS, POLICY & ENVIRONMENT**; a journal of philosophy and geography. Text in English. 1998. 3/yr. GBP 321 combined subscription in United Kingdom to institutions (print & online eds.); EUR 423, USD 530 combined subscription to institutions (print & online eds.) (effective 2012). bk.rev. illus. Index. back issues avail.; reprint service avail. from PSC. **Document type:** *Journal, Academic/Scholarly.* **Description:** Aims to provide a forum for the publication of research and scholarship on all aspects of geographical and environmental ethics.
Formerly (until Jan. 2011): Ethics, Place and Environment (1366-879X); Incorporates (1997-2005): Philosophy amd Geography (1090-3771)
Related titles: Online - full text ed.: ISSN 2155-0093. GBP 289 in United Kingdom to institutions; EUR 381, USD 477 to institutions (effective 2012) (from IngentaConnect).
Indexed: A01, A03, A08, A22, B04, BRD, CA, DIP, E01, E04, E05, ESPM, EnvAb, GEOBASE, GardL, HPNRM, IBR, IBSS, IBZ, P34, PAIS, PhilInd, S02, S03, S21, SCOPUS, SSA, SSAI, SSAb, SSI, SSciA, SUSA, SociolAb, T02, W01, W02, W03.
—IE, Infotrieve, Ingenta. **CCC.**
Published by: Routledge (Subsidiary of: Taylor & Francis Group), 4 Park Sq, Milton Park, Abingdon, Oxon OX14 4RN, United Kingdom. TEL 44-20-70176000, FAX 44-20-70176336, subscriptions@tandf.co.uk, http://www.routledge.com. Adv. contact Linda Hann TEL 44-1344-779945. **Subscr. in N. America to:** Taylor & Francis Inc., Customer Services Dept, 325 Chestnut St, 8th Fl, Philadelphia, PA 19106. TEL 215-625-8900, 800-354-1420, FAX 215-625-2940, customerservice@taylorandfrancis.com; **Subscr. to:** Taylor & Francis Ltd., Journals Customer Service, Sheepen Pl, Colchester, Essex CO3 3LP, United Kingdom. TEL 44-20-70175544, FAX 44-20-70175198.

➤ **ETHICS TODAY.** *see* EDUCATION

170 BEL ISSN 1373-0975
H8
ETHIEK & MAATSCHAPPIJ. Text in Dutch; Summaries in English, French, German. 1956. q. EUR 28.50 to individuals; EUR 45 to institutions; EUR 17.50 to students (effective 2008). bk.rev. charts. index.
Formerly (until 1998): Tijdschrift voor Sociale Wetenschappen (0040-7615)
Indexed: CA, CIS, DIP, FR, IBR, IBZ, KES, P30, P42, PSA, RILM, S02, S03, SCOPUS, SSA, SociolAb, T02.
—Infotrieve, INIST.
Published by: Academia Press, Eekhout 2, Gent, 9000, Belgium. TEL 32-9-2338088, FAX 32-9-2331409, info@academiapress.be, http://www.academiapress.be. Ed. Koen Raes.

170 DEU ISSN 1615-9497
ETHIK IM UNTERRICHT. Text in German. 2001. irreg., latest vol.9, 2009. price varies. **Document type:** *Monographic series, Academic/Scholarly.*
Published by: Waxmann Verlag GmbH, Steinfurter Str 555, Muenster, 48159, Germany. TEL 49-251-265040, FAX 49-251-2650426, info@waxmann.com. Ed. Ursula Reitemeyer.

174.95 DEU
ETHIK IN DEN BIOWISSENSCHAFTEN. Text in German. 2002. irreg., latest vol.10, 2009. price varies. **Document type:** *Monographic series, Academic/Scholarly.*
Published by: (Deutsches Referenzzentrum fuer Ethik in den Biowissenschaften), Verlag Karl Alber, Hermann-Herder-Str 4, Freiburg, 79104, Germany. TEL 49-761-2717436, FAX 49-761-2717212.

174.2 500 DEU ISSN 1862-2410
ETHIK IN DEN WISSENSCHAFTEN. Text in German. 1990. irreg., latest vol.18, 2005. price varies. **Document type:** *Monographic series, Academic/Scholarly.*
Published by: A. Francke Verlag GmbH, Dischinger Weg 5, Tuebingen, 72070, Germany. TEL 49-7071-97970, FAX 49-7071-979711, info@francke.de, http://www.francke.de.

170 610 DEU ISSN 0935-7335
R724 CODEN: ETMEEH
➤ **ETHIK IN DER MEDIZIN.** Text in German. 1989. q. EUR 185, USD 208 combined subscription to institutions (print & online eds.) (effective 2012). adv. reprint service avail. from PSC. **Document type:** *Journal, Academic/Scholarly.* **Description:** Discusses ethical issues encountered in clinical medicine, research and development, and psychology.
Related titles: Microform ed.: (from PQC); Online - full text ed.: ISSN 1437-1618 (from IngentaConnect).
Indexed: A22, A26, E01, FR, P03, P30, PsycInfo, SCI, SCOPUS, W07.
—GNLM, IE, Infotrieve, Ingenta, INIST. **CCC.**
Published by: (Akademie fuer Ethik in der Medizin), Springer (Subsidiary of: Springer Science+Business Media), Tiergartenstr 17, Heidelberg, 69121, Germany. TEL 49-6221-4870, FAX 49-6221-345229. Adv. contact Stephan Kroeck TEL 49-30-827875739. **Subscr. in the Americas to:** Springer New York LLC, Journal Fulfillment, PO Box 2485, Secaucus, NJ 07096. TEL 800-777-4643, 201-348-4033, FAX 201-348-4505, journals-ny@springer.com, http://www.springer.com; **Subscr. to:** Springer Distribution Center, Kundenservice Zeitschriften, Haberstr 7, Heidelberg 69126, Germany. TEL 49-6221-3454303, FAX 49-6221-3454229, subscriptions@springer.com.

170 DEU ISSN 1610-5966
ETHIK IN FORSCHUNG UND PRAXIS. Text in German. 2002. irreg., latest vol.9, 2009. price varies. **Document type:** *Monographic series, Academic/Scholarly.*
Published by: Verlag Dr. Kovac, Leverkusenstr 13, Hamburg, 22761, Germany. TEL 49-40-3988800, FAX 49-40-39888055, info@verlagdrkovac.de.

100 DEU ISSN 1861-4310
ETHIK TRANSDISZIPLINAER. Text in German. 2006. irreg., latest vol.10, 2009. price varies. **Document type:** *Monographic series, Academic/Scholarly.*
Published by: Peter Lang GmbH (Subsidiary of: Peter Lang Publishing Group), Eschborner Landstr 42-50, Frankfurt Am Main, 60489, Germany. TEL 49-69-7807050, FAX 49-69-78070550, zentrale.frankfurt@peterlang.com. Ed. Michael Fischer.

170 CHE ISSN 1422-4496
ETHIK UND POLITISCHE PHILOSOPHIE. Text in German. 1998. irreg., latest vol.14, 2008. price varies. **Document type:** *Monographic series, Academic/Scholarly.*
Published by: Academic Press Fribourg, Perolles 42, Fribourg, 1705, Switzerland. TEL 41-26-4264311, FAX 41-26-4264300, info@paulusedition.ch, http://www.paulusedition.ch/academic_press/.

ETHIK UND RECHT/ETHIQUE ET DROIT/ETICA E DIRITTO. *see* LAW

174.937 DEU ISSN 0936-7772
BJ66
ETHIK UND UNTERRICHT. Text in German. 1990. q. EUR 63; EUR 15 newsstand/cover (effective 2011). adv. **Document type:** *Journal, Academic/Scholarly.*
Indexed: DIP, IBR, IBZ.
Published by: Erhard Friedrich Verlag GmbH, Im Brande 17, Seelze, 30926, Germany. TEL 49-511-400040, FAX 49-511-40004170, info@friedrich-verlag.de, http://www.friedrich-verlag.de. Adv. contact Bianca Kraft. Circ: 2,500 (paid and controlled).

170 USA
ETHIKON SERIES IN COMPARATIVE ETHICS. Text in English. 1996. irreg., latest 2007. price varies. back issues avail. **Document type:** *Monographic series, Academic/Scholarly.* **Description:** Analyzes the role of ethics in various sociopolitical contexts.
Published by: Princeton University Press, 41 William St, Princeton, NJ 08540. TEL 609-258-4900, 800-777-4726, FAX 609-258-6305, cpriday@pupress.co.uk. Ed. Carole Pateman. **Subscr. addr. in US:** California - Princeton Fulfillment Services, Inc., 1445 Lower Ferry Rd, Ewing, NJ 08618. TEL 609-883-1759, 800-777-4726, FAX 609-883-7413, 800-999-1958, orders@cpfsinc.com. **Dist. in Canada, Australia & New Zealand, and Latin America:** University Press Group.; **Dist. in Europe & Africa:** John Wiley & Sons Ltd.

174 658 USA ISSN 0895-5026
K5
ETHIKOS; examining ethical and compliance issues in business. Text in English. 1987. bi-m. USD 195 to non-members; USD 175 to members (effective 2010). adv. bk.rev. back issues avail. **Document type:** *Journal, Trade.* **Description:** Examines ethical issues in business with particular focus on corporate ethics programs, ombudsman offices, codes of conduct, and monitoring ethics.
Incorporates (1991-1998): Corporate Conduct Quarterly (1061-8775)
Related titles: Online - full text ed.
Indexed: A22, P10, P21, P48, P53, P54, PQC.
—BLDSC (3814.675000).
Published by: Ethikos, Inc., 154 E Boston Post Rd, Mamaroneck, NY 10543. TEL 914-381-7475, FAX 914-381-6947. Eds. Andrew W Singer, Joseph E Murphy. Pub. Andrew W Singer. Adv. contact Victoria Theodore.

ETHIOPIQUES. *see* HISTORY—History Of Africa

ETHIQUE & SANTE. *see* PHYSICAL FITNESS AND HYGIENE

172 CAN ISSN 1488-0946
JA79E77
ETHIQUE PUBLIQUE. Text in French. 1999. s-a. **Document type:** *Journal, Academic/Scholarly.*
—**CCC.**
Published by: Editions Liber, 2318, rue Belanger, Montreal, PQ H2G 1C8, Canada. TEL 514-522-3227, FAX 514-522-2007, info@editionsliber.org, http://www.editionsliber.org.

170 230.2 BEL ISSN 0778-6069
➤ **ETHISCHE PERSPECTIEVEN.** Text in Dutch. 1991. q. EUR 24 combined subscription (print & online eds.) (effective 2011). bk.rev. Index. 75 p./no.; **Document type:** *Journal, Academic/Scholarly.* **Description:** Promotes dialogue between fundamental and applied ethics at an international level.
Related titles: Online - full text ed.: ISSN 1783-144X; ◆ English ed.: Ethical Perspectives. ISSN 1370-0049.
—IE.
Published by: (Universite Catholique de Louvain, Overlegcentrum Ethiek/Katholieke Universiteit Leuven), Peeters Publishers, Bondgenotenlaan 153, Leuven, 3000, Belgium. TEL 32-16-235170, FAX 32-16-228500, peeters@peeters-leuven.be, http://www.peeters-leuven.be. Ed. Bart Pattyn.

100 ARG ISSN 0325-5387
ETHOS; revista de filosofia practica. Text in Spanish. 1973. a. USD 45. adv. bk.rev. bibl. **Document type:** *Academic/Scholarly.*
Published by: Instituto de Filosofia Practica, Viamonte, 1596, Buenos Aires, 1055, Argentina. TEL 54-114-3713315. Ed. Julio Guido Soaje Ramos. Adv. contact Maria Lukac de Stier. Circ: 500.

100 300 TUR ISSN 1309-1328
ETHOS: DIALOGUES IN PHILOSOPHY AND SOCIAL SCIENCE. Text in English, Turkish. 2008. s-a. free (effective 2011). **Document type:** *Journal, Academic/Scholarly.*
Media: Online - full text.
Indexed: PhilInd.
Published by: Ethos

170 ESP ISSN 1988-7973
ETICA DE LOS CIUDADANOS. Text in Spanish. 2008. s-a.
Media: Online - full text.
Published by: Fundacion Index, Calle Horno de Marina 2, Granada, 18001, Spain. http://www.index-f.com/fundacion.php.

100 ITA ISSN 1825-5167
BJ4
ETICA & POLITICA/ETHICS & POLITICS. Text in Multiple languages. 1999. s-a. free (effective 2011). **Document type:** *Journal, Academic/Scholarly.* **Description:** It aims at promoting research and reflection, both historically and theoretically, in the field of moral and political philosophy, with no cultural preclusion or adhesion to any philosophical current.
Media: Online - full text.
Indexed: PhilInd.
Published by: Universita degli Studi di Trieste, Dipartimento di Filosofia, Androna Campo Marzio 10, Trieste, 34123, Italy. TEL 39-040-5584314, FAX 39-040-311796, http://www.univ.trieste.it/~dipfilo/vari.html. Ed. P Marrone.

ETICA ED ECONOMIA. *see* BUSINESS AND ECONOMICS

100 CAN ISSN 0708-319X
ETIENNE GILSON SERIES. Text in English. 1979. irreg., latest vol.20, 1997. price varies. back issues avail. **Document type:** *Monographic series, Academic/Scholarly.*
Published by: Pontifical Institute of Mediaeval Studies, 59 Queens Park Crescent E, Toronto, ON M5S 2C4, Canada. pontifex@chass.utoronto.ca, http://www.pims.ca. Circ: 600. **Dist. in Europe by:** Brepols Publishers, Begijnhof 67, Turnhout 2300, Belgium. TEL 32-14-402500, FAX 32-14-428919.

100 NOR ISSN 1890-3991
➤ **ETIKK I PRAKSIS.** Text in Multiple languages. 2007. s-a. adv. **Document type:** *Journal, Academic/Scholarly.*
Related titles: Online - full text ed.: ISSN 1890-4009.
Indexed: A01, T02.
Published by: (Norges Teknisk-Naturvitenskapelige Universitet, Filosofisk Institutt/Norwegian University of Science and Technology, Department of Philosophy), Tapir Akademisk Forlag A/S, Nardoveien 14, Trondheim, 7005, Norway. TEL 47-73-593210, FAX 47-73-593204, post@tapirforlag.no, http://www.tapirforlag.no.

100 CAN ISSN 0826-9920
ETUDES MARITAINIENNES/MARITAIN STUDIES. Text in English, French. 1985. a. **Document type:** *Journal, Academic/Scholarly.* **Description:** Publishes articles on topics and themes in philosophy that Maritain thought important.
Indexed: MLA-IB, PhilInd.
Published by: Association Canadienne Jacques Maritain, c/o Departement de Philosophie, College Dominicain de Philosophie et de Theologie, 96 rue Empress, Ottawa, ON K1R 7G3, Canada. Ed. William Sweet.

100 FRA ISSN 0014-2166
➤ **LES ETUDES PHILOSOPHIQUES.** Text in French; Abstracts in French, English. 1926. q. EUR 90 foreign to institutions (effective 2012). adv. bk.rev. charts; illus. index. reprint service avail. from SCH. **Document type:** *Journal, Academic/Scholarly.* **Description:** Each issue covers a broad philosophical topic or the essential ideas of a great philosophical thinker.
Formerly (until 1927): La Societe d'Etudes Philosophiques du Sud-Est. Bulletin (0996-0996)
Related titles: Online - full text ed.: ISSN 2101-0056 (from PQC).
Indexed: A20, ArtHuCI, CurCont, DIP, FR, IBR, IBRH, IBSS, IBZ, IPB, MLA, MLA-IB, PCI, PhilInd, RASB, RILM, SCOPUS, W07.
—IE, INIST. **CCC.**
Published by: Presses Universitaires de France, 6 Avenue Reille, Paris, 75685, France. TEL 33-1-58103161, FAX 33-1-45897530, revues@puf.com, http://www.puf.com. Ed. Frederic Lefebvre. Circ: 1,500.

184 FRA ISSN 1770-9687
B395
ETUDES PLATONICIENNES. Text in French. 2004. a. back issues avail. **Document type:** *Journal, Academic/Scholarly.*
Published by: (Societe d'Etudes Platoniciennes), Editions Les Belles Lettres, 95 Blvd Raspail, Paris, 75006, France. TEL 33-1-44398421, FAX 33-1-45449288, courrier@lesbelleslettres.com, http://www.lesbelleslettres.com.

100 340 320 USA ISSN 2156-7808
▼ ➤ **ETUDES RICOEURIENNES/ RICOEUR STUDIES.** Abbreviated title: E R R S. Text in English, French. 2010. 2/yr. free (effective 2011). bk.rev. back issues avail. **Document type:** *Journal, Academic/Scholarly.* **Description:** Contains interdisciplinary and original studies on the work of Paul Ricoeur.
Media: Online - full text.
Published by: University of Pittsburgh, University Library System, Coordinator of Library Instruction, 207 Hillman Library, Pittsburgh, PA 15260. TEL 412-648-7732, FAX 412-648-7733, e-journals@mail.pitt.edu, http://www.library.pitt.edu. Eds., Pubs., R&Ps Johann Michel, Scott Davidson.

170 POL ISSN 0014-2263
BJ8.P6
ETYKA. Text in Polish; Summaries in English. 1966. a. price varies. bk.rev. abstr. **Document type:** *Academic/Scholarly.*
Indexed: FR, PhilInd.
—INIST.
Published by: Polska Akademia Nauk, Instytut Filozofii i Socjologii, Nowy Swiat 72, Warsaw, 00330, Poland. TEL 48-22-8267181, FAX 48-22-8267823, secretar@ifispan.waw.pl, http://www.ifispan.waw.pl. Ed. Barbara Skarga. Circ: 1,100.

EUBIOS JOURNAL OF ASIAN AND INTERNATIONAL BIOETHICS. *see* BIOLOGY

100 MEX ISSN 2007-1647
EUPHYIA. Text in Spanish. 2007. s-a. **Document type:** *Journal, Academic/Scholarly.*
Published by: Universidad Autonoma de Aguascalientes, Centro de Ciencias Sociales y Humanidades, Ciudad Universitaria, Edif. 6 Planta Alta, Aguascalientes, Aguascalientes 20131, Mexico. TEL 52-449-9108477, cvargas@correo.uaa.mx, uaa.academia.edu/centros/ccsh/.

100 DEU ISSN 0721-3417
EUROPAEISCHE HOCHSCHULSCHRIFTEN. REIHE 20: PHILOSOPHIE. Text in German. 1970. irreg., latest vol.734, 2010. price varies. **Document type:** *Monographic series, Academic/Scholarly.*
Published by: Peter Lang GmbH (Subsidiary of: Peter Lang Publishing Group), Eschborner Landstr 42-50, Frankfurt Am Main, 60489, Germany. TEL 49-69-7807050, FAX 49-69-78070550, zentrale.frankfurt@peterlang.com, http://www.peterlang.com.

▼ **EUROPEAN JOURNAL FOR PHILOSOPHY OF SCIENCE.** *see* SCIENCES: COMPREHENSIVE WORKS

190 GBR ISSN 0966-8373
B1
➤ **EUROPEAN JOURNAL OF PHILOSOPHY.** Abbreviated title: E J P. Text in English. 1993. q. GBP 436 in United Kingdom to institutions; EUR 554 in Europe to institutions; USD 775 in the Americas to institutions; USD 907 elsewhere to institutions; GBP 502 combined subscription in United Kingdom to institutions (print & online eds.); EUR 638 combined subscription in Europe to institutions (print & online eds.); USD 892 combined subscription in the Americas to institutions (print & online eds.); USD 1,044 combined subscription elsewhere to institutions (print & online eds.) (effective 2012). adv. bk.rev. illus. Index. back issues avail.; reprint service avail. from PSC. **Document type:** *Journal, Academic/Scholarly.*
Related titles: Online - full text ed.: ISSN 1468-0378. GBP 436 in United Kingdom to institutions; EUR 554 in Europe to institutions; USD 775 in the Americas to institutions; USD 907 elsewhere to institutions (effective 2012) (from IngentaConnect).
Indexed: A01, A02, A03, A08, A20, A22, A26, AmHI, ArtHuCI, BrHumI, CA, CurCont, DIP, E01, H07, H14, IBR, IBSS, IBZ, IPB, P02, P10, P48, P53, P54, PCI, PQC, PhilInd, S02, S03, SCOPUS, SociolAb, T02, W07.
—BLDSC (3829.734400), IE, Infotrieve, Ingenta. **CCC.**
Published by: Wiley-Blackwell Publishing Ltd. (Subsidiary of: John Wiley & Sons, Inc.), 9600 Garsington Rd, Oxford, OX4 2DQ, United Kingdom. TEL 44-1865-776868, FAX 44-1865-714591, customerservices@blackwellpublishing.com. Ed. Robert Stern TEL 44-1142-220582. Adv. contact Craig Pickett TEL 44-1865-476267.

100 ITA ISSN 2036-4091
▼ **EUROPEAN JOURNAL OF PRAGMATISM AND AMERICAN PHILOSOPHY.** Text in English. 2009. s-a. free (effective 2011). **Document type:** *Journal, Academic/Scholarly.*
Media: Online - full text.
Published by: Associazione Culturale Pragma, Via Ostiense 234, Rome, 00146, Italy. Ed. Rosa M Calcaterra.

EUROPEAN JUDAISM; a journal for the new Europe. *see* RELIGIONS AND THEOLOGY—Judaic

940 GBR ISSN 1084-8770
D1
➤ **THE EUROPEAN LEGACY**; toward new paradigms. Text in English. 1996. 7/yr. GBP 509 combined subscription in United Kingdom to institutions (print & online eds.); EUR 670, USD 841 combined subscription to institutions (print & online eds.) (effective 2012). adv. back issues avail.; reprint service avail. from PSC. **Document type:** *Journal, Academic/Scholarly.* **Description:** Examines the interplay and impact of the rich European intellectual history on a variety of topics and issues, taking a multidisciplinary approach.
Related titles: Online - full text ed.: ISSN 1470-1316. GBP 458 in United Kingdom to institutions; EUR 603, USD 757 to institutions (effective 2012) (from IngentaConnect).
Indexed: A01, A02, A03, A08, A20, A22, ABS&EES, AmH&L, AmHI, ArtHuCI, CA, DIP, E01, H07, HistAb, IBR, IBSS, IBZ, M02, M10, MLA-IB, P30, P34, P42, PAIS, PSA, PhilInd, RILM, S02, S03, SCOPUS, SociolAb, T02, W07.
—IE, Infotrieve, Ingenta. **CCC.**
Published by: (International Society for the Study of European Ideas USA), Routledge (Subsidiary of: Taylor & Francis Group), 4 Park Sq, Milton Park, Abingdon, Oxon OX14 4RN, United Kingdom. TEL 44-20-70176000, FAX 44-20-70176336, subscriptions@tandf.co.uk, http://www.routledge.com. Eds. David W Lovell, Edna Rosenthal, Erza Talmor TEL 972-3-9386445. **Subscr. in N America to:** Taylor & Francis Inc., Customer Services Dept, 325 Chestnut St, 8th Fl, Philadelphia, PA 19106. TEL 215-625-8900, 800-354-1420, FAX 215-625-2940, customerservice@taylorandfrancis.com; **Subscr. to:** Taylor & Francis Ltd., Journals Customer Service, Sheepen Pl, Colchester, Essex CO3 3LP, United Kingdom. TEL 44-20-70175544, FAX 44-20-70175198, tf.enquiries@tfinforma.com.

➤ **EUROPEAN PERSPECTIVES**; a series in social thought and cultural criticism. *see* ANTHROPOLOGY

➤ **EUROPEAN STUDIES IN PHILOSOPHY OF MEDICINE.** *see* MEDICAL SCIENCES

146.7 128 FRA ISSN 1779-5567
EVEIL & EVOLUTION. Text in French. 2005. q. EUR 30 to individuals (effective 2009). **Document type:** *Magazine, Consumer.*
Related titles: Online - full text ed.
Published by: EnlightenNext Paris, 22 Square de Chatillon, Paris, 75014, France. info.paris@EnlightenNext.org.

EVERGREEN MONTHLY. *see* NEW AGE PUBLICATIONS

EVOLUTION AND COGNITION. *see* PSYCHOLOGY

100 ESP ISSN 1131-6950
EXCERPTA E DISSERTATIONIBUS IN PHILOSOPHIA. Text in Spanish. 1991. a. **Document type:** *Monographic series, Academic/Scholarly.*
Related titles: Online - full text ed.
Indexed: A01, CA, F03, F04, T02.
Published by: Universidad de Navarra, Servicio de Publicaciones, Campus Universitario, Pamplona, 31009, Spain. http://www.unav.es/publicaciones/.

EXCERPTA PHILOLOGICA; filologia griega y latina de la Universidad de Cadiz. *see* CLASSICAL STUDIES

142.7 HUN ISSN 1215-5950
B1
EXISTENTIA; meletai sophias - philosophical papers - bolcseleti tanulmanyok. Text mainly in English, German; Text occasionally in French, Hungarian, Italian. 1991. 4/yr. USD 240 to institutions (effective 2009). adv. bk.rev. Supplement avail. **Document type:** *Journal, Academic/Scholarly.* **Description:** Covers developments in phenomenology, hermeneutical philosophy, as well as contemporary continental philosophy, paying particular attention to investigations that "probe possible points of intersection between continental and Anglo-American traditions.".
Related titles: E-mail ed.; Fax ed.; Online - full text ed.
Indexed: IPB, PhilInd.
Published by: Societas Philosophia Classica, PO Box 554, Budapest, 1374, Hungary. TEL 36-1-3122798, FAX 36-1-3122798. Ed. Ferge Gabor.

142.7 616.89 GBR ISSN 1752-5616
B819.A1
➤ **EXISTENTIAL ANALYSIS.** Text in English. 1989. s-a. free to members (effective 2010). adv. bk.rev. 200 p./no.; back issues avail. **Document type:** *Journal, Academic/Scholarly.* **Description:** Presents papers relating to the analysis of existence from philosophical and psychological-psychotherapeutic perspectives.
Formerly (until 2001): Society for Existential Analysis. Journal (0958-0476)
Related titles: Online - full text ed.: ISSN 2044-0413.
Indexed: A01, A02, A03, A08, A26, CA, E-psyche, I05, P03, P43, PhilInd, PsycInfo, PsycholAb, T02.
—BLDSC (3836.347500), IE, Ingenta.
Published by: Society for Existential Analysis, 70 Selhurst Close, London, SW19 6AZ, United Kingdom. TEL 44-7941-218372, membership@existentialanalysis.co.uk. Eds. Greg Madison, Ian Jones-Healey, Simon Du Plock.

100 USA ISSN 1057-1035
BF637.S4
EXTROPY; the journal of transhumanist thought. Text in English. 1988. q. USD 18 domestic to individuals; USD 22 in Canada & Mexico to individuals; USD 24 elsewhere to individuals; USD 40 domestic to institutions; USD 45 in Canada & Mexico to institutions; USD 60 elsewhere to institutions. adv. bk.rev.; film rev. bibl.; illus. **Document type:** *Magazine, Consumer.* **Description:** Covers futurist philosophy, physical immortality, smart drugs, artificial intelligence and A-life, nanotechnology and others.
Published by: Extropy Institute, 10709 Pointe View Dr, Austin, TX 78738. TEL 512-263-2749, natasha@extropy.org, http://www.extropy.org. Ed. Max More. Circ: 2,500.

EYE OF THE HEART. *see* RELIGIONS AND THEOLOGY

100 CHE ISSN 1424-0602
B791
FACTA PHILOSOPHICA. Text in German. 1999. s-a. CHF 50 domestic; EUR 35 in Germany; EUR 33 in Europe; GBP 31, USD 50 (effective 2010). **Document type:** *Journal, Academic/Scholarly.*
Related titles: Online - full text ed.: EUR 35 to individuals; EUR 70 to institutions (effective 2010).
Indexed: DIP, IBR, IBZ, IPB, PhilInd.
—BLDSC (3863.466250).
Published by: Peter Lang AG (Subsidiary of: Peter Lang Publishing Group), Hochfeldstr 32, Postfach 746, Bern 9, 3000, Switzerland. TEL 41-31-3061717, FAX 41-31-3061727, info@peterlang.com, http://www.peterlang.com. Eds. Alex Burri, Klaus Petrus.

100 301 150 SRB ISSN 0354-4648
FACTA UNIVERSITATIS. SERIES PHILOSOPHY, SOCIOLOGY AND PSYCHOLOGY. Text in English, French, German. 1994. a., latest vol.2, no.9, 2002. **Document type:** *Journal, Academic/Scholarly.*
Indexed: CA, PhilInd, S02, S03, SCOPUS, SociolAb, T02.
—Linda Hall.
Published by: Univerzitet u Nishu/University of Nis, Univerzitetski Trg 2, P.O. Box 123, Nis, 18000. TEL 381-18-547970, FAX 381-18-547950, facta@ni.ac.yu, http://ni.ac.yu. Ed. Momcilo Stojkovic.

100 200 USA ISSN 0739-7046
BR100
➤ **FAITH AND PHILOSOPHY.** Text in English. 1984. q. USD 45 to individuals; USD 79 to institutions; USD 275 combined subscription to institutions (print & online eds.); USD 12 per issue to individuals; USD 20 per issue to institutions; free to members (effective 2010). adv. bk.rev. illus. index. back issues avail.; reprints avail. **Document type:** *Journal, Academic/Scholarly.*
Related titles: Microform ed.: (from PQC); Online - full text ed.: ISSN 2153-3393. USD 225 to institutions (effective 2010).
Indexed: A21, A22, ChrPI, IPB, P30, PCI, PhilInd, R&TA, RASB, RI-1, RI-2.
—BLDSC (3865.511100), IE, Infotrieve, Ingenta. **CCC.**
Published by: (Society of Christian Philosophers), Philosophy Documentation Center, PO Box 7147, Charlottesville, VA 22906. TEL 434-220-3300, FAX 434-220-3301, order@pdcnet.org, http://www.pdcnet.org. Ed. Thomas P Flint. Adv. contact Greg Swope.

➤ **FAR WEST PHILOSOPHY OF EDUCATION SOCIETY JOURNAL.** *see* EDUCATION

➤ **FARHANG.** *see* HUMANITIES: COMPREHENSIVE WORKS

➤ **FEDERAL ETHICS REPORT.** *see* PUBLIC ADMINISTRATION

100 TUR
FELSEFE TARTISMALARI; a Turkish journal of philosophy. Abbreviated title: f t. Text in Turkish. s-a. TRY 850 (effective 2009). **Document type:** *Journal, Academic/Scholarly.* **Description:** Publishes original articles, translations, book reviews, discussions and in memoriam notes about philosophy.
Related titles: English ed.: Philosophical Discussions.
Published by: Bogazici Universitesi/Bogazici University, Felsefe Bolumu, Bebek, Istanbul, 34342, Turkey. bilgi@pandora.com.tr, http://www.pandora.com.tr. Eds. Ilhan Inan, Murat Bac.

FENG SHUI. *see* INTERIOR DESIGN AND DECORATION

100 ITA ISSN 0394-2759
FENOMENOLOGIA E SOCIETA. Text in Italian. 1977. q. EUR 99 in the European Union; EUR 134 elsewhere (effective 2009). **Document type:** *Journal, Academic/Scholarly.*
Indexed: CA, L&LBA, P42, PSA, S02, S03, SCOPUS, SSA, SociolAb, T02.
Published by: Rosenberg & Sellier, Via Andrea Doria 14, Turin, 10123, Italy. TEL 39-011-8127808, FAX 39-011-8127820, info@rosenbergesellier.it, http://www.rosenbergesellier.it. Ed. Giuseppe Pirola.

100 DEU
FERMENTA PHILOSOPHICA. Text in German. 1974. irreg., latest 2008. price varies. **Document type:** *Monographic series, Academic/Scholarly.*
Published by: Verlag Karl Alber, Hermann-Herder-Str 4, Freiburg, 79104, Germany. TEL 49-761-2717436, FAX 49-761-2717212, info@verlag-alber.de.

100 NLD ISSN 0925-0166
B2800 CODEN: MASDDW
➤ **FICHTE - STUDIEN**; Beitraege zur Geschichte und Systematik der Transzendentalphilosophie. Text in German. 1991. irreg., latest vol.31, 2007. price varies. bk.rev. back issues avail. **Document type:** *Monographic series, Academic/Scholarly.*
Related titles: ◆ Supplement(s): Fichte-Studien. Supplementa. ISSN 0927-3816.
Indexed: AmHI, DIP, H07, IBR, IBZ, IPB, P28, P48, P53, P54, PQC, PhilInd, T02.
Published by: (Internationale Johann Gottlieb Fichte Gesellschaft eV/Association Internationale Johann Gottlieb Fichte DEU), Editions Rodopi B.V., Tijnmuiden 7, Amsterdam, 1046 AK, Netherlands. TEL 31-20-6114821, FAX 31-20-4472979, info@rodopi.nl. Ed. Dr. Hartmut Traub. **Dist in France by:** Nordeal, 30 rue de Verlinghem, BP 139, Lambersart 59832, France. TEL 33-3-20099060, FAX 33-3-20929495; **Dist. by:** Rodopi - USA, 606 Newark Ave, 2nd fl, Kenilworth, NJ 07033. TEL 908-497-9031, 800-225-3998, FAX 908-497-9035.

193 NLD ISSN 0927-3816
FICHTE-STUDIEN. SUPPLEMENTA. Text in German. 1993. irreg., latest vol.21, 2006. price varies. back issues avail. **Document type:** *Monographic series, Academic/Scholarly.*
Related titles: ◆ Supplement to: Fichte - Studien. ISSN 0925-0166.
Indexed: AmHI, H07, IPB, T02.
Published by: (Internationale Johann Gottlieb Fichte Gesellschaft eV/Association Internationale Johann Gottlieb Fichte DEU), Editions Rodopi B.V., Tijnmuiden 7, Amsterdam, 1046 AK, Netherlands. TEL 31-20-6114821, FAX 31-20-4472979, info@rodopi.nl. **Dist. addr. in France:** Nordeal, 30 rue de Verlinghem, BP 139, Lambersart 59832, France. TEL 33-3-20099060, FAX 33-3-20929495; **Dist. addr. in the US:** Rodopi - USA, 606 Newark Ave, 2nd fl, Kenilworth, NJ 07033. TEL 908-497-9031, 800-225-3998, FAX 908-497-9035.

100 ITA ISSN 1824-6966
FIERI; annali del Dipartimento di Filosofia, Storia e Critica dei Saperi. Text in Italian. 2004. a. **Document type:** *Journal, Academic/Scholarly.*
Published by: Universita degli Studi di Palermo, Facolta di Lettere e Filosofia, Viale delle Scienze 12, Palermo, 90128, Italy. TEL 39-091-6560225, FAX 39-091-427366.

FILM AND PHILOSOPHY. *see* MOTION PICTURES

100 RUS ISSN 1024-1817
FILOLOGICHESKIE NAUKI. Text in Russian. 1958. bi-m. USD 149 in United States (effective 2006). **Document type:** *Journal, Academic/Scholarly.*
Formerly (until 1991): Nauchnye Doklady Vysshei Shkoly. Filologicheskie Nauki (0130-9730)
Indexed: FR, L11, MLA-IB, RASB.
—East View, INIST.
Published by: (Komitet po Vysshei Shkole Minnauki Rossiiskoi Federatsii), Rossiiskaya Akademiya Estestvennykh Nauk/Russian Academy of Natural Sciences, Varshavskoe Shosse, 8, Moscow, 117105, Russian Federation. TEL 7-095-9542611, FAX 7-095-9547305, info@raen.ru, http://www.raen.ru. **Dist. by:** East View Information Services, 10601 Wayzata Blvd, Minneapolis, MN 55305. TEL 952-252-1201, 800-477-1005, FAX 952-252-1202, info@eastview.com, http://www.eastview.com. **Co-sponsor:** Akademiya Estestvennykh Nauk.

FILOLOGOS/SCHOLAR. *see* CLASSICAL STUDIES

FILOMUSICA; revista de musica culta. *see* MUSIC

128 NLD ISSN 2210-7827
FILOS. Text in Dutch. 1963. s-a.
Former titles (until 2008): Ego (1574-339X); (until 2005): Thema (1568-0495); (until 1999): Ego (1384-0525)
Published by: Dienst Humanistisch Geestelijke Verzorging, Postbus 90701, The Hague, 2597 PC, Netherlands. TEL 31-70-3166289. Ed. Gerjos Hengelaar.

100 CHE ISSN 1661-8386
FILOSOFANDO. Text in Italian. 2006. s-a. **Document type:** *Journal, Academic/Scholarly.*
Published by: Istituto di Filosofia Applicata, Via Giuseppe Buffi 13, Casella Postale 4663, Lugano, 6904, Switzerland. TEL 41-58-6664555, FAX 41-58-6664556, info@filosofia-applicata.ch, http://www.filosofia-applicata.ch.

100 ARG ISSN 0325-805X
FILOSOFAR CRISTIANO. Text in Portuguese, Spanish. 1974. s-a. USD 10. bk.rev.
Formerly (until 1977): Asociacion Latino-Americana de Filosofos Catolicos. Boletin
Published by: Asociacion Catolica Interamericana de Filosofia, Arturo M Bas, 366, Cordoba, 5000, Argentina. Ed. Alberto Caturelli. Circ: 1,200.

100 ITA ISSN 0015-1823
B4
FILOSOFIA. Text in Italian. 1950. 3/yr. adv. bk.rev. bibl. index, cum.index. reprints avail. **Document type:** *Journal, Academic/Scholarly.*
Indexed: A20, A21, A22, ArtHuCI, CCMJ, CurCont, DIP, FR, IBR, IBZ, IPB, MLA-IB, PCI, PhilInd, RASB, RI-1, RI-2.
—IE, INIST.
Published by: Ugo Mursia Editore, Via Melchiorre Gioia 45, Milan, 20124, Italy. TEL 39-02-67378500, FAX 39-02-67378605, info@mursia.com, http://www.mursia.com. Eds. Marzio Pinottini, Vittorio Mathieu.

100 PHL
➤ **FILOSOFIA**; international journal of philosophy. Cover title: Phi Iota Lambda Omicron Sigma Omicron Phi Iota Allpha. Variant title: Philosophia. Text in English. 1971. s-a. USD 55 to individuals; USD 65 to institutions (effective 2005). bk.rev. abstr. 120 p./no.; back issues avail. **Document type:** *Journal, Academic/Scholarly.* **Description:** Publishes scholarly articles reflecting significant qualitative or quantitative researches in Filipino and Asian Philosophy, Continental and Analytic Philosophy, Islamic and other areas in contemporary philosophy. Includes conference reports, notes and comments, philosophical research updates, and activities of philosophical associations or societies, and the like.
Formerly (until 2000): Sofia (0115-8988)
Indexed: A20, ArtHuCI, CurCont, IPB, IPP, PhilInd, W07.
Published by: Philippine National Philosophical Research Society, c/o Philosophy Department, De La Salle University, 2401 Taft Ave, Manila, 1004, Philippines. TEL 63-2-524-4611 ext 546, FAX 63-2-456-9314, gripaldor@dlsu.edu.ph. Eds. Leonora R Dimagiba, Rolando M Gripaldo. R&P Rolando M Gripaldo. Circ: 200 (paid and controlled).

100 ESP ISSN 1989-810X
FILOSOFIA. Variant title: Serie Verde. Filosofía. Text in Spanish. 1981. irreg. price varies. back issues avail. **Document type:** *Monographic series, Academic/Scholarly.*
Published by: Universidad de Deusto, Departamento de Publicaciones, Apdo 1/E, Bilbao, 48080, Spain. TEL 34-94-4139162, FAX 34-94-4456817, publicaciones@deusto.es, http://deusto-publicaciones.es/.

100 BGR
FILOSOFIA. Text in Bulgarian. bi-m. USD 36 foreign (effective 2002). **Document type:** *Journal, Academic/Scholarly.*
Published by: Ministerstvo na Obrazovanieto i Naukata na Republika Bulgaria/Ministry of Education and Sciences of the Republic of Bulgaria, 125 Tzarigradsko Shosse Blvd., Bl. 5, PO Box 336, Sofia, 1113, Bulgaria. TEL 359-2-705298, http://www.minedu.government.bg. **Dist. by:** Sofia Books, ul Silivria 16, Sofia 1404, Bulgaria. TEL 359-2-9586257, info@sofiabooks-bg.com, http://www.sofiabooks-bg.com.

100 ITA ISSN 1591-0660
FILOSOFIA E QUESTIONI PUBBLICHE. Text in Italian. 1995. 3/yr. **Document type:** *Magazine, Consumer.*
Published by: Luiss Bookstore, Via Pola 12, Rome, 00198, Italy. TEL 39-06-85225370, FAX 39-06-85225363, http://www.luissbookstore.it.

FILOSOFIA E SAPERE STORICO. *see* HISTORY

FILOSOFIA E SCIENZA NELL'ETA MODERNA. SER.1. STUDI. *see* SCIENCES: COMPREHENSIVE WORKS

FILOSOFIA E SCIENZA NELL'ETA MODERNA. SER 3. TESTI INEDITI O RARI. *see* SCIENCES: COMPREHENSIVE WORKS

294.54 ITA ISSN 1824-4963
BT40
FILOSOFIA E TEOLOGIA. Text in Italian. 1987. 3/yr. EUR 66 domestic to individuals; EUR 82 domestic to institutions; EUR 102 foreign (effective 2009). **Document type:** *Journal, Academic/Scholarly.* **Description:** Discusses the implication and relationship between ethics and religion.
Indexed: IPB.
Published by: Edizioni Scientifiche Italiane SpA, Via Chiatamone 7, Naples, NA 80121, Italy. TEL 39-081-7645443, FAX 39-081-7646477, info@edizioniesi.it, http://www.edizioniesi.it. Ed. Andrea Milano.

FILOSOFIA PARA NINOS (CD-ROM). *see* EDUCATION

FILOSOFIA POLITICA. *see* POLITICAL SCIENCE

100 ITA
FILOSOFIA PUBBLICA. Text in Italian. 1989. irreg., latest vol.15, 1999. price varies. adv. **Document type:** *Monographic series, Academic/Scholarly.*
Published by: Liguori Editore, Via Posillipo 394, Naples, 80123, Italy. TEL 39-081-7206111, FAX 39-081-7206244, liguori@liguori.it, http://www.liguori.it. Ed. Sebastiano Maffettone.

100 900 300 ITA ISSN 2036-9212
FILOSOFIA, STORIA, SCIENZE SOCIALI. Text in Italian. 2005. irreg. **Document type:** *Monographic series, Academic/Scholarly.*
Published by: (Universita degli Studi di Siena, Facolta di Lettere e Filosofia), Franco Angeli Edizioni, Viale Monza 106, Milan, 20127, Italy. TEL 39-02-2837141, FAX 39-02-26144793, redazioni@francoangeli.it, http://www.francoangeli.it.

100 340 ARG ISSN 1851-5886
FILOSOFIA Y DERECHO. Text in Spanish. 1973. a. **Document type:** *Monographic series, Academic/Scholarly.*
Published by: Editorial Astrea, IA vALLE 1208, Buenos Aires, C1048AAF, Argentina. http://www.astrea.com.ar/.

100 CZE ISSN 0015-1831
B8.C9
➤ **FILOSOFICKY CASOPIS/PHILOSOPHICAL REVIEW.** Text in Czech; Summaries in Multiple languages; Contents page in English, French, German, Russian. 1953. bi-m. CZK 295 domestic; CZK 59 per issue domestic (effective 2008). adv. bk.rev. bibl. index. reprints avail. **Document type:** *Journal, Academic/Scholarly.* **Description:** Examines all aspects of contemporary philosophy as well as the history of philosophy.
Indexed: A20, ASCA, ArtHuCI, BibLing, CurCont, FR, IBR, IBZ, PCI, PhilInd, RASB, SCOPUS, W07.
—INIST.
Published by: Akademie Ved Ceske Republiky, Filozoficky Ustav/Czech Academy of Sciences, Institute of Philosophy, Jilska 1, Prague 1, 110 00, Czech Republic. TEL 420-222-220099, FAX 420-222-220108, filosofia@flu.cas.cz. Ed. Petr Horak. Adv. contact Olga Baranova. Circ: 1,500. **Dist. by:** Kubon & Sagner Buchexport - Import GmbH, Hessstr 39-41, Munich 80798, Germany. TEL 49-89-542180, FAX 49-89-54218218, postmaster@kubon-sagner.de, http://www.kubon-sagner.de.

100 NLD ISSN 0925-9449
FILOSOFIE. Text in Dutch. 1991. bi-m. EUR 28 domestic; EUR 34.50 foreign; EUR 6.25 newsstand/cover (effective 2008). **Document type:** *Magazine, Trade.*
Published by: (Stichting Informatie Filosofie), Uitgeverij Damon, Postbus 2014, Budel, 6020 AA, Netherlands. TEL 31-495-499319, FAX 31-495-499889, info@damon.nl, http://www.damon.nl. Ed. Harry Willemsen.

100 NLD ISSN 0167-2444
FILOSOFIE & PRAKTIJK. Text in Dutch. 1916. 5/yr. EUR 32 domestic; EUR 37 in Belgium; EUR 8.50 newsstand/cover (effective 2008). bk.rev. bibl. **Document type:** *Academic/Scholarly.*
Formerly (until 1980): Amersfoortse Stemmen (0003-1666); Supersedes: Mens en Kosmos
Indexed: IPB.
—IE, Infotrieve.
Published by: (Internationale School voor Wijsbegeerte), Uitgeverij Damon, Postbus 2014, Budel, 6020 AA, Netherlands. TEL 31-495-499319, FAX 31-495-499889, info@damon.nl, http://www.damon.nl. Ed. Ton Vink.

101 NLD ISSN 0928-1789
B8.D8
FILOSOFIE MAGAZINE. Text in Dutch. 1992. 10/yr. EUR 69.50; EUR 7.25 newsstand/cover (effective 2009). adv. bk.rev. illus. back issues avail. **Document type:** *Journal, Academic/Scholarly.* **Description:** Reviews 25 centuries of philosophy in both contemporary and historical contexts.
Related titles: Audio cassette/tape ed.
Published by: Veen Magazines, Postbus 256, Diemen, 1110 AG, Netherlands. TEL 31-20-5310900, FAX 31-20-5310950, http://www.veenmagazines.nl. Ed. Daan Roovers. Pub. Erno Eskens. adv.: B&W page EUR 1,550, color page EUR 2,585; trim 210 x 280. Circ: 18,583.

301.01 LTU ISSN 0235-7186
B8.L6
➤ **FILOSOFIJA, SOCIOLOGIJA.** Text in Lithuanian; Summaries in English. 1955. q. USD 160 foreign (effective 2011). adv. **Document type:** *Journal, Academic/Scholarly.*
Related titles: Online - full text ed.
Indexed: A20, ArtHuCI, CA, PhilInd, S02, S03, SCOPUS, SSCI, SociolAb, T02, W07.
Published by: (Lietuvos Mokslu Akademija/Lithuanian Academy of Sciences, Lietuvos Kulturos Tyrimu Institutas/Lithuanian Culture Research Institute), Lietuvos Mokslu Akademijos Leidykla/Lithuanian Academy of Sciences Publishers, Gedimino pr 3, Vilnius, 2600, Lithuania. TEL 370-2-2626851, FAX 370-2-2613620, leidykla@lma.lt. Ed. Arvydas Matulionis. Circ: 520. **Dist. by:** East View Information Services, 10601 Wayzata Blvd, Minneapolis, MN 55305. TEL 952-252-1201, FAX 952-252-1202, info@eastview.com, http://www.eastview.com.

198 SWE ISSN 0348-7482
B8.S93
FILOSOFISK TIDSKRIFT. Text in Swedish. 1980. q. SEK 200 domestic; SEK 300 elsewhere; SEK 55 per issue (effective 2010). adv. bk.rev. back issues avail. **Document type:** *Journal, Academic/Scholarly.*
Indexed: PCI.
Published by: (Stiftelsen Bokfoerlaget Thales), Thales (Subsidiary of: Stiftelsen Bokfoerlaget Thales), PO Box 50034, Stockholm, 10405, Sweden. TEL 46-8-7596410, info@bokforlagetthales.se, http://www.bokforlagetthales.se. Ed. Lars Bergstroem. **Subscr. to:** Filosofisk Tidskrift.

100 DNK ISSN 0106-0449
➤ **FILOSOFISKE STUDIER.** Text in Multiple languages. 1978. irreg., latest vol.24, 2008. **Document type:** *Monographic series, Academic/Scholarly.*
Related titles: Online - full text ed.: 1995.
Published by: Koebenhavns Universitet, Institut for Medier, Erkendelse og Formidling/Copenhagen University, Department of Media, Cognition and Communication, Njalsgade 80, Copenhagen S, 2300, Denmark. TEL 45-35-328100, FAX 45-35-328850, mef@hum.ku.dk, http://www.filosofi.ku.dk. Eds. Finn Collin, Jan Riis Flor. Circ: 600.

100 RUS
FILOSOFIYA I OBSHCHESTVO. Text in Russian. bi-m. USD 95 in United States.
Address: Smolenskii bulv 20, Moscow, 121002, Russian Federation. TEL 7-095-2015686. Ed. I A Gobozov. **Dist. by:** East View Information Services, 10601 Wayzata Blvd, Minneapolis, MN 55305. TEL 952-252-1201, 800-477-1005, FAX 952-252-1202, info@eastview.com, http://www.eastview.com.

215 RUS ISSN 1560-7488
Q174
➤ **FILOSOFIYA NAUKI/PHILOSOPHY OF SCIENCE.** Text in Russian; Summaries in English. 1995. s-a. RUR 170 per issue domestic; USD 80 foreign (effective 2005). bk.rev. abstr.; bibl.; illus. **Document type:** *Journal, Academic/Scholarly.* **Description:** Includes papers on philosophy, methodology, and logic; extracts from archives.
Published by: (Rossiiskaya Akademiya Nauk, Sibirskoe Otdelenie, Institut Filosofii i Prava/Russian Academy of Sciences, Siberian Branch, Institute of Philosophy and Law), Izdatel'stvo Sibirskogo Otdeleniya Rossiiskoi Akademii Nauk/Publishing House of the Russian Academy of Sciences, Siberian Branch, Morskoi pr 2, a/ya 187, Novosibirsk, 630090, Russian Federation. TEL 7-3832-300570, FAX 7-3832-333755, psb@ad-sbras.nsc.ru. Ed. A P Simanov. Circ: 300 (paid). **Dist. by:** M K - Periodica, ul Gilyarovskogo 39, Moscow 129110, Russian Federation. TEL 7-095-2845008, FAX 7-095-2813798, info@periodicals.ru, http://www.mkniga.ru.

100 RUS ISSN 0869-611X
FILOSOFKIE ISSLEDOVANIYA. Text in Russian. s-a. USD 119.95 in United States.
Related titles: Online - full text ed.
Indexed: RASB.
—BLDSC (0391.325000), East View.
Published by: Moskovskii Filosofskii Fond, Smolenskii bulv 20, Moscow, 121002, Russian Federation. TEL 7-095-2015004. **Dist. by:** East View Information Services, 10601 Wayzata Blvd, Minneapolis, MN 55305. TEL 952-252-1201, 800-477-1005, FAX 952-252-1202, info@eastview.com, http://www.eastview.com.

100 UKR ISSN 0235-7941
B6
FILOSOFS'KA DUMKA/PHILOSOPHICAL THOUGHT; naukovo-teoretychnyi chasopys. Text in Ukrainian; Summaries in English. 1927. bi-m. USD 234 foreign (effective 2011). bibl. **Document type:** *Journal, Academic/Scholarly.*
Former titles: Filosofs'ka i Sotsiolohichna Dumka (1015-2229); (until 1989): Filosofs'ka Dumka (0130-5719)
Related titles: Microfiche ed.: (from EVP).
Indexed: FR, MLA, MLA-IB, RASB.
—East View.
Published by: (Natsional'na Akademiya Nauk Ukrainy, Instytut Filosofii imeni H.H. Skovorody), Natsional'na Akademiya Nauk Ukrainy, 54 Volodymyrska St, Kyiv, 01601, Ukraine. TEL 380-44-234 5167, FAX 380-44-2343243, prez@nas.gov.ua, http://www.nas.gov.ua. Ed. Myroslav Popovych. **Dist. by:** East View Information Services, 10601 Wayzata Blvd, Minneapolis, MN 55305. TEL 952-252-1201, 800-477-1005, FAX 952-252-1202, info@eastview.com, http://www.eastview.com.

100 RUS ISSN 0235-1188
B6
FILOSOFSKIE NAUKI (MOSCOW). Text in Russian. 1958. q. USD 85. bk.rev. bibl.; charts; illus.; stat.
Formerly (until 1987): Nauchnye Doklady Vysshei Shkoly (0130-9749)
Indexed: FR, RASB, RefZh, SOPODA.
—BLDSC (0391.332000), East View, INIST.
Published by: Izdatel'stvo Gumanitarii, Leninskii pr-t 6, k 301, Moscow, 117933, Russian Federation. TEL 7-095-2369707, FAX 7-095-2368402. Ed. V M Silin. Circ: 6,260. **Dist. by:** East View Information Services, 10601 Wayzata Blvd, Minneapolis, MN 55305. TEL 952-252-1201, 800-477-1005, FAX 952-252-1202, info@eastview.com, http://www.eastview.com.

100 SVK ISSN 0046-385X
B6
➤ **FILOZOFIA/PHILOSOPHY.** Text in Slovak; Summaries in English. 1946. 10/yr. EUR 98.50 in Europe; EUR 120 elsewhere (effective 2011). bk.rev. abstr.; bibl. 70 p./no. 2 cols./p.; back issues avail. **Document type:** *Journal, Academic/Scholarly.* **Description:** Offers original papers and articles from various spheres of philosophic creation.
Indexed: A20, AmHI, ArtHuCI, BibLing, CA, CurCont, DIP, FR, H07, IBR, IBZ, P42, PCI, PSA, PhilInd, RASB, SCOPUS, SOPODA, SociolAb, T02, W07.
Published by: (Slovenska Akademia Vied, Filozoficky Ustav/Slovak Academy of Scinces, Institute of Philosophy), Slovak Academic Press Ltd., Nam Slobody 6, PO Box 57, Bratislava, 81005, Slovakia. TEL 421-2-55421729, sap@sappress.sk, http://www.sappress.sk. Ed. Frantisek Novosad. Circ: 450 (paid). **Dist. by:** Slovart G.T.G. s.r.o., Krupinska 4, PO Box 152, Bratislava 85299, Slovakia. TEL 421-2-63839472, FAX 421-2-63839485, info@slovart-gtg.sk, http://www.slovart-gtg.sk.

100 POL ISSN 1230-6894
FILOZOFIA NAUKI. Text in Polish. 1993. q. EUR 67 foreign (effective 2006). **Document type:** *Journal, Academic/Scholarly.*
Indexed: ArtHuCI, CurCont, W07.
Published by: Uniwersytet Warszawski, Instytut Filozofii/Warsaw University, Institute of Philosophy, Krakowskie Przedmiescie 3, Warsaw, 00047, Poland. TEL 48-22-5523705, FAX 48-22-8265734. **Dist. by:** Ars Polona, Obroncow 25, Warsaw 03933, Poland. TEL 48-22-5098609, FAX 48-22-5098610, arspolona@arspolona.com.pl, http://www.arspolona.com.pl.

100 320 SRB
FILOZOFIJA I DRUSTVO. Text in English, Serbian. 1987. 3/yr. **Document type:** *Journal, Academic/Scholarly.*
Related titles: Online - full text ed.: free (effective 2011).
Published by: Institut za Filozofiju i Drustvenu Teoriju Beograd/Institute for Philosophy and Social Theory, Kraljice Natalije 45, Belgrade, 11000. Ed. Predrag Milidrag.

100 HRV ISSN 0351-4706
B6
➤ **FILOZOFSKA ISTRAZIVANJA.** Text in Croatian; Summaries in Croatian, English, German. 1980. q. HRK 150 domestic to individuals; EUR 22 foreign to individuals; HRK 200 domestic to institutions; EUR 30 foreign to institutions (effective 2008). bk.rev. abstr.; bibl.; illus. Index. back issues avail.; reprints avail. **Document type:** *Journal, Academic/Scholarly.* **Description:** Covers current philosophical issues and debates with a wide audience among scholars and students in Croatia and abroad.
Related titles: Online - full text ed.: free (effective 2011); ◆ English ed.: Synthesis Philosophica. ISSN 0352-7875.
Indexed: A20, ArtHuCI, PhilInd, RILM, SCOPUS, W07.
Published by: Hratsko Filozofsko Drustvo/Croatian Philosophical Society, Krcka 1, Zagreb, 10000, Croatia. TEL 385-1-6111808, FAX 385-1-6170682, filozofska-istrazivanja@zg.t-com.hr, http://www.hrfd.hr. Ed., R&P Ante Covic. Pub. Pavo Barisic. Circ: 1,400 (paid).

➤ **FILOZOFSKI FAKULTET - ZADAR. RAZDIO FILOZOFIJE, PSIHOLOGIJE, SOCIOLOGIJE I PEDAGOGIJE. RADOVI.** *see* EDUCATION

100 SVN ISSN 0353-4510
HX8 CODEN: FIVEFV
➤ **FILOZOFSKI VESTNIK/ACTA PHILOSOPHICA.** Text in English, French, German, Slovenian; Summaries in English, French, German. 1980. 3/yr. EUR 20.40 to individuals; EUR 40.80 to institutions (effective 2007). adv. bk.rev. 220 p./no. 1 cols./p.; back issues avail. **Document type:** *Journal, Academic/Scholarly.* **Description:** Provides a forum for discussion of a wide range of issues in contemporary political and social philosophy, history of philosophy, philosophy of law, epistemology and philosophy of science, ethics, aesthetics and cultural critique.
Formerly: Institut za Marksisticne Studije. Vestnik (0351-6881)
Related titles: Online - full text ed.: ISSN 1581-1239. free (effective 2011).
Indexed: A20, A22, ASCA, AmHI, ArtHuCI, CA, CurCont, DIP, FR, H07, IBR, IBZ, IPB, P42, PSA, PhilInd, RASB, RILM, S02, S03, SCOPUS, SOPODA, SociolAb, T02, W07.
—BLDSC (0593.900000), Ingenta, INIST.
Published by: (Slovenska Akademija Znanosti in Umetnosti, Znanstvenoraziskovalni Center, Filozofski Institut/Slovene Academy of Sciences, Scientific Research Center, Institute of Philosophy), Zalozba Z R C/Scientific Research Centre Publishing, Novi trg 2, PO Box 306, Ljubljana, 1001, Slovenia. TEL 386-1-4706474, FAX 386-1-4257794, likar@zrc-sazu.si, zalozba@zrc-sazu.si, http://www.zrc-sazu.si/zalozba. Ed. Peter Klepek. Circ: 800.

➤ **FINANCE ET BIEN COMMUN/FINANCE AND COMMON GOOD.** *see* BUSINESS AND ECONOMICS—Banking And Finance

➤ **FLORENSIA.** *see* RELIGIONS AND THEOLOGY

100 USA ISSN 1535-3656
B1
FLORIDA PHILOSOPHICAL REVIEW. Text in English. 2001. s-a. free (effective 2011).
Media: Online - full text.
Indexed: A39, C27, C29, D03, D04, E13, PhilInd, R14, S14, S15, S18.
Published by: University of Central Florida, Department of Philosophy, Colbourn Hall 4117, Orlando, FL 32816-1352. TEL 407-823-2273, fpr@mail.ucf.edu. Ed. Shelley M. Park.

100 CHE ISSN 1661-5719
BD450
➤ **FLUSSER STUDIES.** Text in Multiple languages. 2005. s-a. free (effective 2011). **Document type:** *Journal, Academic/Scholarly.* **Description:** Seeks to promote scholarship on different aspects of specifically interdisciplinary and multilingual approaches Flusser himself developed in the course of his career as a writer and philosopher.
Media: Online - full text.

Indexed: AmHI, CA, H07, T02. Ed. Rainer Guldin.

105 938 GRC ISSN 1105-221X
FONDATION DE RECHERCHE ET D'EDITIONS DE PHILOSOPHIE NEOHELLENIQUE. SERIE RECHERCHES; Corpus Philosophorum Graecorum Recentiorum. Abbreviated title: Foundation de Recherche et d'Editions de Philosophie Neohellenique(C P G R). Text in French, Greek. 1980. irreg., latest 2001. EUR 30 (effective 2003). 300 p./no.; **Document type:** *Monographic series, Academic/Scholarly.* **Description:** Explores the legacy of Platonic and Aristotelian thought in modern Greek history.
Published by: (Hellenic Society for Philosophical Studies/Societe Hellenique d'Etudes Philosophiques), Evanghelos A. Moutsopoulos Ed. & Pub., 40 Hypsilantou St, Athens, 115 21, Greece. TEL 30-10-725-1212, FAX 30-10-722-7322. Ed. A Stavelas. Pub., R&P Evanghelos A Moutsopoulos.

FONDAZIONE LUIGI FIRPO. STUDI E TESTI. *see* POLITICAL SCIENCE

100 DEU ISSN 1430-9998
FORSCHUNGEN ZUM JUNGHEGELIANISMUS; Quellenkunde, Umkreisforschung, Theorie, Wirkungsgeschichte. Text in German. 1996. irreg., latest vol.17, 2009. price varies. **Document type:** *Monographic series, Academic/Scholarly.*
Published by: Peter Lang GmbH (Subsidiary of: Peter Lang Publishing Group), Eschborner Landstr 42-50, Frankfurt Am Main, 60489, Germany. TEL 49-69-7807050, FAX 49-69-78070550, zentrale.frankfurt@peterlang.com. Eds. Konrad Feilchenfeldt, Lars Lambrecht.

100 001.3 DEU ISSN 0933-6990
FORUM FUER INTERDISZIPLINAERE FORSCHUNG. Text in English, German. 1988. irreg., latest vol.22, 2007. price varies. **Document type:** *Monographic series, Academic/Scholarly.*
Published by: J.H. Roell, Wuerzburgerstr 16, Dettelbach, 97337, Germany. TEL 49-9324-99770, FAX 49-9324-99771, info@roell-verlag.de.

170 DEU ISSN 0937-3861
FORUM INTERDISZIPLINAERE ETHIK. Text in German. 1991. irreg., latest vol.31, 2008. price varies. **Document type:** *Monographic series, Academic/Scholarly.*
Published by: Peter Lang GmbH (Subsidiary of: Peter Lang Publishing Group), Eschborner Landstr 42-50, Frankfurt Am Main, 60489, Germany. TEL 49-69-7807050, FAX 49-69-78070550, zentrale.frankfurt@peterlang.com. Ed. Gerfried Hunold.

100 POL ISSN 1426-1898
B1
FORUM PHILOSOPHICUM. Text in Polish. 1996. a. USD 10 per issue (effective 2003). **Document type:** *Academic/Scholarly.*
Related titles: Online - full content ed.; Online - full text ed.
Indexed: A01, A03, A08, CA, IBR, IBZ, PhilInd, T02.
Published by: Wyzsza Szkola Filozoficzno-Pedagogiczna "Ignatianum", Wydzial Filozof/School of Philosophy and of Education "Ignatianum," Faculty of Philosophy, ul. Kopernika 26, Krakow, 31-501, Poland. TEL 48-12-4294416, FAX 48-12-4295019, filozofia@jezuici.krakow.pl, http://www.ignatianum.edu.pl/filozofia/.

FORUM TEOLOGICZNE. *see* RELIGIONS AND THEOLOGY

100 USA
FORUM TODAY. Text in English. 3/yr. USD 10. adv. illus.
Published by: New Forum, 4176 Greystone, Yorba Linda, CA 92686. Ed. Judith A Christie.

FORUM WIRTSCHAFTSETHIK. *see* BUSINESS AND ECONOMICS

100 AUS ISSN 1832-5203
B2430.F724
➤ **FOUCAULT STUDIES.** Text in English; Text occasionally in French. 2004. s-a. free (effective 2011). bk.rev. **Document type:** *Journal, Academic/Scholarly.* **Description:** Ppublishes work about and inspired by the French philosopher Michel Foucault's work as well as new translations of Foucault's work and reviews of books relating to Foucault.
Media: Online - full text.
Indexed: A39, AmHI, C27, C29, CA, D03, D04, E13, H07, MLA-IB, R14, S02, S03, S14, S15, S18, T02.
Published by: Queensland University of Technology, GPO 2434, Brisbane, QLD 4001, Australia. TEL 61-7-38642111, qutinformation@qut.edu.au.

➤ **FOUNDATIONS OF SCIENCE.** *see* SCIENCES: COMPREHENSIVE WORKS

100 ESP ISSN 1132-3329
FRAGMENTOS DE FILOSOFIA. Variant title: Revista de Fragmentos de Filosofia. Text in Spanish. 1992. irreg., latest vol.4, 1994. **Document type:** *Journal, Academic/Scholarly.*
Related titles: Online - full text ed.
Published by: Universidad de Sevilla, Secretariado de Publicaciones, Calle Porvenir 27, Sevilla, 41013, Spain. TEL 34-95-4487444, FAX 34-95-4487443, secpub10@us.es, http://www.us.es/publius/inicio.html.

100 GBR ISSN 0262-8228
FRANCIS BACON RESEARCH TRUST. JOURNAL; studies in ancient wisdom. Text in English. 1981. irreg. looseleaf. back issues avail. **Document type:** *Journal, Academic/Scholarly.* **Description:** Membership newsletter which discusses Francis Bacon's life, work, and teachings, and their relevance for us today.
Related titles: Online - full text ed.
Published by: Francis Bacon Research Trust, Roses Farm House, Epwell Rd, Upper Tysoe, Warks CV35 0TN, United Kingdom. TEL 44-1295-688185, FAX 44-1295-680770, secretary@fbrt.org.uk, secretary@fbrt.org.uk, http://www.fbrt.org.uk.

255.3 COL ISSN 0120-1468
BR7
FRANCISCANUM; revista de las ciencias del espiritu. Text in Spanish. 1959. 3/yr. COP 9,500, USD 29 (effective 1998). adv. bk.rev. bibl. index, cum.index: 1959-1983. **Document type:** *Monographic series, Academic/Scholarly.* **Description:** Interdisciplinary studies of religion and philosophy.
Indexed: CPL, FR, IPB, OTA, PhilInd, RASB.
—INIST.
Published by: Universidad de San Buenaventura, Bogota, Transversal 26 #172, Bogota, DC 08, Colombia. FAX 57-1-677-3003, http://www.usbbog.edu.co. Ed. Fr Fernando Garzon Ramirez. Pub. Fr. Miguel Angel Builes Uribe. R&P Betty Fernandez. Circ: 3,000.

100 DEU ISSN 0943-4666
B3199.A34
FRANKFURTER ADORNO BLAETTER. Text in German. 1992. irreg., latest vol.8, 2003. price varies. **Document type:** *Monographic series, Academic/Scholarly.*
Indexed: IPB.
Published by: (Theodor-W.-Adorno-Archiv), Edition Text und Kritik in Richard Boorberg Verlag GmbH & Co. KG (Subsidiary of: Richard Boorberg Verlag GmbH und Co. KG), Levelingstr 6A, Munich, 81673, Germany. TEL 49-89-43600012, FAX 49-89-43600019, info@etk-muenchen.de, http://www.etk-muenchen.de. Ed. Rolf Tiedemann.

100 DEU ISSN 1431-1119
B3240.F584
FRANZ-FISCHER-JAHRBUECHER. Variant title: Franz-Fischer-Jahrbuch fuer Philosophie und Paedagogik. Text in German. 1986. a. EUR 24 (effective 2011). **Document type:** *Journal, Academic/Scholarly.*
Formerly (until 1996): Norderstedter Hefte fuer Philosophie und Paedagogik (0937-5627)
Published by: Leipziger Universitaetsverlag GmbH, Oststr 41, Leipzig, 04317, Germany. TEL 49-341-9900440, FAX 49-341-9900440, info@univerlag-leipzig.de.

100 401 800 ITA ISSN 2037-5069
▼ **LA FRECCIA E IL CERCHIO.** Text in Italian, English. 2010. a. **Document type:** *Journal, Academic/Scholarly.*
Published by: (Istituto Italiano per gli Studi Filosofici (I I S F)), La Scuola di Pitagora Editrice, Piazza Santa Maria degli Angeli 1, Naples, 80132, Italy. info@scuoladipitagora.it, http://www.scuoladipitagora.it.

100 USA ISSN 0272-0701
BL2700 CODEN: FRINFM
FREE INQUIRY. Abbreviated title: F I. Text in English. 1980. q. USD 31.50; USD 6.95 per issue (effective 2010). adv. bk.rev.; film rev. illus. cum.index: 1980-1995. back issues avail.; reprints avail. **Document type:** *Magazine, Consumer.* **Description:** Deals with the separation of Church and State and secular humanism. Articles on religion, ethics and moral thought from a secular humanist viewpoint.
Related titles: Microform ed.: (from PQC); Online - full text ed.; ♦ Supplement(s): Secular Humanist Bulletin. ISSN 1063-2611.
Indexed: A01, A02, A03, A08, A22, A26, CA, CCR, CLFP, DIP, E08, FR, G08, H14, I05, I07, IBR, IBZ, LeftInd, MLA-IB, P02, P10, P30, P34, P48, P53, P54, PAIS, PQC, PhilInd, R05, R10, RASB, Reac, S02, S03, S09, S23, SCOPUS, T02.
—BLDSC (4033.321930), IE, Infotrieve, Ingenta, INIST.
Published by: Council for Secular Humanism, 3965 Rensch Rd, Amherst, NY 14228. TEL 716-636-7571, FAX 716-636-1733, info@secularhumanism.org. Eds. Thomas W Flynn, Paul Kurtz. **Subscr. to:** PO Box 664, Amherst, NY 14226.

144 USA
FREE MIND. Text in English. 19??. q. free to members (effective 2010). back issues avail. **Document type:** *Newsletter, Trade.* **Description:** Features articles contain ideas for activism, news of developments, and opinion. Covers information which is published on AHA initiatives, forthcoming conferences and other events, and the profile work of Humanists.
Published by: American Humanist Association, 1777 T St, NW, Washington, DC 20009. TEL 202-238-9088, 800-837-3792, FAX 202-238-9003, aha@americanhumanist.org, http://www.americanhumanist.org/index.html. Ed. Maggie Ardiente.

100 USA
FREE SPIRIT (BROOKLYN); a directory and journal of new realities. Text in English. bi-m. USD 18. **Description:** Presents articles that illustrate the interconnection and interdependence of all things.
Published by: Paul English, Ed. & Pub., 107 Sterling Place, Brooklyn, NY 11217. TEL 718-638-3733, FAX 718-230-3459.

100 GBR ISSN 0016-0687
THE FREETHINKER; the voice of atheism since 1881. Text in English. 1881. m. GBP 15 domestic; GBP 18 foreign (effective 2009). adv. bk.rev. back issues avail. **Document type:** *Journal, Academic/Scholarly.* **Description:** Devoted to topics of interest to humanists and secularists.
Related titles: Microform ed.; Online - full text ed.: free (effective 2009).
Indexed: RASB.
Published by: G W Foote and Company Limited, PO Box 234, Brighton, BN1 4XD, United Kingdom. Ed. Barry Duke.

100 CAN ISSN 1912-7510
THE FREETHINKER'S PRESS. Text in English. 2005. irreg. **Document type:** *Newsletter, Consumer.*
Published by: Toronto Secular Alliance, c/o Canadian Freethought Centre, 216 Beverley St., Toronto, ON M5T 1Z3, Canada. TEL 416-971-5676, into@secularalliance.ca, http://secular.sa.utoronto.ca. Ed. Zachary Fiddes.

100 200 USA ISSN 0882-8512
BL2700
FREETHOUGHT TODAY. Text in English. 1983. 10/yr. USD 20 domestic (effective 2005); USD 27.50 in Canada & Mexico; USD 35 elsewhere (effective 2000). adv. **Document type:** *Newspaper.* **Description:** Chronicles freethought activism, critiques religion and monitors state-church separation.
Related titles: Online - full text ed.
Indexed: APW, AltPI.
Published by: Freedom from Religion Foundation, PO Box 750, Madison, WI 53701. TEL 608-256-8900, FAX 608-256-1116. Ed., R&P Annie Laurie Gaylor. Circ: 3,800 (paid); 400 (controlled).

200 CHE
FREIBURGER MEDIAEVISTISCHE VORTRAEGE. Text in German. 2008. irreg., latest vol.2, 2009. price varies. **Document type:** *Monographic series, Academic/Scholarly.*
Published by: Schwabe und Co. AG, Steinentorstr 13, Basel, 4010, Switzerland. TEL 41-61-2789565, FAX 41-61-2789566, verlag@schwabe.ch, http://www.schwabe.ch.

FREIBURGER ZEITSCHRIFT FUER PHILOSOPHIE UND THEOLOGIE. *see* RELIGIONS AND THEOLOGY—Roman Catholic

100 DEU ISSN 0067-5911
FREIE UNIVERSITAET BERLIN. OSTEUROPA-INSTITUT. PHILOSOPHISCHE UND SOZIOLOGISCHE VEROEFFENTLICHUNGEN. Text in German. 1959. irreg., latest vol.30, 2000. price varies. **Document type:** *Monographic series, Academic/Scholarly.*
Published by: (Freie Universitaet Berlin, Osteuropa-Institut, Freie Universitaet Berlin), Harrassowitz Verlag, Kreuzberger Ring 7b-d, Wiesbaden, 65205, Germany. TEL 49-611-5300, FAX 49-611-530560, verlag@harrassowitz.de, http://www.harrassowitz.de. Eds. Hans Joachim Lieber, Rene Ahlberg. R&P Michael Langfeld. Adv. contact Robert Gietz. Circ: 500.

111.85 DEU
FROMMANN-HOLZBOOG AESTHETIK. Text in German. 2000. irreg., latest vol.3, 2005. price varies. **Document type:** *Monographic series, Academic/Scholarly.*
Published by: Frommann-Holzboog Verlag e.K., Koenig-Karl-Str 27, Stuttgart, 70372, Germany. TEL 49-711-9559690, FAX 49-711-9559691, info@frommann-holzboog.de, http://www.frommann-holzboog.de.

100 DEU
FROMMANN-HOLZBOOG STUDIENTEXTE. Text in German. 2000. irreg., latest vol.8, 2006. price varies. **Document type:** *Monographic series, Academic/Scholarly.*
Published by: Frommann-Holzboog Verlag e.K., Koenig-Karl-Str 27, Stuttgart, 70372, Germany. TEL 49-711-9559690, FAX 49-711-9559691, info@frommann-holzboog.de, http://www.frommann-holzboog.de.

100 340 VEN ISSN 1315-6268
K6
➤ **FRONESIS**; revista de filosofia juridica, social y politica. Text in Spanish; Abstracts in English, Spanish. 1994. 3/yr. USD 30 in Latin America; USD 40 in US & Canada; USD 50 in Europe (effective 2009). cum.index. **Document type:** *Journal, Academic/Scholarly.* **Description:** Dedicated to publishing research works related to legal, political, and social philosophy.
Indexed: A26, AmHI, ESPM, F04, H07, I04, I05, PhilInd, RiskAb, T02.
Published by: Instituto de Filosofia del Derecho, Facultad de Ciencias Juridicas y Politicas, Nucleo Humanistico de la Universidad del Zulia, Sector Ziruma, Maracaibo, 4011, Venezuela. TEL 58-61-596637, FAX 58-61-596657, abozoa@cantv.net. Ed. Elida Aponte Sanchez. Circ: 1,000. **Co-sponsor:** Scientific and Humanisitic Development Council.

➤ **FRONTIERS OF BUSINESS ETHICS.** *see* BUSINESS AND ECONOMICS

100 CHN ISSN 1673-3436
FRONTIERS OF PHILOSOPHY IN CHINA; selected publications from Chinese universities. Text in English. 2006. q. EUR 628, USD 879 to institutions; EUR 685, USD 959 combined subscription to institutions (print & online eds.) (effective 2012). reprint service avail. from PSC. **Document type:** *Journal, Academic/Scholarly.*
Related titles: Online - full text ed.: ISSN 1673-355X. EUR 571, USD 799 to institutions (effective 2012).
Indexed: A22, A26, AmHI, BRD, CA, E01, H07, H08, HAb, HumInd, P10, P27, P28, P48, P53, P54, PQC, PhilInd, SCOPUS, T02, W03, W05.
—BLDSC (4042.046800), IE, Ingenta. **CCC.**
Published by: Gaodeng Jiaoyu Chubanshe/Higher Education Press, 4 Dewai Dajie, Beijing, 100011, China. TEL 86-10-58581863, FAX 86-10-82085552, info@hep.com.cn, http://www.hep.edu.cn/. Ed. Guiren Yuan. **Co-publisher:** Brill.

100 GBR
THE FRONTIERS OF THEORY. Text in English. irreg. price varies. **Document type:** *Journal, Academic/Scholarly.*
Published by: Edinburgh University Press, 22 George Sq, Edinburgh, Scotland EH8 9LF, United Kingdom. TEL 44-131-6504218, FAX 44-131-6503286, journals@eup.ed.ac.uk. Ed. Martin McQuillan.

FUJIAN NONG-LIN DAXUE XUEBAO (ZHEXUE SHEHUI KEXUE BAN)/FUJIAN AGRICULTURE AND FORESTRY UNIVERSITY. JOURNAL (PHILOSOPHY AND SOCIAL SCIENCES). *see* SOCIAL SCIENCES: COMPREHENSIVE WORKS

100 943 DEU
G.W. LEIBNIZ: SAEMTLICHE SCHRIFTEN UND BRIEFE. Text in English, French, German, Latin. 1950. irreg., latest vol.20, 2006. price varies. **Document type:** *Monographic series, Academic/Scholarly.* **Description:** Complete collection of Leibniz's work and correspondence.
Published by: Akademie Verlag GmbH (Subsidiary of: Oldenbourg Wissenschaftsverlag GmbH), Markgrafenstr 12-14, Berlin, 10969, Germany. TEL 49-30-4220060, FAX 49-30-42200657, info@akademie-verlag.de, http://www.akademie-verlag.de.

GEDRAAG JE!. *see* SOCIOLOGY

121 NLD ISSN 1876-1526
GEERT GROTE REEKS VOOR KRITISCHE SPIRITUALITEIT. Text in Dutch. 2008. irreg. **Document type:** *Monographic series, Academic/Scholarly.*
Published by: (Geert Grote Universiteit), Deventer Universitaire Pers, Sandrasteeg 8, Deventer, 7411 KS, Netherlands. TEL 31-570-613663, info@deventeruniversitairepers.nl.

519 DEU ISSN 1612-7919
GEIST, ERKENNTNIS, KOMMUNIKATION. Text in German. 1998. irreg. price varies. **Document type:** *Monographic series, Academic/Scholarly.*
Published by: Mentis Verlag GmbH, Schulze-Delitzsch-Str 19, Paderborn, 33100, Germany. TEL 49-5251-687902, FAX 49-5251-687905, webmaster@mentis.de, http://www.mentis.de.

LE GENRE HUMAN. *see* HUMANITIES: COMPREHENSIVE WORKS

GEORGETOWN JOURNAL OF LEGAL ETHICS. *see* LAW

GERMANISTISCHE BEITRAEGE. *see* HUMANITIES: COMPREHENSIVE WORKS

GESCHICHTE UND PHILOSOPHIE DER MEDIZIN. *see* MEDICAL SCIENCES

170 200 CHE ISSN 1422-2264
GESELLSCHAFT UND ETHIK. Text in German. 1964. irreg. price varies. **Document type:** *Monographic series, Academic/Scholarly.*
Formerly (until 1989): Universitaet Zuerich. Institut fuer Sozialethik. Veroeffentlichungen (0084-5787)
Published by: Universitaet Zuerich, Institut fuer Sozialethik, Zollikerstr 117, Zurich, 8008, Switzerland. TEL 41-44-6348511, FAX 41-44-6348507, akoch@sozethik.uzh.ch, http://www.ethik.uzh.ch/ise.html.

GESHER. *see* RELIGIONS AND THEOLOGY—Judaic

GILBERT LAW SUMMARIES. LEGAL ETHICS. *see* LAW

P

144 NLD
GILSON STUDIES. Text in English. irreg. price varies. **Document type:** *Monographic series, Academic/Scholarly.* **Description:** Aims to foster a greater appreciation of the philosophical and Thomistic realism that was part of Gilson's method of philosophizing.
Related titles: ◆ Series of: Value Inquiry Book Series. ISSN 0929-8436.
Published by: Editions Rodopi B.V., Tijnmuiden 7, Amsterdam, 1046 AK, Netherlands. TEL 31-20-6114821, FAX 31-20-4472979, info@rodopi.nl. Ed. Peter A Redpath. **Dist. by:** Rodopi - USA, 606 Newark Ave, 2nd fl, Kenilworth, NJ 07033. TEL 908-497-9031, FAX 908-497-9035.

100 ITA ISSN 0017-0089
B4
GIORNALE CRITICO DELLA FILOSOFIA ITALIANA. Text in English, French, Italian. 1920. 3/yr. EUR 83 domestic; EUR 99 foreign (effective 2008). bk.rev. bibl. index. **Document type:** *Journal, Academic/Scholarly.*
Indexed: A20, A22, ASCA, ArtHuCI, CurCont, DIP, FR, IBR, IBZ, IPB, MLA, MLA-IB, P30, PCI, PhilInd, RASB, SCOPUS, W07.
—BLDSC (4177.600000), IE, Infotrieve, INIST.
Published by: Casa Editrice Le Lettere, Piazza dei Nerli 8, Florence, FI 50124, Italy. TEL 39-055-2342710, FAX 39-055-2346010, staff@lelettere.it, http://www.lelettere.it. Circ: 800. **Dist. by:** Licosa SpA, Via Duca di Calabria 1-1, Florence, FI 50125, Italy. TEL 39-055-64831, FAX 39-055-641257, licosa@licosa.com, http://www.licosa.com.

100 ITA ISSN 1827-5834
IL GIORNALE DI FILOSOFIA. Text in Italian. 2005. m. **Document type:** *Journal, Consumer.*
Media: Online - full text.
Published by: Il Giornale di Filosofia redazione@giornaledifilosofia.net, http://www.giornaledifilosofia.net.

110 ITA ISSN 0017-0372
B4
➤ **GIORNALE DI METAFISICA.** Text in Italian. 1946; N.S. 1979. 3/yr. EUR 89 combined subscription domestic (print & online eds.); EUR 112 combined subscription in Europe (print & online eds.); EUR 124 combined subscription elsewhere (print & online eds.) (effective 2011). bk.rev. index. **Document type:** *Journal, Academic/Scholarly.*
Related titles: Online - full text ed.: ISSN 1825-6570. 1994.
Indexed: AmHI, DIP, FR, H07, IBR, IBZ, IPB, MLA-IB, PCI, PhilInd, RASB, RILM.
—INIST.
Published by: Tilgher Genova, Via Assarotti 31-15, Genoa, GE 16122, Italy. TEL 39-010-8391140, FAX 39-010-870653, tilgher@tilgher.it. Ed. Giuseppe Nicolaci.

➤ **GIST.** *see* RELIGIONS AND THEOLOGY

100 KOS ISSN 0351-2223
PG9501
GJURMIME ALBANOLOGJIKE. SERIA E SHKENCAVE FILOLOGJIKE/ ALBANOLOGYCAL RESEARCHES: PHILOLOGICAL SCIENCE SERIES. Text in Albanian. 1962. a. **Document type:** *Journal, Academic/Scholarly.*
Suerpsedes in part (in 1970): Gjurmime Albanologjike (0436-0273)
Published by: Instituti Albanologjik i Prishtines, Str. Eqrem Cabej, p.n., Prishtina, 10000, Kosova. TEL 381-38-220822, FAX 381-38-224156, institutialbanologjik@hotmail.com.

181.48 USA ISSN 1089-6902
B132.V3
GLOBAL VEDANTA; voice of the worldwide vedanta movement. Text in English. 1996. q. USD 10 domestic; USD 12 in Canada & Mexico; USD 15 in Central and South America & Europe; USD 17 elsewhere; USD 3 newsstand/cover (effective 2003). **Document type:** *Magazine, Consumer.* **Description:** Contains humorous and serious articles on spiritual life and practices of the world-wide Vedanta movement.
Published by: Viveka Press, 2718 Broadway Ave. E, Seattle, WA 98102-3909. TEL 206-323-1228, FAX 206-329-1791, vivekapress@vedanta-seattle.org, http://www.vedanta-seattle.org. Ed., Pub. Swami Bhaskarananda. R&P Allen R. Freedman. Adv. contact Devra Freedman. Circ: 800 (paid and controlled).

100 CAN ISSN 0316-618X
B1 G557
➤ **GNOSIS**; a journal of philosophic interest. Text in English, French. 1973. a. CAD 3 to individuals; CAD 5 to institutions. adv. bk.rev. **Document type:** *Journal, Academic/Scholarly.* **Description:** Publishes articles on various philosophical subjects, including metaphysics, epistemology, ethics, aesthetics, logic and philosophy of science.
Indexed: PhilInd.
Published by: Concordia University, Philosophy Department/Universite Concordia, 1455 de Maisonneuve Blvd W, Montreal, PQ H3G 1M8, Canada. TEL 514-848-2500. Circ: 150.

100 HRV ISSN 0352-3306
GODISNJAK ZA POVIJEST FILOZOFIJE. Text in Croatian. a.
Indexed: A26.
Published by: (Odjel za Povijest Filozofije), Sveuciliste u Zagrebu, Institut za Povijesne Znanosti, Krcka 1, Zagreb, 41000, Croatia. TEL 041-511-841. Circ: 800.

100 ESP ISSN 1577-9424
GOGOA; Euskal Herriko Unibertsitateko Hizkuntza, Ezagutza, Komunikazio eta Ekintzari buruzko aldizkaria. Text in Basque. 2001. s-a. back issues avail. **Document type:** *Journal, Academic/Scholarly.*
Indexed: L&LBA, PhilInd.
Published by: Universidad del Pais Vasco, Servicio Editorial, Apartado 1397, Bilbao, 48080, Spain. TEL 34-94-6015126, FAX 34-94-4801314, luxedito@lg.ehu.es, http://www.ehu.es/servicios/se_az/.

100 IND
GOKULDAS SANSKRIT SERIES. Text in English, Sanskrit. 1975 (no.4). irreg., latest vol.83, 1990. free (effective 2011).
Published by: Chaukhambha Orientalia, Gokul Bhawan, K 37-109 Gopal Mandir Ln, Varanasi, Uttar Pradesh 221 001, India. TEL 91-542-2333476, FAX 91-542-2334356.

GOOD GOVERNMENT; a journal of political, social & economic comment. *see* BUSINESS AND ECONOMICS—Economic Systems And Theories, Economic History

100 200 USA ISSN 1940-0020
GORGIAS STUDIES IN PHILOSOPHY AND THEOLOGY. Text in English. 2007 (Dec.). irreg., latest 2009. price varies. back issues avail. **Document type:** *Monographic series, Academic/Scholarly.* **Description:** Provides a forum for original scholarship on specific or general theological and philosophical issues.
Published by: Gorgias Press LLC, 954 River Rd, Piscataway, NJ 08854. TEL 732-885-8900, FAX 732-885-8908, helpdesk@gorgiaspress.com, http://www.gorgiaspress.com/bookshop/default.aspx.

GOVERNARE LA PAURA. *see* POLITICAL SCIENCE

100 USA ISSN 0093-4240
B1
➤ **GRADUATE FACULTY PHILOSOPHY JOURNAL.** Abbreviated title: G F P J. Text in English. 1971. s-a. USD 20 to individuals; USD 60 to institutions; USD 76 combined subscription to individuals (print & online eds.); USD 198 combined subscription to institutions (print & online eds.); USD 10 per issue to individuals; USD 30 per issue to institutions (effective 2010). adv. bk.rev. back issues avail. **Document type:** *Journal, Academic/Scholarly.* **Description:** Brings out scholarly essays, lectures, and book reviews in continental philosophy and the history of philosophy.
Related titles: Online - full text ed.: ISSN 2153-9197. USD 60 to individuals; USD 165 to institutions (effective 2010).
Indexed: A22, BibInd, FR, IPB, MLA-IB, P30, PhilInd.
—BLDSC (4206.827000), IE, Infotrieve, Ingenta, INIST.
Published by: (Social Research), Philosophy Documentation Center, PO Box 7147, Charlottesville, VA 22906. TEL 434-220-3300, FAX 434-220-3301, order@pdcnet.org, http://www.pdcnet.org. Adv. contact Greg Swope.

110 FRA ISSN 1760-1711
LES GRANDS MYSTERES DES SCIENCES SACREES. Text in French. 2003. q. **Document type:** *Magazine, Consumer.*
Published by: Export Press, 91 Rue de Turenne, Paris, 75003, France. TEL 33-1-40291451, FAX 33-1-42720743, dir@exportpress.com, http://www.exportpress.com.

110 FRA ISSN 1958-704X
LES GRANDS MYSTERES DES SCIENCES SACREES. HORS-SERIE. Text in French. 2005. a. **Document type:** *Magazine, Consumer.*
Published by: Export Press, 91 Rue de Turenne, Paris, 75003, France. TEL 33-1-40291451, FAX 33-1-42720743, dir@exportpress.com, http://www.exportpress.com.

100 NLD ISSN 0165-9227
B20.6
➤ **GRAZER PHILOSOPHISCHE STUDIEN**; internationale Zeitschrift fuer analytische Philosophie. Text in English, German. 1975. s-a. price varies. bk.rev. back issues avail. **Document type:** *Monographic series, Academic/Scholarly.* **Description:** Publishes original papers discussing topics in modern analytical philosophy.
Related titles: Online - full text ed.: ISSN 1875-6735 (from IngentaConnect).
Indexed: A01, A03, A08, A22, AmHI, CA, CCMJ, DIP, H07, IBR, IBZ, IPB, L&LBA, MathR, PCI, PhilInd, SCOPUS, SOPODA, SociolAb, T02.
—BLDSC (4214.370000), IE, Ingenta. **CCC.**
Published by: Editions Rodopi B.V., Tijnmuiden 7, Amsterdam, 1046 AK, Netherlands. TEL 31-20-6114821, FAX 31-20-4472979, orders-queries@rodopi.nl. Eds. Johannes L Brandl, Leopold Stubenberg, Marian David. Circ: 700. **Dist in France by:** Nordeal, 30 rue de Verlinghem, BP 139, Lambersart 59832, France. TEL 33-3-20099060, FAX 33-3-20929495; **Dist in N America by:** Rodopi - USA, 295 North Michigan Avenue, Suite 1B, Kenilworth, NJ 07033. TEL 908-298-9071, 800-225-3998, FAX 908-298-9075.

307 USA ISSN 0017-3983
GREEN REVOLUTION; a voice for decentralization and balanced living. Text in English. 1943. q. USD 20; USD 22 in Canada; USD 24 elsewhere (effective 1999). bk.rev.; Website rev. charts; illus. reprints avail. **Document type:** *Newsletter, Consumer.* **Description:** Provides information for governing communities about the land. Promotes decentralism, community land trust, permaculture, intentional community, alternative education, alternative money, and geonomic transformation.
Incorporates (1969-1979): Aquarian Research Foundation Newsletter
Related titles: Microform ed.: (from PQC).
Indexed: EIA, EnerInd, NPI, RASB.
Published by: School of Living, 215 Julian Woods Ln., Julian, PA 16844-8617. TEL 610-593-6988, FAX 610-593-6988. Ed. Rebekah Hicks TEL 570-648-0293. Circ: 250 (paid).

GREGORIANUM. *see* RELIGIONS AND THEOLOGY—Roman Catholic

100 DEU ISSN 0232-8925
GREIFSWALDER PHILOSOPHISCHE HEFTE. Variant title: Ernst-Moritz-Arndt-Universitaet Greifswald. Wissenschaftliche Beitraege. Greifswalder Philosophische Hefte. Text in German. 1982. irreg., latest vol.8, 1990. price varies. **Document type:** *Monographic series, Academic/Scholarly.*
Published by: Ernst-Moritz-Arndt-Universitaet Greifswald, Domstr 11, Greifswald, 17487, Germany. TEL 49-3834-861100, FAX 49-3834-861105, rektor@uni-greifswald.de, http://www.uni-greifswald.de.

100 BRA ISSN 2178-1036
▼ **GRIOT.** Text in Portuguese. 2010. s-a. free (effective 2011). **Document type:** *Journal, Academic/Scholarly.*
Media: Online - full text.
Published by: Universidade Federal do Reconcavo da Bahia, Rua Rui Barbosa 710, Centro, Cruz das Almas, BA 44380-000, Brazil. TEL 55-75-36212350. Eds. Jose Joao Neves Barbosa Vicente, Ronaldo Crispim Sena Barros.

GROENLANDSRELATERET FORSKNING OG UDVIKLING; forskningsstatistik. *see* STATISTICS

170 GBR ISSN 1470-854X
GROVE ETHICS SERIES. Text in English. 197?. q. GBP 10; GBP 3.50 per issue (print or online ed.) (effective 2009). back issues avail. **Document type:** *Monographic series, Trade.* **Description:** Provides clear and concise explorations of contemporary ethical issues.
Former titles (until 2000): Grove Ethical Studies (0951-2659); (until 1987): Grove Booklets on Ethics (0305-4241)
Related titles: Online - full text ed.
—BLDSC (4220.530000), IE, Ingenta. **CCC.**
Published by: Grove Books Ltd., Ridley Hall Rd, Cambridge, CB3 9HU, United Kingdom. TEL 44-1223-464748, FAX 44-1223-464849, sales@grovebooks.co.uk.

100 DEU ISSN 1862-1244
GRUNDTHEMEN PHILOSOPHIE. Text in German. 2005. irreg., latest 2011. price varies. **Document type:** *Monographic series, Academic/Scholarly.*
Published by: Walter de Gruyter GmbH & Co. KG, Genthiner Str 13, Berlin, 10785, Germany. TEL 49-30-26005220, FAX 49-30-26005251, info@degruyter.com, http://www.degruyter.de.

GUANGXI DAXUE XUEBAO (ZHEXUE SHEHUI KEXUE BAN)/ GUANGXI UNIVERSITY. JOURNAL (PHILOSOPHY AND SOCIAL SCIENCES). *see* SOCIAL SCIENCES: COMPREHENSIVE WORKS

100 001.3 CHN ISSN 1673-8179
GUANGXI MINZU DAXUE XUEBAO (ZHEXUE SHEHUI KEXUE BAN)/GUANGXI UNIVERSITY FOR NATIONALITIES. JOURNAL (PHILOSOPHY AND SOCIAL SCIENCE EDITION). Text in Chinese. 1978. bi-m. **Document type:** *Journal, Academic/Scholarly.*
Former titles (until 2006): Guangxi Minzu Xueyuan Xuebao (Zhexue Shehui Kexue Ban) (1002-3887); (until 1983): Guangxi Minzu Xueyuan Xuebao (Shehui Kexue Ban)
Related titles: Online - full text ed.
Indexed: RILM.
Published by: Guangxi Minzu Xueyuan/Guangxi University for Nationalities, 188, Daxue Dong Lu, Nanning, 530006, China. TEL 86-771-3260122, FAX 86-771-3263361, http://www.gxun.edu.cn/.

GUANGXI SHIFAN DAXUE XUEBAO (ZHEXUE SHEHUI KEXUE BAN)/GUANGXI NORMAL UNIVERSITY. JOURNAL (PHILOSOPHY AND SOCIAL SCIENCES EDITION). *see* SOCIAL SCIENCES: COMPREHENSIVE WORKS

170 ESP ISSN 1988-7507
GUIAS PARA ENSENANZAS MEDIAS. ETICA. Text in Spanish. 2007. m. **Document type:** *Monographic series, Academic/Scholarly.*
Media: Online - full text.
Published by: Wolters Kluwer Espana - Educacion (Subsidiary of: Wolters Kluwer N.V.), C Collado Mediano 9, Las Rozas, Madrid, 28230, Spain. TEL 34-902-250510, FAX 34-902-250515, cleintes@wkeducacion.es, http://www.wkeducacion.es/index.asp. Ed. Joaquin Gairin.

110 USA
GUIDE TO LOST WONDER; an emanation of the Museum of Lost Wonder. Text in English. 1997. irreg., latest no.10. USD 3 per issue domestic; USD 4 per issue in Canada; USD 5 per issue elsewhere; USD 25 (effective 2005). bibl.; charts; illus. 10 p./no. 3 cols./p.; back issues avail. **Document type:** *Magazine, Consumer.*
Published by: Wonderella Printed, 10145, Berkeley, CA 94709-5145. http://www.onderella.com/pamphlets/lostwonder.htm. Ed. Jeff Hoke.

100 USA ISSN 1948-0873
BP605.G92
THE GURDJIEFF JOURNAL. Text in English. 19??. 3/yr. USD 25 in US & Canada; USD 37 elsewhere (effective 2009). back issues avail. **Document type:** *Journal, Academic/Scholarly.* **Description:** Contains feature articles, essays, interviews and book and film reviews that explores the principles, perspectives and practices of G.I. Gurdjieff's teaching of The Fourth Way.
Formerly (until 1992): Telos
Related titles: Online - full text ed.
Published by: Gurdjieff Legacy, 773 Center Blvd 58, Fairfax, CA 94978. Arete@Gurdjieff-Legacy.Org, http://www.gurdjieff-legacy.org.

H E C FORUM; an interprofessional journal on healthcare institutions' ethical and legal issues. (HealthCare Ethics Committee) *see* HEALTH FACILITIES AND ADMINISTRATION

H O P O S NEWSLETTER. (History of Philosophy of Science) *see* SCIENCES: COMPREHENSIVE WORKS

HANDBOOK OF TEXAS LAWYER AND JUDICIAL ETHICS; attorney tort standards, attorney ethics standards, judicial ethics standards, recusal and disqualification of judges. *see* LAW

160 NLD
HANDBOOK OF THE HISTORY OF LOGIC. Text in English. 2004. irreg., latest vol.5, 2008. price varies. **Document type:** *Monographic series, Academic/Scholarly.*
Related titles: Online - full text ed.: ISSN 1874-5857.
Published by: Elsevier BV, North-Holland (Subsidiary of: Elsevier Science & Technology), Sara Burgerhartstraat 25, Amsterdam, 1055 KV, Netherlands. TEL 31-20-4853911, FAX 31-20-4852457, JournalsCustomerServiceEMEA@elsevier.com, http://www.elsevier.com. Eds. Dov M Gabbay, John Woods.

HANDBOOK OF THE PHILOSOPHY OF SCIENCE. *see* SCIENCES: COMPREHENSIVE WORKS

HANGZHOU SHIFAN DAXUE XUEBAO (SHEHUI KEXUE BAN)/ HANGZHOU TEACHERS COLLEGE. JOURNAL (SOCIAL SCIENCE EDITION). *see* SOCIAL SCIENCES: COMPREHENSIVE WORKS

100 USA ISSN 1062-6239
B1
THE HARVARD REVIEW OF PHILOSOPHY. Text in English. 1991. a. USD 10 domestic to individuals; USD 12 foreign to individuals; USD 50 domestic to institutions; USD 52 foreign to institutions (effective 2010). back issues avail. **Document type:** *Journal, Academic/Scholarly.* **Description:** Publishes philosophical work that is interesting and insightful.
Related titles: Online - full text ed.: ISSN 2153-9154.
Indexed: PhilInd.
—BLDSC (4270.010000), IE, Ingenta.
Published by: Harvard University, Department of Philosophy, c/o Philosophy Tutorial Office, Emerson Hall 303, Cambridge, MA 02138. http://www.fas.harvard.edu/~phildept. Ed. Max Wong.

HASTINGS CENTER REPORT. *see* MEDICAL SCIENCES

HAWLIYYAT KULLIYYAT AL-ADAB/ANNALS OF THE ARTS AND SOCIAL SCIENCES. *see* HUMANITIES: COMPREHENSIVE WORKS

HEBEI DAXUE XUEBAO (SHEHUI ZHEXUE BAN)/HEBEI UNIVERSITY. JOURNAL (PHILOSOPHY & SOCIAL SCIENCES). *see* SOCIAL SCIENCES: COMPREHENSIVE WORKS

190 DEU
HEGEL-DEUTUNGEN. Text in German. 1996. irreg., latest vol.5, 1997. price varies. **Document type:** *Monographic series, Academic/Scholarly.*
Published by: Felix Meiner Verlag GmbH, Richardstr 47, Hamburg, 22081, Germany. TEL 49-40-2987560, FAX 49-40-29875620, info@meiner.de.

182 DEU ISSN 0073-1579
B2900
HEGEL-JAHRBUCH. Text in German. 1961. a. EUR 99.80 (effective 2011). **Document type:** *Journal, Academic/Scholarly.*
Indexed: IPB, PCI, RASB.
Published by: (Hegel-Gesellschaft), Akademie Verlag GmbH (Subsidiary of: Oldenbourg Wissenschaftsverlag GmbH), Markgrafenstr 12-14, Berlin, 10969, Germany. TEL 49-30-4220060, FAX 49-30-42200657, info@akademie-verlag.de.

100 DEU
▼ **HEGEL LECTURES.** Text in English. 2011. irreg. price varies. **Document type:** *Monographic series, Academic/Scholarly.*
Published by: Walter de Gruyter GmbH & Co. KG, Genthiner Str 13, Berlin, 10785, Germany. TEL 49-30-26005220, FAX 49-30-26005251, info@degruyter.com, http://www.degruyter.de.

100 GBR ISSN 0263-5232
B2900
HEGEL SOCIETY OF GREAT BRITAIN. BULLETIN. Text in English. 1978. a. free to members (effective 2009). adv. bk.rev. back issues avail. **Document type:** *Bulletin, Academic/Scholarly.* **Description:** Features articles and reviews on the philosopher G.W.F. Hegel.
Indexed: IPB, PhilInd.
—BLDSC (2554.350000), IE, Ingenta.
Published by: Hegel Society of Great Britain, c/o Katerina Deligiorgi, Arts B 346, Department of Philosophy, University of Sussex, Falmer, Brighton, BN1 9QN, United Kingdom. Ed. Katerina Deligiorgi. adv.: page GBP 50.

190 DEU ISSN 0073-1587
➤ **HEGEL-STUDIEN.** Text in German. 1955. irreg., latest vol.44, 2009. price varies. **Document type:** *Monographic series, Academic/Scholarly.*
Indexed: A20, A22, ASCA, ArtHuCI, BibInd, CurCont, DIP, FR, IBR, IBZ, IPB, MLA-IB, PCI, RASB, SCOPUS, W07.
—IE, Infotrieve, INIST.
Published by: (Deutsche Forschungsgemeinschaft, Hegel Kommission), Felix Meiner Verlag GmbH, Richardstr 47, Hamburg, 22081, Germany. TEL 49-40-2987560, FAX 49-40-29875620, info@meiner.de. R&P Johannes Kambylis.

140 DEU ISSN 0440-5927
HEGEL-STUDIEN. BEIHEFT. Text in German. 1964. irreg., latest vol.54, 2010. price varies. adv. bk.rev. **Document type:** *Monographic series, Academic/Scholarly.*
Formerly: Internationale Vereinigung zur Foerderung des Studiums der Hegelschen Philosophie. Veroeffentlichung
Indexed: DIP, FR, IBR, IBZ, PCI.
—INIST.
Published by: Felix Meiner Verlag GmbH, Richardstr 47, Hamburg, 22081, Germany. TEL 49-40-2987560, FAX 49-40-29875620, info@meiner.de. Circ: 1,000.

193 ITA ISSN 1724-4811
HEGELIANA. Text in Italian. 1991. irreg., latest vol.40, 2004. price varies. **Document type:** *Monographic series, Academic/Scholarly.*
Published by: Edizioni Angelo Guerini e Associati SpA, Viale Angelo Filippetti 28, Milan, MI 20122, Italy. TEL 39-02-582980, FAX 39-02-58298030, info@guerini.it, http://www.guerini.it.

193 DEU ISSN 0939-7779
HEGELIANA; Studien und Quellen zu Hegel und zum Hegelianismus. Text in German. 1991. irreg., latest vol.21, 2008. price varies. **Document type:** *Monographic series, Academic/Scholarly.*
Published by: Peter Lang GmbH (Subsidiary of: Peter Lang Publishing Group), Eschborner Landstr 42-50, Frankfurt Am Main, 60489, Germany. TEL 49-69-7807050, FAX 49-69-78070550, zentrale.frankfurt@peterlang.com, http://www.peterlang.com. Ed. Helmut Schneider.

HEHAI DAXUE XUEBAO (ZHEXUE SHEHUI KEXUE BAN)/HOHAI UNIVERSITY. JOURNAL (PHILOSOPHY AND SOCIAL SCIENCES EDITION). *see* SOCIAL SCIENCES: COMPREHENSIVE WORKS

193 DEU ISSN 1868-3355
▼ **HEIDEGGER FORUM.** Text in German. 2009. irreg., latest vol.4, 2010. price varies. **Document type:** *Monographic series, Academic/Scholarly.*
Published by: Vittorio Klostermann, Frauenlobstr 22, Frankfurt Am Main, 60487, Germany. TEL 49-69-9708160, FAX 49-69-708038, verlag@klostermann.de, http://www.klostermann.de.

100 DEU ISSN 1612-3166
B3279.H49
HEIDEGGER-JAHRBUCH. Text in German. 2004. irreg., latest vol.7, 2009. EUR 38 (effective 2010). **Document type:** *Yearbook, Academic/Scholarly.*
Indexed: IBR, IBZ.
Published by: Verlag Karl Alber, Hermann-Herder-Str 4, Freiburg, 79104, Germany. TEL 49-761-2717436, FAX 49-761-2717212, info@verlag-alber.de. Eds. Alfred Denker, Holger Zaborowski.

100 DEU ISSN 0885-4580
B3279.H49
HEIDEGGER STUDIES/ETUDES HEIDEGGER/HEIDEGGER STUDIEN. Text in German, English, French. 1985. a. EUR 46 (effective 2011). adv. bk.rev. bibl. back issues avail. **Document type:** *Journal, Academic/Scholarly.* **Description:** Dedicated to promoting the understanding of Heidegger's thought through the interpretation of his writings.
Related titles: Online - full text ed.: ISSN 2153-9170. USD 285 to institutions (effective 2010).
Indexed: DIP, IBR, IBZ, IPB, PCI, PhilInd.
—BLDSC (4283.885000), IE, Ingenta.
Published by: Duncker und Humblot GmbH, Carl-Heinrich-Becker-Weg 9, Berlin, 12165, Germany. TEL 49-30-7900060, FAX 49-30-79000631, info@duncker-humblot.de.

100 800 DEU
HEIDELBERGER AKADEMIE DER WISSENSCHAFTEN. PHILOSOPHISCH-HISTORISCHEN KLASSE. SCHRIFTEN. Text in German. irreg., latest 1996. price varies. **Document type:** *Monographic series.*
Published by: (Heidelberger Akademie der Wissenschaften), Universitaetsverlag Winter GmbH, Dossenheimer Landstr 13, Heidelberg, 69121, Germany. TEL 49-6221-770260, FAX 49-6221-770269, info@winter-verlag-hd.de, http://www.winter-verlag-hd.de.

189 DEU
HERDERS BIBLIOTHEK DER PHILOSOPHIE DES MITTELALTERS. Text in German. 2005. irreg., latest vol.20, 2009. price varies. **Document type:** *Monographic series, Academic/Scholarly.*
Published by: Verlag Herder GmbH, Hermann-Herder-Str 4, Freiburg Im Breisgau, 79104, Germany. TEL 49-761-27170, FAX 49-761-2717520, kundenservice@herder.de, http://www.herder.de.

100 700 ROM ISSN 1453-9047
➤ **HERMENEIA**; journal of hermeneutics, art theory and criticism. Text in Romanian, English, French, German. 1998. s-a. **Document type:** *Journal, Academic/Scholarly.*
Related titles: Online - full text ed.: ISSN 2069-8291. free (effective 2011).
Published by: Universitatea "Alexandru Ioan Cuza" din Iasi, Facultatea de Filosofie si Stiinte Social - Politice, 11 Carol I Boulevard, Iasi, 700506, Romania.

820 CHE ISSN 1661-8505
HERMENEIA. Text in German. 2006. a. **Document type:** *Journal, Academic/Scholarly.*
Address: Allmendstr 26, Wohlen, 5610, Switzerland. Eds. Flavio Marelli, Goran Grubacevic, Marc-Andre Kaspar.

100 USA ISSN 1043-5735
HERMENEUTIC COMMENTARIES. Text in English. 1989. irreg., latest vol.2, 2008. price varies. **Document type:** *Monographic series, Academic/Scholarly.* **Description:** Presents commentaries on classical texts with a strong emphasis on the hermeneutic, rather than on the historical, grammatical or stylistic aspects of the texts.
Published by: Peter Lang Publishing, Inc. (Subsidiary of: Peter Lang Publishing Group), 29 Broadway, New York, NY 10006. TEL 212-647-7706, 212-647-7700, 800-770-5264, FAX 212-647-7707, customerservice@plang.com.

HERMENEUTICA. *see* RELIGIONS AND THEOLOGY

100 CHL ISSN 0718-4980
HERMENEUTICA INTERCULTURAL. Text in Spanish. 1987. a. back issues avail. **Document type:** *Journal, Academic/Scholarly.*
Formerly (until 2003): Boletin de Filosofia (0716-601X)
Published by: Universidad Catolica Cardenal Raul Silva Henrique, Departamento de Humanidades y Educacion Media, General Jofre, 462, Santiago, Chile. TEL 56-2-4601100, FAX 56-2-6354193, publicaciones@ucsh.cl, http://www.ucsh.cl/. Ed. Luis Uribe Miranda.

HERMES. *see* SOCIAL SCIENCES: COMPREHENSIVE WORKS

100 ESP ISSN 2171-8857
▼ **HERMES ANALOGICA**; revista interdisciplinaria sobre hermeneutica analogica. Text in Spanish. 2010. a. **Document type:** *Monographic series, Academic/Scholarly.*
Media: Online - full text.
Published by: Centro de Estudios y Analisis Sociales de Galicia, R Novoa Santos 16, Portal 4, 1o. E, Santa Uxia de Riviera, Coruna, 15960, Spain. TEL 34-634-772946, http://ceasga.jimdo.com/. Eds. Juan R. Coca, Mauricio Beuchet.

100 DEU ISSN 0440-7563
HESTIA. Text in German. 1960. irreg., latest vol.22, 2008. price varies. **Document type:** *Monographic series, Academic/Scholarly.*
Indexed: DIP, IBR, IBZ.
Published by: Verlag Koenigshausen und Neumann GmbH, Leistenstr 7, Wuerzburg, 97082, Germany. TEL 49-931-3298700, FAX 49-931-83620, info@koenigshausen-neumann.de, http://koenigshausen-neumann.gebhardt-riegel.de.

THE HEYTHROP JOURNAL; a bi-monthly review of philosophy and theology. *see* RELIGIONS AND THEOLOGY

100 DEU
HINBLICK. Text in German. 2008. irreg., latest vol.4, 2008. price varies. **Document type:** *Monographic series, Academic/Scholarly.*
Published by: Verlag Karl Alber, Hermann-Herder-Str 4, Freiburg, 79104, Germany. TEL 49-761-2717436, FAX 49-761-2717212, info@verlag-alber.de.

HISTOIRE EPISTEMOLOGIE LANGAGE. *see* LINGUISTICS

109 ITA ISSN 1724-6121
B790.5
HISTORIA PHILOSOPHICA. Text in Italian, English, French, Spanish, German; Summaries in English. 2003. a. EUR 395 combined subscription domestic to institutions (print & online eds.); EUR 445 combined subscription foreign to institutions (print & online eds.) (effective 2009). **Document type:** *Journal, Academic/Scholarly.*
Related titles: Online - full text ed.: ISSN 1824-095X.
Indexed: CA, HistAb, T02.
Published by: Fabrizio Serra Editore (Subsidiary of: Accademia Editoriale), c/o Accademia Editoriale, Via Santa Bibbiana 28, Pisa, 56127, Italy. TEL 39-050-542332, FAX 39-050-574888, accademiaeditoriale@accademiaeditoriale.it, http://www.libraweb.net.

100 NLD
HISTORIES AND ADDRESSES OF PHILOSOPHICAL SOCIETIES. Text in English. irreg. price varies. **Document type:** *Monographic series, Academic/Scholarly.* **Description:** Publishes and preserves the presidential and other major addresses of philosophical societies.
Related titles: ◆ Series of: Value Inquiry Book Series. ISSN 0929-8436.
Published by: Editions Rodopi B.V., Tijnmuiden 7, Amsterdam, 1046 AK, Netherlands. TEL 31-20-6114821, FAX 31-20-4472979, info@rodopi.nl. Ed. Richard T Hull. **Dist. by:** Rodopi - USA, 606 Newark Ave, 2nd fl, Kenilworth, NJ 07033. TEL 908-497-9031, FAX 908-497-9035.

HISTORIOGRAPHIA LINGUISTICA; international journal for the history of the language sciences. *see* LINGUISTICS

160 GBR ISSN 0144-5340
BC1
➤ **HISTORY AND PHILOSOPHY OF LOGIC.** Text in English. 1980. q. GBP 535 combined subscription in United Kingdom to institutions (print & online eds.); EUR 707, USD 890 combined subscription to institutions (print & online eds.) (effective 2012). adv. bk.rev. illus. back issues avail.; reprint service avail. from PSC. **Document type:** *Journal, Academic/Scholarly.* **Description:** Concerned with general philosophical questions on logic: existential and ontological aspects, the relationship between classical and nonclassical logics, and the connections between logic and other fields of knowledge, such as mathematics, philosophy of science, epistemology, linguistics, psychology and computing.
Related titles: Online - full text ed.: ISSN 1464-5149. GBP 482 in United Kingdom to institutions; EUR 636, USD 801 to institutions (effective 2012) (from IngentaConnect).
Indexed: A01, A03, A08, A20, A22, ASCA, AmH&L, ArtHuCI, CA, CCMJ, CurCont, DIP, E01, HistAb, I14, IBR, IBZ, IPB, MSN, MathR, PCI, PhilInd, RASB, S01, SCI, SCOPUS, T02, W07, Z02.
—IE, Infotrieve, Ingenta, Linda Hall. **CCC.**
Published by: Taylor & Francis Ltd. (Subsidiary of: Taylor & Francis Group), 4 Park Sq, Milton Park, Abingdon, Oxfordshire OX14 4RN, United Kingdom. TEL 44-20-70176000, FAX 44-20-70176336, subscriptions@tandf.co.uk, http://www.taylorandfrancis.com. Ed. Volker Peckhaus. Adv. contact Linda Hann. **Subscr. in N. America to:** Taylor & Francis Inc., Customer Services Dept, 325 Chestnut St, 8th Fl, Philadelphia, PA 19106. TEL 215-625-8900, 800-354-1420, FAX 215-625-2940, customerservice@taylorandfrancis.com; **Subscr. to:** Journals Customer Service, Sheepen Pl, Colchester, Essex CO3 3LP, United Kingdom. TEL 44-20-70175544, FAX 44-20-70175198, tf.enquiries@tfinforma.com.

➤ **HISTORY AND PHILOSOPHY OF THE LIFE SCIENCES.** *see* BIOLOGY

➤ **HISTORY AND THEORY**; studies in the philosophy of history. *see* HISTORY

190.09 GBR ISSN 0191-6599
D1
➤ **HISTORY OF EUROPEAN IDEAS.** Text in English. 1980. 4/yr. EUR 726 in Europe to institutions; JPY 96,300 in Japan to institutions; USD 811 elsewhere to institutions (effective 2012). adv. bk.rev. abstr. back issues avail.; reprints avail. **Document type:** *Journal, Academic/Scholarly.* **Description:** Devoted to the intellectual history of Europe from the Renaissance onwards. It is interdisciplinary in that it aims to publish papers on the history of ideas in a number of different fields: political and economic thought, philosophy, natural philosophy and science, theology and literature.
Related titles: Microfilm ed.: (from PQC); Online - full text ed.: ISSN 1873-541X (from IngentaConnect, ScienceDirect).
Indexed: A20, A21, A22, A26, ABS&EES, ASCA, AmH&L, AmHI, ArtHuCI, B24, BrHumI, CA, CurCont, FR, H07, HistAb, I05, I13, MLA-IB, P30, P42, PCI, PSA, PhilInd, RASB, RI-1, RI-2, RILM, S02, S03, SCOPUS, SOPODA, SSA, SociolAb, T02, W07.
—BLDSC (4318.138000), IE, Infotrieve, Ingenta, INIST. **CCC.**
Published by: Pergamon (Subsidiary of: Elsevier Science & Technology), The Blvd, Langford Ln, East Park, Kidlington, Oxford OX5 1GB, United Kingdom. TEL 44-1865-843000, FAX 44-1865-843010, JournalsCustomerServiceEMEA@elsevier.com. Ed. Richard Whatmore. **Subscr. to:** Elsevier BV, Radarweg 29, PO Box 211, Amsterdam 1000 AE, Netherlands. TEL 31-20-4853757, FAX 31-20-4853432, http://www.elsevier.nl.

100 USA ISSN 0740-0675
B1
➤ **HISTORY OF PHILOSOPHY QUARTERLY.** Abbreviated title: H P Q. Text in English. 1984. q. USD 55 to individuals; USD 297 to institutions (print or online ed.); USD 331 combined subscription to institutions (print & online eds.) (effective 2011). adv. illus. Index. back issues avail.; reprints avail. **Document type:** *Journal, Academic/Scholarly.* **Description:** Contains papers that cultivate philosophical history with a strong interaction between contemporary and historical concerns.
Related titles: Online - full text ed.: ISSN 2152-1026.
Indexed: A21, A22, DIP, IBR, IBZ, IPB, PCI, PhilInd, RI-1, RI-2.
—BLDSC (4318.394500), IE, Infotrieve, Ingenta. **CCC.**
Published by: University of Illinois Press, 1325 S Oak St, Champaign, IL 61820. TEL 217-333-0950, 866-244-0626, FAX 217-244-8082, journals@uillinois.edu. Ed. Jeffrey Tlumak. Adv. contact Jeff McArdle TEL 217-244-0381.

➤ **HISTORY OF POLITICAL THOUGHT.** *see* POLITICAL SCIENCE

➤ **HJAERNSTORM.** *see* ART

100 330.1 NLD ISSN 0921-5891
B1247
➤ **HOBBES STUDIES.** Text in English, French, Spanish. 1987. a., latest vol.15. EUR 97, USD 135 to institutions; EUR 105, USD 147 combined subscription to institutions (print & online eds.) (effective 2012). adv. bk.rev. back issues avail.; reprint service avail. from PSC. **Document type:** *Journal, Academic/Scholarly.* **Description:** Devoted to the life and works and continuing intellectual heritage of Thomas Hobbes.
Related titles: Online - full text ed.: ISSN 1875-0257. EUR 88, USD 123 to institutions (effective 2012) (from IngentaConnect).
Indexed: A22, AmHI, CA, DIP, E01, H07, IBR, IBZ, IPB, IZBG, P42, PhilInd, RASB, SCOPUS, T02.
—BLDSC (4319.813000), IE. **CCC.**
Published by: Brill, PO Box 9000, Leiden, 2300 PA, Netherlands. TEL 31-71-5353500, FAX 31-71-5317532, cs@brill.nl. Ed. Martin A Bertman. Circ: 250.

100 230 DEU ISSN 1619-666X
HODOS; Wege bildungsbezogener Ethikforschung in Philosophie und Theologie. Text in German. 2002. irreg., latest vol.9, 2009. price varies. **Document type:** *Monographic series, Academic/Scholarly.*
Published by: Peter Lang GmbH (Subsidiary of: Peter Lang Publishing Group), Eschborner Landstr 42-50, Frankfurt Am Main, 60489, Germany. TEL 49-69-7807050, FAX 49-69-78070550, zentrale.frankfurt@peterlang.com.

100 ESP ISSN 2171-6889
▼ **EL HOMBRE A CABALLO.** Text in Spanish. 2010. 3/yr. **Document type:** *Journal, Academic/Scholarly.*

P

Published by: Universidad de Sevilla, Facultad de Filosofia, C Camilo Jose Cela, s-n, Sevilla, 41018, Spain. TEL 34-954-551656, FAX 34-954-551634, jsecfil@us.es, http://centro.us.es/filosofia/web/.

100 CAN ISSN 1181-9227
HORIZONS PHILOSOPHIQUES. Text in French. 1979. s-a.
Formerly (until 1990): Petite Revue de Philosophie (0709-4469)
Indexed: MLA-IB, PhilInd.
—BLDSC (4326.795350).
Published by: College Edouard-Montpetit, 945 Chemin de Chambly, Longueuil, PQ J4H 3M6, Canada. TEL 450-679-2631, http://www.collegeem.qc.ca.

HUAIBEI MEITAN SHIFAN XUYUAN XUEBAO (ZHEXUE SHEHUI KEXUE BAN)/HUABEI COAL INDUSTRY TEACHERS COLLEGE. JOURNAL (PHILOSOPHY AND SOCIAL SCIENCES). *see* SOCIAL SCIENCES: COMPREHENSIVE WORKS

HUAIYIN SHIFAN XUEYUAN XUEBAO (ZHEXUE SHEHUI KEXUE BAN)/HUAIYIN TEACHERS COLLEGE. JOURNAL (SOCIAL SCIENCES EDIITON). *see* SOCIAL SCIENCES: COMPREHENSIVE WORKS

HUBEI DAXUE XUEBAO (ZHEXUE SHEHUI KEXUE BAN). *see* SOCIAL SCIENCES: COMPREHENSIVE WORKS

HUBEI SHIFAN XUEYUAN XUEBAO (ZHEXUE SHEHUI KEXUE BAN)/HUBEI NORMAL UNIVERSITY. JOURNAL (PHILOSOPHY AND SOCIAL SCIENCES). *see* SOCIAL SCIENCES: COMPREHENSIVE WORKS

HUGINN & MUNINN; interstellar messenger. *see* PARAPSYCHOLOGY AND OCCULTISM

HUIZHOU XUEYUAN XUEBAO/HUIZHOU UNIVERSITY. JOURNAL. *see* SOCIAL SCIENCES: COMPREHENSIVE WORKS

170 NLD ISSN 1875-6123
HUMAN. Text in Dutch. 1945. q. EUR 29.50 to individuals; EUR 82.50 to institutions; EUR 24 to students (effective 2010). adv. bk.rev.; film rev.; play rev. illus. **Document type:** *Magazine, Consumer.*
Former titles (until 2008): Humanist (0025-9489); (until 1971): Mens en Wereld
Related titles: Online - full text ed.
Indexed: Acal, MEA&I, PerIslam, SCOPUS.
—IE, Infotrieve.
Published by: (Humanistisch Verbond), Boom Uitgevers Amsterdam, Prinsengracht 747-751, Amsterdam, 1017 JX, Netherlands. TEL 31-20-6226107, FAX 31-20-6253327, info@uitgeverijboom.nl, http://www.uitgeverijboom.nl. Eds. Hedda M Post, Julia S Schmidt.

144 USA ISSN 1559-8926
HUMAN INTEREST. Text in English. 2001. 10/yr. (except Jul. & Aug.). **Document type:** *Newsletter, Consumer.*
Published by: Humanist Association of the Greater Sacramento Area, PO Box 3003, Orangevale, CA 95662-7406. TEL 916-285-9367, http://www.hagsa.org/index1.html.

HUMAN REPRODUCTION AND GENETIC ETHICS. *see* BIOLOGY

100 NLD ISSN 0163-8548
B1 CODEN: HUSTDT
➤ **HUMAN STUDIES**; a journal for philosophy and the social sciences. Text in English. 1978. q. EUR 603, USD 638 combined subscription to institutions (print & online eds.) (effective 2012). adv. bk.rev. illus. index. back issues avail.; reprint service avail. from PSC. **Document type:** *Journal, Academic/Scholarly.* **Description:** Provides a forum for discussion of issues relating to the d ialogue between philosophy and the human sciences, such as the logic of inquiry, methodology, epistemology and fundamental issues.
Related titles: Microform ed.: (from PQC); Online - full text ed.: ISSN 1572-851X (from IngentaConnect).
Indexed: A01, A02, A03, A08, A20, A22, A26, ABS&EES, ASCA, BibInd, BibLing, CA, CurCont, DIP, E01, FamI, IBR, IBSS, IBZ, IPB, L11, MLA, MLA-IB, P10, P27, P28, P30, P42, P46, P48, P53, P54, PCI, PQC, PSA, PhilInd, RASB, RILM, S02, S03, SCOPUS, SOPODA, SSA, SSCI, SociolAb, T02, W07.
—BLDSC (4336.467000), IE, Infotrieve, Ingenta. **CCC.**
Published by: Springer Netherlands (Subsidiary of: Springer Science+Business Media), Van Godewijckstraat 30, Dordrecht, 3311 GX, Netherlands. TEL 31-78-6576050, FAX 31-78-6576474, http://www.springer.com. Eds. L Langsdorf, George Psathas.

➤ **HUMANES LEBEN - HUMANES STERBEN.** *see* MEDICAL SCIENCES

100 USA ISSN 0018-7399
B821.A1
THE HUMANIST; a magazine of critical inquiry and social concern. Text in English. 1941. bi-m. USD 24.95 domestic (effective 2010). adv. bk.rev. illus. index. back issues avail.; reprints avail. **Document type:** *Magazine, Consumer.* **Description:** Covers social and ethical content aimed at educating the public from a secular viewpoint.
Supersedes (in 1941): The Humanist Bulletin (0362-5125); Which superseded (in 1938): The New Humanist (0362-4625); Incorporates (1965-1969): The Ethical Forum (0425-4201); Which was formerly (until 1965): Ethical Culture Today (1947-0371); (until 1964): The Ethical Outlook (1947-0479); (until 1956): The Standard (1947-0363); (until 1914): Ethical Addresses and Ethical Record (1947-0541); Which was formed by the merger of (1899-1904): Ethical Record (1947-0525); (18??-1904): Ethical Addresses (1947-0533)
Related titles: CD-ROM ed.; Microform ed.: (from PQC); Online - full text ed.
Indexed: A01, A02, A03, A08, A20, A21, A22, A25, A26, Acal, AmHI, B04, B14, BRD, BRI, C05, C12, CA, CBRI, CERDIC, CPerI, ChPerI, DIP, E08, ECER, FR, FutSurv, G05, G06, G07, G08, G10, H07, H08, H09, H10, H14, HAb, HumInd, I05, I07, IBR, IBZ, M01, M02, M06, MASUSE, MLA-IB, MRD, MagInd, P02, P05, P06, P10, P13, P27, P28, P30, P34, P48, P53, P54, PAIS, PCI, PMR, PQC, PRA, R03, R04, R05, R06, RASB, RGAb, RGPR, RI-1, RI-2, RILM, S02, S03, S08, S09, S23, SCOPUS, SOPODA, SociolAb, T02, U01, W03, W05, W09.
—BLDSC (4336.519000), IE, Infotrieve, Ingenta. **CCC.**
Published by: American Humanist Association, 1777 T St, NW, Washington, DC 20009. TEL 202-238-9088, 800-837-3792, FAX 202-238-9003, aha@americanhumanist.org, http://www.americanhumanist.org/index.html. Ed. Jennifer Bardi. Adv. contact Ronald E Burr TEL 703-893-3632. Circ: 15,000 (paid).

170 NOR ISSN 0801-6283
HUMANIST. Text in Norwegian. 1978. 4/yr. NOK 200 (effective 2002). **Description:** Contains articles, interviews and debates on outlook on life, morals, and faith.
Formerly (until 1987): Human-Etikk (0332-5970)
Related titles: Online - full text ed.
Published by: Human - Etisk Forbund, St. Olavs Pl., Postboks 7644, Toeyen, Oslo, 0130, Norway. TEL 47-22-11-10-10, FAX 47-22-11-01-40. Ed. Terje Emberland.

170 SWE
HUMANIST-INFO; medlemstidning foer humanisterna. Text in Swedish. 1979. q. **Document type:** *Magazine, Consumer.* **Description:** Focuses on different ethical questions from a non-religious perspective.
Former titles (until 1999): Human-Etik (1101-0703); (until 1989): H E F - Eko (0283-152X); (until 1982): H E F - Nytt
Related titles: Online - full text ed.
Published by: Humanisterna, PO Box 16241, Stockholm, 10324, Sweden. TEL 46-8-50862290, FAX 46-582-105-82, http://www.humanisterna.org.

144 USA ISSN 1054-9633
HUMANIST NEWS & VIEWS. Text in English. 1986. m. USD 20 (effective 2003). bk.rev. **Document type:** *Newsletter, Consumer.* **Description:** Aims to promote a positive philosophy: a better life for all through education, democracy, free speech, reason, and science, without reliance on arbitrary dogmas, revelations and faiths.
Related titles: Microfilm ed.
Published by: Humanist Association of Minnesota, PO Box 582997, Minneapolis, MN 55458-2997. TEL 651-335-3800, president@humanistviews.org, http://www.humanistviews.org. Ed., Pub., R&P Ronald Scribner TEL 952-884-5755. Circ: 400.

144 IND ISSN 0018-7429
➤ **HUMANIST OUTLOOK.** Text in English. 1966. q. bk.rev. bibl. **Document type:** *Journal, Academic/Scholarly.* **Description:** Devoted to the furtherance of human values through an ethics based on human perceptions and capabilities.
Published by: Indian Humanist Union, D-36 First Fl, Jangpura Ext, New Delhi, 110 014, India. TEL 91-44-26862191, humanistindia@gmail.com, http://india.humanists.net/.

144 CAN ISSN 1719-6337
CODEN: MPPAEC
HUMANIST PERSPECTIVES. Text in English. 1967. q. CAD 22 domestic; USD 22 foreign (effective 2006). adv. bk.rev. abstr.; bibl.; charts; illus.; stat. index, cum.index. 40 p./no.; back issues avail.; reprints avail. **Document type:** *Magazine, Consumer.* **Description:** Discusses divergent views and topics covering a large spectrum of human interest from a non-religious perspective.
Formerly (until 2005): Humanist in Canada (0018-7402); Which was formed by the merger of: Montreal Humanist; (1964-1967): Victoria Humanist (0506-8657)
Related titles: Microfilm ed.: (from PQC); Online - full text ed.
Indexed: A26, C03, CBCARef, CBPI, CPerI, CWPI, E08, G08, I05, P48, PQC, PRA, R05, RASB, S09.
Published by: Canadian Humanist Publications, P O Box 3769, Sta C, Ottawa, ON K1Y 4J8, Canada. Ed. Douglas Harding. Pub. Paul Pfalzner. R&P B Piercy. Adv. contact Dan Morrison. B&W page USD 200. Circ: 1,250 (paid).

144 AUS
HUMANIST VIEWPOINTS. Text in English. 1969 (vol.7). m. free to members (effective 2008). bk.rev. back issues avail. **Document type:** *Newsletter, Trade.*
Former titles (until 1979): Viewpoints (0042-5877); (until 1962): New South Wales Humanist Society.Monthly Bulletin
Published by: Humanist Society of New South Wales Inc., PO Box 784, Edgecliff, NSW 2027, Australia. TEL 61-2-95973218, FAX 61-2-95562327, vbien@smartchat.net.au, http://www.hsnsw.asn.au. Ed. Affie Adagio.

144 SWE ISSN 1401-8691
HUMANISTEN. Text in Swedish. 1995. q. SEK 200 to individuals; SEK 300 to institutions (effective 2005). **Document type:** *Magazine, Consumer.*
Related titles: Online - full text ed.
Published by: Humanisterna, PO Box 16241, Stockholm, 10324, Sweden. TEL 46-8-50862290, FAX 46-582-105-82. Eds. Andreas Jonson, Christer Sturmark.

165.74 NLD ISSN 1568-1785
HUMANISTISCH ERFGOED. Text in Dutch. 2000. irreg., latest vol.10. price varies.
Published by: (Het Humanistisch Archief), Uitgeverij Papieren Tijger, Postbus 2599, Breda, 4800 CN, Netherlands. TEL 31-76-5228375, FAX 31-76-5205329, info@papierentijger.org, http://www.papierentijger.org.

HUMANISTISCHE RUNDSCHAU. *see* RELIGIONS AND THEOLOGY

144 DEU ISSN 0046-824X
HUMANISTISCHE UNION. MITTEILUNGEN. Text in German. 1961. q. membership. adv. bk.rev. **Document type:** *Newsletter.*
Published by: Humanistische Union e.V., Griefswalder Str 4, Berlin, 10405, Germany. Ed., Pub., Adv. contact Tobias Baur TEL 49-30-20450256. Circ: 2,000.

100 ISL ISSN 0319-7336
B1450
➤ **HUME STUDIES.** Text in English. 1975. biennial. USD 35 to individuals; USD 50 domestic to institutions; USD 58 foreign to institutions (effective 2005). adv. bk.rev. illus. back issues avail.; reprint service avail. from PSC. **Document type:** *Journal, Academic/Scholarly.* **Description:** An interdisciplinary journal dedicated to publishing important work bearing on the thought of David Hume.
Related titles: Microfiche ed.: (from MML); Microfilm ed.; Microform ed.: (from MML); Online - full text ed.: ISSN 1947-9921.
Indexed: A21, A22, A26, BibInd, DIP, E08, FR, G08, I05, IBR, IBZ, IPB, PCI, PhilInd, R05, RI-1, RI-2, S09.
—BLDSC (4336.650000), IE, Infotrieve, Ingenta, INIST.
Published by: Hume Society, c/o Jane McIntyre, Pall S. Ardal Institute for Hume Studies, University of Akureyri, Solborg, Akureyri, 600, Iceland. president@humesociety.org, http://www.humesociety.org. Eds. Elizabeth S Radcliffe, Kenneth P Winkler. R&P Elizabeth S Radcliffe. Circ: 800 (paid). **Subscr. to:** Philosophy Documentation Center, PO Box 7147, Charlottesville, VA 22906. TEL 434-220-3300, FAX 434-220-3301, order@pdcnet.org, http://www.pdcnet.org.

170 NLD ISSN 1872-3942
HUP PROEFSCHRIFTENREEKS. (Humanistics University Press) Key Title: Proefschriftenreeks. Text in Dutch. 2006. irreg. price varies. **Document type:** *Monographic series, Academic/Scholarly.*
Published by: (Universiteit voor Humanistiek), Uitgeverij S W P, Postbus 257, Amsterdam, 1000 AG, Netherlands. TEL 31-20-3307200, FAX 31-20-3308040, admi@swpbook.co, swp@swpbook.com, http://www.swpbook.com.

190 NLD ISSN 0167-9848
B3279.H94 CODEN: HUSTEU
➤ **HUSSERL STUDIES.** Text in English, German. 1984. 3/yr. EUR 440, USD 463 combined subscription to institutions (print & online eds.) (effective 2012). adv. bk.rev. illus. Index. back issues avail.; reprint service avail. from PSC. **Document type:** *Journal, Academic/Scholarly.* **Description:** Emphasizes the relevance of Husserl's phenomenology for contemporary philosophy and the wider academic field.
Related titles: Microform ed.: (from PQC); Online - full text ed.: ISSN 1572-8501 (from IngentaConnect).
Indexed: A20, A22, A26, ASCA, AmHI, ArtHuCI, BibInd, BibLing, CA, CurCont, DIP, E01, FR, H07, IBR, IBZ, IPB, P28, P48, P53, P54, PCI, PQC, PhilInd, RI-1, RI-2, SCOPUS, T02, W07.
—BLDSC (4337.854000), IE, Infotrieve, Ingenta, INIST. **CCC.**
Published by: Springer Netherlands (Subsidiary of: Springer Science+Business Media), Van Godewijckstraat 30, Dordrecht, 3311 GX, Netherlands. TEL 31-78-6576050, FAX 31-78-6576474, http://www.springer.com. Eds. Sonia Rinofner-Kreidl, Steven Crowell.

100 NLD ISSN 0923-4128
➤ **HUSSERLIANA STUDIENSGABE.** Text in English, German. 1950. irreg., latest vol.38, 2004. price varies. **Document type:** *Monographic series, Academic/Scholarly.*
Published by: (Centre d'Archives Husserl BEL), Springer Netherlands (Subsidiary of: Springer Science+Business Media), Van Godewijckstraat 30, Dordrecht, 3311 GX, Netherlands. TEL 31-78-6576050, FAX 31-78-6576474.

323.4 USA
HYPERBOREAN. Text in English. 1990. bi-m. USD 11. back issues avail. **Description:** Contains original and reprinted articles of interest to freethinkers, anarchists and libertarians.
Related titles: Microfiche ed.
Published by: Hyperborean Micropublishers, 2024 N Manor Dr, Erie, PA 16505. TEL 814-456-6819. Ed. Richard Gaska. Circ: 200.

100 DEU
HYPERNIETZSCHE. Text in Multiple languages. 2001. irreg.
Media: Online - full text.
Published by: Projekt HyperNietzsche, Schellingstr 9, Munich, 80799, Germany. TEL 49-89-21806410, FAX 49-89-218013540, pres@hypernietzsche.org.

100 BRA ISSN 1413-9138
B5
➤ **HYPNOS.** Text in Portuguese, Spanish; Summaries in English. 1996. a., latest vol.8, 2002. BRL 15 domestic; USD 12 foreign (effective 2002). back issues avail. **Document type:** *Academic/Scholarly.*
Indexed: C01, PhilInd.
Published by: (Pontificia Universidade Catolica de Sao Paulo), Edicoes Loyola, Rua 1822, n347 - Ipiranga, Sao Paulo, 04216-000, Brazil. TEL 55-11-69141922. Ed. Rachel Gazolla. Circ: 300 (paid); 700 (controlled).

➤ **HYPOMNEMATA**; Untersuchungen zur Antike und zu ihrem Nachleben. *see* CLASSICAL STUDIES

100 ITA ISSN 1824-9817
I S P F. LABORATORIO; rivista elettronica di testi, saggi e strumenti. (Istituto per la Storia del Pensiero Filosofico) Text in Multiple languages. 2004. s-a. free (effective 2011). **Document type:** *Journal, Academic/Scholarly.*
Media: Online - full text.
Published by: Consiglio Nazionale delle Ricerche (C N R), Istituto per la Storia del Pensiero Filosofico e Scientifico Moderno, Via Porta di Massa 1, Napies, 80133, Italy. TEL 39-081-2535580, FAX 39-081-2535515, info@ispf.ccnr.it.

628 GBR
IAN RAMSEY CENTRE. PUBLICATIONS. Text in English. 1989 (no.2). irreg. **Document type:** *Monographic series, Academic/Scholarly.* **Description:** Studies ethical problems arising from scientific and medical research and practice; examines the underlying philosophical and theological issues. Reviews religious beliefs in relation to the sciences.
Published by: Ian Ramsey Centre, 11 Bevington Rd, Oxford, OX2 6NB, United Kingdom. TEL 44-1865-274548, 44-1865-274717, FAX ian-ramsey-centre@theology.oxford.ac.uk, http://www.ianramseycentre.org/. **Co-sponsor:** University of Wales, Cardiff, Centre for Applied Statistics.

100 POL ISSN 0860-4487
IDEA (BIALYSTOK); studia nad struktura i rozwojem pojec filozoficznych. Text in Polish. 1986. a., latest vol.16, 2004. PLZ 20 per vol. (effective 2005). **Document type:** *Monographic series, Academic/Scholarly.*
Published by: Wydawnictwo Uniwersytetu w Bialymstoku, ul Marii Sklodowskiej-Curie 14, Bialystok, 15097, Poland. TEL 48-85-7457059, FAX 48-85-7457073, ac-dw@uwb.edu.pl.

100 BRA ISSN 1415-4668
IDEACAO. Text in Portuguese. 1997. s-a. back issues avail. **Document type:** *Journal, Academic/Scholarly.*
Published by: Universidade Estadual de Feira de Santana, Nucleo Interdisciplinario de Estudos e Pesquisas Filosoficas, Campus Universitario, BR 166 N. Km. 03, Estrada Feira, Serinha, 43000-000, Brazil. TEL 55-75-2248097, FAX 55-75-2248215, chf@uefs.br, http://www.uefs.br/dchf/.

100 USA ISSN 0046-8541
B823
➤ **IDEALISTIC STUDIES.** Text in English. 1971. 3/yr. USD 35 to individuals; USD 64 to institutions; USD 82 combined subscription to individuals (print & online eds.); USD 250 combined subscription to institutions (print & online eds.); USD 12 per issue to individuals; USD 22 per issue to institutions (effective 2010). adv. bk.rev. bibl.; illus. index. back issues avail.; reprint service avail. from PSC. **Document type:** *Journal, Academic/Scholarly.* **Description:** Provides a forum for the discussion of themes and topics that relate to the tradition and legacy of philosophical idealism.

Related titles: Online - full text ed.: ISSN 2153-8239. USD 56 to individuals; USD 215 to institutions (effective 2010).
Indexed: A01, A03, A08, A20, A21, A22, A26, ASCA, AmHI, ArtHuCI, BibInd, CA, CurCont, DIP, E08, FR, G08, H07, I05, IBR, IBZ, IPB, MLA-IB, PCI, PhilInd, R05, RASB, RI-1, RI-2, S09, SCOPUS, T02, W07.
—BLDSC (4362.382500), IE, Infotrieve, Ingenta, INIST. **CCC.**
Published by: Philosophy Documentation Center, PO Box 7147, Charlottesville, VA 22906. TEL 434-220-3300, FAX 434-220-3301, order@pdcnet.org, http://www.pdcnet.org. Ed. Gary Overvold TEL 508-793-7416. Adv. contact Greg Swope.

141 NLD
IDEALIZATION. Text in English. irreg. price varies. **Document type:** *Monographic series, Academic/Scholarly.*
Related titles: ◆ Series of: Poznan Studies in the Philosophy of the Sciences and the Humanities. ISSN 0303-8157.
Indexed: AmHI, H07.
Published by: Editions Rodopi B.V., Tijnmuiden 7, Amsterdam, 1046 AK, Netherlands. TEL 31-20-6114821, FAX 31-20-4472979, info@rodopi.nl. **Dist. by:** Rodopi - USA, 606 Newark Ave, 2nd fl, Kenilworth, NJ 07033. TEL 908-497-9031, FAX 908-497-9035.

IDEAS IN CONTEXT. *see* HUMANITIES: COMPREHENSIVE WORKS

100 COL ISSN 0120-0062
➤ **IDEAS Y VALORES**; revista colombiana de filosofia. Variant title: Revista Ideas y Valores. Text in English, Spanish. 1951. 3/yr. bk.rev. **Document type:** *Journal, Academic/Scholarly.* **Description:** Publishes articles in the field of philosophy.
Formerly: Ideas
Related titles: Online - full text ed.: ISSN 2011-3668. 2007. free (effective 2011) (from SciELO).
Indexed: A20, ArtHuCI, C01, FR, IBR, IBZ, IPB, PCI, PhilInd, RASB, W07.
Published by: Universidad Nacional de Colombia, Departamento de Filosofia, Edificio 239, Cuidad Universitaria Cra 30, No 45-03, Bogota, Colombia. TEL 57-1-3165384, FAX 57-1-3165279. Ed. Jorge Aurelio Diaz.

100 ITA ISSN 0394-3054
➤ **IDEE.** Text in Multiple languages. 1986. 3/yr. **Document type:** *Journal, Academic/Scholarly.*
Related titles: Online - full text ed.: ISSN 1591-0733. free (effective 2011).
Indexed: PhilInd.
Published by: (Universita degli Studi del Salento, Dipartimento di Filosofia), Universita degli Studi del Salento, Coordinamento S I B A, Viale Gallipoli 49, Lecce, 73100, Italy. TEL 39-083-2291111, http://siba2.unile.it. Ed. Mario Signore.

100 DEU ISSN 1862-1147
➤ **IDEEN UND ARGUMENTE.** Text in German. 2002. irreg., latest 2011. price varies. **Document type:** *Monographic series, Academic/ Scholarly.*
Published by: Walter de Gruyter GmbH & Co. KG, Genthiner Str 13, Berlin, 10785, Germany. TEL 49-30-26005220, FAX 49-30-26005251, info@degruyter.com, http://www.degruyter.de.

190 FRA ISSN 2105-0996
▼ ➤ **IGITUR.** Text in French. 2009. irreg., latest 2011, May. **Document type:** *Journal, Academic/Scholarly.*
Media: Online - full text.
Address: Departement de Philosophie, Chemin la Censive du Tertre, BP 81227, Nantes Cedex 3, 44312, France.

100 BEL ISSN 1846-8551
N1.A1
IKON; journal of iconographic studies. Text in Multiple languages. 2008. a. EUR 61 combined subscription (print & online eds.) (effective 2012). **Document type:** *Journal, Academic/Scholarly.*
Related titles: Online - full text ed.
Published by: (Sveuciliste u Rijeci, Filozofski Fakultet/University of Rijeka, Faculty of Philosophy HRV), Brepols Publishers, Begijnhof 67, Turnhout, 2300, Belgium. TEL 32-14-448020, FAX 32-14-428919, periodicals@brepols.net, http://www.brepols.net.

141 NLD ISSN 1875-2942
IMAGINE. Text in Dutch. 1999. bi-m. EUR 25 (effective 2009). adv. **Document type:** *Magazine, Consumer.*
Formerly (until 2006): De Spirituele Krant (1569-3082)
Address: Haalweide 12, Zaandam, 1507 NL, Netherlands. TEL 31-75-6354439, FAX 31-75-6142308. Ed., Pub. Jan Bongers. adv.: page EUR 1,500; 275 x 377. Circ: 20,000.

155.6 170 USA ISSN 1551-4889
BF818
IN CHARACTER; a journal of everyday virtues. Text in English. 2004. 3/yr. USD 27 domestic; USD 32 in Canada & Mexico; USD 37 elsewhere (effective 2008). illus. **Document type:** *Magazine, Consumer.*
Related titles: Online - full text ed.: ISSN 1551-4919.
Indexed: MLA-IB.
Published by: John Templeton Foundation, 300 Conshohocken State Rd, Ste 500, West Conshohocken, PA 19428. editor@incharacter.org, incharacter@templeton.org. Ed. Mark Oppenheimer.

100 ITA ISSN 2037-9706
INCIPIT. Text in Italian. 2008. irreg. **Document type:** *Monographic series, Academic/Scholarly.*
Published by: (Universita degli Studi di Napoli "Federico II", Facolta di Lettere e Filosofia), Giannini Editore, Via Cisterna dell'Olio 6B, Naples, NA 80134, Italy. tipografia@gianninispa.191.it, http://www.gianninieditore.it.

100 IND ISSN 0970-7794
B130 CODEN: JICPEC
➤ **INDIAN COUNCIL OF PHILOSOPHICAL RESEARCH. JOURNAL.** Abbreviated title: J I C P R. Variant title: I C P R Journal. Text in English. 1983. q. INR 500 domestic to individuals; USD 50 foreign to individuals; INR 1,000 domestic to institutions; USD 100 foreign to institutions; INR 150 per issue domestic; USD 15 per issue foreign (effective 2011). **Document type:** *Journal, Academic/Scholarly.*
Indexed: DIP, IBR, IBZ, PCI, PhilInd.
—BLDSC (4764.400000).
Published by: Indian Council of Philosophical Research, Darshan Bhawan, 36, Tughlakabad Institutional Area, Mehrauli Badarpur Rd, Near Batra Hospital, New Delhi, 110 062, India. TEL 91-11-29901506, FAX 91-11-29964750, icpr@del2.vsnl.net.in. Ed. Mrinal Miri.

100 IND ISSN 0376-415X
B130
➤ **INDIAN PHILOSOPHICAL QUARTERLY.** Text in English. 19??. q. INR 150 domestic to individuals; USD 50 foreign to individuals; INR 300 domestic to institutions; USD 100 foreign to institutions; INR 50 per issue domestic; USD 25 per issue foreign; free to members (effective 2011). bk.rev. **Document type:** *Journal, Academic/Scholarly.* **Description:** Provides space for free and critical writings on any philosophical topic.
Formerly (until 1973): The Philosophical Quarterly
Indexed: BAS, DIP, IBR, IBRH, IBZ, IPB, MLA-IB, PCI, PhilInd, RASB.
—BLDSC (4426.300000), IE, Ingenta.
Published by: University of Poona, Department of Philosophy, Ganeshkhind, Pune, Maharashtra 411 007, India. TEL 91-20-25601315, philosophy@unipune.ac.in, http://www.unipune.ac.in/dept/mental_moral_and_social_science/philosophy/default.htm. Ed. Sharad Deshpande.

190 NLD
INDIGENOUS PHILOSOPHIES OF THE AMERICAS. Text in English. irreg. price varies. **Document type:** *Monographic series, Academic/ Scholarly.*
Related titles: ◆ Series of: Value Inquiry Book Series. ISSN 0929-8436.
Published by: Editions Rodopi B.V., Tijnmuiden 7, Amsterdam, 1046 AK, Netherlands. TEL 31-20-6114821, FAX 31-20-4472979, info@rodopi.nl. Ed. Dr. Anne Waters. **Dist. by:** Rodopi - USA, 606 Newark Ave, 2nd fl, Kenilworth, NJ 07033. TEL 908-497-9031, FAX 908-497-9035.

INDO-IRANIAN JOURNAL. *see* ASIAN STUDIES

100 ITA ISSN 1824-7121
INFORMACION FILOSOFICA. Text in Multiple languages. 2004. irreg. **Document type:** *Journal, Academic/Scholarly.*
Related titles: Online - full text ed.: ISSN 1721-7709. free (effective 2011).
Published by: Angelo Marocco http://www.philosophica.org/asp/redazione.asp.

160 CAN
CODEN: INLOEA
➤ **INFORMAL LOGIC (ONLINE)**; reasoning and argumentation in theory and practice. Text in English. 1978. 3/yr. free (effective 2011). adv. bk.rev. back issues avail. **Document type:** *Journal, Academic/ Scholarly.* **Description:** Publishes articles which advance the dialectic in reasoning and argumentation in theory and practice.
Former titles (until 2008): Informal Logic (Print) (0824-2577); (until 1983): Informal Logic Newsletter (0226-1448)
Media: Online - full text.
Indexed: A20, A39, ArtHuCI, C03, C27, C29, CBCARef, D03, D04, E13, IPB, P48, PQC, PhilInd, R14, S14, S15, S18, SOPODA, SociolAb, W07.
—BLDSC (4481.284000), IE, Ingenta. **CCC.**
Published by: University of Windsor, Department of Philosophy, 401 Sunset Ave, Windsor, ON N9B 3P4, Canada. TEL 519-253-3000, FAX 519-971-3610, http://www.uwindsor.ca/faculty/arts/philosophy/il. Ed., R&P Anthony Blair TEL 519-253-4232. Adv. contact Ralph Johnson.

100 DEU ISSN 1434-5250
INFORMATION PHILOSOPHIE. Text in German. 1972. 5/yr. EUR 32 domestic; EUR 34 foreign (effective 2011). bk.rev. bibl. 194 p./no. 2 cols./p.; back issues avail.; reprint service avail. from SCH. **Document type:** *Journal, Academic/Scholarly.* **Description:** News in philosophy, universities, departments, research and books.
Related titles: Online - full text ed.
Indexed: A22, DIP, IBR, IBZ, PhilInd.
—Infotrieve.
Published by: Verlag Claudia Moser, Hauptstr 42, Loerrach, 79540, Germany. TEL 49-7621-87125, FAX 49-7621-169993. Ed. Peter Moser. Pub., Adv. contact Claudia Moser. Circ: 4,200.

100 ESP
INICIACION FILOSOFICA. Text in Spanish. 1982. irreg., latest 2009. price varies.
Published by: (Universidad de Navarra, Facultad de Filosofia y Letras), Universidad de Navarra, Servicio de Publicaciones, Campus Universitario, Pamplona, 31009, Spain. TEL 34-948-256850, FAX 34-948-256854, http://www.unav.es/publicaciones/.

100 GBR ISSN 0020-174X
B1
➤ **INQUIRY**; an interdisciplinary journal of philosophy. Text in English. 1958. bi-m. GBP 302 combined subscription in United Kingdom to institutions (print & online eds.); EUR 396, USD 498 combined subscription to institutions (print & online eds.) (effective 2012). adv. bk.rev. illus. index. back issues avail.; reprint service avail. from PSC. **Document type:** *Journal, Academic/Scholarly.* **Description:** Publishes scholarly articles, discussions and review discussions in all areas of philosophy.
Related titles: Microform ed.: (from PQC); Online - full text ed.: ISSN 1502-3923. GBP 271 in United Kingdom to institutions; EUR 357, USD 448 to institutions (effective 2012) (from IngentaConnect).
Indexed: A01, A02, A03, A08, A20, A21, A22, A26, A36, ASCA, AmHI, ArtHuCI, B01, B04, B06, B07, B08, B09, BAS, BRD, C11, CA, CurCont, DIP, E01, E08, FR, G08, GH, H04, H07, H08, H13, H14, HAb, HumInd, I05, I13, IBR, IBRH, IBSS, IBZ, INI, IPB, L&LBA, MCR, MLA-IB, P02, P10, P20, P27, P30, P42, P46, P48, P50, P53, P54, PCI, PQC, PSA, PhilInd, R05, RASB, RI-1, RI-2, S09, SCOPUS, SOPODA, SSCI, SWR&A, SociolAb, T02, W03, W07.
—IE, Infotrieve, Ingenta, INIST. **CCC.**
Published by: Routledge (Subsidiary of: Taylor & Francis Group), 4 Park Square, Milton Park, Abingdon, Oxon OX14 4RN, United Kingdom. subscriptions@tandf.co.uk, http://www.routledge.com. Ed. Wayne Martin. Adv. contact Linda Hann TEL 44-1344-779945. Circ: 1,200. **Subscr. to:** Taylor & Francis Ltd., Journals Customer Service, Sheepen Pl, Colchester, Essex CO3 3LP, United Kingdom. TEL 44-20-70175544, FAX 44-20-70175198.

170 USA ISSN 1077-4742
BJ1031
INSIGHTS ON GLOBAL ETHICS. Text in English. 1991. q. USD 45 membership (effective 2005). bk.rev. illus. cum.index. back issues avail. **Document type:** *Newsletter, Trade.* **Description:** Reports on ethical issues, news and projects at the institute.
Published by: Institute for Global Ethics, PO Box 563, Camden, ME 04843. TEL 207-236-6658, FAX 207-236-4014. Ed. Rushworth M Kidder. Pub., R&P Paula Blanchard. Circ: 1,600.

100 ARG ISSN 1666-2849
INSTANTES Y AZARES; escrituras Nietzscheanas. Text in Spanish. 2001. a. **Document type:** *Journal, Academic/Scholarly.*
Related titles: Online - full text ed.: ISSN 1853-2144. free (effective 2011).
Published by: Ediciones La Cebra, Madariaga 159, Buenos Aires, CP 1826, Argentina. edicioneslacebra@gmail.com, http://www.edicioneslacebra.com.ar.

INSTITUT PIERRE BAYLE. STUDIES. *see* HISTORY—History Of Europe

100 AUT
INSTITUT WIENER KREIS. VEROEFFENTLICHUNG. Text in German. 1997. irreg., latest vol.12, 2003. price varies. **Document type:** *Monographic series, Academic/Scholarly.*
Published by: (Institut Wiener Kreis), Springer Wien (Subsidiary of: Springer Science+Business Media), Sachsenplatz 4-6, Vienna, W 1201, Austria. TEL 43-1-3302415-0, FAX 43-1-330242665, books@springer.at, http://www.springer.at. Ed. F Stadler. R&P Angela Foessl TEL 43-1-3302415517. **Subscr. in N. America to:** Springer New York LLC, 233 Spring St, New York, NY 10013. TEL 800-777-4643, FAX 201-348-4505.

INSTITUTE FOR LOGIC, LANGUAGE AND COMPUTATION. PREPUBLICATION SERIES. *see* LINGUISTICS

INSTITUTE OF ASIAN STUDIES. JOURNAL. *see* SOCIOLOGY

100 PRT ISSN 1647-5259
INSTITUTO DE ESTUDOS FILOSOFICOS. PUBLICACOES. SERIE CULTURA PORTUGUESA. Text in Portuguese. 195?. irreg. **Document type:** *Monographic series, Academic/Scholarly.*
Published by: Universidade de Coimbra, Faculdade de Letras, Largo da Porta Ferrea, Coimbra, 3004-530, Portugal. TEL 351-239-859900, FAX 351-239-836733, http://www.uc.pt/fluc/.

INSTITUTO DE FILOSOFIA DEL DERECHO DR. JOSE MANUEL DELGADO OCANDO. BOLETIN. *see* LAW

INSTITUTO DE FILOSOFIA DEL DERECHO DR. JOSE MANUEL DELGADO OCANDO. COLECCION DE CURSOS Y LECCIONES. *see* LAW

INSTITUTO DE FILOSOFIA DEL DERECHO DR. JOSE MANUEL DELGADO OCANDO. COLECCION DE MONOGRAFIAS. *see* LAW

INSTITUTO DE FILOSOFIA DEL DERECHO DR. JOSE MANUEL DELGADO OCANDO. CUADERNO DE TRABAJO. *see* LAW

INSTITUTO DE FILOSOFIA DEL DERECHO DR. JOSE MANUEL DELGADO OCANDO. REVISTA. *see* LAW

100 PRT
INSTITUTO NACIONAL DE INVESTIGACAO CIENTIFICA. TEXTOS CLASSICOS. Text in Portuguese. irreg., latest vol.11, 1981.
Published by: (Instituto Nacional de Investigacao Cientifica), Universidade de Coimbra, Centro de Estudos Classicos y Humanisticos, Faculdade de Letras, Coimbra, 3000-447, Portugal.

INTEGRAL. *see* MUSIC

100 USA ISSN 0730-2355
B945.R234
THE INTELLECTUAL ACTIVIST; an objectivist review. Text in English. 1979. m. USD 48 domestic; USD 63 in Canada & Mexico; USD 69 elsewhere (effective 2010). bk.rev. back issues avail. **Document type:** *Journal, Academic/Scholarly.* **Description:** Examines and evaluates the ideas that influence the whole spectrum of human action - from the immediate practical realities of politics and economics - to the vision of human potential offered by art etc.
Published by: T I A Publications, Inc., PO Box 8086, Charlottesville, VA 22906. TEL 540-967-5531, FAX 540-967-5857. Ed., Pub. Robert Tracinski.

110 615.5 FRA ISSN 1771-6101
INTELLIGENCES DE LA NATURE. Text in French. 2004. irreg. back issues avail. **Document type:** *Monographic series, Consumer.*
Published by: Editions du Fayet, 5 Chemin de la Basse Valiere, Ampuis, 69420, France.

100 USA ISSN 2157-1694
▼ ➤ **INTER-AMERICAN JOURNAL OF PHILOSOPHY.** Text in English, Portuguese, Spanish. 2010. s-a. **Document type:** *Journal, Academic/ Scholarly.* **Description:** Contains peer-reviewed papers on philosophy that relate to peoples in the western hemisphere.
Media: Online - full text.
Published by: Texas A & M University, Department of Philosophy, 314 Bolton Hall, 4237 TAMU, College Station, TX 77843-4237. TEL 979-845-5660, FAX 979-845-0458. Ed. Gregory Pappas.

150 DEU ISSN 1612-6572
INTERAKTIONISTISCHER KONSTRUKTIVISMUS. Text in German. 2004. irreg., latest vol.9, 2010. price varies. **Document type:** *Monographic series, Academic/Scholarly.*
Published by: Waxmann Verlag GmbH, Steinfurter Str 555, Muenster, 48159, Germany. TEL 49-251-265040, FAX 49-251-2650426, info@waxmann.com. Eds. Kersten Reich, Stefan Neubert.

181.45 USA ISSN 1935-8806
➤ **INTERBEING.** Text in English. 2007. 2/yr. adv. back issues avail. **Document type:** *Journal, Academic/Scholarly.* **Description:** Focuses on the publication of research and experiential findings in the field of personal and professional excellence.
Indexed: A12, ABIn, APW, B01, B07, CA, H14, P02, P10, P27, P28, P48, P51, P53, P54, PQC, T02.
Published by: Academy of Spirituality and Professional Excellence, 1712 Elliot Dr, Ste B, Burbank, CA 91504. TEL 818-845-3063, FAX 818-845-3063, jmarques01@earthlink.net. Ed. Joan Marques. adv.: B&W page USD 300, color page USD 650. Circ: 500 (paid).

100 800 MAR
INTERDISCIPLINARITE ETUDES PHILOSOPHIQUES ET LITTERAIRES. Text in French. N.S. 1977. s-a. MAD 30; MAD 15 to students. bk.rev.
Formerly (until 1984): Etudes Philosophiques et Litteraires (0531-1934)
Indexed: MLA-IB.
Published by: Societe de Philosophie du Maroc, B P 25, Temara, Morocco. Ed. F Jamai Lahbabi. Circ: 4,000.

INTERDISCIPLINARY YEARBOOK OF BUSINESS ETHICS. *see* BUSINESS AND ECONOMICS

P

100 DEU
▼ **INTERDISZIPLINAERE PERSPEKTIVEN IN DER PHILOSOPHIE.** Text in German. 2010. irreg. price varies. **Document type:** *Monographic series, Academic/Scholarly.*
Published by: Tectum Wissenschaftsverlag Marburg, Biegenstr 4, Marburg, 35037, Germany. TEL 49-6421-481523, FAX 49-6421-43470, email@tectum-verlag.de. Ed. Ulrich Frey.

INTERDISZIPLINAERER DIALOG - ETHIK IM GESUNDHEITSWESEN. *see* MEDICAL SCIENCES

160 GBR ISSN 1367-0751
QA9.A1
➤ **INTEREST GROUP IN PURE AND APPLIED LOGICS. LOGIC JOURNAL.** Variant title: Logic Journal of the I G P L. Text in English. 1993. bi-m. GBP 648 in United Kingdom to institutions; EUR 970 in Europe to institutions; USD 1,295 in US & Canada to institutions; GBP 648 elsewhere to institutions; GBP 707 combined subscription in United Kingdom to institutions (print & online eds.); EUR 1,058 combined subscription in Europe to institutions (print & online eds.); USD 1,412 combined subscription in US & Canada to institutions (print & online eds.); GBP 707 combined subscription elsewhere to institutions (print & online eds.) (effective 2012). adv. 140 p./no.; back issues avail.; reprint service avail. from PSC. **Document type:** *Journal, Academic/Scholarly.* **Description:** Publishes papers in all areas of pure and applied logic, including pure logical systems, proof theory, nonclassical logics, nonmonotonic logics, numerical and uncertainty reasoning, logic and artificial intelligence, foundations of logic programming, logic and computation, logic and language, and logic engineering.
Former titles (until 1997): I G P L Journal; (until 1995): I G P L Bulletin (0945-9103)
Related titles: Online - full text ed.: ISSN 1368-9894. GBP 589 in United Kingdom to institutions; EUR 882 in Europe to institutions; USD 1,177 in US & Canada to institutions; GBP 589 elsewhere to institutions (effective 2012) (from IngentaConnect).
Indexed: A20, A22, B01, C10, CCMJ, CMCI, E01, H14, MSN, MathR, P10, P30, P48, P53, P54, PQC, SCI, SCOPUS, T02, W07, Z02.
—BLDSC (5292.308290), IE, Ingenta. **CCC.**
Published by: (Interest Group in Pure and Applied Logics), Oxford University Press, Great Clarendon St, Oxford, OX2 6DP, United Kingdom. TEL 44-1865-556767, FAX 44-1865-556646, enquiry@oup.co.uk, http://www.oxfordjournals.org. Eds. Dov M Gabbay TEL 44-20-78482930, Ruy de Queiroz. Pub. Ian McIntosh. **Subscr. in N. America to:** Oxford University Press, 2001 Evans Rd, Cary, NC 27513. TEL 919-677-0977 ext 5777, FAX 919-677-1714, jnlorders@oup-usa.org, http://www.us.oup.com.

183 NLD ISSN 1877-0460
▼ **INTERNATIONAL ARISTOTLE BIBLIOGRAPHY ONLINE.** Text in English. 2009. base vol. plus s-a. updates. EUR 330, USD 450 (effective 2010). **Document type:** *Bibliography.*
Media: Online - full text.
Published by: Brill, PO Box 9000, Leiden, 2300 PA, Netherlands. TEL 31-71-5353500, FAX 31-71-5317532, cs@brill.nl. Ed. Richard Ingardia.

100 USA ISSN 0074-4603
B35
INTERNATIONAL DIRECTORY OF PHILOSOPHY AND PHILOSOPHERS/REPERTOIRE INTERNATIONAL DE LA PHILOSOPHIE ET DES PHILOSOPHES. Text in English. 1965. biennial, latest 2007, 15th ed. USD 175 per issue (effective 2009). **Document type:** *Directory, Academic/Scholarly.* **Description:** Contains edited listings for over 1200 university and college philosophy programs, 220 research centers, 250 professional societies and associations, 690 academic journals, and 540 philosophy publishers in 110 countries.
Related titles: Online - full text ed.
Indexed: RASB.
Published by: Philosophy Documentation Center, PO Box 7147, Charlottesville, VA 22906. TEL 434-220-3300, FAX 434-220-3301, order@pdcnet.org. R&P George Leaman. Adv. contact Greg Swope.

100 GBR ISSN 0929-4589
B821.A1
INTERNATIONAL HUMANIST NEWS. Abbreviated title: I H N. Text in English. 1952. q. GBP 16.50, EUR 25, USD 30 to individuals; GBP 33, EUR 50, USD 60 to institutions; GBP 5 newsstand/cover; free to qualified personnel (effective 2009). bk.rev. back issues avail. **Document type:** *Magazine, Consumer.* **Description:** Contains humanist news and views from around the world.
Former titles (until 1993): International Humanist (0925-1375); (until 1981): International Humanism (0020-692X); (until 1962): International Humanist and Ethical Union. Information Bulletin
Related titles: Online - full text ed.: free (effective 2009).
Indexed: RASB.
Published by: International Humanist and Ethical Union, 1 Gower St, London, WC1E 6HD, United Kingdom. TEL 44-870-2887631, FAX 44-870-2887631, office-iheu@iheu.org, http://www.iheu.org. Ed. Sangeeta Mall.

INTERNATIONAL JOURNAL FOR PHILOSOPHY OF RELIGION. *see* RELIGIONS AND THEOLOGY

100 NLD ISSN 2210-5697
B837
▼ **INTERNATIONAL JOURNAL FOR THE STUDY OF SKEPTICISM.** Text in English. 2011. s-a. EUR 69, USD 97 to institutions; EUR 76, USD 106 combined subscription to institutions (print & online eds.) (effective 2012). **Document type:** *Journal, Academic/Scholarly.*
Related titles: Online - full text ed.: ISSN 2210-5700. EUR 63, USD 88 to institutions (effective 2012) (from IngentaConnect).
—CCC.
Published by: Brill, PO Box 9000, Leiden, 2300 PA, Netherlands. TEL 31-71-5353500, FAX 31-71-5317532, http://www.brill.nl. Ed. Baron Reed.

100 USA ISSN 0739-098X
BJ1
➤ **INTERNATIONAL JOURNAL OF APPLIED PHILOSOPHY.** Abbreviated title: I J A P. Text in English. 1982. s-a. USD 33 to individuals; USD 64 to institutions; USD 78 combined subscription to individuals (print & online eds.); USD 230 combined subscription to institutions (print & online eds.); USD 17 per issue to individuals; USD 32 per issue to institutions (effective 2010). adv. bk.rev. back issues avail.; reprint service avail. from PSC. **Document type:** *Journal, Academic/Scholarly.* **Description:** Brings out philosophical articles dealing with practical issues in business, education, the environment, government, health care, law, psychology, and science.
Formerly (until 1983): Applied Philosophy (0733-155X)
Related titles: Online - full text ed.: ISSN 2153-6910. USD 53 to individuals; USD 192 to institutions; USD 40 to members (effective 2010).
Indexed: A01, A03, A08, A26, AmHI, CA, DIP, E08, FR, G08, H07, I05, IBR, IBSS, IBZ, IPB, MLA-IB, P30, P42, PCI, PSA, PhilInd, R05, S02, S03, S09, SCOPUS, SociolAb, T02.
—BLDSC (4542.090000), IE, Infotrieve, Ingenta, INIST. **CCC.**
Published by: Philosophy Documentation Center, PO Box 7147, Charlottesville, VA 22906. TEL 434-220-3300, FAX 434-220-3301, order@pdcnet.org, http://www.pdcnet.org. Ed. Elliot D Cohen. Adv. contact Greg Swope.

➤ **INTERNATIONAL JOURNAL OF CHILDREN'S SPIRITUALITY.** *see* PSYCHOLOGY

➤ **INTERNATIONAL JOURNAL OF CHINESE & COMPARATIVE PHILOSOPHY.** *see* MEDICAL SCIENCES

➤ **INTERNATIONAL JOURNAL OF ETHICS.** *see* POLITICAL SCIENCE

174.95 305.4 USA ISSN 1937-4585
INTERNATIONAL JOURNAL OF FEMINIST APPROACHES TO BIOETHICS. Text in English. 2008 (Apr.). s-a. USD 128.50 combined subscription to institutions (print & online eds.) (effective 2012). adv. reprint service avail. from PSC. **Document type:** *Journal, Academic/Scholarly.* **Description:** Provides a forum within bioethics for feminist thought and debate.
Related titles: Online - full text ed.: ISSN 1937-4577. USD 84.50 to institutions (effective 2012).
Indexed: A22, E01, P30, S21.
—BLDSC (4542.248000), IE. **CCC.**
Published by: Indiana University Press, 601 N Morton St, Bloomington, IN 47404. TEL 812-855-8817, 800-842-6796, journals@indiana.edu, http://iupress.indiana.edu. Ed. Mary C Rawlinson.

INTERNATIONAL JOURNAL OF GANDHI STUDIES. *see* POLITICAL SCIENCE

▼ **INTERNATIONAL JOURNAL OF INTELLIGENCE ETHICS.** *see* POLITICAL SCIENCE—International Relations

INTERNATIONAL JOURNAL OF INTERNET RESEARCH ETHICS. *see* COMPUTERS—Internet

770 GBR ISSN 0967-2559
B1
➤ **INTERNATIONAL JOURNAL OF PHILOSOPHICAL STUDIES.** Text in English. 1951. 5/yr. GBP 571 combined subscription in United Kingdom to institutions (print & online eds.); EUR 756, USD 950 combined subscription to institutions (print & online eds.) (effective 2012). bk.rev. illus. back issues avail.; reprint service avail. from PSC. **Document type:** *Journal, Academic/Scholarly.*
Formerly (until 1993): Philosophical Studies (0554-0739)
Related titles: Online - full text ed.: International Journal of Philosophical Studies (Online). ISSN 1466-4542. 1999. GBP 514 in United Kingdom to institutions; EUR 680, USD 855 to institutions (effective 2012) (from IngentaConnect).
Indexed: A01, A02, A03, A08, A20, A22, ASCA, AmHI, ArtHuCI, BrHumI, CA, CPL, CurCont, E01, FR, H07, IBSS, IPB, L&LBA, PCI, PhilInd, SCOPUS, T02, W07.
—IE, Infotrieve, Ingenta, INIST. **CCC.**
Published by: Routledge (Subsidiary of: Taylor & Francis Group), 4 Park Square, Milton Park, Abingdon, Oxon OX14 4RN, United Kingdom. info@routledge.co.uk, http://www.routledge.com. Ed. Maria Baghramian. Adv. contact Linda Hann TEL 44-1344-779945. **Subscr. to:** Taylor & Francis Ltd., Journals Customer Service, Sheepen Pl, Colchester, Essex CO3 3LP, United Kingdom. TEL 44-20-70175544, FAX 44-20-70175198, subscriptions@tandf.co.uk.

303.34 255.53 USA
➤ **INTERNATIONAL JOURNAL OF SERVANT-LEADERSHIP.** Text in English. 2005. a. USD 50 to individuals; USD 100 to institutions (effective 2010). back issues avail. **Document type:** *Journal, Academic/Scholarly.* **Description:** Contains essays, theory, and research on servant-leadership to influence the scientific community, in the world of business, political inquiry, and social justice, as well as across the academic disciplines.
Published by: Gonzaga University, 502 E Boone Ave, PO Box 25, Spokane, WA 99258. TEL 800-986-9585, president@gonzaga.edu. Ed. Shann Ferch. **Co-sponsor:** Larry C. Spears Center for Servant-Leadership.

▼ ➤ **INTERNATIONAL JOURNAL OF TECHNOETHICS.** *see* SCIENCES: COMPREHENSIVE WORKS

184 NLD ISSN 1872-5082
B395
➤ **INTERNATIONAL JOURNAL OF THE PLATONIC TRADITION.** Text in English. 2007. 2/yr. EUR 179, USD 251 to institutions; EUR 179, USD 251 combined subscription to institutions (print & online eds.) (effective 2012). reprint service avail. from PSC. **Document type:** *Journal, Academic/Scholarly.* **Description:** Covers all facets of the Platonic tradition (from Thales through Thomas Taylor, and beyond) from all perspectives (including philosophical, historical, religious, etc.) and all corners of the world (Pagan, Christian, Jewish, Islamic, etc.).
Related titles: Online - full text ed.: ISSN 1872-5473 (from IngentaConnect).
Indexed: A22, AmHI, CA, E01, H07, IZBG, SCOPUS, T02.
—IE. **CCC.**
Published by: Brill, PO Box 9000, Leiden, 2300 PA, Netherlands. TEL 31-71-5353500, FAX 31-71-5317532, cs@brill.nl. Ed. John F Finamore.

▼ ➤ **INTERNATIONAL JOURNAL OF THINKING OBJECTIVELY.** *see* COMPUTERS

➤ **INTERNATIONAL JOURNAL OF TRANSPERSONAL STUDIES.** *see* PSYCHOLOGY

➤ **INTERNATIONAL JOURNAL OF YOGA.** *see* PHYSICAL FITNESS AND HYGIENE

➤ **INTERNATIONAL JOURNAL OF YOGA THERAPY.** *see* PHYSICAL FITNESS AND HYGIENE

170 340 600 NLD ISSN 1875-0044
THE INTERNATIONAL LIBRARY OF ETHICS, LAW AND TECHNOLOGY. Text in English. 2008. irreg., latest vol.6, 2010. price varies. **Document type:** *Monographic series, Academic/Scholarly.* **Description:** Provides a forum for the discussion and analysis of emerging technologies that are likely to have a significant impact on the environment, society and/or humanity.
Related titles: Online - full text ed.: ISSN 1875-0036.
Published by: Springer Netherlands (Subsidiary of: Springer Science+Business Media), Van Godewijckstraat 30, Dordrecht, 3311 GX, Netherlands. TEL 31-78-6576050, FAX 31-78-6576474. Eds. A M Cutter, B Gordijn, G E Marchant.

100 USA ISSN 0019-0365
B1
➤ **INTERNATIONAL PHILOSOPHICAL QUARTERLY.** Text in English. 1961. q. USD 37 to individuals; USD 72 to institutions; USD 87 combined subscription to individuals (print & online eds.); USD 260 combined subscription to institutions (print & online eds.); USD 30 in developing nations (effective 2009). adv. bk.rev. illus. index. 128 p./no.; back issues avail.; reprint service avail. from PSC. **Document type:** *Journal, Academic/Scholarly.* **Description:** Presents scholarly research articles in all areas of philosophy; open to creative contemporary pieces, as well as to critical and historical studies. Takes a special interest in the intercultural tradition of theistic and personalistic humanism.
Related titles: Microform ed.: (from PQC); Online - full text ed.: ISSN 2153-8077. USD 60 to individuals; USD 216 to institutions (effective 2009).
Indexed: A01, A02, A03, A08, A20, A21, A22, A26, ABS&EES, ASCA, AmHI, ArtHuCI, B04, BAS, BEL&L, BRD, CA, CBRI, CPL, CurCont, DIP, E08, FR, G08, H07, H08, H09, H10, H14, HAb, HumInd, I05, IBR, IBRH, IBZ, IPB, MEA&I, MLA-IB, P02, P10, P30, P48, P53, P54, PCI, PQC, PhilInd, R05, RASB, RI-1, RI-2, RILM, S05, S09, SCOPUS, T02, W03, W05, W07.
—BLDSC (4544.924800), IE, Infotrieve, Ingenta, INIST. **CCC.**
Published by: Philosophy Documentation Center, PO Box 7147, Charlottesville, VA 22906. TEL 434-220-3300, FAX 434-220-3301, order@pdcnet.org, http://www.pdcnet.org. Ed. Joseph W Koterski. R&P George Leaman. Adv. contact Greg Swope.

100 020 DEU
➤ **INTERNATIONAL REVIEW OF INFORMATION ETHICS.** Abbreviated title: I R I E. Text in Multiple languages. 2004. s-a. free (effective 2011). **Document type:** *Journal, Academic/Scholarly.* **Description:** It envisions an international and intercultural discussion focusing on the ethical impacts of information technology on human practices and thinking, social interaction, other areas of science and research and society itself.
Formerly (until 200?): International Journal of Information Ethics (1614-1687)
Media: Online - full text.
Published by: International Center for Information Ethics, c/o Rafel Capurro, EIC, Wolframstr 32, Stuttgart, 70191, Germany. Ed. Rafael Capurro.

179.1 USA ISSN 1564-0027
INTERNATIONAL SOCIETY FOR ENVIRONMENTAL ETHICS. NEWSLETTER. Text in English. 1990. q. USD 15 domestic membership; USD 20 foreign membership (effective 2002). **Description:** Includes articles and presentation in environmental ethics and environmental philosophy, including some related sciences.
Media: Online - full content.
Published by: International Society for Environmental Ethics, c/o Kristin Shrader-Frechette, University of Notre Dame, Notre Dame, IN 46556. TEL 219-631-7579, FAX 219-631-8209, kristin.shrader-frechette1@nd.edu. Ed. Jack Weir.

▼ **THE INTERNATIONAL SOCIETY OF BUSINESS, ECONOMICS, AND ETHICS BOOK SERIES.** *see* BUSINESS AND ECONOMICS

100 USA ISSN 0270-5664
B1
➤ **INTERNATIONAL STUDIES IN PHILOSOPHY**; interdisciplinary issues in philosophy, interpretation, and culture. Text in English; Text occasionally in French, German, Italian. 1959. q. USD 40 to individuals; USD 75 to institutions (effective 2010). bk.rev. bibl. back issues avail. **Document type:** *Journal, Academic/Scholarly.* **Description:** Features articles and discussions in all areas of philosophy for an international scholarly international audience.
Former titles (until 1974): Studi Internazionali di Filosofia (0039-2979); (until 1969): Filosofia. Fascicolo Internazionale (1124-7142)
Related titles: Online - full text ed.: ISSN 2154-1809. USD 64 to individuals; USD 225 to institutions (effective 2010).
Indexed: A20, A22, AmHI, ArtHuCI, CurCont, DIP, FR, H07, IBR, IBZ, IPB, MLA-IB, PCI, PhilInd, RASB, SCOPUS, T02, W07.
—BLDSC (4549.794300), IE, Infotrieve, Ingenta, INIST. **CCC.**
Published by: (State University of New York at Binghamton), Philosophy Documentation Center, PO Box 7147, Charlottesville, VA 22906. TEL 434-220-3300, FAX 434-220-3301, order@pdcnet.org, http://www.pdcnet.org. Ed. Stephen David Ross. Adv. contact Greg Swope. **Subscr. to:** State University of New York at Binghamton, Department of Philosophy.

215 GBR ISSN 0269-8595
Q174
INTERNATIONAL STUDIES IN THE PHILOSOPHY OF SCIENCE. Text in English. 1986. 3/yr. GBP 802 combined subscription in United Kingdom to institutions (print & online eds.); EUR 1,058, USD 1,328 combined subscription to institutions (print & online eds.) (effective 2012). adv. back issues avail.; reprint service avail. from PSC. **Document type:** *Journal, Academic/Scholarly.* **Description:** Publishes articles by scholars of diverse nationalities on all aspects of the philosophy of science.
Formerly: International Studies in the Philosophy of Science - the Dubrovnik Papers

Related titles: Online - full text ed.: ISSN 1469-9281. GBP 722 in United Kingdom to institutions; EUR 952, USD 1,195 to institutions (effective 2012) (from IngentaConnect).
Indexed: A01, A03, A08, A22, BrHumI, CA, CCMJ, DIP, E01, IBR, IBSS, IBZ, IPB, MSN, MathR, P11, P28, P48, P52, P53, P54, P56, PQC, PerIslam, PhilInd, RASB, S21, SCOPUS, SociolAb, T02, Z02.
—BLDSC (4549.794400), IE, Infotrieve, Ingenta, Linda Hall. **CCC.**
Published by: Routledge (Subsidiary of: Taylor & Francis Group), 4 Park Sq, Milton Park, Abingdon, Oxon OX14 4RN, United Kingdom. TEL 44-20-70176000, FAX 44-20-70176336, subscriptions@tandf.co.uk, http://www.routledge.com. Ed. James W McAllister. Adv. contact Linda Hann TEL 44-1344-779945. **Subscr. to:** Taylor & Francis Ltd., Journals Customer Service, Sheepen Pl, Colchester, Essex CO3 3LP, United Kingdom. TEL 44-20-70175544, FAX 44-20-70175198, tf.enquiries@tfinforma.com.

INTERNATIONAL YOGA GUIDE. *see* RELIGIONS AND THEOLOGY—Hindu

100 DEU ISSN 1865-0171
INTERNATIONALE FEUERBACHFORSCHUNG. Text in German. 2006. irreg., latest vol.4, 2009. price varies. **Document type:** *Monographic series, Academic/Scholarly.*
Published by: Waxmann Verlag GmbH, Steinfurter Str 555, Muenster, 48159, Germany. TEL 49-251-265040, FAX 49-251-2650426, info@waxmann.com. Eds. Francesco Tomasoni, Takayuki Shibata, Ursula Reitemeyer.

100 DEU
INTERNATIONALE GESELLSCHAFT FUER PHILOSOPHISCHE PRAXIS. JAHRBUCH. Text in German. 2005. a. **Document type:** *Journal, Academic/Scholarly.*
Published by: (Internationale Gesellschaft fuer Philosophische Praxis), Lit Verlag, Grevener Str/Fresnostr 2, Muenster, 48159, Germany. TEL 49-251-235091, FAX 49-251-231972, lit@lit-verlag.de, http://www.lit-verlag.de.

100 DEU
▼ **INTERNATIONALE GESELLSCHAFT FUER PHILOSOPHISCHE PRAXIS. SCHRIFTEN.** Text in German. 2009. irreg. price varies. **Document type:** *Monographic series, Academic/Scholarly.*
Published by: (Internationale Gesellschaft fuer Philosophische Praxis), Lit Verlag, Grevener Str/Fresnostr 2, Muenster, 48159, Germany. TEL 49-251-235091, FAX 49-251-231972, lit@lit-verlag.de, http://www.lit-verlag.de.

193 DEU ISSN 1612-037X
INTERNATIONALE GESELLSCHAFT HEGEL-MARX FUER DIALEKTISCHES DENKEN. ANNALEN. Text in German. 1983. irreg., latest vol.12, 2004. price varies. **Document type:** *Monographic series, Academic/Scholarly.*
Formerly (until 2004): Internationale Gesellschaft fuer Dialektische Philosophie. Annalen (0255-3457)
Published by: Peter Lang GmbH (Subsidiary of: Peter Lang Publishing Group), Eschborner Landstr 42-50, Frankfurt Am Main, 60489, Germany. TEL 49-69-7807050, FAX 49-69-78070550, zentrale.frankfurt@peterlang.com.

100 DEU ISSN 1869-6880
▼ **INTERNATIONALE ZEITSCHRIFT FUER PHILOSOPHIE UND PSYCHOSOMATIK.** Text in German, English. 2009. s-a. free (effective 2011). **Document type:** *Journal, Academic/Scholarly. Eds. Joachim Heil, Wolfgang Eirund.*

193 DEU ISSN 1613-0472
B3185
➤ **INTERNATIONALES JAHRBUCH DES DEUTSCHEN IDEALISMUS/ INTERNATIONAL YEARBOOK OF GERMAN IDEALISM.** Text in German, English. 2003. a. EUR 74.95; EUR 84.95 combined subscription (print & online eds.) (effective 2010). adv. reprint service avail. from SCH. **Document type:** *Journal, Academic/Scholarly.*
Description: Provides an international framework for comparative investigation of theories and problems relating to German idealism.
Related titles: Online - full text ed.: ISSN 1613-0480. EUR 74.95 (effective 2010).
Indexed: A26, AmHI, H07, IBR, IBZ, T02.
Published by: Walter de Gruyter GmbH & Co. KG, Genthiner Str 13, Berlin, 10785, Germany. TEL 49-30-260050, FAX 49-30-26005251, info@degruyter.com, http://www.degruyter.com. Eds. Juergen Stolzenberg, Karl Amerks. adv.: page EUR 550; trim 155 x 230. Circ: 350 (controlled).

100 DEU ISSN 1619-7569
INTERNATIONALES JAHRBUCH FUER HERMENEUTIK. Text in German. 2002. a. EUR 99 (effective 2011). **Document type:** *Journal, Academic/Scholarly.*
Published by: Mohr Siebeck GmbH & Co. KG, Wilhelmstr 18, Tuebingen, 72074, Germany. TEL 49-7071-9230, FAX 49-7071-51104, info@mohr.de, http://www.mohr.de.

100 NLD
INTERPRETATION AND TRANSLATION. Text in English. irreg. price varies. **Document type:** *Monographic series, Academic/Scholarly.*
Description: Explores philosophical issues of interpretation and its cultural objects through the publication of theoretical works drawn from philosophy, rhetoric, linguistics, anthropology, religious studies, art history and musicology.
Related titles: ♦ Series of: Value Inquiry Book Series. ISSN 0929-8436.
Published by: Editions Rodopi B.V., Tijnmuiden 7, Amsterdam, 1046 AK, Netherlands. TEL 31-20-6114821, FAX 31-20-4472979, info@rodopi.nl. Ed. Michael Krausz. **Dist. by:** Rodopi - USA, 606 Newark Ave, 2nd fl, Kenilworth, NJ 07033. TEL 908-497-9031, FAX 908-497-9035.

100 DEU
INTERPRETATION UND QUELLEN. Text in German. 2008. irreg., latest vol.2, 2010. price varies. **Document type:** *Monographic series, Academic/Scholarly.*
Published by: Verlag Karl Alber, Hermann-Herder-Str 4, Freiburg, 79104, Germany. TEL 49-761-2717436, FAX 49-761-2717212, info@verlag-alber.de.

160 ITA
INTERPRETAZIONI; collana di filosofia. Text in Italian. irreg., latest vol.28. price varies. **Document type:** *Monographic series, Academic/Scholarly.*
Published by: Edizioni Studium, Via Cassiodoro 14, Rome, 00193, Italy. TEL 39-06-6865846, FAX 39-06-6875456, info@edizionistudium.it, http://www.edizionistudium.it.

100 FRA ISSN 1159-6120
L'INTERROGATION PHILOSOPHIQUE. Text in French. 1992. irreg., latest 2003. price varies. **Document type:** *Monographic series, Academic/Scholarly.*
Published by: Presses Universitaires de France, 6 Avenue Reille, Paris, 75685, France. TEL 33-1-58103161, FAX 33-1-45897530, http://www.puf.com.

INTERVENTI CLASSENSI. *see* ART

180 NLD ISSN 1879-9787
▼ ➤ **INVESTIGATING MEDIEVAL PHILOSOPHY.** Text in English. 2010. irreg., latest vol.2, 2011. EUR 108, USD 154 per vol. (effective 2011). **Document type:** *Monographic series, Academic/Scholarly.*
Related titles: Online - full text ed.: ISSN 1879-9795.
Published by: Brill, PO Box 9000, Leiden, 2300 PA, Netherlands. TEL 31-71-5353500, FAX 31-71-5317532, cs@brill.nl.

100 PAK ISSN 0021-0773
BP80.I6
➤ **IQBAL REVIEW.** Text in English, Urdu. 1960. s-a. (English & Urdu eds.; a., Arabic, Persian & Turkish eds.). PKR 60, USD 15 (effective 1999). adv. bk.rev. **Document type:** *Journal, Academic/Scholarly.*
Description: Publishes research on the life, poetry and thought of the poet-philosopher Muhammad Iqbal, and disseminates his literary, political, philosophical and religious ideas.
Related titles: Arabic ed.; Urdu ed.; Turkish ed.; Persian, Modern ed.
Indexed: BAS, IBR, IBZ, MLA, MLA-IB, PerIslam.
Published by: Iqbal Academy Pakistan, Aiwan-e-Iqbal Complex, 6th Fl., Khayaban-e-Iqbal Rd., Lahore, Pakistan. TEL 92-42-6314510, FAX 92-42-6314496, info@iap.gov.pk. Ed. Muhammed Suheyl Umar. Circ: 1,000.

101 ITA ISSN 1122-7893
IRIDE; filosofia e discussione pubblica. Text in Italian. 198?. 3/yr. EUR 88 combined subscription domestic to institutions (print & online eds.); EUR 140.50 combined subscription foreign to institutions (print & online eds.) (effective 2009). back issues avail. **Document type:** *Journal, Academic/Scholarly.*
Related titles: Online - full text ed.
Indexed: A22, IPB, MLA-IB, PhilInd.
Published by: Societa Editrice Il Mulino, Strada Maggiore 37, Bologna, 40125, Italy. TEL 39-051-256011, FAX 39-051-256034, riviste@mulino.it. Ed. Giovanni Mari.

100 ITA ISSN 2036-3257
B1
▼ ➤ **IRIS**; European journal of philosophy and public debate. Text in English. 2009. s-a. **Document type:** *Journal, Academic/Scholarly.*
Related titles: Online - full text ed.: ISSN 2036-6329. free (effective 2011) (from IngentaConnect).
Indexed: AmHI, CA, H07, P45, P46, T02.
Published by: Firenze University Press, Borgo Albizi 28, Florence, 50122, Italy. TEL 39-055-2743051, FAX 39-055-2743058, info@fupress.com, www.fupress.com/index.asp. Ed. Giovanni Mari.

100 ROM ISSN 2068-4797
IRREGULAR F. Text in English, French, Romanian; Summaries in English. 2008. irreg. (1-2/yr.). free. bk.rev. abstr.; bibl. back issues avail. **Document type:** *Journal, Academic/Scholarly.* **Description:** Publishes work from all areas and traditions of philosophy and theoretical research in social sciences and humanities.
Formerly (until 2011): Irregular (2065-7226)
Media: Online - full text.
Published by: Ifilosofie Online Publishing House ifilosofie.ro@gmail.com. Ed., Pub. Rares Iordache.

170 ESP ISSN 1130-2097
B5
ISEGORIA; revista de filosofia moral y politica. Text in Spanish. 1990. s-a. EUR 28.16 per issue domestic; EUR 37.28 per issue foreign (effective 2010). back issues avail. **Document type:** *Journal, Academic/Scholarly.* **Description:** Aims to open discussion about social sciences, moral, history of philosophy, political philosophy, and religion of philosophy.
Related titles: Online - full text ed.: ISSN 1988-8376. free (effective 2011).
Indexed: A20, ArtHuCI, FR, IPB, P09, PCI, PhilInd, RILM, SCOPUS, W07.
—INIST.
Published by: (Consejo Superior de Investigaciones Cientificas (C S I C), Instituto de Filosofia), Consejo Superior de Investigaciones Cientificas (C S I C), Departamento de Publicaciones, Vitruvio 8, Madrid, 28006, Spain. publ@csic.es, http://www.publicaciones.csic.es.

ISLAMIC PHILOSOPHY, THEOLOGY AND SCIENCE; texts and studies. *see* RELIGIONS AND THEOLOGY—Islamic

100 ITA ISSN 2037-4348
ISONOMIA. Text in Multiple languages. 2002. irreg. **Document type:** *Journal, Academic/Scholarly.*
Media: Online - full text.
Published by: Universita degli Studi di Urbino, Dipartimento di Filosofia, Palazzo Albani, Via Timoteo Viti 10, Urbino, 61029, Italy. http://www.uniurb.it/Filosofia/.

174 NLD ISSN 0925-6733
➤ **ISSUES IN BUSINESS ETHICS.** Text in English. 1990. irreg., latest vol.25, 2008. price varies. **Document type:** *Monographic series, Academic/Scholarly.* **Description:** Focuses on ethical issues in international business.
—BLDSC (4584.139700), IE, Ingenta.
Published by: Springer Netherlands (Subsidiary of: Springer Science+Business Media), Van Godewijckstraat 30, Dordrecht, 3311 GX, Netherlands. TEL 31-78-6576050, FAX 31-78-6576474. Eds. Mollie Painter-Morland, Wim Dubbink.

170 USA ISSN 1091-7772
BJ1031
ISSUES IN ETHICS. Text in English. 1987. a.
Indexed: CPL, P30, SCOPUS.
Published by: Santa Clara University, Markkula Center for Applied Ethics, 500 El Camino Real, Santa Clara, CA 95053. TEL 408-554-5319, ethics@scu.edu. Ed. Miriam Schulman.

100 ITA ISSN 0394-2821
ISTITUTO INTERNAZIONALE JACQUES MARITAIN. NOTES ET DOCUMENTS. Text in Multiple languages. 1975. 3/yr. **Document type:** *Journal, Academic/Scholarly.*
Related titles: Online - full text ed.: ISSN 2035-2719. 2006.
Published by: (Istituto Internazionale Jacques Maritain/Institut International Jacques Maritain), Aracne Editrice, Via Raffaele Garofalo 133 A/B, Rome, 00173, Italy. info@aracneeditrice.it, http://store.aracneeditrice.com.

100 ITA ISSN 1824-5080
ISTITUTO ITALIANO PER GLI STUDI FILOSOFICI. SAGGI. Text in Italian. 2000. irreg. **Document type:** *Monographic series, Academic/Scholarly.*
Published by: Istituto Italiano per gli Studi Filosofici (I I S F), Via Monte di Dio 14, Naples, 80132, Italy. TEL 39-081-7642652, FAX 39-081-7642654, http://www.iisf.it.

100 ITA
ISTITUTO UNIVERSITARIO ORIENTALE. DIPARTIMENTO DI FILOSOFIA E POLITICA. QUADERNI. Text in Italian. 1987. irreg., latest vol.16, 1996. price varies. adv. **Document type:** *Monographic series, Academic/Scholarly.*
Published by: Liguori Editore, Via Posillipo 394, Naples, 80123, Italy. TEL 39-081-7206111, FAX 39-081-7206244, liguori@liguori.it, http://www.liguori.it. Ed. Biagio Degiovanni.

294.54 ITA ISSN 0391-7509
ITALIA FRANCESCANA; rivista internazionale di cultura. Text in Italian. 1926-1991; N.S. 1992. 3/yr. EUR 40 (effective 2009). bk.rev. back issues avail. **Document type:** *Magazine, Consumer.*
Indexed: MLA, MLA-IB.
Published by: Conferenza Italiana Ministri Provinciali Cappuccini, Via Pomponia Grecina, Rome, 00145, Italy. Ed. Francesco Neri. Circ: 800.

100 FRA ISSN 1630-5752
ITINERAIRES DU SAVOIR. Text in French. 2001. irreg. back issues avail. **Document type:** *Monographic series, Academic/Scholarly.*
Published by: Editions Albin Michel, 22 rue Huyghens, Paris, 75014, France. TEL 33-1-42791000, FAX 33-1-43272158, http://www.albin-michel.fr.

ITINERARIOS DE FILOSOFIA DA EDUCACAO. *see* EDUCATION

811.45 CAN ISSN 1719-430X
IYENGAR YOGA CENTRE OF VICTORIA. Text in English. 1984. bi-m. **Document type:** *Newsletter, Consumer.*
Former titles (until 2005): Victoria Yoga Centre. Newsletter (1193-0764); (until 1991): Victoria Yoga Centre Society Newsletter (0829-9293)
Published by: The Iyengar Yoga Centre, #202 - 919 Fort St, Victoria, BC V8V 3K3, Canada. TEL 250-386-9642, FAX 250-386-9682, iyoga@telus.net.

100 296 ISR ISSN 0021-3306
B8.H4
➤ **IYYUN**; the Jerusalem philosophical quarterly. Text in Hebrew, English. 1945. q. USD 30 to individuals; USD 22 to individuals English issues only; USD 35 to institutions; USD 25 to institutions English issues only; USD 15 per issue (effective 2008). bk.rev. index. 120 p./no.; back issues avail. **Document type:** *Journal, Academic/Scholarly.*
Indexed: DIP, FR, IBR, IBZ, IHP, PCI, PhilInd.
—Ingenta, INIST.
Published by: Hebrew University of Jerusalem, S.H. Bergman Centre for Philosophical Studies, Jerusalem, 91905, Israel. TEL 972-2-5883747, FAX 972-2-5322545, TELEX 26458, msevas@mscc.huji.ac.il. Ed. Eddy M Zemach. R&P Eva Shorr TEL 972-2-588-3747. Circ: 700.

➤ **J B S BULLETIN.** (John Birch Society) *see* POLITICAL SCIENCE—International Relations

➤ **J O Y**; investigating the philosophy, science, and spirituality of yoga. (Journal of Yoga) *see* NEW AGE PUBLICATIONS

100 DEU ISSN 0946-9559
B2900
JAHRBUCH FUER HEGELFORSCHUNG. Text in German. 1995. a. EUR 25 (effective 2008). **Document type:** *Journal, Academic/Scholarly.*
Indexed: DIP, IBR, IBZ, IPB, MLA-IB, PhilInd.
Published by: Academia Verlag GmbH, Bahnstr 7, Sankt Augustin, 53757, Germany. TEL 49-2241-345210, FAX 49-2241-345316, kontakt@academia-verlag.de. Ed. Helmut Schneider.

215 DEU ISSN 1619-9588
BL4
JAHRBUCH FUER RELIGIONSPHILOSOPHIE. Text in German. 2002. a. price varies. **Document type:** *Journal, Academic/Scholarly.*
Published by: Vittorio Klostermann, Frauenlobstr 22, Frankfurt Am Main, 60487, Germany. TEL 49-69-9708160, FAX 49-69-708038, verlag@klostermann.de. Ed. Markus Enders.

JAHRBUCH FUER WISSENSCHAFT UND ETHIK. *see* SCIENCES: COMPREHENSIVE WORKS

100 ESP ISSN 0211-495X
JAKIN/SABER. Text in Basque. 1956. bi-m. bk.rev. **Document type:** *Journal, Academic/Scholarly.* **Description:** Offers thought and criticism, analysis of cultural and social agents and events.
Indexed: BibLing, MLA-IB.
Published by: Jakinkizunak, S.L., C. Tolosa Hiribidea 103, Donostia, 20009, Spain. TEL 34-943-218092, FAX 34-943-218207, jakin@jalgi.com. **Dist. by:** Asociacion de Revistas Culturales de Espana, C Covarruvias 9 2o. Derecha, Madrid 28010, Spain. TEL 34-91-3086066, FAX 34-91-3199267, info@arce.es, http://www.arce.es/.

JAPAN ASSOCIATION FOR PHILOSOPHY OF SCIENCE. ANNALS. *see* SCIENCES: COMPREHENSIVE WORKS

100 TWN ISSN 1028-4583
JIE Di XUEKAN/ALETHEIA. Text in Chinese. 1997. m. **Document type:** *Journal, Academic/Scholarly.*
Related titles: Online - full text ed.
Published by: Nanhua Daxue, Zhexuexi/Nanhua University, Department of Philosophy, 32, Chung Keng Li, Dalin, Chiayi 62248, Taiwan. TEL 886-5-2721001 ext 2111, FAX 886-5-2427141, cliou@mail.nhu.edu.tw, http://www.nhu.edu.tw/~philos/.

JIMEI DAXUE XUEBAO (ZHEXUE SHEHUI KEXUE BAN)/JIMEI UNIVERSITY. JOURNAL (PHILOSOPHY AND SOCIAL SCIENCES). *see* SOCIAL SCIENCES: COMPREHENSIVE WORKS

P

100 300 CHN ISSN 1000-5072
AS452.C363
JINAN XUEBAO (ZHEXUE SHEHUI KEXUE BAN)/JINAN UNIVERSITY. JOURNAL (PHILOSOPHY & SOCIAL SCIENCES EDITION). Text in Chinese; Contents page in English. 1979. bi-m. USD 28.20 (effective 2009). adv. bk.rev. **Document type:** *Academic/Scholarly.*
Related titles: Online - full text ed.
—East View, Ingenta.
Published by: Ji'nan Daxue, Xuebao Bianjibu/Jinan University, Journal Editorial Department, Rm. 216, 2nd Fl, Bldg. 75, Shipai, Guangzhou, Guangdong 510632, China. TEL 81-20-8522-0281. Ed., R&P Weiliang Wang. Adv. contact Min Liang. Circ: 3,000. **Dist. outside China by:** China International Book Trading Corp, 35 Chegongzhuang Xilu, Haidian District, PO Box 399, Beijing 100044, China.

JINBUN KAGAKU KENKYU/HUMANITIES: CHRISTIANITY AND CULTURE. *see* HUMANITIES: COMPREHENSIVE WORKS

170 CHN
JINGSHEN WENMING DAOKAN/GUIDE TO SPIRITUAL CIVILIZATION. Text in Chinese. 1989. m. 48 p./no.; **Document type:** *Journal, Academic/Scholarly.*
Formerly (until 199?): Jingshen Wenming Jianshe (1006-1835)
Published by: Zhongguo Renmin Daxue Shubao Ziliao Zhongxin/Renmin University of China, Information Center for Social Sciences, Dongcheng-qu, 3, Zhangzizhong Lu, Beijing, 100007, China. TEL 86-10-84043003, FAX 86-10-64015080. **Dist. in US by:** China Publications Service, PO Box 49614, Chicago, IL 60649. TEL 312-288-3291; **Dist. by:** China International Book Trading Corp, 35 Chegongzhuang Xilu, Haidian District, PO Box 399, Beijing 100044, China. TEL 86-10-68412045, FAX 86-10-68412023, cibtc@mail.cibtc.com.cn, http://www.cibtc.com.cn.

JOBS FOR PHILOSOPHERS. *see* OCCUPATIONS AND CAREERS

JOURNAL FOR COMMUNICATION AND CULTURE. *see* COMMUNICATIONS

THE JOURNAL FOR CULTURAL AND RELIGIOUS THEORY. *see* RELIGIONS AND THEOLOGY

JOURNAL FOR GENERAL PHILOSOPHY OF SCIENCE/ZEITSCHRIFT FUER ALLGEMEINE WISSENSCHAFTSTHEORIE. *see* SCIENCES: COMPREHENSIVE WORKS

JOURNAL FOR THE THEORY OF SOCIAL BEHAVIOUR. *see* PSYCHOLOGY

174.2 616.89 DEU ISSN 1869-8549
RC321
➤ **JOURNAL FUER PHILOSOPHIE UND PSYCHIATRIE.** Text in German. 2008. 2/yr. free (effective 2011). **Document type:** *Journal, Academic/Scholarly.*
Media: Online - full text.
Published by: Pabst Science Publishers, Am Eichengrund 28, Lengerich, 49525, Germany. TEL 49-5484-97234, FAX 49-5484-550, pabst@pabst-publishers.com, http://www.pabst-publishers.de. Ed. Jann Schlimme.

174.957 FRA ISSN 1287-7352
K10
JOURNAL INTERNATIONAL DE BIOETHIQUE/INTERNATIONAL JOURNAL OF BIOETHICS. Text in French. q. EUR 130 (effective 2009). **Document type:** *Journal, Academic/Scholarly.* **Description:** Provides an international review and data bank covering reproductive technology, organ transplants, and sophisticated techniques of reanimation and discusses how they have transformed birth, life, and death.
Former titles (until 1998): Journal International de Bioethique, Ethique, la Vie en Question (1282-3279); Which was formed by the merger of (1990-1997): Journal International de Bioethique (1145-0762); (1991-1997): Ethique (1151-5104); Which supersedes in part (in 1990): Cahier de Droit et d'Ethique Medicale (0997-7368)
Indexed: EMBASE, ExcerpMed, FR, IPB, MEDLINE, P20, P21, P22, P30, P54, PQC, R10, Reac, SCOPUS.
—BLDSC (4542.150500), GNLM, IE, Infotrieve, Ingenta. **CCC.**
Published by: Editions ESKA, 12 Rue du Quatre-Septembre, Paris, 75002, France. TEL 33-1-40942222, FAX 33-1-40942232, eska@eska.fr. Eds. Christian Byk, Dominique Folscheid.

174 330 378 USA ISSN 1941-336X
JOURNAL OF ACADEMIC AND BUSINESS ETHICS. Text in English. 2008. irreg. free (effective 2011). **Document type:** *Journal, Academic/Scholarly.* **Description:** Covers topics related to ethical issues in contemporary business and education. Education issues covered include plagiarism, academic integrity and educational policy, and business topcis include legislative issues, white-collar crime and fraud.
Media: Online - full text.
Indexed: A12, A17, B01, CA, P51, P54, T02.
Published by: Academic and Business Research Institute, PO Box 350997, Jacksonville, FL 32235. staff@aabri.com. Ed. Gina Almerico.

JOURNAL OF AESTHETIC EDUCATION. *see* EDUCATION

JOURNAL OF AESTHETICS AND ART CRITICISM. *see* ART

111.85 700 SWE ISSN 2000-4214
▼ ➤ **JOURNAL OF AESTHETICS AND CULTURE.** Text in English. 2009. irreg. free (effective 2011). Index. back issues avail. **Document type:** *Journal, Academic/Scholarly.* **Description:** Aims to develop inter-disciplinary theoretical models as applied to human science research on aesthetic questions, understood in their broadest meaning, as a means to transcend traditional subject boundaries and to integrate regional, national, international and global perspectives; and finally, to also bridge the gaps between art and technology, between high brow culture and popular culture, and between aesthetics and politics.
Media: Online - full text.
Indexed: A30, A31, T02.
Published by: (Stockholms Universitet, Filmvetenskapliga Institutionen/ Stockholm University, Department of Cinema Studies), Co-Action Publishing, Ripvaegen 7, Jaerfaella, 17564, Sweden. TEL 46-18-4951150, FAX 46-18-4951138, info@co-action.net, http://www.co-action.net. Ed. Astrid Soederbergh Widding. Pub., R&P Anne Bindslev. Adv. contact Caroline Sutton TEL 46-18-4951126.

➤ **JOURNAL OF AFRICAN RELIGION AND PHILOSOPHY**; a journal of religion and philosophy in Africa. *see* RELIGIONS AND THEOLOGY

179.1 NLD ISSN 1187-7863
CODEN: JAEVEI
➤ **JOURNAL OF AGRICULTURAL AND ENVIRONMENTAL ETHICS.** Text in English. 1988. bi-m. EUR 467, USD 482 combined subscription to institutions (print & online eds.) (effective 2012). adv. bk.rev. reprint service avail. from PSC. **Document type:** *Journal, Academic/Scholarly.* **Description:** Creates a forum for discussion of moral issues arising from actual or projected social policies in regard to ethical questions concerning the responsibilities of agricultural producers, the assessment of technological changes affecting farm populations, the utilization of farmland and other resources,the deployment of intensive agriculture, the modification of ecosystems, animal welfare, the professional responsibilities of agrologists, veterinarians, or food scientists, the use of biotechnology, the safety, availability, and affordability of food.
Formerly (until 1991): Journal of Agricultural Ethics (0893-4282)
Related titles: Online - full text ed.: ISSN 1573-322X (from IngentaConnect).
Indexed: A12, A20, A22, A26, A34, A35, A37, A38, ABIn, ASCA, AgBio, Agr, ArtHuCI, B&AI, B&BAb, B01, B04, B07, B10, B19, B25, BA, BIOSIS Prev, BRD, BibLing, BrArAb, C03, C25, CA, CABA, CBCARef, CPerI, CurCont, D01, E01, E04, E05, E11, E12, ESPM, F08, F12, G08, GEOBASE, GH, H14, H16, HPNRM, I05, IAB, IndVet, LT, MaizeAb, MycolAb, N02, N03, N04, OR, P10, P11, P28, P30, P32, P33, P37, P40, P48, P51, P52, P53, P54, P56, PGegResA, PGrRegA, PHN&I, PN&I, PQC, PhilInd, PollutAb, R07, R08, R12, RASB, RI-1, RI-2, RRTA, S04, S10, S12, S13, S16, SCI, SCOPUS, SSCI, SSciA, T02, T04, TAR, VS, W03, W05, W07, W10, W11.
—BLDSC (4919.999500), IE, Infotrieve, Ingenta, INIST. **CCC.**
Published by: Springer Netherlands (Subsidiary of: Springer Science+Business Media), Van Godewijckstraat 30, Dordrecht, 3311 GX, Netherlands. TEL 31-78-6576050, FAX 31-78-6576474, http://www.springer.com. Ed. Richard P Haynes.

▼ ➤ **JOURNAL OF ANIMAL ETHICS.** *see* ANIMAL WELFARE

160 NLD ISSN 1570-8683
➤ **JOURNAL OF APPLIED LOGIC.** Text in English. 2003. 4/yr. EUR 521 in Europe to institutions; JPY 61,600 in Japan to institutions; USD 551 elsewhere to institutions (effective 2012). **Document type:** *Journal, Academic/Scholarly.* **Description:** Contains research in the areas of logic which can be applied in other disciplines, as well as application papers in those disciplines, the unifying theme being logics arising from modelling the human agent.
Related titles: Online - full text ed.: ISSN 1570-8691 (from IngentaConnect, ScienceDirect).
Indexed: A20, A26, A28, APA, BrCerAb, C&ISA, C10, CA, CA/WCA, CCMJ, CIA, CPEI, CerAb, CivEngAb, CorrAb, CurCont, E&CAJ, E11, EEA, EMA, ESPM, EngInd, EnvEAb, H15, I05, Inspec, L&LBA, L11, M&TEA, M09, MBF, METADEX, MSN, MathR, SCI, SCOPUS, SolStAb, T02, T04, W07, WAA, Z02.
—BLDSC (4942.645000), IE, Ingenta, Linda Hall. **CCC.**
Published by: Elsevier BV (Subsidiary of: Elsevier Science & Technology), Radarweg 29, PO Box 211, Amsterdam, 1000 AE, Netherlands. TEL 31-20-4853911, FAX 31-20-4852457, JournalsCustomerServiceEMEA@elsevier.com, http://www.elsevier.nl. Eds. Andrew J Jones, Dev M Gabbay, Jorg Siekmann.

100 GBR ISSN 0264-3758
B1
➤ **JOURNAL OF APPLIED PHILOSOPHY.** Text in English. 1984. q. GBP 549 in United Kingdom to institutions; EUR 696 in Europe to institutions; USD 917 in the Americas to institutions; USD 1,073 elsewhere to institutions; GBP 631 combined subscription in United Kingdom to institutions (print & online eds.); EUR 801 combined subscription in Europe to institutions (print & online eds.); USD 1,055 combined subscription in the Americas to institutions (print & online eds.); USD 1,234 combined subscription elsewhere to institutions (print & online eds.) (effective 2012). adv. bk.rev. index. back issues avail.; reprint service avail. from PSC. **Document type:** *Journal, Academic/Scholarly.* **Description:** Provides a forum for philosophical research which seeks to make a constructive contribution to problems of practical concern.
Related titles: Microfiche ed.; Online - full text ed.: ISSN 1468-5930. GBP 549 in United Kingdom to institutions; EUR 696 in Europe to institutions; USD 917 in the Americas to institutions; USD 1,073 elsewhere to institutions (effective 2012) (from IngentaConnect).
Indexed: A01, A03, A08, A22, A26, AmHI, BAS, BrHumI, CA, E01, FR, H07, H14, IPB, P02, P10, P30, P42, P48, P53, P54, PCI, PQC, PhilInd, R10, RASB, RI-1, RI-2, Reac, S02, S03, SCOPUS, SociolAb, T02.
—BLDSC (4943.800000), IE, Infotrieve, Ingenta, INIST. **CCC.**
Published by: (Society of Applied Philosophy), Wiley-Blackwell Publishing Ltd. (Subsidiary of: John Wiley & Sons, Inc.), 9600 Garsington Rd, Oxford, OX4 2DQ, United Kingdom. TEL 44-1865-776868, FAX 44-1865-714591, customerservices@blackwellpublishing.com. Eds. Alan Carter, Dr. Suzanne Uniacke. Adv. contact Craig Pickett TEL 44-1865-476267. B&W page GBP 445, B&W page USD 823; 135 x 205. Circ: 700.

191 USA ISSN 1526-1018
PS3535.A547
➤ **THE JOURNAL OF AYN RAND STUDIES.** Text in English. 1999. s-a. USD 25 to individuals; USD 45 to institutions; USD 15 newsstand/ cover (effective 2010). adv. back issues avail. **Document type:** *Journal, Academic/Scholarly.* **Description:** Devoted to the study of Ayn Rand and her times.
Indexed: A20, AmHI, ArtHuCI, CA, CurCont, DIP, H07, I13, IBR, IBZ, L06, MLA-IB, P42, PAIS, PhilInd, SCOPUS, T02, W07.
Published by: Journal of Ayn Rand Studies Foundation, PO Box 230052, Brooklyn, NY 11223.

700 GBR ISSN 2045-757X
JOURNAL OF BENTHAM STUDIES. Text in English. 1978. a. bk.rev. back issues avail. **Document type:** *Journal, Academic/Scholarly.* **Description:** Provides a forum to discuss Bentham studies and utilitarian philosophy.
Formerly (until 1988): Bentham Newsletter (0141-190X)
Related titles: Online - full text ed.: free (effective 2009).
Published by: University College London, Bentham Project, University College London, Bentham House, Endsleigh Gardens, London, WC1H 0EG, United Kingdom. TEL 44-20-76791407, library@ucl.ac.uk. Ed. Valerie Wallace.

JOURNAL OF BUDDHIST ETHICS. *see* RELIGIONS AND THEOLOGY—Buddhist

174.4 GBR ISSN 1649-5195
JOURNAL OF BUSINESS ETHICS EDUCATION. Abbreviated title: J B E E. Text in English. 2004. q. GBP 240 domestic to institutions; EUR 360 in Europe to institutions; USD 430 elsewhere to institutions; GBP 250 combined subscription domestic to institutions (print & onilne eds.); EUR 370 combined subscription in Europe to institutions (print & onilne eds.); USD 435 combined subscription elsewhere to institutions (print & onilne eds.) (effective 2010). bk.rev. back issues avail. **Document type:** *Journal, Academic/Scholarly.* **Description:** Features research articles that deal with teaching strategies and educational issues related to business ethics.
Related titles: Online - full text ed.: ISSN 2044-4559. GBP 230 domestic to institutions; EUR 350 in Europe to institutions; USD 415 elsewhere to institutions (effective 2010).
Indexed: P10, P18, P27, P48, P51, P53, P54, PQC.
Published by: NeilsonJournals Publishing, 151 Whitehouse Loan, Edinburgh, EH9 2EY, United Kingdom. TEL 44-131-4473300, FAX 44-131-4640300, pneilson@neilsonjournals.com. Eds. Ken McPhail, Olukunle Iyanda, John Hooker.

181 USA ISSN 0301-8121
B5230
➤ **JOURNAL OF CHINESE PHILOSOPHY.** Text mainly in English. 1973. q. GBP 591 in United Kingdom to institutions; EUR 751 in Europe to institutions; USD 820 in the Americas to institutions; USD 1,157 elsewhere to institutions; GBP 680 combined subscription in United Kingdom to institutions (print & online eds.); EUR 864 combined subscription in Europe to institutions (print & online eds.); USD 943 combined subscription in the Americas to institutions (print & online eds.); USD 1,331 combined subscription elsewhere to institutions (print & online eds.) (effective 2012). adv. bk.rev. illus. Index. back issues avail.; reprint service avail. from PSC. **Document type:** *Journal, Academic/Scholarly.* **Description:** Explores Chinese philosophy and Chinese thought in all phases and stages of articulation and development, providing English-language translations of important materials in the history of Chinese philosophy, offering interpretations and expositions in Chinese philosophy, and publishing comparative studies within Chinese philosophy or in relation to schools of thought in the Western tradition.
Related titles: Online - full text ed.: ISSN 1540-6253. GBP 591 in United Kingdom to institutions; EUR 751 in Europe to institutions; USD 820 in the Americas to institutions; USD 1,157 elsewhere to institutions (effective 2012) (from IngentaConnect).
Indexed: A01, A03, A08, A20, A22, A26, ASCA, AmHI, ArtHuCI, BAS, CA, CurCont, E01, FR, H07, H14, IBR, IBSS, IBZ, IPB, MLA, MLA-IB, P02, P10, P48, P53, P54, PCI, PQC, PhilInd, RASB, RI-1, RI-2, SCOPUS, T02, W07.
—BLDSC (4958.140000), IE, Infotrieve, Ingenta, INIST. **CCC.**
Published by: (International Society for Chinese Philosophy), Wiley-Blackwell Publishing, Inc. (Subsidiary of: Wiley-Blackwell Publishing Ltd.), 111 River St, Hoboken, NJ 07030. TEL 201-748-6000, FAX 201-748-6088, info@wiley.com. Ed. Chung-ying Cheng. Adv. contact Kristin McCarthy TEL 201-748-7683.

➤ **THE JOURNAL OF CLINICAL ETHICS.** *see* MEDICAL SCIENCES

100 USA ISSN 2153-8212
B808.9
▼ ➤ **JOURNAL OF CONSCIOUSNESS EXPLORATION & RESEARCH.** Text in English. 2010. q. free (effective 2010). **Document type:** *Journal, Academic/Scholarly.* **Description:** Features work by scientists, philosophers and other learned scholars on the nature, origin and mechanism of consciousness.
Media: Online - full text.
Published by: QuantumDream, Inc., PO Box 267, Stony Brook, NY 11790-0267. TEL 631-678-1864, hupinghu@quantumbrain.org.

➤ **JOURNAL OF CONSCIOUSNESS STUDIES**; controversies in science & the humanities. *see* PSYCHOLOGY

149.2 GBR ISSN 1476-7430
JOURNAL OF CRITICAL REALISM. Abbreviated title: J C R. Text in English. 1997. q. USD 440 combined subscription in North America to institutions (print & online eds.); GBP 246 combined subscription elsewhere to institutions (print & online eds.) (effective 2012). adv. back issues avail.; reprints avail. **Document type:** *Journal, Academic/Scholarly.* **Description:** Provides a forum for scholars wishing to promote realist emancipatory philosophy, social theory and science on an interdisciplinary and international basis.
Formerly (until 2001): Alethia
Related titles: Online - full text ed.: ISSN 1572-5138. USD 352 in North America to institutions; GBP 196 elsewhere to institutions (effective 2012) (from IngentaConnect).
Indexed: A22, AmHI, CA, E01, H07, IBSS, IZBG, LeftInd, PhilInd, T02.
—BLDSC (4965.642000), IE, Ingenta. **CCC.**
Published by: (International Association for Critical Realism), Equinox Publishing Ltd., Unit S3, Kelham House, 3 Lancaster St, Sheffield, S6 3AF, United Kingdom. TEL 44-114-2725957, FAX 44-560-3459046, journals@equinoxpub.com, http://www.equinoxpub.com/. Ed. Mervyn Hartwig. Adv. contact Val Hall.

174 NLD ISSN 1382-4554
BJ1 CODEN: JETHFC
➤ **THE JOURNAL OF ETHICS**; an international philosophical review. Text in English. 1997. q. EUR 565, USD 615 combined subscription to institutions (print & online eds.) (effective 2012). adv. bk.rev. illus. reprint service avail. from PSC. **Document type:** *Journal, Academic/ Scholarly.* **Description:** Seeks to publish articles on a wide range of topics in ethics, philosophically construed, including such areas as ethical theory, moral, social, political, and legal philosophy.
Related titles: Online - full text ed.: ISSN 1572-8609 (from IngentaConnect).
Indexed: A01, A02, A03, A08, A22, A26, BibLing, CA, E01, E08, FR, G08, I05, IPB, P10, P30, P48, P53, P54, PQC, PhilInd, R10, Reac, S02, S03, S09, SCOPUS, T02.
—BLDSC (4979.568000), IE, Infotrieve, Ingenta, INIST. **CCC.**
Published by: Springer Netherlands (Subsidiary of: Springer Science+Business Media), Van Godewijckstraat 30, Dordrecht, 3311 GX, Netherlands. TEL 31-78-6576050, FAX 31-78-6576474, http://www.springer.com. Ed. J Angelo Corlett.

170 301 340 USA ISSN 1559-3061
HM665
➤ **JOURNAL OF ETHICS & SOCIAL PHILOSOPHY**; online peer-reviewed journal of moral, political and legal philosophy. Abbreviated title: J E S P. Text in English. 2005. irreg. free (effective 2009). **Document type:** *Journal, Academic/Scholarly.* **Description:** Covers philosophical analyses of contemporary ethical, political and legal issues.
Media: Online - full text.
Indexed: A26, AmHI, CA, E08, H07, I05, LRI, PhilInd, S09, T02.
Published by: University of Southern California, Gould School of Law, University Park, Los Angeles, CA 90089. TEL 213-740-6314, FAX 213-740-5502, academicsupport@law.usc.edu, http://lawweb.usc.edu. Eds. James Dreier, Julia Driver, Andrei Marmor.

100 USA ISSN 1541-0099
GN281
➤ **JOURNAL OF EVOLUTION AND TECHNOLOGY.** Short title: J E T. Text in English. 1998. irreg. free (effective 2011). **Document type:** *Journal, Academic/Scholarly.* **Description:** Publishing contemporary research into future science and philosophy.
Formerly: Journal of Transhumanism
Media: Online - full text.
Indexed: A01, A39, C27, C29, CA, D03, D04, E13, R14, S14, S15, S18, T02.
Published by: World Transhumanist Association, c/o James J Hughes, Williams 229B, Trinity College, 300 Summit St, Hartford, CT 06106. TEL 860-297-2376. Ed. Russell Blackford.

100 USA
B1802
➤ **JOURNAL OF FRENCH AND FRANCOPHONE PHILOSOPHY.** Text in English, French. 1989-2000; resumed 2003. s-a. USD 25 to individuals; USD 40 to institutions (effective 2011). adv. bk.rev. back issues avail. **Document type:** *Journal, Academic/Scholarly.* **Description:** Publishes interdisciplinary essays, book reviews, and critical notes on philosophy and related theoretical endeavors in terms of the geography and historical period of the French language.
Former titles (until 2008): Journal of French Philosophy (1936-6280); (until 2006): Societe Americaine de Philosophie de Langue Francaise. Bulletin (1042-6833)
Related titles: Online - full text ed.: ISSN 2155-1162. free.
Indexed: IPB, MLA-IB.
—BLDSC (4986.535500).
Published by: University of Pittsburgh, University Library System, Coordinator of Library Instruction, 207 Hillman Library, Pittsburgh, PA 15260. TEL 412-648-7732, FAX 412-648-7733, e-journals@mail.pitt.edu, http://www.library.pitt.edu. Eds., Pubs., R&Ps John E. Drabinski, Scott Davidson.

➤ **JOURNAL OF GANDHIAN STUDIES.** *see* POLITICAL SCIENCE

➤ **THE JOURNAL OF HOSPITAL ETHICS.** *see* HEALTH FACILITIES AND ADMINISTRATION

➤ **JOURNAL OF HUMAN VALUES.** *see* BUSINESS AND ECONOMICS—Management

181 NLD ISSN 0022-1791
B130
➤ **JOURNAL OF INDIAN PHILOSOPHY.** Text in English. 1970. bi-m. EUR 877, USD 922 combined subscription to institutions (print & online eds.) (effective 2012). adv. bk.rev. illus. Index. reprint service avail. from PSC. **Document type:** *Journal, Academic/Scholarly.* **Description:** Publishes articles dealing with the work of Indian philosophers of the past as well as the creative researches of contemporary scholars.
Related titles: Microform ed.: (from PQC); Online - full text ed.: ISSN 1573-0395 (from IngentaConnect).
Indexed: A20, A21, A22, A26, ASCA, AmHI, ArtHuCI, BAS, BibInd, BibLing, CA, CurCont, DIP, E01, FR, H07, H14, IBR, IBSS, IBZ, IPB, MLA, MLA-IB, P10, P30, P48, P53, P54, PCI, PQC, PhilInd, RASB, RI-1, RI-2, SCOPUS, T02, W07.
—BLDSC (5005.325000), IE, Infotrieve, Ingenta, INIST. **CCC.**
Published by: Springer Netherlands (Subsidiary of: Springer Science+Business Media), Van Godewijckstraat 30, Dordrecht, 3311 GX, Netherlands. TEL 31-78-6576050, FAX 31-78-6576474, http://www.springer.com. Ed. Phyllis Granoff.

➤ **JOURNAL OF INFORMATION, COMMUNICATION & ETHICS IN SOCIETY.** *see* SOCIOLOGY

➤ **JOURNAL OF INFORMATION ETHICS.** *see* LIBRARY AND INFORMATION SCIENCES

100 800 GBR ISSN 2045-8797
➤ **JOURNAL OF INKLINGS STUDIES**; theology-philosophy-literature. Abbreviated title: J I S. Text in English. 2004. s-a. GBP 14.80 domestic to individuals; GBP 17 in Europe to individuals; GBP 19.40 elsewhere to individuals; GBP 62.80 domestic to institutions; GBP 65 in Europe to institutions; GBP 67.40 elsewhere to institutions (effective 2011). back issues avail. **Document type:** *Journal, Academic/Scholarly.* **Description:** Seeks to contribute to the reception of these thinkers in theology, philosophy, and literary studies.
Formerly (until 2011): Oxford University C.S. Lewis Society. Chronicle (1752-0274)
Related titles: Online - full text ed.: ISSN 2045-8800.
Published by: Oxford C.S. Lewis Society, c/o Judith Wolfe, St John's College, Oxford, OX1 3JP, United Kingdom. oulewis@herald.ox.ac.uk, http://sites.google.com/site/lewisinoxford/.

➤ **JOURNAL OF INTEGRAL THEORY AND PRACTICE.** *see* PSYCHOLOGY

174 USA ISSN 1940-1485
HF5387
JOURNAL OF INTERNATIONAL BUSINESS ETHICS. Abbreviated title: J I B E. Text in English. 2008. s-a. back issues avail. **Document type:** *Journal, Trade.* **Description:** Aims to bridge the gap between theory and practice in Corporate Social Responsibility and business ethics theory and practice.
Indexed: A12, A17, ABIn, B01, CA, P48, P51, P53, P54, PQC, T02.
Published by: American Scholars Press, Inc., 3238 Harvest Way, Marietta, GA 30062. TEL 770-973-8732, FAX 678-915-4949, contact@americanscholarspress.com. Ed. Yang Hengda.

100 297 USA ISSN 1536-4569
➤ **JOURNAL OF ISLAMIC PHILOSOPHY.** Text in English. 2005. q. USD 63 combined subscription to individuals (print & online eds.); USD 126 combined subscription to institutions (print & online eds.); USD 25 to individuals; USD 48 to institutions (effective 2010). **Document type:** *Journal, Academic/Scholarly.* **Description:** Provides a forum to scholars, professors, and researchers for the philosophical discussion of topics in Islamic thought.
Related titles: Online - full text ed.: ISSN 1536-4755. USD 50 to individuals; USD 100 to institutions (effective 2010).
Indexed: AmHI, CA, H07, M10, T02.
—INIST.
Published by: Journal of Islamic Philosophy, Inc., 70 Normandy Dr, Wayne, NJ 07470. Eds. Macksood A Aftab, Valerie J Turner. **Subscr. to:** Philosophy Documentation Center, PO Box 7147, Charlottesville, VA 22906. order@pdcnet.org, http://www.pdcnet.org.

001.0685 CAN ISSN 1705-9232
HD30.2
JOURNAL OF KNOWLEDGE MANAGEMENT PRACTICE. Abbreviated title: J K M P. Text in English. 1988. irreg. free (effective 2011). back issues avail. **Document type:** *Journal, Academic/Scholarly.* **Description:** Devoted to collecting serious research about knowledge management and its applications.
Formerly: Journal of Systemic Knowledge Management
Media: Online - full text.
Indexed: A39, C27, C29, D03, D04, E13, R14, S14, S15, S18.
Published by: The Leadership Alliance Inc., 12 Kilpatrick Dr., Hollan Landing, ON L9N 1H6, Canada. Ed. Peter Smith.

JOURNAL OF LOGIC, LANGUAGE AND INFORMATION. *see* LINGUISTICS

100 CAN
➤ **THE JOURNAL OF MACRODYNAMIC STUDIES.** Text in English. 2001. a. free (effective 2011). **Document type:** *Journal, Academic/Scholarly.*
Media: Online - full text.
Published by: Memorial University of Newfoundland, Department of Religious Studies, PO Box 4200, St. John's, NF A1C 5S7, Canada. TEL 709-864-8000, http://www.mun.ca. Ed. Michael Shute.

➤ **THE JOURNAL OF MARKETS & MORALITY.** *see* BUSINESS AND ECONOMICS

➤ **JOURNAL OF MASS MEDIA ETHICS**; exploring questions of media morality. *see* SOCIOLOGY

➤ **JOURNAL OF MEDICAL ETHICS**; an international peer-reviewed journal for health professionals and researchers in medical ethics. *see* MEDICAL SCIENCES

➤ **JOURNAL OF MEDICAL HUMANITIES.** *see* MEDICAL SCIENCES

➤ **THE JOURNAL OF MEDICINE AND PHILOSOPHY**; a forum for bioethics and philosophy of medicine. *see* MEDICAL SCIENCES

111 128 GBR ISSN 1366-4786
BF778
➤ **JOURNAL OF MEMETICS - EVOLUTIONARY MODELS OF INFORMATION TRANSMISSION.** Text in English. 1997. s-a. free (effective 2007). bibl. **Document type:** *Journal, Academic/Scholarly.* **Description:** Seeks to develop the memetic perspective, with space devoted to relevant evolutionary issues and related topics.
Media: Online - full text.
Indexed: A01, A02, A03, A08, B01, B06, B07, B09, C10, CA, CompLI, Inspec, RILM, SCOPUS, T02, Z01.
—**CCC.**
Published by: Manchester Metropolitan University, Centre for Policy Modelling, Aytoun Bldg, Aytoun St, Manchester, Lancs M1 3GH, United Kingdom. TEL 44-161-247-6482, FAX 44-161-247-6802, http://cfpm.org/. Ed. Francis Heylighen.

➤ **THE JOURNAL OF MIND AND BEHAVIOR.** *see* PSYCHOLOGY

100 NLD ISSN 1740-4681
BJ1
➤ **JOURNAL OF MORAL PHILOSOPHY.** Text in English. 2004 (April). 3/yr. EUR 329, USD 461 to institutions; EUR 359, USD 503 combined subscription to institutions (print & online eds.) (effective 2012). adv. reprint service avail. from PSC. **Document type:** *Journal, Academic/Scholarly.* **Description:** Covers all areas of moral, political and legal philosophy, including pure and applied ethics, legal, social and political theory.
Related titles: Online - full text ed.: ISSN 1745-5243. EUR 299, USD 419 to institutions (effective 2012) (from IngentaConnect).
Indexed: A01, A02, A03, A08, A22, ArtHuCI, CA, CurCont, E01, IZBG, P42, PSA, PhilInd, SCOPUS, SSCI, T02, W07.
—IE. **CCC.**
Published by: (University of Sheffield, Department of Philosophy GBR), Brill, PO Box 9000, Leiden, 2300 PA, Netherlands. TEL 31-71-5353500, FAX 31-71-5317532, cs@brill.nl. Ed. Thom Brooks. adv.: B&W page GBP 300; 130 x 200.

155.937 128 USA ISSN 0891-4494
BF789.D4 CODEN: JNDAE7
➤ **JOURNAL OF NEAR-DEATH STUDIES.** Text in English. 1981. q. USD 398 to institutions (effective 2009). adv. bk.rev. illus. reprints avail. **Document type:** *Journal, Academic/Scholarly.* **Description:** Publishes articles on the empirical effects and theoretical implications of near-death experiences.
Formerly (until 1986): Anabiosis: The Journal for Near-Death Studies (0743-6238)
Related titles: Online - full text ed.: ISSN 1573-3661 (from IngentaConnect).
Indexed: A22, A26, AMED, AbAn, CA, DIP, E-psyche, E01, IBR, IBZ, P03, PsycInfo, PsycholAb, S02, S03, SWR&A, T02.
—BLDSC (5021.392000), GNLM, IE, Infotrieve, Ingenta, INIST. **CCC.**
Published by: International Association for Near-Death Studies, 2741 Campus Walk Ave, Bldg 500, Durham, NC 27705-8878. TEL 919-383-7940, FAX 919-383-7940.

193 USA ISSN 0968-8005
B3310
➤ **JOURNAL OF NIETZSCHE STUDIES.** Text in English. 1991. s-a. USD 128 combined subscription to institutions (print & online eds.) (effective 2012). adv. back issues avail.; reprint service avail. from PSC. **Document type:** *Journal, Academic/Scholarly.* **Description:** Contains essays, articles, notices, and reports pertaining to the life, thought, and writings of Friedrich Nietzsche.
Related titles: Online - full text ed.: ISSN 1538-4594. USD 98 to institutions (effective 2012).
Indexed: A01, A03, A08, A22, AmHI, BRD, CA, DIP, E01, H07, H08, HAb, HumInd, IBR, IBZ, MLA-IB, PCI, PhilInd, SCOPUS, T02, W03, W05.
—IE. **CCC.**
Published by: (Friedrich Nietzsche Society GBR), Pennsylvania State University Press, 820 N University Dr, University Support Bldg 1, Ste C, University Park, PA 16802. TEL 814-865-1327, 800-326-9180, FAX 814-863-1408, info@psupress.org. Eds. Christa Davis Acampora, Kendra Boileau. Adv. contact Brian Beer TEL 814-863-5992. **Dist. by:** The Johns Hopkins University Press, PO Box 19966, Baltimore, MD 21211. TEL 410-516-6987, 800-548-1784, FAX 410-516-3866, jrnlcirc@press.jhu.edu, https://www.press.jhu.edu/.

➤ **JOURNAL OF PAN AFRICAN STUDIES (ONLINE).** *see* SOCIOLOGY

160 NLD ISSN 0022-3611
BC51 CODEN: JPLGA7
➤ **JOURNAL OF PHILOSOPHICAL LOGIC.** Text in English. 1972. bi-m. EUR 854, USD 907 combined subscription to institutions (print & online eds.) (effective 2012). adv. illus. Index. reprint service avail. from PSC. **Document type:** *Journal, Academic/Scholarly.* **Description:** Publishes papers that utilize formal methods or that deal with topics in logical theory, such as: contributions to branches of logical theory directly related to philosophical concerns; contributions to philosophical discussions that utilize the machinery of formal logic; discussions of philosophical issues relating tothe logical structure of language; philosophical work relating to specific sciences.
Related titles: Microform ed.: (from PQC); Online - full text ed.: ISSN 1573-0433 (from IngentaConnect).
Indexed: A01, A02, A03, A08, A20, A22, A26, ASCA, AmHI, ArtHuCI, BibLing, CA, CCMJ, CMCI, CurCont, DIP, E01, FR, H07, H14, IBR, IBZ, IPB, L&LBA, MLA, MLA-IB, MSN, MathR, P10, P48, P53, P54, PCI, PQC, PhilInd, RASB, RefZh, SCOPUS, SOPODA, T02, W07, Z02.
—BLDSC (5034.400000), IE, Infotrieve, Ingenta, INIST. **CCC.**
Published by: (Association for Symbolic Logic), Springer Netherlands (Subsidiary of: Springer Science+Business Media), Van Godewijckstraat 30, Dordrecht, 3311 GX, Netherlands. TEL 31-78-6576050, FAX 31-78-6576474, http://www.springer.com. Eds. Hans Van Ditmarsch, John Horty, Krister Segerberg.

100 USA ISSN 1053-8364
B1
➤ **JOURNAL OF PHILOSOPHICAL RESEARCH.** Text and summaries in English, French. 1976. a. USD 35 to individuals; USD 77 to institutions (effective 2009). reprint service avail. from PSC. **Document type:** *Journal, Academic/Scholarly.* **Description:** Publishes original papers in all branches of philosophy and from any philosophical orientation.
Formerly: Philosophy Research Archives (0164-0771)
Related titles: Microfiche ed.; Online - full text ed.: ISSN 2153-7984.
Indexed: A01, A03, A08, A20, A26, AmHI, ArtHuCI, CA, CurCont, DIP, E08, FR, G08, H07, I05, IBR, IBZ, IPB, MLA-IB, P30, PCI, PhilInd, R05, S09, SCOPUS, T02, W07.
—BLDSC (5034.420000), IE, Ingenta, INIST. **CCC.**
Published by: Philosophy Documentation Center, PO Box 7147, Charlottesville, VA 22906. TEL 434-220-3300, FAX 434-220-3301. Ed. Michael DePaul. R&P George Leaman. Circ: 300 (paid).

100 USA ISSN 0022-362X
B1
➤ **JOURNAL OF PHILOSOPHY.** Text in English. 1904. m. USD 45 domestic to individuals; USD 65 foreign to individuals; USD 100 domestic to institutions; USD 120 foreign to institutions; USD 20 domestic to students; USD 40 foreign to students; USD 180 combined subscription domestic to institutions (print & online eds.); USD 200 combined subscription foreign to institutions (print & online eds.) (effective 2009). adv. bk.rev. bibl.; illus. index, cum.index: 1904-1953, 1954-1963, 1964-1988. back issues avail.; reprints avail. **Document type:** *Journal, Academic/Scholarly.* **Description:** Features philosophical articles that explore the borderline between philosophy and other disciplines.
Formerly (until 1921): The Journal of Philosophy, Psychology and Scientific Methods (0160-9335)
Related titles: Microfilm ed.: (from PMC); Online - full text ed.: ISSN 1939-8549.
Indexed: A01, A02, A03, A06, A08, A20, A21, A22, A25, A26, ASCA, AmHI, ArtHuCI, B04, B14, BEL&L, BRD, BRI, CA, CBRI, CCMJ, CurCont, DIP, E08, FR, G08, H07, H08, H09, H10, H14, HAb, HumInd, I05, IBR, IBRH, IBSS, IBZ, IPB, M01, M02, MEA&I, MLA, MLA-IB, MSN, MathR, P02, P10, P13, P30, P48, P53, P54, PCI, PQC, PhilInd, R05, RASB, RI-1, RI-2, S02, S03, S05, S08, S09, SCOPUS, T02, W03, W07.
—BLDSC (5034.500000), IE, Infotrieve, Ingenta, INIST.
Published by: Journal of Philosophy, Inc., c/o John Smylie, 1150 Amsterdam Ave, Mail Code 4972, Columbia University, New York, NY 10027. TEL 212-666-4419, FAX 212-932-3721.

100 NPL ISSN 2072-036X
JOURNAL OF PHILOSOPHY; a cross-disciplinary inquiry. Text in English. 2005. q. adv. back issues avail. **Document type:** *Journal, Academic/Scholarly.* **Description:** Dedicated to bringing together western and non-western humanities through articles, comments, and reviews on philosophy, literature, and literary theory.
Related titles: Online - full text ed.: ISSN 2154-1442. USD 100 (effective 2010).
Indexed: A26, AmHI, E08, H07, I05, MLA-IB, P28, PhilInd, T02.
Published by: Society for Philosophy and Literary Studies of Nepal, PO Box 1158, Kirtipur, Nepal. Ed. Yubraj Aryal. **Subscr. to:** Philosophy Documentation Center.

100 AZE ISSN 2078-1121
▼ ➤ **JOURNAL OF PHILOSOPHY.** Text in English. forthcoming 2011. 3/yr. **Document type:** *Journal, Academic/Scholarly.*
Related titles: Online - full text ed.: forthcoming.
Indexed: AmHI, H07.
Published by: Progress Press Inc., M.Mushfig 4B, Apt.107, Baku, 1006, Azerbaijan. TEL 994-050-6691364, subijar@gmail.com.

100 GHA ISSN 0855-6660
B1
➤ **JOURNAL OF PHILOSOPHY AND CULTURE.** Text in English. s-a. USD 15 foreign to individuals; USD 20 foreign to institutions (effective 2007). **Document type:** *Journal, Academic/Scholarly.* **Description:** Devoted to the promotion of scholarship in philosophy, culture and allied disciplines.

P

Indexed: PhilInd.
Published by: University of Cape Coast, Department of Classics & Philosophy, c/o Dr Raymond N Osei, Editor, Cape Coast, Ghana. TEL 233-42-30945, FAX 233-42-34073, clasphil1@yahoo.com. Ed. Dr. Raymond N Osei.

➤ **JOURNAL OF PHILOSOPHY & SCRIPTURE.** *see* RELIGIONS AND THEOLOGY

100 GBR ISSN 0309-8249
LB1025.2
➤ **JOURNAL OF PHILOSOPHY OF EDUCATION.** Text in English. 1966. q. GBP 665 in United Kingdom to institutions; EUR 843 in Europe to institutions; USD 1,244 in the Americas to institutions; USD 1,451 elsewhere to institutions; GBP 766 combined subscription in United Kingdom to institutions (print & online eds.); EUR 970 combined subscription in Europe to institutions (print & online eds.); USD 1,430 combined subscription in the Americas to institutions (print & online eds.); USD 1,669 combined subscription elsewhere to institutions (print & online eds.) (effective 2012). adv. bk.rev. illus. Index. back issues avail.; reprint service avail. from PSC. **Document type:** *Journal, Academic/Scholarly.* **Description:** Aims to promote rigorous thinking on educational matters and to identify and criticise the ideological forces shaping education.
Former titles (until 1978): Philosophy of Education Society of Great Britain. Proceedings (0306-7114); (until 1971): Philosophy of Education Society of Great Britain. Annual Conference. Proceedings (0048-3923)
Related titles: Microfiche ed.; Online - full text ed.: ISSN 1467-9752. GBP 665 in United Kingdom to institutions; EUR 843 in Europe to institutions; USD 1,244 in the Americas to institutions; USD 1,451 elsewhere to institutions (effective 2012) (from IngentaConnect).
Indexed: A01, A02, A03, A08, A20, A21, A22, A26, ASCA, B29, BRD, CA, CPE, CurCont, E01, E02, E03, E07, E09, EAA, ERI, ERIC, EdA, EdI, FR, H14, IBR, IBZ, P02, P04, P10, P18, P48, P53, P54, PCI, PQC, PhilInd, RI-1, RI-2, SCOPUS, SSCI, T02, W03, W07.
—BLDSC (5034.510000), IE, Infotrieve, Ingenta, INIST. **CCC.**
Published by: (Philosophy of Education Society of Great Britain), Wiley-Blackwell Publishing Ltd. (Subsidiary of: John Wiley & Sons, Inc.), 9600 Garsington Rd, Oxford, OX4 2DQ, United Kingdom. TEL 44-1865-776868, FAX 44-1865-714591, customerservices@blackwellpublishing.com. Ed. Paul Standish.

➤ **JOURNAL OF PHILOSOPHY OF INTERNATIONAL LAW.** *see* LAW—International Law

100 340 USA ISSN 1549-8549
➤ **THE JOURNAL OF PHILOSOPHY, SCIENCE & LAW.** Text in English. 2001. bi-m. free (effective 2011). back issues avail. **Document type:** *Journal, Academic/Scholarly.* **Description:** Dedicated to examining issues in the intersection of applied philosophy, science, and the law.
Media: Online - full text.
Indexed: A39, C27, C29, D03, D04, E13, EMBASE, ExcerpMed, MEDLINE, P30, R14, S14, S15, S18.
Published by: The Journal of Philosophy, Science and Law, c/o Jason Borenstein, School of Public Policy, 685 Cherry St, PO Box 4089, Atlanta, GA 30332-0345. TEL 404-385-2801, FAX 404-385-0504, jason.borenstein@pubpolicy.gatech.edu. Ed. Jason Borenstein.

320.5 GBR ISSN 0963-8016
JA1.A1
➤ **JOURNAL OF POLITICAL PHILOSOPHY.** Text in English. 1993. q. GBP 590 in United Kingdom to institutions; EUR 748 in Europe to institutions; USD 815 in the Americas to institutions; USD 1,155 elsewhere to institutions; GBP 679 combined subscription in United Kingdom to institutions (print & online eds.); EUR 860 combined subscription in Europe to institutions (print & online eds.); USD 938 combined subscription in the Americas to institutions (print & online eds.); USD 1,329 combined subscription elsewhere to institutions (print & online eds.) (effective 2012). adv. illus. back issues avail.; reprint service avail. from PSC. **Document type:** *Journal, Academic/Scholarly.* **Description:** Devoted to the study of theoretical issues arising out of the moral, legal, and political life.
Related titles: Microform ed.: (from PQC); Online - full text ed.: ISSN 1467-9760. GBP 590 in United Kingdom to institutions; EUR 748 in Europe to institutions; USD 815 in the Americas to institutions; USD 1,155 elsewhere to institutions (effective 2012) (from IngentaConnect).
Indexed: A01, A03, A08, A20, A22, A26, ABS&EES, ASCA, CA, CurCont, E01, I13, IBSS, IPB, P30, P34, P42, PSA, PhilInd, S02, S03, SCOPUS, SSCI, SociolAb, T02, W07.
—BLDSC (5040.886000), IE, Infotrieve, Ingenta. **CCC.**
Published by: Wiley-Blackwell Publishing Ltd. (Subsidiary of: John Wiley & Sons, Inc.), 9600 Garsington Rd, Oxford, OX4 2DQ, United Kingdom. TEL 44-1865-776868, FAX 44-1865-714591, customerservices@blackwellpublishing.com. Ed. Robert E Goodin TEL 61-2-6249-2156. Adv. contact Craig Pickett TEL 44-1865-476267.

▼ ➤ **JOURNAL OF RELIGION AND BUSINESS ETHICS.** *see* RELIGIONS AND THEOLOGY

100 GBR ISSN 1479-6651
B1401
JOURNAL OF SCOTTISH PHILOSOPHY. Abbreviated title: J S P. Text in English. 1986. s-a. GBP 78 domestic to institutions; USD 157 in North America to institutions; GBP 86 elsewhere to institutions; GBP 98 combined subscription domestic to institutions (print & online eds.); USD 196 combined subscription in North America to institutions (print & online eds.); GBP 108 combined subscription elsewhere to institutions (print & online eds.) (effective 2012). back issues avail.; reprints avail. **Document type:** *Journal, Academic/Scholarly.* **Description:** Provides a forum for philosophical discussion and historical scholarship on Scottish philosophy, philosophical theology, economic and political thought and related fields from any era of Scottish history.
Formerly (until 2003): Reid Studies (0268-9723)
Related titles: Online - full text ed.: ISSN 1755-2001. USD 128 in North America to institutions; GBP 70 elsewhere to institutions (effective 2012).
Indexed: A01, A03, A08, CA, PhilInd, T02.
—BLDSC (5062.200000). **CCC.**
Published by: (Center for the Study of Scottish Philosophy USA), Edinburgh University Press, 22 George Sq, Edinburgh, Scotland EH8 9LF, United Kingdom. TEL 44-131-6504218, FAX 44-131-6503286, journals@eup.ed.ac.uk. Ed. Gordon Graham. Adv. contact Ruth Allison TEL 44-131-6504220.

301 100 USA ISSN 0047-2786
H1
➤ **JOURNAL OF SOCIAL PHILOSOPHY.** Text in English. 1970. q. USD 491 in the Americas to institutions (print or online ed.); GBP 388 in United Kingdom to institutions (print or online ed.); EUR 493 in Europe to institutions (print or online ed.); USD 761 elsewhere to institutions (print or online ed.); USD 541 combined subscription in the Americas to institutions (print & online eds.); GBP 428 combined subscription in United Kingdom to institutions (print & online eds.); EUR 543 combined subscription in Europe to institutions (print & online eds.); USD 837 combined subscription elsewhere to institutions (print & online eds.) (effective 2010); subscr. includes: Midwest Studies in Philosophy. adv. bk.rev. back issues avail.; reprint service avail. from PSC. **Document type:** *Journal, Academic/Scholarly.* **Description:** Interdisciplinary forum for political debate of moral, legal, political and social issues.
Related titles: Online - full text ed.: ISSN 1467-9833 (from IngentaConnect); ◆ Supplement(s): Midwest Studies in Philosophy. ISSN 0363-6550.
Indexed: A01, A03, A08, A21, A22, A26, ArtHuCI, CA, CurCont, DIP, E01, FR, FamI, IBR, IBZ, P30, P34, P42, PerIslam, PhilInd, RASB, RI-1, RI-2, RILM, S02, S03, SCOPUS, SSCI, SociolAb, T02, W07, W09.
—BLDSC (5064.775000), IE, Infotrieve, Ingenta, INIST. **CCC.**
Published by: (North American Society for Social Philosophy), Wiley-Blackwell Publishing, Inc. (Subsidiary of: Wiley-Blackwell Publishing Ltd.), 111 River St, Hoboken, NJ 07030. TEL 201-748-6000, FAX 201-748-6088, info@wiley.com. Ed. Carol C Gould. Adv. contact Kristin McCarthy TEL 201-748-7683.

100 USA ISSN 0891-625X
B1
➤ **JOURNAL OF SPECULATIVE PHILOSOPHY.** Abbreviated title: J S P. Text in English, French, Dutch, Japanese. 1867. q. USD 166 combined subscription to institutions (print & online eds.) (effective 2012). adv. bk.rev. illus. Index. 80 p./no.; back issues avail.; reprint service avail. from PSC. **Document type:** *Journal, Academic/Scholarly.* **Description:** Brings out essays about basic philosophical questions. Focuses on American philosophy and its relations to a variety of areas.
Related titles: Microform ed.: (from PQC); Online - full text ed.: ISSN 1527-9383. USD 118 to institutions (effective 2012).
Indexed: A01, A03, A08, A22, AmHI, BRD, CA, DIP, E01, H07, H08, HAb, HumInd, IBR, IBZ, IPB, PCI, PhilInd, RASB, SCOPUS, T02, W03, W05.
—BLDSC (5066.142000), IE, Ingenta. **CCC.**
Published by: Pennsylvania State University Press, 820 N University Dr, University Support Bldg 1, Ste C, University Park, PA 16802. TEL 814-865-1327, 800-326-9180, FAX 814-863-1408, info@psupress.org. Eds. John J Stuhr, Vincent M Colapietro. Adv. contact Brian Beer TEL 814-863-5992. **Dist. by:** The Johns Hopkins University Press, PO Box 19966, Baltimore, MD 21211. TEL 410-516-6987; 800-548-1784, FAX 410-516-3866, jrnlcirc@press.jhu.edu, https://www.press.jhu.edu/.

➤ **THE JOURNAL OF SYMBOLIC LOGIC.** *see* MATHEMATICS

➤ **THE JOURNAL OF TEXTUAL REASONING.** *see* RELIGIONS AND THEOLOGY—Judaic

109 USA ISSN 0022-5053
B1
➤ **JOURNAL OF THE HISTORY OF PHILOSOPHY.** Abbreviated title: J H P. Text in Multiple languages, English. 1963. q. USD 123 to institutions; USD 172 combined subscription to institutions (print & online eds.); USD 37 per issue to institutions (effective 2012). adv. bk.rev. charts; illus. Index. 140 p./no.; back issues avail.; reprint service avail. from PSC. **Document type:** *Journal, Academic/Scholarly.* **Description:** Brings out articles, notes, discussions, and reviews about the history of Western philosophy.
Related titles: Microform ed.: (from PQC); Online - full text ed.: ISSN 1538-4586. USD 128 to institutions (effective 2012).
Indexed: A01, A02, A03, A08, A20, A21, A22, A26, ASCA, AmH&L, AmHI, ArtHuCI, B04, BEL&L, BRD, CA, CurCont, DIP, E01, E08, FR, G08, H07, H08, H09, H10, H14, HAb, HistAb, HumInd, I05, I14, IBR, IBSS, IBZ, IPB, MLA-IB, P02, P10, P13, P28, P30, P48, P53, P54, PCI, PQC, PhilInd, RASB, RI-1, RI-2, S09, SCOPUS, T02, W03, W07.
—BLDSC (5001.500000), IE, Infotrieve, Ingenta, INIST. **CCC.**
Published by: The Johns Hopkins University Press, 2715 N Charles St, Baltimore, MD 21218. TEL 410-516-6900, FAX 410-516-6968. Ed. Steven Nadler. Pub. William M Breichner. **Subscr. to:** PO Box 19966, Baltimore, MD 21211. TEL 410-516-6987, 800-548-1784, FAX 410-516-3866, jrnlcirc@press.jhu.edu.

121 NLD ISSN 1872-261X
D16.8
JOURNAL OF THE PHILOSOPHY OF HISTORY. Text in English. 2007. 3/yr. EUR 129, USD 179 to institutions; EUR 140, USD 196 combined subscription to institutions (print & online eds.) (effective 2012). reprint service avail. from PSC. **Document type:** *Journal, Academic/Scholarly.* **Description:** Includes contributions from all branches of philosophy that involve history and historiography, including epistemology, metaphysics, philosophy of language, philosophy of science, aesthetics, and value theory.
Related titles: Online - full text ed.: ISSN 1872-2636. EUR 117, USD 163 to institutions (effective 2012) (from IngentaConnect).
Indexed: A22, AmHI, CA, E01, H07, IZBG, SCOPUS, T02.
—IE. **CCC.**
Published by: Brill, PO Box 9000, Leiden, 2300 PA, Netherlands. TEL 31-71-5353500, FAX 31-71-5317532, cs@brill.nl. Ed. Frank Ankersmit.

JOURNAL OF THE PHILOSOPHY OF SPORT. *see* SPORTS AND GAMES

JOURNAL OF THEORETICAL & PHILOSOPHICAL PSYCHOLOGY. *see* PSYCHOLOGY

JOURNAL OF THOUGHT. *see* SOCIAL SCIENCES: COMPREHENSIVE WORKS

170 NLD ISSN 0022-5363
BD232 CODEN: JVINEP
➤ **THE JOURNAL OF VALUE INQUIRY.** Text in English. 1967. q. EUR 738, USD 780 combined subscription to institutions (print & online eds.) (effective 2012). adv. bk.rev. illus. index. back issues avail.; reprint service avail. from PSC. **Document type:** *Journal, Academic/Scholarly.* **Description:** Covers the stimulation and communication of research in value studies. The essays published in the journal concern the nature, origin, experiences and scope of value in general, as well as problems of value in such fields as culture, aesthetics, religion, social and legal theory or practice, ethics education, and methodology, technology and the sciences.
Related titles: Microform ed.: (from PQC); Online - full text ed.: ISSN 1573-0492 (from IngentaConnect).
Indexed: A12, A13, A20, A22, A26, ABIn, ASCA, AmHI, ArtHuCI, BibLing, CA, CurCont, DIP, E01, E08, FR, G08, H07, H14, I05, IBR, IBRH, IBZ, IPB, MLA-IB, P10, P28, P30, P48, P51, P53, P54, PCI, PQC, PhilInd, RASB, RI-1, RI-2, RILM, S09, SCOPUS, SSCI, T02, W07.
—BLDSC (5072.260000), IE, Infotrieve, Ingenta, INIST. **CCC.**
Published by: Springer Netherlands (Subsidiary of: Springer Science+Business Media), Van Godewijckstraat 30, Dordrecht, 3311 GX, Netherlands. TEL 31-78-6576050, FAX 31-78-6576474, http://www.springer.com. Ed. Thomas Magnell.

➤ **JOURNAL ON AFRICAN PHILOSOPHY.** *see* HISTORY—History Of Africa

➤ **JUKIC;** zbornik radova. *see* RELIGIONS AND THEOLOGY

150 USA ISSN 1945-5186
JUNG HISTORY. Text in English. 2005. s-a. back issues avail. **Document type:** *Newsletter, Consumer.*
Related titles: Online - full text ed.
Published by: Philemon Foundation, PO Box 1239, Carpinteria, CA 93014. info@philemonfoundation.org.

▼ **JURISPRUDENCE;** an international journal of legal and political thought. *see* LAW

100 DEU
▼ **JUVENTAS;** Zeitschrift fuer junge Philosophie. Text in German. 2011 (Jun.). 2/yr. EUR 26; EUR 22 to students; EUR 15 newsstand/cover (effective 2011). **Document type:** *Journal, Academic/Scholarly.*
Published by: Bernstein-Verlag GbR, Endenicher Str 97, Bonn, 53115, Germany. TEL 49-228-9658719, FAX 49-228-9658720, bernstein@bernstein-verlag.de, http://www.bernstein-verlag.de. Eds. Anna-Christina Boell, Bastian Reichardt.

KABBALAH TODAY. *see* RELIGIONS AND THEOLOGY—Judaic

105 FRA ISSN 1148-9227
B2
➤ **KAIROS.** Text in French. 1972. s-a. back issues avail. **Document type:** *Journal, Academic/Scholarly.*
Formerly (until 1990): Philosophie (Toulouse) (0182-7103)
Indexed: FR, IPB, MLA-IB.
—INIST. **CCC.**
Published by: (Universite de Toulouse II (Le Mirail)), Presses Universitaires du Mirail, Universite de Toulouse II (Le Mirail), 5, Allee Antonio Machado, Toulouse, 31058, France. TEL 33-05-61503810, FAX 33-05-61503800, pum@univ-tlse2.fr, http://www.univ-tlse2.fr. Ed. Jean Marie Vaysse.

➤ **KAMEN;** rivista semestrale di poesia e filosofia. *see* LITERATURE—Poetry

100 BRA ISSN 1677-1621
KANT E - PRINTS. Text in English, Spanish, Portuguese. 2002. irreg. **Document type:** *Journal, Academic/Scholarly.* **Description:** All articles contain original research in the area of Kant studies.
Related titles: Online - full text ed.: ISSN 1677-163X. free (effective 2011).
Published by: Brasilian Kant Society, Campinas Section, c/o Philosophy Dept, Pontificial Catholic University of Parana, Campinas, Brazil.

100 DEU
KANT-FORSCHUNGEN. Text in German. 1987. irreg., latest vol.18, 2007. price varies. **Document type:** *Monographic series, Academic/Scholarly.*
Indexed: CCMJ.
Published by: Felix Meiner Verlag GmbH, Richardstr 47, Hamburg, 22081, Germany. TEL 49-40-2987560, FAX 49-40-29875620, info@meiner.de. Eds. R. Brandt, W. Stark. R&P, Adv. contact Johannes Kambylis.

142.3 DEU ISSN 0022-8877
B2750
➤ **KANT STUDIEN;** philosophische Zeitschrift der Kant-Gesellschaft . Text in English, French, German. 1896. q. EUR 187, USD 281 to institutions; EUR 215, USD 323 combined subscription to institutions (print & online eds.) (effective 2012). adv. bk.rev. abstr.; charts; illus. index. back issues avail.; reprint service avail. from SCH. **Document type:** *Journal, Academic/Scholarly.*
Related titles: Online - full text ed.: ISSN 1613-1134. EUR 187, USD 281 to institutions (effective 2012); ◆ Supplement(s): Kantstudien Ergaenzungshefte. ISSN 0340-6059.
Indexed: A20, A22, A26, ASCA, AmHI, ArtHuCI, BibInd, CurCont, DIP, E01, FR, H07, H14, I05, IBR, IBRH, IBZ, IPB, MLA-IB, P10, P28, P48, P53, P54, PCI, PQC, PhilInd, RASB, SCOPUS, T02, W07.
—IE, Infotrieve, Ingenta, INIST. **CCC.**
Published by: (Kant-Gesellschaft), Walter de Gruyter GmbH & Co. KG, Genthiner Str 13, Berlin, 10785, Germany. TEL 49-30-260050, FAX 49-30-26005251, info@degruyter.com, http://www.degruyter.de. Eds. Bernd Dorflinger, Manfred Baum, Thomas M Seebohm. Adv. contact Dietlind Makswitat TEL 49-30-260050. Circ: 1,000 (paid and controlled).

100 GBR ISSN 2045-3396
▼ **KANT STUDIES ONLINE.** Text in English. 2011. free (effective 2011). **Document type:** *Journal, Academic/Scholarly.*
Media: Online - full text.
Published by: KantStudiesOnline Ltd, Apartment 704, 25 Church St, Manchester, M4 1PE, United Kingdom. TEL 44-07595-690493, kantstudiesonline@me.com kantstudiesonline@me.com. Ed. Gary Banham.

120 DEU ISSN 1868-4599
B2750
▼ ➤ **KANT YEARBOOK.** Text in English. 2009. a. EUR 63, USD 95 to institutions; EUR 73, USD 110 combined subscription to institutions (print & online eds.) (effective 2012). **Document type:** *Journal, Academic/Scholarly.* **Description:** Publishes articles on the philosophy of Immanuel Kant.
Related titles: Online - full text ed.: ISSN 1868-4602. EUR 63, USD 95 to institutions (effective 2012).
Indexed: AmHI, H07, T02.
Published by: Walter de Gruyter GmbH & Co. KG, Genthiner Str 13, Berlin, 10785, Germany. TEL 49-30-260050, FAX 49-30-26005251, info@degruyter.com. Ed. Dietmar Heidemann.

142.3 GBR ISSN 1369-4154
B2750
KANTIAN REVIEW. Text in English. 1998 (Mar.). a. GBP 159, USD 244 combined subscription to institutions (print & online eds.) (effective 2012). back issues avail. **Document type:** *Journal, Academic/Scholarly.* **Description:** Contains contemporary work on Kant and Kantian issues and will place an emphasis on those current philosophical debates which reflect a Kantian influence.
Related titles: Online - full text ed.: ISSN 2044-2394. GBP 143, USD 212 to institutions (effective 2012) (from IngentaConnect).
Indexed: I13, IBR, IBZ, PhilInd, SCOPUS.
—Ingenta. **CCC.**
Published by: Cambridge University Press, The Edinburgh Bldg, Shaftesbury Rd, Cambridge, CB2 8RU, United Kingdom. TEL 44-1223-326070, FAX 44-1223-325150, information@cambridge.org. Eds. Graham Bird, Howard Williams, Richard Aquila.

142.3 DEU ISSN 0340-6059
➤ **KANTSTUDIEN ERGAENZUNGSHEFTE.** Text in German. 1906. irreg., latest vol.166, 2011. price varies. **Document type:** *Monographic series, Academic/Scholarly.*
Related titles: ◆ Supplement to: Kant Studien. ISSN 0022-8877.
Published by: Walter de Gruyter GmbH & Co. KG, Genthiner Str 13, Berlin, 10785, Germany. TEL 49-30-260050, FAX 49-30-26005251, info@degruyter.com, http://www.degruyter.de.

141 NLD ISSN 2211-8616
▼ **KARAAT**; magazine voor spiritueel bewustzijn. Text in Dutch. 2010. bi-m. EUR 20; EUR 3.95 newsstand/cover (effective 2011). adv. **Document type:** *Magazine, Consumer.*
Published by: HPG de Cirkel bv, Bolsstraat 6, Bergentheim, 7691 DM, Netherlands. TEL 31-523-852931, hpg.de.cirkel@home.nl.

100 001.3 370.1 800 PHL ISSN 0116-7073
B5221
➤ **KARUNUNGAN**; a journal of philosophy. Text and summaries in English, Tagalog. 1983. a., latest 2002. price varies. adv. bk.rev. bibl. back issues avail.; reprints avail. **Document type:** *Proceedings, Academic/Scholarly.* **Description:** Scholarly articles reflecting significant quantitative or qualitative research from philosophers' convention. Includes speeches, research reports, and "state of the art" papers.
Indexed: IPP.
Published by: University of Santo Tomas Publishing House (U S T P H), Beato Angelico Bldg, Espana, Manila, Philippines. TEL 63-2-7313522 ext 8252/8278, FAX 63-2-7313522, publish@ust.edu.ph, http://www.ust.edu.ph. Ed. Alfred P Co. Circ: 500.

100 ESP ISSN 1888-0592
KATH'AUTON. Text in Multiple languages. 2007. 3/yr. **Document type:** *Journal, Academic/Scholarly.*
Published by: Universidad de Salamanca, Facultad de Filosofia, Delegacion de Alumnos, Edif. F.E.S. Desp. 006, Campus Miguel de Unamuno, Salamanca, 37007, Spain. TEL 34-923-294400, mail@kathauton.eu, http://www.usal.es/~delegacionfilosofia/index2.html. Ed. Ricardo Espinosa Roman.

100 POL
KATOLICKI UNIWERSYTET LUBELSKI. WYDZIAL FILOZOFICZNY. ROZPRAWY. Text in Polish; Summaries in English, French, German. 1957. irreg. price varies. index.
Published by: Katolicki Uniwersytet Lubelski, Towarzystwo Naukowe, ul Gliniana 21, Lublin, 20616, Poland. Circ: 3,150.

100 TUR ISSN 1303-4251
➤ **KAYGI: ULUDAG UNIVERSITY FACULTY OF ARTS AND SCIENCES JOURNAL OF PHILOSOPHY.** Text in English, French, German, Turkish. 2002. s-a. back issues avail. **Document type:** *Journal, Academic/Scholarly.* **Description:** Publishes original articles, translations, book reviews, and discussions on a wide range of issues in contemporary philosophy, history of philosophy, epistemology, ontology, philosophy of language, philosophy of science, cultural critique, ethics, aesthetics, and related matters. The journal is open to different philosophical orientations, styles and schools, and welcomes theoretical dialogue between them.
Related titles: Online - full text ed.
Indexed: I14, MLA-IB, PhilInd.
Published by: Uludag University, Faculty of Arts and Sciences/Uludag(Universitesi Felsefe Bolumu Fen-Edebiyat Fakultesi, Bursa, Gorukle 16059, Turkey. TEL 90-224-2941826, FAX 90-224-2941897, http://felsefe.uludag.edu.tr/www/. Ed. Metin Becermen.

181.07 IRN ISSN 1023-3687
KAYHAN ANDISHEH. Text in Persian, Modern. 1985. 6/yr. USD 154 in North America. **Document type:** *Consumer.* **Description:** Covers topics relating to Islam, Islamic philosophy, and Iranian literature.
Published by: Kayhan Publications, Ferdowsi Ave., P O Box 11365-9631, Tehran, Iran. TEL 98-21-3110251, FAX 98-21-3114228.

KENNEDY INSTITUTE OF ETHICS JOURNAL. *see* MEDICAL SCIENCES

KENNEDY INSTITUTE OF ETHICS. SCOPE NOTE. *see* MEDICAL SCIENCES

KEXUE JISHU YU BIANZHENGFA/SCIENCE, TECHNOLOGY, AND DIALECTICS. *see* SCIENCES: COMPREHENSIVE WORKS

100 CHN ISSN 1001-2729
KEXUE JISHU ZHEXUE/PHILOSOPHY OF SCIENCE AND TECHNOLOGY. Text in Chinese. m. USD 63.80 (effective 2009). **Document type:** *Journal, Academic/Scholarly.*
Related titles: Alternate Frequency ed(s).: Kexue Jishu Zhexue (Nian Kan). a. CNY 193.40, USD 55 (effective 2005).
Published by: Zhongguo Renmin Daxue Shubao Ziliao Zhongxin/Renmin University of China, Information Center for Social Sciences, Dongcheng-qu, 3, Zhangzizhong Lu, Beijing, 100007, China. TEL 86-10-64039458, FAX 86-10-64015080, center@zlzx.org, http://www.zlzx.org/. **Dist. by:** China International Book Trading Corp, 35 Chegongzhuang Xilu, Haidian District, PO Box 399, Beijing 100044, China. TEL 86-10-68412045, FAX 86-10-68412023, cibtc@mail.cibtc.com.cn, http://www.cibtc.com.cn/.

KEXUE YU WUSHENLUN/SCIENCE AND ATHEISM. *see* SCIENCES: COMPREHENSIVE WORKS

KEY WORDS; a journal of cultural materialism. *see* POLITICAL SCIENCE

297.5 IRN ISSN 1560-0874
B753.M84
KHERADNAMEH-E SADRA. Text in Persian, Modern, English. 1995. q. IRR 15,000 domestic; CHF 32 in the Middle East; CHF 37 Europe, Central Asia & India; CHF 42 elsewhere (effective 2003). adv. abstr. 100 p./no.; **Document type:** *Magazine, Academic/Scholarly.* **Description:** Covers all aspects of the Islamic and transcendental philosophy of Mulla Sadra.
Related titles: CD-ROM ed.; Diskette ed.; E-mail ed.; Fax ed.
Indexed: PhilInd.
Address: Bozorgrahe Resalat, 12 Modjtama e Imam Khomeini, PO Box 15875-6919, Tehran, Iran. TEL 98-21-8153210, FAX 98-21-8831817, mullasadra@dpir.com. Ed., Pub. Seyyed Muhammad Khamenei. Circ: 5,000 (paid and controlled).

198.9 DEU ISSN 1430-5372
B4370
➤ **KIERKEGAARD STUDIES.** Text in German, English. 1996. a. EUR 177, USD 266 to institutions; EUR 198, USD 297 combined subscription to institutions (print & online eds.) (effective 2012). reprint service avail. from PSC. **Document type:** *Journal, Academic/Scholarly.*
Related titles: Online - full text ed.: ISSN 1612-9792. EUR 177, USD 266 to institutions (effective 2012); ◆ Supplement(s): Kierkegaard Studies Monograph Series. ISSN 1434-2952.
Indexed: A26, AmHI, H07, PhilInd, T02.
Published by: Walter de Gruyter GmbH & Co. KG, Genthiner Str 13, Berlin, 10785, Germany. TEL 49-30-260050, FAX 49-30-26005251, info@degruyter.com. Eds. Hermann Deuser, Niels J Cappelorn.

198.9 DEU ISSN 1434-2952
➤ **KIERKEGAARD STUDIES MONOGRAPH SERIES.** Text in English, German. 1997. irreg., latest vol.25, 2011. price varies. **Document type:** *Monographic series, Academic/Scholarly.*
Related titles: ◆ Supplement to: Kierkegaard Studies. ISSN 1430-5372. **—CCC.**
Published by: Walter de Gruyter GmbH & Co. KG, Genthiner Str 13, Berlin, 10785, Germany. TEL 49-30-260050, FAX 49-30-26005251, info@degruyter.com, http://www.degruyter.de. Ed. Jon Stewart.

198.9 DNK ISSN 0075-6032
B4377
➤ **KIERKEGAARDIANA.** Text in English, French, German; Summaries in English. 1955. irreg., latest vol.24, 2006. price varies. bk.rev. **Document type:** *Monographic series, Academic/Scholarly.* **Description:** Studies related to Soeren Kierkegaard.
Indexed: A21, DIP, IBR, IBZ, IPB, MLA-IB, PCI, PhilInd, RASB, RI-1, RI-2, RILM.
—BLDSC (5095.135000).
Published by: (Soeren Kierkegaard Selskabet/Soeren Kierkegaard Society), C.A. Reitzels Boghandel & Forlag A/S, Noerregade 20, Copenhagen K, 1165, Denmark. TEL 45-33-122400, FAX 45-33-140270, info@careitzel.com, http://www.careitzel.com. Circ: 500. **Co-sponsor:** National Council of the Humanities.

100 USA ISSN 0023-1568
B1
KINESIS (CARBONDALE); graduate journal of philosophy. Text in English. 1968. s-a. USD 20; USD 10 per issue (effective 2010). bk.rev. back issues avail.; reprints avail. **Document type:** *Journal, Academic/Scholarly.* **Description:** Covers philosophy and articles on other disciplines which are philosophical in nature. Material is written exclusively by graduate students.
Formerly: Kinesis Report (0193-1911)
Related titles: Microform ed.: (from PQC).
Indexed: A22, CWPI, FR, IPB, PCI, PhilInd.
—BLDSC (5096.030000), IE, Ingenta, INIST. **CCC.**
Published by: Southern Illinois University at Carbondale, Philosophy Department, 980 Faner Dr, Rm 3065, Carbondale, IL 62901. TEL 618-536-6641, FAX 618-453-7428, jbrant@siu.edu.

100 AUT ISSN 0259-0743
KLAGENFURTER BEITRAEGE ZUR PHILOSOPHIE. Text in German. 1979. irreg. price varies. **Document type:** *Monographic series.*
Related titles: ◆ Supplement(s): Klagenfurter Beitraege zur Philosophie. Reihe: Diplomarbeiten & Dissertationen. ISSN 0259-4943; ◆ Klagenfurter Beitraege zur Philosophie. Reihe: Referate. ISSN 0259-4978; ◆ Klagenfurter Beitraege zur Philosophie. Reihe: Lehrmaterialen. ISSN 0259-496X; ◆ Klagenfurter Beitraege zur Philosophie. Reihe: Gruppendynamik & Organisationsentwicklung. ISSN 0259-4951.
Published by: Philosophische Gesellschaft Klagenfurt, Universitaetsstrasse 65-67, Klagenfurt, K 9022, Austria. Eds. Christof Subik, Thomas Macho.

100 AUT ISSN 0259-4943
KLAGENFURTER BEITRAEGE ZUR PHILOSOPHIE. REIHE: DIPLOMARBEITEN & DISSERTATIONEN. Text in German. 1979. irreg.
Related titles: ◆ Supplement to: Klagenfurter Beitraege zur Philosophie. ISSN 0259-0743.
Published by: Philosophische Gesellschaft Klagenfurt, Universitaetsstrasse 65-67, Klagenfurt, K 9022, Austria.

100 AUT ISSN 0259-4951
KLAGENFURTER BEITRAEGE ZUR PHILOSOPHIE. REIHE: GRUPPENDYNAMIK & ORGANISATIONSENTWICKLUNG. Text in German. 1979. irreg.
Related titles: ◆ Supplement to: Klagenfurter Beitraege zur Philosophie. ISSN 0259-0743.
Published by: Philosophische Gesellschaft Klagenfurt, Universitaetsstrasse 65-67, Klagenfurt, K 9022, Austria.

100 AUT ISSN 0259-496X
KLAGENFURTER BEITRAEGE ZUR PHILOSOPHIE. REIHE: LEHRMATERIALEN. Text in German. 1979.
Related titles: ◆ Supplement to: Klagenfurter Beitraege zur Philosophie. ISSN 0259-0743.
Published by: Philosophische Gesellschaft Klagenfurt, Universitaetsstrasse 65-67, Klagenfurt, K 9022, Austria.

100 AUT ISSN 0259-4978
KLAGENFURTER BEITRAEGE ZUR PHILOSOPHIE. REIHE: REFERATE. Text in German. 1979.
Related titles: ◆ Supplement to: Klagenfurter Beitraege zur Philosophie. ISSN 0259-0743.
Published by: Philosophische Gesellschaft Klagenfurt, Universitaetsstrasse 65-67, Klagenfurt, K 9022, Austria.

KLINISCHE ETHIK; Biomedizin in Forschung und Praxis. *see* MEDICAL SCIENCES

KNOWLEDGE AND SPACE. *see* SOCIAL SCIENCES: COMPREHENSIVE WORKS

KOERS; bulletin vir Christelike wetenskap - bulletin for Christian scholarship. *see* RELIGIONS AND THEOLOGY—Protestant

100 001.3 DEU
KONKURSBUCH; Zeitschrift fuer Vernunftkritik. Text in German. 1978. 2/yr. EUR 12 per issue (effective 2005). back issues avail. **Document type:** *Academic/Scholarly.*
Published by: Konkursbuchverlag Claudia Gehrke, Hechinger Str 203, Tuebingen, 72072, Germany. TEL 49-7071-78779, FAX 49-7071-763780, office@konkursbuch.com. Ed. Claudia Gehrke.

100 001.3 USA ISSN 1947-3796
JC323
➤ **KONTUREN.** Text in English. 2008. a. free (effective 2011). **Document type:** *Journal, Academic/Scholarly.*
Media: Online - full text.
Published by: University of Oregon, Department of German and Scandinavian, 1250 University of Oregon, Eugene, OR 97403. Ed. Jeffrey S Librett.

100 001.3 ARG ISSN 1669-9092
KONVERGENCIAS; revista de filosofia y culturas en dialogo. Text in Spanish. 2002. 3/yr. **Document type:** *Journal, Academic/Scholarly.*
Media: Online - full text. Ed. Silvia B Aquino.

141 NLD ISSN 0920-6884
KOORDDANSER. Text in Dutch. 1984. m. (11/yr.). EUR 25; EUR 2.50 newsstand/cover (effective 2010). adv. **Document type:** *Newspaper, Consumer.*
Published by: Uitgeverij Koorddanser, Postbus 429, Laren, 1250 AK, Netherlands. TEL 31-35-5336226, FAX 31-35-5384443, http://www.kd.nl. Ed., Pub. Ewald Wagenaar. Adv. contact Willem Swart. page EUR 1,650; trim 299 x 420. Circ: 9,531.

519 DEU
KOPAED MEDIENETHIK. Text in German. 2001. irreg., latest vol.3, 2001. price varies. **Document type:** *Monographic series, Academic/Scholarly.*
Published by: KoPaed Verlag, Pfaelzer-Wald-Str 64, Munich, 81539, Germany. TEL 49-89-68890098, FAX 49-89-6891912, info@kopaed.de.

100 DEU ISSN 0454-448X
KOSMOSOPHIE. Text in German. 1962. irreg., latest vol.7, 1992. price varies. **Document type:** *Monographic series, Academic/Scholarly.*
Published by: (Paracelsus-Kommission), Franz Steiner Verlag GmbH, Birkenwaldstr 44, Stuttgart, 70191, Germany. TEL 49-711-25820, FAX 49-711-2582290, service@steiner-verlag.de, http://www.steiner-verlag.de.

100 NLD ISSN 1875-7103
➤ **KRISIS (ONLINE)**; journal for contemporary philosophy. Text in Dutch, English. 200?. q. free (effective 2011). **Document type:** *Journal, Academic/Scholarly.*
Media: Online - full text.
Published by: Boom Uitgevers Amsterdam, PO Box 400, Meppel, 7940 AK, Netherlands. TEL 31-522-237555, FAX 31-522-253864, info@uitgeverijboom.nl, http://www.uitgeverijboom.nl.

100 BRA ISSN 0100-512X
AS80.A1
➤ **KRITERION**; revista de filosofia. Text in Portuguese, English. 1947. s-a. BRL 30 (effective 2006). **Document type:** *Journal, Academic/Scholarly.* **Description:** Publishes articles in philosophy which have philosophical relevance and promote an interchange of philosophical publications among scholars in Brazil and abroad.
Related titles: Online - full text ed.: free (effective 2011).
Indexed: A20, ArtHuCI, MLA-IB, PhilInd, SCOPUS, W07.
Published by: Universidade Federal de Minas Gerais, Faculdade de Filosofia e Ciencias Humanas, Av Antonio Carlos 6627, Pampulha, Belo Horizonte, MG 31270-901, Brazil. TEL 55-31-34995000, FAX 55-31-34994188. Ed. Virginia Figueireido.

100 AUT ISSN 1019-8288
➤ **KRITERION.** Text in English, German. 1991. irreg., latest vol.18, 2004. EUR 2.50 per vol.; EUR 1.45 per vol. to students (effective 2005). bk.rev. back issues avail. **Document type:** *Journal, Academic/Scholarly.* **Description:** Contributions to contemporary (scientific) philosophy, essays by young philosophers are welcome.
Indexed: DIP, IBR, IBZ, PhilInd, RASB, RILM.
Published by: Universitaet Salzburg, Institut fuer Philosophie, Franziskanergasse 1, Salzburg, Sa 5020, Austria. FAX 43-662-8044629. R&P Philippe Patry TEL 43-662-80446034. Adv. contact Michael Sedlaczek TEL 43-662-80446034. Circ: 250 (controlled).

100 PHL ISSN 1908-7330
B1
➤ **KRITIKE**; an online journal of philosophy. Text in English. 2007. s-a. free (effective 2011). bk.rev. Index. back issues avail. **Document type:** *Journal, Academic/Scholarly.* **Description:** Publish articles and book reviews by local and international authors across the whole range of philosophical topics, but with special emphasis on continental philosophy, analytic philosophy, and east-west comparative philosophy.
Media: Online - full text.
Indexed: AmHI, H07, T02.
Published by: University of Santo Tomas, Faculty of Arts and Letters, Espana, Manila, 1008, Philippines. http://www.ust.edu.ph. Ed., R&P Paolo Bolanos.

P

100 DEU ISSN 2190-3344
▼ **KULTUR & PHILOSOPHIE**; Beitraege, Analysen, Kommentare. Text in German. 2010. irreg., latest vol.2, 2010. price varies. **Document type:** *Monographic series, Academic/Scholarly.*
Published by: Projekt Verlag GbR, Oskar-Hoffmann-Str 25, Bochum, 44789, Germany. TEL 49-234-3251570, FAX 49-234-3251571, lektorat@projektverlag.de.

100 DEU ISSN 0947-0298
KULTUR UND ERKENNTNIS. Text in German. 1985. irreg., latest vol.33, 2007. price varies. back issues avail. **Document type:** *Monographic series, Academic/Scholarly.* **Description:** Covers a wide variety of philosophical topics, ranging from historic drama to anxiety in contemporary academic settings.
Published by: (Heinrich-Heine-Universitaet Duesseldorf, Philosophische Fakultaet), A. Francke Verlag GmbH, Dischinger Weg 5, Tuebingen, 72070, Germany. TEL 49-7071-97970, FAX 49-7071-979711, info@francke.de, http://www.francke.de.

KUNGLIGA VITTERHETS HISTORIE OCH ANTIKVITETS AKADEMIEN. HANDLINGAR. FILOLOGISK-FILOSOFISKA SERIEN/ROYAL ACADEMY OF LETTERS, HISTORY AND ANTIQUITIES. PROCEEDINGS. PHILOLOGICAL - PHILOSOPHICAL SERIES. *see* LINGUISTICS

KUNSTPHILOSOPHIE. *see* ART

100 POL ISSN 1230-4050
B7
KWARTALNIK FILOZOFICZNY. Text in Polish. 1923-1950; resumed 1992. q. EUR 59 foreign (effective 2006). **Document type:** *Journal, Academic/Scholarly.*
Indexed: PhilInd.
Published by: (Uniwersytet Jagiellonski, Instytut Filozofii/Jagiellonian University, Institute of Philosophy, Polska Akademia Umiejetnosci), Wydawnictwo Secesja, ul Sawkowska 17, Krakow, 31016, Poland. kwartfil@grodzki.phils.uj.edu.pl. **Dist. by:** Ars Polona, Obroncow 25, Warsaw 03933, Poland. TEL 48-22-5098609, FAX 48-22-5098610, arspolona@arspolona.com.pl, http://www.arspolona.com.pl.

100 320 UKR ISSN 1728-2632
➤ **KYIVS'KYI NATSIONAL'NYI UNIVERSYTET IMENI TARASA SHEVCHENKA. VISNYK. FILOSOFIYA, POLITOLOHIYA.** Text in Ukrainian. 2000. 20/yr. **Document type:** *Journal, Academic/Scholarly.*
Related titles: ◆ Series: Kyivs'kyi Natsional'nyi Universytet imeni Tarasa Shevchenka. Visnyk. ISSN 1728-3817; ◆ Kyivs'kyi Natsional'nyi Universytet imeni Tarasa Shevchenka. Visnyk. Mizhnarodni Vidnosyny. ISSN 1728-2292; ◆ Kyivs'kyi Natsional'nyi Universytet imeni Tarasa Shevchenka. Visnyk. Yurydychni Nauky. ISSN 1728-2195; ◆ Kyivs'kyi Natsional'nyi Universytet imeni Tarasa Shevchenka. Visnyk. Khimiya. ISSN 1728-2209; ◆ Kyivs'kyi Natsional'nyi Universytet imeni Tarasa Shevchenka. Visnyk. Fizyka. ISSN 1728-2411; ◆ Kyivs'kyi Natsional'nyi Universytet imeni Tarasa Shevchenka. Visnyk. Biolohiya. ISSN 1728-2748; ◆ Kyivs'kyi Natsional'nyi Universytet imeni Tarasa Shevchenka. Visnyk. Ekonomika. ISSN 1728-2667; ◆ Kyivs'kyi Natsional'nyi Universytet imeni Tarasa Shevchenka. Visnyk. Istoriya. ISSN 1728-2640; ◆ Kyivs'kyi Natsional'nyi Universytet imeni Tarasa Shevchenka. Visnyk. Kibernetyka. ISSN 1728-2276; ◆ Kyivs'kyi Natsional'nyi Universytet imeni Tarasa Shevchenka. Visnyk. Problemy Rehulyatsii Fiziolohichnykh Funktsii. ISSN 1728-2624; ◆ Kyivs'kyi Natsional'nyi Universytet imeni Tarasa Shevchenka. Visnyk. Radiofizyka ta Elektronika. ISSN 1728-2306; ◆ Kyivs'kyi Natsional'nyi Universytet imeni Tarasa Shevchenka. Visnyk. Introduktsiya ta Zberezhennya Roslynnogo Riznomanittya. ISSN 1728-2284; ◆ Kyivs'kyi Natsional'nyi Universytet imeni Tarasa Shevchenka. Visnyk. Ukrainoznavstvo. ISSN 1728-2330; ◆ Kyivs'kyi Natsional'nyi Universytet imeni Tarasa Shevchenka. Visnyk. Sotsiolohiya, Psykholohiya, Pedahohika. ISSN 1728-2322; ◆ Kyivs'kyi Natsional'nyi Universytet imeni Tarasa Shevchenka. Visnyk. Literaturoznavstvo, Movoznavstvo, Fol'klorystyka. ISSN 1728-2659; ◆ Kyivs'kyi Natsional'nyi Universytet imeni Tarasa Shevchenka. Visnyk. Astronomiya. ISSN 1728-273X; ◆ Kyivs'kyi Natsional'nyi Universytet imeni Tarasa Shevchenka. Visnyk. Seriya: Fizyko-Matematychni Nauky. ISSN 1812-5409; ◆ Kyivs'kyi Natsional'nyi Universytet imeni Tarasa Shevchenka. Visnyk. Heohrafiya. ISSN 1728-2721; ◆ Kyivs'kyi Natsional'nyi Universytet imeni Tarasa Shevchenka. Visnyk. Heolohiya. ISSN 1728-2713; ◆ Kyivs'kyi Natsional'nyi Universytet imeni Tarasa Shevchenka. Visnyk. Zhurnalistyka. ISSN 1728-2705; ◆ Kyivs'kyi Natsional'nyi Universytet imeni Tarasa Shevchenka. Visnyk. Inozemna Filolohiya. ISSN 1728-2683; ◆ Kyivs'kyi Natsional'nyi Universytet imeni Tarasa Shevchenka. Visnyk. Shidni Movy ta Literatury. ISSN 1728-242X; ◆ Kyivs'kyi Natsional'nyi Universytet imeni Tarasa Shevchenka. Visnyk. Matematyka ta Mekhanika. ISSN 1684-1565.
Published by: (Kyivs'kyi Natsional'nyi Universytet imeni Tarasa Shevchenka, Filosofs'kyi Fakul'tet/Taras Shevchenko National University of Kyiv, Faculty of Philosophy), Vydavnycho-Poligrafichnyi Tsentr Kyivs'kyi Universytet, bul'var Tarasa Shevchenko, 14, ofis 43, Kyiv, 01601, Ukraine. TEL 380-44-2393172, FAX 380-44-2393128. Ed. Anatolii Ye Konvers'kyi.

121.68 AUT ISSN 1561-8927
LABYRINTH; international journal for philosophy, feminist theory and cultural hermeneutics. Text in English, French, Dutch. s-a. **Document type:** *Journal, Academic/Scholarly.* **Description:** Aims to promote philosophical and interdisciplinary value inquiry on values in sex-gender contexts, and hermeneutics of culture and religions.
Related titles: Online - full text ed.
Indexed: PhilInd.
Published by: Institut fuer Axiologische Forschungen/Institute for Axiological Research, Doktorberg 23 E-2, Kaltenleutgeben, N 2391, Austria. TEL 43-2238-70174, iaf@iaf.ac.at, http://www.iaf.ac.at. Ed. Yvanka B Raynova.

100 ESP
LAGUNA; revista de filosofia. Text in Spanish. 1992. s-a. **Document type:** *Journal, Academic/Scholarly.*
Indexed: CA.
Published by: Universidad de la Laguna, Secretariado de Publicaciones, Campus Central, La Laguna-Tenerife, Canary Islands 38071, Spain. TEL 34-922-319198, FAX 34-922-258127, svpubli@ull.es, http://www.ull.es.

100 BEL ISSN 0774-2754
LAICITE. LA PENSEE ET LES HOMMES. Text in French. 1985. irreg. **Document type:** *Journal, Academic/Scholarly.*
Indexed: P30.
Published by: Editions de l'Universite de Bruxelles (Subsidiary of: Universite Libre de Bruxelles), Av Paul Heger 26, CP 163, Brussels, 1000, Belgium. TEL 32-2-650-3799, FAX 32-2-650-3794, editions@admin.ulb.ac.be, http://www.editions-universite-bruxelles.be.

100 MEX ISSN 1870-4662
LAMPARA DE DIOGENES; revista semestral de filosofia. Text in Spanish. 2000. s-a. free (effective 2011). **Document type:** *Journal, Academic/Scholarly.*
Media: Online - full text.
Published by: Benemerita Universidad Autonoma de Puebla, Facultad de Filosofia y Letras, 3 Oriente No 210, Puebla, 72000, Mexico. TEL 52-222-2295500, http://www.buap.mx.

100 305.89171 USA ISSN 1940-0837
B4231
➤ **LANDSHAFT.** Text in English, Russian. 2008 (Winter). s-a. free (effective 2010). **Document type:** *Journal, Academic/Scholarly.* **Description:** Contains articles on philosophy, literature, and culture, with a focus on the intellectual landscape of contemporary Russian thought.
Media: Online - full text.
Published by: University of Pittsburgh, Department of Slavic Languages and Literature, 1417 Cathedral of Learning, Pittsburgh, PA 15260. TEL 412-624-5906, FAX 412-624-9714, slavic@pitt.edu, http://www.pitt.edu/~slavic/about.html.

➤ **LAST RIGHTS.** *see* MEDICAL SCIENCES

110 NLD ISSN 2210-5573
LAUNIANA MAIORA. Text in Dutch. 1996. irreg., latest vol.2, 2010. price varies. **Document type:** *Monographic series, Academic/Scholarly.*
Published by: (Rudolf van Laun Instituut), Deventer Universitaire Pers, Sandrasteeg 8, Deventer, 7411 KS, Netherlands. TEL 31-570-613663, info@deventeruniversitairepers.nl, http://www.deventeruniversitairepers.nl.

111 NLD ISSN 1875-449X
LAUNIANA MINORA. Text in Dutch. 2002. a. EUR 4.35 per vol. (effective 2010).
Published by: (Rudolf van Laun Instituut), Deventer Universitaire Pers, Sandrasteeg 8, Deventer, 7411 KS, Netherlands. TEL 31-570-613663, info@deventeruniversitairepers.nl, http://www.deventeruniversitairepers.nl.

210 CAN ISSN 0023-9054
BX802
➤ **LAVAL THEOLOGIQUE ET PHILOSOPHIQUE.** Abbreviated title: L T P. Text in English, French. 1945. 3/yr. CAD 45 domestic to individuals; CAD 60 foreign to individuals; CAD 70 domestic to institutions; CAD 90 foreign to institutions; CAD 25 domestic to students; CAD 30 foreign to students (effective 2005). bk.rev. bibl. index, cum.index. back issues avail. **Document type:** *Journal, Academic/Scholarly.* **Description:** Offers an interdisciplinary review of theology and philosophy. Presents and discusses the main currents of thought that concern the history of both disciplines and their contribution to modern times.
Related titles: Microfilm ed.: (from BNQ).
Indexed: A20, A21, A22, ASCA, ArtHuCI, C03, CBCARef, CERDIC, CPL, CurCont, DIP, FR, IBR, IBZ, IPB, IZBG, MLA-IB, OTA, P48, PCI, PQC, PdeR, PhilInd, R&TA, RI-1, RI-2, SCOPUS, W07.
—BLDSC (5160.825000), IE, Infotrieve, Ingenta, INIST. **CCC.**
Published by: Universite Laval, Faculte de Theologie et de Sciences Religieuses, Cite Universitaire, Quebec, PQ G1K 7P4, Canada. TEL 418-656-2131 ext.4775, FAX 418-656-7267, ftsr@ftsr.ulaval.ca, http://www.ftsr.ulaval.ca/ftsr/index.html. Eds. Thomas De Koninck, Luc Langlois. R&P Thomas De Koninck. Circ: 1,000.

➤ **LAW & JUSTICE**; the Christian law review. *see* LAW

➤ **LAW AND PHILOSOPHY**; an international journal for jurisprudence and legal philosophy. *see* LAW

➤ **LAW AND PHILOSOPHY LIBRARY.** *see* LAW

➤ **LAWYER AND JUDICIAL ETHICS.** *see* LAW

100 305.4 ESP ISSN 1136-5781
LECTORA; revista de mujeres y textualidad. Text in Multiple languages. 1995. a. **Document type:** *Journal, Academic/Scholarly.*
Indexed: MLA-IB.
Published by: (Universitat de Barcelona, Facultat de Filosofia), Universitat de Barcelona, Servei de Publicacions, Gran Via Corts Catalanes 585, Barcelona, 08007, Spain. TEL 34-93-4021100, http://www.publicacions.ub.es.

LEGAL ETHICS FOR MANAGEMENT AND THEIR COUNSEL. *see* LAW

LEGAL ETHICS IN THE PRACTICE OF LAW. *see* LAW

100 DEU
LEGENDA. Text in German. 1993. irreg., latest vol.7, 2006. price varies. **Document type:** *Monographic series, Academic/Scholarly.* **Description:** Aims to introduce and thereby induce people to read philosophical works.
Published by: Frommann-Holzboog Verlag e.K., Koenig-Karl-Str 27, Stuttgart, 70372, Germany. TEL 49-711-9559690, FAX 49-711-9559691, info@frommann-holzboog.de, http://www.frommann-holzboog.de.

100 DEU ISSN 1868-8969
LEIBNIZ INTERNATIONAL PROCEEDINGS IN INFORMATICS. Text in English. 2008. irreg. free (effective 2011). **Document type:** *Journal, Academic/Scholarly.*
Media: Online - full text.
Published by: Schloss Dagstuhl - Leibniz- Zentrum fuer Informatik, Oktavie Allee, Wadern, 66687, Germany. TEL 49-6871-905127, FAX 49-6871-905133.

100 GBR ISSN 0266-0598
B2550
LEIBNIZ NEWSLETTER. Text in English. 1984. a. GBP 2. **Description:** Reports on research and conferences on Leibniz, and on related 17th and 18th century topics and philosophers.
Address: c/o George MacDonald Ross, Dept. of Philosophy, The University, Leeds, W Yorks LS2 9JT, United Kingdom. TEL 0532-333283.

193 USA ISSN 1524-1556
B2550
➤ **THE LEIBNIZ REVIEW.** Text in English. 19??. a. USD 50 per issue in US & Canada; USD 60 per issue elsewhere; free to members (effective 2010). adv. bk.rev. back issues avail. **Document type:** *Journal, Academic/Scholarly.* **Description:** Publishes articles on the philosophy of Leibniz.
Former titles (until 1999): Leibniz Society Review (1069-5192); (until 1993): Leibniz Society Newsletter & Review; (until 1991): Leibniz Society Newsletter
Related titles: Online - full text ed.: ISSN 2153-9162. USD 150 per issue (effective 2010).
Indexed: DIP, IBR, IBZ, PhilInd.
Published by: Philosophy Documentation Center, PO Box 7147, Charlottesville, VA 22906. TEL 434-220-3300, FAX 434-220-3301, order@pdcnet.org, http://www.pdcnet.org. Ed. Glenn A Hartz TEL 419-755-4354. Adv. contact Greg Swope.

➤ **LEICESTER LITERARY & PHILOSOPHICAL SOCIETY. TRANSACTIONS.** *see* LITERATURE

100 DEU ISSN 0947-2460
LEIPZIGER SCHRIFTEN ZUR PHILOSOPHIE. Text in German. 1995. irreg., latest vol.21, 2010. price varies. **Document type:** *Monographic series, Academic/Scholarly.*
Published by: Leipziger Universitaetsverlag GmbH, Oststr 41, Leipzig, 04317, Germany. TEL 49-341-9900440, FAX 49-341-9900440, info@univerlag-leipzig.de.

100 370 ITA ISSN 1973-039X
L'EMOZIONE DI CONOSCERE E IL DESIDERIO DI ESISTERE/ EMOCION DE CONOCER Y EL DESEO DE EXISTIR/EMOTION TO KNOW AND THE DESIRE TO EXIST. Text in Multiple languages. 2007. q. free (effective 2010). **Document type:** *Journal, Academic/Scholarly.*
Media: Online - full text.
Published by: Universita degli Studi di Bologna, Dipartimento di Scienze dell'Educazione Giovanni Maria Bertin, Via Filippo Re 6, Bologna, 40126, Italy. TEL 39-051-2091666, FAX 39-051-2091489, http://www.scedu.unibo.it. Ed. Nicola Cuomo.

LETRAS DE DEUSTO. *see* HUMANITIES: COMPREHENSIVE WORKS

100 USA ISSN 1554-7000
B2430.L484
➤ **LEVINAS STUDIES**; an annual review. Text in English. 2005. a. USD 35 per issue (effective 2010). adv. back issues avail. **Document type:** *Journal, Academic/Scholarly.*
Related titles: Online - full text ed.: ISSN 2153-8433. USD 105 per issue to institutions (effective 2010).
Indexed: AmHI, H07, T02.
Published by: (Duquesne University Press), Philosophy Documentation Center, PO Box 7147, Charlottesville, VA 22906. TEL 434-220-3300, FAX 434-220-3301, order@pdcnet.org, http://www.pdcnet.org. Ed. Jeffrey Bloechl TEL 617-552-4023. Adv. contact Greg Swope.

➤ **LIAONING DAXUE XUEBAO (ZHEXUE SHEHUI KEXUE BAN)/ LIAONING UNIVERSITY. JOURNAL (PHILOSOPHY AND SOCIAL SCIENCES EDITION).** *see* SOCIAL SCIENCES: COMPREHENSIVE WORKS

301 FRA ISSN 1767-2163
LIBELLES. Text in French. 2004. irreg. back issues avail. **Document type:** *Monographic series, Consumer.*
Published by: Presses Universitaires de France, 6 Avenue Reille, Paris, 75685, France. TEL 33-1-58103161, FAX 33-1-45897530, revues@puf.com.

100 GBR ISSN 0267-7091
LIBERTARIAN ALLIANCE. PHILOSOPHICAL NOTES. Text in English. 1985. irreg., latest 2009. bk.rev.; film rev. bibl. back issues avail. **Document type:** *Monographic series, Trade.*
Related titles: Online - full text ed.: ISSN 2042-2768. free (effective 2009).
Published by: Libertarian Alliance, 2 Lansdowne Row, Ste 35, London, W1J 6HL, United Kingdom. TEL 44-7956-472199. Ed. Nigel Meek.

LIBERTY (PORT TOWNSEND). *see* LITERARY AND POLITICAL REVIEWS

LIBRARY OF CONTEMPORARY THOUGHT; America's most original voices tackle today's most provocative issues. *see* LITERARY AND POLITICAL REVIEWS

100 170 NLD ISSN 1387-6678
LIBRARY OF ETHICS AND APPLIED PHILOSOPHY. Text in English. 1997. irreg., latest vol.21, 2009. price varies. **Document type:** *Monographic series, Academic/Scholarly.* **Description:** Focuses on the field of practical philosophy, including ethics, social and political philosophy, and philosophy of action.
—BLDSC (5198.690000), IE.
Published by: Springer Netherlands (Subsidiary of: Springer Science+Business Media), Van Godewijckstraat 30, Dordrecht, 3311 GX, Netherlands. TEL 31-78-6576050, FAX 31-78-6576474. Ed. Marcus Duewell.

100 USA ISSN 0075-9139
LIBRARY OF LIVING PHILOSOPHERS. Abbreviated title: L L P. Text in English. 1939. irreg., latest vol.32, 2009. price varies. back issues avail. **Document type:** *Monographic series, Academic/Scholarly.* **Description:** Devoted to critical analysis and discussion of some of the world's greatest living philosophers.
—BLDSC (5200.300000).
Published by: Open Court Publishing Co., General Books (Subsidiary of: Carus Publishing Company), 70 E Lake St, Ste 300, Chicago, IL 60601. TEL 800-815-2280, FAX 312-701-1728, opencourt@caruspub.com. **Subscr. to:** 30 Grove St, Ste C, Peterborough, NH 03458. FAX 603-924-7380, customerservice@caruspub.com.

100 200 GBR
LIBRARY OF PHILOSOPHY AND RELIGION. Text in English. 1975. irreg., latest 2006. price varies. back issues avail. **Document type:** *Monographic series.*
Published by: Palgrave Macmillan Ltd. (Subsidiary of: Macmillan Publishers Ltd.), Houndmills, Basingstoke, Hants RG21 6XS, United Kingdom. TEL 44-1256-329242, FAX 44-1256-810526, bookenquiries@palgrave.com, http://www.palgrave.com. **Dist. by:** Palgrave Macmillan, 175 Fifth Ave, New York, NY 10010.

100 808 NLD ISSN 0929-6298
LIBRARY OF RHETORICS. Text in English. 1993. irreg., latest vol.4, 1997. price varies. back issues avail. **Document type:** *Monographic series, Academic/Scholarly.* **Description:** Focuses on the theory of reasoning, literary and legal rhetoric, rhetoric and the humanities, sociology and historical aspects of rhetorical thought, and particular problems in rhetoric and argumentation.
Published by: Springer Netherlands (Subsidiary of: Springer Science+Business Media), Van Godewijckstraat 30, Dordrecht, 3311 GX, Netherlands. TEL 31-78-6576050, FAX 31-78-6576474. Ed. Michel Meyer.

100 SWE ISSN 0459-2603
LIBRARY OF THEORIA. Text in English. 1955. irreg., latest vol.23. price varies. **Document type:** *Monographic series, Academic/Scholarly.*
Indexed: CCMJ.
Published by: Thales (Subsidiary of: Stiftelsen Bokforlaget Thales), PO Box 50034, Stockholm, 10405, Sweden. TEL 46-8-7596410, FAX 46-8-152226, info@bokforlagetthales.se, http://www.bokforlagetthales.se.

LICHTENBERG-JAHRBUCH. *see* BIOGRAPHY

LIER EN BOOG; series of philosophy of art & art theory. *see* ART

172 FRA ISSN 1772-5003
LIEUX D'UTOPIES. Text in French. 2005. irreg. back issues avail. **Document type:** *Monographic series, Consumer.*
Published by: Editions Manucius, 9 Rue Moliere, Houilles, 78800, France. TEL 33-8-74487246, FAX 33-1-39682003, http://www.manucius.com.

179.7 USA ISSN 1097-0878
HQ767.15
LIFE AND LEARNING. Variant title: University Faculty For Life. Proceedings. Text in English. 1992. a. free to members (effective 2010). **Document type:** *Proceedings, Academic/Scholarly.* **Description:** Contains annual conference details.
Published by: University Faculty For Life, 120 New N, Georgetown University, Washington, DC 20057. koterski@fordham.edu.

LIGHT OF CONSCIOUSNESS; journal of spiritual awakening. *see* NEW AGE PUBLICATIONS

100 301 LTU ISSN 2029-0187
HM621
➤ **LIMES.** Text in English; Abstracts in English, Lithuanian. 2008. s-a. EUR 70 (effective 2010). **Document type:** *Journal, Academic/Scholarly.* **Description:** Publishes original papers concerning such fields of the humanities and social sciences as philosophy, political science, history and sociology.
Related titles: Online - full text ed.: ISSN 2029-0209.
Indexed: A01, A26, E08, I05, PSA, SCOPUS, SociolAb.
—CCC.
Published by: (Kulturos, Filosofijos ir Meno Moksliniu Tyrimu Institutas/ Culture, Philosophy and Arts Research Institute, Vilniaus Gedimino Technikos Universitetas, Publishing House "Technika"/Vilnius Gediminas Technical University), Vilniaus Gedimino Technikos Universitetas, Leidykla Technika, Sauletekio aleja 11, Vilnius, 10223, Lithuania. TEL 370-5-2745038, FAX 370-5-2370602, books@vgtu.lt, http://leidykla.vgtu.lt. Ed. Dr. Tomas Kacerauskas.

150 CHL ISSN 0718-1361
LIMITE. Variant title: Revista de Filosofia y Psicologia. Text in Spanish. 1994. a. **Document type:** *Journal, Academic/Scholarly.*
Formerly (until 1999): Revista Universitaria Limite (0717-2338)
Related titles: Online - full text ed.: ISSN 0718-5065. 2006. free (effective 2011).
Indexed: C01, CA, F04, MLA-IB, T02.
Published by: Universidad de Tarapaca, Departamento de Filosofia y Psicologia, Ave Gral Velasquez, 1775, Arica, Chile. TEL 56-58-205100, FAX 56-58-205300, info@uta.cl, http://www.uta.cl/. Circ: 300.

LINDEBLAD. *see* MEDICAL SCIENCES

100 USA ISSN 0075-9554
LINDLEY LECTURE. Text in English. 1961. a. back issues avail. **Document type:** *Monographic series, Academic/Scholarly.*
—BLDSC (5221.030000), IE, Ingenta.
Published by: University of Kansas, Department of Philosophy, 1445 Jayhawk Blvd, Rm 3090, Wescoe Hall, Lawrence, KS 66045. TEL 785-864-3976, eggleston@ku.edu.

LINGUA E STILE. *see* LINGUISTICS

LINGUISTIC AND PHILOSOPHICAL INVESTIGATIONS. *see* LINGUISTICS

LINGUISTICS AND PHILOSOPHY; a journal of natural language syntax, semantics, logic, pragmatics, and processing. *see* LINGUISTICS

LINZER BEITRAEGE ZUR KUNSTWISSENSCHAFT UND PHILOSOPHIE. *see* ART

LINZER PHILOSOPHISCH-THEOLOGISCHE BEITRAEGE. *see* RELIGIONS AND THEOLOGY—Roman Catholic

100 DEU ISSN 1663-7674
▼ **LISBON PHILOSOPHICAL STUDIES.** Text in English. 2010. irreg. price varies. **Document type:** *Monographic series, Academic/Scholarly.* **Description:** Aims to encourage the interchange of arguments and ideas between philosophy and other disciplines.
Published by: Peter Lang GmbH (Subsidiary of: Peter Lang Publishing Group), Eschborner Landstr 42-50, Frankfurt Am Main, 60489, Germany. TEL 49-69-7807050, FAX 49-69-78070550, zentrale.frankfurt@peterlang.com.

LISTY FILOLOGICKE/FOLIA PHILOLOGICA/JOURNAL OF PHILOLOGY; folia philologica. *see* CLASSICAL STUDIES

LITERATURE AND PHILOSOPHY. *see* LITERATURE

LITERATURE AND THE SCIENCES OF MAN. *see* LITERATURE

LITIGATION ETHICS. *see* LAW

LIVE AND LET LIVE; pro-life - animal rights - libertarian. *see* ANIMAL WELFARE

170 NLD
LIVED VALUES, VALUED LIVES. Text in English. irreg. price varies. **Document type:** *Monographic series, Academic/Scholarly.* **Description:** Explores how a person's values help form a person's life, how that life expresses those values, and the principled ways in which intelligent individuals deal with life's vagaries.
Related titles: ◆ Series of: Value Inquiry Book Series. ISSN 0929-8436.
Published by: Editions Rodopi B.V., Tijnmuiden 7, Amsterdam, 1046 AK, Netherlands. TEL 31-20-6114821, FAX 31-20-4472979, info@rodopi.nl. Ed. Richard T Hull. **Dist. by:** Rodopi - USA, 606 Newark Ave, 2nd fl, Kenilworth, NJ 07033. TEL 908-497-9031, FAX 908-497-9035.

LIVING BUDDHISM. *see* RELIGIONS AND THEOLOGY—Buddhist

170 AUS ISSN 1444-6545
LIVING ETHICS. Text in English. 1990. q. AUD 22 to non-members; free to members (effective 2007). **Document type:** *Newsletter, Consumer.* **Description:** Features a diverse array of ethics-related articles to promote ethical reflection and debate.
Formerly (until 2000): City Ethics (1036-9783)
Published by: St. James Ethics Centre, PO Box 3599, Sydney, NSW 2001, Australia. TEL 61-2-92999566, FAX 61-2-92999477, contact@ethics.org.au.

100 GBR ISSN 1476-0290
B1250
➤ **LOCKE STUDIES**; an annual journal of Locke research. Text in English, French, German, Italian. 1970; N.S. 2001. a., latest vol.8, 2008. GBP 30 to individuals (effective 2011). bk.rev. 1970-1999. 1 cols./p.; back issues avail. **Document type:** *Journal, Academic/Scholarly.* **Description:** Contains articles and notes on any aspects of the work or life of the English philosopher and political theorist John Locke (1632-1704) as well as on other related authors.
Formerly (until 2001): Locke Newsletter (0307-2606)
Indexed: FR, PCI, PhilInd.
—BLDSC (5290.301000), INIST.
Published by: Locke Newsletter, Summerfields, 26 The Glade, Escrick, York, YO19 6JH, United Kingdom. TEL 44-1904-728408, http://www.luc.edu/philosophy/lockenewsletter. Ed. Roland Hall.

160 POL ISSN 1425-3305
BC51
➤ **LOGIC AND LOGICAL PHILOSOPHY.** Text in English, Polish. 1993. q. **Document type:** *Journal, Academic/Scholarly.* **Description:** Devoted to philosophical logic and philosophy resulting from application of logical tools to philosophical problems.
Indexed: AmHI, CA, CCMJ, H07, MSN, MathR, PhilInd, T02, Z02.
Published by: (Uniwersytet Mikolaja Kopernika, Katedra Logiki/Nicolaus Copernicus University, Department of Logic), Wydawnictwo Naukowe Uniwersytetu Mikolaja Kopernika/Nicolaus Copernicus University Press, ul Gagarina 39, Torun, 87100, Poland. TEL 48-56-6114295, FAX 48-56-6114705, dwyd@uni.torun.pl, http://www.wydawnictwo.umk.pl. Eds. Andrzej Pietruszczak, Marek Nasieniewski.

100 500 ITA ISSN 1826-1043
LOGIC AND PHILOSOPHY OF SCIENCE. Text in Multiple languages. 2003. s-a. **Document type:** *Journal, Academic/Scholarly.*
Media: Online - full text.
Published by: Universita degli Studi di Trieste, Dipartimento di Filosofia, Androna Campo Marzio 10, Trieste, 34123, Italy. TEL 39-040-5584314, FAX 39-040-311796, http://www.univ.trieste.it/~dipfilo/vari.html.

160 BEL ISSN 0024-5836
BC1 CODEN: LOANAM
➤ **LOGIQUE ET ANALYSE.** Text in Dutch, English, French, German. 1954. q. bk.rev. bibl.; illus. Index. reprints avail. **Document type:** *Journal, Academic/Scholarly.* **Description:** Publishes articles on philosophical and symbolic logic.
Formerly (until 1958): Centre National Belge de Recherches de Logique. Bulletin Interieur (1376-3687)
Indexed: A20, A22, ArtHuCI, CCMJ, DIP, IBR, IBZ, IPB, L&LBA, MLA-IB, MSN, MathR, PCI, PhilInd, RASB, SCOPUS, SOPODA, W07, Z02.
—IE, Linda Hall.
Published by: Nationaal Centrum voor Navorsingen in de Logica/Centre National de Recherches de Logique, c/o Jean-Paul van Bendegem, Vrije Universiteit Brussel, Faculteit Letteren en Wijsbegeer, Sectie Wijsbegeerte, Pleinlaan 2, Brussels, 1050, Belgium. jpvbende@vub.ac.be. Circ: 1,000.

➤ **LOGIQUES SOCIALES. SERIE SOCIOLOGIE DE LA CONNAISSANCE.** *see* SOCIOLOGY

160 DEU ISSN 1435-3415
LOGISCHE PHILOSOPHIE. Text in German. 1998. irreg., latest vol.21, 2010. price varies. **Document type:** *Monographic series, Academic/Scholarly.*
Indexed: CCMJ, MSN, MathR.
Published by: Logos Verlag Berlin, Comeniushof, Gubener Str 47, Berlin, 10243, Germany. TEL 49-30-42851090, FAX 49-30-42851092, redaktion@logos-verlag.de.

100 VEN ISSN 1316-693X
➤ **LOGOI**; revista de filosofia. Text in Spanish, English. 1998. s-a. USD 20 domestic; USD 30 foreign (effective 2008). bk.rev. abstr.; bibl. back issues avail. **Document type:** *Journal, Academic/Scholarly.*
Formerly (until 1998): Cuadernos Venezolanos de Filosofia
Related titles: Online - full text ed.
Indexed: A01, C01, CA, F03, F04, PhilInd, T02.
—CCC.
Published by: Universidad Catolica Andres Bello, Escuela de Filosofia, Apartado Postal 20332, Modulo A-2 Montalban, La Vega, Caracas, 1020, Venezuela. TEL 58-212-4074238, FAX 58-212-4074312, http://www.ucab.edu.ve/ucabnuevo/index.php?pagina=112. Ed. Jose Luis Da Silva. Pub. Emilio Piriz Perez.

➤ **LOGOS (ST. PAUL)**; a journal of Catholic thought and culture. *see* RELIGIONS AND THEOLOGY—Roman Catholic

100 NLD ISSN 1879-7113
▼ **LOGOS (ZUTPHEN).** Text in Dutch. 2009. a. EUR 19 (effective 2010).
Published by: Uitgeverij Kamerling, Moesmate 13, Zutphen, 7206 AC, Netherlands. TEL 31-575-530860, info@kamerling.eu, http://www.kamerling.eu. Eds. Inge Delfin, Steven Dijkstra.

110 ESP ISSN 1575-6866
BD115
➤ **LOGOS. ANALES DEL SEMINARIO DE METAFISICA.** Text in English, French, German, Italian, Spanish. 1966. a., latest vol.43, 2010. EUR 18 domestic; EUR 24 in Europe; EUR 28 elsewhere (effective 2011). adv. bk.rev. bibl. back issues avail. **Document type:** *Journal, Academic/Scholarly.* **Description:** Presents monographic issues on philosophy, metaphysics and the knowledge theory.
Formerly (until 1997): Anales del Seminario de Metafisica (0580-8650)
Related titles: CD-ROM ed.; Online - full text ed.: ISSN 1988-3242. free.
Indexed: FR, H21, IPB, P08, P09, P28, P48, P53, P54, PCI, PQC, PhilInd, SCOPUS.
—INIST.
Published by: (Universidad Complutense de Madrid, Facultad de Filosofia), Universidad Complutense de Madrid, Servicio de Publicaciones, C/ Obispo Trejo 2, Ciudad Universitaria, Madrid, 28040, Spain. TEL 34-91-3941127, FAX 34-91-3941126, servicio.publicaciones@rect.ucm.es, http://www.ucm.es/publicaciones. Eds. Antonio M Lopez Molina, Juan Jose Garcia Norro. Circ: 500.

100 ROM ISSN 2069-0533
▼ **LOGOS & EPISTEME**; an international journal of epistemology. Text in English, French, German. 2010. irreg. free (effective 2011). **Document type:** *Journal, Academic/Scholarly.*
Media: Online - full text.
Published by: Institutul European din Romania/European Institute of Romania, 7-9 Bd Regina Elisabeta, Sector 3, Bucharest, 030016, Romania. TEL 40-21-3142696, FAX 40-21-3142666, ier@ier.ro, http://www.ier.ro.

100 POL ISSN 0867-8308
➤ **LOGOS I ETHOS.** Text in Polish. 1991. s-a. USD 25 foreign (effective 2006). **Document type:** *Journal, Academic/Scholarly.*
Published by: (Papieska Akademia Teologiczna w Krakowie, Wydzial Filozoficzny), Wydawnictwo Naukowe Papieskiej Akademii Teologicznej w Krakowie, ul Franciszkanska 1, pok 037, Krakow, 31004, Poland. wydawnictwo@pat.krakow.pl.

100 200 CAN ISSN 0828-184X
BR1
LONERGAN STUDIES NEWSLETTER. Text in English. 1980. q. CAD 8, USD 6 (effective 1999). bk.rev. bibl. back issues avail. **Document type:** *Newsletter, Academic/Scholarly.* **Description:** Publishes update on Lonergan studies, provides information of related workshops, conferences, seminars and reports on other Lonergan institutes and centers around the world.
Published by: Lonergan Research Institute, 10 St Mary St, Ste 500, Toronto, ON M4Y 1P9, Canada. TEL 416-922-2433, FAX 416-921-1673, bdoranca@yahoo.ca. Ed. Tad Dunne. Circ: 300.

100 JPN ISSN 0288-3929
N7483.F43
LOTUS. Text in Japanese. 1981. a. **Document type:** *Journal, Academic/Scholarly.*
Published by: Nihon Fenollosa Gakkai/Fenollosa Society of Japan, Shiga University, Faculty of Education, 2-5-1 Hiratsu, Otsu, Shiga 520-0862, Japan. TEL 61-775-370081. **Subscr. to:** Bunsei Shoin Booksellers Co., Ltd., 14-7, Hongo 6 Chome, Bunkyo-ku, Tokyo 113-0033, Japan. TEL 81-3-38111683, FAX 81-3-38110296, info@bunsei.co.jp, http://www.bunsei.co.jp/.

212.5 FRA ISSN 0024-6670
➤ **LOTUS BLEU**; revue theosophique. Text in French. 1882. 10/yr. EUR 35 domestic; EUR 38 foreign (effective 2009). bk.rev. **Document type:** *Magazine, Consumer.* **Description:** Publishes philosophical and religious papers.
Formerly (until 1890): Revue Theosophique (1255-9040); Which superseded in part (in 1889): Le Lotus (1255-9032); Which was formerly (until 1887): Revue des Hautes Etudes (1255-9024); (1882-1886): L' Anti-Materialiste (1255-9016); Incorporates (1948-1966): La Vie Theosophique (1255-9067); Which incorporated (1953-1953): La Federation des Branches Theosophiques de l'Ile-de-France. Bulletin (1255-9083); Which was formerly (1952-1953): Ile-de-France (1255-9075)
Published by: Societe Theosophique de France, 4 square Rapp, Paris, 75007, France. TEL 33-1-47052630, FAX 33-1-47055916, editionsadyar@wanadoo.fr, http://www.theosophie-adyar.com. Ed., R&P Danielle Audoin. Circ: 600.

➤ **LOUISIANA CULTURAL VISTAS.** *see* HISTORY—History Of North And South America

100 BEL
LOUVAIN PHILOSOPHICAL STUDIES. Text in English. 1987. irreg., latest vol.16, 2001. price varies. back issues avail. **Document type:** *Monographic series, Academic/Scholarly.*
Published by: Leuven University Press, Blijde Inkomststraat 5, Leuven, 3000, Belgium. TEL 32-16-325345, FAX 32-16-325352, university.press@upers.kuleuven.ac.be, http://www.kuleuven.ac.be/upers. Ed. C Steel.

LOVE; the journal of the human spirit. *see* NEW AGE PUBLICATIONS

LUCA; casopis za filozofiju i sociologiju. *see* SOCIOLOGY

LUDONG DAXUE XUEBAO (ZHESHE BAN)/LUDONG UNIVERSITY JOURNAL (PHILOSOPHY AND SOCIAL SCIENCES EDITION). *see* SOCIAL SCIENCES: COMPREHENSIVE WORKS

100 MEX ISSN 1133-5165
QH331
LUDUS VITALIS; revista de filosofia de las ciencias de la vida. Text in Multiple languages. 1993. s-a. **Document type:** *Magazine, Academic/Scholarly.*
Indexed: B25, BIOSIS Prev, C01, CA, F04, MycolAb, P09, PCI, PhilInd, T02, Z01.
Published by: Centro de Estudios Filosoficos, Politicios y Sociales "Vicente Lombardo Toledano", Calle Lombardo Toledano, 51, Col. Ex-Hacienda de Guadalupe Chimalistac, Mexico, D.F., 01050, Mexico. TEL 52-55-5661-4679, FAX 52-55-5661-1787.

100 DEU
LUDWIG FEUERBACH: GESAMMELTE WERKE. Text in German. 1967. irreg., latest vol.6, 2009. price varies. **Document type:** *Monographic series, Academic/Scholarly.*
Published by: Akademie Verlag GmbH (Subsidiary of: Oldenbourg Wissenschaftsverlag GmbH), Markgrafenstr 12-14, Berlin, 10969, Germany. TEL 49-30-4220060, FAX 49-30-42200657, info@akademie-verlag.de, http://www.akademie-verlag.de. Ed. Werner Schuffenhauer.

LUMEN. *see* HISTORY

170 CHN ISSN 1001-2737
BJ1185.C5
LUNLIXUE/ETHICS. Text in Chinese. 1980. m. USD 79 (effective 2009). 80 p./no.; reprints avail. **Document type:** *Journal, Academic/Scholarly.* **Description:** Contains reprints of articles and research on ethics and related theories.

P

Published by: Zhongguo Renmin Daxue Shubao Ziliao Zhongxin/Renmin University of China, Information Center for Social Sciences, Dongcheng-qu, 3, Zhangzizhong Lu, Beijing, 100007, China. TEL 86-10-64039458, FAX 86-10-64015080, center@zlzx.org, http://www.zlzx.org/. **Dist. by:** China International Book Trading Corp, 35 Chegongzhuang Xilu, Haidian District, PO Box 399, Beijing 100044, China. TEL 86-10-68412045, FAX 86-10-68412023, cibtc@mail.cibtc.com.cn, http://www.cibtc.com.cn.

170 CHN
LUNLIXUE WENZHAI KA/ETHICS ABSTRACTS ON CARDS. Text in Chinese. q. CNY 20 (effective 2004).
Published by: Zhongguo Renmin Daxue Shubao Ziliao Zhongxin/Renmin University of China, Information Center for Social Sciences, Dongcheng-qu, 3, Zhangzizhong Lu, Beijing, 100007, China. TEL 86-10-64039458, FAX 86-10-64015080, center@zlzx.org, http://www.zlzx.org/. **Dist. in the US by:** China Publications Service, PO Box 49614, Chicago, IL 60649. TEL 312-288-3291, FAX 312-288-8570; **Dist. outside of China by:** China International Book Trading Corp, 35 Chegongzhuang Xilu, Haidian District, PO Box 399, Beijing 100044, China. TEL 86-10-68412045, FAX 86-10-68412023, cibtc@mail.cibtc.com.cn, http://www.cibtc.com.cn/.

170 CHN ISSN 1671-9115
LUNLIXUE YANJIU/STUDIES IN ETHICS. Text in Chinese. 2002. bi-m. USD 31.20 (effective 2009). **Document type:** *Journal, Academic/Scholarly.*
—East View.
Address: 36, Lusan Nan Lu, Changsha, 410081, China. TEL 86-731-8872086. **Dist. by:** China International Book Trading Corp, 35 Chegongzhuang Xilu, Haidian District, PO Box 399, Beijing 100044, China. TEL 86-10-68412045, FAX 86-10-68412023, cibtc@mail.cibtc.com.cn, http://www.cibtc.com.cn.

160 CHN ISSN 1001-2524
BC1
LUOJI/LOGIC. Text in Chinese. 1978. bi-m. USD 29 (effective 2009). 64 p./no.; **Document type:** *Journal, Academic/Scholarly.* **Description:** Contains reprints of writings on logic.
Published by: Zhongguo Renmin Daxue Shubao Ziliao Zhongxin/Renmin University of China, Information Center for Social Sciences, Dongcheng-qu, 3, Zhangzizhong Lu, Beijing, 100007, China. TEL 86-10-64039458, FAX 86-10-64015080, center@zlzx.org, http://www.zlzx.org/. **Dist. by:** China International Book Trading Corp, 35 Chegongzhuang Xilu, Haidian District, PO Box 399, Beijing 100044, China. TEL 86-10-68412045, FAX 86-10-68412023, cibtc@mail.cibtc.com.cn, http://www.cibtc.com.cn.

100 USA ISSN 1934-2438
B11
LYCEUM (ONLINE). Text in English. 2007. s-a. free (effective 2011). back issues avail. **Document type:** *Journal, Academic/Scholarly.* **Description:** Features articles for both professionals and students of philosophy about issues in metaphysics, ethics, epistemology, and the history of philosophy.
Media: Online - full text.
Published by: Saint Anselm College, Department of Philosophy, 100 Saint Anselm Dr, Manchester, NH 03102. TEL 603-641-7000, http://www.anselmphilosophy.com/. Ed. Thomas Larson.

100 DEU
M A P. (Mentis Anthologien Philosophie) Text in German. 2002. irreg., latest vol.6, 2003. price varies. **Document type:** *Monographic series, Academic/Scholarly.*
Published by: Mentis Verlag GmbH, Schulze-Delitzsch-Str 19, Paderborn, 33100, Germany. TEL 49-5251-687902, FAX 49-5251-687905, webmaster@mentis.de, http://www.mentis.de.

M H ONLINE. (Medical Humanities) *see* MEDICAL SCIENCES

MACROBIOTICS TODAY. *see* NUTRITION AND DIETETICS

MAGAZIN 2000 PLUS; Kosmos - Erde - Mensch. *see* PARAPSYCHOLOGY AND OCCULTISM

100 ITA ISSN 1592-5919
B5
MAGAZZINO DI FILOSOFIA; quadrimestrale di informazione, bilancio ed esercizio della filosofia. Text in Italian. 2000. 3/yr. EUR 63 combined subscription domestic to institutions (print & online eds.); EUR 87.50 combined subscription foreign to institutions (print & online eds.) (effective 2009). **Document type:** *Journal, Academic/Scholarly.*
Related titles: Online - full text ed.: ISSN 1972-5108.
Published by: (Universita degli Studi di Milano, Facolta di Lettere e Filosofia), Franco Angeli Edizioni, Viale Monza 106, Milan, 20127, Italy. TEL 39-02-2837141, FAX 39-02-26144793, redazioni@francoangeli.it, http://www.francoangeli.it.

MAGICAL BLEND; a transformative journey. *see* NEW AGE PUBLICATIONS

100 HUN ISSN 0025-0090
B8.H8
MAGYAR FILOZOFIAI SZEMLE/HUNGARIAN PHILOSOPHICAL REVIEW. Text in Hungarian; Summaries in English, French, German, Russian. 1957. bi-m. adv. bk.rev. index. **Document type:** *Journal, Academic/Scholarly.*
Indexed: FR, PhilInd, RASB, SCOPUS, SOPODA, SociolAb.
—INIST.
Published by: Okori es Kozepkori Filozofia Tanszek, Pf 107, Budapest, 1364, Hungary. steiger@kludens.elte.hu.

181 IND ISSN 0025-0414
MAHAJANMER LAGNA. Text in Bengali. 1967. w. looseleaf. bk.rev. **Document type:** *Magazine, Trade.*
Published by: Sulekha Press, Arambagh Hooghly, West Bengal, India.

100 ESP ISSN 1576-5113
MANIA. Text in Multiple languages. 1996. irreg. **Document type:** *Journal, Academic/Scholarly.*
Published by: (Universitat de Barcelona, Facultat de Filosofia), Universitat de Barcelona, Servei de Publicacions, Gran Via Corts Catalanes 585, Barcelona, 08007, Spain. TEL 34-93-4021100, http://www.publicacions.ub.es.

160 121 BRA ISSN 0100-6045
B1
➤ **MANUSCRITO**; revista internacional de filosofia. Text in English, French, Portuguese, Spanish. 1977. s-a. BRL 35 domestic; USD 35 foreign (effective 2003). adv. bk.rev. illus.; abstr. 300 p./no.; **Document type:** *Journal, Academic/Scholarly.* **Description:** Publishes original articles about philosophy and history of philosophy.
Indexed: C01, IPB, PhilInd.
Published by: Universidade Estadual de Campinas, Centro de Logica Epistemologia e Historia da Ciencia/State University of Campinas, Center for Logic, Epistemology and History of Science, Cidade Universitaria, Caixa Postal 6133, Campinas, SP 13083-970, Brazil. TEL 55-19-37886518, FAX 55-19-32893269, TELEX 0191150, http://www.unicamp.br/cle/clehc.html. Ed., R&P Michael Wrigley. Adv. contact Marcos Antonio Munoz. B&W page USD 50; 15 x 22. Circ: 700.

100 FRA ISSN 1772-5232
LE MARTEAU SANS MAITRE. Text in French. 2004. irreg. back issues avail. **Document type:** *Monographic series, Consumer.*
Published by: Editions Manucius, 9 Rue Moliere, Houilles, 78800, France. TEL 33-8-74487246, FAX 33-1-39682003, http://www.manucius.com.

MARTIN-GRABMANN-FORSCHUNGSINSTITUT. VEROEFFENTLICHUNGEN. *see* RELIGIONS AND THEOLOGY

100 DEU ISSN 1612-7722
MARTIN-HEIDEGGER-GESELLSCHAFT. SCHRIFTENREIHE. Text in German. 1991. irreg., latest vol.9, 2009. price varies. **Document type:** *Monographic series, Academic/Scholarly.*
Published by: (Martin-Heidegger-Gesellschaft e.V.), Vittorio Klostermann, Frauenlobstr 22, Frankfurt Am Main, 60487, Germany. TEL 49-69-9708160, FAX 49-69-708038, verlag@klostermann.de, http://www.klostermann.de.

100 NLD ISSN 0924-4948
MARTINUS NIJHOFF PHILOSOPHY TEXTS. Text in English. 1979. irreg., latest vol.3, 1981. price varies. **Document type:** *Monographic series, Academic/Scholarly.*
Published by: Springer Netherlands (Subsidiary of: Springer Science+Business Media), Van Godewijckstraat 30, Dordrecht, 3311 GX, Netherlands. TEL 31-78-6576050, FAX 31-78-6576474.

100 CZE ISSN 1211-3034
MASARYKOVA UNIVERZITA. FILOZOFICKA FAKULTA. SPISY/OPERA UNIVERSITATIS MASARYKIANAE BRUNENSIS. FACULTAS PHILOSOPHICA. Key Title: Spisy Masarykovy Univerzity v Brne. Filozoficka Fakulta. Text in Czech, French. 1961. a. price varies. **Document type:** *Monographic series, Academic/Scholarly.*
Formerly (until 1991): Univerzita J.E. Purkyne v Brne. Filozoficka Fakulta. Spisy (0232-0630)
Indexed: L&LBA, MLA-IB, SociolAb.
—INIST.
Published by: (Masarykova Univerzita, Filozoficka Fakulta/Masaryk University, Faculty of Arts), Vydavatelstvi Masarykovy Univerzity, Areal VUT Kravi Hora, Pavilon T, Brno, 60200, Czech Republic. TEL 420-54-9254840, 420-54-1321234, skopal@rect.muni.cz, http://www.muni.cz/press.

MAX WEBER STUDIES. *see* SOCIAL SCIENCES: COMPREHENSIVE WORKS

190 CAN ISSN 0711-0995
MCGILL-QUEEN'S STUDIES IN THE HISTORY OF IDEAS. Variant title: Studies in the History of Ideas. Text in English. 1982. irreg., latest vol.35, 2003. price varies. **Document type:** *Monographic series, Academic/Scholarly.* **Description:** Covers Western intellectual history, from antiquity to the twentieth century.
—BLDSC (5413.429250).
Published by: McGill-Queens's University Press, 3430 McTavish St, Montreal, PQ H3A 1X9, Canada. TEL 514-398-3750, FAX 514-398-4333, mqup@mqup.ca. Ed. Philip J. Cercone. **Dist. by:** CUP Services, PO Box 6525, Ithaca, NY 14851-6525. TEL 800-666-2211, FAX 800-688-2877, orderbook@cupserv.org.

180 USA ISSN 0076-5856
BD493
MEDIAEVAL PHILOSOPHICAL TEXTS IN TRANSLATION. Text in English. 1942. irreg. price varies. back issues avail. **Document type:** *Monographic series, Academic/Scholarly.* **Description:** Covers all the aspects of Medieval studies.
Published by: Marquette University, Memorial Library, Rm 164, P O Box 3141, Milwaukee, WI 53201. TEL 414-288-1564, FAX 414-288-7813, http://www.mu.edu/mupress. **Subscr. to:** Book Masters, Standing Order Dept, 1444 U S Rt 2, Mansfield, OH 44903.

100 POL ISSN 0076-5880
B720
MEDIAEVALIA PHILOSOPHICA POLONORUM. Text in French, German, Latin. 1957. a. price varies. **Document type:** *Academic/Scholarly.* **Description:** Dissertations on philosophical thought in the works of great philosophers, with commentaries.
Indexed: FR, IBR, IBZ, IPB, MLA, MLA-IB, P30, RASB.
Published by: Polska Akademia Nauk, Instytut Filozofii i Socjologii, Nowy Swiat 72, Warsaw, 00330, Poland. TEL 48-22-8267181, FAX 48-22-8267823, secretar@ifispan.waw.pl, http://www.ifispan.waw.pl. Ed. W Senko.

MEDICAL ETHICS ADVISOR. *see* MEDICAL SCIENCES

MEDICAL HUMANITIES; an international peer-reviewed journal for health professionals and researchers in medical humanities. *see* MEDICAL SCIENCES

MEDICINE, HEALTHCARE AND PHILOSOPHY. *see* MEDICAL SCIENCES

▼ **MEDICINE STUDIES**; an international journal for history, philosophy, and ethics of medicine & allied sciences. *see* MEDICAL SCIENCES

519 DEU
MEDIENETHIK. Text in German. 2002. irreg., latest vol.8, 2010. price varies. **Document type:** *Monographic series, Academic/Scholarly.*
Published by: Franz Steiner Verlag GmbH, Birkenwaldstr 44, Stuttgart, 70191, Germany. TEL 49-711-25820, FAX 49-711-2582290, service@steiner-verlag.de, http://www.steiner-verlag.de.

MEDIEVALIA ET HUMANISTICA; studies in medieval and renaissance culture. *see* HISTORY—History Of Europe

109 ITA ISSN 0391-2566
B720
MEDIOEVO (PADUA); rivista di storia della filosofia medievale. Text in Italian. 1975. a., latest vol.17, 1991. EUR 65 domestic (effective 2008). **Document type:** *Monographic series, Academic/Scholarly.*
Indexed: ArtHuCI, DIP, IBR, IBZ, PCI, RILM, W07.
Published by: (Universita degli Studi di Padova, Centro per Ricerche di Filosofia Medievale), Editrice Antenore, Via Valadier 52, Rome, 00193, Italy. TEL 39-06-32600370, FAX 39-06-3223132, antenore@editriceantenore.it, http://www.editriceantenore.it.

MEDIZIN UND ETHIK. *see* MEDICAL SCIENCES

100 DEU
MEDIZIN UND PHILOSOPHIE; Beitraege aus der Forschung. Abbreviated title: M Ph. Text in German. 1995. irreg., latest vol.9, 2007. price varies. **Document type:** *Monographic series, Academic/Scholarly.* **Description:** Contains current topics involving the relationships between medicine and philosophy.
Published by: Frommann-Holzboog Verlag e.K., Koenig-Karl-Str 27, Stuttgart, 70372, Germany. TEL 49-711-9559690, FAX 49-711-9559691, info@frommann-holzboog.de, http://www.frommann-holzboog.de.

MEHQ'RE YERUSHALAYIM B'MAHSHEVET YISRA'EL/JERUSALEM STUDIES IN JEWISH THOUGHT. *see* RELIGIONS AND THEOLOGY—Judaic

100 CHN
MEI YU SHIDAI (SHISHANG BAN)/BEAUTY & TIMES (FASHION EDITION). Text in Chinese. m. CNY 10 newsstand/cover (effective 2006). **Document type:** *Magazine, Consumer.*
Formerly (until 2001): Mei yu Shidai/Beauty & Times (1003-2592)
—East View.
Published by: Zhengzhou Daxue* Meixue Yanjiusuo, 75, Daxue Lu, Zhengzhou, 450052, China. TEL 86-371-7763157.

111.85 CHN ISSN 1001-2567
BH8.C4
MEIXUE/AESTHETICS. Text in Chinese. 1980. m. USD 49.90 (effective 2009). 64 p./no.; **Document type:** *Journal, Academic/Scholarly.* **Description:** Contains articles and researches on aesthetics and its history.
Published by: Zhongguo Renmin Daxue Shubao Ziliao Zhongxin/Renmin University of China, Information Center for Social Sciences, Dongcheng-qu, 3, Zhangzizhong Lu, Beijing, 100007, China. TEL 86-10-64039458, FAX 86-10-64015080, center@zlzx.org, http://www.zlzx.org/. **Dist. by:** China International Book Trading Corp, 35 Chegongzhuang Xilu, Haidian District, PO Box 399, Beijing 100044, China. TEL 86-10-68412045, FAX 86-10-68412023, cibtc@mail.cibtc.com.cn, http://www.cibtc.com.cn.

MELANCHTHON-SCHRIFTEN DER STADT BRETTEN. *see* RELIGIONS AND THEOLOGY

MELITA THEOLOGICA. *see* RELIGIONS AND THEOLOGY

190 PRT ISSN 2108-9329
▼ **MEMOIRES ET DOCUMENTS SUR VOLTAIRE.** Text in French. 2010. irreg. **Document type:** *Academic/Scholarly.*
Published by: La Ligne d'Ombre, Apartado 64, EC Condeixa-a-Nova, Condeixa-a-Nova, 3151-909, Portugal.

111.85 701.17 USA ISSN 1543-7442
MERIDIAN: CROSSING AESTHETICS. Text in English. 1993. irreg., latest 2010. price varies. illus. back issues avail. **Document type:** *Monographic series, Academic/Scholarly.* **Description:** Explore the arts as analytical media to undermine the allures of semblance and do away with the mystifications of immediacy. Going against the tradition of isolationism and reductionism that have characterized recent aesthetic inquiry, this series examines philosophy, literature and its theories, psychoanalysis, ethnology, politics, and history, presenting the arts in their broadest contexts.
Published by: Stanford University Press (Subsidiary of: Stanford University), 1450 Page Mill Rd, Palo Alto, CA 94304. TEL 650-723-9434, FAX 650-725-3457, info@www.sup.org. Ed. Werner Hamacher.

MERLEG; folyoiratok es konyvek szemleje. *see* RELIGIONS AND THEOLOGY

100 ROM ISSN 2067-3655
▼ **META**; research in hermeneutics, phenomenology and practical philosophy. Text in Multiple languages. 2009. s-a. free (effective 2011). **Document type:** *Journal, Academic/Scholarly.*
Media: Online - full text.
Published by: Universitatea "Alexandru Ioan Cuza" din Iasi, Editura Universitatii, str. Pacurari, nr. 9, Iasi, 700511, Romania. TEL 40-232-314947, FAX 40-232-314947, editura@uaic.ro, http://www.editura.uaic.ro/default.php.

100 GBR ISSN 0026-1068
B1
➤ **METAPHILOSOPHY.** Text in English. 1970. 5/yr. GBP 453 in United Kingdom to institutions; EUR 574 in Europe to institutions; USD 939 in the Americas to institutions; USD 1,095 elsewhere to institutions; GBP 522 combined subscription in United Kingdom to institutions (print & online eds.); EUR 661 combined subscription in Europe to institutions (print & online eds.); USD 1,080 combined subscription in the Americas to institutions (print & online eds.); USD 1,260 combined subscription elsewhere to institutions (print & online eds.) (effective 2012). adv. bk.rev. illus. index. back issues avail.; reprint service avail. from PSC. **Document type:** *Journal, Academic/Scholarly.* **Description:** Provides articles and reviews books stressing considerations about philosophy and particular schools, methods, or fields of philosophy.
Related titles: Online - full text ed.: ISSN 1467-9973. 1997. GBP 453 in United Kingdom to institutions; EUR 574 in Europe to institutions; USD 939 in the Americas to institutions; USD 1,095 elsewhere to institutions (effective 2012) (from IngentaConnect).
Indexed: A01, A03, A08, A20, A22, A26, ASCA, AmHI, ArtHuCI, BibInd, CA, CurCont, DIP, E01, FR, H07, IBR, IBZ, IPB, MLA-IB, P42, PCI, PhilInd, RASB, RILM, SCOPUS, SOPODA, SociolAb, T02, W07.
—BLDSC (5701.600000), IE, Infotrieve, Ingenta, INIST. **CCC.**

Published by: (Metaphilosophy Foundation USA), Wiley-Blackwell Publishing Ltd. (Subsidiary of: John Wiley & Sons, Inc.), 9600 Garsington Rd, Oxford, OX4 2DQ, United Kingdom. TEL 44-1865-776868, FAX 44-1865-714591, customerservices@blackwellpublishing.com. Ed. Armen T Marsoobian TEL 203-392-6792. Adv. contact Craig Pickett TEL 44-1865-476267.

100 USA
METAPHORIA. Text in English. 1993. m.
Media: Online - full text.
Address: RR1 Box 1010, Wells, VT 05774. Ed. Jozef Hand Boniakowski.

100 NLD ISSN 1437-2053
B2894
METAPHYSICA; Zeitschrift fuer Ontologie und Metaphysik. Text in English, German. 1999. s-a. EUR 169, USD 228 combined subscription to institutions (print & online eds.) (effective 2012). adv. bk.rev. reprint service avail. from PSC. **Document type:** *Journal, Academic/Scholarly.* **Description:** Devoted to the discussion of ontological and metaphysical issues.
Related titles: Online - full text ed.: ISSN 1874-6373 (from IngentaConnect).
Indexed: A01, A22, A26, CA, E01, E08, H12, IPB, P52, PhilInd, S09, SCOPUS, T02.
—BLDSC (5701.680000), IE, Ingenta. **CCC.**
Published by: Springer Netherlands (Subsidiary of: Springer Science+Business Media), Van Godewijckstraat 30, Dordrecht, 3311 GX, Netherlands. TEL 31-78-6576050, FAX 31-78-6576474, http://www.springer.com. Eds. Erwin Tegtmeier, Uwe Meixner, Rafael Huentelmann.

METAPOLITICA; revista trimestral de teoria y ciencia de la politica. *see* POLITICAL SCIENCE

100 DEU ISSN 0327-0289
B5
METHEXIS; revista international de filosofia antigua. Text in German, English, French. 1988. a. EUR 35 (effective 2008). **Document type:** *Journal, Academic/Scholarly.*
Indexed: DIP, IBR, IBZ, IPB, PhilInd.
Published by: Academia Verlag GmbH, Bahnstr 7, Sankt Augustin, 53757, Germany. TEL 49-2241-345210, FAX 49-2241-345316, kontakt@academia-verlag.de. Eds. Alejandro G. Vigo, Marcelo D. Boeri. Circ: 250 (paid).

018 200 USA ISSN 0736-7392
BD241
➤ **METHOD: JOURNAL OF LONERGAN STUDIES.** Text in English. 1983. s-a. USD 16 to individuals; USD 25 to institutions (effective 2010). bk.rev. back issues avail. **Document type:** *Journal, Academic/Scholarly.*
Indexed: PhilInd, R&TA.
—BLDSC (5745.601000).
Published by: Lonergan Institute at Boston College, Bapst Library, Boston College, 140 Commonwealth Ave, Chestnut Hill, MA 02167. TEL 617-552-8095, legeres@bc.edu. Circ: 300.

100 FRA ISSN 1769-7379
METHODOS (ONLINE); savoirs et textes. Text mainly in Multiple languages. 2001. a. free (effective 2011). back issues avail. **Document type:** *Journal, Academic/Scholarly.*
Formerly (until 2004): Methodos (Print) (1626-0600)
Media: Online - full text.
Indexed: DIP, IBR, IBZ.
—INIST.
Published by: Universite de Lille III, U M R Savoirs, Textes, Langage, B P 60149, Villeneuve d'Ascq, Cedex 59653, France. TEL 33-3-20416512, FAX 33-3-20416414, http://stl.recherche.univ-lille3.fr/.

100 CHL ISSN 0718-2775
METHODUS; revista internacional de filosofia moderna. Text in Spanish. 2005. a. **Document type:** *Monographic series, Academic/Scholarly.*
Published by: Pontificia Universidad Catolica de Chile, Instituto de Filosofia, Avda Bernardo O'Higgins 340, Santiago, Chile. TEL 56-2-3541468, http://www.uc.cl/filosofia/index.html.

METODICKI OGLEDI. *see* EDUCATION

THE MIDWEST QUARTERLY; a journal of contemporary thought. *see* HUMANITIES: COMPREHENSIVE WORKS

100 USA ISSN 0363-6550
MIDWEST STUDIES IN PHILOSOPHY. Text in English. 1976. a. USD 491 in the Americas (print or online ed.) (effective Apr. 2010); GBP 388 in United Kingdom to institutions (print or online ed.); EUR 493 in Europe to institutions (print or online ed.); USD 761 elsewhere to institutions (print or online ed.); USD 541 combined subscription in the Americas to institutions (print & online eds.); GBP 428 combined subscription in United Kingdom to institutions (print & online eds.); EUR 543 combined subscription in Europe to institutions (print & online eds.); USD 837 combined subscription elsewhere to institutions (print & online eds.) (effective 2010); subscr. includes Journal of Social Philosophy. adv. back issues avail.; reprint service avail. from PSC. **Document type:** *Monographic series, Academic/Scholarly.* **Description:** Covers a single theme in philosophy reflecting a wide range of views.
Related titles: Online - full text ed.: ISSN 1475-4975. USD 292 in the Americas to institutions; GBP 232 elsewhere to institutions (effective 2004); included with an institutional subscription to the Journal of Social Philosophy (from IngentaConnect); ◆ Supplement to: Journal of Social Philosophy. ISSN 0047-2786.
Indexed: A01, A03, A08, A20, A22, A26, ASCA, AmHI, CA, E01, FR, H07, IPB, PhilInd, RASB, RILM, SCOPUS, T02.
—BLDSC (5761.447600), IE, Infotrieve, Ingenta, INIST. **CCC.**
Published by: Wiley-Blackwell Publishing, Inc. (Subsidiary of: Wiley-Blackwell Publishing Ltd.), 111 River St, Hoboken, NJ 07030. TEL 201-748-6000, FAX 201-748-6088, info@wiley.com. Eds. Howard K Wettstein, Peter A French.

MILLTOWN STUDIES. *see* RELIGIONS AND THEOLOGY—Roman Catholic

100 150 GBR ISSN 0026-4423
B1
➤ **MIND**; a quarterly review of philosophy. Text in English. 1876. q. GBP 125 in United Kingdom to institutions; EUR 189 in Europe to institutions; USD 239 in US & Canada to institutions; GBP 125 elsewhere to institutions; GBP 137 combined subscription in United Kingdom to institutions (print & online eds.); EUR 206 combined subscription in Europe to institutions (print & online eds.); USD 260 combined subscription in US & Canada to institutions (print & online eds.); GBP 137 combined subscription elsewhere to institutions (print & online eds.) (effective 2012). adv. bk.rev. illus. index, cum.index. 256 p./no.; back issues avail.; reprint service avail. from PSC. **Document type:** *Journal, Academic/Scholarly.* **Description:** Expresses and gives direction to currents of thought in epistemology, the philosophy of language, metaphysics and philosophical psychology.
Related titles: Microform ed.: (from PMC, PQC); Online - full text ed.: ISSN 1460-2113. GBP 114 in United Kingdom to institutions; EUR 172 in Europe to institutions; USD 217 in US & Canada to institutions; GBP 114 elsewhere to institutions (effective 2012) (from IngentaConnect).
Indexed: A01, A02, A03, A08, A20, A22, A25, A26, ASCA, AmHI, ArtHuCI, B04, BRD, BrHumI, CA, CCMJ, CIS, CurCont, DIP, E-psyche, E01, E08, FR, G08, H07, H08, H09, H10, H14, HAb, HumInd, I05, IBR, IBRH, IBZ, IPB, L&LBA, MLA-IB, MSN, MathR, P02, P10, P13, P30, P48, P53, P54, PCI, PQC, PhilInd, R05, RASB, S05, S08, S09, SCOPUS, SOPODA, SociolAb, T02, W03, W07.
—BLDSC (5775.500000), IE, Infotrieve, Ingenta. **CCC.**
Published by: (Mind Association), Oxford University Press, Great Clarendon St, Oxford, OX2 6DP, United Kingdom. TEL 44-1865-556767, FAX 44-1865-556646, enquiry@oup.co.uk, http://www.oxfordjournals.org. Ed. Thomas Baldwin. Pub. Nina Curtis. Adv. contact Linda Hann TEL 44-1344-779945.

100 GBR ISSN 0268-1064
P37 CODEN: MILAEB
➤ **MIND & LANGUAGE.** Text in English. 1986. 5/yr. GBP 567 in United Kingdom to institutions; EUR 719 in Europe to institutions; USD 1,158 in the Americas to institutions; USD 1,354 elsewhere to institutions; GBP 652 combined subscription in United Kingdom to institutions (print & online eds.); EUR 827 combined subscription in Europe to institutions (print & online eds.); USD 1,332 combined subscription in the Americas to institutions (print & online eds.); USD 1,558 combined subscription elsewhere to institutions (print & online eds.) (effective 2012). adv. bk.rev. back issues avail.; reprint service avail. from PSC. **Document type:** *Journal, Academic/Scholarly.* **Description:** In an interdisciplinary way mind and language are studied by researchers of linguistics, philosophy, psychology, artificial intelligence, and cognitive anthropology.
Related titles: Microform ed.; Online - full text ed.: ISSN 1468-0017. GBP 567 in United Kingdom to institutions; EUR 719 in Europe to institutions; USD 1,158 in the Americas to institutions; USD 1,354 elsewhere to institutions (effective 2012) (from IngentaConnect).
Indexed: A01, A03, A08, A20, A22, A26, ASCA, ArtIAb, B07, B21, BibLing, CA, CMM, CurCont, DIP, E-psyche, E01, FR, IBR, IBZ, IPB, Inspec, L&LBA, L11, MLA-IB, NSA, P03, PCI, PhilInd, PsycInfo, PsycholAb, RASB, SCOPUS, SOPODA, SSCI, SociolAb, T02, W07.
—BLDSC (5775.526400), AskIEEE, IE, Infotrieve, Ingenta, INIST. **CCC.**
Published by: Wiley-Blackwell Publishing Ltd. (Subsidiary of: John Wiley & Sons, Inc.), 9600 Garsington Rd, Oxford, OX4 2DQ, United Kingdom. TEL 44-1865-776868, FAX 44-1865-714591, customerservices@blackwellpublishing.com. Adv. contact Craig Pickett TEL 44-1865-476267. B&W page GBP 445, B&W page USD 823; 112 x 190. Circ: 700.

100 IRL ISSN 1393-614X
B1
MINERVA; an internet journal of philosophy. Text in English. 1997. a., latest vol.7, 2003. free (effective 2004). **Document type:** *Journal, Academic/Scholarly.*
Related titles: Online - full text ed.: free (effective 2011).
Indexed: AmHI, CA, H07, PhilInd, T02.
Published by: University of Limerick, Department of Philosophy, South Circular Road, Limerick, Ireland. Ed. Dr. Stephen Thornton.

100 500 USA ISSN 0076-9258
Q175
➤ **MINNESOTA STUDIES IN THE PHILOSOPHY OF SCIENCE.** Text in English. 1956. irreg., latest vol.19, 2006. price varies. index. back issues avail.; reprints avail. **Document type:** *Monographic series, Academic/Scholarly.* **Description:** Publishes essays drawn from research and conferences sponsored by the center.
Indexed: A20, ASCA, PCI, SCOPUS.
—BLDSC (5810.465000). **CCC.**
Published by: (Minnesota Center for Philosophy of Science), University of Minnesota Press, Ste 290, 111 Third Ave S, Minneapolis, MN 55401. TEL 612-627-1970, FAX 612-627-1980. Ed. Ken Waters. Circ: 1,500. **Dist. by:** c/o Chicago Distribution Center, 11030 S Langley Ave, Chicago, IL 60628. ump@umn.edu; Plymbridge Distributors Ltd, Estover Rd, Plymouth, Devon PL6 7PY, United Kingdom. TEL 44-1752-202-301, FAX 44-1752-202-331.

➤ **MIRACLES MAGAZINE**; miracles, mysticism, metaphysics & mirth. *see* NEW AGE PUBLICATIONS

299 DEU ISSN 0944-2405
MIROIR ET IMAGE; philosophische Abhandlungen. Text in German. 1996. irreg., latest vol.9, 2009. price varies. **Document type:** *Monographic series, Academic/Scholarly.*
Published by: Peter Lang GmbH (Subsidiary of: Peter Lang Publishing Group), Eschborner Landstr 42-50, Frankfurt Am Main, 60489, Germany. TEL 49-69-7807050, FAX 49-69-78070550, zentrale.frankfurt@peterlang.com, http://www.peterlang.com. Eds. Lutz Baumann, Maryvonne Perrot.

100 ESP ISSN 1699-2849
MISCELANEA POLIANA. Text in Spanish. 2005. irreg. back issues avail. **Document type:** *Journal, Academic/Scholarly.*
Media: Online - full text.
Published by: Instituto de Estudios Filosoficos Leonardo Polo ieflp@leonardopolo.net.

MISCELLANEA FRANCESCANA; rivista trimestrale di scienze teologiche e di studi francescani. *see* RELIGIONS AND THEOLOGY—Roman Catholic

180 930 DEU ISSN 0544-4128
D101.2
➤ **MISCELLANEA MEDIAEVALIA.** Text in German. 1962. irreg., latest vol.35, 2010. price varies. back issues avail. **Document type:** *Monographic series, Academic/Scholarly.*
Indexed: MLA, MLA-IB, RASB, RI-2.
—**CCC.**
Published by: (Universitaet Koeln, Thomas-Institut), Walter de Gruyter GmbH & Co. KG, Genthiner Str 13, Berlin, 10785, Germany. TEL 49-30-260050, FAX 49-30-26005251, info@degruyter.com, http://www.degruyter.de. Ed. Andreas Speer.

181 NLD ISSN 1875-9386
MODEN CHINESE PHILOSOPHY. Text in English. 2008. irreg., latest vol.3, 2010. price varies. **Document type:** *Monographic series, Academic/Scholarly.*
Published by: Brill, PO Box 9000, Leiden, 2300 PA, Netherlands. TEL 31-71-5353500, FAX 31-71-5317532, cs@brill.nl. Ed. John Makeham.

MODERN INTELLECTUAL HISTORY. *see* LITERARY AND POLITICAL REVIEWS

100 USA ISSN 0026-8402
B1 CODEN: TFCEAU
➤ **MODERN SCHOOLMAN**; a quarterly journal of philosophy. Text in English. 1925. q. USD 40; USD 10 per issue (effective 2010). bk.rev. back issues avail. **Document type:** *Journal, Academic/Scholarly.* **Description:** Promotes historical research and critical analysis of philosophy of all periods: ancient, medieval, Renaissance and modern.
Indexed: A20, A22, ASCA, ArtHuCI, C33, CERDIC, CPL, CurCont, IPB, MEA&I, MLA-IB, P30, PCI, PhilInd, RASB, SCOPUS, W07.
—BLDSC (5896.400000), IE, Infotrieve, Ingenta.
Published by: Saint Louis University, Department of Philosophy, 3800 Lindell Blvd, Rm 130, St. Louis, MO 63108. admitme@slu.edu. Ed. William C Charron.

100 181.45 USA ISSN 1051-127X
➤ **MOKSHA JOURNAL**; the journal of knowledge, enlightenment and freedom. Text in English. 1984. s-a. bibl. back issues avail. **Document type:** *Journal, Academic/Scholarly.*
Related titles: Online - full text ed.
Published by: (Yoga Anand Ashram), Vajra Printing & Publishing, 154 Merrick Rd, Amityville, NY 11701.

141 NLD ISSN 2211-1824
▼ **MOMENTEN VAN GELUK.** Text in Dutch. 2010. a. EUR 14.90 (effective 2010).
Published by: Uitgeverij Meinema, Postbus 29, Zoetermeer, 2700 AA, Netherlands. TEL 31-79-3615481, FAX 31-79-3615489, info@boekencentrum.nl, http://www.uitgeverijmeinema.nl.

174.95 344 AUS ISSN 1321-2753
CODEN: JADEFV
MONASH BIOETHICS REVIEW. Text in English. 1981. q. AUD 82 domestic to individuals; AUD 92 foreign to individuals; AUD 99 domestic to institutions; AUD 115 foreign to institutions (effective 2007). **Document type:** *Journal, Academic/Scholarly.* **Description:** Presents the study of the ethical, social and legal problems arising out of medical and biomedical research.
Formerly (until 1994): Bioethics Review (1036-6482)
Related titles: Online - full text ed.: ISSN 1836-6716.
Indexed: CA, EMBASE, ExcerpMed, MEDLINE, P30, SCOPUS, T02.
—BLDSC (5901.591450), Ingenta.
Published by: Monash University, Centre for Human Bioethics, Monash University, Bldg 11, Monash, VIC 3800, Australia. TEL 61-3-99054275, FAX 61-3-99053279. Eds. Deborah Zion, Justin Oakley.

100 USA ISSN 0026-9662
B1
➤ **THE MONIST**; an international quarterly journal of general philosophical inquiry. Text in English. 1888-1936; resumed 1962. q. USD 35 to individuals; USD 55 to institutions (effective 2010). bk.rev. abstr.; illus. Index. back issues avail.; reprints avail. **Document type:** *Journal, Academic/Scholarly.* **Description:** Contains articles on particular philosophical topics of science.
Related titles: Online - full text ed.: ISSN 2153-3601. USD 70 to individuals; USD 220 to institutions (effective 2010).
Indexed: A01, A02, A03, A08, A20, A21, A22, A26, ASCA, AmHI, ArtHuCI, B04, BRD, C12, CA, CurCont, DIP, E08, FR, G08, H07, H08, H09, H10, H14, HAb, HumInd, I05, IBR, IBZ, IPB, L&LBA, M01, M02, MEA&I, MLA-IB, P02, P10, P28, P30, P42, P48, P53, P54, PAIS, PCI, PQC, PSA, PhilInd, R05, RASB, RI-1, RI-2, RILM, S02, S03, S05, S09, SCOPUS, SOPODA, SociolAb, T02, W03, W05, W07.
—BLDSC (5908.600000), IE, Infotrieve, Ingenta, INIST, Linda Hall.
Published by: Hegeler Institute, c/o George Reisch, 315 Fifth St, Peru, IL 61354. Ed. Dr. Barry Smith.

100 170 CHE ISSN 0026-9727
MONITEUR DU REGNE DE LA JUSTICE; journal bi-mensuel philanthropique et humanitaire, pour le relevement moral et social. Text in French. 1936. s-m. **Document type:** *Magazine, Consumer.*
Related titles: Dutch ed.; English ed.; Spanish ed.; Portuguese ed.; Italian ed.
Published by: Association l'Ange de l'Eternel, Les Amis de l'Homme, 27 route de Valliere, Cartigny, 1236, Switzerland. Ed. R Cavin.

100 DEU ISSN 1862-1260
➤ **MONOGRAPHIEN UND TEXTE ZUR NIETZSCHE-FORSCHUNG.** Text in German. 1972. irreg., latest vol.59, 2011. price varies. **Document type:** *Monographic series, Academic/Scholarly.*
Published by: Walter de Gruyter GmbH & Co. KG, Genthiner Str 13, Berlin, 10785, Germany. TEL 49-30-260050, FAX 49-30-26005251, info@degruyter.com, http://www.degruyter.de. Ed. Guenter Abel.

100 500 001.3 NLD ISSN 1573-4749
MONOGRAPHS-IN-DEBATE. Text in English. 2004 (Jul.). irreg. price varies. **Document type:** *Monographic series, Academic/Scholarly.* **Description:** The special nature of this series arises from the recognition of the dialectical nature of philosophical work. Each volume contains a monograph, followed by peer commentaries and the author's replies.
Related titles: ◆ Series of: Poznan Studies in the Philosophy of the Sciences and the Humanities. ISSN 0303-8157.
Indexed: AmHI, H07, T02.

P

Published by: Editions Rodopi B.V., Tijnmuiden 7, Amsterdam, 1046 AK, Netherlands. TEL 31-20-6114821, FAX 31-20-4472979, info@rodopi.nl. Ed. Dr. Katarzyna Paprzycka.

100 ITA ISSN 2037-5115
PQ2012
▼ ➤ **MONTESQUIEU.IT**; biblioteca elettronica su Montesquieu e dintorni. Summaries in English; Text in French, Spanish, Italian. 2009. a. Index. back issues avail. **Document type:** *Journal, Academic/ Scholarly.*
Related titles: Online - full text ed.: ISSN 2035-5769. free (effective 2011).
Published by: (Universita degli Studi di Bologna, Dipartimento di Filosofia), Casa Editrice C L U E B, Via Marsala 31, Bologna, BO 40126, Italy. TEL 39-051-220736, FAX 39-051-237758, clueb@clueb.com, http://www.clueb.eu/home.html. Ed. Domenico Felice.

170 FRA ISSN 1770-7625
MORALES. Text in French. 1991. irreg. back issues avail. **Document type:** *Monographic series, Consumer.*
Formerly (until 2004): Autrement. Serie Morales (1154-5763)
Published by: Editions Autrement, 77 Rue du Faubourg St Antoine, Paris, 75011, France. TEL 33-1-44738000, FAX 33-1-44730012, contact@autrement.com.

MORALITY AND THE MEANING OF LIFE. *see* RELIGIONS AND THEOLOGY

170 DEU ISSN 1431-7281
MORALTHEOLOGIE - ANTHROPOLOGIE - ETHIK. Text in German. 1997. irreg., latest vol.5, 2003. price varies. **Document type:** *Monographic series, Academic/Scholarly.*
Published by: Peter Lang GmbH (Subsidiary of: Peter Lang Publishing Group), Eschborner Landstr 42-50, Frankfurt Am Main, 60489, Germany. TEL 49-69-7807050, FAX 49-69-78070550, zentrale.frankfurt@peterlang.com, http://www.peterlang.com. Ed. Manfred Balkenohl.

100 RUS ISSN 2072-8530
➤ **MOSKOVSKII GOSUDARSTVENNYI OBLASTNOI UNIVERSITET. VESTNIK. SERIYA FILOSOFSKIE NAUKI.** Variant title: Vestnik M G O U. Seriya Filosofskie Nauki. Text in Russian; Summaries in Russian, English. 2004. q. RUR 1,000 (effective 2011). bibl.; charts; illus.; maps. back issues avail. **Document type:** *Journal, Academic/ Scholarly.* **Description:** Intended for scientists, researchers, teachers of high schools, undergraduate and post graduate students. Publishes results of scientific research in the field of Philosophy, including dissertation research, conferences and seminars.
Related titles: Online - full text ed.
Published by: Moskovskii Gosudarstvennyi Oblastnoi Universitet/ Moscow State Regional University, ul Radio, dom 10A, komn. 98, Moscow, Russian Federation. TEL 7-499-7235631, FAX 7-499-2614341, http://www.mgou.ru. Ed. Vladislav Pesotsky.

100 RUS ISSN 0201-7385
B6
➤ **MOSKOVSKII GOSUDARSTVENNYI UNIVERSITET. VESTNIK. SERIYA 7: FILOSOFIYA.** Text in Russian. 1946. bi-m. USD 174 in North America; USD 252.50 combined subscription in North America (print & online eds.) (effective 2011). bk.rev. bibl. index. **Document type:** *Journal, Academic/Scholarly.*
Supersedes in part: Moskovskii Gosudarstvennyi Universitet. Vestnik. Seriya Ekonomika, Filosofiya (0579-9457)
Related titles: Online - full text ed.
Indexed: CCMJ, FLP, FR, HistAb, IBSS, Inspec, MLA-IB, MSN, MathR, RefZh, Z02.
—INIST.
Published by: (Moskovskii Gosudarstvennyi Universitet im. M.V. Lomonosova, Filosofskii Fakul'tet/M.V. Lomonosov Moscow State University, Department of Philosophy), Izdatel'stvo Moskovskogo Gosudarstvennogo Universiteta im. M. V. Lomonosova/Publishing House of Moscow State University, B Nikitskaya 5/7, Moscow, 103009, Russian Federation. TEL 7-095-2295091, FAX 7-095-2036671, kd_mgu@rambler.ru, http://www.msu.ru/depts/MSUPubl. Ed. V V Mironov. **Dist. by:** East View Information Services, 10601 Wayzata Blvd, Minneapolis, MN 55305. TEL 952-252-1201, 800-477-1005, FAX 952-252-1202, info@eastview.com, http:// www.eastview.com.

100 954 IND ISSN 0027-1543
MOTHER INDIA. Text in English. 1949. m. INR 200 domestic; USD 35 foreign (effective 2011). bk.rev. **Document type:** *Magazine, Academic/Scholarly.* **Description:** Review of culture containing articles, essays, poems and reminiscences by various disciples.
Published by: Sri Aurobindo Ashram Trust, SABDA, Pondicherry, Tamil Nadu 605 002, India. TEL 91-413-2233656, FAX 91-413-2223328, mail@sabda.in, http://www.sriaurobindoashram.org.

180 IND ISSN 0027-2574
MOUNTAIN PATH. Text in English. 1964. q. INR 120 domestic; USD 15 foreign; INR 30 per issue (effective 2011). bk.rev. charts; illus. index. **Document type:** *Journal, Trade.* **Description:** Aims to set forth the wisdom of all religions and all ages, especially as testified to by their saints and mystics, and to clarify the paths available to seekers in the conditions of our modern world.
Indexed: BAS.
Published by: Sri Ramanasramam Charities, c/o V S Ramanan, Sri Ramanasramam PO, Tiruvannamalai, Tamil Nadu 606 603, India. TEL 91-4175-237200.

MOUVEMENT ANTI-UTILITARISTE DANS LES SCIENCE SOCIALES. REVUE SEMESTRIELLE. *see* SOCIOLOGY

100 DEU
MUENCHNER PHILOSOPHISCHE BEITRAEGE. Text in German. 1999. irreg., latest vol.22, 2008. price varies. **Document type:** *Monographic series, Academic/Scholarly.*
Published by: Herbert Utz Verlag GmbH, Adalbertstr 57, Munich, 80799, Germany. TEL 49-89-27779100, FAX 49-89-27779101, utz@utzverlag.com.

100 DEU ISSN 0077-1856
MUENCHNER UNIVERSITAETS-SCHRIFTEN. REIHE DER PHILOSOPHISCHEN FAKULTAET. Text in German. 1965. irreg., latest 2002. price varies. **Document type:** *Monographic series, Academic/Scholarly.*
Published by: Wilhelm Fink Verlag, Juehenplatz 1-3, Paderborn, 33098, Germany. TEL 49-5251-1275, FAX 49-5251-127860, kontakt@fink.de, http://www.fink.de.

320 194 FRA ISSN 0292-0107
HB3
MULTITUDES; revue politique, artistique et philosophique. Text in French. 2000. q. EUR 60 in the European Union to individuals (incl. online); EUR 76 elsewhere to individuals; EUR 80 in the European Union to institutions; EUR 95 elsewhere to institutions; EUR 50 in the European Union to students; EUR 65 elsewhere to students (effective 2008). back issues avail. **Document type:** *Journal, Academic/ Scholarly.*
Related titles: Online - full text ed.
Indexed: IBSS, SCOPUS.
—CCC.
Published by: Association Multitudes, 24 Place Etienne Marcel, Montigny le Bretonneux, 78180, France. TEL 33-1-30572630. **Subscr. to:** Dif'Pop', 21 ter rue Voltaire, Paris 75011, France. TEL 33-1-40242131, FAX 33-1-40241588.

100 DOM
MUSEO DEL HOMBRE DOMINICANO. SERIE CONFERENCIAS PENSAMIENTO DOMINICANO. Text in Spanish. 1974. irreg. DOP 5.
Published by: Museo del Hombre Dominicano, Plaza de la Cultura, Calle Pedro Henriquez Urena, Santo Domingo, Dominican Republic.

100 DOM
MUSEO DEL HOMBRE DOMINICANO. SERIE CONFERENCIAS SOBRE EL PENSAMIENTO DE PEDRO HENRIQUEZ URENA. Text in Spanish. irreg., latest vol.2. DOP 5.
Published by: Museo del Hombre Dominicano, Plaza de la Cultura, Calle Pedro Henriquez Urena, Santo Domingo, Dominican Republic. TEL 687-3622.

▼ **MUSTANG JOURNAL OF BUSINESS AND ETHICS.** *see* BUSINESS AND ECONOMICS

215 USA
MY OPINIONS; incest and illegitimacy. Text in English. 1995. irreg., latest vol.3, 1996. USD 9.95 domestic (effective 2000). back issues avail. **Description:** Philosophical criticism of religion and the Bible's contents. Offers a realistic alternative with an enlightening message.
Published by: Al - Jay Publishing, PMB 105, 439 Westwood Shopping Center, Fayetteville, NC 28314. TEL 800-390-2687. Ed., Pub., R&P Alfred Jordan. **Dist. by:** Barnes & Noble Books.

NAGOYA DAIGAKU BUNGAKUBU KENKYU RONSHU/NAGOYA UNIVERSITY. FACULTY OF LITERATURE. JOURNAL (HISTORY)/ NAGOYA UNIVERSITY. FACULTY OF LITERATURE. JOURNAL (LITERATURE)/NAGOYA UNIVERSITY. FACULTY OF LITERATURE. JOURNAL (PHILOSOPHY). *see* LITERATURE

181.4 USA ISSN 1559-9817
B5131
NAMARUPA; categories of Indian thought. Text in English. 2003. s-a. back issues avail. **Document type:** *Journal, Academic/Scholarly.* **Description:** Contains articles and research on philosophical thought that has emanated from the land and people of India.
Related titles: Online - full text ed.: ISSN 1559-9825. USD 18; USD 2.16 per issue (effective 2011).
Published by: Namarupa, Inc., 430 Broome St, Ste 2, New York, NY 10013. TEL 212-431-3738. Ed. Eddie Stern. Pub. Robert Moses.

NANDAN KANAN. *see* RELIGIONS AND THEOLOGY—Hindu

NANOETHICS; ethics for technologies that converge at the nanoscale. *see* TECHNOLOGY: COMPREHENSIVE WORKS

170 JPN
NANZAN INSTITUTE OF SOCIAL ETHICS MONOGRAPH SERIES. Text in Japanese. 1994. every 3 yrs. free. **Document type:** *Monographic series.*
Published by: Nanzan University, Institute for Social Ethics, 18 Yamazato-cho, Showa-ku, Nagoya, 466-8673, Japan. TEL 81-52-8323111 ext 417, 768, FAX 81-52-8323703, n-ise@nanzan-u.ac.jp, sharink@ic.nanzan-u.ac.jp, http://www.nanzan-u.ac.jp/ISE/ index.html.

174.957 USA ISSN 2157-1732
▼ ➤ **NARRATIVE INQUIRY IN BIOETHICS**; a journal of qualitative research. Abbreviated title: N I B. Text in English. forthcoming 2011. 3/yr. USD 175 to institutions (print or online eds.); USD 245 combined subscription to institutions (print & online eds.); USD 70 per issue to institutions (effective 2012). adv. **Document type:** *Journal, Academic/ Scholarly.* **Description:** Provides a forum for exploring current issues in bioethics through the publication and analysis of personal stories, qualitative and mixed-methods research articles, and case studies.
Related titles: Online - full text ed.: ISSN 2157-1740. forthcoming.
Published by: The Johns Hopkins University Press, 2715 N Charles St, Baltimore, MD 21218. TEL 410-516-6900, FAX 410-516-6968. Ed. James M DuBois. Pub. William M Breichner. **Subscr. to:** PO Box 19966, Baltimore, MD 21211. TEL 410-516-6987, 800-548-1784, FAX 410-516-3866.

174.95 230.2 USA ISSN 1532-5490
QH332
THE NATIONAL CATHOLIC BIOETHICS QUARTERLY. Text in English. 2001. q. USD 48 domestic to individuals; USD 65 foreign to individuals; USD 165 to institutions; free to members (effective 2010). **Document type:** *Journal, Academic/Scholarly.* **Description:** Covers the moral issues arising in health care and the life sciences.
Related titles: Online - full text ed.: ISSN 1938-1646.
Indexed: A01, CPL, H05, P30, R&TA, SCOPUS, T02.
—BLDSC (6021.510960). **CCC.**
Published by: National Catholic Bioethics Center, 6399 Drexel Rd, Philadelphia, PA 19151. TEL 215-877-2660, FAX 215-877-2688, info@ncbcenter.org.

100 GBR
NATIONAL SECULAR SOCIETY. ANNUAL REPORT. Text in English. 1867. a. free to members (effective 2009). back issues avail. **Document type:** *Report, Trade.* **Description:** Contains a report of the National Secular Society's activities.
Related titles: Online - full text ed.: free (effective 2009).
Published by: National Secular Society, 25 Red Lion Sq, London, WC1R 4RL, United Kingdom. TEL 44-20-74043126, FAX 44-870-7628971, enquiries@secularism.org.uk.

NATURAL LANGUAGE SEMANTICS; an international journal of semantics and its interfaces in grammar. *see* LINGUISTICS

100 USA ISSN 1555-4775
Q174
NATURAL PHILOSOPHY ALLIANCE. PROCEEDINGS. Text in English. 2004 (Spr.). a. **Document type:** *Proceedings, Academic/Scholarly.*
Published by: Natural Philosophy Alliance, c/o Don Briddell, 8002-A Dollyhyde Rd, Mount Airy, MD 21771. http://www.worldnpa.org.

NATURE AND CULTURE. *see* BIOLOGY

100 300 MNG ISSN 1001-7623
AS451
NEI MENGGU SHIFAN DAXUE XUEBAO (ZHEXUE SHEHUI KEXUE HANWEN BAN)/INNER MONGOLIA NORMAL UNIVERSITY. JOURNAL (PHILOSOPHY & SOCIAL SCIENCE CHINESE EDITION). Text in Chinese. 1958. bi-m. USD 31.20 (effective 2009). **Document type:** *Academic/Scholarly.*
Related titles: Online - full text ed.; Mongol ed.
—East View, Ingenta.
Published by: Nei Menggu Shifan Daxue, 81, Zhaowuda Lu, Hohhot, Inner Mongolia 010022, Mongolia. TEL 86-471-4393037, http:// nmsdxb.imnu.edu.cn/.

100 DEU
NEUE ONTOLOGISCHE FORSCHUNG. Text in German. 2000. irreg., latest vol.2, 2000. price varies. **Document type:** *Monographic series, Academic/Scholarly.*
Published by: J.H. Roell, Wuerzburgerstr 16, Dettelbach, 97337, Germany. TEL 49-9324-99770, FAX 49-9324-99771, info@roell-verlag.de, http://www.roell-verlag.de.

100 DEU
NEUE PHAENOMENOLOGIE. Text in German. 2005. irreg., latest vol.13, 2010. price varies. **Document type:** *Monographic series, Academic/ Scholarly.*
Published by: Verlag Karl Alber, Hermann-Herder-Str 4, Freiburg, 79104, Germany. TEL 49-761-2717436, FAX 49-761-2717212, info@verlag-alber.de.

230.044 830.6 809.93384 USA ISSN 1048-8545
B3090
NEW ATHENAEUM/NEUES ATHENAEUM. Text in English, German. 1989. a. USD 59.95 per issue domestic; GBP 39.95 per issue in United Kingdom (effective 2010). back issues avail. **Document type:** *Yearbook, Academic/Scholarly.* **Description:** Specializing in Schleiermacher and Schlegel Research and other Nineteenth-Century studies.
Published by: Edwin Mellen Press, 415 Ridge St, PO Box 450, Lewiston, NY 14092. TEL 716-754-2266, FAX 716-754-4056, cservice@mellenpress.com. Ed. Ruth Richardson.

THE NEW ATLANTIS; a journal of technology & society. *see* POLITICAL SCIENCE

111.85 USA
NEW DIRECTIONS IN AESTHETICS. Text in English. 2003. irreg., latest 2008. price varies. adv. back issues avail. **Document type:** *Monographic series, Academic/Scholarly.* **Description:** Contains intriguing and pressing problems in aesthetics and the philosophy of art today.
Published by: Wiley-Blackwell Publishing, Inc. (Subsidiary of: Wiley-Blackwell Publishing Ltd.), 111 River St, Hoboken, NJ 07030. TEL 201-748-6000, FAX 201-748-6088, info@wiley.com, http:// www.wiley.com/. Eds. Berys Gaut, Dominic Mciver Lopes.

109 USA
➤ **NEW FRENCH THOUGHT SERIES.** Text in English. 1994. irreg., latest 2009. price varies. charts; illus. back issues avail. **Document type:** *Monographic series, Academic/Scholarly.* **Description:** Examines topics and issues in French philosophy.
Published by: Princeton University Press, 41 William St, Princeton, NJ 08540. TEL 609-258-4900, 800-777-4726, FAX 609-258-6305, cpriday@pupress.co.uk. Eds. Mark Lilla, Thomas Pavel. **Subscr. addr. in US:** California - Princeton Fulfillment Services, Inc., 1445 Lower Ferry Rd, Ewing, NJ 08618. TEL 609-883-1759, 800-777-4726, FAX 609-883-7413, 800-999-1958, orders@cpfsinc.com. **Dist. addr. in Canada:** University Press Group.; **Dist. addr. in UK:** John Wiley & Sons Ltd.

➤ **NEW FRONTIER**; magazine of transformation. *see* NEW AGE PUBLICATIONS

144 GBR ISSN 0306-512X
AP4
NEW HUMANIST. Text in English. 1885. bi-m. GBP 21 domestic; GBP 25 foreign; GBP 3.95 newsstand/cover domestic; EUR 6 newsstand/ cover in Europe; USD 7 newsstand/cover elsewhere (effective 2009). adv. bk.rev. back issues avail.; reprints avail. **Document type:** *Magazine, Trade.* **Description:** Aims to support and promote humanism and rational inquiry and to oppose religious dogma, irrationalism and bunkum wherever it is found.
Former titles (until 1972): Humanist (0018-7380); (until 1956): Literary Guide; (until 1954): The Literary Guide and Rationalist Review; (until 1894): Watts Literary Guide
Related titles: Microform ed.: (from PQC); Online - full text ed.: GBP 10 to individuals; GBP 150 to institutions (effective 2009).
Indexed: A22, AmHI, BrHumI, CA, H07, MLA-IB, P30, RASB, SCOPUS, T02.
—BLDSC (6084.246000), IE, Infotrieve, Ingenta. **CCC.**
Published by: Rationalist Press Association Ltd., One Gower St, London, WC1E 6HD, United Kingdom. TEL 44-20-74361171, FAX 44-20-70793588, jim.rpa@humanism.org.uk. Ed., Adv. contact Caspar Melville.

100 GBR ISSN 0307-0980
➤ **NEW HUMANITY JOURNAL**; journal for the creative individual - the free and independent thinker. Text in English. 1975. bi-m. GBP 18 in United Kingdom (surface mail); GBP 20 rest of Europe (surface mail); EUR 30 worldwide (surface mail); GBP 22, USD 36 worldwide (airmail) (effective 2000). adv. bk.rev. back issues avail. **Document type:** *Journal, Academic/Scholarly.* **Description:** Integrates the disciplines of science, philosophy, politics, the arts, religion and the humanities to promote closer cooperation and understanding among them.
Published by: New Humanity, 51a York Mansions, Prince Of Wales Dr, London, SW11 4BP, United Kingdom. TEL 44-20-7622-4013, FAX 44-20-7498-0173. Ed., Pub. Johan Henri Quanjer. Adv. contact James Traeger. Circ: 14,000 (paid and controlled).

170 GBR ISSN 1663-0033
▼ **NEW INTERNATIONAL STUDIES IN APPLIED ETHICS.** Text in English. 2009. irreg. price varies. **Document type:** *Monographic series, Academic/Scholarly.* **Description:** Examines the ethical implications of selected areas of public life and concern.
Published by: Peter Lang Ltd. (Subsidiary of: Peter Lang Publishing Group), Evenlode Ct, Main Rd, Long Hanborough, Oxfordshire OX29 8SZ, United Kingdom. TEL 44-1993-880088, FAX 44-1993-882040, info@peterlang.com. Eds. R. John Elford, Simon Robinson.

149.7 AUS
THE NEW LIBERATOR. Text in English. 1966. q. bk.rev.
Formerly (until 2001): The Rationalist News (0156-7594)
Published by: Rationalist Association of New South Wales, PO Box 249, Strawberry Hills, NSW 2012, Australia. Ed., R&P, Adv. contact Peter Hanna.

193 USA ISSN 1091-0239
B3310
➤ **NEW NIETZSCHE STUDIES.** Text in English. 1996. q. USD 125 (effective 2010). bk.rev. back issues avail. **Document type:** *Journal, Academic/Scholarly.*
Related titles: Online - full text ed.: ISSN 2153-8417.
Indexed: IPB, PhilInd.
—BLDSC (6084.804650).
Published by: (Nietzsche Society), Philosophy Documentation Center, PO Box 7147, Charlottesville, VA 22906. FAX 434-220-3301.

100 USA ISSN 1045-4500
QH1 CODEN: ENWEEP
NEW PERSPECTIVES IN PHILOSOPHICAL SCHOLARSHIP; texts and issues. Text in English. 1991. irreg., latest vol.16, 2001. price varies. **Document type:** *Monographic series, Academic/Scholarly.* **Description:** Features innovations in philosophical scholarship on texts and issues in both Eastern and Western philosophy.
Published by: Peter Lang Publishing, Inc. (Subsidiary of: Peter Lang Publishing Group), 29 Broadway, New York, NY 10006. TEL 212-647-7706, 212-647-7700, 800-770-5264, FAX 212-647-7707, customerservice@plang.com. Ed. James Duerlinger.

100 230.94 USA ISSN 0028-6443
BX8701
THE NEW PHILOSOPHY. Text in English. 1898. s-a. USD 25 (effective 2010). bk.rev. cum.index every 3 yrs. back issues avail. **Document type:** *Journal, Academic/Scholarly.* **Description:** Contains articles which addresses philosophical questions and topics that bears the works of Emanuel Swedenborg.
Related titles: Online - full text ed.: free (effective 2010).
Indexed: AESIS, DIP, FR, GeoRef, IBR, IBZ, MLA-IB.
—Ingenta, INIST.
Published by: Swedenborg Scientific Association, PO Box 757, Bryn Athyn, PA 19009. TEL 215-947-0576, FAX 215-914-2986, info@swedenborg-philosophy.org. Ed. Erland J Brock.

100 USA ISSN 0893-6005
NEW STUDIES IN AESTHETICS. Text in English. 1987. irreg., latest vol.39, 2008. price varies. **Document type:** *Monographic series, Academic/Scholarly.* **Description:** Explores the philosophy of art as well as the philosophy of life.
—BLDSC (6088.773000), IE, Ingenta.
Published by: Peter Lang Publishing, Inc. (Subsidiary of: Peter Lang Publishing Group), 29 Broadway, New York, NY 10006. TEL 212-647-7706, 212-647-7700, 800-770-5264, FAX 212-647-7707, customerservice@plang.com. Ed. Robert Ginsberg.

NEW STUDIES IN CHRISTIAN ETHICS. *see* RELIGIONS AND THEOLOGY

193 DEU ISSN 1618-999X
NEW STUDIES IN PHENOMENOLOGY. Text in English. 2002. irreg., latest vol.5, 2008. price varies. **Document type:** *Monographic series, Academic/Scholarly.*
Published by: Peter Lang GmbH (Subsidiary of: Peter Lang Publishing Group), Eschborner Landstr 42-50, Frankfurt Am Main, 60489, Germany. TEL 49-69-7807050, FAX 49-69-78070550, zentrale.frankfurt@peterlang.com. Eds. Christian Lotz, David Carr, Klaus Held.

109 160 NLD ISSN 1879-8578
➤ **NEW SYNTHESE HISTORICAL LIBRARY**; texts and studies in the history of logic and philosophy. Text in English. 1969. irreg., latest vol.64, 2008. price varies. **Document type:** *Monographic series, Academic/Scholarly.* **Description:** Publishes studies in the history of Western philosophy.
Formerly (until vol.37, 1990): Synthese Historical Library (0082-111X)
Indexed: MathR.
—CCC.
Published by: Springer Netherlands (Subsidiary of: Springer Science+Business Media), Van Godewijckstraat 30, Dordrecht, 3311 GX, Netherlands. TEL 31-78-6576050, FAX 31-78-6576474. Ed. Simo Knuuttila.

100 NLD
NEW TRENDS IN PHILOSOPHY. Text in English. irreg. price varies. **Document type:** *Monographic series, Academic/Scholarly.*
Related titles: ◆ Series of: Poznan Studies in the Philosophy of the Sciences and the Humanities. ISSN 0303-8157.
Indexed: AmHI, H07.
Published by: Editions Rodopi B.V., Tijnmuiden 7, Amsterdam, 1046 AK, Netherlands. TEL 31-20-6114821, FAX 31-20-4472979, info@rodopi.nl. Ed. Dr. Katarzyna Paprzycka. **Dist. by:** Rodopi - USA, 606 Newark Ave, 2nd fl, Kenilworth, NJ 07033. TEL 908-497-9031, FAX 908-497-9035.

100 USA ISSN 0733-9542
B3580.A1
➤ **NEW VICO STUDIES.** Text in English. 1983. a. USD 33 per issue to individuals; USD 59 per issue to institutions; USD 78 combined subscription per issue to individuals (print & online eds.); USD 212 combined subscription per issue to institutions (print & online eds.) (effective 2009). adv. bk.rev. back issues avail.; reprint service avail. from PSC. **Document type:** *Journal, Academic/Scholarly.* **Description:** Brings out articles, translations, notes, reports, and book reviews that reflect the current state of the study of the works of Giambattista Vico.
Related titles: Online - full text ed.: ISSN 2153-8255. USD 53 per issue to individuals; USD 177 per issue to institutions (effective 2010).
Indexed: A01, A03, A08, A22, A26, BibInd, CA, DIP, E08, G08, I05, IBR, IBZ, L&LBA, MLA-IB, PCI, PhilInd, RI-1, RI-2, S09, T02.
—CCC.
Published by: (The Institute for Vico Studies), Philosophy Documentation Center, PO Box 7147, Charlottesville, VA 22906. TEL 434-220-3300, FAX 434-220-3301, order@pdcnet.org, http://www.pdcnet.org. Ed. Donald Phillip Verene TEL 404-727-4340. Adv. contact Greg Swope.

100 USA ISSN 1533-7472
B829.5.A1
THE NEW YEARBOOK FOR PHENOMENOLOGY AND PHENOMENOLOGICAL PHILOSOPHY. Variant title: Phenomenology and Phenomenological Philosophy. Text in English. 2001. a. USD 105 per vol. domestic to institutions; USD 115 per vol. foreign to institutions (effective 2009). **Document type:** *Yearbook, Academic/Scholarly.* **Description:** Explores the relation of phenomenology to the history of philosophy, to contemporary philosophical issues and debates, and to work in related fields.
Indexed: PhilInd.
—BLDSC (6089.251500).
Published by: Noesis Press, PO Box 1321, Edmonds, WA 98020. info@noesispress.com. Eds. Burt Hopkins, John J Drummond.

141 NLD ISSN 1878-903X
NEXUS BIBLIOTHEEK/NEXUS LIBRARY. Text in Dutch. 1998. irreg., latest vol.7, 2010. price varies. **Document type:** *Monographic series, Academic/Scholarly.*
Published by: (Nexus Instituut), Uitgeverij Nexus bv, Postbus 90153, Tilburg, 5000 LE, Netherlands. TEL 31-13-4663450, FAX 31-13-4663434, info@nexus-instituut.nl, http://www.nexus-instituut.nl.

193 DEU ISSN 2191-5733
▼ ➤ **NIETZSCHE HEUTE.** Text in German. 2011. irreg., latest vol.3, 2012. price varies. **Document type:** *Monographic series, Academic/Scholarly.*
Published by: Walter de Gruyter GmbH & Co. KG, Genthiner Str 13, Berlin, 10785, Germany. TEL 49-30-260050, FAX 49-30-26005251, info@degruyter.com, http://www.degruyter.de.

100 DEU ISSN 0342-1422
B3310
NIETZSCHE-STUDIEN; internationales Jahrbuch fuer die Nietzsche-Forschung. Text in English, German, French. 1972. a. EUR 219, USD 329 to institutions; EUR 250, USD 375 combined subscription to institutions (print & online eds.) (effective 2012). reprint service avail. from SCH. **Document type:** *Journal, Academic/Scholarly.*
Related titles: Online - full text ed.: ISSN 1613-0790. EUR 219, USD 329 to institutions (effective 2012).
Indexed: A22, A26, AmHI, BibLing, DIP, E01, FR, H07, IBR, IBZ, IPB, MLA, MLA-IB, PCI, PhilInd, RASB, RILM, T02.
—BLDSC (6110.950000), IE, Ingenta, INIST. **CCC.**
Published by: Walter de Gruyter GmbH & Co. KG, Genthiner Str 13, Berlin, 10785, Germany. TEL 49-30-260050, FAX 49-30-26005251, info@degruyter.com, http://www.degruyter.de.

190 DEU ISSN 2191-5741
▼ ➤ **NIETZSCHE TODAY.** Text in English. 2011. irreg., latest vol.3, 2012. price varies. **Document type:** *Monographic series, Academic/Scholarly.*
Published by: Walter de Gruyter GmbH & Co. KG, Genthiner Str 13, Berlin, 10785, Germany. TEL 49-30-260050, FAX 49-30-26005251, info@degruyter.com, http://www.degruyter.de.

100 ITA ISSN 1970-6138
NIETZSCHEANA. Text in Italian. 2004. irreg. price varies. **Document type:** *Monographic series, Academic/Scholarly.*
Published by: Edizioni E T S, Piazza Carrara 16-19, Pisa, Italy. TEL 39-050-29544, FAX 39-050-20158, info@edizioniets.it, http://www.edizioniets.it. Eds. Franco Volpi, Giuliano Campioni.

193 DEU ISSN 1869-5604
NIETZSCHEFORSCHUNG. Text in German. 1990. a. EUR 99.80 (effective 2011). **Document type:** *Journal, Academic/Scholarly.*
Formerly (until 1994): Foerder- und Forschungsgemeinschaft Friedrich Nietzsche. Jahresschrift
Published by: (Nietzsche-Gesellschaft e.V.), Akademie Verlag GmbH (Subsidiary of: Oldenbourg Wissenschaftsverlag GmbH), Markgrafenstr 12-14, Berlin, 10969, Germany. TEL 49-30-4220060, FAX 49-30-42200657, info@akademie-verlag.de.

100 NLD ISSN 0924-4530
➤ **NIJHOFF INTERNATIONAL PHILOSOPHY SERIES.** Text in English. 1976. irreg., latest vol.54, 1997. price varies. **Document type:** *Monographic series, Academic/Scholarly.*
Formerly (until 1989): Melbourne International Philosophy Series (0924-493X)
Indexed: CCMJ, MathR.
Published by: Springer Netherlands (Subsidiary of: Springer Science+Business Media), Van Godewijckstraat 30, Dordrecht, 3311 GX, Netherlands. TEL 31-78-6576050, FAX 31-78-6576474. Ed. Jan T J Srzednicki.

100 FRA ISSN 1275-7691
B2
NOESIS. Text in French. 1997. irreg. **Document type:** *Journal, Academic/Scholarly.*
Related titles: Online - full text ed.: ISSN 1773-0228.
Published by: Centre de Recherches d'Histoire des Idees, Faculte des lettres, art et sciences humaines, 96, boulevard Edouard Herriot, BP 3209, Nice 3, 06204, France. TEL 33-4-93375415, FAX 33-4-93375481.

THE NOETIC JOURNAL. *see* PHYSICS

100 POL ISSN 1230-7858
NOMOS; kwartalnik religioznawczy. Text in Polish. 1992. q. PLZ 11.60 for 6 mos. domestic (effective 2003). **Document type:** *Journal, Academic/Scholarly.*
Published by: (Uniwersytet Jagiellonski, Instytut Religioznawstwa), Zaklad Wydawniczy Nomos, ul Tkacka 5/4, Krakow, 30050, Poland. biuro@nomos.pl, http://www.nomos.pl.

NOOR AL-ISLAM; thiqafiyyah islamiyyah - islamic cultural magazine. *see* RELIGIONS AND THEOLOGY—Islamic

111 DNK ISSN 2000-1452
➤ **NORDIC JOURNAL OF AESTHETICS.** Text in English. 1988. s-a. DKK 300 to individual members; DKK 450 to institutional members; DKK 150 to students; EUR 40 to individual members; EUR 60 to institutional members; EUR 20 to students (effective 2010). cum.index:1988-2001. back issues avail. **Document type:** *Journal, Academic/Scholarly.*
Formerly (until 2008): Nordisk Estetisk Tidskrift (0284-7698)
Related titles: Online - full text ed.: ISSN 2000-9607.
Indexed: MLA-IB, RILM.
Published by: Nordic Society of Aesthetics, c/o Morten Kyndrup, Inst of Aesthetic Studies, Langelandsgade 141, Aarhus C, 8000, Denmark. TEL 45-89-421815, aekag@hum.au.dk, http://www.nsae.au.dk. Ed. Jacob Lund.

190 NLD
NORDIC VALUE STUDIES. Text in English. irreg. price varies. **Document type:** *Monographic series, Academic/Scholarly.* **Description:** Covers philosophical works related to the intellectual traditions and cultural interests of Denmark, Finland, Iceland, Norway and Sweden.
Related titles: ◆ Series of: Value Inquiry Book Series. ISSN 0929-8436.
Published by: Editions Rodopi B.V., Tijnmuiden 7, Amsterdam, 1046 AK, Netherlands. TEL 31-20-6114821, FAX 31-20-4472979, info@rodopi.nl. Ed. Matti Hayry. **Dist. by:** Rodopi - USA, 606 Newark Ave, 2nd fl, Kenilworth, NJ 07033. TEL 908-497-9031, FAX 908-497-9035.

100 943 DEU
NORDRHEIN-WESTFAELISCHE AKADEMIE DER WISSENSCHAFTEN UND DER KUENSTE. GEISTESWISSENSCHAFTEN VORTRAEGE. Text in German. 1953. irreg., latest vol.425, 2010. price varies. back issues avail. **Document type:** *Monographic series, Academic/Scholarly.*
Former titles (until 2009): Nordrhein-Westfaelische Akademie der Wissenschaften. Geisteswissenschaften Vortraege (0944-8810); Rheinisch-Westfaelische Akademie der Wissenschaften. Geisteswissenschaften Vortraege (0172-2093); (until 1971): Arbeitsgemeinschaft fuer Forschung des Landes Nordrhein-Westfalen. Geisteswissenschaften (0570-5649)
Indexed: RASB.
Published by: (Nordrhein-Westfaelische Akademie der Wissenschaften), Verlag Ferdinand Schoeningh GmbH, Postfach 2540, Paderborn, 33055, Germany. TEL 49-5251-1275, FAX 49-5251-127860, info@schoeningh.de, http://www.schoeningh.de.

100 NOR ISSN 0029-1943
CODEN: NGGTAZ
NORSK FILOSOFISK TIDSSKRIFT/NORWEGIAN JOURNAL OF PHILOSOPHY. Text in Norwegian, Swedish, Danish. 1966. q. NOK 498 to individuals; NOK 685 to institutions; NOK 280 to students (effective 2010). adv. bk.rev. bibl. index. **Document type:** *Journal, Academic/Scholarly.*
Related titles: Online - full text ed.: ISSN 1504-2901. 2004. NOK 785 (effective 2010).
Indexed: DIP, IBR, IBZ.
Published by: Universitetsforlaget AS/Scandinavian University Press (Subsidiary of: Aschehoug & Co.), Sehesteds Gate 3, P O Box 508, Sentrum, Oslo, 0105, Norway. TEL 47-24-147500, FAX 47-24-147501, post@universitetsforlaget.no. Ed. Kjersti Fjortoft.

NOTRE DAME JOURNAL OF FORMAL LOGIC. *see* MATHEMATICS

100 USA ISSN 1538-1617
B1
NOTRE DAME PHILOSOPHICAL REVIEWS. Text in English. 2002. irreg.
Media: Online - full content.
Published by: University of Notre Dame, Department of Philosophy, 100 Malloy Hall, Notre Dame, IN 46556-4619. TEL 574-631-6471, FAX 574-631-0588, http://www.nd.edu/~ndphilo/. Ed. Gary Gutting.

100 ZAF
THE NOUMENON JOURNAL; nondual perspectives on transformation. Text in English. 1995. a. ZAR 35 domestic; USD 15 foreign (effective 2006).
Formerly: Noumenon (1024-8501)
Published by: Noumenon Press, PO Box 1280, Wandsbeck, South Africa. TEL 27-31-2627152.

100 USA ISSN 0029-4624
B1
➤ **NOUS.** Text in English. 1967. q. GBP 538 in United Kingdom to institutions (print or online ed.); USD 732 in the Americas to institutions (print or online ed.); EUR 683 in Europe to institutions (print or online ed.); USD 1,054 elsewhere to institutions (print or online ed.); GBP 592 combined subscription in United Kingdom to institutions (print & online eds.); USD 805 combined subscription in the Americas to institutions (print & online eds.); EUR 752 combined subscription in Europe to institutions (print & online eds.); USD 1,160 combined subscription elsewhere to institutions (print & online eds.) (effective 2010); subscr. includes Philosophical Issues and Philosophical Perspectives. adv. bk.rev. illus. index, cum.index. back issues avail.; reprint service avail. from PSC. **Document type:** *Journal, Academic/Scholarly.* **Description:** Publishes critical essays, brief discussions, and important results of philosophic research.
Related titles: Microfilm ed.: (from PQC); Online - full text ed.: ISSN 1468-0068 (from IngentaConnect); ◆ Supplement(s): Philosophical Perspectives. ISSN 1520-8583; ◆ Philosophical Issues. ISSN 1533-6077.
Indexed: A01, A03, A08, A20, A21, A22, A26, AmHI, ArtHuCI, B04, BRD, CA, CCMJ, CurCont, DIP, E01, FR, H07, H08, H14, HAb, HumInd, IBR, IBRH, IBZ, IPB, L&LBA, L05, L06, MSN, MathR, P02, P10, P30, P48, P53, P54, PCI, PQC, PhilInd, RASB, RI-1, RI-2, RILM, SCOPUS, SOPODA, SociolAb, T02, W03, W07.
—BLDSC (6176.310000), IE, Infotrieve, Ingenta, INIST. **CCC.**
Published by: Wiley-Blackwell Publishing, Inc. (Subsidiary of: Wiley-Blackwell Publishing Ltd.), 111 River St, Hoboken, NJ 07030. TEL 201-748-6000, FAX 201-748-6088, info@wiley.com, http://www.wiley.com/WileyCDA/. Ed. Ernest Sosa. Adv. contact Kristin McCarthy TEL 201-748-7683.

190 FRA ISSN 1773-8083
NOUS, LES SANS-PHILOSOPHIE. Text in French. 2005. irreg. back issues avail. **Document type:** *Monographic series, Consumer.*
Published by: L' Harmattan, 5 Rue de l'École Polytechnique, Paris, 75005, France. TEL 33-1-43257651, FAX 33-1-43258203.

111.85 FRA ISSN 1969-2269
BH2
➤ **NOUVELLE REVUE D'ESTHETIQUE.** Text in French; Abstracts in French, English. 1945-2005; resumed 2008. 2/yr. EUR 83 foreign to institutions (effective 2012). bk.rev. bibl.; charts; illus. index. **Document type:** *Journal, Academic/Scholarly.*
Formerly (until 2005): Revue d'Esthetique (0035-2292)
Indexed: A20, A22, ABCT, ASCA, BibInd, DIP, FR, IBR, IBZ, IIMP, IPB, MLA, MLA-IB, MusicInd, PCI, PhilInd, RASB, RILM, SCOPUS.
—IE, Infotrieve, INIST. **CCC.**

P

Published by: (Societe Francaise d'Esthetique), Presses Universitaires de France, 6 Avenue Reille, Paris, 75685, France. TEL 33-1-58103161, FAX 33-1-45897530, revues@puf.com. Ed. Anne Cauquelin.

100 ITA ISSN 0392-2332
AS222.N775
NOUVELLES DE LA REPUBLIQUE DES LETTRES. Text in Italian. 1981. s-a. bk.rev. **Document type:** *Journal, Academic/Scholarly.* **Description:** Covers philosophy, science and art from the Renaissance and the Enlightenment periods.
Indexed: DIP, FR, IBR, IBZ, MLA, MLA-IB, P30, PhilInd.
—INIST.
Published by: (Istituto Italiano per gli Studi Filosofici (I I S F)), Prismi Editrice Politecnica Napoli, Via Francesco Caracciolo 13, Naples, 80122, Italy. TEL 39-081-7612884, FAX 39-081-668339, info@prismi.com, http://www.prismi.com.

100 IRL
NUA NEW THINKING. Text in English. 1996. w. free. adv. **Document type:** *Newsletter.* **Description:** Contains a philosophical exploration of our technological society and aims at management personnel in business and academia.
Media: Online - full text.
Published by: Nua Ltd., Merrion House, Merrion Road, Dublin, 4, Ireland. TEL 353-1-676-8996, FAX 353-1-283-9988. Ed., R&P Gerry McGovern. Adv. contact Oriana LoLacona.

100 ITA
NUOVA CIVILTA DELLE MACCHINE. Text in Italian. 1983. q. EUR 52 (effective 2008). bk.rev. **Document type:** *Magazine, Consumer.*
Indexed: IPB.
Published by: E R I Edizioni R A I (Subsidiary of: R A I - Radiotelevisione Italiana), Via Verdi 16, Turin, TO 10121, Italy. http://www.eri.rai.it.

NUOVA CORRENTE. *see* LITERATURE

100 ITA ISSN 0390-3036
NUOVA STOA; rivista quadrimestrale di studi filosofici. Text in Italian. 1974. 3/yr. bk.rev. reprints avail. **Document type:** *Journal, Academic/Scholarly.*
Published by: Universita degli Studi di Palermo, Facolta di Lettere e Filosofia, Viale delle Scienze 12, Palermo, 90128, Italy. TEL 39-091-6560225, FAX 39-091-427366.

NUOVA UNIVERSALE STUDIUM. *see* LITERATURE

NURSING PHILOSOPHY; an international journal for healthcare professionals. *see* MEDICAL SCIENCES—Nurses And Nursing

100 200 DNK ISSN 0900-1441
DEN NYE DIALOG. Text in Danish. 1980. q. DKK 200 membership; DKK 125 to students (effective 2009). **Document type:** *Magazine, Consumer.* **Description:** Information on religion and new religious movements.
Former titles (until 1985): Dialog (0109-1395); (until 1983): Dialog Nyhedsbrev (0902-3461)
Related titles: Online - full text ed.: ISSN 1902-4711. 200?.
Published by: Dialogcentret, Katrinebergvej 46, Aarhus N, 8200, Denmark. TEL 45-86-105411, FAX 45-86-105416, info@dci.dk.

100 USA ISSN 1559-1905
E169.12
THE OBJECTIVE STANDARD. Text in English. 2006. q. USD 59 combined subscription domestic to individuals print & online eds.; USD 74 combined subscription in Canada & Mexico to individuals print & online eds.; USD 118 combined subscription domestic to institutions print & online eds.; USD 133 combined subscription in Canada & Mexico to institutions print & online eds.; USD 49 combined subscription domestic to students print & online eds.; USD 64 combined subscription in Canada & Mexico to students print & online eds. (effective 2007). back issues avail. **Document type:** *Journal, Academic/Scholarly.*
Related titles: Online - full text ed.: ISSN 1559-1913.
Indexed: A26, G08, I05, P05, P42, PAIS.
Published by: Glen Allen Press, LLC, PO Box 5274, Glen Allen, VA 23058. TEL 804-747-1776, FAX 804-273-0500, http://glenallenpress.com.

100 900 RUS ISSN 2221-2787
▼ ➤ **OBSHCHESTVO: FILOSOFIYA, ISTORIYA, KUL'TURA/SOCIETY: PHILOSOPHY, HISTORY, CULTURE.** Text in Russian; Summaries in Russian, English. 2011. q. free. bk.rev. back issues avail. **Document type:** *Journal, Academic/Scholarly.*
Related titles: Online - full text ed.: ISSN 2223-6449.
Published by: Izdatel'skii Dom HORS, ul Yankovskogo 156, Krasnodar, Russian Federation. TEL 7-861-2901335, dom-hors@mail.ru. Eds. Valerii Kas'yanov, Victoria L Kharseeva.

105 DNK ISSN 0107-7384
ODENSE UNIVERSITY STUDIES IN PHILOSOPHY. Text in Danish, English. 1972. irreg., latest vol.18, 2001. price varies. back issues avail. **Document type:** *Monographic series, Academic/Scholarly.*
Published by: Syddansk Universitetsforlag/University Press of Southern Denmark, Campusvej 55, Odense M, 5230, Denmark. TEL 45-66-157999, FAX 45-66-158126, press@forlag.sdu.dk, http://www.universitypress.dk.

100 ZAF ISSN 0256-0356
ODYSSEY (TOKAI); an adventure in more conscious living. Text in English. 1977. bi-m. ZAR 135 domestic; ZAR 230 in Africa; ZAR 340 elsewhere (effective 2007). adv. bk.rev. tr.lit. back issues avail. **Document type:** *Magazine, Consumer.* **Description:** Covers self-discovery, inspiration and transformation, philosophy, holistic health and nutrition, ecology, metaphysics, personal and spiritual growth and parapsychology.
Incorporates (1999-2004): Namaste (1562-4374)
Published by: Sacred Spaces Publishing House CC, PO Box 30946, Tokai, 7966, South Africa. TEL 27-21-7130018, FAX 27-21-7124665. Ed. Chris Erasmus. Adv. contact Belinda Jamison. color page ZAR 13,463.40; trim 210 x 275. Circ: 6,000.

141 NLD ISSN 2210-5638
▼ **OER.** Text in Dutch. 2010. a. EUR 4 newsstand/cover (effective 2010). adv. **Document type:** *Magazine, Consumer.*
Published by: Uitgeverij Koorddanser, Postbus 429, Laren, 1250 AK, Netherlands. TEL 31-35-5336226, FAX 31-35-5384443. Ed., Pub. Ewald Wagenaar. Adv. contact Willem Swart. page EUR 693; 190 x 277. Circ: 5,000.

OESTERREICHISCHE AKADEMIE DER WISSENSCHAFTEN. PHILOSOPHISCH-HISTORISCHE KLASSE. ANZEIGER. *see* HISTORY—History Of Europe

100 DEU ISSN 1433-1527
OESTERREICHISCHE GESELLSCHAFT FUER PHAENOMENOLOGIE. REIHE. Text in German. 1998. irreg., latest vol.16, 2009. price varies. **Document type:** *Monographic series, Academic/Scholarly.*
Published by: Peter Lang GmbH (Subsidiary of: Peter Lang Publishing Group), Eschborner Landstr 42-50, Frankfurt Am Main, 60489, Germany. TEL 49-69-7807050, FAX 49-69-78070550, zentrale.frankfurt@peterlang.com.

100 AUT ISSN 1019-3251
OESTERREICHISCHEN KARL-JASPERS-GESELLSCHAFT. JAHRBUCH. Text in German. 1988. a. EUR 19 (effective 2005). adv. bk.rev. **Document type:** *Journal, Academic/Scholarly.*
Published by: (Karl-Jaspers-Gesellschaft), StudienVerlag, Erlerstr 10, Innsbruck, 6020, Austria. TEL 43-512-395045, FAX 43-512-39504515, order@studienverlag.at, http://www.studienverlag.at. Eds. Elisabeth Salamun Hybasek, Kurt Salamun. R&P, Adv. contact Markus Hatzer.

190 USA
➤ **OHIO UNIVERSITY PRESS. SERIES IN CONTINENTAL THOUGHT.** Text in English. irreg., latest vol.38. price varies. adv. back issues avail. **Document type:** *Monographic series, Academic/Scholarly.* **Description:** Brings out books that relate to the work of thinkers in the European tradition such as Husserl, Heidegger, Sartre, Merleau-Ponty, Derrida, Foucault, Buber, and others.
Related titles: Online - full text ed.
Published by: Ohio University Press, 19 Cir Dr, The Ridges, Athens, OH 45701. TEL 740-593-1154, FAX 740-593-4536. Ed. Ted Toadvine. **Subscr. to:** Eurospan Group, 3 Henrietta St, Covent Garden, London WC2E 8LU, United Kingdom. TEL 44-20-7240-0856, FAX 44-20-7379-0609, orders@edspubs.co.uk, http://www.eurospanonline.com.

➤ **OIKONOMIA**; rivista di etica e scienze sociali/review of ethics & social sciences. *see* SOCIAL SCIENCES: COMPREHENSIVE WORKS

190 940 BEL
ON THE MAKING OF EUROPE. Text in English. 1992. irreg., latest 2007. price varies. back issues avail. **Document type:** *Monographic series, Academic/Scholarly.* **Description:** Discusses philosophical and ethical issues arising from the integration of Europe, with particular emphasis on studies of people and groups at the margins of the process.
Published by: Peeters Publishers, Bondgenotenlaan 153, Leuven, 3000, Belgium. TEL 32-16-235170, FAX 32-16-228500, http://www.peeters-leuven.be.

ON WINGS. *see* WOMEN'S INTERESTS

ONLINE JOURNAL OF HEALTH ETHICS. *see* MEDICAL SCIENCES

ONLINE NOETIC NETWORK. *see* NEW AGE PUBLICATIONS

170 NLD ISSN 1874-7612
BJ1
➤ **THE OPEN ETHICS JOURNAL.** Text in English. 2008. irreg. free (effective 2011). **Document type:** *Journal, Academic/Scholarly.*
Media: Online - full text.
Indexed: A01, ESPM, RiskAb.
Published by: Bentham Open (Subsidiary of: Bentham Science Publishers Ltd.), PO Box 294, Bussum, AG 1400, Netherlands. TEL 31-35-6923800, FAX 31-35-6980150, subscriptions@bentham.org.

100 051 USA ISSN 2153-5469
OPEN FOR BUSINESS; ideas, culture and technology for the business of life. Text in English. 2001. irreg. free (effective 2010). **Document type:** *Magazine, Consumer.* **Description:** Covers a broad array of subjects with a tech savvy bent and offers readers interesting new commentary every week.
Media: Online - full text.
Published by: Universal Networks http://www.uninetsolutions.com/. Ed. Timothy R Butler.

100 NLD ISSN 1878-447X
▼ ➤ **THE OPEN PHILOSOPHY JOURNAL.** Text in English. forthcoming 2011. irreg. free (effective 2011). **Document type:** *Journal, Academic/Scholarly.* **Description:** Addresses all aspects of philosophy, including metaphysics, epistemology, logic, ethics, political philosophy, aesthetics, ancient philosophy, and the philosophy of religion, science, psychology, mind, language and law.
Media: Online - full text.
Published by: Bentham Open (Subsidiary of: Bentham Science Publishers Ltd.), PO Box 294, Bussum, AG 1400, Netherlands. TEL 31-35-6923800, FAX 31-35-6980150, subscriptions@bentham.org, http://www.bentham.org.

140 230.0071 NZL ISSN 1175-8619
THE OPEN SOCIETY; serving New Zealand's non-religious community since 1927. Text in English. 1927 (July). q. free membership. adv. bk.rev. bibl.; illus. 26 p./no.; back issues avail. **Document type:** *Journal, Academic/Scholarly.* **Description:** A journal on philosophy, science, religion and society.
Former titles (until 2002): New Zealand Rationalist and Humanist (0028-8632); (until 1964): New Zealand Rationalist; (until 1939): The Truth Seeker
Related titles: Supplement(s): 1975. members only.
—**CCC.**
Published by: New Zealand Association of Rationalists & Humanists Inc., 64 Symonds St, Auckland, 1001, New Zealand. TEL 64-9-3735131, FAX 64-9-3798233, heathen@nazarh.org.nz. Eds. Mr. David Ross, Mr. Paul Litterick, Dr. Bill Cooke. R&P Dr. Bill Cooke. Circ: 800.

100 DEU
ORBIS PHAENOMENOLOGICUS. Text in German. irreg. price varies. **Document type:** *Monographic series, Academic/Scholarly.*
Published by: Verlag Koenigshausen und Neumann GmbH, Leistenstr 7, Wuerzburg, 97082, Germany. TEL 49-931-3298700, FAX 49-931-83620, info@koenigshausen-neumann.de, http://koenigshausen-neumann.gebhardt-riegel.de.

149.2 570 DEU ISSN 1438-6909
ORGANISMUS UND SYSTEM. Text in German. 2000. irreg., latest vol.8, 2008. price varies. **Document type:** *Monographic series, Academic/Scholarly.*

Published by: Peter Lang GmbH (Subsidiary of: Peter Lang Publishing Group), Eschborner Landstr 42-50, Frankfurt Am Main, 60489, Germany. TEL 49-69-7807050, FAX 49-69-78070550, zentrale.frankfurt@peterlang.com.

101 SVK ISSN 1335-0668
B6
ORGANON F. Text in Czech, English, Slovak. 1994. q. **Document type:** *Journal, Academic/Scholarly.* **Description:** Publishes works concerning problems of philosophy of language, semiotics, mathematics, and logic, as well as natural and social sciences.
Indexed: A20, ArtHuCI, CurCont, L&LBA, PhilInd, SCOPUS, W07.
Published by: (Slovenska Akademia Vied, Filozoficky Ustav/Slovak Academy of Scinces, Institute of Philosophy, Presovska Univerzita, Filozoficka Fakulta), Vydavatel'stvo Slovenskej Akademie Vied Veda/Veda, Publishing House of the Slovak Academy of Sciences, Dubravska cesta 9, PO Box 106, Bratislava 45, 84005, Slovakia. TEL 421-2-54774253, FAX 421-2-54772682, http://www.veda-sav.sk.

ORIENTIERUNG; katholische Blaetter fuer weltanschauliche Information. *see* RELIGIONS AND THEOLOGY—Roman Catholic

ORIGINS (LOMA LINDA). *see* SCIENCES: COMPREHENSIVE WORKS

100 ITA ISSN 1973-8986
ORIZZONTE FILOSOFICO. Text in Italian. 1974. irreg. **Document type:** *Monographic series, Academic/Scholarly.*
Published by: Cittadella Editrice, Via Ancaiani 3, Assisi, PG 06081, Italy. TEL 39-075-813595, FAX 39-075-813719, http://www.cittadellaeditrice.com.

OSHO TIMES INTERNATIONAL. *see* RELIGIONS AND THEOLOGY—Hindu

100 DEU
OSNABRUECKER PHILOSOPHISCHE SCHRIFTEN. REIHE A: ABHANDLUNGEN. Text in German. 1981-1983; N.S. 1996. irreg., latest vol.3, 2000. price varies. **Document type:** *Monographic series, Academic/Scholarly.*
Published by: V & R Unipress GmbH (Subsidiary of: Vandenhoeck und Ruprecht), Robert-Bosch-Breite 6, Goettingen, 37079, Germany. TEL 49-551-5084303, FAX 49-551-5084333, info@vr-unipress.de, http://www.v-r.de/en/publisher/unipress.

100 DEU ISSN 1610-5761
OSTDEUTSCHE BEITRAEGE ZUR PHILOSOPHISCHEN DISKUSSION. Text in German. 2001. irreg. price varies. **Document type:** *Monographic series, Academic/Scholarly.*
Published by: Weissensee Verlag e.K., Simplonstr 59, Berlin, 10245, Germany. TEL 49-30-29049192, FAX 49-30-27574315, mail@weissensee-verlag.de.

100 SVK ISSN 1336-6556
OSTIUM. Text in Slovak, Czech. 2005. irreg. free (effective 2011). **Document type:** *Journal, Academic/Scholarly.*
Media: Online - full text.
Indexed: AmHI, H07, T02.
Published by: Schola Philosophica, Hlavna 49, Puste Ulany, 92528, Slovakia. scholaphilosophica@yahoo.com. Ed. Reginald Adrian Slavkovsky.

100 USA
OUTLANDER. Text in English. 1994. irreg. USD 1 newsstand/cover domestic (effective 2001). back issues avail.; reprints avail. **Document type:** *Monographic series, Trade.* **Description:** Contains humor, satire and "outlandish" social commentary. Also covers new civilization.
Media: Duplicated (not offset).
Published by: Omdega Press, PO Box 1546, Provincetown, MA 02657. Ed., Pub., R&P Robert Seaver Gebelein. Circ: 50.

100 USA ISSN 0846-8508
➤ **OVERHEARD IN SEVILLE**; bulletin of the Santayana Society. Text in English. 1983. a. **Document type:** *Journal, Academic/Scholarly.* **Description:** Promotes the work of George Santayana and includes scholarly articles and annual updates to the Santayana bibliography.
Related titles: Online - full text ed.: ISSN 2153-7046.
Indexed: PhilInd.
Published by: (Santayana Society), Philosophy Documentation Center, PO Box 7147, Charlottesville, VA 22906. FAX 434-220-3301, order@pdcnet.org, http://www.pdcnet.org.

100 USA ISSN 0030-7580
B2900
➤ **OWL OF MINERVA.** Text in English. 1969. s-a. USD 35 to individuals; USD 48 to institutions; USD 173 combined subscription to institutions (print & online eds.); USD 18 per issue to individuals; USD 24 per issue to institutions; free to members (effective 2010). adv. bk.rev. bibl. cum.index. back issues avail. **Document type:** *Journal, Academic/Scholarly.* **Description:** Features articles, discussions, translations, reviews, and bibliographical information pertaining to Hegel, his predecessors, contemporaries, and successors.
Related titles: Online - full text ed.: ISSN 2153-3385. USD 144 to institutions (effective 2010).
Indexed: A01, A03, A08, A22, A26, AmHI, CA, DIP, E07, E08, G08, H07, I05, IBR, IBZ, IPB, MLA-IB, PCI, PhilInd, S09, T02.
—BLDSC (6320.540000), IE, Ingenta.
Published by: (Hegel Society of America), Philosophy Documentation Center, PO Box 7147, Charlottesville, VA 22906. TEL 434-220-3300, FAX 434-220-3301, order@pdcnet.org, http://www.pdcnet.org. Ed. Ardis B Collins. Adv. contact Greg Swope.

➤ **OXFORD EDITIONS OF CUNEIFORM TEXTS.** *see* ARCHAEOLOGY

➤ **OXFORD LITERARY REVIEW.** *see* LITERATURE

100 GBR ISSN 1754-5463
OXFORD PHILOSOPHICAL MONOGRAPHS. Text in English. 198?. irreg., latest 2009. price varies. back issues avail. **Document type:** *Monographic series, Academic/Scholarly.*
—BLDSC (6321.012450).
Published by: Oxford University Press, Great Clarendon St, Oxford, OX2 6DP, United Kingdom. TEL 44-1865-556767, FAX 44-1865-556646, enquiry@oup.co.uk, http://www.oup-usa.org/catalogs/general/series/.

100 GBR ISSN 0265-7651
B1
➤ **OXFORD STUDIES IN ANCIENT PHILOSOPHY.** Text in English. 1983. s-a. price varies. illus. reprints avail. **Document type:** *Monographic series, Academic/Scholarly.*
Indexed: IPB, P30, PCI, SCOPUS.
—BLDSC (6321.021800), Ingenta.

Published by: Oxford University Press, Great Clarendon St, Oxford, OX2 6DP, United Kingdom. TEL 44-1865-556767, FAX 44-1865-556646, enquiry@oup.co.uk, http://www.oup-usa.org/catalogs/general/series/. Ed. Brad Inwood. **Orders in N. America to:** Oxford University Press, 2001 Evans Rd, Cary, NC 27513. TEL 919-677-0977 ext 5777, 800-852-7323, FAX 919-677-1714, jnlorders@oup-usa.org, http://www.us.oup.com.

190 GBR ISSN 1754-7873
B801
OXFORD STUDIES IN EARLY MODERN PHILOSOPHY. Text in English. 2003. a. price varies. back issues avail. **Document type:** *Monographic series, Academic/Scholarly.*
Published by: Oxford University Press, Great Clarendon St, Oxford, OX2 6DP, United Kingdom. TEL 44-1865-556767, FAX 44-1865-556646, enquiry@oup.co.uk, http://www.oup-usa.org/catalogs/general/series/. Ed. Daniel Garber.

P A T H. *see* RELIGIONS AND THEOLOGY—Roman Catholic

P R O U T PRESS. (Progressive Utilization Theory) *see* GENERAL INTEREST PERIODICALS—United States

100 GBR ISSN 0279-0750
AP2 CODEN: PPHQEJ
➤ **PACIFIC PHILOSOPHICAL QUARTERLY.** Text in English. 1920. q. GBP 276 in United Kingdom to institutions; EUR 350 in Europe to institutions; USD 402 in the Americas to institutions; USD 616 elsewhere to institutions; GBP 317 combined subscription in United Kingdom to institutions (print & online eds.); EUR 403 combined subscription in Europe to institutions (print & online eds.); USD 463 combined subscription in the Americas to institutions (print & online eds.); USD 710 combined subscription elsewhere to institutions (print & online eds.) (effective 2012). adv. bibl.; illus. index. back issues avail.; reprint service avail. from PSC. **Document type:** *Journal, Academic/Scholarly.* **Description:** Presents articles from all areas of philosophy including epistemology, moral philosophy, political philosophy, philosophy of language, philosophy of mind, aesthetics and history of philosophy.
Formerly (until Jan.1980): Personalist (0031-5621)
Related titles: Microform ed.: (from PQC); Online - full text ed.: ISSN 1468-0114. GBP 276 in United Kingdom to institutions; EUR 350 in Europe to institutions; USD 402 in the Americas to institutions; USD 616 elsewhere to institutions (effective 2012) (from IngentaConnect).
Indexed: A01, A02, A03, A08, A20, A22, A26, ASCA, AmHI, ArtHuCI, BEL&L, BRD, CA, CurCont, E01, E08, FR, G08, H07, H08, H09, H10, H14, HAb, HumInd, I05, IBR, IBZ, IPB, MLA-IB, P02, P10, P30, P42, P48, P53, P54, PCI, PQC, PhilInd, R05, RASB, RILM, S09, SCOPUS, SOPODA, SociolAb, T02, W03, W07.
—BLDSC (6330.700000), IE, Ingenta, INIST. **CCC.**
Published by: (University of Southern California, School of Philosophy USA), Wiley-Blackwell Publishing Ltd. (Subsidiary of: John Wiley & Sons, Inc.), 9600 Garsington Rd, Oxford, OX4 2DQ, United Kingdom. TEL 44-1865-776868, FAX 44-1865-714591, customerservices@blackwellpublishing.com.

➤ **PACIFICA**; Australasian theological studies. *see* RELIGIONS AND THEOLOGY

➤ **PAEDAGOGIK UND PHILOSOPHIE.** *see* EDUCATION

100 ESP ISSN 0214-7300
PAIDEIA (MADRID). Text in Spanish. 1980. q. **Document type:** *Journal, Academic/Scholarly.*
Formerly (until 1989): Sociedad Espanola de Profesores de Filosofia de Instituto. Boletin Informativo (0214-7297)
Indexed: IPB, PhilInd.
Published by: Sociedad Espanola de Profesores de Filosofia, C Francos Rodriguez 106, Madrid, 28039, Spain. http://www.filosofia.org/bol/soc/bs005.htm.

PAIDEUSIS (ONLINE). *see* EDUCATION

100 PAK ISSN 0078-8406
PAKISTAN PHILOSOPHICAL CONGRESS. PROCEEDINGS. Text in English. 1954. a. USD 7. **Document type:** *Proceedings.*
Published by: Pakistan Philosophical Congress, Department of Philosophy, University of the Punjab, New Campus, Lahore 20, Pakistan. Ed. Abdul Khaliq. Circ: 900.

100 PAK ISSN 0552-914X
B1
PAKISTAN PHILOSOPHICAL JOURNAL. Text in English. 1962. s-a. USD 7. adv. bk.rev. bibl.
Indexed: BAS, PCI, PhilInd.
Published by: Pakistan Philosophical Congress, Department of Philosophy, University of the Punjab, New Campus, Lahore 20, Pakistan. Ed. Abdul Khaliq. Circ: 1,000.

190 ESP
PAPELES DE TRABAJO. CONFERENCIAS. Text in Spanish. 1995. irreg. price varies. back issues avail. **Document type:** *Monographic series, Academic/Scholarly.*
Published by: Fundacion Jose Ortega y Gasset, Fortuny 53, Madrid, 28010, Spain. TEL 34-91-7004100, FAX 34-91-7003530, comunicacion@fog.es, http://www.ortegaygasset.edu/.

190 ESP
PAPELES DE TRABAJO. ESTUDIOS ORTEGUIANOS. Text in Spanish. 1991. irreg. price varies. back issues avail. **Document type:** *Monographic series, Academic/Scholarly.*
Published by: Fundacion Jose Ortega y Gasset, Fortuny 53, Madrid, 28010, Spain. TEL 34-91-7004100, FAX 34-91-7003530, comunicacion@fog.es, http://www.ortegaygasset.edu/.

PAPIESKI FAKULTET TEOLOGICZNY WE WROCLAWIU. ROZPRAWY NAUKOWE. *see* RELIGIONS AND THEOLOGY—Roman Catholic

100 DEU
PARADEIGMATA; innovative Beitraege zur philosophischen Forschung. Text in German. 1982. irreg., latest vol.30, 2009. price varies. **Document type:** *Monographic series, Academic/Scholarly.*
Published by: Felix Meiner Verlag GmbH, Richardstr 47, Hamburg, 22081, Germany. TEL 49-40-2987560, FAX 49-40-29875620, info@meiner.de. R&P, Adv. contact Johannes Kambylis.

100 ITA ISSN 1120-3404
PARADIGMI; rivista di critica filosofica. Text in Italian. 1983. 3/yr. EUR 67 domestic; EUR 93 foreign (effective 2010). **Document type:** *Journal, Academic/Scholarly.*
Related titles: Online - full text ed.: ISSN 2035-357X. 2008.
Indexed: FR, PhilInd.
Published by: Franco Angeli Edizioni, Viale Monza 106, Milan, 20127, Italy. TEL 39-02-2837141, FAX 39-02-26144793, redazioni@francoangeli.it, http://www.francoangeli.it. Ed. Luigi Formigari.

PARADOXISM. *see* LITERATURE

100 200 IND
PARMARTH. Text in Gujarati. 19??. m. **Description:** Promotes moral ethics of religion and philosophy.
Published by: Jai Hind Publications, Jai Hind Press Bldg, Near Sharda Baug, Rajkot, 360 001, India. TEL 91-281-2440513, FAX 91-281-2448677.

100 AUS ISSN 1834-3287
B1
PARRHESIA; a journal of critical philosophy. Text in English. 2006. s-a. **Document type:** *Journal, Academic/Scholarly.*
Media: Online - full text.
Published by: (University of Melbourne), Parrhesia, PO Box 4272, Parkville, VIC 3052, Australia. contact@parrhesiajournal.org, http://www.parrhesiajournal.org. Eds. Alex Murray, Jon Roffe, Matthew Sharpe.

144 NLD ISSN 2211-8462
▼ **PARTAGE.** Text in Dutch. 2010. s-a. **Document type:** *Journal, Academic/Scholarly.*
Media: Online - full text.
Published by: Universiteit voor Humanistiek, Postbus 797, Utrecht, 3500 AT, Netherlands. TEL 31-30-2390100, FAX 31-30-2340738, info@uvh.nl, http://www.uvh.nl.

100 ESP ISSN 1137-8204
A PARTE REI/JOURNAL OF PHILOSOPHY; revista de filosofia. Text in Spanish. 1997. q. back issues avail. **Document type:** *Magazine, Academic/Scholarly.* **Description:** Aims to be a forum for people interested in philosophy.
Related titles: Online - full text ed.: free (effective 2011).
Published by: Sociedad de Estudios Filosoficos "Juan Blanco"/ Philosophical Studies Society, C Penarroya, 20, Madrid, 28053, Spain. Ed. Carlos Munoz Gutierrez.

PASHTO ACADEMY. MONTHLY JOURNAL. *see* LITERATURE

PATHWAY TO GOD; one God, one world, one humanity. *see* RELIGIONS AND THEOLOGY

100 641.1 USA
PATHWAYS TO HEALTH. Text in English. 1978. 4/yr. USD 25. adv. **Description:** Based on the Edgar Cayce readings, PTH includes holistic health tips, A.R.E. Clinic programs, educational activities and research projects, and Edgar Cayce insights on health.
Published by: A.R.E. Medical Clinic, 4018 N 40th St, Phoenix, AZ 85018. TEL 602-955-0551. Ed. Scott Grady. Circ: 3,500 (controlled).

100 POL ISSN 1508-1834
➤ **PATOS.** Text in Polish. 1999. q. **Document type:** *Journal, Academic/Scholarly.*
Published by: (Papieska Akademia Teologiczna w Krakowie/Pontifical Academy of Theology in Krakow), Wydawnictwo Naukowe Papieskiej Akademii Teologicznej w Krakowie, ul Franciszkanska 1, pok 037, Krakow, 31004, Poland. wydawnictwo@pat.krakow.pl.

➤ **PATRISTICA ET MEDIAEVALIA.** *see* HISTORY

170 USA ISSN 0079-0249
➤ **PAUL ANTHONY BRICK LECTURES.** Text in English. 1960. irreg., latest 2002. price varies. back issues avail. **Document type:** *Monographic series, Academic/Scholarly.*
Published by: University of Missouri Press, 2910 LeMone Blvd, Columbia, MO 65201. TEL 573-882-7641, FAX 573-884-4498, upress@umsystem.edu.

100 USA ISSN 0079-0257
PAUL CARUS LECTURES. Text in English. 1925. irreg., latest vol.21, 2003. price varies. index. back issues avail.; reprints avail. **Document type:** *Monographic series, Academic/Scholarly.*
Published by: (American Philosophical Association), Open Court Publishing Co., General Books (Subsidiary of: Carus Publishing Company), 70 E Lake St, Ste 300, Chicago, IL 60601. TEL 800-815-2280, FAX 312-701-1728, opencourt@caruspub.com. **Subscr. to:** 30 Grove St, Ste C, Peterborough, NH 03458. FAX 603-924-7380, customerservice@caruspub.com.

174.2 USA ISSN 2150-5462
➤ **PENN BIOETHICS JOURNAL.** Abbreviated title: P B J. Text in English. 2005. s-a. free (effective 2009). back issues avail. **Document type:** *Journal, Academic/Scholarly.*
Related titles: Online - full text ed.: ISSN 2150-5470. free (effective 2009).
Indexed: A01, T02.
Published by: University of Pennsylvania, Penn Bioethics Society, 3401 Market St, Ste 320, Philadelphia, PA 19104. penn.bioethics.society@gmail.com, http://www.dolphin.upenn.edu/bioethic/.

101 ESP ISSN 0031-4749
B5
PENSAMIENTO; revista de investigacion e informacion filosofica. Text in Spanish. 1945. q. EUR 32 domestic; EUR 61 in Europe; EUR 68 in Africa; EUR 74 elsewhere (effective 2008). bk.rev. bibl. index. back issues avail. **Document type:** *Journal, Academic/Scholarly.*
Indexed: A20, A22, ASCA, ArtHuCI, CurCont, DIP, FR, IBR, IBZ, IPB, MLA-IB, P09, PCI, PhilInd, RASB, SCOPUS, W07.
—IE, Infotrieve, INIST. **CCC.**
Published by: Universidad Pontificia Comillas de Madrid, Facultade de Filosofia, C Universidad Comillas, 3, Madrid, 28049, Spain. TEL 34-91-7343950, FAX 34-91-7344570, revista@pub.upcomillas.es. Ed. Javier Monserrat.

100 BRA ISSN 2178-843X
▼ **PENSANDO**; revista de filosofia. Text in English, French, Portuguese. 2010. s-a. free (effective 2011). **Document type:** *Journal, Academic/Scholarly.*
Media: Online - full text.
Published by: Universidade Federal do Piaui, Editora, Campus Profa, Cinobelina Elvas, Bom Jesus, Piaui 64900-000, Brazil. http://www.ufpi.edu.br.

300 MEX ISSN 1870-4492
➤ **PENSARES Y QUEHACERES**; revista de politicas de la filosofia. Text in Spanish. 2004. 2/yr. MXN 50 per issue (effective 2007). adv. **Document type:** *Journal, Academic/Scholarly.* **Description:** Contains analyses and reflections on the politics of philosophy in Latin America.
Indexed: C01, PhilInd.
Published by: Sociedad de Estudios Culturales de Nuestra America, Torre de Humanidades II, 8 piso, Ciudad Universitaria, Mexico, D.F., 04510, Mexico. TEL 52-55-56230211, FAX 52-55-56230219, secnacomunicacion@yahoo.com. Ed. Horacio Cerutti Guldberg. R&P Ruben Garcia Clarck. Adv. contact Cecilia Ortega Ibarra. B&W page MXN 6,000, color page MXN 11,000. Circ: 1,000 (paid and controlled).

100 ITA ISSN 2037-9986
▼ **PENSATORI.** Text in Italian. 2009. irreg. **Document type:** *Monographic series, Academic/Scholarly.*
Published by: Carocci Editore, Via Sardegna 50, Rome, 00187, Italy. TEL 39-06-42818417, FAX 39-06-42747931, clienti@carocci.it, http://www.carocci.it.

100 ITA ISSN 1824-4971
IL PENSIERO (NAPLES); rivista di filosofia. Text in Italian. 1956. s-a. EUR 36 domestic to individuals; EUR 41 domestic to institutional members; EUR 61 foreign (effective 2009). **Document type:** *Journal, Academic/Scholarly.*
Indexed: PhilInd.
Published by: Edizioni Scientifiche Italiane SpA, Via Chiatamone 7, Naples, NA 80121, Italy. TEL 39-081-7645443, FAX 39-081-7646477, info@edizioniesi.it, http://www.edizioniesi.it. Ed. Vincenzo Vitiello.

100 ITA ISSN 0394-4131
B4
➤ **PER LA FILOSOFIA**; filosofia e insegnamento. Text in Italian. 1985. 3/yr. EUR 245 combined subscription domestic to institutions (print & online eds.); EUR 345 combined subscription foreign to institutions (print & online eds.) (effective 2009). **Document type:** *Journal, Academic/Scholarly.* **Description:** Confronts philosophical debates on a serious but not overly specialized level. Includes teaching hints and ideas for those in philosophy education.
Related titles: Online - full text ed.: ISSN 1724-059X.
Indexed: IPB, PhilInd.
Published by: Fabrizio Serra Editore (Subsidiary of: Accademia Editoriale), c/o Accademia Editoriale, Via Santa Bibbiana 28, Pisa, 56127, Italy. TEL 39-050-542332, FAX 39-050-574888, accademiaeditoriale@accademiaeditoriale.it, http://www.libraweb.net.

100 ITA
PERCORSI. Text in Italian. 1994. irreg., latest vol.6, 1999. price varies. **Document type:** *Monographic series, Academic/Scholarly.*
Published by: Liguori Editore, Via Posillipo 394, Naples, 80123, Italy. TEL 39-081-7206111, FAX 39-081-7206244, liguori@liguori.it, http://www.liguori.it.

100 ITA ISSN 2036-1068
PERCORSI (PADOVA). Text in Italian. 1999. irreg. **Document type:** *Monographic series, Academic/Scholarly.*
Published by: Universita degli Studi di Verona, Dipartimento di Filosofia, Pedagogia e Psicologia, Lungadige Porta Vittoria 17, Verona, 37129, Italy. http://www.dfpp.univr.it.

▼ **PERFORMING ETHOS**; an international journal of ethics in theatre & performance. *see* THEATER

183 DEU ISSN 1862-1465
PERIPATOI; philologisch-historische Studien zum Aristotelismus. Text in German, English, French. 1971. irreg., latest vol.21, 2008. price varies. **Document type:** *Monographic series, Academic/Scholarly.*
Media: Large Type.
Published by: Walter de Gruyter GmbH & Co. KG, Genthiner Str 13, Berlin, 10785, Germany. TEL 49-30-260050, FAX 49-30-26005251, info@degruyter.com, http://www.degruyter.de. Eds. Juergen Wiesner, R W Sharples, Wolfgang Kullmann.

PERSATUAN PURE LIFE. ANNUAL REPORT. *see* SOCIAL SERVICES AND WELFARE

100 DEU ISSN 1433-4933
PERSEPHONE. Text in German. 1997. irreg., latest vol.5, 2007. price varies. **Document type:** *Monographic series, Academic/Scholarly.*
Published by: Peter Lang GmbH (Subsidiary of: Peter Lang Publishing Group), Eschborner Landstr 42-50, Frankfurt Am Main, 60489, Germany. TEL 49-69-7807050, FAX 49-69-78070550, zentrale.frankfurt@peterlang.com. Eds. Evelin Klein, Hans-Dieter Klein.

174.95 COL ISSN 0123-3122
PERSONA Y BIOETICA. Text in Spanish. s-a. COP 50,000 domestic; USD 42 foreign (effective 2007). **Document type:** *Journal, Academic/Scholarly.*
Related titles: Online - full text ed.
Indexed: A01, C01, CA, F03, F04, H21, P08, P28, P48, P53, P54, PQC, T02.
Published by: Universidad de La Sabana, Facultad de Medicina, Campus Universitario del Puente del Comun, Km 21, Autopista Norte de Bogota, D. C. Edificio H - Oficina, Bogota, Colombia. TEL 57-1-8615555 ext 2609, FAX 57-1-8615555 ext 2626. Ed. Gilberto A. Gamboa Bernal.

PERSONA Y SOCIEDAD. *see* SOCIAL SCIENCES: COMPREHENSIVE WORKS

144 NLD
PERSONALIST STUDIES. Text in English. irreg. price varies. **Document type:** *Monographic series, Academic/Scholarly.*
Related titles: ◆ Series of: Value Inquiry Book Series. ISSN 0929-8436.
Published by: Editions Rodopi B.V., Tijnmuiden 7, Amsterdam, 1046 AK, Netherlands. TEL 31-20-6114821, FAX 31-20-4472979, info@rodopi.nl. Ed. Thomas F Woods. **Dist. by:** Rodopi - USA, 606 Newark Ave, 2nd fl, Kenilworth, NJ 07033. TEL 908-497-9031, FAX 908-497-9035.

100 230 CAN ISSN 0384-8922
PERSPECTIVE (TORONTO, 1967). Text in English. 1967. q. CAD 15, USD 15 (effective 2002). illus. back issues avail. **Document type:** *Newsletter.* **Description:** Promotes and provides information about the ICS and its work on the advancement of Christian scholarship.
Related titles: Online - full text ed.
Indexed: A22.

P

Published by: Institute for Christian Studies, 229 College St, Toronto, ON M5T 1R4, Canada. TEL 416-979-2331, FAX 416-979-2332, email@icscanada.edu. Circ: 6,000.

PERSPECTIVE ON ETHICS AND INTERNATIONAL AFFAIRS; education and studies newsletter. *see* POLITICAL SCIENCE—International Relations

100 IRL ISSN 2009-1842
➤ **PERSPECTIVES**; international postgraduate journal of philosophy. Text in English. 2008. a. **Document type:** *Journal, Academic/Scholarly.*
Related titles: Online - full text ed.: free (effective 2011).
Published by: University College Dublin, School of Philosophy, Newman Building, Belfield, Dublin, 4, Ireland. FAX 353-1-7168258.

801 ISR ISSN 0793-2839
PN1
PERSPECTIVES; revue de l'Universite Hebraique de Jerusalem. Text in French. 1994. irreg., latest vol.14, 2007. USD 27 per issue to non-members; USD 24 per issue to members (effective 2008); 27. **Document type:** *Journal, Academic/Scholarly.*
Formerly: Etudes, Art et Litterature, Universite de Jerusalem
Indexed: DIP, IBR, IBZ, MLA-IB.
Published by: Magnes Press (Subsidiary of: Hebrew University of Jerusalem), Hebrew University, Jerusalem, The Sherman Building for Research Management, PO Box 39099, Jerusalem, 91390, Israel. FAX 972-2-5883688, hubp@h2.hum.huji.ac.il. Ed. Fernande Bartfeld.

190 FRA ISSN 0338-5930
PERSPECTIVES CRITIQUES. Text in French. 1975. irreg. price varies. **Document type:** *Monographic series, Academic/Scholarly.*
—CCC.
Published by: Presses Universitaires de France, 6 Avenue Reille, Paris, 75685, France. TEL 33-1-58103161, FAX 33-1-45897530, revues@puf.com, http://www.puf.com.

190 FRA ISSN 1950-1943
PERSPECTIVES CRITIQUES LA REVUE. Text in French. 2006. s-a. **Document type:** *Journal, Academic/Scholarly.*
Published by: Presses Universitaires de France, 6 Avenue Reille, Paris, 75685, France. TEL 33-1-58103161, FAX 33-1-45897530, revues@puf.com, http://www.puf.com.

100 DEU
PERSPEKTIVEN DER ANALYTISCHEN PHILOSOPHIE. Text in German. 2000. irreg., latest vol.9, 2003. price varies. **Document type:** *Monographic series, Academic/Scholarly.*
Published by: Mentis Verlag GmbH, Schulze-Delitzsch-Str 19, Paderborn, 33100, Germany. TEL 49-5251-687902, FAX 49-5251-687905, webmaster@mentis.de, http://www.mentis.de.

100 NLD ISSN 0171-1288
B3
PERSPEKTIVEN DER PHILOSOPHIE. NEUES JAHRBUCH. Text in English, German. 1969. a., latest vol.33, 2007. price varies. adv. bk.rev. back issues avail. **Document type:** *Journal, Academic/Scholarly.* **Description:** Presents studies on philosophers of all schools.
Formerly (until 1975): Philosophische Perspektiven (0556-4980)
Related titles: Online - full text ed.: ISSN 1875-6778 (from IngentaConnect).
Indexed: A22, AmHI, FR, H07, IPB, PCI, PhilInd, RASB, T02.
—IE, Ingenta, INIST. **CCC.**
Published by: Editions Rodopi B.V., Tijnmuiden 7, Amsterdam, 1046 AK, Netherlands. TEL 31-20-6114821, FAX 31-20-4472979, orders-queries@rodopi.nl. Eds. Martina Scherbel, Wiebke Schrader. **Dist in France by:** Nordeal, 30 rue de Verlinghem, BP 139, Lambersart 59832, France. TEL 33-3-20099060, FAX 33-3-20929495; **Dist in N America by:** Rodopi - USA, 295 North Michigan Avenue, Suite 1B, Kenilworth, NJ 07033. TEL 908-298-9071, 800-225-3998, FAX 908-298-9075.

100 PRT ISSN 1646-5180
PESSOAS E SINTOMAS. Text in Portuguese. 2006. 3/yr. **Document type:** *Journal, Academic/Scholarly.*
Published by: Universidade Catolica Portuguesa, Faculdade de Filosofia, Praca da Faculdade, 1, Braga, 4710-297, Portugal. TEL 351-253-201200, FAX 351-253-201210, jvila-cha@braga.ucp.pt, http://www.rpf.pt.

100 FRA ISSN 2105-4592
▼ **PETITE PHILOSOPHIE DES GRANDES IDEES.** Text in French. 2009. irreg. **Document type:** *Monographic series.*
Published by: Editions Eyrolles, 61 Boulevard Saint-Germain, Paris, 75240, France. http://www.editions-eyrolles.com.

100 CAN ISSN 1911-1576
PHAENEX; journal of existential and phenomenological theory and culture. Text in English, French. 2006. s-a. free (effective 2011). **Document type:** *Journal, Academic/Scholarly.*
Media: Online - full text.
Indexed: A39, C27, C29, D03, D04, E13, PhilInd, R14, S14, S15, S18.
Published by: University of Windsor, 401 Sunset Ave, Windsor, ON N9B 3P4, Canada. TEL 519-253-3000, FAX 519-973-7050, http://www.uwindsor.ca.

142 NLD ISSN 0079-1350
PHAENOMENOLOGICA. Text in English, French, German. 1958. irreg., latest vol.191, 2009. price varies. **Document type:** *Monographic series, Academic/Scholarly.* **Description:** Publishes studies on Husserl's phenomenology and on related thinkers, as well as on the history of phenomenology.
Indexed: RASB, RI-2.
—BLDSC (6441.700000).
Published by: (Centre d'Archives Husserl BEL), Springer Netherlands (Subsidiary of: Springer Science+Business Media), Van Godewijckstraat 30, Dordrecht, 3311 GX, Netherlands. TEL 31-78-6576050, FAX 31-78-6576474. Ed. Ullrich Melle.

142.7 DEU ISSN 0342-8117
B829.5.A1
PHAENOMENOLOGISCHE FORSCHUNGEN/PHENOMENOLOGICAL STUDIES. Text in English, French, German. 1975. a. EUR 96 (effective 2010). bibl. **Document type:** *Journal, Academic/Scholarly.* **Description:** Provides an international forum for all phenomenologically oriented articles and work.
Indexed: DIP, IBR, IBZ, IPB, PhilInd.
—CCC.
Published by: (Deutsche Gesellschaft fuer Phaenomenologische Forschung), Felix Meiner Verlag GmbH, Richardstr 47, Hamburg, 22081, Germany. TEL 49-40-2987560, FAX 49-40-29875620, info@meiner.de, http://www.meiner.de. Eds. Ernst Wolfgang Orth, Karl-Heinz Lembeck.

128 DEU ISSN 1862-2240
PHAINOMENA. Text in German. 1992. irreg., latest vol.13, 2004. price varies. **Document type:** *Monographic series, Academic/Scholarly.*
Published by: Attempto Verlag, Dischingerweg 5, Tuebingen, 72070, Germany. TEL 49-7071-97970, FAX 49-7071-979711, info@attempto-verlag.de, http://www.narr.de.

165.62 SVN ISSN 1318-3362
➤ **PHAINOMENA.** Text in Slovenian. 1992. 2/yr. USD 30 to individuals; USD 60 to institutions; USD 20 newsstand/cover (effective 2003). adv. **Document type:** *Journal, Academic/Scholarly.* **Description:** Publishes articles from the fields of phenomenology, hermeneutics, social hermeneutics, philosophy of religion, theory of science, philosophy of art, history of philosophy and philosophy of culture.
Indexed: AmHI, DIP, IBR, IBZ, L&LBA, PhilInd, SCOPUS, SociolAb.
Published by: (Fenomenolosko Drustvo), Zalozba Nova Revija, Dalmatinova 1, Ljubljana, 1000, Slovenia. TEL 386-1-4334306, FAX 386-1-1334250, info@nova-revija.si, http://www.nova-revija.si. Ed. Andrina Tonkli-Komel. Pub., R&P Dean Komel. adv.: page USD 20. Circ: 400 (paid).

100 CAN ISSN 1496-8533
PHARES; revue philosophique etudiante de l'Universite Laval. Text in French. 2001. irreg. **Document type:** *Journal, Academic/Scholarly.*
Related titles: Online - full text ed.: free (effective 2011).
Indexed: A39, C27, C29, D03, D04, E13, MLA-IB, R14, S14, S15, S18.
Published by: Universite Laval, Faculte de Philosophie, Pavillon Felix-Antoine-Savard, Bureau 644, Quebec, PQ G1K 7P4, Canada. TEL 418-656-2244, FAX 418-656-7267, http://www.fp.ulaval.ca/fp/, fp@fp.ulaval.ca.

PHENOMENEWS; exploring human potential, holistic health and living. *see* NEW AGE PUBLICATIONS

100 USA ISSN 0885-3886
B829.5
PHENOMENOLOGICAL INQUIRY; a review of philosophical ideas and trends. Text mainly in English; Text occasionally in French. 1977. a. (Oct.), latest no.27. USD 65 per issue to individuals; USD 72 per issue to institutions (effective 2011). bk.rev. bibl. back issues avail. **Document type:** *Journal, Academic/Scholarly.*
Formerly (until 1985): Phenomenology Information Bulletin (0278-8322)
Indexed: A22, IPB, MLA-IB, PhilInd, RASB.
—IE, Infotrieve, Ingenta.
Published by: World Phenomenology Institute, 1 Ivy Pointe Way, Hanover, NH 03755. TEL 802-295-3487, FAX 802-295-5963, Wphenomenology@aol.com. Ed. Anna Teresa Tymieniecka.

121 USA ISSN 1524-0193
PHENOMENOLOGY AND LITERATURE. Text in English. 2002. irreg., latest vol.6, 2009. price varies. **Document type:** *Monographic series, Academic/Scholarly.* **Description:** Contains studies of a comparative nature which straddle and/or combine the disciplines of philosophical and literary studies.
Published by: Peter Lang Publishing, Inc. (Subsidiary of: Peter Lang Publishing Group), 29 Broadway, New York, NY 10006. TEL 212-647-7700, 800-770-5264, FAX 212-647-7707, customerservice@plang.com. Ed. Hans Rudnick.

100 CAN ISSN 1913-4711
B829.5.A1
PHENOMENOLOGY & PRACTICE. Text in English. 2007. a. free (effective 2011). **Document type:** *Journal, Academic/Scholarly.*
Formerly (until 1993): Phenomenology & Pedagogy (Print) (0820-9189)
Media: Online - full text.
Indexed: A39, C03, C27, C29, CEI, D03, D04, E13, PQC, R14, S14, S15, S18.
—CCC.
Published by: Thompson Rivers University, 900 McGill Rd, Kamloops, BC V2C 5N3, Canada. Ed. Carina Henricksson.

100 NLD ISSN 1568-7759
➤ **PHENOMENOLOGY AND THE COGNITIVE SCIENCES.** Text in English. 2002 (Jan.). q. EUR 553, USD 572 combined subscription to institutions (print & online eds.) (effective 2012). adv. bk.rev. reprint service avail. from PSC. **Document type:** *Journal, Academic/Scholarly.* **Description:** Covers broadly defined aspects of cognition, including issues that are open to both phenomenological and empirical investigation, including perception, emotion and language.
Related titles: Online - full text ed.: ISSN 1572-8676 (from IngentaConnect).
Indexed: A20, A22, A26, AmHI, ArtHuCI, B21, BibLing, CA, E01, H07, Inspec, NSA, P03, PhilInd, PsycInfo, SCOPUS, T02, W07.
—BLDSC (6449.355300), IE, Infotrieve, Ingenta. **CCC.**
Published by: Springer Netherlands (Subsidiary of: Springer Science+Business Media), Van Godewijckstraat 30, Dordrecht, 3311 GX, Netherlands. TEL 31-78-6576050, FAX 31-78-6576474, http://www.springer.com. Eds. Dan Zahavi, Shaun Gallagher.

100 USA ISSN 1098-3570
BL2747.6
➤ **PHILO.** Text in English. 1998. s-a. USD 35 to individuals; USD 60 to institutions (effective 2010). adv. back issues avail. **Document type:** *Journal, Academic/Scholarly.* **Description:** Aims to publish articles in all fields of philosophy and not devoted to any specific branch of philosophy.
Related titles: Online - full text ed.: ISSN 2154-1639. USD 52 to individuals; USD 150 to institutions (effective 2010).
Indexed: PhilInd, R&TA.
Published by: Philosophy Documentation Center, PO Box 7147, Charlottesville, VA 22906. TEL 434-220-3300, FAX 434-220-3301, order@pdcnet.org, http://www.pdcnet.org. Ed. Paul Draper. Adv. contact Greg Swope.

100 NLD ISSN 1570-095X
PHILO OF ALEXANDRIA COMMENTARY SERIES. Text in English. 2001. irreg., latest vol.2, 2003. price varies. **Document type:** *Monographic series, Academic/Scholarly.*
Indexed: IZBG.
Published by: Brill, PO Box 9000, Leiden, 2300 PA, Netherlands. TEL 31-71-5353500, FAX 31-71-5317532, cs@brill.nl. Ed. Gregory E Sterling.

100 FRA ISSN 1765-7865
LE PHILOSOPHE. Text in French. 2004. irreg. back issues avail. **Document type:** *Monographic series, Consumer.*
Published by: Editions Manucius, 9 Rue Moliere, Houilles, 78800, France. TEL 33-8-74487246, FAX 33-1-39682003, http://www.manucius.com.

100 GBR ISSN 0967-6074
B1
THE PHILOSOPHER. Text in English. 1913. s-a. free to members (effective 2009). bk.rev. **Document type:** *Journal, Academic/Scholarly.* **Description:** Covers the study of philosophy for the general public.
Related titles: Online - full text ed.
Indexed: PdeR.
Published by: Philosophical Society of England, c/o Michael Bavidge, 6 Craighall Dene Rd, Newcastle, NE3 1QR, United Kingdom. M.C.Bavidge@Newcastle.ac.uk. Ed. Martin Cohen.

100 USA
PHILOSOPHER OF CREATIVITY MONOGRAPH SERIES. Text in English. 1984. irreg. price varies. back issues avail. **Document type:** *Monographic series.* **Description:** For researchers at all levels. Explores the nature and structure of creativity.
Published by: Foundation for Philosophy of Creativity, Inc., c/o Larry Cobb, 250 Slippery Rock Rd, Slippery Rock, PA 16057. TEL 724-794-2938. Ed. John C Thomas. **Subscr. to:** University Press of America, 4501 Forbes Blvd., Ste. 200, Lanham, MD 20706. TEL 301-459-3366.

PHILOSOPHERS AND THEIR CRITICS. *see* LINGUISTICS

100 USA ISSN 1533-628X
➤ **PHILOSOPHERS' IMPRINT.** Text in English. 2001. q. free (effective 2011). back issues avail. **Document type:** *Journal, Academic/Scholarly.* **Description:** Contains series of original papers in philosophy.
Media: Online - full text.
Indexed: PhilInd.
Published by: University of Michigan, Library, 435 S State St, An Arbor, MI 48109. TEL 734-764-6285, FAX 734-763-8071, http://www.lib.umich.edu/. Eds. J David Velleman, Stephen Darwall.

100 GBR ISSN 1354-814X
THE PHILOSOPHERS' MAGAZINE. Abbreviated title: T P M. Text in English. 1997. q. GBP 19.99 in UK & North America; GBP 23.99 in Europe; GBP 27.99 elsewhere (effective 2009). adv. bk.rev. back issues avail. **Document type:** *Magazine, Consumer.* **Description:** Features the best in classic and contemporary philosophy.
Related titles: CD-ROM ed.: ISSN 1467-2545. GBP 25 domestic to individuals; USD 39.99 in US & Canada to individuals; GBP 35 elsewhere to individuals; GBP 75 domestic to institutions; USD 99 in US & Canada to institutions; GBP 90 elsewhere to institutions (effective 2009); Online - full text ed.: The Philosophers' Web Magazine. ISSN 1368-7611.
Indexed: PhilInd.
—IE.
Published by: Philosophers' Magazine, 14a St Cross St, London, EC1N 8XA, United Kingdom. TEL 44-20-78411959, FAX 44-20-72421474, jerry@philosophers.co.uk. Ed. Julian Baggini. **Subscr. in N. America:** Philosophy Documentation Center, PO Box 7147, Charlottesville, VA 22906. TEL 434-220-3300, FAX 434-220-3301, pkswope@pdcnet.org, http://www.pdcnet.org.

190 BEL ISSN 0079-1660
PHILOSOPHES CONTEMPORAINS. Text in French. 1948. irreg. price varies. **Document type:** *Monographic series.*
Published by: Universite Catholique de Louvain, Institut Superieur de Philosophie, Pl du Cardinal Marcier 1, Louvain-la-Neuve, 1348, Belgium. TEL 32-10-474613, FAX 32-10-474819.

180 BEL ISSN 0079-1679
➤ **PHILOSOPHES MEDIEVAUX.** Text in English, French, Latin. 1948. irreg., latest 2008. price varies. back issues avail. **Document type:** *Monographic series, Academic/Scholarly.* **Description:** Discusses medieval philosophy and provides translations of texts.
Published by: (Universite Catholique de Louvain, Institut Superieur de Philosophie), Peeters Publishers, Bondgenotenlaan 153, Leuven, 3000, Belgium. TEL 32-16-235170, FAX 32-16-228500, http://www.peeters-leuven.be.

100 ARG ISSN 0031-8000
PHILOSOPHIA. Text in Spanish. 1944. s-a. per issue exchange basis.
Indexed: FR, P09, P30, PCI.
—INIST.
Published by: Universidad Nacional de Cuyo, Instituto de Filosofia, Facultad de Filosofia y Letras, Parque General San Martin, Mendoza, 5500, Argentina.

100 NLD ISSN 0048-3893
B1
PHILOSOPHIA; philosophical quarterly of Israel. Text in English. 1971. q. EUR 356, USD 437 combined subscription to institutions (print & online eds.) (effective 2012). adv. bk.rev. bibl.; charts. reprint service avail. from PSC. **Document type:** *Journal, Academic/Scholarly.* **Description:** Contributions in analytic philosophy (articles, discussion notes, critical studies, book reviews, etc).
Related titles: Online - full text ed.: ISSN 1574-9274 (from IngentaConnect).
Indexed: A20, A22, A26, AmHI, ArtHuCI, B04, BRD, CA, CurCont, DIP, E01, FR, H07, H08, HAb, HumInd, IBR, IBZ, IPB, PhilInd, SCOPUS, T02, W03, W05, W07.
—BLDSC (6461.492000), IE, Ingenta, INIST. **CCC.**
Published by: (Bar-Ilan University ISR, Department of Philosophy ISR), Springer Netherlands (Subsidiary of: Springer Science+Business Media), Van Godewijckstraat 30, Dordrecht, 3311 GX, Netherlands. TEL 31-78-6576050, FAX 31-78-6576474, http://www.springer-sbm.de. Ed. Asa Kasher.

100 USA ISSN 2155-0891
▼ ➤ **PHILOSOPHIA**; a journal of continental feminism. Text in English. 2010 (Aug.). s-a. USD 100 domestic to institutions; USD 200 foreign to institutions (effective 2011). **Document type:** *Journal, Academic/Scholarly.*
Related titles: Online - full text ed.: ISSN 2155-0905. 2010 (Aug.).
Published by: State University of New York Press, 90 State St, Ste 700, Albany, NY 12207. TEL 518-472-5000, FAX 518-472-5038, info@sunypress.edu. Eds. Elaine P Miller, Emily Zakin.

105 GRC
PHILOSOPHIA. Text in English, French, German, Greek. 1971. a. USD 50 (effective 2000). adv. bk.rev. back issues avail. **Document type:** *Journal, Academic/Scholarly.* **Description:** Includes articles about philosophy, the history of philosophy, and the philosophy of right, of literature, and aesthetics.
Published by: Academy of Athens, Research Center for Greek Philosophy/Kentron Erevnis tis Hellenikes Philosophias, 14 Anagnostopoulou St, Athens, 106 73, Greece. TEL 30-1-3600-140, FAX 30-1-3600-140. Ed. E Moutsopoulos. Adv. contact Anna Aravantinou. Circ: 1,000.

199 001.3 USA ISSN 1539-8250
B5300
➤ **PHILOSOPHIA AFRICANA**; analysis of philosophy and issues in Africa and the Black Diaspora. Text in English. s-a. USD 205 to individuals; USD 590 to institutions; USD 650 combined subscription to institutions print & online eds. (effective 2008). adv. bk.rev.; film rev. Index. 120 p./no.; back issues avail. **Document type:** *Journal, Academic/Scholarly.* **Description:** Aims to promote scholarly research and teaching of philosophy from the point of view of African and African Diaspora experience and traditions. Also intends to explore relationships between philosophy and art and literature in Africa and the African Diaspora in dialogue with other cultures of the world.
Former titles (until 2001): African Philosophy (1369-6823); (until 1998): S A P I N A Newsletter (Society for African Philosophy in North America)
Related titles: Online - full text ed.: ISSN 1944-7914. USD 250 (effective 2007) (from IngentaConnect).
Indexed: A01, A03, A08, A20, A22, A26, ASD, AmHI, ArtHuCI, CA, CurCont, DIP, E01, H07, I05, IBR, IBZ, IIBP, IPB, MLA-IB, P42, PhilInd, S02, S03, SCOPUS, SociolAb, T02, W07.
—BLDSC (6461.493500), IE, Ingenta. **CCC.**
Published by: Ball State University, Department of Philosophy and Religious Studies, 2000 W University Ave, NQ 211, Muncie, IN 47306. TEL 765-285-1244, 800-383-8540, FAX 765-285-8980, http://www.bsu.edu/philosophy/. Ed. Kibujjo m Kalumba TEL 765-285-5991.

180 NLD ISSN 0079-1687
➤ **PHILOSOPHIA ANTIQUA.** Text in English, French, German. 1946. irreg., latest vol.114, 2008. price varies. back issues avail. **Document type:** *Monographic series, Academic/Scholarly.* **Description:** Scholarly monographs on topics in ancient philosophy.
Indexed: CCMJ, IZBG, MSN, MathR.
Published by: Brill, PO Box 9000, Leiden, 2300 PA, Netherlands. TEL 31-71-5353500, FAX 31-71-5317532, cs@brill.nl, http://www.brill.nl. R&P Elizabeth Venekamp. **Dist. by:** Turpin Distribution Services Ltd., Pegasus Dr, Stratton Business Park, Biggleswade, Bedfordshire SG18 8QB, United Kingdom. TEL 44-1767-604954, FAX 44-1767-601640, custserv@turpin-distribution.com, http://www.turpin-distribution.com/.

100 170 230 USA ISSN 1529-1634
BR100
➤ **PHILOSOPHIA CHRISTI. SERIES 2.** Text in English. 1978. s-a. free to members (effective 2011). back issues avail. **Document type:** *Journal, Academic/Scholarly.* **Description:** Provides a vehicle for the scholarly discussion of philosophy and philosophical issues in the fields of ethics, theology, and religion.
Former titles (until 1999): Philosophia Christi; (until 1994): Evangelical Philosophical Society. Bulletin
Indexed: A21, PhilInd, R&TA, RI-1.
Published by: Evangelical Philosophical Society, c/o Craig Hazen, Biola University, PO Box 1298, La Mirada, CA 90637. TEL 562-906-4570. Ed. Dr. Craig J Hazen.

510.01 GBR ISSN 0031-8019
QA9 CODEN: PHMAB5
➤ **PHILOSOPHIA MATHEMATICA**; philosophy of mathematics, its learning, and its application. Text in English. 1964-1981 (vol.18); resumed 1986 (2nd series)-1991 (vol.6); resumed 1993 (3rd series). 3/yr. GBP 108 in United Kingdom to institutions; EUR 161 in Europe to institutions; USD 213 in US & Canada to institutions; GBP 108 elsewhere to institutions; GBP 118 combined subscription in United Kingdom to institutions (print & online eds.); EUR 175 combined subscription in Europe to institutions (print & online eds.); USD 233 combined subscription in US & Canada to institutions (print & online eds.); GBP 118 combined subscription elsewhere to institutions (print & online eds.) (effective 2012). adv. bk.rev. index. back issues avail.; reprint service avail. from PSC. **Document type:** *Journal, Academic/Scholarly.* **Description:** Philosophical study in the nature of mathematics. Publishes peer-reviewed new work iurk in philosophy of mathematics, including what can be learned from the study of mathematics, whether under instruction or by research.
Related titles: Online - full text ed.: ISSN 1744-6406. GBP 98 in United Kingdom to institutions; EUR 146 in Europe to institutions; USD 194 in US & Canada to institutions; GBP 98 elsewhere to institutions (effective 2012) (from IngentaConnect).
Indexed: A01, A20, A22, ArtHuCI, C03, CBCARef, CCMJ, E01, H14, IPB, MSN, MathR, P10, P26, P48, P49, P52, P53, P54, PCI, PQC, PhilInd, RASB, S10, SCOPUS, T02, W07, Z02.
—BLDSC (6461.500000), IE, Infotrieve, Ingenta, Linda Hall. **CCC.**
Published by: (Canadian Society for History and Philosophy of Mathematics/Societe Canadienne d'Anthropologie USA), Oxford University Press, Great Clarendon St, Oxford, OX2 6DP, United Kingdom. TEL 44-1865-556767, FAX 44-1865-556646, enquiry@oup.co.uk, http://www.oxfordjournals.org. Ed. Robert S D Thomas.

530 146 DEU ISSN 0031-8027
B3
➤ **PHILOSOPHIA NATURALIS**; Archiv fuer Naturphilosophie und die philosophischen Grenzgebiete der exakten Wissenschaften und Wissenschaftsgeschichte. Text in German. 1950. s-a. EUR 134 to institutions (effective 2010). adv. bk.rev. bibl. index. back issues avail. **Document type:** *Journal, Academic/Scholarly.* **Description:** Discusses topics in the philosophy of natural history and of the history of science.
Related titles: Online - full text ed.: (from IngentaConnect).
Indexed: A22, BibInd, CCMJ, DIP, FR, IBR, IBZ, IPB, MSN, MathR, P30, PCI, PhilInd, RASB.
—IE, Infotrieve, Ingenta, INIST, Linda Hall. **CCC.**
Published by: Vittorio Klostermann, Frauenlobstr 22, Frankfurt Am Main, 60487, Germany. TEL 49-69-9708160, FAX 49-69-708038, verlag@klostermann.de. Ed. Andreas Bartel. Circ: 380 (paid and controlled).

510.1 CHE ISSN 1424-8425
PHILOSOPHIA NATURALIS ET GEOMETRICALIS. Text in French. 2002. irreg., latest vol.6, 2007. price varies. **Document type:** *Monographic series, Academic/Scholarly.*
Indexed: Z02.
Published by: Peter Lang AG (Subsidiary of: Peter Lang Publishing Group), Hochfeldstr 32, Postfach 746, Bern 9, 3000, Switzerland. TEL 41-31-3061717, FAX 41-31-3061727, info@peterlang.com. Ed. Luciano Boi.

185 USA ISSN 1195-8553
➤ **PHILOSOPHIA PERENNIS.** Text in English. 1994. s-a. bk.rev. back issues avail. **Document type:** *Journal, Academic/Scholarly.*
Indexed: PhilInd, RASB.
Published by: Society for Aristotelian Studies, c/o Robert Augros, Treas, St Anselm College, 100 St Anselm Dr, Box 1643, Manchester, NH 03102. http://www.aristotle-aquinas.org. Circ: 160 (paid).

294.54 NLD ISSN 0031-8035
BX9401
PHILOSOPHIA REFORMATA. Text in English. 1936. s-a. EUR 27.50 domestic to individuals; EUR 32.50 foreign to individuals; EUR 55 domestic to institutions; EUR 65 foreign to institutions (effective 2010). bk.rev. bibl. **Document type:** *Journal, Academic/Scholarly.* **Description:** Discusses issues pertaining to Reformation philosophy.
Indexed: A22, AmHI, CERDIC, FR, H07, IPB, MLA-IB, PCI, PhilInd, T02.
—IE, Infotrieve, INIST.
Published by: Stichting voor Reformatorische Wijsbegeerte/Association for Reformational Philosophy, Postbus 3206, Soest, 3760 DE, Netherlands. TEL 31-35-5880205, FAX 31-35-5880981.

100 NLD
PHILOSOPHIA SPINOZAE PERENNIS. Text in Dutch, English, French. 1976. irreg., latest vol.10, 2000. price varies. bibl. index. **Document type:** *Monographic series, Academic/Scholarly.*
Published by: Koninklijke Van Gorcum BV/Royal Van Gorcum BV, PO Box 43, Assen, 9400 AA, Netherlands. TEL 31-592-379555, FAX 31-592-372064, info@vangorcum.nl, http://www.vangorcum.nl.

100 CAN
PHILOSOPHICA. Text in English, French. 1972. irreg. price varies. **Document type:** *Monographic series, Academic/Scholarly.* **Description:** Books on various subjects in the field of philosophy.
Formerly: Collection Philosophica (0824-9474)
Published by: University of Ottawa Press/Presses de l'Universite d'Ottawa, 542 King Edward, Ottawa, ON K1N 6N5, Canada. TEL 613-562-5246, FAX 613-562-5247. Ed. Josiane Ayoub.

100 BEL ISSN 0379-8402
B63
PHILOSOPHICA. Text in Dutch, English, French, German. 1963. s-a. adv. bk.rev. **Document type:** *Journal, Academic/Scholarly.* **Description:** Journal of philosophical inquiry. Each volume is devoted to a current issue in epistemology, philosophy of science, ethics, or social philosophy.
Formerly (until 1974): Studia Philosophica Gandensia (0081-6833)
Indexed: A22, CCMJ, DIP, FR, IBR, IBZ, IPB, L&LBA, MSN, MathR, PhilInd, RILM, SociolAb.
—BLDSC (6461.635000), IE, Ingenta, INIST.
Published by: Universiteit Gent, Department of Philosophy and Moral Science, Blandijnberg 2, Gent, 9000, Belgium. TEL 32-9-2643785, FAX 32-9-2644187, erik.weber@rug.ac.be. Ed. Erik Weber. Circ: 300.

100 300 GBR ISSN 1386-9795
BD418.3
➤ **PHILOSOPHICAL EXPLORATIONS**; an international journal for the philosophy of mind and action. Text in English. 1998. 3/yr. GBP 198 combined subscription in United Kingdom to institutions (print & online eds.); EUR 262, USD 330 combined subscription to institutions (print & online eds.) (effective 2012). adv. back issues avail.; reprint service avail. from PSC. **Document type:** *Journal, Academic/Scholarly.* **Description:** Provides a forum for analytically minded philosophers interested in genuine dialogue with continental philosophy and the (social) sciences in the area of the philosophy of mind and action and related disciplines such as moral psychology, ethics, philosophical anthropology, social philosophy, political philosophy and philosophy of the social sciences.
Related titles: Online - full text ed.: ISSN 1741-5918. GBP 178 in United Kingdom to institutions; EUR 236, USD 296 to institutions (effective 2012) (from IngentaConnect).
Indexed: A01, A02, A03, A08, A20, A22, ArtHuCI, BrHumI, CA, E01, IBR, IBZ, P48, P53, P54, PQC, PhilInd, SCOPUS, T02, W07.
—IE, Ingenta. **CCC.**
Published by: Routledge (Subsidiary of: Taylor & Francis Group), 4 Park Sq, Milton Park, Abingdon, Oxon OX14 4RN, United Kingdom. TEL 44-20-70176000, FAX 44-20-70176336, subscriptions@tandf.co.uk, http://www.routledge.com. Ed. Anthonie Meijers. Adv. contact Linda Hann TEL 44-1344-779945. **Subscr. to:** Taylor & Francis Ltd., Journals Customer Service, Sheepen Pl, Colchester, Essex CO3 3LP, United Kingdom. TEL 44-20-70175544, FAX 44-20-70175198, tf.enquiries@tfinforma.com.

100 USA ISSN 0031-806X
B1
➤ **THE PHILOSOPHICAL FORUM.** Text in English. 1942. q. GBP 290 in United Kingdom to institutions; EUR 367 in Europe to institutions; USD 355 in the Americas to institutions; USD 567 elsewhere to institutions; GBP 333 combined subscription in United Kingdom to institutions (print & online eds.); EUR 422 combined subscription in Europe to institutions (print & online eds.); USD 409 combined subscription in the Americas to institutions (print & online eds.); USD 652 combined subscription elsewhere to institutions (print & online eds.) (effective 2012). adv. bibl.; illus. index. back issues avail.; reprint service avail. from PSC. **Document type:** *Journal, Academic/Scholarly.* **Description:** Examines various philosophical issues and dilemmas from an interdisciplinary standpoint.
Related titles: Online - full text ed.: ISSN 1467-9191. GBP 290 in United Kingdom to institutions; EUR 367 in Europe to institutions; USD 355 in the Americas to institutions; USD 567 elsewhere to institutions (effective 2012) (from IngentaConnect).
Indexed: A01, A02, A03, A08, A20, A22, A26, ASCA, AmHI, ArtHuCI, B04, BRD, CA, CurCont, DIP, E01, E08, FR, G08, H07, H08, H09, H10, H14, HAb, HumInd, I05, IBR, IBZ, IPB, MLA-IB, P02, P10, P30, P42, P48, P53, P54, PCI, PQC, PSA, PhilInd, R05, RASB, RI-1, RI-2, S09, SCOPUS, SociolAb, T02, W03, W07.
—BLDSC (6461.700000), IE, Infotrieve, Ingenta, INIST. **CCC.**
Published by: Wiley-Blackwell Publishing, Inc. (Subsidiary of: Wiley-Blackwell Publishing Ltd.), 111 River St, Hoboken, NJ 07030. TEL 201-748-6000, FAX 201-748-6088, info@wiley.com, http://www.wiley.com/WileyCDA/. Ed. Doug Lackey. Adv. contact Kristin McCarthy TEL 201-748-7683.

100 GBR ISSN 1758-1532
➤ **PHILOSOPHICAL FRONTIERS**; a journal of emerging thought. Text in English. 2006. s-a. GBP 22 domestic to individuals; GBP 24 in Europe to individuals; GBP 26 elsewhere to individuals; GBP 45 domestic to institutions; GBP 50 in Europe to institutions; GBP 55 elsewhere to institutions (effective 2009). back issues avail. **Document type:** *Journal, Academic/Scholarly.* **Description:** Features articles on all aspects of philosophy, especially those that deal with the intersection of philosophy with other academic disciplines.
Related titles: Online - full text ed.: ISSN 1758-1540. 2008.
Indexed: AmHI, H07, PhilInd, T02.
Published by: Progressive Frontiers Press, 30 Hayes Ct, Longford, Gloucester GL2 9AW, United Kingdom. TEL 44-79-75797403, Contact@progressivefrontiers.com, http://www.frontierspublications.com/. Ed. Richard H Corrigan.

105 GRC ISSN 1105-235X
B1
➤ **PHILOSOPHICAL INQUIRY**; international quarterly. Text in English, French, German. 1978. q. USD 60 (effective 2003). adv. bk.rev. bibl. back issues avail. **Document type:** *Journal, Academic/Scholarly.* **Description:** Examines Ancient Greek philosophy, theory of knowledge - epistemology, aesthetics, ethics, philosophy of language, and philosophy of literature.
Related titles: Diskette ed.; Large type ed.
Indexed: FR, PhilInd.
—IE, INIST.
Address: PO Box 3825, Central Post Office, Athens, 102 10, Greece. TEL 301-210-8022349, FAX 301-210-8022949. Ed. D Z Andriopoulos. Pub., R&P D.Z. Andriopoulos. Adv. contact Helen Andriopoulos. B&W page USD 60. Circ: 1,300.

P

100 GBR ISSN 0190-0536
B1
➤ **PHILOSOPHICAL INVESTIGATIONS.** Text in English. 1978. q. GBP 341 in United Kingdom to institutions; EUR 431 in Europe to institutions; USD 752 in the Americas to institutions; USD 877 elsewhere to institutions; GBP 393 combined subscription in United Kingdom to institutions (print & online eds.); EUR 496 combined subscription in Europe to institutions (print & online eds.); USD 865 combined subscription in the Americas to institutions (print & online eds.); USD 1,010 combined subscription elsewhere to institutions (print & online eds.) (effective 2012). adv. bk.rev. illus. index. back issues avail.; reprint service avail. from PSC. **Document type:** *Journal, Academic/Scholarly.* **Description:** Contains articles, discussion, critical notices and reviews on every branch of philosophy.
Related titles: Online - full text ed.: ISSN 1467-9205. GBP 341 in United Kingdom to institutions; EUR 431 in Europe to institutions; USD 752 in the Americas to institutions; USD 877 elsewhere to institutions (effective 2012) (from IngentaConnect).
Indexed: A01, A03, A08, A20, A21, A22, A26, ASCA, AmHI, ArtHuCI, CA, CurCont, E01, FR, H07, IPB, PCI, PhilInd, RASB, RI-1, RI-2, SCOPUS, SOPODA, SociolAb, T02, W07.
—BLDSC (6461.780000), IE, Infotrieve, Ingenta, INIST. **CCC.**
Published by: Wiley-Blackwell Publishing Ltd. (Subsidiary of: John Wiley & Sons, Inc.), 9600 Garsington Rd, Oxford, OX4 2DQ, United Kingdom. TEL 44-1865-776868, FAX 44-1865-714591, customerservices@blackwellpublishing.com. Ed. H O Mounce TEL 44-1792-295190. Adv. contact Craig Pickett TEL 44-1865-476267.

100 USA ISSN 1533-6077
PHILOSOPHICAL ISSUES. Text in English. 1991. a. USD 732 per issue in the Americas (print or online ed.); GBP 538 per issue in United Kingdom (print or online ed.); EUR 683 per issue in Europe (print or online ed.); USD 1,054 per issue elsewhere (print or online ed.); USD 805 combined subscription per issue in the Americas (print & online eds.); GBP 592 combined subscription per issue in United Kingdom (print & online eds.); EUR 752 combined subscription per issue in Europe (print & online eds.); USD 1,160 combined subscription per issue elsewhere (print & online eds.) (effective 2010); subscr. includes Philosophical Perspectives. adv. back issues avail.; reprint service avail. from PSC. **Document type:** *Journal, Academic/Scholarly.*
Related titles: Online - full text ed.: ISSN 1758-2237; ◆ Supplement to: Nous. ISSN 0029-4624.
Indexed: A01, A03, A08, A22, AmHI, CA, CCMJ, E01, FR, H07, L05, L06, MSN, MathR, PCI, PhilInd, T02, Z02.
—BLDSC (6461.789000), IE, INIST. **CCC.**
Published by: Wiley-Blackwell Publishing, Inc. (Subsidiary of: Wiley-Blackwell Publishing Ltd.), 111 River St, Hoboken, NJ 07030. TEL 201-748-6000, FAX 201-748-6088, info@wiley.com. Adv. contact Kristin McCarthy TEL 201-748-7683.

100 ITA ISSN 2037-6707
▼ **PHILOSOPHICAL NEWS.** Text in Italian. 2010. s-a. free (effective 2011). **Document type:** *Journal, Academic/Scholarly.*
Media: Online - full text.

100 ZAF ISSN 0556-8641
➤ **PHILOSOPHICAL PAPERS.** Text in English. 1972. 3/yr. GBP 130 combined subscription in United Kingdom to institutions (print & online eds.); EUR 189, USD 235 combined subscription to institutions (print & online eds.) (effective 2012). adv. back issues avail.; reprint service avail. from PSC. **Document type:** *Journal, Academic/Scholarly.* **Description:** An international journal of philosophy in the broad analytical tradition.
Related titles: CD-ROM ed.; Online - full text ed.: ISSN 1996-8523. GBP 118 in United Kingdom to institutions; EUR 170, USD 212 to institutions (effective 2012); Special ed(s).
Indexed: A20, AmHI, ArtHuCI, CA, CurCont, DIP, FR, H07, IBR, IBZ, ISAP, PCI, PhilInd, RASB, T02, W07.
—BLDSC (6462.200000), IE, Ingenta, INIST. **CCC.**
Address: c/o Dept of Philosophy, Rhodes University, PO Box 94, Grahamstown, 6140, South Africa. TEL 27-46-6038351. Ed. Ward E Jones. Circ: 400.

100 NGA
➤ **PHILOSOPHICAL PAPERS AND REVIEW.** Text in English. m. free (effective 2010). adv. **Document type:** *Journal, Academic/Scholarly.*
Media: Online - full text.
Published by: Academic Journals, PO Box 73023, Victoria Island, Lagos, Nigeria. service@academicjournals.org. Ed. Dr. Joseph Osei.

100 USA ISSN 1520-8583
B1
➤ **PHILOSOPHICAL PERSPECTIVES.** Text in English. 1987. a. USD 732 per issue in the Americas (print or online ed.); GBP 538 per issue in United Kingdom (print or online ed.); EUR 683 per issue in Europe (print or online ed.); USD 1,054 per issue elsewhere (print or online ed.); USD 805 combined subscription per issue in the Americas (print & online eds.); GBP 592 combined subscription per issue in United Kingdom (print & online eds.); EUR 752 combined subscription per issue in Europe (print & online eds.); USD 1,160 combined subscription per issue elsewhere (print & online eds.) (effective 2010); subscr. includes Nous & Philosophical Issues. adv. back issues avail.; reprint service avail. from PSC. **Document type:** *Journal, Academic/Scholarly.*
Related titles: Online - full text ed.: ISSN 1758-2245; ◆ Supplement to: Nous. ISSN 0029-4624.
Indexed: A01, A03, A08, A20, A22, ArtHuCI, CA, CCMJ, CurCont, E01, FR, MSN, MathR, PCI, PhilInd, SCOPUS, T02, W07, Z02.
—BLDSC (6462.255000), IE, INIST. **CCC.**
Published by: Wiley-Blackwell Publishing, Inc. (Subsidiary of: Wiley-Blackwell Publishing Ltd.), 111 River St, Hoboken, NJ 07030. TEL 201-748-6000, FAX 201-748-6088, info@wiley.com, http://www.wiley.com/. Adv. contact Kristin McCarthy TEL 201-748-7683.

100 USA ISSN 1742-8173
➤ **PHILOSOPHICAL PRACTICE**; client counseling, group facilitation, and organizational consulting. Text in English. 2005 (Mar.). 3/yr. USD 180 to institutions; free to members (effective 2009). adv. Index. back issues avail. **Document type:** *Journal, Academic/Scholarly.* **Description:** Covers substantive issues in the areas of client counseling, group facilitation, and organizational consulting.
Related titles: Online - full text ed.: ISSN 1742-8181.
Indexed: A01, A22, CA, E01, PhilInd, T02.
—IE, Ingenta. **CCC.**
Published by: American Philosophical Practitioners Association, The City College of New York, 160 Convent Ave, New York, NY 10031. TEL 212-650-7827, admin@appa.edu. Ed., Adv. contact Lou Marinoff TEL 212-650-7647. page USD 750.

190 NLD
➤ **PHILOSOPHICAL PROBLEMS TODAY/PROBLEMES PHILOSOPHIQUES D'AUJOURD'HUI.** Text in English, French. 1994. irreg., latest vol.3, 2004. price varies. **Document type:** *Monographic series, Academic/Scholarly.* **Description:** Publishes extensive discussions of topical philosophical problems.
Published by: (Institut International de Philosophie FRA), Springer Netherlands (Subsidiary of: Springer Science+Business Media), Van Godewijckstraat 30, Dordrecht, 3311 GX, Netherlands. TEL 31-78-6576050, FAX 31-78-6576474.

➤ **PHILOSOPHICAL PSYCHOLOGY.** *see* PSYCHOLOGY

100 GBR ISSN 0031-8094
➤ **THE PHILOSOPHICAL QUARTERLY.** Text in English. 1950. q. GBP 227 in United Kingdom to institutions; EUR 287 in Europe to institutions; USD 512 in the Americas to institutions; USD 597 elsewhere to institutions; GBP 249 combined subscription in United Kingdom to institutions (print & online eds.); EUR 315 combined subscription in Europe to institutions (print & online eds.); USD 563 combined subscription in the Americas to institutions (print & online eds.); USD 658 combined subscription elsewhere to institutions (print & online eds.) (effective 2012). adv. bk.rev. bibl.; illus. index. back issues avail.; reprint service avail. from PSC. **Document type:** *Journal, Academic/Scholarly.* **Description:** Provides articles from leading international scholars across the range of philosophical study.
Related titles: Microform ed.: (from PQC); Online - full text ed.: ISSN 1467-9213. GBP 222 in United Kingdom to institutions; EUR 281 in Europe to institutions; USD 501 in the Americas to institutions; USD 583 elsewhere to institutions (effective 2012) (from IngentaConnect).
Indexed: A01, A02, A03, A08, A20, A22, A25, A26, ASCA, AmHI, ArtHuCI, B04, BRD, CA, CCMJ, CurCont, DIP, E01, E08, FR, G08, H07, H08, H09, H10, H14, HAb, HumInd, I05, IBR, IBRH, IBZ, IPB, MLA, MLA-IB, MSN, MathR, P02, P10, P30, P48, P53, P54, PCI, PQC, PhilInd, R05, RASB, S02, S03, S08, S09, SCOPUS, SOPODA, SociolAb, T02, W03, W07, WBA, WMB.
—BLDSC (6462.300000), IE, Infotrieve, Ingenta, INIST. **CCC.**
Published by: (Scots Philosophical Club, University of St Andrews), Wiley-Blackwell Publishing Ltd. (Subsidiary of: John Wiley & Sons, Inc.), 9600 Garsington Rd, Oxford, OX4 2DQ, United Kingdom. TEL 44-1865-776868, FAX 44-1865-714591, customerservices@blackwellpublishing.com. Adv. contact Andy Patterson.

100 USA ISSN 0031-8108
B1
➤ **PHILOSOPHICAL REVIEW.** Text in English. 1892. q. USD 33 to individuals; USD 136 to institutions; USD 142 combined subscription to institutions (print & online eds.); USD 34 per issue to institutions (effective 2012). adv. bk.rev. bibl.; illus. index. back issues avail.; reprint service avail. from PSC. **Document type:** *Journal, Academic/Scholarly.* **Description:** Aims to publish scholarly work in all areas of analytic philosophy, with an emphasis on material of general interest to academic philosophers.
Related titles: Microform ed.: (from MIM, PMC, PQC); Online - full text ed.: ISSN 1558-1470. USD 119 to institutions (effective 2012).
Indexed: A01, A02, A03, A06, A08, A20, A22, A25, A26, AmHI, ArtHuCI, B14, BAS, BRD, BRI, CA, CBRI, CurCont, DIP, E08, FR, G08, H07, H08, H09, H10, H14, HAb, HumInd, I05, IBR, IBZ, IPB, MLA, MLA-IB, P02, P10, P13, P30, P48, P53, P54, PCI, PQC, PhilInd, R05, RASB, S02, S03, S05, S08, S09, S23, SCOPUS, SOPODA, SociolAb, T02, W03, W07.
—BLDSC (6462.700000), IE, Infotrieve, Ingenta, INIST. **CCC.**
Published by: (Cornell University, Sage School of Philosophy), Duke University Press, 905 W Main St, Ste 18 B, Durham, NC 27701. TEL 919-688-5134, 888-651-0122, FAX 919-688-2615, 888-651-0124, subscriptions@dukeupress.edu, http://www.dukeupress.edu.

190 NLD ISSN 0031-8116
B21 CODEN: PLSDA3
➤ **PHILOSOPHICAL STUDIES**; an international journal for philosophy in the analytic tradition. Text in English. 1950. 15/yr. (in 5 vols., 3 nos./vol.). EUR 2,488, USD 2,653 combined subscription to institutions (print & online eds.) (effective 2012). adv. bk.rev. illus. Index. back issues avail.; reprint service avail. from PSC. **Document type:** *Journal, Academic/Scholarly.* **Description:** Publishes work in analytical philosophy, particularly in epistemology, philosophical logic, the philosophy of language and ethics.
Related titles: Microform ed.: (from PQC); Online - full text ed.: ISSN 1573-0883 (from IngentaConnect).
Indexed: A01, A02, A03, A08, A20, A21, A22, A26, ASCA, AmHI, ArtHuCI, BibLing, CA, CCMJ, CPL, CurCont, DIP, E01, FR, H07, H14, I05, I13, IBR, IBRH, IBZ, IPB, L&LBA, MLA, MLA-IB, MSN, MathR, P10, P30, P42, P48, P53, P54, PCI, PQC, PhilInd, RASB, RI-1, RI-2, RefZh, S02, S03, SCOPUS, SOPODA, SociolAb, T02, W07.
—BLDSC (6462.900000), IE, Infotrieve, Ingenta, INIST. **CCC.**
Published by: Springer Netherlands (Subsidiary of: Springer Science+Business Media), Van Godewijckstraat 30, Dordrecht, 3311 GX, Netherlands. TEL 31-78-6576050, FAX 31-78-6576474, http://www.springer.com. Ed. Stewart Cohen.

100 300 NLD ISSN 0928-9518
PHILOSOPHICAL STUDIES IN CONTEMPORARY CULTURE. Text in English. 1992. irreg., latest vol.16, 2009. price varies. **Document type:** *Monographic series, Academic/Scholarly.* **Description:** Explores the philosophical issues, concerns, and controversies of contemporary culture.
—BLDSC (6462.932000).
Published by: Springer Netherlands (Subsidiary of: Springer Science+Business Media), Van Godewijckstraat 30, Dordrecht, 3311 GX, Netherlands. TEL 31-78-6576050, FAX 31-78-6576474. Ed. H Tristram Engelhardt Jr.

PHILOSOPHICAL STUDIES IN EDUCATION. *see* EDUCATION

215 NLD ISSN 1877-8542
▼ ➤ **PHILOSOPHICAL STUDIES IN SCIENCE AND RELIGION.** Text in English. 2009. irreg., latest vol.2, 2010. price varies. **Document type:** *Monographic series, Academic/Scholarly.*
Published by: Brill, PO Box 9000, Leiden, 2300 PA, Netherlands. TEL 31-71-5353500, FAX 31-71-5317532, cs@brill.nl. Ed. F LeRon Shults.

100 NLD ISSN 0921-8599
➤ **PHILOSOPHICAL STUDIES SERIES.** Text in English. 1974. irreg., latest vol.112, 2009. price varies. **Document type:** *Monographic series, Academic/Scholarly.*
Formerly (until 1987): Philosophical Studies Series in Philosophy (0169-7323)
Indexed: CCMJ, MathR.
—BLDSC (6462.937000), IE, Ingenta. **CCC.**
Published by: Springer Netherlands (Subsidiary of: Springer Science+Business Media), Van Godewijckstraat 30, Dordrecht, 3311 GX, Netherlands. TEL 31-78-6576050, FAX 31-78-6576474. Ed. Stephen Hetherington.

100 USA ISSN 0276-2080
B1
➤ **PHILOSOPHICAL TOPICS.** Text in English. 1970. s-a. USD 45 in US & Canada to individuals; USD 70 in US & Canada to institutions; USD 85 elsewhere to institutions (effective 2010). adv. illus. back issues avail.; reprints avail. **Document type:** *Journal, Academic/Scholarly.* **Description:** Features articles covering all aspects of philosophy.
Formerly (until 1981): Southwestern Journal of Philosophy (0038-481X)
Related titles: Online - full text ed.: ISSN 2154-154X. USD 195 (effective 2010).
Indexed: A20, A22, FR, IPB, MLA-IB, P30, PCI, PhilInd, RASB.
—BLDSC (6462.947000), IE, Infotrieve, Ingenta, INIST.
Published by: University of Arkansas Press, 105 N McIlroy Ave, Fayetteville, AR 72701. TEL 479-575-3246, 800-626-0090, FAX 479-575-6044. Ed. Edward Minar.

100 DEU ISSN 1860-8337
PHILOSOPHIE (BERLIN). Text in German. 2005. irreg., latest vol.2, 2009. price varies. **Document type:** *Monographic series, Academic/Scholarly.*
Published by: Frank und Timme GmbH, Wittelsbacherstr 27a, Berlin, 10707, Germany. TEL 49-30-88667911, FAX 49-30-86398731, info@frank-timme.de.

100 DEU
PHILOSOPHIE (MUNICH). Text in German. 1995. irreg., latest vol.27, 2010. price varies. **Document type:** *Monographic series, Academic/Scholarly.*
Published by: Herbert Utz Verlag GmbH, Adalbertstr 57, Munich, 80799, Germany. TEL 49-89-27779100, FAX 49-89-27779101, utz@utzverlag.com.

100 FRA ISSN 0294-1805
B2
PHILOSOPHIE (PARIS). Text in French. 1984. q. EUR 32 domestic; EUR 39 foreign (effective 2009). bk.rev. **Document type:** *Journal, Academic/Scholarly.* **Description:** Presents current philosophic works in the Anglo-Saxon world, original French works and interpretations of classical texts.
Indexed: A22, DIP, FR, IBR, IBZ, IPB, RILM.
—IE, Infotrieve, INIST.
Published by: Editions de Minuit, 7 rue Bernard Palissy, Paris, 75006, France. TEL 33-1-44393920, FAX 33-1-45448236, http://www.leseditionsdeminuit.com. Ed. Claude Romano.

100 FRA ISSN 1242-6326
PHILOSOPHIE (VILLENEUVE D'ASCQ). Text in French. 1991. irreg., latest 2009. proce varies. back issues avail. **Document type:** *Monographic series, Academic/Scholarly.*
Published by: Presses Universitaires du Septentrion, Rue du Barreau, BP 30199, Villeneuve d'Ascq, Cedex 59654, France. TEL 33-3-20416693, FAX 33-3-20416690, septentrion@septentrion.com, http://www.septentrion.com.

100 FRA ISSN 1634-4561
PHILOSOPHIE ANTIQUE. Text in Multiple languages. 2001. a. EUR 15 (effective 2009). **Document type:** *Journal, Academic/Scholarly.*
Indexed: IBR, IBZ, PhilInd.
Published by: Presses Universitaires du Septentrion, Rue du Barreau, BP 30199, Villeneuve d'Ascq, Cedex 59654, France. septentrion@septentrion.com, http://www.septentrion.com.

100 FRA ISSN 0768-0805
PHILOSOPHIE D'AUJOURD'HUI. Text in French. 1973. irreg., latest 2009. back issues avail. **Document type:** *Monographic series, Academic/Scholarly.*
Published by: Presses Universitaires de France, 6 Avenue Reille, Paris, 75685, France. TEL 33-1-58103161, FAX 33-1-45897530.

109 DEU ISSN 0943-5921
PHILOSOPHIE DER ANTIKE. Text in German. 1993. irreg., latest vol.30, 2010. price varies. **Document type:** *Monographic series, Academic/Scholarly.*
Published by: (Karl- und Gertrud-Abel-Stiftung), Franz Steiner Verlag GmbH, Birkenwaldstr 44, Stuttgart, 70191, Germany. TEL 49-711-25820, FAX 49-711-2582290, service@steiner-verlag.de, http://www.steiner-verlag.de. R&P Sabine Koerner.

100 DEU
PHILOSOPHIE DES LEBENS - PHILOSOPHIE DES GEISTES. Text in German. 2007. irreg., latest vol.2, 2007. price varies. **Document type:** *Monographic series, Academic/Scholarly.*
Published by: Wehrhahn Verlag, Am Mittelfelde 1, Hannover, 30519, Germany. TEL 49-511-8989806, FAX 49-511-8988245, info@wehrhahn-verlag.de.

174 BEL ISSN 1376-0939
PHILOSOPHIE ET POLITIQUE. Text in French. 1993. irreg., latest vol.18, 2009. price varies. **Document type:** *Monographic series, Academic/Scholarly.*
Related titles: English ed.: Philosophy and Politics. ISSN 1376-0920. 1993.
Published by: P I E - Peter Lang SA, 1 avenue Maurice, 6e etage, Brussels, 1050, Belgium. TEL 32-2-3477236, FAX 32-2-3477237, pie@peterlang.com, http://www.peterlang.net. Ed. Gabriel Fragniere.

100 FRA ISSN 0760-9620
PHILOSOPHIE IMAGINAIRE. Text in French. 1985. s-a. **Document type:** *Monographic series.*
Published by: Editions de L' Eclat, 4 Av. Hoche, Paris, 75008, France. TEL 33-1-45770404, FAX 33-1-45759251, infos@lyber-eclat.net.

100 DEU ISSN 1616-749X
PHILOSOPHIE IN GESCHICHTE UND GEGENWART. Text in German. 2004. irreg., latest vol.2, 2006. price varies. **Document type:** *Monographic series, Academic/Scholarly.*
Published by: Peter Lang GmbH (Subsidiary of: Peter Lang Publishing Group), Eschborner Landstr 42-50, Frankfurt Am Main, 60489, Germany. TEL 49-69-7807050, FAX 49-69-78070550, zentrale.frankfurt@peterlang.com.

100 DEU
PHILOSOPHIE INTERDISZIPLINAER. Text in German. 1999. irreg., latest vol.31, 2010. price varies. **Document type:** *Monographic series, Academic/Scholarly.*
Published by: (Kueser Akademie fuer Europaeische Geistesgeschichte e.V.), S. Roderer Verlag, In der Obern Au 12, Regensburg, 93055, Germany. TEL 49-941-7992270, FAX 49-941-795198, info@roderer-verlag.de.

100 DEU
PHILOSOPHIE INTERKULTURELL. Text in German. 2004. irreg. price varies. **Document type:** *Monographic series, Academic/Scholarly.*
Published by: Frommann-Holzboog Verlag e.K., Koenig-Karl-Str 27, Stuttgart, 70372, Germany. TEL 49-711-9559690, FAX 49-711-9559691, info@frommann-holzboog.de, http://www.frommann-holzboog.de.

100 FRA ISSN 1951-1787
PHILOSOPHIE MAGAZINE. Text in French. 2006. 10/yr. EUR 37 domestic; EUR 46 in Europe; EUR 47 in Africa; EUR 48 DOM-TOM; EUR 47 in the Middle East; EUR 47 in Asia; EUR 48 in North America; EUR 52 elsewhere (effective 2009). **Document type:** *Magazine, Consumer.*
Published by: Philo Editions, Philosophie Magazine, 10, rue Ballu, Paris, 75009, France.

100 DEU ISSN 1611-258X
PHILOSOPHIE, PHAENOMENOLOGIE UND HERMENEUTIK DER WERTE. Text in German. 2004. irreg., latest vol.4, 2009. price varies. **Document type:** *Monographic series, Academic/Scholarly.*
Published by: (Institut fuer Axiologische Forschungen/Institute for Axiological Research AUT), Peter Lang GmbH (Subsidiary of: Peter Lang Publishing Group), Eschborner Landstr 42-50, Frankfurt Am Main, 60489, Germany. TEL 49-69-7807050, FAX 49-69-78070550, zentrale.frankfurt@peterlang.com, http://www.peterlang.com. Ed. Yvanka Raynova.

100 FRA ISSN 2106-5489
▼ **PHILOSOPHIE PRATIQUE.** Text in French. 2010. q. EUR 9.87 (effective 2011). **Document type:** *Magazine, Consumer.*
Published by: Lafont Presse, 53 Rue du Chemin Vert, Boulogne-Billancourt, 92100, France. TEL 33-1-46102121, FAX 33-1-45792211, http://www.lafontpresse.fr.

215 DEU ISSN 0724-4479
PHILOSOPHIE UND GESCHICHTE DER WISSENSCHAFTEN; Studien und Quellen. Text in German. 1984. irreg., latest vol.70, 2009. price varies. **Document type:** *Monographic series, Academic/Scholarly.*
Published by: Peter Lang GmbH (Subsidiary of: Peter Lang Publishing Group), Eschborner Landstr 42-50, Frankfurt Am Main, 60489, Germany. TEL 49-69-7807050, FAX 49-69-78070550, zentrale.frankfurt@peterlang.com, http://www.peterlang.com. Eds. Hans Joerg Sandkuehler, Pirmin Stekeler-Weithofer.

100 DEU
PHILOSOPHIE UND GESELLSCHAFT. Text in German. 1994. irreg., latest vol.13, 2005. price varies. **Document type:** *Monographic series, Academic/Scholarly.*
Published by: Holos Verlag, Breite Str 47, Bonn, 53111, Germany. TEL 49-228-263020, FAX 49-228-212435, info@holos-verlag.de, http://www.holos-verlag.de.

100 DEU
PHILOSOPHIE UND REALISTISCHE PHAENOMENOLOGIE/ PHILOSOPHY AND REALIST PHENOMENOLOGY. Text in German. 1992. irreg., latest vol.18, 2007. price varies. **Document type:** *Monographic series, Academic/Scholarly.*
Published by: Universitaetsverlag Winter GmbH, Dossenheimer Landstr 13, Heidelberg, 69121, Germany. TEL 49-6221-770260, FAX 49-6221-770269, info@winter-verlag-hd.de, http://www.winter-verlag-hd.de.

100 DEU ISSN 0927-4405
PHILOSOPHIE & REPRAESENTATION/PHILOSOPHY & REPRESENTATION. Text in English, German. 1992. irreg., latest vol.11, 2006. price varies. back issues avail. **Document type:** *Monographic series, Academic/Scholarly.*
Published by: Verlag Koenigshausen und Neumann GmbH, Leistenstr 7, Wuerzburg, 97082, Germany. TEL 49-931-3298700, FAX 49-931-83620, info@koenigshausen-neumann.de, http://koenigshausen-neumann.gebhardt-riegel.de.

100 300 DEU ISSN 1618-467X
PHILOSOPHIE UND TRANSKULTURALITAET. Text in French, German. 2002. irreg., latest vol.8, 2010. price varies. **Document type:** *Monographic series, Academic/Scholarly.*
Published by: Peter Lang GmbH (Subsidiary of: Peter Lang Publishing Group), Eschborner Landstr 42-50, Frankfurt Am Main, 60489, Germany. TEL 49-69-7807050, FAX 49-69-78070550, zentrale.frankfurt@peterlang.com.

160 DEU ISSN 1617-3473
B1
PHILOSOPHIEGESCHICHTE UND LOGISCHE ANALYSE. Text in German. 1998. a. EUR 32 (effective 2004). **Document type:** *Monographic series, Academic/Scholarly.* **Description:** Provides a forum for articles in which classical philosophical texts are interpreted by drawing on the resources on modern formal logic.
Indexed: PhilInd.
Published by: Mentis Verlag GmbH, Schulze-Delitzsch-Str 19, Paderborn, 33100, Germany. TEL 49-5251-687902, FAX 49-5251-687905, webmaster@mentis.de, http://www.mentis.de.

100 FRA ISSN 0766-1398
PHILOSOPHIES. Text in French. 1984. irreg. back issues avail. **Document type:** *Monographic series, Academic/Scholarly.*
Published by: Presses Universitaires de France, 6 Avenue Reille, Paris, 75685, France. TEL 33-1-58103161, FAX 33-1-45897530.

190 NLD
PHILOSOPHIES OF THE CARIBBEAN. Text in English. irreg. price varies. **Document type:** *Monographic series, Academic/Scholarly.* **Description:** Publishes philosophical works about issues that concern the Caribbean region.
Related titles: ◆ Series of: Value Inquiry Book Series. ISSN 0929-8436.
Published by: Editions Rodopi B.V., Tijnmuiden 7, Amsterdam, 1046 AK, Netherlands. TEL 31-20-6114821, FAX 31-20-4472979, info@rodopi.nl. Ed. Dr. Eddy Souffrant. **Dist. by:** Rodopi - USA, 606 Newark Ave, 2nd fl, Kenilworth, NJ 07033. TEL 908-497-9031, FAX 908-497-9035.

100 CAN ISSN 0316-2923
B2
PHILOSOPHIQUES. Text in English. 1974. 2/yr. CAD 80 (effective 1998). **Document type:** *Journal, Academic/Scholarly.*
Indexed: A22, DIP, FR, IBR, IBZ, IPB, MLA-IB, PdeR, PhilInd.
—BLDSC (6464.059500), IE, Ingenta, INIST. **CCC.**
Published by: Editions Bellarmin, 165 rue Deslauriers, St Laurent, PQ H4N 2S4, Canada. TEL 514-745-4290.

100 370 DEU
PHILOSOPHISCH-PAEDAGOGISCHES FORUM. Text in German. 1999. irreg., latest vol.2, 2000. price varies. **Document type:** *Monographic series, Academic/Scholarly.*
Published by: Eusl-Verlagsgesellschaft mbH, Archenholdweg 16, Paderborn, 33100, Germany. TEL 49-5251-184099, FAX 49-5251-184102, Eusl-Verlag@eusl.de, http://www.eusl.de.

100 DEU ISSN 0175-6508
PHILOSOPHISCHE ABHANDLUNGEN. Text in German. 1957. irreg., latest vol.102, 2011. price varies. back issues avail. **Document type:** *Monographic series, Academic/Scholarly.* **Description:** Discusses various topics in philosophy.
Indexed: CCMJ, MSN, MathR.
—CCC.
Published by: Vittorio Klostermann, Frauenlobstr 22, Frankfurt Am Main, 60487, Germany. TEL 49-69-9708160, FAX 49-69-708038, verlag@klostermann.de, http://www.klostermann.de.

100 DEU
PHILOSOPHISCHE BROCKEN. Text in German. 1993. irreg., latest vol.4, 1998. price varies. **Document type:** *Monographic series, Academic/Scholarly.*
Published by: J.H. Roell, Wuerzburgerstr 16, Dettelbach, 97337, Germany. TEL 49-9324-99770, FAX 49-9324-99771, info@roell-verlag.de, http://www.roell-verlag.de.

100 DEU ISSN 1439-751X
PHILOSOPHISCHE GRENZGAENGE. Text in German. 2000. irreg. price varies. **Document type:** *Monographic series, Academic/Scholarly.*
Published by: Peter Lang GmbH (Subsidiary of: Peter Lang Publishing Group), Eschborner Landstr 42-50, Frankfurt Am Main, 60489, Germany. TEL 49-69-7807050, FAX 49-69-78070550, zentrale.frankfurt@peterlang.com. Ed. Rudolf Burger.

100 DEU ISSN 2190-4316
▼ **PHILOSOPHISCHE PRAXIS (HAMBURG).** Variant title: Schriftenreihe Philosophische Praxis. Text in German. 2010. irreg. price varies. **Document type:** *Monographic series, Academic/Scholarly.*
Published by: Verlag Dr. Kovac, Leverkusenstr 13, Hamburg, 22761, Germany. TEL 49-40-3988800, FAX 49-40-39888055, info@verlagdrkovac.de.

100 DEU ISSN 1867-1861
PHILOSOPHISCHE PRAXIS (KONSTANZ). Text in German. 2008. irreg. price varies. **Document type:** *Monographic series, Academic/Scholarly.*
Published by: Hartung-Gorre Verlag, Konstanz, 78465, Germany. TEL 49-7533-97227, FAX 49-7533-97228, Hartung.Gorre@t-online.de.

100 DEU ISSN 0031-8159
B3
➤ **PHILOSOPHISCHE RUNDSCHAU;** eine Zeitschrift fuer philosophische Kritik. Text in German. 1953. q. EUR 84 to individuals; EUR 169 to institutions; EUR 44 to students (effective 2012). adv. bk.rev. illus. cum.index. reprint service avail. from SCH. **Document type:** *Journal, Academic/Scholarly.* **Description:** Philosophical journal that follows international philosophical publications, outlines trends, examines schools and research programs.
Related titles: Online - full text ed.: ISSN 1868-7261. 2009 (from IngentaConnect).
Indexed: A20, A22, ASCA, ArtHuCI, BibInd, CurCont, DIP, FR, IBR, IBZ, IPB, MLA-IB, PCI, PhilInd, RASB, SCOPUS, W07.
—IE, Infotrieve, INIST. **CCC.**
Published by: Mohr Siebeck GmbH & Co. KG, Wilhelmstr 18, Tuebingen, 72074, Germany. TEL 49-7071-9230, FAX 49-7071-51104, info@mohr.de. Ed. Bernhard Waldenfels. Adv. contact Tilman Gaebler.

101 DEU ISSN 0935-6053
PHILOSOPHISCHE SCHRIFTEN. Text in German. 1988. irreg., latest vol.76, 2010. price varies. **Document type:** *Monographic series, Academic/Scholarly.*
Published by: Duncker und Humblot GmbH, Carl-Heinrich-Becker-Weg 9, Berlin, 12165, Germany. TEL 49-30-7900060, FAX 49-30-79000631, info@duncker-humblot.de.

100 DEU ISSN 0175-9574
PHILOSOPHISCHE TEXTE UND STUDIEN. Text in German, English. irreg., latest vol.106, 2009. price varies. **Document type:** *Monographic series, Academic/Scholarly.*
Published by: Georg Olms Verlag, Hagentorwall 7, Hildesheim, 31134, Germany. TEL 49-5121-15010, FAX 49-5121-150150, info@olms.de, http://www.olms.de.

100 DEU ISSN 1434-2650
PHILOSOPHISCHE UNTERSUCHUNGEN. Text in German. 1997. irreg., latest vol.26, 2010. price varies. **Document type:** *Monographic series, Academic/Scholarly.*
Published by: Mohr Siebeck GmbH & Co. KG, Wilhelmstr 18, Tuebingen, 72074, Germany. TEL 49-7071-9230, FAX 49-7071-51104, info@mohr.de.

100 DEU ISSN 0031-8175
PHILOSOPHISCHER LITERATURANZEIGER; Ein Referateorgan fuer die Neuerscheinungen der Philosophie und ihrer gesamten Grenzgebiete. Text in German. 1949. q. EUR 125 (effective 2011). adv. bk.rev. abstr.; bibl. index. back issues avail. **Document type:** *Journal, Academic/Scholarly.* **Description:** Includes elaborate reports of new books in philosophy and related fields, published in German and other languages. Also includes comparative philosophical essays.
Indexed: A22, DIP, IBR, IBZ, IPB, PCI, PhilInd, RASB, RILM.
—IE, Infotrieve.
Published by: Vittorio Klostermann, Frauenlobstr 22, Frankfurt Am Main, 60487, Germany. TEL 49-69-9708160, FAX 49-69-708038, verlag@klostermann.de. Eds. Stephan Nachtsheim, Ulrike Bardt. Circ: 590 (paid and controlled).

100 DEU ISSN 0031-8183
B3
➤ **PHILOSOPHISCHES JAHRBUCH.** Text in German. 1888. s-a. EUR 66; EUR 48 to students (effective 2010). bk.rev. abstr.; bibl. reprint service avail. from SCH. **Document type:** *Journal, Academic/Scholarly.* **Description:** Presents philosophical essays from theoretical and practical areas as well as historical analyses and discoveries.
Indexed: A20, A22, ASCA, ArtHuCI, CurCont, DIP, FR, IBR, IBRH, IBZ, IPB, MLA-IB, PCI, PhilInd, RASB, SCOPUS, W07.
—BLDSC (6464.470000), IE, Infotrieve, Ingenta, INIST. **CCC.**
Published by: (Goerres-Gesellschaft), Verlag Karl Alber, Hermann-Herder-Str 4, Freiburg, 79104, Germany. TEL 49-761-2717436, FAX 49-761-2717212, info@verlag-alber.de. Circ: 650.

100 GBR ISSN 0031-8191
B1
➤ **PHILOSOPHY.** Text in English. 1925. q. (plus two supplements). GBP 293, USD 538 to institutions; GBP 299, USD 550 combined subscription to institutions (print & online eds.) (effective 2009). adv. bk.rev. illus. index. back issues avail.; reprint service avail. from PSC. **Document type:** *Journal, Academic/Scholarly.* **Description:** Contains significant articles in the field of philosophy; also serves the philosophical interests of specialists in other fields and those of the general reader.
Formerly (until 1931): Journal of Philosophical Studies (1752-6795)
Related titles: Microform ed.: (from PQC); Online - full text ed.: ISSN 1469-817X. GBP 267, USD 489 to institutions (effective 2009); ◆ Supplement(s): Royal Institute of Philosophy Supplement. ISSN 1358-2461.
Indexed: A01, A02, A03, A08, A20, A21, A22, A26, AC&P, AmHI, ArtHuCI, B04, BAS, BRD, CA, CurCont, DIP, E01, E08, FR, G08, H07, H08, H09, H10, H14, HAb, HumInd, I05, IBR, IBRH, IBZ, IPB, M01, M02, MEA&I, MLA-IB, MSN, MathR, P02, P10, P28, P30, P48, P53, P54, PCI, PQC, PhilInd, PsycholAb, R05, RASB, RI-1, RI-2, S02, S03, S09, SCOPUS, SociolAb, T02, W03, W07.
—BLDSC (6464.500000), IE, Infotrieve, Ingenta, INIST. **CCC.**
Published by: (Royal Institute of Philosophy), Cambridge University Press, The Edinburgh Bldg, Shaftesbury Rd, Cambridge, CB2 8RU, United Kingdom. TEL 44-1223-312393, FAX 44-1223-315052, journals@cambridge.org, http://www.cambridge.org/uk. Ed. Anthony O'Hear. R&P Linda Nicol TEL 44-1223-325702. Adv. contact Rebecca Roberts TEL 44-1223-325083. page GBP 520, page USD 985. Circ: 2,000. **Subscr. to:** Cambridge University Press, 32 Ave of the Americas, New York, NY 10013. TEL 212-337-5000, FAX 212-691-3239, journals_subscriptions@cup.org.

100 GBR ISSN 1754-2596
PHILOSOPHY A-Z SERIES. Text in English. 2005. irreg., latest 2009. price varies. back issues avail. **Document type:** *Monographic series, Academic/Scholarly.* **Description:** Authoritative and concise alphabetical guides intoduce the central concepts of the various branches of philosophy.
Published by: Edinburgh University Press, 22 George Sq, Edinburgh, Scotland EH8 9LF, United Kingdom. TEL 44-131-6504218, FAX 44-131-6503286, journals@eup.ed.ac.uk, http://www.euppublishing.com. Ed. Oliver Leaman.

PHILOSOPHY AND EDUCATION. *see* EDUCATION

PHILOSOPHY AND FOUNDATIONS OF PHYSICS. *see* PHYSICS

100 809 USA ISSN 0190-0013
PN2 CODEN: PHILEL
➤ **PHILOSOPHY AND LITERATURE.** Text in English. 1976. s-a. USD 110 to institutions; USD 154 combined subscription to institutions (print & online eds.); USD 66 per issue to institutions (effective 2012). adv. bk.rev. bibl.; abstr.; illus. Index. 276 p./no.; back issues avail.; reprint service avail. from PSC. **Document type:** *Journal, Academic/Scholarly.* **Description:** Addresses fresh perspectives to two modes of inquiry through its effective interdisciplinary approach to the study of major literary and philosophical texts.
Related titles: Online - full text ed.: ISSN 1086-329X. USD 115 to institutions (effective 2012).
Indexed: A01, A03, A08, A20, A22, ABS&EES, AES, ASCA, AmHI, ArtHuCI, BEL&L, BRI, CA, CBRI, CRCL, CurCont, DIP, E01, FR, H07, H14, IBR, IBRH, IBT&D, IBZ, IPB, L&LBA, LCR, LIFT, MLA, MLA-IB, P02, P10, P28, P48, P53, P54, PCI, PQC, PhilInd, RASB, SCOPUS, SOPODA, SociolAb, T02, W07.
—BLDSC (6464.570000), IE, Infotrieve, Ingenta, INIST. **CCC.**
Published by: (Whitman College), The Johns Hopkins University Press, 2715 N Charles St, Baltimore, MD 21218. TEL 410-516-6900, FAX 410-516-6968. Eds. Denis Dutton TEL 643-366-7001, Garry L Hagberg TEL 845-758-7270. Pub. William M Breichner. **Subscr. to:** PO Box 19966, Baltimore, MD 21211. TEL 410-516-6987, 800-548-1784, FAX 410-516-3866, jrnlcirc@press.jhu.edu.

100 610 NLD ISSN 0376-7418
CODEN: PHIMDN
➤ **PHILOSOPHY AND MEDICINE.** Text in English. 1975. irreg., latest vol.106, 2009. price varies. **Document type:** *Monographic series, Academic/Scholarly.*
Indexed: A22.
—BLDSC (6464.580000), IE, Infotrieve, Ingenta. **CCC.**
Published by: Springer Netherlands (Subsidiary of: Springer Science+Business Media), Van Godewijckstraat 30, Dordrecht, 3311 GX, Netherlands. TEL 31-78-6576050, FAX 31-78-6576474. Ed. H Tristram Engelhardt Jr.

100 142.7 USA ISSN 0031-8205
B1 CODEN: PPHRAI
➤ **PHILOSOPHY AND PHENOMENOLOGICAL RESEARCH.** Abbreviated title: P P R. Text in English. 1940. bi-m. GBP 264 combined subscription in United Kingdom to institutions (print & online eds.); EUR 337 combined subscription in Europe to institutions (print & online eds.); USD 322 combined subscription in the Americas to institutions (print & online eds.); USD 518 combined subscription elsewhere to institutions (print & online eds.) (effective 2012). adv. bk.rev. illus. 256 p./no. 1 cols./p.; back issues avail.; reprint service avail. from PSC. **Document type:** *Journal, Academic/Scholarly.* **Description:** Publishes articles in a wide range of areas including philosophy of mind, epistemology, ethics, metaphysics, and philosophical history of philosophy.
Related titles: Microform ed.: (from PQC); Online - full text ed.: ISSN 1933-1592. GBP 205 in United Kingdom to institutions; EUR 261 in Europe to institutions; USD 253 in the Americas to institutions; USD 401 elsewhere to institutions (effective 2012) (from IngentaConnect).
Indexed: A01, A02, A03, A08, A20, A21, A22, A25, A26, ABS&EES, ASCA, AmHI, ArtHuCI, B04, BRD, CA, CurCont, DIP, E01, E08, G08, H07, H08, H09, H10, HAb, HumInd, I05, IBR, IBRH, IBZ, IPB, L&LBA, MEA&I, MLA, MLA-IB, P30, PCI, PhilInd, PsycholAb, R05, RASB, RI-1, RI-2, RILM, S02, S03, S08, S09, SCOPUS, SOPODA, SociolAb, T02, W03, W07.
—BLDSC (6464.600000), IE, Infotrieve, Ingenta. **CCC.**
Published by: Wiley-Blackwell Publishing, Inc. (Subsidiary of: Wiley-Blackwell Publishing Ltd.), 111 River St, Hoboken, NJ 07030. TEL 201-748-6000, FAX 201-748-6088, info@wiley.com, http://www.wiley.com/WileyCDA/. Ed. Ernest Sosa. Adv. contact Kristin McCarthy TEL 201-748-7683.

P

100 150 NLD
PHILOSOPHY AND PSYCHOLOGY. Text in English. irreg. price varies. **Document type:** *Monographic series, Academic/Scholarly.* **Description:** Publishes philosophical works on the humanistic and valuational areas of psychology.
Related titles: ◆ Series of: Value Inquiry Book Series. ISSN 0929-8436.
Published by: Editions Rodopi B.V., Tijnmuiden 7, Amsterdam, 1046 AK, Netherlands. TEL 31-20-6114821, FAX 31-20-4472979, info@rodopi.nl. Ed. Mark Letteri. **Dist. by:** Rodopi - USA, 606 Newark Ave, 2nd fl, Kenilworth, NJ 07033. TEL 908-497-9031, FAX 908-497-9035.

100 USA
H1
PHILOSOPHY AND PUBLIC POLICY QUARTERLY. Text in English. 1981. q. free (effective 2011). back issues avail. **Document type:** *Journal, Academic/Scholarly.* **Description:** Covers philosophical debate on current public policy choices.
Former titles (until 2001): Institute for Philosophy and Public Policy. Report (1067-2478); (until 1990): Qq (0735-8555)
Related titles: Online - full text ed.: free (effective 2011).
Indexed: A39, AmHI, BRD, C27, C29, D03, D04, E13, P30, PhilInd, R03, R14, RGAb, RGPR, S14, S15, S18, SCOPUS, W03, W05.
—IE, Infotrieve, Ingenta.
Published by: Institute for Philosophy and Public Policy, University of Maryland, 2101 Van Munching Hall, College Park, MD 20742. TEL 301-405-6330, FAX 301-403-4675.

PHILOSOPHY AND RELIGION (AMSTERDAM). *see* RELIGIONS AND THEOLOGY

210 NLD ISSN 0924-7904
➤ **PHILOSOPHY AND RELIGION (LEIDEN);** a comparative yearbook. Text in English. 1989. irreg., latest vol.4, 1998. price varies. back issues avail. **Document type:** *Journal, Academic/Scholarly.* **Description:** Scholarly contributions on topics in comparative religion and philosophy.
Indexed: IBR, IBZ, IZBG.
—BLDSC (6464.680000).
Published by: Brill, PO Box 9000, Leiden, 2300 PA, Netherlands. TEL 31-71-5353500, FAX 31-71-5317532, cs@brill.nl, http://www.brill.nl. Ed. Shlomo Biderman. R&P Elizabeth Venekamp. **Dist. in N. America by:** Brill, PO Box 605, Herndon, VA 20172-0605. TEL 703-661-1585, 800-337-9255, FAX 703-661-1501, cs@brillusa.com; **Dist. by:** Turpin Distribution Services Ltd., Pegasus Dr, Stratton Business Park, Biggleswade, Bedfordshire SG18 8QB, United Kingdom. TEL 44-1767-604954, FAX 44-1767-601640, custserv@turpin-distribution.com, http://www.turpin-distribution.com/.

100 USA ISSN 0031-8213
B1
➤ **PHILOSOPHY AND RHETORIC.** Abbreviated title: P & R. Text in English. 1968. q. USD 165 combined subscription to institutions (print & online eds.) (effective 2012). adv. bk.rev. bibl.; illus. index. back issues avail.; reprint service avail. from PSC. **Document type:** *Journal, Academic/Scholarly.* **Description:** Brings out articles on the relations between philosophy and rhetoric.
Related titles: Microform ed.: (from PQC); Online - full text ed.: ISSN 1527-2079. 1968. USD 118 to institutions (effective 2012).
Indexed: A20, A21, A22, AES, ASCA, AmHI, ArtHuCI, CA, CMM, CurCont, DIP, E01, FR, H07, IBR, IBRH, IBZ, IJCS, IPB, MLA, MLA-IB, PCI, PhilInd, RASB, RI-1, RI-2, S02, S03, SCOPUS, SOPODA, SociolAb, T02, W07.
—BLDSC (6464.800000), IE, Infotrieve, Ingenta, INIST. **CCC.**
Published by: Pennsylvania State University Press, 820 N University Dr, University Support Bldg 1, Ste C, University Park, PA 16802. TEL 814-865-1327, 800-326-9180, FAX 814-863-1408, info@psupress.org. Eds. Gerard A Hauser, Kendra Boileau. Adv. contact Brian Beer TEL 814-863-5992. **Dist. by:** The Johns Hopkins University Press, PO Box 19966, Baltimore, MD 21211. TEL 410-516-6987, 800-548-1784, FAX 410-516-3866, jrnlcirc@press.jhu.edu, https://www.press.jhu.edu/.

100 300 GBR ISSN 0191-4537
AS30
➤ **PHILOSOPHY & SOCIAL CRITICISM**; an international, interdisciplinary journal. Text in English. 1973. 9/yr. USD 1,973, GBP 1,066 combined subscription to institutions (print & online eds.); USD 1,934, GBP 1,045 to institutions (effective 2011). adv. bk.rev. illus. index. back issues avail.; reprint service avail. from PSC. **Document type:** *Journal, Academic/Scholarly.* **Description:** Presents original theoretical contributions to the latest developments in social and political thought, emphasizing the contributions of continental scholarship as it affects international theoretical developments.
Formerly (until 1978): Cultural Hermeneutics (0011-2860)
Related titles: Online - full text ed.: ISSN 1461-734X. USD 1,776, GBP 959 to institutions (effective 2011).
Indexed: A01, A03, A08, A20, A22, ABS&EES, AltPI, ArtHuCI, B07, CA, DIP, E01, FR, H04, I13, IBR, IBSS, IBZ, IBibSS, IPB, LeftInd, MLA-IB, P42, PCI, PSA, PerIslam, PhilInd, RASB, RI-1, RI-2, S02, S03, SCOPUS, SOPODA, SSA, SociolAb, T02, V02, W07.
—BLDSC (6464.810000), IE, Infotrieve, Ingenta, INIST. **CCC.**
Published by: Sage Publications Ltd. (Subsidiary of: Sage Publications, Inc.), 1 Oliver's Yard, 55 City Rd, London, EC1Y 1SP, United Kingdom. TEL 44-20-73248500, FAX 44-20-73248600, info@sagepub.co.uk, http://www.uk.sagepub.com/home.nav. Ed. David Rasmussen. adv.: B&W page GBP 400; 130 x 205. **Subscr. to:** Sage Publications, Inc., 2455 Teller Rd, Thousand Oaks, CA 91320. TEL 805-499-9774, FAX 805-499-0871, journals@sagepub.com.

➤ **PHILOSOPHY & TECHNOLOGY.** *see* SOCIAL SCIENCES: COMPREHENSIVE WORKS

➤ **PHILOSOPHY AND TECHNOLOGY.** *see* TECHNOLOGY: COMPREHENSIVE WORKS

210 USA ISSN 0890-2461
B1
➤ **PHILOSOPHY & THEOLOGY.** Text in English. 1986. s-a. USD 40; free to members (effective 2009). back issues avail.; reprint service avail. from PSC. **Document type:** *Journal, Academic/Scholarly.* **Description:** Addresses all areas of interest to both philosophy and theology.
Related titles: CD-ROM ed.: Philosophy & Theology on CD-ROM: Volumes 1-10; Diskette ed.: USD 15 domestic; USD 25 foreign; Online - full text ed.: ISSN 2153-828X. USD 56 to individuals; USD 120 to institutions (effective 2009).
Indexed: A01, A03, A08, A21, A26, CA, DIP, E08, G08, I05, IBR, IBZ, MLA-IB, P30, PCI, PhilInd, R05, RI-1, RI-2, S09, T02.
—IE. **CCC.**
Published by: Philosophy Documentation Center, PO Box 7147, Charlottesville, VA 22906. TEL 434-220-3300, FAX 434-220-3301, order@pdcnet.org, http://www.pdcnet.org. Ed. James B South. R&P George Leaman. Adv. contact Greg Swope.

100 305.4 NLD
PHILOSOPHY AND WOMEN. Text in English. irreg. price varies. **Document type:** *Monographic series, Academic/Scholarly.* **Description:** Explores intersections between philosophy and women's studies, including feminist philosophy, the works of women philosophers, and philosophical analyses of women's issues.
Related titles: ◆ Series of: Value Inquiry Book Series. ISSN 0929-8436.
Published by: Editions Rodopi B.V., Tijnmuiden 7, Amsterdam, 1046 AK, Netherlands. TEL 31-20-6114821, FAX 31-20-4472979, info@rodopi.nl. Ed. Adrianne McEvoy. **Dist. by:** Rodopi - USA, 606 Newark Ave, 2nd fl, Kenilworth, NJ 07033. TEL 908-497-9031, FAX 908-497-9035.

100 GBR ISSN 2046-9632
PHILOSOPHY AT CAMBRIDGE. Text in English. 2004. a. free to qualified personnel (effective 2011). **Document type:** *Newsletter, Trade.*
Related titles: Online - full text ed.: ISSN 2046-9640.
Published by: University of Cambridge, Faculty of Philosophy, Sidgwick Ave, Cambridge, CB3 9DA, United Kingdom. TEL 44-1223-335090, FAX 44-1223-335091, phil-admin@lists.cam.ac.uk, http://www.phil.cam.ac.uk.

100 USA ISSN 1747-9991
B1
➤ **PHILOSOPHY COMPASS.** Text in English. 2006. m. GBP 561 in United Kingdom to institutions; EUR 714 in Europe to institutions; USD 445 in the Americas to institutions; USD 1,100 elsewhere to institutions (effective 2012). back issues avail. **Document type:** *Journal, Academic/Scholarly.* **Description:** Combines an extensive online reference library with original articles.
Media: Online - full text.
Indexed: A22, A26, BrHumI, E01, PhilInd.
—BLDSC (6464.835550), IE. **CCC.**
Published by: Wiley-Blackwell Publishing, Inc. (Subsidiary of: Wiley-Blackwell Publishing Ltd.), 111 River St, Hoboken, NJ 07030. TEL 201-748-6000, FAX 201-748-6088, info@wiley.com. Ed. Brian Weatherson.

100 USA ISSN 0031-8221
B1
➤ **PHILOSOPHY EAST AND WEST**; a quarterly of comparative philosophy. Abbreviated title: P E W. Text in English. 1951. q. USD 40 domestic to individuals; USD 88 foreign to individuals; USD 80 domestic to institutions; USD 128 foreign to institutions; USD 20 per issue domestic to individuals; USD 32 per issue foreign to individuals; USD 25 per issue domestic to institutions; USD 37 per issue foreign to institutions (effective 2009). adv. bk.rev. illus. index. back issues avail.; reprint service avail. from PSC. **Document type:** *Journal, Academic/Scholarly.* **Description:** Focuses on comparative and Asian philosophy.
Related titles: Microform ed.: (from PQC); Online - full text ed.: ISSN 1529-1898. 2001.
Indexed: A01, A02, A03, A08, A20, A21, A22, A25, A26, ASCA, AmHI, ArtHuCI, B04, BAS, BRD, C12, CA, CurCont, DIP, E01, E08, FR, FamI, G08, H07, H08, H09, H10, H14, HAb, HumInd, I05, I07, I14, IBR, IBRH, IBSS, IBZ, IPB, L&LBA, L05, L06, M01, M02, MEA&I, MLA, MLA-IB, P02, P10, P13, P28, P30, P48, P53, P54, PCI, PQC, PerIslam, PhilInd, R&TA, R05, RASB, RI-1, RI-2, RILM, S02, S03, S07, S08, S09, S23, SCOPUS, SOPODA, SociolAb, T02, W03, W05, W07.
—BLDSC (6464.850000), IE, Infotrieve, Ingenta. **CCC.**
Published by: University of Hawaii Press, Journals Department, 2840 Kolowalu St, Honolulu, HI 96822. TEL 808-956-8255, FAX 808-988-6052, uhpbooks@hawaii.edu. Ed. Roger T Ames. R&P Joel Bradshaw TEL 808-956-6790. Adv. contact Norman Kaneshiro TEL 808-956-8833. page USD 200; 5 x 8. Circ: 775.

➤ **PHILOSOPHY, ETHICS, AND HUMANITIES IN MEDICINE.** *see* MEDICAL SCIENCES

170 GBR ISSN 2043-0736
PHILOSOPHY FOR BUSINESS. Text in English. 2003 (Nov.). m. free (effective 2011). back issues avail. **Document type:** *Journal, Trade.* **Description:** Features articles about philosophical and ethical aspects of business practice.
Media: Online - full text.
Published by: International Society for Philosophers, 45 Wolseley Rd, Sheffield, S8 0ZT, United Kingdom. TEL 44-114-2558631, http://www.isfp.co.uk. Ed. Geoffrey Klempner.

100 DEU
PHILOSOPHY IN INTERNATIONAL CONTEXT/PHILOSOPHIE IM INTERNATIONALEN KONTEXT. Text in German, English. 2006. irreg., latest vol.5, 2009. EUR 24.90 per vol. (effective 2009). **Document type:** *Monographic series, Academic/Scholarly.*
Published by: Lit Verlag, Grevener Str/Fresnostr 2, Muenster, 48159, Germany. TEL 49-251-235091, FAX 49-251-231972, lit@lit-verlag.de. Ed. Hans Lenk.

190 NLD
PHILOSOPHY IN LATIN AMERICA. Text in English. irreg. price varies. **Document type:** *Monographic series, Academic/Scholarly.*
Related titles: ◆ Series of: Value Inquiry Book Series. ISSN 0929-8436.
Published by: Editions Rodopi B.V., Tijnmuiden 7, Amsterdam, 1046 AK, Netherlands. TEL 31-20-6114821, FAX 31-20-4472979, info@rodopi.nl. Ed. Dr. Arleen Salles. **Dist. by:** Rodopi - USA, 606 Newark Ave, 2nd fl, Kenilworth, NJ 07033. TEL 908-497-9031, FAX 908-497-9035.

100 CAN ISSN 1206-5269
B1
PHILOSOPHY IN REVIEW/COMPTES RENDUS PHILOSOPHIQUES. Text in English, French. 1981. 6/yr. CAD 54 domestic to individuals; USD 56 in United States to individuals; USD 58, EUR 63 elsewhere to individuals; CAD 112 domestic to institutions; USD 117 in United States to institutions; USD 118, EUR 125 elsewhere to institutions; CAD 40 domestic to students; USD 45 in United States to students; USD 48, EUR 54 elsewhere to students (effective 2003). adv. bk.rev.; software rev. **Document type:** *Journal, Academic/Scholarly.* **Description:** Book review journal for recent work in philosophy.
Formerly: Canadian Philosophical Reviews (0228-491X)
Indexed: A26, BRI, CBRI, CWPI, DIP, E08, I05, IBR, IBZ, IPB, PhilInd, S09.
—BLDSC (6464.999000), IE, Ingenta. **CCC.**
Published by: Academic Printing and Publishing, 9-3151 Lakeshore Road, Ste 403, Kelowna, BC V1W 3S7, Canada. TEL 250-764-6427, FAX 250-764-6428, app@silk.net. R&P, Adv. contact Sharon Pfenning. Circ: 250.

190 NLD
PHILOSOPHY IN SPAIN. Text in English. irreg. price varies. **Document type:** *Monographic series, Academic/Scholarly.*
Related titles: ◆ Series of: Value Inquiry Book Series. ISSN 0929-8436.
Published by: Editions Rodopi B.V., Tijnmuiden 7, Amsterdam, 1046 AK, Netherlands. TEL 31-20-6114821, FAX 31-20-4472979, info@rodopi.nl. Ed. John R Welch. **Dist. by:** Rodopi - USA, 606 Newark Ave, 2nd fl, Kenilworth, NJ 07033. TEL 908-497-9031, FAX 908-497-9035.

100 USA ISSN 1077-1999
B791
➤ **PHILOSOPHY IN THE CONTEMPORARY WORLD.** Text in English. 1993. s-a. USD 55 to institutions; free to members (effective 2010). adv. back issues avail. **Document type:** *Journal, Academic/Scholarly.* **Description:** Provides a venue for continuing dialogues in applied philosophy, philosophy and public policy, philosophy of the professions, race and gender studies, environmental philosophy, educational philosophy, and a range of multi-cultural issues.
Related titles: Online - full text ed.: ISSN 2153-3377. USD 165 to institutions (effective 2010).
Indexed: A01, A03, A08, AmHI, CA, DIP, H07, IBR, IBSS, IBZ, P42, PSA, PhilInd, S02, S03, SociolAb, T02.
Published by: (Society for Philosophy in the Contemporary World), Philosophy Documentation Center, PO Box 7147, Charlottesville, VA 22906. TEL 434-220-3300, FAX 434-220-3301, order@pdcnet.org, http://www.pdcnet.org. Ed. Andrew Fiala. Adv. contact Greg Swope.

100 GBR ISSN 0961-5970
B1
PHILOSOPHY NOW; a magazine of ideas. Text in English. 1991. bi-m. GBP 24 combined subscription domestic to institutions (print & online eds.); USD 55 combined subscription in United States to institutions (print & online eds.); CAD 86 combined subscription in Canada to institutions (print & online eds.); AUD 96 combined subscription in Australia to institutions (print & online eds.); NZD 106 combined subscription in New Zealand to institutions (print & online eds.); EUR 46 combined subscription in Europe to institutions (print & online eds.); GBP 37 combined subscription elsewhere to institutions (print & online eds.) (effective 2010). adv. bk.rev.; film rev. illus. 56 p./no.; back issues avail. **Document type:** *Magazine, Consumer.* **Description:** Contains articles on all aspects of Western philosophy, as well as book reviews, letters, news, cartoons, and the occasional short story.
Related titles: Online - full text ed.: ISSN 2044-9992.
Indexed: AmHI, BrHumI, CA, DIP, H07, IBR, IBZ, PhilInd, SCOPUS, T02.
—BLDSC (6464.956500), IE, Ingenta. **CCC.**
Address: 43a Jerningham Rd, London, SE14 5NQ, United Kingdom. TEL 44-20-76397314, FAX 44-20-76397314. Ed. Rick Lewis. Adv. contact Jay Sanders.

100 370.1 NLD
PHILOSOPHY OF EDUCATION. Text in English. irreg. price varies. **Document type:** *Monographic series, Academic/Scholarly.*
Related titles: ◆ Series of: Value Inquiry Book Series. ISSN 0929-8436.
Published by: Editions Rodopi B.V., Tijnmuiden 7, Amsterdam, 1046 AK, Netherlands. TEL 31-20-6114821, FAX 31-20-4472979, info@rodopi.nl. Eds. George Allan, Malcolm D Evans. **Dist. by:** Rodopi - USA, 606 Newark Ave, 2nd fl, Kenilworth, NJ 07033. TEL 908-497-9031, FAX 908-497-9035.

301 NLD ISSN 0922-6001
➤ **PHILOSOPHY OF HISTORY AND CULTURE.** Text in English. 1988. irreg., latest vol.27, 2008. price varies. back issues avail. **Document type:** *Monographic series, Academic/Scholarly.*
Indexed: IZBG.
—BLDSC (6464.950500).
Published by: Brill, PO Box 9000, Leiden, 2300 PA, Netherlands. TEL 31-71-5353500, FAX 31-71-5317532, cs@brill.nl, http://www.brill.nl. Ed. Michael Krausz. R&P Elizabeth Venekamp. **Dist. in N. America by:** Brill, PO Box 605, Herndon, VA 20172-0605. TEL 703-661-1585, 800-337-9255, FAX 703-661-1501, cs@brillusa.com; **Dist. by:** Turpin Distribution Services Ltd., Pegasus Dr, Stratton Business Park, Biggleswade, Bedfordshire SG18 8QB, United Kingdom. TEL 44-1767-604954, FAX 44-1767-601640, custserv@turpin-distribution.com, http://www.turpin-distribution.com/.

100 658 GBR ISSN 1740-3812
HD28
➤ **PHILOSOPHY OF MANAGEMENT.** Text in English. 2001. 3/yr. GBP 35, EUR 56, USD 68 to individuals; GBP 250, EUR 400, USD 487 to institutions (effective 2009). bk.rev.; film rev.; software rev.; video rev. back issues avail. **Document type:** *Journal, Academic/Scholarly.* **Description:** Offers a forum for philosophically informed thinking about management in theory and practice. It seeks to define and develop the field of philosophy of management.
Formerly (until 2003): Reason in Practice (1473-589X)
Published by: Reason in Practice Limited, PO Box 217, Oxted, Surrey RH8 8AJ, United Kingdom. TEL 44-1883-715419, FAX 44-1883-717015. Ed., Pub. Nigel Laurie.

➤ **PHILOSOPHY OF MUSIC EDUCATION REVIEW.** *see* MUSIC

➤ **PHILOSOPHY OF PEACE.** *see* POLITICAL SCIENCE—International Relations

➤ **PHILOSOPHY OF SCIENCE.** *see* SCIENCES: COMPREHENSIVE WORKS

100 152.4 NLD
PHILOSOPHY OF SEX AND LOVE. Text in English. irreg. price varies. **Document type:** *Monographic series, Academic/Scholarly.* **Description:** Publishes philosophical works dealing with sexuality, love, friendship, gender, marriage, and related topics.
Related titles: ◆ Series of: Value Inquiry Book Series. ISSN 0929-8436.
Published by: Editions Rodopi B.V., Tijnmuiden 7, Amsterdam, 1046 AK, Netherlands. TEL 31-20-6114821, FAX 31-20-4472979, info@rodopi.nl. Ed. Adrianne McEvoy. **Dist. by:** Rodopi - USA, 606 Newark Ave, 2nd fl, Kenilworth, NJ 07033. TEL 908-497-9031, FAX 908-497-9035.

PHILOSOPHY OF THE SOCIAL SCIENCES. *see* SOCIAL SCIENCES: COMPREHENSIVE WORKS

100 GBR ISSN 2043-0728
PHILOSOPHY PATHWAYS; electronic journal. Text in English. 2001 (Jan.). m. free (effective 2011). back issues avail. **Document type:** *Journal, Academic/Scholarly.* **Description:** Contains articles on a philosophical topic.
Media: Online - full text.
Published by: International Society for Philosophers, 45 Wolseley Rd, Sheffield, S8 0ZT, United Kingdom. TEL 44-114-2558631, http://www.isfp.co.uk. Ed. Geoffrey Klempner.

616.89001 USA ISSN 1071-6076
RC437.5
➤ **PHILOSOPHY, PSYCHIATRY & PSYCHOLOGY.** Abbreviated title: P P P. Text in English. 1994. q. USD 190 to institutions (print or online ed.); USD 266 combined subscription to institutions (print & online eds.); USD 57 per issue to institutions (effective 2011). adv. bk.rev. illus. 92 p./no.; back issues avail.; reprint service avail. from PSC. **Document type:** *Journal, Academic/Scholarly.* **Description:** Focuses on the overlap among three fields, making clinical material and theory more accessible to philosophers.
Related titles: Online - full text ed.: ISSN 1086-3303. 1996.
Indexed: A01, A03, A08, A22, CA, CJPI, DIP, E-psyche, E01, H14, IBR, IBZ, P03, P10, P12, P25, P28, P30, P48, P53, P54, PCI, PQC, PhilInd, PsycInfo, PsycholAb, T02.
—BLDSC (6464.980000), GNLM, IE, Infotrieve, Ingenta. **CCC.**
Published by: (Association for the Advancement of Philosophy and Psychiatry), The Johns Hopkins University Press, 2715 N Charles St, Baltimore, MD 21218. TEL 410-516-6900, FAX 410-516-6968, bjs@press.jhu.edu. Ed. John Z Sadler. Pub. William M Breichner. Circ: 213. **Subscr. to:** PO Box 19966, Baltimore, MD 21211. TEL 410-516-6987, 800-548-1784, FAX 410-516-3866, jrnlcirc@press.jhu.edu. **Co-sponsors:** Royal College of Psychiatrists Philosophy Group, Royal Institute of Philosophy; Association for the Advancement of Philosophy and Psychiatry.

100 USA ISSN 2159-5313
▼ ➤ **PHILOSOPHY STUDY.** Text in English. 2011. m.
Related titles: Online - full text ed.: ISSN 2159-5321.
Published by: David Publishing Co., Inc., 1840 Industrial Dr, Ste 160, Libertyville, IL 60048. TEL 847-281-9822, FAX 847-281-9855, order@davidpublishing.com, http://www.davidpublishing.com.

100 USA ISSN 0031-8256
B1
➤ **PHILOSOPHY TODAY.** Text in English. 1957. q. USD 50 domestic; USD 61 foreign (effective 2010). adv. bk.rev. illus. index. Supplement avail.; back issues avail.; reprints avail. **Document type:** *Journal, Academic/Scholarly.*
Related titles: Microform ed.: (from PQC); Online - full text ed.
Indexed: A01, A02, A03, A08, A20, A22, A25, A26, ASCA, AmHI, ArtHuCI, B04, BRD, CA, CPL, CurCont, E08, FR, G08, H07, H08, H09, H10, H14, HAb, HumInd, I05, IPB, M01, M02, MLA-IB, P02, P10, P13, P28, P48, P53, P54, PCI, PQC, PhilInd, R05, RASB, S08, S09, SCOPUS, T02, W03, W07.
—BLDSC (6465.090000), IE, Infotrieve, Ingenta, INIST.
Published by: DePaul University, Department of Philosophy, 2352 North Clifton Ave, Chicago, IL 60614. TEL 773-325-7267, FAX 773-325-7268. Ed. David Pellauer. Circ: 1,180.

▼ ➤ **PHILOSOPHY AND THEORY IN BIOLOGY.** *see* BIOLOGY

180 NLD ISSN 0031-8868
B1
➤ **PHRONESIS**; a journal for ancient philosophy. Text in English, French, German, Italian. 1956. 4/yr. EUR 296, USD 415 to institutions; EUR 323, USD 452 combined subscription to institutions (print & online eds.) (effective 2012). adv. bk.rev. illus. index. back issues avail.; reprint service avail. from PSC. **Document type:** *Journal, Academic/Scholarly.*
Related titles: Online - full text ed.: ISSN 1568-5284. EUR 269, USD 377 to institutions (effective 2012) (from IngentaConnect).
Indexed: A01, A03, A08, A20, A22, AmHI, ArtHuCI, BibLing, CA, CurCont, DIP, E01, FR, H07, IBR, IBRH, IBZ, IPB, IZBG, PCI, PhilInd, RASB, SCOPUS, T02, W07.
—IE, Infotrieve, Ingenta, INIST. **CCC.**
Published by: Brill, PO Box 9000, Leiden, 2300 PA, Netherlands. TEL 31-71-5353500, FAX 31-71-5317532, cs@brill.nl. Eds. Christopher Gill, Verity Harte. Circ: 1,100. **Dist. by:** Turpin Distribution Services Ltd., Pegasus Dr, Stratton Business Park, Biggleswade, Bedfordshire SG18 8QB, United Kingdom. TEL 44-1767-604954, FAX 44-1767-601640, custserv@turpin-distribution.com, http://www.turpin-distribution.com/.

100 530 DEU ISSN 1863-7388
QC5.56
➤ **PHYSICS & PHILOSOPHY.** Text in English. 2006. irreg. free (effective 2011). **Description:** Aims to foster an interdisciplinary dialogue and establish an international platform for publication of original research at the borderline between physics and philosophy.
Media: Online - full text.
Published by: Technische Universitaet Dortmund, Institut fuer Philosophie und Politikwissenschaft, Emil-Figge-Str 50, Dortmund, 44227, Germany. TEL 49-231-7552835, FAX 49-231-7555896, jansen@fk14.tu-dortmund.de, http://ifpp.fk14.tu-dortmund.de/cms/ifpp/de/institut/index.html. Eds. Brigitte Falkenburg, Wolfgang Rohde.

215 610 509 USA
➤ **PITTSBURGH SERIES IN PHILOSOPHY & HISTORY OF SCIENCE.** Text in English. 1982. irreg., latest vol.3, 1986. price varies. back issues avail. **Document type:** *Monographic series, Academic/Scholarly.* **Description:** Examines philosophical issues in the history of medical and physical sciences.
Related titles: Online - full text ed.
Published by: University of California Press, Book Series, 2120 Berkeley Way, Berkeley, CA 94704. TEL 510-642-4247, FAX 510-643-7127, foundation@ucpress.edu. **Subscr. to:** California - Princeton Fulfillment Services, Inc., 1445 Lower Ferry Rd, Ewing, NJ 08618. TEL 609-883-1759, 800-777-4726, FAX 800-999-1958, orders@cpfsinc.com.

121 USA ISSN 0032-0420
BR1
THE PLAIN TRUTH. Abbreviated title: P T. Text in English. 1934. bi-m. free in US & Canada; USD 29.95 elsewhere; USD 4 per issue (effective 2009). adv. bk.rev. 48 p./no. 3 cols./p.; back issues avail.; reprints avail. **Document type:** *Magazine, Consumer.* **Description:** Revolves around religious themes concerning the Bible and the ministry.
Related titles: Microform ed.: (from PQC).
Indexed: A22, GeoRef, SpeleolAb.
Published by: Plain Truth Ministries, Pasadena, CA 91129. TEL 800-309-4466, FAX 626-358-4846, info@ptm.org. Ed. Greg Albrecht. Adv. contact Skip Dunn TEL 626-298-8013.

100 FRA ISSN 2079-7567
B350
PLATO. Text in Multiple languages. 2001. a. free (effective 2011). **Document type:** *Journal, Academic/Scholarly.*
Media: Online - full text.
Published by: The International Plato Society http://www.platosociety.org.

100 DNK ISSN 0901-2583
➤ **PLATONSELSKABETS SKRIFTSERIE.** Text in Danish. 1974. irreg., latest vol.14, 2007. price varies. **Document type:** *Monographic series, Academic/Scholarly.* **Description:** Publishes individual translations of and studies within philosophical texts.
Published by: Museum Tusculanum Press, c/o University of Copenhagen, Njalsgade 126, Copenhagen S, 2300, Denmark. TEL 45-35-329109, FAX 45-35-329113, info@mtp.dk, http://www.mtp.dk. **Dist. in France by:** Editions Picard, Editions Picard, Paris 75006, France. TEL 33-1-43269778, FAX 33-1-43264264; **Dist. in UK by:** Gazelle Book Services Ltd., White Cross Mills, Hightown, Lancaster LA1 4UU, United Kingdom. TEL 44-1524-68765, FAX 44-1524-63232, sales@gazellebooks.co.uk, http://www.gazellebookservices.co.uk/; **Dist. in US & Canada by:** International Specialized Book Services Inc., 920 NE 58th Ave Ste 300, Portland, OR 97213. TEL 503-287-3093, 800-944-6190, FAX 503-280-8832, orders@isbs.com, http://www.isbs.com/.

190 GBR
➤ **PLI - WARWICK JOURNAL OF PHILOSOPHY.** Text in English. 1989. irreg. GBP 11.95 per issue domestic to individuals; GBP 12.95 per issue in Europe to individuals; GBP 13.95 per issue elsewhere to individuals; GBP 25 per issue domestic to institutions; GBP 26 per issue in Europe to institutions; GBP 27 per issue elsewhere to institutions (effective 2009). bk.rev. back issues avail. **Document type:** *Journal, Academic/Scholarly.* **Description:** Concentrates on contemporary work coming from the post-Kantian and phenomenological traditions.
Published by: University of Warwick, Department of Philosophy, Gibbet Hill Rd, Coventry, Warks CV4 7AL, United Kingdom. TEL 44-24-76523421, FAX 44-24-76523019, l.d.hemsley@warwick.ac.uk, http://www2.warwick.ac.uk/fac/soc/philosophy/.

100 USA ISSN 1930-7365
B830.A1
➤ **THE PLURALIST.** Text in English. 1985. 3/yr. USD 114 combined subscription to institutions (print & online eds.) (effective 2012). adv. bk.rev. back issues avail. **Document type:** *Journal, Academic/Scholarly.* **Description:** Contains scholarly articles address issues associated with being a person in this world, with reviews of philosophical works that are relevant to that theme.
Formerly (until 2006): The Personalist Forum (0889-065X)
Related titles: Online - full text ed.: ISSN 1944-6489. USD 104 to institutions (effective 2012).
Indexed: A20, A21, A22, A26, AmHI, ArtHuCI, B04, CA, CurCont, E01, H07, H08, HAb, HumInd, I05, MLA-IB, PhilInd, RI-1, T02, W03, W05, W07.
—BLDSC (6541.013750), INIST. **CCC.**
Published by: University of Illinois Press, 1325 S Oak St, Champaign, IL 61820. TEL 217-333-0950, 866-244-0626, FAX 217-244-8082, journals@uillinois.edu. Ed. Randall E Auxier TEL 608-453-7437. Adv. contact Jeff McArdle TEL 217-244-0381.

110 FRA ISSN 1952-5788
POCHE ESOTERISME. Text in French. 2006. irreg. back issues avail. **Document type:** *Monographic series, Consumer.*
Published by: Anagramme Editions, 48 Rue des Ponts, Croissy sur Seine, 78290, France. TEL 33-1-39769943, FAX 33-1-39764587, info@anagramme-editions.fr, http://www.anagramme-editions.fr/. **Dist. by:** Volumen, 69 bis Rue de Vaugirard, Paris 75006, France. TEL 33-1-44107575, FAX 33-1-44107580.

POLIS. *see* POLITICAL SCIENCE

100 NLD ISSN 1389-6768
POLISH ANALYTIC PHILOSOPHY. Text in English. 1999. irreg., latest vol.77, 2003. price varies. back issues avail. **Document type:** *Monographic series, Academic/Scholarly.*
Indexed: AmHI, H07, T02.
Published by: Editions Rodopi B.V., Tijnmuiden 7, Amsterdam, 1046 AK, Netherlands. TEL 31-20-6114821, FAX 31-20-4472979, info@rodopi.nl. Ed. Jacek Juliusz Jadacki.

100 POL ISSN 1897-1652
POLISH JOURNAL OF PHILOSOPHY. Text in English. 2007. s-a. EUR 75, GBP 55, USD 100 to institutions (effective 2010). **Document type:** *Journal, Academic/Scholarly.* **Description:** Promotes the best of the living Polish philosophical tradition, especially the Lvov-Warsaw School of analytic philosophy and the phenomenological school of Roman Ingarden.
Related titles: Online - full text ed.: ISSN 2154-3747.
Indexed: PhilInd.
Published by: Uniwersytet Jagiellonski, Instytut Filozofii/Jagiellonian University, Institute of Philosophy, ul Grodzka 52, Krakow, 31-041, Poland. TEL 48-12-4227111, FAX 48-12-4224916, infoiph@iphils.uj.edu.pl, http://www.iphils.uj.edu.pl. Ed. Sebastian Tomasz Kolodziejczyk.

POLITICS, PHILOSOPHY & ECONOMICS. *see* POLITICAL SCIENCE

190 AUT ISSN 1437-6881
➤ **POLITISCHE PHILOSOPHIE UND OEKONOMIE.** Text in German. 1999. irreg., latest 2002. price varies. **Document type:** *Monographic series, Academic/Scholarly.*
Published by: Springer Wien (Subsidiary of: Springer Science+Business Media), Sachsenplatz 4-6, Vienna, W 1201, Austria. TEL 43-1-3302415-0, FAX 43-1-330242665, books@springer.at, http://www.springer.at. Ed. W Pircher. R&P Angela Foessl TEL 43-1-3302415517. **Subscr. to:** Springer New York LLC, 233 Spring St, New York, NY 10013. TEL 800-777-4643, FAX 201-348-4505.

100 AUT ISSN 1560-6325
➤ **POLYLOG**; Zeitschrift fuer interkulturelles philosophieren. Text in German; Summaries in English, Spanish. 1998. 2/yr. adv. bk.rev. back issues avail. **Document type:** *Journal, Academic/Scholarly.* **Description:** Explores interculturality in philosophy and the humanities.
Published by: Wiener Gesellschaft fuer Interkulturelle Philosophie, Meiselstrasse 73-3, Vienna, W 1140, Austria. TEL 43-1-9859153, FAX 43-1-9859461. Ed., R&P, Adv. contact Michael Shorny. Circ: 1,000 (paid).

100 DEU ISSN 1616-2943
B59
➤ **POLYLOG - FORUM FOR INTERCULTURAL PHILOSOPHIZING.** Text in English, Spanish, German. 2000. s-a. back issues avail. **Document type:** *Journal, Academic/Scholarly.* **Description:** Provides an interdisciplinary scholarly forum for philosophical dialogue across cultures.
Media: Online - full text.
Published by: Polylog e.V., Guldeinstrabe 40, Munich, 80339, Germany. office@polylog.org. Eds. Bertold Bernreuter, Kai Kresse.

100 USA
POPULAR CULTURE AND PHILOSOPHY. Abbreviated title: P C P. Text in English. 2000. irreg., latest vol.53, 2010. price varies. back issues avail. **Document type:** *Monographic series, Academic/Scholarly.*
Published by: Open Court Publishing Co., General Books (Subsidiary of: Carus Publishing Company), 70 E Lake St, Ste 300, Chicago, IL 60601. TEL 800-815-2280, FAX 312-701-1728, opencourt@caruspub.com, http://www.opencourtbooks.com. Ed. George A Reisch. **Subscr. to:** 30 Grove St, Ste C, Peterborough, NH 03458. FAX 603-924-7380, customerservice@caruspub.com.

100 300 FRA ISSN 1283-8594
B2
LE PORTIQUE. Text in English. s-a. **Document type:** *Journal, Academic/Scholarly.*
Related titles: Online - full text ed.: ISSN 1777-5280.
Published by: Revue Le Portique, BP 65, Strasbourg Cedex, 67061, France.

190 NLD
POST-COMMUNIST EUROPEAN THOUGHT. Text in English. irreg. price varies. **Document type:** *Monographic series, Academic/Scholarly.*
Related titles: ◆ Series of: Value Inquiry Book Series. ISSN 0929-8436.
Published by: Editions Rodopi B.V., Tijnmuiden 7, Amsterdam, 1046 AK, Netherlands. TEL 31-20-6114821, FAX 31-20-4472979, info@rodopi.nl. Ed. Dane R Gordon. **Dist. by:** Rodopi - USA, 606 Newark Ave, 2nd fl, Kenilworth, NJ 07033. TEL 908-497-9031, FAX 908-497-9035.

100 ITA ISSN 1827-5133
POST FILOSOFIE. Text in Multiple languages. 2005. a. **Document type:** *Journal, Academic/Scholarly.*
Published by: (Universita degli Studi di Bari, Seminario Permanente di Filosofia), Cacucci Editore, Via D Nicolai 39, Bari, 70122, Italy. TEL 39-080-5214220, FAX 39-080-5234777, info@cacucci.it, http://www.cacucci.it. Eds. Francesco Fistetti, Roberto Finelli.

100 VEN ISSN 2220-7333
▼ **POSTCOVENCIONALES**; etica universidad democracia. Text in Spanish. 2010. s-a. **Document type:** *Journal, Academic/Scholarly.*
Media: Online - full text.
Published by: Universidad Central de Venezuela, Facultad de Ciencias Juridicas y Politicas, Ciudad Universitaria, Los Chaguaramos, Caracas, DF 1040, Venezuela. Ed. Levy Farias.

170 USA ISSN 1949-968X
POYNTER CENTER NEWSLETTER. Text in English. 1986. s-a. free (effective 2009). bk.rev. back issues avail. **Document type:** *Newsletter, Academic/Scholarly.* **Description:** Contains reports on center activities and projects.
Related titles: Online - full text ed.: free (effective 2009).
Published by: Poynter Center for the Study of Ethics and American Institutions, 618 E Third St, Bloomington, IN 47405. TEL 812-855-0261, FAX 812-855-3315. Ed. Glenda Murray.

190 NLD ISSN 0303-8157
B1 CODEN: PSSHEY
➤ **POZNAN STUDIES IN THE PHILOSOPHY OF THE SCIENCES AND THE HUMANITIES.** Text in English. 1975. irreg., latest vol.94, 2007. price varies. adv. bk.rev. illus. index. back issues avail. **Document type:** *Monographic series, Academic/Scholarly.* **Description:** Contributes to practicing philosophy as deep as Marxism and as rationality justified as positivism by promoting the development of philosophy which respects the tradition of great philosophical ideas and the manner of philosophical thinking introduced by analytical philosophy.
Related titles: Online - full text ed.: ISSN 1875-7243 (from IngentaConnect); ◆ Series: Idealization; ◆ New Trends in Philosophy; ◆ Monographs-in-Debate. ISSN 1573-4749.
Indexed: AmHI, CCMJ, DIP, FR, H07, IBR, IBZ, PhilInd, T02.
—BLDSC (6579.127000), IE, Ingenta, INIST. **CCC.**
Published by: (Uniwersytet im. Adama Mickiewicza w Poznaniu/Adam Mickiewicz University POL), Editions Rodopi B.V., Tijnmuiden 7, Amsterdam, 1046 AK, Netherlands. TEL 31-20-6114821, FAX 31-20-4472979, orders-queries@rodopi.nl. Eds. Dr. Katarzyna Paprzycka, Leszek Nowak. **Dist in France by:** Nordeal, 30 rue de Verlinghem, BP 139, Lambersart 59832, France. TEL 33-3-20099060, FAX 33-3-20929495; **Dist in N America by:** Rodopi - USA, 295 North Michigan Avenue, Suite 1B, Kenilworth, NJ 07033. TEL 908-298-9071, 800-225-3998, FAX 908-298-9075.

➤ **PRABUDDHA BHARATA/AWAKENED INDIA.** *see* RELIGIONS AND THEOLOGY—Hindu

100 GBR ISSN 1363-3228
➤ **PRACTICAL PHILOSOPHY.** Text in English. 1996. s-a. GBP 10 to individuals; GBP 60 to institutions; free to members (effective 2009). bk.rev. back issues avail. **Document type:** *Journal, Academic/Scholarly.* **Description:** Contains full-length essays and short articles called reflections, and comments section, incluidng writings by leading philosophical practitioners cover a wide variety of topics relevant to philosophical practice, practical philosophy, philosophical counselling, socratic dialogue and philosophy for children. Audience includes mainly philosophers, counselors, and cultural analysts.
Related titles: Online - full text ed.
Published by: Society for Philosophy in Practice, c/o Monica tobon, SPP Administrator, 7 The Friars, Canterbury, Kent CT1 2AS, United Kingdom. admin@society-for-philosophy-in-practice.org. Ed. Bo Meinertsen.

100 DEU ISSN 1615-570X
PRAGMATA; Studien zur Philosophie. Text in German. 2002. irreg., latest vol.3, 2002. price varies. **Document type:** *Monographic series, Academic/Scholarly.*
Published by: Peter Lang GmbH (Subsidiary of: Peter Lang Publishing Group), Eschborner Landstr 42-50, Frankfurt Am Main, 60489, Germany. TEL 49-69-7807050, FAX 49-69-78070550, zentrale.frankfurt@peterlang.com.

100 POL ISSN 0079-4872
B831.3
PRAKSEOLOGIA. Text in Polish; Summaries in English. 1960. q. USD 46 foreign (effective 2003). bk.rev. bibl.; charts. **Document type:** *Academic/Scholarly.* **Description:** Covers philosophical, theoretical, and methodological topics of efficient action.
Formerly (until 1966): Materialy Prakseologiczne
Indexed: AgrLib, RASB.
Published by: Polska Akademia Nauk, Instytut Filozofii i Socjologii, Nowy Swiat 72, Warsaw, 00330, Poland. TEL 48-22-8267181, FAX 48-22-8267823, secretar@ifispan.waw.pl, http://www.ifispan.waw.pl. Ed. Wojciech Gasparski.

100 DEU ISSN 1610-157X
PRAKTISCHE PHILOSOPHIE KONTROVERS. Text in German. 2003. irreg., latest vol.4, 2005. price varies. **Document type:** *Monographic series, Academic/Scholarly.*
Published by: Peter Lang GmbH (Subsidiary of: Peter Lang Publishing Group), Eschborner Landstr 42-50, Frankfurt Am Main, 60489, Germany. TEL 49-69-7807050, FAX 49-69-78070550, zentrale.frankfurt@peterlang.com.

P

181.45 USA ISSN 0149-953X
PRANA YOGA LIFE. Text in English. 1977. irreg. USD 3. adv. bk.rev. illus. back issues avail.
Published by: Prana Yoga Ashram, PO Box 1037, Berkeley, CA 94701. TEL 415-549-2911. Ed. Swami Vignanananda. Circ: 1,500.

100 USA ISSN 0138-0311
BD450
PRAXIOLOGY. Text in English. 1980. irreg., latest vol.17, 2009. USD 59.95, GBP 53.95, CAD 72.95 per issue (effective 2010). back issues avail. **Document type:** *Monographic series, Academic/Scholarly.* **Description:** Examines fundamental issues in the theory of human action, the nature of economics and theoretical issues in disciplines such as design, accounting, market mechanisms, planning and more.
Indexed: RASB.
—CCC.
Published by: Transaction Publishers, 35 Berrue Cir, Piscataway, NJ 08854. TEL 732-445-2280, FAX 732-445-3138, trans@transactionpub.com, http://www.transactionpub.com. Ed. Wojciech W Gasparski.

100 CRI
PRAXIS. Text in Spanish. 1975. q. per issue exchange basis. bibl.; charts; illus.; stat.
Published by: Universidad Nacional, Departamento de Filosofia, c/o Jack Wilson-Pacheco, Coordinacion de Publicaciones y Canje, Centro de Documentacion e Informacion en Filosofia, Heredia, Costa Rica. Circ: 1,000.

100 GBR ISSN 1756-1019
PRAXIS. Text in English. 2007. 3/yr. free (effective 2011). **Document type:** *Journal, Academic/Scholarly.*
Media: Online - full text.
Published by: University of Manchester, Oxford Rd, Manchester, M13 9PL, United Kingdom. TEL 44-161-3066000, http://www.manchester.ac.uk/.

100 COL ISSN 0120-4688
➤ **PRAXIS FILOSOFICA.** Text in English, French, Spanish; Summaries in English, French, Spanish, Portuguese. 1977; N.S. 1990. s-a. COP 30,000 domestic; USD 12 in the Americas; USD 16 elsewhere (effective 2010). bibl. cum.index: 1990-1997. back issues avail.; reprints avail. **Document type:** *Journal, Academic/Scholarly.* **Description:** Publishes articles on philosophical topics such as philosophy of the mind, Spanish philosophy, philosophy of language and multiculturalism.
Related titles: Online - full text ed.: (from SciELO).
Indexed: A26, I04, I05, MLA-IB, PhilInd.
—CCC.
Published by: Universidad del Valle, Departamento de Filosofia, Coiudad Universitaria Melendez, Calle 13 No 100-00, Cali, Colombia. TEL 57-2-3316159, FAX 57-2-3391184. Ed., R&P, Adv. contact German Guerrero Pino. Circ: 300 (paid).

105 BRA ISSN 0103-2283
PRESENCA FILOSOFICA. Text in Portuguese, French; Text occasionally in English. 1974. irreg. USD 25. bibl.
Published by: Sociedade Brasileira de Filosofos Catolicos, Rua Benjamim Constant, 23-420, Gloria, Rio De Janeiro, RJ 20241-150, Brazil. Ed. Tarcisio Meirelles Padilha. Circ: 2,000.

100 FRA ISSN 1166-9993
PRESENCE DE GABRIEL MARCEL. Text in French. 1978. a. EUR 23. bk.rev. **Document type:** *Bulletin.* **Description:** Publishes philosophy, news from around the world concerning Gabriel Marcel and announcements of books about him which have recently been published.
Formerly (until 1991): Presence de Gabriel Marcel. Cahier (0294-6491)
Published by: Association Presence de Gabriel Marcel, 21 rue de Tournon, Paris, 75006, France. TEL 33-1-43268432, FAX 33-1-43545342.

PRESSE-INTER. *see* NEW AGE PUBLICATIONS

100 HRV ISSN 0350-2791
PRILOZI ZA ISTRAZIVANJE HRVATSKE FILOZOFSKE BASTINE. Text in Croatian, Greek, Latin; Summaries in English, French, German, Italian. 1975. s-a. USD 8. bk.rev. back issues avail.
Indexed: A26, DIP, IBR, IBZ, PhilInd, RASB, RILM.
Published by: (Odjel za Povijest Filozofije), Sveuciliste u Zagrebu, Institut za Povijesne Znanosti, Krcka 1, Zagreb, 41000, Croatia. TEL 041 511-841. Ed. Damir Barbaric. Circ: 800.

142.7 NLD ISSN 0924-1965
➤ **PRIMARY SOURCES IN PHENOMENOLOGY.** Text in English. 1987. irreg., latest vol.3, 1990. price varies. **Document type:** *Monographic series, Academic/Scholarly.* **Description:** Presents materials relating to the foundation and background of early phenomenology, with special emphasis on investigations of logical, ontological and related themes, and to the interconnection between phenomenology and other disciplines.
Published by: Springer Netherlands (Subsidiary of: Springer Science+Business Media), Van Godewijckstraat 30, Dordrecht, 3311 GX, Netherlands. TEL 31-78-6576050, FAX 31-78-6576474. Ed. Karl Schuhmann.

➤ **PRINCETON JOURNAL OF BIOETHICS.** *see* BIOLOGY

109 USA
PRINCETON MONOGRAPHS IN PHILOSOPHY. Text in English. 2000. irreg., latest 2009. price varies. back issues avail. **Document type:** *Monographic series, Academic/Scholarly.* **Description:** Explores topics and issues in philosophy.
Published by: Princeton University Press, 41 William St, Princeton, NJ 08540. TEL 609-258-4900, 800-777-4726, FAX 609-258-6305, cpriday@pupress.co.uk. Ed. Harry Frankfurt. **Subscr. addr. in US:** California - Princeton Fulfillment Services, Inc., 1445 Lower Ferry Rd, Ewing, NJ 08618. TEL 609-883-1759, 800-777-4726, FAX 609-883-7413, 800-999-1958, orders@cpfsinc.com. **Dist. addr. in Canada:** University Press Group.; **Dist. addr. in UK:** John Wiley & Sons Ltd.

100 POL ISSN 0867-5392
B6
PRINCIPIA. Text in Polish. 1990. irreg., latest vol.53, 2010. price varies. **Document type:** *Monographic series, Academic/Scholarly.*
Published by: (Uniwersytet Jagiellonski, Instytut Filozofii/Jagiellonian University, Institute of Philosophy), Wydawnictwo Uniwersytetu Jagiellonskiego/Jagiellonian University Press, ul Grodzka 26, Krakow, 31044, Poland. TEL 48-12-4312364, FAX 48-12-4301995, wydaw@if.uj.edu.pl. Ed. Jan Hartman.

100 BRA ISSN 1808-1711
PRINCIPIA; revista internacional de epistemologia. Text in English, French, Portuguese, Spanish. 2003. s-a. free. **Document type:** *Journal, Academic/Scholarly.* **Description:** Publishes papers on contemporary epistemology, philosophy of science and related areas.
Media: Online - full content. **Related titles:** CD-ROM ed.: ISSN 1808-1525. USD 10 per vol. (effective 2008).
Published by: Universidade Federal de Santa Catarina. Nucleo de Epistemologia e Logica, C. P. 476, Florianopolis - SC, 88010-970, Brazil. Ed. Luiz Henrique de Araujo Dutra.

PRINCIPIA CYBERNETICA NEWS. *see* COMPUTERS—Cybernetics

100 BRA ISSN 0104-8694
B5
➤ **PRINCIPIOS;** revista de filosofia. Text in English, French, Portuguese, Spanish. 1994. s-a. free. **Document type:** *Journal, Academic/Scholarly.*
Related titles: Online - full text ed.: ISSN 1983-2109. free (effective 2011).
Indexed: PhilInd.
Published by: Universidade Federal do Rio Grande do Norte, Programa de Pos-Graduacao em Filosofia, Campus Universitario, Lagoa Nova, Natal, RN 59 078-970, Brazil. TEL 55-84-32153566. Ed. Jaimir Conte.

100 CZE ISSN 1212-9097
➤ **PRO-FIL.** Text in Czech. 2000. s-a. free. **Document type:** *Journal, Academic/Scholarly.*
Media: Online - full text.
Published by: Masarykova Univerzita, Filozoficka Fakulta/Masaryk University, Faculty of Arts, Arna Novaka 1, Brno, 60200, Czech Republic. TEL 420-549-491111, FAX 420-549-491520, podatelna@phil.muni.cz, http://www.phil.muni.cz. Ed. Radim Brazda.

174.2 NLD ISSN 1380-3646
PRO VITA HUMANA. Text in Dutch. 1994. 6/yr. EUR 25; EUR 4.50 newsstand/cover (effective 2008). **Document type:** *Magazine, Trade.*
Formed by the merger of (1984-1993): Pro Vita (0929-4872); Which was formerly (1984-1992): Juristenvereniging Pro Vita. Medelingenblad (0926-7905); (1974-1993): Vita Humana (0923-2397); Which was formerly (1974-1982): Nederlands Artsenverbond. Informatiebulletin (0923-2451)
Published by: (Juristenvereniging Pro Vita), Nederlands Artsenverbond, Marijnenlaan 44, Vlijmen, 5251 SC, Netherlands. TEL 31-73-5119072, FAX 31-73-5112956, secretariaat@artsenverbond.nl, http://artsenverbond.nl.

100 001.3 DEU
PROBLEMATA. Text in German. 1971. irreg., latest vol.152, 2005. price varies. **Document type:** *Monographic series, Academic/Scholarly.*
Indexed: MathR.
Published by: Frommann-Holzboog Verlag e.K., Koenig-Karl-Str 27, Stuttgart, 70372, Germany. TEL 49-711-9559690, FAX 49-711-9559691, info@frommann-holzboog.de, http://www.frommann-holzboog.de.

160 ROM ISSN 1454-2366
PROBLEME DE LOGICA. Text in Romanian. 1968. irreg., latest vol.11, 2003. **Document type:** *Monographic series, Academic/Scholarly.*
Published by: (Academia Romana/Romanian Academy), Editura Academiei Romane/Publishing House of the Romanian Academy, Calea 13 Septembrie 13, Sector 5, Bucharest, 050711, Romania. Eds. Calin Candiescu, Crizantema Joja. **Dist. by:** Rodipet S.A., Piata Presei Libere 1, sector 1, PO Box 33-57, Bucharest 3, Romania. TEL 40-21-2226407, 40-21-2224126, rodipet@rodipet.ro.

149.946 DEU ISSN 0933-4483
➤ **PROBLEME DER SEMIOTIK.** Text in German. 1984. irreg., latest vol.20, 2002. price varies. adv. **Document type:** *Monographic series, Academic/Scholarly.*
Published by: Stauffenburg Verlag, Postfach 2525, Tuebingen, 72015, Germany. TEL 49-7071-97300, FAX 49-7071-973030, info@stauffenburg.de. Ed. Roland Posner.

100 LTU ISSN 1392-1126
PROBLEMOS. Text in Lithuanian; Summaries in English, Russian. 1968. s-a. **Document type:** *Monographic series, Academic/Scholarly.*
Formerly (until 1990): Lietuvos T S R Aukstuju Mokyklu Mokslo Darbai. Problemos (0203-7238)
Related titles: Online - full text ed.
Indexed: A20, AmHI, ArtHuCI, CA, CurCont, FR, H07, PhilInd, SCOPUS, T02, W07.
Published by: Vilniaus Universiteto Leidykla, Universiteto g 1, Vilnius, 2734, Lithuania. TEL 370-5-2687260, FAX 370-5-2123939, leidykla@leidykla.vu.lt, http://www.leidykla.vu.lt.

100 USA ISSN 0898-0136
➤ **PROBLEMS IN CONTEMPORARY PHILOSOPHY.** Text in English. 1986. irreg., latest vol.64, 2005. price varies. back issues avail. **Document type:** *Monographic series, Academic/Scholarly.*
—IE, Ingenta.
Published by: Edwin Mellen Press, 415 Ridge St, PO Box 450, Lewiston, NY 14092. TEL 716-754-2266, FAX 716-754-4056, cservice@mellenpress.com.

193
PROCEEDINGS OF THE FRIESIAN SCHOOL. Text in English. 1996. irreg. **Document type:** *Proceedings, Academic/Scholarly.* **Description:** Takes up issues involving all aspects of the Friesian school of philosophy, to promote further development of Kantian philosphy.
Media: Online - full text.
Published by: Los Angeles Valley College, Department of Philosophy, 5800 Fulton Ave, Valley Glen, CA 91401. TEL 818-947-2600, http://www.lavc.edu. Ed. Kelley Ross.

149 USA
PROCESS PERSPECTIVES. Text in English. 1975. 3/yr. looseleaf. USD 21 domestic to non-members; USD 30 foreign to non-members; free to members (effective 2010). 2 cols./p.; back issues avail. **Document type:** *Magazine, Consumer.* **Description:** Covers events and developments relating to the philosophy of Alfred North Whitehead, Charles Hartshorne and other process-relational thinkers.
Formerly (until 1995): Center for Process Studies. Newsletter (0360-618X)
Published by: Claremont School of Theology, Center for Process Studies, 1325 N College Ave, Claremont, CA 91711. TEL 909-621-5330, 800-626-7821, FAX 909-621-2760, sweeney@ctr4process.org. Ed. Ashley Riordan.

192 USA ISSN 0360-6503
BD372
➤ **PROCESS STUDIES.** Text in English. 1971. 2/yr. USD 35 domestic to individuals; USD 45 foreign to individuals; USD 60 domestic to institutions; USD 75 foreign to institutions (effective 2010). adv. bk.rev. abstr. 1 cols./p.; back issues avail.; reprints avail. **Document type:** *Journal, Academic/Scholarly.* **Description:** Covers the process philosophy of Alfred North Whitehead, and its application to other philosophies and other fields, including aesthetics, mathematics, physics, biology, cosmology, history of religion, social science, and literary criticism.
Related titles: Microform ed.: (from PQC); Online - full text ed.: ISSN 2154-3682. 1971.
Indexed: A01, A20, A21, A22, ASCA, CERDIC, CPL, FR, IPB, OTA, PCI, PhilInd, R&TA, RASB, RI-1, RI-2.
—BLDSC (6849.990700), IE, Infotrieve, Ingenta, INIST.
Published by: Claremont School of Theology, Center for Process Studies, 1325 N College Ave, Claremont, CA 91711. TEL 909-621-5330, 800-626-7821, FAX 909-621-2760, journal@ctr4process.org. Ed. Daniel A Dombrowski. adv.: page USD 175. Circ: 900.

➤ **PROEFDIERVRIJ.** *see* ANIMAL WELFARE

170 USA ISSN 1045-8808
PROFESSIONAL ETHICS REPORT. Abbreviated title: P E R. Text in English. 1988. q. bk.rev. cum.index: 1988-1991, 1992-1993. back issues avail. **Document type:** *Newsletter, Trade.* **Description:** Provides a forum for the exchange of information on professional ethics issues that affect a wide range of professions, especially scientists and engineers.
Related titles: Online - full text ed.: free (effective 2009).
Indexed: P30.
Published by: American Association for the Advancement of Science, 1200 New York Ave, NW, Washington, DC 20005. TEL 202-326-6400, FAX 202-371-9849, jlstaana@aaas.org. Ed. Mark S Frankel.

190 NLD ISSN 0924-1930
➤ **PROFILES;** an international series on contemporary philosophers and logicians. Text in English. 1979. irreg., latest vol.8, 1987. price varies. bibl. index. back issues avail. **Document type:** *Monographic series, Academic/Scholarly.*
—CCC.
Published by: Springer Netherlands (Subsidiary of: Springer Science+Business Media), Van Godewijckstraat 30, Dordrecht, 3311 GX, Netherlands. TEL 31-78-6576050, FAX 31-78-6576474.

100 ITA ISSN 1973-1507
PROFILI. TEORIE E OGGETTI DELLA FILOSOFIA. Text in Italian. 1978. irreg., latest vol.39, 1999. price varies. **Document type:** *Monographic series, Academic/Scholarly.*
Formerly: Teorie e Oggetti Serie Rossa; Which supersedes in part: Teorie e Oggetti (0392-2154)
Published by: Liguori Editore, Via Posillipo 394, Naples, 80123, Italy. TEL 39-081-7206111, FAX 39-081-7206244, liguori@liguori.it, http://www.liguori.it.

PROGRESS (MEDFORD). *see* RELIGIONS AND THEOLOGY

100 HRV ISSN 1333-4395
➤ **PROLEGOMENA.** Text in English, Croatian. 2002. s-a. **Document type:** *Journal, Academic/Scholarly.* **Description:** Its principal objective is to introduce novel or underdeveloped fields of philosophical research into the academic community of Croatia.
Related titles: Online - full text ed.: ISSN 1846-0593. free (effective 2011).
Indexed: A20, AmHI, ArtHuCI, CA, CurCont, DIP, H07, IBR, IBZ, PhilInd, SCOPUS, T02, W07.
—IE.
Published by: Society for the Advancement of Philosophy, Ilica Grada Vukovara 68, Soba 106, Zagreb, 10000, Croatia. TEL 385-1-6117962, FAX 385-1-6117963. Ed. Tomislav Bracanovic.

100 CAN
PROLEGOMENA; the University of British Columbia online philosophy journal. Text in English. 2000. s-a.
Media: Online - full content.
Published by: University of British Columbia, Department of Philosophy, Buchanan E370, 1866 Main Mall, Vancouver, BC V6T 1Z1, Canada. Ed. Brad Murray.

100 BRA ISSN 1807-3042
PROMETEUS. FILOSOFIA EM REVISTA. Text in Portuguese. 2004. s-a. **Document type:** *Journal, Academic/Scholarly.*
Related titles: Online - full text ed.: ISSN 2176-5960. free (effective 2011).
Published by: Universidade Federal de Sergipe, Departamento de Filosofia, Avenida Marechal Rondon s/n, Jardim Rosa Elize, Sao Cristoval, Sergipe, 49100-000, Brazil. http://www.ufs.br.

100 320 ITA ISSN 1126-5191
PROSPETTIVA PERSONA; trimestrale di cultura etica e politica. Text in Italian. 1992. q. **Document type:** *Journal, Consumer.*
Published by: Rubbettino Editore, Viale Rosario Rubbettino 10, Soveria Mannelli, CZ 88049, Italy. TEL 39-0968-662034, FAX 39-0968-662055, segreteria@rubbettino.it, http://www.rubbettino.it.

100 ITA ISSN 0552-3702
B4
IL PROTAGORA. Text in Italian. 1959. s-a. EUR 38 domestic; EUR 54 foreign (effective 2009). **Document type:** *Journal, Academic/Scholarly.*
Indexed: IPB, PhilInd.
Published by: Barbieri Edizioni, Via Santa Lucia 1, Manduria, TA 74024, Italy. TEL 39-099-9711142, FAX 39-099-4506141, info@barbierieditore.it, http://www.barbierieditore.it.

301 DEU
➤ **PROTOSOCIOLOGY (ONLINE);** an international journal of interdisciplinary research. Text in English. 1991. 2/yr. EUR 12 per issue (effective 2009). bk.rev. **Document type:** *Journal, Academic/Scholarly.*
Former titles (until 200?): ProtoSociology (CD-ROM) (1611-1281); (until 2002): ProtoSociology (Print) (1434-4319); (until 1996): Protosoziologie (0940-4147)
Media: Online - full text.

Indexed: CA, DIP, IBR, IBZ, L&LBA, PhilInd, S02, S03, SCOPUS, SOPODA, SSA, SociolAb, T02.
—Ingenta.
Published by: Protosociology, Stephan-Heise-Str 56, Frankfurt Am Main, 60488, Germany. TEL 49-69-769461, FAX 49-69-7988465. Ed. Gerhard Preyer. Circ: 500 (paid).

100 POL ISSN 1230-1493
B8.P7
PRZEGLAD FILOZOFICZNY NOWA SERIA. Text in Polish; Summaries in English. 1897-1949; N.S. 1992. q. bk.rev. bibl.
Formerly (until 1949): Przeglad Filozoficzny (0867-1176)
Indexed: RASB.
Published by: Polska Akademia Nauk, Instytut Filozofii i Socjologii, Nowy Swiat 72, Warsaw, 00330, Poland. secretar@ifispan.waw.pl. Ed. Jacek Holowka. **Dist. by:** Ars Polona, Obroncow 25, Warsaw 03933, Poland. **Co-sponsor:** Polska Akademia Nauk, Komitet Nauk Socjologii.

PRZEGLAD RUSYCYSTYCZNY. *see* LINGUISTICS

100 USA ISSN 0887-0373
H96
PUBLIC AFFAIRS QUARTERLY. Abbreviated title: P A Q. Text in English. 1987. q. USD 55 to individuals; USD 297 to institutions (print or online ed.); USD 331 combined subscription to institutions (print & online eds.) (effective 2011). adv. back issues avail.; reprints avail. **Document type:** *Journal, Academic/Scholarly.* **Description:** Aims to advance the ends of philosophical thought and dialogue in all widely used philosophical methodologies, including non-Western methods and those of traditional cultures.
Related titles: Online - full text ed.: ISSN 2152-0542.
Indexed: A22, DIP, FamI, IBR, IBSS, IBZ, P30, PAIS, PhilInd, RASB, RI-1, RI-2, SCOPUS, SociolAb.
—BLDSC (6962.765000), IE, Infotrieve, Ingenta. **CCC.**
Published by: University of Illinois Press, 1325 S Oak St, Champaign, IL 61820. TEL 217-333-0950, 866-244-0626, FAX 217-244-8082, journals@uillinois.edu. Ed. Robert B Talisse. Adv. contact Jeff McArdle TEL 217-244-0381. page USD 225; 4.375 x 7.25. Circ: 250.

PUBLIC INTEGRITY. *see* PUBLIC ADMINISTRATION

100 ROM ISSN 2065-7285
▼ ➤ **PUBLIC REASON.** Text in English. 2009. 3/yr. **Document type:** *Journal, Academic/Scholarly.*
Related titles: Online - full text ed.: ISSN 2065-8958. free (effective 2011).
Indexed: AmHI, H07, T02.
Published by: Universitatea din Bucuresti, Facultatea de Filosofia, 36-46 M Kigalnicenau Bd, Sector 5, Bucharest, 70709, Romania. TEL 40-21-3077300, FAX 40-21-3131760, info@unibuc.ro, http://www.unibuc.ro.

➤ **Q J I.** (Quarterly Journal of Ideology) *see* POLITICAL SCIENCE

➤ **QINGDAO DAXUE SHIFAN XUEYUAN XUEBAO/TEACHERS COLLEGE QINGDAO UNIVERSITY. JOURNAL.** *see* SOCIAL SCIENCES: COMPREHENSIVE WORKS

➤ **QINGHAI SHIFAN DAXUE XUEBAO (ZHEXUE SHEHUI KEXUE BAN)/QINGHAI NORMAL UNIVERSITY. JOURNAL (PHILOSOPHY AND SOCIAL SCIENCE EDITION).** *see* SOCIAL SCIENCES: COMPREHENSIVE WORKS

100 CHN ISSN 1000-0062
AS452.P4417
QINGHUA DAXUE XUEBAO (ZHEXUE SHEHUI KEXUE BAN)/ TSINGHUA UNIVERSITY. JOURNAL (PHILOSOPHY AND SOCIAL SCIENCES). Text in Chinese. 1986. bi-m. USD 40.20 (effective 2009). **Document type:** *Journal, Academic/Scholarly.*
Related titles: Online - full text ed.
—East View.
Published by: Qinghua Daxue, Xuebao Bianjibu/Tsinghua University, Editorial Board, Haidian-qu, Qinghuayuan, 100, Wenxi Lou, Beijing, 100084, China. TEL 86-10-62783533.

QIUSHI XUEKAN/SEEKING TRUTH. *see* SOCIAL SCIENCES: COMPREHENSIVE WORKS

111.85 ITA ISSN 1825-7763
QUADERNI DI ESTETICA. Text in Italian. 2002. irreg. **Document type:** *Monographic series, Academic/Scholarly.*
Published by: Mimesis Edizioni, Via Risorgimento 33, Sesto San Giovanni, MI 20099, Italy. http://www.mimesisedizioni.it.

111.85 ITA ISSN 1972-3342
QUADERNI DI ESTETICA E CRITICA. Text in Italian. 2006. a. **Document type:** *Journal, Academic/Scholarly.*
Published by: Bulzoni Editore, Via dei Liburni 14, Rome, 00185, Italy. TEL 39-06-4455207, FAX 39-06-4450355, bulzoni@bulzoni.it, http://www.bulzoni.it.

100 ITA ISSN 1970-2388
QUADERNI DI FILOSOFIA. Text in Italian. 2002. irreg. price varies. **Document type:** *Journal, Academic/Scholarly.*
Published by: Bibliopolis, Via Vincenzo Arangio Ruiz 83, Naples, NA 80122, Italy. TEL 39-081-664606, FAX 39-081-7616273, info@bibliopolis.it, http://www.bibliopolis.it.

100 370 ESP ISSN 0213-5965
QUADERNS DE FILOSOFIA Y CIENCIA. Text in Multiple languages. 1982. s-a. **Document type:** *Journal, Academic/Scholarly.*
Formerly (until 1984): Cuadernos de Filosofia y Ciencia (0212-2669)
Indexed: CCMJ, MSN, MathR, PhilInd.
Published by: Societat de Filosofia del Pais Valencia, Facultat de Filosofia i Ciencies de l'Educacio, Universitat de Valencia, Avgda Blasco Ibanez 30, Valencia, 40610, Spain. sfpv@uv.es, http://www.uv.es/sfpv/cat/presentacio.htm.

110 BEL ISSN 1379-2547
BD111
QUAESTIO. Variant title: Annuaire d'Histoire de la Metaphysique. Annuario di Storia della Metafisica. Jahrbuch fuer die Geschichte der Metaphysik. Yearbook of the History of Metaphysics. Text in French. 2001. a. EUR 114 combined subscription (print & online eds.) (effective 2012). **Document type:** *Journal, Academic/Scholarly.* **Description:** Examines the ancient origins of metaphysics and its reception, transformation, or rejection into modern and contemporary philosophy.
Related titles: Online - full text ed.
—IE.
Published by: Brepols Publishers, Begijnhof 67, Turnhout, 2300, Belgium. TEL 32-14-448030, FAX 32-14-428919, periodicals@brepols.net, http://www.brepols.net. Eds. Constantino Esposito, Pasquale Porro.

100 DEU
QUAESTIONES; Themen und Gestalten der Philosophie. Text in German. 1991. irreg., latest vol.14, 2003. price varies. **Document type:** *Monographic series, Academic/Scholarly.*
Published by: Frommann-Holzboog Verlag e.K., Koenig-Karl-Str 27, Stuttgart, 70372, Germany. TEL 49-711-9559690, FAX 49-711-9559691, info@frommann-holzboog.de, http://www.frommann-holzboog.de.

100 USA ISSN 2150-5756
▼ **QUAESTIONES DISPUTATAE.** Text in English. 2010. s-a. USD 25 (effective 2010). **Document type:** *Journal, Academic/Scholarly.* **Description:** Addresses significant questions and topics of contemporary philosophic interest. Each issue has a special theme.
Address: 1235 University Blvd, Steubenville, OH 43952. TEL 740-284-5345, mroberts@franciscan.edu.

109 DEU ISSN 0344-8142
B23
➤ **QUELLEN UND STUDIEN ZUR PHILOSOPHIE.** Text in German. 1960. irreg., latest vol.104, 2011. price varies. **Document type:** *Monographic series, Academic/Scholarly.*
Formerly (until 1971): Quellen und Studien zur Geschichte der Philosophie (0481-3618)
Published by: Walter de Gruyter GmbH & Co. KG, Genthiner Str 13, Berlin, 10785, Germany. TEL 49-30-260050, FAX 49-30-26005251, info@degruyter.com, http://www.degruyter.de. Ed. Dominik Perler.

100 NLD ISSN 1011-226X
B1
➤ **QUEST (LEIDEN);** philosophical discussions. Text in English, French. 1987. s-a. USD 15 in Africa to individuals; USD 25 elsewhere to individuals; USD 20 in Africa to institutions; USD 35 elsewhere to institutions (effective 2010). bk.rev. illus. back issues avail.; reprints avail. **Document type:** *Journal, Academic/Scholarly.* **Description:** Endeavors to act as a channel of expression for African thinkers; reflects on the radical transformations taking place. Intended to serve professionals and students of philosophy and intellectuals in other disciplines.
Indexed: ASD, IBSS, PCI, PhilInd, RASB.
—Ingenta.
Published by: (Zambia. University of Zambia ZMB, Department of Philosophy), Quest, c/o Wim van Binsbergen, PO Box 9555, Leiden, 2300 RB, Netherlands. FAX 31-71-5273344.

100 USA ISSN 1541-4760
➤ **QUESTIONS;** philosophy for young people. Text in English. 2001. a. USD 25 per issue to individuals; USD 50 per issue to institutions; USD 58 combined subscription per issue to individuals (print & online eds.); USD 90 combined subscription per issue to institutions (print & online eds.) (effective 2010). adv. back issues avail. **Document type:** *Journal, Academic/Scholarly.* **Description:** Brings out articles offering advice and ideas for teachers and parents interested in facilitating philosophical discussions with young people.
Related titles: Online - full text ed.: ISSN 2154-1183. USD 40 per issue to individuals; USD 75 per issue to institutions (effective 2010).
Indexed: A26, I05, I07.
—**CCC.**
Published by: (Northwest Center for Philosophy for Children), Philosophy Documentation Center, PO Box 7147, Charlottesville, VA 22906. TEL 434-220-3300, FAX 434-220-3301, order@pdcnet.org, http://www.pdcnet.org. Eds. Alison C Reiheld, Rory E Kraft Jr. Adv. contact Greg Swope.

100 FRA ISSN 2105-6188
▼ **R E P H A.** (Revue Etudiante de Philosophie Analytique) Text in French. 2009. s-a. **Document type:** *Journal, Academic/Scholarly.*
Related titles: Online - full text ed.: ISSN 2115-4600. 2011.
Published by: Revue Etudiante de Philosophie Analytique, 66, Rue Didot, Paris, 75014, France. postmaster@repha.fr, http://www.repha.fr.

340 GBR ISSN 0300-211X
B1 CODEN: RAPHEH
➤ **RADICAL PHILOSOPHY.** Text in English. 1972. bi-m. GBP 30 domestic to individuals; GBP 36 in Europe to individuals; GBP 37 elsewhere to individuals; GBP 80 domestic to institutions; GBP 86 in Europe to institutions; GBP 90 elsewhere to institutions (effective 2009). adv. bk.rev. illus. cum.index: nos.1-60. back issues avail. **Document type:** *Journal, Academic/Scholarly.* **Description:** Provides a forum for the theoretical work which was emerging in the wake of the radical movements of the 1960s, in philosophy and other fields.
Indexed: A20, A22, ASCA, AltPI, AmHI, BrHumI, CA, H07, IPB, LeftInd, P42, PCI, PSA, PhilInd, RASB, S02, S03, SCOPUS, SOPODA, SSA, SSCI, SociolAb, T02, W07, W09.
—BLDSC (7228.095000), IE, Infotrieve, Ingenta. **CCC.**
Published by: Radical Philosophy Ltd., c/o Stewart Martin, Trent Park campus, Trent Park campus, Bramley Rd, London, N14 4YZ, United Kingdom. S.C.Martin@mdx.ac.uk. Adv. contact Pater Hallward. page GBP 220. **Subscr. to:** PO Box 2068, Bushey, Herts WD23 3ZF, United Kingdom. TEL 44-20-89509117, tenalps@alliance-media.co.uk.

306 USA ISSN 1388-4441
➤ **RADICAL PHILOSOPHY REVIEW.** Abbreviated title: R P R. Text in English. 1998. s-a. USD 69 per issue to institutions; USD 249 combined subscription per issue to institutions (print & online eds.); free to members (effective 2009). bk.rev. back issues avail.; reprint service avail. from PSC. **Document type:** *Journal, Academic/ Scholarly.* **Description:** Features original articles, special discussions, and reviews that will be of interest to those who share the view that society should be built on cooperation rather than competition, and that social decision-making should be governed by democratic procedures.
Formerly (until 1996): Radical Philosophy Review of Books (1047-8302)
Related titles: Online - full text ed.: ISSN 1569-1659. USD 207 per issue to institutions (effective 2009).
Indexed: A01, A03, A08, AltPI, AmHI, CA, H07, IBR, IBSS, IBZ, LeftInd, MLA-IB, P42, PhilInd, S02, S03, SociolAb, T02.
—BLDSC (7228.095050), INIST. **CCC.**
Published by: (Radical Philosophy Association), Philosophy Documentation Center, PO Box 7147, Charlottesville, VA 22906. TEL 434-220-3300, FAX 434-220-3301, order@pdcnet.org, http://www.pdcnet.org. Ed. Jeffrey Paris TEL 415-422-5116. R&P George Leaman. Adv. contact Greg Swope.

100 USA ISSN 1934-547X
➤ **RADICAL PHILOSOPHY TODAY.** Text in English. 2000. irreg., latest vol.5. USD 26 per issue to individuals; USD 41 per issue to institutions (effective 2009). back issues avail. **Document type:** *Monographic series, Academic/Scholarly.* **Description:** Provides an overview of the current research interests of philosophers working from a range of socially or politically progressive orientations, and each volume is organized around the conference theme.
Related titles: Online - full text ed.: ISSN 2154-1558. USD 35 per issue to individuals; USD 75 per issue to institutions; USD 25 per issue to members (effective 2009).
Indexed: AltPI.
Published by: (Radical Philosophy Association), Philosophy Documentation Center, PO Box 7147, Charlottesville, VA 22906. TEL 434-220-3300, FAX 434-220-3301, order@pdcnet.org, http://www.pdcnet.org. R&P George Leaman. Adv. contact Greg Swope.

100 ITA ISSN 1720-2396
RAGION PRATICA. Text in Italian. 1993. s-a. EUR 69.50 combined subscription domestic to institutions (print & online eds.); EUR 105 combined subscription foreign to institutions (print & online eds.) (effective 2009). **Document type:** *Journal, Academic/Scholarly.*
Related titles: Online - full text ed.
Indexed: IPB.
Published by: Societa Editrice Il Mulino, Strada Maggiore 37, Bologna, 40125, Italy. TEL 39-051-256011, FAX 39-051-256034, riviste@mulino.it. Ed. M Barberis.

100 200 ITA ISSN 1971-0577
RAGIONE & FEDE. Text in Italian. 1984. irreg. **Document type:** *Magazine, Consumer.*
Published by: Edizioni A R E S, Via Antonio Stradivari 7, Milan, 20131, Italy. TEL 39-02-29514202, FAX 39-02-520163, info@ares.mi.it, http://www.ares.mi.it.

RAINBOW RAY FOCUS. *see* NEW AGE PUBLICATIONS

211 FRA ISSN 0033-9075
B2
RAISON PRESENTE. Text in French. 1966. q. EUR 46 to individuals; EUR 80 to institutions (effective 2009). bk.rev.; film rev.
Indexed: CA, FR, GeoRef, IBSS, MLA-IB, P34, P42, PAIS, PSA, S02, S03, SCOPUS, SOPODA, SSA, SociolAb, SpeleolAb, T02.
—BLDSC (7253.221000), INIST. **CCC.**
Published by: Union Rationaliste, 14 rue de l'Ecole Polytechnique, Paris, 75005, France. TEL 33-1-46330350, http://www.union-rationaliste.org. Ed. Jean Paul Thomas.

170 IND ISSN 2013-8393
▼ ➤ **RAMON LLULL JOURNAL OF APPLIED ETHICS.** Text in English. 2010. a. **Document type:** *Journal, Academic/Scholarly.*
Related titles: Online - full text ed.: ISSN 2229-578X. free (effective 2011).
Indexed: A01.
—**CCC.**
Published by: Medknow Publications and Media Pvt. Ltd., B-9, Kanara Business Ctr, Off Link Rd, Ghatkopar (E), Mumbai, Maharastra 400 075, India. TEL 91-22-66491818, FAX 91-22-66491817, publishing@medknow.com, http://www.medknow.com.

100 GBR ISSN 0034-0006
B1
➤ **RATIO;** an international journal of analytic philosophy. Text in English. 1957; N.S. 1988. q. GBP 445 in United Kingdom to institutions; EUR 564 in Europe to institutions; USD 956 in the Americas to institutions; USD 1,112 elsewhere to institutions; GBP 511 combined subscription in United Kingdom to institutions (print & online eds.); EUR 649 combined subscription in Europe to institutions (print & online eds.); USD 1,100 combined subscription in the Americas to institutions (print & online eds.); USD 1,280 combined subscription elsewhere to institutions (print & online eds.) (effective 2012). bk.rev. illus. index. back issues avail.; reprint service avail. from PSC. **Document type:** *Journal, Academic/Scholarly.* **Description:** Provides articles which meet the highest standards of philosophical expertise, while at the same time remaining accessible to readers from a broad range of philosophical disciplines.
Related titles: Online - full text ed.: ISSN 1467-9329. N.S. GBP 445 in United Kingdom to institutions; EUR 564 in Europe to institutions; USD 956 in the Americas to institutions; USD 1,112 elsewhere to institutions (effective 2012) (from IngentaConnect).
Indexed: A01, A03, A08, A20, A22, A26, AmHI, ArtHuCI, BrHumI, CA, CurCont, E01, FR, H07, IBR, IBZ, IPB, MLA-IB, MathR, P42, PCI, PhilInd, RASB, SCOPUS, SOPODA, SociolAb, T02, W07.
—BLDSC (7295.400000), IE, Infotrieve, Ingenta, INIST. **CCC.**
Published by: Wiley-Blackwell Publishing Ltd. (Subsidiary of: John Wiley & Sons, Inc.), 9600 Garsington Rd, Oxford, OX4 2DQ, United Kingdom. TEL 44-1865-776868, FAX 44-1865-714591, customerservices@blackwellpublishing.com. Ed. John G Cottingham TEL 44-1189-318325. Adv. contact Craig Pickett TEL 44-1865-476267.

➤ **RATIO FIDEI;** Beitraege zur philosophischen Rechenschaft der Theologie. *see* RELIGIONS AND THEOLOGY

100 CHE ISSN 0253-3294
RATIO HUMANA. Text in German. 1975. q. CHF 60 (effective 2003). adv. bk.rev. **Document type:** *Journal, Academic/Scholarly.*
Published by: Schweizerische Vereinigung fuer Humanismus, Hohlegasse 6, Postfach 10, Uster, 8612, Switzerland. TEL 41-1-9403850. Ed., Adv. contact Albert Anderes.

RATIO JURIS; an international journal of jurisprudence and philosophy law. *see* LAW

RAW NERVZ HAIKU; a quarterly of haiku and related material. *see* LITERATURE—Poetry

320 ESP ISSN 0212-5978
DP1
➤ **RAZON ESPANOLA.** Text in Spanish. 1983. bi-m. adv. bk.rev. **Document type:** *Magazine, Consumer.*
Indexed: IBR, IBZ, P09, PCI.

P

Published by: Fundacion Balmes, Paseo Santa Maria de la Cabeza 59, 4o D., Madrid, 28045, Spain. TEL 34-1-4744689. Ed. G Fernandez de la Mora. Adv. contact Juana Fernandez Silva. Circ: 3,000.

100 USA ISSN 0882-6196
READING PLUS. Text in English. 1986. irreg., latest vol.16, 1995. price varies. **Document type:** *Monographic series, Academic/Scholarly.*
Description: Presents textual, intertextual, and textural crosscuttings to enhance the re-reading and fresh understanding of classical and modern works.
Published by: Peter Lang Publishing, Inc. (Subsidiary of: Peter Lang Publishing Group), 29 Broadway, New York, NY 10006. TEL 212-647-7706, 212-647-7700, 800-770-5264, FAX 212-647-7707, customerservice@plang.com, http://www.peterlang.com.

100 DEU
▼ **REASON AND NORMATIVITY/RAZON Y NORMATIVIDAD/ VERNUNFT UND NORMATIVITAET**; a series on practical reason, morality and natural law. Text in German. 2010. irreg., latest vol.3, 2011. price varies. **Document type:** *Monographic series, Academic/ Scholarly.*
Published by: Georg Olms Verlag, Hagentorwall 7, Hildesheim, 31134, Germany. TEL 49-5121-15010, FAX 49-5121-150150, info@olms.de.

100 USA ISSN 0363-1893
➤ **REASON PAPERS**; a journal of interdisciplinary normative studies. Text in English. 1974. a. USD 25 per issue (effective 2009). bk.rev. **Document type:** *Journal, Academic/Scholarly.* **Description:** Contains articles on moral, political, legal, and social/cultural philosophy.
Indexed: A26, AmHI, H07, H12, I05, P30, Philind, T02.
—**CCC.**
Address: c/o Aeon Skoble, Department of Philosophy, Bridgewater State College, Bridgewater, MA 02325. TEL 508-531-2460. Ed. Aeon Skoble.

100 ITA ISSN 1826-4654
RECENSIONI FILOSOFICHE. Abbreviated title: ReF. Text in Italian. 2005. m. **Document type:** *Magazine, Consumer.* **Description:** Dedicated to reviewing philosophy texts.
Media: Online - full text.

100 ESP ISSN 1130-6149
RECERCA; revista de pensament i analisi. Text in Spanish, Catalan. 1974. s-a. **Document type:** *Journal, Academic/Scholarly.*
Formerly (until 1989): Millars. Filosofia y Ciencias de la Educacion (0213-5655); Which superseded in part (in 1983): Millars (0210-5683)
Indexed: Philind.
Published by: Universitat Jaume I, Servei de Comunicacio i Publicacions, Edif. de Recorat i Serveis Centrals, Pl. 0, Campus del Riu Sec., Castello de la Plana, 12071, Spain. TEL 34-964-728821, FAX 34-964-728832, publicacions@uji.es, http://sic.uji.es/publ/.

RECHERCHES AUGUSTINIENNES ET PATRISTIQUES. *see* RELIGIONS AND THEOLOGY

100 BEL ISSN 1377-9613
RECHERCHES HUSSERLIENNES. Text in French. 1995. s-a. **Document type:** *Journal, Academic/Scholarly.*
—INIST.
Published by: Facultes Universitaires Saint Louis, Centre de Recherches Phenomenologiques, Boulevard du Jardin Botanique 43, Brussels, 1000, Belgium. TEL 32-2-2117911, FAX 32-2-2117997, http://www.fusl.ac.be/crp/.

202.2 COD
RECHERCHES PHILOSOPHIQUES AFRICAINES. Text in English, French. 1977. a. USD 5. adv. bk.rev.
Formerly (until 1977): Recherches Philosophiques Africaines. Collection
Published by: Faculte Catholique de Kinshasa, BP 1534, Kinshasa-Limite, Congo, Dem. Republic. TEL 78476. Circ: 1,500.

105 401 FRA ISSN 0754-331X
B2
RECHERCHES SUR LA PHILOSOPHIE ET LE LANGAGE. Text in French. 1981. a., latest vol.22. **Document type:** *Academic/Scholarly.*
Indexed: FR, Philind.
—INIST.
Published by: (Groupe de Recherches sur la Philosophie et le Langage), Librairie Philosophique J. Vrin, 6 Place de la Sorbonne, Paris, 75005, France. TEL 33-1-43540347, FAX 33-1-43544818, contact@vrin.fr, http://www.vrin.fr. Ed. Denis Vernant.

100 DEU ISSN 1613-5342
RECHTS-, SOZIAL- UND WIRTSCHAFTSPHILOSOPHIE. Text in German. 1982. irreg., latest vol.21, 2010. price varies. **Document type:** *Monographic series, Academic/Scholarly.*
Published by: Peter Lang GmbH (Subsidiary of: Peter Lang Publishing Group), Eschborner Landstr 42-50, Frankfurt Am Main, 60489, Germany. TEL 49-69-7807050, FAX 49-69-78070550, zentrale.frankfurt@peterlang.com.

340 DEU ISSN 0941-9527
RECHTSPHILOSOPHISCHE HEFTE; Beitraege zur Rechtswissenschaft, Philosophie und Politik. Text in German. 1993. irreg., latest vol.13, 2007. price varies. **Document type:** *Monographic series, Academic/ Scholarly.*
Published by: Peter Lang GmbH (Subsidiary of: Peter Lang Publishing Group), Eschborner Landstr 42-50, Frankfurt Am Main, 60489, Germany. TEL 49-69-7807050, FAX 49-69-78070550, zentrale.frankfurt@peterlang.com, http://www.peterlang.com. Ed. Ulrich Steinvorth.

RECHTSPHILOSOPHISCHE SCHRIFTEN. *see* LAW

100 BRA ISSN 1984-7157
▼ **REDESCRICOES.** Text in Portuguese. 2009. 3/yr. free (effective 2011). **Document type:** *Journal, Academic/Scholarly.*
Media: Online - full text.
Published by: Asociacao Nacional de Pos - Graduacao em Filosofia, Avenida Epitacio Pessoa 1834, Apt 104, Lagoa, Rio de Janeiro, 22411-072, Brazil.

111.85 NLD ISSN 1878-8963
REEKS BURGERHARTLEZINGEN WERKGROEP 18E EEUW. Variant title: Burgerhart Lecture. Burgerhartlezing. Text in Dutch. 2008. a.
Related titles: ◆ Supplement to: De Achttiende Eeuw. ISSN 0929-9890.
Published by: (Werkgroep 18e Eeuw/Institute for the History and Foundations of Science), HoLaPress Communicatie bv, Postbus 130, Valkenswaard, 5550 AC, Netherlands. TEL 31-40-2086000, FAX 31-40-2086009, http://www.holapress.com.

100 GBR ISSN 1462-3943
➤ **REFLECTIVE PRACTICE**; international and multidisciplinary perspectives. Text in English. 2000. 5/yr. GBP 615 combined subscription in United Kingdom to institutions (print & online eds.); EUR 811, USD 1,015 combined subscription to institutions (print & online eds.) (effective 2012). adv. back issues avail.; reprint service avail. from PSC. **Document type:** *Journal, Academic/Scholarly.*
Description: Publishes original work that explores reflection within and on practice, as an individual and collective activity, that concerns personal knowing and transformation, collective regeneration and political activism, reflection and voice, values negotiated meaning, identity and community.
Related titles: Online - full text ed.: ISSN 1470-1103. GBP 553 in United Kingdom to institutions; EUR 730, USD 913 to institutions (effective 2012) (from IngentaConnect).
Indexed: A01, A03, A08, A22, B28, B29, C06, C07, CA, CPE, E01, E03, ERI, P03, P48, P53, P54, PQC, PsycInfo, PsycholAb, T02.
—IE, Infotrieve, Ingenta. **CCC.**
Published by: Routledge (Subsidiary of: Taylor & Francis Group), 4 Park Sq, Milton Park, Abingdon, Oxon OX14 4RN, United Kingdom. TEL 44-20-70176000, FAX 44-20-70176336, subscriptions@tandf.co.uk, http://www.routledge.com. Ed. Tony Ghaye. Adv. contact Linda Hann TEL 44-1344-779945. **Subscr. in N America to:** Taylor & Francis Inc., Customer Services Dept, 325 Chestnut St, 8th Fl, Philadelphia, PA 19106. TEL 215-625-8900, 800-354-1420, FAX 215-625-2940, customerservice@taylorandfrancis.com; **Subscr. to:** Taylor & Francis Ltd., Journals Customer Service, Sheepen Pl, Colchester, Essex CO3 3LP, United Kingdom. TEL 44-20-70175544, FAX 44-20-70175198, tf.enquiries@tfinforma.com.

100 DNK ISSN 0906-4664
REFLEKS. Variant title: Reflex. Tidsskriftet Refleks. Tidsskriftet Reflex. Text in Danish. 1990-2000; resumed 2004. s-a. free. **Document type:** *Journal, Academic/Scholarly.*
Related titles: Online - full text ed.
Indexed: RILM.
Published by: Syddansk Universitet, Institut for Filosofi, Paedagogik og Religionsstudier/University of Southern Denmark, Institute of Philosophy, Education and the Study of Religions, Campusvej 55, Odense M, 5230, Denmark. TEL 45-65-503131, FAX 45-65-502830, ifpr@ifpr.sdu.dk, http://www.sdu.dk/Om_SDU/Institutter_centre/ Ifpr.aspx. Ed. Mette Smoelz Skau.

100 BRA ISSN 0102-0269
➤ **REFLEXAO.** Text in Portuguese; Summaries in English, French. 1975. every 4 mos. BRL 30 domestic; USD 10 foreign (effective 1999). bibl. back issues avail. **Document type:** *Magazine, Academic/Scholarly.*
Indexed: IPB.
Published by: Pontificia Universidade Catolica de Campinas, Instituto de Filosofia, Rua Marechal Deodoro, 1099, Centro, Campinas, SP 13020-904, Brazil. TEL 55-19-7355872, FAX 55-19-7355820, if@acad.puccamp.br. Ed. Constanca Marcondes Cesar.

➤ **REFORMED REVIEW (ONLINE).** *see* RELIGIONS AND THEOLOGY—Protestant

100 DEU
▼ **REINHOLDIANA.** Text in German. 2011. irreg., latest vol.2, 2011. price varies. **Document type:** *Monographic series, Academic/Scholarly.*
Published by: Walter de Gruyter GmbH & Co. KG, Genthiner Str 13, Berlin, 10785, Germany. TEL 49-30-260050, FAX 49-30-26005251, info@degruyter.com, http://www.degruyter.de. Ed. Ernst Otto Onnasch.

128 NLD ISSN 1381-2866
RELEVANT. Text in Dutch. 1975. q. EUR 10 (effective 2009). adv. bk.rev. **Document type:** *Consumer.* **Description:** Discusses issues concerning euthanasia and the right to die for persons with terminal illnesses and their families.
Former titles (until 1994): Euthanasie (0921-2396); (until 1985): Nederlandse Vereniging voor Vrijwillige Euthanasie. Kwartaalblad (0921-240X)
Related titles: Audio cassette/tape ed.
Published by: Nederlandse Vereniging voor Vrijwillige Euthanasie/Dutch Voluntary Euthanasia Society, Postbus 75331, Amsterdam, 1070 AH, Netherlands. TEL 31-20-6200690, FAX 31-20-4207216, euthanasie@nvve.nl, http://www.nvve.nl. Ed. Janneke Vonkeman. Circ: 120,000.

RELIGION AND REASON; method and theory in the study and interpretation of religion. *see* RELIGIONS AND THEOLOGY

RELIGION AND SOCIETY. *see* RELIGIONS AND THEOLOGY

RELIGION IN PHILOSOPHY AND THEOLOGY. *see* RELIGIONS AND THEOLOGY

RELIGION UND AUFKLAERUNG. *see* RELIGIONS AND THEOLOGY

189 BEL
RENCONTRES DE PHILOSOPHIE MEDIEVALE. Text in French. 1991. a., latest vol.9, 2000. price varies. back issues avail. **Document type:** *Proceedings, Academic/Scholarly.*
Published by: (Societe Internationale pour l'Etude de la Philosophie Medievale), Brepols Publishers, Begijnhof 67, Turnhout, 2300, Belgium. FAX 32-14-428919, periodicals@brepols.net.

RENCONTRES INTERNATIONALES DE GENEVE. *see* SOCIAL SCIENCES: COMPREHENSIVE WORKS

100 300 TWN ISSN 1018-189X
AS455.T2575
➤ **RENWEN JI SHEHUI KEXUE JIKAN/JOURNAL OF SOCIAL SCIENCES AND PHILOSOPHY.** Text in Chinese, English. 1988. q. free. **Document type:** *Journal, Academic/Scholarly.* **Description:** Publishes contributions in the fields of philosophy, political science, history, economics social studies and law.
—BLDSC (5064.912850), Ingenta.
Published by: Academia Sinica, Sun Yat-Sen Institute for Social Sciences and Philosophy/Chung Yang Yen Chiu Yuan, Chung Shan Ren Wen Sheh Hui Ko Sheyue Yen Chiu So, Nankang, Taipei, 11529, Taiwan. TEL 886-2-7821693, FAX 886-2-7854160, isspub@gate.sinica.edu.tw, http://www.issp.sinica.edu.tw. Eds. Ching-chong Lai, Tien-wang Tsaur. Circ: 1,000.

➤ **REPORT OF THE ETHICS COUNSELLOR ON THE ACTIVITIES OF THE OFFICE OF THE ETHICS COUNSELLOR/RAPPORT DU CONSEILLER EN ETHIQUE SUR LES ACTIVITES DU BUREAU DU CONSEILLER EN ETHIQUE.** *see* PUBLIC ADMINISTRATION

➤ **REPORTS ON MATHEMATICAL LOGIC.** *see* MATHEMATICS

100 POL ISSN 0324-8712
B1
REPORTS ON PHILOSOPHY. Text in English. 1972. a., latest vol.21, 2004. price varies. **Document type:** *Monographic series, Academic/ Scholarly.*
Formerly (until 1977): Uniwersytet Jagiellonski. Zeszyty Naukowe. Prace Filozoficzne (0137-2424)
Indexed: FR, Philind.
Published by: (Uniwersytet Jagiellonski, Instytut Filozofii/Jagiellonian University, Institute of Philosophy), Wydawnictwo Uniwersytetu Jagiellonskiego/Jagiellonian University Press, ul Grodzka 26, Krakow, 31044, Poland. TEL 48-12-4312364, FAX 48-12-4301995, wydaw@if.uj.edu.pl. Ed. Piotr Mroz.

100 DNK ISSN 1603-8509
B8.D3
➤ **RES COGITANS**; journal of philosophy. Text in Multiple languages. 2004. irreg. free (effective 2011). **Document type:** *Journal, Academic/Scholarly.* **Description:** Aims at providing a forum for philosophical discussion at a high level, but does not require any specific methodology or philosophical orientation.
Media: Online - full text.
Indexed: Philind.
Published by: Syddansk Universitet, Institut for Filosofi, Paedagogik og Religionsstudier/University of Southern Denmark, Institute of Philosophy, Education and the Study of Religions, Campusvej 55, Odense M, 5230, Denmark. TEL 45-65-503334, FAX 45-65-432375, ifpr@ifpr.sdu.dk, http://www.sdu.dk/Om_SDU/Institutter_centre/ Ifpr.aspx. Eds. Soeren Harnow Klausen TEL 45-65-503334, Erich Klawonn.

100 USA ISSN 2155-4838
▼ **RES COGITANS (FOREST GROVE).** Text in English. 2010 (July). a. free (effective 2010). **Document type:** *Journal, Academic/Scholarly.*
Description: Features work by undergraduates in all areas of philosophy.
Media: Online - full text.
Published by: Pacific University, 2043 College Way, Forest Grove, OR 97116. silkroad.pacific@gmail.com, jjbutler@pacificu.edu. Ed. David Boersema.

100 ESP ISSN 1576-4184
RES PUBLICA. Text in Spanish. 1998. s-a. **Document type:** *Journal, Academic/Scholarly.*
Published by: (Universidad de Murcia, Departamento de Filosofia), Universidad de Murcia, Servicio de Publicaciones, Edificio Saavedra Fajardo, C/ Actor Isidoro Maiquez 9, Murcia, 30007, Spain. TEL 34-968-363887, FAX 34-968-363414, http://www.um.es/ publicaciones/.

170 340 NLD ISSN 1356-4765
K18 CODEN: REPUFH
➤ **RES PUBLICA**; a journal of moral, legal and social philosophy. Text in English. 1995. 4/yr. EUR 393, USD 409 combined subscription to institutions (print & online eds.) (effective 2012). adv. reprint service avail. from PSC. **Document type:** *Journal, Academic/Scholarly.*
Description: Takes an interdisciplinary approach to the philosophical analysis of moral, social, and legal issues.
Related titles: Online - full text ed.: ISSN 1572-8692 (from IngentaConnect).
Indexed: A22, A26, AmHI, B04, BRD, BibLing, CA, CLI, DIP, E01, G08, H07, I01, I05, I13, IBR, IBZ, ILP, LRI, P10, P28, P30, P42, P45, P48, P53, P54, PQC, PSA, Philind, R05, S02, S03, SCOPUS, SOPODA, SociolAb, T02, W03, W05.
—BLDSC (7713.890070), IE, Infotrieve, Ingenta. **CCC.**
Published by: (U.K. Association for Legal and Social Philosophy), Springer Netherlands (Subsidiary of: Springer Science+Business Media), Van Godewijckstraat 30, Dordrecht, 3311 GX, Netherlands. TEL 31-78-6576050, FAX 31-78-6576474, http://www.springer.com. Eds. Gideon Calder, Jonathan Seglow.

364.4 CHE ISSN 1422-4437
RES SOCIALIS. Text in French. 1996. irreg., latest vol.37, 2011. price varies. **Document type:** *Monographic series, Academic/Scholarly.*
Published by: Academic Press Fribourg, Perolles 42, Fribourg, 1705, Switzerland. TEL 41-26-4264311, FAX 41-26-4264300, info@paulusedition.ch, http://www.paulusedition.ch/academic_press/.

100 ITA ISSN 1828-7778
RESCOGITANS. Text in Italian. 2005. 3/yr. **Document type:** *Magazine, Consumer.*
Media: Online - full text.
Published by: Fondazione Arnoldo e Alberto Mondadori, Via Riccione 8, Milan, 20156, Italy. TEL 39-02-39273061, FAX 39-02-39273069, info@fondazionemondadori.it, http://www.fondazionemondadori.it.

100 NLD ISSN 0085-5553
B829.5
➤ **RESEARCH IN PHENOMENOLOGY.** Text in English. 1971. a., latest vol.38, 2008. EUR 272, USD 380 to institutions; EUR 296, USD 414 combined subscription to institutions (print & online eds.) (effective 2012). adv. bk.rev. back issues avail.; reprint service avail. from PSC. **Document type:** *Journal, Academic/Scholarly.* **Description:** Deals with phenomenological philosophy in a broad sense, including original phenomenological research, critical and interpretative studies of major phenomenological thinkers, studies relating phenomenological philosophy to other disciplines, and historical studies of special relevance to phenomenological philosophy.
Related titles: Online - full text ed.: ISSN 1569-1640. 1994. EUR 247, USD 345 to institutions (effective 2012) (from IngentaConnect).
Indexed: A01, A02, A03, A08, A20, A22, A25, A26, ASCA, AmHI, ArtHuCI, B04, BRD, CA, CurCont, DIP, E-psyche, E01, E08, FR, G08, H07, H08, H09, H10, H14, HAb, HumInd, I05, IBR, IBZ, IPB, IZBG, M01, M02, P02, P10, P26, P28, P48, P53, P54, PCI, PQC, Philind, R05, RASB, RILM, S08, S09, SCOPUS, T02, W03, W05, W07.
—BLDSC (7755.073000), IE, Ingenta, INIST. **CCC.**
Published by: Brill, PO Box 9000, Leiden, 2300 PA, Netherlands. TEL 31-71-5353500, FAX 31-71-5317532, cs@brill.nl. Ed. John Sallis. adv.: B&W page USD 150; trim 9 x 6. Circ: 200. **Dist. by:** Turpin Distribution Services Ltd., Pegasus Dr, Stratton Business Park, Biggleswade, Bedfordshire SG18 8QB, United Kingdom. TEL 44-1767-604954, FAX 44-1767-601640, custserv@turpin-distribution.com, http://www.turpin-distribution.com/.

100 300 IND ISSN 0048-7325
RESEARCH JOURNAL OF PHILOSOPHY AND SOCIAL SCIENCES. Text in English. 1963. s-a. INR 400 per issue (effective 2011). bk.rev. bibl. **Document type:** *Journal, Trade.*
Indexed: BAS, PhilInd.
Published by: (Meerut University), Anu Books Publishers & Distributors, Shivaji Rd, Near IBP Petrol Pump, Meerut, Uttar Pradesh 250 001, India. TEL 91-121-2657362, journal@anubooks.com, http://www.anubooks.com. Ed. James Van Patten.

RESEARCH ON PROFESSIONAL RESPONSIBILITY AND ETHICS IN ACCOUNTING. *see* BUSINESS AND ECONOMICS—Accounting

170 BEL ISSN 0378-9926
RESEAUX - CIEPHUM; revue interdisciplinaire de philosophie morale et politique. Text in French. 1965. irreg. (approx. 3/yr.). EUR 16 domestic to individuals; EUR 23 foreign to individuals; EUR 30 domestic to institutions; EUR 38 foreign to institutions (effective 2002). bk.rev. bibl. **Document type:** *Journal, Academic/Scholarly.*
Formerly (until 1972): Revue Universitaire de Science Morale (0035-435X)
Indexed: FR, IPB, P30, P42, RI-1, RI-2, S02, S03, SOPODA, T02.
—INIST.
Published by: Universite de Mons - Hainaut, Centre Interdisciplinaire d'Etudes Philosophiques, Pl du Parc 20, Mons, 7000, Belgium. TEL 32-65-335084, FAX 32-65-373054. Ed. Claire Lejeune.

THE RESHAPING OF PSYCHOANALYSIS; from Sigmund Freud to Ernest Becker. *see* PSYCHOLOGY

RESURGENCE; an international magazine for ecological and spiritual thinking. *see* POLITICAL SCIENCE

REVELATIONS OF AWARENESS; the cosmic newsletter. *see* NEW AGE PUBLICATIONS

144 360 USA
REVERENCE. Text in English. 1954. a. USD 15 to members. bk.rev. **Document type:** *Newsletter.* **Description:** Informs interested readers of the Schweitzer Fellowship's activities in support of "reverence for life.".
Formerly: Courier (Boston)
Related titles: Microform ed.: (from PQC).
Published by: Albert Schweitzer Fellowship, 330 Brookline Ave, Boston, MA 02215. TEL 617-667-5111, FAX 617-667-7989. Ed. Maurice Loiselle. Circ: 6,500.

330 IND ISSN 0258-1701
H1
REVIEW JOURNAL OF PHILOSOPHY AND SOCIAL SCIENCE. Text in English. 1977. biennial. INR 500 per issue (effective 2011). **Document type:** *Journal, Trade.*
Indexed: PhilInd.
Published by: Anu Books Publishers & Distributors, Shivaji Rd, Near IBP Petrol Pump, Meerut, Uttar Pradesh 250 001, India. TEL 91-121-2657362, journal@anubooks.com, http://www.anubooks.com. Ed. James Sasso.

REVIEW JOURNAL OF POLITICAL PHILOSOPHY. *see* POLITICAL SCIENCE

100 USA ISSN 1841-5261
➤ **REVIEW OF CONTEMPORARY PHILOSOPHY.** Text in English. 2002. a. bk.rev. tr.lit. back issues avail. **Document type:** *Journal, Academic/Scholarly.* **Description:** Publishes work on a wide variety of topics and a broad range of philosophical disciplines.
Formerly (until 2005): Revista de Filosofie Contemporana (1583-5391)
Related titles: Online - full text ed.
Indexed: A39, AmHI, C27, C29, CA, D03, D04, E13, H07, P02, P10, P28, P48, P53, P54, PQC, R14, S14, S15, S18, T02.
Published by: Addleton Academic Publishers, 30-18 50th St, Woodside, NY 11377. TEL 718-626-6017, sales@addletonacademicpublishers.com.

➤ **REVIEW OF EXISTENTIAL PSYCHOLOGY AND PSYCHIATRY.** *see* PSYCHOLOGY

110 USA ISSN 0034-6632
B1
➤ **THE REVIEW OF METAPHYSICS**; a philosophical quarterly. Text in English. 1947. q. USD 40 domestic to individuals; USD 52 foreign to individuals; USD 60 domestic to institutions; USD 72 foreign to institutions (effective 2010). adv. bk.rev. abstr.; bibl.; illus. index, cum.index: 1947-1967. back issues avail.; reprints avail. **Document type:** *Journal, Academic/Scholarly.* **Description:** Promotes persistent, resolute inquiries into root questions, and technically competent, definitive contributions to philosophical knowledge.
Related titles: CD-ROM ed.: ISSN 1549-4853; Microform ed.: (from PQC); Online - full text ed.: ISSN 2154-1302.
Indexed: A01, A02, A03, A06, A07, A08, A20, A22, A25, A26, A30, A31, AA, ABS&EES, ASCA, AmHI, ArtHuCI, ArtInd, B04, B14, BRD, BRI, CA, CBRI, CERDIC, CurCont, DIP, E08, FR, G08, H07, H08, H09, H10, H14, HAb, HumInd, I05, I14, IBR, IBRH, IBZ, IPB, M01, M02, MLA-IB, P02, P10, P13, P26, P28, P30, P48, P53, P54, PCI, PQC, PhilInd, R05, RASB, RI-1, RI-2, RILM, S05, S08, S09, SCOPUS, SOPODA, SociolAb, T02, W03, W05, W07.
—BLDSC (7793.070000), IE, Infotrieve, Ingenta. **CCC.**
Published by: Philosophy Education Society, Inc., Catholic University of America, Washington, DC 20064. TEL 202-635-8778, 800-255-5924, FAX 202-319-4484. Ed. Jude P Dougherty. Adv. contact Mary Rakow.

100 150 NLD ISSN 1878-5158
▼ ➤ **REVIEW OF PHILOSOPHY AND PSYCHOLOGY.** Text in English. 2010 (Mar.). q. EUR 324 combined subscription to institutions (print & online eds.) (effective 2011). **Document type:** *Journal, Academic/Scholarly.*
Related titles: Online - full text ed.: ISSN 1878-5166 (from IngentaConnect).
Indexed: A26, H12, SCOPUS.
—**CCC.**
Published by: Springer Netherlands (Subsidiary of: Springer Science+Business Media), Van Godewijckstraat 30, Dordrecht, 3311 GX, Netherlands. TEL 31-78-6576050, FAX 31-78-6576474. Ed. Dario Taraborelli.

➤ **REVIEW OF RADICAL POLITICAL ECONOMICS.** *see* BUSINESS AND ECONOMICS—Economic Systems And Theories, Economic History

150 GBR ISSN 1755-0203
QA9.A1
REVIEW OF SYMBOLIC LOGIC. Text in English. 2008. q. GBP 440, USD 740 to institutions; GBP 475, USD 778 combined subscription to institutions (print & online eds.) (effective 2012). adv. back issues avail.; reprint service avail. from PSC. **Document type:** *Journal, Academic/Scholarly.* **Description:** Covers all areas of philosophical logic, non-classical, and algebraic logic, plus applications of these logics in such areas as computer science, linguistics, game theory and decision theory, formal epistemology, and cognitive science.
Related titles: Online - full text ed.: ISSN 1755-0211. GBP 415, USD 655 to institutions (effective 2012).
Indexed: A01, A20, A22, ArtHuCI, CurCont, E01, MSN, SCI, T02, W07.
—IE, Linda Hall. **CCC.**
Published by: (Association for Symbolic Logic USA), Cambridge University Press, The Edinburgh Bldg, Shaftesbury Rd, Cambridge, CB2 8RU, United Kingdom. TEL 44-1223-312393, FAX 44-1223-315052, journals@cambridge.org, http://www.cambridge.org/uk. R&P Linda Nicol TEL 44-1223-325702. Adv. contact Rebecca Roberts TEL 44-1223-325083. B&W page GBP 265, B&W page USD 500.

100 USA ISSN 0899-9937
REVISIONING PHILOSOPHY. Text in English. 1989. irreg., latest vol.27, 2003. price varies. back issues avail. **Document type:** *Monographic series, Academic/Scholarly.* **Description:** Publishes innovative thought in the foundation, aim and objectives of philosophy; approaches to world philosophy and the repositioning of traditional viewpoints.
Published by: Peter Lang Publishing, Inc. (Subsidiary of: Peter Lang Publishing Group), 29 Broadway, New York, NY 10006. TEL 212-647-7706, 212-647-7700, 800-770-5264, FAX 212-647-7707, customerservice@plang.com, http://www.peterlang.com. Ed. David Appelbaum.

REVISTA BRASILEIRA DE BIOETICA. *see* BIOLOGY

100 BRA ISSN 1981-7517
REVISTA CONATUS; filosofia de Spinoza. Text in Portuguese, English, Spanish, French. 2007. s-a. **Document type:** *Journal, Academic/Scholarly.*
Related titles: Online - full text ed.: ISSN 1981-7509. free (effective 2011).
Published by: Universidade Estadual do Ceara, Av Paranjana 1700, Campus do Itaperi, Fortaleza, CE, Brazil. TEL 55-85-31019600, http://www.uece.br.

REVISTA DE DIREITO DO UNIFOA. *see* LAW

121 ARG ISSN 1852-625X
▼ **REVISTA DE EPISTEMOLOGIA Y CIENCIAS HUMANAS.** Text in Spanish. 2009. bi-m. back issues avail. **Document type:** *Journal, Academic/Scholarly.*
Published by: Grupo IANUS, Santa Fe 1261 3o Piso Ofic. 323, Rosario, Argentina. TEL 54-341-4850731.

190 ESP ISSN 1577-0079
B4568.O74
➤ **REVISTA DE ESTUDIOS ORTEGUIANOS.** Abstracts in English; Text and summaries in Spanish. 2000 (Nov.). s-a. EUR 24.04 domestic; EUR 32.74 in Europe; EUR 33.66 in the Americas; EUR 34.86 in Asia. abstr.; illus.; bibl. back issues avail. **Document type:** *Journal, Academic/Scholarly.* **Description:** Provides a forum where the new approaches and research works into the different fields of Ortega's thought, such as philosophy, policy, sociology, art, and literature.
Indexed: PhilInd.
Published by: Fundacion Jose Ortega y Gasset, Fortuny 53, Madrid, 28010, Spain. TEL 34-91-7004100, FAX 34-91-7003530, comunicacion@fog.es. Ed. Javier Zamora Bonilla. Pub. Dr. Ignacio Sanchez Camara. R&P Mrs. Carmen Asenjo. **Dist. by:** Asociacion de Revistas Culturales de Espana, C Covarruvias 9 2o. Derecha, Madrid 28010, Spain. TEL 34-91-3086066, FAX 34-91-3199267, info@arce.es, http://www.arce.es/.

100 BRA ISSN 0104-4443
REVISTA DE FILOSOFIA. Text in Portuguese. 1988. s-a. **Document type:** *Journal, Academic/Scholarly.*
Indexed: A20, ArtHuCI, W07.
Published by: Pontificia Universidade Catolica do Parana, Rua Imaculada Conceicao 1155, Prado Velho, Curitiba, PR 80215-901, Brazil. TEL 55-41-32711515, http://www.pucpr.br.

100 CRI ISSN 0034-8252
B5 CODEN: RFURE5
REVISTA DE FILOSOFIA. Text in Spanish. 1958. 3/yr. adv. bk.rev. index. back issues avail. **Document type:** *Journal, Academic/Scholarly.*
Related titles: Online - full text ed.
Indexed: A01, A26, C01, CA, DIP, F03, F04, FR, H21, I04, I05, IBR, IBZ, IPB, MLA-IB, P08, P42, PSA, PhilInd, RASB, S02, S03, SCOPUS, SOPODA, SociolAb, T02.
—INIST.
Published by: Universidad de Costa Rica, Editorial, Sede Rodrigo Facio Brenes, Montes de Oca, San Jose, Costa Rica. TEL 506-207-4000, FAX 506-224-8214, direccion@editorial.ucr.ac.cr, http://editorial.ucr.ac.cr. Circ: 750.

100 ESP ISSN 0034-8244
B5
➤ **REVISTA DE FILOSOFIA.** Text in Spanish. 1942. s-a. EUR 27 domestic; EUR 36 in Europe; EUR 40 elsewhere (effective 2011). bk.rev. bibl.; charts. back issues avail. **Document type:** *Journal, Academic/Scholarly.* **Description:** Covers philosophical works that reflect scientific activities into the Faculty and the University.
Related titles: CD-ROM ed.: ISSN 1695-5129. EUR 54 to individuals; EUR 72 to institutions (effective 2003); Online - full text ed.: ISSN 1988-284X. free.
Indexed: FR, H21, IBR, IBZ, IPB, MLA-IB, P08, P09, P10, P28, P48, P53, P54, PCI, PQC, PhilInd, RASB.
—INIST.
Published by: (Universidad Complutense de Madrid, Facultad de Filosofia), Universidad Complutense de Madrid, Servicio de Publicaciones, C/ Obispo Trejo 2, Ciudad Universitaria, Madrid, 28040, Spain. TEL 34-91-3941127, FAX 34-91-3941126, servicio.publicaciones@rect.ucm.es, http://www.ucm.es/publicaciones. Ed. Juan Manuel Navarro Cordon. Circ: 1,200.

100 MEX ISSN 0185-3481
B5
REVISTA DE FILOSOFIA. Text in Spanish. 1968. 3/yr. MXN 80 (effective 2010). bk.rev. **Document type:** *Journal, Academic/Scholarly.* **Description:** Includes works in philosophy written by professors at the university and others.
Indexed: C01, FR, IBR, IBZ, MLA-IB, PhilInd.
—INIST.
Published by: (Departamento de Filosofia), Universidad Iberoamericana, Prol Paseo de la Reforma 880, Col Lomas de Santa Fe, Mexico City, DF 01210, Mexico. TEL 52-5-2674043, FAX 52-5-2921274, mariana.espinoza@uia.mx. Ed. Dulce Granja Castro. Circ: 750.

100 VEN ISSN 0798-1171
B5
➤ **REVISTA DE FILOSOFIA.** Text in Spanish. 1972. 3/yr. VEB 30 domestic; USD 30 foreign (effective 2011). bk.rev. bibl. **Document type:** *Journal, Academic/Scholarly.* **Description:** Publishes original papers (studies and essays) on philosophy.
Supersedes (after no.1, 1974): Centro de Estudios Filosoficos. Boletin
Related titles: Online - full text ed.: free (effective 2011).
Indexed: A01, A26, CA, E08, F03, F04, I04, I05, PhilInd, S09, SCOPUS, T02.
Published by: Universidad del Zulia, Centro de Estudios Filosoficos "Adolfo Garcia Diaz", Facultad de Humanidades y Educacion, Apartado 526, Maracaibo, Zulia 4011, Venezuela. Circ: 1,000.

100 CHL ISSN 0034-8236
B5
➤ **REVISTA DE FILOSOFIA (SANTIAGO, 1949).** Text in Spanish. 1949. a. bk.rev. abstr. every several years. 200 p./no. 1 cols./p.; back issues avail. **Document type:** *Journal, Academic/Scholarly.*
Related titles: Online - full text ed.: ISSN 0718-4360. 2007. free (effective 2011) (from SciELO).
Indexed: A01, A26, AmHI, C01, CA, F03, F04, FR, H07, I04, I05, IBR, IBZ, MLA-IB, PhilInd, T02.
—INIST.
Published by: Universidad de Chile, Facultad de Filosofia y Humanidades, Capitan Ignacio Carrerr Pinto 1025, Santiago, Chile. http://www.uchile.cl/facultades/filosofia/frameset.htm. Ed. Carla Cordua.

100 BRA
REVISTA DE FILOSOFIA E CIENCIAS HUMANAS. Text in Portuguese. s-a.?. **Document type:** *Academic/Scholarly.*
Published by: Universidade Federal da Bahia, Faculdade de Filosofia e Ciencias Humanas, Rua Sao Lazaro, 197, Federacao, Salvador, BA 40210-720, Brazil. TEL 071-247-2978.

100 ESP ISSN 1888-7759
REVISTA DE FILOSOFIA: SOLILOQUIOS. Text in Spanish. 2008. q. abstr. back issues avail. **Document type:** *Monographic series, Academic/Scholarly.*
Related titles: CD-ROM ed.
Address: J M M Caminero, Apdo 321, Ciudad Real, 13080, Spain. Ed. J M M Caminero.

100 ARG ISSN 0328-6223
B5
REVISTA DE FILOSOFIA Y TEORIA POLITICA. Text in Spanish. 1950. 9/yr. ARS 20 (effective 2010). bk.rev. bibl. index; cum.index.
Formerly (until 1985): Revista de Filosofia (0034-8228)
Indexed: PSA, PhilInd, RASB, SociolAb.
—INIST.
Published by: Universidad Nacional de la Plata, Facultad de Humanidades y Ciencias de la Educacion, Calle 48 entre 6 y 7, 1er Subsuelo, La Plata, Buenos Aires 1900, Argentina. TEL 54-221-4230125, ceciroz@.fahce.unlp.edu.ar. Circ: 300.

100 ROM ISSN 0034-8260
B8.R8
REVISTA DE FILOSOFIE/REVUE DE PHILOSOPHIE. Text in Romanian; Summaries in French, Russian. 1954. 6/yr. bk.rev. index.
Related titles: Online - full text ed.
Indexed: A20, FR, IBR, IBZ, PhilInd, RASB, S02, S03.
—INIST.
Published by: (Academia Romana/Romanian Academy), Editura Academiei Romane/Publishing House of the Romanian Academy, Calea 13 Septembrie 13, Sector 5, Bucharest, 050711, Romania. TEL 40-21-3188146, FAX 40-21-3182444, edacad@ear.ro, http://www.ear.ro. Ed. Alexandru Surdu. **Dist. by:** Rodipet S.A.

100 ESP ISSN 1136-8071
B93
REVISTA DE HISPANISMO FILOSOFICO. Text in Spanish. 1989. a. back issues avail. **Document type:** *Magazine, Academic/Scholarly.*
Formerly (until 1996): Asociacion de Hispanismo Filosofico. Boletin (1132-0060)
Related titles: Online - full text ed.
Indexed: A20, ArtHuCI, PhilInd, W07.
Published by: Asociacion de Hispanismo Filosofico, Via de los Poblados, s-n, Edif. Indubuilding-Goico, 4o., Madrid, 28033, Spain. secrettaria@ahf-filosofia.es, http://www.ahf-filosofia.es/.

100 ESP ISSN 1134-4717
REVISTA DE PENSAMIENTO CRITICO. Text in Spanish. 1994. q. **Document type:** *Journal, Academic/Scholarly.*
Address: Pere Alegrete, 39 2o., Villafranca del Penedes, Barcelona 08720, Spain.

100 BRA ISSN 1980-8372
REVISTA ELECTRONICA DE ESTUDOS HEGELIANOS. Text in Portuguese. 2004. s-m. back issues avail. **Document type:** *Journal, Academic/Scholarly.*
Media: Online - full text.
Published by: Sociedade Hegel Brasileira, c/o Prof. Alfredo de Oliveira Moraes, Ave Acad. Helio Ramos s-n 15o Andar, Cidade Universitaria, Recife, 50740-530, Brazil. TEL 55-82-21268000, FAX 55-82-21268297, reh@hegelbrasil.org, http://www.hegelbrasil.org/index.htm.

100 ESP ISSN 1133-0902
B721
REVISTA ESPANOLA DE FILOSOFIA MEDIEVAL. Text in Spanish. 1993. a. EUR 10 (effective 2009). back issues avail. **Document type:** *Journal, Academic/Scholarly.*
Related titles: Online - full text ed.
Indexed: IPB, PhilInd, RILM.

P

Published by: (Sociedad Espanola de Filosofia Medieval), Prensas Universitarias de Zaragoza, C/ Pedro Cerbuna 12, Edificio de Ciencias Geologicas, Zaragoza, 50009, Spain. TEL 34-976-761330, FAX 34-976-761063, puz@posta.unizar.es, http://puz.unizar.es.

REVISTA ESTUDIOS; revista trimestral publicada por los frailes de la orden de la merced. *see* RELIGIONS AND THEOLOGY

▼ **REVISTA F I D E S.** (Revista de Filosofia do Diretito, do Estado e da Sociedade) *see* LAW

100 BRA ISSN 1982-6613
➤ **REVISTA FILOSOFIA CAPITAL.** Text in Portuguese. 2006. s-a. free (effective 2011). **Document type:** *Journal, Academic/Scholarly.*
Media: Online - full text.
Published by: Grupo de Pesquisa em Filosofia, Artes e Educacao, Qse 01 Lote 01 SL 104, Taguatinga, DF 72.025-020, Brazil.

100 PRT ISSN 0872-0851
REVISTA FILOSOFICA DE COIMBRA. Text in Portuguese. 1992. s-a. **Document type:** *Journal, Academic/Scholarly.*
Published by: Universidade de Coimbra, Faculdade de Letras, Largo da Porta Ferrea, Coimbra, 3004-530, Portugal. TEL 351-239-859900, FAX 351-239-836733, http://www.uc.pt/fluc/.

100 BRA ISSN 2175-6244
▼ **REVISTA INDICE**; revista eletronica de filosofia. Variant title: Indice. Text in Portuguese. 2009. s-a. free (effective 2011). **Document type:** *Journal, Academic/Scholarly.*
Media: Online - full text.
Published by: Universidade Federal do Rio de Janeiro, Av Pedro Calmon 550, Cidade Universitaria, Rio de Janeiro, 21941-901, Brazil. TEL 55-21-25989600, FAX 55-21-25981605, http://www.ufrj.br.

100 320 ESP ISSN 1132-9432
B65
REVISTA INTERNACIONAL DE FILOSOFIA POLITICA. Text in Spanish. 1993. s-a. EUR 20 domestic; EUR 36.71 in Europe; EUR 47.70 elsewhere (effective 2008). **Document type:** *Journal, Academic/Scholarly.*
Indexed: C01, CA, IPB, P42, PSA, PhilInd, SCOPUS, SociolAb, T02.
Published by: Universidad Nacional de Educacion a Distancia (U N E D), Departamento de Filosofia y Filosofia Moral y Politica, Bravo Murillo 38, Madrid, Spain. rifp@human.uned.es, http://www.uned.es/. Ed. Fernando Quesada Castro.

100 ARG ISSN 0325-0725
B5
REVISTA LATINOAMERICANA DE FILOSOFIA. Text in Spanish, Portuguese; Summaries in English. 1975. s-a. USD 25 foreign to individuals; USD 35 foreign to institutions (effective 2007). bk.rev. back issues avail. **Document type:** *Journal, Academic/Scholarly.* **Description:** Presents unpublished works by Latinamerican philosophers.
Related titles: Online - full text ed.: ISSN 1852-9178. 2010 (from SciELO); Cumulative ed(s).: ISSN 1852-7353 (from SciELO).
Indexed: A22, FR, IBR, IBZ, IPB, P09, PCI, PhilInd.
—IE, Infotrieve, INIST.
Published by: Centro de Investigaciones Filosoficas, Casilla de Correo 5379, Buenos Aires, C 1000 WCB, Argentina. cifrlf@mail.retina.ar. Ed. Mario Presas. Circ: 500.

100 CHL ISSN 0718-3712
REVISTA OBSERVACIONES FILOSOFICAS. Text in Spanish. 2005. s-a. free (effective 2011). **Document type:** *Journal, Academic/Scholarly.*
Media: Online - full text.
Published by: Pontificia Universidad Catolica de Valparaiso, Avenida Brasil 2950, Valparaiso, 4059, Chile. TEL 56-32-273000, FAX 56-32-212746, rector@ucv.cl, http://www.ucv.cl. Ed. Adolfo Vasquez Rocca.

100 BRA ISSN 2178-1176
▼ **REVISTA OPINIAO FILOSOFICA.** Text in Portuguese. 2010. s-a. free (effective 2011). **Document type:** *Journal, Academic/Scholarly.*
Media: Online - full text.
Published by: Sociedade Hegel Brasileira, c/o Prof. Alfredo de Oliveira Moraes, Ave Acad. Helio Ramos s-n 15o Andar, Cidade Universitaria, Recife, 50740-530, Brazil. TEL 55-82-21268000, FAX 55-82-21268297, reh@hegelbrasil.org, http://www.hegelbrasil.org/index.htm.

100 ARG ISSN 1514-5999
Q174
REVISTA PATAGONICA DE FILOSOFIA. Text in Spanish. 1999. s-a. back issues avail. **Document type:** *Academic/Scholarly.*
Related titles: Online - full text ed.
Indexed: PhilInd.
Published by: Fundacion Bariloche, Casilla de Correos 138, San Carlos de Bariloche, Rio Negro 8400, Argentina. TEL 54-2944-422050, FAX 54-2944-462550, fb@bariloche.com.ar, http://www.bariloche.com.ar/fb. Ed. Oscar Nudler.

100 PER ISSN 1024-1531
REVISTA PERUANA DE FILOSOFIA APLICADA. Abbreviated title: R P F A. Text in Spanish. 1994. biennial. **Document type:** *Journal, Academic/Scholarly.*
Published by: Universidad Nacional Mayor de San Marcos, Ciudad Universitaria, Jr Jorge Amezaga s/n, Lima, Peru. TEL 51-1-6197000, secgen@unmsm.edu.pe, http://www.unmsm.edu.pe.

100 CHL ISSN 0716-1913
REVISTA PHILOSOPHICA. Text in Spanish. 1978. a. USD 8 per issue (effective 2005). bk.rev. **Document type:** *Journal, Academic/Scholarly.*
Formerly: Philosophica
Indexed: C01, IPB, P09, PCI.
Published by: (Pontificia Universidad Catolica de Valparaiso), Ediciones Universitarias de Valparaiso, Casilla 1415, Valparaiso, Chile. TEL 56-32-273087, FAX 56-32-273429, euvsa@ucv.cl, http://www.euv.cl/inicioeuv.htm. Ed. Juan Antonio Widow. Circ: 300.

100 BRA ISSN 1982-2928
REVISTA PHILOSOPHOS. Text in Portuguese. s-a. **Document type:** *Journal, Academic/Scholarly.*
Formerly (until 2000): Filosofos (Print) (1414-2236); Which superseded in part (in 1995): Ciencias Humanas em Revista; Which superseded in part (1981-1994): Revista do I C H L (0101-6938)
Media: Online - full content.
Indexed: PhilInd.

Published by: Universidade Federal de Goias, Faculdade de Ciencias Humanas e Filosofia, Caixa Postal 131, Goiania - GO, 74001-970, Brazil. TEL 55-62-35211314, FAX 55-62-35211128.

REVISTA PORTUGUESA DE BIOETICA. *see* BIOLOGY

100 PRT ISSN 0870-5283
B5
➤ **REVISTA PORTUGUESA DE FILOSOFIA.** Text in English, Portuguese, French, German, Spanish; Summaries in English, Portuguese. 1945. q. EUR 37.50 domestic to individuals; EUR 50 foreign to individuals; EUR 47.50 domestic to institutions; EUR 60 foreign to institutions (effective 2006). adv. bk.rev. bibl. index, cum.index: 1945-1994. reprints avail. **Document type:** *Journal, Academic/Scholarly.* **Description:** Publishes articles, commentaries and notes in all areas of philosophy, as well as monographic issues on different philosophical topics and authors.
Related titles: Supplement(s): Revista Portuguesa de Filosofia. Suplemento Bibliografico. ISSN 0035-0400. 1950-suspended.
Indexed: DIP, FR, IBR, IBZ, IPB, MLA, MLA-IB, PhilInd, RI-1, RI-2.
—INIST.
Published by: Universidade Catolica Portuguesa, Faculdade de Filosofia, Praca da Faculdade, 1, Braga, 4710-297, Portugal. TEL 351-253-201200, FAX 351-253-201210, jvila-cha@braga.ucp.pt. Ed., Pub., R&P, Adv. contact Joao J Vila-Cha. Circ: 1,000 (paid and controlled).

➤ **REVISTA ROMANA DE BIOETICA.** *see* BIOLOGY

➤ **REVISTA TEMAS DE BIOETICA.** *see* BIOLOGY—Genetics

100 BRA
➤ **REVISTA TRAGICA**; estudos sobre Nietzsche. Text in Portuguese; Summaries in English, Portuguese. 2008 (Jul.). s-a. free. bk.rev. abstr. back issues avail. **Document type:** *Journal, Academic/Scholarly.* **Description:** Publishes original articles and reviews about Nietzsche's philosophy and its main commentators. It's directed to graduate students, university professors and researchers.
Formerly: Tragica: Estudos Sobre Nietzsche (Print) (1982-5870)
Media: Online - full text. Eds., Pubs. Ana Claudia Gama Barreto, Danilo Bilate, Tiago Barros.

100 056 VEN ISSN 1013-2368
B5
➤ **REVISTA VENEZOLANA DE FILOSOFIA.** Text in Spanish. 1973. s-a. adv. bk.rev. back issues avail. **Document type:** *Journal, Academic/Scholarly.*
Indexed: DIP, FR, IBR, IBZ, IPB, PhilInd.
—INIST.
Published by: Universidad Simon Bolivar, Departamento de Filosofia, Apdo 89000, Caracas, DF 1080-A, Venezuela. TEL 58-02-9063765, FAX 58-02-9063768, rvf@usb.ve. Ed. Javier Sasso. Pub. Alberto Rosales. Adv. contact Fabio Morales. **Co-sponsor:** Sociedad Venezolana de Filosofia.

110 190 FRA ISSN 0035-1571
B2
➤ **REVUE DE METAPHYSIQUE ET DE MORALE.** Text in French; Abstracts in French, English. 1893. q. EUR 83 foreign to institutions (effective 2012). adv. bk.rev. bibl.; illus. reprint service avail. from SCH. **Document type:** *Journal, Academic/Scholarly.*
Related titles: Online - full text ed.: ISSN 2102-5177 (from IDC).
Indexed: A20, A22, ASCA, ArtHuCI, CurCont, FR, IBSS, IPB, MLA, MLA-IB, P30, PCI, PhilInd, RASB, RI-1, RI-2, SCOPUS, W07.
—BLDSC (7933.200000), IE, Infotrieve, Ingenta, INIST. **CCC.**
Published by: (Societe Francaise de Philosophie), Presses Universitaires de France, 6 Avenue Reille, Paris, 75685, France. TEL 33-1-58103161, FAX 33-1-45897530, revues@puf.com, http://www.puf.com. Ed. Isabelle Thomas-Fogiel. Circ: 1,700.

180 BEL ISSN 0771-5420
REVUE DE PHILOSOPHIE ANCIENNE. Text in French. 1983. q. EUR 24.79 (effective 2004).
Indexed: A22, FR, PCI, SCOPUS.
—IE, INIST.
Published by: Editions OUSIA, Rue Bosquet, 37 bte 3, Brussels, 1060, Belgium. TEL 33-2-6471195, FAX 33-2-6473489, ousia@swing.be, http://www.eurorgan.be. Ed. Lambros Couloubaritsis.

REVUE DE PHILOSOPHIE ECONOMIQUE. *see* BUSINESS AND ECONOMICS—Economic Systems And Theories, Economic History

100 FRA ISSN 0035-1776
D1
REVUE DE SYNTHESE. Text in French. 1900. q. EUR 116, USD 144 combined subscription to institutions (print & online eds.) (effective 2012). bk.rev. bibl. index. reprint service avail. from PSC. **Document type:** *Journal, Academic/Scholarly.*
Related titles: Online - full text ed.: ISSN 1955-2343 (from IngentaConnect).
Indexed: A20, A22, A26, ArtHuCI, DIP, E01, E08, EMBASE, ExcerpMed, FR, I14, IBR, IBZ, IPB, MEDLINE, MLA-IB, MSN, MathR, P30, PCI, RASB, SCOPUS, W07.
—IE, INIST, Linda Hall. **CCC.**
Published by: (Centre International de Synthese), Springer France (Subsidiary of: Springer Science+Business Media), 22 Rue de Palestro, Paris, 75002, France. TEL 33-1-53009860, FAX 33-1-53009861, sylvie.kamara@springer.com. Ed. Eric Brian. Circ: 1,000.

REVUE DE THEOLOGIE ET DE PHILOSOPHIE. *see* RELIGIONS AND THEOLOGY

REVUE DE THEOLOGIE ET DE PHILOSOPHIE. CAHIERS. *see* RELIGIONS AND THEOLOGY

100 200 FRA ISSN 0035-2209
B2
REVUE DES SCIENCES PHILOSOPHIQUES ET THEOLOGIQUES. Text in French. 1907. q. USD 120 (effective 2004). bk.rev. index. reprints avail.
Indexed: A20, A21, A22, ASCA, ArtHuCI, BibInd, CERDIC, CurCont, DIP, FR, I14, IBR, IBZ, IPB, IZBG, MLA, MLA-IB, OTA, P30, PCI, PhilInd, R&TA, RASB, RI-1, RI-2, SCOPUS, W07.
—IE, Infotrieve, INIST. **CCC.**
Published by: (Centre d'Etudes du Saulchoir), Librairie Philosophique J. Vrin, 6 place de la Sorbonne, Paris, F-75005, France. TEL 33-1-43540347, FAX 33-1-43544818, contact@vrin.fr, http://www.vrin.fr. Ed. R P Bernard Quelquejeu. Circ: 1,475.

100 FRA ISSN 1760-7507
REVUE D'ETUDES BENTHAMIENNES. Text in English, French. 2006. s-a. free (effective 2011). **Document type:** *Journal, Academic/Scholarly.*
Media: Online - full text.
Published by: (Centre Bentham), Revues.org, 3 Place Victor Hugo, Case no 86, Marseille, 13331, France. TEL 33-4-13550355, FAX 33-4-13550341, http://www.revues.org.

100 BEL ISSN 0048-8143
B1
➤ **REVUE INTERNATIONALE DE PHILOSOPHIE.** Text in English, French. 1938. q. EUR 27.83 (effective 2005). adv. bk.rev. illus. reprints avail. **Document type:** *Journal, Academic/Scholarly.*
Related titles: Microfiche ed.: (from IDC).
Indexed: A20, A22, ASCA, ArtHuCI, BibInd, CurCont, DIP, FR, IBR, IBRH, IBZ, IPB, MLA-IB, MathR, P30, PCI, PhilInd, RASB, SCOPUS, SOPODA, SociolAb, W07.
—BLDSC (7925.119000), IE, Infotrieve, Ingenta, INIST. **CCC.**
Published by: Universa Press, Rue Hoender 24, Wetteren, 9230, Belgium.

100 301 FRA ISSN 1762-6153
AS1
➤ **LA REVUE L I S A.** (Litterature, Histoire des Idees, Images, Societes du Monde Anglophone) Text in French, English. 2003. irreg. free (effective 2011). **Document type:** *Journal, Academic/Scholarly.*
Media: Online - full text.
Indexed: MLA-IB, RILM.
—CCC.
Published by: Universite de Caen, Maison de la Recherche en Sciences Humaines, Esplanade de la Paix, Caen, 14032, France. Ed. Renee Dickason.

294.54 COD
REVUE PHILOSOPHIQUE DE KINSHASA. Text in French, English. 1983. a. USD 70. adv. bk.rev.
Indexed: PLESA.
Published by: Faculte Catholique de Kinshasa, BP 1534, Kinshasa-Limite, Congo, Dem. Republic. TEL 78476. Circ: 1,500.

100 FRA ISSN 0035-3833
B2
➤ **REVUE PHILOSOPHIQUE DE LA FRANCE ET DE L'ETRANGER.** Text in French; Abstracts in French, English. 1876. q. EUR 89 foreign to institutions (effective 2012). bk.rev. abstr.; bibl.; illus. index. reprint service avail. from SCH. **Document type:** *Journal, Academic/Scholarly.*
Related titles: Online - full text ed.
Indexed: A06, A20, ASCA, ArtHuCI, BibInd, CurCont, DIP, FR, H09, H10, I13, IBR, IBRH, IBSS, IBZ, IPB, MLA-IB, P30, PCI, PhilInd, RASB, RILM, S02, S03, S05, SCOPUS, SOPODA, SociolAb, W07.
—INIST. **CCC.**
Published by: Presses Universitaires de France, 6 Avenue Reille, Paris, 75685, France. TEL 33-1-58103161, FAX 33-1-45897530, revues@puf.com, http://www.puf.com. Eds. Dominique Merllie, Yvon Bres.

100 BEL ISSN 0035-3841
B2
➤ **REVUE PHILOSOPHIQUE DE LOUVAIN/BIBLIOGRAFISCH REPERTORIUM VAN DE WIJSBEGEERTE.** Text in French; Summaries in English. 1894. s-a. EUR 70 combined subscription (print & online eds.) (effective 2011). adv. bk.rev. bibl.; illus. index. reprints avail. **Document type:** *Journal, Academic/Scholarly.* **Description:** Review of the international philosophical movement by scholars of the Institute and others as well.
Former titles (until 1946): Revue Neo-Scolastique de Philosophie (0776-555X); (until 1910): Revue Neo-Scolastique (0776-5541)
Related titles: Online - full text ed.: ISSN 1783-1768; ◆ Supplement(s): Repertoire Bibliographique de la Philosophie. ISSN 0034-4567.
Indexed: A20, A22, ASCA, ArtHuCI, BibInd, CPL, CurCont, DIP, FR, I14, IBR, IBZ, IPB, MLA, MLA-IB, P30, PCI, PhilInd, RILM, SCOPUS, W07.
—IE, Infotrieve, INIST.
Published by: (Universite Catholique de Louvain, Institut Superieur de Philosophie), Peeters Publishers, Bondgenotenlaan 153, Leuven, 3000, Belgium. TEL 32-16-235170, FAX 32-16-228500, peeters@peeters-leuven.be, http://www.peeters-leuven.be. Ed. M Ghins. Circ: 1,400. **Co-sponsor:** Fondation Universitaire Belge.

100 160 300 ROM ISSN 1220-5400
B1
REVUE ROUMAINE DE PHILOSOPHIE. Text in Romanian. 1953. 4/yr. ROL 140, USD 52. reprint service avail. from SCH.
Former titles (until 1991): Revue Roumaine de Philosophie et Logique (1220-5486); (until 1990): Revue Roumaine des Sciences Sociales. Serie de Philosophie et Logique (0035-4031); Which superseded in part (in 1964): Revue des Sciences Sociales (0484-8640)
Related titles: Online - full text ed.
Indexed: FR, IPB, PhilInd, RASB.
—INIST.
Published by: (Academia Romana/Romanian Academy), Editura Academiei Romane/Publishing House of the Romanian Academy, Calea 13 Septembrie 13, Sector 5, Bucharest, 050711, Romania. TEL 40-21-3188146, FAX 40-21-3182444, edacad@ear.ro. Ed. G J Gulian. **Dist. by:** Rodipet S.A., Piata Presei Libere 1, sector 1, PO Box 33-57, Bucharest 3, Romania. TEL 40-21-2224126, 40-21-2226407, rodipet@rodipet.ro.

REVUE THOMISTE; revue doctrinale de theologie et de philosophie. *see* RELIGIONS AND THEOLOGY

RHETORIK-FORSCHUNGEN. *see* LITERATURE

RICERCHE STORICHE SALESIANE; rivista semestrale di storia religiosa e civile. *see* RELIGIONS AND THEOLOGY—Roman Catholic

100 700 ITA ISSN 0035-6212
BH4
RIVISTA DI ESTETICA. Text in English, French, Italian. 1956-1973; N.S. 1979. 3/yr. EUR 82 in the European Union; EUR 118 elsewhere (effective 2009). adv. bk.rev. abstr. index. back issues avail. **Document type:** *Journal, Academic/Scholarly.* **Description:** Covers topics related to estetics, word vs. case, rhetoric, philosophy, poetry and anthropology.
Indexed: FR, IPB, MLA, MLA-IB, P30, PhilInd, RASB, RILM.
—IE, INIST.

Published by: Rosenberg & Sellier, Via Andrea Doria 14, Turin, 10123, Italy. TEL 39-011-8127808, FAX 39-011-8127820, info@rosenbergesellier.it, http://www.rosenbergesellier.it. Ed. Maurizio Ferraris. Circ: 1,500.

100 ITA ISSN 0035-6239
B4

RIVISTA DI FILOSOFIA. Text in Italian. 1909. 3/yr. EUR 87 combined subscription domestic to institutions (print & online eds.); EUR 140.50 combined subscription foreign to institutions (print & online eds.) (effective 2009). adv. bk.rev. bibl. index. back issues avail. **Document type:** *Journal, Academic/Scholarly.*
Incorporates (1950-1962): Il Pensiero Critico (0553-6219); Formed by the merger of (1902-1908): Rivista di Filosofia e Scienze Affini (1125-9825); Which was formerly (until 1901): Rivista di Filosofia, Pedagogia e Scienze Affini (1125-9817); (1899-1899): Rivista di Filosofia e Pedagogia (1125-9809); (1899-1908): Rivista Filosofica (1125-9795); Which was formerly (until 1898): Rivista Italiana di Filosofia (1125-9787); (1870-1885): La Filosofia delle Scuole Italiane (1125-9779)
Related titles: Online - full text ed.
Indexed: A22, DIP, FR, IBR, IBZ, IPB, MLA-IB, P30, PCI, PhilInd, RASB.
—IE, Infotrieve, INIST.
Published by: Societa Editrice Il Mulino, Strada Maggiore 37, Bologna, 40125, Italy. TEL 39-051-256011, FAX 39-051-256034, riviste@mulino.it. Ed. Massimo Mori. Circ: 1,500.

149.2 ITA ISSN 0035-6247
B4

RIVISTA DI FILOSOFIA NEO-SCOLASTICA. Text in Italian. 1909. q. EUR 70 domestic to institutions; EUR 120 foreign to institutions (effective 2009). adv. bk.rev. bibl. **Document type:** *Journal, Academic/ Scholarly.* **Description:** Covers various areas in philosophy.
Related titles: Online - full text ed.
Indexed: A20, A22, ASCA, ArtHuCI, CurCont, DIP, FR, IBR, IBZ, IPB, MLA-IB, P30, PCI, PhilInd, RASB, SCOPUS, W07.
—IE, INIST.
Published by: (Universita Cattolica del Sacro Cuore), Vita e Pensiero (Subsidiary of: Universita Cattolica del Sacro Cuore), Largo Gemelli 1, Milan, 20123, Italy. TEL 39-02-72342335, FAX 39-02-72342260, redazione.vp@mi.unicatt.it, http://www.vitaepensiero.it. Ed. Alessandro Ghisalberti. Circ: 850.

109 ITA ISSN 0393-2516
B4

➤ **RIVISTA DI STORIA DELLA FILOSOFIA.** Text in Italian, English, French. 1946; N.S. 1950. s-a. EUR 71.50 combined subscription domestic to institutions (print & online eds.); EUR 121 combined subscription foreign to institutions (print & online eds.) (effective 2009). adv. bk.rev. abstr.; bibl. index. back issues avail. **Document type:** *Journal, Academic/Scholarly.*
Formerly (until 1984): Rivista Critica di Storia della Filosofia (0035-581X); (until 1950): Rivista di Storia della Filosofia (0393-2508)
Related titles: Online - full text ed.: ISSN 1972-5558.
Indexed: A20, A22, ASCA, ArtHuCI, CurCont, DIP, FR, I14, IBR, IBZ, IPB, MLA-IB, P30, PCI, PhilInd, RASB, RI-1, RI-2, SCOPUS, W07.
—IE, Infotrieve, INIST. **CCC.**
Published by: Franco Angeli Edizioni, Viale Monza 106, Milan, 20127, Italy. TEL 39-02-2837141, FAX 39-02-26144793, redazioni@francoangeli.it, http://www.francoangeli.it. Circ: 1,000.

100 ITA ISSN 2035-8873
HX806

RIVISTA DI STUDI UTOPICI. Text in Multiple languages. 2006. s-a. EUR 15 domestic; EUR 20 foreign (effective 2010). **Document type:** *Journal, Academic/Scholarly.*
Related titles: Online - full text ed.: ISSN 2035-8881.
Published by: (Universita degli Studi del Salento, Centro Interuniversitario di Studi Utopici), Carra Editrice, Casella Postale 20, Casarano, LE 73042, Italy. TEL 39-0833-502319, FAX 39-0833-591634, http://www.carraeditrice.it.

RIVISTA INTERNAZIONALE DI FILOSOFIA DEL DIRITTO. *see* LAW

RIVISTA INTERNAZIONALE DI FILOSOFIA DEL DIRITTO. QUADERNI. *see* LAW

100 ITA ISSN 2037-4445

▼ ➤ **RIVISTA ITALIANA DI FILOSOFIA ANALITICA JUNIOR.** Text in Italian, English. 2010. s-a. free (effective 2011). **Document type:** *Journal, Academic/Scholarly.*
Media: Online - full text.
Address: Via Emilo Caldara 34, Soresina, CR 20015, Italy.

100 ITA ISSN 0035-7030
B3640

RIVISTA ROSMINIANA DI FILOSOFIA E DI CULTURA. Text in English, French, Italian, Spanish. 1906; N.S. 1967. q. EUR 40 domestic; EUR 50 foreign (effective 2008). adv. bk.rev. bibl. index. **Document type:** *Journal, Academic/Scholarly.*
Indexed: DIP, FR, IBR, IBZ, IPB, MLA-IB, P30, SOPODA, SociolAb.
—INIST.
Published by: (Centro Internazionale di Studi Rosminiani), Edizioni Rosminiane Sodalitas s.a.s., Corso Umberto 1st, 15, Stresa, VB 28838, Italy. TEL 39-0323-30091, FAX 39-0323-31623, edizioni@rosmini.it. Circ: 600.

100 ITA ISSN 1971-2871

ROCINANTE; studi di filosofia in lingua spagnola. Text in Multiple languages. 2005. a. **Document type:** *Journal, Academic/Scholarly.*
Published by: Citta del Sole Editore, Via Osservatorio 2, Ischia Porto, NA 80077, Italy. TEL 39-081-984332, FAX 39-081-981298.

100 300 POL ISSN 0035-7685
B31 CODEN: RFLZBF

ROCZNIKI FILOZOFICZNE. (In four parts: 1. Metaphysics, Logic, History of Philosophy; 2. Philosophy of Morals, Philosophy of Religion; 3. Natural Philosophy; 4. Psychology) Text in Polish; Summaries in English, French, German. 1948. irreg.?. price varies. bk.rev. index.
Indexed: BibInd, IBR, IBZ, IPB, P30, PCI, PsycholAb, RASB, S02, S03.
—INIST.
Published by: Katolicki Uniwersytet Lubelski, Towarzystwo Naukowe, ul Gliniana 21, Lublin, 20616, Poland. Circ: 720.

100 NLD ISSN 0925-8639

RODOPI PHILOSOPHICAL STUDIES. Text in English. 1993. irreg., latest vol.8, 2007. price varies. back issues avail. **Document type:** *Monographic series, Academic/Scholarly.* **Description:** Publishes South American studies of philosophy.
Indexed: AmHI, H07, T02.
Published by: Editions Rodopi B.V., Tijnmuiden 7, Amsterdam, 1046 AK, Netherlands. TEL 31-20-6114821, FAX 31-20-4472979, info@rodopi.nl. Eds. Ernest Sosa, Carlos Miro Quesada. **Dist in France by:** Nordeal, 30 rue de Verlinghem, BP 139, Lambersart 59832, France. TEL 33-3-20099060, FAX 33-3-20929495; **Dist in N America by:** Rodopi - USA, 606 Newark Ave, 2nd fl, Kenilworth, NJ 07033. TEL 908-497-9031, 800-225-3998, FAX 908-497-9035.

366.4 135.43 MEX ISSN 0035-8266

EL ROSACRUZ. Text in Spanish. 1947. bi-m. USD 9. illus. **Description:** Explores mysticism and philosophy.
Published by: Rosacruz, Calle RIO LERMA 76, Col Cuauhtemoc, Mexico City, DF 06500, Mexico. Pub. Ruben Colomo B. Circ: 17,000 (controlled).

100 DEU

ROSENZWEIG-JAHRBUCH/ROSENZWEIG YEARBOOK. Text in German. 2006. a. EUR 38 (effective 2010). **Document type:** *Journal, Academic/Scholarly.*
Published by: Verlag Karl Alber, Hermann-Herder-Str 4, Freiburg, 79104, Germany. TEL 49-761-2717436, FAX 49-761-2717212, info@verlag-alber.de.

100 DEU

ROSENZWEIGIANA. Text in German. 2006. irreg., latest vol.4, 2009. price varies. **Document type:** *Monographic series, Academic/ Scholarly.*
Published by: Verlag Karl Alber, Hermann-Herder-Str 4, Freiburg, 79104, Germany. TEL 49-761-2717436, FAX 49-761-2717212, info@verlag-alber.de.

110 USA ISSN 0035-8339
BF1623.R7

ROSICRUCIAN DIGEST. Text in English. 1915. s-a. USD 12 to non-members; USD 6 per issue to non-members; free to members (effective 2010). 32 p./no.; **Document type:** *Magazine, Consumer.* **Description:** Publishes articles on philosophy, psychology, metaphysics, and new developments in the arts and sciences.
Formerly (until 19??): Mystic Triangle
Related titles: Online - full text ed.: free (effective 2010).
—Ingenta.
Published by: Rosicrucian Order A M O R C, 1342 Naglee Ave, San Jose, CA 95191. TEL 408-947-3600, FAX 408-947-3677, editorinchief@rosicrucian.org. Circ: 9,000 (paid and free).

100 NLD ISSN 0923-0114

➤ **ROYAL INSTITUTE OF PHILOSOPHY CONFERENCE.** Text in English. 1979. irreg., latest vol.4, 1987. price varies. **Document type:** *Proceedings, Academic/Scholarly.*
—**CCC.**
Published by: (Royal Institute of Philosophy), Springer Netherlands (Subsidiary of: Springer Science+Business Media), Van Godewijckstraat 30, Dordrecht, 3311 GX, Netherlands. TEL 31-78-6576050, FAX 31-78-6576474.

100 GBR ISSN 1358-2461
B11 CODEN: CHASFU

ROYAL INSTITUTE OF PHILOSOPHY SUPPLEMENT. Text in English. 1966. irreg., latest vol.64, 2009. price varies. back issues avail.; reprint service avail. from PSC. **Document type:** *Monographic series, Academic/Scholarly.* **Description:** Contains key philosophical topics arising from the Royal Institute of Philosophy annual conferences and annual lectures.
Former titles (until 1989): Royal Institute of Philosophy. Lecture Series (0957-042X); (until 1982): Royal Institute of Philosophy Lectures (0080-4436)
Related titles: Online - full text ed.: ISSN 1755-3555. 2005; ◆ Supplement to: Philosophy. ISSN 0031-8191.
Indexed: A01, A02, A03, A08, A22, AmHI, CA, DIP, E01, FR, H07, IBR, IBZ, M01, M02, PCI, T02.
—BLDSC (8030.605000), IE, Ingenta, INIST. **CCC.**
Published by: (Royal Institute of Philosophy), Cambridge University Press, The Edinburgh Bldg, Shaftesbury Rd, Cambridge, CB2 8RU, United Kingdom. TEL 44-1223-312393, FAX 44-1223-315052, journals@cambridge.org, http://www.cambridge.org/uk. R&P Linda Nicol TEL 44-1223-325702.

100 POL ISSN 0035-9599
B8.P7

➤ **RUCH FILOZOFICZNY.** Text occasionally in English, German, French; Text mainly in Polish. 1911. q. EUR 46 foreign (effective 2011). bk.rev. abstr.; bibl. index. 150 p./no. 1 cols./p.; back issues avail. **Document type:** *Journal, Academic/Scholarly.* **Description:** Philosophy and history of philosophy including logic and methodology.
Indexed: FR, IBR, IBZ, RASB.
—INIST.
Published by: Polskie Towarzystwo Filozoficzne/Polish Philosophical Society, c/o Uniwersytet Mikolaja Kopernika, Instytut Filozofii, ul. Fosa Staromiejska 1a, Torun, 87100, Poland. olimpiad@ifispan.waw.pl, http://www.ptfilozofia.pl. Eds. Leon Gumanski, Ryszard Wisniewski. Circ: 600 (controlled). **Dist. by:** Ars Polona, Obroncow 25, Warsaw 03933, Poland. TEL 48-22-5098609, FAX 48-22-5098610, arspolona@arspolona.com.pl, http:// www.arspolona.com.pl. **Co-sponsor:** Polska Akademia Nauk, Komitet Badan Naukowych/Polish Academy of Sciences, Committee for Scientific Research.

100 FRA ISSN 1144-0821
B2

RUE DESCARTES. Text in French. 1985. 4/yr. EUR 45 domestic to individuals; EUR 60.14 foreign to individuals; EUR 50 domestic to institutions; EUR 65.14 foreign to institutions (effective 2009). reprint service avail. from SCH. **Document type:** *Journal, Academic/ Scholarly.*
Formerly (until 1991): Le Cahier - College International de Philosophie (0980-1626)
Indexed: FR, IBSS, IPB, PCI.
—IE, Infotrieve.
Published by: (College International de Philosophie), Presses Universitaires de France, 6 Avenue Reille, Paris, 75685, France. TEL 33-1-58103161, FAX 33-1-45897530, revues@puf.com. Ed. Bruno Clement.

RUFFIN SERIES IN BUSINESS ETHICS. *see* BUSINESS AND ECONOMICS

100 ITA ISSN 1970-3554

LA RUOTA. Text in Italian. 1983. irreg. **Document type:** *Monographic series, Academic/Scholarly.*
Published by: Maria Pacini Fazzi Editore, Via dell'Angelo Custode 33, Lucca, 55100, Italy. TEL 39-538-440188, FAX 39-538-464656, mpf@pacinifazzi.it, http://www.pacinifazzi.it. Ed. Silvestro Marcucci.

026 CAN ISSN 0036-0163
B1649 .R94

RUSSELL; the journal of Bertrand Russell studies. Variant title: Russell: the Journal of Bertrand Russell Studies. Text in English. 1971. s-a. USD 45 to individuals; USD 86 to institutions (effective 2008). adv. bk.rev. bibl. back issues avail. **Document type:** *Journal, Academic/ Scholarly.* **Description:** Contains articles and reviews about Bertrand Russell and his work.
Related titles: Online - full text ed.: ISSN 1913-8032.
Indexed: A20, A22, ASCA, ArtHuCI, C03, CBCARef, CurCont, IBRH, IPB, P48, PCI, PQC, PhilInd, SCOPUS, W07.
—BLDSC (8052.660000), IE, Infotrieve, Ingenta.
Published by: McMaster University, Bertrand Russell Research Centre, TSH-619, 1280 Main St W, Hamilton, ON L8S 4M2, Canada. TEL 905-525-9140 ext 24896, FAX 905-577-6930, blackwk@mcmaster.ca. Ed. Kenneth Blackwell. Circ: 350.

100 USA ISSN 1065-9374

RUSSIAN AND EAST EUROPEAN STUDIES IN AESTHETICS AND THE PHILOSOPHY OF CULTURE. Text in English. 1993. irreg., latest vol.4, 1995. price varies. back issues avail. **Document type:** *Monographic series, Academic/Scholarly.* **Description:** Covers art as a social phenomenon, categories of aesthetic analysis, social origins of taste, mathematical aspects of aesthetic analysis, and the material basis of cultural change.
Published by: Peter Lang Publishing, Inc. (Subsidiary of: Peter Lang Publishing Group), 29 Broadway, New York, NY 10006. TEL 212-647-7700, 800-770-5264, FAX 212-647-7707, customerservice@plang.com, http://www.peterlangusa.com. Ed. Willis H Truitt.

100 USA ISSN 1061-1967
B1

➤ **RUSSIAN STUDIES IN PHILOSOPHY.** Abbreviated title: R S P. Text in English. 1962. q. USD 937 combined subscription domestic to institutions (print & online eds.); USD 1,009 combined subscription foreign to institutions (print & online eds.) (effective 2012). adv. illus. index. back issues avail.; reprint service avail. from PSC. **Document type:** *Journal, Academic/Scholarly.* **Description:** Contains English translations of serious Russian work in philosophy, political theory, and social thought.
Formerly (until 1992): Soviet Studies in Philosophy (0038-5883)
Related titles: Online - full text ed.: ISSN 1558-0431. 2004 (June). USD 860 to institutions (effective 2012).
Indexed: A01, A03, A08, A20, A22, ABS&EES, ASCA, AmHI, ArtHuCI, CA, CurCont, DIP, E01, FR, H07, IBR, IBZ, MLA-IB, P30, PCI, PhilInd, SCOPUS, T02, W07.
—BLDSC (8052.931200), IE, Infotrieve, Ingenta, INIST. **CCC.**
Published by: M.E. Sharpe, Inc., 80 Business Park Dr, Armonk, NY 10504. TEL 914-273-1800, 800-541-6563, FAX 914-273-2106, custserv@mesharpe.com. Ed. Marina F Bykova. Adv. contact Barbara Ladd TEL 914-273-1800.

100 500 600 NZL ISSN 1177-1380
Q124.6

THE RUTHERFORD JOURNAL; the New Zealand journal for the history and philosophy of science and technology. Text in English. 2005. irreg. free (effective 2011). **Document type:** *Journal, Academic/ Scholarly.*
Media: Online - full text.
Indexed: A39, C27, C29, D04, E13, S15, S18.
Published by: University of Canterbury, Department of Philosophy, Private Bag 4800, Christchurch, New Zealand. TEL 64-3-3642883. Ed. Jack Copeland.

S A P E R E. (Scripta Antiquitatis Posterioris ad Ethicam Religionemque Pertinentia) *see* RELIGIONS AND THEOLOGY—Other Denominations And Sects

100 ESP ISSN 1885-3617

S I B F. Text in Spanish, English, French, German, Italian. 2005. irreg., latest vol.8, 2007. free (effective 2007). back issues avail. **Document type:** *Journal, Academic/Scholarly.* **Description:** Provides a bibliographical information service for the philosophical community.
Published by: Servicio de Informacion Bibliografica para la Filosofia, c/o Juan Padial, University of Malaga, Faculty of Philosophy and Humanities, Campus de Teatinos, Malaga, 29071, Spain. Ed., Pub. Juan Padial Benticuaga.

S P S C V A NEWSLETTER. *see* MOTION PICTURES

110 FRA ISSN 1779-4676

SACREE PLANETE. Text in French. 2003. bi-m. EUR 25.50 domestic; EUR 28 DOM-TOM; EUR 32 in Europe; EUR 40 elsewhere (effective 2009). back issues avail. **Document type:** *Magazine, Consumer.*
Formerly (until 2005): Stargate Magazine (1765-1565)
Published by: Editions Moan, Le Peuch, Plazac, 24580, France.

100 ITA ISSN 1970-2434

SAGGI. FILOSOFIA. Text in Italian. 2003. irreg. **Document type:** *Monographic series, Academic/Scholarly.*
Published by: Editori Riuniti, c/o The Media Factory, Via Tuscolana 4, Rome, 00182, Italy. TEL 39-06-70614211, FAX 39-06-70613928, http://www.editoririuniti.it.

100 920 AUT ISSN 0259-0794

SALZBURGER BEITRAEGE ZUR PARACELSUSFORSCHUNG. Text in German. 1960. irreg., latest vol.42, 2009. price varies. **Document type:** *Monographic series, Academic/Scholarly.*
Published by: (Internationale Paracelsus-Gesellschaft), Oesterreichischer Kunst- und Kulturverlag, Freundgasse 11, Vienna, 1040, Austria. TEL 43-1-5878551, FAX 43-1-5878552, office@kunstundkulturverlag.at, http://www.kunstundkulturverlag.at.

100 AUT ISSN 0080-5696
B23

SALZBURGER JAHRBUCH FUER PHILOSOPHIE. Text in German. 1957. a. EUR 28 (effective 2010). **Document type:** *Journal, Academic/Scholarly.*
Formerly (until 1960): Salzburger Jahrbuch fuer Philosophie und Psychologie (1012-5868)
Indexed: DIP, FR, IBR, IBZ, IPB, MLA-IB.

P

—INIST.
Published by: Verlag Anton Pustet, Bergstr 12, Salzburg, Sa 5020, Austria. TEL 43-662-87350755, FAX 43-662-87350779, buch@verlag-anton-pustet.at, http://www.verlag-anton-pustet.at.

100 RUS
➤ **SAMARSKII GOSUDARSTVENNYI UNIVERSITET. VESTNIK. GUMANITARNAYA SERIYA. FILOSOFIYA.** Text in Russian. 1995. bi-m. **Document type:** *Journal, Academic/Scholarly.*
Published by: (Samarskii Gosudarstvennyi Universitet), Izdatel'stvo Samarskii Universitet/Publishing House of Samara State University, ul Akademika Pavlova 1, k 209, Samara, 443011, Russian Federation. TEL 7-846-3345406, FAX 7-846-3345406, university-press@ssu.samara.ru, http://publisher.samsu.ru. Ed. G P Yarovoi.

100 USA ISSN 1067-0017
SAN FRANCISCO STATE UNIVERSITY SERIES IN PHILOSOPHY. Text in English. 1993. irreg., latest vol.14, 2007. price varies. back issues avail. **Document type:** *Monographic series, Academic/Scholarly.* **Description:** Designed to encourage philosophers to explore new directions of research in philosophy.
Published by: Peter Lang Publishing, Inc. (Subsidiary of: Peter Lang Publishing Group), 29 Broadway, New York, NY 10006. TEL 212-647-7700, 800-770-5264, FAX 212-647-7707, customerservice@plang.com, http://www.peterlangusa.com. Ed. Anatole Anton.

100 200 ARG ISSN 0036-4703
B4
SAPIENTIA. Text in Spanish. 1946. s-a. ARS 60 domestic; USD 60 foreign (effective 2004). adv. bk.rev. bibl.; charts; illus. index, cum.index: 1946-1992. reprints avail. **Document type:** *Journal, Academic/Scholarly.*
Related titles: Microfilm ed.: (from PQC).
Indexed: C01, CA, CPL, F04, FR, H21, IPB, MLA-IB, P08, P09, PCI, Philind, T02.
—INIST.
Published by: (Pontificia Universidad Catolica Argentina, Facultad de Filosofia y Letras), Pontificia Universidad Catolica Argentina, E D U C A, Av Alicia M de Justo 1400, Buenos Aires, C1107AFD, Argentina. educa@uca.edu.ar, http://www.uca.edu.ar/educa.htm. Ed. Octavio Derisi. Circ: 1,100.

100 200 ITA ISSN 0036-4711
B4
SAPIENZA; rivista internazionale di filosofia e di teologia. Text in Italian. 1948. q. adv. bk.rev. abstr.; bibl. index. **Document type:** *Journal, Academic/Scholarly.*
Indexed: CERDIC, FR, IBR, IBZ, IPB, MLA, MLA-IB, OTA, P30, Philind, RASB.
—INIST.
Published by: Editrice Domenicana Italiana, Via G Marotta 12, Naples, 80133, Italy. http://www.edi.na.it.

142.78 DEU ISSN 1862-166X
SARTRE-GESELLSCHAFT. JAHRBUECHER. Text in German. 2006. irreg., latest vol.2, 2008. price varies. **Document type:** *Monographic series, Academic/Scholarly.*
Published by: (Sartre Gesellschaft e.V.), Peter Lang GmbH (Subsidiary of: Peter Lang Publishing Group), Eschborner Landstr 42-50, Frankfurt Am Main, 60489, Germany. TEL 49-69-7807050, FAX 49-69-78070550, zentrale.frankfurt@peterlang.com. Eds. Peter Knopp, Vincent von Wroblewsky.

142.7 GBR ISSN 1357-1559
B2430.S34
➤ **SARTRE STUDIES INTERNATIONAL;** an interdisciplinary journal of existentialism and contemporary culture. Text in English. 1995. s-a. GBP 101 combined subscription domestic to institutions (print & online eds.); EUR 123 combined subscription in Europe to institutions (print & online eds.); USD 162 combined subscription elsewhere to institutions (print & online eds.) (effective 2011). adv. bk.rev. back issues avail.; reprint service avail. from PSC. **Document type:** *Journal, Academic/Scholarly.* **Description:** Features articles of a multidisciplinary, cross-cultural and international character reflecting the full range and complexity of Sartre's own work.
Related titles: Online - full text ed.: ISSN 1558-5476. GBP 91 domestic to institutions; EUR 111 in Europe to institutions; USD 146 elsewhere to institutions (effective 2011) (from IngentaConnect).
Indexed: A01, A03, A08, A26, B04, BrHumI, CA, E08, G08, I05, L05, L06, MLA-IB, Philind, R05, S09, SCOPUS, SSAI, SSAb, SSI, T02, W03, W05.
—**CCC.**
Published by: (United Kingdom Society for Sartrean Studies, North American Sartre Society USA), Berghahn Books Ltd, 3 Newtec Pl, Magdalen Rd, Oxford, OX4 1RE, United Kingdom. TEL 44-1865-250011, FAX 44-1865-250056, journals@berghahnbooks.com, http://www.berghahnbooks.com. **Dist. in Europe by:** Turpin Distribution Services Ltd., Pegasus Dr, Stratton Business Park, Biggleswade, Bedfordshire SG18 8QB, United Kingdom. TEL 44-1767-604951, FAX 44-1767-601640, berghahnjournalsuk@turpin-distribution.com, http://www.turpin-distribution.com/; **Dist. outside of Europe by:** Turpin Distribution Services Ltd., The Bleachery, 143 W St, New Milford, CT 06776. TEL 860-350-0041, FAX 860-350-0039, berghahnjournalsus@turpin-distribution.com.

105 DEU ISSN 1600-1974
➤ **SATS;** northern european journal of philosophy. Text in English, German. 2000. s-a. EUR 103, USD 155 to institutions; EUR 119, USD 179 combined subscription to institutions (print & online eds.) (effective 2012). bk.rev. back issues avail. **Document type:** *Journal, Academic/Scholarly.*
Related titles: Online - full text ed.: ISSN 1869-7577. EUR 103, USD 155 to institutions (effective 2012).
Indexed: Philind, RILM.
Published by: (Filosofisk Forening i Aarhus/Philosophical Society of Aarhus DNK), Walter de Gruyter GmbH & Co. KG, Genthiner Str 13, Berlin, 10785, Germany. TEL 49-30-260050, FAX 49-30-26005251, info@degruyter.com.

100 294.5 IND ISSN 0972-5016
B59
SATYA NILAYAM; Chennai journal of intercultural philosophy. Text in English. 2002. s-a. bk.rev. back issues avail. **Document type:** *Journal, Academic/Scholarly.* **Description:** Promotes cross-cultural perspective. Each issue has a specific theme and has also a column for current issues to discuss under the heading viewpoints, and reviews or related publications.
Indexed: R&TA.
Published by: Satya Nilayam Research Institute, 201 Kalki Krishnamurthy Rd, Thiruvanmiyur, Chennai, 600 041, India. TEL 91-44-24485879, amaladass24@gmail.com, http://anandamalsnc.com.

100 ITA ISSN 2036-1629
LA SCALA E L'ALBUM. Text in Italian. 2006. irreg. **Document type:** *Monographic series, Academic/Scholarly.*
Published by: Mimesis Edizioni, Via Risorgimento 33, Sesto San Giovanni, MI 20099, Italy. http://www.mimesisedizioni.it. Ed. Luigi Perissinotto.

140 NLD ISSN 2210-8548
SCALA NIEUWSBRIEF. Text in Dutch. 2000. q. EUR 3 newsstand/cover (effective 2010). **Document type:** *Newsletter.*
Published by: Vereniging Scala, Postbus 1330, Roosendaal, 4700 BH, Netherlands.

149.73 577 DEU ISSN 0048-9336
AS181
SCHEIDEWEGE; Jahresschrift fuer skeptisches Denken. Text in German. 1971. a. EUR 28.50 (effective 2012). adv. bk.rev. index. back issues avail. **Document type:** *Journal, Academic/Scholarly.*
Indexed: DIP, IBR, IBZ, MLA-IB, P30.
Published by: S. Hirzel Verlag, Postfach 101061, Stuttgart, 70009, Germany. TEL 49-711-25820, FAX 49-711-2582290, service@hirzel.de, http://www.hirzel.de. Circ: 2,500.

100 ITA ISSN 1973-1582
SCHELLINGHIANA. Text in Italian. 1996. irreg. **Document type:** *Monographic series, Academic/Scholarly.*
Published by: (Istituto Italiano per gli Studi Filosofici (I I S F)), Edizioni Angelo Guerini e Associati SpA, Viale Angelo Filippetti 28, Milan, MI 20122, Italy. TEL 39-02-582980, FAX 39-02-58298030, info@guerini.it, http://www.guerini.it.

100 DEU
SCHELLINGIANA. Text in German. 1989. irreg., latest vol.24, 2009. price varies. **Document type:** *Monographic series, Academic/Scholarly.*
Published by: Frommann-Holzboog Verlag e.K., Koenig-Karl-Str 27, Stuttgart, 70372, Germany. TEL 49-711-9559690, FAX 49-711-9559691, info@frommann-holzboog.de, http://www.frommann-holzboog.de. Ed. Walter E Ehrhardt.

SCHLEIERMACHER-ARCHIV. *see* RELIGIONS AND THEOLOGY

100 DEU ISSN 0080-6935
B3100
SCHOPENHAUER-JAHRBUCH. Text in German. 1948. a. EUR 50 individual membership; EUR 75 institutional membership (effective 2011). bk.rev. reprint service avail. from SCH. **Document type:** *Journal, Academic/Scholarly.* **Description:** Contains articles and research on Schopenhauer's philosophical work.
Indexed: BibInd, DIP, FR, IBR, IBZ, IPB, Philind, RASB, RI-1, RI-2, RILM.
—INIST.
Published by: (Schopenhauer Gesellschaft e.V.), Verlag Koenigshausen und Neumann GmbH, Leistenstr 7, Wuerzburg, 97082, Germany. TEL 49-931-3298700, info@koenigshausen-neumann.de, http://koenigshausen-neumann.gebhardt-riegel.de. Ed. Dr. Margit Ruffing. Circ: 1,912.

SCHRIFTEN ZUR IDEEN- UND WISSENSCHAFTSGESCHICHTE. *see* HISTORY—History Of Europe

174.2 DEU ISSN 1612-0868
SCHRIFTEN ZUR RECHTS- UND STAATSPHILOSOPHIE. Text in German. 2003. irreg., latest vol.10, 2009. price varies. **Document type:** *Monographic series, Academic/Scholarly.*
Published by: Verlag Dr. Kovac, Leverkusenstr 13, Hamburg, 22761, Germany. TEL 49-40-3988800, FAX 49-40-39888055, info@verlagdrkovac.de.

100 DEU ISSN 0932-2434
SCHRIFTEN ZUR TRIADIK UND ONTODYNAMIK. Text in German. 1980. irreg., latest vol.28, 2009. price varies. **Document type:** *Monographic series, Academic/Scholarly.*
Published by: Peter Lang GmbH (Subsidiary of: Peter Lang Publishing Group), Eschborner Landstr 42-50, Frankfurt Am Main, 60489, Germany. TEL 49-69-7807050, FAX 49-69-78070550, zentrale.frankfurt@peterlang.com. Eds. Erwin Schadel, Heinrich Beck.

SCHRIFTENREIHE FUER WIRTSCHAFTS- UND UNTERNEHMENSETHIK. *see* BUSINESS AND ECONOMICS

SCHRIFTENREIHE MEDIZIN - ETHIK - RECHT. *see* MEDICAL SCIENCES

190 NLD ISSN 0925-2657
➤ **SCHRIFTENREIHE ZUR PHILOSOPHIE KARL L POPPERS UND DES KRITISCHEN RATIONALISMUS/SERIES IN THE PHILOSOPHY OF KARL R POPPER AND CRITICAL RATIONALISM.** Text in German, English. 1991. irreg., latest vol.18, 2008. price varies. back issues avail. **Document type:** *Monographic series, Academic/Scholarly.* **Description:** Examines the critical rational philosophy grounded in the work of Karl L Poppers.
—BLDSC (8104.400000).
Published by: Editions Rodopi B.V., Tijnmuiden 7, Amsterdam, 1046 AK, Netherlands. TEL 31-20-6114821, FAX 31-20-4472979, info@rodopi.nl, http://www.rodopi.nl. Ed. Kurt Salamun. **Dist in France by:** Nordeal, 30 rue de Verlinghem, BP 139, Lambersart 59832, France. TEL 33-3-20099060, FAX 33-3-20929495; **Dist. by:** Rodopi - USA, 606 Newark Ave, 2nd fl, Kenilworth, NJ 07033. TEL 908-497-9031, 800-225-3998, FAX 908-497-9035.

▼ ➤ **SCHUTZIAN RESEARCH;** a yearbook of worldly phenomenology and qualitative social science. *see* SOCIAL SCIENCES: COMPREHENSIVE WORKS

100 CHE
▼ **SCHWABE EPICUREA.** Text in German. 2009. irreg., latest vol.2, 2009. price varies. **Document type:** *Monographic series, Academic/Scholarly.*
Published by: Schwabe und Co. AG, Steinentorstr 13, Basel, 4010, Switzerland. TEL 41-61-2789565, FAX 41-61-2789566, verlag@schwabe.ch, http://www.schwabe.ch.

100 CHE
SCHWABE PHILOSOPHICA. Text in German. 2001. irreg., latest vol.12, 2008. price varies. **Document type:** *Monographic series, Academic/Scholarly.*
Published by: Schwabe und Co. AG, Steinentorstr 13, Basel, 4010, Switzerland. TEL 41-61-2789565, FAX 41-61-2789566, verlag@schwabe.ch, http://www.schwabe.ch.

SCIENCE AND CHRISTIAN BELIEF. *see* RELIGIONS AND THEOLOGY

SCIENCE AND ENGINEERING ETHICS. *see* SCIENCES: COMPREHENSIVE WORKS

SCIENCE AND PHILOSOPHY. *see* SCIENCES: COMPREHENSIVE WORKS

200 CAN ISSN 0316-5345
BR1
SCIENCE ET ESPRIT. Text in English. 1948. 3/yr. CAD 30 (effective 2005). bk.rev. index. **Document type:** *Journal, Academic/Scholarly.*
Formerly (until 1968): Sciences Ecclesiastiques (0316-5337)
Indexed: A21, CERDIC, DIP, FR, IBR, IBZ, IPB, IZBG, MLA, MLA-IB, OTA, PdeR, RI-1, RI-2.
—BLDSC (8142.920000), INIST. **CCC.**
Published by: Editions Bellarmin, 165 rue Deslauriers, St Laurent, PQ H4N 2S4, Canada. TEL 514-745-4290, FAX 514-745-4299, editions@fides.qc.ca. Circ: 375.

100 DEU
SCIENTIA ET RELIGIO. Text in German. 2004. irreg., latest vol.7, 2009. price varies. **Document type:** *Monographic series, Academic/Scholarly.*
Published by: Verlag Karl Alber, Hermann-Herder-Str 4, Freiburg, 79104, Germany. TEL 49-761-2717436, FAX 49-761-2717212, info@verlag-alber.de.

100 BRA ISSN 1678-3166
SCIENTIAE STUDIA. Text in Portuguese. 2003. q. **Document type:** *Journal, Academic/Scholarly.*
Related titles: Online - full text ed.: free (effective 2011).
Indexed: Philind.
Published by: Universidade de Sao Paulo, Faculdade de Filosofia, Letras e Ciencias Humanas, Av Professor Luciano Gualberto 315, Butanta, Sao Paulo, SP 05508-010, Brazil.

▼ **SCIENZAEFILOSOFIA.IT.** *see* SCIENCES: COMPREHENSIVE WORKS

100 BRA ISSN 1806-6526
SCINTILLA; revista de filosofia e mistica medieval. Text in Portuguese. 2004. s-a. **Document type:** *Journal, Academic/Scholarly.*
Indexed: AmHI, H07, Philind, T02.
Published by: Faculdade de Filosofia Sao Boaventura, Rua 24 de maio, 135 - Centro, Caixa Postal 6045, Curitiba, PR 80230-080, Brazil. TEL 55-41-21054100, FAX 55-41-21054195, filosofia@saoboaventura.edu.br, http://www.saoboaventura.edu.br.

100 ARG ISSN 1851-8753
SCRIPTA MEDIEVAELIA. Text in Spanish. 2008. s-a. **Document type:** *Journal, Academic/Scholarly.*
Published by: Universidad Nacional del Cuyo, Centro de Estudios Filosoficos Medievales, Centro Universitario C.C. 345, Mendoza, 5500, Argentina. TEL 54-261-4135000, FAX 54-261-4380457, http://ffyl.uncu.edu.ar/spip.php?rubrique168. Ed. Ruben Pereto Rivas.

SCUOLA NORMALE SUPERIORE DI PISA. ANNALI. CLASSE DI LETTERE E FILOSOFIA. *see* HUMANITIES: COMPREHENSIVE WORKS

100 NGA ISSN 0048-9964
SECOND ORDER; an African journal of philosophy. Text in English. 1972. s-a. USD 50. adv. bk.rev. bibl. **Document type:** *Journal, Academic/Scholarly.*
Indexed: MLA-IB.
Published by: Obafemi Awolowo University, Ile Ife, Osun State, Nigeria. TEL 234-36-230290, oauife@oauife.edu.ng, http://www.oauife.edu.ng. Circ: 500.

100 ITA ISSN 1972-2745
SECONDA NAVIGAZIONE. Text in Italian. 1997. a. **Document type:** *Journal, Consumer.*
Published by: Arnoldo Mondadori Editore SpA, Via Mondadori 1, Segrate, 20090, Italy. TEL 39-02-66814363, FAX 39-030-3198412, http://www.mondadori.com.

189 FRA ISSN 1961-6287
LES SECRETS DU TEMPLE. Text in French. 2007. bi-m. **Document type:** *Magazine, Consumer.*
Published by: Societe Highcom, 31 Rue de Rome, Nice, 06100, France.

100 USA ISSN 1529-6261
SEEDS OF UNFOLDING; spiritual ideas for daily living. Text in English. 1982. 3/yr. USD 10; USD 15 foreign (effective 1999). adv. bk.rev.; film rev. back issues avail.
Published by: Cafh Foundation, Inc., 2061 Broadway, New York, NY 10023. TEL 212-724-4260, FAX 914-962-5734, http://www.seedsofunfolding.cafh.org. Ed. Carolyn Cooper. R&P Patricia Colleran. Adv. contact Leonard Ross. **Subscr. to:** 168 W Kerley Rd, Tivoli, NY 10598.

100 DEU
SEELE, EXISTENZ UND LEBEN. Text in German. 2005. irreg., latest vol.14, 2010. price varies. **Document type:** *Monographic series, Academic/Scholarly.*
Published by: Verlag Karl Alber, Hermann-Herder-Str 4, Freiburg, 79104, Germany. TEL 49-761-2717436, FAX 49-761-2717212, info@verlag-alber.de.

100 ITA ISSN 1121-6530
SEGNI E COMPRENSIONE. Text in Italian. 1987. 3/yr. **Document type:** *Journal, Academic/Scholarly.*
Related titles: Online - full text ed.: ISSN 1828-5368. free (effective 2011).
Indexed: Philind.
Published by: (Universita degli Studi del Salento, Dipartimento di Filosofia e Scienze Sociali), Universita degli Studi del Salento, Coordinamento S I B A, Viale Gallipoli 49, Lecce, 73100, Italy. TEL 39-083-2291111, http://siba2.unile.it.

174.95 JPN ISSN 1343-4063
SEIMEI RINRI/JAPAN ASSOCIATION FOR BIOETHICS. JOURNAL. Text in Japanese. 1991. a. **Document type:** *Journal, Academic/ Scholarly.*
Related titles: Online - full text ed.
—BLDSC (8219.747500).
Published by: Nihon Seimei Rinri Gakkai/Japan Association for Bioethics, 2-17-4 Bunkyo-ku, Mukogaoka, Tokyo, 113-0023, Japan. TEL 81-3-62793466, FAX 81-3-62793466.

174.957 COL ISSN 1657-8856
SELECCIONES DE BIOETICA. Text in Spanish. 2002. 3/yr. **Document type:** *Journal, Academic/Scholarly.*
Indexed: A01, CA, F03, F04, T02.
Published by: Pontificia Universidad Javeriana, Instituto de Bioetica, Transversal 4 No. 42-00 Piso 5, Bogota, Colombia. TEL 57-1-3208320, bioetica@javeriana.educ.o, http://www.javeriana.edu.co/bioetica. Ed. Alfonso Llano Escobar.

SELF & SOCIETY; a forum for contemporary psychology. *see* PSYCHOLOGY

181.45 GBR ISSN 0037-1556
SELF-KNOWLEDGE. Text in English. 1935. q. GBP 10, EUR 12, USD 15 (effective 2009). bk.rev. **Document type:** *Journal, Academic/ Scholarly.* **Description:** Contains articles on all aspects of the Yoga philosophy and practice as well as on art, science, history and culture that illustrate spiritual truth and beauty.
Former titles (until 1950): Shanti Sevak; (until 1942): Shanti-Sadan Bulletin
Published by: Shanti Sadan Centre of Adhyatma Yoga, 29 Chepstow Villas, London, W11 3DR, United Kingdom. TEL 44-20-77277846, FAX 44-20-77929817, mail@shantisadan.org.

SEMIKOLON (AARHUS C); tidsskrift for idehistorie, semiotik, filosofi. *see* LITERATURE

SEMIOSIS. *see* LINGUISTICS

153 BEL
SEMIOTIC AND COGNITIVE STUDIES. Text in English, Italian. 1995. irreg., latest vol.7, 2000. price varies. back issues avail. **Document type:** *Monographic series, Academic/Scholarly.* **Description:** Publishes interdisciplinary studies in the fields of cognitive sciences, psychology, psycholinguistics, the philosophy of mind, and artificial intelligence.
Indexed: E-psyche.
Published by: (University of San Marino, International Center for Semiotic and Cognitive Studies), Brepols Publishers, Begijnhof 67, Turnhout, 2300, Belgium. FAX 32-14-428919, periodicals@brepols.net. Eds. Patrizia Violi, Umberto Eco.

SEMIOTIC REVIEW OF BOOKS. *see* HUMANITIES: COMPREHENSIVE WORKS

▼ **SEMIOTICS, COMMUNICATION AND COGNITION.** *see* LINGUISTICS

SEMIQUASI REVIEW. *see* LITERATURE—Poetry

SEQUENCIA; estudos juridicos e politicos. *see* LAW

SERIE DE TEORIA JURIDICA Y FILOSOFIA DEL DERECHO. *see* LAW

100 300 CHN ISSN 1672-4283
SHAANXI SHIFAN DAXUE XUEBAO (ZHEXUE SHEHUI KEXUE BAN)/SHANXI NORMAL UNIVERSITY. JOURNAL (PHILOSOPHY AND SOCIAL SCIENCES EDITION). Text in Chinese. 1960. bi-m. USD 24.60 (effective 2009). **Document type:** *Journal, Academic/ Scholarly.*
Formerly (until 1996): Shaanxi Shi-da Xuebao (Zhexue Shehui Kexue Ban)/Shaanxi Teachers University Journal (1000-5293)
Related titles: Online - full text ed.
Indexed: CA, P42, S02, S03, SCOPUS, SociolAb, T02.
—East View.
Published by: Shaanxi Shifan Daxue/Shaanxi Normal University, Chang'an Nanlu, Box 66, Xi'an, 710062, China. TEL 86-29-85308849.

170 JPN ISSN 1344-0616
SHAKAI TO RINRI. Text in Japanese. 1992. a. free. **Document type:** *Journal, Academic/Scholarly.*
Former titles (until 1996): Shakai Rinri Kenkyu (0918-2209); (until 1991): Nanzan Shakai Rinri Kenkyujo Ronshu/Nanzan Forum for Social Ethics (0911-2812)
Published by: Nanzan University, Institute for Social Ethics, 18 Yamazato-cho, Showa-ku, Nagoya, 466-8673, Japan. TEL 81-52-8323111 ext 417, 768, FAX 81-52-8323703, n-ise@nanzan-u.ac.jp, sharink@ic.nanzan-u.ac.jp, http://www.nanzan-u.ac.jp/ISE/index.html.

SHANDONG DAXUE XUEBAO (ZHEXUE SHEHUI KEXUE BAN)/ SHANDONG UNIVERSITY. JOURNAL (PHILOSOPHY AND SOCIAL SCIENCES). *see* SOCIAL SCIENCES: COMPREHENSIVE WORKS

SHANGHAI JIAOTONG DAXUE XUEBAO (ZHEXUE SHEHUI KEXUE BAN)/SHANGHAI JIAOTONG UNIVERSITY. JOURNAL (PHILOSOPHY AND SOCIAL SCIENCES). *see* SOCIAL SCIENCES: COMPREHENSIVE WORKS

SHANGHAI SHIFAN DAXUE XUEBAO (ZHEXUE SHEHUI KEXUE BAN)/SHANGHAI NORMAL UNIVERSITY. JOURNAL (PHILOSOPHY & SOCIAL SCIENCES). *see* SOCIAL SCIENCES: COMPREHENSIVE WORKS

SHAW; the annual of Bernard Shaw studies. *see* LITERATURE

100 300 CHN ISSN 1671-0304
SHIHEZI DAXUE XUEBAO (ZHEXUE SHEHUI KEXUE BAN)/SHIHEZI UNIVERSITY. JOURNAL (PHILOSOPHY AND SOCIAL SCIENCE). Text in Chinese. 2001. q. USD 24.60 (effective 2009). **Document type:** *Journal, Academic/Scholarly.*
Supersedes: Bingtuan Zhigong Daxue Xuebao (1008-8768)
Related titles: Online - full text ed.
Published by: Shihezi Daxue, Bei-Si Lu, Shihezi, Xinjiang 832003, China. TEL 86-993-2058629, FAX 86-993-2017247.

100 CHN ISSN 1671-4318
SHIJIE ZHEXUE/TRANSLATED PHILOSOPHY SERIES. Variant title: World Philosophy. Text in Chinese. 1956. bi-m. USD 30.60 (effective 2009). **Document type:** *Journal, Academic/Scholarly.*
Formerly (until 2001): Zhexue Yicong/International Philosophy Today (1002-8854)
Related titles: Online - full text ed.
—East View.
Published by: Zhongguo Shehui Kexueyuan, Zhexue Yanjiusuo/Chinese Academy of Social Sciences, Institute of Philosophy, 5 Jianguomennei Dajie, Beijing, 10000732, China. TEL 86-10-65137744 ext 5533, FAX 86-10-65137826. **Dist. by:** China International Book Trading Corp, 35 Chegongzhuang Xilu, Haidian District, PO Box 399, Beijing 100044, China. TEL 86-10-68412045, FAX 86-10-68412023, cibtc@mail.cibtc.com.cn, http://www.cibtc.com.cn.

174.2 NLD ISSN 1871-5184
SIGNALERING ETHIEK EN GEZONDHEID. Text in Dutch, English. 2003. a. free (effective 2009).
Published by: (Centrum voor Ethiek en Gezondheid), Gezondheidsraad/ Health Council of the Netherlands, PO Box 16052, The Hague, 2500 BB, Netherlands. TEL 31-70-3407520, FAX 31-70-3407523, info@gr.nl, http://www.gr.nl.

100 MEX ISSN 1665-1324
SIGNOS FILOSOFICOS. Text in Spanish. 1999. s-a. **Document type:** *Journal, Academic/Scholarly.*
Related titles: Online - full text ed.: free (effective 2011).
Indexed: A01, A26, C01, CA, F03, F04, I04, I05, PhilInd, T02.
Published by: Universidad Autonoma Metropolitana - Iztapalapa, Division de Ciencias Sociales y Humanidades. Departamento de Antropologia, Ave. Michoacan y la Purisima, Col Vicentina, Mexico City, DF 09340, Mexico. TEL 525-77244760, asga@xanum.uam.mx, http://www.iztapalapa.uam.mx/.

100 DNK ISSN 1902-8822
➤ **SIGNS.** Text in English. 2007. irreg. free (effective 2011). **Document type:** *Journal, Academic/Scholarly.* **Description:** Interdisciplinary journal on the semiotics of mind, consciousness, language and culture as well as living and inanimate nature, and possible connections between them. The journal is also transdisciplinary in that it has an interest in the philosophical frameworks forming the specific semiotic outlook on cognitive, communicative and social processes.
Media: Online - full text.
Published by: Danmarks Biblioteksskole, Aalborgafdelingen/Royal School of Library and Information Science, Aalborg, Fredrik Bajersvej, Aalborg OE, 9220, Denmark. TEL 45-98-157922, FAX 45-98-151042, mt@db.dk, http://www.db.dk. Eds. Bent Soerensen, Torkild Thellefsen.

100 600 NLD ISSN 1574-941X
SIMON STEVIN SERIES IN THE PHILOSOPHY OF TECHNOLOGY. Text in English. 2005. irreg., latest vol.7, 2009. **Document type:** *Monographic series, Academic/Scholarly.*
Published by: (Universiteit Twente, Technische Universiteit Eindhoven/ Technical University of Eindhoven), Technische Universiteit Delft/Delft University of Technology, PO Box 5, Delft, 2600 AA, Netherlands. TEL 31-15-2789111, info@tudelft.nl, http://www.tudelft.nl. Eds. Anthonie Meijers, Peter Kroes. **Co-publishers:** Universiteit Twente; Technische Universiteit Eindhoven/Technical University of Eindhoven.

100 CAN ISSN 1718-1747
SIMPLI-CITE. Text in French. 2000. q. CAD 10 to individuals; CAD 20 to institutions (effective 2006). **Document type:** *Newsletter, Consumer.*
Published by: Reseau Quebecois pour la Simplicite Volontaire, 1710, rue Beaudry, local 3.3, Montreal, PQ H2L 3E7, Canada. TEL 514-937-3159, rqsv@simplicitevolontaire.org, http://www.simplicitevolontaire.org.

SINNSPUREN UND WIRTSCHAFT. *see* BUSINESS AND ECONOMICS

100 BRA ISSN 0103-4332
H8
B5
SINTESE. Text in Portuguese; Summaries in English. 1959. 3/yr. BRL 30 domestic; USD 40 foreign (effective 1999). adv. bk.rev. abstr.; bibl. cum.index: vols.1-17 (1974-1990). back issues avail. **Document type:** *Academic/Scholarly.* **Description:** Publishes texts by contemporary philosophers which are of real interest and quality, with a view to enriching the national philosophical culture.
Formerly: Sintese Politica, Economica e Social (0037-5772)
Indexed: C01, CERDIC, DIP, IBR, IBZ, IPB.
Published by: Centro de Estudos Superiores da Companhia de Jesus, Faculdade de Filosofia, Av Dr Cristiano Guimaraes, 2127, Planalto, Belo Horizonte, MG 31720-300, Brazil. TEL 55-31-4991600, FAX 55-31-4991611. Ed. Henrique C L Vaz. Pub., R&P Danilo Mondoni. Adv. contact Airton Santos Gonzaga. Circ: 1,500.

100 ITA ISSN 0037-5888
SISTEMATICA; rivista di filosofia e di filologia. Text in Italian. 1968. q. bk.rev. **Document type:** *Journal, Academic/Scholarly.*
Indexed: MLA-IB.
Published by: Edizioni Pergamena, Viale Gran Sasso 1, Milan, 20131, Italy. TEL 39-02-29523119, FAX 39-02-406069, info@edizionipergamena.it, http://www.edizionipergamena.it.

SIXIANG ZHENGZHI JIAOYU/IDEOLOGICAL AND POLITICAL EDUCATION. *see* EDUCATION

100 DEU ISSN 1105-1582
SKEPSIS. Text in German, English, French. 1990. a. EUR 38.50 (effective 2008). **Document type:** *Journal, Academic/Scholarly.*
Indexed: DIP, IBR, IBZ, PhilInd.
Published by: Academia Verlag GmbH, Bahnstr 7, Sankt Augustin, 53757, Germany. TEL 49-2241-345210, FAX 49-2241-345316, kontakt@academia-verlag.de. Eds. L C Bargeliotes, N Chronis. Circ: 200 (paid).

100 FIN ISSN 0786-2571
SKEPTIKKO. Text in Finnish. 1988. q. back issues avail. **Document type:** *Journal, Academic/Scholarly.*
Published by: Skepsis/The Finnish Skeptics, PO Box 483, Helsinki, 00101, Finland. TEL 358-208-355455, info@skepsis.fi. Ed. Risto K Jarvinen.

SLOW MANAGEMENT. *see* BUSINESS AND ECONOMICS—Management

SOARING SPIRIT. *see* NEW AGE PUBLICATIONS

101 NLD ISSN 1572-459X
SOCIAL AND CRITICAL THEORY. Text in English. 2004. irreg., latest vol.5, 2007. price varies. **Document type:** *Monographic series, Academic/Scholarly.* **Description:** Offers critical and insightful analyses of contemporary societies, as well as explores the many dimensions of the human condition through which critiques can be made.
Indexed: IZBG.
Published by: Brill, PO Box 9000, Leiden, 2300 PA, Netherlands. TEL 31-71-5353500, FAX 31-71-5317532, cs@brill.nl.

100 300 GBR ISSN 0269-1728
BD175
➤ **SOCIAL EPISTEMOLOGY**; a journal of knowledge, culture and policy. Text in English. 1987. q. GBP 528 combined subscription in United Kingdom to institutions (print & online eds.); EUR 699, USD 877 combined subscription to institutions (print & online eds.) (effective 2012). adv. bk.rev. illus. Index. back issues avail.; reprint service avail. from PSC. **Document type:** *Journal, Academic/Scholarly.* **Description:** Provides a forum for philosophical and social scientific enquiry that incorporates the work of scholars from a variety of disciplines who share a concern with the production, assessment and validation of knowledge.
Related titles: Online - full text ed.: ISSN 1464-5297. GBP 475 in United Kingdom to institutions; EUR 629, USD 789 to institutions (effective 2012) (from IngentaConnect).
Indexed: A01, A03, A08, A22, B21, BibInd, CA, DIP, E01, E17, ESPM, FR, IBR, IBZ, IPB, LID&ISL, MLA-IB, P42, PSA, PerIslam, PhilInd, RASB, S02, S03, SCOPUS, SOPODA, SSA, SociolAb, T02.
—IE, Infotrieve, Ingenta, INIST. **CCC.**
Published by: Routledge (Subsidiary of: Taylor & Francis Group), 4 Park Sq, Milton Park, Abingdon, Oxon OX14 4RN, United Kingdom. TEL 44-20-70176000, FAX 44-20-70176336, subscriptions@tandf.co.uk, http://www.routledge.com. Adv. contact Linda Hann TEL 44-1344-779945. **Subscr. addr. in Europe:** Taylor & Francis Ltd., Journals Customer Service, Sheepen Pl, Colchester, Essex CO3 3LP, United Kingdom. TEL 44-20-70175544, FAX 44-20-70175198, tf.enquiries@tfinforma.com; **Subscr. in N. America to:** Taylor & Francis Inc., Customer Services Dept, 325 Chestnut St, 8th Fl, Philadelphia, PA 19106. TEL 800-354-1420, FAX 215-625-2940.

➤ **SOCIAL PHILOSOPHY.** *see* SOCIOLOGY

100 GBR ISSN 0265-0525
H61
➤ **SOCIAL PHILOSOPHY AND POLICY.** Text in English. 1983. s-a. GBP 149, USD 248 to institutions; GBP 159, USD 268 combined subscription to institutions (print & online eds.) (effective 2012). adv. illus. back issues avail.; reprint service avail. from PSC. **Document type:** *Journal, Academic/Scholarly.* **Description:** Takes an interdisciplinary approach to the philosophical underpinnings of enduring social policy debates.
Related titles: Online - full text ed.: ISSN 1471-6437. GBP 135, USD 226 to institutions (effective 2012).
Indexed: A20, A21, A22, ABS&EES, ASCA, ArtHuCI, CA, CurCont, DIP, E01, H14, I13, IBR, IBSS, IBZ, IPB, P02, P10, P28, P30, P34, P42, P46, P48, P53, P54, PAIS, PCI, PQC, PRA, PSA, PerIslam, PhilInd, RASB, RI-1, RI-2, S02, S03, SCOPUS, SOPODA, SSA, SSCI, SociolAb, T02, W07.
—BLDSC (8318.129000), IE, Infotrieve, Ingenta. **CCC.**
Published by: (The Social Philosophy and Policy Foundation USA), Cambridge University Press, The Edinburgh Bldg, Shaftesbury Rd, Cambridge, CB2 8RU, United Kingdom. TEL 44-1223-312393, FAX 44-1223-315052, journals@cambridge.org, http://www.cambridge.org/uk. Eds. Ellen Frankel Paul, Fred D. Miller, Jeffrey Paul. adv.: page GBP 465, page USD 885. Circ: 1,000. **Subscr. to:** Cambridge University Press, 32 Ave of the Americas, New York, NY 10013. TEL 212-337-5000, FAX 212-691-3239, journals_subscriptions@cup.org.

170 USA ISSN 1543-4044
➤ **SOCIAL PHILOSOPHY TODAY.** Text in English. 1988. a. USD 40 per issue to individuals; USD 65 per issue to institutions; USD 80 combined subscription per issue to individuals (print & online eds.); USD 234 combined subscription per issue to institutions (print & online eds.); free to members (effective 2009). back issues avail. **Document type:** *Journal, Academic/Scholarly.* **Description:** Contains a selection of the papers presented at the International Social Philosophy Conference, an annual event held under the auspices of the North American Society for Social Philosophy.
Related titles: Online - full text ed.: ISSN 2153-9448. USD 50 per issue to individuals; USD 195 per issue to institutions (effective 2009).
Indexed: A01, A03, A08, AmHI, CA, H07, IBR, IBZ, P42, PCI, PSA, S02, S03, SCOPUS, SociolAb, T02.
—INIST. **CCC.**
Published by: Philosophy Documentation Center, PO Box 7147, Charlottesville, VA 22906. TEL 434-220-3300, FAX 434-220-3301, order@pdcnet.org, http://www.pdcnet.org. Ed. John Rowan. R&P George Leaman. Adv. contact Greg Swope.

100 NLD ISSN 1571-4993
➤ **SOCIAL, POLITICAL & LEGAL PHILOSOPHY.** Text in English. 2002. irreg., latest vol.8, 2007. price varies. **Document type:** *Monographic series, Academic/Scholarly.* **Description:** Published collections of new essays on topics in social or political or legal philosophy.
Indexed: P02, P10, P48, P53, P54, PQC, S02, S03.
Published by: Editions Rodopi B.V., Tijnmuiden 7, Amsterdam, 1046 AK, Netherlands. TEL 31-20-6114821, FAX 31-20-4472979, info@rodopi.nl. Ed. Dr. Enrique Villanueva.

302.05 GBR ISSN 1035-0330
P99.4.S62
➤ **SOCIAL SEMIOTICS.** Text in English. 1991. q. GBP 648 combined subscription in United Kingdom to institutions (print & online eds.); EUR 847, AUD 766, USD 1,064 combined subscription to institutions (print & online eds.) (effective 2012). adv. bk.rev. back issues avail.; reprint service avail. from PSC. **Document type:** *Journal, Academic/ Scholarly.* **Description:** Connects discourse analysis with contemporary theory, feminist theories, psychoanalysis, deconstruction, and a variety of approaches to cultural studies.
Related titles: Online - full text ed.: ISSN 1470-1219. GBP 583 in United Kingdom to institutions; EUR 762, AUD 690, USD 958 to institutions (effective 2012) (from IngentaConnect).
Indexed: A01, A03, A08, A22, AltPI, AusPAIS, B21, CA, CommAb, E01, E17, ESPM, IBSS, L&LBA, L11, LeftInd, MLA-IB, RILM, S02, S03, SCOPUS, SSA, SociolAb, T02.

P

—IE, Infotrieve, Ingenta. **CCC.**
Published by: Routledge (Subsidiary of: Taylor & Francis Group), 4 Park Sq, Milton Park, Abingdon, Oxon OX14 4RN, United Kingdom. TEL 44-20-70176000, FAX 44-20-70176336, subscriptions@tandf.co.uk, http://www.routledge.com. Adv. contact Linda Hann TEL 44-1344-779945. **Subscr. to:** Taylor & Francis Ltd., Journals Customer Service, Sheepen Pl, Colchester, Essex CO3 3LP, United Kingdom. TEL 44-20-70175544, FAX 44-20-70175198.

100 USA ISSN 0037-802X
H1
➤ **SOCIAL THEORY AND PRACTICE**; an international and interdisciplinary journal of social philosophy. Text in English. 1970. q. USD 28 to individuals; USD 55 to institutions; USD 20 to students; USD 10 per issue to individuals; USD 20 per issue to institutions; USD 8 per issue to students (effective 2010). adv. bk.rev. illus. Index. 176 p./no. 1 cols./p.; back issues avail.; reprints avail. **Document type:** *Journal, Academic/Scholarly.* **Description:** Provides a forum for dicussion of issues in social, political, legal, economic, and moral philosophy.
Related titles: Microfilm ed.: (from PQC); Online - full text ed.: ISSN 2154-123X.
Indexed: A01, A02, A03, A08, A22, A26, ABCPolSci, ABS&EES, AC&P, B04, BRD, C12, CA, DIP, E07, E08, FR, Faml, G08, H09, I05, I13, IBR, IBZ, IPB, L03, M01, M02, MEA&I, MLA-IB, P02, P07, P10, P27, P30, P34, P42, P46, P48, P53, P54, PCI, PQC, PSA, Perlslam, Philind, R05, RASB, RI-1, RI-2, S02, S03, S05, S09, S11, SCOPUS, SOPODA, SSA, SSAI, SSAb, SSI, SociolAb, T02, W01, W02, W03, W05, W09.
—BLDSC (8318.217800), IE, Infotrieve, Ingenta, INIST. **CCC.**
Published by: Florida State University, Department of Philosophy, 151 Dodd Hall, Tallahassee, FL 32306. TEL 850-644-0220, FAX 850-644-3832, journals@mailer.fsu.edu, http://whttp://www.fsu.edu/~philo/. adv.: page USD 95; 5 x 8.

➤ **LA SOCIETA DEGLI INDIVIDUI**; quadrimestrale di teoria sociale e storia delle idee. *see* HUMANITIES: COMPREHENSIVE WORKS

100 ITA ISSN 1129-5643
SOCIETA FILOSOFICA ITALIANA. BOLLETTINO. Text in Italian. 1927. q. free to members. **Document type:** *Bulletin, Consumer.*
Indexed: Philind.
Published by: Societa Filosofica Italiana (S F I), Dipartimento di Studi Filosofici, Universita degli Studi di Roma "La Sapienza", Via Nomentana 118, Rome, 00161, Italy. sfi@getnet.it, http://www.sfi.it.

100 ESP ISSN 1130-4383
B5
SOCIETAT CATALANA DE FILOSOFIA. ANUARI. Text in Multiple languages. 1923. a., latest vol.19, 2008. EUR 20. **Document type:** *Journal, Academic/Scholarly.*
Indexed: Philind.
Published by: Institut d'Estudis Catalans, Carrer del Carme 47, Barcelona, 08001, Spain. TEL 34-932-701620, FAX 34-932-701180, informacio@iecat.net, http://www2.iecat.net.

100 FRA ISSN 0037-9352
B12
SOCIETE FRANCAISE DE PHILOSOPHIE. BULLETIN. Text in French. 1901. 4/yr. USD 50 (effective 2004). bk.rev. back issues avail.; reprint service avail. from SCH.
Indexed: DIP, FR, IBR, IBZ, IPB, PCI, Philind, RASB.
—INIST. **CCC.**
Published by: (Societe Francaise de Philosophie), Librairie Philosophique J. Vrin, 6 place de la Sorbonne, Paris, F-75005, France. TEL 33-1-43540347, FAX 33-1-43544818, contact@vrin.fr, http://www.vrin.fr. Circ: 1,000.

SOCIETY FOR BUSINESS ETHICS. MEMBERSHIP DIRECTORY. *see* BUSINESS AND ECONOMICS

174 USA ISSN 1932-4677
SOCIETY FOR BUSINESS ETHICS. NEWSLETTER. Text in English. 1992. q. free to members (effective 2010). back issues avail. **Document type:** *Newsletter, Academic/Scholarly.*
Related titles: Online - full text ed.: free (effective 2010).
Published by: Society for Business Ethics, PO Box 7147, Charlottesville, VA 22906. TEL 434-220-3300, 800-444-2419, FAX 434-220-3301, order@pdcnet.org. Ed. Jeffery Smith TEL 909-748-8785.

100 USA ISSN 2155-2789
SOCIETY FOR THE ADVANCEMENT OF AMERICAN PHILOSOPHY. NEWSLETTER. Text in English. 1970. 3/yr. free to members (effective 2010). **Document type:** *Newsletter, Academic/Scholarly.* **Description:** Provides information about constitution and bylaws as well as a list of grants associated with the society.
Published by: St. Bonaventure University, 3261 W State Rd, St. Bonaventure,, NY 14778. TEL 716-375-2000, admissions@sbu.edu, http://www.sbu.edu/. Ed. Patrick Dooley.

SOCIO-ECONOMIC PAPERS. *see* RELIGIONS AND THEOLOGY

100 FRA ISSN 1767-3844
LA SOEUR DE L'ANGE. Text in French. 2004. s-a. EUR 18.50 newsstand/cover (effective 2010). **Document type:** *Journal.*
Published by: Le Grand Souffle Editions, 24 Rue Truffaut, Paris, 75017, France. TEL 33-1-42942550, info@legrandsouffle.com.

SOLIDARITY AND IDENTITY/SOLIDARITEIT EN IDENTITEIT. *see* SOCIOLOGY

▼ **SOLIDARITY: THE JOURNAL OF CATHOLIC SOCIAL THOUGHT AND SECULAR ETHICS.** *see* RELIGIONS AND THEOLOGY—Roman Catholic

100 RUS ISSN 2076-9210
SOLOV'YEVSKIE ISSLEDOVANIYA. Text in Russian. 2001. q. **Document type:** *Journal, Academic/Scholarly.*
Related titles: Online - full text ed.
Published by: (Ivanovskii Gosudarstvennyi Energeticheskii Universitet, Kafedra Filosofii), Ivanovskii Gosudarstvennyi Energeticheskii Universitet, ul Rabfakovskaya 34, Ivanovo, Russian Federation. TEL 7-4932-326448, FAX 7-4932-385701, office@ispu.ru, http://ispu.ru. Ed. M V Maksimov TEL 7-4932-269770.

100 TWN
SOOCHOW JOURNAL OF PHILOSOPHICAL STUDIES/DONGWU ZHEXUE XUEBAO. Text in Chinese. 1982-1987; resumed 1992. a. USD 15 per issue. bk.rev.
Former titles (until 1996): Philosophical Research; (until 1992): Chuanxi Lu (1010-0725)
Indexed: Philind.
Published by: (Philosophy Department), Soochow University, Wai Shuang Hsi, Shih Lin, Taipei, Taiwan. FAX 886-2-8801636.

100 ITA
SOPHIA. Text in Italian. 2004. s-a. **Document type:** *Journal, Academic/Scholarly.*
Published by: Edizioni Scientifiche Italiane SpA, Via Chiatamone 7, Naples, NA 80121, Italy. TEL 39-081-7645443, FAX 39-081-7646477, info@edizioniesi.it, http://www.edizioniesi.it. Eds. Giovanni Rossetti, H Kuenkler.

SOPHIA; international journal for philosophy of religion, metaphysical theology and ethics. *see* RELIGIONS AND THEOLOGY

SOPHIA (VIRGINIA); the journal of traditional studies. *see* RELIGIONS AND THEOLOGY

100 DEU
SOPHOS. Text in German. 2008. irreg. price varies. **Document type:** *Monographic series, Academic/Scholarly.*
Published by: Herbert Utz Verlag GmbH, Adalbertstr 57, Munich, 80799, Germany. TEL 49-89-27779100, FAX 49-89-27779101, utz@utzverlag.com.

100 ESP ISSN 1135-1349
B808.5
➤ **SORITES**; digital journal of analytical philosophy. Text in English. 1995. q. **Document type:** *Journal, Academic/Scholarly.*
Media: Online - full text.
Indexed: CCMJ, MSN, MathR, Philind.
Published by: Spanish Institute for Advanced Studies, Center for Analytic Philosophy, Pinar 25, Madrid, 28006, Spain. http://www.ifs.csic.es/sorites/. Ed. Lorenzo Pena.

➤ **SOTER.** *see* RELIGIONS AND THEOLOGY

100 ZAF ISSN 0258-0136
B1 CODEN: SAJPEM
➤ **SOUTH AFRICAN JOURNAL OF PHILOSOPHY.** Text and summaries in English. 1982. q. ZAR 200 in Africa; USD 60 elsewhere (effective 2004). adv. reprints avail. **Document type:** *Journal, Academic/Scholarly.* **Description:** Publishes original contributions in the field of philosophy.
Related titles: Online - full text ed.
Indexed: A01, A02, A03, A08, A20, ASCA, AmHI, ArtHuCI, CA, CurCont, DIP, FR, H07, IBR, IBZ, IPB, ISAP, PCI, Philind, S02, S03, SCOPUS, T02, W07.
—BLDSC (8339.450000), IE, Ingenta, INIST.
Published by: Philosophical Society of Southern Africa (P S S A), c/o Dr. Emma B. Ruttkamp, Department of Philosophy, University of South Africa, PO Box 392, Pretoria, 0003, South Africa. TEL 27-12-4296397, FAX 27-12-4293221, ruttkeb@unisa.ac.za. Ed. D J Louw. Circ: 550.

144 AUS
SOUTH AUSTRALIAN HUMANIST POST. Text in English. 1963. m.
Formerly (until 1973): Humanist Post
Published by: Humanist Society of South Australia Inc., GPO Box 177, Adelaide, SA 5001, Australia. TEL 61-8-82559508.

▼ **SOUTHERN JOURNAL OF BUSINESS AND ETHICS.** *see* BUSINESS AND ECONOMICS

100 USA ISSN 0038-4283
B1
➤ **THE SOUTHERN JOURNAL OF PHILOSOPHY.** Text in English. 1963. q. GBP 150 combined subscription in United Kingdom to institutions (print & online eds.); EUR 175 combined subscription in Europe to institutions (print & online eds.); USD 304 combined subscription elsewhere to institutions (print & online eds.) (effective 2012). illus. index. 200 p./no.; back issues avail.; reprint service avail. from PSC. **Document type:** *Journal, Academic/Scholarly.* **Description:** Serves as a forum for the scholarly discussion of philosophical issues.
Related titles: Microform ed.: (from PQC); Online - full text ed.: ISSN 2041-6962. GBP 127 in United Kingdom to institutions; EUR 150 in Europe to institutions; USD 259 elsewhere to institutions (effective 2012); Supplement(s): Spindel. USD 15 newsstand/cover (effective 2003).
Indexed: A01, A03, A08, A20, A22, ASCA, AmHI, ArtHuCI, BibInd, CA, CurCont, DIP, E01, FR, H07, IBR, IBZ, IPB, MLA-IB, P28, P30, P48, P53, P54, PCI, PQC, Philind, RASB, RI-1, RI-2, SCOPUS, T02, W07.
—BLDSC (8354.280000), IE, Infotrieve, Ingenta, INIST. **CCC.**
Published by: University of Memphis, Department of Philosophy, 327 Clement Hall, Memphis, TN 38152. TEL 901-678-2535, FAX 901-678-4365, philosophy@memphis.edu, http://www.memphis.edu/philosophy/. Ed. Stephan Blatti.

100 USA ISSN 0897-2346
B1
➤ **SOUTHWEST PHILOSOPHY REVIEW.** Text in English. 1937. s-a. free to members (effective 2010). adv. bk.rev. back issues avail. **Document type:** *Journal, Academic/Scholarly.* **Description:** Designed for philosophical inquiry that welcomes contributions from all philosophical perspectives.
Formerly (until 1984): Southwestern Philosophical Society. Newsletter (0038-4925)
Related titles: Online - full text ed.: ISSN 2154-1116.
Indexed: Philind.
—Ingenta.
Published by: (Southwestern Philosophical Society), Philosophy Documentation Center, PO Box 7147, Charlottesville, VA 22906. TEL 434-220-3300, FAX 434-220-3301, order@pdcnet.org, http://www.pdcnet.org. Ed. Todd Stewart TEL 309-438-3757. Adv. contact Greg Swope.

➤ **SOUTHWESTERN JOURNAL OF THEOLOGY.** *see* RELIGIONS AND THEOLOGY

100 300 DEU
▼ **SOZIALPHILOSOPHISCHE STUDIEN.** Text in German. 2010. irreg., latest vol.2, 2010. price varies. **Document type:** *Monographic series, Academic/Scholarly.*
Published by: Transcript, Muehlenstr 47, Bielefeld, 33607, Germany. TEL 49-521-63454, FAX 49-521-61040, live@transcript-verlag.de.

100 DEU ISSN 0178-1367
SOZIALPHILOSOPHISCHE STUDIEN. Text in German. 1984. irreg., latest vol.3, 1985. price varies. **Document type:** *Monographic series, Academic/Scholarly.*
Published by: Wilhelm Fink Verlag, Ohmstr 5, Munich, 80802, Germany. kontakt@fink.de, http://www.fink.de. R&P Marlene Braun.

SOZNANIE I FIZICHESKAYA REAL'NOST'. *see* SOCIAL SCIENCES: COMPREHENSIVE WORKS

SPACES OF UTOPIA. *see* LITERATURE

100 ITA ISSN 2038-6788
▼ **SPAZIO FILOSOFICO.** Text in Multiple languages. 2011. 3/yr. **Document type:** *Magazine, Consumer. Ed. Donatella Mutti.*

100 DEU ISSN 1432-0312
SPEKTRUM PHILOSOPHIE. Text in German. 1996. irreg., latest vol.33, 2009. price varies. **Document type:** *Monographic series, Academic/Scholarly.*
Published by: Ergon Verlag, Keesburgstr 11, Wuerzburg, 97074, Germany. TEL 49-931-280084, FAX 49-931-282872, service@ergon-verlag.de.

100 DEU ISSN 1614-3132
SPEKULATION UND ERFAHRUNG. ABTEILUNG II: UNTERSUCHUNGEN; Texte und Untersuchungen zum deutschen Idealismus. Text in German. 1986. irreg., latest vol.56, 2009. price varies. **Document type:** *Monographic series, Academic/Scholarly.*
Indexed: CCMJ.
Published by: Frommann-Holzboog Verlag e.K., Koenig-Karl-Str 27, Stuttgart, 70372, Germany. TEL 49-711-9559690, FAX 49-711-9559691, info@frommann-holzboog.de, http://www.frommann-holzboog.de.

SPELING. *see* RELIGIONS AND THEOLOGY

SPONTANEOUS GENERATIONS; journal for the history and philosophy of science. *see* HISTORY

SPORT, ETHICS AND PHILOSOPHY. *see* SPORTS AND GAMES

100 NLD ISSN 2211-4548
▼ **SPRINGERBRIEFS IN PHILOSOPHY.** Text in English. 2011. irreg. EUR 49.95 per vol. (effective 2011). **Document type:** *Monographic series, Academic/Scholarly.* **Description:** Covers a broad range of philosophical fields, including philosophy of science, logic, non-Western thinking and Western philosophy.
Related titles: Online - full text ed.: ISSN 2211-4556.
Published by: Springer Netherlands (Subsidiary of: Springer Science+Business Media), Van Godewijckstraat 30, Dordrecht, 3311 GX, Netherlands. TEL 31-78-6576050, FAX 31-78-6576474.

SSU YU YEN/THOUGHT AND WORDS; journal of the humanities and social sciences. *see* HUMANITIES: COMPREHENSIVE WORKS

340 100 DEU
STAATSDISKURSE. Text in German. 2007. irreg., latest vol.14, 2011. price varies. **Document type:** *Monographic series, Academic/Scholarly.*
Published by: Franz Steiner Verlag GmbH, Birkenwaldstr 44, Stuttgart, 70191, Germany. TEL 49-711-25820, FAX 49-711-2582290, service@steiner-verlag.de, http://www.steiner-verlag.de.

378 100 USA ISSN 1943-1880
➤ **STANCE**; an international undergraduate philosophy journal. Text in English. 2008. a. back issues avail. **Document type:** *Journal, Academic/Scholarly.* **Description:** Aims to enrich student learning by providing an opportunity for undergraduate students to have their original scholarly work.
Related titles: Online - full text ed.: ISSN 1943-1899. free (effective 2010).
Indexed: AmHI, H07, Philind.
Published by: Ball State University, 2000 W University Ave, Muncie, IN 47306. TEL 765-289-1241, 800-382-8540, askus@bsu.edu, http://cms.bsu.edu. Ed. Chris Hoover.

100 USA ISSN 1095-5054
B51
STANFORD ENCYCLOPEDIA OF PHILOSOPHY. Text in English. 1997. q. **Document type:** *Journal, Academic/Scholarly.* **Description:** Maintains academic standards while evolving and adapting in response to new research.
Related titles: Online - full text ed.: free (effective 2011).
Published by: Stanford University, Center for the Study of Language and Information, Ventura Hall, Stanford, CA 94305. TEL 650-723-1839, FAX 650-725-2166, csli@csli.stanford.edu, http://www-csli.stanford.edu/.

190 USA
STANFORD SERIES IN PHILOSOPHY. Text in English. 1989. irreg., latest 1993. price varies. back issues avail. **Document type:** *Monographic series, Academic/Scholarly.* **Description:** Examines the teachings and writings of prominent Western philosophers.
Published by: Stanford University Press (Subsidiary of: Stanford University), 1450 Page Mill Rd, Palo Alto, CA 94304. TEL 650-723-9434, FAX 650-725-3457, info@www.sup.org. **Dist. by:** Cambridge University Press, The Edinburgh Bldg, Shaftesbury Rd, Cambridge CB2 8RU, United Kingdom. TEL 44-1223-312393, FAX 44-1223-315052, information@cambridge.org, http://www.cambridge.org/uk; Cambridge University Press Distribution Center, 100 Brookhill Dr, West Nyack, NY 10994. TEL 845-353-7500, FAX 845-353-4141, http://www.cambridge.org.

100 MEX ISSN 2007-1868
▼ **STOA.** Text in Spanish. 2009. s-a. **Document type:** *Journal, Academic/Scholarly.*
Media: Online - full text.
Published by: Universidad Veracruzana, Instituto de Filosofia, Lomas del Estadio s-n, Area de Humanidades, Edif. B Cub. 23, Xalapa, Veracruz 91090, Mexico. TEL 52-228-8152412, FAX 52-228-8421700, dcosta@uv.mx.

101 SWE ISSN 0491-0877
STOCKHOLM STUDIES IN PHILOSOPHY. Text in English. 1957. irreg., latest vol.33, 2009. price varies. back issues avail. **Document type:** *Monographic series, Academic/Scholarly.*
Related titles: ◆ Series of: Acta Universitatis Stockholmiensis. ISSN 0346-6418.
Published by: Stockholms Universitet, Acta Universitatis Stockholmiensis, c/o Stockholms Universitetsbibliotek, Universitetsvaegen 10, Stockholm, 10691, Sweden. TEL 46-8-162800, FAX 46-8-157776, http://www.sub.su.se. Ed. Margaretha Fathli. **Dist. by:** Eddy.se AB, Norra Kyrkogatan 3, Visby 62155, Sweden. TEL 46-498-253900, FAX 46-498-249789, info@eddy.se, order@eddy.se, http://www.eddy.se, http://acta.bokorder.se.

100 SWE ISSN 1100-9667
STOCKHOLM STUDIES IN THE HISTORY OF IDEAS. Text in Swedish; Summaries in English. 1989. irreg., latest vol.7, 2008. price varies. back issues avail. **Document type:** *Monographic series, Academic/ Scholarly.*
Related titles: ◆ Series of: Acta Universitatis Stockholmiensis. ISSN 0346-6418.
Published by: Stockholms Universitet, Acta Universitatis Stockholmiensis, c/o Stockholms Universitetsbibliotek, Universitetsvaegen 10, Stockholm, 10691, Sweden. TEL 46-8-162800, FAX 46-8-157776, http://www.sub.su.se. Ed. Margaretha Fathli. **Dist. by:** Eddy.se AB, Norra Kyrkogatan 3, Visby 62155, Sweden. TEL 46-498-253900, FAX 46-498-249789, info@eddy.se, order@eddy.se, http://www.eddy.se, http:// acta.bokorder.se.

200 ARG ISSN 0049-2353
BX805
➤ **STROMATA**; antigua ciencia y fe. Text in Spanish. 1944. q. (in 2 issues). USD 30 in Latin America; USD 30 elsewhere (effective 2001). adv. bk.rev. abstr.; bibl. cum.index: 1944-1981; 1982-1991; 1992-2001. 400 p./no.; back issues avail. **Document type:** *Journal, Academic/Scholarly.*
Indexed: C01, DIP, FR, H21, IBR, IBZ, IPB, MLA-IB, OTA, P08, PhilInd.
—INIST.
Published by: (Universidad del Salvador, Facultades de Filosofia y Teologia), Asociacion Civil Facultades Loyola, Ave. Mitre 3226, San Miguel, Buenos Aires 1663, Argentina. TEL 52-11-44557992, FAX 52-11-44556442. Ed. Gerardo Losada. Pub. Jorge Seibold. Circ: 1,000.

➤ **STUDI CRITICI SULLE SCIENZE.** *see* SCIENCES: COMPREHENSIVE WORKS

111.85 ITA ISSN 0585-4733
BH4
STUDI DI ESTETICA. Text in Italian. s-a. **Document type:** *Journal, Academic/Scholarly.*
Related titles: Online - full text ed.: ISSN 1825-8646. 2001.
Indexed: DIP, IBR, IBZ, IPB, MLA-IB, RILM.
Published by: Casa Editrice C L U E B, Via Marsala 31, Bologna, BO 40126, Italy. TEL 39-051-220736, FAX 39-051-237758, clueb@clueb.com, http://www.clueb.eu/home.html.

100 ITA ISSN 1123-8623
STUDI EUROPEI. Text in Italian. 1994. a., latest vol.12, 2004. EUR 26 domestic; EUR 34 foreign (effective 2007). **Document type:** *Journal, Academic/Scholarly.*
Published by: (Universita degli Studi di Genova, Dipartimento di Studi sulla Storia del Pensiero Europeo "Michele Federico Sciacca"), Casa Editrice Leo S. Olschki, Viuzzo del Pozzetto 8, Florence, 50126, Italy. TEL 39-055-6530684, FAX 39-055-6530214, celso@olschki.it, http://www.olschki.it. Ed. Maria Adelaide Raschini.

100 ITA ISSN 1124-1047
STUDI FILOSOFICI. Text in Italian. 1978-1981 (vol.4); resumed. a. EUR 26 domestic; EUR 31 foreign (effective 2010). **Document type:** *Journal, Academic/Scholarly.* **Description:** Provides research and comparisons, historical and theoretical, on problems of philosophical, political and scientific thought.
Related titles: Online - full text ed.: ISSN 2038-6613.
Indexed: BibInd, IPB, MLA-IB, PCI, PhilInd.
Published by: (Universita degli Studi di Napoli "L'Orientale"), Bibliopolis, Via Vincenzo Arangio Ruiz 83, Naples, NA 80122, Italy. TEL 39-081-664606, FAX 39-081-7616273, info@bibliopolis.it, http:// www.bibliopolis.it.

STUDI GERMANICI. *see* LITERATURE

190 ITA ISSN 1123-4938
STUDI KANTIANI. Text in Italian. a. EUR 245 combined subscription domestic to institutions (print & online eds.); EUR 295 combined subscription foreign to institutions (print & online eds.) (effective 2009). **Document type:** *Journal, Academic/Scholarly.*
Related titles: Online - full text ed.: ISSN 1724-1812.
Indexed: IPB.
Published by: Fabrizio Serra Editore (Subsidiary of: Accademia Editoriale), c/o Accademia Editoriale, Via Santa Bibbiana 28, Pisa, 56127, Italy. TEL 39-050-542332, FAX 39-050-574888, accademiaeditoriale@accademiaeditoriale.it, http:// www.libraweb.net.

128 ITA ISSN 1971-5684
STUDI TANATOLOGICI/ETUDES THANATOLOGIQUES/ THANATOLOGICAL STUDIES. Text in Multiple languages. 2005. a. **Document type:** *Journal, Academic/Scholarly.*
Published by: Pearson Paravia Bruno Mondadori, Corso Trapani 16, Turin, TO 10139, Italy. TEL 39-011-7502111, FAX 39-011-75021510, http://www.brunomondadori.com.

100 ITA ISSN 2036-8445
STUDIA ANSELMIANA. PHILOSOPHICA. Text in Multiple languages. 1996. irreg. **Document type:** *Monographic series, Academic/ Scholarly.*
Published by: Pontificio Ateneo S. Anselmo, Piazza dei Cavalieri di Malta 5, Rome, 00153, Italy. TEL 39-06-5791320, FAX 39-06-5791366, http://www.santanselmo.org.

100 ITA ISSN 0081-6310
STUDIA ARISTOTELICA. Text in Italian. 1958. irreg., latest vol.12, 1986. price varies. **Document type:** *Monographic series, Academic/ Scholarly.*
Published by: (Universita degli Studi di Padova), Editrice Antenore, Via Valadier 52, Rome, 00193, Italy. TEL 39-06-32600370, FAX 39-06-3223132, antenore@editriceantenore.it, http:// www.editriceantenore.it.

100 500 DEU ISSN 0039-3185
B2550 CODEN: STLBBI
➤ **STUDIA LEIBNITIANA**; Zeitschrift fuer Geschichte der Philosophie und der Wissenschaften. Text in English, German, French. 1969. s-a. EUR 142.40; EUR 113.40 to members; EUR 81.50 per issue (effective 2012). adv. bk.rev. back issues avail.; reprint service avail. from SCH. **Document type:** *Journal, Academic/Scholarly.*
Related titles: ◆ Supplement(s): Studia Leibnitiana. Supplementa. ISSN 0303-5980; ◆ Studia Leibnitiana. Sonderhefte. ISSN 0341-0765.
Indexed: A20, A22, ASCA, ArtHuCI, BibInd, CCMJ, CurCont, DIP, FR, H14, IBR, IBZ, IPB, MLA-IB, MSN, MathR, P10, P28, P30, P48, P53, P54, PCI, PQC, PhilInd, RASB, SCOPUS, SpeleolAb, W07, Z02.
—IE, Ingenta, INIST. **CCC.**
Published by: (Gottfried-Wilhelm-Leibniz-Gesellschaft e.V.), Franz Steiner Verlag GmbH, Birkenwaldstr 44, Stuttgart, 70191, Germany. TEL 49-711-25820, FAX 49-711-2582290, service@steiner-verlag.de. Eds. G H R Parkinson, Heinrich Schepers. R&P Sabine Koerner. Adv. contact Susanne Szoradi. Circ: 420 (paid and controlled).

100 DEU ISSN 0341-0765
STUDIA LEIBNITIANA. SONDERHEFTE. Text in English, German. 1969. irreg., latest vol.39, 2010. price varies. **Document type:** *Monographic series, Academic/Scholarly.*
Related titles: ◆ Supplement to: Studia Leibnitiana. ISSN 0039-3185.
Indexed: MathR.
Published by: (Gottfried Wilhelm Leibniz Gesellschaft, Hannover), Franz Steiner Verlag GmbH, Birkenwaldstr 44, Stuttgart, 70191, Germany. TEL 49-711-25820, FAX 49-711-2582290, service@steiner-verlag.de, http://www.steiner-verlag.de.

100 DEU ISSN 0303-5980
B2550
STUDIA LEIBNITIANA. SUPPLEMENTA. Text in English, French, German. 1968. irreg., latest vol.35, 2010. price varies. **Document type:** *Monographic series, Academic/Scholarly.*
Related titles: ◆ Supplement to: Studia Leibnitiana. ISSN 0039-3185.
Indexed: GeoRef, MathR, SpeleolAb.
—CCC.
Published by: (Gottfried Wilhelm Leibniz Gesellschaft, Hannover), Franz Steiner Verlag GmbH, Birkenwaldstr 44, Stuttgart, 70191, Germany. TEL 49-711-25820, FAX 49-711-2582290, franz.steiner.verlag@t-online.de, http://www.steiner-verlag.de.

160 NLD ISSN 0039-3215
B18.P6 CODEN: SLOGAP
➤ **STUDIA LOGICA**; an international journal for symbolic logic. Text in English. 1953. 9/yr. (in 3 vols., 3 nos./vol.). EUR 1,491, USD 1,570 combined subscription to institutions (print & online eds.) (effective 2012). adv. bk.rev. charts; illus. index. back issues avail.; reprint service avail. from PSC. **Document type:** *Journal, Academic/ Scholarly.* **Description:** Contains papers on all technical issues of contemporary logic, logical systems, their semantics, methodology and application of logic in linguistics, mathematics and other sciences.
Related titles: Microform ed.: (from PQC); Online - full text ed.: ISSN 1572-8730 (from IngentaConnect).
Indexed: A22, A26, BibLing, CA, CCMJ, DIP, E01, FR, IBR, IBZ, IPB, Inspec, L11, MLA-IB, MSN, MathR, PCI, PhilInd, RASB, SCOPUS, T02, Z02.
—BLDSC (8482.975000), AskIEEE, IE, Infotrieve, Ingenta, INIST, Linda Hall. **CCC.**
Published by: (Polska Akademia Nauk, Instytut Filozofii i Socjologii POL), Springer Netherlands (Subsidiary of: Springer Science+Business Media), Van Godewijckstraat 30, Dordrecht, 3311 GX, Netherlands. TEL 31-78-6576050, FAX 31-78-6576474, http://www.springer.com. Ed. Ryszard Wojcicki.

189 POL ISSN 0039-3231
B20.6
STUDIA MEDIEWISTYCZNE. Text in English, German, French, Latin, Polish. 1959. a., latest vol.35, 2000. price varies. **Document type:** *Monographic series, Academic/Scholarly.*
Indexed: FR, IBR, IBZ, MLA, MLA-IB, RASB.
Published by: Polska Akademia Nauk, Instytut Filozofii i Socjologii, Nowy Swiat 72, Warsaw, 00330, Poland. TEL 48-22-8267181, FAX 48-22-8267823, secretar@ifispan.waw.pl. Ed. Z Kuksewicz.

110 POL ISSN 0039-324X
STUDIA METODOLOGICZNE/DISSERTATIONES METHODOLOGICAE. Text in Polish. 1965. s-a. price varies. bk.rev. bibl. index. **Document type:** *Monographic series, Academic/Scholarly.* **Description:** Research papers in Polish, summaries in English, prepared by sociologists, philosophers, historians, psychologists, linguists and others.
Indexed: FR, RASB.
—INIST.
Published by: (Uniwersytet im. Adama Mickiewicza w Poznaniu/Adam Mickiewicz University), Wydawnictwo Naukowe Uniwersytetu im. Adama Mickiewicza/Adam Mickiewicz University Press, ul Fredry 10, Poznan, 61701, Poland. TEL 48-61-8294646, FAX 48-61-8294647, press@amu.edu.pl, http://press.amu.edu.pl. Circ: 380.

100 CZE ISSN 1214-8407
➤ **STUDIA NEOARISTOTELICA.** Text in Multiple languages. 2004. s-a. EUR 35 (effective 2011). back issues avail. **Document type:** *Journal, Academic/Scholarly.* **Description:** Publishes original articles, notes, discussions, translations, and editions on Aristotelian philosophy.
Related titles: Online - full text ed.: ISSN 1804-6843. USD 100 to institutions (effective 2011).
Published by: Jihoceska Univerzita v Ceskych Budejovicich, Teologicka Fakulta/University of South Bohemia in Ceske Budejovice, Faculty of Theology, Knezska 8, Ceske Budejovice, 370 01, Czech Republic. TEL 420-389-033530, http://www.tf.jcu.cz/. Ed. Daniel D. Novotny. **Dist. by:** Kubon & Sagner Buchexport - Import GmbH, PO Box 80328, Munich 80328, Germany. TEL 49-89-542180, FAX 49-89-54218138; Mediaprint-Kapa Pressegrosso, A.S., Vajnorska 137, PO BOX 183, Bratislava 3 830 00, Slovakia. TEL 421-244-458821, FAX 421-244-458819, predplatne@abompkapa.sk, http:// www.mediakapa.sk/.

➤ **STUDIA OECUMENICA FRIBURGENSIA.** *see* RELIGIONS AND THEOLOGY—Roman Catholic

➤ **STUDIA PATAVINA**; rivista di scienze religiose. *see* RELIGIONS AND THEOLOGY

100 200 SWE ISSN 0346-5446
STUDIA PHILOSOPHIAE RELIGIONIS. Text in English. 1973. irreg., latest vol.15, 1989. price varies.
Published by: Uppsala Universitet, Teologiska Institutionen/Uppsala University, Department of Theology, PO Box 511, Uppsala, 75120, Sweden. Ed. Eberhard Herrmann TEL 46-018-471-21-78. **Dist. by:** Almqvist & Wiksell International, PO Box 614, Soedertaelje 15127, Sweden.

100 CHE ISSN 0081-6825
B18.S9
STUDIA PHILOSOPHICA. Text in French, German. 1941. a. CHF 68, EUR 48 (effective 2010). index. reprints avail. **Document type:** *Journal, Academic/Scholarly.*
Related titles: Supplement(s): Studia Philosophica. Supplementum. ISSN 1016-751X. 1946.
Indexed: FR, MLA-IB, PCI, PsycholAb.
—INIST.
Published by: (Societe Suisse de Philosophie), Schwabe und Co. AG, Steinentorstr 13, Basel, 4010, Switzerland. TEL 41-61-2789565, FAX 41-61-2789566, verlag@schwabe.ch, http://www.schwabe.ch.

100 CZE ISSN 1803-7445
➤ **STUDIA PHILOSOPHICA.** Text in Multiple languages. 1953. s-a. EUR 15, USD 20 per issue (effective 2011). bk.rev. **Document type:** *Journal, Academic/Scholarly.* **Description:** Consists of articles on ethics, aesthetics, logics and the history of philosophy.
Former titles (until 2009): Masarykova Univerzita. Filozoficka Fakulta. Sbornik Praci. B: Rada Filozoficka; Univerzita J.E. Purkyne. Filozoficka Fakulta. Sbornik Praci. B: Rada Filozoficka (0231-7664)
Indexed: RASB.
—INIST.
Published by: Masarykova Univerzita, Filozoficka Fakulta/Masaryk University, Faculty of Arts, Arna Novaka 1, Brno, 60200, Czech Republic. TEL 420-549-491111, FAX 420-549-491520, podatelna@phil.muni.cz. Ed. Helena Pavlincova.

100 EST ISSN 1406-0000
B8.E8
➤ **STUDIA PHILOSOPHICA.** Text in English. 1958. a. **Document type:** *Journal, Academic/Scholarly.* **Description:** The history of this journal can be traced back to the Acta et Commentationes Universitatis Tartuensis which was founded in 1893. It is now primarily an electronic journal, although hard copies continue to be sent for free to a number of institutions (note that ISSN Online shows the print edition as ceased since 2006.).
Formerly (until 1991): Tartu Riikliku Ulikooli Toimetised. Trudy po Filosofii (0207-4621)
Related titles: Online - full text ed.: Studia Philosophica Estonica. ISSN 1736-5899. free (effective 2011).
Indexed: FR.
Published by: Tartu Ulikool, Department of Philosophy, Ulikooli 18, Tartu, 50090, Estonia. Ed. Roomet Jakapi.

100 DEU ISSN 0721-5878
STUDIA PHILOSOPHICA ET HISTORICA. Text in German. 1982. irreg., latest vol.27, 2005. price varies. **Document type:** *Monographic series, Academic/Scholarly.*
—CCC.
Published by: Peter Lang GmbH (Subsidiary of: Peter Lang Publishing Group), Eschborner Landstr 42-50, Frankfurt Am Main, 60489, Germany. TEL 49-69-7807050, FAX 49-69-78070550, zentrale.frankfurt@peterlang.com. Ed. Wolfram Hogrebe.

100 SWE ISSN 0585-5497
STUDIA PHILOSOPHICA UPSALIENSIA. Text in Multiple languages. 1965. irreg., latest vol.3, 1996. price varies. **Document type:** *Monographic series, Academic/Scholarly.*
Related titles: ◆ Series of: Acta Universitatis Upsaliensis. ISSN 0346-5462.
Indexed: CIS.
Published by: Uppsala Universitet, Acta Universitatis Upsaliensis/ University Publications from Uppsala, PO Box 256, Uppsala, 75105, Sweden. TEL 46-18-4716804, FAX 46-18-4716804, acta@ub.uu.se, http://www.ub.uu.se/upu/auu/index.html. Ed. Bengt Landgren. **Dist. by:** Almqvist & Wiksell International, PO Box 614, Soedertaelje 15127, Sweden.

100 ESP ISSN 1139-6660
B5
STUDIA POLIANA; revista sobre el pensamiento de Leonardo Polo. Text in Spanish. 1999. a. **Document type:** *Journal, Academic/ Scholarly.*
Indexed: FR, PhilInd, SociolAb.
—INIST.
Published by: (Universidad de Navarra, Facultad de Filosofia y Letras), Universidad de Navarra, Servicio de Publicaciones, Campus Universitario, Pamplona, 31009, Spain. http://www.unav.es/ publicaciones/.

182 DEU ISSN 1869-7143
➤ **STUDIA PRAESOCRATICA.** Text in German. 2007. irreg., latest vol.3, 2012. price varies. **Document type:** *Monographic series, Academic/ Scholarly.*
Published by: Walter de Gruyter GmbH & Co. KG, Genthiner Str 13, Berlin, 10785, Germany. TEL 49-30-260050, FAX 49-30-26005251, info@degruyter.com, http://www.degruyter.de.

➤ **STUDIA PSYCHOLOGICA.** *see* PSYCHOLOGY

100 500 DEU ISSN 0179-3896
B3950
STUDIA SPINOZANA; an international & interdisciplinary series. Text in German. 1985. irreg., latest vol.17, 2009. EUR 30, USD 39.80 (effective 2011). adv. bk.rev. **Document type:** *Journal, Academic/ Scholarly.* **Description:** Contains articles on all aspects of Spinoza's philosophy, including its cultural and intellectual background and influence.
Indexed: DIP, FR, IBR, IBZ, IPB, PCI, PhilInd, RASB.
Published by: (Spinoza-Gesellschaft e.V.), Verlag Koenigshausen und Neumann GmbH, Leistenstr 7, Wuerzburg, 97082, Germany. TEL 49-931-3298700, FAX 49-931-83620, info@koenigshausen-neumann.de, http://koenigshausen-neumann.gebhardt-riegel.de. Ed. Manfred Walther. Circ: 1,000.

174.957 ROM ISSN 2247-0441
➤ **STUDIA UNIVERSITATIS BABES-BOLYAI. BIOETHICA.** Text in English, French, German, Romanian. 2007. s-a. bk.rev. abstr.; bibl.; illus. **Document type:** *Journal, Academic/Scholarly.*
Related titles: Online - full text ed.: ISSN 2065-9504.
Indexed: CA, T02.
Published by: Universitatea "Babes-Bolyai", Studia/Babes-Bolyai University, Studia, 51 Hasdeu Str, Cluj-Napoca, 400371, Romania. TEL 40-264-405352, FAX 40-264-591906, office@studia.ubbcluj.ro. Ed. Ioan Chirila. **Dist by:** "Lucian Blaga" Central University Library, International Exchange Department, Clinicilor st no 2, Cluj-Napoca 400371, Romania. TEL 40-264-597092, FAX 40-264-597633, iancu@bcucluj.ro.

P

100 ROM ISSN 1221-8138
B8.R8
➤ **STUDIA UNIVERSITATIS BABES-BOLYAI. PHILOSOPHIA.** Text in English, French, German, Romanian; Abstracts in English. 1958. 3/yr. exchange basis. bk.rev. abstr.; charts; illus.; stat. cum.index: 1956-1963, 1964-1970. **Document type:** *Journal, Academic/Scholarly.*
Formerly (until 1975): Studia Universitatis "Babes-Bolyai". Series Philosophia (0578-5480); Which superseded in part (in 1975): Studia Universitatis "Babes-Bolyai". Series Philosophia et Oeconomica (1220-0425)
Related titles: Online - full text ed.: ISSN 2065-9407.
Indexed: CA, IBR, IBSS, IBZ, MLA-IB, RASB, T02.
Published by: Universitatea "Babes-Bolyai", Studia/Babes-Bolyai University, Studia, 51 Hasdeu Str, Cluj-Napoca, 400371, Romania. TEL 40-264-405352, FAX 40-264-591906, office@studia.ubbcluj.ro, http://www.studia.ubbcluj.ro. Ed. Ion Copoeru. **Dist by:** "Lucian Blaga" Central University Library, International Exchange Department, Clinicilor st no 2, Cluj-Napoca 400371, Romania. TEL 40-264-597092, FAX 40-264-597633, iancu@bcucluj.ro.

➤ **STUDIEN FUER RELIGION, WISSENSCHAFT UND KUNST.** *see* RELIGIONS AND THEOLOGY

100 DEU ISSN 0585-5802
STUDIEN UND MATERIALEN ZUR GESCHICHTE DER PHILOSOPHIE. Text in German, English, French. 1965. irreg., latest vol.78, 2009. price varies. **Document type:** *Monographic series, Academic/Scholarly.*
Published by: Georg Olms Verlag, Hagentorwall 7, Hildesheim, 31134, Germany. TEL 49-5121-15010, FAX 49-5121-150150, info@olms.de, http://www.olms.de. Ed. Gerhard Funke.

189 NLD ISSN 0169-8028
➤ **STUDIEN UND TEXTE ZUR GEISTESGESCHICHTE DES MITTELALTERS.** Text in English, German. 1950. irreg., latest vol.100, 2008. price varies. back issues avail. **Document type:** *Monographic series, Academic/Scholarly.* **Description:** Scholarly studies on medieval European philosophical texts and issues in the history of philosophy, theology and science in the medieval European world.
Indexed: IZBG.
—GNLM.
Published by: Brill, PO Box 9000, Leiden, 2300 PA, Netherlands. TEL 31-71-5353500, FAX 31-71-5317532, cs@brill.nl, http://www.brill.nl. R&P Elizabeth Venekamp. **Dist. by:** Turpin Distribution Services Ltd., Pegasus Dr, Stratton Business Park, Biggleswade, Bedfordshire SG18 8QB, United Kingdom. TEL 44-1767-604954, FAX 44-1767-601640, custserv@turpin-distribution.com, http://www.turpin-distribution.com/.

170 DEU ISSN 1862-2364
➤ **STUDIEN ZU WISSENSCHAFT UND ETHIK.** Text in German. 2005. irreg., latest vol.5, 2008. price varies. **Document type:** *Monographic series, Academic/Scholarly.*
Media: Large Type.
Published by: Walter de Gruyter GmbH & Co. KG, Genthiner Str 13, Berlin, 10785, Germany. TEL 49-30-260050, FAX 49-30-26005251, info@degruyter.com, http://www.degruyter.de. Eds. Dieter Sturma, Ludwig Siep.

109 DEU
STUDIEN ZUM 18. JAHRHUNDERT. Text in German. 1978. irreg., latest vol.32, 2009. price varies. **Document type:** *Monographic series, Academic/Scholarly.*
Published by: Felix Meiner Verlag GmbH, Richardstr 47, Hamburg, 22081, Germany. TEL 49-40-2987560, FAX 49-40-29875620, info@meiner.de.

170 DEU ISSN 1437-9783
STUDIEN ZUR ETHIK IN OSTMITTELEUROPA. Text in German. 2000. irreg., latest vol.13, 2009. price varies. **Document type:** *Monographic series, Academic/Scholarly.*
Published by: Peter Lang GmbH (Subsidiary of: Peter Lang Publishing Group), Eschborner Landstr 42-50, Frankfurt Am Main, 60489, Germany. TEL 49-69-7807050, FAX 49-69-78070550, zentrale.frankfurt@peterlang.com. Ed. Jan Joerden.

100 NLD ISSN 0928-141X
STUDIEN ZUR INTERKULTURELLEN PHILOSOPHIE/ETUDES DE PHILOSOPHIE INTERCULTURELLE/STUDIES IN INTERCULTURAL PHILOSOPHY. Text in English, German. 1994. irreg., latest vol.17, 2006. price varies. back issues avail. **Document type:** *Monographic series, Academic/Scholarly.* **Description:** Studies philosophy and philosophic schools that cross cultural boundaries.
Indexed: AmHI, H07, T02.
Published by: (Gesellschaft fuer Interkulturelle Philosophie eV/Society for Intercultural Philosophy - Societe pour Philosophie Interculturelle DEU), Editions Rodopi B.V., Tijnmuiden 7, Amsterdam, 1046 AK, Netherlands. TEL 31-20-6114821, FAX 31-20-4472979, info@rodopi.nl. Eds. Henk Oosterling, Hermann-Josef Scheidgen. **Dist in France by:** Nordeal, 30 rue de Verlinghem, BP 139, Lambersart 59832, France. TEL 33-3-20099060, FAX 33-3-20929495; **Dist in N America by:** Rodopi - USA, 606 Newark Ave, 2nd fl, Kenilworth, NJ 07033. TEL 908-497-9031, 800-225-3998, FAX 908-497-9035.

100 NLD ISSN 0167-4102
STUDIEN ZUR OESTERREICHISCHEN PHILOSOPHIE. Text in English, German. 1979. irreg., latest vol.40, 2007. price varies. back issues avail. **Document type:** *Monographic series, Academic/Scholarly.* **Description:** Examines Austrian philosophers and schools of philosophy.
Indexed: AmHI, CCMJ, H07, T02.
Published by: Editions Rodopi B.V., Tijnmuiden 7, Amsterdam, 1046 AK, Netherlands. TEL 31-20-6114821, FAX 31-20-4472979, info@rodopi.nl. Ed. Rudolf Haller. **Dist in France by:** Nordeal, 30 rue de Verlinghem, BP 139, Lambersart 59832, France. TEL 33-3-20099060, FAX 33-3-20929495; **Dist in N America by:** Rodopi - USA, 606 Newark Ave, 2nd fl, Kenilworth, NJ 07033. TEL 908-497-9031, 800-225-3998, FAX 908-497-9035.

100 DEU ISSN 1866-4814
STUDIEN ZUR PHAENOMENOLOGIE UND PRAKTISCHEN PHILOSOPHIE. Text in German. 2006. irreg., latest vol.24, 2011. price varies. **Document type:** *Monographic series, Academic/Scholarly.*
Published by: Ergon Verlag, Keesburgstr 11, Wuerzburg, 97074, Germany. TEL 49-931-280084, FAX 49-931-282872, service@ergon-verlag.de.

109 DEU ISSN 0171-7278
STUDIEN ZUR PHILOSOPHIE DES 18. JAHRHUNDERTS. Text in German. 1976. irreg., latest vol.10, 2004. price varies. **Document type:** *Monographic series, Academic/Scholarly.*
Published by: Peter Lang GmbH (Subsidiary of: Peter Lang Publishing Group), Eschborner Landstr 42-50, Frankfurt Am Main, 60489, Germany. TEL 49-69-7807050, FAX 49-69-78070550, zentrale.frankfurt@peterlang.com, http://www.peterlang.com. Ed. Norbert Hinske.

STUDIEN ZUR THEOLOGISCHEN ETHIK. *see* RELIGIONS AND THEOLOGY

111.85 701.17 SWE ISSN 1100-035X
STUDIES IN AESTHETICS. Text in English, Swedish. 1988. irreg. price varies. **Document type:** *Monographic series, Academic/Scholarly.*
Published by: Lunds Universitet, Department of Philosophy/Lund University, Kungshuset, Lund, 22222, Sweden. TEL 46-46-2227590, FAX 46-46-2224424, fil@fil.lu.se, http://www.fil.lu.se.

178 NLD
STUDIES IN APPLIED ETHICS. Text in English. irreg. price varies. **Document type:** *Monographic series, Academic/Scholarly.*
Related titles: ◆ Series of: Value Inquiry Book Series. ISSN 0929-8436.
Published by: Editions Rodopi B.V., Tijnmuiden 7, Amsterdam, 1046 AK, Netherlands. TEL 31-20-6114821, FAX 31-20-4472979, info@rodopi.nl. Ed. Gerhold K Becker. **Dist. by:** Rodopi - USA, 606 Newark Ave, 2nd fl, Kenilworth, NJ 07033. TEL 908-497-9031, FAX 908-497-9035.

174.2 SWE ISSN 1402-3148
STUDIES IN BIOETHICS AND RESEARCH ETHICS. Text in Multiple languages. 1997. irreg., latest vol.4, 1999. price varies. back issues avail. **Document type:** *Monographic series, Academic/Scholarly.*
Related titles: ◆ Series of: Acta Universitatis Upsaliensis. ISSN 0346-5462.
Published by: Uppsala Universitet, Acta Universitatis Upsaliensis/University Publications from Uppsala, PO Box 256, Uppsala, 75105, Sweden. TEL 46-18-4716804, FAX 46-18-4716804, acta@ub.uu.se, http://www.ub.uu.se/upu/auu/index.html. Ed. Bengt Landgren. **Dist. by:** Almqvist & Wiksell International, PO Box 614, Soedertaelje 15127, Sweden.

STUDIES IN CHRISTIAN ETHICS. *see* RELIGIONS AND THEOLOGY

STUDIES IN COGNITIVE SYSTEMS. *see* PSYCHOLOGY

190 USA ISSN 0893-6919
STUDIES IN CONTEMPORARY CONTINENTAL PHILOSOPHY. Text in English. 1989. irreg., latest vol.3, 1993. price varies. **Document type:** *Monographic series, Academic/Scholarly.* **Description:** Provides a forum for English-language authors of monographs in contemporary continental philosophy.
Published by: Peter Lang Publishing, Inc. (Subsidiary of: Peter Lang Publishing Group), 29 Broadway, New York, NY 10006. TEL 212-647-7700, FAX 212-647-7707, customerservice@plang.com, http://www.peterlang.com. Ed. Galen A Johnson.

108 USA
STUDIES IN CONTEMPORARY GERMAN SOCIAL THOUGHT. Text in English. 19??. irreg. (2-5/yr.). price varies. back issues avail. **Document type:** *Monographic series, Academic/Scholarly.*
Published by: M I T Press, 55 Hayward St, Cambridge, MA 02142. TEL 617-253-5646, FAX 617-258-6779, journals-info@mit.edu.

128 NLD ISSN 1875-2470
STUDIES IN CONTEMPORARY PHENOMENOLOGY. Text in English. 2008. irreg. **Document type:** *Monographic series, Academic/Scholarly.* **Description:** Focuses on the relevance of phenomenology for human life, its relation to the world and contemporary culture.
Indexed: IZBG.
Published by: Brill, PO Box 9000, Leiden, 2300 PA, Netherlands. TEL 31-71-5353500, FAX 31-71-5317532, cs@brill.nl. Ed. Chris Bremmers.

STUDIES IN EAST EUROPEAN THOUGHT. *see* POLITICAL SCIENCE

100 330 DEU ISSN 1431-8822
STUDIES IN ECONOMIC ETHICS AND PHILOSOPHY. Text in English. 1992. irreg., latest vol.40, 2011. price varies. **Document type:** *Monographic series, Academic/Scholarly.* **Description:** Devoted to the investigation of interdisciplinary issues concerning economics, ethics, and philosophy.
Formerly (until 2011): Studies in Economic Ethics and Philosophy (Print) (1431-8822)
Related titles: Online - full text ed.: ISSN 2211-2723.
Published by: Springer Netherlands (Subsidiary of: Springer Science+Business Media), Van Godewijckstraat 30, Dordrecht, 3311 GX, Netherlands. TEL 31-78-6576050, FAX 31-78-6576474. Ed. Peter Koslowski.

142.7 NLD
STUDIES IN EXISTENTIALISM. Text in English. irreg. price varies. **Document type:** *Monographic series, Academic/Scholarly.* **Description:** Covers the thinking of individual existentialists and examines topics of human existence, such as freedom, values, anguish, and interpersonal relationships.
Related titles: ◆ Series of: Value Inquiry Book Series. ISSN 0929-8436.
Published by: Editions Rodopi B.V., Tijnmuiden 7, Amsterdam, 1046 AK, Netherlands. TEL 31-20-6114821, FAX 31-20-4472979, info@rodopi.nl. Ed. Mark Letteri. **Dist. by:** Rodopi - USA, 606 Newark Ave, 2nd fl, Kenilworth, NJ 07033. TEL 908-497-9031, FAX 908-497-9035.

STUDIES IN HISTORY AND PHILOSOPHY OF SCIENCE. *see* SCIENCES: COMPREHENSIVE WORKS

STUDIES IN HISTORY AND PHILOSOPHY OF SCIENCE PART A. *see* SCIENCES: COMPREHENSIVE WORKS

STUDIES IN HISTORY AND PHILOSOPHY OF SCIENCE PART B: STUDIES IN HISTORY AND PHILOSOPHY OF MODERN PHYSICS. *see* PHYSICS

STUDIES IN HISTORY AND PHILOSOPHY OF SCIENCE PART C: STUDIES IN HISTORY AND PHILOSOPHY OF BIOLOGICAL AND BIOMEDICAL SCIENCES. *see* BIOLOGY

100 USA
STUDIES IN HISTORY OF PHILOSOPHY. Text in English. 1986. irreg., latest 2009. price varies. back issues avail. **Document type:** *Monographic series, Academic/Scholarly.*
Published by: Edwin Mellen Press, 415 Ridge St, PO Box 450, Lewiston, NY 14092. TEL 716-754-2266, FAX 716-754-4056, cservice@mellenpress.com.

109 USA ISSN 0956-5078
➤ **STUDIES IN INTELLECTUAL HISTORY AND THE HISTORY OF PHILOSOPHY.** Text in English. 1982. irreg., latest 1997. price varies. back issues avail. **Document type:** *Monographic series, Academic/Scholarly.* **Description:** Examines historical topics in philosophy.
—**CCC.**
Published by: Princeton University Press, 41 William St, Princeton, NJ 08540. TEL 609-258-4900, 800-777-4726, FAX 609-258-6305, cpriday@pupress.co.uk. Eds. David Fate Norton, M A Stewart. **Subscr. addr. in US:** California - Princeton Fulfillment Services, Inc., 1445 Lower Ferry Rd, Ewing, NJ 08618. TEL 609-883-1759, 800-777-4726, FAX 609-883-7413, 800-999-1958, orders@cpfsinc.com. **Dist. addr. in Canada:** University Press Group.; **Dist. addr. in UK:** John Wiley & Sons Ltd.

➤ **STUDIES IN JURISPRUDENCE.** *see* LAW

➤ **STUDIES IN LANGUAGE.** *see* LINGUISTICS

➤ **STUDIES IN LINGUISTICS AND PHILOSOPHY.** *see* LINGUISTICS

➤ **STUDIES IN LOGIC AND PRACTICAL REASONING.** *see* MATHEMATICS

➤ **STUDIES IN LOGIC AND THE FOUNDATIONS OF MATHEMATICS.** *see* MATHEMATICS

100 USA
STUDIES IN MORAL, POLITICAL, AND LEGAL PHILOSOPHY. Text in English. 19??. irreg., latest 1997. price varies. illus. back issues avail. **Document type:** *Monographic series, Academic/Scholarly.*
Published by: Princeton University Press, 41 William St, Princeton, NJ 08540. TEL 609-258-4900, 800-777-4726, FAX 609-258-6305, cpriday@pupress.co.uk. Ed. Marshall Cohen. **Subscr. to:** California - Princeton Fulfillment Services, Inc., 1445 Lower Ferry Rd, Ewing, NJ 08618. TEL 609-883-1759, 800-777-4726, FAX 609-883-7413, 800-999-1958, orders@cpfsinc.com. **Dist. addr. in Canada:** University Press Group.; **Dist. addr. in UK:** John Wiley & Sons Ltd.

141 942 NLD ISSN 1875-029X
STUDIES IN PHILO OF ALEXANDRIA. Text in English. 2003. irreg., latest vol.6, 2011. price varies. **Document type:** *Monographic series, Academic/Scholarly.*
Formerly (until 2008): Ancient Mediterranean and Medieval Texts and Contexts. Studies in Philo of Alexandria and Mediterranean Antiquity (1543-995X)
Indexed: IZBG.
Published by: Brill, PO Box 9000, Leiden, 2300 PA, Netherlands. TEL 31-71-5353500, FAX 31-71-5317532, cs@brill.nl. Eds. Francesca Calabi, Robert M Berchman.

STUDIES IN PHILOSOPHICAL THEOLOGY. *see* RELIGIONS AND THEOLOGY

100 SWE ISSN 1100-4290
STUDIES IN PHILOSOPHY. Text in English, Swedish. 1989. irreg. price varies. **Document type:** *Monographic series, Academic/Scholarly.*
Published by: Lunds Universitet, Department of Philosophy/Lund University, Kungshuset, Lund, 22222, Sweden. TEL 46-46-2227590, FAX 46-46-2224424, fil@fil.lu.se, http://www.fil.lu.se.

STUDIES IN PHILOSOPHY AND EDUCATION; an international quarterly. *see* EDUCATION

100 200 NLD
➤ **STUDIES IN PHILOSOPHY AND RELIGION.** Text in English. 1979. irreg., latest vol.27, 2007. price varies. **Document type:** *Monographic series, Academic/Scholarly.*
Published by: Springer Netherlands (Subsidiary of: Springer Science+Business Media), Van Godewijckstraat 30, Dordrecht, 3311 GX, Netherlands. TEL 31-78-6576050, FAX 31-78-6576474.

100 USA ISSN 0585-6965
B21
STUDIES IN PHILOSOPHY & THE HISTORY OF PHILOSOPHY. Text in English. 1961. irreg., latest vol.51, 2009. price varies. back issues avail.; reprints avail. **Document type:** *Monographic series, Academic/Scholarly.*
Indexed: A22, CCMJ.
—BLDSC (8491.220400), IE, Ingenta. **CCC.**
Published by: Catholic University of America Press, 620 Michigan Ave, NE, 240 Leahy Hall, Washington, DC 20064. TEL 800-537-5487, FAX 202-319-4985, cua-press@cua.edu.

306 170 NLD
STUDIES IN PRAGMATISM AND VALUES. Text in English. irreg. price varies. **Document type:** *Monographic series, Academic/Scholarly.* **Description:** Promotes the study of pragmatism's traditions and figures and the explorations of pragmatic inquiries in all areas of philosophical thought.
Related titles: ◆ Series of: Value Inquiry Book Series. ISSN 0929-8436.
Published by: Editions Rodopi B.V., Tijnmuiden 7, Amsterdam, 1046 AK, Netherlands. TEL 31-20-6114821, FAX 31-20-4472979, info@rodopi.nl. Eds. Harvey Cormier, John R Shook TEL 405-744-9231. **Dist. by:** Rodopi - USA, 606 Newark Ave, 2nd fl, Kenilworth, NJ 07033. TEL 908-497-9031, FAX 908-497-9035.

170 SWE ISSN 1102-0458
STUDIES IN RESEARCH ETHICS. Text in English. 1991. irreg., latest vol.7, 1996. **Document type:** *Monographic series, Academic/Scholarly.*
Published by: Kungliga Vetenskaps- och Vitterhets-Samhaellet i Goeteborg/Royal Society of Arts and Sciences in Gothenburg, c/o Goeteborgs Universitetsbibliotek, PO Box 222, Goeteborg, 40530, Sweden. TEL 46-31-7731733, FAX 46-31-163797.

STUDIES IN SOCIAL JUSTICE. *see* SOCIOLOGY

170 USA
STUDIES IN SOCIAL PHILOSOPHY AND POLICY. Text in English. 1983. irreg., latest 2002. back issues avail. **Document type:** *Monographic series, Academic/Scholarly.*

Published by: (Social Philosophy & Policy Center), Transaction Publishers, 35 Berrue Cir, Piscataway, NJ 08854. TEL 732-445-2280, FAX 732-445-3138, trans@transactionpub.com, http://www.transactionpub.com.

170 USA ISSN 1938-9485
D16.9
➤ **STUDIES IN THE HISTORY OF ETHICS.** Abbreviated title: S H E. Text in English. 2005. irreg. back issues avail. **Document type:** *Journal, Academic/Scholarly.* **Description:** Aims to contribute to the philosophical understanding of perennial problems within ethics.
Media: Online - full text.

109 NLD ISSN 0927-5088
STUDIES IN THE HISTORY OF IDEAS IN THE LOW COUNTRIES. Text in English. 1993. irreg., latest vol.6, 2005. price varies. back issues avail. **Document type:** *Monographic series, Academic/Scholarly.* **Description:** Explores and surveys the history of philosophic ideas and schools in the low countries.
Indexed: T02.
Published by: Editions Rodopi B.V., Tijnmuiden 7, Amsterdam, 1046 AK, Netherlands. TEL 31-20-6114821, FAX 31-20-4472979, info@rodopi.nl. Eds. Hans W Blom, Henri Krop, Wijnand W Mijnhardt. **Dist in France by:** Nordeal, 30 rue de Verlinghem, BP 139, Lambersart 59832, France. TEL 33-3-20099060, FAX 33-3-20929495; **Dist in N America by:** Rodopi - USA, 606 Newark Ave, 2nd fl, Kenilworth, NJ 07033. TEL 908-497-9031, 800-225-3998, FAX 908-497-9035.

109 USA
➤ **STUDIES IN THE HISTORY OF PHILOSOPHY.** Text in English. 1987 (vol.5). irreg., latest 2009. price varies. back issues avail. **Document type:** *Monographic series, Academic/Scholarly.*
Published by: Edwin Mellen Press, 415 Ridge St, PO Box 450, Lewiston, NY 14092. TEL 716-754-2266, FAX 716-754-4056, cservice@mellenpress.com.

190 NLD
STUDIES IN THE HISTORY OF WESTERN PHILOSOPHY. Text in English. irreg. price varies. **Document type:** *Monographic series, Academic/Scholarly.* **Description:** Examines the nature and development of Western philosophical activity from ancient Greece onward.
Related titles: ◆ Series of: Value Inquiry Book Series. ISSN 0929-8436.
Published by: Editions Rodopi B.V., Tijnmuiden 7, Amsterdam, 1046 AK, Netherlands. TEL 31-20-6114821, FAX 31-20-4472979, info@rodopi.nl. Ed. Robert Delfino. **Dist. by:** Rodopi - USA, 606 Newark Ave, 2nd fl, Kenilworth, NJ 07033. TEL 908-497-9031, FAX 908-497-9035.

170 USA ISSN 1086-6809
STUDIES IN THEORETICAL AND APPLIED ETHICS. Text in English. 1998. irreg., latest vol.9, 2002. price varies. **Document type:** *Monographic series, Academic/Scholarly.*
—BLDSC (8491.792350).
Published by: Peter Lang Publishing, Inc. (Subsidiary of: Peter Lang Publishing Group), 29 Broadway, New York, NY 10006. TEL 212-647-7700, FAX 212-647-7707, customerservice@plang.com, http://www.peterlangusa.com. Ed. Sherwin Klein.

STUDIES OF ARGUMENTATION IN PRAGMATICS AND DISCOURSE ANALYSIS. *see* LINGUISTICS

181 954 294 NLD ISSN 0167-4161
➤ **STUDIES OF CLASSICAL INDIA.** Text in English. 1978. irreg., latest vol.13, 1992. price varies. **Document type:** *Monographic series, Academic/Scholarly.* **Description:** Publishes fundamental studies concerning classical Indian civilization.
Published by: Springer Netherlands (Subsidiary of: Springer Science+Business Media), Van Godewijckstraat 30, Dordrecht, 3311 GX, Netherlands. TEL 31-78-6576050, FAX 31-78-6576474. Ed. Bimal K Matilal.

100 700 NLD ISSN 1877-0029
▼ **STUDIES ON THE INTERACTION OF ART, THOUGHT AND POWER.** Text in English. 2009. irreg., latest vol.4, 2011. price varies. **Document type:** *Monographic series, Academic/Scholarly.*
Published by: Brill, PO Box 9000, Leiden, 2300 PA, Netherlands. TEL 31-71-5353500, FAX 31-71-5317532, cs@brill.nl.

SUBTLE ENERGIES AND ENERGY MEDICINE; an interdisciplinary journal of energetic and informational interactions. *see* PHYSICS

SUDHI SAHITYA; a bilingual literary monthly. *see* RELIGIONS AND THEOLOGY—Hindu

SUGHRONA BEMATA. *see* RELIGIONS AND THEOLOGY—Roman Catholic

193 DEU ISSN 1862-2496
SUPPLEMENTA NIETZSCHEANA. Text in German. 1989. irreg., latest vol.7, 2004. price varies. **Document type:** *Monographic series, Academic/Scholarly.*
Published by: Walter de Gruyter GmbH & Co. KG, Genthiner Str 13, Berlin, 10785, Germany. TEL 49-30-260050, FAX 49-30-26005251, info@degruyter.com, http://www.degruyter.de. Eds. Karl Pestalozzi, Wolfgang Mueller-Lauter.

SUPPORTIVE LIFESTYLES NEWS. *see* NEW AGE PUBLICATIONS

100 FRA
SURFACES (PARIS, 1978). Text in French. 1978. irreg.
Published by: Editions Jean Michel Place, 12 rue Pierre et Marie Curie, Paris, 75005, France. Ed. Peter Hoy.

SUZHOU DAXUE XUEBAO (ZHEXUE SHEHUI KEXUE BAN)/SUZHOU UNIVERSITY. JOURNAL (PHILOSOPHY AND SOCIAL SCIENCES). *see* SOCIAL SCIENCES: COMPREHENSIVE WORKS

111.85 USA ISSN 1528-3623
PN2
➤ **SYMBOLISM**; an international annual of critical aesthetics. Text in English. 2000. a. USD 157.50 per issue (effective 2009). bk.rev. bibl.; illus. Index. 500 p./no.; back issues avail.; reprints avail. **Document type:** *Journal, Academic/Scholarly.* **Description:** Articles on the Symbolists and their literature and on the process of symbolizing in a number of eras and contexts.
Indexed: MLA-IB.
—BLDSC (8582.097000).
Published by: A M S Press, Inc., Brooklyn Navy Yard, 63 Flushing Ave, Bldg 292, Unit #221, Brooklyn, NY 11205. FAX 718-875-3800, queries@amspressinc.com. Eds. Klaus Stierstorfer, Rudigier Ahrens.

160 DEU ISSN 0082-0660
BL600
SYMBOLON; Jahrbuch fuer Symbolforschung. Text in German. 1955; N.S. 1972. irreg., latest vol.16, 2007. price varies. index. **Document type:** *Monographic series, Academic/Scholarly.*
Indexed: DIP, IBR, IBZ, PCI, RASB.
Published by: (Gesellschaft fuer Wissenschaftliche Symbolforschung), Peter Lang GmbH (Subsidiary of: Peter Lang Publishing Group), Eschborner Landstr 42-50, Frankfurt Am Main, 60489, Germany. TEL 49-69-7807050, FAX 49-69-78070550, zentrale.frankfurt@peterlang.com. Circ: 1,000.

100 DEU
SYMPOSION. Text in German. 1982. irreg., latest vol.132, 2009. price varies. **Document type:** *Monographic series, Academic/Scholarly.*
Published by: Verlag Karl Alber, Rudolf-Hermann-Herder-Str 4, Freiburg, 79104, Germany. TEL 49-761-2717436, FAX 49-761-2717212, info@verlag-alber.de.

100 USA ISSN 1521-2149
DK32
➤ **SYMPOSION**; a journal of Russian thought. Text in English, French, German, Russian. 1996. a. bk.rev. bibl. 150 p./no.; reprints avail. **Document type:** *Journal, Academic/Scholarly.* **Description:** Contains articles and documents.
Indexed: ABS&EES, CA, MLA-IB, T02.
Published by: Charles Schlacks, Jr., PO Box 1256, Idyllwild, CA 92512. TEL 951-659-4641, info@schlacks.com.

105 CAN ISSN 1480-2333
SYMPOSIUM: CANADIAN JOURNAL OF CONTINENTAL PHILOSOPHY/SYMPOSIUM: REVUE CANADIENNE DE PHILOSOPHIE CONTINENTALE. Text in English, French. 1997. s-a. CAD 55 to individuals; CAD 95 to institutions (effective 2008). adv. bk.rev. back issues avail. **Document type:** *Journal, Academic/Scholarly.*
Formerly (until 2004): Canadian Society for Hermeneutics and Postmodern Thought. Symposium
Indexed: AmHI, H07, IBSS, PhilInd, T02.
Published by: The Canadian Society for Continental Philosophy/La Societe Canadienne de Philosophie Continentale, c/o Antonio Calcagno, Editor, King's University College, 266 Eppworth Ave, London, ON N6A 2M3, Canada. Ed. Antonio Calcagno. adv.: B&W page CAD 100; 6 x 9.

▼ **SYNESIS.** *see* SCIENCES: COMPREHENSIVE WORKS

501 NLD ISSN 0039-7857
AP1 CODEN: SYNTAE
➤ **SYNTHESE**; an international journal for epistemology, methodology and philosophy of science. Text in English. 1936. 15/yr. (in 5 vols., 3 nos./vol.). EUR 2,608, USD 2,728 combined subscription to institutions (print & online eds.) (effective 2012). adv. bk.rev. illus. Index. reprint service avail. from PSC. **Document type:** *Journal, Academic/Scholarly.* **Description:** Publishes articles on the theory of knowledge, the general methodological problems of science, including related issues such as the role of mathematics, statistics and logic in science, and relevant aspects of the history and sociology of science.
Related titles: Microform ed.: (from PQC); Online - full text ed.: ISSN 1573-0964 (from IngentaConnect).
Indexed: A20, A22, A26, ASCA, AmHI, ArtHuCI, B21, BibInd, BibLing, CA, CCMJ, CIS, CMCI, CurCont, DIP, E01, FR, H07, H14, IBR, IBRH, IBZ, IPB, ISR, L&LBA, MLA-IB, MSN, MathR, NSA, P10, P30, P48, P53, P54, PCI, PQC, PhilInd, RASB, RILM, RefZh, SCI, SCOPUS, SOPODA, SSCI, SociolAb, T02, W07, Z02.
—BLDSC (8586.750000), IE, Infotrieve, Ingenta, INIST, Linda Hall. **CCC.**
Published by: Springer Netherlands (Subsidiary of: Springer Science+Business Media), Van Godewijckstraat 30, Dordrecht, 3311 GX, Netherlands. TEL 31-78-6576050, FAX 31-78-6576474, http://www.springer.com. Eds. J F A K van Benthem, John Symons, Vincent F Hendricks.

109 NLD ISSN 0166-6991
QA1
➤ **SYNTHESE LIBRARY**; studies in epistemology, logic, methodology and philosophy of science. Text in English. 1959. irreg., latest vol.344, 2009. price varies. **Document type:** *Monographic series, Academic/Scholarly.* **Description:** Covers the methodology and philosophy of science and epistemology.
Indexed: A22, MathR, RASB.
—BLDSC (8586.757000), IE, Ingenta. **CCC.**
Published by: Springer Netherlands (Subsidiary of: Springer Science+Business Media), Van Godewijckstraat 30, Dordrecht, 3311 GX, Netherlands. TEL 31-78-6576050, FAX 31-78-6576474. Eds. John Symons, Vincent F Hendricks.

100 HRV ISSN 0352-7875
B1
➤ **SYNTHESIS PHILOSOPHICA.** Text in English, German, French; Summaries in English, French, German, Croatian. 1986. s-a. HRK 150 domestic to individuals; EUR 20 foreign to individuals; HRK 200 domestic to institutions; EUR 30 foreign to institutions (effective 2008). bk.rev. abstr.; bibl.; illus. back issues avail.; reprints avail. **Document type:** *Journal, Academic/Scholarly.* **Description:** Aims to establish a network between the various theoretical perspectives in the paradigm of creating orientative knowledge.
Related titles: Online - full text ed.: free (effective 2011); ◆ Croatian ed.: Filozofska Istrazivanja. ISSN 0351-4706.
Indexed: A20, AmHI, ArtHuCI, CA, CurCont, H07, L&LBA, P30, P42, PSA, PhilInd, S02, S03, SCOPUS, SociolAb, T02, W07.
—BLDSC (8586.791000), IE, Ingenta.
Published by: Hrvatsko Filozofsko Drustvo/Croatian Philosophical Society, Krcka 1, Zagreb, 10000, Croatia. TEL 385-1-6111808, FAX 385-1-6170682, filozofska-istrazivanja@zg.t-com.hr, http://www.hrfd.hr. Ed., R&P Ante Covic. Pub. Pavo Barisic. Circ: 1,400 (paid).

100 ITA ISSN 1974-5044
SYZETESIS. Text in Multiple languages. 2008. m. **Document type:** *Journal, Academic/Scholarly.*
Media: Online - full text.
Published by: Associazione Filosofica Syzetesis, Via dei Laterani 36, Rome, 00184, Italy. http://www.syzetesis.it/associazione.html.

SZTUKA I FILOZOFIA. *see* ART

100 USA ISSN 0271-2482
CODEN: RMBRDQ
T A T JOURNAL. Text in English. 1977. a. adv. bk.rev. illus. back issues avail.
Published by: T A T Foundation, PO Box 236, Bellaire, OH 43906. Ed. Louis Khourey.

170 DEU
TA ETHIKA. Text in German. 2005. irreg., latest vol.11, 2010. price varies. **Document type:** *Monographic series, Academic/Scholarly.*
Published by: Herbert Utz Verlag GmbH, Adalbertstr 57, Munich, 80799, Germany. TEL 49-89-27779100, FAX 49-89-27779101, utz@utzverlag.com. Eds. Elke Mack, Nikolaus Knoepffler.

TABONA; revista de prehistoria y de arqueologia y filologia clasicas. *see* ARCHAEOLOGY

TAKING SIDES: CLASHING VIEWS IN BUSINESS ETHICS AND SOCIETY. *see* BUSINESS AND ECONOMICS

TAKING SIDES: CLASHING VIEWS ON BIOETHICAL ISSUES. *see* MEDICAL SCIENCES

100 USA ISSN 0275-7656
BD232
THE TANNER LECTURES ON HUMAN VALUES. Text in English. 1980. a. price varies. back issues avail. **Document type:** *Journal, Academic/Scholarly.* **Description:** Contains the collection of educational and scientific discussions relating to human values.
Indexed: A22, RASB, RI-1, RI-2.
—BLDSC (8602.573000), IE, Ingenta.
Published by: University of Utah Press, 1795 E South Campus Dr, 101, Salt Lake City, UT 84112. glenda.cotter@utah.edu, http://www.uofupress.com.

100 ESP ISSN 0214-6657
B5
TAULA; quaderns de pensament. Text in Spanish, Catalan. 1982. a. **Document type:** *Journal, Academic/Scholarly.*
Published by: (Universitat de les Illes Balears, Department de Filosofia), Universitat de les Illes Balears, Servei de Publicacions i Intercanvi Cientific, Carr. de Valdemosa, Km. 7.5, Palma de Mallorca, 07071, Spain. TEL 34-971-173000, FAX 34-971-173190, dpssec@ps.uib.es, http://www.uib.es.

AL-TAWHID; a quarterly journal of Islamic thought and culture. *see* RELIGIONS AND THEOLOGY—Islamic

170 370 USA ISSN 1544-4031
➤ **TEACHING ETHICS.** Text in English. 2001. s-a. free to members (effective 2010). adv. back issues avail. **Document type:** *Journal, Academic/Scholarly.* **Description:** Explores to ethical issues across the curriculum with particular attention to pedagogical methodology and practice in both academic inquiry and professional practice.
Related titles: Online - full text ed.: ISSN 2154-0551. USD 150 (effective 2010).
Indexed: CA, E03, PhilInd, T02.
Published by: (Society for Ethics Across the Curriculum), Philosophy Documentation Center, PO Box 7147, Charlottesville, VA 22906. TEL 434-220-3300, FAX 434-220-3301, order@pdcnet.org, http://www.pdcnet.org. Eds. Elaine Englehardt, Michael Pritchard. Adv. contact Greg Swope.

P

107.1 USA ISSN 0145-5788
B52
➤ **TEACHING PHILOSOPHY.** Text in English. 1975. q. USD 33 to individuals; USD 86 to institutions; USD 78 combined subscription to individuals (print & online eds.); USD 281 combined subscription to institutions (print & online eds.); USD 9 per issue to individuals; USD 22 per issue to institutions (effective 2010). adv. bk.rev.; film rev. 100 p./no.; back issues avail.; reprint service avail. from PSC. **Document type:** *Journal, Academic/Scholarly.* **Description:** Features practical and theoretical discussion of teaching and learning philosophy.
Related titles: CD-ROM ed.: Twenty-Five Years of Teaching Philosophy on CD-ROM; Online - full text ed.: ISSN 2153-6619. USD 53 to individuals; USD 234 to institutions (effective 2010).
Indexed: A01, A03, A08, A20, A22, A26, ArtHuCI, CA, CPE, CurCont, DIP, E03, E08, E16, ERA, ERI, FR, G08, I05, IBR, IBZ, IPB, MLA-IB, MRD, P30, PCI, PhilInd, RASB, S09, S19, S21, T02, W07.
—BLDSC (8614.298000), IE, Infotrieve, Ingenta, INIST. **CCC.**
Published by: Philosophy Documentation Center, PO Box 7147, Charlottesville, VA 22906. TEL 434-220-3300, FAX 434-220-3301, order@pdcnet.org, http://www.pdcnet.org. Ed. Patrick Boleyn-Fitzgerald. Adv. contact Greg Swope.

100 600 USA
TECHNE: RESEARCH IN PHILOSOPHY AND TECHNOLOGY. Text in English. 1995. 3/yr. free (effective 2010). back issues avail. **Document type:** *Journal, Academic/Scholarly.*
Formerly: Society for Philosophy & Technology Quarterly Electronic Journal (1091-8264)
Media: Online - full text.
Indexed: A09, A10, A39, AmHI, C27, C29, CA, D03, D04, E13, H07, R14, S14, S15, S18, T02, V03, V04.
Published by: Society for Philosophy and Technology, c/o Diane P. Michelfelder, Department of Philosophy, Macalester College, 1600 Grand Ave, St. Paul, MN 55105. TEL 651-696-6141, michelfelder@macalester.edu, http://www.spt.org. Ed. Joseph C Pitt TEL 540-231-5760.

100 DEU
TECHNIKPHILOSOPHIE. Text in German. 2000. irreg., latest vol.22, 2010. price varies. **Document type:** *Journal, Academic/Scholarly.*
Published by: Lit Verlag, Grevener Str/Fresnostr 2, Muenster, 48159, Germany. TEL 49-251-235091, FAX 49-251-231972, lit@lit-verlag.de.

200 100 FRA ISSN 1634-5924
TEILHARD AUJOURD'HUI. Text in French. 2002. 4/yr. EUR 20 (effective 2007). back issues avail. **Document type:** *Journal, Consumer.*
Published by: Association des Amis de Pierre Teilhard de Chardin, B P 90.001, Paris, Cedex 05 75221, France. TEL 33-1-42898476, secretariat@teilhard.org.

100 800 USA ISSN 1087-6456
B11
TELICOM. Text in English. 1975. bi-m. bk.rev. back issues avail. **Document type:** *Journal, Academic/Scholarly.* **Description:** Presents expository writing by those in the 99.9 percentile in their I.Q. Authors must be members to publish.

Published by: International Society for Philosophical Enquiry, c/o Patrick O'Shea, 700 Terr Heights 60, Winona, MN 55987. oshea@ispe-1000.org. Circ: 800.

100 USA ISSN 0090-6514
H1
➤ **TELOS**; a quarterly journal of politics, philosophy, critical theory, culture, and the arts. Text in English. 1968 (May). q. USD 60 domestic to individuals; USD 198 domestic to institutions; USD 290 combined subscription domestic to institutions (print & online eds.); USD 328 combined subscription foreign to institutions (print & online eds.) (effective 2009). adv. bk.rev. illus. back issues avail.; reprints avail. **Document type:** *Journal, Academic/Scholarly.* **Description:** Provides an international forum for discussions of political, social, and cultural change.
Related titles: Microform ed.: (from PQC); Online - full text ed.: ISSN 1940-459X. USD 230 (effective 2009).
Indexed: A01, A02, A03, A08, A21, A22, A26, ABS&EES, AltPI, AmHI, ArtHuCI, C12, CA, CurCont, DIP, E08, FR, G08, H07, H14, HRIR, I05, I13, IBR, IBSS, IBZ, IPB, LeftInd, M01, M02, MEA&I, MLA-IB, P02, P10, P42, P48, P53, P54, PCI, PQC, PSA, PerIslam, PhilInd, R05, RASB, RI-1, RI-2, RILM, S02, S03, S09, SCOPUS, SOPODA, SSA, SSCI, SociolAb, T02, W07.
—BLDSC (8789.350000), IE, Infotrieve, Ingenta, INIST. **CCC.**
Published by: Telos Press Publishing, 431 E 12th St, New York, NY 10009. TEL 212-228-6479, FAX 212-228-6379, telospress@aol.com. Ed. Russell Berman. Circ: 3,000.

170 320 340 ESP ISSN 1132-0877
B843.A1
TELOS; revista iberamericana de estudios utilitaristas. Text in Spanish, Portuguese, English. 1992. q. **Document type:** *Journal, Academic/Scholarly.*
Related titles: Online - full text ed.
Indexed: AmHI, F04, H07, PhilInd, T02.
Published by: Sociedad Iberoamericana de Estudios Utilitaristas, Area de Filosofia Moral, Campos Universitario Sur, Santiago de Compostela, 15782, Spain. TEL 34-981-522060, zfildeca@usc.es, http://www.usc.es/.

TEME; casopis za drustvene nauke. *see* SOCIOLOGY

100 FRA ISSN 1245-2998
B2
LE TEMPS PHILOSOPHIQUE. Text in French. 1995. a., latest 2009. price varies. **Document type:** *Academic/Scholarly.*
Published by: (Universite de Paris X (Paris-Nanterre)), Publidix, 200 av. de la Republique, Nanterre, Cedex 92001, France. TEL 33-1-40977590, FAX 33-1-40975698, publidix@u-paris10.fr.

101 ESP ISSN 0210-1602
B5
➤ **TEOREMA.** Text in Spanish, English. 1971. 3/yr. EUR 35 domestic to individuals; USD 55 foreign to individuals; EUR 55 domestic to institutions; USD 65 foreign to institutions (effective 2009). adv. bk.rev. bibl.; charts. 150 p./no.; back issues avail. **Document type:** *Journal, Academic/Scholarly.*
Related titles: Online - full text ed.; Supplement(s): Limbo. ISSN 1888-1254. 1996.
Indexed: A01, A20, AmHI, ArtHuCI, CA, F03, F04, H07, IPB, MLA-IB, MathR, P09, PCI, PhilInd, RASB, SCOPUS, T02, W07.
—CIS, Linda Hall. **CCC.**
Published by: Editorial Tecnos, Apartado 4437, Murcia, 30080, Spain. TEL 34-98-5104378, lmvaldes@sci.cpd.uniovi.es. Ed., R&P, Adv. contact Luis M Valdes Villanueva.

100 ITA ISSN 1122-1259
B4
TEORIA; rivista di filosofia. Text in English, Italian. 1981. s-a. EUR 30 (effective 2011). adv. bk.rev. **Document type:** *Journal, Academic/Scholarly.*
Indexed: ArtHuCI, CurCont, DIP, IBR, IBZ, IPB, MSN, RASB, W07.
Published by: (Universita degli Studi di Pisa, Dipartimento di Filosofia), Edizioni E T S, Piazza Carrara 16-19, Pisa, Italy. TEL 39-050-29544, FAX 39-050-20158, info@edizioniets.it, http://www.edizioniets.it. Ed. Adriano Fabris. Circ: 1,000.

141 FIN ISSN 0355-8045
TEOSOFI. Text in Finnish. 1920. 6/m. EUR 27 domestic; EUR 30 foreign; EUR 5 per issue foreign (effective 2005). **Document type:** *Journal, Academic/Scholarly.*
Published by: Teosofinen Seura ry, Vironkatu 7 C 2, Helsinki, 00170, Finland. TEL 358-9-1356205, FAX 358-9-1357479, teosofinen-seura@netti.fi. Ed. Erja Lahdenpera.

121 BEL
➤ **TERTIUM DATUR.** Text in Dutch. 1997. irreg., latest 2005. price varies. back issues avail. **Document type:** *Monographic series, Academic/Scholarly.* **Description:** Explores topics in philosophy.
Published by: Peeters Publishers, Bondgenotenlaan 153, Leuven, 3000, Belgium. TEL 32-16-235170, FAX 32-16-228500, http://www.peeters-leuven.be.

▼➤ **TEXTE UND STUDIEN ZUR EUROPAEISCHEN GEISTESGESCHICHTE. REIHE A.** *see* RELIGIONS AND THEOLOGY

▼➤ **TEXTE UND STUDIEN ZUR EUROPAEISCHEN GEISTESGESCHICHTE. REIHE B.** *see* RELIGIONS AND THEOLOGY

215 DEU ISSN 1437-0786
TEXTE UND STUDIEN ZUR WISSENSCHAFTSGESCHICHTE. Text in German. 1999. irreg., latest vol.4, 2009. price varies. **Document type:** *Monographic series, Academic/Scholarly.*
Published by: Georg Olms Verlag, Hagentorwall 7, Hildesheim, 31134, Germany. TEL 49-5121-15010, FAX 49-5121-150150, info@olms.de.

100 DEU ISSN 0174-0474
TEXTE ZUR FORSCHUNG. Text in German. 1971. irreg., latest vol.34, 2009. price varies. **Document type:** *Monographic series, Academic/Scholarly.*
Published by: Wissenschaftliche Buchgesellschaft, Hindenburgstr 40, Darmstadt, 64295, Germany. TEL 49-615-133080, FAX 49-615-1314128, service@wbg-wissenverbindet.de, http://www.wbg-darmstadt.de.

100 AUT ISSN 1433-7185
TEXTE ZUR WISSENSCHAFTLICHEN WELTAUFFASSUNG. Text in German. 1997. irreg. price varies. **Document type:** *Monographic series, Academic/Scholarly.*
Published by: Springer Wien (Subsidiary of: Springer Science+Business Media), Sachsenplatz 4-6, Vienna, W 1201, Austria. TEL 43-1-3302415-0, FAX 43-1-330242665, books@springer.at, http://www.springer.at. R&P Angela Foessl TEL 43-1-3302415517. **Subscr. in N. America to:** Springer New York LLC, 233 Spring St, New York, NY 10013. TEL 800-777-4643, FAX 201-348-4505.

THEMATA. *see* EDUCATION

THEOLOGIE UND PHILOSOPHIE. *see* RELIGIONS AND THEOLOGY—Roman Catholic

THEOLOGY AND MEDICINE. *see* RELIGIONS AND THEOLOGY

THEOPHIL; Zuercher Beitraege zu Religion und Philosophie. *see* RELIGIONS AND THEOLOGY

170 USA ISSN 2156-7174
▼➤ **THEORETICAL & APPLIED ETHICS.** Text in English. 2010. 3/yr. free (effective 2011). **Document type:** *Journal, Academic/Scholarly.*
Media: Online - full text.
Published by: The Society for Moral Inquiry, Philosophy Department, Montclair State University, Montclair, NJ 07043. Ed. Chris Herrera.

➤ **THEORETICAL MEDICINE AND BIOETHICS**; philosophy of medical research and practice. *see* MEDICAL SCIENCES

100 ESP ISSN 0495-4548
B67
➤ **THEORIA**; revista de filosofia, teoria, historia y fundamentos de la ciencia. Text in Spanish, English. 1952. q. EUR 75 to institutions (effective 2009). adv. bk.rev. cum.index: nos.1-20. 210 p./no.; back issues avail. **Document type:** *Journal, Academic/Scholarly.* **Description:** Covers logic, history and philosophy of science, philosophy of language, and cognitive science.
Related titles: Online - full text ed.: ISSN 2171-679X. free (effective 2011).
Indexed: A01, A20, ArtHuCI, CCMJ, CurCont, F04, FR, IECT, L&LBA, L11, MSN, MathR, P09, PCI, PhilInd, SCOPUS, T02, W07, Z02.
—BLDSC (8814.584600), INIST, Linda Hall. **CCC.**
Published by: Universidad del Pais Vasco, Servicio Editorial, Apartado 1397, Bilbao, 48080, Spain. TEL 34-94-6015126, FAX 34-94-4801314, luxedito@lg.ehu.es, http://www.ehu.es/servicios/se_az/. Circ: 700.

100 MEX
THEORIA; revista del Colegio de Filosophia. Cover title: Revista del Colegio de Filosofia. Text in Spanish. q. **Document type:** *Journal, Academic/Scholarly.* **Description:** Includes original articles, interviews and notes on philosophy.
Published by: Universidad Nacional Autonoma de Mexico, Facultad de Filosofia y Letras, Cicuito Interior, Ciudad Universitaria, Mexico, D.F., 04510, Mexico. TEL 52-55-56221833, ffyl@filos.unam.mx, http://www.filos.unam.mx/. Eds. Carlos Pereda, Lizbeth Sagols.

100 GBR ISSN 0040-5825
B1 CODEN: THRAA5
➤ **THEORIA**; a Swedish journal of philosophy. Text in English, French, German, Swedish. 1935. q. GBP 193 combined subscription in United Kingdom to institutions (print & online eds.); EUR 245 combined subscription in Europe to institutions (print & online eds.); USD 356 combined subscription in the Americas to institutions (print & online eds.); USD 378 combined subscription elsewhere to institutions (print & online eds.) (effective 2012). bk.rev. bibl. back issues avail.; reprint service avail. from PSC. **Document type:** *Journal, Academic/Scholarly.* **Description:** Provides research in all areas of philosophy.
Related titles: Online - full text ed.: ISSN 1755-2567. GBP 175 in United Kingdom to institutions; EUR 222 in Europe to institutions; USD 325 in the Americas to institutions; USD 343 elsewhere to institutions (effective 2012).
Indexed: A20, A22, AmHI, ArtHuCI, BEL&L, CA, CCMJ, CurCont, DIP, E-psyche, E01, FR, H07, IBR, IBZ, IPB, L&LBA, MSN, MathR, P30, PCI, PhilInd, PsycholAb, RASB, SCOPUS, SOPODA, SociolAb, T02, W07, Z02.
—IE, Ingenta, INIST. **CCC.**
Published by: Wiley-Blackwell Publishing Ltd. (Subsidiary of: John Wiley & Sons, Inc.), 9600 Garsington Rd, Oxford, OX4 2DQ, United Kingdom. TEL 44-1865-776868, FAX 44-1865-714591, customerservices@blackwellpublishing.com. Ed. Sven Ove Hansson. **Subscr. to:** 1-7 Oldlands Way, PO Box 809, Bognor Regis PO21 9FG, United Kingdom. TEL 44-1865-778054.

➤ **THEORY AND DECISION**; an international journal for multidisciplinary advances in decision sciences. *see* SOCIAL SCIENCES: COMPREHENSIVE WORKS

➤ **THEORY AND DECISION LIBRARY. SERIES A: PHILOSOPHY AND METHODOLOGY OF THE SOCIAL SCIENCES.** *see* SOCIAL SCIENCES: COMPREHENSIVE WORKS

299.934 NLD ISSN 0040-5868
THEOSOFIA; brotherhood, problems of society, religion and occult research. Text in Dutch. 1897. bi-m. EUR 25 domestic (effective 2010). bk.rev. index. 40 p./no.; back issues avail. **Document type:** *Academic/Scholarly.*
Published by: Theosofische Vereniging in Nederland, Tolstraat 154, Amsterdam, 1074 VM, Netherlands. TEL 31-20-6765672, FAX 31-20-6757657, info@theosofie.nl, http://www.theosofie.nl.

299.934 NZL ISSN 1177-8032
THEOSOPHIA. Text in English. 1900. q. NZD 10 domestic to non-members; NZD 15 foreign to non-members; free to members (effective 2008). adv. bk.rev. **Document type:** *Journal, Academic/Scholarly.* **Description:** Explores man's place in the universe through the study of religion, philosophy and science.
Formerly (until 2007): Theosophy in New Zealand (0049-3708)
—**CCC.**
Published by: Theosophical Society in New Zealand, 18 Belvedere St, Epsom, Auckland, 1051, New Zealand. TEL 64-9-5231797, FAX 64-9-5231797. Ed. Jo Barnsdale. Circ: 2,400.

THEOSOPHICAL HISTORY; a quarterly journal of research. *see* RELIGIONS AND THEOLOGY—Other Denominations And Sects

212.5 100 USA ISSN 0040-5906
THEOSOPHY; devoted to the theosophical movement and the brotherhood of humanity, the study of occult science and philosophy and Aryan literature. Text in English. 1912. bi-m. USD 17 (effective 2000). bk.rev. index.
Published by: Theosophy Co., 245 W 33rd St, Los Angeles, CA 90007. TEL 213-748-7244. Ed. Phyllis Ryan. R&P West Vanhorn. Circ: 800.

100 GBR ISSN 1477-1756
B1
THINK (LONDON). Text in English. 2002. 3/yr. GBP 101, USD 186 to institutions; GBP 109, USD 199 combined subscription to institutions (print & online eds.) (effective 2012). adv. back issues avail.; reprint service avail. from PSC. **Document type:** *Journal, Academic/Scholarly.* **Description:** Covers contemporary philosophy and writing by philosophers pre-eminent in their fields.
Related titles: Online - full text ed.: ISSN 1755-1196. GBP 97, USD 179 to institutions (effective 2012).
Indexed: A22, AmHI, B04, E01, H07, H08, HAb, HumInd, IBR, IBZ, P28, P48, P53, P54, PQC, PhilInd, W03.
—INIST. **CCC.**
Published by: (Royal Institute of Philosophy), Cambridge University Press, The Edinburgh Bldg, Shaftesbury Rd, Cambridge, CB2 8RU, United Kingdom. TEL 44-1223-312393, FAX 44-1223-315052, journals@cambridge.org, http://www.cambridge.org/uk. Ed. Dr. Stephen Law. R&P Linda Nicol TEL 44-1223-325702. Adv. contact Rebecca Roberts TEL 44-1223-325083. page GBP 400, page USD 760.

100 USA ISSN 0190-3330
B105.C45
➤ **THINKING**; the journal of philosophy for children. Text in English. 1979. q. USD 35 (effective 2011). bk.rev. charts; illus. Index. back issues avail. **Document type:** *Journal, Academic/Scholarly.* **Description:** Publishes philosophical argument and reflection, classroom transcripts, curricula, empirical research, and reports from the field. Also contains articles in the hermeneutics of childhood, a field of intersecting disciplines including cultural studies, social history, philosophy, art, literature and psychoanalysis.
Related titles: Online - full text ed.
Indexed: A22, B04, BRD, CA, CPE, DIP, E02, E03, ERI, EdA, EdI, FR, IBR, IBZ, PhilInd, T02, W03, W05.
—BLDSC (8820.134000), IE, Infotrieve, Ingenta. **CCC.**
Published by: Institute for the Advancement of Philosophy for Children, Montclair State University, University Hall 2151, Montclair, NJ 07043. TEL 973-655-4278, oylerj@mail.montclair.edu. Ed. Felix Garcia Moriyon.

➤ **THINKING & REASONING.** *see* PSYCHOLOGY

➤ **THOMAS INSTITUUT UTRECHT SERIES.** *see* RELIGIONS AND THEOLOGY

100 DEU ISSN 1864-8703
THOMASIANI. Text in German. 2007. irreg., latest vol.5, 2010. price varies. **Document type:** *Monographic series, Academic/Scholarly.*
Published by: Georg Olms Verlag, Hagentorwall 7, Hildesheim, 31134, Germany. TEL 49-5121-15010, FAX 49-5121-150150, info@olms.de, http://www.olms.de.

THOMIST; a speculative quarterly review. *see* RELIGIONS AND THEOLOGY—Roman Catholic

100 BRA ISSN 1413-893X
THOT. Text in Portuguese. 1975. q. **Document type:** *Newspaper.*
Indexed: RILM.
Published by: Palas Athena, Rua Leoncio de Carvalho, 99, Paraiso, Sao Paulo, 04003-010, Brazil. TEL 55-11-32666188, FAX 55-11-32878941, editor@palasathena.org.br, http://www.palasathena.org.br/.

100 USA
THOUGHTLINE. Text in English. 1954. m. free (effective 2011). **Document type:** *Journal, Academic/Scholarly.*
Related titles: E-mail ed.; Online - full text ed.
Published by: Arcana Workshops, 3916 Sepulveda Blvd Ste 107, Culver City, CA 90230. webdisciple@meditationtraining.org. Circ: 3,000.

212.5 SWE ISSN 0284-4427
TIDLOES VISDOM. Text in Swedish. 1961. q. SEK 100 (effective 2001). bk.rev. 36 p./no. 2 cols./p.; back issues avail. **Document type:** *Newsletter.*
Formerly (until 1987): Teosofi i Norden (0040-3628)
Published by: Theosophical Society in Sweden, Swedish Section, Karlaplan 5 B, Stockholm, 11460, Sweden. TEL 46-8-661-6883, FAX 46-8-661-6883. Ed. Ing-Britt Wiklund. Circ: 300.

TIDSKRIFT FOER POLITISK FILOSOFI. *see* POLITICAL SCIENCE

100 BEL ISSN 1370-575X
TIJDSCHRIFT VOOR FILOSOFIE. Text in Dutch, English, French, German. 1939. q. EUR 75 combined subscription (print & online eds.) (effective 2011). bk.rev. bibl. index, cum.index every 25 yrs. Supplement avail.; reprints avail. **Document type:** *Journal, Academic/Scholarly.* **Description:** Discusses a variety of topics in philosophy.
Formerly (until 1962): Tijdschrift voor Philosophie (0040-750X)
Related titles: Online - full text ed.: ISSN 2031-8952.
Indexed: A20, A22, ASCA, ArtHuCI, BibInd, BibLing, CurCont, DIP, FR, IBR, IBZ, IPB, MLA-IB, PCI, PhilInd, RASB, SCOPUS, W07.
—IE, Infotrieve, INIST. **CCC.**
Published by: Peeters Publishers, Bondgenotenlaan 153, Leuven, 3000, Belgium. TEL 32-16-235170, FAX 32-16-228500, peeters@peeters-leuven.be, http://www.peeters-leuven.be.

TIJDSCHRIFT VOOR GEZONDHEIDSZORG EN ETHIEK. *see* MEDICAL SCIENCES

TIJDSCHRIFT VOOR HUMANISTIEK. *see* LITERARY AND POLITICAL REVIEWS

▼ **TILLICH-FORSCHUNGEN/RECHERCHES SUR TILLICH/TILLICH RESEARCH.** *see* RELIGIONS AND THEOLOGY

TILLICH PREVIEW. *see* RELIGIONS AND THEOLOGY

TILLICH-STUDIEN. *see* RELIGIONS AND THEOLOGY

100 ARG ISSN 1666-485X
TOPICOS; revista de filosofia de Santa Fe. Text in Spanish. 1993. a. **Document type:** *Monographic series, Academic/Scholarly.*
Related titles: Online - full text ed.: ISSN 1668-723X.
Indexed: PhilInd, SCOPUS.
Published by: Asociacion Revista de Filosofia de Santa Fe, Echangue 7151, Santa Fe, 13000, Argentina. TEL 54-342-4603030, revistatopicos@hotmail.com. Ed. Julio De Zan. Circ: 500.

100 MEX ISSN 0188-6649
B5
➤ **TOPICOS.** Text and summaries in English, Spanish. 1991. s-a. MXN 120; USD 15 in North America; USD 20 elsewhere (effective 2002). adv. bk.rev. back issues avail. **Document type:** *Academic/Scholarly.* **Description:** Covers philosophy, metaphysics, logic, ethics, history of philosophy and anthropology.
Indexed: A01, CA, F03, F04, IPB, PhilInd, T02.
Published by: Universidad Panamericana, Departamento de Filosofia, A. Rodin 498, Plaza de Mixcoac, Mexico City, DF 03920, Mexico. http://www.upmx.mx. Ed., Adv. contact Hector Zagal Arreguin.

105 USA ISSN 1051-0362
➤ **TOPICS IN PHILOSOPHY.** Text in English. 1975. irreg., latest vol.2, 2008. price varies. back issues avail. **Document type:** *Monographic series, Academic/Scholarly.*
—CCC.
Published by: University of California Press, Book Series, 2120 Berkeley Way, Berkeley, CA 94704. TEL 510-642-4247, FAX 510-643-7127, foundation@ucpress.edu. **Subscr. to:** California - Princeton Fulfillment Services, Inc., 1445 Lower Ferry Rd, Ewing, NJ 08618. TEL 609-883-1759, 800-777-4726, FAX 800-999-1958, orders@cpfsinc.com.

150 NLD ISSN 0167-7411
B1
➤ **TOPOI**; an international review of philosophy. Text in English. 1982. s-a. EUR 550, USD 585 combined subscription to institutions (print & online eds.) (effective 2012). adv. bk.rev. index. back issues avail.; reprint service avail. from PSC. **Document type:** *Journal, Academic/Scholarly.* **Description:** Publishes articles, reviews and discussions of philosophy and the history of philosophy.
Related titles: Microform ed.: (from PQC); Online - full text ed.: ISSN 1572-8749 (from IngentaConnect).
Indexed: A20, A22, A26, ASCA, AmHI, ArtHuCI, BRD, BibLing, CA, CCMJ, CurCont, E-psyche, E01, FR, H07, H08, HAb, HumInd, IPB, MSN, MathR, PhilInd, RefZh, SCOPUS, T02, W03, W05, W07, Z02.
—BLDSC (8867.499800), IE, Infotrieve, Ingenta, INIST. **CCC.**
Published by: Springer Netherlands (Subsidiary of: Springer Science+Business Media), Van Godewijckstraat 30, Dordrecht, 3311 GX, Netherlands. TEL 31-78-6576050, FAX 31-78-6576474, http://www.springer.com. Ed. Ermanno Bencivenga.

100 370.1 ITA ISSN 2036-5683
▼ **TOPOLOGIK. RIVISTA INTERNAZIONALE DI SCIENZE FILOSOFICHE, PEDAGOGICHE E SOCIALI.** Text in Multiple languages. 2009. s-a. **Document type:** *Journal, Academic/Scholarly.*
Related titles: Online - full text ed.: ISSN 2036-5462. 2006.
Published by: Editrice Luigi Pellegrini, Via de Rada 67c, Cosenza, CS 87100, Italy. TEL 39-0984-795065, FAX 39-0984-792672, http://www.pellegrinieditore.it.

100 808.81 DEU
TOPOS POIETIKOS. Text in German. 2000. irreg., latest vol.3, 2002. price varies. **Document type:** *Monographic series, Academic/Scholarly.*
Published by: Felix Meiner Verlag GmbH, Richardstr 47, Hamburg, 22081, Germany. TEL 49-40-2987560, FAX 49-40-29875620, info@meiner.de. R&P, Adv. contact Johannes Kambylis.

100 POL ISSN 1427-7026
B6
➤ **TORUNSKI PRZEGLAD FILOZOFICZNY.** Text in Polish. 1960. irreg., latest vol.6, 2003. price varies. **Document type:** *Monographic series, Academic/Scholarly.*
Former titles (until 1997): Acta Universitatis Nicolai Copernici. Nauki Humanistyczno-Spoleczne. Filozofia (0208-564X); (until 1979): Uniwersytet Mikolaja Kopernika w Torun. Nauki Humanistyczno-Spoleczne. Zeszyty Naukowe. Filozofia (0083-4475)
Indexed: RASB.
Published by: (Uniwersytet Mikolaja Kopernika/Nicolaus Copernicus University), Wydawnictwo Naukowe Uniwersytetu Mikolaja Kopernika/Nicolaus Copernicus University Press, ul Gagarina 39, Torun, 87100, Poland. TEL 48-56-6114295, FAX 48-56-6114705, dwyd@uni.torun.pl, http://www.wydawnictwo.umk.pl. Ed. Jozef Pawlak.

182 DEU
▼ **TRADITIO PRAESOCRATICA**; Zeugnisse fruehgriechischer Philosophie und ihres Fortlebens. Text in German. 2009. irreg. price varies. **Document type:** *Monographic series, Academic/Scholarly.*
Published by: Walter de Gruyter GmbH & Co. KG, Genthiner Str 13, Berlin, 10785, Germany. TEL 49-30-260050, FAX 49-30-26005251, info@degruyter.com, http://www.degruyter.de.

100 USA ISSN 1057-1027
B945.P584
TRADITION & DISCOVERY. Text in English. 1985. 3/yr. **Document type:** *Journal, Academic/Scholarly.* **Description:** Aims to promote exchange among persons interested in the thought of Michael Polanyi.
Related titles: Online - full text ed.: ISSN 2154-1566. free (effective 2011).
Indexed: A21, A39, AmHI, C27, C29, CA, D03, D04, E13, H07, PhilInd, R14, RI-1, S14, S15, S18, T02.
Published by: The Polanyi Society, c/o Phil Mullins, Missouri Western State University, St Joseph, MO 64507. TEL 816-244-261, FAX 816-271-598. Ed. Phil Mullins.

100 BRA ISSN 0101-3173
B5 CODEN: TFACDH
➤ **TRANS - FORM - ACAO**; revista de filosofia. Text in Portuguese; Summaries in English, Portuguese. 1974-1975; resumed 1980. s-a. BRL 30 domestic; USD 20 foreign (effective 2007). bk.rev. bibl.; abstr. back issues avail. **Document type:** *Journal, Academic/Scholarly.* **Description:** Interdisciplinary approach to the study of philosophy.
Related titles: Online - full text ed.: free (effective 2011).
Indexed: A20, ArtHuCI, C01, CA, DIP, FR, H21, IBR, IBZ, IPB, P08, P42, PSA, PhilInd, S02, S03, SCOPUS, SociolAb, T02, W07.
—INIST.
Published by: Universidade Estadual Paulista, Fundacao Editora U N E S P, Praca da Se 108, Sao Paulo, SP 01001-900, Brazil. TEL 55-11-32427171, cgb@marilia.unesp.br, http://www.unesp.br. Ed. Ricardo Monteagudo. Circ: 1,000.

➤ **TRANSILVANIA.** *see* RELIGIONS AND THEOLOGY

100 DEU ISSN 1619-585X
TREFFPUNKT PHILOSOPHIE. Text in German. 2003. irreg., latest vol.9, 2009. price varies. **Document type:** *Monographic series, Academic/Scholarly.*
Published by: Peter Lang GmbH (Subsidiary of: Peter Lang Publishing Group), Eschborner Landstr 42-50, Frankfurt Am Main, 60489, Germany. TEL 49-69-7807050, FAX 49-69-78070550, zentrale.frankfurt@peterlang.com, http://www.peterlang.com.

160 NLD ISSN 1572-6126
TRENDS IN LOGIC - STUDIA LOGICA LIBRARY. Text in English. 1997. irreg., latest vol.28, 2009. price varies. **Document type:** *Monographic series, Academic/Scholarly.* **Description:** Covers contemporary formal logic an its applications and relations to the other disciplines, including philosophy of science and philosophy of language.
Indexed: CCMJ.
—BLDSC (9049.660200), IE. **CCC.**
Published by: Springer Netherlands (Subsidiary of: Springer Science+Business Media), Van Godewijckstraat 30, Dordrecht, 3311 GX, Netherlands. TEL 31-78-6576050, FAX 31-78-6576474. Ed. Ryszard Wojcicki.

280.4 USA ISSN 1044-6532
THE TRINITY REVIEW. Text in English. 1979. m. free (effective 2010). bk.rev. index: 1978-1988. 4 p./no.; back issues avail.; reprints avail. **Document type:** *Newsletter, Academic/Scholarly.* **Description:** Contains essays in philosophy and theology.
Related titles: Online - full text ed.
Published by: The Trinity Foundation, PO Box 68, Unicoi, TN 37692. TEL 423-743-0199, FAX 423-743-2005.

100 ITA ISSN 2036-542X
TROPOS; rivista di ermeneutica e critica filosofica. Text in Multiple languages. 2008. s-a. **Document type:** *Journal, Academic/Scholarly.*
Published by: Aracne Editrice, Via Raffaele Garofalo 133 A/B, Rome, 00173, Italy. info@aracneeditrice.it, http://store.aracneeditrice.com.

THE TRUMPETER; journal of ecosophy. *see* ENVIRONMENTAL STUDIES

100 USA
TRUTH IN ACTION. Text in English. q. **Document type:** *Newsletter.*
Published by: Seicho-No-Ie Truth of Life Movement, 14527 S Vermont Ave, Gardena, CA 90247. TEL 310-323-8486. Ed. Masayo Tsuruta.

100 USA
TRUTH OF LIFE. Text in English. 12/yr. USD 11. illus.
Published by: Seicho-No-Ie Truth of Life Movement, 14527 S Vermont Ave, Gardena, CA 90247. TEL 310-516-8133. Ed. Masayo Tsuruta.

100 USA ISSN 0041-3712
BL2700
TRUTH SEEKER. Text in English. 1873. s-a. USD 20 domestic; USD 35 foreign (effective 2010). bk.rev. 56 p./no.; **Document type:** *Journal, Academic/Scholarly.* **Description:** Deals with intellectual liberation and civil liberties, focusing on religious and political issues.
Related titles: Online - full text ed.
Indexed: RASB.
Published by: Truth Seeker Co., Inc., 239 S Juniper St, Escondido, CA 92025. http://www.truthseeker.com/. Ed. Bonnie Lange.

128 DEU ISSN 1862-3174
TUEBINGER PHAENOMENOLOGISCHE BIBLIOTHEK. Text in German. 1992. irreg., latest 2008. price varies. **Document type:** *Monographic series, Academic/Scholarly.*
Published by: Attempto Verlag, Dischingerweg 5, Tuebingen, 72070, Germany. TEL 49-7071-97970, FAX 49-7071-979711, info@attempto-verlag.de, http://www.narr.de.

TUEBINGER STUDIEN ZUR THEOLOGIE UND PHILOSOPHIE. *see* RELIGIONS AND THEOLOGY

100 DEU ISSN 0172-858X
TUMULT; Schriften zur Verkehrswissenschaft. Text in German. 1979. s-a. EUR 14.80 newsstand/cover (effective 2006). adv. **Document type:** *Journal, Academic/Scholarly.*
Indexed: IBR, IBZ.
Published by: Philo und Philo Fine Arts GmbH, c/o Europaeische Verlagsanstalt, Bei den Muehren 70, Hamburg, 20457, Germany. TEL 49-40-4501940, FAX 49-40-4501950, info@europaeische-verlagsanstalt.de, http://www.philo-verlag.de.

UDMURTSKII UNIVERSITET. VESTNIK. SERIYA 3: FILOSOHIYA, PSIKHOLOGIYA, PEDAGOGIKA. *see* PSYCHOLOGY

190 DNK ISSN 1604-5203
UDVALGENE VEDROERENDE VIDENSKABELIGE UREDELIGHED. AARSBERETNING. Text in Danish. 1994. a. **Document type:** *Government.*
Formerly (until 2001): Udvalgene Vedroeende Videnskabelige Uredelighed. Beretning (0909-5373)
Related titles: Online - full text ed.: ISSN 1901-1121. 200?; ◆ English ed.: Danish Committee on Scientific Dishonesty. Annual Report. ISSN 1395-0983.
Published by: Forsknings- og Innovationsstyrelsen, Udvalgene Vedroerende Videnskabelige Uredelighed/Danish Agency for Science, Technology and Innovation, Danish Committee on Scientific Dishonesty, c/o Frej Sorento Dichmann, Bredgade 40, Copenhagen K, 1260, Denmark. TEL 45-35-446200, 45-35-446279, FAX 45-35-446201, fi@fi.dk, fdi@fi.dk, http://www.uvvu.dk.

100 200 CAN ISSN 0709-549X
BD331
➤ **ULTIMATE REALITY AND MEANING**; interdisciplinary studies in the philosophy of understanding. Text in English. 1978. q. USD 57.75 in North America to institutions; USD 62.75 elsewhere to institutions (effective 2011). bibl. 128 p./no.; back issues avail. **Document type:** *Journal, Academic/Scholarly.* **Description:** Publishes studies dealing with facts, things, ideas, axioms, persons, and values which people throughout history have considered ultimate, or as horizons, or as supreme value.
Supersedes (in 1976): Institute for Encyclopedia of Human Ideas on Ultimate Reality and Meaning. Newsletter (0315-3002)
Indexed: A20, A21, A22, ABS&EES, ASCA, ArtHuCI, C03, CBCARef, CurCont, DIP, FR, GSS&RPL, IBR, IBZ, IPB, MLA-IB, P48, PCI, PQC, PerIslam, PhilInd, R&TA, RI-1, RI-2, SCOPUS, SOPODA, SociolAb, W07.
—BLDSC (9082.780500), IE, Infotrieve, Ingenta, INIST. **CCC.**
Published by: (International Society for the Study of Human Ideas on Ultimate Reality and Meaning), University of Toronto Press, Journals Division, 5201 Dufferin St, Toronto, ON M3H 5T8, Canada. TEL 416-667-7810, FAX 416-667-7881, journals@utpress.utoronto.ca, http://www.utpress.utoronto.ca. Ed. Mark T DeStephano. Adv. contact Audrey Greenwood TEL 416-667-7777 ext 7766. Circ: 215.

100 SWE ISSN 1650-1748
UMEAA STUDIES IN PHILOSOPHY. Text mainly in English; Text occasionally in Swedish. 2000. irreg., latest vol.8, 2005. **Document type:** *Monographic series, Academic/Scholarly.*
Published by: Umeaa Universitet, Institutionen foer Filosofi och Lingvistik/University of Umeaa. Department of Philosophy and Linguistics, Umeaa Universitet, Umeaa, 90187, Sweden. TEL 46-90-7869546, FAX 46-90-7866377, http://www.ling.umu.se/filing.

UNIVERSAL PROUTIST. *see* NEW AGE PUBLICATIONS

109 ESP ISSN 0211-2337
B5
➤ **UNIVERSIDAD COMPLUTENSE. ANALES DEL SEMINARIO DE HISTORIA DE LA FILOSOFIA.** Text in Spanish. 1980. a., latest vol.27, 2010. EUR 21 domestic; EUR 26 in Europe; EUR 30 elsewhere (effective 2011). back issues avail. **Document type:** *Journal, Academic/Scholarly.* **Description:** Presents scientific articles on historiography and philosophy since the 16th century.
Related titles: CD-ROM ed.: EUR 44 to individuals; EUR 58 to institutions (effective 2003); Online - full text ed.: ISSN 1988-2564. free.
Indexed: A20, ArtHuCI, FR, H14, H21, I14, IPB, P02, P08, P09, P10, P28, P48, P53, P54, PCI, PQC, PhilInd, W07.
—INIST.
Published by: (Universidad Complutense de Madrid, Facultad de Filosofia), Universidad Complutense de Madrid, Servicio de Publicaciones, C/ Obispo Trejo 2, Ciudad Universitaria, Madrid, 28040, Spain. TEL 34-91-3941127, FAX 34-91-3941126, servicio.publicaciones@rect.ucm.es, http://www.ucm.es/publicaciones. Ed. Rafael Ramon Guerrero.

100 ARG
UNIVERSIDAD DE BUENOS AIRES. FACULTAD DE FILOSOFIA Y LETRAS. BOLETIN INFORMATIVO. Text in Spanish. 1998. q. back issues avail.
Media: Online - full text.
Published by: Universidad de Buenos Aires, Facultad de Filosofia y Letras, Puan 470, Buenos Aires, 1406, Argentina. TEL 54-11-44320606, info@filo.uba.ar, http://www.filo.uba.ar.

100 COL ISSN 0120-1492
AS82.M36
UNIVERSIDAD DE CALDAS. FACULTAD DE FILOSOFIA. REVISTA. Text in Spanish; Summaries in English. 1980. q. COP 5,000, USD 6. bk.rev. **Document type:** *Academic/Scholarly.*
Indexed: C01, GeoRef, SpeleolAb.
Published by: Universidad de Caldas, Facultad de Filosofia, Apdo Aereo 275, Manizales, CAL, Colombia. TEL 57-968-857022, FAX 57-968-862520. Ed. Roberto Velez Correa. Circ: 1,000.

100 340 ESP ISSN 0008-7750
B5
UNIVERSIDAD DE GRANADA. CATEDRA FRANCISCO SUAREZ. ANALES. Text in Spanish. 1961. a. EUR 32 per issue (effective 2009). back issues avail. **Document type:** *Monographic series, Academic/Scholarly.*
Indexed: FR, IPB, P09, PCI, PhilInd.
Published by: (Universidad de Granada, Departamento de Filosofia del Derecho), Universidad de Granada, Editorial, Antiguo Colegio Maximo, Campus de Cartuja, Granada, 18071, Spain. TEL 34-958-246220, FAX 34-958-243931, comunicacion@editorialugr.com, http://www.editorialugr.com. Ed. Nicolas M Lopez Calera. Circ: 1,000.

100 URY ISSN 0258-1841
UNIVERSIDAD DE LA REPUBLICA. FACULTAD DE HUMANIDADES Y CIENCIAS. REVISTA. SERIE FILOSOFIA. Text in Spanish. 1979. irreg. per issue exchange basis.
Supersedes in part (in 1979): Universidad de la Republica. Facultad de Humanidades y Ciencias. Revista
Published by: Universidad de la Republica, Facultad de Humanidades y Ciencias de la Educacion, Magallanes 1577, Montevideo, 11200, Uruguay. Ed. Beatriz Martinez Osorio.

100 ESP
UNIVERSIDAD DE SEVILLA. SERIE: FILOSOFIA Y PSICOLOGIA. Text in Spanish. 1990. irreg., latest vol.10, 2001. price varies. back issues avail. **Document type:** *Monographic series, Academic/Scholarly.*
Published by: Universidad de Sevilla, Secretariado de Publicaciones, Calle Porvenir 27, Sevilla, 41013, Spain. TEL 34-95-4487444, FAX 34-95-4487443, secpub10@us.es, http://www.us.es/publius/inicio.html.

100 CHL ISSN 0718-4255
UNIVERSIDAD METROPOLITANA DE CIENCIAS DE LA EDUCACION. DEPARTAMENTO DE FILOSOFIA. ARCHIVOS. Text in Spanish. 2006. a. **Document type:** *Monographic series, Academic/Scholarly.*
Published by: Universidad Metropolitana de Ciencias de la Educacion, Facultad de Filosofia y Educacion, Ave Jose Pedro Alessandri, 774, Santiago, Chile. filosofi@umce.cl, http://www.umce.cl/.

UNIVERSIDAD PONTIFICIA COMILLAS DE MADRID. PUBLICACIONES. SERIE 1: ESTUDIOS. *see* RELIGIONS AND THEOLOGY—Roman Catholic

UNIVERSITA DEGLI STUDI DI PADOVA. FACOLTA DI LETTERE E FILOSOFIA. OPUSCOLI ACCADEMICI. *see* LITERATURE

UNIVERSITA DEGLI STUDI DI PADOVA. FACOLTA DI LETTERE E FILOSOFIA. PUBBLICAZIONI. *see* LITERATURE

UNIVERSITA DEGLI STUDI DI SIENA. FACOLTA DI LETTERE E FILOSOFIA. ANNALI. *see* LITERATURE

100 ITA ISSN 0394-5073
B4
UNIVERSITA DEGLI SUDI DI FIRENZE. DIPARTIMENTO DI FILOSOFIA. ANNALI. Variant title: Annali del Dipartimento di Filosofia. Text in Italian. 1979. a. back issues avail. **Document type:** *Journal, Academic/Scholarly.*
Formerly (until 1984): Universita degli Studi di Firenze. Istituto di Filosofia. Annali

P

Related titles: Online - full text ed.: ISSN 1824-3770. free (effective 2011).
Indexed: AmHI, CA, H07, IBR, IBZ, IPB, P45, P46, T02.
Published by: (Universita degli Studi di Firenze, Dipartimento di Filosofia), Firenze University Press, Borgo Albizi 28, Florence, 50122, Italy. TEL 39-055-2743051, FAX 39-055-2743058, info@fupress.com, www.fupress.com/index.asp. Ed. Andrea Cantini.

100 COL ISSN 0120-5323
B5
UNIVERSITAS PHILOSOPHICA. Text in Spanish. 1983. s-a. COP 19 domestic; USD 40 in Latin America; USD 60 elsewhere (effective 2005).
Indexed: A01, C01, CA, F03, F04, FR, I04, I05, PhilInd, T02.
—INIST.
Published by: Pontificia Universidad Javeriana, Facultad de Filosofia, Carrera 7a, No. 40-62, 4o Piso, Edificio Emilio Arango, SJ, Bogota, Colombia. TEL 57-1-3208320, FAX 57-1-3384532.

100 ROM ISSN 1221-8413
B28.R6
UNIVERSITATEA "AL. I. CUZA" DIN IASI. ANALELE STIINTIFICE. FILOSOFIE. Text in English, French, Romanian, German. 1955. a. free (effective 2011). **Document type:** *Journal, Academic/Scholarly.* **Description:** Covers all areas of philosophy.
Former titles (until 1982): Universitatea "Al. I. Cuza" din Iasi. Analele Stiintifice. Sectiunea 3b: Filozofie (0379-7856); (until 1969): Universitatea "Al. I. Cuza" din Iasi. Analele Stiintifice. Sectiunea 3b: Stiinte Filozofice (0075-353X)
Related titles: Online - full text ed.: ISSN 2067-5437.
Indexed: FR.
Published by: Universitatea "Alexandru Ioan Cuza" din Iasi/"Alexandru Ioan Cuza" University of Iasi, Carol I Boulevard, Iasi, 6600, Romania. Ed. Petru Ioan. Circ: 550. **Subscr. to:** ILEXIM, Str. 13 Decembrie 3, PO Box 136-137, Bucharest 70116, Romania.

100 ROM ISSN 1841-8325
➤ **UNIVERSITATEA DIN CRAIOVA. ANALELE. SERIA: FILOSOFIE.** Text in Romanian. 1997. s-a. USD 10. illus. **Document type:** *Journal, Academic/Scholarly.*
Supersedes in part (in 2005): Universitatea din Craiova. Analele. Seria: Filozofie, Sociologie, Psihologie, Pedagogie (1582-1633); Which was formed by the merger of (1995-1997): Universitatea din Craiova. Analele. Seria: Filozofie, Sociologie (1224-3590); (1996-1997): Universitatea din Craiova. Analele. Seria: Psihologie, Pedagogie (1224-5690)
Indexed: BibLing, PhilInd, RASB.
Published by: Universitatea din Craiova/University of Craiova, Str A.I. Cuza 13, Craiova, 200585, Romania. TEL 40-251-414398, FAX 40-251-411688, relint@central.ucv.ro, http://www.ucv.ro. Ed. Niculae Matasaru.

100 BEL ISSN 0076-1273
UNIVERSITE CATHOLIQUE DE LOUVAIN. INSTITUT SUPERIEUR DE PHILOSOPHIE. COURS PUBLIES. Text in French. 1952. irreg. price varies. **Document type:** *Academic/Scholarly.*
Formerly (until 1964): Universite Catholique de Louvain. Institut Superieur de Philosophie. Cours de Philosophie (0773-1345)
Published by: Universite Catholique de Louvain, Institut Superieur de Philosophie, Pl du Cardinal Marcier 1, Louvain-la-Neuve, 1348, Belgium. TEL 32-10-474613, FAX 32-10-474819.

100 FRA ISSN 0778-4600
B2
L 'UNIVERSITE DE BRUXELLES. L'INSTITUT DE PHILOSOPHIE. ANNALES. Text in French. 1969. a., latest 2009. price varies. bk.rev. bibl. **Document type:** *Monographic series.*
Former titles (until 1990): L' Institut de Philosophie et de Sciences Morales. Annales (0771-4963); (until 1979): L' Institut de Philosophie. Annales (0778-4570)
Indexed: IPB.
Published by: (Universite Libre de Bruxelles BEL, Institut de Philosophie BEL), Librairie Philosophique J. Vrin, 6 place de la Sorbonne, Paris, F-75005, France. TEL 33-1-43540347, FAX 33-1-43544818, contact@vrin.fr, http://www.vrin.fr. Ed. Gilbert Hottois. Circ: 1,000.

100 FRA ISSN 1282-6545
UNIVERSITE DE CAEN. CAHIERS DE PHILOSOPHIE. Key Title: Cahiers de Philosophie de l'Universite de Caen. Text in French. 1982. irreg., latest no.45, 2008. **Document type:** *Academic/Scholarly.*
Former titles (until 1996): Cahiers de Philosophie Politique et Juridique (1144-4924); (until 1984): Cahiers de Philosophie Politique et Juridique de l'Universite de Caen (0759-1810)
Indexed: FR, IBSS, IPB.
—INIST.
Published by: Universite de Caen, Centre de Philosophie Politique et Juridique, Esplanade de la Paix, BP 5186, Caen, 14032, France. TEL 33-231-565500, FAX 33-231-565600. Ed. S Goyard Fabre.

084 FRA ISSN 0751-2902
UNIVERSITE DE FRANCHE-COMTE. CENTRE DE DOCUMENTATION ET DE BIBLIOGRAPHIE PHILOSOPHIQUES. TRAVAUX. Text in French. 1981. irreg. price varies. illus. **Document type:** *Monographic series, Academic/Scholarly.*
Published by: (Universite de Franche-Comte, U F R des Sciences du Langage, de l'Homme et de la Societe, Centre de Documentation et de Bibliographie Philosophiques), Editions Les Belles Lettres, 95 Blvd Raspail, Paris, 75006, France. TEL 33-1-44398421, FAX 33-1-45449288, courrier@lesbelleslettres.com, http://www.lesbelleslettres.com.

100 NOR ISSN 1892-3887
UNIVERSITETET I BERGEN. INSTITUTT FOR FILOSOFI OG FOERSTESEMESTERSTUDIER. SKRIFTSERIE. Variant title: Filosofiske Smuler. Text in Norwegian. 1989. irreg. back issues avail. **Document type:** *Monographic series, Academic/Scholarly.*
Formerly (until 2010): Universitetet i Bergen. Filosofisk Institutt. Skriftserie (0802-4065)
Published by: Universitetet i Bergen, Institutt for Filosofi og Foerstesemesterstudier, PO Box 7805, Bergen, 5020, Norway. TEL 47-55-582382, FAX 47-55-589651, http://www.uib.no.fof.

UNIVERSITY OF LONDON. INSTITUTE OF GERMANIC STUDIES. PUBLICATIONS. *see* LITERATURE

UNIVERZITA KOMENSKEHO. FILOZOFICKA FAKULTA. ZBORNIK: GRAECOLATINA ET ORIENTALIA. *see* CLASSICAL STUDIES

160 SVK
UNIVERZITA KOMENSKEHO. FILOZOFICKA FAKULTA. ZBORNIK: LOGICA ET METHODOLOGICA. Text in English, Slovak. 1989. irreg. free (effective 2005). **Document type:** *Monographic series, Academic/Scholarly.*
Published by: Univerzita Komenskeho, Filozoficka Fakulta, Ustredna Kniznica, Gondova 2, Bratislava, 81801, Slovakia. TEL 421-7-52923608, FAX 421-7-52966016.

100 SVK ISSN 0083-4181
B26
UNIVERZITA KOMENSKEHO. FILOZOFICKA FAKULTA. ZBORNIK: PHILOSOPHICA. Text in Czech, Slovak; Summaries in German, English; Some issues in Multiple languages. 1960. irreg. free domestic (effective 2005). **Document type:** *Academic/Scholarly.*
Incorporates: Univerzita Komenskeho. Ustav Marxismu-Leninizmu. Zbornik: Marxistiska Filozofia
Indexed: RASB.
Published by: Univerzita Komenskeho, Filozoficka Fakulta, Ustredna Kniznica, Gondova 2, Bratislava, 81801, Slovakia. Circ: 700.

100 SRB ISSN 0522-8468
P19
UNIVERZITET U BEOGRADU. FILOZOFSKI FAKULTET. ANALI. Key Title: Anali Filoloskog Fakulteta. Text in Serbian. 1961. a. **Document type:** *Journal, Academic/Scholarly.*
Indexed: MLA-IB.
Published by: Univerzitet u Beogradu, Filozofski Fakultet/University of Belgrade, Faculty of Philosophy, ul Chika Lyubina br 18-20, Belgrade, 11000. TEL 381-11-3281550, FAX 381-11-639356, info@f.bg.ac.yu, http://www.f.bg.ac.yu.

100 SRB ISSN 0374-0730
AS346
UNIVERZITET U NOVOM SADU. FILOZOFSKI FAKULTET. GODISNJAK. Text in Serbian. a. **Document type:** *Yearbook, Academic/Scholarly.*
Indexed: A01.
Published by: Univerzitet u Novom Sadu, Filozofski Fakultet, Dr Zorana Dindica 2, Novi Sad, 21000. TEL 381-21-450690, FAX 381-21-450929.

100 POL ISSN 0083-4246
UNIWERSYTET IM. ADAMA MICKIEWICZA. FILOZOFIA I LOGIKA. Text in Polish. 1961. irreg., latest vol.107, 2010. price varies. bk.rev. **Document type:** *Monographic series, Academic/Scholarly.* **Description:** Contains current research results of the university's scholars, their Ph.D. theses and monographs. Each volume contains the work of one author.
Indexed: FR, RASB.
—INIST.
Published by: Wydawnictwo Naukowe Uniwersytetu im. Adama Mickiewicza/Adam Mickiewicz University Press, ul Fredry 10, Poznan, 61701, Poland. TEL 48-61-8294646, FAX 48-61-8294647, press@amu.edu.pl, http://press.amu.edu.pl. Circ: 600.

100 POL ISSN 1231-0913
B6
➤ **UNIWERSYTET SLASKI W KATOWICACH. PRACE NAUKOWE. FOLIA PHILOSOPHICA.** Text in Polish; Summaries in English, Russian. 1975. irreg., latest vol.28, 2010. price varies. **Document type:** *Monographic series, Academic/Scholarly.* **Description:** Studies on philosophy.
Former titles (until 1993): Uniwersytet Slaski w Katowicach. Prace Naukowe. Prace z Nauk Spolecznych. Folia Philosophica (0867-664X); (until 1984): Uniwersytet Slaski w Katowicach. Prace Naukowe. Prace z Nauk Spolecznych (0208-5437)
Indexed: RASB.
Published by: (Uniwersytet Slaski w Katowicach), Wydawnictwo Uniwersytetu Slaskiego w Katowicach, ul Bankowa 12B, Katowice, 40007, Poland. TEL 48-32-2596915, FAX 48-32-2582735, wydawus@us.edu.pl, https://wydawnictwo.us.edu.pl. Ed. Piotr Laciak.

172 NLD ISSN 2211-1395
UPACT NIEUWS. Text in Dutch. 1982. s-a. **Document type:** *Newsletter, Consumer.*
Former titles (until 2010): E V V Nieuws (2211-1387); (until 2007): Stichting Euro's voor Vrede. Nieuwskrant (1566-9130); (until 1999): Beweging Weigering Defensiebelasting. Nieuwskrant (1384-4245); (until 1996): Beweging Weigering Defensiebelasting. Nieuwsbrief (1381-7299)
Published by: Upact, Postbus 19, Utrecht, 3500 AA, Netherlands. TEL 31-30-2238724, info@upact.nl. Eds. Jalmar Pfeifer, Jephta Peijs. Circ: 1,000 (controlled).

110 USA
UPPER TRIAD. Text in English. 1974. bi-m. free. bk.rev.
Published by: Upper Triad Association, Inc., 825, Madison, NC 27025-0825. TEL 703-443-8289, FAX 703-443-8294. Ed. Peter Hamilton. Circ: 2,000 (controlled).

100 SWE ISSN 0346-6507
UPPSALA STUDIES IN SOCIAL ETHICS. Text in Multiple languages. 1973. irreg., latest vol.27, 2001. price varies. back issues avail. **Document type:** *Monographic series, Academic/Scholarly.*
Related titles: ◆ Series of: Acta Universitatis Upsaliensis. ISSN 0346-5462.
Published by: Uppsala Universitet, Acta Universitatis Upsaliensis/University Publications from Uppsala, PO Box 256, Uppsala, 75105, Sweden. TEL 46-18-4716804, FAX 46-18-4716804, acta@ub.uu.se, http://www.ub.uu.se/upu/auu/index.html. Ed. Bengt Landgren. **Dist. by:** Almqvist & Wiksell International, PO Box 614, Soedertaelje 15127, Sweden.

100 GBR ISSN 0953-8208
B843.A1
➤ **UTILITAS.** Text in English. 1988. q. GBP 198, USD 360 to institutions; GBP 201, USD 362 combined subscription to institutions (print & online eds.) (effective 2012). adv. bk.rev. illus. back issues avail.; reprint service avail. from PSC. **Document type:** *Journal, Academic/Scholarly.* **Description:** Covers all aspects of utilitarian thought and its historical context.
Formed by the merger of (1978-1988): Bentham Newsletter (0141-190X); (1965-1988): Mill News Letter (0026-4253)
Related titles: Online - full text ed.: ISSN 1741-6183. GBP 183, USD 332 to institutions (effective 2012).
Indexed: A01, A03, A08, A12, A20, A22, ABIn, AmHI, ArtHuCI, B07, B16, CA, CurCont, E01, H07, IBR, IBSS, IBZ, IPB, L03, P10, P28, P48, P51, P53, P54, PCI, PQC, PhilInd, T02, W07.
—BLDSC (9135.376700), IE, Infotrieve, Ingenta. **CCC.**
Published by: (Bentham Project, London), Cambridge University Press, The Edinburgh Bldg, Shaftesbury Rd, Cambridge, CB2 8RU, United Kingdom. TEL 44-1223-312393, FAX 44-1223-315052, journals@cambridge.org, http://www.cambridge.org/uk. Ed. Paul Kelly. R&P Linda Nicol TEL 44-1223-325702. Adv. contact Rebecca Roberts TEL 44-1223-325083. page GBP 325, page USD 615. **Subscr. to:** Cambridge University Press, 32 Ave of the Americas, New York, NY 10013. TEL 212-337-5000, FAX 212-691-3239, journals_subscriptions@cup.org.

100 VEN ISSN 1316-5216
H61.15
➤ **UTOPIA Y PRAXIS LATINOAMERICANA**; revista internacional de filosofia iberoamericana y teoria social. Text in Spanish, Portuguese, French; Abstracts in English, Spanish. 1996. q. VEB 200 domestic; USD 120 in Latin America; USD 140 elsewhere (effective 2011). bk.rev. abstr. cum.index: 1996-1998. 150 p./no.; back issues avail.; reprints avail. **Document type:** *Journal, Academic/Scholarly.* **Description:** Looks at social sciences and culture through philosophical analysis and historical interpretation from a Latinoamerican point of view.
Related titles: CD-ROM ed.; Online - full text ed.: free (effective 2011).
Indexed: A01, A26, C01, C32, CA, F03, F04, I04, I05, MLA-IB, P42, PhilInd, S02, S03, T02.
Published by: Universidad del Zulia, Nucleo Luz Punto Fijo, Punto Fijo, Edo Falcon, Venezuela. TEL 58-269-2472158, FAX 58-269-2457587. Ed. Gloria M Comesana-Santalices. Circ: 1,000 (paid).

335.02 USA ISSN 1045-991X
HX806
➤ **UTOPIAN STUDIES.** Text in English. 1987. s-a. USD 147 combined subscription to institutions (print & online eds.) (effective 2012). adv. back issues avail.; reprint service avail. from PSC. **Document type:** *Journal, Academic/Scholarly.* **Description:** Brings out articles on a wide range of subjects related to utopias, utopianism, utopian literature, utopian theory, and intentional communities.
Related titles: Online - full text ed.: ISSN 2154-9648. USD 105 to institutions (effective 2012).
Indexed: A01, A03, A07, A08, A22, A25, A26, A30, A31, AA, AmH&L, AmHI, ArtInd, B04, BRD, CA, E01, E08, G08, H07, H08, HAb, HistAb, HumInd, I05, L05, L06, MLA-IB, P30, P42, R05, S02, S03, S08, S09, T02, W03, W04, W05, W09.
—BLDSC (9135.513020), IE, Infotrieve, Ingenta. **CCC.**
Published by: (Society for Utopian Studies), Pennsylvania State University Press, 820 N University Dr, University Support Bldg 1, Ste C, University Park, PA 16802. TEL 814-865-1327, 800-326-9180, FAX 814-863-1408, info@psupress.org. Eds. Nicole Pohl, Kendra Boileau. Adv. contact Brian Beer TEL 814-863-5992. **Dist. by:** The Johns Hopkins University Press, PO Box 19966, Baltimore, MD 21211. TEL 410-516-6987, 800-548-1784, FAX 410-516-3866, jrnlcirc@press.jhu.edu, https://www.press.jhu.edu/.

335.02 USA
UTOPUS DISCOVERED; a most informal newsletter. Text in English. q. USD 45 individual membership; USD 75 institutional membership (effective 2005); includes subscr. to Utopian Studies journal. **Document type:** *Newsletter.*
Published by: Society for Utopian Studies, c/o Ken Roemer, Dept of English, University of Texas at Arlington, Arlington, TX 76019-0035. TEL 817-272-2729, roemer@uta.edu, http://www.utoronto.ca/utopia.

179 174.95 AUS ISSN 1321-0599
V E BULLETIN. (Voluntary Euthanasia) Text in English. 1984. 3/yr. free to members (effective 2009). bk.rev. back issues avail. **Document type:** *Newsletter, Trade.* **Description:** Promotes a change to the law so that in appropriate circumstances and with defined safeguards a medically assisted or induced death is allowed as an option of last resort in medical practice.
Published by: South Australian Voluntary Euthanasia Society, PO Box 2151, Kent Town, SA 5071, Australia. TEL 61-8-83793421, FAX 61-8-82652287, info@saves.asn.au, http://www.saves.asn.au. Ed. Julia Anaf.

170 ITA ISSN 1724-2037
VALORI. Text in Italian. 2001. m. **Document type:** *Magazine, Consumer.*
Related titles: Online - full text ed.: ISSN 1724-2045.
Published by: Cooperativa Editoriale Etica, Via Copernico 5, Milan, 20125, Italy. http://www.bancaetica.com.

121.8 NLD ISSN 0929-8436
VALUE INQUIRY BOOK SERIES. Abbreviated title: V I B S. Text in English. 1993. irreg., latest vol.199, 2008. price varies. back issues avail. **Document type:** *Monographic series, Academic/Scholarly.* **Description:** Publishes philosophical monographs in all areas of value inquiry, including social and political thought, ethics, applied philosophy, feminism, personalism, religious values, values in education, medical and health values, values in science and technology, humanistic psychology, formal axiology, history of philosophy, post-communist thought, peace theory, law and society, and theory of culture.
Related titles: ◆ Series: African American Philosophy; ◆ Werkmeister Studies; ◆ Cognitive Science; ◆ Contemporary Russian Philosophy; ◆ Daisaku Ikeda Studies; ◆ Gilson Studies; ◆ Hartman Institute Axiology Studies; ◆ Histories and Addresses of Philosophical Societies; ◆ Holocaust and Genocide Studies; ◆ Indigenous Philosophies of the Americas; ◆ Interpretation and Translation; ◆ Lived Values, Valued Lives; ◆ Nordic Value Studies; ◆ Personalist Studies; ◆ Philosophies of the Caribbean; ◆ Philosophy and Psychology; ◆ Philosophy and Religion (Amsterdam); ◆ Philosophy and Women; ◆ Philosophy in Latin America; ◆ Philosophy in Spain; ◆ Philosophy of Education; ◆ Philosophy of Peace; ◆ Philosophy of Sex and Love; ◆ Post-Communist European Thought; ◆ Social Philosophy; ◆ Studies in Applied Ethics; ◆ Studies in Existentialism; ◆ Studies in Jurisprudence; ◆ Studies in Pragmatism and Values; ◆ Studies in the History of Western Philosophy; ◆ Universal Justice; ◆ Values in Bioethics; ◆ Values in Italian Philosophy; ◆ Central-European Value Studies.
Indexed: A01, T02.

Published by: Editions Rodopi B.V., Tijnmuiden 7, Amsterdam, 1046 AK, Netherlands. TEL 31-20-6114821, FAX 31-20-4472979, info@rodopi.nl. **Dist in France by:** Nordeal, 30 rue de Verlinghem, BP 139, Lambersart 59832, France. TEL 33-3-20099060, FAX 33-3-20929495; **Dist in N America by:** Rodopi - USA, 606 Newark Ave, 2nd fl, Kenilworth, NJ 07033. TEL 908-497-9031, 800-225-3998, FAX 908-497-9035.

174.95 NLD

VALUES IN BIOETHICS. Text in English. irreg. price varies. **Document type:** *Monographic series, Academic/Scholarly.* **Description:** Covers medical and nursing ethics, health care ethics, research ethics, environmental ethics, and global bioethics.
Related titles: ◆ Series of: Value Inquiry Book Series. ISSN 0929-8436.
Published by: Editions Rodopi B.V., Tijnmuiden 7, Amsterdam, 1046 AK, Netherlands. TEL 31-20-6114821, FAX 31-20-4472979, info@rodopi.nl. Eds. Matti Hayry, Tuija Takala. **Dist. by:** Rodopi - USA, 606 Newark Ave, 2nd fl, Kenilworth, NJ 07033. TEL 908-497-9031, FAX 908-497-9035.

190 NLD

VALUES IN ITALIAN PHILOSOPHY. Text in English. irreg. price varies. **Document type:** *Monographic series, Academic/Scholarly.*
Related titles: ◆ Series of: Value Inquiry Book Series. ISSN 0929-8436.
Published by: Editions Rodopi B.V., Tijnmuiden 7, Amsterdam, 1046 AK, Netherlands. TEL 31-20-6114821, FAX 31-20-4472979, info@rodopi.nl. Ed. Daniel B Gallagher. **Dist. by:** Rodopi - USA, 606 Newark Ave, 2nd fl, Kenilworth, NJ 07033. TEL 908-497-9031, FAX 908-497-9035.

100 ITA ISSN 1974-7292

VARIAZIONI. Text in Italian. 2005. irreg. **Document type:** *Monographic series, Academic/Scholarly.*
Published by: Rubbettino Editore, Viale Rosario Rubbettino 10, Soveria Mannelli, CZ 88049, Italy. TEL 39-0968-662034, FAX 39-0968-662055, segreteria@rubettino.it, http://www.rubbettino.it.

181.48 GBR ISSN 1355-6436

VEDANTA. Text in English. 1951. bi-m. GBP 9, USD 17.50; GBP 1.50 per issue (effective 2009). bk.rev. **Document type:** *Magazine, Consumer.*
Former titles (until 1995): Vedanta for East and West (0951-127X); (until 1952): Vedanta Bulletin
Related titles: Online - full text ed.: free (effective 2009).
Published by: Ramakrishna Vedanta Centre, Blind Ln, Bourne End, Buckinghamshire SL8 5LF, United Kingdom. TEL 44-1628-526464, FAX 44-1628-532437, vedantauk@talk21.com. Ed. Swami Dayatmananda.

181.48 IND ISSN 0042-2983

➤ **THE VEDANTA KESARI**; the lion of vedanta. Text in English. 1914. m. INR 100, USD 2.26, EUR 1.53 domestic; INR 1,500, USD 33.86, EUR 22.90 foreign (effective 2011). bk.rev. charts; illus.; stat. index, cum.index. 52 p./no. 2 cols./p.; back issues avail. **Document type:** *Journal, Academic/Scholarly.* **Description:** Exposition of Vedanta philosophy.
Formerly (until Apr. 1914): Brahmavadin
Indexed: BAS, PhilInd, RASB.
Published by: Sri Ramakrishna Math, 31, Ramakrishna Math Rd, Mylapore, Chennai, Tamil Nadu 600 004, India. TEL 91-44-24621110, FAX 91-44-24934589, mail@chennaimath.org.

100 340 USA ISSN 0893-4851
K26

➤ **VERA LEX.** Text in English. 2000. a. USD 40 per issue (effective 2010). bk.rev. bibl.; illus. cum.index every 5 yrs. back issues avail. **Document type:** *Journal, Academic/Scholarly.* **Description:** Features to communicate and dialogue on the subject of natural law and natural right.
Indexed: A01, A26, DIP, E08, I01, I05, IBR, IBZ, ILP, PhilInd, T02, W03, W05.
Published by: Pace University Press, 41 Park Row, Rm 1510, New York, NY 10038. TEL 212-346-1405, FAX 212-346-1754, PaceUP@Pace.Edu. Ed. Dr. Richard Connerney.

100 200 ESP ISSN 0042-3718
BX3601

VERDAD Y VIDA; revista de las ciencias del espiritu. Text in Spanish. 1943. q. bk.rev. bibl. index. **Document type:** *Magazine, Consumer.*
Indexed: BAS, CERDIC, DIP, FR, IBR, IBZ, IPB, MLA, MLA-IB, OTA, P09, PCI.
—INIST.
Published by: Franciscanos Espanoles, Joaquin Costa, 36, Madrid, 28002, Spain. TEL 34-91-561-9900, FAX 34-91-561-3990. Ed. P Enrique Chacon Cabello. Circ: 550.

100 ITA ISSN 0391-4186
B4

VERIFICHE; rivista di scienze umane. Text in Italian. 1972. 3/yr. EUR 31 domestic; EUR 36.50 foreign (effective 2009). adv. bk.rev. bibl. back issues avail. **Document type:** *Journal, Academic/Scholarly.* **Description:** Focuses on literary philosophy.
Related titles: Online - full text ed.
Indexed: A20, ASCA, ArtHuCI, CurCont, IBR, IBZ, IPB, W07.
Published by: Associazione Trentina di Scienze Umane, Casella Postale 269, Trento, TN 38100, Italy. TEL 39-0461-1725660. Ed. Mario Rigoni.

100 ITA

VERIFICHE. PUBBLICAZIONI. Text in Italian. 1976. irreg., latest vol.24, 1996. price varies. **Document type:** *Monographic series, Academic/Scholarly.* **Description:** Focuses on philosophy.
Published by: Associazione Trentina di Scienze Umane, Casella Postale 269, Trento, TN 38100, Italy. TEL 39-0461-1725660.

100 ITA

VERIFICHE. QUADERNI. Text in Italian. 1977. irreg., latest vol.7, 1996. price varies. bibl. **Document type:** *Monographic series, Academic/Scholarly.* **Description:** Focuses on philosophy.
Published by: Associazione Trentina di Scienze Umane, Casella Postale 269, Trento, TN 38100, Italy. TEL 39-0461-1725660. Ed. Franco Chiereghin.

100 CHL ISSN 0717-4675

VERITAS; revista de filosofia y teologia. Text in Spanish. 1994. s-a. CLP 8 domestic; USD 40 in the Americas; USD 32 in Europe (effective 2010). back issues avail. **Document type:** *Journal, Academic/Scholarly.*
Related titles: Online - full text ed.: ISSN 0718-9273. 2006. free (effective 2011) (from SciELO).
Indexed: PhilInd.
Published by: Pontificio Seminario Mayor San Rafael Valparaiso, Ruta 68 s-n, Casilla 32, Lo Vazques Casa Blanca, Valparaiso, Chile. TEL 56-32-2741542, FAX 56-32-2741986, editor@revistaveritas.cl. Ed. Mauricio Correa Casanova.

189 CHE ISSN 1021-156X

VESTIGIA. Text in French. 1988. irreg., latest vol.35, 2008. price varies. **Document type:** *Monographic series, Academic/Scholarly.*
Published by: Academic Press Fribourg, Perolles 42, Fribourg, 1705, Switzerland. TEL 41-26-4264311, FAX 41-26-4264300, info@paulusedition.ch, http://www.paulusedition.ch/academic_press/.

374 AUS

VICTORIAN HUMANIST; bulletin of the humanist society of Victoria. Text in English. 1961. m. (10/yr.). AUD 20 to individuals membership (effective 2009). bk.rev. 8 p./no. 2 cols./p.; back issues avail. **Document type:** *Newsletter, Academic/Scholarly.* **Description:** Activities, decisions and policies of the committee, reports of public meetings, humanist ethics and values.
Related titles: Online - full text ed.
Published by: Humanist Society of Victoria Inc., PO Box 1555, Melbourne, VIC 3001, Australia. TEL 61-3-98579717, FAX 61-3-98579466. Ed. Rosslyn Ives. Circ: 100.

190 NLD ISSN 0929-6328
B1

VIENNA CIRCLE INSTITUTE YEARBOOK. Text in English. 1993. a. price varies. **Document type:** *Yearbook, Academic/Scholarly.*
Indexed: CCMJ, MSN, MathR, PhilInd, Z02.
—BLDSC (9235.585600).
Published by: (Institut 'Wiener Kreis'), Springer Netherlands (Subsidiary of: Springer Science+Business Media), Van Godewijckstraat 30, Dordrecht, 3311 GX, Netherlands. TEL 31-78-6576050, FAX 31-78-6576474. Ed. Friedrich Stadler.

VIEWS FROM OFF CENTER. *see* NEW AGE PUBLICATIONS

111.85 401 FRA ISSN 1778-042X

VISIBLE. Text in French. 2005. a., latest 2008. **Document type:** *Monographic series.*
Published by: (Centre de Recherche Semiotiques), Presses Universitaires de Limoges, 39C rue Camille Guerin, Limoges, 87031, France. TEL 33-5-55019535, FAX 33-5-55435629, pulim@unilim.fr.

VISIBLE EVIDENCE SERIES. *see* SOCIOLOGY

100 IND ISSN 0042-7187

VISVA - BHARATI JOURNAL OF PHILOSOPHY. Text in English. 1964. s-a. bk.rev. **Document type:** *Journal, Academic/Scholarly.*
Indexed: IIPL.
—Ingenta.
Published by: Visva-Bharati, Department of Philosophy and Religion, Santiniketan PO, Kolkata, West Bengal 731 235, India. TEL 91-3463-262751, FAX 91-3463-262672, http://www.visva-bharati.ac.in.

VIVARIUM; an international journal for the philosophy and intellectual life of the Middle Ages and Renaissance. *see* HISTORY—History Of Europe

181.48 USA

VIVEKANANDA VEDANTA SOCIETY OF CHICAGO. BULLETINS. Text in English. 1930. m. looseleaf. free to members (effective 2005). back issues avail. **Document type:** *Newsletter, Consumer.* **Description:** Gives schedule of activities at the Vivekananda Vedanta Society and quotations from the society's teachings.
Published by: Vivekananda Vedanta Society, 5423 S Hyde Park Blvd, Chicago, IL 60615. TEL 773-363-0027, FAX 773-667-7882, Info@VedantaSociety-Chicago.org, http://www.vedantasociety-chicago.org/. Ed., R&P Swami Chidananda. Circ: 750.

DE VLAAMSE GIDS. *see* LITERARY AND POLITICAL REVIEWS

100 RUS ISSN 0042-8744
B8.R9

VOPROSY FILOSOFII. Text in Russian; Summaries in English. 1947. m. USD 234 foreign (effective 2005). adv. bk.rev. bibl.; illus. index. reprints avail. **Document type:** *Journal, Academic/Scholarly.*
Related titles: Microfiche ed.: (from EVP); Online - full text ed.
Indexed: A20, ASCA, ArtHuCI, BAS, CA, CDSP, CurCont, DIP, FR, HistAb, IBR, IBZ, L&LBA, MLA-IB, MathR, P30, P42, PSA, PsycholAb, RASB, RILM, S02, S03, SCOPUS, SOPODA, SociolAb, T02, W07.
—East View, INIST. **CCC.**
Published by: (Rossiiskaya Akademiya Nauk/Russian Academy of Sciences, Institut Filosofii), Izdatel'stvo Nauka, Profsoyuznaya ul 90, Moscow, 117864, Russian Federation. TEL 7-095-3347151, FAX 7-095-4202220, secret@naukaran.ru, http://www.naukaran.ru. Circ: 37,000. **Dist. by:** M K - Periodica, ul Gilyarovskogo 39, Moscow 129110, Russian Federation. TEL 7-095-2845008, FAX 7-095-2813798, info@periodicals.ru, http://www.mkniga.ru.

VORLESUNGEN ZUR PHILOSOPHISCHEN PSYCHOLOGIE VON KUNST. *see* ART

100 RUS ISSN 2076-2186
B6

▼ ➤ **VORONEZHSKII GOSUDARSTVENNYI UNIVERSITET. VESTNIK. SERIYA: FILOSOFIYA.** Text in Russian. 2009. s-a. **Document type:** *Journal, Academic/Scholarly.*
Related titles: Online - full text ed.
Published by: Voronezhskii Gosudarstvennyi Universitet, Universitetskaya pl 1, Voronezh, 394693, Russian Federation. TEL 7-4732-207521, FAX 7-4732-208755, http://www.vsu.ru. Ed. A S Kravets.

➤ **VORSCHEIN.** *see* POLITICAL SCIENCE

100 NLD ISSN 1872-1478

DE VRIJDENKER. Text in Dutch. 1970. 10/yr. EUR 33; EUR 10 to students (effective 2010). **Description:** By and for free thinkers.
Formerly (until 2006): De Vrije Gedachte (0166-6614)
Published by: Vrijdenkersvereniging De Vrije Gedachte, Postbus 1087, Rotterdam, 3000 BB, Netherlands. TEL 31-10-4768986, info@devrijegedachte.nl, http://www.devrijegedachte.nl. Ed. Enno Nuy.

105 CHN ISSN 1007-6719

WAIGUO ZHEXUE/FOREIGN PHILOSOPHY. Text in Chinese. 1978. m. USD 63.80 (effective 2009). 112 p./no.; **Document type:** *Journal, Academic/Scholarly.* **Description:** Contains research on all schools of philosophy in the world as well as their development.
Formerly: Waiguo Zhexue yu Zhexueshi/Foreign Philosophy and Its History (1001-2559)
Published by: Zhongguo Renmin Daxue Shubao Ziliao Zhongxin/Renmin University of China, Information Center for Social Sciences, Dongcheng-qu, 3, Zhangzizhong Lu, Beijing, 100007, China. TEL 86-10-64039458, FAX 86-10-64015080, center@zlzx.org, http://www.zlzx.org/. **Dist. by:** China International Book Trading Corp, 35 Chegongzhuang Xilu, Haidian District, PO Box 399, Beijing 100044, China. TEL 86-10-68412045, FAX 86-10-68412023, cibtc@mail.cibtc.com.cn, http://www.cibtc.com.cn.

190 GBR

WARWICK STUDIES IN EUROPEAN PHILOSOPHY. Text in English. 1993. irreg., latest 2004, 2nd ed. price varies. back issues avail. **Document type:** *Monographic series, Academic/Scholarly.* **Description:** Presents the best and most original work being done within the European philosophical tradition.
Published by: Routledge (Subsidiary of: Taylor & Francis Group), 4 Park Sq, Milton Park, Abingdon, Oxon OX14 4RN, United Kingdom. TEL 44-20-70176000, FAX 44-20-70176336, subscriptions@tandf.co.uk, http://www.routledge.com.

100 DEU ISSN 0940-9394
BR4

WEGE OHNE DOGMA. Text in German. 1992. m. EUR 21 (effective 2010). adv. bk.rev. index. **Document type:** *Newsletter, Consumer.*
Formed by the merger of (1962-1992): Freie Religion (0016-0776); (1973-1992): Humanist (0344-1059); Which was formed by the merger of (1957-1973): Freigeistige Aktion (0016-0830); (195?-1973): Freies Denken (0344-161X); (1957-1973): Der Freireligioese (0429-6702)
Indexed: Acal, DIP, IBR, IBZ.
Published by: (Bund Freireligioeser Gemeinden Deutschlands), Freireligioese Verlagsbuchhandlung, T6, 26, Mannheim, 68161, Germany. TEL 49-621-22805, FAX 49-621-28289, FLGBaden@gmx.de. Eds. Holger Behr, Thomas Lasi.

100 DEU

▼ **WELTEN DER PHILOSOPHIE.** Text in German. 2009. irreg., latest vol.3, 2011. price varies. **Document type:** *Monographic series, Academic/Scholarly.*
Published by: Verlag Karl Alber, Hermann-Herder-Str 4, Freiburg, 79104, Germany. TEL 49-761-2717436, FAX 49-761-2717212, info@verlag-alber.de.

100 NLD

WERKMEISTER STUDIES. Text in English. irreg. price varies. **Document type:** *Monographic series, Academic/Scholarly.*
Related titles: ◆ Series of: Value Inquiry Book Series. ISSN 0929-8436.
Published by: Editions Rodopi B.V., Tijnmuiden 7, Amsterdam, 1046 AK, Netherlands. TEL 31-20-6114821, FAX 31-20-4472979, 31-20-447-2979, info@rodopi.nl. Ed. Richard T Hull. **Dist. by:** Rodopi - USA, 606 Newark Ave, 2nd fl, Kenilworth, NJ 07033. TEL 908-497-9031, FAX 908-497-9035.

100 USA ISSN 1040-1415

THE WESLEYAN WOMAN. Text in English. 1980. q.
Published by: Wesleyan Publishing House, PO Box 50434, Indianapolis, IN 46250-0434. Ed. Nancy Heer. Circ: 4,000.

WEST COAST LIBERTARIAN. *see* LITERARY AND POLITICAL REVIEWS

509 NLD ISSN 1566-659X

➤ **THE WESTERN ONTARIO SERIES IN PHILOSOPHY OF SCIENCE.** Variant title: Western Ontario Series. Text in English. 1972. irreg., latest vol.74, 2009. price varies. **Document type:** *Monographic series, Academic/Scholarly.*
Formerly (until 1997): University of Western Ontario. Series in Philosophy of Science (0929-6417)
Indexed: CCMJ.
—BLDSC (9301.620000), IE, Ingenta. **CCC.**
Published by: (University of Western Ontario CAN), Springer Netherlands (Subsidiary of: Springer Science+Business Media), Van Godewijckstraat 30, Dordrecht, 3311 GX, Netherlands. TEL 31-78-6576050, FAX 31-78-6576474. Ed. William Demopoulos.

100 DEU ISSN 0722-8104
B3

WIDERSPRUCH; Zeitschrift fuer Philosophie. Text in German. 1981. s-a. EUR 6 newsstand/cover (effective 2003). adv. **Document type:** *Journal, Academic/Scholarly.*
Indexed: PhilInd.
Published by: Muenchner Gesellschaft fuer Dialektische Philosophie, Tengstr 14, Munich, 80798, Germany. TEL 49-89-2720437. Ed. Manuell Knoll.

100 DEU ISSN 0948-1303

WIENER ARBEITEN ZUR PHILOSOPHIE. REIHE A: UNIVERSITAETSSTUDIEN. Text in German. 1997. irreg., latest vol.3, 2009. price varies. **Document type:** *Monographic series, Academic/Scholarly.*
Published by: Peter Lang GmbH (Subsidiary of: Peter Lang Publishing Group), Eschborner Landstr 42-50, Frankfurt Am Main, 60489, Germany. TEL 49-69-7807050, FAX 49-69-78070550, zentrale.frankfurt@peterlang.com, http://www.peterlang.com. Ed. Stephan Haltmayer.

100 DEU ISSN 0948-1311

WIENER ARBEITEN ZUR PHILOSOPHIE. REIHE B: BEITRAEGE ZUR PHILOSOPHISCHEN FORSCHUNG. Text in German. 1999. irreg., latest vol.20, 2009. price varies. **Document type:** *Monographic series, Academic/Scholarly.*
Published by: Peter Lang GmbH (Subsidiary of: Peter Lang Publishing Group), Eschborner Landstr 42-50, Frankfurt Am Main, 60489, Germany. TEL 49-69-7807050, FAX 49-69-78070550, zentrale.frankfurt@peterlang.com, http://www.peterlang.com. Ed. Stephan Haltmayer.

100 DEU ISSN 0948-132X

WIENER ARBEITEN ZUR PHILOSOPHIE. REIHE C: BEITRAEGE ZUR SOZIALPHILOSOPHIE. Text in German. 2000. irreg., latest vol.2, 2002. price varies. **Document type:** *Monographic series, Academic/Scholarly.*
Published by: Peter Lang GmbH (Subsidiary of: Peter Lang Publishing Group), Eschborner Landstr 42-50, Frankfurt Am Main, 60489, Germany. TEL 49-69-7807050, FAX 49-69-78070550, zentrale.frankfurt@peterlang.com, http://www.peterlang.com. Ed. Stephan Haltmayer.

100 AUT ISSN 0083-999X
B31
WIENER JAHRBUCH FUER PHILOSOPHIE. Text in German. 1968. a. EUR 42.90 (effective 2012). bk.rev. index. **Document type:** *Monographic series, Academic/Scholarly.*
Indexed: DIP, FR, IBR, IBZ, IPB, PCI, PhilInd, RASB.
—INIST.
Published by: Wilhelm Braumueller Universitaets-Verlagsbuchhandlung GmbH, Servitengasse 5, Vienna, 1090, Austria. TEL 43-1-3191159, FAX 43-1-3102805, office@braumueller.at. Circ: 500.

181.4 954 AUT ISSN 0084-0084
PJ5
WIENER ZEITSCHRIFT FUER DIE KUNDE SUEDASIENS UND ARCHIV FUER INDISCHE PHILOSOPHIE. Variant title: Wiener Zeitschrift fuer die Kunde Suedasiens. Text in German. 1957. irreg., latest vol.51, 2009. price varies. 255 p./no.; **Document type:** *Monographic series, Academic/Scholarly.*
Former titles (until 1969): Wiener Zeitschrift fuer die Kunde Sued- und Ostasiens und Archiv fur Indische Philosophie (1027-6203); Archiv fuer Indische Philosophie
Related titles: Online - full text ed.: ISSN 1728-3124. 2003.
Indexed: A21, A22, BAS, BibLing, DIP, FR, IBR, IBZ, MLA-IB, NumL, RI-1, RI-2.
—IE, Ingenta, INIST.
Published by: (Oesterreichische Akademie der Wissenschaften, Kommission fuer Sprachen und Kulturen Suedasiens), Verlag der Oesterreichischen Akademie der Wissenschaften, Postgasse 7/4, Vienna, W 1011, Austria. TEL 43-1-515813402, FAX 43-1-515813400, verlag@oeaw.ac.at, http://www.verlag.oeaw.ac.at. Ed. Gerhard Oberhammer. **Co-sponsor:** Universitaet Wien. Indologisches Institut.

100 300 500 NLD ISSN 0043-5414
WIJSGERIG PERSPECTIEF OP MAATSCHAPPIJ EN WETENSCHAP/ PHILOSOPHICAL PERSPECTIVES ON SOCIETY AND SCIENCE. Text in Dutch. 1960. 4/yr. EUR 47.50 domestic to individuals; EUR 59.50 foreign to individuals; EUR 39.50 domestic to students; EUR 45 foreign to students (effective 2008). adv. bk.rev. **Document type:** *Academic/Scholarly.*
Related titles: Online - full text ed.: ISSN 1875-709X.
Indexed: BAS, IPB, P30.
—IE, Infotrieve.
Published by: Boom Uitgevers Amsterdam, Prinsengracht 747-751, Amsterdam, 1017 JX, Netherlands. TEL 31-20-6226107, FAX 31-20-6253327, info@uitgeverijboom.nl, http://www.uitgeverijboom.nl. Adv. contact Michiel Klaassen TEL 31-20-5200122. page EUR 375; trim 160 x 210. Circ: 850.

100 BEL
WIJSGERIGE VERKENNINGEN. Text in Dutch. 1987. irreg. price varies. **Document type:** *Academic/Scholarly.*
Published by: Leuven University Press, Blijde Inkomststraat 5, Leuven, 3000, Belgium. TEL 32-16-325345, FAX 32-16-325352, university.press@upers.kuleuven.ac.be, http://www.kuleuven.ac.be/upers.

WILLIAM JAMES STUDIES. *see* PSYCHOLOGY

100 DEU ISSN 0935-5200
WISSENSCHAFTLICHE ABHANDLUNGEN UND REDEN ZUR PHILOSOPHIE, POLITIK UND GEISTESGESCHICHTE. Text in German. 1926. irreg., latest vol.60, 2010. price varies. **Document type:** *Monographic series, Academic/Scholarly.*
Published by: Duncker und Humblot GmbH, Carl-Heinrich-Becker-Weg 9, Berlin, 12165, Germany. TEL 49-30-7900060, FAX 49-30-79000631, info@duncker-humblot.de.

100 DEU ISSN 1861-6844
WISSENSCHAFTLICHE BEITRAEGE AUS DEM TECTUM-VERLAG. REIHE PHILOSOPHIE. Text in German. 1999. irreg., latest vol.12, 2009. price varies. **Document type:** *Monographic series, Academic/Scholarly.*
Published by: Tectum Wissenschaftsverlag Marburg, Biegenstr 4, Marburg, 35037, Germany. TEL 49-6421-481523, FAX 49-6421-43470, email@tectum-verlag.de.

100 DEU
WISSENSCHAFTLICHE SCHRIFTENREIHE PHILOSOPHIE. Text in German. 1994. irreg., latest vol.7, 2009. price varies. **Document type:** *Monographic series, Academic/Scholarly.*
Published by: Verlag Dr. Koester, Rungestr 22-24, Berlin, 10179, Germany. TEL 49-30-76403224, FAX 49-30-76403227, verlag-koester@t-online.de.

190 AUT
➤ **WITTGENSTEIN, LUDWIG: WIENER AUSGABE.** Text in German. 1993. irreg., latest vol.11, 2000. price varies. **Document type:** *Monographic series, Academic/Scholarly.*
Published by: Springer Wien (Subsidiary of: Springer Science+Business Media), Sachsenplatz 4-6, Vienna, W 1201, Austria. TEL 43-1-3302415-0, FAX 43-1-330242665, books@springer.at, http://www.springer.at. Ed. Michael Nedo. R&P Angela Foessl TEL 43-1-3302415517. **Subscr. to:** Springer New York LLC, 233 Spring St, New York, NY 10013. TEL 800-777-4643, FAX 201-348-4505.

190 DEU ISSN 1868-7431
B3376.W564
WITTGENSTEIN STUDIEN. NEUE FOLGE. Text in German. 2000. a. EUR 94, USD 141 to institutions; EUR 110, USD 165 combined subscription to institutions (print & online eds.) (effective 2012). **Document type:** *Journal, Academic/Scholarly.*
Formerly (until 2010): Wittgenstein Studien (1439-7668)
Related titles: Online - full text ed.: ISSN 1868-7458. EUR 94, USD 141 to institutions (effective 2012).
Indexed: AmHI, H07, T02.
Published by: (Internationale Ludwig Wittgenstein Gesellschaft e.V.), Walter de Gruyter GmbH & Co. KG, Genthiner Str 13, Berlin, 10785, Germany. TEL 49-30-260050, FAX 49-30-26005251, info@degruyter.com, http://www.degruyter.de.

100 NLD ISSN 1875-4287
WJERKLANK. Text in Frisian. 2007. s-a. EUR 17.50 membership (effective 2009).
Published by: Obe Postma Selskip, Wagnerlaan 7, Enschede, 7522 KH, Netherlands. TEL 31-53-4345511. Eds. Jan Gulmans, Philippus Breuker.

WOMEN IN PHILOSOPHY. *see* WOMEN'S STUDIES

174 330 NLD ISSN 1871-6482
WORKING PAPERS FOR PHILOSOPHY AND ECONOMICS. Text in English. 2006. irreg.
Media: Online - full text.
Published by: Erasmus Institute for Philosophy and Economics, Erasmus University Rotterdam, Department of Philosophy, PO Box 1738, Rotterdam, 3000 DR, Netherlands. TEL 31-10-4088990, FAX 31-10-4089030, eipe@fwb.eur.nl.

100 USA ISSN 0260-4027
B1 CODEN: WOFUDM
➤ **WORLD FUTURES;** the journal of general evolution. Text in French. 1962. 8/yr. GBP 866 combined subscription in United Kingdom to institutions (print & online eds.); EUR 1,145, USD 1,437 combined subscription to institutions (print & online eds.) (effective 2012). adv. bk.rev. bibl.; illus. index. reprint service avail. from PSC. **Document type:** *Journal, Academic/Scholarly.* **Description:** Dedicated to the study of irreversible, nonlinear, system-structuring change in nature and society.
Former titles (until 1981): The Philosophy Forum (0031-823X); (until 1968): Pacific Philosophy Forum (0275-1194)
Related titles: Microform ed.: (from MIM); Online - full text ed.: ISSN 1556-1844. GBP 780 in United Kingdom to institutions; EUR 1,031, USD 1,294 to institutions (effective 2012) (from IngentaConnect).
Indexed: A01, A03, A08, A20, A22, A26, AmHI, B21, BRD, CA, DIP, E01, E08, E17, ESPM, FR, FutSurv, G08, H07, H08, H09, H10, HAb, HumInd, I05, IBR, IBZ, P26, P30, P54, PAIS, PCI, PQC, PerIslam, PhilInd, RASB, S02, S03, S09, SOPODA, SSciA, SociolAb, T02, W03.
—IE, Infotrieve, Ingenta, INIST. **CCC.**
Published by: Taylor & Francis Inc. (Subsidiary of: Taylor & Francis Group), 325 Chestnut St, Ste 800, Philadelphia, PA 19106. TEL 215-625-2940, 800-354-1420, orders@taylorandfrancis.com, http://www.taylorandfrancis.com. Ed. Ervin Laszlo. Adv. contact Linda Hann TEL 44-1344-779945.

➤ **WORLD ORDER;** a Baha'i magazine. *see* RELIGIONS AND THEOLOGY

➤ **WORLD TRIBUNE.** *see* RELIGIONS AND THEOLOGY—Buddhist

➤ **WROCLAWSKI PRZEGLAD TEOLOGICZNY.** *see* RELIGIONS AND THEOLOGY—Roman Catholic

➤ **WUHAN DAXUE XUEBAO (ZHEXUE SHEHUI KEXUE BAN)/ WUHAN UNIVERSITY. JOURNAL (PHILOSOPHY AND SOCIAL SCIENCE EDITION).** *see* SOCIAL SCIENCES: COMPREHENSIVE WORKS

709 POL ISSN 0208-497X
WYDZIAL FILOLOGICZNO-FILOZOFICZNY. PRACE. Text in Polish; Summaries in English, French, German. 1948. irreg., latest vol.36, no.3, 2002. price varies. **Document type:** *Monographic series, Academic/Scholarly.*
Related titles: ◆ Series: Towarzystwo Naukowe w Toruniu. Komisja Historii Sztuki. Teka. ISSN 0082-5514.
Indexed: SOPODA.
Published by: Towarzystwo Naukowe w Toruniu, ul Wysoka 16, Torun, 87100, Poland. TEL 48-56-6223941, tnt.biuro@wp.pl. Circ: 300.

100 CHN ISSN 1000-7660
B804
XIANDAI ZHEXUE/MODERN PHILOSOPHY. Text in Chinese. q. CNY 40 domestic; USD 16.80 foreign (effective 2005). **Document type:** *Journal, Academic/Scholarly.*
Related titles: Online - full text ed.
Address: 135, Xingang Xilu, Zhongshan Daxue Wenkeluo 206, Guangzhou, 510275, China. **Dist. by:** China International Book Trading Corp, 35 Chegongzhuang Xilu, Haidian District, PO Box 399, Beijing 100044, China. TEL 86-10-68412045, FAX 86-10-68412023, cibtc@mail.cibtc.com.cn, http://www.cibtc.com.cn.

XIAOGAN XUEYUAN XUEBAO/XIAOGAN UNIVERSITY. JOURNAL. *see* SOCIAL SCIENCES: COMPREHENSIVE WORKS

XIHUA SHIFAN XUEYUAN XUEBAO (ZHEXUE SHEHUI KEXUE BAN)/SICHUAN NORMAL COLLEGE. JOURNAL. (PHILOSOPHY & SOCIAL SCIENCE EDITION). *see* SOCIAL SCIENCES: COMPREHENSIVE WORKS

XI'NAN ZHENG-FA DAXUE XUEBAO/SOUTHWEST UNIVERSITY OF POLITICAL SCIENCE AND LAW. JOURNAL. *see* LAW

XINJIANG DAXUE XUEBAO (ZHEXUE - RENWEN SHEHUI KEXUE BAN)/XINJIANG UNIVERSITY. JOURNAL (PHILOSOPHY,HUMANITIES & SOCIAL SCIENCE). *see* SOCIAL SCIENCES: COMPREHENSIVE WORKS

XINJIANG SHIFAN DAXUE XUEBAO (ZHEXUE SHEHUI KEXUE BAN). *see* SOCIAL SCIENCES: COMPREHENSIVE WORKS

XUZHOU SHIFAN DAXUE XUEBAO (ZHEXUE SHEHUI KEXUE BAN)/XUZHOU NORMAL UNIVERSITY. JOURNAL (PHILOSOPHY AND SOCIAL SCIENCES EDITION). *see* SOCIAL SCIENCES: COMPREHENSIVE WORKS

YANSHAN DAXUE XUEBAO (ZHEXUE SHEHUI KEXUE BAN). *see* SOCIAL SCIENCES: COMPREHENSIVE WORKS

YANTAI DAXUE XUEBAO (SHEHUI KEXUE BAN)/YANTAI UNIVERSITY. JOURNAL (PHILOSOPHY AND SOCIAL SCIENCE EDITION). *see* SOCIAL SCIENCES: COMPREHENSIVE WORKS

100 CHN ISSN 1002-0772
R723
YIXUE YU ZHEXUE/MEDICINE AND PHILOSOPHY. Text in Chinese. 1980. s-a. USD 62.40 (effective 2009). **Document type:** *Journal, Academic/Scholarly.*
Related titles: Online - full content ed.; Online - full text ed.
Published by: Zhongguo Ziran Bianzhengfa Yanjiuhui/Chinese Society for Dialectics of Nature, 465, Zhongshan Lu, Hekou-qu, Dalian, 116013, China. TEL 86-411-84721530, FAX 86-411-84722033. **Dist. by:** China International Book Trading Corp, 35 Chegongzhuang Xilu, Haidian District, PO Box 399, Beijing 100044, China. TEL 86-10-68412045, FAX 86-10-68412023, cibtc@mail.cibtc.com.cn, http://www.cibtc.com.cn.

YOGA AND HEALTH. *see* PHYSICAL FITNESS AND HYGIENE

181.45 294.54 IND ISSN 0970-1737
➤ **YOGA AND TOTAL HEALTH.** Text in English. 1933. m. INR 150 domestic; USD 25 foreign (effective 2011). bk.rev. abstr.; bibl.; charts; illus. 28 p./no.; back issues avail. **Document type:** *Journal, Trade.* **Description:** Contains articles on Yoga education therapy, Yoga philosophy and techniques, as well as research on cardiac, respiratory, diabetes, orthopaedic problems.
Formerly (until 1984): Yoga Institute. Journal (0044-0493)
Indexed: RASB.
Published by: Yoga Institute, Shri Yogendra Marg, Prabhat Colony, Santacruz (E), Mumbai, Maharashtra 400 055, India. TEL 91-22-26110506, FAX http://www.theyogainstitute.org/, yogainstitute@rediffmail.com. Ed., Pub. Jayadeva Yogendra.

➤ **YOGA INTERNATIONAL.** *see* NEW AGE PUBLICATIONS

181.45 613.7 GBR
YOGA LIFE. Text in English. 1961. 2/yr. GBP 5, USD 10 (effective 1999). bk.rev. illus. **Document type:** *Bulletin.*
Former titles: International Sivananda Yoga Life and Yoga Vacations (0708-076X); International Yoga Life and Yoga Vacations (0381-9043)
Published by: Sivananda Yoga Vedanta Centre, 51 Felsham Rd, London, SW15 1AZ, United Kingdom. TEL 44-181-780-0160, FAX 44-181-780-0128. Ed. Swami Saradananda. Circ: 40,000.

181.45 051 ITA ISSN 1972-6198
YOGA MAGAZINE ITALIA. Text in Italian. 2007. m. **Document type:** *Magazine, Consumer.*
Published by: Play Media Company, Via di Santa Cornelia 5A, Formello, RM 00060, Italy. TEL 39-06-33221250, FAX 39-06-33221235, abbonamenti@playmediacompany.it, http://www.playmediacompany.it.

181.45 IND
YOGA SUDHA/YOGA WING. Text in English. 1984. m. INR 200, USD 5.62 domestic; USD 50 foreign (effective 2011). **Document type:** *Magazine, Academic/Scholarly.* **Description:** Focuses on all aspects of yoga.
Related titles: Online - full text ed.: free (effective 2011).
Published by: Vivekananda Kendra, 40, 7th Cross Atmananda Colony, Sultan Palyam, Bangalore, Karnataka 560 032, India. TEL 91-80-23630773, bangalore@vkendra.org, http://www.vkendra.org. Ed. H R Nagendra.

YOGA THERAPY TODAY. *see* PHYSICAL FITNESS AND HYGIENE

YOKOHAMA KOKURITSU DAIGAKU JINBUN KIYO DAI-1-RUI, TETSUGAKU, SHAKAI KAGAKU/YOKOHAMA NATIONAL UNIVERSITY. HUMANITIES. SECTION 1: PHILOSOPHY AND SOCIAL SCIENCES. *see* SOCIAL SCIENCES: COMPREHENSIVE WORKS

YUNNAN MINZU DAXUE XUEBAO (ZHEXUE SHEHUI KEXUE BAN)/YUNNAN UNIVERSITY OF THE NATIONALITIES. JOURNAL (SOCIAL SCIENCES EDITION). *see* SOCIAL SCIENCES: COMPREHENSIVE WORKS

100 POL ISSN 0867-8286
➤ **ZAGADNIENIA FILOZOFICZNE W NAUCE.** Text in Polish. 1978. s-a. **Document type:** *Journal, Academic/Scholarly.*
Published by: (Papieska Akademia Teologiczna w Krakowie, Wydzial Filozoficzny, Osrodek Badan Interdyscyplinarnych), Wydawnictwo Naukowe Papieskiej Akademii Teologicznej w Krakowie, ul Franciszkanska 1, pok 037, Krakow, 31004, Poland. wydawnictwo@pat.krakow.pl. Ed. Michal Heller.

100 DEU ISSN 0044-2186
N9
➤ **ZEITSCHRIFT FUER AESTHETIK UND ALLGEMEINE KUNSTWISSENSCHAFT.** Text in English, French, German. 1906. s-a. EUR 100 domestic; EUR 105 foreign (effective 2010). bk.rev. reprint service avail. from SCH. **Document type:** *Journal, Academic/ Scholarly.*
Formerly: Jahrbuch fuer Aesthetik
Related titles: Microfiche ed.: (from BHP); Online - full text ed.: (from IngentaConnect).
Indexed: A20, A22, B24, DIP, FR, IBR, IBZ, IPB, MLA-IB, PCI, RASB.
—IE, Infotrieve, INIST. **CCC.**
Published by: Felix Meiner Verlag GmbH, Richardstr 47, Hamburg, 22081, Germany. TEL 49-40-2987560, FAX 49-40-29875620, info@meiner.de. Ed. Philipp Theisohn. Adv. contact Johannes Kambylis. Circ: 600.

100 371.3 DEU
ZEITSCHRIFT FUER DIDAKTIK DER PHILOSOPHIE UND ETHIK. Text in German. 1979. q. **Document type:** *Academic/Scholarly.*
Formerly: Zeitschrift fuer Didaktik der Philosophie
Indexed: IPB, RASB.
Published by: Siebert Verlag, Namedorfstra 1, Hanover, 30539, Germany. Circ: 1,800.

302 AUT ISSN 0044-2763
ZEITSCHRIFT FUER GANZHEITSFORSCHUNG; Philosophie - Gesellschaft - Wirtschaft. Text in German. 1957. q. EUR 14.54 (effective 2003). adv. bk.rev. charts; illus. index. 56 p./no.; **Document type:** *Journal, Academic/Scholarly.*
Related titles: Online - full text ed.
Indexed: DIP, IBR, IBZ, RASB.
Published by: Gesellschaft fuer Ganzheitsforschung, Augasse 2-6, Vienna, W 1090, Austria. TEL 43-1-313364523, FAX 43-1-31336727, j.hanns.pichler@wu-wien.ac.at. Ed., Adv. contact Hubert Verhonig. Circ: 500.

001 DEU ISSN 1863-8937
B3
ZEITSCHRIFT FUER IDEENGESCHICHTE. Text in German. 2007. q. EUR 42; EUR 12.90 newsstand/cover (effective 2011). adv. **Document type:** *Journal, Academic/Scholarly.*
Published by: Verlag C.H. Beck oHG, Wilhelmstr 9, Munich, 80801, Germany. TEL 49-89-381890, FAX 49-89-38189398, bestellung@beck.de, http://www.beck.de. Circ: 2,100 (paid).

ZEITSCHRIFT FUER KATHOLISCHE THEOLOGIE. *see* RELIGIONS AND THEOLOGY—Roman Catholic

100 500 DEU ISSN 1867-1845
B3
➤ **ZEITSCHRIFT FUER KULTURPHILOSOPHIE.** Text in German. 2/yr. EUR 68; EUR 38 newsstand/cover (effective 2010). **Document type:** *Journal, Academic/Scholarly.*
Formerly (until 2007): Dialektik (0939-5512)

Related titles: Online - full text ed.: (from IngentaConnect).
Indexed: DIP, IBR, IBZ, PhilInd, RASB.
Published by: Felix Meiner Verlag GmbH, Richardstr 47, Hamburg, 22081, Germany. TEL 49-40-2987560, FAX 49-40-29875620, info@meiner.de. R&P, Adv. contact Johannes Kambylis.

➤ **ZEITSCHRIFT FUER MEDIZINISCHE ETHIK.** *see* MEDICAL SCIENCES

100 DEU ISSN 0044-3301
B3
➤ **ZEITSCHRIFT FUER PHILOSOPHISCHE FORSCHUNG.** Text in German, English. 1947. q. EUR 89 to individuals; EUR 141 to institutions (effective 2011). adv. bk.rev. bibl.; illus. cum.index every 10 yrs. back issues avail.; reprints avail. **Document type:** *Journal, Academic/Scholarly.* **Description:** Discusses research in various areas of philosophy.
Related titles: Online - full text ed.: (from IngentaConnect).
Indexed: A20, A22, ASCA, AmHI, ArtHuCI, BAS, BibInd, CurCont, DIP, FR, IBR, IBRH, IBZ, IPB, MLA-IB, P30, PCI, PhilInd, RASB, RILM, SCOPUS, W07.
—BLDSC (9480.500000), IE, Infotrieve, Ingenta, INIST.
Published by: Vittorio Klostermann, Frauenlobstr 22, Frankfurt Am Main, 60487, Germany. TEL 49-69-9708160, FAX 49-69-708038, verlag@klostermann.de. Eds. Christof Rapp, Otfried Hoeffe. Circ: 1,200 (paid and controlled).

149.946 DEU ISSN 0170-6241
P99 CODEN: ZESEE3
➤ **ZEITSCHRIFT FUER SEMIOTIK.** Text in German. 1979. q. EUR 68; EUR 27 to students (effective 2010). adv. bk.rev. **Document type:** *Journal, Academic/Scholarly.* **Description:** Covers literature, natural sciences, cultural science, cognitive psychology, media science, and linguistics.
Indexed: A20, A22, ASCA, ArtHuCI, BibLing, CurCont, DIP, IBR, IBZ, MLA-IB, PCI, RASB, RILM, SCOPUS, SOPODA, SociolAb, W07.
—IE, Infotrieve.
Published by: (Deutsche Gesellschaft fuer Semiotik e.V.), Stauffenburg Verlag, Postfach 2525, Tuebingen, 72015, Germany. TEL 49-7071-97300, FAX 49-7071-973030, info@stauffenburg.de. Ed. Roland Posner.

➤ **ZEITSCHRIFT FUER WIRTSCHAFTS- UND UNTERNEHMENSETHIK.** *see* BUSINESS AND ECONOMICS

300 CHN ISSN 1674-604X
ZHELI. Text in Chinese. 2003. m. **Document type:** *Magazine, Consumer.*
Formerly (until 2009): Zhongxue Wenke (1674-2699); Which was formed by the merger of (2001-2003): Zhongxue Wenke (Chuzhong Ban); (2001-2003): Zhongxue Wenke (Gaozhong Ban); Both of which superseded in part (in 2000): Zhongxue Wenke Cankao Ziliao (1002-6371); Which was formerly (until 1986): Zhongxue Wenke Jiaoxue Cankao Ziliao; Which was formed by the merger of (1980-1981): Jiaoxue Cankao Ziliao (Zhongxue Yuwen Ban); (1980-1981): Jiaoxue Cankao Ziliao (Zhongxue Like Ban); Both of which supereseded in part: Jiaoxue Cankao Ziliao (Zhongxue Ban)
Published by: Guangxi Jiaoyu Xueyuan Chubanshe, 37, Jianzheng Lu, Nanning, 530023, China. TEL 86-771-5861162.

ZHENGZHOU DAXUE XUEBAO (ZHEXUE SHEHUI KEXUE BAN)/ ZHENGZHOU UNIVERSITY. JOURNAL (PHILOSOPHY AND SOCIAL SCIENCE EDITION). *see* SOCIAL SCIENCES: COMPREHENSIVE WORKS

100 CHN ISSN 1002-8862
B8.C5
ZHEXUE DONGTAI/PHILOSOPHICAL TRENDS. Text in Chinese. 1987. m. USD 62.40 (effective 2009). **Document type:** *Journal, Academic/Scholarly.*
Related titles: Online - full text ed.
—East View.
Published by: Zhongguo Shehui Kexueyuan, Zhexue Yanjiusuo/Chinese Academy of Social Sciences, Institute of Philosophy, 5 Jianguomennei Dajie, Beijing, 10000732, China. TEL 86-10-65137954. Ed. Ren Jumning. **Dist. by:** China International Book Trading Corp, 35 Chegongzhuang Xilu, Haidian District, PO Box 399, Beijing 100044, China. TEL 86-10-68412045, FAX 86-10-68412023, cibtc@mail.cibtc.com.cn, http://www.cibtc.com.cn.

100 CHN
ZHEXUE LUNCONG. Text in Chinese. bi-m.
Published by: Zhongguo Shehui Kexueyuan, Zhexue Yanjiusuo/Chinese Academy of Social Sciences, Institute of Philosophy, 5 Jianguomennei Dajie, Beijing, 10000732, China. TEL 86-10-65137954. Ed. Li Shubai.

100 CHN ISSN 1000-0216
ZHEXUE YANJIU/PHILOSOPHICAL RESEARCH. Text in Chinese; Contents page in English. 1955. m. USD 74.40 (effective 2009). adv. bk.rev. **Document type:** *Journal, Academic/Scholarly.*
Related titles: Online - full text ed.
—East View, Ingenta.
Published by: Zhongguo Shehui Kexueyuan, Zhexue Yanjiusuo/Chinese Academy of Social Sciences, Institute of Philosophy, 5 Jianguomennei Dajie, Beijing, 10000732, China. TEL 86-10-65137954, FAX 86-10-65137826. **Dist. by:** China International Book Trading Corp, 35 Chegongzhuang Xilu, Haidian District, PO Box 399, Beijing 100044, China. TEL 86-10-68412045, FAX 86-10-68412023, cibtc@mail.cibtc.com.cn, http://www.cibtc.com.cn.

100 CHN ISSN 1001-2710
ZHEXUE YUANLI/PRINCIPLES OF PHILOSOPHY. Text in Chinese. m. USD 138.70 (effective 2009). Index. **Document type:** *Journal, Academic/Scholarly.* **Description:** Reprints papers and articles on philosophical principles.
Published by: Zhongguo Renmin Daxue Shubao Ziliao Zhongxin/Renmin University of China, Information Center for Social Sciences, Dongcheng-qu, 3, Zhangzizhong Lu, Beijing, 100007, China. TEL 86-10-84043003, FAX 86-10-64015080, center@zlzx.org. **Dist. by:** China International Book Trading Corp, 35 Chegongzhuang Xilu, Haidian District, PO Box 399, Beijing 100044, China. TEL 86-10-68412045, FAX 86-10-68412023, cibtc@mail.cibtc.com.cn, http://www.cibtc.com.cn.

ZHONGGUO QINGNIAN/CHINA YOUTH. *see* CHILDREN AND YOUTH—For

181.951 CHN ISSN 1007-6689
B8.C5
ZHONGGUO ZHEXUE/CHINESE PHILOSOPHY. Text in Chinese. 1978. m. USD 91.30 (effective 2009). 104 p./no.; **Document type:** *Journal, Academic/Scholarly.* **Description:** Collects research on contemporary Chinese philosophy and its history.
Former titles (until 1997): Zhongguo Zhexue yu Zhexueshi/Chinese Philosophy and Its History (1007-8835); (until 1995): Zhongguo Zhexueshi (1001-2540)
Indexed: MLA-IB.
Published by: Zhongguo Renmin Daxue Shubao Ziliao Zhongxin/Renmin University of China, Information Center for Social Sciences, Dongcheng-qu, 3, Zhangzizhong Lu, Beijing, 100007, China. TEL 86-10-84043003, FAX 86-10-64015080, center@zlzx.org, http://www.zlzx.org/. **Dist. by:** China International Book Trading Corp, 35 Chegongzhuang Xilu, Haidian District, PO Box 399, Beijing 100044, China. TEL 86-10-68412045, FAX 86-10-68412023, cibtc@mail.cibtc.com.cn, http://www.cibtc.com.cn.

100 CHN ISSN 1004-3462
ZHONGGUO ZHEXUE NIANJIAN (JINGZHUANGBEN)/CHINESE PHILOSOPHICAL ALMANAC (HARDCOVER EDITION). Text in Chinese. a. USD 40 (effective 2009). **Document type:** *Journal, Academic/Scholarly.*
—East View.
Published by: Zhongguo Shehui Kexueyuan, Zhexue Yanjiusuo/Chinese Academy of Social Sciences, Institute of Philosophy, 5 Jianguomennei Dajie, Beijing, 10000732, China.

100 299.51 CHN ISSN 1005-0396
B8.C5
ZHONGGUO ZHEXUESHI/HISTORY OF CHINESE PHILOSOPHY. Text in Chinese. 1978. q. USD 24.80 (effective 2009). **Document type:** *Journal, Academic/Scholarly.* **Description:** Publishes research on the history of Chinese philosophy.
Formerly: Zhongguo Zhexueshi Yanjiu
Related titles: Online - full text ed.
Indexed: MLA-IB.
—East View.
Published by: Zhongguo Zhexueshi Xuehui, 5, Jianguomennei Dajie, Beijing, 100732, China. TEL 86-10-65137744. **Dist. by:** China International Book Trading Corp, 35 Chegongzhuang Xilu, Haidian District, PO Box 399, Beijing 100044, China. TEL 86-10-68412045, FAX 86-10-68412023, cibtc@mail.cibtc.com.cn, http://www.cibtc.com.cn.

ZHONGYANG MINZU DAXUE XUEBAO (ZHEXUE SHEHUI KEXUE BAN)/CENTRAL UNIVERSITY FOR NATIONALITIES. JOURNAL (PHILOSOPHY AND SOCIAL SCIENCES EDITION). *see* SOCIAL SCIENCES: COMPREHENSIVE WORKS

ZIRAN BIANZHENGFA TONGXUN/JOURNAL OF DIALECTICS OF NATURE. *see* SOCIAL SCIENCES: COMPREHENSIVE WORKS

ZMOGUS IR ZODIS/PEOPLE AND THE WORD. *see* LINGUISTICS

ZNAK. *see* RELIGIONS AND THEOLOGY

ZUR DEBATTE. *see* RELIGIONS AND THEOLOGY—Roman Catholic

181 DEU ISSN 1862-8303
ZUSAMMENHAENGE; Jahrbuch fuer asiatische Philosophie. Text in German. 2006. a. **Document type:** *Journal, Academic/Scholarly.*
Published by: Verlag Dr. Kovac, Leverkusenstr 13, Hamburg, 22761, Germany. TEL 49-40-3988800, FAX 49-40-39888055, info@verlagdrkovac.de.

057.8 POL ISSN 0044-5584
BX806.P6
ZYCIE I MYSL/LIFE AND THOUGHT. Text in Polish; Summaries in French. 1950. m. bk.rev.; film rev. bibl.; charts; illus. index.
Indexed: CERDIC, HistAb, MLA-IB, RASB.
Published by: Katolickie Stowarzyszenie Civitas Christiana, Oddzial w Poznaniu, Ul Kramarska 2, Poznan, 61765, Poland. TEL 48-61-532279, FAX 48-61-522139, TELEX 0413631. Ed. Alfred Wawrzyniak. Circ: 1,000. **Dist. by:** Ars Polona, Obroncow 25, Warsaw 03933, Poland.

141 NLD ISSN 2210-3813
▼ **365 GODDELOZE DAGEN.** Text in Dutch. 2010. a. EUR 15.95 (effective 2010).
Published by: Veen Magazines, Postbus 256, Diemen, 1110 AG, Netherlands. TEL 31-20-5310900, FAX 31-20-5310950, http://www.veenmagazines.nl.

PHILOSOPHY—Abstracting, Bibliographies, Statistics

ACTUALIDAD BIBLIOGRAFICA DE FILOSOFIA Y TEOLOGIA; selecciones de libros. *see* RELIGIONS AND THEOLOGY—Abstracting, Bibliographies, Statistics

016.1 GBR ISSN 2153-9596
Z7127
➤ **ANALYTIC PHILOSOPHY.** Text in English. 1960. q. GBP 314 in United Kingdom to institutions; EUR 400 in Europe to institutions; USD 682 in the Americas to institutions; USD 794 elsewhere to institutions; GBP 362 combined subscription in United Kingdom to institutions (print & online eds.); EUR 461 combined subscription in Europe to institutions (print & online eds.); USD 785 combined subscription in the Americas to institutions (print & online eds.); USD 914 combined subscription elsewhere to institutions (print & online eds.) (effective 2012). adv. bk.rev. illus. Index. back issues avail.; reprints avail. **Document type:** *Journal, Academic/Scholarly.* **Description:** Covers extensive discussions of major new publications in all areas of analytic philosophy.
Formerly (until Jan. 2011): Philosophical Books (0031-8051)
Related titles: Online - full text ed.: ISSN 2153-960X. GBP 314 in United Kingdom to institutions; EUR 400 in Europe to institutions; USD 682 in the Americas to institutions; USD 794 elsewhere to institutions (effective 2012) (from IngentaConnect).
Indexed: A01, A03, A08, A20, A22, A26, CA, E01, IBRH, IPB, PCI, PhilInd, RASB, SCOPUS, SOPODA, SociolAb, T02.
—BLDSC (6461.640000), IE, Infotrieve, Ingenta. **CCC.**
Published by: Wiley-Blackwell Publishing Ltd. (Subsidiary of: John Wiley & Sons, Inc.), 9600 Garsington Rd, Oxford, OX4 2DQ, United Kingdom. TEL 44-1865-776868, FAX 44-1865-714591, customerservices@blackwellpublishing.com. Ed. David Sosa. Adv. contact Craig Pickett TEL 44-1865-476267.

100 016 VAT ISSN 0084-7836
BIBLIOGRAPHIA INTERNATIONALIS SPIRITUALITATIS. Text in Multiple languages; Summaries in Latin. 1966. a. price varies. **Document type:** *Bibliography.*
Published by: (Teresianum: Pontificia Facolta Teologica - Pontificio Istituto di Spiritualita ITA), Edizioni del Teresianum, Piazza San Pancrazio 5-A, Rome, 00152, Vatican City. TEL 39-06-58540248, FAX 39-06-58540300, http://www.teresianum.org. Ed. Juan Luis Astigarraga. Circ: 650.

016.1 FRA ISSN 0006-1352
Z7127
BIBLIOGRAPHIE DE LA PHILOSOPHIE/BIBLIOGRAPHY OF PHILOSOPHY. Text in English, French, German, Italian, Spanish. 1937. q. USD 111 domestic; USD 113 foreign (effective 2009). adv. bk.rev. abstr.; bibl. index. 120 p./no.; back issues avail.; reprints avail. **Document type:** *Bulletin, Bibliography.* **Description:** Reviews and analyzes recent books in philosophy from all over the world.
Related titles: CD-ROM ed.
—INIST.
Published by: International Institute of Philosophy, 8 rue Jean Calvin, Paris, 75005, France. TEL 33-1-43363911, FAX 33-1-43540347. Ed. Jean Pierre Cotten. Circ: 1,100. **Subscr. to:** Librairie Philosophique J. Vrin, 6 place de la Sorbonne, Paris F-75005, France. contact@vrin.fr, http://www.vrin.fr.

BIOETHICS THESAURUS (ONLINE). *see* MEDICAL SCIENCES—Abstracting, Bibliographies, Statistics

DIETRICH'S INDEX PHILOSOPHICUS. *see* RELIGIONS AND THEOLOGY—Abstracting, Bibliographies, Statistics

016.11185 016.37 RUS ISSN 0132-8255
Z5069
ESTETICHESKOE VOSPITANIE; referativno-bibliograficheskaya informatsiya. Text in Russian. 1989. q. USD 161 foreign (effective 2010). **Document type:** *Bibliography.* **Description:** Includes abstracts of Russian and foreign publications on different problems in aesthetic education.
Related titles: CD-ROM ed.
Published by: (Rossiiskaya Gosudarstvennaya Biblioteka/Russian State Library), Idatel'stvo Rossiiskoi Gosudarstvennoi Biblioteki Pashkov Dom/Pashkov Dom, Russian State Library Publishing House, Vozdizhenka 3/5, Moscow, 101000, Russian Federation. TEL 7-495-6955953, FAX 7-495-6955953, pashkov_dom@rsl.ru, http://www.rsl.ru/pub.asp. Ed. Tamara Lapteva. Circ: 300. **Dist. by:** East View Information Services, 10601 Wayzata Blvd, Minneapolis, MN 55305. TEL 952-252-1201, 800-477-1005, FAX 952-252-1202, info@eastview.com, http://www.eastview.com.

NEW TITLES IN BIOETHICS (ONLINE). *see* MEDICAL SCIENCES—Abstracting, Bibliographies, Statistics

016.1 RUS
NOVAYA LITERATURA PO SOTSIAL'NYM I GUMANITARNYM NAUKAM. FILOSOFIYA I SOTSIOLOGIYA; bibliograficheskii ukazatel'. Text in Russian. 1992. m. USD 399 in United States (effective 2004). **Document type:** *Bibliography.* **Description:** Contains information about Russian and foreign books on social science and philosophy acquired by the INION library.
Formed by the merger of (1947-1992): Novaya Inostrannaya Literatura po Obshchestvennym Naukam. Filosofiya i Sotsiologiya (0134-2851); (1946-1992): Novaya Sovetskaya Literatura po Obshchestvennym Naukam. Filosofskie Nauki (0134-2789)
Indexed: RASB.
Published by: Rossiiskaya Akademiya Nauk, Institut Nauchnoi Informatsii po Obshchestvennym Naukam, Nakhimovskii pr-t 51/21, Moscow, 117997, Russian Federation. TEL 7-095-1288930, FAX 7-095-4202261, info@inion.ru, http://www.inion.ru. Ed. B P Ginsburg. **Dist. by:** East View Information Services, 10601 Wayzata Blvd, Minneapolis, MN 55305. TEL 952-252-1201, 800-477-1005, FAX 952-252-1202, info@eastview.com, http://www.eastview.com.

016.1 USA
THE PHILOSOPHER'S INDEX. Text in English. base vol. plus q. updates. **Document type:** *Database, Abstract/Index.*
Media: Online - full text. **Related titles:** CD-ROM ed.; ◆ Print ed.: The Philosopher's Index (Print). ISSN 0031-7993.
Published by: Philosopher's Information Center, 1616 E Wooster St, Ste 34, Bowling Green, OH 43402-3478. TEL 419-353-8830, FAX 419-353-8920, info@philinfo.org, http://www.philinfo.org.

100 016 USA ISSN 0031-7993
Z7127 CODEN: PHIXA
THE PHILOSOPHER'S INDEX (PRINT); an international index to philosophical periodicals and books. Text in English, French, German, Italian, Portuguese, Spanish. 1967. q. (plus a. cumulative ed.). USD 119 to individuals quarterly ed. (vol.43); USD 398 to institutions quarterly ed. (vol.43); USD 169 to individuals cumulative ed. (vol.42); USD 419 to institutions cumulative ed. (vol.42) (effective 2010). bk.rev. abstr. index, cum.index. 500 p./no. 2 cols./p.; back issues avail. **Document type:** *Journal, Abstract/Index.* **Description:** Subject and author index with abstracts to philosophy articles, books, contributions to anthologies from more than 40 countries.
Related titles: CD-ROM ed.; ◆ Online - full text ed.: The Philosopher's Index.
Indexed: RASB.
—BLDSC (6461.480000), INIST.
Published by: Philosopher's Information Center, 1616 E Wooster St, Ste 34, Bowling Green, OH 43402-3478. TEL 419-353-8830, FAX 419-353-8920, info@philinfo.org. Ed., R&P Richard H Lineback. Circ: 1,000 (paid).

RELIGION AND PHILOSOPHY COLLECTION. *see* RELIGIONS AND THEOLOGY—Abstracting, Bibliographies, Statistics

016.1 BEL ISSN 0034-4567
Z7127
➤ **REPERTOIRE BIBLIOGRAPHIQUE DE LA PHILOSOPHIE/ BIBLIOGRAFISCH REPERTORIUM VAN DE WIJSBEGEERTE/ INTERNATIONAL PHILOSOPHICAL BIBLIOGRAPHY.** Text in French, Dutch, Catalan, English, German, Italian, Latin, Portuguese, Spanish. 1934. s-a. EUR 200; EUR 500 combined subscription (print & online eds.) (effective 2011). bk.rev. illus. index. 800 p./no.; reprints avail. **Document type:** *Journal, Academic/Scholarly.* **Description:** International bibliography on works, articles and reviews of philosophy.

P

Former titles (until 1949): Revue Philosophique de Louvain. Supplement. Repertoire Bibliographique (1370-5113); (until 1946): Revue Neoscolastique de Philosophie. Repertoire Bibliographique (1370-5105)
Related titles: Online - full content ed.: ISSN 1783-1725; ◆ Supplement to: Revue Philosophique de Louvain. ISSN 0035-3841.
Indexed: DIP, IBR, IBZ, RASB.
Published by: (Universite Catholique de Louvain, Institut Superieur de Philosophie), Peeters Publishers, Bondgenotenlaan 153, Leuven, 3000, Belgium. TEL 32-16-235170, FAX 32-16-228500, peeters@peeters-leuven.be, http://www.peeters-leuven.be. Ed. A Van De Putte. Circ: 1,800.

➤ **SOPHIA**; European databases in the humanities. *see* HISTORY—Abstracting, Bibliographies, Statistics

016.215 RUS
SOTSIAL'NYE I GUMANITARNYE NAUKI. OTECHESTVENNAYA I ZARUBEZHNAYA LITERATURA. FILOSOFIYA; referativnyi zhurnal. Text in Russian. 1992. q. USD 165 in United States (effective 2004). **Document type:** *Abstract/Index.* **Description:** Contains abstracts of foreign and Russian books devoted to philosophy acquired lately by INION.
Formed by the merger of (1973-1992): Obshchestvennye Nauki v S.S.S.R. Filosofskie Nauki (0202-2052); (1972-1992): Obshchestvennye Nauki za Rubezhom. Filosofiya; Which superseded in part: Obshchestvennye Nauki za Rubezhom. Filosofiya i Sotsiologiya (0132-7356)
Indexed: RASB.
—East View.
Published by: Rossiiskaya Akademiya Nauk, Institut Nauchnoi Informatsii po Obshchestvennym Naukam, Nakhimovskii pr-t 51/21, Moscow, 117997, Russian Federation. TEL 7-095-1288930, FAX 7-095-4202261, info@inion.ru, http://www.inion.ru. Ed. A I Panchenko. **Dist. by:** East View Information Services, 10601 Wayzata Blvd, Minneapolis, MN 55305. TEL 952-252-1201, 800-477-1005, FAX 952-252-1202, info@eastview.com, http://www.eastview.com.

016.1 CHN ISSN 1009-7287
ZHEXUE WENZHAI KA/PHILOSOPHY ABSTRACTS ON CARDS. Text in Chinese. q. CNY 20 (effective 2004). **Document type:** *Abstract/Index.*
Published by: Zhongguo Renmin Daxue Shubao Ziliao Zhongxin/Renmin University of China, Information Center for Social Sciences, Dongcheng-qu, 3, Zhangzhizhong Lu, Beijing, 100007, China. TEL 86-10-64039458, FAX 86-10-64015080, center@zlzx.org, http://www.zlzx.org/. **Dist. by:** China International Book Trading Corp, 35 Chegongzhuang Xilu, Haidian District, PO Box 399, Beijing 100044, China. TEL 86-10-68412045, FAX 86-10-68412023, cibtc@mail.cibtc.com.cn, http://www.cibtc.com.cn/; China Publications Service, PO Box 49614, Chicago, IL 60649. TEL 312-288-3291, FAX 312-288-8570.

PHOTOGRAPHY

see also MOTION PICTURES

A D A MAGAZINE. (Art, Design, Architecture) *see* ARCHITECTURE

770 ITA ISSN 1120-205X
TR1
A F T; rivista di storia e fotografia. (Archivio Fotografico Toscano) Text in Italian; Abstracts in English. 1985. s-a. bk.rev. **Document type:** *Magazine, Consumer.* **Description:** Covers research about photography, the study of history of photography, and the preservation, restoration, and cataloguing of photographs.
Related titles: Supplement(s): A F T. Quaderni. 1999.
Published by: Archivio Fotografico Toscano, Via Santa Caterina 17, Prato, 59100, Italy. TEL 39-0574-1835149, FAX 39-0574-1835174, info@aft.it, http://www.aft.it. Ed. Sauro Lusini. **Subscr. to:** Opuslibri, Via Della Torretta, 16, Florence, FI 50137, Italy. TEL 39-55-660833.

771 USA
A I E-THE IMAGING EXECUTIVE NEWSLETTER. Text in English, Spanish, Portuguese. 19??. m. free to members (effective 2009). back issues avail. **Document type:** *Newsletter, Trade.*
Formerly: Colorgram
Published by: (Association of Professional Color Imagers), Photo Marketing Association International, 3000 Picture Pl, Jackson, MI 49201. TEL 517-788-8100, 800-762-9287, FAX 517-788-8371, gpageau@pmai.org, http://www.pmai.org. Circ: 1,700.

770 GBR
A O P AWARDS. Text in English. 1984. a. GBP 10 per issue to non-members; GBP 8 per issue to members (effective 2009). adv. back issues avail. **Document type:** *Journal, Trade.* **Description:** Shows award winning photographs from the members of the association.
Formerly: A F A E P Awards
Published by: Association of Photographers, 81 Leonard St, London, EC2A 4QS, United Kingdom. TEL 44-20-77396669, FAX 44-20-77398707, general@aophoto.co.uk, http://www.the-aop.org/.

770 USA
A P N Y MAGAZINE. Text in English. 1989. 4/yr. free. adv. bk.rev. **Document type:** *Newsletter.* **Description:** Addresses the business and aesthetic concerns of the professional photographer.
Former titles: A P N Y Newsletter; A P A Magazine (1046-4522)
Published by: Advertising Photographers of New York, 27 W 20th St, Rm 601, New York, NY 10011. TEL 212-807-0399, FAX 212-727-8120. Circ: 2,000 (controlled).

AARETS PRESSEFOTO. *see* HISTORY—History Of Europe

ACOUSTICAL IMAGING. *see* PHYSICS—Sound

770 ITA ISSN 1724-9821
ACTA PHOTOGRAPHICA. Text in Italian. 2004. 3/yr. **Document type:** *Magazine, Consumer.*
Published by: Universita degli Studi di Bologna, Bononia University Press, Via Zamboni 33, Bologna, 40126, Italy. http://www.buponline.com.

AD! DICT. *see* ART

770 006.6 FRA ISSN 2103-6780
ADVANCED CREATION. Text in French. 2008. m. EUR 79; EUR 59 to students; EUR 7.90 newsstand/cover (effective 2011). adv. **Document type:** *Magazine, Consumer.*
Formerly (until 2009): Advanced Photoshop (1966-7671)
Published by: Oracom, 168bis-170 Rue Raymond Losserand, Paris, 75014, France. TEL 33-1-44789300, FAX 33-1-44789765, http://www.oracom.fr.

ADVANCED IMAGING; your path to the electronic imaging industry's most important buyers of core technology. *see* COMMUNICATIONS—Computer Applications

770 GBR ISSN 2045-3892
ADVANCED PHOTOGRAPHER. Text in English. 19??. m. GBP 19.95 domestic; GBP 65 foreign (effective 2011). **Document type:** *Magazine, Trade.*
Published by: Bright Publishing, Bright House, 82 High St, Sawston, Cambs CB22 3HJ, United Kingdom. TEL 44-1223-499450, FAX 44-1223-839953, andybrogden@bright-publishing.com, http://www.bright-publishing.com/.

778.53 USA ISSN 0300-7472
TR640
AFTERIMAGE; the journal of media arts and cultural criticism. Text in English. 1972. bi-m. USD 33 domestic to individuals; USD 90 foreign to individuals; USD 100 domestic to institutions; USD 165 foreign to institutions (effective 2009). bk.rev.; film rev.; music rev.; tel.rev.; video rev.; Website rev. illus. Index. back issues avail.; reprints avail. **Document type:** *Journal, Academic/Scholarly.* **Description:** Presents independent critical commentary on issues in media arts, including scholarly research, in-depth and bite-size reviews, and investigative journalism.
Related titles: Microform ed.: (from PQC); Online - full text ed.
Indexed: A01, A02, A03, A06, A07, A08, A09, A10, A15, A22, A26, A27, A30, A31, AA, ABIn, ABM, AmHI, ArtInd, B04, B07, B14, B24, BRD, BRI, CA, CBRI, DIP, E08, F01, F02, G06, G07, G08, H07, I05, I07, IBR, IBZ, IITV, M02, MLA-IB, MRD, P02, P10, P16, P48, P51, P53, P54, PQC, S09, S23, SCOPUS, T02, V02, V03, V04, W03, W05.
—BLDSC (0735.632000), IE, Infotrieve, Ingenta.
Published by: Visual Studies Workshop, 31 Prince St, Rochester, NY 14607. TEL 585-442-8676, FAX 585-442-1992, info@vsw.org. Ed. Karen vanMeenen.

771 GBR ISSN 1475-116X
AG; the international journal of photographic art & practice. Variant title: Ag+ Photographic. Text in English. 1991. q. GBP 37.50 domestic; GBP 43.50 in Europe; GBP 53.50 elsewhere (effective 2009). back issues avail. **Document type:** *Journal, Trade.* **Description:** Focuses on black and white darkroom techniques and fine art printing.
Former titles (until 1999): Ag+ Photographic (1352-3023); (until 1991): Silverprint (0961-9976)
—BLDSC (0735.723000). **CCC.**
Published by: Picture-Box Media Ltd., Dulwich Lodge, 62 Pemberton Rd, East Molesey, Surrey KT8 9LH, United Kingdom. TEL 44-20-89411088, FAX 44-20-89410249, info@ag-photo.co.uk. Ed., Pub. Chris Dickie.

770 ESP
AGFOVAL. Text in Spanish. 1958. q. EUR 6 per issue (effective 2005). back issues avail. **Document type:** *Bulletin.*
Published by: Agrupacion Fotografica Valenciana, Ave Baron de Cancer 25 2o y 4o, Valencia, 46001, Spain. TEL 34-96-3512520, agfoval@agfoval.com, http://www.agfoval.com/. Ed. J Collado Martinez. Adv. contact J. Collado Martinez. Circ: 1,000.

770 392.5 NLD
HET ALBUM. Text in Dutch. a.
Related titles: ◆ Supplement to: Bruid & Bruidegom. ISSN 0926-8812.
Published by: Christiaan Uitgevers, Uraniumweg 17, Amersfoort, 3812 RJ, Netherlands. TEL 31-33-7503500, FAX 31-33-7503501.

ALBUM, LETRAS Y ARTES. *see* ART

ALBUM OF VISUALIZATION. *see* PHYSICS—Optics

770 ITA ISSN 0393-9758
ALMANACCO DI FOTOGRAFARE. Text in Italian. 1968. q. EUR 20 domestic (effective 2008). adv. **Document type:** *Catalog, Consumer.*
Published by: Cesco Ciapanna Editore S.r.l., Via Lipari 8, Rome, 00141, Italy. TEL 39-06-87183441, FAX 39-06-87183995. Circ: 75,000.

770 MEX ISSN 1405-7786
ALQUIMIA. Text in Spanish. 1997. 3/yr. MXN 144 domestic; USD 44 in North America and Central America; USD 48 in South America and Europe; USD 51 elsewhere (effective 2003). adv. bk.rev. index. 46 p./no.; back issues avail. **Document type:** *Magazine, Academic/Scholarly.*
Indexed: C01.
Published by: Instituto Nacional de Antropologia e Historia (I N A H), Cordoba 45, Mexico City 7, DF 06700, Mexico. TEL 52-50-619100, administracion.dg@inah.gob.mx, http://www.inah.gob.mx. Adv. contacts Amanda Rosales Bada, Rosa Laura Hernandez Hernandez.

770 DNK ISSN 0908-3316
ALT OM FOTO & VIDEO. Text in Danish. 1993. 8/yr. illus. **Document type:** *Magazine, Consumer.*
Formed by the merger of (1972-1993): Alt om Foto (0902-2880); Which was formerly (until 1986): Fotokino (0105-8193); Which incorporated (1977-1980): Proffoto (0105-8150); (1966-1993): Foto, Film & Video (0908-052X); Which was formerly (until 1983): Foto og Smalfilm (0015-8747)
Published by: Forlaget Fotoinformation ApS, Bredgade 111, Broenderslev, 9700, Denmark. TEL 45-98-429060, FAX 45-98-484690, mail@fotoinfo.dk. Ed. E Steen Soerensen. Adv. contact E. Steen Soerensen.

770 USA ISSN 1930-5001
ALT PICK MAGAZINE. Text in English. 2003. s-a. **Document type:** *Magazine, Consumer.*
Published by: Storm Editions, Inc., 1123 Broadway, Ste 716, New York, NY 10010. TEL 212-675-4176, FAX 212-675-4403, http://altpick.com/index.php.

770 GBR ISSN 0002-6840
TR1
AMATEUR PHOTOGRAPHER. Text in English. 1884. w. GBP 89.70 domestic; EUR 172.89 in Europe eurozone; GBP 111.46 in Europe non-eurozone; USD 189.57 in United States; GBP 170.65 in Canada; GBP 162.36 elsewhere (effective 2009). adv. bk.rev. illus. s-a index. **Document type:** *Magazine, Consumer.* **Description:** Covers photo technique; includes equipment reviews, news and features.
Related titles: Microform ed.: (from PQC).
Indexed: ChemAb.
—CCC.
Published by: I P C Country & Leisure Media Ltd. (Subsidiary of: I P C Media Ltd.), The Blue Fin Bldg, 110 Southwark St, London, SE1 0SU, United Kingdom. TEL 44-20-31485000. Ed. Damien Demolder TEL 44-20-31484133. Adv. contact Dave Stone TEL 44-20-31482516. page GBP 2,633. Circ: 24,597 (paid). **Dist. by:** MarketForce UK Ltd, The Blue Fin Bldg, 3rd Fl, 110 Southwark St, London SE1 0SU, United Kingdom. TEL 44-20-31483300, FAX 44-20-31488105, salesinnovation@marketforce.co.uk, http://www.marketforce.co.uk/.

AMERICAN CINEMATOGRAPHER; the international journal of film & digital production techniques. *see* MOTION PICTURES

770 USA ISSN 1046-8986
TR1
AMERICAN PHOTO. Variant title: Photo. Text in English. 1978. bi-m. USD 14 domestic; USD 22 foreign (effective 2008). adv. bk.rev. illus. back issues avail.; reprints avail. **Document type:** *Magazine, Consumer.* **Description:** Explores the creative aspects of photography and the persons behind the work for professional, advanced, and newly aspiring photographers. Reviews exhibits and books; examines the working methods of the professionals.
Formerly (until 1990): American Photographer (0161-6854)
Related titles: Online - full text ed.: USD 10 (effective 2008).
Indexed: A01, A02, A03, A07, A08, A09, A10, A22, A25, A26, A27, A30, A31, AA, ASIP, ArtInd, B04, C05, C12, CPerI, E08, G05, G06, G07, G08, G09, I05, M01, M02, MASUSE, MagInd, P02, P10, P16, P48, P53, P54, PCI, PMI, PMR, PQC, S08, S09, V03, V04.
—BLDSC (0850.597000), IE, Ingenta.
Published by: Hachette Filipacchi Media U.S., Inc. (Subsidiary of: Hachette Filipacchi Medias S.A.), 1633 Broadway, New York, NY 10019. TEL 212-767-6000, FAX 212-767-5600, flyedit@hfmus.com, http://www.hfmus.com. Eds. Jack Howard, David Schonauer. Adv. contact Anthony M Ruotolo TEL 212-767-6397. B&W page USD 25,700, color page USD 41,000; trim 9 x 10.88. Circ: 199,159 (paid).

770 USA ISSN 0898-1124
TR23
AMERICAN PHOTOGRAPHY (NEW YORK, N.Y. 1985). Text in English. 1985. a. USD 65 (effective 2005).
Published by: American Photography, 1140 Broadway, 4th Flr, New York, NY 10001. TEL 917-408-9944, FAX 917-591-7770, info@ai-ap.com, http://www.ai-ap.com.

770 USA ISSN 0744-5784
AMERICAN SOCIETY OF MEDIA PHOTOGRAPHERS. BULLETIN. Text in English. 1944. 5/yr. USD 12 (effective 2008). adv. bk.rev. **Document type:** *Bulletin, Trade.* **Description:** Provides information pertaining to the business of professional photography. Published for the members of ASMP, a trade association.
Formerly: American Society of Magazine Photographers. Bulletin (0361-9168)
Published by: American Society of Media Photographers, 150 N 2nd St, Philadelphia, PA 19106-1912. TEL 215-451-2767, FAX 215-451-0880, info@asmp.org. Pub. Lauren Wendle. Adv. contacts Jules Wartell, Richard Wartell. Circ: 7,000 (paid).

ANHUI HUABAO/ANHUI PICTORIAL. *see* GENERAL INTEREST PERIODICALS—China

770 USA ISSN 0003-6420
TR1
APERTURE. Text in English. 1952. q. USD 40 domestic; USD 65 foreign; USD 18.50 newsstand/cover (effective 2008). adv. bk.rev. bibl.; illus. cum.index: vols.1-6 in 1958. reprints avail. **Document type:** *Magazine, Consumer.* **Description:** Devoted to photography as art, contains illustrated profiles of photographers or thematic material.
Related titles: Microfilm ed.: (from PQC); Online - full text ed.
Indexed: A06, A07, A20, A22, A25, A26, A27, A30, A31, AA, ABM, ABS&EES, ASCA, AmHI, ArtHuCI, ArtInd, B04, B24, BRD, CA, CurCont, E08, G08, H07, H08, HAb, HumInd, I05, I14, P02, P10, P13, P48, P53, P54, PQC, S08, S09, SCOPUS, T02, W03, W05, W07.
—BLDSC (1567.880000), IE, Infotrieve, Ingenta.
Published by: Aperture Foundation, Inc., 547 W 27th St, 4th Fl, New York, NY 10001. TEL 212-505-5555, 866-457-4603, FAX 212-475-8790, info@aperture.org, magazine@apeture.org. Ed. Melissa Harris. adv.: B&W page USD 6,300, color page USD 9,100; trim 9.5625 x 10.375. Circ: 664 (controlled); 32,186 (paid). **Subscr. to:** Aperture Customer Service, P O Box 3000, Denville, NJ 07834. TEL 973- 627-5162, 866-457-4603, FAX 212-475-8790.

770 USA
APOGEE PHOTO; the internet's photography magazine. Text in English. 1996. m. free (effective 2010). adv. **Document type:** *Magazine, Consumer.* **Description:** Features photography profiles, photo book reviews as well as essential articles on photography for beginners and young people.
Media: Online - full text.
Published by: Apogee Photo, Inc., 11749 Zenobia Loop, Westminster, CO 80031. TEL 904-619-2010. Ed. Susan Harris. Pub. Michael Fulks. Adv. contact Marla Meier.

779 USA ISSN 0735-5572
TR640
ARCHIVE (TUCSON). Text in English. 1976. a. illus. reprints avail. **Document type:** *Monographic series, Academic/Scholarly.* **Description:** Presents materials from the collection of photographs, negatives and manuscripts in the center's archives.
Formerly (until 1981): Center for Creative Photography. Series
Indexed: A07, A30, A31, AA, ArtInd, B04, B24, CA, T02.
Published by: University of Arizona, Center for Creative Photography, 1030 N Olive Rd, PO Box 210103, Tucson, AZ 85721. TEL 520-621-7968, oncenter@ccp.library.arizona.edu.

770 ESP ISSN 1138-0470
ARCHIVOS DE LA FOTOGRAFIA. Text in Spanish; Summaries in Basque, English. 1995. s-a. **Document type:** *Magazine, Consumer.*
Published by: Photomuseum, San Ignacio 11, Zarautz, 20800, Spain. TEL 34-943-130906, FAX 34-943-831823.

ART CALENDAR; the business magazine for visual artists. *see* ART

ART NEW ZEALAND. *see* ART

770 USA ISSN 2158-0464
▼ **ART SI MAGAZINE.** Text in English. 2009. m. USD 79.99 (effective 2010). adv. back issues avail. **Document type:** *Magazine, Trade.* **Description:** Provides information about artistic nude photography.
Related titles: Online - full text ed.: USD 11.99 (effective 2010).

Published by: Robert W. K. Clark, Ed. & Pub., PO Box 45313, Rio Rancho, NM 87174. Ed., Pub. Robert W K Clark.

770 ESP ISSN 0514-9193
ARTE FOTOGRAFICO. Text in Spanish. 1952. m. adv. bk.rev. illus. back issues avail.
Published by: Cediarte S.A., Santo Angel, 76, Madrid, 28043, Spain. TEL 34-1-3886533, FAX 34-1-7597584. Ed. Antonio Cabello. Circ: 25,000.

ARTIBUS ET HISTORIAE; international journal for visual arts. *see* ART

ARTISTIC TRAVELER; architecture & travel with art & photography. *see* ARCHITECTURE

770 JPN ISSN 0044-9148
ASAHI CAMERA. Text in Japanese. 1926. m. USD 158.50. adv. bk.rev.
Indexed: JTA, RASB.
Published by: Asahi Shimbun Publishing Co., 5-3-2 Tsukiji, Chuo-ku, Tokyo, 104-8011, Japan. Ed. Masami Fujisawa. Circ: 200,000. **Dist. by:** Japan Publications Trading Co., Ltd., Book Export II Dept, PO Box 5030, Tokyo International, Tokyo 101-3191, Japan. TEL 81-3-32923753, FAX 81-3-32920410, infoserials@jptco.co.jp, http://www.jptco.co.jp.

770 BGR ISSN 1310-8611
ATELIE 16. Text in Bulgarian. 1996. s-a. BGL 3.20 newsstand/cover domestic (effective 2002). **Document type:** *Magazine, Consumer.* **Description:** Presents contemporary achievements in some spheres of technology and creativity which are related to photography - layout, computer processing of photographic images, design, Internet, etc. The journal includes creative as well as technical aspects of photography.
Published by: A 16 Konstantin Banderov ST - Plovdiv, 17 Ekzarh Iossif St., Plovdiv, 4000, Bulgaria. TEL 359-32-622516, atelie16@mbox.digsys.bg, http://www.eunet.bg/media. Ed. Konstantin Banderov.

ATLANTIC PACIFIC PRESS; creative writing, art, photography. *see* LITERATURE

AUDIO VIDEO FOTO BILD. *see* COMMUNICATIONS—Video

AUDIO VIDEO FOTO HOY. *see* COMMUNICATIONS—Video

770 AUS ISSN 0004-9964
AUSTRALIAN PHOTOGRAPHY. Text in English. 1950. m. AUD 77 domestic; AUD 90 in New Zealand; AUD 105 in Asia; AUD 140 elsewhere; AUD 6.75 newsstand/cover (effective 2008). adv. bk.rev. charts; illus.; tr.lit. **Document type:** *Magazine, Consumer.* **Description:** Provides relevant advices to photography enthusiasts from beginners through to experienced amateurs; offers forums to display their images in print.
Formerly: Australian Popular Photography
Related titles: Microfiche ed.
Indexed: A30, A31, Pinpoint.
Published by: Yaffa Publishing Group Pty Ltd., 17-21 Bellevue St, Surry Hills, NSW 2010, Australia. TEL 61-2-92812333, FAX 61-2-92812750, info@yaffa.com.au. Ed. Robert Keeley TEL 61-3-96908199. Adv. contact Kerri McNamara TEL 61-2-92138261. B&W page AUD 2,310, color page AUD 3,070; trim 220 x 297. Circ: 8,019. **Subscr. to:** GPO Box 606, Sydney, NSW 2001, Australia.

778.1 USA ISSN 2160-3359
B & W + COLOR. (Black and White) Text in English. 1999. m. adv. back issues avail. **Document type:** *Magazine, Consumer.* **Description:** Contains informative articles for collectors of fine photography.
Formerly (until 2011): B & W Magazine (1522-4805)
Published by: B & W Magazine, PO Box 1529, Ross, CA 94957. FAX 415-382-0587, rosspub@pacbell.net, http://www.bandwmag.com. Adv. contact Ginny Greenfield.

770 GBR
B P I. (British Photographic Industry) Text in English. 19??. m. 36 p./no.; **Document type:** *Magazine, Trade.*
Formerly (until 2007): B P I News (1364-7784); Which incorporated: Panorama
—CCC.
Published by: Archant Specialist Ltd. (Subsidiary of: Archant Group), Archant House, Oriel Rd, Cheltenham, GL50 1BB, United Kingdom. TEL 44-1242-211080, FAX 44-1242-216094, http://www.archant.co.uk/. Circ: 4,300 (controlled).

770 AUT ISSN 0005-8947
DAS BERGMANN-ECHO. Text in German. 1958. bi-m. free.
Published by: (Bergmann-Kameradschaft 137. Inf. Div.), Sepp Sattelberger Editor, Postanschrift, Petzenkirchen, N 3252, Austria.

770 AUS ISSN 1444-9668
BETTER DIGITAL. Text in English. 2001. q. AUD 55; AUD 14.95 newsstand/cover (effective 2008). back issues avail. **Document type:** *Magazine, Consumer.* **Description:** Provides articles on extracting the best from the continuously changing and often confusing technology.
Related titles: Online - full text ed.
Published by: Better Digital Pty, Ltd., PO Box 123, Bondi Junction, NSW 1355, Australia. TEL 61-2-93892465, editorial@betterdigitalonline.com. Ed. Robin Nichols.

770 IND
BETTER PHOTOGRAPHY. Text in English. 19??. m. INR 999 domestic; INR 3,750 foreign; INR 150 per issue (effective 2011). **Document type:** *Magazine, Consumer.* **Description:** Contains articles on photography related techniques, equipment reviews, tests of equipment, photo features, interviews with amateur and professional photographers, as well as the latest news in the industry.
Published by: Infomedia 18 Ltd., A Wing, Ruby House, J K Sawant Marg, Dadar (West), Mumbai, 400 028, India. TEL 91-22-30245000, FAX 91-22-30034499, ho@infomedia18.in. Adv. contact Ruby Roy TEL 91-22-30034582.

770.105 AUS ISSN 1322-7785
BETTER PHOTOGRAPHY. Text in English. 1995. q. AUD 43.80 domestic; AUD 60 foreign (effective 2008). **Document type:** *Magazine, Consumer.* **Description:** Provides articles related to photography that include an insight behind photographers thinking, equipment and technique used, photograph printing and computer manipulation.
Address: PO Box 351, Collaroy Beach, NSW 2097, Australia. TEL 61-2-99716857, FAX 61-2-99716641, eastway@betterphotography.com, http://www.petereastway.com. Ed., Pub. Peter Eastway.

770 USA ISSN 1553-0116
BIG. Text in English. 10/yr. USD 110; USD 15 newsstand/cover domestic; USD 20 newsstand/cover in Canada (effective 2001). **Document type:** *Magazine, Consumer.*
Published by: Big Magazine, Inc., 20 Harrison St, New York, NY 10013-2810. Ed. Michael Fordham. Pub. Marcelo Junemann.

▼ **BILD UND BILD.** *see* ART

770 917.6 USA
BILL STRONG'S MISSISSIPPI PHOTOGRAPHY TRAVEL CULTURE. Text in English. 1995. m. **Description:** Mississippi photographic tour for anyone interested.
Media: Online - full text.
Address: 209 Wildwood Trace, Hattiesburg, MS 39402-2355. Ed. Bill Strong.

770 AUS ISSN 1038-9423
BLACK+WHITE. Variant title: Black & White. Text in English. 1992. bi-m. AUD 20 per issue domestic; AUD 25 per issue in New Zealand; AUD 35 per issue elsewhere; AUD 12.95 newsstand/cover (effective 2008). adv. back issues avail. **Document type:** *Magazine, Consumer.* **Description:** Reflects and anticipates international trends in art, fashion, thought and technology.
Related titles: Online - full text ed.
Published by: Studio Magazines Pty. Ltd., Level 3, 101-111 William St, Sydney, NSW 2011, Australia. TEL 61-2-93601422, FAX 61-2-93609742. Adv. contact Bruce Forster. page AUD 5,800; trim 240 x 325.

770 USA
BLACK & WHITE MAGAZINE; for collectors of fine photography. Abbreviated title: B & W. Text in English. 1999. q. USD 18.80; USD 5.95, CAD 7.95 newsstand/cover (effective 1999). adv. **Document type:** *Magazine, Consumer.* **Description:** Provides a forum for collectors of fine photography.
Published by: Picturama Publications, 930 Bel Marin Keys Blvd, Novato, CA 94949. TEL 415-382-8271. Ed., Pub. Henry Rasmussen. **Subscr. to:** PO Box 700, Arroyo Grande, CA 93420. **Dist. by:** Curtis Circulation Co., 730 River Rd, New Milford, NJ 07646. TEL 201-634-7400, FAX 201-634-7497.

770 USA
BLACK & WHITE WORLD; a celebration of photography. Text in English. 199?. bi-m. illus. **Description:** Features include a black-and-white photo competition, photo of the month, top ten photo Web site listings, discussion forums, and how-to information for beginners and advanced photographers.
Media: Online - full text.
Published by: Resnick Associates Ed., Pub. Mason Resnick.

BLACK CAMERA; an international film journal. *see* MOTION PICTURES

770 700 CAN ISSN 0826-3922
TR654
➤ **BLACKFLASH**; Canadian journal of photo-based and electronic arts production. Text in English. 1983. 3/yr. CAD 18 domestic to individuals; USD 20 foreign to individuals; CAD 26 domestic to institutions; USD 28 foreign to institutions; CAD 6 newsstand/cover (effective 2005). adv. bk.rev.; Website rev.; film rev.; video rev. illus. 48 p./no. 1 cols./p.; back issues avail.; reprints avail. **Document type:** *Magazine, Academic/Scholarly.* **Description:** Features the critical issues surrounding the photographic image. Discusses Canadian and international photography in a critical context.
Formerly (until 1984): Photographers Gallery (0823-2326)
Indexed: A07, A26, A30, A31, AA, ABM, ArtInd, B04, CPerI, E08, G08, I05, S09, SCOPUS, W03, W05.
Published by: Buffalo Berry Press, 12 23rd St E, 2nd Fl, Saskatoon, SK S7K 0H5, Canada. TEL 306-374-5115, FAX 306-665-6568, e. info@blackflash.ca. Ed. Carrie Horachek. R&P, Adv. contact Theo Sims. page CAD 475. Circ: 1,000.

770 USA ISSN 1551-0956
BLIND SPOT. Text in English. 1993. 3/yr. USD 45 domestic; USD 60 in Canada & Mexico; USD 80 elsewhere (effective 2010). adv. illus. back issues avail.; reprints avail. **Document type:** *Magazine, Consumer.* **Description:** Features significant articles on fine art.
Formerly (until 1999): Blind Spot Photography (1068-1647)
Related titles: Online - full text ed.
Indexed: A07, A30, A31, AA, ArtInd, B04.
—BLDSC (2111.318500).
Published by: Blind Spot & Photo-Based Art, Inc, 30 Campus Rd, Annandale-on-Hudson, NY 12504. TEL 845-752-4545, FAX 845-752-4542. Ed., Pub. Dana Faconti. Adv. contact Helena Power.

770 IRL ISSN 2009-339X
▼ **BLOW.** Text in English. 2010. q. **Document type:** *Magazine, Trade.*
Address: 144 Upper Leeson St, Dublin, Ireland. TEL 353-1-6070222, FAX 353-1-6675229, leeson@blow.ie, http://www.blow.ie.

770 910.4 USA
BLUE BOOK: THE DIRECTORY OF GEOGRAPHIC, TRAVEL & DESTINATION STOCK PHOTOGRAPHY. Text in English. biennial. USD 15. **Document type:** *Directory.* **Description:** Lists photo sources for editorial photo buyers. Features descriptions of stock files with location and subject indexes.
Published by: A G Editions, Inc., 41 Union Sq W Ste 523, New York, NY 10003-3208. TEL 212-929-0959, FAX 212-924-4796.

770 USA ISSN 1932-7013
TR820.5
BLUEEYES MAGAZINE. Text in English. 2003. bi-m. **Document type:** *Magazine, Consumer.*
Media: Online - full text.
Published by: John Loomis http://www.blueeyesmagazine.com. Ed. John Loomis.

770 DEU ISSN 0932-7231
BRENNPUNKT; Magazin fuer Photographie. Text in German. 1984. q. EUR 13; EUR 3.80 newsstand/cover (effective 2009). **Document type:** *Magazine, Consumer.*
Published by: Edition Buehrer, Odenwaldstr 26, Berlin, 12161, Germany. TEL 49-30-8533527, http://www.edition-buehrer.de. Ed. Dietmar Buehrer.

770 778.53 GBR ISSN 1477-1020
BRITISH CINEMATOGRAPHER. Text in English. 2002. bi-m. GBP 32 domestic; EUR 58 in Europe; USD 69 elsewhere (effective 2009). adv. bk.rev. **Document type:** *Magazine, Trade.* **Description:** Covers all issues on international cinematography.
Incorporates (1982-2001): Eyepiece (0950-737X); Which was formerly (until 1982): Eyepiece / G B C T News
Related titles: Online - full text ed.
Indexed: F01, F02.
Published by: (British Society of Cinematographers), Guild of British Camera Technicians, Metropolitan Ctr, Bristol Rd, Greenford, Mddx UB6 8GD, United Kingdom. TEL 44-20-88131999, FAX 44-20-88132111, admin@gbct.org, http://www.gbct.org. Ed. Ron Prince. Pubs. Alan Lowne TEL 44-1753-650101, Stuart Walters TEL 44-121-6082300. adv.: page GBP 2,045; bleed 250 x 352.

770 790 GBR ISSN 0007-1196
TR1 CODEN: BRJFAM
BRITISH JOURNAL OF PHOTOGRAPHY; the professional's weekly. Text in English. 1854. w. GBP 90 domestic; GBP 160 in Europe; GBP 200 elsewhere (effective 2009). adv. bk.rev. charts; illus.; mkt.; stat.; tr.lit. index. back issues avail. **Document type:** *Magazine, Consumer.* **Description:** Keeps the professional - and everyone with a serious interest in photography - fully up-to-date with progress in the tools and materials of their craft.
Incorporates (1996-1998): British Journal of Digital Imaging (1364-8373)
Related titles: Microfilm ed.: GBP 160 per vol. 2002 issues (effective 2003) (from PQC, WMP); Online - full text ed.; ◆ Supplement(s): British Journal of Photography. Big Book. ISSN 1465-2951.
Indexed: A06, A07, A22, A27, A30, A31, AA, ABM, ArtInd, B04, B24, BrTechI, ChemAb, E11, Inspec, P10, P26, P48, P53, P54, PQC, PhotoAb, RASB, T04.
—BLDSC (2317.000000), AskIEEE, CASDDS, IE, Infotrieve, Ingenta, INIST, Linda Hall. **CCC.**
Published by: Incisive Photographic Ltd. (Subsidiary of: Incisive Media Plc.), 32-34 Broadwick St, London, United Kingdom. Ed. Simon Bainbridge TEL 44-20-73169416. Pub. Foutella Michael TEL 44-20-73169037. Circ: 8,000 (paid).

770 GBR ISSN 1465-2951
BRITISH JOURNAL OF PHOTOGRAPHY. BIG BOOK. Text in English. 1998. a. **Document type:** *Directory, Trade.* **Description:** Directory of and for the photographic and creative industry, including hire studios, picture libraries, professional labs, and galleries.
Formed by the merger of (1992-1998): British Journal of Photography. Information Directory (0969-6326); (1990-1998): British Journal of Photography. Photographic Services; Which was formerly: British Journal of Photography. Services Guide (0969-3580)
Related titles: ◆ Supplement to: British Journal of Photography. ISSN 0007-1196.
—CCC.
Published by: Incisive Photographic Ltd. (Subsidiary of: Incisive Media Plc.), 32-34 Broadwick St, London, United Kingdom. Ed. Simon Bainbridge TEL 44-20-73169416. Pub. Foutella Michael TEL 44-20-73169037.

771 658.8 GBR ISSN 1474-600X
BUSINESS RATIO REPORT. THE PHOTOGRAPHIC INDUSTRY. Text in English. 1980. a., latest no.29, 2008, Jul. GBP 365 per issue (effective 2010). charts; stat. back issues avail. **Document type:** *Report, Trade.* **Description:** Covers companies active in the photographic industry.
Former titles (until 2001): Business Ratio. The Photographic Industry (1467-4483); (until 1999): Business Ratio Plus: The Photographic Industry (1356-546X); (until 1994): Business Ratio Report: Photographic Equipment and Processing (0954-6731); (until 1988): Business Ratio Report: The Photographic Industry (0261-9369)
Published by: Key Note Ltd. (Subsidiary of: Bonnier Business Information), Harlequin House, 5th Fl, 7 High St, Teddington, Richmond upon Thames, TW11 8EE, United Kingdom. TEL 44-845-5040452, FAX 44-845-5040453, sales@keynote.co.uk.

C; international contemporary art. *see* ART

C-ING MAGAZINE. *see* JOURNALISM

770 GBR ISSN 1748-3565
TR640
C INTERNATIONAL PHOTO MAGAZINE (ENGLISH-CHINESE EDITION). Variant title: C Photo Magazine. Text in English, Chinese. 2005. s-a. GBP 92, EUR 101, USD 140; GBP 53, EUR 57, USD 75 per issue (effective 2009). **Document type:** *Magazine, Consumer.* **Description:** Explore the changes and trends that have shaped the art of photography over the course of its history.
Related titles: ◆ Spanish ed.: C International Photo Magazine (Spanish-Japanese Edition). ISSN 1748-8869.
Published by: Ivory Press Ltd., Riverside One, 22 Hestor Rd, London, SW11 4AN, United Kingdom. TEL 44-20-78010933, FAX 44-20-78019448, enquiries@ivorypress.com.

770 GBR ISSN 1748-8869
C INTERNATIONAL PHOTO MAGAZINE (SPANISH-JAPANESE EDITION). Variant title: C Photo Magazine. Text in Spanish, Japanese. 2005. s-a. GBP 75 (effective 2006). **Document type:** *Magazine, Consumer.* **Description:** Explores the changes and trends that have shaped the art of photography over the course of its history as well as presenting an eclectic overview of contemporary trends. It will also serve as a platform for living artists, with no aesthetic or cultural distinctions.
Related titles: ◆ English ed.: C International Photo Magazine (English-Chinese Edition). ISSN 1748-3565.
Published by: Ivory Press Ltd., Riverside One, 22 Hestor Rd, London, SW11 4AN, United Kingdom. TEL 44-20-78019352, FAX 44-20-78019448, enquiries@ivorypress.com.

770 CAN ISSN 1196-9261
C V PHOTO. Text in English, French. 1985. q. CAD 26 domestic to individuals; USD 33 foreign to individuals; CAD 33 domestic to institutions; CAD 7 newsstand/cover (effective 2000). adv. bk.rev. back issues avail. **Document type:** *Journal, Consumer.* **Description:** Includes theoretical texts on contemporary photography and artists portfolios.
Formerly (until 1992): Ciel Variable (0831-3091)
Related titles: Online - full text ed.
Indexed: SCOPUS.
Published by: Productions Ciel Variable, 4060 boulevard Saint Laurent, Local 301, Montreal, PQ H2W 1Y9, Canada. TEL 514-289-0508, FAX 514-284-6775, vpopuli@cam.org, http://www.cam.org/~vpopuli. Ed. Franck Michel. Pub. Pierre Blache. Adv. contact Marie Josee Jean. Circ: 1,500. **Dist. by:** C M P A, 130 Spadina Ave, Ste 202, Toronto, ON M5V 2L4, Canada. TEL 416-504-0348, FAX 416-504-0437.

P

770 AUS ISSN 1039-7949
CAMERA; film & digital for photorgraphers. Key Title: Australian Camera, Photo, Video, Digital. Text in English. 1979. bi-m. AUD 31.20 in Australia & New Zealand; AUD 58 elsewhere; AUD 6.50 newsstand/cover (effective 2008). adv. bk.rev. back issues avail. **Document type:** *Magazine, Consumer.* **Description:** Popular magazine for photography enthusiasts. Includes techniques, new products, equipment tests, buyers guide.
Former titles (until 1993): Australian Camera and Shooting Video (1320-6672); (until 1991): Australian Camera Craft and Shooting Video (1035-641X); (until 1987): Australian Camera Craft (0158-2658)
—CCC.
Published by: Wolseley Media Pty Ltd., Level 5, 55 Chandos St, PO Box 5555, St. Leonards, NSW 2065, Australia. TEL 61-2-99016100, FAX 61-2-99016198, contactsubs@wolseleymedia.com.au. Circ: 11,500.

770 USA ISSN 0271-1583
TR640
CAMERA ARTS. Text in English. 1980. bi-m. USD 25 (effective 2004). adv. **Document type:** *Magazine, Consumer.*
Indexed: PMI.
—CCC.
Published by: Steve Simmons Photography, PO Box 2328, Corrales, NM 87048. TEL 505-899-8054. Ed. Dave Howard. Pub. Steve Simmons. adv.: B&W page USD 1,400, color page USD 1,900; bleed 8.5 x 10.875. Circ: 125,000.

770 AUT ISSN 1015-1915
TR1
CAMERA AUSTRIA; international. Text in English, German. 1980. q. EUR 45; EUR 140 newsstand/cover (effective 2005). bk.rev. back issues avail. **Document type:** *Magazine, Consumer.* **Description:** Presents artistic and theoretical work in and about photography.
Related titles: Online - full text ed.
Indexed: ABM, DIP, IBR, IBZ, SCOPUS.
—BLDSC (3016.061890).
Published by: Edition Camera Austria, Lendkai 1, Graz, 8020, Austria. TEL 43-316-8155500, FAX 43-316-8155509, office@camera-austria.at. Ed. Christine Frisinghelli. Pub., R&P Manfred Willmann. Adv. contact Heidi Oswald TEL 43-316-81555013. Circ: 3,500.

770 028.5 CAN ISSN 0008-2090
CAMERA CANADA. Text in English. 1969. q. CAD 19.80 to non-members. bk.rev.
Indexed: C03, CBCARef, CBPI, CPerI, G08, PQC.
Published by: Canadian Association for Photographic Art/Association Canadienne d'Art Photographique, 31858 Hopedale Ave., Clearbrook, BC V2T 2G7, Canada. TEL 604-855-4848. Ed. Doug Boult. adv.: B&W page USD 500, color page USD 900; trim 11 x 8.25. Circ: 4,000.

770 AUS ISSN 1323-3408
CAMERA PHOTOGRAPHER'S HANDBOOK. Text in English. 1981. a. AUD 11 per issue in Australia & New Zealand; AUD 19 per issue elsewhere (effective 2008). adv. **Document type:** *Handbook/Manual/Guide, Consumer.* **Description:** Annual guide to imaging tips and techniques.
Formerly: Australia Camera Craft Photographer's Handbook
Published by: Wolseley Media Pty Ltd., Level 5, 55 Chandos St, PO Box 5555, St. Leonards, NSW 2065, Australia. TEL 61-2-99016100, FAX 61-2-99016198, contactsubs@wolseleymedia.com.au, http://www.wolseleymedia.com.au.

CAMERART PHOTO TRADE DIRECTORY. *see* BUSINESS AND ECONOMICS—Trade And Industrial Directories

770 CAN ISSN 1702-062X
CANADIAN CAMERA MAGAZINE. Text in English. 1981 (vol.14). 4/yr. free to members. **Document type:** *Magazine, Consumer.*
Former titles (until 1999): Canadian Camera (1206-3401); (until 1997): Fotoflash Journal (1200-9598); (until 199?): Fotoflash (0318-7500)
Published by: Canadian Association for Photographic Art, c/o Joy McDonell, 47 Bunting Ln, Ottawa, ON K2M 2P7, Canada. Ed. Joy McDonell. Circ: 2,800.

770 JPN
CAPA; active camera magazine. Text in Japanese. 1981. m. JPY 4,200.
Published by: Gakken Co. Ltd., 1-17-15, Nakaikegami, Otaku, Tokyo, 145-0064, Japan. Ed. Shonosuke Abe.

CAPE ROCK; a journal of poetry. *see* LITERATURE—Poetry

778 AUS ISSN 1445-6486
CAPTURE; commercial photography magazine. Text in English. 1963. bi-m. AUD 38.50 domestic; AUD 45 in New Zealand; AUD 55 in Africa; AUD 75 elsewhere; AUD 6.75 newsstand/cover (effective 2008). adv. bk.rev. illus. reprints avail. **Document type:** *Magazine, Trade.* **Description:** Covers all facets of the photographic industry and in particular practical issues such as marketing, training, pricing and rights management.
Former titles (until 2001): Commercial Photography (1329-7821); (until 1996): Commercial Photography Plus Digital Studio (1329-7813); (until 1995): Commercial Photography in Australia (1037-6992); (until 1991): Industrial and Commercial Photography (0313-4393); (until 1974): Industrial Photography and Commercial Camera (0019-8609)
Published by: Yaffa Publishing Group Pty Ltd., 17-21 Bellevue St, Surry Hills, NSW 2010, Australia. TEL 61-2-92812333, FAX 61-2-92812750, info@yaffa.com.au. Ed. Marc Gafen TEL 61-2-92138271. Adv. contact Karen Vaughan Williams TEL 61-2-92138291. B&W page AUD 1,940, color page AUD 2,580; trim 220 x 297. Circ: 2,205. **Subscr. to:** GPO Box 606, Sydney, NSW 2001, Australia.

▼ **CERISE PRESS**; journal of literature, arts & culture. *see* LITERATURE

CHAMPAIGN COUNTY HISTORICAL ARCHIVES HISTORICAL PUBLICATIONS SERIES. *see* HISTORY—History Of North And South America

770 FRA ISSN 0396-8235
CHASSEUR D'IMAGES. Text in French. 1976. 10/yr. EUR 43 (effective 2009). adv. illus. **Document type:** *Magazine, Consumer.*
Related titles: Supplement(s): Nat' Images. ISSN 2106-3478. 2004.
—CCC.
Published by: Editions Jibena, 11 Rue des Lavoirs, Senille, 86100, France. TEL 33-5-49854985, FAX 33-5-49854999. Ed. Guy Michel Cogne. R&P Sandrine Texier. Adv. contact Marie Therese Perissat. Circ: 105,000.

CHENG SHI HUABAO/CITY PICTORIAL. *see* GENERAL INTEREST PERIODICALS—China

778.53 SGP ISSN 0009-6954
CINE NEWS. Text in English. 1970 (vol.11). m. free. adv. illus.
Published by: Singapore Cine Club, 42 Branksome Rd, Singapore, 439580, Singapore. Ed. Paul Gomez. Circ: 1,500.

CINEDOCFILME. *see* MOTION PICTURES

CINEMA 15. *see* MOTION PICTURES

CINEMATOGRAPH. *see* MOTION PICTURES

CLAY PALM REVIEW: ART AND LITERARY MAGAZINE. *see* LITERATURE—Poetry

778.53 USA
TR1
CLOSE-UP. Text in English. 1979. bi-m. free to members (effective 2009). back issues avail. **Document type:** *Newsletter, Trade.*
Former titles (until 2006): George Eastman House - International Museum of Photography and Film. News & Events; (until 1995): George Eastman House - International Museum of Photography and Film. Newsletter; (until 1993): George Eastman House - International Museum of Photography. Newsletter (1055-3886); (until 1986): George Eastman House Newsletter
Related titles: Online - full text ed.: free (effective 2009).
Published by: George Eastman House - International Museum of Photography and Film, 900 East Ave, Rochester, NY 14607. TEL 585-271-3361. Ed. Robyn Hansen.

770 FRA ISSN 2107-2175
▼ **COLLECTION L' AMISOURIS.** Text in French. 2009. irreg. **Document type:** *Monographic series, Consumer.*
Published by: Les Editions de la Souris, 2 Rue Sainte Luce, Les Deux Alpes, 38860, France. leseditionsdelasouris@wanadoo.fr, http://leseditionsdelasouris.over-blog.fr/article-11908795.html.

COLLECTIVE; the project. *see* ART

770 DEU ISSN 0343-3102
COLOR FOTO; Das Profi-Magazin fuer digitale Fotografie. Text in German. 1973. m. EUR 63.90; EUR 5.50 newsstand/cover (effective 2011). adv. **Document type:** *Magazine, Consumer.*
Incorporates (1999-2001): e-photo; (1992-1998): Foto und Labor (0943-1993); Which was formerly (1980-1992): Foto-Hobby-Labor (0721-6939); Formerly (until 1976): Color Foto Journal (0343-3099)
Related titles: Online - full text ed.
Indexed: A22.
—IE, Infotrieve.
Published by: W E K A Media Publishing GmbH, Gruberstr 46a, Poing, 85586, Germany. TEL 49-8121-950, FAX 49-8121-951199, online@wekanet.de, http://www.weka-media-publishing.de. Ed. Werner Luettgens. Adv. contact Michael Hackenberg. Circ: 42,065 (paid and controlled).

COLOR RESEARCH AND APPLICATION. *see* ENGINEERING—Chemical Engineering

770 USA ISSN 0145-899X
TR640
COMBINATIONS; a journal of photography. Text in English. 1977. irreg. USD 5. adv. bk.rev.
Published by: Mary Ann Lynch, Ed. & Pub., 22 Jones St 3F, New York, NY 10014. TEL 212-929-2511. Circ: 1,500.

770 ITA ISSN 1973-2783
COME FOTOGRAFARE. Text in Italian. 2007. bi-m. **Document type:** *Magazine, Consumer.*
Published by: Sprea Editori Srl, Via Torino 51, Cernusco sul Naviglio, MI 20063, Italy. TEL 39-02-92432222, FAX 39-02-92432236, editori@sprea.it, http://www.sprea.it.

770 JPN
COMMERCIAL PHOTO. Text in Japanese. 1980. 12/yr. USD 320.
Published by: Intercontinental Marketing Corp., I.P.O. Box 5056, Tokyo, 100-3191, Japan. TEL 81-3-3661-7458.

333 USA ISSN 1064-640X
TR640
CONTACT SHEET. Text in English. 1977. 5/yr. USD 40 (effective 2004).
Indexed: ABM, SCOPUS.
Published by: Light Work, Robert B Menschel Media Center, 316 Waverly Ave, Syracuse, NY 13244. TEL 315-443-1300, FAX 315-443-6516, http://www.lightwork.org/publications/index.html. Ed. Jeffrey Hoone.

CONTEMPORARY. *see* ART

770 ESP
CONTRA LUZ. Text in Spanish. m.
Published by: Agrupacion Fotografica y Cinematografica de Navarra, Calle Rio Urrobi 3, Pamplona, Navarra 31005, Spain. revista.contraluz@gmail.com, http://www.agrupacionfotonavarra.com/.

770 ITA ISSN 1972-3741
CORSO PRATICO FOTOGRAFIA DIGITALE. Text in Italian. 2007. w. **Document type:** *Magazine, Consumer.*
Published by: Poligrafici Editoriale (Subsidiary of: Monrif Group), Via Enrico Mattei 106, Bologna, BO 40138, Italy. TEL 39-051-6006111, FAX 39-051-6006266, http://www.monrifgroup.net.

CREATIEF MET FOTO'S. *see* ARTS AND HANDICRAFTS

770 GBR ISSN 1756-5316
CREATIVE IMAGE MAKER. Abbreviated title: C I M. Text in English. 2008. m. free (effective 2011). back issues avail. **Document type:** *Magazine, Consumer.*
Media: Online - full text.

CREATIVE QUARTERLY. *see* ART

770 USA
THE CRITICAL EYE. Text in English. bi-m. bk.rev. **Description:** Covers photography and criticism.
Media: Online - full text. **Related titles:** CD-ROM ed.
Published by: Critical Eye, 291 Hermitage St, Philadelphia, PA 19127-1013. gregrubin@thecriticaleye.com, http://www.thecriticaleye.com/. Ed. Gregory Rubin.

780 MEX ISSN 1605-4903
CUARTO OSCURO. Text in Spanish. bi-m. back issues avail.
Media: Online - full text.
Published by: Cuarto Oscuro, SA de CV, Frontera 102, Col. Roma, Mexico, DF, 06700, Mexico. FAX 52-5-2078607, info@cuartooscuro.com. Circ: 10,000.

770 700 USA
D B C C PHOTOGRAPHIC SOCIETY. NEWSLETTER. Text in English. 1978. q. free. adv. bk.rev.
Published by: Daytona Beach Community College, 1200 International Spdy Blvd, Daytona Beach, FL 32114. TEL 904-254-3057. Ed. Ed Davenport. Circ: 2,750.

770 AUS ISSN 1838-4870
▼ **D I**; the interactive publication for image makers. Text in English. 2010. irreg. free (effective 2011). adv. back issues avail. **Document type:** *Magazine, Trade.* **Description:** Designed for all photographers, creative image makers and photoshop, photoshop elements and lightroom users.
Media: Online - full text.
Published by: Dark Glass Media Pty Ltd info@di-magazine.com. Ed. Philip Andrews.

D X N MAGAZINE. *see* LITERATURE—Poetry

770 POL ISSN 1233-2445
TR95.P7
DAGEROTYP. Text in Polish. 1993. a. **Document type:** *Journal, Academic/Scholarly.* **Description:** Covers the history of photography.
Published by: Polska Akademia Nauk, Instytut Sztuki/Polish Academy of Science, Institute of Art, ul Dluga 28, Warsaw, 00950, Poland. TEL 48-22-5048200, FAX 48-22-8313149, ispan@ispan.pl, http://www.ispan.pl.

770 USA
DAGUERREIAN SOCIETY. ANNUAL. Text in English. 1990. a., latest 2000. price varies.
Published by: Daguerreian Society, 3043 West Library Ave, Pittsburgh, PA 15216-2460. TEL 412-343-5525, FAX 412-343-5972, dagsocpgh@aol.com.

770 USA ISSN 1072-8600
TR365
DAGUERREIAN SOCIETY NEWSLETTER; dedicated to the history, science, and art of the daguerreotype. Text in English. 1988. bi-m. USD 50; USD 65 foreign; USD 25 to students (effective 2003). **Document type:** *Newsletter.*
Indexed: ABM, SCOPUS.
Published by: Daguerreian Society, 3043 West Library Ave, Pittsburgh, PA 15216-2460. TEL 412-343-5525, FAX 412-343-5972. Ed., R&P, Adv. contact Mark S Johnson. Circ: 1,100.

770 DNK ISSN 0901-4209
DANSK FOTOGRAFI; kontaktblad. Variant title: Kontaktblad. Text in Danish. 1981 (no.108). 4/yr. DKK 345 membership (effective 2009). adv. illus. **Document type:** *Magazine, Consumer.*
Formerly (until 1986): Selskabet for Dansk Fotografi. Kontaktblad (0108-2558)
Published by: Selskabet for Dansk Fotografi, c/o Per Valentin, Bavnager 57, Oelsted, 3310, Denmark. TEL 45-48280813, info@sdf.dk, http://www.sdf.dk. Ed. Ebbe Rosendahl Kragemosen. Adv. contact Per Valentin.

770 700 USA ISSN 1550-7343
DAYLIGHT MAGAZINE. Text in English. 2003. s-a. USD 30 in US & Canada to individuals; USD 45 in US & Canada to institutions; USD 55 elsewhere (effective 2008). **Document type:** *Magazine, Consumer.*
Published by: Daylight Community Arts Foundation, Inc., PO Box 847, New York, NY 10116. TEL 917-239-8615, FAX 775-908-5587. Eds. Michael Itkoff, Taj Forer.

770 CHN ISSN 0494-4372
DAZHONG SHEYING/POPULAR PHOTOGRAPHY. Text in Chinese. 1958. m. USD 106.80 (effective 2009). **Document type:** *Magazine, Consumer.*
—East View.
Published by: (Zhongguo Sheyingjia Xiehui/China Photographers' Association), Dazhong Sheying Zazhishe, 61 Hongxing Hutong, Dongdan, Beijing, 100005, China. TEL 86-1-557378, FAX 86-10-65130094. **Dist. by:** China International Book Trading Corp, 35 Chegongzhuang Xilu, Haidian District, PO Box 399, Beijing 100044, China. TEL 86-10-68412045, FAX 86-10-68412023, cibtc@mail.cibtc.com.cn, http://www.cibtc.com.cn.

DEAR DAVE. *see* LITERATURE

770 FRA ISSN 1769-9568
DECLIC PHOTO MAGAZINE. Text in French. 2004. m. **Document type:** *Magazine, Consumer.*
Published by: Digicia Media, 14 Rue Soleillet, Paris, 75020, France. TEL 33-1-40337902, FAX 33-1-40337113.

770 JPN
DEJA-VU; a photography quarterly. Text in Japanese. 1992. q. USD 110. adv. illus. **Description:** Each issue focuses on one or two influential contemporary photographers.
Published by: Photo - Planete Co. Ltd., 3-21-14-402 Higashi, Shibuya-ku, Tokyo, 150-0011, Japan. Ed. Iizawa Kohtaro.

DESIGNERS DIGEST; Magazin fuer Gestaltung und Technik. *see* ART

778 SVK ISSN 1336-5754
DIGI REVUE. Text in Slovak. 2004. m. EUR 2.62 newsstand/cover (effective 2009). adv. **Document type:** *Magazine, Trade.*
Published by: Digital Visions, spol. s r.o., Kladnianska 60, Bratislava, 821 05, Slovakia. TEL 421-2-43420956, FAX 421-2-43420958. Ed. Peter Orvisky. Adv. contact Ludmila Gebauerova.

770 CZE
DIGIFOTO. Text in Czech. 2008. 10/yr. CZK 1,009 (effective 2011). adv. **Document type:** *Magazine, Consumer.*
Related titles: Online - full text ed.: CZK 645 (effective 2011).
Published by: Mlada Fronta, Mezi Vodami 1952/9, Prague 4, 14300, Czech Republic. TEL 420-2-25276201, FAX 420-2-25276222, online@mf.cz, http://www.mf.cz. Ed. Petr Lindner. Adv. contact Vera Harvankova.

771 USA ISSN 1523-844X
DIGITAL CAMERA. Text in English. 1998. bi-m. USD 18 domestic; USD 26 in Canada & Mexico; USD 50 elsewhere (effective 2003). **Document type:** *Magazine, Consumer.*
Published by: Aeon Publishing Group, Inc., 88 Sunnyside Blvd, Ste 203, Plainview, NY 11803. TEL 916-684-7904, FAX 916-684-7628. Ed. Shawn Barnett. **Subscr. to:** PO Box 640, Folsom, CA 95763.

778.2 GBR ISSN 2040-5855
DIGITAL CAMERA ESSENTIALS. Text in English. 2002. 13/yr. GBP 41.50 domestic; GBP 70 in Europe; GBP 80 elsewhere; GBP 4 per issue (effective 2010). adv. back issues avail. **Document type:** *Magazine, Consumer.* **Description:** Provides informed opinion and advice on buying the best digital camera from entry-level models to the latest high-tech gears.
Formerly (until 2009): Digital Camera Buyer (1475-0538)
Published by: Imagine Publishing Ltd., Richmond House, 33 Richmond Hill, Bournemouth, Dorset BH2 6EZ, United Kingdom. TEL 44-1202-586200, http://www.imagine-publishing.co.uk. Ed. Debbi Allen TEL 44-1202-586218. Adv. contact James Hanslip TEL 44-1202-586423.

770 USA
DIGITAL IMAGING DIGEST. Text in English. m. free to members (effective 2008). back issues avail. **Document type:** *Newsletter, Trade.* **Description:** Provides time-sensitive information on business tools, emerging technologies and marketing information for firms substantially involved in providing digital imaging products and services.
Formerly: Speciality Lab Update
Related titles: Online - full text ed.
Indexed: CompD.
Published by: (Digital Imaging Market Association), Photo Marketing Association International, 3000 Picture Pl, Jackson, MI 49201. TEL 517-788-8100, FAX 517-788-8371, gpageau@pmai.org. Pub. Gary Pageau. Circ: 6,000 (controlled).

DIGITAL IMAGING TECHNIQUES; an advanced tool for commercial & creative pros. *see* COMPUTERS—Computer Graphics

770 620 USA ISSN 1083-5121
Z286.E43
DIGITAL OUTPUT. Text in English. 1995. m. free to qualified personnel. adv. **Document type:** *Magazine, Trade.*
Related titles: Online - full text ed.
Published by: Doyle Group, 5150 Palm Valley Rd, Ste 103, Ponte Vedra Beach, FL 32082. TEL 904-285-6020, FAX 904-285-9944. Ed. Terry Murphy. Pub. Douglas Apelian.

770 USA ISSN 1545-8520
TR267
DIGITAL PHOTO PRO. Text in English. 2003 (Sept./Oct.). 7/yr. USD 19.97; USD 9 per issue (effective 2011). adv. **Document type:** *Magazine, Consumer.*
Related titles: Online - full text ed.
Published by: Werner Publishing Corporation, 12121 Wilshire Blvd, 12th Fl, Los Angeles, Los Angeles, CA 90025. TEL 310-820-1500, FAX 310-826-5008, http://www.wernerpublishing.com.

770 006.6 AUS ISSN 1327-9432
DIGITAL PHOTOGRAPHY + DESIGN. Text in English. 1995. bi-m. AUD 49.50 domestic; AUD 60 in New Zealand; AUD 70 in Asia; AUD 128 elsewhere; AUD 8.25 newsstand/cover (effective 2008). adv. **Document type:** *Magazine, Consumer.* **Description:** Provides comprehensive test reviews on the latest photography gear such as cameras, software, computers, printers and other peripherals. Also provides step-by-step tutorials to help master the latest imaging techniques.
Published by: Yaffa Publishing Group Pty Ltd., 17-21 Bellevue St, Surry Hills, NSW 2010, Australia. TEL 61-2-92812333, FAX 61-2-92812750, info@yaffa.com.au. Ed. James Ostinga TEL 61-2-92138248. Adv. contact Kerri McNamara TEL 61-2-92138261. B&W page AUD 2,010, color page AUD 2,680; trim 210 x 297. Circ: 5,368.

770 AUS
DIGITAL PHOTOGRAPHY AND IMAGING. Text in English. 199?. bi-m. **Description:** Features articles on digital photography, equipment and image processing.
Media: Online - full text.
Address: Australia. tippine@real.net.au.

778.315 GBR ISSN 2044-7329
▼ **DIGITAL PHOTOGRAPHY ENTHUSIAST.** Abbreviated title: D P E. Text in English. 2010. m. GBP 39 domestic; GBP 69 in Europe; GBP 89 elsewhere; GBP 3.99 per issue (effective 2011). adv. back issues avail. **Document type:** *Magazine, Consumer.* **Description:** Provides the perfect backdrop for today's digital lifestyle.
Related titles: Online - full text ed.
Published by: Select Publisher Services Ltd., PO Box 6337, Bournemouth, Dorset BH1 9EH, United Kingdom. TEL 44-1202-586848, tim@selectps.com, http://www.selectps.com. Ed. Rob Clymo. Adv. contact Tammy Mileson TEL 44-1202-940305.

775 GBR ISSN 1752-1939
DIGITAL S L R USER. (Single Lens Reflex) Text in English. 2006. m. GBP 21; GBP 3.99 newsstand/cover (effective 2009). adv. back issues avail. **Document type:** *Magazine, Consumer.*
Related titles: Online - full text ed.
Published by: Bright Publishing, Bright House, 82 High St, Sawston, Cambs CB22 3HJ, United Kingdom. TEL 44-1223-499450, FAX 44-1223-839953, http://www.bright-publishing.com/. Adv. contact Matt Snow TEL 44-1223-499453.

770 ESP ISSN 0212-8187
DIORAMA; foto y digitografia. Text in Spanish. 1984. 10/yr. **Document type:** *Magazine, Consumer.*
Published by: Ed. Alcocer de Castro S.A., Tembleque, 96, bajo C, Madrid, 28024, Spain. TEL 34-1-7192413, FAX 34-1-7192494. Ed. Jose Alcocer Saez.

DIRIGIDO; revista de cine. *see* MOTION PICTURES

DISCURSOS FOTOGRAFICOS. *see* COMMUNICATIONS

770 FRA ISSN 0419-5361
AG250
DOCUMENTATION PHOTOGRAPHIQUE. Text in French. 1947. 6/yr. EUR 51 (effective 2009). bibl.; illus. **Document type:** *Journal, Government.* **Description:** Treats the themes of history and geography through a photographic view.
Related titles: Microfiche ed.
Indexed: FR, RASB, SpeleolAb.
Published by: Documentation Francaise, 29-31 Quai Voltaire, Paris, Cedex 7 75344, France. FAX 33-1-40157230. Circ: 15,000.

DOSSIER (BROOKLYN). *see* CLOTHING TRADE—Fashions

DOUBLETRUCK MAGAZINE. *see* JOURNALISM

DREAMBOYS. *see* HOMOSEXUALITY

770 NLD ISSN 1879-7679
▼ **E EN V.** Key Title: E & V. Text in Dutch. 2010. bi-m. EUR 59; EUR 12.95 newsstand/cover (effective 2011). **Document type:** *Magazine, Consumer.*
Published by: E & V Magazine, Postbus 134, Wormerveer, 1520 AC, Netherlands. TEL 31-75-6212578, info@evmagazine.nl, http://www.evmagazine.nl.

614.19 USA ISSN 1554-8317
TR822
E P I C JOURNAL; the official publication of the Evidence Photographers International Council. (Evidence Photographers International Council) Text in English. 1968. s-a. free to members (effective 2005). adv. reprints avail. **Document type:** *Journal, Trade.* **Description:** Features articles advancing knowledge in the field of forensic photography.
Formerly (until 199?): Journal of Evidence Photography
Related titles: Microform ed.: (from PQC).
Published by: Evidence Photographers International Council, 600 Main St, Honesdale, PA 18431. TEL 570-253-5450, FAX 570-253-5011. Ed. William Amptman. R&P, Adv. contact Robert F Jennings. page USD 250. Circ: 2,500.

770 USA
EDIT. Text in English. 2004. 2/yr. USD 13.75 (effective 2005). **Document type:** *Magazine, Consumer.* **Description:** Covers the people, trends, issues and ideas that affect photography and filmmaking.
Published by: Getty Images, Inc., 601 N 34th St, Seattle, WA 98103. TEL 206-925-5000, FAX 206-925-5001, feedback@gettyimages.com. Ed. John O'Reilly. Pub. Deb Trevino. Adv. contact Julia Riddiough.

770 AUT ISSN 1993-1557
EDITION FOTOHOF. Text in German. 1990. irreg., latest vol.36, 2009. price varies. **Document type:** *Monographic series, Academic/Scholarly.*
Published by: Otto Mueller Verlag, Ernst-Thun-Str 11, Salzburg, 5020, Austria. TEL 43-662-8819740, FAX 43-662-872387, info@omvs.at, http://www.omvs.at.

770 AUT ISSN 1024-1922
TR1
EIKON; internationale zeitschrift fuer photographie und medienkunst. Text in German. 199?. q. EUR 48 (effective 2004). adv. **Document type:** *Magazine, Trade.* **Description:** Focuses on Austrian and international media arts, with special emphasis on fine art photography and its significance in the intermedial context.
Related titles: Online - full text ed.: ISSN 1605-7872.
Indexed: ABM, SCOPUS.
Published by: (Oesterreichisches Instituts fuer Photographie & Medienkunst), Eikon, Museums Quartier 21, Museumsplatz 1, Steige 6, Top 4, Vienna, 1070, Austria. TEL 43-1-5977088, office@eikon.or.at, http://www.eikon.or.at/. adv.: B&W page EUR 1,141; 210 x 280.

770 USA ISSN 0896-0976
ELECTRONIC PHOTOGRAPHY NEWS. Text in English. 1986. m. free (effective 2005). bk.rev. charts; stat. back issues avail. **Document type:** *Newsletter, Trade.*
Related titles: Online - full text ed.
Published by: E P N Publishing, 70 Southwich Ct, Rochester, NY 14623-2139. TEL 585-292-1690, FAX 585-292-6753, epnpublishing@aol.com. Ed., Pub. John Larish. Circ: 400.

770 USA ISSN 1933-4125
TR1
EMULSION MAGAZINE. Text in English. 2006. q. USD 32 domestic; USD 44 in Canada; USD 54 elsewhere (effective 2007). **Document type:** *Magazine, Consumer.*
Address: PO Box 367, Hurricane, UT 84737. editor@emulsionmagazine.org, http://www.emulsionmagazine.org/index.php.

EMZIN; magazine for culture. *see* ART

770 GBR ISSN 2040-8412
▼ **ENSEMBLE.** Text in English. 2009. a. GBP 3 per issue (effective 2010). **Document type:** *Journal, Trade.* **Description:** Explores a department of over 200 students who can engage their community and stimulate a collective discourse using photography.
Published by: University College Falmouth, Woodlane, Falmouth, Cornwall TR11 4RH, United Kingdom. TEL 44-1326-213794, FAX 44-1326-370725, international@falmouth.ac.uk, http://www.falmouth.ac.uk/. **Co-publisher:** Fotonow.

770 GBR ISSN 1748-5568
EOS MAGAZINE. Text in English. 19??. q. GBP 21.95 domestic; GBP 26.95 in Europe; GBP 31.95 elsewhere (effective 2009). adv. a.index. 80 p./no.; back issues avail. **Document type:** *Magazine, Consumer.* **Description:** Packed with practical advice and technical insights to help photography.
Formerly (until 1993): Canon User
Related titles: Online - full text ed.: GBP 3.95 (effective 2009).
Published by: Robert Scott Associates, The Old Barn, Ball Ln, Tackely, Kidlington, Oxfordshire OX5 3AG, United Kingdom. TEL 44-186-9331741, FAX 44-186-9331641, subscriptions@eos-magazine.com.

770 PRT ISSN 0874-6230
ERZATS. Text in Portuguese. 1999. q. **Document type:** *Magazine, Consumer.*
Published by: Ministerio da Cultura, Centro Portugues de Fotografia, Edificio Cadeia da Relacao, Campos Martires da Patria, Oporto, Portugal. TEL 351-22-2076310, FAX 351-22-2076311, email@cpf.pt, http://www.cpf.pt.

770 FRA ISSN 1270-9050
TR1
ETUDES PHOTOGRAPHIQUES. Text in French, English. 1996. s-a. EUR 40 domestic; EUR 50 foreign (effective 2009 - 2010). **Document type:** *Journal, Academic/Scholarly.*
Related titles: Online - full text ed.: ISSN 1777-5302. free (effective 2011).
Indexed: B24, FR, I14, SCOPUS.
—INIST. **CCC.**
Published by: La Societe Francaise de Photographie, 71 rue de Richelieu, Paris, 75002, France. TEL 33-01-42600598, FAX 33-01-47037539, sfp@wanadoo.fr, http://www.sfp.photographie.com.

770 DEU ISSN 0172-7028
TR640
EUROPEAN PHOTOGRAPHY. Text in English, German. 1980. s-a. EUR 64 for 2 yrs. in Europe; EUR 90 for 2 yrs. elsewhere; EUR 16 newsstand/cover (effective 2008). adv. bk.rev.; software rev.; video rev. bibl.; illus. cum.index. 80 p./no.; back issues avail.; reprints avail. **Document type:** *Magazine, Consumer.* **Description:** International art magazine for contemporary photography and new media.
Related titles: Online - full text ed.
Indexed: A07, A30, A31, AA, ABM, ArtInd, B04, BRD, DIP, IBR, IBZ, SCOPUS, W03, W05.
—**CCC.**
Address: Postfach 080227, Berlin, 10002, Germany. Ed., Pub. Andreas Mueller-Pohle. Adv. contact Bernd Neubauer. B&W page USD 1,200; trim 196 x 255. Circ: 3,800 (paid).

770 USA
EX. CAMERA; a cultural digest of images and ideas. Text in English. 2000. q. USD 28; USD 10 newsstand/cover (effective 2001). **Document type:** *Magazine, Consumer.*
Address: Box 3856, Federick, MD 21705. TEL 301-631-1893, editor@ex-camera.com, http://www.ex-camera.com. Ed. Tom McCluskey. Pub. Kevin Dwyer.

770.5 USA ISSN 0098-8863
TR1
➤ **EXPOSURE (CLEVELAND).** Text in English. 1963. s-a. USD 35 domestic to institutions; USD 50 foreign to institutions; USD 15 per issue to individuals; free to members (effective 2010). adv. bk.rev. bibl.; illus.; abstr. back issues avail.; reprints avail. **Document type:** *Journal, Academic/Scholarly.* **Description:** Photography studies blend insight, critical dialogue, historical perspective and educational issues.
Indexed: A07, A22, A30, A31, AA, ABM, ArtInd, B04, B24, CA, SCOPUS, T02.
—BLDSC (3843.374500), IE, Ingenta.
Published by: Society for Photographic Education, 2530 Superior Ave, #403, Cleveland, OH 44114. TEL 216-622-2733, FAX 216-622-2712, membership@spenational.org. Ed. Carla Williams. Circ: 2,500.

770 NLD
F+D FOTOGRAFIE. Text in Dutch. 1979. 11/yr. EUR 49.95 (effective 2009). adv. illus. **Document type:** *Consumer.*
Formed by the merger of (1997-2007): Digitaal Beeld (1387-3407); (1979-2007): Fotografie (1389-4935); Which was formerly (until 1999): F en D; (until 1991): Foto en Doka (0165-5531)
—IE.
Published by: Blauw Media Uitgeverij B.V., Postbus 1043, Maarssen, 3600 BA, Netherlands. TEL 31-346-574040, FAX 31-346-576056, info@blauwmedia.com, http://www.blauwmediauitgeverij.nl.

778.59 ESP ISSN 0214-2244
F V - FOTO VIDEO ACTUALIDAD. Text in Spanish. 1988. m. adv. bk.rev. 100 p./no.; **Document type:** *Magazine, Consumer.* **Description:** Covers all that pertains to Spanish photography and video. Informs on new techniques, products and applications.
Published by: Omnicon S.A., Hierro, 9 3A 7, Madrid, 28045, Spain. TEL 34-91-5278249, FAX 34-91-5281348, omnicon@skios.es, http://www.omnicon.es/. Circ: 25,000. **Dist. by:** Asociacion de Revistas Culturales de Espana, C Covarruvias 9 2o. Derecha, Madrid 28010, Spain. TEL 34-91-3086066, FAX 34-91-3199267, info@arce.es, http://www.arce.es/.

770 GBR ISSN 1754-0615
F2 FREELANCE PHOTOGRAPHER. Text in English. 1989. bi-m. GBP 29.50 domestic; GBP 34.50 in Europe; GBP 39.50 elsewhere; GBP 5.98 per issue domestic; GBP 7.88 per issue in Europe; GBP 8.95 per issue elsewhere; GBP 4.90 newsstand/cover (effective 2010). adv. bk.rev. illus. back issues avail. **Document type:** *Magazine, Trade.*
Former titles (until 2007): F2 Freelance + Digital (1743-5803); (until 2004): Freelance Photographer (1465-2781); Which was formed by the merger of (1995-1999): Photon (1359-2769); Which was formerly (until 1995): Photo Pro (0956-2745); (1996-1999): 35mm Photographer (1365-6252); F2 Freelance + Digital superseded in part (in 2004): Master Digital Photographer (1740-3847); Which was formerly (until 2001): Master Digital
Related titles: Online - full text ed.
Published by: EC1 Publishing Ltd., Finsbury Business Ctr, 40 Bowling Green Ln, London, EC1R 0NE, United Kingdom. TEL 44-20-74157099, http://www.ec1publishing.com/. Ed. David Land. Pub. Simon James TEL 44-20-76929961. Adv. contact Sulann Staniford-Grainger TEL 44-7827-322466.

770 646.72 NLD ISSN 1878-8246
▼ **FACE & FIGURE.** Text in Dutch. 2009. bi-m. EUR 27 (effective 2011). adv. **Document type:** *Magazine, Consumer.*
Published by: Face & Figure Media, Kasteelstraat 16, Heijen, 6598 BJ, Netherlands. TEL 31-485-513316, FAX 31-485-518461. Circ: 3,250.

770 USA
FAMILY PHOTO. Text in English. 1996. bi-m. USD 19.94; USD 2.95 newsstand/cover (effective 1997). adv. **Document type:** *Magazine, Consumer.*
Published by: Petersen Publishing Co. (New York), 110 Fifth Ave, 2nd Fl, New York, NY 10011. TEL 212-886-3600, FAX 212-886-2810. Ed. Ron Leach. Pub. Jackie Augustine. Adv. contact Kathy Schnieder. Circ: 150,000. **Subscr. to:** PO Box 53210, Boulder, CO 80322-6945.

770 659.1 USA
HF5805
FASHION & PRINT; the Madison Avenue Handbook. Text in English. 1956. a. **Document type:** *Handbook/Manual/Guide, Trade.* **Description:** Specialized yellow pages for the world of advertising, print business and fashion industries and all attendant services.
Formerly (until 2001): Image Makers Source of the Madison Avenue Handbook; Which superseded in part (in 199?): Madison Avenue Handbook (0076-2148)
Published by: Peter Glenn Publications, Inc., 777 E Atlantic Ave, Suite C2337, Delray Beach, FL 33483. TEL 888-332-6700, gregjames@pgdirect.com. Ed. Lauren Gillmore. Pub. Gregory James.

770 ZAF ISSN 0015-3494
FLASH. Text in English. 1956. m. ZAR 5.
Published by: Pretoria Photographic Society, PO Box 3611, Pretoria, 0001, South Africa. Circ: 150.

P

770 NLD ISSN 1570-4874
FOAM; international photography magazine. Text in English. 2002. q. EUR 50 domestic; EUR 55 foreign (effective 2008). adv. **Document type:** *Magazine, Consumer.*
Related titles: Online - full text ed.
Indexed: ABM.
Published by: Foam Magazine B.V., Keizersgracht 609, Amsterdam, 1017 DS, Netherlands. TEL 31-20-5516500, FAX 31-20-5516501, info@foammagazine.nl, editors@foammagazine.nl. Ed. Marloes Krijnen.

770 NLD ISSN 0015-4997
CODEN: FOCUAL
FOCUS (HAARLEM); maandblad voor fotografie en visuele communicatie. Text in Dutch. 1914. 11/yr. EUR 51 domestic; EUR 57 in Belgium (effective 2009). adv. bk.rev.; film rev. illus. index. **Document type:** *Magazine, Consumer.*
Incorporates (in 2006): Digifoto/Foto+ (1871-7497); Which was formed by the 2005 merger of: Digifoto (1574-9177); Foto+ (1871-7489); Both of which superseded in part (1946-2004): Foto (0015-8682)
Related titles: Online - full text ed.
Indexed: A22, ABM.
—IE, Infotrieve.
Published by: Focus Media Groep, Hendrik Figeeweg 1-z, Haarlem, 2031 BJ, Netherlands. TEL 31-23-5348844, FAX 31-23-5423110, focus@focusmedia.nl, http://www.focusmedia.nl. Ed. Dirk van der Spek.

770 USA ISSN 1932-2844
TR640
FOCUS MAGAZINE (BROOKLYN). Text in English. 2005. bi-m. **Document type:** *Magazine, Consumer.*
Published by: Focus Fine Art Photography Magazine, 77 Berry St, Ste #1R, Brooklyn, NY 11211. TEL 718-360-4724, info@focusmag.info, http://www.focusmag.info.

770 POL ISSN 0324-8453
FOTO. Text in Polish. 1953. m. PLZ 127.20 (effective 2002 - 2003). adv. bk.rev. illus. index. **Document type:** *Magazine, Consumer.*
Formerly (until 1975): Fotografia (0324-850X)
Published by: Imphot Photo Imaging Sp. z o.o., ul Hajoty 61, Warsaw, 01821, Poland. foto@foto.com.pl. Ed. Eugenia Herzyk. Circ: 30,000. **Dist. by:** Ars Polona, Obroncow 25, Warsaw 03933, Poland.

778.53 SWE ISSN 1104-5558
FOTO. Text in Swedish. 1992. 11/yr. SEK 390 (effective 2005). adv. 4 cols./p.; **Document type:** *Magazine, Consumer.* **Description:** Presents articles and features on photography and photo equipment.
Formerly (until 1994): Aktuell Fotografi och Foto (1103-0690); Which was formed by the merger of (1989-1992): Foto och Video (1100-4673); (1972-1992): Aktuell Fotografi (0345-0511)
Published by: Allers Foerlag AB, Landskronavaegen 23, Helsingborg, 25185, Sweden. TEL 46-42-173500, FAX 46-42-173682. Ed. Jan Almloef. Adv. contact Lilimor Werre TEL 46-8-6794681. page SEK 28,500; trim 190 x 265. Circ: 25,300.

778.59 ESP ISSN 1134-5993
FOTO. Text in Spanish. 1983. 12/yr. EUR 40 domestic; EUR 87 in Europe; EUR 123 elsewhere. bk.rev. back issues avail. **Document type:** *Magazine, Consumer.* **Description:** Covers photography and video.
Formerly (until 1993): Foto Professional (0211-9552)
Published by: Revista Foto, S.L., Apdo 673, Alicante, 03700, Spain. TEL 34-652-326655. Ed., Pub. Manuel Lopez. Adv. contact Maria Rosa Medel. Circ: 24,000.

770 ROM ISSN 1453-8601
FOTO & MODEL. Text in Romanian. 1997. m. **Document type:** *Magazine, Trade.*
Published by: Hiparion, Str. Mihai Veliciu 15-17, Cluj-Napoca, 3400, Romania. TEL 40-64-411100, FAX 40-64-411700, office@hiparion.ro, http://www.hiparion.com.

770 RUS
FOTO&VIDEO. Text in Russian. 1997. m.
Published by: Izdatel'skii Dom KATMAT, ul Ordzhonikidze 11, Moscow, Russian Federation. TEL 7-495-2344797, FAX 7-495-2344770, info@katmat.ru, http://www.katmat.ru. Ed. Vladimir Neskoromnyi.

770 DEU
FOTO HITS. Text in German. 2005. 10/yr. EUR 25; EUR 2.50 newsstand/cover (effective 2010). adv. **Document type:** *Magazine, Consumer.*
Published by: G F W PhotoPublishing GmbH, Holzstr 2, Duesseldorf, 40221, Germany. TEL 49-211-390090, FAX 49-211-3900955, info@gfw.de, http://www.gfw.de. Ed. Martin Knapp. Adv. contact Ulrich Horst. color page EUR 8,900.

770 DEU ISSN 1436-4255
FOTO HITS DER EINKAUFSFUEHRER; Alles fuers Fotohobby in einem Heft. Text in German. 1994. a. EUR 7.90 newsstand/cover (effective 2010). **Document type:** *Magazine, Consumer.*
Formed by the merger of (19??-1994): Einkaufsfuehrer Spiegelreflex (0941-0341); (19??-1994): Einkaufsfuehrer Kompaktkameras (0941-5904); (19??-1994): Foto-Einkaufsfuehrer Zubehoer (0943-0954); Which was formerly (until 1992): Einkaufsfuehrer Fotozubehoer (0941-0333); (until 1991): Fotozubehoer Journal (0931-086X); (until 1982): Foto-Journal (0344-1210)
Published by: G F W PhotoPublishing GmbH, Holzstr 2, Duesseldorf, 40221, Germany. TEL 49-211-390090, FAX 49-211-3900955, info@gfw.de, http://www.gfw.de. Adv. contact Ulrich Horst.

770 DEU
FOTO HITS FLASHLIGHT. Text in German. 1974. 10/yr. adv. bk.rev. charts; illus.; mkt.; tr.lit. **Document type:** *Magazine, Consumer.*
Former titles (until 2010): Faszination Fotografie; (until 2002): F F - Magazin fuer Fotografie; F F - Foto, Film, Video (0942-296X); (until 1990): F F - Foto und Filmtips (0172-2484); Which was formed by the merger of (1956-1974): Charmant (0009-1820); (19??-1974): Hallo, Photofreunde (0172-2492)
Published by: G F W PhotoPublishing GmbH, Holzstr 2, Duesseldorf, 40221, Germany. TEL 49-211-390090, FAX 49-211-3900955, info@gfw.de. Ed. Martin Knapp. Adv. contact Ulrich Horst. color page EUR 8,900. Circ: 59,274 (paid and controlled).

770 ITA
FOTO IDEA. Text in Italian. 2005. bi-m. **Document type:** *Magazine, Consumer.*
Published by: Acacia Edizioni, Via Copernico 3, Binasco, MI 20082, Italy. http://www.acaciaedizioni.com.

771 POL ISSN 0867-6151
FOTO KURIER; pismo uzytkownikow sprzetu fotograficznego. Text in Polish. 1991. m. PLZ 57.60; PLZ 129.36 foreign (effective 2002). adv. **Document type:** *Consumer.* **Description:** For photo equipment users both professional and amature.
Published by: Agencja Reklamowo-Wydawnicza Foto Kurier, ul. Rzedzinska 23, Warsaw, 01-368, Poland. TEL 48-22-6652433, FAX 48-22-6654179. adv.: page PLZ 1,125; 270 x 190.

770 NLD
FOTO MARKT; vakblad voor de foto-detailhandel, foto-snelservice, foto-vaklabs en vakfotografen. Text in Dutch. 1992. 11/yr. EUR 5 newsstand/cover (effective 2009). adv. bk.rev. illus. **Document type:** *Magazine, Trade.*
Published by: Focus Media Groep, Hendrik Figeeweg 1-z, Haarlem, 2031 BJ, Netherlands. TEL 31-23-5348844, FAX 31-23-5423110, focus@focusmedia.nl, http://www.focusmedia.nl. Ed. Dirk van der Spek. Circ: 5,000.

770 IDN ISSN 0852-596X
FOTO MEDIA. Text in English. 1990. m. **Document type:** *Magazine, Consumer.*
Published by: P T Gramedia, Jalan Palmerah Selatan 22-26, Jakarta, 10270, Indonesia. TEL 62-21-5483008, FAX 62-21-5494035, ulj@gramedia-majalah.com, http://www.gramedia.com. Circ: 10,000.

770 ITA ISSN 0015-8720
FOTO-NOTIZIARIO. Text in Italian. 1946. w. (32/yr.). EUR 10 (effective 2010). adv. bk.rev.; software rev. illus. 58 p./no.; back issues avail. **Document type:** *Magazine, Trade.* **Description:** Covers professional photography, videography and digital images. For professional photographers, photo shops and photofinishers.
Related titles: Online - full text ed.
Published by: Mediaspazio, Via Macedonio Melloni 17, Milan, 20129, Italy. TEL 39-02-718341, FAX 39-02-714067. Ed. Gisella Scattolin.

770 AUT
FOTO OBJEKTIV. Text in German. 6/yr.
Published by: Z B Verlag, Marschallplatz 23-1-21, Vienna, W 1125, Austria. TEL 01-8040474, FAX 01-8044439. Ed. G K Buchberger. Circ: 14,200.

770 BGR ISSN 1311-3178
FOTO OKO. Text in Bulgarian. 1999. bi-m. BGL 33; BGL 5.50 newsstand/cover (effective 2002). **Document type:** *Magazine, Consumer.* **Description:** Devoted to the theory of photography, techniques and practice, news, competitions, etc.
Published by: Photography Information Center, PO Box 162, Sofia, 1606, Bulgaria. TEL 359-2-9885727. Ed. Iglena Ruseva.

770 POL ISSN 1507-4137
TR1
FOTO POZYTYW. Text in Polish. 1999. m. EUR 144 foreign (effective 2006).
Address: ul Jasia i Malgosi 8, Lodz, 94118, Poland. TEL 48-42-6898489, FAX 48-42-6882640. **Dist. by:** Ars Polona, Obroncow 25, Warsaw 03933, Poland. TEL 48-22-5098609, FAX 48-22-5098610, arspolona@arspolona.com.pl, http://www.arspolona.com.pl.

770 ESP
FOTO - VENTAS. Text in Spanish. 1978. 16/yr. adv. back issues avail. **Document type:** *Magazine, Consumer.*
Published by: Fopren S.L., C Comte Borrell, 95, Barcelona, 08015, Spain. TEL 34-93-4253525, FAX 34-93-4241611, fotoventas@fopren.es, http://fotoventasdigital.com/. Ed. Victor Comas. Circ: 5,000 (controlled).

770 BEL ISSN 0777-3625
FOTO VIDEO AUDIO NEWS (DUTCH EDITION). Text in Dutch. 1984. bi-m. free to qualified personnel. adv. illus. 48 p./no.; **Document type:** *Magazine, Trade.* **Description:** Covers news and business developments of interest to all branches of the photo, video and audio trade, including retailers, film processors and photofinishing labs, photographers, manufacturers and importers.
Former titles (until 1989): Foto Film Video News (0777-3617); Foto-Contact (0772-5795)
Related titles: ◆ French ed.: Photo Video Audio News (French Edition). ISSN 0777-3641.
Published by: Mema NV, Wielewaasstraat 20, Wilrijk, 2610, Belgium. TEL 32-3-4480827, FAX 32-3-4480832, pgermeys@skynet.be. Ed., Adv. contact Piet Germeys. B&W page EUR 1,262, color page EUR 2,147; trim 297 x 210. Circ: 3,500 (controlled).

770 NLD ISSN 0165-1692
FOTO VISIE; maandblad voor de fotovakhandel, het minilab en de professionele fotograaf. Text in Dutch. 1971. 10/yr. EUR 39.95 in Netherlands & Belgium; EUR 72.50 elsewhere (effective 2009). adv. abstr.; illus.; mkt.; stat. **Document type:** *Magazine, Trade.*
Published by: Blauw Media Uitgeverij B.V., Postbus 1043, Maarssen, 3600 BA, Netherlands. TEL 31-346-574040, FAX 31-346-576056, info@blauwmedia.com, http://www.blauwmediauitgeverij.nl. Eds. Johan Elzenga, Michiel Mulder. Pub. Henk Louwmans. Adv. contact Gert-Jan Pas TEL 31-314-375631. B&W page EUR 1,185, color page EUR 2,360; trim 210 x 297.

770 DEU
FOTOAGENTUREN UND BILDARCHIVE. Text in English. 1987. a. EUR 25 (effective 2006). **Document type:** *Directory, Trade.* **Description:** Contains over 7,000 addresses, telephone and fax numbers, and e-mail addresses of picture suppliers worldwide.
Former titles (until 2003): Picture Research, Photo Agencies and Libraries; (until 1995): Foto Agenturen und Archive
Related titles: German ed.
Published by: Presse Informations Agentur GmbH, Lothar-von-Kuebel Str 18, Sinzheim, 76547, Germany. TEL 49-7221-3017560, FAX 49-7221-3017570, office@piag.de, http://piag.de.

770 RUS ISSN 1728-189X
FOTODELO. Text in Russian. 2002. m. **Document type:** *Journal, Trade.*
Published by: Izdatel'skii Dom Connect!, ul Dolgorukovskaya 23A, 4 etazh, Moscow, 127006, Russian Federation. TEL 7-095-1051118, FAX 7-095-9785100, post@connect.ru, http://www.connect.ru.

770 DEU
FOTOFORUM. Text in German. bi-m. EUR 37.50; EUR 6.95 newsstand/cover (effective 2006). adv. **Document type:** *Magazine, Consumer.*
Published by: Fotoforum Verlag e.K., Ludwig-Wolker-Str 37, Muenster, 48157, Germany. TEL 49-251-143930, FAX 49-251-143939, info@fotoforum.de. Ed. Martin Breutmann. adv.: B&W page EUR 2,170, color page EUR 3,320; trim 210 x 297. Circ: 13,800 (paid and controlled).

770 DEU ISSN 0720-5260
TR15
FOTOGESCHICHTE; Beitraege zur Geschichte und Aesthetik der Fotografie. Text in German. 1981. q. EUR 64 domestic; EUR 75.13 foreign (effective 2003). bk.rev. index. **Document type:** *Journal, Academic/Scholarly.*
Indexed: ABM, B24, BibInd, DIP, IBR, IBZ, SCOPUS.
Published by: Jonas Verlag, Weidenhaeuser Str 88, Marburg, 35037, Germany. TEL 49-6421-25132, FAX 49-6421-210572, jonas@jonas-verlag.de, http://www.jonas-verlag.de. Ed. Anton Holzer. Circ: 550.

770 ITA
FOTOGRAFARE. Text in Italian. 1967. m. EUR 40 domestic (effective 2008). adv. bk.rev. **Document type:** *Magazine, Consumer.*
Former titles: Fotografare Novita (1125-8098); (until 1982): Fotografare (1125-8071); (until 1977): Fotografe Novita (1125-808X); (until 1972): Fotografe (0015-878X)
Published by: Cesco Ciapanna Editore S.r.l., Via Lipari 8, Rome, 00141, Italy. TEL 39-06-87183441, FAX 39-06-87183995. Circ: 80,000.

770 BRA ISSN 1413-7232
FOTOGRAFE MELHOR; suas melhores fotos comecam aqui. Text in Burmese. 1996. 18/yr. BRL 151.47; BRL 9.90 newsstand/cover (effective 2007). adv. **Document type:** *Magazine, Consumer.* **Description:** Covers equipment, filters, know-how, illumination and production in the photography field.
Published by: Editora Europa Ltda., Rua MMDC 121, Butanta, Sao Paulo, SP 05510-021, Brazil. TEL 55-11-30385050, FAX 55-11-38190538. Ed. Aydano Roriz. Adv. contact Ana Maria Faria de Oliveira. Circ: 23,800 (paid).

770 NOR ISSN 0806-7732
FOTOGRAFI. Text in Norwegian. 1968. 8/yr. adv. bk.rev.
Former titles (until 1995): Fotografi Video (0802-9628); (until 1990): Fotografi (0046-4805)
Published by: Forlaget Fotografi AS, PO Box 28, Snaroeya, 1335, Norway. TEL 47-67-81-86-80, FAX 47-67-81-86-86. Ed. Tore Holten TEL 47-67-81-86-83. Adv. contact John Willy Schulteiss TEL 47-67-81-86-81. color page NOK 22,200; 187 x 268. Circ: 12,000.

770 POL ISSN 1509-9628
TR1
FOTOGRAFIA. Text in Polish. 2000. q. PLZ 18 per issue domestic; USD 8 per issue foreign (effective 2002 - 2003). **Document type:** *Magazine, Consumer.*
Related titles: Online - full content ed.: ISSN 1689-1260.
Published by: Wydawnictwo Kropka, ul Szczecinska 5, Wrzesnia, 62300, Poland. TEL 48-61-4379754. Ed. Zbigniew Tomaszczuk. Circ: 1,000.

770 ESP ISSN 1887-1267
LA FOTOGRAFIA ACTUAL. Text in Spanish. 1989. 6/yr. EUR 26 domestic; EUR 76 foreign (effective 2007). adv. bk.rev. **Document type:** *Consumer.* **Description:** Aims to inform about the most representative images and photographic events.
Formerly (until 1991): Fotografia (1134-9506)
Published by: Artual Ediciones S.L., Calle Paris 150, Entlo. 1a, Barcelona, 08036, Spain. TEL 34-93-4548100, FAX 34-93-4309627, info@la-fotografia.com, http://www.la-fotografia.com/. Ed., Pub. Francs Gori. R&P, Adv. contact Concepcion Alarcon. Circ: 30,000 (paid).

770 ITA ISSN 1970-1942
FOTOGRAFIA & VIDEO DIGITALE PER TUTTI. Text in Italian. 2006. w. **Document type:** *Magazine, Consumer.*
Published by: Rolling Group Srl, Corso Re Umberto 30, Turin, 10128, Italy. info@rollingmedia.it, http://www.rollingmedia.it.

770 ITA ISSN 1594-2449
FOTOGRAFIA REFLEX. Text in Italian. 1980. m. EUR 48 domestic (effective 2009). adv. bk.rev. **Document type:** *Magazine, Consumer.*
Formerly (until 2000): Reflex (0393-473X)
Related titles: Online - full text ed.
Published by: Editrice Reflex s.r.l., Via di Villa Severini 54, Rome, 00191, Italy. TEL 39-06-36308595, FAX 39-06-3295648, segreteria@reflex.it. Circ: 45,000.

770 CZE ISSN 1211-0019
TR1
FOTOGRAFIE MAGAZIN/PHOTOGRAPHY. Text in Czech, Slovak; Summaries in English, German, Russian. 1946. m. CZK 869 domestic (effective 2008). adv. bk.rev. charts; illus. index. **Document type:** *Magazine, Consumer.*
Former titles (until 1993): Fotografie (1211-0256); (until 1991): Ceskoslovenska Fotografie (0009-0549)
Published by: (Spolecnost Pratel Fotografie), ABEBE - Richard Guryca, Letenske namesti 2, Prague 7, 170 00, Czech Republic. Ed. Richard Guryca.

770 DNK ISSN 1600-9797
FOTOGRAFISK AARBOG. Text in Danish. 1979. a. DKK 345 membership (effective 2009). adv. **Document type:** *Yearbook, Consumer.*
Former titles (until 2000): Dansk Fotografi (0901-7453); (until 1982): Selskabet for Dansk Fotografi - Aarskatalog (0107-0363)
Published by: Selskabet for Dansk Fotografi, c/o Per Valentin, Bavnager 57, Oelsted, 3310, Denmark. TEL 45-48280813, info@sdf.dk, http://www.sdf.dk.

770 SWE ISSN 0284-7035
FOTOGRAFISK TIDSKRIFT. Variant title: F. Text in Swedish. 1911. 6/yr. SEK 400 (effective 2004). adv. bk.rev. charts; illus.; tr.lit. index. 52 p./no.; **Document type:** *Magazine, Consumer.*
Former titles (until 1988): Svensk Fotografisk Tidskrift (0039-6540); (until 1916): Svenska Fotografen
Indexed: ABM, ChemAb, SCOPUS.
Published by: Svenska Fotografers Foerbund/Swedish Professional Photographers Association, Upplandsgatan 4, Stockholm, 11123, Sweden. Ed. Goesta Flemming TEL 46-8-7020371. Adv. contact Hans Flygare TEL 46-8-6627500. Circ: 6,000.

770 ITA ISSN 1122-696X
IL FOTOGRAFO. Text in Italian. 1992. m. EUR 39.90 (effective 2011). adv. **Document type:** *Magazine, Consumer.*

Published by: Sprea Editori Srl, Via Torino 51, Cernusco sul Naviglio, MI 20063, Italy. TEL 39-02-92432222, FAX 39-02-92432236, editori@sprea.it, http://www.sprea.it.

770 ITA ISSN 1592-6362
IL FOTOGRAFO DIGITALE. Text in Italian. 2001. m. EUR 39.90 (effective 2009). **Document type:** *Magazine, Consumer.*
Published by: Sprea Editori Srl, Via Torino 51, Cernusco sul Naviglio, MI 20063, Italy. TEL 39-02-92432222, FAX 39-02-92432236, editori@sprea.it, http://www.sprea.it.

770 ITA ISSN 1723-6118
IL FOTOGRAFO DIGITALE ANNUAL. Text in Italian. 2001. a. **Document type:** *Catalog, Consumer.*
Published by: Sprea Editori Srl, Via Torino 51, Cernusco sul Naviglio, MI 20063, Italy. TEL 39-02-92432222, FAX 39-02-92432236, editori@sprea.it, http://www.sprea.it.

FOTOGRAMAS Y VIDEO. *see* MOTION PICTURES

770 ITA ISSN 1121-0346
FOTOLOGIA; studi di storia della fotografia. Text in Italian. 1985. a. price varies. 128 p./no.; **Document type:** *Monographic series, Consumer.*
Published by: (Museo di Storia della Fotografia), Fratelli Alinari SpA, Largo Fratelli Alinari 15, Florence, FI 50123, Italy. TEL 39-055-23951, FAX 39-055-2382857, distribution@alinari.it, http://www.alinari.it.

770 DEU ISSN 0340-6660
FOTOMAGAZIN. Text in German. 1947. m. EUR 5.20 newsstand/cover (effective 2011). adv. bk.rev. illus. index. **Document type:** *Magazine, Consumer.*
Formerly (until 1949): Foto-Spiegel (0174-2485); Incorporates (1966-1981): Film- & Ton-Magazin (0015-1114); (1922-1981): Camera (0008-2074); (1948-1965): Fotopost (0174-2434); Which was formerly: Fotoindustrie (0174-2426)
Indexed: A22, RASB.
—IE, Infotrieve.
Published by: Jahr Top Special Verlag, Troplowitzstr 5, Hamburg, 22529, Germany. TEL 49-40-389060, FAX 49-40-38906300, info@jahr-tsv.de, http://www.jahr-tsv.de. Ed. Franz Raith. Adv. contact Jutta Friedrichsen-Devakar. Circ: 41,748 (paid).

770 778.5 621.389 MEX
FOTOMUNDO. Text in Spanish. 1969. m. MXN 130, USD 15.
Published by: Editorial Mex-Ameris, S.A., Av. Morelos, No. 16, 4 Piso, Mexico City 1, DF, Mexico. Ed. Julio Perales Gay. Circ: 40,000.

778.53 ARG ISSN 0325-7150
FOTOMUNDO. Text in Spanish. 1966. m. adv. bk.rev.; Website rev. back issues avail. **Document type:** *Magazine.*
Related titles: Online - full content ed.
Published by: Ediciones Fotograficas Argentina S.A., Maipu 671, Piso 5, Buenos Aires, 1006, Argentina. TEL 54-114-3222006, FAX 54-114-3222171, fotomundo@fotomundo.com. Ed. Silvia Mangialardi. Circ: 10,000.

770 HUN ISSN 0532-3010
TR640
FOTOMUVESZET. Text in Hungarian; Summaries in English. 1958. q. **Document type:** *Magazine, Consumer.*
Formerly (until 1966): Fenykepmuveszeti Tajekoztato (0200-1551)
Indexed: ABM, RASB, SCOPUS.
Published by: Magyar Fotografiai Szakszajto Alapitvany, Pf. 72, Budapest, 1676, Hungary. TEL 36-1-2913621. Circ: 3,500.

778.53 VEN ISSN 0015-8895
FOTON; fotografia, cine y sonida (photography, amateur movie and sound). Text in Spanish. 1965. m. adv.
Published by: M.G. Ediciones Especializadas, S.A., Av. Maturin, No. 15, Urb. Los Cedros, El Bosque, Caracas, 1050, Venezuela. Ed. Montserrat Giol. Circ: 4,500.

770 NLD ISSN 1871-7802
FOTONICA MAGAZINE. Cover title: Fotonica. Text in Dutch. 1975. q. EUR 39 to individuals; EUR 56 to institutions; EUR 19 to students (effective 2009). adv. **Document type:** *Magazine, Trade.*
Former titles (until 2003): Nederlands Tijdschrift voor Fotonica (0925-5338); (until 1980): Fotonica Mededelingen (0925-5346)
—IE, Infotrieve.
Published by: Photonics Cluster Netherlands, c/o Guus Taminiau, Prins Bernhardstraat 64, Koudekerk aan den Rijn, 2396 GN, Netherlands. info@photonicscluster-nl.org, http://www.photonicscluster-nl.org. Eds. Bob Kruizinga, Erwin Dekker, Guus Taminiau.

770 SWE ISSN 0015-8909
FOTONYHETERNA. Text in Swedish. 1961. 10/yr. SEK 398. adv. bk.rev. charts; illus.; mkt.; pat.; tr.lit.
Incorporating: Scandinavian Journal of Photography and Film
Address: Fack 5111, Stockholm, 10243, Sweden. Ed. Bjoern Sandels. Circ: 5,000.

770 SWE ISSN 2000-5105
▼ **FOTOSIDAN MAGASIN.** Text in Swedish. 2009. bi-m. SEK 379 (effective 2011). adv. **Document type:** *Magazine, Consumer.*
Published by: I D G AB (Subsidiary of: I D G Communications Inc.), Karlbergsvaegen 77-81, Stockholm, 10678, Sweden. TEL 46-8-4536000, FAX 46-8-4536005, kundservice@idg.se, http://www.idg.se. Ed. Magnus Froderberg. Adv. contact Magnus Mu Ray. Circ: 23,000 (paid).

770 CUB
FOTOTECNICA. Text in Spanish. q. USD 8 in North America; USD 10 in South America; USD 12 in Europe; USD 14 elsewhere. illus.
Published by: (Union de Periodistas de Cuba, Secretariado Ejecutivo), Ediciones Cubanas, Obispo 527, Havana, Cuba.

770 920 HUN ISSN 0209-6927
FOTOTEKA. Text in Hungarian. 1981. irreg. HUF 600. **Document type:** *Catalog.* **Description:** Presents photographs of famous Hungarian writers.
Published by: Magyar Irodalmi Muzeum/Musuem of Hungarian Literature, Karolyi Mihaly utca 16, Budapest 5, 1053, Hungary. TEL 36-1-3173611, FAX 36-1-3171722. Ed. Mihaly Praznovszky.

771.3 CZE ISSN 1213-855X
FOTOVIDEO. Text in Czech. 1996. 10/yr. CZK 636; CZK 89 newsstand/cover (effective 2008). adv. **Document type:** *Magazine, Consumer.*
Formerly (until 1999): Advanced Obraz & Zvuk (1211-5312)
Related titles: Online - full text ed.: iFotoVideo. ISSN 1801-4356. 2005.
Published by: Atemi s.r.o., Velvarska 1626 - 45, Prague 6, 160 00, Czech Republic. TEL 420-233-025501, FAX 420-233-025502, info@atemi.cz, http://www.atemi.cz. Ed. Rudolf Stahlich. adv.: page CZK 90,000; trim 203 x 267. Circ: 15,000 (paid and controlled).

770 DEU ISSN 0340-6644
FOTOWIRTSCHAFT; Das Wirtschaftsmagazin fuer die Fotobranche. Text in German. 1950. m. EUR 70.20; EUR 6.35 newsstand/cover (effective 2011). adv. charts; illus.; mkt.; pat.; stat. index. **Document type:** *Magazine, Trade.*
Formerly (until 1975): Fotohaendler (0015-8844)
Indexed: PhotoAb.
Published by: Jahr Top Special Verlag, Troplowitzstr 5, Hamburg, 22529, Germany. TEL 49-40-389060, FAX 49-40-38906300, info@jahr-tsv.de, http://www.jahr-tsv.de. Ed. Franz Raith. Adv. contact Jutta Friedrichsen-Devakar. Circ: 3,080 (paid and controlled).

770 NLD ISSN 1879-5153
▼ **FOUR EYES PHOTOGRAPHY MAGAZINE.** Text in English. 2009. s-a. EUR 3 newsstand/cover (effective 2010). adv. **Document type:** *Magazine, Consumer.*
Published by: Four Eyes Photography & Art, Zaagmolenkade 46, Unit 2, Rotterdam, 3035 KA, Netherlands. TEL 31-6-22471800, info@four-eyes.nl, http://www.four-eyes.nl.

770 USA
TR183
FRAME WORK PRESS; art books and catalogues. Text in English. 1987. s-a. USD 35 domestic to individuals; USD 40 foreign to individuals; USD 45 domestic to institutions; USD 50 foreign to institutions (effective 1999 - 2000). adv. illus. back issues avail.; reprints avail. **Document type:** *Journal, Trade.*
Formerly: Frame / Work (0895-6030); Which was formed by the merger of (1979-1987): Camera Lucida (0740-8641); (1980-1987): Obscura (0273-0235)
Published by: Los Angeles Center for Photographic Studies, 6518 Hollywood Blvd, Los Angeles, CA 90028. TEL 323-466-6232, FAX 323-466-3203. Ed. Tania Martinez Lemke. Adv. contact Anne Yang. Circ: 2,000.

770 FRA ISSN 1625-6433
FRANCE - PHOTOGRAPHIE. Text in French. 1968. bi-m. (5/yr). EUR 30 domestic to non-members; EUR 30 DOM-TOM to non-members; EUR 42 foreign to non-members (effective 2009). Website rev.; bk.rev. 64 p./no.; back issues avail. **Document type:** *Magazine, Consumer.* **Description:** Informs on the activities of photo clubs and photography in general.
Formerly (until 1970): Federation Nationale des Societes Photographiques de France. Bulletin d'Information (1625-6441)
Published by: Federation Photographique, 5 rue Jules Valles, Paris, 75011, France. TEL 33-1-43713040, FAX 33-1-43713877, http://ourworld.compuserve.com/homepage.fpf. Ed., Adv. contact Jean Lamouret. Circ: 5,000.

FREELANCE WRITER'S REPORT. *see* JOURNALISM

770 JPN ISSN 0915-1478
TR196.5.F85
FUJI FILM RESEARCH & DEVELOPMENT. Text in Japanese, English. 1953. a. **Document type:** *Journal, Trade.*
Formerly (until 1988): Fuji Shashin Fuirumu Kenkyu Hokoku (0367-3189)
Indexed: A22, RefZh, SCOPUS.
—BLDSC (4054.847000), IE, Ingenta.
Published by: Fuji Shashin Fuirumu Kabushiki Gaisha, Ashigara Kenkyujo, Gijutsu Shiryoshitsu/Fuji Photo Film Company, Ashigara Research Laboratories, Technical Information Office, 210 Nakanuma, Minami-Ashigara, Kanagawa, 250-0193, Japan. TEL 81-465-741111.

FUJIAN HUABAO/FUJIAN PICTORIAL. *see* GENERAL INTEREST PERIODICALS—China

778.1 USA ISSN 2150-198X
FUTURECLAW. Text in English. 2008. q. USD 72 domestic; USD 225 foreign (effective 2009). back issues avail. **Document type:** *Magazine, Consumer.*
Related titles: Online - full text ed.
Published by: FutureClaw LLC., 113 Church St, Burlington, VT 05401. TEL 802-922-9380, 800-320-9299. Ed. Bobby Mozumder.

G A HOUSES. (Global Architecture) *see* ARCHITECTURE

770 NLD ISSN 1871-8450
G U P. (Guide to Unique Photography) Text in Dutch. 2005. bi-m. EUR 33 domestic; EUR 44 in Europe; EUR 72 elsewhere (effective 2009). adv. **Document type:** *Magazine, Consumer.* **Description:** Covers all aspects of photography, from documentary to fashion, contemporary to historical, and world-famous photographers to young or upcoming talent.
Published by: HUP Editions, Tesselschadestr 15, Amsterdam, 1054 ET, Netherlands.

GADNEY'S GUIDES TO INTERNATIONAL CONTESTS, FESTIVALS & GRANTS IN FILM & VIDEO, PHOTOGRAPHY, TV-RADIO BROADCASTING, WRITING & JOURNALISM. *see* COMMUNICATIONS

GANSU HUABAO/GANSU PICTORIAL. *see* GENERAL INTEREST PERIODICALS—China

770 JPN ISSN 0915-6755
GAZO RABO/IMAGE LAB. Text in Japanese. 1990. m. JPY 18,000; JPY 1,500 newsstand/cover (effective 2006). **Document type:** *Journal, Academic/Scholarly.*
Published by: Nihon Kogyo Shuppan K.K./Japan Industrial Publishing Co., Ltd., 6-3-26 Honkomagome, Bunkyo-ku, Tokyo, 113-0021, Japan. TEL 81-3-39441181, FAX 81-3-39446826, info@nikko-pb.co.jp.

778.315 JPN ISSN 0913-2708
GEKKAN I M/JOURNAL OF IMAGE & INFORMATION MANAGEMENT. Text in Japanese. 1962. m. JPY 12,600 (effective 2008). adv. charts; illus.; mkt.; stat. cum.index. **Document type:** *Journal, Academic/Scholarly.*
Former titles (until 1987): Maikuroshashin/Journal of Micrographics (0287-6655); (until 1983): Maikuro Shashin/Journal of Microphotography (0026-2811); (until 1967): Maikuro Shashin Joho
Related titles: Microfiche ed.: 1962.
—BLDSC (5004.552500).
Published by: Nihon Gazo Joho Manejimento Kyokai/Japan Image & Information Management Association, 2-1-3 Iwamoto-cho, Chiyoda-ku, Wako Bldg 7th. Fl, Tokyo, 101-0032, Japan. TEL 81-3-58217451, FAX 81-3-58217354, kuriyama@jiima.or.jp, http://www.jiima.or.jp/. Ed. Tokuchika Ochiai. Circ: 3,500.

778.53 USA
GEORGE EASTMAN HOUSE - INTERNATIONAL MUSEUM OF PHOTOGRAPHY AND FILM. ANNUAL REPORT. Text in English. 19??. a. back issues avail. **Document type:** *Corporate.*
Published by: George Eastman House - International Museum of Photography and Film, 900 East Ave, Rochester, NY 14607. TEL 585-271-3361, http://www.eastmanhouse.org.

GOLDEN DOLPHIN VIDEO C D MAGAZINE. (Compact Disc) *see* EARTH SCIENCES—Oceanography

770 USA
GORDON'S (YEAR) INTERNATIONAL PHOTOGRAPHY PRICE ANNUAL. Text in English. 1995. a. USD 65. **Document type:** *Directory.* **Description:** Contains over 5000 entries organized by photographer and print title.
Related titles: CD-ROM ed.: 1995.
Published by: Gordon's Art Reference, Inc. (Subsidiary of: L T B Media), 306 W Coronado Rd, Phoenix, AZ 85003-1147. TEL 941-434-6842, FAX 941-434-6969.

770 659 USA
TR690.A1
GRAPHIS PHOTOGRAPHY ANNUAL; the international annual of photography. Text in English, French, German. 1966. a. index. **Document type:** *Journal, Trade.* **Description:** Highlights and showcases notable photography.
Former titles (until 2008): Graphis Photography Journal (1931-8081); Which superseded in part (in 2006): Graphis (0017-3452); (until 2005): PhotoAnnual; (until 2004): Graphis Photo Annual; (until 2000): Photo Annual; (until 1998): Graphis Photo (1016-0507); (until 1987): Photographis (0079-1830)
—BLDSC (4212.527000), IE, Ingenta.
Published by: Graphis Inc., 307 Fifth Ave, 10th Fl, New York, NY 10016. TEL 212-532-9387, FAX 212-213-3229, GraphisOrders@abdintl.com. Circ: 12,500. **Subscr. to:** PO Box 1020, Sewickley, PA 15143-1020. TEL 412-741-3679, 800-209-4234.

GRAPHIS POSTERS. *see* ART

770 USA
GREEN BOOK: THE DIRECTORY OF NATURAL HISTORY AND GENERAL STOCK PHOTOGRAPHY. Text in English. biennial. USD 28. **Document type:** *Directory.* **Description:** Lists photo sources for editorial photo buyers. Features descriptions of stock files and cross-referenced natural history, general stock and geographic indexes.
Published by: A G Editions, Inc., 41 Union Sq W Ste 523, New York, NY 10003-3208. TEL 212-929-0959, FAX 212-924-4796. Ed., Pub. Ann Guilfoyle.

770 USA ISSN 0889-8235
GUILFOYLE REPORT. Text in English. 1982. 10/yr. USD 225 (effective 1998). **Document type:** *Newsletter, Trade.* **Description:** For natural history photographers. Identifies buyers and lists their photo needs. Also discusses equipment, pricing, and professional practices.
Related titles: E-mail ed.; Online - full text ed.
Published by: A G Editions, Inc., 41 Union Sq W Ste 523, New York, NY 10003-3208. TEL 212-929-0959, FAX 212-924-4796. Ed., Pub., R&P Ann Guilfoyle. Circ: 1,000.

770 USA ISSN 1551-4943
HAMBURGER EYES. Text in English. 2001. q. USD 10 newsstand/cover (effective 2006). **Document type:** *Magazine, Consumer.*
Published by: Burgerword Media, P O Box 420546, San Francisco, CA 94142.

770 SWE ISSN 0282-5449
HASSELBLAD FORUM (ENGLISH EDITION). Text in English. 1965. q. **Document type:** *Magazine, Consumer.*
Formerly (until 1985): Hasselblad (English Edition) (0345-4533)
Indexed: ABM, SCOPUS.
Published by: Hasselblad AB, Victor, Pumpgatan 2, Box 220, Goeteborg, 401 23, Sweden. TEL 46-31-102400, FAX 46-31-135074, info@hasselblad.se, http://www.hasselblad.se.

HENAN HUABAO. *see* GENERAL INTEREST PERIODICALS—China

770 GBR ISSN 0308-7298
TR15
➤ **HISTORY OF PHOTOGRAPHY.** Text in English. 1976. q. GBP 408 combined subscription in United Kingdom to institutions (print & online eds.); EUR 542, USD 680 combined subscription to institutions (print & online eds.) (effective 2012). adv. bk.rev. illus. back issues avail.; reprint service avail. from PSC. **Document type:** *Journal, Academic/Scholarly.* **Description:** Devoted to the history and early development of this graphic art form. Covers the earliest uses of photography in exploration, science and war, lives of notable practitioners and inventors; the influence of photography on painting and sculpture; history of photojournalism; and the preservation and restoration of old photographs.
Related titles: Online - full text ed.: ISSN 2150-7295. GBP 367 in United Kingdom to institutions; EUR 488, USD 613 to institutions (effective 2012) (from IngentaConnect).
Indexed: A01, A03, A06, A07, A08, A20, A22, A30, A31, AA, ABCT, ABM, AIAP, ASCA, AmH&L, AmHI, ArtHuCI, ArtInd, B04, B24, BAS, BrHumI, CA, CMM, CurCont, DIP, E01, FR, H07, HistAb, IBR, IBZ, PCI, RASB, RILM, SCOPUS, T02, W07.
—BLDSC (4318.395000), IE, Infotrieve, Ingenta, INIST. **CCC.**
Published by: Routledge (Subsidiary of: Taylor & Francis Group), 4 Park Sq, Milton Park, Abingdon, Oxon OX14 4RN, United Kingdom. TEL 44-20-70176000, FAX 44-20-70176336, subscriptions@tandf.co.uk, http://www.routledge.com. Ed. Graham Smith. Adv. contact Linda Hann TEL 44-1344-779945. **Subscr. in N. America to:** Taylor & Francis Inc., Customer Services Dept, 325 Chestnut St, 8th Fl, Philadelphia, PA 19106. TEL 215-625-8900, 800-354-1420, FAX 215-625-2940, customerservice@taylorandfrancis.com; **Subscr. to:** Taylor & Francis Ltd., Journals Customer Service, Sheepen Pl, Colchester, Essex CO3 3LP, United Kingdom. TEL 44-20-70175544, FAX 44-20-70175198, tf.enquiries@tfinforma.com.

➤ **HJAERNSTORM.** *see* ART

P

770 GBR ISSN 0959-6933
TR690
HOTSHOE INTERNATIONAL; the magazine for today's professional photographer. Text in English. 1980. bi-m. GBP 23 domestic; GBP 30 in Europe; GBP 39 elsewhere; GBP 25 combined subscription domestic; GBP 38 combined subscription in Europe; GBP 41 combined subscription elsewhere (effective 2009). bk.rev.; software rev. illus. back issues avail. **Document type:** *Magazine, Trade.* **Description:** Directed to the advertising, design, and corporate photographer.
Formerly (198?): Hot Shoe (0260-5783)
Related titles: Online - full text ed.: GBP 15 (effective 2009).
Indexed: SCOPUS.
—CCC.
Published by: World Illustrated, 29 - 31 Saffron Hill, London, EC1N 8SW, United Kingdom. TEL 44-20-74216000, FAX 44-20-74216006, admin@worldillustrated.com, http://www.worldillustrated.com/. Ed. Melissa DeWitt.

770 USA ISSN 1942-9436
I HEART MAGAZINE. Text in English. 2008. q. **Document type:** *Magazine, Consumer.* **Description:** Contains a collection of black and white duotone photographs contributed by famous photographers as well as amateurs.
Address: PO Box 777, New York, NY 10108.

I R I S. (International Research for Image Selection) *see* LAW

770 DEU ISSN 1023-8573
I R I S (DEUTSCHE AUSGABE). Text in German. 1995. 10/yr. EUR 230 (effective 2009). reprint service avail. from SCH. **Document type:** *Journal, Academic/Scholarly.*
Related titles: ◆ French ed.: I R I S. ISSN 1023-8557.
Published by: Nomos Verlagsgesellschaft mbH und Co. KG, Waldseestr 3-5, Baden-Baden, 76530, Germany. TEL 49-7221-21040, FAX 49-7221-210427, nomos@nomos.de, http://www.nomos.de.

770 620 686.2 USA
I S & T ANNUAL CONFERENCE. PROCEEDINGS. Text in English. 194?. a., latest 1997. back issues avail. **Document type:** *Proceedings, Academic/Scholarly.*
Formerly: S P S E Annual Conference. Paper Summaries
Published by: Society for Imaging Science and Technology, 7003 Kilworth Ln, Springfield, VA 22151. TEL 703-642-9090, FAX 703-642-9094, info@imaging.org, http://www.imaging.org/ist/index.cfm.

770 620 686.2 USA
I S & T NON-IMPACT PRINTING PROCEEDINGS. Text in English. 198?. a. price varies. **Document type:** *Proceedings, Academic/Scholarly.* **Description:** Covers all aspects of the technology.
Published by: Society for Imaging Science and Technology, 7003 Kilworth Ln, Springfield, VA 22151. TEL 703-642-9090, FAX 703-642-9094, info@imaging.org, http://www.imaging.org/ist/index.cfm.

770 620 686.2 USA
I S & T - S P I E SYMPOSIUM ON ELECTRONIC IMAGING: SCIENCE AND TECHNOLOGY. ABSTRACTS. Text in English. a. back issues avail. **Document type:** *Proceedings, Academic/Scholarly.*
Published by: Society for Imaging Science and Technology, 7003 Kilworth Ln, Springfield, VA 22151. TEL 703-642-9090, FAX 703-642-9094, info@imaging.org, http://www.imaging.org/ist/index.cfm. **Co-sponsor:** S P I E - International Society for Optical Engineering.

770 AUS ISSN 0728-5701
IMAGE. Text in English. 1964. bi-m. adv. bk.rev. **Description:** Contains photographs, articles about photography and society news and information.
Published by: Australian Photographic Society Inc., PO Box 7339, Geelong West, VIC 3218, Australia. TEL 61-3-5243-4440. Ed. Max Leonard. Circ: 1,200.

770 ZAF
IMAGE. Text in Afrikaans, English. m. (except Dec.). adv.
Published by: Photographic Society of Southern Africa, PO Box 370, Edenvale, 1610, South Africa.

770 GBR ISSN 1361-2050
IMAGE (LONDON). Text in English. 1969. m. adv. bk.rev. **Document type:** *Magazine, Trade.*
—CCC.
Published by: Association of Photographers, 81 Leonard St, London, EC2A 4QS, United Kingdom. TEL 44-20-77396669, FAX 44-20-77398707, general@aophoto.co.uk, http://www.the-aop.org/. Circ: 2,500.

778.53 USA ISSN 0536-5465
TR1
➤ **IMAGE (ROCHESTER, 1952)**; journal of photography and motion pictures. Text in English. 1952. 6/yr. free to members (effective 2009). illus. back issues avail.; reprints avail. **Document type:** *Magazine, Trade.* **Description:** Presents scholarly essays and reproductions covering the science, history and art of photography and film.
Related titles: Online - full text ed.
Indexed: A06, A07, A20, A22, A26, A30, A31, AA, ABS&EES, ArtInd, B04, B24, CA, E08, I05, S09, T02.
—Ingenta.
Published by: George Eastman House - International Museum of Photography and Film, 900 East Ave, Rochester, NY 14607. TEL 585-271-3361.

770 USA
IMAGEPACK. Text in English. m. back issues avail. **Document type:** *Newsletter, Trade.*
Published by: (Association of Photo C D Imagers), Photo Marketing Association International, 3000 Picture Pl, Jackson, MI 49201. TEL 517-788-8100, 800-762-9287, FAX 517-788-8371, gpageau@pmai.org, http://www.pmai.org.

770 791 FRA ISSN 1955-6063
IMAGES SPECTACLES PHOTO. Text in French. 2007. bi-m. **Document type:** *Magazine, Consumer.*
Published by: Agence Enguerand, 12 Chemin du Moulin Basset, Saint-Denis, 93200, France. TEL 33-1-58349070, FAX 33-1-58349079, agence@enguerand.com, http://213.215.53.34/agence/login.php.

771 535 GBR ISSN 1368-2199
TR1 CODEN: ISCJFK
➤ **THE IMAGING SCIENCE JOURNAL.** Text in English. 1944. bi-m. GBP 555 combined subscription to institutions (print & online eds.); USD 974 combined subscription in United States to institutions (print & online eds.) (effective 2012). adv. bk.rev. stat.; illus. index. back issues avail.; reprint service avail. from PSC. **Document type:** *Journal, Academic/Scholarly.* **Description:** Embraces conventional chemical, electronic, digital and hybrid imaging systems and processes. Main subject areas are digital imaging, applications, visual perception and image quality, fundamental silver halide processing, photographic gelatins.
Former titles (until 1997): Journal of Photographic Science (0022-3638); (until 1953): Photographic Journal, Section B: Scientific and Technical Photography (0370-0240); Which superseded in part (in 1945): Photographic Journal (1461-9415); Which was formerly (until 1895): Photographic Society of Great Britain. Journal and Transactions (1461-9466); (until 1876): Photographic Journal (1461-9458); (until 1959): Photographic Society of London. Journal (1461-9407)
Related titles: Microform ed.: (from PQC); Online - full text ed.: ISSN 1743-131X. GBP 502 to institutions; USD 880 in United States to institutions (effective 2012) (from IngentaConnect).
Indexed: A&ATA, A01, A03, A08, A20, A22, ASCA, B&BAb, B19, CA, CIN, Cadscan, ChemAb, ChemTitl, CurCont, GALA, ISR, Inspec, LeadAb, PhotoAb, S01, SCI, SCOPUS, T02, W07, Zincscan.
—BLDSC (4368.996555), AskIEEE, CASDDS, IE, Infotrieve, Ingenta, INIST, Linda Hall. **CCC.**
Published by: (The Royal Photographic Society), Maney Publishing, Ste 1C, Joseph's Well, Hanover Walk, Leeds, W Yorks LS3 1AB, United Kingdom. TEL 44-113-2432800, FAX 44-113-3868178, maney@maney.co.uk, http://www.maney.co.uk. Ed. Dr. Ralph Jacobson. adv.: B&W page GBP 800, color page GBP 1,260. **Subscr. in N America to:** Maney Publishing, 875 Massachusetts Ave, 7th Fl, Cambridge, MA 02139. TEL 866-297-5154, FAX 617-354-6875, maney@maneyusa.com.

770 DEU ISSN 1430-1121
IMAGING UND FOTO-CONTACT. Text in German. 1972. m. EUR 4 newsstand/cover (effective 2009). adv. **Document type:** *Magazine, Trade.*
Former titles (until 1996): Foto- und Video-Contact (0942-3702); (until 1992): Foto-Contact (0722-7051)
Published by: C.A.T. Verlag Bloemer GmbH, Freiligrathring 18-20, Ratingen, 40878, Germany. TEL 49-2102-20270, FAX 49-2102-202790, worldofphoto@cat-verlag.de, http://www.cat-verlag.de. Ed. Thomas Bloemer. adv.: B&W page EUR 2,580, color page EUR 4,386. Circ: 7,397 (paid and controlled).

770 ITA ISSN 1592-341X
IMMAGINI FOTOPRATICA. Text in Italian. 1968. a. EUR 10 per issue domestic (effective 2009). bk.rev. 250 p./no.; **Document type:** *Magazine, Trade.* **Description:** Covers photography, technical aspects, cultural events and more.
Formerly (until 1985): Fotopratica (0015-8917)
Published by: Design Diffusion Edizioni, Via Lucano 3, Milan, 20135, Italy. TEL 39-02-5516109, FAX 39-02-59902431, info@designdiffusion.com, http://www.designdiffusion.com. Circ: 22,000.

770 700 DEU
INFOBRIEF: FOTOGRAFIE; ein Kulleraugen Informationsdienst. Text in German. 1994. fortn. looseleaf. EUR 30 (effective 2001). bk.rev.; software rev. back issues avail. **Document type:** *Newsletter, Consumer.*
Formerly: Infofax: Fotografie (0947-8418)
Media: Fax.
Published by: Kulleraugen Verlag, Laaseweg 4, Schellerten, 31174, Germany. TEL 49-5123-4330, FAX 49-5123-2015, redaktion.kulleraugen@epost.de, http://www.kulleraugen-verlag.de. Ed. Hans-Juergen Tast.

770 FRA ISSN 1778-9001
INFRA-MINCE. Text in French. 2005. a. EUR 45 for 3 yrs. (effective 2006). **Document type:** *Journal, Trade.*
Published by: Ecole Nationale Superieure de la Photographie, 16 Rue des Arenes, BP 10149, Arles Cedex, 13631, France. TEL 33-4-90993333, FAX 33-4-90993359.

770 DEU ISSN 0019-0179
INPHO; Das Fachmagazin fuer Entscheider der Imaging- und Consumer Electronics-Branche. Text in German. 1962. 11/yr. EUR 92 domestic; EUR 128 foreign; EUR 7.90 newsstand/cover (effective 2010). adv. bk.rev. illus.; stat. **Document type:** *Magazine, Trade.*
—IE, Infotrieve.
Published by: (Bundesverband des Deutschen Fotofachhandels e.V.), G F W PhotoPublishing GmbH, Holzstr 2, Duesseldorf, 40221, Germany. TEL 49-211-390090, FAX 49-211-3900955, info@gfw.de, http://www.gfw.de.

770 USA ISSN 1527-6007
INTERNATIONAL CINEMATOGRAPHERS GUILD MAGAZINE; film and video techniques magazine. Abbreviated title: I C G Magazine. Text in English. 1929. m. USD 48 domestic; USD 117 foreign; USD 4.95 newsstand/cover (effective 2005). adv. bk.rev. bibl.; illus. **Document type:** *Magazine, Trade.* **Description:** Written by professionals for professionals, covering cinematography and video techniques.
Formerly (until 1999): International Photographer (0020-8299)
Indexed: ChemAb, F01, F02, IBT&D, IIPA, RASB, T02.
—Linda Hall.
Published by: International Cinematographers Guild, 7755 Sunset Blvd, Hollywood, CA 90046. TEL 323-876-0160, FAX 323-876-6383, admin@cameraguild.com, http://www.cameraguild.com. Eds. Andrew Thompson, George Spiro Dibie. Pub. George Spiro Dibie. Adv. contact John P McCarthy. B&W page USD 1,955, color page USD 2,985; trim 11 x 8.5. Circ: 11,500 (paid).

770 USA ISSN 1018-9181
INTERNATIONAL CONGRESS ON HIGH SPEED PHOTOGRAPHY AND PHOTONICS. PROCEEDINGS. Text in English, French, German. 1952. biennial. USD 290 per issue to non-members; USD 220 per issue to members (effective 2010). adv. back issues avail.; reprints avail. **Document type:** *Proceedings, Academic/Scholarly.*
Formerly (until 1978): High Speed Photography (0074-4093)
—CCC.
Published by: (Society of Photo-Optical Instrumentation Engineers), S P I E - International Society for Optical Engineering, PO Box 10, Bellingham, WA 98227. TEL 360-676-3290, 888-504-8171, FAX 360-647-1445, customerservice@spie.org. Eds. Baoli Yao, Wei Zhao, Xun Hou. **Co-sponsor:** Chinese Optical Society.

770 DEU ISSN 0939-8619
INTERNATIONAL CONTACT; independent journal for the international photographic market. Text in German. 1982. bi-m. adv. bk.rev. charts; stat. back issues avail. **Document type:** *Magazine, Trade.*
Published by: C.A.T. Verlag Bloemer GmbH, Freiligrathring 18-20, Ratingen, 40878, Germany. TEL 49-2102-20270, FAX 49-2102-202790, worldofphoto@cat-verlag.de, http://www.cat-verlag.de. Ed. Thomas Bloemer. adv.: B&W page EUR 2,216, color page EUR 3,767. Circ: 11,673 (paid and controlled).

THE INTERNATIONAL DIRECTORY OF PHOTOGRAPHIC EQUIPMENT AND SUPPLIES IMPORTERS. *see* BUSINESS AND ECONOMICS—Trade And Industrial Directories

770 USA ISSN 1935-0414
J P G. (Joint Photographic Experts Group) Text in English. 2005. bi-m. USD 24.99 (effective 2008). adv. illus. **Document type:** *Magazine, Consumer.*
Related titles: Online - full text ed.
Published by: 8020 Publishing, 199 Fremont St 12th Fl, San Francisco, CA 94105. contact@8020publishing.com, http://www.8020publishing.com/. Ed., Pub. Paul Cloutier.

771 JPN ISSN 0021-4345
JAPAN CAMERA TRADE NEWS; monthly information on photographic products, optical instruments and accessories. Text in English. 1950. m. USD 130 (effective 2001). adv. bk.rev. illus.; stat. 12 p./no.; **Document type:** *Journal, Trade.*
Published by: Genyosha Publications Inc., 4-7 Shibuya 2-chome, Shibuya-ku, Tokyo, 150-0002, Japan. TEL 81-3-3407-7521, FAX 81-3-3407-7902, info@genyosha.co.jp, http://www.genyosha.com. Ed. K Eda. Circ: 8,000.

770 FRA ISSN 2107-6545
LE JOURNAL NATURE. Text in French. 2008. irreg. **Document type:** *Magazine, Consumer.*
Media: Online - full text.
Published by: Pacific, Departement Pistes et Sentiers http://www.lejournalnature.com.

770 620 686.2 USA ISSN 1017-9909
TA1632 CODEN: JEIME5
➤ **JOURNAL OF ELECTRONIC IMAGING.** Text in English. 1992. q. USD 510 combined subscription domestic to institutions (print & online eds.); USD 550 combined subscription foreign to institutions (print & online eds.) (effective 2012). adv. bk.rev. abstr.; charts; illus. index. **Document type:** *Journal, Academic/Scholarly.* **Description:** Publishes technical papers in all areas of the field of electronic imaging science and technology.
Related titles: CD-ROM ed.; Online - full text ed.: USD 395 to institutions (effective 2012).
Indexed: A01, A03, A05, A08, A20, A22, A28, APA, AS&TA, AS&TI, ASCA, BrCerAb, C&ISA, C10, CA, CA/WCA, CIA, CMCI, CPEI, CPI, CerAb, CivEngAb, CorrAb, CurCont, E&CAJ, E11, EEA, EMA, EngInd, H15, Inspec, M&TEA, M09, MBF, METADEX, P30, SCI, SCOPUS, SPINweb, SolStAb, T02, T04, W07, WAA.
—BLDSC (4974.940000), AskIEEE, IE, Infotrieve, Ingenta, Linda Hall. **CCC.**
Published by: S P I E - International Society for Optical Engineering, 1000 20th St, Bellingham, WA 98225. TEL 360-676-3290, FAX 360-647-1445, journals@spie.org, http://spie.org. Ed. Dr. Jan P Allebach. adv.: B&W page USD 995, color page USD 1,810; trim 8.5 x 11. Circ: 3,000 (paid). **Co-sponsor:** I S & T - Society for Imaging Science and Technology.

➤ **THE JOURNAL OF EROTIC PHOTOGRAPHY.** *see* MEN'S INTERESTS

770 620 686.2 USA ISSN 1062-3701
TR1 CODEN: JIMTE6
➤ **THE JOURNAL OF IMAGING SCIENCE AND TECHNOLOGY.** Text in English. 1992. bi-m. USD 260 domestic to institutions; USD 290 foreign to institutions (effective 2010). bk.rev. abstr.; bibl.; charts; illus.; pat.; stat.; tr.lit. index. back issues avail.; reprints avail. **Document type:** *Journal, Academic/Scholarly.* **Description:** Covers a broad range of research, development, and applications in imaging.
Formed by the merger of (1984-1991): Journal of Imaging Technology (0747-3583); Which was formerly (1974-1983): Journal of Applied Photographic Engineering (0098-7298); (1985-1991): Journal of Imaging Science (8750-9237); Which was formerly (until 1983): Photographic Science and Engineering (0031-8760); (1950-1957): Photographic Engineering (0554-1085)
Related titles: CD-ROM ed.; Microfilm ed.: (from PQC); Online - full text ed.: ISSN 1943-3522.
Indexed: A&ATA, A20, A22, ASCA, C&ISA, C33, CIN, CIS, CMCI, CPEI, ChemAb, ChemTitl, CurCont, E&CAJ, EngInd, GeoRef, ISMEC, ISR, Inspec, L09, P&BA, P30, PhotoAb, SCI, SCOPUS, SolStAb, SpeleolAb, W07.
—BLDSC (5004.556900), AskIEEE, CASDDS, IE, Infotrieve, Ingenta, INIST, Linda Hall. **CCC.**
Published by: Society for Imaging Science and Technology, 7003 Kilworth Ln, Springfield, VA 22151. TEL 703-642-9090, FAX 703-642-9094, info@imaging.org, http://www.imaging.org/ist/index.cfm. Ed. Melville R V Sahyun. Circ: 2,000 (paid).

➤ **JOURNAL OF PHOTOCHEMISTRY AND PHOTOBIOLOGY, A: CHEMISTRY.** *see* CHEMISTRY—Physical Chemistry

➤ **JOURNAL OF PHOTOCHEMISTRY AND PHOTOBIOLOGY, C: PHOTOCHEMISTRY REVIEWS.** *see* CHEMISTRY—Physical Chemistry

➤ **JUMP CUT**; a review of contemporary media. *see* MOTION PICTURES

770 SWE ISSN 1653-350X
KAMERA & BILD. Text in Swedish. 2003. m. SEK 649 (effective 2011). adv. **Document type:** *Magazine, Consumer.*
Formerly (until 2005): Allt om Digitalfoto (1651-7474)
Published by: Mediaprovider Scandinavia AB, Klarabergsgatan 29, Stockholm, 11121, Sweden. TEL 46-8-54512110, FAX 46-8-54512119, info@mediaprovider.se, http://www.mediaprovider.se. Ed. Elin Parmhed. Adv. contact Per Westman. Circ: 16,000; 9,000 (paid).

770 FIN ISSN 0022-8133
TR1
KAMERALEHTI. Text in Finnish. 1950. 10/yr. adv. bk.rev. index.
Document type: *Magazine, Consumer.*
Related titles: Online - full text ed.
Published by: Kameraseura r.y., Lastenkodingatu 5, Helsinki, 00180, Finland. TEL 358-9-6811490, FAX 358-9-6940166. Ed. Pekka Punkari. Adv. contact Riitta Valkonen. B&W page EUR 1,495, color page EUR 2,800; 210 x 297. Circ: 14,800.

KARTOGRAPHISCHE NACHRICHTEN; Fachzeitschrift fuer Geoinformation und Visualisierung. *see* GEOGRAPHY

770 DNK ISSN 0904-2334
TR640
KATALOG; journal of photography and video. Text in English, Danish. 1988. 3/yr. DKK 400 to individual members; DKK 295 to students; DKK 700 to institutional members (effective 2009). adv. bk.rev. illus. index. back issues avail. **Document type:** *Journal, Consumer.* **Description:** Covers photography,video, and other electronic media through critical and biographical essays, reviews, calendars of exhibitions and events.
Related titles: Online - full content ed.
Indexed: ABM, B24, SCOPUS.
Published by: Museet for Fotokunst/Museum of Photographic Art, Brandts Torv 1, Odense C, 5000, Denmark. TEL 45-65-207030, FAX 45-65-207042, info@brandts.dk, http://www.brandts.dk/foto.

770 USA
KODAK E-MAGAZINE; the online photography magazine. Text in English. 2000. m. **Document type:** *Magazine, Consumer.* **Description:** Contains stories and articles on the power of pictures and the people who make them come alive.
Media: Online - full content.
Published by: Eastman Kodak Co., 343 State St, Rochester, NY 14650. TEL 716-724-4000, FAX 716-724-9624.

KRONIKA; casopis za Slovensko krajevno zgodovino. *see* HISTORY—History Of Europe

KULLERAUGEN; Visuelle Kommunikation. *see* MOTION PICTURES

770.1 SWE ISSN 1653-9443
KVARTALSBREV FRAAN FOTOSEKRETARIATET. Text in Swedish. 2003. q. free. back issues avail. **Document type:** *Newsletter, Consumer.*
Media: Online - full content.
Published by: Nordiska Museet, Fotosekretariatet, PO Box 27820, Stockholm, 11593, Sweden. TEL 46-8-51954750, FAX 46-8-51954619, fotosekretariatet@nordiskamuseet.se.

770 FRA ISSN 1773-6889
LABO NUMERIQUE. Text in French. 2004. irreg. back issues avail. **Document type:** *Monographic series, Consumer.*
Published by: Editions Eyrolles, 61 Boulevard Saint-Germain, Paris, 75240, France.

LAKE SUPERIOR MAGAZINE. *see* HISTORY—History Of North And South America

770 DEU ISSN 0937-3969
TR1
LEICA-FOTOGRAFIE INTERNATIONAL. Text in German. 1949. 8/yr. EUR 60; EUR 6.50 newsstand/cover (effective 2007). adv. bk.rev. bibl.; charts; illus. index. back issues avail. **Document type:** *Magazine, Consumer.*
Formerly (until 1988): Leica Fotografie (0024-0621)
Related titles: English ed.: ISSN 0937-3977.
Indexed: ChemAb, IBR, IBZ, RASB.
—IE. **CCC.**
Published by: (Leica Camera GmbH), I D C Corporate Publishing GmbH, Hammerbrookstr 93, Hamburg, 20097, Germany. TEL 49-40-226211280, FAX 49-40-226211270. Ed. Frank Lohstoeter. Adv. contact Kirstin Ahrndt-Buchholz. B&W page EUR 2,730, color page EUR 4,200; trim 215 x 280. Circ: 11,951 (paid).

770 IRL
LENS. Text in English. 1925. bi-m. membership. adv. bk.rev.
Published by: Photographic Society of Ireland, 38-39 Parnell Sq., Dublin, Ireland. Ed. Joseph Webb. Circ: 600.

770 USA ISSN 1534-2743
LENSWORK. Text in English. 1994. bi-m. USD 39 domestic; USD 49 in Canada & Mexico; USD 78 elsewhere; USD 9.95 newsstand/cover domestic; USD 11.50 newsstand/cover in Canada (effective 2007). back issues avail.
Formerly (until 2000): Lenswork Quarterly (1075-5624)
Related titles: Online - full text ed.
Published by: Lenswork Publishing, 909 3rd St, Anacortes, WA 98221-1502. TEL 360-588-1343, 800-659-2130, FAX 503-905-6111, 800-866-7459, customerservice@lenswork.com. Ed. Brooks Jensen.

770 USA ISSN 1940-5782
LIFE IMAGES. Text in English. 2008 (Jan.). q. USD 59.99 domestic; USD 67.99 in Canada; USD 75.99 elsewhere; USD 14.99 per issue (effective 2008). back issues avail. **Document type:** *Magazine, Consumer.*
Published by: Stampington & Company, LLC., 22992 Mill Creek, Ste B, Laguna Hills, CA 92653. TEL 949-380-7318, 877-782-6737, FAX 949-380-9355, sameditor@stampington.com. Pub. Kellene Giloff.

THE LIFEWRITER'S DIGEST; a newsletter for memoir writers and photo journalers. *see* GENEALOGY AND HERALDRY

770 USA
LIGHT AND SHADE. Text in English. 1916. 9/yr. looseleaf. USD 40. bk.rev. back issues avail. **Document type:** *Newsletter.*
Published by: Pictorial Photographers of America, 299 W 12 St, New York, NY 10014. Ed. Sylvia Mavis. Circ: 100.

770 GBR ISSN 2041-0662
LITEBOOK; the creative lighting magazine. Text in English. 2008 (Jul.). q. free. illus. back issues avail. **Document type:** *Magazine, Trade.* **Description:** Contains interviews and profiles of leading photographers, featured studios, student photographer profiles, photographic equipment reviewed.
Related titles: Online - full text ed.
Published by: Bowens International Ltd., 355-361 Old Rd., Clacton on Sea, Essex CO15 3RH, United Kingdom. TEL 44-1255-422807, FAX 44-1255-436342, info@bowens.co.uk. Ed. David Hollingsworth. Pub. Robert Cook. Circ: 40,000 (controlled). **Dist. by:** PO Box 3128, Tilbrook, Milton Keynes MK7 8JB, United Kingdom. TEL 44-870-4585258, FAX 44-870-4585358, sales@ctdistribution.com.

770 MEX ISSN 0188-8005
TR28
LUNA CORNEA. Text in Spanish. 1993. q. MXN 120; USD 50 foreign. adv. bk.rev. **Document type:** *Monographic series.*
Published by: Consejo Nacional para la Cultura y las Artes, Centro de la Imagen, Plaza de la Ciudadela 2, Centro Historico, Mexico, DF 06040, Mexico. TEL 52-5-7095914, FAX 52-5-7095914. Ed. Patricia Gola. Pub. Pablo Ortiz Monasterio. Adv. contact Sandra Gonzalez. Circ: 6,000.

770 USA
M P EXPOSURE MAGAZINE. Variant title: Model Photographer Exposure Magazine. Text in English. 2005. irreg. free. **Document type:** *Magazine, Trade.* **Description:** Provides information for models, photographers and agents.
Media: Online - full content.

771 CAN
MASTER GUIDE. Text in English. 1992. a. adv. 30 p./no. 2 cols./p.; **Document type:** *Magazine, Trade.* **Description:** Covers trends and the latest technological advancements in photography as well as providing marketing strategies.
Formerly: Photo Retailer (1188-5955)
Published by: Apex Publications Inc., 185 rue St Paul, Quebec, PQ G1K 3W2, Canada. TEL 418-692-2110, FAX 418-692-3392, 800-664-2739. Ed. Don Long. Pub. Curtis Sommerville. R&P Anthony Fleming. Adv. contact Michelle Vella TEL 416-487-9335. B&W page CAD 1,930, color page CAD 2,680; trim 10.88 x 8.25. Circ: 5,250 (controlled).

770 GBR ISSN 2042-0234
MASTER PHOTOGRAPHY. Text in English. 2004. 10/yr. GBP 4.30 newsstand/cover; free to members (effective 2010). back issues avail. **Document type:** *Magazine, Trade.*
Formerly (until 2009): Master Photo Digital (1743-5986); Which was formed by the merger of (2001-2004): Master Digital Photographer (1740-3847); Which was formerly (until 2001): Master Digital; (1982-2004): The Master Photographer (0047-6196)
Related titles: Online - full text ed.: free (effective 2010).
Published by: (The Master Photographers Association), Icon Publications Ltd., Maxwell Pl, Maxwell Ln, Kelso, Roxburghshire TD5 7BB, United Kingdom. TEL 44-1573-226032, FAX 44-1573-226000, iconmags@btconnect.com, http://www.iconpublications.com/. Ed. David Kilpatrick.

771 USA ISSN 1092-7816
TR197
MCBROOM'S CAMERA BLUEBOOK. Text in English. 1991. biennial. USD 29.95. **Document type:** *Directory.* **Description:** Lists descriptions and prices of new and used cameras.
Published by: Amherst Media, Inc., 175 Rano St., Ste. 200, Buffalo, NY 14207-2176. TEL 716-874-4450, FAX 716-874-4508. Ed. Michael McBroom. Circ: 8,000.

778.53 CHE ISSN 1422-1098
MEDIA-EXPERT; la revue suisse au service des photographes et cineastes. Text in French. 1996. 9/yr. CHF 55. adv. bk.rev. illus.
Formed by the merger of (1993-1996): Audio Video Magazine (1421-6043); (1941-1996): Photo-Video-Expert (1421-8380); Which was formerly (until 1987): Photo-Cine-Expert-Video (1421-8410); (until 1978): Nouveau Photo-Cine-Expert (1421-8402); (until 1974): Photo-Cine-Expert (0031-8450); (until 1959): Photo-Expert (1421-8399)
Published by: Editions Jean Spinatsch SA, 13, route de Bellebouche, Corsier-geneva, 1246, Switzerland. Ed. Jean Spinatsch. Circ: 8,500.

MEMORY MAKERS; a community of ideas and inspiration. *see* ARTS AND HANDICRAFTS

778.315 GBR
MICROGRAPHICS AND OPTICAL STORAGE BUYER'S GUIDE. Text in English. 1981. a. GBP 10. adv. illus.
Formerly: Micrographics Year Book (0260-7069)
Published by: G.G. Baker & Associates, c/o Alan Armstrong & Assoc. Ltd., 72 Park Rd, London, NW1 4SH, United Kingdom. Circ: 1,000.

770 USA
MINI LAB FOCUS. Text in English. m. free to members (effective 2008). back issues avail. **Document type:** *Newsletter, Trade.* **Description:** Provides time-sensitive information on business activities and techniques, emerging technologies and marketing information for firms engaged in retail on-site photofinishing.
Published by: Photo Marketing Association International, 3000 Picture Pl, Jackson, MI 49201. TEL 517-788-8100, FAX 517-788-8371, gpageau@pmai.org. Circ: 3,800 (paid).

771 USA ISSN 1052-4142
MINILAB DEVELOPMENTS. Text in English. 1986. bi-m. free. adv. **Document type:** *Journal, Trade.* **Description:** Focuses on how to maintain and build the success of the minilab (on-site retail photofinishing outlet) industry.
Published by: International Minilab Association, Inc., 2627 Grimsley St, Greensboro, NC 27403. TEL 919-854-8088, FAX 919-854-8566. Ed. Bess Lewis. Pub. Roger McManus. Adv. contact Susan Smoot. Circ: 15,466.

MINZU HUABAO/NATIONALITY PICTORIAL. *see* ETHNIC INTERESTS

770 DEU
MIXAGE. Text in German. 1988. 4/yr. EUR 2.90 newsstand/cover (effective 2007). adv. **Document type:** *Magazine, Consumer.*
Published by: Segerer Media Verlag, Rothmahlweg 6, Regensburg, 93055, Germany. TEL 49-941-700505, fotos@manfred-segerer.de, http://www.manfred-segerer.de. Ed., Pub. Manfred Segerer. adv.: page EUR 4,500. Circ: 39,000 (paid and controlled).

THE MOONWORT REVIEW. *see* LITERATURE—Poetry

771 USA
N A P E T NEWS. Text in English. q. free to members (effective 2008). back issues avail. **Document type:** *Newsletter, Trade.* **Description:** Provides information about NAPET activities, information on independent camera repair trends and general retail trends.
Published by: (National Association of Photo Equipment Technicians), Photo Marketing Association International, 3000 Picture Pl, Jackson, MI 49201. TEL 517-788-8100, FAX 517-788-8371, gpageau@pmai.org. Ed., R&P Gary Pageau. Circ: 1,100.

770 NLD ISSN 1877-9816
N C N MAGAZINE. (Nikon Club Nederland) Text in Dutch. 200?. q. EUR 27 (effective 2010). **Document type:** *Magazine, Consumer.*
Formerly (until 2009): Nikon Club Nederland Nieuws (1877-1238)
Published by: Vereniging Nikon Club Nederland, Hoedenmakersveste 5, Arnhem, 6846 BG, Netherlands. bestuur@nikon-club-nederland.nl, http://www.nikon-club-nederland.nl. Ed. Onno Feringa.

741.6 USA ISSN 0893-3170
HF5807.N5
N Y GOLD. (New York) Text in English. 1987. a. **Document type:** *Magazine, Consumer.*
Published by: New York Gold, 10 E 21st St, 14th Fl, New York, NY 10010. TEL 212-254-1000, FAX 212-254-1204.

770 USA
N Y GOLD'S TILT. (New York) Text in English. 2000. s-a. USD 18; USD 20 newsstand/cover (effective 2001). adv. **Document type:** *Magazine, Consumer.*
Published by: New York Gold, 10 E 21st St, 14th Fl, New York, NY 10010. TEL 212-254-1000, FAX 212-254-1204, info@tiltmagazine.com, http://www.tiltmagazine.com. Pub. Arie Kopelman.

NANTAHALA REVIEW. *see* LITERATURE

770 USA ISSN 1049-6602
NATURE PHOTOGRAPHER. Text in English. 1990. q. bk.rev.; Website rev. **Document type:** *Magazine, Consumer.* **Description:** Covers nature photography with both film and digital cameras.
Published by: Nature Photographer Publishing Co. Inc., Box 690518, Quincy, MA 02269. TEL 617-847-0091, FAX 617-847-0952. Circ: 25,000.

NATURE'S BEST PHOTOGRAPHY. *see* CONSERVATION

770 DEU ISSN 1615-3545
NATURFOTO; Magazin fuer Tier- und Naturfotografie. Text in German. 1969. m. EUR 70.60 domestic; EUR 92 foreign; EUR 6.40 newsstand/cover (effective 2007). adv. bk.rev. **Document type:** *Magazine, Trade.*
Former titles (until 2000): Fotografie Draussen (0935-414X); (until 1988): Tier und Naturfotografie (0343-0448)
Published by: Tecklenborg Verlag, Siemenstr 4, Steinfurt, 48565, Germany. TEL 49-2552-92002, FAX 49-2552-920160, info@tecklenborg-verlag.de, http://www.tecklenborg-verlag.de. Ed. Eduard Gossner. Pub. Hubert Tecklenborg. Adv. contact Heike Baumer. B&W page EUR 2,960, color page EUR 4,850. Circ: 26,100 (paid).

770 NOR ISSN 0803-0987
NATURFOTOGRAFEN. Text in Norwegian. 1986. q. NOK 450 membership; NOK 300 to students (effective 2011). adv. **Document type:** *Magazine, Consumer.*
Formerly (until 1989): BioFoto-Nytt (0803-1371)
Published by: BioFoto. Forening for Naturfotografer, Olav Nygaardsvei 49, Oslo, 0688, Norway. TEL 47-41-626295, biofoto@biofoto.no. Ed. Svein Wik.

770 GBR ISSN 0143-036X
TR505
NEW MAGIC LANTERN JOURNAL. Text in English. 1978. irreg. free to members (effective 2009). bk.rev. illus. back issues avail. **Document type:** *Journal, Academic/Scholarly.* **Description:** Contains research papers, commentary, discussion and dialog on all aspects of the Magic Lantern and related optical entertainments and history.
Indexed: CA, F01, F02, T02.
Published by: Magic Lantern Society of Great Britain, S Park, Galphay Rd, Kirkby Malzeard, Ripon, N Yorkshire HG4 3RX, United Kingdom. Ed. Richard Crangle.

NEW ORLEANS REVIEW. *see* LITERATURE

NEW VIRGINIA REVIEW. *see* LITERATURE

770 NZL ISSN 1177-2417
NEW ZEALAND CAMERA. Text in English. 1953. a. NZD 69.99 (effective 2008). adv. bk.rev. illus. index. **Document type:** *Newsletter.* **Description:** Promotes all forms of photography both within New Zealand and overseas.
Former titles (until 2004): Camera (Auckland) (1176-2594); (until 2003): New Zealand Camera (1174-555X); (until 1996): Camera New Zealand (0114-264X); (until 1988): Camera (0110-3989); (until 1977): New Zealand Camera (0048-0118)
Published by: (Photographic Society of New Zealand), Willson Scott Publishing Limited, PO Box 29-527, Christchurch, New Zealand. TEL 64-3-3511535, FAX 64-3-3516173, http://www.willsonscott.biz, publish@willsonscott.biz. Eds. Bevan Tulett, Newell Grenfell, Sally Mason. Circ: 2,000.

775.05 NZL ISSN 1176-6948
NEW ZEALAND D-PHOTO. Variant title: D-Photo. Text in English. 2004. bi-m. NZD 49 domestic; NZD 75 Australia & Pacific; NZD 110 elsewhere; NZD 9.90 newsstand/cover (effective 2008). adv. back issues avail. **Document type:** *Magazine, Consumer.* **Description:** Aimed at both the novice and amateur photographer, it encourages and helps its readers to embrace digital photography through informative articles and creative practice.
Published by: Parkside Media, Herne Bay, PO Box 46020, Auckland, 1147, New Zealand. TEL 64-9-3601480, FAX 64-9-3601470, http://www.parksidemedia.co.nz. Ed. Steve Hart. Pub. Greg Vincent.

770 USA ISSN 0199-2422
TR820
NEWS PHOTOGRAPHER. Text in English. 1946. m. USD 48 domestic to non-members; USD 60 in Canada to non-members; USD 65 elsewhere to non-members; free to members (effective 2010). adv. bk.rev. illus. 48 p./no. 3 cols./p.; back issues avail.; reprints avail. **Document type:** *Magazine, Trade.* **Description:** Presents articles, interviews, profiles, history, and news relating to still and television news photography. Discusses new products and related issues such as electronic imaging.
Incorporates (1976-200?): The Best of Photojournalism (0161-4762); Which was formerly (until 1977): Photojournalism (0363-5996); Formerly (until 1974): National Press Photographer (0027-9935)
Related titles: Microform ed.: (from PQC); Online - full text ed.

P

Indexed: A01, A02, A03, A08, A09, A10, A22, A25, A26, A27, CMM, E08, G06, G07, G08, GALA, I05, M01, M02, P02, P10, P16, P34, P48, P53, P54, PQC, S08, S09, S23, T02, V03, V04.
—IE, Ingenta, Linda Hall.
Published by: National Press Photographers Association, Inc., 3200 Croasdaile Dr, Ste 306, Durham, NC 27705. TEL 919-383-7246, FAX 919-383-7261, info@nppa.org. Ed. Donald R Winslow. Adv. contact Stephanie Holland TEL 301-215-6710 ext 109.

NGHE THUAT DIEN ANH/CINEMATOGRAPHY. *see* MOTION PICTURES

770 JPN ISSN 1344-4425
➤ **NIHON GAZO GAKKAISHI/IMAGING SOCIETY OF JAPAN. JOURNAL.** Text in Japanese; Summaries in English. 1959. q. JPY 8,000. adv. charts; illus. **Document type:** *Journal, Academic/Scholarly.*
Former titles (until 1998): Denshi Shashin Gakkaishi (0387-916X); (until 1979): Denshi Shashin (0011-8478)
Indexed: A22, B&BAb, CIN, ChemAb, ChemTitl, Inspec, JCT, JTA, PhotoAb.
—BLDSC (4759.575000), IE, Ingenta, Linda Hall.
Published by: Imaging Society of Japan/Nihon Gazo Gakkai, c/o Tokyo Institute of Polytechnics, 2-9-5 Hon-cho, Nakano-ku, Tokyo, 164-0012, Japan. TEL 81-3-3373-9576, FAX 81-3-3372-4414. Ed. Masaaki Yokoyama. Circ: 1,500.

770 JPN ISSN 0369-5662
TR1 CODEN: NSGKAP
NIHON SHASHIN GAKKAISHI/SOCIETY OF PHOTOGRAPHIC SCIENCE AND TECHNOLOGY OF JAPAN. JOURNAL. Text in English, Japanese. 1935. bi-m. JPY 7,000 membership (effective 2006). adv. bk.rev. bibl.; charts; illus.; stat. Index. **Document type:** *Journal, Academic/Scholarly.* **Description:** Contains original papers that contribute to the advancement of knowledge and application of photography and imaging directly related sciences.
Incorporates (in 1974): Society of Photographic Science and Technology of Japan. Bulletin (0038-0059); Which was previously (1951-1970): Society of Scientific Photography in Japan. Bulletin (0366-3582)
Indexed: A22, Inspec, PhotoAb.
—BLDSC (4894.850000), AskIEEE, CASDDS, IE, Ingenta, Linda Hall.
Published by: Nihon Shashin Gakkai/Society of Photographic Science and Technology of Japan, c/o Tokyo Institute of Polytechnics, 2-9-5 Honcho, Nakano-ku, Tokyo, 164-8678, Japan. TEL 81-3-33730724, FAX 81-3-32995887, http://wwwsoc.nii.ac.jp/spstj2/. Circ: 1,500.

NIHON SHASHIN SOKURYO GAKKAI. GAKUJUTSU KOENKAI HAPPYO RONBUNSHU. *see* GEOGRAPHY

770.5 GBR ISSN 1365-6821
NIKON PRO. Text in English, French, German, Italian. 1995. 3/yr. GBP 18, EUR 25 (effective 2010). adv. **Document type:** *Magazine, Consumer.* **Description:** Provides readers the inside line on recent and forthcoming equipment launches, while contact information, support and expert tips make the vital link between the brand and its customers.
Related titles: German ed.; Italian ed.; Spanish ed.; French ed.
Published by: (Nikon Europe B.V.), Cedar Communications, 85 Strand, London, WC2R 0WD, United Kingdom. TEL 44-20-75508000, info@cedarcom.co.uk.

770 NOR ISSN 0332-8597
NORSK FOTOGRAFISK TIDSSKRIFT. Text in Norwegian. 1963. q. NOK 350 domestic; NOK 375 elsewhere (effective 2002). adv.
Formerly (until 1979): Norsk Fagfoto (0029-1900); Which was formed by the merger of (1950-1963): Fotohandleren (0801-8340); (1912-1963): Norsk Fotografisk Tidsskrift (0369-5093)
Indexed: ABM, SCOPUS.
Published by: Norges Fotografforbund, Raadhusgt. 20, Oslo, 0151, Norway. TEL 47-22-33-21-15, FAX 47-22-33-21-14. Ed. Roy Gabrielsen.

THE NORTHERN VIRGINIA REVIEW. *see* LITERATURE

770 USA ISSN 0887-5855
N1
NUEVA LUZ; photographic journal. Text in English, Spanish. 1984. 3/yr. USD 65 to institutions (in US and Puerto Rico); USD 75 in Canada & Mexico to institutions; USD 80 elsewhere to institutions (effective 2010). adv. bk.rev. illus. 44 p./no.; back issues avail. **Document type:** *Magazine, Consumer.* **Description:** Publishes portfolios of fine art and documentary work by minority American photographers. Notifies readers of opportunities for grants, exhibits, and awards.
Incorporates (in 1997): Critical Mass (1071-3794)
Published by: En Foco, Inc, 1738 Hone Ave, Bronx, NY 10461. TEL 718-931-9311, FAX 718-409-6445, info@enfoco.org. Ed. Miriam Romais. Adv. contact Marisol Diaz.

770 NZL ISSN 2230-4835
▼ **NZ PHOTOGRAPHER.** Text in English. 2009. m. free (effective 2011). adv. **Document type:** *Magazine, Trade.*
Media: Online - full text.
Published by: Espire Media, Parnell, PO Box 137162, Auckland, 1151, New Zealand. TEL 64-21-866036, alastairn@espiremedia.com, http://www.espiremedia.com/. Ed. Ollie Dale TEL 64-9-5502005. Adv. contact Richard Liew TEL 64-21-994136.

770 FRA ISSN 1959-4720
TR640
O E; La revue de l'oeil public. Text in French, English. 2007. irreg. **Document type:** *Journal, Consumer.*
Published by: Oeil Public, 31 Rue de Tlemcen, Paris, 75020, France. TEL 33-1-43150033, FAX 33-1-43150378, http://www.oeilpublic.com.

770 DNK ISSN 0107-6329
OBJEKTIV. Text in Danish. 1976. 4/yr. DKK 350 domestic membership; DKK 375 foreign membership; DKK 50 per issue (effective 2008). adv. bk.rev. illus. **Document type:** *Magazine, Trade.*
Indexed: B24.
Published by: Dansk Fotohistorisk Selskab, c/o Flemming Berendt, Teglgaardsvej 308, Humlebaek, 3050, Denmark. TEL 45-49-192299, http://www.objektiv.dk/forening/index.html. Ed. Flemming Berendt.

OBSERVATORI DE LA PRODUCCION AUDIOVISUAL. *see* MOTION PICTURES

770 ESP ISSN 1696-0092
OJODEPEZ. Text in Spanish. 2003. q. EUR 35 domestic; EUR 50 in Europe; EUR 55 elsewhere (effective 2008). adv. **Document type:** *Journal, Trade.*
Related titles: Online - full text ed.: ISSN 1696-0106. 2003.
Published by: Asociacion OjodePez para el Fomento de la Imagen Documental, c/ Veronica 13, Madrid, 28014, Spain. TEL 34-91-3601320. Ed. Arianna Rinaldo. Adv. contact Gonzalo Peleaz.

770 USA
ON COLLECTING PHOTOGRAPHS. Text in English. 1983. every 5 yrs. USD 15 domestic; USD 35 foreign (effective 2008). bibl. **Document type:** *Magazine, Consumer.* **Description:** A brief guide for beginning collectors.
Published by: Association of International Photography Art Dealers, 2025 M St, NW, Ste 800, Washington, DC 20036. TEL 202-367-1158, FAX 202-367-2158, info@aipad.com. R&P Kathleen Ewing.

770 USA ISSN 1934-8274
ON-E MAGAZINE. Text in English. 2006. m. **Document type:** *Magazine, Consumer.*
Media: Online - full text.
Published by: FotoHighway TEL 757-214-2685, http://www.fotohighway.com.

770 700 CAN
OPEN SPACE MONOGRAPHS. Text in English. 1976. irreg. price varies. bk.rev.
Formerly: Photography at Open Space Monographs
Published by: Photography at Open Space, 510 Fort St, Victoria, BC V8W 1E6, Canada. Circ: 500.

OSNOVAC. *see* ART

770 USA ISSN 0890-5304
CODEN: ETGAA5
OUTDOOR PHOTOGRAPHER; scenic - travel - wildlife - sports. Text in English. 1985. 11/yr. USD 14.97 domestic; USD 29.97 foreign; USD 7 per issue (effective 2011). illus. back issues avail.; reprints avail. **Document type:** *Magazine, Consumer.* **Description:** Covers the techniques and art of outdoor photography in all settings. Reviews cameras, film, and accessories.
—Ingenta.
Published by: Werner Publishing Corporation, 12121 Wilshire Blvd, 12th Fl, Los Angeles, Los Angeles, CA 90025. TEL 310-820-1500, FAX 310-826-5008, http://www.wernerpublishing.com.

770 ITA ISSN 1594-9184
P C PHOTO. Text in Italian. 1894. m. bk.rev. illus. index. **Document type:** *Magazine, Trade.*
Formerly (until 2002): Progresso Fotografico (0033-0868)
Indexed: ChemAb.
Published by: Editrice Progresso s.r.l., Viale Piceno 14, Milan, 20129, Italy. TEL 39-02-70002222, FAX 39-02-713030, abbonamenti@fotografia.it, http://www.fotografia.it.

770 USA
P D N - PIX. (Photo District News) Text in English. 199?. bi-m. **Document type:** *Journal, Trade.*
Related titles: Online - full text ed.
Published by: Nielsen Business Publications (Subsidiary of: Nielsen Business Media, Inc.), 770 Broadway, 7th Fl, New York, NY 10003. TEL 646-654-5780, 800-697-8859, FAX 646-654-5813, ContactCommunications@nielsen.com, http://www.nielsenbusinessmedia.com.

770 NLD ISSN 0168-9991
P - F; vakblad voor fotografie en imaging. (Professionele Fotografie) Text in Dutch. 1983. 8/yr. EUR 72.50; EUR 9.75 newsstand/cover (effective 2009). adv. bk.rev. **Document type:** *Magazine, Trade.*
Incorporates (1991-1993): Professional Imaging (0928-3846); (1983-1984): F (Amsterdam) (0168-0994)
—IE, Infotrieve.
Published by: Eisma Businessmedia bv, Celsiusweg 41, Postbus 340, Leeuwarden, 8901 BC, Netherlands. TEL 31-58-2954854, FAX 31-58-2954875, businessmedia@eisma.nl, http://www.eisma.nl/businessmedia/index.asp. Eds. Fred van der Ende, Jan van der Schans. Adv. contact Ed Rothuis. color page EUR 2,730, B&W page EUR 1,365; trim 235 x 312. Circ: 9,000.

771 USA ISSN 0031-8531
P M A MAGAZINE; connecting the imaging communities. (Photo Marketing Association) Text in English. 1924. m. (except July/August). USD 50 domestic; USD 55 in Canada; USD 70 elsewhere; USD 5 per issue; free to members (effective 2009). adv. illus. back issues avail. **Document type:** *Magazine, Trade.* **Description:** Designed to help the worldwide photo imaging community to achieve business success and adapt to new technologies.
Former titles (until 2006): Photo Marketing; (until 19??): Photo Developments
Related titles: Online - full text ed.
Indexed: A26, B02, B03, B11, B15, B17, B18, G04, G06, G07, G08, I05.
—IE, Infotrieve.
Published by: Photo Marketing Association International, 3000 Picture Pl, Jackson, MI 49201. TEL 517-788-8100, 800-762-9287, FAX 517-788-8371, gpageau@pmai.org. Pub. Gary Pageau. Adv. contact Jon Rousseau TEL 202-973-6448. B&W page USD 2,370, color page USD 3,300; trim 8.125 x 10.75. Circ: 11,800.

771 USA
P M A NEWSLINE. (Photo Marketing Association) Text in English. w. free to members (effective 2009). back issues avail. **Document type:** *Newsletter, Trade.*
Formerly: Photo Marketing Newsline
Published by: Photo Marketing Association International, 3000 Picture Pl, Jackson, MI 49201. TEL 517-788-8100, 800-762-9287, FAX 517-788-8371, gpageau@pmai.org.

770 USA ISSN 1949-8586
▼ **P O V (KINNELON).** (Point of View) Text in English. 2009. bi-m. USD 10 per issue (effective 2009). **Document type:** *Magazine, Consumer.* **Description:** Features photography from a different point of view.
Media: Online - full content.
Published by: Nick D'Andrea, Ed. & Pub., 80 Fayson Lake Rd, Kinnelon, NJ 07405-3136. TEL 973-768-5735, pov@nickandreaphoto.com, http://nickdandrea.com/Portfolio.cfm?nL=0&nS=6&nK=7307&i=118074#0.

770 CAN
P P O C: PROFESSIONAL PHOTOGRAPHERS OF CANADA - PHOTOGRAPHES PROFESSIONNELS DU CANADA. Text in English, French. 1970 (vol.3). bi-m. adv. bk.rev.; software rev. tr.lit. **Document type:** *Magazine, Trade.*
Former titles: P P O C National News (0048-5462); Professional Photographers of Canada. P P O C News and Comments
Published by: Craig Kelman & Associates Ltd., 3C 2020 Portage Ave, Winnipeg, MB R3J 0K4, Canada. TEL 204-985-9780, FAX 204-985-9795. Ed. Jim E Watson. Adv. contact Michelle Cottyn. B&W page CAD 875; trim 10.75 x 8.25. Circ: 1,600 (controlled). **Co-publisher:** Professional Photographers of Canada.

770 USA ISSN 0030-8277
P S A JOURNAL. Text in English. 1934. m. free to members (effective 2010). adv. bk.rev. abstr.; illus. Index. back issues avail.; reprints avail. **Document type:** *Magazine, Consumer.* **Description:** Promotes the art and science of photography in all its forms.
Formerly (until 1947): Photographic Society of America. Journal (0096-5812); Incorporates (1954-1957): Photographic Science and Technique (0480-4619); Which was formerly (until 1954): P S A Journal, Section B. Photographic Science and Technique (0099-3069)
Related titles: Microform ed.: (from PQC); Online - full text ed.
Indexed: A01, A02, A03, A08, A22, A26, A27, A30, A31, B01, B02, B06, B07, B08, B09, B15, B17, B18, BusI, C12, CA, ChemAb, E08, G04, G05, G06, G07, G08, GALA, I05, I07, M01, M02, MagInd, P02, P10, P48, P53, P54, PQC, RASB, S09, S23, T&II, T02.
—IE, Infotrieve, Ingenta, Linda Hall.
Published by: Photographic Society of America, Inc., 3000 United Founders Blvd, Ste 103, Oklahoma City, OK 73112. TEL 405-843-1437, FAX 405-843-1438, hq@psa-photo.org. Ed. Donna Brennan. Adv. contact Carol Hajek. B&W page USD 1,336, color page USD 2,464; 7 x 10.

770 305.42 USA
P W P NEWSLETTER. Text in English. 1984. bi-m. USD 25 in state; USD 15 out of state. adv. bk.rev. **Document type:** *Newspaper.*
Supersedes: P W P Times
Published by: Professional Women Photographers, c/o Photographics Unlimited, 17 W 17th St, New York, NY 10011-5510. Ed. Meryl Meisler. Circ: 500.

PALATINATE. *see* LITERATURE

778.3 USA ISSN 1090-994X
TR661
PANORAMA (NEW YORK). Text in English. 19??. q. adv. **Document type:** *Magazine, Trade.*
Formerly (until 1995): International Association of Panoramic Photographers (1063-7478)
Published by: International Association of Panoramic Photographers, PO Box 3371, Church St Sta, New York, NY 10008-3371. Ed., Adv. contact Richard Schneider. Pub. Warren Wright. R&P Fred Yake.

770 BRA ISSN 1413-2575
PAPARAZZI. Text in Portuguese. 1995. bi-m. USD 120; BRL 36, USD 20 newsstand/cover (effective 2000). adv.
Related titles: Online - full text ed.
Published by: Paparazzi Estudio Fotografico Ltda., Av Pedroso de Moraes, 99, Pinheiros, Sao Paulo, SP 05419-000, Brazil. TEL 55-11-8165520, FAX 55-11-8165960, cirenza@uol.com, paparazzi@uol.com.br, cirenza@uol.com.brD. Ed., Pub. Carlo Cirenza. Adv. contact Helen Baurich. Circ: 5,000 (paid).

770 ESP ISSN 1136-4831
TR1
PAPEL ALPHA; cuadernos de fotografia. Text in Spanish. 1996. a., latest vol.4, 1999. EUR 9 (effective 2009). **Document type:** *Magazine, Consumer.*
Indexed: I04, I05.
Published by: Universidad de Salamanca, Ediciones, Apartado 325, Salamanca, 37080, Spain. TEL 34-923-294598, FAX 34-923-262579, pedidos@universitas.usal.es, http://www.eusal.es/. Ed. Javier Panera.

770 GBR ISSN 2040-3682
▼ ➤ **PHILOSOPHY OF PHOTOGRAPHY.** Abbreviated title: P O P. Text in English. 2010. s-a. GBP 36, USD 68 to individuals; GBP 132, USD 185 to institutions (effective 2012). adv. **Document type:** *Journal, Academic/Scholarly.* **Description:** Devoted to the scholarly understanding of photography.
Related titles: Online - full text ed.: ISSN 2040-3690. GBP 99, USD 140 (effective 2012).
Indexed: A30, A31, T02.
Published by: Intellect Ltd., The Mill, Parnall Rd, Fishponds, Bristol, BS16 3JG, United Kingdom. TEL 44-117-9589910, FAX 44-117-9589911, info@intellectbooks.com. Eds. Andrew Fisher, Daniel Rubinstein, Pedro Vicente. Pub. Masoud Yazdani. **Dist. by:** Turpin Distribution Services Ltd., Pegasus Dr, Stratton Business Park, Biggleswade, Bedfordshire SG18 8QB, United Kingdom. TEL 44-1767-604951, FAX 44-1767-601640, custserv@turpin-distribution.com, http://www.turpin-distribution.com/.

770 FRA ISSN 1950-9928
PHOT'ART INTERNATIONAL. Text in French. 2006. q. EUR 26 domestic; EUR 35 in the European Union; EUR 45 in Asia & the Pacific; EUR 40 elsewhere (effective 2009). **Document type:** *Magazine, Consumer.*
Published by: Herkadia Creations, Phot' Art International, 15 Place de la Republique, Armentieres, 59280, France. redaction@phot-art.com, http://www.phot-art.com/. Ed. Jacky Martin.

770 FRA ISSN 0399-8568
TR1
PHOTO. Text in French. 1960. 10/yr. EUR 22; EUR 4 newsstand/cover (effective 2008). adv. illus. **Document type:** *Magazine, Consumer.*
Published by: Hachette Filipacchi Medias S.A. (Subsidiary of: Lagardere Media), 149/151 Rue Anatole France, Levallois-Perret, 925340, France. TEL 33-1-413462, FAX 33-1-413469, lgardere@interdeco.fr, http://www.lagardere.com. Circ: 191,908. **Subscr. in N. America to:** Express Magazine, 4011 Blvd Robert, Montreal, PQ H1Z 4H6, Canada. expsmag@expressmag.com.

770 AUS
PHOTO & IMAGING NEWS. Text in English. 1958. bi-m. AUD 44 domestic; AUD 53 in New Zealand; AUD 60 in Asia; AUD 80 elsewhere; AUD 7.95 newsstand/cover (effective 2008). adv. **Document type:** *Magazine, Trade.* **Description:** Provides photo trade news and information on latest issues affecting retailers; offers interview sections with photo industry identities.
Former titles (until 2004): Photo & Imaging Trade News (1446-0289); (until 2001): Photo & Imaging Retailer (1325-7552); (until 1996): Photo & Video Retailer (1036-384X); (until 1991): Photo Retailer (0816-1909); (until 1985): Photo Trade News (0031-8590)
Related titles: Online - full text ed.
—CIS.

Published by: Yaffa Publishing Group Pty Ltd., 17-21 Bellevue St, Surry Hills, NSW 2010, Australia. TEL 61-2-92812333, FAX 61-2-92812750, info@yaffa.com.au, http://www.yaffa.com.au. Ed. Keith Shipton TEL 61-3-54262402. Adv. contact Kerri McNamara TEL 61-2-92138261. B&W page AUD 1,920, color page AUD 2,570; trim 210 x 297. Circ: 3,220. **Subscr. to:** GPO Box 606, Sydney, NSW 2001, Australia.

770 USA
PHOTO DAILY. Text in English. 1988. d. USD 375 (effective 2011). back issues avail. **Document type:** *Newsletter, Consumer.* **Description:** Provides descriptions of the photo needs of photo editors at books and magazines.
Related titles: E-mail ed.; Fax ed.; Online - full text ed.
Published by: PhotoSource International, 1910 35th Rd, Pine Lake Farm, Osceola, WI 54020. TEL 715-248-3800, FAX 715-248-7394, info@photosource.com, http://www.photosource.com.

770 USA ISSN 1045-8158
PHOTO DISTRICT NEWS. Abbreviated title: P D N. Text in English. 1980. m. USD 65 combined subscription domestic (print & online eds.); USD 105 combined subscription in Canada (print & online eds.); USD 125 combined subscription elsewhere (print & online eds.) (effective 2009); USD 7.95 newsstand/cover (effective 2006). **Document type:** *Magazine, Trade.* **Description:** Provides unbiased news and analysis, interviews and portfolios of the latest photographic work.
Supersedes in part (in 198?): Photo District News (0883-766X); Which was formerly: New York Photo District News (0274-7731)
Related titles: Online - full text ed.: USD 65 (effective 2009).
Indexed: A15, A22, ABIn, B02, B07, B15, B16, B17, B18, G04, G06, G07, G08, I05, M01, M02, P10, P48, P51, P53, P54, PQC, T02.
—CIS. **CCC.**
Published by: Nielsen Business Publications (Subsidiary of: Nielsen Business Media, Inc.), 770 Broadway, New York, NY 10003. TEL 646-654-4500, FAX 646-654-5813, ContactCommunications@nielsen.com, http://www.nielsenbusinessmedia.com. Ed. Holly Hughes. Pub. Jeffrey Roberts. Adv. contact Chris O'Hara TEL 212-536-5236. Circ: 33,000 (paid). **Subscr. to:** PO Box 1983, Marion, OH 43305-1983.

771 USA ISSN 1060-4936
TR1 CODEN: PELIE6
PHOTO ELECTRONIC IMAGING; the magazine for photographic, electronic imaging & graphics professionals. Abbreviated title: P E I. Text in English. 1958. m. USD 20; USD 33 in Canada; USD 50 elsewhere. adv. bk.rev. charts; illus.; tr.lit. index. reprints avail. **Document type:** *Magazine, Trade.* **Description:** Serves the field of industrial visual communications.
Former titles (until 1991): Photomethods (0146-0153); (until 1974): Photomethods for Industry (0030-8110)
Related titles: Microform ed.: (from PQC).
Indexed: A&ATA, A22, GALA, IHTDI, SoftBase.
—IE, Infotrieve, Ingenta, Linda Hall.
Published by: Professional Photographers of America, 229 Peachtree St, N E, Ste 2200, Atlanta, GA 30303-2206. TEL 404-522-8600, FAX 404-614-6406. Ed. Kim Brady. Pub. Cameron Bishopp. Adv. contact Donna McMahon. B&W page USD 4,810. Circ: 42,000.

770 USA ISSN 1536-6553
PHOTO IMAGING NEWS. Text in English. 1983. bi-w. USD 150 domestic; USD 175 foreign (effective 2006). bk.rev. stat. 12 p./no.; back issues avail.; reprints avail. **Document type:** *Newsletter, Trade.* **Description:** Marketing, technical, and general information on the worldwide photography and photo processing markets.
Formerly (until 2002): Photofinishing News Letter (0889-2393)
Related titles: Online - full text ed.
Indexed: A10, V03.
Published by: Photofinishing News, Inc., 10915 Bonita Beach Rd, Ste 1091, Bonita Springs, FL 34135-9047. TEL 239-992-4421, FAX 239-992-6328, dfranz@photo-news.com. Ed. Don Franz. Circ: 1,000 (paid and controlled).

770 USA ISSN 1535-9433
PHOTO INDUSTRY REPORTER. Text in English. 18/yr.
Published by: I R M Publications, 7600 Jericho Turnpike, Woodbury, NY 11797. TEL 516-364-0016. Eds., Pubs. Edward Wagner, Rudolf Maschke.

770 USA
PHOTO INSIDER. Text in English. bi-m. USD 11.95 domestic; USD 15.95 in Canada; USD 16.95 elsewhere (effective 2001). **Description:** Contains features on a wide variety of photography subjects, targeting beginning photographers to professionals.
Published by: Unique Photo, Inc., 11 Vreeland Rd, Florham Park, NJ 07932. TEL 973-377-1003, FAX 973-377-2679. Ed. Matthew Sweetwood. Adv. contact Raymond Coppola TEL 561-243-2001.

770 DEU ISSN 1863-1509
PHOTO INTERNATIONAL. Text in German. 1954. bi-m. EUR 45.90 domestic; EUR 55.20 foreign; EUR 7.65 newsstand/cover (effective 2007). adv. **Document type:** *Magazine, Consumer.*
Former titles (until 2006): Photo-Technik International (0176-0785); (until 1984): International Phototechnik (0341-423X)
Published by: Hess Verlag, Trappentreustr 31, Munich, 80339, Germany. Ed. Hans-Eberhard Hess. adv.: B&W page EUR 3,600, color page EUR 5,100. Circ: 14,000 (paid and controlled).

PHOTO INTERPRETATION; images aeriennes et spatiales. *see* GEOGRAPHY

347.7 CZE ISSN 1211-8214
PHOTO LIFE. Text in Czech. 1997. bi-m. CZK 495 (effective 2008). adv. **Document type:** *Magazine, Consumer.*
Published by: B & H Photo-Design, Seydlerova 13, Prague 5, 158 00, Czech Republic. TEL 420-2-51615989, FAX 420-2-51615989. Pub. Jan Karbusicky. **Subscr. to:** SEND Predplatne s.r.o., PO Box 141, Prague 4 140 21, Czech Republic. TEL 420-225-985225, FAX 420-225-341425, send@send.cz, http://www.send.cz.

770 CAN ISSN 0700-3021
TR1
PHOTO LIFE. Text in English. 1976. 6/yr. CAD 27 domestic; USD 23.70 in United States; USD 37.70 elsewhere (effective 2001). adv. bk.rev. 84 p./no. 3 cols./p.; back issues avail. **Document type:** *Magazine, Consumer.* **Description:** Features Canadian news, reviews of the latest equipment, tips and portfolios.
Incorporates (1990-1996): Photo Digest (0843-6029)
Related titles: Microfiche ed.: (from MML); Microform ed.: (from MML); Online - full text ed.
Indexed: A22, C03, CBCARef, CBPI, CPerI, G08, P48, PQC, SCOPUS.
Published by: Apex Publications Inc. (Toronto), One Dundas St, Ste 2500, P O Box 84, Toronto, ON M5G 1Z3, Canada. TEL 800-905-7468, FAX 800-664-2739, sales@photolife.com, http://www.photolife.com. Ed. Mark Price. Pub. Curtis J Sommerville. R&P Anthony Fleming. Adv. contact Michelle Vella TEL 616-487-9335. B&W page CAD 6,914, color page CAD 9,629; trim 10.88 x 8.25. Circ: 81,031.

770 DEU
PHOTO PRESSE. Text in German. 1945. w. EUR 95.60 domestic; EUR 151.20 foreign (effective 2008). adv. **Document type:** *Magazine, Trade.*
Published by: Klie Verlagsgesellschaft mbH, Postfach 1348, Hannover Muenden, 34333, Germany. TEL 49-5541-98490, FAX 49-5541-984999. adv.: B&W page EUR 2,200, color page EUR 3,400. Circ: 8,120 (paid and controlled).

775.05 GBR ISSN 1757-9317
PHOTO PRO MAGAZINE. Text in English. 2006. m. GBP 25.50 (effective 2009). adv. **Document type:** *Magazine, Trade.*
Formerly (until 2008): Digital Photo Pro (1752-2242)
Related titles: Online - full text ed.
Published by: Bright Publishing, Bright House, 82 High St, Sawston, Cambs CB22 3HJ, United Kingdom. TEL 44-1223-499450, FAX 44-1223-839953, http://www.bright-publishing.com/. Adv. contact Matt Snow TEL 44-1223-499453.

770 USA
THE PHOTO REVIEW. Text in English. 1976. q. USD 45 domestic; USD 60 in Canada & Mexico; USD 80 elsewhere (effective 2010); subscr. includes The Photo Review Newsletter. bk.rev. illus. back issues avail. **Document type:** *Journal, Trade.* **Description:** Contains critical reviews of exhibitions, essays, interviews, portfolios of photography and industry news.
Formerly (until 1984): Philadelphia Photo Review (0363-6488)
Indexed: ABM.
Published by: The Photo Review, 140 E Richardson Ave, Ste 301, Langhorne, PA 19047. TEL 215-891-0214, FAX 215-891-9358, info@photoreview.org.

770 USA
THE PHOTO REVIEW NEWSLETTER. Text in English. 19??. 8/yr. USD 45 domestic; USD 60 in Canada & Mexico; USD 80 elsewhere (effective 2010); subscr. includes Photo Review journal. **Document type:** *Newsletter, Trade.* **Description:** Contains exhibition listings from throughout the Mid-Atlantic region (New York, Philadelphia, Pittsburgh, New Jersey, Delaware, Maryland, Virginia, and Washington, DC) and exhibition opportunities and news of interest from throughout the world.
Formerly (until 1984): Philadelphia Photo Review Newsletter
Related titles: Online - full text ed.
Published by: The Photo Review, 140 E Richardson Ave, Ste 301, Langhorne, PA 19047. TEL 215-891-0214, FAX 215-891-9358, info@photoreview.org.

770 CAN ISSN 1916-100X
PHOTO SOLUTION MAGAZINE. Text in French. 1981. bi-m. CAD 27 domestic; USD 27 foreign (effective 2008). adv. bk.rev. cum.index: 1981-1984. back issues avail. **Document type:** *Magazine, Consumer.* **Description:** Includes photographers' profiles, new techniques, equipment reviews. Directed to photography amateurs and pros.
Former titles (until 2008): Photo Selection Magazine (1482-275X); (until 1997): Photo Selection (1187-1725); (until 1991): Nouveau Photo Selection (0848-9807); (until 1990): Photo Selection (0226-9708)
Published by: Apex Publications Inc., 185 rue St Paul, Quebec, PQ G1K 3W2, Canada. TEL 418-692-2110, 800-905-7468, FAX 418-692-3392, publicite@photoselection.com, http://www.photoselection.com. Ed. Xavier Bonacorsi. Pub. Guy J Poirier. Adv. contact Richard Payette. B&W page CAD 3,192, color page CAD 4,436; trim 10.88 x 8.25. Circ: 20,233.

770 DEU
PHOTO TECHNIK INTERNATIONAL. Text in German. 1954. bi-m. EUR 45.90; EUR 7.65 newsstand/cover (effective 2005). adv. bk.rev. charts; illus.; mkt.; tr.lit. **Document type:** *Magazine, Consumer.*
Formerly: International Photo Technik (0020-8280)
Related titles: English ed.
Indexed: PhotoAb, RASB.
—IE. **CCC.**
Published by: Jahr Top Special Verlag, Troplowitzstr 5, Hamburg, 22529, Germany. TEL 49-40-389060, FAX 49-40-38906300, info@jahr-tsv.de, http://www.jahr-tsv.de. Ed. Hans-Eberhard Hess. Adv. contact Gerfried Urban TEL 49-89-68001162. B&W page EUR 3,600, color page EUR 5,100; trim 185 x 248. Circ: 5,371 (paid).

770 USA ISSN 1083-9070
TR287
PHOTO TECHNIQUES. Abbreviated title: P T. Text in English. 1979. bi-m. USD 29.99 domestic; USD 41.99 foreign (effective 2009). adv. bk.rev. charts; illus.; stat. back issues avail.; reprints avail. **Document type:** *Magazine, Consumer.* **Description:** Discusses photographic and darkroom procedures and techniques for serious amateurs and professionals.
Former titles (until 1996): Darkroom and Creative Camera Techniques (1083-9054); (until 1984): Darkroom Techniques (0195-3850)
Related titles: Online - full text ed.: USD 19.99 (effective 2009).
Indexed: IHTDI, PhotoAb.
—**CCC.**
Published by: Preston Publications, 6600 W Touhy Ave, Niles, IL 60714-4588. TEL 847-647-2900, FAX 847-647-1155, circulation@prestonpub.com, http://www.prestonpub.com. Ed. S Lewis. Pub. Tinsley Preston. adv.: B&W page USD 2,200, color page USD 3,200; bleed 8.375 x 11.125. Circ: 18,288.

771 USA ISSN 1082-4189
PHOTO TRADE NEWS; business news for the imaging channel. Text in English. 1937. m. USD 77 domestic; USD 97 in Canada & Mexico; USD 142 elsewhere; free to qualified personnel (effective 2008). adv. bk.rev. illus.; tr.lit. Supplement avail.; back issues avail.; reprints avail. **Document type:** *Magazine, Trade.*
Former titles (until 1995): P T N (1053-8968); (until 1989): Photographic Video Trade News (1054-0601); (until 1987): Photographic Trade News (0031-8779); (until 1941): Photographic Retailing
Related titles: Online - full text ed.
Indexed: A09, A10, A15, ABIn, P48, P51, PQC, PROMT, T02, V03, V04.
—CIS. **CCC.**
Published by: Cygnus Business Media, Inc., 1233 Janesville Ave, PO Box 803, Fort Atkinson, WI 53538. TEL 920-563-6388, FAX 920-563-1702, http://www.cygnusb2b.com. Pub. Ian Littauer TEL 631-963-6242. adv.: B&W page USD 6,315, color page USD 7,960; trim 9 x 10.875. Circ: 14,300.

770 BEL ISSN 0777-3641
PHOTO VIDEO AUDIO NEWS (FRENCH EDITION). Text in French. 1984. bi-m. free to qualified personnel. adv. illus. 48 p./no.; **Document type:** *Magazine, Trade.* **Description:** Covers news and business developments of interest to all branches of the photo, video and audio trade, including retailers, film processing and photofinishing labs, photographers, manufacturers and importers.
Former titles (until 1989): Photo Film Video News (0777-3633); Photo-Contact (0772-5809)
Related titles: ◆ Dutch ed.: Foto Video Audio News (Dutch Edition). ISSN 0777-3625.
Published by: Mema NV, Wielewaasstraat 20, Wilrijk, 2610, Belgium. TEL 32-3-4480827, FAX 32-3-4480832, pgermeys@skynet.be. Ed., Adv. contact Piet Germeys. B&W page EUR 1,262, color page EUR 2,147; trim 297 x 210. Circ: 3,000 (controlled).

770 CHE
PHOTO VIDEO EXPERT. Text in English. 9/yr.
Address: Bellebouche 13, Corsier Ge, 1246, Switzerland. TEL 022-7511653, FAX 022-7511871. Ed. Jean Spinatsch. Circ: 7,500.

770 AUS ISSN 0811-0859
PHOTOFILE. Text in English. 1983. 3/yr. AUD 35 domestic to individuals; AUD 50 in New Zealand to individuals; AUD 70 domestic to institutions; AUD 70 elsewhere (effective 2008). adv. bk.rev. 62 p./no.; back issues avail. **Document type:** *Magazine, Consumer.* **Description:** A photo-art magazine for people interested in photography.
Related titles: Online - full text ed.
Indexed: ABM, AusPAIS, RILM, SCOPUS.
—**CCC.**
Published by: Australian Centre for Photography, 257 Oxford St, Paddington, NSW 2021, Australia. TEL 61-2-93321455, FAX 61-2-93316887, info@acp.org.au, http://acp.au.com. Ed. Ashley Crawford. adv.: B&W page USD 500; 220 x 280. Circ: 5,000 (controlled).

770 USA
PHOTOFOLIO; photography collectors' newsletter. Text in English. 1979. q. USD 20. bk.rev. back issues avail.
Published by: Photocollect, 740 West End Ave, New York, NY 10025. Ed. Alan Klotz. Circ: 500.

PHOTOGRAMMETRIC ENGINEERING AND REMOTE SENSING. *see* GEOGRAPHY

526.982 FIN ISSN 0554-1069
➤ **PHOTOGRAMMETRIC JOURNAL OF FINLAND.** Text in English, German. 1968. a. EUR 20 domestic; EUR 40 elsewhere (effective 2004). adv. back issues avail. **Document type:** *Journal, Academic/Scholarly.*
Indexed: GeoRef.
Published by: (Fotogrammetrian ja Kaukokartoituksen Seura ry (FKS)/Finnish Society of Photogrammetry), Teknillinen Korkeakoulu, Fotogrammetrian Laboratorio/Helsinki University of Technology. Institute of Photogrammetry and Remote Sensing, HUT, PO Box 1200, Espoo, 02015, Finland. TEL 358-9-4513901, FAX 358-9-465077, http://www.hut.fi. Eds. Anita Laiho-Heikkinen TEL 358-9-4513898, Henrik Haggren. **Co-publisher:** Fotogrammetrian ja Kaukokartoituksen Seura ry (FKS)/Finnish Society of Photogrammetry.

➤ **THE PHOTOGRAMMETRIC RECORD**; an international journal of photogrammetry. *see* GEOGRAPHY

770 AUT
DER PHOTOGRAPH. Text in German. 11/yr. **Document type:** *Magazine, Trade.*
Published by: (Landesinnung der Fotografen fuer Wien), Verlag fuer Photographische Literatur A. Barylli, Opernring 6, Vienna, W 1010, Austria. TEL 43-1-5128712, FAX 43-1-5137833, office@photobook.at, http://www.photobook.at. Ed. Andreas Barylli. Circ: 2,600.

770 USA ISSN 1544-9084
PHOTOGRAPH (NEW YORK). Text in English. 1988. bi-m. USD 35 domestic; USD 40 in Canada; USD 70 elsewhere; USD 8 per issue in US & Canada; USD 12 per issue elsewhere (effective 2003). adv. bk.rev. back issues avail. **Document type:** *Directory.* **Description:** Presents a listing of gallery and museum exhibitions, dealers, and booksellers, as well as information about auctions, classes and workshops. Includes a calendar of events.
Former titles (until Sep. 2003): Photography in New York International (1547-6189); (until Sep. 1995): Photography in New York (1040-0346)
Published by: Photography in New York, Inc., 64 W 89th St, New York, NY 10024. TEL 212-787-0401, FAX 212-799-3054, http://www.photography-guide.com. Ed., Pub., R&P, Adv. contact Bill Mindlin. Circ: 9,000.

790.132 332.67 USA ISSN 0271-0838
TR1
THE PHOTOGRAPH COLLECTOR; information, opinion and advice for collectors, curators and dealers. Abbreviated title: T P C. Text in English. 1980. m. looseleaf. USD 149.95 in North America; USD 169.95 elsewhere (effective 2010). bk.rev. back issues avail.; reprints avail. **Document type:** *Newsletter, Trade.* **Description:** Contains news of the photography art market, auction previews and results, gallery, museum, and not-for-profit news, listings of auctions, courses, lectures, and seminars, trade shows and fairs, and limited edition portfolios and books.
Published by: The Photo Review, 140 E Richardson Ave, Ste 301, Langhorne, PA 19047. TEL 215-891-0214, FAX 215-891-9358, info@photoreview.org.

770 FRA ISSN 0369-9560
TR1
LE PHOTOGRAPHE. Text in French. 1910. m. EUR 5.40 newsstand/cover (effective 2004); EUR 50 (effective 2008). adv. **Document type:** *Magazine, Consumer.* **Description:** Magazine for professional photographers and business imaging.
Indexed: PdeR.

P

—CCC.
Published by: Mondadori France, 1 Rue du Colonel Pierre-Avia, Paris, Cedex 15 75754, France. TEL 33-1-41335001, contact@mondadori.fr, http://www.mondadori.fr. Circ: 10,511.

770 USA ISSN 0194-5467
TR1
PHOTOGRAPHER'S FORUM; magazine for the emerging professional. Text in English. 1978. q. USD 15 domestic; USD 19 in Canada; USD 22 elsewhere (effective 2010). adv. bk.rev. illus. 48 p./no. 2 cols./p.; Supplement avail.; reprints avail. **Document type:** *Magazine, Trade.* **Description:** Contains articles on commercial and fine art photography, interviews with master photographers as well as the portfolios of emerging professionals.
Formerly (until 1979): Student Forum (0148-589X)
Indexed: ABM, SCOPUS.
—Ingenta.
Published by: Serbin Communications, Inc., 813 Reddick St, Santa Barbara, CA 93103. TEL 805-963-0439, FAX 805-965-0496, admin@serbin.com, http://www.serbin.com/. Ed. Glen R Serbin. Adv. contact Janice Brown TEL 800-876-6425 ext 241. B&W page USD 2,800, color page USD 4,905; trim 8.375 x 10.875.

770 GBR ISSN 2043-720X
▼ **THE PHOTOGRAPHER'S GUIDE TO TURNING PRO.** Text in English. 2010. q. GBP 14.97 (effective 2010). **Document type:** *Magazine, Trade.*
Published by: Archant Specialist Ltd. (Subsidiary of: Archant Group), Archant House, Oriel Rd, Cheltenham, GL50 1BB, United Kingdom. http://www.archant.co.uk/.

770.99305 NZL ISSN 1171-9214
THE PHOTOGRAPHER'S MAIL. Text in English. 1992. m. NZD 25 domestic; NZD 65 foreign (effective 2008); free per issue domestic retail outlets. adv. illus. **Document type:** *Magazine, Consumer.*
Published by: Parkside Media, Herne Bay, PO Box 46020, Auckland, 1147, New Zealand. TEL 64-9-3601480, FAX 64-9-3601470, http://www.parksidemedia.co.nz. Ed., Adv. contact Tim Steele. Pub. Greg Vincent.

770 USA ISSN 0147-247X
TR12
PHOTOGRAPHER'S MARKET; 2000 places to sell your photographs. Text in English. 1974. a. USD 29.99 (effective 2009). 640 p./no.; **Document type:** *Directory, Trade.* **Description:** Lists 2000 markets open to freelancers. Includes pay structures for electronic usage, interviews with Pulitzer Prize winners, contests and professional organizations.
Incorporates in part (1992-1994): Guide to Literary Agents & Art/Photo Reps (1055-6087); Supersedes in part (in 1977): Artist's and Photographer's Market (0146-8294); Which was formerly (until 197?): Artist's Market (0361-607X)
—BLDSC (6468.870000).
Published by: F + W Media Inc., 4700 E Galbraith Rd, Cincinnati, OH 45236. TEL 513-531-2690, 800-283-0963, FAX 513-531-0798, wds@fwpubs.com, http://www.fwpublications.com. Ed. Donna Poehner.

770 GRC ISSN 0259-7349
PHOTOGRAPHIA. Text in Greek. 1977. q. USD 30 (effective 2000). adv. bk.rev. back issues avail. **Document type:** *Magazine, Consumer.* **Description:** Photographic theory magazine for amateur, advanced, and fine art photographers.
Published by: Moressopoulos S.A., 19 I Peridou, Athens, 105 58, Greece. TEL 30-1-323-4217, FAX 30-1-323-2082, hcp@photography.gr. Ed. Stavros Moressopoulos. Circ: 12,000. **Subscr. to:** PO Box 30 564, Athens 100 33, Greece.

770 USA ISSN 1053-7031
TR6.5
PHOTOGRAPHIC ART MARKET: AUCTION PRICES (YEAR). Text in English. 1981. a. back issues avail. **Document type:** *Trade.* **Description:** For collectors, dealers, curators, and appraisers for buying, selling, appraising, valuing a donation, insuring, or filing an insurance claim.
Formerly: Photographic Art Market Auction Price Results and Analysis
Published by: The Photo Review, 140 E Richardson Ave, Ste 301, Langhorne, PA 19047. TEL 215-891-0214, FAX 215-891-9358, info@photoreview.org.

770 900 CAN ISSN 0704-0024
TR1
PHOTOGRAPHIC CANADIANA. Text in English. 1974. 5/yr. CAD 24 domestic membership; USD 24 foreign membership (effective 2003). bk.rev. illus. index. back issues avail. **Document type:** *Journal, Academic/Scholarly.* **Description:** Provides information on images, photographers, and hardware with an emphasis on Canadian content and perspective.
Indexed: SCOPUS.
Published by: Photographic Historical Society of Canada, RPO Avenue Fairlawn, P O Box 54620, Toronto, ON M5M 4N5, Canada. TEL 416-691-1555, FAX 416-621-0018, phsc@phsc.ca. Ed. Robert Lansdale. Circ: 300 (paid).

770 USA
PHOTOGRAPHIC RESOURCE CENTER. NEWSLETTER. Text in English. 1979. 9/yr. USD 40 to members. adv. bk.rev. **Document type:** *Newsletter.*
Published by: Photographic Resource Center, Boston University, 602 Commonwealth Ave, Boston, MA 02215. TEL 617-353-0700. Circ: 2,500.

770 JPN
THE PHOTOGRAPHIC SOCIETY OF JAPAN. Text in Japanese. 1953. q. (m. until 1996). JPY 1,600 (effective 2001). adv. bk.rev. 24 p./no.; **Document type:** *Journal, Corporate.*
Formerly (until Feb. 1996): Photography in Japan
Published by: Photographic Society of Japan/Nihon Shashin Kyokai, JCII Bldg 4th Fl, 25 Ichiban-cho, Chiyoda-ku, Tokyo, 102-0082, Japan. TEL 81-3-5276-3585, FAX 81-3-5276-3586. Ed., Pub. Minoru Ohnishi. Circ: 1,300.

770 DEU ISSN 1437-4951
TR1
PHOTOGRAPHIE. Text in German. 1977. 10/yr. EUR 45; EUR 5 newsstand/cover (effective 2010). adv. **Document type:** *Magazine, Consumer.*
Related titles: Supplement(s): Photographie Spezial. ISSN 1617-4275. 2000; D V F Journal. ISSN 1617-4070. 1996.
Indexed: A22.
—IE, Infotrieve.
Published by: (Deutscher Verband fuer Fotografie e.V.), Vereinigte Verlagsanstalten GmbH, Hoeherweg 278, Duesseldorf, 40231, Germany. TEL 49-211-73570, FAX 49-211-7357123, info@vva.de, http://www.vva.de.

770 BEL ISSN 0777-3374
PHOTOGRAPHIE OUVERTE. Text in French. 1979. bi-m. bk.rev. **Document type:** *Newsletter, Consumer.* **Description:** News of the museum's activities, exhibitions and collections, and information on notable exhibitions and festivals in Belgium and other countries.
Published by: Musee de la Photographie, Av Paul Pastur 11, Charleroi - Mont-sur March, 6032, Belgium. TEL 32-71-435810, FAX 32-71-364645, http://musee.photo.infonie.be. Ed. Georges Vercheval.

770 GBR ISSN 1754-0763
TR1
➤ **PHOTOGRAPHIES.** Text in English. 2008. s-a. GBP 141 combined subscription in United Kingdom to institutions (print & online eds.); EUR 220, USD 278 combined subscription to institutions (print & online eds.) (effective 2012). adv. back issues avail.; reprint service avail. from PSC. **Document type:** *Journal, Academic/Scholarly.* **Description:** Aims to further develop the history and theory of photography, considering new frameworks for thinking and addressing questions arising from the present context of technological, economic, political and cultural change.
Related titles: Online - full text ed.: ISSN 1754-0771. GBP 127 in United Kingdom to institutions; EUR 199, USD 250 to institutions (effective 2012) (from IngentaConnect).
Indexed: A10, A22, A30, A31, ABM, BrHumI, CA, E01, P10, P48, P53, P54, PQC, T02, V03.
—IE. CCC.
Published by: Routledge (Subsidiary of: Taylor & Francis Group), 4 Park Sq, Milton Park, Abingdon, Oxon OX14 4RN, United Kingdom. TEL 44-20-70176000, FAX 44-20-70176336, subscriptions@tandf.co.uk, http://www.routledge.com. Adv. contact Linda Hann TEL 44-1344-779945. **Subscr. to:** Taylor & Francis Ltd., Journals Customer Service, Sheepen Pl, Colchester, Essex CO3 3LP, United Kingdom. TEL 44-20-70175544, FAX 44-20-70175198.

770 GBR ISSN 1751-4517
TR1
➤ **PHOTOGRAPHY AND CULTURE.** Text in English. 2008 (Jul.). 3/yr. USD 326 combined subscription in North America to institutions (print & online eds.); GBP 167 combined subscription elsewhere to institutions (print & online eds.) (effective 2011). back issues avail.; reprint service avail. from PSC. **Document type:** *Journal, Academic/Scholarly.* **Description:** Aims to interrogate the contextual and historic breadth of photographic practice from a range of informed perspectives and to encourage new insights into the media through original and incisive writing.
Related titles: Online - full text ed.: ISSN 1751-4525. USD 277 in North America; GBP 142 elsewhere (effective 2011) (from IngentaConnect).
Indexed: A07, A30, A31, AA, ABM, ArtInd, B04, CA, T02, W03, W05.
Published by: Berg Publishers (Subsidiary of: Oxford International Publishers Ltd.), 1st Fl Angel Ct, 81 St Clements St, Oxford, Berks OX4 1AW, United Kingdom. TEL 44-1865-245104, FAX 44-1865-791165, enquiry@bergpublishers.com. Eds. Kathy Kubicki, Thy Phu, Val Williams.

770 USA
PHOTOGRAPHY COLLECTORS REPORTS. Text in English. 1990. q. USD 250 (effective 2001). adv. bk.rev. bibl.; charts; mkt.; stat. back issues avail. **Document type:** *Newsletter, Consumer.* **Description:** Covers new books on photography, reviews of exhibitions, photographers, photo reproduction, illustrations, auction results, gallery openings and international exhibits.
Published by: Devin - Adair Publishers, Inc., PO Box A, Old Greenwich, CT 06870. TEL 203-531-7755, FAX 718-359-8568. Ed. W Dows. Pub., R&P R Lourie. Circ: 4,800 (paid and controlled).

770.5 GBR ISSN 1473-4966
PHOTOGRAPHY MONTHLY. Text in English. 2001. m. GBP 24.99 domestic; GBP 40 foreign; GBP 3.95 newsstand/cover (effective 2009). adv. **Document type:** *Magazine, Consumer.*
Related titles: Online - full text ed.: GBP 15 (effective 2009).
—CCC.
Published by: Archant Specialist Ltd. (Subsidiary of: Archant Group), Archant House, Oriel Rd, Cheltenham, GL50 1BB, United Kingdom. TEL 44-1242-211080, FAX 44-1242-216094, http://www.archant.co.uk/. Ed. Roger Payne. Adv. contact Sam Scott-Smith TEL 44-1242-261092.

770 USA
➤ **PHOTOGRAPHY QUARTERLY.** Text in English. 1979. q. USD 25 domestic to non-members; USD 40 in Canada & Mexico to non-members; USD 45 elsewhere to non-members; free to members (effective 2010). adv. bk.rev. cum.index, 1979-1999. back issues avail. **Document type:** *Magazine, Consumer.* **Description:** Contains articles on contemporary artists and visual art.
Formerly (until 1994): Center Quarterly (0890-4634)
Indexed: ABM.
Published by: (Center for Photography at Woodstock), Kenner Printing, 59 Tinker St, Woodstock, NY 12498. TEL 845-679-9957, FAX 845-679-6337, info@cpw.org.

770 USA ISSN 1554-138X
TR12
THE PHOTOGRAPHY SHOW; membership directory and illustrated catalogue. Text in English. 1991. a. USD 25 domestic; USD 45 foreign (effective 2008). adv. illus. index. back issues avail. **Document type:** *Directory, Trade.* **Description:** Catalogs the association's annual event and lists members. Includes index of photographers represented by membership.
Formerly (until 1994): Membership Directory & Illustrated Catalogue (1554-1401)
Published by: Association of International Photography Art Dealers, 2025 M St, NW, Ste 800, Washington, DC 20036. TEL 202-367-1158, FAX 202-367-2158, info@aipad.com. Ed., R&P, Adv. contact Kathleen Ewing. Circ: 7,500.

771 HKG
PHOTOIMAGING YEARBOOK. Text in English. a. adv. **Description:** Covers suppliers of 35mm cameras, digital imaging equipment, binocu-lars, scopes and accessories in Asia.
Published by: ACE Media Co., Ltd., c/o ACE Marketing and Publications Ltd., 10F, Ultragrace Commercial Bldg, 5 Jordan Rd, Kowloon, Hong Kong. adv.: page USD 2,800. Circ: 15,000.

770 CAN ISSN 1047-661X
TR1
PHOTOINFO. Text in English. 1989. q.
Address: #200, 550 Eleventh Ave S W, Calgary, AB T2R 2M7, Canada. support@photoinfo.com.

770 070.49 USA ISSN 0893-5610
TR820
PHOTOJOURNALIST (NEWARK). Text in English. 1969. a. USD 5.20. adv.
Published by: New Jersey Press Photographers Association, c/o New Jersey Newsphotos, PO Box 2562, Newark, NJ 07114. TEL 973-242-1111. Ed. Ray Fisk. Circ: 500.

770 USA
PHOTOKINA NEWS. Text in English. a. **Document type:** *Journal, Trade.*
Published by: P T N Publishing Corp., 445 Broad Hollow Rd, Ste 21, Melville, NY 11747-4722. TEL 516-845-2700, FAX 516-845-7109. Pub. Tom Martin. Circ: 30,000.

770 USA ISSN 0190-1400
PHOTOLETTER. Text in English. 1976. w. USD 275 (effective 2011). 5 p./no. 3 cols./p.; back issues avail. **Document type:** *Newsletter, Consumer.* **Description:** Lists photo needs, deadlines, photo buyer addresses, phone numbers, faxes, and e-mail.
—CCC.
Published by: PhotoSource International, 1910 35th Rd, Pine Lake Farm, Osceola, WI 54020. TEL 715-248-3800, FAX 715-248-7394, info@photosource.com, http://www.photosource.com.

770 IND ISSN 0255-660X
TR810
➤ **PHOTONIRVACHAK.** Variant title: Journal of the Indian Society of Remote Sensing. Text in English. 1973. q. EUR 156, USD 236 combined subscription to institutions (print & online eds.) (effective 2012). reprint service avail. from PSC. **Document type:** *Journal, Academic/Scholarly.* **Description:** Publishes review articles dealing with recent advancements in remote sensing technologies, research papers, brief research letters, etc.
Related titles: Online - full text ed.: ISSN 0974-3006 (from IngentaConnect).
Indexed: A22, ASFA, B21, E01, ESPM, GEOBASE, GeoRef, SCI, SCOPUS, W07.
—IE, INIST. CCC.
Published by: (Indian Society of Remote Sensing), Springer (India) Private Ltd. (Subsidiary of: Springer Science+Business Media), 212, Deen Dayal Upadhyaya Marg, 3rd Fl, Gandharva Mahavidyalaya, New Delhi, 110 002, India. TEL 91-11-45755888, FAX 91-11-45755889. Ed. George Joseph.

770 NLD ISSN 1877-5551
PHOTOQ JAARBOEK. Text in Dutch. 200?. a. price varies.
Published by: Stichting PhotoQ, Admiraal de Ruijterweg 363 III, Amsterdam, 1055 MA, Netherlands. TEL 31-6-55195461, info@photoq.nl, http://www.photoq.nl. Ed. Edie Peters.

770 AUT ISSN 0958-2606
TR1
PHOTORESEARCHER. Text in English. 1990. irreg., latest vol.11, 2008. price varies. **Document type:** *Monographic series, Academic/Scholarly.*
Indexed: ABM, B24.
—CCC.
Published by: European Society for the History of Photography/Europaeischen Gesellschaft fuer die Geschichte der Photographie, Fleischmarkt 16/2/2/31, Vienna, 1010, Austria. TEL 43-1-5137196, office.eshph@aon.at, http://www.donau-uni.ac.at/eshph.

770 FRA ISSN 1962-4786
PHOTOSCHOOL; magazine de la retouche photo a la portee de tous. Text in French. 2008. bi-m. **Document type:** *Magazine, Consumer.*
Published by: One Press, Immeuble Le Melies, 261 Rue de Paris, Montreuil, Cedex 93556, France.

775 006.6 USA ISSN 1548-0399
PHOTOSHOP FIX. Text in English. 2004 (May). m. USD 59 domestic; USD 72.76 in Canada; USD 89 elsewhere (effective 2005). **Document type:** *Newsletter.*
Published by: Dynamic Graphics Group, PO Box 9007, Maple Shade, NJ 08052. TEL 856-380-4122, FAX 856-380-4101, ddn@dgusa.com.

770 USA ISSN 1073-0710
PHOTOSTOCKNOTES. Text in English. 1993. m. looseleaf. USD 35; USD 3.50 per issue (effective 2011). bk.rev.; software rev. index. back issues avail. **Document type:** *Newsletter, Consumer.* **Description:** Provides information and market reports for stock photographers.
Related titles: Online - full text ed.
—CCC.
Published by: PhotoSource International, 1910 35th Rd, Pine Lake Farm, Osceola, WI 54020. TEL 715-248-3800, FAX 715-248-7394, info@photosource.com.

770 ESP ISSN 0211-7029
TR640
➤ **PHOTOVISION.** Text in English, Spanish. 1981. 2/yr. EUR 30 domestic; EUR 40 in Europe; USD 76 elsewhere (effective 2008). adv. index every 6 nos. back issues avail. **Document type:** *Monographic series, Academic/Scholarly.* **Description:** Devoted to creative photography. Issues deal with historical and contemporary themes. Presents the work of international photographers and writers.
Indexed: ABM, SCOPUS.
Published by: Arte y Proyectos Editoriales S.L., Apartado 164, Utrera, Sevilla 41710, Spain. TEL 34-95-4862895. Ed. Joan Fontcuberta. Pub. Ignacio Gonzalez. Circ: 13,000.

770 USA
PHOTOVISION; art & technique. Text in English. 2000. bi-m. USD 24.95; USD 4.95 newsstand/cover (effective 2001). adv. **Document type:** *Magazine, Consumer.*
Published by: H.A.S.T. Publishing, Inc., 233 Sweetgrass Overlook, Crestone, CO 81131. TEL 719-256-5099, FAX 719-256-5099, pvadvert@fone.net, http://www.hastpublishing.com. Ed. Thomas Harrop. Pub. Michael St. Peter.

PICNIC. *see* ART

770 USA
PICTORIALIST. Text in English. 1941. m. looseleaf. membership.
Published by: Photo Pictorialists of Milwaukee, c/o Ellen Worzala, 9703 W Ruby Ave, Wauwatosa, WI 53225-4713. Circ: 75.

770 USA ISSN 1526-3754
TR1
PICTURE (NEW YORK). Text in English. 1996. bi-m. USD 14 domestic; USD 24 foreign (effective 2002). **Document type:** *Magazine, Consumer.*
Published by: Picture Magazine, 41 Union Sq, Ste 504, New York, NY 10003. TEL 212-352-2700, FAX 212-352-2155, picmag@aol.com. Ed. Brock Wylan.

778.1 USA ISSN 2159-869X
PICTURE BUSINESS & DIGITAL GRAPHICS; today's imaging news for tomorrow's imaging retailer. Variant title: Picture Business & Mobile Lifestyle. Text in English. 2004 (Oct). m. free to qualified personnel (effective 2011). adv. reprints avail. **Document type:** *Magazine, Trade.* **Description:** Focuses on the important business issues effecting today's imaging retailer.
Formerly (until 200?): Picture Business (1553-6386)
Related titles: Online - full text ed.: free to qualified personnel (effective 2008).
Indexed: A15, ABIn, P51, PQC.
Published by: North American Publishing Co., 1500 Spring Garden St., 12th Fl, Philadelphia, PA 19130. TEL 215-238-5300, FAX 215-238-5213, magazinecs@napco.com, http://www.napco.com. Ed. Michael McEnaney. Adv. contact Eric Schwartz TEL 215-238-5420.

778.1 USA ISSN 1930-5117
PICTURE BUSINESS DIGITAL CLIQUE. Text in English. 2006 (May). w. free (effective 2008). adv. back issues avail. **Document type:** *Newsletter, Trade.* **Description:** Covers imaging retail trends, innovations and new product announcements making news within the imaging industry.
Media: E-mail.
Published by: North American Publishing Co., 1500 Spring Garden St., 12th Fl, Philadelphia, PA 19130. TEL 215-238-5300, FAX 215-238-5213, magazinecs@napco.com, http://www.napco.com.

PINAKOTEKA. *see* ART

770 USA ISSN 0885-1476
PINHOLE JOURNAL. Text in English. 1985. 3/yr. USD 37.50 domestic; USD 42.50 foreign (effective 2005). **Document type:** *Magazine, Trade.*
Published by: Pinhole Resource, Star Route 15, Box 1355, San Lorenzo, NM 88041. TEL 505-536-9942, pinhole@gilanet.com, http://www.pinholeresource.com/.

770 GBR
PIXEL VIDEO & PHOTOGRAPHY. Text in English. 37/yr.
Address: 36 Stoke Fields, Guildford, Surrey GU1 4LS, United Kingdom. TEL 0483-505351, FAX 0483-505364. Ed. Dennis Taylor. Circ: 3,000.

PLAINS SONG REVIEW; exploring sense of place in the Great Plains. *see* LITERATURE

770 USA ISSN 1943-8311
▼ **PLATES TO PIXELS.** Text in English. 2009. s-a. USD 19.50 (effective 2009).
Address: PO Box 6628, Portland, OR 97228. TEL 503-701-5347, FAX 503-646-1262. Pub. Blue Mitchell.

770 FRA ISSN 1962-3488
POLKA MAGAZINE. Text in French. 2008. bi-m. EUR 20 (effective 2008). **Document type:** *Magazine, Consumer.*
Published by: Polka Images, 27 Rue Jasmin, Paris, 75016, France. contact@polkaimage.com.

770 USA ISSN 1944-0510
TR1
POPULAR PHOTOGRAPHY; the image of today. Text in English. 1937. m. USD 14 domestic; USD 22 foreign (effective 2008). adv. bk.rev. charts; illus.; mkt. index. back issues avail.; reprints avail. **Document type:** *Magazine, Consumer.* **Description:** Covers all aspects of amateur and professional photography, both art and technique. Reviews cameras and accessories.
Former titles (until 2008): Popular Photography & Imaging (1542-0337); (until 2003): Popular Photography (0032-4582); (until 1955): Photography; Popular Photography was incorporated (1949-1989): Modern Photography (0026-8240); Which was formerly (until 1950): Minicam Photography (0096-5863); (until 1941): Minicam
Related titles: Online - full text ed.
Indexed: A&ATA, A01, A02, A03, A08, A09, A10, A11, A22, A23, A24, A25, A26, A30, A31, ARG, Acal, B04, B13, BRD, C05, C12, CBRI, CPerI, ChemAb, ConsI, E08, G05, G06, G07, G08, G09, GALA, GdIns, I05, I07, IHTDI, M01, M02, M06, MASUSE, MagInd, P02, P07, P10, P13, P16, P48, P53, P54, PMI, PMR, PQC, R03, R04, R06, RASB, RGAb, RGPR, S08, S09, T02, TOM, V03, V04, W03, WBA, WMB.
—IE, Ingenta, Linda Hall. **CCC.**
Published by: Hachette Filipacchi Media U.S., Inc. (Subsidiary of: Hachette Filipacchi Medias S.A.), 1633 Broadway, New York, NY 10019. TEL 212-767-6000, FAX 212-767-5600, flyedit@hfmus.com, http://www.hfmus.com. Eds. Jack Howard, Philip Ryan, John Owens. Pub. Richard Rabinowitz. adv.: B&W page USD 60,060, color page USD 77,435; trim 7.88 x 10.5. Circ: 457,132 (paid).

770 GBR ISSN 1354-4446
TR640
PORTFOLIO; the catalogue of contemporary photography in Britain. Text in English. 1988. s-a. GBP 17 domestic to individuals; GBP 25 in Europe to individuals; GBP 30 elsewhere to individuals; GBP 25 domestic to institutions (effective 2003). adv. bk.rev. 72 p./no.; back issues avail. **Document type:** *Journal, Consumer.* **Description:** Features the work of internationally acclaimed photographic artists and portfolios by young and emerging talent.
Former titles (until 1995): Photography; Portfolio Magazine (0960-3913)
Indexed: ABM, B24, SCOPUS.
—**CCC.**
Published by: Photography Workshop Ltd., 43 Candlemaker Row, Edinburgh, EH1 2QB, United Kingdom. TEL 44-131-220-1911, FAX 44-131-226-4287, http://www.portfoliocataglogue.com. Ed., R&P Gloria Chalmers. Adv. contact Elizabeth Parooe. B&W page GBP 700, color page GBP 1,050; trim 195 x 245. Circ: 3,000 (paid).

PORTFOLIO (NEW YORK); the magazine of visual arts. *see* ART

POSMOTRI. *see* GENERAL INTEREST PERIODICALS—Russia

770 GBR ISSN 0032-6445
PRACTICAL PHOTOGRAPHY. Text in English. 1957. 13/yr. GBP 45.70 domestic; GBP 71 foreign; GBP 3.99 newsstand/cover (effective 2009). adv. bk.rev. charts; illus. back issues avail. **Document type:** *Magazine, Consumer.* **Description:** Provides a diverse range of content that teaches photo enthusiasts to take better photos and how to creatively enhance them in Photoshop.
Formerly (until 1959): Popular Photography (British Edition)
—BLDSC (6595.405000), IE. **CCC.**
Published by: H. Bauer Publishing Ltd. (Subsidiary of: Bauer Media Group), Media House, Lynchwood, Peterborough, Cambridgeshire PE2 6EA, United Kingdom. TEL 44-1733-468000, http://www.bauer.co.uk. Ed. Andrew James. Adv. contact Iain Grundy TEL 44-1733-468000. **Subscr. to:** Tower House, Sovereign Park, Market Harborough, Leicestershire LE16 9EF, United Kingdom. TEL 44-1858-438866, subs@greatmagazines.co.uk.

770 CAN ISSN 1492-4137
TR640
PREFIX PHOTO. Text in English; Summaries in French. 2000. 2/yr. CAD 28, USD 35, GBP 21, EUR 31 to individuals; CAD 42, USD 63, GBP 38, EUR 41 to institutions; CAD 18, USD 14.95, GBP 8.95, EUR 12.95 newsstand/cover (effective 2008). adv. bk.rev. back issues avail. **Document type:** *Magazine, Consumer.* **Description:** Consists primarily of portfolio and essay sections. These features are accompanied by book reviews and newsbriefs which provide information and opportunities for professional photographers, including new technological developments. Whether photographic or photo-based, photocollage or photocopied, photogravure or photogram, Prefix Photo seeks to represent the breadth of practices and concepts, old, new, or as yet unimagined, which surround the transformation of light into image.
Indexed: ABM, SCOPUS.
—**CCC.**
Published by: Prefix Institute of Contemporary Art, 401 Richmond St W, Ste 124, Toronto, ON M5V 3A8, Canada. TEL 416-591-0357, FAX 416-591-0358. Ed., Pub., R&P Scott McLeod. adv.: B&W page CAD 599, color page CAD 999; trim 9 x 10.625. Circ: 2,500 (paid).

PRESIDENT AND PLANNER. *see* LAW—Civil Law

PRINTSHOP. *see* PRINTING

770 ITA ISSN 2035-6579
▼ **PROFESSIONAL PHOTO.** Text in Italian. 2009. m. EUR 34.90 (effective 2011). **Document type:** *Magazine, Consumer.*
Published by: Sprea Editori Srl, Via Torino 51, Cernusco sul Naviglio, MI 20063, Italy. TEL 39-02-92432222, FAX 39-02-92432236, editori@sprea.it, http://www.sprea.it.

770 USA ISSN 1528-5286
TR690
PROFESSIONAL PHOTOGRAPHER. Text in English. 1961. m. USD 27 domestic; USD 43 in Canada; USD 63 elsewhere (effective 2005). adv. bk.rev. charts; illus. index. back issues avail.; reprints avail. **Document type:** *Magazine, Trade.* **Description:** Serves professional photographers of all types, including portrait studios, commercial studios, freelancers, industrial photographers, specialists, and manufacturers, distributors, finishers, and others allied to the field.
Former titles (until 1999): Professional Photographer Storytellers (1096-7915); (until 1997): The Professional Photographer (0033-0167); (until 1963): The National Professional Photographer (0734-7529); Which was formed by the merger of (1934-1961): The Professional Photographer (0749-0119); (1907-1961): National Photographer
Related titles: Online - full text ed.
Indexed: A22, GALA, IHTDI.
—Ingenta, Linda Hall.
Published by: (Professional Photographers of America), P P A Publications and Events, Inc., 57 Forsyth St, N W, Ste 1600, Atlanta, GA 30303-2206. TEL 404-522-8600, FAX 404-614-6405. Pub. Andrew N Foster. adv.: B&W page USD 2,515. Circ: 35,000 (paid).

770 GBR ISSN 1472-5339
PROFESSIONAL PHOTOGRAPHER. Text in English. 1961. m. GBP 24.99 domestic; GBP 40 foreign; GBP 3.99 newsstand/cover (effective 2009). adv. bk.rev. illus. index. reprints avail. **Document type:** *Magazine, Trade.*
Former titles (until 1998): Professional Photographer and Digital Pro (1460-1508); (until 1996): Professional Photographer (0144-509X); (until 1980): Industrial and Commercial Photographer (0019-784X)
Related titles: Microform ed.: (from PQC); Online - full text ed.: GBP 15 (effective 2009); ◆ Supplement(s): Directory - Professional Photographer. ISSN 0956-2974.
—IE, Infotrieve, Ingenta. **CCC.**
Published by: Archant Specialist Ltd. (Subsidiary of: Archant Group), Archant House, Oriel Rd, Cheltenham, GL50 1BB, United Kingdom. TEL 44-1242-211080, FAX 44-1242-216094, http://www.archant.co.uk/. Adv. contact Sam Scott-Smith TEL 44-1242-261092. **Dist. by:** Seymour Distribution Ltd, 86 Newman St, London W1T 3EX, United Kingdom. FAX 44-207-396-8002, enquiries@seymour.co.uk.

PROFFSFOTO. *see* COMPUTERS—Computer Graphics

778.53 DEU ISSN 0721-9725
PROFIFOTO; das Magazin fuer professionelle Fotografie und Digital Imaging. Text in German. 1969. 10/yr. EUR 70; EUR 7.80 newsstand/cover (effective 2010). adv. bk.rev. illus.; tr.lit. **Document type:** *Magazine, Trade.*
Formerly (until 1979): Fachkontakt (0721-9709)
Indexed: IBR, IBZ.
—IE, Infotrieve.
Published by: (Arbeitskreis Werbe-, Mode- und Industriefotographie), G F W PhotoPublishing GmbH, Holzstr 2, Duesseldorf, 40221, Germany. TEL 49-211-390090, FAX 49-211-3900955, info@gfw.de, http://www.gfw.de.

770 ZAF ISSN 0033-0329
PROFOTO. Text in English. 1964. m. membership. adv. illus.; tr.lit. **Document type:** *Magazine, Trade.*
Published by: Professional Photographers of Southern Africa, PO Box 47044, Parklands, Johannesburg 2121, South Africa. Ed. Chris Reilly. adv.: B&W page ZAR 2,680, color page ZAR 3,650; trim 210 x 297. Circ: 3,200 (controlled).

770 AUS ISSN 1328-715X
PROPHOTO; the magazine for imaging professionals. Variant title: Professional Photography. Professional Photography in Australasia. Text in English. 1949. 10/yr. AUD 72 domestic; AUD 105 foreign; AUD 7.95 newsstand/cover (effective 2008). adv. bk.rev. back issues avail. **Document type:** *Magazine, Trade.* **Description:** News and views for professional photographers.
Former titles (until 199?): Professional Photography in Australasia (1322-395X); (until 1993): Professional Photography in Australia (1983) (1323-2819); (until 1982): Professional Photography (0159-8880); (until 1979): Professional Photography in Australia (1949) (1323-2800); I.A.P. Professional Photography in Australia (0046-9742)
—**CCC.**
Published by: Wolseley Media Pty Ltd., Level 5, 55 Chandos St, PO Box 5555, St. Leonards, NSW 2065, Australia. TEL 61-2-99016100, FAX 61-2-99016198, contactsubs@wolseleymedia.com.au. Ed. Paul Burrows TEL 61-2-99016157. Adv. contact Diane Preece TEL 61-2-99016151. color page AUD 3,500; trim 235 x 315. Circ: 6,000.

778.3 USA ISSN 1539-4654
TR860
R E S (NEW YORK); film, music, art, design, culture. (Resource) Text in English. 1997. bi-m. USD 24.95 domestic; USD 28.95 in Canada; USD 5.95 newsstand/cover domestic; USD 7.95 newsstand/cover in Canada (effective 2006). adv. **Document type:** *Magazine, Consumer.*
Indexed: A30, A31, F01, F02, T02.
Published by: RES Media Group, 76 Ninth Ave, 11th Fl, New York, NY 10011. TEL 212-320-3750 212/320-3750 212-, FAX 212-320-3709. Ed. Holly Willis. Adv. contact Sue Appelbaum.

R I T TRAINING UPDATE. (Rochester Institute of Technology) *see* PRINTING

770 GBR ISSN 1468-8670
TR1
R P S JOURNAL. Text in English. 1853. m. (10/yr). free to members (effective 2009). bk.rev. bibl.; charts; illus. reprints avail. **Document type:** *Journal, Trade.* **Description:** Contains news, reviews, in-depth articles, a diary of exhibitions and events, and award-winning photography.
Former titles (until 1999): Photographic Journal (0031-8736); (until 1956): Photographic Journal, Section A: Pictorial and General Photography (0370-0224); Which superseded in part (in 1944): Photographic Journal (1461-9415); Which was formerly (until 1895): The Photographic Society of Great Britain. Journal and Transactions (1461-9466); (until 1876): Photographic Journal (1461-9458); (until 1859): The Photographic Society of London. Journal (1461-9407)
Related titles: Microform ed.: (from PQC); Online - full text ed.
Indexed: A06, A07, A22, A30, A31, AA, ABM, ArtInd, B04, BRD, BrTechI, ChemAb, E11, GALA, Inspec, PhotoAb, RASB, SCOPUS, T04, W03, W05, WSCA.
—BLDSC (8036.489000), IE, Ingenta. **CCC.**
Published by: The Royal Photographic Society, Fenton House, 122 Wells Rd, Bath, BA2 3AH, United Kingdom. TEL 44-1225-325733, reception@rps.org, http://www.rps.org.

P

770 USA ISSN 1947-8003
▼ **R SQUARED QUARTERLY.** Variant title: R2 Quarterly. Text in English. 2009. q. USD 36.99; USD 12.99 per issue (effective 2009). **Document type:** *Magazine, Consumer.* **Description:** Journal of photographic artistry by Robert Rhea Photography studios featuring images and interviews.
Published by: Robert Rhea Photography, LLC, 3665 Andrew Jackson Way, Hermitage, TN 37076. TEL 615-713-2025, robert.rhea@robertrheaphotography.com, http://www.robertrheaphotography.com/.

RAILROAD PRESS. *see* HOBBIES

770 USA ISSN 0033-9202
TR1
RANGEFINDER. Text in English. 1952. m. USD 18 (effective 2005). adv. bk.rev. index. **Document type:** *Magazine, Trade.*
Indexed: GALA, IHTDI, PMI, SCOPUS.
Published by: Rangefinder Publishing Co., Inc., 1312 Lincoln Blvd, Santa Monica, CA 90401. TEL 310-451-0090, FAX 310-395-9058, 310-395-9058. Ed. Bill Hurter. Pub. Steve Sheanin. Adv. contact Skip Cohen. B&W page USD 8,250, color page USD 9,200. Circ: 50,500 (controlled).

RECENT RESEARCH DEVELOPMENTS IN PHOTOCHEMISTRY & PHOTOBIOLOGY. *see* CHEMISTRY—Physical Chemistry

REIHE: KULLERAUGEN STUDIUM; die blauen Schnellhefter. *see* MOTION PICTURES

REMOTE SENSING AND DIGITAL IMAGE PROCESSING. *see* COMPUTERS—Computer Graphics

770 CHN
RENMIN SHEYING/PEOPLE'S PHOTOGRAPHY. Text in Chinese. 1983. w. CNY 54 (effective 2004). **Document type:** *Newspaper, Consumer.*
Address: 124, Shuangtasi, Taiyuan, Shanxi 030012, China. TEL 86-351-4297341, FAX 86-351-4290003. **Dist. by:** China International Book Trading Corp, 35 Chegongzhuang Xilu, Haidian District, PO Box 399, Beijing 100044, China. TEL 86-10-68412045, FAX 86-10-68412023, cibtc@mail.cibtc.com.cn, http://www.cibtc.com.cn.

770 CHN ISSN 1002-7211
RENXIANG SHEYING/PORTRAIT PHOTOGRAPHY. Text in Chinese. 1983. bi-m. USD 96 (effective 2009). adv. **Description:** Studies the photographic techniques, and introduces cameras and other related equipment.
Published by: (Shangye-bu/Ministry of Commerce, Yinshi Fuwu-ju/Food Service Bureau), Renxiang Sheying Zazhishe, 45 Fuxingmennei Dajie, Beijing, 100801, China. TEL 86-10-6609-5097. Ed., Adv. contact Yunbiao Ji. Circ: 100,000. **Dist. overseas by:** China Book Import & Export Corp., 16 Gongti Donglu, Chaoyang District, Beijing, China. TEL 86-10-6609-5097.

771 778 FRA ISSN 1167-864X
REPONSES PHOTO. Text in French. 1992. m. EUR 46 (effective 2008). **Document type:** *Magazine, Consumer.*
Published by: Mondadori France, 1 Rue du Colonel Pierre-Avia, Paris, Cedex 15 75754, France. TEL 33-1-41335001, contact@mondadori.fr, http://www.mondadori.fr.

REPRO BULLETIN. *see* PRINTING

778.315 FRA ISSN 0245-3355
REPRODUIRE. Text in French. 1981. m. adv. bk.rev.
Indexed: B03.
—INIST.
Published by: C I P Groupe, 40 rue Sainte-Anne, Paris, 75002, France. FAX 33-1-42963708. Ed. Christian Thiebaut. Circ: 5,000.

770 782.421 USA ISSN 2150-8674
▼ **RESPECT.** Variant title: Respect Magazine. Text in English. 2009. q. USD 7.99 per issue (effective 2009). **Document type:** *Magazine, Consumer.* **Description:** Features photography of hip-hop artists.
Published by: Musinart, LLC, 43 Montgomery Pl, Brooklyn, NY 11215. TEL 815-734-5997, http://musinart.com/.

770 ESP ISSN 2171-2220
▼ **REVISTA FEPFI.** Key Title: Fepfi. Text in Spanish. 2010. bi-m. **Document type:** *Magazine, Consumer.*
Related titles: Online - full text ed.
Published by: Federacion Espanola de Profesionales de la Fotografia y de la Imagen, Calle de Dona Urriaca, Palencia, 34005, Spain. TEL 34-979-100130.

770 CAN ISSN 1718-1305
RIPE. Text in English. 200?. q. CAD 19.95 domestic; CAD 25 in United States; CAD 50 elsewhere; CAD 6.95 per issue domestic (effective 2006). **Document type:** *Magazine, Consumer.*
Published by: Ripe Magazine Society, 214-2001 Wall St, Vancouver, BC V5L 5E4, Canada. info@ripemagazine, http://www.ripemagazine.com/ripeBase/index.php. Ed. Kirsten Craven. Pub. Margus Riga.

770 USA
'ROUND. Text in English. q. USD 11.99 per issue (effective 2011). **Document type:** *Magazine, Trade.* **Description:** Contains articles featuring the best of New York City.
Related titles: Online - full text ed.: ISSN 2160-7818. free (effective 2011).
Published by: Jones Studio Ltd., PO Box 140402, New York, NY 10314. TEL 800-698-5856, info@jonesstudioltd.com, http://www.jonesstudioltd.com/.

770 DEU ISSN 0945-0327
RUNDBRIEF FOTOGRAFIE; sammeln - bewahren - erschliessen - vermitteln. Text in German. 1993. q. EUR 50; EUR 40 to students; EUR 16.50 newsstand/cover (effective 2005). adv. **Document type:** *Journal, Academic/Scholarly.* **Description:** Covers all aspects of managing and maintaining photographic collections in libraries, archives and museums.
Published by: (Museumsverband Baden-Wuerttemberg, Arbeitsgruppe Fotografie im Museum), Fototext Verlag Wolfgang Jaworek, Liststr 7B, Stuttgart, 70180, Germany. TEL 49-711-609021, FAX 49-711-609024, w.jaworek@fototext.s.shuttle.de. Ed. Wolfgang Hesse. Adv. contact Wolfgang Jaworek. page EUR 360; trim 187 x 255. Circ: 660 (paid and controlled).

770 USA ISSN 2161-4121
▼ **RUST QUEENS MAGAZINE.** Text in English. 2010. q. USD 20; USD 8 per issue (effective 2011). **Document type:** *Magazine, Trade.*
Related titles: Online - full text ed.
Published by: Rust Queens Inc., PO Box 504, Pewee Valley, KY 40056. Pub. Sue McNally.

770 USA
S P F E NEWSLETTER. Text in English. m. free to members (effective 2008). back issues avail. **Document type:** *Newsletter, Trade.* **Description:** Provides information to the members of Society of Photo Finishing Engineers.
Published by: (Society of Photo Finishing Engineers), Photo Marketing Association International, 3000 Picture Pl, Jackson, MI 49201. TEL 517-788-8100, FAX 517-788-8371, gpageau@pmai.org. Pub. Ted Fox. R&P Gary Pageau. Circ: 3,200 (paid).

770 330 USA
SALES COUNTER. Text in English. m. free to members (effective 2008). back issues avail. **Document type:** *Newsletter, Trade.* **Description:** Provides tips and information for the sale of photo/digital hardware and services, targeted to the counter-level sales person.
Published by: (Society for Photographic Counselors), Photo Marketing Association International, 3000 Picture Pl, Jackson, MI 49201. TEL 517-788-8100, FAX 517-788-8371, gpageau@pmai.org. Pub. Gary Pageau. Circ: 1,200.

779 JPN
SANGAKU SHASHIN NENKAN. Text in Japanese. 1974. irreg.
Published by: Yama-Kei (Publishers) Co. Ltd., 1-1-33 Shiba-Daimon, Minato-ku, Tokyo, 105-0000, Japan.

770.71 USA
SCHOOL PHOTOGRAPHER. Text in English. m. free to members (effective 2009). back issues avail. **Document type:** *Newsletter, Trade.*
Published by: (Professional School Photographers of America), Photo Marketing Association International, 3000 Picture Pl, Jackson, MI 49201. TEL 517-788-8100, 800-762-9287, FAX 517-788-8371, gpageau@pmai.org. Circ: 900.

770 DEU ISSN 1433-2809
SCHWARZWEISS; das Magazin fuer Fotografie. Text in German. 1991. bi-m. EUR 78 domestic; EUR 82 foreign; EUR 13.55 newsstand/cover (effective 2007). adv. **Document type:** *Magazine, Consumer.*
Published by: Tecklenborg Verlag, Siemenstr 4, Steinfurt, 48565, Germany. TEL 49-2552-92002, FAX 49-2552-920160, info@tecklenborg-verlag.de, http://www.tecklenborg-verlag.de. adv.: B&W page EUR 2,650, color page EUR 4,570; trim 185 x 245. Circ: 6,700 (paid).

SCREEN DIGEST. *see* COMMUNICATIONS—Television And Cable

SCRIBENDI. *see* COLLEGE AND ALUMNI

SCRIVENER CREATIVE REVIEW. *see* LITERATURE

770 CHN ISSN 1002-6770
SHEYING SHIJIE/PHOTOGRAPHY WORLD. Text in Chinese. 198?. m. USD 105.60 (effective 2009). **Document type:** *Magazine, Consumer.*
—East View.
Published by: Sheying Shijie Zazhishe, 57 Xuanwumen Xidajie, Beijing, 100803, China. TEL 86-10-63074848. Ed. Liu Xinning.

770 778.5992 CHN ISSN 1006-4788
SHEYING YU SHEXIANG/PHOTO & VIDEO. Text in Chinese. 1995. m. **Document type:** *Magazine, Consumer.*
Published by: (Zhongguo Kejiao Dianying Dianshi Xiehui/China Film and Video Association), Sheying yu Shexiang Zazhishe, 19, Dengshi Dongkou Nei Wubu Jie, Beijing, 100010, China. TEL 86-10-64097069, FAX 86-10-64097079.

770 CHN ISSN 1004-0153
SHEYING ZHIUOU/PHOTOGRAPHERS' COMPANY. Text in Chinese. 1985. m. USD 106.80 (effective 2009). **Document type:** *Journal, Academic/Scholarly.*
—East View.
Published by: Guangdong Sheng Sheyingjia Xiehui, 2/F, no.14, Xinhepu Siheng Lu, Guangzhou, Guangdong 510080, China. TEL 86-20-87624050, FAX 86-20-87185690. **Dist. by:** China International Book Trading Corp, 35 Chegongzhuang Xilu, Haidian District, PO Box 399, Beijing 100044, China. TEL 86-10-68412045, FAX 86-10-68412023, cibtc@mail.cibtc.com.cn, http://www.cibtc.com.cn.

770 TWN ISSN 1019-9608
SHEYINGJIA ZAZHI/PHOTOGRAPHERS INTERNATIONAL. Text in Chinese, English. 1992. bi-m. TWD 2,200; USD 103 foreign. adv. **Document type:** *Monographic series.*
Indexed: ABM.
Published by: Photographers International, Rm. 1015, 10F, 61 Chungking S. Rd, Sec 1, Taipei, Taiwan. TEL 886-2-2375-1552, FAX 886-2-2331-7659. Ed. Juan I Jong. Pub. Nathalia Juan. R&P Nathalie Juan. Adv. contact Grace Yuan. **Subscr. to:** Box 39-1265, Taipei Post Office, Taipei, Taiwan.

770 USA ISSN 1048-793X
TR640
SHOTS. Text in English. 1986. q. USD 20 domestic to members; USD 25 in Canada to members; USD 40 elsewhere to members (effective 2003). adv. back issues avail. **Document type:** *Magazine, Consumer.* **Description:** Fine-art photography for people worldwide.
Published by: Shots Magazine, c/o Russ Joslin, PO Box 27755, Minneapolis, MN 55427-0755. Ed., Pub. Russ Joslin. Circ: 1,600.

770 USA ISSN 0895-321X
TR197
SHUTTERBUG; tools, techniques & creativity. Variant title: Shutter Bug. Text in English. 1971. m. USD 17.95 domestic; USD 30.95 in Canada; USD 32.95 elsewhere (effective 2008). adv. bk.rev. illus. **Document type:** *Magazine, Consumer.* **Description:** Covers the entire field of photography - film and digital, professionals and students, cutting-edge innovations and collectible classics.
Former titles (until 198?): Shutterbug Ads Photographic News; (until 19??): Shutterbug Ads
Related titles: Online - full text ed.: USD 9 (effective 2008); ◆ Supplement(s): Shutterbug Buying Guide. ISSN 1074-5378.
Indexed: G06, G07, G08, H20, I05, IHTDI, S23.
—Ingenta. **CCC.**
Published by: Source Interlink Companies, 6420 Wilshire Blvd, 10th Fl, Los Angeles, CA 90048. TEL 323-782-2000, FAX 323-782-2585, dheine@sourceinterlink.com, http://www.sourceinterlinkmedia.com. Ed. Kevin McNutly. Pub. Ron Leach TEL 323-782-2207. adv.: B&W page USD 7,420, color page USD 8,245; trim 8 x 10.875. Circ: 109,409 (paid).

770 USA ISSN 1074-5378
SHUTTERBUG BUYING GUIDE. Variant title: Shutter Bug Buying Guide. Text in English. 1994. a. **Document type:** *Magazine, Consumer.*
Related titles: ◆ Supplement to: Shutterbug. ISSN 0895-321X.
Published by: Source Interlink Companies, 6420 Wilshire Blvd, 10th Fl, Los Angeles, CA 90048. TEL 323-782-2000, FAX 323-782-2585, dheine@sourceinterlink.com, http://www.sourceinterlink.com.

770 AUS ISSN 1832-5750
SILVERSHOTZ; the international journal of fine art photography. Text in English. 1998. bi-m. AUD 99 domestic; USD 77 in US & Canada; GBP 39 in United Kingdom; GBP 47 in Europe; GBP 52 elsewhere (effective 2009). adv. back issues avail. **Document type:** *Magazine, Consumer.* **Description:** Covers black and white photography and alternative printing processes.
Formerly (until 2005): Black and White Enthusiast (1445-3460)
Published by: Silvershotz Pty. Ltd., PO Box 797, Maleny, QLD 4552, Australia. TEL 61-7-54435707, FAX 61-7-30090009, info@silvershotz.com. Ed., Pub., R&P, Adv. contact Clive Waring. color page USD 400. Circ: 10,000 (paid and controlled). **Subscr. in Europe & the Americas to:** Silvershotz International.

SKRIEN; filmmagazine voor professionals en connaisseurs. *see* MOTION PICTURES

SLIPSTREAM (NIAGARA FALLS). *see* LITERATURE—Poetry

770.5 USA ISSN 0748-6413
TR1
SOCIETY FOR PHOTOGRAPHIC EDUCATION. QUARTERLY NEWSLETTER. Text in English. q. USD 35 domestic membership; USD 50 elsewhere membership (effective 2003); includes Exposure. adv. **Document type:** *Newsletter.* **Description:** Provides a network for communicating member concerns and for sharing information about job listings, exhibitions and regional and national news.
Published by: Society for Photographic Education, The School for Interdisciplinary Studies, Miami University, 126 Peabody, Oxford, OH 45056. TEL 513-529-8328, FAX 513-529-1532, socphotoed@aol.com, http://www.spenational.org/. Ed. Mary Brown TEL 610-645-9567. R&P James Murphy. Adv. contact Jeannie Pearce. page USD 450; 7.75 x 10.5. Circ: 2,500.

770 USA
SOCIETY OF PHOTOGRAPHER AND ARTIST REPRESENTATIVES. MEMBER DIRECTORY. Text in English. irreg. **Document type:** *Directory.*
Published by: Society of Photographer and Artist Representatives, 60 E 42nd St, 1166, New York, NY 10165-0006. TEL 212-779-7464.

770 700 USA
SOCIETY OF PHOTOGRAPHER AND ARTIST REPRESENTATIVES. NEWSLETTER. Text in English. q. membership only. **Document type:** *Newsletter.*
Published by: Society of Photographer and Artist Representatives, 60 E 42nd St, 1166, New York, NY 10165-0006. TEL 212-779-7464. Circ: (controlled).

770 IRL
SOURCE. Text in English. q. USD 4 (effective 2004).
Address: P O Box 352, Belfast, BTI, Ireland. Eds. John Duncan, Richard West.

770 GBR ISSN 1369-2224
TR59.3
SOURCE MAGAZINE. Text in English. 1992. q. GBP 13 domestic to individuals includes Ireland; EUR 14 in Europe to individuals; GBP 15 elsewhere to individuals; GBP 22 domestic to institutions includes Ireland; EUR 24 in Europe to institutions; GBP 27 elsewhere to institutions; GBP 6 per issue (effective 2009). bk.rev. back issues avail. **Document type:** *Magazine, Consumer.* **Description:** Features contemporary photographic work being produced in Britain and Ireland along with informative critical debate on photographic culture.
Indexed: ABM, SCOPUS.
Address: PO Box 352, Belfast, BT1 2WB, United Kingdom. TEL 44-28-90329691, FAX 44-28-90329691, subs@source.ie. Eds. John Duncan, Richard West.

SOUTHEAST ASIA MICROFILMS NEWSLETTER. *see* HISTORY—History Of Asia

770 USA ISSN 0038-4070
SOUTHERN EXPOSURE (TALLADEGA). Text in English. 1950. q. membership. adv. bk.rev. **Document type:** *Journal, Trade.*
Published by: Southeastern Professional Photographers Association, Inc., PO Box 355, Talladega, AL 35160. TEL 205-362-3485, FAX 205-362-3485. Ed. MaryLee Blankenship. Circ: 5,200.

778.1 305.868 USA
SOUTHWESTERN & MEXICAN PHOTOGRAPHY. Text in English. 1997. irreg. price varies. charts; illus. back issues avail. **Document type:** *Monographic series, Academic/Scholarly.* **Description:** Publishes commentaries on old and contemporary photographs reflecting the lives of ethnic Mexicans in the US.
Formerly (until 199?): The Wittliff Gallery Series
Published by: (Southwest Texas State University, Media Relations and Publications, Wittliff Gallery of Southwestern and Mexican Photography), University of Texas Press, Books Division, PO Box 7819, Austin, TX 78713. TEL 512-471-4034, 800-252-3206, FAX 512-232-7178, 800-687-6046, cs@utpress.utexas.edu. Ed. Bill Wittliff.

SPIRIT. *see* ETHNIC INTERESTS

770.7 USA ISSN 1049-0450
TR1
➤ **SPOT.** Text in English. 1982. s-a. free to members (effective 2011). bk.rev. back issues avail. **Document type:** *Magazine, Consumer.* **Description:** Serves the photographic community as a resource for educational exchange through feature articles, profiles, and exhibitions.
Formerly (until 1984): Image
Published by: Houston Center for Photography, 1441 W Alabama, Houston, TX 77006. TEL 713-529-4755, FAX 713-529-9248, info@hcponline.org, http://www.hcponline.org.

770 USA ISSN 0191-4030
TR780
STEREO WORLD. Text in English. 1974. bi-m. USD 26; USD 38 foreign (effective 1998). adv. bk.rev. **Document type:** *Bulletin.* **Description:** Magazine of stereophotography - everything from the study and collection of historical stereographs to modern 3-D techniques.
Indexed: GeoRef, H20, SpeleolAb, T02.
Published by: National Stereoscopic Association, Inc., PO Box 14801, Columbus, OH 43214. TEL 503-771-4440, FAX 503-771-7176. Ed., R&P, Adv. contact John Dennis. B&W page USD 200. Circ: 3,600 (paid).

770 DEU ISSN 1619-2656
STERN SPEZIAL FOTOGRAFIE. Text in German. 1996. q. EUR 18 newsstand/cover (effective 2010). adv. **Document type:** *Magazine, Consumer.* **Description:** Presents the stories and experiences of world-class photographers along with their portfolios.
Formerly (until 2000): Portfolio (1436-1701)
—**CCC.**
Published by: Gruner + Jahr AG & Co, Am Baumwall 11, Hamburg, 20459, Germany. TEL 49-40-37030, FAX 49-40-37035601, info@gujmedia.de, http://www.guj.de. Adv. contact Helma Spieker. page EUR 4,100. Circ: 10,000 (paid and controlled).

770 791.43 GBR
STOCK FOOTAGE INDEX (YEAR); the index to specialist stock footage libraries & their websites. Text in English. 200?. q. USD 1,300 in US & Canada includes stockfootageonlie; GBP 895 elsewhere includes stockfootageonlie (effective 2009). **Document type:** *Report, Trade.* **Description:** Designed specifically to make footage researchers aware of the specialist footage your company holds.
Related titles: Online - full content ed.: free (effective 2009).
Published by: The Publishing Factory Ltd., 32 Queensway, London, W2 3RX, United Kingdom. TEL 44-20-77274236, FAX 44-20-77924034, production@creativecityonline.com, http://www.creativecityonline.com/. Pub., Adv. contact Robert Prior.

770 GBR
STOCK INDEX U K / EUROPE (YEAR). Text in English. 19??. a. USD 1,190 combined subscription per issue in US & Canada (print & online eds.); GBP 595 combined subscription per issue elsewhere (print & online eds.) (effective 2010). **Document type:** *Directory, Trade.* **Description:** Essential guide to what is available in stock, and how to get hold of it.
Related titles: Online - full content ed.
Published by: The Publishing Factory Ltd., 32 Queensway, London, W2 3RX, United Kingdom. TEL 44-20-77274236, FAX 44-20-77924034, production@creativecityonline.com, http://www.creativecityonline.com/. Pub., Adv. contact Robert Prior.

770 GBR
STOCK INDEX U S A (YEAR). Text in English. 2002. a. USD 1,190 combined subscription per issue in US & Canada (print & online eds.); GBP 595 combined subscription per issue elsewhere (print & online eds.) (effective 2010). **Document type:** *Directory, Trade.* **Description:** Guide to what is available in stock, and how to get hold of it. Contains over 160 fully illustrated pages of specialist stock library details, including full contact information.
Related titles: Online - full content ed.
Published by: The Publishing Factory Ltd., 32 Queensway, London, W2 3RX, United Kingdom. TEL 44-20-77274236, FAX 44-20-77924034, space@creativecityonline.com, http://www.creativecityonline.com/. Pub., Adv. contact Robert Prior.

770.29 USA ISSN 0897-6287
STOCK PHOTO DESKBOOK. Text in English. 1977. a. USD 48.95. adv. **Document type:** *Directory.* **Description:** Lists the names, addresses, telephone, fax, e-mail and website info of U.S. and foreign stock houses, individual, government, and museum sources, freelance picture researchers, CD-ROM producers, and professional associations.
Formerly (until 1989): Stock Photo and Assignment Stock Book (0146-5961)
Published by: Exeter Co., Inc., 767 Winthrop Rd, Teaneck, NJ 07666. TEL 201-692-1743, FAX 201-692-8173. Ed., R&P Adrienne E Lesser. Pub., Adv. contact Stephen Goller.

770 RUS
STRANA LYUBVI. ROMAN V FOTOGRAFIYAKH. Text in Russian. m. USD 139 in United States.
Published by: Post-Shop, Olimpiiskii pr-t 22, Moscow, 129090, Russian Federation. TEL 7-095-9591490, FAX 7-095-9590987. Ed. N N Morgunova. **Dist. by:** East View Information Services, 10601 Wayzata Blvd, Minneapolis, MN 55305. TEL 952-252-1201, 800-477-1005, FAX 952-252-1202, info@eastview.com, http://www.eastview.com.

770 USA ISSN 1930-3920
STUDIES IN PHOTOGRAPHIC ARTS. Text in English. 1990. irreg., latest vol.6, 2005. price varies. back issues avail. **Document type:** *Monographic series, Academic/Scholarly.*
Published by: Edwin Mellen Press, 415 Ridge St, PO Box 450, Lewiston, NY 14092. TEL 716-754-2266, FAX 716-754-4056, cservice@mellenpress.com.

770 GBR ISSN 1462-0510
STUDIES IN PHOTOGRAPHY. Text in English. 1986. a. free to members (effective 2009). adv. bk.rev. back issues avail. **Document type:** *Yearbook, Academic/Scholarly.* **Description:** Provides a forum for critical debate on issues relating to historical and contemporary photography in Scotland.
Former titles (until 1996): Scottish Photography Bulletin (0951-4821); (until 1986): Scottish Society for the History of Photography. Bulletin (0269-1787); (until 1986): Scottish Society for the History of Photography. Newsletter
Published by: Scottish Society for the History of Photography, 1 Queen St, Edinburgh, EH2 1JD, United Kingdom.

771 USA
TR1
STUDIO PHOTOGRAPHY. Abbreviated title: S P. Text in English. 1964. m. free to qualified personnel; USD 53 domestic; USD 97 in Canada & Mexico; USD 142 elsewhere (effective 2008). adv. bk.rev. bibl.; illus. index. Supplement avail.; back issues avail.; reprints avail. **Document type:** *Magazine, Trade.*
Former titles (until 2006): Studio Photography & Design (1097-1181); (until 1998): Studio Photography (0746-0996); (until 1975): Photographic Business and Product News (0031-8728); Studio Photography & Design was incorporated (1952-1997): Commercial Image (1081-3128); Which was formerly (until 1995): Industrial Photography (0019-8595)
Related titles: Online - full text ed.
Indexed: A05, A09, A10, A15, A20, A22, A23, A24, A30, A31, ABIPC, ABIn, AS&TA, AS&TI, B02, B04, B13, B15, B17, B18, C10, G04, G08, GALA, I05, IHTDI, Inspec, P16, P48, P51, P53, P54, PQC, T02, V03, V04.
—IE, Infotrieve, Ingenta, INIST. **CCC.**
Published by: Cygnus Business Media, Inc., 1233 Janesville Ave, PO Box 803, Fort Atkinson, WI 53538. TEL 920-563-6388, FAX 920-563-1702, http://www.cygnusb2b.com. Pub. Ian Littauer TEL 631-963-6242. Adv. contacts Ian Littauer TEL 631-963-6242, Liz Hildenbrand. B&W page USD 6,200, color page USD 10,325; trim 8.5 x 10.875. Circ: 50,008.

770 AUT ISSN 1991-9913
SUBTITLED; for documentary photography. Text in English. 2006. m. **Document type:** *Magazine, Consumer.*
Media: Online - full content.
Address: Versorgungshausstr 32-2, Salzburg, 5023, Austria.

770 ESP
SUPER FOTO NATURALEZA; revista del fotografo de naturaleza. Text in Spanish. m. EUR 4.95 newsstand/cover (effective 2009). adv. **Document type:** *Magazine, Consumer.*
Published by: Grupo V, C Valportillo Primera, 11, Alcobendas, Madrid, 28108, Spain. TEL 34-91-6622137, FAX 34-91-6622654, secretaria@grupov.es, http://www.grupov.es/. Adv. contact Carmina Ferrer. page EUR 4,110; trim 20 x 27. Circ: 32,000.

770 ESP ISSN 1136-5544
SUPER FOTO PRACTICA. Text in Spanish. 1996. m. EUR 3.95 newsstand/cover (effective 2009). adv. **Document type:** *Magazine, Consumer.*
Published by: Grupo V, C Valportillo Primera, 11, Alcobendas, Madrid, 28108, Spain. TEL 34-91-6622137, FAX 34-91-6622654, secretaria@grupov.es. Ed. Martin Gabilondo-Viqueira. adv.: page EUR 4,380; trim 20 x 27. Circ: 32,833.

TAUCHEN; Europas grosse Tauchzeitschrift. *see* SPORTS AND GAMES

770 GBR ISSN 2045-2896
▼ **TECHRADAR CAMERA BUYING GUIDE.** Variant title: Camera Buying Guide. Text in English. 2010. s-a. GBP 7.99 domestic; GBP 8.99 in Europe; GBP 9.99 elsewhere (effective 2011). **Document type:** *Magazine, Trade.* **Description:** Provides information on where to get the best deals on techradar camera buying.
Published by: Future Publishing Ltd., Beauford Ct, 30 Monmouth St, Bath, Avon BA1 2BW, United Kingdom. TEL 44-1225-442244, customerservice@subscription.co.uk, http://www.futureplc.com. **Subscr. to:** 10 Waterside Way, Northampton NN4 7XD, United Kingdom. TEL 44-1604-251045, contact@myfavouritemagazines.co.uk.

TEN THOUSAND WORDS!. *see* MOTION PICTURES

THRESHOLDS (CAMBRIDGE). *see* ART

770 USA
TODAY'S PHOTOGRAPHER INTERNATIONAL. Text in English. 1984. bi-m. USD 17.70 (effective 2000). adv. bk.rev. **Document type:** *Magazine, Trade.* **Description:** Devoted to how to make money with your camera.
Formerly: International Photographer (Lewisville)
Related titles: Online - full text ed.
Published by: (International Freelance Photographer's Organization), American Image, Inc., 6495 Shallowford Rd, Box 777, Lewisville, NC 27023. TEL 336-945-9867, FAX 336-945-3711. Ed., R&P Vonda H Blackburn. Pub. Jack Gallimore. Adv. contact Sarah Hinshaw. B&W page USD 2,992, color page USD 4,631; trim 10.88 x 8.25. Circ: 78,000.

771.46 USA ISSN 1048-4388
TR465
TOPICS IN PHOTOGRAPHIC PRESERVATION. Cover title: AIC/PMG Topics in Photographic Preservation. Text in English. 1986. s-a. **Description:** Provides a means for the exchange of information on experiences and techniques relating to photographic science, conservation, and collections care.
Indexed: A&ATA.
Published by: American Institute for Conservation of Historic and Artistic Works, Photographic Materials Group, 1717 K St., N.W., Suite 200, Washington, DC 20006. TEL 202-452-9545, FAX 202-452-9328, info@aic-faic.org.

770 USA ISSN 2158-2025
TR99
▼ ➤ **TRANS-ASIA PHOTOGRAPHY REVIEW.** Text in English. 2010. s-a. free (effective 2010). **Document type:** *Journal, Academic/Scholarly.* **Description:** Devoted to the discussion of historic and contemporary photography in Asia.
Media: Online - full text.
Published by: (University of Michigan Library, Scholarly Publishing Office), Hampshire College cballantine@hampshire.edu, http://www.hampshire.edu/.

➤ **TRENDS IN PHOTOCHEMISTRY & PHOTOBIOLOGY.** *see* CHEMISTRY—Physical Chemistry

770 791.43 ITA ISSN 0041-4395
TUTTI FOTOGRAFI. Text in Italian. 1969. m. adv. bk.rev. illus. index. **Document type:** *Magazine, Trade.*
Published by: Editrice Progresso s.r.l., Viale Piceno 14, Milan, 20129, Italy. TEL 39-02-70002222, FAX 39-02-713030, abbonamenti@fotografia.it, http://www.fotografia.it.

770 CAN ISSN 1925-3877
▼ **URBANA LEGIO MAGAZINE.** Text in English. 2011. m. free (effective 2011). back issues avail. **Document type:** *Magazine, Trade.*
Media: Online - full text.
Published by: Dioni Pereira, Ed. & Pub., 19-4446 De La Roche St, Montreal, PQ H2J 3J1, Canada.

770 FIN ISSN 0356-8075
VALOKUVAUKSEN VUOSIKIRJA/FINNISH PHOTOGRAPHIC YEARBOOK/FINSK FOTOGRAFISK ARSBOK. Text in English, Finnish, Swedish. 1972. a. adv. illus. **Document type:** *Yearbook.*
Published by: Suomen Valokuvataiteen Museon Saatio/Finnish Museum of Photography, Cable Factory, Tallberginkatu 1 G/85, Helsinki, 00180, Finland. TEL 358-9-6866360, FAX 358-9-68663630, fmp@fmp.fi, http://www.fmp.fi. Ed. Asko Makela. Circ: 4,000.

770 FRA ISSN 1952-076X
LA VIE EN IMAGES. Text in French. 2005. irreg. back issues avail. **Document type:** *Monographic series, Consumer.*
Published by: Editions Palette, 17 C Rue Campagne-Premiere, Paris, 75014, France. TEL 33-1-43201953, FAX 33-1-43203448.

770 DEU ISSN 1861-6445
VIEW; Die besten Bilder des Monats. Variant title: Stern View. Text in German. 2005. m. EUR 38.40; EUR 3.30 newsstand/cover (effective 2011). adv. **Document type:** *Magazine, Consumer.*
Published by: Gruner + Jahr AG & Co, Am Baumwall 11, Hamburg, 20459, Germany. TEL 49-40-37030, FAX 49-40-37035601, info@gujmedia.de, http://www.guj.de. Adv. contact Helma Spieker. Circ: 149,881 (paid and controlled).

770 USA ISSN 1066-6958
TR1
VIEW CAMERA. Text in English. 1988. bi-m. USD 27.50 domestic; USD 48 in Canada (effective 2010). adv. bk.rev. illus. Index. back issues avail.; reprints avail. **Document type:** *Journal, Consumer.*
Related titles: Print ed.: USD 25 (effective 2010).
Indexed: A30, A31, AmHI, H07, SCOPUS, T02.
Published by: Steve Simmons Photography, PO Box 2328, Corrales, NM 87048. TEL 505-899-8054, FAX 505-899-7977, amiles@viewcamera.com, http://www.cameraarts.com. Pub., Adv. contact Steve Simmons. B&W page USD 1,400; 7 x 10. Circ: 16,000.

771.3 USA ISSN 1543-8732
TR263.L4
VIEWFINDER (NORTHBROOK); quarterly journal of the Leica Historical Society of America. Text in English. 1967. q.
Published by: Leica Historical Society of America, c/o LHSA Administrative Manager, 60 Revere Dr. Ste. 500, Northbrook, IL 60062. TEL 847-564-2181, FAX 847-480-9282, admin@lhsa.org, http://www.lhsa.org. Ed. Bill Rosauer.

770 700 USA
VIEWFINDER JOURNAL OF FOCAL POINT GALLERY. Text in English. 1982. a. USD 35 to members (effective 2000). bk.rev. back issues avail. **Document type:** *Catalog.* **Description:** Prints of artwork from and promotional information on the gallery, located in City Island, New York.
Published by: Focal Point Press, 321 City Island Ave, New York, NY 10464. TEL 718-885-1403, FAX 718-885-1403-51. Ed., R&P Ron Terner. Circ: 3,000.

VISUAL RESOURCES; an international journal of documentation. *see* ART

770 DEU ISSN 0720-4841
VISUELL. Text in German, English. 1980. bi-m. EUR 35.70 domestic; EUR 38.70 in Europe; EUR 55.70 elsewhere (effective 2010). adv. **Document type:** *Magazine, Trade.* **Description:** Reports on the progress of the globalization of the picture market.
Incorporates (1996-2009): Visuell International (1438-3012); Which was formerly (1982-1995): Visuell Aktuell (0722-3609)
Related titles: Online - full text ed.
—CCC.
Published by: Presse Informations Agentur GmbH, Lothar-von-Kuebel Str 18, Sinzheim, 76547, Germany. TEL 49-7221-3017560, FAX 49-7221-3017570, office@piag.de, http://piag.de. Ed. Dieter Brinzer. Adv. contact Jutta Maennle. B&W page EUR 1,250, color page EUR 2,000; 162 x 225. Circ: 9,500 (paid and controlled).

770 USA
W P P I MONTHLY. Text in English. 1978. m. USD 75 to members; free to members (effective 2005). back issues avail. **Document type:** *Newsletter, Trade.* **Description:** Provides information on running a wedding photography studio, how-to techniques, business management, and continuing education. Publishes print competition winners.
Former titles: Wedding Photographer; Wedding Photographers International
Published by: (Wedding & Portrait Photographers International), Rangefinder Publishing Co., Inc., 1312 Lincoln Blvd, Santa Monica, CA 90401. TEL 310-451-0090, FAX 310-395-9058, ssheanin@rfpublishing.com, http://www.focusonimagingmag.com/landingpage/index.tml. Ed. Bill Hurter. Circ: 4,500 (paid).

WESTWIND (LOS ANGELES). *see* ART

770 577.51 USA ISSN 1935-7745
TR800
WETPIXEL QUARTERLY. Text in English. 2007. q. USD 45 domestic; USD 55 in Canada & Mexico (effective 2007). **Document type:** *Magazine, Consumer.* **Description:** Devoted to underwater and ocean photography and the conservation of marine life through photographs. Includes profiles and interviews of underwater photographers, and images of rarely seens and sometimes endangered ocean animals.
Published by: Wetpixel LLC, 434 Napa St, Sausalito, CA 94965. TEL 415-332-3655, FAX 415-332-3655, http://www.wetpixel.com. Pub. Eric Cheng.

770 GBR ISSN 1366-5324
WHAT DIGITAL CAMERA. Text in English. 1997. m. GBP 34.49 domestic; USD 81.40 in US & Canada; EUR 62.30 in Europe; GBP 48.30 elsewhere; GBP 3.99 newsstand/cover (effective 2010). adv. back issues avail. **Document type:** *Magazine, Consumer.* **Description:** Features reviews of new cameras and software, scanners and printers as well as covers digital imaging techniques for the intermediate consumer, plus news, 'how to' articles and user profiles.
Incorporates (1994-200?): What Camera (1359-1800); Which superseded in part (in 1994): Amateur Photographer (0002-6840); Which incorporated (1988-1990): What Camera? (0956-148X); Which was formerly (until 1988): Camera Weekly (0264-0988); (until 1982): What Camera Weekly (0144-6320); (until 1980): What Camera? Monthly (0140-7945)
Related titles: Online - full text ed.: GBP 12.87 (effective 2010).
Published by: I P C Country & Leisure Media Ltd. (Subsidiary of: I P C Media Ltd.), The Blue Fin Bldg, 110 Southwark St, London, SE1 0SU, United Kingdom. TEL 44-20-31485000, FAX 44-20-31486439, http://www.ipcmedia.com. Ed. Nigel Atherton TEL 44-20-31484795. Adv. contact Dave Stone TEL 44-20-31482516. page GBP 1,761. Circ: 24,034. **Subscr. to:** Rockwood House, Perrymount Rd, Haywards Heath RH16 3DH, United Kingdom. TEL 44-845-1231231, IPCsubs@quadrantsubs.com, http://www.magazinesdirect.co.uk. **Dist. by:** MarketForce UK Ltd.

WHITE WALL REVIEW. *see* LITERATURE

WHITEFISH REVIEW; art, literature, photography. *see* LITERATURE

770 GBR
WIDESCREEN INTERNATIONAL. Text in English. 1964. bi-m. USD 35. adv. bk.rev.; film rev. back issues avail. **Document type:** *Magazine, Consumer.* **Description:** Panoramic photography, 3-D, stereoscopic, multi-channel sound, multi-projector set-ups.
Formerly: Widescreen
Published by: Widescreen Centre, 48 Dorset St, London, W1H 3FH, United Kingdom. TEL 44-171-935-2580, FAX 44-171-486-1272. Ed., R&P Tony Shapps. Adv. contact Tony Smithson. Circ: 5,000.

770 USA
WOLFPIX; making better pictures a part of your life. Text in English. 2001 (Jun. 29th). bi-m. USD 24.99; USD 4.95 newsstand/cover; USD 6.95 newsstand/cover in Canada (effective 2001). adv. **Document type:** *Magazine, Consumer.* **Description:** Aims to help readers create better pictures by providing articles on taking conventional or digital photos, expert columnists, fun photo projects, and lifestyle features.
Published by: Reedy River Press, Inc., PO Box 26013, Greenville, SC 29615. TEL 864-286-0540, 888-259-3887, FAX 864-286-1056, info@pccreateit.com.

770 GBR ISSN 2045-0524
▼ **WORLD OF PHOTOGRAPHY.** Text in English. 2010. a. **Document type:** *Magazine, Consumer.*
Published by: Archant Specialist Ltd. (Subsidiary of: Archant Group), Archant House, Oriel Rd, Cheltenham, GL50 1BB, United Kingdom. TEL 44-1242-216052, miller.hogg@archant.co.uk, http://www.archant.co.uk/business_specialist.aspx.

770 NLD ISSN 0510-9337
WORLD PRESS PHOTO. Text in Multiple languages. 1958. a. EUR 24 (effective 2009). back issues avail. **Document type:** *Yearbook, Trade.*
Related titles: ◆ German ed.: World Press Photo (Deutsche Ausgabe). ISSN 2210-4313.
Published by: (World Press Photo), Schilt Publishing, Het Sieraad, Postjesweg 1, Amsterdam, 1057 DT, Netherlands. TEL 31-20-6256087, FAX 31-20-6270242, http://www.schiltpublishing.com.

770 070.49 NLD ISSN 2210-4313
▼ **WORLD PRESS PHOTO (DEUTSCHE AUSGABE).** Text in German. 2009. a. EUR 24 (effective 2010).
Related titles: ◆ Multiple languages ed.: World Press Photo. ISSN 0510-9337.
Published by: (World Press Photo), Schilt Publishing, Het Sieraad, Postjesweg 1, Amsterdam, 1057 DT, Netherlands. TEL 31-20-6256087, FAX 31-20-6270242, http://www.schiltpublishing.com.

770 CHN
XIANDAI SHEYING/INPHOTO. Text in Chinese. 1984. q. USD 16. adv. bk.rev. **Description:** Features fine art photographs by both Chinese and foreign photographers. Also includes critics.
Published by: Shenzhen Shi Wenlian/Shengzhen Writers and Artists Federation, 2nd Fl, 13 Guiyuan Rd, Shenzhen, Guangdong 518001, China. TEL 86-755-586168, FAX 86-755-586168. Ed. Li Mei. Circ: 4,000.

770 CHN ISSN 1001-0270
➤ **YINGXIANG JISHU/IMAGE TECHNOLOGY.** Text in Chinese; Abstracts in English. 1989. q. USD 31.20 (effective 2009). adv. bk.rev. **Document type:** *Academic/Scholarly.*

P

Related titles: Online - full text ed.
Indexed: SCOPUS.
—East View.
Published by: Quanguo Qinggong Ganguang Cailiao Keji Qingbao-zhan, 20 Dongting Lu, Hexi-qu, Tianjin 300220, China. TEL 86-22-2834-2934, FAX 86-22-2834-0654. Ed., Adv. contact Zhengeng Wei. **Dist. overseas by:** China International Book Trading Corp, 35 Chegongzhuang Xilu, Haidian District, PO Box 399, Beijing 100044, China. **Co-sponsors:** Chinese Photographic Materials Information Center; Chinese Society of Photographic Science and Engineering.

770 CHN ISSN 1674-0475
TR692 CODEN: YKYGAW
➤ **YINGXIANG KEXUE YU GUANGHUAXUE/IMAGING SCIENCE AND PHOTOCHEMISTRY.** Text in Chinese; Abstracts in Chinese, English. 1983. bi-m. adv. **Document type:** *Journal, Academic/Scholarly.* **Description:** Covers photochemical imaging systems, exposure and development mechanisms, image structure and evaluation, sensitometry of photographic materials, organic photochemistry, photochemistry of polymers, photobiochemistry, photoelectrochemistry at interface, and photocatalysis.
Formerly (until 2007): Ganguang Kexue yu Guanghuaxue/Photographic Science and Photochemistry (1000-3231)
Related titles: Online - full text ed.
Indexed: A28, A32, APA, ASFA, BrCerAb, C&ISA, C33, CA/WCA, CIA, CIN, CerAb, ChemAb, ChemTitl, CivEngAb, CorrAb, E&CAJ, E11, EEA, EMA, ESPM, EngInd, EnvEAb, H15, M&TEA, M09, MBF, METADEX, PhotoAb, RefZh, SCOPUS, SWRA, SolStAb, T04, WAA.
—BLDSC (6471.800000), CASDDS, East View, Linda Hall.
Published by: Zhongguo Kexueyuan Lihua Jishu Yanjiusuo/Chinese Academy of Sciences, Technical Institute of Physics & Chemistry, 2, Zhongguancun Bei Yi-Tiao, Beijing, 100190, China. TEL 86-10-82543683, FAX 86-10-82543682, http://www.ipc.ac.cn/. Circ: 11,000. **Dist. by:** China International Book Trading Corp, 35 Chegongzhuang Xilu, Haidian District, PO Box 399, Beijing 100044, China. TEL 86-10-68412045, FAX 86-10-68412023, cibtc@mail.cibtc.com.cn, http://www.cibtc.com.cn. **Co-sponsor:** Zhongguo Ganguang Kexuehui/Chinese Society for Imaging Science and Technology.

770 CHN ISSN 1673-8101
CODEN: GACAFF
YINGXIANG SHIJUE/DIGITAL CAMERA. Text in Chinese. 1973. m. CNY 192 domestic; USD 48 in Hong Kong, Macau & Taiwan; USD 72 elsewhere (effective 2007). adv. bk.rev. **Document type:** *Magazine, Trade.* **Description:** Provides information on the development, manufacture and application of photosensitive materials. Covers new products, technologies and trends of the market and industrial circle.
Former titles (until 2007): Yingxiang Cailiao/Image Materials (1009-7783); (until 2000): Ganguang Cailiao/Photosensitive Materials (1003-3874)
Related titles: Online - full text ed.
Indexed: CIN, ChemAb, ChemTitl, SCOPUS.
—BLDSC (9418.467900), CASDDS.
Published by: Guanguo Ganguang Cailiao Xinxi Zhan, 6, Yuekai Nan Dajie, Baoding, 071054, China. TEL 86-312-7922172, FAX 86-312-7923008, http://www.imageinfo.com.cn/. Ed. Rongguo Yao. R&P Fengqi Wang. Adv. contact Licheng Du. Circ: 5,000 (paid). **Dist. by:** China International Book Trading Corp, 35 Chegongzhuang Xilu, Haidian District, PO Box 399, Beijing 100044, China. TEL 86-10-68412045, FAX 86-10-68412023, cibtc@mail.cibtc.com.cn, http://www.cibtc.com.cn.

770 CHN ISSN 1009-2250
ZHAOXIANGJI/CAMERAS. Text in Chinese. 1985. bi-m.
Related titles: Online - full text ed.
Published by: Hangzhou Zhaoxiangji Jixie Yanjiusuo, 94 Xi Xi Lu, Hangzhou, Zhejiang 310013, China. TEL 521014. Ed. Wang Zhenkui.

770 CHN ISSN 0529-6420
ZHONGGUO SHEYING/CHINESE PHOTOGRAPHY. Text in Chinese. 1957. m. USD 117.60 (effective 2009). adv. bk.rev. 96 p./no.
Indexed: RASB.
—East View.
Published by: (Zhongguo Sheyingjia Xiehui/China Photographers' Association), Zhongguo Sheying Zazhishe, 61 Hongxing Hutong, Dongdan, Beijing, 100005, China. TEL 86-10-65252277, FAX 86-10-65253197, 86-10-65131859, cphoto@public.bta.net.cn, http://www.cphoto.com.cn. Eds. Bang Liu, Changyun Wu. R&P Bang Liu. Adv. contact Yanjuan Xu. color page USD 4,500; 230 x 260. **Dist. overseas by:** China International Book Trading Corp, 35 Chegongzhuang Xilu, Haidian District, PO Box 399, Beijing 100044, China. TEL 86-10-68412045, FAX 86-10-68412023, cibtc@mail.cibtc.com.cn, http://www.cibtc.com.cn.

770 616.075 CHN ISSN 1007-1482
ZHONGGUO TISHIXUE YU TUXIANG FENXI/CHINESE JOURNAL OF STEREOLOGY AND IMAGE ANALYSIS. Text in Chinese. 1996. q. **Document type:** *Journal, Academic/Scholarly.*
Related titles: Online - full text ed.
Published by: Zhongguo Tishixue Xuehui, Tsinghua Daxue, Gongwuxiguan 113, Beijing, 100084, China.

778.53 RUS ISSN 0869-6144
TR1 CODEN: ZNPFEK
➤ **ZHURNAL NAUCHNOI I PRIKLADNOI FOTOGRAFII.** Text in Russian. 1956. bi-m. RUR 519 for 6 mos. (effective 2003). bibl.; charts; illus. index. **Document type:** *Journal, Academic/Scholarly.*
Formerly (until 1992): Zhurnal Nauchnoi i Prikladnoi Fotografii i Kinematografii (0044-4561)
Indexed: A20, ASCA, CIN, ChemAb, ChemTitl, ISR, Inspec, PhotoAb, SCOPUS.
—BLDSC (0060.999000), CASDDS, INIST, Linda Hall. **CCC.**
Published by: (Rossiiskaya Akademiya Nauk/Russian Academy of Sciences, Institut Khimicheskoi Fiziki im. N.N. Semenova), Izdatel'stvo Nauka, Profsoyuznaya ul 90, Moscow, 117864, Russian Federation. TEL 7-095-3347151, FAX 7-095-4202220, secret@naukaran.ru, http://www.naukaran.ru. Circ: 70,290.

➤ **ZOO (LONDON,1999).** *see* ART

770 ITA ISSN 0393-4330
ZOOM. Text in English. 1980. bi-m. adv. bk.rev. illus. index. **Document type:** *Magazine, Trade.*
Published by: Editrice Progresso s.r.l., Viale Piceno 14, Milan, 20129, Italy. TEL 39-02-70002222, FAX 39-02-713030, abbonamenti@fotografia.it, http://www.fotografia.it. Circ: 20,000.

770 NLD ISSN 1871-7764
ZOOM.NL. Text in Dutch. 2003. 10/yr. EUR 42.95 (effective 2009). adv. **Document type:** *Magazine, Consumer.*
Formerly (until 2005): Zoom Magazine (1571-5582)
Media: Online - full text.
Published by: I D G Communications Nederland BV, Postbus 5446, Haarlem, 2000 GK, Netherlands. TEL 31-23-5461111, FAX 31-23-5461155, info@idg.nl, http://idg.nl. Ed. Remco de Graaf.

770 USA
21ST: THE JOURNAL OF CONTEMPORARY PHOTOGRAPHY. Text in English. 1998. irreg. price varies each volume. **Document type:** *Journal, Academic/Scholarly.* **Description:** Features hand-pulled photogravure images from many of the world?s most highly respected contemporary photographers.
Address: 9 New Venture Dr, #1, South Dennis, MA 02660. TEL 508-398-3000, FAX 508-398-0343. Ed. John Wood. Pub. Steven Albahari.

52ND CITY. *see* ART

PHOTOGRAPHY—Abstracting, Bibliographies, Statistics

016.77 GBR ISSN 0896-100X
TR1
IMAGING ABSTRACTS. Text in English. 1921. bi-m. GBP 902.50 (effective 2010). abstr.; pat. index, cum.index. 80 p./no. 2 cols./p.; back issues avail. **Document type:** *Abstract/Index.* **Description:** Provides comprehensive coverage from around the world on all aspects of imaging science and technology.
Formerly (until 1988): Photographic Abstracts (0031-8701)
Related titles: CD-ROM ed.; Microfiche ed.: (from PMC); Microform ed.: (from PQC); Online - full text ed.: 1975.
—BLDSC (4368.996450), Linda Hall. **CCC.**
Published by: (The Royal Photographic Society, Imaging Science and Technology Group), IntertechPira, Cleeve Rd, Leatherhead, Surrey KT22 7RU, United Kingdom. TEL 44-1372-802000, FAX 44-1372-802079, info@pira-international.com, http://www.pira-international.com/.

770 USA ISSN 1084-2233
HD9708.A1
INTERNATIONAL PHOTO PROCESSING INDUSTRY REPORT. Text in English. 1983. a. USD 1,000 (effective 2001). **Document type:** *Report, Trade.* **Description:** Statistical review of the worldwide photo processing market.
Related titles: Online - full text ed.
Published by: Photofinishing News, Inc., 10915 Bonita Beach Rd, Ste 1091, Bonita Springs, FL 34135-9047. TEL 239-992-4421, FAX 239-992-6328.

770 316.8 ZAF
SOUTH AFRICA. STATISTICS SOUTH AFRICA. CENSUS OF SOCIAL, RECREATIONAL AND PERSONAL SERVICES - PHOTOGRAPHIC STUDIOS. Text in English. irreg., latest 1990. **Document type:** *Government.*
Formerly (until Aug.1998): South Africa. Central Statistical Service. Census of Social, Recreational and Personal Services - Photographic Studios
Published by: Statistics South Africa/Statistieke Suid-Afrika, Private Bag X44, Pretoria, 0001, South Africa. TEL 27-12-3108911, FAX 27-12-3108500, info@statssa.gov.za, http://www.statssa.gov.za.

PHOTOGRAPHY—Computer Applications

775.22 DEU
▼ **ADVANCED PHOTOSHOP**; Das Magazin fuer den professionellen Photoshop-Anwender. Text in German. 2009. 9/yr. EUR 99; EUR 9.90 newsstand/cover (effective 2011). adv. **Document type:** *Magazine, Consumer.*
Published by: Sonic Media Verlag GmbH, Hauptstr 31, Bad Honnef, 53604, Germany. TEL 49-2224-988260, FAX 49-2224-9882679, info@sonic-media-verlag.de, http://www.sonic-media-verlag.de. Ed. Hans-Guenther Beer. Adv. contact Brigitta Reinhart. Circ: 25,000 (paid and controlled).

775.22 NLD ISSN 1875-8665
ADVANCED PHOTOSHOP. Text in Dutch. 2007. 10/yr. EUR 50; EUR 8.95 newsstand/cover (effective 2009). adv. **Document type:** *Magazine, Consumer.*
Published by: F & L Publishing Group B.V., Meijhorst 60-10, Postbus 31331, Nijmegen, 6503 CH, Netherlands. TEL 31-24-3723636, FAX 31-24-3723630, info@fnl.nl, http://www.fnl.nl. Adv. contact Dick Verbeeten. page EUR 2,950; trim 230 x 300.

775.22 GBR ISSN 1748-7277
ADVANCED PHOTOSHOP. Text in English. 2003. m. GBP 62.30 domestic; GBP 70 in Europe; GBP 80 elsewhere; GBP 6 per issue (effective 2010). adv. back issues avail. **Document type:** *Magazine, Consumer.* **Description:** Provides Adobe Photoshop professionals and enthusiasts with informative articles and tips to improve their skills in Photoshop.
Formerly (until 2005): Digital Creative Arts Special Edition (1740-2778)
Published by: Imagine Publishing Ltd., Richmond House, 33 Richmond Hill, Bournemouth, Dorset BH2 6EZ, United Kingdom. TEL 44-1202-586200, http://www.imagine-publishing.co.uk. Ed. Julie Easton TEL 44-1202-586243. Adv. contact Hang Deretz TEL 44-1202-586442.

AUDIO VIDEO FOTO BILD. *see* COMMUNICATIONS—Video

770.285 DEU
▼ **DER BILDBEARBEITER**; Das Praxismagazin fuer Fotografie & Bildbearbeitung. Text in German. 2011. bi-m. EUR 50; EUR 9.90 newsstand/cover (effective 2011). adv. **Document type:** *Magazine, Consumer.*
Published by: Sonic Media Verlag GmbH, Hauptstr 31, Bad Honnef, 53604, Germany. TEL 49-2224-988260, FAX 49-2224-9882679, info@sonic-media-verlag.de, http://www.sonic-media-verlag.de. Ed. Hans-Guenther Beer. Adv. contact Liza Man. Circ: 30,000 (paid).

770 NLD ISSN 2210-5964
▼ **CAMERA EN COMPUTER.** Text in Dutch. 2010. m. EUR 39.95 domestic; EUR 99.95 foreign (effective 2010). **Document type:** *Magazine, Consumer.*
Formed by the merger of (2009-2010): Fotaal (1877-9328); (2009-2010): B-Gates (1878-528X)
Published by: Toptijdschriften, Zeemanstraat 27, Barendrecht, 2991 BG, Netherlands. http://www.toptijdschriften.nl.

770.285 DEU ISSN 2192-5852
CHIP FOTO-VIDEO. Text in German. 2003. m. EUR 49.90; EUR 4.50 newsstand/cover (effective 2011). adv. **Document type:** *Magazine, Consumer.*
Formerly (until 2003): Chip Foto-Video Digital (1614-9424)
Published by: Chip Communications GmbH, Poccistr 11, Munich, 80336, Germany. TEL 49-89-746420, FAX 49-89-74642325. Ed. Florian Schuster. Adv. contact Jochen Lutz. Circ: 62,713 (paid and controlled).

770.285 POL ISSN 1732-7938
CHIP FOTO-VIDEO DIGITAL. Text in German. 2004. m. PLZ 15.50 newsstand/cover (effective 2006). adv. **Document type:** *Magazine, Consumer.*
Published by: Vogel Burda Communications sp. z o.o., ul Topiel 23, Warsaw, 00 342, Poland. TEL 48-22-3201900, FAX 48-22-3201901, pr@vbc.pl, http://www.vbc.pl. adv.: page PLZ 6,600; trim 230 x 300.

770.285 NLD ISSN 1574-6682
CHIP FOTO-VIDEO DIGITAL. Text in Dutch. 2004. 8/yr. EUR 27; EUR 3.75 newsstand/cover (effective 2009). adv. **Document type:** *Magazine, Consumer.*
Published by: F & L Publishing Group B.V., Meijhorst 60-10, Postbus 31331, Nijmegen, 6503 CH, Netherlands. TEL 31-24-3723636, FAX 31-24-3723630, info@fnl.nl. Eds. Ton Heijnen, Wien Feitz. Adv. contact Dick Verbeeten. page EUR 2,950; trim 230 x 300.

770.285 IDN ISSN 1829-9539
CHIP FOTO-VIDEO DIGITAL. Text in Indonesian. q. IDR 29,800 newsstand/cover (effective 2006). adv. **Document type:** *Magazine, Consumer.*
Published by: PT Elex Media Komputindo, Taman Meruya Plaza Blok E/14, No 38-40, Kompleks Taman Meruya Ilir, Jakarta Barat, Indonesia. TEL 62-21-5851473, FAX 62-21-5851475, elexklub@elexmedia.co.id, http://www.elexmedia.co.id.

770.285 THA
CHIP FOTO-VIDEO DIGITAL. Text in Thai. bi-m. adv. **Document type:** *Magazine, Consumer.*
Published by: Vogel Burda Communications (Thailand) Co. Ltd., Phayathai Bldg, Fl 10, Ste 101-104, 31 Phayathai Rd, Rajathewee, Bangkok, 10400, Thailand. TEL 66-2354-16015, FAX 66-2354-1606, http://www.vbc.co.th. Circ: 50,000 (controlled).

770.285 MYS
CHIP PHOTO-VIDEO DIGITAL. Text in English. m. MYR 128 (effective 2006). adv. **Document type:** *Magazine, Consumer.*
Published by: Chip Media Sdn. Bhd., Unit 506, Level 5, Block B, Phileo Damansara 1, Jalan 16/11, Off Jalan Damansara, Petaling Jaya, 46350, Malaysia. TEL 60-3-79578490, FAX 60-3-79578492, ykcheah@chip.com.my, http://www.chip.com.my.

770.285 ITA ISSN 1825-4659
COMPUTER WEEK PHOTO. Text in Italian. 2005. m. **Document type:** *Magazine, Consumer.*
Published by: Sprea Editori Srl, Via Torino 51, Cernusco sul Naviglio, MI 20063, Italy. TEL 39-02-92432222, FAX 39-02-92432236, editori@sprea.it, http://www.sprea.it.

770.285 FRA ISSN 2109-2168
▼ **CREATION PHOTO.** Text in French. 2010. bi-m. EUR 40; EUR 7.90 newsstand/cover (effective 2011). adv. **Document type:** *Magazine, Consumer.*
Related titles: Supplement(s): Creation Photo. Hors-serie. ISSN 2108-338X. 2010.
Published by: Oracom, 168bis-170 Rue Raymond Losserand, Paris, 75014, France. TEL 33-1-44789300, FAX 33-1-44789765, service-client@oracom.fr, http://www.oracom.fr.

770.285 DEU
D-PIXX; fototipps + technik. Text in German. 2005. bi-m. EUR 19.80; EUR 3.30 newsstand/cover (effective 2011). adv. **Document type:** *Magazine, Consumer.*
Published by: Herbert Kaspar Verlagsbuero, Kirchgrundsiedlung 17, Hammelburg, 97762, Germany. TEL 49-9732-5842, FAX 49-9732-5862. Circ: 15,950 (paid).

770 USA ISSN 1935-7117
DARKROOM; the how-to magazine for Adobe Photoshop Lightroom. Text in English. 2007 (Apr.). 8/yr. USD 12.95 newsstand/cover (effective 2007). **Document type:** *Magazine, Consumer.* **Description:** Features tutorials, digital photography techniques, and shortcuts for photographers who use Adobe Photoship Lightroom.
Related titles: Online - full content ed.
Published by: National Association of Photoshop Professionals, 333 Douglas Rd East, Oldsmar, FL 34677. TEL 813-433-5006, 800-738-8513, FAX 813-433-5015, info@photoshopuser.com, http://www.photoshopuser.com.

DESIGN MAGAZINE. *see* COMPUTERS—Computer Graphics

DESIGN MAGAZINE ESPECIAL. *see* COMPUTERS—Computer Graphics

770 DEU ISSN 1617-643X
DIGIFOTO; das Magazin fuer digitale Fotografie. Text in German. 2001. 10/yr. EUR 45.50; EUR 5 newsstand/cover (effective 2001). adv. back issues avail. **Document type:** *Magazine, Consumer.* **Description:** Contains information and reviews on digital photography and related products and services.
Related titles: Online - full text ed.
Published by: Umschau Zeitschriftenverlag Breidenstein GmbH, Otto-Volger-Str 15, Sulzbach, 65843, Germany. TEL 49-69-26000, FAX 49-69-2600629, http://www.broenner-umschau.de. Ed. Norbert Jiptner. Pub. Gerhard Stock. Adv. contact Bernd Pohl TEL 49-69-2600621. color page EUR 4,039.21; trim 195 x 250. Circ: 40,000 (paid).

770.285 DEU
DIGIT!. Text in German. bi-m. EUR 28 domestic; EUR 30 foreign (effective 2007). adv. **Document type:** *Magazine, Consumer.*
Published by: Klie Verlagsgesellschaft mbH, Postfach 1348, Hannover Muenden, 34333, Germany. TEL 49-5541-98490, FAX 49-5541-984999. Ed. Roland Franken. Adv. contact Jutta Kock. B&W page EUR 1,700, color page EUR 2,800; trim 189 x 270. Circ: 5,000 (paid and controlled).

778.3 GBR ISSN 1477-1721
DIGITAL CAMERA. Abbreviated title: Digit. Camera Mag. Text in English. 2002. m. GBP 39.99 domestic; GBP 67.20 in Europe; GBP 75; GBP 86.40 elsewhere; GBP 3.99 newsstand/cover (effective 2010). adv. **Document type:** *Magazine, Consumer.*
Related titles: Online - full text ed.
—CCC.
Published by: Future Publishing Ltd., Beauford Ct, 30 Monmouth St, Bath, Avon BA1 2BW, United Kingdom. TEL 44-1225-442244, FAX 44-1225-446019, customerservice@subscription.co.uk, http://www.futureplc.com. Eds. Ali Jennings, Geoff Harris. Adv. contact Mark Rankine TEL 44-207-0424127. **Subscr. to:** Tower House, Sovereign Park, Market Harborough, Leicestershire LE16 9EF, United Kingdom. TEL 44-844-8481602, FAX 44-1858-438795, future@subscription.co.uk.

770.285 ITA ISSN 1721-6893
DIGITAL CAMERA MAGAZINE. Text in Italian. 2003. m. EUR 44.90 (effective 2009). adv. **Document type:** *Magazine, Consumer.*
Published by: Sprea Editori Srl, Via Torino 51, Cernusco sul Naviglio, MI 20063, Italy. TEL 39-02-92432222, FAX 39-02-92432236, editori@sprea.it, http://www.sprea.it.

770.285 DEU
DIGITAL CAMERA SPECIAL; der Einkaufsberater fuer digitale Fotografie. Text in German. irreg. EUR 7.90 newsstand/cover (effective 2004). adv. **Document type:** *Magazine, Consumer.*
Published by: Pro Verlag Gesellschaft fuer Publikationen mbH, Berner Str 38, Frankfurt Am Main, 60437, Germany. TEL 49-69-5008050, FAX 49-69-5008051, office@proverlag.com, http://www.proverlag.com. adv.: B&W page EUR 2,526, color page EUR 4,800. Circ: 35,000 (paid and controlled).

▼ **DIGITAL INSIGHT.** *see* MEDICAL SCIENCES—Computer Applications

DIGITAL LIFESTYLE MAGAZIN; basics for digital lifestyle. *see* COMMUNICATIONS—Television And Cable

770 GBR ISSN 1474-6883
DIGITAL PHOTO. Text in English. 1997. 13/yr. GBP 61 domestic; GBP 65 foreign; GBP 4.99 newsstand/cover (effective 2009). adv. back issues avail. **Document type:** *Magazine, Consumer.* **Description:** Designed for photographers looking to take and make better pictures. Includes easy-to-follow projects, tips and techniques.
Formerly (until 2001): Digital Photo FX (1460-6801)
Published by: H. Bauer Publishing Ltd. (Subsidiary of: Bauer Media Group), Media House, Lynchwood, Peterborough, Cambridgeshire PE2 6EA, United Kingdom. TEL 44-1733-468000, http://www.bauer.co.uk. Ed. Jon Adams. Adv. contact Iain Grundy TEL 44-1733-468000. **Subscr. to:** Tower House, Sovereign Park, Market Harborough, Leicestershire LE16 9EF, United Kingdom. TEL 44-1858-438866, subs@greatmagazines.co.uk.

770.285 USA ISSN 1948-5557
TR267
DIGITAL PHOTO. Text in English. 1997. 7/yr. USD 11.97 domestic; USD 26.97 foreign; USD 7 per issue (effective 2011). adv. back issues avail. **Document type:** *Magazine, Consumer.* **Description:** Covers the technologies of the computer and photography. Contains step by step instructions, evaluations of new products, tips from professional photographers, and more.
Formerly (until 2009): P C Photo (1094-1673)
Related titles: Online - full text ed.
Indexed: CA, Microcompind, T02.
Published by: Werner Publishing Corporation, 12121 Wilshire Blvd, 12th Fl, Los Angeles, Los Angeles, CA 90025. TEL 310-820-1500, FAX 310-826-5008, http://www.wernerpublishing.com.

778.3 GBR ISSN 1477-6650
DIGITAL PHOTOGRAPHER. Text in English. 2002. m. GBP 52 domestic; GBP 70 in Europe; GBP 80 elsewhere; GBP 5 per issue (effective 2010). adv. back issues avail. **Document type:** *Magazine, Consumer.* **Description:** Provides digital photography enthusiasts and professionals with interviews of leading expert photographers, cutting-edge imagery, practical shooting advice and the very latest high-end digital news and equipment reviews.
Published by: Imagine Publishing Ltd., Richmond House, 33 Richmond Hill, Bournemouth, Dorset BH2 6EZ, United Kingdom. TEL 44-1202-586200, http://www.imagine-publishing.co.uk. Ed. Debbi Allen TEL 44-1202-586218. Adv. contact Jennifer Farrell TEL 44-1202-586430.

778.3 USA ISSN 1532-6012
DIGITAL PHOTOGRAPHER. Variant title: Digital Photographer's Guide to Digital Cameras. Text in English. 1998. bi-m. USD 5.99 per issue (effective 2009). adv. back issues avail. **Document type:** *Magazine, Consumer.* **Description:** Provides comprehensive consumer guides and reviews on all aspects and products involving digital photography.
Published by: Miller Magazines, Inc, 290 Maple Ct, Ste 232, Ventura, CA 93003. TEL 805-644-3824, FAX 805-644-3875, ads4miller@millermags.com, http://www.millermags.com. Adv. contact Scott McLean TEL 623-327-3525. B&W page USD 3,000, color page USD 3,650; trim 8 x 10.75.

770.285 USA ISSN 1948-1829
▼ **DIGITAL PHOTOGRAPHY MONTHLY.** Text in English. 2010 (Jan.). m. **Document type:** *Magazine, Consumer.* **Description:** Features technical information and product reviews for digital photography.
Media: Online - full content.
Published by: The Henrichs Group, 1331 Harvey Mitchell Pkwy S, No 507, College Station, TX 77840. TEL 361-676-3433, carol@henrichs.us.

770.285 GBR
DIGITAL PHOTOGRAPHY TECHNIQUES. Text in English. 2003 (Jun.). m. GBP 5 newsstand/cover (effective 2003). 116 p./no.; **Document type:** *Magazine, Consumer.* **Description:** Covers digital photography techniques, equipments, software and tips for all skill levels.
Published by: Future Publishing Ltd., Beauford Ct, 30 Monmouth St, Bath, Avon BA1 2BW, United Kingdom. TEL 44-1225-442244, FAX 44-1225-446019, customerservice@subscription.co.uk, http://www.futureplc.com. Eds. Dave Taylor, Nick Merritt.

DIGITAL TESTED. *see* COMMUNICATIONS—Television And Cable

770 SWE ISSN 1651-9973
DIGITALFOTO. Text in Swedish. 2003. 13/yr. SEK 649 (effective 2006). adv. back issues avail. **Document type:** *Magazine, Consumer.*
Incorporates (2004-2006): Digital Video (1652-5892)
Published by: First Publishing Group AB, Deltavaegen 3, PO Box 3187, Vaexjoe, 35043, Sweden. TEL 46-470-762400, FAX 46-470-762425, info@firstpublishing.se, http://www.firstpublishing.se. Ed. Peter Hedenfalk. Adv. contact Andreas Bjoerck. color page SEK 39,000; 210 x 285. Circ: 58,500.

770.285 HUN ISSN 1786-0199
DIGITALIS VIDEO & FOTO. Variant title: Chip Digitalis Video & Foto. Text in Hungarian. 2003. q. **Document type:** *Magazine, Consumer.*
Published by: Vogel Burda Communications Kft., Rakoczi ut 1-3, Budapest, 1088, Hungary. TEL 36-1-8883421, FAX 36-1-8883499, rtasnadi@vogelburda.hu, http://www.vogelburda.hu. Circ: 8,000 (controlled).

770.295 SVN ISSN 1581-7946
DIGITALNA KAMERA; revija za digitalno fotografijo. Text in Slovenian. 2004. bi-m. EUR 47.99 (effective 2007). **Document type:** *Magazine, Consumer.*
Published by: VideoToP d.o.o., Trg Revolucije 2, Maribor, 2000, Slovenia. TEL 386-2-3303300, FAX 386-2-3303311, pisma@digitalnakamera.net, http://www.videotop.si.

770.285 DEU ISSN 1866-3214
DIGITALPHOTO; Fachmagazin fuer die Foto-Profis von morgen. Text in German. 2002. m. EUR 69; EUR 58.65 to students; EUR 6.90 newsstand/cover (effective 2011). adv. **Document type:** *Magazine, Consumer.*
Formerly (until 2005): Digital Camera Magazin
Related titles: Online - full text ed.
Published by: Falkemedia, An der Halle 400, Kiel, 24149, Germany. TEL 49-431-2007660, FAX 49-431-20076650, info@falkemedia.de, http://www.falkemedia.de. Ed. Nico Barbat. Pub. Kassian Alexander Goukassian. Adv. contact Sascha Eilers. Circ: 37,145 (paid).

770.285 DEU ISSN 2192-2594
DIGITALPHOTO PHOTOSHOP. Text in German. 2007. bi-m. EUR 49.95; EUR 9.90 newsstand/cover (effective 2011). adv. **Document type:** *Magazine, Consumer.*
Published by: Falkemedia, An der Halle 400, Kiel, 24149, Germany. TEL 49-431-2007660, FAX 49-431-20076650, info@falkemedia.de, http://www.falkemedia.de. Ed. Nico Barbat. Pub. Kassian Alexander Goukassian. Adv. contact Sascha Eilers. Circ: 19,201 (paid and controlled).

DIGITALSTUFF. *see* COMMUNICATIONS—Telephone And Telegraph

DOCMA; Doc Baumanns Magazin fuer digitale Bildbearbeitung. *see* COMPUTERS—Computer Graphics

770.285 USA
EPHOTOZINE. Text in English. 2001. irreg. adv. **Document type:** *Magazine, Consumer.* **Description:** Covers digital photography news, reviews, resources and techniques, including a photo gallery.
Address: mail@ephotozine.com. Ed., Pub. Peter Bargh.

770.285 DEU
FOTO DIGITAL; die neue Welt der Fotografie. Text in German. 1999. 6/yr. EUR 41.40 domestic; EUR 50.40 foreign (effective 2010). adv. **Document type:** *Magazine, Consumer.*
Related titles: Supplement(s): foto Digital Test. 2002. EUR 7.40 newsstand/cover (effective 2003).
Published by: Verlag B. Kaemmer, Georgenstr 19, Munich, 80799, Germany. TEL 49-89-34018900, FAX 49-89-34018901, bk@verlag-kaemmer.de, http://www.verlag-kaemmer.de. Ed. Norbert Jiptner. Adv. contact Stefanie Schlecht. B&W page EUR 3,700, color page EUR 5,000. Circ: 10,500 (paid and controlled).

770.285 DEU ISSN 2191-897X
▼ **FOTO EASY**; Rezepte fuer bessere Fotos. Text in German. 2011. bi-m. EUR 39.90; EUR 7.90 newsstand/cover (effective 2011). adv. **Document type:** *Magazine, Consumer.*
Published by: Falkemedia, An der Halle 400, Kiel, 24149, Germany. TEL 49-431-2007660, FAX 49-431-20076650, info@falkemedia.de, http://www.falkemedia.de. Ed. Daniel Albrecht. Adv. contact Sascha Eilers.

770 DEU
FOTO PRAXIS. Text in German. 2002. 6/yr. EUR 39.60 domestic; EUR 60.90 foreign; EUR 7.80 newsstand/cover (effective 2011). adv. **Document type:** *Magazine, Consumer.*
Published by: Data Becker GmbH & Co. KG, Merowingerstr 30, Duesseldorf, 40223, Germany. TEL 49-211-9331800, FAX 49-211-9331444, info@databecker.de, http://www.databecker.de. Adv. contact Joerg Hausch. Circ: 40,580 (paid and controlled).

770.285 GRC
FOTO-VIDEO ORITI. Text in Greek. 2006. m. EUR 6.95 newsstand/cover (effective 2006). adv. **Document type:** *Magazine, Consumer.*
Published by: Motorpress Hellas (Subsidiary of: Gruner + Jahr AG & Co), 132 Lefkis Str, Krioneri, 14568, Greece. TEL 30-210-6262000, FAX 30-210-6262401, info@motorpress.gr, http://www.motorpress.gr. Circ: 20,000 (paid and controlled).

770.285 ITA ISSN 1593-6422
FOTOCAMERE DIGITALI. Text in Italian. 2001. 8/yr. **Document type:** *Magazine, Consumer.*
Published by: Play Media Company, Via di Santa Cornelia 5A, Formello, RM 00060, Italy. TEL 39-06-33221250, FAX 39-06-33221235, abbonamenti@playmediacompany.it, http://www.playmediacompany.it. Ed. Carlo Chericoni. Pub. Alessandro Ferri. Circ: 40,000 (paid and controlled).

770.285 BRA ISSN 1678-7633
FOTOGRAFE MELHOR DIGITAL. Text in Portuguese. 2003. bi-m. BRL 8.90 newsstand/cover (effective 2007). adv. **Document type:** *Magazine, Consumer.*
Published by: Editora Europa Ltda., Rua MMDC 121, Butanta, Sao Paulo, SP 05510-021, Brazil. TEL 55-11-30385050, FAX 55-11-38190538.

681.3 ITA ISSN 1591-2523
FOTOGRAFIA DIGITALE FACILE. Text in Italian. 2000. 10/yr. EUR 42 (effective 2009). adv. **Document type:** *Magazine, Consumer.*
Published by: Play Media Company, Via di Santa Cornelia 5A, Formello, RM 00060, Italy. TEL 39-06-33221250, FAX 39-06-33221235, abbonamenti@playmediacompany.it, http://www.playmediacompany.it. Circ: 55,000 (paid and controlled).

770.285 DEU ISSN 2192-4155
FOTOTEST; das unabhaengige Magazin fuer digitale Fotografie. Text in German. 2008. bi-m. EUR 30; EUR 5.50 newsstand/cover (effective 2011). adv. **Document type:** *Magazine, Consumer.*
Formerly (until 2011): Spiegelreflex Digital (1869-7755)
Published by: Dr. Landt Verlag, Ammerseestr 61A, Neuried bei Muenchen, 82061, Germany. TEL 49-89-95441416, FAX 49-89-95441292. Ed., Pub. Artur Landt.

770.285 DEU ISSN 0937-101X
IMAGE-SCENE; Handbuch fuer elektronische Fotografie und digitale Bildverarbeitung. Text in German. 1977. a. EUR 8 newsstand/cover (effective 2011). adv. bk.rev. **Document type:** *Magazine, Consumer.* **Description:** Register and handbook of and for the digital imaging scene.
Published by: Verlag Peter Walz, Gustav-Adolf-Str. 144, Berlin, 13086, Germany. TEL 49-30-46998182, FAX 49-3212-1012722, peter.walz@peterwalz.de, http://www.peterwalz.de. Ed. Peter Walz. adv.: B&W page EUR 280, color page EUR 800; trim 210 x 297. Circ: 8,000.

▼ **THE IMAGING CHANNEL**; the business and people of managed print. *see* PRINTING

770 USA ISSN 2155-0425
▼ **IPHONEOGRAPHY.** Text in English. forthcoming 2011. bi-m. USD 6.99 per issue (effective 2010). **Document type:** *Magazine, Consumer.* **Description:** The word's first iphone photography magazine.
Media: Online - full text.
Published by: Type A Design, 7544 Arbor Park Dr, Fort Worth, TX 76120. TEL 817-717-5556, marty@typeadesign.com. Ed., Pub. Marty Yawnick.

LABO NUMERIQUE. *see* PHOTOGRAPHY

MULTIMEDIA. *see* COMMUNICATIONS—Television And Cable

770.285 686.2 USA ISSN 1536-2582
P C CREATE IT. Text in English. 2000 (May 31st). bi-m. USD 24.99; USD 4.99 newsstand/cover (effective 2001). adv. software rev. 76 p./no.; back issues avail. **Document type:** *Magazine, Consumer.*
Published by: Reedy River Press, Inc., PO Box 26013, Greenville, SC 29615. TEL 864-286-0540, 888-259-3887, FAX 864-286-1056. Ed. Linda Dennis. adv.: B&W page USD 2,785; 8.375 x 10.875. Circ: 220,000 (paid).

770 USA ISSN 2155-7624
TR267
PETERSEN'S PHOTOGRAPHIC DIGITAL PHOTOGRAPHY GUIDE. Variant title: Photographic Digital Photography Guide. Text in English. (2008). irreg. **Document type:** *Magazine, Consumer.* **Description:** Includes tutorials, tips and techniques for digital photography.
Published by: Source Interlink Companies, 261 Madison Ave, 6th Fl, New York, NY 10016. TEL 212-915-4000, FAX 212-915-4422, edisupport@sourceinterlink.com, http://www.sourceinterlinkmedia.com.

778.3 NLD ISSN 1877-6183
PHOTO DIGITAAL. Text in Dutch. 2008. 8/yr. EUR 30; EUR 4.95 newsstand/cover (effective 2009). adv. **Document type:** *Magazine, Consumer.*
Published by: F & L Publishing Group B.V., Meijhorst 60-10, Postbus 31331, Nijmegen, 6503 CH, Netherlands. TEL 31-24-3723636, FAX 31-24-3723630, info@fnl.nl, http://www.fnl.nl. Adv. contact Dick Verbeeten. page EUR 2,950; trim 230 x 300.

775.22 ITA ISSN 1723-1191
PHOTOGRAFARE IN DIGITALE. Key Title: Fotografare in Digitale. Text in Italian. 2003. m. EUR 6 newsstand/cover (effective 2008). adv. **Document type:** *Magazine, Consumer.*
Published by: Play Media Company, Via di Santa Cornelia 5A, Formello, RM 00060, Italy. TEL 39-06-33221250, FAX 39-06-33221235, abbonamenti@playmediacompany.it, http://www.playmediacompany.it.

775.22 GBR ISSN 1747-7816
PHOTOSHOP CREATIVE. Text in English. 2005. 13/yr. GBP 62.40 domestic; GBP 70 in Europe; GBP 80 elsewhere; GBP 6 per issue (effective 2010). adv. back issues avail. **Document type:** *Magazine, Consumer.* **Description:** Contains inspirational tutorials covering the whole scope of the software, from creative projects, to practical guides to using tools and techniques.
—CCC.
Published by: Imagine Publishing Ltd., Richmond House, 33 Richmond Hill, Bournemouth, Dorset BH2 6EZ, United Kingdom. TEL 44-1202-586200. Ed. Rosie Tanner. Adv. contact Hang Deretz TEL 44-1202-586442.

775.22 NLD ISSN 1877-6191
PHOTOSHOP CREATIVE. Text in Dutch. 2008. 10/yr. EUR 50; EUR 8.95 newsstand/cover (effective 2009). adv. **Document type:** *Magazine, Consumer.*
Published by: F & L Publishing Group B.V., Meijhorst 60-10, Postbus 31331, Nijmegen, 6503 CH, Netherlands. TEL 31-24-3723636, FAX 31-24-3723630, info@fnl.nl, http://www.fnl.nl. Adv. contact Dick Verbeeten. page EUR 2,950; trim 230 x 300.

PHOTOSHOP ELEMENTS PROFESSIONELL NUTZEN. *see* COMPUTERS—Software

775 005.36 GBR ISSN 1741-3966
PHOTOSHOP FOCUS GUIDE. Text in English. 2003. m. adv. **Document type:** *Magazine, Consumer.*
—CCC.
Published by: Future Publishing Ltd., Beauford Ct, 30 Monmouth St, Bath, Avon BA1 2BW, United Kingdom. TEL 44-1225-442244, FAX 44-1225-446019, customerservice@subscription.co.uk, http://www.futureplc.com.

PHOTOSHOP INSIDE. *see* COMPUTERS—Computer Graphics

775.22 ITA ISSN 1827-7829
PHOTOSHOP MAGAZINE. Text in Italian. 2006. 8/yr. EUR 40 (effective 2009). adv. **Document type:** *Magazine, Consumer.*
Published by: Play Media Company, Via di Santa Cornelia 5A, Formello, RM 00060, Italy. TEL 39-06-33221250, FAX 39-06-33221235, abbonamenti@playmediacompany.it, http://www.playmediacompany.it.

PRATIQUE PHOTOSHOP. *see* COMPUTERS—Software

775.22 POL ISSN 1732-2200
.PSD. Text in Polish. 2004. m. PLZ 239 (effective 2009). adv. **Document type:** *Magazine, Consumer.*
Related titles: Spanish ed.: ISSN 1898-7958. 200?; French ed.: ISSN 1733-2745. 2004.

P

Published by: Software - Wydawnictwo Sp. z o.o., ul Bokserska 1, Warsaw, 02-682, Poland. TEL 48-22-4273530, FAX 48-22-2442459, sdj@software.com.pl, http://www.software.com.pl.

686.43 775 CHN ISSN 1672-495X
SHUZI YU SUOWEI YINGXIANG/DIGITAL & MICROGRAPHIC IMAGING. Text in Chinese. 1989. q. USD 20.80 (effective 2009). **Document type:** *Journal, Academic/Scholarly.*
Formerly (until 2003): Suowei Jishu/Journal of Micrographics (1004-4094)
Related titles: Online - full text ed.
—East View.
Published by: Beijing Dianying Jiexie Yanjiusuo/Beijing Film Machinery Research Institute, Zhaoyang-qu, 2, Tuanjie Hubei Lu, Beijing, 100026, China. TEL 86-10-65826973, FAX 86-10-65822260, http://www.filmtech.com.cn/.

770.285 ITA ISSN 1721-2162
VIDEO DIGITALE FACILE. Text in Italian. 2002. bi-m. adv. **Document type:** *Magazine, Consumer.*
Published by: Play Media Company, Via di Santa Cornelia 5A, Formello, RM 00060, Italy. TEL 39-06-33221250, FAX 39-06-33221235, abbonamenti@playmediacompany.it, http://www.playmediacompany.it. Circ: 40,000 (paid and controlled).

778.3 GBR ISSN 2045-0532
WHICH DIGITAL CAMERA?. Text in English. 1981-200?; N.S. 2004 (Oct.). m. **Document type:** *Magazine, Consumer.*
Former titles (until 200?): Which Camera? Digital (1472-3611); (until 2000): Which Camera? (0263-9106)
—CCC.
Published by: Archant Specialist Ltd. (Subsidiary of: Archant Group), Prospect House, Rouen Rd, Norwich, NR1 1RE, United Kingdom. TEL 44-1603-772772, farine.clarke@archant.co.uk.

770 POL ISSN 1732-3762
ZOOM. Text in Polish. 2004. q. adv. **Document type:** *Magazine, Consumer.*
Published by: I D G Poland S.A., ul Jordanowska 12, PO Box 73, Warsaw, 04-204, Poland. TEL 48-22-3217800, FAX 48-22-3217888, idg@idg.com.pl, http://www.idg.pl. Circ: 15,000 (paid).

PHYSICAL CHEMISTRY

see CHEMISTRY—Physical Chemistry

PHYSICAL FITNESS AND HYGIENE

see also MEDICAL SCIENCES ; NUTRITION AND DIETETICS ; PUBLIC HEALTH AND SAFETY ; SPORTS AND GAMES

A B C NEWSLETTER. *see* MEDICAL SCIENCES—Hematology

613.7 USA ISSN 1082-0361
A C E FITNESSMATTERS. Text in English. 1995. bi-m. USD 19.95 (effective 2005). bk.rev. **Document type:** *Magazine, Consumer.* **Description:** Contains up-to-date information on the latest research and trends in the fitness industry, including fitness-product reviews (i.e. ab rollers, treadmills, aerobic riders).
Published by: American Council on Exercise, 4851 Paramount Dr, San Diego, CA 92123. TEL 858-279-8227, 800-825-3636, FAX 858-279-8064, acepubs@acefitness.org, http://www.acefitness.rog. Ed. Christine J Ekeroth. R&P Holly Yancy. Circ: 37,000.

613.0711 USA ISSN 0002-7952
A C H A ACTION. Text in English. 1970. 4/yr. free membership (effective 2007). adv. **Document type:** *Newsletter.* **Description:** Covers current issues in college health for those interested in student health services.
Formerly: A C H Action; Supersedes: American College Health Association. Newsletter
Related titles: Microform ed.
Published by: American College Health Association, PO Box 28937, Baltimore, MD 21240-8937. TEL 410-859-1500, FAX 410-859-1510. Ed. Rebecca Kerins. Pub. Charley Hartman. Adv. contact Susan Ainsworth. Circ: 4,300.

613.7 AUS ISSN 1328-7133
A C H P E R ACTIVE AND HEALTHY MAGAZINE. (Australian Council for Health Physical Education and Recreation) Text in English. 1994. 3/yr. AUD 50 domestic; AUD 65 foreign (effective 2008). back issues avail. **Document type:** *Magazine, Consumer.* **Description:** Aims to improve the health and life-styles of Australians by the dissemination of classroom ideas, teaching strategies and trends for fitness, health and physical education.
Formerly (until 1996): Active and Healthy (1321-1609); Which was formed by the 1994 merger of: Physical Education Teacher Newsletter; Health and Fitness Newsletter (0814-754X); Health Education and Lifestyle Promotion Newsletter; Which was formerly (until 1991): Health Education and Lifestyle Project Newsletter (1030-8369)
Indexed: SD.
—BLDSC (0676.009000).
Published by: Australian Council for Health, Physical Education and Recreation Inc., 214 Port Rd, PO Box 304, Hindmarsh, SA 5007, Australia. TEL 61-8-83403388, FAX 61-8-83403399, membership@achper.org.au, http://www.achper.org.au/. Adv. contact Lyndall Bryden.

613.7 USA ISSN 1091-5397
RA781
A C S M'S HEALTH & FITNESS JOURNAL. Variant title: Health & Fitness Journal. Text in English. 1997. bi-m. USD 126 domestic to institutions; USD 143 foreign to institutions (effective 2011). adv. back issues avail.; reprints avail. **Document type:** *Journal, Academic/Scholarly.* **Description:** Aims to promote and distribute information on health and fitness.
Related titles: Online - full text ed.: ISSN 1536-593X.
Indexed: A22, C06, C07, C08, CINAHL, E-psyche, FoSS&M, PEI, SCI, SCOPUS, SD, T02, W07.
—BLDSC (0578.950700), IE, Ingenta. **CCC.**
Published by: (American College of Sports Medicine), Lippincott Williams & Wilkins (Subsidiary of: Wolters Kluwer N.V.), 530 Walnut St, Philadelphia, PA 19106. TEL 215-521-8300, FAX 215-521-8902, customerservice@lww.com, http://www.lww.com. Ed. Edward T Howley TEL 865-851-5224. Pub. David Mayers. Adv. contact Christine Kenney TEL 410-528-4106. Circ: 9,732.

613.7 RUS
A I F. ZDOROV'E. (Argumenty i Fakty) Text in Russian. 1994. w. USD 212 foreign (effective 2010). **Document type:** *Newspaper, Consumer.* **Description:** Presents family pedagogy, beauty salon, folk medicine, psychology, new medicines and methods of treatment. Includes free supplement, Family Doctor.
Related titles: Online - full content ed.; ◆ Supplement to: Argumenty i Fakty. ISSN 0204-0476.
Published by: Argumenty i Fakty, ul Elektrozavodskaya 27, str 4, Moscow, 107996, Russian Federation. TEL 7-495-6465757, letters@aif.ru. Ed. V Romanenko. **Dist. by:** East View Information Services, 10601 Wayzata Blvd, Minneapolis, MN 55305. TEL 952-252-1201, 800-477-1005, FAX 952-252-1202, info@eastview.com, http://www.eastview.com.

613.7 AUT
A P A - JOURNAL. GESUNDHEIT. Text in German. w. EUR 380 combined subscription print & online eds. (effective 2003). **Document type:** *Journal, Trade.*
Related titles: Online - full text ed.
Published by: Austria Presse Agentur, Gunoldstr 14, Vienna, W 1190, Austria. TEL 43-1-360600, FAX 43-1-360603099, kundenservice@apa.at, http://www.apa.at.

A S H SMOKING AND HEALTH REVIEW. *see* LAW

613.7 USA
A V A CHECKPOINT. Text in English. m. USD 10 domestic membership (effective 2005). **Document type:** *Magazine, Consumer.* **Description:** To inform clubs of AVA business.
Published by: American Volkssport Association, 1001 Pat Booker Rd., Ste. 101, Universal City, TX 78148-4147. avahq@ava.org.

613.7 330 USA ISSN 1067-1714
A W H P ACTION. Text in English. 1975. q. free for members. adv. **Document type:** *Newsletter.*
Formerly: A F B Action (0891-7450)
Media: Online - full text.
Indexed: SportS.
Published by: Association for Worksite Health Promotion, 60 Revere Dr, Ste 500, Northbrook, IL 60062-1577. TEL 847-480-9574, FAX 847-480-9282. Ed. Patricia Sullivan. Pub. Greg Schultz. R&P, Adv. contact Rick Koepke. Circ: 3,000 (controlled).

613.7 BIH ISSN 1840-2976
➤ **ACTA KINESIOLOGICA.** Text in English; Abstracts in Croatian. 2007. s-a. EUR 15 domestic; EUR 30 foreign (effective 2010). **Document type:** *Journal, Academic/Scholarly.*
Related titles: Online - full text ed.: ISSN 1840-3700. free (effective 2011).
Indexed: A36, B21, CA, ESPM, H&SSA, N03, SD, T02.
Published by: Drustvo Pedagoga Tjelesne i Zdravstvene Kulture, Put za crveni grm bb BiH, Ljubuski-Teskera, Bosnia Herzegovina. TEL 387-39-838399, FAX 387-39-838171. Ed. Zarko Bilic.

796.815 CAN
ACTION MARTIAL ARTS. Text in English. q. CAD 12 domestic; CAD 17 foreign (effective 2004). **Document type:** *Magazine, Consumer.* **Description:** Presents news on world champions, founding fathers, and movie stars. Also includes fitness tips, training secrets, safety tips, interest articles and grading results.
Indexed: SD.
Address: Box 48213, #40 Midlake Blvd SE, Calgary, AB T2X 3C9, Canada. TEL 403-254-5713, FAX 403-256-6159, actionmartialarts@shaw.ca.

ACTIVE TRAVEL CYMRU NEWS. *see* SPORTS AND GAMES—Bicycles And Motorcycles

ACTIVE TRAVEL NEWS. *see* SPORTS AND GAMES—Bicycles And Motorcycles

ADAPTED PHYSICAL ACTIVITY QUARTERLY. *see* EDUCATION—Special Education And Rehabilitation

ADIPOSITAS; Ursachen, Klinik und Folgeerkrankungen. *see* NUTRITION AND DIETETICS

ADVANCE FOR HEALTHY AGING; age management medicine for physicians. *see* MEDICAL SCIENCES

330 613 GBR ISSN 0731-2199
RA410.A1
➤ **ADVANCES IN HEALTH ECONOMICS AND HEALTH SERVICES RESEARCH.** Text in English. 1979. irreg. price varies. **Document type:** *Monographic series, Academic/Scholarly.*
Formerly (until 1981): Research in Health Economics (0197-0690)
Indexed: A22, AHCMS, EMBASE, ExcerpMed, Inpharma, MEDLINE, P30, R10, Reac, SCOPUS.
—BLDSC (0709.008000), GNLM, IE, Infotrieve, Ingenta. **CCC.**
Published by: Emerald Group Publishing Ltd., Howard House, Wagon Ln, Bingley, W Yorks BD16 1WA, United Kingdom. TEL 44-1274-777700, FAX 44-1274-785201, emerald@emeraldinsight.com. Eds. Bjorn Lindgren, Michael Grossman.

613.7 USA
AEROBIC BEAT. Text in English. 1984. bi-m. USD 40; USD 3.33 newsstand/cover (effective 2007). adv. bk.rev.; music rev. **Document type:** *Newsletter.* **Description:** Designed to help in the location of the latest and most appropriate music for aerobic workouts, jogging, step training and other fitness activities done with music.
Address: 7985 Santa Monica Blvd, Ste 109, Los Angeles, CA 90046-5186. TEL 310-659-2503, FAX 213-655-5223. Eds. Ken Alan, Randy Sills.

613 ZAF ISSN 1117-4315
GV201
➤ **AFRICAN JOURNAL FOR PHYSICAL, HEALTH EDUCATION, RECREATION AND DANCE.** Text in English. 1995. s-a. USD 50 in Africa to individuals; USD 80 elsewhere to individuals; USD 100 in Africa to institutions; USD 150 elsewhere to institutions (effective 2007). back issues avail. **Document type:** *Journal, Academic/Scholarly.* **Description:** Provides a forum for physical educators, health educators and dance specialists, and other related professionals in Africa to report their research findings based on the African setting and also exchange ideas among themselves.
Related titles: Online - full text ed.
Indexed: A36, CABA, E12, GH, LT, N02, N03, PEI, R12, RRTA, S21, SD, T02, T05, W11.
—BLDSC (0732.547000), IE.
Published by: University of Venda for Science and Technology, Centre for Biokinetics, Recreation and Sport Science, P.Bag X5050, Thohoyandou, 0950, South Africa. amusalbw@yahoo.com. Ed. L. Amusa.

613.79 DNK ISSN 1902-3375
AFSPAENDING, PSYKOMOTORIK. Text in Danish. 1978. 6/yr. DKK 400; DKK 60 per issue (effective 2009). adv. **Document type:** *Magazine, Trade.*
Former titles (until 2007): Afspaendingspaedagogen (0909-7503); (until 1993): D A P - Danske Afspaendingspaedagoger (0901-7062); (until 1984): D A P (0106-5947)
Published by: Danske Afspaendingspaedagoger, Vesterbrogade 43, 2, Copenhagen V, 1620, Denmark. TEL 45-33-791260, FAX 45-33-791261, dap@dap.dk, http://www.dap.dk. Ed. Ulla Graumann. adv.: page DKK 2,000; 170 x 258.

613.2 613.7 ITA ISSN 1828-4159
AGENDA DELLA SALUTE. Text in Italian. 2006. bi-m. EUR 16 (effective 2008). **Document type:** *Magazine, Consumer.*
Published by: Politecne Srl, Via Don Carlo Botta 7c, Bergamo, 24122, Italy.

AIDS EDUCATION AND PREVENTION; an interdisciplinary journal. (Acquired Immune Deficiency Syndrome) *see* PUBLIC HEALTH AND SAFETY

613.7 POL ISSN 0239-9776
AKADEMIA WYCHOWANIA FIZYCZNEGO IM. EUGENIUSZA PIASECKIEGO W POZNANIU. KRONIKA. Text in Polish. 1956. a., latest vol.38, 2003. PLZ 94 per vol. (effective 2003). **Document type:** *Yearbook, Academic/Scholarly.*
Formerly (until 1973): Wyzsza Szkola Wychowania Fizycznego w Poznaniu. Kronika (0477-7468)
Published by: Akademia Wychowania Fizycznego im. Eugeniusza Piaseckiego w Poznaniu/Eugeniusz Piasecki University School of Physical Education in Poznan, ul Krolowej Jadwigi 27-39, Poznan, 61871, Poland. TEL 48-61-8355092, FAX 48-61-8330087, http://www.awf.poznan.pl.

613.7 POL ISSN 0137-6578
➤ **AKADEMIA WYCHOWANIA FIZYCZNEGO IM. EUGENIUSZA PIASECKIEGO W POZNANIU. ROCZNIKI NAUKOWE.** Summaries in English; Text in Polish; Contents page in Polish, English. 1960. a. PLZ 22 per vol. domestic (effective 2003). **Document type:** *Journal, Academic/Scholarly.*
Published by: Akademia Wychowania Fizycznego im. Eugeniusza Piaseckiego w Poznaniu/Eugeniusz Piasecki University School of Physical Education in Poznan, ul Krolowej Jadwigi 27-39, Poznan, 61871, Poland. TEL 48-61-8355092, http://www.awf.poznan.pl.

613.7 DEU ISSN 1860-4757
AKTIV (MUNICH); Ihr Gesundheitsmagazin der Kaufmaennischen. Text in German. 1940. q. free membership (effective 2008). adv. bk.rev. **Document type:** *Magazine, Consumer.*
Formerly: K K H Journal (0932-1055)
Published by: (Kaufmaennische Krankenkasse - K K H, Hauptverwaltung), BurdaYukom Publishing GmbH (Subsidiary of: Hubert Burda Media Holding GmbH & Co. KG), Konrad-Zuse-Platz 11, Munich, 81829, Germany. TEL 49-89-306200, FAX 49-89-30620100, info@burdayukom.de, http://www.yukom.de. Ed. Dr. Silke Hesse. Adv. contact Adrian Peipp TEL 49-89-92503649. B&W page EUR 11,300, color page EUR 14,500. Circ: 1,300,000 (controlled).

613.7 CZE ISSN 1803-3261
AKTIVNE. Text in Czech. 2008. m. CZK 489 (effective 2008). **Document type:** *Magazine, Consumer.*
Published by: Computer Press a.s., Spielberk Office Centre, Holandska 8, Brno, 639 00, Czech Republic. TEL 420-545-113777, FAX 420-545-113701, webmaster@cpress.cz, http://www.cpress.cz. Ed. Michal Kasparek.

613.2 CAN ISSN 0228-586X
TX341 CODEN: ACOLEL
ALIVE; Canada's natural health & wellness magazine. Text in English. 1975. m. CAD 37 domestic; USD 39 in United States; USD 69 elsewhere (effective 2009). adv. bk.rev. **Document type:** *Magazine, Consumer.* **Description:** Covers nutrition and alternative health information, issues and therapies.
Related titles: Online - full text ed.
Indexed: A04, A33, C04, C05, C06, C07, C11, CA, MEA&I, T02.
—BLDSC (0788.275000). **CCC.**
Published by: Alive Publishing Group, Inc., 100-12751 Vulcan Way, Richmond, BC V6V 3C8, Canada. TEL 800-663-6580, FAX 800-663-6597. Ed., R&P, Adv. contact Terry-Lynn Stone. page CAD 9,975; trim 8.125 x 10.75. Circ: 200,000 (paid).

ALLURE. *see* WOMEN'S INTERESTS

613.7 ZAF ISSN 1991-6124
AMAZING ABS. Text in English. 2006. a.
Published by: Touchline Media, PO Box 16368, Vlaeberg, Cape Town 8018, South Africa. TEL 27-21-4083800, FAX 27-21-4083811, http://www.touchline.co.za.

613.194 USA ISSN 1938-8500
AMERICAN ASSOCIATION FOR NUDE RECREATION. BULLETIN. Text in English. 1951. m. membership. adv. **Document type:** *Newspaper, Consumer.*
Formerly: American Sunbathing Association. Bulletin (0279-8158)
Published by: American Association for Nude Recreation, North American Headquarters, 1703 N Main St, Ste E, Kissimmee, FL 34744. TEL 800-879-6833. R&P Julie Bagby. Adv. contact Kathleen Bokun. Circ: 30,000.

AMERICAN BABY; for expectant and new parents. *see* CHILDREN AND YOUTH—About

AMERICAN BABY. THE FIRST YEAR OF LIFE; a guide to your baby's growth and development month by month. *see* CHILDREN AND YOUTH—About

AMERICAN CURVES. *see* MEN'S INTERESTS

613.7 USA ISSN 0893-5238
CODEN: AAFIEL

AMERICAN FITNESS. Text in English. 1983. bi-m. USD 27 (effective 2007). adv. bk.rev. **Document type:** *Magazine, Trade.* **Description:** Provides news and information concerning health and fitness.
Former titles (until 1987): Aerobics and Fitness (0749-8942); (until 1984): Aerobics and Fitness Association of America. Journal
Related titles: Microform ed.: (from PQC); Online - full text ed.
Indexed: A01, A02, A03, A08, A26, C05, C11, C12, CPerI, E07, E08, G05, G06, G07, G08, H03, H11, H12, H13, I05, I06, I07, M01, M02, M04, M06, MASUSE, P02, P07, P10, P20, P34, P48, P53, P54, PQC, S09, S23, SD, SportS, T02.
—BLDSC (0815.220000), IE, Ingenta.
Published by: Aerobics and Fitness Association of America, 15250 Ventura Blvd, Sherman Oaks, CA 91403. TEL 818-905-0040, FAX 818-990-2118, customerservice@afaa.com, http://www.afaa.com. Ed. Peg Jordan, R.N. Pub. Roscoe Fawcett. R&P Peg Jordan Jordan, R N. Adv. contact Cindy Schofield. Circ: 30,000.

613.7 MEX ISSN 2007-1736

AMERICAN HEALTH & FITNESS. Text in Spanish. 2008. m. MXN 30 newsstand/cover (effective 2011). **Document type:** *Magazine, Consumer.*
Published by: Mina Editores, Circuito Medicos, 13, Ciudad Satelite, Naucalpan de Juaez, Estado de Mexico, 53100, Mexico. TEL 52-55-9114315, http://www.minaeditores.com/. Ed. Lydia Ramos. Circ: 65,000.

AMERICAN HIKER. *see* SPORTS AND GAMES—Outdoor Life

613.7 USA ISSN 1087-3244
RA421

➤ **AMERICAN JOURNAL OF HEALTH BEHAVIOR.** Text in English. 1977. bi-m. USD 128 combined subscription to individuals (print & online eds.); USD 238 combined subscription to institutions (print & online eds.); USD 33 newsstand/cover domestic to individuals; USD 38 newsstand/cover in Canada & Mexico to individuals; USD 46 newsstand/cover elsewhere to individuals; USD 48 newsstand/cover domestic to institutions; USD 50 newsstand/cover in Canada & Mexico to institutions; USD 58 newsstand/cover elsewhere to institutions (effective 2010). bk.rev. illus. index. back issues avail.; reprints avail. **Document type:** *Journal, Academic/Scholarly.* **Description:** Aims to provide a comprehensive understanding of the relationships among personal behavior, social structure and health, and to disseminate knowledge of major behavioral science principles and strategies to assist in designing and implementing programs to prevent disease and promote health.
Formerly (until 1996): Health Values (0147-0353)
Related titles: Microform ed.: (from PQC); Online - full text ed.: ISSN 1945-7359.
Indexed: A01, A03, A04, A08, A20, A22, A26, A29, A36, ASCA, B20, B21, C06, C07, C08, C11, C28, CA, CABA, CHNI, CINAHL, CurCont, D01, E-psyche, E12, EMBASE, ERA, ERIC, ESPM, ExcerpMed, FamI, G10, GH, H04, H05, H11, H12, HPNRM, I05, I10, LT, M12, MEDLINE, N02, N03, NRN, P03, P18, P19, P20, P22, P24, P25, P30, P33, P34, P48, P50, P53, P54, PEI, PQC, PsycInfo, PsycholAb, R08, R10, R12, RRTA, Reac, RiskAb, S02, S03, S13, S16, S20, S21, SCOPUS, SFSA, SOPODA, SSCI, SSciA, SociolAb, T02, T05, TAR, ToxAb, VirolAbstr, W07, W09, W11.
—BLDSC (0824.700000), GNLM, IE, Ingenta. **CCC.**
Published by: P N G Publications, 2205-K Oak Ridge Rd, #115, Oak Ridge, NC 27310. Ed. Elbert D Glover TEL 301-405-2029.

➤ **AMERICAN JOURNAL OF HEALTH EDUCATION.** *see* EDUCATION—Teaching Methods And Curriculum

613.2 USA ISSN 0890-1171
CODEN: AJHPED

➤ **AMERICAN JOURNAL OF HEALTH PROMOTION.** Short title: A J H P. Text in English. 1986. bi-m. USD 177 domestic to institutions; USD 186 in Canada & Mexico to institutions; USD 195 elsewhere to institutions; USD 359 combined subscription domestic to institutions (print & online eds.); USD 368 combined subscription in Canada & Mexico to institutions (print & online eds.); USD 377 combined subscription elsewhere to institutions (print & online eds.) (effective 2010); Health Promotion: Global Perspectives - included. adv. bk.rev.; film rev. abstr.; charts; stat.; illus. back issues avail.; reprints avail. **Document type:** *Journal, Academic/Scholarly.* **Description:** Covers the science and art of helping people change their lifestyle to move toward a state of optimal health.
Incorporates (1997-2002): The Art of Health Promotion
Related titles: Online - full text ed.: USD 359 (effective 2010).
Indexed: A01, A02, A03, A08, A22, A36, ASCA, ASG, ASSIA, B21, C06, C07, C08, CA, CABA, CINAHL, CurCont, D01, E-psyche, E03, E12, EMBASE, ERI, ESPM, ExcerpMed, F08, FR, FamI, GH, H&SSA, H04, H05, LT, MEDLINE, N02, N03, NRN, P03, P04, P30, P33, P34, PAIS, PEI, PSI, PsycInfo, PsycholAb, R08, R09, R10, R12, RRTA, Reac, S02, S03, SCOPUS, SD, SOPODA, SSCI, SociolAb, T02, T05, W07, W11.
—BLDSC (0824.760000), GNLM, IE, Infotrieve, Ingenta, INIST. **CCC.**
Address: PO Box 1254, Troy, MI 48099. TEL 248-682-0707, FAX 248-630-4399, contact@healthpromotionjournal.com. Ed. Michael P O'Donnell. Adv. contact Patti Weber TEL 248-425-2737. B&W page USD 1,125, color page USD 2,030; trim 8.5 x 11. Circ: 2,600. **Subscr. to:** PO Box 15847, North Hollywood, CA 91615. TEL 818-985-0687, 800-783-9913, FAX 818-985-1213, amjcs@magserv.com.

613.7 USA ISSN 1945-4511

AMERICAN JOURNAL OF HEALTH STUDIES (ONLINE). Text in English. 1997. q. USD 94.50 libraries/institutions (effective 2009). **Document type:** *Journal, Academic/Scholarly.* **Description:** Publishes feature articles and commentaries on the history, principles and philosophy of the practice of health education and health promotion.
Media: Online - full text.
Published by: Expert Health Data System, Inc., 12530 Stratford Garden Dr, Silver Spring, MD 20904. Ed. Min Qi Wang TEL 301-405-6652.

613.907 155.3 USA ISSN 1554-6128
HQ56 CODEN: JSETE2

➤ **AMERICAN JOURNAL OF SEXUALITY EDUCATION.** Text in English. 1975-1995; resumed 1997. q. GBP 189 combined subscription in United Kingdom to institutions (print & online eds.); EUR 246, USD 254 combined subscription to institutions (print & online eds.) (effective 2012). bk.rev.; video rev. charts; illus.; stat. reprint service avail. from PSC. **Document type:** *Journal, Academic/Scholarly.* **Description:** Publishes selected research on sex education as well as sex counseling and therapy.
Formerly (until vol.26, no.4, 2004): Journal of Sex Education and Therapy (0161-4576)
Related titles: Online - full text ed.: ISSN 1554-6136. GBP 171 in United Kingdom to institutions; EUR 222, USD 229 to institutions (effective 2012).
Indexed: A01, A02, A03, A08, A22, AC&P, ASCA, AbAn, CA, CDA, CLFP, CPE, DIP, E-psyche, E01, E03, ERI, FamI, H04, IBR, IBZ, L01, L02, M02, MEA&I, MLA-IB, P18, P30, P43, P48, P50, P53, P54, PQC, PsycholAb, S02, S03, S21, SCOPUS, SOPODA, SSA, SWR&A, SociolAb, T02.
—BLDSC (0838.190000), IE, Infotrieve, Ingenta. **CCC.**
Published by: (American Association of Sex Educators, Counselors and Therapists), Routledge (Subsidiary of: Taylor & Francis Group), 325 Chestnut St, Ste 800, Philadelphia, PA 19106. TEL 215-625-8900, 800-354-1420, FAX 215-625-8914, journals@routledge.com, http://www.routledge.com. Ed. William J Taverner. Circ: 2,700.

613.194 USA

AMERICAN NUDIST RESEARCH LIBRARY NEWSLETTER. Text in English. 1980. s-a. looseleaf. USD 12 to members (effective 2000). **Document type:** *Newsletter.*
Published by: American Nudist Research Library, 2950 Sun Cove Dr, Kissimmee, FL 34746. TEL 407-933-2866. Ed. Lyda Hadley. Circ: 400.

613.7 USA ISSN 0003-1259

AMERICAN SOKOL. Text in English. 1879. 9/yr. free to members (effective 2007). adv. illus. **Document type:** *Newsletter, Consumer.* **Description:** Focuses on physical education and cultural activities of members.
Published by: American Sokol Organization, 122 W 22nd St, Oak Brook, IL 60523-1557. TEL 630-368-0771, FAX 630-368-0758, editor@american-sokol.org, http://www.american-sokol.org. Ed. Patricia Satek. R&P Fred Kala. Adv. contact June Pros. Circ: 5,000.

613.7 USA ISSN 0748-7444

THE AMERICAN WANDERER. Text in English. 1974. q. USD 25 to individual members; USD 30 family membership (effective 2005). adv. **Document type:** *Newsletter, Consumer.* **Description:** Covers Association news, national office news, travel and walk as well as health and fitness articles, opinion, columns, photo spreads and international fitness events. Offers chartered club list, upcoming events, and list of award recipients.
Related titles: Supplement(s): Starting Point.
Published by: American Volksport Association, 1001 Pat Booker Rd, Ste 101, Universal City, TX 78148. TEL 210-659-2112, 800-830-9255, FAX 210-659-1212, avahq@ava.org. Circ: 5,000 (paid).

613.7 FIN ISSN 1795-8016

ANANDA; jooga, henkisyys, mietiskely, kasvisruoka. Text in Finnish. 2005. q. EUR 20 (effective 2006). **Document type:** *Magazine, Consumer.*
Published by: Trax Oy, Rauhankatu 21 B, Porvoo, 06100, Finland. TEL 358-5-5695754, toimitus@anandalehti.fi, http://www.anandalehti.fi.

613.7 CHN ISSN 1008-1879

ANMO YU DAOYIN/CHINESE MANIPULATION & QIGONG THERAPY. Text in Chinese. 1985. m.
Published by: Guangdong Sheng Zhongyi Yanjiusuo/Guangdong Provincial Institute Traditional Chinese Medicine, 60, Hengfu Lu, Guangzhou, 510095, China. TEL 86-20-88546498, FAX 86-20-83592829, http://www.tcmgdp.cn/.

613 USA ISSN 0278-4653
RA773

➤ **ANNUAL EDITIONS: HEALTH.** Text in English. 1975. a. USD 22.25 per issue (effective 2010). illus. back issues avail. **Document type:** *Journal, Academic/Scholarly.*
Former titles (1980-1981): Readings in Health (0730-8930); Annual Editions: Readings in Health (0360-9766)
Related titles: Online - full text ed.
Published by: McGraw-Hill, Contemporary Learning Series (Subsidiary of: McGraw-Hill Companies, Inc.), 1221 Ave of the Americas, New York, NY 10020. TEL 212-904-2000, FAX 212-512-2000, customer.service@mcgraw-hill.com, http://www.mhhe.com/cls/.

➤ **ANNUAL EDITIONS: NUTRITION.** *see* NUTRITION AND DIETETICS

613 IND ISSN 0003-6498

APKA SWASTHYA. Text in Hindi. 1953. m. **Document type:** *Report, Academic/Scholarly.*
Published by: Indian Medical Association, I M A House, Indraprastha Marg, New Delhi, 110 002, India. TEL 91-11-23370009, FAX 91-11-23379470, inmedici@vsnl.com, http://www.ima-india.org.

APNEU MAGAZINE. *see* MEDICAL SCIENCES

613.7 DEU

APOTHEKEN SPIEGEL; Gesundheit - Fitness - Wellness. Text in German. 1995. m. adv. **Document type:** *Magazine, Consumer.*
Published by: Apotheken-Spiegel-Verlagsgesellschaft mbH, Edisonstr 3-5, Frankfurt am Main, 60388, Germany. TEL 49-6109-71200, FAX 49-6109-7120222, inbox@as-verlag.com.

613.7 610 DEU ISSN 0402-7108

APOTHEKEN UMSCHAU; das Gesundheits-Magazin. Text in German. 1957. s-m. adv. **Document type:** *Magazine, Consumer.*
Related titles: Online - full text ed.
Published by: Wort und Bild Verlag Konradshoehe GmbH, Konradshoehe, Baierbrunn, 82065, Germany. TEL 49-89-744330, FAX 49-89-74433150, info@wortundbildverlag.de, http://www.wortundbild.de. Eds. Hans Haltmeier, Peter Kanzler. adv.: color page EUR 107,030. Circ: 19,970,000 (controlled).

APPLIED PHYSIOLOGY, NUTRITION AND METABOLISM/PHYSIOLOGIE APPLIQUEE, NUTRITION ET METABOLISME. *see* MEDICAL SCIENCES—Sports Medicine

613.7 640.73 USA

AQUA BUYER'S GUIDE. Text in English. 1979. a. USD 50 (effective 2008). adv. **Document type:** *Directory, Trade.*
Former titles: Aqua Industry Guide; Aqua Buyers Guide; Spa and Sauna Buyers Guide
Related titles: Online - full text ed.
Published by: Athletic Business Publications, Inc., 4130 Lien Rd, Madison, WI 53704-3602. TEL 608-249-0186, 800-722-8764, FAX 608-249-1153, http://www.athleticbusiness.com. Circ: 5,000.

▼ **ARCHIVES OF EXERCISE IN HEALTH AND DISEASE.** *see* MEDICAL SCIENCES

613.7 IND

AROGYA SANJEEVANI. Text in Hindi. 1990. q. INR 204; INR 25 per issue (effective 2011). adv. **Document type:** *Magazine, Consumer.*
Published by: Pioneer Book Co. Pvt. Ltd., C-14, Royal Industrial Estate, 5-B, Naigaum Cross Rd, Wadala, Mumbai, Maharashtra 400 031, India.

613.7 BRA ISSN 0102-7778

ARTUS. Text in Portuguese. 1976. s-a. **Document type:** *Magazine, Trade.* **Description:** Covers all aspects of physical education and sports.
Published by: Universidade Gama Filho, Rua Manoel Vitorino 625, Piedade, Rio de Janeiro, RJ 20748-900, Brazil. TEL 55-21-32137735, FAX 55-21-32137731, http://www.ugf.br.

ASIA-PACIFIC JOURNAL OF HEALTH, PHYSICAL EDUCATION AND RECREATION. *see* EDUCATION

613.7 AUS

▼ ➤ **ASIA-PACIFIC JOURNAL OF HEALTH, SPORT AND PHYSICAL EDUCATION.** Text in English. 2010. bi-m. (3/yr until 2011). AUD 92 domestic; AUD 110 foreign (effective 2011). back issues avail. **Document type:** *Journal, Academic/Scholarly.* **Description:** Publishes articles that engage in critical analysis and discussion of current events relevant to the key defining areas of health, sport and physical education.
Published by: The Australian Council for Health, Physical Education and Recreation Inc., A/Prof. Christopher Hickey, School of Education, Deakin University, Pigdons Rd., Waurn Ponds, VIC 3217, Australia.

613.7 USA ISSN 1939-6678

ASIAN HEALTH GUIDE. Text in English. 2007. m. free (effective 2010). adv. back issues avail. **Document type:** *Guide, Trade.* **Description:** Provides comprehensive information on wellness health practices used in Asian cultures for centuries.
Media: Online - full text.
Published by: Pyramid Media Group, One Penn Plz, Ste 6166, New York, NY 10119. TEL 646-808-9057, info@pyramid.ch, http://www.pyramid.ch.

371.7 HKG ISSN 2075-4604
GV210

➤ **ASIAN JOURNAL OF PHYSICAL EDUCATION & RECREATION.** Text in English, Chinese. 1995. s-a. free (effective 2010). 60 p./no.; reprints avail. **Document type:** *Journal, Academic/Scholarly.*
Former titles (until 2009): Journal of Physical Education & Recreation (1028-7418); (until 1998): P E R S Review (1028-6853)
Indexed: CA, PEI, SD, T02.
—BLDSC (1742.560500), IE.
Published by: Hong Kong Baptist University, Dr. Stephen Hui Research Centre for Physical Recreation & Wellness, Department of Physical Education, 1/F, R5, University Road Campus, Hong Kong, Hong Kong. TEL 852-3411-7805, FAX 852-3411-5757, s62591@hkbu.edu.hk. Ed., R&P Dr. Lobo Luie TEL 582-34115631.

➤ **ATLETICAMENTE.** *see* SPORTS AND GAMES

613.7 USA

AUSTIN FIT MAGAZINE. Text in English. m. adv. back issues avail. **Document type:** *Magazine, Trade.* **Description:** Targets the health and fitness industry of Austin, Texas.
Related titles: Online - full text ed.
Address: 49220, Austin, TX 78765-9220. TEL 512-472-1348, FAX 512-472-7348, afitmag@flash.net, http://www.austinfitmagazine.com. Ed. Georgia Beth Johnson.

613.71 AUS ISSN 1322-8307

AUSTRALIAN IRONMAN; bodybuilding and fitness magazine. Text in English. 1994. m. AUD 75 domestic; AUD 115 foreign (effective 2008). adv. back issues avail. **Document type:** *Magazine, Consumer.* **Description:** Provides information and pictures on weight training, fat loss, muscle building, nutrition, diet modification, recovery, goal setting and sports psychology.
Published by: Blitz Publications, PO Box 4075, Mulgrave, VIC 3170, Australia. TEL 61-3-95748460, FAX 61-3-95748899, info@blitzmag.com.au. Adv. contact Sineade Sullivan.

AUSTRALIAN MEN'S FITNESS. *see* MEN'S HEALTH

613 AUS ISSN 1446-5000

AUSTRALIAN VITAL MAGAZINE; caring for your health. Text in English. 200?. q.
Published by: Shields Media Pty Ltd, 3-5 Bennett St, Ste 2, Ground Fl, East Perth, W.A. 60042, Australia.

613.7 AUS ISSN 1837-2406

▼ **AUSTRALIAN YOGA JOURNAL.** Text in English. 2009. bi-m. AUD 60 domestic; AUD 72 in New Zealand; AUD 7.95 per issue (effective 2011). **Document type:** *Magazine, Consumer.* **Description:** Designed for people who love yoga. Contains information to learn yoga from some of the best teachers in the world, as well as discover healthy recipes, inspirational people and places, to lead a balanced, happy life.
Published by: Odysseus Publishing, PO Box 81, St Leonards, NSW 1590, Australia. TEL 61-2-94391955, FAX 61-2-94391977, info@your-web-domain.com, http://www.odysseus.com.au. Ed. Liz Graham. Pub. Ian Brooks.

AUSTRALIAN YOGA LIFE. *see* NEW AGE PUBLICATIONS

THE AWAKENING. *see* PHILOSOPHY

613.7 SWE ISSN 1100-3839

B & K SPORTS MAGAZINE. Text in Swedish. 1981. m. SEK 398 (effective 2002). adv. 84 p./no. 3 cols./p.; **Description:** Deals with body building, exercise and food, sports injuries.
Published by: B & K Sports Magazine AB, PO Box 3417, Stockholm, 10368, Sweden. TEL 46-8-34-77-00, FAX 46-8-34-63-33. Ed. Ove Rytter. Adv. contact Alexander Jilkke. B&W page SEK 22,600; trim 275 x 185. Circ: 43,000.

P

613.7 POL ISSN 2080-1297
BALTIC JOURNAL OF HEALTH AND PHYSICAL ACTIVITY. Text in English. 1993. s-a. **Document type:** *Journal, Academic/Scholarly.*
Supersedes in part (in 2008): Jedrzej Sniadecki Academy of Physical Education and Sport. Research Yearbook (1730-7988); Which was formerly (until 2000): Jedrzej Sniadecki University School of Physical Education. Research Yearbook (1730-797X); (until 1995): Academy of Physical Education in Gdansk. Research Yearbook (1730-7961)
Related titles: Online - full text ed.: ISSN 2080-9999. free (effective 2011).
Indexed: CA, SD.
Published by: (Akademia Wychowania Fizycznego i Sportu im. Jedrzeja Sniadeckiego/Jedrzej Sniadecki Academy of Physical Education and Sport in Gdansk), Wydawnictwo Uczelniane Akademii Wychowania Fizycznego i Sportu im. Jedrzeja Sniadeckiego, ul. Kazimierza Gorskiego 1, Gdansk, 80336, Poland. TEL 48-58-5547161, kasiadz@awf.gda.pl.

613.7 CHN ISSN 1671-3583
BAOJIAN YIYUAN. Text in Chinese. 2002. m. **Document type:** *Magazine, Consumer.*
Related titles: Online - full text ed.
Published by: Weishengbu Beijing Yiyuan/Beijing Hospital of Health Ministry, 1, Dongchan Dahua Lu, Beijing, 100730, China.

613.7 CHN ISSN 1005-5371
BAOJIAN YU SHENGHUO/HEALTH & LIFE. Text in English. 1993. m. **Document type:** *Magazine, Consumer.*
Published by: Anhui Kexue Jishu Chubanshe/Anhui Science & Tecnology Publishing House, 1118, Shengquan Lu, Zhengwu Wenhua Xin Qu, 9/F, Chuban Chuanmei Guangchang, Hefei, 230071, China. TEL 86-551-3533333, FAX 86-551-3533330, yougoubu@sina.com, http://www.ahstp.net/.

613.7 CZE ISSN 1214-7729
BAZENY A SAUNY. Text in Czech. 2004. q. CZK 294; CZK 49 newsstand/cover (effective 2009). adv. **Document type:** *Magazine, Consumer.*
Published by: Roof Press, s.r.o., Rehorova 10, Prague 3, 130 00, Czech Republic. TEL 420-2-22811104, FAX 420-2-22541428, v.divis@roofpress.cz.

613 USA ISSN 1937-5816
BE WELL (MILFORD). Text in English. 2007. bi-m. USD 19.95 domestic; USD 24.95 in Canada; USD 36.95 elsewhere (effective 2007). **Document type:** *Magazine, Consumer.* **Description:** Includes articles about maintaining a healthy lifestyle, including improving eating habits, increasing excercise and quitting smoking.
Published by: Red Mat Publishing, LLC, PO Box 2387, Milford, CT 06460. TEL 203-876-8618, http://www.redmatpublishing.com.

613.7 USA
BEAUTY HANDBOOK. Text in English. 1982. q. adv. illus. **Document type:** *Magazine, Consumer.* **Description:** Provides information of men and women to improve their own and their families' health and fitness through improving nutrition, reducing stress, and generally engaging in healthful lifestyles.
Formerly: Health Handbook
Published by: Compendium Systems Corporation, 346 N Main St, Port Chester, NY 10573. TEL 914-935-1000, FAX 914-935-1063, editor@beauty-handbook.com. Ed. Melissa Macron. Pub. John McAuliffe.

613.7 370 CHN ISSN 1007-3612
GV201
BEIJING TIYU DAXUE XUEBAO/BEIJING UNIVERSITY OF PHYSICAL EDUCATION. JOURNAL. Text in Chinese. 1966. q. USD 80.40 (effective 2009). **Document type:** *Journal, Academic/Scholarly.*
Formerly (until 1993): Beijing Tiyu Xueyuan Xuebao (1002-834X)
Related titles: Online - full text ed.
Indexed: CA, E03, PEI, SD, T02.
—BLDSC (4707.893500), East View.
Published by: Beijing Tiyu Daxue/Beijing University of Physical Education, Yuanminyuan Nan Lu, Haidian-qu, Beijing, 100084, China. **Dist. by:** China International Book Trading Corp, 35 Chegongzhuang Xilu, Haidian District, PO Box 399, Beijing 100044, China. TEL 86-10-68412045, FAX 86-10-68412023, cibtc@mail.cibtc.com.cn, http://www.cibtc.com.cn.

BELLISSIMA. *see* BEAUTY CULTURE

▼ **BEM!.** *see* PUBLIC HEALTH AND SAFETY

BEST BODY; balance.exercise.style.taste. *see* WOMEN'S HEALTH

613.7 DEU ISSN 0176-8700
BETRIFFT SPORT. Text in German. 1979. bi-m. looseleaf. EUR 45; EUR 8 newsstand/cover (effective 2011). adv. 38 p./no. 2 cols./p.; back issues avail. **Document type:** *Magazine, Consumer.* **Description:** Magazine for physical exercise instructors.
Indexed: DIP, IBR, IBZ.
Published by: Meyer & Meyer Verlag, Von-Coels-Str 390, Aachen, 52080, Germany. TEL 49-241-958100, FAX 49-241-9581010, verlag@m-m-sports.com, http://m-m-sports.de. Circ: 8,500 (paid and controlled).

BETTER HEALTH. *see* PUBLIC HEALTH AND SAFETY

613.7 USA ISSN 8750-1228
BETTER HEALTH (BIRMINGHAM). Text in English. 1984. m. **Document type:** *Magazine, Consumer.*
Indexed: G08, H11, H12.
Published by: University of Alabama at Birmingham, Medical Center, 930 20th St S, Birmingham, AL 35205. TEL 800-822-8816, http://www.health.uab.edu.

613.7 610 USA
BETTER HEALTH (NEW HAVEN). Text in English. 1979. bi-m. USD 15 out of state; free in state (effective 2009). back issues avail. **Document type:** *Magazine, Consumer.* **Description:** Provides informations about health for healthier lives and make better healthcare decisions.
Published by: Saint Raphael Healthcare System, 1450 Chapel St, New Haven, CT 06511. TEL 203-789-3972, FAX 203-789-4053, feedback@srhs.org. Ed. Sharon Napolitano. Pub. David W Benfer.

BEWEGUNG, SPIEL, SPORT. *see* SPORTS AND GAMES

613 LIE ISSN 0006-0429
BEWUSSTER LEBEN; Zeitschrift fuer positive Lebens- und Arbeitsgestaltung, gesunde Ernaehrung und natuerliche Lebensweise. Text in German. 1935. m. CHF 64. bk.rev. bibl.; charts; illus.
Formerly: Leben
Published by: Leben Verlag AG, Vaduz, 9490, Liechtenstein. TEL 41-75-2371051. adv.: page CHF 1,211; 180 x 131. Circ: 25,000.

BEYOND CHANGE; information regarding obesity and obesity surgery. *see* MEDICAL SCIENCES

613 DZA ISSN 1112-5152
RA418.5F3
BIEN-ETRE; le magazine de toute la famille. Text in French. 2004. m. **Document type:** *Magazine, Consumer.*
Published by: Alpha Design, Palais des Expositions, Pins Maritimes, Alger, Algeria. http://www.alpha-dz.com/.

613.7 DEU ISSN 0949-4642
BIO MAGAZIN; Gesundheit fuer Koerper, Geist und Seele. Text in German. 1984. bi-m. EUR 24.90 domestic; EUR 28.80 foreign; EUR 4.50 newsstand/cover (effective 2009). adv. bk.rev. back issues avail. **Document type:** *Magazine, Consumer.* **Description:** Contains information on achieving health through natural means and procedures.
Formerly: Bio Spezial Magazin
Published by: Bio Ritter GmbH, Monatshauserstr 8, Tutzing, 82327, Germany. TEL 49-8158-8022, FAX 49-8158-7142, bioritter@aol.com, http://www.bio-ritter.de. Ed., R&P Monica Ritter. Adv. contact Edith von Hafenbraedl. B&W page EUR 2,450, color page EUR 3,650; trim 184 x 250. Circ: 120,000 (paid and controlled).

613.7 GRC ISSN 1791-325X
GV557
➤ **BIOLOGY OF EXERCISE.** Text in English. 2005. s-a. free (effective 2011). back issues avail. **Document type:** *Journal, Academic/Scholarly.* **Description:** Covers sport injuries, exercise physiology, sport rehabilitation, diseases and exercise, sport psychology, sport nutrition, sport biomechanics, sport pedagogy, sport philosophy, sport sociology, sport recreation and sport management.
Media: Online - full text.
Indexed: A36, CA, CABA, GH, LT, N02, N03, P33, P39, RRTA, SD, T02.
Published by: Simmetria, 80 Iioannou Theologou St, Zografou, Athens 15773, Greece. TEL 30-1301-7702033, FAX 30-0310-7702581, ekdoseissimmetria@yahoo.gr, http://www.simmetria.gr. Ed. Apostolos Stergioulas. Pub. Stavros Athanasopoulos.

613.7 USA ISSN 2159-3949
▼ **BLACK FIT MAGAZINE.** Text in English. 2011. q. USD 5.99 per issue (effective 2011). **Document type:** *Magazine, Consumer.*
Media: Online - full text.
Published by: HonneBunch Publishing, 2201 N Lamar Blvd, Ste 140, Austin, TX 78741. TEL 888-902-1821.

613.7 CZE ISSN 1802-3738
BLESK ZDRAVI. Text in Czech. 2006. m. CZK 23 newsstand/cover (effective 2010). adv. **Document type:** *Magazine, Consumer.*
Published by: Ringier CR, Komunardu 1584/42, Prague 7, 170 00, Czech Republic. TEL 420-2-25977616, FAX 420-2-67097718, info@ringier.cz, http://www.ringier.cz. Ed. Monika Muzikova. Circ: 33,374 (paid).

613.7 646.7 BRA ISSN 0104-1533
BOA FORMA. Text in Portuguese. 1988. m. BRL 84.27; BRL 7.90 newsstand/cover (effective 2010). adv. charts; illus. **Document type:** *Magazine, Consumer.* **Description:** Contains articles on fitness, health, beauty and sports.
Related titles: Online - full text ed.
Published by: Editora Abril, S.A., Avenida das Nacoes Unidas 7221, Pinheiros, Sao Paulo, SP 05425-902, Brazil. TEL 55-11-50872112, FAX 55-11-50872100, abrilsac@abril.com.br, http://www.abril.com.br. adv.: color page BRL 55,800; trim 202 x 266. Circ: 224,264 (paid).

613.7 CHN ISSN 1007-8428
BOAI/FRATERNITY. Text in Chinese. bi-m. CNY 57.60 (effective 2004). **Document type:** *Magazine, Consumer.*
Former titles (until 1992): Zhongguo Hongshizi/Chinese Red Cross (1000-1387); (until 1960): Aiguo Weisheng; Which was formed by the merger of (1957-1958): Jiang Weisheng; (1955-1958): Zhongguo Hongshizi; Which was formerly (1950-1954): Xingzhongguo Hongshizi
Published by: (Zhongguo Hongshizihui/Chinese Red Cross), Zhongguo Hongshizihui Zonghui Baokanshe, 43, Ganmian Hutong, Beijing, 100010, China. TEL 86-10-65254012, 86-10-65254766, FAX 86-10-65238052. **Dist. by:** China International Book Trading Corp, 35 Chegongzhuang Xilu, Haidian District, PO Box 399, Beijing 100044, China. TEL 86-10-68412045, FAX 86-10-68412023, cibtc@mail.cibtc.com.cn, http://www.cibtc.com.cn.

613.7 FIN ISSN 0788-9917
BODAUS; fitness magazine. Text in Finnish. 1983. 8/yr. EUR 44 (effective 2007). adv. **Document type:** *Magazine, Consumer.*
Formerly (until 1989): Bodaus-Lehti (0780-6892)
Published by: Karprint Oy, Vanha Turunrie 371, Huhmari, 03150, Finland. TEL 358-9-41397300, FAX 358-9-41397405, http://www.karprint.fi. Ed. Reetta Ahola. Adv. contact Arja Blom. page EUR 2,052. Circ: 18,000.

613.7 051 USA
BODY BEAUTIFUL; living well in southern california. Text in English. 19??. m. free to qualified personnel (effective 2009). adv. **Document type:** *Magazine, Consumer.* **Description:** Designed to educate readers on ways to improve their image, health and well-being.
Related titles: Online - full text ed.
Published by: Churm Media, 1451 Quail St, Ste 201, Newport Beach, CA 92660. TEL 949-757-1404 ext 303, FAX 949-757-1996, http://www.churmmedia.com. adv.: B&W page USD 1,995.

613.7 USA ISSN 1930-0360
BODY DIALOGUE. Text in English. 1992. s-a. **Document type:** *Newsletter, Consumer.*
Published by: Shintaido of America, PO Box 1979, Novato, CA 94948-1979. info@shintaido.org.

794 DEU ISSN 1437-286X
BODY LIFE. Text in German. 199?. m. EUR 79 (effective 2010). adv. **Document type:** *Magazine, Trade.*
Published by: Health and Beauty Business Media GmbH & Co. KG, Karl-Friedrich-Str 14-18, Karlsruhe, 76133, Germany. TEL 49-721-1650, FAX 49-721-165618, info@health-and-beauty.com, http://www.health-and-beauty.com. Circ: 6,680 (paid and controlled).

613.7 305.4 NLD ISSN 1871-3270
BODY + MIND. WOMAN. Text in Dutch. 1998. m. EUR 19.95 domestic; EUR 39.95 in Belgium; EUR 39.95 in Spain (effective 2010). adv. **Document type:** *Magazine, Consumer.*
Formerly (until 2005): Body en Mind (1389-1103)
Published by: Publi Force, Postbus 229, Alblasserdam, 2950 AE, Netherlands. TEL 31-78-6522700, FAX 31-78-6522701, info@publiforce.nl, http://www.publiforce.nl. adv.: page EUR 2,500; trim 230 x 297. Circ: 22,675.

613.7 613.04244 GBR ISSN 2042-9681
▼ **BODYFIT**; women's workout magazine. Text in English. 2010. m. GBP 37 domestic; GBP 50 in Europe; GBP 60 elsewhere (effective 2010). adv. back issues avail. **Document type:** *Magazine, Consumer.*
Published by: Maze Media Ltd., 25 Phoenix Ct, Hawkins Rd, Colchester, Essex CO2 8JY, United Kingdom. TEL 44-1206-505960. Ed. Naomi Abeykoon. Adv. contact Jay Hurley TEL 44-1206-505488. page GBP 1,100; trim 210 x 297.

613.7 DEU
BODYMEDIA; Fachmagazin fuer Fitness und Wellness. Text in German. 6/yr. EUR 60 domestic; EUR 70 foreign (effective 2007). adv. **Document type:** *Magazine, Trade.*
Published by: Horn Druck und Verlag GmbH & Co. KG, Stegwiesenstr 6-10, Bruchsal, 76646, Germany. TEL 49-7251-978511, FAX 49-7251-978549, N.Tauscher@horn-verlag.de, http://www.horn-verlag.de. Ed. Hubert Horn. Adv. contact Franz Jahn. B&W page EUR 1,710, color page EUR 2,195. Circ: 11,300 (controlled).

613.7 USA ISSN 2155-5788
▼ **BOFI.** (Body Fitness) Variant title: Body Fitness Magazine. Text in English. 2010 (Aug.). q. free (effective 2011). **Document type:** *Magazine, Consumer.* **Description:** Information on fitness, lifestyle, nutrition, training and health.
Published by: BOFIMAG, Inc., 2221 NE 164th St, Ste 398, North Miami Beach, FL 33160. TEL 305-424-1446, carlos@bofimag.com.

613.7 USA ISSN 1092-0129
BOTTOM LINE / HEALTH. Variant title: Bottom Line Health. Text in English. 1987. m. USD 19.95 domestic; USD 56 in Canada (effective 2008). 16 p./no. 3 cols./p.; back issues avail.; reprints avail. **Document type:** *Newsletter, Consumer.* **Description:** Offers consumers valuable expert insider tips on all aspects of personal health and fitness.
Formerly (until 1997): Health Confidential (0894-4172)
Indexed: A01, A02, A03, A08, C06, C07, C08, CINAHL, M01, M02.
Published by: Boardroom, Inc., PO Box 422318, Palm Coast, FL 32142. TEL 800-289-0409, FAX 800-456-3787, editors@boardroom.com, http://www.bottomlinesecrets.com. Ed. Rebecca Shannonhouse. Pub. Martin Edelston. Circ: 30,000.

613.7 USA ISSN 2157-1538
BOTTOM LINE / WEALTH. Text in English. 2008. m. back issues avail. **Document type:** *Newsletter, Consumer.*
Published by: Boardroom, Inc., PO Box 422309, Palm Coast, FL 32142. TEL 800-288-1051, FAX 800-456-3787.

▼ **BRITISH JOURNAL OF WELLBEING**; a new approach to mental and physical health. *see* NEW AGE PUBLICATIONS

613.194 GBR ISSN 0264-0406
BRITISH NATURISM. Abbreviated title: B N. Text in English. 1964. q. GBP 5 per issue to non-members; free to members (effective 2009). adv. illus. back issues avail. **Document type:** *Magazine, Trade.* **Description:** Aims to raise the public profile of naturism, through media work and by lobbying local and national government.
Published by: Central Council for British Naturism, 30-32 Wycliffe Rd, Northampton, NN1 5JF, United Kingdom. TEL 44-1604-620361, http://www.british-naturism.org.uk, FAX 44-1604-230176, headoffice@british-naturism.org.uk. Adv. contact Debbie Knowlson.

613.7 RUS
BUD' ZDOROV!. Text in Russian. 1993. m. USD 110 foreign (effective 2007). **Document type:** *Magazine, Consumer.*
Published by: Izdatel'stvo Shenkman i Synov'ya, ul Sushchevskii Val, dom 5, str 15, Moscow, 127018, Russian Federation. TEL 7-495-9261356. Ed. S B Shenkman. **Dist. by:** East View Information Services, 10601 Wayzata Blvd, Minneapolis, MN 55305. TEL 952-252-1201, 800-477-1005, FAX 952-252-1202, info@eastview.com, http://www.eastview.com.

613.7 DEU ISSN 1617-0911
BUSCHE ERLEBNISGUIDE. Text in German. 2000. a. EUR 19.80 newsstand/cover (effective 2009). adv. **Document type:** *Magazine, Consumer.*
Published by: Busche Verlagsgesellschaft mbH, Schleefstr 1, Dortmund, 44287, Germany. TEL 49-231-444770, FAX 49-231-4447777, info@busche.de, http://www.busche.de. adv.: page EUR 3,100. Circ: 24,924 (paid and controlled).

613.7 613.2 PRT
▼ **C I D E S D BOLETIM INFORMATIVO DA SAUDE.** (Centro de Investigacao em Desporto, Saude e Desenvolvimento Humano) Text in Portuguese. 2009. s-a. **Document type:** *Bulletin, Consumer.*
Published by: Universidade de Tras-os-Montes e Alto Douro, Centro de Investigacao em Desporto, Saude e Desenvolvimento Humano/University of Tras-os-Montes and Alto Douro, Research Centre for Sports Sciences, Health and Human Development, Rua Dr. Manuel Cardona, Vila Real, 5000-558, Portugal. TEL 351-259-330100, FAX 351-259-330169, http://cidesd.org.

C P H A HEALTH DIGEST. *see* PUBLIC HEALTH AND SAFETY

613.9 CAN ISSN 1712-5782
CA SEXPRIME. Text in French. 2005. irreg. **Document type:** *Monographic series, Consumer.*
Published by: Quebec, Ministere de la Sante et des Services Sociaux, 400, boul. Jean-Lesage, bureau 105, Quebec, PQ G1K 8W1, Canada. TEL 418-643-1344, 800-363-1363, http://www.msss.gouv.qc.ca/index.php.

CADERNOS DE SAUDE. *see* PUBLIC HEALTH AND SAFETY

CAHIERS DE LA PUERICULTRICE. *see* CHILDREN AND YOUTH—About

613.7 USA ISSN 1545-8725
➤ **CALIFORNIAN JOURNAL OF HEALTH PROMOTION.** Abbreviated title: C J H P. Text in English. 2003. q. free (effective 2011). back issues avail. **Document type:** *Journal, Academic/Scholarly.*
Description: Covers health education and health promotion practice, teaching, research, and issues of interest to professionals in California and surrounding states.
Media: Online - full text. **Related titles:** CD-ROM ed.: ISSN 1545-8717.
Indexed: R11.
Published by: California State University, Chico, Department of Health and Community Services, Butte Hall 607, Chico, CA 95929. TEL 530-898-6661, FAX 530-898-5107, hcsv@csuchico.edu, http://www.csuchico.edu/hcsv/. Eds. Jie Weiss, Michele Mouttapa.

613.7 CAN ISSN 1911-1150
CANADIAN HEALTH; your partner in healthy living. Text in English. 2006. bi-m. CAD 12 (effective 2009). adv. **Document type:** *Magazine, Consumer.*
Published by: Canadian Medical Association/Association Medicale Canadienne, 1867 Alta Vista Dr, Ottawa, ON K1G 3Y6, Canada. TEL 613-731-8610, 888-855-2555, FAX 613-236-8864, cmamsc@cma.ca, cmamsc@cma.ca, http://www.cma.ca. Ed. Diana Swift. Pub. Steve Ball. adv.: color page CAD 8,470; trim 8.1 x 10.8. Circ: 55,000 (paid and controlled).

CANADIAN JOURNAL OF DIABETES. *see* MEDICAL SCIENCES—Endocrinology

613.7 DEU
CAPITAL-HEALTH MAGAZINE. Text in German. 3/yr. EUR 4 newsstand/cover (effective 2007). adv. **Document type:** *Magazine, Consumer.*
Published by: T M M Marketing und Medien GmbH & Co. KG, Kantstr 151, Berlin, 10623, Germany. TEL 49-30-2062673, FAX 49-30-20626750, mail@tmm.de, http://tmm.de. Ed. Katrin Herzog. adv.: color page EUR 1,650. Circ: 12,000 (paid and controlled).

613.7 CAN ISSN 1487-752X
CAPITAL SANTE. Text in English. 1984. 10/yr. CAD 17.25 domestic; CAD 30 in United States; CAD 3.25 newsstand/cover (effective 2003). adv. **Document type:** *Magazine, Consumer.*
Formerly (until 1998): Sante (0832-6770)
Related titles: Online - full text ed.
Indexed: C05, PdeR, SD.
—**CCC.**
Published by: Transcontinental Media, Inc. (Subsidiary of: Transcontinental, Inc.), 2001 University St, Ste 900, Montreal, PQ H3A 2A6, Canada. TEL 514-499-0561, FAX 514-499-3078, info@transcontinental.ca, http://www.transcontinental-gtc.com/en/home.html. Ed. Jean-Louis Gauthier. Pub. Francine Tremblay. Circ: 49,084.

613.7 FRA ISSN 1764-4666
LES CARNETS DE LA FORME. Text in French. 2002. irreg. back issues avail. **Document type:** *Monographic series, Consumer.*
Published by: Ellebore Editions, B P 60001, Paris, 75560 Cedex 12, France. info@ellebore.fr.

CATALYST (MARIETTA); a publication resource of New Age newsletters, book reviews, personals, holistic health, UFO's and psychic connections. *see* NEW AGE PUBLICATIONS

▼ **CENTRO DE DOCUMENTACAO E BIBLIOTECA / SECRETARIA MUNICIPAL DE ESPORTES, LAZER E RECREACAO. REVISTA ELETRONICA.** *see* SPORTS AND GAMES

613 USA ISSN 2153-2168
RC628
➤ **CHILDHOOD OBESITY.** Text in English. 2005. bi-m. USD 360 domestic to institutions; USD 439 foreign to institutions; USD 432 combined subscription domestic to institutions (print & online eds.); USD 492 combined subscription foreign to institutions (print & online eds.) (effective 2012). adv. reprint service avail. from PSC.
Document type: *Journal, Academic/Scholarly.* **Description:** Focuses on issues surrounding the health hazards that obesity poses and covers practical advice and information about prevention and treatment; interviews with leading obesity experts; concise, up-to-date practical summaries of the latest research; meeting calendar; Internet and web resources; and reviews of both new books and products.
Former titles (until 2010): Obesity and Weight Management (1948-6553); (until 2009): Obesity Management (1545-1712)
Related titles: Online - full text ed.: ISSN 2153-2176. USD 360 to institutions (effective 2012).
Indexed: A22, A26, A36, CABA, D01, E01, E07, GH, H12, I05, N02, N03, P19, P24, P30, PEI, PQC, RA&MP, SCOPUS, W11.
—BLDSC (3172.956500), IE, Ingenta. **CCC.**
Published by: (American Dietetic Association, American Academy of Family Physicians, American College of Sports Medicine, American Association of Diabetes Educators), Mary Ann Liebert, Inc. Publishers, 140 Huguenot St, 3rd Fl, New Rochelle, NY 10801. TEL 914-740-2100, FAX 914-740-2101, 800-654-3237, info@liebertpub.com. Ed. David L Katz. Adv. contact Harriet I Matysko TEL 914-740-2182.

➤ **CHINESE ACADEMIC JOURNALS FULL-TEXT DATABASE. MEDICINE & HYGIENE.** *see* MEDICAL SCIENCES

613.7 640.73 AUS ISSN 1324-8065
CHOICE HEALTH READER. Text in English. 1995. 10/yr. AUD 55 to individuals; AUD 79.20 to institutions (effective 2008). **Document type:** *Magazine, Consumer.* **Description:** Contains information about the latest developments in health, fitness and medical research for consumers.
Former titles (until 1995): Health Reader (1036-8744); (until 1990): The International Health Reader; (until 1984): The Fitness Reader; Fitness Reader
Published by: Australian Consumers' Association, 57 Carrington Rd, Marrickville, NSW 2204, Australia. TEL 61-2-95773399, FAX 61-2-95773377. Eds. Dr. Garry Egger, Dr. Norman Swan. Circ: 4,000.

613.7 BRA ISSN 1519-2512
GV238.R57
CINERGIS. Text in Portuguese. 2000. s-a. BRL 24 (effective 2006). back issues avail. **Document type:** *Journal, Academic/Scholarly.*
Published by: (Universidade de Santa Cruz do Sul, Departamento de Educacao Fisica e Saude), Editora da Universidade de Santa Cruz do Sul, Av Independencia 2293, Barrio Universitario, Santa Cruz do Sul, RS 96815-900, Brazil. TEL 55-51-37177461, FAX 55-51-37177402, editora@unisc.br. Ed. Ruy Jornada Krebs.

CITIUS ALTIUS FORTIUS. *see* SPORTS AND GAMES

613.7 CAN ISSN 1914-7856
CITYHEALTH. Variant title: City Health. Text in English. 2004. bi-m. CAD 29 domestic; CAD 45 foreign (effective 2007). back issues avail. **Document type:** *Magazine, Consumer.*
Published by: Frager Productions, 329 March Road, PO Box 72097, Kanata, ON K2K 2P4, Canada. TEL 613-599-6801, FAX 613-599-6980, www.fragerproductions.com.

613.7 ROM ISSN 2065-6831
CLICK! SANATATE. Text in Romanian. m. ROL 15; ROL 2.49 newsstand/cover (effective 2011). adv. **Document type:** *Magazine, Consumer.*
Related titles: Online - full text ed.: ISSN 2068-813X. 2009.
Published by: Adevarul Holding, Str Fabrica de Glucoza, nr 21, sector 2, Bucharest, Romania. TEL 40-21-4077632, FAX 40-21-4077602, redactie@adevarul.ro, http://www.adevarul.ro. Ed. Delia Sabau.

CLINICAL JOURNAL OF SPORT MEDICINE. *see* MEDICAL SCIENCES—Sports Medicine

CLINICAL KINESIOLOGY (ONLINE). *see* MEDICAL SCIENCES—Physical Medicine And Rehabilitation

CLUB BUSINESS INTERNATIONAL. *see* BUSINESS AND ECONOMICS—Small Business

613.7 USA ISSN 2150-2692
GV428.5
CLUB INDUSTRY. Text in English. 1984. m. USD 59 domestic; USD 67 in Canada; USD 84 elsewhere; free to qualified personnel (effective 2011). adv. tr.lit. back issues avail. **Document type:** *Magazine, Trade.*
Description: Provides fitness business professionals with articles on health and fitness facility management.
Former titles (until 2009): Club Industry's Fitness Business Pro (1552-5503); (until Sep.2004): Club Industry (0747-8283)
Related titles: Online - full text ed.: ISSN 2150-2706. free (effective 2010).
Indexed: A09, A10, A15, ABIn, B01, B04, B06, B07, B09, BPI, BRD, H&TI, H06, P48, P51, PQC, PROMT, S22, T02, V03, V04, W01, W02, W03, W05.
—CIS, Ingenta.
Published by: Penton Media, Inc., 9800 Metcalf Ave, Overland Park, KS 66212. TEL 913-341-1300, FAX 913-967-1898, http://www.penton.com. Ed. Pamela Kufahl.

613.7 AUS
CLUB NETWORK. Text in English. 1991. s-a. free to members (effective 2008). back issues avail. **Document type:** *Newsletter, Consumer.*
Description: Provides information, ideas and advice for fitness club owners and managers.
Former titles (until 2002): Club Fitness Network; (until 2000): Club Network
Related titles: Online - full text ed.: free (effective 2008).
Published by: Australian Fitness Network, PO Box 1606, Crows Nest, NSW 1585, Australia. TEL 61-2-84247200, FAX 61-2-94376511, info@fitnessnetwork.com.au, http://www.fitnessnetwork.com.au/. Ed. Oli Kitchingman TEL 61-2-84247286.

613.7 DEU
▼ **COK YASA**; Aylyk Tuerk-Alman Saolyk Magazini - Deutsch-Tuerkische Gesundheits-Magazin. Text in German, Turkish. 2009 (Nov.). bi-m. adv. **Document type:** *Magazine, Consumer.*
Published by: P A C S Gesellschaft fuer Promotion, Advertising & Communication Services mbH, Gewerbestr 9, Staufen, 79219, Germany. TEL 49-7633-982007, FAX 49-7633-982060, pacs@pacs-online.com, http://www.pacs-online.com. Ed. Nicole Franke-Gricksch. Adv. contact Claudia Haeussler. Circ: 30,000 (controlled).

COME & EAT!. *see* HOME ECONOMICS

613 ITA ISSN 1124-1705
COME STAI; mensile della salute per la famiglia. Text in Italian. 1995. m. EUR 21 domestic (effective 2008). adv. illus. **Document type:** *Magazine, Consumer.* **Description:** Provides health and fitness tips and articles for the whole family.
Published by: Unitop Srl (Subsidiary of: Casa Editrice Universo SpA), Corso di Porta Nuova 3A, Milan, 20121, Italy. FAX 39-02-252007333. Ed. Monica Sori. R&P Elisabetta Savoca TEL 39-02-723311. Adv. contact Luigi Randello. Circ: 124,000 (paid).

COMPARATIVE EXERCISE PHYSIOLOGY; the international journal of exercise physiology, biomechanics and nutrition. *see* SPORTS AND GAMES—Horses And Horsemanship

CONDITION; Ratgebermagazin fuer Lauf- und Ausdauersport. *see* SPORTS AND GAMES

613.7 155.937 USA
THE CONNECTICUT HOSPICE NEWSLETTER; making today count. Text in English. 1979. s-a. free (effective 2007). **Description:** Provides information related to timely medical issues as they impact hospice care; includes features about hospice services.
Related titles: Online - full text ed.
Indexed: E-psyche.
Published by: Connecticut Hospice Inc., 100 Double Beach Rd, Branford, CT 06405. TEL 203-315-7526, 203-315-7500, info@hospice.com, llaucella@hospice.com. Circ: 50,000.

613.7 USA ISSN 1058-0832
CODEN: CREHEI
CONSUMER REPORTS ON HEALTH. Text in English. 1989. m. USD 24 combined subscription (print & online eds.) (effective 2009). illus. Index. back issues avail.; reprints avail. **Document type:** *Newsletter, Consumer.* **Description:** Provides objective facts and clear recommendations to help the reader to make smart decisions about health from nutrition and weight loss to prescription drugs, disease prevention, pain relief and more.
Formerly (until 1991): Consumer Reports Health Letter (1044-3193)
Related titles: Online - full text ed.; ◆ Supplement to: Consumer Reports. ISSN 0010-7174.
Indexed: A01, A02, A03, A08, A11, A15, A22, A26, ABIn, B01, B06, B07, B08, B09, BiolDig, C05, C06, C07, C08, C12, CA, CINAHL, CPerI, G08, H01, H04, H05, H11, H12, H13, I05, M01, M02, M06, MASUSE, P02, P10, P19, P20, P21, P24, P30, P34, P48, P51, P53, P54, PQC, S22, T02, U01.
—BLDSC (3424.551000), CIS, IE, Infotrieve, Ingenta.
Published by: Consumers Union of the United States, Inc., 101 Truman Ave, Yonkers, NY 10703. TEL 914-378-2000, 800-234-1645, FAX 914-378-2900, http://www.consumersunion.org. Eds. Joel Keehn, Ronni Sandroff. Pub. James D Davis. Circ: 360,000. **Subscr. to:** PO Box 56356, Boulder, CO 80322-6356.

CONTACT QUARTERLY; a vehicle for moving ideas. *see* DANCE

613.7 ITA ISSN 1127-4646
CORRERE. Text in Italian. 1981. m. EUR 45 domestic; EUR 98 in Europe; EUR 130 elsewhere (effective 2009). adv. **Document type:** *Magazine, Consumer.*
Published by: Editoriale Sport Italia, Via Masaccio 12, Milan, MI 20149, Italy. TEL 39-02-4815396, FAX 39-02-4690907, http://www.sportivi.it. Circ: 50,000.

613.7 790.1 ESP
CORRICOLARI; el corredor y su mundo. Text in Spanish. 1986. m. adv. illus. back issues avail. **Document type:** *Magazine, Consumer.*
Description: Covers the world of racing: marathons, race courses, athletics, nutrition, and the physiology of sport.
Published by: Outside Comunicacion Integral, P. Marquez de Monistrol, 7, Madrid, 28011, Spain. TEL 34-91-5268080, FAX 34-91-5261012, outside@airelibre.com, http://www.airelibre.com/. Circ: 35,000.

613.7 613.2 ITA ISSN 1120-5016
CORRIERE SALUTE. Text in Italian. 1989. w. **Document type:** *Newspaper, Consumer.*
Related titles: ◆ Supplement to: Corriere della Sera. ISSN 1120-4982.
Published by: R C S Quotidiani (Subsidiary of: R C S Mediagroup), Via San Marco 21, Milan, 20121, Italy. TEL 39-02-25844111, http://www.rcsmediagroup.it.

LA CORSA. *see* SPORTS AND GAMES

613.7 AUS ISSN 1837-7300
▼ **COSMOPOLITAN HEALTH.** Text in English. 2010. a. **Document type:** *Magazine, Trade.*
Published by: A C P Magazines Ltd. (Subsidiary of: P B L Media Pty Ltd.), 54-58 Park St, Sydney, NSW 2000, Australia. TEL 61-2-92828000, FAX 61-2-91263769, research@acpaction.com.au, http://www.acp.com.au. Ed. Franki Hobson.

613.7 CAN ISSN 1701-7173
COURSE CONDUCTOR NEWS. Variant title: C C News. Fitness Appraisal Certification and Accreditation News. Text in English. 2000. a. **Document type:** *Newsletter, Trade.*
Indexed: A15, ABIn, P48, P51, PQC.
Published by: Canadian Society for Exercise Physiology, 185 Somerset St W, Ste 202, Ottawa, ON K2P 0J2, Canada. TEL 613-234-3755, 877-651-3755, FAX 613-234-3565, info@csep.ca, http://www.csep.ca/.

CREATIVE LIVING. *see* LIFESTYLE

613.7 COL ISSN 0123-5761
CUADERNOS DE OCIO. Text in Spanish. q. **Document type:** *Journal, Academic/Scholarly.*
Published by: Universidad de Antioquia, Instituto Universitario de Educacion Fisica y Deporte, Apartado Aereo 1226, Medellin, ANT, Colombia. TEL 57-4-4259267, FAX 57-4-4259261.

613.7 ESP ISSN 1130-4421
CUERPOMENTE; salud y medicina natural. Text in Spanish. 1990. m. EUR 24.95 (effective 2008). **Document type:** *Magazine, Consumer.*
Description: Covers articles about beauty and health for men and women.
Published by: R B A Edipresse, Perez Galdos 36, Barcelona, 08012, Spain. TEL 34-93-4157374, FAX 34-93-2177378, http://www.rbaedipresse.es. Circ: 45,000.

CURRENT HEALTH 1; the beginning guide to health education. *see* EDUCATION—Teaching Methods And Curriculum

CURRENT HEALTH TEENS. *see* EDUCATION—Teaching Methods And Curriculum

D A S H. (Diet, Adventure, Sport and Health) *see* NUTRITION AND DIETETICS

362.1 DEU ISSN 1611-1834
D F G - GRADUIERTENKOLLEG LEBENSTILLE, SOZIALE DIFFERENZEN, GESUNDHEITSFOERDERUNG. BERICHTE. Text in German. 2003. irreg., latest vol.7, 2005. price varies. **Document type:** *Monographic series, Academic/Scholarly.*
Published by: (D F G - Graduiertenkolleg Lebenstille, Soziale Differenzen, Gesundheitsfoerderung), Logos Verlag Berlin, Comeniushof, Gubener Str 47, Berlin, 10243, Germany. TEL 49-30-42851090, FAX 49-30-42851092, redaktion@logos-verlag.de.

613.7 CHN ISSN 1009-6019
DAJIA JIANKANG/GOOD HEALTH FOR ALL. Text in Chinese. 1985. m. CNY 8 per issue (effective 2009).
Former titles (until 2007): Jiankang Xinshiye/The New Health Horizon; (until 2006): Dajia Jiankang (Shang Bian Yue. Shishang Nan Niu)
Published by: Dajia Jiankang Zazhishe, 8, Xinglong Xi Jie, 1-206, Yuanyazhou Meili Huayuan, Beijing, China. TEL 86-10-81663373.

613.7 CHN ISSN 1002-574X
DAZHONG JIANKANG/PUBLIC HEALTH. Text in Chinese. 1985. m. USD 62.40 (effective 2009). **Document type:** *Magazine, Consumer.*
—East View.
Published by: Jiankang Baoshe, Dongzhimen Wai, 6, Xiaojiejia, Beijing, 100027, China. http://www.jkb.com.cn/. Ed. Li Zhimin. **Dist. by:** China International Book Trading Corp, 35 Chegongzhuang Xilu, Haidian District, PO Box 399, Beijing 100044, China. TEL 86-10-68412045, FAX 86-10-68412023, cibtc@mail.cibtc.com.cn, http://www.cibtc.com.cn.

DIABETES DIALOGUE. *see* MEDICAL SCIENCES—Endocrinology

DIET & NUTRITION SOURCEBOOK. *see* NUTRITION AND DIETETICS

613.7 AUS ISSN 1039-3145
DIRECTION; a journal on the Alexander Technique. Text in English. 1984. irreg. free to members (effective 2008). adv. back issues avail.
Document type: *Journal, Trade.* **Description:** For teachers of the Alexander Technique. Each issue explores an application of the work.
Related titles: Online - full text ed.: free to members (effective 2008).
Published by: Direction Journal, PO Box 700, Highett, VIC 3190, Australia. TEL 61-4-1249-7460, info@directionjournal.com. Ed., Pub. Paul B Cook.

DISCOBOBUL. *see* SPORTS AND GAMES

610 DNK ISSN 0904-2369
DIT LAEGEMAGASIN/YOUR MEDICAL MAGAZINE; populaer laegevidenskab for hele familien. Text in Danish. 1987. 9/yr. adv. back issues avail. **Document type:** *Magazine, Consumer.* **Description:** Popular medical magazine for the family which aims at mediating factual medical information to the general public.

P

Formerly (1987): Patientmagasinet (0902-1795)
Related titles: Online - full text ed.: ISSN 1902-4673. 200?; ◆ Supplement to: Laegemagasinet. ISSN 0902-1787.
Published by: Scanpublisher A/S, Emiliekildevej 35, Klampenborg, 2930, Denmark. TEL 45-39-908000, FAX 45-39-908280, info@scanpublisher.dk, http://www.scanpublisher.dk. Eds. Jette Ingerslev, John Vaboe. Adv. contact Tina Lund Larsen. color page DKK 12,560; trim 179 x 231. Circ: 5,400.

613.7 USA
DOCTOM'S ONLINE SELF-CARE JOURNAL. Text in English. 1996. irreg.
Media: Online - full content.
Published by: Harvard Medical School, Center for Clinical Computing, Boston, MA 02115. Ed. Tom Ferguson.

DOE. *see* LIFESTYLE

613.7 CHN
DONGFANG QIGONG/ORIENTAL QIGONG. Text in Chinese. bi-m.
Published by: Beijing Qigong Yanjiuhui/Beijing Qigong Research Society, Gongren Tiyuguan-nei (Inside Beijing Workers Gym), Beijing, 100027, China. TEL 592961. Ed. Xu Yixing.

613.7 613.2 CHN ISSN 1004-5058
DONGFANG YANGSHENG. Text in Chinese. 1992. m. **Document type:** *Magazine, Consumer.*
Published by: Dongfang Yangsheng Jikanshe, 15, Longkun Lu, Zhonghong Dasha A-7, Haikou, 570125, China. TEL 86-898-66735750, FAX 86-898-66746950.

613.7 613.2 ITA ISSN 1973-7165
DOSSIER MEDICINA; rivista medica su benessere e salute. Text in Italian. 2007. q. **Document type:** *Magazine, Consumer.*
Related titles: Online - full text ed.: ISSN 1973-7173.
Published by: Redazione di Dossier Medicina (R D M), Via S Cresimata, Capagatti, PE 65012, Italy. FAX 39-085-9152202. Ed. Cristiana Zappoli.

DR. MARCUS LAUX'S NATURALLY WELL TODAY. *see* ALTERNATIVE MEDICINE

DUNAREA DE JOS UNIVERSITY OF GALATI. ANNALS. PHYSICAL EDUCATION AND SPORT MANAGEMENT, FASCICLE XV/ UNIVERSITATEA "DUNAREA DE JOS" GALATI. ANALELE. FASCICULA XV, EDUCATIE FIZICA SI MANAGEMENT IN SPORT. *see* SPORTS AND GAMES

E L D R MAGAZINE; celebrate aging!. *see* GERONTOLOGY AND GERIATRICS

613.7 FRA ISSN 2105-3014
E P S. LES CAHIERS. (Education Physique et Sportive) Text in French. 1989. s-a. **Document type:** *Magazine, Academic/Scholarly.*
Former titles (until 2008): Academie de Nantes. Les Cahiers E P S (Print) (1281-3605); (until 1996): E P S (1140-4914)
Media: Online - full text.
Indexed: SD.
Published by: (Academie de Nantes), Centre Regional de Documentation Pedagogique de Nantes, Chemin de l'Hebergement, Nantes, 44036, France. http://www.crdp-nantes.cndp.fr.

EATING WELL; where good taste meets good health. *see* FOOD AND FOOD INDUSTRIES

613.7 CHL ISSN 0716-0518
GV239
EDUCACION FISICA CHILE. Text in Spanish. 1929. q. **Document type:** *Journal, Academic/Scholarly.*
Former titles (until 1970): Revista Chilena de Educacion Fisica (0716-3428); (until 1950): Boletin de Educacion Fisica (0716-3436); (until 1031): Educacion Fisica (0716-3444)
Indexed: P30.
Published by: Universidad Metropolitana de Ciencias de la Educacion, Avenida Jose Pedro Alessandri 774, Nunoa, Santiago, Chile. TEL 56-2-412400, FAX 56-2-412723, prensa@umce.cl, http://www.umce.cl.

613.7 ARG ISSN 1514-0105
EDUCACION FISICA Y CIENCIA. Text in Spanish. 1995. a. **Document type:** *Journal, Academic/Scholarly.*
Published by: Universidad Nacional de la Plata, Facultad de Humanidades y Ciencias de la Educacion, Calle 48 entre 6 y 7, 1er Subsuelo, La Plata, Buenos Aires 1900, Argentina. TEL 54-221-4230125, ceciroz@.fahce.unlp.edu.ar, http://www.publicaciones.fahce.unlp.edu.ar.

613.7 HUN ISSN 1786-2434
EGESZSEGFEJLESZTES; educatio sanitaria. Text in Hungarian, English. 1959. bi-m. bk.rev. **Document type:** *Journal, Academic/Scholarly.*
Formerly (until 2004): Egeszsegneveles (0073-4004)
Published by: Orszagos Egeszsegfejlesztesi Intezet/National Institute for Health Development, Nagyvarad ter 2, Pf 433, Budapest, 1096, Hungary. TEL 36-1-4288272, FAX 36-1-4288273, titkarsag@oefi.hu, http://www.oefi.hu. Circ: 4,300.

613.7 USA
EHEALTH. Text in English. 19??. q. **Document type:** *Newsletter, Consumer.* **Description:** Contains articles and features on health and wellness.
Related titles: ◆ Online - full text ed.: eHealth.com.
Published by: McMurry, Inc., 1010 E Missouri Ave, Phoenix, AZ 85014. TEL 602-395-5850, 888-626-8779, FAX 602-395-5853, info@mcmurry.com, http://www.mcmurry.com.

613.7 USA
EHEALTH.COM. Text in English. 200?. q. **Document type:** *Newsletter, Consumer.*
Media: Online - full text. **Related titles:** ◆ Print ed.: eHealth.
Published by: McMurry, Inc., 1010 E Missouri Ave, Phoenix, AZ 85014. TEL 602-395-5850, 888-626-8779, FAX 602-395-5853, info@mcmurry.com, http://www.mcmurry.com.

ELEMENT. *see* NUTRITION AND DIETETICS

613.7 ESP ISSN 1989-8304
▼ **EMASF**; revista digital de educacion fisica. Text in Spanish. 2009. bi-m. free evening (effective 2010). abstr. Index. back issues avail. **Document type:** *Journal, Academic/Scholarly.*
Media: Online - full text.
Address: c/o Juan Carlos Munoz Diaz, Ronda de la Misericordia 5, Jaen, 23009, Spain. TEL 34-660-227717. Ed. Juan Carlos Munoz Diaz.

EMPLOYER HEALTH REGISTER. *see* OCCUPATIONAL HEALTH AND SAFETY

613.7 FRA ISSN 1620-6282
EN JEU. Text in French. 1952. 9/yr. (plus supplements). EUR 25 domestic; EUR 40 foreign (effective 2010). adv. bk.rev. **Document type:** *Magazine, Consumer.*
Former titles (until 2000): Informations U F O L E P - U S E P (0151-1890); (until 1966): U F O L E P Informations (1284-2052)
Published by: Union Francaise des Oeuvres Laiques d'Education Physique, 3 rue Recamier, Paris, Cedex 7 75341, France. TEL 33-1-43589770, FAX 33-1-43589774. Circ: 104,000.

368.382 BEL ISSN 0013-6964
EN MARCHE; le journal de la mutualite chretienne. Text in French. 1948. s-m. adv. bk.rev. charts; illus.; stat. **Description:** Discusses various aspects of health and relevant fields, such as insurance.
Published by: Alliance Nationale des Mutualites Chretiennes, Ch de Haecht 579, BP 40, Bruxelles, 1031, Belgium. TEL 32-2-246-4629, FAX 32-2-246-4630. Ed. Christian van Rompeal. Circ: 480,000.

613.7 ITA ISSN 1970-8610
ENCICLOPEDIA DELLA SALUTE. Text in Italian. 2006. w. **Document type:** *Magazine, Consumer.*
Published by: Poligrafici Editoriale (Subsidiary of: Monrif Group), Via Enrico Mattei 106, Bologna, BO 40138, Italy. TEL 39-051-6006111, FAX 39-051-6006266, http://www.monrifgroup.net.

ENERGY FOR WOMEN; how to energize your life. *see* WOMEN'S HEALTH

613.7 362.1 JPN ISSN 1342-078X
RA565.A1 CODEN: EHPMF7
➤ **ENVIRONMENTAL HEALTH AND PREVENTIVE MEDICINE.** Text in English. 1996. q. EUR 200, USD 266 combined subscription to institutions (print & online eds.) (effective 2012). reprint service avail. from PSC. **Document type:** *Journal, Academic/Scholarly.*
Description: Devoted to the publication of definitive studies including original papers, short communications and review articles, on human health sciences related to biological, physical, chemical, medical, psychosocial, and other various environmental factors.
Related titles: Online - full text ed.: ISSN 1347-4715 (from IngentaConnect).
Indexed: A22, A26, A34, A35, A36, A38, ASFA, AgBio, B21, B25, BIOSIS Prev, CA, CABA, D01, E01, E08, E12, EMBASE, ESPM, ExcerpMed, F08, F11, F12, GH, H&SSA, H16, H17, I11, INIS AtomInd, IndVet, LT, MycolAb, N02, N03, P20, P22, P30, P33, P37, P39, P48, P50, P52, P54, P56, PEI, PHN&I, PQC, PollutAb, R07, R08, R12, R13, RA&MP, RM&VM, RRTA, RiskAb, S09, S13, S16, SCOPUS, SD, T02, T05, ToxAb, TriticAb, VS, W10, W11.
—BLDSC (3791.486000), IE, Ingenta, INIST. **CCC.**
Published by: (Nihon Eisei Gakkai/Japanese Society for Hygiene), Springer Japan KK (Subsidiary of: Springer Science+Business Media), No 2 Funato Bldg, 1-11-11 Kudan-kita, Chiyoda-ku, Tokyo, 102-0073, Japan. TEL 81-3-68317000, FAX 81-3-68317001, orders@springer.jp, http://www.springer.jp. Ed. Akio Koizumi.

➤ **DIE ERSATZKASSE.** *see* SOCIAL SERVICES AND WELFARE

➤ **ERTONG YU JIANKANG/HEALTHY FOR BABY.** *see* CHILDREN AND YOUTH—About

613.7 MNG
ERUUL MEND/HEALTH. Text in Mongol. 1959. q. MNT 160.
Published by: Ministry of Health, Ulan Bator, Mongolia. TEL 976-1-321307, FAX 976-1-321278, TELEX 247 MINHE MH. Ed. T Ochirkhuu. Circ: 25,000.

613.7 PRT ISSN 0872-458X
ESPACO; revista de ciencia do desporto dos paises de lingua portuguesa. Text in Multiple languages. 1993. s-a. **Document type:** *Journal, Academic/Scholarly.*
Published by: Universidade do Porto, Faculdade de Ciencias do Desporto e de Educacao Fisica, Rua D Manuel II, Oporto, 4050-345, Portugal. TEL 351-22-6073500, FAX 351-22-6098736, up@up.pt, http://www.up.pt.

613.7 BRA ISSN 1808-8384
ESPECIAL MASSAGENS. Text in Portuguese. 2005. bi-m. BRL 12.90 newsstand/cover (effective 2007). **Document type:** *Magazine, Consumer.*
Published by: Digerati Comunicacao e Tecnologia Ltda., Rua Haddock Lobo 347, 12o andar, Sao Paulo, 01414-001, Brazil. TEL 55-11-32172600, FAX 55-11-32172617, http://www.digerati.com.br.

613.7 170 FRA ISSN 1765-4629
ETHIQUE & SANTE. Text in French. 2004. q. EUR 183 in Europe to institutions; EUR 166.50 in France to institutions; JPY 28,100 in Japan to institutions; USD 238 elsewhere to institutions (effective 2012). **Document type:** *Journal, Academic/Scholarly.*
Related titles: Online - full text ed.: ISSN 1769-695X (from ScienceDirect).
Indexed: SCOPUS.
—INIST. **CCC.**
Published by: Elsevier Masson (Subsidiary of: Elsevier Health Sciences), 62 Rue Camille Desmoulins, Issy les Moulineaux, Cedex 92442, France. TEL 33-1-71165500, infos@elsevier-masson.fr. Ed. A de Broca.

EUROPEAN INSTITUTE FOR T'AI CHI STUDIES. JOURNAL. *see* SPORTS AND GAMES

613.7 DEU
EVE; Ernaehrung - Vitalitaet - Erleben. Text in German. 2002. bi-m. adv. **Document type:** *Magazine, Consumer.*
Published by: Medienfabrik Guetersloh GmbH, Carl-Bertelsmann-Str 33, Guetersloh, 33311, Germany. TEL 49-5241-2348010, FAX 49-5241-2348022, kontakt@medienfabrik-gt.de, http://www.medienfabrik-gt.de. Circ: 450,000 (controlled).

613.7 613.2 NLD ISSN 1871-790X
EVEAN PLUS. Text in Dutch. 199?. 4/yr. EUR 19.50 (effective 2010).
Formerly (until 2004): Evean Zorg Plus (1572-2724)
Published by: Evean Ledenvereniging, Postbus 900, Meppel, 7940 KE, Netherlands. FAX 31-299-394444, ledenvereniging@evean.nl, http://www.evean.nl.

613.7 TWN
EVERGREEN MONTHLY. Text in Chinese. 1983. m. **Description:** Introduces health care knowledge.
Address: 11 Fl, 2 Pa Teh Rd, Sec3, Taipei, Taiwan. TEL 02-7731665, FAX 02-7416838. Circ: 140,000.

613.7 HKG
EXECUTIVE FITNESS NEWSLETTER. Text in Chinese. 1975. s-m. USD 95. **Document type:** *Newsletter.*
Formerly: Executive Fitness
Published by: Asia Letter Group, GPO Box 10874, Hong Kong, Hong Kong.

EXERCISE & HEALTH; the complete fitness guide for men. *see* MEN'S HEALTH

613.7 USA ISSN 0882-4657
EXERCISE FOR MEN ONLY. Variant title: Exercise. Text in English. 1985. bi-m. USD 31.15 domestic; USD 40.95 foreign; USD 5.99 newsstand/cover (effective 2004). adv. bk.rev. illus. reprints avail. **Document type:** *Magazine, Consumer.*
Published by: Chelo Publishing, Inc., 350 Fifth Ave, Ste 3323, New York, NY 10118. TEL 212-947-4322, FAX 212-563-4774, editorial@exercisegroup.com. Eds. Cheh N Low, Steve Downs. Pub., R&P Cheh N Low. Adv. contact Robert B Rose. B&W page USD 3,970, color page USD 5,290. Circ: 110,258 (paid).

613.7 USA ISSN 0748-3155
QP301
EXERCISE PHYSIOLOGY: CURRENT SELECTED RESEARCH. Text in English. 1985. a. index. back issues avail. **Description:** Research articles on various topics of exercise science and sports medicine.
—GNLM.
Published by: A M S Press, Inc., Brooklyn Navy Yard, 63 Flushing Ave, Bldg 292, Unit #221, Brooklyn, NY 11205. FAX 718-875-3800, queries@amspressinc.com, http://www.amspressinc.com.

EXERCISE STANDARDS AND MALPRACTICE REPORTER. *see* LAW

613.7 USA ISSN 1537-6656
EXPERIENCE LIFE. Text in English. 1998. 10/yr. USD 12.40 (effective 2004). adv. **Document type:** *Magazine, Consumer.*
Formerly (until 2001): Life Time Fitness Experience (1526-6117)
Published by: Life Time Fitness, 6442 City West Pkwy, Eden Prairie, MN 55344. TEL 952-947-0000, FAX 952-947-9137, tlink@lifetimefitness.com. Ed. Pilar Gerasimo. adv.: color page USD 14,300; trim 8.25 x 10.8125.

FACTA UNIVERSITATIS. SERIES PHYSICAL EDUCATION AND SPORT. *see* EDUCATION—Teaching Methods And Curriculum

613.7 TWN
FAMILIES MONTHLY. Text in Chinese. 1976. m. **Description:** Covers family life.
Address: 11th Fl, 2 Pa Teh Rd, Sec3, Taipei, Taiwan. TEL 02-7731665, FAX 02-7416838. Circ: 155,000.

613.7 CAN ISSN 0830-0305
FAMILY HEALTH. Text in English. 1985. bi-m. CAD 15.95 domestic; CAD 4.25 newsstand/cover (effective 2005). adv. **Document type:** *Magazine, Consumer.* **Description:** Informs and increases health consciousness of Albertans through professional information.
Related titles: Online - full text ed.
Indexed: A26, C03, CBCARef, CPerI, G08, I05, P19, P48, PQC, S23.
—CIS. **CCC.**
Address: PO Box 2421, Edmonton, AB T5J 2S6, Canada. TEL 780-429-5189, FAX 780-498-5661.

613.7 CAN ISSN 1920-8855
▼ **FAMILY HEALTH & LIFE.** Abbreviated title: F H L. Text in English. 2010. m. free to qualified personnel (effective 2010). adv. **Document type:** *Magazine, Consumer.* **Description:** Contains articles about health, fitness, body, mind and soul, natural healing and lifestyle.
Related titles: Online - full text ed.: free (effective 2010).
Published by: Agnitio Media Corporation, 69, 601 Shoreline Dr, Mississauga, ON L5B 4K7, Canada. TEL 905-486-0197, 877-644-1194, FAX 877-644-1194. Ed., Pub. Ian Khan. Circ: 5,000 (controlled).

613.7 USA
FAMILY PROGRAMMER. Text in English. m. free. **Description:** Information about the Step-In-Time fitness test and health and fitness awareness.
Formerly (until 1983): T I Source and Logo News
Published by: Bodylog Inc., 34 Maple Ave, Box 8, Armonk, NY 10504.

FARMACIST TIMES. *see* NUTRITION AND DIETETICS

FEMININ UND FIT. *see* WOMEN'S HEALTH

613.7 AUS
FERNWOOD; your healthy living magazine. Text in English. 2006. bi-m. adv. **Document type:** *Magazine, Consumer.* **Description:** Focuses on health and fitness and provides readers with the expert advice necessary to achieve and maintain a healthy, well-balanced lifestyle.
Formerly: Fernwood Essence
Published by: A C P Magazines Ltd. (Subsidiary of: P B L Media Pty Ltd.), 54-58 Park St, Sydney, NSW 2000, Australia. TEL 61-2-92828000, FAX 61-2-91263769, research@acpaction.com.au. Ed. Sandie McPhie. Adv. contact Cara Boatswain TEL 61-2-92639759. color page AUD 7,500; trim 230 x 275. Circ: 71,942.

613.7 BRA ISSN 0103-5150
➤ **FISIOTERAPIA EM MOVIMENTO.** Text in Portuguese. 1989. q.
Related titles: Online - full text ed.: ISSN 1980-5918. free (effective 2011).
Indexed: C06, CINAHL.
Published by: Pontificia Universidade Catolica do Parana, Rua Imaculada Conceicao 1155, Prado Velho, Curitiba, PR 80215-901, Brazil. TEL 55-41-32711515, webmstr@pucpr.br, http://www.pucpr.br. Circ: 1,000.

613.71 USA
FIT & FUN MAGAZINE. Text in English. m. Free to qualified subscribers. adv. **Document type:** *Magazine, Consumer.* **Description:** Provides information on style, health, leisure, events, recreation, dining, golf, biking and fitness for readers in the Chicago western and northwestern suburbs.
Related titles: Online - full text ed.
Published by: Jameson Publishing, Inc., P O Box 2517, Darien, IL 60561. TEL 630-515-1529, FAX 630-515-1062.

613.7 USA ISSN 1933-9305
THE FIT CHRISTIAN; a Christian health & fitness magazine. Text in English. 2004. bi-m. **Document type:** *Magazine, Consumer.*
Media: Online - full text.

Published by: His Work Christian Publishing, PO Box 5732, Ketchikan, AK 99901. TEL 206-274-8474, FAX 614-388-0664, hiswork@hisworkpub.com, http://www.hisworkpub.com/index.html. Pub. Angela J Perez.

613.7 790.1 DEU ISSN 0946-9680
FIT FOR FUN. Text in German. 1994. m. EUR 35.40; EUR 3.30 newsstand/cover (effective 2010). adv. **Document type:** *Magazine, Consumer.*
Related titles: Online - full text ed.
Published by: Verlagsgruppe Milchstrasse (Subsidiary of: Hubert Burda Media Holding GmbH & Co. KG), Mittelweg 177, Hamburg, 22786, Germany. TEL 49-40-41311310, FAX 49-40-41312015, abo@milchstrasse.de, http://www.milchstrasse.de. Ed. Willy Loderhose. Adv. contact Richard Kraus. Circ: 190,435 (paid).

613.7 ITA ISSN 1125-6737
FIT FOR FUN. Text in Italian. 1997. m. adv. illus. **Document type:** *Magazine, Consumer.* **Description:** Offers young, active, sports and fitness-minded readers articles and information on ways to keep fit as part of a fun lifestyle.
Published by: R C S Periodici (Subsidiary of: R C S Mediagroup), Via San Marco 21, Milan, 20121, Italy. TEL 39-2-25844111, FAX 39-2-25845444, info@periodici.rcs.it, http://www.rcsmediagroup.it/siti/periodici.php. Circ: 174,435 (paid). **Dist. in UK by:** Seymour Distribution Ltd, 86 Newman St, London W1T 3EX, United Kingdom. FAX 44-207-396-8002, enquiries@seymour.co.uk.

613.7 DNK ISSN 1903-3176
FIT LIVING. Text in Danish. 2008. m. DKK 499 (effective 2009). adv. **Document type:** *Magazine, Consumer.*
Published by: Egmont Magasiner A/S, Hellerupvej 51, Hellerup, 2900, Denmark. TEL 45-39-457500, FAX 45-39-457404, abo@egmontmagasiner.dk, http://www.egmont-magasiner.dk. Ed. Christina Boelling. Adv. contact Kristina Langberg. page DKK 29,000; trim 208 x 280.

FIT / LOW CARB. *see* NUTRITION AND DIETETICS

FIT PARENT; an active family lifestyle publication. *see* CHILDREN AND YOUTH—For

FIT PREGNANCY. *see* MEDICAL SCIENCES—Obstetrics And Gynecology

FIT PREGNANCY. *see* MEDICAL SCIENCES—Obstetrics And Gynecology

613.7 DEU ISSN 1611-8448
FIT UND FUENFZIG. Text in German. 1990. 6/yr. free newsstand/cover (effective 2011). adv. **Document type:** *Magazine, Consumer.* **Description:** Provides health and fitness tips and advice for those over 50 years of age.
Published by: Marken Verlag GmbH, Hansaring 97, Cologne, 50670, Germany. TEL 49-221-9574270, FAX 49-221-95742777, marken-info@markenverlag.de, http://www.markenverlag.de. Adv. contact Frank Krauthaeuser. page EUR 3,700; trim 148 x 210. Circ: 50,000 (paid and controlled).

613.7 USA ISSN 1932-8842
FIT YOGA. Text in English. 1982. 8/yr. USD 19.95 domestic; USD 34.95 foreign (effective 2008). adv. illus. back issues avail.; reprints avail. **Document type:** *Magazine, Consumer.* **Description:** Guide for exercising women who need continuous motivation and support.
Former titles (until 2005): Fit (1082-5665); (until 1995): New Body (0732-4782)
Published by: Goodman Media Group, Inc., 250 W 57th St, Ste 710, New York, NY 10107. TEL 212-262-2247, FAX 212-400-8620. Ed. Rita Trieger TEL 212-262-2247 ext 303. Pub. Jason Goodman TEL 212-262-2247 ext 307. Adv. contact Brian Kelly TEL 212-262-2247 ext 308. Circ: 25,000 (paid).

613.7 AUS
FITLINK AUSTRALIA. Text in English. 1987. q. **Document type:** *Magazine, Trade.*
Address: 124 Phillip Cresent, Barellan Point, QLD 4306, Australia. TEL 300-557-637, admin@onfit.com.au, http://www.fitlink.com.au/.

FITNESS. *see* WOMEN'S HEALTH

613.04244 USA ISSN 1060-9237
GV482
FITNESS; mind - body - spirit for women. Text in English. 1983. 11/yr. USD 16.97 for 2 yrs. domestic; USD 29.97 in Canada (effective 2009). adv. illus. reprints avail. **Document type:** *Magazine, Consumer.* **Description:** Covers beauty and fashion, health, fitness and wellness for women.
Formerly (until 1992): Family Circle's Fitness Now
Related titles: Online - full text ed.
Indexed: G06, G07, G08, I05.
Published by: Meredith Corporation, 125 Park Ave, 25th Fl, New York, NY 10017. TEL 212-557-6600, FAX 212-455-1345, patrick.taylor@meredith.com, http://www.meredith.com. Eds. Betty Wong, Denise Brodey. Pub. Lee Slattery TEL 212-551-6947. adv.: B&W page USD 108,440, color page USD 138,200; trim 7.875 x 10.5. Circ: 1,574,067 (paid).

613.082 CHN
FITNESS. Text in Chinese. 2003. m. **Document type:** *Magazine, Consumer.*
Published by: G + J - C L I P Publishing Consulting Co. Ltd. (Subsidiary of: Gruner + Jahr AG & Co), Commercial Office Bldg, 4th Fl, No 8 Gongyuan West St, Jianguomennei, Dongcheng District, Beijing, 100005, China. TEL 86-10-65235020, FAX 86-10-65235021, kohl.wolfgang@gjclip.com.cn. Circ: 50,000 (controlled).

613.7 BRA ISSN 1519-9088
FITNESS & PERFORMANCE JOURNAL. Text in Portuguese, English, Spanish. 2001. bi-m. BRL 115 to individual members; BRL 200 to institutional members (effective 2009). **Document type:** *Journal, Academic/Scholarly.*
Related titles: Online - full text ed.: ISSN 1676-5133. 2000.
Indexed: A01, C01, C06, C07, CA, F03, F04, FS&TA, G09, P02, P10, P48, P53, P54, PEI, PQC, SD, T02.
Published by: Colegio Brasileiro de Atividade Fisica, Saude e Esporte, Rua Andre Rocha, 3215, Salas 205 e 207, Jacarepagua, Rio de Janeiro, RJ, Brazil. TEL 55-21-24264309, FAX 55-21-24415340, http://www.cobrase.org.br/. Ed. Jose Fernandes Filho.

613.7 USA ISSN 1549-9030
FITNESS AND PHYSIQUE. Text in English. 2003. s-a. USD 8 (effective 2007). back issues avail. **Document type:** *Magazine, Consumer.*
Formerly (until 2004): Physique Competitor Magazine (1549-9022)
Published by: Fitness & Physique Magazine, PO Box 1006, Bryans Road, MD 20616. TEL 301-375-9273, info@FPmagOnline.com, http://www.physiquecompetitor.com/index.htm.

613.7 USA ISSN 1552-9118
FITNESS AND WELLNESS BUSINESS WEEK. Text in English. 2004. w. USD 2,295 in US & Canada; USD 2,495 elsewhere; USD 2,525 combined subscription in US & Canada (print & online eds.); USD 2,755 combined subscription elsewhere (print & online eds.) (effective 2008). back issues avail. **Document type:** *Newsletter, Trade.*
Related titles: E-mail ed.; Online - full text ed.: ISSN 1552-9126. USD 2,295 combined subscription (online & email eds.); single user (effective 2008).
Indexed: A15, ABIn, B16, H13, P10, P20, P21, P48, P51, P53, P54, PQC.
Published by: NewsRx, 2727 Paces Ferry Rd SE, Ste 2-440, Atlanta, GA 30339. TEL 770-435-8286, 800-726-4550, FAX 770-435-6800, pressrelease@newsrx.com, http://www.newsrx.com. Pub. Susan Hasty TEL 770-507-7777.

FITNESS EXPERT. *see* SPORTS AND GAMES

613.7 613.04244 GBR ISSN 2046-0511
▼ **FITNESS FOR WOMEN.** Text in English. 2011. m. GBP 1.99 per issue (effective 2011). adv. back issues avail. **Document type:** *Magazine, Consumer.*
Published by: Kelsey Publishing Ltd., Cudham Tithe Barn, Berry's Hill, Cudham, Kent TN16 3AG, United Kingdom. TEL 44-1959-541444, FAX 44-1959-541400, info@kelsey.co.uk, http://www.kelsey.co.uk.

613.7 658 USA ISSN 0882-0481
FITNESS MANAGEMENT. Text in English. m. free domestic to qualified personnel; USD 15 in Canada; USD 40 elsewhere (effective 2004). adv. back issues avail. **Document type:** *Magazine, Trade.* **Description:** Presents scientific and professional health fitness and management information in non-technical language to owners, managers and pro shop buyers of commerical community and corporate physical fitness centers.
Indexed: P34, PEI, SD, SportS, T02.
—BLDSC (3948.229200), IE, Ingenta.
Published by: Leisure Publications, Inc., 4160 Wilshire Blvd, Los Angeles, CA 90010. TEL 323-964-4800, FAX 323 964-4835. Ed. Rhodes Tucker Ronale. Pub. Chris Ballard. Adv. contact Scott Christie. B&W page USD 3,985, color page USD 4,960. Circ: 25,000.

613.7 658 DEU
FITNESS MANAGEMENT INTERNATIONAL. Text in German. 1995. bi-m. EUR 37 domestic; EUR 42 foreign; EUR 6 newsstand/cover (effective 2007). adv. bk.rev. back issues avail. **Document type:** *Magazine, Trade.*
Address: Wohlersweg 36, Hamburg, 21079, Germany. TEL 49-40-3009450, FAX 49-40-30096990. Ed., R&P, Adv. contact Birgit Schwarze TEL 49-40-3009450. Pubs. Birgit Schwarze TEL 49-40-3009450, Refit Kamberovic. color page EUR 2,300; trim 210 x 297. Circ: 9,500 (paid).

613.7 USA
FITNESS PLUS MAGAZINE; health and fitness Arizona style. Text in English. m.
Published by: Fitness Plus Inc, 1402 N Miller Rd, Scottsdale, AZ 85257. TEL 480-945-9402, FAX 480-945-2598, fitnesplus@aol.com. Ed. Joan M Elam. Pub. Lori Lippman. Circ: 40,000.

613.7 USA ISSN 1095-4929
FITNESS PRODUCT NEWS; trends and solutions for facility management. Text in English. 6/yr. **Description:** Serving the field of athletic-health clubs, fitness centers, gymnasiums, YMCA-YWCA, rehabilitation-health care centers, sports medicine facilities and others allied to the field.
Published by: Adams Business Media, 2101 S Arlington Heights Rd, Ste 150, Arlington Heights, IL 60005-4142. http://www.abm.net.

613.7 USA ISSN 1543-8406
FITNESS RX FOR MEN. Text in English. 2003. bi-m. USD 17.95 (effective 2003).
Published by: Advanced Research Press, Inc., 690 Route 25A, Setauket, NY 11733. TEL 631-751-9696, 800-653-1151, FAX 631-751-9699, http://www.advancedresearchpress.com/. Ed. Steve Blechman. Pubs. Elyse Blechman, Steve Blechman. Adv. contact Angela Frizalone.

613.7 NZL ISSN 1175-8430
FITNESSLIFE. Text in English. 2002. bi-m. NZD 40 domestic; NZD 79 in Australia; NZD 143.70 elsewhere (effective 2008). adv. **Document type:** *Magazine, Consumer.* **Description:** Provides encouragement and ideas to help individuals reach their fitness and life goals.
Incorporates (2003-2005): Kids Life (1176-4414)
Published by: Tania Greig, Ed. & Pub., Dominion Rd, PO Box 56709, Auckland, New Zealand. TEL 64-9-6230050, FAX 64-9-6230059. Ed., Pub., Adv. contact Tania Greig.

613.7 USA
FITNESSLINK. Text in English. 1996. d.
Published by: FitnessLink Inc., PO Box 213, Eugene, OR 97440. TEL 541-543-0566, FAX 541-242-3577, jacqui@fitnesslinkinc.com, http://fitnesslinkinc.com.

613.7 RUS
➤ **FIZICHESKAYA KUL'TURA: OBRAZOVANIE, TRENIROVKA, VOSPITANIE.** Text in Russian. 1996. q. USD 110 foreign (effective 2007). **Document type:** *Journal, Academic/Scholarly.*
Published by: Rossiiskia Gosudarstvennaya Akademiya Fizicheskoi Kul'tury/Russian State Academy of Physical Culture, Sirenevyi bulv 4, Moscow, 105122, Russian Federation. fkvot@infosport.ru. Ed. V V Kuzin. **Dist. by:** East View Information Services, 10601 Wayzata Blvd, Minneapolis, MN 55305. TEL 952-252-1201, 800-477-1005, FAX 952-252-1202, info@eastview.com, http://www.eastview.com.

613.7 RUS ISSN 0130-5581
FIZICHESKAYA KUL'TURA V SHKOLE; nauchno-metodicheskii zhurnal. Text in Russian. 1958. bi-m. USD 152 foreign (effective 2007). **Document type:** *Journal, Academic/Scholarly.*
—East View.
Published by: Izdatel'stvo Shkola Press, ul Rustaveli, dom 10, korpus 3, Moscow, 127254, Russian Federation. marketing@schoolpress.ru. Ed. A V Komarov. Circ: 16,000. **Dist. by:** East View Information Services, 10601 Wayzata Blvd, Minneapolis, MN 55305. TEL 952-252-1201, 800-477-1005, FAX 952-252-1202, info@eastview.com, http://www.eastview.com.

613.7 378 RUS ISSN 1609-3143
FIZICHESKOE OBRAZOVANIE V VUZAKH. Text in Russian. 1997. q. USD 217 foreign (effective 2007). **Document type:** *Journal, Academic/Scholarly.*
Indexed: RefZh.
—East View.
Published by: Moskovskoe Fizicheskoe Obshchestvo, Leninskii pr-t 53, Moscow, 117924, Russian Federation. TEL 7-095-1326651, FAX 7-095-1357995. Ed. O N Krokhin. **Dist. by:** East View Information Services, 10601 Wayzata Blvd, Minneapolis, MN 55305. TEL 952-252-1201, 800-477-1005, FAX 952-252-1202, info@eastview.com, http://www.eastview.com.

613.7 GBR ISSN 0955-1212
FLEX. Text in English. 1986. m. USD 34.97 domestic; USD 51.97 in Canada; USD 83.97 elsewhere (effective 2009). adv. illus. **Document type:** *Magazine, Consumer.* **Description:** Provides information about body building.
Related titles: Online - full text ed.
Published by: Weider Publishing, 10 Windsor Ct, Clarence Dr, Harrogate, N Yorks HG1 2PE, United Kingdom. TEL 44-1423-504516, FAX 44-1423-561494, mailorder@weideruk.com. Eds. Michael Berg, Allan Donnelly. Adv. contact Mike McErlane TEL 818-226-0158. color page USD 12,300, B&W page USD 9,900; trim 7.75 x 10.5. Circ: 110,000. **Dist. by:** Comag.

613.7 USA ISSN 8750-8915
FLEX; the voice of champions. Variant title: Joe Weider's Flex. Text in English. 1983. m. USD 34.97 domestic; USD 51.97 in Canada; USD 83.97 elsewhere; USD 6.99 newsstand/cover (effective 2009). adv. illus. back issues avail. **Document type:** *Magazine, Consumer.* **Description:** Designed to be the ultimate resource for hardcore bodybuilding industry.
Related titles: Online - full text ed.; Polish ed.: Flex (Polish Edition). ISSN 1428-5487.
Indexed: A22, A26, G05, G06, G07, G08, H03, H11, H12, I05, PEI, SD, T02.
—Ingenta.
Published by: A M I - Weider Publications (Subsidiary of: American Media, Inc.), 21100 Erwin St, Woodland Hills, CA 91367. TEL 818-595-0589, 800-998-0731, FAX 818-884-6910, http://www.americanmediainc.com. Ed. Bolster Mary. adv.: B&W page USD 9,900, color page USD 12,300; trim 7.75 x 10.5. Circ: 110,000. **Subscr. to:** PO Box 37210, Boone, IA 50037.

FOCUS ON FEDERAL EMPLOYEE WORK/LIFE AND WELLNESS PROGRAMS. *see* OCCUPATIONAL HEALTH AND SAFETY

FODOR'S HEALTHY ESCAPES. *see* TRAVEL AND TOURISM

FORMA. *see* WOMEN'S HEALTH

FREUNDIN WELLFIT. *see* WOMEN'S HEALTH

A FRIEND INDEED; for women in the prime of life. *see* WOMEN'S INTERESTS

FRONTIERS OF HEALTH SERVICES MANAGEMENT. *see* HEALTH FACILITIES AND ADMINISTRATION

613.7 CHE ISSN 1422-0970
FUER UNS VITA SANA; Magazin fuer Dialog und Gesundheit. Text in German. 1997. 10/yr. CHF 49.50; CHF 65 in Europe; CHF 82 elsewhere; CHF 5.80 newsstand/cover (effective 2000). adv. **Document type:** *Magazine, Consumer.* **Description:** Contains information, tips and products on healthy lifestyles.
Formed by the merger of (1975-1997): Vita Sana Magazin (1421-4334); (1978-1997): Fuer Uns (1422-111X)
Published by: Vita Sana Verlag AG, Postfach 468, Breganzona, 6932, Switzerland. TEL 41-91-9681110, FAX 41-91-9667183. Adv. contact Markus Mettler. Circ: 102,500 (controlled).

FUKUOKA KYOIKU DAIGAKU KIYO. DAI 5-BUNSATSU, GEIJUTSU, HOKEN TAIIKU, KASEIKA-HEN/FUKUOKA UNIVERSITY OF EDUCATION. BULLETIN. PART V, ARTS, HEALTH AND PHYSICAL EDUCATION AND HOME ECONOMICS. *see* EDUCATION

613.7 GBR ISSN 2046-0589
FUTURE FITNESS; sport and fitness for today's youth. Text in English. 2007. m. GBP 35 domestic; GBP 45 foreign; GBP 2.75 per issue; free to qualified personnel (effective 2011). adv. **Document type:** *Magazine, Trade.* **Description:** Packed with breaking news, features and expert comment and analysis from the burgeoning young fitness market.
Published by: Wharncliffe Publishing Ltd., 47 Church St, Barnsley, S Yorkshire S70 2AS, United Kingdom. TEL 44-1226-734639, FAX 44-1226-734478, editorial@wharncliffepublishing.co.uk, http://www.wharncliffepublishing.co.uk. Adv. contact Tony Barry TEL 44-1226-734333.

613.7 USA
➤ **THE G A H P E R D JOURNAL.** Text in English. 1968. 3/yr. USD 30 to institutions; USD 12 newsstand/cover (effective 2010). **Document type:** *Journal, Academic/Scholarly.* **Description:** Addresses critical issues of daily physical education for K-12, nutrition education, and school wellness policies to combat the overweight and obesity epidemic in children.
Published by: Georgia Association for Health, Physical Education, Recreation and Dance, 520 Greenridge Circle, Stone Mountain, GA 30083. Ed. Mike Tenoschok.

613.7 IRN ISSN 1735-4242
GAM/HA-YI TUSIAH DAR AMUZISH-I PIZISHKI/STRIDES IN DEVELOPMENT OF MEDICAL EDUCATION. Text in Persian, Modern. 2004. s-a. **Document type:** *Journal, Academic/Scholarly.*
Related titles: Online - full text ed.: ISSN 2008-272X. free (effective 2011).
Published by: Kerman University of Medical Sciences/Danishgah-i Ulum-i Pizishki, Jahad Blvd., Kerman, Iran. TEL 98-341-2263725, FAX 98-341-2263725, http://www.kmu.ac.ir.

615.85 USA ISSN 2161-783X
▼ ➤ **GAMES FOR HEALTH**; research, development, and clinical applications. Text in English. 2012. bi-m. USD 1,445 combined subscription domestic (print & online eds.); USD 1,661 combined subscription foreign (print & online eds.) (effective 2012). adv. **Document type:** *Journal, Academic/Scholarly.* **Description:** Details the development, use, and applications of game technology for improving physical and mental health and well-being.

P

Related titles: Online - full text ed.: ISSN 2161-7856. USD 1,295 (effective 2012).
Published by: Mary Ann Liebert, Inc. Publishers, 140 Huguenot St, 3rd Fl, New Rochelle, NY 10801. TEL 914-740-2100, FAX 914-740-2101, 800-654-3237, info@liebertpub.com. Ed. Bill Ferguson TEL 914-740-2246. Adv. contact Harriet I Matysko TEL 914-740-2182.

613.7 POL ISSN 1232-1907
GAZETA O ZDROWIU I URODZIE. Text in Polish. 1993. irreg.
Related titles: ◆ Supplement to: Gazeta Wyborcza. ISSN 0860-908X.
Published by: Agora S.A., ul Czerska 8/10, Warsaw, 00732, Poland. TEL 48-22-6994301, FAX 48-22-6994603, http://www.agora.pl.

GEEZERJOCK. *see* SPORTS AND GAMES

362.1 DEU
GESUND UND VITAL. Text in German. m. EUR 36.50 (effective 2006). adv. **Document type:** *Magazine, Consumer.*
Published by: Media Dialog Verlag, Am Bahndamm 2, Ortenberg, 63683, Germany. TEL 49-6041-823390, FAX 49-6041-8233920, info@media-dialog.com, http://www.media-dialog.com. adv.: page EUR 8,000. Circ: 280,000 (controlled).

362.1 DEU ISSN 0942-3427
GESUNDE MEDIZIN; das Magazin fuer mehr Wohlbefinden. Text in German. 1989. m. EUR 2 newsstand/cover (effective 2010). adv. **Document type:** *Magazine, Consumer.*
Published by: P A C S Gesellschaft fuer Promotion, Advertising & Communication Services mbH, Gewerbestr 9, Staufen, 79219, Germany. TEL 49-7633-982007, FAX 49-7633-982060, pacs@pacs-online.com, http://www.pacs-online.com. Ed. Nicole Franke-Gricksch. Adv. contact Thomas Tritschler.

613 AUT ISSN 0250-3689
GESUNDHEIT; das Magazin fuer Lebensqualitaet. Text in German. 1970. 11/yr. EUR 33.60 domestic; EUR 42.80 foreign (effective 2007). adv. bk.rev. **Document type:** *Magazine, Consumer.*
Published by: Verlag Gesundheit GmbH, Achauerstr 49a, Leopoldsdorf, W 2335, Austria. TEL 43-2235-447450, FAX 43-2235-44745213, gesundheit@gesundheit.co.at. Ed. Susanna Sklenar. Pub. Ilse Koenigstetter. Adv. contact Elisabeth Plenk. Circ: 70,000.

613 DEU ISSN 0935-7742
GESUNDHEIT (BADEN-BADEN). Text in German. 1949. q. free membership (effective 2008). adv. bk.rev. illus. **Document type:** *Magazine, Consumer.*
Former titles (until 1988): Gesundheit in Betrieb und Familie (0016-9269); (until 1969): Gesundheit (0935-7734)
Related titles: Microform ed.: (from PQC).
Published by: Agis Verlag GmbH, Ooser Luisenstr 23, Baden-Baden, 76532, Germany. TEL 49-7221-95750, FAX 49-7221-66810, info@agis-verlag.de, http://www.agis-verlag.de. Ed. Karin Grochowiak. Adv. contact Wolfgang Jacob. Circ: 2,700,000.

GESUNDHEIT IN DER EINEN WELT; Nachrichten aus der Aerzlichen Mission. *see* RELIGIONS AND THEOLOGY

613.7 CHE ISSN 1423-5536
GESUNDHEIT-SPRECHSTUNDE. Text in German. 1998. fortn. CHF 3.80 newsstand/cover (effective 2009). adv. **Document type:** *Magazine, Consumer.* **Description:** Presents articles and information on leading and maintaining a healthy and active lifestyle.
Published by: Ringier AG, Dufourstr 49, Zuerich, 8008, Switzerland. TEL 41-44-2596262, FAX 41-44-2598665, info@ringier.ch, http://www.ringier.ch. Ed. Regula Kaech. adv.: page CHF 13,125; trim 224 x 298. Circ: 86,952 (paid).

GESUNDHEIT UND ERZIEHUNG FUER MEIN KIND; Der aktuelle Ratgeber fuer die gesunde Entwicklung Ihres Kindes im Alter von 0 bis 6 Jahren. *see* CHILDREN AND YOUTH—About

613 CHE ISSN 0016-9285
GESUNDHEITSNACHRICHTEN. Text in German. 1944. 11/yr. CHF 36 (effective 2007). adv. bk.rev. **Document type:** *Newsletter, Consumer.*
Published by: Verlag A. Vogel, Roggwil, 9325, Switzerland. TEL 41-71-4546161, FAX 41-71-4546162, c.umbricht@verlag-avogel.ch. Ed. Claudia Rawer. Circ: 65,000.

613.7 DEU
GESUNDHEITSPROFI. Text in German. 1995. m. EUR 112 domestic; EUR 138 foreign (effective 2011). adv. **Document type:** *Magazine, Trade.*
Published by: Verlag Otto Sternefeld GmbH, Oberkasseler Str 100, Duesseldorf, 40545, Germany. TEL 49-211-577080, FAX 49-211-5770812, sk.vertrieb@sternefeld.de, http://www.sternefeld.de. Circ: 4,800 (paid and controlled).

613.7 DEU
GESUNDHEITSPROFI DIREKT. Text in German. 1995. s-a. included into subsc. to GesundheitsProfi. adv. **Document type:** *Magazine, Trade.*
Published by: Verlag Otto Sternefeld GmbH, Oberkasseler Str 100, Duesseldorf, 40545, Germany. TEL 49-211-577080, FAX 49-211-5770812, sk.vertrieb@sternefeld.de. adv.: B&W page EUR 2,500, color page EUR 3,580. Circ: 30,000 (controlled).

613.7 AUT
DER GEWICHTHEBER. Text in German. 1954. 6/yr. EUR 24 domestic; EUR 33 foreign (effective 2005). **Document type:** *Magazine, Consumer.*
Formerly: Kraftsportmagazin Gewichtheben
Related titles: Diskette ed.
Published by: Oesterreichischer Gewichtheberverband, Hauffgasse 2-1-10, Vienna, W 1112, Austria. TEL 43-1-7497061, FAX 43-1-7497062, oegv@aon.at, http://www.gewichtheben.net. Ed. Gerhard Peya.

614 RUS ISSN 0016-9900
CODEN: GISAAA
GIGIENA I SANITARIYA/HYGIENE AND SANITATION. Text in Russian; Summaries in English. 1922. bi-m. USD 138 foreign (effective 2005). adv. bk.rev.; Website rev. bibl. index. reprints avail. **Document type:** *Journal, Academic/Scholarly.* **Description:** Publishes papers on all the branches of hygienic science and sanitary practice.
Indexed: A22, A34, A35, A36, A37, A38, AgBio, B21, B25, BIOSIS Prev, BP, C25, CABA, CIN, CISA, ChemAb, ChemTitl, D01, DentInd, E12, EMBASE, ESPM, ExcerpMed, F08, F09, F12, FCA, FS&TA, GH, H16, H17, I10, I11, IndMed, IndVet, LT, MEDLINE, MycolAb, N02, N03, N04, OR, P30, P32, P33, P37, P38, P39, P40, PGrRegA, PHN&I, PST, R07, R08, R10, R13, RA&MP, RM&VM, RRTA, Reac, RefZh, S13, S16, SCOPUS, SoyAb, T05, ToxAb, TriticAb, VS, W10, W11, WBSS.
—BLDSC (0048.000000), CASDDS, East View, GNLM, IE, Infotrieve, Ingenta, INIST, Linda Hall. **CCC.**
Published by: Izdatel'stvo Meditsina/Meditsina Publishers, ul B Pirogovskaya, d 2, str 5, Moscow, 119435, Russian Federation. TEL 7-095-2483324, meditsina@mtu-net.ru, http://www.medlit.ru. Ed. Gennadii I Rumyantsev. Pub. A M Stochik. R&P V Sinitsina. Adv. contact O A Fadeeva TEL 7-095-923-51-40. Circ: 2,500. **Dist. by:** M K - Periodica, ul Gilyarovskogo 39, Moscow 129110, Russian Federation. TEL 7-095-2845008, FAX 7-095-2813798, info@periodicals.ru, http://www.mkniga.ru.

GLOBAL HEALTH DIRECTORY. *see* MEDICAL SCIENCES

GLOBAL HEALTH PROMOTION/PROMOTION ET EDUCATION. *see* PUBLIC HEALTH AND SAFETY

613.7 CAN ISSN 1702-8396
GLOW. Text in English. 1984. bi-m. CAD 3.50 newsstand/cover (effective 2007). adv. **Document type:** *Magazine, Consumer.*
Former titles (until 2002): Images (1204-2765); (until 1995): Canadian Images (1204-265X); (until 1994): Canadian Images, Beauty, Fashion & Style (1196-1007); (until 1993): Images (0826-5127)
Related titles: Online - full text ed.
Indexed: C03, CBCARef, GW, PQC.
Published by: Rogers Publishing Ltd./Les Editions Rogers Limitee, One Mount Pleasant Rd, 8th Fl, Toronto, ON M4Y 2Y5, Canada. TEL 416-764-2866, FAX 416-764-2863, http://www.rogerspublishing.ca. adv.: B&W page CAD 19,940; trim 200 x 273. Circ: 430,000.

613.7 613.2 ITA ISSN 2036-9638
▼ **GOCCE DI BENESSERE.** Text in Italian. 2010. w. **Document type:** *Magazine, Consumer.*
Published by: Poligrafici Editoriale (Subsidiary of: Monrif Group), Via Enrico Mattei 106, Bologna, BO 40138, Italy. TEL 39-051-6006111, FAX 39-051-6006266, http://www.monrifgroup.net.

613.7 USA ISSN 1933-7752
GOING BONKERS?; the self-help magazine with a sense of humor. Text in English. 2007. q. USD 24.95 in US & Canada; USD 54.95 elsewhere; USD 6.95 newsstand/cover domestic; USD 8.95 newsstand/cover in Canada (effective 2008). illus. **Document type:** *Magazine, Consumer.* **Description:** Provides educational, entertaining and motivational information on self-help.
Indexed: C11, G05, G06, G07, I05.
Published by: Going Bonkers, LLC., 2210 Highland Knolls, PO Box 6190, Katy, TX 77450. TEL 281-492-1605, FAX 281-754-4458. Ed. J Carol Pereyra.

▼ **GOLF & WELLNESS.** *see* SPORTS AND GAMES—Ball Games

GOLF FITNESS. *see* SPORTS AND GAMES—Ball Games

613.7 AUS
GOOD HEALTH & MEDICINE. Text in English. 2007. m. AUD 54.95 domestic; AUD 88.95 in New Zealand; AUD 109.95 elsewhere; AUD 6.70 newsstand/cover (effective 2008). adv. **Document type:** *Magazine, Consumer.* **Description:** Covers the latest news and views in traditional/alternative medicine, emotional health, beauty, nutrition, weight management, body image and fitness.
Formerly: Good Medicine (1449-6194)
Published by: A C P Magazines Ltd. (Subsidiary of: P B L Media Pty Ltd.), 54-58 Park St, Sydney, NSW 2000, Australia. TEL 61-2-92828000, FAX 61-2-91263769, research@acpaction.com.au, http://www.acp.com.au. Ed. Catherine Marshall. Adv. contact Simone Aquilina TEL 61-2-92828420. color page AUD 9,625; trim 205 x 275. Circ: 65,099. **Subscr. to:** Magshop, Reply Paid 4967, Sydney, NSW 2001, Australia. TEL 61-2-136116, subs@magstore.com.au, http://shop.magstore.com.au.

GOVERNMENT RECREATION & FITNESS. *see* LEISURE AND RECREATION

613.7 613.2 ITA ISSN 2036-6116
▼ **IL GRANDE ATLANTE DELLA SALUTE.** Text in Italian. 2009. w. **Document type:** *Magazine, Consumer.*
Published by: Poligrafici Editoriale (Subsidiary of: Monrif Group), Via Enrico Mattei 106, Bologna, BO 40138, Italy. TEL 39-051-6006111, FAX 39-051-6006266, http://www.monrifgroup.net.

GREAT ACTIVITIES. *see* EDUCATION

613.194 GBR
THE GROVE. Text in English. 1949. 2/yr. adv. bk.rev. **Document type:** *Bulletin, Consumer.* **Description:** Information on facilities for naturist recreation in Great Britain and elsewhere.
Published by: Naturist Foundation, Naturist Headquarters, Orpington, Kent BR5 4ET, United Kingdom. marsha.majors@hotmail.co.uk, http://www.naturistfoundation.org/. Ed. Peter Fallows. R&P, Adv. contact Christine Ashford. Circ: 750.

GUANGZHOU TIYU XUEYUAN XUEBAO/GUANGZHOU PHYSICAL EDUCATION INSTITUTE. JOURNAL. *see* EDUCATION

613 ESP ISSN 1888-0991
GUIA PREVENIR SALUD. Text in Spanish. 1994. m. adv. **Document type:** *Magazine, Consumer.* **Description:** Provides practical information and advice on health and nutrition.
Formerly (until 2006): Guia Prevenir (1575-2623)
Published by: Globus Comunicacion (Subsidiary of: Bonnier AB), Covarrubias 1, Madrid, 28010, Spain. TEL 34-91-4471202, FAX 34-91-4471043, txhdez@globuscom.es, http://www.globuscom.es. Ed. Ricardo Lopez. adv.: color page EUR 3,880; trim 13.5 x 18.7.

GUIDE TO YOGA TEACHERS AND CLASSES. *see* NEW AGE PUBLICATIONS

613.7 CHN ISSN 1001-1226
GUOWAI YIXUE (WEISHENGXUE FENCE)/FOREIGN MEDICAL SCIENCES (HYGIENICS). Text in Chinese. 1974. bi-m. USD 24.60 (effective 2009). back issues avail. **Document type:** *Journal, Academic/Scholarly.*
Related titles: Online - full text ed.
—East View.
Published by: Weishengbu, Yixue Xinxi Gongzuo Guanli Weiyuanhui, 29, Nanwei Lu, Beijing, 100050, China. TEL 86-10-63028739. **Dist. by:** China International Book Trading Corp, 35 Chegongzhuang Xilu, Haidian District, PO Box 399, Beijing 100044, China. TEL 86-10-68412045, FAX 86-10-68412023, cibtc@mail.cibtc.com.cn, http://www.cibtc.com.cn.

GURL. *see* WOMEN'S INTERESTS

613.7 USA
H E - XTRA. Text in English. 19??. s-a. free to members (effective 2010). adv. **Document type:** *Newsletter, Trade.* **Description:** Seeks to advance health by encouraging, supporting, and assisting health professionals concerned with health promotion through education and other systematic strategies.
Published by: American Association for Health Education, 1900 Association Dr, Reston, VA 20191. TEL 703-476-3400, 800-213-7193, aahe@aahperd.org. Ed. Linda M Moore TEL 703-476-3437.

613.7 SWE ISSN 2000-4354
▼ **HAELSA & VETENSKAP.** Text in Swedish. 2009. q. SEK 150 (effective 2010). adv. **Document type:** *Magazine, Consumer.*
Related titles: Online - full text ed.
Published by: Laekartidningen Foerlag AB, Oester Malmsgatan 40, PO Box 5603, Stockholm, 11486, Sweden. TEL 46-8-7903530, FAX 46-8-207435. Ed. Karin Bergqvist. Adv. contact Ulfa Jansson TEL 46-8-7903547. Circ: 33,000 (controlled).

HARMONIE & BIEN-ETRE. *see* PSYCHOLOGY

051 USA ISSN 1052-1577
RC81.A1 CODEN: HHLEET
THE HARVARD HEALTH LETTER. Text in English. 1975. m. USD 29 combined subscription (print & online eds.) (effective 2009). illus. index. back issues avail.; reprints avail. **Document type:** *Newsletter, Consumer.* **Description:** Provides medical research articles and advice necessary for a healthy life.
Formerly (until 1990): Harvard Medical School Health Letter (0161-7486)
Related titles: Online - full text ed.: ISSN 1557-5616. USD 25 (effective 2009).
Indexed: A01, A02, A03, A08, A11, A22, A26, Agr, B04, BRD, BiolDig, C05, C06, C07, C08, C11, C12, CA, CHNI, CINAHL, CPerI, ConsI, E08, EMBASE, ExcerpMed, G05, G06, G07, G08, H03, H04, H11, H12, H13, HlthInd, I05, I07, M01, M02, M06, MASUSE, MEDLINE, MagInd, P02, P10, P20, P30, P48, P53, P54, PQC, R03, R10, RGAb, RGPR, Reac, S09, S23, SCOPUS, SportS, T02, W03, WBA, WMB.
—BLDSC (4267.127000), CASDDS, GNLM, IE, Ingenta. **CCC.**
Published by: Harvard Health Publications Group (Subsidiary of: Harvard Medical School), 10 Shattuck St, Ste 612, Boston, MA 02115. TEL 877-649-9457, hhp@hms.harvard.edu, http://www.health.harvard.edu. Eds. Peter Wehrein, Anthony L Komaroff.

613 USA ISSN 1059-938X
RA773
HEALTH; vital information with a human touch. Text in English. 1992. 10/yr. USD 12.97 domestic; CAD 20.97 in Canada; USD 3.99 newsstand/cover (effective 2008). adv. bk.rev. charts; illus.; stat. back issues avail.; reprints avail. **Document type:** *Magazine, Trade.* **Description:** Provides reliable, up-to-date health and medical information for consumers.
Formed by the merger of (1990-1992): In Health (1047-0549); (1969-1991): Health (0279-3547); Which was formerly (1969-1981): Family Health (0014-7249); Which incorporated (1950-1976): Today's Health (0040-8514); Which was formerly: Hygeia (0096-1876)
Related titles: Online - full text ed.
Indexed: A01, A02, A03, A04, A08, A09, A10, A11, A22, A25, A26, ARG, AcaI, B04, BRD, BiolDig, C03, C05, C06, C07, C08, C11, C12, CBCARef, CHNI, CINAHL, CLFP, CMM, CPerI, ConsI, E08, G03, G05, G06, G07, G08, GSA, GSI, GeoRef, H03, H04, H11, H12, H13, HlthInd, I05, I06, I07, M01, M02, MASUSE, MLA-IB, MagInd, P02, P06, P10, P13, P20, P26, P30, P34, P48, P53, P54, PEI, PMR, PQC, R03, R04, R06, RGAb, RGPR, S02, S03, S08, S09, S23, SCOPUS, SD, SpeleolAb, SportS, T02, TOM, U01, V02, V03, V04, W03.
—IE, Infotrieve, Ingenta, Linda Hall. **CCC.**
Published by: Southern Progress Corp. (Subsidiary of: Time Warner Inc.), 2100 Lakeshore Dr, Birmingham, AL 35209. TEL 205-445-6000, FAX 205-445-8655, http://www.southernprogress.com. Pub. Renee Tulenko. adv.: B&W page USD 88,200, color page USD 98,200; trim 8 x 10.75. Circ: 1,365,650 (paid).

613.7 344 USA ISSN 0897-3598
KF3821.A15
HEALTH ADVOCATE. Text in English. 1971. 4/yr. USD 85 (effective 2005). bk.rev. **Document type:** *Newsletter.* **Description:** Covers legal aspects of current health care issues, including Medicaid, managed care, access to health care, and more.
Former titles (until 1982): N H E L P Health Advocate (0272-7102); (until 1980): Health Law Newsletter (0160-7227)
Indexed: MCR.
Published by: National Health Law Program, 2639 S La Cienega Blvd, Los Angeles, CA 90034. TEL 310-204-6010, FAX 310-204-0891, nhelp@healthlaw.org, http://www.healthlaw.org. Ed. Laurence Lavin. R&P, Adv. contact Brendan McTaggart TEL 202-289-7661. Circ: 1,700.

613.194 GBR ISSN 0017-8888
HEALTH AND EFFICIENCY. Abbreviated title: H & E. Text in English, French, German. 1899. m. GBP 27, GBP 30, GBP 37; GBP 2.60 newsstand/cover (effective 1999). adv. bk.rev. illus. **Document type:** *Magazine, Consumer.* **Description:** News, views and reflections on the nudist and naturist scene, including areas where nudity and naked living are accepted.
Related titles: Online - full text ed.
Published by: New Freedom Publications Ltd., Bow House Business Centre, 153-159 Bow Rd, London, E3 2SE, United Kingdom. TEL 44-181-983-3011, FAX 44-181-983-6322. Ed. Helen Ludbrook. R&P J Hendy Smith. Adv. contact Jacklyn Knight. page GBP 800; 190 x 275. Circ: 130,000. **Dist. by:** M M C Ltd., Octagon House, White Hart Meadows, Ripley, Woking, Surrey GU23 6HR, United Kingdom. TEL 44-1483-211222, FAX 44-1483-224541.

613.7 GBR ISSN 0957-5928
HEALTH AND FITNESS; all you need for life!. Text in English. 1984. m. GBP 29.99 domestic; GBP 62.40 in Europe; GBP 70 elsewhere (effective 2006). adv. illus. back issues avail. **Document type:** *Magazine, Consumer.* **Description:** Informs readers of the many ways in which to maintain one's health and fitness through exercise, good nutrition, and a healthy lifestyle.
Formerly (until 1989): Fitness
—BLDSC (4274.811500), IE.
Published by: Future Publishing Ltd., Beauford Ct, 30 Monmouth St, Bath, Avon BA1 2BW, United Kingdom. TEL 44-1225-442244, FAX 44-1225-446019, customerservice@subscription.co.uk, http://www.futureplc.com. Circ: 558,000.

613.7 USA
HEALTH AND FITNESS SPORTS MAGAZINE. Text in English. 1985. m. adv. 84 p./no. 4 cols./p.; **Document type:** *Magazine, Consumer.* **Description:** Promotes living a fit and active lifestyle necessary for achieving personal health and wellness.
Address: 1502 Augusta, Ste 230, Houston, TX 77057. TEL 713-552-9991, FAX 713-552-9997. Ed. Rod Evans. Pub. Pat Monfrey. Adv. contact Wendy Reeves. color page USD 4,060. Circ: 50,000.

613 USA ISSN 1057-9273
HEALTH & HEALING. Variant title: Dr. Julian Whitaker's Health and Healing. Text in English. 1991. m. looseleaf. USD 39.99 (effective 2011). adv. Supplement avail. **Document type:** *Newsletter, Consumer.*
Related titles: Online - full text ed.: USD 9.95 (effective 2011).
—CCC.
Published by: Healthy Directions, LLC. (Subsidiary of: Phillips International, Inc.), 95 Old Shoals Rd, Arden, NC 28704. TEL 866-748-7513, feedback@healthydirections.com, http://www.healthydirections.com.

613.7 ZAF
HEALTH & HYGIENE. Text in English. ZAR 85.50 (effective 2000). adv. **Document type:** *Journal, Trade.*
Published by: Malnor (Pty) Ltd., Private Bag X20, Auckland Park, Johannesburg 2006, South Africa. TEL 27-11-7263081, FAX 27-11-7263017, malnor@iafrica.com. Ed. Cornelia Fick. R&P Ken Nortje. adv.: color page ZAR 5,495, B&W page ZAR 4,445; trim 210 x 297.

613.7 664 IND
HEALTH & NUTRITION. Text in English. 1989. m. adv. **Document type:** *Magazine, Consumer.*
Published by: Magna Publishing Company Ltd., Magna House, 100 E Old Prabhadevi Rd, Prabhadevi, Mumbai, Maharashtra 400 025, India. TEL 91-22-67091234, FAX 91-22-24306523.

613.7 IRL
HEALTH & NUTRITION. Text in English. q. adv. **Document type:** *Magazine, Consumer.*
Published by: Eireann Healthcare Publications, 25-26 Windsor Pl., Dublin, 2, Ireland. TEL 353-1-4753300, FAX 353-1-4753311, mhenderson@eireannpublications.ie, http://www.eireannpublications.ie. adv.: B&W page EUR 1,251, color page EUR 1,422. Circ: 3,350 (paid and controlled).

HEALTH AND PHYSICAL EDUCATION/HOKEN TAIIKU KYOSHITSU. *see* EDUCATION

HEALTH AND QUALITY OF LIFE OUTCOMES. *see* PUBLIC HEALTH AND SAFETY

613.9 USA ISSN 1054-2957
RA788
HEALTH AND SEXUALITY. Text in English. 1990. q. USD 3 newsstand/cover (effective 2006). **Document type:** *Magazine, Consumer.*
Indexed: P30.
Published by: Association of Reproductive Health Professionals, 2401 Pennsylvania Ave, N.W., Suite 350, Washington, DC 20037. TEL 202-466-3825, FAX 202-466-3826, http://www.arhp.org.

613.7 USA ISSN 0898-3569
HEALTH & YOU. Text in English. 1985. q. 32 p./no.; back issues avail. **Document type:** *Magazine, Consumer.* **Description:** Contains general health and wellness publication for consumers covering fitness, nutrition, and prevention.
Indexed: C06, C07, C08, CHNI, CINAHL.
—BLDSC (4274.914000), IE, Ingenta.
Published by: StayWell Custom Communications, 909 Davis St, Ste 600, Evanston, IL 60201. TEL 800-543-3854, info@staywellcustom.com, http://www.staywellcustom.com.

613 GBR ISSN 0965-4283
RA440.3.G7
➤ **HEALTH EDUCATION.** Abbreviated title: H E. Text in English. 1996. bi-m. EUR 4,519 combined subscription in Europe (print & online eds.); USD 5,129 combined subscription in the Americas (print & online eds.); GBP 3,259 combined subscription in the UK & elsewhere (print & online eds.); AUD 6,389 combined subscription in Australasia (print & online eds.) (effective 2012). adv. reprint service avail. from PSC. **Document type:** *Journal, Academic/Scholarly.* **Description:** Disseminates good practice in health education, particularly with regard to children's and young people.
Related titles: Online - full text ed.: ISSN 1758-714X (from IngentaConnect).
Indexed: A22, A26, A34, A36, A37, ASSIA, B14, B28, CABA, CPE, D01, E01, E08, E09, E12, E16, ERA, ERIC, EmerIntel, G08, GH, H12, I05, IndVet, LT, M12, N02, N03, P02, P03, P10, P18, P19, P21, P33, P37, P48, P50, P53, P54, PEI, PQC, PsycInfo, R08, R12, RRTA, S09, S13, S19, S20, S21, SCOPUS, T05, V05, VS, W11.
—BLDSC (4274.968700), IE, Infotrieve, Ingenta. **CCC.**
Published by: Emerald Group Publishing Ltd., Howard House, Wagon Ln, Bingley, W Yorks BD16 1WA, United Kingdom. TEL 44-1274-777700, FAX 44-1274-785201, information@emeraldinsight.com. Ed. Dr. Katherine Weare TEL 44-23-8059-3707. Pub. Kate Snowden. **Subscr. addr. in N America:** Emerald Group Publishing Limited, One Mifflin Pl, Ste 400, Harvard Sq, Cambridge, MA 02138. TEL 617-576-5782, 888-309-7810, FAX 617-576-5883.

➤ **HEALTH EDUCATION JOURNAL.** *see* PUBLIC HEALTH AND SAFETY

➤ **HEALTH LAW DIGEST.** *see* LAW

➤ **HEALTH LAW JOURNAL.** *see* LAW

➤ **HEALTH MARKETING QUARTERLY.** *see* PUBLIC HEALTH AND SAFETY

➤ **HEALTH PHYSICS;** the radiation safety journal. *see* MEDICAL SCIENCES

613.7 CAN ISSN 1715-6165
THE HEALTH Q. Text in English. 2005. m. **Document type:** *Newsletter, Consumer.*
Media: Online - full text. **Related titles:** Print ed.: ISSN 1715-6157. 2005.
Published by: The Health-Q Consulting http://www.thehq.ca/index.php.

HEALTH SCIENCE; living in harmony with nature. *see* NUTRITION AND DIETETICS

613.7 USA
HEALTH SHOPPER. Text in English. q. adv. **Description:** Provides current health information; covers nutrition and diets.
Published by: Swanson Health Products, 4075 40th Ave S., Fargo, ND 58104-3912. TEL 800-437-4148.

613.7 USA ISSN 0741-9368
HEALTHCARE MARKETING REPORT; the national newspaper on healthcare marketing. Text in English. m. USD 215 domestic; USD 255 foreign (effective 2005). **Document type:** *Newspaper, Trade.*
Related titles: Online - full text ed.
Published by: H M R Publications Group, PO Box 76002, Atlanta, GA 30358-1002. TEL 770-457-6105, FAX 770-457-4606, info@hmrpublicationsgroup.com. Ed. Beverly Seitz. Circ: 1,900.

362.1 USA
HEALTHOLOGY. Text in English. 1999. m. **Description:** Includes news that communicates health information between health care professionals and the public.
Media: Online - full text.
Published by: Healthology, LLC, 500 Fashion Ave., # 14, New York, NY 10018-4502. TEL 212-431-5100. Ed. Steven Haimowitz.

613.7 USA ISSN 1051-8770
RC81.A1
HEALTHWISE HANDBOOK (U.S. EDITION). Text in English. 1976. irreg., latest 2006, 17th ed. USD 7.50 per issue (effective 2012). **Document type:** *Handbook/Manual/Guide, Consumer.* **Description:** Aims to help people make better health decisions, offering tips on how to save money and providing a personal window to the Web.
Related titles: Regional ed(s).: Healthwise Handbook (Canadian Edition). ISSN 1559-8756. 1998.
Published by: Healthwise, 2601 N Bogus Basin Rd, Boise, ID 83702. TEL 800-706-9646, https://www.healthwise.org/. Ed. Donald W Kemper.

613.7 USA
HEALTHY & FIT. Text in English. 2005. m. USD 18 (effective 2007). **Document type:** *Magazine, Consumer.*
Indexed: PEI.
Address: 1600 Tuttle Rd., Mason, MI 48854. TEL 517-256-1077, FAX 517-913-6004. Ed., Pub., Adv. contact Tim Kissman. Circ: 12,000.

610 051 USA ISSN 2150-9921
HEALTHY BEGINNINGS. Text in English. 2006. m. free (effective 2009). adv. back issues avail. **Document type:** *Magazine, Consumer.* **Description:** Provides advice on nutrition, fitness, natural healing, alternative medicine, organic, green living and sustainability, natural beauty, personal growth, family health, pet health, spirituality, supplements and more.
Related titles: Online - full text ed.: ISSN 2150-993X.
Published by: Dawn M. Gowery, Ed. & Pub., PO Box 19041, Reno, NV 89511. TEL 775-828-4547, FAX 775-828-1305. Ed., Pub. Dawn M Gowery.

613 JPN
HEALTHY FAMILY. Text in Japanese. 1976. bi-m. JPY 3,420.
Published by: Shufu-to-Seikatsu Sha Ltd., 3-5-7 Kyobashi, Chuo-ku, Tokyo, 104-8357, Japan. Ed. Kyoshi Inoue.

613.7 USA
HEALTHY LIVING N Y C. Text in English. m. **Document type:** *Magazine, Consumer.*
Published by: H L Productions, Llc., P O Box 8061, New York, NY 10116. Ed. Michael Long. Pub. Justin J Luciani.

613.7 USA
HEALTHY MIND, HEALTHY BODY. Text in English. q. **Document type:** *Bulletin.* **Description:** Provides information that helps Oxford Health Plan members lead healthier lives and make better healthcare decisions.
Published by: (Oxford Health Plans), J S A Communications, LLC, 3732 Mt Diablo Blvd., Ste. 395, Lafayette, CA 94549-3637. TEL 510-283-5525, FAX 510-283-5515. Ed. Victoria Manassero. Pub. Barry Freilicher.

613.7 NZL ISSN 1170-6058
HEALTHY OPTIONS. Text in English. 1984. m. NZD 62 domestic; NZD 84 in Australia & South Pacific; NZD 90 elsewhere (effective 2008). bk.rev. tr.lit. 88 p./no.; back issues avail. **Document type:** *Magazine, Consumer.* **Description:** Provides information on New Zealand's natural health and environmental issues.
Related titles: Online - full text ed.: ISSN 1177-5718.
Published by: Healthy Options Ltd., 100 Grage Rd, PO Box 13209, Tauranga, New Zealand. TEL 64-7-5700560, FAX 64-7-5700360. Ed., Pub. Janice-Ann Priest. Adv. contact Alan Morton TEL 64-7-5700560 ext 201. Circ: 18,000.

613.7 USA ISSN 1092-1974
RA776.5
HEART & SOUL. Text in English. 1993-2003; resumed 2004. bi-m. USD 18 domestic; USD 34 in Canada; USD 48 elsewhere (effective 2009). adv. bk.rev.; music rev. illus. reprints avail. **Document type:** *Magazine, Consumer.* **Description:** Aims to promote the physical, mental, spiritual and financial well-being of today's African-American woman.
Formerly (until 1994): Rodale's Heart and Soul (1072-7345)
Indexed: GW, IIBP, M01, M02.
—Ingenta.
Published by: Heart and Soul Enterprises, 2514 Maryland Ave, Baltimore, MD 21218. TEL 800-834-8813. Pub. Edwin V Avent. adv.: B&W page USD 17,527, color page USD 21,400; trim 8.125 x 10.875. Circ: 300,000.

HEART, HEALTH & NUTRITION. *see* MEDICAL SCIENCES

HEART-HEALTHY LIVING. *see* NUTRITION AND DIETETICS

613.7 CHN ISSN 1008-3596
HEBEI TIYU XUEYUAN XUEBAO/HEBEI INSTITUTE OF PHYSICAL EDUCATION. JOURNAL. Text in Chinese. 1987. q. CNY 10 newsstand/cover (effective 2006).
Related titles: Online - full text ed.
Indexed: PEI.
Published by: Hebei Tiyu Xueyuan, 82, Xuefu Lu, Shijiazhuang, 050041, China. TEL 86-311-5337572, FAX 86-311-6839726.

613 DNK ISSN 0018-0149
HELSE; familiens laegemagasin. Text in Danish. 1955. 10/yr. DKK 219 (effective 2009). adv. back issues avail. **Document type:** *Magazine, Consumer.*
Incorporates (1985-1989): Dig! (0901-8832); (1982-1990): Hejsa (0905-1554); Which was formerly (until 1989): Helses Boerneblad (0108-934X); (until 1983): Boerne Bladet (0109-0143)
Related titles: Online - full text ed.: ISSN 1902-5025. 2007.
Published by: Helse - Active Living A/S, Frederiksberg Runddel 1, Frederiksberg, 2000, Denmark. TEL 45-35-250525, FAX 45-35-268760, helse@helse.dk. Eds. Christina Alfthan, Jesper Bo Bendtsen. Adv. contact Bitten Hesse. Circ: 290,000 (paid and controlled).

613.7 DNK ISSN 1903-8461
HELSEJOB. Text in Danish. 1955. bi-m. adv. **Document type:** *Magazine, Consumer.* **Description:** About health and work.
Formerly (until 2009): Arbejdsliv (1902-3669); Which superseded in part (in 2007): Helse (0018-0149)
Related titles: Online - full text ed.: ISSN 1903-847X. 2007.
Published by: Helse - Active Living A/S, Frederiksberg Runddel 1, Frederiksberg, 2000, Denmark. TEL 45-35-250525, FAX 45-35-268760, helse@helse.dk. Eds. Christina Alfthan, Jesper Bo Bendtsen. Adv. contact Bitten Hesse. page DKK 16,000. Circ: 25,000.

613 IND ISSN 0018-0491
HERALD OF HEALTH. Text in English. 1924. m. INR 200; INR 15 per issue (effective 2011). adv. bk.rev. illus.; stat. **Document type:** *Magazine, Consumer.*
Published by: (Seventh-Day Adventists USA), Oriental Watchman Publishing House, Salisbury Park, PO Box 1417, Pune, Maharashtra 411 037, India. TEL 91-20-24261441, FAX 91-20-24261638.

613.7 MEX
HERCULES MODERNO. Text in Spanish. 1980. fortn. MXN 150, USD 80. adv. illus. **Description:** Covers bodybuilding, nutrition, kinesiology, training, psychology and health.
Published by: (Federacion Internacional de Fisioconstructores (IFBB)), Editormex Mexicano S.A., Avda. Rodolfo Gaona, Edif. 82-B-203, Lomas de Sotelo, Mexico City, DF 11200, Mexico. TEL 557-07-92, FAX 525-395-65-64. Ed. Javier Barrigo. Circ: 45,000.

613.7 USA ISSN 1550-2880
GV546.6.W64
HERS; for women who want more out of fitness. Text in English. 2000. bi-m. USD 17.97 domestic; USD 21.97 in Canada; USD 28.97 elsewhere (effective 2008). adv. back issues avail. **Document type:** *Magazine, Consumer.* **Description:** Provides tips, advice and instruction for women who want more out of fitness.
Formerly (until 2004): Muscle & Fitness Hers (1526-9140)
Related titles: Online - full text ed.
Indexed: A26, G05, G06, G07, G08, H11, H12, I05, I07, M02, MASUSE, SD.
Published by: A M I - Weider Publications (Subsidiary of: American Media, Inc.), 1 Park Ave, 3d Fl, New York, NY 10016. TEL 212-545-4800, FAX 212-448-9890, http://www.amilink.com. Ed. Vince Scalisi. Pub. David Pecker. Adv. contact Aaron Woloff TEL 212-743-6614. color page USD 10,710, B&W page USD 8,630; trim 8.25 x 10.875. Circ: 100,000.

HIDEAWAYS BEAUTY SPECIAL. *see* TRAVEL AND TOURISM

616.398 JPN ISSN 1343-229X
HIMAN KENKYU/JAPAN SOCIETY FOR THE STUDY OF OBESITY. JOURNAL. Text in Japanese. 1995. 3/yr. membership. **Document type:** *Journal, Academic/Scholarly.*
—BLDSC (4315.015000).
Published by: Nihon Himan Gakkai/Japan Society for the Study of Obesity, 2F, 1 Gohkan, Shimbashi Ekimae Bldg., 1, 2-20-15 Shimbashi, Minato-ku, Tokyo, 105-0004, Japan. TEL 86-3-35722590, FAX 86-3-35754748, jasso-webmaster@kk-kyowa.co.jp, http://wwwsoc.nii.ac.jp/jasso/.

HOCHSCHULSPORT. *see* SPORTS AND GAMES

HOCHSCHULSPORT: BILDUNG UND WISSENSCHAFT. *see* SPORTS AND GAMES

613 JPN ISSN 0018-3342
HOKEN NO KAGAKU/HEALTH CARE. Text in Japanese. 1959. m. JPY 13,125 newsstand/cover (effective 2010). Index. **Document type:** *Journal, Academic/Scholarly.*
—BLDSC (4274.937000).
Published by: (Health Science Research Association/Hoken Kagaku Kenkyukai), Kyorin Shoin, 4-2-1 Yushima, Bunkyo-ku, Tokyo, 113-0034, Japan. TEL 81-3-38114887, FAX 81-3-38119148, info@kyorin-shoin.co.jp. Circ: 710.

HOKURIKU KOSHU EISEI GAKKAISHI/HOKURIKU JOURNAL OF PUBLIC HEALTH. *see* PUBLIC HEALTH AND SAFETY

613.7 USA
HOME GYM MAGAZINE. Text in English. 2007. q. USD 11.99 (effective 2008). adv. **Document type:** *Magazine, Consumer.* **Description:** Covers home fitness. Aims to educate readers on all their fitness options and to show that exercising from home is an excellent long-term investment in their health.
Address: PO Box 1677, Simi Valley, CA 93062. TEL 805-581-1220, FAX 866-502-1220. Ed. Loran Lewis. Pub., Adv. contact Charlie Flora. color page USD 4,400; trim 8.375 x 10.875. Circ: 40,000.

613.7 USA ISSN 1078-2389
HOME HEALTH LINE; the home care industry's national independent newsletter. Text in English. 1975. w. (48/yr.). USD 437 (effective 2005). adv. index. back issues avail. **Document type:** *Newsletter, Consumer.*
Related titles: Online - full text ed.
—CCC.
Address: 11300 Rockville Pike, Ste 1100, Rockville, MD 20852-3030. TEL 301-816-8950, FAX 301-816-8945. Ed. Lisa Mann. Adv. contact Terry Gray. Circ: 2,800.

HOME HEALTHCARE NURSE. *see* MEDICAL SCIENCES

613.7 ITA ISSN 1970-4852
HOME WELLNESS. Text in Italian. 2007. q. EUR 28 (effective 2011). **Document type:** *Magazine, Consumer.*
Published by: Editrice Il Campo, Via Giovanni Amendola 11, Bologna, BO 40121, Italy. TEL 39-051-255544, FAX 39-051-255360, customer@fitnesstrends.com, http://www.ilcampo.it.

P

301.16 613.7 USA ISSN 0891-3374
HOPE HEALTH LETTER. Text in English. 1978. m. looseleaf. USD 25 (effective 2007). illus. **Document type:** *Newsletter.* **Description:** Covers many subjects on health including smoking, exercise, family matters, substance abuse, stress management, diet, self-care, health-care, cost-containment. Written for all levels.
Formerly (until 1986): Hope Newsletter
Published by: Hope Heart Institute, 1710 E Jefferson St, Seattle, WA 98122. TEL 206-903-2001, FAX 206-903-2001, info@hopeheart.org. Ed. Carol P Garzona. **Dist. by:** Hope Health, 350 E Michigan Ave, Ste 301, Kalamazoo, MI 49007-3851. TEL 800-334-4094, info@HopeHealth.com, http://www.hopehealth.com.

613.7 616.1 USA
HORIZONS (LIVINGSTON). Text in English. q. free. illus. **Document type:** *Journal, Consumer.* **Description:** Offers cancer patients and their families advice on the treatment and prevention of cancer. Provides news of the Cancer Center and related departments at Saint Barnabas Medical Center, along with sponsored programs.
Published by: Saint Barnabas Medical Center, Cancer Center, Dept of Public Relations, 95 Old Short Hills Rd, Livingston, NJ 07039. Ed. Lydia T Dorsky.

613.7 790.1 PRT ISSN 0870-0184
HORIZONTE; revista de educacao fisica e desporto. Text in Portuguese. 1984. bi-m. **Document type:** *Magazine, Trade.*
Published by: Livros Horizonte, Rua da Chagas 17, Lisbon, 1200-106, Portugal. TEL 351-213-466917, geral@livroshorizonte.pt, http://www.livroshorizonte.pt.

613.7 646 ITA ISSN 2035-4614
HOUSEHOLD AND PERSONAL CARE TODAY. Abbreviated title: H P C. Text in English. 2004. q. **Document type:** *Magazine, Consumer.*
Related titles: Online - full text ed.: ISSN 2035-4738.
—BLDSC (4334.878500).
Published by: Tekno Scienze, Viale Brianza 22, Milan, 20127, Italy. TEL 39-02-26809375, FAX 39-02-2847226, http://www.teknoscienze.com. Ed. Carla Scesa.

613.7 POL ISSN 1732-3991
➤ **HUMAN MOVEMENT.** Text in English. 1999. s-a. PLZ 27 domestic to individuals; EUR 27 foreign to individuals; PLZ 55 domestic to institutions; EUR 55 foreign to institutions (effective 2008). **Document type:** *Journal, Academic/Scholarly.*
Formerly (until 2004): Czlowiek i Ruch (1508-5287)
Related titles: Online - full text ed.: ISSN 1899-1955. free (effective 2011).
Indexed: CA, PEI, R09, R10, Reac, SCOPUS, SD, T02.
—BLDSC (4336.206500), IE.
Published by: Akademia Wychowania Fizycznego we Wroclawiu/ University School of Physical Education in Wroclaw, ul Banacha 11, Wroclaw, 51617, Poland. TEL 48-71-3473121, http://www.awf.wroc.pl. Ed. Ryszard Panfil.

➤ **HUMAN MOVEMENT SCIENCE.** *see* MEDICAL SCIENCES

➤ **HUMAN SEXUALITY SUPPLEMENT.** *see* EDUCATION—Teaching Methods And Curriculum

➤ **HYGIENETOWN.** *see* MEDICAL SCIENCES—Dentistry

613 GBR ISSN 0018-8263
THE HYGIENIST (FRINTON-ON-SEA). Text in English. 1959. q. GBP 10.50 domestic membership; GBP 12.50 in Europe membership; USD 23 elsewhere membership (effective 2009). bk.rev. **Document type:** *Newsletter, Consumer.*
Published by: British Natural Hygiene Society, Shalimar, 3 Harold Grove, Frinton-on-Sea, Essex C013 9BD, United Kingdom. TEL 44-1255-672823, 44-1636-682941, http://www.drsidhwa.com/bnhs/. Ed. Keki R Sidhwa. Circ: 300.

613.7 USA
I C H P E R - S D CONGRESS PROCEEDINGS. Text in English. ceased; resumed 1958. biennial. price varies. **Document type:** *Proceedings.* **Description:** Covers physical fitness.
Former titles: I C H P E R Congress Proceedings; I C H P E R Congress Reports (0074-4417)
Indexed: SportS.
Published by: International Council on Health, Physical Education, Recreation, Sport and Dance, 1900 Association Dr, Reston, VA 20191. TEL 703-476-3462, FAX 703-476-9527.

613.7 USA ISSN 1930-4595
GV201
➤ **I C H P E R - S D JOURNAL OF RESEARCH IN HEALTH, PHYSICAL EDUCATION, RECREATION, SPORT AND DANCE.** (International Council for Health, Physical Education, Recreation, Sport and Dance) Variant title: The I C H P E R - S D Journal of Research. Text in English, Spanish, German, French, Arabic. 2006. s-a. free to members (effective 2011). adv. 64 p./no.; reprints avail. **Document type:** *Journal, Academic/Scholarly.* **Description:** Contains articles, research papers, worldwide developments in the professional areas of sport, dance and physical fitness.
Indexed: CA, E02, E03, ERI, EdA, EdI, P02, P10, P18, P24, P48, P53, P54, P55, PEI, PQC, SD, SportS, T02, W03, W05.
—BLDSC (4802.218000), Ingenta. **CCC.**
Published by: International Council for Health, Physical Education and Recreation, Sport, and Dance, 1900 Association Dr, Reston, VA 20191. TEL 703-476-3462, FAX 703-476-9527, ichper@aahperd.org. Ed. Steven C Wright TEL 603-862-4408.

613.7 USA ISSN 1548-419X
RA781
I D E A FITNESS JOURNAL; for professionals who inspire the world to fitness. Text in English. 2004. 10/yr. USD 5 (effective 2004). 116 p./no.; **Document type:** *Magazine, Trade.* **Description:** Contains comprehensive sections on personal training, group exercise, nutrition and mind-body fitness along with in-depth CEC features and columns that cover news, exercise science, career strategies, membership updates, business information, program design, management tips, personal enrichment, equipment updates, and more.
Formed by the merger of (1998-2004): I D E A Health & Fitness Source (1096-8156); (1990-2004): I D E A Personal Trainer (1068-087X)
Related titles: Online - full text ed.
Indexed: A26, C06, C07, CA, E08, G05, G06, G07, G08, H11, H12, I05, PEI, S09, SD, T02.
—BLDSC (4362.371625). **CCC.**
Published by: (International Dance-Exercise Association), I D E A Health & Fitness Association, 10455 Pacific Center Court, San Diego, CA 92121-4339. TEL 858-535-8979 ext 7, 800-999-4332 ext 7, FAX 858-535-8234, contact@ideafit.com. Ed. Sandy Webster.

613.7 USA ISSN 1073-7952
I D E A FITNESS MANAGER NEWSLETTER. Text in English. 5/yr. membership. **Document type:** *Newsletter.* **Description:** Offers fitness business owners, program directors and managers information needed to build business, support staff and be effective administrators.
—**CCC.**
Published by: (International Dance-Exercise Association), I D E A Health & Fitness Association, 10455 Pacific Center Court, San Diego, CA 92121-4339. TEL 858-535-8979 ext 7, 800-999-4332 ext 7, FAX 858-535-8234, contact@ideafit.com. Ed. Patricia Ryan. Pub. Peter Davis. Circ: 5,000.

613.7 USA
I D E A TRAINER SUCCESS. Text in English. 2004. 5/yr. Subscr. incld. with membership. **Document type:** *Newsletter, Trade.* **Description:** Contains articles and tips from industry-leading PFTs and business owners, offering insights, strategies and directions on topics such as starting up a business, reinvigorating an existing business, sales and marketing, finance and money management, leveraging services, systems implementation, software, hardware and other technology, liability and risk management and interpersonal skill-building and communication.
Indexed: SD.
Published by: (International Dance-Exercise Association), I D E A Health & Fitness Association, 10455 Pacific Center Court, San Diego, CA 92121-4339. TEL 858-535-8979 ext 7, 800-999-4332 ext 7, FAX 858-535-8234, contact@ideafit.com.

613.7 DNK ISSN 0902-1620
I FORM. Text in Danish. 1987. 18/yr. DKK 725 (effective 2008). adv. back issues avail. **Document type:** *Magazine, Consumer.* **Description:** News and tips on the medicin, nutrition, psychology and active involvement needed to stay in shape.
Related titles: Online - full text ed.
—**CCC.**
Published by: Bonnier Publications AS, Strandboulevarden 130, Copenhagen OE, 2100, Denmark. TEL 45-39-172000, FAX 45-39-290199, bp@bp.bonnier.dk, http://www.bonnierpublications.com. Ed. Tina Gundorph Joergensen. adv.: color page DKK 39,000. Circ: 63,089 (paid).

613.7 USA ISSN 1062-2764
➤ **ILLINOIS JOURNAL OF HEALTH, PHYSICAL EDUCATION, RECREATION AND DANCE.** Variant title: I A H P E R D Journal. Text in English. 1967. s-a. free to members (effective 2011). bk.rev. **Document type:** *Journal, Academic/Scholarly.* **Description:** Publishes articles, research reports, innovative programs, articles with practical applications or implications for HPERD educators and professionals, trend and issue articles, IAHPERD grant summaries and book/software reviews.
Formerly (until 1983): Illinois Journal of Health, Physical Education and Recreation (0019-2074)
Indexed: CA, IBT&D, PEI, SD, T02.
Published by: Illinois Association for Health, Physical Education, Recreation and Dance, PO Box 1326, Jacksonville, IL 62651. TEL 217-245-6413, FAX 217-245-5261, iahperd@iahperd.org.

613.7 CAN ISSN 1486-1976
IMPACT (CALGARY). Text in English. 1991. bi-m. CAD 19.50 (effective 2005). **Document type:** *Magazine, Consumer.* **Description:** Covers areas of fitness, health, nutrition, sports medicine, research, food, etc.
Formerly (until 1996): Impact Magazine (1486-1968)
Published by: Impact Productions Inc., 2007 - 2 St S W, Calgary, AB, Canada. TEL 403-228-0605, FAX 403-228-0627.

IMPRINT MAGAZINE; mind, body, soul. *see* NEW AGE PUBLICATIONS

INCLEAN; delivering sustainable cleaning information. *see* CLEANING AND DYEING

613.7 USA ISSN 1949-9809
GV201
INDIANA A H P E R D JOURNAL. (Association for Health, Physical Education, Recreation & Dance) Text in English. 1994. 3/yr. membership. adv. **Document type:** *Journal, Academic/Scholarly.* **Description:** Provides information to educators and community leaders in health, physical education, recreation, dance, and sports. Includes articles on current events, new teaching methods, and curriculum developments.
Published by: Indiana Association for Health, Physical Education, Recreation & Dance, 2007 Wilno Dr, Marion, IN 46952. indianaahperd@aol.com, http://www.indiana-ahperd.org/. adv.: page USD 250; 8.5 x 11.

616.398 616.8526 USA ISSN 1551-2118
RA645.O23
INFORMATION PLUS REFERENCE SERIES. WEIGHT IN AMERICA; obesity, eating disorders, and other health risks. Text in English. 2004. biennial. USD 49 per issue (effective 2008). **Document type:** *Monographic series, Academic/Scholarly.* **Description:** Provides a compilation of current and historical statistics, with analysis, on aspects of one contemporary social issue.
Related titles: Online - full text ed.; ◆ Series of: Information Plus Reference Series.
Published by: Gale (Subsidiary of: Cengage Learning), 27500 Drake Rd, Farmington Hills, MI 48331. TEL 248-699-4253, 800-877-4253, FAX 877-363-4253, gale.customerservice@cengage.com, http://gale.cengage.com.

613.7 GRC ISSN 1790-3041
➤ **INQUIRIES IN SPORT & PHYSICAL EDUCATION.** Text in Greek; Abstracts in English. 2003. irreg. free (effective 2011). **Document type:** *Journal, Academic/Scholarly.* **Description:** Covers all aspects related to the promotion of health and quality of life through exercise and physical activity and related to leisure and sport management.
Media: Online - full text.
Indexed: A36, CA, CABA, GH, LT, N02, N03, PEI, R09, RRTA, SD, T02.
Published by: Hellenic Academy of Physical Education, University of Thessaly, Trikala, Greece. Ed. Yannis Theodorakis.

613.7 CAN ISSN 1923-4120
INSIDE FITNESS MAGAZINE. Abbreviated title: I F M. Text in English. 2006. bi-m. adv. back issues avail. **Document type:** *Magazine, Consumer.* **Description:** Helps athletes, models and trainers to stay healthy, and fitness.
Published by: IFM Media Inc., 414 N service Rd, 3rd Fl, Oakville, ON L6H 5R2, Canada. TEL 905-901-1512, FAX 905-901-1494, info@ifmmedia.com, http://www.ifmmedia.com/. Ed. Jonathan Chaimberg. Pub. Terry Frendo. Adv. contact Michelle Shaw.

INSTITUTION OF MECHANICAL ENGINEERS. PROCEEDINGS. PART P: JOURNAL OF SPORTS, ENGINEERING AND TECHNOLOGY/ JOURNAL OF SPORTS, ENGINEERING AND TECHNOLOGY. *see* SPORTS AND GAMES

613.7 USA ISSN 1529-1944
➤ **THE INTERNATIONAL ELECTRONIC JOURNAL OF HEALTH EDUCATION.** Abbreviated title: I E J H E. Text in English. 1998. a. (updated weekly). free (effective 2011). adv. back issues avail. **Document type:** *Journal, Academic/Scholarly.* **Description:** Presents a complete text of articles ranging from research to theory-based manuscripts as well as series of interviews with legends in the field of health education, promotion, and behavior.
Media: Online - full text.
Indexed: A26, A36, A39, B21, BRD, C06, C07, C08, C27, C29, CA, CABA, CINAHL, D01, D03, D04, E02, E03, E07, E12, E13, ERI, ERIC, ESPM, EdA, EdI, GH, H&SSA, H12, I05, LT, N02, N03, PEI, R12, R14, RRTA, RiskAb, S14, S15, S18, T02, T05, TAR, W03, W05, W11.
—**CCC.**
Published by: American Association for Health Education, 1900 Association Dr, Reston, VA 20191. TEL 703-476-3437, 800-321-0789, FAX 703-476-9527, aahe@aahperd.org. Ed. W William Chen.

797.21 USA ISSN 1932-9997
➤ **INTERNATIONAL JOURNAL OF AQUATIC RESEARCH AND EDUCATION.** Text in English. 2007. q. USD 368 domestic to institutions; USD 378 foreign to institutions; USD 426 combined subscription domestic to institutions (print & online eds.); USD 436 combined subscription foreign to institutions (print & online eds.) (effective 2012). adv. **Document type:** *Journal, Academic/Scholarly.* **Description:** Publishes original aquatic research, as well as information related to aquatic education and instructional practices, use of aquatic facilities and technology, aquatic health and safety practices, and factors surrounding and influencing aquatic participation.
Related titles: Online - full text ed.: ISSN 1932-9253. USD 368 to institutions (effective 2012).
Indexed: A36, CA, CABA, E12, GH, LT, N02, N03, PEI, R09, RRTA, S13, S16, SD, T02, T05, W11.
—BLDSC (4542.103100), IE. **CCC.**
Published by: Human Kinetics, 1607 N Market St, Champaign, IL 61820. TEL 800-747-4457, FAX 217-351-2674, orders@hkusa.com. Ed. Stephen Langendorfer TEL 419-372-0221. R&P Martha Gullo TEL 217-403-7534. Adv. contact Amy Bleich TEL 217-403-7803.

➤ **THE INTERNATIONAL JOURNAL OF BEHAVIORAL NUTRITION AND PHYSICAL ACTIVITY.** *see* PSYCHOLOGY

613.7 USA ISSN 1939-795X
QP301
➤ **INTERNATIONAL JOURNAL OF EXERCISE SCIENCE.** Text in English. 2008 (Jan.). q. free (effective 2011). **Document type:** *Journal, Academic/Scholarly.* **Description:** Aims to engage undergraduate and graduate students in scholarly activity as authors and reviewers as they develop into professionals.
Media: Online - full text.
Indexed: CA, P30, PEI, SD, T02.
Published by: Western Kentucky University, 1906 College Heights Blvd, Bowling Green, KY 42101. TEL 270-745-0111, western@wku.edu, http://www.wku.edu. Eds. James W Navalta, Scott T Lyons.

613.7 IND ISSN 0973-2152
➤ **INTERNATIONAL JOURNAL OF FITNESS.** Text in English. 2005. s-a. INR 2,200 for 3 yrs. domestic; USD 145 for 3 yrs. foreign (effective 2010). adv. **Document type:** *Journal, Academic/Scholarly.*
Indexed: CA, P30, PEI, SD, T02.
Published by: Fitness Society of India, c/o Prof S R Gangopadhyay, 404 Shivalik Apartments, Opp AIR, Gandhi Rd, Gwalior, Madhya Pradesh 474 002, India. TEL 91-751-2342557, FAX 91-751-2342557, srgango@fsionline.org. Ed. Ms. Maria Francesca Piacentini. adv.: B&W page INR 6,000; 180 x 245.

613.7071 GBR ISSN 1463-5240
RA421 CODEN: IHPEFR
➤ **INTERNATIONAL JOURNAL OF HEALTH PROMOTION AND EDUCATION.** Text in English. 1962. q. free to members (effective 2009). bk.rev. index. **Document type:** *Journal, Academic/Scholarly.* **Description:** Serves as a platform for new ideas and practical research, publishing research articles for a wide range of health and teaching professionals.
Former titles (until 1998): International Journal of Health Education (1368-1222); (until 1997): Institute of Health Education. Journal (0307-3289)
Indexed: A22, A26, A34, A36, B28, C06, C07, C08, CA, CABA, CINAHL, CPE, D01, E12, EMBASE, ERA, ExcerpMed, GH, H12, H17, I05, IndVet, LT, M12, N02, N03, P33, PN&I, R08, R12, RRTA, S20, S21, SCOPUS, T02, T05, TAR, V05, VS, W11.
—BLDSC (4542.277700), GNLM, IE, Ingenta. **CCC.**
Published by: Institute of Health Promotion and Education, c/o Helen Draper, School of Dentistry, University of Manchester, Higher Cambridge St, Manchester, M15 6FH, United Kingdom. honsec@ihpe.org.uk. Ed. Stephen S Palmer TEL 44-20-82934114.

➤ **INTERNATIONAL JOURNAL OF OBESITY.** *see* NUTRITION AND DIETETICS

➤ **INTERNATIONAL JOURNAL OF PHYSICAL EDUCATION/ INTERNATIONALE ZEITSCHRIFT FUER SPORTPAEDAGOGIK.** *see* EDUCATION—Teaching Methods And Curriculum

➤ **INTERNATIONAL JOURNAL OF QUALITATIVE STUDIES ON HEALTH AND WELL-BEING.** *see* MEDICAL SCIENCES

613.7 617.1 JPN ISSN 1348-1509
➤ **INTERNATIONAL JOURNAL OF SPORT AND HEALTH SCIENCE.** Text in English. 2003. a. membership. **Document type:** *Journal, Academic/Scholarly.*
Related titles: Online - full text ed.: ISSN 1880-4012.

Indexed: PEI.
—BLDSC (4542.680550).
Published by: Nihon Taiiku Gakkai/Japan Society of Physical Education, Health and Sport Sciences, Kishi Memorial Hall, 1-1-1 Jinnan, Shibuya-ku, Tokyo, 150-8050, Japan. TEL 81-3-34812427, FAX 81-3-34812428, http://wwwsoc.nii.ac.jp/jspe3/index.htm.

613.7 612 USA ISSN 1555-0265
RC1235
➤ **INTERNATIONAL JOURNAL OF SPORTS PHYSIOLOGY AND PERFORMANCE.** Abbreviated title: I J S P P. Text in English. 2006 (Mar.). q. USD 368 domestic to institutions; USD 378 foreign to institutions; USD 426 combined subscription domestic to institutions (print & online eds.); USD 436 combined subscription foreign to institutions (print & online eds.) (effective 2012). adv. **Document type:** *Journal, Academic/Scholarly.* **Description:** Publishes authoritative research in sports physiology and related disciplines, with an emphasis on work having direct practical applications in enhancing sports performance in sports physiology and related disciplines.
Related titles: Online - full text ed.: ISSN 1555-0273. USD 368 to institutions (effective 2012).
Indexed: C06, C07, CA, EMBASE, ExcerpMed, MEDLINE, P30, PEI, R09, R10, Reac, SCI, SCOPUS, SD, T02, W07.
—BLDSC (4542.681310), IE, Ingenta. **CCC.**
Published by: Human Kinetics, 1607 N Market St, Champaign, IL 61820. TEL 800-747-4457, FAX 217-351-2674, orders@hkusa.com. Ed. Carl Foster TEL 608-785-8687. R&P Martha Gullo TEL 217-403-7534. Adv. contact Amy Bleich TEL 217-403-7803.

613.7 CAN ISSN 1206-7857
➤ **INTERNATIONAL JOURNAL OF SPORTS, TOURISM & PHYSICAL EDUCATION.** Text in Arabic, English. 1997. q. CAD 400 (effective 2006). adv. bk.rev. **Document type:** *Journal, Academic/Scholarly.* **Description:** Designed for concise, cooperative publication of simple and creative ideas for family and youth development.
Published by: M.I. Ismail, Ed. & Pub., 9 Finsh DDO, Montreal, PQ H9A 3G9, Canada. TEL 514-626-9800, ismail.csc@usa.net. Ed., Pub. M I Ismail TEL 965-918-9996.

613.7 USA ISSN 1916-257X
RM721
➤ **INTERNATIONAL JOURNAL OF THERAPEUTIC MASSAGE & BODYWORK**; research, education & practice. Abbreviated title: I J T M B. Text in English. 2008. q. free (effective 2011). **Document type:** *Journal, Academic/Scholarly.*
Media: Online - full text.
Indexed: C06, C07, SCOPUS.
Published by: Massage Therapy Foundation, 500 Davis St, Ste 900, Evanston, IL 60201. TEL 847-869-5019, FAX 847-864-1178, info@massagetherapyfoundation.org, http://www.massagetherapyfoundation.org. Ed. Thomas Findley TEL 973-676-1000 ext 2713.

613.2 IND ISSN 0973-6131
BL1238.52
➤ **INTERNATIONAL JOURNAL OF YOGA.** Abbreviated title: I J O Y. Text in English. 2007. s-a. INR 1,500 domestic; USD 150 foreign to individuals; USD 200 foreign to institutions; INR 1,800 combined subscription domestic (print & online eds.); USD 180 combined subscription foreign to individuals (print & online eds.); USD 240 combined subscription foreign to institutions (print & online eds.); INR 938 per issue domestic; USD 125 per issue foreign (effective 2011). adv. **Document type:** *Journal, Academic/Scholarly.* **Description:** Covers yoga and its applications in the areas of medicine, physical sciences, spirituality, management and education. Audience includes: health professionals and others working in the fields of yoga and spirituality, life sciences, physical sciences, education and management and humanities.
Related titles: Online - full text ed.: ISSN 2231-2714. INR 1,200 domestic; USD 120 foreign to individuals; USD 160 foreign to institutions (effective 2011).
Indexed: A26, C11, CA, E08, I05, P10, P30, P48, P53, P54, PQC, S09, T02.
—IE. **CCC.**
Published by: (Swami Vivekananda Yoga Anusandhana Samsthana), Medknow Publications and Media Pvt. Ltd., B-9, Kanara Business Ctr, Off Link Rd, Ghatkopar (E), Mumbai, Maharastra 400 075, India. TEL 91-22-66491816, FAX 91-22-66491817, http://www.medknow.com. Ed. Nagendra H R.

181.45 294.54 USA ISSN 1531-2054
➤ **INTERNATIONAL JOURNAL OF YOGA THERAPY.** Abbreviated title: I J Y T. Text in English. 1990. a. USD 200 domestic to institutions; USD 230 foreign to institutions; USD 250 combined subscription domestic to institutions (print & online eds.); USD 280 combined subscription foreign to institutions (print & online eds.); free to members (effective 2011); subscr. includes Yoga Therapy Today. adv. back issues avail. **Document type:** *Journal, Academic/Scholarly.*
Formerly (until 1999): International Association of Yoga Therapists. Journal (1524-2617)
Related titles: Online - full text ed.: USD 200 to institutions (effective 2011).
Indexed: A04, C11, CA, PEI, T02.
—BLDSC (4542.701950).
Published by: International Association of Yoga Therapists, PO Box 12890, Prescott, AZ 86304. TEL 928-541-0004, mail@iayt.org. Ed. Kelly McGonigal.

➤ **INTERNATIONAL REVIEW OF SPORT AND EXERCISE PSYCHOLOGY.** *see* PSYCHOLOGY

➤ **INTERNATIONAL SOCIETY OF SPORTS NUTRITION. JOURNAL.** *see* NUTRITION AND DIETETICS

613 USA ISSN 0047-1496
GV546.5
IRONMAN. Text in English. 1936. m. USD 29.95 domestic; USD 5.99 newsstand/cover domestic; CAD 6.99 newsstand/cover in Canada (effective 2000). adv. bk.rev. charts; illus.; tr.lit. **Document type:** *Magazine, Consumer.*
Indexed: PEI.
Published by: IronMan Publishing, 1701 Ives Ave, Oxnard, CA 93033-1866. TEL 805-385-3500, FAX 805-385-3515. Ed. Stephen Holman. Pub., R&P John Balik TEL 805-385-3500 ext 318. Adv. contacts Helen Yu, Warren Wanderer. Circ: 230,000.

613 RUS
IRONMAN MAGAZINE (MOSCOW). Text in Russian. m.
Related titles: Online - full content ed.
Published by: E A M Sport Service, Ul Krzhizhanovskogo 14, korp 3, Moscow, 117218, Russian Federation. TEL 7-095-1292082.

ISOKINETICS AND EXERCISE SCIENCE. *see* MEDICAL SCIENCES—Sports Medicine

JEWISH VEGETARIAN. *see* NUTRITION AND DIETETICS

613.7 CHN ISSN 1002-8803
JIAN YU MEI/FITNESS AND BEAUTY. Text in Chinese. 1980. m. USD 74.40 (effective 2009). **Document type:** *Magazine, Consumer.*
—East View.
Published by: Zhongguo Tiyubao Yezongshe, 8, Tiyuguan Lu, Chongwen-qu, Beijing, 100061, China. TEL 86-10-67131583, FAX 86-10-67103006. **Dist. by:** China International Book Trading Corp, 35 Chegongzhuang Xilu, Haidian District, PO Box 399, Beijing 100044, China. TEL 86-10-68412045, FAX 86-10-68412023, cibtc@mail.cibtc.com.cn, http://www.cibtc.com.cn.

613.7 CHN
JIANGNAN BAOJIAN BAO. Text in Chinese. 2002. w. **Document type:** *Consumer.*
Published by: Wuxi Ribao Baoye Jituan, 1, Xueqian Donglu, Xinwen Dasha, Wuxi, Jiangsu 214002, China. TEL 86-510-2757557, wxrb@wxrb.com. **Dist. by:** China International Book Trading Corp, 35 Chegongzhuang Xilu, Haidian District, PO Box 399, Beijing 100044, China. TEL 86-10-68412045, FAX 86-10-68412023, cibtc@mail.cibtc.com.cn, http://www.cibtc.com.cn.

613.7 CHN ISSN 1005-7803
JIANGSU WEISHENG SHIYE GUANLI/JIANGSU HEALTH CARE MANAGEMENT. Variant title: Jiangsu Hygienic Undertakings and Management. Text in Chinese. 1990. bi-m. USD 31.20 (effective 2009). **Document type:** *Journal, Academic/Scholarly.*
Related titles: Online - full text ed.
—East View.
Published by: Jiangsu Sheng Weishengting, 42, Zhongyang Lu, Nanjing, 210008, China. **Dist. by:** China International Book Trading Corp, 35 Chegongzhuang Xilu, Haidian District, PO Box 399, Beijing 100044, China. TEL 86-10-68412045, FAX 86-10-68412023, cibtc@mail.cibtc.com.cn, http://www.cibtc.com.cn.

613.7 CHN ISSN 1002-297X
JIANKANG/HEALTH MAGAZINE. Text in Chinese. 1980. m. USD 43.20 (effective 2009). adv. **Document type:** *Magazine, Government.* **Description:** Covers general medical and disease prevention knowledge.
Related titles: Online - full text ed.
—East View.
Published by: Beijing Shi Jibeing Yufang Kongzhi Zhongxin/Beijing Center for Disease Prevention and Control, Dongcheng-qu, 16, Hepingli Zhongjie, Beijing, 100013, China. TEL 86-10-64201826, FAX 86-10-84255225, http://www.bjcdc.org. Circ: 100,000. **Dist. by:** China International Book Trading Corp, 35 Chegongzhuang Xilu, Haidian District, PO Box 399, Beijing 100044, China. TEL 86-10-68412045, FAX 86-10-68412023, cibtc@mail.cibtc.com.cn, http://www.cibtc.com.cn.

613.2 CHN
JIANKANG BAO/HEALTH NEWSPAPER. Text in Chinese. 1931. d. (Mon.-Fri.). CNY 222, USD 80.40 (effective 2005). **Document type:** *Newspaper, Consumer.*
Indexed: INI.
Published by: Jiankang Baoshe, Dongzhimen Wai, 6, Xiaojiejia, Beijing, 100027, China. TEL 86-10-64620055. **Dist. by:** China International Book Trading Corp, 35 Chegongzhuang Xilu, Haidian District, PO Box 399, Beijing 100044, China. TEL 86-10-68412045, FAX 86-10-68412023, cibtc@mail.cibtc.com.cn, http://www.cibtc.com.cn.

613.7 CHN ISSN 1006-415X
JIANKANG BOLAN/HEALTH REVIEW. Text in Chinese. USD 30 (effective 2009). **Document type:** *Magazine, Consumer.* **Description:** Provides information on health, life style, diets, love and other related subjects.
Address: 630, Xincheng Rd., Rm 1005, Zhejiang CDC Bldg. 1003, Hangzhou, 310004, China. TEL 86-571-87115241, FAX 86-571-87115242. **Dist. by:** China International Book Trading Corp, 35 Chegongzhuang Xilu, Haidian District, PO Box 399, Beijing 100044, China. TEL 86-10-68412045, FAX 86-10-68412023, cibtc@mail.cibtc.com.cn, http://www.cibtc.com.cn.

613.7 CHN ISSN 1009-9409
JIANKANG NUHAI/SUNSHINE GIRL. Text in Chinese. 1985. m. CNY 7.20. **Document type:** *Magazine, Consumer.*
Formerly (until 2000): Qingchun yu Jiankang/Youth and Health (1005-5487)
Published by: Shanghai Jiankang Jiaoyusuo, 394, Zhoushan Lu, Shanghai, 200082, China. TEL 86-21-65460177, FAX 86-21-65861526. Circ: 200,000.

613.7 028.5 CHN ISSN 1002-3089
JIANKANG SHAONIAN HUABAO/HEALTHY CHILDREN'S PICTORIAL. Text in Chinese. 1985. bi-m. **Document type:** *Journal, Academic/Scholarly.*
Published by: Beijing Shi Weishengju, 45, Dong Siliu Tiao, Dongcheng-qu, Beijing, 100007, China. TEL 86-10-8401491, FAX 86-10-8408491.

613.7 CHN ISSN 1005-4596
JIANKANG SHIJIE/HEALTH WORLD. Text in Chinese. 1979. m. USD 62.40 (effective 2009). **Document type:** *Magazine, Consumer.*
—East View.
Address: 15, Deshengmen Dajie, #1 Bldg., Unit 3, Rm. 601, Beijing, 100088, China. TEL 86-10-82292929 ext 612, FAX 86-10-82292833.

613.7 CHN ISSN 1002-431X
JIANKANG TIANDI/HEALTH WORLD. Text in Chinese. 1979. m. USD 48 (effective 2009). **Document type:** *Journal, Academic/Scholarly.*
Address: 36, Hongqi Lu, Baoding, 071000, China. TEL 86-312-5086669. **Dist. by:** China International Book Trading Corp, 35 Chegongzhuang Xilu, Haidian District, PO Box 399, Beijing 100044, China. TEL 86-10-68412045, FAX 86-10-68412023, cibtc@mail.cibtc.com.cn, http://www.cibtc.com.cn.

613.7 CHN ISSN 1674-6449
JIANKANG YANJIU/HEALTH RESEARCH. Text in Chinese. 1978. bi-m. CNY 10 (effective 2010). **Document type:** *Journal, Academic/Scholarly.*
Former titles (until 2008): Hangzhou Shifan Xueyuan Xuebao (Yixue Ban)/Hangzhou Teachers College (Medical Edition). Journal; (until 2005): Hangzhou Yixue Gaodeng Zhuanke Xuexiao Xuebao/Hangzhou Medical College. Journal (1008-4894)
Related titles: Online - full text ed.
Published by: Hangzhou Shifan Xueyuan Xueshu Jikanshe/Hangzhou Teachers College, 16, Xuelin Jie, Xiasha Gaojiaoyuan, Hangzhou, 310036, China. TEL 86-571-28865871, FAX 86-571-28865871.

613.7 CHN ISSN 1002-7270
RA773
JIANKANG ZHINAN (ZHONG LAO NAN)/GUIDE TO HEALTH. Text in Chinese. 1988. bi-m. USD 39.60 (effective 2009). **Document type:** *Magazine, Consumer.*
Published by: Quanguo Laoganbu Jiankang Zhidao Weiyuanhui/National Health Committee for Senior Officials, c/o Beijing Daxue, Yixue Bu, Beingli Lou 251, Beijing, 100083, China. TEL 86-10-82801682. Ed. Jun-Bo Zhi. **Dist. by:** China International Book Trading Corp, 35 Chegongzhuang Xilu, Haidian District, PO Box 399, Beijing 100044, China. TEL 86-10-68412045, FAX 86-10-68412023, cibtc@mail.cibtc.com.cn, http://www.cibtc.com.cn.

613.7 CHN ISSN 1674-1412
JIANKANG ZHONGGAO/HEALTH ADVICE. Text in Chinese. 2008. m. **Document type:** *Magazine, Consumer.*
Published by: Guangdong Sheng Chuban Jituan Youxian Gongsi/Guangdong Provincial Publishing Group, 472, Huanshi Dong Lu, Yuehai Dasha 11/F., Guangzhou, 510075, China. http://www.gdpg.com.cn.

613.7 CHN ISSN 1000-9701
JIEFANGJUN JIANKANG/P L A HEALTH. Text in Chinese. 1987. bi-m. USD 12.60 (effective 2009). **Document type:** *Journal, Academic/Scholarly.*
Related titles: Online - full text ed.
—East View.
Address: 36, Wenhua Donglu, Jinan, 250014, China. **Dist. by:** China International Book Trading Corp, 35 Chegongzhuang Xilu, Haidian District, PO Box 399, Beijing 100044, China. TEL 86-10-68412045, FAX 86-10-68412023, cibtc@mail.cibtc.com.cn, http://www.cibtc.com.cn.

JOSAI DAIGAKU KENKYU NENPO. SHIZEN KAGAKU HEN/JOSAI UNIVERSITY BULLETIN OF LIBERAL ARTS. NATURAL SCIENCE, HEALTH AND PHYSICAL EDUCATION. *see* HUMANITIES: COMPREHENSIVE WORKS

JOURNAL OF AGING AND PHYSICAL ACTIVITY. *see* GERONTOLOGY AND GERIATRICS

613.7 USA ISSN 0744-8481
RA564.5
➤ **JOURNAL OF AMERICAN COLLEGE HEALTH.** Text in English. 1952. 8/yr. GBP 235 combined subscription in United Kingdom to institutions (print & online eds.); EUR 310, USD 387 combined subscription to institutions (print & online eds.) (effective 2012). adv. bk.rev. charts; illus. index. 2 cols./p.; back issues avail.; reprint service avail. from PSC. **Document type:** *Journal, Academic/Scholarly.* **Description:** Covers developments and research in this broad field, including administration, clinical and preventive medicine, environmental health and safety, nursing diagnosis, pharmacy, and sports medicine.
Former titles (until 1982): American College Health Association. Journal (0164-4300); (until 1962): Student Medicine (0096-7149)
Related titles: CD-ROM ed.; Microform ed.; Online - full text ed.: ISSN 1940-3208. GBP 211 in United Kingdom to institutions; EUR 279, USD 348 to institutions (effective 2012).
Indexed: A01, A02, A03, A08, A20, A22, A26, ASCA, ASSIA, B04, BRD, C06, C07, C08, C11, CA, CINAHL, CISA, CLFP, CWI, ChemAb, CurCont, DIP, E-psyche, E02, E03, E06, E07, E08, EAA, EMBASE, ERI, ERIC, EdA, EdI, ExcerpMed, FamI, G08, H04, H11, H12, HEA, HospLI, I05, IBR, IBZ, INI, IndMed, M01, M02, M06, MEDLINE, P03, P04, P07, P18, P19, P20, P22, P24, P25, P30, P34, P43, P48, P53, P54, PEI, PQC, PsycInfo, PsycholAb, R10, Reac, S02, S03, S04, S09, SCOPUS, SD, SSCI, T02, THA, W03, W05, W07.
—BLDSC (4927.231000), GNLM, IE, Infotrieve, Ingenta, INIST. **CCC.**
Published by: (American College Health Association), Routledge (Subsidiary of: Taylor & Francis Group), 325 Chestnut St, Ste 800, Philadelphia, PA 19106. TEL 215-625-8900, FAX 215-625-2940, journals@routledge.com, http://www.routledge.com. **Co-sponsor:** Helen Dwight Reid Educational Foundation.

➤ **JOURNAL OF BIOENERGETICS AND BIOMEMBRANES.** *see* BIOLOGY—Biochemistry

➤ **JOURNAL OF CONSUMER HEALTH ON THE INTERNET.** *see* COMPUTERS—Internet

613 610 USA ISSN 1044-2790
THE JOURNAL OF HEALTH & HEALING. Text in English. 1975. q. USD 12 domestic; USD 18 in Canada; USD 32 elsewhere (effective 2010). charts; illus. index. back issues avail. **Document type:** *Journal, Academic/Scholarly.* **Description:** Emphasizes whole health for the whole person - physically, mentally, socially, and spiritually.
Formerly (until 19??): Wildwood Echoes
Published by: Wildwood Lifestyle Center & Hospital, 435 Lifestyle Ln, Wildwood, GA 30757.

613.7 200 USA ISSN 0885-4726
BV4335
➤ **JOURNAL OF HEALTH CARE CHAPLAINCY.** Abbreviated title: J H C C. Text in English. 1987. s-a. GBP 251 combined subscription in United Kingdom to institutions (print & online eds.); EUR 326, USD 323 combined subscription to institutions (print & online eds.) (effective 2012). adv. bk.rev. 120 p./no. 1 cols./p.; back issues avail.; reprint service avail. from PSC. **Document type:** *Journal, Academic/Scholarly.* **Description:** Promotes both foundational and applied interdisciplinary research related to chaplaincy as practiced in community hospitals, medical centers, nursing homes, and other health care institutions.
Related titles: Microfiche ed.: (from PQC); Microform ed.; Online - full text ed.: ISSN 1528-6916. GBP 226 in United Kingdom to institutions; EUR 293, USD 291 to institutions (effective 2012).
Indexed: A01, A03, A21, A22, C06, C07, C08, CA, CINAHL, E01, EMBASE, ExcerpMed, FamI, INI, IndMed, J01, M02, MEDLINE, P30, P50, PerIslam, R&TA, RI-1, RI-2, S02, S03, SCOPUS, T02.
—GNLM, IE. **CCC.**

P

Published by: Routledge (Subsidiary of: Taylor & Francis Group), 325 Chestnut St, Ste 800, Philadelphia, PA 19106. TEL 215-625-8900, 800-354-1420, FAX 215-625-8914, journals@routledge.com, http://www.routledge.com. Ed. Kevin Flannelly. adv.: B&W page USD 315, color page USD 550; trim 4.375 x 7.125. Circ: 277 (paid).

613.7 POL ISSN 1640-5544
JOURNAL OF HUMAN KINETICS. Text in English. 1999. s-a. EUR 32 foreign (effective 2006). **Document type:** *Journal, Academic/Scholarly.*
Formerly (until 1999): Antropomotoryka (0860-9853)
Indexed: P30, SCI, SCOPUS, W07.
—BLDSC (5003.416600), IE, Ingenta.
Published by: (Polska Akademia Nauk, Komitet Nauk o Kulturze Fizycznej/Polish Academy of Science, Committee of Physical Culture), Akademia Wychowania Fizycznego w Katowicach, Katedra Nauk Biologicznych/Academy of Physical Education in Katowice, ul Raciborska 1, Katowice, 40065, Poland. TEL 48-32-2075100. Ed. Jan Szopa. **Dist. by:** Ars Polona, Obroncow 25, Warsaw 03933, Poland. TEL 48-22-5098609, FAX 48-22-5098610, arspolona@arspolona.com.pl, http://www.arspolona.com.pl. **Co-sponsor:** International Association of Sport Kinetics.

JOURNAL OF LONGEVITY; when traditional & scientific approaches to aging come together. *see* GERONTOLOGY AND GERIATRICS

613.7 USA ISSN 1546-5381
JOURNAL OF MARTIAL ARTS & HEALING. Text in English. 2005. s-a. USD 25 domestic; USD 32 foreign (effective 2007). **Document type:** *Magazine, Consumer.* **Description:** Features information about how martial arts and meditation contribute to physical and mental health.
Address: 26B E Park Dr, Athens, OH 45701. TEL 740-593-7915, threetreasures@frognet.net. Ed. Frances Gander.

▼ **JOURNAL OF MID - LIFE HEALTH.** *see* MEDICAL SCIENCES

613.7 USA ISSN 1543-3080
GV481
➤ **JOURNAL OF PHYSICAL ACTIVITY & HEALTH.** Text in English. 2004 (Jan.). 8/yr. USD 606 combined subscription domestic to institutions (print & online eds.); USD 621 combined subscription foreign to institutions (print & online eds.) (effective 2012). adv. **Document type:** *Journal, Academic/Scholarly.* **Description:** Publishes research articles and papers examining the relationship between physical activity and health, studying physical activity as an exposure as well as an outcome.
Related titles: Online - full text ed.: ISSN 1543-5474. 2004 (Jan.). USD 566 to institutions (effective 2012).
Indexed: CA, CurCont, EMBASE, ExcerpMed, MEDLINE, P03, P30, PEI, PsycInfo, R09, R10, Reac, SCOPUS, SD, SSCI, T02, W07.
—BLDSC (5035.600000), IE, Ingenta. **CCC.**
Published by: Human Kinetics, 1607 N Market St, Champaign, IL 61820. TEL 800-747-4457, FAX 217-351-2674, orders@hkusa.com, http://www.humankinetics.com. Eds. Harold W Kohl III, Jennifer M Hootman. R&P Martha Gullo TEL 217-403-7534. Adv. contact Amy Bleich TEL 217-403-7803. Circ: 458 (paid).

613.7 617.1 NGA
➤ **JOURNAL OF PHYSICAL EDUCATION AND SPORT MANAGEMENT.** Text in English. m. free (effective 2010). adv. **Document type:** *Journal, Academic/Scholarly.*
Media: Online - full text.
Published by: Academic Journals, PO Box 73023, Victoria Island, Lagos, Nigeria. service@academicjournals.org. Eds. Chung Pak-kwong, Nader Rahnamg, Dr. Van Hung.

➤ **JOURNAL OF PHYSICAL EDUCATION, RECREATION AND DANCE.** *see* EDUCATION—Teaching Methods And Curriculum

➤ **THE JOURNAL OF SPORTS MEDICINE AND PHYSICAL FITNESS**; a journal on applied physiology, biomechanics, preventive medicine, sports medicine and traumatology, sports psychology. *see* MEDICAL SCIENCES—Sports Medicine

➤ **JOURNAL OF STRENGTH AND CONDITIONING RESEARCH.** *see* MEDICAL SCIENCES—Sports Medicine

➤ **JOURNAL OF TOURISM CHALLENGES AND TRENDS.** *see* TRAVEL AND TOURISM

➤ **JOURNAL OF UNDERGRADUATE KINESIOLOGY RESEARCH.** *see* MEDICAL SCIENCES—Physical Medicine And Rehabilitation

796 613.7 FIN ISSN 0782-4971
JUOKSIJA. Text in Finnish. 1971. 10/yr. EUR 54 domestic; EUR 61 foreign (effective 2005). adv. bk.rev. 96 p./no. 3 cols./p.; **Document type:** *Magazine, Consumer.* **Description:** Devoted to running, cross-country skiing, and physical fitness.
Published by: Kustannusyhtio Juoksija Oy, Olympic Stadium, Etelakaare B 10, Helsinki, 00250, Finland. TEL 358-9-4342040, FAX 358-9-43420444. Ed. Ari Paunonen TEL 358-9-43420413. Pub., R&P Tapio Pekola. Adv. contact Ilkka Kalermo. B&W page EUR 920, color page EUR 2,800; trim 185 x 260. Circ: 13,000.

613.7 USA ISSN 1536-5549
A K W A MAGAZINE. Text in English. 1986. bi-m. free to members (effective 2010). adv. back issues avail. **Document type:** *Magazine, Consumer.*
Formerly (until 2001): The A K W A Letter (1091-5249)
Published by: Aquatic Exercise Association, Inc., PO Box 1609, Nokomis, FL 34274. TEL 941-486-8600, 888-232-9283, FAX 941-486-8820, info@aeawave.com, http://www.aeawave.com.

613.7 TWN
KANGJIAN ZAZHI/COMMON HEALTH. Text in Chinese. 2000. m. TWD 1,800 (effective 2002). **Document type:** *Magazine, Consumer.*
Related titles: Online - full content ed.: ISSN 1606-724X.
Published by: Tianxia Zazhi/Common Wealth Magazine Co., 104 Songjiang Road, no.87, 4F, Taipei, Taiwan. TEL 886-2-2662-0332, FAX 886-2-2662-6048.

613 JPN
KENKO/HEALTH. Text in Japanese. 1976. m. JPY 6,840 domestic; JPY 12,480 foreign (effective 2001). adv. bk.rev. **Document type:** *Consumer.*
Formerly: Watashi no Kenko - My Health
Published by: Shufunotomo Co. Ltd., 2-9 Kanda-Surugadai, Chiyoda-ku, Tokyo, 101-8911, Japan. TEL 81-3-5280-7541, FAX 81-3-5280-7441. Ed. Yuuichiro Takahashi. Circ: 140,000.

613.7 USA
KENTUCKIANA HEALTHFITNESS MAGAZINE. Text in English. m. **Document type:** *Magazine, Consumer.* **Description:** Covers health and fitness issues.
Media: Online - full text.
Address: P O Box 436387, Louisville, KY 40253-6387. FAX 502-245-4098. Ed. Barbara Day.

KENTUCKY ASSOCIATION FOR HEALTH, PHYSICAL EDUCATION, RECREATION AND DANCE. JOURNAL. *see* EDUCATION

613.7 658.8 GBR
KEY NOTE MARKET REPORT: HEALTH CLUBS AND LEISURE CENTRES. Variant title: Health Clubs and Leisure Centres Market Report. Text in English. 1994. irreg., latest 2009, Jan. GBP 460 per issue (effective 2010). **Document type:** *Report, Trade.* **Description:** Provides an overview of a specific UK market segment and includes executive summary, market definition, market size, industry background, competitor analysis, current issues, forecasts, company profiles, and more.
Formerly (until 1999): Key Note Report: Health Clubs and Leisure Centres (1354-179X)
Related titles: CD-ROM ed.; Online - full text ed.
Published by: Key Note Ltd. (Subsidiary of: Bonnier Business Information), Harlequin House, 5th Fl, 7 High St, Teddington, Richmond upon Thames, TW11 8EE, United Kingdom. TEL 44-845-5040452, FAX 44-845-5040453, info@keynote.co.uk.

613.7 USA ISSN 2162-1845
KI MOMENTS. Text in English. 2005. m. free (effective 2011). **Document type:** *Newsletter, Trade.*
Media: E-mail.
Published by: Judy Ringer, Ed. & Pub., 76 Park St, Portsmouth, NH 03801. TEL 603-431-8560, judy@judyringer.com, http://www.judyringer.com.

613.7 NLD ISSN 1877-9778
KIJKKEZ GEZONDHEIDSZORG. Text in Dutch. 2008. s-a. free (effective 2010). adv.
Published by: Uitgeverij Maypress, Postbus 53, Heerhugowaard, 1700 AB, Netherlands. TEL 31-72-5715013, FAX 31-72-5715214, maypress@maypress.nl, http://www.maypress.nl.

613.7 SVN ISSN 1318-2269
➤ **KINESIOLOGIA SLOVENICA**; scientific journal on sport. Text in Slovenian. 1992. s-a. EUR 20 in Europe; EUR 50 elsewhere (effective 2008). **Document type:** *Journal, Academic/Scholarly.* **Description:** Publishes empirical and theoretical contributions related to the science of physical activity, human movement, exercise, and sport.
Indexed: CA, SD, T02.
—BLDSC (5096.010000).
Published by: Univerza v Ljubljani, Fakulteta za Sport, Institut za Kineziologijo, Gortanova 22, Ljubljana, Slovenia. TEL 386-1-5207700, FAX 386-1-5207750. Ed. Milan Coh.

613.7 HRV ISSN 1331-1441
QP303
➤ **KINESIOLOGY.** Text in English. 1996. s-a. **Document type:** *Journal, Academic/Scholarly.*
Supersedes in part (in 1996): Kineziologija (0351-1057)
Indexed: A01, A02, A03, A08, A26, CA, FoSS&M, I05, P03, P30, PEI, PsycInfo, PsycholAb, R09, SCI, SCOPUS, SD, SSCI, T02, W07.
—BLDSC (5096.020200).
Published by: Sveuciliste u Zagrebu, Kinezioloski Fakultet, Horvacanski zavoj 15, Zagreb, Croatia. TEL 385-1-3658666, FAX 385-1-3658646, dekanat@kif.hr, http://www.kif.hr.

613.7 DEU
KIRROYAL. Text in German. 2005. bi-m. EUR 9.60; EUR 2.40 newsstand/cover (effective 2008). adv. **Document type:** *Magazine, Consumer.*
Formerly (until 2006): Chiemroyal
Published by: Weilacher Werbung Verlag PR, Hafnerstr 13, Bad Aibling, 83043, Germany. TEL 49-8061-392788, office@kirroyal.eu, http://www.weilacher.de. adv.: page EUR 2,400. Circ: 20,000 (paid and controlled).

613 DEU
KNEIPP JOURNAL. Text in German. 1891. m. EUR 2.50 newsstand/cover (effective 2007). adv. bk.rev. illus. **Document type:** *Magazine, Consumer.*
Formerly: Kneipp Blaetter (0023-2254)
—CCC.
Published by: Kneipp Verlag GmbH, Adolf Scholz Allee 6-8, Bad Woerishofen, 86825, Germany. TEL 49-8247-3002102, FAX 49-8247-3002164, kneippverlag@t-online.de, http://www.kneippverlag.de. Ed. Ulf Fink. R&P Beate Seesslen. Adv. contact Annette Kersting. B&W page EUR 3,095, color page EUR 4,800. Circ: 110,981 (paid and controlled).

613.7 AUT
KNEIPP ZEITSCHRIFT; das oesterreichische Gesundheitsmagazin. Text in German. 10/yr. EUR 25 membership (effective 2007). **Document type:** *Magazine, Consumer.*
Former titles: Kneipp Magazin (1013-2147); (until 1981): Das Oesterreichische Kneipp-Magazin (0250-5428); (until 1974): Oesterreichisches Kneipp Jahrbuch
Published by: Oesterreichischer Kneippbund, Kunigundenweg 10, Leoben, St 8700, Austria. TEL 43-3842-21718, FAX 43-3842-2171819, office@kneippbund.at. Ed. Waltraud Ruth. Adv. contact Monika Brunner. Circ: 57,000 (controlled).

613.7 POL ISSN 1732-0895
KONSYLIARZ. Text in Polish. 2004. m. PLZ 60 (effective 2006). **Document type:** *Magazine, Consumer.*
Published by: ViMedia, ul Marii Konopnickiej 6, Warsaw, 00-491, Poland. biuro@vimedia.com.pl, http://www.vimedia.com.pl. Ed. Mateusz Kuczabsky. Adv. contact Sylwia Guzowska.

613 FIN ISSN 0787-9385
KOTILAAKARI. Text in Finnish. 1889. 10/yr. EUR 58.60 (effective 2005). adv. illus. **Document type:** *Magazine, Consumer.* **Description:** Features diverse, challenging contents and a holistic approach to health.
Former titles (until 1978): T H Kotilaakari (0355-1903); (until 1975): Terveydenhoitolehti (0040-3903); (until 1896): Suomen Terveydenhoitolehti; Incorporates (1936-1995): Terveys (0040-3911)
Published by: Yhtyneet Kuvalehdet Oy/United Magazines Ltd., Maistraatinportti 1, Helsinki, 00015, Finland. TEL 358-9-15661, FAX 358-9-145650, http://www.kuvalehdet.fi. Ed. Taina Salomaa. Circ: 60,000.

613.7 JPN
KOTOBUKI/LONGEVITY. Text in Japanese. 1981. m. JPY 6,930 (effective 2007). **Document type:** *Magazine, Consumer.*
Published by: Doraggu Magajin/Drugmagazine Co., Ltd., 2-3-15 Nihonbashihoncho, Chuo-ku, Tokyo, 103-0023, Japan. TEL 81-3-32414661, FAX 81-3-32414594.

613.7 ESP ISSN 1579-5225
KRONOS; la revista cientifica de actividad fisica y deporte. Text in Spanish. 2002. s-a. **Document type:** *Journal, Academic/Scholarly.*
Indexed: CA, F04, SD, T02.
Published by: Universidad Europea de Madrid, Facultad de Ciencias de la Actividad Fisica y el Deporte, Tajos s/n, Villaviciosa de Odon, Madrid, Spain. TEL 34-91-2115200, uem@uem.es, http://www.uem.es.

613.7 POL ISSN 0137-7671
KULTURA FIZYCZNA. Text in Polish. bi-m. **Document type:** *Journal, Academic/Scholarly.*
Indexed: P30.
Published by: Akademia Wychowania Fizycznego Jozefa Pilsudskiego w Warszawie, ul Marymoncka 34, Warsaw, 00968, Poland. TEL 48-22-8340431, http://www.awf.edu.pl.

613.7 IND
KUMUDAM HEALTH. Text in Tamil. bi-m. adv. back issues avail. **Document type:** *Magazine, Consumer.*
Related titles: Online - full text ed.
Published by: Kumudam Publications Pvt. Ltd., 151 Purasawalkam High Rd, Chennai, Tamil Nadu 600 010, India. TEL 91-44-26422146, FAX 91-44-26425041, kumudam@vsnl.com.

613.717 DEU ISSN 0863-3371
LAUFZEIT; Das Monatsjournal fuer alle Freunde des Laufens. Text in German. 1990. 11/yr. EUR 27 domestic; EUR 38 foreign; EUR 3 newsstand/cover (effective 2009). adv. **Document type:** *Magazine, Consumer.*
Incorporates (2003-2006): Fit mit Walking
Related titles: Online - full text ed.
Published by: Laufzeit Verlags GmbH, Danziger Str 219, Berlin, 10407, Germany. TEL 49-30-4235066, FAX 49-30-4241717. Ed. Wolfgang Weising. Adv. contact Matthias Thiel. B&W page EUR 1,250, color page EUR 2,030; trim 185 x 257. Circ: 15,973 (paid and controlled).

613.7 DEU
LEBENS(T)RAEUME; Das Magazin fuer Gesundheit und Bewusstsein. Text in German. 10/yr. EUR 30; EUR 3 newsstand/cover (effective 2009). adv. **Document type:** *Magazine, Trade.*
Published by: Lebens-t-raeume, Stumpenstr 1, Villingen, 78052, Germany. TEL 49-7721-63315, FAX 49-7721-74306. Ed. Wolfgang Maiworm. Adv. contact Ursel Maiworm. B&W page EUR 1,500, color page EUR 1,980; trim 210 x 297. Circ: 12,000 (paid and controlled).

LEHRHILFEN FUER DEN SPORTUNTERRICHT. *see* EDUCATION—Teaching Methods And Curriculum

LEPA & ZDRAVA. *see* WOMEN'S INTERESTS

LIFE EXTENSION; the ultimate source for new health and medical findings from around the world. *see* ALTERNATIVE MEDICINE

613.7 CAN ISSN 1916-6230
LIFE TRENDS; your health and wellness magazine. Text in English. 2008. q. CAD 10.44 (effective 2010). adv. **Document type:** *Magazine, Consumer.* **Description:** Provides articles on timely and important health issues for the entire family, including health information for seniors.
Related titles: Online - full text ed.: free (effective 2010).
Published by: Merritt House Publishing Inc., 133 Richmond St, Ste 301, Toronto, ON M5H 2L3, Canada. TEL 416-703-4449, sales@merritthousemedia.com. Eds. Barb Kovacs, Kathy Bassi. Adv. contact Janet Byers TEL 905-714-9571.

613.7 CAN ISSN 1182-0489
LIFELINES (SASKATOON). Text in English. 1989. irreg. CAD 15 (effective 2000). **Document type:** *Monographic series, Academic/Scholarly.*
Published by: (Saskatchewan Health Educators Association), Saskatchewan Teachers' Federation, 2317 Arlington Ave., Saskatoon, SK S7J 2H8, Canada. stf@stf.sk.ca.

LIFELINES (TORONTO); the voice of Toronto's vegetarian community. *see* NUTRITION AND DIETETICS

613.7 USA ISSN 1946-1690
▼ **LIVE FIT E-ZINE.** Text in English. 2009. m. free (effective 2009). back issues avail. **Document type:** *Magazine, Consumer.*
Media: Online - full content.
Published by: Ron Betta, Pub ron@livefitezine.com.

LIVING FIT. *see* WOMEN'S HEALTH

613 USA
LIVING HEALTHY. Text in English. 2/yr. **Document type:** *Magazine, Consumer.*
Published by: (Blue Cross Blue Shield of Michigan), The Pohly Co., 99 Bedford St, Fl 5, Boston, MA 02111. TEL 617-451-1700, 800-383-0888, FAX 617-338-7767, info@pohlyco.com, http://www.pohlyco.com. Circ: 1,850,000 (controlled).

362 USA ISSN 2151-8173
LIVINGRIGHT (NEENAH); health & wellness awareness program. Text in English. 2008. m. USD 179 (effective 2009). **Document type:** *Bulletin, Consumer.* **Description:** Contains the tools for educating employees on one specific topic such as blood pressure education, nutrition, saving your vision, cancer control, better sleep, heart health, and many more.
Related titles: Online - full text ed.: ISSN 2151-8181.
Published by: J.J. Keller & Associates, Inc., 3003 Breezewood Ln, PO Box 368, Neenah, WI 54957. TEL 877-564-2333, FAX 800-727-7516, sales@jjkeller.com.

613.7 613.2 FRA ISSN 1960-8462
LONG LIFE. Text in French. 2007. bi-m. **Document type:** *Magazine, Consumer.*
Published by: Editions Riva, 16 Rue de la Fontaine-au-Roi, Paris, 75011, France.

613.7 USA ISSN 0890-4189
GV510.U5
LOOKING FIT. Text in English. 1986. m. **Document type:** *Magazine, Trade.* **Description:** For health conscious tanning and full service salon management.
Related titles: Online - full text ed.
Published by: Virgo Publishing, Llc, PO Box 40079, Phoenix, AZ 85067. TEL 480-990-1101, FAX 480-990-0819, jsiefert@vpico.com, http://www.vpico.com. Ed. Karen Butler TEL 480-990-1101 ext 2251. Circ: 20,000 (paid and controlled).

613.7 CAN
LOOKING GREAT. Text in English. q. CAD 14.95 (effective 2005). **Document type:** *Magazine, Consumer.* **Description:** Designed to help you develop ways to look and feel better according to your own terms, whether to regain what you had or protect what you've got.
Published by: August Communications, 225-530 Century St, Winnipeg, MB R3H 0Y4, Canada. TEL 204-957-0265, 888-573-1136, FAX 204-957-0217, 866-957-0217, info@august.ca.

LUDICA PEDAGOGICA. *see* EDUCATION—Teaching Methods And Curriculum

613.7 910.09 USA ISSN 1553-0698
RA794
LUXURY SPAFINDER MAGAZINE. Text in English. 1987. bi-m. USD 19 domestic; USD 29 in Canada; USD 34 elsewhere (effective 2005). adv. maps. **Document type:** *Magazine, Consumer.* **Description:** Contains information on the world's great spas and fitness resorts for health, fitness and beauty enthusiasts.
Formerly: Spa Finder (1088-9027)
Published by: Spa Finders - Travel Arrangements Ltd., 91 Fifth Ave, New York, NY 10003-3039. TEL 212-924-6800, FAX 212-924-7240. Ed. Frank Van Patten. Pubs. Frank Van Patten, Jed Horowitz. Adv. contact Jed Horowitz. B&W page USD 9,500, color page USD 9,900; trim 10.75 x 8.5. Circ: 150,000.

613.7 RUS ISSN 1682-7090
M K ZDOROV'YE. Text in Russian. 2000. m. **Document type:** *Newspaper, Consumer.*
Related titles: Online - full content ed.
Published by: Moskovskii Komsomolets, ul 1905 goda, dom 7, Moscow, 123995, Russian Federation. TEL 7-095-2532094, podpiska@mk.ru.

613.2 SWE ISSN 0346-6280
MAA BRA; specialtidningen foer kropp & sjael. Text in Swedish. 1976. m. SEK 360 (effective 2005). adv. 4 cols./p.; **Document type:** *Magazine, Consumer.* **Description:** Presents articles and features on how to lead a healthy life without sacrificing pleasure.
Published by: Allers Foerlag AB, Landskronavaegen 23, Helsingborg, 25185, Sweden. TEL 46-42-173500, FAX 46-42-173682, http://www.allersforlag.se. Ed. Inger Ridstroem. Adv. contact Lilimor Werre TEL 46-8-6794681. page SEK 51,000; trim 190 x 265. Circ: 123,200 (paid).

AL-MAGALLAT AL-'ILMIYYAT LI-'ULUM AL-TARBIYYAT AL-BADANIYYAT WA-AL-RIYYADIYYAT/SCIENTIFIC JOURNAL FOR PHYSICAL EDUCATION AND SPORTS SCIENCES. *see* EDUCATION—Higher Education

613 DEU
DAS MAGAZIN AUS IHRER APOTHEKE. Text in German. m. **Document type:** *Magazine, Consumer.*
Formerly (until 2005): Das Wellness-Magazin aus Ihrer Apotheke
Published by: M K V Medienkontor Verlagsgesellschaft mbH & Co. KG, Rathausstr 28, Bargteheide, 22941, Germany. TEL 49-4532-28670, FAX 49-4532-286750, info@mkv-medienkontor.de, http://www.mkv-apotheken-kombi.de. Circ: 1,198,000 (controlled).

646.7 POL ISSN 1734-5456
MAGAZYN EDEN. Text in Polish. 2005. m. PLZ 72 (effective 2006). adv. **Document type:** *Magazine, Consumer.*
Published by: ViMedia, ul Marii Konopnickiej 6, Warsaw, 00-491, Poland. biuro@vimedia.com.pl, http://www.vimedia.com.pl. Ed. Danuta Zdanowicz. Adv. contact Sylwia Guzowska.

613 JPN
MAINICHI RAIFU/MAINICHI LIFE. Text in Japanese. 1970. m. JPY 550 newsstand/cover (effective 2008). **Document type:** *Magazine, Consumer.*
Published by: Mainichi Shinbunsha/Mainichi Newspapers, 1-1-1 Hitotsubashi, Chiyoda-ku, Tokyo, 100-8051, Japan. TEL 81-3-32120321. Ed. Yasuo Miyazawa.

613.7 CAN ISSN 1206-0011
MANITOBA PHYSICAL EDUCATION TEACHERS' ASSOCIATION. JOURNAL. Text in English. 197?. q. **Document type:** *Journal, Academic/Scholarly.*
Former titles (until 1988): M P E T A Journal (1483-7595); (until 1985): Manitoba Physical Education Teachers' Association (0706-0882); (until 1977): Manitoba Physical Education Teachers' Association. Newsletter (0384-7462); (until 1975): C A H P E R Journal. Manitoba Branch (0315-9302)
Indexed: C03, CEI, P48, PQC.
Published by: Manitoba Physical Education Teachers' Association, 200 Main St, Suite 303, Winnipeg, MB R2C 4M2, Canada. TEL 204-926-8357, FAX 204-925-5703, mpeta@shaw.ca.

MARKETING HEALTH SERVICES. *see* BUSINESS AND ECONOMICS—Marketing And Purchasing

THE MARTIAL ARTS JOURNAL; the online magazine uniting martial artists worldwide. *see* SPORTS AND GAMES

790 USA ISSN 1090-7122
MARYLAND SPORTS, HEALTH & FITNESS MAGAZINE. Text in English. bi-m. adv.
Published by: Frontline Communications Group, 8268 Streamwood Dr, Baltimore, MD 21208. TEL 410-922-1158. Adv. contact Greg Osita.

615.82 USA ISSN 1544-8827
MASSAGE AND BODYWORK; nuturing body, mind & spirit. Text in English. 1988. bi-m. USD 26 in US & Canada; USD 75 elsewhere (effective 2010). adv. music rev.; video rev.; bk.rev. tr.lit. 168 p./no.; back issues avail. **Document type:** *Magazine, Consumer.* **Description:** For an International audience of massage, bodywork, somatic and esthetic therapy professionals. The latest research, historical perspectives massage techniques, business information, professional trends and a variety of regularly featured columns keep the audience in touch with their work, their clients and their health.
Former titles (until 1997): Massage and Bodywork Quarterly (1066-9337); Associated Bodywork and Massage Professionals News (1053-458X)
Related titles: Diskette ed.; Online - full text ed.
Indexed: A04, A10, AMED, C06, C07, C08, CINAHL, R09, SD, T02, V03. —BLDSC (5388.692470), IE, Ingenta.
Published by: Associated Bodywork and Massage Professionals Inc., 25188 Genesee Trail Rd, Ste 200, Golden, CO 80401. TEL 800-458-2267, FAX 800-667-8260, http://www.abmp.com. Ed. Leslie A. Young. Adv. contact Angie Parris-Raney. B&W page USD 2,635, color page USD 3,530; trim 8.25 x 10.875. Circ: 75,623 (paid). **Dist. by:** IPD, 3360 Industrial Rd, Harrisburg, PA 17110.

613.7 USA
MAXIMUM FITNESS. Text in English. 2000. bi-m. USD 14.97 domestic; USD 19.97 in Canada; USD 39.97 newsstand/cover (effective 2006). adv. illus. **Document type:** *Magazine, Consumer.*
Formerly (until Jan. 2006): American Health & Fitness (1533-6352)
Published by: Canusa Products, Inc., 205 McKinley St, Hollywood, FL 33020. http://www.ahfmag.com. Ed. Matt Nicholls.

613.7 CAN ISSN 1911-6225
MAXIMUM FITNESS FOR MEN. Text in English. 2006. q. CAD 11.97 (effective 2007). **Document type:** *Magazine, Consumer.*
Published by: Maximum Fitness, 5775 McLaughlin Rd., Mississauga, ON L5R 3P7, Canada.

613.7 USA ISSN 1091-367X
GV436 CODEN: MPESFC
➤ **MEASUREMENT IN PHYSICAL EDUCATION AND EXERCISE SCIENCE.** Abbreviated title: M P E E S. Text in English. 1997. q. GBP 384 combined subscription in United Kingdom to institutions (print & online eds.); EUR 512, USD 644 combined subscription to institutions (print & online eds.) (effective 2012). adv. back issues avail.; reprint service avail. from PSC. **Document type:** *Journal, Academic/Scholarly.* **Description:** Covers research, test development, and evaluation of theoretical and methodological issues in measurement and statistics as they apply to physical education and exercise science.
Related titles: Online - full text ed.: ISSN 1532-7841. GBP 345 in United Kingdom to institutions; EUR 461, USD 579 to institutions (effective 2012).
Indexed: A01, A02, A03, A08, A22, A26, A36, C06, C07, C11, CA, CABA, E-psyche, E01, EMBASE, ERIC, ExcerpMed, GH, H04, H12, H13, I05, LT, N02, N03, P03, P10, P20, P48, P53, P54, PEI, PQC, PsycInfo, PsycholAb, R09, R12, RRTA, SCOPUS, SD, T02. —BLDSC (5413.567300), IE, Infotrieve, Ingenta. **CCC.**
Published by: (American Association for Active Lifestyles and Fitness), Routledge (Subsidiary of: Taylor & Francis Group), 325 Chestnut St, Ste 800, Philadelphia, PA 19106. TEL 800-354-1420, FAX 215-625-2940, journals@routledge.com, http://www.routledge.com. Ed. Eddie T C Lam. Adv. contact Linda Hann TEL 44-1344-779945.

613 USA ISSN 0749-9973
R118.4.U6
MEDICAL AND HEALTH INFORMATION DIRECTORY. Text in English. 1978. triennial (in 3 vols.). USD 845 base vol(s). (effective 2006). **Document type:** *Directory, Trade.* **Description:** Provides guidance to organizations, agencies, institutions, services and information sources in medicine and health-related fields.
Related titles: Online - full text ed.
Published by: Gale (Subsidiary of: Cengage Learning), 27500 Drake Rd, Farmington Hills, MI 48331. TEL 248-699-4253, 800-877-4253, FAX 248-699-8035, gale.customerservice@cengage.com, http://gale.cengage.com. Ed. Bridgett Travers.

MEDICAL CORPS INTERNATIONAL; forum for military medicine and pharmacy. *see* MEDICAL SCIENCES

362.12 USA
MEDICALSPAS; the healthy aging business review. Text in English. bi-m. adv. **Document type:** *Magazine, Trade.*
Published by: Medical Spas Review, PO Box 220, Houlton, ME 04730-0220. TEL 866-450-9768, FAX 866-450-2546. Pub. Peter Cole TEL 866-450-9768. adv.: color page USD 3,165; trim 8.5 x 11. Circ: 32,735.

613 USA
MEDICINE SHOPPE TALK. Text in English. 2001. q. adv. **Document type:** *Magazine, Consumer.*
Published by: MediZine, Inc., 500 Fifth Ave, Ste 1900, New York, NY 10110. TEL 212-695-2223, requestinfo@medizine.com, http://www.medizine.com.

MEDIZINI. *see* CHILDREN AND YOUTH—For

MEGALIFE; life enhancing. *see* SPORTS AND GAMES

613.7 FIN ISSN 1459-5311
MEIDAN SAUNA/FINNISH SAUNA; kylpijan erikoislehti. Text in Finnish. 2003. 4/yr. EUR 16 (effective 2007). adv. **Document type:** *Magazine, Consumer.*
Published by: Karprint Oy, Vanha Turunrie 371, Huhmari, 03150, Finland. TEL 358-9-41397300, FAX 358-9-41397405, http://www.karprint.fi. Ed. Mari Ahola-Aalto. Adv. contact Arja Blom. page EUR 2,050. Circ: 20,000.

613.7 USA ISSN 1043-8475
CODEN: SPOKAV
MEMPHIS HEALTH CARE NEWS. Text in English. fortn. **Document type:** *Journal, Trade.*
—**CCC.**
Published by: Mid-South Communications, Inc., 88 Union, Rm 200, Memphis, TN 38103-5100. TEL 901-526-2007, FAX 901-526-5240. Ed. Deborah Dubois. Circ: 12,601.

613.7 USA ISSN 1547-3147
AP2
MEN'S EDGE. Text in English. 2004 (Feb/Mar). m. USD 5 newsstand/cover (effective 2009). adv. **Document type:** *Magazine, Consumer.*
Published by: Future U S, Inc. (Subsidiary of: Future Publishing Ltd.), 4000 Shoreline Ct, Ste 400, South San Francisco, CA 94080. TEL 650-872-1642, FAX 650-872-1643, http://www.futureus.com.

613.7 790 USA ISSN 1059-9169
MEN'S EXERCISE; the fitness guide for today's man. Text in English. 1990. bi-m. USD 17.75 domestic; USD 22.75 foreign; USD 4.95 newsstand/cover (effective 2005). adv. **Document type:** *Magazine, Consumer.* **Description:** Provides complete training routines and programs that help men build muscles, lose weight, stay fit, and look better.
Published by: Pumpkin Press, Inc., 350 Fifth Ave, Ste 3323, New York, NY 10118. TEL 212-947-4322, FAX 212-563-4774. Ed. Steve Downs. Pub. Cheh N Low. Adv. contact Robert B Rose. Circ: 150,000 (paid). **Dist. in UK by:** Seymour Distribution Ltd, 86 Newman St, London W1T 3EX, United Kingdom. FAX 44-207-396-8002, enquiries@seymour.co.uk.

MEN'S FITNESS. *see* MEN'S HEALTH

MENTAL HEALTH AND PHYSICAL ACTIVITY. *see* PSYCHOLOGY

613.7 ITA ISSN 1971-8888
MENTECORPO. Variant title: Riza MenteCorpo. Text in Italian. 2007. m. EUR 42 (effective 2010). **Document type:** *Magazine, Consumer.*
Published by: Edizioni Riza, Via Luigi Anelli 1, Milan, 20122, Italy. TEL 39-02-5845961, info@riza.it, http://www.riza.it.

613.7 615.5 CAN ISSN 1718-3758
METROLAND LIVE IT!; Canada's new health & wellness magazine. Variant title: Live It!. Text in English. 2006. q. **Document type:** *Magazine, Consumer.*
Published by: Metroland Media Group Ltd. (Subsidiary of: Torstar Corp.), 10 Tempo Ave, Willowdale, ON M2H 2N8, Canada. TEL 416-493-1300, FAX 416-493-0623, http://www.metroland.com.

MICHIGAN RUNNER. *see* SPORTS AND GAMES—Outdoor Life

613.7 CHN ISSN 1674-9561
▼ **MINGYI/RENOWNED DOCTOR.** Text in Chinese. 2010. m. CNY 108; CNY 9 per issue (effective 2011). back issues avail. **Document type:** *Magazine, Consumer.*
Related titles: Online - full text ed.
Published by: Guangdong Keji Chubanshe, 55, Zhongshan Dadao Xi, Tianhe-qu, Huanan Shifan Daxue Gaoxiao Jiaoshi Cun C-3104, Guangdong, 510631, China. TEL 86-20-85533963, FAX 86-20-85533963, http://www.gdstp.com.cn/.

613.7 ITA
MISSIONE SALUTE; bimestrale di cultura e salute sul mondo della sanita. Text in Italian. 1988. bi-m. adv. 84 p./no.; **Document type:** *Magazine, Consumer.*
Published by: Provincia Lombardo Veneta dei Camilliani d'Italia, Via Francesco Nava, 31, Milan, MI 20159, Italy. TEL 39-02-69516156, FAX 39-02-69516157, missionesalute.camillians@interbusiness.it. Circ: 20,000.

613.7 792.8 USA ISSN 1058-6288
GV224.A1
MISSOURI JOURNAL OF HEALTH, PHYSICAL EDUCATION, RECREATION AND DANCE. Text in English. 1980. a.
Indexed: CA, PEI, SD, T02.
Published by: Missouri Association for Health, Physical Education, Recreation and Dance, 1220 W Crestview, Maryville, MO 64468. TEL 660-582-7378, FAX 660-582-7380, jmahperd@asde.net, http://hes.truman.edu/moahperd. Ed. Lynn Imergoot.

613.7 CZE ISSN 1214-3871
MOJE ZDRAVI. Text in Czech. 2003. m. CZK 390 (effective 2011). adv. **Document type:** *Magazine, Consumer.*
Published by: Mlada Fronta, Mezi Vodami 1952/9, Prague 4, 14300, Czech Republic. TEL 420-2-25276201, FAX 420-2-25276222, online@mf.cz. Ed. Marie Hejlova. Adv. contact Sarka Kamarytova.

MON BEBE. *see* CHILDREN AND YOUTH—About

051 613.7 USA
MONMOUTH HEALTH & LIFE; the good living magazine. Text in English. 2002. bi-m. USD 3.95 per issue (effective 2009). adv. **Document type:** *Magazine, Consumer.* **Description:** Provides a local look at the county's resources in entertainment, recreation, shopping and services.
Published by: Wainscot Media, 110 Summit Ave, Montvale, NJ 07645. TEL 201-571-2244, FAX 201-782-5319, http://www.wainscotmedia.com. Pub. Suzanne Tron TEL 212-756-5049. adv.: color page USD 2,900; trim 8.875 x 10.75. Circ: 41,000.

613.7 051 USA
MORRIS HEALTH & LIFE; the good living magazine. Text in English. 2002. bi-m. USD 3.95 per issue (effective 2007). adv. **Document type:** *Magazine, Consumer.* **Description:** Provides a resource for information on medical care and healthy lifestyle choices.
Published by: (Saqint Clare's Health System), Wainscot Media, 110 Summit Ave, Montvale, NJ 07645. TEL 201-571-2244, FAX 201-782-5319, http://www.wainscotmedia.com. Ed. Jason Jason Kontos. Pub. Suzanne Tron TEL 212-756-5049. adv.: color page USD 3,265; trim 8.375 x 10.875. Circ: 49,647.

613.7 DEU ISSN 0170-5792
MOTORIK; Zeitschrift fuer Motopaedagogik und Mototherapie. Text in German. q. EUR 46.80; EUR 42.80 to students; EUR 11 newsstand/cover (effective 2010). adv. **Document type:** *Journal, Academic/Scholarly.*
Indexed: DIP, IBR, IBZ, SD, SportS.
—BLDSC (5978.174000), GNLM. **CCC.**
Published by: (Aktionkreis Psychomotorik e.V.), Hofmann Bauverlag GmbH, Steinwasenstr 6-8, Schorndorf, 73614, Germany. TEL 49-7181-4020, FAX 49-7181-402111, info@hofmann-bauverlag.de. Ed. Klaus Fischer.

613.7 ESP ISSN 0214-0071
MOTRICIDAD. Text in Spanish. 1987. s-a. **Document type:** *Journal, Academic/Scholarly.*
Related titles: Online - full text ed.: ISSN 2172-2862. 199?. free (effective 2011).
Indexed: A36, CABA, GH, LT, N02, N03.
Published by: Universidad de Granada, Facultad de Ciencias de la Actividad Fisica y el Deporte, Cuesta del Hospicio s/n, Granada, 18071, Spain. http://www.deporte.ugr.es.

MOTRICIDADE. *see* SPORTS AND GAMES

MOTUS CORPORIS. *see* MEDICAL SCIENCES

MOVING MATTERS. *see* EDUCATION—Teaching Methods And Curriculum

MPULS; Magazin fuers Sportliche. *see* SPORTS AND GAMES

613.7 USA ISSN 1078-0661
MS. FITNESS; fitness lifestyle for today's active woman. Text in English. 1993. q. USD 15.96 domestic; USD 18 in Canada; USD 36 elsewhere (effective 2003). adv. bk.rev. illus. reprints avail. **Document type:** *Magazine, Consumer.* **Description:** Fitness lifestyle for today's active woman.

P

Published by: Wally Boyko Productions, Inc., PO Box 2378, Corona, CA 91718-2378. TEL 909-371-0606, FAX 909-371-0608, http://www.getbig.com/magazine/msfit/msfit.com. Ed. Greta Blackburn. Pub. Wally Boyko. Circ: 150,000.

613.7 GBR ISSN 0955-1387
MUSCLE AND FITNESS. Text in English. 1988. m. GBP 29.97 domestic; GBP 41.97 in Europe; GBP 59.97 elsewhere (effective 2009). adv. illus. **Document type:** *Magazine, Consumer.* **Description:** Offers persons engaged or interested in body building features and tips on general training, nutrition, and fitness.
Published by: Weider Publishing, 10 Windsor Ct, Clarence Dr, Harrogate, N Yorks HG1 2PE, United Kingdom. TEL 44-1423-504516, FAX 44-1423-561494, mailorder@weideruk.com. Adv. contact Samantha Lund TEL 44-1423-550848. page GBP 1,670; trim 200 x 267. Circ: 97,000. **Dist. by:** Comag.

613.7 USA ISSN 0744-5105
GV481
MUSCLE & FITNESS; your ultimate source for training & nutrition. Variant title: Joe Weider's Muscle & Fitness. Text in English. 1939. m. USD 34.97 domestic; USD 51.97 in Canada; USD 66.97 elsewhere; USD 6.99 newsstand/cover (effective 2009). adv. illus. reprints avail. **Document type:** *Magazine, Consumer.* **Description:** Designed for dynamic men and women who are not only looking for strength training and nutrition advice but are also interested in maintaining an active lifestyle outside the gym.
Formerly (until 198?): Joe Weider's Muscle
Related titles: Online - full text ed.; Polish ed.: ISSN 1230-6118; Finnish ed.: ISSN 1238-4755; Italian ed.: ISSN 1121-385X.
Indexed: A11, A22, A26, B07, C05, C11, CPerI, G05, G06, G07, G08, G09, H03, H11, H12, H13, HlthInd, I05, I07, M01, M02, M06, MASUSE, MagInd, P02, P10, P19, P20, P48, P53, P54, PEI, PQC, S23, SD, SportS, T02, U01.
—IE, Infotrieve, Ingenta.
Published by: A M I - Weider Publications (Subsidiary of: American Media, Inc.), 21100 Erwin St, Woodland Hills, CA 91367. TEL 818-595-0589, 800-998-0731, FAX 818-884-6910, http://www.americanmediainc.com. Ed. Vince Scalisi. Pub. David Pecker. adv.: B&W page USD 36,145; color page USD 44,840; trim 7.75 x 10.5. Circ: 425,000. **Subscr. to:** PO Box 37208, Boone, IA 50037.

613.7 SVK ISSN 1335-7867
MUSCLE & FITNESS. Text in Slovak. 1991. m. EUR 29 (effective 2011). adv. **Document type:** *Magazine, Consumer.*
Address: PO Box 40, Bratislava, 82012, Slovakia. TEL 421-2-43334169, FAX 421-2-43339752. Ed. Ludovit Major. Adv. contact Petra Siskova Kobezdova.

613.7 ZAF ISSN 1728-9130
MUSCLE EVOLUTION. Text in English. 2003. m. ZAR 167.80 (effective 2006). **Document type:** *Magazine, Consumer.*
Published by: Muscle Evolution cc, Postnet Suite 99, Private Bag X8, North Riding, 2162, South Africa.

613.7 USA ISSN 1079-2465
MUSCLE MEDIA; training guide. Text in English. 10/yr. USD 23.97 domestic; USD 48.97 foreign (effective 2003). adv. **Document type:** *Magazine, Consumer.* **Description:** Provides information and advice on how to build and maintain a healthy body and lifestyle.
Related titles: Online - full text ed.
Published by: Muscle Media, Inc., 555 Corporate Circle, Golden, CO 80401. TEL 303-271-1002, 800-967-3462, FAX 303-604-3462, info@musclemedia.com, http://www.musclemedia.com.

796.41 USA
MUSCLEZINE. Text in English. 1995. bi-m. USD 18; USD 3.50 newsstand/cover (effective 1997). adv. bk.rev.; software rev.; video rev. **Document type:** *Newspaper, Consumer.* **Description:** Deals with fitness, bodybuilding, health, and nutrition.
Related titles: Online - full text ed.
Published by: N Y Z Media, Inc., 330 E 35th St, Ste 32, New York, NY 10016. Ed., Pub., Adv. contact Scott Harrah. page USD 700; trim 14 x 10.

613 796.41 USA
MUSCULAR DEVELOPMENT. Cover title: Muscular Development Magazine. Text in English. 1964. m. USD 49.97 domestic; USD 79.97 foreign (effective 2007). adv. charts; illus.; tr.lit. **Document type:** *Magazine, Consumer.* **Description:** Offers comprehensive coverage of bodybuilding, sports nutrition, muscular development and strength training.
Former titles (until 1999): All Natural Muscular Development; (until 1997): Muscular Development Fitness and Health; Muscular Development (0047-8415)
Related titles: Online - full text ed.: USD 14.99 (effective 2007).
Indexed: SportS.
—Ingenta.
Published by: Advanced Research Press, Inc., 690 Route 25A, Setauket, NY 11733. TEL 631-751-9696, 800-653-1151, FAX 631-751-9699, http://www.advancedresearchpress.com/. Ed. Alan Paul. Pub. Steve Blechman. R&P Roy Ulin. Adv. contact Angela Frizalone. Circ: 125,000 (paid). **Dist. in UK by:** Seymour Distribution Ltd, 86 Newman St, London W1T 3EX, United Kingdom. TEL 44-20-73968000, FAX 44-20-73968002.

613 RUS
MUSCULAR DEVELOPMENT (MOSCOW). Text in Russian. bi-m.
Published by: E A M Sport Service, Ul Krzhizhanovskogo 14, korp 3, Moscow, 117218, Russian Federation. TEL 7-095-1292082.

613.7 646.75 USA
N B A F MAGAZINE. (National Bodybuilding and Fitness) Text in English. m. free. **Document type:** *Magazine, Consumer.* **Description:** Dedicated to people who are interested in improving their strength, physique, health and fitness - or are simply intrigued by the art and sport of bodybuilding.
Media: Online - full text. Ed. Jim Eddy.

613.7 USA ISSN 2157-7358
N S C A'S PERFORMANCE TRAINING JOURNAL. Text in English. 2002. bi-m. free (effective 2010). back issues avail. **Document type:** *Journal, Trade.* **Description:** Contains strength and conditioning topics based on sound research and practices.
Media: Online - full text.
Published by: National Strength and Conditioning Association, 1885 Bob Johnson Dr, Colorado Springs, CO 80906. TEL 719-632-6722, 800-815-6826, FAX 719-632-6367, nsca@nsca-lift.org. Ed. T Jeff Chandler. Pub. Keith Cinea.

613.7 USA
THE N S P I BUSINESS OWNERS. Text in English. 4/yr. membership. **Document type:** *Newsletter.*
Formerly (until 1998): Team S P I News
Published by: National Spa & Pool Institute, 2111 Eisenhower Ave, Alexandria, VA 22314. TEL 703-838-0083. Eds. Barbara Brady, Ken Suzuki. R&P Barbara Brady. Circ: 4,500.

613.7 USA
NATIONAL STRENGTH & CONDITIONING ASSOCIATION BULLETIN. Abbreviated title: N S C A Bulletin. Text in English. bi-m. free membership (effective 2007). bk.rev. back issues avail. **Document type:** *Bulletin.* **Description:** Keeps readers informed about the latest products, current industry events, and upcoming conferences.
Related titles: Online - full text ed.
Indexed: SD, SportS.
Published by: National Strength and Conditioning Association, 1885 Bob Johnson Dr, Colorado Springs, CO 80906. TEL 719-632-6722, FAX 719-632-6367, nsca@nsca-lift.org. Ed. Lori Marker. Adv. contact Kris Clark. Circ: 16,000. **Subscr. to:** Allen Press Inc., PO Box 7075, Lawrence, KS 66044. TEL 785-843-1235, FAX 785-843-1274.

613.7 DEU
▼ **NATUERLICH GESUND**; Ernaehrung, Fitness, Wellness. Text in German. 2010. m. adv. **Document type:** *Magazine, Consumer.*
Published by: Apotheken-Spiegel-Verlagsgesellschaft mbH, Edisonstr 3-5, Frankfurt am Main, 60388, Germany. TEL 49-6109-71200, FAX 49-6109-7120222, inbox@as-verlag.com, http://www.as-verlag.com.

613.7 CHE ISSN 1661-3643
NATUERLICH GESUND. Text in German. 1997. 8/yr. CHF 55; CHF 7.50 newsstand/cover (effective 2010). adv. **Document type:** *Magazine, Consumer.*
Formerly (until 2004): Heilpraxis-Magazin (1660-8623)
Published by: Medical Tribune AG, Urs-Graf-Str 8, Postfach 368, Basel, 4020, Switzerland. TEL 41-61-3125566, FAX 41-61-3125560, stomasi@medical-tribune.ch, http://www.medical-tribune.ch.

613 CHE ISSN 1660-8976
NATUERLICH LEBEN. Text in German. 1939. 11/yr. CHF 49 domestic; CHF 59 foreign (effective 2008). adv. **Document type:** *Magazine, Consumer.*
Former titles (until 2004): Kneipp (0023-2246); (until 1965): Schweizerische Kneipp-Schrift (1422-030X)
Published by: (Schweizer Kneippverband), Effingerhof AG, Storchengasse 15, Brugg, 5201, Switzerland. TEL 41-56-4607777, FAX 41-56-4607780, info@effingerhof.ch, http://www.effingerhof.ch. adv.: B&W page CHF 2,100, color page CHF 3,150; trim 210 x 297. Circ: 17,500 (paid).

613 DEU
NATUERLICH NATUR. Text in German. 2/yr. EUR 6; EUR 3.50 newsstand/cover (effective 2008). adv. **Document type:** *Magazine, Trade.*
Published by: ckmedien Verlags-Gesellschaft mbH, Von Laue Str 12, Euskirchen, 53881, Germany. TEL 49-2255-94110, FAX 49-2255-941111. Pub. Claudia Kersten. adv.: page EUR 985. Circ: 5,500 (paid and controlled).

613.7 USA ISSN 1071-555X
NATURAL BODYBUILDING AND FITNESS. Text in English. 1988. q. USD 12.90 (effective 2007). adv. **Document type:** *Magazine, Consumer.*
Formerly (until 1993): Natural Physique (1044-6583)
Published by: Chelo Publishing, Inc., 350 Fifth Ave, Ste 3323, New York, NY 10118. TEL 212-947-4322, FAX 212-563-4774. Ed., R&P Cheh N Low. Adv. contact Robert B Rose.

NATURAL HEALTH. *see* ALTERNATIVE MEDICINE

613.05 GBR ISSN 2040-4840
NATURAL HEALTH (COLCHESTER). Text in English. 2000. m. GBP 35 domestic; GBP 42 in Europe; GBP 52.50 elsewhere (effective 2009). adv. **Document type:** *Magazine, Consumer.* **Description:** Designed for health-conscious women who seek optimum wellness in mind, body and spirit.
Former titles (until 2008): Natural Health & Beauty (1748-0833); (until 2005): Natural Health & Well-Being (1471-101X)
—CCC.
Published by: Aceville Publications Ltd., 21-23 Phoenix Ct, Hawkins Rd, Colchester, Essex CO2 8JY, United Kingdom. TEL 44-1206-505962, FAX 44-1206-505915, aceville@servicehelpline.co.uk, http://www.aceville.com. Ed. Emma Van Hinsbergh TEL 44-1206-508618. Adv. contact Belinda Buckle TEL 44-1206-506237. **Subscr. to:** 800 Guillat Ave, Kent Science Park, Sittingbourne, Kent ME9 8GU, United Kingdom. TEL 44-844-8150036, FAX 44-845-4567143.

NATURAL HEALTH AND VEGETARIAN LIFE. *see* NUTRITION AND DIETETICS

NATURAL LIVING MAGAZINE. *see* LIFESTYLE

613.7 USA
NATURAL MUSCLE MAGAZINE. Text in English. 1996. m. USD 24.95 subscr - home delivery; free newsstand/cover at gyms, health food stores (effective 2007). **Document type:** *Magazine, Consumer.* **Description:** Information on all aspects of natural bodybuilding, training, weightlifting, and supplements.
Address: 4203 Arborwood Lane, Tampa, FL 33618. totalh@aol.com. Pub. Debbie Baigrie. Circ: 65,000 (paid and free).

613.7 GBR ISSN 2042-8286
NATURALLY GOOD HEALTH; get more from your local health store. Abbreviated title: N G H. Text in English. 2007. q. free (effective 2010). adv. back issues avail. **Document type:** *Magazine, Consumer.*
Related titles: Online - full text ed.: ISSN 2042-8294. free (effective 2010).
Published by: Target Publishing Ltd., The Old Dairy, Hudsons Farm, Fieldgate Ln, Ugley Green, Bishops Stortford, Essex CM22 6HJ, United Kingdom. TEL 44-1279-810080, FAX 44-1279-810081, info@targetpublishing.com, http://www.targetpublishing.com. Ed. Rachel Symonds TEL 44-1279-810088. Adv. contact Ruth Dodsley TEL 44-1279-810084.

NATURALLY GOOD MAGAZINE; a voice in the wilderness of hope and truth. *see* MEDICAL SCIENCES

613.7 DEU
NATURE FITNESS; Nordic Fitness, Wandern und gesundes Leben. Text in German. 2005. bi-m. EUR 16; EUR 3.50 newsstand/cover (effective 2007). adv. **Document type:** *Magazine, Consumer.*
Address: Ahornweg 3, Aitrang, 87648, Germany. TEL 49-8343-9239940, FAX 49-8343-923179. Ed., Pub. Ulrich Pramann. adv.: B&W page EUR 4,100, color page EUR 5,800. Circ: 75,000 (paid and controlled).

613 DEU ISSN 1613-3943
DIE NATURHEILKUNDE. Text in German. 1924. bi-m. EUR 36; EUR 6.90 newsstand/cover (effective 2008). adv. bk.rev. tr.lit. **Document type:** *Magazine, Consumer.*
Formerly (until 2004): Gesundes Leben (0016-9250); Which incorporated (1955-1964): Heilkunde, Heilwege (1430-9343)
Indexed: AMED.
—BLDSC (6048.075000), GNLM, IE, Ingenta.
Published by: Forum Medizin Verlagsgesellschaft mbH, Muehlenweg 144, Wilhelmshaven, 26384, Germany. TEL 49-4421-7556616, FAX 49-4421-7556610, info@forum-medizin.de, http://www.forum-medizin.de. Pub. Holger Wehner. adv.: color page EUR 3,205, B&W page EUR 2,015; trim 178 x 246. Circ: 13,212 (paid and controlled).

613.7 USA ISSN 0895-0911
NATURIST LIFE INTERNATIONAL. Text in English. 1987. q. USD 25 (effective 1999). back issues avail. **Description:** Family-oriented magazine promoting nude living.
Published by: Naturist Life International, Inc., PO Box 300 U, Troy, VT 05868-0300. TEL 802-744-6565. Ed. Jim C Cunningham. Circ: 1,700 (paid).

613 DNK ISSN 1602-0219
NATURLI. Text in Danish. 2002. 8/yr. DKK 340 (effective 2004). adv. bk.rev. illus. index. **Document type:** *Magazine, Consumer.*
Formed by the merger of (1881-2002): Sundhedsbladet (0039-5366); (1988-2002): Sund og Rask (0904-6518)
Published by: Forlaget Mediegruppen ApS, Porschevej 12, P B Box 436, Vejle, 7100, Denmark. TEL 45-75-841200, FAX 45-75-841229, info@naturli.dk. Eds. Malene Tonning, Jakob Christensen. Adv. contact Mette Baastrup. color page DKK 22,500; 210 x 280. Circ: 30,000.

613.7 ALB
NENA DHE FEMIJA. Text in Albanian. 3/yr.
Published by: Ministria e Shendetesise/Ministry of Health, Bulevardi "Bajram Curri" nr 1, Tirana, Albania. TEL 355-43-62937, http://www.moh.gov.al.

646.72 613.7 FRA ISSN 1961-0149
NESS; the wellness business magazine. Text in French. 2007. bi-m. **Document type:** *Magazine, Trade.*
Published by: Promep, 1198 Av. Maurice Donat, Bat. A, Mougins, 06250, France. TEL 33-4-93062623.

613.7 AUS
NETWORK E-NEWS. Text in English. m. free (effective 2008). back issues avail. **Document type:** *Newsletter, Consumer.* **Description:** Features the lastest research findings from around the globe, industry trends and announcements, latest training and choreography information.
Media: Online - full text.
Published by: Australian Fitness Network, PO Box 1606, Crows Nest, NSW 1585, Australia. TEL 61-2-84247200, FAX 61-2-94376511, info@fitnessnetwork.com.au. Ed. Oli Kitchingman TEL 61-2-84247286.

NEW BEGINNINGS (SCHAUMBURG). *see* CHILDREN AND YOUTH—About

▼ **NEW JERSEY NAMASTE NEWS.** *see* LIFESTYLE

NEW LIFE; America's guide to a healthy life, body, spirit. *see* NEW AGE PUBLICATIONS

613.7 USA
NEW LIVING. Text in English. 1991. m. USD 12.95 (effective 2000). adv. bk.rev. **Document type:** *Newspaper.*
Published by: Christine Lynn Harvey, Ed. & Pub., PO Box 1519, Stony Brook, NY 11790. TEL 516-751-8819, FAX 516-751-8910. Ed., Pub., R&P Christine Lynn Harvey. Adv. contact Bill Stevens. B&W page USD 1,295. Circ: 100,000.

NEW MEDICAL THERAPIES BRIEFS. OBESITY. *see* MEDICAL SCIENCES

613.7 NZL ISSN 1172-6687
NEW ZEALAND FITNESS. Variant title: Fitness. Text in English. 1989. bi-m. NZD 46 (effective 2008). adv. bk.rev. back issues avail. **Document type:** *Magazine, Consumer.* **Description:** For active gym goers and people interested in keeping fit and healthy.
Formerly (until 1991): Fitness (0114-2623)
Related titles: Online - full text ed.
Indexed: INZP.
Published by: Methode Media Ltd., PO Box 105-483, Auckland, 1143, New Zealand. TEL 64-9-3660404, FAX 64-9-3660402, info@methode.co.nz. Ed., Pub. Lorraine Thomson. Adv. contact Peter Murphy. Circ: 25,000.

613.7 NZL ISSN 1179-8858
▼ **NEW ZEALAND GOOD HEALTH.** Text in English. 2010. m. adv. **Document type:** *Magazine, Consumer.*
Published by: A C P Magazines, Private Bag 92512, Auckland, 1036, New Zealand. TEL 64-9-3082700, FAX 64-9-3082878, http://www.acpmedia.co.nz/ACPMagazines/tabid/66/Default.aspx.

613.7 AUT
NEWS LEBEN. Text in German. 2004. 10/yr. EUR 19.90 (effective 2006). adv. **Document type:** *Magazine, Consumer.*
Published by: Verlagsgruppe News Gesellschaft mbH (Subsidiary of: Gruner + Jahr AG & Co), Taborstr 1-3, Vienna, W 1020, Austria. TEL 43-1-213129011, FAX 43-1-213121650, redaktion@news.at, http://www.news.at. adv.: page EUR 9,500. Circ: 66,683 (paid).

NIHON DAIGAKU. KEIZAIGAKU KENKYUKAI.KENKYU KIYO. IPPAN KYOIKU, GAIKOKUGO, HOKEN TAIIKU/NIHON UNIVERSITY. ECONOMIC AND COMMERCIAL RESEARCH SOCIETY. RESEARCH BULLETIN. LIBERAL ARTS. *see* EDUCATION

613 JPN ISSN 0021-5082
CODEN: NEZAAQ
NIHON EISEIGAKU ZASSHI/JAPANESE JOURNAL OF HYGIENE. Text in Japanese; Abstracts in English. 1946. bi-m. subscr. incld. with membership. adv. **Document type:** *Journal, Academic/Scholarly.*
Incorporates (1923-1962): Kokumin Eisei/Japanese Journal of the Nation's Health (0368-6353)
Related titles: Online - full text ed.: ISSN 1882-6482.

Indexed: A22, CISA, EMBASE, ExcerpMed, FS&TA, INI, INIS AtomInd, IndMed, MEDLINE, P30, R10, Reac, SCOPUS.
—BLDSC (4655.300000), CASDDS, GNLM, IE, Infotrieve, Ingenta, INIST. **CCC.**
Published by: Nihon Eisei Gakkai/Japanese Society for Hygiene, 1-15-1, Kitasato,, Sagamihara, Kanagawa 228-8555, Japan. eisei@med.kitasato-u.ac.jp, http://www.nacos.com/jsh/main/. Ed. K Morimoto. Circ: 2,700.

613.7 JPN
NIKKEI HEALTH. Text in Japanese. 1998. m. JPY 490 newsstand/cover. adv. **Document type:** *Consumer.* **Description:** Urban lifestyle magazine focusing on health for men in their 30's to 50's. Targets businessmen who are concerned about maintaining their health.
Published by: Nikkei Business Publications Inc. (Subsidiary of: Nihon Keizai Shimbun, Inc.), 2-7-6 Hirakawa-cho, Chiyoda-ku, Tokyo, 102-8622, Japan. TEL 81-3-5210-8311, FAX 81-3-5210-8530, info@nikkeibp-america.com. Ed. Ichiro Higuchi. Pub. Hitoshi Sawai. adv.: B&W page JPY 600,000, color page JPY 800,000; trim 210 x 280. Circ: 62,598. **Dist. in America by:** Nikkei Business Publications America Inc., 575 Fifth Ave, 20th Fl, New York, NY 10017.

613.7 USA ISSN 1930-0743
NOEXCUSESGYM.COM. Text in English. 2005. w. **Document type:** *Newsletter, Consumer.*
Media: Online - full text.
Published by: Marcela Vanhara Ed. Marcela Vanharova TEL 702-353-0168.

613.7 USA ISSN 1081-8928
NORTHWEST HEALTH. Text in English. 1958. q. USD 12 (effective 2005). bk.rev. 20 p./no. 2 cols./p.; **Document type:** *Magazine, Consumer.* **Description:** Covers health and fitness life-styles for western Washington State.
Formerly (until 1995): View (Seattle) (0504-264X)
Related titles: Online - full text ed.
Published by: Group Health Cooperative, 521 Wall St, Seattle, WA 98121. Ed. Pat Bailey. Pub. Clarice Hutchison. Circ: 300,000 (controlled).

613.7 ITA ISSN 1120-4931
IL NUOVO CLUB; attualita e management dei circoli sportivi e palestre. Text in Italian. 1989. bi-m. EUR 39 domestic; EUR 78 in Europe; EUR 90 elsewhere (effective 2011). adv. bk.rev. **Document type:** *Magazine, Trade.*
Published by: Editrice Il Campo, Via Giovanni Amendola 11, Bologna, BO 40121, Italy. TEL 39-051-255544, FAX 39-051-255360, customer@fitnesstrends.com, http://www.ilcampo.it. Ed. Franco Maestrami. Circ: 15,000.

NURSING SPECTRUM - FLORIDA EDITION. *see* MEDICAL SCIENCES—Nurses And Nursing

NUTRIDATE (ONLINE); class room support for teachers since 1990. *see* NUTRITION AND DIETETICS

NUTRITION AND HEALTH. *see* NUTRITION AND DIETETICS

NUTRITION NEWS (RIVERSIDE). *see* NUTRITION AND DIETETICS

613.7 NOR ISSN 1891-2265
DET NYE SHAPE UP. Text in Norwegian. 1984. 6/yr. NOK 199 (effective 2011). adv. **Document type:** *Magazine, Consumer.*
Formerly (until 2009): Shape-Up (0803-222X)
Published by: Hjemmet Mortensen AS, Gullhaugveien 1, Nydalen, Oslo, 0441, Norway. TEL 47-22-585000, FAX 47-22-585959, firmapost@hm-media.no, http://www.hm-media.no.

613.7 USA
O A LIFELINE. Text in English. m. USD 6 (effective 2004). illus. **Description:** Focuses on recovery from compulsive eating and other disorders.
Published by: Overeaters Anonymous, 2190 190 St, Box 6190, Torrance, CA 90504.

613.7 ITA ISSN 1825-9375
O K LA SALUTE PRIMA DI TUTTO. Text in Italian. 2005. m. EUR 30 (effective 2008). **Document type:** *Magazine, Consumer.*
Published by: R C S Periodici (Subsidiary of: R C S Mediagroup), Via San Marco 21, Milan, 20121, Italy. TEL 39-2-25844111, FAX 39-2-25845444, info@periodici.rcs.it, http://www.rcsmediagroup.it/siti/periodici.php. Ed. Eliana Liotta.

OBESITY; a research journal. *see* MEDICAL SCIENCES

613.7 616.398 USA ISSN 1531-6386
OBESITY, FITNESS, AND WELLNESS WEEK. Text in English. 2000. w. USD 2,595 in US & Canada; USD 2,795 elsewhere; USD 2,825 combined subscription in US & Canada (print & online eds.); USD 3,055 combined subscription elsewhere (print & online eds.) (effective 2007). **Document type:** *Newsletter, Trade.* **Description:** Focuses on all aspects of obesity and related fitness and health issues including adipogenesis, bariatrics, diet, nutrition and exercise, genetics, alternative and complimentary medicines, and type 2 diabetes.
Related titles: CD-ROM ed.: USD 2,295 (effective 2008); Online - full text ed.: ISSN 1532-4664. USD 2,595 (effective 2007).
Indexed: A26, CWI, G08, H11, H12, H13, I05, I06, I07, M06, P10, P19, P20, P24, P48, P50, P53, P54, PQC, S06, S23.
—CIS.
Published by: NewsRx, 2727 Paces Ferry Rd SE, Ste 2-440, Atlanta, GA 30339. TEL 770-435-8286, 800-726-4550, FAX 770-435-6800, pressrelease@newsrx.com, http://www.newsrx.com. Pub. Susan Hasty TEL 770-507-7777.

OBESITY RESEARCH & CLINICAL PRACTICE. *see* MEDICAL SCIENCES

OBESITY REVIEWS. *see* NUTRITION AND DIETETICS

616.398 USA
OBESITYHELP. Text in English. 2003 (Jun.). q. USD 25 (effective 2003). **Description:** Covers the treatment and other aspects of morbid obesity, including bariatric surgery, exercise, clinical comorbidities, and obesity discrimination.
Address: c/o Melissa Reed, 57 Hillsboro-Viola Rd, Hillsboro, TN 37342. TEL 800-709-1293. **Subscr. to:** c/o Tammy Colter, 530 South Lake Ave #289, Pasadena, CA 91101. FAX 931-596-4592.

OCCUPATIONAL HEALTH; a journal for the occupational health team. *see* MEDICAL SCIENCES—Nurses And Nursing

OESTERREICHISCHES JUGENDROTKREUZ. ARBEITSBLAETTER. *see* SOCIAL SERVICES AND WELFARE

OLYMPIAN'S NEWS. *see* SPORTS AND GAMES

OLYMPIC HEALTH NEWS. *see* MEDICAL SCIENCES—Sports Medicine

613.7 USA ISSN 1932-8788
GV743
ONSITE FITNESS. Text in English. 2006. bi-m. **Document type:** *Magazine, Consumer.*
Published by: Virtual Productions, LLC, 40101 Monterey Ave. Ste B-1 #328, Rancho Mirage, CA 92270. TEL 760-779-0917, FAX 760-862-9096, http://www.onsite-fitness.com. Pub. Chris Ballard.

OOSAKA JOSHI DAIGAKU KIYO. KISO RIGAKU HEN, TAIIKUGAKU HEN/OSAKA WOMEN'S UNIVERSITY. BULLETIN. SERIES OF NATURAL SCIENCE, PHYSICAL EDUCATION. *see* SCIENCES: COMPREHENSIVE WORKS

613.7 ITA ISSN 1121-3264
OPTIMA SALUTE. Text in Italian. 1990. m. (10/yr.). free; distributed by pharmacies. adv. **Document type:** *Magazine, Consumer.*
Published by: Edioptima Srl, Via Calabria 18-20, Redecesio di Segrate, MI 20090, Italy. TEL 39-2-76017397, FAX 39-2-76014959. Circ: 245,000.

613.7 613.2 USA
OPTIMUM WELLNESS. Text in English. 2005. m. **Document type:** *Magazine, Consumer.* **Description:** Provides information on natural and organic living.
Indexed: P02.
Published by: Active Interest Media, 300 Continental Blvd, Ste 650, El Segundo, CA 90245. TEL 310-356-4100, FAX 310-356-4110.

OREGON DISTANCE RUNNER. *see* SPORTS AND GAMES

ORTOPEDICI E SANITARI. *see* MEDICAL SCIENCES—Orthopedics And Traumatology

613.7 USA ISSN 1948-044X
OUTLOOK BY THE BAY; the magazine for the savvy senior. Text in English. 2007. bi-m. USD 24.95; free to qualified personnel (effective 2009). adv. back issues avail. **Document type:** *Magazine, Consumer.* **Description:** Features articles on lifestyle, finances, health, nutrition, housing or activities devoted to the interests of the active Chesapeake Bay area senior.
Related titles: Online - full text ed.: ISSN 1948-0512. free (effective 2009).
Published by: OutLook by the Bay, LLC, 626-C Admiral Cochran Dr, Ste 608, Annapolis, MD 21401. TEL 410-849-3000, FAX 410-630-3838. Ed., Pub. Tecla Emerson Murphy.

PARKS & RECREATION CANADA/PARCS & LOISIRS. *see* LEISURE AND RECREATION

613.7 USA ISSN 1947-7481
RZ201
PATHWAYS TO FAMILY WELLNESS. Text in English. 2004. q. USD 24.95 domestic to non-members; USD 34.95 in Canada to non-members; AUD 24.95 in Australia to non-members; USD 44.95 elsewhere to non-members; free to members (effective 2010). adv. back issues avail. **Document type:** *Magazine, Consumer.* **Description:** Provides articles relevant to family's well-being.
Published by: International Chiropractic Pediatric Associaton, 327 N Middletown Rd, Media, PA 19063. TEL 610-565-2360, FAX 610-565-3567, info@icpa4kids.com, http://www.icpa4kids.com. adv.: page USD 1,500; bleed 8.5 x 11. **Co-publisher:** Holistic Pediatric Association.

PATHWAYS TO HEALTH. *see* PHILOSOPHY

613.7 USA ISSN 1089-4349
PAUZ. Text in English. 1992. bi-m. USD 8. bk.rev.; film rev. charts; stat. **Description:** Includes articles relating to traditional and alternative health, poetry, legal aid for laypeople, psychological articles for mid-lifers, etc. Aimed at audience over 30.
Formerly (until 1996): Backfence Quarterly (1069-739X)
Published by: Punkin - Xpress, 827 Central Ave, Ste 263, Dover, NH 03820. TEL 603-467-2177. Ed. Lz Giammarco. Circ: 2,000.

PEDAL UPDATE. *see* SPORTS AND GAMES—Bicycles And Motorcycles

PELIZZA'S POSITIVE PRINCIPLES FOR BETTER LIVING. *see* PSYCHOLOGY

613.7 612.3 USA
PERSONAL CARE NEWS. Text in English. fortn. free. **Document type:** *Newsletter.*
Media: Online - full text.
Published by: E G W Publishing Co., 4075 Papazian Way, #208, Fremont, CA 94538. TEL 510-668-0269, FAX 510-668-0280, support@egw.com, http://www.egw.com.

613 USA ISSN 1523-780X
GV428.7
PERSONAL FITNESS PROFESSIONAL; helping you prosper as a fitness proffesional. Abbreviated title: P F P. Text in English. 1999. 9/yr. USD 36 domestic; USD 60 in Canada & Mexico; USD 80 elsewhere; free to qualified personnel (print or online ed.) (effective 2009). adv. back issues avail.; reprints avail. **Document type:** *Magazine, Consumer.* **Description:** Provides relevant, useful information to enable fitness professionals to be successful financially through sound business practices and training expertise.
Related titles: Online - full text ed.
Published by: R B Publishing, Inc., 2901 International Ln, Ste 200, Madison, WI 53704. TEL 608-241-8777, 800-536-1992, FAX 608-241-8666, ron@rbpub.com, http://www.rbpub.com. Ed. Shelby Murphy. Pub. Ron Brent TEL 608-442-5062. **Subscr. to:** PO Box 259098, Madison, WI 53725.

PERSPECTIVES IN PUBLIC HEALTH. *see* SOCIAL SERVICES AND WELFARE

613.7 DEU
PHARMA AKTUELL GESUNDHEITSMAGAZIN. Text in German. bi-m. EUR 18; EUR 1.50 newsstand/cover (effective 2008). adv. **Document type:** *Magazine, Consumer.*
Published by: Pharma Aktuell Verlagsgruppe GmbH, Lehmweg 11, Varel, 26316, Germany. TEL 49-4451-950395, FAX 49-4451-950390. Ed. Kerstin Paulsen. Adv. contact Barbara Bepler. B&W page EUR 6,825, color page EUR 8,253; trim 210 x 297. Circ: 126,300 (paid and controlled).

613 CAN ISSN 1918-8927
GV201
▼ **PHENEX JOURNAL/REVUE PHENEPS.** Text in English, French. 2010. irreg. free (effective 2011). **Document type:** *Journal, Academic/Scholarly.*
Media: Online - full text.
Published by: Physical and Health Education Canada, 301-2197 Riverside Drive, Ottawa, ON K1H 7X3, Canada. TEL 613-523-1348, FAX 613-523-1206.

613.7 USA ISSN 1520-8397
PHYSICAL. Text in English. 1998. m. USD 15.98 (effective 2000). adv. **Document type:** *Magazine, Consumer.* **Description:** Provides information and motivation for high-energy activities and sports nutrition.
Related titles: Online - full text ed.
Indexed: PEI.
Published by: Franklin Publications (Subsidiary of: Basic Media Group), 11050 Santa Monica Blvd, Los Angeles, CA 90025. TEL 310-445-7500.

613.7 POL ISSN 2081-2221
PHYSICAL CULTURE AND SPORT STUDIES AND RESEARCH. Text in English. 2008. a. **Document type:** *Journal, Academic/Scholarly.*
Related titles: Online - full text ed.: ISSN 1899-4849. free (effective 2011) (from Versita).
Published by: Akademia Wychowania Fizycznego Jozefa Pilsudskiego w Warszawie, ul Marymoncka 34, Warsaw, 00968, Poland. TEL 48-22-8340431, FAX 48-22-8640646, bwz@awf.edu.pl, http://www.awf.edu.pl.

PHYSICAL EDUCATION AND SPORT PEDAGOGY. *see* EDUCATION—Teaching Methods And Curriculum

PHYSICAL EDUCATION MATTERS. *see* EDUCATION—Teaching Methods And Curriculum

613.7 BRA ISSN 1807-9407
PILATES. Text in Portuguese. 2005. bi-m. BRL 29.90 newsstand/cover (effective 2007). **Document type:** *Magazine, Consumer.*
Published by: Digerati Comunicacao e Tecnologia Ltda., Rua Haddock Lobo 347, 12o andar, Sao Paulo, 01414-001, Brazil. TEL 55-11-32172600, FAX 55-11-32172617, http://www.digerati.com.br.

613.7 FRA ISSN 1961-6600
PILATES & STRETCHING MAGAZINE. Text in French. 2007. q. **Document type:** *Magazine, Consumer.*
Published by: Societe Francaise de Revues, 80 Av. du General-de-Gaulle, Neuilly-sur-Seine, 92200, France. http://www.michel-buh.com/catalogue/index.php.

613.7 USA ISSN 1549-6937
PILATES STYLE. Text in English. 2004. bi-m. USD 19.95 domestic; USD 34.95 foreign; USD 4.99 newsstand/cover (effective 2008). adv. back issues avail. **Document type:** *Magazine, Consumer.* **Description:** Dedicated to this exciting field, with essential information and tips for a healthy, active lifestyle.
Related titles: Online - full text ed.; Supplement(s): Pilates Style Annual. ISSN 1943-8656.
Published by: Goodman Media Group, Inc., 250 W 57th St, Ste 710, New York, NY 10107. TEL 212-262-2247, FAX 212-400-8620, info@goodmanmediagroup.com, http://www.goodmanmediagroup.com. Ed. Suzanne Gerber. Adv. contact Brian Kelly TEL 212-262-2247 ext 308. B&W page USD 4,660, color page USD 6,925; trim 8 x 10.875.

613.7 613.2 ITA ISSN 2037-2736
▼ **PIU SALUTE MAGAZINE.** Text in Italian. 2009. m. **Document type:** *Magazine, Consumer.*
Published by: Edizioni Mimosa, Piazza E de Angeli 9, Milan, 20146, Italy. TEL 39-02-3650507, FAX 39-02-48110494, segreteria@edizionimimosa.it, http://www.edizionimimosa.it.

613 GBR
POSITIVE HEALTH (ONLINE). Text in English. 1996. m. adv. back issues avail. **Document type:** *Magazine, Consumer.* **Description:** Provides a blend of expertly written features, case reports, research and topical news written directly for practitioners and consumers of complementary medicine.
Media: Online - full text.
Published by: Positive Health Publications Ltd., c/o Compass Internet Ltd, 32 Brindle Grove, Ramsgate, Kent CT11 8BN, United Kingdom. TEL 44-1843-855113, FAX 44-1843-855107, admin@compassinternet.com. Ed. Dr. Sandra Goodman TEL 44-1843-855114.

158 USA ISSN 1545-2778
POSITIVE THINKING; attitude is everything. Text in English. 2003. bi-m. USD 14.97 domestic; USD 16.97 in Canada; USD 20.97 elsewhere (effective 2007). adv. **Document type:** *Magazine, Consumer.*
Indexed: M02, T02.
Published by: Center for Positive Thinking, 16 E 34th St, New York, NY 10016. TEL 212-251-8100. Ed. Amy Wong. Pub. Janine Scolpino. Adv. contact James Sammartino. **Subscr. to:** PO Box 1475, Carmel, NY 10512. TEL 888-297-2970, customerservice@positivethinkingmag.com.

POTSDAMER STUDIEN ZUR GESCHICHTE VON SPORT UND GESUNDHEIT. *see* SPORTS AND GAMES

613.7 USA ISSN 2150-5411
▼ **POWER MAGAZINE.** Text in English. 2009. bi-m. USD 29 domestic; USD 65 elsewhere (effective 2010). **Document type:** *Magazine, Consumer.* **Description:** Features information on training, equipment, meets, nutrition, and interviews with powerlifters.
Published by: Andee Bell, Ed. & Pub., 609 Crystal Springs Dr, Woodland, CA 95776. TEL 530-661-7585, andeebell@sbcglobal.net.

613 FRA ISSN 1968-2905
PRATIQUE SANTE. Text in French. 2008. q. EUR 44 for 2 yrs. (effective 2010). **Document type:** *Magazine, Consumer.*
Published by: Lafont Presse, 53 Rue du Chemin Vert, Boulogne-Billancourt, 92100, France. TEL 33-1-46102121, FAX 33-1-45792211, http://www.lafontpresse.fr.

613.7 DEU ISSN 0170-060X
PRAXIS DER PSYCHOMOTORIK; Zeitschrift fuer Bewegungserziehung. Text in German. 1976. q. EUR 34; EUR 8.80 newsstand/cover (effective 2011). adv. bk.rev. abstr.; charts; illus. index. back issues avail. **Document type:** *Journal, Academic/Scholarly.* **Description:** Deals with the importance of movement in a child's education and development. Covers dance, sport, play, and the physically handicapped.
Indexed: DIP, IBR, IBZ, RefZh, SD.
—GNLM, IE.

P

Published by: Verlag Modernes Lernen Borgmann KG, Schleefstr 14, Dortmund, 44287, Germany. TEL 49-231-128008, FAX 49-231-125640, info@verlag-modernes-lernen.de. Ed. Dorothea Becker. Pub. Dieter Borgmann. Circ: 4,717 (paid and controlled).

613 ESP ISSN 1133-3782
PREVENIR ES SALUD. Text in Spanish. 1992. m. EUR 19.20 domestic; EUR 43 in Europe; EUR 47 elsewhere (effective 2009). adv. **Document type:** *Magazine, Consumer.*
Published by: Globus Comunicacion (Subsidiary of: Bonnier AB), Covarrubias 1, Madrid, 28010, Spain. TEL 34-91-4471202, FAX 34-91-4471043, txhdez@globuscom.es, http://www.globuscom.es. Ed. Amalia Mosquera. adv.: page EUR 4,392; trim 13.5 x 18.7. Circ: 17,880.

613 USA ISSN 0032-8006
RA421 CODEN: PRVEAT
PREVENTION. Text in English. 1950. m. USD 21.97 domestic; USD 32 in Canada; USD 42.97 elsewhere (effective 2011). adv. bk.rev. illus. index. back issues avail.; reprints avail. **Document type:** *Magazine, Consumer.* **Description:** Reports on new developments in nutrition, preventive medicine, fitness, natural living and drugless therapies. Emphasis is on practicality and self-improvement.
Related titles: Microform ed.: (from PQC); Online - full text ed.; ◆ Esperanto ed.: Prevention en Espanol. ISSN 1529-370X.
Indexed: A01, A02, A03, A04, A08, A11, A22, A26, ARG, AgeL, B04, BRD, C05, C12, CHNI, CPerI, E04, E05, E07, E08, G03, G05, G06, G07, G08, GSA, GSI, H03, H11, H12, H13, HlthInd, I05, I06, I07, JHMA, M01, M02, M06, MASUSE, MagInd, P02, P07, P10, P13, P19, P20, P26, P48, P50, P53, P54, PMR, PQC, R03, R06, RGAb, RGPR, S06, S09, S23, T02, TOM, U01, W03, W05.
—GNLM, IE, Infotrieve, Ingenta, Linda Hall.
Published by: Rodale, Inc., 33 E Minor St, Emmaus, PA 18098. TEL 610-967-5171, info@rodale.com, http://www.rodaleinc.com. Ed. Diane J Salvatore.

613.7 305.4 613.04244 AUS ISSN 1839-0455
▼ **PREVENTION.** Text in English. 2009. m. AUD 78 domestic; AUD 75 in New Zealand; AUD 110 elsewhere (effective 2011). adv. **Document type:** *Magazine, Consumer.* **Description:** Provides healthy lifestyle information for and about Australian women 40+.
Published by: Pacific Magazines Pty Ltd., Media City, 8 Central Ave, Eveleigh, NSW 2015, Australia. TEL 61-2-93942000, http://www.pacificpubs.com.au. Adv. contact Amie Lane-Smith TEL 61-2-93942033. Circ: 61,379. **Subscr. to:** GPO Box 4983, Sydney, NSW 2001, Australia. TEL 61-2-82965425, 300-668-118, FAX 61-2-92793161, 300-300-517, subscriptions@pacificmags.com.au, http://www.subscribetoday.com.au.

613.7 ROM ISSN 1843-567X
PREVENTION. Text in Romanian. 2007. m. adv. **Document type:** *Magazine, Consumer.*
Published by: Liberis Publications Romania SRL, Maria Rosetti St, 49 A, sector 2, Bucharest, 020482, Romania. TEL 40-316-900611, FAX 40-316-900615, office@liberis.ro. Ed. Dorina Slaveanu. Adv. contact Janina Paun. Circ: 30,000 (paid).

613.7 GRC ISSN 1790-5583
PREVENTION. Text in Greek. 2005. m. adv. **Document type:** *Magazine, Consumer.*
Published by: Liberis Publications S.A./Ekdoseon Lymperi A.E., Ioannou Metaxa 80, Karelas, Koropi 19400, Greece. TEL 30-210-6688000, FAX 30-210-6688300, info@liberis.gr, http://www.liberis.gr. Ed. Katerina Vourlaki. Circ: 32,527 (paid and controlled).

613.7 MEX ISSN 1529-370X
PREVENTION EN ESPANOL. Text in Esperanto. 1999. m. adv. **Document type:** *Magazine, Consumer.* **Description:** Covers breakthroughs in medical research, alternative health, herbs, nutrition, fitness, and weight loss.
Related titles: ◆ English ed.: Prevention. ISSN 0032-8006.
Published by: Editorial Televisa, Vasco de Quiroga 2000, Edificio E, Colonia Santa Fe, Mexico City, DF 01210, Mexico. TEL 52-55-52612761, FAX 52-55-52612704, info@editorialtelevisa.com, http://www.esmas.com/editorialtelevisa/. Circ: 60,000 (paid).

613.7 USA
PREVENTION GUIDE. WEIGHT LOSS. Text in English. a. USD 495 per issue (effective 2009). adv. **Document type:** *Magazine, Consumer.*
Published by: Rodale, Inc., 33 E Minor St, Emmaus, PA 18098. TEL 610-967-5171, FAX 610-967-8963, customer_service@rodale.com, http://www.rodaleinc.com.

PRINCESS HERBAL. *see* ALTERNATIVE MEDICINE

613.7 AUS
PROFESSOR TRIM'S WAISTLINE. Text in English. 2004. q. free to members (effective 2008). back issues avail. **Document type:** *Newsletter, Consumer.* **Description:** Provides information for any fitness professional who works with clients or participants seeking assistance with weight management.
Related titles: Online - full text ed.: free to members (effective 2008).
Published by: Australian Fitness Network, PO Box 1606, Crows Nest, NSW 1585, Australia. TEL 61-2-84247200, FAX 61-2-94376511, info@fitnessnetwork.com.au. Ed. Oli Kitchingman TEL 61-2-84247286.

613.7 RUS
➤ **PROFILAKTICHESKAYA MEDITSINA/DISEASES PREVENTION AND HEALTH PROMOTION**; nauchno-prakticheskii zhurnal. Text in Russian. 1997. bi-m. USD 266 in North America (effective 2010). reprints avail. **Document type:** *Journal, Academic/Scholarly.*
Formerly (until 2009): Profilaktika Zabolevanii i Ukreplenie Zdorov'ya (1726-6130)
Related titles: Online - full content ed.
Indexed: RefZh.
Published by: Media Sfera, Dmitrovskoe shosse 46, korp 2, etazh 4, P.O. Box 54, Moscow, 127238, Russian Federation. TEL 7-095-4824329, FAX 7-095-4824312, podpiska@mediasphera.ru, http://mediasphera.ru. Ed. Rafael D Oganov. Circ: 2,000 (paid).

➤ **PROGRESS IN OBESITY RESEARCH (YEAR).** *see* MEDICAL SCIENCES

613.7 DEU ISSN 1433-6413
PROVITA. Text in German. 1997. bi-m. EUR 4.50 newsstand/cover (effective 2008). adv. **Document type:** *Magazine, Trade.*
—**CCC.**

Published by: Muehlen Verlag, Zum Wasserbaum 13, Salzhemmendorf, 31020, Germany. TEL 49-5153-5810, FAX 49-5153-5711, muehlen-verlag@t-online.de. adv.: B&W page EUR 2,100, color page EUR 3,360. Circ: 21,512 (paid and controlled).

PSICOLOGIA DELLA SALUTE; quadrimestrale di psicologia e scienze della salute. *see* PSYCHOLOGY

PSYCHOLOGY AND SOCIOLOGY OF SPORT: CURRENT SELECTED RESEARCH. *see* PSYCHOLOGY

PSYCHOLOGY OF SPORT AND EXERCISE. *see* PSYCHOLOGY

PUERTO RICO. DEPARTMENT OF HEALTH. BOLETIN ESTADISTICO. *see* SOCIAL SERVICES AND WELFARE

PUERTO RICO. DEPARTMENT OF HEALTH. INFORME ESTADISTICO DE FACILIDADES DE SALUD. *see* HEALTH FACILITIES AND ADMINISTRATION

613.7 CHE ISSN 1424-6082
PULS-DOSSIER. Text in German. 1996. irreg. CHF 28 newsstand/cover. **Document type:** *Consumer.*
Published by: K I Media GmbH, Hottingerstr 12, Postfach 75, Zurich, 8024, Switzerland. TEL 41-1-2661717, FAX 41-1-2661700, http://www.ki-media.ch. Adv. contact Yvonne Mueller.

613.7 CHE ISSN 1424-6090
PULS-TIP. Text in German. 1994. 11/yr. CHF 24; CHF 2.90 newsstand/cover (effective 2000). adv. **Document type:** *Magazine, Consumer.* **Description:** Contains articles and features on maintaining a healthy lifestyle.
Published by: K I Media GmbH, Hottingerstr 12, Postfach 75, Zurich, 8024, Switzerland. TEL 41-1-2661717, FAX 41-1-2661700, http://www.ki-media.ch. Ed. Tobias Frey. Adv. contact Yvonne Mueller. B&W page CHF 7,995, color page CHF 10,800; trim 209 x 287. Circ: 140,763 (paid).

613.7 GBR ISSN 2046-2735
▼ **PURE HEALTH MAGAZINE**; the world of personal care ingredients. Abbreviated title: P H M. Text in English. 2009. q. free to qualified personnel (effective 2011). adv. back issues avail. **Document type:** *Magazine, Trade.* **Description:** Provides scientific and technical information for cosmetic scientists, formulating chemists, dermatologists, microbiologists, marketing personnel, production staff and senior executives working in the personal care industry.
Related titles: Online - full text ed.: free (effective 2011).
Indexed: S22.
Published by: Via Media Ltd., Wesley House, Bull Hill, Leatherhead, Surrey KT22 7AH, United Kingdom. TEL 44-1372-364120, FAX 44-1372-364121, info@via-medialtd.com, http://www.via-medialtd.com/. Ed. Kevin Robinson TEL 44-1392-202591. Pub. Miranda Docherty TEL 44-1372-364122. Circ: 18,000.

613.7 USA ISSN 1539-1264
PURE POWER; when training + science = peak performance. Text in English. 2001 (July). bi-m. USD 26.95 (effective 2004). **Document type:** *Magazine, Consumer.*
Indexed: A01, SD.
Published by: Body Intellect, Inc., PO Box 77066, Colorado Springs, CO 80970. TEL 719-597-3525, FAX 719-638-6107. Ed., Pub. Dr. Dan Wagman, PhD, CSCS. Adv. contact Ms. Christine Smith TEL 719-942-9620.

613.7 CHN ISSN 1000-0895
RM727.C54
QIGONG YU KEXUE/QIGONG AND SCIENCE. Text in Chinese. m. CNY 12. **Description:** Presents different theories and practice of different schools of qigong in China and abroad. Introduces the applications of this deep-breathing excercise to medical treatment, sports and education.
Published by: (Guangdongsheng Qigong Kexue Yanjiu Xiehui/Guangdong Qigong Science Research Association), Qigong yu Kexue Zazhishe, P.O. Box 343, Guangzhou, Guangdong 510030, China. **Dist. overseas by:** Jiangsu Publications Import & Export Corp., 56 Gao Yun Ling, Nanjing, Jiangsu, China.

613.85 USA
QUIT SMOKING REPORT EZINE. Text in English. 1998. bi-m. free. back issues avail. **Document type:** *Newsletter, Consumer.* **Description:** Contains quit smoking tips, encouragement, success stories from other smokers, questions, pleas for help, plus information about products on how to quit smoking.
Media: Online - full text.
Published by: Quit Smoking Company, 3675 Glennvale Court, Cummings, GA 30041. TEL 770-346-9222, FAX 770-475-5007.

613.7 ESP ISSN 1133-0619
R E D. REVISTA DE ENTRENAMIENTO DEPORTIVO. Text in Spanish. 1987. q. back issues avail. **Document type:** *Magazine, Trade.*
Indexed: PEI.
Published by: Boidecanto SL, Almirante Eulate 6, La Coruna, 15011, Spain. TEL 34-981-254355.

RADIANCE ONLINE. *see* WOMEN'S INTERESTS

614 USA
RADIUS; for health, healing, happiness. Text in English. 2005. q. USD 14.95 (effective 2006). adv. **Document type:** *Magazine, Consumer.* **Description:** Addresses those aspects of human life that contribute to well being, health, and happiness and covers topics on nutrition, exercise, and mental health.
Published by: Radius Magazine, c/o Dev M Brar, MD, Pub., 12766 Hamilton Crossing Blvd, Carmel, IN 46032. TEL 317-334-7777, 866-334-7777, FAX 317-569-1403. adv.: B&W page USD 6,500, color page USD 10,000; trim 8.375 x 10.875.

613 DEU ISSN 1438-2865
RATGEBER AUS IHRER APOTHEKE. Text in German. 1922. s-m. free (effective 2010). adv. bk.rev. illus. **Document type:** *Magazine, Consumer.*
Former titles (until 1999): Ratgeber aus der Apotheke (0722-9062); (until 1972): Ratgeber fuer Kranke und Gesunde (0033-9997)
Published by: Gebr. Storck GmbH & Co. Verlags-oHG, Duisburger Str 375, Oberhausen, 46049, Germany. TEL 49-208-8480211, FAX 49-208-8480238, kalender@storckverlag.de, http://www.storckverlag.de.

613.7 305.896 USA
REAL HEALTH. Text in English. q. USD 9.97 (effective 2007). **Document type:** *Magazine, Consumer.* **Description:** Designed for African-American. Covers health, including fitness, nutrition, parenting and more.

Indexed: PEI.
Published by: Poz Publishing, LLC, 500 Fifth Ave, Ste 320, New York, NY 10110. TEL 212-242-2163, FAX 212-675-8505, webmaster@poz.com, http://www.poz.com.

RECRUITMENT DIRECTIONS. *see* OCCUPATIONS AND CAREERS

613.7 USA ISSN 0270-1367
GV201 CODEN: PMBIDB
➤ **RESEARCH QUARTERLY FOR EXERCISE AND SPORT.** Abbreviated title: R Q E S. Text in English. 1930. q. USD 105 in US & Canada to non-members; USD 117 elsewhere to non-members; USD 260 in US & Canada to institutions (print or online ed.); USD 272 elsewhere to institutions; USD 295 combined subscription in US & Canada to institutions (print & online eds.); USD 307 combined subscription elsewhere to institutions (print & online eds.); free to members (effective 2010). adv. bibl.; charts; illus.; abstr. index, cum.index every 10 yrs.: 1930-1969 (in 4 vols.). 120 p./no.; reprints avail. **Document type:** *Journal, Academic/Scholarly.* **Description:** Features research articles in the art and science of human movement that lead to the development of theory or the application of new techniques.
Incorporates (1965-1974): Abstracts of Research Papers (0587-4890); Former titles (until 1980): American Alliance for Health, Physical Education, Recreation and Dance. Research Quarterly (0034-5377); (until 1979): American Alliance for Health, Physical Education, and Recreation. Research Quarterly (1067-1315); (until 1974): American Association for Health, Physical Education, and Recreation. Research Quarterly (1067-1188); (until 1939): American Association for Health and Physical Education. Research Quarterly; (until 1937): American Physical Education Association. Research Quarterly.
Related titles: Microform ed.: (from PMC); ISSN 0364-9857 (from PQC); Online - full text ed.: (from IngentaConnect); Supplement(s).
Indexed: A01, A02, A03, A08, A20, A22, A25, A26, AMED, ASCA, B04, BRD, BiolDig, C06, C07, C33, CA, CIS, CurCont, DIP, E02, E03, E06, E07, E08, EMBASE, ERI, ERIC, EdA, EdI, ErgAb, ExcerpMed, FR, FoSS&M, G05, G06, G07, G08, H04, H11, H12, H13, I05, I07, IBR, IBZ, IndMed, Inpharma, M01, M02, M06, MEDLINE, NRN, P02, P07, P10, P13, P18, P19, P20, P22, P24, P26, P30, P48, P50, P53, P54, P55, PEI, PQC, PsycholAb, R09, RASB, RILM, S02, S03, S08, S09, S23, SCI, SCOPUS, SD, SSCI, SportS, T02, W03, W07, W09.
—BLDSC (7759.172000), GNLM, IE, Infotrieve, Ingenta, INIST. **CCC.**
Published by: American Alliance for Health, Physical Education, Recreation, and Dance, 1900 Association Dr, Reston, VA 20191. TEL 703-476-3400, 800-213-7193, FAX 703-476-9527, info@aahperd.org. Ed. Mark G Fischman.

613.7 BRA ISSN 1413-3482
REVISTA BRASILEIRA DE ATIVIDADE FISICA & SAUDE. Text in Portuguese. 1995. q. **Document type:** *Magazine, Trade.*
Published by: Associacao dos Professores de Educacao Fisica de Londrina, c/o Abdallah Achour Junior, Caixa Postal 642, Londrina, PR 86100-001, Brazil.

REVISTA BRASILEIRA DE CIENCIAS DA SAUDE. *see* MEDICAL SCIENCES

613.1 BRA ISSN 1415-8426
REVISTA BRASILEIRA DE CINEANTROPOMETRIA & DESEMPENHO HUMANO. Text in Portuguese. 1998. s-a. BRL 50 (effective 2006). **Document type:** *Journal, Academic/Scholarly.*
Related titles: Online - full text ed.: ISSN 1980-0037. free (effective 2011).
Indexed: CA, PEI, SD, T02.
Published by: Universidade Federal de Santa Catarina, Centro de Desportos, Campus Universitario - Trindade, CP 476, Florianopolis, SC 88040-900, Brazil. TEL 55-48-3318562, FAX 55-48-3319927, http://www.cds.ufsc.br. Ed. Paula Mercedes Vilanova Ilha.

613.7 BRA ISSN 1677-8510
REVISTA BRASILEIRA DE FISIOLOGIA DO EXERCICIO. Text in Portuguese. 2002. s-a. **Document type:** *Magazine, Trade.*
Published by: Editora Sprint, Rua Guapiara 28, Tijuca, Rio de Janeiro, 20521-180, Brazil. TEL 55-21-22648080, sprint@sprint.com.br.

REVISTA CHILENA DE DOCENCIA E INVESTIGACION EN SALUD. *see* EDUCATION

REVISTA CUBANA DE HIGIENE Y EPIDEMIOLOGIA. *see* PUBLIC HEALTH AND SAFETY

REVISTA DE EDUCACAO FISICA. *see* EDUCATION—Teaching Methods And Curriculum

613.7 ESP ISSN 1133-0546
REVISTA DE EDUCACION FISICA; renovacion de teoria y practica. Text in Spanish. 1985. bi-m. back issues avail. **Document type:** *Journal, Academic/Scholarly.*
Published by: Boidecanto SL, Almirante Eulate 6, La Coruna, 15011, Spain. TEL 34-981-254355.

613.7 ARG ISSN 1851-0175
REVISTA YOGA FACIL. Text in Spanish. 2007. m.
Published by: Producciones Publiexpress, Magallanes 1346, Buenos Aires, C1288ABB, Argentina. TEL 54-11-43031484, FAX 54-11-43031280, rrhh@publiexpress.com.ar, http://www.publiexpress.com.ar/.

613 ITA ISSN 0035-6921
RA421 CODEN: RIIGAV
RIVISTA ITALIANA D'IGIENE. Text in Italian; Summaries in English, Italian. 1941. bi-m. EUR 67 domestic; EUR 83 foreign (effective 2011). bibl.; charts; illus.; stat. index. **Document type:** *Journal, Academic/Scholarly.*
Indexed: ChemAb, ChemTitl, P30, RefZh.
—CASDDS, GNLM, INIST.
Published by: (Universita degli Studi di Pisa, Dipartimento di Patologia Sperimentale), Edizioni Plus - Universita di Pisa (Pisa University Press), Lungarno Pacinotti 43, Pisa, Italy. TEL 39-050-2212056, FAX 39-050-2212945, http://www.edizioniplus.it.

613.7 GBR ISSN 1360-497X
ROSEMARY CONLEY DIET & FITNESS. Text in English. 1996. 9/m. GBP 19.99 domestic; GBP 32 in Europe; GBP 40 elsewhere (effective 2009). adv. back issues avail. **Document type:** *Magazine, Consumer.* **Description:** Promotes health and well-being through special exercise and diet plans and examples. Includes special interest stories, celebrity interviews, entertainment articles, and fashion spreads.
—**CCC.**

Published by: Quorn House Publishing Ltd., Quorn House, Meeting St, Quorn, Leics LE12 8EX, United Kingdom. TEL 44-1509-620222, FAX 44-1509-621046, editorial@rosemaryconley.com.

613.2 USA ISSN 0898-5162
GV1061
RUNNING & FITNEWS. Text in English. bi-m. USD 25 to members; USD 40 to libraries (effective 2002). bk.rev. charts; illus. index. back issues avail.; reprints avail. **Document type:** *Newsletter, Consumer.* **Description:** Dedicated to helping runners and recreational athletes get the most from their exercise program by providing information on exercise, nutrition, training, sports medicine, injury prevention and long-term health.
Former titles (until 1984): Running and Fitness (0279-2214); (until 1981): Jogger (0164-694X)
Related titles: Online - full text ed.
Indexed: A01, A02, A03, A08, A26, C06, C07, C08, C11, CA, CINAHL, G05, G06, G07, G08, H03, H04, H11, H12, I05, I06, I07, M02, P19, P24, P48, PQC, S23, SD, SportS, T02.
Published by: American Running Association, 4405 East West Hwy, Ste 405, Bethesda, MD 20814. TEL 301-913-9517, FAX 301-913-9520, run@americanrunning.org. R&P David Watt. Circ: 15,000 (paid); 20,000 (controlled).

613.717 GBR ISSN 1472-4545
RUNNING FITNESS. Text in English. m. GBP 43.20 domestic; GBP 49.44 in Europe; GBP 54.96 elsewhere (effective 2009). back issues avail. **Document type:** *Magazine, Consumer.* **Description:** Contains advice with everything from training to returning from injury and covers all aspects of running.
Formerly (until 2000): Today's Runner (0268-4977)
Published by: Kelsey Publishing Ltd., Cudham Tithe Barn, Berry's Hill, Cudham, Kent TN16 3AG, United Kingdom. TEL 44-1959-541444, FAX 44-1959-541400, info@kelsey.co.uk, http://www.kelsey.co.uk.

S I I CSALUD. (Sociedad Iberoamericana de Informacion Cientifica) *see* MEDICAL SCIENCES

613.7 USA
S R L A NEWSLETTER. Text in English. 2003. bi-m. free to members. **Document type:** *Newsletter, Trade.* **Description:** Provides SRLA updates, recent cases, article citations pertaining to sport and recreation law and book citations.
Related titles: Online - full text ed.
Published by: Sports and Recreation Law Association, 1845 Fairmount, Wichita State University, Wichita, KS 67260. TEL 316-978-5445, mary.myers@wichita.edu, http://web.me.com/staceyaltman12/SRLA/Home.html. Ed. Paul M Anderson.

S T A P S. (Sciences et Techniques des Activites Physiques et Sportives) *see* MEDICAL SCIENCES—Sports Medicine

613.7 USA
ST. RAPHAEL'S BETTER HEALTH. Text in English. 1978. bi-m. USD 11. adv. bk.rev.
Published by: Institute for Better Health, 1384 Chapel St, New Haven, CT 06511. TEL 203-789-4089. Ed. Paul J Taylor. Circ: 120,000.

SALUD PARA TODOS. *see* CHILDREN AND YOUTH—For

613 ARG ISSN 0329-1421
RA773
SALUD VITAL. Text in Spanish. 1997. m. adv. **Document type:** *Magazine, Consumer.* **Description:** Devoted to health care and a commitment to quality of life.
Related titles: Online - full text ed.
Published by: Editorial Perfil S.A., Chacabuco 271, Buenos Aires, Buenos Aires 1069, Argentina. TEL 54-11-4341-9000, FAX 54-11-4341-9090, correo@perfil.com.ar, http://www.perfil.com.ar. Ed. Alejandro Wolfenson. Circ: 24,000 (paid).

SALUD(I)CIENCIA. *see* MEDICAL SCIENCES

SALUTE NATURALE; la nuova via del vivere bene. *see* ALTERNATIVE MEDICINE

▼ **SALUTE NATURALE EXTRA.** *see* ALTERNATIVE MEDICINE

613.7 POL ISSN 1429-1568
SAMO ZDROWIE; piekno - sila - witalnosc. Text in Polish. 1997. m. PLZ 1.99 newsstand/cover (effective 2010). adv. **Document type:** *Magazine, Consumer.*
Published by: Hubert Burda Media, ul Warecka 11a, Warsaw, 00034, Poland. TEL 48-22-4488000, FAX 48-22-4488001, kontakt@burdamedia.pl. Ed. Anna Mandes. Adv. contact Katarzyna Krzywinska-Grzybek TEL 48-22-4488459.

SANISSIMI. *see* MEDICAL SCIENCES

613.7 RUS ISSN 1994-4683
➤ **SANKT-PETERBURGSKII GOSUDARSTVENNYI UNIVERSITET FIZICHESKOI KUL'TURY IM. P.F. LESGAFTA. UCHENYE ZAPISKI/SCIENTIFIC NOTES OF THE LESGAFT NATIONAL STATE UNIVERSITY OF PHYSICAL EDUCATION, SPORT AND HEALTH.** Text in Russian, English. 1944. m. free. bk.rev. abstr.; bibl.; illus. Index. back issues avail. **Document type:** *Journal, Academic/Scholarly.* **Description:** Publishes scientific articles on actual problems of pedagogics and psychology. Covers problems of the theory and technique of physical training and sports, medical and biological problems of physical training, scientific research results of both experimental and theoretical character.
Formerly (until 2006): Gosudarstvennyi Institut Fizicheskoi Kul'tury im. P.F. Lesgafta. Uchenye Zapiski (0459-0465)
Related titles: Online - full text ed.
Published by: Sankt-Peterburgskii Gosudarstvennyi Universitet Fizicheskoi Kul'tury im. P.F. Lesgafta/Lesgaft National State University of Physical Education, Sport and Health, ul Dekabristov 35, St. Petersburg, Russian Federation. TEL 7-812-7141084, FAX 7-812-7141084, chistiakov52@mail.ru, http://lesgaft.spb.ru. Ed. V A Talmazov.

➤ **SANTE FAMILLE MAGAZINE.** *see* HANDICAPPED—Visually Impaired

613.7 FRA ISSN 0397-0329
SANTE MAGAZINE. Text in French. 1976. m. EUR 25 domestic (effective 2007). **Document type:** *Magazine, Consumer.* **Description:** Offers short articles and advice on every day health issues.
Related titles: Online - full text ed.: Santemagazine.fr. ISSN 1952-4676. **—CCC.**
Published by: Uni-Editions SAS, 22 Rue Letellier, Paris, Cedex 15 75739, France. TEL 33-1-43234572, FAX 33-1-43236112, http://www.uni-editions.com. Circ: 418,555.

▼ **SANTE REVUE SENIORS.** *see* GERONTOLOGY AND GERIATRICS

613.2 613.7 FRA ISSN 1960-7377
SANTE ZEN. Text in French. 2007. bi-m. **Document type:** *Magazine, Consumer.*
Published by: Editions Montefiori, 128 Rue de la Boetie, Paris, 75008, France. TEL 33-800-913-853, contact@santezen.fr.

SATSANG. *see* AGRICULTURE

613 BRA ISSN 0104-1568
SAUDE!; e vital!. Key Title: Saude e Vital. Variant title: Viva Vida com Saude. Text in Portuguese. 1983. m. BRL 96.12; BRL 8.90 newsstand/cover (effective 2010). adv. charts; illus. **Document type:** *Magazine, Consumer.* **Description:** For active, health-conscious readers. Contains information on the world of health, nutrition and related fields.
Related titles: Online - full text ed.
Published by: Editora Abril, S.A., Avenida das Nacoes Unidas 7221, Pinheiros, Sao Paulo, SP 05425-902, Brazil. TEL 55-11-50872112, FAX 55-11-50872100, abrilsac@abril.com.br, http://www.abril.com.br. adv.: page USD 22,000; 134 x 190. Circ: 219,195 (paid).

613 DEU
SAUNA - POOL - AMBIENTE. Text in German. 2004. bi-m. EUR 18; EUR 3.50 newsstand/cover (effective 2007). adv. **Document type:** *Magazine, Consumer.*
Published by: Michael E. Brieden Verlag GmbH, Gartroper Str 42, Duisburg, 47138, Germany. TEL 49-203-42920, FAX 49-203-4292149, info@brieden.de, http://www.brieden.de. Ed. Vera Sattler. adv.: B&W page EUR 3,330, color page EUR 5,410. Circ: 30,000 (controlled).

613 DEU ISSN 1862-8206
SAUNA UND BAEDERPRAXIS. Text in German. 1991. q. EUR 24 domestic; EUR 32 foreign; EUR 7 newsstand/cover (effective 2008). adv. **Document type:** *Magazine, Trade.*
Formerly (until 2006): Saunabetrieb und Baederpraxis (0945-5698)
Published by: Sauna-Matti GmbH, Kavalleriestr 9, Bielefeld, 33602, Germany. TEL 49-521-9667914, FAX 49-521-9667919, info@sauna-matti.de, http://www.sauna-matti.de. Ed. Rolf-Andreas Pieper. Adv. contact Hans-Juergen Gensow. B&W page EUR 1,395, color page EUR 1,840. Circ: 8,000 (paid and controlled).

SCHORERMAGAZINE. *see* HOMOSEXUALITY

613.7 DEU ISSN 1869-8387
▼ **SCHRIFTEN ZUR BEWEGUNGSWISSENSCHAFT.** Text in German. 2010. irreg. price varies. **Document type:** *Monographic series, Academic/Scholarly.*
Published by: Verlag Dr. Kovac, Leverkusenstr 13, Hamburg, 22761, Germany. TEL 49-40-3988800, FAX 49-40-39888055, info@verlagdrkovac.de, http://www.verlagdrkovac.de.

SCIENTIFIC JOURNAL IN SPORT AND EXERCISE. *see* SPORTS AND GAMES

613.7 368.382 DEU
SECURVITAL; das Magazin fuer Alternativen im Versicherungs- und Gesundheitswesen. Text in German. 2003. 5/yr. adv. **Document type:** *Magazine, Consumer.*
Published by: Securvita, Luebeckertordamm 1-3, Hamburg, 20099, Germany. TEL 49-40-3860800, FAX 49-40-38608090, mail@securvita.de. Ed. Norbert Schnorbach. Circ: 254,000 (controlled).

613.7 JPN ISSN 0582-4176
RA421 CODEN: SEEIAY
SEIKATSU EISEI/URBAN LIVING AND HEALTH ASSOCIATION. JOURNAL. Text in Japanese. 1957. bi-m. **Document type:** *Journal, Academic/Scholarly.*
Related titles: Online - full text ed.
—BLDSC (4912.280000). **CCC.**
Published by: Oosaka Seikatsu Eisei Kyokai/Urban Living and Health Association, Osaka City Institute of Public Health & Environmental Sciences, 8-34 Tojo-cho, Tennoji-ku, Osaka, 543-0026, Japan. TEL 81-6-67713085, FAX 81-6-67735086, http://ss7.inet-osaka.or.jp/~oeisei99/.

SETUBAL. GUIA DA SAUDE. *see* HEALTH FACILITIES AND ADMINISTRATION

613.7 CHN ISSN 1009-9840
SHANDONG TIYU KEJI/SHANDONG SPORTS SCIENCE & TECHNOLOGY. Text in Chinese. 1979. q. CNY 10 newsstand/cover (effective 2006). **Document type:** *Journal, Academic/Scholarly.*
Related titles: Online - full text ed.
Indexed: PEI.
Address: 122, Jing-Shi-Lu, Ji'nan, 250002, China. TEL 86-531-2026224, FAX 86-531-2072215.

SHANDONG TIYU XUEYUAN XUEBAO/SHANDONG PHYSICAL EDUCATION INSTITUTE. JOURNAL. *see* EDUCATION—Teaching Methods And Curriculum

613.7 CHN ISSN 1008-8571
SHANXI SHI-DA TIYU XUEYUAN XUEBAO/SHANXI TEACHERS UNIVERSITY. PHYSICAL EDUCATION INSTITUTE. JOURNAL. Text in Chinese. 1986. q. USD 16.40 (effective 2009). **Document type:** *Journal, Academic/Scholarly.*
Related titles: Online - full text ed.
Indexed: PEI.
—East View.
Published by: Shanxi Shifan Daxue/Shanxi Teachers University, 1, Gongyuan Jie, Linfen, Shanxi 041004, China. TEL 86-357-2051625.

SHAOLIN YU TAIJI. *see* SPORTS AND GAMES

SHAPE. *see* WOMEN'S HEALTH

SHAPE. *see* WOMEN'S HEALTH

SHAPE. *see* WOMEN'S HEALTH

SHAPE. *see* WOMEN'S HEALTH

613.7 SGP
SHAPE (SINGAPORE EDITION). Text in English. m. SGD 48 (effective 2008). **Document type:** *Magazine, Consumer.*
Published by: S P H Magazines Pte Ltd. (Subsidiary of: Singapore Press Holdings Ltd.), 82 Genting Ln Level 7, Media Centre, Singapore, 349567, Singapore. TEL 65-6319-6319, FAX 65-6319-6345, sphmag@sph.com.sg, http://www.sphmagazines.com.sg/.

SHAPE SOUTH AFRICA. *see* WOMEN'S HEALTH

613.7 ZAF ISSN 1991-6132
SHAPE. THE COMPLETE WORKOUT GUIDE. Text in English. 2006. a. ZAR 49.95 (effective 2007).
Published by: Touchline Media, PO Box 16368, Vlaeberg, Cape Town 8018, South Africa. TEL 27-21-4083800, FAX 27-21-4083811, http://www.touchline.co.za.

613.7 DEU ISSN 0949-2380
SHAPE UP. Text in German. 1992. bi-m. EUR 17.60 domestic; EUR 27 in Europe; EUR 3.25 newsstand/cover (effective 2007). adv. **Document type:** *Magazine, Consumer.*
Published by: Shape Up Verlagsgesellschaft mbH, Immenhorst 14D, Norderstedt, 22850, Germany. TEL 49-40-63916629, FAX 49-40-63916827. adv.: page EUR 8,400. Circ: 148,000 (paid and controlled).

613.7 DEU
SHAPE UP TRAINER'S ONLY. Text in German. 2004. bi-m. EUR 16.30 (effective 2007). adv. **Document type:** *Magazine, Trade.*
Published by: Shape Up Verlagsgesellschaft mbH, Immenhorst 14D, Norderstedt, 22850, Germany. TEL 49-40-63916629, FAX 49-40-63916827. adv.: page EUR 1,369. Circ: 16,000 (paid and controlled).

613.7 362.41 GBR
SHAPING UP. Text in English. 19??. m. GBP 0.50 per issue (effective 2009). **Document type:** *Magazine, Consumer.* **Description:** Provides information about health and fitness, product reviews, articles on alternative therapies, and tips on keeping in shape.
Media: Braille. **Related titles:** Diskette ed.; E-mail ed.
Published by: Royal National Institute of Blind People, 105 Judd St, London, WC1H 9NE, United Kingdom. TEL 44-20-73881266, FAX 44-20-73882034, helpline@rnib.org.uk, http://www.rnib.org.uk.

613.7 CHN ISSN 1009-3613
SHENGHUO YU JIANKANG/LIFE & HEALTH. Text in Chinese. 2000. m. USD 36 (effective 2009). **Document type:** *Journal, Academic/Scholarly.*
Related titles: Online - full text ed.
—East View.
Published by: Renmin Weisheng Chubanshe/People's Medical Publishing House, Fangqunyuan 3-qu, No.3 Bldg., Beijing, 100078, China. TEL 86-10-67617325, FAX 86-10-67653157.

SHENYANG TIYU XUEYUAN XUEBAO/SHENYANG SPORT UNIVERSITY. JOURNAL. *see* EDUCATION

796 PAK ISSN 1991-8410
GV204.P18
➤ **THE SHIELD**; research journal of physical education and sports science. Text in English. 2006. a. PKR 150 newsstand/cover domestic to individuals; USD 10 newsstand/cover foreign to individuals; USD 300 newsstand/cover domestic to libraries; USD 15 newsstand/cover foreign to libraries (effective 2010). **Document type:** *Journal, Academic/Scholarly.* **Description:** Publishes articles and research on health, physical education, sports science and other related disciplines.
Indexed: B21, ESPM, H&SSA, PEI, SD, T02.
Published by: University of Sindh, Faculty of Social Sciences, Allama I.I.Kazi Campus, Sindh, 76080, Pakistan. TEL 92-22-2771681 ext 2091, dean@social.usindh.edu.pk, http://social.usindh.edu.pk. Eds. Darlene Kaluka, Yasmeen Iqbal, Parveen Shah. R&P Iqbal Qureshi.

613.972 JPN ISSN 0037-4113
SHONI HOKEN KENKYU/JOURNAL OF CHILD HEALTH. Text in Japanese. 1933. bi-m. bk.rev. stat. Index. **Document type:** *Journal, Academic/Scholarly.*
Published by: Nihon Shoni Hoken Kenkyukai/Japanese Society of Child Health, 1-12 Katamachi, Shinjuku-ku, Fujita Bldg. 4F, Tokyo, 160-0001, Japan. TEL 81-3-33594964, FAX 81-3-33594906, jsch-soc@umin.ac.jp, http://plaza.umin.ac.jp/~jschild/.

613.7 370 CHN ISSN 1009-783X
SHOUDU TIYU XUEYUAN XUEBAO/CAPITAL INSTITUTE OF PHYSICAL EDUCATION. JOURNAL. Text in Chinese. 1989. bi-m. USD 37.20 (effective 2009). **Document type:** *Journal, Academic/Scholarly.*
Formerly: Beijing Tiyu Shifan Xueyuan Xuebao/Beijing Teachers College of Physical Education. Journal (1008-2220)
Related titles: Online - full text ed.; ◆ Supplement(s): Tiyu Jiaoxue. ISSN 1005-2410.
Indexed: CA, PEI, SD, T02.
—BLDSC (4723.202000).
Published by: Shoudu Tiyu Xueyuan, 11, San-Huan Xi Lu, Beijing, 100088, China.

SICHERHEITSBEAUFTRAGTER; Zeitschrift fuer Unfallverhuetung und Arbeitssicherheit. *see* BUSINESS AND ECONOMICS—Labor And Industrial Relations

SICHERHEITSINGENIEUR; Zeitschrift fuer Arbeitssicherheit. *see* BUSINESS AND ECONOMICS—Labor And Industrial Relations

SILENT SPORTS. *see* SPORTS AND GAMES

SIMPLY BETTER. *see* LIFESTYLE

SLIM AT HOME. *see* NUTRITION AND DIETETICS

SLIMMING. *see* NUTRITION AND DIETETICS

613.7 USA ISSN 1938-128X
▼ **SO BE FIT.** Text in English. 2009 (Jan.). bi-m. USD 29.95 (effective 2009). adv. **Document type:** *Magazine, Consumer.* **Description:** Provides advice on topics of fitness, nutrition, health and sports for men and women of South Florida.
Related titles: Online - full text ed.: ISSN 1938-1298.
Published by: M P G Publishing, 1201 Brickell Ave, Ste 320, Miami, FL 33131. TEL 305-375-9595, FAX 305-375-9596. Pub. Marta Montenegro. adv.: color page USD 6,509.07; trim 9 x 10.875. Circ: 1,005 (paid).

613.7 USA ISSN 1088-7482
SO YOUNG!; dedicated to a youthful body, mind and spirit. Text in English. 1996. q. USD 35 in US & Canada (effective 2005). adv. bk.rev.; music rev. illus. 12 p./no.; back issues avail. **Document type:** *Newsletter, Consumer.* **Description:** Informs on holistic self-help, cutting-edge, and anti-aging information. Covers all aspects of anti-aging: beauty, diet, nutrition, hormone replacement therapy, exercise, and medical breakthroughs.
Published by: Anti-Aging Press, Inc., PO Box 142174, Coral Gables, FL 33114. TEL 305-662-3928, 800-SO-YOUNG, FAX 305-661-4123. Ed., R&P Julia M Busch. Circ: 500 (paid); 500 (controlled).

P

SOCIEDADE PORTUGUESA DE EDUCACAO FISICA. BOLETIM. *see* SPORTS AND GAMES

613.7 JPN
SOKAI. Text in Japanese. 1974. m. **Document type:** *Consumer.*
Published by: Kodansha Ltd., 2-12-21 Otowa, Bunkyo-ku, Tokyo, 112-8001, Japan. TEL 81-3-3946-6201, FAX 81-3-3944-9915, TELEX J34509 KODANSHA, http://www.toppan.co.jp/kodansha, http://www.kodansha.co.jp. Ed. Masaaki Kajiyama. Circ: 250,000.

SOKOL POLSKI/POLISH FALCON. *see* ETHNIC INTERESTS

613 USA ISSN 0147-5231
QP448
SOMATICS; magazine - journal of the mind - body arts and sciences. Text in English. 1976. s-a. USD 20 domestic to individuals; USD 27 in Canada & Mexico to individuals; USD 33 elsewhere to individuals; USD 25 domestic to institutions (effective 2005). adv. bk.rev. back issues avail. **Description:** Publishes articles for professionals and laypersons in the mind and body field. Covers issues relating to holistic health care, fitness, movement, dance, psychology and philosophy.
Indexed: E-psyche, PhilInd, PsycholAb, SD.
—GNLM.
Published by: Novato Institute for Somatic Research and Training, 1516 Grant Avenue, Ste 212, Novato, CA 94945. TEL 415-892-0617, FAX 415-892-4388. Ed. Eleanor Criswell Hanna TEL 415-897-0336. Circ: 1,300.

613.9 ZAF ISSN 1819-2041
SOUTH AFRICAN FITNESS PROFESSIONALS. Text in English. 2006. q. ZAR 236 domestic; ZAR 380 foreign (effective 2006). adv. **Document type:** *Magazine, Consumer.*
Published by: Definitive Africa Media, 312 Gibraltar House, Regent Rd, Sea Point, Cape Town, 8005, South Africa. TEL 27-21-4340184, FAX 27-21-4342074, media@definitiveafricamedia.co.za. Ed. Steve Kruger. Pub. Christine Maritz.

613.122 USA
SPA MAGAZINE. Text in English. bi-m. USD 12 domestic; USD 30 in Canada; USD 36 elsewhere (effective 2005). bk.rev. **Document type:** *Magazine, Consumer.* **Description:** Covers the latest advances in self-care, beauty, healthy living and relaxation.
Related titles: Supplement(s): Spa Worldwide Guide. USD 9.95.
Published by: Islands Media Corp., 6267 Carpinteria Ave, Ste 200, Carpinteria, CA 93013. TEL 805-745-7100, FAX 805-745-7105, islands@islands.com, http://www.islandsmedia.com. Ed. Elizabeth Mazurski. Circ: 67,000 (paid).

613.7 USA
SPA SPECS; resources for health and well-being. Text in English. 1990. bi-m. USD 59. adv. back issues avail. **Document type:** *Newsletter.* **Description:** Covers trends in preventative medicine, health and fitness, nutrition, body work, and beauty.
Published by: Spa Specs International, 21548 Hyde Rd, Sonoma, CA 95476. TEL 707-939-0101. Ed., Pub. Eva M Jensch. Circ: 1,200.

613.7 RUS
SPID-INFO ZDOROV'E. Text in Russian. m. RUR 96 for 6 mos. domestic (effective 2004). **Document type:** *Newspaper, Consumer.*
Published by: Izdatel'stvo S-Info, A-ya 42, Moscow, 125284, Russian Federation. TEL 7-095-7969294, FAX 7-095-2520920, s-info@si.ru. **Subscr. to:** Unicont Enterprises Inc., 1340 Centre St, Ste 209, Newton, MA 02459. TEL 800-763-7475, FAX 617-964-8753, podpiska@unipressa.com.

613.7 DEU ISSN 0171-6298
SPIRIDON LAUFMAGAZIN. Text in German. 1975. m. EUR 36; EUR 3.50 newsstand/cover (effective 2007). adv. bk.rev. illus. index. back issues avail. **Document type:** *Magazine, Consumer.*
Published by: Spiridon Verlags GmbH, Dorfstr 18, Erkrath, 40699, Germany. TEL 49-211-726364, FAX 49-211-786823. Ed., Pub. Manfred Steffny. Adv. contact Nicole Uhr. B&W page EUR 1,200, color page EUR 2,040; trim 184 x 257. Circ: 11,500 (paid and controlled).

SPIRITUALITY & HEALTH; the soul body connection. *see* ALTERNATIVE MEDICINE

SPLASH! (COLORADO SPRINGS). *see* SPORTS AND GAMES

613.082 FIN ISSN 1458-7122
SPORT. Text in Finnish. 2002. 10/yr. EUR 64 (effective 2009). **Document type:** *Magazine, Consumer.* **Description:** Contains articles and features on physical training, nutrition and beauty for active women.
Published by: Sanoma Magazines Finland Corporation, Lapinmaentie 1, Helsinki, 00350, Finland. TEL 358-9-1201, FAX 358-9-1205171, info@sanomamagazines.fi, http://www.sanomamagazines.fi. Circ: 34,046 (paid and controlled).

SPORT AND EXERCISE PSYCHOLOGY REVIEW. *see* PSYCHOLOGY

613.7105 GBR ISSN 1754-3444
THE SPORT AND EXERCISE SCIENTIST. Text in English. 2004. q. free membership. adv. back issues avail. **Document type:** *Journal, Academic/Scholarly.* **Description:** Aims to provide up-to-date information to those with an interest in sport and exercise sciences and to support excellence in the delivery of sport and exercise science practice, teaching and learning, and research.
Related titles: Online - full text ed.: ISSN 1754-3452.
Indexed: R09, SD, T02.
—BLDSC (8419.364180).
Published by: British Association of Sport and Exercise Sciences (BASES), Rm GO7 and G08, Leeds Metropolitan University, Carnegie Faculty of Sport and Education, Fairfax Hall, Headingly Campus, Beckett Park, Leeds, LS6 3QS, United Kingdom. TEL 44-113-2836162, FAX 44-113-2836163. Ed. Andy Lane. Adv. contact Debbie Pearce TEL 44-113-8126162.

SPORT & MEDICINA. *see* MEDICAL SCIENCES—Sports Medicine

SPORT & GENEESKUNDE; the Flemish/Dutch journal of sports medicine. *see* MEDICAL SCIENCES—Sports Medicine

SPORT F M. *see* SPORTS AND GAMES

613.7 GBR ISSN 1757-0840
SPORT I Q (14-16 EDITION). (Intelligence Quotient) Text in English. 2008. 3/yr. GBP 69 (effective 2010). adv. back issues avail. **Document type:** *Magazine, Consumer.*
Formerly (until 2008): Balls (14-16 Edition)
Media: Online - full text.
Published by: Sport I Q Publications Ltd., 101 Aberdeen Ave, Manadon Park, Plymouth, Devon PL5 3UN, United Kingdom. TEL 44-8459-569688, info@sport-iq.com. Ed. Harvey Grout.

613.7 GBR ISSN 1757-0859
SPORT I Q (16-19 EDITION). (Intelligence Quotient) Text in English. 2006. 3/yr. adv. back issues avail. **Document type:** *Magazine, Consumer.*
Formerly (until 2008): Balls (16-19 Edition) (1757-0883); Which superseded in part (in 2007): Balls (1753-8173)
Related titles: Online - full text ed.: ISSN 1757-0867. GBP 69 (effective 2010).
Published by: Sport I Q Publications Ltd., 101 Aberdeen Ave, Manadon Park, Plymouth, Devon PL5 3UN, United Kingdom. TEL 44-8459-569688, info@sport-iq.com. Ed. Stuart Taylor.

613.7 796 DEU ISSN 1728-5666
SPORT SCIENCE & PHYSICAL EDUCATION BULLETIN. Text in English. 199?. 3/yr. free. adv. 68 p./no. 3 cols./p.; back issues avail. **Document type:** *Bulletin.* **Description:** Aims to provide a forum for ICSSPE members and other contributors to share news and experiences, raise issues for discussion, develop international and external links and promote events.
Supersedes in part (in 2003): I C S S P E Bulletin (Print) (1563-3632)
Media: Online - full text.
Published by: International Council of Sport Science and Physical Education, Hanns-Braun-Strasse Friesenhaus II, Berlin, 14053, Germany. TEL 49-30-36418850, FAX 49-30-8056386, icsspe@icsspe.org, http://www.icsspe.org. Ed. Tamie Devine. Circ: 2,000 (controlled).

613.7 ITA ISSN 1824-7490
GV557
➤ **SPORT SCIENCES FOR HEALTH.** Text in English. 2004. 4/yr. EUR 269, USD 308 combined subscription to institutions (print & online eds.) (effective 2012). reprint service avail. from PSC. **Document type:** *Journal, Academic/Scholarly.* **Description:** Publishes reports of experimental and clinical research on the physiology and pathophysiology of physical exercise with special focus on the mechanism through which exercise can prevent or treat chronic-degenerative disease, contributing to health maintenance in the population.
Related titles: Online - full text ed.: ISSN 1825-1234 (from IngentaConnect).
Indexed: A01, A03, A22, A26, B21, BRD, CA, E01, E08, ESPM, G03, G08, GSA, GSI, H&SSA, H11, I05, PEI, R09, S04, S09, SCOPUS, SD, T02, W03, W05.
—BLDSC (8419.645800), IE, Ingenta. **CCC.**
Published by: Springer Italia Srl (Subsidiary of: Springer Science+Business Media), Via Decembrio 28, Milan, 20137, Italy. TEL 39-02-54259722, FAX 39-02-55193360, springer@springer.it. Ed. Giuliano Pizzini.

➤ **SPORTEX DYNAMICS**; the publication for professionals seeking sporting excellence. *see* MEDICAL SCIENCES—Sports Medicine

617.1 613.7 GBR ISSN 2040-4794
SPORTEX HEALTH. Text in English. 2000. q. GBP 59 to individuals; GBP 175 to institutions (effective 2010). adv. **Document type:** *Magazine, Trade.* **Description:** Focuses on the promotion of physical activity for health.
Formerly (until 2008): HealthEX Specialist (1744-9375); Which superseded in part (in 2004): SportEX Health (1471-8154)
Related titles: Online - full text ed.: GBP 50 (effective 2010).
Indexed: C06, C07, C08, C11, CA, CINAHL, SD, T02.
—**CCC.**
Published by: Centor Publishing, 88 Nelson Rd, Wimbledon, SW19 1HX, United Kingdom. TEL 44-845-6521906, FAX 44-845-6521907, subs@sportex.net. Ed. Jackie Cresswell. Pub. Tor Davies. Adv. contact Paul Harris.

SPORTEX MEDICINE. *see* MEDICAL SCIENCES—Sports Medicine

SPORTGERICHT. *see* SPORTS AND GAMES

SPORTKADER NIEUWSBRIEF (ONLINE). *see* EDUCATION—Special Education And Rehabilitation

SPORTLOJA. *see* SPORTS AND GAMES

SPORTS BIOMECHANICS. *see* SPORTS AND GAMES

SPORTS MEDICINE BULLETIN (ONLINE). *see* MEDICAL SCIENCES—Sports Medicine

613.7 USA
SPRY. Text in English. 2008 (Sep.). m. adv. **Document type:** *Magazine, Consumer.* **Description:** Offers information and authoritative articles on health, diet, recreation and leisure activities that contribute to a satisfying and healthful lifestyle.
Published by: Publishing Group of America, 60 E 42nd St, Ste 1111, New York, NY 10165. TEL 212-478-1900, FAX 646-865-1921, http://www.pubgroupofamerica.com/. Pub. Bob Mattone TEL 212-478-1922. Adv. contact Erica Schultz TEL 312-396-4090. B&W 1/2 page USD 330,375, color page USD 359,100; trim 9.188 x 10. Circ: 9,000,000.

613.7 ITA ISSN 1120-527X
STARBENE. Text in Italian. 1978. m. EUR 18.50 (effective 2009). adv. **Document type:** *Magazine, Consumer.*
Published by: Arnoldo Mondadori Editore SpA, Via Mondadori 1, Segrate, 20090, Italy. TEL 39-02-66814363, FAX 39-030-3198412, infolibri@mondadori.it, http://www.mondadori.com. Ed. Cristina Merlino. Circ: 323,870 (paid).

613.7 DEU ISSN 1860-1375
STERN GESUND LEBEN; Das Magazin fuer Koerper, Geist und Seele. Variant title: Gesund Leben. Text in German. 2003. bi-m. EUR 5.90 newsstand/cover (effective 2010). adv. **Document type:** *Magazine, Consumer.*
Published by: Gruner + Jahr AG & Co, Am Baumwall 11, Hamburg, 20459, Germany. TEL 49-40-37030, FAX 49-40-37035601, info@gujmedia.de, http://www.guj.de. Adv. contact Helma Spieker. page EUR 13,200. Circ: 80,269 (paid).

613.7 USA ISSN 1524-1602
GV514
➤ **STRENGTH AND CONDITIONING JOURNAL.** Abbreviated title: S & C. Text in English. 1979. bi-m. USD 179 domestic to institutions; USD 212 foreign to institutions (effective 2011). adv. bk.rev. charts; illus.; stat. Index. 80 p./no.; back issues avail.; reprints avail. **Document type:** *Journal, Academic/Scholarly.* **Description:** Brings out articles that report both the practical applications of research findings and the knowledge gained by experienced professionals.
Former titles (until 1999): Strength and Conditioning (1073-6840); (until 1994): N S C A Journal (1073-2721); (until 1993): National Strength & Conditioning Association Journal (0744-0049); (until 1981): National Strength Coaches Association Journal (0199-610X)
Related titles: Online - full text ed.: ISSN 1533-4295.
Indexed: A22, ASCA, C06, C07, C08, CA, CINAHL, DIP, E01, ErgAb, FoSS&M, H13, IBR, IBZ, P02, P10, P19, P20, P24, P30, P48, P50, P53, P54, PEI, PQC, R09, SCI, SCOPUS, SD, SportS, T02, W07.
—BLDSC (8474.119970), IE, Infotrieve, Ingenta. **CCC.**
Published by: (National Strength and Conditioning Association), Lippincott Williams & Wilkins (Subsidiary of: Wolters Kluwer N.V.), 530 Walnut St, Philadelphia, PA 19106. TEL 215-521-8300, FAX 215-521-8902, customerservice@lww.com, http://www.lww.com. Ed. T Jeff Chandler. Pub. Terry Materese. Adv. contact Bob Williams TEL 215-521-8394. Circ: 27,608.

613.7 ROM ISSN 1453-4223
GV201
➤ **STUDIA UNIVERSITATIS BABES-BOLYAI. EDUCATIO ARTIS GYMNASTICAE.** Text in English. 1993. q. exchange basis. bk.rev. abstr.; bibl.; charts; illus. **Document type:** *Journal, Academic/Scholarly.*
Formerly (until 1994): Studia Universitatis "Babes-Bolyai". Educatia Physica (1224-1652)
Related titles: Online - full text ed.: ISSN 2065-9547.
Indexed: CA, T02.
Published by: Universitatea "Babes-Bolyai", Studia/Babes-Bolyai University, Studia, 51 Hasdeu Str, Cluj-Napoca, 400371, Romania. TEL 40-264-405352, FAX 40-264-591906, office@studia.ubbcluj.ro, http://www.studia.ubbcluj.ro. Eds. Rares Ciocoi-Pop, Vasile Bogdan. **Dist by:** "Lucian Blaga" Central University Library, International Exchange Department, Clinicilor st no 2, Cluj-Napoca 400371, Romania. TEL 40-264-597092, FAX 40-264-597633, iancu@bcucluj.ro.

➤ **STUDIES IN HEALTH AND HUMAN SERVICES.** *see* PUBLIC HEALTH AND SAFETY

613.7 POL ISSN 0867-1079
GV557
➤ **STUDIES IN PHYSICAL CULTURE AND TOURISM.** Text in English. 1990. s-a. PLZ 28 domestic; EUR 7 foreign (effective 2004). bk.rev. back issues avail. **Document type:** *Journal, Academic/Scholarly.* **Description:** Covers all domains of physical culture: experimental laboratory studies on physiology and motor performance, methodology of sport, physical education and health promotion, leisure, recreation and tourism, history of physical culture and sport.
Indexed: A10, A36, A37, CA, CABA, F08, F12, GH, H&TI, H06, LT, N02, N03, PEI, RRTA, SD, T02, V03, W11.
Published by: Akademia Wychowania Fizycznego im. Eugeniusza Piaseckiego w Poznaniu/Eugeniusz Piasecki University School of Physical Education in Poznan, ul Krolowej Jadwigi 27-39, Poznan, 61871, Poland. TEL 48-61-8355092. Eds. Piotr Krutki, Wojciech Liponski. Circ: 120 (paid); 80 (controlled).

613.7 790.1 FIN ISSN 0356-1070
CODEN: RADKEY
STUDIES IN SPORT, PHYSICAL EDUCATION AND HEALTH. Text in English, Finnish. 1971. irreg., latest vol.9, 1976. per issue exchange basis. **Document type:** *Monographic series, Consumer.*
Published by: Jyvaskylan Yliopisto/University of Jyvaskyla, PO Box 35, Jyvaskyla, 40014, Finland. TEL 941-601-371, FAX 603-371. Eds. Harri Suominen, Juhani Kirjonen. Circ: 450.

612.044 790.072 ZAF ISSN 0379-9069
➤ **SUID-AFRIKAANSE TYDSKRIF VIR NAVORSING IN SPORT, LIGGAAMLIKE OPVOEDKUNDE EN ONTSPANNING/SOUTH AFRICAN JOURNAL FOR RESEARCH IN SPORT, PHYSICAL EDUCATION AND RECREATION.** Text in Afrikaans, English; Summaries in English. 1978. s-a. ZAR 100 domestic; USD 50 foreign (effective 2007). bk.rev. back issues avail. **Document type:** *Journal, Academic/Scholarly.* **Description:** Aimed at scientists involved in the areas of physical fitness, sport, sports medicine, movement education and recreation.
Related titles: Online - full text ed.
Indexed: A36, CA, CABA, E12, GH, ISAP, LT, N02, N03, R12, RRTA, SCOPUS, SD, SSCI, SportS, T02, T05, W07.
—BLDSC (8053.668500), IE.
Published by: University of Stellenbosch, Department of Sport Science, Private Bag X1, Maiteland, 7602, South Africa. TEL 27-21-8084915, FAX 27-21-8084817. Ed. F J G Van der Merwe. Circ: 600.

613 NOR ISSN 0332-7434
SUNNHETSBLADET. Text in Norwegian. 1881. 11/yr. NOK 340 (effective 2007). adv. bk.rev. **Document type:** *Magazine, Consumer.*
—**CCC.**
Published by: Norsk Bokforlag A-S, Vik Senter, Roeyse, 3530, Norway. TEL 47-32-461550, FAX 47-32-461551, salg@noskbokforlag.no, http://www.norskbokforlag.no. Ed. Per de Lange. Adv. contact Dagfinn Moeller Nielsen. color page NOK 10,000. Circ: 6,167 (controlled).

SWIMMING POOLS TODAY. *see* SPORTS AND GAMES—Outdoor Life

613.7 CZE ISSN 1212-1061
T P. (Telovychovny Pracovnik) Text in Czech. 1957. m. adv. illus. Supplement avail. **Document type:** *Magazine.* **Description:** Covers sports and games activity of union members.
Formerly (until 1993): Telovychovny Pracovnik (0040-2850)
Indexed: RASB.
Published by: Cesky Svaz Talesne Vychovy/Czech Sport Association, Zatopkova 100/2, Prague 6, 16017, Czech Republic. TEL 420-2-33017333, FAX 420-2-33358467, cstv@cstv.cz. Ed., R&P, Adv. contact Eva Fiserova. Circ: 5,000.

T'AI CHI; the leading international magazine of T'ai Chi Ch'uan. *see* ASIAN STUDIES

TAI CHI & ALTERNATIVE HEALTH. *see* ASIAN STUDIES

TAIIKU NO KAGAKU/JOURNAL OF HEALTH, PHYSICAL EDUCATION AND RECREATION. *see* EDUCATION—Teaching Methods And Curriculum

TAIIKUGAKU KENKYU/JAPAN JOURNAL OF PHYSICAL EDUCATION, HEALTH AND SPORT SCIENCES. *see* EDUCATION

TAIJIQUAN & QIGONG JOURNAL. *see* SPORTS AND GAMES

610 613.7 JPN ISSN 0039-906X
➤ **TAIRYOKU KAGAKU/JAPANESE JOURNAL OF PHYSICAL FITNESS AND SPORTS MEDICINE.** Text in English, Japanese. 1950. bi-m. membership. adv. **Document type:** *Journal, Academic/Scholarly.*
Formerly: Japanese Journal of Physical Fitness
Related titles: Online - full text ed.
Indexed: ASCA, B21, B25, BIOSIS Prev, CA, ESPM, FoSS&M, H&SSA, MycolAb, PEI, R09, SCI, SCOPUS, SD, T02, W07.
—BLDSC (4657.420000).
Published by: Nihon Tairyoku Igakkai/Japanese Society of Physical Fitness and Sports Medicine, Association for Supporting Academic Societies, 26-1-B03, Kaitai-cho, Shinjyuku, Tokyo, 162-0802, Japan. TEL 81-3-52066065, FAX 81-3-52066008. Circ: 4,800.

613.7 JPN ISSN 0389-9071
CODEN: TAKNAS
TAIRYOKU KENKYU/PHYSICAL FITNESS RESEARCH INSTITUTE. BULLETIN. Variant title: Tairyoku Igaku Kenkyujo Hokoku. Text in Japanese. 1963. 3/yr. **Document type:** *Bulletin, Academic/Scholarly.*
Indexed: B25, BIOSIS Prev, MycolAb, SCOPUS.
—BLDSC (2684.007000).
Published by: Meiji Seimei Kosei Jigyodan, Tairyoku Igaku Kenkyujo/ Meiji Life Foundation of Health and Welfare, Physical Fitness Research Institute, 150, Tobuki, Hachioji, Tokyo, 192-0001, Japan. TEL 81-426-911163, FAX 81-426-915559.

613.7 ESP ISSN 1577-0834
TANDEM; didactica de la educacion fisica. Text in Spanish. 2000. q. EUR 58.50 domestic; EUR 88 foreign (effective 2009). **Document type:** *Magazine, Trade.*
Published by: Editoral Grao, C Hurtado, 29, Barcelona, 08022, Spain. TEL 34-93-4080464, FAX 34-93-3524337, web@grao.com, http://www.grao.com.

TARZAN. *see* MEN'S INTERESTS

613.7 USA
TENNESSEE ASSOCIATION OF HEALTH, PHYSICAL EDUCATION, RECREATION AND DANCE. NEWSLETTER. Text in English. 196?. s-a. free to members (effective 2007). **Document type:** *Newsletter, Consumer.*
Former titles: Tennessee Journal of Health, Physical Education, Recreation and Dance (0890-1597); Tennessee Journal of Health, Physical Education, and Recreation
Indexed: SportS.
Published by: Tennessee Association of Health, Physical Education, Recreation and Dance, c/o Chris Ayres, Executive Director, 120 Tami Dr., Johnson City, TN 37601. TEL 423-547-9780, FAX 423-547-0868, ed@tahperd.us, http://www.tahperd.us. Ed. Ruth Henry.

613.7 EST ISSN 1406-300X
TERVIS PLUSS. Text in Estonian. 1998. m. EUR 24.48; EUR 2.40 newsstand/cover (effective 2011). adv. **Document type:** *Magazine, Consumer.*
Published by: Ajakirjade Kirjastus, Maakri 23A, Tallinn, 10145, Estonia. TEL 372-666-2600, FAX 372-666-2557, sekr@kirjastus.ee, http://www.kirjastus.ee. Ed. Evelin Kivilo-Paas. adv.: page EEK 14,500; trim 210 x 280.

613.7 USA
TESTOSTERONE; muscle with attitude. Text in English. bi-m. USD 29.95; USD 4.99 newsstand/cover (effective 2001). adv. **Document type:** *Magazine, Consumer.* **Description:** Provides information and articles on building a bigger and stronger body.
Published by: Testosterone Publishing, LLC, PO Box 60310, Colorado Springs, CO 80960-0310. TEL 719-473-5500, 800-530-1940, FAX 719-473-7700, 888-556-2727. Ed. T C Luoma.

613.7 USA
➤ **TEXAS ASSOCIATION H P E R D JOURNAL.** Text in English. 1954. 3/yr. free to members (effective 2010). adv. back issues avail. **Document type:** *Journal, Academic/Scholarly.* **Description:** Designed to serve education from kindergarten through college.
Former titles (until 1985): T A H P E R D Journal (0889-0846); (until 1983): T A H P E R Journal; (until 195?): Texas Association for Health, Physical Education, and Recreation. News Bulletin
Indexed: CA, PEI, SD, SportS, T02.
Published by: Texas Association for Health, Physical Education, Recreation and Dance, 7910 Cameron Rd, Austin, TX 78754. TEL 512-459-1299, FAX 512-459-1290, tahperd@tahperd.org.

613.7 155.916 USA ISSN 0040-5914
RM737 CODEN: TRJOED
➤ **THERAPEUTIC RECREATION JOURNAL.** Text in English. 1967. q. USD 52 domestic to members; USD 56 foreign to members; USD 72 domestic to non-members; USD 96 foreign to non-members; USD 88 to libraries (effective 2010). bk.rev. illus. Index. back issues avail.; reprints avail. **Document type:** *Journal, Academic/Scholarly.*
Related titles: Microform ed.: (from PQC); Online - full text ed.
Indexed: A22, A36, A37, C06, C07, C08, CA, CABA, CINAHL, E-psyche, E03, E12, ERI, FamI, GH, LT, N02, P03, P18, P24, P25, P30, P48, P53, P54, PEI, PQC, PsycInfo, PsycholAb, R09, R12, RRTA, SD, SOPODA, SociolAb, SportS, T02, T05.
—BLDSC (8814.672100), GNLM, IE, Infotrieve, Ingenta. **CCC.**
Published by: (National Therapeutic Recreation Society), National Recreation and Park Association, 22377 Belmont Ridge Rd, Ashburn, VA 20148. TEL 703-858-0784, FAX 703-858-0794, customerservice@nrpa.org.

796 CHN ISSN 1005-0000
TIANJIN TIYU XUEYUAN XUEBAO/TIANJIN INSTITUTE OF PHYSICAL EDUCATION. JOURNAL. Text in Chinese. 1986. q. USD 40.20 (effective 2009). **Document type:** *Journal, Academic/Scholarly.*
Related titles: Online - full text ed.
Indexed: CA, PEI, SD, T02.
—BLDSC (4908.628000), East View.
Published by: Tianjin Tiyu Xueyuan/Tianjin Institute of Physical Education, Hexi District, 51, Weijin Nan Road, Tianjin, 300381, China. TEL 86-22-2301-2636.

TIMISOARA PHYSICAL EDUCATION AND REHABILITATION JOURNAL. *see* EDUCATION

TIYU JIAOXUE/TEACHING & LEARNING OF PHYSICAL EDUCATION. *see* EDUCATION

613.7 CHN ISSN 1007-7413
TIYU KEXUE YANJIU/SPORTS SCIENCES RESEARCHES. Text in Chinese. 1984. q. CNY 6 newsstand/cover (effective 2006). **Document type:** *Journal, Academic/Scholarly.*
Related titles: Online - full text ed.
Indexed: PEI.
Published by: Jimei Daxue/Jimei University, 1, Jimeijicen Lu, Xiamen, 361021, China. TEL 86-592-6180707, FAX 86-592-6181242.

TIYU KEYAN/SPORTS SCIENCE RESEARCH. *see* MEDICAL SCIENCES—Sports Medicine

613.7 CHN ISSN 1006-7116
TIYU XUEKAN/JOURNAL OF PHYSICAL EDUCATION. Text in Chinese; Abstracts in English. 1995. m. USD 80.40 (effective 2009). **Document type:** *Journal, Academic/Scholarly.*
Formerly (until 1994): Tiyuxue Tongxun
Related titles: Online - full text ed.
Indexed: A36, CA, CABA, E12, F08, F12, GH, LT, N02, N03, O01, P32, PEI, PHN&I, R12, RRTA, SD, T02, T05, TAR, W11.
—BLDSC (5036.201000).
Published by: Huanan Shifan Daxue/South China Normal University, 303 Public Physical Education Bldg., Guangzhou, 510631, China. TEL 86-20-85211412, FAX 86-20-85210629, http://www.scnu.edu.cn/. Eds. Jin-Xian Song, Wen-Xuan Yang, Yuan-yuan Li. **Dist. by:** China International Book Trading Corp, 35 Chegongzhuang Xilu, Haidian District, PO Box 399, Beijing 100044, China. TEL 86-10-68412045, FAX 86-10-68412023, cibtc@mail.cibtc.com.cn, http://www.cibtc.com.cn. **Co-sponsor:** Huanan Ligong Daxue/South China University of Technology.

613.7 USA ISSN 1534-2212
TO YOUR HEALTH. Text in English. 1998. m. USD 19.95 domestic; USD 29.95 in Canada (effective 2009). **Document type:** *Magazine, Consumer.*
Related titles: Online - full text ed.
Indexed: I05, S23.
Published by: M P A Media, PO Box 4139, Huntington Beach, CA 92605-4139. TEL 714-230-3150, 800-324-7758, FAX 714-899-4273, editorial@mpamedia.com, http://www.mpamedia.com. Ed. Ramon McLeod.

613.7 USA
TO YOUR HEALTH!; the magazine of healing and hope. Text in English. 1989. bi-m. USD 25 (effective 1997). adv. bk.rev. illus.
Address: 280 Lowndes Ave., Apt. 110, Huntingtn Sta, NY 11746-1258. TEL 718-921-3131, FAX 718-921-0183. Ed., Pub., R&P Bernice Stock. Circ: 73,000.

613.7 USA ISSN 1531-8044
TODAY'S HEALTH AND WELLNESS. Text in English. 2000. 5/yr. free to members (effective 2008). adv. 80 p./no.; back issues avail. **Document type:** *Magazine, Consumer.* **Description:** Focuses on overall balance in life and contains instruction on both western and complementary healthcare.
Published by: North American Media Group, Inc. (Subsidiary of: North American Membership Group, Inc.), 12301 Whitewater Dr, Minnetonka, MN 55343. TEL 952-936-9333, 800-922-4888, FAX 952-936-9755, namghq@namginc.com, http://www.northamericanmediagroup.com/. Ed. Claire Lewis. Pub. Lee Sarles TEL 952-988-7114. adv.: B&W page USD 7,165, color page USD 10,463; trim 7.75 x 10.5. Circ: 182,445.

TODOVIDA. *see* ALTERNATIVE MEDICINE

613.7 ITA ISSN 1123-3532
TOP SALUTE; il giornale della prevenzione. Text in Italian. 1986. m. (10/yr.). **Document type:** *Magazine, Consumer.*
Formerly (until 1993): Forma
Published by: Alberto Peruzzo Editore Srl, Via Ercole Marelli 165, Sesto San Giovanni, MI 20099, Italy. TEL 39-02-242021, FAX 39-02-2485736. Circ: 250,000.

613.7 FRA ISSN 1152-7137
TOP SANTE. Text in French. 1990. m. EUR 21.60 (effective 2008). **Document type:** *Magazine, Consumer.*
Published by: Mondadori France, 1 Rue du Colonel Pierre-Avia, Paris, Cedex 15 75754, France. TEL 33-1-46484848, contact@mondadori.fr, http://www.mondadori.fr.

TOP TIMES; das Sportmagazin. *see* SPORTS AND GAMES

613.7 SRB ISSN 1452-8517
TOP ZDRAVLJE. Text in Serbian. 2007. m. CSD 420; CSD 35 newsstand/cover (effective 2011). adv. **Document type:** *Magazine, Consumer.*
Published by: Color Media International, Temerinska 102, Novi Sad, 21000. TEL 381-21-4897100, FAX 381-21-4897126, milan.sobot@color.rs, http://www.color.rs. Ed. Natasa Veletic. Adv. contact Goran Radulovic.

613.2 USA
TOPS NEWS. Text in English. 1949. 9/yr. free to members (effective 2009). **Document type:** *Magazine, Consumer.* **Description:** News and features about weight-control and nutrition. Covers activities of the organization.
Published by: Tops Club Inc., 4575 S Fifth St, PO Box 070360, Milwaukee, WI 53207. TEL 414-482-4620, topsinteractive@tops.org, http://www.tops.org.

613.7 USA ISSN 1072-4788
TOTAL WELLNESS. Text in English. 1993. m. USD 25 (effective 2009). **Document type:** *Newsletter, Consumer.* **Description:** Aims to promote general good health among employees and their families.
Published by: Rutherford Publishing, 1600 Lake Air Dr, Waco, TX 76710. TEL 254-751-1194, 800-815-2323, FAX 254-776-5561, rpublish@rpublish.com. Ed. Kimberly Denman. Pub. Ronnie Marroquin.

TOTAL WELLNESS. *see* BEAUTY CULTURE

613.7 615.53 USA
TOUCH FOR HEALTH. Text in English. 1982. q. USD 20. adv. bk.rev. **Document type:** *Newsletter.* **Description:** Offers commentary and news concerning holistic health promotion, wellness, healing, kinesiology, acupressure, subtle energies, world views and beliefs.
Published by: Touch for Health Education, Inc., 6162 La Gloria Dr, Malibu, CA 90265-3105. TEL 310-589-5269, thie@touch4health.com, http://www.touch4health.com. Ed. John F Thie. R&P John Thie. Circ: 2,000.

794 DEU ISSN 1437-255X
TRAINER. Text in German. 1996. bi-m. EUR 42 (effective 2010); EUR 51 foreign (effective 2006). adv. **Document type:** *Magazine, Trade.*
Published by: Health and Beauty Business Media GmbH & Co. KG, Karl-Friedrich-Str 14-18, Karlsruhe, 76133, Germany. TEL 49-721-1650, FAX 49-721-165618, info@health-and-beauty.com, http://www.health-and-beauty.com. Circ: 6,946 (paid and controlled).

TRANS-HEALTH; the online magazine of health and fitness for transsexual and transgendered people. *see* HOMOSEXUALITY

TRIATHLON AND MULTI-SPORT MAGAZINE. *see* SPORTS AND GAMES

613.7 DEU
TRIATHLON MAGAZIN. Text in German. 1985. 4/yr. adv. bk.rev. index. back issues avail. **Document type:** *Magazine, Consumer.*
Published by: Spiridon Verlags GmbH, Dorfstr 18, Erkrath, 40699, Germany. TEL 49-211-726364, FAX 49-211-786823. Ed., Pub. Manfred Steffny. Adv. contact Nicole Uhr. B&W page EUR 1,200, color page EUR 2,040. Circ: 4,000 (controlled).

TSPORT; impianti sportivi e ricreativi, piscine, fitness e arredo urbano. *see* SPORTS AND GAMES

TURISMO&BENESSERE. *see* TRAVEL AND TOURISM

U E M / REVISTA DA EDUCACAO FISICA. (Universidade Estadual de Maringa) *see* EDUCATION—Teaching Methods And Curriculum

613.194 NLD ISSN 1874-0197
UIT!. Text in Dutch. 1961. 4/yr. EUR 18; EUR 7.75 newsstand/cover (effective 2008). adv. bk.rev. illus. **Document type:** *Consumer.*
Formerly (until 2007): Naturisme (0028-0968)
Published by: Stichting Naturistische Uitgaven/Dutch Federation of Naturist Organisations, Postbus 1767, Amersfoort, 3800 BT, Netherlands. TEL 31-33-2533050, FAX 31-33-2533060, office@nfn.nl, http://www.nfn.nl/. Circ: 42,000.

ULTIMATE M M A. (Mixed Martial Arts) *see* SPORTS AND GAMES

613.7 GBR ISSN 0957-0616
ULTRA-FIT. Cover title: Ultra-FIT Magazine. Text in English. 1989. 9/yr. GBP 25; GBP 3.99 per issue (effective 2009). adv. bk.rev. tr.lit. back issues avail. **Document type:** *Magazine, Consumer.* **Description:** Covers all aspects of personal fitness, from exercise to nutrition to emotional well-being.
Indexed: SD.
Published by: Ultra-Fit Publications, Champions House, 5 Princes St, Penzance, Cornwall TR18 2NL, United Kingdom. TEL 44-1736-350204, FAX 44-1736-368587. **Dist. by:** Comag Specialist Division.

P

613.7 AUS
ULTRA FIT MAGAZINE. Text in English. 1985. 9/yr. AUD 59; AUD 7.95 newsstand/cover (effective 2008). adv. bk.rev.; Website rev. back issues avail. **Document type:** *Magazine, Consumer.* **Description:** Provides nutritional information, exercise and fitness advice, new product and medical information, celebrity profiles and human interest stories.
Former titles (until 2002): Australian Ultra-Fit; (until 1997): Ultra-Fit Australia (1321-1536); (until 1990): Australian Fitness and Training (1031-4105); (until 1987): Australian Workout (0815-6980)
Indexed: SD.
Published by: Ultra Fit Australia, PO Box 880, Newport, NSW 2106, Australia. TEL 61-2-99993384, FAX 61-2-99993385. Ed. Rosemary Marchese. Adv. contact Adrian Buckley TEL 61-2-99990234. page AUD 2,500; trim 210 x 297. Circ: 25,000.

UNG. *see* CHILDREN AND YOUTH—For

UNIVERSIDAD DE CARABOBO. FACULTAD DE CIENCIAS. REVISTA. *see* MEDICAL SCIENCES

613.7 ESP ISSN 1139-7101
UNIVERSIDAD DE ZARAGOZA. ESCUELA UNIVERSITARIA DE CIENCIAS DE LA SALUD. ANALES. Text in Spanish. 1998. a. **Document type:** *Journal, Academic/Scholarly.*
Published by: Universidad de Zaragoza, Escuela Universitaria de Ciencias de la Salud, C/ Domingo Miral s/n, Zaragoza, Spain. TEL 34-976-761751, FAX 34-976-761752, http://www.unizar.es.

613 ITA ISSN 1827-4161
UNIVERSITA DEGLI STUDI DI MILANO. ISTITUTO D'IGIENE. QUADERNI. Text in Italian. 1979. irreg. **Document type:** *Monographic series, Academic/Scholarly.*
Published by: Universita degli Studi di Milano, Istituto d'Igiene, Via C Pascal 36, Milan, Italy. TEL 39-02-50315111, FAX 39-02-50315100.

UNIVERSITATEA "OVIDIUS" CONSTANTA. ANALELE. SERIE EDUCATIE FIZICA SI SPORT. *see* SPORTS AND GAMES

613.7 USA ISSN 0748-9234
RA773 CODEN: UCWLE9
UNIVERSITY OF CALIFORNIA, BERKELEY. WELLNESS LETTER; the newsletter of nutrition, fitness, and stress management. Text in English. 1984. m. USD 24 (effective 2009). illus. back issues avail.; reprints avail. **Document type:** *Newsletter, Consumer.* **Description:** Features significant a news articles nutrition, fitness and self care for a healthy life.
Related titles: Online - full text ed.
Indexed: A01, A02, A03, A08, A25, A26, BiolDig, C06, C07, C08, CA, CINAHL, ConsI, E08, G05, G06, G07, G08, H03, H11, H12, H13, HlthInd, I05, I07, M01, M02, MagInd, P02, P10, P13, P20, P48, P53, P54, PQC, S08, S09, T02.
—BLDSC (9104.436000). **CCC.**
Published by: (University of California, Berkeley, School of Public Health), Health Letter Associates, Prince St Sta, PO Box 412, New York, NY 10012. **Subscr. to:** PO Box 420148, Palm Coast, FL 32142. TEL 800-829-9170.

613.7 MEX ISSN 0188-395X
UNO MISMO; sensibilidad conciencia compromiso. Text in Spanish. 1990. m. **Description:** Covers the enrichment of the body, mind and spirit.
Published by: Editorial Samra S.A. de C.V., Lucio Blanco 435, Azcapotzalco, Mexico City, DF 02400, Mexico.

613.7 USA
UPDATE (RESTON). Text in English. 1970. 6/yr. USD 45 domestic to institutions; USD 48.15 in Canada to institutions; USD 53 elsewhere to institutions (effective 2007). reprints avail. **Document type:** *Newsletter, Trade.* **Description:** Provides news of activities, programs, and professionals of A A H P E R D.
Former titles: Alliance Update (0273-8023); A A H P E R D Update (0199-932X); A A H P E R Update (0194-9446)
Indexed: SportS.
—CCC.
Published by: American Alliance for Health, Physical Education, Recreation, and Dance, 1900 Association Dr, Reston, VA 20191. TEL 703-476-3400, 800-213-7193, FAX 703-476-9527, info@aahperd.org. Circ: 28,000.

613.7 790.1 USA ISSN 0739-4586
➤ **V A H P E R D JOURNAL.** Text in English. 1978. s-a. 50 p./no.; back issues avail. **Document type:** *Journal, Academic/Scholarly.*
Indexed: A26, I05, SD, SportS, T02.
Published by: Virginia Association for Health, Physical Education and Dance, c/o Henry Castelvecchi, 7812 Falling Hill Terr, Chesterfield, VA 23832. TEL 804-519-6343, info@vahperd.org, http://www.vahper.org.

613 613.7 052 AUS
V O I C E. (Victory Over Incontinence/Continence Education) Text in English. 1999. q. bk.rev. 16 p./no. 7 cols./p.; **Document type:** *Newspaper.* **Description:** Increases awareness and knowledge of incontinence problems and treatment. For parents of bedwetters, aged persons and prostate sufferers.
Published by: (Australian Continence Foundation), The Victorian Senior, PO Box 1899, Geelong, VIC 3220, Australia. TEL 03-5221-9051, FAX 03-5221-9052.

613.7 FIN ISSN 1238-4283
VALMENTAJA. Text in Finnish. 1978. 6/yr. EUR 30 (effective 2005). adv. **Document type:** *Magazine, Trade.*
Former titles (until 1995): Valmennus ja Kunto (0789-0095); (until 1990): V K - Lehti (0783-3636); (until 1986): Valmennus ja Kuntoila (0780-8860); (until 1983): Valmennuslehti (0357-2072)
Related titles: Online - full text ed.
Published by: Suomen Valmentajat ry, Ratavartijankatu 2, Helsinki, 00520, Finland. TEL 358-9-25101370, FAX 358-9-1463987. Ed. Antero Kujala TEL 358-9-25101373. adv.: B&W page EUR 1,009, color page EUR 1,296. Circ: 9,584.

VEGETARIAN VOICE. *see* NUTRITION AND DIETETICS

613.2 USA ISSN 0749-3509
R773
VIBRANT LIFE; a magazine for healthful living. Text in English. 1904. bi-m. USD 15 (effective 2009). adv. bk.rev. abstr.; charts; illus. Index. 32 p./no. 3 cols./p.; reprints avail. **Document type:** *Magazine, Consumer.* **Description:** Features lifestyle tips, vegetarian recipes and medical news.
Former titles (until 1985): Your Life and Health (0279-2680); (until 1981): Life and Health (0024-3035); Which incorporated: Health; (until 1916): Health and Temperance; (until 1915): Life and Health; (until 1904): Pacific Health Journal
Related titles: Online - full text ed.
Indexed: A22, A26, C06, C07, C08, C11, CA, CCR, CHNI, CINAHL, G06, G07, G08, G09, H11, H12, HlthInd, I05, P10, P19, P24, P48, P53, P54, PQC, T02.
Published by: Review and Herald Publishing Association, 55 W Oak Ridge Dr, Hagerstown, MD 21740. TEL 301-393-3000, FAX 301-393-4055, info@rhpa.org, http://www.rhpa.org. Ed. Charles Mills TEL 301-393-4019. Adv. contact Genia Blumenberg TEL 301-393-3170. B&W page USD 886, color page USD 1,440; bleed 8.125 x 10.625. Circ: 30,000.

613.7 ARG
VIDA FELIZ. Text in Spanish. 1899. m. USD 15.50. illus.
Published by: (Iglesia Adventista del Septimo Dia), Asociacion Casa Editora Sudamericana, Ave. San Martin, 4555, Florida, Buenos Aires 1602, Argentina. TEL 54-114-7602426, FAX 54-114-7618455. Ed. Ricardo Bentancur. Circ: 30,000.

613.7 DEU
VIGO! BLEIBGESUND. Text in German. bi-m. adv. **Document type:** *Magazine, Consumer.*
Published by: W D V Gesellschaft fuer Medien & Kommunikation mbH & Co. OHG, Siemensstr 6, Bad Homburg, 61352, Germany. TEL 49-6172-6700, FAX 49-6172-670144, info@wdv.de, http://www.wdv.de. adv.: page EUR 12,000; trim 190 x 260. Circ: 1,110,803 (controlled).

613.7 USA ISSN 0886-6554
VIM & VIGOR. Text in English. 1985. q. USD 2.95 per issue (effective 2009). adv. bk.rev. tr.lit. back issues avail. **Document type:** *Magazine, Consumer.* **Description:** Directed to health-conscious people who are interested in a variety of health issues including diagnosis, treatment, diet, fitness, and exercise.
Published by: McMurry, Inc., 1010 E Missouri Ave, Phoenix, AZ 85014. TEL 888-626-8779, FAX 602-395-5853, http://www.mcmurry.com. Eds. Jill Schildhouse, Joann Gometz. Pub. Phil Titolo TEL 212-626-6835. adv.: B&W page USD 38,845, color page USD 50,010. Circ: 1,300,000.

VISIONARY. *see* MEDICAL SCIENCES—Ophthalmology And Optometry

613 GRC ISSN 1108-6033
VITA. Text in Greek. 1997. m. adv. **Document type:** *Magazine, Consumer.* **Description:** Aims to inform and educate on vital health-related issues, healthy lifestyles, and physical fitness options.
Published by: Lambrakis Press SA, Panepistimiou 18, Athens, 106 72, Greece. TEL 30-1-3686-452, FAX 30-1-3686-445, dolinfo@dol.gr, http://www.dol.gr. Circ: 44,714 (paid).

614.004 POL ISSN 1505-9294
VITA. Text in Polish. 1998. m. PLZ 35.88 domestic; USD 12.50 foreign (effective 2010). adv. **Document type:** *Magazine, Consumer.* **Description:** Provides health news, advice and solutions to improve one's life and well-being.
Published by: Edipresse Polska S A, ul Wiejska 19, Warsaw, 00-480, Poland. TEL 48-22-5842516, FAX 48-22-5842500, info@edipresse.pl, http://www.edipresse.pl. Ed. Agnieszka Swiecka. adv.: page PLZ 25,500; 133 x 189. Circ: 72,677 (paid).

613 ITA ISSN 0042-7268
VITA E SALUTE; rivista mensile di medicina preventiva. Text in Italian. 1952. m. EUR 32 (effective 2009). adv. bk.rev. charts; illus. index. **Document type:** *Magazine, Consumer.*
Published by: Edizioni A D V, Via Chiantigiana, 30, Falciani, Impruneta, FI 50023, Italy. TEL 39-055-2326291, FAX 39-055-2326241, info@edizioniadv.it, http://www.edizioniadv.it. Ed. Ennio Battista. Circ: 40,000.

VITAL; Michigan's health & fitness magazine. *see* WOMEN'S INTERESTS

613 DEU ISSN 0507-1747
VITAL. Text in German. 1969. m. EUR 30; EUR 2.50 newsstand/cover (effective 2011). adv. **Document type:** *Magazine, Consumer.*
Formerly: Vital Gesundheit, Freizeit, Lebensfreude
Published by: Jahreszeiten Verlag GmbH (Subsidiary of: Ganske Verlagsgruppe), Possmoorweg 5, Hamburg, 22301, Germany. TEL 49-40-27170, FAX 49-40-27172056, jahreszeitenverlag@jalag.de, http://www.jalag.de. Ed. Joy Jensen. Adv. contact Kristin Kettler. Circ: 255,464 (paid). **Dist. in UK by:** Seymour Distribution Ltd, 86 Newman St, London W1T 3EX, United Kingdom. TEL 44-20-73968000, FAX 44-20-73968002.

613.7 USA
VITALIDA AHORA. Text in Spanish. 19??. q. **Document type:** *Newsletter, Consumer.* **Description:** Covers health and wellness items of interest to Spanish-speaking communities.
Published by: McMurry, Inc., 1010 E Missouri Ave, Phoenix, AZ 85014. TEL 602-395-5850, 888-626-8779, FAX 602-395-5853, info@mcmurry.com, http://www.mcmurry.com.

613.7 SVK ISSN 1335-9134
VITALITA. Text in Slovak. 2002. m. EUR 1.13 newsstand/cover (effective 2011). adv. **Document type:** *Magazine, Consumer.*
Address: Strojnicka 8, Bratislava, 82105, Slovakia. TEL 421-911-281099, vitalita@stonline.sk. Ed. Michal Opeta. Adv. contact Martina Tejkalova. Circ: 23,500 (paid).

613 USA ISSN 1074-5831
VITALITY. Text in English. 1986. m. USD 13.90 to individuals (effective 2011). bk.rev. 20 p./no.; **Document type:** *Magazine, Consumer.* **Description:** Features health diet, fitness, parenting, and personal productivity.
Published by: Health Ink & Vitality Communications, 780 Township Line Rd, Yardley, PA 19067. TEL 800-524-1176, FAX 267-685-2983. Circ: 495,000 (controlled).

VITALITY. *see* NUTRITION AND DIETETICS

613.7 BRA ISSN 1806-3551
VIVA LEVE. Text in Portuguese. 2004. m. BRL 58.80 (effective 2006). adv. **Document type:** *Magazine, Consumer.*
Published by: Editora Escala Ltda., Av Prof Ida Kolb, 551, Casa Verde, Sao Paulo, 02518-000, Brazil. TEL 55-11-38552100, FAX 55-11-38579643, escala@escala.com.br, http://www.escala.com.br.

613.7 DEU
VIVE - GESUNDHEIT ERLEBEN!. Text in German. fortn. adv. **Document type:** *Magazine, Consumer.*
Published by: Vivesco Apotheken-Partner GmbH, Solmsstrasse 25, Frankfurt am Main, 60486, Germany. TEL 49-69-7191850, FAX 49-69-719185115, info@vivesco.de, http://www.vivesco-partner.de. adv.: page EUR 4,600. Circ: 180,000 (controlled).

613.7 646.7 ITA
VIVER SANI E BELLI; settimanale di salute e bellezza. Text in Italian. 1992. w. adv. illus. **Document type:** *Magazine, Consumer.* **Description:** Offers women advice on enhancing and maintaining their health and beauty.
Published by: D.E. Didieffe s.r.l. (Subsidiary of: Casa Editrice Universo SpA), Corso di Porta Nuova 3A, Milan, MI 20121, Italy. TEL 39-02-636751, FAX 39-02-252007333. Circ: 227,800.

613 ESP ISSN 1697-7122
VIVIR CON SALUD; la revista decana del naturismo espanol. Key Title: Vivir. Text in Spanish. 1953. 5/yr. EUR 20 (effective 2009). bk.rev. bibl.; illus.; tr.mk. index. 56 p./no.; back issues avail. **Document type:** *Magazine, Consumer.*
Former titles (until 1979): Vivir (0042-7578); (until 1953): Consejos para Vivir con Salud (1697-7130)
Published by: (Centro de Estudios Naturistas), Ediciones CEDEL, Mallorca 257, Barcelona, 08008, Spain. TEL 34-93-4877349, FAX 34-93-4873145, centrocool@mixmail.com, http://www.centrodeestudiosnaturistas.com/. Ed. Jose Avila. Pub. Gabriel Alomar. Circ: 5,000.

613.7 FIN ISSN 0780-1122
VOI HYVIN. Text in Finnish. 1986. 8/yr. EUR 69.60 domestic; EUR 72 in Europe; EUR 77.60 elsewhere (effective 2005). adv. **Document type:** *Magazine, Consumer.* **Description:** Provides information on healthy living.
Published by: A-Lehdet Oy, Risto Rytin tie 33, Helsinki, 00081, Finland. TEL 358-9-75961, FAX 358-9-7598600, a-tilaus@a-lehdet.fi. Ed. Jaana-Mirjam Mustavuori. adv.: color page EUR 3,700; 187 x 241. Circ: 60,009 (controlled).

613.7 DEU ISSN 0944-3509
WAERLAND. Text in German. 1953. 6/yr. EUR 25 (effective 2010). adv. **Document type:** *Magazine, Consumer.*
Formerly (until 1991): Waerland-Monatshefte (0507-794X)
Published by: Guenter Albert Ulmer Verlag, Hauptstr. 16, Tuningen, 78609, Germany. TEL 49-7464-98740, FAX 49-7464-3054, info@ulmertuningen.de. Circ: 5,000 (controlled).

613.7 DEU
WALKING. Text in German. q. EUR 2.90 newsstand/cover (effective 2008). adv. **Document type:** *Magazine, Consumer.*
Published by: Sportagentur WAG's, Badenweiler Str 2-4, Freiburg, 79117, Germany. TEL 49-761-211720, FAX 49-761-2117211. adv.: B&W page EUR 3,360, color page EUR 4,320; trim 210 x 297. Circ: 46,000 (paid and controlled).

WEG ZUR GESUNDHEIT; Zeitschrift fuer Biochemie und natuerliche Gesundheitspflege. *see* BIOLOGY—Biochemistry

613.7 CAN ISSN 1712-7076
WEIGHT LOSS DOCTOR. Text in English. 2002. m. CAD 99 (effective 2006). **Document type:** *Newsletter, Consumer.*
Published by: Lombardi Publishing Corp., 8555 Jane St, Concord, ON L4K 5N9, Canada. TEL 905-760-9929, FAX 905-264-9619, http://www.lombardipublishing.com.

WEIGHT WATCHERS; das schlanke Frauenmagazin. *see* NUTRITION AND DIETETICS

WEIGHT WATCHERS MAGAZINE. *see* NUTRITION AND DIETETICS

613.7 GBR ISSN 0309-8095
WEIGHT WATCHERS MAGAZINE. Text in English. 1977. m. GBP 30 domestic; GBP 36.95 foreign; GBP 2.60 per issue (effective 2009). bk.rev. **Document type:** *Magazine, Consumer.* **Description:** Full of motivational hints and tips to keep you on track whilst reaching goal. It contains great inspirational success stories, reader offers, up-to-date features and the latest new foods.
Related titles: Supplement(s): Body Beautiful. ISSN 0959-9053.
Indexed: HlthInd.
—CCC.
Published by: Weight Watchers UK Limited, Millennium House, Ludlow Rd, Maidenhead, Berks SL6 2SL, United Kingdom. uk.help@weightwatchers.co.uk. Ed. Pat Kane.

613.7 USA
WEIGHTLIFTING U S A. Text in English. 1983. q. USD 20 domestic; USD 30 foreign (effective 2000). adv. bk.rev. back issues avail. **Document type:** *Newsletter.* **Description:** Covers USA weightlifting, coaching, health and fitness, sports medicine, and local, national, and international competition results.
Published by: U S A Weightlifting Federation, One Olympic Plaza, Colorado Springs, CO 80909-5764. TEL 719-578-4508, FAX 719-578-4741. Ed., Adv. contact James J Fox. R&P Laurie Lopez. Circ: 3,300.

613.7 CHN ISSN 1000-8020
WEISHENG YANJIU/JOURNAL OF HYGIENE RESEARCH. Text in Chinese. 1972. bi-m. USD 43.80 (effective 2009). **Document type:** *Journal, Academic/Scholarly.*
Related titles: Online - full text ed.
Indexed: EMBASE, ExcerpMed, IndMed, MEDLINE, P30, R10, Reac, RefZh, SCOPUS.
—BLDSC (5004.200000).
Address: Xuanwu-qu, 29, Nanwei Lu, Beijing, 100050, China. **Dist. by:** China International Book Trading Corp, 35 Chegongzhuang Xilu, Haidian District, PO Box 399, Beijing 100044, China. TEL 86-10-68412045, FAX 86-10-68412023, cibtc@mail.cibtc.com.cn, http://www.cibtc.com.cn.

WEISHENG ZHIYE JIAOYU/HEALTH VOCATIONAL EDUCATION. *see* EDUCATION

613.7 USA ISSN 1559-4955
WELL BEING JOURNAL; heralding the integration of medicine with physical, mental, emotional, spiritual & social aspects of healing. Text in English. 1991. bi-m. USD 24 domestic; USD 34 in Canada; USD 36 in Mexico; USD 48 elsewhere; USD 6.50 newsstand/cover (effective 2005). illus. back issues avail. **Document type:** *Journal, Academic/Scholarly.* **Description:** Dedicated to publishing quality information on natural, alternative and complementary medicine. Publishes articles on natural healing, nutrition, herbs, and spirituality and its relation to health.
Published by: Well Being, Inc., P O Box 739, North Bend, WA 98045. TEL 888-532-3117, FAX 425-888-0375. Ed. Scott Miners.

613.7 613.2 USA
WELL MAGAZINE. Text in English. s-a. adv. **Document type:** *Magazine, Consumer.* **Description:** Features articles on fitness and exercise, leisure and lifestyle, medical, new and progressive resources, nutrition and local events for the communities of southeastern Wisconsin.
Published by: Nei-Turner Media Group, 93 W Geneva St, PO Box 1080, Williams Bay, WI 53191. TEL 262-245-1000, 800-386-3228, FAX 262-245-2000, info@ntmediagroup.com. Ed. Anne Celano Frohna. Pub. Gary Nei. Adv. contact Jane Trenchard Backes TEL 262-245-1000 ext 110. Circ: 40,000 (free).

613.7 AUS ISSN 1328-7540
WELLBEING MAGAZINE; personal and planetary healing. Variant title: International WellBeing. Text in English. 1984. bi-m. AUD 48 domestic; AUD 84 in New Zealand; AUD 131 in Asia; AUD 155 elsewhere (effective 2009). adv. bk.rev. back issues avail. **Document type:** *Magazine, Consumer.* **Description:** Features in-depth expert articles for total health of mind, body and soul as well as helpful techniques and inspiration for experiencing the best of what life has to offer.
Formerly (until 1995): Australian WellBeing (0812-8227)
Indexed: A11, M01, M02, WBA, WMB.
—CCC.
Published by: Universal WellBeing, Inc., Private Bag 154, N Ryde, NSW 2113, Australia. TEL 61-2-98870311, 300-303-414, FAX 61-2-98785553, rpamilar@universalmagazines.com.au. Eds. Chelsea Hunter TEL 61-2-98870640, Terry Robson TEL 61-2-98870320. Adv. contact Margaret Sherrard TEL 61-2-98870641.

WELLNESS. *see* WOMEN'S HEALTH

613.7 DEU
WELLNESS. Text in German. 4/yr. EUR 6.40 newsstand/cover (effective 2002). adv. **Document type:** *Magazine, Consumer.*
Published by: mbverlag GmbH, Leobener Str 30, Stuttgart, 70469, Germany. adv.: B&W page EUR 3,300, color page EUR 4,910. Circ: 70,000 (paid and controlled).

WELLNESS BOUND. *see* LIFESTYLE

613.7 CHE ISSN 1660-5004
WELLNESS LIVE. Text in German. 2003. 3/yr. CHF 36 (effective 2010). adv. **Document type:** *Magazine, Consumer.*
Published by: Flash Media GmbH, Sonnenstr 8, Au SG, 9434, Switzerland. TEL 41-71-7449490, FAX 41-71-7449491, info@flashmedia.ch. Ed. Nicole Caloz Schnyder. Adv. contact Harald Fessler. Circ: 30,000 (paid).

610 613.7 USA ISSN 1085-7125
WELLNESS PROGRAM MANAGEMENT ADVISOR. Text in English. 1996. m. USD 257 (effective 2008). Index. back issues avail. **Document type:** *Newsletter, Trade.* **Description:** Designed to help professionals manage their organizations' health promotion and wellness programs more effectively by demonstrating return on investment, incentive and disincentive programs, overcoming barriers to success, industry trends, and in-depth profiles of wellness programs around the country.
—CCC.

Published by: Health Resources Publishing, PO Box 456, Allenwood, NJ 08720. TEL 732-292-1100, 800-516-4343, FAX 732-292-1111, hrp@healthrespubs.com, http://www.healthrespubs.com.

613.7 CAN ISSN 1187-7472
RA776
WELLSPRING. Text in English. 1990. 3/yr. **Document type:** *Magazine, Trade.* **Description:** Provides information on best practices, topical issues, recent research, and policy in the active living/physical activity field.
Formerly (until 1991): Alberta Centre for Well-Being. Newsletter (1187-7480)
Related titles: Online - full text ed.
Indexed: A01, SD.
Published by: Alberta Centre for Active Living, 3rd Fl, 11759 Groat Rd, Edmonton, AB T5M 3K6, Canada. TEL 780-427-6949, 800-661-4551, FAX 780-455-2092, active.living@ualberta.ca.

613.7 DEU
WIE GEHT'S. Text in German. 2005. bi-m. adv. **Document type:** *Magazine, Consumer.*
Published by: Fincke Werbung, Schulstr 24, Reinsbuettel, 25764, Germany. TEL 49-4833-45540, FAX 49-4833-455454, info@fincke-werbung.de, http://www.fincke-werbung.de. Ed., Pub. Silvia Fincke-Bartsch. Adv. contact Nadine Hoelk. B&W page EUR 1,530, color page EUR 1,980. Circ: 20,000 (controlled).

613.7 USA ISSN 0043-5856
THE WINGED FOOT; the magazine of the New York atheletic club. Text in English. 1892. m. USD 30; USD 2.50 per issue (effective 2004). adv. bk.rev.; dance rev.; music rev.; play rev. illus. **Document type:** *Magazine, Consumer.* **Description:** Covers subject matter of interest to members of the New York Atheletic Club.
Published by: New York Athletic Club, 180 Central Park S, New York, NY 10019. TEL 212-247-5100, FAX 212-247-7063. Ed., Pub., R&P James J O'Brien TEL 212-767-7061. Adv. contact Christine Murphy. B&W page USD 970, color page USD 1,660; trim 10.88 x 8.13. Circ: 8,000 (paid).

613.7 DEU ISSN 1861-9886
WISSEN UND GESUNDHEIT; Das Magazin fuer mehr Lebensqualitaet. Text in German. 2006. 4/yr. EUR 13, USD 17 to institutions (effective 2012). adv. **Document type:** *Magazine, Consumer.*
—CCC.
Published by: Med.Komm - Verlag fuer medizinische Kommunikation (Subsidiary of: Springer Science+Business Media), Neumarkter Str 43, Munich, 81673, Germany. TEL 49-89-43721362, FAX 49-89-43721360, knorre@medkomm.de, http://www.medkomm.de. Ed. Dr. Monika von Berg. Adv. contact Barbara Kanters. B&W page EUR 3,450, color page EUR 5,090; trim 174 x 230. Circ: 72,000 (paid).

613.7 AUT
WOCHE GESUND. Text in German. w. free. adv. **Document type:** *Consumer.* **Description:** Provides weekly articles and features that provide assistance in leading a healthy and happy life.
Media: Online - full text.
Published by: Das Gruene Haus, Langenzersdorf, N 2103, Austria. TEL 43-2244-292370, FAX 43-2244-292373, verlag@gruenehaus.at. Ed. Dieter Altermiller.

613.71082 GBR ISSN 1752-6310
WOMEN'S FITNESS. Text in English. 2002. m. GBP 2.50 newsstand/cover (effective 2009). back issues avail. **Document type:** *Magazine, Consumer.* **Description:** Aimed at ordinary women seeking to lose weight and tone up through regular exercise and a healthy diet and features workouts, exercise hints and tips and nutrition advice.
Formerly (until 2006): Personal Trainer for Women (1476-5780)
Related titles: Online - full text ed.
Published by: Trojan Publishing Ltd., 3rd Fl, 207 Old St, London, EC1V 9NR, United Kingdom. TEL 44-20-76086300, FAX 44-20-76086320, info@trojanpublishing.co.uk, http://www.trojanpublishing.co.uk/. Ed. Joanna Knight TEL 44-20-76086350. Adv. contact Nicola Shubrook TEL 44-20-76086444.

WOMEN'S SPORTS EXPERIENCE. *see* SPORTS AND GAMES

613.7 GBR ISSN 2046-0570
WORK OUT. Text in English. 1993. m. GBP 40 domestic; GBP 50 foreign; GBP 3 per issue; free to qualified personnel (effective 2011). adv. **Document type:** *Magazine, Trade.* **Description:** Covers news, authoritative views and latest products, services and innovations from the UK, Europe for the fitness industry.
Published by: Wharncliffe Publishing Ltd., 47 Church St, Barnsley, S Yorkshire S70 2AS, United Kingdom. TEL 44-1226-734639, FAX 44-1226-734478, editorial@wharncliffepublishing.co.uk, http://www.wharncliffepublishing.co.uk. Adv. contact Tony Barry TEL 44-1226-734333.

WORLD LEISURE JOURNAL. *see* LEISURE AND RECREATION

THE WORLD OF A S P. *see* SPORTS AND GAMES

WUDANG. *see* SPORTS AND GAMES

WUHAN TIYUAN XUEBAO/WUHAN INSTITUTE OF PHYSICAL EDUCATION. JOURNAL. *see* EDUCATION

WYCHOWANIE FIZYCZNE I SPORT. *see* EDUCATION—Teaching Methods And Curriculum

WYCHOWANIE FIZYCZNE I ZDROWOTNE. *see* EDUCATION—Teaching Methods And Curriculum

613.7 CHN ISSN 1001-747X
➤ **XI'AN TIYU XUEYUAN XUEBAO/XI'AN INSTITUTE OF PHYSICAL EDUCATION. JOURNAL.** Text in Chinese; Summaries in English. 1984. bi-m. USD 31.20 (effective 2009). bk.rev. **Document type:** *Journal, Academic/Scholarly.* **Description:** Covers the latest achievement, technology and experiment of teaching, training and scientific research in physical education, teaching methods and curriculum, sports medicine, physical chemistry and sports news from China.
Related titles: CD-ROM ed.; Online - full text ed.
Indexed: CA, PEI, SD, T02.
—BLDSC (4917.469860).
Published by: Xi'an Tiyu Xueyuan/Xi'an Institute of Physical Education, 65, Hanguan Lu, Xi'an, Shaanxi 710068, China. TEL 86-29-88409449, http://www.xaipe.edu.cn/index.htm. Ed. Kai Zhu. Circ: 600.

➤ **XINLI YUEKAN/PSYCHOLOGIES.** *see* PSYCHOLOGY

613.7 CAN
Y M C A WEEKLY NEWS. (Young Men's Christian Association) Text in English. w.
Published by: Vancouver Downtown Young Men's Christian Association, 955 Burrard St, Vancouver, BC V6Z 1Y2, Canada. TEL 604-681-0221. Ed. Terry Connolly. Circ: 1,000.

613.7 CHN ISSN 1671-1734
GV505
YANGSHENG YUEKAN/BREATH EXERCISE. Text in Chinese. 1980. m. USD 32.40 (effective 2009). **Document type:** *Journal, Academic/Scholarly.*
Formerly (until 2000): Qigong/Health Preserving (1000-825X)
Related titles: Online - full text ed.
—East View.
Published by: Zhejiang-sheng Zhongyiyao Yanjiuyuan/Zhejiang Academy of Traditional Chinese Medicine, 132, Tianmushan Lu, Hangzhou, Zhejiang 310007, China. TEL 86-571-8842882, FAX 86-571-8845196.

YINSHI NAN NU/EAT & TRAVEL WEEKLY. *see* HOTELS AND RESTAURANTS

613.2 GBR ISSN 0953-2161
YOGA AND HEALTH. Text in English. 1975. m. GBP 30 domestic; GBP 35 in Europe excluding U.K; GBP 41 elsewhere (effective 2009). adv. bk.rev. back issues avail. **Document type:** *Magazine, Consumer.* **Description:** Features on health issues, complementary therapies and healthy nutrition suggestions.
Formerly (until 1988): Yoga Today (0308-3349)
Published by: Yoga Today Ltd., Seaford, PO Box 2130, Sussex, BN25 9BF, United Kingdom. TEL 44-1323-872466, subs@yogaandhealthmag.co.uk. Ed. Jane Sill TEL 44-207-4805456. Adv. contact Simon Briant TEL 44-1273-594455. B&W page GBP 950, color page GBP 1,195; trim 190 x 261. Circ: 15,000 (paid and controlled).

613.704 BRA ISSN 1807-3093
YOGA & SAUDE. Text in Portuguese. 2004. bi-m. BRL 14.90 newsstand/cover. **Document type:** *Magazine, Consumer.*
Published by: Digerati Comunicacao e Tecnologia Ltda., Rua Haddock Lobo 347, 12o andar, Sao Paulo, 01414-001, Brazil. TEL 55-11-32172600, FAX 55-11-32172617, http://www.digerati.com.br.

YOGA AND TOTAL HEALTH. *see* PHILOSOPHY

613.7 USA ISSN 1935-5890
YOGA BEAN. Text in English. 2006. m. **Document type:** *Newsletter, Consumer.*
Media: Online - full text.
Published by: Yoga Bean, LLC TEL 610-805-6724, tina@yogabean.net. Ed., Pub. Tina R LeMar.

613.7 USA ISSN 1544-0907
YOGA FOR EVERYBODY. Text in English. 2004 (Apr.). q. USD 17.97 domestic; USD 25.97 foreign (effective 2004).
Published by: E G W Publishing Co., 4075 Papazian Way, #208, Fremont, CA 94538. TEL 510-668-0269, FAX 510-668-0280, http://www.egw.com. Ed. Kelly Townsend.

YOGA JOURNAL. *see* NEW AGE PUBLICATIONS

613.7 ESP
YOGA JOURNAL. Text in Spanish. 2006. m. EUR 31.80 domestic; EUR 73 foreign (effective 2009). adv. **Document type:** *Magazine, Consumer.*
Published by: Globus Comunicacion (Subsidiary of: Bonnier AB), Covarrubias 1, Madrid, 28010, Spain. TEL 34-91-4471202, txhdez@globuscom.es, http://www.globuscom.es. Ed. Pepa Castro. adv.: page EUR 3,872; trim 19.8 x 27.

YOGA LIFE. *see* PHILOSOPHY

YOGA MAGAZINE. *see* NEW AGE PUBLICATIONS

181.45 USA
YOGA THERAPY TODAY. Text in English. 2005. 3/yr. USD 75 membership (effective 2009). adv. **Document type:** *Bulletin, Trade.* **Description:** Provides practical ideas, inspiration, and support for yoga professionals.
Formerly (until 2009): Yoga Therapy in Practice (1945-7235)
Related titles: Online - full text ed.: ISSN 1945-7294.
Indexed: A04, C11, R09, SD, T02.
—BLDSC (9418.723800), IE.
Published by: International Association of Yoga Therapists, 115 S McCormick St, Ste 3, Prescott, AZ 86303. TEL 928-541-0004, FAX 928-541-0182, mail@iayt.org. Ed. Julie Deife. Adv. contact Madeline Groves.

613.7 DEU ISSN 1430-3345
YOGA UND GANZHEITLICHE GESUNDHEIT. Text in German. 1996. q. EUR 20 domestic; EUR 25 foreign (effective 2010). charts; illus. 24 p./no. 2 cols./p.; back issues avail. **Document type:** *Newsletter, Consumer.* **Description:** Covers the technical, psychological, philosophical, medical, scientific, and emotional aspects of yoga.
Published by: Hella Naura Verlag, Gerckensplatz 18, Hamburg, 22339, Germany. TEL 49-40-464997. Ed. Hella Naura. Circ: 300.

613.7 181 USA ISSN 1091-8841
YOGA WORLD. Text in English. 1997. bi-m. **Document type:** *Magazine, Consumer.*
Related titles: Online - full text ed.
Indexed: A04, C11.
Published by: The Yoga Research Center, P O Box 1386, Lower Lake, CA 95457. TEL 707-928-9898, FAX 707-928-4738.

613.7 USA
YOGAMOM MAGAZINE. Text in English. 2008. q. USD 19.80; USD 4.95 newsstand/cover (effective 2008). adv. **Description:** For women seeking to blend a more natural and healthy lifestyle into the reality of their daily lives.
Published by: YogaMom LLC, Box 872, Brewton, AL 36427. TEL 251-867-3500, FAX 251-867-6600, info@yogamommagazine.com, http://www.yogamonmagazine.com. Ed., Pub. Celina Miller. adv.: color page USD 3,000; trim 9 x 10.875.

613.7 USA
YOU24; the power of what you can be. Text in English. 2007 (Jan.). 3/yr. free (effective 2009). **Document type:** *Magazine, Consumer.*
Related titles: Online - full text ed.
Published by: (24 Hour Fitness), Rodale, Inc., 33 E Minor St, Emmaus, PA 18098. TEL 610-967-5171, FAX 610-967-8963, customer_service@rodale.com, http://www.rodaleinc.com.

613.7 USA
YOUR HEALTH DAILY. Text in English. 1997. d. **Document type:** *Magazine, Consumer.*
Media: Online - full content.
Published by: New York Times Company, 620 8th Ave, New York, NY 10018. TEL 212-556-1234, FAX 212-556-7088, letters@nytimes.com, http://www.nytimes.com.

613.7 GBR ISSN 2046-3243
▼ **YOUR HEALTHY LIVING.** Abbreviated title: Y H L. Text in English. 2009. 11/yr. GBP 21 (effective 2011). adv. back issues avail. **Document type:** *Magazine, Consumer.* **Description:** Helps people to lead healthier life by focusing on products such as natural, organic, fair-trade, vegetarian, vegan and eco-friendly food products etc.
Related titles: Online - full text ed.: free (effective 2011).
Published by: J H N Productions Ltd., 15 Burton End, W Wickham, Cambridge, Cambs CB21 4SD, United Kingdom. Ed. Tracy McLoughlin. Pub. Carlota Hudgell. Adv. contact Heidi Thoday.

613.7 RUS
ZDOROV'YE DETEI. Text in Russian. 1994. s-m. USD 292 in United States (effective 2007). **Document type:** *Newspaper, Trade.*
Related titles: ◆ Supplement to: Pervoe Sentyabrya.
Published by: Pervoe Sentyabrya, ul Kievskaya 24, Moscow, 121165, Russian Federation. TEL 7-499-2494758, FAX 7-499-2493184, podpiska@1september.ru, http://www.1september.ru. **Dist. by:** East View Information Services, 10601 Wayzata Blvd, Minneapolis, MN 55305. TEL 952-252-1201, 800-477-1005, FAX 952-252-1202, info@eastview.com, http://www.eastview.com.

613 057.87 SVK ISSN 0044-1953
ZDRAVIE; fit, krasa, pohoda. Text in Slovak. 1945. m. EUR 14.30; EUR 1.32 newsstand/cover (effective 2011). adv. bk.rev. illus. **Document type:** *Magazine, Consumer.* **Description:** Covers beauty culture, birth control, health aids, medical sciences, men's health, psychology, rational nutrition, and healthy lifestyles.
Formerly: Zdravie Ludu
Related titles: Online - full content ed.: ISSN 1336-2615.
Published by: Spolocnost 7 Plus s.r.o., Panonska cesta 7, Bratislava 5, 85232, Slovakia. TEL 421-2-32153111, FAX 421-2-32153376, predplatne@7plus.sk, http://www.7plus.sk. Ed. Drahoslava Vyzinkarova TEL 421-2-32153301. Adv. contact Jana Gressova. Circ: 100,000 (paid and controlled).

761 SVK ISSN 1336-8745
ZDRAVIE.SK. Text in Slovak. 2004. d. adv. **Document type:** *Consumer.*
Formerly (until 2006): Svet Zdravia (1336-7455)
Media: Online - full content.
Published by: Sanding spol. s.r.o., Radnicne Namestie 1, Bratislava, 821 05, Slovakia. TEL 421-905-610549, http://www.sanding.sk.

610 POL ISSN 0137-8066
ZDROWIE. Text in Polish. 1925. m. PLZ 59.10 (effective 2011). adv. **Document type:** *Magazine, Consumer.*
Former titles (until 1949): Jestem na Stanowisku w Czasie Pokoju i Wojny (1640-7075); (until 1947): Jestem w Czasie Pokoju i Wojny na Stanowisku (1640-7067); (until 1938): Polski Czerwony Krzyz (1640-7059); (until 1925): Czerwony Krzyz (1640-7040)
Published by: Wydawnictwo Murator Sp. z o.o., ul Deblinska 6, Warsaw, 04187, Poland. TEL 48-22-5905000, FAX 48-22-5905444, klienci@murator.com.pl, http://www.murator.com.pl. Ed. Izabella Radecka. adv.: page PLZ 16,800; trim 180 x 232.

ZEST. *see* WOMEN'S INTERESTS

ZHONG LAO NIAN BAOJIAN YIXUE/HEALTH FOR THE ELDERLY AND MIDDLE-AGED. *see* GERONTOLOGY AND GERIATRICS

613.7 CHN ISSN 1005-0515
ZHONGGUO JIANKANG YUEKAN/CHINA HEALTH. Text in Chinese. 1982. m. USD 62.40 (effective 2009). **Document type:** *Magazine, Consumer.* **Description:** Covers health, marriage, disease prevention, education and other public health related issues.
Formerly: Zhongguo Weisheng Huakan/China Health Pictorial (1002-2783)
Related titles: Online - full text ed.
—East View.
Published by: Zhongguo Jiankang Yuekan Zazhishe, 252, Shayang Lu, Shenyang, 110055, China. TEL 86-24-23395363, FAX 86-24-23395363 ext 801.

613.7 CHN ISSN 1001-2001
RM735.A1
ZHONGGUO KANGFU/CHINESE JOURNAL OF REHABILITATION. Text in Chinese. 1986. bi-m. **Document type:** *Journal, Academic/Scholarly.*
Related titles: Online - full text ed.: (from WanFang Data Corp.).
—BLDSC (9512.738840), East View.
Published by: Huazhong Keji Daxue Tongji Yixueyuan/Huazhong University of Science and Technology, Tongji Medical College, 1095 Jiefang Dadao, Wuhan, 430030, China. TEL 86-27-83662666, FAX 86-27-83662686, http://www.tjmu.edu.cn/. **Dist. by:** China International Book Trading Corp, 35 Chegongzhuang Xilu, Haidian District, PO Box 399, Beijing 100044, China. TEL 86-10-68412045, FAX 86-10-68412023, cibtc@mail.cibtc.com.cn, http://www.cibtc.com.cn.

613.7 CHN ISSN 1000-8268
RA781.8
ZHONGGUO QIGONG. Text in Chinese. 1986. m. USD 36. adv.
Published by: Hebei Beidaihe Qigong Kangfu Yiyuan, 198 Dongjing Lu, Beidaihe-qu, Qinhuandao, Hebei 066100, China. TEL 86-33-5404-1257. Ed. Ding Rui Ming. Circ: 70,000. **Co-sponsor:** Zhongguo Qigong Keyan Hui.

613.7 370 CHN ISSN 1000-9817
ZHONGGUO XUEXIAO WEISHENG/JOURNAL OF CHINESE SCHOOL HEALTH. Text in Chinese. 1980. m. **Document type:** *Journal, Academic/Scholarly.*
Formerly (until 1989): Xuexiao Weisheng/Journal of School Health (1000-3622)
Related titles: Online - full text ed.
—BLDSC (9512.827420), East View.
Published by: (Zhonghua Yufang Yixuehui/China Preventive Medicine Association), Zhongguo Xuexiao Weisheng Zazhishe, Shengli Zhonglu, Bengbu Er-Zhong, Bengbu, 233000, China. TEL 86-552-2054276.

P

613.7 CHN ISSN 1009-8011
RM727.C54
ZHONGHUA YANGSHENG BAOJIAN/CHINESE BREATH EXERCISE. Text in Chinese. 1982. m. USD 32.40 (effective 2009). **Document type:** *Academic/Scholarly.*
Formerly (until 2001): Zhonghua Qigong (1000-4610)
Related titles: Online - full text ed.
—East View.
Published by: Beijing Zhongyiyao Daxue/Beijing University of Chinese Medicine, 11 Bei San Huan Dong Lu, Chao Yang District, Beijing, 100029, China. TEL 86-10-64286904, FAX 86-10-64220034, bucmpo@public.bta.net.cn, http://www.bjucmp.edu.cn/. **Dist. by:** China International Book Trading Corp, 35 Chegongzhuang Xilu, Haidian District, PO Box 399, Beijing 100044, China. TEL 86-10-68412045, FAX 86-10-68412023, cibtc@mail.cibtc.com.cn, http://www.cibtc.com.cn.

ZORG & WELZIJN; opiniemagazine voor de sector zorg en welzijn. *see* SOCIAL SERVICES AND WELFARE

ZUKUNFT JETZT. *see* SOCIAL SERVICES AND WELFARE

ZWANGER & ZO. *see* WOMEN'S INTERESTS

613.7 USA
24; everyday fitness for everyday body. Text in English. 2004. q. USD 2.95 per issue (effective 2004). adv. **Document type:** *Magazine, Consumer.*
Published by: 24 Hour Fitness, 12647 Alcosta Blvd, #500, San Ramon, CA 94583. TEL 818-783-7945, 800-432-6348, FAX 818-783-2387, vsanzone@24mag.com. Pub. Vito Sanzone. adv.: B&W page USD 16,280, color page USD 19,155; trim 9.125 x 10.875.

PHYSICAL FITNESS AND HYGIENE—Abstracting, Bibliographies, Statistics

613.7021 AUS
AUSTRALIA. BUREAU OF STATISTICS. HOW AUSTRALIANS MEASURE UP (ONLINE). Text in English. 1995. irreg., latest 1995. free (effective 2009). **Description:** Presents findings from an analysis comparing Australian's self-reported height, weight and body mass index recorded in the 1995 national health survey with measured height, weight and body mass index from the 1995 national nutrition survey. Findings are presented by a range of demographic and physical characteristics.
Formerly: Australia. Bureau of Statistics. How Australians Measure Up (Print)
Media: Online - full text.
Published by: Australian Bureau of Statistics, Locked Bag 10, Belconnen, ACT 2616, Australia. TEL 61-2-92684909, 300-135-070, FAX 61-2-92684654, client.services@abs.gov.au.

613.7021 AUS
AUSTRALIA. BUREAU OF STATISTICS. OCCASIONAL PAPER: CIGARETTE SMOKING AMONG INDIGENOUS AUSTRALIANS (ONLINE). Text in English. 1995. irreg. free (effective 2009). **Document type:** *Government.* **Description:** Aims to present accounts of developments and research work or analysis of an experimental nature as to encourage discussion and comment.
Formerly: Australia. Bureau of Statistics. Occasional Paper: Cigarette Smoking among Indigenous Australians (Print)
Media: Online - full text.
Published by: Australian Bureau of Statistics, Locked Bag 10, Belconnen, ACT 2616, Australia. TEL 61-2-92684909, 61-2-62527037, 300-135-070, FAX 61-2-62528103, client.services@abs.gov.au.

613.7021 AUS
AUSTRALIA. BUREAU OF STATISTICS. OCCASIONAL PAPER: OVERWEIGHT AND OBESITY, INDIGENOUS AUSTRALIANS (ONLINE). Text in English. 1998. irreg. free (effective 2009). **Document type:** *Government.* **Description:** Presents information on the distributions of height, weight and body mass index (BMI) in a large, nationally representative sample of Indigenous Australians aged 5 years and over.
Formerly: Australia. Bureau of Statistics. Occasional Paper: Overweight and Obesity, Indigenous Australians (Print)
Media: Online - full text.
Published by: Australian Bureau of Statistics, Locked Bag 10, Belconnen, ACT 2616, Australia. TEL 61-2-92684909, 61-2-62527037, 300-135-070, FAX 61-2-62528103, client.services@abs.gov.au.

613.7021 AUS
AUSTRALIA. BUREAU OF STATISTICS. OCCASIONAL PAPER: SELF-ASSESSED HEALTH STATUS, INDIGENOUS AUSTRALIANS (ONLINE). Text in English. 1997. irreg. free (effective 2009). **Document type:** *Government.* **Description:** Aims to present accounts of developments and research work or analysis of an experimental nature so as to encourage discussion and comment.
Formerly: Australia. Bureau of Statistics. Occasional Paper: Self-Assessed Health Status, Indigenous Australians (Print)
Media: Online - full text.
Published by: Australian Bureau of Statistics, Locked Bag 10, Belconnen, ACT 2616, Australia. TEL 61-2-92684909, 61-2-62527037, 300-135-070, FAX 61-2-62528103, client.services@abs.gov.au.

613.7021 AUS ISSN 1441-2004
RA553
AUSTRALIA. BUREAU OF STATISTICS. THE HEALTH AND WELFARE OF AUSTRALIA'S ABORIGINAL AND TORRES STRAIT ISLANDER PEOPLES. Text in English. 1997. biennial. AUD 65 per issue (effective 2009). back issues avail. **Document type:** *Government.* **Description:** Presents the latest data on the health and welfare of Australia's Aboriginal and Torres Strait Islander peoples, as well as information about their socioeconomic circumstances.
Related titles: Online - full text ed.: free (effective 2009).
Published by: Australian Bureau of Statistics, Locked Bag 10, Belconnen, ACT 2616, Australia. TEL 61-2-92684909, 61-2-62527037, 300-135-070, FAX 61-2-62528103, client.services@abs.gov.au. **Co-sponsor:** Australian Institute of Health and Welfare.

HAWAII. DEPARTMENT OF HEALTH. RESEARCH AND STATISTICS OFFICE. R & S REPORT. *see* POPULATION STUDIES—Abstracting, Bibliographies, Statistics

613.7 790 USA ISSN 1547-1284
QP303
KINESIOLOGY ABSTRACTS. Text in English. 1949. a. See prices for Microfiche and Online editions. abstr. cum.index: 1949-1999. back issues avail. **Document type:** *Bulletin, Abstract/Index.* **Description:** Serves as an index to a collection of microfiches representing dissertations and theses in the area of physical education, sport and exercise science, health, dance and recreational studies.
Former titles (until Apr. 2003): Health, Physical Education and Recreation, Exercise and Sport Sciences Microform Publications Bulletin (1526-1956); (until 1992): Health, Physical Education and Recreation Microform Publications Bulletin (0090-5119); (until 1972): Health, Physical Education, and Recreation Microcard Bulletin (0017-906X); (until 1964): Health and Physical Education Microcard Bulletin (0732-4804); (until 1955): Health and Physical Education Microcards (0732-4790)
Related titles: Microfiche ed.: USD 1,663 (effective 2006); Online - full text ed.: 1993. USD 1,500 (effective 2006).
Indexed: CA, PEI, SD, T02.
Published by: (University of Oregon, International Institute for Sport & Human Performance), University of Oregon, International Institute for Sport & Human Performance, Kinesiology Publications, 1243 University of Oregon, Eugene, OR 97403-1243. TEL 541-346-4117, FAX 541-346-0935, dgorman@oregon.uoregon.edu. Ed. Henriette Heiny.

613 016 USA
N T I S ALERTS: HEALTH CARE. (National Technical Information Service) Text in English. 19??. s-m. USD 255 in North America; USD 332 elsewhere (effective 2011). index. back issues avail. **Document type:** *Newsletter, Government.* **Description:** Reports on methodology, health services, facilities utilization and health needs. Also covers health care assessment quality assurance, forecasting and measurement methods and legislation and regulations.
Former titles: Abstract Newsletter: Health Care; Abstract Newsletter: Health Planning and Health Services Research; Weekly Abstract Newsletter: Health Planning and Health Services Research; (until 1987): Weekly Government Abstracts. Health Planning and Health Services Research (0199-9974); (until 1979): Weekly Government Abstracts. Health Planning (0017-9086)
Related titles: Microform ed.: (from NTI).
—GNLM.
Published by: U.S. Department of Commerce, National Technical Information Service, 5301 Shawnee Rd, Alexandria, VA 22312. TEL 703-605-6000, 800-553-6847, info@ntis.gov.

613.7 CAN ISSN 1498-0940
PHYSICAL & HEALTH EDUCATION JOURNAL. Short title: C A H P E R D Journal. Text in English, French. 1933. 4/yr. CAD 65 domestic to individuals; CAD 118 foreign to individuals; CAD 100 domestic to institutions; CAD 118 foreign to institutions (effective 1999). adv. bk.rev. illus. **Document type:** *Journal, Academic/Scholarly.*
Former titles (until 2000): Canadian Association for Health, Physical Education, Recreation and Dance. Journal (1201-2319); (until 1994): Canadian Association for Health, Physical Education and Recreation. Journal (0834-1915); (until 1984): C A H P E R Journal (0226-5478); (until 1968): Canadian Association for Health, Physical Education and Recreation. Journal (0008-2899)
Media: Duplicated (not offset). **Related titles:** Microfilm ed.: (from MML); Online - full text ed.
Indexed: A22, A26, C03, CA, CBPI, CEI, CPerI, G08, I05, P19, P48, P50, PEI, PQC, SD, SportS, T02.
—BLDSC (6475.273500), GNLM, IE, Ingenta. **CCC.**
Published by: Canadian Association for Health, Physical Education, Recreation and Dance, 2197 Riverside Dr, Ste 403, Ottawa, ON K1H 7X3, Canada. TEL 613-523-1348, FAX 613-523-1206, info@cahperd.ca, http://www.cahperd.ca. Ed. Andrea Grantham. Circ: 2,200.

SPORTDISCUS WITH FULL TEXT. *see* SPORTS AND GAMES—Abstracting, Bibliographies, Statistics

613.7 CHN ISSN 1002-3674
ZHONGGUO WEISHENG TONGJI/CHINESE JOURNAL OF HEALTH STATISTICS. Text in Chinese. 1984. bi-m. USD 24.60 (effective 2009). **Document type:** *Journal, Academic/Scholarly.*
Related titles: Online - full text ed.
—BLDSC (3180.345300), East View.
Published by: Zhongguo Yike Daxue/China Medical University, 92 Er-ma Lu, Hepin Qu Bei, Shenyang, 110001, China. TEL 86-24-23256666 ext 5170, http://www.cmu.edu.cn/. **Dist. by:** China International Book Trading Corp, 35 Chegongzhuang Xilu, Haidian District, PO Box 399, Beijing 100044, China. TEL 86-10-68412045, FAX 86-10-68412023, cibtc@mail.cibtc.com.cn, http://www.cibtc.com.cn.

PHYSICAL MEDICINE AND REHABILITATION

see MEDICAL SCIENCES—Physical Medicine And Rehabilitation

PHYSICALLY IMPAIRED

see HANDICAPPED—Physically Impaired

PHYSICS

see also PHYSICS—Computer Applications ; PHYSICS—Electricity ; PHYSICS—Heat ; PHYSICS—Mechanics ; PHYSICS—Nuclear Physics ; PHYSICS—Optics ; PHYSICS—Sound

530 SGP ISSN 0218-2203
A A P P S BULLETIN. (Association of Asia Pacific Physical Societies) Text in English. 1991. bi-m. **Document type:** *Bulletin, Academic/Scholarly.* **Description:** Reports major happenings in the physics community to bring to the attention of the scientists in the Asia Pacific region those events or activities which take place outside the region but which may have important bearings on this community.
Related titles: Online - full text ed.: 2003. free (effective 2011).
Published by: Association of Asia Pacific Physical Societies Circ: 5,000.

A C O NEWSLETTER. *see* MEDICAL SCIENCES—Psychiatry And Neurology

530 USA ISSN 2158-3226
▼ ➤ **A I P ADVANCES.** Text in English. 2011 (Mar.). free (effective 2011). **Document type:** *Journal, Academic/Scholarly.* **Description:** Focuses on applied research in the physical sciences.
Media: Online - full text.
Published by: American Institute of Physics, 1 Physics Ellipse, College Park, MD 20740. TEL 301-209-3100, FAX 301-209-0843, aipinfo@aip.org, http://www.aip.org.

530 USA ISSN 0094-243X
CODEN: APCPCS
A I P CONFERENCE PROCEEDINGS. Text in English. 1970-1993; N.S. irreg. price varies based on number of users. bibl.; charts; illus.; stat. back issues avail. **Document type:** *Proceedings, Academic/Scholarly.*
Related titles: Online - full text ed.: A I P Conference Proceedings. ISSN 1551-7616. 1970; Optical Disk - DVD ed.: ISSN 1935-0465.
Indexed: A01, A02, A03, A08, A22, A28, A33, APA, BrCerAb, C&ISA, CA, CA/WCA, CCMJ, CIA, CIS, CPI, CerAb, ChemAb, CivEngAb, CorrAb, E&CAJ, E11, EEA, EMA, ESPM, EnvEAb, GeoRef, H15, INIS AtomInd, Inspec, M&TEA, M09, MBF, METADEX, MSN, MathR, P30, P34, PhysBer, S01, SCOPUS, SolStAb, SpeleolAb, T02, T04, TM, WAA, Z02.
—BLDSC (0773.430000), AskIEEE, CASDDS, IE, Ingenta, INIST. **CCC.**
Published by: American Institute of Physics, 1 Physics Ellipse, College Park, MD 20740. TEL 301-209-3100, aipinfo@aip.org, http://www.aip.org. **Subscr. to:** PO Box 503284, St Louis, MO 63150. TEL 516-576-2270, 800-344-6902, FAX 516-349-9704, subs@aip.org, http://librarians.aip.org. **Dist. by:** Springer New York LLC, 233 Spring St, New York, NY 10013. TEL 212-460-1500, FAX 212-460-1575, service-ny@springer.com, http://www.springer.com/.

530 USA ISSN 1931-3012
A I P CONFERENCE PROCEEDINGS. ACCELERATORS & BEAMS. Text in English. 200?. irreg., latest 2010. adv. back issues avail. **Document type:** *Proceedings, Academic/Scholarly.*
Media: Online - full text. **Related titles:** Print ed.: USD 256 per vol. (effective 2010); ◆ Series: A I P Conference Proceedings. Atomic, Molecular & Statistical Physics. ISSN 1931-3039; ◆ A I P Conference Proceedings. Astronomy & Astrophysics. ISSN 1931-3020; ◆ A I P Conference Proceedings. Plasma Physics. ISSN 1931-3071; ◆ A I P Conference Proceedings. Mathematical & Statistical Physics. ISSN 1931-3055; ◆ A I P Conference Proceedings. Materials Physics & Applications. ISSN 1931-3047; ◆ A I P Conference Proceedings. Nuclear & High Energy Physics. ISSN 1931-3063; A I P Conference Proceedings. ISSN 1551-7616. 1970.
—**CCC.**
Published by: American Institute of Physics, 1 Physics Ellipse, College Park, MD 20740. TEL 301-209-3100, FAX 301-209-0843, aipinfo@aip.org, http://www.aip.org. **Subscr. to:** PO Box 503284, St Louis, MO 63150. TEL 516-576-2270, 800-344-6902, FAX 516-349-9704, subs@aip.org.

530 520 USA ISSN 1931-3020
A I P CONFERENCE PROCEEDINGS. ASTRONOMY & ASTROPHYSICS. Text in English. 200?. irreg. adv. back issues avail. **Document type:** *Proceedings, Academic/Scholarly.*
Media: Online - full text. **Related titles:** Print ed.; ◆ Series: A I P Conference Proceedings. Atomic, Molecular & Statistical Physics. ISSN 1931-3039; ◆ A I P Conference Proceedings. Accelerators & Beams. ISSN 1931-3012; ◆ A I P Conference Proceedings. Plasma Physics. ISSN 1931-3071; ◆ A I P Conference Proceedings. Mathematical & Statistical Physics. ISSN 1931-3055; ◆ A I P Conference Proceedings. Materials Physics & Applications. ISSN 1931-3047; ◆ A I P Conference Proceedings. Nuclear & High Energy Physics. ISSN 1931-3063; A I P Conference Proceedings. ISSN 1551-7616. 1970.
—**CCC.**
Published by: American Institute of Physics, 1 Physics Ellipse, College Park, MD 20740. TEL 301-209-3100, FAX 301-209-0843, aipinfo@aip.org, http://www.aip.org.

530.41 USA ISSN 1931-3039
A I P CONFERENCE PROCEEDINGS. ATOMIC, MOLECULAR & STATISTICAL PHYSICS. Text in English. 200?. irreg. adv. back issues avail. **Document type:** *Proceedings, Academic/Scholarly.*
Media: Online - full text. **Related titles:** Print ed.; ◆ Series: A I P Conference Proceedings. Astronomy & Astrophysics. ISSN 1931-3020; ◆ A I P Conference Proceedings. Accelerators & Beams. ISSN 1931-3012; ◆ A I P Conference Proceedings. Plasma Physics. ISSN 1931-3071; ◆ A I P Conference Proceedings. Mathematical & Statistical Physics. ISSN 1931-3055; ◆ A I P Conference Proceedings. Materials Physics & Applications. ISSN 1931-3047; ◆ A I P Conference Proceedings. Nuclear & High Energy Physics. ISSN 1931-3063; A I P Conference Proceedings. ISSN 1551-7616. 1970.
—**CCC.**
Published by: American Institute of Physics, 1 Physics Ellipse, College Park, MD 20740. TEL 301-209-3100, FAX 301-209-0843, aipinfo@aip.org, http://www.aip.org.

530 USA ISSN 1931-3047
A I P CONFERENCE PROCEEDINGS. MATERIALS PHYSICS & APPLICATIONS. Text in English. 200?. irreg. adv. back issues avail. **Document type:** *Proceedings, Academic/Scholarly.*
Media: Online - full text. **Related titles:** Print ed.; ◆ Series: A I P Conference Proceedings. Astronomy & Astrophysics. ISSN 1931-3020; ◆ A I P Conference Proceedings. Accelerators & Beams. ISSN 1931-3012; ◆ A I P Conference Proceedings. Plasma Physics. ISSN 1931-3071; ◆ A I P Conference Proceedings. Atomic, Molecular & Statistical Physics. ISSN 1931-3039; ◆ A I P Conference Proceedings. Mathematical & Statistical Physics. ISSN 1931-3055; ◆ A I P Conference Proceedings. Nuclear & High Energy Physics. ISSN 1931-3063; A I P Conference Proceedings. ISSN 1551-7616. 1970.
—**CCC.**
Published by: American Institute of Physics, 1 Physics Ellipse, College Park, MD 20740. TEL 301-209-3100, FAX 301-209-0843, aipinfo@aip.org, http://www.aip.org.

A I P CONFERENCE PROCEEDINGS. MATHEMATICAL & STATISTICAL PHYSICS. *see* MATHEMATICS

530.44 USA ISSN 1931-3071
A I P CONFERENCE PROCEEDINGS. PLASMA PHYSICS. Text in English. 200?. irreg. adv. back issues avail. **Document type:** *Proceedings, Academic/Scholarly.*
Media: Online - full text. **Related titles:** Print ed.; ◆ Series: A I P Conference Proceedings. Astronomy & Astrophysics. ISSN 1931-3020; ◆ A I P Conference Proceedings. Accelerators & Beams. ISSN 1931-3012; ◆ A I P Conference Proceedings. Nuclear & High Energy Physics. ISSN 1931-3063; ◆ A I P Conference Proceedings. Atomic, Molecular & Statistical Physics. ISSN 1931-3039; ◆ A I P Conference Proceedings. Mathematical & Statistical Physics. ISSN 1931-3055; ◆ A I P Conference Proceedings. Materials Physics & Applications. ISSN 1931-3047; A I P Conference Proceedings. ISSN 1551-7616. 1970.
—CCC.
Published by: American Institute of Physics, 1 Physics Ellipse, College Park, MD 20740. TEL 301-209-3100, FAX 301-209-0843, aipinfo@aip.org, http://www.aip.org.

530 IND ISSN 0976-0954
▼ **A N U JOURNAL OF PHYSICAL SCIENCES.** Text in English. 2009. s-a. **Document type:** *Journal, Academic/Scholarly.*
Published by: Acharya Nagarjuna University, Nagarjuna Nagar, Guntur, Andhra Pradesh 522 510, India. TEL 91-863-2293007, FAX 91-863-2293378, http://www.nagarjunauniversity.ac.in.

530 USA ISSN 1058-8132
CODEN: ANWSEN
A P S NEWS. Text in English. 1992. m. free domestic to members; USD 15 foreign to members (effective 2010). **Document type:** *Newsletter, Trade.* **Description:** Contains news of the society and of its divisions, topical groups, sections, and forums; advance information on meetings of the society; and reports to the society by its committees and task forces, as well as opinions.
Supersedes in part: American Physical Society. Bulletin (0003-0503)
Related titles: Online - full text ed.
Indexed: A22.
—IE, Infotrieve, Linda Hall.
Published by: American Physical Society, One Physics Ellipse, College Park, MD 20740. TEL 301-209-3200, FAX 301-209-0865, subs@aps.org. Ed. Alan Chodos. **Subscr. to:** APS Subscription Services, Ste. 1N01, 2 huntington Quadrangle, Melville, NY 11747-4502. TEL 800-344-6902.

A R I; an interdisciplinary journal of physical and engineering sciences. *see* EARTH SCIENCES—Geology

530 ITA ISSN 1020-7007
QC1.I6285
ABDUS SALAM INTERNATIONAL CENTRE FOR THEORETICAL PHYSICS. ANNUAL REPORT. Text in English. 1964. a. free. **Document type:** *Corporate.*
Formerly (until 1965): International Centre for Theoretical Physics. Report (0538-5415)
Published by: Abdus Salam International Centre for Theoretical Physics, Strada Costiera 11, Trieste, TS 34014, Italy. pub_off@ictp.trieste.it, http://www.ictp.trieste.it. Circ: 450.

ABHANDLUNGEN AUS DER HAMBURGER STERNWARTE. *see* ASTRONOMY

530 SWE ISSN 1654-9163
THE ABRAHAM ZELMANOV JOURNAL; the journal for general relativity, gravitation and cosmology. Variant title: Tidskriften Abraham Zelmanov. Text in English. 2008. a. **Document type:** *Journal, Academic/Scholarly.*
Related titles: Online - full text ed.; free (effective 2011).
Published by: The Abraham Zelmanov Journal Ed. Dmitri Rabounski.

530 510 600 MDA
CODEN: IZFMBL
ACADEMIA DE STIINTE A REPUBLICII MOLDOVA. BULETINUL. FIZICA SI TEHNICA. Text in Romanian, Russian. 1951. 3/yr. USD 30.
Formerly (until 1989): Academia de Stiinte a R.S.S. Moldova. Buletinul. Fizica si Tehnika (0236-3097); Supersedes in part (in 1968): Akademiya Nauk Moldovskoi S.S.R. Izvestiya. Seriya Fiziko-Tekhnicheskikh i Matematicheskikh Nauk (0321-169X)
Indexed: ChemAb, MathR, Z02.
—CASDDS, INIST, Linda Hall.
Published by: Academia de Stiinte a Moldovej, Biblioteca Stiintifica Centrala, Bd Stefan cel Mare 1, Chisinau, 2001, Moldova. http://www.asm.md/altstruc/library.

530 TWN ISSN 0304-5293
QC1 CODEN: RIPSD3
ACADEMIA SINICA. INSTITUTE OF PHYSICS. ANNUAL REPORT/ CHUNG YANG YEN CHIU YUAN WU LI HSUEH YEN CHIU SO NIEN PAO. Text in Chinese. 1970. a. per issue exchange basis. bk.rev.
Indexed: CIN, ChemAb, ChemTitl, Inspec.
—AskIEEE, CASDDS.
Published by: Academia Sinica, Institute of Physics/Chung Yang Yen Chiu Yuan, Wu Li Hsueh Yen Chiu So, Nankang, Taipei, 11529, Taiwan. FAX 02-783-4187. Ed. E K Lin. Circ: 500.

538 USA
ACADEMIC PRESS SERIES IN MAGNETISM. Text in English. irreg., latest 2004. price varies. **Document type:** *Monographic series, Academic/Scholarly.*
Published by: Academic Press (Subsidiary of: Elsevier Science & Technology), 525 B St, Ste 1900, San Diego, CA 92101-4495. TEL 619-231-6616, FAX 619-699-6422, JournalCustomerService-usa@elsevier.com, http://www.elsevierdirect.com/imprint.jsp?iid=5.

ACCADEMIA ROVERETANA DEGLI AGIATI. ATTI. FASC. B: CLASSE DI SCIENZE MATEMATICHE, FISICHE E NATURALI. *see* SCIENCES: COMPREHENSIVE WORKS

530 IND ISSN 0253-7257
CODEN: JSOIDI
➤ **ACOUSTICAL SOCIETY OF INDIA. JOURNAL.** Text in English. 1973. q. INR 500 to non-members; free to members (effective 2011). **Document type:** *Journal, Trade.*
Related titles: Online - full text ed.: free (effective 2011).
Indexed: AcoustA, ChemAb, Inspec.
—CASDDS, Ingenta.
Published by: Acoustical Society of India, c/o Shri. P. V. S. Ganesh Kumar, Naval science & Technological Laboratory, Visakhapatnam, 530 027, India. TEL 91-891-2586390, asi.india@yahoo.co.in, http://www.acousticsindia.org. Ed. V Mohanan TEL 91-11-45608112.

530 IND ISSN 0253-732X
QC1 CODEN: ACIPD2
ACTA CIENCIA INDICA. PHYSICS. Text in English. 1974. q. bk.rev. bibl.; charts. **Document type:** *Journal, Academic/Scholarly.*
Supersedes in part (in 1979): Acta Ciencia Indica (0379-5411)
Indexed: CCMJ, CIN, ChemAb, ChemTitl, Inspec, MSN, MathR.
—BLDSC (0611.373000), AskIEEE, CASDDS, IE, Ingenta, INIST, Linda Hall.
Published by: (Society for the Progress of Science), Pragati Prakashan, 240, Western Kutchery Rd, Meerut, Uttar Pradesh, India. TEL 91-121-2643636, FAX 91-121-2663838, info@pragatiprakashan.in, http://pragatiprakashan.in. **Subscr. to:** I N S I O Scientific Books & Periodicals.

530 POL ISSN 0209-3316
ACTA MAGNETICA. Text and summaries in English. 1983. a. price varies. back issues avail. **Document type:** *Monographic series, Academic/Scholarly.* **Description:** Covers all aspects of physics.
Published by: (Uniwersytet im. Adama Mickiewicza w Poznaniu, Instytut Fizyki/Institute of Physics), Wydawnictwo Naukowe Uniwersytetu im. Adama Mickiewicza/Adam Mickiewicz University Press, ul Fredry 10, Poznan, 61701, Poland. TEL 48-61-8294646, FAX 48-61-8294647, press@amu.edu.pl, http://press.amu.edu.pl. Ed. Grzegorz Kamieniarz. Circ: 280.

ACTA MATHEMATICA SCIENTIA. *see* MATHEMATICS

530 540 HUN ISSN 0567-7947
QC1 CODEN: APDBAN
ACTA PHYSICA ET CHIMICA DEBRECINA. Variant title: Acta Physica et Chimica Debrecina. Text in English. 1954. a., latest vol.33. 120 p./no.; reprints avail. **Document type:** *Journal, Academic/Scholarly.*
Formerly (until 1963): Acta Universitatis Debreceniensis. Series Physica et Chimica (0365-7930); Which superseded in part (in 1962): Acta Universitatis Debreceniensis (0365-7817)
Media: Large Type (12 pt.).
Indexed: CIN, ChemAb, ChemTitl, GeoRef, SpeleolAb.
—INIST, Linda Hall.
Published by: Kossuth Lajos Tudomanyegyetem, PF 37, Debrecen, 4010, Hungary. Ed. R Gaspar.

530 POL ISSN 0587-4246
QC1 CODEN: ATPLB6
➤ **ACTA PHYSICA POLONICA. SERIES A: GENERAL PHYSICS, PHYSICS OF CONDENSED MATTER, OPTICS AND QUANTUM ELECTRONICS, ATOMIC AND MOLECULAR PHYSICS, APPLIED PHYSICS.** Text in Multiple languages. 1932. m. EUR 370 foreign (effective 2011). bibl.; charts; illus. index. **Document type:** *Journal, Academic/Scholarly.*
Supersedes in part: Acta Physica Polonica (0001-673X)
Related titles: Online - full text ed.: ISSN 1898-794X. free (effective 2011).
Indexed: A01, A22, ASCA, ApMecR, BPRC&P, C33, CA, CIN, CPEI, Cadscan, ChemAb, ChemTitl, CurCont, EngInd, GeoRef, INIS AtomInd, ISR, Inspec, LeadAb, MathR, MinerAb, SCI, SCOPUS, SpeleolAb, T02, W07, Zincscan.
—BLDSC (0650.050000), AskIEEE, CASDDS, IE, Infotrieve, Ingenta, INIST, Linda Hall. **CCC.**
Published by: Polska Akademia Nauk, Instytut Fizyki/Polish Academy of Sciences, Institute of Physics, Al Lotnikow 32-46, Warsaw, 02668, Poland. TEL 48-22-8436601, FAX 48-22-8430926, appol@ifpan.edu.pl. Ed. Witold D Dobrowolski. **Dist. by:** Ars Polona, Obroncow 25, Warsaw 03933, Poland. TEL 48-22-5098609, FAX 48-22-5098610, arspolona@arspolona.com.pl, http://www.arspolona.com.pl.

530 POL ISSN 0587-4254
QC770 CODEN: APOBBB
➤ **ACTA PHYSICA POLONICA. SERIES B: ELEMENTARY PARTICLE PHYSICS, NUCLEAR PHYSICS, STATISTICAL PHYSICS, THEORY OF RELATIVITY, FIELD THEORY.** Text in English. 1932. m. EUR 330 foreign; EUR 370 foreign (with Supplement) (effective 2011). bk.rev. index. back issues avail. **Document type:** *Journal, Academic/Scholarly.*
Supersedes in part: Acta Physica Polonica (0001-673X)
Related titles: Microfiche ed.: (from BHP); Online - full text ed.: ISSN 1509-5770. free (effective 2011); Supplement(s): Acta Physica Polonica. Series B: Proceedings Supplement. ISSN 1899-2358. 2008.
Indexed: A01, A22, ASCA, ApMecR, C33, CA, CCMJ, CIN, CPEI, Cadscan, ChemAb, ChemTitl, CurCont, EngInd, INIS AtomInd, ISR, Inspec, LeadAb, MSN, MathR, MinerAb, SCI, SCOPUS, T02, W07, Z02, Zincscan.
—BLDSC (0650.060000), AskIEEE, CASDDS, IE, Infotrieve, Ingenta, INIST, Linda Hall.
Published by: (Uniwersytet Jagiellonski, Instytut Fizyki/Jagellonian University, Institute of Physics), Wydawnictwo Uniwersytetu Jagiellonskiego/Jagiellonian University Press, ul Grodzka 26, Krakow, 31044, Poland. TEL 48-12-4312364, FAX 48-12-4301995, wydaw@if.uj.edu.pl, http://www.wuj.pl. Ed. Michal Praszalowicz. **Co-sponsor:** Polska Akademia Umiejetnosci.

530 SVK ISSN 0323-0465
QC1 CODEN: APSVCO
➤ **ACTA PHYSICA SLOVACA**; journal for experimental and theoretical physics. Text and summaries in English. 1951. bi-m. EUR 208 foreign (effective 2010). bk.rev. abstr.; bibl.; charts; illus. back issues avail. **Document type:** *Journal, Academic/Scholarly.* **Description:** Publishes original scientific and special works from all areas of physics, especially physics of solid substances, nuclear and subnuclear physics, as well as borderline areas such as biophysics and physical electronics.
Formerly (until 1973): Fyzika'lny Casopis (0532-9132)
Related titles: Online - full text ed.: ISSN 1336-040X.
Indexed: ASCA, CIN, Cadscan, ChemAb, ChemTitl, CurCont, IBR, IBZ, INIS AtomInd, ISR, Inspec, LeadAb, MathR, PhysBer, SCI, SCOPUS, W07, Zincscan.
—BLDSC (0650.630000), AskIEEE, CASDDS, IE, Ingenta, INIST, Linda Hall.
Published by: Slovenska Akademia Vied, Fyzikalny Ustav/Slovak Academy of Sciences, Institute of Physics, Dubravska cesta 9, Bratislava, 842 28, Slovakia. TEL 421-7-59410501, FAX 421-7-54776085, Danka.Haasova@savba.sk, http://www.fu.sav.sk. Ed. Vladimir Buzek. Circ: 300 (paid); 100 (controlled). **Dist. by:** Slovart G.T.G. s.r.o., Krupinska 4, PO Box 152, Bratislava 85299, Slovakia. TEL 421-2-63839472, FAX 421-2-63839485, info@slovart-gtg.sk, http://www.slovart-gtg.sk.

530 SVK ISSN 0231-889X
QC1 CODEN: APUCED
ACTA PHYSICA UNIVERSITATIS COMENIANAE. Text in English. 1957. irreg.
Formerly (until 1983): Acta Facultatis Rerum Naturalium Universitatis Comenianae. Physica (0524-2355)
Indexed: Inspec.
—INIST, Linda Hall.
Published by: Univerzita Komenskeho, Matematicko-Fizikalna Fakulta, Mlynska Dolina, Bratislava, 84248, Slovakia. TEL 421-7-65428981, FAX 421-7-65428981.

530 POL ISSN 0867-2997
➤ **ACTA PHYSICAE SUPERFICIERUM.** Text in English. 1990. s-a. **Document type:** *Journal, Academic/Scholarly.*
Published by: (Uniwersytet Lodzki, Wydzial Fizyki i Informatyki Stosowanej, Katedra Fizyki Ciala Stalego/University of Lodz, Faculty of Physics and Applied Informatics, Solid State Physics Department), Wydawnictwo Uniwersytetu Lodzkiego/Lodz University Press, ul Lindleya 8, Lodz, 90-131, Poland. TEL 48-42-6655861, FAX 48-42-6655861, wdwul@uni.lodz.pl, http://www.wydawnictwo.uni.lodz.pl. Ed. Leszek Wojczak.

539.7 FIN ISSN 0355-2721
QC1 CODEN: APSSDG
ACTA POLYTECHNICA SCANDINAVICA. P H. APPLIED PHYSICS SERIES. Text and summaries in English. 1958. irreg. (4-5/yr.). price varies. index, cum.index: 1958-1994. back issues avail.; reprints avail. **Document type:** *Monographic series, Academic/Scholarly.* **Description:** Presents research results in physical engineering and technical physics.
Formerly (until 1976): Acta Polytechnica Scandinavica. Physics Including Nucleonics Series (0001-6888)
Related titles: Microfilm ed.: (from PQC).
Indexed: A22, ASCA, Cadscan, ChemAb, GeoRef, ICEA, Inspec, LeadAb, SCOPUS, SoftAbEng, SpeleolAb, Zincscan.
—AskIEEE, CASDDS, IE, Ingenta, INIST, Linda Hall. **CCC.**
Published by: Teknillistieteelliset Akatemiat/Finnish Academies of Technology, Mariankatu 8 B 11, Helsinki, 00170, Finland. TEL 358-9-2782400, FAX 358-9-2782177, facte@facte.com. Ed. Mauri Luukkala. Circ: 500.

P

ACTA TRIBOLOGICA. *see* ENGINEERING—Mechanical Engineering

ACTA UNIVERSITATIS CAROLINAE. MATHEMATICA ET PHYSICA. *see* MATHEMATICS

530 CZE ISSN 0231-9772
QC1
➤ **ACTA UNIVERSITATIS PALACKIANAE OLOMUCENSIS. FACULTAS RERUM NATURALIUM. PHYSICA.** Text in Multiple languages. 1973. irreg. price varies. **Document type:** *Monographic series, Academic/Scholarly.*
Formerly (until 1983): Univerzita Palackeho v Olomouci. Prirodovedecka Fakulta. Sbornik Praci. Fyzika (0231-6145)
Indexed: Z02.
—INIST, Linda Hall.
Published by: Univerzita Palackeho v Olomouci, Prirodovedecka Fakulta, tr Svobody 26, Olomouc, 77146, Czech Republic. TEL 420-58-5634060, FAX 420-58-5634002, dekanat.prf@upol.cz, http://www.upol.cz/fakulty/prf.

➤ **ADSORPTION.** *see* ENGINEERING—Chemical Engineering

530 SGP ISSN 1793-1002
ADVANCED SERIES IN APPLIED PHYSICS. Text in English. 1988. irreg., latest vol.5, 2004. price varies. back issues avail. **Document type:** *Monographic series, Academic/Scholarly.*
Published by: World Scientific Publishing Co. Pte. Ltd., 5 Toh Tuck Link, Singapore, 596224, Singapore. TEL 65-6466-5775, FAX 65-6467-7667, wspc@wspc.com.sg, http://www.worldscientific.com. Eds. A J Campillo, Richard K Chang. **Dist. by:** World Scientific Publishing Co., Inc., 27 Warren St, Ste 401-402, Hackensack, NJ 07601. TEL 201-487-9655, 800-227-7562, FAX 201-487-9656, 888-977-2665, wspc@wspc.com; World Scientific Publishing Ltd., 57 Shelton St, London WC2H 9HE, United Kingdom. TEL 44-207-8360888, FAX 44-207-8362020, sales@wspc.co.uk.

530 SGP
ADVANCED SERIES IN FULLERENES. Text in English. 1992. irreg., latest vol.5, 1997. price varies. back issues avail. **Document type:** *Monographic series, Academic/Scholarly.*
Published by: World Scientific Publishing Co. Pte. Ltd., 5 Toh Tuck Link, Singapore, 596224, Singapore. TEL 65-6466-5775, FAX 65-6467-7667, wspc@wspc.com.sg, http://www.worldscientific.com. **Dist. in Europe by:** World Scientific Publishing Ltd., 57 Shelton St, London WC2H 9HE, United Kingdom. TEL 44-207-8360888, FAX 44-207-8362020, sales@wspc.co.uk; **Dist. in US by:** World Scientific Publishing Co., Inc., 27 Warren St, Ste 401-402, Hackensack, NJ 07601. TEL 201-487-9655, 800-227-7562, FAX 201-487-9656, 888-977-2665, wspc@wspc.com.

530 510 SGP ISSN 0218-0340
ADVANCED SERIES IN MATHEMATICAL PHYSICS. Text in English. 1987. irreg., latest vol.28, 2008. price varies. back issues avail. **Document type:** *Monographic series, Academic/Scholarly.*
Indexed: CCMJ.
Published by: World Scientific Publishing Co. Pte. Ltd., 5 Toh Tuck Link, Singapore, 596224, Singapore. TEL 65-6466-5775, FAX 65-6467-7667, wspc@wspc.com.sg, http://www.worldscientific.com. Eds. D H Phong, Huzihiro Araki, Victor Kac. **Dist. by:** World Scientific Publishing Co., Inc., 27 Warren St, Ste 401-402, Hackensack, NJ 07601. TEL 201-487-9655, 800-227-7562, FAX 201-487-9656, 888-977-2665, wspc@wspc.com; World Scientific Publishing Ltd., 57 Shelton St, London WC2H 9HE, United Kingdom. TEL 44-207-8360888, FAX 44-207-8362020, sales@wspc.co.uk.

530 SGP ISSN 1793-1045
ADVANCED SERIES IN NONLINEAR DYNAMICS. Text in English. 1991. irreg., latest vol.26, 2009. price varies. back issues avail. **Document type:** *Monographic series, Academic/Scholarly.*
Indexed: CCMJ.
Published by: World Scientific Publishing Co. Pte. Ltd., 5 Toh Tuck Link, Singapore, 596224, Singapore. TEL 65-6466-5775, FAX 65-6467-7667, wspc@wspc.com.sg, http://www.worldscientific.com. Ed. R S MacKay. **Dist. by:** World Scientific Publishing Co., Inc., 27 Warren St, Ste 401-402, Hackensack, NJ 07601. TEL 201-487-9655, 800-227-7562, FAX 201-487-9656, 888-977-2665, wspc@wspc.com; World Scientific Publishing Ltd., 57 Shelton St, London WC2H 9HE, United Kingdom. TEL 44-207-8360888, FAX 44-207-8362020, sales@wspc.co.uk.

530 SGP ISSN 0218-0324
CODEN: ASDPEM
ADVANCED SERIES ON DIRECTIONS IN HIGH ENERGY PHYSICS. Text in English. 1988. irreg., latest vol.21, 2010. price varies. back issues avail. **Document type:** *Monographic series, Academic/Scholarly.* **Description:** Covers reviews of important developments in each sector of high energy physics and is of use to all researchers.
Indexed: CIN, ChemAb, ChemTitl, Z02.
—BLDSC (0696.927340), CASDDS.
Published by: World Scientific Publishing Co. Pte. Ltd., 5 Toh Tuck Link, Singapore, 596224, Singapore. TEL 65-6466-5775, FAX 65-6467-7667, wspc@wspc.com.sg, http://www.worldscientific.com. **Dist. by:** World Scientific Publishing Ltd., 57 Shelton St, London WC2H 9HE, United Kingdom. TEL 44-207-8360888, FAX 44-207-8362020, sales@wspc.co.uk; World Scientific Publishing Co., Inc., 27 Warren St, Ste 401-402, Hackensack, NJ 07601. TEL 201-487-9655, 800-227-7562, FAX 201-487-9656, 888-977-2665, wspc@wspc.com.

530 SGP ISSN 1793-1495
ADVANCED SERIES ON THEORETICAL PHYSICAL SCIENCE. Text in English. 1993. irreg., latest vol.10, 2006. price varies. back issues avail. **Document type:** *Journal, Academic/Scholarly.*
Published by: World Scientific Publishing Co. Pte. Ltd., 5 Toh Tuck Link, Singapore, 596224, Singapore. TEL 65-6466-5775, FAX 65-6467-7667, wspc@wspc.com.sg, http://www.worldscientific.com. Eds. Dai Yuan-Ben, Hao Bai-Lin, Su Zhao-Bin. **Dist. by:** World Scientific Publishing Co., Inc., 27 Warren St, Ste 401-402, Hackensack, NJ 07601. TEL 201-487-9655, 800-227-7562, FAX 201-487-9656, 888-977-2665, wspc@wspc.com; World Scientific Publishing Ltd., 57 Shelton St, London WC2H 9HE, United Kingdom. TEL 44-207-8360888, FAX 44-207-8362020, sales@wspc.co.uk.

530 BGR ISSN 1313-1311
QC20
➤ **ADVANCED STUDIES IN THEORETICAL PHYSICS.** Text in English, French. 2007. q. free (effective 2008). back issues avail. **Document type:** *Journal, Academic/Scholarly.* **Description:** Publishes original research papers in all areas of theoretical physics and related mathematical physics.
Related titles: Online - full text ed.: free (effective 2011).
Indexed: CCMJ, MSN, MathR, SCOPUS, Z02.
Published by: Hikari Ltd., Rui planina str 4, vh 7, et 5, Ruse, 7005, Bulgaria. TEL 359-82-580962, hikari@m-hikari.com. Ed., Pub., R&P, Adv. contact Emil Minchev.

➤ **ADVANCES AND APPLICATIONS IN FLUID MECHANICS.** *see* ENGINEERING—Hydraulic Engineering

➤ **ADVANCES IN ASTROBIOLOGY AND BIOGEOPHYSICS.** *see* ASTRONOMY

530 541 USA ISSN 0065-2385
QD453 CODEN: ADCPAA
➤ **ADVANCES IN CHEMICAL PHYSICS.** Text in English. 1958. irreg., latest vol.144, 2010. price varies. adv. back issues avail. **Document type:** *Monographic series, Academic/Scholarly.* **Description:** Contains developments in classical density functional theory, nonadiabatic chemical dynamics in intermediate and intense laser fields, and bilayers and their simulation.
Related titles: Online - full text ed.: ISSN 1934-4791.
Indexed: A22, ASCA, C13, C33, CCMJ, CIN, ChemAb, ChemTitl, ISR, SCI, SCOPUS, W07.
—BLDSC (0703.550000), CASDDS, IE, Ingenta, INIST, Linda Hall. **CCC.**
Published by: John Wiley & Sons, Inc., 111 River St, Hoboken, NJ 07030. TEL 201-748-6000, FAX 201-748-6088, info@wiley.com, http://www.wiley.com/WileyCDA/. Ed. Stuart A Rice.

➤ **ADVANCES IN COLLOID AND INTERFACE SCIENCE.** *see* CHEMISTRY—Physical Chemistry

530 USA ISSN 2159-1709
ADVANCES IN CONDENSED MATTER AND MATERIALS RESEARCH. Text in English. 2001. irreg., latest vol.10, 2011. price varies. back issues avail. **Document type:** *Monographic series, Trade.* **Description:** Presents a collection of papers which explores the current and cutting edge research into the condensed matter field.
Published by: Nova Science Publishers, Inc., 400 Oser Ave, Ste 1600, Hauppauge, NY 11788. TEL 631-231-7269, FAX 631-231-8175, journals@novapublishers.com.

530.094 USA ISSN 1687-8108
➤ **ADVANCES IN CONDENSED MATTER PHYSICS.** Text in English. 2008. irreg. USD 395 (effective 2011). **Document type:** *Journal, Academic/Scholarly.* **Description:** Publishes original research articles as well as review articles in all areas of condensed matter physics.
Related titles: Online - full text ed.: ISSN 1687-8124. 2008. free (effective 2011).
Indexed: A26, C10, CA, E08, I05, P52, SCOPUS, T02.
Published by: Hindawi Publishing Corporation, 410 Park Ave, 15th Fl, PMB 287, New York, NY 10022. FAX 866-446-3294, orders@hindawi.com.

530 USA ISSN 1560-9324
ADVANCES IN CONDENSED MATTER SCIENCE. Text in English. 2000. irreg. **Document type:** *Monographic series, Academic/Scholarly.* **Description:** Includes topics in condensed matter science such as spectroscopy of solids, semiconductors, and nanostructures.
Related titles: Online - full text ed.: ISSN 2153-9952.
Published by: C R C Press, LLC (Subsidiary of: Taylor & Francis Group), 6000 Broken Sound Pkwy, NW, Ste 300, Boca Raton, FL 33487. TEL 561-994-0555, FAX 561-989-9732, journals@crcpress.com.

530 SGP
ADVANCES IN DISORDERED SEMICONDUCTORS. Text in English. 1989. irreg., latest vol.3, 1990. price varies. back issues avail. **Document type:** *Monographic series, Academic/Scholarly.*
Indexed: CIN, ChemAb, ChemTitl.
Published by: World Scientific Publishing Co. Pte. Ltd., 5 Toh Tuck Link, Singapore, 596224, Singapore. TEL 65-6466-5775, FAX 65-6467-7667, wspc@wspc.com.sg, http://www.worldscientific.com. Ed. H Fritzsche. **Dist. by:** World Scientific Publishing Co., Inc., 27 Warren St, Ste 401-402, Hackensack, NJ 07601. TEL 201-487-9655, 800-227-7562, FAX 201-487-9656, 888-977-2665, wspc@wspc.com; World Scientific Publishing Ltd., 57 Shelton St, London WC2H 9HE, United Kingdom. TEL 44-207-8360888, FAX 44-207-8362020, sales@wspc.co.uk.

530 USA ISSN 1687-7357
➤ **ADVANCES IN HIGH ENERGY PHYSICS.** Text in English. 2007. irreg. USD 495 (effective 2011). **Document type:** *Journal, Academic/Scholarly.* **Description:** Publishes reviews and original research papers of wide interest in all fields of high energy physics.
Related titles: Online - full text ed.: ISSN 1687-7365. 2007. free (effective 2011).
Indexed: A01, A26, A28, A39, APA, BrCerAb, C&ISA, C27, C29, CA, CA/WCA, CCMJ, CIA, CerAb, CivEngAb, CorrAb, CurCont, D03, D04, E&CAJ, E08, E11, E13, E14, EEA, EMA, ESPM, EnvEAb, H15, I05, M&TEA, M09, MBF, METADEX, MSN, MathR, P52, R14, S14, S15, S18, SCI, SolStAb, T02, T04, W07, WAA, Z02.
Published by: Hindawi Publishing Corporation, 410 Park Ave, 15th Fl, PMB 287, New York, NY 10022. FAX 866-446-3294, info@hindawi.com.

➤ **ADVANCES IN IMAGING AND ELECTRON PHYSICS.** *see* ENGINEERING—Electrical Engineering

530.1 668.9 USA ISSN 2162-531X
▼ ➤ **ADVANCES IN MATERIALS PHYSICS AND CHEMISTRY.** Text in English. 2011. q. **Document type:** *Journal, Academic/Scholarly.* **Description:** Contains rapid communications, full-length original research, review articles and comments on interrelationships among synthesis, micro/nanostructures, properties, processing and performance of materials science, physics, and chemistry.
Related titles: Online - full text ed.: ISSN 2162-5328. free (effective 2011).
Published by: Scientific Research Publishing, Inc., PO Box 54821, Irvine, CA 92619. service@scirp.org. Ed. Zhiwen Chen.

➤ **ADVANCES IN MATERIALS SCIENCE AND ENGINEERING.** *see* ENGINEERING—Engineering Mechanics And Materials

530 510 USA ISSN 1687-9120
➤ **ADVANCES IN MATHEMATICAL PHYSICS.** Text in English. 2008. irreg. USD 195 (effective 2011). **Document type:** *Journal, Academic/Scholarly.* **Description:** Publishes original research articles as well as review articles in all areas of mathematical physics.
Related titles: Online - full text ed.: ISSN 1687-9139. 2008. free (effective 2011).
Indexed: A26, C10, CA, E08, I05, MSN, P49, P52, T02.
Published by: Hindawi Publishing Corporation, 410 Park Ave, 15th Fl, PMB 287, New York, NY 10022. FAX 215-893-4392, 866-446-3294, orders@hindawi.com.

530 GBR ISSN 0001-8732
QC1 CODEN: ADPHAH
➤ **ADVANCES IN PHYSICS.** Text in English. 1952. bi-m. GBP 3,239 combined subscription in United Kingdom to institutions (print & online eds.); EUR 4,278, USD 5,373 combined subscription to institutions (print & online eds.) (effective 2012). adv. charts; illus. back issues avail.; reprint service avail. from PSC. **Document type:** *Journal, Academic/Scholarly.* **Description:** Aims to meet the need for review papers in the major branches of condensed-matter physics.
Related titles: Microform ed.; Online - full text ed.: ISSN 1460-6976. 1999. GBP 2,915 in United Kingdom to institutions; EUR 3,850, USD 4,835 to institutions (effective 2012) (from IngentaConnect).
Indexed: A01, A02, A03, A08, A22, A28, APA, ASCA, BrCerAb, C&ISA, CA, CA/WCA, CIA, CIN, CPEI, CerAb, ChemAb, ChemTitl, CivEngAb, CorrAb, CurCont, E&CAJ, E01, E11, EEA, EMA, ESPM, EngInd, EnvEAb, GeoRef, H15, IBR, IBZ, ISMEC, ISR, IndMed, Inspec, M&TEA, M09, MBF, METADEX, MSCI, MathR, P26, P52, P54, P56, PQC, PhysBer, S01, SCI, SCOPUS, SolStAb, SpeleolAb, T02, T04, VirolAbstr, W07, WAA.
—AskIEEE, CASDDS, IE, Infotrieve, Ingenta, INIST, Linda Hall. **CCC.**
Published by: Taylor & Francis Ltd. (Subsidiary of: Taylor & Francis Group), 4 Park Sq, Milton Park, Abingdon, Oxfordshire OX14 4RN, United Kingdom. TEL 44-20-70176000, FAX 44-20-70176336, subscriptions@tandf.co.uk, http://www.taylorandfrancis.com. Eds. J M F Gunn, Kevin S Bedell, David Sherrington. **Subscr. addr. in US:** Taylor & Francis Inc., Customer Services Dept, 325 Chestnut St, 8th Fl, Philadelphia, PA 19106. TEL 215-625-8900, 800-354-1420, FAX 215-625-2940, customerservice@taylorandfrancis.com; **Subscr. to:** Journals Customer Service, Sheepen Pl, Colchester, Essex CO3 3LP, United Kingdom. TEL 44-20-70175544, FAX 44-20-70175198, tf.enquiries@tfinforma.com.

530.41 DEU ISSN 1438-4329
QC176.A1 CODEN: ASSPFU
➤ **ADVANCES IN SOLID STATE PHYSICS.** Text in English. 1954. irreg., latest vol.48, 2009. price varies. **Document type:** *Monographic series, Academic/Scholarly.* **Description:** Directed toward all scientists at universities and in industry who wish to obtain an overview and to keep informed on the latest developments in solid state physics.
Fomer titles (until 1999): Festkorperprobleme (0430-3393); (until 1962): Halbleiterprobleme (0506-6743)
Related titles: Online - full text ed.: ISSN 1617-5034. 2001.
Indexed: ASCA, IBR, IBZ, ISR, Inspec, SCOPUS.
—BLDSC (0711.440000), IE, Ingenta. **CCC.**
Published by: Springer (Subsidiary of: Springer Science+Business Media), Tiergartenstr 17, Heidelberg, 69121, Germany. TEL 49-6221-4870, FAX 49-6221-345229, subscriptions@springer.com. Ed. Rolf Haug.

530 NLD
➤ **ADVANCES IN SOLID STATE TECHNOLOGY.** Text in English. 1985. irreg., latest vol.5, 1991. price varies. back issues avail. **Document type:** *Monographic series, Academic/Scholarly.*
Published by: Springer Netherlands (Subsidiary of: Springer Science+Business Media), Van Godewijckstraat 30, Dordrecht, 3311 GX, Netherlands. TEL 31-78-6576050, FAX 31-78-6576474.

➤ **ADVANCES IN THEORETICAL AND MATHEMATICAL PHYSICS.** *see* MATHEMATICS

539 USA ISSN 1097-0002
CODEN: AXRAAA
➤ **ADVANCES IN X-RAY ANALYSIS (CD-ROM).** Variant title: Annual Conference on Applications of X-Ray Analysis. Proceedings. Text in English. 1957. a. USD 170 per issue (effective 2010). **Document type:** *Proceedings, Academic/Scholarly.* **Description:** Features on the work of leading scientists in the field of X-ray materials analysis.
Formerly (until 1997): Advances in X-Ray Analysis (Print) (0376-0308)
Media: CD-ROM.
Indexed: A22, AESIS, C33, CIN, ChemAb, ChemTitl, GeoRef, INIS AtomInd, Inspec, SpeleolAb.
—BLDSC (0712.201000), Linda Hall. **CCC.**
Published by: International Centre for Diffraction Data, 12 Campus Blvd, Newton Square, PA 19073. TEL 610-325-9814, 866-378-9331, FAX 610-325-9823, info@icdd.com, http://www.icdd.com.

➤ **AEROSOL AND AIR QUALITY RESEARCH.** *see* ENGINEERING—Chemical Engineering

530 USA ISSN 1948-0229
▼ ➤ **AFRICAN JOURNAL OF PHYSICS.** Text in English. 2009. 5/yr. USD 100; USD 30 per issue (effective 2009). **Document type:** *Journal, Academic/Scholarly.* **Description:** Articles on physics by African scientists worldwide.
Related titles: CD-ROM ed.: ISSN 1948-0245. 2009; Online - full text ed.: ISSN 1948-0237. 2009.
Published by: African Physical Society, 1601 E Market St, Greensboro, NC 27411. TEL 336-285-2113, gutaye@ncat.edu, http://sirius-c.ncat.edu/asn/afps/index.html.

530 ITA ISSN 1970-4097
QC1
AFRICAN PHYSICAL REVIEWS. Text in Italian. 2007. a. free (effective 2011). **Document type:** *Journal, Academic/Scholarly.*
Media: Online - full text.
Published by: Abdus Salam International Centre for Theoretical Physics, Strada Costiera 11, Trieste, TS 34014, Italy. TEL 39-040-2240575, FAX 39-040-224163, pub_off@ictp.trieste.it, http://www.ictp.trieste.it.

530 510 551 TJK ISSN 1023-8581
Q60 CODEN: IANNES
AKADEMIAI ILMHOI CUMHURII TOCIKISTON. SU'BAI ILMHOI FIZIKAU MATEMATIKA VA KIMIE. AHBORI. Text in Russian. 1967. q. charts; illus.
Formerly (until 1992): Akademiya Nauk Tadzhikskoi S.S.R. Izvestiya. Otdelenie Fiziko-Matematicheskikh i Geologo-Khimicheskikh Nauk (0002-3485)
Indexed: GeoRef, MathR, SpeleolAb, Z02.
—CASDDS.
Published by: Akademiai Ilmhoi Cumhurii Tocikiston/Academy of Sciences of the Republic of Tajikistan, 33 Rudaki Ave, Dushanbe, 734025, Tajikistan. TEL 992-372-215083, FAX 992-372-214911, ulmas@tajik.net.

AKADEMIE DER WISSENSCHAFTEN ZU GOETTINGEN. ABHANDLUNGEN. MATHEMATISCH-PHYSIKALISCHE KLASSE. DRITTE FOLGE. *see* MATHEMATICS

530 551 TKM
QC1 CODEN: ITUFAW
AKADEMIYA NAUK TURKMENISTANA. IZVESTIYA. SERIYA FIZIKO-TEKHNICHESKIKH, KHIMICHESKIKH I GEOLOGICHESKIKH NAUK. Text in Russian. 1960. bi-m. USD 15. charts; illus. index.
Formerly (until 1992): Akademiya Nauk Turkmenskoi S.S.R. Izvestiya. Seriya Fiziko-Tekhnicheskikh, Khimicheskikh i Geologicheskikh Nauk (0002-3507)
Indexed: CIS, ChemAb, MathR, SpeleolAb, Z02.
—CASDDS, INIST, Linda Hall. **CCC.**
Published by: Turkmenistan Ylymlar Akademiasynyn/Academy of Sciences of Turkmenistan, Gogolya ul 15, Ashkhabad, 744000, Turkmenistan. Circ: 500.

ALKALMAZOTT MATEMATIKAI LAPOK. *see* MATHEMATICS

530 USA ISSN 0569-5686
QC1 CODEN: AIPABW
AMERICAN INSTITUTE OF PHYSICS. ANNUAL REPORT. Text in English. 19??. a. free (effective 2010). adv. **Document type:** *Journal, Academic/Scholarly.*
Related titles: Online - full text ed.: free (effective 2010); ◆ Supplement to: Physics Today. ISSN 0031-9228.
Indexed: GeoRef.
—Linda Hall.
Published by: American Institute of Physics, 1 Physics Ellipse, College Park, MD 20740. TEL 301-209-3100, FAX 301-209-0843, aipinfo@aip.org.

530 USA ISSN 1048-1338
QC9.U5
AMERICAN INSTITUTE OF PHYSICS. HISTORY NEWSLETTER. Variant title: Center for History of Physics Newsletter. Text in English. 1964. s-a. free (effective 2011). adv. bibl. cum.index. back issues avail. **Document type:** *Newsletter, Academic/Scholarly.* **Description:** Acts scholarly publication for historians of science, archivists, physicists.
Former titles (until 1988): American Institute of Physics. Center for History of Physics. Newsletter (0148-5857); (until 1972): American Institute of Physics. Center for History and Philosophy of Physics. Newsletter (0008-9060); (until 1966): American Institute of Physics. Newsletter (0569-5708)
Related titles: Online - full text ed.
Indexed: GeoRef, SpeleolAb.
—INIST, Linda Hall. **CCC.**
Published by: American Institute of Physics, 1 Physics Ellipse, College Park, MD 20740. TEL 301-209-3100, FAX 301-209-0843, aipinfo@aip.org, http://www.aip.org. Ed. Gregory A Good. **Subscr. to:** PO Box 503284, St Louis, MO 63150. TEL 516-576-2270, 800-344-6902, FAX 516-349-9704, subs@aip.org.

530.071 USA ISSN 0002-9505
QC1 CODEN: AJPIAS
➤ **AMERICAN JOURNAL OF PHYSICS.** Abbreviated title: A J P. Text in English. 1933. m. USD 682 domestic to institutions; USD 717 foreign to institutions; USD 62, USD 74 per issue to institutions; free to members (effective 2010). adv. bk.rev. illus.; bibl. cum.index: vols.1-20 (1933-1952), vols.21-30 (1953-1963), vols.31-40 (1963-1972), (1983-1992). back issues avail.; reprints avail. **Document type:** *Journal, Academic/Scholarly.* **Description:** Features articles devoted to the educational and cultural aspects of physics.
Formerly (until 1940): American Physics Teacher (0096-0322)
Related titles: Microform ed.; Online - full text ed.
Indexed: A01, A02, A03, A05, A08, A20, A22, A23, A24, A25, A26, ABIPC, AS&TA, AS&TI, ASCA, AcoustA, B04, B13, BRD, C10, CA, CCMJ, CIN, CPI, Cadscan, ChemAb, ChemTitl, CurCont, E03, E06, E07, E08, G01, G03, G08, GPAA, GSA, GSI, HECAB, I05, IBR, IBZ, INIS AtomInd, ISR, Inspec, LeadAb, MLA-IB, MSN, MathR, P02, P10, P13, P26, P30, P48, P52, P53, P54, P56, PQC, PhilInd, PhysBer, RILM, RefZh, S01, S08, S09, S10, SCI, SCOPUS, SPINweb, T02, W01, W02, W03, W07, Z02, Zincscan.
—BLDSC (0833.000000), AskIEEE, CASDDS, IE, Infotrieve, Ingenta, INIST, Linda Hall. **CCC.**
Published by: American Association of Physics Teachers, One Physics Ellipse, College Park, MD 20740. TEL 301-209-3300, FAX 301-209-0845, webmaster@aapt.org, http://www.aapt.org. Ed. Jan Tobochnik. adv.: B&W page USD 1,016, color page USD 1,820; trim 8.25 x 11. Circ: 7,300. **Subscr. to:** American Institute of Physics, PO Box 503284, St Louis, MO 63150. TEL 800-344-6902, subs@aip.org.

530 USA ISSN 0003-0503
QC1 CODEN: BAPSA6
AMERICAN PHYSICAL SOCIETY. BULLETIN. Text in English. 1956. irreg. abstr. index. **Document type:** *Bulletin, Academic/Scholarly.*
Related titles: Microfilm ed.; Online - full text ed.
Indexed: A20, A22, A28, APA, BrCerAb, C&ISA, CA/WCA, CIA, CerAb, ChemAb, CivEngAb, CorrAb, CurPA, E&CAJ, E11, EEA, EMA, H15, INIS AtomInd, M&TEA, M09, MBF, METADEX, PhysBer, SolStAb, T04, WAA.
—BLDSC (2391.000000), IE, Infotrieve, Ingenta, INIST, Linda Hall. **CCC.**
Published by: American Physical Society, One Physics Ellipse, College Park, MD 20740. TEL 301-209-3200, FAX 301-209-0865. **Subscr. to:** American Institute of Physics, PO Box 503284, St Louis, MO 63150. TEL 800-344-6902, subs@aip.org, http://librarians.aip.org.

530 USA ISSN 1088-0348
QC1
AMERICAN PHYSICAL SOCIETY. MEMBERSHIP DIRECTORY. Text in English. 199?. biennial. **Document type:** *Directory, Consumer.*
—Linda Hall.
Published by: American Physical Society, One Physics Ellipse, College Park, MD 20740. TEL 301-209-3200, FAX 301-209-0865.

530 ROM ISSN 0254-8895
QC1
ANALELE UNIVERSITATII BUCURESTI. FIZICA. Text and summaries in Multiple languages. 1969. a.
Supersedes in part (1974-1976): Analele Universitatii Bucuresti. Stiintele Naturii (0254-8887); Which was formed by the merger of (1969-1973): Analele Universitatii Bucuresti. Chimie (0068-3140); (1969-1973): Analele Universitatii Bucuresti. Biologie Animala (0068-3124); (1969-1973): Analele Universitatii Bucuresti. Biologie Vegetala (0068-3132); (1969-1973): Analele Universitatii Bucuresti. Geografie (0068-3191); (1969-1973): Analele Universitatii Bucuresti. Geologie (0068-3183); (1969-1973): Analele Universitatii Bucuresti. Fizica (0068-3108); (1969-1973): Analele Universitatii Bucuresti. Matematica - Mecanica (0068-3272)
Indexed: CIN, ChemAb, ChemTitl, Inspec.
—BLDSC (0869.410000), AskIEEE, INIST, Linda Hall.
Published by: Universitatea din Bucuresti, Bd. Gh. Gheorghiu-Dej 64, Bucharest, Romania.

▼ **ANALYSIS AND MATHEMATICAL PHYSICS.** *see* MATHEMATICS

530 DEU ISSN 1616-3427
ANGEWANDTE FESTKOERPERPHYSIK. Text in German. 2000. irreg., latest vol.2, 2001. price varies. **Document type:** *Monographic series, Academic/Scholarly.*
Published by: Bochumer Universitaetsverlag GmbH, Querenburger Hoehe 281, Bochum, 44801, Germany. TEL 49-234-9719780, FAX 49-234-9719786, bou@bou.de, http://bou.de.

530 DEU ISSN 0003-3804
QC1 CODEN: ANPYA2
➤ **ANNALEN DER PHYSIK.** Text in English. 1790. 10/yr. GBP 615 in United Kingdom to institutions; EUR 987 in Europe to institutions; USD 1,205 elsewhere to institutions; GBP 708 combined subscription in United Kingdom to institutions (print & online eds.); EUR 1,136 combined subscription in Europe to institutions (print & online eds.); USD 1,386 combined subscription elsewhere to institutions (print & online eds.) (effective 2011). charts; illus. index. reprint service avail. from PSC. **Document type:** *Journal, Academic/Scholarly.* **Description:** Offers a forum covering the entire field of experimental, computational, applied, and theoretical physics.
Former titles (until 1799): Neues Journal der Physik (0369-4542); (until 1795): Journal der Physik (0863-6516)
Related titles: Online - full text ed.: ISSN 1521-3889. GBP 615 in United Kingdom to institutions; EUR 987 in Europe to institutions; USD 1,205 elsewhere to institutions (effective 2011).
Indexed: A20, A22, ASCA, CCMJ, CIN, CPEI, Cadscan, ChemAb, ChemTitl, CurCont, EngInd, GeoRef, IBR, IBZ, INIS AtomInd, ISR, Inspec, LeadAb, MSN, MathR, P30, RefZh, SCI, SCOPUS, SpeleolAb, TM, W07, Z02, Zincscan.
—BLDSC (0912.000000), AskIEEE, CASDDS, IE, Infotrieve, Ingenta, INIST, Linda Hall. **CCC.**
Published by: Wiley - V C H Verlag GmbH & Co. KGaA (Subsidiary of: John Wiley & Sons, Inc.), Postfach 101161, Weinheim, 69451, Germany. TEL 49-6201-606400, FAX 49-6201-606184, subservice@wiley-vch.de. Ed. Ulrich Eckern. R&P Claudia Rutz.

530 CHE ISSN 1424-0637
QC1 CODEN: AHPJFM
➤ **ANNALES HENRI POINCARE.** Text in English, French, German, Italian. 2000. 8/yr. EUR 898, USD 1,056 combined subscription to institutions (print & online eds.) (effective 2012). adv. bk.rev. charts; illus.; pat. index. back issues avail.; reprint service avail. from PSC. **Document type:** *Journal, Academic/Scholarly.* **Description:** Aims to serve the international scientific community in theoretical and mathematical physics by collecting and publishing original research papers.
Formed by the merger of (1928-2000): Helvetica Physica Acta (0018-0238); (1983-2000): Institut Henri Poincare. Annales: Physique Theorique (0246-0211); Which was formerly: Institut Henri Poincare. Annales. Section A: Physique Theorique (0020-2339); Which superseded in part (1930-1964): Institut Henri Poincare. Annales (0365-320X)
Related titles: Microfilm ed.: (from PMC, PQC); Online - full text ed.: ISSN 1424-0661 (from IngentaConnect).
Indexed: A01, A03, A08, A22, A26, ASCA, CA, CCMJ, CIN, CMCI, ChemAb, ChemTitl, CurCont, E01, GeoRef, ISR, Inspec, MSN, MathR, PhysBer, RefZh, SCI, SCOPUS, ST&MA, SpeleolAb, T02, W07, Z02.
—BLDSC (0917.550000), AskIEEE, CASDDS, IE, Infotrieve, Ingenta, INIST, Linda Hall. **CCC.**
Published by: (Schweizerische Physikalische Gesellschaft), Birkhaeuser Verlag AG (Subsidiary of: Springer Science+Business Media), Viaduktstr 42, Postfach 133, Basel, 4051, Switzerland. TEL 41-61-2050707, FAX 41-61-2050799, info@birkhauser.ch, http://www.birkhauser.ch/journals. Ed. Vincent Rivasseau. **Subscr. in the Americas to:** Springer New York LLC, Journal Fulfillment, PO Box 2485, Secaucus, NJ 07096. TEL 201-348-4033, 800-777-4643, FAX 201-348-4505, journals@birkhauser.com; **Subscr. to:** Springer Distribution Center, Kundenservice Zeitschriften, Haberstr 7, Heidelberg 69126, Germany. TEL 49-6221-3454303, FAX 49-6221-3454229, birkhauser@springer.de.

530 POL ISSN 0137-6861
QC1 CODEN: AUMADZ
➤ **ANNALES UNIVERSITATIS MARIAE CURIE-SKLODOWSKA. SECTIO AAA. PHYSICA.** Text in English, French, Polish; Summaries in English, Polish. 1978. irreg., latest vol.58, 2011. price varies. **Document type:** *Journal, Academic/Scholarly.*
Supersedes in part (in 1979): Annales Universitatis Mariae Curie-Sklodowska. Section AA. Physica et Chemica (0137-1819)
Related titles: Online - full text ed.
Indexed: CIN, ChemAb, ChemTitl, GeoRef, INIS AtomInd.
—CASDDS, INIST, Linda Hall.
Published by: (Uniwersytet Marii Curie-Sklodowskiej w Lublinie, Instytut Fizyki), Wydawnictwo Uniwersytetu Marii Curie-Sklodowskiej w Lublinie, Pl Marii Curie-Sklodowskiej 5, Lublin, 20031, Poland. TEL 48-81-5375304, press@ramzes.umcs.lublin.pl, http://www.press.umcs.lublin.pl. Ed. Karol I Wysokinski. Circ: 575.

530 USA ISSN 0003-4916
QC1 CODEN: APNYA6
➤ **ANNALS OF PHYSICS.** Text in English. 1957. m. EUR 6,419 in Europe to institutions; JPY 670,100 in Japan to institutions; USD 5,012 elsewhere to institutions (effective 2012). adv. charts; illus. index. back issues avail.; reprints avail. **Document type:** *Journal, Academic/Scholarly.* **Description:** Presents original work in all areas of basic physics research. Features papers on particular topics spanning theory, methodology, and applications.
Related titles: Online - full text ed.: ISSN 1096-035X (from IngentaConnect, ScienceDirect).
Indexed: A01, A03, A08, A22, A26, ASCA, C33, CA, CCMJ, CIN, Cadscan, ChemAb, ChemTitl, CurCont, E01, I05, IBR, IBZ, INIS AtomInd, ISR, Inspec, LeadAb, MSN, MathR, P10, P48, P52, P53, P54, P56, PQC, RefZh, S01, S10, SCI, SCOPUS, T02, W07, Z02, Zincscan.
—BLDSC (1043.500000), AskIEEE, CASDDS, IE, Infotrieve, Ingenta, INIST, Linda Hall. **CCC.**
Published by: Academic Press (Subsidiary of: Elsevier Science & Technology), 3251 Riverport Ln, Maryland Heights, MO 63043. TEL 314-447-8010, FAX 314-447-8030, JournalCustomerService-usa@elsevier.com, http://www.elsevierdirect.com/imprint.jsp?iid=5. Ed. Frank Wilczek.

➤ **ANNUAL REVIEW OF ASTRONOMY AND ASTROPHYSICS.** *see* ASTRONOMY

530 USA ISSN 1947-5454
QC173.45
▼ ➤ **ANNUAL REVIEW OF CONDENSED MATTER PHYSICS.** Text in English. 2010 (Jan.). a. USD 272 combined subscription per issue to institutions (print & online eds.); USD 227 per issue to institutions (print or online ed.) (effective 2012). back issues avail. **Document type:** *Journal, Academic/Scholarly.* **Description:** Features yearly synthesis and reviews of topics in condensed matter physics.
Related titles: Online - full text ed.: ISSN 1947-5462. 2010 (Jan.).
Indexed: SCI, W07.
—CCC.
Published by: Annual Reviews, PO Box 10139, Palo Alto, CA 94303. TEL 650-493-4400, FAX 650-424-0910, 800-523-8635, service@annualreviews.org. Eds. James S Langer TEL 805-893-7597, Samuel Gubins.

530 621 USA ISSN 1049-0787
QA901 CODEN: ARHTED
➤ **ANNUAL REVIEW OF HEAT TRANSFER.** Text in English. 1987. a. USD 235 per issue to individuals; USD 1,200 per issue to institutions (effective 2010). adv. back issues avail.; reprints avail. **Document type:** *Proceedings, Academic/Scholarly.* **Description:** Covers areas such as radiation and combustion, micro/nanoscale heat transfer, phase change and heat pipes, porous media, materials processing and laser materials interactions, and energy systems.
Formerly (until 1990): Annual Review of Numerical Fluid Mechanics and Heat Transfer (0892-6883)
Indexed: Z02.
—BLDSC (1522.565680), CASDDS, Linda Hall. **CCC.**
Published by: Begell House Inc., 50 Cross Hwy, Redding, CT 06896. TEL 203-938-1300, FAX 203-938-1304, orders@begellhouse.com. Eds. Gang Chen, Vish Prasad, Yogesh Jaluria TEL 732-445-2248.

531.14 USA
ANNUAL SUMMARY OF PROGRESS IN GRAVITATION SCIENCES. Text in English. 1974. a. membership. adv. bk.rev. abstr.; bibl.; charts; illus.; pat.; stat. **Document type:** *Corporate.*
Published by: (Ensanian Physicochemical Institute), Minas Ensanian Corporation, PO Box 98, Eldred, PA 16731. TEL 814-225-3296. Ed. Minas Ensanian. Circ: 100 (controlled).

530 AUT ISSN 0937-9347
QC762 CODEN: APMREI
➤ **APPLIED MAGNETIC RESONANCE.** Text in English. 1990. 8/yr. EUR 1,832, USD 2,197 combined subscription to institutions (print & online eds.) (effective 2012). adv. abstr. back issues avail.; reprint service avail. from PSC. **Document type:** *Journal, Academic/Scholarly.* **Description:** Provides an international forum for the application of magnetic resonance in physics, chemistry, biology, medicine, geochemistry, ecology, engineering, and related fields. Emphasizes new applications of the technique, and new experimental methods.
Related titles: Online - full text ed.: ISSN 1613-7507 (from IngentaConnect).
Indexed: A22, A26, ASCA, CCI, CIN, CPEI, ChemAb, ChemTitl, CurCont, E01, GeoRef, ISR, Inspec, P30, RefZh, SCI, SCOPUS, SpeleolAb, VITIS, W07.
—BLDSC (1573.500000), AskIEEE, CASDDS, IE, Infotrieve, Ingenta, Linda Hall. **CCC.**
Published by: Springer Wien (Subsidiary of: Springer Science+Business Media), Sachsenplatz 4-6, Vienna, W 1201, Austria. TEL 43-1-33024150, FAX 43-1-3302426, journals@springer.at, http://www.springer.at. Ed. Kev M Salikhov. Adv. contact Irene Hofmann. B&W page EUR 1,290; 170 x 230. Circ: 1,000 (paid). **Subscr. in the Americas to:** Springer New York LLC, Journal Fulfillment, PO Box 2485, Secaucus, NJ 07096. TEL 800-777-4643, 201-348-4033, FAX 201-348-4505, journals-ny@springer.com, http://www.springer.com; **Subscr. to:** Springer Distribution Center, Kundenservice Zeitschriften, Haberstr 7, Heidelberg 69126, Germany. TEL 49-6221-3454303, FAX 49-6221-3454229, subscriptions@springer.com.

530 621.3 DEU ISSN 2190-5509
▼ ➤ **APPLIED NANOSCIENCE.** Text in English. 2011. free (effective 2011). **Document type:** *Journal, Academic/Scholarly.* **Description:** Publishes research on state of the art nanoscience and the application of emerging nanotechnologies.
Related titles: Online - full text ed.: ISSN 2190-5517. 2011.
Published by: SpringerOpen (Subsidiary of: Springer Science+Business Media), Tiergartenstr 17, Heidelberg, 69121, Germany. info@springeropen.com, http://www.springeropen.com.

530 USA ISSN 1080-9198
CODEN: APPYEK
APPLIED PHYSICS. Text in English. 1993. irreg., latest 2003. price varies. back issues avail. **Document type:** *Monographic series, Trade.*
Formerly (until 1994): Applied Physics Series
—BLDSC (1576.335000), CASDDS. **CCC.**
Published by: C R C Press, LLC (Subsidiary of: Taylor & Francis Group), 6000 Broken Sound Pky, NW, Ste 300, Boca Raton, FL 33487. TEL 800-272-7737, FAX 800-374-3401, orders@crcpress.com.

621 530 DEU ISSN 0947-8396
QC1 CODEN: APAMFC
➤ **APPLIED PHYSICS A;** materials science & processing. Text in English. 1973. 16/yr. EUR 5,418, USD 6,295 combined subscription to institutions (print & online eds.) (effective 2012). adv. abstr.; charts; illus. index. reprint service avail. from PSC. **Document type:** *Journal, Academic/Scholarly.* **Description:** Covers primarily the condensed state, including surface science and engineering.
Former titles: Applied Physics A: Solids and Surfaces (0721-7250); Supersedes in part (in 1981): Applied Physics (0340-3793); Which superseded: Zeitschrift fuer Angewandte Physik (0044-2283)
Related titles: Microform ed.: (from PQC); Online - full text ed.: ISSN 1432-0630 (from IngentaConnect).
Indexed: A01, A02, A03, A08, A20, A22, A26, ASCA, C24, C33, CA, CIN, CISA, CPEI, Cadscan, ChemAb, ChemTitl, CurCont, E01, EngInd, FR, IBR, IBZ, INIS AtomInd, ISR, ISRS, Inspec, LeadAb, MSCI, P30, PhotoAb, PhysBer, RefZh, S01, SCI, SCOPUS, T02, TM, W07, Zincscan.
—BLDSC (1576.360000), AskIEEE, CASDDS, IE, Infotrieve, Ingenta, INIST, Linda Hall. **CCC.**
Published by: (Deutsche Physikalische Gesellschaft), Springer (Subsidiary of: Springer Science+Business Media), Tiergartenstr 17, Heidelberg, 69121, Germany. TEL 49-6221-4870, FAX 49-6221-345229. Ed. Michael Stuke. Adv. contact Stephan Kroeck TEL 49-30-827875739. **Subscr. in the Americas to:** Springer New York LLC, Journal Fulfillment, PO Box 2485, Secaucus, NJ 07096. TEL 201-348-4033, 800-777-4643, FAX 201-348-4505, journals-ny@springer.com, http://www.springer.com; **Subscr. to:** Springer Distribution Center, Kundenservice Zeitschriften, Haberstr 7, Heidelberg 69126, Germany. TEL 49-6221-3454303, FAX 49-6221-3454229, subscriptions@springer.com.

621 530 DEU ISSN 0946-2171
QC1 CODEN: APBOEM
➤ **APPLIED PHYSICS B;** lasers and optics. Text in English. 16/yr. EUR 5,269, USD 6,122 combined subscription to institutions (print & online eds.) (effective 2012). adv. back issues avail.; reprint service avail. from PSC. **Document type:** *Journal, Academic/Scholarly.*
Formerly: Applied Physics. B: Photophysics and Laser Chemistry (0721-7269); Supersedes in part (in 1981): Applied Physics (0340-3793)
Related titles: Microform ed.: (from PQC); Online - full text ed.: ISSN 1432-0649 (from IngentaConnect).
Indexed: A01, A02, A03, A08, A20, A22, A26, ASCA, BPRC&P, C&ISA, C24, C33, CA, CIN, CPEI, ChemAb, ChemTitl, CurCont, E&CAJ, E01, EngInd, IBR, IBZ, ISMEC, ISR, Inspec, MSCI, P30, PhotoAb, S01, SCI, SCOPUS, SolStAb, T02, TM, VITIS, W07.
—BLDSC (1576.375000), AskIEEE, CASDDS, IE, Infotrieve, Ingenta, INIST, Linda Hall. **CCC.**

P

Published by: (Deutsche Physikalische Gesellschaft), Springer (Subsidiary of: Springer Science+Business Media), Tiergartenstr 17, Heidelberg, 69121, Germany. TEL 49-6221-4870, FAX 49-6221-345229. Ed. Frank Traeger. Adv. contact Stephan Kroeck TEL 49-30-827875739. **Subscr. in the Americas to:** Springer New York LLC, Journal Fulfillment, PO Box 2485, Secaucus, NJ 07096. TEL 201-348-4033, 800-777-4643, FAX 201-348-4505, journals-ny@springer.com, http://www.springer.com; **Subscr. to:** Springer Distribution Center, Kundenservice Zeitschriften, Haberstr 7, Heidelberg 69126, Germany. TEL 49-6221-3454303, FAX 49-6221-3454229, subscriptions@springer.com.

530 JPN ISSN 1882-0778
CODEN: APEPC4

APPLIED PHYSICS EXPRESS. Text in English. 1962. m. JPY 180,000 combined subscription includes Japanese Journal of Applied Physics (print & online eds.) (effective 2008). **Description:** Provides quick and up-to-date and concise reports on new findings in applied physics.
Supersedes (in 2008): Japanese Journal of Applied Physics. Part 2, Letters & Express Lettres (0021-4922)
Related titles: Online - full text ed.: ISSN 1882-0786.
Indexed: C33, CPEI, CurCont, MSCI, RefZh, SCI, SCOPUS, W07.
—BLDSC (1576.392000), IE, INIST, Linda Hall.
Published by: (Japan Society of Applied Physics/Oyo Butsuri Gakkai), Institute of Pure and Applied Physics, da Vinci Yushima 5F, 2-31-22 Yushima, Bunkyo-ku, Tokyo, 113-0034, Japan. TEL 81-3-58443291, FAX 81-3-58443290, subscription@ipap.jp, http://www.ipap.jp.

621 530 USA ISSN 0003-6951
QC1 CODEN: APPLAB

➤ **APPLIED PHYSICS LETTERS.** Abbreviated title: A P L. Text in English. 1962. w. price varies based on the number of users. adv. charts; illus. index, cum.index: 1977-1981, 1982-1986. back issues avail.; reprints avail. **Document type:** *Journal, Academic/Scholarly.* **Description:** Concise up to date reports of new findings in applied physics. Includes coverage of experimental and theoretical research in condensed matter, semiconductors, superconductivity, optics, solid state lasers, nonlinear optics, surfaces, thin films, materials and device properties.
Related titles: CD-ROM ed.: ISSN 1520-8842; Microfiche ed.; Online - full text ed.: ISSN 1077-3118.
Indexed: A01, A02, A03, A05, A08, A22, AS&TA, AS&TI, ASCA, AcoustA, B04, B07, B10, C10, C13, C33, CA, CIN, CPEI, CPI, Cadscan, ChemAb, ChemTitl, CurCont, EngInd, GPAA, GeoRef, IBR, IBZ, INIS AtomInd, ISR, Inspec, LeadAb, MSCI, P30, PhotoAb, PhysBer, RefZh, S01, SCI, SCOPUS, SPINweb, SpeleolAb, T02, W07, Zincscan.
—BLDSC (1576.400000), AskIEEE, CASDDS, IE, Infotrieve, Ingenta, INIST, Linda Hall. **CCC.**
Published by: American Institute of Physics, 1 Physics Ellipse, College Park, MD 20740. TEL 301-209-3100, aipinfo@aip.org, http://www.aip.org. Ed. Nghi Q Lam TEL 630-252-4200. Adv. contact Mary Ellen Mormile TEL 516-576-2461. **Subscr. to:** PO Box 503284, St Louis, MO 63150. TEL 516-576-2270, 800-344-6902, FAX 516-349-9704, subs@aip.org, http://librarians.aip.org.

530 CAN ISSN 1916-9639

▼ ➤ **APPLIED PHYSICS RESEARCH.** Text in English. 2009. s-a. software rev. abstr.; bibl. back issues avail. **Document type:** *Journal, Academic/Scholarly.* **Description:** Covers applied physics, theoretical physics, particle physics and nuclear physics, atomic and molecular physics, plasma physics, condensed matter physics, acoustics, optics, radiophysics, electromagnetism, thermodynamics, quantum electronics, high energy physics, environmental physics, mechanics and engineering.
Related titles: Online - full text ed.: free (effective 2011).
Indexed: A01, A26, CPerI, I05, P10, P48, P51, P52, P53, P54, PQC, T02.
Published by: Canadian Center of Science and Education, 4915 Bathurst St, Unit 209-309, Toronto, ON M2R 1X9, Canada. TEL 416-208-4027, FAX 416-208-4028, info@ccsenet.org, http://www.ccsenet.org. Ed. Lily Green. **Subscr. to:** JournalBuy.com, Rm. 666, 118 Chongqing S. Rd., Qingdao 266032, China. TEL 86-532-86069259, FAX 86-532-95105198 ext 81082, order@journalbuy.com, http://www.journalbuy.com/.

621 USA ISSN 1931-9401
QC1

➤ **APPLIED PHYSICS REVIEWS.** Text in English. 2007. a. price varies based on the number of users. **Document type:** *Journal, Academic/Scholarly.* **Description:** Carries review articles of important and current topics of experimental or theoretical research in applied physics and applications of physics to other branches of science and engineering.
Media: Online - full text.
—CCC.
Published by: American Institute of Physics, 1 Physics Ellipse, College Park, MD 20740. TEL 301-209-3100, FAX 301-209-0843, aipinfo@aip.org, http://www.aip.org. Ed. John M Poate TEL 303-384-2375. **Subscr. to:** PO Box 503284, St Louis, MO 63150. TEL 516-576-2270, 800-344-6902, FAX 516-349-9704, subs@aip.org.

➤ **ARAB GULF JOURNAL OF SCIENTIFIC RESEARCH.** *see* SCIENCES: COMPREHENSIVE WORKS

➤ **ARKHIMEDES.** *see* MATHEMATICS

530 ARM ISSN 1829-1171
QC1

➤ **ARMENIAN JOURNAL OF PHYSICS.** Text in English. 2008. irreg. free (effective 2011). **Document type:** *Journal, Academic/Scholarly.*
Media: Online - full text.
Indexed: A01.
Published by: National Academy of Sciences of the Republic of Armenia, 24, Marshall Baghramian Ave, Yerevan, 375019, Armenia. TEL 374-10-527031, FAX 374-10-569281, academy@sci.am, http://www.sci.am.

530 ARG ISSN 0327-358X

ASOCIACION FISICA DE ARGENTINA. ANALES. Text in Spanish. 1990. a. **Document type:** *Proceedings, Academic/Scholarly.*
Published by: Asociacion Fisica Argentina, C.C. 62, La Plata, 1900, Argentina. TEL 54-221-4247201, FAX 54-221-4236335, secretaria@fisica.org.ar, http://www.fisica.org.ar/. Ed. Roberto Gratton.

530 EGY ISSN 1687-4900

ASSIUT UNIVERSITY JOURNAL OF PHYSICS. Text in English. 1988. s-a. free (effective 2004). **Document type:** *Journal, Academic/Scholarly.*
Formerly (until 2005): Assuit University. Faculty of Science. Bulletin: A. Physics (1110-0958); Supersedes in part (in 1988): Assiut University. Faculty of Science. Bulletin: A. Physics and Mathematics (1010-268X); Which was formerly (until 1982): Assiut University. Faculty of Science. Bulletin. Section A: Natural Science (0253-1143); Which superseded in part (in 1979): Assiut University. Bulletin of Science and Technology (0379-3389)
Indexed: CCMJ, GeoRef, MSN, MathR, Z02.
—INIST.
Published by: Assiut University, Faculty of Science, PO Box 71516, Assiut, Egypt. TEL 20-88-411376, FAX 20-88-342708, science@aun.edu.eg, http://www.aun.eun.eg. Ed. Dr. Hassan Mohamed Hassan El-Hawary.

530 PRT ISSN 1646-804X

ASSOCIATION EURATOM - I S T. ANNUAL REPORT. (Instituto Superior Tecnico) Text in English. 2002. a. **Document type:** *Report, Trade.*
Published by: Universidade Tecnica de Lisboa, Instituto Superior Tecnico (I S T), Av Rovisco Pais 1, Lisbon, 1049-001, Portugal. TEL 351-218-417000, FAX 351-218-499242, http://www.ist.utl.pt.

ASTROFIZIKA. *see* ASTRONOMY

ASTRONOMY & ASTROPHYSICS. *see* ASTRONOMY

THE ASTRONOMY AND ASTROPHYSICS REVIEW. *see* ASTRONOMY

530 SGP ISSN 2010-0868

ASTROPARTICLE, PARTICLE, SPACE PHYSICS, RADIATION INTERACTION, DETECTORS AND MEDICAL PHYSICS APPLICATIONS. Text in English. 2002. irreg., latest vol.5, 2010. price varies. back issues avail. **Document type:** *Monographic series, Academic/Scholarly.* **Description:** Provides coverage of investigations, physics requirements, survey of technologies and performance of detectors employed or to be employed in fundamental and particle physics experiments at accelerators, underground laboratories, submarine facilities, and in space environment.
Published by: World Scientific Publishing Co. Pte. Ltd., 5 Toh Tuck Link, Singapore, 596224, Singapore. TEL 65-6466-5775, FAX 65-6467-7667, wspc@wspc.com.sg, http://www.worldscientific.com. Eds. Claude Leroy, Pier-Giorgio Rancoita. **Dist. by:** World Scientific Publishing Co., Inc., 27 Warren St, Ste 401-402, Hackensack, NJ 07601. TEL 201-487-9655, 800-227-7562, FAX 201-487-9656, 888-977-2665, wspc@wspc.com; World Scientific Publishing Ltd., 57 Shelton St, London WC2H 9HE, United Kingdom. TEL 44-207-8360888, FAX 44-207-8362020, sales@wspc.co.uk.

ASTROPARTICLE PHYSICS. *see* ASTRONOMY

ASTROPHYSICAL BULLETIN. *see* ASTRONOMY

THE ASTROPHYSICAL JOURNAL; an international review of astronomy and astronomical physics. *see* ASTRONOMY

THE ASTROPHYSICAL JOURNAL SUPPLEMENT SERIES. *see* ASTRONOMY

ASTROPHYSICS. *see* ASTRONOMY

ASTROPHYSICS AND SPACE SCIENCE; an international journal of astronomy, astrophysics and space science. *see* ASTRONOMY

ASTROPHYSICS AND SPACE SCIENCE LIBRARY; a series of books on the developments of space science and of general astronomy and astrophysics published in connection with the journal Space Science Reviews. *see* ASTRONOMY

ASTROPHYSICS AND SPACE SCIENCES TRANSACTIONS (ONLINE). *see* ASTRONOMY

ASTROPHYSICS AND SPACE SCIENCES TRANSACTIONS (PRINT). *see* ASTRONOMY

ATELIERS. *see* CHILDREN AND YOUTH—For

530 CAN ISSN 1207-0203

L'ATTRACTEUR. Text in French. 1995. s-a. **Description:** Presents articles, reviews and news on physics.
Media: Online - full text.
Published by: Universite de Sherbrooke, Departement de Physique, 2500 boul Universite, Sherbrooke, PQ J1K 2R1, Canada. TEL 819-821-7055, FAX 819-821-8046.

AUGSBURGER SCHRIFTEN ZUR MATHEMATIK, PHYSIK UND INFORMATIK. *see* MATHEMATICS

AUSTRALASIAN PHYSICAL & ENGINEERING SCIENCES IN MEDICINE. *see* MEDICAL SCIENCES

530 AUS ISSN 0084-7518

AUSTRALIAN NATIONAL UNIVERSITY, CANBERRA. RESEARCH SCHOOL OF PHYSICAL SCIENCES AND ENGINEERING. RESEARCH PAPER. Text in English. irreg. AUD 10 per issue (effective 1999). **Document type:** *Monographic series, Academic/Scholarly.*
Formerly: Australian National University, Canberra. Research School of Physical Sciences. Research Paper
Indexed: AESIS.
Published by: Australian National University, Research School of Physical Sciences and Engineering, Bldg 60, ANU Campus, Canberra, ACT 0200, Australia. TEL 61-2-61250361, FAX 61-2-61252966.

530 AUS

AUSTRALIAN NATIONAL UNIVERSITY. RESEARCH SCHOOL OF PHYSICAL SCIENCES AND ENGINEERING. ANNUAL REPORT (ONLINE). Text in English. 1972. a. free. back issues avail. **Document type:** *Report, Academic/Scholarly.* **Description:** Provides comprehensive record of the School's activities for the year.
Former titles: Australian National University. Research School of Physical Sciences and Engineering. Annual Report (Print); Australian National University. Research School of Physical Sciences. Annual Report (0155-624X)
Media: Online - full content.
Published by: Australian National University, Research School of Physical Sciences and Engineering, Bldg 60, ANU Campus, Canberra, ACT 0200, Australia. TEL 61-2-61252361, FAX 61-2-61252966. Circ: 600.

530 AUS ISSN 1837-5375
QC1 CODEN: ANZPET

AUSTRALIAN PHYSICS. Text in English. 1964. bi-m. free w/ membership. adv. bk.rev. charts; illus. **Document type:** *Journal, Academic/Scholarly.* **Description:** Information on physics for the professional for research and teaching purposes.
Former titles (until 2005): The Physicist (1835-212X); (until 1999): The Australian & New Zealand Physicist (1036-3831); (until 1991): Australian Physicist (0004-9972)
Indexed: AEI, ASI, CPEI, ChemAb, EngInd, Inspec, SCOPUS.
—AskIEEE, CASDDS, Ingenta, Linda Hall.
Published by: Australian Institute of Physics, 1/21 Vale St, North Melbourne, VIC 3051, Australia. TEL 61-3-9326 6669, FAX 61-3-9328 2670, physics@raci.org.au. Ed. John Daicopoulos.

AUSZUEGE AUS DEN EUROPAEISCHEN PATENTANMELDUNGEN. TEIL 2A. PHYSIK, OPTIK, AKUSTIK, FEINMECHANIK/EXTRACTS FROM EUROPEAN PATENT APPLICATIONS. PART 2A. PHYSICS, PRECISION ENGINEERING, OPTICS, ACOUSTICS. *see* PATENTS, TRADEMARKS AND COPYRIGHTS—Abstracting, Bibliographies, Statistics

540 ARG ISSN 1515-1565

AVANCES EN ANALISIS POR TECNICAS DE RAYOS X. Text in Spanish. 1987. biennial. ARS 20 newsstand/cover (effective 2005). **Document type:** *Monographic series, Academic/Scholarly.*
Published by: Universidad Nacional de Cordoba, Facultad de Matematicas, Astronomia y Fisica, Ciudad Universitaria, Medina Allende y Haya de la Torre, Cordoba, 5000, Argentina. TEL 54-351-4334051, FAX 54-351-4334054, http://www.famaf.unc.edu.ar/. Ed. Jorge Trincavelli. Circ: 110.

530 510 520 EGY ISSN 2090-1623

AL-AZHAR BULLETIN OF SCIENCE. BASIC SCIENCE SECTOR. PHYSICS, MATHEMATICS AND ASTRONOMY. Text in English. 1990. s-a. **Document type:** *Bulletin, Academic/Scholarly.*
Supersedes in part (in 2007): Al- Azhar Bulletin of Science (1110-2535)
Published by: Al-Azhar University, Faculty of Science, Al-Nasr Rd, Nasr City, Cairo, Egypt. TEL 20-2-4028752.

B W K; das Energie-Fachmagazin. (Brennstoff, Waerme, Kraft) *see* ENERGY

530 GRC ISSN 1301-8329

BALKAN PHYSICS LETTERS. Text in English. 4/yr.
Indexed: Inspec.
Published by: (Bogazici Universitesi, Faculty of Economics and Administrative Sciences TUR), Balkan Physical Union, c/o Athan Lambros, Department of Physics, Aristoteles University, Thessaloniki, 54006, Greece. lambros@kelifos.physics.auth.gr. Ed. E Rizaoglu.

BAO PO/BLASTING. *see* ENGINEERING—Chemical Engineering

662.2 CHN ISSN 1001-1455
QD516 CODEN: BAYCE7

BAOZHA YU CHONGJI/EXPLOSION AND SHOCK WAVES. Text in Chinese. 1981. bi-m. CNY 10 per issue (effective 2011). **Document type:** *Journal, Academic/Scholarly.*
Related titles: Online - full text ed.
Indexed: A22, CPEI, EngInd, SCOPUS.
—BLDSC (3842.305000), East View, IE, Ingenta.
Published by: (Zhongguo Lixue Xuehui, Sichuan Sheng Lixue Xuehui, Zhongguo Gongcheng Wuli Yanjiuyuan Liuti Wuli Yanjiusuo/China Academy of Engineering Physics, Institute of Fluid Physics), Baozha yu Chongji Bianjibu, 919 Xinxiang 110 Fenxiang, Mianyang, Sichuan 621900, China. TEL 86-816-2486197, FAX 86-816-2282695.

530 621.3 DEU
CODEN: BJNEAH

▼ ➤ **BEILSTEIN JOURNAL OF NANOTECHNOLOGY.** Text in English. 2010. irreg. free (effective 2010). **Document type:** *Journal, Academic/Scholarly.* **Description:** Publishes original articles on all aspects of nanoscience and nanotechnology.
Media: Online - full text.
Indexed: C33.
Published by: Beilstein - Institut zur Foerderung der Chemischen Wissenschaften, Trakehner Str 7/9, Frankfurt am Main, 60487, Germany. TEL 49-69-716732, FAX 49-69-716732, info@beilstein-institut.de, http://www.beilstein-institut.de. Ed. Thomas Schimmel.

➤ **BELORUSSKII GOSUDARSTVENNYI UNIVERSITET. VESTNIK. SERIYA 1. FIZIKA, MATEMATIKA, INFORMATIKA/BELORUSSIAN STATE UNIVERSITY. PROCEEDINGS. SERIES 1. PHYSICS, MATHEMATICS, COMPUTER SCIENCE.** *see* MATHEMATICS

530 DEU ISSN 0945-0793

BERICHTE AUS DER HOCHFREQUENZTECHNIK. Text in German. 1994. irreg., latest 2009. price varies. **Document type:** *Monographic series, Academic/Scholarly.*
Published by: Shaker Verlag GmbH, Kaiserstr 100, Herzogenrath, 52134, Germany. TEL 49-2407-95960, FAX 49-2407-95969, info@shaker.de.

530 DEU ISSN 1864-6379

BERICHTE UEBER VERTEILTE MESSSYSTEME. Text in German. 2007. irreg., latest vol.6, 2009. price varies. **Document type:** *Monographic series, Academic/Scholarly.*
Published by: Shaker Verlag GmbH, Kaiserstr 100, Herzogenrath, 52134, Germany. TEL 49-2407-95960, FAX 49-2407-95969, info@shaker.de, http://www.shaker.de.

530 USA ISSN 1930-9864

THE BEST TEST PREPARATION FOR THE ADVANCED PLACEMENT EXAMINATIONS. A P PHYSICS B & C. (Advanced Placement) Variant title: A P Physics B & C. Text in English. 19??. irreg., latest 2009, 6th ed. USD 18.95 per issue (effective 2009). **Document type:** *Guide, Consumer.* **Description:** Provides comprehensive subject review of every physics B & C topic on the AP exam.
Published by: Research & Education Association, Inc., 61 Ethel Rd W, Piscataway, NJ 08854. TEL 732-819-8880, FAX 732-819-8808, info@rea.com. Ed. S Brehmer.

530 SGP ISSN 2010-2879

▼ **BIENNIAL REVIEWS OF THE THEORY OF MAGNETIZED PLASMAS.** Text in English. 2009. irreg., latest vol.1, 2009. price varies. **Document type:** *Monographic series, Academic/Scholarly.*

Published by: World Scientific Publishing Co. Pte. Ltd., 5 Toh Tuck Link, Singapore, 596224, Singapore. TEL 65-6466-5775, FAX 65-6467-7667, wspc@wspc.com.sg, http://www.worldscientific.com. Eds. Patrick H Diamond, Xavier Garbet, Yanick Sarazin. **Dist. by:** World Scientific Publishing Co., Inc., 27 Warren St, Ste 401-402, Hackensack, NJ 07601. TEL 201-487-9655, 800-227-7562, FAX 201-487-9656, 888-977-2665, wspc@wspc.com; World Scientific Publishing Ltd., 57 Shelton St, London WC2H 9HE, United Kingdom. TEL 44-207-8360888, FAX 44-207-8362020, sales@wspc.co.uk.

538.36 USA ISSN 0192-6020
QH324.9.M2 CODEN: BMGRDB

➤ **BIOLOGICAL MAGNETIC RESONANCE.** Text in English. 1978. irreg., latest vol.29, 2010. price varies. back issues avail. **Document type:** *Monographic series, Academic/Scholarly.*
Indexed: CIN, ChemAb, ChemTitl, P30.
—BLDSC (2076.550000), CASDDS, Ingenta, Linda Hall. **CCC.**
Published by: Springer New York LLC (Subsidiary of: Springer Science+Business Media), 233 Spring St, New York, NY 10013. TEL 212-460-1500, FAX 212-460-1575, service-ny@springer.com.

➤ **BIOMASS BULLETIN.** *see* ENERGY

530 USA ISSN 1932-1058
TP248.13

BIOMICROFLUIDICS. Text in English. 2007 (Jan.). q. price varies based on the number of users. back issues avail. **Document type:** *Journal, Academic/Scholarly.* **Description:** Disseminates novel microfluidic techniques with diagnostic, medical, biological, pharmaceutical, environmental, and chemical applications.
Media: Online - full text.
Indexed: A01, B25, B26, BIOSIS Prev, CA, Inspec, MycolAb, P30, SCI, SCOPUS, T02, W07.
—Linda Hall. **CCC.**
Published by: American Institute of Physics, 1 Physics Ellipse, College Park, MD 20740. TEL 301-209-3100, aipinfo@aip.org, http://www.aip.org. Eds. Hsueh-Chia Chang TEL 574-631-5697, Leslie Y Yeo TEL 61-3-99053834. **Subscr. to:** PO Box 503284, St Louis, MO 63150. TEL 516-576-2270, 800-344-6902, FAX 516-349-9704, subs@aip.org, http://librarians.aip.org.

530 SGP ISSN 1793-0480
QH505

BIOPHYSICAL REVIEWS AND LETTERS. Abbreviated title: B R L. Text in English. 2006 (Jan.). q. SGD 829, USD 513, EUR 402 combined subscription to institutions (print & online eds.) (effective 2012). adv. back issues avail. **Document type:** *Journal, Academic/Scholarly.* **Description:** Features research papers, review articles and brief communications in the field of experimental and theoretical Biophysics.
Related titles: Online - full text ed.: ISSN 1793-7035. SGD 754, USD 466, EUR 365 to institutions (effective 2012).
Indexed: A01, A22, B&BAb, B19, B21, BIOSIS Prev, CA, CTA, ChemoAb, E01, EMBASE, ExcerpMed, MycolAb, NSA, P30, SCOPUS, T02.
—BLDSC (2089.410100), IE.
Published by: World Scientific Publishing Co. Pte. Ltd., 5 Toh Tuck Link, Singapore, 596224, Singapore. TEL 65-6466-5775, FAX 65-6467-7667, wspc@wspc.com.sg, http://www.worldscientific.com. **Dist. by:** World Scientific Publishing Co., Inc., 27 Warren St, Ste 401-402, Hackensack, NJ 07601. TEL 201-487-9655, 800-227-7562, FAX 201-487-9656, 888-977-2665, wspc@wspc.com; World Scientific Publishing Ltd., 57 Shelton St, London WC2H 9HE, United Kingdom. TEL 44-207-8360888, FAX 44-207-8362020, sales@wspc.co.uk.

BIPOLAR - B I C M O S CIRCUITS AND TECHNOLOGY MEETING. PROCEEDINGS. *see* ELECTRONICS

530 SVN ISSN 1580-4992

➤ **BLEJSKE DELAVNICE IZ FIZIKE/BLED WORKSHOPS IN PHYSICS;** bled workshops in physics. Text in Slovenian, English. 1999. s-a. free to members (effective 2006). adv. abstr.; charts. back issues avail. **Document type:** *Journal, Academic/Scholarly.*
Related titles: Online - full content ed.
Published by: Drustvo Matematikov, Fizikov in Astronomov/Society of Mathematicians, Physicists and Astronomers, Jadranska ulica 19, pp 2964, Ljubljana, 1001, Slovenia. TEL 386-1-2512005, 386-1-4232460, FAX 386-1-2517281, tajnik@dmfa.si, http://www.dmfa.si. Ed. Mr. Mitja Rosina. Adv. contact Mr. Vladimir Bensa. Circ: 100.

▼ ➤ **BRAIN AND COSMOS.** *see* MEDICAL SCIENCES—Psychiatry And Neurology

530 USA ISSN 0103-9733
QC1 CODEN: BJPHE6

➤ **BRAZILIAN JOURNAL OF PHYSICS.** Text in English. 1971. q. EUR 171, USD 210 combined subscription to institutions (print & online eds.) (effective 2012). bk.rev. charts. back issues avail. **Document type:** *Journal, Academic/Scholarly.* **Description:** Original research work and review articles in physics.
Formerly (until 1992): Revista Brasileira de Fisica (0374-4922)
Related titles: Online - full text ed.: ISSN 1678-4448.
Indexed: C01, CIN, ChemAb, ChemTitl, CurCont, INIS AtomInd, ISR, Inspec, RefZh, SCI, SCOPUS, W07.
—BLDSC (2277.419550), AskIEEE, CASDDS, IE, Ingenta, INIST, Linda Hall. **CCC.**
Published by: (Sociedade Brasileira de Fisica BRA), Springer New York LLC (Subsidiary of: Springer Science+Business Media), 233 Spring St, New York, NY 10013. TEL 212-460-1500, FAX 212-460-1575, journals@springer-ny.com, http://www.springer.com. Ed. Silvio R A Salinas. Circ: 1,700.

530 BGR ISSN 1310-0157
QC1 CODEN: BJPHD5

BULGARIAN JOURNAL OF PHYSICS. Text in English. 1974. 3/yr. USD 125 foreign (effective 2002). illus.; bibl.; charts. reprint service avail. from IRC. **Document type:** *Journal, Academic/Scholarly.*
Formerly: Bulgarskii Fizicheskii Zhurnal (0323-9217); Which was formed by the merger of: Bulgarska Akademiia na Naukite. Fizicheskii Institut. Izvestiia (0525-0706); Bulgarska Akademiia na Naukite. Institut po Elektronika. Izvestiia (0525-079X)
Indexed: BSLMath, CCMJ, CIN, ChemAb, ChemTitl, GeoRef, INIS AtomInd, Inspec, MSN, MathR, PhysBer, RefZh, Z02.
—AskIEEE, CASDDS, Ingenta, INIST, Linda Hall. **CCC.**
Published by: (Bulgarska Akademiya na Naukite/Bulgarian Academy of Sciences), Akademichno Izdatelstvo Prof. Marin Drinov/Prof. Marin Drinov Academic Publishing House, Akad G Bonchev 6, Sofia, 1113, Bulgaria. Ed. M Mateev. Circ: 520. **Dist. by:** Pensoft Publishers, Akad G Bonchev 6, Sofia 1113, Bulgaria. TEL 359-2-716451, FAX 359-2-704508, info@pensoft.net, http://www.pensoft.net.

530 IND ISSN 0970-6569
QC1 CODEN: BPASC4

➤ **BULLETIN OF PURE & APPLIED SCIENCES. SECTION D: PHYSICS.** Text in English. 1982. s-a. INR 1,000, USD 60, GBP 30 (effective 2011). bk.rev. 80 p./no.; back issues avail. **Document type:** *Journal, Academic/Scholarly.* **Description:** Research papers related with Physics.
Supersedes in part (in 1983): Bulletin of Pure & Applied Sciences (0970-4604)
Media: Large Type (11 pt.).
Indexed: A26, E08, I05, S06, S09.
—Ingenta, Linda Hall. **CCC.**
Published by: A.K. Sharma, Ed. & Pub., 115 R P S, D D A Flats, Mansarover Park, Shahdara, New Delhi, 110 032, India. TEL 91-921-2200909, info@bpas.in. Circ: 600.

530 JPN ISSN 0525-2997
QC173.28 CODEN: BUSKB2

BUSSEI KENKYU/MATERIAL SCIENCE STUDY. Text in English, Japanese; Summaries in Japanese. 1963. m. JPY 19,200 domestic; JPY 21,300 foreign (effective 2002). Index. 150 p./no.; **Document type:** *Journal, Academic/Scholarly.*
Indexed: ChemAb, JPI.
—BLDSC (2934.975000), INIST, Linda Hall.
Published by: Bussei Kenkyu Kankokai, c/o Yukawa Hall, Kyoto University, Kyoto-shi, 606-8502, Japan. TEL 81-75-753-7051, 81-75-722-3540, FAX 81-75-722-6339. Ed. Hisao Hayakawa. Pub., R&P Bussei Kenkyu Kankoukai TEL 81-75-722-3540. Circ: 350.

530 JPN ISSN 0385-9843
QC176.A1 CODEN: BUDADZ

BUSSEIKEN DAYORI/INSTITUTE FOR SOLID STATE PHYSICS. NEWS. Text in English, Japanese. 1957. bi-m.
—CASDDS.
Published by: University of Tokyo, Institute for Solid State Physics/Tokyo Daigaku Bussei Kenkyujo, Kashiwanoha, Kashiwa-shi, Chiba, 277-8581, Japan. http://www.issp.u-tokyo.ac.jp/.

530 JPN ISSN 0029-0181
QC1.N56 CODEN: NBGSAW

BUTSURI/PHYSICS. Variant title: Nihon Butsuri Gakkaishi. Text in Japanese. 1946. m. JPY 28,000 (effective 2004). adv. bk.rev. abstr.; bibl.; charts; illus. **Document type:** *Bulletin, Academic/Scholarly.* **Description:** Publishes original papers in all fields of physics.
Indexed: GeoRef, INIS AtomInd, JTA, SpeleolAb.
—CASDDS, Linda Hall. **CCC.**
Published by: Physical Society of Japan/Nihon Butsuri Gakkai, 5F, Eishin-kaihatsu Bldg., 5-34-3 Shimbashi, Minato-ku, Tokyo, 105-0004, Japan. TEL 81-3-34342671, FAX 81-3-34320997, pubpub@jps.or.jp, http://wwwsoc.nii.ac.jp/jps/index-j.html. Ed. A Hosoya. Circ: 19,000.

530.07 JPN ISSN 0385-6992

➤ **BUTSURI KYOIKU/PHYSICS EDUCATION SOCIETY OF JAPAN. JOURNAL.** Text in Japanese. 1953. 6/yr. JPY 10,000 to non-members; JPY 8,000 to members. adv. bk.rev. **Document type:** *Academic/Scholarly.*
—**CCC.**
Published by: Physics Education Society of Japan/Nihon Butsuri Kyoiku Gakkai, Koishikawa Yubinkyoku, P.O. Box 29, Tokyo, 112, Japan. TEL 81-3-3942-0875. Ed. Akira Akabane. Pub. Koichi Shimoda. R&P Shoichi Kinoshita. Adv. contact Kazumasa Yagi. Circ: 1,700.

530 JPN ISSN 0912-4446

➤ **BUTSURIGAKUSHI/JOURNAL FOR THE HISTORY OF PHYSICS.** Text in Japanese. 1986. a. **Document type:** *Academic/Scholarly.*
Published by: Butsurigakushi Kenkyukai/Study Group of the History of Physics, c/o Tomohiro Hyodo, Faculty of Business Administration, Ritsumeikan University, 56-1 Tojiin-Kita-Machi, Kita-ku, Kyoto-shi, 603-8346, Japan. TEL 81-75-465-1111, FAX 81-75-465-7883. Ed. Tomohiro Hyodo. Circ: 250.

➤ **C R C HANDBOOK OF CHEMISTRY AND PHYSICS.** *see* CHEMISTRY

530 305.4 USA ISSN 0897-3539

C S W P GAZETTE. (Committee on the Status of Women in Physics) Text in English. 19??. s-a. free to members (effective 2010). back issues avail. **Document type:** *Newsletter, Academic/Scholarly.* **Description:** Covers CSWP activities and programs, book reviews, statistical reports, and articles on programs designed to increase the participation of women and girls in science.
Related titles: Online - full text ed.: free (effective 2010).
Published by: American Physical Society, Committee on the Status of Women in Physics, One Physics Ellipse, College Park, MD 20740. TEL 301-209-3200, FAX 301-209-0865. Ed. Saeqa Vrtilek.

530 BRA ISSN 1677-2334

CADERNO BRASILEIRO DE ENSINO DE FISICA. Text in Portuguese, Spanish. 1984. q. **Document type:** *Journal, Academic/Scholarly.*
Formerly (until 2010): Caderno Catarinense de Ensino de Fisica (0102-3594)
Indexed: C01, CA, T02.
Published by: Universidade Federal de Santa Catarina, Departamento de Fisica, Bairro Trindade, Campus Universitario, Florianopolis, 88040-900, Brazil. TEL 55-48-37219885, fsccef@fsc.ufsc.br, http://www.fsc.ufsc.br.

CAIRO UNIVERSITY. FACULTY OF SCIENCE. BULLETIN. A: PHYSICAL SCIENCES/NASHRAT KULLIYYAT AL-'ULUM. JAMI'AT AL-QAHIRAT. A: AL-'ULUM AL-TABI'IYYAT. *see* SCIENCES: COMPREHENSIVE WORKS

530 GBR

➤ **CAMBRIDGE LECTURE NOTES IN PHYSICS.** Text in English. 1994. irreg., latest vol.15, 2002. price varies. back issues avail. **Document type:** *Monographic series, Academic/Scholarly.* **Description:** Provides a vehicle for the publication of informal lecture note volumes in all areas of theoretical and experimental physics.
Indexed: CCMJ, SpeleolAb.
Published by: University of Cambridge, Press Syndicate, The Old Schools, Trinity Ln, Cambridge, CB2 1TN, United Kingdom. TEL 44-1223-332300, communications@admin.cam.ac.uk, http://www.cam.ac.uk/univ/works/syndicate.html. Eds. Julia Yeomans, Peter Goddard.

530 510 GBR ISSN 0269-8242
CODEN: CMMPED

CAMBRIDGE MONOGRAPHS ON MATHEMATICAL PHYSICS. Text in English. 1973. irreg. price varies. back issues avail.; reprints avail. **Document type:** *Monographic series, Trade.* **Description:** Provides introductory accounts of specialised topics in mathematical and theoretical physics for graduate students and research workers.
Indexed: CCMJ, Inspec, MathR, PhysBer.
Published by: Cambridge University Press, The Edinburgh Bldg, Shaftesbury Rd, Cambridge, CB2 8RU, United Kingdom. TEL 44-1223-312393, FAX 44-1223-315052, journals@cambridge.org, http://www.cambridge.org/uk. Eds. D R Nelson, P V Landshoff, S Weinberg. R&P Linda Nicol TEL 44-1223-325702.

530 520 GBR

CAMBRIDGE MONOGRAPHS ON PLASMA PHYSICS. Text in English. 1950. irreg., latest 2005. price varies. back issues avail.; reprints avail. **Document type:** *Monographic series, Academic/Scholarly.* **Description:** Provides high-quality research level texts in plasma physics.
Formerly (until 1993): Cambridge Monographs on Physics
Indexed: Inspec.
Published by: Cambridge University Press, The Edinburgh Bldg, Shaftesbury Rd, Cambridge, CB2 8RU, United Kingdom. TEL 44-1223-312393, FAX 44-1223-315052, journals@cambridge.org, http://www.cambridge.org/uk. Eds. I H Hutchinson, K I Hopcraft, M G Haines. R&P Linda Nicol TEL 44-1223-325702.

CAMBRIDGE PHILOSOPHICAL SOCIETY. MATHEMATICAL PROCEEDINGS. *see* MATHEMATICS

530 GBR ISSN 0964-6752

CAMBRIDGE SOLID STATE SCIENCE SERIES. Text in English. 1979. irreg., latest 2007. price varies. back issues avail.; reprints avail. **Document type:** *Monographic series, Academic/Scholarly.* **Description:** Aims to provide accounts of the properties of solids both from a phenomenological and a theoretical viewpoint.
Published by: Cambridge University Press, The Edinburgh Bldg, Shaftesbury Rd, Cambridge, CB2 8RU, United Kingdom. TEL 44-1223-312393, FAX 44-1223-315052, journals@cambridge.org, http://www.cambridge.org/uk. Eds. D R Clarke, I M Ward, S Suresh. R&P Linda Nicol TEL 44-1223-325702.

P

530 CAN ISSN 0008-4204
CODEN: CJPHAD

➤ **CANADIAN JOURNAL OF PHYSICS/JOURNAL CANADIEN DE PHYSIQUE.** Text mainly in English; Text occasionally in French. 1929. m. CAD 945 to institutions; CAD 1,185 combined subscription to institutions (print & online eds.) (effective 2011). adv. bibl.; illus. index. back issues avail.; reprints avail. **Document type:** *Journal, Academic/Scholarly.*
Related titles: Microfiche ed.: (from MML); Microform ed.: (from MML, PMC, PQC); Online - full text ed.: ISSN 1208-6045. CAD 790 to institutions (effective 2011) (from IngentaConnect).
Indexed: A01, A02, A03, A05, A08, A22, A26, A28, ABIPC, APA, AS&TA, AS&TI, ASCA, ASFA, AcoustA, B04, B10, BRD, BrCerAb, BullT&T, C&ISA, C03, C05, C10, C23, C33, CA, CA/WCA, CBCARef, CIA, CIN, CPEI, CPerI, Cadscan, CerAb, ChemAb, ChemTitl, CivEngAb, CorrAb, CurCont, E&CAJ, E01, E04, E05, E08, E11, EEA, EMA, ESPM, EngInd, EnvEAb, G08, GeoRef, H15, I05, IBR, IBZ, INIS AtomInd, ISR, Inspec, LeadAb, M&GPA, M&TEA, M09, MBF, METADEX, MathR, P10, P26, P30, P48, P52, P53, P54, P56, PQC, PetrolAb, PhotoAb, PhysBer, RefZh, S01, S06, S10, SCI, SCOPUS, SolStAb, SpeleolAb, T02, T04, W03, W05, W07, WAA, Z02, Zincscan.
—BLDSC (3034.000000), AskIEEE, CASDDS, CIS, IE, Infotrieve, Ingenta, INIST, Linda Hall. **CCC.**
Published by: (Canadian Association of Physicists, National Research Council Canada (N R C)/Conseil National de Recherches Canada (C N R C)), N R C Research Press, 1200 Montreal Rd, Bldg M-55, Ottawa, ON K1A 0R6, Canada. TEL 613-993-9084, 800-668-1222, FAX 613-952-7656, pubs@nrc-cnrc.gc.ca, http://pubs.nrc-cnrc.gc.ca. Ed. Michael Steinitz. adv.: B&W page CAD 675; trim 11 x 8.5. Circ: 777.

530 SGP

CANBERRA INTERNATIONAL PHYSICS SUMMER SCHOOLS. (Several vols. in this series are out of print.) Text in English. 1990. irreg., latest vol.16, 2005. price varies. back issues avail. **Document type:** *Monographic series, Academic/Scholarly.*
Published by: World Scientific Publishing Co. Pte. Ltd., 5 Toh Tuck Link, Singapore, 596224, Singapore. TEL 65-6466-5775, FAX 65-6467-7667, wspc@wspc.com.sg, http://www.worldscientific.com. Ed. Robert L Dewar. **Dist. by:** World Scientific Publishing Co., Inc., 1060 Main St, River Edge, NJ 07661. wspc@wspc.com; World Scientific Publishing Ltd., 57 Shelton St, London WC2H 9HE, United Kingdom. TEL 44-207-8360888, FAX 44-207-8362020, sales@wspc.co.uk.

538 CHL ISSN 0717-7275

CARTA GEOLOGICA DE CHILE. SERIE GEOFISICA. Text in Spanish. 2001. irreg. USD 20 (effective 2003). bk.rev. bibl.; illus.; maps. **Document type:** *Monographic series, Government.*
Formed by the merger of (1980-2001): Carta Magnetica de Chile (0716-095X); (1998-2001): Carta Gravimetrica de Chile (0717-2796)
Related titles: CD-ROM ed.
Published by: Servicio Nacional de Geologia y Mineria, Ave. Santa Maria, 104, Providencia, Santiago, Chile. TEL 56-2-737-5050, FAX 56-2-735-6960. Ed. Constantino Mpodozis. Circ: 1,000.

530 MEX ISSN 0187-6449

CATALOGO DE PROGRAMAS Y RECURSOS HUMANOS EN FISICA. Text in Spanish. 1987. a. price varies. **Document type:** *Yearbook, Trade.*
Related titles: CD-ROM ed.; Online - full text ed.
Published by: Sociedad Mexicana de Fisica, A.C., Apartado Postal 70-348, Coyoacan, Mexico City, DF 04511, Mexico. smf@hp.fciencias.unam.mx, http://www.smf.mx.

530 POL ISSN 1644-3608
CENTRAL EUROPEAN JOURNAL OF PHYSICS. Text in English. 2002. bi-m. EUR 1,132 combined subscription to institutions (print & online eds.) (effective 2011). **Document type:** *Journal, Academic/Scholarly.* **Description:** Provides an international medium for the publication of research results and reviews in all areas of physics.
Media: Online - full text. **Related titles:** Print ed.: ISSN 1895-1082.
Indexed: APA, C&ISA, CorrAb, E&CAJ, EEA, Inspec, SCOPUS, SolStAb, WAA.
—Ingenta. **CCC.**
Published by: Versita, ul Druga Poprzeczna, 9, Warsaw, 00-951, Poland. TEL 48-22-7015015, FAX 48-22-4335126, info@versita.com. Ed. Vladimir Zakharov. Pub. Jacek Ciesielski. **Dist. by:** Springer, Haber Str 7, Heidelberg 69126, Germany. TEL 49-6221-3454303, FAX 49-6221-3454229, service@springer.de. **Co-publisher:** Springer.

530 CZE ISSN 0009-0700
QC1 CODEN: CKCFAH
CESKOSLOVENSKY CASOPIS PRO FYZIKU. Text and summaries in Czech, Slovak; Summaries in English. 1950. bi-m. CZK 456; CZK 70 per issue (effective 2008). bk.rev. charts; illus. index. 70 p./no. 2 cols./p.; **Document type:** *Journal, Academic/Scholarly.* **Description:** Contains review articles, ideas and opinions, and reports. Also includes interviews with leading physicists, and articles on the history of physics and the philosophy of science.
Formerly (until 1971): Ceskoslovensky Casopis pro Fyziku. Sekce A
Indexed: CIN, ChemAb, ChemTitl, GeoRef, INIS AtomInd, Inspec, MathR, PhysBer, SpeleolAb.
—AskIEEE, CASDDS, INIST, Linda Hall.
Published by: Akademie Ved Ceske Republiky, Fyzikalni Ustav/Czech Academy of Sciences, Institute of Physics, Na Slovance 2, Prague, 18221, Czech Republic. TEL 420-266053111, FAX 420-286890527, http://www.fzu.cz. Ed. Libor Juha TEL 420-286589325. Circ: 1,450.

530 535 ROM ISSN 1584-8663
QC611.98.C53
CHALCOGENIDE LETTERS. Text in English. 2004. irreg. free (effective 2011). **Document type:** *Journal, Academic/Scholarly.* **Description:** Publishes scientific articles of interest for the community of chalcogeniders.
Media: Online - full text.
Indexed: A01, CA, MSCI, SCI, SCOPUS, T02, W07.
Published by: Institutul National de Cercetare-Dezvoltare Pentru Fizica Materialelor/National Institute of Research and Development of Materials Physics, PO Box MG-7, Bucharest, 077125, Romania. TEL 40-21-4930195, FAX 40-21-4930267, frunza@infim.ro, http://www.infim.ro.

530 USA ISSN 1054-1500
Q172.5.C45 CODEN: CHAOEH
➤ **CHAOS;** an interdisciplinary journal of nonlinear science. Text in English. 1991. q. price varies based on the number of users. adv. back issues avail.; reprints avail. **Document type:** *Journal, Academic/Scholarly.* **Description:** Features research articles, brief reports, and solicited technical reviews from physics, mathematics, engineering, chemistry, biology and other disciplines in which nonlinear phenomena play an important role.
Related titles: CD-ROM ed.: ISSN 1527-2443; Microform ed.; Online - full text ed.: ISSN 1089-7682. price varies based on the number of users.
Indexed: A01, A03, A05, A08, A20, A22, AS&TA, AS&TI, ApMecR, B04, C10, CA, CCMJ, CMCI, CPI, CurCont, EMBASE, ExcerpMed, INIS AtomInd, ISR, Inspec, MEDLINE, MSN, MathR, P30, S01, SCI, SCOPUS, SPINweb, T02, W07, Z02.
—BLDSC (3129.715000), AskIEEE, CASDDS, IE, Ingenta, INIST, Linda Hall. **CCC.**
Published by: American Institute of Physics, 1 Physics Ellipse, College Park, MD 20740. TEL 301-209-3100, aipinfo@aip.org, http://www.aip.org. Ed. David K Campbell. **Subscr. to:** PO Box 503284, St Louis, MO 63150. TEL 516-576-2270, 800-344-6902, FAX 516-349-9704, subs@aip.org, http://librarians.aip.org.

➤ **CHEMICAL PHYSICS.** *see* CHEMISTRY—Physical Chemistry

➤ **THE CHEMICAL PHYSICS OF SOLID SURFACES.** *see* CHEMISTRY—Physical Chemistry

➤ **CHEMICAL PHYSICS RESEARCH JOURNAL.** *see* CHEMISTRY

➤ **CHEMICAL SOCIETY OF JAPAN. SYMPOSIUM ON PHYSICAL AND CHEMICAL ASPECTS OF ULTRASOUND. PROCEEDINGS/ONPA NO BUSSEI TO KAGAKU TORONKAI KOEN RONBUNSHU.** *see* CHEMISTRY

530 USA ISSN 0069-3294
➤ **CHICAGO LECTURES IN PHYSICS.** Text in English. 1963. irreg., latest 1994. price varies. reprints avail. **Document type:** *Proceedings, Academic/Scholarly.*
Indexed: CCMJ.
Published by: University of Chicago, 5801 S Ellis Ave, Chicago, IL 60637. TEL 773-702-7899. Ed. Robert M Wald.

➤ **CHINESE JOURNAL OF AERONAUTICS.** *see* AERONAUTICS AND SPACE FLIGHT

530 540 GBR ISSN 1674-0068
QD450 CODEN: CJCPA6
CHINESE JOURNAL OF CHEMICAL PHYSICS. Abbreviated title: C J C P. Text in English. 1988. bi-m. GBP 615 combined subscription to institutions (print & online eds.) (effective 2010). 96 p./no.; reprints avail. **Document type:** *Journal, Academic/Scholarly.* **Description:** Reports new and original experimental and theoretical research on interdisciplinary areas with a strong chemistry and physics foundation.
Formerly (until 2007): Huaxue Wuli Xuebao (1003-7713)
Related titles: Online - full text ed.: GBP 586 to institutions (effective 2010).
Indexed: C33, CCI, CIN, ChemAb, ChemTitl, RefZh, SCI, SCOPUS, W07.
—BLDSC (3180.299200), CASDDS, East View, IE, Ingenta, Linda Hall. **CCC.**
Published by: (Chinese Physical Society CHN), Institute of Physics Publishing Ltd., Dirac House, Temple Back, Bristol, BS1 6BE, United Kingdom. TEL 44-117-9297481, FAX 44-117-9301178, custserv@iop.org, http://publishing.iop.org/.

530 TWN ISSN 0577-9073
QC1 CODEN: CJOPAW
➤ **CHINESE JOURNAL OF PHYSICS.** Key Title: Zhongguo Wuli Xuekan. Text in English. 1963. q. USD 150 (effective 2005). **Document type:** *Journal, Academic/Scholarly.* **Description:** Publishes reviews, regular articles, and refereed conference papers in: general physics, gravitation and astrophysics, elementary particles and fields, nuclear physics, atomic, molecular, and optical physics, fluid and plasma physics, statistical and nonlinear physics, condensed matter physics, and cross disciplinary physics.
Related titles: Online - full text ed.: free (effective 2011).
Indexed: A22, CCMJ, CurCont, ISR, Inspec, MSN, MathR, SCI, SCOPUS, W07.
—BLDSC (3180.500000), IE, Ingenta, Linda Hall.
Published by: Zhonghua Minguo Wuli Xuehui/Physical Society of the Republic of China, PO BOX 23-30, Taipei, 106, Taiwan. TEL 886-2-23634923, FAX 886-2-23626538. Ed. Ming-Kong Fung.

530 GBR ISSN 1674-1056
QC1
CHINESE PHYSICS B/ZHONGGUO WULI B. Text in English. 1992. m. GBP 909 combined subscription to institutions (print & online eds.) (effective 2010). back issues avail. **Document type:** *Journal, Academic/Scholarly.* **Description:** Features the latest developments in all fields of physics in China.
Former titles (until 2008): Chinese Physics (Overseas Edition) (1009-1963); (until 2000): Acta Physica Sinica (Overseas Edition) (1004-423X)
Related titles: Microfiche ed.: USD 1,072 in the Americas; GBP 545 elsewhere (effective 2007); Online - full text ed.: ISSN 1741-4199. GBP 866 to institutions (effective 2010) (from IngentaConnect); ◆ Chinese ed.: Wuli Xuebao. ISSN 1000-3290.
Indexed: A01, A03, A08, A22, ASCA, CA, CIN, CPEI, ChemAb, ChemTitl, CurCont, EngInd, ISR, Inspec, M&GPA, RefZh, SCI, SCOPUS, T02, W07.
—AskIEEE, CASDDS, IE, Infotrieve, Ingenta, Linda Hall. **CCC.**
Published by: (Chinese Physical Society CHN), Institute of Physics Publishing Ltd., Dirac House, Temple Back, Bristol, BS1 6BE, United Kingdom. TEL 44-117-9297481, FAX 44-117-9301178, custserv@iop.org, http://publishing.iop.org/. Ed. Ouyang Zhong-Can. **Subscr. in the Americas to:** American Institute of Physics, PO Box 503284, St Louis, MO 63150. FAX 516-349-9704, subs@aip.org.

530 GBR ISSN 0256-307X
QC1 CODEN: CPLEEU
➤ **CHINESE PHYSICS LETTERS/ZHONGGUO WULI KUAIBAO.** Text in English. 1984. m. GBP 623 combined subscription to institutions (print & online eds.) (effective 2010). abstr.; bibl.; illus. back issues avail. **Document type:** *Journal, Academic/Scholarly.* **Description:** Features the latest developments in all fields of physics in China.
Related titles: Microfiche ed.: USD 735 in the Americas; GBP 373 elsewhere (effective 2007); Online - full text ed.: ISSN 1741-3540. GBP 593 to institutions (effective 2010) (from IngentaConnect).
Indexed: A01, A03, A08, A22, ASCA, CA, CIN, ChemAb, ChemTitl, CurCont, GeoRef, INIS AtomInd, ISR, Inspec, M&GPA, SCI, SCOPUS, T02, W07.
—BLDSC (3181.048400), AskIEEE, CASDDS, IE, Infotrieve, Ingenta, INIST, Linda Hall. **CCC.**
Published by: (Chinese Physical Society CHN), Institute of Physics Publishing Ltd., Dirac House, Temple Back, Bristol, BS1 6BE, United Kingdom. TEL 44-117-9297481, FAX 44-117-9301178, custserv@iop.org, http://publishing.iop.org/. Ed. Bang-Fen Zhu. **Subscr. in Japan to:** Maruzen Co., Ltd., 3-10 Nihonbashi, 2-Chome, Chuo-ku, Tokyo 103, Japan. TEL 81-3-32723884, FAX 81-3-32723923, journal@maruzen.co.jp; **Subscr. in the Americas to:** American Institute of Physics, PO Box 503284, St Louis, MO 63150. TEL 516-576-2270, 800-344-6902, FAX 516-349-9704, subs@aip.org.

530 GBR ISSN 0264-9381
QC178 CODEN: CQGRDG
➤ **CLASSICAL AND QUANTUM GRAVITY.** Text in English. 1984. s-m. GBP 2,642 combined subscription to institutions (print & online eds.) (effective 2010). Index. back issues avail. **Document type:** *Journal, Academic/Scholarly.* **Description:** Covers gravitational physics, cosmotology, geometry and field theory.
Related titles: Microfiche ed.: USD 3,270 in the Americas to institutions; GBP 1,664 elsewhere to institutions (effective 2007); Online - full text ed.: ISSN 1361-6382. GBP 2,517 to institutions (effective 2010) (from IngentaConnect).
Indexed: A01, A03, A08, A22, ASCA, CA, CCMJ, CIN, ChemAb, ChemTitl, CurCont, INIS AtomInd, ISR, Inspec, M&GPA, MSN, MathR, RefZh, SCI, SCOPUS, T02, W07, Z02.
—BLDSC (3274.534200), AskIEEE, CASDDS, IE, Infotrieve, Ingenta, INIST, Linda Hall. **CCC.**
Published by: (Institute of Physics), Institute of Physics Publishing Ltd., Dirac House, Temple Back, Bristol, BS1 6BE, United Kingdom. TEL 44-117-9297481, FAX 44-117-9301178, custserv@iop.org, http://publishing.iop.org/. Ed. C M Will. **Subscr. in N. America to:** American Institute of Physics, PO Box 503284, St Louis, MO 63150. TEL 516-576-2270, 800-344-6902, FAX 516-349-9704, subs@aip.org

530 620.1 NLD ISSN 0922-7725
➤ **COHESION AND STRUCTURE.** Text in English. 1988. irreg., latest vol.4, 1995. price varies. back issues avail. **Document type:** *Monographic series, Academic/Scholarly.* **Description:** Discusses chemical cohesion and structure from experimental, theoretical, and applied perspectives.
Related titles: Online - full text ed.
—CCC.
Published by: Elsevier BV, North-Holland (Subsidiary of: Elsevier Science & Technology), Sara Burgerhartstraat 25, Amsterdam, 1055 KV, Netherlands. TEL 31-20-4853911, FAX 31-20-4852457, JournalsCustomerServiceEMEA@elsevier.com, http://www.elsevier.com. Eds. D Pettifor, F R de Boer. **Subscr. to:** Elsevier BV, Radarweg 29, PO Box 211, Amsterdam 1000 AE, Netherlands. TEL 31-20-4853757, FAX 31-20-4853432.

530 510 540 610 FIN ISSN 0788-5717
Q60 CODEN: CPMCET
COMMENTATIONES PHYSICO-MATHEMATICAE ET CHEMICO-MEDICAE. Text in English. 1923. irreg. price varies. charts; illus. index. **Document type:** *Monographic series, Academic/Scholarly.*
Formerly (until 1991): Commentationes Physico-Mathematicae (0069-6609); Incorporates (1980-1990): Commentationes Physico-Mathematicae. Dissertationes (0358-9307)
Indexed: CIS, ChemAb, GeoRef, ISR, Inspec, PhysBer, SpeleolAb, Z02.
—AskIEEE, CASDDS, INIST, Linda Hall.
Published by: Suomen Tiedeseura/Finnish Society of Sciences and Letters, Mariagatan 5, Helsinki, 00170, Finland. TEL 358-9-633005, FAX 358-9-661065. Circ: 600.

530 510 DEU ISSN 0010-3616
QC20 CODEN: CMPHAY
➤ **COMMUNICATIONS IN MATHEMATICAL PHYSICS.** Text in English. 1965. 24/yr. EUR 5,051, USD 5,025 combined subscription to institutions (print & online eds.) (effective 2012). adv. bibl.; charts; illus. index. back issues avail.; reprint service avail. from PSC. **Document type:** *Journal, Academic/Scholarly.* **Description:** Features physics papers with mathematical content. Covers a broad spectrum of topics, from classical to quantum physics.
Related titles: Microform ed.: (from PQC); Online - full text ed.: ISSN 1432-0916 (from IngentaConnect).
Indexed: A01, A02, A03, A08, A22, A26, ASCA, CA, CCMJ, CIS, CMCI, CurCont, E01, INIS AtomInd, ISR, Inspec, M05, MSN, MathR, PhysBer, RefZh, SCI, SCOPUS, T02, W07, Z02.
—BLDSC (3361.100000), AskIEEE, IE, Infotrieve, Ingenta, INIST, Linda Hall. **CCC.**
Published by: Springer (Subsidiary of: Springer Science+Business Media), Tiergartenstr 17, Heidelberg, 69121, Germany. TEL 49-6221-4870, FAX 49-6221-345229. Ed. Dr. M Aizenman. Adv. contact Stephan Kroeck TEL 49-30-827875739. **Subscr. in the Americas to:** Springer New York LLC, Journal Fulfillment, PO Box 2485, Secaucus, NJ 07096. TEL 201-348-4033, 800-777-4643, FAX 201-348-4505, journals-ny@springer.com, http://www.springer.com; **Subscr. to:** Springer Distribution Center, Kundenservice Zeitschriften, Haberstr 7, Heidelberg 69126, Germany. TEL 49-6221-3454303, FAX 49-6221-3454229, subscriptions@springer.com.

➤ **COMMUNICATIONS IN NUMBER THEORY AND PHYSICS.** *see* MATHEMATICS

530 VNM ISSN 0868-3166
QC1 CODEN: CMPYEL
COMMUNICATIONS IN PHYSICS. Text in English. 1973. q. **Description:** Publishes research and review articles in all fields of physics.
Former titles (until 1991): Tap San Vat Ly/Journal of Physics (0378-8822); Tap Chi Vat Ly (0378-8814)
Indexed: INIS AtomInd.
Published by: Institute for Nuclear Science and Technique, Hoang Quoc Viet, Nghia Do, Cau Giay, PO Box 5T-160, Hanoi, Viet Nam. TEL 84-4-7564926, FAX 84-4-8363295. Ed. Dao Vong Duc.

530 GBR ISSN 0253-6102
QC19.2 CODEN: CTPHDI
➤ **COMMUNICATIONS IN THEORETICAL PHYSICS/LILUN WULI.** Text in English. 1981. 12/yr. GBP 528 combined subscription to institutions (print & online eds.) (effective 2010). **Document type:** *Journal, Academic/Scholarly.* **Description:** Covers multifarious aspects of theoretical research in physics, such as atomic and molecular physics, condensed matter and statistical physics, plasma and fluid theory, nuclear theory, particle physics, and quantum field theory.
Related titles: Online - full text ed.: ISSN 1572-9494. GBP 503 to institutions (effective 2010) (from IngentaConnect).
Indexed: A22, ASCA, CCMJ, CurCont, ISR, Inspec, MSN, MathR, RefZh, SCI, SCOPUS, W07, Z02.
—BLDSC (3363.458000), AskIEEE, CASDDS, IE, Infotrieve, Ingenta, INIST, Linda Hall. **CCC.**
Published by: (Chinese Academy of Sciences, Institute of Theoretical Physics CHN), Institute of Physics Publishing Ltd., Dirac House, Temple Back, Bristol, BS1 6BE, United Kingdom. TEL 44-117-9297481, FAX 44-117-9301178, custserv@iop.org, http://publishing.iop.org/. Ed. Ho Tso-Hsiu.

530 NLD ISSN 1568-5543
COMPOSITE INTERFACES (ONLINE). Text in English. 200?. bi-m. EUR 1,498, USD 2,037 to institutions (effective 2012).
Media: Online - full text (from IngentaConnect).
—CCC.
Published by: V S P (Subsidiary of: Brill), Brill Academic Publishers, PO Box 9000, Leiden, 2300 PA, Netherlands. TEL 31-71-5353500, FAX 31-71-5317532, marketing@brill.nl, http://www.brill.nl.

539 GBR ISSN 1096-598X
TK7871.99.C65 CODEN: COSEFP
➤ **COMPOUND SEMICONDUCTOR.** Text in English. 1995. 8/yr. GBP 105 domestic; EUR 158 in Europe; USD 198 in United States; GBP 138 elsewhere; GBP 4.50 per issue; free (effective 2010). adv. back issues avail. **Document type:** *Magazine, Academic/Scholarly.* **Description:** Provides in-depth, timely information on current developments within the global compound semiconductor industry. Coverage includes manufacturing and research, devices and materials, markets and applications, and all other aspects of compound semiconductor technology and production.
Related titles: Online - full text ed.: ISSN 2042-7328. 1995. free (effective 2010).
Indexed: EngInd, Inspec, SCOPUS.
—BLDSC (3366.229730), Infotrieve. **CCC.**
Published by: Angel Business Communications Ltd., Unit 6, Bow Ct, Fletchworth Gate, Burnsall Rd, Coventry, CV5 6SP, United Kingdom. TEL 44-2476-718970, FAX 44-2476-718971, ask@angelbcl.co.uk, http://www.angelbc.co.uk. Ed. David Ridsdale TEL 44-1923-690210. Pub. Jackie Cannon TEL 44-1923-690205. adv.: page GBP 5,460, page USD 9,050, page EUR 6,030; trim 210 x 297.

530 HUN
COMPUTATIONAL AND APPLIED PHYSICS. Text in English. a. **Description:** Publishes research papers on theoretical and applied physics, with special emphasis on computational physics low energy quantum mechanics.
Formerly: University of Miskolc. Publications. Physics (1585-2768); Which superseded in part (in 1999): University of Miskolc. Publications. Series D. Natural Sciences (1219-283X); Which was formerly (until 1994): Technical University for Heavy Industry. Publications. Series D. Natural Sciences (0133-2929); Which superseded in part (in 1976): Nehezipari Muszaki Egyetem

Idegennyelvu Kozlemenyei (0369-4852); Which was formerly (until 1960): Soproni Muszaki Egyetemi Karok Banyamernoki es Foldmernoki Karok Kozlemenyei (0371-1099); (until 1955): Banya- es Kohomernoki Osztaly Kozlemenyei (0367-6412); (until 1934): Soproni M Kir. Banyamernoki es Erdomernoki Foiskola Banyaszati es Kohaszati Osztalyanak Kozlemenyei (0324-4474)
—Linda Hall.
Published by: Miskolci Egyetem/University of Miskolc, Miskolc, 3515, Hungary. TEL 36-46-565111, http://www.uni-miskolc.hu.

530 GBR ISSN 2044-9283
COMPUTATIONAL AND EXPERIMENTAL METHODS IN STRUCTURES. Text in English. 2008. irreg., latest vol.4, 2010. price varies. back issues avail. **Document type:** *Monographic series, Academic/Scholarly.* **Description:** Provides fundamental concepts of experimental and computational methods and their relevance to real world problems.
Published by: Imperial College Press (Subsidiary of: World Scientific Publishing Co. Pte. Ltd.), 57 Shelton St, Covent Garden, London, WC2H 9HE, United Kingdom. TEL 44-20-78360888, FAX 44-20-78362020, edit@icpress.co.uk, http://www.icpress.co.uk/. Ed. M H Aliabadi. **Dist. by:** World Scientific Publishing Co., Inc., 27 Warren St, Ste 401-402, Hackensack, NJ 07601. TEL 201-487-9655, 800-227-7562, FAX 201-487-9656, 888-977-2665, wspc@wspc.com; World Scientific Publishing Ltd.

COMPUTATIONAL MATHEMATICS AND MATHEMATICAL PHYSICS. *see* MATHEMATICS

COMPUTER MODELLING AND NEW TECHNOLOGIES. *see* COMPUTERS

CONCEPTS IN MAGNETIC RESONANCE. PART A. *see* MEDICAL SCIENCES—Radiology And Nuclear Medicine

CONCEPTS IN MAGNETIC RESONANCE. PART B: MAGNETIC RESONANCE ENGINEERING. *see* MEDICAL SCIENCES—Radiology And Nuclear Medicine

530 UKR ISSN 1607-324X
➤ **CONDENSED MATTER PHYSICS.** Text in English; Text occasionally in Ukrainian. 1993. q. USD 200 foreign (effective 2010). adv. bk.rev. 200 p./no.; reprints avail. **Document type:** *Journal, Academic/Scholarly.* **Description:** Contains original and review articles in the field of statistical mechanics and thermodynamics of equilibrium and nonequilibrium processes, relativistic mechanics of interacting particle systems.
Related titles: Online - full content ed.: free (effective 2011).
Indexed: A01, CA, CurCont, Inspec, P30, RefZh, SCI, SCOPUS, T02, W07.
—BLDSC (3405.707000), Linda Hall. **CCC.**
Published by: Natsional'na Akademiya Nauk Ukrainy, Instytut Fizyky Kondensovanykh System/National Academy of Sciences of Ukraine, the Institute for Condensed Matter Physics, 1 Svientsitskii St, Lviv, 79011, Ukraine. TEL 380-322-761978, FAX 380-322-761158, cmp@icmp.lviv.ua. Ed. Ihor Yukhnovskii. Circ: 200 (paid).

530 548 USA ISSN 0893-861X
QC173.4.C65 CODEN: CMTHEO
➤ **CONDENSED MATTER THEORIES.** Text in English. 1986. irreg., latest vol.21, 2008. USD 198 per vol. (effective 2012). back issues avail. **Document type:** *Monographic series, Academic/Scholarly.* **Description:** Covers new theoretical developments in solid-state physics of condensed matter.
Indexed: CIN, ChemAb, ChemTitl.
—BLDSC (3405.710000), CASDDS, IE, Ingenta, Linda Hall. **CCC.**
Published by: Nova Science Publishers, Inc., 400 Oser Ave, Ste 1600, Hauppauge, NY 11788. TEL 631-231-7269, FAX 631-231-8175, main@novapublishers.com. Eds. Atsushi Hosaka, Hiroshi Toki, Hisazumi Akai.

538 USA
CONFERENCE ON MAGNETISM AND MAGNETIC MATERIALS. PROCEEDINGS. Variant title: Proceedings of the Annual Conference on Magnetism and Magnetic Materials. Text in English. 19??. a. adv. back issues avail. **Document type:** *Proceedings, Academic/Scholarly.*
Formerly (until 1977): Magnetism and Magnetic Materials
—CCC.
Published by: American Institute of Physics, 1 Physics Ellipse, College Park, MD 20740. TEL 301-209-3100, FAX 301-209-0843, aipinfo@aip.org, http://www.aip.org.

530 POL ISSN 0208-9947
CODEN: PCPIDB
CONFERENCES IN PHYSICS. PROCEEDINGS. Text in English. 1981. 3/w.
Indexed: Inspec.
Published by: (Polska Akademia Nauk, Instytut Fizyki/Polish Academy of Sciences, Institute of Physics), Zaklad Narodowy Im. Ossolinskich, Ul Szewska 37, Wroclaw, 50139, Poland.

530 NLD ISSN 1572-0934
CONTEMPORARY CONCEPTS OF CONDENSED MATTER SCIENCE. Text in English. 2006. irreg., latest vol.3, 2008. price varies. **Document type:** *Monographic series, Academic/Scholarly.*
Related titles: Online - full text ed.: ISSN 2212-1196.
Indexed: SCOPUS.
—CCC.
Published by: Elsevier BV (Subsidiary of: Elsevier Science & Technology), Radarweg 29, PO Box 211, Amsterdam, 1000 AE, Netherlands. TEL 31-20-4853911, FAX 31-20-4852457, JournalsCustomerServiceEMEA@elsevier.com.

530 GBR ISSN 0010-7514
QC1 CODEN: CTPHAF
➤ **CONTEMPORARY PHYSICS.** Text in English. 1959. bi-m. GBP 846 combined subscription in United Kingdom to institutions (print & online eds.); EUR 1,121, USD 1,407 combined subscription to institutions (print & online eds.) (effective 2012). adv. bk.rev. bibl.; charts; illus. index. back issues avail.; reprint service avail. from PSC. **Document type:** *Journal, Academic/Scholarly.* **Description:** Presents articles on important developments in physics that can be read and understood by anyone with an interest and fundamental grasp of physics.
Related titles: Microform ed.: (from MIM, PMC); Online - full text ed.: ISSN 1366-5812. 1997. GBP 761 in United Kingdom to institutions; EUR 1,009, USD 1,267 to institutions (effective 2012) (from IngentaConnect).
Indexed: A01, A02, A03, A08, A22, A26, A28, APA, ASCA, B04, BRD, BrCerAb, C&ISA, CA, CA/WCA, CIA, CIN, CerAb, ChemAb, ChemTitl, CivEngAb, CorrAb, CurCont, E&CAJ, E01, E08, E11, EEA, EMA, ESPM, EnvEAb, G01, G03, G08, GSA, GSI, GeoRef, H15, I05, ISR, Inspec, M&TEA, M09, MBF, METADEX, P02, P10, P26, P48, P52, P53, P54, P56, PQC, PhotoAb, PhysBer, S01, S09, S10, SCI, SCOPUS, SolStAb, SpeleolAb, T02, T04, W03, W07, WAA.
—AskIEEE, CASDDS, IE, Infotrieve, Ingenta, INIST, Linda Hall. **CCC.**
Published by: Taylor & Francis Ltd. (Subsidiary of: Taylor & Francis Group), 4 Park Sq, Milton Park, Abingdon, Oxfordshire OX14 4RN, United Kingdom. TEL 44-20-70176000, FAX 44-20-70176336, subscriptions@tandf.co.uk, http://www.taylorandfrancis.com. Ed. Peter L Knight. Adv. contact Linda Hann. **Subscr. in N. America to:** Taylor & Francis Inc., Customer Services Dept, 325 Chestnut St, 8th Fl, Philadelphia, PA 19106. TEL 215-625-8900, 800-354-1420, FAX 215-625-2940, customerservice@taylorandfrancis.com; **Subscr. to:** Journals Customer Service, Sheepen Pl, Colchester, Essex CO3 3LP, United Kingdom. TEL 44-20-70175544, FAX 44-20-70175198, tf.enquiries@tfinforma.com.

530.44 DEU ISSN 0863-1042
QC717.6 CODEN: CPPHEP
➤ **CONTRIBUTIONS TO PLASMA PHYSICS.** Text in English. 1961. 10/yr. GBP 1,856 in United Kingdom to institutions; EUR 2,848 in Europe to institutions; USD 3,635 elsewhere to institutions; GBP 2,042 combined subscription in United Kingdom to institutions (print & online eds.); EUR 3,134 combined subscription in Europe to institutions (print & online eds.); USD 3,999 combined subscription elsewhere to institutions (print & online eds.) (effective 2010). illus. index. reprint service avail. from PSC. **Document type:** *Journal, Academic/Scholarly.* **Description:** Publishes original papers and reviews on plasma physics and gas discharges, including their diagnosis and applications.
Formerly (until 1985): Beitraege aus der Plasmaphysik (0005-8025)
Related titles: Online - full text ed.: ISSN 1521-3986. GBP 1,856 in United Kingdom to institutions; EUR 2,848 in Europe to institutions; USD 3,635 elsewhere to institutions (effective 2010).
Indexed: A22, ASCA, CIN, ChemAb, ChemTitl, CurCont, IBR, IBZ, INIS AtomInd, ISR, Inspec, MathR, PhysBer, RefZh, SCI, SCOPUS, T02, W07.
—BLDSC (3461.116000), AskIEEE, CASDDS, IE, Infotrieve, Ingenta, INIST, Linda Hall. **CCC.**
Published by: Wiley - V C H Verlag GmbH & Co. KGaA (Subsidiary of: John Wiley & Sons, Inc.), Postfach 101161, Weinheim, 69451, Germany. TEL 49-6201-606400, FAX 49-6201-606184, subservice@wiley-vch.de. Eds. G Fussmann, T Klinger, W Ebeling. **Subscr. in the Americas to:** John Wiley & Sons, Inc., 111 River St, Hoboken, NJ 07030. TEL 201-748-6645, subinfo@wiley.com, http://www.wiley.com/WileyCDA/; **Subscr. outside Germany, Austria & Switzerland to:** John Wiley & Sons Ltd., The Atrium, Southern Gate, Chichester, West Sussex PO19 8SQ, United Kingdom. TEL 44-1243-779777, FAX 44-1243-775878, cs-journals@wiley.com.

530 SWE ISSN 0348-9329
CODEN: CSPLDN
COSMIC AND SUBATOMIC PHYSICS REPORT. Text in English. 1971. irreg. **Document type:** *Monographic series, Academic/Scholarly.*
Formerly (until 1977): Cosmic Ray Physics Report
—BLDSC (3477.200800).
Published by: Lunds Universitet, Fysiska Institutionen/Lund University, Department of Physics, P O Box 117, Lund, 22100, Sweden. TEL 46-46-2224124, FAX 46-46-2224709, http://www.lth.se/fysik.

530 510 SGP ISSN 0219-6077
COSMOS. Text in English. 2005. s-a. SGD 67, USD 67, EUR 67 combined subscription to institutions (print & online eds.) (effective 2012). adv. back issues avail. **Document type:** *Journal, Academic/Scholarly.* **Description:** Brings out review articles, articles on new research results, or a combination of both, with the aim of promoting multidisciplinary research in science and mathematics.
Related titles: Online - full text ed.: ISSN 1793-7051. SGD 61, USD 61, EUR 61 to institutions (effective 2012).
Indexed: A01, A22, CA, CCMJ, E01, MSN, MathR, T02.
—IE.
Published by: World Scientific Publishing Co. Pte. Ltd., 5 Toh Tuck Link, Singapore, 596224, Singapore. TEL 65-6466-5775, FAX 65-6467-7667, wspc@wspc.com.sg, http://www.worldscientific.com. Ed. Andrew Wee Thye Shen. **Dist. by:** World Scientific Publishing Co., Inc., 27 Warren St, Ste 401-402, Hackensack, NJ 07601. TEL 201-487-9655, 800-227-7562, FAX 201-487-9656, 888-977-2665, wspc@wspc.com; World Scientific Publishing Ltd., 57 Shelton St, London WC2H 9HE, United Kingdom. TEL 44-207-8360888, FAX 44-207-8362020, sales@wspc.co.uk.

CRACKING THE A P PHYSICS B EXAM. (Advanced Placement) *see* EDUCATION—Higher Education

CRACKING THE S A T PHYSICS SUBJECT TEST. *see* EDUCATION—Higher Education

530.41 USA ISSN 1040-8436
QC176.A1 CODEN: CCRSDA
➤ **CRITICAL REVIEWS IN SOLID STATE AND MATERIALS SCIENCES.** Text in English. 1970. q. GBP 667 combined subscription in United Kingdom to institutions (print & online eds.); EUR 882, USD 1,107 combined subscription to institutions (print & online eds.) (effective 2012). adv. bibl.; charts; illus. Index. back issues avail.; reprint service avail. from PSC. **Document type:** *Journal, Academic/Scholarly.* **Description:** Reviews articles in theoretical and experimental solid state materials science including new and emerging areas in a variety of disciplines.
Former titles (until 1980): C R C Critical Reviews in Solid State and Materials Sciences (0161-1593); (until 1977): C R C Critical Reviews in Solid State Sciences (0011-085X)
Related titles: Online - full text ed.: ISSN 1547-6561. GBP 600 in United Kingdom to institutions; EUR 794, USD 996 to institutions (effective 2012) (from IngentaConnect).
Indexed: A01, A03, A08, A22, A28, APA, ASCA, B01, B06, B07, B09, BrCerAb, C&ISA, C33, CA, CA/WCA, CIA, CIN, CPEI, CerAb, ChemAb, ChemTitl, CivEngAb, CorrAb, CurCont, E&CAJ, E01, E11, EEA, EMA, ESPM, EngInd, EnvEAb, H15, ISR, Inspec, M&TEA, M09, MBF, METADEX, MSCI, P15, P26, P48, P52, P54, P56, PQC, RefZh, S01, SCI, SCOPUS, SolStAb, T02, T04, W07, WAA.
—AskIEEE, CASDDS, IE, Infotrieve, Ingenta, INIST, Linda Hall. **CCC.**
Published by: Taylor & Francis Inc. (Subsidiary of: Taylor & Francis Group), 325 Chestnut St, Ste 800, Philadelphia, PA 19106. TEL 215-625-2940, 800-354-1420, orders@taylorandfrancis.com, http://www.taylorandfrancis.com. Ed. Wolfgang Sigmund. Adv. contact Linda Hann TEL 44-1344-779945. Circ: 570.

530 NLD ISSN 1567-1739
QC1
➤ **CURRENT APPLIED PHYSICS.** Text in English. 2001. 6/yr. EUR 710 in Europe to institutions; JPY 94,200 in Japan to institutions; USD 792 elsewhere to institutions (effective 2012). **Document type:** *Journal, Academic/Scholarly.* **Description:** Covers all fields of applied science, investigating the physics of advanced materials for future applications.
Related titles: Online - full text ed.: (from IngentaConnect, ScienceDirect).
Indexed: A01, A03, A08, A26, A28, APA, BrCerAb, C&ISA, CA, CA/WCA, CIA, CPEI, CerAb, CivEngAb, CorrAb, CurCont, E&CAJ, E11, EEA, EMA, ESPM, EngInd, EnvEAb, H15, I05, Inspec, M&TEA, M09, MBF, METADEX, MSCI, RefZh, S01, SCI, SCOPUS, SolStAb, T02, T04, W07, WAA.
—BLDSC (3494.204500), IE, Ingenta. **CCC.**
Published by: Elsevier BV (Subsidiary of: Elsevier Science & Technology), Radarweg 29, PO Box 211, Amsterdam, 1000 AE, Netherlands. TEL 31-20-4853911, FAX 31-20-4852457, JournalsCustomerServiceEMEA@elsevier.com, http://www.elsevier.nl. Ed. Tae Won Noh.

➤ **CURRENT OPINION IN SOLID STATE & MATERIALS SCIENCE.** *see* ENGINEERING—Electrical Engineering

530 NLD ISSN 0922-503X
➤ **CURRENT PHYSICS - SOURCES AND COMMENTS.** Text in English. 1988. irreg., latest vol.10, 1992. price varies. back issues avail. **Document type:** *Monographic series, Academic/Scholarly.* **Description:** Presents a selection of essential source material on contemporary topics in elementary-particle physics.
Indexed: Inspec.
Published by: Elsevier BV, North-Holland (Subsidiary of: Elsevier Science & Technology), Sara Burgerhartstraat 25, Amsterdam, 1055 KV, Netherlands. TEL 31-20-4853911, FAX 31-20-4852457, JournalsCustomerServiceEMEA@elsevier.com, http://www.elsevier.com. **Subscr. to:** Elsevier BV, Radarweg 29, PO Box 211, Amsterdam 1000 AE, Netherlands. TEL 31-20-4853757, FAX 31-20-4853432.

530 USA ISSN 2154-3119
▼ ➤ **CURRENT RESEARCH IN PHYSICS.** Text in English. 2010 (Apr.). s-a. **Document type:** *Journal, Academic/Scholarly.* **Description:** Publishes original research articles in the field of physics (pure and applied). Scope of the journal includes: atomic and molecular physics, condensed matter, elementary particles and nuclear physics, gases, fluid dynamics and plasmas, electromagnetism and optics, mathematical physics, and interdisciplinary, classical and applied physics.
Related titles: Online - full text ed.
Published by: Academic Journals Inc., 224, 5th Ave, No 2218, New York, NY 10001. TEL 845-863-0090, FAX 845-591-0669, academicjournals@gmail.com.

530 IND ISSN 0972-4818
CURRENT TOPICS IN ACOUSTICAL RESEARCH. Text in English. 1994. a. EUR 134.10 in Europe; JPY 17,582 in Japan; USD 149 elsewhere (effective 2010). **Document type:** *Journal, Academic/Scholarly.* **Description:** Contains review articles and original papers reporting the results of experimental and theoretical work in the interdisciplinary subject area of sound in its widest sense.
Related titles: CD-ROM ed.
Indexed: A28, APA, ASFA, BrCerAb, C&ISA, CA/WCA, CIA, CerAb, CivEngAb, CorrAb, E&CAJ, E11, EEA, EMA, ESPM, EnvEAb, H15, Inspec, M&TEA, M09, MBF, METADEX, OceAb, SolStAb, T04, WAA.
—Linda Hall.
Published by: Research Trends (P) Ltd., T.C. 17 / 250 (3), Chadiyara Rd, Poojapura, Trivandrum, Kerala 695 012, India. TEL 91-471-2344424, FAX 91-471-2344423, info@researchtrends.net.

530 DEU ISSN 0418-9833
QC789.G32
D E S Y (YEAR). Text in German. 1973. a. **Document type:** *Journal, Trade.*
Formerly (until 1993): D E S Y Journal (0938-801X)
—BLDSC (3576.600000).
Published by: Deutsches Elektronen-Synchrotron, Notkestr 85, Hamburg, 22607, Germany. TEL 49-40-89980, FAX 49-40-89983282, desypr@desy.de, http://www.desy.de. Ed. Petra Folkerts.

621 USA ISSN 2154-8242
▼ **D O E OFFICE OF SCIENCE AMERICAN RECOVERY & REINVESTMENT ACT NEWSLETTER.** (Department of Energy) Text in English. 2009. m. free (effective 2010). back issues avail. **Document type:** *Newsletter, Trade.*
Media: Online - full text.
Published by: U.S. Department of Energy, Office of Science, 1000 Independence Ave, SW, Washington, DC 20585. TEL 202-586-5430, FAX 202-586-4403, The.Secretary@hq.doe.gov.

DANESHMAND. *see* ENGINEERING

530 CHN ISSN 1000-0712
DAXUE WULI/COLLEGE PHYSICS. Text in Chinese. 1982. m. USD 62.40 (effective 2009). **Document type:** *Journal, Academic/Scholarly.*
Related titles: Online - full text ed.
—East View.
Published by: Beijing Shifan Daxue/Beijing Normal University, Keji Lou C-qu, Rm. 701, Beijing, 100875, China. TEL 86-10-58808024, FAX 86-10-58805411.

▼ **DE GRUYTER STUDIES IN MATHEMATICAL PHYSICS.** *see* MATHEMATICS

DELTA; matematyczno-fizyczno-astronomiczny miesiecznik popularny. *see* MATHEMATICS

530 GRC
DEMOKRITOS NATIONAL CENTER FOR SCIENTIFIC RESEARCH. DEMO. Text in Greek. irreg. **Document type:** *Monographic series.*
Formerly (until 1993): Demokritos National Research Center for Physical Sciences. Demo
Published by: Demokritos National Center for Scientific Research, PO Box 60228, Hagia Paraskevi, Athens 153 10, Greece.

530 DEU ISSN 1439-5215
DENK-SCHRIFTEN. Text in German. 2000. irreg., latest vol.9, 2006. price varies. **Document type:** *Monographic series, Academic/Scholarly.*
Published by: Bochumer Universitaetsverlag GmbH, Querenburger Hoehe 281, Bochum, 44801, Germany. TEL 49-234-9719780, FAX 49-234-9719786, bou@bou.de, http://bou.de.

530 DEU ISSN 0420-0195
DEUTSCHE PHYSIKALISCHE GESELLSCHAFT. VERHANDLUNGEN. Text and summaries in English, German. 1966. irreg. (5-10/yr.). EUR 30 to non-members (effective 2009). adv. **Document type:** *Monographic series, Academic/Scholarly.*
Related titles: Online - full text ed.
Indexed: Inspec.
—INIST, Linda Hall. **CCC.**
Published by: Deutsche Physikalische Gesellschaft, Hauptstr 5, Bad Honnef, 53604, Germany. TEL 49-2224-92320, FAX 49-2224-923250, dpg@dpg-physik.de, http://www.dpg-physik.de. Circ: (controlled).

502.825 CHN ISSN 1000-6281
QH212.E4
➤ **DIANZI XIANWEI XUEBAO/CHINESE ELECTRON MICROSCOPY SOCIETY. JOURNAL.** Text in Chinese. 1982. bi-m. **Document type:** *Journal, Academic/Scholarly.*
Related titles: Online - full text ed.
Indexed: A22.
—BLDSC (4729.255000), IE, Ingenta.
Published by: Zhongguo Dianzi Xianweijing Xuehui/Chinese Electron Microscopy Society, 13 Beiertiao Zhongguancun, PO Box 2724, Beijing, 100080, China. TEL 86-10-82671519, tsxie@imr.ac.cn, http://www.cems.synl.ac.cn/. Ed. Jun-en Yao.

530 DEU ISSN 1862-4138
QC185
➤ **DIFFUSION FUNDAMENTALS.** Text in English. 2005. irreg. free (effective 2011). **Document type:** *Journal, Academic/Scholarly.* **Description:** Covers the fields of diffusion and transport.
Media: Online - full text.
Address: c/o Joerg Kaerger, Editor, Universitaet Leipzig, Faculty of Physics and Earth Science, Linnerstr 5, Leipzig, 04103, Germany. TEL 49-341-9732500, FAX 49-341-9732549, kaerger@uni-leipzig.de. Ed. Joerg Kaerger.

➤ **DIGEST JOURNAL OF NANOMATERIALS AND BIOSTRUCTURES.** *see* BIOLOGY—Biotechnology

➤ **DIMENSIO.** *see* MATHEMATICS

530 SGP ISSN 0217-9148
DIRECTIONS IN CHAOS. Text in English. 1990. irreg., latest vol.7, 1998. price varies. back issues avail. **Document type:** *Monographic series, Academic/Scholarly.*
Indexed: CCMJ.
Published by: World Scientific Publishing Co. Pte. Ltd., 5 Toh Tuck Link, Singapore, 596224, Singapore. TEL 65-6466-5775, FAX 65-6467-7667, wspc@wspc.com.sg, http://www.worldscientific.com. Ed. Hao Bailin. **Dist. by:** World Scientific Publishing Co., Inc., 27 Warren St, Ste 401-402, Hackensack, NJ 07601. TEL 201-487-9655, 800-227-7562, FAX 201-487-9656, 888-977-2665, wspc@wspc.com; World Scientific Publishing Ltd., 57 Shelton St, London WC2H 9HE, United Kingdom. TEL 44-207-8360888, FAX 44-207-8362020, sales@wspc.co.uk.

530 548 NLD ISSN 1572-4859
➤ **DISLOCATIONS IN SOLIDS.** Text in English. 1978. irreg., latest vol.14, 2008. price varies. **Document type:** *Monographic series, Academic/Scholarly.* **Description:** Offers a comprehensive review of the entire study of dislocations in solid matter.
Related titles: Online - full text ed.
Indexed: SCOPUS.
—CCC.
Published by: Elsevier BV, North-Holland (Subsidiary of: Elsevier Science & Technology), Sara Burgerhartstraat 25, Amsterdam, 1055 KV, Netherlands. TEL 31-20-4853911, FAX 31-20-4852457, JournalsCustomerServiceEMEA@elsevier.com, http://www.elsevier.com. **Subscr. to:** Elsevier BV, Radarweg 29, PO Box 211, Amsterdam 1000 AE, Netherlands. TEL 31-20-4853757, FAX 31-20-4853432.

530 RUS ISSN 1028-3358
QC1 CODEN: DOPHFU
DOKLADY PHYSICS. Text in English. 1933. m. EUR 3,815, USD 4,632 combined subscription to institutions (print & online eds.) (effective 2012). index. back issues avail. **Document type:** *Journal, Academic/Scholarly.* **Description:** Each issue comprises thirty, four-page papers on topics essential in general physics and on such areas as technical physics, mathematical physics, mechanics, aerodynamics, crystallography and elasticity theory.
Former titles (until 1998): Physics - Doklady (1063-7753); Soviet Physics - Doklady (0038-5689)
Related titles: Online - full text ed.: ISSN 1562-6903 (from IngentaConnect); ◆ Partial translation of: Rossiiskaya Akademiya Nauk. Doklady. ISSN 0869-5652.
Indexed: A01, A02, A03, A08, A20, A22, A26, AcoustA, ApMecR, C33, CA, CCMJ, CPEI, CPI, CurCont, E01, EngInd, GPAA, GeoRef, Inspec, MSN, MathR, MinerAb, PhysBer, S01, SCI, SCOPUS, SPINweb, SpeleolAb, T02, W07, Z02.
—BLDSC (0411.355000), AskIEEE, East View, IE, Infotrieve, Ingenta, INIST, Linda Hall. **CCC.**
Published by: (Rossiiskaya Akademiya Nauk/Russian Academy of Sciences), M A I K Nauka - Interperiodica (Subsidiary of: Pleiades Publishing, Inc.), Profsoyuznaya ul 90, Moscow, 117997, Russian Federation. TEL 7-095-3347420, FAX 7-095-3360666, compmg@maik.ru, http://www.maik.ru. Ed. Yurii S Osipov. **Distr. in the Americas by:** Springer New York LLC, Journal Fulfillment, PO Box 2485, Secaucus, NJ 07096. TEL 212-460-1500, 800-777-4643, FAX 201-348-4505; **Distr. outside of the Americas by:** Springer, Haber Str 7, Heidelberg 69126, Germany. TEL 49-6221-3454303, service@springer.de.

530 IRL ISSN 0070-7414
QC1 CODEN: CDIAAH
DUBLIN INSTITUTE FOR ADVANCED STUDIES. COMMUNICATIONS. SERIES A. Text in English. 1943. irreg., latest vol.28, 1984. price varies. **Document type:** *Monographic series.*
Indexed: Inspec, MathR, PhysBer.
—AskIEEE.
Published by: Dublin Institute for Advanced Studies, 10 Burlington Rd., Dublin, 4, Ireland. TEL 353-1-6680748, FAX 353-1-680561.

DYES AND PIGMENTS. *see* CHEMISTRY

E A R SE L EPROCEEDINGS. *see* EARTH SCIENCES

530 JPN ISSN 1348-0391
QD506.A1
E-JOURNAL OF SURFACE SCIENCE AND NANOTECHNOLOGY. Text in English. 2003. d. free (effective 2011). back issues avail. **Document type:** *Journal, Academic/Scholarly.* **Description:** Contains research papers on fundamental theory and experiments at frontiers of science and technology relating to surfaces, interfaces, thin films, fine particles, nanowires, nanotubes, and other nanometer-scale structures, and their interdisciplinary areas such as crystal growth, vacuum technology, and so on.
Media: Online - full content. **Related titles:** Online - full text ed.
Indexed: A39, C27, C29, CPEI, D03, D04, E13, EngInd, Inspec, R14, S14, S15, S18, SCOPUS.
Published by: Surface Science Scociety of Japan, Hongo Corporation 402, 2-40-13 Hongo, Bunkyo-ku, Tokyo, 113-0033, Japan. TEL 81-3-38120266, FAX 81-3-38122897, ejssnt@sssj.org, http://www.sssj.org/. Ed. Ayahiko Ichimiya.

530 FRA ISSN 2100-014X
QC1
▼ **E P J WEB OF CONFERENCES.** (European Physical Journal) Text in English. 2009. irreg. free (effective 2012).
Media: Online - full text.
—Linda Hall.
Published by: E D P Sciences, 17 Ave du Hoggar, Parc d'Activites de Courtaboeuf, BP 112, Cedex A, Les Ulis, F-91944, France. TEL 33-1-69187575, FAX 33-1-69860678, http://www.edpsciences.org.

EARTH, PLANETS AND SPACE. *see* EARTH SCIENCES

EAST-WEST JOURNAL OF MATHEMATICS. *see* BIOLOGY

ECLETICA QUIMICA. *see* CHEMISTRY

530 SGP
EDOARDO AMALDI FOUNDATION SERIES. Text in English. 1995. irreg., latest vol.4. price varies. back issues avail. **Document type:** *Monographic series, Academic/Scholarly.*
Published by: World Scientific Publishing Co. Pte. Ltd., 5 Toh Tuck Link, Singapore, 596224, Singapore. TEL 65-6466-5775, FAX 65-6467-7667, wspc@wspc.com.sg, http://www.worldscientific.com. **Dist. by:** World Scientific Publishing Co., Inc., 1060 Main St, River Edge, NJ 07661. wspc@wspc.com; World Scientific Publishing Ltd., 57 Shelton St, London WC2H 9HE, United Kingdom. TEL 44-207-8360888, FAX 44-207-8362020, sales@wspc.co.uk.

530 EGY ISSN 1110-0214
QC1 CODEN: EJPHB2
➤ **EGYPTIAN JOURNAL OF PHYSICS/AL-MAGALLAT AL-MISRIYYAT LIL-FIIZIQAA.** Text in English; Summaries in English, Arabic. 1970. s-a. USD 112 (effective 2002). abstr.; charts. reprint service avail. from IRC. **Document type:** *Journal, Academic/Scholarly.*
Formerly (until 1971): United Arab Republic Journal of Physics (0372-3763)
Indexed: AcoustA, CIN, ChemAb, ChemTitl, INIS AtomInd, Inspec, PhysBer, SpeleolAb.
—CASDDS, INIST.
Published by: (Egyptian Physical Society, Research Department), National Information and Documentation Centre (NIDOC), Tahrir St., Dokki, Awqaf P.O., Giza, Egypt. TEL 20-2-3371696, FAX 20-2-3371746. Ed. Dr. Abdel-Maqssoud Muhammad El-Nadi. Circ: 1,000.

530 540 EGY ISSN 1012-5566
QC176.A1
EGYPTIAN JOURNAL OF SOLIDS. Text in English. s-a. EGP 10 per issue domestic to members; EGP 25 per issue domestic to institutions; USD 25 per issue foreign (effective 2008). **Document type:** *Journal, Academic/Scholarly.*
Related titles: Online - full text ed.
Indexed: A01, A03, A08, CA, Inspec, S01, T02.
—Ingenta, Linda Hall.
Published by: (Egyptian Materials Research Society), National Information and Documentation Centre (NIDOC), Tahrir St., Dokki, Awqaf P.O., Giza, Egypt. TEL 20-2-701696, 20-2-3371696.

ELECTRICAL LINE; Western Canada's electrical trade magazine. *see* ENERGY

537.5 NLD ISSN 0929-5054
CODEN: ELWAFY
➤ **ELECTROMAGNETIC WAVES;** recent developments in research. Text in English. 1992. irreg., latest vol.2, 1995. price varies. back issues avail. **Document type:** *Monographic series, Academic/Scholarly.* **Description:** Publishes comprehensive review articles on aspects of fundamental physics and research in electromagnetic wave phenomena in a wide range of materials.
—BLDSC (3699.555000), CASDDS.
Published by: Elsevier BV (Subsidiary of: Elsevier Science & Technology), Radarweg 29, PO Box 211, Amsterdam, 1000 AE, Netherlands. TEL 31-20-4853911, FAX 31-20-4852457, JournalsCustomerServiceEMEA@elsevier.com, http://www.elsevier.nl.

531.112 CAN
➤ **ELECTRONIC JOURNAL OF COMPUTATIONAL KINEMATICS.** Text in English. 1999. irreg. free. back issues avail. **Document type:** *Journal, Academic/Scholarly.* **Description:** Features kinematics research involving intensive computation not only of the numerical type, but also of a symbolic or geometric nature.
Media: Online - full text.
Published by: McGill University, Department of Mechanical Engineering, 817 Sherbrooke St W, Montreal, PQ H3A 2K6, Canada. TEL 514-398-6315, FAX 514-398-7348. **Co-sponsor:** International Federation on the Theory of Machines and Mechanisms.

530 UAE ISSN 1729-5254
QC1
➤ **ELECTRONIC JOURNAL OF THEORETICAL PHYSICS.** Text in English. 2004. s-a. free (effective 2011). **Document type:** *Journal, Academic/Scholarly.* **Description:** Publishes original research papers, comments and brief reviews on all aspects of Theoretical and Mathematical Physics, and Theoretical Astrophysics.
Media: Online - full text.
Indexed: A01, CA, SCOPUS, T02, Z02.
Address: PO Box 48210, Abu Dhabi, United Arab Emirates. Ed. A J Sakaji.

➤ **ELEKTRONENMIKROSKOPIE.** *see* BIOLOGY—Microscopy

➤ **ENERGY SOURCES. PART A. RECOVERY, UTILIZATION, AND ENVIRONMENTAL EFFECTS.** *see* ENERGY

➤ **ENERGY SOURCES. PART B. ECONOMICS, PLANNING, AND POLICY.** *see* ENERGY

➤ **ENERGY TODAY.** *see* ENERGY

621 JPN ISSN 0286-3162
ENERUGI SOGO KOGAKU. Text in Japanese. 1978. q.
Indexed: INIS AtomInd.
Published by: Enerugi Sogo Kogaku Kenkyujo/Institute of Applied Energy, Tokyo, Shimbashi SY Bldg, 1-14-2 Nishi-Shimbashi, Minato-ku, Tokyo, 105-0003, Japan. TEL 81-3-35088894, FAX 81-3-35011735, http://www.iae.or.jp/.

530 541 USA ISSN 0013-8533
ENSANIAN PHYSICOCHEMICAL INSTITUTE. JOURNAL. Text in English. 1969. q. membership. bk.rev. abstr.; bibl.; charts; illus.; pat. index, cum.index. **Document type:** *Corporate.*
Media: Duplicated (not offset).
Published by: Ensanian Physicochemical Institute, PO Box 98, Eldred, PA 16731. TEL 814-225-3296. Ed. Minas Ensanian. Circ: 250.

333.714 541 LTU ISSN 1392-740X
CODEN: FZATAH
➤ **ENVIRONMENTAL AND CHEMICAL PHYSICS/APLINKOS FIZIKA.** Text and summaries in English. 1973. q. **Document type:** *Journal, Academic/Scholarly.* **Description:** Covers problems of the atmosphere's and hydrosphere's pollution by radioactive and chemical substances.
Former titles (until 1999): Environmental Physics (1392-4168); (until 1997): Atmospheric Physics Atmospheros Fizika (1392-0332); (until 1994): Fizika Atmosfery (0135-1419)
Indexed: CIN, ChemAb, ChemTitl, GeoRef, SpeleolAb.
—CASDDS, INIST, Linda Hall.
Published by: Fizikos Institutas/Institute of Physics, A. Gostauto 12, Vilnius, 2600, Lithuania. TEL 3702-621058, FAX 3702-617070, romanska@ktl.mii.lt. Ed. A Undzenas.

540 CRI
ESPACIO VIRTUAL DE LA FISICA. Text in Spanish. 2001. q.
Media: Online - full text.
Published by: Instituto Tecnologico de Costa Rica, Apdo 159, Cartago, 7050, Costa Rica. TEL 506-552-5333, FAX 506-551-5348, http://www.itcr.ac.cr/. Ed. Alvaro Amador.

▼ **EURASIAN JOURNAL OF PHYSICS AND CHEMISTRY EDUCATION.** *see* EDUCATION

530 DEU ISSN 0531-7401
EUROPAEISCHE HOCHSCHULSCHRIFTEN. REIHE 12: PHYSIK. Text in German. 1968. irreg., latest vol.8, 1981. price varies. **Document type:** *Monographic series, Academic/Scholarly.*
Published by: Peter Lang GmbH (Subsidiary of: Peter Lang Publishing Group), Eschborner Landstr 42-50, Frankfurt Am Main, 60489, Germany. TEL 49-69-7807050, FAX 49-69-78070550, zentrale.frankfurt@peterlang.com, http://www.peterlang.com.

530 GBR ISSN 0143-0807
QC1 CODEN: EJPHD4
➤ **EUROPEAN JOURNAL OF PHYSICS.** Text in English. 1980. bi-m. GBP 594 combined subscription to institutions (print & online eds.) (effective 2010). adv. bk.rev. bibl.; illus.; charts. Index. back issues avail. **Document type:** *Journal, Academic/Scholarly.* **Description:** Publishes educational and scholarly studies in physics and closely related sciences at the university level.
Related titles: Microfiche ed.: USD 743 in North America; GBP 374 elsewhere (effective 2007); Online - full text ed.: ISSN 1361-6404. GBP 566 to institutions (effective 2010) (from IngentaConnect).
Indexed: A01, A03, A08, A20, A22, AcoustA, BiolDig, CA, CCMJ, CIN, CPEI, ChemAb, ChemTitl, CurCont, ERIC, EngInd, INIS AtomInd, Inspec, M&GPA, MSN, MathR, PhysBer, RefZh, SCI, SCOPUS, T02, W07, Z02.
—BLDSC (3829.735000), AskIEEE, CASDDS, IE, Infotrieve, Ingenta, INIST, Linda Hall. **CCC.**
Published by: (Institute of Physics), Institute of Physics Publishing Ltd., Dirac House, Temple Back, Bristol, BS1 6BE, United Kingdom. TEL 44-117-9297481, FAX 44-117-9301178, custserv@iop.org, http://publishing.iop.org/. Ed. A I M Rae. Pub. Andrea Pomroy. **Subscr. in the US, Canada & Mexico to:** American Institute of Physics, PO Box 503284, St Louis, MO 63150. TEL 516-576-2270, 800-344-6902, FAX 516-349-9704, subs@aip.org. **Co-sponsor:** European Physical Society.

▼ ➤ **EUROPEAN JOURNAL OF PHYSICS EDUCATION.** *see* EDUCATION

➤ **EUROPEAN PHYSICAL JOURNAL A. HADRONS AND NUCLEI.** *see* PHYSICS—Nuclear Physics

621 530 FRA ISSN 1286-0042
QC1 CODEN: EPAPFV
➤ **THE EUROPEAN PHYSICAL JOURNAL - APPLIED PHYSICS.** Text in English. 1998. m. GBP 1,784, EUR 1,962, USD 2,600 combined subscription to institutions (print & online eds.) (effective 2012). bk.rev. charts; illus. index. back issues avail. **Document type:** *Journal, Academic/Scholarly.* **Description:** Publishes articles on original measurements relative to known phenomena or experimental methods in physics.
Incorporates in part (1903-2000): Anales de Fisica (1133-0376); Formed by the 1998 merger of: Journal de Physique III (1155-4320); Which was formerly: Revue de Physique Appliquee (0035-1687); Microscopy Microanalysis Microstructures (1154-2799); Which was formerly (until 1989): Journal de Microscopie et de Spectroscopie Electroniques (0395-9279); Which superseded in part: Journal de Microscopie (0021-7921)
Related titles: Online - full text ed.: ISSN 1286-0050. GBP 1,515, EUR 1,667, USD 2,167 to institutions (effective 2012).
Indexed: A20, A22, A28, APA, ASCA, BrCerAb, C&ISA, CA, CA/WCA, CIA, CPEI, Cadscan, CerAb, ChemAb, CivEngAb, CorrAb, CurCont, E&CAJ, E11, EEA, EMA, ESPM, EngInd, EnvEAb, GeoRef, H15, IBR, IBZ, INIS AtomInd, ISR, Inspec, LeadAb, M&TEA, M09, MBF, METADEX, PhysBer, RefZh, SCI, SCOPUS, SolStAb, SpeleolAb, T02, T04, TM, W07, WAA, Zincscan.

—BLDSC (3794.339150), AskIEEE, CASDDS, GNLM, IE, Infotrieve, Ingenta, INIST, Linda Hall. **CCC.**

Published by: E D P Sciences, 17 Ave du Hoggar, Parc d'Activites de Courtaboeuf, BP 112, Cedex A, Les Ulis, F-91944, France. TEL 33-1-69187575, FAX 33-1-69860678, subscribers@edpsciences.org, http://www.edpsciences.org. Ed. B Drevillon. Circ: 3,500. **Dist. by:** Cambridge University Press, The Edinburgh Bldg, Shaftesbury Rd, Cambridge CB2 8RU, United Kingdom. TEL 44-1223-312393, FAX 44-1223-315052, information@cambridge.org.

536.44 DEU ISSN 1434-6028
QC173.45 CODEN: EPJBFY

➤ **EUROPEAN PHYSICAL JOURNAL B. CONDENSED MATTER AND COMPLEX SYSTEMS.** Text in English. 1998. s-m. EUR 3,680, USD 4,736 combined subscription to institutions (print & online eds.) (effective 2012). adv. illus. Index. back issues avail.; reprint service avail. from PSC. **Document type:** *Journal, Academic/Scholarly.* **Description:** Presents papers on the physical properties of crystalline, disordered, and amorphous solids, and on classical and quantum liquids.

Incorporates in part (1903-2000): Anales de Fisica (1133-0376); Formed by the merger of (1963-1998): Journal de Physique I (1155-4304); Which was formerly (until 1991): Journal de Physique (0302-0738); (until 1962): Jopurnal de Physique et le Radium (0368-3842); (1963-1998): Zeitschrift fuer Physik B: Condensed Matter (0722-3277); Which was formerly (until 1980): Zeitschrift fuer Physik B (Condensed Matter and Quanta) (0340-224X); (until 1973): Physik der Kondensierten Materie - Physique de la Matiere Condensee - Physics of Condensed Matter (0031-9236); (1771-1998): Societa Italiana di Fisica. Nuovo Cimento D (0392-6737); Which superseded in part (in 1982): Nuovo Cimento (0029-6341); Which was formerly (until 1885): Il Cimento (1124-1845); (until 1843): Miscellanee di Chimica, Fisica e Storia Naturale (1124-1829); Which superseded in part (in 1843): Giornale Toscano di Scienze Mediche Fisiche e Naturali (1124-1810); Which was formerly (until 1840): Nuovo Giornale dei Letterati (1124-1802); (until 1822): Accademia Italiana di Scienze Lettere ed Arti. Giornale Scientifico e Letterario (1124-1799); (until 1810): Giornale Pisano di Letteratura, Scienze ed Arti (1124-1780); (until 1807): Giornale Pisano dei Letterati (1124-1772); (until 1806): Nuovo Giornale dei Letterati (1124-1764); (until 1820): Giornale dei Letterati (1124-1756)

Related titles: Microform ed.: (from PMC, PQC); Online - full text ed.: ISSN 1434-6036 (from IngentaConnect).

Indexed: A01, A02, A03, A08, A20, A22, A26, ASCA, C33, CA, CCMJ, CIN, CPEI, ChemAb, ChemTitl, CurCont, E01, EngInd, FR, GeoRef, IBR, IBZ, INIS AtomInd, ISR, Inspec, M&GPA, MSCI, MSN, MathR, P30, PhysBer, RefZh, SCI, SCOPUS, SpeleolAb, T02, W07, Z02.

—BLDSC (3829.779212), AskIEEE, CASDDS, IE, Infotrieve, Ingenta, INIST, Linda Hall. **CCC.**

Published by: Springer (Subsidiary of: Springer Science+Business Media), Tiergartenstr 17, Heidelberg, 69121, Germany. TEL 49-6221-4870, FAX 49-6221-345229. Eds. Alois Loidl, Frank Schweitzer, Luciano Colombo. **Subscr. in the Americas to:** Springer New York LLC, Journal Fulfillment, PO Box 2485, Secaucus, NJ 07096. TEL 800-777-4643, 201-348-4033, FAX 201-348-4505, journals-ny@springer.com, http://www.springer.com; **Subscr. to:** Springer Distribution Center, Kundenservice Zeitschriften, Haberstr 7, Heidelberg 69126, Germany. TEL 49-6221-3454303, FAX 49-6221-3454229, subscriptions@springer.com.

530 DEU ISSN 1434-6044
QC1 CODEN: EPCFFB

➤ **EUROPEAN PHYSICAL JOURNAL C. PARTICLES AND FIELDS.** Text in English. 1979. 20/yr. (in 4 vols., 5 nos./vol.). EUR 5,614, USD 7,074 combined subscription to institutions (print & online eds.) (effective 2012). adv. illus. Index. reprint service avail. from PSC. **Document type:** *Journal, Academic/Scholarly.* **Description:** Covers experimental and theoretical particle physics.

Incorporates in part (1903-2000): Anales de Fisica (1133-0376); (1855-1999): Societa Italiana di Fisica. Nuovo Cimento. A. Nuclei, Paticles and Fields (1124-1861); Which was formerly (until 1982): Societa Italiana di Fisica. Nuovo Cimento. A (1124-1853); (until 1971): Nuovo Cimento A (0369-3546); Which superseded in part (in 1965): Nuovo Cimento (0029-6341); Formerly (until 1997): Zeitschrift fuer Physik C. Particles and Fields (0170-9739)

Related titles: Microform ed.: (from PMC, PQC); Online - full text ed.: ISSN 1434-6052 (from IngentaConnect).

Indexed: A01, A02, A03, A08, A22, A26, ASCA, C33, CA, CCMJ, CIN, CMCI, ChemAb, ChemTitl, CurCont, E01, INIS AtomInd, ISR, Inspec, MSN, MathR, PhysBer, SCI, SCOPUS, T02, TM, W07.

—BLDSC (3829.779214), AskIEEE, CASDDS, IE, Infotrieve, Ingenta, INIST, Linda Hall. **CCC.**

Published by: Springer (Subsidiary of: Springer Science+Business Media), Tiergartenstr 17, Heidelberg, 69121, Germany. TEL 49-6221-4870, FAX 49-6221-345229. Eds. G Weiglein, S Bethke. **Subscr. in the Americas to:** Springer New York LLC, Journal Fulfillment, PO Box 2485, Secaucus, NJ 07096. TEL 800-777-4643, 201-348-4033, FAX 201-348-4505, journals-ny@springer.com, http://www.springer.com; **Subscr. to:** Springer Distribution Center, Kundenservice Zeitschriften, Haberstr 7, Heidelberg 69126, Germany. TEL 49-6221-3454303, FAX 49-6221-3454229, subscriptions@springer.com.

530 DEU ISSN 1434-6060
QC1 CODEN: EPJDF6

➤ **EUROPEAN PHYSICAL JOURNAL D. ATOMIC, MOLECULAR, OPTICAL AND PLASMA PHYSICS.** Text in English. 1998. 15/yr. EUR 2,889, USD 3,150 combined subscription to institutions (print & online eds.) (effective 2012). adv. illus. Index. back issues avail.; reprint service avail. from PSC. **Document type:** *Journal, Academic/Scholarly.* **Description:** Encompasses the entire field of atomic, molecular, cluster, and chemical physics.

Incorporates (1951-2007): Czechoslovak Journal of Physics (0011-4626); Incorporates in part (1903-2000): Anales de Fisica (1133-0376); Formed by the merger of (1991-1998): Journal de Physique II (1155-4312); (1986-1998): Zeitschrift fuer Physik D. Atoms, Molecules and Clusters (0178-7683); Supersedes in part (1982-1999): Societa Italiana di Fisica. Nuovo Cimento D (0392-6737); Which incorporated in part (1855-1965): Nuovo Cimento (0029-6341); Which superseded (1843-1847): Cimento (1124-1845); Miscellanee de Chimica, Fisica e Storia Naturale (1124-1829); Which superseded in part (in 1843): Giornale Toscano di Scienze Mediche Fisiche e Naturali (1124-1810); (until 1840): Nuovo Giornale dei Letterati (1124-1802); Which superseded (in 1822): Accademia Italiana di Scienze Lettere ed Arti. Giornale Scientifico e Letterario (1124-1799); (until 1809): Giornale Pisano di Letteratura, Scienze ed Arti (1124-1780); (until 1807): Giornale Pisano dei Letterati (1124-1772); (1802-1806): Nuovo Giornale dei Letterati (1124-1764); Which superseded (1771-1796): Giornale dei Letterati (1124-1756)

Related titles: Online - full text ed.: ISSN 1434-6079 (from IngentaConnect).

Indexed: A01, A02, A03, A08, A22, A26, ASCA, C33, CA, CCMJ, CIN, ChemAb, ChemTitl, CurCont, E01, IBR, IBZ, INIS AtomInd, ISR, Inspec, MSN, MathR, RefZh, SCI, SCOPUS, SpeleolAb, T02, W07.

—BLDSC (3829.779220), AskIEEE, CASDDS, IE, Infotrieve, Ingenta, INIST, Linda Hall. **CCC.**

Published by: Springer (Subsidiary of: Springer Science+Business Media), Tiergartenstr 17, Heidelberg, 69121, Germany. TEL 49-6221-4870, FAX 49-6221-345229. Eds. C Fabre, Franco A Gianturco, K H Becker. Circ: 700. **Subscr. in the Americas to:** Springer New York LLC, Journal Fulfillment, PO Box 2485, Secaucus, NJ 07096. TEL 800-777-4643, 201-348-4033, FAX 201-348-4505, journals-ny@springer.com, http://www.springer.com; **Subscr. to:** Springer Distribution Center, Kundenservice Zeitschriften, Haberstr 7, Heidelberg 69126, Germany. TEL 49-6221-3454303, FAX 49-6221-3454229, subscriptions@springer.com.

530 DEU ISSN 1292-8941
QC173.458.S62 CODEN: EPJSFH

➤ **EUROPEAN PHYSICAL JOURNAL E. SOFT MATTER.** Text in English. 2000. m. EUR 2,532, USD 3,033 combined subscription to institutions (print & online eds.) (effective 2012). adv. reprint service avail. from PSC. **Document type:** *Journal, Academic/Scholarly.* **Description:** Provides a common platform and audience for all scientists involved in soft matter science.

Formed by the merger of part of (1998-2000): European Physical Journal. B. Condensed Matter Physics (1434-6028); part of (1992-2000): Anales de Fisica (1133-0376); Which was formed by the merger of (1903-1992): Anales de Fisica. Serie A: Fenomenos e Interacciones (0211-6243); (1903-1992): Anales de Fisica. Serie B: Aplicaciones, Metodos e Instrumentos (0211-6251); Both of which superseded in part (in 1981): Anales de Fisica (0365-4818); Which was formerly (until 1968): Real Sociedad Espanola de Fisica y Quimica. Anales. Serie A: Fisica (0034-0871); Which superseded in part (in 1948): Anales de Fisica y Quimica (0365-2351); Which was formerly (until 1941): Sociedad Espanola de Fisica y Quimica. Anales (0365-6675)

Related titles: Microform ed.; Online - full text ed.: ISSN 1292-895X (from IngentaConnect).

Indexed: A01, A02, A03, A08, A22, A26, B&BAb, B19, B21, C33, CA, CPEI, CurCont, E01, EMBASE, EngInd, ExcerpMed, ISR, Inspec, MEDLINE, P30, R10, Reac, RefZh, SCI, SCOPUS, T02, W07.

—BLDSC (3829.779230), IE, Infotrieve, Ingenta, INIST, Linda Hall. **CCC.**

Published by: (Societa Italiana di Fisica (S I F) ITA), Springer (Subsidiary of: Springer Science+Business Media), Haber Str 7, Heidelberg, 69126, Germany. Eds. Frank Juelicher, Georg Maret, Richard A Jones. **Subscr. in the Americas to:** Springer New York LLC, Journal Fulfillment, PO Box 2485, Secaucus, NJ 07096. TEL 800-777-4643, 201-348-4033, FAX 201-348-4505, journals-ny@springer.com, http://www.springer.com; **Subscr. to:** Springer Distribution Center, Kundenservice Zeitschriften, Haberstr 7, Heidelberg 69126, Germany. TEL 49-6221-3454303, FAX 49-6221-3454229, subscriptions@springer.com.

530 DEU ISSN 2102-6459
QC1 CODEN: ANPHAJ

➤ **EUROPEAN PHYSICAL JOURNAL H.** Text and summaries in English, French. 1816. q. EUR 562, USD 760 combined subscription to institutions (print & online eds.) (effective 2012). bk.rev. illus. index. back issues avail.; reprints avail. **Document type:** *Journal, Academic/Scholarly.* **Description:** Covers the basics of atomic and molecular physics, condensed matter, nuclear physics and astrophysics.

Formerly (until 2009): Annales de Physique (0003-4169); Which superseded in part (in 1914): Annales de Chimie et de Physique (0365-1444)

Related titles: Microfilm ed.: (from PMC); Online - full text ed.: ISSN 2102-6467. 1998.

Indexed: A22, A28, APA, ASCA, BrCerAb, C&ISA, CA/WCA, CIA, CIN, Cadscan, CerAb, ChemAb, ChemTitl, CivEngAb, CorrAb, CurCont, E&CAJ, E11, EEA, EMA, ESPM, EnvEAb, GeoRef, H15, ISR, Inspec, LeadAb, M&TEA, M09, MBF, METADEX, MathR, P30, RefZh, SCI, SCOPUS, SolStAb, SpeleolAb, T02, T04, VITIS, W07, WAA, Zincscan.

—BLDSC (0993.000000), AskIEEE, CASDDS, IE, Infotrieve, Ingenta, INIST, Linda Hall. **CCC.**

Published by: Springer (Subsidiary of: Springer Science+Business Media), Tiergartenstr 17, Heidelberg, 69121, Germany. TEL 49-6221-4870, FAX 49-6221-345229, subscriptions@springer.de. Ed. Wolf Beiglboeck.

530 DEU ISSN 2190-5444

➤ **EUROPEAN PHYSICAL JOURNAL PLUS.** Text in English. m. EUR 1,075, USD 1,322 to institutions (effective 2012). **Document type:** *Journal, Academic/Scholarly.* **Description:** Provides a new forum for the setting and improvement of standards, procedures and performance in experimental and observational physics, computational physics, and theoretical physics.

Media: Online - full text.

Indexed: CurCont, SCI, W07.

—IE. **CCC.**

Published by: Springer (Subsidiary of: Springer Science+Business Media), Tiergartenstr 17, Heidelberg, 69121, Germany. TEL 49-6221-4870, FAX 49-6221-345229, subscriptions@springer.com. Ed. Luisa Cifarelli.

530 DEU ISSN 1951-6355
QC1 CODEN: JPICEI

➤ **THE EUROPEAN PHYSICAL JOURNAL. SPECIAL TOPICS.** Variant title: Journal de Physique IV. Proceedings. Text in English. 1966. 14/yr. EUR 2,004, USD 2,436 combined subscription to institutions (print & online eds.) (effective 2012). reprint service avail. from PSC. **Document type:** *Journal, Academic/Scholarly.* **Description:** Devoted to the publication of topical issues in fields related to the pure and applied physical sciences, including complex systems, physical biology, chemistry and materials science.

Former titles (until 2007): Journal de Physique IV (1155-4339); (until 1991): Journal de Physique. Colloque (0449-1947)

Related titles: Online - full text ed.: The European Physical Journal. Special Topics (Online). ISSN 1951-6401 (from IngentaConnect).

Indexed: A20, A22, A26, A28, APA, ASCA, BrCerAb, C&ISA, CA/WCA, CIA, CIN, CerAb, ChemAb, ChemTitl, CivEngAb, CorrAb, CurCont, E&CAJ, E01, E11, EEA, EMA, ESPM, EngInd, EnvEAb, GeoRef, H15, I05, INIS AtomInd, ISMEC, ISR, Inspec, M&TEA, M09, MBF, METADEX, P30, RefZh, SCI, SCOPUS, SolStAb, SpeleolAb, T04, TM, VITIS, W07, WAA.

—BLDSC (3829.779240), AskIEEE, CASDDS, IE, Infotrieve, Ingenta, INIST, Linda Hall. **CCC.**

Published by: (Societe Francaise de Physique FRA), Springer (Subsidiary of: Springer Science+Business Media), Tiergartenstr 17, Heidelberg, 69121, Germany. TEL 49-6221-4870, FAX 49-6221-345229, subscriptions@springer.com, http://www.springer.de.

530 FRA ISSN 0295-5075
QC1 CODEN: EULEEJ

➤ **EUROPHYSICS LETTERS**; a letters journal exploring the frontiers of physics. Abbreviated title: E P L. Text in English. 1986. 24/yr. EUR 2,520 combined subscription in the European Union (print & online eds.); EUR 2,581 combined subscription elsewhere (print & online eds.) (effective 2012). back issues avail. **Document type:** *Journal, Academic/Scholarly.* **Description:** Highlights new ideas, experimental methods, theoretical treatments and results of interest to the physics community.

Formed by the merger of (1974-1986): Journal de Physique. Lettres (0302-072X); (1969-1986): Societa Italiana di Fisica. Lettere al Nuovo Cimento (0375-930X); Which was formerly (until 1971): Lettere al Nuovo Cimento (0024-1318)

Related titles: Microfiche ed.; Online - full text ed.: ISSN 1286-4854. EUR 1,983 (effective 2011) (from IngentaConnect).

Indexed: A20, A22, A28, APA, ASCA, AcoustA, BrCerAb, C&ISA, CA, CA/WCA, CCMJ, CIA, CIN, CerAb, ChemAb, ChemTitl, CivEngAb, CorrAb, CurCont, E&CAJ, E11, EEA, EMA, ESPM, EnvEAb, GeoRef, H15, INIS AtomInd, ISR, Inspec, M&TEA, M09, MBF, METADEX, MSN, MathR, P30, RefZh, SCI, SCOPUS, SolStAb, SpeleolAb, T02, T04, W07, WAA.

—BLDSC (3830.419000), AskIEEE, CASDDS, IE, Infotrieve, Ingenta, INIST, Linda Hall. **CCC.**

Published by: (Societa Italiana di Fisica (S I F) ITA), E D P Sciences, 17 Ave du Hoggar, Parc d'Activites de Courtaboeuf, BP 112, Cedex A, Les Ulis, F-91944, France. TEL 33-1-69187575, FAX 33-1-69860678, subscribers@edpsciences.org, http://www.edpsciences.org. Circ: 1,500. **Co-sponsor:** European Physical Society.

530 FRA ISSN 0531-7479
QC1 CODEN: EUPNAS

EUROPHYSICS NEWS. Text in English. 1969. 6/yr. EUR 95 combined subscription in the European Union (print & online eds.); EUR 113 combined subscription elsewhere (print & online eds.) (effective 2012). adv. **Document type:** *Journal, Academic/Scholarly.*

Formerly: Europhysics Review

Related titles: Online - full text ed.: ISSN 1432-1092. 1969. free (effective 2011).

Indexed: A22, A28, APA, BrCerAb, C&ISA, CA/WCA, CIA, CIN, CerAb, ChemAb, ChemTitl, CivEngAb, CorrAb, E&CAJ, E11, EEA, EMA, ESPM, EnvEAb, H15, Inspec, M&TEA, M09, MBF, METADEX, SCOPUS, SolStAb, T04, WAA.

—AskIEEE, CASDDS, IE, Infotrieve, INIST, Linda Hall.

Published by: (European Physical Society NLD), E D P Sciences, 17 Ave du Hoggar, Parc d'Activites de Courtaboeuf, BP 112, Cedex A, Les Ulis, F-91944, France. TEL 33-1-69187575, FAX 33-1-69860678, subscribers@edpsciences.org, http://www.edpsciences.org. Ed. T Chapman. Circ: 26,700. **Dist. by:** Springer, Haber Str 7, Heidelberg 69126, Germany.

530 USA ISSN 1079-4042
CODEN: EMPSFQ

➤ **EXPERIMENTAL METHODS IN THE PHYSICAL SCIENCES.** Text in English. 1959. irreg., latest vol.43, 2009. USD 215 per vol. (effective 2010). adv. back issues avail.; reprints avail. **Document type:** *Monographic series, Academic/Scholarly.* **Description:** Discusses the use of optical resonators and lasers to make sensitive spectroscopic measurements.

Formerly (until 1995): Methods of Experimental Physics (0076-695X)

Related titles: Online - full text ed.

Indexed: CIN, ChemAb, ChemTitl, GeoRef, Inspec, PhysBer, SCOPUS, SpeleolAb.

—BLDSC (3839.770000), CASDDS, IE, Ingenta, INIST. **CCC.**

Published by: Academic Press (Subsidiary of: Elsevier Science & Technology), 3251 Riverport Ln, Maryland Heights, MO 63043. TEL 314-447-8010, FAX 314-447-8030, JournalCustomerService-usa@elsevier.com, http://www.elsevierdirect.com/imprint.jsp?iid=5.

➤ **F A C E N A.** (Facultad de Ciencias Exactas y Naturales e Agrimensura) *see* BIOLOGY

➤ **F G M NEWS.** (Functionally Gradient Materials) *see* TECHNOLOGY: COMPREHENSIVE WORKS

➤ **F & S.** (Filtrieren und Separieren) *see* CHEMISTRY

530 540 600 SRB ISSN 0354-4656

FACTA UNIVERSITATIS. SERIES PHYSICS, CHEMISTRY AND TECHNOLOGY. Text in English, French, German. 1994. irreg., latest vol.2, no.2, 2000. **Document type:** *Journal, Academic/Scholarly.*

Related titles: Online - full text ed.: free (effective 2011).

Indexed: RefZh.

—Linda Hall.

Published by: Univerzitet u Nishu/University of Nis, Univerzitetski Trg 2, P.O. Box 123, Nis, 18000. TEL 381-18-547970, FAX 381-18-547950, facta@ni.ac.yu, http://ni.ac.yu. Ed. Ivan Mancev.

530 CHN ISSN 1000-0720
QD71 CODEN: FENSE4

FENXI SHIYANSHI/ANALYTICAL LABORATORY. Text in Chinese. 1932. bi-m. USD 80.40 (effective 2009). **Description:** Publishes information on analysis chemistry, combining theory with practice and research with application.

Related titles: Online - full text ed.

Indexed: A28, A32, A40, APA, BrCerAb, C&ISA, CA/WCA, CIA, CerAb, CivEngAb, CorrAb, E&CAJ, E11, EEA, EMA, ESPM, EnvEAb, GeoRef, H15, M&TEA, M09, MBF, METADEX, SolStAb, T04, WAA.

—East View, IE, Linda Hall.

Published by: Zhongguo Youse Jinshu Xuehui/Chinese Society of Nonferrous Metal, 2 Xinjiekouwai Dajie, Beijing, 100088, China. TEL 86-10-62028395, FAX 86-10-62025838, mnfirgb@public.bta.net.cn.

530 CHN ISSN 1001-3555
QD505 CODEN: FECUEN
FENZI CUIHUA/JOURNAL OF MOLECULAR CATALYSIS. Text in Chinese. 1987. bi-m. USD 53.40 (effective 2009). **Document type:** *Journal, Academic/Scholarly.*
Related titles: Online - full content ed.; Online - full text ed.
Indexed: C33, RefZh.
—BLDSC (5020.703000), East View.
Published by: (Zhongguo Huaxuehui/Chinese Chemical Society, Zhongguo Kexueyuan Lanzhou Huaxue Wuli Yanjiusuo), Kexue Chubanshe/Science Press, 16 Donghuang Cheng Genbei Jie, Beijing, 100717, China. TEL 86-10-64000246, FAX 86-10-64030255, http://www.sciencep.com/. Ed. Shu-Ben Li. **Dist. by:** China International Book Trading Corp, 35 Chegongzhuang Xilu, Haidian District, PO Box 399, Beijing 100044, China. TEL 86-10-68412045, FAX 86-10-68412023, cibtc@mail.cibtc.com.cn, http://www.cibtc.com.cn.

530 USA ISSN 0015-0193
QC595 CODEN: FEROA8
➤ **FERROELECTRICS.** Text in English. 1970. 16/yr. GBP 14,229 combined subscription in United Kingdom to institutions (print & online eds.); EUR 17,417, USD 21,870 combined subscription to institutions (print & online eds.) (effective 2012). adv. bk.rev. index. reprint service avail. from PSC. **Document type:** *Journal, Academic/Scholarly.* **Description:** Publishes experimental, theoretical, and applied papers aimed at understanding ferroelectrics and related materials.
Related titles: CD-ROM ed.: ISSN 1026-7484. 1995; Microform ed.; Online - full text ed.: ISSN 1563-5112. GBP 12,807 in United Kingdom to institutions; EUR 15,675, USD 19,683 to institutions (effective 2012) (from IngentaConnect).
Indexed: A01, A03, A08, A22, A28, APA, BrCerAb, C&ISA, C33, CA, CA/WCA, CCI, CIA, CPEI, Cadscan, CerAb, ChemAb, CivEngAb, CorrAb, CurCont, E&CAJ, E01, E11, EEA, EMA, ESPM, EngInd, EnvEAb, H15, IBR, IBZ, ISMEC, ISR, Inspec, LeadAb, M&TEA, M09, MBF, METADEX, MSCI, P26, P52, P54, P56, PQC, PhysBer, S01, SCI, SCOPUS, SolStAb, T02, T04, TM, W07, WAA, Zincscan.
—BLDSC (3908.400000), AskIEEE, IE, Infotrieve, Ingenta, INIST, Linda Hall. **CCC.**
Published by: Taylor & Francis Inc. (Subsidiary of: Taylor & Francis Group), 325 Chestnut St, Ste 800, Philadelphia, PA 19106. TEL 215-625-2940, 800-354-1420, orders@taylorandfrancis.com, http://www.taylorandfrancis.com. Ed. George W Taylor. Adv. contact Linda Hann TEL 44-1344-779945.

530 AUT ISSN 0177-7963
QC1 CODEN: FBSYEQ
➤ **FEW-BODY SYSTEMS.** Text in English. 1947; N.S. 1986. 8/yr. EUR 1,375, USD 1,649 combined subscription to institutions (print & online eds.) (effective 2012). adv. bk.rev. charts; illus.; abstr. index. back issues avail.; reprint service avail. from PSC. **Document type:** *Journal, Academic/Scholarly.* **Description:** Devoted to the publication of original research work, both experimental and theoretical, in the field of few-body systems.
Formerly (until 1986): Acta Physica Austriaca (0001-6713)
Related titles: Microform ed.: N.S. (from PQC); Online - full text ed.: ISSN 1432-5411. N.S. (from IngentaConnect); ◆ Supplement(s): Few-Body Systems. Supplementum. ISSN 0177-8811.
Indexed: A01, A03, A08, A22, A26, ASCA, CA, Cadscan, ChemAb, CurCont, E01, IBR, IBZ, INIS AtomInd, ISR, Inspec, LeadAb, MathR, P02, P26, P48, P52, P54, P56, PQC, PhysBer, RefZh, SCI, SCOPUS, T02, W07, Z02, Zincscan.
—AskIEEE, CASDDS, IE, Infotrieve, Ingenta, INIST, Linda Hall. **CCC.**
Published by: Springer Wien (Subsidiary of: Springer Science+Business Media), Sachsenplatz 4-6, Vienna, W 1201, Austria. TEL 43-1-33024150, FAX 43-1-330242426, journals@springer.at. Ed. Ben Bakker. Adv. contact Irene Hofmann. B&W page EUR 1,290; 170 x 230. Circ: 500 (paid). **Subscr. in the Americas to:** Springer New York LLC, Journal Fulfillment, PO Box 2485, Secaucus, NJ 07096. TEL 800-777-4643, 201-348-4033, FAX 201-348-4505, journals-ny@springer.com, http://www.springer.com; **Subscr. to:** Springer Distribution Center, Kundenservice Zeitschriften, Haberstr 7, Heidelberg 69126, Germany. TEL 49-6221-3454303, FAX 49-6221-3454229, subscriptions@springer.com.

530 AUT ISSN 0177-8811
CODEN: FBSSE8
FEW-BODY SYSTEMS. SUPPLEMENTUM. Text in English. 1965; N.S. 1986. irreg., latest vol.14, 2003. price varies. adv. reprints avail. **Document type:** *Monographic series, Academic/Scholarly.* **Description:** Publishes selected papers of conferences in the field of few-body systems.
Formerly (until no.27, 1985): Acta Physica Austriaca. Supplement (0065-1559)
Related titles: Microform ed.: N.S. (from PQC); ◆ Supplement to: Few-Body Systems. ISSN 0177-7963.
Indexed: INIS AtomInd, Inspec, MathR.
—BLDSC (3914.145100), AskIEEE, CASDDS, INIST. **CCC.**
Published by: Springer Wien (Subsidiary of: Springer Science+Business Media), Sachsenplatz 4-6, Vienna, W 1201, Austria. TEL 43-1-3302415-0, FAX 43-1-330242665, journals@springer.at. Ed. Ben Bakker. R&P Angela Foessl TEL 43-1-3302415517. Adv. contact Michael Katzenberger TEL 43-1-3302415220. B&W page EUR 1,000; 120 x 190. **Subscr. in the Americas to:** Springer New York LLC, Journal Fulfillment, PO Box 2485, Secaucus, NJ 07096. TEL 201-348-4033, 800-777-4643, FAX 201-348-4505, journals-ny@springer.com, orders@springer-ny.com.

530 ITA
FISICA. Text in Italian. 1987. irreg., latest vol.6, 1999. price varies. **Document type:** *Monographic series, Academic/Scholarly.*
Published by: Liguori Editore, Via Posillipo 394, Naples, 80123, Italy. TEL 39-081-7206111, FAX 39-081-7206244, liguori@liguori.it, http://www.liguori.it.

530.15 ARG ISSN 0326-7512
FISICA. Text in Spanish. 1985. 2/yr. USD 4 per issue (effective 1998). bk.rev. **Document type:** *Academic/Scholarly.* **Description:** Includes articles on history, philosophy, tools and more.
—Linda Hall.
Published by: Zagier & Urruty Publicaciones, P.O. Box 94, Sucursal 19, Buenos Aires, 1419, Argentina. TEL 54-114-5721050, FAX 54-114-5725766. Ed. Sergio Zagier. Circ: 1,500.

530 620 TUR ISSN 1013-7815
FIZIK MUHENDISLIGI/JOURNAL OF PHYSICS ENGINEERING. Text in Turkish. 1977. q. **Document type:** *Journal, Academic/Scholarly.*
Published by: T M M O B Chamber of Turkish Physics Engineering, Kat 3, Yenisehir, Konur Sokak 4, Ankara, 06450, Turkey.

530 BGR
FIZIKA. Text in Bulgarian. 1976. bi-m. USD 36 foreign (effective 2002). **Document type:** *Journal, Academic/Scholarly.*
Published by: Ministerstvo na Obrazovanieto i Naukata na Republika Bulgaria/Ministry of Education and Sciences of the Republic of Bulgaria, 125 Tzarigradsko Shosse Blvd., Bl. 5, PO Box 336, Sofia, 1113, Bulgaria. TEL 359-2-705298, http://www.minedu.government.bg. **Dist. by:** Sofia Books, ul Silivria 16, Sofia 1404, Bulgaria. TEL 359-2-9586257, info@sofiabooks-bg.com, http://www.sofiabooks-bg.com.

530 HRV ISSN 1330-0008
QC1 CODEN: FIZAE4
FIZIKA A; a journal of experimental and theoretical physics. Text in English. 1969. q. USD 40 (effective 2000). Supplement avail. **Document type:** *Journal, Academic/Scholarly.* **Description:** Publishes results of original experimental or theoretical research work on classical physics, atomic and molecular physics, condensed matter physics, and plasma physics.
Supersedes in part (in 1992): Fizika (0015-3206)
Related titles: CD-ROM ed.: ISSN 1333-8390. 2001; Online - full text ed.: ISSN 1333-9125. 1998. free (effective 2011).
Indexed: CIN, ChemAb, ChemTitl, Inspec, PhysBer, RefZh, SpeleolAb.
—BLDSC (3949.110000), AskIEEE, CASDDS, IE, Ingenta, INIST, Linda Hall.
Published by: Hrvatsko Fizikalno Drustvo/Croatian Physical Society, Bijenicka 32, Zagreb, 10000, Croatia. FAX 385-1-4680336. Ed. K Ilakovac. Circ: 500.

530 HRV ISSN 1330-0016
QC1 CODEN: FIZBE7
FIZIKA B; a journal of experimental and theoretical physics. Text in English. 1969. q. USD 40 (effective 2000). **Document type:** *Journal, Academic/Scholarly.* **Description:** Publishes results of original experimental or theoretical research work on general and nuclear physics, and particles and fields.
Supersedes in part (in 1992): Fizika (0015-3206)
Related titles: Online - full text ed.: free (effective 2011).
Indexed: CIN, ChemAb, ChemTitl, Inspec, RefZh.
—BLDSC (3949.120000), AskIEEE, CASDDS, IE, Ingenta, INIST, Linda Hall.
Published by: Hrvatsko Fizikalno Drustvo/Croatian Physical Society, Bijenicka 32, Zagreb, 10000, Croatia. Ed. K Ilakovac.

FIZIKA I KHIMIYA OBRABOTKI MATERIALOV. *see* ENGINEERING—Engineering Mechanics And Materials

530.44 RUS ISSN 0367-2921
QC717.6 CODEN: FIPLDK
FIZIKA PLAZMY (MOSCOW, 1975). Text in Russian. 1975. m. USD 614 foreign (effective 2010). illus. **Document type:** *Journal, Academic/Scholarly.* **Description:** Emphasizes theoretical and experimental studies of plasma, with particular emphasis on plasma confinement systems.
Related titles: Online - full text ed.; ◆ English Translation: Plasma Physics Reports. ISSN 1063-780X.
Indexed: CIN, ChemAb, ChemTitl, INIS AtomInd, Inspec, RefZh.
—CASDDS, East View, Linda Hall. **CCC.**
Published by: (Rossiiskaya Akademiya Nauk/Russian Academy of Sciences), Izdatel'stvo Nauka, Profsoyuznaya ul 90, Moscow, 117864, Russian Federation. TEL 7-095-3347151, FAX 7-095-4202220, secret@naukaran.ru, http://www.naukaran.ru. **Dist. by:** East View Information Services, 10601 Wayzata Blvd, Minneapolis, MN 55305. TEL 952-252-1201, 800-477-1005, FAX 952-252-1202, info@eastview.com, http://www.eastview.com.

530 520 571.45 UKR ISSN 1680-6921
FIZIKA SOZNANIYA I ZHYZNI, KOSMOLOGIYA I ASTROFIZIKA. Text in Russian, English; Summaries in English. 2001. q. USD 32 domestic; USD 88 foreign; USD 22 newsstand/cover (effective 2002). index. back issues avail. **Document type:** *Journal, Academic/Scholarly.*
Related titles: English ed.: Physics of Consciousness and Life, Cosmology and Astrophysics. ISSN 1680-7057. 2002.
—East View.
Published by: Mezhdunarodnyi Institut Sotsioniki/International Socionics Institute, a/s 23, Kiev, 02206, Ukraine. TEL 380-44-5580935, physics@socionics.ibc.com.ua, admin@socionics.ibc.com.ua, http://www.socionics.ibc.com.ua/esocint.html. Eds. A. V. Dr. Bukalov, M. V. Dr. Kurik, V. P. Prof. Kaznacheev, Yu. N. Dr. Levchuk. Circ: 300 (paid).

530 RUS ISSN 0367-3294
QC176.A1 CODEN: FTVTAC
➤ **FIZIKA TVERDOGO TELA.** Text in Russian, English. 1959. m. USD 660 foreign (effective 2011). charts; illus. index. **Document type:** *Journal, Academic/Scholarly.* **Description:** Publishes articles about solid state optics, solid state acoustics, electronic and vibrational spectra, phase transition, ferroelectricity, magnetism, and superconductivity.
Related titles: Online - full text ed.: ISSN 1726-7498. 1997; ◆ English Translation: Physics of the Solid State. ISSN 1063-7834.
Indexed: ASCA, AcoustA, CIN, Cadscan, ChemAb, ChemTitl, CorrAb, INIS AtomInd, ISR, Inspec, LeadAb, RefZh, SCOPUS, WAA, Zincscan.
—BLDSC (0389.905000), AskIEEE, CASDDS, East View, Infotrieve, INIST, Linda Hall. **CCC.**
Published by: (Rossiiskaya Akademiya Nauk, Fiziko-tekhnicheskii Institut im. A.F. Ioffe, Rossiiskaya Akademiya Nauk/Russian Academy of Sciences), Izdatel'stvo Nauka, Sankt-Peterburgskoe Otdelenie, Mendeleevskaya liniya 1, St Petersburg, 199034, Russian Federation. TEL 7-812-3286291. Ed. B P Zakharchenya.

530.071 371.3 RUS ISSN 0130-5522
QC1 CODEN: FIZSAK
FIZIKA V SHKOLE. Text in Russian; Summaries in English, Russian. 1934. bi-m. USD 139 foreign (effective 2007). adv. bk.rev. back issues avail. **Document type:** *Journal, Academic/Scholarly.* **Description:** Provides methodology and instructions in teaching physics.
Indexed: RefZh.
—East View.
Published by: Izdatel'stvo Shkola Press, ul Rustaveli, dom 10, korpus 3, Moscow, 127254, Russian Federation. marketing@schoolpress.ru. Ed. S V Tret'yakova. Pub., R&P Irina Kozlova TEL 7-095-2195287. Adv. contact Vladimir Kolyshev. Circ: 29,000. **Dist. by:** East View Information Services, 10601 Wayzata Blvd, Minneapolis, MN 55305. TEL 952-252-1201, 800-477-1005, FAX 952-252-1202, info@eastview.com, http://www.eastview.com.

530 HUN ISSN 0015-3257
QC1 CODEN: FISZA6
➤ **FIZIKAI SZEMLE.** Text in Hungarian. 1891. m. charts. index. **Document type:** *Journal, Academic/Scholarly.*
Related titles: Online - full content ed.: ISSN 1588-0540.
Indexed: CIN, ChemAb, ChemTitl, INIS AtomInd, Inspec.
—CASDDS, Linda Hall.
Published by: Eotvos Lorand Fizikai Tarsulat/Roland Eotvos Physical Society, Fo utca 68, Budapest II, 1027, Hungary. TEL 36-1-2018682, mail.elft@mtesz.hu, http://www.kfki.hu/elft. Ed. Nemeth Judit.

530 510 BGR ISSN 0015-3265
CODEN: FMBMAC
FIZIKO-MATEMATICHESKO SPISANIE. Contents page in English, Russian. 195?. q. BGL 5.70, USD 7. bk.rev. bibl.; illus. index, cum.index: vols.1-10, 1968. reprint service avail. from IRC.
Indexed: CIS, ChemAb, MathR, Z02.
—CASDDS, INIST, Linda Hall.
Published by: (Bulgarska Akademiya na Naukite/Bulgarian Academy of Sciences, Fizicheski i Matematicheski Institut), Sofiiski Universitet Sv. Kliment Ohridski, Universitetsko Izdatelstvo/Sofia University St. Kliment Ohridski University Press, Akad G Bonchev 6, Sofia, 1113, Bulgaria. Ed. L Iliev. Circ: 780. **Dist. by:** Hemus, 6 Rouski Blvd., Sofia 1000, Bulgaria.

530 371.3 POL ISSN 0426-3383
CODEN: FISZD9
FIZYKA W SZKOLE. Text in Polish. 1955. 6/yr. PLZ 101.43 domestic; EUR 57 foreign (effective 2011). bk.rev.; software rev.; Website rev. bibl.; illus. 64 p./no.; **Document type:** *Journal, Academic/Scholarly.* **Description:** Publishes articles on the theory and practice of teaching physics and astronomy, with discussions of school syllabi and research methodology in physics. Provides information on the latest developments in modern physics, astrophysics and technology, and presents new concepts in teaching physics.
Indexed: AgrLib.
—CASDDS.
Published by: (Poland. Ministerstwo Edukacji Narodowej), Dr. Josef Raabe Spolka Wydawnicza z o.o., ul Kurpinskiego 55a, Warsaw, 02-733, Poland. TEL 48-22-8430660, FAX 48-22-8433317, raabe@raabe.com.pl, http://www.raabe.com.pl. **Dist. by:** Ars Polona, Obroncow 25, Warsaw 03933, Poland. TEL 48-22-5098609, FAX 48-22-5098610, arspolona@arspolona.com.pl, http://www.arspolona.com.pl.

530 FRA
QC1 CODEN: AFLBDU
FONDATION LOUIS DE BROGLIE. ANNALES. Text and summaries in English, French. 1975. q. EUR 100 domestic to institutions; EUR 110 foreign to institutions (effective 2011). bk.rev. back issues avail. **Document type:** *Journal, Academic/Scholarly.* **Description:** Journal of theoretical physics, primarily intended for the publication of lectures given at the foundation's seminars. Also presents articles on wave mechanics, the foundation of microphysics, wave and quantum mechanics.
Related titles: Online - full text ed.: ISSN 2108-6397. 200?.
Indexed: CCMJ, CPEI, EngInd, Inspec, MSN, MathR, SCOPUS, Z02.
—AskIEEE, Ingenta, INIST.
Published by: Fondation Louis de Broglie, 23 Rue Marsoulan, Paris, 75012, France. TEL 33-1-40020008, FAX 33-1-40049707, inst.louisdebroglie@free.fr, http://www.fondationlouisdebroglie.org. Eds. Daniel Fargue, Xavier Oudet.

FORMULA. *see* CHEMISTRY

530 DEU ISSN 0015-8208
QC1 CODEN: FPYKA6
➤ **FORTSCHRITTE DER PHYSIK/PROGRESS OF PHYSICS.** Text in English. 1953. 10/yr. GBP 1,905 in United Kingdom to institutions; EUR 2,975 in Europe to institutions; USD 3,733 elsewhere to institutions; GBP 2,192 combined subscription in United Kingdom to institutions (print & online eds.); EUR 3,421 combined subscription in Europe to institutions (print & online eds.); USD 4,293 combined subscription elsewhere to institutions (print & online eds.) (effective 2012). charts; illus. index. reprint service avail. from PSC. **Document type:** *Journal, Academic/Scholarly.* **Description:** Devoted to the theoretical and experimental study of the fundamental constituents of matter and their interactions.
Related titles: Microfilm ed.: (from BHP); Online - full text ed.: ISSN 1521-3978. GBP 1,905 in United Kingdom to institutions; EUR 2,975 in Europe to institutions; USD 3,733 elsewhere to institutions (effective 2012).
Indexed: A22, ASCA, CA, CCMJ, CIN, ChemAb, ChemTitl, CurCont, IBR, IBZ, INIS AtomInd, ISR, Inspec, MSN, MathR, PhysBer, RefZh, SCI, SCOPUS, T02, W07, Z02.
—BLDSC (6873.458200), AskIEEE, CASDDS, IE, Infotrieve, Ingenta, INIST, Linda Hall. **CCC.**
Published by: Wiley - V C H Verlag GmbH & Co. KGaA (Subsidiary of: John Wiley & Sons, Inc.), Postfach 101161, Weinheim, 69451, Germany. TEL 49-6201-606400, FAX 49-6201-606184, subservice@wiley-vch.de. Ed. Dr. Dieter Luest. **Subscr. in the Americas to:** John Wiley & Sons, Inc., 111 River St, Hoboken, NJ 07030. TEL 201-748-6645, subinfo@wiley.com; **Subscr. outside Germany, Austria & Switzerland to:** John Wiley & Sons Ltd., The Atrium, Southern Gate, Chichester, West Sussex PO19 8SQ, United Kingdom. TEL 44-1243-779777, FAX 44-1243-775878.

530 POL ISSN 1234-4729
FOTON. Text in Polish. 1991. q. PLZ 31.50 (effective 2011). **Document type:** *Journal, Academic/Scholarly.*
Related titles: Online - full text ed.
Published by: (Uniwersytet Jagiellonski, Instytut Fizyki/Jagiellonian University, Institute of Physics), Wydawnictwo Uniwersytetu Jagiellonskiego/Jagiellonian University Press, ul Grodzka 26, Krakow, 31044, Poland. TEL 48-12-4312364, FAX 48-12-4301995, wydaw@if.uj.edu.pl, http://www.wuj.pl. Ed. Zofia Golab-Meyer. **Co-sponsors:** Polskie Towarzystwo Fizyczne, Sekcja Nauczycielska; Uniwersytet Jagiellonski, Fundacja Edukacji Informatycznej.

530 USA ISSN 0015-9018
QC1 CODEN: FNDPA4
➤ **FOUNDATIONS OF PHYSICS**; an international journal devoted to the conceptual bases and fundamental theories of modern physics. Text in English. 1970. m. EUR 2,488, USD 2,665 combined subscription to institutions (print & online eds.) (effective 2012). adv. bk.rev. illus. Index. back issues avail.; reprint service avail. from PSC. **Document type:** *Journal, Academic/Scholarly.* **Description:** Examines in detail the logical, methodological, and philosophical premises of theories and procedures in modern physics.
Incorporates (1988-2006): Foundations of Physics Letters (0894-9875)
Related titles: Microfilm ed.: (from PQC); Online - full text ed.: ISSN 1572-9516 (from IngentaConnect).
Indexed: A01, A02, A03, A08, A20, A22, A26, ASCA, B04, BRD, BibLing, CA, CCMJ, Cadscan, CurCont, E01, E08, G03, G08, GSA, GSI, I05, IBR, IBZ, INIS AtomInd, ISR, Inspec, LeadAb, MSN, MathR, PhilInd, PhysBer, RASB, RefZh, S04, S09, SCI, SCOPUS, T02, W03, W05, W07, Z02, Zincscan.
—BLDSC (4025.400000), AskIEEE, IE, Infotrieve, Ingenta, INIST, Linda Hall. **CCC.**
Published by: Springer New York LLC (Subsidiary of: Springer Science+Business Media), 233 Spring St, New York, NY 10013. TEL 212-460-1500, FAX 212-460-1575, service-ny@springer.com. Ed. Gerard 't Hooft.

530 NOR ISSN 0015-9247
CODEN: FYVDAX
FRA FYSIKKENS VERDEN. Text in Norwegian. 1939. q. NOK 120 to individuals; NOK 60 to students; NOK 40 per issue (effective 2007). adv. bk.rev. charts; illus. index. **Document type:** *Journal, Academic/ Scholarly.*
Indexed: ChemAb, INIS AtomInd, Inspec.
—AskIEEE, CASDDS, Linda Hall. **CCC.**
Published by: Norsk Fysisk Selskap, Institutt for Fysikk, NTNU, Trondheim, 7491, Norway. TEL 47-73-590726, FAX 47-73-597710, henning.hansen@phys.ntnu.no, http://www.norskfysikk.no. Eds. Finn Ingebretsen, Oeivin Holter. Adv. contact Karl Maaseide TEL 47-22-855668.

530 GBR ISSN 0016-0032
CODEN: JFINAB
➤ **FRANKLIN INSTITUTE. JOURNAL**; engineering and applied mathematics. Text in English. 1826. 10/yr. EUR 2,228 in Europe to institutions; JPY 295,800 in Japan to institutions; USD 2,505 elsewhere to institutions (effective 2012). adv. bk.rev. charts; illus.; stat. s-a. index, cum.index every 10 yrs.; vols.1-280 (1826-1965) in 8 vols. back issues avail.; reprints avail. **Document type:** *Journal, Academic/Scholarly.* **Description:** Covers aricles in the field of engineering and interdisciplinary mathematics.
Former titles (until 1828): Franklin Journal and American Mechanics' Magazine (0093-7029); (until 1826): American Mechanics' Magazine (2155-8760); (until 1825): Mechanics' Magazine
Related titles: Microfiche ed.: (from MIM); Microfilm ed.: (from PQC); Microform ed.: (from PMC); Online - full text ed.: ISSN 1879-2693 (from IngentaConnect, ScienceDirect).
Indexed: A01, A03, A08, A22, A23, A24, A26, ASCA, ApMecR, B&BAb, B13, B19, C&ISA, CA, CCMJ, CEA, CEABA, CIS, CPEI, CompAb, CurCont, CybAb, E&CAJ, EngInd, GeoRef, I05, IBR, IBZ, Inspec, L09, MLA-IB, MSN, MathR, P30, PetrolAb, PhotoAb, PsycholAb, RASB, S&VD, S01, SCI, SCOPUS, SolStAb, SpeleolAb, T02, TCEA, W07, WSCA, Z02.
—BLDSC (4755.000000), AskIEEE, CASDDS, IE, Infotrieve, Ingenta, INIST, Linda Hall, PADDS. **CCC.**
Published by: (Franklin Institute USA), Pergamon (Subsidiary of: Elsevier Science & Technology), The Blvd, Langford Ln, East Park, Kidlington, Oxford OX5 1GB, United Kingdom. TEL 44-1865-843000, FAX 44-1865-843010, JournalsCustomerServiceEMEA@elsevier.com. Ed. Rabinder Madan. **Subscr. to:** Elsevier BV, Radarweg 29, PO Box 211, Amsterdam 1000 AE, Netherlands. TEL 31-20-4853757, FAX 31-20-4853432, http://www.elsevier.nl.

530 SGP
FRONTIERS IN SOLID STATE SCIENCES. Text in English. 1993. irreg., latest vol.2, 1993. price varies. back issues avail. **Document type:** *Monographic series, Academic/Scholarly.*
Published by: World Scientific Publishing Co. Pte. Ltd., 5 Toh Tuck Link, Singapore, 596224, Singapore. TEL 65-6466-5775, FAX 65-6467-7667, wspc@wspc.com.sg, http://www.worldscientific.com. Eds. L C Gupta, M Multani. **Dist. by:** World Scientific Publishing Co., Inc., 27 Warren St, Ste 401-402, Hackensack, NJ 07601. TEL 201-487-9655, 800-227-7562, FAX 201-487-9656, 888-977-2665, wspc@wspc.com; World Scientific Publishing Ltd., 57 Shelton St, London WC2H 9HE, United Kingdom. TEL 44-207-8360888, FAX 44-207-8362020, sales@wspc.co.uk.

530 NLD ISSN 1876-2778
▼ **FRONTIERS OF NANOSCIENCE.** Text in English. 2009. irreg., latest vol.3, 2011. price varies. **Document type:** *Monographic series, Academic/Scholarly.*
Related titles: Online - full text ed.: ISSN 1876-276X.
Published by: Elsevier BV (Subsidiary of: Elsevier Science & Technology), Radarweg 29, PO Box 211, Amsterdam, 1000 AE, Netherlands. TEL 31-20-4853911, FAX 31-20-4852457, http:// www.elsevier.com.

530 CHN ISSN 1673-3487
➤ **FRONTIERS OF PHYSICS IN CHINA**; selected publications from Chinese universities. Text in English. 2006. q. EUR 483, USD 600 combined subscription to institutions (print & online eds.) (effective 2010). reprint service avail. from PSC. **Document type:** *Journal, Academic/Scholarly.* **Description:** Contains review articles and research papers on physics carried out in Chinese universities. Covers all main branches of physics, both theoretical and applied, including physics of particles and field theory; astrophysics and cosmology; condensed matter physics; statistical physics and nonlinear science; physics of plasmas; atomic, molecular and optical physics; nuclear physics and accelerator physics; physics of low-dimension and mesoscopic system, surface physics; nanostructures and functional materials; quantum information physics; gravitation.
Related titles: Microform ed.: (from PQC); Online - full text ed.: ISSN 1673-3606.
Indexed: A22, A26, CurCont, E01, SCI, SCOPUS, W07.
—IE, Ingenta. **CCC.**
Published by: Gaodeng Jiaoyu Chubanshe/Higher Education Press, 4 Dewai Dajie, Beijing, 100011, China. TEL 86-10-58581863, FAX 86-10-82085552, info@hep.edu.cn, http://www.hep.edu.cn/. Ed. Kuang-ta Chao. **Subscr. outside of China to:** Springer New York LLC, Journal Fulfillment, PO Box 2485, Secaucus, NJ 07096. TEL 201-348-4033, FAX 201-348-4505, orders@springer-ny.com, http://www.springer.com/. **Co-publisher:** Springer New York LLC.

621 USA ISSN 1524-5349
FUEL CELL TECHNOLOGY NEWS. Text in English. 1998 (Oct.). m. USD 550 domestic; USD 600 foreign (effective 2006). **Document type:** *Newsletter, Trade.* **Description:** Contains the latest news in fuel cell technology, manufacturing, applications, and investments.
Formerly: Cell Therapy News
Related titles: Online - full text ed.
Indexed: B02, B15, B17, B18, G04, G06, G07, G08, I05.
Published by: Business Communications Co., Inc., 40 Washington St, Ste 110, Wellesley, MA 02481. TEL 781-489-7301, FAX 781-489-7308, sales@bccresearch.com, http://www.bccresearch.com. Ed. Patrick Wier. Pub. Louis Naturman.

530 NLD ISSN 0168-1222
CODEN: FTPHDH
➤ **FUNDAMENTAL THEORIES OF PHYSICS**; an international series of monographs on the fundamental theories of physics: their clarification, development and application. Text in English. 1982. irreg., latest vol.160, 2009. price varies. **Document type:** *Monographic series, Academic/Scholarly.* **Description:** Covers the clarification, development and application of the fundamental theories of physics.
Indexed: CCMJ, CIS, Inspec, Z02.
—BLDSC (4056.086000), CASDDS, IE, Ingenta.
Published by: Springer Netherlands (Subsidiary of: Springer Science+Business Media), Van Godewijckstraat 30, Dordrecht, 3311 GX, Netherlands. TEL 31-78-6576050, FAX 31-78-6576474. Eds. Alwyn Van Der Merwe, G C Ghirardi, V Petkov.

539 FRA ISSN 0769-1343
CODEN: NOGAE5
G A N I L. NOUVELLES. (Grand Accelerateur National d'Ions Lourds) Text in French. 198?. q.
Indexed: INIS AtomInd.
Published by: Grand Accelerateur National d'Ions Lourds, BP 55027, Caen, 14076 Cedex 5, France. TEL 33-2-31454647, FAX 33-2-31454665. Eds. Gerard Auger, Monique Bex.

530 USA ISSN 1047-4811
QC630 CODEN: GAELEN
➤ **GALILEAN ELECTRODYNAMICS.** Text in English. 1990. bi-m. USD 40 to individuals; USD 80 to corporations (effective 2010). bk.rev. abstr.; charts; illus.; bibl. Cumulative index published yearly. Also on web. 20 p./no. 2 cols./p.; back issues avail. **Document type:** *Journal, Academic/Scholarly.* **Description:** Aims to publish high-quality scientific papers that discuss challenges to accepted orthodoxy in physics, especially in the realm of relativity theory, both special and general.
Related titles: Online - full text ed.
Indexed: Inspec, RefZh.
—BLDSC (4067.445000), AskIEEE, IE, Ingenta.
Published by: Space Time Analyses, Ltd., 141 Rhinecliff St, Arlington, MA 02476. Ed., Pub. Cynthia K Whitney.

530 DNK ISSN 0108-0954
QC1 CODEN: GMMADB
GAMMA; tidsskrift for fysik. Text in Danish. 1971. q. free (effective 2004). bk.rev. cum index 1995. back issues avail. **Document type:** *Academic/Scholarly.* **Description:** Aimed at students, teachers and researchers in all aspects of physics.
Related titles: Online - full text ed.: 1989.
Published by: Koebenhavns Universitet, Niels Bohr Institutet/University of Copenhagen, Niels Bohr Institut, Blegdamsvej 17, Copenhagen OE, 2100, Denmark. eksp-blv@nbi.ku.dk, http://www.nbi.ku.dk. Ed. Katrine Rudee Laub TEL 45-36-325519. Circ: 3,000.

GAOFENZI TONGBAO/POLYMER BULLETIN. *see* CHEMISTRY

GAUSS-GESELLSCHAFT. MITTEILUNGEN. *see* ASTRONOMY

530 PRT ISSN 0367-3561
CODEN: GAFIAF
GAZETA DE FISICA. Text in Portuguese. 1946. q.
Related titles: Online - full text ed.
Indexed: INIS AtomInd.
Published by: Sociedade Portuguesa de Fisica, Avenida da Republica N 37 4 Andar, Lisbon, 1050-187, Portugal. TEL 351-21-7993665, FAX 351-21-7952349, secretariado@spf.pt, http://www.spf.pt/.

533.5 FRA ISSN 1638-802X
QC166
➤ **LA GAZETTE DU VIDE.** Text and summaries in English, French. 1946. 3/yr. adv. bk.rev. bibl.; abstr.; charts; illus. index. Supplement avail. **Document type:** *Monographic series, Academic/Scholarly.* **Description:** Presents scientific papers, technical texts, news and new products in the field of vacuum technology, list of next conferences in the field, presentation of laboratories, employment information.
Former titles (until 2003): Le Vide (1266-0167); (until 1995): Vide, les Couches Minces (0223-4335); (until 1979): Vide (0042-5281)
Related titles: Online - full text ed.: ISSN 2108-6400.
Indexed: A22, APA, ASCA, C&ISA, CIN, ChemAb, CorrAb, E&CAJ, EEA, INIS AtomInd, Inspec, SCOPUS, SolStAb, WAA.
—AskIEEE, CASDDS, IE, Infotrieve, Ingenta, INIST, Linda Hall. **CCC.**
Published by: Societe Francaise du Vide, 19 rue du Renard, Paris, 75004, France. TEL 33-1-5301-9030, FAX 33-1-4278-6320. Ed. Bernard Agius. Adv. contact Veronique Pfohl. Circ: 4,000.

530 USA ISSN 0001-7701
QC173.6 CODEN: GRGVA8
➤ **GENERAL RELATIVITY AND GRAVITATION.** Text in English. 1962. m. EUR 2,442, USD 2,566 combined subscription to institutions (print & online eds.) (effective 2012). adv. bk.rev. charts; illus. Index. back issues avail.; reprint service avail. from PSC. **Document type:** *Journal, Academic/Scholarly.* **Description:** Presents letters, research papers, review articles and comments on all theoretical and experimental aspects of modern general relativity and gravitation and its extensions, plus book reviews, related mathematical topics, results and techniques.
Formerly (until 1970): Bulletin on General Relativity and Gravitation (0573-049X)
Related titles: Microfilm ed.: (from PQC); Online - full text ed.: ISSN 1572-9532 (from IngentaConnect).
Indexed: A01, A03, A08, A22, A26, ASCA, BibLing, CA, CCMJ, CurCont, E01, ISR, Inspec, M&GPA, MSN, MathR, PhysBer, RefZh, SCI, SCOPUS, T02, W07, Z02.
—BLDSC (4109.650000), AskIEEE, IE, Infotrieve, Ingenta, INIST, Linda Hall. **CCC.**
Published by: (International Society on General Relativity and Gravitation), Springer New York LLC (Subsidiary of: Springer Science+Business Media), 233 Spring St, New York, NY 10013. TEL 212-460-1500, FAX 212-460-1575, service-ny@springer.com. Eds. G F R Ellis, H Nicolai.

➤ **GEOLOGIAN TUTKIMUSKESKUS. YDINJATTEIDEN SIJOITUSTUTKIMUKSET. TIEDONANTO Y S T/GEOLOGICAL SURVEY OF FINLAND. NUCLEAR WASTE DISPOSAL RESEARCH. REPORT Y S T.** *see* EARTH SCIENCES—Geology

530 ITA ISSN 0017-0283
QC1 CODEN: GFSIAD
GIORNALE DI FISICA. Text in Italian. 1956. q. EUR 78 to members; EUR 98 to non-members (effective 2008). **Document type:** *Journal, Academic/Scholarly.* **Description:** Intended for secondary school teachers of physics. Presents information on educational techniques and the history of physics.
Related titles: Online - full text ed.: ISSN 1827-6156. 1965.
Indexed: CIN, ChemAb, ChemTitl, Inspec.
—AskIEEE, CASDDS, Linda Hall.
Published by: Societa Italiana di Fisica (S I F), Via Saragozza 12, Bologna, 40123, Italy. TEL 39-051-331554, FAX 39-051-581340, subscriptions@sif.it. Ed. Angela Oleandri.

530.0711 USA ISSN 1533-5445
QC30
GRADUATE PROGRAMS IN PHYSICS, ASTRONOMY AND RELATED FIELDS. Text in English. 1970. a. USD 76 per issue to non-members; USD 66 per issue to members (effective 2010). adv. back issues avail. **Document type:** *Journal, Academic/Scholarly.* **Description:** Provides information on nearly every U.S. doctoral program in physics and astronomy, plus data on most major master's programs in these fields.
Formerly (until 1978): Graduate Programs: Physics, Astronomy, and Related Fields (Year) (0147-1821)
—**CCC.**
Published by: American Institute of Physics, 1 Physics Ellipse, College Park, MD 20740. TEL 301-209-3100, FAX 301-209-0843, aipinfo@aip.org. **Subscr. to:** PO Box 503284, St Louis, MO 63150. TEL 516-576-2270, 800-344-6902, FAX 516-349-9704, subs@aip.org.

530 USA ISSN 0938-037X
GRADUATE TEXTS IN CONTEMPORARY PHYSICS. Text in English. 1986. irreg., latest 2000. price varies. back issues avail.; reprints avail. **Document type:** *Monographic series, Academic/Scholarly.*
Formerly (until 1986): Contemporary Physics
Indexed: CCMJ.
Published by: Springer New York LLC (Subsidiary of: Springer Science+Business Media), 233 Spring St, New York, NY 10013. TEL 212-460-1500, FAX 212-473-6272.

531.14 523.1 RUS ISSN 0202-2893
➤ **GRAVITATION & COSMOLOGY.** Text in English; Abstracts and contents page in Russian. 1995. q. EUR 407, USD 542 combined subscription to institutions (print & online eds.) (effective 2012). abstr. 80 p./no. 2 cols./p.; reprints avail. **Document type:** *Journal, Academic/Scholarly.* **Description:** Includes papers in theoretical (classical and quantum) and experimental gravity; relativistic astrophysics and cosmology; exact solutions and modern mathematical methods in gravitation and cosmology, including Lie groups, geometry and topology; unification theories including gravity; fundamental physical constants and related topics.
Related titles: Online - full text ed.: ISSN 1995-0721 (from IngentaConnect).
Indexed: A22, A26, CCMJ, CurCont, E01, E08, Inspec, MSN, MathR, RefZh, S09, SCI, SCOPUS, W07, Z02.
—East View, IE. **CCC.**
Published by: (Ministry of Science and Technological Policy of Russia, Peoples' Friendship University, Institute of Gravitation and Cosmology), M A I K Nauka - Interperiodica (Subsidiary of: Pleiades Publishing, Inc.), Profsoyuznaya ul 90, Moscow, 117997, Russian Federation. TEL 7-095-3361600, FAX 7-095-3360666, compmg@maik.ru. Ed. Vitaly Melnikov. **Dist. by:** East View Information Services, 10601 Wayzata Blvd, Minneapolis, MN 55305. TEL 952-252-1201, 800-477-1005, FAX 952-252-1202, info@eastview.com, http://www.eastview.com. **Co-sponsor:** Russian Gravitational Society.

539 CHE ISSN 0432-7136
GROUPEMENT D'INFORMATIONS MUTUELLES A M P E R E. BULLETIN. Text in French. 1952. q.
Published by: Groupement d'Informations Mutuelles A M P E R E, ETH Zurich, Laboratorium fur Physikalische Chemie, ETH-Honggerberg, HCI, Zurich, CH-8093, Switzerland. TEL 411-632-4401, FAX 411-632-1621. Ed. Beat H Meier.

621.361 CHN ISSN 1004-8138
GUANGPU SHIYANSHI/CHINESE JOURNAL OF SPECTROSCOPY LABORATORY. Text in Chinese. 1984. bi-m. **Document type:** *Journal, Academic/Scholarly.*
Related titles: Online - full text ed.
Indexed: A28, APA, BrCerAb, C&ISA, CA/WCA, CIA, CerAb, CivEngAb, CorrAb, E&CAJ, E11, EEA, EMA, ESPM, EnvEAb, H15, M&TEA, M09, MBF, METADEX, SolStAb, T04, WAA.
—BLDSC (3180.676700), East View, Linda Hall.
Published by: (Zhongguo Kexueyuan Guocheng Gongcheng Yanjiusuo), Kexue Chubanshe/Science Press, 16 Donghuang Cheng Genbei Jie, Beijing, 100717, China.

530 CHN ISSN 1003-7551
GUANGXI WULI/GUANGXI PHYSICS. Text in Chinese. 1980. bi-m. CNY 2.50 newsstand/cover (effective 2006). **Document type:** *Journal, Academic/Scholarly.*
Related titles: Online - full text ed.
Address: Wangcheng, Guilin, 541001, China. TEL 86-773-2822288 ext 3157.

GUIAS PARA ENSENANZAS MEDIAS. FISICA Y QUIMICA. *see* CHEMISTRY

P

530 USA ISSN 0162-5519
QC793.5.H322 CODEN: HAJODX
➤ **HADRONIC JOURNAL.** Text in English. 1978. bi-m. USD 250 (effective 2010). back issues avail. **Document type:** *Journal, Academic/Scholarly.*
Related titles: ◆ Supplement(s): Hadronic Journal. Supplement. ISSN 0882-5394.
Indexed: A22, CCMJ, CIN, ChemAb, ChemTitl, ISR, Inspec, MSN, MathR, PhysBer, RefZh, Z02.
—BLDSC (4237.700000), AskIEEE, CASDDS, IE, Infotrieve, Ingenta, INIST, Linda Hall.
Published by: Hadronic Press, Inc., 35246 US 19 N, No 215, Palm Harbor, FL 34684. TEL 727-934-9593, FAX 727-934-9275, hadronic@tampabay.rr.com. Ed. Ruggero Maria Santilli.

530 USA ISSN 0882-5394
QC793.5.H32 CODEN: HJSUEO
➤ **HADRONIC JOURNAL. SUPPLEMENT.** Text in English. 1985. q. USD 150 (effective 2010). back issues avail. **Document type:** *Journal, Academic/Scholarly.*
Related titles: ◆ Supplement to: Hadronic Journal. ISSN 0162-5519.
Indexed: CCMJ, CIN, ChemAb, ChemTitl, Inspec, MSN, MathR, PhysBer, Z02.
—BLDSC (4237.701000), AskIEEE, CASDDS, Linda Hall.
Published by: Hadronic Press, Inc., 35246 US 19 N, No 215, Palm Harbor, FL 34684. TEL 727-934-9593, FAX 727-934-9275, hadronic@tampabay.rr.com. Ed. Ruggero Maria Santilli.

530 JPN
HAKUMAKU HYOMEN BUTSURI SEMINA/JAPAN SOCIETY OF APPLIED PHYSICS. THIN FILM AND SURFACE PHYSICS SEMINAR. Text in English, Japanese; Summaries in English. 1970. a. JPY 4,000.
Published by: Japan Society of Applied Physics/Oyo Butsuri Gakkai, Kudan-Kita Bldg 5th Fl, 1-12-3 Kudan-Kita, Chiyoda-ku, Tokyo, 102-0073, Japan.

621.55 KOR ISSN 1225-8822
HAN-GUG JIN-GONG HAG-HOEJI/KOREAN VACUUM SOCIETY. JOURNAL. Text in Korean. 1992. q. membership. **Document type:** *Journal, Academic/Scholarly.*
Related titles: Online - full text ed.
—BLDSC (4812.349100).
Published by: Han-gug Jin-gong Hag-hoe/Korean Vacuum Society, Korean Science & Technology Center, Room 805, 635-4 Yeogsam Dong, Kangham Ku, Seoul, 135-703, Korea, S. TEL 82-2-567-9486, FAX 82-2-556-5675, khip@khip.co.kr, http://www.kvs.or.kr.

530 NLD ISSN 1574-0641
HANDAI NANOPHOTONICS. Text in English. irreg., latest vol.3, 2007. price varies. **Document type:** *Monographic series, Academic/Scholarly.*
Indexed: SCOPUS.
—BLDSC (4241.670000). **CCC.**
Published by: Elsevier BV (Subsidiary of: Elsevier Science & Technology), Radarweg 29, PO Box 211, Amsterdam, 1000 AE, Netherlands. TEL 31-20-4853911, FAX 31-20-4852457, JournalsCustomerServiceEMEA@elsevier.com, http://www.elsevier.com. Eds. Hiroshi Masuhara, Satoshi Kawata.

HANDBOOK OF MAGNETIC MATERIALS. *see* METALLURGY

530.41 NLD ISSN 1573-4323
HANDBOOK OF METAL PHYSICS. Text in English. 2004. irreg., latest vol.5, 2009. price varies. **Document type:** *Monographic series, Academic/Scholarly.*
Published by: Elsevier BV (Subsidiary of: Elsevier Science & Technology), Radarweg 29, PO Box 211, Amsterdam, 1000 AE, Netherlands. TEL 31-20-4853911, FAX 31-20-4852457, JournalsCustomerServiceEMEA@elsevier.com, http://www.elsevier.com. Ed. Prasanta Misra.

530.44 NLD ISSN 0169-2852
➤ **HANDBOOK OF PLASMA PHYSICS.** Text in Dutch. 1983. irreg., latest vol.3, 1991. price varies. **Document type:** *Monographic series, Academic/Scholarly.* **Description:** Acts as an encyclopedic reference by compiling information on techniques, applications, and developments in the field of plasma physics.
Indexed: Inspec.
Published by: Elsevier BV (Subsidiary of: Elsevier Science & Technology), Radarweg 29, PO Box 211, Amsterdam, 1000 AE, Netherlands. TEL 31-20-4853911, FAX 31-20-4852457, JournalsCustomerServiceEMEA@elsevier.com, http://www.elsevier.nl. Eds. M N Rosenbluth, R Z Sagdeev.

530 NLD
HANDBOOK OF STABLE ISOTOPE ANALYTICAL TECHNIQUES. Text in English. 2007. irreg., latest vol.1, 2007. **Document type:** *Monographic series, Academic/Scholarly.*
Related titles: Online - full text ed.: ISSN 1874-5830.
Published by: Elsevier BV (Subsidiary of: Elsevier Science & Technology), Radarweg 29, PO Box 211, Amsterdam, 1000 AE, Netherlands. TEL 31-20-4853911, FAX 31-20-4852457, http://www.elsevier.com. Ed. Pier de Groot.

530 NLD
HANDBOOK OF SURFACE SCIENCE. Text in English. 1996. irreg., latest vol.3, 2008. price varies. **Document type:** *Monographic series, Academic/Scholarly.* **Description:** Covers solid surfaces and their interactions with foreign species.
Published by: Elsevier BV (Subsidiary of: Elsevier Science & Technology), PO Box 1527, Amsterdam, 1000, Netherlands. JournalsCustomerServiceEMEA@elsevier.com, http://www.elsevier.com. Eds. N V Richardson, Stephen Holloway.

530 USA
HANDBOOK OF VAPOR PRESSURE. Text in English. irreg., latest vol.4, 1995. price varies. **Document type:** *Monographic series, Academic/Scholarly.*
Related titles: Online - full text ed.: ISSN 1874-8813.
Published by: Gulf Professional Publishing (Subsidiary of: Elsevier Science & Technology), 3251 Riverport Ln, Maryland Heights, MO 63043. TEL 314-453-7010, FAX 314-453-7095, http://www.elsevier.com.

539.735 NLD
➤ **HANDBOOK ON SYNCHROTRON RADIATION.** Text in English. 1983. irreg., latest vol.4, 1991. price varies. back issues avail. **Document type:** *Monographic series, Academic/Scholarly.* **Description:** Discusses applications of synchrotron radiation in various areas of physics and chemistry and examines properties of sources, elements of instrumentation, and applications to biological and medical research.
Published by: Elsevier BV, North-Holland (Subsidiary of: Elsevier Science & Technology), Sara Burgerhartstraat 25, Amsterdam, 1055 KV, Netherlands. TEL 31-20-4853911, FAX 31-20-4852457, JournalsCustomerServiceEMEA@elsevier.com, http://www.elsevier.com. **Subscr. to:** Elsevier BV, Radarweg 29, PO Box 211, Amsterdam 1000 AE, Netherlands. TEL 31-20-4853757, FAX 31-20-4853432.

530.1 669 NLD ISSN 1573-4366
➤ **HANDBOOK ON THE PHYSICS AND CHEMISTRY OF RARE EARTHS.** Text in English. 1978. irreg., latest vol.41, 2011. price varies. cum.index: vols.1-15 in 1993. back issues avail. **Document type:** *Monographic series, Academic/Scholarly.* **Description:** Publishes original reviews of technological advances and research relating to the lanthanide series of rare earth metals, related alloys and compounds, and applications of these elements in all industries.
Indexed: Inspec, SpeleolAb.
Published by: Elsevier BV, North-Holland (Subsidiary of: Elsevier Science & Technology), Sara Burgerhartstraat 25, Amsterdam, 1055 KV, Netherlands. TEL 31-20-4853911, FAX 31-20-4852457, JournalsCustomerServiceEMEA@elsevier.com, http://www.elsevier.com. Eds. Jean-Claude Buenzli, Karl A Gschneider, Vitalij Pecharsky. **Subscr. to:** Elsevier BV, Radarweg 29, PO Box 211, Amsterdam 1000 AE, Netherlands. TEL 31-20-4853757, FAX 31-20-4853432.

➤ **HANGKONG XUEBAO/ACTA AERONAUTICA ET ASTRONAUTICA SINICA.** *see* AERONAUTICS AND SPACE FLIGHT

➤ **HANNENG CAILIAO/ENERGETIC MATERIALS.** *see* ENERGY

530 ARM
CODEN: IAAFF8
HAYASTANY GUITOUTYUNNERY AZGAYIN ACADEMIA. TEGHEKAGIR. FIZIKA/AKADEMIYA NAUK ARMENII. IZVESTIYA. SERIYA FIZIKA. Text in Armenian. 1966. bi-m. charts; illus. index. **Document type:** *Proceedings, Academic/Scholarly.*
Formerly: Akademiya Nauk Armyanskoi S.S.R. Izvestiya. Seriya Fizika (0002-3035)
Related titles: ◆ English Translation: Journal of Contemporary Physics. ISSN 1068-3372.
Indexed: CIS, ChemAb, INIS AtomInd, Inspec, MathR, PhysBer, RefZh.
—AskIEEE, CASDDS, East View, INIST, Linda Hall.
Published by: Hayastany Guitoutyunnery Azgayin Academia/National Academy of Sciences of the Republic of Armenia, Marshal Bagramyan Ave 24b, Erevan, 375019, Armenia. TEL 78852-524580, FAX 78852-151087, academy@sci.am. Ed. Vladimir M Aroutounian. Circ: 820.

HELSINKI UNIVERSITY OF TECHNOLOGY. LABORATORY OF STRUCTURAL ENGINEERING AND BUILDING PHYSICS. PUBLICATIONS/TEKNILLINEN KORKEAKOULU. TALONRAKENNUSTEKNIIKAN LABORATORIO. JULKAISU. *see* ENGINEERING—Civil Engineering

530 540 JPN ISSN 0386-3034
QC1 CODEN: JHPCAR
HIROSHIMA UNIVERSITY. JOURNAL OF SCIENCE. SERIES A. PHYSICS AND CHEMISTRY. Text in English. 1961. 3/yr. **Document type:** *Journal, Academic/Scholarly.*
Formerly (until 1971): Hiroshima University. Journal of Science. Series A-2. Physics and Chemistry (0439-173X); Which superseded in part (1930-1961): Hiroshima University. Journal of Science. Series A. Mathematics, Physics, Chemistry (0386-3018)
Indexed: Inspec.
—IE, Ingenta, INIST, Linda Hall.
Published by: Hiroshima University, Faculty of Science/Hiroshima Daigaku Rigakubu Chikyu Wakuseisisutemugaku, 1-3-1 Kagamiyama, Higashihiroshima, 739-8526, Japan. FAX 81-82-4240709, http://www.hiroshima-u.ac.jp.

HISTORICAL STUDIES IN THE NATURAL SCIENCES. *see* SCIENCES: COMPREHENSIVE WORKS

HOSHASEN KAGAKU (TOKYO)/RADIATION CHEMISTRY. *see* CHEMISTRY

HOSHASEN KAGAKU TORONKAI KOEN YOSHISHU/PROCEEDINGS OF SYMPOSIUM ON RADIATION CHEMISTRY. *see* CHEMISTRY—Physical Chemistry

530 NLD ISSN 0924-8099
➤ **LES HOUCHES SUMMER SCHOOL PROCEEDINGS.** Key Title: Houches (Amsterdam). Text in English, French. 1951. irreg., latest vol.82, 2005. price varies. back issues avail. **Document type:** *Proceedings, Academic/Scholarly.* **Description:** Publishes research in all areas of physics presented at the Les Houches summer school.
Formerly: Ecole d'Ete de Physique Theorique. Les Houches
Related titles: Online - full text ed.
Indexed: CCMJ, GeoRef, Inspec, MSN, MathR, SpeleolAb.
—Ingenta. **CCC.**
Published by: (Ecole d'Ete de Physique Theorique, Les Houches), Elsevier BV (Subsidiary of: Elsevier Science & Technology), Radarweg 29, PO Box 211, Amsterdam, 1000 AE, Netherlands. TEL 31-20-4853911, FAX 31-20-4852457, JournalsCustomerServiceEMEA@elsevier.com, http://www.elsevier.com.

530 370 CHN ISSN 1673-1875
HUNAN ZHONGXUE WULI/HUNAN MIDDLE SCHOOL PHYSICS. Text in Chinese. 1987. bi-m. CNY 72; CNY 6 per issue (effective 2009). **Document type:** *Journal, Academic/Scholarly.*
Published by: (Hunan Shifan Daxue/Hunan Normal University), Hunan Zhongxue Wuli Zazhishe, 36, Yuelu Lu, Hunan Shifan Daxue, Wuli yu Xinxi Kexue Xueyuan, Keyuan Lou 402, Changsha, 410081, China. TEL 86-731-88872575. **Co-sponsor:** Hunan Sheng Wuli Xuehui.

530 HUN ISSN 0133-5502
HUNGARIAN ACADEMY OF SCIENCES. CENTRAL RESEARCH INSTITUTE FOR PHYSICS. YEARBOOK/MAGYAR TUDOMANYOS AKADEMIA. KOZPONTI FIZIKAI KUTATO INTEZET. EVKONYV. Text in English. 1971. s-a. avail. on exchange basis only.
Indexed: ChemAb, Inspec.
Published by: Magyar Tudomanyos Akademia, Kozponti Fizikai Kutato Intezet, PO Box 76, Budapest, 1325, Hungary. Ed. T Dolinszky. Circ: 1,400.

HYDROGEN & FUEL CELL LETTER. *see* CHEMISTRY—Inorganic Chemistry

530 JPN ISSN 0388-5321
CODEN: HYKAET
HYOMEN KAGAKU/SURFACE SCIENCE SOCIETY OF JAPAN. JOURNAL. Text in Japanese; Summaries in English. 1980. m. Subscr. incld. with membership. **Document type:** *Journal, Academic/Scholarly.* **Description:** Contains research papers on fundamental theory and experiments at frontiers of science and technology relating to surfaces, interfaces, thin films, fine particles, nanowires, nanotubes, and other nanometer-scale structures, and their interdisciplinary areas such as crystal growth, vacuum technology, and so on.
Related titles: Online - full text ed.
Indexed: A22, CIN, ChemAb, ChemTitl, INIS AtomInd, RefZh.
—BLDSC (4904.473000), CASDDS, IE, Ingenta. **CCC.**
Published by: Nihon Hyomen Kagakukai/Surface Science Society of Japan, Hongo Corporation 402, 2-40-13 Hongo, Bunkyo-ku, Tokyo, 113-0033, Japan. TEL 81-3-38120266, FAX 81-3-38122897, sssj@t3.rim.or.jp. Ed. Ayahiko Ichimiya.

530 540 JPN
HYOMEN KAGAKU KISO KOZA/TEXTBOOK OF LECTURES ON SURFACE SCIENCE. Text in Japanese. a. **Document type:** *Academic/Scholarly.*
Published by: Nihon Hyomen Kagakukai/Surface Science Society of Japan, Hongo Corporation 402, 2-40-13 Hongo, Bunkyo-ku, Tokyo, 113-0033, Japan. TEL 81-3-38120266, FAX 81-3-38122897. Ed. T Ohiwa. R&P Toshio Ogino.

530 540 JPN
HYOMEN KAGAKU KOEN TAIKAI KOEN YOSHISHU/SURFACE SCIENCE SOCIETY OF JAPAN. ABSTRACTS OF MEETINGS. Text in Japanese. 1982. a. **Document type:** *Academic/Scholarly.*
Published by: Nihon Hyomen Kagakukai/Surface Science Society of Japan, Hongo Corporation 402, 2-40-13 Hongo, Bunkyo-ku, Tokyo, 113-0033, Japan. TEL 81-3-38120266, FAX 81-3-38122897.

530 540 JPN
HYOMEN KAGAKU SEMINA/TEXTBOOK OF SEMINAR ON SURFACE SCIENCE. Text in Japanese. a. **Document type:** *Academic/Scholarly.*
Published by: Nihon Hyomen Kagakukai/Surface Science Society of Japan, Hongo Corporation 402, 2-40-13 Hongo, Bunkyo-ku, Tokyo, 113-0033, Japan. TEL 81-3-38120266, FAX 81-3-38122897. Ed. T Ohiwa. R&P Toshio Ogino.

530 NLD ISSN 0304-3843
QC762 CODEN: HYINDN
➤ **HYPERFINE INTERACTIONS.** Text in English. 1975. 21/yr. (in 7 vols.). EUR 3,459, USD 3,584 combined subscription to institutions (print & online eds.) (effective 2012). adv. reprint service avail. from PSC. **Document type:** *Journal, Academic/Scholarly.* **Description:** Publishes international research on solid-state physics, atomic physics, nuclear physics, and relevant chemistry.
Incorporates (1987-1992): Muon Catalyzed Fusion (0259-9805)
Related titles: Online - full text ed.: ISSN 1572-9540 (from IngentaConnect).
Indexed: A01, A03, A08, A20, A22, A26, BibLing, C33, CA, CIN, Cadscan, ChemAb, ChemTitl, E01, GeoRef, ISR, Inspec, LeadAb, P30, PhysBer, RefZh, SCOPUS, SpeleolAb, T02, Zincscan.
—BLDSC (4352.625000), AskIEEE, CASDDS, IE, Infotrieve, Ingenta, INIST, Linda Hall. **CCC.**
Published by: Springer Netherlands (Subsidiary of: Springer Science+Business Media), Van Godewijckstraat 30, Dordrecht, 3311 GX, Netherlands. TEL 31-78-6576050, FAX 31-78-6576474, http://www.springer.com. Eds. Guido Langouche, Hans-Juergen Kluge.

530 SGP ISSN 0218-0243
CODEN: ISTPEK
THE I C T P SERIES IN THEORETICAL PHYSICS. (International Centre for Theoretical Physics) Text in English. 1984. irreg., latest vol.16, 2000. price varies. 404 p./no.; back issues avail. **Document type:** *Monographic series, Academic/Scholarly.* **Description:** Brings out the proceedings volumes of summer schools held at ICTP since 1985.
Indexed: CCMJ.
—CASDDS.
Published by: (Abdus Salam International Centre for Theoretical Physics ITA, International Atomic Energy Agency AUT), World Scientific Publishing Co. Pte. Ltd., 5 Toh Tuck Link, Singapore, 596224, Singapore. TEL 65-6466-5775, FAX 65-6467-7667, wspc@wspc.com.sg, http://www.worldscientific.com. **Dist. by:** World Scientific Publishing Ltd., 57 Shelton St, London WC2H 9HE, United Kingdom. TEL 44-207-8360888, FAX 44-207-8362020, sales@wspc.co.uk; World Scientific Publishing Co., Inc., 27 Warren St, Ste 401-402, Hackensack, NJ 07601. TEL 201-487-9655, 800-227-7562, FAX 201-487-9656, 888-977-2665, wspc@wspc.com.

530 621.3 USA ISSN 1099-4734
TK7872.F44
I E E E INTERNATIONAL SYMPOSIUM ON APPLICATIONS OF FERROELECTRICS. (Institute of Electrical and Electronics Engineers) Variant title: I E E E International Symposium on Applications of Ferroelectrics. Proceedings. Text in English. 1975. a. adv. back issues avail. **Document type:** *Proceedings, Academic/Scholarly.*
Formerly (until 1979): I E E E Symposium on Applications of Ferroelectrics. Proceedings
Related titles: Online - full text ed.
—CCC.
Published by: I E E E, 445 Hoes Ln, Piscataway, NJ 08855. contactcenter@ieee.org, http://www.ieee.org.

I E E E MICROWAVE AND WIRELESS COMPONENTS LETTERS. (Institute of Electrical and Electronics Engineers) *see* ENGINEERING—Electrical Engineering

I E E E PARTICLE ACCELERATOR CONFERENCE. (Institute of Electrical and Electronics Engineers) *see* ENGINEERING—Electrical Engineering

621.3 USA ISSN 1540-7977
TK1001
I E E E POWER & ENERGY MAGAZINE. (Institute of Electrical and Electronics Engineers) Variant title: Power and Energy Magazine. Text in English. 2003. bi-m. USD 430; USD 535 combined subscription (print & online eds.) (effective 2012). back issues avail.; reprints avail. **Document type:** *Journal, Academic/Scholarly.* **Description:** Features articles with a focus on advanced concepts, technologies, and practices associated with all aspects of electric power from a technical perspective in synergy with non-technical areas such as business, environmental, and social concerns.
Formed by the merger of (1988-2003): I E E E Computer Applications in Power (0895-0156); (1981-2003): I E E E Power Engineering Review (0272-1724)
Related titles: Online - full text ed.: ISSN 1558-4216. USD 390 (effective 2012).
Indexed: A22, A28, APA, BrCerAb, C&ISA, CA/WCA, CIA, CPEI, CerAb, CivEngAb, CorrAb, CurCont, E&CAJ, E11, EEA, EMA, ESPM, EngInd, EnvEAb, H15, Inspec, M&TEA, M09, MBF, METADEX, RefZh, SCI, SCOPUS, SolStAb, T04, W07, WAA.
—BLDSC (4363.014500), IE, INIST, Linda Hall. **CCC.**
Published by: I E E E, 445 Hoes Ln, Piscataway, NJ 08854. TEL 732-981-0060, 800-678-4333, FAX 732-562-6380, contactcenter@ieee.org, http://www.ieee.org. Ed. Melvin I Olken TEL 212-982-8286. Adv. contact Barry LeCerf TEL 913-663-1112. **Co-sponsor:** I E E E Power & Energy Society.

I E E E TRANSACTIONS ON APPLIED SUPERCONDUCTIVITY. (Institute of Electrical and Electronics Engineers) *see* ELECTRONICS

530.44 USA ISSN 0093-3813
TA2001 CODEN: ITPSBD
I E E E TRANSACTIONS ON PLASMA SCIENCE. (Institute of Electrical and Electronics Engineers) Text in English. 1973. bi-m. USD 1,285; USD 1,605 combined subscription (print & online eds.) (effective 2012). adv. bk.rev. index. back issues avail.; reprints avail. **Document type:** *Journal, Academic/Scholarly.* **Description:** Examines all aspects of plasma science and engineering.
Related titles: CD-ROM ed.; Microfiche ed.; Online - full text ed.: ISSN 1939-9375. USD 1,170 (effective 2012).
Indexed: A01, A02, A03, A05, A08, A20, A22, A26, A28, APA, AS&TA, AS&TI, ASCA, B01, B04, B06, B07, B09, BrCerAb, C&ISA, C10, CA, CA/WCA, CIA, CIN, CPEI, CerAb, ChemAb, ChemTitl, CivEngAb, CorrAb, CurCont, E&CAJ, E08, E11, EEA, EMA, ESPM, EngInd, EnvEAb, G01, G08, H15, I05, IBR, IBZ, INIS AtomInd, ISMEC, ISR, Inspec, M&TEA, M05, M06, M09, MBF, METADEX, MSCI, MathR, P02, P10, P26, P30, P47, P48, P52, P53, P54, P56, PQC, PhysBer, RefZh, S01, S09, S10, SCI, SCOPUS, SolStAb, T02, T04, TM, W07, WAA.
—BLDSC (4363.212000), AskIEEE, CASDDS, IE, Infotrieve, Ingenta, INIST, Linda Hall. **CCC.**
Published by: I E E E, 445 Hoes Ln, Piscataway, NJ 08854. TEL 732-981-0060, 800-678-4333, FAX 732-562-6380, contactcenter@ieee.org, http://www.ieee.org. Eds. Steven J Gitomer TEL 505-988-5751, Dawn Melley. **Subscr. to:** Universal Subscription Agency, Pvt. Ltd.; Maruzen Co., Ltd. **Co-sponsor:** Nuclear and Plasma Sciences Society.

530 DEU ISSN 0939-592X
I F F - FERIENKURSES. VORLESUNGSMANUSKRIPTE. (Institut fuer Festkoerperforschung) Text in German. 1986. a. **Document type:** *Monographic series, Academic/Scholarly.*
—IE, Ingenta.
Published by: (Institut fuer Festkoerperforschung, Kernforschungsanlage Juelich) Forschungszentrum Juelich GmbH, Leo-Brandt-Str, Juelich, 52428, Germany. TEL 49-2461-614662, FAX 49-2461-614666, info@fz-juelich.de, http://www.fz-juelich.de.

I F S NEWSLETTER. *see* ENERGY—Nuclear Energy

621 JPN
I P A P CONFERENCE SERIES. Text in English. irreg., latest 2001. price varies. **Document type:** *Monographic series, Academic/Scholarly.* **Description:** Includes papers presented at scientific and technology conferences, symposiums and meetings around the world.
Published by: Institute of Pure and Applied Physics, Toyokaiji Bldg, no.12, 6-9-6 Shinbashi, Minato-ku, Tokyo, 105-0004, Japan. TEL 81-3-3432-4308, FAX 81-3-3432-0728, subscription@ipap.jp, http://www.ipap.jp.

I R M A LECTURES IN MATHEMATICS AND THEORETICAL PHYSICS. (Institut de Recherche Mathematique Avancee) *see* MATHEMATICS

530 USA ISSN 2090-6064
▼ ➤ **I S R N NANOTECHNOLOGY.** (International Scholarly Research Network) Text in English. 2011. **Document type:** *Journal, Academic/Scholarly.* **Description:** Publishes original research articles as well as review articles in all areas of nanotechnology.
Related titles: Online - full text ed.: ISSN 2090-6072. 2011. free (effective 2011).
Published by: Hindawi Publishing Corporation, 410 Park Ave, 15th Fl, PMB 287, New York, NY 10022. FAX 215-893-4392, 866-446-3294, info@hindawi.com.

530 IND
THE I U P JOURNAL OF PHYSICS. Text in English. 2008. q. INR 625 combined subscription domestic (print & online eds.); USD 32 combined subscription foreign (print & online eds.) (effective 2011). adv. back issues avail. **Document type:** *Journal, Academic/Scholarly.* **Description:** Focuses on the areas of thermodynamics and statistical mechanics, electromagnetism, hydrodynamics, classical and quantum mechanics, special and general relativity, elasticity, astrophysics and cosmology, etc.
Formerly (until 2009): The I C F A I University Journal of Physics (0974-1380)
Related titles: Online - full text ed.
Indexed: A01, CA, T02.
Published by: (Institute of Chartered Financial Analysts of India), I C F A I University Press, Plot # 53, Nagarjuna Hills, Panjagutta, Hyderabad, 500 082, India. TEL 91-40-23430448, FAX 91-40-23430447, info@iupindia.in. Ed. E N Murthy. **Subscr. to:** Plot # 126, Maalaxmi Towers, Beside Nikhil Hospital, Srinagar Colony, Hyderabad 500 073, India. TEL 91-40-23423101, FAX 91-40-23423111, serv@iupindia.in.

530 GBR ISSN 1793-1231
IMPERIAL COLLEGE PRESS ADVANCED PHYSICS TEXTS. Text in English. 2005. irreg., latest vol.3, 2005. price varies. back issues avail. **Document type:** *Monographic series, Academic/Scholarly.*
Published by: Imperial College Press (Subsidiary of: World Scientific Publishing Co. Pte. Ltd.), 57 Shelton St, Covent Garden, London, WC2H 9HE, United Kingdom. TEL 44-20-78360888, FAX 44-20-78362020, edit@icpress.co.uk, http://www.icpress.co.uk/. **Dist. by:** World Scientific Publishing Ltd.; World Scientific Publishing Co., Inc., 27 Warren St, Ste 401-402, Hackensack, NJ 07601. TEL 201-487-9655, 800-227-7562, FAX 201-487-9656, 888-977-2665, wspc@wspc.com.

530 IND ISSN 0973-1458
CODEN: IJPNCV
➤ **INDIAN JOURNAL OF PHYSICS.** Text in English. 2004. m. EUR 439 combined subscription to institutions (print & online eds.) (effective 2011). bk.rev. **Document type:** *Journal, Academic/Scholarly.* **Description:** Contains original scientific research results in the form of full papers and short notes. It emphasizes both fundamental and applied research work in Physics.
Formed by the merger of (1977-2004): Indian Journal of Physics. Part A (0252-9262); (1977-2004): Indian Journal of Physics. Part B (0252-9254); Both of which superseded in part (in 1977): Indian Journal of Physics and Proceedings of the Indian Association for the Cultivation of Science (0019-5480); Which was formerly (1915-1926): Indian Association for the Cultivation of Science. Proceedings (0369-9897)
Related titles: Online - full text ed.: ISSN 0974-9845 (from IngentaConnect).
Indexed: A20, C33, CurCont, Inspec, RefZh, SCI, W07.
—BLDSC (4419.905000), IE, Ingenta, INIST.
Published by: (Indian Association for the Cultivation of Science), Springer (India) Private Ltd. (Subsidiary of: Springer Science+Business Media), 212, Deen Dayal Upadhyaya Marg, 3rd Fl, Gandharva Mahavidyalaya, New Delhi, 110 002, India. TEL 91-11-45755888, FAX 91-11-45755889. Eds. A Ghosh, Deb S Ray. Circ: 600. **Subscr. to:** I N S I O Scientific Books & Periodicals, PO Box 7234, Indraprastha HPO, New Delhi 110 002, India. iihm@ap.nic.in, http://iihm.ap.nic.in/.

530 IND ISSN 0019-5596
QC1 CODEN: IJOPAU
➤ **INDIAN JOURNAL OF PURE & APPLIED PHYSICS.** Abbreviated title: I J P A P. Text in English. 1963. m. USD 550 (effective 2009). bk.rev. bibl.; charts; illus. index. back issues avail. **Document type:** *Journal, Academic/Scholarly.* **Description:** Provides original research communication in all branches of physics.
Related titles: Online - full text ed.: ISSN 0975-1041. free (effective 2011).
Indexed: A20, A22, A28, APA, ASCA, ASFA, AcoustA, ApMecR, BrCerAb, C&ISA, C33, CA/WCA, CIA, CIN, CTE, Cadscan, CerAb, ChemAb, ChemTitl, CivEngAb, CorrAb, CurCont, E&CAJ, E11, EEA, EMA, ESPM, EnvEAb, GeoRef, H15, IBR, IBZ, INIS AtomInd, ISA, ISR, Inspec, LeadAb, M&TEA, M09, MBF, METADEX, MathR, PhysBer, SCI, SCOPUS, SolStAb, SpeleolAb, T04, W07, WAA, Zincscan.
—BLDSC (4420.700000), AskIEEE, CASDDS, IE, Infotrieve, Ingenta, INIST, Linda Hall.
Published by: National Institute of Science Communication and Information Resources (N I S C A I R), Dr. K.S. Krishnan Marg, New Delhi, 110 012, India. TEL 91-11-25841647, FAX 91-11-25847062, http://www.niscair.res.in/. Ed. Poonam Bhatt. Circ: 1,200. **Co-sponsor:** Indian National Science Academy.

530 IND ISSN 0019-5693
QC1 CODEN: IJTPAL
INDIAN JOURNAL OF THEORETICAL PHYSICS. Text in Bengali, English. 1953. q. INR 500 domestic; USD 100 foreign (effective 2011). bk.rev. back issues avail. **Document type:** *Journal, Academic/Scholarly.*
Indexed: ApMecR, CIN, ChemAb, ChemTitl, INIS AtomInd, Inspec, MathR, PhysBer.
—AskIEEE, CASDDS, INIST, Linda Hall.
Published by: Institute of Theoretical Physics, Bignan Kutir, 4-1 Mohan Bagan Lane, Kolkata, West Bengal 700 004, India. admin@itphy.org, www.itphy.org. **Subscr. to:** I N S I O Scientific Books & Periodicals, PO Box 7234, Indraprastha HPO, New Delhi 110 002, India.

553.5 IND ISSN 0970-2334
CODEN: BIVSES
INDIAN VACUUM SOCIETY. BULLETIN. Text in English. 1970. q. bk.rev. **Document type:** *Bulletin, Trade.* **Description:** Contains research papers, review articles and articles on vacuum science and technology.
Formerly (until 1985): V A C News (0254-7848)
Indexed: INIS AtomInd, Inspec.
—AskIEEE, Linda Hall.
Published by: Indian Vacuum Society, c/o Shrikrishna Gupta, Bhabha Atomic Research Centre, Mumbai, Maharashtra 400 085, India. TEL 91-22-25559592. Ed. Dr. K G Bhushan TEL 91-22-25592909. **Subscr. to:** I N S I O Scientific Books & Periodicals, PO Box 7234, Indraprastha HPO, New Delhi 110 002, India.

530 IDN ISSN 1410-8860
QC47.I53
INDONESIAN PHYSICAL SOCIETY. PHYSICS JOURNAL. Text in English. 1996. irreg. **Document type:** *Journal, Academic/Scholarly.* **Description:** Consists of 3 sub-fields with different volume numbers: Applied Physics, Educational Physics and Theoretical Physics.
Related titles: Online - full text ed.: 2004.
Published by: Indonesian Physical Society, Pusat Penelitian Fisika L I P I, Kompleks PUSPIPTEK, Serpong, Tangerang, 15310, Indonesia. TEL 62-021-7560570, FAX 62-021-7560554, redaksi@hfi.fisika.net. Eds. L T Handoko, Terry Mart.

530 ROM ISSN 1454-5837
INGINERIA ILUMINATULUI. Text in Romanian. 1999. q. **Document type:** *Journal, Academic/Scholarly.*
Related titles: Online - full text ed.: free (effective 2011).
Published by: Universitatea Tehnica Cluj-Napoca, Str Constantin Daicoviciou 15, Cluj-Napoca, 400020, Romania. TEL 40-264-401200, FAX 40-264-592055, http://www.utcluj.ro.

530 USA
INSIDE SCIENCE NEWS SERVICE. Text in English. 19??. w. free. **Document type:** *Newsletter, Trade.* **Description:** Provides news content for syndication by news organizations, delivering articles, graphics, audio and videos.
Incorporates (19??-2009): Physics News Update
Media: E-mail. **Related titles:** Online - full text ed.
Published by: American Institute of Physics, 1 Physics Ellipse, College Park, MD 20740. TEL 301-209-3100, FAX 301-209-0843, aipinfo@aip.org, http://www.aip.org.

INSTITUT FOR STUDIET AF MATEMATIK OG FYSIK SAMT DERES FUNKTIONER I UNDERVISNING FORSKNING OG ANVENDELSE. TEKSTER/INSTITUTE OF STUDIES IN MATHEMATICS AND PHYSICS, AND THEIR FUNCTIONS IN EDUCATION, RESEARCH AND APPLICATION. TEXT. *see* MATHEMATICS

L'INSTITUT HENRI POINCARE. ANNALES (C). ANALYSE NON LINEAIRE. *see* MATHEMATICS

INSTITUT ROYAL METEOROLOGIQUE DE BELGIQUE. BULLETIN MENSUEL: OBSERVATIONS IONOSPHERIQUES ET DU RAYONNEMENT COSMIQUE/KONINKLIJK METEOROLOGISCHE INSTITUUT VAN BELGIE. MAANDBULLETIN: WAARNEMINGEN VAN DE IONOSFEER EN DE KOSMISCHE STRALING. *see* METEOROLOGY

530 SGP
THE INSTITUTE FOR NUCLEAR THEORY. PROCEEDINGS. Text in English. 1992. irreg., latest vol.16, 2009. price varies. back issues avail. **Document type:** *Monographic series, Academic/Scholarly.*
Published by: World Scientific Publishing Co. Pte. Ltd., 5 Toh Tuck Link, Singapore, 596224, Singapore. TEL 65-6466-5775, FAX 65-6467-7667, wspc@wspc.com.sg, http://www.worldscientific.com. Eds. Ernest M Henley, Wick C Haxton. **Dist. by:** World Scientific Publishing Co., Inc., 27 Warren St, Ste 401-402, Hackensack, NJ 07601. TEL 201-487-9655, 800-227-7562, FAX 201-487-9656, 888-977-2665, wspc@wspc.com; World Scientific Publishing Ltd., 57 Shelton St, London WC2H 9HE, United Kingdom. TEL 44-207-8360888, FAX 44-207-8362020, sales@wspc.co.uk.

INSTITUTE OF PHYSICS AND ENGINEERING IN MEDICINE. REPORT. *see* MEDICAL SCIENCES—Radiology And Nuclear Medicine

530 GBR ISSN 0951-3248
CODEN: IPCSEP
➤ **INSTITUTE OF PHYSICS CONFERENCE SERIES.** Text in English. 1967. irreg., latest vol.169, 2009. **Document type:** *Proceedings, Academic/Scholarly.*
Former titles (until 1985): Institute of Physics. Conference Series (0305-2346); (until 1971): Institute of Physics and the Physical Society. Conference Series (0537-9504)
Related titles: Microform ed.: (from PMC).
Indexed: A22, ASCA, CIN, ChemAb, ChemTitl, GeoRef, ISR, Inspec, PhysBer, SCOPUS, SpeleolAb.
—BLDSC (3409.950000), CASDDS, IE, Infotrieve, Ingenta, INIST. **CCC.**
Published by: (Institute of Physics), Institute of Physics Publishing Ltd., Dirac House, Temple Back, Bristol, BS1 6BE, United Kingdom. TEL 44-117-9297481, FAX 44-117-9301178, custserv@iop.org, http://publishing.iop.org/.

P

620.5 GBR ISSN 1740-3499
T174.7
INSTITUTION OF MECHANICAL ENGINEERS. PROCEEDINGS. PART N: JOURNAL OF NANOENGINEERING AND NANOSYSTEMS. Text in English. 2004. q. USD 992 combined subscription in North America to institutions (print & online eds.); GBP 571 combined subscription elsewhere to institutions (print & online eds.) (effective 2011). reprint service avail. from PSC. **Document type:** *Journal, Academic/Scholarly.* **Description:** Dedicated to the particular aspects of nanoscale engineering, science, and technology that involve the descriptions of nanoscale systems.
Related titles: Online - full text ed.: ISSN 2041-3092. USD 894 in North America to institutions; GBP 514 elsewhere to institutions (effective 2011); ♦ Series: Institution of Mechanical Engineers. Proceedings.
Indexed: A22, A28, APA, BrCerAb, C&ISA, CA/WCA, CIA, CPEI, CerAb, CivEngAb, CorrAb, E&CAJ, E01, E11, EEA, EMA, ESPM, EnvEAb, H15, Inspec, M&TEA, M09, MBF, METADEX, P26, P48, P52, P54, P56, PQC, SolStAb, T04, WAA.
—BLDSC (6724.905000), IE, Ingenta, Linda Hall. **CCC.**
Published by: (Institution of Mechanical Engineers), Sage Publications Ltd. (Subsidiary of: Sage Publications, Inc.), 1 Oliver's Yard, 55 City Rd, London, EC1Y 1SP, United Kingdom. TEL 44-20-73248500, FAX 44-20-73248600, info@sagepub.co.uk, http://www.uk.sagepub.com/home.nav.

530 ROM
INSTITUTUL DE SUBINGINERI ORADEA. LUCRARI STIINTIFICE: SERIA FIZICA. Text in Romanian; Text occasionally in English, French; Summaries in Romanian, French, German. 1967. a. **Document type:** *Academic/Scholarly.*
Formerly: Institutul Pedagogic Oradea. Lucrari Stiintifice: Seria Fizica; Which superseded in part (in 1973): Institutul Pedagogic Oradea. Lucrari Stiintifice: Seria Matematica, Fizica, Chimie; Which superseded (in 1971): Institutul Pedagogic Oradea. Lucrari Stiintifice: Seria A si Seria B; (in 1969): Institutul Pedagogic Oradea. Lucrari Stiintifice
Published by: Universitatea din Oradea, Facultatea de Inginerie Electrica si Tehnologia Informatiei, Strada Universitatii 1, Oradea, 410087, Romania.

INSTITUTUL POLITEHNIC DIN IASI. BULETINUL. SECTIA MATEMATICA, MECANICA, FIZICA/POLYTECHNIC INSTITUTE OF IASI. MATHEMATICS. BULLETIN. THEORETICAL MECHANICS. PHYSICS. *see* MATHEMATICS

INTERACTIONS ACROSS PHYSICS AND EDUCATION. *see* EDUCATION—Teaching Methods And Curriculum

530 NLD ISSN 1573-4285
INTERFACE SCIENCE AND TECHNOLOGY. Text in English. 2004. irreg., latest vol.16, 2009. price varies. **Document type:** *Monographic series, Academic/Scholarly.*
Indexed: SCOPUS.
—BLDSC (4533.460050). **CCC.**
Published by: Elsevier BV (Subsidiary of: Elsevier Science & Technology), Radarweg 29, PO Box 211, Amsterdam, 1000 AE, Netherlands. TEL 31-20-4853911, FAX 31-20-4852457, JournalsCustomerServiceEMEA@elsevier.com, http://www.elsevier.com. Ed. A Hubbard.

538 USA ISSN 2150-4598
TK454.4.M3 CODEN: DICODA
INTERMAG. Variant title: International Magnetics Conference. Text in English. 19??. irreg., latest 2006. adv. back issues avail.; reprints avail. **Document type:** *Proceedings, Trade.* **Description:** Covers all areas of basic science, applied science and engineering as they pertain to magnetism.
Former titles (until 2006): Intermag Asia; (until 2005): International Magnetics Conference. Digests of the Intermag Conference; (until 2000): International Magnetics Conference. Digest (0074-6843); (until 1970): Abstracts of the Intermag Conference (0538-6160)
Related titles: CD-ROM ed.; Microfiche ed.; Online - full text ed.: ISSN 2150-4601.
Indexed: EngInd, SCOPUS.
—CASDDS. **CCC.**
Published by: I E E E, 445 Hoes Ln, Piscataway, NJ 08854. TEL 732-981-0060, 800-678-4333, FAX 732-562-6380, customer.service@ieee.org, http://www.ieee.org. **Co-sponsor:** I E E E Magnetics Society.

INTERNATIONAL JOURNAL OF COMPUTATIONAL METHODS. *see* MATHEMATICS

530 KOR ISSN 2093-9655
▼ ➤ **INTERNATIONAL JOURNAL OF ENERGY, INFORMATION AND COMMUNICATIONS.** Text in English. 2011. q. bk.rev. Index. back issues avail.; reprints avail. **Document type:** *Journal, Academic/Scholarly.* **Description:** Coves the recent progress in the area of energy, information and communications. Topics include: Energy (Energy systems; electric power systems; renewable energy systems; energy economics & policy). Information (Intelligent and knowledge-based systems; agent and multi-agent systems; autonomic and autonomous systems; software and algorithms). Communications (Communication networks and services; web intelligence and applications; human interfaces). Information & Communications in Energy Systems (Smart grids; cyber security in energy systems; information & communication technologies in energy systems; energy management system in buildings).
Related titles: Online - full text ed.: free.
Published by: Science and Engineering Research Support Society, Rm.402, Man-Je Bldg., 449-8 Ojung-Dong, Daedoek-Gu, Daejon, Korea, S. TEL 82-42-6298373, FAX 82-42-6298383. Ed. Tetsuo Kinoshita.

530 SGP ISSN 0219-8878
QC19.2
INTERNATIONAL JOURNAL OF GEOMETRIC METHODS IN MODERN PHYSICS. Abbreviated title: I J G M M P. Text in English. 2004 (June). 8/yr. SGD 1,142, USD 708, EUR 594 combined subscription to institutions (print & online eds.) (effective 2012). adv. back issues avail. **Document type:** *Journal, Academic/Scholarly.* **Description:** Brings out communications, research and review articles devoted to the application of geometric methods (including differential geometry, algebraic geometry, global analysis and topology) to quantum field theory etc.
Related titles: Online - full text ed.: ISSN 1793-6977. SGD 1,038, USD 644, EUR 540 to institutions (effective 2012).
Indexed: A01, A22, A28, APA, BrCerAb, C&ISA, CA, CA/WCA, CCMJ, CIA, CMCI, CerAb, CivEngAb, CorrAb, CurCont, E&CAJ, E01, E11, EEA, EMA, ESPM, EnvEAb, H15, M&TEA, M09, MBF, METADEX, MSN, MathR, SCI, SCOPUS, SolStAb, T02, T04, W07, WAA, Z02.
—BLDSC (4542.266550), IE, Ingenta, Linda Hall. **CCC.**
Published by: World Scientific Publishing Co. Pte. Ltd., 5 Toh Tuck Link, Singapore, 596224, Singapore. TEL 65-6466-5775, FAX 65-6467-7667, wspc@wspc.com.sg, http://www.worldscientific.com. **Dist. by:** World Scientific Publishing Co., Inc., 27 Warren St, Ste 401-402, Hackensack, NJ 07601. TEL 201-487-9655, 800-227-7562, FAX 201-487-9656, 888-977-2665, wspc@wspc.com; World Scientific Publishing Ltd., 57 Shelton St, London WC2H 9HE, United Kingdom. TEL 44-207-8360888, FAX 44-207-8362020, sales@wspc.co.uk.

530 621.3 USA ISSN 1943-0876
▼ **INTERNATIONAL JOURNAL OF GREEN NANOTECHNOLOGY: PHYSICS AND CHEMISTRY.** Text in English. 2009 (Mar.). s-a. USD 259, GBP 129, EUR 207 combined subscription to institutions (print & online eds.) (effective 2010). adv. reprints avail. **Document type:** *Journal, Academic/Scholarly.* **Description:** Focuses on the important challenges and latest advances in the chemistry, physics, biology, engineering, and other scientific aspects of green nanotechnology as well as on their societal impact and the policies that have been or should be developed to address them.
Related titles: Online - full text ed.: ISSN 1943-0884. 2009 (Mar.).
Indexed: B&BAb, B19, CA, G02, T02.
—**CCC.**
Published by: Taylor & Francis Inc. (Subsidiary of: Taylor & Francis Group), 325 Chestnut St, Ste 800, Philadelphia, PA 19106. TEL 215-625-2940, 800-354-1420, orders@taylorandfrancis.com, http://www.taylorandfrancis.com. Ed. Kattesh V Katti. Adv. contact Linda Hann TEL 44-1344-779945.

INTERNATIONAL JOURNAL OF HEAT AND MASS TRANSFER. *see* ENGINEERING—Mechanical Engineering

INTERNATIONAL JOURNAL OF HYDROGEN ENERGY. *see* ENERGY

530 USA ISSN 0899-9457
TK8315 CODEN: IJITEG
➤ **INTERNATIONAL JOURNAL OF IMAGING SYSTEMS AND TECHNOLOGY.** Text in English. 1989. q. GBP 697 in United Kingdom to institutions; EUR 882 in Europe to institutions; USD 1,240 in United States to institutions; USD 1,324 in Canada & Mexico to institutions; USD 1,366 elsewhere to institutions; GBP 802 combined subscription in United Kingdom to institutions (print & online eds.); EUR 1,015 combined subscription in Europe to institutions (print & online eds.); USD 1,427 combined subscription in United States to institutions (print & online eds.); USD 1,511 combined subscription in Canada & Mexico to institutions (print & online eds.); USD 1,553 combined subscription elsewhere to institutions (print & online eds.) (effective 2012). adv. back issues avail.; reprint service avail. from PSC. **Document type:** *Journal, Academic/Scholarly.* **Description:** Covers current information pertinent to engineers and specialists working with imaging technology.
Related titles: Microform ed.: (from PQC); Online - full text ed.: ISSN 1098-1098. GBP 633 in United Kingdom to institutions; EUR 801 in Europe to institutions; USD 1,240 elsewhere to institutions (effective 2012).
Indexed: A01, A22, ASCA, B&BAb, B19, CA, CMCI, CPEI, CurCont, EngInd, GeoRef, Inspec, P30, SCI, SCOPUS, SpeleolAb, T02, W07.
—BLDSC (4542.299000), AskIEEE, IE, Infotrieve, Ingenta, INIST, Linda Hall. **CCC.**
Published by: John Wiley & Sons, Inc., 111 River St, Hoboken, NJ 07030. TEL 201-748-6000, FAX 201-748-6088, info@wiley.com, http://www.wiley.com/WileyCDA/. Eds. Larry Shepp TEL 732-445-1143, Zang-Hee Cho TEL 949-824-5905. Adv. contact Kim Thompkins TEL 212-850-6921. **Subscr. outside the Americas to:** John Wiley & Sons Ltd., The Atrium, Southern Gate, Chichester, West Sussex PO19 8SQ, United Kingdom. TEL 44-1243-779777, FAX 44-1243-775878, cs-journals@wiley.com.

➤ **INTERNATIONAL JOURNAL OF MATHEMATICAL SCIENCES.** *see* MATHEMATICS

➤ **INTERNATIONAL JOURNAL OF MATHEMATICS AND MATHEMATICAL SCIENCES.** *see* MATHEMATICS

530 SGP ISSN 0217-751X
QC793 CODEN: IMPAEF
➤ **INTERNATIONAL JOURNAL OF MODERN PHYSICS A;** particles and fields; gravitation; cosmology; nuclear physics. Abbreviated title: I J M P A. Text in English. 1986. 32/yr. SGD 11,948, USD 7,406, EUR 6,225 combined subscription to institutions (print & online eds.) (effective 2012). adv. back issues avail. **Document type:** *Journal, Academic/Scholarly.* **Description:** Covers particle and field physics, nuclear physics, gravitation and cosmology.
Related titles: Online - full text ed.: ISSN 1793-656X. SGD 10,862, USD 6,733, EUR 5,659 to institutions (effective 2012).
Indexed: A01, A03, A08, A22, ASCA, CA, CCMJ, CIN, ChemAb, ChemTitl, CurCont, E01, E04, E05, ISR, Inspec, MSN, MathR, P30, S01, SCI, SCOPUS, T02, W07, Z02.
—BLDSC (4542.365200), AskIEEE, CASDDS, IE, Infotrieve, Ingenta, INIST. **CCC.**
Published by: World Scientific Publishing Co. Pte. Ltd., 5 Toh Tuck Link, Singapore, 596224, Singapore. TEL 65-6466-5775, FAX 65-6467-7667, wspc@wspc.com.sg, http://www.worldscientific.com. **Dist. by:** World Scientific Publishing Co., Inc., 27 Warren St, Ste 401-402, Hackensack, NJ 07601. TEL 201-487-9655, 800-227-7562, FAX 201-487-9656, 888-977-2665, wspc@wspc.com; World Scientific Publishing Ltd., 57 Shelton St, London WC2H 9HE, United Kingdom. TEL 44-207-8360888, FAX 44-207-8362020, sales@wspc.co.uk.

530 SGP ISSN 0217-9792
QC173.4.C65 CODEN: IJPBEV
➤ **INTERNATIONAL JOURNAL OF MODERN PHYSICS B;** condensed matter physics; statistical physics; applied physics. Abbreviated title: I J M P B. Text in English. 1987. 32/yr. SGD 9,055, USD 5,636, EUR 4,714 combined subscription to institutions (print & online eds.) (effective 2012). adv. back issues avail. **Document type:** *Journal, Academic/Scholarly.* **Description:** Provides review and research articles on condensed matter, statistical and applied physics at graduate and post-graduate levels.
Related titles: Online - full text ed.: ISSN 1793-6578. SGD 8,232, USD 5,124, EUR 4,285 to institutions (effective 2012).
Indexed: A01, A03, A08, A20, A22, A28, APA, ASCA, BrCerAb, C&ISA, CA, CA/WCA, CCMJ, CIA, CIN, CerAb, ChemAb, ChemTitl, CivEngAb, CorrAb, CurCont, E&CAJ, E01, E11, EEA, EMA, ESPM, EnvEAb, H15, INIS AtomInd, ISR, Inspec, M&GPA, M&TEA, M09, MBF, METADEX, MSN, MathR, S01, SCI, SCOPUS, SolStAb, T02, T04, W07, WAA, Z02.
—BLDSC (4542.365210), AskIEEE, CASDDS, IE, Infotrieve, Ingenta, INIST. **CCC.**
Published by: World Scientific Publishing Co. Pte. Ltd., 5 Toh Tuck Link, Singapore, 596224, Singapore. TEL 65-6466-5775, FAX 65-6467-7667, wspc@wspc.com.sg, http://www.worldscientific.com. Eds. Rongjia Tao, W Schommers TEL 49-7247-822432, Yu Peng Wang. **Dist. by:** World Scientific Publishing Co., Inc., 27 Warren St, Ste 401-402, Hackensack, NJ 07601. TEL 201-487-9655, 800-227-7562, FAX 201-487-9656, 888-977-2665, wspc@wspc.com; World Scientific Publishing Ltd., 57 Shelton St, London WC2H 9HE, United Kingdom. TEL 44-207-8360888, FAX 44-207-8362020, sales@wspc.co.uk.

530 500 SGP ISSN 0129-1831
QC52 CODEN: IJMPEO
➤ **INTERNATIONAL JOURNAL OF MODERN PHYSICS C;** computational physics and physical computation. Abbreviated title: I J M P C. Text in English. 1990. m. SGD 3,189, USD 2,001, EUR 1,613 combined subscription to institutions (print & online eds.) (effective 2012). adv. back issues avail. **Document type:** *Journal, Academic/Scholarly.* **Description:** Brings out both review and research articles on the use of computers to advance knowledge in the physical sciences and the use of physical analogies in computation.
Incorporates (1994-2001): Annual Reviews of Computational Physics
Related titles: Online - full text ed.: ISSN 1793-6586. SGD 2,899, USD 1,819, EUR 1,466 to institutions (effective 2012).
Indexed: A01, A03, A08, A22, ASCA, C10, C23, CA, CCMJ, CMCI, CompLI, CurCont, E01, ISR, Inspec, MSN, MathR, RefZh, S01, SCI, SCOPUS, T02, W07, Z02.
—BLDSC (4542.365220), AskIEEE, IE, Infotrieve, Ingenta. **CCC.**
Published by: World Scientific Publishing Co. Pte. Ltd., 5 Toh Tuck Link, Singapore, 596224, Singapore. TEL 65-6466-5775, FAX 65-6467-7667, wspc@wspc.com.sg, http://www.worldscientific.com. **Dist. by:** World Scientific Publishing Ltd., 57 Shelton St, London WC2H 9HE, United Kingdom. TEL 44-207-8360888, FAX 44-207-8362020, sales@wspc.co.uk; World Scientific Publishing Co., Inc., 27 Warren St, Ste 401-402, Hackensack, NJ 07601. TEL 201-487-9655, 800-227-7562, FAX 201-487-9656, 888-977-2665, wspc@wspc.com.

530 SGP ISSN 2010-1945
▼ **INTERNATIONAL JOURNAL OF MODERN PHYSICS: CONFERENCE SERIES.** Text in English. forthcoming 2011. irreg. free (effective 2012). **Document type:** *Proceedings, Academic/Scholarly.*
Media: Online - full text.
Published by: World Scientific Publishing Co. Pte. Ltd., 5 Toh Tuck Link, Singapore, 596224, Singapore. TEL 65-6466-5775, FAX 65-6467-7667, wspc@wspc.com.sg, http://www.worldscientific.com. **Subscr. to:** Farrer Rd, PO Box 128, Singapore 912805, Singapore. **Dist. by:** World Scientific Publishing Ltd., 57 Shelton St, London WC2H 9HE, United Kingdom. TEL 44-207-8360888, FAX 44-207-8362020, sales@wspc.co.uk.; World Scientific Publishing Co., Inc., 27 Warren St, Ste 401-402, Hackensack, NJ 07601. TEL 201-487-9655, 800-227-7562, FAX 201-487-9656, 888-977-2665.

530 SGP ISSN 0218-2718
QB460 CODEN: IMPDEO
➤ **INTERNATIONAL JOURNAL OF MODERN PHYSICS D;** gravitation, astrophysics and cosmology. Abbreviated title: I J M P D. Text in English. 1992. 14/yr. SGD 3,121, USD 1,909, EUR 1,577 combined subscription to institutions (print & online eds.) (effective 2012). adv. back issues avail. **Document type:** *Journal, Academic/Scholarly.* **Description:** Features research and review articles on theoretical, observational, and experimental findings in the fields of gravitation, astrophysics and cosmology.
Related titles: Online - full text ed.: ISSN 1793-6594. SGD 2,837, USD 1,799, EUR 1,434 to institutions (effective 2012).
Indexed: A01, A03, A08, A22, A28, APA, ASCA, BrCerAb, C&ISA, CA, CA/WCA, CCMJ, CIA, CerAb, CivEngAb, CorrAb, CurCont, E&CAJ, E01, E11, EEA, EMA, ESPM, EnvEAb, H15, ISR, Inspec, M&GPA, M&TEA, M09, MBF, METADEX, MSN, MathR, S01, SCI, SCOPUS, SolStAb, T02, T04, W07, WAA, Z02.
—BLDSC (4542.365230), AskIEEE, IE, Infotrieve, Ingenta, Linda Hall. **CCC.**
Published by: World Scientific Publishing Co. Pte. Ltd., 5 Toh Tuck Link, Singapore, 596224, Singapore. TEL 65-6466-5775, FAX 65-6467-7667, wspc@wspc.com.sg, http://www.worldscientific.com. **Dist. by:** World Scientific Publishing Co., Inc., 27 Warren St, Ste 401-402, Hackensack, NJ 07601. TEL 201-487-9655, 800-227-7562, FAX 201-487-9656, 888-977-2665, wspc@wspc.com; World Scientific Publishing Ltd., 57 Shelton St, London WC2H 9HE, United Kingdom. TEL 44-207-8360888, FAX 44-207-8362020, sales@wspc.co.uk.

➤ **INTERNATIONAL JOURNAL OF MULTIPHASE FLOW.** *see* ENGINEERING—Mechanical Engineering

530 GBR ISSN 1750-9548
➤ **THE INTERNATIONAL JOURNAL OF MULTIPHYSICS.** Abbreviated title: I J M. Text in English. 2007 (Jan.). q. GBP 272; GBP 297 combined subscription (print & online eds.) (effective 2012). **Document type:** *Journal, Academic/Scholarly.* **Description:** Addresses the latest advances in theoretical developments, numerical modelling and industrial applications which will promote the concept of simultaneous engineering.
Related titles: Online - full text ed.: 2007. GBP 253 (effective 2012).
Indexed: A01, A28, APA, BrCerAb, C&ISA, CA, CA/WCA, CIA, CerAb, CivEngAb, CorrAb, E&CAJ, E11, EEA, EMA, ESPM, EnvEAb, H15, M&TEA, M09, MBF, METADEX, RefZh, SolStAb, T02, T04, WAA.
—BLDSC (4542.367000), IE, Ingenta.
Published by: Multi-Science Publishing Co. Ltd., 5 Wates Way, Brentwood, Essex CM15 9TB, United Kingdom. TEL 44-1277-244632, FAX 44-1277-223453, info@multi-science.co.uk. Ed. M Moatamedi.

▼ ➤ **INTERNATIONAL JOURNAL OF NANOMECHANICS SCIENCE AND TECHNOLOGY.** *see* ENGINEERING

530 621.3 USA ISSN 1941-6318
T174.7
▼ ➤ **INTERNATIONAL JOURNAL OF NANOTECHNOLOGY AND MOLECULAR COMPUTATION.** Text in English. 2009 (1st q.). q. USD 210 to individuals; USD 595 to institutions; USD 275 combined subscription to individuals (print & online eds.); USD 860 combined subscription to institutions (print & online eds.) (effective 2012). **Document type:** *Journal, Academic/Scholarly.* **Description:** Publishes research in all areas of nanotechnology and molecular computation.
Related titles: Online - full text ed.: ISSN 1941-6326. USD 140 to individuals; USD 595 to institutions (effective 2012).
—BLDSC (4542.369285), IE.
Published by: (Information Resources Management Association), I G I Global, 701 E Chocolate Ave, Ste 200, Hershey, PA 17033. TEL 717-533-8845 ext 100, 866-342-6657, FAX 717-533-8661, cust@igi-global.com. Ed. Bruce MacLennan.

501.5118 GBR ISSN 1749-3889
INTERNATIONAL JOURNAL OF NONLINEAR SCIENCE. Abbreviated title: I J N S. Text in English. 2006. bi-m. GBP 272 to institutions; GBP 40 to members; GBP 43 per issue (effective 2010). **Document type:** *Journal, Academic/Scholarly.* **Description:** Publishes original research papers and reviews on nonlinear science and applications, including the field of mathematics, physics, biology, engineering, economics, social sciences, and other areas of science.
Related titles: Online - full text ed.: ISSN 1749-3897. free (effective 2010).
Indexed: CCMJ, MSN, MathR, RefZh, Z02.
—BLDSC (4542.395500), IE, Ingenta.
Published by: World Academic Union (World Academic Press), 113 Academic House, Mill Lane, Wavertree Technology Park, Liverpool, L13 4AH, United Kingdom. TEL 44-870-7779498, journals@worldacademicunion.com, http://www.worldacademicunion.com/. Ed. BoLing Guo.

530 NGA ISSN 1992-1950
QC1
➤ **INTERNATIONAL JOURNAL OF PHYSICAL SCIENCES.** Text in English. 2006 (July). m. free (effective 2011). adv. **Document type:** *Journal, Academic/Scholarly.* **Description:** Covers intelligence, neural processing, nuclear and particle physics, geophysics, physics in medicine and biology, plasma physics, semiconductor science and technology, etc.
Media: Online - full text.
Indexed: A32, A34, A36, A37, AgrForAb, BA, C25, C30, CABA, E12, ESPM, F08, F11, F12, FCA, GH, H16, H17, I11, IndVet, M&GPA, MaizeAb, N02, N03, O01, OR, P32, P33, P37, P39, P40, PGegResA, PHN&I, PN&I, PollutAb, R07, R08, R11, R12, RA&MP, S13, S16, S17, SCI, SCOPUS, SWRA, T05, TAR, VS, W07.
Published by: Academic Journals, PO Box 73023, Victoria Island, Lagos, Nigeria. service@academicjournals.org. Eds. Huisheng Peng, Zafar Iqbal.

530 CHE ISSN 2077-0391
▼ ➤ **INTERNATIONAL JOURNAL OF PHYSICS.** Text in English. forthcoming 2011. q. free (effective 2011). **Document type:** *Journal, Academic/Scholarly.*
Media: Online - full text.
Published by: M D P I AG, Postfach, Basel, 4005, Switzerland. TEL 41-61-6837734, FAX 41-61-3028918, http://www.mdpi.org/.

530 IND ISSN 0973-1776
➤ **INTERNATIONAL JOURNAL OF PURE AND APPLIED PHYSICS.** Abbreviated title: I J P A P. Text in English. 2005. q. INR 3,000 domestic to libraries; USD 480 foreign to libraries; USD 520 combined subscription foreign to libraries (print & online eds.) (effective 2011). back issues avail. **Document type:** *Journal, Academic/Scholarly.* **Description:** Publishes quality original research papers, comprehensive review articles, survey articles, book reviews, dissertation abstracts in pure Physics and its applications in the bradest sense. Dedicated to the proliferation and dissemination of scholarly research results covering all disciplines and branches of Physics and its applications.
Related titles: Online - full text ed.: ISSN 0974-4843. USD 460 to libraries (effective 2011).
Indexed: A01, CA, T02.
Published by: Research India Publications, D1/71, Top Fl, Rohini Sec-16, New Delhi, 110 089, India. TEL 91-11-65394240, FAX 91-11-27297815, info@ripublication.com. Ed. Ossama M M El-Shazly.

530 SGP ISSN 0219-7499
QA76.889
➤ **INTERNATIONAL JOURNAL OF QUANTUM INFORMATION.** Abbreviated title: I J Q I. Text in English. 2003 (Mar.). 8/yr. SGD 812, USD 537, EUR 408 combined subscription to institutions (print & online eds.) (effective 2012). adv. back issues avail. **Document type:** *Journal, Academic/Scholarly.* **Description:** Covers the interdisciplinary scientific research in quantum information, computation and communication theory.
Related titles: Online - full text ed.: ISSN 1793-6918. SGD 738, USD 488, EUR 371 to institutions (effective 2012).
Indexed: A01, A22, A28, APA, BrCerAb, C&ISA, CA, CA/WCA, CIA, CMCI, CerAb, CivEngAb, CorrAb, CurCont, E&CAJ, E01, E11, EEA, EMA, ESPM, EnvEAb, H15, M&TEA, M09, MBF, METADEX, SCI, SCOPUS, SolStAb, T02, T04, W07, WAA, Z02.
—BLDSC (4542.516000), IE, Ingenta, Linda Hall. **CCC.**
Published by: World Scientific Publishing Co. Pte. Ltd., 5 Toh Tuck Link, Singapore, 596224, Singapore. TEL 65-6466-5775, FAX 65-6467-7667, wspc@wspc.com.sg, http://www.worldscientific.com. **Dist. by:** World Scientific Publishing Ltd., 57 Shelton St, London WC2H 9HE, United Kingdom. TEL 44-207-8360888, FAX 44-207-8362020, sales@wspc.co.uk; World Scientific Publishing Co., Inc., 27 Warren St, Ste 401-402, Hackensack, NJ 07601. TEL 201-487-9655, 800-227-7562, FAX 201-487-9656, 888-977-2665, wspc@wspc.com.

➤ **INTERNATIONAL JOURNAL OF RADIATION BIOLOGY.** *see* MEDICAL SCIENCES—Oncology

530 USA ISSN 0020-7748
QC1 CODEN: IJTPBM
➤ **INTERNATIONAL JOURNAL OF THEORETICAL PHYSICS.** Text in English. 1968. m. EUR 2,854, USD 2,950 combined subscription to institutions (print & online eds.) (effective 2012). adv. abstr.; bibl.; charts; illus. Index. back issues avail.; reprint service avail. from PSC. **Document type:** *Journal, Academic/Scholarly.* **Description:** Features original research and reviews in theoretical physics and related fields, such as mathematics and biological sciences.
Related titles: Microfilm ed.: (from PQC); Online - full text ed.: ISSN 1572-9575 (from IngentaConnect).
Indexed: A01, A02, A03, A08, A20, A22, A26, ASCA, BibLing, CA, CCMJ, CIN, ChemAb, ChemTitl, CurCont, E01, ISR, Inspec, MSN, MathR, PhilInd, PhysBer, SCI, SCOPUS, T02, W07, Z02.
—BLDSC (4542.695000), AskIEEE, CASDDS, IE, Infotrieve, Ingenta, INIST, Linda Hall. **CCC.**
Published by: Springer New York LLC (Subsidiary of: Springer Science+Business Media), 233 Spring St, New York, NY 10013. TEL 212-460-1500, FAX 212-460-1575, service-ny@springer.com. Ed. Heinrich Saller.

530 USA ISSN 1525-4674
QC20.7.G76
INTERNATIONAL JOURNAL OF THEORETICAL PHYSICS, GROUP THEORY AND NONLINEAR OPTICS. Text in English. 1993. q. USD 800 to institutions; USD 1,200 combined subscription to institutions (print & online eds.) (effective 2012). **Document type:** *Journal, Academic/Scholarly.* **Description:** Publishes manuscripts reporting theoretical concepts and developments in physics.
Incorporates (1992-1999): Nova Journal of Theoretical Physics; Formerly: Journal of Group Theory in Physics (1070-2458)
Related titles: Online - full text ed.: USD 800 to institutions (effective 2012).
Indexed: CCMJ, MSN, MathR, RefZh, Z02.
—INIST.
Published by: Nova Science Publishers, Inc., 400 Oser Ave, Ste 1600, Hauppauge, NY 11788. TEL 631-231-7269, FAX 631-231-8175, main@novapublishers.com. Eds. Guoping Zhang, Renat R Letfullin, Thomas George.

530 620 USA
INTERNATIONAL KHARKOV SYMPOSIUM ON PHYSICS AND ENGINEERING OF MICROWAVES, MILLIMETER AND SUB-MILLIMETER WAVES. Text in English. 19??. triennial. adv. back issues avail.; reprints avail. **Document type:** *Proceedings, Trade.*
Related titles: Online - full text ed.
Published by: I E E E, 445 Hoes Ln, Piscataway, NJ 08854. TEL 732-981-0060, 800-678-4333, FAX 732-562-6380, customer.service@ieee.org, http://www.ieee.org.

530 USA ISSN 1971-680X
INTERNATIONAL REVIEW OF PHYSICS. Text in English. 2007. bi-m. EUR 210 to individuals; EUR 240 to institutions (effective 2010). back issues avail. **Document type:** *Journal, Academic/Scholarly.* **Description:** Brings out theoretical and applied papers on all aspects of Physics.
Related titles: CD-ROM ed.: ISSN 1971-6796. EUR 120 to individuals; EUR 150 to institutions (effective 2010).
Indexed: A01, CA, T02.
Published by: Praise Worthy Prize, 2959 Ruth Rd, Wantag, NY 11793. info@praiseworthyprize.com.

530 THA ISSN 1906-862X
➤ **INTERNATIONAL SCHOOL BANGKOK JOURNAL OF PHYSICS.** Text in English. 2007. s-a. free (effective 2011). **Document type:** *Journal, Academic/Scholarly.*
Media: Online - full text.
Published by: International School Bangkok, 39/7 Sol Nichada Thani, Somakee Road, Pakkret, Nonthaburi, 11120, Thailand. TEL 66-2-9635800, FAX 66-2-5835432.

530 SGP
INTERNATIONAL SCHOOL FOR ADVANCED STUDIES LECTURE SERIES. Text in English. 1985. irreg., latest vol.3, 1985. price varies. back issues avail. **Document type:** *Monographic series, Academic/Scholarly.*
Published by: World Scientific Publishing Co. Pte. Ltd., 5 Toh Tuck Link, Singapore, 596224, Singapore. TEL 65-6466-5775, FAX 65-6467-7667, wspc@wspc.com.sg, http://www.worldscientific.com. **Dist. by:** World Scientific Publishing Ltd., 57 Shelton St, London WC2H 9HE, United Kingdom. TEL 44-207-8360888, FAX 44-207-8362020, sales@wspc.co.uk; World Scientific Publishing Co., Inc., 27 Warren St, Ste 401-402, Hackensack, NJ 07601. TEL 201-487-9655, 800-227-7562, FAX 201-487-9656, 888-977-2665, wspc@wspc.com.

530 NLD ISSN 0074-784X
CODEN: PIPFA7
INTERNATIONAL SCHOOL OF PHYSICS "ENRICO FERMI." PROCEEDINGS. Variant title: Enrico Fermi International School of Physics. Text in English. 1953. irreg., latest vol.169, 2008. price varies. back issues avail.; reprints avail. **Document type:** *Proceedings, Academic/Scholarly.* **Description:** Collects papers presented at conferences during sessions of the international summer school, covering specialized topics in physics, including classical and quantum physics, condensed matter, mathematical physics, and other related areas.
Former titles: Scuola Internazionale di Fisica "Enrico Fermi". Rendiconti, Corso (0375-7595); (until 1960): Scuola Internazionale di Fisica "Enrico Fermi". Rendiconti (0370-7253); Supersedes: International School of Physics "Ettore Majorana". Proceedings (0074-7858)
Related titles: Online - full text ed.: ISSN 1879-8195.
Indexed: A22, CCMJ, CIN, ChemAb, ChemTitl, GeoRef, Inspec, MSN, MathR, SpeleolAb.
—BLDSC (6733.900000), CASDDS, IE, Ingenta, Linda Hall. **CCC.**
Published by: (Societa Italiana di Fisica (S I F) ITA), I O S Press, Nieuwe Hemweg 6B, Amsterdam, 1013 BG, Netherlands. TEL 31-20-6883355, FAX 31-20-6870039, info@iospress.nl. **Subscr. to:** I O S Press, Inc, 4502 Rachael Manor Dr, Fairfax, VA 22032-3631. sales@iospress.com. **Dist. by:** Ohmsha Ltd.

530 ITA
INTERNATIONAL SCHOOL OF PLASMA PHYSICS PIERO CALDIROLA. PROCEEDINGS. Text in English. 1987. irreg., latest vol.19, 2001. price varies. **Document type:** *Proceedings, Academic/Scholarly.*
Published by: (International School of Plasma Physics Piero Caldirola), Editrice Compositori Srl, Via Stalingrado 97-2, Bologna, 40128, Italy. TEL 39-051-3540111, FAX 39-051-327877, 1865@compositori.it, http://www.compositori.it.

530 GBR ISSN 0950-5563
CODEN: ISMPFK
➤ **INTERNATIONAL SERIES OF MONOGRAPHS ON PHYSICS.** Text in English. 1930. irreg., latest 2007. price varies. back issues avail. **Document type:** *Monographic series, Academic/Scholarly.*
Indexed: Inspec, MathR.
—BLDSC (4549.260650).
Published by: Oxford University Press, Great Clarendon St, Oxford, OX2 6DP, United Kingdom. TEL 44-1865-556767, FAX 44-1865-556646, enquiry@oup.co.uk, http://www.oup-usa.org/catalogs/general/series/.

➤ **INTERNATIONAL SERIES ON ADVANCES IN SOLID STATE ELECTRONICS AND TECHNOLOGY.** *see* ENGINEERING

621 RUS ISSN 1815-3712
INTERNATIONAL SIBERIAN WORKSHOPS AND TUTORIALS ON ELECTRON DEVICES AND MATERIALS. Text in English. 2004. a.
—**CCC.**
Published by: Novosibirskii Gosudartvennyi Tekhnicheskii Universitet, pr-kt Karla Marksa 20, Novosibirsk, 630092, Russian Federation. TEL 7-383-3465001, FAX 7-383-3460209, webmaster@nstu.ru, http://www.nstu.ru.

530 USA ISSN 1938-5358
TK7867.2
INTERNATIONAL SYMPOSIUM ON ELECTROMAGNETIC COMPATIBILITY AND ELECTROMAGNETIC ECOLOGY. PROCEEDINGS. Text in English. 1995. biennial, latest 2007. adv. back issues avail.; reprints avail. **Document type:** *Proceedings, Academic/Scholarly.*
Related titles: Online - full text ed.
Published by: I E E E, 445 Hoes Ln, Piscataway, NJ 08854. TEL 732-981-0060, 800-678-4333, FAX 732-562-6380, customer.service@ieee.org, http://www.ieee.org.

530.44 USA
INTERNATIONAL SYMPOSIUM ON PLASMA PROCESS-INDUCED DAMAGE. Text in English. 1996. a., latest 2003. adv. back issues avail.; reprints avail. **Document type:** *Proceedings, Trade.*
Related titles: Online - full text ed.
Published by: I E E E, 445 Hoes Ln, Piscataway, NJ 08854. TEL 732-981-0060, 800-678-4333, FAX 732-562-6380, customer.service@ieee.org, http://www.ieee.org.

523.01 SGP
INTERNATIONAL WORKSHOP ON THE IDENTIFICATION OF DARK MATTER. PROCEEDINGS. Text in English. a. **Document type:** *Proceedings, Academic/Scholarly.*
Published by: (University of Sheffield, Department of Physics and Astronomy GBR), World Scientific Publishing Co. Pte. Ltd., 5 Toh Tuck Link, Singapore, 596224, Singapore. TEL 65-6466-5775, FAX 65-6467-7667, wspc@wspc.com.sg, http://www.worldscientific.com. Eds. Neil J C Spooner, Vitaly Kudryavtsev.

▼ **INVENTI RAPID NANOTECH & BIONIC ENGG.** *see* ENGINEERING—Electrical Engineering

621 RUS
INZHENERNAYA FIZIKA. Text in Russian. 1999. q. USD 512 foreign (effective 2006). **Document type:** *Journal, Trade.*
Published by: NauchTekhLitIzdat, Alymov per, dom 17, str 2, Moscow, 107258, Russian Federation. TEL 7-095-2690004, FAX 7-095-3239010, pribor@tgizdat.ru. **Dist. by:** East View Information Services, 10601 Wayzata Blvd, Minneapolis, MN 55305. TEL 952-252-1201, 800-477-1005, FAX 952-252-1202, info@eastview.com, http://www.eastview.com.

INZHENERNO-FIZICHESKII ZHURNAL. *see* ENGINEERING

537.56 660.2972 DEU ISSN 0947-7047
CODEN: IONIFA
➤ **IONICS;** international journal of ionics. Text in English. 1995. bi-m. EUR 769, USD 932 combined subscription to institutions (print & online eds.) (effective 2012). adv. bk.rev. 80 p./no. 2 cols./p.; back issues avail.; reprint service avail. from PSC. **Document type:** *Journal, Academic/Scholarly.* **Description:** Contributes to the fundamental scientific understanding and technological aspects of ionics, an interdisciplinary field of physics, chemistry, materials science, engineering and other related areas.
Related titles: Online - full text ed.: ISSN 1862-0760 (from IngentaConnect).
Indexed: A22, A26, APIAb, C33, CCI, CPEI, ChemAb, E01, I05, Inspec, MSCI, P30, SCI, SCOPUS, TM, W07.
—BLDSC (4564.834800), CASDDS, IE, Ingenta, INIST. **CCC.**
Published by: (Institute for Ionics), Springer (Subsidiary of: Springer Science+Business Media), Tiergartenstr 17, Heidelberg, 69121, Germany. TEL 49-6221-4870, FAX 49-6221-345229, subscriptions@springer.com. Eds. E Wachsman TEL 352-846-2991, W Weppner. Circ: 250.

➤ **IOWA AGRICULTURE AND HOME ECONOMICS EXPERIMENT STATION. RESEARCH BULLETIN.** *see* AGRICULTURE

530 IRN ISSN 1682-6957
IRANIAN JOURNAL OF PHYSICS RESEARCH/MAJALLAH - 'I PIZHUHISH - I FIZIK I IRAN. Text in English, Persian, Modern. 1996. s-a. **Document type:** *Journal, Academic/Scholarly.*
Related titles: Online - full text ed.: free (effective 2011).
Indexed: A01.
Published by: Isfahan University of Technology, Mechanical Engineering Department, J A F M Office, Isfahan, 84156-83111, Iran. TEL 98-311-3915803, FAX 98-311-3915805.

530 ITA ISSN 1973-2260
ISOMORPH LETTERS. Text in English. 2007. irreg. **Document type:** *Journal, Academic/Scholarly.*
Media: Online - full text.
Published by: Universita degli Studi di Udine, Diaprtimento di Fisica, Via delle Scienze 208, Udine, 33100, Italy. TEL 39-043-2558210, http://www.fisica.uniud.it. Ed. Hans Grassmann.

ISOTOPES IN ENVIRONMENTAL AND HEALTH STUDIES. *see* CHEMISTRY

530 ISR ISSN 0374-2687
ISRAEL PHYSICAL SOCIETY. BULLETIN. Text in English. 1971. irreg., latest 2005. **Document type:** *Bulletin, Academic/Scholarly.* **Description:** Provides abstracts of the annual meetings.
Indexed: INIS AtomInd, Inspec.
Published by: Israel Physical Society, c/o Dept. of Physics, Ben-Gurion University, Beer-Sheva, 84105, Israel. TEL 972-8-6461567, 972-8-6461764, FAX 972-8-6472904, 972-8-6472864.

530 RUS ISSN 0021-3411
QC1 CODEN: IVUFAC
➤ **IZVESTIYA VYSSHIKH UCHEBNYKH ZAVEDENII. FIZIKA.** Text in Russian; Contents page in English. 1957. m. USD 394 foreign (effective 2005). charts; illus. index, cum.index: 1957-1967. **Document type:** *Journal, Academic/Scholarly.*
Related titles: ◆ English Translation: Russian Physics Journal. ISSN 1064-8887.
Indexed: CCMJ, CIN, Cadscan, ChemAb, ChemTitl, INIS AtomInd, ISR, Inspec, LeadAb, MSN, MathR, PhysBer, RefZh, SCOPUS, Z02, Zincscan.
—BLDSC (0077.900000), AskIEEE, CASDDS, East View, INIST, Linda Hall. **CCC.**
Published by: Tomskii Gosudarstvennyi Universitet/Tomsk State University, Pl Revolyutsii, 1, Tomsk, 634050, Russian Federation. TEL 7-3822-233335. Ed. Aleksandr Potekaev. Circ: 2,200. **Dist. by:** East View Information Services, 10601 Wayzata Blvd, Minneapolis, MN 55305. TEL 952-252-1201, 800-477-1005, FAX 952-252-1202, info@eastview.com, http://www.eastview.com.

530 RUS ISSN 0869-6632
RA978.R8
IZVESTIYA VYSSHIKH UCHEBNYKH ZAVEDENII. PRIKLADNAYA I NELINEINAYA DINAMIKA; nauchno-tekhnicheskii zhurnal. Text in Russian. 1993. bi-m. **Description:** Publishes theoretical articles and reviews on nonlinear dynamics, oscillations and waves, bifurcations in different systems.
Related titles: ◆ English Translation: Applied Nonlinear Dynamics. ISSN 1078-7550.
Indexed: Inspec, RefZh, Z02.
Published by: Izdatelstvo Uchebno-Nauchnyi Tsentr "Kolledzh", Astrakhanskaya, 83, Saratov, 410026, Russian Federation. TEL 7-8452-514298, FAX 7-8452-240446, and@ccollege.saratov.su. Ed. Yu. Gulyaev.

530 621.384 RUS ISSN 0021-3462
QC661 CODEN: IVYRAY
IZVESTIYA VYSSHIKH UCHEBNYKH ZAVEDENII. RADIOFIZIKA. Text in Russian; Summaries in English. 1958. m. USD 305 foreign (effective 2005). charts; illus. index. **Document type:** *Journal, Academic/Scholarly.* **Description:** Covers aspects of radio physics. Generalizes experience in investigation of single-frequency generation stability of external cavity injection lasers, in determining the influence of intensive amplitude pump fluctuations on one-circuit parametric amplifier noise characteristics, etc.
Related titles: ◆ English Translation: Radiophysics and Quantum Electronics. ISSN 0033-8443.
Indexed: A28, APA, BrCerAb, C&ISA, CA/WCA, CCMJ, CIA, CIN, CIS, CerAb, ChemAb, ChemTitl, CivEngAb, CorrAb, E&CAJ, E11, EEA, EMA, GeoRef, H15, Inspec, M&TEA, M09, MBF, METADEX, MSN, MathR, PhysBer, RefZh, SCOPUS, SolStAb, SpeleolAb, T04, WAA.
—BLDSC (0077.760000), AskIEEE, CASDDS, East View, INIST, Linda Hall. **CCC.**
Published by: (Nizhegorodskii Gosudarstvennyi Universitet, Nauchno-Issledovatel'skii Radiofizicheskii Institut), Izdatel'stvo Nizhegorodskogo Gosudarstvennogo Universiteta, pr-kt Gagarina 23, Nizhnii Novgorod, 603950, Russian Federation. TEL 7-8312-657923, FAX 7-8312-658592, http://www.unn.ru/rus/books/stat_main.htm. Ed. V L Ginzburg. **Dist. by:** East View Information Services, 10601 Wayzata Blvd, Minneapolis, MN 55305. TEL 952-252-1201, 800-477-1005, FAX 952-252-1202, info@eastview.com, http://www.eastview.com.

P

IZVESTIYA VYSSHIKH UCHEBNYKH ZAVEDENII. SEVERO-KAVKAZSKII REGION. ESTESTVENNYE NAUKI/NORTH-CAUCASUS SCIENTIFIC CENTER OF HIGH SCHOOL. NATURAL SCIENCES. NEWS. *see* MATHEMATICS

531.14 JPN ISSN 0915-3616
J A S M A: JOURNAL OF THE JAPAN SOCIETY OF MICROGRAVITY APPLICATION. Text in Japanese. 1984. q. JPY 5,000 membership (effective 2005). **Document type:** *Journal, Academic/Scholarly.*
Formerly (until 1989): Nihon Maikurogurabiti Oyo Gakkai Kaiho
—BLDSC (4808.005000), Linda Hall. **CCC.**
Published by: Nihon Maikurogurabiti Oyo Gakkai/Japan Society of Microgravity Application, c/o WORDS Publishing House, 2-62-8-507 Higashi Ikebukuro, Toshima-ku, Tokyo, 170-0013, Japan. TEL 81-3-59501290, FAX 81-3-59501292, jasma@words-smile.com, http://www.jasma.info/. Ed. Kazuhiko Kuribayashi.

572 USA ISSN 1931-9223
J C P: BIOCHEMICAL PHYSICS. (Journal of Chemical Physics) Text in English. 2007. m. price varies based on the number of users. **Document type:** *Journal, Academic/Scholarly.*
Media: Online - full text.
—CCC.
Published by: American Institute of Physics, 1 Physics Ellipse, College Park, MD 20740. TEL 301-209-3100, FAX 301-209-0843, aipinfo@aip.org, http://www.aip.org. Ed. Marsha I Lester TEL 215-573-2112.

530 RUS ISSN 0021-3640
QC1 CODEN: JTPLA2
➤ **J E T P LETTERS.** (Journal of Theoretical and Experimental Physics) Text in English. 1965. s-m. EUR 3,480, USD 4,225 combined subscription to institutions (print & online eds.) (effective 2012). illus. Index. back issues avail.; reprints avail. **Document type:** *Journal, Academic/Scholarly.* **Description:** Timely, topical short papers, emphasizing fundamental theoretical and experimental research in all fields of physics.
Related titles: Online - full text ed.: J E T P Letters Online. ISSN 1090-6487 (from IngentaConnect); ◆ Translation of: Pis'ma v Zhurnal Eksperimental'noi i Teoreticheskoi Fiziki. ISSN 0370-274X.
Indexed: A01, A03, A08, A20, A22, A26, ASCA, AcoustA, ApMecR, C33, CA, CPI, Cadscan, ChemAb, CurCont, E01, GPAA, IBR, IBZ, INIS AtomInd, ISR, Inspec, LeadAb, PhysBer, S01, SCI, SCOPUS, SPINweb, T02, W07, Zincscan.
—BLDSC (0412.741000), AskIEEE, East View, IE, Infotrieve, Ingenta, INIST, Linda Hall. **CCC.**
Published by: M A I K Nauka - Interperiodica (Subsidiary of: Pleiades Publishing, Inc.), Profsoyuznaya ul 90, Moscow, 117997, Russian Federation. TEL 7-095-3347420, FAX 7-095-3360666, compmg@maik.ru. Ed. Vsevolod F Gantmakher. **Distr. in the Americas by:** Springer New York LLC, Journal Fulfillment, PO Box 2485, Secaucus, NJ 07096. TEL 212-460-1500, 800-777-4643, FAX 201-348-4505; **Distr. outside of the Americas by:** Springer, Haber Str 7, Heidelberg 69126, Germany. TEL 49-6221-3454303, FAX 49-6221-3454229, subscriptions@springer.com, http://www.springer.de.

530 JPN ISSN 0914-9090
CODEN: JJSEEW
J J A P SERIES. Text in English. 1988. a. **Document type:** *Journal, Academic/Scholarly.*
Indexed: CIN, ChemAb, ChemTitl.
—CASDDS.
Published by: Japanese Journal of Applied Physics, Daini Toyokaiji Bldg, 4-24-8 Shinbashi, Minato-ku, Tokyo, 105-0004, Japan. FAX 81-3-3432-0728. Eds. Atsushi Koma, Yoshinobu Aoyagi.

J P JOURNAL OF SOLIDS AND STRUCTURES. *see* ENGINEERING—Civil Engineering

530 JPN
J S A P INTERNATIONAL. (Japan Society of Applied Physics) Text in English. 2000. s-a. **Document type:** *Journal, Academic/Scholarly.*
Related titles: ◆ Japanese ed.: Oyo Buturi. ISSN 0369-8009.
Indexed: Inspec.
Published by: Japan Society of Applied Physics/Oyo Butsuri Gakkai, Kudan-Kita Bldg 5th Fl, 1-12-3 Kudan-Kita, Chiyoda-ku, Tokyo, 102-0073, Japan. TEL 81-3-32381041, FAX 81-3-32216245, http://www.jsap.or.jp.

J S M P NEWS. (Japan Society of Medical Physics) *see* MEDICAL SCIENCES

530 JPN
JAPAN SOCIETY OF APPLIED PHYSICS. THIN FILM AND SURFACE PHYSICS DIVISION. NEWSLETTER. Text in Japanese. bi-m.
Published by: (Thin Film and Surface Physics Division), Japan Society of Applied Physics/Oyo Butsuri Gakkai, Kudan-Kita Bldg 5th Fl, 1-12-3 Kudan-Kita, Chiyoda-ku, Tokyo, 102-0073, Japan.

621 530 JPN
TA4 CODEN: JJAPB6
➤ **JAPANESE JOURNAL OF APPLIED PHYSICS.** Text in English. 1962. m. JPY 180,000 combined subscription to institutions includes Applied Physics Express (print & online eds.) (effective 2006). illus. Index. reprints avail. **Document type:** *Journal, Academic/Scholarly.* **Description:** Contains research papers in the field of applied physics.
Supersedes (in 2008): Japanese Journal of Applied Physics: Part 1. Regular Papers & Short Notes (0021-4922)
Related titles: Microform ed.; Online - full text ed.; Supplement(s):.
Indexed: A&ATA, AcoustA, ApicAb, C&ISA, C33, CIN, Cadscan, ChemAb, ChemTitl, CorrAb, E&CAJ, EngInd, GeoRef, INIS AtomInd, ISMEC, ISR, Inspec, JCT, JTA, LeadAb, PhotoAb, PhysBer, SCOPUS, SPINweb, SolStAb, SpeleolAb, TM, WAA, Zincscan.
—BLDSC (4650.880600), AskIEEE, CASDDS, IE, Infotrieve, Ingenta, INIST, Linda Hall. **CCC.**
Published by: (Japan Society of Applied Physics/Oyo Butsuri Gakkai), Institute of Pure and Applied Physics, da Vinci Yushima 5F, 2-31-22 Yushima, Bunkyo-ku, Tokyo, 113-0034, Japan. TEL 81-3-58443291, FAX 81-3-58443290, subscription@ipap.jp, http://www.ipap.jp. Eds. Akihiro Kono, Yoshiaki Nakano. Circ: 3,900. **Co-sponsor:** Physical Society of Japan/Nihon Butsuri Gakkai.

530 DEU
▼ **JENAER BEITRAEGE ZUR GESCHICHTE DER PHYSIK.** Text in German. 2010. irreg. price varies. **Document type:** *Monographic series, Academic/Scholarly.*
Published by: G N T Verlag, Schlosstr. 1, Diepholz, 49356, Germany. TEL 49-5441-927129, FAX 49-5441-927127, service@gnt-verlag.de.

530 SGP
JERUSALEM WINTER SCHOOL FOR THEORETICAL PHYSICS. (vol.1-4, 6-8 out of print) Text in English. 1986. irreg., latest vol.9. price varies. back issues avail. **Document type:** *Monographic series, Academic/Scholarly.*
Published by: World Scientific Publishing Co. Pte. Ltd., 5 Toh Tuck Link, Singapore, 596224, Singapore. TEL 65-6466-5775, FAX 65-6467-7667, wspc@wspc.com.sg, http://www.worldscientific.com. **Dist. by:** World Scientific Publishing Ltd., 57 Shelton St, London WC2H 9HE, United Kingdom. TEL 44-207-8360888, FAX 44-207-8362020, sales@wspc.co.uk; World Scientific Publishing Co., Inc., 27 Warren St, Ste 401-402, Hackensack, NJ 07601. TEL 201-487-9655, 800-227-7562, FAX 201-487-9656, 888-977-2665, wspc@wspc.com.

JIKI KYOMEI IGAKKAI PUROGURAMU/SOCIETY OF MAGNETIC RESONANCE IN MEDICINE. PROCEEDINGS OF ANNUAL CONFERENCE. *see* MEDICAL SCIENCES—Radiology And Nuclear Medicine

530 JPN ISSN 0913-7785
JINRUI DOTAI GAKKAI KAIHO/HUMAN ERGOLOGY SOCIETY. NEWSLETTER. Text in Japanese. 1970. 3/yr. **Document type:** *Newsletter.* **Description:** Contains news of the organization.
Address: Rodo Kagaku Kenkyujo, 8-14 Sugao 2-chome, Miyamae-ku, Kawasaki-shi, Kanagawa-ken 216-0015, Japan.

530 CHN ISSN 1001-246X
QC19.2
JISUAN WULI/CHINESE JOURNAL OF COMPUTATIONAL PHYSICS. Text in Chinese. 1984. bi-m. USD 40.20 (effective 2009). **Document type:** *Journal, Consumer.*
Related titles: Online - full text ed.
Indexed: A22, CPEI, EngInd, SCOPUS.
—BLDSC (3180.308000), East View, IE, Ingenta.
Address: PO Box 8009, Beijing, 100088, China. TEL 86-10-62014411ext 2647, 2292 & 2171, FAX 86-10-62010108.

530 621 USA ISSN 0270-5214
TA1 CODEN: JHADDQ
➤ **JOHNS HOPKINS A P L TECHNICAL DIGEST.** (Applied Physics Laboratory) Text in English. 1961. q. free to qualified personnel (effective 2011). bk.rev. charts; illus. **Document type:** *Journal, Academic/Scholarly.* **Description:** Highlights work performed at the Johns Hopkins University Applied Physics Laboratory for its sponsors, and to the scientific and engineering communitites, defense establishment; academia, and industry.
Supersedes (in 1980): A P L Technical Digest (0001-2211)
Related titles: Online - full text ed.: ISSN 1930-0530. free (effective 2011).
Indexed: A22, A28, APA, ASCA, ASFA, B21, BrCerAb, C&ISA, CA/WCA, CIA, CIN, CPEI, CerAb, ChemAb, ChemTitl, CivEngAb, CorrAb, CurCont, E&CAJ, E11, EEA, EMA, ESPM, EngInd, EnvEAb, GeoRef, H15, ISMEC, Inspec, M&GPA, M&TEA, M09, MBF, METADEX, NSA, OceAb, P30, SCI, SCOPUS, SolStAb, SpeleolAb, T04, W07, WAA.
—BLDSC (4671.530000), AskIEEE, CASDDS, IE, Ingenta, INIST, Linda Hall.
Published by: Johns Hopkins University, Applied Physics Laboratory, 11100 Johns Hopkins Rd, Laurel, MD 20723. TEL 443-778-5000, FAX 240-228-5000. Ed. David M Silver.

530 JOR ISSN 1994-7607
QC1
➤ **JORDAN JOURNAL OF PHYSICS/AL-MAGALLAT AL-URDUNIYYAT LI-L-FIZIYA.** Text in Arabic, English. 2008. q. JOD 8 domestic to individuals; EUR 40 foreign to individuals; JOD 12 domestic to institutions; EUR 60 foreign to institutions (effective 2009). Index. back issues avail. **Document type:** *Journal, Academic/Scholarly.*
Related titles: Online - full text ed.: ISSN 1994-7615.
Published by: Yarmouk University, Deanship of Research and Graduate Studies, c/o Prof. Ibrahim O. Abu Al-Jarayesh, EIC, Irbid, Jordan. TEL 962-2-7211111, FAX 962-2-7211199, yarmouk@yu.edu.jo, http://graduatestudies.yu.edu.jo/graduate/. Ed. Ibrahim O Abu Al-Jarayesh.

530 FRA
JOURNAL DE PHYSIQUE ARCHIVES. Text in French, English. irreg. EUR 650 (effective 2012). **Document type:** *Academic/Scholarly.*
Description: 135 years and 48,000 articles.
Media: Online - full text.
Published by: E D P Sciences, 17 Ave du Hoggar, Parc d'Activites de Courtaboeuf, BP 112, Cedex A, Les Ulis, F-91944, France. TEL 33-1-69187575, FAX 33-1-69860678, http://www.edpsciences.org.

668.3 USA ISSN 0021-8464
QC183 CODEN: JADNAJ
➤ **THE JOURNAL OF ADHESION.** Text in English. 1969. m. GBP 3,767 combined subscription in United Kingdom to institutions (print & online eds.); EUR 3,896, USD 4,892 combined subscription to institutions (print & online eds.) (effective 2012). adv. bk.rev. charts; illus. index. reprint service avail. from PSC. **Document type:** *Journal, Academic/Scholarly.* **Description:** Provides a forum for discussion of the basic and applied problems in adhesion.
Related titles: CD-ROM ed.: ISSN 1026-5414. 1995; Microform ed.; Online - full text ed.: ISSN 1545-5823. GBP 3,390 in United Kingdom to institutions; EUR 3,506, USD 4,403 to institutions (effective 2012) (from IngentaConnect).
Indexed: A01, A03, A08, A22, A28, ABIPC, APA, ASCA, ApMecR, BrCerAb, C&ISA, C24, C33, CA, CA/WCA, CIA, CPEI, CerAb, ChemAb, CivEngAb, CorrAb, CurCont, E&CAJ, E01, E11, EEA, EMA, ESPM, EngInd, EnvEAb, H15, ISR, Inspec, M&TEA, M09, MBF, METADEX, MSCI, P30, P31, R18, S01, SCI, SCOPUS, SolStAb, T02, T04, W07, WAA, WSCA.
—BLDSC (4918.935000), IE, Infotrieve, Ingenta, INIST, Linda Hall. **CCC.**
Published by: Taylor & Francis Inc. (Subsidiary of: Taylor & Francis Group), 325 Chestnut St, Ste 800, Philadelphia, PA 19106. TEL 215-625-2940, 800-354-1420, orders@taylorandfrancis.com, http://www.taylorandfrancis.com. Ed. Louis H Sharpe. Adv. contact Linda Hann TEL 44-1344-779945.

530 540 GBR ISSN 1479-4810
JOURNAL OF ADVANCES IN CHEMICAL PHYSICS. Text in English. 1983. m. GBP 2,400 (effective 2009). **Document type:** *Journal, Academic/Scholarly.*
Former titles (until 2003): Chemical Physics Reports (1074-1550); (until 1994): Soviet Journal of Chemical Physics (0733-2831)
Related titles: ◆ Russian ed.: Khimicheskaya Fizika. ISSN 0207-401X.
Indexed: Inspec, SCOPUS.
—Ingenta. **CCC.**
Published by: Cambridge International Science Publishing Ltd., 7 Meadow Walk, Great Abington, Cambridge, CB1 6AZ, United Kingdom. TEL 44-1223-893295, FAX 44-1223-894539, cisp@cisp-publishing.com, http://www.cisp-publishing.com/. Pub. Mr. Victor Riecansky.

JOURNAL OF ALLOYS AND COMPOUNDS. *see* METALLURGY

JOURNAL OF APPLIED MECHANICS AND TECHNICAL PHYSICS. *see* ENGINEERING—Engineering Mechanics And Materials

530 540 USA ISSN 0021-8979
QC1 CODEN: JAPIAU
➤ **JOURNAL OF APPLIED PHYSICS.** Text in English. 1931. s-m. price varies based on the number of users. adv. charts; illus. Index. back issues avail.; reprints avail. **Document type:** *Journal, Academic/Scholarly.* **Description:** Publishes results of original physics research with applications to other fields.
Formerly (until 1937): Physics (0148-6349); Which incorporated (1929-1932): Journal of Rheology (0097-0360)
Related titles: CD-ROM ed.: ISSN 1520-8850; Microform ed.; Online - full text ed.: ISSN 1089-7550. price varies based on the number of users.
Indexed: A01, A02, A03, A05, A08, A20, A22, A23, A24, A26, ABIPC, AS&TA, AS&TI, ASCA, AcoustA, ApMecR, B04, B07, B10, B13, C10, C13, C33, CA, CIN, CPEI, CPI, Cadscan, ChemAb, ChemTitl, CurCont, E08, EngInd, G01, G08, GPAA, GeoRef, GeotechAb, I05, IBR, IBZ, INIS AtomInd, ISR, Inspec, LeadAb, MSCI, MathR, P30, PetrolAb, PhotoAb, RefZh, S01, S09, SCI, SCOPUS, SPINweb, SpeleolAb, T02, TM, W07, Zincscan.
—BLDSC (4944.000000), AskIEEE, CASDDS, IE, Infotrieve, Ingenta, INIST, Linda Hall, PADDS. **CCC.**
Published by: American Institute of Physics, 1 Physics Ellipse, College Park, MD 20740. TEL 301-209-3100, aipinfo@aip.org, http://www.aip.org. Ed. James P Viccaro TEL 630-252-8700. **Subscr. to:** PO Box 503284, St Louis, MO 63150. TEL 516-576-2270, 800-344-6902, FAX 516-349-9704, subs@aip.org, http://librarians.aip.org.

➤ **JOURNAL OF ATMOSPHERIC AND SOLAR - TERRESTRIAL PHYSICS.** *see* EARTH SCIENCES—Geophysics

▼ ➤ **JOURNAL OF CHARACTERIZATION AND DEVELOPMENT OF NOVEL MATERIALS.** *see* CHEMISTRY

▼ ➤ **JOURNAL OF CHEMICAL, BIOLOGICAL AND PHYSICAL SCIENCES**; an international peer review E3 journal of sciences. *see* CHEMISTRY

530 541 USA ISSN 0021-9606
CODEN: JCPSA6
➤ **THE JOURNAL OF CHEMICAL PHYSICS.** Abbreviated title: J C P. Text in English. 1933. w. (48/yr.). price varies based on the number of users. adv. charts; illus. Index. back issues avail.; reprints avail. **Document type:** *Journal, Academic/Scholarly.* **Description:** Publishes original research at the interface between physics and chemistry.
Related titles: CD-ROM ed.: ISSN 1520-9032. USD 5,065 combined subscription to institutions CD-ROM & online eds. (effective 2006); Microfiche ed.; Microfilm ed.; Online - full text ed.: ISSN 1089-7690. price varies based on the number of users.
Indexed: A01, A02, A03, A08, A22, A23, A24, ABIPC, ApMecR, B07, B13, BPRC&P, BullT&T, C13, C24, C33, CA, CCI, CEA, CIN, CIS, CPEI, CPI, ChemAb, ChemTitl, CurCR, CurCont, E&PHSE, EMBASE, EngInd, ExcerpMed, GP&P, GPAA, GeoRef, IBR, IBZ, INIS AtomInd, ISR, Inspec, MEDLINE, MSB, MathR, OffTech, P30, PetrolAb, PhysBer, R10, R16, Reac, RefZh, S01, SCI, SCOPUS, SPINweb, SpeleolAb, T02, TCEA, W07.
—BLDSC (4957.000000), AskIEEE, CASDDS, IE, Infotrieve, Ingenta, INIST, Linda Hall, PADDS. **CCC.**
Published by: American Institute of Physics, 1 Physics Ellipse, College Park, MD 20740. TEL 301-209-3100, aipinfo@aip.org, http://www.aip.org. Ed. Marsha I Lester TEL 215-573-2112. **Subscr. to:** PO Box 503284, St Louis, MO 63150. TEL 516-576-2270, 800-344-6902, FAX 516-349-9704, subs@aip.org, http://librarians.aip.org.

530 621.3 USA ISSN 1546-1955
T174.7 CODEN: JCTNAB
➤ **JOURNAL OF COMPUTATIONAL AND THEORETICAL NANOSCIENCE.** Text in English. 2004 (Mar.). m. USD 2,680; USD 3,880 combined subscription (print & online eds.) (effective 2010). back issues avail. **Document type:** *Journal, Academic/Scholarly.* **Description:** Brings out research papers in all fundamental and applied research aspects of computational and theoretical nanoscience and nanotechnology dealing with chemistry, physics, materials science, engineering, and biology/medicine.
Related titles: Online - full text ed.: ISSN 1546-1963. USD 3,680 (effective 2010) (from IngentaConnect).
Indexed: A28, APA, B&BAb, B19, BrCerAb, C&ISA, C33, CA/WCA, CCI, CIA, CPEI, CerAb, CivEngAb, CorrAb, CurCont, E&CAJ, E11, EEA, EMA, ESPM, EngInd, EnvEAb, H15, Inspec, M&TEA, M09, MBF, METADEX, MSCI, P30, RefZh, SCI, SCOPUS, SolStAb, T04, W07, WAA.
—BLDSC (4963.453000), IE, Ingenta. **CCC.**
Published by: American Scientific Publishers, 26650 The Old Rd, Ste 208, Valencia, CA 91381. TEL 661-799-7200, FAX 661-254-1207, order@aspbs.com. Ed. Dr. Wolfram Schommers TEL 49-7247-822432. **Subscr. to:** 25650 N Lewis Way, Stevenson Ranch, CA 91381.

530 USA ISSN 1068-3372
QC1 CODEN: JCOPEU
➤ **JOURNAL OF CONTEMPORARY PHYSICS.** Text in English. 1984. bi-m. EUR 1,989, USD 2,410 combined subscription to institutions (print & online eds.) (effective 2012). abstr.; illus. back issues avail. **Document type:** *Journal, Academic/Scholarly.* **Description:** Covers superconductivity, semiconductors, optics, electromagnetic waves, elementary particles, and mathematical physics.
Formerly (until 1991): Soviet Journal of Contemporary Physics (8755-4585)
Related titles: Online - full text ed.: ISSN 1934-9378; ◆ Translation of: Hayastany Guitoutyunnery Azgayin Academia. Teghekagir. Fizika.
Indexed: A22, A26, E01, E08, Inspec, S09, SCI, W07.
—BLDSC (0414.260000), AskIEEE, IE, Ingenta. **CCC.**

Published by: (National Academy of Sciences of the Republic of Armenia ARM), Allerton Press, Inc. (Subsidiary of: Pleiades Publishing, Inc.), 18 W 27th St, New York, NY 10001. TEL 646-424-9686, FAX 646-424-9695, journals@allertonpress.com. Ed. Vladimir M Aroutiounian.

530 520 GBR ISSN 1475-7516
QB980

➤ **JOURNAL OF COSMOLOGY AND ASTROPARTICLE PHYSICS.** Abbreviated title: J C A P. Text in English. 2003. m. GBP 1,002 to institutions (effective 2010). back issues avail. **Document type:** *Journal, Academic/Scholarly.* **Description:** Encompasses theoretical, observational and experimental areas as well as computation and simulation. It covers the latest developments in the theory of all fundamental interactions and their cosmological implications (e.g. M-theory and cosmology, brane cosmology).
Media: Online - full text (from IngentaConnect).
Indexed: CCMJ, CurCont, Inspec, M&GPA, MSN, MathR, RefZh, SCI, SCOPUS, W07, Z02.
—BLDSC (4965.430450), Linda Hall. **CCC.**
Published by: (Institute of Physics, Scuola Internazionale Superiore di Studi Avanzati (S I S S A)/International School of Advanced Studies ITA), Institute of Physics Publishing Ltd., Dirac House, Temple Back, Bristol, BS1 6BE, United Kingdom. TEL 44-117-9297481, FAX 44-117-9301178, custserv@iop.org, http://publishing.iop.org/. **Subscr. in N. America to:** American Institute of Physics, PO Box 503284, St Louis, MO 63150. TEL 516-576-2270, 800-344-6902, FAX 516-349-9704.

➤ **JOURNAL OF DYNAMICAL AND CONTROL SYSTEMS.** *see* ENGINEERING—Industrial Engineering

530 NLD ISSN 0920-5071
QC660.5 CODEN: JEWAE5

➤ **JOURNAL OF ELECTROMAGNETIC WAVES AND APPLICATIONS.** Text in English. 1987. 18/yr. EUR 2,910, USD 3,958 to institutions; EUR 3,174, USD 4,317 combined subscription to institutions (print & online eds.) (effective 2012). adv. back issues avail.; reprint service avail. from PSC. **Document type:** *Journal, Academic/Scholarly.* **Description:** Presents original papers and review articles on new theories, methodology, and computational results about electromagnetic wave theory and its various applications.
Related titles: Online - full text ed.: ISSN 1569-3937. EUR 2,645, USD 3,598 to institutions (effective 2012) (from IngentaConnect).
Indexed: A01, A03, A08, A22, ASCA, CA, CCMJ, CPEI, CurCont, E01, Englnd, GeoRef, IZBG, Inspec, MSN, MathR, S01, SCI, SCOPUS, SpeleolAb, T02, W07, Z02.
—BLDSC (4974.850000), AskIEEE, IE, Infotrieve, Ingenta, INIST, Linda Hall. **CCC.**
Published by: V S P (Subsidiary of: Brill), Brill Academic Publishers, PO Box 9000, Leiden, 2300 PA, Netherlands. TEL 31-71-5353500, FAX 31-71-5317532, vsppub@brill.nl. Ed. W C Chew. **Dist. by:** Turpin Distribution Services Ltd., Pegasus Dr, Stratton Business Park, Biggleswade, Bedfordshire SG18 8QB, United Kingdom. TEL 44-1767-604800, FAX 44-1767-601640, custserv@turpin-distribution.com, http://www.turpin-distribution.com/.

530 USA ISSN 0737-0652
TP270.A1 CODEN: JOEMDK

➤ **JOURNAL OF ENERGETIC MATERIALS.** Text in English. 1983. q. GBP 428 combined subscription in United Kingdom to institutions (print & online eds.); EUR 569, USD 713 combined subscription to institutions (print & online eds.) (effective 2012). adv. abstr.; bibl.; charts. reprint service avail. from PSC. **Document type:** *Journal, Academic/Scholarly.* **Description:** Forum of scientific and technical interchange in the disciplines of explosives, propellants, and pyrotechnics.
Related titles: Online - full text ed.: ISSN 1545-8822. GBP 386 in United Kingdom to institutions; EUR 512, USD 642 to institutions (effective 2012) (from IngentaConnect).
Indexed: A01, A03, A08, A22, A28, APA, BrCerAb, C&ISA, C33, CA, CA/WCA, CCI, CIA, CIN, CerAb, ChemAb, ChemTitl, CivEngAb, CorrAb, CurCont, E&CAJ, E01, E11, EEA, EMA, ESPM, EnvEAb, H15, M&TEA, M09, MBF, METADEX, MSCI, P26, P52, P54, P56, PQC, RefZh, SCI, SCOPUS, SolStAb, T02, T04, W07, WAA.
—CASDDS, IE, Infotrieve, Ingenta, INIST, Linda Hall. **CCC.**
Published by: Taylor & Francis Inc. (Subsidiary of: Taylor & Francis Group), 325 Chestnut St, Ste 800, Philadelphia, PA 19106. TEL 215-625-2940, 800-354-1420, orders@taylorandfrancis.com, http://www.taylorandfrancis.com. Ed. James Short. Adv. contact Linda Hann TEL 44-1344-779945.

➤ **JOURNAL OF ENGINEERING PHYSICS AND THERMOPHYSICS.** *see* ENGINEERING

530 621 RUS ISSN 1810-2328
TJ265 CODEN: RJETER

➤ **JOURNAL OF ENGINEERING THERMOPHYSICS.** Text in English. 1991. q. (in 1 vol., 4 nos./vol.). EUR 867, USD 1,033 combined subscription to institutions (print & online eds.) (effective 2012). adv. back issues avail. **Document type:** *Journal, Academic/Scholarly.* **Description:** Publishes original English language articles of archival nature based on the research conducted at research institutes in Russia and CIS. Focuses on experimental work, theory, analysis and computational studies which enhances the basic understanding of thermophysics relevant to engineering or the environment.
Formerly (until 2002): Russian Journal of Engineering Thermophysics (1051-8053)
Related titles: Online - full text ed.: ISSN 1990-5432 (from IngentaConnect).
Indexed: A22, A26, ApMecR, ChemAb, ChemTitl, E01, E08, S09, SCI, SCOPUS, W07.
—BLDSC (8052.709700), CASDDS, East View, IE, Ingenta. **CCC.**
Published by: (Rossiiskaya Akademiya Nauk, Sibirskoe Otdelenie, Institut Teplofiziki im. S.S. Kutateladze), M A I K Nauka - Interperiodica (Subsidiary of: Pleiades Publishing, Inc.), Profsoyuznaya ul 90, Moscow, 117997, Russian Federation. TEL 7-095-3361600, FAX 7-095-3360666, compmg@maik.ru. Ed. Vladimir E Nakoryalov. **Dist. by:** East View Information Services, 10601 Wayzata Blvd, Minneapolis, MN 55305. TEL 952-252-1201, 800-477-1005, FAX 952-252-1202, info@eastview.com, http://www.eastview.com.

530 RUS ISSN 1063-7761
QC1 CODEN: JTPHES

➤ **JOURNAL OF EXPERIMENTAL AND THEORETICAL PHYSICS.** Text in English. 1955. m. EUR 6,802, USD 8,247 combined subscription to institutions (print & online eds.) (effective 2012). charts; illus. index. back issues avail.; reprints avail. **Document type:** *Journal, Academic/Scholarly.* **Description:** Presents papers emphasizing fundamental and experimental research in all fields of physics - from solid state to elementary particles and cosmology.
Formerly: Soviet Physics - J E T P (0038-5646)
Related titles: Online - full text ed.: ISSN 1090-6509 (from IngentaConnect); ◆ Translation of: Zhurnal Eksperimental'noi i Teoreticheskoi Fiziki. ISSN 0044-4510.
Indexed: A01, A02, A03, A08, A22, A26, AcoustA, ApMecR, C33, CA, CCMJ, CPEI, CPI, ChemAb, CurCont, E01, Englnd, GPAA, IBR, IBZ, INIS AtomInd, ISR, Inspec, MSN, MathR, PhysBer, S01, SCI, SCOPUS, SPINweb, T02, TM, W07, Z02.
—BLDSC (0414.500000), AskIEEE, CASDDS, East View, IE, Infotrieve, Ingenta, INIST, Linda Hall. **CCC.**
Published by: (Rossiiskaya Akademiya Nauk/Russian Academy of Sciences), M A I K Nauka - Interperiodica (Subsidiary of: Pleiades Publishing, Inc.), Profsoyuznaya ul 90, Moscow, 117997, Russian Federation. TEL 7-095-3347420, FAX 7-095-3360666, compmg@maik.ru. Ed. A F Andreev. **Distr. in the Americas by:** Springer New York LLC, Journal Fulfillment, PO Box 2485, Secaucus, NJ 07096. TEL 212-460-1500, 800-777-4643, FAX 201-348-4505; **Dist. by:** Springer, Haber Str 7, Heidelberg 69126, Germany. TEL 49-6221-3454303, FAX 49-6221-3454229, subscriptions@springer.com, http://www.springer.de.

➤ **JOURNAL OF FLUID MECHANICS.** *see* ENGINEERING—Hydraulic Engineering

530 540 GBR ISSN 2046-9888

▼ **JOURNAL OF FOUNDATIONS OF PHYSICS AND CHEMISTRY.** Text in English. 2011. bi-m. GBP 50, USD 80, EUR 58 to individuals; GBP 180, USD 290, EUR 210 to institutions (effective 2011). **Document type:** *Journal, Academic/Scholarly.*
Published by: (Alpha Institute for Advanced Studies), Cambridge International Science Publishing Ltd., 7 Meadow Walk, Great Abington, Cambridge, CB1 6AZ, United Kingdom. TEL 44-1223-893295, FAX 44-1223-894539, cisp@cisp-publishing.com, http://www.cisp-publishing.com/. Ed. Myron Evans.

JOURNAL OF GEOMETRY AND PHYSICS. *see* MATHEMATICS

JOURNAL OF GEOMETRY AND SYMMETRY IN PHYSICS. *see* MATHEMATICS

531.14 USA ISSN 1077-9248
QP82.2.G7

➤ **JOURNAL OF GRAVITATIONAL PHYSIOLOGY.** Text in English. 1994. s-a. USD 32 to non-members; free to members (effective 2011). **Document type:** *Journal, Academic/Scholarly.* **Description:** Contains research and information on the effects on cells and physiological organs and systems of humans, animals and plants of changes in the magnitude and directions of the gravitational force environment.
Indexed: B&BAb, B21, CTA, ChemoAb, EMBASE, ExcerpMed, MEDLINE, NSA, P30, SCOPUS, VirolAbstr.
—BLDSC (4996.505000), IE, Ingenta, INIST, Linda Hall.
Published by: (International Society for Gravitational Physiology, International Gravitational Physiology Meeting), Galileo Foundation, PO Box 157, Davis, CA 95617. TEL 530-752-9698, FAX 530-752-5851, cafuller@usdavis.edu.

530 DEU ISSN 1029-8479
QC793.3.H5 CODEN: JHEPFG

➤ **THE JOURNAL OF HIGH ENERGY PHYSICS (ONLINE).** Abbreviated title: J H E P. Text in English. 1997. m. EUR 1,950, USD 2,498 to institutions (effective 2012). back issues avail. **Document type:** *Journal, Academic/Scholarly.* **Description:** Aims to explore the area of high-energy physics in a broad sense.
Media: Online - full text.
Indexed: A22, CCMJ, E01, Inspec, MSN, MathR, SCOPUS.
—BLDSC (4998.375000), Linda Hall. **CCC.**
Published by: Springer (Subsidiary of: Springer Science+Business Media), Tiergartenstr 17, Heidelberg, 69121, Germany. TEL 49-6221-4870, FAX 49-6221-345229, subscriptions@springer.com. **Co-sponsor:** Scuola Internazionale Superiore di Studi Avanzati (S I S S A)/International School of Advanced Studies.

530 NLD ISSN 1001-6058
TC171 CODEN: JOUHEI

➤ **JOURNAL OF HYDRODYNAMICS.** Text in English. 1989. bi-m. EUR 518 in Europe to institutions; JPY 75,100 in Japan to institutions; USD 656 elsewhere to institutions (effective 2012). **Document type:** *Journal, Academic/Scholarly.* **Description:** Provides up-to-date information about various aspects of hydrodynamic research especially in China, including theoretical, experimental and computational techniques plus field measurement.
Related titles: Online - full text ed.: (from ScienceDirect); Chinese ed.: Shuidong Lixue Yanjiu yu Jinzhan. ISSN 1000-4874.
Indexed: A28, APA, ApMecR, BrCerAb, C&ISA, CA, CA/WCA, CIA, CPEI, CerAb, CivEngAb, CorrAb, E&CAJ, E11, EEA, EMA, ESPM, Englnd, EnvEAb, H15, M&TEA, M09, MBF, METADEX, PollutAb, RefZh, SCI, SCOPUS, SWRA, SolStAb, T02, T04, W07, WAA, Z02.
—IE, Ingenta, Linda Hall. **CCC.**
Published by: Elsevier BV (Subsidiary of: Elsevier Science & Technology), Radarweg 29, PO Box 211, Amsterdam, 1000 AE, Netherlands. TEL 31-20-4853911, FAX 31-20-4852457, JournalsCustomerServiceEMEA@elsevier.com, http://www.elsevier.nl. Ed. D X Zhu.

530 USA ISSN 0022-2348
QD380 CODEN: JMAPBR

➤ **JOURNAL OF MACROMOLECULAR SCIENCE: PART B - PHYSICS.** Text in English. 1966. bi-m. GBP 3,763 combined subscription in United Kingdom to institutions (print & online eds.); EUR 4,969, USD 6,238 combined subscription to institutions (print & online eds.) (effective 2012). adv. reprint service avail. from PSC. **Document type:** *Journal, Academic/Scholarly.* **Description:** Devoted to the publication of significant fundamental contributions to the physics of macromolecular solids and liquids.
Supersedes in part (in 1967): Journal of Macromolecular Chemistry (0449-2730)
Related titles: Microform ed.: (from RPI); Online - full text ed.: ISSN 1525-609X. GBP 3,386 in United Kingdom to institutions; EUR 4,472, USD 5,614 to institutions (effective 2012) (from IngentaConnect).
Indexed: A01, A03, A08, A22, A28, A29, APA, ASCA, B20, B21, BrCerAb, C&ISA, C24, C33, CA, CA/WCA, CCI, CIA, CPEI, CerAb, ChemAb, ChemTitl, CivEngAb, CorrAb, CurCR, CurCont, E&CAJ, E01, E11, EEA, EMA, ESPM, Englnd, EnvEAb, H15, I10, ISMEC, ISR, Inspec, M&TEA, M09, MBF, METADEX, MSCI, R16, R18, S01, SCI, SCOPUS, SolStAb, T02, T04, TM, VirolAbstr, W07, WAA.
—BLDSC (5010.770000), AskIEEE, CASDDS, IE, Infotrieve, Ingenta, INIST, Linda Hall. **CCC.**
Published by: Taylor & Francis Inc. (Subsidiary of: Taylor & Francis Group), 325 Chestnut St, Ste 800, Philadelphia, PA 19106. TEL 215-625-2940, 800-354-1420, orders@taylorandfrancis.com, http://www.taylorandfrancis.com. Adv. contact Linda Hann TEL 44-1344-779945.

538.36 USA ISSN 1090-7807
QC762 CODEN: JMARF3

➤ **JOURNAL OF MAGNETIC RESONANCE.** Abbreviated title: J M R. Text in English. 1969. m. EUR 6,309 in Europe to institutions; JPY 658,900 in Japan to institutions; USD 4,976 elsewhere to institutions (effective 2012). adv. abstr.; bibl.; charts; illus. index. back issues avail.; reprints avail. **Document type:** *Journal, Academic/Scholarly.* **Description:** Provides current information on the theory, techniques, methods of spectral analysis and interpretation, spectral correlations, and results of magnetic resonance spectroscopy.
Formed by the merger of (1993-1997): Journal of Magnetic Resonance - Series A (1064-1858); (1993-1997): Journal of Magnetic Resonance - Series B (1064-1866); Both of which superseded in part (1969-1993): Journal of Magnetic Resonance (0022-2364)
Related titles: Online - full text ed.: ISSN 1096-0856 (from IngentaConnect, ScienceDirect).
Indexed: A01, A03, A08, A20, A22, A26, A28, ABIPC, AESIS, APA, ASCA, B&BAb, B19, B21, BPRC&P, BioEngAb, BrCerAb, C&ISA, C24, C33, CA, CA/WCA, CIA, CPEI, Cadscan, CerAb, ChemAb, CivEngAb, CorrAb, CurCont, E&CAJ, E01, E11, EEA, EMA, EMBASE, ESPM, Englnd, EnvEAb, ExcerpMed, GeoRef, H15, I05, ISR, IndMed, Inspec, LeadAb, M&TEA, M09, MBF, MEDLINE, METADEX, NSA, P30, R10, Reac, RefZh, S01, SCI, SCOPUS, SolStAb, T02, T04, TM, VITIS, W07, WAA, Zincscan.
—BLDSC (5010.790000), AskIEEE, CASDDS, IE, Infotrieve, Ingenta, INIST, Linda Hall. **CCC.**
Published by: Academic Press (Subsidiary of: Elsevier Science & Technology), 3251 Riverport Ln, Maryland Heights, MO 63043. TEL 314-447-8010, FAX 314-447-8030, JournalCustomerService-usa@elsevier.com, http://www.elsevierdirect.com/imprint.jsp?iid=5. Ed. S J Opella.

538 NLD ISSN 0304-8853
QC750 CODEN: JMMMDC

➤ **JOURNAL OF MAGNETISM AND MAGNETIC MATERIALS.** Text in English. 1975. 24/yr. EUR 9,390 in Europe to institutions; JPY 1,246,700 in Japan to institutions; USD 10,501 elsewhere to institutions (effective 2012). adv. charts; illus. cum.index. back issues avail.; reprints avail. **Document type:** *Journal, Academic/Scholarly.* **Description:** Covers the whole spectrum of topics from basic magnetism to the technology and applications of magnetic materials and magnetic recording.
Related titles: Microform ed.: (from PQC); Online - full text ed.: ISSN 1873-4766 (from IngentaConnect, ScienceDirect).
Indexed: A01, A03, A08, A22, A26, A28, APA, ASCA, BrCerAb, C&ISA, C13, C24, C33, CA, CA/WCA, CCI, CIA, CIN, CPEI, Cadscan, CerAb, ChemAb, ChemTitl, CivEngAb, CorrAb, CurCont, E&CAJ, E11, EEA, EMA, ESPM, Englnd, EnvEAb, GeoRef, H15, I05, INIS AtomInd, ISMEC, ISR, Inspec, LeadAb, M&TEA, M09, MBF, METADEX, MSCI, P30, PhysBer, RefZh, S01, SCI, SCOPUS, SolStAb, SpeleolAb, T02, T04, TM, W07, WAA, Zincscan.
—BLDSC (5010.793000), AskIEEE, CASDDS, IE, Infotrieve, Ingenta, INIST, Linda Hall. **CCC.**
Published by: (European Physical Society), Elsevier BV, North-Holland (Subsidiary of: Elsevier Science & Technology), Sara Burgerhartstraat 25, Amsterdam, 1055 KV, Netherlands. TEL 31-20-4853911, FAX 31-20-4852457, JournalsCustomerServiceEMEA@elsevier.com. Ed. S D Bader. **Subscr. to:** Elsevier BV, Radarweg 29, PO Box 211, Amsterdam 1000 AE, Netherlands. TEL 31-20-4853757, FAX 31-20-4853432.

➤ **JOURNAL OF MATERIALS RESEARCH.** *see* ENGINEERING—Engineering Mechanics And Materials

➤ **JOURNAL OF MATHEMATICAL AND PHYSICAL SCIENCES.** *see* MATHEMATICS

530 CHE ISSN 1422-6928
QA901

➤ **JOURNAL OF MATHEMATICAL FLUID MECHANICS.** Text in English. 1999. q. EUR 378, USD 424 combined subscription to institutions (print & online eds.) (effective 2012). back issues avail.; reprint service avail. from PSC. **Document type:** *Journal, Academic/Scholarly.* **Description:** Provides a forum for the publication of high-quality peer-reviewed papers on the mathematical theory of fluid mechanics, with special regards to the Navier-Stokes equations.
Related titles: Online - full text ed.: ISSN 1422-6952 (from IngentaConnect).
Indexed: A22, A26, ApMecR, CA, CCMJ, CMCI, CPEI, CurCont, E01, Englnd, FLUIDEX, GEOBASE, MSN, MathR, RefZh, SCI, SCOPUS, T02, W07, Z02.
—BLDSC (5012.382000), IE, Infotrieve, Ingenta. **CCC.**
Published by: Birkhaeuser Verlag AG (Subsidiary of: Springer Science+Business Media), Viaduktstr 42, Postfach 133, Basel, 4051, Switzerland. TEL 41-61-2050707, FAX 41-61-2050799, info@birkhauser.ch, http://www.birkhauser.ch/journals. Eds. Giovanni P Galdi TEL 412-624-4846, John G Heywood TEL 604-822-6074, Rolf Rannacher TEL 49-6221-545331. **Subscr. in the Americas to:** Springer New York LLC, Journal Fulfillment, PO Box 2485, Secaucus, NJ 07096. TEL 201-348-4033, 800-777-4643, FAX 201-348-4505, journals@birkhauser.com; **Subscr. to:** Springer Distribution Center, Kundenservice Zeitschriften, Haberstr 7, Heidelberg 69126, Germany. TEL 49-6221-3454303, FAX 49-6221-3454229, birkhauser@springer.de.

P

500 USA ISSN 0022-2488
QC20 CODEN: JMAPAQ

➤ **JOURNAL OF MATHEMATICAL PHYSICS.** Abbreviated title: J M P. Text in English. 1960. m. price varies based on the number of users. adv. abstr.; bibl.; charts; illus. Index. back issues avail.; reprints avail. **Document type:** *Journal, Academic/Scholarly.* **Description:** Publishes original research covering developments in the mathematical formulation of physical theories, mathematical methods for the solution of physical problems, and mathematical ideas suitable for physical applications.
Related titles: CD-ROM ed.: ISSN 1527-2427; Microfiche ed.; Online - full text ed.: ISSN 1089-7658. price varies based on the number of users.
Indexed: A01, A02, A03, A08, A22, ASCA, CA, CCMJ, CIS, CMCI, CPI, ChemAb, CurCont, GPAA, IBR, IBZ, INIS AtomInd, ISR, Inspec, MSN, MathR, P02, P10, P30, P48, P49, P52, P53, P54, P56, PQC, PhysBer, RefZh, S01, S10, SCI, SCOPUS, SPINweb, T02, W07, Z02.
—BLDSC (5012.400000), AskIEEE, CASDDS, IE, Infotrieve, Ingenta, INIST, Linda Hall. **CCC.**
Published by: American Institute of Physics, 1 Physics Ellipse, College Park, MD 20740. TEL 301-209-3100, aipinfo@aip.org, http://www.aip.org. Ed. Bruno L Z Nachtergaele TEL 530-754-8092. **Subscr. to:** PO Box 503284, St Louis, MO 63150. TEL 516-576-2270, 800-344-6902, FAX 516-349-9704, subs@aip.org, http://librarians.aip.org.

➤ **JOURNAL OF MATHEMATICAL SCIENCES.** *see* MATHEMATICS

530 610 IND ISSN 0971-6203
CODEN: JMPHFE

JOURNAL OF MEDICAL PHYSICS. Text in English. 1975. q. INR 1,200 domestic to individuals; USD 120 foreign to individuals; INR 2,400 domestic to institutions; USD 240 foreign to institutions; INR 1,500 combined subscription domestic to individuals (print & online eds.); USD 145 combined subscription foreign to individuals (print & online eds.); INR 2,900 combined subscription domestic to institutions (print & online eds.); USD 285 combined subscription foreign to institutions (print & online eds.) (effective 2011). adv. bk.rev. **Document type:** *Journal, Academic/Scholarly.* **Description:** Covers the practice of medical physics in developing countries.
Formerly (until 1996): Medical Physics Bulletin (0971-040X)
Related titles: Online - full text ed.: ISSN 1998-3913. INR 1,000 domestic to individuals; USD 95 foreign to individuals; INR 2,000 domestic to institutions; USD 195 foreign to institutions (effective 2011).
Indexed: A01, A26, CA, E08, EMBASE, ExcerpMed, G08, H11, H12, I05, INIS AtomInd, Inspec, P10, P30, P48, P52, P53, P54, PQC, S09, SCOPUS, T02.
—IE. **CCC.**
Published by: (Association of Medical Physicists of India), Medknow Publications and Media Pvt. Ltd., B-9, Kanara Business Ctr, Off Link Rd, Ghatkopar (E), Mumbai, Maharastra 400 075, India. TEL 91-22-66491816, FAX 91-22-66491817, http://www.medknow.com. Ed. A S Pradhan.

530 USA ISSN 2153-1196
QC1

▼ ➤ **JOURNAL OF MODERN PHYSICS.** Abbreviated title: J M P. Text in English. 2009. q. **Document type:** *Journal, Academic/Scholarly.*
Related titles: Online - full text ed.: ISSN 2153-120X. free (effective 2011).
Indexed: A26, I05, P52.
Published by: Scientific Research Publishing, Inc., 5005 Paseo Segovia, Irvine, CA 92603. service@scirp.org.

620.5 CHE ISSN 1662-5250
T174.7

➤ **JOURNAL OF NANO RESEARCH.** Text in English. 2008. 4/yr. EUR 278; EUR 310 combined subscription (print & online eds.) (effective 2009). **Document type:** *Journal, Academic/Scholarly.* **Description:** Provides up-to-date information on all developments and progresses being made in nanoscience and nanotechnology.
Related titles: CD-ROM ed.: ISSN 1661-9889. 2008; Online - full text ed.: ISSN 1661-9897. 2008. EUR 278 (effective 2009).
Indexed: A20, CPEI, MSCI, RefZh, SCI, SCOPUS, W07.
—BLDSC (5021.173025), IE.
Published by: Trans Tech Publications Ltd., Laubisrutistr 24, Stafa-Zurich, 8712, Switzerland. TEL 41-1-9221022, FAX 41-44-9221033, info@ttp.net. Ed. Harold W Kroto.

530 USA ISSN 1687-4110

➤ **JOURNAL OF NANOMATERIALS.** Text in English. 2006. irreg. USD 395 (effective 2011). **Document type:** *Journal, Academic/Scholarly.* **Description:** Aims to bring science and applications together on nanoscale and nanostructured materials with emphasis on synthesis, processing, characterization, and applications of materials containing true nanosize dimensions or nanostructures that enable novel/enhanced properties or functions.
Related titles: Online - full text ed.: ISSN 1687-4129. free (effective 2011).
Indexed: A01, A26, A28, A39, APA, B&BAb, B19, BrCerAb, C&ISA, C27, C29, CA, CA/WCA, CIA, CerAb, CivEngAb, CorrAb, CurCont, D03, D04, E&CAJ, E08, E11, E13, EEA, EMA, ESPM, EnvEAb, H15, I05, M&TEA, M09, MBF, METADEX, MSCI, P52, R14, RefZh, S09, S14, S15, S18, SCI, SCOPUS, SolStAb, T02, T04, W07, WAA.
—IE.
Published by: Hindawi Publishing Corporation, 410 Park Ave, 15th Fl, PMB 287, New York, NY 10022. FAX 215-893-4392, 866-446-3294, info@hindawi.com. Ed. Michael Hu.

531.16 NLD ISSN 1388-0764
TA418.78 CODEN: JNARFA

JOURNAL OF NANOPARTICLE RESEARCH; an interdisciplinary forum for nanoscale science and technology. Text in English. 1999. 8/yr. EUR 1,173, USD 1,221 combined subscription to institutions (print & online eds.) (effective 2012). adv. reprint service avail. from PSC. **Document type:** *Journal, Academic/Scholarly.* **Description:** Disseminates knowledge of the physical, chemical and biological phenomena and processes in structures that have at least one lengthscale ranging from molecular to approximately 100 nm (or submicron in some situations), and exhibit improved and novel properties that are a direct result of their small size.
Related titles: Online - full text ed.: ISSN 1572-896X (from IngentaConnect).
Indexed: A01, A20, A22, A26, B&BAb, B19, B21, BibLing, CA, CCI, CPEI, CurCont, E01, EMBASE, ESPM, EngInd, ExcerpMed, Inspec, MSCI, P30, RefZh, SCI, SCOPUS, T02, ToxAb, W07.
—BLDSC (5021.174000), IE, Infotrieve, Ingenta, Linda Hall. **CCC.**
Published by: Springer Netherlands (Subsidiary of: Springer Science+Business Media), Van Godewijckstraat 30, Dordrecht, 3311 GX, Netherlands. TEL 31-78-6576050, FAX 31-78-6576474, http://www.springer.com. Ed. Mihail C Roco.

620.5 USA ISSN 1533-4880
T174.7 CODEN: JNNOAR

➤ **JOURNAL OF NANOSCIENCE AND NANOTECHNOLOGY.** Abbreviated title: J N N. Text and summaries in English. 2001. m. USD 3,280; USD 4,480 combined subscription (print & online eds.) (effective 2010). bk.rev. abstr.; illus. 120 p./no.; back issues avail. **Document type:** *Journal, Academic/Scholarly.* **Description:** Covers research activities in all areas of nanoscience and nanotechnology into a single reference source.
Related titles: Online - full text ed.: ISSN 1533-4899. USD 4,280 (effective 2010) (from IngentaConnect).
Indexed: A28, APA, B&BAb, B19, BrCerAb, C&ISA, C33, CA/WCA, CCI, CIA, CPEI, CerAb, ChemAb, CivEngAb, CorrAb, CurCont, E&CAJ, E11, EEA, EMA, EMBASE, ESPM, EngInd, EnvEAb, ExcerpMed, H15, Inspec, M&TEA, M09, MBF, MEDLINE, METADEX, MSCI, P30, R10, Reac, RefZh, SCI, SCOPUS, SolStAb, T04, TM, VITIS, W07, WAA.
—BLDSC (5021.174500), IE, Ingenta, INIST, Linda Hall. **CCC.**
Published by: American Scientific Publishers, 26650 The Old Rd, Ste 208, Valencia, CA 91381. TEL 661-799-7200, FAX 661-254-1207, order@aspbs.com. Ed. Hari Singh Nalwa.

530 USA ISSN 1687-9503

➤ **JOURNAL OF NANOTECHNOLOGY.** Text in English. 2008. irreg. USD 295 (effective 2011). **Document type:** *Journal, Academic/Scholarly.* **Description:** Publishes original research articles as well as review articles in all areas of nanotechnology.
Formerly (until 2009): Research Letters in Nanotechnology (1687-6849)
Related titles: Online - full text ed.: ISSN 1687-9511. 2008. free (effective 2011).
Indexed: C10, CA, P52, T02.
Published by: Hindawi Publishing Corporation, 410 Park Ave, 15th Fl, PMB 287, New York, NY 10022. FAX 215-893-4392, 866-446-3294, info@hindawi.com.

➤ **JOURNAL OF NATURAL SCIENCES AND MATHEMATICS.** *see* SCIENCES: COMPREHENSIVE WORKS

530 541 NLD ISSN 0022-3093
CODEN: JNCSBJ

➤ **JOURNAL OF NON-CRYSTALLINE SOLIDS.** Text in Dutch. 1969. 54/yr. EUR 9,471 in Europe to institutions; JPY 1,256,300 in Japan to institutions; USD 10,645 elsewhere to institutions (effective 2012). adv. bk.rev. charts; illus.; stat. cum.index. back issues avail.; reprints avail. **Document type:** *Journal, Academic/Scholarly.* **Description:** Publishes review articles and research papers on oxide and non-oxide glasses, amorphous semiconductors, non-crystalline films such as those prepared by vapor-deposition, glass ceramics and glassy composites.
Related titles: Microform ed.: (from PQC); Online - full text ed.: ISSN 1873-4812 (from IngentaConnect, ScienceDirect).
Indexed: A01, A03, A08, A20, A22, A26, A28, APA, ASCA, BrCerAb, C&ISA, C13, C24, C33, CA, CA/WCA, CCI, CIA, CMCI, CPEI, Cadscan, CerAb, ChemAb, ChemTitl, CivEngAb, CorrAb, CurCont, E&CAJ, E11, EEA, EMA, ESPM, EngInd, EnvEAb, FR, GeoRef, H15, I05, IBR, IBZ, ISMEC, ISR, Inspec, LeadAb, M&TEA, M09, MBF, METADEX, MSCI, P30, PhysBer, PsycholAb, RefZh, S01, SCI, SCOPUS, SolStAb, SpeleolAb, T02, T04, TM, W07, WAA, Zincscan.
—BLDSC (5022.830000), AskIEEE, CASDDS, IE, Infotrieve, Ingenta, INIST, Linda Hall. **CCC.**
Published by: Elsevier BV, North-Holland (Subsidiary of: Elsevier Science & Technology), Sara Burgerhartstraat 25, Amsterdam, 1055 KV, Netherlands. TEL 31-20-4853911, FAX 31-20-4852457, JournalsCustomerServiceEMEA@elsevier.com. Ed. J H Simmons. **Subscr. to:** Elsevier BV, Radarweg 29, PO Box 211, Amsterdam 1000 AE, Netherlands. TEL 31-20-4853757, FAX 31-20-4853432, http://www.elsevier.nl.

530 510 SGP ISSN 1402-9251
QC20.7.N6

➤ **JOURNAL OF NONLINEAR MATHEMATICAL PHYSICS.** Abbreviated title: J N M P. Text in English. 1994. q. SGD 790, USD 526, EUR 405 combined subscription to institutions (print & online eds.) (effective 2012). adv. bk.rev. back issues avail. **Document type:** *Journal, Academic/Scholarly.* **Description:** Brings out research, along with notes and reviews on fundamental mathematical and computational methods in mathematical physics.
Related titles: Online - full text ed.: ISSN 1776-0852. SGD 718, USD 478, EUR 368 to institutions (effective 2012).
Indexed: A01, A22, A39, C27, C29, CA, CCMJ, CIS, CMCI, CurCont, D03, D04, E01, E13, MSN, MathR, R14, S14, S15, S18, SCI, SCOPUS, T02, W07, Z02.
—BLDSC (5022.838200), IE, Ingenta.
Published by: World Scientific Publishing Co. Pte. Ltd., 5 Toh Tuck Link, Singapore, 596224, Singapore. TEL 65-6466-5775, FAX 65-6467-7667, wspc@wspc.com.sg, http://www.worldscientific.com. Ed. Norbert Euler TEL 46-920-491073. **Dist. by:** World Scientific Publishing Co., Inc., 27 Warren St, Ste 401-402, Hackensack, NJ 07601. TEL 201-487-9655, 800-227-7562, FAX 201-487-9656, 888-977-2665, wspc@wspc.com; World Scientific Publishing Ltd., 57 Shelton St, London WC2H 9HE, United Kingdom. TEL 44-207-8360888, FAX 44-207-8362020, sales@wspc.co.uk. **Co-publisher:** Atlantis Press.

530 USA ISSN 0938-8974
QC20.7.N6 CODEN: JNSCEK

➤ **JOURNAL OF NONLINEAR SCIENCE.** Text in English. 1991. bi-m. (in 1 vol., 6 nos./vol.). EUR 1,138, USD 1,207 combined subscription to institutions (print & online eds.) (effective 2012). adv. back issues avail.; reprint service avail. from PSC. **Document type:** *Journal, Academic/Scholarly.* **Description:** Brings out papers that augment the fundamental ways that describe, model, and predict nonlinear phenomena.
Related titles: Online - full text ed.: ISSN 1432-1467 (from IngentaConnect).
Indexed: A01, A03, A08, A22, A26, ASCA, ApMecR, CA, CCMJ, CMCI, CPEI, CurCont, E01, EngInd, ISR, MSN, MathR, RefZh, S01, SCI, SCOPUS, T02, W07, Z02.
—BLDSC (5022.839000), CASDDS, IE, Infotrieve, Ingenta, Linda Hall. **CCC.**
Published by: Springer New York LLC (Subsidiary of: Springer Science+Business Media), 233 Spring St, New York, NY 10013. TEL 212-460-1500, FAX 212-460-1575, service@springer-ny.com, http://www.springer.com/. Ed. Jerrold E Marsden. **Subscr. to:** Journal Fulfillment, PO Box 2485, Secaucus, NJ 07096. TEL 201-348-4033, FAX 201-348-4505, journals-ny@springer.com.

➤ **THE JOURNAL OF ORGONOMY.** *see* MEDICAL SCIENCES—Psychiatry And Neurology

➤ **JOURNAL OF PHYSICAL AND CHEMICAL REFERENCE DATA.** *see* CHEMISTRY

➤ **JOURNAL OF PHYSICAL AND CHEMICAL REFERENCE DATA. MONOGRAPH.** *see* CHEMISTRY

▼ ➤ **JOURNAL OF PHYSICAL MATHEMATICS.** *see* MATHEMATICS

530 UKR ISSN 1027-4642
QC1 CODEN: ZFDOFY

➤ **JOURNAL OF PHYSICAL STUDIES.** Text in English, Ukrainian. 1996. q. UAK 48 domestic; USD 120 foreign (effective 2003). bk.rev. charts; illus. reprints avail. **Document type:** *Journal, Academic/Scholarly.* **Description:** Covers various fields of physics, including condensed matter physics, nuclear, atomic, and molecular physics.
Related titles: Online - full text ed.: free (effective 2011).
Indexed: A01, CCMJ, INIS AtomInd, Inspec, MSN, MathR, RefZh, SCOPUS, Z02.
—BLDSC (5036.214500), CASDDS, East View. **CCC.**
Published by: Zakhidno-Ukrains'ke Fizychne Tovarystvo/West Ukrainian Physical Society, 12 Drahomanov St, Lviv, 79005, Ukraine. TEL 380-322-740113, FAX 380-322-727981, editor@jps.frank.lviv.ua, http://www.ktf.franko.lviv.ua/. Ed. Ivan Vakarchuk. **Co-sponsor:** Ivan Franko National University of Lviv.

530 IND ISSN 0976-7673

▼ ➤ **JOURNAL OF PHYSICS.** Text in English. 2010. s-a. USD 425 (effective 2011). **Document type:** *Journal, Academic/Scholarly.* **Description:** Publishes all the latest research articles, reviews and letters in all areas of physics.
Related titles: Online - full text ed.: ISSN 0976-7681. free (effective 2011).
Published by: Bioinfo Publications, 49/F-72, Vighnahar Complex, Front of Overseas Bank, Sector 12, Kharghar, Navi Mumbai, 410 210, India. TEL 91-22-27743967, FAX 91-22-66736413, editor@bioinfo.in, subscription@bioinfo.in.

530 GBR ISSN 1751-8113
CODEN: JPHAC5

➤ **JOURNAL OF PHYSICS A: MATHEMATICAL AND THEORETICAL.** Text in English. 1958. 50/yr. GBP 4,788 combined subscription to institutions (print & online eds.) (effective 2010). bibl.; charts; illus.; abstr. index. back issues avail. **Document type:** *Journal, Academic/Scholarly.* **Description:** Examines classical and quantum mechanics, chaotic and complex systems, statistical physics, quantum information and computation, classical and quantum integrable systems, classical and quantum field theory.
Formerly (until 2007): Journal of Physics A: Mathematical and General (Print) (0305-4470); Which superseded in part (in 1975): Journal of Physics A: Mathematical, Nuclear and General (0301-0015); Which was formerly (until 1973): Journal of Physics. A, Proceedings of the Physical Society. General (0022-3689); Which superseded in part (in 1968): Physical Society. Proceedings (0370-1328); Which was formed by the merger of (1874-1957): Physical Society. Proceedings. Section A (0370-1298); (1874-1957): Physical Society. Proceedings. Section B (0370-1301); Both of which superseded in part (in 1949): Physical Society. Proceedings (0959-5309); Which was formerly (until 1926): Physical Society of London. Proceedings (1478-7814); Physical Society. Proceedings incorporated (1900-1932): Optical Society. Transactions (1475-4878)
Related titles: Microfiche ed.: USD 5,914 in North America; GBP 3,016 elsewhere (effective 2007); Microfilm ed.; Online - full text ed.: ISSN 1751-8121. 1996. GBP 4,560 to institutions (effective 2010) (from IngentaConnect).
Indexed: A01, A03, A08, A20, A22, ASCA, ApMecR, CA, CCMJ, CIN, CIS, CMCI, ChemAb, ChemTitl, CurCont, GeoRef, INIS AtomInd, ISR, Inspec, MSN, MathR, P30, PhysBer, RefZh, SCI, SCOPUS, ST&MA, SpeleolAb, T02, W07, Z02.
—BLDSC (5036.237400), AskIEEE, CASDDS, IE, Infotrieve, Ingenta, INIST, Linda Hall. **CCC.**
Published by: (Institute of Physics), Institute of Physics Publishing Ltd., Dirac House, Temple Back, Bristol, BS1 6BE, United Kingdom. TEL 44-117-9297481, FAX 44-117-9301178, custserv@iop.org, http://publishing.iop.org/. Ed. Murray T Batchelor TEL 61-2-61252044. **Subscr. addr. in US:** American Institute of Physics, PO Box 503284, St Louis, MO 63150. TEL 516-576-2270, 800-344-6902, FAX 516-349-9704, subs@aip.org.

530 540 GBR ISSN 0022-3697
QC176.A1 CODEN: JPCSAW

➤ **JOURNAL OF PHYSICS AND CHEMISTRY OF SOLIDS.** Text in English, French, German. 1956. 12/yr. EUR 5,820 in Europe to institutions; JPY 773,100 in Japan to institutions; USD 6,513 elsewhere to institutions (effective 2012). bk.rev. illus. Index. back issues avail.; reprints avail. **Document type:** *Journal, Academic/Scholarly.* **Description:** Covers all aspects of the fundamental physics and chemistry of the solid state.
Formerly (until 1963): Physics and Chemistry of Solids (0369-8726)
Related titles: Microfiche ed.: (from MIM); Microfilm ed.: (from PQC); Online - full text ed.: ISSN 1879-2553 (from IngentaConnect, ScienceDirect).
Indexed: A01, A03, A08, A20, A22, A26, ASCA, AcoustA, ApMecR, BullT&T, C&ISA, C24, C33, CA, CCI, CIN, CPEI, Cadscan, ChemAb, ChemTitl, CurCR, CurCont, E&CAJ, EngInd, GeoRef, I05, ISR, Inspec, LeadAb, MSCI, P30, PhysBer, R16, RefZh, S01, SCI, SCOPUS, SolStAb, SpeleolAb, T02, TM, W07, Zincscan.
—BLDSC (5036.500000), AskIEEE, CASDDS, IE, Infotrieve, Ingenta, INIST, Linda Hall. **CCC.**
Published by: Pergamon (Subsidiary of: Elsevier Science & Technology), The Blvd, Langford Ln, East Park, Kidlington, Oxford OX5 1GB, United Kingdom. TEL 44-1865-843000, FAX 44-1865-843010, JournalsCustomerServiceEMEA@elsevier.com. Eds. A Bansil, K Prassides, Y Iwasa. **Subscr. to:** Elsevier BV, Radarweg 29, PO Box 211, Amsterdam 1000 AE, Netherlands. TEL 31-20-4853757, FAX 31-20-4853432, http://www.elsevier.nl.

530.41 GBR ISSN 0953-4075
QC770 CODEN: JPAPEH
➤ **JOURNAL OF PHYSICS B: ATOMIC, MOLECULAR AND OPTICAL PHYSICS.** Text in English. 1958. s-m. GBP 3,422 combined subscription to institutions (print & online eds.) (effective 2010). bibl.; illus.; charts. Index. back issues avail. **Document type:** *Journal, Academic/Scholarly.* **Description:** Publishes research papers, Fast Track Communications (FTCs), topical reviews and tutorial articles.
Incorporates (1989-2005): Journal of Optics B: Quantum and Semiclassical Optics (1464-4266); Which was formerly (until 1999): Quantum and Semiclassical Optics (1355-5111); (until 1995): Quantum Optics (0954-8998); Former titles (until 1988): Journal of Physics B: Atomic and Molecular Physics (0022-3700); (until 1969): Journal of Physics B: Proceedings of the Physical Society. Atomic and Molecular Physics (0368-3508); Which superseded in part (in 1968): Physical Society. Proceedings (0370-1328); Which was formed by the merger of (1874-1957): Proceedings of the Physical Society. Section A (0370-1298); (1874-1957): Proceedings of the Physical Society. Section B (0370-1301); Both of which superseded in part (in 1949): Physical Society. Proceedings (0959-5309); Which was formerly (until 1926): Physical Society of London. Proceedings (1478-7814); Physical Society. Proceedings incorporated (1900-1932): Optical Society. Transactions (1475-4878)
Related titles: Microfiche ed.: USD 4,223 in North America; GBP 2,155 elsewhere (effective 2007); Online - full text ed.: ISSN 1361-6455. 1996. GBP 3,259 to institutions (effective 2010) (from IngentaConnect).
Indexed: A01, A03, A08, A22, A28, APA, ASCA, ApMecR, BrCerAb, BullT&T, C&ISA, C24, C33, CA, CA/WCA, CCMJ, CIA, CIN, CPEI, Cadscan, CerAb, ChemAb, ChemTitl, CivEngAb, CorrAb, CurCont, E&CAJ, E11, EEA, EMA, ESPM, EngInd, EnvEAb, H15, INIS AtomInd, ISR, Inspec, LeadAb, M&TEA, M09, MBF, METADEX, MSB, MSN, MathR, P30, PhysBer, RefZh, SCI, SCOPUS, SolStAb, T02, T04, W07, WAA, Zincscan.
—BLDSC (5036.238400), AskIEEE, CASDDS, IE, Infotrieve, Ingenta, INIST, Linda Hall. **CCC.**
Published by: (Institute of Physics), Institute of Physics Publishing Ltd., Dirac House, Temple Back, Bristol, BS1 6BE, United Kingdom. TEL 44-117-9297481, FAX 44-117-9301178, custserv@iop.org, http://publishing.iop.org/. Ed. J-M Rost. Pub. Julia Dickinson. **Subscr. addr. in US:** American Institute of Physics, PO Box 503284, St Louis, MO 63150. TEL 516-576-2270, 800-344-6902, FAX 516-349-9704, subs@aip.org.

530.41 GBR ISSN 0953-8984
QC173.4.C65 CODEN: JCOMEL
➤ **JOURNAL OF PHYSICS: CONDENSED MATTER.** Text in English. 1989. 50/yr. GBP 6,323 combined subscription to institutions (print & online eds.) (effective 2010). bibl.; charts; illus. Index. 1 cols./p.; back issues avail. **Document type:** *Journal, Academic/Scholarly.* **Description:** Reports experimental and theoretical studies of the structural, thermal, mechanical, electrical, magnetic and optical properties of condensed matter, including crystals, quasicrystals and liquid crystals; amorphous and polymeric materials, alloys and metalic materials; liquids.
Formed by the merger of (1970-1989): Journal of Physics F: Metal Physics (0305-4608); Which was formerly (until 1971): Metal Physics (0369-1608); (1957-1989): Journal of Physics C: Solid State Physics (0022-3719); Which was formerly (until 1968): Journal of Physics C: Proceedings of the Physical Society. Solid State Physics (0368-3516); Which superseded in part (in 1967): Physical Society. Proceedings (0370-1328); Which was formed by the merger of (1874-1957): Physical Society. Proceedings. Section A (0370-1298); (1874-1957): Physical Society. Proceedings. Section B (0370-1301); Both of which superseded in part (in 1949): Physical Society. Proceedings (0959-5309); Which was formerly (until 1926): Physical Society of London. Proceedings (1478-7814); Physical Society. Proceedings incorporated (1900-1932): Optical Society. Transactions (1475-4878)
Related titles: Microfiche ed.: USD 7,774 in North America; GBP 3,982 elsewhere (effective 2007); Microfilm ed.; Online - full text ed.: ISSN 1361-648X. GBP 6,022 to institutions (effective 2010) (from IngentaConnect).
Indexed: A20, A22, A28, APA, ASCA, AcoustA, ApMecR, BrCerAb, C&ISA, C13, C24, C33, CA/WCA, CCI, CIA, CIN, CPEI, Cadscan, CerAb, ChemAb, ChemTitl, CivEngAb, CorrAb, CurCont, E&CAJ, E11, EEA, EMA, ESPM, EngInd, EnvEAb, GeoRef, H15, INIS AtomInd, ISMEC, ISR, Inspec, LeadAb, M&TEA, M09, MBF, MEDLINE, METADEX, MSCI, MathR, P30, PhysBer, RefZh, SCI, SCOPUS, SolStAb, SpeleolAb, T04, TM, W07, WAA, Zincscan.
—BLDSC (5036.800000), AskIEEE, CASDDS, IE, Infotrieve, Ingenta, INIST, Linda Hall. **CCC.**
Published by: (Institute of Physics), Institute of Physics Publishing Ltd., Dirac House, Temple Back, Bristol, BS1 6BE, United Kingdom. TEL 44-117-9297481, FAX 44-117-9301178, custserv@iop.org, http://publishing.iop.org/. Ed. D K Ferry. **U.S. subscr. to:** American Institute of Physics, PO Box 503284, St Louis, MO 63150. TEL 516-576-2270, 800-344-6902, FAX 516-349-9704, subs@aip.org.

530 GBR ISSN 1742-6596
JOURNAL OF PHYSICS: CONFERENCE SERIES (ONLINE). Text in English. 2004. a. free (effective 2011). back issues avail. **Document type:** *Monographic series, Academic/Scholarly.*
Media: Online - full text.
Indexed: Inspec.
—BLDSC (5036.223000), Linda Hall. **CCC.**
Published by: Institute of Physics Publishing Ltd., Dirac House, Temple Back, Bristol, BS1 6BE, United Kingdom. TEL 44-117-9297481, FAX 44-117-9301178, custserv@iop.org, http://publishing.iop.org/. Pub. Graham Douglas TEL 44-117-9301280.

530 621 GBR ISSN 0022-3727
QC1 CODEN: JPAPBE
➤ **JOURNAL OF PHYSICS D: APPLIED PHYSICS.** Text in English. 1950. 50/yr. GBP 2,583 combined subscription to institutions (print & online eds.) (effective 2010). bibl.; charts; illus. Index. back issues avail. **Document type:** *Journal, Academic/Scholarly.* **Description:** Explores the theoretical and experimental aspects of physics, as applied to interdisciplinary science, engineering or industry.
Former titles (until 1970): British Journal of Applied Physics. Journal of Physics D (0262-8171); (until 1968): British Journal of Applied Physics (0508-3443)
Related titles: Microfiche ed.: USD 2,708 in North America; GBP 1,376 elsewhere (effective 2007); Microfilm ed.; Online - full text ed.: ISSN 1361-6463. GBP 2,246 to institutions (effective 2010) (from IngentaConnect).
Indexed: A01, A03, A05, A08, A20, A22, A23, A24, A28, ABIPC, APA, AS&TA, AS&TI, ASCA, AcoustA, B04, B13, BrCerAb, C&ISA, C10, C33, CA, CA/WCA, CIA, CIN, CISA, CPEI, CTE, Cadscan, CerAb, ChemAb, ChemTitl, CivEngAb, CorrAb, CurCont, E&CAJ, E11, EEA, EMA, ESPM, EngInd, EnvEAb, GeoRef, H15, IBR, IBZ, INIS AtomInd, ISMEC, ISR, Inspec, LeadAb, M&TEA, M09, MBF, METADEX, MSB, P30, PhotoAb, R18, RefZh, SCI, SCOPUS, SolStAb, SpeleolAb, T02, T04, TM, W07, WAA, Zincscan.
—BLDSC (5036.240000), AskIEEE, CASDDS, IE, Infotrieve, Ingenta, INIST, Linda Hall. **CCC.**
Published by: (Institute of Physics), Institute of Physics Publishing Ltd., Dirac House, Temple Back, Bristol, BS1 6BE, United Kingdom. TEL 44-117-9297481, FAX 44-117-9301178, custserv@iop.org, http://publishing.iop.org/. Ed. P I Bhattacharya. Pub. Sarah Quin. **Subscr. addr. in US:** American Institute of Physics, PO Box 503284, St Louis, MO 63150. TEL 516-576-2270, 800-344-6902, FAX 516-349-9704, subs@aip.org.

➤ **JOURNAL OF PHYSICS G: NUCLEAR AND PARTICLE PHYSICS.** *see* PHYSICS—Nuclear Physics

530 330 USA ISSN 1945-8193
JOURNAL OF PHYSICS RESEARCH. Text in English. 2008. w. USD 2,295 in US & Canada; USD 2,495 elsewhere; USD 2,525 combined subscription in US & Canada (print & online eds.); USD 2,755 combined subscription elsewhere (print & online eds.) (effective 2011). adv. back issues avail. **Document type:** *Newsletter, Trade.* **Description:** Reports on the companies involved in a range of applied physics, including business involved in satellite imaging and mineral exploration, global space programs, and astronomy.
Related titles: E-mail ed.; Online - full text ed.: ISSN 1945-8207. USD 2,295 combined subscription (online & e-mail eds.) (effective 2011).
Indexed: A26, E08, H11, I05, P26, P48, P52, P54, P56, PQC, S09.
Published by: NewsRx, 2727 Paces Ferry Rd SE, Ste 2-440, Atlanta, GA 30339. TEL 770-435-8286, 800-726-4550, FAX 770-435-6800, pressrelease@newsrx.com, http://www.newsrx.com. Pub., Adv. contact Susan Hasty TEL 770-507-7777.

JOURNAL OF PHYSICS TEACHER EDUCATION ONLINE. *see* EDUCATION—Teaching Methods And Curriculum

530.44 GBR ISSN 0022-3778
QC718 CODEN: JPLPBZ
➤ **JOURNAL OF PLASMA PHYSICS.** Text in English. 1967. bi-m. GBP 1,075, USD 1,890 to institutions; GBP 1,092, USD 2,021 combined subscription to institutions (print & online eds.) (effective 2012). adv. bk.rev. bibl.; charts; illus. index. back issues avail.; reprint service avail. from PSC. **Document type:** *Journal, Academic/Scholarly.* **Description:** Features primary research articles in plasma physics, both theoretical and experimental, and its applications to fusion, laboratory plasmas and communications devices.
Related titles: Microform ed.: (from PQC); Online - full text ed.: ISSN 1469-7807. GBP 1,028, USD 1,722 to institutions (effective 2012).
Indexed: A01, A03, A08, A22, ASCA, ApMecR, CA, CIN, CPEI, ChemAb, ChemTitl, CurCont, E01, EngInd, IBR, IBZ, ISR, Inspec, M&GPA, P26, P48, P52, P54, P56, PQC, PhysBer, RefZh, SCI, SCOPUS, T02, W07.
—BLDSC (5040.550000), AskIEEE, CASDDS, IE, Infotrieve, Ingenta, INIST, Linda Hall. **CCC.**
Published by: Cambridge University Press, The Edinburgh Bldg, Shaftesbury Rd, Cambridge, CB2 8RU, United Kingdom. TEL 44-1223-312393, FAX 44-1223-315052, journals@cambridge.org, http://www.cambridge.org/uk. Ed. Padma Kant Shukla. R&P Linda Nicol TEL 44-1223-325702. Adv. contact Rebecca Roberts TEL 44-1223-325083. page GBP 445, page USD 845. Circ: 400. **Subscr. to:** Cambridge University Press, 32 Ave of the Americas, New York, NY 10013. TEL 212-337-5000, FAX 212-691-3239, journals_subscriptions@cup.org.

➤ **JOURNAL OF PYROTECHNICS.** *see* ENGINEERING—Chemical Engineering

621.38 USA ISSN 1949-4882
▼ ➤ **JOURNAL OF QUANTUM ELECTRONICS AND SPINTRONICS.** Text in English. 2010 (Jan.). q. USD 295 to institutions; USD 442 combined subscription to institutions (print & online eds.) (effective 2012). **Document type:** *Journal, Academic/Scholarly.*
Related titles: Online - full text ed.: USD 295 to institutions (effective 2012).
Published by: Nova Science Publishers, Inc., 400 Oser Ave, Ste 1600, Hauppauge, NY 11788. TEL 631-231-7269, FAX 631-231-8175, main@novapublishers.com. Ed. M I Miah.

530 SRB ISSN 1450-7404
JOURNAL OF RESEARCH IN PHYSICS. Text in English. 1981.
Formerly (until 1998): Prirodno-Matematicki Fakultet. Zbornik Radova . Serija za Fiziku (0352-0889)
Indexed: Inspec.
Published by: Univerzitet u Novom Sadu, Prirodno-Matematicki Fakultet, Institut za Fiziku, Trg Dositeja-Obradovica 3, Novi Sad, 21000. TEL 381-21-55-630, FAX 381-21-55-662.

JOURNAL OF RUSSIAN LASER RESEARCH. *see* ENGINEERING

JOURNAL OF SOL-GEL SCIENCE AND TECHNOLOGY. *see* ENGINEERING—Engineering Mechanics And Materials

530 CHE ISSN 1664-039X
▼ **JOURNAL OF SPECTRAL THEORY.** Text in English. 2010. q. EUR 238 combined subscription (print & online eds.) (effective 2012). **Document type:** *Journal, Academic/Scholarly.* **Description:** Focuses on spectral theory and its many areas of application.
Related titles: Online - full text ed.: ISSN 1664-0403. 2010. EUR 198 (effective 2012).
Published by: European Mathematical Society Publishing House, Seminar for Applied Mathematics, ETH-Zentrum FLI C4, Fliederstr 23, Zurich, 8092, Switzerland. TEL 41-44-6323436, FAX 41-44-6321104, hintermann@ems-ph.org. Ed. E. Brian Davies.

▼ **JOURNAL OF SPORT AND PHYSICS.** *see* SPORTS AND GAMES

530 USA ISSN 0022-4715
QC175 CODEN: JSTPSB
➤ **JOURNAL OF STATISTICAL PHYSICS.** Text in English. 1969. 21/yr. EUR 4,084, USD 4,190 combined subscription to institutions (print & online eds.) (effective 2012). adv. back issues avail.; reprint service avail. from PSC. **Document type:** *Journal, Academic/Scholarly.* **Description:** Publishes original and review articles in the fields of statistical mechanics and thermodynamics of equilibrium and nonequilibrium processes.
Related titles: Microfilm ed.: (from PQC); Online - full text ed.: ISSN 1572-9613 (from IngentaConnect).
Indexed: A01, A02, A03, A08, A20, A22, A26, ASCA, ApMecR, BibLing, CA, CCMJ, CIS, CMCI, CompAb, CurCont, E01, ISR, Inspec, MSN, MathR, P30, PhysBer, RefZh, SCI, SCOPUS, ST&MA, T02, W07, Z02.
—BLDSC (5066.840000), AskIEEE, IE, Infotrieve, Ingenta, INIST, Linda Hall. **CCC.**
Published by: Springer New York LLC (Subsidiary of: Springer Science+Business Media), 233 Spring St, New York, NY 10013. TEL 212-460-1500, FAX 212-460-1575, service-ny@springer.com, http://www.springer.com/. Ed. Joel L Lebowitz.

530 USA ISSN 1557-1939
CODEN: JSNMBN
➤ **JOURNAL OF SUPERCONDUCTIVITY AND NOVEL MAGNETISM.** Text in English. 1988. 8/yr. EUR 1,463, USD 1,498 combined subscription to institutions (print & online eds.) (effective 2012). adv. bibl. back issues avail.; reprint service avail. from PSC. **Document type:** *Journal, Academic/Scholarly.* **Description:** Provides a forum for the publication of original articles on all aspects of the science and technology of superconductivity.
Formerly (until 2006): Journal of Superconductivity (0896-1107)
Related titles: Microfilm ed.: (from PQC); Online - full text ed.: ISSN 1557-1947 (from IngentaConnect).
Indexed: A01, A03, A05, A08, A22, A26, A28, APA, AS&TA, AS&TI, ASCA, B04, BRD, BibLing, BrCerAb, C&ISA, C10, C33, CA, CA/WCA, CIA, CIN, CPEI, CerAb, ChemAb, ChemTitl, CivEngAb, CorrAb, CurCont, E&CAJ, E01, E11, E14, EEA, EIA, EMA, ESPM, EngInd, EnvEAb, H15, ISR, Inspec, M&TEA, M09, MBF, METADEX, MSCI, RefZh, S04, SCI, SCOPUS, SolStAb, T02, T04, W03, W05, W07, WAA.
—BLDSC (5067.118050), AskIEEE, CASDDS, IE, Infotrieve, Ingenta, INIST, Linda Hall. **CCC.**
Published by: Springer New York LLC (Subsidiary of: Springer Science+Business Media), 233 Spring St, New York, NY 10013. TEL 212-460-1500, FAX 212-460-1575, service-ny@springer.com, http://www.springer.com/. Eds. Stuart A Wolf, Vladimir Z Kresin. **Subscr. to:** Journal Fulfillment, PO Box 2485, Secaucus, NJ 07096. TEL 201-348-4033, FAX 201-348-4505, journals-ny@springer.com.

530 548 USA ISSN 1063-4576
TA418.45
➤ **JOURNAL OF SUPERHARD MATERIALS.** Text in English. 1983. bi-m. EUR 2,440, USD 2,954 combined subscription to institutions (print & online eds.) (effective 2012). abstr.; charts; illus. back issues avail. **Document type:** *Journal, Academic/Scholarly.* **Description:** Covers properties of superhard materials and their industrial uses, production technology, synthetic diamonds, superhard tools, powders and pastes, physical chemistry of superhard materials.
Formerly (until 1992): Soviet Journal of Superhard Materials (0739-8425)
Related titles: Online - full text ed.: ISSN 1934-9408; ◆ Translation of: Sverkhtverdye Materialy. ISSN 0203-3119.
Indexed: A22, A26, E01, E08, Inspec, MSCI, S09, SCI, SCOPUS, W07.
—BLDSC (0415.380000), East View, IE, Ingenta, INIST, Linda Hall. **CCC.**
Published by: (Natsional'na Akademiya Nauk Ukrainy UKR, Otdelenie Fiziko-Tekhnicheskikh Materialov UKR), Allerton Press, Inc. (Subsidiary of: Pleiades Publishing, Inc.), 18 W 27th St, New York, NY 10001. TEL 646-424-9686, FAX 646-424-9695, journals@allertonpress.com. Ed. Nikolai V Novikov.

530 JPN ISSN 1341-1756
JOURNAL OF SURFACE ANALYSIS. Text in Japanese. 1995. 3/yr. JPY 4,000 (effective 2006). back issues avail.; reprints avail. **Document type:** *Journal, Academic/Scholarly.*
Related titles: Online - full text ed.: ISSN 1347-8400.
—BLDSC (5067.355000), IE, Ingenta.
Published by: Hyomen Bunseki Kenkyukai/Surface Analysis Society of Japan, c/o Shigeo Tanuma, Materials Engineering Lab., NIMS, 1-2-1 Sengen, Tsukuba, 305-0047, Japan. TEL 81-29-8592801, http://www.sasj.gr.jp/jpn-index.html.

530 IRN ISSN 0378-1046
QC801 CODEN: JESPCS
JOURNAL OF THE EARTH AND SPACE PHYSICS. Text and summaries in English, Persian, Modern, French, German. 1972. s-a. adv. charts; stat. **Document type:** *Academic/Scholarly.*
Indexed: AJEE, GeoRef, SpeleolAb.
—INIST, Linda Hall.
Published by: University of Teheran, Institute of Geophysics, Amirabad-e Shomali Ave., Tehran, 14394, Iran. Ed. Bahram Akasheh.

530 USA ISSN 0887-8722
TL900 CODEN: JTHTEO
➤ **JOURNAL OF THERMOPHYSICS AND HEAT TRANSFER;** devoted to thermophysics and heat transfer. Text in English. 1987. q. USD 685 domestic to non-members (print or online ed.); USD 725 foreign to non-members; USD 790 combined subscription domestic to non-members (print & online eds.); USD 835 combined subscription foreign to non-members (print & online eds.); USD 55 combined subscription domestic to members (print & online eds.); USD 75 combined subscription foreign to members (print & online eds.) (effective 2009). adv. charts; illus. index. back issues avail.; reprints avail. **Document type:** *Journal, Academic/Scholarly.* **Description:** Features original research papers disclosing new technical knowledge and exploratory developments and applications based on new knowledge in the science and technology of thermophysics and heat transfer.
Related titles: Microform ed.; Online - full text ed.: ISSN 1533-6808.
Indexed: A22, A28, APA, ASCA, ApMecR, BrCerAb, C&ISA, C33, CA/WCA, CIA, CIN, CMCI, CPEI, CerAb, ChemAb, ChemTitl, CivEngAb, CorrAb, CurCont, E&CAJ, E11, EEA, EMA, ESPM, EngInd, EnvEAb, FLUIDEX, H15, ISMEC, ISR, Inspec, M&TEA, M09, MBF, METADEX, MSCI, RefZh, SCI, SCOPUS, SolStAb, T04, W07, WAA, Z02.

P

—BLDSC (5069.099300), CASDDS, IE, Infotrieve, Ingenta, INIST, Linda Hall. **CCC.**

Published by: American Institute of Aeronautics and Astronautics, Inc., 1801 Alexander Bell Dr, Ste 500, Reston, VA 20191. TEL 703-264-7500, 800-639-2422, FAX 703-264-7551, custserv@aiaa.org. Ed. Alfred L Crosbie.

530 GBR ISSN 1468-5248
QA913 CODEN: JTOUAO

➤ **JOURNAL OF TURBULENCE.** Abbreviated title: J O T. Text in English. 2000. irreg. GBP 513 in United Kingdom to institutions; EUR 680, USD 853 to institutions (effective 2012). adv. back issues avail. **Document type:** *Journal, Academic/Scholarly.* **Description:** Provides a digital forum for theoretical, numerical and experimental studies aimed at understanding, predicting and controlling fluid turbulence, the last great problem of classical physics.

Media: Online - full content. **Related titles:** Online - full text ed.: (from IngentaConnect).

Indexed: A01, A03, A08, A22, A28, APA, ASFA, ApMecR, BrCerAb, C&ISA, CA, CA/WCA, CCMJ, CIA, CerAb, CivEngAb, CorrAb, CurCont, E&CAJ, E01, E11, EEA, EMA, ESPM, EnvEAb, FLUIDEX, GEOBASE, H15, Inspec, M&GPA, M&TEA, M09, MBF, METADEX, MSN, MathR, SCI, SCOPUS, SolStAb, T02, T04, W07, WAA, Z02.

—BLDSC (5071.260000), IE, Infotrieve, Ingenta, Linda Hall. **CCC.**

Published by: Taylor & Francis Ltd. (Subsidiary of: Taylor & Francis Group), 4 Park Sq, Milton Park, Abingdon, Oxfordshire OX14 4RN, United Kingdom. TEL 44-20-70176000, FAX 44-20-70176336, subscriptions@tandf.co.uk, http://www.taylorandfrancis.com. Eds. Charles Meneveau, Gregory L Eyinks, Shiyi Chen. **Subscr. in N America to:** Taylor & Francis Inc., Customer Services Dept, 325 Chestnut St, 8th Fl, Philadelphia, PA 19106. TEL 215-625-8900, 800-354-1420, FAX 215-625-2940, customerservice@taylorandfrancis.com; **Subscr. outside N America to:** Journals Customer Service, Sheepen Pl, Colchester, Essex CO3 3LP, United Kingdom. TEL 44-20-70175544, FAX 44-20-70175198, tf.enquiries@tfinforma.com.

530 USA
CODEN: JURPF2

➤ **JOURNAL OF UNDERGRADUATE RESEARCH IN PHYSICS (ONLINE).** Abbreviated title: J U R P. Text in English. 1982. a. free (effective 2010). bk.rev. back issues avail. **Document type:** *Journal, Academic/Scholarly.* **Description:** Devoted to research work done by undergraduate students in physics and related fields.

Formerly (until 2002): Journal of Undergraduate Research in Physics (Print) (0731-3764)

—Infotrieve, Ingenta.

Published by: (American Institute of Physics), Guilford College, Department of Physics, 5800 W Friendly Ave, Greensboro, NC 27410. TEL 336-316-2000, its@guilford.edu, http://www.guilford.edu/academics/departments/physics/. Ed. Dwight E Neunschwander. **Co-sponsor:** Society of Physics Students.

533.5 USA ISSN 1553-1813
TJ940 CODEN: JVTAD6

➤ **JOURNAL OF VACUUM SCIENCE & TECHNOLOGY. A: INTERNATIONAL JOURNAL DEVOTED TO VACUUM, SURFACES, AND FILMS.** Text in English. 1964. 6/yr. price varies based on the number of users. adv. bk.rev. charts; illus. Index. back issues avail. **Document type:** *Journal, Academic/Scholarly.* **Description:** Designed for engineers, physicists, chemists, materials scientists, microelectronics specialists, and technicians working in all areas of vacuum science, surfaces, microelectronics and thin film materials science.

Formerly (until 2003): Journal of Vacuum Science and Technology. Part A. Vacuum, Surfaces and Films (0734-2101); Which superseded in part (in 1983): Journal of Vacuum Science and Technology (0022-5355)

Related titles: CD-ROM ed.: ISSN 1071-8028. USD 1,601 combined subscription domestic to institutions print, online & CD-ROM eds.; USD 1,655 combined subscription to institutions in the Americas & the Caribbean for print, online & CD-ROM eds.; USD 1,703 combined subscription elsewhere to institutions print, online & CD-ROM eds. (effective 2006); Microform ed.: (from PQC); Online - full text ed.: ISSN 1944-2807. price varies based on the number of users.

Indexed: A20, A22, ASCA, C10, C13, C24, C33, CA, CPEI, CPI, Cadscan, ChemAb, ChemTitl, CurCont, EngInd, GPAA, IBR, IBZ, INIS AtomInd, IPackAb, ISR, Inspec, LeadAb, MSCI, P30, PhotoAb, PhysBer, RefZh, SCI, SCOPUS, SPINweb, T02, TM, W07, Zincscan.

—BLDSC (5072.210100), AskIEEE, CASDDS, IE, Infotrieve, Ingenta, INIST, Linda Hall. **CCC.**

Published by: (American Vacuum Society), American Institute of Physics, 1 Physics Ellipse, College Park, MD 20740. TEL 301-209-3100, aipinfo@aip.org, http://www.aip.org. Ed. G Lucovsky TEL 919-515-3301. **Subscr. to:** PO Box 503284, St Louis, MO 63150. TEL 516-576-2270, 800-344-6902, FAX 516-349-9704, subs@aip.org.

533.5 USA ISSN 1071-1023
TJ940 CODEN: JVSTBM

➤ **JOURNAL OF VACUUM SCIENCE AND TECHNOLOGY. PART B. MICROELECTRONICS AND NANOMETER STRUCTURES.** Text in English. 1964. 6/yr. price varies based on the number of users. adv. bk.rev. charts; illus. Index. back issues avail. **Document type:** *Journal, Academic/Scholarly.* **Description:** Covers microelectronics, microlithography, materials processing and characterization, nanometer structures and devices.

Formerly (until 1991): Journal of Vacuum Science and Technology. Part B. Microelectronics Processing and Phenomena (0734-211X); Which superseded in part (in 1983): Journal of Vacuum Science and Technology (0022-5355)

Related titles: CD-ROM ed.: USD 1,601 combined subscription domestic print, online & CD-ROM eds.; USD 1,655 combined subscription in the Americas & the Caribbean for print, online & CD-ROM eds.; USD 1,703 combined subscription elsewhere print, online & CD-ROM eds. (effective 2006); Microform ed.: (from PQC); Online - full text ed.: ISSN 1520-8567. price varies based on the number of users.

Indexed: A22, ASCA, C10, C13, C24, C33, CA, CIN, CPEI, CPI, Cadscan, ChemAb, ChemTitl, CurCont, EngInd, IBR, IBZ, INIS AtomInd, ISR, Inspec, LeadAb, MSCI, P30, PhotoAb, RefZh, SCI, SCOPUS, SPINweb, T02, TM, W07, Zincscan.

—BLDSC (5072.210130), AskIEEE, CASDDS, IE, Ingenta, INIST, Linda Hall. **CCC.**

Published by: (American Vacuum Society), American Institute of Physics, 1 Physics Ellipse, College Park, MD 20740. TEL 301-209-3100, FAX 301-209-0843, aipinfo@aip.org, http://www.aip.org. Ed. Gary E McGuire. **Subscr. to:** PO Box 503284, St Louis, MO 63150. TEL 516-576-2270, 800-344-6902, FAX 516-349-9704, subs@aip.org.

530 VEN ISSN 1856-6847
QC173.5

JOURNAL OF VECTOR RELATIVITY. Text in English, Spanish. 2006. irreg. free (effective 2011). **Document type:** *Journal, Academic/Scholarly.* **Description:** Covers experimental, theoretical and mathematical aspects of physics envisioned mainly, but not only, under the optics of the theory of vectorial relativity.

Media: Online - full text.

Published by: Journal of Vectorial Relativity Ed. J G Quintero.

530 620 NLD ISSN 0895-3996
QC480.8 CODEN: JXSTE5

➤ **JOURNAL OF X-RAY SCIENCE AND TECHNOLOGY.** Text in English. 1988. q. USD 671 combined subscription in North America (print & online eds.); EUR 480 combined subscription elsewhere (print & online eds.) (effective 2012). back issues avail. **Document type:** *Journal, Academic/Scholarly.* **Description:** Articles on recent developments in x-ray sources: synchrotons and x-ray lasers; x-ray image formation; x-ray spectroscopy; and x-ray physics.

Related titles: Online - full text ed.: ISSN 1095-9114 (from IngentaConnect).

Indexed: A01, A03, A08, A22, A26, CA, CPEI, CurCont, E01, EMBASE, EngInd, ExcerpMed, I05, Inspec, MEDLINE, P30, S01, SCI, SCOPUS, T02, TM, W07.

—BLDSC (5072.705000), AskIEEE, CASDDS, IE, Infotrieve, Ingenta. **CCC.**

Published by: I O S Press, Nieuwe Hemweg 6B, Amsterdam, 1013 BG, Netherlands. TEL 31-20-6883355, FAX 31-20-6870019, info@iospress.nl. Ed. Wei R Chan. **Subscr. to:** I O S Press, Inc, 4502 Rachael Manor Dr, Fairfax, VA 22032-3631. sales@iospress.com; Globe Publication Pvt. Ltd., C-62 Inderpuri, New Delhi 100 012, India; Kinokuniya Co Ltd., Shinjuku 3-chome, Shinjuku-ku, Tokyo 160-0022, Japan.

530 MYS ISSN 0128-0333
QC1 CODEN: JFMAEU

➤ **JURNAL FIZIK MALAYSIA.** Text in English. 1976. q. USD 40 to individuals; USD 80 to libraries (effective 2002). back issues avail. **Document type:** *Journal, Academic/Scholarly.*

Former titles (until 1984): Buletin Fizik (0126-9674); (until 1980): Suara Fizikawan (0126-6640)

Indexed: ChemAb, ChemTitl, INIS AtomInd, Inspec.

—CASDDS, IE, Ingenta, Linda Hall.

Published by: Malaysian Institute of Physics/Institut Fizik Malaysia, c/o Physics Department, University of Malaysia, Kuala Lumpur, 50603, Malaysia. TEL 603-7594385, 603-7594288, FAX 603-9259637, TELEX 39845-MA-UNIMAL, wcs@fizik.um.edu.my, http://foe.mmu.edu.my/ifm/. Ed. C S Wong. R&P C.S. Wong. Circ: 500.

530 USA ISSN 1949-1441

▼ ➤ **K B M JOURNAL OF PHYSICS & PHYSICAL SCIENCES.** Text in English. 2010 (Jan.). q. free (effective 2010). **Document type:** *Journal, Academic/Scholarly.* **Description:** Includes research and reviews in all areas of physics and physical sciences.

Media: Online - full content.

Published by: K B M Scientific Publishing, Ltd, 971 Pepperwood Dr, Fayetteville, NC 28331-9331. TEL 910-672-1114, info@kbm-scientific-publishing.org.

530 JPN ISSN 1344-1299
QC789.2.J32

K E K HIGH ENERGY ACCELERATOR RESEARCH ORGANIZATION. ANNUAL REPORT. Text in English. 1971. a. **Document type:** *Government.*

Former titles (until 1997): National Laboratory for High Energy Physics. Annual Report (1343-1064); (until 1981): K E K Annual Report

Indexed: INIS AtomInd.

—BLDSC (5089.212000).

Published by: Koenerugi Kasokuki Kenkyu Kiko/High Energy Accelerator Research Organization, 1-1, Oho, Tsukuba-shi, Ibaraki-ken 305-0801, Japan. TEL 81-298-64-5137, FAX 81-298-64-4604, adm-journhushiryou1@ccgemail.kek.jp.

530 JPN

K E K NEWS/KOENERUGIKEN GEPPO. Text in Japanese. 1972. m. **Document type:** *Government.*

Formerly (until 1997): National Laboratory for High Energy Physics. Monthly Bulletin

Related titles: English ed.: ISSN 1343-3547. 1997.

Published by: (Kenkyu Kyoryoku Daiichi Kakari/Laboratory Services Division I), Koenerugi Kasokuki Kenkyu Kiko/High Energy Accelerator Research Organization, 1-1, Oho, Tsukuba-shi, Ibaraki-ken 305-0801, Japan. TEL 81-298-64-5137, FAX 81-298-64-4604, http://www.kek.jp.

530 JPN

K E K PREPRINT. Text in English. 1971. irreg. **Document type:** *Monographic series, Academic/Scholarly.*

Published by: Koenerugi Kasokuki Kenkyu Kiko/High Energy Accelerator Research Organization, 1-1, Oho, Tsukuba-shi, Ibaraki-ken 305-0801, Japan. TEL 81-298-64-5137, FAX 81-298-64-4604, adm-journhushiryou1@ccgemail.kek.jp.

530 JPN

K E K PROCEEDINGS. Text in English, Japanese. 1991. irreg. **Document type:** *Proceedings.*

Indexed: CIN, ChemAb, ChemTitl.

Published by: Koenerugi Kasokuki Kenkyu Kiko/High Energy Accelerator Research Organization, 1-1, Oho, Tsukuba-shi, Ibaraki-ken 305-0801, Japan. TEL 81-298-64-5137, FAX 81-298-64-4604, adm-journhushiryou1@ccgemail.kek.jp, http://www.kek.jp.

530 JPN

K E K PROGRESS REPORT. Text in English. 1983. irreg. **Document type:** *Government.*

Published by: Koenerugi Kasokuki Kenkyu Kiko/High Energy Accelerator Research Organization, 1-1, Oho, Tsukuba-shi, Ibaraki-ken 305-0801, Japan. TEL 81-298-64-5137, FAX 81-298-64-4604, adm-journhushiryou1@ccgemail.kek.jp.

530 JPN

K E K REPORT. Text in English, Japanese. 1971. irreg. **Document type:** *Government.*

Indexed: ChemAb, ChemTitl.

Published by: Koenerugi Kasokuki Kenkyu Kiko/High Energy Accelerator Research Organization, 1-1, Oho, Tsukuba-shi, Ibaraki-ken 305-0801, Japan. TEL 81-298-64-5137, FAX 81-298-64-4604, adm-journhushiryou1@ccgemail.kek.jp, http://www.kek.jp.

530 SGP

KATHMANDU SUMMER SCHOOL LECTURE NOTES. Text in English. 1990. irreg. **Document type:** *Monographic series, Academic/Scholarly.*

Published by: World Scientific Publishing Co. Pte. Ltd., 5 Toh Tuck Link, Singapore, 596224, Singapore. TEL 65-6466-5775, FAX 65-6467-7667, series@wspc.com.sg, wspc@wspc.com.sg, http://www.worldscientific.com.

530 510 RUS ISSN 1815-6088

➤ **KAZANSKII GOSUDARSTVENNYI UNIVERSITET. UCHENYE ZAPISKI. SERIYA FIZIKO-MATEMATICHESKIE NAUKI.** Text in Russian, English. 1925. q. RUR 880 domestic (effective 2011). bk.rev. abstr.; bibl.; charts; illus. back issues avail. **Document type:** *Journal, Academic/Scholarly.* **Description:** Publishes results of scientific research (in the form of original articles, reviews and short communications) in various fields of physical and mathematical sciences.

Supersedes in part (in 2005): Kazanskii Gosudarstvennyi Universitet imeni V.I. Ul'yanova-Lenina. Uchenye Zapiski (1029-5704)

Related titles: Online - full text ed.

—Linda Hall.

Published by: (Kazanskii Gosudarstvennyi Universitet/Kazan State University), Izdatel'stvo Kazanskogo Universiteta, 1/37 Professor Nuzhin St, Kazan, 420008, Russian Federation. TEL 7-843-2926560, FAX 7-843-2337334, pressksu@mail.ru, http://www.ksu.ru/structur/izdat.htm. Ed. Il'shat R Gafurov. Circ: 100 (paid); 200 (controlled).

➤ **KEISHA KINO ZAIRYO SHINPOJUMU KOENSHU/SYMPOSIUM OF FUNCTIONALLY GRADIENT MATERIALS FORUM. PROCEEDINGS.** *see* TECHNOLOGY: COMPREHENSIVE WORKS

530 548 JPN

KESSHO KOGAKU BUNKAKAI KENKYUKAI/DIVISION OF MATERIALS SCIENCE AND CRYSTAL TECHNOLOGY. PROCEEDINGS. Text in Japanese. s-a. **Document type:** *Proceedings, Academic/Scholarly.*

Published by: Oyo Butsuri Gakkai, Kessho Kogaku Bunkakai/Japan Society of Applied Physics, Division of Crystals Science and Technology, 1-12-13 Kudan Kita Chiyoda-ku, Tokyo, 102-0073, Japan. TEL 81-3-32381043, FAX 81-3-32216245, divisions@jsap.or.jp, http://annex.jsap.or.jp/kessho/.

530 540 UKR ISSN 2079-1704

▼ ➤ **KHIMIYA, FIZYKA TA TEKHNOLOGIYA POVERHNI/CHEMISTRY, PHYSICS AND TECHNOLOGY OF SURFACE.** Text in Ukrainian, Russian, English. 2009. q. abstr.; bibl.; charts; illus. Index. back issues avail. **Document type:** *Journal, Academic/Scholarly.* **Description:** Features the results of studies on actual problems of chemistry, physics, and technology of solid surfaces, physical and chemical processes at interfaces as well as on nanosystems preparation techniques and property examinations.

Related titles: Online - full text ed.

Indexed: RefZh.

Published by: Natsional'na Akademiya Nauk Ukrainy, Instytut Khimii Poverhni im O.O. Chuika/National Academy of Sciences of Ukraine, Chuiko Institute of Surface Chemistry, vul Generala Naumova 17, ofis 154, Kyiv, 03164, Ukraine. TEL 380-44-4229626, FAX 380-44-4243567, http://www.isc.gov.ua. Ed. Nikolai Kartel.

➤ **KINEMATICS AND PHYSICS OF CELESTIAL BODIES.** *see* ASTRONOMY

530.13 USA ISSN 1937-5093
QC174.9

KINETIC AND RELATED MODELS. Abbreviated title: K R M. Text in English. 2008 (Mar.). q. USD 496 combined subscription (print & online eds.) (effective 2010). adv. back issues avail. **Document type:** *Journal, Academic/Scholarly.* **Description:** Features papers of original research in the areas of kinetic equations spanned from mathematical theory to numerical analysis, simulations and modelling.

Related titles: Online - full text ed.: ISSN 1937-5077. 2008 (Mar.). USD 426 (effective 2010).

Indexed: CCMJ, CurCont, MSN, MathR, SCI, W07, Z02.

Published by: American Institute of Mathematical Sciences, PO Box 2604, Springfield, MO 65801. TEL 417-886-0559, FAX 417-886-0559, general@aimsciences.org, http://aimsciences.org. Eds. Pierre Degond, Seiji Ukai, Tong Yang.

530 510 520 SVN ISSN 1408-1547

KNJIZNICA SIGMA. Text in Slovenian. 1959. s-a. back issues avail. **Document type:** *Monographic series.*

Related titles: Online - full content ed.

Published by: Drustvo Matematikov, Fizikov in Astronomov/Society of Mathematicians, Physicists and Astronomers, Jadranska ulica 19, pp 2964, Ljubljana, 1001, Slovenia. TEL 386-1-4232460, FAX 386-1-2517281, tajnik@dmfa.si, http://www.dmfa.si. Ed. Matjaz Omladic. Adv. contact Mr. Vladimir Bensa. Circ: 500.

530 JPN

KOBAYASI RIGAKU KENKYUJO REPOTO/KOBAYASHI INSTITUTE OF PHYSICAL RESEARCH. ANNUAL REPORT. Text in English, Japanese. 1989. a.

Formerly: Kobayashi Rigaku Kenkyujo Repoto (0918-8088)

Published by: Kobayashi Rigaku Kenkyujo/Kobayashi Institute of Physical Research, 20-41 Higashi-Moto-Machi 3-chome, Kokubunji-shi, Tokyo-to 185-0022, Japan.

530 JPN

KOBAYASI RIKEN NYUSU/KOBAYASHI INSTITUTE OF PHYSICAL RESEARCH. NEWS. Text in Japanese. 1983. q.

Formerly: Kobayashi Riken Nyusu

Published by: Kobayashi Rigaku Kenkyujo/Kobayashi Institute of Physical Research, 20-41 Higashi-Moto-Machi 3-chome, Kokubunji-shi, Tokyo-to 185-0022, Japan.

530 JPN ISSN 0389-0260

KOCHI UNIVERSITY. FACULTY OF SCIENCE. MEMOIRS. SERIES B, PHYSICS. Text in English. 1980. a. **Document type:** *Journal, Academic/Scholarly.*

Published by: Kochi University, Faculty of Science/Kochi Daigaku Rigakubu, 5-1 Akebono-cho 2-chome, Kochi-shi, 780-8072, Japan.

KONGELIGE DANSKE VIDENSKABERNES SELSKAB. MATEMATISK - FYSISKE MEDDELELSER. *see* MATHEMATICS

531.1134 KOR

➤ **KOREA - AUSTRALIA RHEOLOGY JOURNAL.** Text in English. 1989. q. EUR 303, USD 373 combined subscription to institutions (print & online eds.) (effective 2012). **Document type:** *Journal, Academic/Scholarly.*
Formerly: Yu-byeon-hag (1226-119X)
Related titles: Online - full text ed.: ISSN 2093-7660.
Indexed: CCI, MSCI, SCI, SCOPUS, W07.
—**CCC.**
Published by: Korean Society of Rheology/Han-gug Yubyeon Haghoe, Sue 806, The Korea Science and Technology Center, 635-4 Yeoksam-dong, Kangnam-gu, Seoul, 135-703, Korea, S. TEL 82-2-34525117, FAX 82-2-34525119, ksr@ksr.or.kr. Eds. Hyungsu Kim, Ravi P Jagadeeshan. **Dist. outside of Australia & Korea by:** Springer, Haber Str 7, Heidelberg 69126, Germany. TEL 49-6221-3454303, FAX 49-6221-3454229, subscriptions@springer.com. **Co-publisher:** Springer. **Co-sponsor:** Australian Society of Rheology.

530 KOR ISSN 0374-4884
QC1 CODEN: JKPSDV

➤ **KOREAN PHYSICAL SOCIETY. JOURNAL.** Text in English. 1968. m. membership. 120 p./no.; back issues avail.; reprints avail. **Document type:** *Journal, Academic/Scholarly.* **Description:** Contains original papers in experimental and theoretical physics.
Indexed: A22, CurCont, GeoRef, INIS AtomInd, ISR, Inspec, P30, SCI, SCOPUS, W07.
—BLDSC (4812.342000), IE, Ingenta, INIST, Linda Hall.
Published by: Han'guk Mulli Hakhoe/Korean Physical Society, Kangnam-Gu, Yuksam-Dong 635-4, Seoul, 135703, Korea, S. TEL 82-2-5564737, FAX 82-2-5541643. Ed. Uhm Jung-In. Pub. Song Hee-Sung. Circ: 1,000 (paid); 200 (controlled).

530 RUS

KOSMICHESKII VEK. Text in Russian. 1993. q. RUR 2,125 domestic; USD 85 foreign (effective 2001). bk.rev.
Address: Ul Butyrskaya 6, kv 166, Moscow, 125015, Russian Federation. TEL 7-095-2852871, FAX 7-095-2175224. Ed. A V Myagchenkov. **Dist. by:** East View Information Services, 10601 Wayzata Blvd, Minneapolis, MN 55305. TEL 952-252-1201, 800-477-1005, FAX 952-252-1202, info@eastview.com, http://www.eastview.com.

539 SWE ISSN 0368-6213
Q9 CODEN: KMOSAE

KOSMOS. Text in Swedish. 1921. a. SEK 190 (effective 2004).
Indexed: INIS AtomInd.
Published by: (Svenska Fysikersamfundet), Swedish Science Press, PO Box 118, Uppsala, 75104, Sweden. TEL 46-18-365566, FAX 46-18-365277, info@ssp.nu, http://www.swedsciencepress.se. Ed. Leif Karlsson.

530 510.71 HUN ISSN 1215-9247
QA11.A1

➤ **KOZEPISKOLAI MATEMATIKAI ES FIZIKAI LAPOK.** Text in Hungarian. 1894. 9/yr. HUF 1,890; USD 35 foreign (effective 2000). adv. bk.rev. abstr.; illus. back issues avail. **Document type:** *Academic/Scholarly.* **Description:** Includes articles concerning problems in mathematics and physics for high school students and teachers.
Formerly (until 1991): Kozepiskolai Matematikai Lapok (0133-1833); Supersedes (1925-1939): Kozepiskolai Matematikai es Fizikai Lapok (0200-9188); (1894-1914): Kozepiskolai Matematikai Lapok (0200-917X)
Related titles: CD-ROM ed.; Online - full text ed.
—Linda Hall.
Published by: R. Eotvoes Physical Society, Fo utca 68, II emelet 241, Budapest, 1027, Hungary. TEL 36-1-201-8682, FAX 36-1-2018682. Ed., Adv. contact Vera Ola'h. Pub. Adam Kovach. B&W page HUF 60,000. Circ: 5,000. **Dist. by:** Roland Eotvoes Physical, Hungary.

➤ **KUMAMOTO JOURNAL OF MATHEMATICS.** *see* MATHEMATICS

530 JPN ISSN 0303-4070
QC1 CODEN: PRKUBN

KUMAMOTO UNIVERSITY. DEPARTMENT OF PHYSICS. PHYSICS REPORTS. Text in English. 1973. biennial. free. **Document type:** *Report, Academic/Scholarly.* **Description:** Presents technical research reports in physics from the university.
Indexed: CCMJ, ChemAb, ChemTitl, GeoRef, MSN, MathR, SpeleolAb.
—CASDDS, INIST, Linda Hall.
Published by: Kumamoto Daigaku, Rigakubu Butsuri Kyoshitsu/Kumamoto University, Faculty of Science, Department of Physics, 39-1 Kurokami 2-chome, Kumamoto-shi, 860-0862, Japan. TEL 81-96-342-3351, FAX 81-96-342-3351. Circ: 400.

530 520 550 DNK ISSN 0905-8893
QC1 CODEN: KVANEU

➤ **KVANT**; tidsskrift for fysik og astronomi. Text in Danish. 1902. 4/yr. DKK 165 (effective 2008). adv. bk.rev. bibl. cum.index: vols.1-75. 42 p./no. 2 cols./p.; back issues avail. **Document type:** *Magazine, Academic/Scholarly.* **Description:** Contains articles on progress in physics, astrophysics, geophysics, earth system science, and climate.
Formerly (until 1990): Fysisk Tidsskrift (0016-3392)
Related titles: Online - full text ed.
Indexed: ChemAb, Inspec.
—AskIEEE, CASDDS, Linda Hall.
Published by: Dansk Fysisk Selskab, c/o Joergen Schou, D T U Fotonik, Risoe Campus, Roskilde, 4000, Denmark. TEL 45-46-774755, FAX 45-46-774765, dfs@nbi.dk, http://dfs.nbi.dk. Ed., Adv. contact Michael Cramer Andersen TEL 45-22-672642. B&W page DKK 3,000; 21 x 29.5. Circ: 2,500. **Co-sponsors:** Dansk Geofysisk Forening; Astronomisk Selskab i Danmark/Astronomical Society in Denmark; Selskabet for Naturlaerens Udbredelse.

➤ **KVANTOVAYA ELEKTRONIKA (KYIV).** *see* ENGINEERING—Electrical Engineering

530 UKR ISSN 1728-2411
QC47.U383

➤ **KYIVS'KYI NATSIONAL'NYI UNIVERSYTET IMENI TARASA SHEVCHENKA. VISNYK. FIZYKA.** Text in Ukrainian. 1961. s-a. **Document type:** *Journal, Academic/Scholarly.* **Description:** Publishes results of experimental and theoretical investigations in the fields of physics of metals, optics, molecular physics and thermophysics, nuclear physics.
Former titles (until 1999): Kievskii Universitet. Vestnik. Fizika (0259-6482); (until 1977): Kyivs'kyi Universytet. Visnyk. Fizyka (0372-607X); Which superseded in part (in 1967): Kyivs'kyi Universytet. Visnyk. Seriya Fizyky ta Khimii (1563-1729); Which superseded in part (in 1962): Kyivs'kyi Universytet. Visnyk. Seriya Astronomii, Fizyky ta Khimii (1563-1710)
Related titles: ◆ Series: Kyivs'kyi Natsional'nyi Universytet imeni Tarasa Shevchenka. Visnyk. ISSN 1728-3817; ◆ Kyivs'kyi Natsional'nyi Universytet imeni Tarasa Shevchenka. Visnyk. Mizhnarodni Vidnosyny. ISSN 1728-2292; ◆ Kyivs'kyi Natsional'nyi Universytet imeni Tarasa Shevchenka. Visnyk. Yurydychni Nauky. ISSN 1728-2195; ◆ Kyivs'kyi Natsional'nyi Universytet imeni Tarasa Shevchenka. Visnyk. Khimiya. ISSN 1728-2209; ◆ Kyivs'kyi Natsional'nyi Universytet imeni Tarasa Shevchenka. Visnyk. Biolohiya. ISSN 1728-2748; ◆ Kyivs'kyi Natsional'nyi Universytet imeni Tarasa Shevchenka. Visnyk. Ekonomika. ISSN 1728-2667; ◆ Kyivs'kyi Natsional'nyi Universytet imeni Tarasa Shevchenka. Visnyk. Istoriya. ISSN 1728-2640; ◆ Kyivs'kyi Natsional'nyi Universytet imeni Tarasa Shevchenka. Visnyk. Kibernetyka. ISSN 1728-2276; ◆ Kyivs'kyi Natsional'nyi Universytet imeni Tarasa Shevchenka. Visnyk. Problemy Rehulyatsii Fiziolohichnyh Funktsii. ISSN 1728-2624; ◆ Kyivs'kyi Natsional'nyi Universytet imeni Tarasa Shevchenka. Visnyk. Radiofizyka ta Elektronika. ISSN 1728-2306; ◆ Kyivs'kyi Natsional'nyi Universytet imeni Tarasa Shevchenka. Visnyk. Filosofiya, Politolohiya. ISSN 1728-2632; ◆ Kyivs'kyi Natsional'nyi Universytet imeni Tarasa Shevchenka. Visnyk. Introduktsiya ta Zberezhennya Roslynnogo Riznomanittya. ISSN 1728-2284; ◆ Kyivs'kyi Natsional'nyi Universytet imeni Tarasa Shevchenka. Visnyk. Ukrainoznavstvo. ISSN 1728-2330; ◆ Kyivs'kyi Natsional'nyi Universytet imeni Tarasa Shevchenka. Visnyk. Sotsiolohiya, Psykholohiya, Pedahohika. ISSN 1728-2322; ◆ Kyivs'kyi Natsional'nyi Universytet imeni Tarasa Shevchenka. Visnyk. Literaturoznavstvo, Movoznavstvo, Fol'klorystyka. ISSN 1728-2659; ◆ Kyivs'kyi Natsional'nyi Universytet imeni Tarasa Shevchenka. Visnyk. Astronomiya. ISSN 1728-273X; ◆ Kyivs'kyi Natsional'nyi Universytet imeni Tarasa Shevchenka. Visnyk. Seriya: Fizyko-Matematychni Nauky. ISSN 1812-5409; ◆ Kyivs'kyi Natsional'nyi Universytet imeni Tarasa Shevchenka. Visnyk. Heohrafiya. ISSN 1728-2721; ◆ Kyivs'kyi Natsional'nyi Universytet imeni Tarasa Shevchenka. Visnyk. Heolohiya. ISSN 1728-2713; ◆ Kyivs'kyi Natsional'nyi Universytet imeni Tarasa Shevchenka. Visnyk. Zhurnalistyka. ISSN 1728-2705; ◆ Kyivs'kyi Natsional'nyi Universytet imeni Tarasa Shevchenka. Visnyk. Inozemna Filolohiya. ISSN 1728-2683; ◆ Kyivs'kyi Natsional'nyi Universytet imeni Tarasa Shevchenka. Visnyk. Shidni Movy ta Literatury. ISSN 1728-242X; ◆ Kyivs'kyi Natsional'nyi Universytet imeni Tarasa Shevchenka. Visnyk. Matematyka ta Mekhanika. ISSN 1684-1565.
—Linda Hall.
Published by: (Kyivs'kyi Natsional'nyi Universytet imeni Tarasa Shevchenka, Fizychnyi Fakul'tet/Taras Shevchenko National University of Kyiv, Faculty of Physics), Vydavnycho-Polihrafichnyi Tsentr Kyivs'kyi Universytet, bul'var Tarasa Shevchenko, 14, ofis 43, Kyiv, 01601, Ukraine. TEL 380-44-2393172. Ed. Leonid A Bulavin.

530 510 UKR ISSN 1812-5409
QC1

➤ **KYIVS'KYI NATSIONAL'NYI UNIVERSYTET IMENI TARASA SHEVCHENKA. VISNYK. SERIYA: FIZYKO-MATEMATYCHNI NAUKY.** Text in Ukrainian. 1998. q. **Document type:** *Journal, Academic/Scholarly.*
Related titles: Online - full text ed.: ISSN 2218-2055; ◆ Series: Kyivs'kyi Natsional'nyi Universytet imeni Tarasa Shevchenka. Visnyk. Matematyka ta Mekhanika. ISSN 1684-1565; ◆ Kyivs'kyi Natsional'nyi Universytet imeni Tarasa Shevchenka. Visnyk. Yurydychni Nauky. ISSN 1728-2195; ◆ Kyivs'kyi Natsional'nyi Universytet imeni Tarasa Shevchenka. Visnyk. Khimiya. ISSN 1728-2209; ◆ Kyivs'kyi Natsional'nyi Universytet imeni Tarasa Shevchenka. Visnyk. Fizyka. ISSN 1728-2411; ◆ Kyivs'kyi Natsional'nyi Universytet imeni Tarasa Shevchenka. Visnyk. Biolohiya. ISSN 1728-2748; ◆ Kyivs'kyi Natsional'nyi Universytet imeni Tarasa Shevchenka. Visnyk. Ekonomika. ISSN 1728-2667; ◆ Kyivs'kyi Natsional'nyi Universytet imeni Tarasa Shevchenka. Visnyk. Istoriya. ISSN 1728-2640; ◆ Kyivs'kyi Natsional'nyi Universytet imeni Tarasa Shevchenka. Visnyk. Kibernetyka. ISSN 1728-2276; ◆ Kyivs'kyi Natsional'nyi Universytet imeni Tarasa Shevchenka. Visnyk. Problemy Rehulyatsii Fiziolohichnyh Funktsii. ISSN 1728-2624; ◆ Kyivs'kyi Natsional'nyi Universytet imeni Tarasa Shevchenka. Visnyk. Radiofizyka ta Elektronika. ISSN 1728-2306; ◆ Kyivs'kyi Natsional'nyi Universytet imeni Tarasa Shevchenka. Visnyk. Filosofiya, Politolohiya. ISSN 1728-2632; ◆ Kyivs'kyi Natsional'nyi Universytet imeni Tarasa Shevchenka. Visnyk. Introduktsiya ta Zberezhennya Roslynnogo Riznomanittya. ISSN 1728-2284; ◆ Kyivs'kyi Natsional'nyi Universytet imeni Tarasa Shevchenka. Visnyk. Ukrainoznavstvo. ISSN 1728-2330; ◆ Kyivs'kyi Natsional'nyi Universytet imeni Tarasa Shevchenka. Visnyk. Sotsiolohiya, Psykholohiya, Pedahohika. ISSN 1728-2322; ◆ Kyivs'kyi Natsional'nyi Universytet imeni Tarasa Shevchenka. Visnyk. Literaturoznavstvo, Movoznavstvo, Fol'klorystyka. ISSN 1728-2659; ◆ Kyivs'kyi Natsional'nyi Universytet imeni Tarasa Shevchenka. Visnyk. Astronomiya. ISSN 1728-273X; ◆ Kyivs'kyi Natsional'nyi Universytet imeni Tarasa Shevchenka. Visnyk. Heohrafiya. ISSN 1728-2721; ◆ Kyivs'kyi Natsional'nyi Universytet imeni Tarasa Shevchenka. Visnyk. Heolohiya. ISSN 1728-2713; ◆ Kyivs'kyi Natsional'nyi Universytet imeni Tarasa Shevchenka. Visnyk. Zhurnalistyka. ISSN 1728-2705; ◆ Kyivs'kyi Natsional'nyi Universytet imeni Tarasa Shevchenka. Visnyk. Inozemna Filolohiya. ISSN 1728-2683; ◆ Kyivs'kyi Natsional'nyi Universytet imeni Tarasa Shevchenka. Visnyk. Shidni Movy ta Literatury. ISSN 1728-242X; ◆ Kyivs'kyi Natsional'nyi Universytet imeni Tarasa Shevchenka. Visnyk. Mizhnarodni Vidnosyny. ISSN 1728-2292; ◆ Kyivs'kyi Natsional'nyi Universytet imeni Tarasa Shevchenka. Visnyk. ISSN 1728-3817.
Published by: (Kyivs'kyi Natsional'nyi Universytet imeni Tarasa Shevchenka/National Taras Shevchenko University of Kyiv), Vydavnycho-Poligrafichnyi Tsentr Kyivs'kyi Universytet, bul'var Tarasa Shevchenko, 14, ofis 43, Kyiv, 01601, Ukraine. TEL 380-44-2393172, FAX 380-44-2393128. Ed. Anatolii Anisimov.

539 621.48 JPN ISSN 0917-1746
QD450 CODEN: KDGHEI

KYOTO DAIGAKU GENSHIRO JIKKENSHO GAKUJUTSU KOENKAI HOUBUNSHU/KYOTO UNIVERSITY. RESEARCH REACTOR INSTITUTE. PROCEEDINGS OF THE SCIENTIFIC MEETING. Text in Japanese; Summaries in English. 1967. a. free. **Document type:** *Proceedings, Academic/Scholarly.* **Description:** Includes proceedings from general lectures as well as those from special projects such as the KURRI project.
Indexed: CIN, ChemAb, ChemTitl, INIS AtomInd.
—BLDSC (6849.039000), CASDDS.
Published by: Kyoto Daigaku, Genshiro Jikkensho Gakujutsu Kokai Iinkai, Sennani-gun, Kumatori-cho, Osaka 590-0494, Japan. Circ: 500.

530.1 JPN ISSN 1345-0700
QC173.96

KYOTO UNIVERSITY. FACULTY OF ENGINEERING. QUANTUM SCIENCE AND ENGINEERING CENTER. ANNUAL REPORT. Text in English. 1999. a.
Indexed: INIS AtomInd.
Published by: Kyoto University, Faculty of Engineering, Quantum Science and Engineering Center, Gokasho, Uji, Kyoto, 611-0011, Japan.

530.44 JPN

KYOTO UNIVERSITY. PLASMA PHYSICS LABORATORY. ANNUAL REVIEW. Text in English. 1978. a.
Published by: Kyoto University, Plasma Physics Laboratory, Gokasho, Uji-shi, Kyoto-Fu 611-0011, Japan.

530.44 JPN

KYOTO UNIVERSITY. PLASMA PHYSICS LABORATORY. RESEARCH REPORT. Text in English. irreg.
Published by: Kyoto University, Plasma Physics Laboratory, Gokasho, Uji-shi, Kyoto-Fu 611-0011, Japan.

530 370 MEX ISSN 1870-9095
QC30

➤ **LATIN - AMERICAN JOURNAL OF PHYSICS EDUCATION.** Abbreviated title: L A J P E. Text in English, Spanish, Portuguese. 2007. 3/yr. free (effective 2011). **Document type:** *Journal, Academic/Scholarly.*
Media: Online - full text.
Indexed: E03, T02.
Published by: Instituto Politecnico Nacional, Unidad Profesional Zacatenco, Del Gustavo A Madero, Mexico City, DF 07738, Mexico. TEL 52-5729-6000, FAX 52-5729-51132.

➤ **LATIN AMERICAN JOURNAL OF SOLIDS AND STRUCTURES.** *see* ENGINEERING—Civil Engineering

530 600 LVA ISSN 0868-8257
TA4 CODEN: LJPSED

➤ **LATVIJAS FIZIKAS UN TEHNISKO ZINATNU ZURNALS/LATVIAN JOURNAL OF PHYSICS AND TECHNICAL SCIENCES.** Text in Latvian. 1964. bi-m. EUR 84 to institutions (effective 2011). adv. charts; illus. index. back issues avail. **Document type:** *Journal, Academic/Scholarly.* **Description:** Covers solid state physics, nuclear physics, energetics, electrical engineering, thermophysics, gas hydrodynamics, and environmental studies (pollution, toxicology and environmental safety, waste management).
Former titles: Latvijas Zinatnu Akademijas. Fizikas un Tehnisko Zinatnu Serija; Akademiya Nauk Latviiskoi S.S.R. Izvestiya. Seriya Fizicheskikh i Tekhnicheskikh Nauk (0321-1673)
Related titles: CD-ROM ed.: 2000; Online - full text ed.: 2000. free (effective 2011).
Indexed: A01, CA, CIN, ChemAb, ChemTitl, INIS AtomInd, Inspec, RefZh, SCOPUS, T02, Z02.
—AskIEEE, CASDDS, INIST, Linda Hall. **CCC.**
Published by: Latvijas Zinatnu Akademijas, Fizikalas Energetikas Instituts/Latvian Academy of Sciences, Institute of Physical Energetics, Aizkraukles 21, Riga, 1006, Latvia. TEL 371-6-7552011, FAX 371-6-7550839, fei@edi.lv. Ed. Juris Ekmanis. Circ: 300 (paid and controlled).

530 USA ISSN 1068-3356
QC1 CODEN: BLPIEN

➤ **LEBEDEV PHYSICS INSTITUTE. BULLETIN.** Text in English. 1974. m. EUR 2,332, USD 2,821 combined subscription to institutions (print & online eds.) (effective 2012). abstr. index. back issues avail. **Document type:** *Journal, Academic/Scholarly.* **Description:** Covers all areas of theoretical and applied physics, emphasis on lasers, optics, superconductivity, and plasma physics.
Formerly (until 1992): Soviet Physics - Lebedev Institute Reports (0364-2321)
Related titles: Online - full text ed.: ISSN 1934-838X; Translation of: Kratkie Soobshcheniya po Fizike. ISSN 0455-0595.
Indexed: A22, A26, E01, E08, Inspec, PhysBer, S09, SCI, SCOPUS, W07.
—BLDSC (0409.280000), AskIEEE, East View, IE, Infotrieve, Ingenta, INIST, Linda Hall. **CCC.**
Published by: (Rossiiskaya Akademiya Nauk, Institut Fiziki im. P.N. Lebedeva/Russian Academy of Sciences, P.N. Lebedev Physics Institute RUS), Allerton Press, Inc. (Subsidiary of: Pleiades Publishing, Inc.), 18 W 27th St, New York, NY 10001. TEL 646-424-9686, FAX 646-424-9695, journals@allertonpress.com. Ed. Oleg N Krokhin.

530.1 NLD ISSN 0377-9017
QC19.2 CODEN: LMPHDY

➤ **LETTERS IN MATHEMATICAL PHYSICS**; a journal for the rapid dissemination of short contributions in the field of mathematical physics. Short title: L M P. Text in English. 1975. 12/yr. (in 4 vols., 3 nos./vol.). EUR 1,329, USD 1,395 combined subscription to institutions (print & online eds.) (effective 2012). adv. reprint service avail. from PSC. **Document type:** *Journal, Academic/Scholarly.* **Description:** Provides a vehicle for the rapid communication of short contributions and contains the letters and, occasionally, short review articles and research projects in the fields of: modern group theory and applications to physics; quantum-field theory; mathematical models for physical systems; classical, quantum and statistical mechanics; relativity and gravitation, etc.
Related titles: Microform ed.: (from PQC); Online - full text ed.: ISSN 1573-0530 (from IngentaConnect); ◆ Series: Mathematical Physics Studies. ISSN 0921-3767.

Indexed: A&AAb, A01, A03, A08, A22, A26, ASCA, B21, BibLing, CA, CCMJ, CIS, CMCI, ChemAb, CurCont, E01, IBR, IBZ, ISR, Inspec, MSN, MathR, PhysBer, RefZh, SCI, SCOPUS, T02, W07, Z02.
—BLDSC (5185.170154), AskIEEE, CASDDS, IE, Infotrieve, Ingenta, INIST, Linda Hall. **CCC.**
Published by: Springer Netherlands (Subsidiary of: Springer Science+Business Media), Van Godewijckstraat 30, Dordrecht, 3311 GX, Netherlands. TEL 31-78-6576050, FAX 31-78-6576474, http://www.springer.com. Eds. Daniel Sternheimer, Massimo Porrati, Maxim Kontsevich.

530 BEL
LEUVEN NOTES IN MATHEMATICAL AND THEORETICAL PHYSICS. SERIES A, MATHEMATICAL PHYSICS. Text in English. 1989. irreg., latest vol.9, 1998. price varies. back issues avail. **Document type:** *Monographic series, Academic/Scholarly.*
Published by: Leuven University Press, Blijde Inkomststraat 5, Leuven, 3000, Belgium. TEL 32-16-325345, FAX 32-16-325352, university.press@upers.kuleuven.ac.be, http://www.kuleuven.ac.be/upers.

530 BEL
LEUVEN NOTES IN MATHEMATICAL AND THEORETICAL PHYSICS. SERIES B, THEORETICAL PARTICLE PHYSICS. Text in English. 1990. irreg., latest vol.6, 1996. price varies. back issues avail. **Document type:** *Monographic series, Academic/Scholarly.*
Indexed: CCMJ.
Published by: Leuven University Press, Blijde Inkomststraat 5, Leuven, 3000, Belgium. TEL 32-16-325345, FAX 32-16-325352, university.press@upers.kuleuven.ac.be, http://www.kuleuven.ac.be/upers.

537.5 CHN ISSN 1007-5461
QC685 CODEN: LDXUFI
LIANGZI DIANZI XUEBAO/CHINESE JOURNAL OF QUANTUM ELECTRONICS. Text in Chinese; Abstracts in Chinese, English. 1984. bi-m. (q. until 1997). CNY 180; CNY 30 per issue (effective 2010). **Document type:** *Journal, Academic/Scholarly.*
Formerly (until 1997): Liangzi Dianzixue (1001-7577)
Related titles: Online - full text ed.
Indexed: A22, A28, APA, BrCerAb, C&ISA, CA/WCA, CIA, CerAb, CivEngAb, CorrAb, E&CAJ, E11, EEA, EMA, ESPM, EnvEAb, H15, Inspec, M&TEA, M09, MBF, METADEX, RefZh, SolStAb, T04, WAA.
—BLDSC (3180.615000), East View, IE, Ingenta, Linda Hall.
Published by: (Zhongguo Guangxue Xuehui, Jichu Guangxue Zhuanye Weiyuanhui), Kexue Chubanshe/Science Press, 16 Donghuang Cheng Genbei Jie, Beijing, 100717, China. TEL 86-10-64000246, FAX 86-10-64030255. Ed. Zhiben Gong.

530 CHN ISSN 1007-6654
QC446.15
LIANGZI GUANGXUE XUEBAO/ACTA SINICA QUANTUM OPTICA. Text in English. 1995. q. USD 12 (effective 2009). **Document type:** *Journal, Academic/Scholarly.*
Related titles: Online - full content ed.; Online - full text ed.
Indexed: RefZh.
Published by: Shanxi Daxue, Guangdian Yanjiusuo/Shanxi University, College of physics & Electronics Engineering, Taiyuan, 030006, China. TEL 86-351-7010688, FAX 86-351-7011500.

LICHTENBERG-JAHRBUCH. *see* BIOGRAPHY

530 LTU ISSN 1648-8504
QC1 CODEN: LFRMA7
➤ **LITHUANIAN JOURNAL OF PHYSICS.** Text in English, Russian; Summaries in English, Lithuanian, Russian. 1961. bi-m. EUR 150 foreign (effective 2011). bibl.; charts; illus. **Document type:** *Journal, Academic/Scholarly.* **Description:** Deals with semiconductor physics, spectroscopy and laser radiation.
Former titles (until 2000): Lietuvos Fizikos Zhurnalas (1392-1932); (until 1993): Litovskii Fizicheskii Sbornik (0024-2969)
Related titles: Online - full text ed.
Indexed: A28, APA, BrCerAb, C&ISA, CA/WCA, CIA, CIN, CerAb, ChemAb, ChemTitl, CivEngAb, CorrAb, E&CAJ, E11, EEA, EMA, H15, Inspec, M&TEA, M09, MBF, METADEX, SCI, SCOPUS, SolStAb, T04, W07, WAA.
—BLDSC (5277.430000), AskIEEE, CASDDS, INIST, Linda Hall. **CCC.**
Published by: (Lietuvos Fiziku Draugija/Lithuanian Physical Society), Lietuvos Mokslu Akademijos Leidykla/Lithuanian Academy of Sciences Publishers, Gedimino pr 3, Vilnius, 2600, Lithuania. TEL 370-2-2626851, FAX 370-2-2613620, leidykla@lma.lt, http://www.lmaleidykla.lt. Ed. Evaldas Tornau. Circ: 600.

530 DEU ISSN 1433-8351
QC173.5
➤ **LIVING REVIEWS IN RELATIVITY.** Text in English. 1998 (Jan). irreg. free (effective 2011). bk.rev. back issues avail. **Document type:** *Journal, Academic/Scholarly.* **Description:** Specializes in publishing and maintaining current reviews of research in all areas of relativity. It is offered as a free service to the scientific community.
Media: Online - full text.
Indexed: A01, A03, CA, CCMJ, CurCont, Inspec, MSN, MathR, SCI, SCOPUS, T02, W07, Z02.
Published by: Max-Planck-Institut fuer Gravitationsphysik, Am Muehlenberg 1, Potsdam, 14476, Germany. TEL 49-331-56770, FAX 49-331-5677298, webteam@aei.mpg.de, http://www.aei.mpg.de. Ed. Bernard Schutz.

➤ **LIVING REVIEWS IN SOLAR PHYSICS.** *see* ASTRONOMY

530 510 USA ISSN 2150-8895
R838.5
▼ **M C A T PHYSICS AND MATH REVIEW.** (Medical College Admission Test) Text in English. 2010 (Jul.). biennial. USD 45 per issue (effective 2011). **Document type:** *Monographic series, Academic/Scholarly.* **Description:** Presents study guides and questions for the math and physics sections of the MCAT.
Published by: Princeton Review Publishing, L.L.C. (Subsidiary of: Random House Inc.), 1745 Broadway, New York, NY 10019. TEL 212-782-9000, 800-733-3000, princetonreview@randomhouse.com.

M R S BULLETIN. *see* ENGINEERING—Engineering Mechanics And Materials

620 USA ISSN 1946-4274
M R S ONLINE PROCEEDINGS. Variant title: M R S Online Proceedings Library. Text in English. 1980. irreg. (approx. 50/yr.). GBP 4,305, USD 6,455 to institutions (effective 2012). **Document type:** *Monographic series, Academic/Scholarly.* **Description:** Features over 65,000 peer-reviewed papers presented at Materials Research Society Meetings.
Media: Online - full text. **Related titles:** ◆ Print ed.: Materials Research Society Symposium Proceedings. ISSN 0272-9172.
—CCC.
Published by: (Materials Research Society), Cambridge University Press, 32 Ave of the Americas, New York, NY 10013. TEL 212-337-5000, FAX 212-691-3239, information@cambridge.org, http://us.cambridge.org.

MAGNETIC RESONANCE IN MEDICINE. *see* MEDICAL SCIENCES—Radiology And Nuclear Medicine

538 USA ISSN 1938-0828
➤ **MAGNETICS BUSINESS & TECHNOLOGY E-REPORT.** Text in English. 2004. m. free (effective 2011). back issues avail. **Document type:** *Newsletter, Trade.* **Description:** Covers product, company and industry news in the magnetics market.
Media: Online - full text.
Published by: Webcom Communications Corp., 7355 E Orchard Rd, Ste 100, Greenwood Village, CO 80111. TEL 720-528-3770, 800-803-9488, FAX 720-528-3771, http://www.infowebcom.com. Ed., Pub. David Webster.

530 JPN ISSN 0285-0192
QC750 CODEN: NOJGD3
MAGNETICS SOCIETY OF JAPAN. JOURNAL/NIHON OYO JIKI GAKKAISHI. Text in English. 1977. 7/yr. (12/yr. until 2005; issue no.6 has pt.1 & 2.). JPY 2,000 per issue. **Document type:** *Journal, Academic/Scholarly.*
Incorporates (2001-2005): Magnetics Society of Japan. Transactions (1346-7948)
Related titles: Online - full text ed.: ISSN 1880-4004; ◆ Supplement(s): Magnetics Society of Japan. Journal. Supplement. ISSN 1341-7290.
Indexed: A22, ChemAb, INIS AtomInd, Inspec.
—BLDSC (4819.180000), CASDDS, IE, Ingenta, INIST. **CCC.**
Published by: Magnetics Society of Japan/Nihon Oyo Jiki Gakkai, Mitsui Sumitomo Kaijo Surugadai Bldg 6F, 3-11, Kanda Surugadai, Chiyoda-ku, Tokyo, 101-0062, Japan. TEL 81-3-52810106, FAX 81-3-52810107, msj@bj.wakwak.com, http://wwwsoc.nii.ac.jp/msj2/.

530 JPN ISSN 1341-7290
MAGNETICS SOCIETY OF JAPAN. JOURNAL. SUPPLEMENT. Text in English. 1987. irreg. **Document type:** *Monographic series.*
Related titles: ◆ Supplement to: Magnetics Society of Japan. Journal. ISSN 0285-0192.
Published by: Magnetics Society of Japan/Nihon Oyo Jiki Gakkai, Mitsui Sumitomo Kaijo Surugadai Bldg 6F, 3-11, Kanda Surugadai, Chiyoda-ku, Tokyo, 101-0062, Japan. TEL 81-3-52810106, FAX 81-3-52810107, msj@bj.wakwak.com, http://wwwsoc.nii.ac.jp/msj2/.

530 JPN ISSN 1880-7208
QC750
MAGUNE/MAGNETICS JAPAN. Text in Japanese. 2006. m. **Document type:** *Journal, Academic/Scholarly.*
Supersedes in part (in 2006): Nihon Oyo Jiki Gakkaishi/Magnetic Society of Japan. Journal (0285-0192); Which incorporated (2001-2005): Magnetics Society of Japan. Transactions (1346-7948)
Indexed: RefZh.
—BLDSC (5340.217060).
Published by: Magnetics Society of Japan/Nihon Oyo Jiki Gakkai, Mitsui Sumitomo Kaijo Surugadai Bldg 6F, 3-11, Kanda Surugadai, Chiyoda-ku, Tokyo, 101-0062, Japan. TEL 81-3-52810106, FAX 81-3-52810107, msj@bj.wakwak.com, http://wwwsoc.nii.ac.jp/msj2/.

530.071 IRN ISSN 0254-9611
QC1
MAJALLAH-I FIZIK/IRANIAN JOURNAL OF PHYSICS. Text in Persian, Modern; Contents page in English. 1983. q. IRR 16,000 domestic; GBP 24 in the Middle East; GBP 26 in Europe; GBP 31 elsewhere (effective 2001). bk.rev. **Document type:** *Journal, Academic/Scholarly.* **Description:** Aims to maintain personal communication among Farsi speaking physicists. Deals with educational and cultural aspects of physics. Reports on the most recent developments in fundamental and applied physics.
Published by: Markaz-i Nashr-i Danishgahi/Iran University Press, 85 Park Ave., P O Box 15875-4748, Tehran, Iran. TEL 98-21-8713232, FAX 98-21-8725954, TELEX 213636-8-D5300, pobox@iup-ir.com. Ed. R Mansouri. Circ: 4,000.

530 SGP ISSN 1793-1487
MAJOR AMERICAN UNIVERSITIES PHD QUALIFYING QUESTIONS AND SOLUTIONS. PHYSICS. Text in English. 1990. irreg., latest 2000. price varies. back issues avail. **Document type:** *Monographic series, Academic/Scholarly.*
Published by: World Scientific Publishing Co. Pte. Ltd., 5 Toh Tuck Link, Singapore, 596224, Singapore. TEL 65-6466-5775, FAX 65-6467-7667, wspc@wspc.com.sg, http://www.worldscientific.com. **Dist. by:** World Scientific Publishing Ltd., 57 Shelton St, London WC2H 9HE, United Kingdom. TEL 44-207-8360888, FAX 44-207-8362020, sales@wspc.co.uk; World Scientific Publishing Co., Inc., 27 Warren St, Ste 401-402, Hackensack, NJ 07601. TEL 201-487-9655, 800-227-7562, FAX 201-487-9656, 888-977-2665, wspc@wspc.com.

530 550 MYS ISSN 1394-3065
Q1 CODEN: MJSBFN
MALAYSIAN JOURNAL OF SCIENCE. SERIES B: PHYSICAL & EARTH SCIENCES. Text in English. 1972. 2/yr. **Document type:** *Journal, Academic/Scholarly.* **Description:** Covers original research, communications and reviews in the fields of physical and earth sciences.
Supersedes in part (in 1995): Malaysian Journal of Science (0126-7906)
Indexed: A34, A35, A36, A37, A38, ASFA, AgBio, AgrForAb, B21, BA, BP, C25, C30, CABA, CIN, ChemAb, ChemTitl, D01, E12, ESPM, F08, F11, F12, FCA, G11, GH, H16, H17, I11, INIS AtomInd, IndVet, N02, N03, N04, O01, OR, P32, P33, P40, PGegResA, PGrRegA, PHN&I, R07, R08, R11, R12, R13, RA&MP, RM&VM, S12, S13, S16, S17, SCOPUS, SWRA, SoyAb, T05, TAR, VS, W10.
—CASDDS, Linda Hall.
Published by: (University of Malaya, Faculty of Science), University of Malaya/Perpustakaan Universiti Malaya, Lembah Pantai, Kuala Lumpur, 59100, Malaysia. http://www.um.edu.my. Ed. Dr. Yong Hoi Sen.

530 GBR ISSN 0953-3206
MALVERN PHYSICS SERIES. Text in English. 1986. irreg., latest 2000. price varies. back issues avail. **Document type:** *Monographic series, Academic/Scholarly.*
Indexed: Inspec.
Published by: Routledge (Subsidiary of: Taylor & Francis Group), 4 Park Sq, Milton Park, Abingdon, Oxon OX14 4RN, United Kingdom. TEL 44-20-7017-6000, FAX 44-20-7017-6336, subscriptions@tandf.co.uk.

530 520 USA
MASTER'S SERIES IN PHYSICS AND ASTRONOMY. Text in English. 200?. irreg. **Document type:** *Monographic series, Academic/Scholarly.* **Description:** Features monographs on topics in physics and astronomy.
Related titles: Online - full text ed.: ISSN 2154-8803.
Published by: C R C Press, LLC (Subsidiary of: Taylor & Francis Group), 6000 Broken Sound Pky, NW, Ste 300, Boca Raton, FL 33487. TEL 561-994-0555, FAX 561-989-9732, journals@crcpress.com, http://www.crcpress.com.

MATEMATIKA, FYZIKA, INFORMATIKA; casopis pro zakladni a stredni skoly. *see* EDUCATION

530 RUS ISSN 0130-3678
MATERIALOVEDENIE. Text in Russian. 1974. irreg.
Published by: Voronezhskii Gosudarstvennyi Tekhnicheskii Universitet/ Voronezh State Technical University, 14, Moskovskii Prospekt, Voronezh, 394026, Russian Federation.

530 NLD ISSN 0167-577X
TA401 CODEN: MLETDJ
➤ **MATERIALS LETTERS.** Text in English. 1982. 30/yr. EUR 3,323 in Europe to institutions; JPY 441,100 in Japan to institutions; USD 3,738 elsewhere to institutions (effective 2012). back issues avail. **Document type:** *Journal, Academic/Scholarly.* **Description:** Covers the spectrum of materials science, from solid-state physics to materials technology.
Related titles: Microform ed.: (from PQC); Online - full text ed.: ISSN 1873-4979 (from IngentaConnect, ScienceDirect).
Indexed: A01, A03, A08, A20, A22, A26, A28, APA, ASCA, B21, BrCerAb, C&ISA, C24, C33, CA, CA/WCA, CCI, CIA, CIN, CPEI, CerAb, ChemAb, ChemTitl, CivEngAb, CorrAb, CurCont, E&CAJ, E11, EEA, EMA, ESPM, EngInd, EnvEAb, FR, GeoRef, H15, I05, I10, ISMEC, ISR, Inspec, M&TEA, M09, MBF, METADEX, MSCI, P30, PhysBer, RefZh, S01, SCI, SCOPUS, SolStAb, SpeleolAb, T02, T04, W07, WAA.
—BLDSC (5396.002000), AskIEEE, CASDDS, IE, Infotrieve, Ingenta, INIST, Linda Hall. **CCC.**
Published by: (Materials Research Society), Elsevier BV (Subsidiary of: Elsevier Science & Technology), Radarweg 29, PO Box 211, Amsterdam, 1000 AE, Netherlands. TEL 31-20-4853911, FAX 31-20-4852457, JournalsCustomerServiceEMEA@elsevier.com. Eds. G L Messing, J Hojo, L S Shvindlerman. **Subscr. to:** Radarweg 29, PO Box 211, Amsterdam 1000 AE, Netherlands. TEL 31-20-4853757, FAX 31-20-4853432.

530 540 620 USA ISSN 0272-9172
CODEN: MRSPDH
MATERIALS RESEARCH SOCIETY SYMPOSIUM PROCEEDINGS. Text in English. 1980. irreg. (approx. 50/yr.). free to members (effective 2009). reprints avail. **Document type:** *Proceedings, Academic/Scholarly.*
Related titles: ◆ Online - full text ed.: M R S Online Proceedings. ISSN 1946-4274.
Indexed: A22, A28, APA, BrCerAb, C&ISA, C13, C33, CA/WCA, CCMJ, CIA, CIN, CerAb, ChemAb, ChemTitl, CivEngAb, CorrAb, E&CAJ, E11, EEA, EMA, ESPM, EngInd, EnvEAb, GeoRef, H15, INIS AtomInd, ISMEC, Inspec, M&TEA, M09, MBF, METADEX, P30, PhysBer, SCOPUS, SolStAb, SpeleolAb, T04, TM, WAA.
—BLDSC (5396.412000), CASDDS, IE, Infotrieve, Ingenta, INIST. **CCC.**
Published by: Materials Research Society, 506 Keystone Dr, Warrendale, PA 15086. TEL 724-779-3003, FAX 724-779-8313, info@mrs.org, http://www.mrs.org/publications/books.

MATERIALS SCIENCE AND ENGINEERING R: REPORTS. *see* ENGINEERING—Engineering Mechanics And Materials

530 541 CHE ISSN 0255-5476
TA401.3 CODEN: MSFOEP
➤ **MATERIALS SCIENCE FORUM.** Text in English. 1973. 30/yr. EUR 2,340 (effective 2004). **Document type:** *Journal, Academic/Scholarly.* **Description:** Deals with materials science topics.
Formerly (until 1984): Diffusion and Defect Monograph Series (0250-9776); Incorporates (1975-1992): Crystal Properties and Preparation (1013-5049); Which was formerly (until 1986): Mechanical and Corrosion Properties. Series B. Single Crystal Properties (0252-1067); Which superseded in part (in 1982): Mechanical and Corrosion Properties (0250-9784); Which was formerly (until 1979): Mechanical Properties (0361-2821)
Related titles: Supplement(s): Journal of Metastable and Nanocrystalline Materials. ISSN 1422-6375. 1999.
Indexed: A22, A28, APA, B&BAb, B19, BrCerAb, C&ISA, C13, CA/WCA, CIA, CerAb, ChemAb, ChemTitl, CivEngAb, CorrAb, E&CAJ, E11, EEA, EMA, ESPM, EngInd, EnvEAb, GeoRef, H15, INIS AtomInd, Inspec, M&TEA, M09, MBF, METADEX, RefZh, SCOPUS, SolStAb, SpeleolAb, T04, TM, WAA.
—BLDSC (5396.435700), AskIEEE, CASDDS, IE, Ingenta, INIST, Linda Hall. **CCC.**
Published by: Trans Tech Publications Ltd., Laubisrutistr 24, Stafa-Zurich, 8712, Switzerland. TEL 41-1-9221022, FAX 41-1-9221033, info@ttp.net, http://www.ttp.ch. Eds. Fred H Wohlbier, Graeme Murch, Yiu-Wing Mai. Circ: 800 (paid and controlled).

530 CZE ISSN 1211-5894
QD901
➤ **MATERIALS STRUCTURE IN CHEMISTRY, BIOLOGY, PHYSICS AND TECHNOLOGY.** Text in English, Czech, Slovak. 1984. q. **Document type:** *Journal, Academic/Scholarly.*
Formerly (until 1994): Materials Science in Chemistry, Biology, Physics and Technology. Bulletin (1210-8529)
Related titles: Online - full text ed.: free (effective 2011).

Published by: Kristalograficka Spolecnost/Czech and Slovak Crystallographic Association, Heyrovskeho 2, Prague, 162 06, Czech Republic. Ed. Radovan Cerny.

510 530 NLD ISSN 1385-0172
QC19.2 CODEN: MPAGFO

➤ **MATHEMATICAL PHYSICS, ANALYSIS AND GEOMETRY.** Text in English. 1997. q. EUR 397, USD 416 combined subscription to institutions (print & online eds.) (effective 2012). adv. reprint service avail. from PSC. **Document type:** *Journal, Academic/Scholarly.* **Description:** Publishs papers presenting new mathematical results in mathematical physics, and geometry with particular reference to: mathematical problems of statistical phyics, fluids, etc.; complex function theory; operators in function space, especically operator algebras; ordinary and partial differential equations; differential and algebraic geometry.
Related titles: Online - full text ed.: ISSN 1572-9656 (from IngentaConnect).
Indexed: A22, A26, BibLing, CA, CCMJ, CMCI, E01, Inspec, MSN, MathR, RefZh, SCI, SCOPUS, T02, W07, Z01.
—BLDSC (5402.576300), IE, Infotrieve, Ingenta. **CCC.**
Published by: Springer Netherlands (Subsidiary of: Springer Science+Business Media), Van Godewijckstraat 30, Dordrecht, 3311 GX, Netherlands. TEL 31-78-6576050, FAX 31-78-6576474, http://www.springer.com. Eds. Alexander Its, Anne Boutet de Monvel, Henry McKean.

➤ **MATHEMATICAL PHYSICS AND APPLIED MATHEMATICS.** *see* MATHEMATICS

➤ **MATHEMATICAL PHYSICS ELECTRONIC JOURNAL.** *see* MATHEMATICS

530 510 NLD ISSN 0921-3767
QC20

➤ **MATHEMATICAL PHYSICS STUDIES.** Text in English. 1977. irreg., latest vol.28, 2007. price varies. **Document type:** *Monographic series, Academic/Scholarly.*
Related titles: ◆ Series of: Letters in Mathematical Physics. ISSN 0377-9017.
Indexed: A22, CCMJ, CIS, Inspec, MathR, Z02.
Published by: Springer Netherlands (Subsidiary of: Springer Science+Business Media), Van Godewijckstraat 30, Dordrecht, 3311 GX, Netherlands. TEL 31-78-6576050, FAX 31-78-6576474. Eds. Daniel Sternheimer, Massimo Porrati, Maxim Kontsevich, V B Matveev.

➤ **MATHEMATICAL PROCEEDINGS OF THE ROYAL IRISH ACADEMY.** *see* MATHEMATICS

530 GBR ISSN 1081-2865
TA405 CODEN: MMESFP

➤ **MATHEMATICS AND MECHANICS OF SOLIDS.** Abbreviated title: M M S. Text in English. 1996. 8/yr. USD 2,229, GBP 1,311 combined subscription to institutions (print & online eds.); USD 2,184, GBP 1,285 to institutions (effective 2011). adv. 112 p./no.; back issues avail.; reprint service avail. from PSC. **Document type:** *Journal, Academic/Scholarly.* **Description:** Publishes original research that elucidates the mechanical behavior of solids, with particular emphasis on mathematical principles.
Related titles: Online - full text ed.: ISSN 1741-3028. USD 2,006, GBP 1,180 to institutions (effective 2011).
Indexed: A01, A02, A03, A08, A22, A26, A28, APA, ApMecR, B07, BrCerAb, C&ISA, CA, CA/WCA, CCMJ, CIA, CMCI, CPEI, CerAb, CivEngAb, CorrAb, CurCont, E&CAJ, E01, E08, E11, EEA, EMA, ESPM, EngInd, EnvEAb, G01, G08, H04, H15, I05, Inspec, M&TEA, M09, MBF, METADEX, MSCI, MSN, MathR, P10, P26, P48, P49, P52, P53, P54, P56, PQC, S01, S09, S10, SCI, SCOPUS, SolStAb, T02, T04, V02, W07, WAA, Z02.
—BLDSC (5405.220000), AskIEEE, IE, Ingenta, INIST, Linda Hall. **CCC.**
Published by: Sage Publications Ltd. (Subsidiary of: Sage Publications, Inc.), 1 Oliver's Yard, 55 City Rd, London, EC1Y 1SP, United Kingdom. TEL 44-20-73248500, FAX 44-20-73248600, info@sagepub.co.uk, http://www.uk.sagepub.com/home.nav. Ed. David J Steigmann. adv.: B&W page GBP 400; 140 x 210. **Subscr. in the Americas to:** Sage Publications, Inc., 2455 Teller Rd, Thousand Oaks, CA 91320. TEL 805-499-9774, FAX 805-499-0871, journals@sagepub.com.

➤ **MATHEMATISCHE SEMESTERBERICHTE.** *see* MATHEMATICS

➤ **MATSUSHITA TECHNICAL JOURNAL.** *see* ENGINEERING—Electrical Engineering

➤ **MAX-PLANCK-INSTITUT FUER PHYSIK. WERNER-HEISENBERG-INSTITUT. JAHRESBERICHT.** *see* ASTRONOMY

➤ **MEASUREMENT.** *see* METROLOGY AND STANDARDIZATION

530 GBR ISSN 1368-6550

MEASUREMENT GOOD PRACTICE GUIDE. Text in English. 1997. irreg., latest vol.103, 2007. price varies. **Document type:** *Monographic series, Academic/Scholarly.*
—BLDSC (5413.563500). **CCC.**
Published by: National Physical Laboratory, Hampton Rd, Teddington, Middlesex TW11 0LW, United Kingdom. TEL 44-20-89773222, FAX 44-20-89436458, enquiry@npl.co.uk, http://www.npl.co.uk.

MEASUREMENT SCIENCE AND TECHNOLOGY. *see* INSTRUMENTS

MECHANICS AND PHYSICS OF DISCRETE SYSTEMS. *see* ENGINEERING—Mechanical Engineering

MEDICAL PHYSICS. *see* MEDICAL SCIENCES

MEDICAL SCIENCE SERIES. *see* MEDICAL SCIENCES

530 JPN ISSN 0910-0717
CODEN: MUKKDH

➤ **MEIDAI UCHUSAN KENKYUSHITSU KIJI/NAGOYA UNIVERSITY. SOLAR-TERRESTRIAL ENVIRONMENT LABORATORY. COSMIC RAY SECTION. PROCEEDINGS.** Text in Japanese. 1947. a. per issue exchange basis. adv. cum.index: 1947-2003. **Document type:** *Journal, Academic/Scholarly.*
Indexed: ChemAb, Inspec, JTA.
—AskIEEE, CASDDS.
Published by: (Cosmic Ray Section), Nagoya University, Solar-Terrestrial Environment Laboratory, Chikusa-ku, Nagoya-shi, Aichi-ken 464-8601, Japan. TEL 81-52-789-4314, FAX 81-52-789-4313. Ed., R&P, Adv. contact Yasushi Muraki.

➤ **MEISEI DAIGAKU KENKYU KIYO. RIKOGAKUBU/MEISEI UNIVERSITY. RESEARCH BULLETIN. PHYSICAL SCIENCES AND ENGINEERING.** *see* ENGINEERING

➤ **METALLOFIZIKA I NOVEISHIE TEKHNOLOGII**; an international research journal. *see* METALLURGY

➤ **METHODS OF SURFACE CHARACTERIZATION.** *see* CHEMISTRY—Electrochemistry

530 JPN

MICROPROCESS CONFERENCE. DIGEST OF PAPERS. Text in English. 1988. a.
Published by: Japan Society of Applied Physics/Oyo Butsuri Gakkai, Kudan-Kita Bldg 5th Fl, 1-12-3 Kudan-Kita, Chiyoda-ku, Tokyo, 102-0073, Japan.

MINUFIYA UNIVERSITY. SCIENTIFIC JOURNAL OF FACULTY OF SCIENCE. MATH AND PHYSICS/GAMI'AT AL-MUNUFIYYAT. KULLIYYAT AL-'ULUM. AL-MAGALLAT AL-'ILLMIYYAT. RIYADIYAT WA-FIZYA. *see* MATHEMATICS

530 MEX

MISCELANEA DE LA FISICA. Text in Spanish. 1995. q.
Related titles: Online - full text ed.
Published by: Universidad Autonoma Metropolitana - Azcapotzalco, Departamento de Humanidades, Ave. San Pablo 180, Col Reynosa Tamaulipas, Mexico, D.F., DF 02200, Mexico. TEL 52-5-53189125, FAX 52-5-53947506, cshenlinea@correo.azc.uam.mx, http://www.cshenlinea.azc.uam.mx/index.html/. Ed. Juarez H Garcia Orozco.

530 GBR ISSN 0965-0393
TA407 CODEN: MSMEEU

➤ **MODELLING AND SIMULATION IN MATERIALS SCIENCE AND ENGINEERING.** Text in English. 1992. 8/yr. GBP 623 combined subscription to institutions (print & online eds.) (effective 2010). bk.rev. Index. back issues avail. **Document type:** *Journal, Academic/Scholarly.* **Description:** Covers the whole range of methods and applications of modeling and simulation in materials science and engineering.
Related titles: Microfiche ed.: USD 773 in North America; GBP 392 elsewhere (effective 2007); Microform ed.; Online - full text ed.: ISSN 1361-651X. GBP 593 to institutions (effective 2010) (from IngentaConnect).
Indexed: A01, A03, A08, A22, A28, APA, ApMecR, BrCerAb, C&ISA, CA, CA/WCA, CIA, CIN, CIS, CMCI, CPEI, CerAb, ChemAb, ChemTitl, CivEngAb, CorrAb, CurCont, E&CAJ, E01, E11, EEA, EMA, ESPM, EngInd, EnvEAb, H15, ISR, Inspec, M&TEA, M09, MBF, METADEX, MSCI, RefZh, SCI, SCOPUS, SolStAb, T02, T04, W07, WAA.
—BLDSC (5883.531980), AskIEEE, CASDDS, IE, Infotrieve, Ingenta, Linda Hall. **CCC.**
Published by: (Institute of Physics), Institute of Physics Publishing Ltd., Dirac House, Temple Back, Bristol, BS1 6BE, United Kingdom. TEL 44-117-9297481, FAX 44-117-9301178, custserv@iop.org, http://publishing.iop.org/. Ed. W A Curtin. **Subscr. addr. in US:** American Institute of Physics, PO Box 503284, St Louis, MO 63150. FAX 516-349-9704, subs@aip.org.

530.4 NLD ISSN 0167-7837
CODEN: MPCSDY

➤ **MODERN PROBLEMS IN CONDENSED MATTER SCIENCES.** Text in English. 1982. irreg., latest vol.34, 1992. price varies. back issues avail. **Document type:** *Monographic series, Academic/Scholarly.* **Description:** Offers English-language translations from the Russian of research into the challenges that condensed matter poses.
Indexed: Inspec.
Published by: Elsevier BV, North-Holland (Subsidiary of: Elsevier Science & Technology), Sara Burgerhartstraat 25, Amsterdam, 1055 KV, Netherlands. TEL 31-20-4853911, FAX 31-20-4852457, JournalsCustomerServiceEMEA@elsevier.com, http://www.elsevier.com. Eds. A Maradudin, V M Agranovich. **Subscr. to:** Elsevier BV, Radarweg 29, PO Box 211, Amsterdam 1000 AE, Netherlands. TEL 31-20-4853757, FAX 31-20-4853432.

➤ **MOLECULAR PHYSICS**; an international journal at the interface between chemistry and physics. *see* CHEMISTRY—Physical Chemistry

530 540 GBR ISSN 0969-3386
CODEN: MPCMFI

➤ **MONOGRAPHS ON THE PHYSICS AND CHEMISTRY OF MATERIALS.** Text in English. 1948. irreg., latest 2009. price varies. **Document type:** *Monographic series, Academic/Scholarly.*
Indexed: Inspec.
—CASDDS. **CCC.**
Published by: Oxford University Press, Great Clarendon St, Oxford, OX2 6DP, United Kingdom. TEL 44-1865-556767, FAX 44-1865-556646, enquiry@oup.co.uk, http://www.oup-usa.org/catalogs/general/series/.

530 USA ISSN 0027-1349
Q4 CODEN: MUPBAC

➤ **MOSCOW UNIVERSITY PHYSICS BULLETIN.** Text in English. 1966. bi-m. EUR 2,390, USD 2,894 combined subscription to institutions (print & online eds.) (effective 2012). charts; illus.; abstr. index. back issues avail. **Document type:** *Journal, Academic/Scholarly.* **Description:** Covers all main areas of physics research, with an emphasis on new ideas and novel approaches.
Related titles: Online - full text ed.: ISSN 1934-8460; ◆ Translation of: Moskovskii Gosudarstvennyi Universitet. Vestnik. Seriya 3: Fizika i Astronomiya. ISSN 0579-9392.
Indexed: A22, A26, E01, E08, Inspec, MathR, S09, SCI, SCOPUS, W07, Z02.
—BLDSC (0416.240000), AskIEEE, East View, IE, Ingenta, INIST, Linda Hall. **CCC.**
Published by: (Moskovskii Gosudarstvennyi Universitet im. M.V. Lomonosova/M.V. Lomonosov Moscow State University RUS), Allerton Press, Inc. (Subsidiary of: Pleiades Publishing, Inc.), 18 W 27th St, New York, NY 10001. TEL 646-424-9686, FAX 646-424-9695, journals@allertonpress.com. Ed. Vladimir I Trukhin.

530 510 RUS ISSN 2072-8387

➤ **MOSKOVSKII GOSUDARSTVENNYI OBLASTNOI UNIVERSITET. VESTNIK. SERIYA FIZIKA-MATEMATIKA.** Variant title: Vestnik M G O U. Seriya Fizika-Matematika. Text in Russian; Summaries in Russian, English. 2004. q. bibl.; charts; illus.; maps. back issues avail. **Document type:** *Journal, Academic/Scholarly.* **Description:** Intended for scientists, researchers, teachers of high schools, undergraduate and post graduate students. Publishes results of scientific research in the fields of Physics and Mathematics, including dissertation research, conferences and seminars.
Related titles: Online - full text ed.
Indexed: RefZh.
Published by: Moskovskii Gosudarstvennyi Oblastnoi Universitet/ Moscow State Regional University, ul Radio, dom 10A, komn. 98, Moscow, Russian Federation. TEL 7-499-7235631, FAX 7-499-2614341, http://www.mgou.ru. Ed. Anatoliy Bugrimov.

530 520 RUS ISSN 0579-9392
Q60 CODEN: VMUFAO

MOSKOVSKII GOSUDARSTVENNYI UNIVERSITET. VESTNIK. SERIYA 3: FIZIKA I ASTRONOMIYA. Text in Russian; Contents page in English. 1960. bi-m. USD 194 in North America; USD 279 combined subscription in North America (print & online eds.) (effective 2011). bk.rev. bibl. index. **Document type:** *Journal, Academic/Scholarly.*
Supersedes in part (1956-1959): Moskovskii Gosudarstvennyi Universitet. Vestnik. Seriya Matematiki, Mekhaniki, Astronomii, Fiziki, Khimii (0579-9376)
Related titles: Online - full text ed.; ◆ English Translation: Moscow University Physics Bulletin. ISSN 0027-1349.
Indexed: C&ISA, CIN, ChemAb, CorrAb, E&CAJ, GeoRef, Inspec, MathR, PhysBer, RASB, RefZh, SCOPUS, SolStAb, SpeleolAb, WAA.
—BLDSC (0032.450000), AskIEEE, CASDDS, East View, INIST, Linda Hall. **CCC.**
Published by: (Moskovskii Gosudarstvennyi Universitet im. M.V. Lomonosova, Fizicheskii Fakul'tet/M.V. Lomonosov Moscow State University, Department of Physics), Izdatel'stvo Moskovskogo Gosudarstvennogo Universiteta im. M. V. Lomonosova/Publishing House of Moscow State University, B Nikitskaya 5/7, Moscow, 103009, Russian Federation. TEL 7-095-2295091, FAX 7-095-2036671, kd_mgu@rambler.ru, http://www.msu.ru/depts/MSUPubl. Ed. Vladimir I Trukhin. **Dist. by:** East View Information Services, 10601 Wayzata Blvd, Minneapolis, MN 55305. TEL 952-252-1201, 800-477-1005, FAX 952-252-1202, info@eastview.com, http://www.eastview.com.

530 KOR ISSN 1013-7017

MULLI KYOYUK/PHYSICS TEACHING. Text in Korean. 1983. s-a. membership. **Document type:** *Academic/Scholarly.*
Indexed: Inspec.
Published by: Han'guk Mulli Hakhoe/Korean Physical Society, Kangnam-Gu, Yuksam-Dong 635-4, Seoul, 135703, Korea, S. TEL 82-2-5564737, FAX 82-2-5541643, http://www.kps.or.kr.

530 571.4 NLD ISSN 1874-6500

N A T O SCIENCE FOR PEACE AND SECURITY SERIES. B: PHYSICS AND BIOPHYSICS. (North Atlantic Treaty Organization) Text in English. 2005. irreg., latest 2008. price varies. **Document type:** *Proceedings, Academic/Scholarly.* **Description:** Covers scientific solutions to security threats arising from nuclear and conventional agents and weapons.
Formerly (until 2008): N A T O Security Through Science Series. B: Physics and Biophysics (Print) (1871-465X)
Related titles: Online - full text ed.: ISSN 1874-6535.
Indexed: CCMJ, GeoRef, MSN, MathR, SCOPUS.
—IE.
Published by: (North Atlantic Treaty Organization (N A T O) BEL), Springer Netherlands (Subsidiary of: Springer Science+Business Media), Van Godewijckstraat 30, Dordrecht, 3311 GX, Netherlands. TEL 31-78-6576050, FAX 31-78-6576474.

533.5 NLD ISSN 0169-9431
CODEN: NDVTBN

N E V A C BLAD/DUTCH VACUUM SOCIETY. JOURNAL. Text in Dutch. 1963. 4/yr. EUR 25 domestic; EUR 35 foreign (effective 2009). adv. bk.rev. charts; illus.; pat. **Document type:** *Newsletter, Academic/Scholarly.* **Description:** Studies vacuum technology and its applications.
Former titles (until 1983): Nederlandse Vacuumvereniging. Mededelingenblad (0169-9482); (until 1982): Nederlands Tijdschrift voor Vacuumtechniek - Dutch Journal of Vacuum Technology (0047-9233)
Indexed: A22, ChemAb, Inspec.
—CASDDS, IE, Infotrieve, Linda Hall.
Published by: Nederlandse Vacuumvereniging/Dutch Vacuum Society, c/o Ad Ettema, Specs Nanotechnology, Delftechpark 26, Delft, 2628 XH, Netherlands. TEL 31-15-2600406, FAX 31-15-2600405, http://www.nevac.nl. Eds. B J Kooi, G Palasantzas.

530 NLD

N I K H E F ANNUAL REPORT (ONLINE). (Nationaal Instituut voor Kernfysica en Hoge-Energiefysica) Text in Dutch. 1946. a. **Document type:** *Corporate.*
Former titles (until 1998): N I K H E F Annual Report (Print); National Instituut voor Kernfysica en Hoge-Energiefysica; Instituut voor Kernphysisch Onderzoek. Annual Report
Media: Online - full text.
Published by: Nationaal Instituut voor Subatomaire Fysica/National Institute for Subatomic Physics, Postbus 41882, Amsterdam, 1009 DB, Netherlands. TEL 31-20-5922000, FAX 31-20-5925155, info@nikhef.nl.

530 GBR ISSN 1754-2944

N P L REPORT ON O P. Text in English. 2004. irreg., latest 2009, Aug. free (effective 2009). **Document type:** *Monographic series, Academic/Scholarly.*
Formerly (until 2007): N P L Report on D Q L - O R (1744-0610)
Related titles: Online - full text ed.
—BLDSC (6180.515000).
Published by: National Physical Laboratory, Hampton Rd, Teddington, Middlesex TW11 0LW, United Kingdom. TEL 44-20-89773222, FAX 44-20-86140446, enquiry@npl.co.uk, http://www.npl.co.uk.

P

530 GBR
N P L SCIENCE REVIEW. Text in English. 1900. a. free (effective 2009). back issues avail. **Document type:** *Journal, Trade.* **Description:** Provides overviews of the quality and breadth of the work we carry out and the passion our staff have for science that makes an impact.
Former titles (until 2008): N P L Annual Review; (until 1996): N P L Annual Report; N P L News (0143-1536)
Related titles: Online - full text ed.
Indexed: A22, Inspec, WSCA.
—AskIEEE. **CCC.**
Published by: National Physical Laboratory, Hampton Rd, Teddington, Middlesex TW11 0LW, United Kingdom. TEL 44-20-89773222, FAX 44-20-86140446, enquiry@npl.co.uk.

621 531.6 DEU ISSN 2192-2543
▼ ➤ **NANO ENERGY AND NANO ENVIRONMENT.** Text in English. forthcoming 2012. q. EUR 500 to institutions; EUR 600 combined subscription to institutions (print & online eds.) (effective 2012). **Document type:** *Journal, Academic/Scholarly.*
Related titles: Online - full text ed.: ISSN 2192-2551. forthcoming 2012. EUR 500 to institutions (effective 2012).
Published by: Walter de Gruyter GmbH & Co. KG, Genthiner Str 13, Berlin, 10785, Germany. TEL 49-30-260050, FAX 49-30-26005251, info@degruyter.com, http://www.degruyter.de. Ed. L Q Wang.

530 USA
➤ **NANO-EXPRESS.** Text in English. 2003. m. **Document type:** *Magazine, Consumer.* **Description:** Devoted to providing information on technological advances, applications, and business news to nanotechnology professionals.
Related titles: Online - full text ed.: free (effective 2011).
Published by: Texas State University - San Marcos, Nanoparticles Applications Center, Department of Physics, San Marcos, TX 78666. TEL 512-245-0587, FAX 512-245-8233, spencer@txstate.edu.

530 621.3 IND ISSN 0974-7494
NANO SCIENCE & NANO TECHNOLOGY; an Indian journal. Text in English. 4/yr. INR 2,400 domestic; USD 240 foreign (effective 2011). **Document type:** *Journal, Academic/Scholarly.* **Description:** Contains fundamental research papers on all branches of the theory and practise of nano science & nano technology.
Related titles: Online - full text ed.
Published by: Trade Science, Inc., 126, Prasheel Park, SanjayRaj Farm House, Nr. Saurashtra University, Rajkot, Gujarat 360 005, India. tsijournals@tsijournals.com.

530 CHE ISSN 2079-4991
▼ ➤ **NANOMATERIALS.** Text in English. 2011. q. free (effective 2011). **Document type:** *Journal, Academic/Scholarly.*
Media: Online - full text.
Published by: M D P I AG, Postfach, Basel, 4005, Switzerland. TEL 41-61-6837734, FAX 41-61-3028918, http://www.mdpi.org/. Ed. Thomas Nann.

530 621.3 HUN ISSN 1787-4033
➤ **NANOPAGES**; interdisciplinary journal of nano science and technology. Text in English. 2005. q. (in 1 vol., 4 nos./vol.). EUR 108, USD 148 (effective 2012). 120 p./no.; **Document type:** *Journal, Academic/Scholarly.*
Related titles: Online - full text ed.: ISSN 1788-0718. free (effective 2012).
Indexed: RefZh, SCOPUS.
—BLDSC (9830.024000), IE.
Published by: (Szegedi Tudomanyegyetem, Alkalmazott es Kornyezeti Kemiai Tanszek Kemiai Tanszek/University of Szeged, Department of Applied and Environmental Chemistry), Akademiai Kiado Rt. (Subsidiary of: Wolters Kluwer N.V.), Prielle Kornelia u 19/D, Budapest, 1117, Hungary. TEL 36-1-4648222, FAX 36-1-4648221, journals@akkrt.hu, http://www.akademiai.com. Ed. Imre Kiricsi.

530 USA ISSN 1528-8528
NANOPARTICLE NEWS. Text in English. 1998. bi-w. USD 550 (effective 2005). **Document type:** *Newsletter, Trade.* **Description:** Dedicated to bringing its readers the latest news in the fine, ultrafine and nano powder industry.
Formerly: Fine Particle Technology News
Related titles: Online - full content ed.: USD 632.50 (effective 2005); Online - full text ed.: USD 4,995 (effective 2008).
Indexed: B02, B15, B17, B18, G04, G06, G07, G08.
Published by: Business Communications Co., Inc., 40 Washington St, Ste 110, Wellesley, MA 02481. TEL 781-489-7301, FAX 781-489-7308, sales@bccresearch.com, http://www.bccresearch.com. Ed. Alan Hall. Pub. Louis Naturman.

530 621.3 NLD ISSN 2210-6812
▼ **NANOSCIENCE & NANOTECHNOLOGY - ASIA.** Text in English. 2011. s-a. USD 370 to institutions (print & online ed.) (effective 2012). adv. **Document type:** *Journal, Academic/Scholarly.* **Description:** Publishes authoritative reviews and original research reports, written by experts in the field from Asia, including Japan in all the most recent advances in nanoscience and nanotechnology.
Related titles: Online - full text ed.: ISSN 2210-6820.
—CCC.
Published by: Bentham Science Publishers Ltd., PO Box 294, Bussum, 1400 AG, Netherlands. TEL 31-35-6923800, FAX 31-35-6980150, sales@bentham.org. Eds. Atta-ur Rahman TEL 92-21-34824924, Jinlong Gong. **Subscr. to:** Bentham Science Publishers Ltd., c/o Richard E Morrissy, PO Box 446, Oak Park, IL 60301. TEL 312-413-5867, FAX 312-996-7107, subscriptions@bentham.org.

▼ **NANOSCIENCE AND NANOTECHNOLOGY LETTERS.** *see* ENGINEERING—Electrical Engineering

620.5 MYS ISSN 2180-1304
▼ ➤ **NANOSCIENCES AND NANOTECHNOLOGIES.** Text in English. 2010. bi-m. MYR 3,700 domestic to individuals; USD 1,200 foreign to individuals; MYR 4,642 domestic to institutions; USD 1,500 foreign to institutions (effective 2011). bk.rev. abstr.; bibl. Index. back issues avail. **Document type:** *Journal, Academic/Scholarly.* **Description:** Publishes articles on new scientific and technological findings, reviews, current scientific research in the area relevant to nanoscience and nanotechnology.
Related titles: Online - full text ed.
Published by: Computer Science Journals, M-3-19 Plaza Damas, Sri Hartamas, Kuala Lumpur, 50480, Malaysia. Ed. Massimo Lazzari. Pub. M.N. Tahir.

620 UKR ISSN 1816-5230
QC176.8.N35
➤ **NANOSYSTEMY, NANOMATERIALY, NANOTEKHNOLOHII**; zbirnyk naukovykh prats'. Text in Ukrainian, English. 2003. q. USD 137 in United States (effective 2007). **Document type:** *Journal, Academic/Scholarly.*
Indexed: RefZh.
—BLDSC (0119.140750), Linda Hall.
Published by: Natsional'na Akademiya Nauk Ukrainy, Instytut Metalofizyky/National Academy of Sciences of the Ukraine, Institute of Metal Physics, bulvar Akad Vernadskogo 36, Kyiv, 103142, Ukraine. TEL 380-44-4241221, FAX 380-44-4242561, tatar@imp.kiev.ua, http://www.imp.kiev.ua. Adv. contact V A Tatarenko. **Dist. by:** East View Information Services, 10601 Wayzata Blvd, Minneapolis, MN 55305. TEL 952-252-1201, 800-477-1005, FAX 952-252-1202, info@eastview.com, http://www.eastview.com.

530 621.3 RUS ISSN 1995-0780
NANOTECHNOLOGIES IN RUSSIA. Text in English. 2006. 3/yr. EUR 1,534, USD 2,042 combined subscription to institutions (print & online eds.) (effective 2012). **Document type:** *Journal, Academic/Scholarly.* **Description:** Focuses on basic issues of the structure and properties of nanoscale objects and nanomaterials.
Related titles: Online - full text ed.: ISSN 1995-0799 (from IngentaConnect).
Indexed: A22, A26, CPEI, E01, E08, S09.
—East View, IE. **CCC.**
Published by: M A I K Nauka - Interperiodica (Subsidiary of: Pleiades Publishing, Inc.), Profsoyuznaya ul 90, Moscow, 117997, Russian Federation. TEL 7-095-3361600, FAX 7-095-3360666, compmg@maik.ru. Ed. Mikhail Alfimov.

530 621.3 GBR ISSN 0957-4484
T174.7 CODEN: NNOTER
➤ **NANOTECHNOLOGY.** Text in English. 1990. 50/yr. GBP 2,391 combined subscription to institutions (print & online eds.) (effective 2010). Index. back issues avail. **Document type:** *Journal, Academic/Scholarly.* **Description:** Aims to promote the dissemination of research and improve understanding among the engineering, fabrications, optics, electronics, materials science, biology, and medical communities.
Related titles: Microfiche ed.: USD 2,100 in North America; GBP 1,069 elsewhere (effective 2007); Online - full text ed.: ISSN 1361-6528. GBP 2,277 to institutions (effective 2010) (from IngentaConnect).
Indexed: A01, A03, A08, A22, A28, APA, ASCA, B&BAb, B19, B21, BioEngAb, BrCerAb, C&ISA, CA, CA/WCA, CIA, CIN, CPEI, CerAb, ChemAb, ChemTitl, CivEngAb, CorrAb, CurCont, E&CAJ, E11, EEA, EMA, EMBASE, ESPM, EngInd, EnvEAb, ExcerpMed, H15, ISMEC, ISR, Inspec, M&TEA, M09, MBF, MEDLINE, METADEX, MSCI, P30, RefZh, SCI, SCOPUS, SolStAb, T02, T04, W07, WAA.
—BLDSC (6015.335540), AskIEEE, CASDDS, IE, Infotrieve, Ingenta, INIST, Linda Hall. **CCC.**
Published by: (Institute of Physics), Institute of Physics Publishing Ltd., Dirac House, Temple Back, Bristol, BS1 6BE, United Kingdom. TEL 44-117-9297481, FAX 44-117-9301178, custserv@iop.org, http://publishing.iop.org/. Ed. Mark Reed. **Subscr. in US, Canada & Mexico to:** American Institute of Physics, PO Box 503284, St Louis, MO 63150. TEL 516-576-2270, 800-344-6902, FAX 516-349-9704, subs@aip.org.

530 621.3 IND ISSN 0976-7630
▼ ➤ **NANOTECHNOLOGY AND NANOSCIENCE.** Text in English. 2010. s-a. USD 425 (effective 2011). **Document type:** *Journal, Academic/Scholarly.* **Description:** Publishes all the latest research articles, reviews and letters in all areas of nanotechnology and nanoscience.
Related titles: Online - full text ed.: ISSN 0976-7649. free (effective 2011).
Published by: Bioinfo Publications, 49/F-72, Vighnahar Complex, Front of Overseas Bank, Sector 12, Kharghar, Navi Mumbai, 410 210, India. TEL 91-22-27743967, FAX 91-22-66736413, editor@bioinfo.in, subscription@bioinfo.in.

530 621.3 338 USA ISSN 1945-8231
NANOTECHNOLOGY BUSINESS JOURNAL. Text in English. 2008. w. USD 2,295 in US & Canada; USD 2,495 elsewhere; USD 2,525 combined subscription in US & Canada (print & online eds.); USD 2,755 combined subscription elsewhere (print & online eds.) (effective 2011). adv. back issues avail. **Document type:** *Newsletter, Trade.*
Related titles: E-mail ed.; Online - full text ed.: ISSN 1945-824X. USD 2,295 combined subscription (online & e-mail eds.) (effective 2011).
Indexed: A15, A26, ABIn, B02, B15, B17, B18, G04, H11, I05, P10, P17, P26, P48, P49, P51, P52, P53, P54, PQC.
Published by: NewsRx, 2727 Paces Ferry Rd SE, Ste 2-440, Atlanta, GA 30339. TEL 770-435-8286, 800-726-4550, FAX 770-435-6800, pressrelease@newsrx.com, http://www.newsrx.com. Pub., Adv. contact Susan Hasty TEL 770-507-7777.

621 ITA ISSN 2038-968X
▼ ➤ **NANOTECHNOLOGY DEVELOPMENT.** Text in English. 2010. irreg. **Document type:** *Journal, Academic/Scholarly.*
Media: Online - full text.
Published by: Pagepress, Via Giuseppe Belli 4, Pavia, 27100, Italy. TEL 39-0382-1751762, FAX 39-0382-1750481.

530 CHE ISSN 1660-6795
T174.7
NANOTECHNOLOGY PERCEPTIONS; a review of ultraprecision engineering and nanotechnology. Text in English. 2005. 3/yr. CHF 108 to individuals; CHF 360 to institutions (effective 2006). **Document type:** *Journal, Academic/Scholarly.*
Indexed: Inspec, SCOPUS.
Published by: Collegium Basilea, Hochstr 51, Basel, 4053, Switzerland. cb@unibas.ch, http://www.unibas.ch/colbas/ems.htm. Ed. Jeremy Ramsden.

530 621.3 USA ISSN 1935-2484
T174.7
NANOTECHNOLOGY RESEARCH JOURNAL. Text in English. 2007. q. USD 295 to institutions; USD 442 combined subscription to institutions (print & online eds.) (effective 2012). **Document type:** *Journal, Academic/Scholarly.*
Related titles: Online - full text ed.: 2007. USD 295 to institutions (effective 2012).
Indexed: RefZh.
Published by: Nova Science Publishers, Inc., 400 Oser Ave, Ste 1600, Hauppauge, NY 11788. TEL 631-231-7269, FAX 631-231-8175, main@novapublishers.com. Ed. Frank Columbus.

530 620 DEU ISSN 2191-9089
▼ ➤ **NANOTECHNOLOGY REVIEWS.** Text in English. forthcoming 2012. bi-m. EUR 398 to institutions; EUR 458 combined subscription to institutions (print & online eds.) (effective 2012). **Document type:** *Journal, Academic/Scholarly.*
Related titles: Online - full text ed.: ISSN 2191-9097. forthcoming 2012. EUR 398 to institutions (effective 2012).
Published by: Walter de Gruyter GmbH & Co. KG, Genthiner Str 13, Berlin, 10785, Germany. TEL 49-30-260050, FAX 49-30-26005251, info@degruyter.com, http://www.degruyter.de. Ed. Challa Kumar.

530 GBR ISSN 1177-8903
T174.7
➤ **NANOTECHNOLOGY, SCIENCE AND APPLICATIONS.** Text in English. 2008. irreg. free (effective 2011). **Document type:** *Journal, Academic/Scholarly.* **Description:** Focuses on the science of nanotechnology in a wide range of industrial and academic applications.
Media: Online - full text.
Indexed: P30, SCOPUS.
—CCC.
Published by: Dove Medical Press Ltd., Beechfield House, Winterton Way, Macclesfield, SK11 0JL, United Kingdom. TEL 44-1625-509130, FAX 44-1625-617933. Ed. Dmitri Litvinov.

➤ **NATIONAL ACADEMY OF SCIENCES, INDIA. PROCEEDINGS. SECTION A. PHYSICAL SCIENCES.** *see* SCIENCES: COMPREHENSIVE WORKS

530 JPN ISSN 0917-1185
QC718.5.C65 CODEN: AIFSE5
NATIONAL INSTITUTE FOR FUSION SCIENCE. ANNUAL REPORT. Text in English. 1989. a. **Document type:** *Corporate.*
Indexed: INIS AtomInd, RefZh.
—CCC.
Published by: National Institute for Fusion Science, Research Information Center/Kaku Yugo Kagaku Kenkyujo, 322-6 Oroshi-cho, Toki, Gifu-ken 509-5292, Japan. TEL 81-572-58-2066. Ed. Chusei Namba.

530 JPN ISSN 0915-6348
CODEN: RNPSE5
NATIONAL INSTITUTE FOR FUSION SCIENCE. RESEARCH REPORT. P R O C SERIES. (Proceedings of Conferences) Text in English. 1962. a. free (effective 2005). **Document type:** *Monographic series, Academic/Scholarly.*
Formerly (until 1990): Nagoya University. Institute of Plasma Physics. Research Report (0469-4732)
Indexed: Inspec, RefZh.
—BLDSC (7762.722437), CASDDS. **CCC.**
Published by: National Institute for Fusion Science, Research Information Center/Kaku Yugo Kagaku Kenkyujo, 322-6 Oroshi-cho, Toki, Gifu-ken 509-5292, Japan. TEL 81-572-58-2066, FAX 81-572-58-2607, bunken@nifs.ac.jp. Ed. Chusei Namba.

539.76 621.48 JPN ISSN 0915-6356
NATIONAL INSTITUTE FOR FUSION SCIENCE. RESEARCH REPORT. TECH SERIES. Key Title: Research Report N I F S. TECH Series. Text in English. 1990. irreg. **Document type:** *Report, Academic/Scholarly.*
Indexed: Inspec.
—BLDSC (7762.722440).
Published by: National Institute for Fusion Science, Research Information Center/Kaku Yugo Kagaku Kenkyujo, 322-6 Oroshi-cho, Toki, Gifu-ken 509-5292, Japan. TEL 81-572-58-2066. Ed. Chusei Namba.

NATIONAL INSTITUTE OF STANDARDS AND TECHNOLOGY. JOURNAL OF RESEARCH. *see* METROLOGY AND STANDARDIZATION

530 510 UKR ISSN 1025-6415
CODEN: DNAUFL
NATSIONAL'NA AKADEMIYA NAUK UKRAINY. DOPOVIDI; naukovyi zhurnal. Text in Russian, Ukrainian; Summaries in English. 1991. m. USD 135; USD 300 foreign. bk.rev. bibl.; charts; illus. index. **Document type:** *Journal, Academic/Scholarly.*
Former titles (until 1994): Dopovidi Akademii Nauk Ukraini (1024-767X); (until 1992): Akademiya Nauk Ukrainskoi S.S.R. Doklady (0868-8044); Which was formed by the merger of (1979-1991): Akademiya Nauk Ukrainskoi S.S.R. Doklady. Seriya B. Geologicheskie, Khimicheskie i Biologicheskie Nauki (0201-8454); (1979-1991): Akademiya Nauk Ukrainskoi S.S.R. Doklady. Seriya A. Fiziko-Matematicheskie i Tekhnicheskie Nauki (0201-8446); Which was formerly (1967-1978): Akademiya Nauk Ukrainskoi R.S.R. Seriya A. Fiziko-Tekhnichni ta Matematychni Nauki (0002-3531)
Indexed: A33, ASFA, B21, BIOSIS Prev, C33, CCMJ, CIN, CIS, ChemAb, ChemTitl, CompR, ESPM, GeoRef, INIS AtomInd, Inspec, MSN, MathR, MycolAb, PhysBer, RASB, RefZh, SpeleolAb, Z02.
—BLDSC (0055.927000), CASDDS, East View, INIST, Linda Hall. **CCC.**
Published by: Natsional'na Akademiya Nauk Ukrainy, Prezydium/ National Academy of Sciences of Ukraine, Presidium, Ul Tereshchenkovskaya 3, Kiev, Ukraine. TEL 380-44-224-7118. Circ: 500. **US dist. addr.:** East View Information Services, 10601 Wayzata Blvd, Minneapolis, MN 55305. TEL 952-252-1201, 800-477-1005, FAX 952-252-1202, info@eastview.com, http://www.eastview.com.

530 510 KAZ ISSN 1991-346X
Q4 CODEN: IAKFBK
NATSIONAL'NAYA AKADEMIYA NAUK RESPUBLIKI KAZAKHSTAN. IZVESTIYA. SERIYA FIZIKO-MATEMATICHESKAYA/NATIONAL ACADEMY OF SCIENCES OF THE REPUBLIC OF KAZAKHSTAN. PROCEEDINGS. PHYSICS AND MATHEMATICS SERIES. Text in Russian. 1963. bi-m. USD 365 foreign (effective 2007). charts. index. **Document type:** *Proceedings, Academic/Scholarly.*
Former titles (until 2002): Ministerstvo Nauki Akademii Nauk Respubliki Kazakhstan. Izvestiya. Seriya Fiziko-Matematicheskaya (1029-3310); (until 1996): Kazakstan Respublikasy Ulttyk Gylym Akademiasynyn Habarlary. Seriya Fiziko-Matematiceskaya (1027-9903); (until 1992): Akademiya Nauk Kazakhskoi S.S.R. Izvestiya. Seriya Fiziko-Matematicheskaya (0002-3191)
Indexed: C&ISA, CCMJ, CIS, ChemAb, CorrAb, E&CAJ, INIS AtomInd, MSN, MathR, SolStAb, WAA, Z02.
—CASDDS, East View, INIST, Linda Hall.

Published by: (Kazakhstan Respublikasy Gylym Zane Zogary Bilim Ministrliginn. Kazakhstan Respublikasy Ulttyk Gylym Akademiiasynyn/ Ministry of Education and Science of the Republic of Kazakhstan, National Academy of Sciences of the Republic of Kazakhstan), Gylym, Pushkina 111-113, Almaty, 480100, Kazakstan. TEL 3272-611877. **Dist. by:** East View Information Services, 10601 Wayzata Blvd, Minneapolis, MN 55305. TEL 952-252-1201, 800-477-1005, FAX 952-252-1202, info@eastview.com, http://www.eastview.com.

530 510 BLR ISSN 1561-2430
QC1 CODEN: VBSFA5

➤ **NATSIYANAL'NAYA AKADEMIYA NAVUK BELARUSI. VESTSI. SERYYA FIZIKA-MATEMATYCHNYKH NAVUK/NATIONAL ACADEMY OF SCIENCES OF BELARUS. PROCEEDINGS. SERIES OF PHYSICAL AND MATHEMATICAL SCIENCES/ NATSIONAL'NAYA AKADEMIYA NAUK BELARUSI. IZVESTIYA. SERIYA FIZIKO-MATEMATIHESKIKH NAUK.** Text in Russian, Belorussian; Summaries in English, Russian. 1965. q. bibl.; charts; illus. index. **Document type:** *Journal, Academic/Scholarly.* **Description:** Presents papers on general and theoretical physics, including optics, as well as the main branches of mathematics and computer science.
Former titles (until 1998): Akademiya Navuk Belarusi. Vestsi. Seryya Fizika-Matematychnykh Navuk (1024-591X); (until 1992): Akademiya Navuk Belarusskai S.S.R. Vestsi. Seryya Fizika-Matematychnykh Navuk (0002-3574)
Indexed: CCMJ, CIS, INIS AtomInd, MSN, MathR, Z02.
—CASDDS, East View, INIST, Linda Hall.
Published by: (Natsiyanal'naya Akademiya Navuk Belarusi/National Academy of Sciences of Belarus), Vydavetstvo Belaruskaya Navuka/Publishing House Belaruskaya Navuka, ul F. Skaryny, 40, Minsk, 220141, Belarus. TEL 375-17-2633700, FAX 375-17-2637618, belnauka@infonet.by, http://www.belnauka.by. Ed. Sergey B Ablameiko. Circ: 270.

530 BLR ISSN 1561-8358
CODEN: VABFAF

➤ **NATSIYANAL'NAYA AKADEMIYA NAVUK BELARUSI. VESTSI. SERYYA FIZIKA-TECHNICHNYKH NAVUK/NATIONAL ACADEMY OF SCIENCES OF BELARUS. PROCEEDINGS. SERIES OF PHYSICAL AND TECHNICAL SCIENCES/NATSIONAL'NAYA AKADEMIYA NAUK BELARUSI. IZVESTIYA. SERIYA FIZIKO-TEKHNICHESKIKH NAUK.** Text in Russian, Belorussian; Summaries in English. 1956. q. bibl.; charts; illus. index. **Document type:** *Journal, Academic/Scholarly.* **Description:** Presents papers on the heavy machinery industry, reliability and longevity of machines, physics of strength and plasticity, applied physics, pressure and thermal treatment of metals and other materials.
Former titles (until 1998): Akademiya Navuk Belarusi. Vestsi. Seryya Fizika-Technichnykh Navuk (1024-5901); (until 1992): Akademiya Navuk Belarusskai S.S.R. Vestsi. Seryya Fizika-Technichnykh Navuk (0002-3566)
Indexed: ChemAb, CorrAb, INIS AtomInd, WAA.
—BLDSC (0037.832000), CASDDS, INIST, Linda Hall. **CCC.**
Published by: (Natsiyanal'naya Akademiya Navuk Belarusi/National Academy of Sciences of Belarus), Vydavetstvo Belaruskaya Navuka/Publishing House Belaruskaya Navuka, ul F. Skaryny, 40, Minsk, 220141, Belarus. TEL 375-17-2633700, FAX 375-17-2637618, belnauka@infonet.by, http://www.belnauka.by. Ed. S A Zhdanok. Circ: 220.

530 GBR ISSN 1748-3387
TP248.25.N35 CODEN: NNAABX

➤ **NATURE NANOTECHNOLOGY.** Text in English. 2006. m. EUR 3,214 in Europe to institutions; USD 4,048 in the Americas to institutions; GBP 2,077 to institutions in the UK & elsewhere (effective 2011). adv. back issues avail.; reprints avail. **Document type:** *Journal, Academic/ Scholarly.* **Description:** Covers research into the design, characterization and production of structures, devices and systems that involve the manipulation and control of materials and phenomena at atomic, molecular and macromolecular scales.
Related titles: Online - full text ed.: ISSN 1748-3395.
Indexed: A01, A20, B&BAb, B19, B21, C33, CA, CurCont, EMBASE, ExcerpMed, Inspec, MEDLINE, MSCI, P20, P22, P30, PQC, R10, Reac, RefZh, SCI, SCOPUS, T02, W07.
—BLDSC (6047.039000), IE, Ingenta. **CCC.**
Published by: Nature Publishing Group (Subsidiary of: Macmillan Publishers Ltd.), The MacMillan Bldg, 4 Crinan St, London, N1 9XW, United Kingdom. TEL 44-20-78334000, FAX 44-20-78334640. Ed. Peter Rodgers. Adv. contact Andy Douglas TEL 44-22-78434975. **Subscr. to:** Brunel Rd, Houndmills, Basingstoke, Hamps RG21 6XS, United Kingdom. TEL 44-1256-329242, FAX 44-1256-812358, subscriptions@nature.com.

530 GBR ISSN 1745-2473
QC1 CODEN: NPAHAX

➤ **NATURE PHYSICS.** Text in English. 2005 (Oct.). m. EUR 3,214 in Europe to institutions; USD 4,048 in the Americas to institutions; GBP 2,077 to institutions in the UK & elsewhere (effective 2011). adv. back issues avail.; reprints avail. **Document type:** *Journal, Academic/ Scholarly.* **Description:** Provides information for the physics community through the publication of commentaries, research highlights, news & views, reviews and correspondence.
Related titles: Online - full text ed.: ISSN 1745-2481.
Indexed: A01, A20, B21, C33, CA, CurCont, Inspec, NSA, P26, P30, P48, P52, P54, P56, PQC, SCI, SCOPUS, T02, W07.
—IE, Ingenta. **CCC.**
Published by: Nature Publishing Group (Subsidiary of: Macmillan Publishers Ltd.), The MacMillan Bldg, 4 Crinan St, London, N1 9XW, United Kingdom. TEL 44-20-78334000, FAX 44-20-78334640. Ed. Alison Wright. Adv. contact Andy Douglas TEL 44-22-78434975. **Subscr. to:** Brunel Rd, Houndmills, Basingstoke, Hamps RG21 6XS, United Kingdom. TEL 44-1256-329242, FAX 44-1256-812358, subscriptions@nature.com.

530 616.8 TUR ISSN 1303-5150
NEUROQUANTOLOGY; an interdisciplinary journal of neuroscience and quantum physics. Text in English, Turkish. 2002. irreg. **Document type:** *Journal, Academic/Scholarly.* **Description:** Designed to bring to you a critical analysis of the best of the world neuroscience and quantum physics literature, written by neuroscientist and physicist.
Media: Online - full text.
Indexed: A01, A20, CA, EMBASE, ExcerpMed, NSCI, SCI, SCOPUS, T02, W07.

NEW DIAMOND AND FRONTIER CARBON TECHNOLOGY; an international journal on newdiamond, frontier carbon and related materials. *see* ENGINEERING—Mechanical Engineering

530 ITA
NEW FROM I C T P. (International Centre for Theoretical Physics) Text in English. 1984. q. free (effective 2008). back issues avail. **Document type:** *Newsletter, Corporate.* **Description:** Designed to keep ICTP scientists and staff informed on past and future activities at ICTP and initiatives in their home countries.
Formerly (until 2001): International Centre for Theoretical Physics. News
Related titles: Online - full text ed.
Published by: Abdus Salam International Centre for Theoretical Physics, Strada Costiera 11, Trieste, TS 34014, Italy. pub_off@ictp.trieste.it, http://www.ictp.trieste.it. Ed. Dr. Daniel Schaffer. Circ: 2,000 (controlled).

530 GBR ISSN 1367-2630
QC1 CODEN: NJOPFM

➤ **NEW JOURNAL OF PHYSICS.** Abbreviated title: N J P. Text in English. 1998. m. free (effective 2011). abstr.; illus. back issues avail. **Document type:** *Journal, Academic/Scholarly.* **Description:** Publishes original research in all areas of physics.
Media: Online - full text.
Indexed: A01, A03, A08, A20, A39, C27, C29, CA, CCMJ, CPEI, CurCont, D03, D04, E13, EngInd, INIS AtomInd, Inspec, MSN, MathR, P30, R14, RefZh, S14, S15, S18, SCI, SCOPUS, T02, W07, Z02.
—Infotrieve, Ingenta, Linda Hall. **CCC.**
Published by: (Deutsche Physikalische Gesellschaft DEU, Institute of Physics), Institute of Physics Publishing Ltd., Dirac House, Temple Back, Bristol, BS1 6BE, United Kingdom. TEL 44-117-9297481, FAX 44-117-9301178, custserv@iop.org, http://publishing.iop.org/. Ed. Eberhard Bodenschatz. **Co-sponsor:** German Physical Society/ Deutsche Physikalische Gesellschaft.

➤ **NEWS OF SCIENCE.** *see* CHEMISTRY

530 DEU ISSN 1435-7151
NICHTLINEARE UND STOCHASTISCHE PHYSIK. Text in English, German. 1998. irreg., latest vol.11, 2007. price varies. **Document type:** *Monographic series, Academic/Scholarly.*
Published by: Logos Verlag Berlin, Comeniushof, Gubener Str 47, Berlin, 10243, Germany. TEL 49-30-42851090, FAX 49-30-42851092, redaktion@logos-verlag.de. Ed. Lutz Schimansky-Geier.

530 NLD
➤ **NIELS BOHR - COLLECTED WORKS.** Text in English. 1972. irreg., latest vol.12, 2007. price varies. back issues avail. **Document type:** *Monographic series, Academic/Scholarly.*
Published by: Elsevier BV, North-Holland (Subsidiary of: Elsevier Science & Technology), Sara Burgerhartstraat 25, Amsterdam, 1055 KV, Netherlands. TEL 31-20-4853911, FAX 31-20-4852457, JournalsCustomerServiceEMEA@elsevier.com, http://www.elsevier.com. Ed. E Ruedinger. **Subscr. to:** Elsevier BV, Radarweg 29, PO Box 211, Amsterdam 1000 AE, Netherlands. TEL 31-20-4853757, FAX 31-20-4853432.

530 NGA ISSN 1596-0862
NIGERIA JOURNAL OF PURE AND APPLIED PHYSICS. Text in English. 2000. irreg. USD 25 (effective 2004). **Description:** Publishes original results of research in all branches of pure and applied physics.
Related titles: Online - full text ed.
Published by: Federal University of Technology, Department of Physics, PMB 704, Akure, Ondo State, Nigeria. TEL 234-32-241305, dare@gannetcity.net. Ed. Moses Oludare Ajewole.

530 JPN ISSN 1342-8349
NIHON BUTSURI GAKKAI KOEN GAIYOSHU/PHYSICAL SOCIETY OF JAPAN. MEETING ABSTRACTS. Text mainly in Japanese; Text occasionally in English. 1952. s-a. JPY 1,600 for Part 1; JPY 2,300 for Part 2; JPY 2,400 for Part 3; JPY 1,800 for Part 4. **Document type:** *Abstract/Index.*
Published by: Physical Society of Japan/Nihon Butsuri Gakkai, Rm 211 Kikai-shinko Bldg, 3-5-8 Shiba-Koen, Minato-ku, Tokyo, 105-0011, Japan. FAX 81-3-3432-0997, http://wwwsoc.nii.ac.jp/jps/index-j.html.

530 JPN ISSN 1340-8100
NIHON OYO JIKI GAKKAI GAKUJUTSU KOEN GAIYOSHU/ANNUAL CONFERENCE ON MAGNETICS IN JAPAN. DIGESTS. Text in English, Japanese. a. JPY 5,000. **Document type:** *Proceedings, Academic/Scholarly.*
—BLDSC (3588.380100).
Published by: Magnetics Society of Japan/Nihon Oyo Jiki Gakkai, Mitsui Sumitomo Kaijo Surugadai Bldg 6F, 3-11, Kanda Surugadai, Chiyoda-ku, Tokyo, 101-0062, Japan. TEL 81-3-52810106, FAX 81-3-52810107, msj@bj.wakwak.com, http://wwwsoc.nii.ac.jp/msj2/.

530 JPN ISSN 1340-7562
NIHON OYO JIKI GAKKAI KENKYUKAI SHIRYO/MAGNETICS SOCIETY OF JAPAN. PAPERS OF TECHNICAL MEETING. Text in Japanese; Summaries in English. 1977. irreg. **Document type:** *Academic/Scholarly.*
—BLDSC (6112.915300).
Published by: Magnetics Society of Japan/Nihon Oyo Jiki Gakkai, Mitsui Sumitomo Kaijo Surugadai Bldg 6F, 3-11, Kanda Surugadai, Chiyoda-ku, Tokyo, 101-0062, Japan. TEL 81-3-52810106, FAX 81-3-52810107, msj@bj.wakwak.com, http://wwwsoc.nii.ac.jp/msj2/.

540 JPN ISSN 0287-864X
NIHON RIKAGAKU KYOKAI. KENKYU KIYO. Text in Japanese. 1968. a. JPY 1,500. **Document type:** *Bulletin.* **Description:** Research bulletin of the society.
Published by: Nihon Rikagaku Kyokai/Japan Society of Physics and Chemistry Education, 11-2-206 Sugamo 1-chome, Toshima-ku, Tokyo, 170-0002, Japan. Circ: 800.

539 JPN ISSN 0388-0125
QC976.A3
NIIGATA AIRGLOW OBSERVATORY. BULLETIN. Text in English. 1972. a. per issue exchange basis.
Published by: (Fuzoku Chokoso Taikiko Kansokujo), Niigata Daigaku, Rigakubu/Niigata University, Faculty of Science, 8050 Igarashi Nino-cho, Niigata-shi, Nigata-ken 950-21, Japan.

530 540 JPN ISSN 0286-7125
CODEN: NIRID7
NIIGATA RIKAGAKU/JOURNAL OF PHYSICS AND CHEMISTRY OF NIIGATA. Text in Japanese. a. abstr. **Description:** Contains original articles, reviews, commentary, and news.
Indexed: CIN, ChemAb, ChemTitl.
—CASDDS.
Published by: Niigata-ken Rikagaku Gijutsu Shokuin Kyogikai, Niigata-ken Eisei Kogai Kenkyujo, 314-1 Sowa, Niigata-shi, Niigata-ken 950-21, Japan.

530 JPN ISSN 0371-2699
NIIGATA UNIVERSITY. FACULTY OF SCIENCE. SCIENCE REPORTS. SERIES B: PHYSICS. Text in Multiple languages. 1964. irreg. per issue exchange basis.
Published by: Niigata Daigaku, Rigakubu/Niigata University, Faculty of Science, 8050 Igarashi Nino-cho, Niigata-shi, Nigata-ken 950-21, Japan.

530 571 100 150 USA ISSN 1094-0359
B808.9

➤ **THE NOETIC JOURNAL.** Text in English. 1997. q. bk.rev. abstr.; bibl.; charts; illus. 200 p./no.; back issues avail.; reprints avail. **Document type:** *Journal, Academic/Scholarly.* **Description:** Provides an international forum specializing in the physical basis of consciousness, including aspects of Extended Electromagnetic Theory, de Broglie-Bohm and Relativistic Quantum Field Theory, Quantum Computing, Astrophysics, Cosmology, Superstring (M, F-Theory), Philosophy of Mind and Cartesian Dualism.
Related titles: CD-ROM ed.: ISSN 1528-3739. 2002. USD 31 to individuals; USD 45 to institutions (effective 2002); Online - full text ed.
Published by: (The International Noetic University), The Noetic Press, c/o R L Amoroso, 608 Jean St, Oakland, CA 94610. noeticpress@mindspring.com, http://www.mindspring.com/ ~noeticpress/. Ed. Dr. Richard L Amoroso.

530 510 BLR ISSN 1561-4085
➤ **NONLINEAR PHENOMENA IN COMPLEX SYSTEMS.** Text in English. 1998. q. USD 196 combined subscription (print & online eds.) (effective 2007). 104 p./no. 2 cols./p.; **Document type:** *Journal, Academic/Scholarly.* **Description:** Covers the experimental, computational, and theoretical aspects of phase transitions, critical phenomena, bifurcations, chaos, fluctuation phenomena, pattern formation, fractals and complexity in all areas of science.
Related titles: Online - full text ed.: ISSN 1817-2458.
Indexed: CA, CCMJ, Inspec, MSN, MathR, RefZh.
—BLDSC (6117.316870), IE, Ingenta.
Published by: (Belorusskii Gosudarstvennyi Universitet/Belorussian State University, Natsiyanal'naya Akademiya Navuk Belarusi, Instytut Fiziki imya B I Styapanava/National Academy of Sciences of Belarus, B I Stepanov Institute of Physics, Univerza v Mariboru, Center za Uporabno Matematiko in Teoreticno Fiziko/University of Maribor, Center for Applied Mathematics and Theoretical Physics SVN), Education and Upbringing Publishing, ul Korolja 16, Minsk, 220004, Belarus. Ed. Viatcheslav I. Kuvshinov. Circ: 150 (paid).

➤ **NONLINEARITY.** *see* MATHEMATICS

➤ **NORDIC JOURNAL OF BUILDING PHYSICS**; acta physica aedificiorum. *see* BUILDING AND CONSTRUCTION

530 NLD ISSN 0927-5029
➤ **NORTH-HOLLAND DELTA SERIES.** Text in English. 1989. irreg., latest 2002. price varies. back issues avail. **Document type:** *Monographic series, Academic/Scholarly.*
Published by: Elsevier BV, North-Holland (Subsidiary of: Elsevier Science & Technology), Sara Burgerhartstraat 25, Amsterdam, 1055 KV, Netherlands. TEL 31-20-4853911, FAX 31-20-4852457, JournalsCustomerServiceEMEA@elsevier.com, http://www.elsevier.com. **Subscr. to:** Elsevier BV, Radarweg 29, PO Box 211, Amsterdam 1000 AE, Netherlands. TEL 31-20-4853757, FAX 31-20-4853432.

530 NLD ISSN 0925-5818
➤ **NORTH-HOLLAND PERSONAL LIBRARY.** Text in English. 1985. irreg., latest 2005. price varies. back issues avail. **Document type:** *Monographic series, Academic/Scholarly.*
Indexed: CIS.
Published by: Elsevier BV, North-Holland (Subsidiary of: Elsevier Science & Technology), Sara Burgerhartstraat 25, Amsterdam, 1055 KV, Netherlands. TEL 31-20-4853911, FAX 31-20-4852457, JournalsCustomerServiceEMEA@elsevier.com, http://www.elsevier.com. **Subscr. to:** Elsevier BV, Radarweg 29, PO Box 211, Amsterdam 1000 AE, Netherlands. TEL 31-20-4853757, FAX 31-20-4853432.

➤ **NOTES ON NUMERICAL FLUID MECHANICS AND MULTIDISCIPLINARY DESIGN.** *see* ENGINEERING—Hydraulic Engineering

➤ **NUCLEAR FUSION/FUSION NUCLEAIRE.** *see* PHYSICS—Nuclear Physics

530 ITA ISSN 2037-4895
CODEN: NIFBAP
IL NUOVO CIMENTO B. Text in English, French, German; Summaries in English, Italian, Russian. 1771. m. **Document type:** *Journal, Academic/Scholarly.* **Description:** Covers general topics in classical areas of phenomenology. Includes plasma and electric discharges, fundamental astronomy and astrophysics.
Former titles (until 2009): Societa Italiana di Fisica. Nuovo Cimento B. Basic Topics in Physics (1594-9982); (until 1985): Societa Italiana di Fisica. Nuovo Cimento B. Relativity, Classical and Statistical Physics (1124-1888); (until 1982): Societa Italiana di Fisica. Nuovo Cimento B (1124-187X); (until 1971): Nuovo Cimento B (0369-3554); Which superseded in part (in 1965): Nuovo Cimento (0029-6341); Which was formerly (until 1847): Cimento (1124-1845); (until 1847): Miscellanee de Chimica, Fisica e Storia Naturale (1124-1829); Which superseded in part (in 1843): Giornale Toscano di Scienze Mediche Fisiche e Naturali (1124-1810); Which was formerly (until 1840): Nuovo Giornale dei Letterati (1124-1802); Which superseded (in 1822): Accademia Italiana di Scienze Lettere ed Arti. Giornale Scientifico e Letterario (1124-1799); Which was formerly (until 1810): Giornale Pisano di Letteratura, Scienze ed Arti (1124-1780); (until 1807): Giornale Pisano dei Letterati (1124-1772); (until 1806): Nuovo Giornale dei Letterati (1124-1764); Which superseded in part (in 1796): Giornale dei Letterati (1124-1756)
Related titles: Online - full text ed.: ISSN 1826-9877.
Indexed: A22, ASCA, CCMJ, ChemAb, CurCont, INIS AtomInd, ISR, Inspec, MSN, MathR, PhysBer, SCI, SCOPUS.
—BLDSC (6185.200000), AskIEEE, IE, Infotrieve, Ingenta, INIST, Linda Hall. **CCC.**

P

Published by: Societa Italiana di Fisica (S I F), Via Saragozza 12, Bologna, 40123, Italy. TEL 39-051-331554, FAX 39-051-581340, subscriptions@sif.it. Ed. Angela Oleandri.

530 551 ITA ISSN 2037-4909
CODEN: NIFCAS

IL NUOVO CIMENTO C. Text in English, French, German; Summaries in English, Italian, Russian. 1855. bi-m. **Document type:** *Journal, Academic/Scholarly.* **Description:** Covers geophysics and space physics.
Former titles (until 2009): Societa Italiana di Fisica. Nuovo Cimento C. Colloquia on Physics (1124-1896); (until 1981): Nuovo Cimento C (0390-5551); Supersedes in part (in 1965): Nuovo Cimento (0029-6341); Which superseded (1843-1847): Cimento (1124-1845); Miscellanee de Chimica, Fisica e Storia Naturale (1124-1829); Which superseded in part (in 1843): Giornale Toscano di Scienze Mediche Fisiche e Naturali (1124-1810); (until 1840): Nuovo Giornale dei Letterati (1124-1802); Which superseded (in 1822): Accademia Italiana di Scienze Lettere ed Arti. Giornale Scientifico e Letterario (1124-1799); (until 1809): Giornale Pisano di Letteratura, Scienze ed Arti (1124-1780); (until 1807): Giornale Pisano dei Letterati (1124-1772); (1802-1806): Nuovo Giornale dei Letterati (1124-1764); Which superseded (1771-1796): Giornale dei Letterati (1124-1756)
Related titles: Online - full text ed.: ISSN 1826-9885.
Indexed: A20, A22, ASCA, ASFA, CIN, ChemAb, ChemTitl, GeoRef, INIS AtomInd, Inspec, M&GPA, OceAb, P30, SCOPUS, SpeleolAb.
—BLDSC (6185.250000), AskIEEE, CASDDS, IE, Infotrieve, Ingenta, INIST, Linda Hall. **CCC.**
Published by: Societa Italiana di Fisica (S I F), Via Saragozza 12, Bologna, 40123, Italy. TEL 39-051-331554, FAX 39-051-581340, subscriptions@sif.it. Ed. Angela Oleandri.

530 ITA ISSN 0393-4578
CODEN: FITEDJ

IL NUOVO SAGGIATORE. Text mainly in Italian. 1958. bi-m. free to members (effective 2009). **Document type:** *Journal, Academic/Scholarly.* **Description:** Publishes news on recent studies from Italian and foreign universities and laboratories, as well as from industrial laboratories.
Incorporates (1978-1990): Fisica e Tecnologia (0391-9757); Formerly (until 1984): Societa Italiana di Fisica. Bollettino (0037-8801)
Related titles: Online - full text ed.: ISSN 1827-6148. 1985.
Indexed: GeoRef, Inspec, SpeleolAb.
—CASDDS, INIST, Linda Hall.
Published by: Societa Italiana di Fisica (S I F), Via Saragozza 12, Bologna, 40123, Italy. TEL 39-051-331554, FAX 39-051-581340, subscriptions@sif.it. Ed. Angela Oleandri.

OBZORNIK ZA MATEMATIKO IN FIZIKO. *see* MATHEMATICS

530 SWE ISSN 1652-148X

OEREBRO STUDIES IN PHYSICS. Text in English. 2003. irreg., latest vol.1, 2003. SEK 180 per issue (effective 2006). **Document type:** *Monographic series, Academic/Scholarly.*
Published by: Oerebro Universitet, Universitetsbiblioteket/University of Oerebro. University Library, Fakultetsgatan 1, Oerebro, 70182, Sweden. TEL 46-19-303240, FAX 46-19-331217, biblioteket@ub.oru.se. Ed. Joanna Jansdotter.

539 USA ISSN 2151-8688

ONTARGET. Text in English. 19??. irreg. free (effective 2009). back issues avail. **Document type:** *Newsletter, Trade.*
Media: Online - full content.
Published by: Thomas Jefferson National Accelerator Facility, 12000 Jefferson Ave, Newport News, VA 23606. TEL 757-269-7100, FAX 757-269-7363.

530 JPN ISSN 0918-1156

OOSAKA DAIGAKU KYOKUGEN BUSSHITSU KENKYU SENTA HOKOKUSHO/OSAKA UNIVERSITY. RESEARCH CENTER FOR EXTREME MATERIALS. REPORT. Text in English, Japanese; Summaries in English. 1990. a.
Published by: Oosaka Daigaku, Kyokugen Bussitsu Kenkyu Senta/ Osaka University, Research Center for Extreme Materials, 1-1 Machikaneyama-cho, Toyonaka-shi, Osaka-fu 560-0043, Japan.

530 NLD ISSN 1874-1835
QC1

➤ **THE OPEN APPLIED PHYSICS JOURNAL.** Text in English. 2008. irreg. free (effective 2011). **Document type:** *Journal, Academic/ Scholarly.* **Description:** Covers experimental and theoretical applications of physics to all branches of science.
Media: Online - full text.
Indexed: C10, M&GPA.
Published by: Bentham Open (Subsidiary of: Bentham Science Publishers Ltd.), PO Box 294, Bussum, AG 1400, Netherlands. TEL 31-35-6923800, FAX 31-35-6980150, subscriptions@bentham.org. Ed. Franco Cacialio.

➤ **THE OPEN CHEMICAL PHYSICS JOURNAL.** *see* CHEMISTRY

530 NLD ISSN 1874-186X
QC173.45

➤ **THE OPEN CONDENSED MATTER PHYSICS JOURNAL.** Text in English. 2008. irreg. free (effective 2011). **Document type:** *Journal, Academic/Scholarly.*
Media: Online - full text.
Published by: Bentham Open (Subsidiary of: Bentham Science Publishers Ltd.), PO Box 294, Bussum, AG 1400, Netherlands. TEL 31-35-6923800, FAX 31-35-6980150, subscriptions@bentham.org. Ed. Gianfranco Pacchioni.

➤ **THE OPEN NANOMEDICINE JOURNAL.** *see* MEDICAL SCIENCES

530 NLD ISSN 1874-415X
QC770

➤ **THE OPEN NUCLEAR & PARTICLE PHYSICS JOURNAL.** Text in English. 2008. irreg. free (effective 2009). **Document type:** *Journal, Academic/Scholarly.*
Media: Online - full text.
Published by: Bentham Open (Subsidiary of: Bentham Science Publishers Ltd.), PO Box 294, Bussum, AG 1400, Netherlands. TEL 31-35-6923800, FAX 31-35-6980150, subscriptions@bentham.org. Eds. Bennie Ward, Eduardo Guendelman.

530.44 NLD ISSN 1876-5343
QC717.6

➤ **THE OPEN PLASMA PHYSICS JOURNAL.** Text in English. 2008. irreg. free (effective 2011). **Document type:** *Journal, Academic/ Scholarly.*
Media: Online - full text.
Indexed: A01.
Published by: Bentham Open (Subsidiary of: Bentham Science Publishers Ltd.), PO Box 294, Bussum, AG 1400, Netherlands. TEL 31-35-6923800, FAX 31-35-6980150, subscriptions@bentham.org.

530 620 NLD ISSN 1876-5378

▼ ➤ **THE OPEN SUPERCONDUCTORS JOURNAL.** Text in English. 2009. irreg. free (effective 2011). **Document type:** *Journal, Academic/Scholarly.* **Description:** Presents current developments in the field of experimental and theoretical research on superconductors and the applications of superconductivity.
Media: Online - full text.
Indexed: C10.
Published by: Bentham Open (Subsidiary of: Bentham Science Publishers Ltd.), PO Box 294, Bussum, AG 1400, Netherlands. TEL 31-35-6923800, FAX 31-35-6980150, subscriptions@bentham.org, http://www.bentham.org. Ed. Y Zhao.

541.345 NLD ISSN 1876-5319
QC173.4.S94

➤ **THE OPEN SURFACE SCIENCE JOURNAL.** Text in English. 2008. irreg. free (effective 2011). **Document type:** *Journal, Academic/ Scholarly.*
Media: Online - full text.
Indexed: A01.
Published by: Bentham Open (Subsidiary of: Bentham Science Publishers Ltd.), PO Box 294, Bussum, AG 1400, Netherlands. TEL 31-35-6923800, FAX 31-35-6980150, subscriptions@bentham.org.

➤ **ORGONOMIC FUNCTIONALISM**; a journal devoted to the work of Wilhelm Reich. *see* MEDICAL SCIENCES—Psychiatry And Neurology

➤ **OSSERVATORIO ASTROFISICO DI ARCETRI. OSSERVAZIONI E MEMORIE.** *see* ASTRONOMY

➤ **OTTAWA R & D REPORT.** *see* ENGINEERING

530 JPN

OYO BUTSURI GAKKAI GAKUJUTSU KOENKAI KO EN YOKOSHU/ JAPAN SOCIETY OF APPLIED PHYSICS. AUTUMN MEETING. EXTENDED ABSTRACTS. Text in Japanese. irreg. **Document type:** *Monographic series, Academic/Scholarly.*
Published by: Japan Society of Applied Physics/Oyo Butsuri Gakkai, Kudan-Kita Bldg 5th Fl, 1-12-3 Kudan-Kita, Chiyoda-ku, Tokyo, 102-0073, Japan. TEL 81-3-32381041, FAX 81-3-32216245, customer@jjap.or.jp, http://www.jsap.or.jp.

530 JPN ISSN 0369-8009
QC1 CODEN: OYBSA9

OYO BUTURI/JOURNAL OF APPLIED PHYSICS. Variant title: Oyo Butsuri. Text in Japanese; Abstracts in English. 1932. m. JPY 10,000 membership; Subscr. incld. with membership. adv. **Document type:** *Journal, Academic/Scholarly.* **Description:** Contains mainly reviews and interpretive articles.
Related titles: ◆ English ed.: J S A P International.
Indexed: AcoustA, ChemAb, ChemTitl, INIS AtomInd, Inspec, JPI.
—BLDSC (6321.086000), AskIEEE, CASDDS, INIST, Linda Hall. **CCC.**
Published by: Japan Society of Applied Physics/Oyo Butsuri Gakkai, Kudan-Kita Bldg 5th Fl, 1-12-3 Kudan-Kita, Chiyoda-ku, Tokyo, 102-0073, Japan. TEL 81-3-32381041, FAX 81-3-32216245, jsapcent@mb.infoweb.or.jp. adv.: page JPY 130,000. Circ: 23,000.

530 JPN

OYO DENSHI BUSSEI BUNKAKAI KENKYU HOKOKU/JAPAN SOCIETY OF APPLIED PHYSICS. SOLID STATE PHYSICS AND APPLICATION DIVISION. BULLETIN. Text in Japanese. 5/yr. **Document type:** *Bulletin, Academic/Scholarly.*
Published by: Oyo Butsuri Gakkai, Oyo Denshi Bussei Bunkakai/Japan Society of Applied Physics, Solid State Physics and Application Division, 1-12-13 Kudan Kita Chiyoda-ku, Tokyo, 102-0073, Japan. nisitani@mns.kyutech.ac.jp, http://annex.jsap.or.jp/support/division/ ohden/index.html.

530 GBR ISSN 1754-0410
QC770

➤ **P M C PHYSICS A.** Text in English. 2007. irreg. free (effective 2011). back issues avail. **Document type:** *Journal, Academic/Scholarly.* **Description:** Publishes articles on high-energy & nuclear physics, cosmology, gravity & astroparticle physics and also the instrumentation & data analysis of results in these areas.
Media: Online - full text.
Indexed: A01, A26, A39, C27, C29, CA, CCMJ, D03, D04, E13, H12, I05, MSN, MathR, R14, S14, S15, S18, SCOPUS, T02, Z02.
—**CCC.**
Published by: PhysMath Central (Subsidiary of: BioMed Central Ltd.), Fl 6, 236 Gray's Inn Rd, London, WC1X 8HB, United Kingdom. TEL 44-20-31922000, FAX 44-20-31922010, info@physmathcentral.com. Ed. Ken Peach.

530.1 GBR ISSN 1754-0429

➤ **P M C PHYSICS B.** Text in English. 2007. irreg. free (effective 2011). back issues avail. **Document type:** *Journal, Academic/Scholarly.* **Description:** Covers atomic and molecular physics, optics, quantum physics and semiconductors.
Media: Online - full text.
Indexed: A01, A26, A39, C27, C29, CA, CPEI, D03, D04, E13, I05, R14, S06, S14, S15, S18, SCOPUS, T02.
—**CCC.**
Published by: PhysMath Central (Subsidiary of: BioMed Central Ltd.), Fl 6, 236 Gray's Inn Rd, London, WC1X 8HB, United Kingdom. TEL 44-20-31922000, FAX 44-20-31922010, info@physmathcentral.com. Eds. Peter Hatton, Stephen Buckman.

➤ **PACKAGING, TRANSPORT, STORAGE & SECURITY OF RADIOACTIVE MATERIAL.** *see* TRANSPORTATION

530 ARG ISSN 1852-4249
QC1

▼ **PAPERS IN PHYSICS.** Text in English. 2009. irreg. free (effective 2011). **Document type:** *Journal, Academic/Scholarly.*
Media: Online - full text.
Published by: Instituto de Fisica de Liquidos y Sistemas Biologicos, Calle 59, Numero 789, La Plata, Argentina. TEL 54-221-4233283, FAX 54-221-4257317. Ed. Luis Ariel Pugnaloni.

538.3 RUS ISSN 0202-2257

PARAMAGNITNYI REZONANS. Text in Russian. irreg. illus.
Indexed: ChemAb.
—INIST.
Published by: Kazanskii Gosudarstvennyi Universitet/Kazan State University, 18 Kremlyovskaya St, Kazan, 420008, Russian Federation.

530 JPN ISSN 0911-4815
Q4

PARITI/PARITY. Text in Japanese. 1985. m. JPY 1,200 per issue.
Published by: Maruzen Co., Ltd./Maruzen Kabushikikaisha, 3-10 Nihonbashi 2-chome, Chuo-ku, Tokyo, 103-0027, Japan. TEL 81-3-3272-7211, FAX 81-3-3278-1937.

530 JPN ISSN 0913-137X

PARITI. BESSATSU SHIRIZU/PARITY. SPECIAL ISSUE. Text in Japanese. 1986. irreg. JPY 2,800 per issue.
Published by: Maruzen Co., Ltd./Maruzen Kabushikikaisha, 3-10 Nihonbashi 2-chome, Chuo-ku, Tokyo, 103-0027, Japan. TEL 81-3-3272-7211, FAX 81-3-3278-1937.

530 DEU ISSN 0934-0866
TA418.78 CODEN: PPCHEZ

➤ **PARTICLE & PARTICLE SYSTEMS CHARACTERIZATION**; an international journal devoted to the measure and description of particle and bulk properties in dispersed systems. Text in English. 1983. bi-m. GBP 993 in United Kingdom to institutions; EUR 1,465 in Europe to institutions; USD 1,946 elsewhere to institutions; GBP 1,093 combined subscription in United Kingdom to institutions (print & online eds.); EUR 1,612 combined subscription in Europe to institutions (print & online eds.); USD 2,141 combined subscription elsewhere to institutions (print & online eds.) (effective 2010). adv. bk.rev. reprint service avail. from PSC. **Document type:** *Journal, Academic/Scholarly.*
Formerly (until 1988): Particle Characterization (0176-2265)
Related titles: Online - full text ed.: ISSN 1521-4117. GBP 993 in United Kingdom to institutions; EUR 1,465 in Europe to institutions; USD 1,946 elsewhere to institutions (effective 2010).
Indexed: A22, A28, APA, ASCA, BrCerAb, C&ISA, CA/WCA, CEABA, CIA, CPEI, CerAb, ChemAb, ChemTitl, CivEngAb, CorrAb, CurCont, E&CAJ, E11, EEA, EMA, ESPM, EngInd, EnvEAb, H15, Inspec, M&TEA, M09, MBF, METADEX, MSCI, SCI, SCOPUS, SolStAb, T04, W07, WAA.
—BLDSC (6407.310000), AskIEEE, CASDDS, IE, Infotrieve, Ingenta, INIST, Linda Hall. **CCC.**
Published by: Wiley - V C H Verlag GmbH & Co. KGaA (Subsidiary of: John Wiley & Sons, Inc.), Postfach 101161, Weinheim, 69451, Germany. TEL 49-6201-606400, FAX 49-6201-606184, info@wiley-vch.de, http://www.wiley-vch.de. Ed. Hans-Joachim Schmid. Circ: 650. **Subscr. in the Americas to:** John Wiley & Sons, Inc., 111 River St, Hoboken, NJ 07030. TEL 201-748-6645, subinfo@wiley.com; **Subscr. outside Germany, Austria & Switzerland to:** John Wiley & Sons Ltd., The Atrium, Southern Gate, Chichester, West Sussex PO19 8SQ, United Kingdom. TEL 44-1243-779777, FAX 44-1243-775878, http://onlinelibrary.wiley.com/.

➤ **PARTICLE PHYSICS AND ASTRONOMY RESEARCH COUNCIL. OPERATING PLAN.** *see* ASTRONOMY

530 NZL ISSN 1178-640X

▼ ➤ **PARTICLE PHYSICS INSIGHTS.** Text in English. 2010. irreg. free (effective 2011). **Document type:** *Journal, Academic/Scholarly.* **Description:** Covers all aspects of particle or high energy physics.
Media: Online - full text.
—**CCC.**
Published by: Libertas Academica Ltd., PO Box 300-874, Mairangi Bay, Auckland, 0751, New Zealand. TEL 64-9-4763930, FAX 64-9-3531397, editorial@la-press.com. Ed. Hanna Moussa.

539.72 NLD ISSN 1674-2001
TP156.P3

PARTICUOLOGY; science and technology of particles. Text in English. 2003. bi-m. EUR 285 in Europe to institutions; JPY 37,700 in Japan to institutions; USD 318 elsewhere to institutions (effective 2012). **Document type:** *Journal, Academic/Scholarly.*
Formerly (until 2008): China Particuology (1672-2515)
Related titles: Online - full text ed.: ISSN 2210-4291 (from ScienceDirect).
Indexed: A22, A28, APA, BrCerAb, C&ISA, CA/WCA, CIA, CPEI, CerAb, CivEngAb, CorrAb, E&CAJ, E01, E11, EEA, EMA, ESPM, EnvEAb, H15, M&TEA, M09, MBF, METADEX, MSCI, PollutAb, RefZh, SCI, SCOPUS, SolStAb, T04, W07, WAA.
—BLDSC (6407.559750), East View, IE, Linda Hall. **CCC.**
Published by: (Chinese Society of Particuology/Zhongguo Keli Xuehui CHN), Elsevier BV (Subsidiary of: Elsevier Science & Technology), Radarweg 29, PO Box 211, Amsterdam, 1000 AE, Netherlands. TEL 31-20-4853911, FAX 31-20-4852457, JournalsCustomerServiceEMEA@elsevier.com, http:// www.elsevier.nl. Ed. Mooson Kwauk.

530 NLD ISSN 0923-1749

PERSPECTIVES IN CONDENSED MATTER PHYSICS. Text in English. 1989. irreg., latest vol.7, 1993. price varies. **Document type:** *Monographic series, Academic/Scholarly.*
Published by: Springer Netherlands (Subsidiary of: Springer Science+Business Media), Van Godewijckstraat 30, Dordrecht, 3311 GX, Netherlands. TEL 31-78-6576050, FAX 31-78-6576474.

530 GBR ISSN 0141-1594
QC176.8.P45 CODEN: PHTRDP

➤ **PHASE TRANSITIONS**; a multinational journal. Text in English. 1979. m. GBP 5,273 combined subscription in United Kingdom to institutions (print & online eds.); EUR 5,134, USD 6,449 combined subscription to institutions (print & online eds.) (effective 2012). adv. bk.rev. charts; illus. back issues avail.; reprint service avail. from PSC. **Document type:** *Journal, Academic/Scholarly.* **Description:** Provides a focus for papers on most aspects of phase transitions in condensed matter.
Related titles: CD-ROM ed.: ISSN 1026-7700. 1995; Microform ed.; Online - full text ed.: ISSN 1029-0338. 1996. GBP 4,746 in United Kingdom to institutions; EUR 4,621, USD 5,804 to institutions (effective 2012) (from IngentaConnect).
Indexed: A01, A03, A08, A20, A22, A28, APA, ASCA, BrCerAb, C&ISA, C33, CA, CA/WCA, CCI, CIA, CPEI, Cadscan, CerAb, ChemAb, CivEngAb, CorrAb, CurCR, CurCont, E&CAJ, E01, E11, EEA, EMA, ESPM, EngInd, EnvEAb, H15, IBR, IBZ, ISR, Inspec, LeadAb, M&TEA, M09, MBF, METADEX, MSCI, P26, P52, P54, P56, PQC, PhysBer, R16, RefZh, S01, SCI, SCOPUS, SolStAb, T02, T04, W07, WAA, Zincscan.
—AskIEEE, IE, Infotrieve, Ingenta, INIST, Linda Hall. **CCC.**

Published by: Taylor & Francis Ltd. (Subsidiary of: Taylor & Francis Group), 4 Park Sq, Milton Park, Abingdon, Oxfordshire OX14 4RN, United Kingdom. TEL 44-20-70176000, FAX 44-20-70176336, subscriptions@tandf.co.uk, http://www.taylorandfrancis.com. Ed. J Kreisel. Adv. contact Linda Hann. **Subscr. to:** Journals Customer Service, Sheepen Pl, Colchester, Essex CO3 3LP, United Kingdom. TEL 44-20-70175544, FAX 44-20-70175198, tf.enquiries@tfinforma.com.

530 GBR ISSN 1478-6435
QC173.45 CODEN: PMHABF

➤ **PHILOSOPHICAL MAGAZINE (LONDON, 2003).** Text in English. 2003. 36/yr. GBP 4,976 combined subscription in United Kingdom to institutions (print & online eds.); EUR 6,564, USD 8,245 combined subscription to institutions (print & online eds.) (effective 2012). adv. back issues avail.; reprint service avail. from PSC. **Document type:** *Journal, Academic/Scholarly.* **Description:** Publishes contributed articles and critical reviews in the field of condensed matter describing original results, theories and concepts relating to the structure and properties of crystalline materials, ceramics, polymers, glasses, amorphous films, composites and soft matter.

Formed by the merger of (1995-2003): Philosophical Magazine A: Physics of Condensed Matter, Structure, Defects and Mechanical Properties (1364-2804); Which was formerly (1798-1995): Philosophical Magazine A: Physics of Condensed Matter. Defects and Mechanical Properties (0141-8610); (1995-2003): Philosophical Magazine B: Physics of Condensed Matter, Statistical Mechanics, Electronic, Optical and Magnetic Properties (1364-2812); Which was formerly (1986-1995): Philosophical Magazine B: Physics of Condensed Matter, Structural, Electronic, Optical and Magnetic Properties (0958-6644); (1798-1986): Philosophical Magazine B: Physics of Condensed Matter, Electronics, Optical and Magnetic Properties (0141-8637); Both of which superseded in part (in 1978): Philosophical Magazine (0031-8086); Which was formerly (until 1945): The London, Edinburgh and Dublin Philosophical Magazine and Journal of Science (1941-5982); (until 1840): The London and Edinburgh Philosophical Magazine and Journal of Science (1941-5966); (until 1832): The Philosophical Magazine (1941-5850); Which incorporated (1824-1832): Edinburgh Journal of Science (0367-0287); (1813-1826): Annals of Philosophy (0365-4915)

Related titles: Online - full text ed.: ISSN 1478-6443. 2003. GBP 4,478 in United Kingdom to institutions; EUR 5,908, USD 7,420 to institutions (effective 2012) (from IngentaConnect).

Indexed: A01, A03, A08, A22, A28, APA, BrCerAb, C&ISA, C33, CA, CA/WCA, CIA, CPEI, CerAb, ChemAb, CivEngAb, CorrAb, CurCont, E&CAJ, E01, E11, EEA, EMA, ESPM, EngInd, EnvEAb, GeoRef, H15, Inspec, M&TEA, M09, MBF, METADEX, MSCI, P26, P52, P54, P56, PCI, PQC, S01, SCI, SCOPUS, SolStAb, T02, T04, TM, W07, WAA.

—IE, Ingenta, INIST, Linda Hall. **CCC.**

Published by: (European Physical Society FRA), Taylor & Francis Ltd. (Subsidiary of: Taylor & Francis Group), 4 Park Sq, Milton Park, Abingdon, Oxfordshire OX14 4RN, United Kingdom. TEL 44-20-70176000, FAX 44-20-70176336, subscriptions@tandf.co.uk, http://www.taylorandfrancis.com. Eds. A L Greer, K M Knowles, P S Riseborough. **US subscr. addr.:** Taylor & Francis Inc., Customer Services Dept, 325 Chestnut St, 8th Fl, Philadelphia, PA 19106. TEL 215-625-8900, 800-354-1420, FAX 215-625-2940, customerservice@taylorandfrancis.com; **Subscr. to:** Journals Customer Service, Sheepen Pl, Colchester, Essex CO3 3LP, United Kingdom. TEL 44-20-70175544, FAX 44-20-70175198, tf.enquiries@tfinforma.com.

530 GBR ISSN 0950-0839
QC173.4.C65 CODEN: PMLEEG

➤ **PHILOSOPHICAL MAGAZINE LETTERS**; structure and properties of condensed matter. Text and summaries in English, French, German. 1798. m. GBP 811 combined subscription in United Kingdom to institutions (print & online eds.); EUR 1,070, USD 1,345 combined subscription to institutions (print & online eds.) (effective 2012). adv. index. back issues avail.; reprint service avail. from PSC. **Document type:** *Journal, Academic/Scholarly.* **Description:** Publishes short contributions covering original research in the broad field of condensed matter physics.

Supersedes in part (in 1995): Philosophical Magazine. A. Physics of Condensed Matter. Defects and Mechanical Properties (0141-8610); (in 1987): Philosophical Magazine. B. Physics of Condensed Matter. Electronic, Optical and Magnetic Properties (0141-8637); Both of which superseded (in 1978): Philosophical Magazine (0031-8086); Which was formerly (until 1945): The London, Edinburgh and Dublin Philosophical Magazine and Journal of Science (1941-5982); (until 1840): The London and Edinburgh Philosophical Magazine and Journal of Science (1941-5966); (until 1832): The Philosophical Magazine (1941-5850); (until 1827): The Philosophical Magazine and Journal (1941-5818); (until 1814): The Philosophical Magazine

Related titles: Microfiche ed.; Online - full text ed.: ISSN 1362-3036. GBP 730 in United Kingdom to institutions; EUR 963, USD 1,211 to institutions (effective 2012) (from IngentaConnect).

Indexed: A01, A03, A08, A22, A28, APA, ASCA, B07, BrCerAb, C&ISA, C24, C33, CA, CA/WCA, CIA, CPEI, CerAb, ChemAb, ChemTitl, CivEngAb, CorrAb, CurCont, E&CAJ, E01, E11, EEA, EMA, ESPM, EngInd, EnvEAb, GeoRef, H15, ISR, Inspec, M&TEA, M09, MBF, METADEX, MSCI, P30, PCI, SCI, SCOPUS, SolStAb, T02, T04, W07, WAA.

—AskIEEE, CASDDS, IE, Infotrieve, Ingenta, INIST, Linda Hall. **CCC.**

Published by: (European Physical Society FRA), Taylor & Francis Ltd. (Subsidiary of: Taylor & Francis Group), 4 Park Sq, Milton Park, Abingdon, Oxfordshire OX14 4RN, United Kingdom. TEL 44-20-70176000, FAX 44-20-70176336, subscriptions@tandf.co.uk, http://www.taylorandfrancis.com. Ed. E A Davis. Adv. contact Linda Hann. **Subscr. in N. America to:** Taylor & Francis Inc., Customer Services Dept, 325 Chestnut St, 8th Fl, Philadelphia, PA 19106. TEL 215-625-8900, 800-354-1420, FAX 215-625-2940, customerservice@taylorandfrancis.com.

530 NLD ISSN 1871-1774

PHILOSOPHY AND FOUNDATIONS OF PHYSICS. Text in English. 2006. irreg., latest vol.4, 2008. price varies. **Document type:** *Monographic series, Academic/Scholarly.*

Related titles: Online - full text ed.: ISSN 2212-201X.

Indexed: MSN, SCOPUS.

—**CCC.**

Published by: Elsevier BV (Subsidiary of: Elsevier Science & Technology), Radarweg 29, PO Box 211, Amsterdam, 1000 AE, Netherlands. TEL 31-20-4853911, FAX 31-20-4852457, JournalsCustomerServiceEMEA@elsevier.com, http://www.elsevier.com.

530 JPN ISSN 1344-6320
QC793.5.P422

PHOTON FACTORY ACTIVITY REPORT. PART A. HIGH LIGHTS AND FACILITY REPORT. Text in English. 1983. a. **Document type:** *Government.*

Supersedes in part (in 1999): Photon Factory Activity Report (0912-1803)

Published by: (Hoshako Kenkyu Shisetsu/Photon Factory), Koenerugi Kasokuki Kenkyu Kiko/High Energy Accelerator Research Organization, 1-1, Oho, Tsukuba-shi, Ibaraki-ken 305-0801, Japan. TEL 81-298-64-5137, FAX 81-298-64-4604, adm-journhushiryou1@ccgemail.kek.jp, http://www.kek.jp.

530 JPN ISSN 1344-6339

PHOTON FACTORY ACTIVITY REPORT. PART B. USERS' REPORT. Text in English. a. **Document type:** *Government.*

Supersedes in part (in 1999): Photon Factory Actvity Report (0912-1803)

Published by: (Hoshako Kenkyu Shisetsu/Photon Factory), Koenerugi Kasokuki Kenkyu Kiko/High Energy Accelerator Research Organization, 1-1, Oho, Tsukuba-shi, Ibaraki-ken 305-0801, Japan. TEL 81-298-64-5137, FAX 81-298-64-4604, adm-journhushiryou1@ccgemail.kek.jp, http://www.kek.jp.

530 USA ISSN 1387-974X
TK5103.59

➤ **PHOTONIC NETWORK COMMUNICATIONS.** Text in English. 1999. bi-m. EUR 708, USD 718 combined subscription to institutions (print & online eds.) (effective 2012). adv. back issues avail.; reprint service avail. from PSC. **Document type:** *Journal, Academic/Scholarly.* **Description:** Brings out papers presenting research results, major achievements, and trends involving all-optical communication networks.

Related titles: Online - full text ed.: ISSN 1572-8188 (from IngentaConnect).

Indexed: A22, A26, BibLing, C10, CA, CMCI, CPEI, CurCont, E01, EngInd, ISR, Inspec, SCI, SCOPUS, T02, W07.

—BLDSC (6474.315600), IE, Infotrieve, Ingenta. **CCC.**

Published by: Springer New York LLC (Subsidiary of: Springer Science+Business Media), 233 Spring St, New York, NY 10013. TEL 212-460-1500, FAX 212-460-1575, service-ny@springer.com, http://www.springer.com/. Ed. Harmen R van As. **Subscr. to:** Journal Fulfillment, PO Box 2485, Secaucus, NJ 07096. TEL 201-348-4033, FAX 201-348-4505, journals-ny@springer.com.

530 540 NLD ISSN 1569-4410
TA1501

PHOTONICS AND NANOSTRUCTURES; fundamentals and applications. Text in English. 2003. 4/yr. EUR 442 in Europe to institutions; JPY 44,200 in Japan to institutions; USD 420 elsewhere to institutions (effective 2012). **Document type:** *Journal, Academic/Scholarly.* **Description:** Deals with photonic crystals and photonic band gaps.

Related titles: Online - full content ed.: ISSN 1569-4429; Online - full text ed.: (from IngentaConnect, ScienceDirect).

Indexed: A26, CA, CPEI, CurCont, EngInd, I05, Inspec, MSCI, RefZh, SCI, SCOPUS, T02, W07.

—BLDSC (6474.315800), IE, Ingenta, INIST. **CCC.**

Published by: Elsevier BV (Subsidiary of: Elsevier Science & Technology), Radarweg 29, PO Box 211, Amsterdam, 1000 AE, Netherlands. TEL 31-20-4853911, FAX 31-20-4852457, JournalsCustomerServiceEMEA@elsevier.com, http://www.elsevier.nl. Eds. E Ozbay, H Benisty, T F Krauss.

530 CAN ISSN 0710-0140

PHYS 13 NEWS. Text in English. 1971. 4/yr. CAD 10; USD 12 in United States; USD 15 elsewhere (effective 1999). adv. bk.rev. **Document type:** *Newsletter.* **Description:** Items of interest to high school and first-year university physics students and teachers.

Published by: University of Waterloo, Department of Physics, 200 University Ave. W, Waterloo, ON N2L 3G1, Canada. TEL 519-885-1211, FAX 519-746-8115. Ed. Jim Leslie. Pub. Debbie Guenther. adv.: B&W page USD 300. Circ: 4,000.

530 NLD ISSN 0378-4371
QC1 CODEN: PHYSAG

➤ **PHYSICA A: STATISTICAL MECHANICS AND ITS APPLICATIONS.** Text in English. 1934. 24/yr. EUR 6,973 in Europe to institutions; JPY 926,600 in Japan to institutions; USD 7,797 elsewhere to institutions (effective 2012). charts. index. back issues avail.; reprints avail. **Document type:** *Journal, Academic/Scholarly.* **Description:** Publishes research in the field of statistical mechanics and its applications. Areas covered include: random systems, fluids and soft condensed matter, dynamical processes, fundamental and general methods, models, biological applications, econophysics, interdisciplinary applications, complex systems, and networks.

Supersedes in part (in 1975): Physica (0031-8914); Which was formed by the merger of (1921-1933): Physica. Nederlandsch Tijdschrift voor Natuurkunde (0370-2707); (1866-1933): Archives Neerlandaises des Sciences Exactes et Naturelles. Serie 3a: Sciences Exactes (0365-5024); Which superseded in part (in 1912): Archives Neerlandaises des Sciences Exactes et Naturelles (0365-5059)

Related titles: Microform ed.: (from PQC); Online - full text ed.: ISSN 1873-2119 (from IngentaConnect, ScienceDirect).

Indexed: A01, A03, A08, A20, A22, A26, A33, ASCA, ApMecR, CA, CCMJ, CIN, CIS, CMCI, CPEI, Cadscan, ChemAb, ChemTitl, CurCont, EngInd, I05, IBR, IBZ, ISR, Inspec, LeadAb, MSN, MathR, P30, P34, PhysBer, RefZh, S01, SCI, SCOPUS, T02, W07, Z02, Zincscan.

—BLDSC (6475.010000), AskIEEE, CASDDS, IE, Infotrieve, Ingenta, INIST, Linda Hall. **CCC.**

Published by: Elsevier BV, North-Holland (Subsidiary of: Elsevier Science & Technology), Sara Burgerhartstraat 25, Amsterdam, 1055 KV, Netherlands. TEL 31-20-4853911, FAX 31-20-4852457, JournalsCustomerServiceEMEA@elsevier.com. **Subscr. to:** Elsevier BV, Radarweg 29, PO Box 211, Amsterdam 1000 AE, Netherlands. TEL 31-20-4853757, FAX 31-20-4853432.

531 621.3 NLD ISSN 0921-4526
QC1 CODEN: PHYBE3

➤ **PHYSICA B: CONDENSED MATTER.** Text in English. 1934. 24/yr. EUR 7,571 in Europe to institutions; JPY 1,005,400 in Japan to institutions; USD 8,470 elsewhere to institutions (effective 2012). back issues avail.; reprints avail. **Document type:** *Journal, Academic/Scholarly.* **Description:** Contains papers, both experimental and theoretical, in the realm of the physics of condensed matter. Examples of topics covered in the journal are low temperature physics (e.g. superconductivity and properties of liquid and solid helium), fundamental research on novel materials (e.g. rare earth and actinide compounds) as well as modern techniques of condensed matter research (e.g. neutron scattering), and mesoscopic physics.

Supersedes in part (in 1988): Physica B en C (0378-4363); Which superseded in part (in 1975): Physica (0031-8914); Which was formed by the merger of (1921-1933): Physica. Nederlandsch Tijdschrift voor Natuurkunde (0370-2707); (1866-1933): Archives Neerlandaises des Sciences Exactes et Naturelles. Serie 3A: Sciences Exactes (0365-5024); Which superseded in part (in 1912): Archives Neerlandaises des Sciences Exactes et Naturelles (0365-5059)

Related titles: Microform ed.: (from PQC); Online - full text ed.: ISSN 1873-2135 (from IngentaConnect, ScienceDirect).

Indexed: A01, A03, A08, A20, A22, A26, A28, APA, ASCA, BrCerAb, C&ISA, C13, C33, CA, CA/WCA, CIA, CPEI, CerAb, ChemAb, ChemTitl, CivEngAb, CorrAb, CurCont, E&CAJ, E11, EEA, EMA, ESPM, EngInd, EnvEAb, GeoRef, H15, I05, IBR, IBZ, ISMEC, ISR, Inspec, M&TEA, M09, MBF, METADEX, MSCI, RefZh, S01, SCI, SCOPUS, SolStAb, T02, T04, W07, WAA.

—BLDSC (6475.015000), AskIEEE, CASDDS, IE, Infotrieve, Ingenta, INIST, Linda Hall. **CCC.**

Published by: Elsevier BV, North-Holland (Subsidiary of: Elsevier Science & Technology), Sara Burgerhartstraat 25, Amsterdam, 1055 KV, Netherlands. TEL 31-20-4853911, FAX 31-20-4852457, JournalsCustomerServiceEMEA@elsevier.com. Eds. F R de Boer, L Degiorgi, R Jochemsen. **Subscr. to:** Elsevier BV, Radarweg 29, PO Box 211, Amsterdam 1000 AE, Netherlands. TEL 31-20-4853757, FAX 31-20-4853432.

530 621.3 NLD ISSN 0921-4534
CODEN: PHYCE6

➤ **PHYSICA C: SUPERCONDUCTIVITY AND ITS APPLICATIONS.** Text in English. 1934. 24/yr. EUR 9,319 in Europe to institutions; JPY 1,237,400 in Japan to institutions; USD 10,424 elsewhere to institutions (effective 2012). illus.; tr.lit. index. back issues avail.; reprints avail. **Document type:** *Journal, Academic/Scholarly.* **Description:** Serves as a rapid channel for publications on superconductivity, its applications and related subjects. Contains papers on the theoretical issues of superconductivity, reports on measurements of a wide variety of physical properties of superconducting materials, as well as the phenomena occurring in the vortex state of type-II superconductors. Publishes articles on all aspects of superconductivity relevant to applications, including large-scale applications (power and high magnetic fields), superconducting electronics, and materials research aimed at such applications, with special emphasis on the physical background, studied both experimentally and theoretically.

Supersedes in part (in 1988): Physica B en C (0378-4363); Which superseded in part (in 1975): Physica (0031-8914); Which was formed by the merger of (1921-1933): Physica. Nederlandsch Tijdschrift voor Natuurkunde (0370-2707); (1866-1933): Archives Neerlandaises des Sciences Exactes et Naturelles. Serie 3a: Sciences Exactes (0365-5024); Which superseded in part (in 1912): Archives Neerlandaises des Sciences Exactes et Naturelles (0365-5059)

Related titles: Microform ed.: (from PQC); Online - full text ed.: ISSN 1873-2143 (from IngentaConnect, ScienceDirect).

Indexed: A01, A03, A08, A22, A26, A28, APA, ASCA, BrCerAb, C&ISA, C13, C33, CA, CA/WCA, CIA, CIN, CPEI, CerAb, ChemAb, ChemTitl, CivEngAb, CorrAb, CurCont, E&CAJ, E11, EEA, EMA, ESPM, EngInd, EnvEAb, H15, I05, ISMEC, ISR, Inspec, M&TEA, M09, MBF, METADEX, MSCI, RefZh, S01, SCI, SCOPUS, SolStAb, T02, T04, TM, W07, WAA.

—BLDSC (6475.025000), AskIEEE, CASDDS, IE, Infotrieve, Ingenta, INIST, Linda Hall. **CCC.**

Published by: Elsevier BV, North-Holland (Subsidiary of: Elsevier Science & Technology), Sara Burgerhartstraat 25, Amsterdam, 1055 KV, Netherlands. TEL 31-20-4853911, FAX 31-20-4852457, JournalsCustomerServiceEMEA@elsevier.com. Eds. S Maekawa, V Maroni, W K Kwok. **Subscr. to:** Elsevier BV, Radarweg 29, PO Box 211, Amsterdam 1000 AE, Netherlands. TEL 31-20-4853757, FAX 31-20-4853432, http://www.elsevier.nl.

531 621.3 NLD ISSN 0167-2789
QC1 CODEN: PDNPDT

➤ **PHYSICA D: NONLINEAR PHENOMENA.** Text in English. 1980. 24/yr. EUR 6,266 in Europe to institutions; JPY 833,100 in Japan to institutions; USD 7,010 elsewhere to institutions (effective 2012). back issues avail. **Document type:** *Journal, Academic/Scholarly.* **Description:** Publishes papers and review articles reporting experiments, techniques and ideas which advance the understanding of nonlinear phenomena in general. Contributions of this type in the recent literature have dealt with: wave motion in physical, chemical and biological systems; chaotic motion in models relevant to turbulence, physical and biological phenomena governed by nonlinear field equations; instability, bifurcation, pattern formation and cooperative phenomena.

Related titles: Microform ed.: (from PQC); Online - full text ed.: ISSN 1872-8022 (from IngentaConnect, ScienceDirect).

Indexed: A01, A03, A08, A20, A22, A26, A28, APA, ASCA, ApMecR, BrCerAb, C&ISA, CA, CA/WCA, CCMJ, CIA, CIS, CMCI, CPEI, CerAb, ChemAb, ChemTitl, CivEngAb, CompR, CorrAb, CurCont, E&CAJ, E11, EEA, EMA, ESPM, EngInd, EnvEAb, GeoRef, H15, I05, ISR, Inspec, M&TEA, M09, MBF, METADEX, MSN, MathR, P30, RefZh, S01, SCI, SCOPUS, SolStAb, SpeleolAb, T02, T04, W07, WAA, Z02.

—BLDSC (6475.030000), AskIEEE, CASDDS, IE, Infotrieve, Ingenta, INIST, Linda Hall. **CCC.**

P

Published by: Elsevier BV, North-Holland (Subsidiary of: Elsevier Science & Technology), Sara Burgerhartstraat 25, Amsterdam, 1055 KV, Netherlands. TEL 31-20-4853911, FAX 31-20-4852457, JournalsCustomerServiceEMEA@elsevier.com. **Subscr. to:** Elsevier BV, Radarweg 29, PO Box 211, Amsterdam 1000 AE, Netherlands. TEL 31-20-4853757, FAX 31-20-4853432.

530 NLD ISSN 1386-9477
QC176.8.N35 CODEN: PELNFM

➤ **PHYSICA E: LOW-DIMENSIONAL SYSTEMS AND NANOSTRUCTURES.** Text in English. 1997. 10/yr. EUR 1,803 in Europe to institutions; JPY 239,100 in Japan to institutions; USD 2,020 elsewhere to institutions (effective 2012). back issues avail.; reprints avail. **Document type:** *Journal, Academic/Scholarly.* **Description:** Contains papers and review articles on the fundamental and applied aspects of physics in low-dimensional systems, including semiconductor heterostructures, mesoscopic systems, quantum wells and superlattices, two-dimensional electron systems, and quantum wires and dots.
Related titles: Online - full text ed.: ISSN 1873-1759 (from IngentaConnect, ScienceDirect).
Indexed: A01, A03, A08, A22, A26, C10, CA, CPEI, CurCont, EngInd, I05, ISR, Inspec, MSCI, P30, RefZh, S01, SCI, SCOPUS, T02, W07.
—BLDSC (6475.035000), CASDDS, IE, Infotrieve, Ingenta, INIST, Linda Hall. **CCC.**
Published by: Elsevier BV, North-Holland (Subsidiary of: Elsevier Science & Technology), Sara Burgerhartstraat 25, Amsterdam, 1055 KV, Netherlands. TEL 31-20-4853911, FAX 31-20-4852457, JournalsCustomerServiceEMEA@elsevier.com. Eds. C Schueller, J Nitta, T Chakraborty. **Subscr. to:** Elsevier BV, Radarweg 29, PO Box 211, Amsterdam 1000 AE, Netherlands. TEL 31-20-4853757, FAX 31-20-4853432.

➤ **PHYSICA MEDICA**; an international journal devoted to the applications of physics to medicine and biology. *see* MEDICAL SCIENCES

530 GBR ISSN 0031-8949
QC1 CODEN: PHSTBO

➤ **PHYSICA SCRIPTA**; an international journal for experimental and theoretical physics. Text in English. 1872. m. GBP 1,307 combined subscription (print & online eds.) (effective 2010). charts; stat. Index. back issues avail.; reprint service avail. from PSC. **Document type:** *Journal, Academic/Scholarly.* **Description:** Concentrates on experimental and theoretical physics, with a dominant international contribution. Contains strong components of atomic, molecular and optical physics, plasma physics, condensed matter physics and mathematical physics.
Incorporates (1961-1977): Physica Norvegica (0031-8930); Which superseded in part (in 1962): Archiv for Mathematik og Naturvidenskab (0365-4524); (1965-1975): Physica Fennica (0031-8922); Formerly (until 1974): Arkiv for Fysik (0365-2440); Which superseded in part (in 1949): Arkiv foer Matematik, Astronomi och Fysik (0365-4133); Which was formerly (until 1903): Svenska Vetenskaps-Akademiens Handlingar. Afdelning I, Mathematik, Astronomi, Mekanik, Fysik, Meteorologi och Beslagtade Amnen. Bihang (0284-7949); Which superseded in part (in 1886): Kongliga Svenska Vetenskaps-Akademiens Handlingar. Bihang (0284-7280)
Related titles: Microfiche ed.: USD 1,298 in the Americas; GBP 748 elsewhere (effective 2006); Online - full text ed.: ISSN 1402-4896. GBP 1,245 to institutions (effective 2010); ◆ Supplement(s): Physica Scripta. Topical Issues. ISSN 0281-1847.
Indexed: A22, ASCA, ApMecR, C&ISA, C33, CCMJ, CIN, CPEI, Cadscan, ChemAb, ChemTitl, CurCont, E&CAJ, EngInd, GeoRef, IBR, IBZ, INIS AtomInd, ISMEC, ISR, Inspec, LeadAb, MSN, MathR, PhysBer, RefZh, SCI, SCOPUS, SolStAb, SpeleolAb, W07, Z02, Zincscan.
—BLDSC (6475.150000), AskIEEE, CASDDS, IE, Infotrieve, Ingenta, INIST, Linda Hall. **CCC.**
Published by: (Kungliga Vetenskapsakademien/Royal Swedish Academy of Sciences SWE), Institute of Physics Publishing Ltd., Dirac House, Temple Back, Bristol, BS1 6BE, United Kingdom. TEL 44-117-9297481, FAX 44-117-9301178, custserv@iop.org, http://publishing.iop.org/. Ed. Roger Wappling. Pub. Graeme Watt. **Co-sponsor:** Academies of Sciences and Physical Societies of Denmark, Finland, Iceland, Norway and Sweden.

530 SWE ISSN 0281-1847
QC1 CODEN: PHSTER

➤ **PHYSICA SCRIPTA. TOPICAL ISSUES.** Text in Swedish. 1982. irreg. (incl. in subscr. to Physica Scripta). **Document type:** *Proceedings, Academic/Scholarly.*
Related titles: Online - full text ed.; ◆ Supplement to: Physica Scripta. ISSN 0031-8949.
Indexed: A22, C33, ChemAb, ChemTitl, EngInd, INIS AtomInd, Inspec, SCOPUS, Z02.
—BLDSC (6475.151000), AskIEEE, CASDDS, IE, Infotrieve, Ingenta, INIST. **CCC.**
Published by: Kungliga Vetenskapsakademien/Royal Swedish Academy of Sciences, PO Box 50005, Stockholm, 10405, Sweden. TEL 46-8-6739500, FAX 46-8-155670, http://www.kva.se. Ed. Roger Waeppling TEL 46-8-6739528.

530.41 DEU ISSN 1862-6319

PHYSICA STATUS SOLIDI. A: APPLICATIONS AND MATERIALS SCIENCE (ONLINE). Text in English. 2001. 15/yr. GBP 4,876 in United Kingdom to institutions; EUR 7,339 in Europe to institutions; USD 9,555 elsewhere to institutions (effective 2012). **Document type:** *Journal, Academic/Scholarly.*
Formerly (until 2005): Physica Status Solidi. A: Applied Research (Online) (1521-396X)
Media: Online - full text. **Related titles:** ◆ Print ed.: Physica Status Solidi. A: Applications and Materials Science (Print). ISSN 1862-6300.
—**CCC.**
Published by: Wiley - V C H Verlag GmbH & Co. KGaA (Subsidiary of: John Wiley & Sons, Inc.), Postfach 101161, Weinheim, 69451, Germany. TEL 49-6201-606400, FAX 49-6201-606184, info@wiley-vch.de, http://www.wiley-vch.de.

530.41 DEU ISSN 1862-6300
QC176.A1 CODEN: PSSABA

➤ **PHYSICA STATUS SOLIDI. A: APPLICATIONS AND MATERIALS SCIENCE (PRINT).** Text in English. 1961. 15/yr. (in 6 vols.). GBP 4,876 in United Kingdom to institutions; EUR 7,339 in Europe to institutions; USD 9,555 elsewhere to institutions (effective 2012). charts; illus. index. 300 p./no. 1 cols./p.; back issues avail.; reprint service avail. from PSC. **Document type:** *Journal, Academic/Scholarly.* **Description:** Covers the preparation, structural analysis, and numerical simulation of advanced materials, nanostructures, surfaces and interfaces, as well as properties of such materials and structures relevant for device applications (magnetic, electromechanical, or electronic devices, photonics, spintronics, sensors..).
Formerly (until 2005): Physica Status Solidi. A: Applied Research (Print) (0031-8965); Which superseded in part (in 1970): Physica Status Solidi (0031-8957)
Related titles: ◆ Online - full text ed.: Physica Status Solidi. A: Applications and Materials Science (Online). ISSN 1862-6319.
Indexed: A22, A28, APA, ASCA, BrCerAb, C&ISA, C33, CA/WCA, CIA, CPEI, Cadscan, CerAb, ChemAb, ChemTitl, CivEngAb, CorrAb, CurCont, E&CAJ, E11, EEA, EMA, EngInd, GeoRef, H15, IBR, IBZ, INIS AtomInd, ISR, Inspec, LeadAb, M&TEA, M09, MBF, METADEX, MSCI, P30, PhysBer, RefZh, SCI, SCOPUS, SolStAb, SpeleolAb, T02, T04, TM, W07, WAA, Zincscan.
—AskIEEE, CASDDS, IE, Infotrieve, Ingenta, INIST, Linda Hall. **CCC.**
Published by: Wiley - V C H Verlag GmbH & Co. KGaA (Subsidiary of: John Wiley & Sons, Inc.), Postfach 101161, Weinheim, 69451, Germany. TEL 49-6201-606400, FAX 49-6201-606184, subservice@wiley-vch.de, http://www.wiley-vch.de. **Subscr. in the Americas to:** John Wiley & Sons, Inc., 111 River St, Hoboken, NJ 07030. TEL 201-748-6645, subinfo@wiley.com.

530.41 DEU ISSN 0370-1972
QC176.A1 CODEN: PSSBBD

➤ **PHYSICA STATUS SOLIDI. B: BASIC RESEARCH.** Text in English. 1961. 15/yr. (in 6 vols.). GBP 4,876 in United Kingdom to institutions; EUR 7,339 in Europe to institutions; USD 9,555 elsewhere to institutions (effective 2012). abstr.; bibl.; charts; illus. index. 300 p./no. 1 cols./p.; back issues avail.; reprint service avail. from PSC. **Document type:** *Journal, Academic/Scholarly.*
Supersedes in part (in 1970): Physica Status Solidi (0031-8957)
Related titles: Online - full text ed.: ISSN 1521-3951. GBP 4,876 in United Kingdom to institutions; EUR 7,339 in Europe to institutions; USD 9,555 elsewhere to institutions (effective 2012).
Indexed: A22, A28, APA, ASCA, BrCerAb, C&ISA, C33, CA/WCA, CIA, CIN, Cadscan, CerAb, ChemAb, ChemTitl, CivEngAb, CorrAb, CurCont, E&CAJ, E11, EEA, EMA, ESPM, EnvEAb, H15, IBR, IBZ, INIS AtomInd, ISR, Inspec, LeadAb, M&TEA, M09, MBF, METADEX, MSCI, RefZh, SCI, SCOPUS, SolStAb, T02, T04, TM, W07, WAA, Zincscan.
—BLDSC (6475.230000), AskIEEE, CASDDS, IE, Infotrieve, Ingenta, INIST, Linda Hall. **CCC.**
Published by: Wiley - V C H Verlag GmbH & Co. KGaA (Subsidiary of: John Wiley & Sons, Inc.), Postfach 101161, Weinheim, 69451, Germany. TEL 49-6201-606400, FAX 49-6201-606184, info@wiley-vch.de, subservice@wiley-vch.de, http://www.wiley-vch.de. **Subscr. in the Americas to:** John Wiley & Sons, Inc., 111 River St, Hoboken, NJ 07030. TEL 201-748-6645, subinfo@wiley.com; **Subscr. outside Germany, Austria & Switzerland to:** John Wiley & Sons Ltd., The Atrium, Southern Gate, Chichester, West Sussex PO19 8SQ, United Kingdom. TEL 44-1243-779777, FAX 44-1243-775878.

530 DEU ISSN 1862-6351
QC176.A1 CODEN: PSSCGL

➤ **PHYSICA STATUS SOLIDI. C: CURRENT TOPICS IN SOLID STATE PHYSICS.** Text in English. 2002. 15/yr. Part C is only avail. as a part of subscr. package. reprint service avail. from PSC. **Document type:** *Journal, Academic/Scholarly.* **Description:** Aims at the timely dissemination of scientific results in rapidly evolving specific areas of solid state physics and materials science.
Formerly (until 2006): Physica Status Solidi. C: Conferences and Critical Reviews (1610-1634)
Related titles: Online - full text ed.: ISSN 1610-1642.
Indexed: A28, APA, BrCerAb, C&ISA, C33, CA/WCA, CIA, CerAb, CivEngAb, CorrAb, E&CAJ, E11, EEA, EMA, ESPM, EnvEAb, H15, Inspec, M&TEA, M09, MBF, METADEX, RefZh, SCOPUS, SolStAb, T04, TM, WAA.
—BLDSC (6475.235000), IE, Ingenta, INIST, Linda Hall. **CCC.**
Published by: Wiley - V C H Verlag GmbH & Co. KGaA (Subsidiary of: John Wiley & Sons, Inc.), Postfach 101161, Weinheim, 69451, Germany. TEL 49-6201-606400, FAX 49-6201-606184, info@wiley-vch.de, http://www.wiley-vch.de.

530 DEU ISSN 1862-6254
QC176.A1 CODEN: PSSRCS

PHYSICA STATUS SOLIDI. RAPID RESEARCH LETTERS. Text in English. 2007. bi-m. GBP 787 in United Kingdom to institutions; EUR 1,099 in Europe to institutions; USD 1,541 elsewhere to institutions (effective 2012). reprint service avail. from PSC. **Document type:** *Journal, Academic/Scholarly.* **Description:** Communicates important findings with a high degree of novelty and need for express publication, as well as other results of immediate interest to the solid state physics and materials science community.
Related titles: Online - full text ed.: ISSN 1862-6270. 2007. GBP 787 in United Kingdom to institutions; EUR 1,099 in Europe to institutions; USD 1,541 elsewhere to institutions (effective 2012).
Indexed: A28, APA, BrCerAb, C&ISA, C33, CA/WCA, CIA, CPEI, CerAb, CivEngAb, CorrAb, CurCont, E&CAJ, E11, EEA, EMA, ESPM, EnvEAb, H15, Inspec, M&TEA, M09, MBF, METADEX, MSCI, RefZh, SCI, SCOPUS, SolStAb, T04, WAA.
—BLDSC (6475.235500), IE, INIST, Linda Hall.
Published by: Wiley - V C H Verlag GmbH & Co. KGaA (Subsidiary of: John Wiley & Sons, Inc.), Postfach 101161, Weinheim, 69451, Germany. TEL 49-6201-606400, FAX 49-6201-606184, info@wiley-vch.de, http://www.wiley-vch.de. Ed. Martin Stutzmann.

530 570 GBR ISSN 1478-3975

➤ **PHYSICAL BIOLOGY.** Text in English. 2004. q. GBP 585 to institutions (effective 2010). back issues avail. **Document type:** *Journal, Academic/Scholarly.* **Description:** Promotes a unified biological physics, one that joins biology with the traditionally more quantitative fields of physics, chemistry, computer science and engineering.
Media: Online - full text. **Related titles:** Print ed.: ISSN 1478-3967. GBP 680 combined subscription to institutions (effective 2010).
Indexed: BIOBASE, EMBASE, ExcerpMed, IABS, Inspec.
—Linda Hall.
Published by: Institute of Physics Publishing Ltd., Dirac House, Temple Back, Bristol, BS1 6BE, United Kingdom. TEL 44-117-9297481, FAX 44-117-9301178, custserv@iop.org, http://publishing.iop.org/. Ed. Terence Hwa.

621.382 NLD ISSN 1874-4907

➤ **PHYSICAL COMMUNICATION.** Text in English. 2008. 4/yr. EUR 396 in Europe to institutions; JPY 64,300 in Japan to institutions; USD 474 elsewhere to institutions (effective 2012). **Document type:** *Journal, Academic/Scholarly.*
Related titles: Online - full text ed.: ISSN 1876-3219 (from ScienceDirect).
Indexed: CA, SCOPUS, T02.
—IE. **CCC.**
Published by: Elsevier BV (Subsidiary of: Elsevier Science & Technology), Radarweg 29, PO Box 211, Amsterdam, 1000 AE, Netherlands. TEL 31-20-4853911, FAX 31-20-4852457, JournalsCustomerServiceEMEA@elsevier.com. Ed. I F Akyildiz.

530.07 IND

PHYSICAL RESEARCH LABORATORY, AHMEDABAD: ANNUAL REPORT. Text in English. 1954. a. illus. **Document type:** *Report, Corporate.*
Published by: Physical Research Laboratory, Navrangpura, Ahmedabad, Gujarat 380 009, India. TEL 91-79-26314000, FAX 91-79-26314900, info@prl.res.in, http://www.prl.res.in/.

530 USA ISSN 1050-2947
QC1 CODEN: PLRAAN

➤ **PHYSICAL REVIEW A (ATOMIC, MOLECULAR AND OPTICAL PHYSICS).** Text in English. 1893. m. USD 2,375 combined subscription domestic to institutions academic (print & online eds.); USD 2,635 combined subscription foreign to institutions academic (print & online eds.) (effective 2011). bibl.; illus. s-a. index. back issues avail.; reprints avail. **Document type:** *Journal, Academic/Scholarly.* **Description:** Contains articles on fundamental concepts of quantum mechanics, atomic and molecular structure and dynamics, collisions and interactions, molecular clusters, atomic and molecular processes in electromagnetic fields, and quantum optics.
Formerly (until 1989): Physical Review A (General Physics) (0556-2791); Which superseded in part (in 1970): Physical Review (0031-899X)
Related titles: CD-ROM ed.; Microfiche ed.: (from BHP); Online - full text ed.: ISSN 1094-1622. USD 1,645 to institutions academic (effective 2011).
Indexed: A22, AESIS, ASCA, ApMecR, C13, C33, CCMJ, CMCI, CPEI, CPI, Cadscan, ChemAb, CurCont, EngInd, GeoRef, IBR, IBZ, INIS AtomInd, ISR, Inspec, LeadAb, MSB, MSN, MathR, P30, PhysBer, RefZh, SCI, SCOPUS, SPINweb, SpeleolAb, W07, Zincscan.
—BLDSC (6476.020000), AskIEEE, CASDDS, IE, Infotrieve, Ingenta, INIST, Linda Hall. **CCC.**
Published by: American Physical Society, One Physics Ellipse, College Park, MD 20740. TEL 301-209-3200, FAX 301-209-0865, subs@aps.org, http://www.aps.org. Eds. Gordon W.F. Drake, Margaret Malloy. **Subscr. to:** APS Subscription Services, Ste. 1N01, 2 huntington Quadrangle, Melville, NY 11747-4502. TEL 800-344-6902.

530 USA ISSN 1098-0121
QC176.A1 CODEN: PRBMDO

➤ **PHYSICAL REVIEW B (CONDENSED MATTER AND MATERIALS PHYSICS).** Text in English. 1893. 48/yr. USD 6,270 combined subscription domestic to institutions academic (print & online eds.); USD 6,990 combined subscription foreign to institutions academic (print & online eds.) (effective 2011). bibl.; illus. s-a. index. back issues avail.; reprints avail. **Document type:** *Journal, Academic/Scholarly.* **Description:** Specializes in condensed-matter phenomena; covers structural phase transitions, mechanical properties and defects, dynamics, latice effects, quantum solids and liquids, magnetism, superfluidity and superconductivity.
Former titles (until 1998): Physical Review B (Condensed Matter) (0163-1829); (until Jul.1978): Physical Review B (Solid State) (0556-2805); Which superseded in part (in 1970): Physical Review (0031-899X)
Related titles: CD-ROM ed.; Microfiche ed.; Online - full text ed.: ISSN 1550-235X. USD 4,195 to institutions (effective 2011).
Indexed: A22, ABIPC, AESIS, ASCA, ApMecR, C13, C33, CMCI, CPI, Cadscan, ChemAb, ChemTitl, CurCont, GeoRef, IBR, IBZ, INIS AtomInd, ISR, Inspec, LeadAb, MSB, MSCI, MathR, P30, PhotoAb, PhysBer, RefZh, SCI, SCOPUS, SPINweb, SpeleolAb, W07, Zincscan.
—BLDSC (6476.050000), AskIEEE, CASDDS, IE, Ingenta, INIST, Linda Hall. **CCC.**
Published by: American Physical Society, One Physics Ellipse, College Park, MD 20740. TEL 301-209-3200, FAX 301-209-0865, subs@aps.org, http://www.aps.org. Ed. P D Adams. **Subscr. to:** APS Subscription Services, Ste. 1N01, 2 huntington Quadrangle, Melville, NY 11747-4502. TEL 800-344-6902.

530 USA ISSN 1539-3755
QC174.7 CODEN: PRESCM

➤ **PHYSICAL REVIEW E (STATISTICAL, NONLINEAR, AND SOFT MATTER PHYSICS).** Text in English. 1893. m. USD 3,550 combined subscription domestic to institutions academic (print & online eds.); USD 3,890 combined subscription foreign to institutions academic (print & online eds.) (effective 2011). illus. Index. reprints avail. **Document type:** *Journal, Academic/Scholarly.* **Description:** Reports on results of research in statistical physics, plasmas, fluids, and related interdisciplinary topics.
Formerly (until 2001): Physical Review E (Statistical Physics, Plasmas, Fluids, and Related Interdisciplinary Topics) (1063-651X); Which superseded in part (in 1993): Physical Review A (Atomic, Molecular and Optical Physics) (1050-2947); Which was formerly (until 1990): Physical Review A (General Physics) (0556-2791); Which superseded in part (in 1970): Physical Review (0031-899X)
Related titles: CD-ROM ed.; Microfiche ed.: (from PQC); Online - full text ed.: ISSN 1550-2376. USD 2,470 to institutions (effective 2011).
Indexed: A20, A22, ASCA, C13, C33, CCMJ, CIN, CMCI, CPEI, CPI, ChemAb, ChemTitl, CurCont, EMBASE, EngInd, ExcerpMed, INIS AtomInd, ISR, IndMed, Inspec, MEDLINE, MSN, MathR, P30, R10, Reac, RefZh, SCI, SCOPUS, SPINweb, W07, Z02.
—BLDSC (6476.070500), AskIEEE, CASDDS, IE, Infotrieve, Ingenta, INIST, Linda Hall. **CCC.**

Published by: American Physical Society, One Physics Ellipse, College Park, MD 20740. TEL 301-209-3200, FAX 301-209-0865, subs@aps.org, http://www.aps.org. Eds. Gary S. Grest, Margaret Malloy. **Subscr. to:** APS Subscription Services, Ste. 1N01, 2 huntington Quadrangle, Melville, NY 11747-4502. TEL 800-344-6902.

530 USA ISSN 1539-0748
QC1

PHYSICAL REVIEW FOCUS. Text in English. 1998. s-a. free (effective 2010). back issues avail. **Document type:** *Journal, Academic/Scholarly.* **Description:** Features explanation of selected physics research published in the APS journals.
Media: Online - full text.
—Linda Hall.
Published by: American Physical Society, One Physics Ellipse, College Park, MD 20740. TEL 301-209-3200, FAX 301-209-0865, help@aps.org, http://www.aps.org. Ed. David Ehrenstein.

530 USA ISSN 0031-9007
QC1 CODEN: PRLTAO

➤ **PHYSICAL REVIEW LETTERS.** Text in English. 1958. w. USD 3,610 combined subscription domestic to institutions academic (print & online eds.); USD 3,920 combined subscription foreign to institutions academic (print & online eds.) (effective 2011). abstr.; illus. cum.index: 1956-1976. back issues avail.; reprints avail. **Document type:** *Journal, Academic/Scholarly.* **Description:** Provides rapid publication of short reports of significant fundamental research in all fields of physics.
Related titles: CD-ROM ed.: ISSN 1092-0145; Microfiche ed.; Online - full text ed.: ISSN 1079-7114. USD 2,605 to institutions (effective 2011).
Indexed: A20, A22, AESIS, ASCA, AcoustA, ApMecR, C13, C33, CCMJ, CMCI, CPEI, CPI, Cadscan, ChemAb, ChemTitl, CurCont, EMBASE, EngInd, ExcerpMed, GeoRef, IBR, IBZ, INIS AtomInd, ISR, IndMed, Inspec, LeadAb, MEDLINE, MSN, MathR, P30, PhotoAb, PhysBer, R10, Reac, RefZh, SCI, SCOPUS, SPINweb, SpeleolAb, W07, Z02, Zincscan.
—BLDSC (6476.200000), AskIEEE, CASDDS, IE, Infotrieve, Ingenta, INIST, Linda Hall, PADDS. **CCC.**
Published by: American Physical Society, One Physics Ellipse, College Park, MD 20740. TEL 301-209-3200, FAX 301-209-0865, subs@aps.org, http://www.aps.org. Eds. George Basbas, Jack Sandweiss, Reinhardt B. Schuhmann, Stanley G. Brown. **Subscr. to:** APS Subscription Services, Ste. 1N01, 2 huntington Quadrangle, Melville, NY 11747-4502. TEL 800-344-6902.

530 USA ISSN 1098-4402
QC787.P3 CODEN: PRABFM

➤ **PHYSICAL REVIEW SPECIAL TOPICS - ACCELERATORS AND BEAMS.** Text in English. 1998. m. free (effective 2011). **Document type:** *Journal, Academic/Scholarly.* **Description:** Features articles that cover the full range of accelerator science and technology: subsystem and component technologies; beam dynamics; applications of accelerators; and design, operation, and improvement of accelerators used in science and industry.
Media: Online - full text.
Indexed: CPI, CurCont, Inspec, SCI, SCOPUS, SPINweb, W07.
—Infotrieve, Linda Hall.
Published by: American Physical Society, One Physics Ellipse, College Park, MD 20740. TEL 301-209-3200, FAX 301-209-0865, help@aps.org, http://www.aps.org. Eds. Frank Zimmermann, Gene D Sprouse.

530 USA ISSN 1554-9178
QC30

PHYSICAL REVIEW SPECIAL TOPICS - PHYSICS EDUCATION RESEARCH. Text in English. q. **Document type:** *Journal, Academic/Scholarly.*
Related titles: Online - full text ed.: free (effective 2011).
Indexed: A39, C27, C29, CurCont, D03, D04, E13, ERIC, Inspec, R14, S14, S15, S18, SCI, SCOPUS, SSCI, W07.
—Linda Hall.
Published by: American Physical Society, One Physics Ellipse, College Park, MD 20740. TEL 301-209-3200, FAX 301-209-0865, http://www.aps.org. Ed. Robert Beichner.

530 USA

▼ ➤ **PHYSICAL REVIEW X.** Text in English. forthcoming 2011 (Fall). irreg. free (effective 2011). **Document type:** *Journal, Academic/Scholarly.* **Description:** Provides open access, primary research covering all of physics and its application to related fields.
Media: Online - full text.
Published by: American Physical Society, One Physics Ellipse, College Park, MD 20740. TEL 301-209-3200, FAX 301-209-0865, help@aps.org, http://www.aps.org. Ed. Jorge Pullin.

530 NLD ISSN 0921-318X

➤ **PHYSICAL SCIENCES DATA.** Text in Dutch. 1978. irreg., latest vol.45, 1998. price varies. **Document type:** *Monographic series, Academic/Scholarly.* **Description:** Reports on research in chemistry and other physical sciences.
Related titles: Online - full text ed.
Indexed: A22, ChemAb, IMMAb, Inspec.
—INIST. **CCC.**
Published by: Elsevier BV (Subsidiary of: Elsevier Science & Technology), Radarweg 29, PO Box 211, Amsterdam, 1000 AE, Netherlands. TEL 31-20-4853911, FAX 31-20-4852457, JournalsCustomerServiceEMEA@elsevier.com, http://www.elsevier.nl.

530 JPN ISSN 0031-9015
QC1 CODEN: JUPSAU

➤ **PHYSICAL SOCIETY OF JAPAN. JOURNAL.** Text in English. 1946. m. JPY 86,000 combined subscription for print & online eds. (effective 2006). abstr.; charts; illus. cum.index. Supplement avail.; back issues avail.; reprints avail. **Document type:** *Journal, Academic/Scholarly.* **Description:** Publishes original papers in all fields of physics. Intended to secure prompt publication of important new discoveries in physics.
Formerly: Physico-Mathematical Society of Japan. Proceedings (0370-1239)
Related titles: CD-ROM ed.: 2001 (vol.70). JPY 32,000 (effective 2004); Online - full text ed.: ISSN 1347-4073; Supplement(s): International Symposium on Advanced Science Research. Proceedings. 2001 (Mar.). JPY 12,000 to non-members; JPY 10,000 to members (effective until Mar. 2001); JPY 13,000 to non-members; JPY 11,000 to members (effective Apr. 2001).
Indexed: A22, AcoustA, ApMecR, C13, C33, CCMJ, CIN, CMCI, ChemAb, ChemTitl, CurCont, GeoRef, INIS AtomInd, ISR, Inspec, JCT, JTA, MSN, MathR, PhotoAb, PhysBer, RefZh, SCI, SCOPUS, SpeleolAb, W07, Z02.
—BLDSC (4842.000000), AskIEEE, CASDDS, IE, Infotrieve, Ingenta, INIST, Linda Hall. **CCC.**
Published by: (Physical Society of Japan/Nihon Butsuri Gakkai), Institute of Pure and Applied Physics, Toyokaiji Bldg, no.12, 6-9-6 Shinbashi, Minato-ku, Tokyo, 105-0004, Japan. TEL 81-3-3432-4308, FAX 81-3-3432-0728, subscription@ipap.jp. Ed. H Shiba. Circ: 2,600.

530 JPN ISSN 0375-9598

PHYSICAL SOCIETY OF JAPAN. JOURNAL. SUPPLEMENT. Text in Japanese. irreg. price varies. **Document type:** *Academic/Scholarly.*
—INIST.
Published by: Physical Society of Japan/Nihon Butsuri Gakkai, Rm 211 Kikai-shinko Bldg, 3-5-8 Shiba-Koen, Minato-ku, Tokyo, 105-0011, Japan. FAX 81-3-3432-0997, http://wwwsoc.nii.ac.jp/jps/index-j.html.

530 BEL ISSN 0770-0520
CODEN: PHMAD7

PHYSICALIA MAGAZINE. Text in Multiple languages. 1978. q. EUR 25 (effective 2004).
Indexed: INIS AtomInd.
—BLDSC (6476.353400).
Published by: Belgische Natuurkundige Vereniging/Societe Belge de Physique, c/o Johan Ingels, BIRA-IASB, Ringlaan 3, Ukkel, 1180, Belgium. TEL 32-2-3730378, FAX 32-2-3748423, http://infnu07.rug.ac.be/bps/bpshome.htm. Ed. Robert Vandenberghe.

530 ISR

PHYSICAPLUS. Text in English. irreg., latest no.10. **Document type:** *Magazine, Academic/Scholarly.*
Media: Online - full text.
Published by: Israel Physical Society, c/o Department of Physics, Technion, Haifa, 32000, Israel. TEL 972-4-829-3551, FAX 972-4-829-5755, http://physics.technion.ac.il/~ips/web. Ed. Dr. Alex Manes.

530 USA ISSN 1943-2879

➤ **PHYSICS**; spotlighting exceptional research. Text in English. 2008. w. **Document type:** *Journal, Academic/Scholarly.* **Description:** Features expert commentaries written by active researchers who are asked to explain the results to physicists in other subfields.
Media: Online - full content.
—Linda Hall.
Published by: American Physical Society, One Physics Ellipse, College Park, MD 20740. TEL 301-209-3200, FAX 301-209-0865, subs@aps.org, http://www.aps.org. Ed. David Voss.

530 SVK ISSN 0139-9861
CODEN: PHAPDQ

PHYSICS AND APPLICATIONS. Text in English. a. price varies.
Formerly: High Energy Particle Physics
Indexed: ChemAb.
—CASDDS.
Published by: (Slovenska Akademia Vied/Slovak Academy of Sciences), Vydavatel'stvo Slovenskej Akademie Vied Veda/Veda, Publishing House of the Slovak Academy of Sciences, Dubravska cesta 9, PO Box 106, Bratislava 45, 84005, Slovakia. Ed. Mikulas Blazek. **Dist. by:** Slovart G.T.G. s.r.o., Krupinska 4, PO Box 152, Bratislava 85299, Slovakia. TEL 421-2-63839472, FAX 421-2-63839485, http://www.slovart-gtg.sk.

PHYSICS AND CHEMISTRY OF MATERIALS TREATMENT. *see* ENGINEERING—Engineering Mechanics And Materials

PHYSICS & PHILOSOPHY. *see* PHILOSOPHY

530 USA ISSN 1049-4162
QC29

PHYSICS AND SOCIETY. Text in English. 1972. q. free to members (effective 2010). bk.rev. back issues avail. **Document type:** *Newsletter, Academic/Scholarly.* **Description:** Presents letters, articles, reviews, news, and commentary on the relations of physics to society.
Formerly: Forum on Physics and Society. Newsletter (1049-4170)
Related titles: Online - full text ed.: free (effective 2010).
Published by: American Physical Society, Forum on Physics and Society, 1 Physics Ellipse, College Park, MD 20740. TEL 301-209-3200, FAX 301-209-0865. Ed. Cameron Reed.

530.071 GBR ISSN 0031-9120
QC30 CODEN: PHEDA7

➤ **PHYSICS EDUCATION.** Text in English. 1966. bi-m. GBP 300 combined subscription to institutions (print & online eds.) (effective 2010). bk.rev.; software rev.; video rev.; Website rev. charts; illus. Index. back issues avail. **Document type:** *Journal, Academic/Scholarly.* **Description:** Provides reliable treatments of difficult subjects and clear explanations of new and established concepts in physics to aid in the teaching of physics to students 16 to 21 years old.
Related titles: Microfiche ed.: USD 368 in the Americas; GBP 189 elsewhere (effective 2007); Microfilm ed.; Online - full text ed.: ISSN 1361-6552. GBP 285 to institutions (effective 2010) (from IngentaConnect).
Indexed: A01, A03, A08, A22, AEI, B29, BiolDig, CA, CPE, ChemAb, E03, E16, ERA, ERI, ERIC, HECAB, Inspec, MRD, PhysBer, RILM, RefZh, S21, SCOPUS, T02, V05.
—BLDSC (6478.530000), AskIEEE, CASDDS, IE, Infotrieve, Ingenta, INIST, Linda Hall. **CCC.**
Published by: (Institute of Physics), Institute of Physics Publishing Ltd., Dirac House, Temple Back, Bristol, BS1 6BE, United Kingdom. TEL 44-117-9297481, FAX 44-117-9301178, custserv@iop.org, http://publishing.iop.org/. Ed. Gary Williams. **Subscr. in N. America to:** American Institute of Physics, PO Box 503284, St Louis, MO 63150. TEL 516-576-2270, 800-344-6902, FAX 516-349-9704, subs@aip.org.

530 CAN ISSN 0836-1398
QC1 CODEN: PHESEM

➤ **PHYSICS ESSAYS.** Text in English; Abstracts in French. 1988. q. USD 407 combined subscription to institutions (print & online eds.) (effective 2009). adv. bk.rev. 150 p./no. 2 cols./p.; back issues avail. **Document type:** *Journal, Academic/Scholarly.* **Description:** Dedicated to theoretical and experimental aspects of fundamental problems in physics.
Related titles: Online - full text ed.: USD 350 (effective 2009).
Indexed: A01, A03, A08, A20, A22, A26, ASCA, CA, CCMJ, CIN, ChemAb, ChemTitl, E08, I05, Inspec, MSN, MathR, P43, SCOPUS, T02.
—BLDSC (6478.560000), AskIEEE, CASDDS, IE, Ingenta, Linda Hall. **CCC.**
Published by: Physics Essays Publication, 2012 Woodglen Cres, Ottawa, ON K1J 6G4, Canada. TEL 819-457-2161, FAX 819-457-1020. Ed. E Panarella. Adv. contact Ken Charbonneau TEL 819-777-0548. Circ: 200.

530 CAN ISSN 0031-9147

PHYSICS IN CANADA/PHYSIQUE AU CANADA. Text in English, French. 1944. 6/yr. CAD 40 domestic; USD 40 in United States; USD 45 elsewhere (effective 2007). adv. bk.rev. charts; illus. index. reprints avail. **Document type:** *Journal, Academic/Scholarly.*
Supersedes in part: Canadian Association of Physicists. Annual Report; Incorporates (in 1952): Canadian Association of Physicists. Bulletin (0380-6669); Which was formerly (until 1947): Canadian Association of Professional Physicists. Bulletin (0380-6677)
Related titles: Microfiche ed.: (from MML); Microfilm ed.: (from MML); Microform ed.: (from MML).
Indexed: A22, C03, CBCARef, P48, P52, P56, PQC.
Published by: Canadian Association of Physicists, 150 Louis Pasteur Ave, Ste 112, McDonald Bldg, Ottawa, ON K1N 6N5, Canada. TEL 613-562-5614, FAX 613-562-5615, cap@physics.uottawa.ca, http://www.cap.ca. Ed. Bela Joos TEL 613-562-5800 ext 6755.

571.45 GBR ISSN 0031-9155
QH505 CODEN: PHMBA7

➤ **PHYSICS IN MEDICINE AND BIOLOGY.** Text in English; Abstracts in English, French, German. 1956. s-m. GBP 1,893 combined subscription to institutions (print & online eds.) (effective 2010). bk.rev. illus. Index. back issues avail.; reprint service avail. from IRC. **Document type:** *Journal, Academic/Scholarly.* **Description:** Covers the use of physical agents such as ionizing and non-ionizing radiation, electromagnetic fields and ultrasound in diagnosis, therapy and radiobiology; corresponding physical methods of dosimetry; associated hazards and protection requirements.
Related titles: Microfiche ed.: USD 2,303 in the Americas; GBP 1,193 elsewhere (effective 2007); Microfilm ed.; Online - full text ed.: ISSN 1361-6560. GBP 1,803 to institutions (effective 2010) (from IngentaConnect).
Indexed: A01, A03, A08, A22, A34, A36, ASCA, B25, BIOSIS Prev, CA, CABA, CPEI, ChemAb, ChemTitl, CurCont, DokArb, E12, EMBASE, EngInd, ExcerpMed, FR, GH, IBR, IBZ, INIS AtomInd, ISR, IndMed, IndVet, Inpharma, Inspec, MEDLINE, MycolAb, N02, N03, P30, PN&I, RefZh, SCI, SCOPUS, T02, TM, VS, W07.
—BLDSC (6478.800000), AskIEEE, CASDDS, GNLM, IE, Infotrieve, Ingenta, INIST, Linda Hall. **CCC.**
Published by: (Institute of Physics), Institute of Physics Publishing Ltd., Dirac House, Temple Back, Bristol, BS1 6BE, United Kingdom. TEL 44-117-9297481, FAX 44-117-9301178, custserv@iop.org, http://publishing.iop.org/. Ed. S Webb. **Subscr. in the US, Canada & Mexico to:** American Institute of Physics, PO Box 503284, St Louis, MO 63150. TEL 516-576-2270, 800-344-6902, FAX 516-349-9704, subs@aip.org. **Co-sponsors:** Institute of Physics, Engineering and Medicine; European Federation of Organizations for Medical Physics; International Organization for Medical Physics.

530 CHE ISSN 1422-6944
QC1 CODEN: PHPEF2

➤ **PHYSICS IN PERSPECTIVE.** Text in English. 1999. q. EUR 301, USD 343 combined subscription to institutions (print & online eds.) (effective 2012). reprint service avail. from PSC. **Document type:** *Journal, Academic/Scholarly.* **Description:** Conveys to a broad spectrum of readers a deeper understanding and appreciation of the way physics is conducted, of its content and application, and of the profound influence that physics has had in changing our conception of the natural world and in shaping our modern scientific and technological culture.
Related titles: Online - full text ed.: ISSN 1422-6960 (from IngentaConnect).
Indexed: A01, A03, A08, A20, A22, A26, CA, CCMJ, CurCont, E01, Inspec, MSN, MathR, S01, SCI, SCOPUS, SSCI, T02, W07, Z02.
—BLDSC (6478.878500), IE, Infotrieve, Ingenta, Linda Hall. **CCC.**
Published by: Birkhaeuser Verlag AG (Subsidiary of: Springer Science+Business Media), Viaduktstr 42, Postfach 133, Basel, 4051, Switzerland. TEL 41-61-2050707, FAX 41-61-2050799, info@birkhauser.ch, http://www.birkhauser.ch/journals. Eds. Dr. John Rigden TEL 301-209-3124, Dr. Roger H Stuewer TEL 612-624-8073. **Subscr. in the Americas to:** Springer New York LLC, Journal Fulfillment, PO Box 2485, Secaucus, NJ 07096. TEL 201-348-4033, 800-777-4643, FAX 201-348-4505, journals@birkhauser.com; **Subscr. to:** Springer Distribution Center, Kundenservice Zeitschriften, Haberstr 7, Heidelberg 69126, Germany. TEL 49-6221-3454303, FAX 49-6221-3454229, birkhauser@springer.de.

530 IND ISSN 0253-7583
QC1 CODEN: PNEWD7

PHYSICS NEWS. Text in English. 1970. q. free to members (effective 2011). adv. bk.rev. charts; illus.; stat. index. back issues avail. **Document type:** *Bulletin.*
Indexed: CIN, ChemAb, ChemTitl, INIS AtomInd.
—CASDDS.
Published by: Indian Physics Association, PRIP Shed, Rm No 4, Trombay, Mumbai, 400005, India. TEL 91-22-25505138, ipa.india@gmail.com. Ed. Dipan Ghosh. **Subscr. address:** Editor, Physics News, Tata Institute of Fundamental Research, Homi Bhabha Rd., Mumbai, Maharashtra 400 005, India; **Subscr. to:** I N S I O Scientific Books & Periodicals, PO Box 7234, Indraprastha HPO, New Delhi 110 002, India.

530 USA

PHYSICS NEWS PREVIEW; the American institute of physics index of physics topics. Text in English. 19??. irreg. illus. **Document type:** *Monographic series, Academic/Scholarly.*
Media: Online - full text.
Published by: (American Institute of Physics), American Physical Society, One Physics Ellipse, College Park, MD 20740. TEL 301-209-3200, FAX 301-209-0865, help@aps.org, http://www.aps.org.

530 USA ISSN 0891-4524

PHYSICS OF ATOMS AND MOLECULES. Text in English. 1979. irreg., latest 2005. price varies. back issues avail. **Document type:** *Monographic series, Academic/Scholarly.*

Indexed: Inspec.
—CCC.
Published by: Springer New York LLC (Subsidiary of: Springer Science+Business Media), 233 Spring St, New York, NY 10013. TEL 212-460-1500, FAX 212-460-1575, service-ny@springer.com. Eds. Hans Kleinpoppen, Philip G Burke.

530.44 USA ISSN 1070-6631
QC150 CODEN: PHFLE6
➤ **PHYSICS OF FLUIDS.** Text in English. 1958. m. price varies based on the number of users. adv. illus. Index. back issues avail.; reprints avail. **Document type:** *Journal, Academic/Scholarly.* **Description:** Devoted to original contributions to the physics of fluids covering kinetic theory, statistical mechanics, structure and general physics of gases, liquids, and other fluids, as well as certain basic aspects of physics of fluids bordering geophysics, astrophysics, biophysics, and other related science fields.
Formerly (until 1994): Physics of Fluids A: Fluid Dynamics (0899-8213); Which superseded in part (in 1989): Physics of Fluids (0031-9171)
Related titles: CD-ROM ed.; Microfiche ed.; Online - full text ed.: ISSN 1089-7666. price varies based on the number of users.
Indexed: A01, A03, A08, A20, A22, ABIPC, AESIS, ASCA, ASFA, AcoustA, ApMecR, B21, C24, C33, CA, CCMJ, CMCI, CPEI, CPI, ChemAb, ChemTitl, CurCont, EngInd, FLUIDEX, GeoRef, IBR, IBZ, INIS AtomInd, ISR, Inspec, M&GPA, MSN, MathR, P30, RefZh, S01, SCI, SCOPUS, SPINweb, SpeleolAb, T02, W07, Z02.
—BLDSC (6478.600000), AskIEEE, CASDDS, IE, Infotrieve, Ingenta, INIST, Linda Hall. **CCC.**
Published by: American Institute of Physics, 1 Physics Ellipse, College Park, MD 20740. TEL 301-209-3100, aipinfo@aip.org, http://www.aip.org. Eds. John Kim TEL 310-825-4393, L Gary Leal. **Subscr. to:** PO Box 503284, St Louis, MO 63150. TEL 516-576-2270, 800-344-6902, FAX 516-349-9704, subs@aip.org, http://librarians.aip.org.

➤ **PHYSICS OF LIFE REVIEWS.** *see* BIOLOGY

530.44 USA ISSN 1070-664X
QC717.6 CODEN: PHPAEN
➤ **PHYSICS OF PLASMAS.** Text in English. 1958. m. price varies based on the number of users. adv. illus. Index. back issues avail.; reprints avail. **Document type:** *Journal, Academic/Scholarly.* **Description:** Devoted to original contributions to and reviews of the physics of plasma, including magnetofluid mechanics, kinetic theory and statistical mechanics of fully and partially ionized gases.
Formerly (until 1994): Physics of Fluids B: Plasma Physics (0899-8221); Which superseded in part (in 1989): Physics of Fluids (0031-9171)
Related titles: CD-ROM ed.: ISSN 1527-2419; Microfiche ed.; Online - full text ed.: ISSN 1089-7674. price varies based on the number of users.
Indexed: A01, A03, A08, A22, ABIPC, ASCA, C33, CA, CCMJ, CIN, CPEI, CPI, ChemAb, ChemTitl, CurCont, EngInd, IBR, IBZ, INIS AtomInd, ISR, Inspec, MSN, MathR, P30, RefZh, S01, SCI, SCOPUS, SPINweb, T02, W07.
—BLDSC (6478.879000), AskIEEE, CASDDS, IE, Infotrieve, Ingenta, INIST, Linda Hall. **CCC.**
Published by: American Institute of Physics, 1 Physics Ellipse, College Park, MD 20740. TEL 301-209-3100, aipinfo@aip.org, http://www.aip.org. Ed. Ronald C Davidson TEL 609-243-3552. **Subscr. to:** PO Box 503284, St Louis, MO 63150. TEL 516-576-2270, 800-344-6902, FAX 516-349-9704, subs@aip.org, http://librarians.aip.org.

539 UKR ISSN 1023-2427
QH505 CODEN: PHALFG
PHYSICS OF THE ALIVE/FIZIKA ZIVOGO. Variant title: Physics of the Alive, Biophysics and Beyond. Text in English, Ukrainian. 1993. q. **Description:** Covers the transition from traditional biophysics to physics of the alive, through the application of synergetical and quantum mechanical principles.
Indexed: Inspec.
—Linda Hall.
Published by: Scientific Research Center Vidhuk, 61-B Volodymyrska Str, Kiev, 252033, Ukraine. Ed. Sergei P. Sit'ko. **Co-sponsor:** Ukrainian Biophysical Society.

530.41 RUS ISSN 1063-7834
QC176 CODEN: PSOSED
➤ **PHYSICS OF THE SOLID STATE.** Text in English. 1959. m. EUR 7,077, USD 8,575 combined subscription to institutions (print & online eds.) (effective 2012). bibl.; charts; illus. index. back issues avail. **Document type:** *Journal, Academic/Scholarly.* **Description:** Publishes articles about solid state optics, solid state acoustics, electronic and vibrational spectra, phase transition, ferroelectricity, magnetism, and superconductivity.
Formerly (until 1992): Soviet Physics - Solid State (0038-5654)
Related titles: Microform ed.; Online - full text ed.: ISSN 1090-6460 (from IngentaConnect); ◆ Translation of: Fizika Tverdogo Tela. ISSN 0367-3294.
Indexed: A01, A02, A03, A08, A22, A26, AcoustA, C33, CA, CPI, ChemAb, CurCont, E01, GPAA, IBR, IBZ, ISR, Inspec, MSCI, MathR, PhysBer, S01, SCI, SCOPUS, SPINweb, T02, W07.
—BLDSC (0416.866000), AskIEEE, CASDDS, East View, IE, Infotrieve, Ingenta, INIST, Linda Hall. **CCC.**
Published by: (Rossiiskaya Akademiya Nauk/Russian Academy of Sciences), M A I K Nauka - Interperiodica (Subsidiary of: Pleiades Publishing, Inc.), Profsoyuznaya ul 90, Moscow, 117997, Russian Federation. TEL 7-095-3361600, FAX 7-095-3360666, compmg@maik.ru, http://www.maik.ru. Ed. A A Kaplyanskii. **Dist. in the Americas by:** Springer New York LLC, Journal Fulfillment, PO Box 2485, Secaucus, NJ 07096. TEL 212-460-1500, FAX 201-348-4505; **Distl outside of the Americas by:** Springer, Haber Str 7, Heidelberg 69126, Germany. TEL 49-6221-3454303, FAX 49-6221-3454229.

530 USA ISSN 1541-308X
QA935
➤ **PHYSICS OF WAVE PHENOMENA.** Text in English. 1993. q. EUR 786, USD 954 combined subscription to institutions (print & online eds.) (effective 2012). abstr.; charts; illus. back issues avail. **Document type:** *Journal, Academic/Scholarly.* **Description:** Publishes original contributions to the general and nonlinear theory of vibrations, wave theory and experiments, optics, acoustics, radiophysics, laser physics, and spectroscopy.
Formerly (until 2002): Physics of Vibrations (1069-1227)
Related titles: Online - full text ed.: ISSN 1934-807X.
Indexed: A22, A26, E01, E08, Inspec, RefZh, S09, SCI, W07.
—BLDSC (6479.170000), East View, IE, Ingenta. **CCC.**
Published by: Allerton Press, Inc. (Subsidiary of: Pleiades Publishing, Inc.), 18 W 27th St, New York, NY 10001. TEL 646-424-9686, FAX 646-424-9695, journals@allertonpress.com. Ed. Fyodor V Bunkin.

530 NLD ISSN 1875-3892
PHYSICS PROCEDIA. Text in English. 2008. m. **Document type:** *Proceedings, Academic/Scholarly.*
Media: Online - full text (from ScienceDirect).
Indexed: CA, MSN, T02.
—BLDSC (6475.125000), IE. **CCC.**
Published by: Elsevier BV (Subsidiary of: Elsevier Science & Technology), Radarweg 29, PO Box 211, Amsterdam, 1000 AE, Netherlands. JournalsCustomerServiceEMEA@elsevier.com, http://www.elsevier.nl.

530 NLD ISSN 0370-1573
QC1 CODEN: PRPLCM
➤ **PHYSICS REPORTS.** Text in Dutch. 1971. 90/yr. EUR 6,783 in Europe to institutions; JPY 899,600 in Japan to institutions; USD 7,589 elsewhere to institutions (effective 2012). illus. Index. back issues avail.; reprints avail. **Document type:** *Journal, Academic/Scholarly.* **Description:** Presents short review articles on recent developments in all fields of physics, including particle and field physics, nuclear, molecular, plasma and condensed matter physics, geophysics, interdisciplinary papers, and applications.
Incorporates (1983-1991): Computer Physics Reports (0167-7977); (1972-1975): Case Studies in Atomic Physics (0300-4503)
Related titles: Microform ed.: (from PQC); Online - full text ed.: ISSN 1873-6270 (from IngentaConnect, ScienceDirect).
Indexed: A01, A03, A08, A20, A22, A26, ASCA, CA, CCMJ, CIN, ChemAb, ChemTitl, CurCont, GeoRef, I05, ISR, Inspec, MSN, MathR, P30, PhysBer, RefZh, S01, SCI, SCOPUS, SpeleolAb, T02, W07, Z02.
—BLDSC (6478.885000), AskIEEE, CASDDS, IE, Infotrieve, Ingenta, INIST, Linda Hall. **CCC.**
Published by: Elsevier BV, North-Holland (Subsidiary of: Elsevier Science & Technology), Sara Burgerhartstraat 25, Amsterdam, 1055 KV, Netherlands. TEL 31-20-4853911, FAX 31-20-4852457, JournalsCustomerServiceEMEA@elsevier.com. Ed. M P Kamionkowski. **Subscr.:** Elsevier BV, Radarweg 29, PO Box 211, Amsterdam 1000 AE, Netherlands. TEL 31-20-4853757, FAX 31-20-4853432.

530 USA ISSN 2090-2220
➤ **PHYSICS RESEARCH INTERNATIONAL.** Text in English. 2007. irreg. USD 195 (effective 2011). **Document type:** *Journal, Academic/Scholarly.* **Description:** Publishes original research articles as well as review articles in all areas of physics.
Formerly (until 2009): Research Letters in Physics (1687-689X)
Related titles: Online - full text ed.: ISSN 2090-2239. 2007. free (effective 2011).
Indexed: A01, SCOPUS, T02.
Published by: Hindawi Publishing Corporation, 410 Park Ave, 15th Fl, PMB 287, New York, NY 10022. FAX 866-446-3294, hindawi@hindawi.com, info@hindawi.com.

530 GBR ISSN 0959-8472
PHYSICS REVIEW. Text in English. 1991. 4/yr. GBP 26.95 domestic; GBP 33 in Europe; GBP 38 elsewhere (effective 2010). adv. **Document type:** *Magazine, Academic/Scholarly.*
Related titles: Online - full text ed.: free to qualified personnel (effective 2010).
Indexed: A26, A28, APA, BrCerAb, BrTechI, C&ISA, CA/WCA, CIA, CerAb, CivEngAb, CorrAb, E&CAJ, E11, EEA, EMA, ESPM, EnvEAb, G05, G06, G07, G08, H15, I05, I06, I07, M&TEA, M09, MBF, METADEX, S06, S23, SolStAb, T04, WAA.
—Linda Hall. **CCC.**
Published by: Philip Allan Updates, Market Pl, Deddington, Banbury, Oxon OX15 0SE, United Kingdom. TEL 44-1869-338652, FAX 44-1869-337590, sales@philipallan.co.uk. **Subscr. to:** Turpin Distribution, Pegasus Dr, Stratton Business Park, Biggleswade, Bedfordshire SG18 8TQ, United Kingdom. TEL 44-1767-604974, FAX 44-845-0095840, custserv@turpin-distribution.com.

530.071 USA ISSN 0031-921X
QC30 CODEN: PHTEAH
➤ **THE PHYSICS TEACHER.** Text in English. 1963. m. USD 434 domestic to institutions; USD 469 foreign to institutions; USD 55 per issue domestic to institutions; USD 67 per issue foreign to institutions; free to members (effective 2010). adv. bk.rev.; film rev.; Website rev. charts; illus. index. 64 p./no.; back issues avail.; reprints avail. **Document type:** *Journal, Academic/Scholarly.* **Description:** Focuses on teaching introductory physics at all levels. tutorial papers, articles on pedagogy, current research or news in physics; articles on history and philosophy and biographies.
Related titles: Microform ed.; Online - full text ed.: ISSN 1943-4928.
Indexed: A01, A02, A03, A08, A22, A25, A26, B04, B14, BRD, BRI, CA, CPE, CPI, ChemAb, E02, E03, E06, E07, E08, E09, ERI, EdA, EdI, G03, G08, GSA, GSI, GeoRef, I05, INIS AtomInd, Inspec, M01, M02, MRD, P02, P04, P07, P10, P18, P48, P53, P54, PQC, PhysBer, S01, S06, S08, S09, SPINweb, T02, W03.
—BLDSC (6478.900000), CASDDS, IE, Infotrieve, Ingenta, Linda Hall. **CCC.**
Published by: American Association of Physics Teachers, One Physics Ellipse, College Park, MD 20740. TEL 301-209-3300, FAX 301-209-0845, webmaster@aapt.org, http://www.aapt.org. Ed. Karl Mamola. Adv. contact Robert Finnegan. B&W page USD 1,016, color page USD 1,520; trim 8.125 x 10.75. Circ: 10,300 (paid).

530.071 IND
THE PHYSICS TEACHER. Text in English. 1958. q. free to members (effective 2011). bk.rev. back issues avail. **Document type:** *Journal, Academic/Scholarly.*
Indexed: MRD.
Published by: Indian Physical Society, IACS Campus, 2-3 Raja Subodh Mallik Rd, Kolkata, West Bengal 700 032, India. TEL 91-33-24734971 ext 144.

530 USA ISSN 0031-9228
QC1 CODEN: PHTOAD
➤ **PHYSICS TODAY.** Text in English. 1948. m. price varies based on the number of users. bk.rev. bibl.; charts; illus.; stat. Index. back issues avail.; reprints avail. **Document type:** *Journal, Academic/Scholarly.* **Description:** Provides original articles and ground-breaking research in physics and related sciences. Offers fresh perspectives on contemporary technical innovations, basic and applied research, history of science, education, and science policy.
Related titles: Microfiche ed.: USD 360 domestic; USD 390 foreign (effective 2006); Online - full text ed.: ISSN 1945-0699; ◆ Supplement(s): American Institute of Physics. Annual Report. ISSN 0569-5686.
Indexed: A&ATA, A01, A02, A03, A05, A08, A09, A10, A11, A20, A22, A23, A24, A25, A26, A28, APA, AS&TA, AS&TI, ASCA, AcaI, ApMecR, B04, B05, B07, B10, B13, B14, BRD, BRI, BiolDig, BrCerAb, BrTechI, C&ISA, C05, C10, C12, C13, CA, CA/WCA, CBRI, CEABA, CIA, CIN, CPI, CPerI, Cadscan, CerAb, ChemAb, ChemTitl, CivEngAb, CorrAb, CurCont, CurPA, E&CAJ, E08, E11, EEA, EIA, EMA, ESPM, EngInd, EnvEAb, G01, G03, G05, G06, G07, G08, GALA, GSA, GSI, GeoRef, H15, I05, IBR, IBZ, INIS AtomInd, ISR, Inspec, LeadAb, M&GPA, M&TEA, M01, M02, M06, M09, MASUSE, MBF, METADEX, MSN, MagInd, P02, P10, P13, P26, P30, P34, P48, P52, P53, P54, P56, PQC, PRA, PhysBer, R03, R04, RGAb, RGPR, RILM, RefZh, S01, S08, S09, S10, SCI, SCOPUS, SPINweb, SolStAb, SpeleolAb, T02, T04, TOM, U01, V02, V03, V04, W03, W07, WAA, WBA, WMB, Zincscan.
—BLDSC (6479.000000), AskIEEE, CASDDS, IE, Infotrieve, Ingenta, INIST, Linda Hall. **CCC.**
Published by: American Institute of Physics, 1 Physics Ellipse, College Park, MD 20740. TEL 301-209-3100, aipinfo@aip.org, http://www.aip.org. Adv. contact Randy Nanna TEL 301-209-3040. **Subscr. to:** PO Box 503284, St Louis, MO 63150. TEL 516-576-2270, 800-344-6902, FAX 516-349-9704, subs@aip.org, http://librarians.aip.org.

530 GBR ISSN 1063-7869
QC1 CODEN: PHUSEY
➤ **PHYSICS - USPEKHI.** Text in English. 1918. m. USD 2,972 combined subscription in United States to institutions (print & online eds.); GBP 1,651 combined subscription elsewhere to institutions (print & online eds.); USD 297 per issue in United States to institutions; USD 165 per issue elsewhere to institutions (effective 2012). adv. bibl.; charts; abstr. index. 105 p./no. 2 cols./p.; back issues avail. **Document type:** *Journal, Academic/Scholarly.* **Description:** Covers a wide spectrum of the world's scientific research in physics and associated fields.
Formerly (until 1993): Soviet Physics - Uspekhi (0038-5670)
Related titles: CD-ROM ed.: 1997; E-mail ed.; Online - full text ed.: ISSN 1468-4780. USD 2,675 in United States to institutions; GBP 1,486 elsewhere to institutions (effective 2012); ◆ Translation of: Uspekhi Fizicheskikh Nauk. ISSN 0042-1294.
Indexed: A01, A03, A08, A22, A28, APA, AcoustA, BrCerAb, C&ISA, CA, CA/WCA, CIA, CPEI, CPI, CerAb, CivEngAb, CorrAb, CurCont, E&CAJ, E11, EEA, EMA, EngInd, GeoRef, H15, IBR, IBZ, ISR, Inspec, M&TEA, M09, MBF, METADEX, MathR, PhysBer, SCI, SCOPUS, SolStAb, SpeleolAb, T02, T04, W07, WAA.
—BLDSC (0416.867000), AskIEEE, CASDDS, IE, Infotrieve, Ingenta, INIST, Linda Hall. **CCC.**
Published by: (Rossiiskaya Akademiya Nauk, Institut Fiziki im. P.N. Lebedeva/Russian Academy of Sciences, P.N. Lebedev Physics Institute RUS), Turpion Ltd., 207 Brondesbury Park, London, NW2 5JN, United Kingdom. TEL 44-20-84590066, FAX 44-20-84516454, admin@turpion.org. Ed. L V Keldysh. **Dist. addr.:** Turpin Distribution Services Ltd. **Co-publisher:** Turpion - Moscow Ltd.

530 USA ISSN 1944-2653
PHYSICS WEEK. Text in English. 2008 (Jan.). w. USD 2,295 in US & Canada; USD 2,495 elsewhere; USD 2,525 combined subscription in US & Canada (print & online eds.); USD 2,755 combined subscription elsewhere (print & online eds.) (effective 2011). adv. back issues avail. **Document type:** *Newsletter, Trade.* **Description:** Compiles the latest research in all areas of physics, including laser physics, polymer physics, astrophysics, macromolecular physics, geophysics and theoretical physics.
Related titles: E-mail ed.; Online - full text ed.: ISSN 1944-2661. USD 2,295 combined subscription (online & e-mail eds.) (effective 2011).
Indexed: I05, P26, P48, P52, P54, P56, PQC.
Published by: NewsRx, 2727 Paces Ferry Rd SE, Ste 2-440, Atlanta, GA 30339. TEL 770-435-8286, 800-726-4550, FAX 770-435-6800, pressrelease@newsrx.com, http://www.newsrx.com. Pub., Adv. contact Susan Hasty TEL 770-507-7777.

530 GBR ISSN 0953-8585
QC1 CODEN: PHWOEW
➤ **PHYSICS WORLD.** Text in English. 1988. m. USD 1,295 combined subscription to institutions (print & online eds.) (effective 2009). adv. bk.rev. charts; illus. index. back issues avail.; reprints avail. **Document type:** *Journal, Academic/Scholarly.* **Description:** For all physicists: those in industry, government, education or academia, pure or applied physics, in engineering or business.
Formed by the merger of (1950-1988): Physics Bulletin (0031-9112); Which was formerly (until 1968): Institute of Physics and the Physical Society. Bulletin; (until 1962): Great Britain. Institute of Physics. Bulletin; (1970-1988): Physics in Technology (0305-4624); Which was formerly (until 1973): Review of Physics in Technology (0034-6683)
Related titles: Microfiche ed.; Microfilm ed.; Online - full text ed.
Indexed: A20, A22, A33, AESIS, ASCA, BiolDig, C&ISA, ChemAb, ChemTitl, CorrAb, CurCont, E&CAJ, EngInd, GeoRef, INIS AtomInd, Inspec, PhilInd, PhysBer, SCI, SCOPUS, SolStAb, SpeleolAb, TM, W07, WAA.
—BLDSC (6479.200000), AskIEEE, CASDDS, IE, Infotrieve, Ingenta, INIST, Linda Hall. **CCC.**
Published by: (Institute of Physics), Institute of Physics Publishing Ltd., Dirac House, Temple Back, Bristol, BS1 6BE, United Kingdom. TEL 44-117-9297481, FAX 44-117-9301178, custserv@iop.org, http://publishing.iop.org/. Ed. Matin Durrani. Pub. Jo Nicholas TEL 44-117-9301029. Adv. contact Edward Jost TEL 44-117-9301026. B&W page GBP 2,990, color page GBP 3,735; trim 213 x 282. Circ: 34,495.

530 DEU ISSN 1616-2811
PHYSIK. Text in German. 2000. irreg. price varies. **Document type:** *Monographic series, Academic/Scholarly.*

Published by: Bochumer Universitaetsverlag GmbH, Querenburger Hoehe 281, Bochum, 44801, Germany. TEL 49-234-9719780, FAX 49-234-9719786, bou@bou.de, http://bou.de.

530 DEU
PHYSIK IN HOHEN MAGNETFELDERN. Text in German. 1996. irreg., latest vol.27, 2004. price varies. **Document type:** *Monographic series, Academic/Scholarly.*
Published by: Hartung-Gorre Verlag, Konstanz, 78465, Germany. TEL 49-7533-97227, FAX 49-7533-97228, Hartung.Gorre@t-online.de. Ed. Peter Wyder.

530 DEU ISSN 0031-9252
QC1 CODEN: PHUZAH
PHYSIK IN UNSERER ZEIT. Text in German. 1969. bi-m. GBP 132 in United Kingdom to institutions; EUR 247 in Europe to institutions; USD 259 elsewhere to institutions; GBP 153 combined subscription in United Kingdom to institutions (print & online eds.); EUR 284 combined subscription in Europe to institutions (print & online eds.); USD 298 combined subscription elsewhere to institutions (print & online eds.) (effective 2012). adv. bk.rev.; software rev.; Website rev. charts; illus. index. reprint service avail. from PSC. **Document type:** *Journal, Academic/Scholarly.* **Description:** Provides an in-depth overview of the latest scientific findings in physics as well as related fields.
Related titles: Microform ed.; Online - full text ed.: ISSN 1521-3943. GBP 132 in United Kingdom to institutions; EUR 247 in Europe to institutions; USD 259 elsewhere to institutions (effective 2012).
Indexed: A22, CIN, ChemAb, ChemTitl, Inspec, PhilInd, PhysBer, TM.
—CASDDS, IE, Infotrieve, Ingenta, INIST, Linda Hall. **CCC.**
Published by: Wiley - V C H Verlag GmbH & Co. KGaA (Subsidiary of: John Wiley & Sons, Inc.), Postfach 101161, Weinheim, 69451, Germany. TEL 49-6201-606400, FAX 49-6201-606184, info@wiley-vch.de, http://www.wiley-vch.de. Ed. Hans-Joachim Schlichting. adv.: B&W page EUR 2,740, color page EUR 4,120. Circ: 5,752 (paid and controlled).

530 DEU ISSN 1617-9439
CODEN: TEBIDX
➤ **PHYSIK JOURNAL.** Text in German. 1944. m. GBP 177 in United Kingdom to institutions; EUR 360 in Europe to institutions; USD 348 elsewhere to institutions (effective 2012). adv. bk.rev. abstr.; charts; illus. index. reprint service avail. from PSC. **Document type:** *Journal, Academic/Scholarly.* **Description:** Reports on new developments and progress in basic physics, applied physics and technology.
Former titles (until 2002): Physikalische Blaetter (0031-9279); (until 1947): Neue Physikalische Blaetter (0342-4480); (until 1946): Physikalische Blaetter (0342-4472)
Related titles: Online - full text ed.: ISSN 1619-6597.
Indexed: A22, CEABA, ChemAb, ChemTitl, IBR, IBZ, Inspec, PhysBer, TM.
—BLDSC (6479.759500), AskIEEE, CASDDS, IE, Ingenta, INIST, Linda Hall. **CCC.**
Published by: (Deutsche Physikalische Gesellschaft), Wiley - V C H Verlag GmbH & Co. KGaA (Subsidiary of: John Wiley & Sons, Inc.), Postfach 101161, Weinheim, 69451, Germany. TEL 49-6201-606400, FAX 49-6201-606184, subservice@wiley-vch.de, info@wiley-vch.de, http://www.wiley-vch.de. Ed. Stefan Jorda. Adv. contact Aenne Anders TEL 49-6201-606552. B&W page EUR 5,300, color page EUR 6,950. Circ: 52,443 (paid and controlled). **Subscr. in the Americas to:** John Wiley & Sons, Inc., 111 River St, Hoboken, NJ 07030. TEL 201-748-6645, subinfo@wiley.com, http://www.wiley.com/WileyCDA/; **Subscr. outside Germany, Austria & Switzerland to:** John Wiley & Sons Ltd., The Atrium, Southern Gate, Chichester, West Sussex PO19 8SQ, United Kingdom. TEL 44-1243-779777, FAX 44-1243-775878, cs-agency@wiley.com, http://onlinelibrary.wiley.com/.

➤ **PHYSIOLOGICAL MEASUREMENT.** *see* MEDICAL SCIENCES

530 RUS ISSN 0370-274X
QC1 CODEN: PZETAB
PIS'MA V ZHURNAL EKSPERIMENTAL'NOI I TEORETICHESKOI FIZIKI. Text in Russian. 1965. s-m. RUR 930 for 6 mos. domestic (effective 2004). **Document type:** *Journal, Academic/Scholarly.* **Description:** Timely, topical short papers, emphasizing fundamental theoretical and experimental research in all fields of physics.
Formerly (until 1993): Soviet Technical Physics Letters (0360-120X)
Related titles: ◆ English Translation: J E T P Letters. ISSN 0021-3640.
Indexed: CorrAb, GeoRef, INIS AtomInd, Inspec, RefZh, SpeleolAb, WAA.
—BLDSC (0129.488000), East View, INIST, Linda Hall.
Published by: (American Institute of Physics USA), Izdatel'stvo Nauka, Profsoyuznaya ul 90, Moscow, 117864, Russian Federation. TEL 7-095-3347151, FAX 7-095-4202220, secret@naukaran.ru, http://www.naukaran.ru.

530.05 RUS ISSN 0320-0116
QC1 CODEN: PZTFDD
PIS'MA V ZHURNAL TEKHNICHESKOI FIZIKI. Text in Russian. 1975. m. USD 624 foreign (effective 2011). **Document type:** *Journal, Academic/Scholarly.* **Description:** Rapid publication on developments in theoretical and experimental physics with potential technological applications.
Related titles: Online - full text ed.: ISSN 1726-7471; ◆ English Translation: Technical Physics Letters. ISSN 1063-7850.
Indexed: CorrAb, INIS AtomInd, Inspec, RefZh, WAA.
—East View, INIST, Linda Hall. **CCC.**
Published by: (Rossiiskaya Akademiya Nauk, Fiziko-tekhnicheskii Institut im. A.F. Ioffe), Izdatel'stvo Nauka, Profsoyuznaya ul 90, Moscow, 117864, Russian Federation. TEL 7-095-3347151, FAX 7-095-4202220, secret@naukaran.ru, http://www.naukaran.ru.

530.44 JPN ISSN 1880-6821
➤ **PLASMA AND FUSION RESEARCH.** Text in English. 2006. s-a. free (effective 2009). **Document type:** *Journal, Academic/Scholarly.* **Description:** Covers plasma science and technology, including basic plasma physics and new trends, magnetic confinement fusion, magnetic confinement fusion, inertial confinement fusion, fusion engineering, and applied plasma physics.
Media: Online - full content.
Published by: Purazuma Kaku Yugo Gakkai/Japan Society of Plasma Science and Nuclear Fusion Research, 20-29 Nishiki 2-chome, Naka-ku, Nagoya-shi, Aichi-ken 460-0003, Japan. TEL 81-52-7353185, FAX 81-52-7353485, http://www.nifs.ac.jp/jspf/. Ed. Terai Takayuki.

➤ **PLASMA CHEMISTRY & PLASMA PROCESSING.** *see* ENGINEERING—Chemical Engineering

530 GBR ISSN 1051-9998
TA2001 CODEN: PDOPEZ
➤ **PLASMA DEVICES AND OPERATIONS.** Text in English. 1990. q. GBP 1,389, EUR 1,761, USD 2,211 combined subscription to institutions (print & online eds.) (effective 2009). adv. back issues avail.; reprint service avail. from PSC. **Document type:** *Journal, Academic/Scholarly.* **Description:** Covers plasma technology, engineering, and applications; plasma source and pulsed plasma devices; plasma accelerators and pulsed plasma heating systems.
Related titles: CD-ROM ed.: ISSN 1026-7735; Microform ed.; Online - full text ed.: ISSN 1029-4929. GBP 1,320, EUR 1,673, USD 2,100 to institutions (effective 2009) (from IngentaConnect).
Indexed: A01, A03, A08, A22, CA, CPEI, CurCont, E01, EngInd, MSCI, S01, SCI, SCOPUS, T02, W07.
—IE, Infotrieve, Ingenta. **CCC.**
Published by: Taylor & Francis Ltd. (Subsidiary of: Taylor & Francis Group), 4 Park Sq, Milton Park, Abingdon, Oxfordshire OX14 4RN, United Kingdom. TEL 44-20-70176000, FAX 44-20-70176336, subscriptions@tandf.co.uk, http://www.taylorandfrancis.com. Ed. V A Glukhikh. Adv. contact Linda Hann. **Subscr. to:** Journals Customer Service, Sheepen Pl, Colchester, Essex CO3 3LP, United Kingdom. TEL 44-20-70175544, FAX 44-20-70175198, tf.enquiries@tfinforma.com.

530.44 GBR ISSN 0741-3335
QC770 CODEN: PPCFET
➤ **PLASMA PHYSICS AND CONTROLLED FUSION.** Text in English; Text occasionally in French, German. 1954. m. GBP 1,916 combined subscription to institutions (print & online eds.) (effective 2010). bk.rev. bibl.; illus.; abstr.; charts. Index. back issues avail.; reprints avail. **Document type:** *Journal, Academic/Scholarly.* **Description:** Covers all aspects of the physics of hot, highly-ionized plasmas including results of current experimental and theoretical research on all aspects of the physics of high-temperature plasmas and of controlled nuclear fusion, including the basic phenomena in highly-ionized gases in the laboratory, in the ionosphere and in space, in magnetic-confinement and inertial-confinement fusion as well as related diagnostic methods.
Former titles (until 1984): Plasma Physics (0032-1028); (until 1967): Journal of Nuclear Energy. Part C, Plasma Physics, Accelerators, Thermonuclear Research (0368-3281); Which superseded in part (in 1959): Journal of Nuclear Energy (0891-3919)
Related titles: Microfiche ed.: USD 2,374 in the Americas; GBP 1,206 elsewhere (effective 2007) (from MIM, PQC); Online - full text ed.: ISSN 1361-6587. 1996. GBP 1,824 to institutions (effective 2010) (from IngentaConnect).
Indexed: A01, A03, A05, A08, A22, A23, A24, AS&TA, AS&TI, ASCA, ApMecR, B13, C10, CA, CPEI, ChemAb, ChemTitl, CurCont, EngInd, INIS AtomInd, ISR, Inspec, RefZh, SCI, SCOPUS, T02, W07.
—BLDSC (6528.720000), AskIEEE, CASDDS, IE, Infotrieve, Ingenta, INIST, Linda Hall. **CCC.**
Published by: (Institute of Physics), Institute of Physics Publishing Ltd., Dirac House, Temple Back, Bristol, BS1 6BE, United Kingdom. TEL 44-117-9297481, FAX 44-117-9301178, custserv@iop.org, http://publishing.iop.org/. Ed. R O Dendy. Pub. Caroline Wilkinson. **Subscr. in N. America to:** American Institute of Physics, PO Box 503284, St Louis, MO 63150. TEL 516-576-2270, 800-344-6902, FAX 516-349-9704, subs@aip.org.

530.44 RUS ISSN 1063-780X
QC717.6 CODEN: PPHREM
➤ **PLASMA PHYSICS REPORTS.** Text in English. 1975. m. EUR 4,667, USD 5,650 combined subscription to institutions (print & online eds.) (effective 2012). abstr.; bibl.; charts; illus. index. back issues avail. **Document type:** *Journal, Academic/Scholarly.* **Description:** Emphasizes theoretical and experimental studies of plasma, with particular emphasis on plasma confinement systems.
Formerly: Soviet Journal of Plasma Physics (0360-0343)
Related titles: Microform ed.; Online - full text ed.: ISSN 1562-6938 (from IngentaConnect); ◆ Translation of: Fizika Plazmy (Moscow, 1975). ISSN 0367-2921.
Indexed: A01, A03, A08, A22, A26, ASCA, CA, CurCont, E01, GPAA, INIS AtomInd, ISR, Inspec, PhysBer, S01, SCI, SCOPUS, SPINweb, T02, W07.
—BLDSC (0416.900500), AskIEEE, East View, IE, Infotrieve, Ingenta, INIST, Linda Hall. **CCC.**
Published by: (Rossiiskaya Akademiya Nauk/Russian Academy of Sciences), M A I K Nauka - Interperiodica (Subsidiary of: Pleiades Publishing, Inc.), Profsoyuznaya ul 90, Moscow, 117997, Russian Federation. TEL 7-095-3347420, FAX 7-095-3360666, compmg@maik.ru. Ed. Vitalii D Shafranov. **Dist. in the Americas by:** Springer New York LLC, Journal Fulfillment, PO Box 2485, Secaucus, NJ 07096. TEL 212-460-1500, FAX 201-348-4505; **Dist. outside of the Americas by:** Springer, Haber Str 7, Heidelberg 69126, Germany. TEL 49-6221-3454303, FAX 49-6221-3454229.

530.44 DEU ISSN 1612-8850
QD381.8 CODEN: PPPLA6
➤ **PLASMA PROCESSES AND POLYMERS.** Text in English. 2004. m. GBP 1,019 in United Kingdom to institutions; EUR 1,545 in Europe to institutions; USD 1,995 elsewhere to institutions; GBP 1,172 combined subscription in United Kingdom to institutions (print & online eds.); EUR 1,777 combined subscription in Europe to institutions (print & online eds.); USD 2,294 combined subscription elsewhere to institutions (print & online eds.) (effective 2012). reprint service avail. from PSC. **Document type:** *Journal, Academic/Scholarly.* **Description:** Publishes articles on low-temperature plasma sources and processes operating at pressures ranging from partial vacuum to atmospheric.
Related titles: Online - full text ed.: ISSN 1612-8869. GBP 1,019 in United Kingdom to institutions; EUR 1,545 in Europe to institutions; USD 1,995 elsewhere to institutions (effective 2012).
Indexed: A28, APA, BrCerAb, C&ISA, C33, CA/WCA, CCI, CIA, CPEI, CerAb, CivEngAb, CorrAb, CurCont, E&CAJ, E11, EEA, EMA, EngInd, H15, Inspec, M&TEA, M09, MBF, METADEX, MSCI, P30, SCI, SCOPUS, SolStAb, T04, TM, W07, WAA.
—BLDSC (6528.781000), IE, Ingenta, INIST, Linda Hall. **CCC.**
Published by: Wiley - V C H Verlag GmbH & Co. KGaA (Subsidiary of: John Wiley & Sons, Inc.), Postfach 101161, Weinheim, 69451, Germany. TEL 49-6201-606400, FAX 49-6201-606184, info@wiley-vch.de. Ed. Joern Ritterbusch.

530 GBR ISSN 0963-0252
QC717.6 CODEN: PSTEEU
➤ **PLASMA SOURCES SCIENCE AND TECHNOLOGY.** Abbreviated title: P S S T. Text in English. 1992. bi-m. GBP 566 combined subscription to institutions (print & online eds.) (effective 2010). back issues avail. **Document type:** *Journal, Academic/Scholarly.* **Description:** Reports on non-fusion plasma sources which operate at all ranges of pressure and density including neutral and non-neutral plasma sources; positive and negative ion sources; free radical sources; microwave, RF, direct current, laser and electron beam excited sources; resonant sources; plasmas for etching, deposition, polymerization, sintering; plasma sources for accelerators; lighting applications; plasma sources for medical physics; plasma sources for lasers.
Related titles: Microfiche ed.: USD 563 in the Americas; GBP 288 elsewhere (effective 2007); Online - full text ed.: ISSN 1361-6595. GBP 436 to institutions (effective 2010) (from IngentaConnect).
Indexed: A01, A03, A08, A22, ASCA, CA, CIN, CPEI, ChemAb, ChemTitl, CurCont, EngInd, ISR, Inspec, RefZh, SCI, SCOPUS, T02, W07.
—BLDSC (6528.782150), AskIEEE, CASDDS, IE, Infotrieve, Ingenta, INIST, Linda Hall. **CCC.**
Published by: (Institute of Physics), Institute of Physics Publishing Ltd., Dirac House, Temple Back, Bristol, BS1 6BE, United Kingdom. TEL 44-117-9297481, FAX 44-117-9301178, custserv@iop.org, http://publishing.iop.org/. Ed. Mark J Kushner. Pub. Caroline Wilkinson. **Subscr. addr. in the US, Canada & Mexico:** American Institute of Physics, PO Box 503284, St Louis, MO 63150. TEL 516-576-2270, 800-344-6902, FAX 516-349-9704, subs@aip.org.

530 621.3 NLD ISSN 1572-6061
➤ **PLASMA TECHNOLOGY.** Text in English. 1985. irreg., latest vol.4, 1992. price varies. back issues avail. **Document type:** *Monographic series, Academic/Scholarly.* **Description:** Explores physics and engineering applications of plasma technology.
Published by: Elsevier BV (Subsidiary of: Elsevier Science & Technology), Radarweg 29, PO Box 211, Amsterdam, 1000 AE, Netherlands. TEL 31-20-4853911, FAX 31-20-4852457, JournalsCustomerServiceEMEA@elsevier.com, http://www.elsevier.nl.

530 USA ISSN 1557-1955
QC176.8.P55
➤ **PLASMONICS.** Text in English. 2006. q. USD 588 combined subscription to institutions (print & online eds.) (effective 2011). back issues avail.; reprint service avail. from PSC. **Document type:** *Journal, Academic/Scholarly.* **Description:** Covers theory, physics, and applications of surface plasmons in metals, and rapidly emerging areas of nanotechnology, biophotonics, sensing, biochemistry and medicine.
Related titles: Online - full text ed.: ISSN 1557-1963 (from IngentaConnect).
Indexed: A01, A22, A26, CCI, CurCont, E01, MSCI, P30, SCI, SCOPUS, T02, W07.
—BLDSC (6528.790130), IE, Ingenta. **CCC.**
Published by: Springer New York LLC (Subsidiary of: Springer Science+Business Media), 233 Spring St, New York, NY 10013. TEL 212-460-1500, service-ny@springer.com, http://www.springer.com/. Ed. Chris D Geddes.

➤ **POLISH ACADEMY OF SCIENCES. BULLETIN. MATHEMATICS.** *see* MATHEMATICS

➤ **POLISH JOURNAL OF MEDICAL PHYSICS AND ENGINEERING.** *see* MEDICAL SCIENCES

530 POL ISSN 0072-0364
QC1
POLITECHNIKA GDANSKA. ZESZYTY NAUKOWE. FIZYKA. Text in English, Polish; Summaries in Russian. 1967. irreg. price varies. bibl.; charts; illus. **Document type:** *Monographic series, Academic/Scholarly.*
—INIST, Linda Hall.
Published by: Politechnika Gdanska/Gdansk University of Technology, ul Narutowicza 11-12, Gdansk, 80233, Poland. **Dist. by:** Osrodek Rozpowszechniania Wydawnictw Naukowych PAN, Palac Kultury i Nauki, Warsaw 00901, Poland.

POLITECHNIKA SLASKA. ZESZYTY NAUKOWE. MATEMATYKA - FIZYKA. *see* MATHEMATICS

530 POL ISSN 0324-8380
CODEN: PIFWA8
POLITECHNIKA WARSZAWSKA. INSTYTUT FIZYKI. PRACE. Text in English, Polish. 1967. irreg., latest no.48, 1999. price varies. **Document type:** *Monographic series, Academic/Scholarly.*
Indexed: ChemAb.
—CASDDS, Linda Hall.
Published by: (Politechnika Warszawska, Instytut Fizyki), Oficyna Wydawnicza Politechniki Warszawskiej/Publishing House of the Warsaw University of Technology, ul Polna 50, Warsaw, 00644, Poland. oficyna@wpw.pw.edu.pl. Ed. Waclaw Jakubowski.

POLYTECHNICAL UNIVERSITY OF BUCHAREST. SCIENTIFIC BULLETIN. SERIES A: APPLIED MATHEMATICS AND PHYSICS. *see* MATHEMATICS

530 PRT ISSN 0048-4903
CODEN: POPYA4
PORTUGALIAE PHYSICA. Text and summaries in English, French. 1943-1975; resumed 1979. s-a. USD 24 to individuals; USD 60 to libraries.
Indexed: ChemAb, GeoRef, Inspec, MathR, PhysBer, SpeleolAb.
—AskIEEE, CASDDS, INIST, Linda Hall.
Published by: Sociedade Portuguesa de Fisica, Laboratorio de Fisica, Praca Gomes Teixeira, Porto, 4000, Portugal. TEL 2-325937. Ed. J M Machado da Silva. Circ: 950.

534 POL ISSN 0032-5430
QC1 CODEN: PSTFAT
➤ **POSTEPY FIZYKI.** Text in Polish; Abstracts in English. 1950. bi-m. EUR 50 foreign (effective 2011). illus. **Document type:** *Journal, Academic/Scholarly.* **Description:** Addressed to the Polish community of physicists. Presents the latest research in physics, as well as reports on important events, reviews of academic publications, etc.
Indexed: B22, CIN, ChemAb, ChemTitl, Inspec, PhysBer.
—AskIEEE, CASDDS, INIST, Linda Hall.

P

Published by: Polskie Towarzystwo Fizyczne/Polish Physical Society, ul Hoza 69, Warsaw, 00681, Poland. TEL 48-22-5532154, FAX 48-22-6212668, ptf@fuw.edu.pl, http://ptf.fuw.edu.pl. Circ: 1,000. **Dist. by:** Ars Polona, Obroncow 25, Warsaw 03933, Poland. TEL 48-22-5098609, FAX 48-22-5098610, arspolona@arspolona.com.pl, http://www.arspolona.com.pl.

539 621 RUS ISSN 1028-0960 CODEN: PFKMDJ
POVERKHNOST'. RENTGENOVSKIE, SINKHROTRONNYE I NEJTRONNYE ISSLEDOVANIYA. Text in Russian. 1982. m.
Description: Covers theoretical and experimental research in physics, chemistry, and the mechanics of solid surfaces.
Formerly (until 1996): Poverkhnost'. Fizika, Khimiia, Mekhanika (0207-3528)
Indexed: C33, CorrAb, INIS AtomInd, RefZh, SCOPUS, WAA.
—East View, INIST, Linda Hall. **CCC.**
Published by: Rossiiskaya Akademiya Nauk/Russian Academy of Sciences, Profsoyuznaya ul., 90, Moscow, 117864, Russian Federation. http://www.ras.ru.

530 IND ISSN 0304-4289
QC1 CODEN: PRAMCI
➤ **PRAMANA**; journal of physics. Text in English. 1973. m. EUR 443, USD 536 combined subscription to institutions (print & online eds.) (effective 2012). illus. s-a. index. 120 p./no. 1 cols./p.; back issues avail.; reprint service avail. from PSC. **Document type:** *Journal, Academic/Scholarly.* **Description:** Contains research papers, brief reports, rapid communications, and review articles.
Related titles: Microform ed.: 1973 (from PQC); Online - full text ed.: ISSN 0973-7111 (from IngentaConnect).
Indexed: A01, A20, A22, A26, A28, APA, ASCA, ApMecR, BrCerAb, C&ISA, CA, CA/WCA, CIA, CIN, CPEI, CerAb, ChemAb, ChemTitl, CivEngAb, CorrAb, CurCont, E&CAJ, E01, E11, EEA, EMA, EngInd, GeoRef, H12, H15, I05, IBR, IBZ, INIS AtomInd, ISMEC, ISR, Inspec, M&TEA, M09, MBF, METADEX, P30, PhysBer, SCI, SCOPUS, SolStAb, SpeleolAb, T02, T04, W07, WAA.
—BLDSC (6601.300000), AskIEEE, CASDDS, IE, Infotrieve, Ingenta, INIST, Linda Hall. **CCC.**
Published by: Indian Academy of Sciences, C.V. Raman Ave, Sadashivanagar, PO Box 8005, Bangalore, Karnataka 560 080, India. TEL 91-80-22661200, FAX 91-80-23616094, http://www.ias.ac.in. Ed. Rohini M Godbole. Circ: 1,000. **Subscr. to:** I N S I O Scientific Books & Periodicals, PO Box 7234, Indraprastha HPO, New Delhi 110 002, India. iihm@ap.nic.in, http://iihm.ap.nic.in/. **Co-publisher:** Springer (India) Private Ltd.

530.07 DEU ISSN 1617-5689
PRAXIS DER NATURWISSENSCHAFTEN - PHYSIK IN DER SCHULE. Text in German. 2000. 8/yr. EUR 63.20 to individuals; EUR 47.20 to students; EUR 9.50 newsstand/cover (effective 2009). adv. bk.rev. **Document type:** *Journal, Academic/Scholarly.*
Formed by the merger of (1963-2000): Physik in der Schule (0031-9244); (1969-2000): Praxis der Naturwissenschaften. Physik (0177-8374); Which was formerly (until 1980): Praxis der Naturwissenschaften. Physik im Unterricht der Schulen (0342-8729); (until 1973): Praxis der Naturwissenschaften. Teil 1, Physik (0342-8710)
Indexed: IBR, IBZ.
Published by: Aulis-Verlag Deubner GmbH und Co. KG, Antwerpener Str 6-12, Cologne, 50672, Germany. TEL 49-221-9514540, FAX 49-221-95145460, info@aulis.de. R&P Wolfgang Deubner. Adv. contact Ulrike Lennertz. B&W page EUR 920, color page EUR 1,715. Circ: 4,500 (paid).

PRESEK; list za mlade matematike, fizike, astronome in racunalnikarje. *see* SCIENCES: COMPREHENSIVE WORKS

530 USA ISSN 2153-8301
QC173.59.S65
▼ ➤ **PRESPACETIME JOURNAL.** Text in English. 2010. q. free (effective 2010). **Description:** Features research by physicists, mathematicians and other scientists on the origin, nature and mechanism of spacetime and its possible connection to a prespacetime.
Media: Online - full text.
Published by: QuantumDream, Inc., PO Box 267, Stony Brook, NY 11790-0267. TEL 631-678-1864, hupinghu@quantumbrain.org.

530 RUS
PRIKLADNAYA FIZIKA. Text in Russian. q. USD 99.95 in United States.
Indexed: RASB.
Published by: V.I.M.I., Volokolamskoe shosse 77, Moscow, 123584, Russian Federation. TEL 7-095-4911306, FAX 7-095-4916820. **Dist. by:** East View Information Services, 10601 Wayzata Blvd, Minneapolis, MN 55305. TEL 952-252-1201, 800-477-1005, FAX 952-252-1202, info@eastview.com, http://www.eastview.com.

PRINCETON LANDMARKS IN MATHEMATICS AND PHYSICS. *see* MATHEMATICS

PRINCETON SERIES IN ASTROPHYSICS. *see* ASTRONOMY

530 USA ISSN 1052-8083
➤ **PRINCETON SERIES IN PHYSICS.** Text in English. 1953. irreg., latest 2001. price varies. illus. back issues avail.; reprints avail. **Document type:** *Monographic series, Academic/Scholarly.* **Description:** Examines topics in all areas of physics.
Formerly (until 1971): Investigations in Physics (0075-0220)
Indexed: CCMJ, Inspec, MathR.
—**CCC.**
Published by: Princeton University Press, 41 William St, Princeton, NJ 08540. TEL 609-258-4900, 800-777-4726, FAX 609-258-6305, cpriday@pupress.co.uk. Ed. Sam B Treiman. **Subscr. to:** California - Princeton Fulfillment Services, Inc., 1445 Lower Ferry Rd, Ewing, NJ 08618. TEL 609-883-1759, 800-777-4726, FAX 609-883-7413, 800-999-1958, orders@cpfsinc.com. **Dist. by:** University Press Group.; John Wiley & Sons Ltd.

530 NLD ISSN 1877-8569
▼ **PROGRESS IN COLLOID AND INTERFACE SCIENCE.** Text in English. 2009. irreg., latest vol.2, 2011. price varies. **Document type:** *Monographic series, Academic/Scholarly.*
Published by: Brill, PO Box 9000, Leiden, 2300 PA, Netherlands. TEL 31-71-5353500, FAX 31-71-5317532, cs@brill.nl. Eds. L Liggieri, R Miller.

530 SGP
PROGRESS IN HIGH TEMPERATURE SUPERCONDUCTIVITY. Text in English. 1987. irreg., latest vol.33. price varies. **Document type:** *Monographic series, Academic/Scholarly.*
Indexed: CIN, ChemAb, ChemTitl, Inspec.
Published by: World Scientific Publishing Co. Pte. Ltd., 5 Toh Tuck Link, Singapore, 596224, Singapore. TEL 65-6466-5775, FAX 65-6467-7667, wspc@wspc.com.sg, http://www.worldscientific.com. **Dist. by:** World Scientific Publishing Co., Inc., 27 Warren St, Ste 401-402, Hackensack, NJ 07601. TEL 201-487-9655, 800-227-7562, FAX 201-487-9656, 888-977-2665, wspc@wspc.com; World Scientific Publishing Ltd., 57 Shelton St, London WC2H 9HE, United Kingdom. TEL 44-207-8360888, FAX 44-207-8362020, sales@wspc.co.uk.

530 USA ISSN 1544-9998 CODEN: PRPHEC
PROGRESS IN MATHEMATICAL PHYSICS. Text in English. 1980. irreg. price varies. adv. back issues avail.; reprints avail. **Document type:** *Monographic series, Academic/Scholarly.*
Formerly (until 2001): Progress in Physics (0736-7422)
Indexed: CCMJ, ChemAb, Inspec, MathR.
—BLDSC (6868.916000), CASDDS, IE, Ingenta.
Published by: Birkhaeuser Boston (Subsidiary of: Springer Science+Business Media), 233 Spring St, New York, NY 10013. TEL 212-460-1500, FAX 212-460-1575, service-ny@springer.com, http://www.springer.com/birkhauser. **Dist. by:** Springer New York LLC.

530 USA ISSN 1555-5534
QC1
➤ **PROGRESS IN PHYSICS.** Text in English. 2005. q. back issues avail. **Document type:** *Journal, Academic/Scholarly.* **Description:** Covers advanced studies in theoretical and experimental physics, including related themes from mathematics.
Related titles: Online - full text ed.: ISSN 1555-5615. 2005. free (effective 2011).
Indexed: A01, A26, A28, A39, APA, BrCerAb, C&ISA, C27, C29, CA, CA/WCA, CCMJ, CIA, CerAb, CivEngAb, CorrAb, D03, D04, E&CAJ, E08, E11, E13, EEA, EMA, ESPM, EnvEAb, G08, H15, I05, Inspec, M&TEA, M09, MBF, METADEX, MSN, MathR, P26, P48, P52, P54, P56, PQC, R14, RefZh, S06, S09, S14, S15, S18, SolStAb, T02, T04, WAA, Z02.
—IE.
Address: c/o Prof Florentin Smarandache, Department of Mathematics and Science, University of New Mexico, 200 College Rd, Gallup, NM 87301. Ed. Dmitri Rabounski.

530 GBR ISSN 0079-6816
QD506 CODEN: PSSFBP
➤ **PROGRESS IN SURFACE SCIENCE.** Text in English. 1971. 12/yr. EUR 2,288 in Europe to institutions; JPY 303,800 in Japan to institutions; USD 2,561 elsewhere to institutions (effective 2012). back issues avail. **Document type:** *Journal, Academic/Scholarly.* **Description:** Contains review articles from all disciplines where surfaces and interfaces play an important role.
Related titles: Microfilm ed.: (from PQC); Online - full text ed.: ISSN 1878-4240 (from IngentaConnect, ScienceDirect).
Indexed: A01, A03, A08, A22, A26, A28, APA, ASCA, BrCerAb, C&ISA, C24, C33, CA, CA/WCA, CCI, CIA, CIN, CPEI, CerAb, ChemAb, ChemTitl, CivEngAb, CorrAb, CurCont, E&CAJ, E11, EEA, EMA, ESPM, EngInd, EnvEAb, H15, I05, ISR, Inspec, M&TEA, M09, MBF, METADEX, MSCI, P30, PhysBer, R16, RefZh, S01, SCI, SCOPUS, SolStAb, T02, T04, W07, WAA.
—BLDSC (6924.575000), AskIEEE, CASDDS, IE, Infotrieve, Ingenta, INIST. **CCC.**
Published by: Pergamon (Subsidiary of: Elsevier Science & Technology), The Blvd, Langford Ln, East Park, Kidlington, Oxford OX5 1GB, United Kingdom. TEL 44-1865-843000, FAX 44-1865-843010, JournalsCustomerServiceEMEA@elsevier.com. Ed. H Petek. **Subscr. to:** Elsevier BV, Radarweg 29, PO Box 211, Amsterdam 1000 AE, Netherlands. TEL 31-20-4853757, FAX 31-20-4853432, http://www.elsevier.nl.

➤ **PROGRESS OF CRYOGENICS AND ISOTOPES SEPARATION.** *see* CHEMISTRY

530 JPN ISSN 0033-068X
QC1 CODEN: PTPKAV
➤ **PROGRESS OF THEORETICAL PHYSICS/RIRON BUTSURIGAKU NO SHINPO.** Text in English. 1946. m. JPY 86,400 to institutions (effective 2006). cum.index: vol.89-100 (1993-1998); vol.77-88 (1987-1992); vol.67-76 (1982-1986); vol.57-66 (1977-1981); vol.37-56 (1967-1976); vol.21-36 (1959-1966); vol.1-20 (1946-1958). back issues avail. **Document type:** *Journal, Academic/Scholarly.* **Description:** Publishes papers in such areas as particles and fields, nuclear physics, solid state physics, statistical physics, astrophysics and cosmology.
Related titles: Online - full text ed.: ISSN 1347-4081; ◆ Supplement(s): Progress of Theoretical Physics. Supplement. ISSN 0375-9687.
Indexed: A22, ASCA, CCMJ, ChemAb, ChemTitl, CurCont, GeoRef, INIS AtomInd, ISR, Inspec, JCT, JTA, MSN, MathR, PhysBer, RefZh, SCI, SCOPUS, SpeleolAb, W07, Z02.
—BLDSC (6924.600000), AskIEEE, CASDDS, IE, Infotrieve, Ingenta, INIST, Linda Hall. **CCC.**
Published by: Institute of Pure and Applied Physics, Toyokaiji Bldg, no.12, 6-9-6 Shinbashi, Minato-ku, Tokyo, 105-0004, Japan. TEL 81-3-3432-4308, FAX 81-3-3432-0728, subscription@ipap.jp, http://www.ipap.jp. **Co-sponsors:** Physical Society of Japan/Nihon Butsuri Gakkai; Yukawa Institute for Theoretical Physics.

530 JPN ISSN 0375-9687 CODEN: PTPSEP
➤ **PROGRESS OF THEORETICAL PHYSICS. SUPPLEMENT.** Text in English. 1955. 4/yr. incld. with subscr. to Progress of Theoretical Physics. back issues avail. **Document type:** *Journal, Academic/Scholarly.* **Description:** Covers the developments in various fields of fundamental physics.
Related titles: ◆ Supplement to: Progress of Theoretical Physics. ISSN 0033-068X.
Indexed: A20, A22, ASCA, CCMJ, CIN, ChemAb, ChemTitl, CurCont, INIS AtomInd, ISR, Inspec, MSN, MathR, RefZh, SCI, SCOPUS, SpeleolAb, W07, Z02.
—BLDSC (6924.601000), AskIEEE, CASDDS, IE, Ingenta, INIST, Linda Hall. **CCC.**
Published by: Yukawa Institute for Theoretical Physics, c/o Yukawa Hall, Kyoto University, Kyoto, 606-8502, Japan. TEL 81-722-3540, FAX 81-75-722-6339. **Co-sponsor:** Physical Society of Japan/Nihon Butsuri Gakkai.

➤ **PSYCHOTRONIC VIDEO.** *see* COMMUNICATIONS—Video

530.44 621.381 JPN
PURAZUMA PUROSESHINGU KENKYUKAI PUROSHIDINGUSU/ PLASMA PROCESSING. Text in English, Japanese; Summaries in English. a. **Document type:** *Journal, Academic/Scholarly.*
Published by: Oyo Butsuri Gakkai, Purazuma Erekutoronikusu Kenkyukai/Japan Society of Applied Physics, Division of Plasma Electronics, 1-12-13 Kudan Kita Chiyoda-ku, Tokyo, 102-0073, Japan. TEL 81-3-32381043, FAX 81-3-32216245, divisions@jsap.or.jp, http://annex.jsap.or.jp/plasma/.

THE PYROTECHNIC LITERATURE SERIES. *see* ENGINEERING—Chemical Engineering

THE PYROTECHNIC REFERENCE SERIES. *see* ENGINEERING—Chemical Engineering

530 ITA ISSN 1594-9974
QUADERNI DI STORIA DELLA FISICA. Text in Italian. 1997. irreg., latest vol.8, 2001. price varies. **Document type:** *Journal, Academic/ Scholarly.*
Related titles: Online - full text ed.: ISSN 1827-6164.
Published by: Societa Italiana di Fisica (S I F), Via Saragozza 12, Bologna, 40123, Italy. TEL 39-051-331554, FAX 39-051-581340, subscriptions@sif.it. Ed. Angela Oleandri.

621.38 GBR ISSN 1063-7818
TK8300 CODEN: QUELEZ
➤ **QUANTUM ELECTRONICS.** Text in English. 1971. m. USD 4,325 combined subscription in United States to institutions (print & online eds.); GBP 2,404 combined subscription elsewhere to institutions (print & online eds.); USD 433 per issue in United States to institutions; GBP 240 per issue elsewhere to institutions (effective 2012). bibl.; charts; illus.; stat. index. 100 p./no. 2 cols./p.; back issues avail. **Document type:** *Journal, Academic/Scholarly.* **Description:** Covers all aspects of laser research and its applications.
Formerly (until 1993): Soviet Journal of Quantum Electronics (0049-1748)
Related titles: CD-ROM ed.: 1997; E-mail ed.; Online - full text ed.: ISSN 1468-4799. USD 3,893 in United States to institutions; GBP 2,164 elsewhere to institutions (effective 2012); ◆ Translation of: Kvantovaya Elektronika (Moscow). ISSN 0368-7147.
Indexed: A01, A03, A08, A22, C33, CA, CIN, CPEI, CPI, ChemAb, ChemTitl, CurCont, EngInd, GPAA, ISR, Inspec, MSCI, SCI, SCOPUS, T02, TM, W07.
—BLDSC (0420.528000), AskIEEE, CASDDS, IE, Infotrieve, Ingenta, INIST, Linda Hall. **CCC.**
Published by: (Rossiiskaya Akademiya Nauk/Russian Academy of Sciences RUS, Rossiiskaya Akademiya Nauk, Institut Fiziki im. P.N. Lebedeva/Russian Academy of Sciences, P.N. Lebedev Physics Institute RUS), Turpion Ltd., 207 Brondesbury Park, London, NW2 5JN, United Kingdom. TEL 44-20-84590066, FAX 44-20-84516454, admin@turpion.org. Ed. Oleg N Krokhin. **Dist. addr.:** Turpin Distribution Services Ltd. **Co-publisher:** Turpion - Moscow Ltd.

530 USA ISSN 1533-7146
QA76.889 CODEN: QICUAW
➤ **QUANTUM INFORMATION & COMPUTATION.** Abbreviated title: Q I C. Text in English. 2001 (July). m. USD 270 combined subscription to individuals (print & online eds.); USD 680 combined subscription to institutions (print & online eds.) (effective 2011). back issues avail.; reprints avail. **Document type:** *Journal, Academic/Scholarly.* **Description:** Publishes papers in all areas of quantum information processing.
Related titles: Online - full text ed.
Indexed: CCMJ, CMCI, CurCont, Inspec, MSN, MathR, SCI, SCOPUS, W07, Z02.
—BLDSC (7168.547000), IE, Linda Hall.
Published by: Rinton Press, Inc., 565 Edmund Terr, Paramus, NJ 07652. TEL 201-261-9408, FAX 201-261-7374, editorial@rintonpress.com.

530 USA ISSN 2160-1119
RADIATIONS. Text in English. 1930. s-a. free (effective 2011). **Document type:** *Magazine, Trade.*
Related titles: Online - full text ed.: ISSN 2160-1127.
Published by: American Institute of Physics, 1 Physics Ellipse, College Park, MD 20740. TEL 301-209-3007, FAX 301-209-0839, aipinfo@aip.org, http://www.aip.org. Ed. Dwight E Neuenschwander.

522.682 530 USA ISSN 2152-274X
QB475.A1
▼ ➤ **RADIO PHYSICS AND RADIO ASTRONOMY.** Text in English. 2010. q. USD 681 to institutions; USD 714 combined subscription to institutions (print & online eds.) (effective 2010). **Document type:** *Journal, Academic/Scholarly.* **Description:** Presents articles on investigations in radio physics and electronic engineering, radio astronomy, and astrophysics.
Related titles: Online - full text ed.: ISSN 2152-2758; ◆ English ed.: Radio Physics and Radio Astronomy. ISSN 1027-9636.
Published by: Begell House Inc., 50 Cross Hwy, Redding, CT 06896. TEL 203-938-1300, FAX 203-938-1304, orders@begellhouse.com. Ed. Leonid M Lytvynenko.

530 522.682 UKR ISSN 1027-9636
➤ **RADIO PHYSICS AND RADIO ASTRONOMY.** Text in English. 1995. q. **Document type:** *Journal, Academic/Scholarly.* **Description:** Features articles on investigations in radio physics and electronic engineering, radio astronomy, and astrophysics.
Related titles: ◆ English ed.: Radio Physics and Radio Astronomy. ISSN 2152-274X.
Indexed: RefZh.
Published by: National Academy of Sciences of Ukraine, Institute of Radio Astronomy, 4 st Krasnoznamennaya, Kharkiv, 61002, Ukraine. TEL 380 (57) 700-3092, danilen@ira.kharkov.ua.

620.1 519.2 NLD ISSN 0925-5850
➤ **RANDOM MATERIALS AND PROCESSES.** Text in English. 1990. irreg., latest vol.5, 1994. price varies. back issues avail. **Document type:** *Monographic series, Academic/Scholarly.* **Description:** Explores this class of phenomena, ranging from the pure mathematical interest to those of direct engineering relevance.

Published by: Elsevier BV, North-Holland (Subsidiary of: Elsevier Science & Technology), Sara Burgerhartstraat 25, Amsterdam, 1055 KV, Netherlands. TEL 31-20-4853911, FAX 31-20-4852457, JournalsCustomerServiceEMEA@elsevier.com, http://www.elsevier.com. **Subscr. to:** Elsevier BV, Radarweg 29, PO Box 211, Amsterdam 1000 AE, Netherlands.

530 510 SGP ISSN 2010-3263

▼ **RANDOM MATRICES: THEORY AND APPLICATION.** Text in English. 2011. q. back issues avail. **Document type:** *Journal, Academic/Scholarly.* **Description:** Publishes original papers on all aspects regarding random matrices, both theory and applications. Topics include: Spectral theory, new ensembles (those not generally considered in classical random matrix theory), and applications to a wide variety of areas, including high dimensional data analysis, wireless communications, finance, and economics.
Related titles: Online - full text ed.: ISSN 2010-3271. free.
Published by: World Scientific Publishing Co. Pte. Ltd., 5 Toh Tuck Link, Singapore, 596224, Singapore. TEL 65-6466-5775, FAX 65-6467-7667, wspc@wspc.com.sg, http://www.worldscientific.com. Eds. Yang Chen, Zhidong Bai. **Subscr. to:** Farrer Rd, PO Box 128, Singapore 912805, Singapore. TEL 65-382-5663, FAX 65-382-5919. **Dist. by:** World Scientific Publishing Ltd., 57 Shelton St, London WC2H 9HE, United Kingdom. TEL 44-207-8360888, FAX 44-207-8362020, sales@wspc.co.uk.; World Scientific Publishing Co., Inc., 27 Warren St, Ste 401-402, Hackensack, NJ 07601. TEL 201-487-9655, 800-227-7562, FAX 201-487-9656, 888-977-2665.

RAUM UND ZEIT; die neue Dimension der Wissenschaft. *see* MEDICAL SCIENCES

530 USA ISSN 0891-4680
CODEN: RPTOER

READINGS FROM PHYSICS TODAY. Text in English. 1984. irreg. **Document type:** *Monographic series.*
Indexed: Inspec.
Published by: Springer New York LLC (Subsidiary of: Springer Science+Business Media), 233 Spring St, New York, NY 10013. TEL 212—460-1500, FAX 212-460-1575, http://www.springer.com/.

530 621.3 NLD ISSN 1872-2105
T174.7 CODEN: RPNEBW

➤ **RECENT PATENTS ON NANATECHNOLOGY.** Text in English. 2006. 3/yr. USD 930 to institutions (print or online ed.) (effective 2012). adv. back issues avail.; reprints avail. **Document type:** *Journal, Academic/Scholarly.* **Description:** Publishes review articles by experts on recent patents on nanotechnology. Includes a selection of important and recent annotated patents on nanotechnology.
Related titles: Online - full text ed.: (from IngentaConnect).
Indexed: A01, A28, APA, B&BAb, B19, BrCerAb, C&ISA, C33, CA, CA/WCA, CIA, CPEI, CerAb, CivEngAb, CorrAb, E&CAJ, E11, EEA, EMA, EMBASE, ESPM, EnvEAb, ExcerpMed, H15, M&TEA, M09, MBF, MEDLINE, METADEX, P30, SCI, SCOPUS, SolStAb, T02, T04, W07, WAA.
—IE, Ingenta. **CCC.**
Published by: Bentham Science Publishers Ltd., PO Box 294, Bussum, 1400 AG, Netherlands. TEL 31-35-6923800, FAX 31-35-6980150, sales@bentham.org. Eds. Eduardo Ruiz-Hitzky, Pilar Aranda. **Subscr. to:** Bentham Science Publishers Ltd., c/o Richard E Morrissy, PO Box 446, Oak Park, IL 60301. TEL 312-413-5867, FAX 312-996-7107, subscriptions@bentham.org.

530 NLD ISSN 1877-9123

▼ **RECENT PATENTS ON NANOMEDICINE.** Text in English. 2011. 2/yr. USD 570 to institutions (effective 2012). adv. **Document type:** *Journal, Academic/Scholarly.* **Description:** Publishes review articles by experts on recent patents on nanomedicine.
Related titles: Online - full text ed.: ISSN 1877-9131.
—CCC.
Published by: Bentham Science Publishers Ltd., PO Box 294, Bussum, 1400 AG, Netherlands. TEL 31-35-6923800, FAX 31-35-6980150, sales@bentham.org. Ed. Victor M Meneses. **Subscr. to:** Bentham Science Publishers Ltd., c/o Richard E Morrissy, PO Box 446, Oak Park, IL 60301. TEL 312-413-5867, FAX 312-996-7107, subscriptions@bentham.org.

621 IND

RECENT RESEARCH DEVELOPMENTS IN APPLIED PHYSICS. Text in English. 1998. a. **Document type:** *Monographic series, Academic/Scholarly.*
Published by: Transworld Research Network, T C 37-661 (2), Fort Post Office, Trivandrum, Kerala 695 023, India. TEL 91-471-2452918, FAX 91-471-2573051, ggcom@vsnl.com, http://www.trnres.com.

530 IND

RECENT RESEARCH DEVELOPMENTS IN MAGNETICS. Text in English. 2000. a. **Document type:** *Monographic series, Academic/Scholarly.*
Published by: Transworld Research Network, T C 37-661 (2), Fort Post Office, Trivandrum, Kerala 695 023, India. TEL 91-471-2452918, FAX 91-471-2573051, ggcom@vsnl.com, http://www.trnres.com.

530 541 IND

RECENT RESEARCH DEVELOPMENTS IN NON-CRYSTALLINE SOLIDS. Text in English. 2001. a. **Document type:** *Monographic series, Academic/Scholarly.*
Published by: Transworld Research Network, T C 37-661 (2), Fort Post Office, Trivandrum, Kerala 695 023, India. TEL 91-471-2452918, FAX 91-471-2573051, ggcom@vsnl.com, http://www.trnres.com.

530 IND

RECENT RESEARCH DEVELOPMENTS IN PHYSICS. Text in English. 2000. a. **Document type:** *Monographic series, Academic/Scholarly.*
Published by: Transworld Research Network, T C 37-661 (2), Fort Post Office, Trivandrum, Kerala 695 023, India. TEL 91-471-2452918, FAX 91-471-2573051, ggcom@vsnl.com, http://www.trnres.com.

530 IND

RECENT RESEARCH DEVELOPMENTS IN SOLID STATE IONICS. Text in English. 2003. a. **Document type:** *Monographic series, Academic/Scholarly.*
Published by: Transworld Research Network, T C 37-661 (2), Fort Post Office, Trivandrum, Kerala 695 023, India. TEL 91-471-2452918, FAX 91-471-2573051, ggcom@vsnl.com, http://www.trnres.com.

RECENT RESEARCH DEVELOPMENTS IN STATISTICAL PHYSICS. *see* PHYSICS—Abstracting, Bibliographies, Statistics

533.5 IND

RECENT RESEARCH DEVELOPMENTS IN VACUUM SCIENCE & TECHNOLOGY. Text in English. 1999. a. **Document type:** *Monographic series, Academic/Scholarly.*
Published by: Transworld Research Network, T C 37-661 (2), Fort Post Office, Trivandrum, Kerala 695 023, India. TEL 91-471-2452918, FAX 91-471-2573051, ggcom@vsnl.com, http://www.trnres.com.

530 ESP ISSN 1988-7930

RECURSOS DE FISICA. Text in Multiple languages. 2007. s-a. back issues avail. **Document type:** *Journal, Academic/Scholarly.*
Media: Online - full text.
Published by: Societat Catalana de Fisica, Carrer del Carme, 47, Barcelona, 08001, Spain. TEL 34-93-3248583, FAX 34-93-2701180, scfis@iec.cat, http://www.scf-iec.org/. Ed. Josep Ametlla.

530 FRA ISSN 1953-793X
CODEN: BFPYAP

REFLETS DE LA PHYSIQUE. Text in French. 1881. 5/yr. charts; illus.; stat. Supplement avail. **Document type:** *Journal, Academic/Scholarly.* **Description:** Lists all congresses to take place as well as all relevant information about them.
Formerly (until 2006): Societe Francaise de Physique. Bulletin (0037-9360)
Related titles: Online - full text ed.: ISSN 2102-6777.
Indexed: CIN, ChemAb, ChemTitl, INIS AtomInd.
—CASDDS, INIST, Linda Hall. **CCC.**
Published by: (Societe Francaise de Physique), E D P Sciences, 17 Ave du Hoggar, Parc d'Activites de Courtaboeuf, BP 112, Cedex A, Les Ulis, F-91944, France. TEL 33-1-69187575, FAX 33-1-69860678, http://www.edpsciences.org.

621 CHE ISSN 2072-4292
G70.4

▼ **REMOTE SENSING.** Text in English. 2009. q. free (effective 2011). **Document type:** *Journal, Academic/Scholarly.* **Description:** Covers all aspects of the remote sensing process, from instrument design and signal processing to the retrieval of geophysical parameters and their application in geosciences.
Media: Online - full text.
Indexed: A01, A34, A37, A38, AgrForAb, C25, C30, CABA, E12, F08, F11, F12, FCA, G11, GH, H16, I11, LT, MaizeAb, N02, O01, P32, P40, R07, R11, R12, R13, S12, S13, S16, SoyAb, T02, TAR, W10, W11.
Published by: M D P I AG, Postfach, Basel, 4005, Switzerland. TEL 41-61-6837734, FAX 41-61-3028918, http://www.mdpi.org/.

530 ITA ISSN 0392-4130

RENDICONTI ACCADEMIA NAZIONALE DELLE SCIENZE DETTA DEI XL. MEMORIE DI SCIENZE FISICHE E NATURALI. Text in Italian. 1782. a. **Document type:** *Journal, Academic/Scholarly.*
Supersedes in part (in 1979): Rendiconti della Accademia Nazionale dei XL (0370-3460); Which had former titles (until 1950): Rendiconti Societa Italiana delle Scienze detta Accademia dei XL (0391-0733); (until 1948): Memorie della Societa Italiana delle Scienze detta dei XL (1123-2978); (until 1928): Memorie di Matematica e di Scienze Fisiche e Naturali della Societa Italiana delle Scienze detta dei XL (1123-296X); (until 1913): Memorie di Matematica e di Fisica della Societa Italiana delle Scienze (1123-2951); (until 1799): Memorie di Matematica e di Fisica della Societa Italiana (1123-2943)
Indexed: GeoRef, Z02.
—INIST, Linda Hall.
Published by: Accademia Nazionale delle Scienze detta del XL, Via L Spallanzani 7, Rome, 00161, Italy. TEL 39-06-44250054, FAX 39-06-44250465, segreteria@accademiaxl.it, http://www.accademiaxl.it/.

530 FIN ISSN 1239-4327

REPORT SERIES IN PHYSICAL SCIENCES. Text in English. 1967. irreg. **Document type:** *Monographic series, Academic/Scholarly.*
Formerly (until 1996): University of Oulu. Department of Physics. Report (0356-1852)
Indexed: Inspec.
Published by: Oulun Yliopisto, Fysikaalisten Tieteiden Laitos/University of Oulu. Department of Physical Sciences, PO Box 3000, Oulu, 90014, Finland. TEL 358-8-553-1280, FAX 358-8-553-1287, physics@oulu.fi, http://physics.oulu.fi.

530.1 GBR ISSN 0034-4877
QC19.2 CODEN: RMHPBE

➤ **REPORTS ON MATHEMATICAL PHYSICS.** Text in English. 1970. 6/yr. EUR 1,608 in Europe to institutions; JPY 213,600 in Japan to institutions; USD 1,799 elsewhere to institutions (effective 2012). back issues avail. **Document type:** *Journal, Academic/Scholarly.* **Description:** Features papers in theoretical physics presenting a rigorous mathematical approach to problems of quantum and classical mechanics and field theories, relativity and gravitation, statistical physics and mathematical foundations of physical theories.
Related titles: Microform ed.; Online - full text ed.: ISSN 1879-0674 (from IngentaConnect, ScienceDirect).
Indexed: A01, A03, A08, A22, A26, A28, APA, ApMecR, BrCerAb, C&ISA, CA, CA/WCA, CCMJ, CIA, CIS, CMCI, CerAb, CivEngAb, CorrAb, CurCont, E&CAJ, E11, EEA, EMA, ESPM, EnvEAb, H15, I05, Inspec, M&TEA, M09, MBF, METADEX, MSN, MathR, RefZh, S01, SCI, SCOPUS, SolStAb, T02, T04, W07, WAA, Z02.
—BLDSC (7660.510000), AskIEEE, CASDDS, IE, Infotrieve, Ingenta, INIST, Linda Hall. **CCC.**
Published by: (Uniwersytet Mikolaja Kopernika/Nicolaus Copernicus University POL), Pergamon (Subsidiary of: Elsevier Science & Technology), The Blvd, Langford Ln, East Park, Kidlington, Oxford OX5 1GB, United Kingdom. TEL 44-1865-843000, FAX 44-1865-843010, JournalsCustomerServiceEMEA@elsevier.com. Ed. A Jamiolkowski. **Subscr. to:** Elsevier BV, Radarweg 29, PO Box 211, Amsterdam 1000 AE, Netherlands. TEL 31-20-4853757, FAX 31-20-4853432, http://www.elsevier.nl.

530 GBR ISSN 0034-4885
QC3 CODEN: RPPHAG

➤ **REPORTS ON PROGRESS IN PHYSICS.** Text in English. 1934. m. GBP 1,684 combined subscription to institutions (print & online eds.) (effective 2010). bibl.; charts; illus. cum.index. back issues avail. **Document type:** *Journal, Academic/Scholarly.* **Description:** Provides a foundation of reviews for all research libraries and an overview of physics for other libraries.
Related titles: Microfiche ed.: USD 2,074 in the Americas; GBP 1,061 elsewhere (effective 2007); Microfilm ed.; Online - full text ed.: ISSN 1361-6633. GBP 1,604 to institutions (effective 2010) (from IngentaConnect); Alternate Frequency ed(s).: q. USD 2,600 in North America to institutions; GBP 1,311 elsewhere to institutions (effective 2005).
Indexed: A&ATA, A01, A03, A08, A20, A22, ASCA, ApMecR, CA, CCMJ, Cadscan, ChemAb, ChemTitl, CurCont, GeoRef, IBR, IBZ, INIS AtomInd, ISR, Inspec, LeadAb, MSN, MathR, P30, PhysBer, RefZh, SCI, SCOPUS, SpeleolAb, T02, W07, Zincscan.
—BLDSC (7665.500000), AskIEEE, CASDDS, IE, Infotrieve, Ingenta, INIST, Linda Hall. **CCC.**
Published by: (Institute of Physics), Institute of Physics Publishing Ltd., Dirac House, Temple Back, Bristol, BS1 6BE, United Kingdom. TEL 44-117-9297481, FAX 44-117-9301178, custserv@iop.org, http://publishing.iop.org/. Ed. Laura H Greene. **Subscr. in N. America to:** American Institute of Physics, PO Box 503284, St Louis, MO 63150. TEL 516-576-2270, 800-344-6902, FAX 516-349-9704, subs@aip.org.

➤ **RESEARCH IN ASTRONOMY AND ASTROPHYSICS.** *see* ASTRONOMY

➤ **RESEARCH INSTITUTE FOR MATHEMATICAL SCIENCES. PUBLICATIONS.** *see* MATHEMATICS

530 USA ISSN 1819-3463

➤ **RESEARCH JOURNAL OF PHYSICS.** Text in English. 2007. q. USD 900 to individuals; USD 1,100 to institutions; USD 300 per issue (effective 2007). **Document type:** *Journal, Academic/Scholarly.* **Description:** Contains research articles, rapid communications, and review articles contributed by recognized experts in Canada and abroad.
Related titles: Online - full text ed.
Indexed: A01, CA, T02.
Published by: Academic Journals Inc., 224, 5th Ave, No 2218, New York, NY 10001. FAX 888-777-8532, support@scialert.com, http://www.academicjournalsinc.com/.

530 SGP ISSN 0129-055X
QC19.2 CODEN: RMPHEX

➤ **REVIEWS IN MATHEMATICAL PHYSICS**; a journal for survey and expository articles in the field of mathematical physics. Abbreviated title: R M P. Text in English. 1989. 10/yr. SGD 3,120, USD 1,933, EUR 1,623 combined subscription to institutions (print & online eds.) (effective 2012). adv. back issues avail. **Document type:** *Journal, Academic/Scholarly.* **Description:** Contains survey and expository articles in mathematical physics.
Related titles: Online - full text ed.: ISSN 1793-6659. SGD 2,836, USD 1,757, EUR 1,475 to institutions (effective 2012).
Indexed: A01, A03, A08, A22, ASCA, CA, CCMJ, CMCI, CurCont, E01, ISR, Inspec, M05, MSN, MathR, S01, SCI, SCOPUS, T02, W07, Z02.
—AskIEEE, IE, Infotrieve, Ingenta, Linda Hall. **CCC.**
Published by: World Scientific Publishing Co. Pte. Ltd., 5 Toh Tuck Link, Singapore, 596224, Singapore. TEL 65-6466-5775, FAX 65-6467-7667, wspc@wspc.com.sg, http://www.worldscientific.com. Ed. J Yngvason. **Dist. by:** World Scientific Publishing Co., Inc., 27 Warren St, Ste 401-402, Hackensack, NJ 07601. TEL 201-487-9655, 800-227-7562, FAX 201-487-9656, 888-977-2665, wspc@wspc.com; World Scientific Publishing Ltd., 57 Shelton St, London WC2H 9HE, United Kingdom. TEL 44-207-8360888, FAX 44-207-8362020, sales@wspc.co.uk.

➤ **REVIEWS OF GEOPHYSICS.** *see* EARTH SCIENCES—Geophysics

539 USA ISSN 0034-6861
QC1 CODEN: RMPHAT

➤ **REVIEWS OF MODERN PHYSICS.** Text in English. 1929. q. USD 630 combined subscription domestic to institutions academic (print & online eds.); USD 660 combined subscription foreign to institutions academic (print & online eds.) (effective 2011). bibl.; illus. cum.index: vols.1-27 (1929-1955); vols.28-45 (1956-1973); vols.46-53 (1974-1981). back issues avail.; reprints avail. **Document type:** *Journal, Academic/Scholarly.* **Description:** Seeks to enhance communication among physicists by publishing comprehensive scholarly reviews of significant topics, as well as colloquia and tutorial articles in rapidly developing fields of physics.
Related titles: Microfiche ed.; Microform ed.: (from MIM); Online - full text ed.: ISSN 1539-0756. 1997. USD 455 domestic to institutions (effective 2011).
Indexed: A01, A03, A05, A08, A22, A23, A24, A26, AS&TA, AS&TI, ASCA, ApMecR, B04, B13, BRD, C10, C13, CA, CCMJ, CMCI, CPEI, CPI, ChemAb, ChemTitl, CurCont, E08, EngInd, G03, G08, GSA, GSI, GeoRef, INIS AtomInd, ISR, IndMed, Inspec, MSN, MathR, P30, PhysBer, RefZh, S09, SCI, SCOPUS, SPINweb, SpeleolAb, T02, W03, W07.
—BLDSC (7793.300000), AskIEEE, CASDDS, IE, Infotrieve, Ingenta, INIST, Linda Hall. **CCC.**
Published by: American Physical Society, One Physics Ellipse, College Park, MD 20740. TEL 301-209-3200, FAX 301-209-0865, subs@aps.org, http://www.aps.org. Ed. Alan Chodos. **Subscr. to:** APS Subscription Services, Ste. 1N01, 2 huntington Quadrangle, Melville, NY 11747-4502. TEL 800-344-6902.

530.44 USA ISSN 0080-2050
QC718 CODEN: RPLPAK

➤ **REVIEWS OF PLASMA PHYSICS.** Text in English. 1965. irreg., latest vol.24, 2008. price varies. back issues avail. **Document type:** *Monographic series, Academic/Scholarly.* **Description:** English translations of research originally published in Russian.
Related titles: Online - full text ed.: ISSN 1574-8952.
Indexed: A22, Inspec.
—Ingenta. **CCC.**
Published by: Consultants Bureau (Subsidiary of: Springer New York LLC), 233 Spring St, New York, NY 10013. TEL 212-460-1500, FAX 212-460-1575, service-ny@springer.com. Eds. Maria Aksentieva, Oleg G Bakunin, Vitalii D Shafranov.

530 BOL ISSN 1562-3823

REVISTA BOLIVIANA DE FISICA. Text in Spanish. 1995. a. back issues avail. **Document type:** *Monographic series, Academic/Scholarly.*
Related titles: Online - full text ed.: (from SciELO).
Indexed: C01.
Published by: Universidad Mayor de San Andres, Instituto de Investigaciones Fisicas, Casilla 8635, La Paz, Bolivia. TEL 591-2-792999, FAX 591-2-792622. Ed. Alfonso Velarde.

P

530 371.3 BRA ISSN 1806-1117
REVISTA BRASILEIRA DE ENSINO DE FISICA. Text in Portuguese. 1979. m. **Document type:** *Journal, Academic/Scholarly.*
Formerly (until 1992): Revista de Ensino de Fisica (0102-4744)
Related titles: Online - full text ed.: ISSN 1806-9126. 2001. free (effective 2011).
Indexed: A28, APA, BrCerAb, C&ISA, CA/WCA, CIA, CerAb, CivEngAb, CorrAb, E&CAJ, E11, EEA, EMA, H15, M&TEA, M09, MBF, METADEX, SCI, SCOPUS, SolStAb, T04, W07, WAA.
Published by: Sociedade Brasileira de Fisica, Caixa Postal 66328, Sao Paulo, SP 05389-970, Brazil. TEL 55-11-3816-4132.

530 COL ISSN 0120-2650
REVISTA COLOMBIANA DE FISICA. Text in English, French, Italian, Portuguese, Spanish. 1965. s-a. **Document type:** *Journal, Academic/Scholarly.*
Related titles: Online - full text ed.: free (effective 2011).
Indexed: A01, C01, CA, F03, F04, Inspec, T02.
Published by: Sociedad Colombiana de Fisica, Instituto Interdisciplinario de las Ciencias, Universidad del Quindio, Avenida Bolivar Calle 12 Norte, Armenia Quindio, Colombia. TEL 7460183, socofi@uniquindio.edu.co, http://www.sociedadcolombianadefisica.org.co, http://www.uniquindio.edu.co/scf/. Ed. Roberto Enrique Martinez.

530 CUB ISSN 0253-9268
CODEN: RECFD7
REVISTA CUBANA DE FISICA. Text in Spanish; Summaries in English, Spanish. 1981. 3/yr. back issues avail. **Document type:** *Journal, Academic/Scholarly.*
Related titles: Online - full text ed.: free (effective 2011).
Indexed: A01, A26, C01, C32, CA, CIN, ChemAb, ChemTitl, F03, F04, I04, INIS AtomInd, T02.
—CASDDS.
Published by: (Universidad de La Habana, Direccion de Informacion Cientifica y Tecnica), Ediciones Cubanas, Obispo 527, Havana, Cuba. Ed. Maria Sanchez Colina.

530.7 ARG ISSN 0326-7091
REVISTA DE ENSENANZA DE LA FISICA. Text in Spanish. 1985. s-a. ARS 20 to individuals; ARS 40 to institutions (effective 2010). back issues avail. **Document type:** *Journal, Academic/Scholarly.*
Published by: Asociacion de Profesores de Fisica de la Argentina, Ave Pellegrini, 250, Rosario, Santa Fe S2000BTP, Argentina. TEL 54-341-4802649, http://www.apfa.org.ar/. Ed. Graciela Utges. Circ: 500.

530 ESP ISSN 1131-5326
REVISTA DE FISICA. Text in Spanish. 1991. s-a. EUR 5 (effective 2009). back issues avail. **Document type:** *Journal, Academic/Scholarly.*
Related titles: Online - full text ed.
Indexed: IECT, Inspec, RILM.
Published by: (Societat Catalana de Fisica), Institut d'Estudis Catalans, Carrer del Carme 47, Barcelona, 08001, Spain. TEL 34-932-701620, FAX 34-932-701180, informacio@iecat.net, http://www2.iecat.net. Ed. Josep Campmany i Guillot.

530 BRA ISSN 0102-6895
REVISTA DE FISICA APLICADA E INSTRUMENTACAO. Text in English, French, Portuguese, Spanish. 1985. q. USD 50 (effective 2002).
Description: Publishes experimental and theoretical papers in physics and their applications to other sciences, engineering, and industry.
Indexed: C01, INIS AtomInd, Inspec.
Published by: Sociedade Brasileira de Fisica, Caixa Postal 66328, Sao Paulo, SP 05389-970, Brazil. TEL 55-11-3816-4132, http://sbf.if.usp.br. Ed. Joao Alziro Herz da Jornada.

530 PER ISSN 1605-7724
REVISTA DE INVESTIGACION DE FISICA. Text in Spanish. 1999. irreg.
Related titles: Online - full text ed.: ISSN 1728-2977.
Indexed: INIS AtomInd.
Published by: (Universidad Nacional Mayor de San Marcos, Facultad de Ciencias Fisicas), Universidad Nacional Mayor de San Marcos, Ciudad Universitaria, Jr Jorge Amezaga s/n, Lima, Peru. http://www.unmsm.edu.pe.

530.15 ARG ISSN 0080-2360
QA1
REVISTA DE MATEMATICA Y FISICA TEORICA. SERIE A. Text in Spanish, French, German, Italian, English; Summaries in English. 1940. a. USD 15. bk.rev. index.
Indexed: CIS, MathR, Z02.
Published by: Universidad Nacional de Tucuman, Facultad de Ciencias Exactas y Tecnologia, Avda. Independencia 1800, San Miguel de Tucuman, Tucuman, Argentina. FAX 81311462, TELEX 61249-FDCET-AR. Eds. Constantino Grosse, Raul Luccioni. Circ: 250.

530 ESP ISSN 0213-862X
➤ **REVISTA ESPANOLA DE FISICA.** Text in Spanish. 1987. q. adv. **Document type:** *Journal, Academic/Scholarly.* **Description:** Addresses the community of physicists.
Indexed: GeoRef, IECT, INIS AtomInd, SpeleolAb.
—Linda Hall.
Published by: Real Sociedad Espanola de Fisica, Facultad de Ciencias Fisicas, Universidad Complutense, Madrid, 28040, Spain. TEL 34-91-3944359, FAX 34-91-3944350, rsef@fis.ucm.es, http://www.rsef.org/. Ed. Eloisa Lopez Perez. Adv. contact Isabel Munoz. Circ: 3,000.

530 ESP ISSN 1888-2188
REVISTA IBEROAMERICANA DE FISICA. Text in Spanish. 2006. a. **Document type:** *Journal, Academic/Scholarly.*
Published by: Real Sociedad Espanola de Fisica, Facultad de Ciencias Fisicas, Universidad Complutense, Madrid, 28040, Spain. TEL 34-91-3944359, FAX 34-91-5433879.

530 MEX ISSN 0035-001X
QC1 CODEN: RMXFAT
➤ **REVISTA MEXICANA DE FISICA.** Text and summaries in English, Spanish. 1952. bi-m. bibl.; charts; illus. index. Supplement avail. **Document type:** *Journal, Academic/Scholarly.* **Description:** Original papers in physics: research, education, and instrumentation.
Related titles: Online - full text ed.: ISSN 1870-3542. free (effective 2011).
Indexed: A&AAb, A22, ASCA, C01, CCMJ, ChemAb, ChemTitl, CurCont, INIS AtomInd, ISR, Inspec, M&GPA, MSN, MathR, PhysBer, RefZh, SCI, SCOPUS, W07, Z02.
—BLDSC (7866.300000), AskIEEE, CASDDS, IE, Ingenta, INIST, Linda Hall.
Published by: Sociedad Mexicana de Fisica, A.C., Apartado Postal 70-348, Coyoacan, Mexico City, DF 04511, Mexico. smf@hp.fciencias.unam.mx, http://www.smf.mx.

530 PER ISSN 1022-0194
REVISTA PERUANA DE FISICA. Text in Spanish. 1990. irreg. **Document type:** *Journal, Academic/Scholarly.*
Published by: Sociedad Peruana de Fisica, Las Camelias 491, Of 403, San Isidro, Lima, Peru. http://www.soperfi.org.pe.

531.11 FRA ISSN 1763-5152
RHEOLOGIE. Text in French. 1955. s-a. **Document type:** *Journal, Academic/Scholarly.*
Former titles (until 2002): Cahiers de Rheologie (1149-0039); (until 1987): Groupe Francais de Rheologie. Cahiers (0373-5699); (until 1961): Groupe Francais d'Etudes de Rheologie. Cahier (0429-3312)
Indexed: GeoRef, Inspec.
—INIST, Linda Hall.
Published by: Groupe Francais de Rheologie, Laboratoire de Rheologie, 1301 Rue de la Piscine, Domaine Universitaire, B.P. 53, Grenoble, Cedex 09 38041, France. TEL 33-4-76825171, http://legfr.org. Ed. Ahmed Allal.

531.11 NLD ISSN 0169-3107
CODEN: RHSEE4
RHEOLOGY SERIES. Text in English. 1984. irreg., latest vol.8, 1999. price varies. back issues avail. **Document type:** *Monographic series, Academic/Scholarly.* **Description:** Covers research and applications in the science of rheology.
Related titles: Online - full text ed.
Indexed: Inspec, SCOPUS.
—BLDSC (7960.590000), CASDDS, IE. **CCC.**
Published by: Elsevier BV (Subsidiary of: Elsevier Science & Technology), Radarweg 29, PO Box 211, Amsterdam, 1000 AE, Netherlands. TEL 31-20-4853911, FAX 31-20-4852457, JournalsCustomerServiceEMEA@elsevier.com, http://www.elsevier.nl.

530 JPN ISSN 0913-543X
CODEN: RIJOFV
RIGAKU JOURNAL. Text in English. 1984. s-a. **Document type:** *Journal, Academic/Scholarly.*
—CASDDS.
Published by: Rigaku Denki K.K./Rigaku Corp., 3-9-12 Matsubara-cho, Akishima-shi, Tokyo-to 196-0003, Japan. TEL 0425-45-8139, FAX 0425-46-7090. Ed. Tomohiko Watanabe.

RIKAGAKKAISHI/JOURNAL OF PHYSICS, CHEMISTRY AND EARTH SCIENCE. *see* SCIENCES: COMPREHENSIVE WORKS

ROMANIAN ACADEMY. PROCEEDINGS. SERIES A: MATHEMATICS, PHYSICS, TECHNICAL SCIENCES, INFORMATION SCIENCE. *see* MATHEMATICS

530 ROM ISSN 1221-146X
QC1 CODEN: RJPHEC
➤ **ROMANIAN JOURNAL OF PHYSICS.** Text in English, French. 1956. 10/yr. adv. bk.rev. charts; illus. index. **Document type:** *Journal, Academic/Scholarly.* **Description:** Includes papers and short notes in all fields of physics.
Former titles (until 1992): Revue Roumaine de Physique (0035-4090); (until 1964): Revue de Physique (0370-6818); Which superseded in part (in 1956): Revue des Mathematiques et de Physique (1220-4765); Which superseded in part (in 1954): La Science dans la Republique Populaire Roumaine (1220-4757)
Related titles: Online - full text ed.
Indexed: C33, CCMJ, Cadscan, ChemAb, ChemTitl, GeoRef, INIS AtomInd, Inspec, LeadAb, MSN, MathR, PhysBer, RefZh, SCI, SCOPUS, SpeleolAb, W07, Z02, Zincscan.
—BLDSC (8019.638950), AskIEEE, CASDDS, IE, Ingenta, INIST, Linda Hall.
Published by: (Academia Romana/Romanian Academy), Editura Academiei Romane/Publishing House of the Romanian Academy, Calea 13 Septembrie 13, Sector 5, Bucharest, 050711, Romania. TEL 40-21-3188146, FAX 40-21-3182444, edacad@ear.ro, http://www.ear.ro. Ed. A Sandulescu. Adv. contact R Calboreanu. Circ: 600. **Dist. by:** Rodipet S.A., Piata Presei Libere 1, sector 1, PO Box 33-57, Bucharest 3, Romania. TEL 40-21-2224126, 40-21-2226407, rodipet@rodipet.ro.

530 ROM ISSN 1221-1451
QC1 CODEN: RORPED
ROMANIAN REPORT IN PHYSICS. Text in Romanian. 1950. 10/yr. bk.rev. illus. index.
Formerly (until 1992): Studii si Cercetari de Fizica (0039-3940)
Related titles: Online - full text ed.
Indexed: CCMJ, CIN, ChemAb, ChemTitl, INIS AtomInd, Inspec, MSN, MathR, PhysBer, RefZh, SCI, SCOPUS, W07, Z02.
—BLDSC (8019.668000), AskIEEE, CASDDS, IE, Ingenta, Linda Hall.
Published by: (Academia Romana/Romanian Academy), Editura Academiei Romane/Publishing House of the Romanian Academy, Calea 13 Septembrie 13, Sector 5, Bucharest, 050711, Romania. TEL 40-21-3188146, FAX 40-21-3182444, edacad@ear.ro, http://www.ear.ro. Ed. Ioan Jovit Popescu. **Dist. by:** Rodipet S.A., Piata Presei Libere 1, sector 1, PO Box 33-57, Bucharest 3, Romania. TEL 40-21-2226407, 40-21-2224126, rodipet@rodipet.ro.

530 551.46 RUS ISSN 0233-9390
CODEN: TIOSEL
ROSSIISKAYA AKADEMIYA NAUK. INSTITUT OBSHCHEI FIZIKI. TRUDY. Text in Russian. 1986. irreg. RUR 6,000. adv. **Document type:** *Proceedings.*
Formerly: Akademiya Nauk S.S.S.R. Institut Obshchei Fiziki. Trudy (1011-0399)
Indexed: CCMJ, CIN, ChemAb, ChemTitl.
—CASDDS, INIST, Linda Hall.
Published by: (Rossiiskaya Akademiya Nauk/Russian Academy of Sciences, Institut Obshchei Fiziki), Fizmatlit Publishing House (Subsidiary of: Pleiades Publishing, Inc.), Leninskii pr-t 15, Moscow, 117071, Russian Federation. TEL 7-095-1326089, FAX 7-095-1326089. Ed. Alexander M Prokhorov. **Subscr. to:** Akademkniga, B Cherkasskii per 2-10, Moscow 103624, Russian Federation.

530 RUS ISSN 1026-3489
AS262 CODEN: IRAFEO
➤ **ROSSIISKAYA AKADEMIYA NAUK. IZVESTIYA. SERIYA FIZICHESKAYA.** Text in Russian. m. RUR 1,050 for 6 mos. domestic (effective 2004). **Document type:** *Journal, Academic/Scholarly.*
Formerly (until 1992): Akademiya Nauk S.S.S.R. Izvestiya. Seriya Fizicheskaya (0367-6765); Which superseded in part (in 1936): Akademiya Nauk S.S.S.R. Otdelenie Matematicheskikh i Estestvennykh Nauk. Izvestiya (0367-9586)
Related titles: ◆ English Translation: Russian Academy of Sciences. Physics Bulletin. ISSN 1062-8738.
Indexed: C33, GeoRef, INIS AtomInd, Inspec, RefZh, SCOPUS, SpeleolAb, Z02.
—BLDSC (0082.308000), CASDDS, East View, INIST, Linda Hall. **CCC.**
Published by: (Rossiiskaya Akademiya Nauk/Russian Academy of Sciences), Izdatel'stvo Nauka, Profsoyuznaya ul 90, Moscow, 117864, Russian Federation. TEL 7-095-3347151, FAX 7-095-4202220, secret@naukaran.ru, http://www.naukaran.ru.

530 620 GBR ISSN 1364-503X
Q41 CODEN: PTRMAD
➤ **ROYAL SOCIETY OF LONDON. PHILOSOPHICAL TRANSACTIONS A. MATHEMATICAL, PHYSICAL AND ENGINEERING SCIENCES.** Variant title: Royal Society. Philosophical Transactions. Mathematical, Physical and Engineering Sciences. Text in English. 1665. bi-w. GBP 2,731, EUR 3,551 combined subscription in Europe to institutions (print & online eds.); USD 5,175 combined subscription in US & Canada to institutions (print & online eds.); GBP 2,957, USD 5,302 combined subscription elsewhere to institutions (print & online eds.) (effective 2012). back issues avail.; reprint service avail. from PSC. **Document type:** *Proceedings, Academic/Scholarly.* **Description:** Brings out reports of the society's renowned discussion meetings, specially selected theme issues and reviews. Contains papers on mathematics, engineering and earth sciences.
Former titles (until 1996): Royal Society of London. Philosophical Transactions. Physical Sciences and Engineering (0962-8428); (until 1990): Royal Society of London. Philosophical Transactions. Series A. Mathematical and Physical Sciences (0080-4614); (until 1933): Royal Society of London. Philosophical Transactions. Series A. Containing Papers of a Mathematical or Physical Character (0264-3952); (until 1897): Royal Society of London. Philosophical Transactions A (0264-3820); Which superseded in part (in 1887): Royal Society of London. Philosophical Transactions (0261-0523); Which was formerly (until 1776): Royal Society of London. Philosophical Transactions (0260-7085); (until 1682): Royal Society of London. Philosophical Collections (0369-8696); (until 1679): Royal Society of London. Philosophical Transactions (0370-2316)
Related titles: Microfiche ed.: (from IDC); Microform ed.: (from PMC); Online - full text ed.: ISSN 1471-2962. GBP 2,101, EUR 2,732 in Europe to institutions; USD 3,981 in US & Canada to institutions; GBP 2,275, USD 4,079 elsewhere to institutions (effective 2012).
Indexed: A01, A03, A08, A20, A22, A34, A35, A36, A37, A38, AESIS, ASCA, ASFA, ApMecR, B21, BA, BrArAb, BrGeoL, C25, C30, CA, CABA, CCMJ, CIN, CIS, CPEI, ChemAb, ChemTitl, CurCont, E01, E12, EIA, EMBASE, EnvAb, EnvInd, ExcerpMed, F08, F12, GH, GeoRef, H09, H10, I11, IBR, IBZ, IMMAb, ISR, Inspec, LT, M&GPA, MEDLINE, MSN, MathR, MinerAb, N02, NSA, P30, P32, P33, PCI, PetrolAb, R08, RRTA, RefZh, S05, S13, S16, SCI, SCOPUS, SpeleolAb, T02, T05, W07, W11, Z02.
—BLDSC (6462.990000), AskIEEE, CASDDS, IE, Infotrieve, Ingenta, INIST, Linda Hall, PADDS. **CCC.**
Published by: The Royal Society Publishing, 6-9 Carlton House Terr, London, SW1Y 5AG, United Kingdom. TEL 44-20-74512500, FAX 44-20-79761837, sales@royalsociety.org, http://royalsocietypublishing.org. Ed. Dave Garner. **Subscr. to:** Portland Customer Services, Commerce Way, Colchester CO2 8HP, United Kingdom. TEL 44-1206-796351, FAX 44-1206-799331, sales@portland-services.com, http://www.portlandpress.com.

➤ **ROZHLEDY MATEMATICKO-FYZIKALNI.** *see* MATHEMATICS

➤ **RUSSIAN ACADEMY OF SCIENCES. COLLOID JOURNAL.** *see* CHEMISTRY—Physical Chemistry

530 USA ISSN 1062-8738
QC1 CODEN: BRSPEX
➤ **RUSSIAN ACADEMY OF SCIENCES. PHYSICS BULLETIN/ IZVESTIYA ROSSIISKOI AKADEMII NAUK. SERIYA FIZICHESKAYA.** Text in English. 1954. m. EUR 3,854, USD 4,666 combined subscription to institutions (print & online eds.) (effective 2012). abstr.; illus. back issues avail. **Document type:** *Journal, Academic/Scholarly.* **Description:** Each issue provides conference proceedings in a specific area, such as atomic and molecular physics, nuclear physics, laser technology, optics, luminescence, and condensed matter.
Formerly (until 1992): Academy of Sciences of the U S S R. Bulletin. Physical Series (0001-432X)
Related titles: Online - full text ed.: ISSN 1934-9432; ◆ Translation of: Rossiiskaya Akademiya Nauk. Izvestiya. Seriya Fizicheskaya. ISSN 1026-3489.
Indexed: A22, A26, CPEI, ChemAb, E01, E08, EngInd, IBR, IBZ, Inspec, S09, SCOPUS, Z02.
—BLDSC (0409.350000), AskIEEE, East View, IE, Infotrieve, Ingenta, INIST, Linda Hall. **CCC.**
Published by: (Rossiiskaya Akademiya Nauk/Russian Academy of Sciences RUS), Allerton Press, Inc. (Subsidiary of: Pleiades Publishing, Inc.), 18 W 27th St, New York, NY 10001. TEL 646-424-9686, FAX 646-424-9695, journals@allertonpress.com. Ed. Andrei V Gaponov-Grekhov.

530 510 RUS ISSN 1061-9208
QC19.2 CODEN: RJMPEL
➤ **RUSSIAN JOURNAL OF MATHEMATICAL PHYSICS.** Text in English. 1993. q. EUR 1,202, USD 1,458 combined subscription to institutions (print & online eds.) (effective 2012). back issues avail. **Document type:** *Journal, Academic/Scholarly.* **Description:** Covers functional analysis, linear and partial differential equations, algebras, modern differential and algebraic geometry and topology, representations of Lie groups, dynamic systems, and control theory.
Related titles: Online - full text ed.: ISSN 1555-6638. 2006 (from IngentaConnect).
Indexed: A22, A26, ASCA, CCMJ, CurCont, E01, MSN, MathR, SCI, SCOPUS, W07, Z02.
—BLDSC (8052.713200), East View, IE, Infotrieve, Ingenta. **CCC.**

Published by: M A I K Nauka - Interperiodica (Subsidiary of: Pleiades Publishing, Inc.), Profsoyuznaya ul 90, Moscow, 117997, Russian Federation. TEL 7-095-3347420, FAX 7-095-3360666, compmg@maik.ru, http://www.maik.ru. Ed. Viktor P Maslov. R&P Vladimir I Vasil'ev. **Dist. in the Americas by:** Springer New York LLC, Journal Fulfillment, PO Box 2485, Secaucus, NJ 07096. TEL 212-460-1500, FAX 201-348-4505; **Dist. outside of the Americas by:** Springer, Haber Str 7, Heidelberg 69126, Germany. TEL 49-6221-3454303, FAX 49-6221-3454229.

530 USA ISSN 1064-8887
QC1 CODEN: RPJOEB
➤ **RUSSIAN PHYSICS JOURNAL.** Text in English. 1965. 10/yr. EUR 4,863, USD 4,948 combined subscription to institutions (print & online eds.) (effective 2012). adv. back issues avail.; reprint service avail. from PSC. **Document type:** *Journal, Academic/Scholarly.* **Description:** Covers all aspects of research in applied physics, placing emphasis on work with practical applications in solid-state physics, optics, and magnetism.
Formerly (until 1992): Soviet Physics Journal (0038-5697)
Related titles: Microfilm ed.: (from PQC); Online - full text ed.: ISSN 1573-9228 (from IngentaConnect); ◆ Translation of: Izvestiya Vysshikh Uchebnykh Zavedenii. Fizika. ISSN 0021-3411.
Indexed: A01, A03, A08, A22, A26, ApMecR, BibLing, CA, CCMJ, ChemTitl, E01, Inspec, MSN, MathR, SCI, SCOPUS, T02, W07, Z02.
—BLDSC (0420.778500), AskIEEE, CASDDS, East View, IE, Infotrieve, Ingenta, INIST, Linda Hall. **CCC.**
Published by: (Nizhegorodskii Gosudarstvennyi Universitet, Nauchno-Issledovatel'skii Radiofizicheskii Institut RUS), Springer New York LLC (Subsidiary of: Springer Science+Business Media), 233 Spring St, New York, NY 10013. TEL 212-460-1500, FAX 212-460-1575, service-ny@springer.com, http://www.springer.com. Ed. Alexander I Potekaev.

➤ **RYUTAI RIKIGAKU KOENKAI KOENSHU/SYMPOSIUM ON FLUID MECHANICS. PROCEEDINGS.** *see* ENGINEERING—Hydraulic Engineering

530 370 USA ISSN 2155-6040
QC32
▼ **S A T SUBJECT TEST. PHYSICS.** (Scholastic Aptitude Test) Text in English. 2010 (Aug.). triennial. **Document type:** *Handbook/Manual/Guide, Academic/Scholarly.*
Published by: Barron's Educational Series, Inc., 250 Wireless Blvd, Hauppage, NY 11788. TEL 800-645-3476, FAX 631-434-3723, barrons@barronseduc.com, http://www.barronseduc.com.

530 USA ISSN 2160-1305
QC1
THE S P S OBSERVER. Text in English. 19??. q. free (effective 2011). **Document type:** *Magazine, Trade.* **Description:** Contains articles, physics problems, society news and announcements, meeting information, outreach articles, and breaking news in physics and related sciences.
Formerly (until 200?): S P S Newsletter
Related titles: Online - full text ed.: ISSN 2160-1313.
Published by: American Institute of Physics, 1 Physics Ellipse, College Park, MD 20740. TEL 301-209-3007, FAX 301-209-0839, aipinfo@aip.org, http://www.aip.org. Ed. Dwight E Neuenschwander. **Co-publisher:** Society of Physics Students.

530 USA ISSN 2090-116X
QC1
S R X PHYSICS. (Scholarly Research Exchange) Text in English. 2008. irreg. free (effective 2011). **Document type:** *Journal, Academic/Scholarly.*
Media: Online - full text.
Published by: Scholarly Research Exchange (S R X) (Subsidiary of: Hindawi Publishing Corporation), 410 Park Ave, 15th Fl, #287, New York, NY 10022.

530 KOR ISSN 0374-4914
QC1 CODEN: NWPYA4
SAE MULLI/NEW PHYSICS. Text in Korean. 1961. bi-m. membership. **Document type:** *Journal, Academic/Scholarly.*
Indexed: ChemAb, ChemTitl, INIS AtomInd, Inspec.
—BLDSC (8062.920500).
Published by: Han'guk Mulli Hakhoe/Korean Physical Society, Kangnam-Gu, Yuksam-Dong 635-4, Seoul, 135703, Korea, S. TEL 82-2-5564737, FAX 82-2-5541643, jkps@mulli.kps.or.kr.

SAGA DAIGAKU RIKOGAKUBU SHUHO/SAGA UNIVERSITY. FACULTY OF SCIENCE AND ENGINEERING. REPORTS. *see* ENGINEERING

SAITAMA MATHEMATICAL JOURNAL. *see* MATHEMATICS

530 RUS
➤ **SAMARSKII GOSUDARSTVENNYI UNIVERSITET. VESTNIK. ESTESTVENNONAUCHNAYA SERIYA. FIZIKA/SAMARA STATE UNIVERSITY. VESTNIK. NATURAL SCIENCE SERIES. PHYSICS.** Text in Russian; Summaries in English. 1995. bi-m. **Document type:** *Journal, Academic/Scholarly.*
Published by: (Samarskii Gosudarstvennyi Universitet), Izdatel'stvo Samarskii Universitet/Publishing House of Samara State University, ul Akademika Pavlova 1, k 209, Samara, 443011, Russian Federation. TEL 7-846-3345406, FAX 7-846-3345406, university-press@ssu.samara.ru, http://publisher.samsu.ru. Ed. Dr. I A Noskov.

530 540 RUS ISSN 1024-8579
AS262 CODEN: VLUFBI
➤ **SANKT-PETERBURGSKII UNIVERSITET. VESTNIK. SERIYA 4. FIZIKA, KHIMIYA.** Text in Russian; Summaries in English. 1946. q. USD 208 foreign (effective 2010). bk.rev. charts; illus. index. **Document type:** *Journal, Academic/Scholarly.*
Formerly (until 1992): Leningradskii Universitet. Vestnik. Seriya Fizika i Khimiya (0024-0826)
Related titles: Microfiche ed.: (from BHP); Microform ed.: (from EVP).
Indexed: CIN, ChemAb, GeoRef, Inspec, MathR, RASB, RefZh, SpeleolAb.
—BLDSC (0032.758700), CASDDS, Linda Hall. **CCC.**
Published by: (Sankt-Peterburgskii Gosudarstvennyi Universitet, Nauchno-Issledovatel'skii Institut Fiziki imeni V.A. Foka), Izdatel'skii Dom Sankt-Peterburgskogo Gosudarstvennogo Universiteta, V.O., 6-ya liniya, dom 11/21, komn 319, St Petersburg, 199004, Russian Federation. TEL 7-812-3252604, press@unipress.ru, http://www.unipress.ru. Ed. N A Gulyaeva. Circ: 1,340. **Dist. by:** East View Information Services, 10601 Wayzata Blvd, Minneapolis, MN 55305. TEL 952-252-1201, 800-477-1005, FAX 952-252-1202, info@eastview.com, http://www.eastview.com.

530 USA ISSN 1930-8574
QC32
SAT SUBJECT TEST. PHYSICS. Text in English. 2005. a. USD 19 per issue (effective 2010). **Document type:** *Handbook/Manual/Guide, Academic/Scholarly.*
Published by: Kaplan Inc. (Subsidiary of: Washington Post Co.), 888 7th Ave, New York, NY 10106. TEL 212-997-5886, mrelations@kaplan.com, http://www.kaplan.com.

SCIEN TECH/SAGA DAIGAKU RIKOGAKUBU KOHO. *see* ENGINEERING

530 SGP
THE SCIENCE AND CULTURE SERIES - ADVANCED SCIENTIFIC CULTURE. Text in English. 2001. irreg., latest vol.3, 2001. price varies. back issues avail. **Document type:** *Monographic series, Academic/Scholarly.*
Related titles: ◆ Series: The Science and Culture Series - Astrophysics; ◆ The Science and Culture Series - Ethology; ◆ The Science and Culture Series - Materials Science; ◆ The Science and Culture Series - Spectroscopy; ◆ The Science and Culture Series - Nuclear Strategy and Peace Technology; ◆ The Science and Culture Series - Physics; ◆ The Science and Culture Series - Medicine.
Published by: World Scientific Publishing Co. Pte. Ltd., 5 Toh Tuck Link, Singapore, 596224, Singapore. TEL 65-6466-5775, FAX 65-6467-7667, wspc@wspc.com.sg, http://www.worldscientific.com. **Dist. by:** World Scientific Publishing Ltd., 57 Shelton St, London WC2H 9HE, United Kingdom. TEL 44-207-8360888, FAX 44-207-8362020, sales@wspc.co.uk; World Scientific Publishing Co., Inc., 27 Warren St, Ste 401-402, Hackensack, NJ 07601. TEL 201-487-9655, 800-227-7562, FAX 201-487-9656, 888-977-2665, wspc@wspc.com.

THE SCIENCE AND CULTURE SERIES - ASTROPHYSICS. *see* ASTRONOMY

530 SGP
THE SCIENCE AND CULTURE SERIES - PHYSICS. Variant title: International School of Solid State Physics. Proceeding of the (Number) Course of. Text in English. 1992. irreg., latest 2010, Epioptics 10. price varies. back issues avail. **Document type:** *Monographic series, Academic/Scholarly.* **Description:** Consists of the proceedings of international workshops, seminars, schools, etc. and reports, proposals, studies, etc. of working group meetings under the responsibility of the President of the World Federation of Scientists.
Related titles: ◆ Series: The Science and Culture Series - Advanced Scientific Culture; ◆ The Science and Culture Series - Astrophysics; ◆ The Science and Culture Series - Ethology; ◆ The Science and Culture Series - Spectroscopy; ◆ The Science and Culture Series - Medicine; ◆ The Science and Culture Series - Nuclear Strategy and Peace Technology; ◆ The Science and Culture Series - Materials Science.
Published by: World Scientific Publishing Co. Pte. Ltd., 5 Toh Tuck Link, Singapore, 596224, Singapore. TEL 65-6466-5775, FAX 65-6467-7667, wspc@wspc.com.sg, http://www.worldscientific.com. Ed. A Zichichi. **Dist. by:** World Scientific Publishing Ltd., 57 Shelton St, London WC2H 9HE, United Kingdom. TEL 44-207-8360888, FAX 44-207-8362020, sales@wspc.co.uk; World Scientific Publishing Co., Inc., 27 Warren St, Ste 401-402, Hackensack, NJ 07601. TEL 201-487-9655, 800-227-7562, FAX 201-487-9656, 888-977-2665, wspc@wspc.com.

530 SGP
THE SCIENCE AND CULTURE SERIES - SPECTROSCOPY. Text in English. 2001. irreg., latest 2001. price varies. **Document type:** *Monographic series, Academic/Scholarly.* **Description:** Describes advances in both experimental and theoretical treatments in the field of energy transfer processes that are relevant to various fields, such as spectroscopy, laser technology, phosphors, artificial solar energy conversion, and photobiology.
Related titles: ◆ Series: The Science and Culture Series - Advanced Scientific Culture; ◆ The Science and Culture Series - Astrophysics; ◆ The Science and Culture Series - Ethology; ◆ The Science and Culture Series - Physics; ◆ The Science and Culture Series - Medicine; ◆ The Science and Culture Series - Nuclear Strategy and Peace Technology; ◆ The Science and Culture Series - Materials Science.
Published by: World Scientific Publishing Co. Pte. Ltd., 5 Toh Tuck Link, Singapore, 596224, Singapore. TEL 65-6466-5775, FAX 65-6467-7667, wspc@wspc.com.sg, http://www.worldscientific.com. Ed. A Zichichi. **Dist. by:** World Scientific Publishing Ltd., 57 Shelton St, London WC2H 9HE, United Kingdom. TEL 44-207-8360888, FAX 44-207-8362020, sales@wspc.co.uk; World Scientific Publishing Co., Inc., 27 Warren St, Ste 401-402, Hackensack, NJ 07601. TEL 201-487-9655, 800-227-7562, FAX 201-487-9656, 888-977-2665, wspc@wspc.com.

SCIENCE CHINA MATHEMATICS. *see* MATHEMATICS

530 520 CHN ISSN 1674-7348
QC1
➤ **SCIENCE CHINA PHYSICS, MECHANICS & ASTRONOMY.** Text in English. 1950. m. EUR 997, USD 1,230 combined subscription to institutions (print & online eds.) (effective 2012). reprint service avail. from PSC. **Document type:** *Journal, Academic/Scholarly.*
Former titles (until 2010): Science in China. Series G: Physics, Mechanics & Astronomy; Science in China. Series G: Physics and Astronomy (1672-1799); Which superseded in part (in 2003): Science in China. Series A: Mathematics, Physics and Astronomy (1006-9283)
Related titles: Online - full text ed.: ISSN 1869-1927; ◆ Chinese ed.: Zhongguo Kexue. G Ji: Wulixue, Tianwenxue. ISSN 1672-1780.
Indexed: A20, A22, A26, A28, APA, BrCerAb, C&ISA, CA/WCA, CCMJ, CIA, CPEI, CerAb, CivEngAb, CorrAb, CurCont, E&CAJ, E01, E11, EEA, EMA, ESPM, EngInd, EnvEAb, H15, ISR, M&GPA, M&TEA, M09, MBF, METADEX, MSN, MathR, RefZh, SCI, SCOPUS, SolStAb, T04, W07, WAA, Z02.
—BLDSC (8141.654600), IE, Ingenta, INIST, Linda Hall. **CCC.**
Published by: Zhongguo Kexue Zazhishe/Science in China Press, 16 Donghuangchenggen North Street, Beijing, 100717, China. TEL 86-10-64015835, sale@scichina.com, http://www.scichina.com/. Ed. Ding-Sheng Wang. **Dist. by:** Springer New York LLC, Journal Fulfillment, PO Box 2485, Secaucus, NJ 07096. TEL 212-460-1500, FAX 201-348-4505, journals-ny@springer.com; Springer, Haber Str 7, Heidelberg 69126, Germany. TEL 49-6221-3454303, FAX 49-6221-3454229, subscriptions@springer.com. **Co-publisher:** Springer. **Co-sponsors:** Chinese Academy of Sciences/Zhongguo Kexueyuan; National Natural Science Foundation of China.

530 GBR ISSN 0964-9565
SCOPE (YORK). Text in English. 1951. q. GBP 35 to non-members; GBP 10 per issue to non-members; free to members (effective 2009). adv. bk.rev. **Document type:** *Magazine, Trade.*
Formerly: H P A Bulletin
Published by: Institute of Physics and Engineering in Medicine, Fairmount House, 230 Tadcaster Rd, York, YO24 1ES, United Kingdom. TEL 44-1904-610821, FAX 44-1904-612279, office@ipem.ac.uk. Ed. Marc E Miquel TEL 44-207-6018232. Adv. contact Oliver Kirkman TEL 44-1727-739184.

SCUOLA NORMALE SUPERIORE DI PISA. ANNALI. CLASSE DI SCIENZE. *see* MATHEMATICS

SEARCHLITES. *see* ASTRONOMY

530 JPN ISSN 1342-1492
SEIDENKI GAKKAI KOEN RONBUNSHU/INSTITUTE OF ELECTROSTATICS. PROCEEDINGS OF ANNUAL MEETING. Text in English, Japanese; Summaries in English. a. JPY 7,000. **Document type:** *Proceedings.*
Published by: Seidenki Gakkai/Institute of Electrostatics Japan, c/o Sharum '80 4F, 1-3, Hongo 4-chome, Bunkyo-ku, Tokyo, 113-0033, Japan. TEL 81-3-3815-4171.

530 JPN ISSN 0386-2550
QC570
SEIDENKI GAKKAISHI. Text in English, Japanese; Summaries in English. 1977. bi-m. **Document type:** *Journal, Academic/Scholarly.*
Indexed: JPI.
—BLDSC (4775.545000). **CCC.**
Published by: Seidenki Gakkai/Institute of Electrostatics Japan, c/o Sharum '80 4F, 1-3, Hongo 4-chome, Bunkyo-ku, Tokyo, 113-0033, Japan. TEL 81-3-3815-4171, www-admin@streamer.t.u-tokyo.ac.jp, http://streamer.t.u-tokyo.ac.jp/~iesj/homepage-e.html.

SELECTA MATHEMATICA. *see* MATHEMATICS

530 USA
➤ **SELECTED TOPICS IN SUPERCONDUCTIVITY.** Text in English. 1994. irreg., latest 2001. price varies. back issues avail. **Document type:** *Monographic series, Academic/Scholarly.* **Description:** Discusses contemporary issues in the science and technology of superconductivity, including applications and techniques of current interest.
Published by: Springer New York LLC (Subsidiary of: Springer Science+Business Media), 233 Spring St, New York, NY 10013. TEL 212-460-1500, FAX 212-460-1575, service-ny@springer.com. Ed. Stuart A Wolf.

537.622 RUS ISSN 1063-7826
QC612.S4 CODEN: SMICES
➤ **SEMICONDUCTORS.** Text in English. 1967. m. EUR 6,705, USD 8,125 combined subscription to institutions (print & online eds.) (effective 2012). index. back issues avail. **Document type:** *Journal, Academic/Scholarly.* **Description:** Covers semiconductor theory, transport phenomena, optics, magneto-optics, and electro-optics in semiconductors, lasers, and semiconductor surface physics.
Formerly: Soviet Physics - Semiconductors (0038-5700)
Related titles: Microform ed.; Online - full text ed.: ISSN 1090-6479 (from IngentaConnect); ◆ Translation of: Fizika i Tekhnika Poluprovodnikov. ISSN 0015-3222.
Indexed: A01, A03, A08, A22, A26, ASCA, C33, CA, CPI, ChemAb, CurCont, E01, E14, GPAA, I05, IBR, IBZ, INIS AtomInd, ISR, Inspec, MSCI, PhysBer, S01, SCI, SCOPUS, SPINweb, T02, TM, W07.
—BLDSC (0420.805800), AskIEEE, CASDDS, East View, IE, Infotrieve, Ingenta, INIST, Linda Hall. **CCC.**
Published by: (Rossiiskaya Akademiya Nauk/Russian Academy of Sciences, Sankt-Peterburgskoe Otdelenie), M A I K Nauka - Interperiodica (Subsidiary of: Pleiades Publishing, Inc.), Profsoyuznaya ul 90, Moscow, 117997, Russian Federation. TEL 7-095-3361600, FAX 7-095-3360666, compmg@maik.ru, http://www.maik.ru. Ed. Robert Suris. **Dist. in the Americas by:** Springer New York LLC, Journal Fulfillment, PO Box 2485, Secaucus, NJ 07096. TEL 212-460-1500, FAX 201-348-4505; **Dist. outside of the Americas by:** Springer, Haber Str 7, Heidelberg 69126, Germany. TEL 49-6221-3454303, FAX 49-6221-3454229.

➤ **SENSOR TECHNOLOGY.** *see* COMPUTERS—Cybernetics

530 JPN ISSN 0914-4935
TA165 CODEN: SENMER
➤ **SENSORS AND MATERIALS;** an international journal on sensor technology. Text in English. 1989. 8/yr. JPY 36,750, USD 350 (effective 2005). 60 p./no.; back issues avail. **Document type:** *Journal, Academic/Scholarly.* **Description:** Publishes contributions describing original work in the experimental and theoretical fields, aimed at understanding sensing technology, related materials, associated phenomena, and applied systems.
Indexed: A22, A28, APA, ASCA, BrCerAb, C&ISA, CA/WCA, CIA, CerAb, ChemAb, ChemTitl, CivEngAb, CorrAb, E&CAJ, E11, EEA, EMA, ESPM, EnvEAb, H15, Inspec, M&TEA, M09, MBF, METADEX, MSCI, SCI, SCOPUS, SolStAb, T04, TM, VITIS, W07, WAA.
—BLDSC (8241.785400), AskIEEE, CASDDS, IE, Ingenta, INIST, Linda Hall.
Published by: M Y U, Scientific Publishing Division, 1-23-3-303 Sendagi, Bunkyo-ku, Tokyo, 113-0022, Japan. TEL 81-3-38227374, FAX 81-3-38278547, myukk@myu-inc.jp, http://www.myu-inc.jp/myukk/index.html. Ed. Susumu Sugiyama.

➤ **SERIE DI MATEMATICA E FISICA.** *see* MATHEMATICS

530 USA
SERIES IN CONDENSED MATTER PHYSICS. Text in English. irreg. **Document type:** *Monographic series, Academic/Scholarly.* **Description:** Features monographs on topics such as thermodynamics, fluids, superconductivity, semiconductors and other topics in condensed matter physics.

P

Related titles: Online - full text ed.: ISSN 2155-2533.
Published by: C R C Press, LLC (Subsidiary of: Taylor & Francis Group), 6000 Broken Sound Pky, NW, Ste 300, Boca Raton, FL 33487. TEL 561-994-0555, FAX 561-989-9732, journals@crcpress.com, http://www.crcpress.com.

539 DEU ISSN 1438-0609
SERIES IN MICROSYSTEMS. Text in English. 1999. irreg., latest vol.27, 2010. price varies. **Document type:** *Monographic series, Academic/Scholarly.*
—BLDSC (8250.163380).
Published by: Hartung-Gorre Verlag, Konstanz, 78465, Germany. TEL 49-7533-97227, FAX 49-7533-97228, Hartung.Gorre@t-online.de. Eds. J Brugger, M Gijs, P A Besse.

530 SGP
SERIES IN MODERN CONDENSED MATTER PHYSICS. Text in English. 1992. irreg., latest vol.13, 2008. price varies. back issues avail. **Document type:** *Monographic series, Academic/Scholarly.* **Description:** Covers the development of modern condensed matter physics.
Published by: World Scientific Publishing Co. Pte. Ltd., 5 Toh Tuck Link, Singapore, 596224, Singapore. TEL 65-6466-5775, FAX 65-6467-7667, wspc@wspc.com.sg, http://www.worldscientific.com. Eds. Igor Dzyaloshinski, S Lundqvist, Yu Lu. **Dist. by:** World Scientific Publishing Co., Inc., 27 Warren St, Ste 401-402, Hackensack, NJ 07601. TEL 201-487-9655, 800-227-7562, FAX 201-487-9656, 888-977-2665, wspc@wspc.com; World Scientific Publishing Ltd., 57 Shelton St, London WC2H 9HE, United Kingdom. TEL 44-207-8360888, FAX 44-207-8362020, sales@wspc.co.uk.

530 DEU ISSN 1433-8165
SERIES IN QUANTUM ELECTRONICS. Text in German. 1997. irreg., latest vol.50, 2010. price varies. **Document type:** *Monographic series, Academic/Scholarly.*
Published by: Hartung-Gorre Verlag, Konstanz, 78465, Germany. TEL 49-7533-97227, FAX 49-7533-97228, Hartung.Gorre@t-online.de.

530 SGP ISSN 1793-1479
SERIES IN SOFT CONDENSED MATTER. Text in English. 2008. irreg., latest vol.2, 2009. price varies. back issues avail. **Document type:** *Monographic series, Academic/Scholarly.* **Description:** Covers a large number of diverse aspects, both theoretical and experimental, and a variety of types of publications on all areas of "soft condensed matter".
Published by: World Scientific Publishing Co. Pte. Ltd., 5 Toh Tuck Link, Singapore, 596224, Singapore. TEL 65-6466-5775, FAX 65-6467-7667, wspc@wspc.com.sg, http://www.worldscientific.com. Eds. David Andelman, Gunter Reiter. **Dist. by:** World Scientific Publishing Co., Inc., 27 Warren St, Ste 401-402, Hackensack, NJ 07601. TEL 201-487-9655, 800-227-7562, FAX 201-487-9656, 888-977-2665, wspc@wspc.com; World Scientific Publishing Ltd., 57 Shelton St, London WC2H 9HE, United Kingdom. TEL 44-207-8360888, FAX 44-207-8362020, sales@wspc.co.uk.

530 SGP ISSN 1793-1460
SERIES ON ADVANCES IN QUANTUM MANY-BODY THEORY. Text in English. 1998. irreg., latest vol.11, 2008. price varies. back issues avail. **Document type:** *Monographic series, Academic/Scholarly.* **Description:** Covers research and reports on the advances of quantum many-body theory applications, and also contains the proceedings of the international conference on recent progress in many-body theories.
Published by: World Scientific Publishing Co. Pte. Ltd., 5 Toh Tuck Link, Singapore, 596224, Singapore. TEL 65-6466-5775, FAX 65-6467-7667, wspc@wspc.com.sg, http://www.worldscientific.com. Ed. R F Bishop. **Dist. by:** World Scientific Publishing Co., Inc., 27 Warren St, Ste 401-402, Hackensack, NJ 07601. TEL 201-487-9655, 800-227-7562, FAX 201-487-9656, 888-977-2665, wspc@wspc.com; World Scientific Publishing Ltd., 57 Shelton St, London WC2H 9HE, United Kingdom. TEL 44-207-8360888, FAX 44-207-8362020, sales@wspc.co.uk.

530 SGP ISSN 1793-1452
SERIES ON ATMOSPHERIC, OCEANIC AND PLANETARY PHYSICS. Text in English. 1999. irreg., latest vol.4, 2008. price varies. back issues avail. **Document type:** *Monographic series, Academic/Scholarly.*
Published by: World Scientific Publishing Co. Pte. Ltd., 5 Toh Tuck Link, Singapore, 596224, Singapore. TEL 65-6466-5775, FAX 65-6467-7667, wspc@wspc.com.sg, http://www.worldscientific.com. Ed. F W Taylor. **Dist. by:** World Scientific Publishing Co., Inc., 27 Warren St, Ste 401-402, Hackensack, NJ 07601. TEL 201-487-9655, 800-227-7562, FAX 201-487-9656, 888-977-2665, wspc@wspc.com; World Scientific Publishing Ltd., 57 Shelton St, London WC2H 9HE, United Kingdom. TEL 44-207-8360888, FAX 44-207-8362020, sales@wspc.co.uk.

530 SGP
SERIES ON BIOPHYSICS AND BIOCYBERNETICS. Text in English. 1998. irreg., latest vol.12, 2002. price varies. back issues avail. **Document type:** *Monographic series, Academic/Scholarly.*
Published by: World Scientific Publishing Co. Pte. Ltd., 5 Toh Tuck Link, Singapore, 596224, Singapore. TEL 65-6466-5775, FAX 65-6467-7667, wspc@wspc.com.sg, http://www.worldscientific.com. Ed. Cloe Taddei-Ferretti. **Dist. by:** World Scientific Publishing Co., Inc., 27 Warren St, Ste 401-402, Hackensack, NJ 07601. TEL 201-487-9655, 800-227-7562, FAX 201-487-9656, 888-977-2665, wspc@wspc.com; World Scientific Publishing Ltd., 57 Shelton St, London WC2H 9HE, United Kingdom. TEL 44-207-8360888, FAX 44-207-8362020, sales@wspc.co.uk.

530 GBR ISSN 1755-7453
▼ **SERIES ON COMPLEXITY SCIENCE.** Text in English. forthcoming 2011. irreg. **Document type:** *Monographic series, Academic/Scholarly.* **Description:** Presents theoretical and phenomenological treatises spanning the diverse and evolving field of complexity research including mathematics, biology, engineering, neuroscience, social science and others.
Published by: Imperial College Press (Subsidiary of: World Scientific Publishing Co. Pte. Ltd.), 57 Shelton St, Covent Garden, London, WC2H 9HE, United Kingdom. TEL 44-20-78360888, FAX 44-20-78362020, edit@icpress.co.uk, http://www.icpress.co.uk/. Ed. Henrik Jeldtoft Jensen. **Dist. by:** World Scientific Publishing Co., Inc., 27 Warren St, Ste 401-402, Hackensack, NJ 07601. TEL 201-487-9655, 800-227-7562, FAX 201-487-9656, 888-977-2665, wspc@wspc.com; World Scientific Publishing Ltd.

530 SGP ISSN 0218-0332
SERIES ON DIRECTIONS IN CONDENSED MATTER PHYSICS. Text in English. 1986. irreg., latest vol.19, 2009. price varies. back issues avail. **Document type:** *Monographic series, Academic/Scholarly.*
Indexed: CCMJ, Inspec.
—BLDSC (9360.006000). **CCC.**
Published by: World Scientific Publishing Co. Pte. Ltd., 5 Toh Tuck Link, Singapore, 596224, Singapore. TEL 65-6466-5775, FAX 65-6467-7667, wspc@wspc.com.sg, http://www.worldscientific.com. **Dist. by:** World Scientific Publishing Co., Inc., 27 Warren St, Ste 401-402, Hackensack, NJ 07601. TEL 201-487-9655, 800-227-7562, FAX 201-487-9656, 888-977-2665, wspc@wspc.com; World Scientific Publishing Ltd., 57 Shelton St, London WC2H 9HE, United Kingdom. TEL 44-207-8360888, FAX 44-207-8362020, sales@wspc.co.uk.

530 SGP ISSN 1793-1215
SERIES ON NEUTRON TECHNIQUES AND APPLICATIONS. Text in English. 1997. irreg., latest vol.4, 2009. price varies. back issues avail. **Document type:** *Monographic series, Academic/Scholarly.*
Published by: World Scientific Publishing Co. Pte. Ltd., 5 Toh Tuck Link, Singapore, 596224, Singapore. TEL 65-6466-5775, FAX 65-6467-7667, wspc@wspc.com.sg, http://www.worldscientific.com. **Dist. by:** World Scientific Publishing Co., Inc., 27 Warren St, Ste 401-402, Hackensack, NJ 07601. TEL 201-487-9655, 800-227-7562, FAX 201-487-9656, 888-977-2665, wspc@wspc.com; World Scientific Publishing Ltd., 57 Shelton St, London WC2H 9HE, United Kingdom. TEL 44-207-8360888, FAX 44-207-8362020, sales@wspc.co.uk.

530 621.3 GBR ISSN 0955-9019
CODEN: SSSTF2
SERIES ON SEMICONDUCTOR SCIENCE AND TECHNOLOGY. Text in English. 1989. irreg., latest vol.16, 2008. price varies. back issues avail. **Document type:** *Monographic series, Academic/Scholarly.*
—BLDSC (8250.202280), CASDDS.
Published by: Oxford University Press, Great Clarendon St, Oxford, OX2 6DP, United Kingdom. TEL 44-1865-556767, FAX 44-1865-556646, enquiry@oup.co.uk, http://www.oup-usa.org/catalogs/general/series/. **Orders in N. America to:** Oxford University Press, 2001 Evans Rd, Cary, NC 27513. TEL 919-677-0977 ext 5777, 800-852-7323, FAX 919-677-1714, jnlorders@oup-usa.org, http://www.us.oup.com.

530 JPN ISSN 0559-8516
TJ940 CODEN: SHINAM
SHINKU/VACUUM SOCIETY OF JAPAN. JOURNAL. Text in Japanese; Summaries in English. 1958. m. free to members. **Document type:** *Journal, Academic/Scholarly.*
Indexed: APA, C&ISA, CIN, CPEI, ChemAb, ChemTitl, CorrAb, E&CAJ, EEA, EngInd, INIS AtomInd, Inspec, SCOPUS, SolStAb, WAA.
—AskIEEE, CASDDS, INIST, Linda Hall. **CCC.**
Published by: Nihon Shinku Kyokai/Vacuum Society of Japan, 306 Kikai Shinko Kaikan Bldg., 3-5-8 Shiba Koen, Minato-ku, Tokyo, 105-0011, Japan. TEL 81-3-34314395, FAX 81-3-34335371, ofc-vsj@vacuum-jp.org, http://wwwsoc.nii.ac.jp/vsj/. Ed. Nobuo Saito.

530 JPN
SHINKU NI KANSURU RENGO KOENKAI KOEN YOKOSHU/JOINT SYMPOSIA ON VACUUM. PREPRINTS. Text in Japanese. 1960. a. membership.
Published by: Nihon Shinku Kyokai/Vacuum Society of Japan, 306 Kikai Shinko Kaikan Bldg., 3-5-8 Shiba Koen, Minato-ku, Tokyo, 105-0011, Japan. Ed. Nobuo Saito.

SHITING JISHU/CHINA AVPHILE. *see* ELECTRONICS

SHUXUE WULI XUEBAO (A JI). *see* MATHEMATICS

SIAULIAI MATHEMATICAL SEMINAR. *see* MATHEMATICS

SIGNAL PROCESSING; an international journal. *see* COMMUNICATIONS

530 SGP ISSN 0217-4251
CODEN: SJPHEN
SINGAPORE JOURNAL OF PHYSICS. Text in English. 1973. bi-m.
Formerly (until 1984): I P S Bulletin (0129-2587)
Indexed: INIS AtomInd, Inspec.
—Linda Hall.
Published by: Institute of Physics Singapore, c/o Department of Physics, National University of Singapore, Lower Kent Ridge Rd, Singapore, 119260, Singapore. TEL 65-874-2618, FAX 65-777-6126, ips@www.physics.nus.edu.sg.

530 370 CZE ISSN 1211-1511
➤ **SKOLSKA FYZIKA.** Text in Czech. 1993. q. CZK 300 domestic (effective 2009). **Document type:** *Journal, Academic/Scholarly.*
Published by: Zapadoceska Univezita v Plzni, Fakulta Pedagogicka, Katedra Obecne Fyziky, Klatovska 51, Plzen, 30614, Czech Republic. TEL 420-377-636303, http://www.kof.zcu.cz. Ed. Vaclav Havel. **Co-sponsor:** Jednota Ceskych Matematiku a Fyziku.

534 GBR ISSN 0964-1726
TA418.9.S62 CODEN: SMSTER
➤ **SMART MATERIALS AND STRUCTURES.** Text in English. 1992. bi-m. GBP 943 combined subscription to institutions (print & online eds.) (effective 2010). abstr.; illus. Index. back issues avail. **Document type:** *Journal, Academic/Scholarly.* **Description:** Covers technical advances in smart materials and structures systems, from acoustic to electromagnetic fields.
Related titles: Microfiche ed.: USD 615 in the Americas; GBP 317 elsewhere (effective 2007); Online - full text ed.: ISSN 1361-665X. GBP 898 to institutions (effective 2010) (from IngentaConnect).
Indexed: A22, A28, APA, ASCA, ApMecR, BrCerAb, C&ISA, CA, CA/WCA, CIA, CIN, CPEI, CerAb, ChemAb, ChemTitl, CivEngAb, CorrAb, CurCont, E&CAJ, E11, EEA, EMA, ESPM, EngInd, EnvEAb, H15, ISR, Inspec, M&TEA, M09, MBF, METADEX, MSCI, R18, RefZh, SCI, SCOPUS, SolStAb, T02, T04, W07, WAA.
—BLDSC (8310.193520), AskIEEE, CASDDS, IE, Infotrieve, Ingenta, INIST, Linda Hall. **CCC.**
Published by: (Institute of Physics), Institute of Physics Publishing Ltd., Dirac House, Temple Back, Bristol, BS1 6BE, United Kingdom. TEL 44-117-9297481, FAX 44-117-9301178, custserv@iop.org, http://publishing.iop.org/. Ed. E Garcia. Pub. Ian Forbes. **Subscr. in N. America to:** American Institute of Physics, PO Box 503284, St Louis, MO 63150. TEL 516-576-2270, 800-344-6902, FAX 516-349-9704, subs@aip.org, http://librarians.aip.org.

530 540 USA ISSN 1949-4823
TA418.9.C6
▼ ➤ **SMART NANOCOMPOSITES.** Text in English. 2010 (Jan.). q. USD 245 to institutions; USD 367 to institutions (print & online eds.) (effective 2012). **Document type:** *Journal, Academic/Scholarly.* **Description:** Presents new research on smart materials and composite nanostructured materials, including the physics and physical chemistry of surfaces, interfaces, thin films and coatings, nanoparticles and other nanostructures.
Related titles: Online - full text ed.: USD 245 to institutions (effective 2012).
Published by: Nova Science Publishers, Inc., 400 Oser Ave, Ste 1600, Hauppauge, NY 11788. TEL 631-231-7269, FAX 631-231-8175, journals@novapublishers.com.

530 MEX ISSN 0187-4713
QC1 CODEN: BSMFBB
SOCIEDAD MEXICANA DE FISICA. BOLETIN. Text in English. 1987. q. free to members.
—Linda Hall.
Published by: Sociedad Mexicana de Fisica, A.C., Apartado Postal 70-348, Coyoacan, Mexico City, DF 04511, Mexico. smf@hp.fciencias.unam.mx, http://www.smf.mx. Ed. Jose Luis Cordoba Frunz. Circ: 1,700.

530 ITA ISSN 1122-1437
CODEN: CPISEN
SOCIETA ITALIANA DI FISICA. ATTI DI CONFERENZE/ITALIAN PHYSICAL SOCIETY. CONFERENCE PROCEEDINGS. Text in Italian. 1985. irreg., latest vol.73, 2001. price varies. **Document type:** *Proceedings, Academic/Scholarly.*
Indexed: CIN, ChemAb, ChemTitl, GeoRef.
—BLDSC (3409.770700), CASDDS, IE, Ingenta.
Published by: Societa Italiana di Fisica (S I F), Via Saragozza 12, Bologna, 40123, Italy. TEL 39-051-331554, FAX 39-051-581340, subscriptions@sif.it.

530 ITA ISSN 0393-697X
QC1 CODEN: RNUCAC
➤ **SOCIETA ITALIANA DI FISICA. RIVISTA DEL NUOVO CIMENTO.** Text in English. 1969. m. charts. back issues avail. **Document type:** *Monographic series, Academic/Scholarly.* **Description:** Deals with topics of particular interest in the different fields of physics.
Formerly (until 1971): Rivista del Nuovo Cimento (0035-5917)
Related titles: Online - full text ed.: ISSN 1826-9850. 2000.
Indexed: A22, ASCA, ApMecR, CIN, CMCI, ChemAb, ChemTitl, CurCont, GeoRef, INIS AtomInd, ISR, Inspec, MathR, SCI, SCOPUS, SpeleolAb, W07.
—BLDSC (7991.500000), AskIEEE, CASDDS, IE, Ingenta, INIST, Linda Hall. **CCC.**
Published by: Societa Italiana di Fisica (S I F), Via Saragozza 12, Bologna, 40123, Italy. TEL 39-051-331554, FAX 39-051-581340, subscriptions@sif.it. Ed. Angela Oleandri.

533.5 FRA
➤ **SOCIETE FRANCAISE DU VIDE. PROCEEDINGS.** Text in English, French. 3/yr. adv. **Document type:** *Proceedings, Academic/Scholarly.* **Description:** Presents proceedings from 3 conferences whose subjects are: Materials for Advanced Metallization, Plasma Processes, Adhesion.
Published by: Societe Francaise du Vide, 19 rue du Renard, Paris, 75004, France. TEL 33-1-5301-9030, FAX 33-1-4278-6320, http://www.vide.org. Ed. Bernard Agius. Adv. contact Veronique Pfohl.

530 BGR ISSN 1310-0130
SOFIISKI UNIVERSITET SV. KLIMENT OHRIDSKI. FIZICHESKI FAKULTET. GODISHNIK. KNIGA 1. FIZIKA. Text in Bulgarian. 1982. a.
Supersedes in part (in 1992): Sofiiskii Universitet Sv. Kliment Ohridski. Fizicheski fakultet. Godishnik (0584-0279)
Indexed: CCMJ, INIS AtomInd, Inspec, MSN, MathR, RefZh.
—INIST, Linda Hall.
Published by: Sofiiski Universitet Sv. Kliment Ohridski, Universitetsko Izdatelstvo/Sofia University St. Kliment Ohridski University Press, Akad G Bonchev 6, Sofia, 1113, Bulgaria. TEL 359-2-9792914.

SOFT MATTER. *see* CHEMISTRY

SOLAR PHYSICS; a journal for solar and solar-stellar research and the study of solar terrestrial physics. *see* ASTRONOMY

SOLAR SYSTEM RESEARCH. *see* ASTRONOMY

530.41 GBR ISSN 0038-1098
QC176.A1 CODEN: SSCOA4
➤ **SOLID STATE COMMUNICATIONS.** Text in English. 1963. 48/yr. EUR 5,315 in Europe to institutions; JPY 705,800 in Japan to institutions; USD 5,946 elsewhere to institutions (effective 2012). adv. bk.rev. charts; illus. index. back issues avail.; reprints avail. **Document type:** *Journal, Academic/Scholarly.* **Description:** Features original experimental and theoretical research on the physical and chemical properties of solids and condensed systems.
Related titles: Microfiche ed.: (from MIM); Microfilm ed.: (from PQC); Online - full text ed.: ISSN 1879-2766 (from IngentaConnect, ScienceDirect).
Indexed: A01, A03, A08, A22, A26, A28, APA, ASCA, AcoustA, ApMecR, BrCerAb, C&ISA, C13, C24, C33, CA, CA/WCA, CIA, CIN, CPEI, CerAb, ChemAb, ChemTitl, CivEngAb, CorrAb, CurCont, E&CAJ, E11, EEA, EMA, ESPM, EngInd, EnvEAb, GeoRef, H15, I05, ISMEC, ISR, Inspec, M&TEA, M09, MBF, METADEX, MSCI, P30, PhysBer, RefZh, S01, SCI, SCOPUS, SolStAb, SpeleolAb, T02, T04, TM, W07, WAA.
—BLDSC (8327.378000), AskIEEE, CASDDS, IE, Infotrieve, Ingenta, INIST, Linda Hall. **CCC.**
Published by: Pergamon (Subsidiary of: Elsevier Science & Technology), The Blvd, Langford Ln, East Park, Kidlington, Oxford OX5 1GB, United Kingdom. TEL 44-1865-843000, FAX 44-1865-843010, JournalsCustomerServiceEMEA@elsevier.com. Ed. A Pinczuk. adv.: color page USD 1,350. **Subscr. to:** Elsevier BV, Radarweg 29, PO Box 211, Amsterdam 1000 AE, Netherlands. TEL 31-20-4853757, FAX 31-20-4853432, http://www.elsevier.nl.

530 NLD ISSN 0167-2738
QC176.A1 CODEN: SSIOD3

➤ **SOLID STATE IONICS.** Text in English. 1980. 40/yr. EUR 5,167 in Europe to institutions; JPY 686,900 in Japan to institutions; USD 5,809 elsewhere to institutions (effective 2012). adv. index. reprints avail. **Document type:** *Journal, Academic/Scholarly.* **Description:** Devoted to the physics, chemistry and materials science of diffusion in mass transport and reactivity of solids.
Incorporates (1985-1989): Reactivity of Solids (0168-7336)
Related titles: Microform ed.: (from PQC); Online - full text ed.: ISSN 1872-7689 (from IngentaConnect, ScienceDirect).
Indexed: A01, A03, A08, A22, A26, A28, APA, ASCA, BrCerAb, C&ISA, C24, C33, CA, CA/WCA, CCI, CIA, CIN, CPEI, CerAb, ChemAb, ChemTitl, CivEngAb, CorrAb, CurCont, E&CAJ, E11, EEA, EMA, ESPM, EngInd, EnvEAb, GeoRef, H15, I05, ISMEC, ISR, Inspec, M&TEA, M09, MBF, METADEX, MSCI, PhysBer, RefZh, S01, SCI, SCOPUS, SolStAb, SpeleolAb, T02, T04, TM, W07, WAA.
—BLDSC (8327.386000), AskIEEE, CASDDS, IE, Infotrieve, Ingenta, INIST, Linda Hall. **CCC.**
Published by: Elsevier BV, North-Holland (Subsidiary of: Elsevier Science & Technology), Sara Burgerhartstraat 25, Amsterdam, 1055 KV, Netherlands. TEL 31-20-4853911, FAX 31-20-4852457, JournalsCustomerServiceEMEA@elsevier.com. Ed. J Maier. **Subscr.:** Elsevier BV, Radarweg 29, PO Box 211, Amsterdam 1000 AE, Netherlands. TEL 31-20-4853757, FAX 31-20-4853432.

530 USA ISSN 0081-1947
QC173 CODEN: SSPHAE

➤ **SOLID STATE PHYSICS.** Text in English. 1955. irreg., latest vol.61, 2009. USD 250 per vol. (effective 2010). index, cum.index: vols.1-11 (1955-1960). back issues avail.; reprints avail. **Document type:** *Monographic series, Academic/Scholarly.*
Related titles: Online - full text ed.
Indexed: A22, ASCA, C13, ISR, Inspec, SCI, SCOPUS, SpeleolAb, W07.
—BLDSC (8327.400000), CASDDS, IE, Infotrieve, Ingenta, INIST, Linda Hall. **CCC.**
Published by: Academic Press (Subsidiary of: Elsevier Science & Technology), 3251 Riverport Ln, Maryland Heights, MO 63043. TEL 314-447-8010, FAX 314-447-8030, JournalCustomerService-usa@elsevier.com, http://www.elsevierdirect.com/imprint.jsp?iid=5. Ed. E P Wohlfarth.

➤ **SOLID-STATE SCIENCE AND TECHNOLOGY LIBRARY.** *see* ELECTRONICS

531 NLD ISSN 1874-7906
SOLIDS PROCESSING BENELUX. Text in Dutch. 2005. bi-m. adv. **Document type:** *Magazine, Trade.*
Published by: Vezor Media, Postbus 106, Doetinchem, 7000 AC, Netherlands. TEL 31-314-346688, FAX 31-84-2207821, http://www.vezor.nl. Ed. Henk Klein Gunnewiek TEL 31-314-344143. Pubs. Hans Schouten, Henk Klein Gunnewiek TEL 31-314-344143. Circ: 7,000.

SOSEI TO KAKO/JAPAN SOCIETY FOR TECHNOLOGY OF PLASTICITY. JOURNAL. *see* TECHNOLOGY: COMPREHENSIVE WORKS

SOURCES AND STUDIES IN THE HISTORY OF MATHEMATICS AND PHYSICAL SCIENCES. *see* MATHEMATICS

530 USA ISSN 0930-8989
QC3 CODEN: SPPPEL
SPRINGER PROCEEDINGS IN PHYSICS. Text in English. 1984. irreg., latest vol.135, 2010. price varies. back issues avail.; reprints avail. **Document type:** *Monographic series.*
Indexed: A22, CIN, ChemAb, ChemTitl, Inspec, Z02.
—BLDSC (8424.726500), CASDDS, IE, Ingenta, INIST. **CCC.**
Published by: Springer New York LLC (Subsidiary of: Springer Science+Business Media), 233 Spring St, New York, NY 10013. TEL 212-460-1500, FAX 212-460-1575, service-ny@springer.com.

530 541 USA ISSN 0172-6218
QD450 CODEN: SSCPDA
SPRINGER SERIES IN CHEMICAL PHYSICS. Text in English. 1978. irreg., latest vol.98, 2010. price varies. back issues avail.; reprints avail. **Document type:** *Monographic series.*
Indexed: A22, C&ISA, CCMJ, CIN, ChemAb, ChemTitl, E&CAJ, GeoRef, ISMEC, Inspec, PhysBer, SCOPUS, SolStAb, SpeleolAb.
—BLDSC (8424.755000), CASDDS, IE, Ingenta, INIST. **CCC.**
Published by: Springer New York LLC (Subsidiary of: Springer Science+Business Media), 233 Spring St, New York, NY 10013. TEL 212-460-1500, FAX 212-460-1575, service-ny@springer.com.

530 USA ISSN 0933-033X
CODEN: SSMSE2
SPRINGER SERIES IN MATERIALS SCIENCE. Text in English. 1986. irreg., latest vol.142, 2010. price varies. back issues avail.; reprints avail. **Document type:** *Monographic series.*
Indexed: ChemAb, ChemTitl.
—BLDSC (8424.766600), CASDDS, IE, Ingenta. **CCC.**
Published by: Springer New York LLC (Subsidiary of: Springer Science+Business Media), 233 Spring St, New York, NY 10013. TEL 212-460-1500, FAX 212-460-1575, service-ny@springer.com.

530 USA ISSN 0171-1873
CODEN: SSSSDV
SPRINGER SERIES IN SOLID STATE SCIENCES. Text in English. 1978. irreg., latest vol.166, 2010. price varies. back issues avail.; reprints avail. **Document type:** *Monographic series.*
Indexed: A22, CCMJ, CIS, ChemAb, ChemTitl, GeoRef, Inspec, PhysBer, SpeleolAb, Z02.
—BLDSC (8424.775000), CASDDS, IE, Ingenta, INIST. **CCC.**
Published by: Springer New York LLC (Subsidiary of: Springer Science+Business Media), 233 Spring St, New York, NY 10013. TEL 212-460-1500, FAX 212-460-1575, service-ny@springer.com.

530 USA ISSN 0931-5195
CODEN: SSSSEW
SPRINGER SERIES IN SURFACE SCIENCES. Text in English. 1986. irreg., latest vol.45, 2010. price varies. back issues avail.; reprints avail. **Document type:** *Monographic series.*
Indexed: A22, CIN, ChemAb, ChemTitl, GeoRef, Inspec.
—BLDSC (8424.777200), CASDDS, IE, Ingenta. **CCC.**
Published by: Springer New York LLC (Subsidiary of: Springer Science+Business Media), 233 Spring St, New York, NY 10013. TEL 212-460-1500, FAX 212-460-1575, service-ny@springer.com. Eds. Douglas L Mills, Gerhard Ertl, Hans Luth.

530 DEU ISSN 1615-5653
SPRINGER SERIES ON ATOMIC, OPTICAL, AND PLASMA PHYSICS. Text in English. 1985. irreg., latest vol.58, 2010. price varies. **Document type:** *Monographic series, Academic/Scholarly.* **Description:** Covers in a comprehensive manner theory and experiment in the entire field of atoms and molecules and their interaction with electromagnetic radiation.
Formerly (until 2004): Springer Series on Atoms and Plasmas (0177-6495)
Related titles: Online - full text ed.
Indexed: Inspec, MSN.
—BLDSC (8424.744500), IE. **CCC.**
Published by: Springer (Subsidiary of: Springer Science+Business Media), Tiergartenstr 17, Heidelberg, 69121, Germany. TEL 49-6221-4870, FAX 49-6221-345229, subscriptions@springer.com. Eds. U Becker, W E Baylis.

539 DEU ISSN 0081-3869
QC1 CODEN: STPHBM

➤ **SPRINGER TRACTS IN MODERN PHYSICS.** Text in German. 1964. irreg., latest vol.239, 2010. price varies. back issues avail.; reprints avail. **Document type:** *Monographic series, Academic/Scholarly.* **Description:** Provides comprehensive and critical reviews of topics of current interest in physics.
Formerly (until 1965): Ergebnisse der Exacten Naturwissenschaften (0367-0325)
Related titles: Online - full text ed.: ISSN 1615-0430.
Indexed: A22, ASCA, CCMJ, ISR, Inspec, MSN, MathR, PhysBer, SCOPUS, Z02.
—BLDSC (8424.800000), CASDDS, IE, Ingenta, INIST, Linda Hall. **CCC.**
Published by: Springer (Subsidiary of: Springer Science+Business Media), Tiergartenstr 17, Heidelberg, 69121, Germany. TEL 49-6221-4870, FAX 49-6221-345229, subscriptions@springer.com, http://www.springer.com. **Orders in N. America to:** Order Department, PO Box 25, Secaucus, NJ 07096-9812. TEL 201-348-4505, 201-348-4033.

➤ **STANDARD TIME & FREQUENCY SERVICE BULLETIN.** *see* METROLOGY AND STANDARDIZATION

➤ **STATISTICAL INFERENCE FOR STOCHASTIC PROCESSES**; an international journal devoted to time series analysis and the statistics of continuous time processes and dynamical systems. *see* MATHEMATICS

539 GBR ISSN 1545-2255
TA630
STRUCTURAL CONTROL AND HEALTH MONITORING; the bulletin of A C S. Text in English. 1994. 8/yr. GBP 282 in United Kingdom to institutions; EUR 358 in Europe to institutions; USD 554 elsewhere to institutions; GBP 311 combined subscription in United Kingdom to institutions (print & online eds.); EUR 394 combined subscription in Europe to institutions (print & online eds.); USD 610 combined subscription elsewhere to institutions (print & online eds.) (effective 2010). adv. back issues avail.; reprint service avail. from PSC. **Document type:** *Journal, Academic/Scholarly.* **Description:** The aim of this journal is to provide a forum in which survey articles and original research in the field of structural control can be communicated rapidly, towards a cross-fertilization of information and ideas. An important aim is to achieve a balance between academic material and practical applications.
Incorporates (1997-2007): Progress in Structural Engineering and Materials (1365-0556); Formerly (until 2004): Journal of Structural Control (1122-8385)
Related titles: Online - full text ed.: ISSN 1545-2263. GBP 282 in United Kingdom to institutions; EUR 358 in Europe to institutions; USD 554 elsewhere to institutions (effective 2010).
Indexed: A20, A28, APA, B21, BrCerAb, C&ISA, CA/WCA, CIA, CPEI, CerAb, CivEngAb, CorrAb, CurCont, E&CAJ, E11, EEA, EMA, ESPM, EngInd, EnvEAb, H&SSA, H15, HRIS, M&TEA, M09, MBF, METADEX, S01, SCI, SCOPUS, SolStAb, T04, W07, WAA.
—IE, Linda Hall. **CCC.**
Published by: (European Association for the Control of Structures ITA), John Wiley & Sons Ltd. (Subsidiary of: John Wiley & Sons, Inc.), 1-7 Oldlands Way, PO Box 808, Bognor Regis, West Sussex PO21 9FF, United Kingdom. TEL 44-1865-778315, FAX 44-1243-843232, cs-journals@wiley.com, http://eu.wiley.com/WileyCDA/. Ed. Lucia Faravelli. **Subscr. to:** 1-7 Oldlands Way, PO Box 809, Bognor Regis, West Sussex PO21 9FG, United Kingdom. TEL 44-1865-778054, cs-agency@wiley.com.

530 540 NLD
STRUCTURE AND DYNAMICS OF MOLECULAR SYSTEMS. Text in English. 1985. irreg., latest vol.2, 1986. price varies. **Document type:** *Monographic series, Academic/Scholarly.*
Published by: Springer Netherlands (Subsidiary of: Springer Science+Business Media), Van Godewijckstraat 30, Dordrecht, 3311 GX, Netherlands. TEL 31-78-6576050, FAX 31-78-6576474.

530 ROM ISSN 0258-8730
QC1 CODEN: SBBPAJ

➤ **STUDIA UNIVERSITATIS BABES-BOLYAI. PHYSICA.** Text in English, French, German, Romanian. 1957. s-a. exchange basis. abstr.; bibl.; stat.; charts; illus. **Document type:** *Journal, Academic/Scholarly.*
Formerly (until 1975): Studia Universitatis "Babes-Bolyai". Series Physica (0370-8578); Which superseded in part (in 1970): Studia Universitatis "Babes-Bolyai". Series Mathematica-Physica (0039-3436); Which superseded in part (in 1962): Studia Universitatis "Babes-Bolyai". Series 1: Matematica, Fizica, Chimie (0578-5413); Which superseded in part (in 1958): Buletinul Universitatilor "V Babes si Bolyai" Cluj. Seria Stiintele Naturii (0365-9216)
Related titles: Online - full text ed.: ISSN 2065-9415.
Indexed: CA, CIN, ChemAb, ChemTitl, MathR, RefZh, T02, Z02.
—CASDDS, INIST, Linda Hall.
Published by: Universitatea "Babes-Bolyai", Studia/Babes-Bolyai University, Studia, 51 Hasdeu Str, Cluj-Napoca, 400371, Romania. TEL 40-264-405352, FAX 40-264-591906, office@studia.ubbcluj.ro. Ed. Onuc Cozar. **Dist by:** "Lucian Blaga" Central University Library, International Exchange Department, Clinicilor st no 2, Cluj-Napoca 400371, Romania. TEL 40-264-597092, FAX 40-264-597633, iancu@bcucluj.ro.

530 DEU ISSN 1614-8967
STUDIEN ZUM PHYSIK- UND CHEMIELERNEN. Text in German. 2000. irreg., latest vol.113, 2011. price varies. **Document type:** *Monographic series, Academic/Scholarly.*
Formerly (until 2005): Studien zum Physiklernen (1435-5280)
Published by: Logos Verlag Berlin, Comeniushof, Gubener Str 47, Berlin, 10243, Germany. TEL 49-30-42851090, FAX 49-30-42851092, redaktion@logos-verlag.de. Eds. Hans Niederrer, Helmut Fischler.

STUDIES IN APPLIED MATHEMATICS (MALDEN). *see* MATHEMATICS

530.9 GBR ISSN 1355-2198
QC6.9

➤ **STUDIES IN HISTORY AND PHILOSOPHY OF SCIENCE PART B: STUDIES IN HISTORY AND PHILOSOPHY OF MODERN PHYSICS.** Text in English. 1995 (vol.26). 4/yr. EUR 637 in Europe to institutions; JPY 84,400 in Japan to institutions; USD 711 elsewhere to institutions (effective 2012). illus. Index. back issues avail.; reprints avail. **Document type:** *Journal, Academic/Scholarly.* **Description:** Devoted to all aspects of the history and philosophy of modern physics broadly understood, including physical aspects of astronomy, chemistry and other non-biological sciences.
Related titles: Microform ed.: (from PQC); Online - full text ed.: ISSN 1879-2502 (from IngentaConnect, ScienceDirect).
Indexed: A01, A03, A08, A20, A22, A26, AmH&L, ArtHuCI, CA, CCMJ, CurCont, DIP, HistAb, I05, IBR, IBZ, IPB, MSN, MathR, PhilInd, S01, SCI, SCOPUS, T02, W07.
—BLDSC (8490.651900), IE, Infotrieve, Ingenta, Linda Hall. **CCC.**
Published by: Pergamon (Subsidiary of: Elsevier Science & Technology), The Blvd, Langford Ln, East Park, Kidlington, Oxford OX5 1GB, United Kingdom. TEL 44-1865-843000, FAX 44-1865-843010, JournalsCustomerServiceEMEA@elsevier.com. **Subscr. to:** Elsevier BV, Radarweg 29, PO Box 211, Amsterdam 1000 AE, Netherlands. TEL 31-20-4853757, FAX 31-20-4853432, http://www.elsevier.nl.

530 NLD ISSN 1383-7303
CODEN: SISCFH

➤ **STUDIES IN INTERFACE SCIENCE.** Text in English. 1995. irreg., latest vol.23, 2006. price varies. back issues avail. **Document type:** *Monographic series, Academic/Scholarly.* **Description:** Publishes contributions describing and reviewing recent theoretical and experimental developments in interface science.
Related titles: Online - full text ed.: ISSN 2212-0815.
Indexed: SCOPUS.
—BLDSC (8490.740600), CASDDS. **CCC.**
Published by: Elsevier BV (Subsidiary of: Elsevier Science & Technology), Radarweg 29, PO Box 211, Amsterdam, 1000 AE, Netherlands. TEL 31-20-4853911, FAX 31-20-4852457, JournalsCustomerServiceEMEA@elsevier.com, http://www.elsevier.nl. Eds. D Moebius, R Miller.

530.1 NLD ISSN 0925-8582

➤ **STUDIES IN MATHEMATICAL PHYSICS.** Text in English. 1990. irreg., latest vol.7, 1997. price varies. back issues avail. **Document type:** *Monographic series, Academic/Scholarly.* **Description:** Discusses new techniques, ideas, and methods in physics, offering sound mathematics and a high didactical quality.
Related titles: Online - full text ed.
Indexed: CCMJ, Z02.
—BLDSC (8491.049000). **CCC.**
Published by: Elsevier BV, North-Holland (Subsidiary of: Elsevier Science & Technology), Sara Burgerhartstraat 25, Amsterdam, 1055 KV, Netherlands. TEL 31-20-4853911, FAX 31-20-4852457, JournalsCustomerServiceEMEA@elsevier.com, http://www.elsevier.com. Eds. E de Jager, E van Groesen. **Subscr. to:** Elsevier BV, Radarweg 29, PO Box 211, Amsterdam 1000 AE, Netherlands. TEL 31-20-4853757, FAX 31-20-4853432.

530 SGP ISSN 8756-4475
CODEN: SUSEE4
THE SUBNUCLEAR SERIES. Text in English. 1963-1992 (vol.29); N.S. 1994. irreg., latest vol.46. price varies. back issues avail. **Document type:** *Monographic series, Academic/Scholarly.* **Description:** Presents the proceedings of the International School of Nuclear Physics.
Indexed: CIN, ChemAb, ChemTitl, Inspec.
—CASDDS, INIST.
Published by: World Scientific Publishing Co. Pte. Ltd., 5 Toh Tuck Link, Singapore, 596224, Singapore. TEL 65-6466-5775, FAX 65-6467-7667, wspc@wspc.com.sg, http://www.worldscientific.com. Ed. A Zichichi. **Dist. by:** World Scientific Publishing Ltd., 57 Shelton St, London WC2H 9HE, United Kingdom. TEL 44-207-8360888, FAX 44-207-8362020, sales@wspc.co.uk; World Scientific Publishing Co., Inc., 27 Warren St, Ste 401-402, Hackensack, NJ 07601. TEL 201-487-9655, 800-227-7562, FAX 201-487-9656, 888-977-2665, wspc@wspc.com.

615.89 110 USA ISSN 1099-6591

➤ **SUBTLE ENERGIES AND ENERGY MEDICINE**; an interdisciplinary journal of energetic and informational interactions. Text in English. 1990. 3/yr. USD 50 (effective 2011). bk.rev. abstr.; charts; illus.; stat. back issues avail. **Document type:** *Journal, Academic/Scholarly.* **Description:** Concerns the study of subtle energies and energy medicine, self-regulation and alternative therapies.
Formerly (until 1996): Subtle Energies (1084-2209)
—BLDSC (8503.537000), IE, Ingenta.
Published by: International Society for the Study of Subtle Energies and Energy Medicine, 2770 Arapaho Rd Ste 132, Lafayette, CO 80026. TEL 303-425-4625, FAX 866-269-0972, info@issseem.org. Ed. Bernard O Williams.

530 510 PRK ISSN 0371-0688
QA1 CODEN: SKMOAW
SUHAK KWA MULLI. Variant title: Soohak Kwa Moolli. Text in Korean. 1957. q.
—CASDDS.
Published by: Korean Academy of Sciences, Physics and Mathematics Committee, Pyongyang, Korea, N.

530 540 620 GBR ISSN 0953-2048
QC611.9 CODEN: SUSTEF

➤ **SUPERCONDUCTOR SCIENCE & TECHNOLOGY.** Text in English. 1988. m. GBP 863 combined subscription to institutions (print & online eds.) (effective 2010). back issues avail. **Document type:** *Journal, Academic/Scholarly.* **Description:** Provides a forum for chemists, physicists, materials scientists, and electronics and electrical engineers involved in any aspect of the science and technology of superconductors, both conventional and the new ceramic materials.
Related titles: Microfiche ed.: USD 1,065 in the Americas; GBP 544 elsewhere (effective 2007); Online - full text ed.: ISSN 1361-6668. GBP 822 to institutions (effective 2010) (from IngentaConnect).

P

Indexed: A01, A03, A05, A08, A20, A22, A28, APA, AS&TA, AS&TI, ASCA, B04, BrCerAb, C&ISA, C10, C24, C33, CA, CA/WCA, CIA, CIN, CPEI, CerAb, ChemAb, ChemTitl, CivEngAb, CorrAb, CurCont, E&CAJ, E11, EEA, EIA, EMA, ESPM, EngInd, EnvAb, EnvEAb, H15, INIS AtomInd, ISR, Inspec, M&TEA, M09, MBF, METADEX, MSCI, RefZh, SCI, SCOPUS, SolStAb, T02, T04, W07, WAA.
—BLDSC (8547.075500), AskIEEE, CASDDS, IE, Infotrieve, Ingenta, INIST, Linda Hall. **CCC.**
Published by: (Institute of Physics), Institute of Physics Publishing Ltd., Dirac House, Temple Back, Bristol, BS1 6BE, United Kingdom. TEL 44-117-9297481, FAX 44-117-9301178, custserv@iop.org, http://publishing.iop.org/. Ed. D P Hampshire. **Subscr. addr. in US:** American Institute of Physics, PO Box 503284, St Louis, MO 63150. TEL 516-576-2270, 800-344-6902, FAX 516-349-9704, subs@aip.org.

530 USA ISSN 0894-7635
QC612.S8
SUPERCONDUCTOR WEEK; the newsletter of record in the field of superconductivity. Text in English. 1987. 24/yr. USD 437 in US & Canada; USD 556 elsewhere; USD 15 newsstand/cover (effective 2007). 8 p./no.; back issues avail. **Document type:** *Magazine, Trade.* **Description:** Covers news of superconductor and cryogenics applications, commercialization, markets, products, and business.
Related titles: Online - full text ed.
Published by: Peregrine Communications, PO Box 13002, Portland, OR 97213-0002. TEL 503-232-5466, FAX 646-218-4618. Ed. Mark Bitterman. Pub. Jennifer L Turner.

530 MEX ISSN 1665-3521
SUPERFICIES Y VACIOS. Text in Spanish. 1989. q. back issues avail. **Document type:** *Journal, Academic/Scholarly.*
Related titles: Online - full text ed.: free (effective 2011).
Indexed: F04.
Published by: Sociedad Mexicana de Ciencia y Tecnologia de Superficies y Materiales, Cinvestav - Depto. de Fisica, Apto. Postal 14-740, Mexico, D.F., 07000, Mexico. TEL 52-5-7473828, alex@fis.cinvestav.mx, http://www.smcsyv.org.mx/principal/. Ed. Maximo Lopez Miranda.

SUPERLATTICES AND MICROSTRUCTURES. *see* CHEMISTRY

530.44 JPN
SUPESU PURAZUMA KENKYUKAI. Text in English, Japanese. 1970. a.
Published by: (Space Plasma Study Group), Institute of Space and Aeronautical Science/Uchu Kagaku Kenkyujo, 1-1 Yoshinodai 3-chome, Sagamihara-shi, Kanagawa-ken 229-0022, Japan.

SURFACE INVESTIGATION: X-RAY, SYNCHROTRON AND NEUTRON TECHNIQUES. *see* ENGINEERING—Mechanical Engineering

541.345 NLD ISSN 0039-6028
CODEN: SUSCAS
➤ **SURFACE SCIENCE.** Text in English, French, German; Summaries in English. 1964. 24/yr. EUR 11,025 in Europe to institutions; JPY 1,463,800 in Japan to institutions; USD 12,333 elsewhere to institutions (effective 2012). adv. bk.rev. bibl.; charts; illus. index. reprints avail. **Document type:** *Journal, Academic/Scholarly.* **Description:** Deals with theoretical and experimental studies in the physics and chemistry of surfaces.
Incorporates (1980-1990): Surface Science Letters (0167-2584)
Related titles: Microform ed.: (from PQC); Online - full text ed.: (from IngentaConnect, ScienceDirect).
Indexed: A01, A03, A08, A22, A26, A28, APA, ASCA, BrCerAb, C&CR, C&ISA, C13, C24, C33, CA, CA/WCA, CCI, CIA, CIN, CPEI, CerAb, ChemAb, ChemTitl, CivEngAb, CorrAb, CurCR, CurCont, E&CAJ, E11, EEA, EMA, ESPM, EngInd, EnvEAb, GeoRef, H15, I05, IBR, IBZ, ISMEC, ISR, Inspec, M&TEA, M09, MBF, METADEX, MSB, MSCI, P30, PhotoAb, PhysBer, R16, RefZh, S01, SCI, SCOPUS, SolStAb, SpeleolAb, T02, T04, TM, W07, WAA.
—BLDSC (8547.950000), AskIEEE, CASDDS, IE, Infotrieve, Ingenta, INIST, Linda Hall. **CCC.**
Published by: Elsevier BV, North-Holland (Subsidiary of: Elsevier Science & Technology), Sara Burgerhartstraat 25, Amsterdam, 1055 KV, Netherlands. TEL 31-20-4853911, FAX 31-20-4852457, JournalsCustomerServiceEMEA@elsevier.com, http://www.elsevier.nl/homepage/about/us/regional_sites.htt. Ed. C T Campbell. **Subscr. to:** Elsevier BV, Radarweg 29, PO Box 211, Amsterdam 1000 AE, Netherlands. TEL 31-20-4853757, FAX 31-20-4853432.

530 NLD ISSN 0167-5729
QC173.4.S94 CODEN: SSREDI
➤ **SURFACE SCIENCE REPORTS.** Text in English. 1981. 12/yr. EUR 1,883 in Europe to institutions; JPY 250,100 in Japan to institutions; USD 2,104 elsewhere to institutions (effective 2012). adv. back issues avail.; reprints avail. **Document type:** *Journal, Academic/Scholarly.* **Description:** Contains papers on the properties of surfaces and interfaces of metals, semiconductors and insulators, with emphasis on fundamental aspects of solid and liquid interfaces, their atomic and electronic structure.
Related titles: Microform ed.: (from PQC); Online - full text ed.: (from IngentaConnect, ScienceDirect).
Indexed: A01, A03, A08, A22, A26, A28, APA, ASCA, BrCerAb, C&ISA, C24, C33, CA, CA/WCA, CCI, CIA, CIN, CPEI, CerAb, ChemAb, ChemTitl, CivEngAb, CorrAb, CurCR, CurCont, E&CAJ, E11, EEA, EMA, ESPM, EngInd, EnvEAb, H15, I05, ISMEC, ISR, Inspec, M&TEA, M09, MBF, METADEX, MSCI, PhysBer, R16, RefZh, S01, SCI, SCOPUS, SolStAb, T02, T04, W07, WAA.
—BLDSC (8547.950530), AskIEEE, CASDDS, IE, Infotrieve, Ingenta, INIST, Linda Hall. **CCC.**
Published by: Elsevier BV, North-Holland (Subsidiary of: Elsevier Science & Technology), Sara Burgerhartstraat 25, Amsterdam, 1055 KV, Netherlands. TEL 31-20-4853911, FAX 31-20-4852457, JournalsCustomerServiceEMEA@elsevier.com. Ed. W H Weinberg. **Subscr. to:** Elsevier BV, Radarweg 29, PO Box 211, Amsterdam 1000 AE, Netherlands. TEL 31-20-4853757, FAX 31-20-4853432.

530 USA ISSN 1055-5269
QC173.4.S94 CODEN: SSSPEN
➤ **SURFACE SCIENCE SPECTRA**; an international journal devoted to archiving surface science spectra of technological and scientific interest. Text in English. 1991. q. adv. index. back issues avail. **Document type:** *Journal, Academic/Scholarly.* **Description:** Publishes complete records of original surface spectroscopic data.
Related titles: Microform ed.; Online - full text ed.: ISSN 1520-8575.
Indexed: C10, CA, CIN, CPI, ChemAb, ChemTitl, Inspec, SPINweb, T02.
—AskIEEE, CASDDS, Infotrieve, Ingenta, INIST. **CCC.**
Published by: (American Vacuum Society), American Institute of Physics, 1 Physics Ellipse, College Park, MD 20740. TEL 301-209-3100, FAX 301-209-0843, aipinfo@aip.org, http://www.aip.org. Eds. James E Castle, Rick Haasch, S W Gaarenstroom. **Subscr. to:** PO Box 503284, St Louis, MO 63150. TEL 516-576-2270, 800-344-6902, FAX 516-349-9704, subs@aip.org.

530 SRB ISSN 0352-7859
QC1 CODEN: SFNAEW
SVESKE FIZICKIH NAUKA/LECTURES IN PHYSICAL SCIENCES. Text in Serbian. 1988. irreg., latest vol.8, no.2, 1995. **Document type:** *Journal, Academic/Scholarly.* **Description:** Reviews current topics in modern physics.
Indexed: INIS AtomInd.
Published by: Institut za Fiziku/Institute of Physics, PO Box 57, Belgrade, 11001. TEL 381-11-3160260, FAX 381-11-3162190, info@phy.bg.ac.yu, http://www.phy.bg.ac.yu.

SWEDISH INSTITUTE OF SPACE PHYSICS. I R F SCIENTIFIC REPORT. *see* EARTH SCIENCES—Geophysics

530 USA ISSN 1931-8367
QC793
SYMMETRY; dimensions of particle physics. Text in English. 2004. bi-m. free to qualified personnel (effective 2010). back issues avail. **Document type:** *Magazine, Government.* **Description:** Contains information about particle physics and its connections to other aspects of life and science, from interdisciplinary collaborations to policy to culture.
Related titles: Online - full text ed.: ISSN 1931-8375. free (effective 2010).
Indexed: BiolDig.
Published by: (Stanford Linear Accelerator Center), Fermi National Accelerator Laboratory, PO Box 500, Batavia, IL 60510. TEL 630-840-3351, FAX 630-840-8780, fermilab@fnal.gov, http://www.fnal.gov. Ed., Pub. Judy Jackson.

SYNTHETIC METALS. *see* ENGINEERING—Engineering Mechanics And Materials

TAMPEREEN TEKNILLINEN YLIOPISTO. FYSIIKAN LAITOS. RAPORTTI/TAMPERE UNIVERSITY OF TECHNOLOGY. INSTITUTE OF PHYSICS. REPORT. *see* ENGINEERING—Electrical Engineering

TECHMAX; Neugierig auf Wissenschaft. *see* TECHNOLOGY: COMPREHENSIVE WORKS

530 RUS ISSN 1063-7842
QC1 CODEN: TEPHEX
➤ **TECHNICAL PHYSICS.** Text in English. 1931. m. EUR 6,240, USD 7,559 combined subscription to institutions (print & online eds.) (effective 2012). bibl.; charts; illus. index. back issues avail. **Document type:** *Journal, Academic/Scholarly.* **Description:** Simultaneous translation of Russian works in applied physics, especially on instrumentation and measurement techniques. Particular emphasis is on plasma physics.
Formerly: Soviet Physics - Technical Physics (0038-5662)
Related titles: Online - full text ed.: ISSN 1090-6525 (from IngentaConnect); ◆ Translation of: Zhurnal Tekhnicheskoi Fiziki. ISSN 0044-4642.
Indexed: A01, A02, A03, A08, A22, A26, AcoustA, ApMecR, C33, CA, CPI, ChemAb, CurCont, E01, GPAA, IBR, IBZ, ISR, Inspec, MSB, MathR, PhysBer, S01, SCI, SCOPUS, SPINweb, T02, W07.
—BLDSC (0425.899600), AskIEEE, CASDDS, East View, IE, Infotrieve, Ingenta, INIST, Linda Hall. **CCC.**
Published by: (Sankt-Peterburgskoe Otdelenie), M A I K Nauka - Interperiodica (Subsidiary of: Pleiades Publishing, Inc.), Profsoyuznaya ul 90, Moscow, 117997, Russian Federation. TEL 7-095-3347420, FAX 7-095-3360666, compmg@maik.ru. Ed. V V Afrosimov. **Dist. in the Americas by:** Springer New York LLC; **Dist. outside the Americas by:** Springer.

530.05 RUS ISSN 1063-7850
QC1 CODEN: TPLEED
➤ **TECHNICAL PHYSICS LETTERS.** Text in English. 1975. m. EUR 4,025, USD 4,881 combined subscription to institutions (print & online eds.) (effective 2012). bibl.; charts; illus. index. back issues avail. **Document type:** *Journal, Academic/Scholarly.* **Description:** Provides for the rapid publication of developments in theoretical and experimental physics with potential technological applications.
Formerly: Soviet Technical Physics Letters (0360-120X)
Related titles: Online - full text ed.: ISSN 1090-6533 (from IngentaConnect); ◆ Translation of: Pis'ma v Zhurnal Tekhnicheskoi Fiziki. ISSN 0320-0116.
Indexed: A01, A02, A03, A08, A20, A22, A26, AcoustA, C33, CA, ChemAb, CurCont, E01, GPAA, IBR, IBZ, ISR, Inspec, PhysBer, S01, SCI, SCOPUS, SPINweb, T02, TM, W07.
—BLDSC (0425.899800), AskIEEE, CASDDS, East View, IE, Infotrieve, Ingenta, INIST, Linda Hall. **CCC.**
Published by: M A I K Nauka - Interperiodica (Subsidiary of: Pleiades Publishing, Inc.), Profsoyuznaya ul 90, Moscow, 117997, Russian Federation. TEL 7-095-3347420, FAX 7-095-3360666, compmg@maik.ru. Ed. Zhores I Alferov. **Dist. in the Americas by:** Springer New York LLC, Journal Fulfillment, PO Box 2485, Secaucus, NJ 07096. TEL 212-460-1500, FAX 201-348-4505; **Dist. outside of the Americas by:** Springer, Haber Str 7, Heidelberg 69126, Germany. TEL 49-6221-3454303, FAX 49-6221-3454229.

530 ITA ISSN 2035-5831
▼ **TECHNICAL, SCIENTIFIC AND RESEARCH REPORTS.** Text in Multiple languages. 2009. a. **Document type:** *Monographic series, Academic/Scholarly.*
Media: Online - full text.
Published by: Consiglio Nazionale delle Ricerche (C N R), Istituto di Fisica Applicata "Nino Carrara", Via Madonna del Piano 10, Sesto Fiorentino, FI 50019, Italy. TEL 39-055-52251, FAX 39-055-5225000, http://www.ifac.cnr.it.

530 POL ISSN 1505-1013
QC1 CODEN: ZNPFDJ
➤ **TECHNICAL UNIVERSITY OF LODZ. SCIENTIFIC BULLETIN. PHYSICS.** Text in English; Summaries in English, Polish. 1973. a., latest vol.22, 2002. price varies. **Document type:** *Journal, Academic/Scholarly.* **Description:** Publishes articles on solid state physics: physical properties of solid monocrystals, organic solids, liquid crystals, semiconducting and insulating compounds as well as the interaction between laser light and matter.
Formerly (until 1995): Politechnika Lodzka. Zeszyty Naukowe. Fizyka (0137-2564)
Indexed: B22, CIN, ChemAb, ChemTitl, Inspec.
—AskIEEE, CASDDS, Linda Hall.
Published by: (Politechnika Lodzka/Technical University of Lodz), Wydawnictwo Politechniki Lodzkiej, ul Wolczanska 223, Lodz, 93005, Poland. TEL 48-22-6840793, 48-42-6312087, 48-42-6840793. Ed. Cecylia Malinowska-Adamska TEL 48-42-6313662. Circ: 186. **Dist. by:** Ars Polona, Obroncow 25, Warsaw 03933, Poland. TEL 48-22-5098609, FAX 48-22-5098610, arspolona@arspolona.com.pl, http://www.arspolona.com.pl.

➤ **TECNO LOGICA.** *see* CHEMISTRY

➤ **TECSCAN JOURNAL. LAERM.** *see* ENGINEERING—Abstracting, Bibliographies, Statistics

➤ **TEHUDA/RESONANCE**; physics teacher's journal. *see* EDUCATION—Teaching Methods And Curriculum

530 671.52 UKR ISSN 0235-3474
TA410
TEKHNICHESKAYA DIAGNOSTIKA I NERAZRUSHAYUSHCHII KONTROL'/TECHNICAL DIAGNOSTICS AND NONDESTRUCTIVE TESTING; nauchno-teoreticheskii zhurnal. Text in Russian; Contents page in English. 1989. q. USD 52 foreign (effective 2005). **Document type:** *Journal, Academic/Scholarly.* **Description:** Presents the latest achievements in the field of technical diagnostics and NDT (acoustic emission, magnetic, eddy current, radiowave, thermal, optical, radiation and dye penetrate methods). Also deals with the procedures used to evaluate and predict the strength of welded structures.
Related titles: ◆ English Translation: Technical Diagnostics and Nondestructive Testing.
Indexed: C&ISA, CorrAb, Djerelo, E&CAJ, RefZh, SCOPUS, SolStAb, WAA.
—BLDSC (0180.352800), East View, Linda Hall.
Published by: (Natsional'na Akademiya Nauk Ukrainy, Instytut Elektrozvaryuvannya im. EO Patona), Paton Publishing House, E.O. Paton Welding Institute, vul Bozhenko, 11, Kyi, 03680, Ukraine. TEL 380-44-2276302, FAX 380-44-2680486, journal@paton.kiev.ua. Ed. B E Paton.

621 UKR ISSN 2075-8391
➤ **TEKHNIKA I PRIBORY S V CH.** (Sverhvysokaya Chastota) Text in Russian; Contents page in Russian, English, Ukrainian. 2007. s-a. **Document type:** *Journal, Academic/Scholarly.*
Published by: (Odes'kyi Politechnichnyi Universytet (Odessa Polytechnical University), Izdatel'stvo Politekhperiodika, a/ya 17, Odessa, 65044, Ukraine. TEL 380-48-7281850, FAX 380-48-7284946, tkea@optima.com.ua.

530 510 RUS ISSN 0564-6162
QC20 CODEN: TMFZAL
TEORETICHESKAYA I MATEMATICHESKAYA FIZIKA. Text in Russian. 1969. m. USD 420 foreign (effective 2006). **Document type:** *Journal, Academic/Scholarly.* **Description:** Disseminates developments in theoretical physics, along with mathematical problems related to the field.
Related titles: ◆ English Translation: Theoretical and Mathematical Physics. ISSN 0040-5779.
Indexed: CCMJ, ChemAb, CorrAb, INIS AtomInd, Inspec, MSN, MathR, RefZh, WAA, Z02.
—East View, INIST, Linda Hall.
Published by: (Rossiiskaya Akademiya Nauk, Otdelenie Matematiki/Russian Academy of Sciences, Department of Mathematics), Izdatel'stvo Nauka, Profsoyuznaya ul 90, Moscow, 117864, Russian Federation. TEL 7-095-3347151, FAX 7-095-4202220, secret@naukaran.ru, http://www.naukaran.ru. **Dist. by:** M K - Periodica, ul Gilyarovskogo 39, Moscow 129110, Russian Federation. TEL 7-095-2845008, FAX 7-095-2813798, info@periodicals.ru, http://www.mkniga.ru.

536 RUS ISSN 0040-3644
QC277 CODEN: TVYTAP
TEPLOFIZIKA VYSOKIKH TEMPERATUR. Text in Russian. 1963. bi-m. RUR 1,130 for 6 mos. domestic (effective 2004). bk.rev. bibl. index. **Document type:** *Journal, Academic/Scholarly.* **Description:** Examines theoretical and experimental results of research in high-temperature phyciscs, as they apply to modern engineering problems.
Related titles: Online - full text ed.; ◆ English Translation: High Temperature. ISSN 0018-151X.
Indexed: BullT&T, C&ISA, ChemAb, CorrAb, E&CAJ, INIS AtomInd, Inspec, RefZh, SCOPUS, SolStAb, TM, WAA.
—BLDSC (0178.850000), AskIEEE, CASDDS, East View, INIST, Linda Hall. **CCC.**
Published by: (Rossiiskaya Akademiya Nauk, Otdelenie Fiziko-tekhnicheskikh Problem Energetiki), Izdatel'stvo Nauka, Profsoyuznaya ul 90, Moscow, 117864, Russian Federation. TEL 7-095-3347151, FAX 7-095-4202220, secret@naukaran.ru, http://www.naukaran.ru.

530 DEU ISSN 1615-3766
TEUBNER STUDIENBUECHER PHYSIK. Text in German. 197?. irreg., latest 2008. price varies. **Document type:** *Monographic series, Academic/Scholarly.*
Published by: Vieweg und Teubner Verlag (Subsidiary of: Springer Fachmedien Wiesbaden GmbH), Abraham-Lincoln-Str 46, Wiesbaden, 65189, Germany. TEL 49-611-78780, FAX 49-611-7878400, info@viewegteubner.de, http://www.viewegteubner.de.

530 DEU ISSN 0233-0911
CODEN: TTPHE2
TEUBNER-TEXTE ZUR PHYSIK. Text in German. 1984. irreg., latest vol.35, 2000. price varies. **Document type:** *Monographic series, Academic/Scholarly.*
Indexed: CIN, ChemAb, ChemTitl.
—BLDSC (8798.289000), CASDDS, Ingenta. **CCC.**
Published by: Vieweg und Teubner Verlag (Subsidiary of: Springer Fachmedien Wiesbaden GmbH), Abraham-Lincoln-Str 46, Wiesbaden, 65189, Germany. TEL 49-611-78780, FAX 49-611-7878400, http://www.viewegteubner.de.

530 510 USA ISSN 0040-5779
QC20 CODEN: TMPHAH
➤ **THEORETICAL AND MATHEMATICAL PHYSICS.** Text in English. 1969. m. EUR 4,648, USD 4,781 combined subscription to institutions (print & online eds.) (effective 2012). adv. back issues avail.; reprint service avail. from PSC. **Document type:** *Journal, Academic/Scholarly.* **Description:** Covers topics such as quantum field theory and theory of elementary particles, fundamental problems of nuclear physics, many-body problems and statistical physics, nonrelativistic quantum mechanics, and basic problems of gravitation theory.
Related titles: Online - full text ed.: ISSN 1573-9333 (from IngentaConnect); ◆ Translation of: Teoreticheskaya i Matematicheskaya Fizika. ISSN 0564-6162.
Indexed: A01, A03, A08, A22, A26, ApMecR, BibLing, CA, CCMJ, CIN, CMCI, ChemAb, ChemTitl, CurCont, E01, ISR, Inspec, MSN, MathR, SCI, SCOPUS, T02, W07, Z02.
—BLDSC (0426.250000), AskIEEE, East View, IE, Infotrieve, Ingenta, INIST, Linda Hall. **CCC.**
Published by: (Rossiiskaya Akademiya Nauk/Russian Academy of Sciences RUS), Springer New York LLC (Subsidiary of: Springer Science+Business Media), 233 Spring St, New York, NY 10013. TEL 212-460-1500, FAX 212-460-1575, service-ny@springer.com, http://www.springer.com. Eds. Anatoly A Logunov, V V Zharinov.

530 USA ISSN 1864-5879
THEORETICAL AND MATHEMATICAL PHYSICS. Text in English. 1976. irreg., latest 2010. price varies. back issues avail.; reprints avail. **Document type:** *Monographic series, Academic/Scholarly.* **Description:** Devoted to monographs dealing with all aspects of established research fields in theoretical physics, except those related to Astrophysics.
Formerly (until 2006): Texts and Monographs in Physics (0172-5998)
Indexed: CCMJ, CIS, Inspec, MSN, MathR.
Published by: Springer New York LLC (Subsidiary of: Springer Science+Business Media), 233 Spring St, New York, NY 10013. TEL 212-460-1500, FAX 212-460-1575, service-ny@springer.com.

530.425 NLD ISSN 0924-6118
CODEN: TATPFG
➤ **THEORY AND APPLICATIONS OF TRANSPORT IN POROUS MEDIA.** Text in English. 1987. irreg., latest vol.22, 2008. price varies. **Document type:** *Monographic series, Academic/Scholarly.* **Description:** Aims to provide an understanding of the phenomena of transport, modeling them at different scales, coping with the uncertainties that are inherent in such models, especially as a result of spatial heterogeneity, and solving the models in order to provide information for management and decision-making.
Indexed: GeoRef, SpeleolAb, Z02.
—BLDSC (8814.626200), CASDDS, IE, Ingenta. **CCC.**
Published by: Springer Netherlands (Subsidiary of: Springer Science+Business Media), Van Godewijckstraat 30, Dordrecht, 3311 GX, Netherlands. TEL 31-78-6576050, FAX 31-78-6576474. Ed. Jacob Bear.

530 USA ISSN 1543-5016
QC176.A1 CODEN: THFIF8
➤ **THIN FILMS AND NANOSTRUCTURES.** Text in English. 1963. irreg., latest 2009. index. back issues avail.; reprints avail. **Document type:** *Journal, Academic/Scholarly.*
Former titles (until 2002): Thin Films (1079-4050); (until 1995): Physics of Thin Films (0079-1970)
Related titles: Online - full text ed.
Indexed: A22, CIN, ChemAb, ChemTitl, Inspec, SCOPUS.
—BLDSC (8820.111000), CASDDS, IE, Ingenta, INIST, Linda Hall. **CCC.**
Published by: Academic Press (Subsidiary of: Elsevier Science & Technology), 3251 Riverport Ln, Maryland Heights, MO 63043. TEL 314-447-8010, FAX 314-447-8030, JournalCustomerService-usa@elsevier.com, http://www.elsevierdirect.com/imprint.jsp?iid=5. Eds. Deborah Taylor, V Agranovich.

541.345 CHE ISSN 0040-6090
CODEN: THSFAP
➤ **THIN SOLID FILMS.** Text in English. 1968. 46/yr. EUR 13,366 in Europe to institutions; JPY 1,773,400 in Japan to institutions; USD 14,952 elsewhere to institutions (effective 2012). adv. bk.rev. bibl.; illus. index. back issues avail. **Document type:** *Journal, Academic/Scholarly.* **Description:** Serves scientists and engineers working in the fields of thin-film synthesis, characterization, and applications.
Related titles: Microform ed.: (from PQC); Online - full text ed.: ISSN 1879-2731 (from IngentaConnect, ScienceDirect).
Indexed: A01, A03, A08, A22, A26, A28, APA, ASCA, BrCerAb, C&ISA, C10, C13, C24, C33, CA, CA/WCA, CCI, CIA, CPEI, CerAb, ChemAb, ChemTitl, CivEngAb, CorrAb, CurCont, E&CAJ, E11, EEA, EMA, ESPM, EngInd, EnvEAb, H15, I05, IBR, IBZ, ISMEC, ISR, Inspec, M&TEA, M09, MBF, METADEX, MSB, MSCI, P30, PhotoAb, PhysBer, RefZh, S01, SCI, SCOPUS, SolStAb, T02, T04, TM, VITIS, W07, WAA.
—BLDSC (8820.120000), AskIEEE, CASDDS, IE, Infotrieve, Ingenta, INIST, Linda Hall. **CCC.**
Published by: Elsevier S.A., PO Box 564, Lausanne 1, 1001, Switzerland. TEL 41-21-3207381, FAX 41-21-3235444. Ed. J E Greene. **Subscr. to:** Elsevier BV, Radarweg 29, PO Box 211, Amsterdam 1000 AE, Netherlands. TEL 31-20-4853757, FAX 31-20-4853432, JournalsCustomerServiceEMEA@elsevier.com, http://www.elsevier.nl.

530 510 USA
THIS WEEK'S FINDS IN MATHEMATICAL PHYSICS. Text in English. 1993. w. bk.rev. back issues avail. **Document type:** *Journal, Academic/Scholarly.* **Description:** Contains reviews of articles and books as well as; exposition of mathematics and physics.
Related titles: Online - full text ed.: free (effective 2011).
Published by: University of California, Riverside, Department of Mathematics, 900 University Ave, Riverside, CA 92521. TEL 951-827-3113, FAX 951-827-7314, http://mathdept.ucr.edu/.

530 JPN ISSN 0916-2860
QC150
TOHOKU DAIGAKU RYUTAI KAGAKU KENKYUJO HOKOKU/ TOHOKU UNIVERSITY. INSTITUTE OF FLUID SCIENCE. MEMOIRS. Text in Japanese. 1949. a. free. **Document type:** *Academic/Scholarly.*
Formerly (until 1990): Institute of High Speed Mechanics. Report
Indexed: INIS AtomInd.
Published by: Tohoku Daigaku, Ryutai Kagaku Kenkyujo/Tohoku University, Institute of Fluid Science, 1-1 Katahira 2-chome, Aoba-ku, Sendai-shi, Miyagi-ken 980-0812, Japan. TEL 81-22-217-5312, FAX 81-22217-5311. Ed., R&P Junji Tani. Circ: 700.

530 JPN ISSN 0916-2879
TA357 CODEN: RIFUES
TOHOKU UNIVERSITY. INSTITUTE OF FLUID SCIENCE. REPORTS. Text in English. 1990. a. free. **Document type:** *Report, Academic/Scholarly.*
Formerly (until vol.1, 1990): Tohoku University. Institute of High Mechanics. Report (0370-5315)
Indexed: Inspec, RefZh.
—AskIEEE, Linda Hall.
Published by: Tohoku University, Institute of Fluid Science/Tohoku Daigaku Ryutai Kagaku Kenkyujo, 1-1 Katahira 2-chome, Aoba-ku, Sendai-shi, Miyagi-ken 980-0812, Japan. TEL 81-22-217-5312, FAX 81-22-217-5311. Ed. S. Kamiyama. R&P S Kamiyama. Circ: 700.

530 540 JPN ISSN 0040-8808
Q77.T55 CODEN: SRTAA6
➤ **TOHOKU UNIVERSITY. SCIENCE REPORTS OF THE RESEARCH INSTITUTES. SERIES A: PHYSICS, CHEMISTRY, AND METALLURGY/TOHOKU DAIGAKU KENKYUJO HOKOKU. A-SHU: BUTSURIGAKU, KAGAKU, YAKINGAKU.** Text in English. 1949. s-a. per issue exchange basis. charts; illus. index, cum.index every 10 yrs. **Document type:** *Report, Academic/Scholarly.*
Related titles: Microform ed.: (from PMC).
Indexed: ASCA, Cadscan, ChemAb, ChemTitl, GeoRef, IMMAb, Inspec, JCT, JTA, LeadAb, SCOPUS, SpeleolAb, Zincscan.
—AskIEEE, CASDDS, Ingenta, INIST, Linda Hall.
Published by: Tohoku Daigaku, Kenkyujo Rengokai/Tohoku University, Association of the Research Institutes, 4-1 Seiryo-cho, Aoba-ku, Sendai-shi, Miyagi-ken 980-0872, Japan. FAX 022-264-7984. Ed. Hiroyasu Fujimori. Circ: 1,250.

530 540 520 JPN ISSN 0388-5607
Q77 CODEN: SRTAD9
TOHOKU UNIVERSITY. SCIENCE REPORTS. SERIES 8: PHYSICS AND ASTRONOMY. Text in English, French, German. 1911. q. per issue exchange basis. charts; illus.; stat. Index. **Document type:** *Journal, Academic/Scholarly.*
Supersedes (in 1980): Tohoku University. Science Reports. Series 1: Physics, Chemistry, Astronomy (0040-8778)
Related titles: Microform ed.: 1911 (from PMC).
Indexed: ChemAb, GeoRef, INIS AtomInd, Inspec, MathR, SpeleolAb, Z02.
—BLDSC (8156.900000), AskIEEE, CASDDS, IE, Ingenta, INIST, Linda Hall.
Published by: Tohoku University, c/o Satoshi Watamura, Department of Physics, Graduate School of Science, Sendai, 980-8578, Japan. FAX 81-22-2177740. Eds. Makoto Tosa, Toshihiro Kawakatsu, Yu Fujii. Circ: 800.

530 JPN ISSN 0910-0709
TOKYO DAIGAKU DAIGAKUIN RIGAKUKEIKENKYUKA RIGAKUBU BUTSURIGAKU KYOSHITSU NENJI KENKYU/UNIVERSITY OF TOKYO. SCHOOL OF SCIENCE. DEPARTMENT OF PHYSICS. ANNUAL REPORT. Text in English, Japanese. 1966. a. **Document type:** *Bulletin.*
Published by: (Rigakubu, Butsurigaku Kyoshitsu), Tokyo Daigaku, Daigakuin Rigakukeikenyuka, 3-1 Hongo 7-chome, Bunkyo-ku, Tokyo, 113-0033, Japan.

530 621 DEU ISSN 0303-4216
QC3 CODEN: TAPHD4
➤ **TOPICS IN APPLIED PHYSICS.** Text in English. 1974. irreg., latest vol.117, 2010. price varies. reprints avail. **Document type:** *Monographic series, Academic/Scholarly.* **Description:** Presents a comprehensive survey of a selected topic within the area of applied physics.
Related titles: Online - full text ed.: ISSN 1437-0859.
Indexed: A22, ASCA, ChemAb, ISR, Inspec, PhysBer, SCI, SCOPUS, W07, Z02.
—BLDSC (8867.420000), CASDDS, IE, Ingenta, INIST. **CCC.**
Published by: Springer (Subsidiary of: Springer Science+Business Media), Tiergartenstr 17, Heidelberg, 69121, Germany. TEL 49-6221-4870, FAX 49-6221-345229, subscriptions@springer.com. Ed. Dr. Claus E Ascheron.

530 540 JPN ISSN 0372-039X
CODEN: TOKHA6
TOYODA KENKYU HOKOKU/TOYODA PHYSICAL AND CHEMICAL RESEARCH INSTITUTE. REPORTS. Text in Japanese; Summaries in English. 1942. a. abstr.
Indexed: ChemAb, INIS AtomInd, JPI.
—BLDSC (7619.665000).
Published by: Toyoda Rikagaku Kenkyujo/Toyoda Physical and Chemical Research Institute, 41-1 Yokomichi-Nagakute, Aichi-gun, Nagakute-cho, Aichi-ken 480-1100, Japan.

530 FRA ISSN 0765-0019
TK5102.5
➤ **TRAITEMENT DU SIGNAL**; signal, image, parole. Text in French; Summaries in English, French. 1964. 4/yr. (plus 2 special nos.). EUR 132 in Europe to individuals; EUR 160 elsewhere to individuals (effective 2008). bk.rev. bibl.; illus. index. back issues avail. **Document type:** *Journal, Academic/Scholarly.* **Description:** Focuses on the scientific aspects of new scientific and technical results.
Formerly (until 1984): C E T H E D E C. Revue (0035-2535)
Related titles: Online - full text ed.: ISSN 1958-5608.
Indexed: A22, GeoRef, INIS AtomInd, Inspec, MathR, SCI, SpeleolAb, W07, Z02.
—BLDSC (8883.767000), AskIEEE, IE, Infotrieve, Ingenta, INIST, Linda Hall. **CCC.**
Published by: (Groupe de Recherche et d'Etude de Traitement du Signal et des Images (GRETSI)), Presses Universitaires de Grenoble, 1041 Rue des Residences, Grenoble, 38040, France. TEL 33-4-76825651, FAX 33-4-76827835, pug@oug.fr, http://www.pug.fr. Ed. Jean-Louis Lacoume. Circ: 700.

➤ **TRANSPORT IN POROUS MEDIA.** see CHEMISTRY

530.13 USA ISSN 0041-1450
QC175.2 CODEN: TTSPB4
➤ **TRANSPORT THEORY AND STATISTICAL PHYSICS.** Text in English. 1971. 7/yr. GBP 1,871 combined subscription in United Kingdom to institutions (print & online eds.); EUR 2,472, USD 3,103 combined subscription to institutions (print & online eds.) (effective 2012). adv. reprint service avail. from PSC. **Document type:** *Journal, Academic/Scholarly.* **Description:** Covers mathematical concepts and techniques to encourage a productive, interdisciplinary exchange of ideas.
Related titles: Microform ed.: (from RPI); Online - full text ed.: ISSN 1532-2424. GBP 1,684 in United Kingdom to institutions; EUR 2,225, USD 2,793 to institutions (effective 2012) (from IngentaConnect).
Indexed: A01, A03, A08, A22, CA, CCMJ, CIN, CMCI, ChemAb, CurCont, E01, Inspec, MSN, MathR, P30, PhysBer, RefZh, S01, SCI, SCOPUS, T02, W07, Z02.
—BLDSC (9025.965000), AskIEEE, CASDDS, IE, Infotrieve, Ingenta, INIST, Linda Hall. **CCC.**
Published by: Taylor & Francis Inc. (Subsidiary of: Taylor & Francis Group), 325 Chestnut St, Ste 800, Philadelphia, PA 19106. TEL 215-625-2940, 800-354-1420, orders@taylorandfrancis.com, http://www.taylorandfrancis.com. Eds. James P Holloway, John J Dorning.

➤ **TRANSYLVANIA UNIVERSITY OF BRASOV. BULLETIN. SERIES B**; mathematics, economic sciences, philology, medicine, physics, chemistry, sports. see MATHEMATICS

530 315 IND ISSN 0972-480X
TRENDS IN STATISTICAL PHYSICS. Text in English. 2001. a. EUR 134.10 in Europe; JPY 17,852 in Japan; USD 149 elsewhere (effective 2010). **Document type:** *Journal, Academic/Scholarly.* **Description:** Publishes review articles, original research papers and short communications in the field of statistical mechanics, thermodynamics and its applications.
Related titles: CD-ROM ed.
Indexed: A28, APA, CA/WCA, CIA, CivEngAb, E11, EEA, EMA, H15, MBF, T04.
Published by: Research Trends (P) Ltd., T.C. 17 / 250 (3), Chadiyara Rd, Poojapura, Trivandrum, Kerala 695 012, India. TEL 91-471-2344424, FAX 91-471-2344423, info@researchtrends.net.

533.5 IND ISSN 0972-4486
TRENDS IN VACUUM SCIENCE & TECHNOLOGY. Text in English. 1993. a. EUR 134.10 in Europe; JPY 17,852 in Japan; USD 149 elsewhere (effective 2010). **Document type:** *Journal, Academic/Scholarly.* **Description:** Publishes critical reviews and original papers on latest advances in the many areas which require the production and control of a working environment at pressure below one atmosphere.
Related titles: CD-ROM ed.
Indexed: A28, APA, BrCerAb, C&ISA, CA/WCA, CIA, CerAb, CivEngAb, CorrAb, E&CAJ, E11, EEA, EMA, ESPM, EnvEAb, H15, Inspec, M&TEA, M09, MBF, METADEX, SolStAb, T04, WAA.
Published by: Research Trends (P) Ltd., T.C. 17 / 250 (3), Chadiyara Rd, Poojapura, Trivandrum, Kerala 695 012, India. TEL 91-471-2344424, FAX 91-471-2344423, info@researchtrends.net.

TRIBOLOGY (LEEDS); materials, surfaces & interfaces. see METALLURGY

TRIBOLOGY AND INTERFACE ENGINEERING SERIES. see ENGINEERING—Mechanical Engineering

TROMSOE GEOPHYSICAL OBSERVATORY. REPORTS. see METEOROLOGY

530 SGP
▼ **TSINGHUA REPORT AND REVIEW IN PHYSICS.** Text in English. 2010. irreg., latest vol.1, 2010. price varies. **Document type:** *Monographic series, Academic/Scholarly.*
Published by: World Scientific Publishing Co. Pte. Ltd., 5 Toh Tuck Link, Singapore, 596224, Singapore. TEL 65-6466-5775, FAX 65-6467-7667, wspc@wspc.com.sg, http://www.worldscientific.com. Ed. Bang-Fen Zhu. **Dist. by:** World Scientific Publishing Co., Inc., 27 Warren St, Ste 401-402, Hackensack, NJ 07601. TEL 201-487-9655, 800-227-7562, FAX 201-487-9656, 888-977-2665, wspc@wspc.com; World Scientific Publishing Ltd., 57 Shelton St, London WC2H 9HE, United Kingdom. TEL 44-207-8360888, FAX 44-207-8362020, sales@wspc.co.uk.

530 JPN ISSN 0915-5317
QC1
TSUKUBA DAIGAKU BUTSURIGAKUKEI NENJI KENKYU HOKOKU/ UNIVERSITY OF TSUKUBA. INSTITUTE OF PHYSICS. ANNUAL REPORT. Text in Japanese. 1988. a.
Published by: Tsukuba Daigaku, Butsurigakukei/University of Tsukuba. Institute of Physics, 1-1 Tenno-Dai 1-chome, Tsukuba-shi, Ibaraki-ken 305-0006, Japan.

530 TUR ISSN 1300-0101
QC1 CODEN: TJPHEY
➤ **TURKISH JOURNAL OF PHYSICS.** Text and summaries in English. 3/yr. TRY 48 domestic; EUR 30 foreign (effective 2011). **Document type:** *Journal, Academic/Scholarly.*
Former titles (until 1994): Doga Turkish Journal of Physics (1010-7630); (until 1985): Doga Bilim Dergisi. Seri A1. Matematik, Fizik, Kimya, Astronomi (1011-0941); (until 1984): Doga bilim Dergisi. Seri A, Temel Bilimler (0254-5497); Which superseded in part (in 1980): Doga (0250-5169)
Related titles: Online - full text ed.: ISSN 1303-6122. free (effective 2011).
Indexed: A01, A02, A03, A08, CA, CPEI, ChemAb, EngInd, INIS AtomInd, Inspec, S01, SCOPUS, T02.
—BLDSC (9072.484000), AskIEEE, CASDDS, Ingenta, Linda Hall.
Published by: Scientific and Technical Research Council of Turkey - TUBITAK/Turkiye Bilimsel ve Teknik Arastirma Kurumu, Akademik Yayinlar Mudurlugu, Ataturk Bulvari No.221, Kavaklidere / Ankara, 06100, Turkey. TEL 90-312-4685300, FAX 90-312-4270493, bdym.abone@tubitak.gov.tr, http://www.tubitak.gov.tr. Ed. Dr. A Nihat Berker.

530 540 RUS
➤ **UDMURTSKII UNIVERSITET. VESTNIK. SERIYA 4: FIZIKA I KHIMIYA.** Text in Russian. 2008. s-a. RUR 200 per issue (effective 2010). **Document type:** *Journal, Academic/Scholarly.*
Related titles: Online - full text ed.

P

Published by: Udmurtskii Gosudarstvennyi Universitet/Udmurt State University, Universitetskaya Str., 1, Izhevsk, 426034, Russian Federation. TEL 7-341-682061, ob@uni.udm.ru, http://v4.udsu.ru. Ed. Nikolai Leonov.

530 GBR ISSN 0960-6068
CODEN: UJPKAG

UKRAINIAN JOURNAL OF PHYSICS. Abbreviated title: U J P. Text in English. 1956. m. back issues avail. **Document type:** *Journal, Academic/Scholarly.*
Related titles: Online - full text ed.: free (effective 2011).
Indexed: C33, Inspec.
—AskIEEE.
Published by: (Ukrainian Physical Society UKR, Natsional'na Akademiya Nauk Ukrainy UKR), Riecansky Science Publishing Co., 7 Meadow Walk, Great Abington, Cambridge, CB1 6AZ, United Kingdom.

530 UKR ISSN 0372-400X
CODEN: UFIZAW

➤ **UKRAINS'KYI FIZYCHNYI ZHURNAL/UKRAINIAN JOURNAL OF PHYSICS**; naukovyi zhurnal. Text in Ukrainian, English. 1956. m. USD 368 foreign (effective 2004). bk.rev. bibl.; charts; illus. index. 136 p./no. 2 cols./p.; **Document type:** *Journal, Academic/Scholarly.*
Formerly: Ukrainskii Fizicheskii Zhurnal (0202-3628)
Related titles: Diskette ed.
Indexed: ASCA, ChemAb, Djerelo, INIS AtomInd, Inspec, MSN, MathR, PhysBer, SCOPUS.
—IE, INIST, Linda Hall. **CCC.**
Published by: Natsional'na Akademiya Nauk Ukrainy, Instytut Teoretychnoi Fizyky im M. M. Boholyubova/National Academy of Sciences of Ukraine, M. M. Bogolyubov Institute of Theoretical Physics, Metrolohichna vul 14-6, Kiev, 252143, Ukraine. TEL 380-44-2665362, FAX 380-44-2665998, ujphys@iop.kiev, http://ujp.bitp.kiev. Circ: 300 (paid).

530 NLD ISSN 0304-3991
CODEN: ULTRD6

➤ **ULTRAMICROSCOPY.** Text in Dutch. 1975. 12/yr. EUR 2,825 in Europe to institutions; JPY 374,800 in Japan to institutions; USD 3,160 elsewhere to institutions (effective 2012). back issues avail.; reprints avail. **Document type:** *Journal, Academic/Scholarly.* **Description:** Covers all fundamental and technical aspects pertaining to ultramicroscopic elucidation of structure, ranging from particle optics to radiation interaction.
Related titles: Microform ed.: (from PQC); Online - full text ed.: ISSN 1879-2723 (from IngentaConnect, ScienceDirect).
Indexed: A01, A03, A08, A20, A22, A26, A28, APA, ASCA, B&BAb, B19, B25, BIOSIS Prev, BrCerAb, C&ISA, C24, C33, CA, CA/WCA, CIA, CMCI, CPEI, CerAb, ChemAb, CivEngAb, CorrAb, CurCont, E&CAJ, E11, EEA, EMA, EMBASE, ESPM, EngInd, EnvEAb, ExcerpMed, GeoRef, H15, I05, ISR, IndMed, Inpharma, Inspec, M&TEA, M09, MBF, MEDLINE, METADEX, MycolAb, P30, PhotoAb, PhysBer, R10, Reac, RefZh, S01, SCI, SCOPUS, SolStAb, SpeleolAb, T02, T04, TM, W07, WAA.
—BLDSC (9082.783000), AskIEEE, CASDDS, IE, Infotrieve, Ingenta, INIST, Linda Hall. **CCC.**
Published by: Elsevier BV (Subsidiary of: Elsevier Science & Technology), Radarweg 29, PO Box 211, Amsterdam, 1000 AE, Netherlands. TEL 31-20-4853911, FAX 31-20-4852457, JournalsCustomerServiceEMEA@elsevier.com. Ed. P Midgley. **Subscr. to:** Radarweg 29, PO Box 211, Amsterdam 1000 AE, Netherlands. TEL 31-20-4853757, FAX 31-20-4853432.

➤ **ULTRASONIC IMAGING**; an international journal. *see* MEDICAL SCIENCES—Radiology And Nuclear Medicine

530 KOR ISSN 1013-7009
UNGYONG MULLI/KOREAN APPLIED PHYSICS. Text in Korean. 1988. bi-m. membership. **Document type:** *Academic/Scholarly.*
Indexed: ChemAb, INIS AtomInd, Inspec.
Published by: Han'guk Mulli Hakhoe/Korean Physical Society, Kangnam-Gu, Yuksam-Dong 635-4, Seoul, 135703, Korea, S. TEL 82-2-5564737, FAX 82-2-5541643, http://www.kps.or.kr.

UNION MATEMATICA ARGENTINA. REVISTA. *see* MATHEMATICS

530 ITA ISSN 0533-0386
QC1
UNIVERSITA DI FERRARA. ANNALI. SEZIONE 14: FISICA SPERIMENTALE E TEORICA. Text in Italian, English. 1936. a. price varies. **Document type:** *Journal, Academic/Scholarly.*
Supersedes in part (in 1951): Universita di Ferrara. Annali (0365-7833)
—Linda Hall.
Published by: Universita degli Studi di Ferrara, Via Savonarola 9, Ferrara, 44100, Italy. TEL 39-0532-293111, FAX 39-0532-293031, http://www.unife.it.

UNIVERSITA DI MODENA E REGGIO EMILIA. SEMINARIO MATEMATICO E FISICO. ATTI. *see* MATHEMATICS

530 ROM ISSN 0041-9141
QC1 CODEN: AUZFAA
UNIVERSITATEA "AL. I. CUZA" DIN IASI. ANALELE STIINTIFICE. SECTIUNEA 1B: FIZICA. Text in English, French, German, Russian. 1955. a. ROL 35. bk.rev. abstr.; charts; illus. **Description:** Review articles, original papers, short notes and book reviews on physics.
Indexed: ChemAb, Inspec, MathR, Z02.
—AskIEEE, CASDDS, INIST, Linda Hall.
Published by: Universitatea "Alexandru Ioan Cuza" din Iasi/"Alexandru Ioan Cuza" University of Iasi, Carol I Boulevard, Iasi, 6600, Romania. Ed. M Sandulovici. Circ: 250. **Subscr. to:** ILEXIM, Str. 13 Decembrie 3, PO Box 136-137, Bucharest 70116, Romania.

530 ROM
CODEN: AUTFDH

➤ **UNIVERSITATEA DE VEST DIN TIMISOARA. ANALELE. SERIA STIINTE FIZICE.** Text in English. 1963. s-a. ROL 100,000 (effective 2003). bk.rev. **Document type:** *Journal, Academic/Scholarly.*
Former titles: Universitatea din Timisoara. Analele. Stiinte Fizice (0257-7488); (until vol.22, 1982): Universitatea din Timisoara. Analele. Stiinte Fizico-Chimice (0082-4453)
Indexed: CIN, ChemAb, ChemTitl.
—CASDDS, INIST.
Published by: (Universitatea de Vest din Timisoara, Facultatea de Fizica), Universitatea de Vest din Timisoara/West University of Timisoara, Blvd. Vasile Parvan 4, Timisoara, Timis 300223, Romania. TEL 40-256-494068, FAX 40-256-201458, http://www.uvt.ro. Ed. Gheorghe Ardelean.

➤ **UNIVERSITATEA DIN CRAIOVA. ANNALS: ELECTRICAL AND CONTROL SYSTEMS SERIES.** *see* ENGINEERING—Electrical Engineering

530 ROM ISSN 1224-5097
UNIVERSITATEA DIN ORADEA. ANALELE. FASCICULA FIZICA. Text in Romanian. 1976. a. **Document type:** *Journal, Academic/Scholarly.*
Supersedes in part (in 1991): Universitatea din Oradea. Analele. Fascicula Fizica (1221-1257); Which superseded in part (in 1990): Institutul de Invatament Superior Oradea. Lucrari Stiintifice. Serie A. Stiinte Tehnice, Matematica, Fizica, Chimie, Geografie (0254-8593)
Published by: Editura Universitatii din Oradea/University of Oradea Publishing House, Str Universitatii 1, Geotermal Bldg., 2nd Fl., Oradea, Jud.Bihor 410087, Romania. TEL 40-259-408113, FAX 40-259-432789, editura@uoradea.ro, http://webhost.uoradea.ro/editura/.

530 ROM
UNIVERSITATEA DIN TIMISOARA. FACULTATEA DE FIZICA. PUBLICATIONS. Text in Romanian. irreg.
Formerly (until 1989): Universitatea din Timisoara. Facultatea de Stiinte ale Naturii. Sectia Fizica. Publications
Published by: (Universitatea de Vest din Timisoara, Facultatea de Fizica), Universitatea de Vest din Timisoara/West University of Timisoara, Blvd. Vasile Parvan 4, Timisoara, Timis 300223, Romania.

UNIVERSITATEA PETROL - GAZE DIN PLOESTI. SERIA MATEMATICA, INFORMATICA, FIZICA. BULETINUL. *see* MATHEMATICS

UNIVERSITATEA POLITEHNICA DIN TIMISOARA. BULETINUL STIINTIFIC. SERIA MATEMATICA, FIZICA/POLITEHNICA UNIVERSITY OF TIMISOARA. SCIENTIFIC BULLETIN. TRANSACTIONS ON MATHEMATICS AND PHYSICS. *see* MATHEMATICS

530.711 FRA ISSN 1294-0348
UNIVERSITES. PHYSIQUE. Text in French. 1998. irreg. back issues avail. **Document type:** *Monographic series, Consumer.*
Related titles: ◆ Series of: Universites. ISSN 1258-195X.
Published by: Editions Ellipses, 8-10 Rue de La Quintinie, Paris, 75740 Cedex 15, France. TEL 33-1-56566410, FAX 33-1-45310767, edito@editions-ellipses.fr.

UNIVERSITEXTS. *see* MATHEMATICS

UNIVERSITY OF ANKARA. FACULTY OF SCIENCE. COMMUNICATIONS. SERIES A2-A3: PHYSICS, ENGINEERING PHYSICS, ELECTRONIC ENGINEERING AND ASTRONOMY. *see* ENGINEERING

530 620 SRB ISSN 0354-0162
TK1 CODEN: PFEPEX
UNIVERSITY OF BELGRADE. FACULTY OF ELECTRICAL ENGINEERING. PUBLICATIONS. SERIES: ENGINEERING PHYSICS/UNIVERZITETA U BEOGRADU. ELEKTROTEHNICKI FAKULTET. PUBLIKACIJE. SERIJA: TEHNICKA FIZIKA. Text in English, German, Russian; Summaries in Serbo-Croatian. 1961. a. bk.rev. **Document type:** *Journal, Academic/Scholarly.*
Former titles (unti 1991): Tehnicka Fizika (0350-0594); (until 1973): Zavod za Fiziku. Radovi (0376-2114)
Indexed: ChemAb, INIS AtomInd, Inspec, MathR.
—AskIEEE, CASDDS, INIST, Linda Hall.
Published by: Univerzitet u Beogradu, Elektrotehnicki Fakultet/University of Belgrade, Faculty of Electrical Engineering, Bulevar Revolucije 73, Belgrade, 11000. TEL 381-11-3218, FAX 381-11-3218-681, http://www.etf.bg.ac.yu. Circ: 1,000.

530 520 CAN
UNIVERSITY OF BRITISH COLUMBIA. PHYSICS SOCIETY. JOURNAL. Text in English. 1960. a. CAD 3 to non-members. adv. back issues avail. **Description:** Review of papers from undergraduates in physics, astronomy, and geophysics.
Published by: University of British Columbia, Physics Society, Dept of Physics, 6224 Agriculture Rd, Vancouver, BC V6T 2A6, Canada. TEL 604-228-2211. Ed. Aaron Drake. Circ: 150.

530 FIN
UNIVERSITY OF JYVASKYLA. DEPARTMENT OF PHYSICS. PREPRINTS. Text in Finnish. 1969. irreg. (5-6/yr.). per issue exchange basis. **Document type:** *Academic/Scholarly.*
Formerly (until 1984): Jyvaskylan Yliopisto. Department of Physics. Research Report (0075-465X)
Media: Duplicated (not offset).
Published by: Jyvaskylan Yliopisto, Department of Physics/Jyvaskyla University, PL 35, Jyvaskyla, 40351, Finland. FAX 358-41-602351. Ed. Soili Leskinen. Circ: 130.

530 PNG ISSN 0085-4735
UNIVERSITY OF PAPUA NEW GUINEA. DEPARTMENT OF PHYSICS. TECHNICAL PAPER. Text in English. 1968. irreg. free.
Published by: University of Papua New Guinea, Department of Physics, University of Papua New Guinea, PO Box 4820, University Post Office, Port Moresby, Papua New Guinea. Circ: 75.

530 ROM ISSN 1454-5071
QC1
➤ **UNIVERSITY OF PETROSANI. ANNALS. PHYSICS.** Text in English. 1999. a. ROL 7.09 domestic; USD 2.92 foreign; free to qualified personnel (effective 2007). bk.rev. charts; abstr.; bibl. 100 p./no.; back issues avail.; reprints avail. **Document type:** *Proceedings, Academic/Scholarly.* **Description:** Publishes original studies in the field of magnetic fluids, superconductors and lasers.
Related titles: CD-ROM ed.; Online - full text ed.; ◆ Series: University of Petrosani. Annals. Mining Engineering. ISSN 1454-9174; ◆ University of Petrosani. Annals. Electrical Engineering. ISSN 1454-8518; ◆ University of Petrosani. Annals. Mechanical Engineering. ISSN 1454-9166.
—**CCC.**
Published by: Universitatea din Petrosani, Str. Universitatii, nr 20, Petrosani, 332006, Romania. TEL 40-254-542994, FAX 40-254-543491, rector@upet.ro, http://www.upet.ro. Eds. Ioan-Lucian Bolundut, Vasile Iusan. Circ: 80 (paid); 70 (controlled).

538 534 USA
UNIVERSITY OF TEXAS AT AUSTIN. APPLIED RESEARCH LABORATORIES. TECHNICAL REPORT. Text in English. irreg.
Published by: University of Texas at Austin, Applied Research Laboratories, PO Box 8029, Austin, TX 78713-8029. TEL 512-835-3200, FAX 512-835-3259, http://www.arlut.utexas.edu/.

530 JPN ISSN 0082-4798
QC176
UNIVERSITY OF TOKYO. INSTITUTE FOR SOLID STATE PHYSICS. TECHNICAL REPORT. SERIES A. Text in English. 1959. irreg. **Document type:** *Report, Academic/Scholarly.* **Description:** Reprints articles published in scientific journals.
Published by: University of Tokyo, Institute for Solid State Physics/Tokyo Daigaku Bussei Kenkyujo, Kashiwanoha, Kashiwa-shi, Chiba, 277-8581, Japan. http://www.issp.u-tokyo.ac.jp/.

530 JPN ISSN 0082-4801
UNIVERSITY OF TOKYO. INSTITUTE FOR SOLID STATE PHYSICS. TECHNICAL REPORT. SERIES B. Text in English. 1960. irreg. **Document type:** *Report, Academic/Scholarly.* **Description:** Original papers and other data not intended for publication elsewhere.
Published by: University of Tokyo, Institute for Solid State Physics/Tokyo Daigaku Bussei Kenkyujo, Kashiwanoha, Kashiwa-shi, Chiba, 277-8581, Japan. http://www.issp.u-tokyo.ac.jp/.

530 JPN ISSN 0917-754X
UNIVERSITY OF TOKYO. INTERNATIONAL CENTER FOR ELEMENTARY PARTICLE PHYSICS. Variant title: U T - I C E P P. Text in English. irreg.
Published by: (International Center for Elementary Particle Physics), University of Tokyo/Tokyo Daigaku Soryushi Butsuri Kokusai Kenkyu Senta, 3-1, Hongo 7-chome, Bunkyo-ku, Tokyo 113, Japan.

621 USA
UNIVERSITY OF WASHINGTON. APPLIED PHYSICS LABORATORY. REPORT. Text in English. irreg.
Published by: University of Washington, Applied Physics Laboratory, 1013 NE 40th St, Box 355640, Seattle, WA 98105-6698. TEL 206-543-1300, FAX 206-543-6785, http://www.apl.washington.edu.

621 USA
UNIVERSITY OF WASHINGTON. APPLIED PHYSICS LABORATORY. TECHNICAL REPORT. Text in English. irreg.
Published by: University of Washington, Applied Physics Laboratory, 1013 NE 40th St, Box 355640, Seattle, WA 98105-6698. TEL 206-543-1300, FAX 206-543-6785, http://www.apl.washington.edu.

530 POL ISSN 0554-825X
CODEN: UPMFAS
UNIWERSYTET IM. ADAMA MICKIEWICZA. FIZYKA. Text in Polish. 1961. irreg., latest vol.83, 2010. price varies. **Document type:** *Monographic series, Academic/Scholarly.* **Description:** Contains current physics research results, Ph.D. theses, and monographs of the university's scholars. Each volume contains the work of one author.
Formerly (until 1970): Uniwersytet im. Adama Mickiewicza w Poznaniu. Wydzial Matematyki, Fizyki i Chemii. Prace. Seria Fizyka (0860-1992)
Indexed: ChemAb, ChemTitl.
—BLDSC (9120.460000), CASDDS, Linda Hall.
Published by: (Uniwersytet im. Adama Mickiewicza w Poznaniu/Adam Mickiewicz University), Wydawnictwo Naukowe Uniwersytetu im. Adama Mickiewicza/Adam Mickiewicz University Press, ul Fredry 10, Poznan, 61701, Poland. TEL 48-61-8294646, FAX 48-61-8294647, press@amu.edu.pl, http://press.amu.edu.pl. Circ: 330.

530 POL
QC1 CODEN: ZNWFBI
UNIWERSYTET OPOLSKI. ZESZYTY NAUKOWE. FIZYKA. Text in Polish; Summaries in English. 1963. irreg., latest 2000. price varies. **Document type:** *Monographic series, Academic/Scholarly.*
Formerly (until 1994): Wyzsza Szkola Pedagogiczna, Opole. Zeszyty Naukowe. Seria A. Fizyka (0078-5385)
Indexed: ChemAb, MathR.
—CASDDS.
Published by: Wydawnictwo Uniwersytetu Opolskiego, ul Sienkiewicza 33, Opole, 45037, Poland. TEL 48-77-4410878, wydawnictwo@uni.opole.pl, http://www.wydawnictwo.uni.opole.pl/. Eds. Bozena Pedzisz, Danuta Tokar.

530.071 DEU
UNTERRICHT PHYSIK; Beitraege zu seinen fachlichen, methodischen und didaktischen Problemen. Text in German. 1967. 6/yr. EUR 70.60; EUR 15 newsstand/cover (effective 2011). adv. index, cum.index. **Document type:** *Journal, Academic/Scholarly.*
Former titles: Naturwissenschaften im Unterricht Physik (0946-2147); (until 1990): Physikunterricht (0031-9295)
Published by: Erhard Friedrich Verlag GmbH, Im Brande 17, Seelze, 30926, Germany. TEL 49-511-400040, FAX 49-511-40004170, info@friedrich-verlag.de. Adv. contact Bianca Kraft. Circ: 5,500 (paid and controlled).

530 RUS ISSN 0042-1294
QC1 CODEN: UFNAAG
➤ **USPEKHI FIZICHESKIKH NAUK.** Text in Russian. 1918. m. RUR 18,000 domestic (effective 2011). adv. bk.rev. bibl.; charts; illus. index. **Document type:** *Journal, Academic/Scholarly.* **Description:** Publishes reviews of advances in physical science and of the current state of most topical problems in physics and in associated fields.
Related titles: CD-ROM ed.; Online - full text ed.: free (effective 2011); ◆ English Translation: Physics - Uspekhi. ISSN 1063-7869.
Indexed: A20, CIN, ChemAb, ChemTitl, GeoRef, INIS AtomInd, ISR, IndMed, Inspec, MathR, PhysBer, RASB, RefZh, SCOPUS, SpeleolAb.
—BLDSC (0387.000000), AskIEEE, CASDDS, East View, INIST, Linda Hall. **CCC.**
Published by: Rossiiskaya Akademiya Nauk, Institut Fiziki im. P.N. Lebedeva/Russian Academy of Sciences, P.N. Lebedev Physics Institute, Leninskii prosp 53, Moscow, 119991, Russian Federation. TEL 7-095-1351311, FAX 7-095-1358860, ke@sci.lebedev.ru. Ed. Leonid L Keldysh. Circ: 1,200.

621 669 UKR ISSN 1608-1021
➤ **USPEKHI FIZIKI METALLOV**; a research journal. Text in English, Russian, Ukrainian. 2000. q. EUR 28 in Europe; USD 34 elsewhere (effective 2005). **Document type:** *Journal, Academic/Scholarly.* **Description:** Publishes scientific reviews of results of experimental and theoretical investigations in range of physics and technologies of metals, alloys, and com-pounds with metallic properties.
Indexed: A28, APA, BrCerAb, C&ISA, CA/WCA, CIA, CerAb, CivEngAb, CorrAb, E&CAJ, E11, EEA, EMA, ESPM, EnvEAb, H15, M&TEA, M09, MBF, METADEX, RefZh, SolStAb, T04, WAA.
—BLDSC (0386.750000), East View, Linda Hall.

Published by: Natsional'na Akademiya Nauk Ukrainy, Instytut Metalofizyky/National Academy of Sciences of the Ukraine, Institute of Metal Physics, bulvar Akad Vernadskogo 36, Kyiv, 103142, Ukraine. TEL 380-44-4241221, FAX 380-44-4242561, mfint@imp.kiev.ua, tatar@imp.kiev.ua, http://www.imp.kiev.ua. Ed. A P Shpak. Adv. contact V A Tatarenko.

530 RUS ISSN 0301-1798
CODEN: UFZNAD

USPEKHI FIZIOLOGICHESKIKH NAUK. Text in Russian. q. RUR 930 for 6 mos. domestic; USD 150 foreign (effective 2004). **Document type:** *Journal, Academic/Scholarly.*
Indexed: B25, BIOSIS Prev, CPEI, ChemAb, EMBASE, ExcerpMed, IndMed, MEDLINE, MycolAb, P30, R10, Reac, RefZh, SCOPUS, Z01.
—CASDDS, East View, GNLM, INIST, Linda Hall. **CCC.**
Published by: Izdatel'stvo Nauka, Profsoyuznaya ul 90, Moscow, 117864, Russian Federation. TEL 7-095-3347151, FAX 7-095-4202220, secret@naukaran.ru, http://www.naukaran.ru. **Dist. by:** M K - Periodica, ul Gilyarovskogo 39, Moscow 129110, Russian Federation. TEL 7-095-2845008, FAX 7-095-2813798, info@periodicals.ru, http://www.mkniga.ru.

530 510 UZB ISSN 1025-8817
QC1 CODEN: UFZHEX

UZBEKSKII FIZICHESKII ZHURNAL. Text in English, Russian. 1957. bi-m.
Supersedes in part (in 1992): Akademiya Nauk Uzbekistana. Izvestiya. Seriya Fiziko-Matematicheskikh Nauk; Which was formerly: Akademiya Nauk Uzbekskoi S.S.R. Izvestiya. Seriya Fiziko-Matematicheskikh Nauk (0131-8012)
Indexed: CIN, ChemAb, MathR, RefZh.
—CASDDS, East View, INIST, Linda Hall.
Published by: (O'zbekiston Respublikasi Fanlar Akademiyasi/Academy of Sciences of Uzbekistan), Izdatel'stvo Fan, Ya Gulyamov ul 70, k 105, Tashkent, 700047, Uzbekistan.

530 510 UZB ISSN 1027-3433
QA1 CODEN: IUZFAU

UZBEKSKII MATEMATICHESKII ZHURNAL/UZBEKISTON MATEMATIKA ZHURNALI. Text in English, Russian; Summaries in English, Uzbek. 1957. bi-m.
Supersedes in part (in 1996): Akademiya Nauk Uzbekistana. Izvestiya. Seriya Fiziko-Matematicheskikh Nauk; Which was formerly: Akademiya Nauk Uzbekskoi S.S.R. Izvestiya. Seriya Fiziko-Matematicheskikh Nauk (0131-8012)
Indexed: ChemAb, MSN, MathR.
—CASDDS, INIST, Linda Hall.
Published by: (O'zbekiston Respublikasi Fanlar Akademiyasi/Academy of Sciences of Uzbekistan), Izdatel'stvo Fan, Ya Gulyamov ul 70, k 105, Tashkent, 700047, Uzbekistan.

533.5 016 GBR ISSN 0042-207X
QC166 CODEN: VACUAV

➤ **VACUUM**; surface engineering, surface instrumentation & vacuum technology. Text in English. 1951. 12/yr. EUR 3,668 in Europe to institutions; JPY 486,900 in Japan to institutions; USD 4,103 elsewhere to institutions (effective 2012). bk.rev. abstr.; illus. index. back issues avail. **Document type:** *Journal, Academic/Scholarly.* **Description:** Covers all theoretical, methodological, experimental and applied aspects of vacuum science and technology, including instrumentation and developments in related disciplines.
Related titles: Microfilm ed.: (from PQC); Online - full text ed.: ISSN 1879-2715 (from IngentaConnect, ScienceDirect).
Indexed: A&ATA, A01, A03, A05, A08, A20, A22, A23, A24, A26, AS&TA, AS&TI, ASCA, B04, B13, C&ISA, C10, C24, C33, CA, CIN, CPEI, ChemAb, ChemTitl, CurCont, E&CAJ, EngInd, FR, I05, IBR, IBZ, ISMEC, ISR, Inspec, MSB, MSCI, PhysBer, RefZh, S01, SCI, SCOPUS, SolStAb, T02, TM, W07.
—BLDSC (9139.000000), AskIEEE, CASDDS, IE, Infotrieve, Ingenta, INIST, Linda Hall. **CCC.**
Published by: Pergamon (Subsidiary of: Elsevier Science & Technology), The Blvd, Langford Ln, East Park, Kidlington, Oxford OX5 1GB, United Kingdom. TEL 44-1865-843000, FAX 44-1865-843010, JournalsCustomerServiceEMEA@elsevier.com, http://www.elsevier.nl. Eds. G J Exarhos TEL 509-375-2440, J S Colligon TEL 44-161-2471452, L G Hultman. **Subscr. to:** Elsevier BV, Radarweg 29, PO Box 211, Amsterdam 1000 AE, Netherlands. TEL 31-20-4853757, FAX 31-20-4853432, http://www.elsevier.nl.

533.5 621.55 DEU ISSN 0947-076X
CODEN: VFPREO

VAKUUM IN FORSCHUNG UND PRAXIS. Text in German; Summaries in English, French, German. 1951. bi-m. GBP 206 in United Kingdom to institutions; EUR 355 in Europe to institutions; USD 404 elsewhere to institutions; GBP 237 combined subscription in United Kingdom to institutions (print & online eds.); EUR 409 combined subscription in Europe to institutions (print & online eds.); USD 465 combined subscription elsewhere to institutions (print & online eds.) (effective 2012). adv. bk.rev. charts; illus. index, cum.index every 20 yrs. reprint service avail. from PSC. **Document type:** *Journal, Academic/Scholarly.* **Description:** Reports on new trends in research and development involving vacuum technology.
Former titles (until 1995): Vakuum in der Praxis (0934-9758); (until 1989): Vakuum-Technik (0042-2266); (until 1954): Glas- und Hochvakuum-Technik (0367-469X)
Related titles: Online - full text ed.: ISSN 1522-2454. GBP 206 in United Kingdom to institutions; EUR 355 in Europe to institutions; USD 404 elsewhere to institutions (effective 2012).
Indexed: A22, A28, APA, BrCerAb, C&ISA, CA/WCA, CIA, CIN, CPEI, CerAb, ChemAb, CivEngAb, CorrAb, E&CAJ, E11, EEA, EMA, ESPM, EngInd, EnvEAb, H15, IBR, IBZ, INIS AtomInd, Inspec, M&TEA, M09, MBF, METADEX, SCOPUS, SolStAb, T04, TM, WAA.
—BLDSC (9140.880000), CASDDS, IE, Infotrieve, Ingenta, INIST, Linda Hall. **CCC.**
Published by: Wiley - V C H Verlag GmbH & Co. KGaA (Subsidiary of: John Wiley & Sons, Inc.), Postfach 101161, Weinheim, 69451, Germany. TEL 49-6201-606400, FAX 49-6201-606184, info@wiley-vch.de, subservice@wiley-vch.de, http://www.wiley-vch.de. Ed. Norbert Kaiser. Adv. contact Aenne Anders TEL 49-6201-606552. color page EUR 4,470, B&W page EUR 3,300. Circ: 2,890 (paid and controlled). **Subscr. in the Americas to:** John Wiley & Sons, Inc., 111 River St, Hoboken, NJ 07030. TEL 201-748-6645, subinfo@wiley.com, http://www.wiley.com/WileyCDA/; **Subscr. outside Germany, Austria & Switzerland to:** John Wiley & Sons Ltd., The Atrium, Southern Gate, Chichester, West Sussex PO19 8SQ, United Kingdom. TEL 44-1243-779777, FAX 44-1243-775878, cs-agency@wiley.com, http://onlinelibrary.wiley.com/.

533.5 669 SVN ISSN 0351-9716

VAKUUMIST; casopis za vakuumsko znanost, tehniko in tehnologije, vakuumsko metalurgijo, tanke plasti, povrsine in fiziko plazme. Text in Slovenian; Text occasionally in English. 1981. q. looseleaf. adv. cum.index. back issues avail. **Document type:** *Journal, Trade.*
Published by: Drustvo za Vakuumsko Tehniko Slovenije/Slovenian Society for Vacuum Technique, Teslova 30, Ljubljana, 1000, Slovenia. TEL 386-1-4776600, FAX 386-1-4264578, info@dvts.si, http://www.dvts.si. Ed. Miha Cekada. Circ: 400.

530 RUS ISSN 1609-5375

➤ **VESTNIK MOLODYCH UCHENYCH. FIZICHESKIYE NAUKI.** Text in Russian. 1997. s-a. **Document type:** *Journal, Academic/Scholarly.*
Related titles: Online - full text ed.: ISSN 1609-5421. 2000.
Published by: Redaktsiya Zhurnala Vestnik Molodych Uchenych, 1-ya Krasnoarmeiskaya Ul., dom 1, Sankt-Peterburg, 198005, Russian Federation. vmu@peterlink.ru. Ed. V Gurskii TEL 7-812-2519092, ext 44. **Co-sponsors:** Rossiiskaya Akademiya Nauk, Sankt-Peterburgskii Nauchnyi Tsentr; Sovet Rektorov Vuzov Sankt-Peterburga; Ministerstvo Obrazovaniya i Nauki Rossiiskoi Federatsii/Ministry of Education and Science of the Russian Federation.

➤ **VESTNIK SAMARSKOGO GOSUDARSTVENNOGO TEKHNICHESKOGO UNIVERSITETA. SERIYA: FIZIKO-MATEMATICHESKIE NAUKI.** *see* MATHEMATICS

537.623 USA ISSN 1553-9636
QC611.9

VIRTUAL JOURNAL OF APPLICATIONS OF SUPERCONDUCTIVITY. Text in English. 2001. s-m. back issues avail. **Document type:** *Journal, Academic/Scholarly.* **Description:** Contains articles that were previously published in participating source journals and that fall within the scope of applications of superconductivity to electronics and large-scale systems.
Media: Online - full text.
Published by: American Institute of Physics, 1 Physics Ellipse, College Park, MD 20740. TEL 301-209-3100, FAX 301-209-0843, aipinfo@aip.org, http://www.aip.org. Ed. John R Clem. **Co-sponsor:** American Physical Society.

530 570 USA ISSN 1553-9628

➤ **VIRTUAL JOURNAL OF BIOLOGICAL PHYSICS RESEARCH.** Text in English. 2000. s-m. adv. Index. back issues avail. **Document type:** *Journal, Academic/Scholarly.* **Description:** Contains articles that appeared in the participating source journal and fall within a number of contemporary topical areas in biological physics research.
Media: Online - full text.
Published by: (American Institute of Physics), American Physical Society, One Physics Ellipse, College Park, MD 20740. TEL 301-209-3200, FAX 301-209-0865, help@aps.org, http://www.aps.org. Ed. Robert H Austin.

530 USA ISSN 1553-9644

➤ **VIRTUAL JOURNAL OF NANOSCALE SCIENCE & TECHNOLOGY.** Text in English. 2000. w. adv. abstr. back issues avail. **Document type:** *Journal, Academic/Scholarly.* **Description:** Contains articles that was published in one of the participating source journals and that fall within a number of contemporary topical areas in the science and technology of nanometer-scale structures.
Media: Online - full text.
Published by: (American Institute of Physics), American Physical Society, One Physics Ellipse, College Park, MD 20740. TEL 301-209-3200, FAX 301-209-0865, help@aps.org, http://www.aps.org. Ed. David Awschalom.

530 540 571.4 USA ISSN 1553-9601
QC689.5.L37

VIRTUAL JOURNAL OF ULTRAFAST SCIENCE. Text in English. 2002. m. free (effective 2010). back issues avail. **Document type:** *Journal, Academic/Scholarly.* **Description:** Contains articles that have appeared in one of the participating source journals and that fall within a number of contemporary topical areas as they pertain to ultrafast phenomena.
Media: Online - full text.
Published by: American Institute of Physics, 1 Physics Ellipse, College Park, MD 20740. TEL 301-209-3100, FAX 301-209-0843, aipinfo@aip.org, http://www.aip.org. Ed. Philip H Bucksbaum.

530 RUS

➤ **VOPROSY ATOMNOI NAUKI I TEKHNIKI. SERIYA: MATEMATICHESKOE MODELIROVANIE FIZICHESKIKH PROTSESSOV.** Text in Russian; Summaries in Russian, English. q. **Document type:** *Journal, Academic/Scholarly.*
Published by: Federal'noe Gosudarstvennoe Unitarnoe Predpriyatie Rossiiskii Federal'nyi Yadernyi Tsentr, Vserossiiskii Nauchno-Issledovatel'skii Institut Eksperimental'noi Fiziki, prospekt Mira 37, Sarov, Nizhegorodskaya oblast 607188, Russian Federation. TEL 7-83130-44802, FAX 7-83130-29494, staff@vniief.ru.

530 RUS

VOPROSY ATOMNOI NAUKI I TEKHNIKI. SERIYA: TEORETICHESKAYA I PRIKLADNAYA FIZIKA. Text in Russian; Summaries in Russian, English. 3/yr. RUR 200 per issue (effective 2011). **Document type:** *Journal, Academic/Scholarly.*
Published by: Federal'noe Gosudarstvennoe Unitarnoe Predpriyatie Rossiiskii Federal'nyi Yadernyi Tsentr, Vserossiiskii Nauchno-Issledovatel'skii Institut Eksperimental'noi Fiziki, prospekt Mira 37, Sarov, Nizhegorodskaya oblast 607188, Russian Federation. TEL 7-83130-44802, FAX 7-83130-29494, staff@vniief.ru. Ed. Yu A Trutnev.

530 510 RUS ISSN 1609-0705

➤ **VORONEZHSKII GOSUDARSTVENNYI UNIVERSITET. VESTNIK. SERIYA: FIZIKA, MATEMATIKA.** Text in Russian. 1993. irreg. **Document type:** *Journal, Academic/Scholarly.*
Supersedes in part (in 1999): Voronezhskii Gosudarstvennyi Universitet. Vestnik. Seriya: Estestvennye Nauki (1682-7341)
Related titles: Online - full text ed.
Indexed: RefZh, Z02.
Published by: Voronezhskii Gosudarstvennyi Universitet, Universitetskaya pl 1, Voronezh, 394693, Russian Federation. TEL 7-4732-207521, FAX 7-4732-208755, http://www.vsu.ru. Ed. V G Zvyagin.

530 NLD ISSN 0165-2125
QA927 CODEN: WAMOD9

➤ **WAVE MOTION.** Text in English. 1979. 8/yr. EUR 1,150 in Europe to institutions; JPY 153,000 in Japan to institutions; USD 1,288 elsewhere to institutions (effective 2012). adv. bibl.; illus. index, cum.index. back issues avail. **Document type:** *Journal, Academic/Scholarly.* **Description:** Stimulates interaction between workers in various research areas in which wave propagation phenomena play a dominant role.
Related titles: Microform ed.: (from PQC); Online - full text ed.: (from IngentaConnect, ScienceDirect).
Indexed: A01, A03, A08, A22, A26, A28, APA, ASCA, ASFA, AcoustA, ApMecR, BrCerAb, C&ISA, CA, CA/WCA, CCMJ, CIA, CMCI, CPEI, CerAb, CivEngAb, CorrAb, CurCont, E&CAJ, E11, EEA, EMA, ESPM, EngInd, EnvEAb, FLUIDEX, GEOBASE, GeoRef, H15, I05, ISMEC, ISR, Inspec, M&GPA, M&TEA, M09, MBF, METADEX, MSN, MathR, P30, PhysBer, RefZh, S&VD, S01, SCI, SCOPUS, SolStAb, SpeleolAb, T02, T04, W07, WAA, Z02.
—BLDSC (9280.765000), AskIEEE, IE, Infotrieve, Ingenta, INIST, Linda Hall. **CCC.**
Published by: Elsevier BV (Subsidiary of: Elsevier Science & Technology), Radarweg 29, PO Box 211, Amsterdam, 1000 AE, Netherlands. TEL 31-20-4853911, FAX 31-20-4852457, JournalsCustomerServiceEMEA@elsevier.com, http://www.elsevier.nl. Ed. J D Achenbach. **Subscr.:** Radarweg 29, PO Box 211, Amsterdam 1000 AE, Netherlands. TEL 31-20-4853757, FAX 31-20-4853432.

530 USA

WAVELET ANALYSIS AND ITS APPLICATIONS. Text in English. 1992. irreg., latest vol.10, 1998. price varies. **Document type:** *Monographic series, Academic/Scholarly.*
Related titles: Online - full text ed.: ISSN 1874-608X.
Published by: Academic Press (Subsidiary of: Elsevier Science & Technology), 3251 Riverport Ln, Maryland Heights, MO 63043. TEL 314-447-8010, FAX 314-447-8030, http://www.elsevierdirect.com/imprint.jsp?iid=5.

P

530 GBR ISSN 1745-5049

WAVES IN RANDOM AND COMPLEX MEDIA (ONLINE). Text in English. 1996. q. GBP 485 in United Kingdom to institutions; EUR 641, USD 805 to institutions (effective 2012). **Document type:** *Journal, Academic/Scholarly.*
Formerly (until 2005): Waves in Random Media (Online) (1361-6676)
Media: Online - full text (from IngentaConnect). **Related titles:** Microfiche ed.: USD 495 in the Americas; GBP 250 elsewhere (effective 2004); ◆ Print ed.: Waves in Random and Complex Media (Print). ISSN 1745-5030.
—BLDSC (9280.775750). **CCC.**
Published by: Taylor & Francis Ltd. (Subsidiary of: Taylor & Francis Group), 4 Park Sq, Milton Park, Abingdon, Oxfordshire OX14 4RN, United Kingdom. TEL 44-1235-828600, FAX 44-1235-829000, info@tandf.co.uk, http://www.tandf.co.uk/journals.

530 GBR ISSN 1745-5030
QC669 CODEN: WRMEEV

➤ **WAVES IN RANDOM AND COMPLEX MEDIA (PRINT).** Text in English. 1991. q. GBP 539 combined subscription in United Kingdom to institutions (print & online eds.); EUR 711, USD 894 combined subscription to institutions (print & online eds.) (effective 2012). adv. back issues avail.; reprint service avail. from PSC. **Document type:** *Journal, Academic/Scholarly.* **Description:** Provides a forum for papers on new and original theory in wave propagation and scattering in random media, as well as experimental or numerical studies demonstrating basic principles and theories.
Formerly (until 2005): Waves in Random Media (0959-7174)
Related titles: Microfiche ed.: USD 495 in the Americas; GBP 250 elsewhere (effective 2004); ◆ Online - full text ed.: Waves in Random and Complex Media (Online). ISSN 1745-5049.
Indexed: A01, A03, A08, A22, A28, APA, ASCA, ASFA, ApMecR, BrCerAb, C&ISA, CA, CA/WCA, CCMJ, CIA, CIS, CPEI, CerAb, CivEngAb, CorrAb, CurCont, E&CAJ, E01, E11, EEA, EMA, ESPM, EngInd, EnvEAb, GeoRef, H15, ISR, Inspec, M&GPA, M&TEA, M09, MBF, METADEX, MSN, MathR, SCI, SCOPUS, SolStAb, T02, T04, W07, WAA, Z02.
—BLDSC (9280.775750), AskIEEE, IE, Infotrieve, Ingenta, INIST, Linda Hall. **CCC.**
Published by: Taylor & Francis Ltd. (Subsidiary of: Taylor & Francis Group), 4 Park Sq, Milton Park, Abingdon, Oxfordshire OX14 4RN, United Kingdom. TEL 44-20-70176000, FAX 44-20-70176336, subscriptions@tandf.co.uk, http://www.taylorandfrancis.com. Ed. Michael A Fiddy. Adv. contact Linda Hann. **Subscr. in N America to:** Taylor & Francis Inc., Customer Services Dept, 325 Chestnut St, 8th Fl, Philadelphia, PA 19106. TEL 215-625-8900, 800-354-1420, FAX 215-625-2940, customerservice@taylorandfrancis.com; **Subscr. outside N America to:** Journals Customer Service, Sheepen Pl, Colchester, Essex CO3 3LP, United Kingdom. TEL 44-20-70175544, FAX 44-20-70175198, tf.enquiries@tfinforma.com.

530 DEU ISSN 1861-7778

WISSENSCHAFTLICHE BEITRAEGE AUS DEM TECTUM-VERLAG. REIHE PHYSIK. Text in German. 1999. irreg. price varies. **Document type:** *Monographic series, Academic/Scholarly.*
Published by: Tectum Wissenschaftsverlag Marburg, Biegenstr 4, Marburg, 35037, Germany. TEL 49-6421-481523, FAX 49-6421-43470, email@tectum-verlag.de, http://www.tectum-verlag.de.

530 DEU ISSN 1431-0228

WISSENSCHAFTLICHE SCHRIFTENREIHE PHYSIK. Text in German. 1993. irreg., latest vol.72, 2004. price varies. **Document type:** *Monographic series, Academic/Scholarly.*
Published by: Verlag Dr. Koester, Rungestr 22-24, Berlin, 10179, Germany. TEL 49-30-76403224, FAX 49-30-76403227, verlag-koester@t-online.de, http://www.verlag-koester.de.

530 USA ISSN 2160-6919

▼ ➤ **WORLD JOURNAL OF CONDENSED MATTER PHYSICS.** Abbreviated title: W J C M P. Text in English. 2011. q. USD 156 (effective 2011). **Document type:** *Journal, Academic/Scholarly.* **Description:** Covers the whole of condensed matter physics including soft condensed matter and nanostructures.

Related titles: Online - full text ed.: ISSN 2160-6927. free (effective 2011).
Published by: Scientific Research Publishing, Inc., PO Box 54821, Irvine, CA 92619. service@scirp.org. Ed. Ravindran Ponniah.

530 USA ISSN 1531-0809
QC5
WORLD OF PHYSICS. Text in English. 2001. irreg. (in 2 vols.). USD 215 per issue (effective 2008). back issues avail. **Document type:** *Monographic series, Academic/Scholarly.* **Description:** Provides a subject-specific guide to concepts, theories, discoveries, pioneers and issues.
Published by: Gale (Subsidiary of: Cengage Learning), 27500 Drake Rd, Farmington Hills, MI 48331. TEL 248-699-4253, 800-347-4253, FAX 800-414-5043, gale.customerservice@cengage.com, http://gale.cengage.com.

530 SGP ISSN 1793-1037
WORLD SCIENTIFIC LECTURE NOTES IN COMPLEX SYSTEMS. Text in English. 2003 (May). irreg., latest vol.10, 2009. price varies. back issues avail. **Document type:** *Monographic series, Academic/Scholarly.* **Description:** Aims to promote the exchange of information between scientists working in different fields, who are involved in the study of complex systems.
Published by: World Scientific Publishing Co. Pte. Ltd., 5 Toh Tuck Link, Singapore, 596224, Singapore. TEL 65-6466-5775, FAX 65-6467-7667, wspc@wspc.com.sg, http://www.worldscientific.com. Ed. A S Mikhailov. **Dist. by:** World Scientific Publishing Co., Inc., 27 Warren St, Ste 401-402, Hackensack, NJ 07601. TEL 201-487-9655, 800-227-7562, FAX 201-487-9656, 888-977-2665, wspc@wspc.com; World Scientific Publishing Ltd., 57 Shelton St, London WC2H 9HE, United Kingdom. TEL 44-207-8360888, FAX 44-207-8362020, sales@wspc.co.uk.

530 SGP ISSN 0218-026X
WORLD SCIENTIFIC LECTURE NOTES IN PHYSICS. Text in English. 1985. irreg., latest vol.81, 2010. price varies. back issues avail. **Document type:** *Monographic series, Academic/Scholarly.* **Description:** Focuses on historical accounts of the progress of different aspects of physics, collections of scientific papers of eminent physicists, and works or festschrifts dedicated to the physicists of this century.
Indexed: CIN, ChemAb, ChemTitl.
—BLDSC (9360.003000), IE, Ingenta.
Published by: World Scientific Publishing Co. Pte. Ltd., 5 Toh Tuck Link, Singapore, 596224, Singapore. TEL 65-6466-5775, FAX 65-6467-7667, wspc@wspc.com.sg, http://www.worldscientific.com. **Dist. by:** World Scientific Publishing Co., Inc., 27 Warren St, Ste 401-402, Hackensack, NJ 07601. TEL 201-487-9655, 800-227-7562, FAX 201-487-9656, 888-977-2665, wspc@wspc.com; World Scientific Publishing Ltd., 57 Shelton St, London WC2H 9HE, United Kingdom. TEL 44-207-8360888, FAX 44-207-8362020, sales@wspc.co.uk.

530 SGP ISSN 1793-1207
WORLD SCIENTIFIC SERIES IN 20TH CENTURY PHYSICS. (vol.23: Selected Papers of Kun Hang (With Commentary)) Text in English. 1992. irreg., latest vol.42, 2009. price varies. back issues avail. **Document type:** *Monographic series, Academic/Scholarly.* **Description:** Focuses on historical accounts of the progress of different aspects of physics, collections of important scientific papers of physicists, and works or festschrifts dedicated to the physicists of this century.
Indexed: CCMJ.
Published by: World Scientific Publishing Co. Pte. Ltd., 5 Toh Tuck Link, Singapore, 596224, Singapore. TEL 65-6466-5775, FAX 65-6467-7667, wspc@wspc.com.sg, http://www.worldscientific.com. **Dist. by:** World Scientific Publishing Co., Inc., 27 Warren St, Ste 401-402, Hackensack, NJ 07601. TEL 201-487-9655, 800-227-7562, FAX 201-487-9656, 888-977-2665, wspc@wspc.com; World Scientific Publishing Ltd., 57 Shelton St, London WC2H 9HE, United Kingdom. TEL 44-207-8360888, FAX 44-207-8362020, sales@wspc.co.uk.

WORLD SCIENTIFIC SERIES IN ASTRONOMY AND ASTROPHYSICS. *see* ASTRONOMY

530 540 SGP ISSN 1793-0936
WORLD SCIENTIFIC SERIES IN CONTEMPORARY CHEMICAL PHYSICS. Text in English. 1993. irreg., latest vol.26, 2008. price varies. back issues avail. **Document type:** *Monographic series, Academic/Scholarly.*
Published by: World Scientific Publishing Co. Pte. Ltd., 5 Toh Tuck Link, Singapore, 596224, Singapore. TEL 65-6466-5775, FAX 65-6467-7667, wspc@wspc.com.sg, http://www.worldscientific.com. **Dist. by:** World Scientific Publishing Co., Inc., 27 Warren St, Ste 401-402, Hackensack, NJ 07601. TEL 201-487-9655, 800-227-7562, FAX 201-487-9656, 888-977-2665, wspc@wspc.com; World Scientific Publishing Ltd., 57 Shelton St, London WC2H 9HE, United Kingdom. TEL 44-207-8360888, FAX 44-207-8362020, sales@wspc.co.uk.

530 SGP ISSN 2010-2828
WORLD SCIENTIFIC SERIES ON ATOMIC, MOLECULAR AND OPTICAL PHYSICS. Text in English. 1993. irreg., latest vol.3, 2004. price varies. back issues avail. **Document type:** *Monographic series, Academic/Scholarly.*
Published by: World Scientific Publishing Co. Pte. Ltd., 5 Toh Tuck Link, Singapore, 596224, Singapore. TEL 65-6466-5775, FAX 65-6467-7667, wspc@wspc.com.sg, http://www.worldscientific.com. Ed. Phillip L Gould. **Dist. by:** World Scientific Publishing Co., Inc., 27 Warren St, Ste 401-402, Hackensack, NJ 07601. TEL 201-487-9655, 800-227-7562, FAX 201-487-9656, 888-977-2665, wspc@wspc.com; World Scientific Publishing Ltd., 57 Shelton St, London WC2H 9HE, United Kingdom. TEL 44-207-8360888, FAX 44-207-8362020, sales@wspc.co.uk.

WORLDPOWER AND ENERGY. *see* ENERGY

530 CHN ISSN 0379-4148
QC1 CODEN: WULIAL
➤ **WULI/PHYSICS.** Text in Chinese. 1951. m. USD 106.80 (effective 2009). adv. bk.rev. **Document type:** *Journal, Academic/Scholarly.* **Description:** Introduces modern physics in simple language. Reports on developments in new branches of physics, new theories, phenomena, materials, experimental techniques and methods, and the application of physics in economic construction in China.
Related titles: Online - full text ed.
Indexed: CIN, ChemAb, ChemTitl, INIS AtomInd, Inspec, RefZh.
—AskIEEE, CASDDS, East View, IE, Ingenta, Linda Hall.
Published by: (Zhongguo Wuli Xuehui/Chinese Physical Society, Zhongguo Kexueyuan Wuli Yanjiusuo/Chinese Academy of Sciences, Institute of Physics), Kexue Chubanshe/Science Press, 16 Donghuang Cheng Genbei Jie, Beijing, 100717, China. TEL 86-10-64000246, FAX 86-10-64030255, http://www.sciencep.com/. Circ: 21,000. **Dist. by:** China International Book Trading Corp, 35 Chegongzhuang Xilu, Haidian District, PO Box 399, Beijing 100044, China. TEL 86-10-68412045, FAX 86-10-68412023, cibtc@mail.cibtc.com.cn, http://www.cibtc.com.cn.

530.071 CHN ISSN 1002-0748
WULI JIAOXUE/PHYSICS TEACHING. Text in Chinese. 1978. m. USD 49.20 (effective 2009). adv. bk.rev. Index. back issues avail. **Document type:** *Journal, Academic/Scholarly.* **Description:** Covers teaching material and teaching methods, and suggests physics problems and experiments. Includes information on teaching abroad, new developments in physics, and observations on physics in daily life.
—East View.
Published by: Zhongguo Wuli Xuehui/Chinese Physical Society, 3663, Zhongshan Beilu, Shanghai, 200062, China. Circ: 40,000.

530 CHN
WULI SHIYAN/PHYSICS EXPERIMENTATION. Text in Chinese. 1980. m. CNY 7 newsstand/cover (effective 2006). **Document type:** *Journal, Academic/Scholarly.*
Related titles: Online - full text ed.
Published by: Dongbei Shifan Daxue/Northeast Normal University, 5268 Renmin Dajie, Changchun, 130024, China. TEL 86-431-5269569, FAX 86-431-5709573. Ed. Yu Fuchun.

530 TWN
WULI SHUANYUEKAN. Text in Chinese. bi-m.
Former titles: Wulihui Xuekan; Wuli Jikan; Zhonghua Minguo Wuli Xuehui Tongxun
Published by: Zhonghua Minguo Wuli Xuehui/Physical Society of the Republic of China, PO BOX 23-30, Taipei, 106, Taiwan. TEL 886-2-23634923, FAX 886-2-23626538.

530 CHN ISSN 0509-4038
CODEN: WLTPAJ
WULI TONGBAO/PHYSICS BULLETIN. Text in Chinese. 1982. m. USD 49.20 (effective 2009).
Indexed: CIN, ChemAb, ChemTitl, Inspec.
—AskIEEE, CASDDS.
Published by: Hebei Sheng Wuli Xuehui/Physics Society of Hebei Province, Hebei Daxue - Hebei University, 1 Hezuo Lu, Baoding, Hebei 071002, China. TEL 5025052. Ed. Wu Zuren. Circ: 10,000.
Co-sponsor: Hebei University.

530 CHN ISSN 1000-3290
QC1 CODEN: WLHPAR
➤ **WULI XUEBAO/ACTA PHYSICA SINICA.** Text in Chinese; Summaries in English. 1933. m. USD 506.40 (effective 2009). adv. **Document type:** *Journal, Academic/Scholarly.* **Description:** Covers physics research in mainland China, including surface physics, excitation, and amorphous physics.
Related titles: Online - full text ed.; ◆ English ed.: Chinese Physics B. ISSN 1674-1056.
Indexed: A22, C33, CCMJ, CIN, ChemAb, CurCont, EngInd, INIS AtomInd, ISR, Inspec, MSN, MathR, PhysBer, SCI, SCOPUS, W07, Z02.
—BLDSC (0650.500000), CASDDS, East View, IE, Ingenta, INIST, Linda Hall.
Published by: Zhongguo Wuli Xuehui/Chinese Physical Society, PO Box 603, Beijing, 100080, China. TEL 86-10-82649019, FAX 86-10-82649027. Circ: 11,000. **Dist. by:** China International Book Trading Corp, 35 Chegongzhuang Xilu, Haidian District, PO Box 399, Beijing 100044, China. TEL 86-10-68412045, FAX 86-10-68412023, cibtc@mail.cibtc.com.cn, http://www.cibtc.com.cn.

530 620 CHN ISSN 1009-7104
WULI YU GONGCHENG/PHYSICS AND ENGINEERING. Text in Chinese. 1985. bi-m. USD 24 (effective 2009). **Document type:** *Journal, Academic/Scholarly.*
Formerly (until 2000): Gongke Wuli (1004-2873)
Related titles: Online - full text ed.
—East View.
Published by: Qinghua Daxue Chubanshe/Tsinghua University Press, Yan Dasha A, Beijing, 100084, China. TEL 86-10-62789753.

621.361 JPN ISSN 1883-3578
➤ **X-RAY STRUCTURE ANALYSIS ONLINE.** Text in English. 2003. m. free (effective 2011). **Document type:** *Journal, Academic/Scholarly.*
Formerly (until 2009): Analytical Sciences. X-ray Structure Analysis Online (1348-2238); Which superseded in part (in 2003): Analytical Sciences (Online) (1348-2246)
Media: Online - full content.
Indexed: SCOPUS.
—CCC.
Published by: Nihon Bunseki Kagakkai/Japan Society for Analytical Chemistry, 1-26-2 Nishigotanda, Shinagawa, Tokyo, 141-0031, Japan. TEL 81-3-34903351, FAX 81-3-34903572, analytsci@jsac.or.jp, http://wwwsoc.nii.ac.jp/jsac/. Ed. T. Imasaka.

530 USA ISSN 2161-0916
XIANDAI WULI/MODERN PHYSICS. Text in Chinese; Abstracts in English. q. **Document type:** *Journal, Academic/Scholarly.*
Related titles: Online - full text ed.: free (effective 2011).
Published by: Hansi Chubanshe/Hans Publishers, 40 E. Main St., Box 275, Newark, DE 19711. TEL 926408-329-4591. Ed. Jinfeng Jia.

530 CHN ISSN 1001-0610
QC1 CODEN: XWZHEF
XIANDAI WULI ZHISHI/MODERN PHYSICS. Text in Chinese. 1976. bi-m. USD 24.60 (effective 2009). adv. **Document type:** *Journal, Academic/Scholarly.*
Formerly: Gaoneng Wuli - High Energy Physics
Related titles: Online - full text ed.
—East View, Linda Hall.
Published by: (Zhongguo Kexueyuan Gaoneng Wuli Yanjiusuo/Chinese Academy of Sciences, Institute of High Energy Physics), Kexue Chubanshe/Science Press, 16 Donghuang Cheng Genbei Jie, Beijing, 100717, China. TEL 86-10-64000246, FAX 86-10-64030255, http://www.sciencep.com/. Circ: 10,000. **Dist. by:** China International Book Trading Corp, 35 Chegongzhuang Xilu, Haidian District, PO Box 399, Beijing 100044, China. TEL 86-10-68412045, FAX 86-10-68412023, cibtc@mail.cibtc.com.cn, http://www.cibtc.com.cn.

530 USA ISSN 2160-7567
▼ **YINGYONG WULI/APPLIED PHYSICS.** Text in Chinese; Abstracts in English. 2011. q. **Document type:** *Journal, Academic/Scholarly.*
Related titles: Online - full text ed.: ISSN 2160-7575. free (effective 2011).
Published by: Hansi Chubanshe/Hans Publishers, 40 E. Main St., Box 275, Newark, DE 19711. TEL 926408-329-4591. Eds. Jiyuan Tu, Qiren Zhang, Shuyi Zhang.

ZEITSCHRIFT FUER ANGEWANDTE MATHEMATIK UND PHYSIK/ JOURNAL DES MATHEMATIQUES ET DE PHYSIQUE APPLIQUEES/JOURNAL OF APPLIED MATHEMATICS AND PHYSICS. *see* MATHEMATICS

530 541 523.01 DEU ISSN 0932-0784
QC1 CODEN: ZNASEI
➤ **ZEITSCHRIFT FUER NATURFORSCHUNG. SECTION A: A JOURNAL OF PHYSICAL SCIENCES.** Text in English. 1946. m. EUR 683 combined subscription domestic (print & online eds.); EUR 696 combined subscription foreign (print & online eds.) (effective 2010). adv. bk.rev. charts; illus. index. 100 p./no.; **Document type:** *Journal, Academic/Scholarly.* **Description:** Contains contributions from all areas of physical sciences including mathematical physics, physical chemistry, cosmophysics and geophysics.
Former titles (until 1987): Zeitschrift fuer Naturforschung. Section A: Physics, Physical Chemistry, Cosmic Physics (0340-4811); (until 1971): Zeitschrift fuer Naturforschung. Ausgabe A (0044-3166); Which superseded in part (in 1947): Zeitschrift fuer Naturforschung (0372-9516)
Related titles: Online - full text ed.: ISSN 1865-7109. EUR 656 (effective 2010).
Indexed: A22, ASCA, BullT&T, C33, CCI, CCMJ, CIN, ChemAb, ChemTitl, CurCR, CurCont, GeoRef, INIS AtomInd, ISR, Inspec, MSN, MathR, PhysBer, R16, SCI, SCOPUS, SpeleolAb, W07, Z02.
—BLDSC (9474.000000), AskIEEE, CASDDS, IE, Infotrieve, Ingenta, INIST, Linda Hall. **CCC.**
Published by: Verlag der Zeitschrift fuer Naturforschung, Postfach 2645, Tuebingen, 72016, Germany. TEL 49-7071-31555, FAX 49-7071-360571, zna@znaturforsch.com, http://znaturforsch.com. Ed. Siegfried Grossmann. Circ: 600.

530 520 CHN ISSN 1672-1780
QC1
➤ **ZHONGGUO KEXUE. G JI: WULIXUE, TIANWENXUE.** Text in Chinese. 1950. m. CNY 1,440; CNY 120 per issue (effective 2009). **Document type:** *Journal, Academic/Scholarly.*
Supersedes in part (in 2003): Zhongguo Kexue. A Ji (Shuxue, Wulixue, Tianwenxue, Jishu kexue) (1000-3126)
Related titles: Online - full content ed.: USD 50 (effective 2003); Online - full text ed.; ◆ English ed.: Science China Physics, Mechanics & Astronomy. ISSN 1674-7348.
—East View.
Published by: (Chinese Academy of Sciences/Zhongguo Kexueyuan), Zhongguo Kexue Zazhishe/Science in China Press, 16 Donghuangchenggen North Street, Beijing, 100717, China. TEL 86-10-64015835, sale@scichina.com, http://www.scichina.com/. Ed. Ding-Sheng Wang. **Dist. in the Americas by:** Springer New York LLC, Journal Fulfillment, PO Box 2485, Secaucus, NJ 07096. TEL 212-460-1500, FAX 201-348-4505, journals-ny@springer.com; **Dist. outside the Americas by:** Springer, Haber Str 7, Heidelberg 69126, Germany. TEL 49-6221-3454303, FAX 49-6221-3454229, subscriptions@springer.com, http://www.springer.de.

➤ **ZHONGGUO YIXUE WULIXUE ZAZHI/CHINESE JOURNAL OF MEDICAL PHYSICS.** *see* MEDICAL SCIENCES

530 373 CHN ISSN 1009-2927
QC30
ZHONGXUE WULI JIAOYUXUE/TEACHING AND LEARNING OF PHYSICS IN MIDDLE SCHOOL. Text in Chinese. 1980. bi-m. USD 49.90 (effective 2009). 64 p./no.; **Document type:** *Journal, Academic/Scholarly.* **Description:** Covers secondary school physics education, teaching methods and curriculum.
Formerly (until 199?): Zhongxue Wuli Jiaoxue (1001-294X)
Published by: Zhongguo Renmin Daxue Shubao Ziliao Zhongxin/Renmin University of China, Information Center for Social Sciences, Dongcheng-qu, 3, Zhangzizhong Lu, Beijing, 100007, China. TEL 86-10-64039458, FAX 86-10-64015080, center@zlzx.org, http://www.zlzx.org/. **Dist. in US by:** China Publications Service, PO Box 49614, Chicago, IL 60649. TEL 312-288-3291, FAX 312-288-8570; **Dist. by:** China International Book Trading Corp, 35 Chegongzhuang Xilu, Haidian District, PO Box 399, Beijing 100044, China. TEL 86-10-68412045, FAX 86-10-68412023, cibtc@mail.cibtc.com.cn, http://www.cibtc.com.cn.

ZHONGXUESHENG SHU LI HUA (CHUZHONG BAN BA-NAN JI)/SCHOOL JOURNAL OF MATHEMATICS, PHYSICS AND CHEMISTRY (JUNIOR HIGH SCHOOL EDITION). *see* MATHEMATICS

ZHONGXUESHENG SHU LI HUA (CHUZHONG BAN QI-NAN JI)/ SCHOOL JOURNAL OF MATHEMATICS, PHYSICS AND CHEMISTRY (JUNIOR HIGH SCHOOL EDITION). *see* MATHEMATICS

ZHONGXUESHENG SHU LI HUA (CHUZHONG BAN ZHONGKAO BAN)/SCHOOL JOURNAL OF MATHEMATICS, PHYSICS AND CHEMISTRY (JUNIOR HIGH SCHOOL EDITION). *see* MATHEMATICS

ZHONGXUESHENG SHU LI HUA (GAOZHONG BAN)/MATH, PHYSICS & CHEMISTRY FOR MIDDLE SCHOOL STUDENTS (MIDDLE SCHOOL EDITION). *see* EDUCATION—Teaching Methods And Curriculum

ZHONGXUESHENG SHU LI HUA (JIAOYUXUE JIAOYAN BAN). *see* MATHEMATICS

530.071 CHN
ZHONGXUESHENG WULI YUANDI/PHYSICS FOR MIDDLE SCHOOL STUDENTS. Text in Chinese. bi-m. CNY 2.50.
Published by: Fujian Society of Physics, Physics Department, Fuzhou University, Fuzhou, Fujian 350002, China. TEL 710845. Ed. Qiu Jinzhang. **Dist. overseas by:** Jiangsu Publications Import & Export Corp., 56 Gao Yun Ling, Nanjing, Jiangsu, China.

530 RUS ISSN 0044-4510
CODEN: ZETFA7
ZHURNAL EKSPERIMENTAL'NOI I TEORETICHESKOI FIZIKI. Text in Russian; Summaries in English. 1931. m. RUR 1,540 for 6 mos. domestic (effective 2004). charts; illus. index. **Document type:** *Journal, Academic/Scholarly.* **Description:** Presents papers, emphasizing fundamental theoretical and experimental research in all fields of physics-from solid state to elementary particles and cosmology.
Related titles: Microform ed.: (from PMC); ◆ English Translation: Journal of Experimental and Theoretical Physics. ISSN 1063-7761.
Indexed: ASCA, CIN, ChemAb, ChemTitl, CorrAb, GeoRef, INIS AtomInd, ISR, Inspec, MSN, MathR, PhysBer, RefZh, SCOPUS, SpeleolAb, WAA.
—BLDSC (0068.000000), AskIEEE, CASDDS, East View, GNLM, INIST, Linda Hall. **CCC.**
Published by: (Rossiiskaya Akademiya Nauk/Russian Academy of Sciences), Izdatel'stvo Nauka, Profsoyuznaya ul 90, Moscow, 117864, Russian Federation. TEL 7-095-3347151, FAX 7-095-4202220, secret@naukaran.ru, http://www.naukaran.ru. Circ: 2,700.

530 RUS ISSN 0044-4642
QC1 CODEN: ZTEFA3
➤ **ZHURNAL TEKHNICHESKOI FIZIKI.** Text in Russian. 1931. m. USD 540 foreign (effective 2011). charts; illus. index. **Document type:** *Journal, Academic/Scholarly.* **Description:** Contains practical information on all aspects of applied physics, especially instrumentation and measurement techniques.
Related titles: Online - full text ed.: ISSN 1726-748X; ◆ English Translation: Technical Physics. ISSN 1063-7842.
Indexed: ASCA, CIN, ChemAb, ChemTitl, CorrAb, GeoRef, INIS AtomInd, Inspec, PhysBer, RefZh, SpeleolAb, WAA.
—BLDSC (0066.000000), AskIEEE, CASDDS, INIST, Linda Hall. **CCC.**
Published by: (Rossiiskaya Akademiya Nauk, Fiziko-tekhnicheskii Institut im. A.F. Ioffe), Izdatel'stvo Nauka, Profsoyuznaya ul 90, Moscow, 117864, Russian Federation. TEL 7-095-3347151, FAX 7-095-4202220, secret@naukaran.ru, http://www.naukaran.ru. Circ: 4,000.

➤ **ZHURNAL VYCHISLITEL'NOI MATEMATIKI I MATEMATICHESKOI FIZIKI.** *see* MATHEMATICS

539 USA ISSN 1942-664X
Q11
1663. Text in English. 2007. irreg.
Related titles: Online - full text ed.: ISSN 1942-6631.
—Linda Hall.
Published by: Los Alamos National Laboratory, Mail Stop M711, Los Alamos, NM 87545. TEL 505-667-1447, FAX 505-665-4408. Ed. Jay Schecker.

PHYSICS—Abstracting, Bibliographies, Statistics

534.021 AUS
AUSTRALIA. BUREAU OF STATISTICS. AUDIOLOGY AND AUDIOMETRY SERVICES, AUSTRALIA (ONLINE). Text in English. 1997. irreg., latest 1998. free (effective 2009). **Document type:** *Government.* **Description:** Contains detailed information on audiology and audiometry businesses in Australia. Data include income, expense and employment profiles as well as information concerning business structure and the types of activities undertaken.
Formerly: Australia. Bureau of Statistics. Audiology and Audiometry Services, Australia (Print)
Media: Online - full text.
Published by: Australian Bureau of Statistics, Locked Bag 10, Belconnen, ACT 2616, Australia. TEL 61-2-92684909, 300-135-070, FAX 61-2-92684654, client.services@abs.gov.au.

534.021 AUS
AUSTRALIA. BUREAU OF STATISTICS. SOUND RECORDING STUDIOS, AUSTRALIA (ONLINE). Text in English. 1996. irreg., latest 1997. free (effective 2009). **Document type:** *Government.* **Description:** Contains an economic picture of the Australian sound recording studio industry for the 1996-97 financial year, including final figures on employment, income and expenses.
Formerly: Australia. Bureau of Statistics. Sound Recording Studios, Australia (Print)
Media: Online - full text.
Published by: Australian Bureau of Statistics, Locked Bag 10, Belconnen, ACT 2616, Australia. TEL 61-2-92684909, 300-135-070, FAX 61-2-92684654, client.services@abs.gov.au.

681 016 HUN ISSN 0231-0643
AUTOMATIZALASI, SZAMITASTECHNIKAI ES MERESTECHNIKAI SZAKIRODALMI TAJEKOZTATO/AUTOMATION, COMPUTING. COMPUTERS & MEASUREMENT ABSTRACTS. Text in Hungarian. 1948. m. HUF 9,700. abstr. index.
Supersedes: Muszaki Lapszemle. Fizika, Meres- es Muszertechnika, Automatika - Technical Abstracts. Physics, Measurement and Instrument Technology, Automation (0027-500X)
Published by: Orszagos Muszaki Informacios Kozpont es Konyvtar/ National Technical Information Centre and Library, Muzeum utca 17, PO Box 12, Budapest, 1428, Hungary. Ed. Pal Konyves Toth. Circ: 420. **Subscr. to:** Kultura, PO Box 149, Budapest 1389, Hungary.

535 USA ISSN 0195-4911
CODEN: CAASDD
C A SELECTS. ATOMIC SPECTROSCOPY. Text in English. s-w. USD 385 to non-members; USD 115 to members; USD 575 combined subscription to individuals (print & online eds.) (effective 2011). **Document type:** *Abstract/Index.* **Description:** Covers atomic absorption, emission, and fluorescence in optical regions, i.e., infrared, visible, and ultraviolet; applications in spectrochemical analysis.
Related titles: Online - full text ed.: USD 380 to non-members; USD 114 to members (effective 2011).
Published by: Chemical Abstracts Service (Subsidiary of: American Chemical Society), 2540 Olentangy River Rd, Columbus, OH 43210-0012. TEL 614-447-3600, FAX 614-447-3713, help@cas.com, http://caselects.cas.org. **Subscr. to:** PO Box 3012, Columbus, OH 43210. TEL 800-753-4227, FAX 614-447-3751.

535 USA ISSN 0146-4450
CODEN: CSESDN
C A SELECTS. ELECTRON & AUGER SPECTROSCOPY. Text in English. s-w. USD 385 to non-members (print or online ed.); USD 115 to members; USD 575 combined subscription to individuals (print & online eds.) (effective 2011). **Document type:** *Abstract/Index.* **Description:** Covers x-ray photoelectron, photoexcitation, and photoemission spectroscopy.
Related titles: Online - full text ed.: USD 380, USD 114 (effective 2011).
Published by: Chemical Abstracts Service (Subsidiary of: American Chemical Society), 2540 Olentangy River Rd, Columbus, OH 43210-0012. TEL 614-447-3600, FAX 614-447-3713, help@cas.com, http://caselects.cas.org. **Subscr. to:** PO Box 3012, Columbus, OH 43210. TEL 800-753-4227, FAX 614-447-3751.

535 USA ISSN 0190-9436
CODEN: CISAD3
C A SELECTS. INFRARED SPECTROSCOPY (PHYSICOCHEMICAL ASPECTS). Text in English. s-w. USD 385 to non-members; USD 115 to members; USD 575 combined subscription to individuals (print & online eds.) (effective 2011). **Document type:** *Abstract/Index.* **Description:** Covers applied and physicochemical aspects of infrared spectroscopy; infrared lasers; infrared spectroscopic determination of organic and inorganic substances.
Related titles: Online - full text ed.: USD 380 to non-members; USD 114 to members (effective 2011).
Published by: Chemical Abstracts Service (Subsidiary of: American Chemical Society), 2540 Olentangy River Rd, Columbus, OH 43210-0012. TEL 614-447-3600, FAX 614-447-3713, help@cas.com, http://caselects.cas.org. **Subscr. to:** PO Box 3012, Columbus, OH 43210. TEL 800-753-4227, FAX 614-447-3751.

535 USA ISSN 0895-5867
CODEN: CSNMEH
C A SELECTS. NONLINEAR OPTICAL MATERIALS. Text in English. 1988. s-w. USD 385 to non-members; USD 115 to members; USD 575 combined subscription to individuals (print & online eds.) (effective 2011). **Document type:** *Abstract/Index.* **Description:** Covers materials with nonlinear optical properties; applications of these materials in optical communications, laser, waveguides, electrooptical devices, and photoelectric devices.
Related titles: Online - full text ed.: USD 380 to non-members; USD 114 to members (effective 2011).
Published by: Chemical Abstracts Service (Subsidiary of: American Chemical Society), 2540 Olentangy River Rd, Columbus, OH 43210-0012. TEL 614-447-3600, FAX 614-447-3713, help@cas.com, http://caselects.cas.org. **Subscr. to:** PO Box 3012, Columbus, OH 43210. TEL 800-753-4227, FAX 614-447-3751.

535 USA ISSN 0195-5063
CODEN: COPMDW
C A SELECTS. OPTICAL AND PHOTOSENSITIVE MATERIALS. Text in English. s-w. USD 385 to non-members; USD 115 to members; USD 575 combined subscription to individuals (print & online eds.) (effective 2011). **Document type:** *Abstract/Index.* **Description:** Covers light absorbing, transmitting, and reflective materials: films, coatings, glasses, fibers, mirrors, polarizers, solar collectors.
Related titles: Online - full text ed.: USD 380 to non-members; USD 114 to members (effective 2011).
Published by: Chemical Abstracts Service (Subsidiary of: American Chemical Society), 2540 Olentangy River Rd, Columbus, OH 43210-0012. TEL 614-447-3600, FAX 614-447-3713, help@cas.com, http://caselects.cas.org. **Subscr. to:** PO Box 3012, Columbus, OH 43210. TEL 800-753-4227, FAX 614-447-3751.

C A SELECTS PLUS. MASS SPECTROMETRY. *see* CHEMISTRY—Abstracting, Bibliographies, Statistics

C A SELECTS. THERMAL ANALYSIS. *see* CHEMISTRY—Abstracting, Bibliographies, Statistics

535 USA ISSN 0162-7872
CODEN: CSXSDG
C A SELECTS. X-RAY ANALYSIS & SPECTROSCOPY. Text in English. s-w. USD 385 to non-members; USD 115 to members; USD 575 combined subscription to individuals (print & online eds.) (effective 2011). **Document type:** *Abstract/Index.* **Description:** Covers x-ray techniques in chemical analysis, for example, electron microprobe.
Related titles: Online - full text ed.: USD 380 to non-members; USD 114 to members (effective 2011).
Published by: Chemical Abstracts Service (Subsidiary of: American Chemical Society), 2540 Olentangy River Rd, Columbus, OH 43210-0012. TEL 614-447-3600, FAX 614-447-3713, help@cas.com, http://caselects.cas.org. **Subscr. to:** PO Box 3012, Columbus, OH 43210. TEL 800-753-4227, FAX 614-447-3751.

539.7 016 AUT ISSN 1011-2545
C I N D A; an index to the literature on microscopic neutron data. Text in English. 1965. a. price varies. **Document type:** *Bibliography.*
Related titles: Online - full text ed.
Published by: International Atomic Energy Agency/Agence Internationale de l'Energie Atomique, Wagramer Str 5, Postfach 100, Vienna, W 1400, Austria. TEL 43-1-2600-0, FAX 43-1-2600-29302, sales.publications@iaea.org, http://www.iaea.org. Circ: 1,500 (paid). **Co-sponsors:** U.S.A. National Nuclear Data Center; IAEA Nuclear Data Section; N.E.A. Databank; Russian Nuclear Data Centre.

CURRENT CONTENTS: PHYSICAL, CHEMICAL & EARTH SCIENCES. *see* CHEMISTRY—Abstracting, Bibliographies, Statistics

530 016 520 GBR ISSN 0011-3786
QC5.5 CODEN: CPPHAL
CURRENT PAPERS IN PHYSICS. Text in English. 1966. 24/yr. USD 2,090 in the Americas to institutions (print or online ed.); GBP 1,205 elsewhere to institutions (print or online ed.) (effective 2010). **Document type:** *Abstract/Index.* **Description:** Designed to alert scientists and engineers to information in the fields of pure and applied physics and related subjects and gives the titles and full details of the bibliographic reference of each article contained in Physics Abstracts.
Related titles: Online - full text ed.
—CASDDS. **CCC.**
Published by: The Institution of Engineering and Technology, Michael Faraday House, Stevenage, Herts SG1 2AY, United Kingdom. TEL 44-1438-313311, FAX 44-1438-765526, journals@theiet.org.

ENERGIAIPARI ES ENERGIAGAZDALKODASI TAJEKOZTATO/ POWER ENGINEERING ABSTRACTS. *see* ENERGY—Abstracting, Bibliographies, Statistics

539.7 016 CHE ISSN 0304-2871
EUROPEAN ORGANIZATION FOR NUCLEAR RESEARCH. LIST OF SCIENTIFIC PUBLICATIONS/CONSEIL EUROPEEN POUR LA RECHERCHE NUCLEAIRE. LISTE DES PUBLICATIONS SCIENTIFIQUES. Text in English. 1955. irreg. free. **Document type:** *Monographic series, Academic/Scholarly.*
Former titles: European Organization for Nuclear Research. Repertoire des Communications Scientifiques - Index of Scientific Publications (0423-7781); European Organization for Nuclear Research. Repertoire des Publications Scientifiques - Index of Scientific Publications
—INIST.
Published by: C E R N - European Organization for Nuclear Research/ Organisation Europeenne pour la Recherche Nucleaire, C E R N, Geneva 23, 1211, Switzerland.

530 FRA ISSN 0378-2271
QC1 CODEN: ECABDW
EUROPHYSICS CONFERENCE ABSTRACTS. Text in French. irreg. (8-10/yr.). price varies. **Document type:** *Journal, Abstract/Index.*
Indexed: PhysBer.
—BLDSC (3830.415000), IE, Ingenta, Linda Hall.
Published by: European Physical Society, 6 rue des Freres Lumiere, Mulhouse, 68200, France. TEL 33-3-89329440, FAX 33-3-89329449, webmaster@eps.org.

539.7 USA
FUELS AND MATERIALS FACILITIES. Text in English. 19??. irreg. **Document type:** *Handbook/Manual/Guide, Government.*
Published by: (U.S. Nuclear Regulatory Commission), U.S. Department of Commerce, National Technical Information Service, 5301 Shawnee Rd, Alexandria, VA 22312. TEL 703-605-6000, info@ntis.gov.

536 621 USA ISSN 1543-3056
HEAT TRANSFER - RECENT CONTENTS (ONLINE). Text in English. 1992. 6/yr. USD 54 to non-members; USD 24 to members (effective 2003). **Description:** Lists the tables of contents of the world's most important heat transfer research journals.
Formerly (until 2003): Heat Transfer - Recent Contents (Print) (1063-1313)
Media: Online - full content. **Related titles:** Online - full text ed.
—Linda Hall. **CCC.**
Published by: A S M E International, Three Park Ave, New York, NY 10016. TEL 800-843-2763, infocentral@asme.org, http:// www.asme.org. Ed. S V Garimella.

539.2 JPN
HOSHASEN RIYO KENKYU SEIKA HOKOKUKAI KOEN YOSHI/ ABSTRACTS OF RESEARCH RESULTS OF RADIATION UTILIZATION. Text in Japanese. a.
Published by: Nihon Genshiryoku Kenkyujo, Takasaki Kenkyujo/Japan Atomic Energy Research Institute, Takasaki Radiation Chemistry Research Establishment, 1233 Watanuki-Machi, Takasaki-shi, Gunma-ken 370-1207, Japan.

539.7 016 AUT
Z7144.N8 CODEN: INAXAC
I N I S ATOMINDEX (ONLINE). (International Nuclear Information System) Text in English; Summaries in English, French, Russian, Spanish. 1959. base vol. plus q. updates. EUR 800 to individuals; EUR 400 in developing nations to individuals; EUR 4,000 to institutions; EUR 2,000 in developing nations to institutions (effective 2005). **Document type:** *Database, Abstract/Index.*
Formerly (until 1997): I N I S Atomindex (Print) (0004-7139); (until 1968): List of References on Nuclear Energy (1011-2707); I N I S Atomindex (Print) incorporates (1948-1976): United States. Energy Research and Development Administration. Nuclear Science Abstracts (0029-5612); Which was formed by the 1948 merger of: Abstracts of Declassified Documents; Guide to Published Research on Atomic Energy
Media: Online - full text. **Related titles:** CD-ROM ed.
Indexed: P30.
—Linda Hall. **CCC.**
Published by: International Atomic Energy Agency/Agence Internationale de l'Energie Atomique, Wagramer Str 5, Postfach 100, Vienna, W 1400, Austria. TEL 43-1-26000, 43-1-260022883, FAX 43-1-260029882, 43-1-26007, inis@iaea.org. **Dist. in U.S. by:** Bernan Associates, Bernan, 4611-F Assembly Dr., Lanham, MD 20706-4391.

INSPEC. *see* ENGINEERING—Abstracting, Bibliographies, Statistics

ISRAEL PHYSICAL SOCIETY. BULLETIN. *see* PHYSICS

539.7 JPN
J A I F ANNUAL CONFERENCE ABSTRACTS. Text in English. 1968. a.
Published by: Japan Atomic Industrial Forum/Nihon Genshiryoku Sangyo Kaigi, Toshin Bldg, 1-1-13 Shinbashi, Minato-ku, Tokyo, 105-0004, Japan.

JOURNAL OF STATISTICAL MECHANICS: THEORY AND EXPERIMENT. *see* PHYSICS—Mechanics

530 016 JPN ISSN 0011-3336
Z7143
KAGAKU GIJUTSU BUNKEN SOKUHO. BUTSURI, OYOBUTSURI-HEN/CURRENT BIBLIOGRAPHY ON SCIENCE AND TECHNOLOGY: PURE AND APPLIED PHYSICS. Text in Japanese. 1959. s-m. JPY 312,480 (effective 2006). index. **Document type:** *Bibliography.*
Related titles: CD-ROM ed.: ISSN 1341-3333. 1995. JPY 240,345 (effective 2006); Online - full text ed.
Published by: Japan Science and Technology Agency/Kagaku Gijutsu Shinko Jigyodan, 5-3, Yonbancho, Chiyoda-ku, Tokyo, Saitama 102-8666, Japan. TEL 81-3-52148401, FAX 81-3-52148400, http://www.jst.go.jp/. Circ: 500.

530 668.4 GBR ISSN 0950-4753
KEY ABSTRACTS - ADVANCED MATERIALS. Text in English. 1987. m. USD 625 in the Americas to institutions (print or online ed.); GBP 365 elsewhere to institutions (print or online ed.); USD 11,275 in the Americas to institutions all 22 Key Abstracts; (print or online ed.); GBP 6,424 elsewhere to institutions all 22 Key Abstracts; (print or online ed.) (effective 2010). index. **Document type:** *Abstract/Index.* **Description:** Covers the preparation, structure, properties and testing of ceramics, refractories, composite materials, polymers and glasses, and porous materials.
Related titles: Online - full text ed.

P

Published by: The Institution of Engineering and Technology, Michael Faraday House, Stevenage, Herts SG1 2AY, United Kingdom. TEL 44-1438-313311, FAX 44-1438-765526, journals@theiet.org.

536.7 GBR ISSN 0953-1262
QC618.S8
KEY ABSTRACTS - HIGH-TEMPERATURE SUPERCONDUCTORS. Text in English. 1989. m. USD 625 in the Americas to institutions (print or online ed.); GBP 365 elsewhere to institutions (print or online ed.); USD 11,275 in the Americas to institutions all 22 Key Abstracts; (print or online ed.); GBP 6,424 elsewhere to institutions all 22 Key Abstracts; (print or online ed.) (effective 2010). **Document type:** *Abstract/Index.*
Related titles: Online - full text ed.
—**CCC.**
Published by: The Institution of Engineering and Technology, Michael Faraday House, Stevenage, Herts SG1 2AY, United Kingdom. TEL 44-1438-313311, FAX 44-1438-765526, journals@theiet.org.

016.62138 GBR ISSN 0950-4826
KEY ABSTRACTS - OPTOELECTRONICS. Text in English. 1975. m. USD 625 in the Americas to institutions (print or online ed.); GBP 365 elsewhere to institutions (print or online ed.); USD 11,275 in the Americas to institutions all 22 Key Abstracts; (print or online ed.); GBP 6,424 elsewhere to institutions all 22 Key Abstracts; (print or online ed.) (effective 2010). index. **Document type:** *Abstract/Index.*
Description: Covers fiberoptics, integrated optoelectronics, electro-optic devices, lasers and their applications, nonlinear optics, and holography.
Supersedes in part (in 1987): Key Abstracts - Solid State Devices (0306-5537)
Related titles: Online - full text ed.
Published by: The Institution of Engineering and Technology, Michael Faraday House, Stevenage, Herts SG1 2AY, United Kingdom. TEL 44-1438-313311, FAX 44-1438-765526, journals@theiet.org.

539.7 USA
MATERIALS AND PLANT PROTECTION. Text in English. 19??. irreg. **Document type:** *Handbook/Manual/Guide, Government.*
Published by: (U.S. Nuclear Regulatory Commission), U.S. Department of Commerce, National Technical Information Service, 5301 Shawnee Rd, Alexandria, VA 22312. TEL 703-605-6000, info@ntis.gov.

620.5 SWE ISSN 2000-5121
T174.7
➤ **NANO REVIEWS.** Text in English. irreg. free (effective 2011). back issues avail. **Document type:** *Journal, Academic/Scholarly.*
Description: Publishes comprehensive and critical review articles in addition to short communications in all areas of nanoscience, nanotechnology, nanobiotechnology, and single-molecules from basic science to applied aspects of chemistry, physics, biology, medicine, and engineering.
Media: Online - full text.
Indexed: A01, T02.
Published by: Co-Action Publishing, Ripvaegen 7, Jaerfaella, 17564, Sweden. TEL 46-18-4951150, FAX 46-18-4951138, info@co-action.net, http://www.co-action.net. Ed. Vasudevanpillai Biju. Pub. Anne Bindslev. Adv. contact Caroline Sutton TEL 46-18-4951126.

536 JPN
NETSU SOKUTEI TORONKAI KOEN YOSHISHU/ABSTRACTS OF JAPANESE CALORIMETRY CONFERENCE. Text in English, Japanese. 1965. a. **Document type:** *Abstract/Index.*
Published by: Nihon Netsu Sokutei Gakkai/Japan Society of Calorimetry and Thermal Analysis, Miyazawa Bldg 601, 1-6-7 Iwamoto-cho, Chiyoda-ku, Tokyo, 101-0032, Japan. FAX 81-3-58217439, netsu@mbd.nifty.com.

535.84 JPN
NIHON BUNKO GAKKAI SHINPOJUMU KOEN YOSHISHU/ SPECTROSCOPICAL SOCIETY OF JAPAN. ABSTRACTS OF SYMPOSIA. Text in English, Japanese. 2/yr. adv. **Document type:** *Abstract/Index.*
Published by: Nihon Bunko Gakkai/Spectroscopical Society of Japan, Clean Bldg, 1-13 Kanda-Awaji-cho, Chiyoda-ku, Tokyo, 101-0063, Japan. http://wwwsoc.nii.ac.jp/spsj/. Ed. Yoshihiro F Mizugai. Adv. contact Kagaku Gijutsu Sha.

532 JPN
NIHON REOROJI GAKKAI NENKAI KOEN YOKOSHU/ABSTRACTS OF ANNUAL MEETING ON RHEOLOGY. Text in Japanese. 1974. a. **Document type:** *Abstract/Index.*
Published by: Nihon Reoroji Gakkai/Society of Rheology, Japan, 3F, Bldg no.6, Kyoto Research Park, 1, Chudoji-Awata, Shimogyo-ku, Kyoto, 600-8815, Japan.

535 JPN
OYO SUPEKUTOROMETORI TOKYO TORONKAI KOEN YOSHISHU/ ABSTRACTS OF PAPERS PRESENTED AT THE TOKYO SYMPOSIA ON THE APPLIED SPECTROMETRY. Text in Japanese. 1965. a. **Document type:** *Abstract/Index.*
Published by: Oyo Butsuri Gakkai Hoshasen Bunkakai/Japan Society of Applied Physics, 1-12-3 Kudan-Kita, Chiyoda-ku, Tokyo, 102-0073, Japan.

530 016 USA ISSN 0094-0003
Z7143 CODEN: PRPIEF
PHYSICAL REVIEW - INDEX. Text in English. a. **Document type:** *Abstract/Index.*
Related titles: Online - full text ed.
—Linda Hall. **CCC.**
Published by: American Physical Society, One Physics Ellipse, College Park, MD 20740. TEL 301-209-3200, FAX 301-209-0865, subs@aps.org, http://www.aps.org. **Subscr. to:** APS Subscription Services, Ste. 1N01, 2 huntington Quadrangle, Melville, NY 11747-4502. TEL 800-344-6902.

530 016 GBR ISSN 0036-8091
QC1 CODEN: PYASAF
PHYSICS ABSTRACTS. Abbreviated title: P A. Variant title: INSPEC Section A. Science Abstracts. Section A. Text in English. 1895. 24/yr. USD 18,410 in the Americas to institutions (print or online ed.); GBP 10,865 elsewhere to institutions (print or online ed.) (effective 2010). abstr.; illus. index, cum.index every 4 yrs. reprints avail. **Document type:** *Abstract/Index.* **Description:** Covers recently published primary research in all areas of physics, including particle, nuclear, atomic, molecular, fluid, plasma and solid-state physics, biophysics, geophysics, astrophysics, measurement, and instrumentation.
Formerly (until 1941): Science Abstracts. Series A. Physics Abstracts (0300-8460); Which superseded in part (in 1903): Science Abstracts (0370-8861); Which was formerly (until 1898): Abstracts of physical Papers from Foreign Sources (0960-1147)
Related titles: CD-ROM ed.; Online - full text ed.
—BLDSC (6477.000000), CASDDS, INIST, Linda Hall. **CCC.**
Published by: The Institution of Engineering and Technology, Michael Faraday House, Stevenage, Herts SG1 2AY, United Kingdom. TEL 44-1438-313311, FAX 44-1438-765526, journals@theiet.org. **US subscr. addr.:** INSPEC, Inc.

539.7 USA ISSN 0360-6309
POWER REACTORS. Text in English. 19??. irreg. **Document type:** *Handbook/Manual/Guide, Government.*
Published by: (U.S. Nuclear Regulatory Commission), U.S. Department of Commerce, National Technical Information Service, 5301 Shawnee Rd, Alexandria, VA 22312. TEL 703-605-6000, info@ntis.gov.

530 IND
RECENT RESEARCH DEVELOPMENTS IN STATISTICAL PHYSICS. Text in English. 2000. a. **Document type:** *Monographic series, Academic/Scholarly.*
Published by: Transworld Research Network, T C 37-661 (2), Fort Post Office, Trivandrum, Kerala 695 023, India. TEL 91-471-2452918, FAX 91-471-2573051, ggcom@vsnl.com, http://www.trnres.com.

016.534 RUS ISSN 0208-1520
REFERATIVNYI ZHURNAL. AKUSTIKA; vypusk svodnogo toma. Text in Russian. 1954. m. USD 345.60 foreign (effective 2011). **Document type:** *Journal, Abstract/Index.*
Related titles: CD-ROM ed.; Online - full text ed.
—East View.
Published by: VINITI RAN, ul Usievicha 20, Moscow, 125190, Russian Federation. TEL 7-499-1526113, FAX 7-499-9430060, dir@viniti.ru, http://www.viniti.ru. **Dist. by:** Informnauka Ltd., Ul Usievicha 20, Moscow 125190, Russian Federation. alfimov@viniti.ru.

016.53 RUS ISSN 0034-2343
CODEN: RZFZAM
REFERATIVNYI ZHURNAL. FIZIKA; svodnyi tom. Text in Russian. 1953. m. USD 4,836 foreign (effective 2011). **Document type:** *Journal, Abstract/Index.*
Related titles: CD-ROM ed.; Online - full text ed.
Indexed: ChemAb.
—CASDDS, East View, Linda Hall. **CCC.**
Published by: VINITI RAN, ul Usievicha 20, Moscow, 125190, Russian Federation. TEL 7-499-1526113, FAX 7-499-9430060, dir@viniti.ru, http://www.viniti.ru. Ed. Boris Kadomtsev. **Dist. by:** Informnauka Ltd., Ul Usievicha 20, Moscow 125190, Russian Federation. alfimov@viniti.ru.

016.53 RUS ISSN 0207-1401
REFERATIVNYI ZHURNAL. FIZIKA ELEMENTARNYKH CHASTITS I TEORIYA POLEI; vypusk svodnogo toma. Text in Russian. 1954. m. USD 1,088.40 foreign (effective 2011). **Document type:** *Journal, Abstract/Index.*
Related titles: CD-ROM ed.; Online - full text ed.
—East View.
Published by: VINITI RAN, ul Usievicha 20, Moscow, 125190, Russian Federation. TEL 7-499-1526113, FAX 7-499-9430060, dir@viniti.ru, http://www.viniti.ru. **Dist. by:** Informnauka Ltd., Ul Usievicha 20, Moscow 125190, Russian Federation. alfimov@viniti.ru.

016.53 RUS ISSN 0203-6002
REFERATIVNYI ZHURNAL. FIZIKA GAZOV I ZHIDKOSTEI: TERMODINAMIKA I STATISTICHESKAYA FIZIKA; vypusk svodnogo toma. Text in Russian. 1958. m. USD 541.20 foreign (effective 2011). **Document type:** *Journal, Abstract/Index.*
Related titles: CD-ROM ed.; Online - full text ed.
—East View.
Published by: VINITI RAN, ul Usievicha 20, Moscow, 125190, Russian Federation. TEL 7-499-1526113, FAX 7-499-9430060, dir@viniti.ru, http://www.viniti.ru. **Dist. by:** Informnauka Ltd., Ul Usievicha 20, Moscow 125190, Russian Federation. alfimov@viniti.ru.

016.53 RUS
▼ **REFERATIVNYI ZHURNAL. FIZIKA NANOOB'EKTOV I NANOTEKHNOLOGIYA**; vypusk svodnogo toma. Text in Russian. 2009. m. USD 1,070.40 foreign (effective 2011). **Document type:** *Journal, Abstract/Index.*
Related titles: CD-ROM ed.; Online - full text ed.
Published by: VINITI RAN, ul Usievicha 20, Moscow, 125190, Russian Federation. TEL 7-499-1526113, FAX 7-499-9430060, dir@viniti.ru, http://www.viniti.ru.

016.53044 RUS ISSN 0203-6010
REFERATIVNYI ZHURNAL. FIZIKA PLAZMY; vypusk svodnogo toma. Text in Russian. 1954. m. USD 620.40 foreign (effective 2011). **Document type:** *Journal, Abstract/Index.*
Related titles: CD-ROM ed.; Online - full text ed.
—East View.
Published by: VINITI RAN, ul Usievicha 20, Moscow, 125190, Russian Federation. TEL 7-499-1526113, FAX 7-499-9430060, dir@viniti.ru, http://www.viniti.ru. **Dist. by:** Informnauka Ltd., Ul Usievicha 20, Moscow 125190, Russian Federation. alfimov@viniti.ru.

016.53 RUS ISSN 0235-8867
REFERATIVNYI ZHURNAL. FIZIKA TVERDYKH TEL: ELEKTRICHESKIE SVOISTVA; vypusk svodnogo toma. Text in Russian. 1954. m. USD 855.60 foreign (effective 2011). **Document type:** *Journal, Abstract/Index.*
Related titles: CD-ROM ed.; Online - full text ed.
—East View.
Published by: VINITI RAN, ul Usievicha 20, Moscow, 125190, Russian Federation. TEL 7-499-1526113, FAX 7-499-9430060, dir@viniti.ru, http://www.viniti.ru. **Dist. by:** Informnauka Ltd., Ul Usievicha 20, Moscow 125190, Russian Federation. alfimov@viniti.ru.

016.538 RUS ISSN 0235-8859
REFERATIVNYI ZHURNAL. FIZIKA TVERDYKH TEL: MAGNITNYE SVOISTVA; vypusk svodnogo toma. Text in Russian. 1954. m. USD 432 foreign (effective 2011). **Document type:** *Journal, Abstract/Index.*
Related titles: CD-ROM ed.; Online - full text ed.
—East View.
Published by: VINITI RAN, ul Usievicha 20, Moscow, 125190, Russian Federation. TEL 7-499-1526113, FAX 7-499-9430060, dir@viniti.ru, http://www.viniti.ru. **Dist. by:** Informnauka Ltd., Ul Usievicha 20, Moscow 125190, Russian Federation. alfimov@viniti.ru.

016.53 RUS ISSN 0208-1679
REFERATIVNYI ZHURNAL. FIZIKA TVERDYKH TEL: STRUKTURA I DINAMIKA RESHETKI; vypusk svodnogo toma. Text in Russian. 1954. m. USD 1,189.20 foreign (effective 2011). **Document type:** *Journal, Abstract/Index.*
Related titles: CD-ROM ed.; Online - full text ed.
Published by: VINITI RAN, ul Usievicha 20, Moscow, 125190, Russian Federation. TEL 7-499-1526113, FAX 7-499-9430060, dir@viniti.ru, http://www.viniti.ru. **Dist. by:** Informnauka Ltd., Ul Usievicha 20, Moscow 125190, Russian Federation. alfimov@viniti.ru.

016.531 RUS ISSN 0203-5146
REFERATIVNYI ZHURNAL. KOMPLEKSNYE I SPETSYAL'NYE RAZDELY MEKHANIKI; vypusk svodnogo toma. Text in Russian. 1953. m. USD 759.60 foreign (effective 2011). **Document type:** *Journal, Abstract/Index.*
Related titles: CD-ROM ed.; Online - full text ed.
—East View.
Published by: VINITI RAN, ul Usievicha 20, Moscow, 125190, Russian Federation. TEL 7-499-1526113, FAX 7-499-9430060, dir@viniti.ru, http://www.viniti.ru. **Dist. by:** Informnauka Ltd., Ul Usievicha 20, Moscow 125190, Russian Federation. alfimov@viniti.ru.

016.53 016.6213 RUS ISSN 0235-215X
REFERATIVNYI ZHURNAL. KVANTOVAYA ELEKTRONIKA. KRIOELEKTRONIKA. GOLOGRAFIYA; vypusk svodnogo toma. Text in Russian. 1955. m. USD 535.20 foreign (effective 2011). **Document type:** *Journal, Abstract/Index.*
Related titles: CD-ROM ed.; Online - full text ed.
—East View.
Published by: VINITI RAN, ul Usievicha 20, Moscow, 125190, Russian Federation. TEL 7-499-1526113, FAX 7-499-9430060, dir@viniti.ru, http://www.viniti.ru. Ed. Yurii Arskii. **Dist. by:** Informnauka Ltd., Ul Usievicha 20, Moscow 125190, Russian Federation. alfimov@viniti.ru.

016.531 RUS ISSN 0202-9693
REFERATIVNYI ZHURNAL. MEKHANIKA DEFORMIRUEMOGO TVERDOGO TELA; vypusk svodnogo toma. Text in Russian. 1953. m. USD 686.40 foreign (effective 2011). **Document type:** *Journal, Abstract/Index.*
Related titles: CD-ROM ed.; Online - full text ed.
—East View.
Published by: VINITI RAN, ul Usievicha 20, Moscow, 125190, Russian Federation. TEL 7-499-1526113, FAX 7-499-9430060, dir@viniti.ru, http://www.viniti.ru. **Dist. by:** Informnauka Ltd., Ul Usievicha 20, Moscow 125190, Russian Federation. alfimov@viniti.ru.

016.531 RUS ISSN 0202-9707
REFERATIVNYI ZHURNAL. MEKHANIKA ZHIDKOSTI I GAZA; vypusk svodnogo toma. Text in Russian. 1953. m. USD 661.20 foreign (effective 2011). **Document type:** *Journal, Abstract/Index.*
Related titles: CD-ROM ed.; Online - full text ed.
—East View.
Published by: VINITI RAN, ul Usievicha 20, Moscow, 125190, Russian Federation. TEL 7-499-1526113, FAX 7-499-9430060, dir@viniti.ru, http://www.viniti.ru. **Dist. by:** Informnauka Ltd., Ul Usievicha 20, Moscow 125190, Russian Federation. alfimov@viniti.ru.

016.53 RUS ISSN 0207-138X
REFERATIVNYI ZHURNAL. OBSHCHIE VOPROSY FIZIKI I FIZICHESKOGO EKSPERIMENTA; vypusk svodnogo toma. Text in Russian. 1954. m. USD 354 foreign (effective 2011). **Document type:** *Journal, Abstract/Index.*
Related titles: CD-ROM ed.; Online - full text ed.
—East View.
Published by: VINITI RAN, ul Usievicha 20, Moscow, 125190, Russian Federation. TEL 7-499-1526113, FAX 7-499-9430060, dir@viniti.ru, http://www.viniti.ru. **Dist. by:** Informnauka Ltd., Ul Usievicha 20, Moscow 125190, Russian Federation. alfimov@viniti.ru.

016.531 RUS ISSN 0202-9715
REFERATIVNYI ZHURNAL. OBSHCHIE VOPROSY MEKHANIKI. OBSHCHAYA MEKHANIKA; vypusk svodnogo toma. Text in Russian. 1953. m. USD 181.20 foreign (effective 2011). **Document type:** *Journal, Abstract/Index.*
Related titles: CD-ROM ed.; Online - full text ed.
—East View.
Published by: VINITI RAN, ul Usievicha 20, Moscow, 125190, Russian Federation. TEL 7-499-1526113, FAX 7-499-9430060, dir@viniti.ru, http://www.viniti.ru. **Dist. by:** Informnauka Ltd., Ul Usievicha 20, Moscow 125190, Russian Federation. alfimov@viniti.ru.

016.53584 RUS ISSN 0235-8875
REFERATIVNYI ZHURNAL. OPTIKA I YADERNAYA FIZIKA; vypusk svodnogo toma. Text in Russian. 1954. m. USD 1,438.80 foreign (effective 2011). **Document type:** *Journal, Abstract/Index.*
Related titles: CD-ROM ed.; Online - full text ed.
—East View.
Published by: VINITI RAN, ul Usievicha 20, Moscow, 125190, Russian Federation. TEL 7-499-1526113, FAX 7-499-9430060, dir@viniti.ru, http://www.viniti.ru. **Dist. by:** Informnauka Ltd., Ul Usievicha 20, Moscow 125190, Russian Federation. alfimov@viniti.ru.

016.53 RUS ISSN 0202-9979
REFERATIVNYI ZHURNAL. RADIOFIZIKA I FIZICHESKIE OSNOVY ELEKTRONIKI; vypusk svodnogo toma. Text in Russian. 1954. m. USD 627.80 foreign (effective 2011). **Document type:** *Journal, Abstract/Index.*
Related titles: CD-ROM ed.; Online - full text ed.
—East View.
Published by: VINITI RAN, ul Usievicha 20, Moscow, 125190, Russian Federation. TEL 7-499-1526113, FAX 7-499-9430060, dir@viniti.ru, http://www.viniti.ru. **Dist. by:** Informnauka Ltd., Ul Usievicha 20, Moscow 125190, Russian Federation. alfimov@viniti.ru.

016.53 RUS
▼ **REFERATIVNYI ZHURNAL. SPINTRONIKA**; vypusk svodnogo toma. Text in Russian. 2009 (Jan.). m. USD 339.60 foreign (effective 2011). **Document type:** *Journal, Abstract/Index.*
Related titles: CD-ROM ed.; Online - full text ed.
Published by: VINITI RAN, ul Usievicha 20, Moscow, 125190, Russian Federation. TEL 7-499-1526113, FAX 7-499-9430060, dir@viniti.ru, http://www.viniti.ru.

016.538 RUS ISSN 0235-6856
REFERATIVNYI ZHURNAL. SVERKHPROVODIMOST'; vypusk svodnogo toma. Text in Russian. 1989. m. USD 684 foreign (effective 2011). **Document type:** *Journal, Abstract/Index.*

Formerly (until 1990): Referativnyi Zhurnal. Sverkhprovodimost' s Ponomernym Avtorskim Ukazatelem, Ukazatelem Istochnikov (0235-6015)
Related titles: CD-ROM ed.; Online - full text ed.
—East View.
Published by: VINITI RAN, ul Usievicha 20, Moscow, 125190, Russian Federation. TEL 7-499-1526113, FAX 7-499-9430060, dir@viniti.ru, http://www.viniti.ru. **Dist. by:** Informnauka Ltd., Ul Usievicha 20, Moscow 125190, Russian Federation. alfimov@viniti.ru.

016.535 RUS
REFERATIVNYI ZHURNAL. VOLOKONNO-OPTICHESKAYA SVYAZ'; vypusk svodnogo toma. Text in Russian. 1987. m. USD 276 foreign (effective 2011). **Document type:** *Journal, Abstract/Index.*
Formerly: Referativnyi Zhurnal. Volokonno-Opticheskie Systemy (0234-9647)
Related titles: CD-ROM ed.; Online - full text ed.
—East View.
Published by: VINITI RAN, ul Usievicha 20, Moscow, 125190, Russian Federation. TEL 7-499-1526113, FAX 7-499-9430060, dir@viniti.ru. Ed. Yurii Arskii. **Dist. by:** Informnauka Ltd., Ul Usievicha 20, Moscow 125190, Russian Federation. alfimov@viniti.ru.

016.539 RUS ISSN 0203-6037
REFERATIVNYI ZHURNAL. YADERNAYA FIZIKA I FIZIKA YADERNYKH REAKTOROV; vypusk svodnogo toma. Text in Russian. 1953. m. USD 994.80 foreign (effective 2011). **Document type:** *Journal, Abstract/Index.*
Related titles: CD-ROM ed.; Online - full text ed.
—East View.
Published by: VINITI RAN, ul Usievicha 20, Moscow, 125190, Russian Federation. TEL 7-499-1526113, FAX 7-499-9430060, dir@viniti.ru, http://www.viniti.ru. **Dist. by:** Informnauka Ltd., Ul Usievicha 20, Moscow 125190, Russian Federation. alfimov@viniti.ru.

531 JPN
REOROJI TORONKAI KOEN YOSHISHU/ABSTRACTS OF SYMPOSIUM ON RHEOLOGY. Text in English, Japanese. 1952. a. **Document type:** *Abstract/Index.*
Published by: Nihon Reoroji Gakkai/Society of Rheology, Japan, 3F, Bldg no.6, Kyoto Research Park, 1, Chudoji-Awata, Shimogyo-ku, Kyoto, 600-8815, Japan.

535 JPN ISSN 0913-6355
REZA GAKKAI GAKUJUTSU KOENKAI NENJI TAIKAI KOEN YOKOSHU/LASER SOCIETY OF JAPAN. ANNUAL MEETING. DIGEST OF TECHNICAL PAPERS. Text in English, Japanese. 1981. a.
Published by: Reza Gakkai/Laser Society of Japan, 2-6 Yamada-Oka, Suita, Osaka 565-0871, Japan. TEL 81-6-68783070, FAX 81-6-68783088, http://wwwsoc.nii.ac.jp/lsj/.

016.535 JPN
REZA KAGAKU/ABSTRACTS OF RIKEN SYMPOSIUM ON LASER SCIENCE. Text in English, Japanese. a. **Document type:** *Abstract/Index.*
Indexed: ChemAb, ChemTitl.
Published by: (Reza Kagaku Kenkyu Gurupu), Institute of Physical and Chemical Research, Laser Science Group/Reza Kagaku Kenkyu Gurupu, Irikagaku Kenkyujo, 2-1 Hirosawa, Wako-shi, Saitama-ken 351-0198, Japan. TEL 81-48-462-1111, FAX 81-48-462-4714.

532 016 GBR ISSN 0035-452X
QC189 CODEN: RHABA3
RHEOLOGY ABSTRACTS. Text in English. 1958. q. free to members (effective 2009). adv. bk.rev. reprints avail. **Document type:** *Abstract/Index.* **Description:** Covers all papers describing work within the science of rheology, the study of deformation and flow.
Supersedes in part (in 19??): British Society of Rheology. Bulletin; Which was formerly (1946-1950): British Rheologists Club. Bulletin
Related titles: Microfilm ed.: 1958 (from PQC); Online - full text ed.; ♦ Supplement(s): Rheology Bulletin. ISSN 1469-4999.
—Linda Hall.
Published by: British Society of Rheology, c o Dr Oliver Guy Harlen, School of Mathematics, University of Leeds, Leeds, LS2 9JT, United Kingdom. TEL 44-1133-435189, FAX 44-1133-435090, oliver@maths.leeds.ac.uk. Ed. Dr. Nick Hudson TEL 44-141-5482162. Circ: 1,300.

530 540 JPN ISSN 0557-0220
QC1
RIKAGAKU KENKYUJO KENKYU NENPO/I P C R ANNUAL REPORTS OF RESEARCH ACTIVITIES. Text in Japanese. 1964. a. abstr. **Document type:** *Directory, Academic/Scholarly.*
Indexed: INIS AtomInd.
—Linda Hall.
Published by: Rikagaku Kenkyusho/Institute of Physical and Chemical Research, 2-1 Hirosawa, Wako shi, Saitama ken 3510106, Japan. TEL 81-48-462-1111, FAX 81-48-462-4714.

530 540 JPN ISSN 0916-619X
RIKEN NYUSU/RIKEN NEWS. Text in Japanese. 1968. m. **Document type:** *Academic/Scholarly.* **Description:** Contains information on current research.
Formerly (until 1989): Rikagaku Kenkyujo Nyusu (0285-6611)
Published by: Institute of Physical and Chemical Research/Rikagaku Kenkyujo, 2-1 Hirosawa, Wako, Saitama 351-0198, Japan. TEL 81-48-4621111, FAX 81-48-4621554.

531 016 USA ISSN 0896-5900
TK7800 CODEN: SSABER
SOLID STATE AND SUPERCONDUCTIVITY ABSTRACTS. Text in English. 1957. q. (plus a. index CD). USD 2,345 combined subscription (includes a. cum. index on CD-ROM) (effective 2011). bk.rev. abstr.; bibl. Index. back issues avail. **Document type:** *Abstract/Index.* **Description:** Covers theory, production and application of solid state materials, with emphasis on superconductivity.
Former titles: Solid State Abstracts Journal; Solid State Abstracts (0038-108X); Incorporates: Science Research Abstracts Journal. Laser and Electro-Optic Reviews, Quantum Electronics, Unconventional Energy Sources; Science Research Abstracts Journal. Superconductivity, Magnetohydrodynamics and Plasma, Theoretical Physics (0361-3321); Which was formerly: Science Research Abstracts, Part A. MHD and Plasma, Superconductivity and Research, and Theoretical Physics; Which incorporated: Theoretical Physics Journal (0049-3678)
—Linda Hall.
Published by: ProQuest LLC (Bethesda) (Subsidiary of: Cambridge Information Group), 7200 Wisconsin Ave, Ste 715, Bethesda, MD 20814. TEL 301-961-6798, 800-843-7751, FAX 301-961-6799, journals@csa.com. Ed. Evelyn Beck. Pub. Ted Caris. **Co-publisher:** Elsevier Engineering Information, Inc.

539.7 USA
TRANSPORTATION (ALEXANDRIA). Text in English. 19??. irreg. price varies. back issues avail. **Document type:** *Report, Government.*
Indexed: EIA, EnvAb.
Published by: (U.S. Nuclear Regulatory Commission), U.S. Department of Commerce, National Technical Information Service, 5301 Shawnee Rd, Alexandria, VA 22312. TEL 703-605-6000, info@ntis.gov, http://www.ntis.gov.

539.7 USA
U S NUCLEAR REGULATORY COMMISSION REGULATORY GUIDE SERIES: DIVISION 10 - GENERAL. Text in English. 19??. irreg. back issues avail. **Document type:** *Monographic series, Government.*
Related titles: Online - full text ed.: free (effective 2011).
Published by: (U.S. Nuclear Regulatory Commission), U.S. Department of Commerce, National Technical Information Service, 5301 Shawnee Rd, Alexandria, VA 22312. TEL 703-605-6000, 800-553-6847, info@ntis.gov, http://www.ntis.gov.

535.84 CHN ISSN 1004-8073
ZHONGGUO GUANGXUE YU YINGYONG GUANGXUE WENZHAI/ CHINESE OPTICS AND APPLIED OPTICS ABSTRACTS. Text in Chinese. 1985. bi-m. USD 53.40 (effective 2009). **Document type:** *Journal, Academic/Scholarly.*
Related titles: Online - full text ed.
—BLDSC (9512.734262), East View.
Published by: Zhongguo Kexueyuan Changchun Guangxue Jingmei Jijie Yanjiusuo/Chinese Academy of Sciences, Changchun Institute of Optics, Fine Mechanics and Physics, 140 Renming Street, PO Box 1024, Changchun, 130022, China. TEL 86-481-6176853, FAX 86-431-5682346, ciomp@ciomp.ac.cn, http://www.ciomp.ac.cn:8111/welcome.htm. Circ: 50,000.

530 CHN ISSN 1000-8802
ZHONGGUO WULI WENZHAI/CHINESE PHYSICS ABSTRACTS. Text in Chinese. 1986. bi-m. USD 312. **Document type:** *Abstract/Index.*
Published by: Zhongguo Kexueyuan Wenxian Qingbao Zhongxin/ Chinese Academy of Sciences, Documentation and Information Center, 8 Kexueyuan Nanlu, Zhongguancun, Beijing, 100080, China. TEL 86-1-6256-2547, FAX 86-1-6256-6846. Ed. Liu Zaili. Circ: 2,000. **Dist. by:** China International Book Trading Corp, 35 Chegongzhuang Xilu, Haidian District, PO Box 399, Beijing 100044, China. TEL 86-10-68412045, FAX 86-10-68412023, cibtc@mail.cibtc.com.cn, http://www.cibtc.com.cn.

PHYSICS—Computer Applications

APPLIED COMPUTATIONAL ELECTROMAGNETICS SOCIETY. JOURNAL. *see* PHYSICS—Electricity

APPLIED COMPUTATIONAL ELECTROMAGNETICS SOCIETY. NEWSLETTER (ONLINE). *see* PHYSICS—Electricity

530.285 HKG ISSN 1815-2406
QC19.2
➤ **COMMUNICATIONS IN COMPUTATIONAL PHYSICS.** Text in English. 19??. q. USD 500 combined subscription print & online eds. (effective 2007). **Document type:** *Journal, Academic/Scholarly.*
Related titles: Online - full text ed.: ISSN 1991-7120. 2006. USD 420 (effective 2007).
Indexed: A28, APA, BrCerAb, C&ISA, CA/WCA, CCMJ, CIA, CerAb, CivEngAb, CorrAb, CurCont, E&CAJ, E11, EEA, EMA, H15, M&TEA, M09, MBF, METADEX, MSN, MathR, P30, SCI, SCOPUS, SolStAb, T04, W07, WAA, Z02.
—BLDSC (3359.543000), IE.
Published by: Global Science Press, Rm 2303, Office Tower Convention Plaza, 1 Harbour Rd, Wanchai, Hong Kong, Hong Kong. TEL 852-2911-1267, FAX 852-2911-1200, info@global-sci.org, http://www.global-sci.org. Ed. Xian-Tu He.

➤ **COMPLEX SYSTEMS.** *see* MATHEMATICS—Computer Applications

530.285 NLD ISSN 0010-4655
QC52 CODEN: CPHCBZ
➤ **COMPUTER PHYSICS COMMUNICATIONS.** Text in English. 1969. 12/yr. EUR 6,702 in Europe to institutions; JPY 889,900 in Japan to institutions; USD 7,533 elsewhere to institutions (effective 2012). adv. bk.rev.; software rev. charts; illus. Index. back issues avail.; reprints avail. **Document type:** *Journal, Academic/Scholarly.* **Description:** Publishes research papers in computational physics and physical chemistry, and closely related areas in computational science, computer programs, review articles on selected topics, proceedings of topical conferences in the field, thematic issues, and comments on previous publications in the journal.
Related titles: CD-ROM ed.: Computer Physics Communications Program Library. ISSN 1386-9485. EUR 6,444 in Europe to institutions; JPY 855,700 in Japan to institutions; USD 7,243 elsewhere to institutions (effective 2009); Online - full text ed.: ISSN 1879-2944 (from IngentaConnect, ScienceDirect).
Indexed: A01, A03, A08, A22, A26, A28, APA, ASCA, BrCerAb, C&ISA, C10, C33, CA, CA/WCA, CCMJ, CIA, CIN, CIS, CMCI, CPEI, CerAb, ChemAb, ChemTitl, CivEngAb, CompAb, CompLI, CompR, CorrAb, CurCont, CybAb, E&CAJ, E11, EEA, EMA, ESPM, EngInd, EnvEAb, GeoRef, H15, I05, ISMEC, ISR, Inspec, M&TEA, M09, MBF, METADEX, MSN, MathR, P30, PhysBer, RefZh, S01, SCI, SCOPUS, SolStAb, SpeleolAb, T02, T04, W07, WAA, Z02.
—BLDSC (3394.150000), AskIEEE, CASDDS, IE, Infotrieve, Ingenta, INIST, Linda Hall. **CCC.**
Published by: Elsevier BV, North-Holland (Subsidiary of: Elsevier Science & Technology), Sara Burgerhartstraat 25, Amsterdam, 1055 KV, Netherlands. TEL 31-20-4853911, FAX 31-20-4852457, JournalsCustomerServiceEMEA@elsevier.com, http://www.elsevier.nl/homepage/about/us/regional_sites.htt. **Subscr. to:** Elsevier BV, Radarweg 29, PO Box 211, Amsterdam 1000 AE, Netherlands. TEL 31-20-4853757, FAX 31-20-4853432.

530.285 USA ISSN 1521-9615
Q183.9 CODEN: CSENFA
➤ **COMPUTING IN SCIENCE & ENGINEERING;** the bimonthly magazine of computational tools and method. Abbreviated title: C i S E. Text in English. 1999. bi-m. USD 710; USD 830 combined subscription (print & online eds.) (effective 2012). adv. back issues avail.; reprints avail. **Document type:** *Journal, Academic/Scholarly.*
Formed by the merger of (1987-1999): Computers in Physics (0894-1866); (1984-1999): I E E E Computational Science and Engineering (1070-9924)
Related titles: Online - full text ed.: ISSN 1558-366X. USD 645 (effective 2012).
Indexed: A05, A20, A22, A28, APA, AS&TA, AS&TI, B04, BiolDig, BrCerAb, C&ISA, C10, CA, CA/WCA, CIA, CMCI, CPEI, CPI, CerAb, CivEngAb, CompAb, CompLI, CompR, CorrAb, CurCont, E&CAJ, E11, EEA, EMA, ESPM, EngInd, EnvEAb, GeoRef, H15, Inspec, M&TEA, M09, MBF, METADEX, P30, RefZh, SCI, SCOPUS, SPINweb, SolStAb, T02, T04, TM, W07, WAA.
—BLDSC (3395.126500), IE, Infotrieve, Ingenta, INIST, Linda Hall. **CCC.**
Published by: American Institute of Physics, 1 Physics Ellipse, College Park, MD 20740. TEL 301-209-3100, aipinfo@aip.org, http://www.aip.org. Ed. Isabel Beichl. Adv. contact Marian Anderson. **Subscr. to:** PO Box 503284, St Louis, MO 63150. TEL 516-576-2270, 800-344-6902, FAX 516-349-9704, subs@aip.org, http://librarians.aip.org. **Co-publisher:** I E E E.

530.285 SGP ISSN 0218-396X
TA365 CODEN: JCOAEJ
➤ **JOURNAL OF COMPUTATIONAL ACOUSTICS.** Abbreviated title: J C A. Text in English. 1993. q. SGD 1,223, USD 745, EUR 638 combined subscription to institutions (print & online eds.) (effective 2012). adv. bk.rev. back issues avail. **Document type:** *Journal, Academic/Scholarly.* **Description:** Provides a forum for the dissemination of information in the field of computational acoustics.
Related titles: Online - full text ed.: ISSN 1793-6489. SGD 1,112, USD 677, EUR 580 to institutions (effective 2012).
Indexed: A01, A03, A08, A10, A22, ASFA, ApMecR, C10, C23, CA, CCMJ, CMCI, CompLI, CurCont, E01, ISR, Inspec, M&GPA, MSN, MathR, OceAb, S01, SCI, SCOPUS, T02, TM, V03, W07, Z02.
—BLDSC (4963.440000), AskIEEE, IE, Ingenta. **CCC.**
Published by: (International Association for Mathematics and Computers in Simulation USA), World Scientific Publishing Co. Pte. Ltd., 5 Toh Tuck Link, Singapore, 596224, Singapore. TEL 65-6466-5775, FAX 65-6467-7667, wspc@wspc.com.sg, http://www.worldscientific.com. Eds. Chin-Sang Chiu, D Lee TEL 352-674-9350, Michael J Buckingham. **Dist. by:** World Scientific Publishing Co., Inc., 27 Warren St, Ste 401-402, Hackensack, NJ 07601. TEL 201-487-9655, 800-227-7562, FAX 201-487-9656, 888-977-2665, wspc@wspc.com; World Scientific Publishing Ltd., 57 Shelton St, London WC2H 9HE, United Kingdom. TEL 44-207-8360888, FAX 44-207-8362020, sales@wspc.co.uk.

P

530 USA ISSN 0021-9991
QC20 CODEN: JCTPAH
➤ **JOURNAL OF COMPUTATIONAL PHYSICS.** Text in English. 1966. 24/yr. EUR 7,846 in Europe to institutions; JPY 819,200 in Japan to institutions; USD 6,215 elsewhere to institutions (effective 2012). adv. abstr.; charts; illus. index. back issues avail.; reprints avail. **Document type:** *Journal, Academic/Scholarly.* **Description:** Covers the computational aspects of physical problems.
Related titles: Online - full text ed.: ISSN 1090-2716 (from IngentaConnect, ScienceDirect).
Indexed: A01, A03, A08, A22, A26, A28, APA, ASCA, ASFA, ApMecR, BMT, BrCerAb, C&ISA, CA, CA/WCA, CCMJ, CIA, CIN, CMCI, CerAb, ChemAb, ChemTitl, CivEngAb, CompR, CorrAb, CurCont, E&CAJ, E01, E11, EEA, EMA, ESPM, EnvEAb, GeoRef, H15, I05, IBR, IBZ, INIS AtomInd, ISR, Inspec, M&GPA, M&TEA, M09, MBF, METADEX, MSN, MathR, P30, PhysBer, RefZh, S01, SCI, SCOPUS, SolStAb, SpeleolAb, T02, T04, W07, WAA, Z02.
—BLDSC (4963.500000), AskIEEE, CASDDS, IE, Infotrieve, Ingenta, INIST, Linda Hall. **CCC.**
Published by: Academic Press (Subsidiary of: Elsevier Science & Technology), 3251 Riverport Ln, Maryland Heights, MO 63043. TEL 314-447-8010, FAX 314-447-8030, JournalCustomerService-usa@elsevier.com, http://www.elsevierdirect.com/imprint.jsp?iid=5. Ed. G Tryggvason.

627 GBR ISSN 1468-4349
QC150 CODEN: PCFDAB
➤ **PROGRESS IN COMPUTATIONAL FLUID DYNAMICS;** an international journal. Abbreviated title: P C F D. Text in English. 2001. 6/yr. EUR 593 to institutions (print or online ed.); EUR 830 combined subscription to institutions (print & online eds.) (effective 2012). bk.rev. charts; illus.; abstr.; bibl.; stat. **Document type:** *Journal, Academic/Scholarly.* **Description:** Provides an international forum and refereed authoritative source of information in the field of computational fluid dynamics.
Related titles: Online - full text ed.: ISSN 1741-5233 (from IngentaConnect).
Indexed: A26, A28, A37, APA, ApMecR, B02, B15, B17, B18, BA, BrCerAb, C&ISA, C23, CA, CA/WCA, CABA, CCMJ, CIA, CPEI, CerAb, CivEngAb, CorrAb, CurCont, E&CAJ, E08, E11, E12, EEA, EMA, ESPM, EngInd, EnvEAb, F08, F11, FLUIDEX, G04, G08, GH, H15, I05, ICEA, Inspec, M&GPA, M&TEA, M09, MBF, METADEX, MSN, MathR, S09, S13, S16, SCI, SCOPUS, SolStAb, T02, T04, W07, WAA, Z02.
—BLDSC (6867.822000), IE, Ingenta, INIST, Linda Hall. **CCC.**
Published by: Inderscience Publishers, PO Box 735, Olney, Bucks MK46 5WB, United Kingdom. TEL 44-1234-240519, FAX 44-1234-240515, editorial@inderscience.com. Ed. Dr. M A Dorgham. **Subscr. to:** World Trade Centre Bldg, 29 Rte de Pre-Bois, Case Postale 856, Geneva 15 1215, Switzerland. FAX 41-22-7910885, subs@inderscience.com.

530 NLD ISSN 1879-4661
▼ **PROGRESS IN COMPUTATIONAL PHYSICS.** Variant title: P i C P. Text in English. 2010. irreg. **Document type:** *Monographic series, Academic/Scholarly.* **Description:** Focuses on interdisciplinary computational perspectives of current physical challenges, new numerical techniques for the solution of mathematical wave equations and describes certain real-world applications.
Media: Online - full text.
Published by: Bentham Science Publishers Ltd., PO Box 294, Bussum, 1400 AG, Netherlands. TEL 31-35-6923800, FAX 31-35-6980150, sales@bentham.org, http://www.bentham.org. Ed. Matthias Ehrhardt.

534 SGP
➤ **THEORETICAL AND COMPUTATIONAL ACOUSTICS.** Variant title: I M A C S Symposium on Theoretical Computational Acoustics. Proceedings(International Association for Mathematics and Computers in Simulation). Text in English. 1986. irreg. (approx biennial), latest 2005. price varies. back issues avail. **Document type:** *Proceedings, Academic/Scholarly.*
Formerly: Computational Acoustics
Related titles: Online - full text ed.
Published by: (International Association for Mathematics and Computers in Simulation USA), World Scientific Publishing Co. Pte. Ltd., 5 Toh Tuck Link, Singapore, 596224, Singapore. wspc@wspc.com.sg, http://www.worldscientific.com. **Dist. by:** World Scientific Publishing Ltd., 57 Shelton St, London WC2H 9HE, United Kingdom.

530.285 USA ISSN 1553-961X
QA76.889
➤ **VIRTUAL JOURNAL OF QUANTUM INFORMATION.** Text in English. 2001. m. back issues avail. **Document type:** *Journal, Academic/Scholarly.* **Description:** Covers a number of contemporary topical areas in quantum information, including quantum computing, cryptography, error correction, and theoretical and experimental investigations of entanglement.
Media: Online - full text.
Published by: (American Institute of Physics), American Physical Society, One Physics Ellipse, College Park, MD 20740. TEL 301-209-3200, FAX 301-209-0865, help@aps.org, http://www.aps.org. Ed. David DiVincenzo.

➤ **WINDOWS ON ACOUSTICS.** *see* PHYSICS—Sound

PHYSICS—Electricity

537 SGP ISSN 1365-9200
A E S I E A P GOLDBOOK (YEAR). (Association of the Electricity Supply Industry of East Asia and the Western Pacific) Text in English. 1997. a. **Document type:** *Handbook/Manual/Guide, Trade.* **Description:** A desktop reference guide on the Electricity Industry in the Asia-Pacific region covering the latest market trends and detailed regional overview of the power industry. Contains country snapshots providing visual statistics at a glance, easy to read articles on finance, risk, tariff, fuels, privatization and deregulation. Updated company directory featuring only those companies which are active in the region; and a section with a full utility website directory.
Related titles: Online - full text ed.
Published by: (A E S I E A P TWN), Charlton Media Group, 15B Stanley St, Singapore, 068734, Singapore. TEL 65-6223-7660, FAX 65 6223 0132, abf@charltonmedia.com, http://www.charltonmedia.com/. Ed., Pub. Timothy Charlton.

537 USA ISSN 1941-420X
A P L: ORGANIC ELECTRONICS AND PHOTONICS. (Applied Physics Letters) Text in English. 198?. m. free (effective 2010). back issues avail. **Document type:** *Journal, Academic/Scholarly.*
Media: Online - full text.
—CCC.
Published by: American Institute of Physics, 1 Physics Ellipse, College Park, MD 20740. TEL 301-209-3100, FAX 301-209-0843, aipinfo@aip.org, http://www.aip.org. Ed. Nghi Q Lam TEL 630-252-4200.

537 530 USA ISSN 1054-4887
QC759.6 CODEN: JCSOED
➤ **APPLIED COMPUTATIONAL ELECTROMAGNETICS SOCIETY. JOURNAL.** Abbreviated title: A C E S Journal. Text in English. 1986. bi-m. free to members (effective 2010). index, cum.index: 1986-1991. back issues avail.; reprints avail. **Document type:** *Journal, Academic/Scholarly.* **Description:** Features publication of unsuccessful efforts in applied computational electromagnetics.
Supersedes in part (in 1989): Applied Computational Electromagnetics Society. Journal and Newsletter
Related titles: Online - full text ed.: ISSN 1943-5711.
Indexed: A01, CPEI, CurCont, EngInd, FR, GeoRef, Inspec, SCI, SCOPUS, W07.
—BLDSC (1571.936900), AskIEEE, IE, Ingenta, Linda Hall.
Published by: Applied Computational Electromagnetics Society, Inc., c/o Osama Mohammed, ECE Department, Florida International University, 10555 W Flagler St, EAS-3983, Miami, FL 33174. TEL 305-348-3040, mohammed@fiu.edu. Ed. Atef Elsherbeni TEL 662-915-5382.

537 530 USA ISSN 1943-5738
APPLIED COMPUTATIONAL ELECTROMAGNETICS SOCIETY. NEWSLETTER (ONLINE). Text in English. 1986. s-a. free to members (effective 2010). back issues avail. **Document type:** *Newsletter, Trade.* **Description:** Covers membership informed activities of the ACES.
Media: Online - full text.
Published by: Applied Computational Electromagnetics Society, Inc., c/o Osama Mohammed, ECE Department, Florida International University, 10555 W Flagler St, EAS-3983, Miami, FL 33174. TEL 305-348-3040, mohammed@fiu.edu. Ed. Alistair Duffy.

L'ARTISAN ELECTRICIEN ELECTRONICIEN. *see* ELECTRONICS

AUSZUEGE AUS DEN EUROPAEISCHEN PATENTANMELDUNGEN. TEIL 2B. ELEKTROTECHNIK/EXTRACTS FROM EUROPEAN PATENT APPLICATIONS. PART 2B. ELECTRICITY. *see* PATENTS, TRADEMARKS AND COPYRIGHTS—Abstracting, Bibliographies, Statistics

AUSZUEGE AUS DEN EUROPAEISCHEN PATENTSCHRIFTEN. TEIL 2. ELEKTROTECHNIK, PHYSIK, FEINMECHANIK UND OPTIK, AKUSTIK. *see* PATENTS, TRADEMARKS AND COPYRIGHTS—Abstracting, Bibliographies, Statistics

621.38152 CHN ISSN 1001-5868
TK7871.85
BANDAOTI GUANGDIAN/SEMICONDUCTOR OPTOELECTRONICS. Text in Chinese. 1976. bi-m. USD 53.40 (effective 2009). back issues avail. **Document type:** *Academic/Scholarly.*
Related titles: Online - full text ed.
Indexed: A22, EngInd, Inspec, SCOPUS.
—BLDSC (8238.789000), East View, IE, Ingenta.
Published by: Chongqing Guangdian Jishu Yanjiusuo, 14, Nanping Huayuan Lu, Chongqing, 400060, China. TEL 86-23-62806174, FAX 86-23-62814485 ext 3148.

537 CHN ISSN 1671-8410
BIANLIU JISHU YU DIANLI QIANYIN/CONVERTER TECHNOLOGY & ELECTRIC TRACTION. Text in Chinese. 1978. bi-m. CNY 4 newsstand/cover (effective 2006). **Document type:** *Journal, Academic/Scholarly.*
Published by: Zhuzhou Shidai Jituan Gongsi/Zhuzhou Times Electric Group, Shidai Lu, Zhuzhou, 412001, China. TEL 86-733-8498892, FAX 86-733-8498852, http://www.zelri.com.cn/.

CHUGOKU CHIHO DENRYOKU KISHO GAIHO/CHUGOKU DISTRICT. REPORT OF THE POWER AND WEATHER. *see* METEOROLOGY

537 JPN
DENKI NO KAGAKKAN NENPO/ELECTRIC SCIENCE MUSEUM. ANNUAL REPORT. Text in Japanese. a. **Document type:** *Corporate.*
Published by: Chubu Denryoku K.K., Denki no Kagakukan/Chubu Electric Power Co., Inc., Electric Science Museum, 2-5 Sakae 2-chome, Naka-ku, Nagoya-shi, Aichi-ken 460-0008, Japan.

DENRYOKU TO KISHO/POWER AND WEATHER COORDINATING COMMITTEE. ANNUAL REPORT. *see* METEOROLOGY

537 USA ISSN 1096-9993
ELECTRICITY. Text in English. 1997. q. USD 15 (effective 2001). adv. tr.lit. back issues avail. **Document type:** *Magazine, Trade.* **Description:** Provides information about the electric industry and its activities, including meetings and events.
Published by: (Electric Association), Slack Attack Advertising, 5113 Monona Dr., Monona, WI 53716-2719. TEL 608-222-7630, FAX 608-222-0262. Ed., R&P Don Glays TEL 630-724-0200. Pub. Barbara Slack. Adv. contact Beth Vander Grinten. B&W page USD 880, color page USD 1,155; trim 10.88 x 8.38. **Subscr. to:** Electric Association, 4100 Madison St., Ste. 4, Hillside, IL 60162-1760. TEL 630-724-0200.

537 USA ISSN 1070-4698
QC759.6 CODEN: PELREX
➤ **ELECTROMAGNETIC WAVES.** Variant title: P I E R. Progress in Electromagnetic Research. Text in English. 1989. 11/yr. back issues avail. **Document type:** *Journal, Academic/Scholarly.* **Description:** Covers all aspects of electromagnetic theory and applications.
Formerly (until 1994): Progress in Electromagnetics Research (1043-626X)
Related titles: Online - full text ed.: ISSN 1559-8985. free (effective 2011).
Indexed: CIN, CPEI, ChemAb, ChemTitl, GeoRef, Inspec, SCOPUS.
—BLDSC (3699.556000), CASDDS.
Published by: Electromagnetics Academy, 77 Massachusetts Ave, Rm 26-319, Cambridge, MA 02139. FAX 617-258-8766, tpc@piers.org, http://www.emacademy.mit.edu. Ed. Weng Cho Chew TEL 852-2859-2800.

➤ **ELECTROMAGNETIC WAVES**; recent developments in research. *see* PHYSICS

➤ **ELEKTRICHESTVO.** *see* ENERGY—Electrical Energy

537 614.7 NLD ISSN 1871-3785
ELEKTROMAGNETISCHE VELDEN/ELECTROMAGNETIC FIELDS. Text in Dutch, English. 2001. a.
Published by: Gezondheidsraad/Health Council of the Netherlands, PO Box 16052, The Hague, 2500 BB, Netherlands. TEL 31-70-3407520, FAX 31-70-3407523, info@gr.nl, http://www.gr.nl.

ELEKTROMAGNITNYE VOLNY I ELEKTRONNYE SISTEMY/ELECTROMAGNETIC WAVES & ELECTRONIC SYSTEMS. *see* ELECTRONICS

537.5 621.3 UKR ISSN 1562-2991
➤ **ELEKTROMAGNITNYE YAVLENIYA/ELECTROMAGNETIC PHENOMENA.** Text in Russian. 1998. q. USD 400 foreign; USD 100 newsstand/cover foreign (effective 2007). **Document type:** *Journal, Academic/Scholarly.*
—BLDSC (0398.754300).
Published by: Instytut Elektromahnitnykh Doslidzhen'/Institute for Electromagnetic Research, A.S. 4580, Kharkiv 22, 61022, Ukraine. emph@emph.com.ua, http://iemr.com.ua. Ed. Yu V Tkach.

➤ **EXTRACTS FROM EUROPEAN PATENT SPECIFICATIONS. PART 2. ELECTRICITY, PHYSICS, PRECISION ENGINEERING, OPTICS AND ACOUSTICS.** *see* PATENTS, TRADEMARKS AND COPYRIGHTS—Abstracting, Bibliographies, Statistics

537 UKR ISSN 1560-8034
FIZIKA NAPIVPROVIDNIKIV KVANTOVA TA OPTOELEKTRONIKA/SEMICONDUCTOR PHYSICS, QUANTUM ELECTRONICS & OPTOELECTRONICS. Text in English, Ukrainian. 1998. q. USD 122 (effective 2002). **Document type:** *Journal, Academic/Scholarly.* **Description:** Covers hetero- and low-dimensional structures, linear and nonlinear solid-state optics; optoelectronics and optoelectronic devices, physics of microelectronic devices, quantum electronics, semiconductor physics, and sensors.
Related titles: CD-ROM ed.; Online - full text ed.: ISSN 1605-6582.
Indexed: A01, A03, A08, A28, APA, BrCerAb, C&ISA, C10, CA, CA/WCA, CIA, CerAb, CivEngAb, CompLI, CorrAb, E&CAJ, E11, EEA, EMA, H15, Inspec, M&TEA, M09, MBF, METADEX, SolStAb, T02, T04, TM, WAA.
—BLDSC (8238.792000), IE, Ingenta, Linda Hall.
Published by: Natsional'na Akademiya Nauk Ukrainy, Instytut Fizyky Napivprovidnykiv/National Academy of Sciences Ukraine, Institute of Semiconductor Physics, 45 Prospect Nauky, Kiev, 03028, Ukraine. TEL 380-44-265-62-05, FAX 380-44-265-54-30, journal@isp.kiev.ua. Ed. Sergey V. Svechnikov.

537 CHN ISSN 1001-1609
TK452 CODEN: GADIE9
GAOYA DIANQI/HIGH VOLTAGE APPARATUS. Text in Chinese; Abstracts in English. 1958. bi-m. USD 31.20 (effective 2009). **Document type:** *Journal, Academic/Scholarly.*
Related titles: Online - full text ed.
Indexed: A28, APA, BrCerAb, C&ISA, CA/WCA, CIA, CerAb, CivEngAb, CorrAb, E&CAJ, E11, EEA, EMA, ESPM, EngInd, EnvEAb, H15, Inspec, M&TEA, M09, MBF, METADEX, RefZh, SCOPUS, SolStAb, T04, WAA.
—BLDSC (4069.407000), East View.
Published by: Xi'an Gaoya Dianqi Yanjiusuo/Xi'an High Voltage Apparatus Research Institute, Dept. of High Voltage Apparatus, 18, Xi Er-Huan North Part, Xi'an, 710077, China. TEL 86-29-84225621, 86-29-84221958, FAX 86-29-84225621. Ed. Ye Xue. **Dist. by:** China International Book Trading Corp, 35 Chegongzhuang Xilu, Haidian District, PO Box 399, Beijing 100044, China. TEL 86-10-68412045, FAX 86-10-68412023, cibtc@mail.cibtc.com.cn, http://www.cibtc.com.cn.

537 USA ISSN 1523-3472
QC585.8.G38
GASEOUS DIELECTRICS. Text in English. 197?. irreg., latest vol.10, 2004. price varies. back issues avail. **Document type:** *Magazine, Trade.* **Description:** Covers recent advances and developments in a wide range of basic, applied, and industrial areas of gaseous dielectrics.
Published by: Springer New York LLC (Subsidiary of: Springer Science+Business Media), 233 Spring St, New York, NY 10013. TEL 212-460-1500, FAX 212-460-1575, service-ny@springer.com, http://www.springer.com/.

537 GBR ISSN 1574-1818
QC717.6
HIGH ENERGY DENSITY PHYSICS. Text in English. 2006. q. EUR 522 in Europe to institutions; JPY 70,100 in Japan to institutions; USD 659 elsewhere to institutions (effective 2012). adv. back issues avail.; reprints avail. **Document type:** *Journal, Academic/Scholarly.* **Description:** Coves original experimental and related theoretical work studying the physics of matter and radiation under extreme conditions.
Related titles: Online - full text ed.: ISSN 1878-0563 (from ScienceDirect).
Indexed: A26, CA, CurCont, I05, Inspec, SCI, SCOPUS, T02, W07.
—IE, Ingenta. **CCC.**
Published by: Elsevier Advanced Technology (Subsidiary of: Elsevier Science & Technology), The Blvd, Langford Ln, Kidlington, Oxon OX5 1GB, United Kingdom. TEL 44-1865-843434, FAX 44-1865-843970, http://www.elsevier.nl. Eds. Richard W Lee, Steven Rose.

537 JPN ISSN 0911-8713
HODEN KENKYU/JAPAN RESEARCH GROUP OF ELECTRICAL DISCHARGES. JOURNAL. Text in Japanese. 1958. irreg.
Published by: Hoden Kenkyu Gurupu/Japan Research Group of Electrical Discharges, Seikei Daigaku Kogakubu, Denki Denshi Kogakka, 3-1 Kitamachi-Kichijoji 3-chome, Musashino-shi, Tokyo-to 180-0000, Japan.

537 USA
I E E E INTERNATIONAL CONFERENCE ON SEMICONDUCTOR ELECTRONICS. PROCEEDINGS. (Institute of Electrical and Electronics Engineers) Text in English. 19??. biennial. adv. back issues avail. **Document type:** *Proceedings, Trade.*
Related titles: Online - full text ed.
Published by: I E E E, 445 Hoes Ln, Piscataway, NJ 08855. contactcenter@ieee.org, http://www.ieee.org.

537 USA
I E E E SEMICONDUCTING AND INSULATING MATERIALS CONFERENCE. PROCEEDINGS. (Institute of Electrical and Electronics Engineers) Text in English. 1980. a., latest 2004. adv. back issues avail. **Document type:** *Proceedings, Trade.*
Formerly (until 1996): I E E E Semi-Insulating III-V Materials
Published by: (France. Centre National de la Recherche Scientifique FRA), I E E E, 445 Hoes Ln, Piscataway, NJ 08855. contactcenter@ieee.org, http://www.ieee.org.

537 USA ISSN 1065-2221
TK7871.85 CODEN: ASTSFA
I E E E SEMICONDUCTOR THERMAL MEASUREMENT AND MANAGEMENT SYMPOSIUM. PROCEEDINGS. (Institute of Electrical and Electronics Engineers) Text in English. 1984. a. adv. back issues avail. **Document type:** *Proceedings, Trade.*
Formerly (until 1991): I E E E Semiconductor Thermal and Temperature Measurement Symposium
Related titles: Online - full text ed.
Indexed: EngInd, SCOPUS.
—CCC.
Published by: I E E E, 445 Hoes Ln, Piscataway, NJ 08855. contactcenter@ieee.org, http://www.ieee.org.

537 USA
INTERNATIONAL CONFERENCE ON COMPUTATIONAL ELECTROMAGNETICS AND ITS APPLICATION. PROCEEDINGS. Text in English. 1999. irreg., latest 2004. adv. back issues avail.; reprints avail. **Document type:** *Proceedings, Trade.*
Related titles: Online - full text ed.
Published by: I E E E, 445 Hoes Ln, Piscataway, NJ 08854. TEL 732-981-0060, 800-678-4333, FAX 732-562-6380, customer.service@ieee.org, http://www.ieee.org. **Co-sponsor:** I E E E, Beijing Section.

537 USA
INTERNATIONAL CONFERENCE ON ELECTROMAGNETIC INTERFERENCE AND COMPATIBILITY. PROCEEDINGS. Text in English. 1995. biennial. adv. back issues avail.; reprints avail. **Document type:** *Proceedings, Trade.*
Related titles: Online - full text ed.
Published by: I E E E, 445 Hoes Ln, Piscataway, NJ 08854. TEL 732-981-0060, 800-678-4333, FAX 732-562-6380, customer.service@ieee.org, http://www.ieee.org. **Co-sponsor:** I E E E Industrial Electronics Society.

537 USA
INTERNATIONAL CONFERENCE ON HIGH POWER PARTICLE BEAMS. PROCEEDINGS. Text in English. 1998. a. (in 2 vols.). adv. reprints avail. **Document type:** *Proceedings, Trade.* **Description:** Covers material processes, aerospace, radar, communications, medical, military, pulse power, particle beams.
Related titles: Online - full text ed.
Published by: I E E E, 445 Hoes Ln, Piscataway, NJ 08854. TEL 732-981-0060, 800-678-4333, FAX 732-562-6380, customer.service@ieee.org, http://www.ieee.org.

536 USA ISSN 1094-2734
TK2950
INTERNATIONAL CONFERENCE ON THERMOELECTRICS. Variant title: I E E E / I T S International Conference on Thermoelectrics. Proceedings. Text in English. 1992. a. back issues avail. **Document type:** *Proceedings, Academic/Scholarly.*

Formerly (until 1994): International Conference on Thermoelectrics. Proceedings (1078-9642)
Related titles: Online - full text ed.
Published by: (International Thermoelectric Society), I E E E Components, Packaging, and Manufacturing Technology Society, CPMT Society Executive Office, 445 Hoes Ln, PO Box 1331, Piscataway, NJ 08855. TEL 732-562-5528, FAX 732-981-1769, mtickman@calypso.ieee.org, http://www.cpmt.org/.

537 USA ISSN 1545-827X
TK7871.85
INTERNATIONAL SEMICONDUCTOR CONFERENCE. PROCEEDINGS. Text in English. 1995. a. adv. back issues avail.; reprints avail. **Document type:** *Proceedings, Trade.*
Related titles: Online - full text ed.
Published by: I E E E, 445 Hoes Ln, Piscataway, NJ 08854. TEL 732-981-0060, 800-678-4333, FAX 732-562-6380, customer.service@ieee.org, http://www.ieee.org.

537 535 USA ISSN 2153-3253
INTERNATIONAL SYMPOSIUM ON ELECTRETS. PROCEEDINGS. Text in English. 19??. triennial. adv. back issues avail.; reprints avail. **Document type:** *Proceedings, Trade.* **Description:** Provides an opportunity to review recent developments in the field of electrets from the point of view of both physical phenomena and applications.
Formerly (until 1985): I E E E International Workshop on Electric Charges in Dielectrics. Charge Storage, Charge Transport, and Electrostatics with their Applications
Related titles: Online - full text ed.: ISSN 2153-327X.
Published by: I E E E, 445 Hoes Ln, Piscataway, NJ 08854. TEL 732-981-0060, 800-678-4333, FAX 732-562-6380, customer.service@ieee.org, http://www.ieee.org.

621.38152 KOR ISSN 1229-6368
TK7871.85
JEONJA GONGHAGHOE NONMUNJI. SD/INSTITUTE OF ELECTRONICS ENGINEERS OF KOREA. JOURNAL. SD. Text in English, Korean. 2000. m. membership (effective 2008). **Document type:** *Journal, Academic/Scholarly.* **Description:** Covers packaging semiconductor materials and parts, light waves and quantum electronics, SoC design, and PCB and packaging.
Supersedes in part (in 2000): Jeonja Gonghaghoe Nonmunji. S (1226-5837); Which superseded in part (in 1990): Jeonja Gonghaghoe Nonmunji (1016-135X); Which was formerly (until 1963): Korea Institute of Electronics Engineers. Journal (0379-7848)
Indexed: Inspec.
—BLDSC (4775.536000).
Published by: Daehan Jeonja Gonghaghoe/Institute of Electronics Engineers of Korea, 635-4 Yucksam-dong, Kangnam-gu, Seoul, 135-703, Korea, S. TEL 82-2-5530255, FAX 82-2-5526093, ieek@ieek.or.kr, http://www.ieek.or.kr.

JOURNAL OF ATMOSPHERIC ELECTRICITY. *see* METEOROLOGY

537 621.3 USA ISSN 1942-0730
QC759.6
▼ **JOURNAL OF ELECTROMAGNETIC ANALYSIS AND APPLICATIONS.** Abbreviated title: JEMAA. Text in English. 2009 (May). m. back issues avail. **Document type:** *Journal, Academic/Scholarly.* **Description:** Publishes four categories of original technical reports: papers, communications, reviews, and discussions.
Related titles: Online - full text ed.: ISSN 1942-0749. free (effective 2010).
Indexed: A26, C10, CompD, E08, I05, P26, P52, P54, P56, S09, T02.
Published by: Scientific Research Publishing, Inc., PO Box 54821, Irvine, CA 92619. TEL 408-329-4591, service@scirp.org, http://www.scirp.org. Eds. James L Drewniak, Yuanzhang Sun.

KOATSU TORONKAI KOEN YOSHISHU/HIGH PRESSURE CONFERENCE OF JAPAN. PROGRAMME AND ABSTRACTS OF PAPERS. *see* ENGINEERING

KOATSURYOKU NO KAGAKU TO GIJUTSU/REVIEW OF HIGH PRESSURE SCIENCE AND TECHNOLOGY. *see* ENGINEERING

537 JPN
KYOYUDENTAI OYO KAIGI KOEN YOKOSHU/ABSTRACTS OF THE MEETING ON FERROELECTRIC MATERIALS AND THEIR APPLICATIONS. Text in Japanese. 1977. a. **Document type:** *Abstract/Index.*
Published by: Kyoyudentai Oyo Kaigi Un'ei Iinkai/Organizing Committee of the Meeting on Ferroelectric Materials and Their Applications, Kyoto Daigaku Kogakubu, Denshi Kogaku Kyoshitsu, Yoshidahon-Machi, Sakyo-ku, Kyoto-shi, 606-8317, Japan.

537 JPN ISSN 0386-0884
N G K REBYU/N G K REVIEW. Text in Japanese; Summaries in English. 1976. a.
Formed by the merger of (1975-1976): N G K Denki Nyusu (0386-0876); (1969-1976): Gaishi Rebyu (0386-0868); Which was formerly (1952-1963): Nichigai Rebyu (0549-155X)
Published by: Nippon Gaishi K.K., 2-56 Suda-cho, Mizuho-ku, Nagoya-shi, Aichi-ken 467-0871, Japan.

537 JPN ISSN 0386-5843
N G K REVIEW. OVERSEAS EDITION. Text in English. 1977. a.
Published by: Nippon Gaishi K.K., 2-56 Suda-cho, Mizuho-ku, Nagoya-shi, Aichi-ken 467-0871, Japan.

ORGANIC ELECTRONICS. *see* ENGINEERING—Electrical Engineering

537 USA ISSN 1931-7360
QC759.6
➤ **P I E R S ONLINE.** (Progress in Electromagnetics Research Symposium) Text in English. 2005. 8/yr. free (effective 2009). back issues avail. **Document type:** *Journal, Academic/Scholarly.* **Description:** Provides speedy and timely publication for reporting progress and recent advances in the modern development of electromagnetic theory and its new and exciting applications.
Media: Online - full content.
Published by: Electromagnetics Academy, 77 Massachusetts Ave, Rm 26-319, Cambridge, MA 02139. FAX 617-258-8766, tpc@piers.org, http://www.emacademy.mit.edu.

537 FRA ISSN 2105-0716
▼ **P V DIRECT.** (Photovoltaics) Text in English. 2010. free (effective 2012). **Document type:** *Journal, Academic/Scholarly.*
Media: Online - full text.
Published by: E D P Sciences, 17 Ave du Hoggar, Parc d'Activites de Courtaboeuf, BP 112, Cedex A, Les Ulis, F-91944, France. TEL 33-1-69187575, FAX 33-1-69860678, http://www.edpsciences.org. Ed. Pere Roca i Cabarrocas.

POLITECHNIKA WARSZAWSKA. PRACE NAUKOWE. ELEKTRYKA. *see* ENGINEERING—Electrical Engineering

537 USA ISSN 1937-6472
QC759.6
➤ **PROGRESS IN ELECTROMAGNETICS RESEARCH B.** Text in English. 2008. irreg. free (effective 2011). back issues avail. **Document type:** *Journal, Academic/Scholarly.* **Description:** Covers all aspects of electromagnetic theory and applications.
Media: Online - full text.
Indexed: SCOPUS.
Published by: Electromagnetics Academy, 77 Massachusetts Ave, Rm 26-319, Cambridge, MA 02139. FAX 617-258-8766, tpc@piers.org, http://www.emacademy.mit.edu. Ed. Weng Cho Chew TEL 852-2859-2800.

537 USA ISSN 1937-8718
QC759.6
➤ **PROGRESS IN ELECTROMAGNETICS RESEARCH C.** Text in English. 2008. irreg. free (effective 2011). back issues avail. **Document type:** *Journal, Academic/Scholarly.* **Description:** Covers all aspects of electromagnetic theory and applications.
Media: Online - full text.
Indexed: CPEI.
Published by: Electromagnetics Academy, 77 Massachusetts Ave, Rm 26-319, Cambridge, MA 02139. FAX 617-258-8766, tpc@piers.org, http://www.emacademy.mit.edu. Ed. Weng Cho Chew TEL 852-2859-2800.

537 USA ISSN 1937-6480
➤ **PROGRESS IN ELECTROMAGNETICS RESEARCH LETTERS.** Text in English. 2008. irreg. free (effective 2011). back issues avail. **Document type:** *Journal, Academic/Scholarly.* **Description:** Covers all aspects of electromagnetic theory and applications.
Media: Online - full text.
Published by: Electromagnetics Academy, 77 Massachusetts Ave, Rm 26-319, Cambridge, MA 02139. FAX 617-258-8766, tpc@piers.org, http://www.emacademy.mit.edu. Ed. Weng Cho Chew TEL 852-2859-2800.

537 USA ISSN 1937-8726
QC759.6
➤ **PROGRESS IN ELECTROMAGNETICS RESEARCH M.** Text in English. 2008. irreg. free (effective 2011). back issues avail. **Document type:** *Journal, Academic/Scholarly.* **Description:** Covers all aspects of electromagnetic theory and applications.
Media: Online - full text.
Indexed: CPEI.
Published by: Electromagnetics Academy, 77 Massachusetts Ave, Rm 26-319, Cambridge, MA 02139. FAX 617-258-8766, tpc@piers.org, http://www.emacademy.mit.edu. Ed. Weng Cho Chew TEL 852-2859-2800.

537 USA ISSN 1559-9450
PROGRESS IN ELECTROMAGNETICS RESEARCH SYMPOSIUM. Abbreviated title: P I E R S. Text in English. 19??. s-a. back issues avail. **Document type:** *Proceedings, Academic/Scholarly.*
Media: Optical Disk - DVD. **Related titles:** Online - full text ed.: free (effective 2010).
Published by: Electromagnetics Academy, 77 Massachusetts Ave, Rm 26-319, Cambridge, MA 02139. FAX 617-258-8766, tpc@piers.org, http://www.emacademy.mit.edu.

RADIO SCIENCE. *see* EARTH SCIENCES—Geophysics

REDES ENERGETICAS NACIONAIS. RELATORIO E CONTAS. *see* PUBLIC ADMINISTRATION

REFERATIVNYI ZHURNAL. FIZIKA TVERDYKH TEL: ELEKTRICHESKIE SVOISTVA; vypusk svodnogo toma. *see* PHYSICS—Abstracting, Bibliographies, Statistics

SCANFAX. *see* ENGINEERING—Electrical Engineering

SEMICONDUCTOR INDUSTRY ASSOCIATION. (YEAR) ANNUAL REPORT & DIRECTORY. *see* ELECTRONICS

621.38152 USA
SEMICONDUCTOR INNOVATION LETTER. Text in English. 2002. bi-m. **Document type:** *Newsletter, Academic/Scholarly.* **Description:** Contains analysis, insight, news, and evaluation of the semiconductor industry and the technology economy. Provides reporting of latest innovation emerging from corporate and university R and D departments.
Media: E-mail.
Published by: (Massachusetts Institute of Technology), Dow Jones Newsletters (Subsidiary of: Dow Jones Newswires), 1155 Ave of the Americas, 7th Fl, New York, NY 10036. TEL 212-597-5716, http://www.dowjones.com.

SEMICONDUCTOR NEWS. *see* ENGINEERING—Electrical Engineering

537 CHE ISSN 0924-4247
TK7881.2 CODEN: SAAPEB
➤ **SENSORS AND ACTUATORS A: PHYSICAL**; an international journal devoted to research and development of physical and chemical transducers. Text in English. 1981. 16/yr. EUR 4,417 in Europe to institutions; JPY 586,000 in Japan to institutions; USD 4,941 elsewhere to institutions (effective 2012). back issues avail. **Document type:** *Journal, Academic/Scholarly.* **Description:** Covers all aspects of research and development of solid-state devices for transducing physical signals.
Supersedes in part (in 1990): Sensors and Actuators (0250-6874)
Related titles: Microform ed.: (from PQC); Online - full text ed.: ISSN 1873-3069 (from IngentaConnect, ScienceDirect).
Indexed: A01, A03, A08, A20, A22, A26, A28, APA, ASCA, B&BAb, B19, BrCerAb, C&ISA, C24, C33, CA, CA/WCA, CADCAM, CIA, CPEI, CerAb, ChemAb, ChemTitl, CivEngAb, CorrAb, CurCont, CybAb, E&CAJ, E11, EEA, EIA, EMA, ESPM, EnerInd, EngInd, EnvEAb, H15, I05, ISMEC, ISR, Inspec, M&TEA, M09, MBF, METADEX, P30, RefZh, RoboAb, S01, SCI, SCOPUS, SolStAb, T02, T04, TM, Telegen, W07, WAA.
—BLDSC (8241.785200), AskIEEE, CASDDS, IE, Infotrieve, Ingenta, INIST, Linda Hall. **CCC.**
Published by: Elsevier S.A., PO Box 564, Lausanne 1, 1001, Switzerland. TEL 41-21-3207381, FAX 41-21-3235444. Ed. P J French. **Subscr. to:** Elsevier BV, Radarweg 29, PO Box 211, Amsterdam 1000 AE, Netherlands. TEL 31-20-4853757, FAX 31-20-4853432, JournalsCustomerServiceEMEA@elsevier.com, http://www.elsevier.nl.

▼ ➤ **SERIES ON COMPLEXITY, NONLINEARITY AND CHAOS.** *see* MATHEMATICS

➤ **STUDIES IN APPLIED ELECTROMAGNETICS AND MECHANICS.** *see* ENGINEERING—Electrical Engineering

537 RUS ISSN 0868-488X
QH45.5
SVET: PRIRODA I CHELOVEK. Text in Russian. 1981. m. USD 149 in United States.
Formerly (until 1990): Priroda i Chelovek (0203-4867)
—BLDSC (0160.898400).
Address: Ul Marshala Rybalko 8, Moscow, 123060, Russian Federation. TEL 7-095-1942089, FAX 7-095-1942029. Ed. V I Zakharenkov. **Dist. by:** East View Information Services, 10601 Wayzata Blvd, Minneapolis, MN 55305. TEL 952-252-1201, 800-477-1005, FAX 952-252-1202, info@eastview.com, http://www.eastview.com.

537 USA ISSN 2152-2685
▼ **SYNTHESIS SERIES IN COMPUTATIONAL ELECTROMAGNETICS.** Text in English. 2010. irreg. **Document type:** *Monographic series, Academic/Scholarly.* **Description:** Selected works from the Synthesis Digital Library on computational electromagnetics and antennas.
Published by: Morgan & Claypool Publishers, 1537 4th St, Ste 228, San Rafael, CA 94901. TEL 888-822-9942, FAX 802-864-7626, info@morganclaypool.com, http://www.morganclaypool.com. Ed. Dr. Constantine A Balanis.

TAIKI DENKI GAKKAISHI/SOCIETY OF ATMOSPHERIC ELECTRICITY OF JAPAN. JOURNAL. *see* METEOROLOGY

537 FIN ISSN 1797-4585
TEKNILLINEN KORKEAKOULU. RADIOTIETEEN JA -TEKNIIKAN LAITOS. OPPIMATERIAALISARJA. Text in Finnish. 1993. irreg. **Document type:** *Monographic series, Academic/Scholarly.*
Former titles (until 2008): Teknillinen Korkeakoulu. Sahkomagnetiikan Laboratorio. Oppimateriaalisarja (1456-7776); (until 1999): Teknillinen Korkeakoulu. Sahko- ja Tietoliikennetekniikan Osasto. Sahkomagnetiikan Laboratorio. Oppimateriaalisarja (1455-190X); (until 1996): Teknillinen Korkeakoulu. Sahko- ja tietoliikennetekniikan Osasto. Sahkomagnetiikan Laboratorio. Oppimateriaalisarja (1236-7028)
Related titles: Online - full text ed.
Indexed: B04, BRD, L07, RGAb, W03, W05.
Published by: Teknillinen Korkeakoulu, Radiotieteen ja -tekniikan Laitos/Helsinki University of Technology. Department of Radio Science and Engineering, Otakaari 5 A, PO Box 3000, Espoo, 0215, Finland. TEL 358-9-4512251, FAX 358-9-4522152, http://radio.tkk.fi/fi/.

537 621.3 JPN ISSN 0387-4990
TOKYO DAIGAKU CHOKOATSU DENSHI KENBIKYOSHITSU NENPO/UNIVERSITY OF TOKYO. ANNUAL REPORT OF HIGH VOLTAGE ELECTRON MICROSCOPE. Text in English, Japanese. 1976. a.
Published by: Tokyo Daigaku, Kogakubu Sogo Shikenjo Chokoatsu Denshi Kenbikyoshitsu/University of Tokyo, Engineering Research Institute, High Voltage Electron Microscopy Laboratory, 11-16 Yayoi 2-chome, Bunkyo-ku, Tokyo, 113-0032, Japan.

537 USA
WAFERNEWS; the semiconductor equipment and material breifing. Text in English. 19??. s-w. free to qualified personnel (effective 2009). back issues avail. **Document type:** *Newsletter, Trade.* **Description:** Features exclusive news stories and analysis, as well as in-depth financial and market coverage of the semiconductor equipment and materials industry.
Formerly: WaferNews Confidential
Media: E-mail.
Published by: PennWell Corporation, 98 Spit Brook Rd, Nashua, NH 03062. TEL 603-891-9447, Headquarters@PennWell.com, http://www.pennwell.com.

537.5 UKR ISSN 2077-6772
AS264.A1
➤ **ZURNAL NANO TA ELEKTRONNOI FIZIKI.** Text in Ukrainian, Russian. 1994. m. **Document type:** *Journal, Academic/Scholarly.*
Formerly (until 2009): Sums'kyi Derzhavnyi Universytet. Visnyk (1817-9215)
Related titles: Online - full text ed.: ISSN 1817-9290. free (effective 2011).
Indexed: RefZh.
Published by: Sums'kyi Derzhavnyi Universytet/Sumy State University, vul Ryms'kogo-Korsakova 2, Sumy, 40007, Ukraine. TEL 380-542-640657.

PHYSICS—Heat

536 USA
A I A A - A S M E THERMOPHYSICS AND HEAT TRANSFER CONFERENCE. PROCEEDINGS. (American Institute of Aeronautics and Astronautics - American Society of Mechanical Engineers) Text in English. 19??. irreg., latest 2006. USD 850 per issue to non-members; USD 750 per issue to members (effective 2009). back issues avail. **Document type:** *Proceedings.*
Related titles: CD-ROM ed.: USD 750 per issue to non-members; USD 410 per issue to members (effective 2009); Online - full text ed.: USD 750 per issue to non-members; USD 150 per issue to members (effective 2009).
Published by: (American Society of Mechanical Engineers), American Institute of Aeronautics and Astronautics, Inc., 1801 Alexander Bell Dr, Ste 500, Reston, VA 20191. TEL 703-264-7500, 800-639-2422, FAX 703-264-7551, custserv@aiaa.org.

P

621.3813 ITA ISSN 1754-8179
A M P E R E NEWSLETTER (ONLINE). (Association for Microwave Power in Europe for Research and Education) Text in English. 1994. q. free to members (effective 2009). back issues avail. **Document type:** *Newsletter, Trade.* **Description:** Covers short topical articles written by experts in the field. Includes conference reports, a calendar of events and news items on various aspects of radio frequency and microwave energy usage in the ISM frequency band.
Formerly (until Dec.2006): A M P E R E Newsletter (Print) (1361-8598)
Media: Online - full text.
Published by: A M P E R E Europe Ltd., c/o Cristina Leonelli, General Secretariat, DIMA, University of Modena and Reggio Emilia, Via Vignolese 905, Modena, 41100, Italy. contact@ampereeurope.org. Ed. Ricky Metaxas.

621.59 536.56 USA ISSN 0065-2482
TP490 CODEN: ACYEAC
➤ **ADVANCES IN CRYOGENIC ENGINEERING (PART A & B).** Variant title: Cryogenic Engineering Conference Proceedings. Text in English. 1954. irreg. (2 nos./vol.), latest vol.43, 1998. price varies. back issues avail. **Document type:** *Proceedings, Academic/Scholarly.*
Indexed: A22, CIN, ChemAb, ChemTitl, EIA, EnvAb, Inspec, P30, SCOPUS.
—BLDSC (0704.200000), CASDDS, IE, Infotrieve, Ingenta, INIST. **CCC.**
Published by: Springer New York LLC (Subsidiary of: Springer Science+Business Media), 233 Spring St, New York, NY 10013. TEL 212-460-1500, FAX 212-460-1575, service-ny@springer.com.

536.2 USA ISSN 0065-2717
QC320.A1 CODEN: AHTRAR
➤ **ADVANCES IN HEAT TRANSFER.** Text in English. 1964. irreg., latest vol.41, 2009. USD 198 per vol. (effective 2010). index. back issues avail.; reprints avail. **Document type:** *Monographic series, Academic/Scholarly.* **Description:** Provides an overview of review articles on topics of current interest. Bridges the gap between academic researchers and practitioners in industry.
Related titles: Online - full text ed.: ◆ Supplement(s): Advances in Heat Transfer. Supplement. ISSN 1043-6952.
Indexed: A22, ApMecR, CIN, ChemAb, ChemTitl, GeoRef, Inspec, SCOPUS, SpeleolAb.
—BLDSC (0709.010000), CASDDS, IE, Infotrieve, Ingenta, INIST, Linda Hall. **CCC.**
Published by: Academic Press (Subsidiary of: Elsevier Science & Technology), 3251 Riverport Ln, Maryland Heights, MO 63043. TEL 314-447-8010, FAX 314-447-8030, JournalCustomerService-usa@elsevier.com, http://www.elsevierdirect.com/imprint.jsp?iid=5. Eds. Avram Bar-Cohen, George Greene, Young Cho.

➤ **AMERICAN SOCIETY OF MECHANICAL ENGINEERS. HEAT TRANSFER DIVISION. NEWSLETTER.** *see* ENGINEERING—Engineering Mechanics And Materials

536 GBR ISSN 1359-4311
TJ260 CODEN: ATENFT
➤ **APPLIED THERMAL ENGINEERING.** Text in English. 1981. 18/yr. EUR 2,595 in Europe to institutions; JPY 344,600 in Japan to institutions; USD 2,904 elsewhere to institutions (effective 2012). abstr. back issues avail.; reprints avail. **Document type:** *Journal, Academic/Scholarly.* **Description:** Features original, high-quality research papers and ancillary features, spanning activities ranging from fundamental research to trouble-shooting in existing plant and equipment.
Former titles (until vol.16, 1996): Heat Recovery Systems and C H P (Combined Heat and Power) (0890-4332); (until 1987): Journal of Heat Recovery Systems (0198-7593)
Related titles: Microfilm ed.: (from PQC); Online - full text ed.: ISSN 1873-5606 (from IngentaConnect, ScienceDirect).
Indexed: A22, A26, A28, APA, APIAb, ASCA, ApMecR, B01, B06, B07, B09, BrCerAb, C&ISA, CA, CA/WCA, CEA, CEABA, CIA, CIN, CPEI, CerAb, ChemAb, ChemTitl, CivEngAb, CorrAb, CurCont, E&CAJ, E11, EEA, EIA, EMA, ESPM, EnerInd, EngInd, EnvAb, EnvEAb, FPRD, H15, I05, Inspec, M&TEA, M09, MBF, METADEX, RefZh, SCI, SCOPUS, SolStAb, T02, T04, TCEA, TM, VITIS, W07, WAA.
—BLDSC (1580.101000), AskIEEE, CASDDS, IE, Infotrieve, Ingenta, INIST, Linda Hall. **CCC.**
Published by: Pergamon (Subsidiary of: Elsevier Science & Technology), The Blvd, Langford Ln, East Park, Kidlington, Oxford OX5 1GB, United Kingdom. TEL 44-1865-843000, FAX 44-1865-843010, JournalsCustomerServiceEMEA@elsevier.com. Ed. David A Reay. **Subscr. to:** Elsevier BV, Radarweg 29, PO Box 211, Amsterdam 1000 AE, Netherlands. TEL 31-20-4853757, FAX 31-20-4853432, http://www.elsevier.nl.

536 541 POL ISSN 1231-0956
TJ265 CODEN: ATERD5
➤ **ARCHIVES OF THERMODYNAMICS.** Text in English. 1980. q. EUR 64 foreign (effective 2006). bk.rev. abstr.; bibl.; charts; illus. 130 p./no. 1 cols./p.; back issues avail. **Document type:** *Journal, Academic/Scholarly.* **Description:** Includes papers on thermodynamics, heat and mass transfer.
Formerly (until 1991): Archiwum Termodynamiki (0208-418X)
Related titles: Online - full text ed.: ISSN 2083-6023. free (effective 2011).
Indexed: A01, ApMecR, B22, CA, CIN, CPEI, ChemAb, ChemTitl, EngInd, Inspec, RefZh, SCOPUS, T02.
—CASDDS, Linda Hall.
Published by: Polska Akademia Nauk, Oddzial w Gdansku, Instytut Maszyn Przeplywowych/Polish Academy of Sciences, Institute of Fluid-Flow Machinery, ul Fiszera 14, Gdansk, 80952, Poland. TEL 48-58-3411271, FAX 48-58-3416144, esli@imp.gda.pl, http://www.imp.gda.pl. Ed. Jaroslaw Mikielewicz. Circ: 250. **Dist. by:** Ars Polona, Obroncow 25, Warsaw 03933, Poland. TEL 48-22-5098609, FAX 48-22-5098610, arspolona@arspolona.com.pl, http://www.arspolona.com.pl. **Co-sponsor:** Polska Akademia Nauk, Komitet Termodynamiki i Spalania.

➤ **CAILIAO RECHULI XUEBAO/TRANSACTIONS OF MATERIALS AND HEAT TREATMENT.** *see* METALLURGY

536.7 541.36 NLD ISSN 0927-5878
➤ **CHEMICAL THERMODYNAMICS.** Text in English. 1992. irreg., latest vol.9, 2005. price varies. back issues avail. **Document type:** *Monographic series, Academic/Scholarly.* **Description:** Investigates the thermodynamic properties of specific elements.
—BLDSC (3151.784000). **CCC.**
Published by: Elsevier BV (Subsidiary of: Elsevier Science & Technology), Radarweg 29, PO Box 211, Amsterdam, 1000 AE, Netherlands. TEL 31-20-4853911, FAX 31-20-4852457, JournalsCustomerServiceEMEA@elsevier.com, http://www.elsevier.nl.

621.59 USA ISSN 1085-5262
COLD FACTS. Text in English. 1985. q. USD 60 domestic; USD 85 foreign (effective 2000). adv. bk.rev. 30 p./no.; back issues avail. **Document type:** *Magazine, Trade.* **Description:** For those interested in all applications of extremely low temperatures (cryogenics).
Published by: Cryogenic Society of America, c/o Huget Advertising, Inc, 1033 South Blvd, Ste 13, Oak Park, IL 60302. TEL 708-383-6220, FAX 708-383-9337. Ed. Laurie Huget. Adv. contact Karen Kozlowski. Circ: 700 (paid); 3,000 (controlled).

536 333.79 660 GBR ISSN 1364-7830
QD516 CODEN: CTMOFQ
➤ **COMBUSTION THEORY AND MODELLING.** Text in English. 1997. bi-m. GBP 498 combined subscription in United Kingdom to institutions (print & online eds.); EUR 659, USD 829 combined subscription to institutions (print & online eds.) (effective 2012). adv. back issues avail.; reprint service avail. from PSC. **Document type:** *Journal, Academic/Scholarly.* **Description:** Provides a forum for the publication and dissemination of scientific articles that apply mathematical theory, modelling, numerical simulation and experimental techniques to the study of combustion.
Related titles: Microfiche ed.: USD 289 in the Americas; GBP 149 elsewhere (effective 2004); Online - full text ed.: ISSN 1741-3559. GBP 448 in United Kingdom to institutions; EUR 594, USD 746 to institutions (effective 2012) (from IngentaConnect).
Indexed: A01, A03, A08, A22, A28, APA, ApMecR, BrCerAb, C&ISA, CA, CA/WCA, CCMJ, CIA, CMCI, CPEI, CerAb, CivEngAb, CorrAb, CurCont, E&CAJ, E01, E11, E14, EEA, EMA, ESPM, EngInd, EnvEAb, FLUIDEX, H15, ISR, Inspec, M&TEA, M09, MBF, METADEX, MSN, MathR, SCI, SCOPUS, SolStAb, T02, T04, W07, WAA, Z02.
—IE, Infotrieve, Ingenta, Linda Hall. **CCC.**
Published by: Taylor & Francis Ltd. (Subsidiary of: Taylor & Francis Group), 4 Park Sq, Milton Park, Abingdon, Oxfordshire OX14 4RN, United Kingdom. TEL 44-20-70176000, FAX 44-20-70176336, subscriptions@tandf.co.uk, http://www.taylorandfrancis.com. Eds. Mitchell D Smooke, Moshe Matalon. Adv. contact Linda Hann. **Subscr. in N America to:** Taylor & Francis Inc., Customer Services Dept, 325 Chestnut St, 8th Fl, Philadelphia, PA 19106. TEL 215-625-8900, 800-354-1420, FAX 215-625-2940, customerservice@taylorandfrancis.com; **Subscr. outside N America to:** Journals Customer Service, Sheepen Pl, Colchester, Essex CO3 3LP, United Kingdom. TEL 44-20-70175544, FAX 44-20-70175198.

536 USA
COMPUTATIONAL AND PHYSICAL PROCESSES IN MECHANICS AND THERMAL SCIENCE. Text in English. 200?. irreg. **Document type:** *Monographic series, Academic/Scholarly.* **Description:** Features monographs on mechanics, thermal science and heat transfer.
Related titles: Online - full text ed.: ISSN 2154-9818.
Published by: C R C Press, LLC (Subsidiary of: Taylor & Francis Group), 6000 Broken Sound Pky, NW, Ste 300, Boca Raton, FL 33487. TEL 561-994-0555, FAX 561-989-9732, journals@crcpress.com, http://www.crcpress.com.

536 USA ISSN 1940-2503
QC310.15
COMPUTATIONAL THERMAL SCIENCES. Text in English. 2008 (Mar.). bi-m. USD 646; USD 129 per issue (effective 2010). adv. back issues avail.; reprints avail. **Document type:** *Journal, Academic/Scholarly.* **Description:** Provides a forum for the exchange of ideas, methods and results in computational thermodynamics, fluid dynamics, heat transfer and mass transfer in solids, liquids and gases, with applications in areas such as energy, manufacturing and the environment.
Related titles: Online - full text ed.: ISSN 1940-2554.
Indexed: CPEI, ESPM, EnvEAb, FLUIDEX.
Published by: Begell House Inc., 50 Cross Hwy, Redding, CT 06896. TEL 203-938-1300, FAX 203-938-1304, orders@begellhouse.com. Eds. Graham de Vahl Davis, Ivan V Egorov.

CONGRES INTERNATIONAL DU FROID. ACTES/INTERNATIONAL CONGRESS OF REFRIGERATION. PROCEEDINGS. *see* HEATING, PLUMBING AND REFRIGERATION

536.7 DEU ISSN 0935-1175
QA808.2 CODEN: CMETEJ
➤ **CONTINUUM MECHANICS AND THERMODYNAMICS**; analysis of complex materials and judicious evaluation of the environment. Text in English. 1989. 8/yr. EUR 1,444, USD 1,771 combined subscription to institutions (print & online eds.) (effective 2012). adv. reprint service avail. from PSC. **Document type:** *Journal, Academic/Scholarly.* **Description:** Provides information on observed phenomena and presents models that are based on principles of mechanics, thermodynamics and statistical thermodynamics.
Related titles: Microform ed.: (from PQC); Online - full text ed.: ISSN 1432-0959 (from IngentaConnect).
Indexed: A01, A03, A08, A22, A26, ASCA, ApMecR, CA, CCMJ, CMCI, CPEI, CurCont, E01, EngInd, ISR, Inspec, MSCI, MSN, MathR, P02, P26, P48, P52, P54, P56, PQC, RefZh, SCI, SCOPUS, T02, W07, Z02.
—BLDSC (3425.730000), AskIEEE, CASDDS, IE, Infotrieve, Ingenta, INIST, Linda Hall. **CCC.**
Published by: Springer (Subsidiary of: Springer Science+Business Media), Tiergartenstr 17, Heidelberg, 69121, Germany. TEL 49-6221-4870, FAX 49-6221-345229. Eds. I Mueller, K Hutter, Lev Truskinovsky, Stefan Seelecke. **Subscr. in the Americas to:** Springer New York LLC, Journal Fulfillment, PO Box 2485, Secaucus, NJ 07096. TEL 800-777-4643, 201-348-4033, FAX 201-348-4505, journals-ny@springer.com, http://www.springer.com; **Subscr. to:** Springer Distribution Center, Kundenservice Zeitschriften, Haberstr 7, Heidelberg 69126, Germany. TEL 49-6221-3454303, FAX 49-6221-3454229, subscriptions@springer.com.

➤ **CRYOGAS INTERNATIONAL**; the source of timely and relevant information for the industrial gas and cryogenics industries. *see* ENGINEERING—Mechanical Engineering

536.56 GBR ISSN 0011-2275
TP480 CODEN: CRYOAX
➤ **CRYOGENICS.** Text in English. 1960. 12/yr. EUR 2,657 in Europe to institutions; JPY 353,000 in Japan to institutions; USD 2,971 elsewhere to institutions (effective 2012). adv. bk.rev. abstr.; bibl.; illus. index. back issues avail.; reprints avail. **Document type:** *Journal, Academic/Scholarly.* **Description:** Provides international coverage of cryoengineering, cryoplastics and low-temperature engineering and research.
Related titles: Microform ed.: (from PQC); Online - full text ed.: ISSN 1879-2235 (from IngentaConnect, ScienceDirect); Supplement(s): Proceedings of the International Cryogenic Engineering Conference. ISSN 0308-5422.
Indexed: A01, A03, A05, A08, A22, A23, A24, A26, A28, APA, AS&TA, AS&TI, ASCA, AcoustA, ApMecR, B04, B13, BioEngAb, BrCerAb, BrTechI, C&ISA, C10, C33, CA, CA/WCA, CEA, CIA, CIN, CIS, CMCI, CPEI, CerAb, ChemAb, ChemTitl, CivEngAb, CorrAb, CurCont, E&CAJ, E11, EEA, EMA, ESPM, EngInd, EnvEAb, F&EA, GasAb, H15, I05, IBR, IBZ, ISMEC, ISR, Inspec, M&TEA, M09, MBF, METADEX, P30, PhysBer, RefZh, S01, SCI, SCOPUS, SolStAb, T02, T04, TCEA, TM, W07, WAA.
—BLDSC (3490.150000), AskIEEE, CASDDS, IE, Infotrieve, Ingenta, INIST, Linda Hall. **CCC.**
Published by: Pergamon (Subsidiary of: Elsevier Science & Technology), The Blvd, Langford Ln, East Park, Kidlington, Oxford OX5 1GB, United Kingdom. TEL 44-1865-843000, FAX 44-1865-843010, JournalsCustomerServiceEMEA@elsevier.com. Eds. L Bottura, S W Van Sciver, Tomiyoshi Haruyama. **Subscr. to:** Elsevier BV, Radarweg 29, PO Box 211, Amsterdam 1000 AE, Netherlands. TEL 31-20-4853757, FAX 31-20-4853432, http://www.elsevier.nl.

536 JPN ISSN 1344-8692
DENNETSU/HEAT TRANSFER SOCIETY OF JAPAN. JOURNAL. Text in English. 1962. bi-m.
Formerly (until 1998): Dennetsu Kenkyu (0910-7851)
Related titles: Online - full text ed.
—BLDSC (4757.982000). **CCC.**
Published by: Nihon Dennetsu Gakkai/Heat Transfer Society of Japan, 16-16, Yushima 2, Bunkyo-ku, Tokyo, 113-0034, Japan. office@htsj.or.jp.

621.59 CHN ISSN 1000-6516
TP480
➤ **DIWEN GONGCHENG/CRYOGENICS.** Text in Chinese; Abstracts in Chinese, English. 1979. bi-m. CNY 60, USD 60; CNY 10 per issue (effective 2009). **Document type:** *Journal, Academic/Scholarly.* **Description:** Covers the latest developments of theoretical and applied researches in the fields of cryogenics.
Related titles: Online - full text ed.
Published by: Zhongguo Hangtian Keji Jituan Gongsi, Beijing Hangtian Shiyan Jishu Yanjiusuo, PO Box 7205-27, Beijing, 100074, China. TEL 86-10-68375354. Circ: 1,000.

536.56 CHN ISSN 1000-3258
QC277.9 CODEN: DWXUES
➤ **DIWEN WULI XUEBAO/CHINESE JOURNAL OF LOW TEMPERATURE PHYSICS.** Text in Chinese; Summaries in English. 1978. bi-m. USD 20.80 (effective 2009). adv. **Document type:** *Journal, Academic/Scholarly.* **Description:** Publishes research papers in physics from China and the world. Topics include low-temperature physics and technology, and superconductors.
Formerly: Acta Physica Temperaturae Humilis Sinica: Cryophysics (0253-3634)
Related titles: Online - full text ed.
Indexed: A22, CIN, ChemAb, ChemTitl, Inspec.
—BLDSC (3180.368000), AskIEEE, CASDDS, East View, IE, Ingenta, INIST, Linda Hall.
Published by: (Zhongguo Kexue Jishu Daxue/China University of Science and Technology), Kexue Chubanshe/Science Press, 16 Donghuang Cheng Genbei Jie, Beijing, 100717, China. http://www.sciencep.com/. Ed. Xi-Xian Yao. Circ: 6,000. **Dist. by:** China International Book Trading Corp, 35 Chegongzhuang Xilu, Haidian District, PO Box 399, Beijing 100044, China. TEL 86-10-68412045, FAX 86-10-68412023, cibtc@mail.cibtc.com.cn, http://www.cibtc.com.cn.

536.73 CHE ISSN 1099-4300
CODEN: ENTRFG
➤ **ENTROPY**; international and interdisciplinary journal of entropy and information studies. Text in English. 1999. m. USD 30 to individuals; USD 100 to institutions (effective 2002). bk.rev. back issues avail. **Document type:** *Journal, Academic/Scholarly.* **Description:** Publishes reviews, research papers and short notes on general aspects of entropy and information concepts as used in statistical mechanics, thermodynamics, and symmetry.
Related titles: CD-ROM ed.; Online - full text ed.: free (effective 2011).
Indexed: A01, A20, CA, CCMJ, CurCont, Inspec, MSN, MathR, P30, SCI, SCOPUS, T02, W07, Z02.
Published by: M D P I AG, Postfach, Basel, 4005, Switzerland. TEL 41-61-6837734, FAX 41-61-3028918. Circ: 2,000 (controlled).

536 USA ISSN 0891-6152
TJ260 CODEN: EXHTEV
➤ **EXPERIMENTAL HEAT TRANSFER**; an international journal. Text in English. 1987. q. GBP 487 combined subscription in United Kingdom to institutions (print & online eds.); EUR 643, USD 809 combined subscription to institutions (print & online eds.) (effective 2012). adv. back issues avail.; reprint service avail. from PSC. **Document type:** *Journal, Academic/Scholarly.* **Description:** Provides a forum for experimentally based high quality research articles and communications in the general area of heat-mass transfer and the related fluid dynamics.
Related titles: Microform ed.: (from PQC); Online - full text ed.: ISSN 1521-0480. GBP 438 in United Kingdom to institutions; EUR 578, USD 728 to institutions (effective 2012) (from IngentaConnect).
Indexed: A01, A03, A08, A22, A28, ABIPC, APA, ApMecR, BrCerAb, C&ISA, CA, CA/WCA, CIA, CIN, CPEI, CerAb, ChemAb, ChemTitl, CivEngAb, CorrAb, E&CAJ, E01, E11, E14, EEA, EIA, EMA, ESPM, EngInd, EnvEAb, H15, ISMEC, Inspec, M&TEA, M09, MBF, METADEX, P26, P52, P54, P56, PQC, RefZh, S01, SCI, SCOPUS, SolStAb, T02, T04, W07, WAA.
—AskIEEE, CASDDS, IE, Infotrieve, Ingenta, INIST, Linda Hall. **CCC.**

Published by: Taylor & Francis Inc. (Subsidiary of: Taylor & Francis Group), 325 Chestnut St, Ste 800, Philadelphia, PA 19106. TEL 215-625-8900, FAX 215-625-8914, orders@taylorandfrancis.com, http://www.taylorandfrancis.com. Ed. Dimos Poulikakos.

536 531 RUS ISSN 0430-6228
CODEN: FGVZA7

FIZIKA GORENIYA I VZRYVA/COMBUSTION, EXPLOSION AND SHOCK WAVES. Text in Russian. 1965. bi-m. RUR 580 for 6 mos. domestic; USD 185 foreign (effective 2005). **Document type:** *Journal, Academic/Scholarly.* **Description:** Covers solid, gas and dispersed system combustion, detonation waves in condensed explosives, heterogeneous systems and gases, high temperature self-propagating synthesis, explosive welding, and hypervelocity impact.
Related titles: Online - full text ed.; ◆ English ed.: Combustion, Explosion and Shock Waves. ISSN 0010-5082.
Indexed: C&ISA, C33, ChemAb, CorrAb, E&CAJ, GeoRef, Inspec, RefZh, SCOPUS, SolStAb, SpeleolAb, WAA.
—BLDSC (0389.720000), East View, INIST, Linda Hall. **CCC.**
Published by: (Rossiiskaya Akademiya Nauk, Sibirskoe Otdelenie/ Russian Academy of Sciences, Siberian Branch), Izdatel'stvo Sibirskogo Otdeleniya Rossiiskoi Akademii Nauk/Publishing House of the Russian Academy of Sciences, Siberian Branch, Morskoi pr 2, a/ya 187, Novosibirsk, 630090, Russian Federation. TEL 7-3832-300570, FAX 7-3832-333755, psb@ad-sbras.nsc.ru. Ed. V V Mitrofanov. Circ: 365. **Dist. by:** Informnauka Ltd., Ul Usievicha 20, Moscow 125190, Russian Federation. alfimov@viniti.ru.

536.56 UKR ISSN 0132-6414
QC278 CODEN: FNTEDK

➤ **FIZYKA NYZ'KYKH TEMPERATUR**; naukovyi zhurnal. Text in Russian; Summaries in English. 1975. m. USD 360 foreign (effective 2005). adv. bk.rev. illus. **Document type:** *Journal, Academic/ Scholarly.* **Description:** Presents papers, brief reports and letters to the editor bringing original findings, surveys of the most important problems of low-temperature physics.
Formerly: Fizika Nizkikh Temperatur
Related titles: Online - full text ed.: ISSN 1816-0328. 2002. free (effective 2011); ◆ English Translation: Low Temperature Physics. ISSN 1063-777X.
Indexed: A28, APA, ASCA, BrCerAb, C&ISA, CA/WCA, CIA, CIN, CPEI, Cadscan, CerAb, ChemAb, ChemTitl, CivEngAb, CorrAb, Djerelo, E&CAJ, E11, EEA, EMA, EngInd, H15, INIS AtomInd, ISR, Inspec, LeadAb, M&TEA, M09, MBF, METADEX, PhysBer, RefZh, SolStAb, T04, WAA, Zincscan.
—AskIEEE, CASDDS, East View, INIST, Linda Hall. **CCC.**
Published by: Natsional'na Akademiya Nauk Ukrainy, Fizyko-Tekhnichnyi Instytut Nyz'kykh Temperatur im. B.I. Verkina/Ukrainian Academy of Sciences, B. Verkin Institute for Low Temperature Physics and Engineering, pr-kt Lenina 47, Kharkov, 61103, Ukraine. TEL 380-57-3402223, FAX 380-57-3403370, ilt@ilt.kharkov.ua, http:// www.ilt.kharkov.ua. Ed. V V Eremenko.

536.7 CHN ISSN 0253-231X
QC310.15 CODEN: KCJPDF

➤ **GONGCHENG REWULI XUEBAO/JOURNAL OF ENGINEERING THERMOPHYSICS.** Text in Chinese. 1980. bi-m. USD 213.60 (effective 2009). adv. **Document type:** *Journal, Academic/Scholarly.* **Description:** Publishes original papers on engineering thermodynamics, aerothermodynamics of heat engines, heat and mass transfer, combustion, thermophysical properties of matter, and techniques related to thermophysical property measurement and experimentation.
Related titles: Online - full content ed.; Online - full text ed.
Indexed: A22, CPEI, ChemAb, EngInd, SCOPUS.
—BLDSC (4979.240000), CASDDS, East View, IE, Ingenta, Linda Hall.
Published by: (Zhongguo Gongcheng Rewuli Xuehui/Chinese Society of Engineering Thermophysics), Kexue Chubanshe/Science Press, 16 Donghuang Cheng Genbei Jie, Beijing, 100717, China. TEL 86-10-64000246, FAX 86-10-64030255. Ed. Rui-xian Cai. Circ: 6,000. **In US:** Science Press New York Ltd., 63-117 Alderton St, Rego Park, NY 11373. TEL 718-459-4638; **Dist. by:** China International Book Trading Corp, 35 Chegongzhuang Xilu, Haidian District, PO Box 399, Beijing 100044, China. TEL 86-10-68412045, FAX 86-10-68412023, cibtc@mail.cibtc.com.cn, http://www.cibtc.com.cn.

536 NLD ISSN 1573-4374

HANDBOOK OF THERMAL ANALYSIS AND CALORIMETRY. Text in English. 1998. irreg., latest vol.5, 2008. price varies. **Document type:** *Monographic series, Academic/Scholarly.* **Description:** Covers the theory, fundamentals and diverse applications of thermal analysis and calorimetry.
Indexed: SCOPUS.
Published by: Elsevier BV (Subsidiary of: Elsevier Science & Technology), Radarweg 29, PO Box 211, Amsterdam, 1000 AE, Netherlands. TEL 31-20-4853911, FAX 31-20-4852457, JournalsCustomerServiceEMEA@elsevier.com, http:// www.elsevier.com. Ed. Patrick Gallagher.

536 USA

HANDBOOK OF THERMAL CONDUCTIVITY. Text in English. 1995. irreg., latest vol.3, 1995. price varies. **Document type:** *Monographic series, Academic/Scholarly.*
Related titles: Online - full text ed.: ISSN 1874-8783.
Published by: Gulf Professional Publishing (Subsidiary of: Elsevier Science & Technology), 3251 Riverport Ln, Maryland Heights, MO 63043. TEL 314-453-7010, FAX 314-453-7095, http:// www.elsevier.com.

536.4 532 DEU ISSN 0947-7411
TJ260 CODEN: HMTRF8

➤ **HEAT AND MASS TRANSFER**; Waerme- und Stoffuebertragung. Text in English, German. 1968. m. EUR 3,574, USD 4,365 combined subscription to institutions (print & online eds.) (effective 2012). adv. bibl.; charts; illus. back issues avail.; reprint service avail. from PSC. **Document type:** *Journal, Academic/Scholarly.* **Description:** Experimental and theoretical research on the problems of heat and mass transfer.
Formerly: Waerme- und Stoffuebertragung (0042-9929)
Related titles: Microform ed.: (from PQC); Online - full text ed.: ISSN 1432-1181 (from IngentaConnect).
Indexed: A01, A03, A08, A22, A26, ASCA, ApMecR, C24, CA, CEABA, CIN, CPEI, ChemAb, ChemTitl, CurCont, E01, E14, EngInd, INIS AtomInd, ISR, Inspec, PetrolAb, RefZh, SCI, SCOPUS, T02, TCEA, TM, W07.
—BLDSC (4275.405000), AskIEEE, CASDDS, IE, Infotrieve, Ingenta, INIST, Linda Hall, PADDS. **CCC.**
Published by: Springer (Subsidiary of: Springer Science+Business Media), Tiergartenstr 17, Heidelberg, 69121, Germany. TEL 49-6221-4870, FAX 49-6221-345229. Ed. Andrea Luke. adv.: B&W page EUR 700, color page EUR 1,740. Circ: 360 (paid and controlled). **Subscr. in N. America to:** Springer New York LLC, Journal Fulfillment, PO Box 2485, Secaucus, NJ 07096. TEL 201-348-4033, 800-777-4643, FAX 201-348-4505, journals-ny@springer.com, http://www.springer.com; **Subscr. to:** Springer Distribution Center, Kundenservice Zeitschriften, Haberstr 7, Heidelberg 69126, Germany. TEL 49-6221-3454303, FAX 49-6221-3454229, subscriptions@springer.com.

➤ **HEAT TRANSFER - ASIAN RESEARCH (ONLINE).** *see* ENGINEERING—Mechanical Engineering

➤ **HEAT TRANSFER - ASIAN RESEARCH (PRINT).** *see* ENGINEERING—Mechanical Engineering

➤ **HEAT TRANSFER - RECENT CONTENTS (ONLINE).** *see* PHYSICS—Abstracting, Bibliographies, Statistics

➤ **HEAT TRANSFER RESEARCH.** *see* ENGINEERING—Mechanical Engineering

536.57 RUS ISSN 0018-151X
QC276 CODEN: HITEA4

➤ **HIGH TEMPERATURE.** Text in English. 1963. bi-m. EUR 5,591, USD 5,214 combined subscription to institutions (print & online eds.) (effective 2012). back issues avail.; reprint service avail. from PSC. **Document type:** *Journal, Academic/Scholarly.* **Description:** Examines theoretical and experimental results of research in high-temperature physics, as they apply to modern engineering problems.
Formerly: High Temperature Physics
Related titles: Microfilm ed.: (from PQC); Online - full text ed.: ISSN 1608-3156; ◆ Translation of: Teplofizika Vysokikh Temperatur. ISSN 0040-3644.
Indexed: A01, A03, A08, A22, A26, ASCA, ApMecR, BibLing, C24, C33, CA, CEA, CIN, CPEI, ChemAb, ChemTitl, CurCont, E01, E14, EnerRA, EngInd, IBR, IBZ, ISR, Inspec, MSCI, SCI, SCOPUS, T02, TCEA, W07.
—BLDSC (0412.087000), AskIEEE, CASDDS, East View, IE, Infotrieve, Ingenta, INIST, Linda Hall. **CCC.**
Published by: (Rossiiskaya Akademiya Nauk/Russian Academy of Sciences), M A I K Nauka - Interperiodica (Subsidiary of: Pleiades Publishing, Inc.), Profsoyuznaya ul 90, Moscow, 117997, Russian Federation. TEL 7-095-3347420, FAX 7-095-3360666, compmg@maik.ru, http://www.maik.ru. Ed. Vladimir E Fortov.

536 620 540 USA ISSN 0018-1544
QC276 CODEN: HTHPAK

➤ **HIGH TEMPERATURES - HIGH PRESSURES.** Text in English. 1969. q. EUR 148 in Europe to individuals; JPY 19,859 in Japan to individuals; USD 157 elsewhere to individuals; EUR 635 combined subscription in Europe to institutions (print & online eds.); JPY 76,372 combined subscription in Japan to institutions (print & online eds.); USD 766 combined subscription elsewhere to institutions (print & online eds.) (effective 2011). adv. bk.rev. index. back issues avail.; reprints avail. **Document type:** *Journal, Academic/Scholarly.* **Description:** Brings out research papers related to thermophysical properties of matter, including thermal and transport properties.
Related titles: CD-ROM ed.; Online - full text ed.: ISSN 1472-3441.
Indexed: A01, A22, A28, APA, BrCerAb, C&ISA, C33, CA, CA/WCA, CIA, CIN, CerAb, ChemAb, ChemTitl, CivEngAb, CorrAb, E&CAJ, E11, EEA, EMA, GeoRef, H15, IBR, IBZ, Inspec, M&TEA, M09, MBF, METADEX, MinerAb, PhysBer, RefZh, SCOPUS, SolStAb, SpeleolAb, T02, T04, WAA.
—BLDSC (4307.369500), AskIEEE, CASDDS, IE, Infotrieve, Ingenta, INIST, Linda Hall. **CCC.**
Published by: Old City Publishing, Inc., 628 N 2nd St, Philadelphia, PA 19123. TEL 215-925-4390, FAX 215-925-4371, info@oldcitypublishing.com. Eds. Ivan Egry TEL 49-2203-6012844, Jean-Francois Sacadura TEL 33-472-438153.

536 IND ISSN 0379-0479
CODEN: IJCRDD

INDIAN JOURNAL OF CRYOGENICS; a quarterly publication for basic & applied low temperatures. Abbreviated title: I J C. Text in English. 1976. q. bk.rev. abstr.; bibl. back issues avail. **Document type:** *Journal, Academic/Scholarly.* **Description:** Reviews, research papers, short communications on cryogenics and allied subjects.
Formerly: National Symposia on Cryogenics. Proceedings
Indexed: CIN, ChemAb, ChemTitl, Inspec, PhysBer.
—AskIEEE, CASDDS, INIST, Linda Hall.
Published by: Indian Cryogenics Council, Inter University Accelerator Ctr, Aruna Asaf Ali Marg, New Delhi, 110 067, India. TEL 91-11-26893955, FAX 91-11-26893666, roy@nsc.res.in, http:// www.iuac.ernet.in/iccwebsite/icc.html. **Co-sponsor:** Advanced Centre of Cryogenic Research Calcutta.

INDUSTRIAL COMBUSTION. *see* ENGINEERING—Industrial Engineering

INSTITUT INTERNATIONAL DU FROID. BULLETIN/INTERNATIONAL INSTITUTE OF REFRIGERATION. BULLETIN. *see* HEATING, PLUMBING AND REFRIGERATION

INSTITUT INTERNATIONAL DU FROID. COMPTES RENDUS DE REUNIONS DE COMMISSIONS/INTERNATIONAL INSTITUTE OF REFRIGERATION. PROCEEDINGS OF COMMISSION MEETINGS. *see* HEATING, PLUMBING AND REFRIGERATION

INTERNATIONAL CONFERENCE ON THERMOELECTRICS. *see* PHYSICS—Electricity

536 621 USA ISSN 0142-727X
TJ260 CODEN: IJHFD2

➤ **INTERNATIONAL JOURNAL OF HEAT AND FLUID FLOW.** Text in English. 1971. bi-m. EUR 1,619 in Europe to institutions; JPY 214,900 in Japan to institutions; USD 1,817 elsewhere to institutions (effective 2012). adv. bk.rev. abstr.; bibl.; charts; illus.; stat. index. back issues avail.; reprints avail. **Document type:** *Journal, Academic/Scholarly.* **Description:** Covers experimental aspects of engineering thermodynamics, heat transfer and fluid dynamics relevant to industrial applications.
Formerly (until 1979): Heat and Fluid Flow (0046-7138)
Related titles: Microform ed.: N.S. (from PQC); Online - full text ed.: ISSN 1879-2278. N.S. (from IngentaConnect, ScienceDirect).
Indexed: A01, A03, A08, A22, A26, A28, APA, ASCA, ApMecR, BrCerAb, C&ISA, C10, C24, CA, CA/WCA, CEA, CIA, CIN, CPEI, CerAb, ChemAb, ChemTitl, CivEngAb, CorrAb, CurCont, E&CAJ, E11, EEA, EMA, ESPM, EngInd, EnvEAb, FLUIDEX, FPRD, H15, I05, IBuildSA, ISR, Inspec, M&TEA, M09, MBF, METADEX, MSCI, PhysBer, RefZh, S01, SCI, SCOPUS, SolStAb, T02, T04, TCEA, W07, WAA.
—BLDSC (4542.279000), AskIEEE, CASDDS, IE, Infotrieve, Ingenta, INIST, Linda Hall. **CCC.**
Published by: Elsevier Inc. (Subsidiary of: Elsevier Science & Technology), 1600 John F Kennedy Blvd, Philadelphia, PA 19103. TEL 215-239-3900, FAX 215-238-7883, JournalCustomerService-usa@elsevier.com. Eds. B E Launder TEL 44-161-3063801, N Kasagi TEL 81-3-58416417, T B Gatski TEL 757-810-3694.

536 ITA ISSN 0392-8764
CODEN: HETEEE

INTERNATIONAL JOURNAL OF HEAT AND TECHNOLOGY/CALORE E TECNOLOGIA. Key Title: Heat and Technology. Text in English. 1983. s-a. EUR 135 in the European Union; EUR 150 elsewhere (effective 2011). adv. **Document type:** *Journal, Academic/Scholarly.*
Indexed: A22, ApMecR, CIN, CPEI, ChemAb, ChemTitl, EngInd, Inspec, SCOPUS, Z02.
—AskIEEE, CASDDS, Linda Hall. **CCC.**
Published by: Edizioni E T S, Piazza Carrara 16-19, Pisa, Italy. TEL 39-050-29544, FAX 39-050-20158, info@edizioniets.it, http:// www.edizioniets.it. Ed. Enrico Lorenzini. Circ: 1,000.

536 669 USA ISSN 1061-3862
TA401 CODEN: ISHSE3

➤ **INTERNATIONAL JOURNAL OF SELF-PROPAGATING HIGH-TEMPERATURE SYNTHESIS.** Text in English. 1992. q. EUR 1,072, USD 1,297 combined subscription to institutions (print & online eds.) (effective 2012). abstr.; charts; illus. back issues avail. **Document type:** *Journal, Academic/Scholarly.* **Description:** Offers materials scientists, physical and chemical engineers, and metallurgists articles on the new technology of "SHS," the unique process for the production of advanced materials based on solid-state combustion utilizing internally generated chemical energy.
Related titles: Online - full text ed.: ISSN 1934-788X.
Indexed: A22, A26, CIN, ChemAb, ChemTitl, E01, E08, Inspec, RefZh, S09.
—BLDSC (4542.544650), AskIEEE, CASDDS, East View, IE, Ingenta. **CCC.**
Published by: Allerton Press, Inc. (Subsidiary of: Pleiades Publishing, Inc.), 18 W 27th St, New York, NY 10001. TEL 646-424-9686, FAX 646-424-9695, journals@allertonpress.com. Ed. Alexander G Merzhanov.

▼ ➤ **INTERNATIONAL JOURNAL OF THERMAL & ENVIRONMENTAL ENGINEERING.** *see* ENGINEERING

536.7 621.4 FRA ISSN 1290-0729
TJ260 CODEN: IJTSFZ

➤ **INTERNATIONAL JOURNAL OF THERMAL SCIENCES.** Short title: I J T S. Text in English; Summaries in English, French. 1962. 12/yr. EUR 1,362 in Europe to institutions; JPY 181,000 in Japan to institutions; USD 1,532 elsewhere to institutions (effective 2012). adv. bk.rev. abstr.; bibl.; charts; stat. back issues avail.; reprints avail. **Document type:** *Journal, Academic/Scholarly.* **Description:** Publishes original articles on the phenomena of heat and mass transfer, systems, and energy processes, as well as applications related to processes and products in the industrial, construction, transportation and environmental sectors.
Formerly (until 1999): Revue Generale de Thermique (0035-3159)
Related titles: Online - full text ed.: (from IngentaConnect, ScienceDirect).
Indexed: A01, A03, A08, A20, A22, A26, A28, APA, ASCA, ApMecR, BrCerAb, C&ISA, CA, CA/WCA, CEA, CIA, CIN, CISA, CPEI, CerAb, ChemAb, ChemTitl, CivEngAb, CorrAb, CurCont, E&CAJ, E11, EEA, EMA, ESPM, EngInd, EnvEAb, F&EA, FR, GasAb, GeoRef, H15, I05, IBuildSA, INIS AtomInd, Inspec, M&TEA, M09, MBF, METADEX, MSCI, RefZh, S01, SCI, SCOPUS, SolStAb, SpeleolAb, T02, T04, VITIS, W07, WAA.
—BLDSC (4542.695170), CASDDS, IE, Infotrieve, Ingenta, INIST, Linda Hall. **CCC.**
Published by: (Societe Francaise des Thermiciens), Elsevier Masson (Subsidiary of: Elsevier Health Sciences), 62 Rue Camille Desmoulins, Issy les Moulineaux, Cedex 92442, France. TEL 33-1-71165500, FAX 33-1-71165600, infos@elsevier-masson.fr, http://www.elsevier-masson.fr. Eds. D Gobin, U Gross, Y Bayazitoglu. Circ: 1,200.

536.7 TUR ISSN 1301-9724

➤ **INTERNATIONAL JOURNAL OF THERMODYNAMICS.** Text in English. 1998. q. USD 30 to individuals; USD 120 to institutions (effective 2009). **Document type:** *Journal, Academic/Scholarly.* **Description:** Serves as a forum and central source of reference for applied and theoretical thermodynamics with emphasis on the dissemination of technical information of permanent interest, particularly in current applications and proposed improvement in industry.
Formerly (until 2003): International Journal of Applied Thermodynamics
Related titles: Online - full text ed.: free (effective 2011).
Indexed: C10, CA, CPEI, EngInd, SCOPUS, T02.
—IE, Ingenta.
Published by: Internaional Centre for Applied Thermodynamics, Faculty of Mechanical Engineering, Istanbul Technical University, Gumussuyu, Istanbul, 80191, Turkey. TEL 90-212-2518737, FAX 90-212-2450795, mknicat@itu.edu.tr, mknijat@itu.edu.tr, info@icatweb.org. Ed. M R von Spakovsky.

536 USA ISSN 0195-928X
QC192 CODEN: IJTHDY

➤ **INTERNATIONAL JOURNAL OF THERMOPHYSICS**; journal of thermophysical properties and thermophysics and its applications. Text in English. 1980. bi-m. EUR 2,501, USD 2,583 combined subscription to institutions (print & online eds.) (effective 2012). adv. back issues avail.; reprint service avail. from PSC. **Document type:** *Journal, Academic/Scholarly.* **Description:** Provides a medium for the publication of papers in thermophysics, assisting both generators and users of thermophysical properties data.
Related titles: Microfilm ed.: (from PQC); Online - full text ed.: ISSN 1572-9567 (from IngentaConnect).

P

Indexed: A01, A03, A08, A22, A26, A28, APA, ASCA, BibLing, BrCerAb, C&ISA, C24, C33, CA, CA/WCA, CCI, CEABA, CIA, CIN, CPEI, CerAb, ChemAb, ChemTitl, CivEngAb, CorrAb, CurCR, CurCont, E&CAJ, E01, E11, EEA, EMA, ESPM, EngInd, EnvEAb, H15, ISR, Inspec, M&TEA, M09, MBF, METADEX, MSCI, P30, PhysBer, R16, RefZh, SCI, SCOPUS, SolStAb, T02, T04, W07, WAA.
—BLDSC (4542.695200), AskIEEE, CASDDS, IE, Infotrieve, Ingenta, INIST, Linda Hall. **CCC.**
Published by: Springer New York LLC (Subsidiary of: Springer Science+Business Media), 233 Spring St, New York, NY 10013. TEL 212-460-1500, FAX 212-460-1575, service-ny@springer.com. Ed. William M Haynes.

536.7 TUR ISSN 1300-3615
ISI BILIMI VE TEKNIGI DERGISI/JOURNAL OF THERMAL SCIENCES AND TECHNOLOGY. Text in Turkish. 1978. q. TRY 25 membership (effective 2010). **Document type:** *Journal, Academic/Scholarly.*
Indexed: A01, CA, CPEI, SCI, SCOPUS, T02, W07.
Address: TIBTD Makina Muhendisligi, Bolumu ODTU, Ankara, 06531, Turkey. TEL 90-312-5823424, FAX 90-312-2308434, hasmet@gazi.edu.tr, bzuysal@tibtd.org.tr. Ed. Nuri Yucel.

J P JOURNAL OF HEAT AND MASS TRANSFER. *see* ENERGY

536.7 USA ISSN 2090-1968
➤ **JOURNAL OF COMBUSTION.** Text in English. 2007. q. USD 295 (effective 2011). **Document type:** *Journal, Academic/Scholarly.* **Description:** Contains research from the broad areas of combustion, energy, and chemically reacting systems involving high-, moderate- and low-temperature phenomena.
Formerly (until 2008): International Journal of Reacting Systems (1687-6016)
Related titles: Online - full text ed.: ISSN 2090-1976. free (effective 2011).
Indexed: A01, A26, CA, E14, I05, P52, S06, T02.
—IE.
Published by: Hindawi Publishing Corporation, 410 Park Ave, 15th Fl, PMB 287, New York, NY 10022. FAX 866-446-3294, hindawi@hindawi.com. Ed. Suresh Aggarwal.

➤ **JOURNAL OF FLOW VISUALIZATION AND IMAGE PROCESSING.** *see* ENGINEERING—Mechanical Engineering

➤ **THE JOURNAL OF HIGH ENERGY PHYSICS (ONLINE).** *see* PHYSICS

536.56 USA ISSN 0022-2291
QC278 CODEN: JLTPAC
➤ **JOURNAL OF LOW TEMPERATURE PHYSICS.** Text in English. 1969. 11/yr. EUR 3,184, USD 3,282 combined subscription to institutions (print & online eds.) (effective 2012). adv. back issues avail.; reprint service avail. from PSC. **Document type:** *Journal, Academic/Scholarly.* **Description:** Brings out papers and review articles on fundamental theoretical and experimental research developments in all areas of cryogenics and low temperature physics.
Related titles: Microfilm ed.: (from PQC); Online - full text ed.: ISSN 1573-7357 (from IngentaConnect).
Indexed: A01, A03, A08, A22, A26, A28, APA, ASCA, ApMecR, BibLing, BrCerAb, BullT&T, C&ISA, C33, CA, CA/WCA, CIA, CPEI, Cadscan, CerAb, ChemAb, ChemTitl, CivEngAb, CorrAb, CurCont, E&CAJ, E01, E11, EEA, EMA, ESPM, EngInd, EnvEAb, H15, IBR, IBZ, INIS AtomInd, ISMEC, ISR, Inspec, LeadAb, M&TEA, M09, MBF, METADEX, MSCI, PhysBer, RefZh, SCI, SCOPUS, SolStAb, T02, T04, W07, WAA, Zincscan.
—BLDSC (5010.570000), AskIEEE, CASDDS, IE, Infotrieve, Ingenta, INIST, Linda Hall. **CCC.**
Published by: Springer New York LLC (Subsidiary of: Springer Science+Business Media), 233 Spring St, New York, NY 10013. TEL 212-460-1500, FAX 212-460-1575, service-ny@springer.com, http://www.springer.com/. Eds. Horst Meyer, Mikko Paalanen, Neil Sullivan. **Subscr. to:** Journal Fulfillment, PO Box 2485, Secaucus, NJ 07096. TEL 201-348-4033, FAX 201-348-4505, journals-ny@springer.com.

536.7 USA
TK2970
➤ **JOURNAL OF MAGNETOHYDRODYNAMICS, PLASMA AND SPACE RESEARCH;** an international journal. Text in English. 1988. q. USD 925 to institutions; USD 1,387 combined subscription to institutions (print & online eds.) (effective 2012). back issues avail.; reprints avail. **Document type:** *Journal, Academic/Scholarly.* **Description:** Provides a forum for the international treatment of magnetohydrodynamics, implications for related technologies, and fundamental aspects of special interest to engineers.
Former titles: Journal of Magnetohydrodynamics and Plasma Research (1083-4729); (until 1994): Magnetohydrodynamics (0891-9801)
Related titles: Microform ed.: (from PQC); Online - full text ed.: USD 925 to institutions (effective 2012).
Indexed: ChemAb, ChemTitl, RefZh.
—CASDDS, INIST, Linda Hall. **CCC.**
Published by: Nova Science Publishers, Inc., 400 Oser Ave, Ste 1600, Hauppauge, NY 11788. TEL 631-231-7269, FAX 631-231-8175, main@novapublishers.com.

536 DEU ISSN 0340-0204
QC318.I7 CODEN: JNETDY
➤ **JOURNAL OF NON-EQUILIBRIUM THERMODYNAMICS;** thermophysical, chemical and biochemical processes. Text and summaries in English. 1976. q. EUR 986, USD 1,479 to institutions; EUR 1,135, USD 1,703 combined subscription to institutions (print & online eds.) (effective 2012). adv. abstr.; charts. back issues avail.; reprint service avail. from PSC. **Document type:** *Journal, Academic/Scholarly.* **Description:** Emphasizes the experimental investigation of non-equilibrium phenomena, the measurement of transport coefficients, the physical foundations of non-equilibrium thermodynamics & the engineering approach to non-equilibrium problems.
Related titles: Online - full text ed.: ISSN 1437-4358. 1999. EUR 986, USD 1,479 to institutions (effective 2012).
Indexed: A01, A03, A08, A22, A26, ASCA, ApMecR, CA, CIN, CPEI, ChemAb, ChemTitl, CurCont, E01, EngInd, FLUIDEX, I05, IBR, IBZ, ISMEC, ISR, Inspec, PhysBer, SCI, SCOPUS, T02, W07, Z02.
—BLDSC (5022.837000), AskIEEE, CASDDS, IE, Infotrieve, Ingenta, INIST, Linda Hall. **CCC.**
Published by: Walter de Gruyter GmbH & Co. KG, Genthiner Str 13, Berlin, 10785, Germany. TEL 49-30-260050, FAX 49-30-26005251, info@degruyter.com. Eds. Wolfgang Muschik, Juergen U Keller. Adv. contact Dietlind Makswitat TEL 49-30-260050. B&W page EUR 250; trim 125 x 210. Circ: 200 (paid and controlled).

536.7 CHN ISSN 1003-2169
QC310.15 CODEN: JTSCES
➤ **JOURNAL OF THERMAL SCIENCE/REKEXUE XUEBAO;** international journal of thermal and fluid sciences. Text in English. 1992. q. EUR 590, USD 716 combined subscription to institutions (print & online eds.) (effective 2012). reprint service avail. from PSC. **Document type:** *Journal, Academic/Scholarly.* **Description:** Publishes original papers on experimental, numerical and theoretical investigations in the major areas of thermal and fluid sciences.
Related titles: Online - full text ed.: ISSN 1993-033X.
Indexed: A22, A26, ApMecR, CIN, CPEI, ChemAb, ChemTitl, E01, EngInd, SCI, SCOPUS, W07.
—CASDDS, East View, IE, Ingenta. **CCC.**
Published by: (Chinese Academy of Sciences, Institute of Engineering Thermophysics), Kexue Chubanshe/Science Press, 16 Donghuang Cheng Genbei Jie, Beijing, 100717, China. TEL 86-10-64000246, FAX 86-10-64030255. **Dist. outside of China by:** Springer, Haber Str 7, Heidelberg 69126, Germany. TEL 49-6221-3454303, FAX 49-6221-3454229, subscriptions@springer.com. **Co-publisher:** Springer.

536 JPN ISSN 1880-5566
➤ **JOURNAL OF THERMAL SCIENCE AND TECHNOLOGY.** Text in English. 2006. q. free. **Document type:** *Journal, Academic/Scholarly.*
Media: Online - full text.
Indexed: SCI, SCOPUS, W07.
—CCC.
Published by: (Nihon Dennetsu Gakkai/Heat Transfer Society of Japan), Japan Society of Mechanical Engineers/Nihon Kikai Gakkai, Shinanomachi-Rengakan Bldg, 35 Shinano-Machi, Shinjuku-ku, Tokyo, 160-0016, Japan. wwwadmin@jsme.or.jp, http://www.jsme.or.jp/.

536 USA ISSN 1059-9630
TS653 CODEN: JTTEE5
➤ **JOURNAL OF THERMAL SPRAY TECHNOLOGY.** Text in English. 1992. 5/yr. EUR 1,581, USD 1,920 combined subscription to institutions (print & online eds.) (effective 2012). adv. bk.rev. abstr.; bibl.; charts; illus.; pat.; stat.; tr.lit. index. back issues avail.; reprint service avail. from PSC. **Document type:** *Journal, Academic/Scholarly.* **Description:** Covers the latest research, product, equipment and process developments in thermal spray technology; applications; problem-solving; literature; patents; technical case studies.
Related titles: Microfiche ed.; Microfilm ed.; Online - full text ed.: ISSN 1544-1016 (from IngentaConnect).
Indexed: A01, A22, A26, A28, APA, ASCA, BrCerAb, C&ISA, CA, CA/WCA, CIA, CIN, CPEI, CerAb, ChemAb, ChemTitl, CivEngAb, CorrAb, CurCont, E&CAJ, E01, E11, EEA, EMA, ESPM, EngInd, EnvEAb, H15, I05, ISR, Inspec, M&TEA, M09, MBF, METADEX, MSCI, P52, P56, SCI, SCOPUS, SolStAb, T02, T04, TM, W07, WAA, Weldasearch.
—BLDSC (5069.098700), AskIEEE, CASDDS, IE, Infotrieve, Ingenta, INIST, Linda Hall. **CCC.**
Published by: (A S M International), Springer New York LLC (Subsidiary of: Springer Science+Business Media), 233 Spring St, New York, NY 10013. TEL 212-460-1500, FAX 212-460-1575, service-ny@springer.com, http://www.springer.com. Ed. Christian Moreau.

536.7 USA ISSN 1687-9244
➤ **JOURNAL OF THERMODYNAMICS.** Text in English. 2008. irreg. USD 195 (effective 2011). **Document type:** *Journal, Academic/Scholarly.* **Description:** Publishes original research articles as well as review articles in all areas of thermodynamics.
Related titles: Online - full text ed.: ISSN 1687-9252. 2008. free (effective 2011).
Indexed: C10, CA, P52, T02.
Published by: Hindawi Publishing Corporation, 410 Park Ave, 15th Fl, PMB 287, New York, NY 10022. FAX 215-893-4392, 866-446-3294, orders@hindawi.com.

536 JPN ISSN 0387-1096
CODEN: KGAKDH
KOON GAKKAISHI/HIGH TEMPERATURE SOCIETY. JOURNAL. Text in Japanese; Abstracts in English. 1975. 7/yr. JPY 4,500; JPY 1,500 newsstand/cover (effective 2001). abstr. 60 p./no.; back issues avail. **Document type:** *Journal, Academic/Scholarly.*
Related titles: Online - full text ed.
Indexed: A22, A28, APA, BrCerAb, C&ISA, CA/WCA, CIA, CIN, CerAb, ChemAb, ChemTitl, CivEngAb, CorrAb, E&CAJ, E11, EEA, EMA, ESPM, EnvEAb, H15, INIS AtomInd, JPI, M&TEA, M09, MBF, METADEX, SolStAb, T04, WAA.
—BLDSC (4758.095000), CASDDS, IE, Ingenta, Linda Hall. **CCC.**
Published by: Kook Gakkai/High Temperature Society, c/o JWRI, OSaka University, 11-1 Mihogaoka Ibaraki-shi, Osaka, 567-0047, Japan. TEL 81-6-6879-8698, FAX 81-6-6878-3110. Ed. T Iida. Circ: 600.

536.56 USA ISSN 1063-777X
QC278 CODEN: LTPHEG
➤ **LOW TEMPERATURE PHYSICS;** an english translation of fizika nizhkikh temperatur. Abbreviated title: L T P. Text in English. 1975. m. price varies based on the number of users. adv. bibl.; charts; illus. Index. back issues avail. **Document type:** *Journal, Academic/Scholarly.* **Description:** Publishes results of experimental and theoretical studies at low - mainly liquid helium - temperatures.
Formerly (until 1993): Soviet Journal of Low Temperature Physics (0360-0335)
Related titles: Microform ed.; Online - full text ed.: ISSN 1090-6517; ◆ Translation of: Fizyka Nyz'kykh Temperatur. ISSN 0132-6414.
Indexed: A01, A03, A08, A22, CA, CPI, CurCont, GPAA, ISR, Inspec, MSCI, PhysBer, S01, SCI, SCOPUS, SPINweb, T02, W07.
—BLDSC (0415.598000), AskIEEE, CASDDS, IE, Infotrieve, Ingenta, INIST, Linda Hall. **CCC.**
Published by: (Natsional'na Akademiya Nauk Ukrainy, Fizyko-Tekhnichnyi Instytut Nyz'kykh Temperatur im. B.I. Verkina/Ukrainian Academy of Sciences, B. Verkin Institute for Low Temperature Physics and Engineering UKR), American Institute of Physics, 1 Physics Ellipse, College Park, MD 20740. TEL 301-209-3100, aipinfo@aip.org, http://www.aip.org. Ed. Viktor V Eremenko. **Subscr. to:** PO Box 503284, St Louis, MO 63150. TEL 516-576-2270, 800-344-6902, FAX 516-349-9704, subs@aip.org, http://librarians.aip.org.

536.56 JPN ISSN 0385-3683
QC277.9
LOW TEMPERATURE SCIENCE. SERIES A. DATA REPORT. Text in Japanese; Abstracts in English. 1969. a. per issue exchange basis. **Document type:** *Academic/Scholarly.*
Indexed: GeoRef, SpeleolAb.
—Linda Hall.
Published by: Hokkaido University, Institute of Low Temperature Science, North 19, West 8, Kita-ku, Sapporo, 060-0819, Japan. FAX 81-11-706-7142, TELEX 932261 ILTSHU J. Eds. Nishimura Koichi, Yamada Tomomi.

536 620.1 USA ISSN 1556-7265
TJ260 CODEN: MTENFP
➤ **NANOSCALE AND MICROSCALE THERMOPHYSICAL ENGINEERING.** Text in English. 1997. q. GBP 631 combined subscription in United Kingdom to institutions (print & online eds.); EUR 833, USD 1,047 combined subscription to institutions (print & online eds.) (effective 2012). adv. reprint service avail. from PSC. **Document type:** *Journal, Academic/Scholarly.* **Description:** Covers the basic science and engineering of nanoscale and microscale energy conversion, transport, storage, mass transport, and reactions.
Formerly (until 2006): Microscale Thermophysical Engineering (1089-3954)
Related titles: Online - full text ed.: ISSN 1556-7273. GBP 568 in United Kingdom to institutions; EUR 750, USD 942 to institutions (effective 2012) (from IngentaConnect).
Indexed: A01, A03, A08, A22, A28, APA, ApMecR, BrCerAb, C&ISA, CA, CA/WCA, CIA, CPEI, CerAb, CivEngAb, CorrAb, CurCont, E&CAJ, E01, E11, EEA, EMA, ESPM, EngInd, EnvEAb, H15, ISR, M&TEA, M09, MBF, METADEX, MSCI, P26, P52, P54, P56, PQC, S01, SCI, SCOPUS, SolStAb, T02, T04, TM, W07, WAA.
—CASDDS, IE, Infotrieve, Ingenta, INIST, Linda Hall. **CCC.**
Published by: Taylor & Francis Inc. (Subsidiary of: Taylor & Francis Group), 325 Chestnut St, Ste 800, Philadelphia, PA 19106. TEL 215-625-2940, 800-354-1420, orders@taylorandfrancis.com, http://www.taylorandfrancis.com. Ed. Kenneth Goodson. Adv. contact Linda Hann TEL 44-1344-779945.

536 JPN ISSN 0913-946X
CODEN: NEBUE4
➤ **NETSU BUSSEI/JAPAN JOURNAL OF THERMOPHYSICAL PROPERTIES.** Text in Japanese; Summaries in English, Japanese. 1987. q. JPY 6,000 membership (effective 2005). **Document type:** *Journal, Academic/Scholarly.*
Indexed: A28, APA, BrCerAb, C&ISA, CA/WCA, CIA, CIN, CerAb, ChemAb, ChemTitl, CivEngAb, CorrAb, E&CAJ, E11, EEA, EMA, ESPM, EnvEAb, H15, M&TEA, M09, MBF, METADEX, SolStAb, T04, WAA.
—BLDSC (4648.332000), CASDDS, Linda Hall. **CCC.**
Published by: Nihon Netsu Bussei Gakkai/Japan Society of Thermophysical Properties, 4-3-16 Jonan, Faculty of Engineering, Yamagata University, Department of Mechanical Systems Engineering, Yonezawa, 992-8510, Japan. TEL 81-238-263236, FAX 81-238-263205, http://www.netsubussei.jp/public_html/index.html.

536 JPN ISSN 0386-2615
QD79.T38 CODEN: NESOD2
NETSU SOKUTEI/CALORIMETRY AND THERMAL ANALYSIS. Text in English, Japanese. 1974. q. free to members. **Document type:** *Journal, Academic/Scholarly.* **Description:** Contains original papers, short notes, review articles, lectures, commentary and other various information for Calorimetry and Thermal Analysis and its related fields.
Indexed: A28, APA, BrCerAb, C&ISA, CA/WCA, CIA, CerAb, ChemAb, ChemTitl, CivEngAb, CorrAb, E&CAJ, E11, EEA, EMA, ESPM, EnvEAb, H15, Inspec, M&TEA, M09, MBF, METADEX, RefZh, SolStAb, T04, WAA.
—AskIEEE, CASDDS, Linda Hall. **CCC.**
Published by: Nihon Netsu Sokutei Gakkai/Japan Society of Calorimetry and Thermal Analysis, Miyazawa Bldg 601, 1-6-7 Iwamoto-cho, Chiyoda-ku, Tokyo, 101-0032, Japan. FAX 81-3-58217439, netsu@mbd.nifty.com, http://wwwsoc.nii.ac.jp/jscta/.

NETSU SOKUTEI TORONKAI KOEN YOSHISHU/ABSTRACTS OF JAPANESE CALORIMETRY CONFERENCE. *see* PHYSICS—Abstracting, Bibliographies, Statistics

536 624 JPN ISSN 1340-3354
NIHON NETSU RYUTAI KOGAKKAI RONBUNSHU/JAPAN SOCIETY OF HEAT AND FLUID ENGINEERING. TRANSACTIONS. Text in English, Japanese; Summaries in English. 1986. a.
Published by: Nihon Netsu Ryutai Kogakkai/Japan Society of Heat and Fluid Engineering, Nihon Daigaku Seisan Kogakubu Suri Kogakka, 2-1 Izumi-cho 1-chome, Narashino-shi, Chiba-ken 275-0006, Japan.

536 535 600 JPN ISSN 0916-7900
CODEN: NSGKET
➤ **NIHON SEKIGAISEN GAKKAISHI/JAPAN SOCIETY OF INFRARED SCIENCE AND TECHNOLOGY. JOURNAL.** Text in Japanese. 1976. a. JPY 5,000 membership (effective 2005). adv. **Document type:** *Journal, Academic/Scholarly.* **Description:** Contains original papers and reviews on infrared science and technology.
Formerly (until 1991): Sekigaisen Gijutsu - Infrared Society of Japan. Proceedings (0386-8044)
Indexed: Inspec.
—AskIEEE, CASDDS, Linda Hall. **CCC.**
Published by: Nihon Sekigaisen Gakkai/Japan Society of Infrared Science and Technology, Osaka Prefecture University, Department of Physical Electronics, 1-1 Gakuen-cho, Sakai, Osaka 599-8531, Japan. TEL 81-72-2549263, FAX 81-72-2549908, horinaka@pe.osakafu-u.ac.jp. Ed. Y Itakura. Adv. contact Y Tsunawaki. Circ: 1,000.

536 JPN ISSN 0387-4419
QC277.9
OOSAKA DAIGAKU TEION SENTA DAYORI/OSAKA UNIVERSITY. LOW TEMPERATURE CENTER. NEWS. Text in Japanese. 1973. q. **Document type:** *Newsletter.*
Published by: Oosaka Daigaku, Teion Senta, 2-1 Yamada-Oka, Suita-shi, Osaka-fu 565-0871, Japan. TEL 81-6-850-6691, FAX 81-6-879-7986, takeuchi@rcem.osaka-u.ac.jp, momose@ele.eng.osaka-u.ac.jp. Ed. Kazuo Murase.

536.7 NLD ISSN 1874-396X
QC310.15
➤ **THE OPEN THERMODYNAMICS JOURNAL.** Text in English. 2007. irreg. free (effective 2011). **Document type:** *Journal, Academic/Scholarly.* **Description:** Covers all areas of experimental and applied thermodynamics.
Media: Online - full text.
Indexed: A01, A28, APA, BrCerAb, C&ISA, CA, CA/WCA, CIA, CerAb, CivEngAb, CorrAb, E&CAJ, E11, EEA, EMA, ESPM, H15, M&TEA, M09, MBF, METADEX, SolStAb, T02, T04, WAA.
Published by: Bentham Open (Subsidiary of: Bentham Science Publishers Ltd.), PO Box 294, Bussum, AG 1400, Netherlands. TEL 31-35-6923800, FAX 31-35-6980150, subscriptions@bentham.org. Ed. J C Jones.

➤ **PETROCHEMICAL EQUIPMENT.** *see* ENGINEERING—Chemical Engineering

➤ **PHYSICA B: CONDENSED MATTER.** *see* PHYSICS

536.56 USA ISSN 0079-6417
QC277.9 CODEN: PLTPAA
➤ **PROGRESS IN LOW TEMPERATURE PHYSICS.** Text in Dutch. 1955. irreg., latest vol.16, 2008. price varies. **Document type:** *Monographic series, Academic/Scholarly.* **Description:** Publishes reviews of of recent developments in low-temperature physics.
Related titles: Online - full text ed.
Indexed: ChemAb, ChemTitl, Inspec, SCOPUS.
—CASDDS, INIST. **CCC.**
Published by: J A I Press Inc. (Subsidiary of: Elsevier Science & Technology), 360 Park Ave S, New York, NY 10010. TEL 212-989-5800, FAX 212-633-3990, usinfo-f@elsevier.com, http://www.elsevier.com. Ed. W P Halperin.

536 FRA ISSN 1768-6733
QUANTITATIVE INFRA RED THERMOGRAPHY JOURNAL. Abbreviated title: Q I R T Journal. Text in French. 2004. s-a. **Document type:** *Journal, Academic/Scholarly.*
Related titles: Online - full text ed.: ISSN 2116-7176.
Published by: Lavoisier, 14 rue de Provigny, Cachan, 94236, France. TEL 33-1-47406700, FAX 33-1-47406702, info@lavoisier.fr, http://www.lavoisier.fr.

541 CHN ISSN 1006-8740
CODEN: RKJIFR
➤ **RANSHAO KEXUE YU JISHU/JOURNAL OF COMBUSTION SCIENCE AND TECHNOLOGY.** Text in Chinese. 1995. bi-m. **Document type:** *Journal, Academic/Scholarly.*
Related titles: Online - full text ed.: (from WanFang Data Corp.).
Indexed: CPEI, EngInd, SCOPUS.
—BLDSC (4960.650000), CASDDS, East View.
Published by: Tianjin Daxue Jikan Zhongxin/Academic Journals Publishing Center of Tianjin University, 92, Weijin Lu NanKai, Tianjin, 300072, China. TEL 86-22-27406721, FAX 86-22-27403448, tdxbeb@tju.edu.cn, http://www2.tju.edu.cn/orgs/journal/default.htm.

➤ **REFERATIVNYI ZHURNAL. FIZIKA GAZOV I ZHIDKOSTEI: TERMODINAMIKA I STATISTICHESKAYA FIZIKA**; vypusk svodnogo toma. *see* PHYSICS—Abstracting, Bibliographies, Statistics

536 CHN ISSN 1671-8097
QC310.15
REKEXUE YU JISHU/JOURNAL OF THERMAL SCIENCE AND TECHNOLOGY. Text in Chinese. 2002. q. USD 20 (effective 2009). **Document type:** *Journal, Academic/Scholarly.*
Related titles: Online - full text ed.; Ed.
Indexed: A28, APA, BrCerAb, C&ISA, CA/WCA, CIA, CerAb, CivEngAb, CorrAb, E&CAJ, E11, EEA, EMA, ESPM, EnvEAb, H15, M&TEA, M09, MBF, METADEX, RefZh, SolStAb, T04, WAA.
—BLDSC (7352.039600), East View, Linda Hall.
Address: Ganshizi-qu, 2, Linggong Lu, Dalian, Liaoning 116024, China.

SCIENCE ET TECHNIQUE DU FROID. *see* HEATING, PLUMBING AND REFRIGERATION

STUDIES OF HIGH TEMPERATURE SUPERCONDUCTORS; advances in research and applications. *see* CHEMISTRY—Electrochemistry

536.56 JPN ISSN 0389-2441
CODEN: CRYEB4
➤ **TEION KOGAKU/CRYOGENIC SOCIETY OF JAPAN. JOURNAL.** Text in Japanese; Summaries in English. 1966. m. JPY 9,000 membership (effective 2005). 80 p./no.; back issues avail. **Document type:** *Journal, Academic/Scholarly.*
Related titles: Online - full text ed.: ISSN 1880-0408.
Indexed: CIN, ChemAb, ChemTitl, INIS AtomInd, RefZh.
—BLDSC (4732.559000), CASDDS, Linda Hall. **CCC.**
Published by: Teion Kogakkai/Cryogenic Society of Japan, Palais d'or Hongo 302, Hongo 6-12-8, Bunkyo-ku, Tokyo, 113-0033, Japan. TEL 81-3-38184539, FAX 81-3-38184573, LDJ04246@nifty.ne.jp, http://www.csj.or.jp/jcryo/index.html. Circ: 600 (paid).

536.56 621.59 JPN ISSN 0919-5998
TEION KOGAKU CHODENDO GAKKAI KOEN GAIYOSHU/MEETING ON CRYOGENICS AND SUPERCONDUCTIVITY. PRCEEDINGS. Text in English, Japanese. s-a. JPY 9,000 membership (effective 2005). abstr. 300 p./no.; back issues avail. **Document type:** *Proceedings, Academic/Scholarly.*
Formerly (until 1991): Teion Kogaku Chodendo Gakkai Yokoshu
—BLDSC (8764.505000).
Published by: Teion Kogakkai/Cryogenic Society of Japan, Palais d'or Hongo 302, Hongo 6-12-8, Bunkyo-ku, Tokyo, 113-0033, Japan. TEL 81-3-38184539, FAX 81-3-38184573. Circ: 500.

536.7 RUS ISSN 0869-8635
QC320.16 CODEN: TEAEFI
TEPLOFIZIKA I AEROMEKHANIKA. Text in Russian. 1994. q. RUR 385 domestic for 4 mos.; USD 120 foreign (effective 2005). bk.rev. charts; illus. index. **Document type:** *Journal, Academic/Scholarly.* **Description:** Publishes articles of both theoretical and applied nature, studies on numerical and theoretical simulation, experimental data, and new engineering principles.
Former titles (until 1994): Sibirskii Fiziko-tekhnicheskii Zhurnal (0869-1339); (until 1990): Akademiya Nauk S.S.S.R. Sibirskoe Otdelenie. Izvestiya. Seriya Tekhnicheskikh Nauk (0002-3434)
Related titles: ♦ English ed.: Thermophysics and Aeromechanics. ISSN 0869-8643.
Indexed: CIN, ChemAb, ChemTitl, Inspec, MathR, RefZh.
—AskIEEE, CASDDS, East View, INIST, Linda Hall. **CCC.**
Published by: (Rossiiskaya Akademiya Nauk, Sibirskoe Otdelenie, Institut Teplofiziki im. S.S. Kutateladze), Izdatel'stvo Sibirskogo Otdeleniya Rossiiskoi Akademii Nauk/Publishing House of the Russian Academy of Sciences, Siberian Branch, Morskoi pr 2, a/ya 187, Novosibirsk, 630090, Russian Federation. TEL 7-3832-300570, FAX 7-3832-333755, psb@ad-sbras.nsc.ru. Ed. E P Volchkov. Circ: 200. **Dist. by:** Informnauka Ltd., Ul Usievicha 20, Moscow 125190, Russian Federation. alfimov@viniti.ru.

536.7 ITA
TERMODINAMICA APPLICATA. Text in Italian. 1975. irreg., latest vol.11, 1995. price varies. **Document type:** *Monographic series, Trade.*
Published by: Liguori Editore, Via Posillipo 394, Naples, 80123, Italy. TEL 39-081-7206111, FAX 39-081-7206244, liguori@liguori.it, http://www.liguori.it.

TERMOTEHNIKA. *see* ENERGY

THERMAL NEWS E-REPORT. *see* ENGINEERING—Electrical Engineering

THERMAL SCIENCE. *see* ENERGY

536 JPN ISSN 0918-9963
TJ260
THERMAL SCIENCE AND ENGINEERING. Text in English, Japanese. 1993. bi-m. back issues avail. **Document type:** *Journal, Academic/Scholarly.*
Indexed: INIS AtomInd.
—BLDSC (8814.789750).
Published by: Nihon Dennetsu Gakkai/Heat Transfer Society of Japan, 16-16, Yushima 2, Bunkyo-ku, Tokyo, 113-0034, Japan. office@htsj.or.jp.

531 617.1 615.82 AUT ISSN 1560-604X
➤ **THERMOLOGY INTERNATIONAL.** Text in English. 1991. q. EUR 38 domestic to non-members; EUR 56, USD 68 foreign to non-members (effective 2005). **Document type:** *Journal, Academic/Scholarly.*
Former titles (until 1999): European Journal of Thermology (1028-2238); (until 1997): Thermologie Osterreich (1021-4356)
Indexed: EMBASE, ExcerpMed, R10, Reac, SCOPUS.
Published by: (Ludwig Boltzmann Research Institute for Physical Diagnostics, Austrian Society of Thermology), UHLEN Verlagsgesellschaft m.b.H., Lichtgasse 10, Vienna, 1150, Austria. TEL 43-1-8923546, FAX 43-1-892354622, info@skifuehrer.at. Ed. Kurt Ammer.

536 JPN ISSN 0911-1743
➤ **THERMOPHYSICAL PROPERTIES/NIHON NETSU BUSSEI SHINPOJUMU KOEN RONBUNSHU.** Text in English, Japanese; Summaries in English. 1980. a. JPY 4,000. **Document type:** *Journal, Academic/Scholarly.*
Indexed: A28, APA, BrCerAb, C&ISA, CA/WCA, CIA, CerAb, CivEngAb, CorrAb, E&CAJ, E11, EEA, EMA, H15, M&TEA, M09, MBF, METADEX, SolStAb, T04, WAA.
—BLDSC (8814.889000), Ingenta. **CCC.**
Published by: Nihon Netsu Bussei Gakkai/Japan Society of Thermophysical Properties, 4-3-16 Jonan, Faculty of Engineering, Yamagata University, Department of Mechanical Systems Engineering, Yonezawa, 992-8510, Japan. TEL 81-258-466000, FAX 81-258-466972.

536.7 RUS ISSN 0869-8643
THERMOPHYSICS AND AEROMECHANICS. Text in English. 1994. q. EUR 1,247, USD 1,517 combined subscription to institutions (print & online eds.) (effective 2012). **Document type:** *Journal, Academic/Scholarly.* **Description:** Publishes articles of both theoretical and applied nature, studies on numerical and theoretical simulation, experimental data, and new engineering principles.
Related titles: Online - full content ed.: ISSN 1531-8699; Online - full text ed.: (from IngentaConnect); ♦ Russian ed.: Teplofizika i Aeromekhanika. ISSN 0869-8635.
Indexed: A22, A26, ApMecR, E01, SCI, SCOPUS, W07.
—East View, IE, Ingenta. **CCC.**
Published by: (Rossiiskaya Akademiya Nauk, Sibirskoe Otdelenie, Institut Teplofiziki im. S.S. Kutateladze), M A I K Nauka - Interperiodica (Subsidiary of: Pleiades Publishing, Inc.), Profsoyuznaya ul 90, Moscow, 117997, Russian Federation. TEL 7-095-3347420, FAX 7-095-3360666, compmg@maik.ru, http://www.maik.ru. Ed. E P Volchkov. **Dist. in the Americas by:** Springer New York LLC, Journal Fulfillment, PO Box 2485, Secaucus, NJ 07096. TEL 212-460-1500, FAX 201-348-4505; **Dist. outside of the Americas by:** Springer, Haber Str 7, Heidelberg 69126, Germany. TEL 49-6221-3454303, FAX 49-6221-3454229.

536.56 JPN ISSN 1341-1810
CODEN: TSDAEG
➤ **TOKYO DAIGAKU TEOIN SENTA DAYORI/UNIVERSITY OF TOKYO. CRYOGENIC CENTER. REPORT.** Text in Japanese. 1966. 2/yr. free. **Document type:** *Academic/Scholarly.*
—CASDDS.
Published by: Tokyo Daigaku, Teion Senta/University of Tokyo, Cryogenic Center, 11-16 Yayoi 2-chome, Bunkyo-ku, Tokyo, 113-0032, Japan. TEL 81-3-3812-2111, FAX 81-3-3815-8389. Ed., R&P Kunimitsu Uchinokura. Circ: 500 (controlled).

➤ **TRATAMIENTOS TERMICOS.** *see* METALLURGY

536 IND ISSN 0973-2446
TRENDS IN HEAT AND MASS TRANSFER. Text in English. 1991. a. EUR 134.10 in Europe; JPY 17,582 in Japan; USD 149 elsewhere (effective 2010). **Document type:** *Journal, Academic/Scholarly.* **Description:** Contains critical reviews and original research articles in the field of heat and mass transfer.
Formerly (until 2007): Trends in Heat, Mass & Momentum Transfer (0972-4842)
Related titles: CD-ROM ed.
Indexed: A28, APA, BrCerAb, C&ISA, CA/WCA, CIA, CerAb, CivEngAb, CorrAb, E&CAJ, E11, EEA, EMA, ESPM, EnvEAb, H15, M&TEA, M09, MBF, METADEX, SolStAb, T04, WAA.
—BLDSC (9049.622000).
Published by: Research Trends (P) Ltd., T.C. 17 / 250 (3), Chadiyara Rd, Poojapura, Trivandrum, Kerala 695 012, India. TEL 91-471-2344424, FAX 91-471-2344423, info@researchtrends.net.

536 GRC ISSN 1790-5044
W S E A S TRANSACTIONS ON HEAT AND MASS TRANSFER. Text in English. 2006 (Jan.). q. EUR 300 to individuals; EUR 400 to institutions (effective 2005). **Document type:** *Journal, Academic/Scholarly.*
Indexed: A28, APA, BrCerAb, C&ISA, CA/WCA, CIA, CerAb, CivEngAb, CorrAb, E&CAJ, E11, EEA, EMA, H15, Inspec, M&TEA, M09, MBF, METADEX, SCOPUS, SolStAb, T04, WAA.
—IE, Ingenta.
Published by: World Scientific and Engineering Academy and Society, Ag Ioannou Theologou 17-23, Zographou, Athens 15773, Greece. TEL 30-210-7473313, FAX 30-210-7473314, http://www.wseas.org. Ed. Nikolai Kobasko.

PHYSICS—Mechanics

A I A A - A S M E THERMOPHYSICS AND HEAT TRANSFER CONFERENCE. PROCEEDINGS. (American Institute of Aeronautics and Astronautics - American Society of Mechanical Engineers) *see* PHYSICS—Heat

ACTA MECHANICA. *see* ENGINEERING—Mechanical Engineering

531 DEU ISSN 0567-7718
QA801 CODEN: AMESFT
➤ **ACTA MECHANICA SINICA.** Text in English. 1985. bi-m. EUR 905, USD 1,052 combined subscription to institutions (print & online eds.) (effective 2012). adv. abstr.; charts; illus. back issues avail.; reprint service avail. from PSC. **Document type:** *Journal, Academic/Scholarly.* **Description:** Covers all branches of mechanics. Includes research treatises, experimental technology and methods, brief accounts of research work, studies on the history of mechanics, and academic discussions.
Related titles: Online - full text ed.: ISSN 1614-3116 (from IngentaConnect); ♦ Translation of: Lixue Xuebao. ISSN 0459-1879.
Indexed: A22, A26, A28, APA, ASCA, ApMecR, BrCerAb, C&ISA, CA/WCA, CCMJ, CIA, CMCI, CPEI, CerAb, CivEngAb, CorrAb, CurCont, E&CAJ, E01, E11, EEA, EMA, ESPM, EngInd, EnvEAb, H15, ISR, Inspec, M&TEA, M09, MBF, METADEX, MSN, MathR, P30, RefZh, SCI, SCOPUS, SolStAb, T04, W07, WAA, Z02.
—BLDSC (0632.600000), AskIEEE, IE, Ingenta, INIST, Linda Hall. **CCC.**
Published by: (Chinese Society of Theoretical and Applied Mechanics CHN), Springer (Subsidiary of: Springer Science+Business Media), Tiergartenstr 17, Heidelberg, 69121, Germany. TEL 49-6221-4870, FAX 49-6221-345229, subscriptions@springer.com. Eds. Huajian Gao, Shiyi Chen. Circ: 6,000.

P

531 CHN ISSN 0894-9166
TA349 CODEN: ASSIE8
➤ **ACTA MECHANICA SOLIDA SINICA.** Text in English. 1988. q. USD 71.20 (effective 2009). bk.rev. abstr. back issues avail. **Document type:** *Journal, Academic/Scholarly.* **Description:** Covers all fields of theoretical and applied mechanics, such as the classical fields of elasticity, plasticity, vibrations, structures, rigid body dynamics, hydrodynamics, gas dynamics, and the newly emerging fields of micro/nano mechanics, smart materials and structures, and issues at the interface of mechanics and materials.
Related titles: Microform ed.: (from PQC); Online - full text ed.: ISSN 1860-2134 (from ScienceDirect); ♦ Chinese ed.: Guti Lixue Xuebao. ISSN 0254-7805.
Indexed: ASCA, ApMecR, CA, CCMJ, CPEI, EngInd, MSCI, MSN, SCI, SCOPUS, T02, W07.
—BLDSC (0632.610500), IE, Ingenta, INIST, Linda Hall. **CCC.**
Published by: Chinese Society for Theoretical and Applied Mechanics, No 15, BeiSiHuanXi Rd, Beijing, 100190, China. TEL 86-10-62559209, FAX 86-10-62559588, office@cstam.org.cn, http://www.cstam.org.cn. Ed. Shou-Wen Yu.

➤ **ACTA TECHNICA C S A V.** (Czech Science Advanced Views) *see* ENGINEERING

▼ ➤ **ADVANCES IN APPLIED MATHEMATICS AND MECHANICS.** *see* MATHEMATICS

530 620.1 USA ISSN 0065-2156
TA350 CODEN: AAMCAY
➤ **ADVANCES IN APPLIED MECHANICS.** Text in English. 1948. irreg., latest vol.43, 2009. USD 198 per vol. (effective 2010). adv. index. back issues avail.; reprints avail. **Document type:** *Journal, Academic/Scholarly.* **Description:** Covers the major developments in the field of fluid and solid mechanics are scattered throughout an array of scientific journals, making it often difficult to find what the real advances are, especially for a researcher new to the field.
Related titles: Online - full text ed.; Supplement(s): Rarefied Gas Dynamics.
Indexed: A22, A29, ASCA, ApMecR, B20, B21, CCMJ, ESPM, ISR, Inspec, MathR, SCI, SCOPUS, W07, Z02.
—BLDSC (0699.000000), CASDDS, IE, Infotrieve, Ingenta, INIST, Linda Hall. **CCC.**
Published by: Academic Press (Subsidiary of: Elsevier Science & Technology), 3251 Riverport Ln, Maryland Heights, MO 63043. TEL 314-447-8010, FAX 314-447-8030, JournalCustomerService-usa@elsevier.com, http://www.elsevierdirect.com/imprint.jsp?iid=5. Eds. Erik van der Giessen, Hassan Aref. Adv. contact Tino DeCarlo TEL 212-633-3815.

532 SGP ISSN 1793-8503
▼ **ADVANCES IN COMPUTATIONAL FLUID DYNAMICS.** Text in English. forthcoming 2011. irreg. **Document type:** *Monographic series, Academic/Scholarly.* **Description:** Covers advances in computational fluid dynamics in various areas, including computer simulation of fluid flow, heat transfer and associated phenomena in nature as well as in engineering analysis and design.

Published by: World Scientific Publishing Co. Pte. Ltd., 5 Toh Tuck Link, Singapore, 596224, Singapore. TEL 65-6466-5775, FAX 65-6467-7667, wspc@wspc.com.sg, http://www.worldscientific.com. Eds. Remi Abgrall, Chang Shu TEL 65-6516-6476, Chi-Wang Shu TEL 401-863-2549. **Dist. by:** World Scientific Publishing Co., Inc., 27 Warren St, Ste 401-402, Hackensack, NJ 07601. TEL 201-487-9655, 800-227-7562, FAX 201-487-9656, 888-977-2665, wspc@wspc.com; World Scientific Publishing Ltd., 57 Shelton St, London WC2H 9HE, United Kingdom. TEL 44-207-8360888, FAX 44-207-8362020, sales@wspc.co.uk.

531 BGR ISSN 1313-6550
QC120
➤ **ADVANCES IN THEORETICAL AND APPLIED MECHANICS.** Text in English. 2008. irreg. free (effective 2011). **Document type:** *Journal, Academic/Scholarly.*
Media: Online - full text.
Indexed: Z02.
Published by: Hikari Ltd., Rui planina str 4, vh 7, et 5, Ruse, 7005, Bulgaria. TEL 359-82-580962, hikari@m-hikari.com.

533 RUS ISSN 0320-9377
AERODINAMIKA RAZREZHENNYKH GAZOV/RAREFIED GAS AERODYNAMICS. Text in Russian. 1963. irreg.
—Linda Hall.
Published by: Izdatel'skii Dom Sankt-Peterburgskogo Gosudarstvennogo Universiteta, V.O., 6-ya liniya, dom 11/21, komn 319, St Petersburg, 199004, Russian Federation. TEL 7-812-3252604, press@unipress.ru, http://www.unipress.ru.

532 USA ISSN 0066-4189
QC145 CODEN: ARVFA3
➤ **ANNUAL REVIEW OF FLUID MECHANICS.** Text in English. 1969. a. USD 272 combined subscription per issue to institutions (print & online eds.); USD 227 per issue to institutions (print or online ed.) (effective 2012). bibl.; charts; illus.; abstr. index, cum.index. back issues avail.; reprint service avail. from PSC. **Document type:** *Journal, Academic/Scholarly.* **Description:** Reviews synthesize and filter the vast amount of primary research to identify the principal contributiions in the field of fluid mechanics.
Related titles: Microfilm ed.: (from PQC); Online - full text ed.: ISSN 1545-4479.
Indexed: A01, A03, A08, A22, A26, A28, A33, ABIPC, APA, ASCA, ASFA, ApMecR, BrCerAb, C&ISA, CA, CA/WCA, CCMJ, CIA, CPEI, CerAb, ChemAb, CivEngAb, CorrAb, CurCont, E&CAJ, E08, E11, EEA, EMA, ESPM, EngInd, EnvEAb, FLUIDEX, FR, GEOBASE, GeoRef, H15, I05, IBR, IBZ, ISR, Inspec, M&GPA, M&TEA, M09, MBF, METADEX, MRD, MSN, MathR, P26, P30, P48, P52, P54, P56, PQC, PhysBer, S01, SCI, SCOPUS, SWRA, SolStAb, SpeleolAb, T02, T04, TCEA, W07, WAA.
—BLDSC (1522.540000), CASDDS, IE, Infotrieve, Ingenta, INIST, Linda Hall. **CCC.**
Published by: Annual Reviews, PO Box 10139, Palo Alto, CA 94303. TEL 650-493-4400, FAX 650-424-0910, 800-523-8635, service@annualreviews.org. Eds. Parviz Moin TEL 650-723-9713, Stephen H Davis TEL 847-491-3345, Samuel Gubins.

➤ **APPLIED MATHEMATICS AND MECHANICS.** *see* MATHEMATICS

531.1134 DEU ISSN 1430-6395
CODEN: RHEOEW
➤ **APPLIED RHEOLOGY**; Fliessverhalten steuern. Text in English, German. 1991-1997; resumed 1999. bi-m. EUR 130 to individuals; EUR 225 to institutions (effective 2009). adv. **Document type:** *Journal, Academic/Scholarly.* **Description:** Covers the science of the deformation and flow of soft matter, with special interest in experimental and computational advances in the characterization and understanding of complex fluids, including their nonequilibrium dynamic and structural behaviors.
Formerly (until 1996): Rheology (0939-5059)
Related titles: Online - full text ed.: ISSN 1617-8106.
Indexed: ASCA, CEABA, CIN, ChemAb, ChemTitl, CurCont, FLUIDEX, Inspec, MSCI, SCI, SCOPUS, TM, W07, WSCA.
—BLDSC (1576.577800), CASDDS, IE, Infotrieve, Ingenta. **CCC.**
Published by: Kerschensteiner Verlag GmbH, Moerickestr 4, Lappersdorf, 93138, Germany. TEL 49-941-891720, FAX 49-941-897451, dolp-partner@t-online.de. Eds. Martin Kroeger, Peter Fischer. adv.: B&W page EUR 1,500, color page EUR 2,000; trim 190 x 280. Circ: 1,603 (controlled).

621 531 POL ISSN 0373-2029
TA350 CODEN: AVMHBR
➤ **ARCHIVES OF MECHANICS.** Text in English. 1973. bi-m. EUR 217 foreign (effective 2011). abstr.; bibl.; charts; illus. **Document type:** *Journal, Academic/Scholarly.* **Description:** Provides a forum for original research on mechanics of solids, fluids and discrete systems, including the development of mathematical methods for solving mechanical problems.
Formerly: Archiwum Mechaniki Stosowanej (0004-0800)
Related titles: Online - full text ed.
Indexed: A01, A22, A28, APA, ApMecR, B22, BrCerAb, C&ISA, CA, CA/WCA, CCMJ, CEA, CIA, CIN, CerAb, ChemAb, ChemTitl, CivEngAb, CorrAb, CurCont, E&CAJ, E11, EEA, EMA, ESPM, EnvEAb, GeoRef, GeotechAb, H15, ISR, Inspec, M&TEA, M09, MBF, METADEX, MSCI, MSN, MathR, PhysBer, S&VD, SCI, SCOPUS, SolStAb, SpeleolAb, T02, T04, TCEA, W07, WAA, Z02.
—BLDSC (1637.470000), AskIEEE, CASDDS, IE, Ingenta, INIST, Linda Hall.
Published by: Polska Akademia Nauk, Instytut Podstawowych Problemow Techniki/Polish Academy of Sciences, Institute of Fundamental Technological Research, ul Pawinskiego 5b, Warsaw, 02-106, Poland. TEL 48-22-8261281, publikac@ippt.gov.pl, http://www.ippt.gov.pl. Ed. Boguslaw Lempkowski. Circ: 790. **Dist. by:** Ars Polona, Obroncow 25, Warsaw 03933, Poland. TEL 48-22-5098609, FAX 48-22-5098610, arspolona@arspolona.com.pl, http://www.arspolona.com.pl.

531 BGR ISSN 1310-4772
➤ **BALKAN TRIBOLOGICAL ASSOCIATION. JOURNAL.** Text in English. 1995. s-a. EUR 280 in Europe; USD 350 elsewhere (effective 2006). adv. bk.rev. **Document type:** *Journal, Academic/Scholarly.* **Description:** Contains original papers and reviews in tribotechnics, tribomechanics, tribochemistry, biotribology, and lubrication.
Indexed: SCI, SCOPUS, W07.
—BLDSC (4707.642000), IE, Ingenta, Linda Hall.
Published by: (Balkan Tribological Association SRB), Scientific Bulgarian Communications, 7 Nezabravka St, PO Box 249, Sofia, 1113, Bulgaria. scibulcom@global.bg. Ed., Pub., Adv. contact Slavi Ivanov.

➤ **BAUPHYSIK.** *see* BUILDING AND CONSTRUCTION

532 PER ISSN 2079-0147
C E D I T REVISTA DE INVESTIGACION. (Centro de Desarrollo e Investigacion en Termofluidos) Text in Spanish. 2008. s-a. back issues avail. **Document type:** *Journal, Academic/Scholarly.*
Media: Online - full text.
Published by: Universidad Nacional Mayor de San Marcos, Escuela de Ingenieria de Mecanica de Fluidos, Ciudad Universitaria, Ave Venezuela, s-n, Lima, Peru. TEL 51-1-619700, cedit@unmsm.edu.pe, http://www.unmsm.edu.pe/mecanica/imf.htm.

531 FRA ISSN 0399-0001
C E T I M INFORMATIONS. (Centre Technique des Industries Mecaniques) Text in French. 1967. q. **Document type:** *Journal, Academic/Scholarly.*
Related titles: Online - full text ed.
Indexed: A22.
—BLDSC (3123.840000), IE, Ingenta, INIST, Linda Hall.
Published by: Centre Technique des Industries Mecaniques, 52 av Felix Louat, Senlis Cedex, 60304, France. TEL 33-3-44673136, FAX 33-3-44673539, http://www.cetim.fr.

531 510 GBR
CAMBRIDGE MONOGRAPHS ON MECHANICS. Text in English. 1952. irreg. price varies. back issues avail.; reprints avail. **Document type:** *Monographic series, Academic/Scholarly.* **Description:** Covers such areas as wave propagation, fluid dynamics, theoretical geophysics, combustion and the mechanics of solids.
Formerly (until 19??): Cambridge Monographs on Mechanics and Applied Mathematics (0960-2933)
Indexed: CCMJ, MathR.
Published by: Cambridge University Press, The Edinburgh Bldg, Shaftesbury Rd, Cambridge, CB2 8RU, United Kingdom. TEL 44-1223-312393, FAX 44-1223-315052, journals@cambridge.org, http://www.cambridge.org/uk. Eds. E J Hinch, M J Ablowitz, Stephen H Davis. R&P Linda Nicol TEL 44-1223-325702.

531 DEU ISSN 1860-482X
COMPUTATIONAL FLUID AND SOLID MECHANICS. Text in English. 2003. irreg., latest vol.3, 2005. price varies. **Document type:** *Monographic series, Academic/Scholarly.* **Description:** Publishes monographs, textbooks, and reference books on any subject of computational fluid dynamics, computational solid and structural mechanics, and computational multiphysics dynamics.
Published by: Springer (Subsidiary of: Springer Science+Business Media), Tiergartenstr 17, Heidelberg, 69121, Germany. TEL 49-6221-4870, FAX 49-6221-345229, subscriptions@springer.com, http://www.springer.com.

COMPUTER ASSISTED MECHANICS AND ENGINEERING SCIENCES. *see* ENGINEERING—Mechanical Engineering

532 SGP
▼ **CONTEMPORARY CHALLENGES IN MATHEMATICAL FLUID DYNAMICS AND ITS APPLICATIONS.** Text in English. 2010. irreg., latest vol.1, 2010. price varies. **Document type:** *Monographic series, Academic/Scholarly.*
Published by: World Scientific Publishing Co. Pte. Ltd., 5 Toh Tuck Link, Singapore, 596224, Singapore. TEL 65-6466-5775, FAX 65-6467-7667, wspc@wspc.com.sg, http://www.worldscientific.com. Ed. Giovanni Paolo Galdi. **Dist. by:** World Scientific Publishing Co., Inc., 27 Warren St, Ste 401-402, Hackensack, NJ 07601. TEL 201-487-9655, 800-227-7562, FAX 201-487-9656, 888-977-2665, wspc@wspc.com; World Scientific Publishing Ltd., 57 Shelton St, London WC2H 9HE, United Kingdom. TEL 44-207-8360888, FAX 44-207-8362020, sales@wspc.co.uk.

CONTINUUM MECHANICS AND THERMODYNAMICS; analysis of complex materials and judicious evaluation of the environment. *see* PHYSICS—Heat

531 POL
CODEN: CZTEAY
CZASOPISMO TECHNICZNE. SERIA M: MECHANIKA. Text in Polish; Contents page in Multiple languages. 1877; N.S. 1961. irreg. PLZ 20 (effective 2000). bk.rev. charts; illus. index. **Document type:** *Academic/Scholarly.*
Supersedes in part: Czasopismo Techniczne (0011-4561); Which was formerly (until 1883): Dzwignia (1230-2791)
—CASDDS, Linda Hall.
Published by: Politechnika Krakowska im. Tadeusza Kosciuszki/Tadeusz Kosciuszko Cracow University of Technology, ul Warszawska 24, Krakow, 31155, Poland. TEL 48-12-6374289, FAX 48-12-6374289. Ed. Elzbieta Nachlik. Adv. contact Ewa Malochleb. Circ: 12,000.

D C A M M REPORT. (Danish Center for Applied Mathematics and Mechanics) *see* MATHEMATICS

531 UKR
DNIPROPETROVS'KYI NATSIONAL'NYI UNIVERSYTET. VISNYK. SERIYA MEKHANIKA. Text in Ukrainian, Russian. 1998. irreg., latest vol.7, 2003. price varies. **Document type:** *Journal, Academic/Scholarly.*
Published by: Dnipropetrovs'kyi Natsional'nyi Universytet, Mekhaniko-Matematychnyi Fakul'tet, Kafedra Aerohidromekhaniky, vul Kazakova 4a, korpus #14, Dnipropetrovs'k, 49050, Ukraine. TEL 380-562-466333.

531 621 UKR ISSN 0419-8719
CODEN: DVSGBJ
DVIGATELI VNUTRENNEGO SGORANIYA/DVYHUNY VNUTRISHNYOHO SHORYANNYA/INTERNAL COMBUSTION ENGINES; vseukrainskii nauchno-tekhnicheskii zhurnal. Text in Ukrainian. 1965. irreg. free. bk.rev. abstr.; bibl.; charts; illus. **Document type:** *Journal, Academic/Scholarly.* **Description:** Designed for researchers and specialist in field of ICE. Covers construction, exploitation, production technology and calculation of the ICE.
—CASDDS, Linda Hall.
Published by: Natsional'nyi Tekhnichnyi Universytet "Kharkivs'kyi Politekhnichnyi Instytut", Kafedra Dvyhuny Vnutrishyoho Shoryannya/National Technical University "Kharkiv Polytechnical Institute", Department of Internal Combustion Engines, vul Frunze, 21, Kharkiv, 61002, Ukraine. TEL 380-57-7074034, dvs@kpi.kharkov.ua. Ed. Andrey Marchenko. Pub. Inna Rykova.

531 NLD ISSN 1389-1057
E P O APPLIED TECHNOLOGY SERIES. (European Patent Office) Text in English. 1984. irreg., latest vol.12, 1993. price varies. **Document type:** *Monographic series, Trade.*
Indexed: Inspec.
Published by: (European Patent Office DEU), Elsevier BV (Subsidiary of: Elsevier Science & Technology), Radarweg 29, PO Box 211, Amsterdam, 1000 AE, Netherlands. TEL 31-20-4853911, FAX 31-20-4852457, JournalsCustomerServiceEMEA@elsevier.com, http://www.elsevier.nl.

531 CHE
E R C O F T A C BULLETIN. (European Research Community on Flow Turbulence and Combustion) Text in English. q. CHF 80 to members; CHF 185 to non-members (effective 2001).
Published by: European Research Community on Flow, Turbulence and Combustion, Coordination Centre, Lausanne, 1015, Switzerland. TEL 41-21-693-5307, ercoftac@epfl.ch, http://imhefwww.epfl.ch/ERCOFTAC/. Ed. A G Hutton.

531 NLD ISSN 1382-4309
E R C O F T A C SERIES. Text in English. 1995. irreg., latest vol.12, 2008. price varies. back issues avail. **Document type:** *Proceedings, Academic/Scholarly.* **Description:** Covers all aspects of fluid mechanics.
Indexed: CCMJ, GeoRef, MSN.
—BLDSC (3794.939300), IE, Ingenta.
Published by: (European Research Community on Flow, Turbulence and Combustion), Springer Netherlands (Subsidiary of: Springer Science+Business Media), Van Godewijckstraat 30, Dordrecht, 3311 GX, Netherlands. TEL 31-78-6576050, FAX 31-78-6576474. Eds. Rene Oliemans, Wolfgang Rodi.

531 CZE ISSN 1802-1484
➤ **ENGINEERING MECHANICS**; journal for theoretical and applied mechanics. Text in Czech, English. 1994. bi-m. EUR 60 (effective 2008). **Document type:** *Journal, Academic/Scholarly.* **Description:** Examines theoretical, computational and experimental mechanics, including solid mechanics, fluid mechanics, thermodynamics, dynamics and stability of discrete and continuous systems, and acoustics, experimental methods, diagnostic methods, fracture mechanics.
Formerly (until 2005): Inzenyrska Mechanika (1210-2717)
Published by: Association for Engineering Mechanics, Technicka 2, Brno, 61669, Czech Republic. TEL 420-541-142866, FAX 420-541-142867. Ed. Ctirad Kratochvil. Pub. Pavel Heriban.

531 FRA ISSN 0997-7538
QA801 CODEN: EJASEV
➤ **EUROPEAN JOURNAL OF MECHANICS A - SOLIDS.** Text in English. 1977. 6/yr. EUR 891 in Europe to institutions; JPY 118,500 in Japan to institutions; USD 1,001 elsewhere to institutions (effective 2012). adv. abstr. back issues avail.; reprints avail. **Document type:** *Journal, Academic/Scholarly.* **Description:** Publishes articles in all areas of solid mechanics from the physical and mathematical basis to materials engineering, technological applications, and methods of modern computational mechanics, both pure and applied research.
Supersedes in part (in 1989): Journal de Mecanique Theorique et Appliquee (0750-7240); Which was formed by the 1982 merger of: Journal de Mecanique (0021-7832); Journal de Mecanique Appliquee (0399-0842)
Related titles: Microform ed.: (from PQC); Online - full text ed.: ISSN 1873-7285 (from IngentaConnect, ScienceDirect).
Indexed: A01, A03, A08, A22, A26, A28, APA, ASCA, ASFA, AcoustA, ApMecR, BrCerAb, C&ISA, CA, CA/WCA, CCMJ, CIA, CMCI, CPEI, CerAb, CivEngAb, CorrAb, CurCont, E&CAJ, E11, EEA, EMA, ESPM, EngInd, EnvEAb, GeoRef, H15, I05, INIS AtomInd, ISR, Inspec, M&TEA, M09, MBF, METADEX, MSCI, MSN, MathR, RefZh, S01, SCI, SCOPUS, SolStAb, SpeleolAb, T02, T04, TM, W07, WAA, Z02.
—BLDSC (3829.731300), AskIEEE, CASDDS, IE, Infotrieve, Ingenta, INIST, Linda Hall. **CCC.**
Published by: Elsevier Masson (Subsidiary of: Elsevier Health Sciences), 62 Rue Camille Desmoulins, Issy les Moulineaux, Cedex 92442, France. TEL 33-1-71165500, FAX 33-1-71165600, infos@elsevier-masson.fr, http://www.elsevier-masson.fr. Ed. V. Tvergaard. Circ: 1,600.

531 FRA ISSN 0997-7546
QA901 CODEN: EJBFEV
➤ **EUROPEAN JOURNAL OF MECHANICS B - FLUIDS.** Text in English. 1977. 6/yr. EUR 762 in Europe to institutions; JPY 101,200 in Japan to institutions; USD 855 elsewhere to institutions (effective 2012). adv. abstr. back issues avail. **Document type:** *Journal, Academic/Scholarly.* **Description:** Publishes theoretical, computational and experimental papers in all fundamental research areas of fluid mechanics.
Supersedes in part (in 1989): Journal de Mecanique Theorique et Appliquee (0750-7240); Which was formed by the 1982 merger of: Journal de Mecanique (0021-7832); Journal de Mecanique Appliquee (0399-0842)
Related titles: Online - full text ed.: ISSN 1873-7390 (from IngentaConnect, ScienceDirect).
Indexed: A01, A03, A08, A22, A26, A28, APA, ASCA, ASFA, ApMecR, BrCerAb, C&ISA, CA, CA/WCA, CCMJ, CIA, CPEI, CerAb, CivEngAb, CorrAb, CurCont, E&CAJ, E11, EEA, EMA, ESPM, EngInd, EnvEAb, GeoRef, H15, I05, INIS AtomInd, ISR, Inspec, M&GPA, M&TEA, M09, MBF, METADEX, MSN, MathR, P30, RefZh, S01, SCI, SCOPUS, SolStAb, SpeleolAb, T02, T04, TM, W07, WAA, Z02.
—BLDSC (3829.731310), AskIEEE, CASDDS, IE, Infotrieve, Ingenta, INIST, Linda Hall. **CCC.**
Published by: Elsevier Masson (Subsidiary of: Elsevier Health Sciences), 62 Rue Camille Desmoulins, Issy les Moulineaux, Cedex 92442, France. TEL 33-1-71165500, FAX 33-1-71165600, infos@elsevier-masson.fr, http://www.elsevier-masson.fr. Eds. F Dias, J.F. van Heijst. Circ: 1,600.

532 USA
F P S MEMBERSHIP DIRECTORY AND ANNUAL REPORT. Text in English. 1991. a. adv. **Document type:** *Directory.* **Description:** Provides a list of members and their certifications, information on the society and its activities, rosters of Chapters and members, lists of board and committee members, and annual financial information.

Published by: Fluid Power Society, 1420, Cherry Hill, NJ 08034-0054. TEL 414-257-0910, FAX 414-257-4092. Adv. contact Juli Kwakenat. Circ: 3,000 (controlled).

531 629.892 SRB ISSN 0354-2009
FACTA UNIVERSITATIS. SERIES MECHANICS, AUTOMATIC CONTROL AND ROBOTICS. Text in English, French, German. 1991. irreg., latest vol.3, no.12, 2002. **Document type:** *Journal, Academic/ Scholarly.*
Indexed: ApMecR, CCMJ, MSN, MathR, P30, Z02.
—Linda Hall.
Published by: Univerzitet u Nishu/University of Nis, Univerzitetski Trg 2, P.O. Box 123, Nis, 18000. TEL 381-18-547970, FAX 381-18-547950, facta@ni.ac.yu, http://ni.ac.yu. Ed. Katica R Hedrih.

531 RUS ISSN 0130-5611
FIZICHESKAYA MEKHANIKA. Text in Russian. 1974. irreg., latest vol.7, 1998. price varies. abstr.; bibl.; charts. **Document type:** *Monographic series, Academic/Scholarly.*
Indexed: ChemAb.
—Linda Hall.
Published by: Izdatel'skii Dom Sankt-Peterburgskogo Gosudarstvennogo Universiteta, V.O., 6-ya liniya, dom 11/21, komn 319, St Petersburg, 199004, Russian Federation. TEL 7-812-3252604, press@unipress.ru, http://www.unipress.ru. Circ: 2,000.

531 RUS ISSN 1683-805X
TA417.6 CODEN: FMIEAN
FIZICHESKAYA MEZOMEKHANIKA. Text in Russian. 1998. bi-m. RUR 275 for 6 mos. domestic; USD 198 foreign (effective 2005). **Document type:** *Journal, Academic/Scholarly.*
Related titles: ◆ English ed.: Physical Mesomechanics. ISSN 1029-9599.
Indexed: A22, RefZh, SCOPUS.
—BLDSC (0390.775000). **CCC.**
Published by: (Siberian Branch of Russian Academy of Sciences, Institute of Strength Physics and Materials Science), Izdatel'stvo Sibirskogo Otdeleniya Rossiiskoi Akademii Nauk/Publishing House of the Russian Academy of Sciences, Siberian Branch, Morskoi pr 2, a/ya 187, Novosibirsk, 630090, Russian Federation. TEL 7-3832-300570, FAX 7-3832-333755, psb@ad-sbras.nsc.ru, http://www-psb.ad-sbras.nsc.ru. Ed. Mr. Victor E Panin. **Dist. by:** M K - Periodica, ul Gilyarovskogo 39, Moscow 129110, Russian Federation. TEL 7-095-2845008, FAX 7-095-2813798, info@periodicals.ru, http://www.mkniga.ru.

FIZIKA GORENIYA I VZRYVA/COMBUSTION, EXPLOSION AND SHOCK WAVES. *see* PHYSICS—Heat

531 UKR ISSN 0203-4654
QC281 CODEN: FTVDBX
➤ **FIZIKA I TEKHNIKA VYSOKIKH DAVLENII**; Ukrainian scientific journal. Text in English, Russian; Summaries in English. 1980. q. UAK 85 domestic; USD 80 foreign (effective 1999). bk.rev. 140 p./no. 1 cols./p.; **Document type:** *Journal, Academic/Scholarly.*
Indexed: C&ISA, ChemAb, CorrAb, Djerelo, E&CAJ, INIS AtomInd, SolStAb, WAA.
—CASDDS, INIST.
Published by: Natsional'na Akademiya Nauk Ukrainy, Donets'kyi Fizyko-Tekhnichnyi Instytut/Ukrainian National Academy of Sciences, Donetsk Physical & Technical Institute, Vul R Lyuksemburg 72, Donetsk, 83114, Ukraine. TEL 380-622-554202, FAX 380-622-550127. Eds. E A Zavadskii, V N Varyukhin. Circ: 150. **Dist. by:** Idea Ltd., Vul Artyoma 84, Donetsk 83055, Ukraine. info@idea.donetsk.ua, http://www.idea.com.ua.

➤ **FIZIKO-KHIMICHESKA MEKHANIKA/PHYSICO-CHEMICAL MECHANICS.** *see* CHEMISTRY—Physical Chemistry

541 531 UKR ISSN 0430-6252
CODEN: FKMMAJ
➤ **FIZYKO-KHIMICHNA MEKHANIKA MATERIALIV/FIZIKO-KHIMICHESKAYA MEKHANIKA MATERIALOV/ PHYSICOCHEMICAL MECHANICS OF MATERIALS**; mizhnarodnyi naukovo-tekhnichnyi zhurnal. Text in English, Russian, Ukrainian. 1965. bi-m. USD 349 foreign (effective 2004). adv. 128 p./no. 1 cols./p.; back issues avail.; reprints avail. **Document type:** *Journal, Academic/Scholarly.* **Description:** Covers mechanics of materials, fracture mechanics with respect to corrosive environment, corrosion and corrosion protections, nondestructive testing.
Related titles: ◆ English Translation: Materials Science. ISSN 1068-820X.
Indexed: A28, APA, BrCerAb, C&ISA, CA/WCA, CEABA, CIA, CIN, CerAb, ChemAb, ChemTitl, CivEngAb, CorrAb, Djerelo, E&CAJ, E11, EEA, EMA, H15, INIS AtomInd, Inspec, M&TEA, M09, MBF, METADEX, RefZh, SCOPUS, SolStAb, T04, WAA.
—BLDSC (0390.010000), AskIEEE, CASDDS, East View, INIST, Linda Hall. **CCC.**
Published by: Fizyko-Mekhanichnyi Institut im. G.V. Karpenka, vul Naukova 5, Lviv, 290601, Ukraine. TEL 380-322-654230, FAX 380-322-649427, pcmm@ah.ipm.lviv.ua. Ed. V V Panasiuk. Adv. contact R R Kokot. Circ: 300. **Dist. by:** East View Information Services, 10601 Wayzata Blvd, Minneapolis, MN 55305. TEL 952-252-1201, 800-477-1005, FAX 952-252-1202, info@eastview.com, http://www.eastview.com.

532 USA ISSN 1081-7107
TA357
FLOW CONTROL; the magazine of fluid handling systems. Text in English. 1995. m. free to qualified personnel (print or online ed.) (effective 2008). adv. back issues avail. **Document type:** *Magazine, Trade.* **Description:** Focuses on the fluid handling process with information on such topics as system design, operation, maintanance and new technologies that measure, control and contain liquids and gases.
Related titles: Online - full text ed.
Indexed: A09, A10, B01, B07, T02, V03, V04.
—IE.
Published by: Grand View Media Group, Inc. (Subsidiary of: EBSCO Industries, Inc.), 200 Croft St, Ste 1, Birmingham, AL 35242. TEL 888-431-2877, FAX 205-408-3797, webmaster@grandviewmedia.com, http://www.gvmg.com. Ed. Matt Migliore TEL 610-828-1711. Pub. John P Harris TEL 205-408-3765. adv.: color page USD 9,560, B&W page USD 8,060; bleed 8.125 x 11. Circ: 35,000.

532 USA
FLUID CONTROLS INSTITUTE. NEWS & VIEWS. Text in English. 1965. q. **Document type:** *Newsletter.*
Published by: Fluid Controls Institute, 1300 Sumner Ave, Cleveland, OH 44115. TEL 216-241-7333. Ed. Chris Johnson. Circ: 125.

532 620 RUS ISSN 0015-4628
TA357 CODEN: FLDYAH
➤ **FLUID DYNAMICS.** Text in English. 1966. bi-m. EUR 5,554, USD 5,718 combined subscription to institutions (print & online eds.) (effective 2012). bk.rev. back issues avail.; reprint service avail. from PSC. **Document type:** *Journal, Academic/Scholarly.* **Description:** Publishes theoretical, computational, and applied research in the fields of aeromechanics, hydrodynamics, plasma dynamics, and biomechanics of continuous media.
Related titles: Microfilm ed.: (from PQC); Online - full text ed.: ISSN 1573-8507 (from IngentaConnect).
Indexed: A01, A03, A08, A22, A26, ApMecR, BibLing, CA, CCMJ, CEA, E01, EnerRA, FLUIDEX, FR, Inspec, MSN, MathR, PetrolAb, PhysBer, S01, SCI, SCOPUS, T02, TCEA, W07, Z02.
—BLDSC (0411.753000), AskIEEE, CASDDS, East View, IE, Infotrieve, Ingenta, INIST, Linda Hall. **CCC.**
Published by: (Rossiiskaya Akademiya Nauk/Russian Academy of Sciences), M A I K Nauka - Interperiodica (Subsidiary of: Pleiades Publishing, Inc.), Profsoyuznaya ul 90, Moscow, 117997, Russian Federation. TEL 7-095-3347420, FAX 7-095-3360666, compmg@maik.ru, http://www.maik.ru. Ed. Gorimir Ghernyi. **Subscr. to:** Springer Netherlands, Journals Department, PO Box 322, Dordrecht, Netherlands. TEL 31-78-6576392, FAX 31-78-6576474.

532 620.1064 USA ISSN 1555-256X
QC150
FLUID DYNAMICS & MATERIALS PROCESSING. Abbreviated title: F D M P. Text in English. 2005. q. (in 1 vol., 4 nos./vol.). USD 1,000 (print & online eds.) (effective 2010). **Document type:** *Journal, Academic/ Scholarly.* **Description:** Covers some "frontier" aspects of materials science and, in particular, the most modern and advanced processes for the production of inorganic (semiconductors and metal alloys), organic (protein crystals) materials and "living" (in vitro) biological tissues, with emphasis on the fluid-dynamic conditions under which they are operated.
Related titles: Online - full text ed.: ISSN 1555-2578.
Indexed: A28, APA, BrCerAb, C&ISA, CA/WCA, CCMJ, CIA, CPEI, CerAb, CivEngAb, CorrAb, E&CAJ, E11, EEA, EMA, ESPM, EnvEAb, H15, M&TEA, M09, MBF, METADEX, MSN, MathR, SCOPUS, SolStAb, T04, WAA, Z02.
Published by: Tech Science Press, 81 E Main St, Forsyth 488, GA 31029 . TEL 478-992-8737, FAX 661-420-8080, sale@techscience.com. Ed. Dr. Marcello Lappa.

531 620.1 NLD ISSN 0926-5112
CODEN: FMAPFL
FLUID MECHANICS AND ITS APPLICATIONS. Text in English. 1990. irreg., latest vol.92, 2009. price varies. **Document type:** *Monographic series, Academic/Scholarly.* **Description:** Focuses on subjects in which fluid mechanics plays a fundamental role, as well as the more tradiational applications of aeronautics, hydraulics, and heat and mass transfer.
Indexed: CCMJ, CIN, ChemAb, ChemTitl, MSN, Z02.
—BLDSC (3962.039000), CASDDS, IE, Ingenta. **CCC.**
Published by: Springer Netherlands (Subsidiary of: Springer Science+Business Media), Van Godewijckstraat 30, Dordrecht, 3311 GX, Netherlands. TEL 31-78-6576050, FAX 31-78-6576474. Ed. R J Moreau.

FLUID POWER CERTIFICATION BOARD. CERTIFICATION DIRECTORY; accredited fluid power educational institutions and instructors and certified fluid power mechanics, technicians, specialists and engineers. *see* BUSINESS AND ECONOMICS—Trade And Industrial Directories

532 NLD ISSN 1874-7914
FLUIDS PROCESSING BENELUX. Text in Dutch. 2006. bi-m. adv. **Document type:** *Magazine, Trade.*
Published by: Vezor Media, Postbus 106, Doetinchem, 7000 AC, Netherlands. TEL 31-314-346688, FAX 31-84-2207821, http://www.vezor.nl. Ed. Christien Nuboer TEL 31-315-231702. Pubs. Hans Schouten, Henk Klein Gunnewiek TEL 31-314-344143. Circ: 6,000.

FONDATION LOUIS DE BROGLIE. ANNALES. *see* PHYSICS

G A M M MITTEILUNGEN. *see* MATHEMATICS

533 CHN ISSN 1000-5773
QC280 CODEN: GWXUER
➤ **GAOYA WULI XUEBAO/CHINESE JOURNAL OF HIGH PRESSURE PHYSICS.** Text in Chinese; Abstracts in English. 1987. q. USD 20.80 (effective 2009). 80 p./no.; **Document type:** *Journal, Academic/ Scholarly.* **Description:** Publishes scholarly research in the field of high-pressure physics.
Related titles: Online - full content ed.; Online - full text ed.
Indexed: A22, CPEI, EngInd, SCOPUS.
—BLDSC (3180.351000), East View, IE, Ingenta.
Published by: Sichuan-sheng Kexue Jishu Xiehui, PO Box 919-110, Mainyang, 621900, China. TEL 86-816-2490042, FAX 86-816-2272695. Ed. Fu-qian Jing. **Dist. by:** China International Book Trading Corp, 35 Chegongzhuang Xilu, Haidian District, PO Box 399, Beijing 100044, China. TEL 86-10-68412045, FAX 86-10-68412023, cibtc@mail.cibtc.com.cn, http://www.cibtc.com.cn/. **Co-sponsors:** Sichuan-sheng Wuli Xuehui; Zhongguo Wuli Xuehui/Chinese Physical Society.

531 CHN ISSN 0254-7805
➤ **GUTI LIXUE XUEBAO.** Text in Chinese. 1980. q. USD 44.40 (effective 2009). 128 p./no.; **Document type:** *Academic/Scholarly.*
Related titles: Online - full content ed.; Online - full text ed.; ◆ English ed.: Acta Mechanica Solida Sinica. ISSN 0894-9166.
Indexed: CPEI, Inspec, SCOPUS.
—BLDSC (0632.610000), AskIEEE, East View, IE, Ingenta, Linda Hall.
Published by: Huazhong Gongxue Yuan/Huazhong University of Science and Technology, Huazhong Ligong Daxue, Yujiashan, Wuchang-qu, Wuhan, Hubei 430074, China. TEL 86-27-8701154. Ed. Shou-Wen Yu.

531 JPN
HAKAI RIKIGAKU SHINPOJUMU KOEN RONBUNSHU/SYMPOSIUM ON FRACTURE AND FRACTURE MECHANICS. PROCEEDINGS. Text in Japanese; Summaries in English. irreg. **Document type:** *Proceedings.*
Published by: Nihon Zairyo Gakkai/Society of Materials Science Japan, 1-101 Yoshida-izumidono-cho, Sakyo-ku, Kyoto, 606-8301, Japan. TEL 81-75-7615321, FAX 81-75-7615325.

532 NLD
HANDBOOK OF MATHEMATICAL FLUID DYNAMICS. Text in English. 2002. irreg., latest vol.4, 2007. price varies. **Document type:** *Monographic series, Academic/Scholarly.*
Related titles: Online - full text ed.: ISSN 1874-5792.
Published by: Elsevier BV, North-Holland (Subsidiary of: Elsevier Science & Technology), Sara Burgerhartstraat 25, Amsterdam, 1055 KV, Netherlands. TEL 31-20-4853911, FAX 31-20-4852457, http://www.elsevier.com. Eds. D Serre, S Friedlander.

HEAT AND MASS TRANSFER; Waerme- und Stoffuebertragung. *see* PHYSICS—Heat

531 GBR ISSN 0895-7959
QC280 CODEN: HPRSEL
➤ **HIGH PRESSURE RESEARCH**; an international journal. Text in English. 1988. q. GBP 2,870 combined subscription in United Kingdom to institutions (print & online eds.); EUR 2,936, USD 3,690 combined subscription to institutions (print & online eds.) (effective 2012). adv. back issues avail.; reprint service avail. from PSC. **Document type:** *Journal, Academic/Scholarly.* **Description:** Dedicated solely to research in high pressure science and technology. Provides a forum for experimental and theoretical advances.
Related titles: CD-ROM ed.; Microform ed.; Online - full text ed.: ISSN 1477-2299. GBP 2,583 in United Kingdom to institutions; EUR 2,643, USD 3,321 to institutions (effective 2012) (from IngentaConnect).
Indexed: A01, A03, A08, A22, A28, APA, ASCA, BrCerAb, C&ISA, CA, CA/WCA, CIA, CPEI, CerAb, CivEngAb, CorrAb, CurCont, E&CAJ, E01, E11, EEA, EMA, ESPM, EngInd, EnvEAb, H15, Inspec, M&TEA, M09, MBF, METADEX, P26, P30, P54, PQC, RefZh, S01, SCI, SCOPUS, SolStAb, T02, T04, VITIS, W07, WAA.
—BLDSC (4307.355650), AskIEEE, IE, Infotrieve, Ingenta, Linda Hall. **CCC.**
Published by: (European High Pressure Research Group), Taylor & Francis Ltd. (Subsidiary of: Taylor & Francis Group), 4 Park Sq, Milton Park, Abingdon, Oxfordshire OX14 4RN, United Kingdom. TEL 44-20-70176000, FAX 44-20-70176336, subscriptions@tandf.co.uk, http://www.taylorandfrancis.com. Ed. Stefan Klotz. Adv. contact Linda Hann. **Subscr. in N. america to:** Taylor & Francis Inc., Customer Services Dept, 325 Chestnut St, 8th Fl, Philadelphia, PA 19106. TEL 215-625-8900, 800-354-1420, FAX 215-625-2940, customerservice@taylorandfrancis.com; **Subscr. to:** Journals Customer Service, Sheepen Pl, Colchester, Essex CO3 3LP, United Kingdom. TEL 44-20-70175544, FAX 44-20-70175198, tf.enquiries@tfinforma.com.

532 GBR ISSN 2044-7264
▼ **I C P FLUID MECHANICS.** Text in English. 2010. irreg., latest vol.2. price varies. back issues avail. **Document type:** *Monographic series, Academic/Scholarly.*
Published by: Imperial College Press (Subsidiary of: World Scientific Publishing Co. Pte. Ltd.), 57 Shelton St, Covent Garden, London, WC2H 9HE, United Kingdom. TEL 44-20-78360888, FAX 44-20-78362020, edit@icpress.co.uk, http://www.icpress.co.uk/. **Dist. by:** World Scientific Publishing Co., Inc., 27 Warren St, Ste 401-402, Hackensack, NJ 07601. TEL 201-487-9655, 800-227-7562, FAX 201-487-9656, 888-977-2665, wspc@wspc.com.

531 GBR ISSN 1757-8981
▼ ➤ **I O P CONFERENCE SERIES: MATERIALS SCIENCE AND ENGINEERING.** (Institute of Physics) Text in English. 2009. irreg. free (effective 2011). **Document type:** *Proceedings, Academic/Scholarly.*
Related titles: Online - full text ed.: ISSN 1757-899X. 2009. free (effective 2011).
—BLDSC (4565.243500).
Published by: Institute of Physics Publishing Ltd., Dirac House, Temple Back, Bristol, BS1 6BE, United Kingdom. TEL 44-117-9297481, FAX 44-117-9301178, custserv@iop.org, http://publishing.iop.org/.

531 NLD ISSN 1875-3507
I U T A M BOOKSERIES. Text in English. 2007. irreg., latest vol.30, 2010. price varies. **Document type:** *Monographic series, Academic/ Scholarly.*
Published by: (International Union of Theoretical and Applied Mechanics FRA), Springer Netherlands (Subsidiary of: Springer Science+Business Media), Van Godewijckstraat 30, Dordrecht, 3311 GX, Netherlands. TEL 31-78-6576050, FAX 31-78-6576474. Eds. G M L Gladwell, R J Moreau.

532 533 627 621.69 AUS ISSN 1447-1132
INMOTION. Text in English. 2002 (Oct.). bi-m. free to qualified personnel (effective 2008). adv. **Document type:** *Magazine, Trade.* **Description:** Covers the fluid power, pumps and motion control industrial technology sectors in both Australia and New Zealand, and delivers new product information to the engineers, maintenance staff, plant managers and senior managers.
Formed by the merger of (1995-2002): What's New in Hydraulics & Pneumatics (1324-3128); (1999-2002): Pumping Technologies (1441-9718)
Related titles: Online - full text ed.; Supplement(s): Industrial Workwear Solutions.
Published by: Westwick-Farrow Pty. Ltd., Locked Bag 1289, Wahroonga, NSW 2076, Australia. TEL 61-2-94872700, FAX 61-2-94891265, admin@westwick-farrow.com.au, http://www.westwick-farrow.com.au. Eds. Carolyn Jackson, Janette Woodhouse. Pub. Adrian Farrow. adv.: color page AUD 4,526, B&W page AUD 4,076. Circ: 8,135.

INSTITUTUL POLITEHNIC DIN IASI. BULETINUL. SECTIA MATEMATICA, MECANICA, FIZICA/POLYTECHNIC INSTITUTE OF IASI. MATHEMATICS. BULLETIN. THEORETICAL MECHANICS. PHYSICS. *see* MATHEMATICS

620.419 USA ISSN 1071-6769
TA416.5.U6
➤ **INTERNATIONAL DIRECTORY OF TESTING LABORATORIES.** Text in English. 1988. a. USD 76 (effective 2008). **Document type:** *Directory, Trade.* **Description:** Contains lab information that is updated annually to reflect new capabilities and equipment.
Formerly (until 1992): Directory of Testing Laboratories (0895-7886)
—**CCC.**
Published by: A S T M International, 100 Barr Harbor Dr, PO Box C700, W Conshohocken, PA 19428. TEL 610-832-9500, 800-262-1373, FAX 610-832-9555, service@astm.org. Ed. Erin McElrone.

▼ ➤ **INTERNATIONAL JOURNAL OF APPLIED MECHANICS.** *see* ENGINEERING—Mechanical Engineering

P

531 GBR ISSN 1061-8562
QA911 CODEN: IJCFEC
➤ **INTERNATIONAL JOURNAL OF COMPUTATIONAL FLUID DYNAMICS.** Abbreviated title: I J C F D. Text in English. 1993. 10/yr. GBP 1,626 combined subscription in United Kingdom to institutions (print & online eds.); EUR 1,707, USD 2,144 combined subscription to institutions (print & online eds.) (effective 2012). adv. back issues avail.; reprint service avail. from PSC. **Document type:** *Journal, Academic/Scholarly.* **Description:** Publishes advances in the field of fluid dynamics for the aeronautics, astronautics, astrophysics, environmental, hydrodynamics, and power and process fields.
Related titles: CD-ROM ed.: ISSN 1026-7417. 1995; Online - full text ed.: ISSN 1029-0257. 1996. GBP 1,463 in United Kingdom to institutions; EUR 1,536, USD 1,930 to institutions (effective 2012) (from IngentaConnect).
Indexed: A01, A03, A08, A22, A28, APA, ASCA, ApMecR, BrCerAb, C&ISA, CA, CA/WCA, CCMJ, CIA, CMCI, CerAb, CivEngAb, CorrAb, CurCont, E&CAJ, E01, E04, E05, E11, EEA, EMA, ESPM, EnvEAb, H15, M&TEA, M09, MBF, METADEX, MSN, MathR, P26, P30, P47, P49, P52, P54, P56, PQC, S01, SCI, SCOPUS, SolStAb, T02, T04, W07, WAA, Z02.
—BLDSC (4542.173705), IE, Infotrieve, Ingenta, Linda Hall. **CCC.**
Published by: Taylor & Francis Ltd. (Subsidiary of: Taylor & Francis Group), 4 Park Sq, Milton Park, Abingdon, Oxfordshire OX14 4RN, United Kingdom. TEL 44-20-70176000, FAX 44-20-70176336, subscriptions@tandf.co.uk, http://www.taylorandfrancis.com. Eds. Awatef Hamed, Charles Hirsch, Wagdi G Habashi. **Subscr. in N America to:** Taylor & Francis Inc., Customer Services Dept, 325 Chestnut St, 8th Fl, Philadelphia, PA 19106. TEL 215-625-8900, 800-354-1420, FAX 215-625-2940, customerservice@taylorandfrancis.com; **Subscr. to:** Journals Customer Service, Sheepen Pl, Colchester, Essex CO3 3LP, United Kingdom. TEL 44-20-70175544, FAX 44-20-70175198, tf.enquiries@tfinforma.com.

532 GBR ISSN 1756-8315
▼ ➤ **INTERNATIONAL JOURNAL OF EMERGING MULTIDISCIPLINARY FLUID SCIENCES.** Abbreviated title: I J E M F S. Text in English. 2009 (Mar.). q. GBP 272; GBP 283 combined subscription (print & online eds.) (effective 2012). **Document type:** *Journal, Academic/Scholarly.* **Description:** Features fluid related research articles spanning various disciplines of physics, engineering and biology.
Related titles: Online - full text ed.: ISSN 1756-8323. GBP 245 (effective 2012).
Indexed: A01, CPEI, FLUIDEX, T02.
Published by: Multi-Science Publishing Co. Ltd., 5 Wates Way, Brentwood, Essex CM15 9TB, United Kingdom. TEL 44-1277-244632, FAX 44-1277-223453, info@multi-science.co.uk. Ed. Dr. S D Sharma.

532 GBR ISSN 1756-8250
▼ ➤ **INTERNATIONAL JOURNAL OF FLOW CONTROL.** Text in English. 2009 (Mar.). q. GBP 272; GBP 283 combined subscription (print & online eds.) (effective 2012). **Document type:** *Journal, Academic/Scholarly.* **Description:** Features articles that encompass theoretical, computational and experimental fluid dynamics, acoustics, control theory, physics, chemistry, biology and mathematics.
Related titles: Online - full text ed.: ISSN 1756-8269. GBP 245 (effective 2012).
Indexed: A01, CPEI, FLUIDEX, T02.
Published by: Multi-Science Publishing Co. Ltd., 5 Wates Way, Brentwood, Essex CM15 9TB, United Kingdom. TEL 44-1277-244632, FAX 44-1277-223453, info@multi-science.co.uk. Ed. Dr. Surya Raghu.

532 AUS ISSN 1327-1660
QC150
➤ **INTERNATIONAL JOURNAL OF FLUID DYNAMICS.** Text in English. 1997. q. illus. back issues avail.; reprints avail. **Document type:** *Journal, Academic/Scholarly.*
Media: Online - full text.
Indexed: GeoRef, Z02.
Published by: Monash University, Bldg 31, Department of Mechanical and Aerospace Engineering, Monash University, Melbourne, VIC 3800, Australia. TEL 61-3-99053545, FAX 61-3-99051825, http://www.eng.monash.edu.au/mecheng/.

▼ ➤ **INTERNATIONAL JOURNAL OF MICROSCALE AND NANOSCALE THERMAL AND FLUID TRANSPORT PHENOMENA.** *see* ENGINEERING

531 620.1 GBR ISSN 0020-7683
TA349 CODEN: IJSOAD
➤ **INTERNATIONAL JOURNAL OF SOLIDS AND STRUCTURES.** Text in English. 1965. 26/yr. EUR 8,056 in Europe to institutions; JPY 1,069,600 in Japan to institutions; USD 9,010 elsewhere to institutions (effective 2012). adv. charts; illus. back issues avail.; reprints avail. **Document type:** *Journal, Academic/Scholarly.* **Description:** Features original research on the mechanics of solids and structures as a field of applied science and engineering.
Related titles: Microform ed.: (from PQC); Online - full text ed.: ISSN 1879-2146 (from IngentaConnect, ScienceDirect).
Indexed: A01, A03, A08, A22, A26, A28, AJEE, APA, ASCA, ApMecR, BrCerAb, C&ISA, CA, CA/WCA, CCMJ, CIA, CPEI, CerAb, ChemAb, CivEngAb, CorrAb, CurCont, E&CAJ, E11, EEA, EMA, ESPM, EngInd, EnvEAb, GeoRef, GeotechAb, H15, I05, ICEA, ISMEC, ISR, Inspec, JOF, M&TEA, M09, MBF, METADEX, MSCI, MSN, MathR, PhysBer, RefZh, S&VD, S01, SCI, SCOPUS, SoftAbEng, SolStAb, SpeleolAb, T02, T04, TM, W07, WAA, Z02.
—BLDSC (4542.650000), AskIEEE, IE, Infotrieve, Ingenta, INIST, Linda Hall. **CCC.**
Published by: Pergamon (Subsidiary of: Elsevier Science & Technology), The Blvd, Langford Ln, East Park, Kidlington, Oxford OX5 1GB, United Kingdom. TEL 44-1865-843000, FAX 44-1865-843010, JournalsCustomerServiceEMEA@elsevier.com. Eds. D A Hills TEL 44-1865-273119, S Kyriakides TEL 512-471-0568. **Subscr. to:** Elsevier BV, Radarweg 29, PO Box 211, Amsterdam 1000 AE, Netherlands. TEL 31-20-4853757, FAX 31-20-4853432, http://www.elsevier.nl.

532 IND ISSN 0975-8399
▼ ➤ **INTERNATIONAL JOURNAL OF STABILITY AND FLUID MECHANICS.** Abbreviated title: I J S F M. Text and summaries in English. 2010. s-a. USD 40 to individuals; USD 60 to institutions (effective 2011). abstr.; bibl.; charts; illus.; stat.; tr.lit. cum. index. back issues avail.; reprints avail. **Document type:** *Journal, Academic/Scholarly.* **Description:** Publishes research papers on mathematical theory of fluid mechanics.
Related titles: Online - full text ed.; Optical Disk - DVD ed.
Indexed: A01.
Published by: Association for the Advancement in Combinatorial Sciences, A-9 Gagan Enclave, Rohta Rd, Meerut, Uttar Pradesh, India. TEL 91-121-2682738, ultimateworld2050@gmail.com. Ed. Hari Kishan. Pub., R&P S R Singh.

➤ **INTERNATIONAL WORKSHOP ON ADVANCED MOTION CONTROL.** *see* COMPUTERS—Automation

671.52 POL ISSN 1426-1723
TA418.76 CODEN: PLOCAE
INZYNIERIA POWIERZCHNI/SURFACE ENGINEERING. Text in Polish; Summaries in English. 1996. q. EUR 94 foreign (effective 2006). bk.rev. abstr.; pat. 80 p./no. 2 cols./p.; back issues avail.; reprints avail. **Document type:** *Journal, Academic/Scholarly.* **Description:** Covers all aspects or research and technological topics on heat treatment and corrosion protection of metals with required fundamental investigations of physical metalurgy of surface layers.
Formed by the merger of (1973-1994): Powloki Ochronne (0137-3846); (1987-1994): Metaloznawstwo. Obrobka Cieplna. Inzynieria Powierzchni (0860-7583)
Related titles: E-mail ed.; Fax ed.
Indexed: A28, APA, B22, BrCerAb, C&ISA, CA/WCA, CEABA, CIA, CIN, CerAb, ChemAb, ChemTitl, CivEngAb, CoppAb, CorrAb, E&CAJ, E11, EEA, EMA, ESPM, EnvEAb, H15, M&TEA, M09, MBF, METADEX, SolStAb, T04, WAA.
—BLDSC (4563.682000), CASDDS, INIST, Linda Hall.
Published by: Instytut Mechaniki Precyzyjnej, Duchnicka 3, Warsaw, 01796, Poland. TEL 48-22-5602600, FAX 48-22-6634332, info@imp.edu.pl, http://www.imp.edu.pl. Eds. Aleksander Nakonieczny, Henryk Andrzejewski. Circ: 400. **Dist. by:** Ars Polona, Obroncow 25, Warsaw 03933, Poland. TEL 48-22-5098609, FAX 48-22-5098610, arspolona@arspolona.com.pl, http://www.arspolona.com.pl.

JAPAN SOCIETY OF FLUID MECHANICS. PROCEEDINGS. *see* ENGINEERING—Hydraulic Engineering

681 621.38 535 CZE ISSN 0447-6441
TS500 CODEN: JMKOA5
JEMNA MECHANIKA A OPTIKA/PRECISION MECHANICS AND OPTICS. Text in Czech; Summaries in English, German, Russian. 1956. m. EUR 10 per issue (effective 2008). charts; illus. **Document type:** *Journal, Academic/Scholarly.*
Indexed: CISA, Inspec.
—AskIEEE, INIST, Linda Hall.
Published by: Akademie Ved Ceske Republiky, Fyzikalni Ustav/Czech Academy of Sciences, Institute of Physics, Kabelikova 1, Prerov, 75058, Czech Republic. TEL 420-581-242151, FAX 420-581-204731, cscasfyz@fzu.cz, http://www.fzu.cz. Ed. Jaroslav Nevrala. Circ: 1,650. **Co-sponsor:** S P I E - International Society for Optical Engineering.

531 621 HUN ISSN 1586-2070
QA801
JOURNAL OF COMPUTATIONAL AND APPLIED MECHANICS. Text in English. 2000. s-a. **Document type:** *Journal, Academic/Scholarly.* **Description:** The aim of the journal is to publish research papers on theoretical and applied mechanics.
Related titles: Online - full text ed.: 2000. free (effective 2011).
Indexed: CCMJ, MSN, MathR, Z02.
—Linda Hall.
Published by: Miskolci Egyetem/University of Miskolc, Miskolc, 3515, Hungary. TEL 36-46-565111, http://www.uni-miskolc.hu. Ed. Istvan Paczelt.

JOURNAL OF FLOW VISUALIZATION AND IMAGE PROCESSING. *see* ENGINEERING—Mechanical Engineering

531 NLD ISSN 0377-0257
QA901 CODEN: JNFMDI
➤ **JOURNAL OF NON-NEWTONIAN FLUID MECHANICS.** Text in English. 1976. 24/yr. EUR 3,989 in Europe to institutions; JPY 530,400 in Japan to institutions; USD 4,464 elsewhere to institutions (effective 2012). adv. bk.rev. Index. back issues avail.; reprints avail. **Document type:** *Journal, Academic/Scholarly.* **Description:** For those working on basic rheological science and applications.
Related titles: Microform ed.: (from PQC); Online - full text ed.: ISSN 1873-2631 (from IngentaConnect, ScienceDirect).
Indexed: A01, A03, A08, A22, A26, A28, APA, ASCA, ApMecR, BrCerAb, C&ISA, C24, C33, CA, CA/WCA, CEA, CEABA, CIA, CMCI, CPEI, CerAb, ChemAb, ChemTitl, CivEngAb, CorrAb, CurCont, E&CAJ, E&PHSE, E11, EEA, EMA, ESPM, EngInd, EnvEAb, FLUIDEX, GP&P, GeoRef, H15, I05, ISMEC, ISR, Inspec, M&TEA, M09, MBF, METADEX, OffTech, P30, PetrolAb, PhysBer, R18, RefZh, S01, SCI, SCOPUS, SolStAb, SpeleolAb, T02, T04, TCEA, W07, WAA, Z02.
—BLDSC (5022.842000), AskIEEE, CASDDS, IE, Infotrieve, Ingenta, INIST, Linda Hall, PADDS. **CCC.**
Published by: Elsevier BV (Subsidiary of: Elsevier Science & Technology), Radarweg 29, PO Box 211, Amsterdam, 1000 AE, Netherlands. TEL 31-20-4853911, FAX 31-20-4852457, JournalsCustomerServiceEMEA@elsevier.com, http://www.elsevier.nl. Eds. G H McKinley, R Keunings.

532 USA ISSN 0148-6055
QC189 CODEN: JORHD2
➤ **JOURNAL OF RHEOLOGY.** Text in English. 1957. bi-m. USD 550 combined subscription domestic; USD 575 combined subscription elsewhere (effective 2010). adv. back issues avail.; reprints avail. **Document type:** *Journal, Academic/Scholarly.* **Description:** Presents experimental results, phenomenological models, and microscopic theories dealing with the rheological behavior of complex materials.
Formerly (until 1978): Society of Rheology. Transactions (0038-0032)
Related titles: Microform ed.: (from PQC); Online - full text ed.
Indexed: A01, A22, ABIPC, ASCA, ApMecR, C24, C33, CA, CIN, CPEI, CPI, ChemAb, ChemTitl, CurCont, EngInd, FS&TA, GeoRef, INIS AtomInd, ISR, Inspec, MSCI, P&BA, P30, R18, SCI, SCOPUS, SPINweb, SpeleolAb, T02, W07, Z02.
—BLDSC (5052.051000), AskIEEE, CASDDS, GNLM, IE, Infotrieve, Ingenta, INIST, Linda Hall. **CCC.**
Published by: Society of Rheology, c/o Faith A Morrison, Department of Chemical Engineering, Michigan Technological University, 1400 Townsend Dr, Houghton, MI 49931. TEL 906-487-2050, FAX 906-487-3213, fmorriso@mtu.edu, http://www.rheology.org/sor/. Ed. John F Brady.

531.021 GBR ISSN 1742-5468
QC174.7
➤ **JOURNAL OF STATISTICAL MECHANICS: THEORY AND EXPERIMENT.** Abbreviated title: J S T A T. Text in English. 2004. m. GBP 668 to institutions (effective 2010). back issues avail. **Document type:** *Journal, Academic/Scholarly.* **Description:** Brings together cutting-edge research in all aspects of statistical physics particularly emphasising experimental work that impacts on fundamental aspects of the subject.
Media: Online - full content. **Related titles:** Microfiche ed.: USD 705 to institutions (effective 2007).
Indexed: A20, CCMJ, CMCI, CurCont, Inspec, MSN, MathR, P30, RefZh, SCI, SCOPUS, W07, Z02.
—Linda Hall. **CCC.**
Published by: (Scuola Internazionale Superiore di Studi Avanzati (S I S S A)/International School of Advanced Studies ITA), Institute of Physics Publishing Ltd., Dirac House, Temple Back, Bristol, BS1 6BE, United Kingdom. TEL 44-117-9297481, FAX 44-117-9301178, custserv@iop.org, http://publishing.iop.org/.

531 IND ISSN 0970-1893
QD506.A1 CODEN: JSSTE4
JOURNAL OF SURFACE SCIENCE AND TECHNOLOGY. Text in English. 1985. q. INR 800 domestic; USD 200 foreign (effective 2011). **Document type:** *Journal, Academic/Scholarly.*
Related titles: Online - full text ed.: ISSN 0976-9412.
Indexed: A22, SCOPUS.
—BLDSC (5067.360000), IE, Ingenta, INIST, Linda Hall.
Published by: Indian Society for Surface Science and Technology, Department of Chemistry, Jadavpur University, Kolkata, 700 032, India. TEL 91-33-24146411, FAX 91-33-24146266, http://www.issstindia.org/. **Subscr. to:** I N S I O Scientific Books & Periodicals, PO Box 7234, Indraprastha HPO, New Delhi 110 002, India.

531 620.1 GBR ISSN 0022-5096
TA350 CODEN: JMPSA8
➤ **JOURNAL OF THE MECHANICS AND PHYSICS OF SOLIDS.** Text in English. 1952. 12/yr. EUR 4,253 in Europe to institutions; JPY 564,800 in Japan to institutions; USD 4,758 elsewhere to institutions (effective 2012). bk.rev. charts; illus. index. back issues avail. **Document type:** *Journal, Academic/Scholarly.* **Description:** Focuses on research, theory and practice on the properties of construction materials, from the fields of mathematics, engineering, materials science, and physics.
Related titles: Microfilm ed.: (from PQC); Online - full text ed.: ISSN 1873-4782 (from IngentaConnect, ScienceDirect).
Indexed: A01, A03, A05, A08, A22, A26, A28, APA, AS&TA, AS&TI, ASCA, ApMecR, B04, BrCerAb, C&ISA, C10, C24, CA, CA/WCA, CCMJ, CIA, CIN, CMCI, CPEI, Cadscan, CerAb, ChemAb, ChemTitl, CivEngAb, CorrAb, CurCont, E&CAJ, E11, EEA, EMA, ESPM, EngInd, EnvEAb, GeoRef, GeotechAb, H15, I05, IBR, IBZ, ISR, Inspec, LeadAb, M&TEA, M09, MBF, METADEX, MSCI, MSN, MathR, P30, RefZh, S01, SCI, SCOPUS, SolStAb, SpeleolAb, T02, T04, TM, W07, WAA, Z02, Zincscan.
—BLDSC (5016.000000), AskIEEE, CASDDS, IE, Infotrieve, Ingenta, INIST, Linda Hall. **CCC.**
Published by: Pergamon (Subsidiary of: Elsevier Science & Technology), The Blvd, Langford Ln, East Park, Kidlington, Oxford OX5 1GB, United Kingdom. TEL 44-1865-843000, FAX 44-1865-843010, JournalsCustomerServiceEMEA@elsevier.com. Eds. H Gao TEL 401-863-2626, K Bhattacharya TEL 626-395-3389. **Subscr. to:** Elsevier BV, Radarweg 29, PO Box 211, Amsterdam 1000 AE, Netherlands. TEL 31-20-4853757, FAX 31-20-4853432, http://www.elsevier.nl.

531 620.1 BGR ISSN 0861-6663
JOURNAL OF THEORETICAL AND APPLIED MECHANICS. Text in English, Bulgarian. 1970. q. USD 65 (effective 2002). **Description:** Publishes original research papers and invited survey articles in all areas of mechanics, preferably accessible to a broad public.
Formerly (until 1990): Teoretichna i Prilozhna Mekhanika (0204-6148)
Indexed: CCMJ, CIS, GeoRef, MSN, MathR, RefZh, Z02.
—INIST, Linda Hall.
Published by: (Bulgarska Akademiya na Naukite, Institute of Mechanics, Bulgarska Akademiya na Naukite, National Committee of Theoretical and Applied Mechanics), Sofiiski Universitet Sv. Kliment Ohridski, Universitetsko Izdatelstvo/Sofia University St. Kliment Ohridski University Press, 15 Tsar Osvoboditel Blvd., Sofia, 1504, Bulgaria. Ed. S. Radev. **Dist. by:** Sofia Books, ul Silivria 16, Sofia 1404, Bulgaria. TEL 359-2-9586257, info@sofiabooks-bg.com, http://www.sofiabooks-bg.com.

JOURNAL OF THEORETICAL AND APPLIED MECHANICS. *see* ENGINEERING—Engineering Mechanics And Materials

531 621.381 DEU ISSN 1343-8875
➤ **JOURNAL OF VISUALIZATION.** Text in English. 1998. q. EUR 706, USD 954 combined subscription to institutions (print & online eds.) (effective 2012). illus. reprint service avail. from PSC. **Document type:** *Journal, Academic/Scholarly.* **Description:** Develops and advances applications and techniques of visualization, an imaging science using computer techniques to make the invisible visible.
Related titles: Online - full text ed.: ISSN 1875-8975.
Indexed: A01, A03, A08, A20, A22, A28, APA, B07, BrCerAb, C&ISA, CA, CA/WCA, CIA, CMCI, CerAb, CivEngAb, CorrAb, CurCont, E&CAJ, E01, E11, EEA, EMA, ESPM, EnvEAb, H15, IBR, IBZ, Inspec, M&TEA, M09, MBF, METADEX, S01, SCI, SCOPUS, SolStAb, T02, T04, W07, WAA.
—BLDSC (5072.496500), IE, Infotrieve, Ingenta, Linda Hall. **CCC.**
Published by: (Visualization Society of Japan JPN), Springer (Subsidiary of: Springer Science+Business Media), Tiergartenstr 17, Heidelberg, 69121, Germany. TEL 49-6221-4870, FAX 49-6221-345229, subscriptions@springer.com. Circ: 500.

531 RUS ISSN 1682-3532
TH418.9.C6 CODEN: CMDEF4
JOURNAL ON COMPOSITE MECHANICS AND DESIGN. Text in English. 1995. q. USD 395 (effective 2002). **Document type:** *Journal, Academic/Scholarly.* **Description:** Interdisciplinary journal combining problems and achievements of various fields in an attempt to clarify the mechanics of advanced composite materials. Major emphasis is on the mechanics of complex media and composite materials technologies.
Formerly (until 2001): Composite Mechanics and Design (1086-7252)
Related titles: ◆ Russian ed.: Mekhanika Kompozitsionnykh Materialov i Konstruktsii. ISSN 1029-6670.
Indexed: ApMecR, Inspec.
Published by: Rossiiskaya Akademiya Nauk, Institut Prikladnoi Mekhaniki/Russian Academy of Sciences, Institute of Applied Mechanics, Leninskii prospect 32A, Moscow, 119991, Russian Federation. TEL 7-095-9381845, FAX 7-095-9380711, iam@ipsun.ras.ru. **Co-sponsor:** Rossiiskaya Akademiya Nauk, Otdeleniye Problem Mashinostroyeniya, Mekhaniki i Protsessov Upravleniya/Russian Academy of Sciences, Division of Machine Engineering, Mechanics and Control Processes Problems.

531 JPN
KEISAN RIKIGAKU SHINPOJUMU HOBUNSHU/SYMPOSIUM ON COMPUTATIONAL MECHANICS. Text in English, Japanese. 1987. a. **Document type:** *Proceedings.*
Published by: Union of Japanese Scientists and Engineers/Nihon Kagaku Gijutsu Renmei, 5-10-11 Sendagaya, Shibuya-ku, Tokyo, 151-0051, Japan.

531 CHN ISSN 0258-1825
QA930
➤ **KONGQI DONGLIXUE XUEBAO/ACTA AERODYNAMICA SINICA.** Text in Chinese; Abstracts in English. 1980. q. USD 37.20 (effective 2009). abstr.; charts. 120 p./no.; back issues avail. **Document type:** *Journal, Academic/Scholarly.* **Description:** Contains scientific papers on research and development of aerodynamics and related disciplines.
Related titles: Online - full text ed.
Indexed: A28, APA, BrCerAb, C&ISA, CA/WCA, CIA, CPEI, CerAb, CivEngAb, CorrAb, E&CAJ, E11, EEA, EMA, ESPM, EngInd, EnvEAb, H15, M&TEA, M09, MBF, METADEX, SCOPUS, SolStAb, T04, WAA.
—East View, Linda Hall.
Published by: Zhongguo Kongqi Dongli Yanjiu yu Fazhan Zhongxin/ China Aerodynamics R & D Center (CARDC), PO Box 211, Mianyang, Sichuan 621000, China. TEL 86-816-2463287, FAX 86-816-2463138. Circ: 5,000. **Dist. overseas by:** China International Book Trading Corp, 35 Chegongzhuang Xilu, Haidian District, PO Box 399, Beijing 100044, China. TEL 86-10-68412045, FAX 86-10-68412023, cibtc@mail.cibtc.com.cn, http://www.cibtc.com.cn.

531 JPN ISSN 0454-4544
QC176.A1 CODEN: KOTBA2
KOTAI BUTSURI/SOLID STATE PHYSICS. Text in Japanese. 1955. m. JPY 2,000 per issue.
Formerly (until 966): Kinzoku Butsuri/Metal physics (0453-9206)
Indexed: A22, CIN, ChemAb, ChemTitl, GeoRef, INIS AtomInd, Inspec, JTA.
—BLDSC (8327.410000), AskIEEE, IE, Ingenta, Linda Hall.
Published by: AGNE Gijutsu Center, Kitamura Bldg, 1-25, Minamiaoyama 5-chome, Minato-ku, Tokyo, 107-0062, Japan.

KYIVS'KYI NATSIONAL'NYI UNIVERSYTET IMENI TARASA SHEVCHENKA. VISNYK. MATEMATYKA TA MEKHANIKA. *see* MATHEMATICS

531 JPN
KYUSHU UNIVERSITY. TANDEM ACCELERATOR LABORATORY. REPORT. Text in English. 1980. irreg.
Published by: Kyushu University, Faculty of Science, Tandem Accelerator Laboratory, 6-10-1 Hakozaki, Higashi-ku, Fukuoks City, 812-8581, Japan. TEL 81-92-6422707, FAX 81-92-6422710, http://www.kutl.kyushu-u.ac.jp/.

LATIN AMERICAN APPLIED RESEARCH. *see* CHEMISTRY

531 CHN ISSN 1000-0992
QC120 CODEN: LIJIEE
➤ **LIXUE JINZHAN/ADVANCES IN MECHANICS.** Text in Chinese. 1971. q. USD 133.20 (effective 2009). **Document type:** *Academic/ Scholarly.*
Related titles: Online - full text ed.
Indexed: ApMecR, Z02.
—East View.
Published by: Zhongguo Kexueyuan Lixue Yanjiusuo/Chinese Academy of Sciences, Institute of Mechanics, 15 Zhongguancun Lu, Beijing, 100080, China. TEL 2554108, FAX 86-1-2561284, TELEX 222554 MEHAS CN. Ed. Tan Haosheng. **Dist. outside China by:** China International Book Trading Corp, 35 Chegongzhuang Xilu, Haidian District, PO Box 399, Beijing 100044, China. TEL 86-10-68412045, FAX 86-10-68412023, cibtc@mail.cibtc.com.cn, http:// www.cibtc.com.cn.

531 CHN ISSN 0459-1879
TA352 CODEN: LHHPAE
➤ **LIXUE XUEBAO/ACTA MECHANICA SINICA.** Variant title: Chinese Journal of Theoretical Applied Mechanics. Text in Chinese; Summaries in English. 1957. bi-m. USD 240 (effective 2009). adv. **Document type:** *Journal, Academic/Scholarly.* **Description:** Publishes original theses on mechanics and its branches, including research treatises, experimental technology and methodology, brief accounts of research work, studies on the history of mechanics, and academic discussions.
Related titles: Online - full text ed.; ◆ English Translation: Acta Mechanica Sinica. ISSN 0567-7718.
Indexed: CCMJ, CPEI, ChemAb, EngInd, GeoRef, Inspec, MSN, MathR, SCOPUS, Z02.
—BLDSC (0632.500000), AskIEEE, CASDDS, East View, IE, Ingenta, INIST, Linda Hall.
Published by: Zhongguo Kexueyuan Lixue Yanjiusuo/Chinese Academy of Sciences, Institute of Mechanics, 15 Zhongguancun Lu, Beijing, 100080, China. TEL 86-10-62554107, FAX 86-10-62559588, imech@imech.ac.cn, http://www.imech.ac.cn/. Circ: 11,000. **Dist. by:** China International Book Trading Corp, 35 Chegongzhuang Xilu, Haidian District, PO Box 399, Beijing 100044, China. TEL 86-10-68412045, FAX 86-10-68412023, cibtc@mail.cibtc.com.cn, http://www.cibtc.com.cn.

➤ **LIXUE YU SHIJIAN/MECHANICS AND PRACTICE.** *see* ENGINEERING—Mechanical Engineering

➤ **MATERIALOVEDENIE.** *see* ENGINEERING—Industrial Engineering

533 DEU ISSN 0436-1199
CODEN: MPSBBR
MAX-PLANCK-INSTITUT FUER STROEMUNGSFORSCHUNG. BERICHT. Text mainly in German. irreg. price varies. **Document type:** *Monographic series, Academic/Scholarly.*
Indexed: Inspec.
—Linda Hall. **CCC.**
Published by: Max-Planck-Institut fuer Stroemungsforschung, Bunsenstr 10, Goettingen, 37073, Germany. TEL 49-551-51760, FAX 49-551-5176704, mpisf@gwdg.de, http://www.mpisf.mpg.de.

531 620.1 NLD ISSN 0025-6455
QA801 CODEN: MECCB9
➤ **MECCANICA.** Text in English. 1966. bi-m. EUR 1,208, USD 1,279 combined subscription to institutions (print & online eds.) (effective 2012). adv. bk.rev. charts; illus. index. back issues avail.; reprint service avail. from PSC. **Document type:** *Journal, Academic/ Scholarly.* **Description:** Explores fundamental and applications issues in established and emerging areas of mechanics research.
Related titles: Microform ed.: (from PQC); Online - full text ed.: ISSN 1572-9648 (from IngentaConnect).
Indexed: A22, A26, A28, APA, ASCA, ApMecR, BibLing, BrCerAb, C&ISA, C10, CA, CA/WCA, CCMJ, CIA, CPEI, CerAb, ChemAb, CivEngAb, CorrAb, CurCont, E&CAJ, E01, E11, EEA, EMA, ESPM, EngInd, EnvEAb, GeoRef, H15, I05, IBR, IBZ, ICEA, ISR, Inspec, M&TEA, M09, MBF, METADEX, MSN, MathR, P30, RefZh, S&VD, SCI, SCOPUS, SolStAb, SpeleolAb, T02, T04, TM, W07, WAA, Z02.
—BLDSC (5415.770000), AskIEEE, IE, Infotrieve, Ingenta, INIST, Linda Hall. **CCC.**
Published by: (Associazione Italiana per Meccanica Teoretica ed Applicata ITA), Springer Netherlands (Subsidiary of: Springer Science+Business Media), Van Godewijckstraat 30, Dordrecht, 3311 GX, Netherlands. TEL 31-78-6576050, FAX 31-78-6576474, http://www.springer.com. Ed. Vincenzo Parenti Castelli.

531 510 USA ISSN 0076-5783
TA349
MECHANICS. Text in English. 1970. 10/yr. USD 15. adv. bk.rev.
Published by: American Academy of Mechanics, c/o John Dundurs, Ed, Department of Civil Engineering, Northwestern University, Evanston, IL 60201. TEL 312-491-4034. Circ: 1,300.

MECHANICS AND MATHEMATICAL METHODS - SERIES OF HANDBOOKS. *see* MATHEMATICS

531 USA ISSN 0025-6544
QC176.A1 CODEN: MESOBN
➤ **MECHANICS OF SOLIDS/MEKHANIKA TVERDOGO TELA.** Text in English. 1965. bi-m. EUR 2,757, USD 3,340 combined subscription to institutions (print & online eds.) (effective 2012). abstr.; charts; illus. index. back issues avail. **Document type:** *Journal, Academic/ Scholarly.* **Description:** Provides reports on research being conducted at leading Russian institutions for advanced studies in applied and theoretical mechanics in isotropic and anisotropic media.
Formerly (until 1965): Soviet Engineering Journal (0584-5440)
Related titles: Online - full text ed.: ISSN 1934-7936; ◆ Translation of: Rossiiskaya Akademiya Nauk. Izvestiya. Mekhanika Tverdogo Tela. ISSN 1026-3519.
Indexed: A22, A26, ApMecR, E01, E08, Inspec, MathR, S09, SCI, SCOPUS, W07.
—BLDSC (0415.850000), AskIEEE, East View, IE, Infotrieve, Ingenta, INIST, Linda Hall. **CCC.**
Published by: (Rossiiskaya Akademiya Nauk/Russian Academy of Sciences RUS), Allerton Press, Inc. (Subsidiary of: Pleiades Publishing, Inc.), 18 W 27th St, New York, NY 10001. TEL 646-424-9686, FAX 646-424-9695, journals@allertonpress.com. Ed. Dmitry M Klimov.

531 620.1 NLD ISSN 1385-2000
CODEN: MTDMFH
➤ **MECHANICS OF TIME DEPENDENT MATERIALS;** an international journal devoted to the time-dependent behaviour of materials and structures. Text in English. 1997. q. EUR 563, USD 585 combined subscription to institutions (print & online eds.) (effective 2012). adv. reprint service avail. from PSC. **Document type:** *Journal, Academic/ Scholarly.* **Description:** Promotes the transfer of knowledge between various disciplines that deal with the properties of time-dependent solid materials but approach these from different angles. Among these disciplines are: Mechanical engineering, aerospace engineering, chemical engineering, rheology, materials science, polymer physics, design, and others.
Related titles: Online - full text ed.: ISSN 1573-2738 (from IngentaConnect).
Indexed: A22, A26, A28, APA, ApMecR, BibLing, BrCerAb, C&ISA, CA, CA/WCA, CIA, CPEI, CerAb, CivEngAb, CorrAb, CurCont, E&CAJ, E01, E11, EEA, EMA, ESPM, EngInd, EnvEAb, H15, I05, Inspec, M&TEA, M09, MBF, METADEX, MSCI, RefZh, SCI, SCOPUS, SolStAb, T02, T04, TM, W07, WAA.
—BLDSC (5424.166000), CASDDS, IE, Infotrieve, Ingenta, INIST, Linda Hall. **CCC.**
Published by: Springer Netherlands (Subsidiary of: Springer Science+Business Media), Van Godewijckstraat 30, Dordrecht, 3311 GX, Netherlands. TEL 31-78-6576050, FAX 31-78-6576474, http://www.springer.com. Eds. Igor Emri, Wolfgang G Knauss.

531 LTU ISSN 1392-1207
TA357
➤ **MECHANIKA.** Text in Lithuanian, English. 1995. q. USD 420 foreign (effective 2006). **Document type:** *Journal, Academic/Scholarly.*
Indexed: A01, A26, A28, APA, B02, B15, B17, B18, BrCerAb, C&ISA, CA, CA/WCA, CIA, CPEI, CerAb, CivEngAb, CorrAb, E&CAJ, E08, E11, EEA, EMA, ESPM, EngInd, EnvEAb, G04, H15, I05, Inspec, M&TEA, M09, MBF, METADEX, RefZh, SCI, SCOPUS, SolStAb, T02, T04, W07, WAA.
—BLDSC (5424.204000).
Published by: (Kauno Technologijos Universitetas, Transporto Inzinerijos Katedra), Kauno Technologijos Universitetas/Kaunas University of Technology, K Donelaicio g 73, Kaunas, 44029, Lithuania. TEL 370-37-300000, http://www.ktu.lt. Ed. Mykolas Daunys.

531 LVA ISSN 0203-1272
TA455.P58 CODEN: MKMADT
➤ **MEKHANIKA KOMPOZITNYKH MATERIALOV.** Text in Russian; Summaries in English. 1965. bi-m. USD 304 foreign (effective 2005). bk.rev. index. **Document type:** *Journal, Academic/Scholarly.* **Description:** Publishing the latest results on composite mechanics gained by scientists from Commonwealth of Independent States (the former USSR).
Formerly: Mekhanika Polimerov (0025-8865)
Related titles: ◆ English Translation: Mechanics of Composite Materials. ISSN 0191-5665.
Indexed: CIN, ChemAb, ChemTitl, CorrAb, Inspec, SCOPUS, WAA.
—BLDSC (0114.275000), CASDDS, INIST, Linda Hall. **CCC.**
Published by: Latvijas Universitate, Polimeru Mehanikas Instituts/ University of Latvia, Institute of Polymer Mechanics, 23 Aizkraukles St, Riga, 1006, Latvia. TEL 371-7-551145, FAX 371-7-820467, polmech@pmi.lv. Ed. Vitauts Tamuzs. Circ: 70,569. **Dist. by:** M K - Periodica, ul Gilyarovskogo 39, Moscow 129110, Russian Federation. TEL 7-095-2845008, FAX 7-095-2813798, info@periodicals.ru, http://www.mkniga.ru.

531 RUS ISSN 1029-6670
MEKHANIKA KOMPOZITSIONNYKH MATERIALOV I KONSTRUKTSII; vserossiiskii nauchnyi zhurnal. Text in Russian. 1995. q. **Document type:** *Journal, Academic/Scholarly.* **Description:** Interdisciplinary journal combining problems and achievements of various fields in an attempt to clarify the mechanics of advanced composite materials. Major emphasis is on the mechanics of complex media and composite materials technologies.
Related titles: ◆ English ed.: Journal on Composite Mechanics and Design. ISSN 1682-3532.
Indexed: CorrAb, Inspec, RefZh, WAA.
—East View.
Published by: Rossiiskaya Akademiya Nauk, Institut Prikladnoi Mekhaniki/Russian Academy of Sciences, Institute of Applied Mechanics, Leninskii prospect 32A, Moscow, 119991, Russian Federation. TEL 7-095-9381845, FAX 7-095-9380711, iam@ipsun.ras.ru. **Co-sponsor:** Rossiiskaya Akademiya Nauk, Otdeleniye Problem Mashinostroyeniya, Mekhaniki i Protsessov Upravleniya/Russian Academy of Sciences, Division of Machine Engineering, Mechanics and Control Processes Problems.

621.3 NLD ISSN 1873-1988
➤ **METAMATERIALS.** Text in English. 2007. 4/yr. EUR 402 in Europe to institutions; JPY 57,400 in Japan to institutions; USD 402 elsewhere to institutions (effective 2012). **Document type:** *Journal, Academic/ Scholarly.*
Related titles: Online - full text ed.: (from ScienceDirect).
Indexed: A28, APA, BrCerAb, C&ISA, CA/WCA, CIA, CPEI, CerAb, CivEngAb, CorrAb, E&CAJ, E11, EEA, EMA, ESPM, EnvEAb, H15, M&TEA, M09, MBF, METADEX, SCOPUS, SolStAb, T02, T04, WAA.
—IE. **CCC.**
Published by: Elsevier BV (Subsidiary of: Elsevier Science & Technology), Radarweg 29, PO Box 211, Amsterdam, 1000 AE, Netherlands. TEL 31-20-4853911, FAX 31-20-4852457, JournalsCustomerServiceEMEA@elsevier.com.

531 CUB ISSN 1026-048X
T4
METANICA. Text in Spanish. 1975. bi-m. USD 10 in North America; USD 13 in South America; USD 15 in Europe; USD 21 elsewhere. **Document type:** *Bulletin, Trade.*
Formerly: Tecnica Popular (0138-8800)
Published by: Ministerio de la Industria Sidero Mecanica, 36 A No. 712th 7ma y 42,, La Playa, Ciudad de La Playa, Cuba. TELEX 512160. Ed. Mercedes Esber Mulles. Circ: 5,000. **Dist. by:** Ediciones Cubanas, Obispo 527, Havana, Cuba.

MICROFLUIDICS AND NANOFLUIDICS. *see* ENGINEERING—Mechanical Engineering

531 CHN ISSN 1004-0595
TJ1075.A2 CODEN: MAXUE7
MOCAXUE XUEBAO/TRIBOLOGY. Text in Chinese. q. USD 79.80 (effective 2009). **Document type:** *Journal, Academic/Scholarly.*
Related titles: Online - full text ed.
Indexed: A22, A28, APA, BrCerAb, C&ISA, CA/WCA, CIA, CPEI, CerAb, ChemAb, ChemTitl, CivEngAb, CorrAb, E&CAJ, E11, EEA, EMA, ESPM, EngInd, EnvEAb, GeoRef, H15, M&TEA, M09, MBF, METADEX, SCOPUS, SolStAb, T04, WAA.
—BLDSC (9050.216900), CASDDS, East View, IE, Ingenta.
Published by: (Zhongguo Kexueyuan Lanzhou Huaxue Wuli Yanjiusuo), Kexue Chubanshe/Science Press, 16 Donghuang Cheng Genbei Jie, Beijing, 100717, China. TEL 86-10-64000246, FAX 86-10-64030255, http://www.sciencep.com/. **Dist. by:** China International Book Trading Corp, 35 Chegongzhuang Xilu, Haidian District, PO Box 399, Beijing 100044, China. TEL 86-10-68412045, FAX 86-10-68412023, cibtc@mail.cibtc.com.cn, http://www.cibtc.com.cn.

531 USA ISSN 0027-1330
TA349 CODEN: MUVMB8
➤ **MOSCOW UNIVERSITY MECHANICS BULLETIN.** Text in English. 1966. bi-m. EUR 2,275, USD 2,756 combined subscription to institutions (print & online eds.) (effective 2012). abstr.; bibl.; illus. index. back issues avail. **Document type:** *Journal, Academic/ Scholarly.* **Description:** Presents articles on a variety of aspects of mechanics, with emphasis on the analytical and approximated analytical methods of current research being conducted.
Related titles: Online - full text ed.: ISSN 1934-8452; ◆ Partial translation of: Moskovskii Gosudarstvennyi Universitet. Vestnik. Seriya 1: Matematika i Mekhanika. ISSN 0579-9368.
Indexed: A22, A26, ApMecR, E01, E08, S09, Z02.
—East View, IE, Ingenta, INIST, Linda Hall. **CCC.**
Published by: (Moskovskii Gosudarstvennyi Universitet im. M.V. Lomonosova/M.V. Lomonosov Moscow State University RUS), Allerton Press, Inc. (Subsidiary of: Pleiades Publishing, Inc.), 18 W 27th St, New York, NY 10001. TEL 646-424-9686, FAX 646-424-9695, journals@allertonpress.com. Ed. Oleg B Lupanov.

➤ **MOSKOVSKII GOSUDARSTVENNYI UNIVERSITET. VESTNIK. SERIYA 1: MATEMATIKA I MEKHANIKA.** *see* MATHEMATICS

531 USA ISSN 0889-3934
MOTION; guide to electronic motion control. Text in English. 1985. bi-m. USD 36. adv. **Document type:** *Handbook/Manual/Guide, Trade.* **Description:** Covers industrial and aerospace-related electronic motion control.
Indexed: EIA.
—Linda Hall.
Published by: Motion Corporation, P O Box 21730, Carson City, NV 89721-1730. TEL 775-246-9292, FAX 775-246-9222, http://www.motion.org. Ed. Sandra Falk. Circ: 33,000.

531 NLD ISSN 1384-5640
QA843 CODEN: MSDYFC
➤ **MULTIBODY SYSTEM DYNAMICS.** Text in English. 1997. 8/yr. EUR 915, USD 946 combined subscription to institutions (print & online eds.) (effective 2012). adv. reprint service avail. from PSC. **Document type:** *Journal, Academic/Scholarly.* **Description:** Reports original contributions describing significant developments of different topics in multibody system dynamics through a single journal. Mathematical foundations, numerical procedures, experimental results, software development and applications of this of this field are of interest to the readers.
Related titles: Online - full text ed.: ISSN 1573-272X (from IngentaConnect).
Indexed: A22, A26, ApMecR, BibLing, CA, CCMJ, CPEI, CurCont, E01, EngInd, ISR, Inspec, MSN, MathR, P30, RefZh, S&VD, S01, SCI, SCOPUS, T02, W07, Z02.
—BLDSC (5983.081300), IE, Infotrieve, Ingenta, Linda Hall. **CCC.**
Published by: Springer Netherlands (Subsidiary of: Springer Science+Business Media), Van Godewijckstraat 30, Dordrecht, 3311 GX, Netherlands. TEL 31-78-6576050, FAX 31-78-6576474, http://www.springer.com. Ed. Jorge A C Ambrosio.

➤ **NAGARE/JAPAN SOCIETY OF FLUID MECHANICS. JOURNAL.** *see* ENGINEERING—Hydraulic Engineering

➤ **NANOTECHNOLOGY WEEKLY.** *see* BIOLOGY—Biotechnology

531 621 UKR ISSN 2078-9130
CODEN: DNPRAE
➤ **NATSIONAL'NYI TEKHNICHESKII UNIVERSITET "KHAR'KOVSKII POLITEKHNICHESKII INSTITUT". VESTNIK. DINAMIKA I PROCHNOST' MASHIN/NATSIONAL'NYI TEKHNICHNYI UNIVERSYTET "KHARKIVS'KYI POLITEKHNICHNYI INSTYTUT". VISNYK. DYNAMIKA I MITSNIST' MASHYN.** Text in Ukrainian, Russian. 1965. s-a. **Document type:** *Journal, Academic/Scholarly.*
Formerly (until 2001): Dinamika i Prochnost' Mashin (0419-1544)
Related titles: Online - full text ed.
Indexed: C&ISA, CorrAb, E&CAJ, SolStAb, WAA.
—Linda Hall.
Published by: Natsional'nyi Tekhnicheskii Universitet "Kharkovskii Politekhnicheskii Institut"/National Technical University "Kharkiv Polytechnical Institute", vul Frunze 21, Kharkiv, 310002, Ukraine. TEL 380-572-7076212, http://www.kpi.kharkov.ua. Ed. Oleg Morachkovskii.

➤ **NIHON REOROJI GAKKAI NENKAI KOEN YOKOSHU/ABSTRACTS OF ANNUAL MEETING ON RHEOLOGY.** *see* PHYSICS—Abstracting, Bibliographies, Statistics

532 JPN ISSN 0387-1533
QC189.5.A1 CODEN: NRGIAC
➤ **NIHON REOROJI GAKKAISHI/SOCIETY OF RHEOLOGY, JAPAN. JOURNAL.** Text in Japanese. 1973. q. free to members. 80 p./no.; **Document type:** *Journal, Academic/Scholarly.* **Description:** Contains original and review articles, information for all SRJ events, and reports of overseas meetings.
Related titles: Online - full text ed.: free (effective 2011).
Indexed: A20, A22, A39, C27, C29, C33, CCI, CIN, ChemAb, ChemTitl, D03, D04, E13, JPI, MSCI, R14, S14, S15, S18, SCI, SCOPUS, W07.
—BLDSC (4896.860000), CASDDS, IE, Ingenta, Linda Hall. **CCC.**
Published by: Nihon Reoroji Gakkai/Society of Rheology, Japan, 3F, Bldg no.6, Kyoto Research Park, 1, Chudoji-Awata, Shimogyo-ku, Kyoto, 600-8815, Japan. TEL 81-75-3158687, FAX 81-75-3158688, byr06213@nifty.ne.jp. Ed. Yukuo Nanzai TEL 81-6-66052667.

➤ **NONLINEAR DYNAMICS AND SYSTEMS THEORY.** *see* MATHEMATICS

532 SWE
NORDIC RHEOLOGY SOCIETY. ANNUAL TRANSACTIONS. Text in English. a. **Document type:** *Proceedings, Academic/Scholarly.*
Related titles: Online - full text ed.
—BLDSC (1536.637980).
Published by: Nordic Rheology Society, c/o Mikael Rigdahl, Chalmers Universiy of Technology, Goeteborg, 41296, Sweden. TEL 46-31-7721309, FAX 46-31-7721313, mikael.rigdahl@chalmers.se, http://www.sik.se/nrs.

531 RUS
NOVYE PROMYSHLENNYE KATALOGI. PRIBORY. AVTOMATIKA. TELEMEKHANIKA I VYCHISLITEL'NAYA TEKHNIKA. Text in Russian. m. USD 365 in United States.
Published by: Rossiiskii N.I.I. Problem Transporta, Lubyanskii pr 5, Moscow, 101820, Russian Federation. TEL 7-095-9254609, FAX 7-095-2002203. **Dist. by:** East View Information Services, 10601 Wayzata Blvd, Minneapolis, MN 55305. TEL 952-252-1201, 800-477-1005, FAX 952-252-1202, info@eastview.com, http://www.eastview.com.

P M T F. (Prikladnaya Mekhanika i Tekhnicheskaya Fizika) *see* ENGINEERING—Mechanical Engineering

531 534 DEU ISSN 0179-0595
P T B-BERICHT. MECHANIK UND AKUSTIK. (Physikalisch-Technische Bundesanstalt) Variant title: P T B-Bericht. MA. Text in English, German. 1971. irreg., latest vol.82, 2007. price varies. **Document type:** *Monographic series, Academic/Scholarly.*
Formed by the merger of (1971-1987): P T B-Bericht. Abteilung Mechanik (0341-6720); (1973-1986): P T B-Bericht. Abteilung Akustik (0340-8639)
Indexed: Inspec.
—BLDSC (1927.008000). **CCC.**
Published by: (Physikalisch-Technische Bundesanstalt), Wirtschaftsverlag N W - Verlag fuer Neue Wissenschaft GmbH, Buergermeister-Smidt-Str 74-76, Bremerhaven, 27568, Germany. TEL 49-471-945440, FAX 49-471-9454477, info@nw-verlag.de, http://www.nw-verlag.de.

531 USA ISSN 1029-9599
TA417.6 CODEN: FMIEAN
➤ **PHYSICAL MESOMECHANICS.** Text in English. 1998. bi-m. EUR 688 in Europe to institutions; JPY 112,000 in Japan to institutions; USD 940 elsewhere to institutions (effective 2012). adv. 120 p./no. 2 cols./p.; back issues avail.; reprints avail. **Document type:** *Journal, Academic/Scholarly.* **Description:** Brings out papers on structural, physical, mechanical properties of materials, computer methods of physical mesomechanics of heterogeneous media, and non-destructive testing methods etc.
Related titles: Online - full text ed.: ISSN 1990-5424 (from ScienceDirect); ◆ Russian ed.: Fizicheskaya Mezomekhanika. ISSN 1683-805X.
Indexed: A22, CA, CurCont, MSCI, SCI, SCOPUS, T02, W07.
—BLDSC (6475.660000), East View, IE, Ingenta. **CCC.**
Published by: (Siberian Branch of Russian Academy of Sciences, Institute of Strength Physics and Materials Science RUS), Elsevier Inc. (Subsidiary of: Elsevier Science & Technology), 1600 John F Kennedy Blvd, Philadelphia, PA 19103. TEL 215-239-3900, FAX 215-238-7883, JournalCustomerService-usa@elsevier.com. Eds. Victor E Panin, W Panin. Adv. contact Janine Castle TEL 44-1865-843844.

532 540 GBR ISSN 0031-9104
QD541 CODEN: PCLQAC
➤ **PHYSICS AND CHEMISTRY OF LIQUIDS**; an international journal. Text in French. 1968. bi-m. GBP 3,140 combined subscription in United Kingdom to institutions (print & online eds.); EUR 3,340, USD 4,198 combined subscription to institutions (print & online eds.) (effective 2012). adv. reprint service avail. from PSC. **Document type:** *Journal, Academic/Scholarly.* **Description:** Publishes experimental and theoretical papers aimed at furthering the understanding of the liquid state. The coverage embraces the whole spectrum of liquids, from simple monatomic liquids and their mixtures, through charged liquids of all kinds.
Related titles: CD-ROM ed.: ISSN 1026-7727. 1995; Microform ed.: (from MIM); Online - full text ed.: ISSN 1029-0451. 1996. GBP 2,826 in United Kingdom to institutions; EUR 3,007, USD 3,778 to institutions (effective 2012) (from IngentaConnect).
Indexed: A01, A03, A08, A22, ASCA, ApMecR, C24, C33, CA, CPEI, ChemAb, CurCR, CurCont, E01, EngInd, FLUIDEX, IBR, IBZ, ISR, Inspec, P52, PhysBer, R16, S01, SCI, SCOPUS, T02, W07.
—AskIEEE, IE, Infotrieve, Ingenta, INIST. **CCC.**
Published by: Taylor & Francis Ltd. (Subsidiary of: Taylor & Francis Group), 4 Park Sq, Milton Park, Abingdon, Oxfordshire OX14 4RN, United Kingdom. TEL 44-1235-828600, FAX 44-1235-829000, info@tandf.co.uk. Ed. Norman H March. **Subscr. to:** Journals Customer Service, Sheepen Pl, Colchester, Essex CO3 3LP, United Kingdom. TEL 44-20-70175544, FAX 44-20-70175198, tf.enquiries@tfinforma.com.

530 541.2 NLD ISSN 0924-6339
CODEN: PMLSEO
➤ **PHYSICS AND CHEMISTRY OF MATERIALS WITH LOW-DIMENSIONAL STRUCTURES.** Text in English. 1976. irreg., latest vol.25, 2004. price varies. **Document type:** *Monographic series, Academic/Scholarly.* **Description:** Aims to provide a clear and comprehensive overview of the wide properties of phases characterized by low-dimensional structures.
Formed by the 1989 merger of: Physics and Chemistry of Materials with Low-Dimensional Structures. Series C: Molecular Structures (0924-459X); Physics and Chemistry of Materials with Low-Dimensional Structures. Series B: Quasi-One-Dimensional Structures (0924-4581); Physics and Chemistry of Materials with Low-Dimensional Structures. Series A: Layered Structures (0924-4573); Which was formerly (until 1986): Physics and Chemistry of Materials with Layered Structures (0378-1917)
Indexed: ChemAb, ChemTitl.
—BLDSC (6478.215030), CASDDS, IE, Ingenta.
Published by: Springer Netherlands (Subsidiary of: Springer Science+Business Media), Van Godewijckstraat 30, Dordrecht, 3311 GX, Netherlands. TEL 31-78-6576050, FAX 31-78-6576474. Eds. E Mooser, F Levy.

531 POL ISSN 0372-9486
POLITECHNIKA KRAKOWSKA. ZESZYTY NAUKOWE. MECHANIKA. Text in Polish; Summaries in English, French, German, Russian. 1956. irreg. price varies. bibl.; charts; illus. **Document type:** *Monographic series, Academic/Scholarly.*
Indexed: MathR.
—Linda Hall.
Published by: Politechnika Krakowska im. Tadeusza Kosciuszki/Tadeusz Kosciuszko Cracow University of Technology, ul Warszawska 24, Krakow, 31155, Poland. TEL 48-12-6374289, FAX 48-12-6374289. Ed. Elzbieta Nachlik. Adv. contact Ewa Malochleb. Circ: 200.

531 621 POL ISSN 1733-1919
TJ145
POLITECHNIKA POZNANSKA. ZESZYTY NAUKOWE. BUDOWA MASZYN I ZARZADZANIE PRODUKCJI. Text in English, Polish; Summaries in English. 1958. irreg., latest vol.8, 2009. price varies. 100 p./no.; **Document type:** *Monographic series, Academic/Scholarly.* **Description:** Contains research notes and information covering all fields of design, manufacturing and exploitation of machinery in mechanical engineering.
Formerly (until 2004): Politechnika Poznanska. Zeszyty Naukowe. Mechanika (0079-4538)
Indexed: B22.
Published by: (Politechnika Poznanska), Wydawnictwo Politechniki Poznanskiej, Pl M Sklodowskiej Curie 2, Poznan, 60965, Poland. TEL 48-61-6653516, FAX 48-61-6653583, office_ed@put.poznan.pl, http://www.ed.put.poznan.pl. Ed. Zenon Ignaszak. Circ: 120.

POWER TRANSMISSION AND MOTION CONTROL. *see* ENGINEERING—Hydraulic Engineering

POWER TRANSMISSION ENGINEERING. *see* ENGINEERING—Hydraulic Engineering

531 UKR ISSN 1561-9087
CODEN: GDMKBA
PRIKLADNAYA GIDROMEKHANIKA. Text in Russian. 1965. s-a.
Formerly (until 1999): Gidromekhanika (0367-4088)
Indexed: CCMJ, GeoRef, Inspec, MSN, MathR, RefZh, SpeleolAb, Z02.
—AskIEEE, CASDDS, INIST, Linda Hall. **CCC.**
Published by: (Institut Gidrodinamiki), Natsional'na Akademiya Nauk Ukrainy, 54 Volodymyrska St, Kyiv, 01601, Ukraine. TEL 380-44-234 5167, FAX 380-44-2343243, prez@nas.gov.ua, http://www.nas.gov.ua. Ed. Viktor T Hrinchenko. **Dist. by:** M K - Periodica, ul Gilyarovskogo 39, Moscow 129110, Russian Federation. TEL 7-095-2845008, FAX 7-095-2813798, info@periodicals.ru, http://www.mkniga.ru.

PRIKLADNAYA MATEMATIKA I MEKHANIKA. *see* MATHEMATICS

532 IND
RECENT RESEARCH DEVELOPMENTS IN FLUID DYNAMICS. Text in English. 2000. a. **Document type:** *Monographic series, Academic/Scholarly.*
Published by: Transworld Research Network, T C 37-661 (2), Fort Post Office, Trivandrum, Kerala 695 023, India. TEL 91-471-2452918, FAX 91-471-2573051, ggcom@vsnl.com, http://www.trnres.com.

REFERATIVNYI ZHURNAL. KOMPLEKSNYE I SPETSYAL'NYE RAZDELY MEKHANIKI; vypusk svodnogo toma. *see* PHYSICS—Abstracting, Bibliographies, Statistics

REFERATIVNYI ZHURNAL. MEKHANIKA DEFORMIRUEMOGO TVERDOGO TELA; vypusk svodnogo toma. *see* PHYSICS—Abstracting, Bibliographies, Statistics

REFERATIVNYI ZHURNAL. MEKHANIKA ZHIDKOSTI I GAZA; vypusk svodnogo toma. *see* PHYSICS—Abstracting, Bibliographies, Statistics

REFERATIVNYI ZHURNAL. OBSHCHIE VOPROSY MEKHANIKI. OBSHCHAYA MEKHANIKA; vypusk svodnogo toma. *see* PHYSICS—Abstracting, Bibliographies, Statistics

REOROJI TORONKAI KOEN YOSHISHU/ABSTRACTS OF SYMPOSIUM ON RHEOLOGY. *see* PHYSICS—Abstracting, Bibliographies, Statistics

531 621 UKR ISSN 2078-7405
CODEN: RZITAJ
➤ **REZANIE I INSTRUMENT V TEKHNOLOGICHESKIH SISTEMAH/ CUTTING AND TOOLS IN TECHNOLOGICAL SYSTEMS.** Text in Ukrainian, Russian, English, German. 1970. s-a. free to qualified personnel. bk.rev. back issues avail. **Document type:** *Journal, Academic/Scholarly.*
Formerly (until 1995): Rezanie i Instrument (0370-808X)
—CASDDS, Linda Hall.
Published by: Natsional'nyi Tekhnicheskii Universitet "Kharkovskii Politekhnicheskii Institut"/National Technical University "Kharkiv Polytechnical Institute", vul Frunze 21, Kharkiv, 310002, Ukraine. TEL 380-572-7076212, FAX 380-572-7076601, http://www.kpi.kharkov.ua. Ed. Anatolii Grabchenko. Pub. Leonid Tovazhnyanskii.

532 DEU ISSN 0035-4511
QC189 CODEN: RHEAAK
➤ **RHEOLOGICA ACTA**; an international journal of rheology. Text in English. 1958. bi-m. EUR 3,092, USD 3,683 combined subscription to institutions (print & online eds.) (effective 2012). adv. charts. back issues avail.; reprint service avail. from PSC. **Document type:** *Journal, Academic/Scholarly.* **Description:** Publishes papers in all core areas of fluid and solid rheology.
Related titles: Microform ed.: (from PQC); Online - full text ed.: ISSN 1435-1528 (from IngentaConnect).
Indexed: A01, A03, A08, A22, A26, ASCA, ApMecR, C33, CA, CEA, CEABA, CIN, ChemAb, ChemTitl, CurCont, E01, FLUIDEX, FS&TA, GeoRef, GeotechAb, IBR, IBZ, ISR, Inspec, MSCI, MathR, PetrolAb, R18, RefZh, SCI, SCOPUS, SpeleolAb, T02, W07, WSCA, Z02.
—BLDSC (7960.300000), AskIEEE, CASDDS, IE, Infotrieve, Ingenta, INIST, Linda Hall, PADDS. **CCC.**
Published by: Springer (Subsidiary of: Springer Science+Business Media), Tiergartenstr 17, Heidelberg, 69121, Germany. TEL 49-6221-4870, FAX 49-6221-345229. Eds. D Vlassopoulos, H Winter TEL 413-545-0922. Circ: 2,000. **Subscr. in the Americas to:** Springer New York LLC, Journal Fulfillment, PO Box 2485, Secaucus, NJ 07096. TEL 800-777-4643, 201-348-4033, FAX 201-348-4505, journals-ny@springer.com, http://www.springer.com; **Subscr. to:** Springer Distribution Center, Kundenservice Zeitschriften, Haberstr 7, Heidelberg 69126, Germany. TEL 49-6221-3454303, FAX 49-6221-3454229, subscriptions@springer.com.

532 USA ISSN 0035-4538
RHEOLOGY BULLETIN. Text in English. 1929. s-a. free to members (effective 2010). back issues avail. **Document type:** *Bulletin, Trade.* **Description:** Contains society affairs and matters of general interest to rheologists.
Former titles (until 1941): Rheology Leaflet (0099-5916); (until 1937): Journal of Rheology (0097-0360)
Related titles: Online - full text ed.: free (effective 2010).
—Linda Hall. **CCC.**
Published by: Society of Rheology, c/o Faith A Morrison, Department of Chemical Engineering, Michigan Technological University, 1400 Townsend Dr, Houghton, MI 49931. TEL 906-487-2050, FAX 906-487-3213, fmorriso@mtu.edu. Ed. Faith Morrison.

532 GBR ISSN 1469-4999
CODEN: BBRHAO
RHEOLOGY BULLETIN. Text in English. 1946. q. free to members (effective 2009). adv. **Document type:** *Bulletin, Academic/Scholarly.* **Description:** Contains reports on conferences and other society activities, review articles on rheological topics, information on future meetings and general notes and news.
Former titles (until 1998): British Society of Rheology. Bulletin (0045-3145); (until 1950): British Rheologists Club. Bulletin
Related titles: Online - full text ed.; ◆ Supplement to: Rheology Abstracts. ISSN 0035-452X.
Indexed: Inspec.
Published by: British Society of Rheology, c o Dr Oliver Guy Harlen, School of Mathematics, University of Leeds, Leeds, LS2 9JT, United Kingdom. TEL 44-1133-435189, FAX 44-1133-435090, oliver@maths.leeds.ac.uk. Ed. Dr. Xue-Feng Yuan TEL 44-161-3064887. Circ: 600.

ROSSIISKAYA AKADEMIYA NAUK. INSTITUT MATEMATIKI I MEKHANIKI. TRUDY. *see* MATHEMATICS

532 533 RUS ISSN 0568-5281
➤ **ROSSIISKAYA AKADEMIYA NAUK. IZVESTIYA. MEKHANIKA ZHIDKOSTI I GAZA.** Text in Russian. 1966. bi-m. USD 298 foreign (effective 2005). **Document type:** *Journal, Academic/Scholarly.* **Description:** Deals with theoretical and experimental research in fluid dynamics, magnetic hydrodynamics, plasma dynamics including boundary layer problems of gas flow with chemical reactions, problems of hydrodynamic stability, turbulence, savitation etc.
Indexed: CCMJ, CorrAb, GeoRef, Inspec, MSN, MathR, RefZh, SCOPUS, WAA, Z02.
—East View, INIST, Linda Hall, PADDS. **CCC.**
Published by: Izdatel'stvo Nauka, Profsoyuznaya ul 90, Moscow, 117864, Russian Federation. TEL 7-095-3347151, FAX 7-095-4202220, secret@naukaran.ru, http://www.naukaran.ru. **Dist. by:** East View Information Services, 10601 Wayzata Blvd, Minneapolis, MN 55305. TEL 952-252-1201, 800-477-1005, FAX 952-252-1202, info@eastview.com, http://www.eastview.com.

531 RUS
➤ **SAMARSKII GOSUDARSTVENNYI UNIVERSITET. VESTNIK. ESTESTVENNONAUCHNAYA SERIYA. MEKHANIKA/SAMARA STATE UNIVERSITY. VESTNIK. NATURAL SCIENCE SERIES. MECHANICS.** Text in Russian; Summaries in English. 1995. bi-m. **Document type:** *Journal, Academic/Scholarly.*
Published by: (Samarskii Gosudarstvennyi Universitet), Izdatel'stvo Samarskii Universitet/Publishing House of Samara State University, ul Akademika Pavlova 1, k 209, Samara, 443011, Russian Federation. TEL 7-846-3345406, FAX 7-846-3345406, university-press@ssu.samara.ru, http://publisher.samsu.ru. Ed. Dr. I A Noskov.

531 DEU ISSN 0933-8047
SEIBT OBERFLAECHENTECHNIK. Text in English, German. 1988. a. **Document type:** *Directory, Trade.*
Related titles: CD-ROM ed.; Online - full text ed.
Published by: Seibt Verlag GmbH (Subsidiary of: Hoppenstedt Publishing GmbH), Havelstr 9, Darmstadt, 64295, Germany. TEL 49-6151-380120, FAX 49-6151-380468, info@seibt.com, http://www.seibt.com. Circ: 8,000.

531 SGP ISSN 0218-0235
SERIES IN THEORETICAL & APPLIED MECHANICS. Text in English. 1986. irreg., latest vol.11, 1990. price varies. back issues avail. **Document type:** *Monographic series, Academic/Scholarly.*
Indexed: Z02.
Published by: World Scientific Publishing Co. Pte. Ltd., 5 Toh Tuck Link, Singapore, 596224, Singapore. TEL 65-6466-5775, FAX 65-6467-7667, wspc@wspc.com.sg, http://www.worldscientific.com. **Dist. by:** World Scientific Publishing Ltd., 57 Shelton St, London WC2H 9HE, United Kingdom. TEL 44-207-8360888, FAX 44-207-8362020, sales@wspc.co.uk; World Scientific Publishing Co., Inc., 27 Warren St, Ste 401-402, Hackensack, NJ 07601. TEL 201-487-9655, 800-227-7562, FAX 201-487-9656, 888-977-2665, wspc@wspc.com.

531 SGP ISSN 0218-0111
SERIES ON ADVANCES IN STATISTICAL MECHANICS. (Vols. published out of sequence. Latest published vol.8 (2005). Vol.15 published in 2002.) Text in English. 1985. irreg., latest vol.17, 2009. price varies. back issues avail. **Document type:** *Monographic series, Academic/Scholarly.* **Description:** Covers the interesting topics of contemporary statistical mechanics, as well as its main areas of application, with readable books, which are written in didactic style.
Indexed: CCMJ, MSN, MathR.
—BLDSC (8250.149000), IE, Ingenta.
Published by: World Scientific Publishing Co. Pte. Ltd., 5 Toh Tuck Link, Singapore, 596224, Singapore. TEL 65-6466-5775, FAX 65-6467-7667, wspc@wspc.com.sg, http://www.worldscientific.com. Ed. Davide Cassi. **Dist. by:** World Scientific Publishing Ltd., 57 Shelton St, London WC2H 9HE, United Kingdom. TEL 44-207-8360888, FAX 44-207-8362020, sales@wspc.co.uk; World Scientific Publishing Co., Inc., 27 Warren St, Ste 401-402, Hackensack, NJ 07601. TEL 201-487-9655, 800-227-7562, FAX 201-487-9656, 888-977-2665, wspc@wspc.com.

531 CHN ISSN 0254-0053
CODEN: SHLIDP
SHANGHAI LIXUE/SHANGHAI MECHANICS. Text in Chinese. 1980. q. USD 18.80 (effective 2009). bk.rev. **Document type:** *Academic/Scholarly.*
—CASDDS, East View.
Published by: Shanghai Lixue Xuehui/Shanghai Society of Mechanics, 1239 Siping Rd, Tongji Daxue, Jiegou Lilun Yanjiusuo, Shanghai, 200092, China. TEL 86-21-65983708, FAX 86-21-62734708. Ed. Wang Rongchang. Circ: 1,000.

531 CHN ISSN 1672-9897
TA357.5.M43
➤ **SHIYAN LIUTI LIXUE/JOURNAL OF EXPERIMENTS IN FLUID MECHANICS.** Text in Chinese; Abstracts in Chinese, English. 1987. q. USD 20.80 (effective 2009). **Document type:** *Journal, Academic/Scholarly.* **Description:** Contains scientific papers on new research and development of the aerodynamics, fluid mechanics, data acquisition, processing and control, and more.
Former titles (until 2005): Liuti Lixue Shiyan yu Celiang/Experiments and Measurements in Fluid Mechanics (1007-3124); Qidong Shiyan yu Celiang Kongzhi/Aerodynamic Experiment and Measurement and Control (1001-1641)
Related titles: Online - full content ed.; Online - full text ed.
Indexed: A28, APA, BrCerAb, C&ISA, CA/WCA, CIA, CPEI, CerAb, CivEngAb, CorrAb, E&CAJ, E11, EEA, EMA, H15, M&TEA, M09, MBF, METADEX, SCOPUS, SolStAb, T04, WAA.
—BLDSC (8267.297575), East View, Linda Hall.
Published by: (Zhongguo Kexue Jishu Xiehui/China Association for Science and Technology), Zhongguo Kongqi Dongli Yanjiu yu Fazhan Zhongxin/China Aerodynamics R & D Center (CARDC), PO Box 211, Mianyang, Sichuan 621000, China. TEL 86-816-2463142, FAX 86-816-2463138. Ed. Le Jialin. **Dist. by:** China International Book Trading Corp, 35 Chegongzhuang Xilu, Haidian District, PO Box 399, Beijing 100044, China. TEL 86-10-68412045, FAX 86-10-68412023, cibtc@mail.cibtc.com.cn, http://www.cibtc.com.cn. **Co-sponsor:** Zhongguo Kongqi Dongli Xuehui/Chinese Aerodynamics Research Society.

531 CHN ISSN 1001-4888
TA349
SHIYAN LIXUE/EXPERIMENTAL MECHANICS. Text in Chinese. q. USD 37.20 (effective 2009).
Related titles: Online - full text ed.
Indexed: AcoustA.
—East View.
Published by: Zhongguo Lixue Xuehui/Chinese Society of Theoretical and Applied Mechanics, Zhongguo Keji Daxue, 96 Jinzhai Road, Hefei, Anhui 230026, China. http://www.cstam.org.cn/. Ed. Jia Youquan.

531 DEU ISSN 0938-1287
QC168.85.S45 CODEN: SHWAEN
➤ **SHOCK WAVES**; an international journal on shock waves, detonations and explosions. Text in English. 1990. bi-m. EUR 1,016, USD 1,207 combined subscription to institutions (print & online eds.) (effective 2012). adv. back issues avail.; reprint service avail. from PSC. **Document type:** *Journal, Academic/Scholarly.* **Description:** Emphasizes both theoretical and experimental research on shock-wave phenomena in gases, liquids, solids, and two-phase media.
Related titles: Online - full text ed.: ISSN 1432-2153 (from IngentaConnect).
Indexed: A01, A03, A08, A22, A26, ASCA, AcoustA, ApMecR, CA, CurCont, E01, Inspec, RefZh, SCI, SCOPUS, T02, TM, W07, Z02.
—BLDSC (8267.485400), AskIEEE, IE, Infotrieve, Ingenta, Linda Hall. **CCC.**
Published by: Springer (Subsidiary of: Springer Science+Business Media), Tiergartenstr 17, Heidelberg, 69121, Germany. TEL 49-6221-4870, FAX 49-6221-345229. Ed. K Takayama. **Subscr. in the Americas to:** Springer New York LLC, Journal Fulfillment, PO Box 2485, Secaucus, NJ 07096. TEL 800-777-4643, 201-348-4033, FAX 201-348-4505, journals-ny@springer.com, http://www.springer.com; **Subscr. to:** Springer Distribution Center, Kundenservice Zeitschriften, Haberstr 7, Heidelberg 69126, Germany. TEL 49-6221-3454303, FAX 49-6221-3454229, subscriptions@springer.com.

620.1 531 NLD ISSN 0925-0042
CODEN: SMAPFS
➤ **SOLID MECHANICS AND ITS APPLICATIONS.** Text in English. 1990. irreg., latest vol.168, 2009. price varies. bibl. back issues avail. **Document type:** *Monographic series, Academic/Scholarly.* **Description:** Covers the entire scope of solid mechanics, including the foundation of mechanics, variational formulations, computational mechanics, vibrations of solids and structures, dynamical systems and chaos, theories of elasticity, plasticity and viscoelasticity, composite materials, and others.
Indexed: CA, CCMJ, CIN, CIS, ChemAb, ChemTitl, MSN, T02, Z02.
—BLDSC (8327.352000), CASDDS, IE, Ingenta. **CCC.**
Published by: Springer Netherlands (Subsidiary of: Springer Science+Business Media), Van Godewijckstraat 30, Dordrecht, 3311 GX, Netherlands. TEL 31-78-6576050, FAX 31-78-6576474. Ed. G M L Gladwell.

531 USA ISSN 1076-4046
QC787.S9
STANFORD SYNCHROTRON RADIATION LABORATORY. ACTIVITY REPORT. Text in English. a. **Document type:** *Corporate.*
Published by: Stanford University, Stanford Synchrotron Radiation Laboratory, PO Box 4349, MS-69, Stanford, CA 94309. TEL 415-926-4000. Eds. Katherine Cantwell, Lisa Dunn.

531 NLD ISSN 0922-5382
➤ **STUDIES IN APPLIED MECHANICS.** Text in Dutch. 1979. irreg., latest vol.50, 2005. price varies. **Document type:** *Monographic series, Academic/Scholarly.* **Description:** Examines research in applied mechanics.
Related titles: Online - full text ed.
Indexed: CCMJ, GeoRef, Inspec, SCOPUS, SpeleolAb.
—BLDSC (8489.480500), IE, Ingenta, INIST. **CCC.**
Published by: Elsevier BV (Subsidiary of: Elsevier Science & Technology), Radarweg 29, PO Box 211, Amsterdam, 1000 AE, Netherlands. TEL 31-20-4853911, FAX 31-20-4852457, JournalsCustomerServiceEMEA@elsevier.com, http://www.elsevier.nl. Ed. I Elishakov.

531 NLD ISSN 0167-2991
CODEN: SSCTDM
➤ **STUDIES IN SURFACE SCIENCE AND CATALYSIS.** Text in English. 1976. irreg., latest vol.174, 2008. price varies. back issues avail. **Document type:** *Monographic series, Academic/Scholarly.* **Description:** Disseminates current research in surface science and catalysis.
Related titles: Online - full text ed.
Indexed: A22, ASCA, CIN, ChemAb, ChemTitl, GeoRef, Inspec, P30, SCOPUS, SpeleolAb.
—BLDSC (8491.783000), CASDDS, IE, Ingenta, INIST, Linda Hall. **CCC.**
Published by: Elsevier BV (Subsidiary of: Elsevier Science & Technology), Radarweg 29, PO Box 211, Amsterdam, 1000 AE, Netherlands. TEL 31-20-4853911, FAX 31-20-4852457, JournalsCustomerServiceEMEA@elsevier.com, http://www.elsevier.nl. Ed. Gabriele Centi.

➤ **SYKTYVKARSKII GOSUDARSTVENNYI UNIVERSITET. VESTNIK. SERIYA 1. MATEMATIKA, MEKHANIKA, INFORMATIKA.** *see* MATHEMATICS

532 USA ISSN 0082-0849
SYMPOSIUM ON NAVAL HYDRODYNAMICS. PROCEEDINGS. Text in English. 1956. biennial. price varies.
Indexed: BMT.
Published by: U.S. Department of the Navy, Office of Naval Research, 800 North Quincy, Arlington, VA 22217. TEL 202-545-6700.

TECHNISCHE MECHANIK; Wissenschaftliche Zeitschrift fuer Grundlagen und Anwendungen der Festkoerper- und Stroemungsmechanik. *see* ENGINEERING

TEPLOFIZIKA I AEROMEKHANIKA. *see* PHYSICS—Heat

TEST ENGINEERING & MANAGEMENT. *see* AERONAUTICS AND SPACE FLIGHT

531 NLD ISSN 0167-8442
TA409 CODEN: AMROBA
➤ **THEORETICAL AND APPLIED FRACTURE MECHANICS.** (In 2 parts: Fracture Mechanics Technology; Mechanics and Physics of Fracture) Text in Dutch. 1984. 6/yr. EUR 1,416 in Europe to institutions; JPY 187,900 in Japan to institutions; USD 1,589 elsewhere to institutions (effective 2012). back issues avail. **Document type:** *Journal, Academic/Scholarly.* **Description:** Part one emphasizes material characterization techniques and translation of specimen data to design. Part two publishes original research on material damage leading to crack growth or fracture in materials such as metal alloys, polymers, composites, rocks, ceramics and related substances.
Related titles: Microform ed.: (from PQC); Online - full text ed.: ISSN 1872-7638 (from IngentaConnect, ScienceDirect).
Indexed: A01, A03, A08, A22, A26, A28, APA, ASCA, ApMecR, B21, BrCerAb, C&ISA, CA, CA/WCA, CIA, CIN, CPEI, CerAb, ChemAb, ChemTitl, CivEngAb, CorrAb, CurCont, E&CAJ, E11, EEA, EMA, ESPM, EngInd, EnvEAb, FLUIDEX, GeoRef, H15, I05, ISMEC, Inspec, M&TEA, M09, MBF, METADEX, MSCI, RefZh, S01, SCI, SCOPUS, SolStAb, SpeleolAb, T02, T04, W07, WAA.
—BLDSC (8814.551850), AskIEEE, CASDDS, IE, Infotrieve, Ingenta, INIST, Linda Hall. **CCC.**
Published by: Elsevier BV (Subsidiary of: Elsevier Science & Technology), Radarweg 29, PO Box 211, Amsterdam, 1000 AE, Netherlands. TEL 31-20-4853911, FAX 31-20-4852457, JournalsCustomerServiceEMEA@elsevier.com, http://www.elsevier.nl. Ed. G C Sih.

531 SRB ISSN 1450-5584
➤ **THEORETICAL AND APPLIED MECHANICS/TEORIJSKA I PRIMENJENA MEHANIKA**; an international journal. Text in English. 1976. q. **Document type:** *Journal, Academic/Scholarly.* **Description:** Aimed to publish contributions from all fields of theoretical and applied mechanics including experimental contributions.
Formerly (until 1997): Teorijska i Primenjena Mehanika (0353-8249)
Related titles: Online - full text ed.: free (effective 2011).
Indexed: ApMecR, MSN, MathR, SCOPUS, SpeleolAb.
—INIST.
Published by: Drustvo za Mehaniku Srbije/Serbian Society of Mechanics, University of Belgrade, Faculty of Mechanical Engineering, 27 Marta 80, Belgrade, 11120. TEL 381-11-3370372, FAX 381-11-3370364, ysm@ysm.org.yu, http://www.ysm.org.yu. Ed. Milan Micunovic.

P

531 JPN ISSN 1348-0693
TA350
THEORETICAL AND APPLIED MECHANICS JAPAN (PRINT). Text in English. 1953. a. JPY 20,000. **Document type:** *Journal, Academic/Scholarly.*
Former titles (until 2001): Theoretical and Applied Mechanics (Print) (0285-6042); (until 1970): Japan National Congress for Applied Mechanics. Proceedings (0448-8660)
Related titles: Online - full text ed.: Theoretical and Applied Mechanics Japan (Online). ISSN 1349-4244.
Indexed: CPEI, EngInd, SCOPUS, Z02.
—BLDSC (8814.552200), IE, Ingenta.
Published by: Science Council Of Japan, Japan National Committee for Theoretical and Applied Mechanics/Nihon Gakujutsu Kaigi, Rikigaku Kenkyu Renraku Iinkai, Ropongi 7-22-34, Minato-ku, Tokyo, 106-8555, Japan. hokusensha@mvd.biglobe.ne.jp, s245@scj.go.jp.

531 USA ISSN 2095-0349
▼ ➤ **THEORETICAL AND APPLIED MECHANICS LETTERS.** Text in English. 2011. bi-m. free (effective 2011). **Document type:** *Journal, Academic/Scholarly.* **Description:** Publishes research in all aspects of theoretical and applied mechanics as well as other interdisciplinary researches including aerospace and aeronautical engineering, coastal and ocean engineering, environment and energy engineering, material and structure engineering, biomedical engineering, mechanical and transportation engineering, and civil and hydraulic engineering.
Related titles: Online - full text ed.: 2011.
—**CCC.**
Published by: American Institute of Physics, 1 Physics Ellipse, College Park, MD 20740. TEL 301-209-3100, aipinfo@aip.org, http://www.aip.org. Eds. Jiachun Li, Yonggang Huang. **Co-publisher:** Chinese Society of Theoretical and Applied Mechanics.

532 DEU ISSN 0935-4964
QA911 CODEN: TCFDEP
➤ **THEORETICAL AND COMPUTATIONAL FLUID DYNAMICS.** Text in English. 1989. bi-m. EUR 1,343, USD 1,621 combined subscription to institutions (print & online eds.) (effective 2012). adv. back issues avail.; reprint service avail. from PSC. **Document type:** *Journal, Academic/Scholarly.* **Description:** Presents original research in theoretical and computational fluid dynamics aimed at elucidating flow physics.
Related titles: Microform ed.: (from PQC); Online - full text ed.: ISSN 1432-2250 (from IngentaConnect).
Indexed: A01, A03, A08, A22, A26, A28, APA, ASCA, ApMecR, BrCerAb, C&ISA, C10, CA, CA/WCA, CIA, CPEI, CerAb, ChemAb, CivEngAb, CorrAb, CurCont, E&CAJ, E01, E11, EEA, EMA, ESPM, EngInd, EnvEAb, FLUIDEX, GEOBASE, H15, INIS AtomInd, ISR, Inspec, M&TEA, M09, MBF, METADEX, P02, P10, P16, P26, P48, P49, P52, P53, P54, P56, PQC, RefZh, S10, SCI, SCOPUS, SolStAb, T02, T04, W07, WAA, Z02.
—BLDSC (8814.552280), AskIEEE, CASDDS, IE, Infotrieve, Ingenta, INIST, Linda Hall. **CCC.**
Published by: Springer (Subsidiary of: Springer Science+Business Media), Tiergartenstr 17, Heidelberg, 69121, Germany. TEL 49-6221-4870, FAX 49-6221-345229. Ed. M Y Hussaini. **Subscr. in the Americas to:** Springer New York LLC, Journal Fulfillment, PO Box 2485, Secaucus, NJ 07096. TEL 800-777-4643, 201-348-4033, FAX 201-348-4505, journals-ny@springer.com, http://www.springer.com; **Subscr. to:** Springer Distribution Center, Kundenservice Zeitschriften, Haberstr 7, Heidelberg 69126, Germany. TEL 49-6221-3454303, FAX 49-6221-3454229, subscriptions@springer.com.

533 RUS
TRUDY TSAGI. Text in Russian. 36/yr. USD 882.95 in United States.

Published by: Tsentral'nyi Aerogidrodinamicheskii Institut im. N.E. Zhukovskogo, Ul Radio 17, Moscow, 107005, Russian Federation. TEL 7-095-2634039. **Dist. by:** East View Information Services, 10601 Wayzata Blvd, Minneapolis, MN 55305. TEL 952-252-1201, 800-477-1005, FAX 952-252-1202, info@eastview.com, http://www.eastview.com.

533 RUS ISSN 0321-3439
TL570 CODEN: UZTAAG
TSENTRAL'NYI AEROGIDRODINAMICHESKII INSTITUT IM. N.E. ZHIKOVSKOGO. UCHENYE ZAPISKI. Text in Russian. q. USD 545 in United States.
Related titles: ◆ English ed.: Ts A G I Science Journal. ISSN 1948-2590.
Indexed: RefZh.
—CASDDS, East View, Linda Hall.
Published by: Tsentral'nyi Aerogidrodinamicheskii Institut im. N.E. Zhukovskogo, Ul Radio 17, Moscow, 107005, Russian Federation. TEL 7-095-2634039. **Dist. by:** East View Information Services, 10601 Wayzata Blvd, Minneapolis, MN 55305. TEL 952-252-1201, 800-477-1005, FAX 952-252-1202, info@eastview.com, http://www.eastview.com.

533 RUS
TSENTRAL'NYI AEROGIDRODINAMICHESKII INSTITUT. NOVOSTI. Text in Russian. m. USD 399.95 in United States. **Document type:** *Academic/Scholarly.*
Address: Ul Radio 17, Moscow, 107005, Russian Federation. TEL 7-095-2634039. **Dist. by:** East View Information Services, 10601 Wayzata Blvd, Minneapolis, MN 55305. TEL 952-252-1201, 800-477-1005, FAX 952-252-1202, info@eastview.com, http://www.eastview.com.

U L V A C TECHNICAL JOURNAL. (ULtimate in VACuum) *see* ENGINEERING—Mechanical Engineering

531 627 ROM ISSN 1222-5525
UNIVERSITATEA DIN ORADEA. ANALELE. FASCICULA MECANICA. SECTIUNEA MASINI HIDRAULICE, MASINI TERMICE SI TERMOTEHNICE. Text in Romanian. 1976. a. **Document type:** *Journal, Academic/Scholarly.*
Supersedes in part (in 1991): Universitatea din Oradea. Analele. Fascicula Mecanica (1221-1303); Which superseded in part (in 1991): Institutul de Invatamant Superior Oradea. Lucrari Stiintifice. Serie A. Stiinte Technice, Matematica, Fizica, Chimie, Geografie (0254-8593)
Published by: Editura Universitatii din Oradea/University of Oradea Publishing House, Str Universitatii 1, Geotermal Bldg., 2nd Fl., Oradea, Jud.Bihor 410087, Romania. TEL 40-259-408113, FAX 40-259-432789, editura@uoradea.ro, http://webhost.uoradea.ro/editura/.

531 620.1 ROM ISSN 1222-5533
UNIVERSITATEA DIN ORADEA. ANALELE. FASCICULA MECANICA. SECTIUNEA MASINI UNELTE, ROBOTI INDUSTRIALI SI SISTEME FLEXIBLE DE PRELUCRARE. Text in Romanian. 1976. a. **Document type:** *Journal, Academic/Scholarly.*
Supersedes in part (in 1991): Universitatea din Oradea. Analele. Fascicula Mecanica (1221-1303); Which superseded in part (in 1990): Institutul de Invatamant Superior Oradea. Lucrari Stiintifice. Serie A. Stiinte Technice, Matematica, Fizica, Chimie, Geografie (0254-8593)
Published by: Editura Universitatii din Oradea/University of Oradea Publishing House, Str Universitatii 1, Geotermal Bldg., 2nd Fl., Oradea, Jud.Bihor 410087, Romania. TEL 40-259-408113, FAX 40-259-432789, editura@uoradea.ro, http://webhost.uoradea.ro/editura/.

531 620.1 ROM ISSN 1222-5517
UNIVERSITATEA DIN ORADEA. ANALELE. FASCICULA MECANICA. SECTIUNEA MECANISME, ORGANE DE MASINI, TRIBOLOGIE, MECANICA FINA, ROBOTI, DESEN. Text in Romanian. 1976. a. **Document type:** *Journal, Academic/Scholarly.*
Supersedes in part (in 1991): Universitatea din Oradea. Analele. Fascicula Mecanica (1221-1303); Which superseded in part (in 1990): Institutul de Invatamant Superior Oradea. Lucrari Stiintifice. Serie A. Stiinte Technice, Matematica, Fizica, Chimie, Geografie (0254-8593)
Published by: Editura Universitatii din Oradea/University of Oradea Publishing House, Str Universitatii 1, Geotermal Bldg., 2nd Fl., Oradea, Jud.Bihor 410087, Romania. TEL 40-259-408113, FAX 40-259-432789, editura@uoradea.ro, http://webhost.uoradea.ro/editura/.

532 621 SVN ISSN 1318-7279
VENTIL/JOURNAL FOR FLUID POWER AND AUTOMATION; revija za fluidno tehniko in avtomatizacijo. Text in Slovenian. 1988. q. EUR 16.69 (effective 2007). **Document type:** *Journal, Academic/Scholarly.*
Formerly (until 1993): Odbor za Fluidno Tehniko. Bilten (1408-2411)
Indexed: Inspec.
—BLDSC (9154.506000).
Published by: Slovensko Drustvo za Fluidno Tehniko, Univerza v Ljubljani, Fakulteta za Strojnistvo, Urednistvo Revije Ventil, Askereeva 6, PO Box 394, Ljubljana, 1000, Slovenia. TEL 386-1-4771704, FAX 386-1-4771761. Ed. Niko Herakovie. Circ: 1,000.

VESTNIK MOLODYCH UCHENYCH. PRIKLADNAYA MATEMATIKA I MEKHANIKA. *see* MATHEMATICS

W I T TRANSACTIONS ON ENGINEERING SCIENCES. (Wessex Institute of Technology) *see* ENGINEERING

531 GRC ISSN 1991-8747
W S E A S TRANSACTIONS ON APPLIED AND THEORETICAL MECHANICS. Text in English. 2007. q. EUR 100 to individuals; EUR 200 to institutions (effective 2007). **Document type:** *Journal, Academic/Scholarly.*
Indexed: A28, APA, BrCerAb, C&ISA, CA/WCA, CIA, CPEI, CerAb, CivEngAb, CorrAb, E&CAJ, E11, EEA, EMA, H15, Inspec, M&TEA, M09, MBF, METADEX, SolStAb, T04, WAA.
—IE.
Published by: World Scientific and Engineering Academy and Society, Ag Ioannou Theologou 17-23, Zographou, Athens 15773, Greece. TEL 30-210-7473313, FAX 30-210-7473314, http://www.wseas.org. Ed. Olga Martin.

531 GRC ISSN 1790-5087
➤ **W S E A S TRANSACTIONS ON FLUID MECHANICS.** Text in English. 2006 (Jan.). q. EUR 300 to individuals; EUR 400 to institutions (effective 2005). **Document type:** *Journal, Academic/Scholarly.*
Indexed: A28, APA, BrCerAb, C&ISA, CA/WCA, CIA, CerAb, CivEngAb, CorrAb, E&CAJ, E11, EEA, EMA, H15, Inspec, M&TEA, M09, MBF, METADEX, SCOPUS, SolStAb, T04, WAA.
—IE.
Published by: World Scientific and Engineering Academy and Society, Ag Ioannou Theologou 17-23, Zographou, Athens 15773, Greece. TEL 30-210-7473313, FAX 30-210-7473314, http://www.wseas.org. Ed. Siavash H Sohrab.

531 USA ISSN 2160-049X
▼ ➤ **WORLD JOURNAL OF MECHANICS.** Abbreviated title: W J M. Text in English. 2011. q. USD 156 (effective 2011). back issues avail. **Document type:** *Journal, Academic/Scholarly.* **Description:** Covers general field of mechanics and motions including solids, structures and fluids and their interaction.
Related titles: Online - full text ed.: ISSN 2160-0503. free (effective 2011).
Published by: Scientific Research Publishing, Inc., PO Box 54821, Irvine, CA 92619. service@scirp.org.

531 621 CHN ISSN 1000-6915
CODEN: YLGXF5
➤ **YANSHI LIXUE YU GONGCHENG XUEBAO/JOURNAL OF ROCK MECHANICS AND ENGINEERING.** Text in Chinese; Summaries in Chinese, English. 1982. m. USD 213.60 (effective 2009). adv. bk.rev. abstr.; charts; illus. back issues avail. **Document type:** *Academic/Scholarly.* **Description:** Contains academic papers to represent the new achievements, theories, methods, experiments and trends of rock mechanics and rock engineering mainly in China.
Related titles: ◆ CD-ROM ed.: Chinese Academic Journals Full-Text Database. Science & Engineering, Series A. ISSN 1007-8010; E-mail ed.; Fax ed.; Online - full text ed.
Indexed: A28, APA, BrCerAb, C&ISA, CA/WCA, CIA, CPEI, CerAb, CivEngAb, CorrAb, E&CAJ, E11, EEA, EMA, EngInd, GeoRef, H15, M&TEA, M09, MBF, METADEX, SCOPUS, SolStAb, T04, WAA.
—BLDSC (3180.674700), East View, Linda Hall.
Published by: Institute of Rock and Soil Mechanics, Chinese Academy of Sciences, Wuhan, Hubei, 430071, China. TEL 86-27-8786-9250, FAX 86-27-8786-3386. Ed. Weishen Zhu. R&P, Adv. contact Kejun Wang. B&W page CNY 2,500, color page CNY 5,000; trim 297 x 210. Circ: 3,000 (paid). **Dist. overseas by:** China International Book Trading Corp, 35 Chegongzhuang Xilu, Haidian District, PO Box 399, Beijing 100044, China. **Co-sponsor:** Chinese Society for Rock Mechancis and Enginnering.

➤ **YINGYONG SHUXUE HE LIXUE.** *see* MATHEMATICS

531 CHN ISSN 1000-3835
ZHENDONG YU CHONGJI/VIBRATION AND SHOCK. Text in Chinese. q. USD 74.40 (effective 2009).
Related titles: Online - full text ed.
Indexed: A28, APA, BrCerAb, C&ISA, CA/WCA, CIA, CPEI, CerAb, CivEngAb, CorrAb, E&CAJ, E11, EEA, EMA, ESPM, EngInd, EnvEAb, H15, M&TEA, M09, MBF, METADEX, SCOPUS, SolStAb, T04, WAA.
—BLDSC (9512.664600), East View.
Published by: Zhongguo Zhendong Gongcheng Xuehui/Chinese Vibration Engineering Society, 121 Nanjiang Lu, Shanghai, 200011, China. TEL 3774325. Ed. Huang Wenhu.

PHYSICS—Nuclear Physics

539.7 USA ISSN 1931-3063
A I P CONFERENCE PROCEEDINGS. NUCLEAR & HIGH ENERGY PHYSICS. Text in English. 200?. irreg. adv. back issues avail. **Document type:** *Proceedings, Academic/Scholarly.*
Media: Online - full text. **Related titles:** Print ed.; ◆ Series: A I P Conference Proceedings. Astronomy & Astrophysics. ISSN 1931-3020; ◆ A I P Conference Proceedings. Accelerators & Beams. ISSN 1931-3012; ◆ A I P Conference Proceedings. Plasma Physics. ISSN 1931-3071; ◆ A I P Conference Proceedings. Atomic, Molecular & Statistical Physics. ISSN 1931-3039; ◆ A I P Conference Proceedings. Mathematical & Statistical Physics. ISSN 1931-3055; ◆ A I P Conference Proceedings. Materials Physics & Applications. ISSN 1931-3047; A I P Conference Proceedings. ISSN 1551-7616. 1970.
—CCC.
Published by: American Institute of Physics, 1 Physics Ellipse, College Park, MD 20740. TEL 301-209-3100, FAX 301-209-0843, aipinfo@aip.org, http://www.aip.org.

539.7 USA ISSN 1931-5015
A P S SCIENCE. (Advanced Photon Source) Text in English. a., latest 2006. free (effective 2007). **Document type:** *Guide, Academic/Scholarly.*
Media: Online - full text. **Related titles:** Print ed.: ISSN 1931-5007.
Published by: Argonne National Laboratory (Subsidiary of: U.S. Department of Energy, Office of Industrial Technologies), 9700 S Cass Ave, Energy Systems Division, Bldg. 362, Argonne, IL 60439. TEL 708-252-1877, FAX 708-252-7653, http://www.anl.gov.

539 USA ISSN 1049-250X
QC173 CODEN: AAMPE9
ADVANCES IN ATOMIC, MOLECULAR AND OPTICAL PHYSICS. Text in English. 1965. irreg., latest vol.57, 2009. USD 218 per vol. (effective 2010). adv. index. back issues avail.; reprints avail. **Document type:** *Journal, Academic/Scholarly.* **Description:** Covers all aspects of developments in the general area of atomic, molecular and optical physics.
Formerly (until 1989): Advances in Atomic and Molecular Physics (0065-2199)
Related titles: Online - full text ed.
Indexed: A22, ASCA, C33, CIN, ChemAb, ChemTitl, ISR, Inspec, PhysBer, SCI, SCOPUS, W07.
—BLDSC (0699.810000), CASDDS, IE, Ingenta, INIST, Linda Hall. **CCC.**
Published by: Academic Press (Subsidiary of: Elsevier Science & Technology), 3251 Riverport Ln, Maryland Heights, MO 63043. TEL 314-447-8010, FAX 314-447-8030, JournalCustomerService-usa@elsevier.com, http://www.elsevierdirect.com/imprint.jsp?iid=5. Eds. C C Lin, E Arimondo, P R Berman.

539.7 621.48 USA ISSN 0065-2989
TK9001 CODEN: ANUTAC
➤ **ADVANCES IN NUCLEAR SCIENCE AND TECHNOLOGY.** Text in English. 1962. irreg., latest vol.26, 1999. price varies. index. back issues avail. **Document type:** *Monographic series, Academic/Scholarly.* **Description:** Presents reviews of the developments in nuclear science and engineering, from both theoretical and applied perspectives.
Indexed: A22, CIN, ChemAb, ChemTitl, Inspec.
—BLDSC (0709.500000), CASDDS, IE, INIST, Linda Hall. **CCC.**
Published by: Springer New York LLC (Subsidiary of: Springer Science+Business Media), 233 Spring St, New York, NY 10013. TEL 212-460-1500, FAX 212-460-1575, service-ny@springer.com.

539.2 SGP ISSN 1793-6179
➤ **ADVANCES IN SYNCHROTRON RADIATION.** Abbreviated title: A S R. Text in English. 2008. irreg., latest vol.1, 2008. SGD 564, USD 362, EUR 266 combined subscription to institutions (print & online eds.) (effective 2012). adv. **Document type:** *Journal, Academic/Scholarly.* **Description:** Provides a place for any research work involving synchrotron radiation, from generation to applications, theoretical and experimental.
Related titles: Online - full text ed.: ISSN 1793-7124. SGD 513, USD 329, EUR 242 to institutions (effective 2012).
Indexed: A22, E01.
Published by: World Scientific Publishing Co. Pte. Ltd., 5 Toh Tuck Link, Singapore, 596224, Singapore. TEL 65-6466-5775, FAX 65-6467-7667, wspc@wspc.com.sg, http://www.worldscientific.com. Ed. Herbert O Moser. **Dist. by:** World Scientific Publishing Co., Inc., 27 Warren St, Ste 401-402, Hackensack, NJ 07601. TEL 201-487-9655, 800-227-7562, FAX 201-487-9656, 888-977-2665, wspc@wspc.com; World Scientific Publishing Ltd., 57 Shelton St, London WC2H 9HE, United Kingdom. TEL 44-207-8360888, FAX 44-207-8362020, sales@wspc.co.uk.

539 USA ISSN 1868-2146
QC173 CODEN: ANUPBZ
➤ **ADVANCES IN THE PHYSICS OF PARTICLES AND NUCLEI.** Abbreviated title: A P P N. Text in English. 1968. irreg., latest vol.30, 2010. price varies. back issues avail. **Document type:** *Monographic series, Academic/Scholarly.*
Formerly (until 2007): Advances in Nuclear Physics (0065-2970)
Related titles: Online - full text ed.: ISSN 1861-440X.
Indexed: ASCA, CIN, ChemAb, ChemTitl, ISR, Inspec, PhysBer, SCI, SCOPUS, W07.
—CASDDS, Ingenta, Linda Hall. **CCC.**
Published by: Springer New York LLC (Subsidiary of: Springer Science+Business Media), 233 Spring St, New York, NY 10013. TEL 212-460-1500, FAX 212-460-1575, service-ny@springer.com. Eds. Dieter Haidt, Douglas H Beck, John W Negele.

539.2 BEL ISSN 1784-0171
AGENCE FEDERALE DE CONTROLE NUCLEAIRE. RAPPORT ANNUEL. Text in French. 2002. a. **Document type:** *Government.*
Related titles: ◆ Dutch ed.: Federaal Agentschap voor Nucleaire Controle. Jaarverslag. ISSN 1784-018X.
Published by: Agence Federale de Controle Nucleaire (A F C N)/Federaal Agentschap voor Nucleaire Controle, 36 Rue Ravensteinstraat, Bruxelles, 1000, Belgium. TEL 32-2-2892111, FAX 32-2-2892112, http://www.fanc.fgov.be.

539 USA ISSN 0163-8998
QC770 CODEN: ARPSDF
➤ **ANNUAL REVIEW OF NUCLEAR AND PARTICLE SCIENCE.** Text in English. 1951. a. USD 272 combined subscription per issue to institutions (print & online eds.); USD 227 per issue to institutions (print or online ed.) (effective 2012). bibl.; charts; abstr. index, cum.index. back issues avail.; reprint service avail. from PSC. **Document type:** *Journal, Academic/Scholarly.* **Description:** Reviews filter and synthesize primary research to identify the principal contributions in the field of nuclear and particle science.
Formerly (until 1978): Annual Review of Nuclear Science (0066-4243)
Related titles: Microfilm ed.: (from PQC); Online - full text ed.: ISSN 1545-4134.
Indexed: A01, A03, A08, A22, A26, ASCA, C13, C33, CA, CIN, Cadscan, ChemAb, ChemTitl, CurCont, E08, EIA, EnvAb, GeoRef, I05, IBR, IBZ, INIS AtomInd, ISR, Inspec, LeadAb, MRD, P26, P30, P48, P52, P54, P56, PQC, PhysBer, S01, SCI, SCOPUS, SpeleolAb, T02, W07, Zincscan.
—BLDSC (1523.900000), CASDDS, GNLM, IE, Ingenta, INIST, Linda Hall. **CCC.**
Published by: Annual Reviews, PO Box 10139, Palo Alto, CA 94303. TEL 650-493-4400, FAX 650-424-0910, 800-523-8635, service@annualreviews.org. Eds. Barry R Holstein TEL 413-545-0320, Samuel Gubins.

539.2 RUS
APPARATURA I NOVOSTI RADIATSIONNYKH IZMERENII. Abbreviated title: A N R I. Text in Russian. 2000. q. USD 105 foreign (effective 2004). **Document type:** *Journal, Academic/Scholarly.* **Description:** Covers equipment and news of radiation measurements.
Published by: Vserossiiskii Nauchno-Issledovatel'skii Institut Fiziko-Tekhnicheskikh i Radiotekhnicheskikh Izmerenii, Moskovskaya oblast, Solnechnogorskii rayon, p. Mendeleevo, Russian Federation. TEL 7-095-5350862, director@vniiftri.ru, http://www.vniiftri.ru. Ed. A N Martynyuk. **Dist. by:** East View Information Services, 10601 Wayzata Blvd, Minneapolis, MN 55305. TEL 952-252-1201, 800-477-1005, FAX 952-252-1202, info@eastview.com, http://www.eastview.com.

539 616 GBR ISSN 0969-8043
QC770 CODEN: ARISEF
➤ **APPLIED RADIATION AND ISOTOPES.** Text in English. 1956. 12/yr. EUR 3,230 in Europe to institutions; JPY 429,300 in Japan to institutions; USD 3,616 elsewhere to institutions (effective 2012). bk.rev. charts; illus. index. back issues avail.; reprints avail. **Document type:** *Journal, Academic/Scholarly.* **Description:** Features papers relating to the production, measurement and application of radionuclides and radiation in all branches of science and technology.
Incorporates (1987-1995): Nuclear Geophysics (0969-8086); Which was formerly (until 1993): International Journal of Radiation Applications and Instrumentation. Part E: Nuclear Geophysics (0886-0130); Former titles (until 1993): International Journal of Radiation Applications and Instrumentation. Part A: Applied Radiation and Isotopes (0883-2889); (until 1985): International Journal of Applied Radiation and Isotopes (0020-708X)

Related titles: Microfilm ed.: (from PQC); Online - full text ed.: ISSN 1872-9800 (from IngentaConnect, ScienceDirect).
Indexed: A01, A03, A08, A20, A22, A26, A40, AESIS, ASCA, ASFA, B21, BIOBASE, BPRC&P, C&ISA, C24, C33, CA, CCI, CIN, CPEI, ChemAb, ChemTitl, CurCR, CurCont, DBA, E&CAJ, E11, EIA, EMBASE, ESPM, EngInd, EnvAb, EnvInd, ExcerpMed, FS&TA, GeoRef, H&SSA, I05, IABS, INIS AtomInd, ISR, IndMed, Inspec, MEDLINE, MOS, NPU, P30, PetrolAb, PollutAb, R10, R16, Reac, RefZh, S01, SCI, SCOPUS, SWRA, SolStAb, SpeleolAb, T02, T04, ToxAb, ViroIAbstr, W07.
—BLDSC (1576.565000), AskIEEE, CASDDS, GNLM, IE, Infotrieve, Ingenta, INIST, Linda Hall, PADDS. **CCC.**
Published by: Pergamon (Subsidiary of: Elsevier Science & Technology), The Blvd, Langford Ln, East Park, Kidlington, Oxford OX5 1GB, United Kingdom. TEL 44-1865-843000, FAX 44-1865-843010, JournalsCustomerServiceEMEA@elsevier.com. Eds. B E Zimmerman, R P Hugtenburg. **Subscr. to:** Elsevier BV, Radarweg 29, PO Box 211, Amsterdam 1000 AE, Netherlands. TEL 31-20-4853757, FAX 31-20-4853432, http://www.elsevier.nl.

539.7 ITA ISSN 1827-1383
ASIMMETRIE. Text in Italian. 2005. q. **Document type:** *Journal, Academic/Scholarly.*
Related titles: Online - full text ed.: ISSN 1827-6873.
Published by: Istituto Nazionale di Fisica Nucleare (I N F N), Piazza dei Caprettari 70, Rome, 00186, Italy. TEL 39-06-6840031, FAX 39-06-68307924, prot_AC@infn.it, http://www.infn.it.

539.7 RUS
➤ **ATOM.** Text in Russian. 1994. q. USD 156 foreign (effective 2006). **Document type:** *Journal, Academic/Scholarly.*
Published by: Federal'noe Gosudarstvennoe Unitarnoe Predpriyatie Rossiiskii Federal'nyi Yadernyi Tsentr, Vserossiiskii Nauchno-Issledovatel'skii Institut Eksperimental'noi Fiziki, prospekt Mira 37, Sarov, Nizhegorodskaya oblast 607188, Russian Federation. TEL 7-83130-44802, FAX 7-83130-29494, staff@vniief.ru.

539.7 AUT ISSN 1018-5577
QC718.5.P5 CODEN: APIFEU
ATOMIC AND PLASMA-MATERIAL INTERACTION DATA FOR FUSION. Text in English. 1991. a. **Description:** Provides data on atomic, molecular, particle-surface and plasma-material interaction processes.
Related titles: ◆ Supplement to: Nuclear Fusion. ISSN 0029-5515.
Indexed: Inspec.
—BLDSC (1769.361000).
Published by: International Atomic Energy Agency/Agence Internationale de l'Energie Atomique, Wagramer Str 5, Postfach 100, Vienna, W 1400, Austria. TEL 43-1-2600-21731, FAX 43-1-2600-7.

539.7 JPN
ATOMIC COLLISION RESEARCH IN JAPAN. PROGRESS REPORT. Text and summaries in English. 1971. a. JPY 3,000, USD 20. back issues avail.
Published by: Society for Atomic Collision Research/Genshi Shototsu Kenkyu Kyokai, Jochi Daigaku Rikogakubu, Butsurigakka Genshi Butsurigaku Kenkyushitsu, 7-1 Kioi-cho, Chiyoda-ku, Tokyo, 102-0094, Japan. FAX 81-3-3238-3341. Ed. Y Awaya. Circ: 500.

539 USA ISSN 0092-640X
QC173 CODEN: ADNDAT
➤ **ATOMIC DATA AND NUCLEAR DATA TABLES.** Text in English. 1973. bi-m. EUR 1,811 in Europe to institutions; JPY 189,300 in Japan to institutions; USD 1,425 elsewhere to institutions (effective 2012). adv. abstr.; bibl.; charts; illus.; stat. index. back issues avail.; reprints avail. **Document type:** *Journal, Academic/Scholarly.* **Description:** Presents compilations of experimental and theoretical information in atomic physics, nuclear physics, and closely related fields.
Formed by the merger of (1969-1973): Atomic Data (0004-7082); (1971-1973): Nuclear Data Tables (0090-0214); Which was formerly (until 1971): Nuclear Data Tables. Section A (0090-5518); (until 1968): Nuclear Data. Section A (0550-306X); (until 1965): U S Atomic Energy Commission. Nuclear Data Tables (0564-9064); (until 1959): New Nuclear Data
Related titles: Online - full text ed.: ISSN 1090-2090 (from IngentaConnect, ScienceDirect).
Indexed: A01, A03, A08, A22, A26, ASCA, CA, CCI, CIN, ChemAb, ChemTitl, CurCont, E01, E14, I05, INIS AtomInd, ISR, Inspec, PhysBer, RefZh, S01, SCI, SCOPUS, T02, W07.
—BLDSC (1769.375000), AskIEEE, CASDDS, IE, Infotrieve, Ingenta, INIST, Linda Hall. **CCC.**
Published by: Academic Press (Subsidiary of: Elsevier Science & Technology), 3251 Riverport Ln, Maryland Heights, MO 63043. TEL 314-447-8010, FAX 314-447-8030, JournalCustomerService-usa@elsevier.com, http://www.elsevierdirect.com/imprint.jsp?iid=5. Ed. D R Schultz. Adv. contact Tino DeCarlo TEL 212-633-3815. Circ: (controlled).

539.7 CHE ISSN 2076-3360
▼ ➤ **ATOMIC SCIENCES.** Text in English. forthcoming 2011. q. free (effective 2011). **Document type:** *Journal, Academic/Scholarly.*
Media: Online - full text.
Published by: M D P I AG, Postfach, Basel, 4005, Switzerland. TEL 41-61-6837734, FAX 41-61-3028918, http://www.mdpi.org/.

539.14 HUN ISSN 0231-3596
CODEN: AREAE9
ATOMKI ANNUAL REPORT. Variant title: Hungarian Academy of Sciences. Institute of Nuclear Research. Annual Report. Text in English. 1982. a.
Indexed: INIS AtomInd.
Published by: Magyar Tudomanyos Akademia, Atommagkutato Intezete/Hugarian Academy of Sciences. Institute of Nuclear Research, PO Box 51, Debrecen, 4001, Hungary. TEL 36-52-417266, FAX 36-52-416181.

539.7 CHE ISSN 2218-2004
▼ ➤ **ATOMS.** Text in English. forthcoming 2009. q. free (effective 2011). **Document type:** *Journal, Academic/Scholarly.*
Media: Online - full text.
Published by: M D P I AG, Postfach, Basel, 4005, Switzerland. TEL 41-61-6837734, FAX 41-61-3028918, http://www.mdpi.org/.

➤ **B A D. DOKLADI/BGNS TRANSACTIONS.** *see* ENERGY—Nuclear Energy

539.2 IND ISSN 0976-2108
B A R C NEWSLETTER. Text in English. 1980. bi-m. back issues avail. **Document type:** *Newsletter, Academic/Scholarly.*
Related titles: Online - full text ed.: ISSN 0976-2116.
Indexed: Inspec, RefZh.
—BLDSC (1863.480000).
Published by: Bhabha Atomic Research Centre, Scientific Information Resource Division, Trombay, Mumbai, Maharashtra 400 085, India. TEL 91-22-25505050, FAX 91-22-25505151. Ed., Pub. K Bhanumurthy.

539.2 SWE ISSN 1101-5268
CODEN: BAKGEH
BAKGRUND. Text in Swedish. 1988. irreg.
Indexed: INIS AtomInd.
Published by: Karnkraftsakerhet och Utbildning AB, Analysgruppen, Box 1039, Nykoping, 611 29, Sweden. TEL 46-155-263500, FAX 46-155-263074, analys@ksu.se, http://www.analyse.se.

539.2 KOR ISSN 0253-4231
RA1231.R2 CODEN: BBHCDU
BANGSA'SEON BANG'EO HAGHOEJI/KOREAN ASSOCIATION OF RADIATION PROTECTION. JOURNAL. Text in Korean. 1976. 3/yr. membership. **Document type:** *Journal, Academic/Scholarly.*
Indexed: Inspec.
Published by: Daehan Bangsa'seon Bang'eo Haghoe/Korean Association for Radiation Protection, Radiation Health Research, 388-1 Ssangmon-3dong, Dobong-gu, Seoul, 138-736, Korea, S. TEL 82-2-34996642, FAX 82-2-34996699, webmaster@karp.or.kr, http://www.karp.or.kr/index.html.

539.72 USA
BEAM LINE. Text in English. q. free. illus. **Description:** Covers particle physics.
Media: Online - full text.
Published by: Stanford Linear Accelerator Center, 2575 Sand Hill Rd, Menlo Park, CA 94025. guesthouse@stanford.edu, http://www6.slac.stanford.edu. Eds. Bill Kirk, Rene Donaldson.

539.7 DEU ISSN 0944-2952
BERICHTE DES FORSCHUNGSZENTRUMS JUELICH. Text mainly in German. 1960. irreg. price varies. **Document type:** *Monographic series, Academic/Scholarly.*
Formerly (until 1990): Berichte der Kernforschungsanlage Juelich (0366-0885)
Indexed: FR, GeoRef, Inspec, TM.
—BLDSC (1919.650000), IE, Ingenta, INIST. **CCC.**
Published by: Forschungszentrum Juelich GmbH, Leo-Brandt-Str, Juelich, 52428, Germany. TEL 49-2461-610, FAX 49-2461-618100, info@fz-juelich.de, http://www.fz-juelich.de.

539.2 JPN ISSN 0385-0560
QC172 CODEN: BURTDQ
BUNSHIKEN RETAZU/INSTITUTE FOR MOLECULAR SCIENCE. LETTERS. Text in English, Japanese. 1976. s-a. **Document type:** *Newsletter.*
—CASDDS.
Published by: Okazaki National Research Institutes, Institute for Molecular Science/Okazaki Kokuritsu Kyodo Kenkyu Kiko Bunshi Kagaku Kenkyujo, 38 Nishigonaka-Myodaiji-cho, Okazaki-shi, Aichi-ken 444-0000, Japan.

539.2 621.48 FRA ISSN 1166-7648
C E A TECHNOLOGIES. (Commissariat a l'Energie Atomique) Text in French. 1991. 5/yr. free to qualified personnel (effective 2004).
Related titles: Online - full content ed.: ISSN 1625-9734.
Indexed: INIS AtomInd.
Published by: Commissariat a l'Energie Atomique, Direction de la Recherche Technologique, BP 6, Fontenay aux Roses, 92265, France. TEL 33-1-46547080, http://www-dea.cea.fr/.

539.7 GBR ISSN 0304-288X
QC770 CODEN: CECOA2
➤ **C E R N COURIER**; international journal of high-energy physics. Text in English. 1959. m. (10/yr.). free to qualified personnel (effective 2011). adv. bibl.; charts; illus. back issues avail. **Document type:** *Journal, Academic/Scholarly.* **Description:** Designed for personnel of member-state governments, institutes and laboratories affiliated with CERN.
Related titles: Online - full text ed.: ISSN 2077-9550; French ed.: Courrier C E R N. ISSN 0374-2288.
Indexed: Inspec, RefZh.
—AskIEEE, Ingenta.
Published by: (C E R N - European Organization for Nuclear Research/Organisation Europeenne pour la Recherche Nucleaire CHE), Institute of Physics Publishing Ltd., Dirac House, Temple Back, Bristol, BS1 6BE, United Kingdom. TEL 44-117-9297481, FAX 44-117-9301178, custserv@iop.org, http://publishing.iop.org/. Ed. Christine Sutton. Adv. contact Edward Jost TEL 44-117-9301026. B&W page GBP 3,240, color page GBP 4,260; trim 213 x 282.

539.7 CHE ISSN 0366-5690
CODEN: CEHEAV
C E R N - H E R A REPORTS. Text in English. 1969. irreg. free. **Document type:** *Report, Academic/Scholarly.*
Related titles: Microfiche ed.
Indexed: Inspec.
—CASDDS, INIST.
Published by: C E R N - European Organization for Nuclear Research/Organisation Europeenne pour la Recherche Nucleaire, C E R N, Geneva 23, 1211, Switzerland.

539.7 CHE ISSN 0007-8328
CODEN: CERNA6
C E R N REPORTS. Text in English. 1955. irreg. free. **Document type:** *Report, Academic/Scholarly.*
Indexed: A22, CIN, ChemAb, ChemTitl, Inspec.
—BLDSC (3120.110000), CASDDS, IE, Ingenta, INIST.
Published by: C E R N - European Organization for Nuclear Research/Organisation Europeenne pour la Recherche Nucleaire, C E R N, Geneva 23, 1211, Switzerland.

539.7 CHE ISSN 0531-4283
QC770
C E R N SCHOOL OF PHYSICS. PROCEEDINGS. Text in English. 1962. a. free. **Document type:** *Proceedings.*
Indexed: Inspec.
Published by: C E R N - European Organization for Nuclear Research/Organisation Europeenne pour la Recherche Nucleaire, C E R N, Geneva 23, 1211, Switzerland. Circ: 3,500.

539.7 363.1 FRA ISSN 1961-4144
C R I I R A D. DOSSIERS CLEFS. (Commission de Recherche et d'Information Independantes sur la Radioactivite) Text in French. 2007. irreg. **Document type:** *Newsletter.*
Published by: Commission de Recherche et d'Information Independantes sur la Radioactivite (C R I I R A D), 471 av. Victor Hugo, Valence, 26000, France. FAX 33-4-75812648.

C Y R I C ANNUAL REPORT. (Cyclotron Radioisotope Center) *see* MEDICAL SCIENCES—Radiology And Nuclear Medicine

539.7 GBR ISSN 0965-6200
CODEN: CMPCEN
CAMBRIDGE MONOGRAPHS ON PARTICLE PHYSICS, NUCLEAR PHYSICS AND COSMOLOGY. Text in English. 1992. irreg. price varies. back issues avail.; reprints avail. **Document type:** *Monographic series, Trade.* **Description:** Covers all aspects of particle physics, nuclear physics, cosmology, and the interfaces between them.
Indexed: CCMJ, CIN, ChemAb, ChemTitl, Z02.
—BLDSC (3015.965600).
Published by: Cambridge University Press, The Edinburgh Bldg, Shaftesbury Rd, Cambridge, CB2 8RU, United Kingdom. TEL 44-1223-312393, FAX 44-1223-315052, journals@cambridge.org, http://www.cambridge.org/uk. Eds. P V Landshoff, T Ericson. R&P Linda Nicol TEL 44-1223-325702.

539.7 CHN ISSN 1001-6031
CODEN: CJNPEV
➤ **CHINESE JOURNAL OF NUCLEAR PHYSICS.** Text in English. q. USD 165 (effective 2000). **Document type:** *Journal, Academic/Scholarly.* **Description:** Devoted to experimental and theoretical nuclear physics, including nuclear structure and spectroscopy, nuclear reactions of light and heavy ions, nuclear fission and fusion, and nuclear interactions. Reports developments in China and abroad.
Indexed: CIN, ChemAb, ChemTitl, Inspec, SCOPUS.
—CASDDS, INIST.
Published by: (China Institute of Atomic Energy), Kexue Chubanshe/Science Press, 16 Donghuang Cheng Genbei Jie, Beijing, 100717, China. TEL 86-10-64000246, FAX 86-10-64030255, TELEX 22536 NBO CN. **Dist. overseas by:** China National Publications Import & Export Corp., 16 Gongti Dong Lu, Chaoyang-qu, PO Box 88, Beijing 100020, China. TEL 86-1-506-3101, 86-1-506-6688. **Co-sponsor:** Chinese Nuclear Physics Society.

539.7 GBR ISSN 1674-1137
QC793 CODEN: CPCHCQ
➤ **CHINESE PHYSICS C, HIGH ENERGY PHYSICS AND NUCLEAR PHYSICS.** Text in English. 1977. m. GBP 660 combined subscription to institutions (print & online eds.) (effective 2010). back issues avail. **Document type:** *Journal, Academic/Scholarly.* **Description:** Covers physics research in China, including quantum field theory, particle physics, cosmic radiation, nuclear physics and accelerators, thermodynamics, etc.
Formerly (until 2008): Gaoneng Wuli yu Hewuli (0254-3052); Supersedes (1988-1997): High Energy Physics and Nuclear Physics (0899-9996)
Related titles: Online - full text ed.: GBP 627 to institutions (effective 2010) (from IngentaConnect); ◆ Chinese ed.: High Energy Physics & Nuclear Physics. ISSN 0899-9996.
Indexed: A20, A22, ASCA, C33, CurCont, Inspec, RefZh, SCI, SCOPUS, W07.
—BLDSC (9512.825710), IE, Linda Hall. **CCC.**
Published by: (Chinese Society of High Energy Physics CHN), Institute of Physics Publishing Ltd., Dirac House, Temple Back, Bristol, BS1 6BE, United Kingdom. TEL 44-117-9297481, FAX 44-117-9301178, custserv@iop.org, http://publishing.iop.org/. Ed. Zheng Zhi-Peng. **Dist. by:** China International Book Trading Corp, 35 Chegongzhuang Xilu, Haidian District, PO Box 399, Beijing 100044, China. TEL 86-10-68412045, FAX 86-10-68412023, cibtc@mail.cibtc.com.cn, http://www.cibtc.com.cn.

539.7 JPN
CHODENDO ENERUGI CHOZO KENKYUKAI/SUPERCONDUCTING MAGNETIC ENERGY STORAGE. Text in Japanese. 1986. s-a.
Address: 9-9 Tokodai 5-chome, Tsukuba-shi, Ibaraki-ken 300-2635, Japan.

539.7 JPN
CHODENDO ENERUGI CHOZO KENKYUKAI KENKYU HOKOKUSHO/RESEARCH ASSOCIATION OF SUPERCONDUCTING MAGNETIC ENERGY STORAGE. RESEARCH REPORT. Text in Japanese. 1986. a.
Published by: Chodendo Enerugi Chozo Kenkyukai/Research Association of Superconducting Magnetic Energy Storage, 9-9 Tokodai 5-chome, Tsukuba-shi, Ibaraki-ken 300-2635, Japan.

539.7 JPN ISSN 1340-3818
CODEN: CMKHED
CHODENDO KAGAKU KENKYU SENTA HOKOKU/RESEARCH INSTITUTE OF SUPERCONDUCTIVITY. ANNUAL REPORT. Text in English, Japanese; Summaries in English. 1984; N.S. 1994. a. **Document type:** *Journal, Academic/Scholarly.* **Description:** Discusses superconducting magnets and related topics.
Formerly (until 1994): Chodendo Magunetto Kenkyu Senta Hokoku - Research Institute for Superconducting Magnets. Annual Report (0914-6318)
Indexed: ChemAb.
—CASDDS.
Published by: (Fuzoku Chodendo Kagaku Kenkyu Senta), Kyushu Daigaku, Kogakubu/Kyushu University, Faculty of Engineering, Research Institute of Superconductivity, 10-1 Hakozaki 6-chome, Higashi-ku, Fukuoka-shi, 812-0053, Japan. TEL 092-632-2438, FAX 092-651-7399. Ed. K Funatei.

539.7 541.38 GBR
E S R F NEWS. (European Synchrotron Radiation Facility) Text in English. 1987. q. free to members. **Document type:** *Magazine, Trade.*
Formerly (until 2008): E S R F Newsletter (1011-9310)
Related titles: Online - full text ed.
Indexed: Inspec.
Published by: (European Synchrotron Radiation Facility, Information Office FRA), Institute of Physics Publishing Ltd., Dirac House, Temple Back, Bristol, BS1 6BE, United Kingdom. TEL 44-117-9297481, FAX 44-117-9301178, custserv@iop.org, http://publishing.iop.org/. Ed. Dominique Cornuejols. Circ: 10,000.

P

EGYPTIAN JOURNAL OF RADIATION SCIENCES & APPLICATIONS/ AL-MAGALLAT AL-MISRIYYAT LIL-'ULUM AL-IS'AA'IYYAT WA TATBIQATIHAA. *see* MEDICAL SCIENCES—Radiology And Nuclear Medicine

ENVIRONMENTAL RADIOACTIVITY IN THE NETHERLANDS. *see* ENVIRONMENTAL STUDIES

539.7 DEU ISSN 1434-6001
QC770 CODEN: EPJAFV
➤ **EUROPEAN PHYSICAL JOURNAL A. HADRONS AND NUCLEI.** Text in English. 1920. m. EUR 3,617, USD 4,343 combined subscription to institutions (print & online eds.) (effective 2012). adv. charts; illus. reprint service avail. from PSC. **Document type:** *Journal, Academic/ Scholarly.* **Description:** Devoted to original research in experimental and theoretical physics on hadron and nuclear structure.
Incorporates (2004-2006): Acta Physica Hungarica. B. Quantum Electronics (1589-9535); (1951-2006): Acta Physica Hungarica. A. Heavy Ion Physics (1219-7580); Which was formerly (until 1994): Acta Physica Hungarica (0231-4428); (until 1982): Acta Physica Academiae Scientiarum Hungaricae (0001-6705); (until 1949): Hungarica Acta Physica (0367-6382); Incorporated in part (1903-2000): Anales de Fisica (1133-0376); (1855-1999): Societa Italiana di Fisica. Nuovo Cimento. A. Nuclei, Particles and Fields (1124-1861); Which was formerly (until 1982): Societa Italiana di Fisica. Nuovo Cimento A (1124-1853); (until 1971): Nuovo Cimento A (0369-3546); Which superseded in part (in 1965): Nuovo Cimento (0029-6341); Former titles (until 1997): Zeitschrift fuer Physik A. Hadrons and Nuclei (0939-7922); (until 1991): Zeitschrift fuer Physik. Section A. Atomic Nuclei (0930-1151); (until 1986): Zeitschrift fuer Physik. Section A: Atoms and Nuclei (0340-2193); Zeitschrift fuer Physik (0044-3328)
Related titles: Microform ed.: (from PMC, PQC); Online - full text ed.: ISSN 1434-601X. 2003 (from IngentaConnect).
Indexed: A01, A02, A03, A08, A22, A26, ASCA, C33, CA, CIN, ChemAb, ChemTitl, CurCont, E01, I05, INIS AtomInd, ISR, Inspec, M&GPA, MathR, P30, PhysBer, RefZh, SCI, SCOPUS, T02, TM, W07.
—BLDSC (3829.779210), AskIEEE, CASDDS, IE, Infotrieve, Ingenta, INIST, Linda Hall. **CCC.**
Published by: (Deutsche Physikalische Gesellschaft), Springer (Subsidiary of: Springer Science+Business Media), Tiergartenstr 17, Heidelberg, 69121, Germany. TEL 49-6221-4870, FAX 49-6221-345229. Ed. Enzo De Sanctis. Adv. contact Stephan Kroeck TEL 49-30-827875739. **Subscr. in the Americas to:** Springer New York LLC, Journal Fulfillment, PO Box 2485, Secaucus, NJ 07096. TEL 800-777-4643, 201-348-4033, FAX 201-348-4505, journals-ny@springer.com, http://www.springer.com; **Subscr. to:** Springer Distribution Center, Kundenservice Zeitschriften, Haberstr 7, Heidelberg 69126, Germany. TEL 49-6221-3454303, FAX 49-6221-3454229, subscriptions@springer.com.

539.2 BEL ISSN 1784-018X
FEDERAAL AGENTSCHAP VOOR NUCLEAIRE CONTROLE. JAARVERSLAG. Text in Dutch. 2002. a. **Document type:** *Government.*
Related titles: ◆ French ed.: Agence Federale de Controle Nucleaire. Rapport Annuel. ISSN 1784-0171.
Published by: Agence Federale de Controle Nucleaire (A F C N)/Federaal Agentschap voor Nucleaire Controle, 36 Rue Ravensteinstraat, Bruxelles, 1000, Belgium. TEL 32-2-2892111, FAX 32-2-2892112.

539.7 RUS ISSN 0367-2026
QC770 CODEN: FECAAR
➤ **FIZIKA ELEMENTARNYKH CHASTITS I ATOMNOGO YADRA.** Text in Russian. 1970. bi-m. USD 207 (effective 2010). **Document type:** *Journal, Academic/Scholarly.* **Description:** Contains articles or experimental and theoretical research in high-energy and nuclear physics and related instrumentation.
Related titles: Online - full text ed.; ◆ English Translation: Physics of Particles and Nuclei. ISSN 1063-7796.
Indexed: INIS AtomInd, Inspec, RefZh.
—East View, INIST, Linda Hall.
Published by: (Rossiiskaya Akademiya Nauk, Ob'yedinennyi Institut Yadernyh Issledovanii/Russian Academy of Sciences, Joint Institute of Nuclear Research), Izdatel'stvo Nauka, Profsoyuznaya ul 90, Moscow, 117864, Russian Federation. TEL 7-095-3347151, FAX 7-095-4202220, secret@naukaran.ru, http://www.naukaran.ru. Ed. V G Kadyshevskii. **Dist. by:** East View Information Services, 10601 Wayzata Blvd, Minneapolis, MN 55305. TEL 952-252-1201, 800-477-1005, FAX 952-252-1202, info@eastview.com, http://www.eastview.com.

539.2 CHN ISSN 1000-8187
TK9152 CODEN: FUFAEM
FUSHE FANGHU/RADIATION PROTECTION. Text in Chinese. 1981. bi-m. USD 31.20 (effective 2009). **Document type:** *Journal, Academic/Scholarly.*
Related titles: Online - full text ed.
Indexed: INIS AtomInd.
—East View.
Address: PO Box 120, Taiyuang, 030006, China. TEL 86-351-2203446, FAX 86-351-7020407. **Dist. by:** China International Book Trading Corp, 35 Chegongzhuang Xilu, Haidian District, PO Box 399, Beijing 100044, China. TEL 86-10-68412045, FAX 86-10-68412023, cibtc@mail.cibtc.com.cn, http://www.cibtc.com.cn.

539.7 CHN ISSN 1004-6356
FUSHE FANGHU TONGXUE/RADIATION PROTECTION BULLETIN. Text in Chinese. 1981. bi-m. CNY 30; CNY 5 per issue (effective 2010). **Document type:** *Journal, Academic/Scholarly.*
Related titles: Online - full text ed.
Published by: Zhongguo Fushe Fanghu Yanjiuyuan/China Institute for Radiation Protection, PO Box 120, Taiyuan, 030006, China. TEL 86-351-2203447, FAX 86-351-2203623.

539.1 DEU ISSN 0171-4546
G S I REPORT. Text in German. 1979. irreg. **Document type:** *Monographic series, Academic/Scholarly.*
Formed by the merger of (1971-1979): G S I Bericht A (0171-4562); (1971-1979): G S I Bericht J (0171-4570); (1971-1979): G S I Bericht M (0171-4589); (1971-1979): G S I Bericht P (0171-192X); (1971-1979): G S I Bericht Pa (0171-4597); (1971-1979): G S I Bericht PB (0171-4600); (1971-1979): G S I Bericht Pk (0171-4619); (1971-1979): G S I Bericht T (0171-4627); (1971-1979): G S I Bericht Tr (0171-4635); Which all superseded in part (in 1974): G S I Bericht (0171-4554)
Published by: Gesellschaft fuer Schwerionenforschung mbH, Planckstr 1, Darmstadt, 64291, Germany. TEL 49-6159-710, FAX 49-6159-712785, press@gsi.de, http://www.gsi.de.

539.1 DEU
QC787.L5 CODEN: GSIRDG
G S I SCIENTIFIC REPORT (ONLINE). Text in English. 1977. a. free. **Document type:** *Journal, Academic/Scholarly.* **Description:** Contains information on basic and applied research in physics and related natural science disciplines using a heavy ion accelerator facility.
Formerly (until 200?): G S I Scientific Report (Print) (0174-0814); Which superseded in part (in 1980): Gesellschaft fuer Schwerionenforschung. Jahresbericht (0173-1440)
Media: Online - full text.
Published by: Gesellschaft fuer Schwerionenforschung mbH, Planckstr 1, Darmstadt, 64291, Germany. TEL 49-6159-710, FAX 49-6159-712785, press@gsi.de.

539.2 JPN ISSN 0912-4063
GENSHI SHOTOTSU SAKYURA/SOCIETY FOR ATOMIC COLLISION RESEARCH. CIRCULAR. Text in Japanese. 1968. bi-m.
Published by: Genshi Shototsu Kenkyu/Society for Atomic Collision Research, Jochi Daigaku Rikogakubu, Butsurigakka Genshi Butsurigaku Kenkyushitsu, 7-1 Kioi-cho, Chiyoda-ku, Tokyo, 102-0094, Japan.

539.7 JPN ISSN 0367-4169
CODEN: GEKEAM
GENSHIKAKU KENKYU/NUCLEAR STUDY. Text in English, Japanese. 1955. 6/yr. membership. **Document type:** *Journal, Academic/ Scholarly.*
Indexed: CIN, ChemAb, ChemTitl, INIS AtomInd.
—CASDDS.
Published by: Kakudan/Nuclear Physics Forum, c/o Tokushi Shibata, Unit for Proton Accelerator Facilities, Japan Atomic Energy Agency, Tokai, 319-1195, Japan. TEL 81-48-4621111, FAX 81-48-4624641, kakudan@kakudan.rcnp.osaka-u.ac.jp, http://kakudan.rcnp.osaka-u.ac.jp/~kakudan/. Ed. Tokushi Shibata.

539.7 JPN ISSN 0915-4418
GENSHIRO JIKKENJO DAYORI/RESEARCH REACTOR INSTITUTE. NEWS. Text in Japanese. 1988. q. free to qualified personnel. **Document type:** *Newsletter.* **Description:** Contains news of the joint use program of the Institute.
Published by: Kyoto Daigaku, Genshiro Jikkenjo/Kyoto University, Research Reactor Institute, Sennan-gun, Kumatori-cho, Osaka 590-0494, Japan. TEL 81-724-51-2312, FAX 81-724-51-2620, shiroya@kuca.rri.kyoto-u.ac.jp, kyodo@post1.rri.kyoto-u.ac.jp. Ed. Seiji Shiroya.

539.7 JPN
GENSHIRYOKU ANZEN HAKUSHO/WHITE PAPER OF NUCLEAR SAFETY. Text in Japanese. 1981. a. JPY 3,500 (effective 2000). **Document type:** *Government.*
Published by: (Japan. Sorifu Genshiryoku Anzen Iinkai/Prime Minister's Office, Nuclear Safety Commission), Okurasho Insatsukyoku/Ministry of Finance, Printing Bureau, 2-4 Toranomon 2-chome, Minato-ku, Tokyo, 105-0001, Japan. **Subscr. to:** Government Publications Service Center, 2-1 Kasumigaseki 1-chome, Chiyoda-ku, Tokyo 100-0013, Japan.

539.7 JPN ISSN 0387-9674
GENSHIRYOKU ANZEN IINKAI GEPPO/NUCLEAR SAFETY COMMISSION. MONTHLY REPORT. Text in Japanese. 1978. m. per issue price varies.
Indexed: INIS AtomInd.
Published by: (Japan. Kagaku Gijutsucho/Science and Technology Agency, Planning Bureau, Genshiryoku Anzenkyoku/Nuclear Safety Bureau), Okurasho Insatsukyoku/Ministry of Finance, Printing Bureau, 2-4 Toranomon 2-chome, Minato-ku, Tokyo, 105-0001, Japan.

539.7 JPN
GENSHIRYOKU ANZENSEI KENKYU NO GENJO/PROGRESS OF NUCLEAR SAFETY RESEARCH. Text in Japanese. 1973. a.
Published by: Nihon Genshiryoku Kenkyujo, Anzen Shiken Kenkyu Senta/Japan Atomic Energy Research Institute, Nuclear Safety Research Center, 2-4 Shirane-Shirakata, Naka-gun, Tokai-mura, Ibaraki-ken 319-1100, Japan.

539.7 JPN
GENSHIRYOKU KAIGAI INFORMATION. Text in Japanese. 2/m. membership. **Document type:** *Newsletter.*
Formerly (until 1995): Beikoku Genshiryoku Joho - Nuclear Activity News in U.S.A.
Published by: Genshiryoku Anzen Kenkyu Kyokai/Nuclear Safety Research Association, 18-7 Shimbash 5-chome, Minato-ku, Tokyo, 105-0000, Japan. TEL 81-3-5470-1984.

539.7 JPN
GENSHIRYOKU RIYO JISSEKI HOKOKU/RIKKYO UNIVERSITY. INSTITUTE FOR ATOMIC ENERGY. ANNUAL REPORT OF REACTOR FACILITIES. Text in English, Japanese. 1965. a. free. back issues avail.
Published by: Rikkyo Daigaku, Genshiryoku Kenkyujo/Rikkyo University, Institute for Atomic Energy, 5-1 Naga-Saka 2-chome, Yokosuka-shi, Kanagawa-ken 240-0101, Japan. TEL 81-468-56-3131, FAX 81-458-56-7576. Pub. Kenji Gen.

539.7 CHN ISSN 0258-0934
QC795.5 CODEN: HDYUEC
HEDIANZIXUE YU TANCE JISHU/NUCLEAR ELECTRONICS AND DETECTION TECHNOLOGY. Text in Chinese. 1981. bi-m. USD 40.20 (effective 2009). **Document type:** *Journal, Academic/Scholarly.*
Related titles: Online - full text ed.
Indexed: A22, EngInd, INIS AtomInd, SCOPUS.
—BLDSC (6180.631000), East View, IE, Ingenta.
Address: PO Box 8800, Beijing, 100020, China. TEL 86-10-65810509. **Dist. by:** China International Book Trading Corp, 35 Chegongzhuang Xilu, Haidian District, PO Box 399, Beijing 100044, China. TEL 86-10-68412045, FAX 86-10-68412023, cibtc@mail.cibtc.com.cn, http://www.cibtc.com.cn.

HEHUAXUE YU FANGSHE HUAXUE/JOURNAL OF NUCLEAR AND RADIOCHEMISTRY. *see* CHEMISTRY

530.44 CHN ISSN 0254-6086
QC790.95 CODEN: HYDWDP
HEJUBIAN YU DENGLIZITIWULI/NUCLEAR FUSION AND PLASMA PHYSICS. Text in Chinese. 1981. q. USD 16.40 (effective 2009). **Document type:** *Journal, Academic/Scholarly.*
Related titles: Online - full text ed.
Indexed: EngInd, INIS AtomInd, Inspec, SCOPUS.
—BLDSC (6180.775000).
Address: PO Box 432, Chengdu, 610041, China. TEL 86-28-2932483, FAX 86-28-2932202. **Dist. by:** China International Book Trading Corp, 35 Chegongzhuang Xilu, Haidian District, PO Box 399, Beijing 100044, China. TEL 86-10-68412045, FAX 86-10-68412023, cibtc@mail.cibtc.com.cn, http://www.cibtc.com.cn.

539.7 JPN
HERIKARUKEI NO TOJIKOME/CONFINEMENT OF HELICAL SYSTEM. Text in English, Japanese. irreg.
Published by: Kyoto University, Plasma Physics Laboratory, Gokasho, Uji-shi, Kyoto-Fu 611-0011, Japan.

539 TWN ISSN 0029-5647
QC770 CODEN: HTKHAB
HEZI KEXUE/NUCLEAR SCIENCE JOURNAL. Text in Chinese, English. 1957. bi-m. free. adv. bk.rev. **Document type:** *Journal, Academic/ Scholarly.* **Description:** International medium for the publication of original studies, technical notes and review articles in the field of peaceful use of nuclear energy and technology.
Indexed: ChemAb, ChemTitl, E04, E05, EnerRev, IBR, IBZ, Inspec.
—CASDDS, Ingenta, INIST.
Published by: Chung Hua Nuclear Society, 67, Ln 144, Keelung Rd, Sec 4, Taipei, 107, Taiwan. TEL 886-3-4711400. Ed. Dr. Yung Chien Tong. Pub. Dr. Ching Piao Hu. R&P, Adv. contact Dr. Yung-chien Tong TEL 886-3-4711400 ext 5300. Circ: 1,200.

539.7 CHE ISSN 1424-2729
Z675.P49
HIGH ENERGY PHYSICS LIBRARIES WEBZINE. Abbreviated title: H E P Libraries Webzine. Text in English, French. 2000. 3/yr. free (effective 2009). **Document type:** *Magazine, Academic/Scholarly.* **Description:** Covers the fields of high energy physics, astronomy and mathematics.
Media: Online - full text. **Related titles:** E-mail ed.
Indexed: T02.
Published by: C E R N - European Organization for Nuclear Research/ Organisation Europeenne pour la Recherche Nucleaire, C E R N, Geneva 23, 1211, Switzerland. http://www.cern.ch. Ed. Corrado Pettenati.

539.2 JPN ISSN 0285-3604
CODEN: HOSHDJ
HOSHASEN/IONIZING RADIATION. Text in English, Japanese; Summaries in English. 1974. 3/yr. JPY 4,000 membership (effective 2005). adv. **Document type:** *Journal, Academic/Scholarly.*
Indexed: CIN, ChemAb, ChemTitl, INIS AtomInd.
—CASDDS. **CCC.**
Published by: Oyo Butsuri Gakkai, Hoshasen Bunkakai./Japan Society of Applied Physics, Division of Radiation Science, Kudan-Kita Bldg. 5th Fl., 1-12-3 Kudan-Kita, Chiyoda-ku, Tokyo, 102, Japan. TEL 81-3-32381041, FAX 81-3-32216245, http://annex.jsap.or.jp/ radiation/radiation.html.

539.2 JPN ISSN 0912-5116
HOSHASEN JIKKENJO DAYORI/RADIATION LABORATORY NEWS. Text in Japanese. 1985. s-a.
Published by: (Fuzoku Hoshasen Jikkenjo), Oosaka Daigaku, Sangyo Kagaku Kenkyujo/Osaka University, Institute of Science and Industrial Research, Radiation Laboratory, 8-1 Mihogaoka, Ibaraki-shi, Osaka-fu 567-0047, Japan.

539.2 JPN
HOSHASEN KANRISHITSU NENPO/RADIOLOGICAL HEALTH OFFICE. ANNUAL REPORT. Text in Japanese. 1965. a.
Published by: (Hoshasen Kanrishitsu), Tokyo Daigaku, Genshiryoku Kenkyu Sogo Senta/University of Tokyo, Research Center for Nuclear Science and Technology, Radiological Health Office, 11-16 Yayoi 2-chome, Bunkyo-ku, Tokyo, 113-0032, Japan.

HOSHASEN RIYO KENKYU SEIKA HOKOKUKAI KOEN YOSHI/ ABSTRACTS OF RESEARCH RESULTS OF RADIATION UTILIZATION. *see* PHYSICS—Abstracting, Bibliographies, Statistics

539.2 JPN
HOSHASEN RIYO KENKYUKAI HOKOKUSHO, AISOTOPU RIYO GURUPU/RESEARCH REPORT OF UTILIZATION OF RADIATION BY ISOTOPE USER'S GROUP. Text in Japanese. a. JPY 7,000 (effective 2003). **Document type:** *Yearbook, Academic/Scholarly.*
Published by: Nihon Genshiryoku Sangyo Kaigi/Japan Atomic Industrial Forum, Daiishi-Chojiya Bldg, 1-2-13 shiba-Diamon, Minato-ku, Tokyo, 105-8605, Japan. TEL 81-3-57770750, FAX 81-3-57770760, http://www.jaif.or.jp.

539.2 JPN
HOSHASEN RIYO KENKYUKAI HOKOKUSHO, SHOSHA RIYO GURUPU/RESEARCH REPORT OF UTILIZATION OF RADIATION BY IRRADIATION THERAPY GROUP. Text in Japanese. a. JPY 7,000 (effective 2003). **Document type:** *Yearbook, Academic/ Scholarly.*
Published by: Nihon Genshiryoku Sangyo Kaigi/Japan Atomic Industrial Forum, Daiishi-Chojiya Bldg, 1-2-13 shiba-Diamon, Minato-ku, Tokyo, 105-8605, Japan. TEL 81-3-57770750, FAX 81-3-57770760, http://www.jaif.or.jp.

539.2 JPN ISSN 0286-8873
➤ **HOSHASEN TO SANGYO/RADIATION AND INDUSTRIES.** Text in Japanese. 1976. 3/yr. JPY 620 per issue (effective 1998). adv. **Document type:** *Academic/Scholarly.*
Published by: Hoshasen Riyo Shinko Kyokai/Radiation Application Development Association, JAERI, 1233 Watanuki-Machi, Takasaki-shi, Gunma-ken 370-1207, Japan. TEL 81-27-346-1639, FAX 81-346-9822. Ed. Waichiro Kawakami. R&P, Adv. contact Kunimitsu Yagi.

363.7 539.7 362.1 610 GBR ISSN 1473-6691
RA1231.R2 CODEN: JIOCAT

➤ **I C R U JOURNAL.** (International Commission on Radiation Units and Measurements) Text in English. 1956. s-a. GBP 246 in United Kingdom to institutions; EUR 370 in Europe to institutions; USD 468 in US & Canada to institutions; GBP 246 elsewhere to institutions; GBP 269 combined subscription in United Kingdom to institutions (print & online eds.); EUR 403 combined subscription in Europe to institutions (print & online eds.); USD 510 combined subscription in US & Canada to institutions (print & online eds.); GBP 269 combined subscription elsewhere to institutions (print & online eds.) (effective 2012). adv. bk.rev. 250 p./no. 2 cols./p.; back issues avail.; reprints avail. **Document type:** *Journal, Academic/Scholarly.* **Description:** Publishes reports on important and topical subjects within the field of radiation science and measurement.

Formerly (until 2001): I C R U Reports (0579-5435)

Related titles: Online - full text ed.: ISSN 1742-3422. GBP 224 in United Kingdom to institutions; EUR 336 in Europe to institutions; USD 425 in US & Canada to institutions; GBP 224 elsewhere to institutions (effective 2012) (from IngentaConnect).

Indexed: A01, A22, E01, EnvAb, Inspec, R10, Reac, SCOPUS, T02.

—BLDSC (4362.090000), IE, INIST, Linda Hall. **CCC.**

Published by: (International Commission on Radiation Units and Measurements (ICRU) USA), Oxford University Press, Great Clarendon St, Oxford, OX2 6DP, United Kingdom. TEL 44-1865-556767, FAX 44-1865-556646, enquiry@oup.co.uk, http://www.oxfordjournals.org.

➤ **I S T E C JOURNAL.** *see* ELECTRONICS

621.484 USA

INERTIAL CONFINEMENT FUSION QUARTERLY REPORT. Text in English. q. back issues avail. **Description:** Reports selected current research within the program, in major areas of investigation including fusion target theory and design.

Media: Online - full text.

Published by: (Inertial Confinement Fusion Program), University of California, Lawrence Livermore National Security LLC, 7000 East Ave, PO Box 808, Livermore, CA 94551-0808.

539.2 JPN

INSTITUTE FOR MOLECULAR SCIENCE. ANNUAL REVIEW. Text in English. 1978. a. **Document type:** *Journal, Academic/Scholarly.*

Published by: Okazaki National Research Institutes, Institute for Molecular Science/Okazaki Kokuritsu Kyodo Kenkyu Kiko Bunshi Kagaku Kenkyujo, 38 Nishigonaka-Myodaiji-cho, Okazaki-shi, Aichi-ken 444-0000, Japan.

538.2 JPN

INSTITUTE FOR MOLECULAR SCIENCE. COMPUTER CENTER REPORT/OKAZAKI KOKURITSU KYODO KENKYU KIKO BUNSHI KAGAKU KENKYUJO DENSHI KEISANKI SENTA REPOTO. Text in English, Japanese. 1980. a. **Document type:** *Report, Academic/Scholarly.*

Published by: (Computer Center), Okazaki National Research Institutes, Institute for Molecular Science/Okazaki Kokuritsu Kyodo Kenkyu Kiko Bunshi Kagaku Kenkyujo, 38 Nishigonaka-Myodaiji-cho, Okazaki-shi, Aichi-ken 444-0000, Japan.

539.7 570 JPN ISSN 0285-1962

INSTITUTE OF RADIATION BREEDING. TECHNICAL NEWS. Text in English, Japanese. 1969. irreg. **Document type:** *Monographic series, Academic/Scholarly.*

—Linda Hall.

Published by: Ministry of Agriculture & Forestry, National Institute of Agrobiological Science, Institute of Radiation Breeding, 2425, Kamimurata, Hitachiohmiya, Ibaraki 319-2293, Japan. TEL 81-295-521138, FAX 81-295-531075, irbwww@nias.affrc.go.jp, http://www.irb.affrc.go.jp/index.html.

539.722 IND ISSN 0074-3046

INTERNATIONAL CONFERENCE ON COSMIC RAYS. PROCEEDINGS. Text in English. 1984. irreg. bk.rev. **Document type:** *Proceedings, Academic/Scholarly.*

Published by: Tata Institute of Fundamental Research, Homi Bhabha Rd, Mumbai, Maharashtra 400 005, India. TEL 91-22-22782000, FAX 91-22-22804610, root@crl.tifr.res.in, http://www.tifr.res.in.

539.75 USA

INTERNATIONAL CONFERENCE ON THE PHYSICS OF ELECTRONIC AND ATOMIC COLLISIONS. ABSTRACTS OF CONTRIBUTED PAPERS AND INVITED PAPERS. Variant title: Electronic and Atomic Collisions. Physics of Electronic and Atomic Collisions. Text in English. 1958. irreg., latest 1987, 15th, Brighton. USD 150. **Document type:** *Proceedings.*

Formerly: International Conference on the Physics of Electronic and Atomic Collisions. Papers (0074-333X)

Indexed: Inspec.

Published by: International Union of Pure and Applied Physics, Commission on Atomic and Molecular Physics and Spectroscopy, c/o Norman Bardsley, Sec, L 296, Box 800, Livermore, CA 94550. TEL 510-422-1100. Circ: 1,500. **Subscr. to:** Elsevier BV, Radarweg 29, PO Box 211, Amsterdam 1000 AE, Netherlands. TEL 31-20-4853757, FAX 31-20-4853432, JournalsCustomerServiceEMEA@elsevier.com, http://www.elsevier.nl.

539.764 FRA

INTERNATIONAL EUROPEAN CONFERENCE ON HIGH ENERGY PHYSICS. PROCEEDINGS. Text in English. biennial. **Document type:** *Proceedings, Academic/Scholarly.*

Published by: European Physical Society, 6 rue des Freres Lumiere, Mulhouse, 68200, France. TEL 33-389-329440, FAX 33-389-329449, webmaster@eps.org, http://www.eps.org.

INTERNATIONAL JOURNAL OF LOW RADIATION. *see* ENVIRONMENTAL STUDIES

539.7 SGP ISSN 0218-3013
QC770 CODEN: IMPEER

➤ **INTERNATIONAL JOURNAL OF MODERN PHYSICS E**; nuclear physics. Abbreviated title: I J M P E. Text in English. 1992. m. SGD 2,250, USD 1,408, EUR 1,137 combined subscription to institutions (print & online eds.) (effective 2012). adv. back issues avail. **Document type:** *Journal, Academic/Scholarly.* **Description:** Brings out research papers as well as review articles both in theoretical and experimental nuclear physics, including articles devoted to the interface between particle and nuclear and between astrophysics and nuclear physics.

Related titles: Online - full text ed.: ISSN 1793-6608. SGD 2,045, USD 1,280, EUR 1,034 to institutions (effective 2012).

Indexed: A01, A03, A08, A22, A28, APA, ASCA, BrCerAb, C&ISA, CA, CA/WCA, CIA, CerAb, CivEngAb, CorrAb, CurCont, E&CAJ, E01, E11, E14, EEA, EMA, ESPM, EnvEAb, H15, Inspec, M&TEA, M05, M09, MBF, METADEX, S01, SCI, SCOPUS, SolStAb, T02, T04, W07, WAA.

—BLDSC (4542.365240), AskIEEE, IE, Infotrieve, Ingenta, Linda Hall. **CCC.**

Published by: World Scientific Publishing Co. Pte. Ltd., 5 Toh Tuck Link, Singapore, 596224, Singapore. TEL 65-6466-5775, FAX 65-6467-7667, wspc@wspc.com.sg, http://www.worldscientific.com. **Dist. by:** World Scientific Publishing Co., Inc., 27 Warren St, Ste 401-402, Hackensack, NJ 07601. TEL 201-487-9655, 800-227-7562, FAX 201-487-9656, 888-977-2665, wspc@wspc.com; World Scientific Publishing Ltd., 57 Shelton St, London WC2H 9HE, United Kingdom. TEL 44-207-8360888, FAX 44-207-8362020, sales@wspc.co.uk.

539.7 643 SGP ISSN 0129-0835
QD96.X2 CODEN: IJPXET

➤ **INTERNATIONAL JOURNAL OF P I X E.** (Particle-Induced X-ray Emission) Abbreviated title: I J P I X E. Text in English. 1991. q. SGD 1,199, USD 754, EUR 605 combined subscription to institutions (print & online eds.) (effective 2012). adv. back issues avail. **Document type:** *Journal, Academic/Scholarly.* **Description:** Brings out papers and reviews in various aspects of particle-induced X-ray emission (PIXE).

Related titles: Online - full text ed.: ISSN 1793-6616. SGD 1,090, USD 685, EUR 550 to institutions (effective 2012).

Indexed: A01, A03, A08, A40, C33, CA, ChemAb, E11, ESPM, INIS AtomInd, PollutAb, S01, T02, T04.

—BLDSC (4542.467300), CASDDS, IE, Ingenta. **CCC.**

Published by: World Scientific Publishing Co. Pte. Ltd., 5 Toh Tuck Link, Singapore, 596224, Singapore. TEL 65-6466-5775, FAX 65-6467-7667, wspc@wspc.com.sg, http://www.worldscientific.com. Ed. K Ishii. **Dist. by:** World Scientific Publishing Co., Inc., 27 Warren St, Ste 401-402, Hackensack, NJ 07601. TEL 201-487-9655, 800-227-7562, FAX 201-487-9656, 888-977-2665, wspc@wspc.com; World Scientific Publishing Ltd., 57 Shelton St, London WC2H 9HE, United Kingdom. TEL 44-207-8360888, FAX 44-207-8362020, sales@wspc.co.uk.

539.7 SGP ISSN 0217-9474
CODEN: IRNPEH

INTERNATIONAL REVIEW OF NUCLEAR PHYSICS. Text in English. 1985. irreg., latest vol.9, 2004. price varies. back issues avail. **Document type:** *Monographic series, Academic/Scholarly.*

Indexed: CIN, ChemAb, ChemTitl, Inspec.

—CASDDS.

Published by: World Scientific Publishing Co. Pte. Ltd., 5 Toh Tuck Link, Singapore, 596224, Singapore. TEL 65-6466-5775, FAX 65-6467-7667, wspc@wspc.com.sg, http://www.worldscientific.com. Eds. E Osnes, T T S Kuo. **Dist. by:** World Scientific Publishing Co., Inc., 27 Warren St, Ste 401-402, Hackensack, NJ 07601. TEL 201-487-9655, 800-227-7562, FAX 201-487-9656, 888-977-2665, wspc@wspc.com; World Scientific Publishing Ltd., 57 Shelton St, London WC2H 9HE, United Kingdom. TEL 44-207-8360888, FAX 44-207-8362020, sales@wspc.co.uk.

539.752 JPN ISSN 0285-5518
QD466.5 CODEN: ISNEDO

ISOTOPE NEWS. Text in Japanese. 1952. m. JPY 8,700 to members (effective 2000). **Document type:** *Academic/Scholarly.*

Indexed: JTA, RefZh.

Published by: Japan Radioisotope Association/Nihon Aisotope Kyokai, 2-28-45 Honkomagome, Bunkyo-ku, Tokyo, 113-0021, Japan. TEL 81-3-53958021, FAX 81-3-53958051.

539.7 RUS ISSN 0204-3327

IZVESTIYA VYSSHIKH UCHEBNYKH ZAVEDENII. YADERNAYA ENERGETIKA; nauchno-tekhnicheskii zhurnal. Text in Russian; Abstracts in English. 1993. bi-m.

Indexed: RefZh.

—BLDSC (0078.070000).

Published by: Institut Atomnoi Energetiki, Studgorodok, 1, Obninsk, 249020, Russian Federation. TEL 7-8439-70361.

J A I F ANNUAL CONFERENCE ABSTRACTS. *see* PHYSICS—Abstracting, Bibliographies, Statistics

JAARUITGAVE STRALINGSBESCHERMING. *see* PUBLIC HEALTH AND SAFETY

539.7 USA ISSN 1687-9228

➤ **JOURNAL OF ATOMIC, MOLECULAR, AND OPTICAL PHYSICS.** Text in English. 2008. irreg. USD 395 (effective 2011). **Document type:** *Journal, Academic/Scholarly.* **Description:** Publishes original research articles as well as review articles in all areas of atomic, molecular, and optical physics.

Related titles: Online - full text ed.: ISSN 1687-9236. free (effective 2011).

Indexed: A01, CA, P52, T02.

Published by: Hindawi Publishing Corporation, 410 Park Ave, 15th Fl, PMB 287, New York, NY 10022. FAX 215-893-4392, 866-446-3294, orders@hindawi.com.

539.7 NLD ISSN 1023-8166

➤ **JOURNAL OF NEUTRON RESEARCH.** Text in English. 1995. q. USD 905 combined subscription in North America to institutions (print & online eds.); EUR 688 combined subscription elsewhere to institutions (print & online eds.) (effective 2011). adv. back issues avail.; reprints avail. **Document type:** *Journal, Academic/Scholarly.* **Description:** Publishes original research papers of both experimental and theoretical nature in three areas of specialization in neutron research: engineering science, neutron instrumentation and techniques, and reactor or spallation source technology.

Related titles: Online - full text ed.: ISSN 1477-2655 (from IngentaConnect).

Indexed: A01, A03, A08, A22, CA, E01, S01, T02.

—BLDSC (5022.320000), IE, Infotrieve, Ingenta. **CCC.**

Published by: I O S Press, Nieuwe Hemweg 6B, Amsterdam, 1013 BG, Netherlands. TEL 31-20-6883355, FAX 31-20-6870019, info@iospress.nl, http://www.iospress.nl. Ed. C J Carlile.

539.2 EGY ISSN 1687-420X
QC770

➤ **JOURNAL OF NUCLEAR AND RADIATION PHYSICS.** Text in English. 2005. s-a. **Document type:** *Journal, Academic/Scholarly.* **Description:** Publishes research in all fields of nuclear and radiation physics including particle physics, high energy physics, nuclear models and structure, nuclear reactions and spectroscopy, neutron and reactor physics, environmental radiation physics, medical radiation physics and radiation measurement and dosimetry.

Related titles: Online - full text ed.: free (effective 2011).

Published by: Egyptian Nuclear Physics Association, 3 Ahmed El Zomor St, Nasr City, Cairo, 11787, Egypt. TEL 20-2-4021018, FAX 20-2-2876031. Ed. M N H Comsan.

➤ **JOURNAL OF NUCLEAR AND RADIOCHEMICAL SCIENCES.** *see* MEDICAL SCIENCES—Radiology And Nuclear Medicine

621.48 NLD ISSN 0022-3115
CODEN: JNUMAM

➤ **JOURNAL OF NUCLEAR MATERIALS.** Text in English, French, German. 1959. 36/yr. EUR 8,359 in Europe to institutions; JPY 1,110,200 in Japan to institutions; USD 9,397 elsewhere to institutions (effective 2012). adv. bk.rev. charts; illus. cum.index. back issues avail. **Document type:** *Journal, Academic/Scholarly.* **Description:** Publishes papers covering the field of materials research related to nuclear fission and fusion reactor technologies.

Related titles: Microform ed.: (from PQC); Online - full text ed.: ISSN 1873-4820 (from IngentaConnect, ScienceDirect).

Indexed: A01, A03, A08, A20, A22, A26, A28, APA, ASCA, ApMecR, B21, BrCerAb, BullT&T, C&ISA, C33, CA, CA/WCA, CIA, CIN, CPEI, Cadscan, CerAb, ChemAb, ChemTitl, CivEngAb, CorrAb, CurCont, E&CAJ, E11, EEA, EIA, EMA, ESPM, EngInd, EnvAb, EnvEAb, EnvInd, F&EA, GeoRef, H&SSA, H15, I05, INIS AtomInd, ISMEC, ISR, Inspec, LeadAb, M&TEA, M09, MBF, METADEX, MSCI, PhysBer, PollutAb, RefZh, S01, SCI, SCOPUS, SolStAb, SpeleolAb, T02, T04, W07, WAA, Zincscan.

—BLDSC (5023.200000), AskIEEE, CASDDS, IE, Infotrieve, Ingenta, INIST, Linda Hall. **CCC.**

Published by: Elsevier BV, North-Holland (Subsidiary of: Elsevier Science & Technology), Sara Burgerhartstraat 25, Amsterdam, 1055 KV, Netherlands. TEL 31-20-4853911, FAX 31-20-4852457, JournalsCustomerServiceEMEA@elsevier.com. Eds. C Lemaignan, L K Mansur, S Ishino. **Subscr. to:** Elsevier BV, Radarweg 29, PO Box 211, Amsterdam 1000 AE, Netherlands. TEL 31-20-4853757, FAX 31-20-4853432, http://www.elsevier.nl.

539 621.48 JPN ISSN 0022-3131
QC770 CODEN: JNSTAX

➤ **JOURNAL OF NUCLEAR SCIENCE AND TECHNOLOGY/NIHON GENSHIRYOKU GAKKAI OBUN RONBUNSHI.** Text in English. 1964. m. free to members. adv. abstr.; charts; illus. Index. reprints avail. **Document type:** *Journal, Academic/Scholarly.* **Description:** Contains submitted research papers and commissioned papers in all fields of nuclear engineering for peaceful applications and contributions to society.

Related titles: Online - full text ed.

Indexed: A22, A28, APA, ASCA, BPRC&P, BrCerAb, C&ISA, C24, C33, CA/WCA, CADCAM, CIA, CPEI, CerAb, ChemAb, ChemTitl, CivEngAb, CorrAb, CurCont, E&CAJ, E04, E05, E11, EEA, EIA, EMA, ESPM, EngInd, EnvAb, EnvEAb, FR, H15, IBR, IBZ, INIS AtomInd, ISMEC, ISR, Inspec, JTA, M&TEA, M09, MBF, METADEX, P30, SCI, SCOPUS, SolStAb, T04, TM, W07, WAA.

—BLDSC (5023.500000), AskIEEE, CASDDS, IE, Infotrieve, Ingenta, INIST, Linda Hall. **CCC.**

Published by: Nihon Genshiryoku Gakkai/Atomic Energy Society of Japan, 2-3-7 Shinbashi, Minato-ku, Tokyo, 105-0004, Japan. TEL 81-3-35081261, FAX 81-3-35816128, atom@aesj.or.jp, http://wwwsoc.nii.ac.jp/aesj/. Circ: 1,350. **Subscr. to:** Maruzen Co., Ltd., Import & Export Dept, PO Box 5050, Tokyo International, Tokyo 100-3191, Japan. TEL 81-3-3278-9256, 81-3-3273-3234. **Dist. by:** Japan Publications Trading Co., Ltd., Book Export II Dept, PO Box 5030, Tokyo International, Tokyo 101-3191, Japan. TEL 81-3-32923753, FAX 81-3-32920410, infoserials@jptco.co.jp, http://www.jptco.co.jp.

539.7 GBR ISSN 0954-3899
QC770 CODEN: JPGPED

➤ **JOURNAL OF PHYSICS G: NUCLEAR AND PARTICLE PHYSICS.** Text in English. 1958. m. GBP 2,126 combined subscription to institutions (print & online eds.) (effective 2010). bibl.; charts; illus. Index. back issues avail. **Document type:** *Journal, Academic/Scholarly.* **Description:** Explores theoretical and experimental topics in the physics of elementary particles and fields, intermediate energy and cosmic rays.

Formerly (until 1989): Journal of Physics G: Nuclear Physics (0305-4616); Which superseded in part (in 1974): Journal of Physics A: Mathematical Nuclear and General (0301-0015); Which was formerly (until 1973): Journal of Physics A: Proceedings of the Physical Society. General (0022-3689); Which superseded in part (in 1968): Physical Society. Proceedings (0370-1328); Which was formed by the merger of (1874-1958): Physical Society. Proceedings. Section A (0370-1298); (1874-1958): Physical Society. Proceedings. Section B (0370-1301); Both of which superseded in part (in 1949): Physical Society. Proceedings (0959-5309); Which was formerly (until 1926): Physical Society of London. Proceedings (1478-7814)

Related titles: Microfiche ed.: USD 2,629 in North America; GBP 1,339 elsewhere (effective 2007); Microfilm ed.; Online - full text ed.: ISSN 1361-6471. 1996. GBP 2,025 to institutions (effective 2010) (from IngentaConnect).

Indexed: A01, A03, A08, A22, ASCA, C33, CA, CIN, Cadscan, ChemAb, ChemTitl, CurCont, GeoRef, INIS AtomInd, ISR, Inspec, LeadAb, MathR, P30, PhysBer, RefZh, SCI, SCOPUS, SpeleolAb, T02, W07, Zincscan.

—BLDSC (5036.219000), AskIEEE, CASDDS, IE, Ingenta, INIST, Linda Hall. **CCC.**

Published by: (Institute of Physics), Institute of Physics Publishing Ltd., Dirac House, Temple Back, Bristol, BS1 6BE, United Kingdom. TEL 44-117-9297481, FAX 44-117-9301178, custserv@iop.org, http://publishing.iop.org/. Ed. A B Balantekin. **Subscr. addr. in US:** American Institute of Physics, PO Box 503284, St Louis, MO 63150. TEL 516-576-2270, 800-344-6902, FAX 516-349-9704, subs@aip.org.

P

539.735 USA ISSN 0909-0495
QC793.5.E627 CODEN: JSYRES
➤ **JOURNAL OF SYNCHROTRON RADIATION.** Text in English. 1994. bi-m. GBP 761 in United Kingdom to institutions; EUR 966 in Europe to institutions; USD 1,280 elsewhere to institutions; GBP 875 combined subscription in United Kingdom to institutions (print & online eds.); EUR 1,111 combined subscription in Europe to institutions (print & online eds.); USD 1,473 combined subscription elsewhere to institutions (print & online eds.) (effective 2012). adv. charts; illus. reprint service avail. from PSC. **Document type:** *Journal, Academic/Scholarly.*
Related titles: Online - full text ed.: ISSN 1600-5775. GBP 761 in United Kingdom to institutions; EUR 966 in Europe to institutions; USD 1,280 elsewhere to institutions (effective 2012) (from IngentaConnect).
Indexed: A01, A03, A08, A20, A22, A26, A28, APA, ASCA, BrCerAb, C&ISA, CA, CA/WCA, CIA, CIN, CPEI, CerAb, ChemAb, ChemTitl, CivEngAb, CorrAb, CurCont, E&CAJ, E01, E11, EEA, EMA, EMBASE, ESPM, EngInd, EnvEAb, ExcerpMed, H15, I05, INIS AtomInd, ISR, Inspec, M&TEA, M09, MBF, MEDLINE, METADEX, P30, R10, Reac, S01, SCI, SCOPUS, SolStAb, T02, T04, W07, WAA.
—BLDSC (5068.035000), AskIEEE, CASDDS, IE, Infotrieve, Ingenta, INIST, Linda Hall. **CCC.**
Published by: (International Union of Crystallography GBR), Wiley-Blackwell Publishing, Inc. (Subsidiary of: Wiley-Blackwell Publishing Ltd.), Commerce Pl, 350 Main St, Malden, MA 02148. TEL 781-388-8200, FAX 781-388-8210, info@wiley.com, http://www.wiley.com/WileyCDA/. Eds. Aake Kvick, G E Ice. Adv. contact Andrea Sharpe.

539.7 JPN
KAKU YUGO KENKYU KAIHATSU NO GENJO/STATUS OF NUCLEAR FUSION RESEARCH AND DEVELOPMENT. Text in Japanese. 1975. a. free. **Document type:** *Corporate.* **Description:** Describes the progress and achievements of fusion research and development at JAERI, basically during a year. It also includes the domestic and international collaboration on fusion research.
Published by: Nihon Genshiryoku Kenkyujo, Naka Kenkyujo/Japan Atomic Energy Research Institute, Naka Fusion Research Establishment, 801 Muko-Uyama, Naka-gun, Naka-machi, Ibaraki-ken 311-0102, Japan. http://www.naka.jaeri.go.jp. Ed. Yasushi Seki. Circ: 3,500.

539.7 JPN
KAKU YUGO RENGO KOENKAI YOKOSHU/PREPRINTS OF JOINT CONFERENCE ON NUCLEAR FUSION. Text in Japanese. 1978. a.
Published by: Purazuma Kaku Yugo Gakkai/Japan Society of Plasma Science and Nuclear Fusion Research, 20-29 Nishiki 2-chome, Naka-ku, Nagoya-shi, Aichi-ken 460-0003, Japan. TEL 81-52-7353185, FAX 81-52-7353485, http://www.nifs.ac.jp/jspf/.

539.7 JPN ISSN 0915-6704
➤ **KAKU YUUGOU KAGAKU KENKYUSHO NYUSU/NATIONAL INSTITUTE FOR FUSION SCIENCE. NEWS.** Text in Japanese. 1989. m. free. **Document type:** *Academic/Scholarly.*
—**CCC.**
Published by: Kaku Yuugou Kagaku Kenkyusho/National Institute for Fusion Science, 322-6 Oroshi-cho, Toki-shi, Gifu-ken 509-5202, Japan. TEL 81-572-58-2222, FAX 81-572-58-2601, TELEX 0447-3691 NIFSJ. Circ: 2,650 (controlled).

539.7 JPN ISSN 0385-2105
QC770 CODEN: TLNRBV
KAKURIKEN KENKYU HOKOKU/LABORATORY OF NUCLEAR SCIENCE. RESEARCH REPORT. Text in English, Japanese. 1968. s-a.
Indexed: CIN, ChemAb, ChemTitl, INIS AtomInd.
—CASDDS.
Published by: (Fuzoku Genshikaku Rigaku Kenkyu Shisetsu), Tohoku Daigaku, Rigakubu/Tohoku University, Faculty of Science, Laboratory of Nuclear Science, 2-1 Mikamine 1-chome, Taihaku-ku, Sendai-shi, Miyagi-ken 982-0826, Japan.

539.7 ITA ISSN 1828-8545
L N L ANNUAL REPORT. (Laboratori Nazionali di Legnaro) Text in English. 1978. a. **Document type:** *Government.*
Related titles: CD-ROM ed.: ISSN 1828-8553. 2000; Online - full text ed.: ISSN 1828-8561. 2000.
Published by: Istituto Nazionale di Fisica Nucleare (I N F N), Piazza dei Caprettari 70, Rome, 00186, Italy. TEL 39-06-6840031, FAX 39-06-68307924, prot_AC@infn.it, http://www.infn.it.

539.7 FRA
LABORATOIRE DE PHYSIQUE SUBATOMIQUE ET DE COSMOLOGIE DE GRENOBLE. RAPPORT D'ACTIVITE. Text in French; Summaries in English. 1982. biennial. free. back issues avail. **Document type:** *Corporate.*
Former titles (until 2002): Institut des Sciences Nucleaires Grenoble. Rapport d'Activite (0399-127X); (until 1981): Universite Scientifique et Medical de Grenoble. Institut des Sciences Nucleaires. Rapport Annuel (0399-1261)
Related titles: Online - full text ed.
—INIST.
Published by: Laboratoire de Physique Subatomique et de Cosmologie de Grenoble, 53 rue des Martyrs, Grenoble, Cedex 38026, France. TEL 33-4-76284000, FAX 33-4-76284004, http://lpsc.in2p3.fr. Ed. Joel Chauvin. Circ: 500.

539.7 RUS
➤ **MAGNETIC RESONANCE IN SOLIDS.** Text in English. 1997. a. free. **Document type:** *Journal, Academic/Scholarly.* **Description:** Published articles ob magnetic resonance in solids and related phenomena.
Media: Online - full content.
Published by: Kazanskii Gosudarstvennyi Universitet/Kazan State University, 18 Kremlyovskaya St, Kazan, 420008, Russian Federation. TEL 7-843-2926977, FAX 7-843-2924448, public.mail@ksu.ru, http://www.ksu.ru. **Co-sponsor:** International Society of Magnetic Resonance.

543.0877 DEU ISSN 0968-5243
CODEN: MRBMEQ
➤ **MAGNETIC RESONANCE MATERIALS IN PHYSICS, BIOLOGY AND MEDICINE.** Key Title: Magma. Text in English. 1993. bi-m. EUR 659, USD 771 combined subscription to institutions (print & online eds.) (effective 2012). adv. bk.rev. back issues avail.; reprint service avail. from PSC. **Document type:** *Journal, Academic/Scholarly.* **Description:** Presents the latest research, development, and application of techniques in magnetic resonance imaging and spectroscopy.
Which was previously announced as: Magma Magnetic Resonance Materials
Related titles: Online - full text ed.: ISSN 1352-8661 (from IngentaConnect).
Indexed: A22, A26, ASCA, AmHI, B&BAb, B19, B21, BIOBASE, BioEngAb, CA, CIN, ChemAb, ChemTitl, CurCont, E01, EMBASE, ExcerpMed, H07, IABS, IndMed, Inspec, MEDLINE, P26, P30, P48, P52, P54, P56, PQC, R10, Reac, RefZh, SCI, SCOPUS, T02, W07.
—BLDSC (5334.854000), AskIEEE, CASDDS, GNLM, IE, Infotrieve, Ingenta. **CCC.**
Published by: (European Society for Magnetic Resonance in Medicine and Biology GBR), Springer (Subsidiary of: Springer Science+Business Media), Tiergartenstr 17, Heidelberg, 69121, Germany. TEL 49-6221-4870, FAX 49-6221-345229, orders-hd-individuals@springer.com. Ed. Dr. Patrick J Cozzone. **Subscr. to:** Springer New York LLC, Journal Fulfillment, PO Box 2485, Secaucus, NJ 07096. TEL 201-348-4033, 800-777-4643, FAX 201-348-4505, journals-ny@springer.com, http://www.springer.com.

539.2 IRN ISSN 1735-1871
MAJALLAH-I 'ULUM VA FUNUN-I HASTAH-I/JOURNAL OF NUCLEAR SCIENCE AND TECHNOLOGY. Text in English, Persian, Modern. 1983. q. IRR 45,000; IRR 20,000 to students (effective 2005). **Description:** Publishes research findings in the field of nuclear science, technology, and related topics.
Formerly (until 2004): Nashriyyah-i 'ilmi Sazman-i Inirzhi-i Atumi-i Iran/Atomic Energy Organization of Iran. Scientific Bulletin (1015-8545)
Indexed: INIS AtomInd.
—BLDSC (5023.499900).
Published by: Sazman-i Inirzhi-i Atumi-i Iran/Atomic Energy Organization of Iran, PO Box 14155-1339, Tehran, Iran. TEL 98-21-8009439, FAX 98-21-8026500. Ed. V Ahmadi.

539.7 USA
MICHIGAN STATE UNIVERSITY. NATIONAL SUPERCONDUCTING CYCLOTRON LABORATORY (PUBLICATION). Text in English. 1964 (no.21). irreg., latest vol.700, 1989. **Document type:** *Monographic series.*
Formerly: Michigan State University. Department of Physics. Cyclotron Project (Publication) (0076-8146)
Published by: Michigan State University, Superconducting Cyclotron Laboratory, 1 Cyclotron, East Lansing, MI 48824-1321. TEL 517-355-9671. Circ: 300.

539.2 SRB ISSN 1450-5835
MIKROTALASNA REVIJA/MICROWAVE REVIEW. Text in Serbian. 1994. s-a. **Document type:** *Journal, Academic/Scholarly.*
Formerly (until1996): Informator Jugoslovenske IEEE MTT Sekcije (0354-7124)
Related titles: Online - full text ed.: free (effective 2011).
Published by: Society for Microwave Technique, Technologies and Systems, Kneza Milosa 9, Belgrade, 11000. Ed. Zlatica Marinkovic.

539.7 SGP ISSN 0217-7323
QC770 CODEN: MPLAEQ
➤ **MODERN PHYSICS LETTERS A.** Abbreviated title: M P L A. Text in English. 1986. 40/yr. SGD 8,031, USD 4,855, EUR 4,184 combined subscription to institutions (print & online eds.) (effective 2012). adv. back issues avail. **Document type:** *Journal, Academic/Scholarly.* **Description:** Contains research papers covering current research development in particle and field physics, nuclear physics, cosmology and gravitation.
Related titles: Online - full text ed.: ISSN 1793-6632. SGD 7,301, USD 4,414, EUR 3,804 to institutions (effective 2012).
Indexed: A01, A03, A08, A20, A22, ASCA, CA, CCMJ, ChemAb, ChemTitl, CurCont, E01, ISR, Inspec, MSN, MathR, S01, SCI, SCOPUS, T02, W07, Z02.
—BLDSC (5890.835000), AskIEEE, CASDDS, IE, Infotrieve, Ingenta. **CCC.**
Published by: World Scientific Publishing Co. Pte. Ltd., 5 Toh Tuck Link, Singapore, 596224, Singapore. TEL 65-6466-5775, FAX 65-6467-7667, wspc@wspc.com.sg, http://www.worldscientific.com. **Dist. by:** World Scientific Publishing Co., Inc., 27 Warren St, Ste 401-402, Hackensack, NJ 07601. TEL 201-487-9655, 800-227-7562, FAX 201-487-9656, 888-977-2665, wspc@wspc.com; World Scientific Publishing Ltd., 57 Shelton St, London WC2H 9HE, United Kingdom. TEL 44-207-8360888, FAX 44-207-8362020, sales@wspc.co.uk.

539.7 SGP ISSN 0217-9849
QC173.4.C65 CODEN: MPLBET
➤ **MODERN PHYSICS LETTERS B;** condensed matter physics; statistical physics and applied physics. Abbreviated title: M P L B. Text in English. 1987. 32/yr. SGD 6,216, USD 3,911, EUR 3,236 combined subscription to institutions (print & online eds.) (effective 2012). adv. back issues avail. **Document type:** *Journal, Academic/Scholarly.* **Description:** Covers condensed matter physics, statistical physics and applied physics at the post-graduate level.
Related titles: Online - full text ed.: ISSN 1793-6640. SGD 5,651, USD 3,555, EUR 2,942 to institutions (effective 2012).
Indexed: A01, A03, A08, A22, ASCA, C33, CA, CCMJ, ChemAb, ChemTitl, CurCont, E01, ISR, Inspec, MSCI, MSN, MathR, S01, SCI, SCOPUS, T02, W07, Z02.
—BLDSC (5890.835100), AskIEEE, CASDDS, IE, Infotrieve, Ingenta, INIST. **CCC.**
Published by: World Scientific Publishing Co. Pte. Ltd., 5 Toh Tuck Link, Singapore, 596224, Singapore. TEL 65-6466-5775, FAX 65-6467-7667, wspc@wspc.com.sg, http://www.worldscientific.com. Eds. Rongjia Tao, W Schommers TEL 49-7247-822432, Wang Yu Peng. **Dist. by:** World Scientific Publishing Co., Inc., 27 Warren St, Ste 401-402, Hackensack, NJ 07601. TEL 201-487-9655, 800-227-7562, FAX 201-487-9656, 888-977-2665, wspc@wspc.com; World Scientific Publishing Ltd., 57 Shelton St, London WC2H 9HE, United Kingdom. TEL 44-207-8360888, FAX 44-207-8362020, sales@wspc.co.uk.

539.7 NLD ISSN 1381-1991
QH506 CODEN: MODIF4
➤ **MOLECULAR DIVERSITY.** Text in English. 1995. q. EUR 659, USD 670 combined subscription to institutions (print & online eds.) (effective 2012). adv. reprint service avail. from PSC. **Document type:** *Journal, Academic/Scholarly.* **Description:** Publishes both short and full papers, perspectives, news and reviews dealing with all aspects of the generation of molecular diversity, application of diversity for screening against alternative targets of all types (biological, biophysical, technological), analysis of results obtained and their application in various scientific disciplines and approaches.
Incorporates (1994-2003): Letters in Peptide Science (0929-5666)
Related titles: Online - full text ed.: ISSN 1573-501X (from IngentaConnect).
Indexed: A22, A26, Agr, B21, B25, BIOSIS Prev, BibLing, C33, CCI, CIN, ChemAb, ChemTitl, CurCont, E01, EMBASE, ExcerpMed, I05, IndMed, Inpharma, MEDLINE, MycolAb, NucAcAb, P20, P22, P26, P30, P48, P52, P54, P56, PQC, R10, Reac, RefZh, SCI, SCOPUS, W07.
—BLDSC (5900.817357), CASDDS, GNLM, IE, Infotrieve, Ingenta, INIST. **CCC.**
Published by: Springer Netherlands (Subsidiary of: Springer Science+Business Media), Van Godewijckstraat 30, Dordrecht, 3311 GX, Netherlands. TEL 31-78-6576050, FAX 31-78-6576474, http://www.springer.com. Ed. Guillermo A Morales.

539.19 POL ISSN 1505-1250
MOLECULAR PHYSICS REPORTS. Text in English. 1984. q. PLZ 66.77, EUR 17 (effective 2005). **Document type:** *Journal, Academic/Scholarly.*
Formerly (until 1994): Postepy Fizyki Molekularnej (0860-5874)
Indexed: Inspec.
—IE, Ingenta.
Published by: Polska Akademia Nauk, Instytut Fizyki Molekularnej/Polish Academy of Sciences, Institute of Molecular Physics, ul Mariana Smoluchowskiego 17, Poznan, 60-179, Poland. TEL 48-61-8695100, FAX 48-61-8684524, graja@ifmpan.poznan.pl, http://www.ifmpan.poznan.pl. Ed. Narcyz Pislewski. **Dist. by:** Ars Polona, Obroncow 25, Warsaw 03933, Poland. TEL 48-22-5098609, FAX 48-22-5098610, arspolona@arspolona.com.pl, http://www.arspolona.com.pl. **Co-sponsor:** Polska Akademia Nauk, Komitet Fizyki/Polish Academy of Sciences, Committee of Physics.

MUTATION BREEDING REVIEW. *see* AGRICULTURE—Crop Production And Soil

539.7 621.48 JPN ISSN 0915-633X
N I F S SERIES. RESEARCH REPORT. (National Institute for Fusion Science) Text in English. 1990. irreg. **Document type:** *Monographic series.*
Indexed: Inspec, RefZh.
—BLDSC (7762.722430). **CCC.**
Published by: National Institute for Fusion Science, Research Information Center/Kaku Yugo Kagaku Kenkyujo, 322-6 Oroshi-cho, Toki, Gifu-ken 509-5292, Japan. TEL 81-572-58-2066, FAX 81-572-58-2607.

539.76 JPN ISSN 0915-6364
QC303
NATIONAL INSTITUTE FOR FUSION SCIENCE. RESEARCH REPORT. DATA SERIES. Key Title: Research Report N I F S - Data Series. Text in English. 1990. irreg. **Document type:** *Report, Academic/Scholarly.*
Indexed: Inspec, RefZh.
—BLDSC (7762.722434). **CCC.**
Published by: National Institute for Fusion Science, Research Information Center/Kaku Yugo Kagaku Kenkyujo, 322-6 Oroshi-cho, Toki, Gifu-ken 509-5292, Japan. TEL 81-572-58-2066. Ed. Chusei Namba.

539.76 JPN ISSN 0915-6372
QC793.3.B4
NATIONAL INSTITUTE FOR FUSION SCIENCE. RESEARCH REPORT. MEMO SERIES. Key Title: Research Report N I F S - Memo Series. Text in Japanese; Summaries in English, Japanese. 1991. irreg. **Document type:** *Academic/Scholarly.*
—BLDSC (7762.722436). **CCC.**
Published by: National Institute for Fusion Science, Research Information Center/Kaku Yugo Kagaku Kenkyujo, 322-6 Oroshi-cho, Toki, Gifu-ken 509-5292, Japan. TEL 81-572-58-2066. Ed. Chusei Namba.

539.2 GBR ISSN 0308-5430
NATIONAL RADIOLOGICAL PROTECTION BOARD. REPORT. Text in English. irreg. **Document type:** *Report, Trade.*
Indexed: Inspec.
Published by: Health Protection Agency, Radiation Protection Division, Centre for Radiation, Chemical and Environmental Hazards, Chilton, Didcot, Oxon OX11 0RQ, United Kingdom. TEL 44-1235-831600, FAX 44-1235-833891, nrpb@hpa-rp.org.uk, http://www.hpa.org.uk/radiation/.

539.7 621.48 KAZ ISSN 1729-7516
NATSIONAL'NYI YADERNYI TSENTR RESPUBLIKI KAZAKHSTAN. VESTNIK/N N C R K. BULLETIN. Key Title: Vestnik N A C R K. Text in English, Russian. 2000. q. **Description:** Focuses on nuclear power engineering development in Kazakhstan, radiation ecology matters, conversion of former nuclear test site infrastructures, and non-proliferation issues.
Related titles: Online - full text ed.: ISSN 1729-7885.
Indexed: INIS AtomInd.
Published by: Natsional'nyi Yadernyi Tsentr Respubliki Kazakhstan/National Nuclear Center of the Republic of Kazakhstan, Kurchatov, Kazakstan. http://www.nnc.kz.

NEDERLANDS TIJDSCHRIFT VOOR STRALINGSBESCHERMING. *see* PUBLIC HEALTH AND SAFETY

539.7 POL ISSN 1689-9571
NEUTRINO. Text in Polish. 2008. q. **Document type:** *Journal, Academic/Scholarly.*
Published by: (Uniwersytet Jagiellonski, Instytut Fizyki/Jagellonian University, Institute of Physics, Polskie Towarzystwo Fizyczne, Sekcja Nauczycielska), Wydawnictwo Uniwersytetu Jagiellonskiego/Jagiellonian University Press, ul Grodzka 26, Krakow, 31044, Poland. TEL 48-12-4312364, FAX 48-12-4301995, wydaw@if.uj.edu.pl, http://www.wuj.pl. Ed. Zofia Golab-Meyer.

539.7 USA ISSN 1044-8632
QC793.5.N462 CODEN: NTNEEJ

➤ **NEUTRON NEWS.** Text in English. 1990. q. GBP 550 combined subscription in United Kingdom to institutions (print & online eds.); EUR 725, USD 911 combined subscription to institutions (print & online eds.) (effective 2012). adv. reprint service avail. from PSC. **Document type:** *Journal, Academic/Scholarly.* **Description:** Focuses on the use of neutron beams, for both diffraction and inelastic scattering.
Related titles: Microform ed.; Online - full text ed.: ISSN 1931-7352. GBP 495 in United Kingdom to institutions; EUR 652, USD 820 to institutions (effective 2012) (from IngentaConnect).
Indexed: A01, A22, CA, E01, INIS AtomInd, P52, T02.
—IE, Ingenta. **CCC.**
Published by: Taylor & Francis Inc. (Subsidiary of: Taylor & Francis Group), 325 Chestnut St, Ste 800, Philadelphia, PA 19106. TEL 215-625-2940, 800-354-1420, orders@taylorandfrancis.com, http://www.taylorandfrancis.com. Ed. Herma Buttner. Adv. contact Maureen Williams.

539.7 USA ISSN 2157-0868

NEUTRON SCIENCES PROGRESS REPORT. Text in English. 2007. bi-m. free (effective 2010). back issues avail. **Document type:** *Report, Government.* **Description:** Contains reports about the studies in science by providing capabilities for research using neutrons.
Formerly (until 2009): Neutron Sciences Progress at Oak Ridge National Laboratory (2157-085X)
Media: Online - full text.
Published by: Oak Ridge National Laboratory, Neutron Sciences, Oak Ridge National Laboratory, PO Box 2008, Oak Ridge, TN 37831. TEL 865-574-1301, neutronscience@ornl.gov.

539.2 JPN

NIHON AISOTOPU HOSHASEN SOGO KAIGI RONBUNSHU/JAPAN CONFERENCE ON RADIATION AND RADIOISOTOPES. PROCEEDINGS. Text in English, Japanese; Summaries in English. 1956. biennial. JPY 13,000 (effective 2003). **Document type:** *Proceedings, Academic/Scholarly.*
Indexed: CIN, ChemAb, ChemTitl.
Published by: Nihon Genshiryoku Sangyo Kaigi/Japan Atomic Industrial Forum, Daiishi-Chojiya Bldg, 1-2-13 shiba-Diamon, Minato-ku, Tokyo, 105-8605, Japan. TEL 81-3-57770750, FAX 81-3-57770760, http://www.jaif.or.jp.

539.2 JPN ISSN 1347-1503

NIHON HOUSHASEN ANZEN KANRI GAKKAISHI/JAPANESE JOURNAL OF RADIATION SAFETY MANAGEMENT. Text in Japanese. 2001. s-a. **Document type:** *Journal, Academic/Scholarly.*
Related titles: Online - full text ed.
—BLDSC (6112.627500).
Published by: Japanese Society of Radiation Safety Management/Nihon Houshasen Anzen Kanri Gakkai, Nagoya University, Radioisotope Research Center, Radiation Sciences Division, Furo-cho Chikusa-ku, Nagoya, 464-8602, Japan. TEL 81-52-7892569, FAX 81-52-7895048, maekoshi@met.nagoya-u.ac.jp, http://www.ric.nagoya-u.ac.jp/JRSM/index.html.

539.7 JPN ISSN 0369-4305
RC78.A1 CODEN: NIPHAP

NIPPON HOSHASEN GIJUTSU GAKKAI ZASSHI/JAPANESE JOURNAL OF RADIOLOGICAL TECHNOLOGY. Text in Japanese. 1944. m. back issues avail. **Document type:** *Journal, Academic/Scholarly.*
Related titles: Online - full text ed.: ISSN 1881-4883.
Indexed: A22, B&BAb, EMBASE, ExcerpMed, INIS AtomInd, MEDLINE, P30, R10, Reac, SCOPUS.
—BLDSC (4658.500000), IE, Ingenta.
Published by: Nihon Hoshasen Gijutsu Gakkai/Japanese Society of Radiological Technology, View-Fort Gojokarasuma, 167 Higashikazariya-cho, Shinmachi-higashiiru, Gojodori, Shimogyo-ku, Kyoto, 600-8107, Japan. TEL 81-75-354-8989, FAX 81-75-352-2556, office@jsrt.or.jp.

539.7 ITA ISSN 1592-7822

NOTIZIARIO NEUTRONI E LUCE DI SINCROTRONE. Text in English. 1996. s-a. **Document type:** *Journal, Academic/Scholarly.* **Description:** Aims to provide a focus in instrumentation and techniques over all the spectral ranges relevant to neutron and synchrotron radiation research.
Related titles: Online - full text ed.
Published by: Consiglio Nazionale delle Ricerche (C N R)/Italian National Research Council, Piazzale Aldo Moro 7, Rome, 00185, Italy. TEL 39-06-49931, FAX 39-06-4461954, http://www.cnr.it. Ed. C Andreani.

539.7 621.48 KOR ISSN 1738-5733
QC770 CODEN: WJHKAW

NUCLEAR ENGINEERING AND TECHNOLOGY. Variant title: Wonjaryok Hakhoeji. Text in English. 1969. bi-m. membership. bk.rev. back issues avail. **Document type:** *Journal, Academic/Scholarly.* **Description:** Covers all aspects of the application and theory of nuclear science and technology.
Formerly (until 2005): Korean Nuclear Society. Journal (0372-7327)
Related titles: Online - full text ed.
Indexed: A22, INIS AtomInd, Inspec, RefZh, SCI, SCOPUS, W07.
—BLDSC (6180.714500), IE, Ingenta, Linda Hall.
Published by: Korean Nuclear Society/Han'gug Wonja'lyeog Haghoe, Nutopia Bldg., 342-1 Jangae-dong, Daejeon, 305-308, Korea, S. TEL 82-42-8262613, FAX 82-42-8262617, kns@nanum.kaeri.re.kr. Ed. Poong Hyun Seong.

539.7 530.44 GBR ISSN 0029-5515
QC791 CODEN: NUFUAU

➤ **NUCLEAR FUSION/FUSION NUCLEAIRE.** Text and summaries in English. 1960. m. GBP 991 combined subscription to institutions (print & online eds.) (effective 2010). bk.rev. abstr.; bibl.; charts; illus. Index. back issues avail.; reprints avail. **Document type:** *Journal, Academic/Scholarly.* **Description:** Contains all aspects of research relevant to controlled thermonuclear fusion including, production, heating and confinement of high temperature plasmas, as well as the physical properties of such plasmas and the experimental or theoretical methods of exploring or explaining them.
Related titles: Microfiche ed.: USD 1,054 in the Americas; GBP 664 elsewhere (effective 2007) (from PQC); Online - full text ed.: ISSN 1741-4326. GBP 943 to institutions (effective 2010) (from IngentaConnect); ◆ Supplement(s): Atomic and Plasma-Material Interaction Data for Fusion. ISSN 1018-5577.
Indexed: A01, A03, A08, A22, ASCA, ApMecR, C&ISA, C33, CA, CIN, CPEI, ChemAb, ChemTitl, CurCont, E&CAJ, EngInd, FR, IBR, IBZ, INIS AtomInd, ISMEC, ISR, Inspec, PhysBer, RefZh, SCI, SCOPUS, SolStAb, T02, W07.
—BLDSC (6180.760000), AskIEEE, CASDDS, IE, Infotrieve, Ingenta, INIST, Linda Hall. **CCC.**
Published by: Institute of Physics Publishing Ltd., Dirac House, Temple Back, Bristol, BS1 6BE, United Kingdom. TEL 44-117-9297481, FAX 44-117-9301178, custserv@iop.org, http://publishing.iop.org/. Ed. P Thomas. **Subscr. in the US, Canada & Mexico to:** American Institute of Physics, PO Box 503284, St Louis, MO 63150. TEL 516-576-2270, 800-344-6902, FAX 516-349-9704, subs@aip.org. **Co-publisher:** International Atomic Energy Agency/Agence Internationale de l'Energie Atomique.

539 NLD ISSN 0168-9002
QC785.5 CODEN: NIMAER

➤ **NUCLEAR INSTRUMENTS & METHODS IN PHYSICS RESEARCH. SECTION A: ACCELERATORS, SPECTROMETERS, DETECTORS, AND ASSOCIATED EQUIPMENT.** Text in English, French, German; Summaries in English. 1957. 42/yr. EUR 11,176 in Europe to institutions; JPY 1,483,100 in Japan to institutions; USD 12,501 elsewhere to institutions (effective 2012). adv. bk.rev. illus. index. back issues avail.; reprints avail. **Document type:** *Journal, Academic/Scholarly.* **Description:** Publishes papers on particle accelerators and other devices producing and measuring nuclear radiations.
Supersedes in part (in 1984): Nuclear Instruments and Methods in Physics Research (0167-5087); Which was formerly (until 1981): Nuclear Instruments and Methods (0029-554X); (until 1958): Nuclear Instruments (0369-643X)
Related titles: Microform ed.: (from PQC); Online - full text ed.: ISSN 1872-9576 (from IngentaConnect, ScienceDirect).
Indexed: A&ATA, A01, A03, A08, A20, A22, A26, A33, A40, ASCA, C&ISA, C33, CA, CIN, CMCI, CPEI, Cadscan, ChemAb, ChemTitl, CompAb, CurCont, E&CAJ, EIA, EnerInd, EngInd, EnvAb, EnvInd, GeoRef, I05, INIS AtomInd, ISMEC, ISR, Inspec, LeadAb, P30, P34, PhysBer, RefZh, S01, SCI, SolStAb, SpeleolAb, T02, TM, W07, Zincscan.
—BLDSC (6180.861300), AskIEEE, CASDDS, IE, Infotrieve, Ingenta, INIST, Linda Hall. **CCC.**
Published by: Elsevier BV, North-Holland (Subsidiary of: Elsevier Science & Technology), Sara Burgerhartstraat 25, Amsterdam, 1055 KV, Netherlands. TEL 31-20-4853911, FAX 31-20-4852457, JournalsCustomerServiceEMEA@elsevier.com. Ed. W Barletta. **Subscr. to:** Elsevier BV, Radarweg 29, PO Box 211, Amsterdam 1000 AE, Netherlands. TEL 31-20-4853757, FAX 31-20-4853432, http://www.elsevier.nl.

539.7 NLD ISSN 0168-583X
CODEN: NIMBEU

➤ **NUCLEAR INSTRUMENTS & METHODS IN PHYSICS RESEARCH. SECTION B: BEAM INTERACTIONS WITH MATERIALS AND ATOMS.** Text in English. 1957. 24/yr. EUR 10,980 in Europe to institutions; JPY 1,457,900 in Japan to institutions; USD 12,283 elsewhere to institutions (effective 2012). adv. bk.rev. illus. Index. back issues avail.; reprints avail. **Document type:** *Journal, Academic/Scholarly.* **Description:** Covers all aspects of the interaction of energetic beams with atoms, molecules and aggregate forms of matter.
Supersedes in part (in 1984): Nuclear Instruments and Methods in Physics Research (0167-5087); Which was formerly (until 1981): Nuclear Instruments and Methods (0029-554X); (until 1958): Nuclear Instruments (0369-643X)
Related titles: Microform ed.: (from PQC); Online - full text ed.: ISSN 1872-9584 (from IngentaConnect, ScienceDirect).
Indexed: A01, A03, A08, A20, A22, A26, A28, A40, AESIS, APA, ASCA, BrCerAb, C&ISA, C33, CA, CA/WCA, CIA, CPEI, CerAb, ChemAb, ChemTitl, CivEngAb, CompAb, CorrAb, CurCont, E&CAJ, E11, EEA, EMA, ESPM, EngInd, EnvEAb, EnvInd, GeoRef, H15, I05, INIS AtomInd, ISR, Inspec, M&TEA, M09, MBF, METADEX, MSB, MSCI, P30, RILM, RefZh, S01, SCI, SCOPUS, SolStAb, SpeleolAb, T02, T04, TM, VITIS, W07, WAA.
—BLDSC (6180.861320), AskIEEE, CASDDS, IE, Infotrieve, Ingenta, INIST, Linda Hall. **CCC.**
Published by: Elsevier BV (Subsidiary of: Elsevier Science & Technology), Radarweg 29, PO Box 211, Amsterdam, 1000 AE, Netherlands. TEL 31-20-4853911, FAX 31-20-4852457, JournalsCustomerServiceEMEA@elsevier.com. Eds. C Trautmann, Lynn E Rehn, M B H Breese. **Subscr. to:** Radarweg 29, PO Box 211, Amsterdam 1000 AE, Netherlands. TEL 31-20-4853757, FAX 31-20-4853432.

➤ **NUCLEAR MEDICINE AND BIOLOGY.** *see* MEDICAL SCIENCES—Radiology And Nuclear Medicine

539.7 GBR ISSN 1061-9127
QC770

➤ **NUCLEAR PHYSICS NEWS.** Text in English. 1990. q. GBP 571 combined subscription in United Kingdom to institutions (print & online eds.); EUR 755, USD 947 combined subscription to institutions (print & online eds.) (effective 2012). adv. back issues avail.; reprint service avail. from PSC. **Document type:** *Journal, Academic/Scholarly.* **Description:** Provides information on modern research in nuclear physics.
Formerly (until 1991): European Nuclear Physics News (1050-6896)
Related titles: Microform ed.; Online - full text ed.: ISSN 1931-7336. GBP 514 in United Kingdom to institutions; EUR 679, USD 853 to institutions (effective 2012) (from IngentaConnect).
Indexed: A01, A03, A08, A22, CA, E01, E14, P52, T02.
—IE, Ingenta. **CCC.**
Published by: (Nuclear Physics European Collaboration Committee CHE), Taylor & Francis Ltd. (Subsidiary of: Taylor & Francis Group), 4 Park Sq, Milton Park, Abingdon, Oxfordshire OX14 4RN, United Kingdom. TEL 44-20-70176000, FAX 44-20-70176336, subscriptions@tandf.co.uk, http://www.taylorandfrancis.com. Ed. Gabriele-Elisabeth Koerner TEL 49-89-28912293. Adv. contacts Linda Hann, Maureen Williams. **Subscr. to:** Journals Customer Service, Sheepen Pl, Colchester, Essex CO3 3LP, United Kingdom. TEL 44-20-70175544, FAX 44-20-70175198, tf.enquiries@tfinforma.com.

539 NLD ISSN 0375-9474
QC173 CODEN: NUPABL

➤ **NUCLEAR PHYSICS, SECTION A.** Text in English, French, German. 1956. 68/yr. EUR 8,058 in Europe to institutions; JPY 1,069,600 in Japan to institutions; USD 9,015 elsewhere to institutions (effective 2012). adv. bk.rev. charts. index. back issues avail. **Document type:** *Journal, Academic/Scholarly.* **Description:** Covers the domain of general nuclear physics together with intermediate energy and heavy-ion physics and astrophysics.
Supersedes in part (in 1967): Nuclear Physics (0029-5582)
Related titles: Microform ed.: (from PQC); Online - full text ed.: ISSN 1873-1554 (from IngentaConnect, ScienceDirect).
Indexed: A01, A03, A08, A22, A26, ASCA, C33, CA, CIN, Cadscan, ChemAb, ChemTitl, CurCont, I05, INIS AtomInd, ISR, Inspec, LeadAb, MathR, P30, PhysBer, RefZh, S01, SCI, SCOPUS, T02, W07, Z02, Zincscan.
—BLDSC (6182.010000), AskIEEE, CASDDS, IE, Infotrieve, Ingenta, INIST, Linda Hall. **CCC.**
Published by: Elsevier BV, North-Holland (Subsidiary of: Elsevier Science & Technology), Sara Burgerhartstraat 25, Amsterdam, 1055 KV, Netherlands. TEL 31-20-4853911, FAX 31-20-4852457, JournalsCustomerServiceEMEA@elsevier.com. Eds. A Gal, G E Brown. **Subscr. to:** Elsevier BV, Radarweg 29, PO Box 211, Amsterdam 1000 AE, Netherlands. TEL 31-20-4853757, FAX 31-20-4853432, http://www.elsevier.nl.

539 NLD ISSN 0550-3213
QC173 CODEN: NUPBBO

➤ **NUCLEAR PHYSICS, SECTION B.** Text in Dutch. 1956. 54/yr. EUR 6,620 in Europe to institutions; JPY 879,400 in Japan to institutions; USD 7,405 elsewhere to institutions (effective 2012). index. back issues avail.; reprints avail. **Document type:** *Journal, Academic/Scholarly.* **Description:** Focuses on the domain of high energy physics and quantum field theory, and includes sections on cosmology, astrophysics and gravitation, computer simulations in physics and methods in theoretical physics.
Supersedes in part (in 1967): Nuclear Physics (0029-5582)
Related titles: Microform ed.: (from PQC); Online - full text ed.: ISSN 1873-1562 (from IngentaConnect, ScienceDirect); ◆ Supplement(s): Nuclear Physics, Section B, Proceedings Supplements. ISSN 0920-5632.
Indexed: A01, A03, A08, A22, A26, ASCA, C13, C33, CA, CCMJ, ChemAb, ChemTitl, CurCont, I05, INIS AtomInd, ISR, Inspec, MSN, MathR, PhysBer, RefZh, S01, SCI, SCOPUS, T02, W07, Z02.
—BLDSC (6182.020000), AskIEEE, CASDDS, IE, Infotrieve, Ingenta, INIST, Linda Hall. **CCC.**
Published by: Elsevier BV, North-Holland (Subsidiary of: Elsevier Science & Technology), Sara Burgerhartstraat 25, Amsterdam, 1055 KV, Netherlands. TEL 31-20-4853911, FAX 31-20-4852457, JournalsCustomerServiceEMEA@elsevier.com. Eds. G Altarelli, W Bartel. **Subscr.:** Elsevier BV, Radarweg 29, PO Box 211, Amsterdam 1000 AE, Netherlands. TEL 31-20-4853757, FAX 31-20-4853432, http://www.elsevier.nl.

539.7 NLD ISSN 0920-5632
QC770 CODEN: NPBSE7

➤ **NUCLEAR PHYSICS, SECTION B, PROCEEDINGS SUPPLEMENTS.** Text in English. 1987. 12/yr. EUR 3,996 in Europe to institutions; JPY 530,900 in Japan to institutions; USD 4,471 elsewhere to institutions (effective 2012). back issues avail. **Document type:** *Proceedings, Academic/Scholarly.* **Description:** Proceedings of large international conferences and specialized meetings in the field of high energy physics, covering developments in experimental and particle theory physics, hadronic physics, cosmology, astrophysics and gravitation, field theory, and statistical systems.
Related titles: Microform ed.: (from PQC); Online - full text ed.: ISSN 1873-3832 (from IngentaConnect, ScienceDirect); ◆ Supplement to: Nuclear Physics, Section B. ISSN 0550-3213.
Indexed: A01, A03, A08, A22, A26, A33, C33, CA, CCMJ, CIN, ChemAb, ChemTitl, I05, INIS AtomInd, ISR, Inspec, MSN, MathR, RefZh, S01, SCOPUS, T02, Z02.
—BLDSC (6182.050000), AskIEEE, CASDDS, IE, Infotrieve, Ingenta, INIST, Linda Hall. **CCC.**
Published by: Elsevier BV (Subsidiary of: Elsevier Science & Technology), Radarweg 29, PO Box 211, Amsterdam, 1000 AE, Netherlands. TEL 31-20-4853911, FAX 31-20-4852457, JournalsCustomerServiceEMEA@elsevier.com. **Subscr. to:** Radarweg 29, PO Box 211, Amsterdam 1000 AE, Netherlands. TEL 31-20-4853757, FAX 31-20-4853432.

539.7 USA ISSN 0147-2909

NUCLEAR REGULATORY COMMISSION ISSUANCES. Text in English. 1961. m. s-a & q. indexes. **Document type:** *Government.* **Description:** Contains opinions, decisions, denials, memorandum and orders of the Commission, the Atomic Safety and Licensing Appeal Board, the Atomic Safety and Licensing Board, and the Administrative Law Judge.
Formerly (until 1975): Atomic Energy Commission Reports. Opinions and Decisions of the Atomic Energy Commission with Selected Orders (0501-6355)
Published by: U.S. Nuclear Regulatory Commission, Washington, DC 20555. TEL 301-415-7000, 800-368-5642.

539.7 NLD ISSN 1001-8042
TK9001 CODEN: NSETEC

➤ **NUCLEAR SCIENCE AND TECHNIQUES.** Text in English. 1990. bi-m. (q. until 1994). EUR 422 in Europe to institutions; JPY 61,200 in Japan to institutions; USD 538 elsewhere to institutions (effective 2008). adv. 64 p./no.; **Document type:** *Journal, Academic/Scholarly.* **Description:** Publishes new and important results of researches and applications in all branches of nuclear science and technology as well as their interdiscipline studies in materials, automation, life, medicine, agriculture, earth, oceanology, environment, archaeology, energy resource sciences, etc.
Related titles: Online - full text ed.: ISSN 2210-3147; ◆ Chinese ed.: Hejishu. ISSN 0253-3219.
Indexed: C&ISA, CIN, ChemAb, ChemTitl, E&CAJ, EngInd, INIS AtomInd, Inspec, RefZh, SCI, SCOPUS, SolStAb, W07.
—BLDSC (6183.157000), AskIEEE, CASDDS, IE, Ingenta.
Published by: (Chinese Nuclear Society CHN), Elsevier BV (Subsidiary of: Elsevier Science & Technology), Radarweg 29, PO Box 211, Amsterdam, 1000 AE, Netherlands. TEL 31-20-4853911, FAX 31-20-4852457, JournalsCustomerServiceEMEA@elsevier.com. Ed. De-Zhang Zhu.

P

539 621.48 USA ISSN 0029-5450
TK9001 CODEN: NUTYBB
➤ **NUCLEAR TECHNOLOGY.** Abbreviated title: N T. Text in English. 1965. m. USD 1,870 combined subscription in North America to institutions (print & online eds.); USD 1,918 combined subscription elsewhere to institutions (print & online eds.); USD 165 combined subscription per issue in North America to institutions (print & online eds.); USD 174 combined subscription per issue elsewhere to institutions (print & online eds.) (effective 2009). bk.rev. charts; illus.; stat. index. reprints avail. **Document type:** *Journal, Academic/Scholarly.* **Description:** Presents information on all areas of the practical application of nuclear science. Topics include all aspects of reactor technology: operations, safety materials, instrumentation, fuel, and waste management.
Former titles (until 1971): Nuclear Applications and Technology (0550-3043); (until 1969): Nuclear Applications (0894-0401)
Related titles: Online - full text ed.: ISSN 1943-7471.
Indexed: A&ATA, A05, A22, A23, A24, A28, APA, AS&TI, ASCA, B04, B13, B21, BrCerAb, C&ISA, C10, C33, CA, CA/WCA, CADCAM, CIA, CIN, CMCI, CPEI, Cadscan, CerAb, ChemAb, ChemTitl, CivEngAb, CorrAb, CurCont, E&CAJ, E11, E14, EEA, EIA, EMA, ESPM, EngInd, EnvAb, EnvEAb, F&EA, FR, GeoRef, H&SSA, H15, IBR, IBZ, INIS AtomInd, ISMEC, ISR, Inspec, LeadAb, M&TEA, M09, MBF, METADEX, P30, PollutAb, RASB, SCI, SCOPUS, SolStAb, SpeleolAb, T02, T04, W07, WAA, Zincscan.
—BLDSC (6183.520000), AskIEEE, CASDDS, IE, Infotrieve, Ingenta, INIST, Linda Hall. **CCC.**
Published by: American Nuclear Society, Inc., 555 N Kensington Ave, La Grange Park, IL 60526. TEL 708-352-6611, 800-323-3044, FAX 708-352-0499, members@ans.org, http://www.ans.org. Ed. Nicholas Tsoulfanidis TEL 708-579-8281. **Subscr. to:** 97781 Eagle Way, Chicago, IL 60678. TEL 708-352-6611, FAX 708-352-0499, subs@ans.org. **Co-sponsor:** European Nuclear Society.

➤ **NUKLEONIKA**; the international journal of nuclear research. *see* ENERGY—Nuclear Energy

539 JPN
O U L N S. ANNUAL REPORT. (Osaka University Laboratory of Nuclear Studies) Text in English. 1962. a. exchange basis. 200 p./no.; back issues avail. **Document type:** *Bulletin, Trade.* **Description:** Reports research activities from various divisions of O.U.L.N.S.
Formerly (until 1998): Osaka University. Laboratory of Nuclear Studies. Annual Report (0473-4580)
Published by: Osaka University, Laboratory of Nuclear Studies/Oosaka Daigaku Rigaku-Kenkyu-Ka Genshikaku Kenkyu Shisetsu, 1-1 Machikaneyama-cho, Toyonaka-shi, Osaka-fu 560-0043, Japan. FAX 81-6-6850-5516. Eds. A Sakaguchi, A Sato, R Hazama, Y Fujita. R&P Y Fujita. Circ: 300.

OAK RIDGE NATIONAL LABORATORY. REVIEW; the laboratory's research and development magazine. *see* ENERGY

539.7 JPN ISSN 0919-3952
CODEN: ODCEEX
OOSAKA DAIGAKU CHODENDO EREKUTORONIKUSU KENKYU SENTA HOKOKU/OSAKA UNIVERSITY. RESEARCH CENTER FOR SUPERCONDUCTING MATERIALS AND ELECTRONICS. ANNUAL PROGRESS REPORT. Text in Japanese; Summaries in English. 1981. a. **Document type:** *Academic/Scholarly.*
Formerly (until 1990): Osaka Daigaku Chodendo Kogaku Jikken Senta Hokoku - Osaka University. Laboratory for Applied Superconductivity. Annual Progress Report
Indexed: ChemAb, ChemTitl.
—CASDDS.
Published by: Oosaka Daigaku, Chodendo Erekutoronikusu Kenkyu Senta, 2-1 Yamada-Oka, Suita-shi, Osaka-fu 565-0871, Japan.

539.7 530.1 USA ISSN 2162-2450
▼ ➤ **OPEN JOURNAL OF MICROPHYSICS.** Abbreviated title: O J M. Text in English. 2011. q. USD 156 (effective 2011). **Document type:** *Journal, Academic/Scholarly.* **Description:** Provides a platform for scientists and academicians all over the world to promote, share, and discuss various new issues and developments in different areas of microphysics.
Related titles: Online - full text ed.: ISSN 2162-2469. free (effective 2011).
Published by: Scientific Research Publishing, Inc., PO Box 54821, Irvine, CA 92619. service@scirp.org.

539.1 GBR ISSN 0956-9545
OXFORD SERIES ON NEUTRON SCATTERING IN CONDENSED MATTER. Text in English. 1989. irreg., latest vol.15, 2008. price varies. back issues avail. **Document type:** *Monographic series, Academic/Scholarly.*
Published by: Oxford University Press, Great Clarendon St, Oxford, OX2 6DP, United Kingdom. TEL 44-1865-556767, FAX 44-1865-556646, enquiry@oup.co.uk, http://www.oup-usa.org/catalogs/general/series/. **Orders in N. America to:** Oxford University Press, 2001 Evans Rd, Cary, NC 27513. TEL 919-677-0977 ext 5777, 800-852-7323, FAX 919-677-1714, jnlorders@oup-usa.org, http://www.us.oup.com.

539.7 GBR
OXFORD SERIES ON SYNCHROTRON RADIATION. Text in English. 1996. irreg., latest 2009. price varies. back issues avail. **Document type:** *Monographic series, Academic/Scholarly.*
—BLDSC (6321.019800).
Published by: Oxford University Press, Great Clarendon St, Oxford, OX2 6DP, United Kingdom. TEL 44-1865-556767, FAX 44-1865-556646, enquiry@oup.co.uk, http://www.oup-usa.org/catalogs/general/series/.

539.2 DEU ISSN 0341-6747
CODEN: PARADH
P T B-BERICHT. RADIOAKTIVITAET. (Physikalisch-Technische Bundesanstalt) Text in English, German. 1971. irreg., latest vol.51, 2006. price varies. **Document type:** *Monographic series, Academic/Scholarly.*
Indexed: GeoRef, Inspec.
Published by: (Physikalisch-Technische Bundesanstalt), Wirtschaftsverlag N W - Verlag fuer Neue Wissenschaft GmbH, Buergermeister-Smidt-Str 74-76, Bremerhaven, 27568, Germany. TEL 49-471-945440, FAX 49-471-9454477, info@nw-verlag.de, http://www.nw-verlag.de.

539 PHL ISSN 0079-1490
QC770 CODEN: PNUJAB
PHILIPPINES NUCLEAR JOURNAL. Text in English. 1966. a. USD 20. **Document type:** *Government.*
Indexed: INIS AtomInd, IPP.
—Linda Hall.
Published by: Philippine Nuclear Research Institute, Commonwealth Ave, Diliman, Quezon City, Philippines. FAX 63-2-920-1646. Ed. Teresa Y Nazarea. R&P Alumanda M Delarosa TEL 63-2-929-6011. Circ: 500.

539.2 JPN ISSN 0916-0604
PHOTON FACTORY NEWS. Text in Japanese. 1983. q. **Document type:** *Newsletter.*
Published by: (Hoshako Kenkyu Shisetsu/Photon Factory), Koenerugi Kasokuki Kenkyu Kiko/High Energy Accelerator Research Organization, 1-1, Oho, Tsukuba-shi, Ibaraki-ken 305-0801, Japan. TEL 81-298-64-5137, FAX 81-298-64-4604, adm-journhushiryou1@ccgemail.kek.jp, http://www.kek.jp.

539.7 USA ISSN 0556-2813
QC770 CODEN: PRVCAN
➤ **PHYSICAL REVIEW C (NUCLEAR PHYSICS).** Text in English. 1970. m. USD 1,325 combined subscription domestic to institutions academic (online & print eds.); USD 1,450 combined subscription foreign to institutions academic (online & print eds.) (effective 2011). bibl.; illus. s-a. index. back issues avail.; reprints avail. **Document type:** *Journal, Academic/Scholarly.* **Description:** Contains research articles reporting experimental and theoretical results in all aspects of nuclear physics.
Supersedes in part (1893-1969): Physical Review (0031-899X)
Related titles: CD-ROM ed.; Microfiche ed.: (from BHP); Online - full text ed.: ISSN 1089-490X. USD 945 to institutions academic (effective 2011).
Indexed: A22, ASCA, ApMecR, C13, C33, CIN, CPI, Cadscan, ChemAb, ChemTitl, CurCont, IBR, IBZ, INIS AtomInd, ISR, Inspec, LeadAb, MathR, P30, PhysBer, RefZh, SCI, SCOPUS, SPINweb, W07, Zincscan.
—BLDSC (6476.060000), AskIEEE, CASDDS, IE, Infotrieve, Ingenta, INIST, Linda Hall. **CCC.**
Published by: American Physical Society, One Physics Ellipse, College Park, MD 20740. TEL 301-209-3200, FAX 301-209-0865, subs@aps.org, http://www.aps.org. Ed. Benjamin F. Gibson. **Subscr. to:** APS Subscription Services, Ste. 1N01, 2 huntington Quadrangle, Melville, NY 11747-4502. TEL 800-344-6902.

539.7 USA ISSN 1550-7998
QC721 CODEN: PRDPC8
➤ **PHYSICAL REVIEW D (PARTICLES, FIELDS, GRAVITATION AND COSMOLOGY).** Text in English. 1893. 24/yr. USD 4,935 combined subscription domestic to institutions academic (print & online eds.); USD 5,370 combined subscription foreign to institutions academic (print & online eds.) (effective 2011). bibl.; illus. s-a. index. back issues avail.; reprints avail. **Document type:** *Journal, Academic/Scholarly.* **Description:** Covers elementary particle physics, field theory, relativity and cosmology.
Formerly (until 2004): Physical Review. D. Particles and Fields (0556-2821); Which superseded in part (in 1970): Physical Review (0031-899X)
Related titles: CD-ROM ed.; Microfiche ed.: (from BHP); Online - full text ed.: ISSN 1089-4918. USD 3,690 to institutions (effective 2011).
Indexed: A22, ASCA, ApMecR, C13, C33, CCMJ, CPI, ChemAb, ChemTitl, CurCont, IBR, IBZ, INIS AtomInd, ISR, Inspec, MSN, MathR, P30, PhysBer, RefZh, SCI, SCOPUS, SPINweb, W07, Z02.
—BLDSC (6476.070100), AskIEEE, CASDDS, IE, Ingenta, INIST, Linda Hall. **CCC.**
Published by: American Physical Society, One Physics Ellipse, College Park, MD 20740. TEL 301-209-3200, FAX 301-209-0865, subs@aps.org, http://www.aps.org. Eds. D. L. Nordstrom, Erick J. Weinberg. **Subscr. to:** APS Subscription Services, Ste. 1N01, 2 huntington Quadrangle, Melville, NY 11747-4502. TEL 800-344-6902.

539.7 GBR
CODEN: ASRGDU
➤ **PHYSICS AND TECHNOLOGY OF PARTICLE AND PHOTON BEAMS.** Text in English. 1978. irreg., latest 2002. price varies. **Document type:** *Monographic series, Academic/Scholarly.*
Formerly (until 1994): Accelerators and Storage Rings Series (0272-5088)
—BLDSC (6478.273000).
Published by: Taylor & Francis Ltd. (Subsidiary of: Taylor & Francis Group), 4 Park Sq, Milton Park, Abingdon, Oxfordshire OX14 4RN, United Kingdom. TEL 44-1235-828600, FAX 44-1235-829000, info@tandf.co.uk, http://www.tandf.co.uk/journals.

539.7 NLD ISSN 0375-9601
QC1 CODEN: PYLAAG
➤ **PHYSICS LETTERS. SECTION A: GENERAL, ATOMIC AND SOLID STATE PHYSICS.** Key Title: Physics Letters A. Text in Dutch. 1962. 48/yr. EUR 6,183 in Europe to institutions; JPY 821,200 in Japan to institutions; USD 6,915 elsewhere to institutions (effective 2012). illus. Index. back issues avail.; reprints avail. **Document type:** *Journal, Academic/Scholarly.* **Description:** Covers all fields of physics, excluding nuclear and particle physics.
Supersedes in part (in 1967): Physics Letters (0031-9163)
Related titles: Microform ed.: (from PQC); Online - full text ed.: ISSN 1873-2429 (from IngentaConnect, ScienceDirect).
Indexed: A01, A03, A08, A22, A26, A28, APA, ASCA, AcoustA, BrCerAb, C&ISA, C33, CA, CA/WCA, CCMJ, CIA, CMCI, Cadscan, CerAb, ChemAb, CivEngAb, CorrAb, CurCont, E&CAJ, E11, EEA, EMA, ESPM, EnvEAb, GeoRef, H15, I05, ISR, Inspec, LeadAb, M&TEA, M09, MBF, METADEX, MSN, MathR, P30, PhilInd, PhysBer, RefZh, S01, SCI, SCOPUS, SolStAb, SpeleolAb, T02, T04, W07, WAA, Z02, Zincscan.
—BLDSC (6478.761000), AskIEEE, CASDDS, IE, Infotrieve, Ingenta, INIST, Linda Hall. **CCC.**
Published by: Elsevier BV, North-Holland (Subsidiary of: Elsevier Science & Technology), Sara Burgerhartstraat 25, Amsterdam, 1055 KV, Netherlands. TEL 31-20-4853911, FAX 31-20-4852457, JournalsCustomerServiceEMEA@elsevier.com. Eds. A R Bishop, C R Doering, V M Agranovich. **Subscr.:** Elsevier BV, Radarweg 29, PO Box 211, Amsterdam 1000 AE, Netherlands. TEL 31-20-4853757, FAX 31-20-4853432.

539.7 NLD ISSN 0370-2693
QC1 CODEN: PYLBAJ
➤ **PHYSICS LETTERS. SECTION B: NUCLEAR, ELEMENTARY PARTICLE AND HIGH-ENERGY PHYSICS.** Key Title: Physics Letters B. Text in English. 1962. 60/yr. EUR 4,763 in Europe to institutions; JPY 633,300 in Japan to institutions; USD 5,329 elsewhere to institutions (effective 2012). illus. Index. reprints avail. **Document type:** *Journal, Academic/Scholarly.* **Description:** Presents new results in nuclear and particle physics.
Supersedes in part (in 1967): Physics Letters (0031-9163)
Related titles: Microform ed.: (from PQC); Online - full text ed.: ISSN 1873-2445 (from IngentaConnect, ScienceDirect).
Indexed: A01, A03, A08, A20, A22, A26, ASCA, C13, C33, CA, CCMJ, Cadscan, ChemAb, CompR, CurCont, I05, ISR, Inspec, LeadAb, MSN, MathR, P30, PhysBer, RefZh, S01, SCI, SCOPUS, T02, W07, Z02, Zincscan.
—BLDSC (6478.762000), AskIEEE, CASDDS, IE, Infotrieve, Ingenta, INIST, Linda Hall. **CCC.**
Published by: Elsevier BV, North-Holland (Subsidiary of: Elsevier Science & Technology), Sara Burgerhartstraat 25, Amsterdam, 1055 KV, Netherlands. TEL 31-20-4853911, FAX 31-20-4852457, JournalsCustomerServiceEMEA@elsevier.com, http://www.elsevier.nl/homepage/about/us/regional_sites.htt. Eds. L Rolandi, M Doser, W D Schlatter. **Subscr.:** Elsevier BV, Radarweg 29, PO Box 211, Amsterdam 1000 AE, Netherlands. TEL 31-20-4853757, FAX 31-20-4853432.

539 RUS ISSN 1063-7788
QC770 CODEN: PANUEO
➤ **PHYSICS OF ATOMIC NUCLEI.** Text in English. 1965. m. EUR 6,628, USD 8,028 combined subscription to institutions (print & online eds.) (effective 2012). charts; stat. back issues avail. **Document type:** *Journal, Academic/Scholarly.* **Description:** Covers studies of few-body nuclear systems, usual, exotic and superheavy nuclei, heavy ion collisions, hadron-nuclear interactions, and hadronic and quark-gluon matter at high temperature and density.
Formerly (until 1993): Soviet Journal of Nuclear Physics (0038-5506)
Related titles: Microform ed.; Online - full text ed.: ISSN 1562-692X (from IngentaConnect); ◆ Translation of: Yadernaya Fizika. ISSN 0044-0027.
Indexed: A01, A02, A03, A08, A20, A22, A26, ASCA, C33, CA, CCMJ, CPI, ChemAb, CurCont, E01, E04, E05, E14, GPAA, I05, INIS AtomInd, ISR, Inspec, MSN, MathR, PhysBer, S01, SCI, SCOPUS, SPINweb, T02, W07, Z02.
—BLDSC (0416.826000), AskIEEE, East View, IE, Infotrieve, Ingenta, INIST, Linda Hall. **CCC.**
Published by: (Rossiiskaya Akademiya Nauk/Russian Academy of Sciences), M A I K Nauka - Interperiodica (Subsidiary of: Pleiades Publishing, Inc.), Profsoyuznaya ul 90, Moscow, 117997, Russian Federation. TEL 7-095-3347420, FAX 7-095-3360666, compmg@maik.ru. Ed. Yurii G Abov. **Dist. in the Americas by:** Springer New York LLC, Journal Fulfillment, PO Box 2485, Secaucus, NJ 07096. TEL 212-460-1500, FAX 201-348-4505; **Dist. outside of the Americas by:** Springer, Haber Str 7, Heidelberg 69126, Germany. TEL 49-6221-3454303, FAX 49-6221-3454229.

539.7 RUS ISSN 0204-3467
QC175.4.A1 CODEN: PLDSFC
➤ **PHYSICS OF LOW-DIMENSIONAL STRUCTURES.** Text in English, Russian. 12/yr. USD 180 foreign to individuals; USD 340 foreign for institutions and libraries. **Document type:** *Journal, Academic/Scholarly.* **Description:** Presents papers in the field of solid state sciences and ultra-high vacuum technologies dealing with atomic clusters, chains, interfaces, overlayers, heterostructure and nanostructures.
Indexed: CurCont, Inspec, MSCI, SCOPUS.
—BLDSC (6478.768000), IE, Ingenta.
Published by: (Rossiiskaya Akademiya Nauk, Institut Fiziki Tverdogo Tela/Russian Academy of Sciences, Institute of Solid State Physics), V S V Co. Ltd., P O Box 11, Moscow, 105523, Russian Federation. Ed. V A Grazhulis.

539.7 RUS ISSN 1063-7796
QC793 CODEN: PPNUER
➤ **PHYSICS OF PARTICLES AND NUCLEI.** Text in English. 1970 (vol.3). bi-m. USD 4,064 in North America; USD 4,317 elsewhere (effective 2004). bibl.; charts; illus. index. back issues avail. **Document type:** *Journal, Academic/Scholarly.* **Description:** Contains articles or experimental and theoretical research in high-energy and nuclear physics and related instrumentation.
Formerly: Soviet Journal of Particles and Nuclei (0090-4759)
Related titles: Microform ed.; ◆ Translation of: Fizika Elementarnykh Chastits i Atomnogo Yadra. ISSN 0367-2026.
Indexed: A22, A26, ASCA, CIN, CPI, ChemAb, ChemTitl, CurCont, E01, I05, Inspec, MathR, PhysBer, SCI, SCOPUS, SPINweb, W07.
—BLDSC (0416.863000), AskIEEE, CASDDS, IE, Infotrieve, Ingenta, INIST. **CCC.**
Published by: (American Institute of Physics USA), M A I K Nauka - Interperiodica (Subsidiary of: Pleiades Publishing, Inc.), Profsoyuznaya ul 90, Moscow, 117997, Russian Federation. TEL 7-095-3347420, FAX 7-095-3360666, compmg@maik.ru, http://www.maik.ru. Ed. Vladimir G Kadyshevskii. R&P Vladimir I Vasil'ev. **Subscr. to:** Interperiodica, PO Box 1831, Birmingham, AL 35201-1831. TEL 205-995-1567, 800-633-4931, FAX 205-995-1588.

539.7 RUS ISSN 1547-4771
QC793
PHYSICS OF PARTICLES AND NUCLEI LETTERS/PIS'MA O FIZIKE ELEMENTARNYKH CHASTITS I ATOMNOGO YADRA. Text in English, Russian. 1984. bi-m. USD 4,064 in North America; USD 4,317 elsewhere (effective 2004). **Document type:** *Journal, Academic/Scholarly.* **Description:** Covers the results of applied, experimental, methodical, scientific, and theoretical research conducted in the areas of physics, radiology, ecology, and nuclear medicine.
Formerly (until 2000): Kratkie Soobscheniya O I Y A I (0234-5366)
Related titles: Online - full text ed.: ISSN 1531-8567 (from IngentaConnect).
Indexed: A22, A26, E01, I05, Inspec, SCOPUS.
—BLDSC (0416.863100), IE, Ingenta. **CCC.**

Published by: (Joint Institute for Nuclear Research), M A I K Nauka - Interperiodica (Subsidiary of: Pleiades Publishing, Inc.), Profsoyuznaya ul 90, Moscow, 117997, Russian Federation. TEL 7-095-3347420, FAX 7-095-3360666, compmg@maik.ru. Ed. A. M. Baldin. **Subscr. to:** Interperiodica, PO Box 1831, Birmingham, AL 35201-1831. TEL 205-995-1567, 800-633-4931, FAX 205-995-1588.

539.7 UKR ISSN 1682-9344
➤ **PROBLEMS OF ATOMIC SCIENCE AND TECHNOLOGY. SERIES: PLASMA PHYSICS.** Text in English, Russian, Ukrainian. 1999. bi-m. **Document type:** *Journal, Academic/Scholarly.*
Indexed: SCOPUS.
Published by: Natsional'nyi Nauchnyi Tsentr Kharkovskii Fiziko-Tekhnicheskii Institut/National Science Center, Kharkov Institut of Physics and Technology, 1, Akademicheskaya Str, Kharkov, 61108, Ukraine. TEL 38-57-3356895, publisher@kipt.kharkov.ua, http://vant.kipt.kharkov.ua.

➤ **PROGRESS IN NUCLEAR MAGNETIC RESONANCE SPECTROSCOPY.** *see* CHEMISTRY—Analytical Chemistry

539.7 GBR ISSN 0146-6410
QC770 CODEN: PPNPDB
➤ **PROGRESS IN PARTICLE AND NUCLEAR PHYSICS.** Text in English. 1950. 4/yr. EUR 1,806 in Europe to institutions; JPY 240,000 in Japan to institutions; USD 2,022 elsewhere to institutions (effective 2012). index. back issues avail. **Document type:** *Journal, Academic/Scholarly.* **Description:** Aims to discuss new developments in the field at a level suitable for the general nuclear and particle physicist and also, in greater technical depth, to explore the most important advances in these areas.
Formerly (until 1978): Progress in Nuclear Physics (0079-659X)
Related titles: Microfilm ed.: (from PQC); Online - full text ed.: ISSN 1873-2224 (from IngentaConnect, ScienceDirect).
Indexed: A01, A03, A08, A22, A26, ASCA, C24, CA, CPEI, ChemAb, ChemTitl, CurCont, EngInd, I05, INIS AtomInd, ISR, Inspec, PhysBer, RefZh, S01, SCI, SCOPUS, T02, W07.
—BLDSC (6872.400000), AskIEEE, CASDDS, IE, Infotrieve, Ingenta, Linda Hall. **CCC.**
Published by: Pergamon (Subsidiary of: Elsevier Science & Technology), The Blvd, Langford Ln, East Park, Kidlington, Oxford OX5 1GB, United Kingdom. TEL 44-1865-843000, FAX 44-1865-843010, JournalsCustomerServiceEMEA@elsevier.com. Ed. Amand Faessler TEL 49-7071-2976370. **Subscr. to:** Elsevier BV, Radarweg 29, PO Box 211, Amsterdam 1000 AE, Netherlands. TEL 31-20-4853757, FAX 31-20-4853432, http://www.elsevier.nl.

539.764 JPN
PURAZUMA KAKU YUGO GAKKAI NENKAI YOKAI YOKOSHU/JAPAN SOCIETY OF PLASMA SCIENCES AND NUCLEAR FUSION RESEARCH. PREPRINTS OF ANNUAL MEETING. Text in English, Japanese. 1984. a. JPY 1,500.
Published by: Purazuma Kaku Yugo Gakkai/Japan Society of Plasma Science and Nuclear Fusion Research, 20-29 Nishiki 2-chome, Naka-ku, Nagoya-shi, Aichi-ken 460-0003, Japan. TEL 81-52-7353185, FAX 81-52-7353485, http://www.nifs.ac.jp/jspf/.

539.7 JPN ISSN 0918-7928
CODEN: PKYGE5
➤ **PURAZUMA KAKU YUGO GAKKAISHI/JOURNAL OF PLASMA AND FUSION RESEARCH.** Text in English, Japanese; Summaries in English. 1958. m. membership. **Document type:** *Journal, Academic/Scholarly.*
Formerly (until Feb.1993): Kaku Yugo Kenkyu - Nuclear Fusion (0451-2375)
Related titles: Online - full text ed.
Indexed: CIN, ChemAb, ChemTitl, INIS AtomInd, JPI.
—BLDSC (5040.548000), CASDDS. **CCC.**
Published by: Purazuma Kaku Yugo Gakkai/Japan Society of Plasma Science and Nuclear Fusion Research, 20-29 Nishiki 2-chome, Naka-ku, Nagoya-shi, Aichi-ken 460-0003, Japan. TEL 81-52-7353185, FAX 81-52-7353485, http://www.nifs.ac.jp/jspf/.

539.7 JPN
R C N P ANNUAL REPORT. Text and summaries in English. 1976. a. back issues avail. **Document type:** *Academic/Scholarly.*
Published by: Research Center for Nuclear Physics, Osaka University, 10-1 Mihogaoka, Ibaraki-shi, Osaka-fu 567-0047, Japan. TEL 81-6-879-8929, FAX 81-6-879-8899.

539 JPN ISSN 1344-3879
R I K E N - A F - N P. (Rikagaku Kenkyujo - Accelerator Facility - Nuclear Physics) Text in English. 1970. irreg. **Document type:** *Monographic series, Academic/Scholarly.*
Former titles: Riken. Cyclotron Report; I P C R Cyclotron Report
Published by: Institute of Physical and Chemical Research, Cyclotron Laboratory/Rikagaku Kenkyujo, Saikurotoron Kenkyushitsu, 2-1 Hirosawa, Wako-shi, Saitama-ken 351-0106, Japan. FAX 81-484-62-1554, TELEX 02962818-RIKEN-J.

R S O MAGAZINE. (Radiation Safety Officer) *see* OCCUPATIONAL HEALTH AND SAFETY

539.9 GBR ISSN 1042-0150
QD601.A1 CODEN: REDSEI
➤ **RADIATION EFFECTS AND DEFECTS IN SOLIDS.** Text in English. 1989. m. GBP 4,586 combined subscription in United Kingdom to institutions (print & online eds.); EUR 4,827, USD 6,061 combined subscription to institutions (print & online eds.) (effective 2012). adv. back issues avail.; reprint service avail. from PSC. **Document type:** *Journal, Academic/Scholarly.* **Description:** Publishes experimental and theoretical papers of both a fundamental and applied nature that contribute to the understanding of phenomena or defects induced by the interaction of all types of radiation with condensed matter.
Formed by the merger of (1969-1989): Radiation Effects (0033-7579); (1982-1989): Crystal Lattice Defects and Amorphous Materials (0732-8699); Which was formerly (1969-1982): Crystal Lattice Defects (0011-2305)
Related titles: CD-ROM ed.; Microform ed.; Online - full text ed.: ISSN 1029-4953. GBP 4,128 in United Kingdom to institutions; EUR 4,344, USD 5,455 to institutions (effective 2012) (from IngentaConnect).
Indexed: A01, A03, A08, A20, A22, A28, APA, ASCA, BrCerAb, C&ISA, C33, CA, CA/WCA, CIA, CPEI, CerAb, ChemAb, CivEngAb, CorrAb, CurCont, E&CAJ, E01, E04, E05, E11, EEA, EMA, ESPM, EngInd, EnvEAb, GeoRef, H15, IBR, IBZ, ISR, Inspec, M&TEA, M09, MBF, METADEX, MSCI, P26, P30, P52, P54, P56, PQC, S01, SCI, SCOPUS, SolStAb, SpeleolAb, T02, T04, W07, WAA.
—BLDSC (7227.957100), AskIEEE, CASDDS, IE, Infotrieve, Ingenta, INIST, Linda Hall. **CCC.**
Published by: Taylor & Francis Ltd. (Subsidiary of: Taylor & Francis Group), 4 Park Sq, Milton Park, Abingdon, Oxfordshire OX14 4RN, United Kingdom. TEL 44-20-70176000, FAX 44-20-70176336, subscriptions@tandf.co.uk, http://www.taylorandfrancis.com. Ed. D Fink. Adv. contact Linda Hann. **Subscr. to:** Journals Customer Service, Sheepen Pl, Colchester, Essex CO3 3LP, United Kingdom. TEL 44-20-70175544, FAX 44-20-70175198, tf.enquiries@tfinforma.com.

539.7 GBR ISSN 1350-4487
QC787.N78 CODEN: RMEAEP
➤ **RADIATION MEASUREMENTS.** Text in English. 1977. 10/yr. EUR 1,780 in Europe to institutions; JPY 236,300 in Japan to institutions; USD 1,989 elsewhere to institutions (effective 2012). abstr. index. back issues avail. **Document type:** *Journal, Academic/Scholarly.* **Description:** Provides a forum for the presentation of the latest developments in the broad field of ionizing radiation detection and measurement and publishes original papers on both fundamental and applied research.
Former titles (until 1994): Nuclear Tracks and Radiation Measurements (0969-8078); (until 1993): International Journal of Radiation Applications and Instrumentation. Part D: Nuclear Tracks and Radiation Measurements (1359-0189); (until 1986): Nuclear Tracks and Radiation Measurements (0735-245X); (until 1982): Nuclear Tracks (0191-278X); (until 1979): Nuclear Track Detection (0145-224X)
Related titles: Microfilm ed.: (from PQC); Online - full text ed.: (from IngentaConnect, ScienceDirect).
Indexed: A01, A03, A08, A20, A22, A26, ASCA, ASFA, B21, C33, CA, CIN, CPEI, ChemAb, ChemTitl, CurCont, ESPM, EngInd, FR, GeoRef, H&SSA, I05, INIS AtomInd, ISMEC, ISR, Inspec, M&GPA, P30, PhysBer, PollutAb, RefZh, S01, SCI, SCOPUS, SpeleolAb, T02, ToxAb, W07.
—BLDSC (7227.973000), AskIEEE, CASDDS, IE, Infotrieve, Ingenta, INIST, Linda Hall. **CCC.**
Published by: Pergamon (Subsidiary of: Elsevier Science & Technology), The Blvd, Langford Ln, East Park, Kidlington, Oxford OX5 1GB, United Kingdom. TEL 44-1865-843000, FAX 44-1865-843010, JournalsCustomerServiceEMEA@elsevier.com. Eds. F d'Errico, I Bailiff. **Subscr. to:** Elsevier BV, Radarweg 29, PO Box 211, Amsterdam 1000 AE, Netherlands. TEL 31-20-4853757, FAX 31-20-4853432, http://www.elsevier.nl.

539 541 GBR ISSN 0969-806X
QD601.A1 CODEN: RPCHDM
➤ **RADIATION PHYSICS AND CHEMISTRY.** Text in English, French, German, Russian. 1969. 12/yr. EUR 2,644 in Europe to institutions; JPY 350,500 in Japan to institutions; USD 2,955 elsewhere to institutions (effective 2012). adv. bk.rev. abstr. back issues avail. **Document type:** *Journal, Academic/Scholarly.* **Description:** Features papers dealing with the interaction of ionizing radiation with matter, the resultant physical and chemical changes, and the mechanisms involved, as well as papers dealing with applications and techniques.
Former titles (until 1993): International Journal of Radiation Applications and Instrumentation. Part C: Radiation Physics and Chemistry (1359-0197); (until 1986): Radiation Physics and Chemistry (0146-5724); (until 1977): International Journal for Radiation Physics and Chemistry (0020-7055)
Related titles: Microfilm ed.: (from PQC); Online - full text ed.: ISSN 1879-0895 (from IngentaConnect, ScienceDirect).
Indexed: A01, A03, A08, A20, A22, A26, A28, APA, ASCA, ASFA, B21, BrCerAb, C&ISA, C24, C33, CA, CA/WCA, CCI, CIA, CIN, CPEI, CerAb, ChemAb, ChemTitl, CivEngAb, CorrAb, CurCR, CurCont, E&CAJ, E11, EEA, EMA, EMBASE, ESPM, EngInd, EnvEAb, ExcerpMed, FR, H15, I05, INIS AtomInd, ISMEC, ISR, Inspec, M&TEA, M09, MBF, METADEX, MSCI, P30, PollutAb, R10, R16, Reac, RefZh, S01, SCI, SCOPUS, SolStAb, T02, T04, TM, W07, WAA.
—BLDSC (7227.984000), CASDDS, IE, Infotrieve, Ingenta, INIST, Linda Hall. **CCC.**
Published by: Pergamon (Subsidiary of: Elsevier Science & Technology), The Blvd, Langford Ln, East Park, Kidlington, Oxford OX5 1GB, United Kingdom. TEL 44-1865-843000, FAX 44-1865-843010, JournalsCustomerServiceEMEA@elsevier.com. Eds. Arne Miller, L. Wojnarovits, P M Bergstrom. **Subscr. to:** Elsevier BV, Radarweg 29, PO Box 211, Amsterdam 1000 AE, Netherlands. TEL 31-20-4853757, FAX 31-20-4853432, http://www.elsevier.nl.

363.7 GBR ISSN 0144-8420
R905 CODEN: RPDODE
➤ **RADIATION PROTECTION DOSIMETRY.** Abbreviated title: R P D. Text in English. 1981. 20/yr. GBP 1,693 in United Kingdom to institutions; EUR 2,541 in Europe to institutions; USD 3,388 in US & Canada to institutions; GBP 1,693 elsewhere to institutions; GBP 1,847 combined subscription in United Kingdom to institutions (print & online eds.); EUR 2,772 combined subscription in Europe to institutions (print & online eds.); USD 3,696 combined subscription in US & Canada to institutions (print & online eds.); GBP 1,847 combined subscription elsewhere to institutions (print & online eds.) (effective 2012). adv. bk.rev. 96 p./no. 2 cols./p.; back issues avail.; reprints avail. **Document type:** *Journal, Academic/Scholarly.* **Description:** Provides international coverage of biological aspects, physical concepts, external and internal dosimetry and monitoring, environmental and work place monitoring, as well as dosimetry monitoring related to the protection of patients.
Related titles: Online - full text ed.: ISSN 1742-3406. GBP 1,524 in United Kingdom to institutions; EUR 2,287 in Europe to institutions; USD 3,049 in US & Canada to institutions; GBP 1,524 elsewhere to institutions (effective 2012) (from IngentaConnect).
Indexed: A22, A34, A36, A37, ASCA, ASFA, B&BAb, B19, B21, BioEngAb, C24, C25, CA, CABA, CIN, ChemAb, ChemTitl, CurCont, D01, DIP, E01, E04, E05, E11, E12, EIA, EMBASE, ESPM, EnerInd, EnvAb, EnvInd, ExcerpMed, F08, F11, F12, FCA, FR, GH, H&SSA, H16, I11, IBR, IBZ, INIS AtomInd, ISR, IndVet, Inspec, LT, MEDLINE, N02, N03, P30, P33, P38, PGrRegA, PHN&I, PollutAb, R07, R08, R10, R11, R12, RRTA, Reac, RefZh, S12, S13, S16, SCI, SCOPUS, SoyAb, T02, T04, T05, TAR, ToxAb, TriticAb, VS, W07, W11.
—BLDSC (7227.993000), AskIEEE, CASDDS, GNLM, IE, Infotrieve, Ingenta, INIST, Linda Hall. **CCC.**
Published by: (Ramtrans Publishing), Oxford University Press, Great Clarendon St, Oxford, OX2 6DP, United Kingdom. TEL 44-1865-556767, FAX 44-1865-556646, enquiry@oup.co.uk, http://www.oxfordjournals.org. Ed. Dr. J C McDonald.

➤ **RADIATION PROTECTION MANAGEMENT;** the journal of applied health physics. *see* OCCUPATIONAL HEALTH AND SAFETY

615.842 USA ISSN 0033-7587
QC770 CODEN: RAREAE
➤ **RADIATION RESEARCH.** Text in English. 1954. m. USD 760 combined subscription in US & Canada to institutions; USD 860 combined subscription elsewhere to institutions; free to members (effective 2010). adv. bibl.; charts; illus. index. back issues avail. **Document type:** *Journal, Academic/Scholarly.* **Description:** Publishes original articles on the physical, chemical, and biological effects of radiation and on related subjects in the areas of physics, chemistry, biology, and medicine.
Related titles: Online - full text ed.: ISSN 1938-5404.
Indexed: A22, A28, A34, A35, A36, A37, ABS&EES, APA, ASCA, ASFA, AgBio, B21, B25, B27, BIOSIS Prev, BrCerAb, C&ISA, C25, C33, CA/WCA, CABA, CIA, CIN, CTA, CerAb, ChemAb, ChemTitl, ChemoAb, CivEngAb, CorrAb, CurCont, D01, DentInd, E&CAJ, E01, E04, E05, E11, E12, EEA, EMA, EMBASE, ESPM, EnerRev, EnvEAb, ExcerpMed, FCA, FR, GH, H15, IBR, IBZ, INIS AtomInd, ISR, IndMed, IndVet, Inpharma, Inspec, Kidney, M&TEA, M09, MBF, MEDLINE, METADEX, MycolAb, N02, N03, N04, NSA, P30, P32, P33, P40, PGegResA, PGrRegA, R10, RM&VM, Reac, SCI, SCOPUS, SolStAb, SoyAb, T04, T05, THA, ToxAb, VS, W07, W10, WAA.
—BLDSC (7228.000000), AskIEEE, CASDDS, GNLM, IE, Infotrieve, Ingenta, INIST, Linda Hall. **CCC.**
Published by: Radiation Research Society, 810 E 10th St, Lawrence, KS 66044 . TEL 800-627-0326, FAX 785-843-6153, info@radres.org. Ed. Sara Rockwell TEL 203-785-2963. **Subscr. to:** Allen Press Inc.

539.2 JPN ISSN 1347-1511
RADIATION SAFETY MANAGEMENT. Text in English. 2002. s-a. **Document type:** *Journal, Academic/Scholarly.*
—BLDSC (7228.011800).
Published by: Japanese Society of Radiation Safety Management/Nihon Houshasen Anzen Kanri Gakkai, Nagoya University, Radioisotope Research Center, Radiation Sciences Division, Furo-cho Chikusa-ku, Nagoya, 464-8602, Japan. TEL 81-52-7892569, FAX 81-52-7895048, maekoshi@met.nagoya-u.ac.jp, http://www.ric.nagoya-u.ac.jp/JRSM/index.html. Ed. Takayoshi Yamamoto.

539.2 PRT ISSN 0874-7016
RADIOPROTECCAO. Text in Portuguese. 1999. s-a. EUR 35 (effective 2004).
Indexed: INIS AtomInd.
—BLDSC (7240.033000).
Published by: Sociedade Portuguesa de Proteccao contra Radiacoes, Rua 5 de Outubro Lote 33 1E, Sao Joao da Talha, 2695-697, Portugal. TEL 351-21-9552062, FAX 351-21-9942077, geral@sppcr.online.pt, http://www.sppcr.online.pt/.

REFERATIVNYI ZHURNAL. YADERNAYA FIZIKA I FIZIKA YADERNYKH REAKTOROV; vypusk svodnogo toma. *see* PHYSICS—Abstracting, Bibliographies, Statistics

539 JPN ISSN 0289-842X
RIKAGAKU KENKYUJO ACCELERATOR PROGRESS REPORT/ RIKAGAKU KENKYUSHO KASOKUKI NENJI HOKOKU. Short title: R I K E N Accelerator Progress Report. Text in English. 1967. a. JPY 5,000. **Document type:** *Corporate.*
Former titles: I P C R Accelerator Progress Report; I P C R Cyclotron Progress Report
—Linda Hall.
Published by: Rikagaku Kenkyusho/Institute of Physical and Chemical Research, 2-1 Hirosawa, Wako shi, Saitama ken 3510106, Japan. TEL 81-48-462-1111, FAX 81-48-462-4714, 81-48-465-8048, hensan@postman.riken.go.jp, http://www.riken.go.jp.

539.7 JPN
RIKOGAKU NI OKERU DOI GENSO KENKYU HAPPYOKAI YOSHISHU/ANNUAL MEETING ON RADIOISOTOPES IN THE PHYSICAL SCIENCES AND INDUSTRIES. Text in Japanese. 1964. a.
Published by: Oyo Butsuri Gakkai Hoshasen Bunkakai/Japan Society of Applied Physics, 1-12-3 Kudan-Kita, Chiyoda-ku, Tokyo, 102-0073, Japan.

539.2 FRA ISSN 0982-8303
RISQUE ET PREVENTION. Text in French. 1987. a. **Document type:** *Bulletin.*
Indexed: INIS AtomInd.
Published by: Centre d'Etude sur l'Evaluation de la Protection dans le Domaine Nucleaire, BP 48, Fontenay-aux-Roses, 92263, France. TEL 33-1-58357467.

530 ROM
➤ **ROMANIAN PHYSICAL SOCIETY. NATIONAL CONFERENCE FOR PHYSICS. ABSTRACTS.** Text in Romanian. a. free. **Document type:** *Proceedings, Academic/Scholarly.*
Formerly (until 1990): Institutul de Fizica Atomica. Sesiunea Stiintifica Anuala de Comunicari; Program si Rezumate
Published by: Institutul de Fizica Atomica, PO Box MG-6, Bucharest-magurele, Romania. TEL 40-1-6807040, FAX 40-1-6122247. **Co-sponsor:** Romanian Physical Society.

539.2 JPN ISSN 0917-432X
CODEN: SKGJEP
S R KAGAKU GIJUTSU JOHO/S R SCIENCE AND TECHNOLOGY INFORMATION. Text in Japanese. 1991. m.
Published by: Kokido Hihari Kagaku Kenkyu Senta/Japan Synchrotron Radiation Research Institute, 1-1-1 Kouto Mikazuki-cho, Sayo-gun, Hyogo 679-5198, Japan. http://www.spring8.or.jp/index.html.

SCIENCE AND TECHNOLOGY OF NUCLEAR INSTALLATIONS. *see* ENERGY—Nuclear Energy

539.752 ARG ISSN 0327-3849
RA569 CODEN: SERAEB
SEGURIDAD RADIOLOGICA. Text in Spanish. 1983. q.
Formerly (until 1990): Sociedad Argentina de Radioproteccion. Boletin (0327-0009)
Indexed: INIS AtomInd.
Published by: Sociedad Argentina de Radioproteccion, Av del Libertador 8250, Buenos Aires, 1429, Argentina. sar@sede.arn.gov.ar.

P

SHIJIE HEDIZHI KEXUE/WORLD NUCLEAR GEOSCIENCE. *see* EARTH SCIENCES—Geology

539.76 JPN ISSN 0371-1838
QC793 CODEN: SOKEAK
SORYUSHIRON KENKYU/STUDY OF ELEMENTARY PARTICLES. Text in English, Japanese. 1948. m. JPY 14,400 domestic; JPY 16,500 foreign (effective 2003). abstr.; charts; illus. vol. index. 100 p./no.; back issues avail. **Document type:** *Journal, Academic/Scholarly.*
Indexed: RefZh.
—CASDDS, Linda Hall.
Published by: (Soryushiron Gurupu/Research Group on the Theory of Particle and Nuclear Physics), Soryushiron Kenkyu Henshubu, c/o Yukawa Hall, Kyoto University, Kyoto-shi, 606-8502, Japan. TEL 81-75-722-3540, FAX 81-75-722-6339. Ed. Naoki Sasakura. Circ: 400.

539.2 JPN ISSN 1347-104X
SPRING-8 NEMPOU. Text in English, Japanese. 1994. a.
Formerly (until 2002): SPring-8 Annual Report (1342-3053)
Indexed: INIS AtomInd.
Published by: Houshakou Riyou Kenkyuu Sokushin Kikou Koukido Hikari Kagaku Kenkyuu Senta/Japan Synchrotron Radiation Research Institute, 1-1-1 Kouto Mikazui-cho, Sayo-gun, Hyogo, 679-5198, Japan. TEL 81-791-582798.

539.2 JPN ISSN 1341-9668
SPRING-8 RIYOSHA JOHO/SPRING-8 INFORMATION. Text in Japanese. 1996. bi-m.
Indexed: INIS AtomInd.
Published by: Houshakou Riyou Kenkyuu Sokushin Kikou Koukido Hikari Kagaku Kenkyuu Senta/Japan Synchrotron Radiation Research Institute, 1-1-1 Kouto Mikazui-cho, Sayo-gun, Hyogo, 679-5198, Japan. TEL 81-791-582798.

539.2 JPN
SPRING EITO NYUSU/JAPAN SYNCHROTRON RADIATION RESEARCH INSTITUTE. NEWS. Text in Japanese. 1989. q. **Document type:** *Academic/Scholarly.*
Published by: Kokido Hihari Kagaku Kenkyu Senta/Japan Synchrotron Radiation Research Institute, 1-1-1 Kouto Mikazuki-cho, Sayo-gun, Hyogo 679-5198, Japan. http://www.spring8.or.jp/index.html.

539.2 JPN
SYNCHROTRON RADIATION LABORATORY. ACTIVITY REPORT. Text in English. a.
Published by: University of Tokyo, Institute for Solid State Physics/Tokyo Daigaku Bussei Kenkyujo, Kashiwanoha, Kashiwa-shi, Chiba, 277-8581, Japan. http://www.issp.u-tokyo.ac.jp/.

539.7 GBR ISSN 0894-0886
QC793.5.E627
➤ **SYNCHROTRON RADIATION NEWS.** Text in English. 1988. bi-m. GBP 693 combined subscription in United Kingdom to institutions (print & online eds.); EUR 914, USD 1,146 combined subscription to institutions (print & online eds.) (effective 2012). adv. back issues avail.; reprint service avail. from PSC. **Document type:** *Journal, Academic/Scholarly.* **Description:** Addresses the needs of synchrotron users worldwide.
Related titles: Microform ed.; Online - full text ed.: ISSN 1931-7344. GBP 623 in United Kingdom to institutions; EUR 823, USD 1,032 to institutions (effective 2012) (from IngentaConnect).
Indexed: A01, A03, A08, A22, A28, APA, BrCerAb, C&ISA, CA, CA/WCA, CIA, CerAb, CivEngAb, CorrAb, E&CAJ, E01, E11, EEA, EMA, ESPM, EnvEAb, H15, INIS AtomInd, Inspec, M&TEA, M09, MBF, METADEX, P30, P52, S01, SolStAb, T02, T04, WAA.
—IE, Ingenta, Linda Hall. **CCC.**
Published by: Taylor & Francis Ltd. (Subsidiary of: Taylor & Francis Group), 4 Park Sq, Milton Park, Abingdon, Oxfordshire OX14 4RN, United Kingdom. TEL 44-20-70176000, FAX 44-20-70176336, subscriptions@tandf.co.uk, http://www.taylorandfrancis.com. Ed. Heather Wagner. Adv. contacts Linda Hann, Maureen Williams. **Subscr. to:** Journals Customer Service, Sheepen Pl, Colchester, Essex CO3 3LP, United Kingdom. TEL 44-20-70175544, FAX 44-20-70175198, tf.enquiries@tfinforma.com.

539 CAN
T R I U M F ANNUAL REPORT SCIENTIFIC ACTIVITIES. (Tri-University Meson Facility) Text in English. 1967. a. free.
Formerly (until 1980): T R I U M F Annual Report (0082-6367)
Published by: T R I U M F, 4004 Wesbrook Mall, Vancouver, BC V6T 2A3, Canada. TEL 604-222-1047, FAX 604-222-1074, annrep@triumf.ca, http://www.triumf.ca/annrep. Ed. Dr. Martin Comyn.

539 CAN
T R I U M F FINANCIAL AND ADMINISTRATIVE ANNUAL REPORT. Text in English. 1980. a. free. **Document type:** *Corporate.* **Description:** Financial summary and review of current pure and applied research projects in subatomic physics at T R I U M F.
Published by: Tri-University Meson Facility, 4004 Wesbrook Mall, Vancouver, BC V6T 2A3, Canada. TEL 604-222-7354, FAX 604-222-1074. Ed., R&P Michael LaBrooy. Circ: 2,000.

TAIKI HOSHANO KANSOKU SEISEKI/BULLETIN OF ATMOSPHERIC RADIOACTIVITY. *see* METEOROLOGY

539.7 630 JPN ISSN 0916-8621
CODEN: TNDHE2
TOKYO NOGYO DAIGAKU AISOTOPU SENTA KENKYU HOKOKU/ TOKYO UNIVERSITY OF AGRICULTURE. ISOTOPE CENTER. BULLETIN. Text in English, Japanese; Summaries in English. 1980. irreg. **Document type:** *Bulletin.*
Indexed: CIN, ChemAb.
—CASDDS.
Published by: Tokyo Nogyo Daigaku, Aisotopu Senta, 1-1 Sakuragaoka 1-chome, Setagaya-ku, Tokyo, 156-0054, Japan.

539.7 CHN ISSN 1000-7512
QD466.5
TONGWEISU/JOURNAL OF ISOTOPES. Text in English. 1988. q. USD 16.40 (effective 2009). **Document type:** *Journal, Academic/Scholarly.*
Related titles: Online - full text ed.
Indexed: INIS AtomInd.
—BLDSC (5008.550810), East View.
Address: PO Box 275-65, Beijing, 102413, China. TEL 86-10-69357885, FAX 86-10-69357524. **Dist. by:** China International Book Trading Corp, 35 Chegongzhuang Xilu, Haidian District, PO Box 399, Beijing 100044, China. TEL 86-10-68412045, FAX 86-10-68412023, cibtc@mail.cibtc.com.cn, http://www.cibtc.com.cn.

539.735 JPN ISSN 0911-5730
QC787.S9
U V S O R ACTIVITY REPORT. (Ultraviolet Synchrotron Orbital Radiation Facility) Text in English. 1984. a. **Document type:** *Report, Academic/ Scholarly.*
Published by: Okazaki National Research Institutes, Institute for Molecular Science/Okazaki Kokuritsu Kyodo Kenkyu Kiko Bunshi Kagaku Kenkyujo, 38 Nishigonaka-Myodaiji-cho, Okazaki-shi, Aichi-ken 444-0000, Japan.

539.2 JPN
UCHU HOSHASEN SHINPOJUMU/SYMPOSIUM ON COSMIC RADIATION. Text in Japanese. 1972. a.
Published by: Institute of Space and Aeronautical Science/Uchu Kagaku Kenkyujo, 1-1 Yoshinodai 3-chome, Sagamihara-shi, Kanagawa-ken 229-0022, Japan.

539.758 JPN ISSN 1343-0297
QC793.5.N4628 CODEN: ARNRF4
UNIVERSITY OF TOKYO. INSTITUTE FOR SOLID STATE PHYSICS. NEUTRON SCATTERING LABORATORY. ACTIVITY REPORT ON NEUTRON SCATTERING RESEARCH. Text in English. 1994. a.
Indexed: INIS AtomInd.
Published by: University of Tokyo, Institute for Solid State Physics/Tokyo Daigaku Bussei Kenkyujo, Kashiwanoha, Kashiwa-shi, Chiba, 277-8581, Japan. http://www.issp.u-tokyo.ac.jp/.

539 USA ISSN 1935-4061
▼ **VIRTUAL JOURNAL OF ATOMIC QUANTUM FLUIDS.** Text in English. 2009 (Jul.). m. free (effective 2011). back issues avail. **Document type:** *Journal, Academic/Scholarly.* **Description:** Contains articles fall within a range of topical areas involving atomic quantum fluids.
Media: Online - full text.
Published by: (American Physical Society), American Institute of Physics, 1 Physics Ellipse, College Park, MD 20740. TEL 301-209-3100, FAX 301-209-0843, aipinfo@aip.org, http://www.aip.org. Ed. Wolfgang Ketterle.

VOPROSY ATOMNOI NAUKI I TEKHNIKI. SERIYA: FIZIKA RADIATSIONNOGO VOZDEISTVIYA NA RADIOELEKTRONNUYU APPARATURU. *see* ELECTRONICS

621.48 539.2 UKR ISSN 0134-5400
TA418.6
VOPROSY ATOMNOI NAUKI I TEKHNIKI. SERIYA: FIZIKA RADIATSIONNYKH POVREZHDENII I RADIATSIONNOYE MATERIALOVEDENIYE/PROBLEMS OF NUCLEAR SCIENCE AND ENGINEERING. SERIES: PHYSICS OF RADIATION DAMAGE AND RADIATION MATERIALS SCIENCE. Text in Russian. 1974. a. **Document type:** *Journal, Academic/Scholarly.* **Description:** Covers aspects of radiation defects in crystals, effect of radiation on structure and properties of materials, materials for nuclear reactors, equipment, and research methods.
Indexed: C&ISA, CorrAb, E&CAJ, INIS AtomInd, Inspec, SolStAb, WAA.
—Linda Hall. **CCC.**
Published by: Khar'kovskii Fiziko-Tekhnicheskii Institut, Natsional'nyi Nauchnyi Tsentr/Kharkov Institute of Physics and Technology, National Science Center, ul Akademicheskaya, 1, Khar'kov, 61108, Ukraine. TEL 380-572-3356895, FAX 380-572-351688, http://www.kipt.kharkov.ua/.

539.7 RUS
➤ **VOPROSY ATOMNOI NAUKI I TEKHNIKI. SERIYA: FIZIKA YADERNYKH REAKTOROV.** Text in Russian; Summaries in Russian, English. s-a. **Document type:** *Journal, Academic/Scholarly.*
Published by: Federal'noe Gosudarstvennoe Unitarnoe Predpriyatie Rossiiskii Federal'nyi Yadernyi Tsentr, Vserossiiskii Nauchno-Issledovatel'skii Institut Eksperimental'noi Fiziki, prospekt Mira 37, Sarov, Nizhegorodskaya oblast 607188, Russian Federation. TEL 7-83130-44802, FAX 7-83130-29494, staff@vniief.ru.

539.7 RUS ISSN 0202-3822
➤ **VOPROSY ATOMNOI NAUKI I TEKHNIKI. SERIYA: TERMOYADERNYI SINTEZ.** Text in Russian; Summaries in English, Russian. 1978. q. USD 40 foreign (effective 2011). bk.rev. abstr.; bibl.; charts. back issues avail. **Document type:** *Journal, Academic/ Scholarly.* **Description:** Publishes results of theoretical and experimental studies of fusion technological problems, projects of large facilities and economical aspects, results of conferences and international cooperation.
Related titles: Online - full text ed.
Indexed: RefZh.
Published by: Koordinatsionnyi Tsentr Upravlyaemyi Termoyadernyi Sintez - Mezhdunarodnye Proekty/International Fusion Project Coordinating Centre (Fusion-Centre), Pl. Kurchatova 1, Moscow, 123182, Russian Federation. TEL 7-499-1969831, FAX 7-499-9430023, alb@fc.iterru.ru, http://www.iterru.ru/FusionCentre/welcomfc.html. Ed. E P Velikhov. Circ: 300 (paid and controlled).

539.7 UKR ISSN 1562-6016
➤ **VOPROSY ATOMNOI NAUKI I TEKHNIKI. SERIYA: YADERNO-FIZICHESKIE ISSLEDOVANIYA.** Text in Russian. 1999. q. USD 585 foreign (effective 2011). **Document type:** *Journal, Academic/ Scholarly.*
Related titles: Online - full text ed.
Indexed: RefZh, SCI, W07.
—BLDSC (0041.730390).
Published by: Khar'kovskii Fiziko-Tekhnicheskii Institut, Natsional'nyi Nauchnyi Tsentr/Kharkov Institute of Physics and Technology, National Science Center, ul Akademicheskaya, 1, Khar'kov, 61108, Ukraine. TEL 380-572-3356895, FAX 380-572-351688, publisher@kipt.kharkov.ua, http://www.kipt.kharkov.ua/. Ed. I M Neklyudov. Circ: 250. **Dist. by:** East View Information Services, 10601 Wayzata Blvd, Minneapolis, MN 55305. TEL 952-252-1201, FAX 952-252-1202, info@eastview.com, http://www.eastview.com.

539.7 USA ISSN 2161-6795
▼ ➤ **WORLD JOURNAL OF NUCLEAR SCIENCE AND TECHNOLOGY.** Abbreviated title: W J N S T. Text in English. 2011. q. USD 117 (effective 2011). **Document type:** *Journal, Academic/ Scholarly.* **Description:** Provides a platform for publication of articles about nuclear science and technology and its applications.
Related titles: Online - full text ed.: ISSN 2161-6809. free (effective 2011).
Published by: Scientific Research Publishing, Inc., PO Box 54821, Irvine, CA 92619. service@scirp.org.

621.3848 CHN ISSN 1004-7859
TK6573
XIANDAI LEIDA/MODERN RADAR. Text in Chinese. 1979. m. USD 49.20 (effective 2009). **Document type:** *Journal, Academic/Scholarly.*
Related titles: Online - full text ed.
Indexed: A28, APA, BrCerAb, C&ISA, CA/WCA, CIA, CerAb, CivEngAb, CorrAb, E&CAJ, E11, EEA, EMA, ESPM, EnvEAb, H15, M&GPA, M&TEA, M09, MBF, METADEX, RefZh, SolStAb, T04, WAA.
—BLDSC (5894.770000), East View, Linda Hall.
Published by: Nanjing Dianzi Jishu Yanjiusuo/Nanjing Research Institute of Electronics Technology, PO Box 1313-110, Nanjing, 210013, China. TEL 86-25-83772727, FAX 86-25-83716482. Ed. Ling Chen.

539.7 UKR ISSN 1818-331X
➤ **YADERNA FIZYKA TA ENERHETYKA/NUCLEAR PHYSICS AND ATOMIC ENERGY.** Text in Ukrainian, Russian, English. 2000. q. **Document type:** *Journal, Academic/Scholarly.*
Formerly (until 2006): Instytut Yadernyh Doslidzhen'. Zbirnyk Naukovykh Prats' (1606-6723)
Related titles: Online - full text ed.: ISSN 2074-0565. free (effective 2011).
Indexed: SCOPUS.
—Linda Hall.
Published by: Natsional'na Akademiya Nauk Ukrainy, Instytut Yadernykh Doslidzhen', prospekt Nauky, 47, Kyiv, 03680, Ukraine. TEL 380-44-5252349, FAX 380-44-5254463, interdep@kinr.kiev.ua, http://www.kinr.kiev.ua. Ed. Ivan Vyshnevs'kyi.

539 RUS ISSN 0044-0027
QC770 CODEN: IDFZA7
YADERNAYA FIZIKA. Text in Russian. 1965. m. RUR 1,380 for 6 mos. domestic (effective 2004). charts. index. **Document type:** *Journal, Academic/Scholarly.* **Description:** Covers the experimental and theoretical strudies of nuclear physics: nuclear structure, spectra, and properties; radiation, fission, and nuclear reactions and symmetries; hadrons; particle collisions at high and superhigh energies; quark models, supersymmetry and supergravity, astrophysics and cosmology.
Related titles: Online - full text ed.; ◆ English Translation: Physics of Atomic Nuclei. ISSN 1063-7788.
Indexed: CIN, ChemAb, ChemTitl, INIS AtomInd, Inspec, PhysBer, RefZh.
—BLDSC (0399.780000), AskIEEE, CASDDS, East View, INIST, Linda Hall. **CCC.**
Published by: (Rossiiskaya Akademiya Nauk/Russian Academy of Sciences), Izdatel'stvo Nauka, Profsoyuznaya ul 90, Moscow, 117864, Russian Federation. TEL 7-095-3347151, FAX 7-095-4202220, secret@naukaran.ru, http://www.naukaran.ru. Circ: 1,000.

539.7 CHN ISSN 1009-1327
QA319
YINGYONG FANHAN FENXI XUEBAO/ACTA ANALYSIS FUNCTIONALIS APPLICATA. Text in Chinese. 1999. q. USD 20.80 (effective 2009). **Document type:** *Journal, Academic/Scholarly.*
Related titles: Online - full text ed.
Indexed: CCMJ, MSN, MathR, RefZh, Z02.
—BLDSC (0593.850000), East View.
Published by: (Zhongguo Yuanzineng Kexue Yanjiuyuan/China Institute of Atomic Energy), Kexue Chubanshe/Science Press, 16 Donghuang Cheng Genbei Jie, Beijing, 100717, China. TEL 86-10-64000246, FAX 86-10-64030255, http://www.sciencep.com/. Ed. Min-Zhu Yang. **Dist. by:** China International Book Trading Corp, 35 Chegongzhuang Xilu, Haidian District, PO Box 399, Beijing 100044, China. TEL 86-10-68412045, FAX 86-10-68412023, cibtc@mail.cibtc.com.cn, http://www.cibtc.com.cn.

539.7 CHN ISSN 1007-4627
CODEN: HEDOEW
➤ **YUANZI HEWULI PINGLUN/NUCLEAR PHYSICS REVIEW.** Text in Chinese; Abstracts in English. 1984. q. USD 35.60 (effective 2009). **Document type:** *Academic/Scholarly.* **Description:** Features specialists' reviews for the field of nuclear physics.
Formerly (until 1997): He Wuli Dongtai - Trends in Nuclear Physics (1003-9988)
Related titles: Online - full text ed.
Indexed: CIN, ChemAb, ChemTitl, INIS AtomInd.
—BLDSC (6182.423000), CASDDS.
Published by: (Zhongguo Kexueyuan/Chinese Academy of Sciences, Jindai Wuli Yanjiusuo/Institute of Modern Physics), Editorial Board of Nuclear Physics Review, P.O. Box 31, Lanzhou, Gansu 730000, China. TEL 86-931-8828960, FAX 86-931-8881100, TELEX 72153 IMP AS CN. Ed. Genming Jin. Circ: 1,200.

539.7 CHN ISSN 1000-0364
CODEN: YYFXEM
YUANZI YU FENZI WULI XUEBAO/JOURNAL OF ATOMIC AND MOLECULAR PHYSICS. Text in Chinese. 1984. q. USD 53.40 (effective 2009). **Document type:** *Journal, Academic/Scholarly.*
Related titles: Online - full text ed.
Indexed: INIS AtomInd.
—East View.
Published by: Zhongguo Wuli Xuehui/Chinese Physical Society, PO Box 603, Beijing, 100080, China. TEL 86-10-82649019, cps@aphy.iphy.ac.cn, http://www.cps-net.org.cn/. **Dist. by:** China International Book Trading Corp, 35 Chegongzhuang Xilu, Haidian District, PO Box 399, Beijing 100044, China. TEL 86-10-68412045, FAX 86-10-68412023, cibtc@mail.cibtc.com.cn, http://www.cibtc.com.cn.

539.7 JPN ISSN 0917-0731
YUKAI/FUSION SCIENCE ASSOCIATION. NEWS. Text in Japanese. 1990. irreg. (3-4/yr.). free. **Document type:** *Newsletter.* **Description:** Covers the latest news on fusion science and general science.
Published by: Kaku Yugo Kagaku Kenkyukai/Fusion Science Association, 14-12 Higashi-Sakura 1-chome, Higashi-ku, Nagoya-shi, Aichi-ken 461-0005, Japan. TEL 81-52-953-9846, FAX 81-52-953-9846. Eds. Noriyuki Inoue, Ritsuko Kondo.

PHYSICS—Optics

621.36 USA
TK6592.O6
ACQUISITION, TRACKING, POINTING, AND LASER SYSTEMS TECHNOLOGIES. Text in English. 1987. a. USD 70 per issue to non-members; USD 53 per issue to members (effective 2010). adv. back issues avail.; reprints avail. **Document type:** *Proceedings, Academic/Scholarly.*
Formerly (until 2007): Acquisition, Tracking, and Pointing (1050-5784)
—CCC.
Published by: S P I E - International Society for Optical Engineering, PO Box 10, Bellingham, WA 98227. TEL 360-676-3290, 888-504-8171, FAX 360-647-1445, customerservice@spie.org. Eds. Steven L Chodos, William E Thompson.

ADVANCED FUNCTIONAL MATERIALS. see CHEMISTRY—Electrochemistry

535.84 SGP ISSN 0218-0227
QD96.M65 CODEN: AMPSEF
ADVANCES IN MULTI-PHOTON PROCESSES AND SPECTROSCOPY. Text in English. 1984. irreg., latest vol.19, 2010. price varies. back issues avail. **Document type:** *Monographic series, Academic/Scholarly.* **Description:** Aims to publish a series that contains review papers readable not only by active researchers in the areas of multi-photon processes and spectroscopy, but also by those who are not experts in the field but who intend to enter the field.
Indexed: CIN, ChemAb, ChemTitl.
—BLDSC (0709.454000), CASDDS. **CCC.**
Published by: World Scientific Publishing Co. Pte. Ltd., 5 Toh Tuck Link, Singapore, 596224, Singapore. TEL 65-6466-5775, FAX 65-6467-7667, wspc@wspc.com.sg, http://www.worldscientific.com. Ed. S H Lin. **Dist. by:** World Scientific Publishing Co., Inc., 27 Warren St, Ste 401-402, Hackensack, NJ 07601. TEL 201-487-9655, 800-227-7562, FAX 201-487-9656, 888-977-2665, wspc@wspc.com; World Scientific Publishing Ltd., 57 Shelton St, London WC2H 9HE, United Kingdom. TEL 44-207-8360888, FAX 44-207-8362020, sales@wspc.co.uk.

535 NLD ISSN 1871-0018
ADVANCES IN NANO-OPTICS AND NANO-PHOTONICS. Text in English. 2006. irreg., latest vol.2, 2007. price varies. **Document type:** *Monographic series, Academic/Scholarly.*
Published by: Elsevier BV (Subsidiary of: Elsevier Science & Technology), Radarweg 29, PO Box 211, Amsterdam, 1000 AE, Netherlands. TEL 31-20-4853911, FAX 31-20-4852457, JournalsCustomerServiceEMEA@elsevier.com, http://www.elsevier.com.

535 USA ISSN 1687-6393
➤ **ADVANCES IN OPTICAL TECHNOLOGIES.** Text in English. 2007. irreg. USD 495 (effective 2011). **Document type:** *Journal, Academic/Scholarly.*
Related titles: Online - full text ed.: ISSN 1687-6407. free (effective 2011).
Indexed: A26, C10, CA, E08, I05, P52, T02.
—IE.
Published by: Hindawi Publishing Corporation, 410 Park Ave, 15th Fl, PMB 287, New York, NY 10022. FAX 866-446-3294, info@hindawi.com. Ed. H John Caulfield.

535 USA ISSN 1943-8206
▼ ➤ **ADVANCES IN OPTICS AND PHOTONICS.** Text in English. 2009. q. USD 489 (effective 2012). **Document type:** *Journal, Academic/Scholarly.*
Media: Online - full content.
—Linda Hall.
Published by: Optical Society of America, 2010 Massachusetts Ave, NW, Washington, DC 20036. TEL 202-416-1907, FAX 202-416-6140, info@osa.org, http://www.osa.org. Ed. Bahaa Saleh.

535 USA ISSN 1687-563X
➤ **ADVANCES IN OPTOELECTRONICS.** Text in English. 2007. irreg. USD 295 (effective 2011). **Document type:** *Journal, Academic/Scholarly.* **Description:** Aims to accelerate worldwide recognition, dissemination and utilization of the most recent findings and achievements in optoelectronics.
Related titles: Online - full text ed.: ISSN 1687-5648. free (effective 2011).
Indexed: A26, A28, A39, APA, BrCerAb, C&ISA, C10, C27, C29, CA, CA/WCA, CIA, CerAb, CivEngAb, CorrAb, D03, D04, E&CAJ, E11, E13, EEA, EMA, ESPM, EnvEAb, H15, I05, M&TEA, M09, MBF, METADEX, P52, R14, S06, S14, S15, S18, SCOPUS, SolStAb, T02, T04, WAA.
—IE.
Published by: Hindawi Publishing Corporation, 410 Park Ave, 15th Fl, PMB 287, New York, NY 10022. FAX 866-446-3294, info@hindawi.com.

535 HUN ISSN 1419-6301
TR845 CODEN: KEHTAS
AKUSZTIKAI SZEMLE/ACOUSTICAL REVIEW. Text in Hungarian; Summaries in English, German, Russian. 1955. bi-m. adv. charts; illus. **Document type:** *Journal, Academic/Scholarly.*
Formerly (until 1995): Kep- es Hangtechnika (0023-0480)
Indexed: Inspec, PhotoAb, RILM.
—AskIEEE, CASDDS, Linda Hall.
Published by: Optikai, Akusztikai, Film- es Szinhaztechnikai Tudomanyos Egyesulet, Fo utca 68, Budapest, 1027, Hungary. http://www.opakfi.hu. Circ: 900.

535 JPN ISSN 0919-4630
ALBUM OF VISUALIZATION. Text in Japanese; Summaries in English. 1984. a. JPY 35,000 to non-members; JPY 15,000 to members (effective 2006). **Document type:** *Journal, Academic/Scholarly.* **Description:** Covers visualization technology and computer-aided visualization.
Formerly: Nagare no Kashika Shashinshu - Photographic Journal of Flow Visualization (0914-3408)
Published by: Kashika Joho Gakkai/Visualization Society of Japan, 3-29-20 Kamijujo, Kita-ku, Tokyo, 114-0034, Japan. TEL 81-3-59935020, FAX 81-3-59935026, info@vsj.or.jp. Circ: 500.

535 USA ISSN 1087-6146
TK6592.S95
ALGORITHMS FOR SYNTHETIC APERTURE RADAR IMAGERY. Text in English. 1994. a. USD 80 per issue to non-members; USD 60 per issue to members (effective 2010). adv. back issues avail.; reprints avail. **Document type:** *Journal, Academic/Scholarly.*
—CCC.
Published by: S P I E - International Society for Optical Engineering, PO Box 10, Bellingham, WA 98227. TEL 360-676-3290, 888-504-8171, FAX 360-647-1445, customerservice@spie.org. Eds. Edmund G Zelnio, Frederick D Garber.

535.84 547 USA ISSN 1044-0305
QD96.M3 CODEN: JAMSEF
➤ **AMERICAN SOCIETY FOR MASS SPECTROMETRY. JOURNAL.** Text in English. 1990. 12/yr. EUR 508, USD 624 combined subscription to institutions (print & online eds.) (effective 2012). adv. illus. Index. back issues avail.; reprints avail. **Document type:** *Journal, Academic/Scholarly.* **Description:** Covers the fundamentals and applications of mass spectrometry. Principal focus is on research papers that present new and significant findings in all fields of scientific inquiry in which mass spectrometry can play a role.
Related titles: Online - full text ed.: ISSN 1879-1123 (from ScienceDirect).
Indexed: A01, A03, A08, A22, A26, A28, A40, APA, ASCA, B21, BrCerAb, C&ISA, C24, C33, CA, CA/WCA, CCI, CIA, CIN, CPEI, CerAb, ChemAb, ChemTitl, CivEngAb, CorrAb, CurCR, CurCont, E&CAJ, E11, EEA, EIA, EMA, EMBASE, ESPM, EngInd, EnvAb, EnvEAb, ExcerpMed, FS&TA, H15, I05, ISR, IndMed, Inspec, M&TEA, M09, MBF, MEDLINE, METADEX, MSB, NucAcAb, P30, R10, R16, Reac, RefZh, S01, SCI, SCOPUS, SolStAb, T02, T04, W07, WAA.
—BLDSC (4692.920000), AskIEEE, CASDDS, GNLM, IE, Infotrieve, Ingenta, INIST, Linda Hall. **CCC.**
Published by: (American Society for Mass Spectrometry), Springer New York LLC (Subsidiary of: Springer Science+Business Media), 233 Spring St, New York, NY 10013. TEL 212-460-1500, FAX 212-460-1575, journals-ny@springer.com. Ed. Michael L Gross. Circ: 5,110 (paid).

535 USA ISSN 0066-4103
QC490 CODEN: NMRPAJ
➤ **ANNUAL REPORTS ON N M R SPECTROSCOPY.** Text in English. 1968. a., latest vol.68, 2009. USD 224 per vol. (effective 2010). adv. back issues avail.; reprints avail. **Document type:** *Journal, Academic/Scholarly.* **Description:** For chemists and physicists to study the structure and dynamics of molecules.
Formerly (until 1970): Annual Review of N M R Spectroscopy (0066-4235).
Related titles: Online - full text ed.
Indexed: A22, C33, CIN, ChemAb, ChemTitl, Inspec, SCI, SCOPUS, W07.
—BLDSC (1513.400000), CASDDS, GNLM, IE, Ingenta, INIST, Linda Hall. **CCC.**
Published by: Academic Press (Subsidiary of: Elsevier Science & Technology), 3251 Riverport Ln, Maryland Heights, MO 63043. TEL 314-447-8010, FAX 314-447-8030, JournalCustomerService-usa@elsevier.com, http://www.elsevierdirect.com/imprint.jsp?iid=5. Ed. Graham Webb. Adv. contact Tino DeCarlo TEL 212-633-3815.

535 620 USA ISSN 1042-4687
TJ212.2
APPLICATIONS OF DIGITAL IMAGE PROCESSING. Text in English. 1977. a., latest 2007. adv. back issues avail.; reprints avail. **Document type:** *Proceedings, Academic/Scholarly.* **Description:** Theoretical approaches, specialized architectures, image coding, medical and various industrial applications.
—CCC.
Published by: (Society of Photo-Optical Instrumentation Engineers), S P I E - International Society for Optical Engineering, PO Box 10, Bellingham, WA 98227. TEL 360-676-3290, 888-504-8171, FAX 360-647-1445, customerservice@spie.org. Ed. Andrew G Tescher.

502.8 DEU ISSN 1860-0034
APPLIED ELECTRON MICROSCOPY/ANGEWANDTE ELEKTRONENMIKROSKOPIE. Text in English, German. 2004. irreg., latest vol.8, 2009. price varies. **Document type:** *Monographic series, Academic/Scholarly.*
Published by: Logos Verlag Berlin, Comeniushof, Gubener Str 47, Berlin, 10243, Germany. TEL 49-30-42851090, FAX 49-30-42851092, redaktion@logos-verlag.de. Ed. Josef Zweck.

535 USA ISSN 1559-128X
QC350
➤ **APPLIED OPTICS.** Abbreviated title: A O. Text in English. 2004. 36/yr. USD 4,987 combined subscription domestic to institutions (print & online eds.); USD 5,207 combined subscription in Canada to institutions (print & online eds.); USD 5,472 combined subscription elsewhere to institutions (print & online eds.) (effective 2012). adv. bk.rev. charts; illus.; pat.; abstr. cum.index: vols.1-36. back issues avail.; reprints avail. **Document type:** *Journal, Academic/Scholarly.*
Formed by the merger of (1990-2004): Applied Optics. Information Processing (1540-8973); (1995-2004): Applied Optics. Optical Technology and Biomedical Optics (1540-8981); (1991-2004): Applied Optics. Lasers, Photonics, and Environmental Optics (1540-899X); All of which superseded (1962-1990): Applied Optics (0003-6935)
Related titles: Online - full text ed.: ISSN 2155-3165. 1995. USD 3,907 to institutions (effective 2012).
Indexed: A05, A20, A22, A23, A24, A26, ABIPC, AIA, AS&TA, AS&TI, ASCA, ASFA, AcoustA, B&BAb, B04, B10, B13, B21, BioEngAb, C&ISA, C10, C13, CADCAM, CIN, CMCI, CPEI, Cadscan, ChemAb, ChemTitl, CompAb, CurCont, E&CAJ, E08, EMBASE, EngInd, ExcerpMed, FR, G08, GALA, GeoRef, I05, IBR, IBZ, INIS AtomInd, ISR, Inspec, LeadAb, M&GPA, MEDLINE, OceAb, P30, PhotoAb, PhysBer, R10, Reac, RefZh, S09, SCI, SCOPUS, SPINweb, SolStAb, SpeleolAb, TM, W07, Zincscan.
—BLDSC (1576.250000), AskIEEE, CASDDS, IE, Infotrieve, Ingenta, INIST, Linda Hall. **CCC.**
Published by: Optical Society of America, 2010 Massachusetts Ave, NW, Washington, DC 20036. TEL 202-416-1907, FAX 202-416-6140, info@osa.org, http://www.osa.org. Ed. Joseph N Mait.

535.84 USA ISSN 0570-4928
QC450 CODEN: APSRBB
➤ **APPLIED SPECTROSCOPY REVIEWS**; an international journal of principles, methods, and applications. Text in English. 1966. bi-m. GBP 1,921 combined subscription in United Kingdom to institutions (print & online eds.); EUR 2,536, USD 3,183 combined subscription to institutions (print & online eds.) (effective 2012). adv. charts; stat. reprint service avail. from PSC. **Document type:** *Journal, Academic/Scholarly.* **Description:** Provides information on principles, methods and applications of spectroscopy for the researcher and also presents discussions that relate physical concepts to chemical applications.
Related titles: Microform ed.: (from RPI); Online - full text ed.: ISSN 1520-569X. GBP 1,728 in United Kingdom to institutions; EUR 2,282, USD 2,865 to institutions (effective 2012) (from IngentaConnect).
Indexed: A01, A03, A08, A20, A22, A40, ASCA, B21, BibInd, CA, CCI, CIN, CPEI, Cadscan, ChemAb, ChemTitl, CurCont, E01, ESPM, EngInd, GeoRef, ISR, Inspec, LeadAb, MSCI, P26, P54, PQC, S01, SCI, SCOPUS, SWRA, SpeleolAb, T02, W07, Zincscan.
—AskIEEE, CASDDS, IE, Infotrieve, Ingenta, Linda Hall. **CCC.**
Published by: Taylor & Francis Inc. (Subsidiary of: Taylor & Francis Group), 325 Chestnut St, Ste 800, Philadelphia, PA 19106. TEL 215-625-2940, 800-354-1420, orders@taylorandfrancis.com, http://www.taylorandfrancis.com. Ed. Joseph Sneddon. Adv. contact Linda Hann TEL 44-1344-779945. Circ: 400.

535.84 IND ISSN 0971-9237
ASIAN JOURNAL OF SPECTROSCOPY. Text in English. 1997. q. **Document type:** *Journal, Academic/Scholarly.*
Related titles: Online - full text ed.
Indexed: SCOPUS.
—BLDSC (1742.577000).
Published by: Spectral-Force Publications, 32 E C Rd, Dehra Dun, 248 001, India. TEL 91-135-654386, FAX 91-1662-276240, jeff.church@tft.csiro.au.

525 USA
ASIAN SYMPOSIUM ON INFORMATION DISPLAY. PROCEEDINGS. Text in English. 199?. irreg., latest vol.9, 2006. price varies. back issues avail. **Document type:** *Proceedings, Trade.*
Published by: Society for Information Display, 1475 S Bascom Ave, Ste 114, Campbell, CA 95008. TEL 408-879-3901, FAX 408-879-3833, office@sid.org, http://www.sid.org.

AUSZUEGE AUS DEN EUROPAEISCHEN PATENTANMELDUNGEN. TEIL 2A. PHYSIK, OPTIK, AKUSTIK, FEINMECHANIK/EXTRACTS FROM EUROPEAN PATENT APPLICATIONS. PART 2A. PHYSICS, PRECISION ENGINEERING, OPTICS, ACOUSTICS. see PATENTS, TRADEMARKS AND COPYRIGHTS—Abstracting, Bibliographies, Statistics

535 621.39 RUS ISSN 0320-7102
CODEN: AVMEBI
➤ **AVTOMETRIYA.** Text and summaries in English, Russian. 1965. bi-m. RUR 580 for 6 mos. domestic; USD 163 foreign (effective 2005). back issues avail. **Document type:** *Journal, Academic/Scholarly.* **Description:** Covers solid state physics, optics and holygraphy applications to computers and measurement techniques; physical and applied aspects of micro- and optoelectronics; laser information technologies; systems and components.
Related titles: E-mail ed.; ◆ English ed.: Optoelectronics, Instrumentation and Data Processing. ISSN 8756-6990.
Indexed: C&ISA, CorrAb, E&CAJ, Inspec, RefZh, SCOPUS, SolStAb, WAA.
—BLDSC (0002.800000), East View, INIST, Linda Hall. **CCC.**
Published by: (Rossiiskaya Akademiya Nauk, Sibirskoe Otdelenie, Institut Avtomatiki i Elektrometrii), Izdatel'stvo Sibirskogo Otdeleniya Rossiiskoi Akademii Nauk/Publishing House of the Russian Academy of Sciences, Siberian Branch, Morskoi pr 2, a/ya 187, Novosibirsk, 630090, Russian Federation. TEL 7-3832-300570, FAX 7-3832-333755, psb@ad-sbras.nsc.ru, http://www-psb.ad-sbras.nsc.ru. Ed. Semen T Vas'kov. Circ: 300. **Dist. by:** Informnauka Ltd., Ul Usievicha 20, Moscow 125190, Russian Federation. alfimov@viniti.ru.

621.36 DEU ISSN 0945-084X
BERICHTE AUS DER LASERTECHNIK. Text in German. 1993. irreg., latest 2008. price varies. **Document type:** *Monographic series, Academic/Scholarly.*
Published by: Shaker Verlag GmbH, Kaiserstr 100, Herzogenrath, 52134, Germany. TEL 49-2407-95960, FAX 49-2407-95969, info@shaker.de.

BIO-OPTICS WORLD; advances in lasers, optics, and imaging for the life sciences. see BIOLOGY—Biotechnology

631.3 USA
▼ ➤ **BIOMEDICAL OPTICS EXPRESS.** Text in English. 2010 (Aug.). m. free (effective 2012). **Document type:** *Journal, Academic/Scholarly.* **Description:** Focuses on biomedical optics and photonics.
Media: Online - full text.
Published by: Optical Society of America, 2010 Massachusetts Ave, NW, Washington, DC 20036. TEL 202-416-1907, FAX 202-416-6140, info@osa.org, http://www.osa.org. Ed. Joseph A Izatt.

▼ ➤ **BIOOPTICS WORLD.** see MEDICAL SCIENCES—Ophthalmology And Optometry

535 541 CHN ISSN 1000-4556
QC762 CODEN: BOZAE2
➤ **BOPUXUE ZAZHI/CHINESE JOURNAL OF MAGNETIC RESONANCE.** Text in Chinese, English. 1983. q. USD 26.80 (effective 2009). adv. abstr.; bibl.; charts; illus. 96 p./no.; back issues avail. **Document type:** *Journal, Academic/Scholarly.* **Description:** Covers results of scientific research, new techniques and applications in magnetic resonance spectroscopy.
Related titles: ◆ CD-ROM ed.: Chinese Academic Journals Full-Text Database. Science & Engineering, Series A. ISSN 1007-8010; Online - full content ed.; Online - full text ed.
Indexed: A22, C33, CIN, ChemAb, ChemTitl, RefZh.
—BLDSC (3180.369200), CASDDS, East View, IE, Ingenta.
Published by: Wuhan Institute of Physics and Mathematics, PO Box 71010, Wuhan, 430071, China. magres@wipm.ac.cn. Ed. Maili Lu. R&P Shizhen Mao TEL 86-27-87197126. adv.: B&W page USD 100. Circ: 600 (paid); 200 (controlled).

535 JPN
BUNKAKAI NIHON KOGAKKAI SAMA SEMINA RONBUNSHU/OPTICAL SOCIETY OF JAPAN. PROCEEDINGS OF THE SUMMER SEMINAR. Text in English, Japanese; Summaries in English. a. **Document type:** *Proceedings.*

Published by: (Optical Society of Japan), Japan Society of Applied Physics/Oyo Butsuri Gakkai, Kudan-Kita Bldg 5th Fl, 1-12-3 Kudan-Kita, Chiyoda-ku, Tokyo, 102-0073, Japan.

535.84 JPN ISSN 0038-7002
QC450 CODEN: BUKKAT
BUNKO KENKYU/SPECTROSCOPICAL SOCIETY OF JAPAN. JOURNAL. Text in Japanese; Summaries in English. 1951. bi-m. membership. adv. bk.rev. bibl.; charts; illus. Index. **Document type:** *Journal, Academic/Scholarly.*
Indexed: A22, AESIS, CIN, ChemAb, ChemTitl, INIS AtomInd, Inspec, JTA, RefZh.
—BLDSC (4902.500000), AskIEEE, CASDDS, IE, Ingenta, INIST, Linda Hall. **CCC.**
Published by: Nihon Bunko Gakkai/Spectroscopical Society of Japan, Clean Bldg, 1-13 Kanda-Awaji-cho, Chiyoda-ku, Tokyo, 101-0063, Japan. TEL 81-3-32532747, FAX 81-3-32532740, bunko-jimu@mbm.nifty.com. Ed. Yoshihiro F Mizugai. Adv. contact Kagaku Gijutsu Sha. Circ: 2,000.

535 617.7 658.8 GBR ISSN 1474-3191
BUSINESS RATIO REPORT. THE OPTICAL INDUSTRY. Text in English. 1980. a., latest no.29, 2008, Jun. GBP 365 per issue (effective 2010). charts; stat. back issues avail. **Document type:** *Report, Trade.* **Description:** Covers companies active in the optical industry.
Former titles (until 2001): Business Ratio. The Optical Industry (1470-7152); (until 2000): Business Ratio Plus: Optical Industry (1354-8735); (until 1994): Business Ratio Report. Optical Industry (0261-9172)
Published by: Key Note Ltd. (Subsidiary of: Bonnier Business Information), Harlequin House, 5th Fl, 7 High St, Teddington, Richmond upon Thames, TW11 8EE, United Kingdom. TEL 44-845-5040452, FAX 44-845-5040453, sales@keynote.co.uk.

535 GBR ISSN 0959-6208
CODEN: CSMOEI
CAMBRIDGE STUDIES IN MODERN OPTICS. Text in English. 1983. irreg., latest vol.25, 2006. price varies. back issues avail.; reprints avail. **Document type:** *Monographic series, Academic/Scholarly.* **Description:** Contains books on all aspects of theoretical and applied modern optics.
Indexed: CIN, ChemAb, ChemTitl.
—CASDDS.
Published by: Cambridge University Press, The Edinburgh Bldg, Shaftesbury Rd, Cambridge, CB2 8RU, United Kingdom. TEL 44-1223-312393, FAX 44-1223-315052, journals@cambridge.org, http://www.cambridge.org/uk. Eds. A Miller, P L Knight. R&P Linda Nicol TEL 44-1223-325702. Adv. contact Rebecca Roberts TEL 44-1223-325083.

535.84 CAN ISSN 1205-6685
CODEN: CJASFA
➤ **CANADIAN JOURNAL OF ANALYTICAL SCIENCES AND SPECTROSCOPY.** Text in English, French. 1963. q. CAD 190 domestic; CAD 200 foreign (effective 2000). adv. bk.rev. charts; illus. index. reprints avail. **Document type:** *Journal, Academic/Scholarly.* **Description:** For all branches of fundamental and applied spectroscopy.
Former titles (until 1996): Canadian Journal of Applied Spectroscopy (1183-7306); (until 1990): Canadian Journal of Spectroscopy (0045-5105); Supersedes: Canadian Spectroscopy (0008-5057)
Indexed: A22, A28, A40, ABIPC, APA, ASCA, BrCerAb, C&ISA, CA/WCA, CIA, CIN, Cadscan, CerAb, ChemAb, ChemTitl, CivEngAb, CorrAb, E&CAJ, E11, EEA, EMA, GeoRef, H15, INIS AtomInd, ISR, Inspec, LeadAb, M&TEA, M09, MBF, METADEX, MSB, SCOPUS, SolStAb, SpeleolAb, T04, WAA, Zincscan.
—BLDSC (3028.400000), AskIEEE, CASDDS, IE, Infotrieve, Ingenta, INIST, Linda Hall. **CCC.**
Published by: Canadian Society for Analytical Sciences and Spectroscopy, c/o Marc M Lamoureux, Dept of Chemistry, St Mary's University, Halifax,, NS B3H 3C3, Canada. http://csass.org. Ed. Ricardo Aroca TEL 519-253-3000 ext 3528. Circ: 1,500.

535.84 CAN ISSN 0381-5447
QC451
CANADIAN SPECTROSCOPIC NEWS. Text in English. 1971. 3/yr. free to members. bk.rev. bibl. **Document type:** *Newsletter.*
Related titles: Online - full content ed.
Published by: Canadian Society for Analytical Sciences and Spectroscopy, c/o Marc M Lamoureux, Dept of Chemistry, St Mary's University, Halifax,, NS B3H 3C3, Canada. TEL 902-420-5652, FAX 902-496-8104, marc.lamoureux@smu.ca. Ed. Marc M Lamoureux. Circ: 400.

CHALCOGENIDE LETTERS. *see* PHYSICS

535.58 CHN ISSN 1671-7694
QC350 CODEN: CJOEE3
➤ **CHINESE OPTICS LETTERS.** Text in English. 1992. m. USD 1,179 combined subscription in United States (print & online eds.); USD 1,234 combined subscription in Canada & Mexico (print & online eds.); USD 1,304 combined subscription elsewhere (print & online eds.) (effective 2012). 96 p./no.; **Document type:** *Journal, Academic/Scholarly.* **Description:** Contains research papers in the field of laser science and electro-optics.
Formerly: Chinese Journal of Lasers (1004-2822)
Related titles: Online - full text ed.; ◆ Chinese ed.: Zhongguo Jiguang. ISSN 0258-7025.
Indexed: A28, APA, BrCerAb, C&ISA, CA/WCA, CIA, CPEI, CerAb, CivEngAb, CorrAb, E&CAJ, E11, EEA, EMA, EngInd, H15, Inspec, M&TEA, M09, MBF, METADEX, SCI, SCOPUS, SolStAb, T04, W07, WAA.
—BLDSC (3181.032500), East View, IE, Ingenta. **CCC.**
Published by: Chinese Optical Society, PO Box 800-211, Shanghai, 201800, China. TEL 86-21-69918198, FAX 86-21-69918800. **Subscr. to:** Optical Society of America, PO Box 1976, Baltimore, MD 21290-8329. elec@osa.org, http://www.osa.org.

535 640 JPN
COLOR. Text in Japanese. 1969. q.
Published by: Japan Color Research Institute/Nihon Shikisai Kenkyujo, 1-19 Nishi-Azabu 3-chome, Minato-ku, Tokyo, 106-0031, Japan.

535 USA
CONFERENCE ON LASERS AND ELECTRO-OPTICS (YEAR). Variant title: C L E O (Year). Text in English. 1980. biennial. adv. back issues avail. **Document type:** *Proceedings, Trade.*
Former titles (until 2003): Conference on Lasers and Electro-optics. Technical Digest; (until 2000): Conference on Lasers and Electro-optics. Summaries of Papers Presented at the Conference on Lasers and Electro-optics (Postconference Edition) (1054-0393); (until 1988): Conference on Lasers and Electro-optics. Digest of Technical Papers (Postconference Edition) (1054-0377); (until 1987): Conference on Lasers and Electro-optics. Digest of Technical Papers; Which was formed by the merger of (19??-1981): I E E E / O S A Conference on Laser Engineering and Applications. Digest of Technical Papers (0099-121X); (1976-1981): Conference on Laser and Electrooptical Systems. Digest of Technical Papers
Related titles: Online - full text ed.
—BLDSC (4363.012500). **CCC.**
Published by: I E E E, 445 Hoes Ln, Piscataway, NJ 08855. contactcenter@ieee.org, http://www.ieee.org.

621.36 USA
CONFERENCE ON LASERS AND ELECTRO-OPTICS EUROPE. PROCEEDINGS. Text in English. 1994. biennial. back issues avail. **Document type:** *Proceedings, Trade.* **Description:** Provides a forum for an update and review of a wide range of laser and electro-optics disciplines including device development, systems engineering and applications.
Related titles: Online - full text ed.
Published by: I E E E, 445 Hoes Ln, Piscataway, NJ 08855. contactcenter@ieee.org, http://www.ieee.org. **Co-sponsor:** I E E E Lasers and Electro-Optics Society.

535 621.36 USA ISSN 1097-2137
TA1750
CONFERENCE ON OPTOELECTRONIC AND MICROELECTRONIC MATERIALS AND DEVICES. PROCEEDINGS. Text in English. 19??. biennial. adv. back issues avail. **Document type:** *Proceedings, Trade.*
Related titles: Online - full text ed.
—CCC.
Published by: I E E E, 445 Hoes Ln, Piscataway, NJ 08855. contactcenter@ieee.org, http://www.ieee.org.

621.36 USA ISSN 0589-7483
CORNING RESEARCH. Text in English. a. **Document type:** *Report, Trade.*
Indexed: C&ISA, CorrAb, E&CAJ, SolStAb, WAA.
—Linda Hall.
Published by: Corning, Inc., One Riverfront Plaza, Corning, NY 14831-0001. TEL 607-974-9000.

535 DNK ISSN 0901-4632
D O P S - NYT. Text in Danish; Text occasionally in English. 1986. q. DKK 250 to individual members; DKK 1,650 to institutions; DKK 75 to students (effective 2008). adv. bk.rev. back issues avail. **Document type:** *Journal, Academic/Scholarly.*
Indexed: Inspec.
—BLDSC (3619.501000), AskIEEE, IE, Ingenta.
Published by: Dansk Optisk Selskab/Danish Optical Society, c/o Pia Joergensen, Ingenioerhoejskolen i Aarhus, Dalgas Ave. 2, Aarhus C, 8000, Denmark. Ed. Mike van der Poel TEL 45-45-253660. Adv. contact Karsten Rottwitt. page DKK 3,208.

535 621.3 CHN ISSN 1671-637X
DIANGUANG YU KONGZHI/ELECTRONICS OPTICS & CONTROL. Text in Chinese. 1970. m. CNY 240, USD 120; CNY 20 per issue (effective 2009). **Document type:** *Journal, Academic/Scholarly.*
Former titles (until 1986): Jizai Huokong/Airborne Fire Control; (until 1981): Hangkong Huokong Yicong/Airborne Fire Control Translations
Related titles: Online - full text ed.
Indexed: A28, APA, BrCerAb, C&ISA, CA/WCA, CIA, CerAb, CivEngAb, CorrAb, E&CAJ, E11, EEA, EMA, ESPM, EnvEAb, H15, M&TEA, M09, MBF, METADEX, SolStAb, T04, WAA.
—BLDSC (3580.121700), Linda Hall.
Published by: Zhongguo Hangkong Gongye Jituan Zhonggongsi, Luoyang Dian-Guang Shebei Yanjiusuo/Luoyang Institute of Electro-Optical Equipment of Aviation Industry Corporation of China (AVIC), PO Box 017-16, Luoyang, 471009, China. TEL 86-379-63327293, FAX 86-379-63938146, http://www.lieoe.com/. Ed. Hong-man Liu. Circ: 1,200.

621.36 GBR ISSN 2041-9023
▼ **E L I COURIER.** Text in English. 2009. q. back issues avail. **Document type:** *Newsletter, Trade.* **Description:** Contains information about extreme light infrastructure project, its physics and its participants to scientific research in lasers' field.
Related titles: Online - full text ed.: free (effective 2011).
Published by: (Extreme Light Infrastructure), Institute of Physics Publishing Ltd., Dirac House, Temple Back, Bristol, BS1 6BE, United Kingdom. TEL 44-117-9297481, FAX 44-117-9301178, http://publishing.iop.org/.

E M L A LASER HEALTH JOURNAL. (European Medical Laser Association) *see* MEDICAL SCIENCES—Experimental Medicine, Laboratory Technique

535.58 621.329 GBR ISSN 0013-4589
QC371 CODEN: EOPTA4
ELECTRO OPTICS. Text in English. 1968. bi-m. GBP 170; free to qualified personnel (effective 2009). adv. tr.lit. back issues avail. **Document type:** *Magazine, Trade.* **Description:** Contains news regarding lasers, optoelectronics, fiber optics, sensors, imaging displays and optics.
Incorporates (1968-1969): Laser Review
Related titles: Online - full text ed.: free (effective 2009).
Indexed: C10, ISR, Inspec.
—AskIEEE, IE, Infotrieve.
Published by: Europa Science Ltd., The Spectrum Bldg, Michael Young Ctr, Purbeck Rd, Cambridge, CB2 8PD, United Kingdom. TEL 44-1223-211208, FAX 44-1223-211107, tom.wilkie@europascience.com, http://www.europascience.com. Ed. Warren Clark TEL 44-1223-211196. Adv. contact Chris Lawrence TEL 44-1223-211158. Circ: 19,853.

ELECTRONIC MATERIALS AND PACKAGING; the newsletter of advanced electronic packaging. *see* ELECTRONICS

ELECTRONICAST PHOTONICS. *see* COMPUTERS—Computer Networks

535 USA ISSN 2161-2072
▼ **ENERGY EXPRESS.** Text in English. 2010. bi-m. free (effective 2012). back issues avail. **Document type:** *Journal, Academic/Scholarly.*
Media: Online - full text. **Related titles:** ◆ Supplement to: Optics Express. ISSN 1094-4087.
Published by: Optical Society of America, 2010 Massachusetts Ave, NW, Washington, DC 20036. TEL 202-223-8130, FAX 202-223-1096, info@osa.org, http://www.osa.org. Ed. Bernard Kippelen.

EUROLASER; Zeitschrift fuer die industrielle Laseranwendung. *see* ENGINEERING—Industrial Engineering

EUROPEAN FIBER OPTICS REPORT. *see* COMPUTERS—Computer Networks

535 DEU ISSN 1022-0151
EUROPEAN OPTICAL SOCIETY. ANNUAL MEETINGS DIGEST SERIES. Text in English. 1993. a. **Document type:** *Proceedings, Trade.*
—CCC.
Published by: European Optical Society, c/o Laser Zentrum Hannover, Hollerithallee 8, Hannover, 30419, Germany. TEL 49-511-2788115, FAX 49-511-2788119, bindig@myeos.org, http://www.myeos.org.

535 DEU ISSN 1990-2573
QC350
➤ **EUROPEAN OPTICAL SOCIETY. JOURNAL. RAPID PUBLICATIONS.** Text in English. 2006. irreg. free (effective 2011). adv. abstr.; bibl.; illus. Index. back issues avail. **Document type:** *Journal, Academic/Scholarly.*
Media: Online - full text.
Indexed: CurCont, SCI, SCOPUS, W07.
—CCC.
Published by: European Optical Society, c/o Laser Zentrum Hannover, Hollerithallee 8, Hannover, 30419, Germany. TEL 49-511-2788159, FAX 49-511-2788119, http://www.myeos.org. Ed. Mario Bertolotti. Pub. Hans Peter Herzig. Adv. contact Silke Kramprich.

535 USA
EUROPEAN QUANTUM ELECTRONICS CONFERENCE. PROCEEDINGS. Text in English. 19??. irreg., latest 2005. back issues avail. **Document type:** *Proceedings, Trade.* **Description:** Provides a forum for an update and review of a wide range of laser and electro-optics disciplines including device development, systems engineering and applications.
Formerly (until 1994): European Conference on Quantum Electronics. Proceedings
Related titles: Online - full text ed.
Published by: (Optical Society of America), I E E E, 445 Hoes Ln, Piscataway, NJ 08855. contactcenter@ieee.org, http://www.ieee.org.

535 USA ISSN 1091-6083
EUROPHONICS; european coverage of product developments in optics, lasers, imaging, fibre optics, electro-optics and optoelectronics. Text in German. 1996. bi-m. free to qualified personnel. adv. **Document type:** *Magazine, Trade.* **Description:** Provides in-depth coverage of the European photonics industry, reporting on business and technology news, new applications and techniques, conferences and exhibitions.
Indexed: TM.
Published by: Laurin Publishing Co., Inc., Berkshire Common, PO Box 4949, Pittsfield, MA 01202. TEL 413-499-0514, FAX 413-442-3180, http://www.europhotonics.com. adv.: B&W page USD 3,560, color page USD 5,120; trim 213 x 285.

EXTRACTS FROM INTERNATIONAL PATENT APPLICATIONS. PART 2: ELECTRICITY, PHYSICS, PRECISION ENGINEERING, OPTICS AND ACOUSTICS. *see* PATENTS, TRADEMARKS AND COPYRIGHTS—Abstracting, Bibliographies, Statistics

535.84 CHN ISSN 1000-7032
QC476.4 CODEN: FAXUEW
FAGUANG XUEBAO/CHINESE JOURNAL OF LUMINESCENCE. Text in Chinese; Abstracts in Chinese, English. 1980. bi-m. USD 106.80 (effective 2009). **Document type:** *Journal, Academic/Scholarly.* **Description:** Covers physics of luminescence, optical properties of solids, laser spectroscopy, light emitting devices, optoelectronics and photonics, and more.
Related titles: Online - full content ed.; Online - full text ed.
Indexed: A22, A28, APA, BrCerAb, C&ISA, CA/WCA, CIA, CPEI, CTE, CerAb, CivEngAb, CorrAb, E&CAJ, E11, EEA, EMA, ESPM, EnvEAb, H15, Inspec, M&TEA, M09, MBF, METADEX, RefZh, SCOPUS, SolStAb, T04, WAA.
—BLDSC (3180.369000), East View, IE, Ingenta, Linda Hall.
Published by: (Zhongguo Wuli Xuehui, Faguang Kexuehui), Kexue Chubanshe/Science Press, 16 Donghuang Cheng Genbei Jie, Beijing, 100717, China. TEL 86-10-64000246, FAX 86-10-64030255, http://www.sciencep.com/. Circ: 1,000 (paid). **Dist. by:** China International Book Trading Corp, 35 Chegongzhuang Xilu, Haidian District, PO Box 399, Beijing 100044, China. TEL 86-10-68412045, FAX 86-10-68412023, cibtc@mail.cibtc.com.cn, http://www.cibtc.com.cn.

621.36 DEU
FASERINSTITUT BREMEN. FORSCHUNGSBERICHTE. Variant title: Forschungsberichte aus dem Faserinstitut Bremen. Text in German. 2001. irreg. **Document type:** *Monographic series, Academic/Scholarly.*
Published by: Faserinstitut Bremen e.V., Gebaeude IW 3, Am Biologischen Garten 2, Bremen, 28359, Germany. TEL 49-421-2189329, FAX 49-421-2183110, sekretariat@faserinstitut.de, http://www.faserinstitut.de.

621.36 DEU ISSN 1611-3861
FASERINSTITUT BREMEN. SCIENCE-REPORT. Variant title: Science-Report aus dem Faserinstitut Bremen. Text in German. 2003. irreg., latest vol.4, 2009. price varies. **Document type:** *Monographic series, Academic/Scholarly.*
Published by: (Faserinstitut Bremen e.V.), Logos Verlag Berlin, Comeniushof, Gubener Str 47, Berlin, 10243, Germany. TEL 49-30-42851090, FAX 49-30-42851092, redaktion@logos-verlag.de.

535 USA ISSN 0146-8030
TA1800 CODEN: FOIOD2
➤ **FIBER AND INTEGRATED OPTICS**; a journal stressing components, systems, and future trends. Text in English. 1977. bi-m. GBP 701 combined subscription in United Kingdom to institutions (print & online eds.); EUR 928, USD 1,165 combined subscription to institutions (print & online eds.) (effective 2012). adv. abstr. index. back issues avail.; reprint service avail. from PSC. **Document type:** *Journal, Academic/Scholarly.* **Description:** Focuses on fiberoptic developments and in-depth surveys. Achieves a balance between scientific developments in integrated optics, systems, manufacturing and applications of optical fibers. Includes articles on economics and market trends.
Incorporates: International Journal of Optoelectronics (0952-5432)
Related titles: Online - full text ed.: ISSN 1096-4681. GBP 631 in United Kingdom to institutions; EUR 835, USD 1,048 to institutions (effective 2012) (from IngentaConnect).
Indexed: A01, A03, A08, A22, A28, APA, ASCA, AcoustA, B01, B06, B07, B09, BrCerAb, C&ISA, C23, CA, CA/WCA, CIA, CIN, CPEI, CerAb, ChemAb, ChemTitl, CivEngAb, CorrAb, CurCont, E&CAJ, E01, E11, EEA, EMA, ESPM, EngInd, EnvEAb, H15, Inspec, JCLA, M&TEA, M09, MBF, METADEX, MSCI, P26, P54, PQC, PhysBer, RefZh, S01, SCI, SCOPUS, SolStAb, T02, T04, W07, WAA.
—AskIEEE, CASDDS, IE, Infotrieve, Ingenta, INIST, Linda Hall. **CCC.**
Published by: Taylor & Francis Inc. (Subsidiary of: Taylor & Francis Group), 325 Chestnut St, Ste 800, Philadelphia, PA 19106. TEL 215-625-2940, 800-354-1420, orders@taylorandfrancis.com, http://www.taylorandfrancis.com. Ed. Dr. Henri Hodara. Adv. contact Linda Hann TEL 44-1344-779945.

➤ **FIBER OPTIC INDUSTRY GLOBAL QUARTERLY REVIEW.** *see* COMPUTERS—Computer Networks

535 USA ISSN 1051-1946
FIBER OPTIC SENSORS AND SYSTEMS; monthly newsletter on worldwide developments in fiber optic sensors and systems. Short title: F O S S. Variant title: Fiber Optics Sensors and Systems Newsletter. Text in English. 1987. m. looseleaf. USD 695 in US & Canada; USD 745 elsewhere (effective 2008). back issues avail. **Document type:** *Newsletter, Trade.* **Description:** Covers optics applications to sensors, technology, applications, markets, patents, products, and business developments.
Related titles: E-mail ed.: USD 695 single user (effective 2008); Online - full text ed.
Indexed: CompD.
—IE, Infotrieve. **CCC.**
Published by: Information Gatekeepers, Inc., 320 Washington St, Ste 302, Brighton, MA 02135. TEL 617-782-5033, 800-323-1088, FAX 617-782-5735, info@igigroup.com. Ed. Dr. Hui Pan. Pub. Dr. Paul Polishuk.

535 GBR ISSN 1740-7192
FIBER SYSTEMS. AMERICA & ASIA. Text in English. 2000. 7/yr. adv. back issues avail. **Document type:** *Magazine, Trade.* **Description:** Provides high-quality, independent global coverage across all sectors of the optical communications supply chain.
Formerly (until 2003): FiberSystems International (1471-552X)
—CCC.
Published by: Institute of Physics Publishing Ltd., Dirac House, Temple Back, Bristol, BS1 6BE, United Kingdom. TEL 44-117-9297481, FAX 44-117-9301178, custserv@iop.org, http://publishing.iop.org/.

FIBEROPTIC PRODUCT NEWS BUYER'S GUIDE. *see* BUSINESS AND ECONOMICS—Trade And Industrial Directories

FIBRESYSTEMS EUROPE. *see* COMMUNICATIONS—Computer Applications

535 509 ITA ISSN 0391-2051
QC350 CODEN: AFDGA2
➤ **FONDAZIONE GIORGIO RONCHI. ATTI.** Text in English, French, German, Italian. 1946. bi-m. EUR 143 domestic; EUR 157 foreign (effective 2009). bk.rev. charts; illus. index, cum.index every 5 yrs: vols.1-28 (1946-1973). **Document type:** *Journal, Academic/Scholarly.*
Former titles (until 1975): Atti della Fondazione Giorgio Ronchi (0365-236X); (until 1952): Atti della Fondazione Giorgio Ronchi (0015-606X)
Related titles: E-mail ed.; Fax ed.
Indexed: ChemAb, Inspec, OphLit, PsycholAb, RefZh.
—AskIEEE, CASDDS, INIST, Linda Hall.
Published by: Fondazione Giorgio Ronchi, Via San Felice a Ema, 20, Florence, FI 50125, Italy.

➤ **FRONTIERS OF OPTOELECTRONICS IN CHINA.** *see* ENGINEERING—Electrical Engineering

535 CHN
GUANG DE SHIJIE/WORLD OF LIGHT. Text in Chinese. bi-m.
Published by: Zhongguo Guang Xuehui, Zhejiang Daxue, Zheda Lu, Hangzhou, Zhejiang 310027, China. TEL 572244. Ed. Tang Jinfa.

535 CHN ISSN 1673-1255
GUANGDIAN JISHU YINGYONG/ELECTRO-OPTIC TECHNOLOGY APPLICATION. Text in Chinese; Abstracts in Chinese, English. 1982. bi-m. CNY 60, USD 60; CNY 10 per issue (effective 2009). **Document type:** *Journal, Abstract/Index.* **Description:** Covers the latest developments of theoretical and applied researches in the fields of optoelectronics.
Former titles (until 2003): Guangdian Duikang yu Wuyuan Ganrao/ Electro-optics Countermeasures & Passive Jam; (until 1993): Guangdian Ganrao yu Guangdian Duikang
Related titles: Online - full text ed.
Published by: Dongbei Dianzi Jishu Yanjiushu/Northeast Research Institute of Electronics Technology, PO Box 31-19, Jinzhou, Liaoning Province 121000, China. TEL 86-416-2835782, FAX 86-416-2817016.

535.58 CHN ISSN 1005-0086
TA1750
GUANGDIANZI - JIGUANG/JOURNAL OF OPTRONICS-LASER. Text in Chinese. 1990. m. USD 106.80 (effective 2009). adv. **Document type:** *Academic/Scholarly.* **Description:** Covers opt-electronic integration & fiber application techniques, opt-electr information processing, optical computing & optical neural network, opt-electro measurement, laser medicine, laser biology, and laser applications.
Related titles: Online - full text ed.
Indexed: CPEI, EngInd, SCOPUS.
—East View.
Published by: Tianjin Daxue Jidian Fenxiao/Tianjin Institute of Technology, 47 Yingjian Rd, Yangliuqing, Tianjin 300380, China. TEL 86-22-23679707, FAX 86-22-23657134, baenxu@public.tpt.tj.cn. Ed. Enxu Ba. Adv. contact Wang Meilin. **Dist. outside China by:** China International Book Trading Corp, 35 Chegongzhuang Xilu, Haidian District, PO Box 399, Beijing 100044, China. **Co-sponsors:** National Natural Science Foundation of China, Information Science Department; Optoelectronic Committee of Chinese Optic Society.

535.84 CHN ISSN 1000-0593
QC450 CODEN: GYGFED
➤ **GUANGPUXUE YU GUANGPU FENXI/SPECTROSCOPY AND SPECTRAL ANALYSIS.** Text in Chinese; Abstracts in English. 1981. bi-m. CNY 480; CNY 40 per issue (effective 2011). adv. film rev.; software rev. abstr.; bibl.; illus. reprints avail. **Document type:** *Academic/Scholarly.* **Description:** Covers laser spectroscopy measurements, molecular spectroscopy, atomic emission spectrometry, coupled plasma, X-ray fluorescence spectrometry, instrumentation and physics-optics.
Formerly (until 1982): Yuanzi Guangpu Fenxi
Related titles: Online - full text ed.
Indexed: A20, A22, A40, C33, CCI, CIN, CPEI, ChemAb, ChemTitl, EMBASE, EngInd, ExcerpMed, GeoRef, IndMed, MEDLINE, P30, R10, Reac, RefZh, SCI, SCOPUS, SpeleolAb, VITIS, W07.
—BLDSC (8411.114400), CASDDS, East View, IE, Ingenta.
Published by: (Zhongguo Guangxue Xuehui/Chinese Optical Society), Beijing Daxue Chubanshe/Peking University Press, 205, Chengfu Lu, Haidian-qu, Beijing, 100871, China. TEL 86-10-62752024, fd@pup.pku.edu.cn, http://cbs.pku.edu.cn/. adv.: page USD 150. Circ: 4,000.

➤ **GUANGXIAN YU DIANLAN/OPTICAL FIBRE AND CABLE.** *see* ENGINEERING—Electrical Engineering

➤ **GUANGXUE JINGMI GONGCHENG.** *see* ENGINEERING

535 CHN ISSN 1002-1582
GUANGXUE JISHU/OPTICAL TECHNIQUE. Text in Chinese. 1975. bi-m. CNY 38 per issue (effective 2011). 52 p./no.; **Document type:** *Journal, Academic/Scholarly.*
Formerly: Guangxue Gongyi
Related titles: Online - full text ed.
Indexed: EngInd, SCOPUS.
—BLDSC (6273.388000), East View, IE, Ingenta.
Published by: Beijing Ligong Daxue Guangdian Xueyuan/Beijing Institute of Technology, School of Optoelectronics, 5, Zhongguancun Nan Dajie, Haidian-qu, Beijing, 100081, China. TEL 86-10-68948720, FAX 86-10-68948720, http://optoelectronic.bit.edu.cn/. **Dist. overseas by:** China International Book Trading Corp, 35 Chegongzhuang Xilu, Haidian District, PO Box 399, Beijing 100044, China. TEL 86-10-68412045, FAX 86-10-68412023, cibtc@mail.cibtc.com.cn, http://www.cibtc.com.cn. **Co-sponsor:** Zhongguo Beifang Guangdian Gongye Zonggongsi/China Opto-Electro Industries Co., Ltd. (OEC).

535 CHN ISSN 0253-2239
QC350 CODEN: GUXUDC
GUANGXUE XUEBAO/ACTA OPTICA SINICA. Text mainly in Chinese; Summaries in Chinese, English; Text occasionally in English. 1981. m. USD 213.60 (effective 2009). adv. **Document type:** *Journal, Academic/Scholarly.* **Description:** Covers new concepts, new results and new advances in the field of optics and lasers.
Related titles: ◆ CD-ROM ed.: Chinese Academic Journals Full-Text Database. Science & Engineering, Series A. ISSN 1007-8010; Online - full text ed.
Indexed: A22, A28, APA, BrCerAb, C&ISA, CA/WCA, CIA, CIN, CPEI, CerAb, ChemAb, ChemTitl, CivEngAb, CorrAb, E&CAJ, E11, EEA, EMA, EngInd, H15, Inspec, M&TEA, M09, MBF, METADEX, RefZh, SCOPUS, SolStAb, T04, WAA.
—BLDSC (0641.790000), CASDDS, East View, IE, Ingenta, Linda Hall.
Published by: (Zhongguo Guangxue Xuehui/Chinese Optical Society), Kexue Chubanshe/Science Press, 16 Donghuang Cheng Genbei Jie, Beijing, 100717, China. TEL 86-10-64000246, FAX 86-10-64030255, http://www.sciencep.com/. Ed. Deheng Wang. adv.: page USD 150; trim 210 x 297. **Dist. by:** China International Book Trading Corp, 35 Chegongzhuang Xilu, Haidian District, PO Box 399, Beijing 100044, China. TEL 86-10-68412045, FAX 86-10-68412023, cibtc@mail.cibtc.com.cn, http://www.cibtc.com.cn.

GUANGXUE YIQI/OPTICAL INSTRUMENTS. *see* INSTRUMENTS

535 CHN ISSN 1672-3392
GUANGXUE YU GUANGDIAN JISHU/OPTICS & OPTOELECTRONIC TECHNOLOGY. Text in Chinese. 2003. bi-m. USD 53.40 (effective 2009). **Document type:** *Journal, Academic/Scholarly.*
Related titles: Online - full text ed.
—East View.
Published by: Huazhong Guangdian Jishu Yanjiusuo/Huazhong Institute of Electro-Optics, 981, Xiongchu Dadao, Wuhan, 430073, China. TEL 86-27-87801633 ext 2351, FAX 86-27-87803196.

535 CHN ISSN 1004-4213
TA1501 CODEN: GUXUED
GUANGZI XUEBAO/ACTA PHOTONICA SINICA. Text in Chinese; Abstracts in English. 1972. m. USD 186 (effective 2009).
Formerly (until 1992): Gaosu Sheying yu Guangzixue - High Speed Photography and Photonics (1001-0955)
Related titles: Online - full content ed.; Online - full text ed.
Indexed: A22, A28, APA, BrCerAb, C&ISA, CA/WCA, CIA, CIN, CerAb, ChemAb, ChemTitl, CivEngAb, CorrAb, E&CAJ, E11, EEA, EMA, ESPM, EngInd, EnvEAb, H15, Inspec, M&TEA, M09, MBF, METADEX, RefZh, SCOPUS, SolStAb, T04, WAA.
—BLDSC (0648.630000), AskIEEE, CASDDS, East View, IE, Ingenta.
Published by: (Zhongguo Guangxue Xuehui/Chinese Optical Society), Kexue Chubanshe/Science Press, 16 Donghuang Cheng Genbei Jie, Beijing, 100717, China. TEL 86-10-64000246, FAX 86-10-64030255, http://www.sciencep.com/. Ed. Xun Hou.

621.366 GBR
GYBE; the laser sailing magazine. Text in English. 1993. q. free to members. adv. **Document type:** *Magazine, Consumer.*
Published by: U K Laser Association, Eddie Mays, Ed., Sheridan, Rutland Gardens, Bursledon, Southampton, SO31 8FZ, United Kingdom. TEL 44-2380-402194, FAX 44-7766-568150. Ed. Eddie Mays. adv.: B&W page GBP 250, color page GBP 400.

HAKIM FASHION EYEWEAR MAGAZINE. *see* CLOTHING TRADE—Fashions

535 USA
HANDBOOK OF OPTICAL CONSTANTS OF SOLIDS. Text in English. 1997. irreg., latest vol.5, 1998. price varies. **Document type:** *Monographic series, Academic/Scholarly.*
Related titles: Online - full text ed.: ISSN 1874-5814.
Published by: Academic Press (Subsidiary of: Elsevier Science & Technology), 3251 Riverport Ln, Maryland Heights, MO 63043. TEL 314-447-8010, FAX 314-447-8030, http://www.elsevierdirect.com/imprint.jsp?iid=5. Ed. Edward Palik.

535 KOR ISSN 1225-6285
HAN'GUG GWANGHAG HOEJI. Variant title: Hankook Kwanghak Hoeji. Text in Korean. 1990. bi-m. **Document type:** *Journal, Academic/Scholarly.*
Indexed: Inspec.
—BLDSC (4262.108000).
Published by: Han'gug Gwanghaghoe/Optical Society of Korea, 811, 635-4 Yucksam-dong, Kangnam-gu, Seoul, 135-703, Korea, S. TEL 82-2-34526560, FAX 82-2-34526561, osk@osk.or.kr, http://www.osk.or.kr.

535 JPN ISSN 0917-026X
HIKARI ARAIANSU/OPTICAL ALLIANCE. Text in Japanese. 1990. m. JPY 19,000; JPY 2,000 newsstand/cover (effective 2006). **Document type:** *Magazine, Academic/Scholarly.*
—BLDSC (6273.160500).
Published by: Nihon Kogyo Shuppan K.K./Japan Industrial Publishing Co., Ltd., 6-3-26 Honkomagome, Bunkyo-ku, Tokyo, 113-0021, Japan. TEL 81-3-39441181, FAX 81-3-39446826, info@nikko-pb.co.jp.

535.58 USA ISSN 0895-9080
HOLOGRAPHY NEWS. Text in English. 1987. 10/yr. (except Jan. & Aug.). GBP 347 in United Kingdom; EUR 580 in Europe; USD 557 elsewhere (effective 2002). back issues avail.
Related titles: Online - full text ed.
Indexed: B02, B15, B17, B18, CompD, G04, G06, G07, G08, I05.
Address: 5650 Greenwood Plaza Blvd., Ste 225K, Greenwood Village, CO 80111.

535 CHN ISSN 1001-8891
HONGWAI JISHU/INFRARED TECHNOLOGY. Text in Chinese. 1979. bi-m. USD 62.40 (effective 2009). **Document type:** *Consumer.*
Related titles: Online - full text ed.
Indexed: SCOPUS.
—BLDSC (4499.513000), East View, IE, Ingenta.
Published by: Kunming Wuli Yanjiusuo/Kunming Institute of Physics, P.O. Box 500, Kunming, Yunnan 650223, China. Ed. Su Junhong. **Dist. overseas by:** China International Book Trading Corp, 35 Chegongzhuang Xilu, Haidian District, PO Box 399, Beijing 100044, China.

535 CHN ISSN 1001-9014
TA1570 CODEN: HHXUEZ
HONGWAI YU HAOMIBO XUEBAO/JOURNAL OF INFRARED AND MILLIMETER WAVES. Text in Chinese; Text occasionally in English; Abstracts in Chinese, English. 1982. bi-m. CNY 60; CNY 10 per issue (effective 2011). back issues avail. **Document type:** *Journal, Academic/Scholarly.*
Formerly (until 1991): Hongwai Yanjiu (1001-9464)
Related titles: Online - full text ed.: free (effective 2011).
Indexed: A22, A28, APA, BrCerAb, C&ISA, CA/WCA, CIA, CIN, CPEI, CerAb, ChemAb, ChemTitl, CivEngAb, CorrAb, CurCont, E&CAJ, E11, EEA, EMA, ESPM, EngInd, EnvEAb, H15, Inspec, M&TEA, M09, MBF, METADEX, RefZh, SCI, SCOPUS, SolStAb, T04, W07, WAA.
—BLDSC (5006.850000), AskIEEE, CASDDS, East View, IE, Ingenta, Linda Hall.
Published by: (Zhongguo Kexueyuan Shanghai Jishu Wuli Yanjiusuo/ Shanghai Institute of Technical Physics of the Chinese Academy of Sciences, Zhongguo Guangxue Xuehui (Shanghai)), Kexue Chubanshe/Science Press, 16 Donghuang Cheng Genbei Jie, Beijing, 100717, China. TEL 86-10-64000246, FAX 86-10-64030255, http://www.sciencep.com/. Ed. Jun-Hao Chu. **Dist. by:** China International Book Trading Corp, 35 Chegongzhuang Xilu, Haidian District, PO Box 399, Beijing 100044, China. TEL 86-10-68412045, FAX 86-10-68412023, cibtc@mail.cibtc.com.cn, http://www.cibtc.com.cn.

HONGWAI YU JIGUANG GONGCHENG/INFRARED AND LASER ENGINEERING. *see* AERONAUTICS AND SPACE FLIGHT

535.58 USA ISSN 0899-9406
I E E E INTERNATIONAL SEMICONDUCTOR LASER CONFERENCE. CONFERENCE DIGEST. (Institute of Electrical and Electronics Engineers) Text in English. 1967. biennial. adv. back issues avail. **Document type:** *Proceedings, Trade.* **Description:** Covers all aspects of semiconductor injection laser technology.
Formerly (until 1988): I E E E International Semiconductor Laser Conference. Program and Abstract
Related titles: CD-ROM ed.; Microfiche ed.; Online - full text ed.
Indexed: EngInd, Inspec, SCOPUS.
—CCC.
Published by: I E E E, 445 Hoes Ln, Piscataway, NJ 08855. contactcenter@ieee.org, http://www.ieee.org. **Co-sponsor:** Laser and Electro-Optics Society.

I E E E JOURNAL OF QUANTUM ELECTRONICS. (Institute of Electrical and Electronics Engineers) *see* ELECTRONICS

621.36 USA
I E E E L E O S. (Institute Of Electrical And Electronics Engineers Lasers & Electro-Optics Society) Text in English. 1986. bi-m. USD 25 to members (effective 2005). adv. **Document type:** *Newsletter, Trade.* **Description:** Covers the application of lasers, optical devices, optical fibers, and associated lightwave technology in systems and subsystems in which quantum electronic devices are a key element.
Published by: (Lasers and Electro-Optics Society), I E E E Media, 445 Hoes Ln, Piscataway, NJ 08854. TEL 732-562-3946, FAX 732-981-1855, ss.ieeemedia@ieee.org, http://www.ieee.org/ieeemedia, http://www.spectrum.ieee.org/ieeemedia/select.html. adv.: B&W page USD 1,050; trim 7.875 x 10.75. Circ: 7,919.

621.36 USA ISSN 1092-8081
TA1671
I E E E LASERS AND ELECTRO-OPTICS SOCIETY. ANNUAL MEETING. (Institute of Electrical and Electronics Engineers) Text in English. 19??. a. adv. back issues avail. **Document type:** *Proceedings, Trade.*

Related titles: Online - full text ed.
Indexed: EngInd, SCOPUS.
—**CCC.**
Published by: I E E E, 445 Hoes Ln, Piscataway, NJ 08855. contactcenter@ieee.org, http://www.ieee.org.

535 USA ISSN 1943-0655
TA1501
▼ **I E E E PHOTONICS JOURNAL.** Text in English. 2009 (Feb.). bi-m. USD 945 (effective 2012). adv. back issues avail.; reprints avail. **Document type:** *Journal, Academic/Scholarly.* **Description:** Provides quantum electronics and optics to accelerate progress in the generation of novel photon sources and in their utilization in emerging applications at the micro and nano scales spanning from the far-infrared/THz to the x-ray region of the electromagnetic spectrum.
Media: Online - full text. **Related titles:** CD-ROM ed.: ISSN 1943-0647. 2009 (Feb.).
Indexed: CPEI, CurCont, P30, RefZh, SCI, SCOPUS, W07.
—BLDSC (4363.013250), IE. **CCC.**
Published by: (Institute of Electrical and Electronics Engineers, Inc., Photonics Society), I E E E, 445 Hoes Ln, Piscataway, NJ 08854. TEL 732-981-0060, 800-678-4333, FAX 732-562-6380, contactcenter@ieee.org, http://www.ieee.org. Ed. Carmen S Menoni TEL 970-491-8659.

621 USA ISSN 1949-128X
TA1501
I E E E PHOTONICS SOCIETY NEWS. (Institute of Electrical and Electronics Engineers) Text in English. 19??. bi-m. free to members (effective 2009). adv. back issues avail. **Document type:** *Newsletter, Trade.* **Description:** Features original and significant papers relating to photonic- light-wave components and applications, laser physics and systems, and laser-electro-optic technology.
Former titles (until 2009): I E E E L E O S Newsletter (1538-2354); (until 200?): L E O S Newsletter (1060-3301)
Related titles: Online - full text ed.: free (effective 2009).
—**CCC.**
Published by: Institute of Electrical and Electronics Engineers, Inc., Photonics Society, 3 Park Ave, 17th Fl, New York, NY 10016. TEL 212-419-7900, FAX 212-752-4929. Adv. contact Felicia Spagnoli TEL 732-562-6334.

535.58 USA ISSN 1041-1135
TA1501
I E E E PHOTONICS TECHNOLOGY LETTERS. (Institute of Electrical and Electronics Engineers) Abbreviated title: P T L. Text in English. 1989. s-m. USD 1,690; USD 2,115 combined subscription (print & online eds.) (effective 2012). adv. back issues avail.; reprints avail. **Document type:** *Journal, Academic/Scholarly.* **Description:** Covers original research relevant to photonics technology; laser and electro-optic technology, laser physics and systems, and photonic - lightwave components and applications.
Related titles: CD-ROM ed.; Microfiche ed.; Online - full text ed.: ISSN 1941-0174. USD 1,535 (effective 2012).
Indexed: A22, A28, APA, ASCA, BrCerAb, C&ISA, CA/WCA, CIA, CPEI, CerAb, CivEngAb, CorrAb, CurCont, E&CAJ, E11, EEA, EMA, ESPM, EngInd, EnvEAb, H15, INIS AtomInd, ISMEC, ISR, Inspec, M&TEA, M09, MBF, METADEX, MSCI, P30, RefZh, SCI, SCOPUS, SolStAb, T04, W07, WAA.
—BLDSC (4363.013500), AskIEEE, IE, Infotrieve, Ingenta, INIST, Linda Hall. **CCC.**
Published by: I E E E, 445 Hoes Ln, Piscataway, NJ 08854. TEL 732-981-0060, 800-678-4333, FAX 732-562-6380, contactcenter@ieee.org, http://www.ieee.org. Eds. El-Hang Lee TEL 82-32-8607764, Dawn Melley.

535 621.38 GBR ISSN 1751-8768
TA1750 CODEN: IPOPE8
➤ **I E T OPTOELECTRONICS.** Text in English. 1985. bi-m. GBP 606, USD 1,167; GBP 727, USD 1,400 combined subscription (effective 2011). adv. back issues avail. **Document type:** *Journal, Academic/Scholarly.* **Description:** Covers displays, guided optical waves, and integrated optics; holography; light sources, optical modulation and multiplexing, nonlinear optics and optical computing; optical amplifiers; communication systems, fibers and fiber sensors, cables and connectors, information theory and materials; photodetectors and optical receivers.
Former titles (until 2007): I E E Proceedings - Optoelectronics (1350-2433); (until 1994): I E E Proceedings - Part J (Optoelectronics) (0267-3932)
Related titles: Online - full text ed.: ISSN 1751-8776. GBP 589, USD 1,155 (effective 2011).
Indexed: A01, A03, A05, A08, A22, APA, AS&TA, AS&TI, ASCA, B01, B06, B07, B09, BrTechI, C&ISA, C10, CA, CIN, CPEI, ChemAb, ChemTitl, CorrAb, CurCont, E&CAJ, EEA, EngInd, IBR, IBZ, ISR, Inspec, RefZh, S01, SCI, SCOPUS, SolStAb, T02, TM, W07, WAA.
—BLDSC (4363.252900), AskIEEE, CASDDS, IE, Infotrieve, Ingenta, INIST, Linda Hall. **CCC.**
Published by: The Institution of Engineering and Technology, Michael Faraday House, Stevenage, Herts SG1 2AY, United Kingdom. TEL 44-1438-313311, FAX 44-1438-765526, journals@theiet.org, http://www.theiet.org/. Ed. Richard V Penty TEL 44-1223-748358. Adv. contact Louise Hall TEL 44-1438-767351. **Subscr. to:** Publication Sales Dept, PO Box 96, Stevenage SG1 2SD, United Kingdom. TEL 44-1438-767328, FAX 44-1438-767375, sales@theiet.org.

➤ **THE IMAGING SCIENCE JOURNAL.** *see* PHOTOGRAPHY

535 FRA ISSN 0758-5756
INFORM'OPTIQUE; revue de liaison bimestrielle entre les professionnels de l'optique. Text in French. 1971. 10/yr. EUR 65 domestic; EUR 99 in the European Union; EUR 99 in Switzerland; EUR 140 elsewhere (effective 2009). adv. bk.rev. **Document type:** *Magazine, Trade.*
Published by: Societe Inform' Optique, 18 rue Mozart, Clichy, 92110, France. TEL 33-1-47305890, FAX 33-1-47305971. Ed. Jennifer Ivore. Circ: 2,750; 2,750 (paid).

535 NLD ISSN 1350-4495
QC457 CODEN: IPTEEY
➤ **INFRARED PHYSICS & TECHNOLOGY.** Text in English. 1961. 6/yr. EUR 1,743 in Europe to institutions; JPY 231,600 in Japan to institutions; USD 1,951 elsewhere to institutions (effective 2012). adv. bk.rev. illus.; abstr. index. back issues avail.; reprints avail. **Document type:** *Journal, Academic/Scholarly.* **Description:** Covers detectors, solid state photoconductors, multi-element and image tubes, optical materials and systems, polarizers, filters, infrared properties of solids, liquids, and gases, and all types of lasers.
Formerly (until 1994): Infrared Physics (0020-0891)
Related titles: Microfilm ed.: (from PQC); Online - full text ed.: (from IngentaConnect, ScienceDirect).
Indexed: A01, A03, A08, A22, A26, ASCA, AcoustA, C&ISA, C24, CA, CIN, CPEI, Cadscan, ChemAb, ChemTitl, CurCont, E&CAJ, EngInd, GeoRef, I05, ISMEC, ISR, Inspec, LeadAb, M&GPA, MSCI, P30, PhysBer, S01, SCI, SCOPUS, SolStAb, SpeleolAb, T02, TM, W07, Zincscan.
—BLDSC (4499.410000), AskIEEE, CASDDS, IE, Infotrieve, Ingenta, INIST, Linda Hall. **CCC.**
Published by: Elsevier BV (Subsidiary of: Elsevier Science & Technology), Radarweg 29, PO Box 211, Amsterdam, 1000 AE, Netherlands. TEL 31-20-4853911, FAX 31-20-4852457, JournalsCustomerServiceEMEA@elsevier.com, http://www.elsevier.nl. Ed. Dr. H N Rutt.

535 570.282 DEU ISSN 1431-8059
TS510 CODEN: INNOFL
INNOVATION (ENGLISH EDITION); the magazine from Carl Zeiss. Text in English. 1991. 2/yr. free (effective 2009). charts; illus. **Document type:** *Magazine, Consumer.* **Description:** Provides information about the activities of the company, the application of Zeiss instruments, history, new products, business orders, cooperative ventures and technology.
Formerly (until 1996): Zeiss Information with Jena Review (0941-7567); Which was formed by merger of (1962-1991): Zeiss Information (0044-2054); Which was formerly (1953-1962): Zeiss-Werkzeitschrift (English Edition) (0176-9626); (1956-1991): Jena Review (0448-9497)
Related titles: Online - full text ed.; German ed.: Innovation (German Edition). ISSN 1436-1833. 1991.
Indexed: CIN, CRIA, CRICC, ChemAb, ChemTitl, GeoRef, IBR, IBZ, Inspec, PhotoAb, SpeleolAb.
—BLDSC (4515.480245), AskIEEE, CASDDS, IE, Ingenta, INIST, Linda Hall. **CCC.**
Published by: Carl Zeiss Jena GmbH, Carl-Zeiss-Promenade 10, Jena, 07745, Germany. TEL 49-3641-640, FAX 49-3641-642856, info@zeiss.de, http://www.zeiss.de. Ed. Silke Schmid. Circ: 72,000.

535 USA ISSN 0731-2911
QC495
INTER-SOCIETY COLOR COUNCIL NEWS. Text in English. 1933. bi-m. USD 60; USD 80 foreign (effective 1998). bk.rev.; film rev. charts; illus.; pat.; stat. index. **Document type:** *Newsletter.*
Formerly: Inter-Society Color Council Newsletter (0300-7588)
Media: Duplicated (not offset).
Indexed: GALA.
Published by: Inter-Society Color Council, c/o Cynthia Starke, 11491 Sunset Hills Rd, Reston, VA 20190. TEL 609-895-7427, FAX 609-895-7461. Ed. Gultekin Celikiz. Circ: 1,000 (controlled).

539.7 USA
INTERNATIONAL CONFERENCE ON EXPERIMENTAL MESON SPECTROSCOPY. PROCEEDINGS. (Published in A I P Conference Proceedings, Particles and Fields subseries) Text in English. irreg. bibl.; illus. **Document type:** *Proceedings, Academic/Scholarly.*
Related titles: Online - full text ed.
Published by: Springer New York LLC (Subsidiary of: Springer Science+Business Media), 233 Spring St, New York, NY 10013. TEL 212-460-1500, FAX 212-460-1575, http://www.springer.com/.

669.79 535 USA ISSN 1092-8669
INTERNATIONAL CONFERENCE ON INDIUM PHOSPHIDE AND RELATED MATERIALS. PROCEEDINGS. Text in English. 1988. a. adv. back issues avail.; reprints avail. **Document type:** *Proceedings, Trade.*
Related titles: Online - full text ed.
Indexed: EngInd, SCOPUS.
—IE, Ingenta. **CCC.**
Published by: I E E E, 445 Hoes Ln, Piscataway, NJ 08854. TEL 732-981-0060, 800-678-4333, FAX 732-562-6380, customer.service@ieee.org, http://www.ieee.org.

535 USA
INTERNATIONAL CONFERENCE ON INTEGRATED OPTICS AND OPTICAL FIBER COMMUNICATION. PROCEEDINGS. Text in English. 199?. a. adv. back issues avail.; reprints avail. **Document type:** *Proceedings, Trade.*
Related titles: Online - full text ed.
Published by: I E E E, 445 Hoes Ln, Piscataway, NJ 08854. TEL 732-981-0060, 800-678-4333, FAX 732-562-6380, customer.service@ieee.org, http://www.ieee.org.

535 USA
INTERNATIONAL CONFERENCE TRANSPARENT OPTICAL NETWORK. PROCEEDINGS. Text in English. 19??. a. adv. back issues avail.; reprints avail. **Document type:** *Proceedings, Trade.*
Related titles: Online - full text ed.
Published by: I E E E, 445 Hoes Ln, Piscataway, NJ 08854. TEL 732-981-0060, 800-678-4333, FAX 732-562-6380, customer.service@ieee.org, http://www.ieee.org.

INTERNATIONAL JOURNAL FOR ION MOBILITY SPECTROMETRY. *see* CHEMISTRY—Analytical Chemistry

535.84 NLD ISSN 1387-3806
QC454 CODEN: IMSPF8
➤ **INTERNATIONAL JOURNAL OF MASS SPECTROMETRY.** Text in English, French, German. 1968. 30/yr. EUR 5,495 in Europe to institutions; JPY 729,500 in Japan to institutions; USD 6,146 elsewhere to institutions (effective 2012). adv. bk.rev. charts. index. back issues avail. **Document type:** *Journal, Academic/Scholarly.* **Description:** Contains papers dealing with fundamental aspects of mass spectrometry and ion processes, and the application of mass spectrometric techniques to specific problems in chemistry and physics.
Former titles (until 1998): International Journal of Mass Spectrometry and Ion Processes (0168-1176); (until 1983): International Journal of Mass Spectrometry and Ion Physics (0020-7381)
Related titles: Microform ed.: (from PQC); Online - full text ed.: ISSN 1873-2798 (from IngentaConnect, ScienceDirect).
Indexed: A01, A03, A08, A20, A22, A26, A40, ASCA, BPRC&P, C24, C33, CA, CCI, CIN, ChemAb, ChemTitl, CurCR, CurCont, GeoRef, I05, ISR, Inspec, MSB, P30, PhysBer, R16, RefZh, S01, SCI, SCOPUS, SpeleolAb, T02, VITIS, W07.
—AskIEEE, CASDDS, IE, Infotrieve, Ingenta, INIST, Linda Hall. **CCC.**
Published by: Elsevier BV (Subsidiary of: Elsevier Science & Technology), Radarweg 29, PO Box 211, Amsterdam, 1000 AE, Netherlands. TEL 31-20-4853911, FAX 31-20-4852457, JournalsCustomerServiceEMEA@elsevier.com, http://www.elsevier.nl. Eds. H Schwarz, S A McLuckey.

621.381 USA ISSN 1553-0396
➤ **INTERNATIONAL JOURNAL OF MICROWAVE AND OPTICAL TECHNOLOGY.** Abbreviated title: I J M O T. Text in English. 2006. bi-m. USD 200 in Africa to institutions except South Africa; USD 400 elsewhere to institutions; USD 50 per issue in Africa to institutions except South Africa; USD 70 per issue elsewhere to institutions (effective 2011). back issues avail. **Document type:** *Journal, Academic/Scholarly.* **Description:** Provides a forum for discussion in fields of microwave technology, microwave photonics and optical technology.
Media: Online - full text.
Address: c/o Banmali S. Rawat, Dept of Electrical Engineering, Univeristy of Nevada, Reno, NV 89557. rawat@ee.unr.edu. Ed. Banmali S Rawat.

➤ **INTERNATIONAL JOURNAL OF MICROWAVE SCIENCE AND TECHNOLOGY.** *see* ENGINEERING—Electrical Engineering

535 USA ISSN 1687-9384
➤ **INTERNATIONAL JOURNAL OF OPTICS.** Text in English. 2008. irreg. USD 195 (effective 2011). **Document type:** *Journal, Academic/Scholarly.* **Description:** Publishes original research articles as well as review articles in all areas of optics.
Incorporates (2007-2011): Advances in Nonlinear Optics (1687-7276); Formerly (until 2009): Research Letters in Optics (1687-8175)
Related titles: Online - full text ed.: ISSN 1687-9392. 2008. free (effective 2011).
Indexed: C10, CA, P52, T02.
Published by: Hindawi Publishing Corporation, 410 Park Ave, 15th Fl, PMB 287, New York, NY 10022. FAX 215-893-4392, 866-446-3294, info@hindawi.com.

535.84 USA ISSN 1687-9449
➤ **INTERNATIONAL JOURNAL OF SPECTROSCOPY.** Text in English. 2008. irreg. USD 395 (effective 2011). **Document type:** *Journal, Academic/Scholarly.* **Description:** Publishes original research articles as well as review articles in all areas of spectroscopy.
Related titles: Online - full text ed.: ISSN 1687-9457. 2008. free (effective 2011).
Indexed: A01, CA, P52, T02.
Published by: Hindawi Publishing Corporation, 410 Park Ave, 15th Fl, PMB 287, New York, NY 10022. FAX 215-893-4392, 866-446-3294, orders@hindawi.com.

➤ **INTERNATIONAL JOURNAL ON WIRELESS & OPTICAL COMMUNICATIONS.** *see* COMMUNICATIONS

621.36 USA
INTERNATIONAL SEMICONDUCTOR LASER CONFERENCE. PROCEEDINGS. Text in English. 19??. biennial. adv. back issues avail.; reprints avail. **Document type:** *Proceedings, Trade.*
Related titles: Online - full text ed.
Published by: I E E E, 445 Hoes Ln, Piscataway, NJ 08854. TEL 732-981-0060, 800-678-4333, FAX 732-562-6380, customer.service@ieee.org, http://www.ieee.org.

INTERNATIONAL SYMPOSIUM ON ELECTRETS. PROCEEDINGS. *see* PHYSICS—Electricity

INTERNATIONAL TOPIC MEETING ON MICROWAVE PHOTONICS. *see* ELECTRONICS

530 JPN ISSN 0916-3492
J A S C O REPORT. Text in Japanese. 1989. m. JPY 200 per issue.
Formed by the merger of (1982-1989): I R Report (0911-6478); (1979-1989): L C Family (0389-5270); Which was formerly (1963-1979): J A S C OReport (0389-5262)
—BLDSC (4663.141800). **CCC.**
Published by: Japan Spectroscopic Corporation/Nihon Bunko Kogyo K.K., 2967-5 Ishikawa-Machi, Hachioji-shi, Tokyo-to 192-0032, Japan.

535 681.1 DEU ISSN 0075-272X
Q185
JAHRBUCH FUER OPTIK UND FEINMECHANIK. Text in German. 1954. a. EUR 54.90 (effective 2010). adv. **Document type:** *Journal, Academic/Scholarly.*
—**CCC.**
Published by: Fachverlag Schiele und Schoen GmbH, Markgrafenstr 11, Berlin, 10969, Germany. TEL 49-30-2537520, FAX 49-30-2517248, service@schiele-schoen.de, http://www.schiele-schoen.de. Circ: 3,000.

JAPAN/PACIFIC RIM FIBER OPTICS REPORT. *see* COMPUTERS—Computer Networks

JEMNA MECHANIKA A OPTIKA/PRECISION MECHANICS AND OPTICS. *see* PHYSICS—Mechanics

621.366 CHN ISSN 1001-3806
QC976.L36 CODEN: JJISEO
JIGUANG JISHU/LASER TECHNOLOGY. Text in Chinese. 1987. bi-m. USD 48 (effective 2009). 112 p./no.; **Document type:** *Journal, Abstract/Index.* **Description:** Provides in-depth reports on research achievements and application advances of laser technology.
Related titles: Online - full content ed.; Online - full text ed.
Indexed: A28, APA, BrCerAb, C&ISA, CA/WCA, CIA, CerAb, CivEngAb, CorrAb, E&CAJ, E11, EEA, EMA, ESPM, EnvEAb, H15, Inspec, M&TEA, M09, MBF, METADEX, RefZh, SCOPUS, SolStAb, T04, WAA.
—BLDSC (5156.647000), East View.

Published by: (Xinan Jishu Wuli Yanjiusuo), Jiguang Jishu Bianweihui, P.O. Box 238, Chengdu, Sichuan 610041, China. TEL 86-28-68011091, FAX 86-28-522-2120. Ed., Adv. contact Su Wang. **Dist. overseas by:** China International Book Trading Corp, 35 Chegongzhuang Xilu, Haidian District, PO Box 399, Beijing 100044, China.

535.58 CHN ISSN 1006-4125
JIGUANG YU GUANGDIANZIXUE JINZHAN/LASER & OPTOELECTRONICS PROGRESS. Text in Chinese. 1964. m. CNY 25 per issue (effective 2010). **Document type:** *Academic/Scholarly.*
Formerly (until 1995): Guowai Jiguang/Foreign Lasers
Related titles: Online - full text ed.
Published by: Zhongguo Kexueyuan Shanghai Guangxue Jingmi Jixie Yanjiusuo/Shanghai Institute of Optics and Fine Mechanics, Chinese Academy of Sciences, 390, Qinghe Lu, Jiading-qu, Shanghai, 201800, China. TEL 86-21-69918166, FAX 86-21-69918705, siom@mail.shcnc.ac.cn, http://www.siom.cas.cn/. Circ: 1,000.

535.58 621.329 CHN ISSN 1001-5078
TA1671 CODEN: JIHOEY
JIGUANG YU HONGWAI/LASER & INFRARED. Text in Chinese; Abstracts in English. 1971. bi-m. USD 85.20 (effective 2009). **Description:** Covers optics, opto-electronics technology and application.
Related titles: Online - full text ed.
Indexed: SCOPUS.
—BLDSC (5156.518400).
Published by: (Huabei Guangdian Jishu Yanjiusuo/North China Research Institute of Electro-Optics), Jiguang yu Hongwai Bianjibu, PO Box 8511, Beijing, 100015, China. TEL 86-10-4362761, FAX 86-10-436-3226. Ed. Chenhua Yang. **Dist. overseas by:** China International Book Trading Corp, 35 Chegongzhuang Xilu, Haidian District, PO Box 399, Beijing 100044, China.

621.36 CHN ISSN 0253-2743
TA1671 CODEN: JIZAEE
JIGUANG ZAZHI/LASER JOURNAL. Text in Chinese. 1975. bi-m. USD 31.20 (effective 2009). **Document type:** *Academic/Scholarly.* **Description:** Publishes papers on laser techniques and their applications in industry, medicine and science.
Related titles: Online - full text ed.
Indexed: C&ISA, E&CAJ, SCOPUS, SolStAb.
—CASDDS, East View.
Published by: Chongqing Shi Guangxue Jixie Yanjiusuo, 35 Yuzhou Rd, Shiqiaopu, Chongqing, Sichuan 430039, China. TEL 023-686042911. Ed. Zhicheng Yang. Circ: 2,000 (paid). **Dist. outside China by:** China National Publishing Industry Trading Corporation, PO Box 782, Beijing 100011, China.

535 USA ISSN 1931-3195
➤ **JOURNAL OF APPLIED REMOTE SENSING.** Text in English. 2007 (Jan.). m. (frequent updates). USD 305 to institutions (effective 2012). **Document type:** *Journal, Academic/Scholarly.* **Description:** Covers the concepts, information, and progress of the remote sensing community, including past, current, and future remote sensing programs and experiments.
Media: Online - full text. **Related titles:** CD-ROM ed.
Indexed: CPEI, CurCont, SCI, SCOPUS, W07.
—**CCC.**
Published by: S P I E - International Society for Optical Engineering, 1000 20th St, Bellingham, WA 98225. TEL 360-676-3290, 888-504-8171, FAX 360-647-1445, journals@spie.org. Ed. Dr. Wei Gao TEL 970-491-3609.

535.84 543.085 USA ISSN 0021-9037
QD95 CODEN: JASYAP
➤ **JOURNAL OF APPLIED SPECTROSCOPY.** Text in English. 1965. bi-m. EUR 4,611, USD 4,791 combined subscription to institutions (print & online eds.) (effective 2012). adv. back issues avail.; reprint service avail. from PSC. **Document type:** *Journal, Academic/Scholarly.* **Description:** Covers reports on key applications of spectroscopy in chemistry, physics, metallurgy, and biology.
Related titles: Microfilm ed.: (from PQC); Online - full text ed.: ISSN 1573-8647 (from IngentaConnect); ◆ Translation of: Zhurnal Prikladnoi Spektroskopii. ISSN 0514-7506.
Indexed: A01, A03, A08, A22, A26, ApMecR, BibLing, C33, CA, CCI, CIN, ChemAb, ChemTitl, E01, GeoRef, I05, Inspec, PhysBer, S01, SCI, SCOPUS, SpeleolAb, T02, W07.
—BLDSC (0414.200000), AskIEEE, CASDDS, East View, IE, Infotrieve, Ingenta, INIST, Linda Hall. **CCC.**
Published by: Springer New York LLC (Subsidiary of: Springer Science+Business Media), 233 Spring St, New York, NY 10013. TEL 212-460-1500, FAX 212-460-1575, service-ny@springer.com. Ed. N A Borisevich.

➤ **JOURNAL OF ATOMIC, MOLECULAR, AND OPTICAL PHYSICS.** *see* PHYSICS—Nuclear Physics

535 610.284 USA ISSN 1083-3668
R857.O6 CODEN: JBOPFO
➤ **JOURNAL OF BIOMEDICAL OPTICS.** Text in English. 1996. m. (bi-m. until 2011). USD 805 combined subscription domestic to institutions (print & online eds.); USD 925 combined subscription foreign to institutions (print & online eds.) (effective 2012). adv. illus. **Document type:** *Journal, Academic/Scholarly.* **Description:** Applications of modern optics technology to biomedical research.
Related titles: CD-ROM ed.; Online - full text ed.: ISSN 1560-2281. USD 615 to institutions (effective 2012).
Indexed: A01, A03, A08, A22, A28, APA, B25, BIOSIS Prev, BrCerAb, C&ISA, CA, CA/WCA, CIA, CIN, CPEI, CPI, CerAb, ChemAb, ChemTitl, CivEngAb, CorrAb, CurCont, E&CAJ, E11, EEA, EMA, EMBASE, EngInd, ExcerpMed, H15, IndMed, Inpharma, Inspec, M&TEA, M09, MBF, MEDLINE, METADEX, MycolAb, P30, R10, Reac, SCI, SCOPUS, SPINweb, SolStAb, T02, T04, W07, WAA.
—BLDSC (4953.760000), AskIEEE, CASDDS, GNLM, IE, Infotrieve, Ingenta, Linda Hall. **CCC.**
Published by: S P I E - International Society for Optical Engineering, 1000 20th St, Bellingham, WA 98225. TEL 360-676-3290, FAX 360-647-1445, spie@spie.org. Ed. Lihong V Wang. **Co-sponsor:** International Biomedical Optics Society.

535.84 NLD ISSN 0368-2048
QC454.E4 CODEN: JESRAW
➤ **JOURNAL OF ELECTRON SPECTROSCOPY AND RELATED PHENOMENA.** Text in English, French, German. 1973. 21/yr. EUR 4,328 in Europe to institutions; JPY 574,800 in Japan to institutions; USD 4,842 elsewhere to institutions (effective 2012). adv. bk.rev. charts; illus. index. back issues avail. **Document type:** *Journal, Academic/Scholarly.* **Description:** Publishes experimental, theoretical, and applied work in the field of electron spectroscopy, covering such topics as surfaces, interfaces, and thin films; semiconductor physics and chemistry; materials science; solid-state physics; atomic and molecular physics; and synchrotron radiation science.
Related titles: Microform ed.: (from PQC); Online - full text ed.: ISSN 1873-2526 (from IngentaConnect, ScienceDirect).
Indexed: A01, A03, A08, A20, A22, A26, A28, APA, ASCA, B&BAb, B19, BrCerAb, C&ISA, C13, C24, C33, CA, CA/WCA, CCI, CIA, CIN, CPEI, CerAb, ChemAb, ChemTitl, CivEngAb, CorrAb, CurCont, E&CAJ, E11, EEA, EMA, ESPM, EngInd, EnvEAb, H15, I05, INIS AtomInd, ISR, Inspec, M&TEA, M09, MBF, METADEX, P30, PhysBer, RefZh, S01, SCI, SCOPUS, SolStAb, T02, T04, W07, WAA.
—BLDSC (4974.900000), AskIEEE, CASDDS, IE, Infotrieve, Ingenta, INIST, Linda Hall. **CCC.**
Published by: Elsevier BV (Subsidiary of: Elsevier Science & Technology), Radarweg 29, PO Box 211, Amsterdam, 1000 AE, Netherlands. TEL 31-20-4853911, FAX 31-20-4852457, JournalsCustomerServiceEMEA@elsevier.com, http://www.elsevier.nl. Eds. A P Hitchcock, J J Pireaux, N Kosugi.

535.58 USA ISSN 1546-900X
➤ **JOURNAL OF HOLOGRAPHY AND SPECKLE.** Abbreviated title: J O H A S. Text in English. 2004 (Mar.). s-a. USD 580; USD 1,280 combined subscription (print & online eds.) (effective 2010). back issues avail. **Document type:** *Journal, Academic/Scholarly.* **Description:** Brings out communications, research papers and reviews encompassing the fundamental and applied research in all areas of holography, and speckle.
Related titles: Online - full text ed.: ISSN 1546-9018. 2004. USD 1,080 (effective 2010) (from IngentaConnect).
Indexed: CPEI, SCOPUS.
—BLDSC (5002.750000), Ingenta. **CCC.**
Published by: American Scientific Publishers, 26650 The Old Rd, Ste 208, Valencia, CA 91381. TEL 661-799-7200, FAX 661-254-1207, order@aspbs.com. Ed. H John Caulfield TEL 615-329-8785.

535 USA ISSN 1866-6892
TA1570 CODEN: IJIWDO
➤ **JOURNAL OF INFRARED, MILLIMETER AND TERAHERTZ WAVES.** Text in English. 1980. m. EUR 1,785, USD 1,853 combined subscription to institutions (print & online eds.) (effective 2012). adv. illus. back issues avail.; reprint service avail. from PSC. **Document type:** *Journal, Academic/Scholarly.* **Description:** Reports original research in millimeter, submillimeter, and far infrared theory, techniques, devices, systems, spectroscopy, and applications.
Formerly (until 2009): International Journal of Infrared and Millimeter Waves (0195-9271)
Related titles: Microfilm ed.: (from PQC); Online - full text ed.: ISSN 1866-6906 (from IngentaConnect).
Indexed: A01, A03, A08, A22, A26, A28, APA, ASCA, BibLing, BrCerAb, C&ISA, CA, CA/WCA, CIA, CIN, CPEI, CerAb, ChemAb, ChemTitl, CivEngAb, CorrAb, CurCont, E&CAJ, E01, E11, EEA, EMA, ESPM, EngInd, EnvEAb, H15, I05, ISMEC, ISR, Inspec, M&TEA, M09, MBF, METADEX, MSCI, P30, PhysBer, SCI, SCOPUS, SolStAb, T02, T04, TM, W07, WAA.
—BLDSC (4542.305000), AskIEEE, CASDDS, IE, Infotrieve, Ingenta, INIST, Linda Hall. **CCC.**
Published by: Springer New York LLC (Subsidiary of: Springer Science+Business Media), 233 Spring St, New York, NY 10013. TEL 212-460-1500, FAX 212-460-1575, service-ny@springer.com. Eds. Martin Koch, Toshitaka Idehara.

621.329 USA ISSN 1042-346X
TA1671 CODEN: JLAPEN
➤ **JOURNAL OF LASER APPLICATIONS.** Abbreviated title: J L A. Text in English. 1976. q. price varies based on the number of users. adv. bk.rev. abstr.; bibl.; charts; illus. index. back issues avail.; reprints avail. **Document type:** *Journal, Academic/Scholarly.* **Description:** Publishes basic and applied papers dealing with the diverse applications of laser-electro-optics.
Formerly (until 1988): Topics of Laser Applications
Related titles: Online - full text ed.: ISSN 1938-1387.
Indexed: A22, A28, APA, ASCA, BrCerAb, C&ISA, CA/WCA, CIA, CIN, CPEI, CPI, CerAb, ChemAb, ChemTitl, CivEngAb, CorrAb, CurCont, E&CAJ, E01, E11, EEA, EMA, ESPM, EngInd, EnvEAb, H15, Inspec, M&TEA, M09, MBF, METADEX, P30, SCI, SCOPUS, SPINweb, SolStAb, T04, TM, W07, WAA.
—BLDSC (5010.103000), CASDDS, IE, Infotrieve, Ingenta, Linda Hall. **CCC.**
Published by: (Laser Institute of America), American Institute of Physics, 1 Physics Ellipse, College Park, MD 20740. TEL 301-209-3100, aipinfo@aip.org, http://www.aip.org. Ed. Reinhart Poprawe. Circ: 1,300. **Subscr. to:** PO Box 503284, St Louis, MO 63150. TEL 516-576-2270, 800-344-6902, FAX 516-349-9704, subs@aip.org, http://librarians.aip.org.

621.36 JPN ISSN 1880-0688
CODEN: JLMOA8
➤ **JOURNAL OF LASER MICRO NANOENGINEERING.** Text in English. 2006. q. free. **Document type:** *Journal, Academic/Scholarly.*
Media: Online - full text.
Indexed: C33, CurCont, SCI, T02, W07.
Published by: Reza Netsu Kako Kenkyukai/Japan Laser Processing Society, c/o Ms. Hiromi Inoue, Katayama Lab., JWRI-Joining & Welding Research Institute, Osaka University, 11-1 Mihogaoka, Ibaraki, Osaka 567-0047, Japan.

535 JPN ISSN 0387-8805
TH7700 CODEN: JLEVDQ
JOURNAL OF LIGHT & VISUAL ENVIRONMENT. Text in English. 1977. q. JPY 3,000 (effective 2004). back issues avail. **Document type:** *Journal, Academic/Scholarly.* **Description:** Contains papers and general reports, covering light sources, vision, color, radiometry, lighting design, and all other fields of lighting engineering.
Related titles: Online - full text ed.: ISSN 1349-8398. free (effective 2011).
Indexed: A39, C27, C29, CPEI, ChemAb, D03, D04, E13, EngInd, Inspec, R14, S14, S15, S18, SCOPUS.
—BLDSC (5010.471000), AskIEEE, CASDDS, Ingenta, Linda Hall. **CCC.**
Published by: Illuminating Engineering Institute of Japan/Shomei Gakkai, Suitaya Bldg 3F, 2-8-4 Kanda Tsukasa-cho, Chiyoda-ku, Tokyo, 101-0048, Japan. TEL 81-3-52940101, FAX 81-3-52940102, ieijedit@sepia.ocn.ne.jp, http://www.ieij.or.jp/index.html. Ed. Satoru Kawai.

535 USA ISSN 0733-8724
TA1501 CODEN: JLTEDG
JOURNAL OF LIGHTWAVE TECHNOLOGY. Text in English. 1983. m. USD 2,550 combined subscription in the Americas (print & online eds.); USD 2,650 combined subscription elsewhere (print & online eds.) (effective 2012). adv. back issues avail.; reprints avail. **Document type:** *Journal, Academic/Scholarly.* **Description:** Original papers reporting theoretical and-or experimental results that advance the technological base of guided-wave technology.
Related titles: Microfiche ed.; Online - full text ed.: ISSN 1558-2213. USD 1,890 (effective 2012).
Indexed: A22, A28, APA, ASCA, BrCerAb, C&ISA, CA/WCA, CADCAM, CIA, CIN, CMCI, CPEI, CerAb, ChemAb, ChemTitl, CivEngAb, CorrAb, CurCont, E&CAJ, E11, EEA, EMA, ESPM, EngInd, EnvEAb, H15, ISMEC, ISR, Inspec, M&TEA, M09, MBF, METADEX, RefZh, SCI, SCOPUS, SolStAb, T04, TelAb, W07, WAA.
—BLDSC (5010.474000), AskIEEE, CASDDS, IE, Infotrieve, Ingenta, INIST, Linda Hall. **CCC.**
Published by: I E E E, 445 Hoes Ln, Piscataway, NJ 08854. TEL 732-981-0060, 800-678-4333, FAX 732-562-6380, contactcenter@ieee.org, http://www.ieee.org. Eds. Connie Chang-Hasnain, Dawn Melley. **Subscr. to:** Optical Society of America. **Co-publisher:** Optical Society of America.

535 NLD ISSN 0022-2313
QC476.4 CODEN: JLUMA8
➤ **JOURNAL OF LUMINESCENCE.** Text in English, French, German; Summaries in English. 1970. 12/yr. EUR 3,256 in Europe to institutions; JPY 432,100 in Japan to institutions; USD 3,641 elsewhere to institutions (effective 2012). adv. bk.rev. bibl.; charts; illus. index, cum.index. back issues avail. **Document type:** *Journal, Academic/Scholarly.* **Description:** Provides a means of communication between scientists in different disciplines who share a common interest in the electronic excited state of molecular, ionic and covalent system, whether crystalline, amorphous, or liquid.
Related titles: Microform ed.: (from PQC); Online - full text ed.: ISSN 1872-7883 (from IngentaConnect, ScienceDirect).
Indexed: A01, A03, A08, A22, A26, ASCA, BPRC&P, C&ISA, C24, C33, CA, CCI, CIN, CPEI, Cadscan, ChemAb, ChemTitl, CurCont, E&CAJ, EngInd, GeoRef, I05, IBR, IBZ, INIS AtomInd, ISR, Inspec, LeadAb, P30, PhysBer, RefZh, S01, SCI, SCOPUS, SolStAb, SpeleolAb, T02, W07, Zincscan.
—BLDSC (5010.650000), AskIEEE, CASDDS, IE, Infotrieve, Ingenta, INIST, Linda Hall. **CCC.**
Published by: Elsevier BV, North-Holland (Subsidiary of: Elsevier Science & Technology), Sara Burgerhartstraat 25, Amsterdam, 1055 KV, Netherlands. TEL 31-20-4853911, FAX 31-20-4852457, JournalsCustomerServiceEMEA@elsevier.com. Ed. R S Meltzer. **Subscr. to:** Elsevier BV, Radarweg 29, PO Box 211, Amsterdam 1000 AE, Netherlands. TEL 31-20-4853757, FAX 31-20-4853432, http://www.elsevier.nl.

553 537.5 USA ISSN 1932-5150
TK7874 CODEN: JMMMGF
➤ **JOURNAL OF MICRO/NANOLITHOGRAPHY, M E M S, AND M O E M S.** Variant title: Journal of Micro/Nanolithography, Micro Electro Mechanical Systems, and Micro Optical Electro Mechanical System. Text and summaries in English. 2002. q. USD 510 combined subscription domestic (print & online eds.); USD 550 combined subscription foreign (print & online eds.) (effective 2012). adv. abstr.; charts; illus. **Document type:** *Journal, Academic/Scholarly.* **Description:** Publishes papers on the development of lithographic, fabrication, packaging and integration technologies necessary to address the future needs of the electronics, micro-opto-electro-mechanical and photonics industries.
Formerly (until 2007): Journal of Microlithography, Microfabrication, and Microsystems (1537-1646)
Related titles: CD-ROM ed.; Online - full text ed.: ISSN 1932-5134. USD 395 to institutions (effective 2012).
Indexed: A01, A03, A08, A28, APA, BrCerAb, C&ISA, CA, CA/WCA, CIA, CPEI, CerAb, CivEngAb, CorrAb, CurCont, E&CAJ, E11, EEA, EMA, EngInd, H15, Inspec, M&TEA, M09, MBF, METADEX, MSCI, SCI, SCOPUS, SolStAb, T02, T04, W07, WAA.
—BLDSC (5019.256000), IE, Ingenta, Linda Hall. **CCC.**
Published by: S P I E - International Society for Optical Engineering, 1000 20th St, Bellingham, WA 98225. TEL 360-676-3290, FAX 360-647-1445, journals@spie.org. Ed. Burn J Lin.

535 GBR ISSN 0950-0340
QC350 CODEN: JMOPEW
➤ **JOURNAL OF MODERN OPTICS.** Abbreviated title: J M O. Text in English. 1953. 21/yr. GBP 5,286 combined subscription in United Kingdom to institutions (print & online eds.); EUR 6,975, USD 8,760 combined subscription to institutions (print & online eds.) (effective 2012). adv. bk.rev. illus. index. back issues avail.; reprint service avail. from PSC. **Document type:** *Journal, Academic/Scholarly.* **Description:** Aims to cover both the fundamental and applied aspects of contemporary research worldwide on such topics as nonlinear and quantum optics; laser physics, coherence and speckle; optical fibres and thin films; integrated optics and electro-optics; and optical design and testing.
Formerly (until 1987): Optica Acta (0030-3909)
Related titles: Microform ed.; Online - full text ed.: ISSN 1362-3044. 1996. GBP 4,758 in United Kingdom to institutions; EUR 6,277, USD 7,884 to institutions (effective 2012) (from IngentaConnect).
Indexed: A01, A03, A08, A22, A28, APA, ASCA, B01, B06, B07, B09, BrCerAb, C&ISA, C23, CA, CA/WCA, CCMJ, CIA, CPEI, CerAb, ChemAb, ChemTitl, CivEngAb, CorrAb, CurCont, E&CAJ, E01, E11, EEA, EMA, ESPM, EngInd, EnvEAb, H15, IBR, IBZ, ISR, IndMed, Inspec, M&TEA, M09, MBF, METADEX, MSN, MathR, P26, P30, P52, P54, P56, PQC, PhotoAb, PhysBer, S01, SCI, SCOPUS, SolStAb, T02, T04, W07, WAA, Z02.
—AskIEEE, CASDDS, GNLM, IE, Infotrieve, Ingenta, INIST, Linda Hall. **CCC.**

P

Published by: Taylor & Francis Ltd. (Subsidiary of: Taylor & Francis Group), 4 Park Sq, Milton Park, Abingdon, Oxfordshire OX14 4RN, United Kingdom. TEL 44-20-70176000, FAX 44-20-70176336, subscriptions@tandf.co.uk, http://www.taylorandfrancis.com. Ed. Jon Marangos. Adv. contact Linda Hann. **Subscr. in N. America to:** Taylor & Francis Inc., Customer Services Dept, 325 Chestnut St, 8th Fl, Philadelphia, PA 19106. TEL 215-625-8900, 800-354-1420, FAX 215-625-2940, customerservice@taylorandfrancis.com; **Subscr. to:** Journals Customer Service, Sheepen Pl, Colchester, Essex CO3 3LP, United Kingdom. TEL 44-20-70175544, FAX 44-20-70175198, tf.enquiries@tfinforma.com.

535.84 543.1 USA ISSN 0022-2852
QC451 CODEN: JMOSA3

➤ **JOURNAL OF MOLECULAR SPECTROSCOPY.** Text in English. 1957. m. EUR 4,995 in Europe to institutions; JPY 521,800 in Japan to institutions; USD 3,923 elsewhere to institutions (effective 2012). adv. bibl.; charts; illus. index. back issues avail. **Document type:** *Journal, Academic/Scholarly.* **Description:** Presents experimental and theoretical articles on all subjects relevant to molecular spectroscopy and its modern applications.

Related titles: Online - full text ed.: ISSN 1096-083X (from IngentaConnect, ScienceDirect).

Indexed: A01, A03, A08, A22, A26, ABIPC, ASCA, BullT&T, C&ISA, C24, C33, CA, CCI, CIN, CPEI, ChemAb, ChemTitl, CurCR, CurCont, E&CAJ, E01, EngInd, GeoRef, I05, ISMEC, ISR, Inspec, P30, PhysBer, R16, RefZh, S01, SCI, SCOPUS, SolStAb, T02, W07.

—BLDSC (5020.750000), AskIEEE, CASDDS, IE, Infotrieve, Ingenta, INIST, Linda Hall. **CCC.**

Published by: Academic Press (Subsidiary of: Elsevier Science & Technology), 3251 Riverport Ln, Maryland Heights, MO 63043. TEL 314-447-8010, FAX 314-447-8030, JournalCustomerService-usa@elsevier.com, http://www.elsevierdirect.com/imprint.jsp?iid=5. Ed. T A Miller.

535 USA ISSN 1934-2608

➤ **JOURNAL OF NANOPHOTONICS.** Text in English. 2007 (Jan.). m. (frequent updates). USD 305 to institutions (effective 2012). **Document type:** *Journal, Academic/Scholarly.* **Description:** Focuses on the fabrication and application of nanostructures that either generate or manipulate light from the infrared to the ultraviolet regimes.

Media: Online - full text. **Related titles:** CD-ROM ed.

Indexed: CPEI, CurCont, P30, SCI, SCOPUS, W07.

—CCC.

Published by: S P I E - International Society for Optical Engineering, 1000 20th St, Bellingham, WA 98225. TEL 360-676-3290, 888-504-8171, FAX 360-647-1445, journals@spie.org. Ed. Dr. Akhlesh Lakhtakia TEL 814-863-4319.

535 SGP ISSN 0218-8635
QC446.15 CODEN: IJNOEQ

➤ **JOURNAL OF NONLINEAR OPTICAL PHYSICS AND MATERIALS.** Abbreviated title: J N O P M. Text in English. 1992. q. SGD 1,976, USD 1,208, EUR 1,032 combined subscription to institutions (print & online eds.) (effective 2012). adv. back issues avail. **Document type:** *Journal, Academic/Scholarly.* **Description:** Covers research and development in nonlinear interactions of light with matter, including fundamental nonlinear optical processes, novel nonlinear material properties, guided waves and solutions, intense field phenomena, and their applications in laser and coherent lightwave amplification, guiding, switching, modulation, communication and information processing.

Formerly (until 1995): International Journal of Nonlinear Optical Physics (0218-1991)

Related titles: Online - full text ed.: ISSN 1793-6624. SGD 1,796, USD 1,098, EUR 938 to institutions (effective 2012).

Indexed: A01, A03, A08, A22, A28, APA, ASCA, BrCerAb, C&ISA, CA, CA/WCA, CIA, CIN, CerAb, ChemAb, ChemTitl, CivEngAb, CorrAb, CurCont, E&CAJ, E01, E11, EEA, EMA, ESPM, EnvEAb, H15, Inspec, M&TEA, M09, MBF, METADEX, S01, SCI, SCOPUS, SolStAb, T02, T04, W07, WAA.

—BLDSC (5022.838500), AskIEEE, CASDDS, IE, Infotrieve, Ingenta, Linda Hall. **CCC.**

Published by: World Scientific Publishing Co. Pte. Ltd., 5 Toh Tuck Link, Singapore, 596224, Singapore. TEL 65-6466-5775, FAX 65-6467-7667, wspc@wspc.com.sg, http://www.worldscientific.com. Ed. Iam-Choon Khoo. **Dist. by:** World Scientific Publishing Co., Inc., 27 Warren St, Ste 401-402, Hackensack, NJ 07601. TEL 201-487-9655, 800-227-7562, FAX 201-487-9656, 888-977-2665, wspc@wspc.com; World Scientific Publishing Ltd., 57 Shelton St, London WC2H 9HE, United Kingdom. TEL 44-207-8360888, FAX 44-207-8362020, sales@wspc.co.uk.

535 USA ISSN 1943-0620
TK5103.59

JOURNAL OF OPTICAL COMMUNICATIONS AND NETWORKING. Abbreviated title: J O C N. Variant title: I E E E/ O S A Journal of Optical Communications and Networking. Text in English. 2002. q. USD 2,135; USD 2,620 combined subscription (print & online eds.) (effective 2012). adv. back issues avail.; reprints avail. **Document type:** *Journal, Academic/Scholarly.* **Description:** Dedicated to disseminating advances in the state-of-the-art of optical communications networks.

Formerly (until 2009): Journal of Optical Networking (1536-5379)

Related titles: Online - full text ed.: ISSN 1943-0639. USD 1,940 (effective 2012).

Indexed: CMCI, CPEI, CurCont, EngInd, Inspec, RefZh, SCI, SCOPUS, W07.

—BLDSC (4363.012550), IE. **CCC.**

Published by: (Optical Society of America), I E E E, 445 Hoes Ln, Piscataway, NJ 08854. TEL 732-981-0060, 800-678-4333, FAX 732-562-6380, contactcenter@ieee.org, http://www.ieee.org. Eds. Keren Bergman, Vincent Chan.

535 USA ISSN 1070-9762
TS510 CODEN: JOTEE4

➤ **JOURNAL OF OPTICAL TECHNOLOGY.** Abbreviated title: J O T. Text in English. 1966. m. USD 3,286 combined subscription domestic to institutions (print & online eds.); USD 3,336 combined subscription in Canada to institutions (print & online eds.); USD 3,426 combined subscription elsewhere to institutions (print & online eds.) (effective 2011). back issues avail. **Document type:** *Journal, Academic/Scholarly.* **Description:** Contains theoretical and experimental research articles concerning many phases of optical, space and astronomical engineering.

Formerly (until 1994): Soviet Journal of Optical Technology (0038-5514)

Related titles: Online - full text ed.: ISSN 1091-0786. USD 2,907 (effective 2011); ◆ Translation of: Opticheskii Zhurnal.

Indexed: A20, A22, APA, ASCA, C&ISA, CPEI, CPI, CorrAb, CurCont, E&CAJ, EEA, EngInd, GPAA, Inspec, PhotoAb, PhysBer, SCI, SCOPUS, SPINweb, SolStAb, TM, W07, WAA.

—BLDSC (0415.219000), AskIEEE, CASDDS, IE, Infotrieve, Ingenta, INIST, Linda Hall. **CCC.**

Published by: (Opticheskii Institut im. S.I. Vavilova RUS), Optical Society of America, 2010 Massachusetts Ave, NW, Washington, DC 20036. TEL 202-416-1907, FAX 202-416-6140, info@osa.org, http://www.osa.org. Ed. A S Tibilov.

535 GBR ISSN 2040-8978
QC350 CODEN: JOAOF8

➤ **JOURNAL OF OPTICS.** Text in English. 1999. m. GBP 821 combined subscription to institutions (print & online eds.) (effective 2010). adv. bk.rev. annual index. back issues avail. **Document type:** *Journal, Academic/Scholarly.* **Description:** Examines all aspects of research within modern and classical optics.

Formerly (until 2010): Journal of Optics A: Pure and Applied Optics (1464-4258); Which was formed by the merger of (1992-1999): Pure and Applied Optics (0963-9659); (1977-1999): Journal of Optics (0150-536X); Which was formerly (until 1977): Nouvelle Revue d'Optique (0335-7368); (until 1973): Nouvelle Revue d'Optique Appliquee (0029-4780); (until 1970): Revue d'Optique Theorique et Instrumentale (0035-2489)

Related titles: Microfiche ed.: 1992. USD 1,020 in North America; GBP 517 elsewhere (effective 2007); Online - full text ed.: ISSN 2040-8986. GBP 782 to institutions (effective 2010) (from IngentaConnect).

Indexed: A01, A03, A08, A20, A22, A28, APA, ASCA, BrCerAb, C&ISA, CA, CA/WCA, CIA, CPEI, CerAb, ChemAb, CivEngAb, CorrAb, CurCont, E&CAJ, E11, EEA, EMA, ESPM, EngInd, EnvEAb, GeoRef, H15, IBR, IBZ, ISR, Inspec, M&TEA, M09, MBF, METADEX, RefZh, SCI, SCOPUS, SolStAb, SpeleolAb, T02, T04, W07, WAA.

—BLDSC (5026.359500), AskIEEE, CASDDS, IE, Infotrieve, Ingenta, INIST, Linda Hall. **CCC.**

Published by: (Institute of Physics), Institute of Physics Publishing Ltd., Dirac House, Temple Back, Bristol, BS1 6BE, United Kingdom. TEL 44-117-9297481, FAX 44-117-9301178, custserv@iop.org, http://publishing.iop.org/. Ed. Nikolay Zheludev. Pub. Claire Bedrock. Adv. contact David Iddon TEL 44-117-9301032. **Co-sponsor:** European Optical Society.

535 IND ISSN 0972-8821

➤ **JOURNAL OF OPTICS.** Text in English. 1972. q. EUR 235, USD 352 combined subscription to institutions (print & online eds.) (effective 2012). adv. bk.rev. index. back issues avail.; reprint service avail. from PSC. **Document type:** *Journal, Academic/Scholarly.* **Description:** Publishes research papers on results of original and applied research of sufficient merit in all branches of optical physics and technology such as science of vision, colour, photometry, illumination, optical/opto-electronic materials and devices, optical testing and standardisation, spectroscopy, lasers, holography, fibre optics, non-linear optics, optical and opto-electronic systems and instruments, image processing, optical computing etc.

Related titles: Microform ed.: (from PQC); Online - full text ed.: ISSN 0974-6900 (from IngentaConnect).

Indexed: A22, CADCAM, CPEI, ChemAb, E01, EngInd, ISR, Inspec, PhotoAb, RefZh, SCOPUS.

—BLDSC (5026.360000), Ingenta, Linda Hall. **CCC.**

Published by: (Optical Society of India), Springer (India) Private Ltd. (Subsidiary of: Springer Science+Business Media), 212, Deen Dayal Upadhyaya Marg, 3rd Fl, Gandharva Mahavidyalaya, New Delhi, 110 002, India. TEL 91-11-45755888, FAX 91-11-45755889. Ed. A Basuray. Circ: 600. **Subscr. to:** I N S I O Scientific Books & Periodicals, PO Box 7234, Indraprastha HPO, New Delhi 110 002, India. iihm@ap.nic.in, http://iihm.ap.nic.in/.

535 534 USA
CODEN: JOIREM

JOURNAL OF OPTICS RESEARCH. Text in English. 1990. q. USD 680 to institutions; USD 1,020 combined subscription to institutions (print & online eds.) (effective 2012). **Document type:** *Journal, Academic/Scholarly.* **Description:** Provides a forum for the international treatment of all aspects of optics.

Formerly: Optical and Acoustical Review (1050-3315)

Related titles: Online - full text ed.: USD 680 to institutions (effective 2012).

Indexed: A22, RefZh.

—CASDDS, IE, Ingenta.

Published by: Nova Science Publishers, Inc., 400 Oser Ave, Ste 1600, Hauppauge, NY 11788. TEL 631-231-7269, FAX 631-231-8175, main@novapublishers.com.

535.84 GBR ISSN 0022-4073
QC451 CODEN: JQSRAE

➤ **JOURNAL OF QUANTITATIVE SPECTROSCOPY & RADIATIVE TRANSFER.** Text in English, French, German, Russian. 1961. 18/yr. EUR 6,535 in Europe to institutions; JPY 867,400 in Japan to institutions; USD 7,308 elsewhere to institutions (effective 2012). bk.rev. charts; illus. index. back issues avail. **Document type:** *Journal, Academic/Scholarly.* **Description:** Covers spectral line shapes and widths, quantitative spectroscopic techniques for environmental studies, radiant energy emissions for plasmas and spectroscopic studies involving lasers.

Related titles: Microfilm ed.: (from PQC); Online - full text ed.: ISSN 1879-1352 (from IngentaConnect, ScienceDirect).

Indexed: A01, A03, A08, A20, A22, A26, A28, A33, APA, ASCA, ApMecR, BrCerAb, C&ISA, C24, C33, CA, CA/WCA, CIA, CIN, CPEI, Cadscan, CerAb, ChemAb, ChemTitl, CivEngAb, CorrAb, CurCont, E&CAJ, E11, EEA, EMA, ESPM, EngInd, EnvEAb, GEOBASE, GeoRef, H15, I05, INIS AtomInd, ISR, Inspec, LeadAb, M&GPA, M&TEA, M09, MBF, METADEX, P30, PhysBer, RefZh, S01, SCI, SCOPUS, SolStAb, SpeleolAb, T02, T04, W07, WAA, Zincscan.

—BLDSC (5043.700000), AskIEEE, CASDDS, IE, Infotrieve, Ingenta, INIST, Linda Hall. **CCC.**

Published by: Pergamon (Subsidiary of: Elsevier Science & Technology), The Blvd, Langford Ln, East Park, Kidlington, Oxford OX5 1GB, United Kingdom. TEL 44-1865-843000, FAX 44-1865-843010, JournalsCustomerServiceEMEA@elsevier.com. Eds. Laurence Se Rothman TEL 617-495-7474, Michael I Mishchenko TEL 212-678-5590, Pinar Menguc TEL 859-257-6336 ext 8065. **Subscr. to:** Elsevier BV, Radarweg 29, PO Box 211, Amsterdam 1000 AE, Netherlands. TEL 31-20-4853757, FAX 31-20-4853432, http://www.elsevier.nl.

➤ **KEY ABSTRACTS - OPTOELECTRONICS.** *see* PHYSICS—Abstracting, Bibliographies, Statistics

535 JPN ISSN 0910-9854

KODANSEIGAKU RONBUNSHU/JAPAN SOCIETY FOR PHOTOELASTICITY. PROCEEDINGS. Text in Japanese. 1979. a. **Document type:** *Proceedings.*

—CCC.

Published by: Nihon Kodansei Gakkai/Japan Society for Photoelasticity, Nihon Gakkai Jimu Senta, 16-9 Honkomagome 5-chome, Bunkyo-ku, Tokyo, 113-0021, Japan.

535 JPN ISSN 0389-6625
TA1501 CODEN: KOGAD5

KOGAKU/JAPANESE JOURNAL OF OPTICS. Text in English, Japanese; Summaries in English. 1972. m. JPY 9,600 for membership to individuals; JPY 15,000 to institutions (effective 2004). **Document type:** *Journal, Academic/Scholarly.* **Description:** Includes both reviews and original papers on various aspects of optics.

—CASDDS. **CCC.**

Published by: (Optical Society of Japan), Japan Society of Applied Physics/Oyo Butsuri Gakkai, Kudan-Kita Bldg 5th Fl, 1-12-3 Kudan-Kita, Chiyoda-ku, Tokyo, 102-0073, Japan.

535 JPN

KOGAKU GO GAKKAI KANSAI SHIBU RENGO KOENKAI YOKOSHU/KANSAI BRANCHES FIVE SOCIETIES ON OPTICS. JOINT CONVENTION RECORD. Text in Japanese. a.

Published by: Kogaku Go Gakkai Kansai Shibu, c/o Shomei Gakkai Kansai Shibu, Chuo Denki Kurabu, 1-25 Dojima-Hama 2-chome, Kita-ku, Osaka-shi, 530-0000, Japan.

535 RUS ISSN 0368-7147

KVANTOVAYA ELEKTRONIKA (MOSCOW)/QUANTUM ELECTRONICS. Text in Russian. 1971. m. USD 735 foreign (effective 2005). **Document type:** *Journal, Academic/Scholarly.* **Description:** Covers lasers and their applications.

Related titles: Online - full text ed.: 1997; ◆ English Translation: Quantum Electronics. ISSN 1063-7818.

Indexed: Inspec, RefZh, SCOPUS.

—BLDSC (0088.580000), East View, INIST, Linda Hall.

Published by: (Rossiiskaya Akademiya Nauk, Institut Fiziki im. P.N. Lebedeva/Russian Academy of Sciences, P.N. Lebedev Physics Institute), Izdatel'stvo Radio i Svyaz', Kuznetskii Most 20/6, Moscow, 103031, Russian Federation. TEL 7-095-9258436, FAX 7-095-9245290, elsv@garnet.ru. Ed. O N Krokhin. **Dist. by:** East View Information Services, 10601 Wayzata Blvd, Minneapolis, MN 55305. TEL 952-252-1201, 800-477-1005, FAX 952-252-1202, info@eastview.com, http://www.eastview.com.

L A N/PREMISES COMPONENTS QUARTERLY REPORTS. (Local Area Networks) *see* COMPUTERS—Computer Networks

535.58 DEU ISSN 0178-7225

LASER. Text in English. 1985. 4/yr. EUR 65 domestic; EUR 75 foreign (effective 2009). adv. **Document type:** *Journal, Academic/Scholarly.*

Published by: b-Quadrat Verlags GmbH & Co. KG, Kolpingstr 46, Kaufering, 86916, Germany. TEL 49-8191-96410, FAX 49-8191-964141, info@b-quadrat.de. Ed. Wolfgang Klinker. Pub. Gisela Mengling. Adv. contact Werner Duda. B&W page EUR 3,400, color page EUR 4,450; trim 178 x 257. Circ: 11,523 (controlled).

535 GBR ISSN 0263-0346
QC689.5.L37 CODEN: LPBEDA

➤ **LASER AND PARTICLE BEAMS;** pulse power & high energy densities. Text in English. 1983. q. GBP 703, USD 1,275 to institutions; GBP 787, USD 1,441 combined subscription to institutions (print & online eds.) (effective 2012). adv. bk.rev. back issues avail.; reprint service avail. from PSC. **Document type:** *Journal, Academic/Scholarly.* **Description:** Provides a forum for physicists and engineers to pool the findings of their research on the generation of high-intensity laser and particle beams and their interaction with matter.

Related titles: Online - full text ed.: ISSN 1469-803X. GBP 643, USD 1,175 to institutions (effective 2012).

Indexed: A22, ASCA, C&ISA, C33, CA, CIN, CPEI, ChemAb, ChemTitl, CurCont, E&CAJ, E01, EIA, EngInd, IBR, IBZ, ISMEC, ISR, Inspec, P26, P48, P52, P54, P56, PQC, PhysBer, RefZh, SCI, SCOPUS, SolStAb, T02, W07.

—BLDSC (5156.518800), AskIEEE, CASDDS, IE, Infotrieve, Ingenta, INIST, Linda Hall. **CCC.**

Published by: Cambridge University Press, The Edinburgh Bldg, Shaftesbury Rd, Cambridge, CB2 8RU, United Kingdom. TEL 44-1223-312393, FAX 44-1223-315052, journals@cambridge.org, http://www.cambridge.org/uk. Ed. Dieter H H Hoffmann. R&P Linda Nicol TEL 44-1223-325702. Adv. contact Rebecca Roberts TEL 44-1223-325083. page GBP 445, page USD 845. Circ: 600. **Subscr. to:** Cambridge University Press, 32 Ave of the Americas, New York, NY 10013. TEL 212-337-5000, FAX 212-691-3239, journals_subscriptions@cup.org.

621.36 DEU ISSN 1863-8880

➤ **LASER & PHOTONICS REVIEWS.** Text in English. 2007. bi-m. GBP 939 in United Kingdom to institutions; EUR 1,101 in Europe to institutions; USD 1,539 elsewhere to institutions (effective 2012). reprint service avail. from PSC. **Document type:** *Journal, Academic/Scholarly.* **Description:** Covers the current range of laser physics and photonics, both theoretical and experimental, from recent research to specific developments and novel applications.

Related titles: Online - full text ed.: ISSN 1863-8899. GBP 939 in United Kingdom to institutions; EUR 1,101 in Europe to institutions; USD 1,539 elsewhere to institutions (effective 2012).
Indexed: A28, APA, BrCerAb, C&ISA, CA/WCA, CIA, CPEI, CerAb, CivEngAb, CorrAb, CurCont, E&CAJ, E11, EEA, EMA, ESPM, EnvEAb, H15, Inspec, M&TEA, M09, MBF, METADEX, MSCI, P30, RefZh, SCI, SCOPUS, SolStAb, T04, W07, WAA.
—BLDSC (5156.518880), IE, INIST, Linda Hall.
Published by: Wiley - V C H Verlag GmbH & Co. KGaA (Subsidiary of: John Wiley & Sons, Inc.), Postfach 101161, Weinheim, 69451, Germany. TEL 49-6201-606400, FAX 49-6201-606184, info@wiley-vch.de, http://www.wiley-vch.de. Ed. Guido W Fuchs.

535.58 USA ISSN 0278-6273
QD701 CODEN: LSCHDB
➤ **LASER CHEMISTRY.** Text in French. 1982. irreg. USD 195 (effective 2011). **Document type:** *Journal, Academic/Scholarly.* **Description:** Its focus is in the area of fundamental studies and applications within the field of laser chemical physics and spectroscopy.
Related titles: Online - full text ed.: ISSN 1476-3516. free (effective 2011) (from IngentaConnect).
Indexed: A01, A22, A26, A28, A39, APA, ASCA, BrCerAb, C&ISA, C27, C29, C33, CA, CA/WCA, CIA, CerAb, ChemAb, CivEngAb, CorrAb, D03, D04, E&CAJ, E11, E13, EEA, EMA, ESPM, EnvEAb, H15, I05, Inspec, M&TEA, M09, MBF, METADEX, P52, R14, S14, S15, S18, SCOPUS, SolStAb, T02, T04, WAA.
—AskIEEE, IE, Infotrieve, Ingenta, INIST. **CCC.**
Published by: Hindawi Publishing Corporation, 410 Park Ave, 15th Fl, PMB 287, New York, NY 10022. FAX 866-446-3294, info@hindawi.com. Ed. Costas Fotakis.

535.58 621.329 USA ISSN 1043-8092
TA1501 CODEN: LFWOE8
LASER FOCUS WORLD; international resource for technology and applications in the global photonics industry. Text in English. 1965. m. USD 150 domestic; USD 200 in Canada; USD 250 elsewhere; USD 15 newsstand/cover (effective 2008); includes Buyers Guide. adv. illus. Supplement avail.; back issues avail. **Document type:** *Magazine, Trade.* **Description:** Provides global coverage of optoelectronic technologies, applications and markets.
Former titles (until Dec.1988): Laser Focus (0740-2511); (until 1983): Laser Focus with Fiberoptic Technology (0275-1399); (until 1981): Laser Focus with Fiberoptic Communications (0190-1451); (until 1978): Laser Focus (0023-8589); Incorporates (in 1983): Electro-Optics (0745-5003); Which was formerly (until 1969): Electro-Optical Systems Design (0424-8457)
Related titles: Online - full text ed.: free to qualified personnel.
Indexed: A01, A03, A05, A08, A09, A10, A20, A22, A23, A24, A26, A28, ABIPC, APA, AS&TA, AS&TI, ASCA, B01, B02, B03, B04, B06, B07, B08, B09, B10, B11, B13, B15, B17, B18, BrCerAb, C&ISA, C10, C12, CA, CA/WCA, CADCAM, CIA, CIN, CPEI, CerAb, ChemAb, ChemTitl, CivEngAb, CorrAb, CurCont, E&CAJ, E11, EEA, EMA, ESPM, EngInd, EnvEAb, FR, G04, G06, G07, G08, GeoRef, H15, I05, ISR, Inspec, M&TEA, M01, M02, M09, MBF, METADEX, MicrocompInd, P02, P10, P16, P26, P48, P52, P53, P54, P56, PQC, RoboAb, S01, S06, S10, S22, SCI, SCOPUS, SoftBase, SolStAb, SpeleolAb, T02, T04, TM, V03, V04, W07, WAA.
—BLDSC (5156.530610), AskIEEE, CASDDS, IE, Infotrieve, Ingenta, INIST, Linda Hall. **CCC.**
Published by: PennWell Corporation, 1421 S Sheridan Rd, Tulsa, OK 74112. TEL 918-835-3161, 800-331-4463, FAX 918-831-9804, patrickM@pennwell.com, http://www.pennwell.com. Eds. Barbara Goode TEL 603-891-9194, Stephen G Anderson TEL 603-891-9320. adv.: B&W page USD 11,250, color page USD 13,450; trim 8 x 10.5. Circ: 70,002.

658.0029 USA
LASER FOCUS WORLD BUYERS' GUIDE. Text in English. 1964. a. USD 125 domestic; USD 155 in Canada; USD 185 elsewhere; USD 15 per issue domestic; USD 20 per issue in Canada; USD 25 per issue elsewhere; free to qualified personnel (effective 2009). back issues avail. **Document type:** *Magazine, Trade.* **Description:** Provides global coverage of optoelectronic technologies, applications and markets.
Former titles: Laser Focus - Electro Optics Buyers' Guide (8755-1616); Laser Focus Buyers' Guide (0075-8027); (until 1970): Laser Marketers' and Buyers' Guide
Related titles: Online - full text ed.: USD 75; free to qualified personnel (effective 2009).
—Linda Hall. **CCC.**
Published by: PennWell Corporation, 1421 S Sheridan Rd, Tulsa, OK 74112. TEL 918-835-3161, 800-331-4463, FAX 918-831-9804, Headquarters@PennWell.com, http://www.pennwell.com. Ed. Greg Reed. Pub. Marsha Robertson. Adv. contact Jane Harrod. Circ: 50,000.

535.3 621.36 NLD ISSN 0921-8564
➤ **LASER HANDBOOK.** Text in English. 1972. irreg., latest vol.6, 1990. price varies. charts; stat. back issues avail. **Document type:** *Monographic series, Academic/Scholarly.* **Description:** Reports investigations into applications of lasers in applied and theoretical physics research.
Published by: Elsevier BV, North-Holland (Subsidiary of: Elsevier Science & Technology), Sara Burgerhartstraat 25, Amsterdam, 1055 KV, Netherlands. TEL 31-20-4853911, FAX 31-20-4852457, JournalsCustomerServiceEMEA@elsevier.com, http://www.elsevier.com. **Subscr. to:** Elsevier BV, Radarweg 29, PO Box 211, Amsterdam 1000 AE, Netherlands. TEL 31-20-4853757, FAX 31-20-4853432.

535.58 DEU ISSN 0945-8875
LASER-MAGAZIN. Text in German. 1984. bi-m. EUR 70 domestic; EUR 75.50 foreign; EUR 15 newsstand/cover (effective 2006). adv. **Document type:** *Magazine, Trade.*
Indexed: Inspec, TM.
Published by: Magazin Verlag Hightech Publications KG, Jaegerweg 14, Bad Nenndorf, 31542, Germany. TEL 49-5723-5534, FAX 49-5723-76212, kontakt@magazin-verlag.de, http://www.magazin-verlag.de. adv.: B&W page EUR 2,475, color page EUR 3,795; trim 185 x 270. Circ: 9,601 (paid and controlled).

535.58 RUS ISSN 1054-660X
QC685 CODEN: LAPHEJ
➤ **LASER PHYSICS**; international journal. Text in English. 1990. m. EUR 3,650, USD 4,408 combined subscription to institutions (print & online eds.) (effective 2012). **Document type:** *Journal, Academic/Scholarly.* **Description:** Covers the whole range of questions of modern laser physics and quantum electronics, emphasizing physical effects in various media (solid, gaseous, liquid) leading to the generation of laser radiation.
Related titles: Online - full text ed.: ISSN 1555-6611 (from IngentaConnect).
Indexed: A22, A26, ASCA, CIN, CPEI, ChemAb, ChemTitl, CurCont, E01, EngInd, I05, Inspec, P30, SCI, SCOPUS, W07.
—BLDSC (5156.606000), AskIEEE, CASDDS, East View, IE, Infotrieve, Ingenta, INIST. **CCC.**
Published by: (Rossiiskaya Akademiya Nauk/Russian Academy of Sciences), M A I K Nauka - Interperiodica (Subsidiary of: Pleiades Publishing, Inc.), Profsoyuznaya ul 90, Moscow, 117997, Russian Federation. TEL 7-095-3347420, FAX 7-095-3360666, compmg@maik.ru, http://www.maik.ru. Ed. Pavel Pashinin. **Dist. by:** Springer, Haber Str 7, Heidelberg 69126, Germany. TEL 49-6221-3454303, FAX 49-6221-3454229; Springer New York LLC, Journal Fulfillment, PO Box 2485, Secaucus, NJ 07096. TEL 212-460-1500, FAX 201-348-4505.

531.64 DEU ISSN 1612-2011
QC685
➤ **LASER PHYSICS LETTERS.** Text in English. 2004. m. GBP 1,092 in United Kingdom to institutions; EUR 1,665 in Europe to institutions; USD 2,141 elsewhere to institutions; GBP 1,256 combined subscription in United Kingdom to institutions (print & online eds.); EUR 1,915 combined subscription in Europe to institutions (print & online eds.); USD 2,463 combined subscription elsewhere to institutions (print & online eds.) (effective 2012). reprint service avail. from PSC. **Document type:** *Journal, Academic/Scholarly.* **Description:** Covers the broad range of contemporary laser physics from fundamental research to specific developments and new applications in adjacent fields of science.
Related titles: Online - full text ed.: ISSN 1612-202X. GBP 1,092 in United Kingdom to institutions; EUR 1,665 in Europe to institutions; USD 2,141 elsewhere to institutions (effective 2012).
Indexed: CurCont, Inspec, RefZh, SCI, SCOPUS, W07.
—BLDSC (5156.607300), IE, Ingenta. **CCC.**
Published by: Wiley - V C H Verlag GmbH & Co. KGaA (Subsidiary of: John Wiley & Sons, Inc.), Postfach 101161, Weinheim, 69451, Germany. TEL 49-6201-606400, FAX 49-6201-606184, info@wiley-vch.de, http://www.wiley-vch.de.

531.64 DEU ISSN 1613-7728
➤ **LASER TECHNIK JOURNAL.** Text in German. 2004 (Apr.). bi-m. GBP 72 in United Kingdom to institutions; EUR 128 in Europe to institutions; USD 141 elsewhere to institutions (effective 2012). adv. reprint service avail. from PSC. **Document type:** *Journal, Academic/Scholarly.*
Related titles: Online - full text ed.: ISSN 1863-9119.
—IE.
Published by: Wiley - V C H Verlag GmbH & Co. KGaA (Subsidiary of: John Wiley & Sons, Inc.), Postfach 101161, Weinheim, 69451, Germany. TEL 49-6201-606400, FAX 49-6201-606184, info@wiley-vch.de, http://www.wiley-vch.de. Ed. Francisco Velasco TEL 49-30-47031323. Pub. Andreas Thoss TEL 49-30-47031350. Adv. contact Aenne Anders TEL 49-6201-606552. B&W page EUR 3,400; trim 185 x 260. Circ: 10,000 (controlled).

535.58 DEU ISSN 1610-3521
TA1671 CODEN: LASPEO
LASER UND PHOTONIK. Text in German. 1989. 5/yr. EUR 64 combined subscription (print & online eds.); EUR 20.80 newsstand/cover (effective 2011). adv. **Document type:** *Journal, Trade.*
Formerly (until 2002): Laser Praxis (0937-7069)
Related titles: Online - full text ed.; English ed.: Laser and Photonics. ISSN 1865-5475. 2008. EUR 64; EUR 20.80 newsstand/cover (effective 2010).
Indexed: CEABA, Inspec, SCOPUS.
—IE, Infotrieve, INIST. **CCC.**
Published by: Carl Hanser Verlag GmbH & Co. KG, Kolbergerstr 22, Munich, 81679, Germany. TEL 49-89-998300, FAX 49-89-984809, info@hanser.de, http://www.hanser.de. Ed. Matthias Laasch. Adv. contact Regine Schmidt. Circ: 15,540 (paid and controlled).

621.329 USA ISSN 0898-1507
TA367.5 CODEN: LAENEG
➤ **LASERS IN ENGINEERING.** Text in English. 1991. bi-m. EUR 333 in Europe to individuals; JPY 37,889 in Japan to individuals; USD 374 elsewhere to individuals; EUR 1,623 combined subscription in Europe to institutions (print & online eds.); JPY 187,347 combined subscription in Japan to institutions (print & online eds.); USD 1,987 combined subscription elsewhere to institutions (print & online eds.) (effective 2011). adv. back issues avail. **Document type:** *Journal, Academic/Scholarly.* **Description:** Brings out research articles, reviews, short communications and letters on all aspects relating to the applications of lasers in the different branches of engineering and related disciplines.
Related titles: CD-ROM ed.: ISSN 1026-7069; Microform ed.; Online - full text ed.: ISSN 1029-029X (from IngentaConnect).
Indexed: A01, A22, A28, APA, ASCA, BrCerAb, C&ISA, CA, CA/WCA, CIA, CPEI, CerAb, CivEngAb, CorrAb, CurCont, E&CAJ, E01, E11, EEA, EMA, ESPM, EngInd, EnvEAb, H15, M&TEA, M09, MBF, METADEX, MSCI, SCI, SCOPUS, SolStAb, T02, T04, TM, W07, WAA.
—BLDSC (5156.674000), IE, Infotrieve, Ingenta, Linda Hall. **CCC.**
Published by: Old City Publishing, Inc., 628 N 2nd St, Philadelphia, PA 19123. TEL 215-925-4390, FAX 215-925-4371, info@oldcitypublishing.com. Eds. B L Mordike, Jonathan Lawrence.

➤ **LASERS IN MEDICAL SCIENCE.** *see* MEDICAL SCIENCES

➤ **LASERS IN SURGERY AND MEDICINE.** *see* MEDICAL SCIENCES—Surgery

➤ **LATIN AMERICAN FIBER OPTICS REPORT.** *see* COMPUTERS—Computer Networks

535 RUS
LAZERNYE NOVOSTI/LASER NEWS. Text in Russian. q. USD 99.95 in United States.
Published by: Firma Polius Marketing, Ul Vedenskogo 3, Moscow, 117342, Russian Federation. TEL 7-095-3330389, FAX 7-095-3330256. Ed. Yu G D'yakova. **Dist. by:** East View Information Services, 10601 Wayzata Blvd, Minneapolis, MN 55305. TEL 952-252-1201, 800-477-1005, FAX 952-252-1202, info@eastview.com, http://www.eastview.com.

535 USA ISSN 1933-9518
▼ **LIGHT & MATTER.** Text in English. forthcoming 2011 (Nov.). m. free (effective 2009). **Document type:** *Journal, Academic/Scholarly.* **Description:** Includes research on light emission and absorption, optomagnetics, photonics, plasmonics, lasers and optics.
Media: Online - full content.
Published by: Science Observer, 414-3 Galleria Dr, San Jose, CA 95134. TEL 408-772-5658, derek_cunningham@scienceobserver.com, http://www.scienceobserver.com.

LIGHTING DESIGN + APPLICATION. *see* ENGINEERING—Electrical Engineering

LIGHTWAVE EUROPE. *see* COMMUNICATIONS

LYS. *see* ENGINEERING—Electrical Engineering

535.38 025 FRA ISSN 1761-9955
M O S; le magazine de l'archivage et de la gestion d'informations. (Memoires Optiques et Systemes) Text in French. 1982. 10/yr. EUR 137 domestic; EUR 165 foreign (effective 2008). adv. bk.rev. back issues avail. **Document type:** *Magazine, Trade.*
Former titles (until 1998): Memoires Optiques et Systemes (0990-7939); (until 1988): Memoires Optiques (0755-432X)
Indexed: B03.
—INIST.
Published by: Arca Editions, B.P. 303, Vannes, Cedex 56008, France. TEL 33-2-97478306, FAX 33-2-97474946. Ed. Francis Pelletier. Pub., R&P, Adv. contact Martine Corre. Circ: 5,000.

535.84 USA ISSN 0277-7037
QC454.M3 CODEN: MSRVD3
➤ **MASS SPECTROMETRY REVIEWS.** Text in English. 1982. bi-m. GBP 1,044 in United Kingdom to institutions; EUR 1,320 in Europe to institutions; USD 1,918 in United States to institutions; USD 2,002 in Canada & Mexico to institutions; USD 2,044 elsewhere to institutions; GBP 1,202 combined subscription in United Kingdom to institutions (print & online eds.); EUR 1,519 combined subscription in Europe to institutions (print & online eds.); USD 2,206 combined subscription in United States to institutions (print & online eds.); USD 2,290 combined subscription in Canada & Mexico to institutions (print & online eds.); USD 2,332 combined subscription elsewhere to institutions (print & online eds.) (effective 2012). adv. bk.rev. back issues avail.; reprint service avail. from PSC. **Document type:** *Journal, Academic/Scholarly.* **Description:** Publishes current research on mass spectrometry instrumentation and application in chemistry, biology, environmental science, medicine, agriculture, engineering and physics.
Related titles: Microform ed.: (from PQC); Online - full text ed.: ISSN 1098-2787. 1997. GBP 980 in United Kingdom to institutions; EUR 1,239 in Europe to institutions; USD 1,918 elsewhere to institutions (effective 2012).
Indexed: A20, A22, A40, AESIS, ASCA, Agr, B&BAb, B19, BIOSIS Prev, C24, CCI, CIN, CPEI, ChemAb, ChemTitl, CurCont, EMBASE, EngInd, ExcerpMed, GeoRef, ISR, IndMed, MEDLINE, MSB, MycolAb, P30, R10, Reac, RefZh, SCI, SCOPUS, SpeleolAb, T02, W07.
—BLDSC (5388.250000), CASDDS, IE, Infotrieve, Ingenta, INIST, Linda Hall. **CCC.**
Published by: John Wiley & Sons, Inc., 111 River St, Hoboken, NJ 07030. TEL 201-748-6000, FAX 201-748-6088, info@wiley.com, http://www.wiley.com/WileyCDA/. Eds. Carlito B Lebrilla, Dominic M Desiderio. Pub. Kim Thompkins TEL 212-850-6921. **Subscr. outside the Americas to:** John Wiley & Sons Ltd., The Atrium, Southern Gate, Chichester, West Sussex PO19 8SQ, United Kingdom. TEL 44-1243-779777, 800-243407, FAX 44-1243-775878, cs-journals@wiley.com.

➤ **MECHATRONIK**; Design - Entwicklung - Integration. *see* ENGINEERING

502.8 USA
MICROSCOPY SOCIETY OF AMERICA. DIRECTORY. Text in English. 1996. biennial. USD 45 domestic to members; USD 58 foreign to members (effective 2000). **Document type:** *Directory.* **Description:** Listing of Microscopy Society of America members.
Media: Online - full text.
Published by: Microscopy Society of America, 230 E Ohio St, Ste 400, Chicago, IL 60611. TEL 800-538-3672, FAX 312-644-8557. Circ: 5,000.

MICROSCOPY SOCIETY OF SOUTHERN AFRICA. PROCEEDINGS/ MIKROSKOPIEVERENIGING VAN SUIDELIKE AFRIKA. VERRIGTINGS. *see* BIOLOGY—Microscopy

621.381 681 USA ISSN 0895-2477
TK7876 CODEN: MOTLEO
➤ **MICROWAVE & OPTICAL TECHNOLOGY LETTERS.** Text in English. 1988. 12/yr. GBP 1,961 in United Kingdom to institutions; EUR 2,480 in Europe to institutions; USD 3,590 in United States to institutions; USD 3,758 in Canada & Mexico to institutions; USD 3,842 elsewhere to institutions; GBP 2,257 combined subscription in United Kingdom to institutions (print & online eds.); EUR 2,854 combined subscription in Europe to institutions (print & online eds.); USD 4,128 combined subscription in United States to institutions (print & online eds.); USD 4,296 combined subscription in Canada & Mexico to institutions (print & online eds.); USD 4,380 combined subscription elsewhere to institutions (print & online eds.) (effective 2012). adv. back issues avail.; reprint service avail. from PSC. **Document type:** *Journal, Academic/Scholarly.* **Description:** Publishes original short papers and letters on theoretical, applied, and system results in the RF, Microwave, and Millimeter Waves.
Related titles: Microform ed.: (from PQC); Online - full text ed.: ISSN 1098-2760. 1996. GBP 1,832 in United Kingdom to institutions; EUR 2,317 in Europe to institutions; USD 3,590 elsewhere to institutions (effective 2012).
Indexed: A01, A22, A28, APA, ASCA, BrCerAb, C&ISA, CA, CA/WCA, CIA, CPEI, CerAb, CivEngAb, CorrAb, CurCont, E&CAJ, E11, EEA, EMA, ESPM, EngInd, EnvEAb, H15, ISMEC, Inspec, M&TEA, M09, MBF, METADEX, P30, RefZh, SCI, SCOPUS, SolStAb, T02, T04, W07, WAA.

P

—BLDSC (5761.071500), AskIEEE, IE, Infotrieve, Ingenta, INIST, Linda Hall. **CCC.**
Published by: John Wiley & Sons, Inc., 111 River St, Hoboken, NJ 07030. FAX 201-748-6088, info@wiley.com, http://www.wiley.com/WileyCDA/. Ed. Kai Chang. **Subscr. outside the Americas to:** John Wiley & Sons Ltd. cs-journals@wiley.com.

535 629.892 USA ISSN 1018-9149
TJ211.415
MOBILE ROBOTS. Text in English. 1986. a., latest 2004. adv. back issues avail.; reprints avail. **Document type:** *Proceedings, Academic/Scholarly.*
—Ingenta. **CCC.**
Published by: S P I E - International Society for Optical Engineering, PO Box 10, Bellingham, WA 98227. TEL 360-676-3290, 888-504-8171, FAX 360-647-1445, customerservice@spie.org. Ed. Douglas W Gage.

535 USA ISSN 0163-9587
QC490 CODEN: MERJD5
MOESSBAUER EFFECT REFERENCE AND DATA JOURNAL. Text in English. 1978. 10/yr. USD 1,200 combined subscription (print & online eds.) (effective 2010). abstr.; bibl.; charts. Index. 30 p./no.; Supplement avail.; back issues avail. **Document type:** *Journal, Academic/Scholarly.* **Description:** Provides information on Mossbauer spectroscopy.
Related titles: Magnetic Tape ed.; Online - full content ed.: USD 500 (effective 2010); ◆ Supplement(s): Moessbauer Effect Reference and Data Journal. Index.
Published by: University of North Carolina at Asheville, Mossbauer Effect Data Center, 206 Rhoades Hall, CPO 2311, One University Heights, Asheville, NC 28804. TEL 828-251-6617, FAX 828-232-5179, medc@unca.edu.

535 JPN ISSN 0913-5510
MYU. (Cover title is the lower case Greek letter Mu.) Text in Japanese. 1987. s-a. **Document type:** *Journal, Academic/Scholarly.*
Published by: Meisei Daigaku, Bussei Kenkyu Senta/Meisei University, Material Science Research Center, 2-1-1, Hodokubo, Hino, Tokyo 191-8506, Japan. TEL 81-42-5915094, FAX 81-42-5917551, http://msrc.amrc.meisei-u.ac.jp/.

578 535 JPN
NAGOYA DAIGAKU DENSHI KOGAKU KENKYU NO AYUMI/PROGRESS IN ELECTRON OPTICS RESEARCH. Text in English, Japanese. 1973. a. free. **Document type:** *Newsletter, Academic/Scholarly.*
Published by: Nagoya Daigaku, Hyakuman Boruto Denshi Kenbikyo Kenkyushitsu/Nagoya University, 1000KV Electron Microscopy Laboratory, Furo-cho, Chikusa-ku, Nagoya-shi, Aichi-ken 464-0814, Japan. TEL 81-52-789-3154, FAX 81-52-789-3155. Ed. Michio Iseki. Circ: 500.

535 GBR ISSN 1749-4885
TA1501 CODEN: NPAHBY
➤ **NATURE PHOTONICS.** Text in English. 2007 (Jan.). m. EUR 3,214 in Europe to institutions; USD 4,048 in the Americas to institutions; GBP 2,077 to institutions in the UK & elsewhere (effective 2011). adv. back issues avail.; reprints avail. **Document type:** *Journal, Academic/Scholarly.* **Description:** Covers all aspects of research into the fundamental properties of light and how it interacts with matter through to the latest designs of optoelectronic device and emerging applications that exploit photons.
Related titles: Online - full text ed.: ISSN 1749-4893.
Indexed: A01, B&BAb, B19, C33, CA, CurCont, P30, SCI, SCOPUS, T02, W07.
—BLDSC (6047.172000), IE, Ingenta, INIST. **CCC.**
Published by: Nature Publishing Group (Subsidiary of: Macmillan Publishers Ltd.), The MacMillan Bldg, 4 Crinan St, London, N1 9XW, United Kingdom. TEL 44-20-78334000, FAX 44-20-78334640. Ed. Olivier Graydon. Adv. contact Andy Douglas TEL 44-22-78434975. **Subscr. to:** Brunel Rd, Houndmills, Basingstoke, Hamps RG21 6XS, United Kingdom. TEL 44-1256-329242, FAX 44-1256-812358, subscriptions@nature.com.

535.84 JPN
NIHON BUNKO GAKKAI. KAKI SEMINA/SPECTROSCOPICAL SOCIETY OF JAPAN. SUMMER SEMINAR. Text in Japanese. a. adv. **Document type:** *Proceedings.*
Published by: Nihon Bunko Gakkai/Spectroscopical Society of Japan, Clean Bldg, 1-13 Kanda-Awaji-cho, Chiyoda-ku, Tokyo, 101-0063, Japan. http://wwwsoc.nii.ac.jp/spsj/. Ed. Yoshihiro F Mizugai. Adv. contact Kagaku Gijutsu Sha.

NIHON BUNKO GAKKAI SHINPOJUMU KOEN YOSHISHU/SPECTROSCOPICAL SOCIETY OF JAPAN. ABSTRACTS OF SYMPOSIA. *see* PHYSICS—Abstracting, Bibliographies, Statistics

535 JPN
NIHON KODANSEI GAKKAI KAIHO/JAPAN SOCIETY FOR PHOTOELASTICITY. JOURNAL. Text in Japanese. 1980. 3/yr.
Published by: Nihon Kodansei Gakkai/Japan Society for Photoelasticity, Nihon Gakkai Jimu Senta, 16-9 Honkomagome 5-chome, Bunkyo-ku, Tokyo, 113-0021, Japan.

535 JPN ISSN 0910-9862
NIHON KODANSEI GAKKAI KENKYU HAPPYO KOENKAI KOEN RONBUNSHU/PROCEEDINGS OF THE SYMPOSIUM ON PHOTOELASTICITY. Text in Japanese. 1980. a. **Document type:** *Proceedings.*
Published by: Nihon Kodansei Gakkai/Japan Society for Photoelasticity, Nihon Gakkai Jimu Senta, 16-9 Honkomagome 5-chome, Bunkyo-ku, Tokyo, 113-0021, Japan.

NIHON SEKIGAISEN GAKKAISHI/JAPAN SOCIETY OF INFRARED SCIENCE AND TECHNOLOGY. JOURNAL. *see* PHYSICS—Heat

535 JPN
NIHON SHIKISAI GAKKAI NYUZU/C S A J NEWS. Text in Japanese. bi-m. **Document type:** *Newsletter.*
Published by: Nihon Shikisai Gakkai/Color Science Association of Japan, 3-17-42 Shimo-ochiai, Shinjuku-ku, Tokyo, 161-0033, Japan. TEL 81-3-35657716, FAX 81-3-35657717, ren-net@vega.ocn.ne.jp, http://wwwsoc.nii.ac.jp/color/.

535 JPN ISSN 0389-9357
NIHON SHIKISAI GAKKAISHI/COLOR SCIENCE ASSOCIATION OF JAPAN. JOURNAL. Text in Japanese; Summaries in English, Japanese. 1972. 3/yr. JPY 2,000 per issue. **Document type:** *Academic/Scholarly.*
Published by: Nihon Shikisai Gakkai/Color Science Association of Japan, 3-17-42 Shimo-ochiai, Shinjuku-ku, Tokyo, 161-0033, Japan. TEL 81-3-35657716, FAX 81-3-35657717, ren-net@vega.ocn.ne.jp, http://wwwsoc.nii.ac.jp/color/.

NIPPON LASER IGAKKAISHI/JAPAN SOCIETY FOR LASER MEDICINE. JOURNAL. *see* MEDICAL SCIENCES

535 USA
NONLINEAR OPTICS: MATERIALS, FUNDAMENTALS AND APPLICATIONS. Text in English. 19??. irreg., latest 2000. adv. back issues avail.; reprints avail. **Document type:** *Proceedings, Trade.*
Related titles: Online - full text ed.
Published by: I E E E, 445 Hoes Ln, Piscataway, NJ 08854. TEL 732-981-0060, 800-678-4333, FAX 732-562-6380, customer.service@ieee.org, http://www.ieee.org.

535 USA ISSN 1543-0537
QC446.15 CODEN: MCLOEB
➤ **NONLINEAR OPTICS, QUANTUM OPTICS**; concepts in modern optics. Text in English. 1966. q. EUR 135 in Europe to individuals; JPY 19,859 in Japan to individuals; USD 149 elsewhere to individuals; EUR 503 combined subscription in Europe to institutions (print & online eds.); JPY 82,584 combined subscription in Japan to institutions (print & online eds.); USD 793 combined subscription elsewhere to institutions (print & online eds.) (effective 2011). adv. 80 p./no.; back issues avail. **Document type:** *Journal, Academic/Scholarly.* **Description:** Brings out papers reporting research, review articles and communications.
Incorporates (in 2003): Concepts in Modern Optics (1539-9958); Supersedes in part (in 2002): Molecular Crystals and Liquid Crystals Science and Technology. Section B: Nonlinear Optics (1058-7268); Which was formerly (until 1992): Nonlinear Optics (1053-3729); Which superseded in part (in 1991): Molecular Crystals and Liquid Crystals Incorporating Nonlinear Optics (1044-1859); Which was formerly (until 1987): Molecular Crystals and Liquid Crystals (0026-8941); (until 1969): Molecular Crystals (0369-1152)
Related titles: CD-ROM ed.; Microform ed.; Online - full text ed.: ISSN 1944-8325 (from IngentaConnect).
Indexed: A01, A22, CA, CPEI, E01, EngInd, Inspec, SCOPUS, T02.
—BLDSC (6117.316798), AskIEEE, IE, Ingenta, INIST, Linda Hall. **CCC.**
Published by: Old City Publishing, Inc., 628 N 2nd St, Philadelphia, PA 19123. TEL 215-925-4390, FAX 215-925-4371, info@oldcitypublishing.com. Ed. Takayoshi Kobayashi.

➤ **O PLUS E.** *see* ELECTRONICS

535 NLD ISSN 1874-3285
QC350
➤ **THE OPEN OPTICS JOURNAL.** Text in English. 2007. irreg. free (effective 2011). **Document type:** *Journal, Academic/Scholarly.*
Media: Online - full text.
Indexed: A01, A28, APA, BrCerAb, C&ISA, CA/WCA, CIA, CerAb, CivEngAb, CorrAb, E&CAJ, E11, EEA, EMA, ESPM, H15, M&TEA, M09, MBF, METADEX, SolStAb, T04, WAA.
Published by: Bentham Open (Subsidiary of: Bentham Science Publishers Ltd.), PO Box 294, Bussum, AG 1400, Netherlands. TEL 31-35-6923800, FAX 31-35-6980150, subscriptions@bentham.org. Ed. Yang Zhao.

➤ **OPHTHALMIC AND PHYSIOLOGICAL OPTICS.** *see* MEDICAL SCIENCES—Ophthalmology And Optometry

535.58 621.329 USA
OPROELECTRONICS REPORT (ONLINE); the market outlook in lasers and opto-electronics. Text in English. 1965. s-m. USD 315 (effective 2009). adv. **Document type:** *Newsletter, Trade.* **Description:** Covers national and international business news and market trends and tracks technology advances to interpret business implications.
Former titles: Oproelectronics Report (Print) (1522-2837); (until 1998): Laser Report (0023-8600)
Media: Online - full text. **Related titles:** E-mail ed.
Indexed: B02, B15, B17, B18, G04, G06, G07, G08, I05.
—IE. **CCC.**
Published by: PennWell Corporation, 1421 S Sheridan Rd, Tulsa, OK 74112. TEL 918-835-3161, 800-331-4463, FAX 918-831-9804, Headquarters@PennWell.com, http://www.pennwell.com. Ed. David Kales. Circ: 400.

535 POL ISSN 0078-5466
QC350 CODEN: OPAPBZ
➤ **OPTICA APPLICATA (ONLINE).** Text in English; Summaries in Russian. 1971. q. free (effective 2011). **Document type:** *Journal, Academic/Scholarly.* **Description:** Papers on diffraction theory, quantum optics, holography, scientific photography and technology of manufacturing optical elements.
Formerly (until 2008): Optica Applicata (Print)
Media: Online - full text.
Indexed: A01, A22, ASCA, B22, CA, CIN, CPEI, Cadscan, ChemAb, ChemTitl, CurCont, EngInd, Inspec, LeadAb, PhysBer, SCI, SCOPUS, T02, W07, Zincscan.
—BLDSC (6273.050000), AskIEEE, CASDDS, IE, Infotrieve, Ingenta, Linda Hall.
Published by: (Politechnika Wroclawska/Wroclaw University of Technology), Politechnika Wroclawska, Oficyna Wydawnicza/Wroclaw University of Technology, Wybrzeze Wyspianskiego 27, Wroclaw, 50370, Poland. TEL 48-71-3202994, FAX 48-71-3282940, oficwyd@pwr.wroc.pl, http://www.oficyna.pwr.wroc.pl. Ed. Waclaw Urbanczzyk.

535 ESP ISSN 0030-3917
QC350 CODEN: OPAPAY
OPTICA PURA Y APLICADA. Text in English, French, Spanish; Summaries in English, Spanish. 1968. 3/yr. adv. bk.rev. index, cum.index. back issues avail. **Document type:** *Journal, Academic/Scholarly.*
Related titles: Microfilm ed.; Online - full text ed.: ISSN 2171-8814. 1996. free (effective 2011).
Indexed: A&ATA, ChemAb, IBR, IBZ, IECT, Inspec, PhysBer, SCOPUS.
—AskIEEE, CASDDS, Linda Hall. **CCC.**
Published by: (Consejo Superior de Investigaciones Cientificas (C S I C), Instituto de Optica "Daza de Valdes"), Sociedad Espanola de Optica, Serrano, 121, Madrid, 28006, Spain. TEL 34-915-616800, FAX 34-915-645557.

535 621.3 USA ISSN 0306-8919
TA1671 CODEN: OQELDI
➤ **OPTICAL AND QUANTUM ELECTRONICS.** Abbreviated title: O Q E. Text in Dutch. 1969. q. EUR 2,461, USD 2,592 combined subscription to institutions (print & online eds.) (effective 2012). adv. bk.rev. charts; illus. index. back issues avail.; reprint service avail. from PSC. **Document type:** *Journal, Academic/Scholarly.* **Description:** Provides a forum for research papers, tutorial reviews, and letters in such fields as optical physics, optical engineering, and optoelectronics.
Formerly (until 1975): Opto-Electronics (0030-4077)
Related titles: Online - full text ed.: ISSN 1572-817X (from IngentaConnect).
Indexed: A01, A22, A26, A28, APA, ASCA, BibLing, BrCerAb, C&ISA, CA, CA/WCA, CIA, CPEI, CerAb, ChemAb, ChemTitl, CivEngAb, CorrAb, CurCont, E&CAJ, E01, E11, EEA, EMA, ESPM, EngInd, EnvEAb, H15, I05, ISMEC, ISR, Inspec, M&TEA, M09, MBF, METADEX, PhysBer, RefZh, SCI, SCOPUS, SolStAb, T02, T04, TM, W07, WAA.
—BLDSC (6273.170000), AskIEEE, CASDDS, IE, Infotrieve, Ingenta, INIST, Linda Hall. **CCC.**
Published by: Springer New York LLC (Subsidiary of: Springer Science+Business Media), 233 Spring St, New York, NY 10013. TEL 212-460-1500, FAX 212-460-1575, service-ny@springer.com, http://www.springer.com/. Eds. John Dudley, Trevor M Benson. **Subscr. to:** Journal Fulfillment, PO Box 2485, Secaucus, NJ 07096. TEL 201-348-4033, FAX 201-348-4505, journals-ny@springer.com.

535 GBR ISSN 1364-4173
OPTICAL DIAGNOSTICS IN ENGINEERING. Text in English. 1996. q. **Document type:** *Newsletter.* **Description:** Includes technical papers and animations by optical specialists worldwide.
Media: Online - full text.
Address: United Kingdom. TEL 44-131-451-3156, FAX 44-131-447-8660. Ed. Ian Grant.

535 USA ISSN 0091-3286
TR692.5 CODEN: OPEGAR
➤ **OPTICAL ENGINEERING.** Text in English. m. USD 1,055 combined subscription domestic to institutions (print & online eds.); USD 1,175 combined subscription foreign to institutions (print & online eds.) (effective 2012). adv. bk.rev. abstr.; charts; illus.; tr.lit. index, cum.index: vols.1-23 in 1985, vols.24-28 in 1990. 300 p./no. 2 cols./p.; reprints avail. **Document type:** *Journal, Academic/Scholarly.* **Description:** Covers engineering, design, production and applications of optical, electro-optical, fiberoptic, laser, as well as photographic components and systems.
Former titles (until 1972): S P I E Journal (0036-1860); (until 1962): S P I E Newsletter (0099-3093)
Related titles: CD-ROM ed.; Online - full text ed.: ISSN 1560-2303. 1998. USD 815 to institutions (effective 2012).
Indexed: A01, A03, A05, A08, A20, A22, A23, A24, A28, APA, AS&TA, AS&TI, ASCA, B04, B10, B13, BrCerAb, C&ISA, C10, CA, CA/WCA, CIA, CIN, CIS, CMCI, CPEI, CPI, CerAb, ChemAb, ChemTitl, CivEngAb, CorrAb, CurCont, E&CAJ, E11, EEA, EMA, EngInd, GeoRef, H15, IBR, IBZ, ISR, Inspec, M&TEA, M09, MBF, METADEX, P30, PhotoAb, PhysBer, SCI, SCOPUS, SPINweb, SolStAb, SpeleolAb, T02, T04, TM, W07, WAA.
—BLDSC (6273.180000), AskIEEE, CASDDS, IE, Ingenta, INIST, Linda Hall. **CCC.**
Published by: S P I E - International Society for Optical Engineering, 1000 20th St, Bellingham, WA 98225. TEL 360-676-3290, FAX 360-647-1445, spie@spie.org, http://spie.org. Ed. Dr. Ron C Driggers. adv.: B&W page USD 1,365, color page USD 2,180; trim 8.5 x 11. Circ: 9,000 (controlled).

621.36 USA ISSN 1068-5200
TA1800 CODEN: OFTEFV
➤ **OPTICAL FIBER TECHNOLOGY.** Text in English. 1994. bi-m. EUR 813 in Europe to institutions; JPY 85,200 in Japan to institutions; USD 643 elsewhere to institutions (effective 2012). adv. back issues avail.; reprints avail. **Document type:** *Journal, Academic/Scholarly.* **Description:** Presents innovations in optical fiber technology, including new applications in data processing.
Related titles: Online - full text ed.: ISSN 1095-9912 (from IngentaConnect, ScienceDirect).
Indexed: A01, A03, A08, A22, A26, CA, CPEI, CurCont, E01, EngInd, I05, ISR, Inspec, RefZh, S01, SCI, SCOPUS, T01, T02, TM, TTI, W07.
—BLDSC (6273.184700), AskIEEE, IE, Infotrieve, Ingenta. **CCC.**
Published by: Academic Press (Subsidiary of: Elsevier Science & Technology), 3251 Riverport Ln, Maryland Heights, MO 63043. TEL 314-447-8010, FAX 314-447-8030, JournalCustomerService-usa@elsevier.com, http://www.elsevierdirect.com/imprint.jsp?iid=5. Ed. Bertrand Desthieux. Adv. contact Tino DeCarlo TEL 212-633-3815.

535 NLD ISSN 0925-3467
QC374 CODEN: OMATET
➤ **OPTICAL MATERIALS.** Text in English. 1991. 12/yr. EUR 1,447 in Europe to institutions; JPY 192,100 in Japan to institutions; USD 1,625 elsewhere to institutions (effective 2012). **Document type:** *Journal, Academic/Scholarly.* **Description:** Publishes original papers and review articles on the design, synthesis, characterization and applications of optical materials. Focuses on materials systems, optical phenomena in materials, and devices.
Related titles: Microform ed.: (from PQC); Online - full text ed.: ISSN 1873-1252 (from IngentaConnect, ScienceDirect).
Indexed: A01, A03, A08, A20, A22, A26, ASCA, C&ISA, C10, C24, CA, CIN, CPEI, ChemAb, ChemTitl, CompLI, CurCont, E&CAJ, EngInd, I05, ISMEC, ISR, Inspec, MSCI, P30, RefZh, S01, SCI, SCOPUS, SolStAb, T02, TM, W07.
—BLDSC (6273.328000), AskIEEE, CASDDS, IE, Infotrieve, Ingenta, INIST, Linda Hall. **CCC.**
Published by: Elsevier BV, North-Holland (Subsidiary of: Elsevier Science & Technology), Sara Burgerhartstraat 25, Amsterdam, 1055 KV, Netherlands. TEL 31-20-4853911, FAX 31-20-4852457, JournalsCustomerServiceEMEA@elsevier.com. Ed. G Boulon. **Subscr. to:** Elsevier BV, Radarweg 29, PO Box 211, Amsterdam 1000 AE, Netherlands. TEL 31-20-4853757, FAX 31-20-4853432, http://www.elsevier.nl.

535 USA ISSN 1060-992X
TK7895.M4 CODEN: OMNNE8
➤ **OPTICAL MEMORY & NEURAL NETWORKS**; information optics. Text in English. 1992. q. EUR 833, USD 1,010 combined subscription to institutions (print & online eds.) (effective 2012). abstr.; charts; illus.
Document type: *Journal, Academic/Scholarly.* **Description:** Covers the fundamental principles of optical memory, including mechanisms of optical information recording and physical characteristics of photosensitive materials and structures. Includes applied research directed at the realization of optical memory systems for data storage and processing.
Related titles: Online - full text ed.: ISSN 1934-7898.
Indexed: A22, A26, CPEI, E01, E08, H12, Inspec, S09, SCOPUS.
—BLDSC (6273.328900), AskIEEE, East View, IE, Infotrieve, Ingenta, INIST. **CCC.**
Published by: Allerton Press, Inc. (Subsidiary of: Pleiades Publishing, Inc.), 18 W 27th St, New York, NY 10001. TEL 646-424-9686, FAX 646-424-9695, journals@allertonpress.com. Ed. Andrei L Mikaelian.

621.36 USA ISSN 1935-3839
OPTICAL NETWORKS. Text in English. 2007. irreg., latest 2009.
Document type: *Monographic series, Academic/Scholarly.*
Description: Emphasizes both optical communications and networks, including both theoretical and applied books.
Related titles: Online - full text ed.: ISSN 1935-3847. 2007.
Published by: Springer New York LLC (Subsidiary of: Springer Science+Business Media), 233 Spring St, New York, NY 10013. TEL 212-460-1500, FAX 212-460-1575, service-ny@springer.com. Eds. Biswanath Mukherjee, Alex Greene.

535 JPN ISSN 1340-6000
CODEN: OPREFN
➤ **OPTICAL REVIEW.** Text in English. 1994. bi-m. EUR 1,064, USD 1,290 combined subscription to institutions (print & online eds.) (effective 2012). adv. back issues avail.; reprint service avail. from PSC. **Document type:** *Journal, Academic/Scholarly.*
Related titles: Online - full text ed.: ISSN 1349-9432 (from IngentaConnect).
Indexed: A01, A03, A08, A22, A26, ASCA, CA, CIN, CMCI, ChemAb, ChemTitl, CurCont, E01, I05, Inspec, P30, RefZh, S01, SCI, SCOPUS, T02, W07.
—BLDSC (6273.369000), AskIEEE, CASDDS, IE, Infotrieve, Ingenta, INIST. **CCC.**
Published by: Optical Society of Japan, Kudan-Kita Bldg 5F, 1-12-3 Kudan-Kita, Chiyoda-ku, Tokyo, 102-0073, Japan. FAX 81-3-3814-1363. Ed. Ken-ichi Ueda. **Subscr. in the Americas to:** Springer New York LLC, Journal Fulfillment, PO Box 2485, Secaucus, NJ 07096. TEL 800-777-4643, 201-348-4033, FAX 201-348-4505, journals-ny@springer.com, http://www.springer.com; **Subscr. to:** Springer Distribution Center, Kundenservice Zeitschriften, Haberstr 7, Heidelberg 69126, Germany. TEL 49-6221-3454303, FAX 49-6221-3454229, subscriptions@springer.com. **Dist. by:** Japan Publications Trading Co., Ltd., Book Export II Dept, PO Box 5030, Tokyo International, Tokyo 101-3191, Japan. TEL 81-3-32923753, FAX 81-3-32920410, infoserials@jptco.co.jp, http://www.jptco.co.jp.
Co-publisher: Springer Japan KK.

539.11 USA ISSN 1050-7264
OPTICAL SCIENCE AND ENGINEERING SERIES. Text in English. 19??. irreg., latest 2009, 2nd ed. price varies. **Document type:** *Monographic series, Academic/Scholarly.*
Formerly (until 1986): A I P Conference Proceedings. Subseries on Optical Science and Engineering
Related titles: Online - full text ed.
—CCC.
Published by: C R C Press, LLC (Subsidiary of: Taylor & Francis Group), 6000 Broken Sound Pky, NW, Ste 300, Boca Raton, FL 33487. TEL 800-272-7737, FAX 800-374-3401, orders@crcpress.com.

535 USA ISSN 1084-7529
QC350 CODEN: JOAOD6
➤ **OPTICAL SOCIETY OF AMERICA. JOURNAL A: OPTICS, IMAGE SCIENCE, AND VISION.** Abbreviated title: J O S A A. Text in English. 1984. m. USD 2,630 combined subscription domestic (print & online eds.); USD 2,715 combined subscription in Canada (print & online eds.); USD 2,800 combined subscription elsewhere (print & online eds.) (effective 2012). adv. illus. Index. back issues avail.; reprints avail. **Document type:** *Journal, Academic/Scholarly.* **Description:** Covers basic research on optical phenomena. Includes atmospheric, physiological and statistical optics; image processing; scattering and coherence theory, machine and color vision; design and diffraction.
Formerly (until 1993): Optical Society of America. Journal A, Optics and Image Science (0740-3232); Which superseded in part (in 1983): Optical Society of America. Journal (0030-3941); Which superseded in part (in 1929): Optical Society of America. Journal. Review of Scientific Instruments (0093-4119); Which was formerly (until 1922): Optical Society of America. Journal (0093-5433)
Related titles: Microfiche ed.; Microfilm ed.; Online - full text ed.: ISSN 1520-8532. USD 2,049 (effective 2012).
Indexed: A05, A20, A22, ABIPC, AS&TA, AS&TI, ASCA, ApMecR, B04, C&ISA, C10, CA, CCMJ, CIN, CIS, CPEI, CPI, ChemAb, ChemTitl, CurCont, E&CAJ, E-psyche, EMBASE, EngInd, ErgAb, ExcerpMed, GALA, INIS AtomInd, ISMEC, ISR, IndMed, Inspec, MEDLINE, MSN, MathR, P30, PhysBer, PsycholAb, R10, Reac, RefZh, SCI, SCOPUS, SPINweb, SolStAb, SpeleolAb, T02, TM, W07.
—BLDSC (4837.010100), AskIEEE, CASDDS, GNLM, IE, Infotrieve, Ingenta, INIST, Linda Hall. **CCC.**
Published by: Optical Society of America, 2010 Massachusetts Ave, NW, Washington, DC 20036. TEL 202-416-1907, FAX 202-416-6140, info@osa.org, http://www.osa.org. Ed. Franco Gori.

535 USA ISSN 0740-3224
QC392 CODEN: JOBPDE
➤ **OPTICAL SOCIETY OF AMERICA. JOURNAL B: OPTICAL PHYSICS.** Text in English. 1984. m. USD 2,630 combined subscription domestic (print & online eds.); USD 2,715 combined subscription in Canada (print & online eds.); USD 2,800 combined subscription elsewhere (print & online eds.) (effective 2012). adv. illus. Index. back issues avail.; reprints avail. **Document type:** *Journal, Academic/Scholarly.* **Description:** Contains artilces about research on the fundamentals of the interaction of radiation with matter such as quantum optics, nonlinear optics, and laser physics.
Supersedes in part (in 1983): Optical Society of America. Journal (0030-3941); Which superseded in part (in 1929): Optical Society of America. Journal. Review of Scientific Instruments (0093-4119); Which was formerly (until 1922): Optical Society of America. Journal (0093-5433)
Related titles: Microfiche ed.; Microfilm ed.; Online - full text ed.: ISSN 1520-8540. 1995. USD 2,049 (effective 2012).
Indexed: A05, A22, APA, AS&TA, AS&TI, ASCA, ApMecR, B04, C&ISA, C10, C33, CA, CADCAM, CCMJ, CIN, CPEI, CPI, ChemAb, ChemTitl, CorrAb, CurCont, E&CAJ, EEA, EngInd, GALA, INIS AtomInd, ISR, Inspec, MSN, MathR, P30, PhotoAb, PhysBer, PsycholAb, RefZh, SCI, SCOPUS, SPINweb, SolStAb, SpeleolAb, T02, TM, W07, WAA.
—BLDSC (4837.010110), AskIEEE, CASDDS, GNLM, IE, Infotrieve, Ingenta, INIST, Linda Hall. **CCC.**
Published by: Optical Society of America, 2010 Massachusetts Ave, NW, Washington, DC 20036. TEL 202-416-1907, FAX 202-416-6140, info@osa.org, http://www.osa.org. Ed. Henry M Van Driel.

535 KOR ISSN 1226-4776
QC350
OPTICAL SOCIETY OF KOREA. JOURNAL. Text in English. 1997. s-a.
Document type: *Journal, Academic/Scholarly.*
Related titles: Online - full text ed.: ISSN 2093-6885.
Indexed: CPEI, Inspec, P30, SCI, SCOPUS, W07.
—BLDSC (4837.105000), IE, Ingenta.
Published by: Han'gug Gwanghaghoe/Optical Society of Korea, 811, 635-4 Yucksam-dong, Kangnam-gu, Seoul, 135-703, Korea, S. TEL 82-2-34526560, FAX 82-2-34526561, osk@osk.or.kr, http://www.osk.or.kr.

535 RUS
QC350 CODEN: OPMPAQ
OPTICHESKII ZHURNAL. Text in Russian. 1931. m. USD 189. index.
Document type: *Academic/Scholarly.*
Formerly: Optiko-Mekhanicheskaya Promyshlennost' (0030-4042)
Related titles: ◆ English Translation: Journal of Optical Technology. ISSN 1070-9762.
Indexed: ChemAb, ChemTitl, Inspec, RefZh.
—AskIEEE, CASDDS, INIST, Linda Hall. **CCC.**
Published by: Opticheskii Institut im. S.I. Vavilova, Tuchkov per 1, St Petersburg, 199034, Russian Federation. TEL 812-2183986. Ed. M M Miroshnikov. **Dist. by:** East View Information Services, 10601 Wayzata Blvd, Minneapolis, MN 55305. TEL 952-252-1201, 800-477-1005, FAX 952-252-1202, info@eastview.com, http://www.eastview.com.

621.36 GBR ISSN 1757-1804
CODEN: OLEEEV
OPTICS & LASER EUROPE. Abbreviated title: O L E. Text in English. 1992. m. GBP 125 domestic to individuals; EUR 181 in Europe to individuals; USD 225 in United States to individuals; free to qualified personnel (effective 2009). adv. tr.lit. back issues avail. **Document type:** *Journal, Academic/Scholarly.* **Description:** Provides news, commentary, features, and user applications.
Formerly (until 2006): Opto and Laser Europe (0966-9809); Which incorporated (1984-19??): Opto and Laser Products
Related titles: Microfiche ed.; Microform ed.; Online - full text ed.
Indexed: Inspec.
—BLDSC (6273.436000), AskIEEE, IE, Ingenta. **CCC.**
Published by: (Institute of Physics), Institute of Physics Publishing Ltd., Dirac House, Temple Back, Bristol, BS1 6BE, United Kingdom. TEL 44-117-9297481, FAX 44-117-9301178, custserv@iop.org, http://publishing.iop.org/. Ed. Jacqueline Hewett. Pub. Susan Curtis TEL 44-117-9301035. Adv. contact Rob Fisher. B&W page USD 7,505, color page USD 9,380, B&W page GBP 4,170, color page GBP 5,210; trim 213 x 282. Circ: 26,766.

535.58 621.39 GBR ISSN 0030-3992
QC350 CODEN: OLTCAS
➤ **OPTICS & LASER TECHNOLOGY.** Text in English. 1968. 8/yr. EUR 1,540 in Europe to institutions; JPY 204,600 in Japan to institutions; USD 1,724 elsewhere to institutions (effective 2012). adv. bk.rev. charts; illus.; pat. index. back issues avail. **Document type:** *Journal, Academic/Scholarly.* **Description:** Provides a vehicle for a broad range of high quality research and review papers on the development and application of optics and lasers.
Formerly (until 1970): Optics Technology (0374-3926)
Related titles: Microform ed.: (from PQC); Online - full text ed.: ISSN 1879-2545 (from IngentaConnect, ScienceDirect).
Indexed: A01, A03, A08, A20, A22, A26, A28, APA, ASCA, BrCerAb, BrTechI, C&ISA, C10, CA, CA/WCA, CIA, CIN, CPEI, CerAb, ChemAb, ChemTitl, CivEngAb, CorrAb, CurCont, E&CAJ, E11, EEA, EMA, ESPM, EngInd, EnvEAb, FR, H15, I05, IBR, IBZ, ISR, Inspec, M&TEA, M09, MBF, METADEX, PhotoAb, PhysBer, S01, SCI, SCOPUS, SolStAb, T02, T04, TM, VITIS, W07, WAA.
—BLDSC (6273.440000), AskIEEE, CASDDS, IE, Infotrieve, Ingenta, INIST, Linda Hall. **CCC.**
Published by: Elsevier Ltd (Subsidiary of: Elsevier Science & Technology), The Blvd, Langford Ln, Kidlington, Oxford, OX5 1GB, United Kingdom. TEL 44-1865-843000, FAX 44-1865-843010, journalscustomerserviceemea@elsevier.com. Eds. M A Karim TEL 757-683-3460, S James. **Subscr. to:** Elsevier BV, Radarweg 29, PO Box 211, Amsterdam 1000 AE, Netherlands. TEL 31-20-4853757, FAX 31-20-4853432, http://www.elsevier.nl.

535.58 621.39 GBR ISSN 0143-8166
TA367.5 CODEN: OLENDN
➤ **OPTICS AND LASERS IN ENGINEERING.** Text in English. 1980. 12/yr. EUR 2,444 in Europe to institutions; JPY 324,200 in Japan to institutions; USD 2,732 elsewhere to institutions (effective 2012). adv. bk.rev. charts; illus. index. back issues avail. **Document type:** *Journal, Academic/Scholarly.* **Description:** Provides a forum for interchange of information on developments and applications of optical techniques and laser technology in engineering.
Related titles: Microform ed.: (from PQC); Online - full text ed.: ISSN 1873-0302 (from IngentaConnect, ScienceDirect).
Indexed: A01, A03, A08, A22, A26, A28, APA, ASCA, ApMecR, BrCerAb, C&ISA, CA, CA/WCA, CIA, CMCI, CPEI, CerAb, CivEngAb, CorrAb, CurCont, E&CAJ, E11, EEA, EMA, ESPM, EngInd, EnvEAb, FR, GeoRef, H15, I05, ISMEC, ISR, Inspec, M&TEA, M09, MBF, METADEX, P30, PhotoAb, PhysBer, S01, SCI, SCOPUS, SolStAb, SpeleolAb, T02, T04, TM, W07, WAA.
—BLDSC (6273.443000), AskIEEE, IE, Infotrieve, Ingenta, INIST, Linda Hall. **CCC.**
Published by: Elsevier Ltd (Subsidiary of: Elsevier Science & Technology), The Blvd, Langford Ln, Kidlington, Oxford, OX5 1GB, United Kingdom. TEL 44-1865-843000, FAX 44-1865-843010, journalscustomerserviceemea@elsevier.com. Eds. A K Asundi, P K Rastogi. **Subscr. to:** Elsevier BV, Radarweg 29, PO Box 211, Amsterdam 1000 AE, Netherlands. FAX 31-20-4853432, JournalsCustomerServiceEMEA@elsevier.com, http://www.elsevier.nl.

535 USA ISSN 1557-5837
OPTICS AND PHOTONICS. Text in English. 1995. irreg., latest 2008. price varies. **Document type:** *Monographic series, Academic/Scholarly.*
Published by: Academic Press (Subsidiary of: Elsevier Science & Technology), 525 B St, Ste 1900, San Diego, CA 92101-4495. TEL 619-231-6616, FAX 619-699-6422, JournalCustomerService-usa@elsevier.com, http://www.elsevierdirect.com/imprint.jsp?iid=5.

535 USA ISSN 2160-8881
▼ ➤ **OPTICS AND PHOTONICS JOURNAL.** Abbreviated title: O P J. Text in English. 2011. q. USD 156 (effective 2011). **Document type:** *Journal, Academic/Scholarly.* **Description:** Devoted to challenging and innovating methods and techniques related to the development of optics and photonics materials, characterization and applications.
Related titles: Online - full text ed.: ISSN 2160-889X. free (effective 2011).
Published by: Scientific Research Publishing, Inc., PO Box 54821, Irvine, CA 92619. service@scirp.org. Ed. Bouzid Menaa.

535 SGP ISSN 1793-7140
OPTICS AND PHOTONICS LETTERS (ONLINE). Abbreviated title: O P L. Text in English. 2008. m. free (effective 2012). adv. back issues avail. **Document type:** *Journal, Academic/Scholarly.* **Description:** Provides dissemination of results in various fields of optics and photonics, with emphasis on short communications.
Formerly: Optics and Photonics Letters (Print) (1793-5288)
Media: Online - full text.
Indexed: A22, E01.
Published by: World Scientific Publishing Co. Pte. Ltd., 5 Toh Tuck Link, Singapore, 596224, Singapore. TEL 65-6466-5775, FAX 65-6467-7667, wspc@wspc.com.sg, http://www.worldscientific.com. Eds. Hugo Thienpont, Larry X C Yuan, Michael A Fiddy. **Dist. by:** World Scientific Publishing Ltd., 57 Shelton St, London WC2H 9HE, United Kingdom. TEL 44-207-8360888, FAX 44-207-8362020, sales@wspc.co.uk; World Scientific Publishing Co., Inc., 27 Warren St, Ste 401-402, Hackensack, NJ 07601. TEL 201-487-9655, 800-227-7562, FAX 201-487-9656, 888-977-2665, wspc@wspc.com.

535 USA ISSN 1047-6938
TA1501 CODEN: OPPHEL
OPTICS & PHOTONICS NEWS. Abbreviated title: O P N. Text in English. 1975. m. USD 141 combined subscription domestic (print & online eds.); USD 166 combined subscription in Canada & Mexico (print & online eds.); USD 176 combined subscription elsewhere (print & online eds.) (effective 2012). adv. illus. Index. back issues avail.; reprints avail. **Document type:** *Journal, Academic/Scholarly.*
Description: Provides in-depth coverage of recent developments in the field of optics and offers busy professionals the tools they need to succeed in the optics industry, as well as informative pieces on a variety of topics such as science and society, education, technology and business.
Formerly (until 1990): Optics News (0098-907X)
Related titles: Online - full text ed.: ISSN 1541-3721. USD 127 (effective 2012); Supplement(s): O P N Trends.
Indexed: A20, A22, ABIPC, CurCont, EngInd, GALA, Inspec, PhysBer, SCOPUS, SPINweb.
—BLDSC (6273.450000), AskIEEE, CASDDS, IE, Infotrieve, Ingenta, INIST, Linda Hall. **CCC.**
Published by: Optical Society of America, 2010 Massachusetts Ave, NW, Washington, DC 20036. TEL 202-416-1907, FAX 202-416-6140, info@osa.org, http://www.osa.org. Pub. John Childs. Adv. contact Anne Jones TEL 202-416-1942. B&W page USD 2,900, color page USD 4,900; trim 8.125 x 10.875.

535.84 RUS ISSN 0030-400X
QC350 CODEN: OPSUA3
➤ **OPTICS AND SPECTROSCOPY.** Text in English. 1959. m. EUR 3,902, USD 4,726 combined subscription to institutions (print & online eds.) (effective 2012). bibl.; charts; illus.; tr.lit. s-a. index. back issues avail.
Document type: *Journal, Academic/Scholarly.* **Description:** Covers Russian research in optical phenomena ranging from molecular and atomic spectroscopy of gases through solid-state phenomena to physical optics.
Related titles: Online - full text ed.: ISSN 1562-6911 (from IngentaConnect); ◆ Translation of: Optika i Spektroskopiya. ISSN 0030-4034.
Indexed: A01, A03, A08, A22, A26, ABIPC, ApMecR, C33, CA, CCI, CPEI, CPI, ChemAb, CurCont, E01, EngInd, GPAA, GeoRef, I05, INIS AtomInd, ISR, Inspec, PhotoAb, PhysBer, S01, SCI, SCOPUS, SPINweb, SpeleolAb, T02, W07.
—BLDSC (0416.650000), AskIEEE, East View, IE, Infotrieve, Ingenta, INIST. **CCC.**
Published by: (Rossiiskaya Akademiya Nauk, Sankt-Peterburgskoe Otdelenie), M A I K Nauka - Interperiodica (Subsidiary of: Pleiades Publishing, Inc.), Profsoyuznaya ul 90, Moscow, 117997, Russian Federation. TEL 7-095-3347420, FAX 7-095-3360666, compmg@maik.ru, http://www.maik.ru. Ed. Evgenii B Aleksandrov.
Distr. in the Americas by: Springer New York LLC, Journal Fulfillment, PO Box 2485, Secaucus, NJ 07096. TEL 212-460-1500, FAX 201-348-4505; **Distr. outside of the Americas by:** Springer, Haber Str 7, Heidelberg 69126, Germany. TEL 49-6221-3454303, FAX 49-6221-3454229.

535 NLD ISSN 0030-4018
QC350 CODEN: OPCOB8
➤ **OPTICS COMMUNICATIONS.** Text in English, French, German; Summaries in English. 1969. 24/yr. EUR 7,467 in Europe to institutions; JPY 991,600 in Japan to institutions; USD 8,352 elsewhere to institutions (effective 2012). adv. illus. index. back issues avail.; reprints avail. **Document type:** *Journal, Academic/Scholarly.*
Description: Covers all fields of fundamental research in optics, both theoretical and experimental.
Related titles: Microform ed.: (from PQC); Online - full text ed.: ISSN 1873-0310 (from IngentaConnect, ScienceDirect).

P

Indexed: A01, A03, A08, A20, A22, A26, ASCA, C&ISA, C24, C33, CA, CADCAM, CPEI, ChemAb, ChemTitl, CurCont, E&CAJ, EngInd, GeoRef, I05, IBR, IBZ, ISMEC, ISR, Inspec, P30, PhotoAb, RefZh, S01, SCI, SCOPUS, SolStAb, SpeleolAb, T02, TM, W07.
—BLDSC (6273.600000), AskIEEE, CASDDS, IE, Infotrieve, Ingenta, INIST, Linda Hall. **CCC.**
Published by: Elsevier BV, North-Holland (Subsidiary of: Elsevier Science & Technology), Sara Burgerhartstraat 25, Amsterdam, 1055 KV, Netherlands. TEL 31-20-4853911, FAX 31-20-4852457, JournalsCustomerServiceEMEA@elsevier.com. Eds. B J Eggleton, S Kawata, W P Schleich. **Subscr. to:** Elsevier BV, Radarweg 29, PO Box 211, Amsterdam 1000 AE, Netherlands. TEL 31-20-4853757, FAX 31-20-4853432, http://www.elsevier.nl.

621.36 USA ISSN 1094-4087
QC350 CODEN: OPEXFF
➤ **OPTICS EXPRESS.** Text in English. 1997. bi-w. free (effective 2012). back issues avail. **Document type:** *Journal, Academic/Scholarly.* **Description:** Covers original research in optical science and technology.
Media: Online - full content. **Related titles:** CD-ROM ed.; ◆ Supplement(s): Energy Express. ISSN 2161-2072.
Indexed: A20, CPEI, CPI, CurCont, EMBASE, EngInd, ExcerpMed, Inspec, MEDLINE, P30, R10, Reac, SCI, SCOPUS, SPINweb, TM, VITIS, W07.
—Linda Hall. **CCC.**
Published by: Optical Society of America, 2010 Massachusetts Ave, NW, Washington, DC 20036. TEL 202-416-1907, FAX 202-416-6140, info@osa.org, http://www.osa.org. Ed. Martijn de de Sterke.

535 USA ISSN 1936-9808
QC350
OPTICS JOURNAL. Text in English. 2007 (Jul.). w. free (effective 2011). **Document type:** *Journal, Academic/Scholarly.*
Media: Online - full content.
Address: 112 Applegrove Dr, Rochester, NY 14612. TEL 585-228-7286. Ed. F J Duarte.

535 USA ISSN 0146-9592
CODEN: OPLEDP
➤ **OPTICS LETTERS.** Abbreviated title: O L. Text in English. 1977. s-m. USD 2,880 combined subscription domestic to institutions (print & online eds.); USD 2,965 combined subscription in Canada to institutions (print & online eds.); USD 3,070 combined subscription elsewhere to institutions (print & online eds.) (effective 2012). illus. Index. back issues avail.; reprints avail. **Document type:** *Journal, Academic/Scholarly.* **Description:** Covers the latest research in optical science, including atmospheric optics, quantum electronics, fourier optics, integrated optics, and fiber optics.
Related titles: CD-ROM ed.; Online - full text ed.: ISSN 1539-4794. USD 2,200 to institutions (effective 2012).
Indexed: A05, A20, A22, AS&TA, AS&TI, ASCA, B10, C&ISA, C10, CA, CIN, CPEI, CPI, Cadscan, ChemAb, ChemTitl, CurCont, E&CAJ, EMBASE, EngInd, ExcerpMed, GALA, IBR, IBZ, INIS AtomInd, ISMEC, ISR, Inspec, LeadAb, MEDLINE, P30, PhotoAb, PhysBer, R10, Reac, RefZh, SCI, SCOPUS, SPINweb, SolStAb, T02, W07, Zincscan.
—BLDSC (6273.650000), AskIEEE, CASDDS, IE, Infotrieve, Ingenta, INIST, Linda Hall. **CCC.**
Published by: Optical Society of America, 2010 Massachusetts Ave, NW, Washington, DC 20036. TEL 202-416-1907, FAX 202-416-6140, info@osa.org, http://www.osa.org. Ed. Alan E Willner.

535 DEU ISSN 0030-4026
QC350 CODEN: OTIKAJ
➤ **OPTIK.** Text in English. 1946. 12/yr. EUR 2,533 in Europe to institutions; EUR 2,272 to institutions in Germany, Austria and Switzerland; JPY 336,000 in Japan to institutions; USD 2,676 elsewhere to institutions (effective 2012). adv. bk.rev. bibl.; illus. index. **Document type:** *Journal, Academic/Scholarly.*
Related titles: Online - full text ed.: (from IngentaConnect, ScienceDirect); Supplement(s):.
Indexed: A01, A03, A08, A22, A26, ASCA, C&ISA, CA, CPEI, ChemAb, ChemTitl, CurCont, E&CAJ, E01, EngInd, GeoRef, I05, IBR, IBZ, ISR, Inspec, MathR, P30, PhotoAb, PhysBer, RefZh, SCI, SCOPUS, SolStAb, SpeleolAb, T02, TM, W07.
—BLDSC (6274.000000), AskIEEE, CASDDS, IE, Infotrieve, Ingenta, INIST, Linda Hall. **CCC.**
Published by: (Deutsche Gesellschaft fuer angewandte Optik e.V./German Society of Applied Optics, Deutsche Gesellschaft fuer Elektronenmikroskopie e.V.), Urban und Fischer Verlag (Subsidiary of: Elsevier GmbH), Loebdergraben 14a, Jena, 07743, Germany. TEL 49-3641-626430, FAX 49-3641-626432, info@urbanfischer.de, http://www.urbanundfischer.de. Ed. Theo Tschudi. Adv. contact Eva Kraemer TEL 49-89-5383704. Circ: 650 (paid and controlled). **Non-German speaking countries subscr. to:** Nature Publishing Group, Brunel Rd, Houndmills, Basingstoke, Hamps RG21 6XS, United Kingdom. TEL 44-1256-302629, FAX 44-1256-476117, subscriptions@nature.com **Co-sponsor:** European Optical Society.

535 RUS ISSN 0869-5695
QC974.5
OPTIKA ATMOSFERY I OKEANA. Text in Russian. 1987. m. USD 750 in Europe; USD 765 in North America; USD 785 elsewhere (effective 2000 - 2001). adv. **Document type:** *Academic/Scholarly.* **Description:** Covers optical and acoustic wave propagation in the atmosphere; spectroscopy of atmospheric gases; optics of random media; remote sensing of the atmosphere, hydrosphere, and underlying surface; atmospheric radiation, optical weather and climate.
Formerly (until 1992): Optika Atmosfery (0235-277X)
Related titles: ◆ English ed.: Atmospheric and Oceanic Optics. ISSN 1024-8560.
Indexed: M&GPA, RefZh.
—Ingenta, INIST, Linda Hall.
Published by: Rossiiskaya Akademiya Nauk, Sibirskoe Otdelenie, Institut Optiki Atmosfery, Akademicheskii pr-t 1, Tomsk, 634055, Russian Federation. FAX 7-3822-259086. Ed., R&P V R Zuev. Pub. Sergei Kasyanov. Adv. contact S B Ponomareva.

535.84 RUS ISSN 0030-4034
QC350 CODEN: OPSPAM
OPTIKA I SPEKTROSKOPIYA. Text in Russian. 1956. m. RUR 1,190 for 6 mos. domestic (effective 2004). charts; illus. index, cum.index every 5 yrs. **Document type:** *Journal, Academic/Scholarly.* **Description:** Covers Russian research in optical phenomena ranging from molecular and atomic spectroscopy of gases through solid-state phenomena to physical optics.
Related titles: Online - full text ed.; ◆ English Translation: Optics and Spectroscopy. ISSN 0030-400X.
Indexed: ASCA, CIN, ChemAb, ChemTitl, GeoRef, ISR, Inspec, RefZh, SCOPUS, SpeleolAb.
—BLDSC (0128.000000), CASDDS, East View, INIST, Linda Hall. **CCC.**
Published by: (Rossiiskaya Akademiya Nauk, Sankt-Peterburgskoe Otdelenie, Rossiiskaya Akademiya Nauk/Russian Academy of Sciences), Izdatel'stvo Nauka, Profsoyuznaya ul 90, Moscow, 117864, Russian Federation. TEL 7-095-3347151, FAX 7-095-4202220, secret@naukaran.ru, http://www.naukaran.ru. Circ: 2,600.

OPTOELECTRONICS, IMAGING AND SENSING SERIES. *see* ENGINEERING—Electrical Engineering

535 DEU ISSN 1673-1905
OPTOELECTRONICS LETTERS. Text in English. 2007. 3/yr. EUR 800, USD 973 combined subscription to institutions (print & online eds.) (effective 2012). reprint service avail. from PSC. **Document type:** *Journal, Academic/Scholarly.* **Description:** Aims to promote international academic exchange in the fields of Photonics and Optoelectronics in China and abroad, through the rapid reporting of new and important experimental results.
Related titles: Online - full text ed.: ISSN 1993-5013.
Indexed: A22, A26, CPEI, E01, H12, I05, RefZh, SCOPUS.
—IE, Ingenta. **CCC.**
Published by: Springer (Subsidiary of: Springer Science+Business Media), Tiergartenstr 17, Heidelberg, 69121, Germany. TEL 49-6221-4870, FAX 49-6221-345229, subscriptions@springer.com. Ed. En-xu Ba.

OPTOMAGAZINE. *see* MEDICAL SCIENCES—Ophthalmology And Optometry

535.58 621.3 JPN ISSN 0286-9659
TA1750 CODEN: OPUTDD
OPUTORONIKUSU/OPTRONICS. Text in Japanese. 1982. m. USD 230. adv. **Document type:** *Trade.*
Indexed: ChemAb.
—BLDSC (6276.600000), CASDDS.
Published by: Oputoronikususha/Optronics Co., Ltd., Sunken Bldg, 5-5 Shinogawa-Machi, Shinjuku-ku, Tokyo, 162-0814, Japan. TEL 03-3269-3550, FAX 03-3269-2551. Ed. Takashi Kawajiri. Pub. Naoki Ueno. Adv. contact Tetsuo Ohsawa. Circ: 12,000.

OYO SUPEKUTOROMETORI TOKYO TORONKAI KOEN YOSHISHU/ ABSTRACTS OF PAPERS PRESENTED AT THE TOKYO SYMPOSIA ON THE APPLIED SPECTROMETRY. *see* PHYSICS—Abstracting, Bibliographies, Statistics

535.58 DEU ISSN 1674-9251
▼ ➤ **PHOTONIC SENSORS.** Text in English. 2011. q. EUR 418, USD 514 combined subscription to institutions (print & online eds.) (effective 2012). **Document type:** *Journal, Academic/Scholarly.* **Description:** Reports on new developments in photonic sensing and technology.
Related titles: Online - full text ed.: ISSN 2190-7439. 2011.
Indexed: SCOPUS.
—CCC.
Published by: SpringerOpen (Subsidiary of: Springer Science+Business Media), Tiergartenstr 17, Heidelberg, 69121, Germany. info@springeropen.com, http://www.springeropen.com. Ed. Yun-Jiang Rao.

535.029 USA ISSN 2155-3378
TS511.U6
PHOTONICS BUYERS' GUIDE. Text in English. 1954. a. (in 4 vols.). USD 60 combined subscription per issue in US & Canada (print & CD-ROM eds.); USD 84 combined subscription per issue elsewhere (print & CD-ROM eds.) (effective 2010). adv. **Document type:** *Directory, Trade.* **Description:** Four-volume buyers' guide and reference for the photonics industry.
Former titles (until 2010): Photonics Directory (1044-1425); (until 1989): Optical Industry and Systems Purchasing Directory (0191-0647); Which superseded in part (in 1978): Optical Industry and Systems Directory (0078-5474); Which was formerly (until 1963): The Optical Industry Directory (0735-0244)
Related titles: CD-ROM ed.: ISSN 1551-4749. USD 15 per issue in US & Canada; USD 30 per issue elsewhere (effective 2009); Online - full text ed.: ISSN 2155-3386.
Indexed: Inspec.
—Ingenta.
Published by: Laurin Publishing Co., Inc., Berkshire Common, PO Box 4949, Pittsfield, MA 01202. TEL 413-499-0514, FAX 413-442-3180, info@photonics.com.

535 USA ISSN 1539-3623
PHOTONICS COMPONENTS AND SUBSYSTEMS. Text in English. 2002 (Jan). m. USD 695 in US & Canada; USD 745 elsewhere (effective 2008). **Document type:** *Newsletter, Trade.* **Description:** Provides worldwide coverage of technology, markets, and applications.
Related titles: E-mail ed.: USD 695 (effective 2008); Online - full text ed.: ISSN 1539-3828.
Indexed: CompD.
Published by: Information Gatekeepers, Inc., 320 Washington St, Ste 302, Brighton, MA 02135. TEL 617-782-5033, 800-323-1088, FAX 617-782-5735, info@igigroup.com. Ed. Dr. Hui Pan. Pub. Dr. Paul Polishuk.

535 POL ISSN 2080-2242
▼ ➤ **PHOTONICS LETTERS OF POLAND.** Text in English. 2009. q. free (effective 2011). **Document type:** *Journal, Academic/Scholarly.*
Media: Online - full text.
Published by: Polskie Stowarzyszenie Fotoniczne/Photonics Society of Poland, Warsaw University of Technology, Faculty of Physics, Koszykowa 75, Warsaw, 00-662, Poland. http://photonics.pl.

535 USA ISSN 0731-1230
TS510 CODEN: PHSAD3
PHOTONICS SPECTRA. Text in English. 1967. m. free to qualified personnel (effective 2009). adv. index. back issues avail.; reprints avail. **Document type:** *Magazine, Trade.* **Description:** Covers the latest applications, news and technology advances in the field of optics, lasers, imaging, fiber optics, electro-optics and photonic component manufacturing.
Formerly (until 1982): Optical Spectra (0030-395X); Which superseded (in 1967): News and Notes of the Optical Industry
Related titles: Online - full text ed.
Indexed: A20, A22, A26, A28, APA, ASCA, ApMecR, BiolDig, BrCerAb, C&ISA, CA/WCA, CADCAM, CIA, CPEI, CerAb, ChemAb, CivEngAb, CorrAb, CurCont, E&CAJ, E11, EEA, EMA, ESPM, EngInd, EnvEAb, G08, GALA, GeoRef, H15, I05, IBR, IBZ, Inspec, M&TEA, M09, MBF, METADEX, P30, RefZh, SCI, SCOPUS, SolStAb, SpeleolAb, T04, TM, TelAb, W07, WAA.
—BLDSC (6474.317000), AskIEEE, CASDDS, IE, Infotrieve, Ingenta, INIST, Linda Hall. **CCC.**
Published by: Laurin Publishing Co., Inc., Berkshire Common, PO Box 4949, Pittsfield, MA 01202. TEL 413-499-0514, FAX 413-442-3180, info@photonics.com. adv.: B&W page USD 11,295, color page USD 13,345; bleed 213 x 281.

535.58 USA
PHOTONICS TECH BRIEFS. Abbreviated title: P T B. Text in English. 1993. 8/yr. adv. back issues avail. **Document type:** *Magazine, Trade.* **Description:** Covers laser components and systems, electro-optics, fiber optics and imaging technology, as well as new commercial products and company profiles.
Formerly: Laser Tech Briefs
Published by: Associated Business Publications International, 1466 Broadway, Ste 910, New York, NY 10036. TEL 212-490-3999, 800-944-6272, FAX 212-986-7864, info@abpi.net, http://www.abpi.net. Ed. Bruce Bennett. adv.: B&W page USD 5,200, color page USD 6,695. Circ: 190,346.

535.28 DEU ISSN 1432-9778
TA1501
PHOTONIK; Fachzeitschrift fuer die optischen Technologien. Text and summaries in German, English. 1994. 6/yr. EUR 69.90 domestic; EUR 86 foreign; EUR 15 newsstand/cover (effective 2008). adv. bk.rev. tr.lit.; tr.mk. 76 p./no. 4 cols./p.; **Document type:** *Magazine, Trade.*
Formerly (until 1995): Telegramm; Incorporates (1969-2002): LaserOpto (1437-3041); Which was formerly (until 1999): Laser und Optoelektronik (0722-9003); (until 1982): Laser und Elektro-Optik (0344-5186); (until 1971): Laser (0023-8554)
Indexed: A22, IBR, IBZ, TM.
—BLDSC (6474.317370), IE, Ingenta, Linda Hall. **CCC.**
Published by: A T Fachverlag GmbH, Saarlandstr 28, Fellbach, 70734, Germany. TEL 49-711-9529510, FAX 49-711-95295199, at@at-fachverlag.de, http://www.at-fachverlag.de. Ed. Johannes Kuppe. Pub., R&P Werner Page. Adv. contact Norbert Schoene TEL 49-711-95295120. color page EUR 5,178, B&W page EUR 4,128; trim 185 x 264. Circ: 19,505 (paid and free).

535 FRA ISSN 1629-4475
PHOTONIQUES. Text in French. 2001. 6/yr. EUR 66.35 domestic; EUR 80.57 in the European Union; EUR 95 elsewhere (effective 2012). **Document type:** *Journal, Academic/Scholarly.*
—INIST.
Published by: (Societe Francaise d'Optique), E D P Sciences, 17 Ave du Hoggar, Parc d'Activites de Courtaboeuf, BP 112, Cedex A, Les Ulis, F-91944, France. TEL 33-1-69187575, FAX 33-1-69860678, http://www.edpsciences.org. Ed. Francoise Metivier.

PLASTIC OPTICAL FIBER. *see* COMMUNICATIONS

535 USA ISSN 0277-786X
PROCEEDINGS OF S P I E - INTERNATIONAL SOCIETY FOR OPTICAL ENGINEERING. (Society of Photo-Optical Instrumentation Engineers) Text in English. 1971. a. **Document type:** *Proceedings, Academic/Scholarly.*
Formerly (until 1981): Society of Photo-optical Instrumentation Engineers. Proceedings (0361-0748)
Related titles: Online - full text ed.: ISSN 1996-756X.
Indexed: A28, APA, C13, CA/WCA, CIA, CivEngAb, E11, EEA, EMA, ESPM, EnvEAb, H15, MBF, T04.
—BLDSC (6823.100000). **CCC.**
Published by: S P I E - International Society for Optical Engineering, 1000 20th St, Bellingham, WA 98225. TEL 360-676-3290, 888-504-8171, FAX 360-647-1445, spie@spie.org.

535 NLD ISSN 0079-6638
QC351 CODEN: POPTAN
➤ **PROGRESS IN OPTICS.** Text in English. 1961. irreg., latest vol.51, 2008. price varies. index, cum.index: vols.1-32 in vol.32. **Document type:** *Monographic series, Academic/Scholarly.* **Description:** Reviews developments and research in all areas of optics.
Indexed: A22, ASCA, ISR, Inspec, PhysBer, SCI, SCOPUS, W07.
—BLDSC (6871.700000), CASDDS, IE, Infotrieve, Ingenta, INIST, Linda Hall. **CCC.**
Published by: Elsevier BV, North-Holland (Subsidiary of: Elsevier Science & Technology), Sara Burgerhartstraat 25, Amsterdam, 1055 KV, Netherlands. TEL 31-20-4853911, FAX 31-20-4852457, JournalsCustomerServiceEMEA@elsevier.com, http://www.elsevier.com. Ed. E Wolf. **Subscr. to:** Elsevier BV, Radarweg 29, PO Box 211, Amsterdam 1000 AE, Netherlands. TEL 31-20-4853757, FAX 31-20-4853432.

➤ **REFERATIVNYI ZHURNAL. OPTIKA I YADERNAYA FIZIKA**; vypusk svodnogo toma. *see* PHYSICS—Abstracting, Bibliographies, Statistics

➤ **REFERATIVNYI ZHURNAL. VOLOKONNO-OPTICHESKAYA SVYAZ'**; vypusk svodnogo toma. *see* PHYSICS—Abstracting, Bibliographies, Statistics

525 JPN
RESEARCH COMMITTEE FOR GRAPHIC SIMULATION AND VISUALIZATION OF MULTIPHASE FLOW. PROCEEDINGS. Text in English, Japanese. 1988. 4/yr. **Document type:** *Proceedings.*

Published by: Japan Society of Multiphase Flow, Research Committee for Graphic Simulation and Visualization of Multiphase Flow/Nihon Konsoryu Gakkai Konsoryu no Gurafikku Shimyureshon to Kashika ni Kansuru Kenkyukai, Tsukuba Daigaku Kozo Kogakukei, Matsui Kenkyushitsu, 1-1 Tenno-Dai 1-chome, Tsukuba-shi, Ibaraki-ken 305-0006, Japan.

535.8 DEU
RESOLUTION. Variant title: Wild Leitz Scientific and Technical Information. Text in English. 1998. s-a. free. **Document type:** *Newsletter.* **Description:** Covers microscopical science and applications of microscope systems.
Formerly (until 2005): Scientific and Technical Information (CD-ROM) (1612-7552); Which was formed by the merger of (196?-1998): Scientific and Technical Information (Print) (0176-8603); (1989-1998): Mitteilungen fuer Wissenschaft und Technik (Print) (0340-5117); Which was formerly (1958-1988): Leitz-Mitteilungen fuer Wissenschaft und Technik (0457-4176)
Related titles: Online - full text ed.: 2001. free.
Indexed: Inspec.
Published by: Leica Microsystems AG, Ernst-Leitz-Str 17-37, Wetzlar, 35578, Germany. TEL 49-6441-290, FAX 49-6441-292590, http://www.leica-microsystems.com.

REZA GAKKAI GAKUJUTSU KOENKAI NENJI TAIKAI KOEN YOKOSHU/LASER SOCIETY OF JAPAN. ANNUAL MEETING. DIGEST OF TECHNICAL PAPERS. *see* PHYSICS—Abstracting, Bibliographies, Statistics

535 JPN
REZA GAKKAI KENKYUKAI HOKOKU; Laser Society of Japan. Reports on Topical Meeting. Text in Japanese. 5/yr.
Published by: Reza Gakkai/Laser Society of Japan, 2-6 Yamada-Oka, Suita, Osaka 565-0871, Japan.

535 JPN
REZA GIJUTSU SOGO KENKYUJO JIGYO HOKOKUSHO/INSTITUTE FOR LASER TECHNOLOGY. REPORT. Text in Japanese. a.
Published by: Reza Gijutsu Sogo Kenkyujo/Institute for Laser Technology, Osaka Kagaku Gijutsu Senta Biru, 8-4, Utsubohon-machi 1-chome, Nishi-ku, Osaka-shi, Osaka 500, Japan.

535 JPN
REZA GIJUTSU SOGO KENKYUJO NENPO/INSTITUTE FOR LASER TECHNOLOGY. ANNUAL PROGRESS REPORT. Text in English, Japanese; Summaries in English. a.
Published by: Reza Gijutsu Sogo Kenkyujo/Institute for Laser Technology, Kagaku Gijutsu Senta Biru, 8-4 Utsubohon-Machi 1-chome, Nishi-ku, Osaka-shi, 550-0004, Japan.

REZA KAGAKU/ABSTRACTS OF RIKEN SYMPOSIUM ON LASER SCIENCE. *see* PHYSICS—Abstracting, Bibliographies, Statistics

621.36 JPN ISSN 1881-6797
REZA KAKOU GAKKAISHI/JAPAN LASER PROCESSING SOCIETY. JOURNAL. Text in Japanese. 2001. 4/yr. membership. **Document type:** *Journal, Academic/Scholarly.*
Formerly: Reza Netsu Kako Kenkyukai Shiryo
Related titles: Online - full text ed.
Published by: Reza Netsu Kako Kenkyukai/Japan Laser Processing Society, Osaka University, Katayama Lab., JWRI-Joining & Welding Research Institute, 11-1 Mihogaoka, Ibaraki, Osaka 567-0047, Japan. TEL 81-6-68798642, FAX 81-6-68798642.

535 JPN ISSN 0387-0200
TA1671 CODEN: REKEDA
➤ **REZA KENKYU/REVIEW OF LASER ENGINEERING.** Text in Japanese. 1973. m. JPY 21,600 (effective 2004). **Document type:** *Journal, Academic/Scholarly.* **Description:** Contains original papers, reviews, and other significant reports on laser-related topics.
Related titles: Online - full text ed.
Indexed: A22, ChemAb, ChemTitl, INIS AtomInd, Inspec, JPI.
—BLDSC (7791.160000), AskIEEE, CASDDS, IE, Ingenta, Linda Hall. **CCC.**
Published by: Reza Gakkai/Laser Society of Japan, 2-6 Yamada-Oka, Suita, Osaka 565-0871, Japan.

535 JPN ISSN 0914-9805
REZA KUROSU/LASER CROSS. Text in Japanese. 1988. m.
Published by: Reza Gijutsu Sogo Kenkyujo/Institute for Laser Technology, Osaka Kagaku Gijutsu Senta Biru, 8-4, Utsubohon-machi 1-chome, Nishi-ku, Osaka-shi, Osaka 500, Japan.

535 JPN ISSN 0913-1361
REZA KYOKAI UINTA SEMINA/JAPAN SOCIETY OF LASER TECHNOLOGY. WINTER SEMINAR. Text in Japanese. a.
Published by: Reza Kyokai/Japan Society of Laser Technology, Chuo Daigaku Rikogakubu Seimitsu Kikai Kogakka, Kawasumi Kenkyushitsu, Koishikawa Yubinkyoku, P.O. Box 27, Tokyo, 112, Japan.

535 JPN ISSN 0916-7277
REZA KYOKAISHI/LASER. Text in Japanese. 1974. bi-m.
Published by: Reza Kyokai/Japan Society of Laser Technology, Chuo Daigaku Rikogakubu Seimitsu Kikai Kogakka, Kawasumi Kenkyushitsu, Koishikawa Yubinkyoku, P.O. Box 27, Tokyo, 112, Japan.

535 JPN
REZA NO KISO TO SONO OYO. Text in Japanese. a.
Published by: Reza Gakkai/Laser Society of Japan, 2-6 Yamada-Oka, Suita, Osaka 565-0871, Japan.

621.36 USA ISSN 1936-4954
S I A M JOURNAL ON IMAGING SCIENCES. Text in English. 2008. q. USD 337 to institutions (effective 2012). back issues avail. **Document type:** *Journal, Academic/Scholarly.* **Description:** Highlights the commonality of methodology, models, and algorithms among diverse application areas of imaging sciences.
Media: Online - full text.
Indexed: C10, CA, CPEI, CurCont, MSN, P30, SCI, T02, W07, Z02.
—Linda Hall. **CCC.**
Published by: Society for Industrial and Applied Mathematics, 3600 Market St, 6th Fl, Philadelphia, PA 19104. TEL 215-382-9800, 800-447-7426, FAX 215-386-7999, siam@siam.org. Ed. Guillermo Sapiro TEL 612-625-1343. Pub. David K Marshall.

535 USA ISSN 1050-0529
S P I E MILESTONE SERIES. (Society of Photo-optical Instrumentation Engineers) Text in English. 1985. irreg. price varies. adv. back issues avail.; reprints avail. **Document type:** *Monographic series, Academic/Scholarly.* **Description:** Selected reprints of key papers from the world literature covering important discoveries and developments in optics.
Indexed: A22.
—IE, Ingenta, INIST. **CCC.**
Published by: S P I E - International Society for Optical Engineering, PO Box 10, Bellingham, WA 98227. TEL 360-676-3290, 888-504-8171, FAX 360-647-1445, customerservice@spie.org.

S P I E PROFESSIONAL. (Society of Photo-Optical Instrumentation Engineers) *see* ENGINEERING

535 USA ISSN 1946-3251
QC350
▼ ➤ **S P I E REVIEWS.** (Society of Photo-Optical Instrumentation Engineers) Text in English. 2009. irreg. free (effective 2012). reprints avail. **Document type:** *Journal, Academic/Scholarly.* **Description:** Covers the state of the art of emerging and rapidly evolving photonics technologies and their applications.
Media: Online - full text.
—Linda Hall.
Published by: S P I E - International Society for Optical Engineering, PO Box 10, Bellingham, WA 98227. TEL 360-676-3290, 888-504-8171, FAX 360-647-1445, customerservice@spie.org. Ed. William T Rhodes TEL 561-297-2338.

621.36 DEU ISSN 1864-614X
SCHRIFTENREIHE LASERTECHNIK. Text in German. 2006. irreg., latest vol.4, 2010. price varies. **Document type:** *Monographic series, Academic/Scholarly.*
Published by: Cuvillier Verlag, Nonnenstieg 8, Goettingen, 37075, Germany. TEL 49-551-547240, FAX 49-551-5472421, info@cuvillier.de.

535 CHN ISSN 1007-0206
TK7871.85
SEMICONDUCTOR PHOTONICS AND TECHNOLOGY. Text in English. 1995. q. USD 35.60 (effective 2009). **Document type:** *Journal, Academic/Scholarly.*
Related titles: Online - full text ed.
—BLDSC (8238.791000), East View.
Published by: Zhongguo Dianzi Keji Jituan Gongsi Di-44 Yanjiusuo/China Electronics Technology Group Corp. (CETC) No.44 Research Institute, 14, Pinghuayuan Lu, 44-suo, Chongqing, 400060, China. http://www.coeri.com/main.asp.

SENSOR LETTERS. *see* ENGINEERING—Electrical Engineering

535 621.3 GBR ISSN 0964-0339
SENSORS SERIES. Variant title: Adam Hilger Series on Sensors. Text in English. 1987. irreg. **Document type:** *Monographic series, Academic/Scholarly.*
Indexed: Inspec.
Published by: (Institute of Physics), Institute of Physics Publishing Ltd., Dirac House, Temple Back, Bristol, BS1 6BE, United Kingdom. TEL 44-117-9297481, FAX 44-117-9301178, custserv@iop.org, http://publishing.iop.org/.

535 JPN ISSN 0915-1079
SENTAN GIJUTSU KOENKAI/LECTURE ON ADVANCED LASER TECHNOLOGY. Text in Japanese. 1988. irreg. JPY 2,000 per issue.
Published by: Reza Gijutsu Sogo Kenkyujo/Institute for Laser Technology, Kagaku Gijutsu Senta Biru, 8-4 Utsubohon-Machi 1-chome, Nishi-ku, Osaka-shi, 550-0004, Japan.

535 CHN ISSN 1000-8713
QD79.C4 CODEN: SEPUER
➤ **SEPU/CHINESE JOURNAL OF CHROMATOGRAPHY.** Text in Chinese; Abstracts in Chinese, English. 1984. bi-m. CNY 90, USD 90; CNY 15 per issue (effective 2009). adv. **Document type:** *Journal, Academic/Scholarly.* **Description:** Contains review articles, research papers on theories and experiments in the field of chromatography.
Related titles: Online - full text ed.: ISSN 1872-2059.
Indexed: A22, A28, A32, A40, AESIS, APA, B&BAb, B19, B21, BrCerAb, C&ISA, C33, CA/WCA, CIA, CerAb, ChemAb, CivEngAb, CorrAb, E&CAJ, E11, EEA, EMA, EMBASE, ESPM, EnvEAb, ExcerpMed, H15, IndMed, M&TEA, M09, MBF, MEDLINE, METADEX, NucAcAb, P30, R10, Reac, RefZh, SCOPUS, SWRA, SolStAb, T04, ToxAb, WAA.
—BLDSC (3180.299800), CASDDS, IE, Infotrieve, Ingenta, Linda Hall.
Published by: (Zhongguo Kexueyuan Dalian Huaxue Wuli Yanjiusuo/Chinese Academy of Sciences, Dalian Institute of Chemical Physics), Kexue Chubanshe/Science Press, 16 Donghuang Cheng Genbei Jie, Beijing, 100717, China. TEL 86-10-64000246, FAX 86-10-64030255, http://www.sciencep.com/. Ed. Yu-kui Zhang. adv.: B&W page USD 750; trim 145 x 220. Circ: 5,000.

535 SGP
SERIES IN NONLINEAR OPTICS. Text in English. 1993. irreg., latest vol.3. price varies. back issues avail. **Document type:** *Monographic series, Academic/Scholarly.*
Published by: World Scientific Publishing Co. Pte. Ltd., 5 Toh Tuck Link, Singapore, 596224, Singapore. TEL 65-6466-5775, FAX 65-6467-7667, wspc@wspc.com.sg, http://www.worldscientific.com. Ed. Iam-Choon Khoo. **Dist. by:** World Scientific Publishing Co., Inc., 27 Warren St, Ste 401-402, Hackensack, NJ 07601. TEL 201-487-9655, 800-227-7562, FAX 201-487-9656, 888-977-2665, wspc@wspc.com; World Scientific Publishing Ltd., 57 Shelton St, London WC2H 9HE, United Kingdom. TEL 44-207-8360888, FAX 44-207-8362020, sales@wspc.co.uk.

535 SGP ISSN 2010-2313
SERIES IN OPTICS AND PHOTONICS. Text in English. 1989. irreg., latest vol.7, 2009. price varies. back issues avail. **Document type:** *Monographic series, Academic/Scholarly.*
Indexed: CIN, ChemAb, ChemTitl.
Published by: World Scientific Publishing Co. Pte. Ltd., 5 Toh Tuck Link, Singapore, 596224, Singapore. TEL 65-6466-5775, FAX 65-6467-7667, wspc@wspc.com.sg, http://www.worldscientific.com. Ed. S L Chin. **Dist. by:** World Scientific Publishing Co., Inc., 27 Warren St, Ste 401-402, Hackensack, NJ 07601. TEL 201-487-9655, 800-227-7562, FAX 201-487-9656, 888-977-2665, wspc@wspc.com; World Scientific Publishing Ltd., 57 Shelton St, London WC2H 9HE, United Kingdom. TEL 44-207-8360888, FAX 44-207-8362020, sales@wspc.co.uk.

535 USA
SPECIAL REFLECTIONS. Text in English. irreg. adv. **Document type:** *Newsletter.* **Description:** Collects, analyzes, and disseminates information on infrared and electro-optical technology with an emphasis on military applications.
Media: Online - full text.
Published by: (U.S. Department of Defense, Infrared Information Analysis Center), E R I M International, PO Box 134008, Ann Arbor, MI 48113-4008. TEL 734-994-1200, FAX 734-994-5550. Ed. Rodney C Anderson. Adv. contact Nancy Hall.

SPECTROCHIMICA ACTA PART A: MOLECULAR AND BIOMOLECULAR SPECTROSCOPY. *see* CHEMISTRY—Analytical Chemistry

SPECTROCHIMICA ACTA PART B: ATOMIC SPECTROSCOPY. *see* CHEMISTRY—Analytical Chemistry

SPECTROSCOPIC PROPERTIES OF INORGANIC & ORGANOMETALLIC COMPOUNDS. *see* CHEMISTRY

535 JPN
SPECTROSCOPICAL SOCIETY OF JAPAN. ABSTRACTS OF THE MEETING/NIHON BUNKO GAKKAI KOEN YOSHISHU. Text in English, Japanese. irreg. (approx. 2/yr.). JPY 1,000, USD 10 (effective 1998). **Document type:** *Abstract/Index.*
Published by: Spectroscopical Society of Japan/Nihon Bunko Gakkai, 1-13 Kanda-Awaji-cho, Chiyoda-ku, Tokyo, 101-0063, Japan. TEL 81-3-3253-2747. Ed. Yoshihiro F Mizugai.

535.84 USA ISSN 0038-7010
QD95 CODEN: SPLEBX
➤ **SPECTROSCOPY LETTERS**; an international journal for rapid communication. Text in English. 1968. 8/yr. GBP 1,767 combined subscription in United Kingdom to institutions (print & online eds.); EUR 2,332, USD 2,930 combined subscription to institutions (print & online eds.) (effective 2012). adv. charts. reprint service avail. from PSC. **Document type:** *Journal, Academic/Scholarly.* **Description:** Provides vital coverage of fundamental developments, new or improved instrumentation, spectroscopic diagnostics, and applications of spectroscopy across all disciplines.
Related titles: Microform ed.: (from RPI); Online - full text ed.: ISSN 1532-2289. GBP 1,590 in United Kingdom to institutions; EUR 2,099, USD 2,636 to institutions (effective 2012) (from IngentaConnect).
Indexed: A01, A03, A08, A22, A28, APA, ASCA, B&BAb, B19, B21, BrCerAb, C&ISA, C33, CA, CA/WCA, CCI, CIA, CIN, CerAb, ChemAb, ChemTitl, CivEngAb, CorrAb, CurCR, CurCont, E&CAJ, E01, E11, EEA, EMA, ESPM, EnvEAb, GeoRef, H15, IBR, IBZ, ISR, Inspec, M&TEA, M09, MBF, METADEX, NucAcAb, R16, S01, SCI, SCOPUS, SolStAb, SpeleolAb, T02, T04, W07, WAA.
—AskIEEE, CASDDS, IE, Infotrieve, Ingenta, INIST, Linda Hall. **CCC.**
Published by: Taylor & Francis Inc. (Subsidiary of: Taylor & Francis Group), 325 Chestnut St, Ste 800, Philadelphia, PA 19106. TEL 215-625-2940, 800-354-1420, orders@taylorandfrancis.com, http://www.taylorandfrancis.com. Ed. Robert Michel. Adv. contact Linda Hann TEL 44-1344-779945.

P

535 USA ISSN 0490-4176
CODEN: SPSKDK
SPEX SPEAKER. Text in English. 1955. q. adv. charts; stat.
Indexed: GeoRef, SpeleolAb.
—CASDDS, Linda Hall.
Published by: Spex Industries Inc., 3880 Park Ave, Edison, NJ 08820. TEL 201-549-7144, FAX 201-549-5125. Ed. Ray Kaminski. Circ: 15,000.

535 USA ISSN 0342-4111
CODEN: SSOSDB
SPRINGER SERIES IN OPTICAL SCIENCES. Text in English. 1976. irreg., latest vol.158, 2010. price varies. back issues avail.; reprints avail. **Document type:** *Monographic series.*
Related titles: Online - full text ed.: ISSN 1556-1534.
Indexed: A22, CIN, ChemAb, ChemTitl, Inspec, PhysBer, SCOPUS.
—BLDSC (8424.770000), CASDDS, IE, Ingenta, INIST. **CCC.**
Published by: Springer New York LLC (Subsidiary of: Springer Science+Business Media), 233 Spring St, New York, NY 10013. TEL 212-460-1500, FAX 212-460-1575, service-ny@springer.com. Ed. William T Rhodes.

535 621.3 DEU ISSN 1437-0379
SPRINGER SERIES IN PHOTONICS. Text in English. 1999. irreg., latest vol.13, 2006. price varies. **Document type:** *Monographic series, Academic/Scholarly.* **Description:** Covers the entire field of photonics, including theory, experiment, and the technology of photonic devices.
—BLDSC (8424.771350), IE, Ingenta.
Published by: Springer (Subsidiary of: Springer Science+Business Media), Tiergartenstr 17, Heidelberg, 69121, Germany. TEL 49-6221-4870, FAX 49-6221-345229, subscriptions@springer.com. Eds. B Monemar, T Kamiya.

535 540 JPN ISSN 0562-4096
STUDIES OF COLOR/SHIKISAI KENKYU. Text in Japanese; Summaries in English. 1954. s-a.
Published by: Japan Color Research Institute/Nihon Shikisai Kenkyujo, 1-19 Nishi-Azabu 3-chome, Minato-ku, Tokyo, 106-0031, Japan.

535.84 543.085 IND ISSN 0972-4516
TRENDS IN APPLIED SPECTROSCOPY. Text in English. 1993. a. EUR 134.10 in Europe; JPY 17,852 in Japan; USD 149 elsewhere (effective 2010). **Document type:** *Journal, Academic/Scholarly.* **Description:** Contains review articles, mini-reviews and original communications dealing with the latest information on the principles, methods and applications of all diverse branches of spectroscopy.
Related titles: CD-ROM ed.
Indexed: A28, APA, ASFA, BrCerAb, C&ISA, CA/WCA, CIA, CerAb, CivEngAb, CorrAb, E&CAJ, E11, EEA, EMA, ESPM, EnvEAb, H15, Inspec, M&TEA, M09, MBF, METADEX, SolStAb, T04, WAA.
—BLDSC (9049.542200), Linda Hall.
Published by: Research Trends (P) Ltd., T.C. 17 / 250 (3), Chadiyara Rd, Poojapura, Trivandrum, Kerala 695 012, India.

535 USA ISSN 1094-5695
CODEN: OTOPFZ
TRENDS IN OPTICS AND PHOTONICS SERIES. Key Title: O S A Trends in Optics and Photonics. Text in English. 1996. irreg. price varies. bibl. **Document type:** *Proceedings, Academic/Scholarly.* **Description:** Includes papers from recent conferences, selected reprints, invited articles, and topical overviews.

Related titles: Online - full text ed.
Indexed: EngInd, SCOPUS.
—CCC.
Published by: Optical Society of America, 2010 Massachusetts Ave, NW, Washington, DC 20036. TEL 202-416-1907, FAX 202-416-6140, info@osa.org, http://www.osa.org. Circ: 300.

535.58 USA ISSN 1017-6993
CODEN: TTOEEM
TUTORIAL TEXTS IN OPTICAL ENGINEERING. Text in English. 198?. irreg., latest 2007. price varies. **Document type:** *Monographic series, Academic/Scholarly.*
Indexed: Inspec.
—BLDSC (9076.174720), IE, Ingenta, INIST. **CCC.**
Published by: S P I E - International Society for Optical Engineering, 1000 20th St, Bellingham, WA 98225. TEL 360-676-3290, FAX 360-647-1445, spie@spie.org, http://spie.org. Ed. Hugo Weichel.

535 UKR ISSN 1609-1833
➤ **UKRAINIAN JOURNAL OF PHYSICAL OPTICS/UKRAINS'KYI ZHURNAL FIZYCHNOI OPTYKY.** Text in Ukrainian, English. 2000. q. **Document type:** *Journal, Academic/Scholarly.* **Description:** Contains original and review articles in the field of crystal optics, piezo-, electro-, magneto-, acoustooptics, optical properties of solids and liquids in the course of phase transitions, nonlinear optics, etc.
Related titles: Online - full content ed.: ISSN 1816-2002. free (effective 2011).
Indexed: A01, Inspec, RefZh, SCI, SCOPUS, T02, W07.
—East View, IE.
Published by: Ministerstvo Osvity i Nauky Ukrainy, Instytut Fizychnoi Optyky/Ministry of Education and Science of Ukraine, Institute of Physical Optics, vul Dragomanova 23, Lviv, 79005, Ukraine. TEL 380-322-725781, FAX 380-322-723831, ifo@ifo.lviv.ua. Ed. Orest Vlokh.

➤ **THE VIRTUAL JOURNAL FOR BIOMEDICAL OPTICS.** *see* BIOLOGY

535 USA ISSN 1018-8770
TA1632
VISUAL COMMUNICATIONS AND IMAGE PROCESSING. Text in English. 1986. a. USD 170 per issue to non-members; USD 130 per issue to members (effective 2010). adv. back issues avail.; reprints avail. **Document type:** *Proceedings, Academic/Scholarly.*
—CCC.
Published by: S P I E - International Society for Optical Engineering, PO Box 10, Bellingham, WA 98227. TEL 360-676-3290, 888-504-8171, FAX 360-647-1445, customerservice@spie.org. Eds. Feng Wu, Houqiang Li, Pascal Frossard.

535 USA ISSN 1687-7632
➤ **X-RAY OPTICS AND INSTRUMENTATION.** Text in English. 2008. irreg. USD 195 (effective 2011). **Document type:** *Journal, Academic/Scholarly.* **Description:** Aims to promote research and technology development in x-ray optics, sources, detectors, and systems.
Related titles: Online - full text ed.: ISSN 1687-7640. 2008. free (effective 2011).
Indexed: C10, CA, P52, SCOPUS, T02.
Published by: Hindawi Publishing Corporation, 410 Park Ave, 15th Fl, PMB 287, New York, NY 10022. FAX 215-893-4392, 866-446-3294, orders@hindawi.com. Ed. Carolyn MacDonald.

621.3815422 CHN ISSN 1007-2780
TK7872.L56 CODEN: YYXIFY
YEJING YU XIANSHI/CHINESE JOURNAL OF LIQUID CRYSTAL AND DISPLAYS. Text in Chinese; Abstracts in English. 1996. q. USD 79.80 (effective 2009). **Document type:** *Journal, Academic/Scholarly.*
Related titles: Online - full content ed.; Online - full text ed.
Indexed: A28, APA, BrCerAb, C&ISA, CA/WCA, CIA, CerAb, CivEngAb, CorrAb, E&CAJ, E11, EEA, EMA, ESPM, EnvEAb, H15, Inspec, M&TEA, M09, MBF, METADEX, RefZh, SolStAb, T04, WAA.
—BLDSC (3180.367500), East View, Linda Hall.
Published by: Changchun Guangxue Jingmi Jijie yu Wuli Yanjiusuo/ Changchun Institute of Optics, Fine Mechanics and Physics (Subsidiary of: Zhongguo Kexueyuan/Chinese Academy of Sciences), 140, Renmin Dajie, Changchun, 130022, China. TEL 86-431-5684692 ext 2534, FAX 86-431-5682346, ciomp@ms.ciom.ac.cn.

535 CHN ISSN 1002-2082
TA1501 CODEN: YGUAE4
YINGYONG GUANGXUE/JOURNAL OF APPLIED OPTICS. Text in Chinese. 1980. bi-m. USD 66.60 (effective 2009). **Document type:** *Journal, Academic/Scholarly.*
Related titles: Online - full text ed.
Indexed: A28, APA, BrCerAb, C&ISA, CA/WCA, CIA, CerAb, CivEngAb, CorrAb, E&CAJ, E11, EEA, EMA, ESPM, EnvEAb, H15, Inspec, M&TEA, M09, MBF, METADEX, RefZh, SolStAb, T04, WAA.
—East View.
Published by: Zhongguo Bingqi Gongye Di-205 Yanjiusuo/The No.205 Research Institute of China Ordnance Industry, 9 Dianzisanlu Road, Xi'an, 710065, China. TEL 86-29-88288172, FAX 86-29-88288000. Ed. Da-jun Yang.

535.58 CHN ISSN 1000-372X
TA1501 CODEN: WHUXEO
YINGYONG JIGUANG/APPLIED LASERS. Text in Chinese. 1981. bi-m. USD 31.20 (effective 2009). adv.
Related titles: Online - full text ed.
Indexed: A22, C33, SCOPUS.
—BLDSC (1573.240000), East View, IE, Ingenta.
Published by: (Shanghai Jiguang Jishu Yanjiusuo), Shanghai Shiji Jishu Chuban Gufen Youxian Gongsi, Kexue Jishu Chubanshe/Shanghai Scientific and Technical Publishers, 450 Ruijin Er Rd, Shanghai, 200020, China. Ed. Shao Ziwen. Adv. contact Lin Qingbai. page USD 300. Circ: 3,000. **Subscr. to:** Yingyong Jiguang Bianjibu, 770 Yishan Rd, Shanghai 200233, China. TEL 86-21-4700560, FAX 86-21-4700037.

535 CHN ISSN 1004-440X
T55.4
ZHAOMING GONGCHENG XUEBAO/INDUSTRIAL ENGINEERING JOURNAL. Text in Chinese. 1992. q. USD 26 (effective 2009). **Document type:** *Journal, Academic/Scholarly.*
Related titles: Online - full text ed.
Indexed: Inspec.
Published by: Zhongguo Zhaoming Xuehui/China Illuminating Engineering Society, 12 Guanghua Lu, Zhaoyang-qu, Beijing, 100020, China. TEL 86-10-65830997, FAX 86-10-65812194.

535 CHN ISSN 1004-2997
CODEN: ZXHUBO
ZHIPU XUEBAO/CHINESE MASS SPECTROMETRY SOCIETY. JOURNAL. Text in Chinese. 1980. bi-m. CNY 60; CNY 10 per issue (effective 2009). **Document type:** *Journal, Academic/Scholarly.*
Former titles (until 1986): Zhipuxue Zazhi; (until 1983): Zhipu/Mass Spectrometry
Related titles: Online - full text ed.
Indexed: A40, C33, RefZh.
Published by: Zhongguo Zhipu Xuehui/China Mass Spectrometry Society, PO Box 275 (65), Beijing, 102413, China. TEL 86-10-69357734, FAX 86-10-69357285, cmss@ciae.ac.cn, http://www.cmss.org.cn/. Ed. Lan-sun Zheng.

ZHONGGUO GUANGXUE YU YINGYONG GUANGXUE WENZHAI/ CHINESE OPTICS AND APPLIED OPTICS ABSTRACTS. *see* PHYSICS—Abstracting, Bibliographies, Statistics

535.58 CHN ISSN 0258-7025
QC685 CODEN: ZHJIDO
ZHONGGUO JIGUANG/CHINESE JOURNAL OF LASERS. Text in Chinese. 1974. m. USD 186 (effective 2009). **Document type:** *Journal, Academic/Scholarly.*
Related titles: Online - full text ed.; ◆ English ed.: Chinese Optics Letters. ISSN 1671-7694.
Indexed: A22, A28, APA, BrCerAb, C&ISA, CA/WCA, CIA, CIN, CPEI, CerAb, ChemAb, ChemTitl, CivEngAb, CorrAb, E&CAJ, E11, EEA, EMA, ESPM, EngInd, EnvEAb, H15, Inspec, M&TEA, M09, MBF, METADEX, RefZh, SCOPUS, SolStAb, T04, WAA.
—BLDSC (3180.366000), AskIEEE, CASDDS, East View, IE, Ingenta, Linda Hall.
Published by: (Zhongguo Guangxue Xuehui/Chinese Optical Society), Kexue Chubanshe/Science Press, 16 Donghuang Cheng Genbei Jie, Beijing, 100717, China. TEL 86-10-64000246, FAX 86-10-64030255, http://www.sciencep.com/. **Dist. by:** China International Book Trading Corp, 35 Chegongzhuang Xilu, Haidian District, PO Box 399, Beijing 100044, China. TEL 86-10-68412045, FAX 86-10-68412023, cibtc@mail.cibtc.com.cn, http://www.cibtc.com.cn.

ZHONGGUO JIGUANG YIXUE ZAZHI/CHINESE JOURNAL OF LASER MEDICINE & SURGERY. *see* MEDICAL SCIENCES

535.84 543.085 BLR ISSN 0514-7506
CODEN: ZPSBAX
➤ **ZHURNAL PRIKLADNOI SPEKTROSKOPII.** Text in Russian. 1964. bi-m. **Document type:** *Journal, Academic/Scholarly.* **Description:** Publishes original papers and short communications in the field of applied spectroscopy and related topics, including: atomic spectroscopy, molecular spectroscopy, laser spectroscopy, luminescence, radio spectroscopy, etc.
Related titles: ◆ English Translation: Journal of Applied Spectroscopy. ISSN 0021-9037.
Indexed: AESIS, INIS AtomInd, Inspec, RefZh.
—East View, INIST, Linda Hall. **CCC.**
Published by: (Natsiyanal'naya Akademiya Navuk Belarusi, Instytut Malekulyarnai i Atamnai Fiziki/National Academy of Sciences of Belarus, Institute of Molecular and Atomic Physics, Natsiyanal'naya Akademiya Navuk Belarusi, Instytut Fiziki imya B I Styapanava/ National Academy of Sciences of Belarus, B I Stepanov Institute of Physics), Vydavetstvo Belaruskaya Navuka/Publishing House Belaruskaya Navuka, ul F. Skaryny, 40, Minsk, 220141, Belarus. TEL 375-17-2633700, FAX 375-17-2637618, belnauka@infonet.by. Ed. Nikolai Borisevich.

PHYSICS—Sound

see also SOUND RECORDING AND REPRODUCTION

534 DEU ISSN 1866-3052
AACHENER BEITRAEGE ZUR TECHNISCHEN AKUSTIK. Text in German. 2002. irreg., latest vol.10, 2010. price varies. **Document type:** *Monographic series, Academic/Scholarly.*
Published by: Logos Verlag Berlin, Comeniushof, Gubener Str 47, Berlin, 10243, Germany. TEL 49-30-42851090, FAX 49-30-42851092, redaktion@logos-verlag.de.

534 774 USA ISSN 0270-5117
QC244.5 CODEN: ACIGD9
➤ **ACOUSTICAL IMAGING.** Variant title: International Symposium on Acoustical Holography and Imaging. Proceedings. Text in English. 1973. irreg., latest vol.29, 2010. price varies. back issues avail. **Document type:** *Proceedings, Academic/Scholarly.* **Description:** Contains emphasis for the symposium is the exchange of ideas and experience among researchers in different areas of acoustical imaging.
Former titles (until 19??): Acoustical Imaging: Recent Advances in Visualization and Characterization; (until 1978): Acoustical Holography (0065-0870)
Indexed: A22, AcoustA, CIN, ChemAb, ChemTitl, GeoRef, Inspec, SpeleolAb.
—BLDSC (0578.692000), CASDDS, GNLM, IE, Ingenta, INIST. **CCC.**
Published by: Springer New York LLC (Subsidiary of: Springer Science+Business Media), 233 Spring St, New York, NY 10013. TEL 212-460-1500, FAX 212-460-1575, service-ny@springer.com.

534 RUS ISSN 1063-7710
QC221 CODEN: AOUSEK
➤ **ACOUSTICAL PHYSICS.** Text in English. 1955. bi-m. EUR 2,838, USD 3,431 combined subscription to institutions (print & online eds.) (effective 2012). bibl.; charts; illus. index. back issues avail. **Document type:** *Journal, Academic/Scholarly.* **Description:** Reveals results of studies in acoustic signal processing, radiation and scattering, ultrasonics and hypersonics and underwater sound.
Formerly (until 1993): Soviet Physics - Acoustics (0038-562X)
Related titles: Online - full text ed.: ISSN 1562-6865 (from IngentaConnect); ◆ Translation of: Akusticheskii Zhurnal. ISSN 0320-7919.
Indexed: A01, A03, A08, A20, A22, A26, ASCA, ASFA, AcoustA, ApMecR, CA, CPEI, CPI, CurCont, E01, EngInd, FR, GPAA, ISR, Inspec, MathR, NPPA, P30, PhysBer, S01, SCI, SCOPUS, SPINweb, SpeleolAb, T02, W07.
—BLDSC (0404.570000), AskIEEE, East View, IE, Infotrieve, Ingenta, INIST, Linda Hall. **CCC.**
Published by: (Rossiiskaya Akademiya Nauk/Russian Academy of Sciences), M A I K Nauka - Interperiodica (Subsidiary of: Pleiades Publishing, Inc.), Profsoyuznaya ul 90, Moscow, 117997, Russian Federation. TEL 7-095-3347420, FAX 7-095-3360666, compmg@maik.ru. Ed. Oleg Rudenko. **Distr. in the Americas by:** Springer New York LLC, Journal Fulfillment, PO Box 2485, Secaucus, NJ 07096. TEL 212-460-1500, 800-777-4643, FAX 201-348-4505; **Distr. outside of the Americas by:** Springer, Haber Str 7, Heidelberg 69126, Germany. TEL 49-6221-3454303, FAX 49-6221-3454229, subscriptions@springer.com.

534 JPN ISSN 1346-3969
QC221 CODEN: JASED2
➤ **ACOUSTICAL SCIENCE AND TECHNOLOGY.** Text in English. 1980. bi-m. USD 65. adv. bk.rev. **Document type:** *Journal, Academic/ Scholarly.* **Description:** Contains technical papers, and news of the society.
Formerly (until 2001): Acoustical Society of Japan. Journal (0388-2861)
Related titles: Online - full content ed.: ISSN 1347-5177. 2000. free (effective 2011); Online - full text ed.; ◆ Japanese ed.: Nihon Onkyo Gakkaishi. ISSN 0369-4232.
Indexed: A22, ASFA, AcoustA, B21, CPEI, EngInd, Inspec, L&LBA, NSA, RefZh, SCOPUS.
—BLDSC (0578.694400), AskIEEE, IE, Ingenta, INIST, Linda Hall. **CCC.**
Published by: Nihon Onkyo Gakkai/Acoustical Society of Japan, Nakaura 5th-Bldg., 2-18-20 Sotokanda, Chiyoda-ku, Tokyo, 101-0021, Japan. FAX 81-3-52561022, KYM05145@nifty.ne.jp, http://www.asj.gr.jp/. Ed. Eiichi Miyasaka. Adv. contact Sadaoki Furui. Circ: 4,000.

534 USA ISSN 0001-4966
QC221 CODEN: JASMAN
➤ **ACOUSTICAL SOCIETY OF AMERICA. JOURNAL.** Abbreviated title: J A S A. Text in English. 1929. m. USD 1,865 combined subscription domestic to institutions (print & online eds.); USD 1,990 combined subscription in the Americas to institutions (print & online eds.); USD 2,010 combined subscription elsewhere to institutions (print & online eds.); free to members (effective 2009). adv. abstr.; illus.; pat. index, cum.index: vols.1-94, 1929-1993. 700 p./no. 2 cols./p.; back issues avail.; reprints avail. **Document type:** *Journal, Academic/Scholarly.* **Description:** Covers all phases of research and engineering of interest to acoustical scientists and engineers like linear and nonlinear acoustics; aeroacoustics, underwater sound and acoustical oceanography; ultrasonics and quantum acoustics; architectural and structural acoustics and vibration; speech, music and noise; psychology and physiology of hearing; engineering acoustics, sound transducers and measurements; bioacoustics, animal bioacoustics and bioresponse to vibration.
Related titles: CD-ROM ed.: ISSN 1520-9024; Microfiche ed.: USD 1,685 (effective 2006); Online - full text ed.: ISSN 1520-8524. USD 1,710 to institutions (effective 2009); ◆ Supplement(s): References to Contemporary Papers in Acoustics. ISSN 0163-0970; Acoustical Society of America. Program of the Meeting. ISSN 0163-0962.
Indexed: A01, A05, A20, A22, A23, A24, ABIPC, AJEE, AS&TA, AS&TI, ASCA, ASFA, AcoustA, AnBeAb, ApMecR, B04, B13, B21, B25, BIOBASE, BIOSIS Prev, BibLing, C10, CA, CDA, CIN, CMCI, CPEI, CPI, CTA, Cadscan, ChemAb, ChemTitl, CurCont, DentInd, E-psyche, EIA, EMBASE, EnerInd, EngInd, EnvAb, ErgAb, ExcerpMed, FR, GPAA, GeoRef, HRIS, IABS, IBR, IBZ, INIS AtomInd, ISR, IndMed, Inpharma, Inspec, L&LBA, L09, L11, LeadAb, M&GPA, M11, MEDLINE, MLA-IB, MathR, MycolAb, NBA, NPPA, NSA, OceAb, P30, PetrolAb, PhysBer, PsycholAb, R10, RILM, Reac, RefZh, S&VD, S02, S03, SCI, SCOPUS, SOPODA, SPINweb, SpeleolAb, T02, TM, W07, W08, WildRev, Z01, Z02, Zincscan.
—BLDSC (4675.000000), AskIEEE, CASDDS, GNLM, IE, Infotrieve, Ingenta, INIST, Linda Hall, PADDS. **CCC.**
Published by: Acoustical Society of America, 2 Huntington Quadrangle, Ste 1NO1, Melville, NY 11747. TEL 516-576-2360, FAX 516-576-2377, asa@aip.org. Ed. Allan D Pierce. Adv. contact Mary Ellen Mormile TEL 516-576-2461. B&W page USD 1,045, color page USD 2,095; bleed 8.5 x 11.25. Circ: 9,000. **Subscr. to:** American Institute of Physics, PO Box 503284, St Louis, MO 63150. TEL 516-576-2270, 800-344-6902, FAX 516-349-9704, subs@aip.org, http://librarians.aip.org.

534 AUS ISSN 0814-6039
➤ **ACOUSTICS AUSTRALIA.** Text in English. 1972. 3/yr. AUD 58.08 domestic; AUD 69.30 foreign (effective 2010). adv. bk.rev. **Document type:** *Journal, Academic/Scholarly.* **Description:** Covers acoustics research, applied acoustics, hearing, noise, community and environmental acoustics, architectural and musical acoustics, vibration, underwater and physical acoustics.
Formerly: Australian Acoustical Society. Bulletin (0310-1029)
Indexed: A01, A22, AcoustA, CA, CPEI, EngInd, HRIS, Inspec, P30, RILM, SCI, SCOPUS, T02, W07.
—BLDSC (0578.697100), AskIEEE, IE, Ingenta, Linda Hall. **CCC.**
Published by: Australian Acoustical Society, PO Box 2173, Goolwa, SA 5214, Australia. generalsecretary@acoustics.asn.au, http://www.acoustics.asn.au/index.php. Ed. N Kessissoglou. Circ: 500.

534 GBR ISSN 0308-437X
CODEN: ACOBEP
ACOUSTICS BULLETIN. Text in English. 1974. bi-m. GBP 120; GBP 20 per issue (effective 2011). adv. bk.rev. illus.; charts; bibl. **Document type:** *Bulletin, Academic/Scholarly.* **Description:** Written for research establishments covering all aspects of acoustics including aerodynamic noise, the environment, speech, underwater vibrations.
Indexed: A22, AcoustA, CPEI, EngInd, Inspec, RILM, RefZh, SCOPUS.
—BLDSC (0578.697300), AskIEEE, IE, Ingenta. **CCC.**
Published by: Institute of Acoustics, 77A St Peter's St, St Albans, Herts AL1 3BN, United Kingdom. TEL 44-1727-848195, FAX 44-1727-850553, http://www.ioa.org.uk. Ed. I F Bennett TEL 44-161-4872225. Adv. contact Dennis Baylis TEL 33-562-709925. Circ: 2,300.

534 USA ISSN 1557-0215
QC221 CODEN: ATCODK
ACOUSTICS TODAY. Text in English. 2005. q. free to members (effective 2011). adv. back issues avail.; reprints avail. **Document type:** *Journal, Academic/Scholarly.* **Description:** Contains technical articles about and related to acoustics.
Related titles: Online - full text ed.: ISSN 1557-0223.
—BLDSC (0578.697680), INIST, Linda Hall. **CCC.**

Published by: Acoustical Society of America, 2 Huntington Quadrangle, Ste 1NO1, Melville, NY 11747. TEL 516-576-2360, FAX 516-576-2377, asa@aip.org, http://asa.aip.org. Ed. Dick Stern. Adv. contact Deborah Bott TEL 516-576-2430. B&W page USD 2,020, color page USD 3,010; trim 8.5 x 11. Circ: 10,000.

ACOUSTIQUE ET TECHNIQUES. *see* ENVIRONMENTAL STUDIES—Pollution

534 DEU ISSN 1610-1928
QC221 CODEN: ACUSAY
➤ **ACUSTICA UNITED WITH ACTA ACUSTICA.** Text in English. 1996. bi-m. EUR 1,070; EUR 212 per issue (effective 2012). adv. bk.rev. illus. index. **Document type:** *Journal, Academic/Scholarly.*
Formerly (until 2001): Acta Acustica United with Acustica (1436-7947); Which was formed by the merger of (1936-1996): Acustica (0001-7884); Which was formerly (until 1951): Akustische Zeitschrift (0365-382X); (1968-1996): Acta Acustica (1022-4793); Which was formerly (until 1993): Journal d'Acoustique (0988-4319); Revue d'Acoustique (0557-7713)
Related titles: Online - full text ed.: ISSN 1861-9959 (from IngentaConnect).
Indexed: A20, A22, ASCA, AcoustA, ApMecR, B21, CISA, CPEI, ChemAb, CurCont, EIA, EnerInd, EngInd, EnvAb, ErgAb, GeoRef, IBR, IBZ, ICEA, ISR, Inspec, L&LBA, MLA-IB, MathR, NSA, RILM, RefZh, SCI, SCOPUS, SOPODA, SpeleolAb, TM, W07, Z02.
—BLDSC (0587.600000), AskIEEE, CASDDS, IE, Ingenta, INIST, Linda Hall. **CCC.**
Published by: (European Acoustics Association), S. Hirzel Verlag, Postfach 101061, Stuttgart, 70009, Germany. TEL 49-711-25820, FAX 49-711-2582290, service@hirzel.de, http://www.hirzel.de. Ed. Dick Botteldooren. Circ: 3,000 (paid).

➤ **ADVANCES IN ACOUSTIC MICROSCOPY.** *see* BIOLOGY—Microscopy

534 USA ISSN 1687-6261
➤ **ADVANCES IN ACOUSTICS AND VIBRATION.** Text in English. 2007. q. USD 495 (effective 2011). **Document type:** *Journal, Academic/Scholarly.* **Description:** Covers original research and development work in the area of acoustics and vibration.
Related titles: Online - full text ed.: ISSN 1687-627X. free (effective 2011).
Indexed: A01, A26, CA, ESPM, EnvEAb, I05, P52, S06, T02.
—IE.
Published by: Hindawi Publishing Corporation, 410 Park Ave, 15th Fl, PMB 287, New York, NY 10022. FAX 866-446-3294, info@hindawi.com. Ed. M Osman Tohki.

534 JPN
AKOSUTIKKU EMISSHON SOGO KONFARENSU RONBUNSHU/ NATIONAL CONFERENCE ON ACOUSTIC EMISSION. PROCEEDINGS. Text in Japanese. 1977. biennial. JPY 7,000. adv. **Document type:** *Proceedings.*
Published by: Nihon Hihakai Kensa Kyokai/Japanese Society for Non-Destructive Inspection, Natsume No 5 Bldg 4th Fl, 67 Kanda-Sakumagashi, Chiyoda-ku, Tokyo, 101-0026, Japan. TEL 81-3-5821-5105, FAX 81-3-3863-6524. Ed. Teruo Kishi.

534 RUS ISSN 0320-7919
QC221 CODEN: AKZHAE
➤ **AKUSTICHESKII ZHURNAL.** Text in Russian; Contents page in English. 1955. bi-m. USD 451 foreign (effective 2010). bk.rev. bibl.; charts; illus. index. **Document type:** *Journal, Academic/Scholarly.*
Related titles: Online - full text ed.; ◆ English Translation: Acoustical Physics. ISSN 1063-7710.
Indexed: CIN, CPEI, ChemAb, ChemTitl, GeoRef, Inspec, MathR, RefZh, SCOPUS, SpeleolAb.
—AskIEEE, CASDDS, East View, INIST, Linda Hall. **CCC.**
Published by: (Rossiiskaya Akademiya Nauk/Russian Academy of Sciences), Izdatel'stvo Nauka, Profsoyuznaya ul 90, Moscow, 117864, Russian Federation. TEL 7-095-3347151, FAX 7-095-4202220, secret@naukaran.ru, http://www.naukaran.ru. Ed. O V Rudenko. Circ: 2,180. **Dist. by:** East View Information Services, 10601 Wayzata Blvd, Minneapolis, MN 55305. TEL 952-252-1201, 800-477-1005, FAX 952-252-1202, info@eastview.com, http://www.eastview.com.

534 GBR ISSN 0003-682X
CODEN: AACOBL
➤ **APPLIED ACOUSTICS.** Text in English, French, German. 1968. 12/yr. EUR 2,279 in Europe to institutions; JPY 302,400 in Japan to institutions; USD 2,547 elsewhere to institutions (effective 2012). adv. bk.rev. illus.; abstr. index. back issues avail. **Document type:** *Journal, Academic/Scholarly.* **Description:** Provides information for those concerned with the design of buildings, measurements and control of industrial noise and vibration, transportation noise, hearing, the understanding of the acoustics of musical instruments, and the propagation of sound through the atmosphere and under water.
Related titles: Microform ed.: (from PQC); Online - full text ed.: ISSN 1872-910X (from IngentaConnect, ScienceDirect).
Indexed: A01, A03, A08, A20, A22, A26, A28, APA, ASCA, AcoustA, ApMecR, BCIRA, BMT, BrCerAb, C&ISA, CA, CA/WCA, CADCAM, CIA, CISA, CMM, CPEI, CerAb, CivEngAb, CorrAb, CurCont, DSHAb, E&CAJ, E11, EEA, EMA, ESPM, EngInd, EnvAb, EnvEAb, EnvInd, GeoRef, H15, I05, Inspec, M&TEA, M09, MBF, METADEX, NPPA, PhysBer, RILM, RefZh, S&VD, S01, SCI, SCOPUS, SolStAb, T02, T04, TM, W07, WAA.
—BLDSC (1571.400000), AskIEEE, IE, Infotrieve, Ingenta, INIST, Linda Hall. **CCC.**
Published by: Pergamon (Subsidiary of: Elsevier Science & Technology), The Blvd, Langford Ln, East Park, Kidlington, Oxford OX5 1GB, United Kingdom. TEL 44-1865-843000, FAX 44-1865-843010, JournalsCustomerServiceEMEA@elsevier.com. Ed. K Attenborough. **Subscr. to:** Elsevier BV, Radarweg 29, PO Box 211, Amsterdam 1000 AE, Netherlands. TEL 31-20-4853757, FAX 31-20-4853432, http://www.elsevier.nl.

534 POL ISSN 0137-5075
QC221 CODEN: AACODN
ARCHIVES OF ACOUSTICS. Text in English. 1976. q. EUR 129 foreign (effective 2011). abstr.; bibl.; illus. **Document type:** *Journal, Academic/Scholarly.* **Description:** Publishes original research papers from all areas of acoustics and abstracts from some specialized acoustical conferences.
Indexed: A22, AcoustA, ApMecR, BibLing, CPEI, EngInd, Inspec, NPPA, PhysBer, SCI, SCOPUS, W07, Z02.
—BLDSC (1630.800000), AskIEEE, CASDDS, IE, Ingenta, INIST, Linda Hall.
Published by: (Polska Akademia Nauk, Komitet Akustyki), Polska Akademia Nauk, Instytut Podstawowych Problemow Techniki/Polish Academy of Sciences, Institute of Fundamental Technological Research, ul Pawinskiego 5b, Warsaw, 02-106, Poland. TEL 48-22-8261281, FAX 48-22-8269815, publikac@ippt.gov.pl, http://www.ippt.gov.pl. Ed. Bozena Kostek. Circ: 360. **Dist. by:** Ars Polona, Obroncow 25, Warsaw 03933, Poland. TEL 48-22-5098609, FAX 48-22-5098610, arspolona@arspolona.com.pl, http://www.arspolona.com.pl.

534 DEU ISSN 0171-4147
AUDIO; Das Magazin fuer HiFi, Surround, High End, Musik. Text in German. 1977. m. EUR 61.90; EUR 5.30 newsstand/cover (effective 2011). adv. bk.rev. index. back issues avail. **Document type:** *Magazine, Consumer.*
Related titles: Online - full text ed.
Indexed: ISR.
Published by: W E K A Media Publishing GmbH, Gruberstr 46a, Poing, 85586, Germany. TEL 49-8121-950, FAX 49-8121-951199, online@wekanet.de, http://www.weka-media-publishing.de. Ed. Lothar Brandt. Adv. contact Michael Hackenberg. Circ: 31,291 (paid).

AUSTRALIA. BUREAU OF STATISTICS. AUDIOLOGY AND AUDIOMETRY SERVICES, AUSTRALIA (ONLINE). *see* PHYSICS—Abstracting, Bibliographies, Statistics

AUSTRALIA. BUREAU OF STATISTICS. SOUND RECORDING STUDIOS, AUSTRALIA (ONLINE). *see* PHYSICS—Abstracting, Bibliographies, Statistics

534 AUS ISSN 1446-0998
AUSTRALIAN ACOUSTICAL SOCIETY. ANNUAL CONFERENCE. Text in English. 1999. a. AUD 50 per issue (effective 2008). back issues avail. **Document type:** *Proceedings, Academic/Scholarly.*
Formerly (until 2001): Australian Acoustical Society. Proceedings of Annual Conference (Print) (1446-098X)
Media: CD-ROM.
Published by: Australian Acoustical Society, PO Box 903, Castlemaine, VIC 3450, Australia. generalsecretary@acoustics.asn.au, http://www.acoustics.asn.au/index.php.

534 DEU
BERICHTE AUS DER AKUSTIK. Text in German. 2003. irreg., latest 2010. price varies. **Document type:** *Monographic series, Academic/Scholarly.*
Published by: Shaker Verlag GmbH, Kaiserstr 100, Herzogenrath, 52134, Germany. TEL 49-2407-95960, FAX 49-2407-95969, info@shaker.de.

534 DNK ISSN 0007-2621
TK1 CODEN: BKTRAP
BRUEL & KJAER TECHNICAL REVIEW. Text in English. 1949-1990 (vol.2); resumed 1994. irreg. free. bibl.; charts. cum.index every 5 yrs. back issues avail. **Document type:** *Monographic series, Academic/Scholarly.* **Description:** Collection of technical, scientific articles including theory, measurement techniques, and instrumentation for acousticians and vibration engineers.
Related titles: Online - full text ed.
Indexed: CISA, IBR, IBZ, Inspec.
—**CCC.**
Published by: Bruel og Kjaer Industri A-S, Skodsborgvej 307, Naerum, 2850, Denmark. TEL 45-45-800500, FAX 45-77-412030, info@bksv.com.

534 720 GBR ISSN 1351-010X
TH1725 CODEN: BAUCAH
➤ **BUILDING ACOUSTICS.** Text in English. 1994. q. GBP 225; GBP 247 combined subscription (print & online eds.) (effective 2012). **Document type:** *Journal, Academic/Scholarly.* **Description:** Provides a forum for scientists and engineers concerned with research and development for acoustic enhancement and noise control in buildings.
Related titles: Online - full text ed.: GBP 220 (effective 2012).
Indexed: A28, APA, AcoustA, BrCerAb, C&ISA, C10, CA, CA/WCA, CIA, CerAb, CivEngAb, CorrAb, E&CAJ, E11, EEA, EMA, ESPM, EnvEAb, H15, Inspec, M&TEA, M09, MBF, METADEX, SolStAb, T02, T04, WAA.
—BLDSC (2359.320500), IE, Infotrieve, Ingenta. **CCC.**
Published by: Multi-Science Publishing Co. Ltd., 5 Wates Way, Brentwood, Essex CM15 9TB, United Kingdom. TEL 44-1277-244632, FAX 44-1277-223453, info@multi-science.co.uk. Ed. George Dodd.

534 BEL ISSN 0775-2024
BULLETIN D'ACOUSTIQUE. Text in French. 1959. s-a. **Document type:** *Bulletin, Trade.*
Formerly (until 1985): Electroacoustique (0422-888X)
Indexed: Inspec.
—INIST.
Published by: Universite de Liege, Boulevard du Rectorat 7, Liege, 4000, Belgium. http://www.ulg.ac.be.

534 CAN ISSN 0711-6659
TD891 CODEN: CAACDX
CANADIAN ACOUSTICS/ACOUSTIQUE CANADIENNE. Text in English, French. 1973. q. free to members; CAD 60 to institutions (effective 2005). adv. bk.rev. charts. back issues avail. **Document type:** *Proceedings, Academic/Scholarly.*
Formerly (until Jan. 1982): Acoustics and Noise Control in Canada (0229-2238)
Indexed: A22, ASFA, AcoustA, B21, CPEI, ESPM, EngInd, H&SSA, IHD, Inspec, OceAb, PollutAb, SCOPUS.
—BLDSC (3016.476000), AskIEEE, IE, Ingenta, Linda Hall. **CCC.**
Published by: Canadian Acoustical Association, P O Box 74068, Ottawa, ON K1M 2H9, Canada. TEL 613-993-0102, FAX 613-954-5984, http://caa-aca.ca. Ed. Ramani Ramakrishnan. adv.: page USD 175. Circ: 500.

534 CHN ISSN 0217-9776
➤ **CHINESE JOURNAL OF ACOUSTICS.** Text in English. 1982. q. USD 965 per vol. in US & Canada; USD 1,200 per vol. elsewhere (effective 2007). adv. abstr.; illus. back issues avail. **Document type:** *Journal, Academic/Scholarly.* **Description:** Covers acoustical research in China, including physical acoustics, underwater sound, and electroacoustics.
Related titles: Microform ed.; Online - full text ed.; ◆ Translation of: Shengxue Xuebao. ISSN 0371-0025.
Indexed: ApMecR.
—**CCC.**
Published by: Zhongguo Kexueyuan Shengxue Yanjiusuo/Chinese Academy of Sciences, Institute of Acoustics, 17 Zhongguancun Street, Haidian, Beijing, 100080, China. FAX 86-10-62553898, http://www.ioa.ac.cn/. Circ: 6,000.

534.55 JPN ISSN 0916-2410
CHOONPA TECHNO/ULTRASONIC TECHNOLOGY. Text in Japanese. 1989. bi-m. JPY 18,000; JPY 4,000 newsstand/cover (effective 2006). **Document type:** *Journal, Academic/Scholarly.*
Published by: Nihon Kogyo Shuppan K.K./Japan Industrial Publishing Co., Ltd., 6-3-26 Honkomagome, Bunkyo-ku, Tokyo, 113-0021, Japan. TEL 81-3-39441181, FAX 81-3-39446826, info@nikko-pb.co.jp.

COMMUNICATIONS AND SIGNAL PROCESSING. *see* COMMUNICATIONS

534 JPN
CONFERENCE ON SOLID STATE DEVICES & MATERIALS. EXTENDED ABSTRACTS. Text in English. 1969. a. JPY 35,000, USD 420. **Document type:** *Abstract/Index.*
Published by: (Japan Butsuri Gakkai/Japan Society of Applied Physics, Kotai Soshi Zairyo Konfarensu/Solid State Devices and Materials), Business Center for Academic Societies Japan/Nihon Gakkai Jimu Senta, 5-16-19 Honkomagome, Bunkyo-ku, Tokyo, 113-0021, Japan. **Dist. by:** International Marketing Corp., I.P.O. Box 5056, Tokyo 100-30, Japan. FAX 81-3-3667-9646.

DELPHI. THE MULTIPLE REMOVAL AND STRUCTURAL IMAGING PROJECT. (Delft Philosophy on Inversion) *see* EARTH SCIENCES—Geophysics

DELPHI. THE RESERVOIR CHARACTERIZATION AND FLOW SIMULATION PROJECT. *see* EARTH SCIENCES

534 USA
ECHOES (MELVILLE). Text in English. 1991. q. free to members (effective 2009). back issues avail. **Document type:** *Newsletter, Academic/Scholarly.* **Description:** Covers current and topical happenings of general interest and features articles about current research and personalities.
Related titles: Online - full content ed.
Published by: Acoustical Society of America, 2 Huntington Quadrangle, Ste 1NO1, Melville, NY 11747. TEL 516-576-2360, FAX 516-576-2377, asa@aip.org. Eds. Thomas Rossing TEL 516-576-2360, Dick Stern.

534 USA ISSN 1930-8876
TK7871.85
EUROPEAN SOLID STATE DEVICE RESEARCH CONFERENCE. PROCEEDINGS. Abbreviated title: E S S D E R C. Variant title: I E E E European Solid State Device Research Conference. Proceedings. Text in English. 19??. a. adv. back issues avail. **Document type:** *Proceedings, Academic/Scholarly.*
Former titles (until 1993): European Solid State Device Research Conference. Solid State Device Research. Proceedings; (until 1991): European Solid State Device Research Conference. Papers; (until 1988): European Solid State Device Research Conference. Solid State Device; (until 1972): European Semiconductor Device Research Conference. Solid State Devices
Related titles: Online - full text ed.
—**CCC.**
Published by: I E E E, 445 Hoes Ln, Piscataway, NJ 08855. contactcenter@ieee.org, http://www.ieee.org.

534 DEU ISSN 0720-2253
FORTSCHRITTE DER AKUSTIK. Text in German. 1971. a. EUR 53.50 (effective 2009). **Document type:** *Journal, Academic/Scholarly.*
—BLDSC (4018.640000), IE, Ingenta.
Published by: Deutsche Gesellschaft fuer Akustik e.V., Voltastr 5, Gebaeude 10-6, Berlin, 13355, Germany. TEL 49-30-46069463, FAX 49-30-46069470, dega@dega-akustik.de, http://www.dega-akustik.de.

620.23 USA
HANDBOOK OF NOISE AND VIBRATION CONTROL. Text in English. 1970. irreg., latest 2007, Oct. USD 210 per vol. (effective 2009). **Document type:** *Handbook/Manual/Guide, Trade.*
Published by: John Wiley & Sons, Inc., 111 River St, Hoboken, NJ 07030. TEL 201-748-6000, FAX 201-748-5915, uscs-wis@wiley.com. Ed. Malcolm Crocker.

534 USA ISSN 1546-6523
TK7876
HIGH FREQUENCY POSTGRADUATE STUDENT COLLOQUIUM. Text in English. 1995. a., latest 2005. **Document type:** *Proceedings.*
Related titles: Online - full text ed.: ISSN 1558-4607.
Indexed: EngInd.
Published by: (I E E E, United Kingdom and Republic of Ireland Section GBR, I E E E Microwave Theory and Techniques Society), I E E E Service Center, 445 Hoes Ln, Piscataway, NJ 08855. TEL 908-981-0060, 800-678-4333, FAX 732-562-6380, contactcenter@ieee.org, http://www.ieee.org/.

534 DEU ISSN 0933-1980
HOERAKUSTIK. Text in German. 1965. m. EUR 131 domestic; EUR 161.15 foreign; EUR 55 to students; EUR 10 newsstand/cover (effective 2007). adv. bk.rev. bibl.; illus. **Document type:** *Magazine, Trade.*
Formerly: Hoergeraete-Akustiker (0178-4536)
Published by: Median-Verlag von Killisch-Horn GmbH, Hauptstr 64, Heidelberg, 69117, Germany. TEL 49-6221-905090, FAX 49-6221-9050920, info@median-verlag.de, http://www.median-verlag.de. adv.: B&W page EUR 1,255, color page EUR 2,140. Circ: 2,900 (paid and controlled).

I E E E INTERNATIONAL FREQUENCY CONTROL SYMPOSIUM & EXPOSITION. PROCEEDINGS. (Institute of Electrical and Electronics Engineers) *see* ELECTRONICS

620.2 USA
I E E E INTERNATIONAL ULTRASONICS SYMPOSIUM. PROCEEDINGS. (Institute of Electrical and Electronics Engineers) Text in English. 1962. a. adv. back issues avail. **Document type:** *Proceedings, Academic/Scholarly.* **Description:** Covers discoveries, recent advances, new devices, new techniques and their application in all area of sound.

P

Former titles (until 1999): I E E E Ultrasonics Symposium. Proceedings (1051-0117); (until 1984): I E E E Ultrasonics Symposium. Proceedings (0090-5607)
Related titles: CD-ROM ed.; Microfiche ed.; Online - full text ed.
Indexed: A22, A28, APA, AcoustA, BrCerAb, C&ISA, CA/WCA, CIA, CerAb, ChemAb, CivEngAb, CorrAb, E&CAJ, E11, EEA, EMA, EngInd, GeoRef, H15, ISMEC, Inspec, M&TEA, M09, MBF, METADEX, SCOPUS, SolStAb, T04, WAA.
—CASDDS, IE, Ingenta. **CCC.**
Published by: I E E E, 445 Hoes Ln, Piscataway, NJ 08855. contactcenter@ieee.org, http://www.ieee.org. **Co-sponsor:** Ultrasonics, Ferroelectrics, and Frequency Control Society.

534 USA ISSN 1053-5888
TK5981 CODEN: ISPRE6
I E E E SIGNAL PROCESSING MAGAZINE. (Institute of Electrical and Electronics Engineers) Text in English. 1970. bi-m. USD 940; USD 1,175 combined subscription (print & online eds.) (effective 2012). adv. back issues avail.; reprints avail. **Document type:** *Magazine, Academic/Scholarly.* **Description:** Features articles on signal processing research and applications, as well as columns and forums on issues of interest.
Former titles (until 1991): I E E E A S S P Magazine (0740-7467); (until 1984): I E E E Acoustics, Speech, and Signal Processing Newsletter; (until 1974): I E E E Audio and Electroacoustics Newsletter
Related titles: CD-ROM ed.; Microfiche ed.; Online - full text ed.: ISSN 1558-0792. USD 855 (effective 2012).
Indexed: A20, A22, A28, AIA, APA, ASCA, BrCerAb, C&ISA, CA/WCA, CIA, CMCI, CPEI, CerAb, CivEngAb, CorrAb, CurCont, E&CAJ, E11, EEA, EMA, ESPM, EngInd, EnvEAb, H15, ISR, Inspec, M&TEA, M09, MBF, METADEX, P30, RefZh, SCI, SCOPUS, SolStAb, T04, TM, W07, WAA.
—BLDSC (4363.066520), AskIEEE, IE, Infotrieve, Ingenta, INIST, Linda Hall. **CCC.**
Published by: I E E E, 445 Hoes Ln, Piscataway, NJ 08854. TEL 732-981-0060, 800-678-4333, FAX 732-562-6380, contactcenter@ieee.org, http://www.ieee.org. Eds. Li Deng, Dawn Melley. **Co-sponsor:** Acoustics, Speech, and Signal Processing Society.

534 USA ISSN 0885-3010
QC244 CODEN: ITUCER
I E E E TRANSACTIONS ON ULTRASONICS, FERROELECTRICS AND FREQUENCY CONTROL. (Institute of Electrical and Electronics Engineers) Text in English. 1954. m. USD 1,140; USD 1,425 combined subscription (print & online eds.) (effective 2012). adv. bk.rev. abstr.; illus. index. back issues avail.; reprints avail. **Document type:** *Journal, Academic/Scholarly.* **Description:** Discusses theory, design and application in generation, transmission and detection of bulk and surface mechanical waves.
Former titles (until 1986): I E E E Transactions on Sonics and Ultrasonics (0018-9537); (until 1964): I E E E Transactions on Ultrasonics Engineering (0893-6706); (until 1963): I R E Transactions on Ultrasonics Engineering (0096-1019); (until 1955): I R E Professional Group on Ultrasonics Engineering. Transactions (0277-626X)
Related titles: CD-ROM ed.; Microfiche ed.; Online - full text ed.: ISSN 1525-8955. USD 1,035 (effective 2012).
Indexed: A01, A02, A03, A08, A22, A26, A28, APA, ASCA, BrCerAb, C&ISA, CA, CA/WCA, CIA, CMCI, CPEI, CerAb, ChemAb, CivEngAb, CorrAb, CurCont, E&CAJ, E08, E11, EEA, EMA, EMBASE, ESPM, EngInd, EnvEAb, ExcerpMed, FR, G01, G08, H15, I05, ISMEC, ISR, Inspec, M&TEA, MO5, M06, M09, MBF, MEDLINE, METADEX, MathR, P30, RefZh, S01, S09, SCI, SCOPUS, SolStAb, T02, T04, TM, W07, WAA.
—BLDSC (4363.227500), AskIEEE, CASDDS, IE, Infotrieve, Ingenta, INIST, Linda Hall. **CCC.**
Published by: I E E E, 445 Hoes Ln, Piscataway, NJ 08854. TEL 732-981-0060, 800-678-4333, FAX 732-562-6380, contactcenter@ieee.org, http://www.ieee.org. Ed. Jian-Yu Lu TEL 419-530-8079. **Subscr. to:** Universal Subscription Agency, Pvt. Ltd.; Maruzen Co., Ltd. **Co-sponsor:** Ultrasonics, Ferroelectronics and Frequency Control Society.

534 621.395 USA ISSN 1931-1168
TK7881.4
I E E E WORKSHOP ON APPLICATIONS OF SIGNAL PROCESSING TO AUDIO AND ACOUSTICS. (Institute of Electrical and Electronics Engineers) Short title: Applications of Signal Processing to Audio and Acoustics. Text in English. 19??. biennial. adv. back issues avail.; reprints avail. **Document type:** *Proceedings, Trade.* **Description:** Provides an informal environment for the discussion of problems in audio and acoustics and the signal processing techniques applied to these problems.
Formerly (until 1999): I E E E A S S P Workshop on Applications of Signal Processing to Audio and Acoustics
Related titles: CD-ROM ed.: ISSN 1947-1610; Online - full text ed.: ISSN 1947-1629.
—CCC.
Published by: I E E E, 445 Hoes Ln, Piscataway, NJ 08854. TEL 732-981-0060, 800-678-4333, FAX 732-562-6380, customer.service@ieee.org, http://www.ieee.org.

534 GBR
I S V R TECHNICAL MEMORANDA. (Institute of Sound and Vibration Research) Text in English. 19??. irreg., latest no.985, 2009. free (effective 2009). back issues avail. **Document type:** *Monographic series, Academic/Scholarly.* **Description:** Provides information about nonlinear shaping of a spectral excitation matrix for a linear road/tyre interaction stochastic analysis.
Related titles: Online - full text ed.
Published by: University of Southampton, Institute of Sound and Vibration Research, University Rd, Southampton, Hants SO17 1BJ, United Kingdom. TEL 44-23-80592294, FAX 44-23-80593190, enquiries@isvr.soton.ac.uk.

534 GBR
I S V R TECHNICAL REPORTS. (Institute of Sound and Vibration Research) Text in English. 19??. irreg., latest vol.328, 2009. free (effective 2009). back issues avail. **Document type:** *Monographic series, Academic/Scholarly.* **Description:** Features investigations of acoustic wave propagation in a liquid-filled cylindrical tube with and without bubbles.
Related titles: Online - full text ed.
Published by: University of Southampton, Institute of Sound and Vibration Research, University Rd, Southampton, Hants SO17 1BJ, United Kingdom. TEL 44-23-80592294, FAX 44-23-80593190, enquiries@isvr.soton.ac.uk.

534 GBR ISSN 1478-6095
INSTITUTE OF ACOUSTICS. PROCEEDINGS (CD-ROM). Text in English. N.S. 1972. irreg. free to members (effective 2010). abstr. **Document type:** *Proceedings, Academic/Scholarly.* **Description:** Presents research on various topics in applied acoustics.
Former titles (until 2002): Institute of Acoustics. Proceedings (Print) (0309-8117); (until 1977): British Acoustical Society. Proceedings (0374-4108)
Media: CD-ROM.
Indexed: AcoustA, Inspec, P30.
—BLDSC (6714.600700), Ingenta, INIST. **CCC.**
Published by: Institute of Acoustics, 77A St Peter's St, St Albans, Herts AL1 3BN, United Kingdom. TEL 44-1727-848195, FAX 44-1727-850553, ioa@ioa.org.uk.

534 JPN ISSN 0386-8761
INSTITUTE OF NOISE CONTROL ENGINEERING. JOURNAL. Text in Japanese. 1972. bi-m. JPY 16,100 (effective 2001). adv. **Document type:** *Bibliography.*
Published by: Institute of Noise Control Engineering, c/o Kobayashi Institute of Physical Research, 3-20-41 Higashi-Moto-Machi, Kokubunji-shi, Tokyo-to 185-0022, Japan. TEL 0423-25-1652, FAX 0423-27-3847. Ed. E Invi.

INTERNATIONAL JOURNAL OF ACOUSTICS AND VIBRATION. *see* ENGINEERING—Mechanical Engineering

534 GBR ISSN 1475-472X
➤ **THE INTERNATIONAL JOURNAL OF AEROACOUSTICS.** Text in English. 2002 (Mar.). 6/yr. GBP 428; GBP 450 combined subscription (print & online eds.) (effective 2012). **Document type:** *Journal, Academic/Scholarly.* **Description:** Features developments in all areas of fundamental and applied aero-acoustics.
Related titles: Online - full text ed.: 2002. GBP 412 (effective 2012).
Indexed: A01, A03, A08, A28, APA, BrCerAb, C&ISA, CA, CA/WCA, CIA, CerAb, CivEngAb, CorrAb, CurCont, E&CAJ, E11, EEA, EMA, ESPM, EnvEAb, H15, Inspec, M&TEA, M09, MBF, METADEX, RefZh, S01, SCI, SolStAb, T02, T04, W07, WAA.
—BLDSC (4541.577150), IE, Ingenta, Linda Hall. **CCC.**
Published by: Multi-Science Publishing Co. Ltd., 5 Wates Way, Brentwood, Essex CM15 9TB, United Kingdom. TEL 44-1277-244632, FAX 44-1277-223453, info@multi-science.co.uk. Ed. Dr. Ganesh Raman TEL 312-567-3554.

534 USA
CODEN: ARLOFJ
➤ **J A S A EXPRESS LETTERS.** (Journal of the Acoustical Society of America) Abbreviated title: J A S A - E L. (As of 2006, Express Letters are published online as they are accepted for publication and also appear monthly as a special section in the Journal of the Acoustical Society of America (print and CD-ROM editions.)) Text in English. 1929. m. back issues avail. **Document type:** *Journal, Academic/Scholarly.* **Description:** Provides rapid and open dissemination of important new research results and technical discussion in all fields of acoustics.
Formerly (until 2005): Acoustics Research Letters Online (1529-7853)
Media: Online - full text.
Indexed: A20, Inspec, P30, SCOPUS.
—Linda Hall. **CCC.**
Published by: Acoustical Society of America, 2 Huntington Quadrangle, Ste 1NO1, Melville, NY 11747. TEL 516-576-2360, FAX 516-576-2377, asa@aip.org, http://asa.aip.org. Ed. Wilson D Keith.

534 GBR ISSN 1461-3484
➤ **JOURNAL OF LOW FREQUENCY NOISE VIBRATION AND ACTIVE CONTROL.** Abbreviated title: L F N V & A C. Variant title: Low Frequency Noise Vibration and Active Control. Text in English. 1982. q. GBP 273; GBP 298 combined subscription (print & online eds.) (effective 2012). **Document type:** *Journal, Academic/Scholarly.* **Description:** Discusses low frequency noise and vibration, their effects on man, animals, the environment, and active and passive methods of control.
Formerly (until 1997): Journal of Low Frequency Noise and Vibration (0263-0923)
Related titles: Online - full text ed.: GBP 267 (effective 2012).
Indexed: A01, A22, A28, APA, ASCA, ApMecR, BrCerAb, C&ISA, CA, CA/WCA, CIA, CPEI, CerAb, CivEngAb, CorrAb, E&CAJ, E11, EEA, EMA, ESPM, EnvAb, EnvEAb, H15, Inspec, M&TEA, M09, MBF, METADEX, NPPA, S&VD, SCI, SCOPUS, SolStAb, T02, T04, W07, WAA.
—BLDSC (5010.566000), AskIEEE, IE, Ingenta, INIST, Linda Hall. **CCC.**
Published by: Multi-Science Publishing Co. Ltd., 5 Wates Way, Brentwood, Essex CM15 9TB, United Kingdom. TEL 44-1277-244632, FAX 44-1277-223453, info@multi-science.co.uk. Ed. Dr. W Tempest.

534 610 JPN ISSN 1346-4523
JOURNAL OF MEDICAL ULTRASONICS. Text in English. 1997. q. EUR 267, USD 375 combined subscription to institutions (print & online eds.) (effective 2012). reprint service avail. from PSC. **Document type:** *Journal, Academic/Scholarly.* **Description:** Provides information on research and new developments across the field of ultrasound in medicine and biology.
Supersedes in part (in 2000): Journal of Medical Ultrasonics (Tokyo, 1997) (1344-1388); Which was formerly (until 1996): Choonpa Igaku/Japanese Journal of Medical Ultrasonics (0287-0592)
Related titles: Online - full text ed.: ISSN 1613-2254 (from IngentaConnect); ◆ Japanese ed.: Chouompa Igaku. ISSN 1346-1176.
Indexed: A22, A26, E01, EMBASE, ExcerpMed, R10, Reac, SCI, SCOPUS, W07.
—BLDSC (5017.090500), IE, Ingenta. **CCC.**
Published by: (Nihon Chouompa Gakkai/Japan Society of Ultrasonics in Medicine), Springer Japan KK (Subsidiary of: Springer Science+Business Media), No 2 Funato Bldg, 1-11-11 Kudan-kita, Chiyoda-ku, Tokyo, 102-0073, Japan. TEL 81-3-68317000, FAX 81-3-68317001, orders@springer.jp, http://www.springer.jp. Ed. Nobuyuki Taniguchi.

JOURNAL OF OPTICS RESEARCH. *see* PHYSICS—Optics

534 IND ISSN 0256-4637
➤ **JOURNAL OF PURE AND APPLIED ULTRASONICS.** Text in English. 1979. q. INR 2,200 domestic; USD 200 foreign (effective 2011). bk.rev. index. back issues avail. **Document type:** *Journal, Academic/Scholarly.*
Indexed: Inspec.
—BLDSC (5043.682000), AskIEEE, IE, Ingenta.
Published by: (Ultrasonics Society of India), Scientific Publishers, 5-A, New Pali Rd, PO Box 91, Jodhpur, Rajasthan 342 001, India. TEL 91-291-2433323, FAX 91-291-2624154, info@scientificpub.com, http://www.scientificpub.com.

534 GBR ISSN 0022-460X
QC221 CODEN: JSVIAG
➤ **JOURNAL OF SOUND AND VIBRATION.** Abbreviated title: J S V. Text in English. 1964. 50/yr. EUR 9,469 in Europe to institutions; JPY 1,022,900 in Japan to institutions; USD 8,458 elsewhere to institutions (effective 2012). adv. bk.rev. bibl.; charts; illus. index. back issues avail.; reprints avail. **Document type:** *Journal, Academic/Scholarly.* **Description:** Examines experimental and theoretical work concerning all aspects of sound vibration.
Incorporates: Advances in Physical Acoustics
Related titles: Online - full text ed.: ISSN 1095-8568. USD 7,880 to institutions (effective 2009) (from IngentaConnect, ScienceDirect).
Indexed: A01, A03, A08, A20, A22, A26, A28, AJEE, APA, ASCA, ASFA, AcoustA, ApMecR, B21, BMT, BrCerAb, BrRB, C&ISA, CA, CA/WCA, CCMJ, CIA, CIS, CISA, CMCI, CPEI, CerAb, CivEngAb, CorrAb, CurCont, E&CAJ, E01, E11, EEA, EMA, ESPM, EngInd, EnvEAb, ErgAb, F&EA, H&SSA, H15, HRIS, I05, IBR, IBZ, ICEA, ISMEC, ISR, Inspec, M&GPA, M&TEA, M09, MBF, METADEX, MSN, MathR, NPPA, P30, PollutAb, RefZh, S&VD, S01, SCI, SCOPUS, SolStAb, T02, T04, TM, W07, WAA, Z02.
—BLDSC (5065.850000), AskIEEE, IE, Infotrieve, Ingenta, INIST, Linda Hall. **CCC.**
Published by: Elsevier Ltd (Subsidiary of: Elsevier Science & Technology), The Blvd, Langford Ln, Kidlington, Oxford, OX5 1GB, United Kingdom. TEL 44-1865-843000, FAX 44-1865-843010, customerserviceau@elsevier.com. Ed. C L Morfey.

530 POL ISSN 0324-8313
TA355 CODEN: JTPHDR
➤ **JOURNAL OF TECHNICAL PHYSICS.** Text in English. 1959. q. USD 160 foreign (effective 2011). abstr.; charts; illus. **Document type:** *Journal, Academic/Scholarly.* **Description:** Devoted mainly to the application of the phenomenological and continuum physics idea in: mechanics, thermodynamics, electrodynamics, coupled mechanical, electromagnetic and thermal fields, plasmaphysics, and superconductivity.
Formerly (until 1975): Proceedings of Vibrations Problems (0032-9576)
Indexed: A28, APA, AcoustA, ApMecR, B22, BrCerAb, C&ISA, CA/WCA, CCMJ, CIA, CIN, CerAb, ChemAb, ChemTitl, CivEngAb, CorrAb, E&CAJ, E11, EEA, EMA, ESPM, EnvEAb, GeoRef, H15, INIS AtomInd, Inspec, M&TEA, M09, MBF, METADEX, MSN, MathR, PhysBer, SolStAb, SpeleolAb, T04, WAA, Z02.
—BLDSC (5068.291000), AskIEEE, CASDDS, IE, Ingenta, INIST, Linda Hall. **CCC.**
Published by: Polska Akademia Nauk, Instytut Podstawowych Problemow Techniki/Polish Academy of Sciences, Institute of Fundamental Technological Research, ul Pawinskiego 5b, Warsaw, 02-106, Poland. TEL 48-22-8261281, FAX 48-22-8269815, publikac@ippt.gov.pl, http://www.ippt.gov.pl. Ed. Zbigniew Peradzynski. Circ: 600.

➤ **JOURNAL OF ULTRASOUND IN MEDICINE.** *see* MEDICAL SCIENCES—Radiology And Nuclear Medicine

534 GBR ISSN 1077-5463
TA355 CODEN: JVCOFX
➤ **JOURNAL OF VIBRATION AND CONTROL.** Abbreviated title: J V C. Text in English. 1995. 14/yr. USD 2,410, GBP 1,418 combined subscription to institutions (print & online eds.); USD 2,362, GBP 1,390 to institutions (effective 2011). adv. charts; illus. 160 p./no.; back issues avail.; reprint service avail. from PSC. **Document type:** *Journal, Academic/Scholarly.* **Description:** Encompasses all linear and nonlinear vibration phenomena occurring in mechanical, structural, aeronautical, materials, oceanographic, electrical, control, chemical, biological, electromagnetic, and environmental fields.
Incorporates (1993-1996): Modal Analysis (1066-0763); Which was formerly (1986-1992): The International Journal of Analytical and Experimental Modal Analysis (0886-9367)
Related titles: Online - full text ed.: ISSN 1741-2986. USD 2,169, GBP 1,276 to institutions (effective 2011).
Indexed: A01, A02, A03, A08, A22, A26, A28, APA, ASFA, ApMecR, B07, B21, BrCerAb, C&ISA, CA, CA/WCA, CCMJ, CIA, CPEI, CerAb, CivEngAb, CorrAb, CurCont, E&CAJ, E01, E08, E11, EEA, EMA, ESPM, EngInd, EnvEAb, G01, G08, H&SSA, H04, H15, I05, ICEA, Inspec, M&TEA, M09, MBF, METADEX, MSN, MathR, P02, P10, P26, P48, P52, P53, P54, P56, PQC, S&VD, S01, S09, S10, SCI, SCOPUS, SolStAb, T02, T04, V02, W07, WAA, Z02.
—BLDSC (5072.465000), AskIEEE, IE, Infotrieve, Ingenta, Linda Hall. **CCC.**
Published by: Sage Publications Ltd. (Subsidiary of: Sage Publications, Inc.), 1 Oliver's Yard, 55 City Rd, London, EC1Y 1SP, United Kingdom. TEL 44-20-73248500, FAX 44-20-73248600, info@sagepub.co.uk, http://www.uk.sagepub.com/home.nav. Ed. Ali Nayfeh. adv.: B&W page GBP 450; 160 x 215. **Subscr. in the Americas to:** Sage Publications, Inc., 2455 Teller Rd, Thousand Oaks, CA 91320. TEL 805-499-9774, FAX 805-499-0871, journals@sagepub.com.

534 JPN
KENKYU JOSEI JIGYO JOSEI KENKYU SEIKA HOKOKU GAIYO/ SOUND TECHNOLOGY PROMOTION FOUNDATION. RESEARCH REPORT. Text in Japanese. a.
Published by: Saundo Gijutsu Shinko Zaidan/Sound Technology Promotion Foundation, 36-4 Yoyogi 1-chome, Shibuya-ku, Tokyo, 151-0053, Japan.

534 DEU ISSN 1863-4672
TD891
LAERMBEKAEMPFUNG; Zeitschrift fuer Akustik, Schallschutz und Schwingungstechnik. Text in German. 1954. bi-m. EUR 191.50 domestic; EUR 202.50 foreign; EUR 36 per issue (effective 2010). adv. bk.rev. abstr.; charts; illus.; tr.lit. back issues avail.; reprints avail. **Document type:** *Magazine, Trade.* **Description:** Carries material that addresses the physical, psychological, social and economic effects of noise.
Former titles (until 2006): Zeitschrift fuer Laermbekaempfung (0174-1098); (until 1980): Kampf dem Laerm (0022-8249)
Related titles: Microform ed.: (from PQC); Online - full text ed.: ISSN 1436-4999.
Indexed: A22, AcoustA, DokStr, IBR, IBZ, SCOPUS, TM.
—BLDSC (5155.972000), GNLM, IE, Infotrieve, Ingenta, INIST. **CCC.**
Published by: (Deutscher Arbeitsring fuer Laermbekaempfung e.V.), Springer V D I Verlag GmbH & Co. KG, VDI-Platz 1, Duesseldorf, 40468, Germany. TEL 49-211-61030, FAX 49-211-6103300, info@technikwissen.de, http://www.technikwissen.de. Ed. Elisabeth Zimmermann TEL 49-211-6103343. Adv. contact Gabriele Jahn TEL 49-211-6103378. B&W page EUR 1,620, color page EUR 2,700; trim 210 x 297. Circ: 1,806 (paid and controlled).

534 USA ISSN 1939-800X
QC221
➤ **MEETINGS ON ACOUSTICS. PROCEEDINGS.** Text in English. 2007. irreg. free (effective 2010). back issues avail. **Document type:** *Proceedings, Academic/Scholarly.*
Media: Online - full text.
Indexed: P30.
—CCC.
Published by: Acoustical Society of America, 2 Huntington Quadrangle, Ste 1NO1, Melville, NY 11747. TEL 516-576-2360, FAX 516-576-2377, asa@aip.org, http://asa.aip.org. Ed. Allan D Pierce.

534 USA
N C A C NEWSLETTER. Text in English. 1970. q. membership. **Document type:** *Newsletter.*
Published by: National Council of Acoustical Consultants, 66 Morris Ave, Ste 1A, Springfield, NJ 07081-1409. TEL 201-564-5859, FAX 201-564-7480. Ed. Jerry Lilly. Circ: 500.

534 JPN
NATIONAL CONFERENCE ON ACOUSTIC EMISSION. TRANSACTIONS. Text in English. a.
Published by: Nihon Hi-hakai Kensa Kyokai/Japanese Society for Non-Destructive Inspection, MBR 99 4th Fl, 67 Kanda-Sakumagashi, Chiyoda-ku, Tokyo, 101-0026, Japan. TEL 81-3-58215105, FAX 81-3-38636524, acd@jsndi.or.jp, http://wwwsoc.nii.ac.jp/jsndi/.

534 JPN ISSN 1340-3168
NIHON ONKYO GAKKAI KENKYU HAPPYOKAI KOEN RONBUNSHU/ ACOUSTICAL SOCIETY OF JAPAN. PROCEEDINGS OF THE ANNUAL MEETINGS. Text in Japanese. 1952. s-a. JPY 7,000.
Published by: Nihon Onkyo Gakkai/Acoustical Society of Japan, Nakaura 5th-Bldg., 2-18-20 Sotokanda, Chiyoda-ku, Tokyo, 101-0021, Japan. FAX 81-3-52561022, KYM05145@nifty.ne.jp, http://www.asj.gr.jp/.

534 JPN ISSN 0369-4232
CODEN: NIOGAH
➤ **NIHON ONKYO GAKKAISHI/ACOUSTICAL SOCIETY OF JAPAN. JOURNAL.** Text in Japanese. 1936. m. free to members. **Document type:** *Journal, Academic/Scholarly.*
Related titles: Online - full content ed.; ◆ English ed.: Acoustical Science and Technology. ISSN 1346-3969.
Indexed: Inspec, JPI, MLA-IB, RefZh.
—AskIEEE, Linda Hall. **CCC.**
Published by: Nihon Onkyo Gakkai/Acoustical Society of Japan, Nakaura 5th-Bldg., 2-18-20 Sotokanda, Chiyoda-ku, Tokyo, 101-0021, Japan. FAX 81-3-52561022, KYM05145@nifty.ne.jp, http://www.asj.gr.jp/.

534 363.74 GBR ISSN 0144-7785
NOISE & VIBRATION BULLETIN. Abbreviated title: N V B. Variant title: N V B. Noise & Vibration Bulletin. Text in English. 1970. m. GBP 293 (effective 2012). bk.rev. **Document type:** *Bulletin, Academic/ Scholarly.* **Description:** Features articles that cover the effects on the human and animal organism, instrumentation standards and regulations; mechanisms involved in road and rail transport, aircraft, domestic and other noise sources; reduction and control.
Formerly (until 1971): Noise & Vibration Bulletin (0029-0947)
Indexed: A01, AcoustA, ESPM, EnvAb, HRIS, NPPA, PollutAb.
—BLDSC (6115.850000), IE, Ingenta. **CCC.**
Published by: Multi-Science Publishing Co. Ltd., 5 Wates Way, Brentwood, Essex CM15 9TB, United Kingdom. TEL 44-1277-244632, FAX 44-1277-223453, info@multi-science.co.uk. Eds. B R V Hughes, H G Leventhall.

534 GBR ISSN 0950-8163
TJ179
NOISE & VIBRATION IN INDUSTRY. Abbreviated title: N V I. Text in English. 1986. q. GBP 262 (effective 2012). **Document type:** *Journal, Academic/Scholarly.* **Description:** Covers the effects of noise and vibration on individuals at work, the effects of vibration on machines and buildings, the impact of industrially-generated noise on the community, hearing protection, audiology and audiometry.
Formerly: Noise and Vibration for Works Managers
Indexed: A01, A28, APA, B21, BrCerAb, C&ISA, CA, CA/WCA, CIA, CerAb, CivEngAb, CorrAb, E&CAJ, E11, EEA, EMA, ESPM, EnvAb, EnvEAb, H&SSA, H15, M&TEA, M09, MBF, METADEX, PollutAb, SolStAb, T02, T04, WAA.
Published by: Multi-Science Publishing Co. Ltd., 5 Wates Way, Brentwood, Essex CM15 9TB, United Kingdom. TEL 44-1277-244632, FAX 44-1277-223453, info@multi-science.co.uk. Ed. B R V Hughes.

534 GBR ISSN 0957-4565
TD891 CODEN: NVWOE6
NOISE & VIBRATION WORLDWIDE. Text in English. 1970. 11/yr. GBP 290; GBP 315 combined subscription (print & online eds.) (effective 2012). bk.rev. charts; illus.; tr.lit. Index. **Document type:** *Journal, Academic/Scholarly.* **Description:** Covers all the latest developments and applications in noise and vibration control.
Former titles (until 1989): Noise & Vibration Control - Worldwide (0143-6481); (until 1980): Noise Control, Vibration Isolation (0142-0933); (until 1978): Noise Control, Vibration and Insulation (0309-8230); (until 1975): Noise Control and Vibration Reduction (0374-3888)
Related titles: Microform ed.; Online - full text ed.: GBP 283 (effective 2012).
Indexed: A01, A22, A28, APA, AcoustA, B21, BMT, BrCerAb, C&ISA, CA, CA/WCA, CIA, CISA, CPEI, Cadscan, CerAb, CivEngAb, CorrAb, E&CAJ, E11, EEA, EMA, ESPM, EngInd, EnvAb, EnvEAb, F&EA, H&SSA, H15, IBuildSA, Inspec, LeadAb, M&TEA, M09, MBF, METADEX, P34, PollutAb, SCOPUS, SolStAb, T02, T04, TM, WAA, Zincscan.
—BLDSC (6115.865000), AskIEEE, IE, Infotrieve, Ingenta, INIST, Linda Hall. **CCC.**
Published by: Multi-Science Publishing Co. Ltd., 5 Wates Way, Brentwood, Essex CM15 9TB, United Kingdom. TEL 44-1277-244632, FAX 44-1277-223453, info@multi-science.co.uk. Ed. W O Hughes.

534 363.74 GBR ISSN 1475-4738
NOISE NOTES. Text in English. 2002 (Jan). q. GBP 195; GBP 207 combined subscription (print & online eds.) (effective 2012). **Document type:** *Journal, Academic/Scholarly.* **Description:** Covers all aspects of noise in the context of its being an environmental nuisance.
Related titles: Online - full text ed.: GBP 182 (effective 2012).
Indexed: A28, APA, BrCerAb, C&ISA, CA, CA/WCA, CIA, CerAb, CivEngAb, CorrAb, E&CAJ, E04, E05, E11, EEA, EMA, ESPM, EnvEAb, H15, Inspec, M&TEA, M09, MBF, METADEX, SolStAb, T02, T04, WAA.
—BLDSC (6116.078000), IE, Ingenta. **CCC.**
Published by: Multi-Science Publishing Co. Ltd., 5 Wates Way, Brentwood, Essex CM15 9TB, United Kingdom. TEL 44-1277-244632, FAX 44-1277-223453. Ed. B R V Hughes.

534 JPN ISSN 0912-7283
ONGAKU ONKYO KENKYUKAI SHIRYO/ACOUSTICAL SOCIETY OF JAPAN. TECHNICAL COMMITTEES. TRANSACTIONS. Text mainly in Japanese; Text occasionally in English. 1982. irreg.
Published by: Nihon Onkyo Gakkai/Acoustical Society of Japan, Nakaura 5th-Bldg., 2-18-20 Sotokanda, Chiyoda-ku, Tokyo, 101-0021, Japan. FAX 81-3-52561022, KYM05145@nifty.ne.jp, http://www.asj.gr.jp/.

534 616.21 NLD ISSN 1874-8376
QC244.2
➤ **THE OPEN ACOUSTICS JOURNAL.** Text in English. 2008. irreg. free (effective 2011). **Document type:** *Journal, Academic/Scholarly.* **Description:** Covers all areas of pure and applied acoustics.
Media: Online - full text.
Indexed: A01.
Published by: Bentham Open (Subsidiary of: Bentham Science Publishers Ltd.), PO Box 294, Bussum, AG 1400, Netherlands. TEL 31-35-6923800, FAX 31-35-6980150, subscriptions@bentham.org. Ed. Juan Manuel Gorriz Saez.

534 NLD ISSN 1574-3519
OPEN BIJEENKOMST. Text in Dutch. a.
Published by: Nederlands Akoestisch Genootschap/Acoustical Society of the Netherlands, PO Box 1475, Nieuwegein, 3430 BL, Netherlands. TEL 31-30-8509707, FAX 31-30-2341754, secr@nag-acoustics.nl, http://www.nag-acoustics.nl.

P T B-BERICHT. MECHANIK UND AKUSTIK. (Physikalisch-Technische Bundesanstalt) *see* PHYSICS—Mechanics

534 RUS ISSN 0202-2354
QC670
PROBLEMY DIFRAKTSII I RASPROSTRANENIYA VOLN/PROBLEMS OF DIFFRACTION AND SPREADING OF WAVES. Text in Russian. 1962. irreg., latest vol.28, 2000. abstr.; bibl. **Document type:** *Monographic series, Academic/Scholarly.*
—Linda Hall. **CCC.**
Published by: Izdatel'skii Dom Sankt-Peterburgskogo Gosudarstvennogo Universiteta, V.O., 6-ya liniya, dom 11/21, komn 319, St Petersburg, 199004, Russian Federation. TEL 7-812-3252604, press@unipress.ru, http://www.unipress.ru. Circ: 900.

534 JPN
PROGRESS IN ACOUSTIC EMISSION. Text in English. biennial. JPY 15,000 (effective 2000). **Document type:** *Proceedings.*
Published by: Nihon Hihakai Kensa Kyokai/Japanese Society for Non-Destructive Inspection, Natsume No 5 Bldg 4th Fl, 67 Kanda-Sakumagashi, Chiyoda-ku, Tokyo, 101-0026, Japan. TEL 81-3-5821-5105, FAX 81-3-3863-6524. Ed. Teruo Kishi.

REFERATIVNYI ZHURNAL. AKUSTIKA; vypusk svodnogo toma. *see* PHYSICS—Abstracting, Bibliographies, Statistics

534 USA ISSN 0163-0970
QC225.15 CODEN: RCACD8
REFERENCES TO CONTEMPORARY PAPERS IN ACOUSTICS. Text in English. 1975. a. includes with subscr. to Acoustical Society of America. Journal. **Document type:** *Magazine, Trade.*
Related titles: ◆ Supplement to: Acoustical Society of America. Journal. ISSN 0001-4966.
—INIST. **CCC.**
Published by: Acoustical Society of America, 2 Huntington Quadrangle, Ste 1NO1, Melville, NY 11747. TEL 516-576-2360, FAX 516-576-2377, asa@aip.org, http://asa.aip.org. **Dist. by:** American Institute of Physics.

534.55 ESP ISSN 0210-3680
REVISTA DE ACUSTICA. Text and summaries in English, Spanish. 1970. q. adv. bk.rev. bibl. **Document type:** *Magazine, Academic/Scholarly.*
Related titles: Microfilm ed.
Indexed: IECT, RILM, RefZh.
Published by: Sociedad Espanola de Acustica/Spanish Society of Acoustics, Serrano, 144, Madrid, 28006, Spain. TEL 261-88-06, TELEX 4117651, secretaria@sea-acustica.es. Ed. Antonio Calvo Manzano. Circ: 1,000.

534 ITA ISSN 0393-1110
RIVISTA ITALIANA DI ACUSTICA. Text in Multiple languages. 1977. q. free to members (effective 2008). **Document type:** *Journal, Academic/Scholarly.*
Published by: Associazione Italiana di Acustica, c/o CNR-IMAMOTER, Via Canal Bianco 28, Cassana, FE 44044, Italy. TEL 39-0532-735618, FAX 39-0532-735666, http://www.associazioneitalianadiacustica.it.

534 ROM ISSN 1584-7284
➤ **ROMANIAN JOURNAL OF ACOUSTICS AND VIBRATION.** Text in English. s-a. EUR 25 domestic; EUR 50 foreign (effective 2010). adv. bk.rev. back issues avail. **Document type:** *Journal, Academic/ Scholarly.* **Description:** Contains articles, technical notes, letters-to-the-editor, calendar, and announcements. Covers: Active noise control, active vibration control, aero acoustics, architectural acoustics, boundary element and finite element methods, condition monitoring and diagnostics, passive and active damping, environmental noise, human response to sound and vibration, inverse methods, low frequency noise and vibration, machinery noise and vibration control, materials for noise and vibration control, measurement techniques, mechanisms of human hearing, modal analysis, musical acoustics, noise control elements, non-destructive testing, non-linear acoustics and vibration, numerical methods, occupational noise exposure and control, outdoor sound propagation, scattering of sound, signal processing, sound intensity, sound sources, sound transmission, energy statistical analysis, structural acoustics and vibration, structural intensity, transportation vibration and noise, underwater acoustics, vibration and shock, vibration sources, and wavelet analysis.
Related titles: CD-ROM ed.; Online - full text ed.
Published by: Romanian Society of Acoustics/Societatea Romana de Acustica, 266 Pantelimon St., Bucharest, 021652, Romania. TEL 40-21-2550734, ovidiu@icecon.ro, http://www.sra.ro/index.html. Ed., Pub., R&P Polidor Bratu. Circ: 100.

534 CHN ISSN 1000-3630
QC221
SHENGXUE JISHU/TECHNICAL ACOUSTICS. Text in Chinese. 1982. q. USD 24.60 (effective 2009). adv. bk.rev. **Document type:** *Academic/ Scholarly.* **Description:** Covers ultrasonics, bio-medical ultrasonics, underwater sound, architectural acoustics, audio engineering, noise control, physiological and psychological acoustics.
Related titles: Online - full text ed.
Indexed: A22, SCOPUS.
—BLDSC (8256.411600), IE, Ingenta.
Published by: Shanghai Acouctics Society, Shanghai Acouctics Laboratory of of Chinese Academy of Sciences, 456 Xiaomuqiao Rd, Shanghai, 200032, China. TEL 86-21-6404-8159, FAX 86-21-6417-4106. Eds. Jiqing Wang, Shaosong Feng. R&P Shaosong Feng. Adv. contact Hongying Li. **Dist. overseas by:** China National Publishing Industry Trading Corporation, PO Box 782, Beijing 100011, China. **Co-sponsor:** Tongji University, Institute of Acoustics.

534 CHN ISSN 0371-0025
QC221 CODEN: SHGHAS
➤ **SHENGXUE XUEBAO/CHINESE JOURNAL OF ACOUSTICS.** Text in Chinese; Summaries in English. 1964. bi-m. USD 31.20 (effective 2009). adv. **Document type:** *Academic/Scholarly.* **Description:** Contains original papers and brief communications on acoustical research in mainland China and abroad, including physical acoustics, underwater sound, electroacoustics, and manufacture of instruments.
Related titles: Online - full text ed.; ◆ English Translation: Chinese Journal of Acoustics. ISSN 0217-9776.
Indexed: A22, A28, APA, ApMecR, BrCerAb, C&ISA, CA/WCA, CIA, CPEI, CerAb, CivEngAb, CorrAb, E&CAJ, E11, EEA, EMA, ESPM, EngInd, EnvEAb, H15, Inspec, M&TEA, M09, MBF, METADEX, MathR, PhysBer, SCOPUS, SolStAb, T04, WAA.
—BLDSC (0587.200000), AskIEEE, CASDDS, East View, IE, Ingenta, INIST, Linda Hall.
Published by: (Acoustical Society of China, Zhongguo Kexueyuan Shengxue Yanjiusuo/Chinese Academy of Sciences, Institute of Acoustics), Kexue Chubanshe/Science Press, 16 Donghuang Cheng Genbei Jie, Beijing, 100717, China. TEL 86-10-64000246, FAX 86-10-64030255, http://www.sciencep.com/. Circ: 6,000. **Dist. by:** China International Book Trading Corp, 35 Chegongzhuang Xilu, Haidian District, PO Box 399, Beijing 100044, China. TEL 86-10-68412045, FAX 86-10-68412023, cibtc@mail.cibtc.com.cn, http://www.cibtc.com.cn.

534.5 620.11 NLD ISSN 1070-9622
TA355 CODEN: SHVIE8
➤ **SHOCK AND VIBRATION**; shock and vibration control - crashworthiness - structural dynamics - impact engineering - sound. Text in English. 1994. bi-m. USD 1,009 combined subscription in North America (print & online eds.); EUR 720 combined subscription elsewhere (print & online eds.) (effective 2012). adv. back issues avail. **Document type:** *Journal, Academic/Scholarly.* **Description:** Publishes original research on shock and vibration, covering sound, structural dynamics, impact biodynamics, crashworthiness, and earthquake engineering.
Related titles: Microform ed.: (from PQC); Online - full text ed.: ISSN 1875-9203 (from IngentaConnect).
Indexed: A01, A03, A08, A22, A28, APA, ASCA, ASFA, ApMecR, B21, BrCerAb, C&ISA, CA, CA/WCA, CIA, CPEI, CerAb, CivEngAb, CorrAb, CurCont, E&CAJ, E01, E11, EEA, EMA, ESPM, EngInd, EnvEAb, GeoRef, H&SSA, H15, ICEA, Inspec, M&TEA, M09, MBF, METADEX, RiskAb, S&VD, S01, SCI, SCOPUS, SolStAb, T02, T04, W07, WAA.
—BLDSC (8267.457000), IE, Infotrieve, Ingenta, Linda Hall. **CCC.**
Published by: I O S Press, Nieuwe Hemweg 6B, Amsterdam, 1013 BG, Netherlands. TEL 31-20-6883355, FAX 31-20-6870019, info@iospress.nl. Ed. Daniel J Inman. Circ: 500. **Subscr. to:** I O S Press, Inc, 4502 Rachael Manor Dr, Fairfax, VA 22032-3631. iosbooks@iospress.com; Globe Publication Pvt. Ltd., C-62 Inderpuri, New Delhi 100 012, India. TEL 91-11-579-3211, 91-11-579-3212, custserve@globepub.com, http://www.globepub.com; Kinokuniya Co Ltd., Shinjuku 3-chome, Shinjuku-ku, Tokyo 160-0022, Japan. FAX 81-3-3439-1094, journal@kinokuniya.co.jp, http://www.kinokuniya.co.jp.

534 CAN ISSN 0847-1223
SOUND RECORDING. Text in English. 1984. a. CAD 24, USD 29 domestic; USD 34 foreign. **Document type:** *Government.* **Description:** Provides details on all aspects of the sound recording survey, a census of all record and label companies in Canada.
Formerly (until 1987): Sound Recording Preliminary Statistics (0830-8373)

P

Published by: Statistics Canada, Operations and Integration Division (Subsidiary of: Statistics Canada/Statistique Canada), Circulation Management, 120 Parkdale Ave, Ottawa, ON K1A 0T6, Canada. TEL 613-951-7277, 800-267-6677, FAX 613-951-1584.

534 USA
T M I JOURNAL. Text in English. 1983. s-a. free to members (effective 2010). abstr. back issues avail. **Document type:** *Journal, Academic/Scholarly.* **Description:** Covers research in and applications of the Hemi-Sync sound technology in various professional arenas.
Former titles (until 2009): Hemi - Sync Journal; Breakthrough
Related titles: Online - full text ed.: free (effective 2010).
Published by: The Monroe Institute, 365 Roberts Mountain Rd, Faber, VA 22938. TEL 434-361-1252, 866-881-3440, FAX 434-361-1237, info@monroeinstitute.org. Eds. Ann Vaughan, Shirley N Bliley.

534 RUS ISSN 1819-2408
TA365
➤ **TECHNICHESKAYA AKUSTIKA (ONLINE).** Text in English, Russian. 1992. irreg. free (effective 2011). **Document type:** *Journal, Academic/Scholarly.* **Description:** Covers all subjects related to acoustics.
Formerly (until 2001): Technicheskaya Akustika (Print) (0869-4583)
Media: Online - full content.
Indexed: A01, T02.
Published by: (Vostochnoevropeiskaya Assotsiatsiya Akustikov), Tekhnicheskaya Akustika, Moskovskoe shosse 44, Moscow, 196158, Russian Federation. TEL 7-812-7236801, FAX 7-812-7279323.

534 NLD ISSN 0041-624X
TA367 CODEN: ULTRA3
➤ **ULTRASONICS.** Text in English. 1963. 8/yr. EUR 1,625 in Europe to institutions; JPY 216,200 in Japan to institutions; USD 1,821 elsewhere to institutions (effective 2012). adv. bk.rev. abstr.; bibl.; illus. index. back issues avail. **Document type:** *Journal, Academic/Scholarly.* **Description:** Covers the field of ultrasonics and its applications: transducers, nondestructive testing, signal processing.
Related titles: Microform ed.: (from PQC); Online - full text ed.: ISSN 1874-9968 (from IngentaConnect, ScienceDirect).
Indexed: A01, A03, A05, A08, A22, A23, A24, A26, ABIPC, AS&TA, AS&TI, ASCA, AcoustA, ApMecR, B13, BCIRA, BrRB, C&ISA, C10, CA, CISA, CPEI, ChemAb, CurCont, E&CAJ, EMBASE, EngInd, ExcerpMed, HRIS, ISMEC, ISR, IndMed, Inspec, MEDLINE, MLA-IB, P30, R10, Reac, RefZh, S01, SCI, SCOPUS, SolStAb, SpeleolAb, T02, TM, W07.
—BLDSC (9082.796000), AskIEEE, CASDDS, GNLM, IE, Infotrieve, Ingenta, INIST, Linda Hall. **CCC.**
Published by: Elsevier BV (Subsidiary of: Elsevier Science & Technology), Radarweg 29, PO Box 211, Amsterdam, 1000 AE, Netherlands. TEL 31-20-4853911, FAX 31-20-4852457, JournalsCustomerServiceEMEA@elsevier.com, http://www.elsevier.nl. Ed. Dr. W Sachse.

534 541 NLD ISSN 1350-4177
QD801 CODEN: ULSOER
➤ **ULTRASONICS SONOCHEMISTRY.** Text in English. 1994. 6/yr. EUR 728 in Europe to institutions; JPY 96,300 in Japan to institutions; USD 811 elsewhere to institutions (effective 2012). adv. bk.rev. back issues avail. **Document type:** *Journal, Academic/Scholarly.* **Description:** Contains research papers on power ultrasound, cavitation, sonoelectrochemistry, sonoluminescence, mechanochemistry and aspects of surface-surface interactions.
Related titles: Microfilm ed.: (from PQC); Online - full text ed.: ISSN 1873-2828. 199? (from IngentaConnect, ScienceDirect).
Indexed: A01, A03, A05, A08, A22, A26, AS&TA, AS&TI, ASCA, C10, C24, C33, CA, CCI, CIN, CPEI, ChemAb, ChemTitl, CurCR, CurCont, EMBASE, EngInd, ExcerpMed, I05, IndMed, Inspec, MEDLINE, P30, R10, R16, Reac, RefZh, S01, SCI, SCOPUS, T02, W07.
—BLDSC (9082.805000), CASDDS, GNLM, IE, Infotrieve, Ingenta, INIST, Linda Hall. **CCC.**
Published by: Elsevier BV (Subsidiary of: Elsevier Science & Technology), Radarweg 29, PO Box 211, Amsterdam, 1000 AE, Netherlands. TEL 31-20-4853911, FAX 31-20-4852457, JournalsCustomerServiceEMEA@elsevier.com, http://www.elsevier.nl. Ed. T Mason.

➤ **ULTRASOUND IN MEDICINE & BIOLOGY.** *see* BIOLOGY

➤ **UNIVERSITY OF TEXAS AT AUSTIN. APPLIED RESEARCH LABORATORIES. TECHNICAL REPORT.** *see* PHYSICS

534 POL ISSN 0554-8039
UNIWERSYTET IM. ADAMA MICKIEWICZA. AKUSTYKA. Text in Polish. 1972. irreg., latest vol.16, 2008. price varies. **Document type:** *Monographic series, Academic/Scholarly.*
Formerly: Uniwersytet im. Adama Mickiewicza w Poznaniu. Wydzial Matematyki, Fizyki i Chemii. Prace. Seria Akustyka
—Linda Hall.
Published by: Wydawnictwo Naukowe Uniwersytetu im. Adama Mickiewicza/Adam Mickiewicz University Press, ul Fredry 10, Poznan, 61701, Poland. TEL 48-61-8294646, FAX 48-61-8294647, press@amu.edu.pl, http://press.amu.edu.pl. Ed. Aleksandr Sek.

W S E A S TRANSACTIONS ON ACOUSTICS AND MUSIC. *see* MUSIC

534 GRC
➤ **W S E A S TRANSACTIONS ON SIGNAL PROCESSING.** Text in English. 2005. m. EUR 300 to individuals; EUR 400 to institutions (effective 2005). **Document type:** *Journal, Academic/Scholarly.*
Indexed: Inspec.
Published by: World Scientific and Engineering Academy and Society, Ag Ioannou Theologou 17-23, Zographou, Athens 15773, Greece. TEL 30-210-7473313, FAX 30-210-7473314, http://www.wseas.org. Ed. Nikos Mastorakis.

➤ **WIDESCREEN INTERNATIONAL.** *see* PHOTOGRAPHY

534 GBR
WINDOWS ON ACOUSTICS. Text in English. bi-m. software rev. illus. **Document type:** *Newsletter.* **Description:** Reviews software used in acoustic applications and research.
Published by: AcSoft Ltd., 8B Wingbury Courtyard, Leighton Rd, Wingrave, Aylesbury, HP22 4LW, United Kingdom. TEL 44-1296-682686, FAX 44-1296-682860, sales@acsoft.co.uk, http://www.acsoft.co.uk/.

534 CHN ISSN 1000-310X
➤ **YINGYONG SHENGXUE/APPLIED ACOUSTICS.** Text in Chinese. 1981. bi-m. USD 40.20 (effective 2009). adv. **Document type:** *Journal, Academic/Scholarly.* **Description:** Aims to present concrete applications of acoustics in various branches of China's economy. Popularizes basic knowledge of acoustics and reports on academic developments in China and other countries.
Related titles: Online - full text ed.
—East View, Linda Hall.
Published by: (Zhongguo Shengxue Xuehui), Kexue Chubanshe/ Science Press, 16 Donghuang Cheng Genbei Jie, Beijing, 100717, China. TEL 86-10-64000246, FAX 86-10-64030255, http://www.sciencep.com/. Circ: 11,000. **Dist. by:** China International Book Trading Corp, 35 Chegongzhuang Xilu, Haidian District, PO Box 399, Beijing 100044, China. TEL 86-10-68412045, FAX 86-10-68412023, cibtc@mail.cibtc.com.cn, http://www.cibtc.com.cn.

534 DEU ISSN 1435-4691
CODEN: AUKADP
ZEITSCHRIFT FUER AUDIOLOGIE/AUDIOLOGICAL ACOUSTICS. Text in English, German. 1962. 4/yr. EUR 53 domestic; EUR 60 foreign (effective 2009). adv. bk.rev. bibl.; charts; illus. index. **Document type:** *Journal, Academic/Scholarly.*
Former titles (until 1998): Audiologische Akustik (0172-8261); Zeitschrift fuer Hoergeraete Akustik (0044-2860)
Indexed: AcoustA, Inspec, NBA, TM.
—BLDSC (9453.251500), AskIEEE, GNLM, IE, Ingenta, INIST, Linda Hall. **CCC.**
Published by: (Deutsche Gesellschaft fuer Audiologie e.V.), Median-Verlag von Killisch-Horn GmbH, Hauptstr 64, Heidelberg, 69117, Germany. TEL 49-6221-905090, FAX 49-6221-9050920, info@median-verlag.de, http://www.median-verlag.de. adv.: B&W page EUR 790, color page EUR 1,480. Circ: 2,150 (paid and controlled).

PHYSIOLOGY

see BIOLOGY—Physiology

PLASTICS

see also CHEMISTRY—Physical Chemistry ; ENGINEERING—Chemical Engineering

668.4 658 GBR
A M I'S (YEAR) EUROPEAN PLASTICS INDUSTRY REPORT. (Applied Market Information) Text in English. 1994. a. GBP 465, EUR 555, USD 720 (effective 2009). stat. **Document type:** *Report, Trade.* **Description:** Provides a complete, easy to use overview of the trends and developments in the European thermoplastics industry.
Former titles (until 2005): A M I's (Year) West European Plastics Industry Report (1468-7224); (until 1996): West European Plastics Industry Handbook (1367-1405)
—BLDSC (0859.196500).
Published by: Applied Market Information Ltd., AMI House, 45-47 Stokes Croft, Bristol, BS1 3PQ, United Kingdom. TEL 44-117-9249442, FAX 44-117-9892128, info@amiplastics.com.

668.4 GBR ISSN 0306-3747
TP1142
ADDITIVES FOR POLYMERS. Text in English. 1971. m. EUR 1,346 in Europe to institutions; JPY 178,600 in Japan to institutions; USD 1,505 elsewhere to institutions (effective 2010). adv. bk.rev. Index. back issues avail.; reprints avail. **Document type:** *Newsletter, Academic/Scholarly.* **Description:** Summarizes information on new products and materials (including patents), new manufacturing techniques and processes, and new applications. Also industry and market news and the strategies of key players in this sector.
Related titles: Microform ed.: (from PQC); Online - full text ed.: ISSN 1873-5312. 199? (from IngentaConnect, ScienceDirect).
Indexed: A01, A03, A08, CA, EngInd, R18, S01, SCOPUS, T01, T02, TTI.
—BLDSC (0679.500000), IE, Infotrieve, Ingenta. **CCC.**
Published by: Elsevier Advanced Technology (Subsidiary of: Elsevier Science & Technology), PO Box 150, Kidlington, OX5 1AS, United Kingdom. TEL 44-1865-843000, FAX 44-1865-843971, http://www.elsevier.com. Ed. Caroline Edser TEL 44-1905-773004. **Subscr. to:** Elsevier BV, Radarweg 29, PO Box 211, Amsterdam 1000 AE, Netherlands. TEL 31-20-4853757, FAX 31-20-4853432, JournalsCustomerServiceEMEA@elsevier.com, http://www.elsevier.nl.

668.4 540 DEU ISSN 1619-1919
TP967 CODEN: ADHAES
ADHAESION - KLEBEN & DICHTEN. Text in German. 193?. 10/yr. EUR 234; EUR 93 to students (effective 2010). adv. bk.rev. abstr.; bibl.; charts; illus.; mkt.; pat. index. reprint service avail. from PSC. **Document type:** *Magazine, Trade.*
Former titles (until 2001): Kleben & Dichten (0943-1454); (until 1992): Adhaesion (0001-8198); (until 1957): Gelatine, Leim, Klebstoffe (0367-472X)
Indexed: A22, ABIPC, CEABA, CIN, CLL, ChemAb, ChemTitl, EngInd, IBR, IBZ, IPackAb, P&BA, PST, R18, RefZh, SCOPUS, TM, WSCA.
—CASDDS, IE, Ingenta, INIST, Linda Hall. **CCC.**
Published by: Vieweg und Teubner Verlag (Subsidiary of: Springer Fachmedien Wiesbaden GmbH), Abraham-Lincoln-Str 46, Wiesbaden, 65189, Germany. TEL 49-611-78780, FAX 49-611-7878400, info@viewegteubner.de, http://www.viewegteubner.de.

668.4 JPN ISSN 0037-0495
CODEN: STHKAO
ADHESION AND ADHESIVES/SETCHAKU. Text in Japanese. 1957. m. JPY 7,800. adv. charts; illus.
Indexed: CIN, ChemAb, ChemTitl, R18.
—CASDDS, Linda Hall.
Published by: High Polymer Publishing Association/Kobunshi Kankokai, Chiekoin-Sagura, Marutamachi, Kamikyoku, Kyoto-shi, 602, Japan. Ed. Hitoshi Okuda.

668.4 666 GBR ISSN 0951-953X
ADVANCED COMPOSITES BULLETIN. Text in English. 1987. m. GBP 497, USD 910 combined subscription (effective 2010). adv. bk.rev. abstr.; charts; illus.; pat. back issues avail. **Document type:** *Newsletter, Trade.* **Description:** Contains information on new materials, applications, processing and company news. Reports on technological and business opportunities in composites industry.
Related titles: E-mail ed.; Online - full text ed.: ISSN 1878-6855.
Indexed: A28, APA, BrCerAb, C&ISA, CA/WCA, CIA, CerAb, CivEngAb, CorrAb, E&CAJ, E11, EEA, EMA, ESPM, EnvEAb, H15, I05, M&TEA, M09, MBF, METADEX, R18, SCOPUS, SolStAb, T04, WAA, WTA.
—BLDSC (0696.838500), IE, Infotrieve, Ingenta, Linda Hall. **CCC.**
Published by: International Newsletters Ltd., 9A Victoria Sq, Droitwich, Worcs WR9 8DE, United Kingdom. TEL 44-870-1657210, FAX 44-870-1657212, in@intnews.com, http://www.intnews.com. Ed. James Bakewell. Adv. contact David Kay TEL 44-1273-423512.

668.4 USA ISSN 0963-6935
➤ **ADVANCED COMPOSITES LETTERS.** Text in Greek. 1992. bi-m. EUR 360 combined subscription in Europe to institutions (print & online eds.); GBP 280 combined subscription in United Kingdom to institutions (print & online eds.); USD 600 combined subscription elsewhere to institutions (print & online eds.) (effective 2011). 30 p./no. 2 cols./p.; **Document type:** *Journal, Academic/Scholarly.* **Description:** Covers the selection, design, processing and manufacture of fiber-reinforced materials.
Related titles: Online - full text ed.
Indexed: A28, APA, ASCA, ApMecR, BrCerAb, C&ISA, CA/WCA, CIA, CPEI, CerAb, CivEngAb, CorrAb, E&CAJ, E11, EEA, EMA, ESPM, EngInd, EnvEAb, H15, Inspec, M&TEA, M09, MBF, METADEX, MSCI, R18, SCI, SCOPUS, SolStAb, T04, W07, WAA.
—BLDSC (0696.839200), AskIEEE, IE, Ingenta, Linda Hall. **CCC.**
Published by: A B C - C L I O, PO Box 291846, Kettering, OH 45429. TEL 800-771-5579, FAX 937-890-0221, customerservice@abc-clio.com, http://www.abc-clio.com. **Dist. by:** Turpin Distribution Services Ltd., Pegasus Dr, Stratton Business Park, Biggleswade, Bedfordshire SG18 8QB, United Kingdom. TEL 44-1767-604800, FAX 44-1767-601640, custserv@turpin-distribution.com, http://www.turpin-distribution.com/.

668.4 USA ISSN 0730-6679
TP1101 CODEN: APTYD5
➤ **ADVANCES IN POLYMER TECHNOLOGY.** Text in English. 1981. q. GBP 869 in United Kingdom to institutions; EUR 1,099 in Europe to institutions; USD 1,618 in United States to institutions; USD 1,674 in Canada & Mexico to institutions; USD 1,702 elsewhere to institutions; GBP 1,001 combined subscription in United Kingdom to institutions (print & online eds.); EUR 1,264 combined subscription in Europe to institutions (print & online eds.); USD 1,861 combined subscription in United States to institutions (print & online eds.); USD 1,917 combined subscription in Canada & Mexico to institutions (print & online eds.); USD 1,945 combined subscription elsewhere to institutions (print & online eds.) (effective 2012). adv. charts; illus.; pat.; stat. back issues avail.; reprint service avail. from PSC. **Document type:** *Journal, Academic/Scholarly.* **Description:** Presents developments in polymeric materials, production and processing methods, and equipment and product design.
Formerly (until 1982): Advances in Plastics Technology (0272-9504)
Related titles: Microform ed.: (from PQC); Online - full text ed.: ISSN 1098-2329. 19??. GBP 826 in United Kingdom to institutions; EUR 1,045 in Europe to institutions; USD 1,618 elsewhere to institutions (effective 2012).
Indexed: A22, A28, APA, ASCA, BrCerAb, C&ISA, C33, CA/WCA, CCI, CIA, CIN, CPEI, CerAb, ChemAb, ChemTitl, CivEngAb, CorrAb, CurCont, E&CAJ, E11, EEA, EMA, ESPM, EngInd, EnvEAb, H15, ISMEC, Inspec, M&TEA, M09, MBF, METADEX, MSCI, R18, RefZh, SCI, SCOPUS, SolStAb, T01, T04, TM, TTI, W07, WAA.
—BLDSC (0710.610000), AskIEEE, CASDDS, IE, Infotrieve, Ingenta, Linda Hall. **CCC.**
Published by: (Polymer Processing Institute), John Wiley & Sons, Inc., 111 River St, Hoboken, NJ 07030. TEL 201-748-6000, FAX 201-748-6088, info@wiley.com, http://www.wiley.com/WileyCDA/. Ed. Theodore Davidson TEL 973-642-4582. Adv. contact Kim Thompkins TEL 212-850-6921. **Subscr. outside the Americas to:** John Wiley & Sons Ltd.

➤ **ANNUAL BOOK OF A S T M STANDARDS. VOLUME 04.10. WOOD.** (American Society for Testing and Materials) *see* ENGINEERING—Engineering Mechanics and Materials

➤ **ANNUAL BOOK OF A S T M STANDARDS. VOLUME 08.01. PLASTICS (1): D256 - D3159.** (American Society for Testing and Materials) *see* ENGINEERING—Engineering Mechanics And Materials

➤ **ANNUAL BOOK OF A S T M STANDARDS. VOLUME 08.02. PLASTICS (2): D3222 - D5083.** (American Society for Testing and Materials) *see* ENGINEERING—Engineering Mechanics And Materials

➤ **ANNUAL BOOK OF A S T M STANDARDS. VOLUME 08.04. PLASTIC PIPE AND BUILDING PRODUCTS.** (American Society for Testing and Materials) *see* ENGINEERING—Engineering Mechanics And Materials

668.4 BRA
ANUARIO BRASILEIRO DO PLASTICO. Text in Portuguese. 1984. a. BRL 250, USD 250 (effective 2000). adv. back issues avail. **Document type:** *Directory.*
Published by: Editora Q D Ltda., Rua Conselheiro Brotero, 589 Cj 11-1o Andar, B Funda, Sao Paulo, SP 01154-001, Brazil. TEL 55-11-826-6899, FAX 55-11-825-8192. Eds., Pubs. Denisard Gerola da Silva Pinto, Emanuel Fairbanks. Adv. contact Rogerio Barbato. page USD 4,568.96; trim 275 x 205. Circ: 10,000.

668.4 SGP ISSN 0966-1867
ASIAN PLASTICS NEWS. Text in English. 1988. 10/yr. SGD 350 (effective 2007). adv. back issues avail. **Document type:** *Magazine, Trade.* **Description:** Focuses on the processing technology, raw materials and machinery hardware used in Asia and often sourced in Europe.
Indexed: B03, CBNB, R18.
—**CCC.**

Published by: Asian Plastic News Publishing and Fulfillment Pte Ltd. (Subsidiary of: Emap Communications Ltd.), 79C Duxton Rd, Singapore, 089538, Singapore. TEL 65-62222933, FAX 65-62222551. Ed. Keith Boi. Adv. contact Karen Hewitt TEL 44-20-82775516.

ASSOCIATION FRANCAISE DES INGENIEURS ET CADRES DU CAOUTCHOUC ET DES PLASTIQUES. ANNUAIRE. *see* RUBBER

BIOMEDICAL MATERIALS (DROITWICH). *see* MEDICAL SCIENCES

668.4 678.2 GBR ISSN 0307-6164
HD9661.G7
BRITISH PLASTICS AND RUBBER MAGAZINE. Text in English. 1970. m. GBP 75 domestic; GBP 110 foreign (effective 2004). adv. bk.rev. charts; illus.; tr.lit. 52 p./no. 3 cols./p.; reprints avail. **Document type:** *Magazine, Trade.* **Description:** Monitors technical developments from around the world for the benefit of senior managers in British polymer processing companies.
Former titles (until 1975): Polymer Age (0142-5110); (until 1974): P R T - Polymer Age (0032-387X); Which incorporated (1920-1969): Rubber & Plastics Age (0370-7695); Which was formerly (until 1954): Rubber Age and Synthetics (0370-3614); (until 1944): Rubber Age (0370-761X)
Related titles: Online - full text ed.
Indexed: A22, A28, APA, BrCerAb, C&ISA, CA/WCA, CIA, Cadscan, CerAb, CivEngAb, CorrAb, E&CAJ, E11, EEA, EMA, ESPM, EngInd, EnvEAb, FR, G08, H15, I05, IPackAb, KES, LeadAb, M&TEA, M09, MBF, METADEX, R18, SCOPUS, SolStAb, T04, WAA, Zincscan.
—BLDSC (2337.300000), IE, Infotrieve, Ingenta, INIST, Linda Hall. **CCC.**
Published by: M C M Publishing Ltd., 37 Nelson Rd, Caterham, Surrey CR3 5PP, United Kingdom. TEL 44-1883-347059, FAX 44-1883-341350, ken@mcmpublishing.co.uk. Ed., Pub., R&P Ken Grace. Adv. contact Geraldine Chiverton. Circ: 11,400.

BUSINESS RATIO REPORT. PLASTICS PACKAGING MANUFACTURERS. *see* PACKAGING

668.4 GBR ISSN 1472-6726
BUSINESS RATIO REPORT. PLASTICS PROCESSORS (YEAR). Text in English. 1974. irreg., latest no.29, 2003, Sep. GBP 365 per issue (effective 2010). charts; stat. **Document type:** *Report, Trade.* **Description:** Covers companies active as plastics processors.
Former titles (until 2000): Business Ratio. Plastics Processors (1468-3725); (until 1999): Business Ratio Plus: Plastics Processors (1356-6946); (until 1994): Business Ratio Report: Plastics Processors (0261-9393)
Published by: Key Note Ltd. (Subsidiary of: Bonnier Business Information), Harlequin House, 5th Fl, 7 High St, Teddington, Richmond upon Thames, TW11 8EE, United Kingdom. TEL 44-845-5040452, FAX 44-845-5040453, sales@keynote.co.uk.

668.4 IND
C I P E T PIMES. (Central Institute of Plastics Engineering & Technology) Text in English. 1992. q. **Document type:** *Bulletin, Government.*
Formely (until 20??): C I P E T Bulletin (0972-6578)
—BLDSC (3198.742400).
Published by: C I P E T Corporate, T.V.K Industrial Estate, Guindy, Chennai, Tamil Nadu 600 032, India. TEL 91-44-22254780, FAX 91-44-22254787, cipetchn@eth.net, http://cipet.gov.in.

668.4 CAN ISSN 0008-4778
CODEN: CNPLAJ
CANADIAN PLASTICS. Text in English. 1943. 13/yr. CAD 66.95 domestic; USD 74.95 in United States; USD 116.95 elsewhere (effective 2008). adv. charts; illus.; stat.; tr.lit. **Document type:** *Magazine, Trade.* **Description:** Serving Canadian plastics industry with news and feature articles on plastics markets and technology.
Related titles: Microfiche ed.: (from MML); Microfilm ed.: (from MML); Microform ed.: (from MML); Online - full text ed.
Indexed: A09, A10, A12, A15, A17, A22, A28, ABIn, APA, B01, B02, B03, B06, B07, B08, B09, B11, B17, B18, BrCerAb, C&ISA, C03, C05, CA, CA/WCA, CBCABus, CBPI, CIA, CPerI, CerAb, ChemAb, CivEngAb, CorrAb, E&CAJ, E11, EEA, EMA, ESPM, EnvEAb, G04, H15, KES, M&TEA, M09, MBF, METADEX, P48, P51, P52, P53, P54, PQC, PROMT, R18, S22, SolStAb, T02, T04, V03, V04, WAA.
—CASDDS, IE, Infotrieve, Linda Hall. **CCC.**
Published by: Business Information Group, 12 Concorde Pl, Ste 800, Toronto, ON M3C 4J2, Canada. TEL 416-442-2122, 800-668-2374, FAX 416-442-2191, orders@businessinformationgroup.ca, http://www.businessinformationgroup.ca. Ed. Dean Dussault TEL 514-843-2309. Pub. Judith Nancekivell TEL 416-510-5116. adv.: B&W page USD 3,850, color page USD 5,505. Circ: 10,566 (controlled).

668.4 CAN ISSN 0068-9459
TP986.A1
CANADIAN PLASTICS DIRECTORY AND BUYER'S GUIDE. Text in English. 1959. a. CAD 99 domestic; USD 99 foreign (effective 2008). **Document type:** *Directory, Trade.* **Description:** Lists plastics processors and products, suppliers of raw material, machinery and equipment, mold, tool and die makers, suppliers to moldmakers, services and associations.
—Linda Hall.
Published by: Business Information Group, 12 Concorde Pl, Ste 800, Toronto, ON M3C 4J2, Canada. TEL 416-442-2122, 800-668-2374, FAX 416-442-2191, orders@businessinformationgroup.ca, http://www.businessinformationgroup.ca.

668.4 USA
CARD MANUFACTURING. Text in English. 1990. 8/yr. USD 75; free to members (effective 2005). adv. bk.rev. illus.; tr.lit. back issues avail.; reprints avail. **Document type:** *Magazine, Trade.* **Description:** Supports, promotes and encourages the success and growth of companies and organizations that participate in the plastic card industry - including manufacturers, industry suppliers and service providers.
Formerly: Transaction Times
Published by: International Card Manufacturers Association, 191 Clarksville Rd, Princeton Junction, NJ 08550. TEL 609-799-4900, FAX 609-799-7032, mkmetcalf@icma.com, http://www.icma.com. Circ: 3,500 (paid and controlled).

668.4 658 USA ISSN 1942-8014
CAST POLYMER CONNECTION. Text in English. 1975. q. free in North America; USD 35 elsewhere (effective 2008). adv. **Document type:** *Magazine, Trade.* **Description:** Contains association news and promotions, government regulatory updates, technical articles as well as news items that affect the cast polymer industry.
Formerly: Cultured Marble News
Published by: International Cast Polymer Association, 1010 N Glebe Rd, Ste 450, Arlington, VA 22201. TEL 703-525-0320, FAX 703-525-0743, http://www.icpa-hq.com. Ed. Jeanne Molumbyd. R&P Jeanne Molumby. Adv. contact Jeanny Molumbay. B&W page USD 2,220, color page USD 2,610; trim 11 x 8.5. Circ: 2,000.

668.4 660.284 GBR ISSN 0262-4893
TP1183.F6 CODEN: CELPDJ
➤ **CELLULAR POLYMERS.** Text in English. 1978. bi-m. GBP 455, USD 744.84, EUR 504.60 (effective 2010). bk.rev. illus.; abstr. back issues avail.; reprints avail. **Document type:** *Journal, Academic/Scholarly.* **Description:** Covers developments over the full range of foam polymers, from elastomeric material to rigid plastics.
Formerly (until 1982): The European Journal of Cellular Plastics (0162-7600)
Related titles: Online - full text ed.: ISSN 1478-2421.
Indexed: A22, A26, A28, APA, BrCerAb, C&ISA, C33, CA/WCA, CCI, CIA, CPEI, CerAb, ChemAb, CivEngAb, CorrAb, CurCR, CurCont, E&CAJ, E11, EEA, EMA, ESPM, EngInd, EnvEAb, H15, I05, M&TEA, M09, MBF, METADEX, MSCI, P10, P26, P48, P52, P53, P54, PQC, R16, R18, S10, SCI, SCOPUS, SolStAb, T04, W07, WAA.
—BLDSC (3097.935000), CASDDS, IE, Infotrieve, Ingenta, INIST, Linda Hall. **CCC.**
Published by: iSmithers, Shawbury, Shrewsbury, Shrops SY4 4NR, United Kingdom. TEL 44-1939-250383, FAX 44-1939-251118, info@ismithers.net. Ed. V Kumar.

➤ **CHEMICALS & POLYMERS NEWS.** *see* PETROLEUM AND GAS

668.4 CHE
DAS CHEMIE- UND KUNSTSTOFF-JAHRBUCH DER SCHWEIZ. Text in German. 1965. a. CHF 38 (effective 2004). adv. bk.rev. **Document type:** *Yearbook, Trade.*
Former titles (until 2003): Jahrbuch Kunststoffe: Synthetics (1420-5645); (until 1993): Jahrbuch Kunststoffe: Plastics (0255-6936)
Published by: Vogt-Schild AG, Zuchwilerstr 21, Solothurn, 4501, Switzerland. TEL 41-32-6247111, FAX 41-65-247235, a.widmer@vsonline.ch, http://www.vsonline.ch. Eds. Alfred Widmer, Marianne Flury. Adv. contact Hansruedi Spiri. B&W page CHF 2,340, color page CHF 3,440; trim 185 x 260. Circ: 6,000.

668.4 HKG ISSN 1021-1330
➤ **CHINA PLASTIC AND RUBBER JOURNAL/ZHONGGUO CUOLIAO XIANGJIAO;** a plastic and rubber journal for P.R. China. Text in Chinese; Contents page in Chinese, English. 1982. bi-m. HKD 455 domestic; USD 90 in Asia; USD 100 elsewhere (effective 2003). adv. abstr.; charts; illus.; stat. 80 p./no.; back issues avail.; reprints avail. **Document type:** *Journal, Academic/Scholarly.* **Description:** Contains information on foreign advanced technology and market trends in the plastic and rubber industries for readers in the PRC.
Published by: (National Council of Light Industry, Institute of Plastics Processing and Application), Yashi Chuban Gongsi/Adsale Publishing Ltd., 4-F, Stanhope House, 734 King's Rd, North Point, Hong Kong. TEL 852-2811-8891, FAX 852-2516-5119, circulation@adsalepub.com.hk. Ed. Mabel Tang. Pub. Annie Chu. Adv. contact Janet Tong TEL 852-2516-3380. B&W page USD 3,060, color page USD 4,480; trim 280 x 215. Circ: 29,670 (controlled).
Co-sponsors: China United Rubber Corporation; Ministry of Chemical Industry, China Association of Rubber Industry.

➤ **CHINESE MARKETS FOR PLASTIC ADDITIVES.** *see* BUSINESS AND ECONOMICS—Marketing And Purchasing

➤ **CHINESE MARKETS FOR PLASTIC COMPOUNDING.** *see* BUSINESS AND ECONOMICS—Marketing And Purchasing

➤ **CHINESE MARKETS FOR REINFORCED PLASTICS.** *see* BUSINESS AND ECONOMICS—Marketing And Purchasing

668.4 USA ISSN 0888-1227
TA418.9.C6
THE COMPOSITES AND ADHESIVES NEWSLETTER. Text in English. 1984. q. USD 190 domestic; USD 210 foreign (effective 2004); includes Flash News Reports. adv. bk.rev. 20 p./no.; back issues avail. **Document type:** *Newsletter.* **Description:** Covers composite and adhesive materials. Includes information on new applications, potential problems, technology developments, as well as industry news about companies, schools, and professional societies. Includes Flash News Reports.
Related titles: Online - full text ed.
Indexed: APA, C&ISA, CorrAb, E&CAJ, EEA, R18, SolStAb, WAA.
—BLDSC (3365.515000), Linda Hall. **CCC.**
Published by: T - C Press (Subsidiary of: Technology Conferences), 36006, Los Angeles, CA 90036-0006. TEL 323-938-6923, FAX 323-938-6923. Ed., R&P George Epstein. Adv. contact Sue Stone. Circ: 300 (paid and controlled).

668.4 USA
CODEN: COFAFG
COMPOSITES MANUFACTURING. Text in English. 1986. m. free in North America; USD 55 foreign (effective 2005). adv. **Document type:** *Magazine, Trade.* **Description:** Serves composites manufacturers involved in all segments of the composites industry, including architectural, bath, cast polymer, corrosion, custom molding, marine, and transportation.
Former titles (until 2005): Composites Fabrication (1084-841X); (until May 1994): Fabrication News
Indexed: A28, APA, BrCerAb, C&ISA, CA/WCA, CIA, CerAb, CivEngAb, CorrAb, E&CAJ, E11, EEA, EMA, ESPM, EnvEAb, H15, M&TEA, M09, MBF, METADEX, SolStAb, T04, WAA.
—Linda Hall.
Published by: Composites Fabricators Association, 1010 N Glebe Rd, Ste 450, Arlington, VA 22201-5761. TEL 703-525-0511, FAX 703-525-0743, http://www.cfa-hq.org. Ed. Andy Rusnak. Pub. Melanie Henniksen. R&P Nola Kende Long. Adv. contact Kale Dimantora. B&W page USD 1,188, color page USD 2,064; trim 11 x 8.5. Circ: 5,000.

668.4 USA ISSN 1935-3316
COMPOSITES RESEARCH JOURNAL. Text in English. 2007. q. USD 65 (effective 2007). **Document type:** *Magazine, Trade.*
Media: Online - full content.
Published by: Composites Fabricators Association, 1010 N Glebe Rd, Ste 450, Arlington, VA 22201-5761. TEL 703-525-0511, FAX 703-525-0743, info@acmanet.org. Ed. Andrew Rusnak. Pub. Tom Dobbins.

664 USA ISSN 1083-4117
TA418.9.C6
COMPOSITES TECHNOLOGY; engineering and manufacturing solutions. Text in English. 1995. bi-m. free to qualified personnel (effective 2005). adv. **Document type:** *Magazine, Trade.* **Description:** Deals with design and manufacture technology and applications for products and components made wiyh FRP composites materials.
Indexed: A01, A28, APA, BrCerAb, C&ISA, CA/WCA, CIA, CerAb, CivEngAb, CorrAb, E&CAJ, E11, EEA, EMA, H15, HRIS, M&TEA, M09, MBF, METADEX, R18, SCOPUS, SolStAb, T04, WAA, WTA.
—BLDSC (3365.680000), Linda Hall.
Published by: Ray Publishing, 4891 Independence St, Ste 270, Wheat Ridge, CO 80033-6714. TEL 303-467-1776, FAX 303-467-1777, http://www.raypubs.com. Ed., Pub. Judith Ray Hazen. R&P Jusith Ray Hazen. Adv. contact Bill Parkers. Circ: 29,000.

668.4 DEU ISSN 1618-0062
DEUTSCHES KUNSTSTOFF-INSTITUT. JAHRESBERICHT. Text in German. 1964. a. free (effective 2009). **Document type:** *Newsletter, Trade.* **Description:** Presents research results and coming events at the German Plastics Institute.
Formerly (until 2001): Deutsches Kunststoff-Institut. Mitteilungen (0936-0352)
Published by: Deutsches Kunststoff-Institut, Schlossgartenstr 6, Darmstadt, 64289, Germany. TEL 49-6151-162104, FAX 49-6151-292855, central@dki.tu-darmstadt.de, http://www.dki.tu-darmstadt.de.

E P E. (European Production Engineering) *see* ENGINEERING—Mechanical Engineering

668.4 338.094 GBR ISSN 1352-223X
E U R O M A P ECONOMIC SURVEY. (European Plastics and Rubber Machinery Manufacturers Association) Text in English. 1989. a. free to members (effective 2010). charts; stat. **Document type:** *Report, Trade.* **Description:** Features statistical information on production, UK sales, imports and exports on plastics, and rubber-processing machinery.
Published by: (European Plastics and Rubber Machinery Manufacturers Association DEU), British Plastics Federation, 5 - 6 Bath Pl, Rivington St, London, EC2A 3JE, United Kingdom. TEL 44-20-74575000, FAX 44-20-74575020, reception@bpf.co.uk, http://www.bpf.co.uk.
Co-sponsor: European Plastics and Rubber Machinery Manufacturers Association.

P

ELASTOMERS AND COMPOSITES. *see* RUBBER

ELASTOMERY. *see* ENGINEERING—Chemical Engineering

668.4 USA ISSN 1935-777X
HD9661.U62
ENGINEERED PLASTICS. Text in English. 1997. irreg. USD 3,900 per issue (print or online ed.) (effective 2011). back issues avail. **Document type:** *Monographic series, Trade.*
Related titles: Online - full text ed.
Published by: The Freedonia Group, Inc., 767 Beta Dr, Cleveland, OH 44143. TEL 440-684-9600, 800-927-5900, FAX 440-646-0484, info@freedoniagroup.com.

668.4 678.2 FRA ISSN 1774-9131
EURO TELEX. MECANIQUE. Variant title: Eurotelex. Mecanique. Text in French. 1997. 11/yr. bk.rev. **Document type:** *Trade.* **Description:** Reviews plastic manufacturing.
Formerly (until 2001): Telex Mecanique, Chaudronnerie, Machine Outil, Plastiques et Caoutchoucs (1280-794X); Which was formed by the merger of (1995-1997): Telex Plastiques et Caoutchoucs (1268-9092); (198?-1997): Telex. Mecanique, Chaudronnerie, Machine Outil (1167-8569)
Published by: Groupe Alain Thirion, 58 rue d'Alsace, Epinal, 88000, France. TEL 33-3-29291212, FAX 33-3 29354154. Ed. Alain Thirion. Circ: 18,000.

668.4 DEU
EUROPAEISCHER WIRTSCHAFTSDIENST. KUNSTSTOFF. Text in German. 1962. w. EUR 465 (effective 2009). adv. **Document type:** *Bulletin, Trade.*
Formerly (until 1988): Europaeischer Wirtschaftsdienst. Kunststoff-Dienst
Published by: (Europaeischer Wirtschaftsdienst), E U W I D - Europaeischer Wirtschaftsdienst GmbH, Bleichstr 20-22, Gernsbach, 76593, Germany. TEL 49-7224-9397572, FAX 49-7224-9397901, service@euwid.com, http://www.euwid.de. Adv. contact Sven Roth. B&W page EUR 570, color page EUR 1,470; trim 189 x 260. Circ: 1,080 (paid and controlled).

668.4 GBR
EUROPEAN PLASTICS AND RUBBER DIRECTORY (CD-ROM). Text in English, French, Italian, Spanish. 19??. a. price varies. adv. 736 p./no. 2 cols./p.; **Document type:** *Directory, Trade.*
Media: CD-ROM.
Published by: iSmithers, Shawbury, Shrewsbury, Shrops SY4 4NR, United Kingdom. TEL 44-1939-250383, FAX 44-1939-251118, info@ismithers.net, http://www.ismithers.net.

668.4 GBR ISSN 0306-3534
TP1101 CODEN: EUPNBT
EUROPEAN PLASTICS NEWS. Abbreviated title: E P N. Text in English. 1929. m. GBP 220 in Europe; GBP 240 elsewhere; free in Europe to qualified personnel (effective 2010). adv. bk.rev. charts; illus.; tr.mk. back issues avail.; reprints avail. **Document type:** *Magazine, Trade.* **Description:** Covers developments and events within Europe's plastics industry.
Former titles (until 1974): Europlastics Monthly (0367-1488); (until 1972): British Plastics (0007-1625); (until 1945): British Plastics and Moulded Products Trader
Related titles: Microform ed.: (from PMC, PQC); Online - full text ed.: EuropeanPlasticsNews.com.
Indexed: A22, A23, A24, B02, B03, B13, B15, B17, B18, BMT, CBNB, CIN, CISA, Cadscan, ChemAb, ChemTitl, G04, G08, I05, IPackAb, Inspec, KES, LeadAb, PST, R18, SCOPUS, Zincscan.
—BLDSC (3829.787000), CASDDS, IE, Infotrieve, Ingenta, INIST, Linda Hall. **CCC.**
Published by: Crain Communications, Ltd., Carolyn House, 4th Fl, Ste 1, 26 Dingwall Rd, Croydon, CR0 9XF, United Kingdom. TEL 44-20-82539600, http://www.crain.co.uk. Ed. Chris Smith TEL 44-20-82539614. Adv. contact Steve Crowhurst TEL 44-20-82539603. page GBP 4,850, page EUR 6,400, page USD 8,800; trim 210 x 297. Circ: 13,695.

668.4 DEU
EXTRUSION. Text in German. 1995. 8/yr. EUR 15 newsstand/cover (effective 2007). adv. **Document type:** *Magazine, Trade.*
Indexed: TM.
Published by: V M Verlag, Gleueler Str 373, Cologne, 50935, Germany. TEL 49-221-439256, FAX 49-221-438121. Ed. Fritz Vollmer. Adv. contact Guenther Merkel. page EUR 2,800. Circ: 3,995 (paid and controlled).

668.4 NLD ISSN 1229-9197
TP1101 CODEN: FPIOA6
FIBERS AND POLYMERS. Text in Korean. 2000. q. EUR 808, USD 1,080 combined subscription to institutions (print & online eds.) (effective 2012). reprint service avail. from PSC. **Document type:** *Magazine, Trade.*
Related titles: Online - full text ed.: ISSN 1875-0052.
Indexed: A22, A26, CCI, E01, E08, MSCI, P52, S09, SCI, SCOPUS, TM, W07.
—BLDSC (3914.698500), IE, Ingenta. **CCC.**
Published by: (Korean Fiber Society KOR), Springer Netherlands (Subsidiary of: Springer Science+Business Media), Van Godewijckstraat 30, Dordrecht, 3311 GX, Netherlands. TEL 31-78-6576050, FAX 31-78-6576474, http://www.springer.com. Ed. Won Ho Jo. **Subscr. to:** Springer Distribution Center, Kundenservice Zeitschriften, Haberstr 7, Heidelberg 69126, Germany. TEL 49-6221-3454303, FAX 49-6221-3454229, subscriptions@springer.com.

668.9 730 NLD ISSN 2211-3673
▼ **FROM POLYMER TO ART.** Variant title: Polymer Art Magazine. Text in English. 2011. q. EUR 47; EUR 11.95 newsstand/cover (effective 2011). **Document type:** *Magazine, Consumer.*
Published by: Total Pre Press bv, Johan Enschedeweg 15, Uithoorn, 1422 DR, Netherlands. TEL 31-297-531739, FAX 31-297-540926, info@totalpress.nl, http://www.totalpress.nl.

668.4 DEU ISSN 0948-4914
GENAU; Fachzeitung fuer das holz und kunststoffverarbeitende Handwerk. Text in German. 1976. 10/yr. EUR 18.50; EUR 3 newsstand/cover (effective 2010). adv. **Document type:** *Magazine, Trade.*
—**CCC.**
Published by: (Bundesverband des Holz- und Kunststoffverarbeitende Industrie), Schluetersche Verlagsgesellschaft mbH und Co. KG, Hans-Boeckler-Allee 7, Hannover, 30173, Germany. TEL 49-511-85500, FAX 49-511-85501100, info@schluetersche.de. Ed. Irmke Froemling. Adv. contact Sabine Kalner. B&W page EUR 3,770, color page EUR 4,520; trim 200 x 284. Circ: 20,323 (paid and controlled).

668.4 CHN ISSN 1001-3539
TP1101
GONGCHENG SUOLIAO YINGYONG/ENGINEERING PLASTICS APPLICATION. Text in Chinese. 1973. m. USD 62.40 (effective 2009). 96 p./no.; **Document type:** *Journal, Academic/Scholarly.* **Description:** Covers research developments and manufacturing or engineering design of resins, plastics, composites, functional materials and their products.
Related titles: Online - full text ed.
—BLDSC (3766.350000), East View.
Published by: Gongcheng Suoliao Yingyong Zazhishe, PO Box 108, Jinan, Shandong 250031, China. Ed. Anyuan Sun. **Dist. overseas by:** China International Book Trading Corp, 35 Chegongzhuang Xilu, Haidian District, PO Box 399, Beijing 100044, China.

668.4 JPN ISSN 0387-0936
TP977 CODEN: GOSJBC
GOSEI JUSHI/PLASTICS. Text in Japanese. 1947. m. JPY 12,875.
Indexed: CIN, ChemAb, ChemTitl.
—CASDDS.
Published by: Nihon Gosei Jushi Gijutsu Kyokai/Japan Society of Plastics Technology, 10-18 Ginza 2-chome, Chuo-ku, Tokyo, 104-0061, Japan. TEL 81-3-3542-0261, FAX 81-3-3543-0619.

668.4 MEX
GUIA DE LA INDUSTRIA: HULE, PLASTICOS Y RESINAS/RUBBER, PLASTICS AND RESINS GUIDE. Text in English, Spanish. 1964. a. USD 80. adv. index avail. on the Internet. **Document type:** *Directory.* **Description:** Lists over 1200 suppliers of raw materials, machinery and services. Lists 900 products, services and materials. Indexes 1300 rubber and plastics items manufacturers in the country. Includes English-Spanish product index.
Former titles: Hule, Plasticos y Resinas (Annual); Plasticos y Resinas (Annual)
Published by: Informatica Cosmos, S.A. de C.V., Calz. del Hueso 122-A1, Col. Ex-Hacienda Coapa, Mexico City, DF 14300, Mexico. TEL 52-5-677-48-68, FAX 52-5-679-3575. Ed., Pub. Raul Macazaga. Adv. contact Mary Christen. B&W page USD 1,000; trim 274 x 211. Circ: 5,000.

668.4 ARG
GUIA DEL PLASTICO. Text in Spanish. 1952. 6/yr.
Published by: Camara Argentina de la Industria Plastica, Jeronimo Salguero 1939, Buenos Aires, 1425, Argentina. TEL 54-114-8265480. Circ: 5,000.

GUIDE PLASTIQUES ET CAOUTCHOUC. *see* BUSINESS AND ECONOMICS—Trade And Industrial Directories

GUMA, ELASTOMERY, PRZETWORTSTWO. *see* ENGINEERING—Chemical Engineering

668.4 CHN ISSN 1002-5219
GUOWAI SULIAO/WORLD PLASTICS. Text in Chinese. m. CNY 288 (effective 2008). **Document type:** *Magazine, Trade.*
Related titles: Online - full text ed.
Published by: Guowai Suliao Zazhishe, Rm. 139, no. 6 Changan Jie, Beijing, 100740, China. TEL 86-10-65254996, FAX 86-10-65251538.

668.4 CHE ISSN 0073-0084
HANDBUCH DER INTERNATIONALEN KUNSTSTOFFINDUSTRIE/INTERNATIONAL PLASTICS DIRECTORY/MANUEL INTERNATIONAL DES PLASTIQUES. Text in French, German, English; Index in French, German, English. 1958. every 10 yrs. CHF 600. index.
Published by: Verlag fuer Internationale Wirtschaftsliteratur GmbH, Postfach 28, Zuerich, 8047, Switzerland. FAX 41-1-4010545. Ed. Walter Hirt.

668.4 CHN ISSN 1002-1396
TP977
HECHENG SHUZHI JI SULIAO/SYNTHETIC RESIN AND PLASTICS. Text in Chinese. 1984. bi-m. USD 31.20 (effective 2009). **Document type:** *Journal, Academic/Scholarly.*
Related titles: Online - full text ed.
Indexed: Englnd, SCOPUS.
—East View.
Address: PO Box 10041, Beijing, 102500, China. TEL 86-10-69341924, FAX 86-10-69341930.

668.4 USA ISSN 1081-9223
TA418.9.C6
HIGH-PERFORMANCE COMPOSITES; design and manufacturing solutions for industry. Text in English. 1993. bi-m. USD 30 domestic to non-members; USD 40 in Canada to non-members; USD 62 elsewhere to non-members (effective 2003). adv. back issues avail. **Document type:** *Magazine, Trade.* **Description:** Deals with design and manufacturing technology and practical application examples for products and componentd made with or using advnced composite nmaterials.
Indexed: A01, A28, APA, BrCerAb, C&ISA, CA/WCA, CIA, CerAb, CivEngAb, CorrAb, E&CAJ, E11, EEA, EMA, ESPM, EnvEAb, H15, M&TEA, M09, MBF, METADEX, RefZh, SCOPUS, SolStAb, T04, WAA, WTA.
—BLDSC (4307.338584), IE, Ingenta, Linda Hall.
Published by: Ray Publishing, 4891 Independence St, Ste 270, Wheat Ridge, CO 80033-6714. TEL 303-467-1776, FAX 303-467-1777. Ed., Pub., R&P Judith Ray Hazen. Adv. contact Bill Parker. Circ: 22,000.

668.4 GBR ISSN 0264-7753
TP1101
HIGH PERFORMANCE PLASTICS. Text in English. 1983. m. GBP 497, USD 910 combined subscription (effective 2010). adv. bk.rev. illus.; stat. back issues avail. **Document type:** *Newsletter, Trade.* **Description:** Covers market and industry news, new materials and processing, performance applications, environmental issues, technological developments and an events calendar.
Related titles: E-mail ed.; Online - full text ed.: ISSN 1878-7010.
Indexed: A28, APA, BrCerAb, C&ISA, CA/WCA, CBNB, CIA, CerAb, CivEngAb, CorrAb, E&CAJ, E11, EEA, EMA, ESPM, EnvEAb, H15, I05, M&TEA, M09, MBF, METADEX, R18, SolStAb, T04, WAA.
—BLDSC (4307.338650), IE, Infotrieve, Ingenta, INIST, Linda Hall. **CCC.**
Published by: International Newsletters Ltd., 9A Victoria Sq, Droitwich, Worcs WR9 8DE, United Kingdom. TEL 44-870-1657210, FAX 44-870-1657212, in@intnews.com, http://www.intnews.com. Ed. James Bakewell. Adv. contact David Kay TEL 44-1273-423512.

HUNTSMAN POLYURETHANES REVIEW. *see* ENGINEERING—Engineering Mechanics And Materials

668.4 USA
I A P D MAGAZINE; the voice of plastics distribution. Text in English. 1986. bi-m. USD 70 to non-members (effective 1999). adv. **Document type:** *Magazine, Trade.*
Formerly: N A P D Magazine
Indexed: APA, C&ISA, CIA, CorrAb, E&CAJ, EEA, SolStAb, WAA.
Published by: International Association of Plastics Distributors, 4707 College Blvd., Ste. 105, Leawood, KS 66211-1667. TEL 913-345-1005, FAX 913-345-1006. Ed. Deborah Hamlin. R&P Janet Thill. Adv. contact Dana Roseberry. B&W page USD 2,885. Circ: 10,000.

INDUSTRY CONTACTS. *see* BUSINESS AND ECONOMICS—Trade And Industrial Directories

668.4 USA ISSN 1071-362X
INJECTION MOLDING. Abbreviated title: I M M. Text in English. 1993. m. free in US & Canada to qualified personnel (effective 2008). adv. bk.rev. back issues avail. **Document type:** *Magazine, Trade.* **Description:** Designed to target all the stages and levels of the injection molding process from design to manufacture to market.
Related titles: Online - full text ed.
Indexed: A28, APA, BrCerAb, C&ISA, CA/WCA, CIA, CerAb, CivEngAb, CorrAb, E&CAJ, E11, EEA, EMA, ESPM, EnvEAb, G08, H15, I05, M&TEA, M09, MBF, METADEX, R18, SolStAb, T04, WAA.
—BLDSC (4514.355000), Linda Hall. **CCC.**
Published by: Canon Communications LLC (Subsidiary of: Apprise Media LLC), 11444 W Olympic Blvd, Ste 900, Los Angeles, CA 90064. TEL 310-445-4200, FAX 310-445-4299, info@cancom.com, http://www.cancom.com. Ed. Rob Neilly. Pub. Kevin O'Grady. adv.: B&W page USD 7,880, color page USD 8,670; bleed 8.125 x 11. Circ: 41,040.

668.4 GBR ISSN 1462-0278
INJECTION MOULDING ASIA. Text in English. 1998. q. includes subscr. with Plastics and Rubber Asia. **Document type:** *Magazine, Trade.* **Description:** Features specific articles of direct interest to injection moulders, thus creating a unique editorial and advertising environment for companies that supply injection moulding technology and materials.
Related titles: Online - full text ed.; ◆ Supplement to: Plastics and Rubber Asia. ISSN 1360-1245.
Indexed: B03, R18.
—CIS.
Published by: Airports Publishing Network, The Stables, Willow Ln, Paddock Wood, Kent TN12 6PF, United Kingdom. TEL 44-1892-839202, FAX 44-1892-839210.

668.4 ESP
INSTITUTO DE CIENCIA Y TECNOLOGIA DE POLIMEROS. MEMORIA. Text in Spanish. a. **Document type:** *Monographic series, Academic/Scholarly.*
Published by: Instituto de Estudios Documentales sobre Ciencia y Tecnologia (I E D C Y T), Ciencia y Tecnologia, Joaquin Costa 22, Madrid, 28002, Spain. TEL 34-91-5635482, FAX 34-91-5642644, http://www.cindoc.csic.es.

INTERNATIONAL BOTTLER AND PACKER. *see* BEVERAGES

THE INTERNATIONAL DIRECTORY OF PLASTIC AND PLASTIC PRODUCTS IMPORTERS. *see* BUSINESS AND ECONOMICS—Trade And Industrial Directories

668.4 GBR ISSN 0143-7496
TP967 CODEN: IJAADK
➤ **INTERNATIONAL JOURNAL OF ADHESION AND ADHESIVES.** Text in English. 1980. 8/yr. EUR 1,255 in Europe to institutions; JPY 166,800 in Japan to institutions; USD 1,406 elsewhere to institutions (effective 2012). adv. bk.rev. abstr.; bibl.; charts; illus.; stat. index. back issues avail. **Document type:** *Journal, Academic/Scholarly.* **Description:** Covers design of joints, stress analysis, surface preparation, dynamic properties, manufacturing technology, and industrial and academic developments in sealants and adhesives.
Related titles: Microform ed.: (from PQC); Online - full text ed.: ISSN 1879-0127 (from IngentaConnect, ScienceDirect).
Indexed: A01, A03, A08, A20, A22, A26, A28, ABIPC, APA, ASCA, ApMecR, BrCerAb, C&ISA, C24, C33, CA, CA/WCA, CIA, CPEI, CerAb, ChemAb, CivEngAb, CorrAb, CurCont, E&CAJ, E11, EEA, EMA, ESPM, Englnd, EnvEAb, GeoRef, H15, HRIS, I05, IPackAb, Inspec, M&TEA, M09, MBF, METADEX, MSCI, P31, R18, RefZh, S01, SCI, SCOPUS, SolStAb, T01, T02, T04, TM, TTI, W07, WAA, WSCA.
—BLDSC (4541.560000), CASDDS, IE, Infotrieve, Ingenta, INIST, Linda Hall. **CCC.**
Published by: Elsevier Ltd (Subsidiary of: Elsevier Science & Technology), The Blvd, Langford Ln, Kidlington, Oxford, OX5 1GB, United Kingdom. TEL 44-1865-843000, FAX 44-1865-843010. Eds. L S Penn, J Comyn, R D Adams. **Subscr. to:** Elsevier BV, Radarweg 29, PO Box 211, Amsterdam 1000 AE, Netherlands. TEL 31-20-4853757, FAX 31-20-4853432, JournalsCustomerServiceEMEA@elsevier.com, http://www.elsevier.nl.

668.4 IND ISSN 0972-656X
➤ **INTERNATIONAL JOURNAL OF PLASTICS TECHNOLOGY.** Text in English. 2002. 2/yr. EUR 155, USD 231 combined subscription to institutions (print & online eds.) (effective 2012). reprint service avail. from PSC. **Document type:** *Journal, Academic/Scholarly.* **Description:** Covers research and developments in the areas of polymeric materials, blends & alloys, composites, nanocomposites, plastics processing, mould & product design, recycling and application development. Disseminate research advancements in the areas of polymer/plastics engineering & technology.
Related titles: Online - full text ed.: ISSN 0975-072X (from IngentaConnect).
Indexed: A22, E01, P52, SCOPUS.
—BLDSC (4542.470100), IE. **CCC.**
Published by: Springer (India) Private Ltd. (Subsidiary of: Springer Science+Business Media), 212, Deen Dayal Upadhyaya Marg, 3rd Fl, Gandharva Mahavidyalaya, New Delhi, 110 002, India. TEL 91-11-45755888, FAX 91-11-45755889. Ed. S K Nayak.

668.4 DEU ISSN 0930-777X
TP1080 CODEN: IPPREJ
➤ **INTERNATIONAL POLYMER PROCESSING.** Text in English. 1986. 5/yr. EUR 648; EUR 155.80 newsstand/cover (effective 2011). adv. bk.rev. charts; illus. **Document type:** *Journal, Academic/Scholarly.* **Description:** Publishes articles on the science of processing thermoplastics, thermosets, elastomers and fibers.
Indexed: A22, A28, APA, ASCA, BrCerAb, C&ISA, C33, CA/WCA, CIA, CIN, CerAb, ChemAb, ChemTitl, CivEngAb, CorrAb, CurCR, CurCont, E&CAJ, E11, EEA, EMA, H15, ISR, M&TEA, M09, MBF, METADEX, MSCI, R16, R18, SCI, SCOPUS, SolStAb, T04, TM, W07, WAA.
—BLDSC (4544.965800), CASDDS, IE, Infotrieve, Ingenta, Linda Hall. **CCC.**
Published by: (Polymer Processing Society), Carl Hanser Verlag GmbH & Co. KG, Kolbergerstr 22, Munich, 81679, Germany. TEL 49-89-998300, FAX 49-89-984809, info@hanser.de. Ed. A N Hrymak. Adv. contact Heike Herchenroether-Rosenstein. Circ: 2,000.

668.4 540 GBR ISSN 0307-174X
QD380
INTERNATIONAL POLYMER SCIENCE AND TECHNOLOGY. Text in English. 1974. m. GBP 1,065, USD 1,743.41, EUR 1,181.09 (effective 2010). abstr.; charts; illus. back issues avail. **Document type:** *Journal, Academic/Scholarly.* **Description:** Contains English translations of papers selected from eight foreign rubber and plastics journals, primarily Russian, Japanese, Hungarian and German.
Formed by the merger of: Soviet Plastics; Soviet Rubber Technology
Related titles: Online - full text ed.: ISSN 1478-2405.
Indexed: A22, A26, I05, P10, P26, P48, P52, P53, P54, PQC, R18, S10, TM.
—BLDSC (4544.965900), IE, Infotrieve, Ingenta, INIST, Linda Hall. **CCC.**
Published by: iSmithers, Shawbury, Shrewsbury, Shrops SY4 4NR, United Kingdom. TEL 44-1939-250383, FAX 44-1939-251118, info@ismithers.net, http://www.ismithers.net. Ed. Kate Evans TEL 44-1939-252455.

668.4 678.2 FRA ISSN 1639-965X
CODEN: PRFTDV
J E C COMPOSITES. Text in Multiple languages. 1963. bi-m. free. adv. **Document type:** *Magazine, Trade.*
Former titles (until 2003): Composites International (1627-3486); (until 2000): Composites (0754-0876); (until 1983): Plastiques Renforces, Fibres de Verre Textile (0240-9917)
Related titles: Online - full text ed.
Indexed: A28, APA, ASCA, BrCerAb, C&ISA, CA/WCA, CIA, CerAb, CivEngAb, CorrAb, E&CAJ, E11, EEA, EMA, ESPM, EnvEAb, H15, M&TEA, M09, MBF, METADEX, R18, SCOPUS, SolStAb, T04, WAA, WTA.
—BLDSC (4663.465665), CASDDS, IE, Ingenta, INIST, Linda Hall. **CCC.**
Published by: Journal and Exhibition Composites (JEC), 25 Bd. de l'Amiral Bruix, Paris, 75016, France. TEL 33-1-58361501, FAX 33-1-58361514. Ed. Frederique Mutel. R&P Jean Christian Lerat. Adv. contacts Claudie Devooght, Judith Blacker. Circ: 31,349.

668.4 DEU ISSN 1864-3450
JOINING PLASTICS/FUEGEN VON KUNSTSTOFFEN. Text in English, German. 2007. 4/yr. EUR 58 (effective 2011). adv. **Document type:** *Magazine, Trade.*
Published by: D V S Verlag GmbH, Aachener Str 172, Duesseldorf, 40223, Germany. TEL 49-211-15910, FAX 49-211-1591150, verlag@dvs-hg.de, http://www.dvs-verlag.de. Ed. Paul-Robert Hoene. Adv. contact Iris Jansen.

THE JOURNAL OF ADHESION. *see* PHYSICS

668.4 NLD ISSN 0169-4243
TP967 CODEN: JATEE8
➤ **JOURNAL OF ADHESION SCIENCE AND TECHNOLOGY**; the international journal of theoretical and basic aspects of adhesion science and its applications in all areas of technology. Text in English. 1987. 16/yr. EUR 2,741, USD 3,658 to institutions; EUR 2,990, USD 3,990 combined subscription to institutions (print & online eds.) (effective 2012). adv. bk.rev. index. back issues avail.; reprint service avail. from PSC. **Document type:** *Journal, Academic/Scholarly.* **Description:** Covers theoretical and basic aspects of adhesion science and its applications in all areas of technology.
Related titles: Online - full text ed.: ISSN 1568-5616. EUR 2,492, USD 3,325 to institutions (effective 2012) (from IngentaConnect).
Indexed: A01, A03, A08, A22, A28, APA, ASCA, ApMecR, BrCerAb, C&ISA, C24, C33, CA, CA/WCA, CIA, CPEI, CerAb, ChemAb, CivEngAb, CorrAb, CurCR, CurCont, E&CAJ, E01, E11, EEA, EMA, ESPM, EngInd, EnvEAb, H15, ISR, IZBG, Inspec, M&TEA, M09, MBF, METADEX, MSCI, P&BA, P30, PQC, R16, R18, S01, SCI, SCOPUS, SolStAb, T01, T02, T04, TM, TTI, W07, WAA, WSCA.
—BLDSC (4918.936000), AskIEEE, CASDDS, IE, Infotrieve, Ingenta, INIST, Linda Hall. **CCC.**
Published by: V S P (Subsidiary of: Brill), Brill Academic Publishers, PO Box 9000, Leiden, 2300 PA, Netherlands. TEL 31-71-5353500, FAX 31-71-5317532, marketing@brill.nl. Ed. K L Mittal.

668.44 GBR ISSN 0021-955X
TP1183.F6 CODEN: JCUPAM
➤ **JOURNAL OF CELLULAR PLASTICS.** Text in English. 1965. bi-m. USD 1,314, GBP 773 combined subscription to institutions (print & online eds.); USD 1,288, GBP 758 to institutions (effective 2011). adv. bk.rev. charts; illus.; pat.; stat. index. back issues avail.; reprint service avail. from PSC. **Document type:** *Journal, Academic/Scholarly.* **Description:** Reports on new research and developments in the area of foamed plastics covering: chemistry, processing, properties, and applications.
Related titles: E-mail ed.; Microform ed.: (from PQC); Online - full text ed.: ISSN 1530-7999. USD 1,183, GBP 696 to institutions (effective 2011).
Indexed: A01, A03, A08, A15, A22, A28, ABIn, APA, ASCA, ApMecR, B07, BrCerAb, C&ISA, CA, CA/WCA, CIA, CIN, CPEI, CerAb, ChemAb, ChemTitl, CivEngAb, CorrAb, CurCont, E&CAJ, E01, E11, EEA, EMA, ESPM, EngInd, EnvEAb, H04, H15, IPackAb, M&TEA, M09, MBF, METADEX, MSCI, P51, PQC, R18, S01, SCI, SCOPUS, SolStAb, T02, T04, TM, V02, W07, WAA.
—BLDSC (4955.050000), CASDDS, IE, Infotrieve, Ingenta, INIST, Linda Hall. **CCC.**
Published by: Sage Publications Ltd. (Subsidiary of: Sage Publications, Inc.), 1 Oliver's Yard, 55 City Rd, London, EC1Y 1SP, United Kingdom. FAX 44-20-73248600, info@sagepub.co.uk, http://www.uk.sagepub.com/home.nav. Eds. Chul B Park, S T Lee. adv.: B&W page GBP 550; 130 x 205. **Subscr. in the Americas to:** Sage Publications, Inc., 2455 Teller Rd, Thousand Oaks, CA 91320. TEL 805-499-9774, FAX 805-499-0871, journals@sagepub.com.

668.4 GBR ISSN 0095-2443
TA455.P5 CODEN: JEPLAX
➤ **JOURNAL OF ELASTOMERS AND PLASTICS.** Abbreviated title: J E P. Text in English. 1969. bi-m. USD 1,483, GBP 872 combined subscription to institutions (print & online eds.); USD 1,453, GBP 855 to institutions (effective 2011). adv. charts. index. back issues avail.; reprint service avail. from PSC. **Document type:** *Journal, Academic/Scholarly.* **Description:** Reports on the chemistry, processing, properties and applications of synthetic and natural rubber.
Formerly (until 1974): Journal of Elastoplastics (0022-071X)
Related titles: E-mail ed.; Microform ed.: (from PQC); Online - full text ed.: ISSN 1530-8006. USD 1,335, GBP 785 to institutions (effective 2011).
Indexed: A01, A03, A08, A15, A22, A28, ABIn, APA, ApMecR, B07, BrCerAb, C&ISA, CA, CA/WCA, CIA, CIN, CPEI, CerAb, ChemAb, ChemTitl, CivEngAb, CorrAb, CurCR, CurCont, E&CAJ, E01, E11, EEA, EMA, ESPM, EngInd, EnvEAb, H04, H15, M&TEA, M09, MBF, METADEX, MSCI, P51, PQC, R16, R18, S01, SCI, SCOPUS, SolStAb, T02, T04, V02, W07, WAA.
—BLDSC (4973.289000), CASDDS, IE, Infotrieve, Ingenta, INIST, Linda Hall. **CCC.**
Published by: Sage Publications Ltd. (Subsidiary of: Sage Publications, Inc.), 1 Oliver's Yard, 55 City Rd, London, EC1Y 1SP, United Kingdom. TEL 44-20-73248500, FAX 44-20-73248600, info@sagepub.co.uk, http://www.uk.sagepub.com/home.nav. Ed. Heshmat A Aglan. adv.: B&W page GBP 450; 130 x 205. **Subscr. in the Americas to:** Sage Publications, Inc., 2455 Teller Rd, Thousand Oaks, CA 91320. TEL 805-499-9774, FAX 805-499-0871, journals@sagepub.com.

➤ **JOURNAL OF INDUSTRIAL TEXTILES.** *see* TEXTILE INDUSTRIES AND FABRICS

668.4 GBR ISSN 8756-0879
CODEN: JPFSEH
➤ **JOURNAL OF PLASTIC FILM AND SHEETING.** Text in English. 1985. q. USD 1,115, GBP 656 combined subscription to institutions (print & online eds.); USD 1,093, GBP 643 to institutions (effective 2011). adv. abstr.; bibl.; illus. back issues avail.; reprint service avail. from PSC. **Document type:** *Journal, Academic/Scholarly.* **Description:** Reports on polymer science, processing and applications for plastic films.
Related titles: E-mail ed.; Online - full text ed.: ISSN 1530-8014. USD 1,004, GBP 590 to institutions (effective 2011).
Indexed: A01, A03, A08, A22, A28, A34, A37, APA, ASCA, B07, BrCerAb, C&ISA, CA, CA/WCA, CABA, CIA, CIN, CPEI, CerAb, ChemAb, ChemTitl, CivEngAb, CorrAb, E&CAJ, E01, E11, EEA, EMA, ESPM, EngInd, EnvEAb, FS&TA, GH, H04, H15, H16, IPackAb, M&TEA, M09, MBF, MSCI, N02, N04, O01, PHN&I, R12, R18, S01, S13, S16, SCI, SCOPUS, SolStAb, T01, T02, T04, TAR, TM, TTI, V02, W07, W11, WAA.
—BLDSC (5040.695000), CASDDS, IE, Infotrieve, Ingenta, INIST, Linda Hall. **CCC.**
Published by: Sage Publications Ltd. (Subsidiary of: Sage Publications, Inc.), 1 Oliver's Yard, 55 City Rd, London, EC1Y 1SP, United Kingdom. TEL 44-20-73248500, FAX 44-20-73248600, info@sagepub.co.uk, http://www.uk.sagepub.com/home.nav. Ed. James P Harrington. adv.: B&W page GBP 450; 130 x 205. **Subscr. in the Americas to:** Sage Publications, Inc., 2455 Teller Rd, Thousand Oaks, CA 91320. TEL 805-499-9774, FAX 805-499-0871, journals@sagepub.com.

668.4 NLD ISSN 1022-9760
CODEN: JPOREP
➤ **JOURNAL OF POLYMER RESEARCH.** Text in English. 1994. bi-m. EUR 458, USD 467 combined subscription to institutions (print & online eds.) (effective 2012). adv. back issues avail.; reprint service avail. from PSC. **Document type:** *Journal, Academic/Scholarly.* **Description:** Devoted to all aspects of polymer science.
Related titles: Online - full text ed.: ISSN 1572-8935 (from IngentaConnect).
Indexed: A01, A02, A03, A08, A22, A26, A28, APA, Agr, BibLing, BrCerAb, C&ISA, C33, CA, CA/WCA, CCI, CIA, CPEI, CerAb, ChemAb, CivEngAb, CorrAb, CurCR, CurCont, E&CAJ, E01, E11, EEA, EMA, ESPM, EngInd, EnvEAb, H15, I05, M&TEA, M09, MBF, METADEX, MSCI, P52, R16, R18, RefZh, SCI, SCOPUS, SolStAb, T01, T02, T04, TTI, W07, WAA.
—BLDSC (5040.999000), IE, Infotrieve, Ingenta, Linda Hall. **CCC.**
Published by: Springer Netherlands (Subsidiary of: Springer Science+Business Media), Van Godewijckstraat 30, Dordrecht, 3311 GX, Netherlands. TEL 31-78-6576050, FAX 31-78-6576474, http://www.springer.com. Ed. Show-An Chen.

➤ **JOURNAL OF REINFORCED PLASTICS & COMPOSITES.** *see* ENGINEERING—Engineering Mechanics And Materials

668.4 GBR ISSN 0892-7057
TA418.9.C6 CODEN: JTMAEQ
➤ **JOURNAL OF THERMOPLASTIC COMPOSITE MATERIALS.** Text in English. 1988. 8/yr. GBP 1,092, USD 1,855 to institutions; GBP 1,114, USD 1,893 combined subscription to institutions (print & online eds.) (effective 2012). index. back issues avail.; reprint service avail. from PSC. **Document type:** *Journal, Academic/Scholarly.* **Description:** Reports on the technology of thermoplastic - matrix composite material.
Related titles: Online - full text ed.: ISSN 1530-7980. GBP 1,003, USD 1,074 to institutions (effective 2012).
Indexed: A01, A03, A08, A22, A28, APA, ASCA, ApMecR, B07, BrCerAb, C&ISA, CA, CA/WCA, CIA, CIN, CMCI, CPEI, CerAb, ChemAb, ChemTitl, CivEngAb, CorrAb, CurCont, E&CAJ, E01, E11, EEA, EMA, ESPM, EngInd, EnvEAb, H04, H15, Inspec, M&TEA, M09, MBF, METADEX, MSCI, R18, S01, SCI, SCOPUS, SolStAb, T02, T04, TM, V02, W07, WAA.
—BLDSC (5069.099400), CASDDS, IE, Infotrieve, Ingenta, Linda Hall. **CCC.**
Published by: (American Society for Composites USA), Sage Publications Ltd. (Subsidiary of: Sage Publications, Inc.), 1 Oliver's Yard, 55 City Rd, London, EC1Y 1SP, United Kingdom. TEL 44-20-73248500, FAX 44-20-73248600, info@sagepub.co.uk, http://www.uk.sagepub.com/home.nav. Ed. John W Gillespie Jr.

668.4 USA ISSN 1083-5601
TP1180.V48 CODEN: JVATF4
➤ **JOURNAL OF VINYL & ADDITIVE TECHNOLOGY.** Text in English. 1979. q. GBP 412 in United Kingdom to institutions; EUR 521 in Europe to institutions; USD 723 in United States to institutions; USD 779 in Canada & Mexico to institutions; USD 807 elsewhere to institutions; GBP 475 combined subscription in United Kingdom to institutions (print & online eds.); EUR 600 combined subscription in Europe to institutions (print & online eds.); USD 833 combined subscription in United States to institutions (print & online eds.); USD 889 combined subscription in Canada & Mexico to institutions (print & online eds.); USD 917 combined subscription elsewhere to institutions (print & online eds.) (effective 2012). adv. charts; illus. index. back issues avail.; reprint service avail. from PSC. **Document type:** *Journal, Academic/Scholarly.* **Description:** Covers the fields of polymer modifiers and additives, vinyl polymers and selected review papers.
Formerly (until 1995): Journal of Vinyl Technology (0193-7197)
Related titles: Online - full text ed.: ISSN 1548-0585. GBP 369 in United Kingdom to institutions; EUR 467 in Europe to institutions; USD 723 elsewhere to institutions (effective 2012).
Indexed: A22, A28, APA, ASCA, BrCerAb, C&ISA, C33, CA/WCA, CIA, CPEI, CerAb, ChemAb, ChemTitl, CivEngAb, CorrAb, CurCont, E&CAJ, E11, EEA, EMA, ESPM, EngInd, EnvEAb, H15, M&TEA, M09, MBF, METADEX, MSCI, P16, P26, P48, P52, P53, P54, PQC, R18, SCI, SCOPUS, SolStAb, T04, W07, WAA.
—BLDSC (5072.483500), CASDDS, IE, Infotrieve, Ingenta, INIST, Linda Hall. **CCC.**
Published by: (Society of Plastics Engineers, Inc.), John Wiley & Sons, Inc., 111 River St, Hoboken, NJ 07030. TEL 201-748-6000, FAX 201-748-6088, info@wiley.com, http://www.wiley.com/WileyCDA/. Ed. William H Starnes. Pub., Adv. contact Kim Thompkins TEL 212-850-6921.

➤ **JUZHI GONGYE/POLYESTER INDUSTRY.** *see* BUSINESS AND ECONOMICS

668.4 DEU ISSN 0451-1646
K MITTEILUNGEN. Text in German. 1950. m. membership. adv. bk.rev. abstr.; bibl.; stat. **Document type:** *Newsletter.*
Published by: Gesamtverband Kunststoffverarbeitende Industrie e.V., Froschpfort 16, Montabaur, 56410, Germany. FAX 49-2602-4308. Ed. Reinhard Ackermann. Circ: 3,000 (controlled).

K R V NACHRICHTEN. (Kunststoffrohrverband) *see* ENGINEERING—Engineering Mechanics And Materials

668.4 DEU ISSN 1436-6401
K: ZEITUNG. Text in German. 1969. fortn. EUR 154, EUR 162 (effective 2010). adv. bk.rev. illus.; stat. index. **Document type:** *Newspaper, Trade.*
Former titles (until 1999): K: Plastic und Kautschuk Zeitung (0342-7099); (until 1976): K-Platic-Zeitung, K W, Kunststoff- und Kautschuk-Woche (0342-7137)
—Linda Hall. **CCC.**
Published by: Giesel Verlag GmbH (Subsidiary of: Schluetersche Verlagsgesellschaft mbH und Co. KG), Rehkamp 3, Isernhagen, 30916, Germany. TEL 49-511-73040, FAX 49-511-7304157, giesel@giesel.de, http://www.giesel.de. Circ: 16,000 (paid and controlled).

KAMI INSATSU PURASUCHIKKU GOMU SEIHIN TOUKEI GEPPOU/ MONTHLY REPORT OF PAPER, PRINTING, PLASTICS PRODUCTS AND RUBBER PRODUCTS STATISTICS. *see* PAPER AND PULP

668.4 658.8 GBR ISSN 1460-8294
KEY NOTE MARKET REPORT: PLASTICS PROCESSING. Variant title: Plastics Processing Market Report. Text in English. 19??. irreg., latest 2003, Jul. GBP 360 per issue (effective 2010). **Document type:** *Report, Trade.* **Description:** Provides an overview of a specific UK market segment and includes executive summary, market definition, market size, industry background, competitor analysis, current issues, forecasts, company profiles, and more.
Formerly (until 1997): Key Note Report: Plastics Processing (0267-4696)
Related titles: CD-ROM ed.; Online - full text ed.
Published by: Key Note Ltd. (Subsidiary of: Bonnier Business Information), Harlequin House, 5th Fl, 7 High St, Teddington, Richmond upon Thames, TW11 8EE, United Kingdom. TEL 44-845-5040452, FAX 44-845-5040453, info@keynote.co.uk.

KLOECKNER WERKE HEUTE; Maschinenbau, Kunststoff Verarbeitung. *see* METALLURGY

668.4 POL ISSN 1641-8611
TA418.9.C6
KOMPOZYTY/COMPOSITES. Text in Polish, English. 2001. a.
Indexed: B22.
Published by: (Polskie Towarzystwo Materialow Kompozytowych/Polish Society for Composite Materials), Politechnika Czestochowska, Ul J.H. Dabrowskiego 69, Czestochowa, 42200, Poland. TEL 48-34-3255211, http://adm.pcz.czest.pl.

668.4 NLD ISSN 0167-9597
CODEN: KRUBDV
KUNSTSTOF EN RUBBER; monthly review on plastics. Text in Dutch. 1948. m. (11/yr.). EUR 174.50 domestic; EUR 198.50 foreign; EUR 77.50 to students (effective 2009). adv. bk.rev. abstr.; charts; illus.; tr.lit. **Document type:** *Magazine, Trade.*
Formerly (until 1983): Plastica (0032-1095)
Indexed: A22, CBNB, CIN, ChemAb, ChemTitl, IPackAb.
—BLDSC (5130.795000), CASDDS, IE, Infotrieve, Ingenta, INIST.
Published by: (T N O, Chemistry), Media Business Press BV, Postbus 8632, Rotterdam, 3009 AP, Netherlands. TEL 31-10-2894078, FAX 31-10-2894076, info@mbp.nl, http://www.mbp.nl/. Ed. Wim Danhof TEL 31-10-2894043. Pub. Suzanne Wanders. Adv. contact Stefan Prins. B&W page EUR 1,572, color page EUR 2,537; trim 210 x 297. Circ: 2,214.

668.4 NLD ISSN 1382-385X
KUNSTSTOF MAGAZINE. Text in Dutch. 1990. 9/yr. EUR 116 domestic; EUR 124 in Belgium (effective 2009). adv. illus. 48 p./no.; **Document type:** *Magazine, Trade.*
Indexed: R18.
—IE, Infotrieve.
Published by: (Nederlandse Federatie voor Kunststoffen/Netherlands Plastics Federation), Koggeschip Vakbladen B.V., Hettenheuvelweg 41-43, Postbus 1198, Amsterdam, 1000 BD, Netherlands. TEL 31-20-6916666, FAX 31-20-6960396, http://www.koggeschip-vakbladen.nl. Ed. Pierre D F van Daalen. Pub. Anthony van Trigt. adv.: B&W page EUR 1,870, color page EUR 3,165; trim 210 x 297. Circ: 4,079.

668.4 DEU ISSN 0075-7276
DIE KUNSTSTOFF-INDUSTRIE UND IHRE HELFER. Text in German. 1952. a. USD 51 (effective 2000). **Document type:** *Directory.*
Related titles: CD-ROM ed.; Online - full text ed.
Published by: Industrieschau-Verlagsgesellschaft mbH, Postfach 100262, Darmstadt, 64202, Germany. TEL 49-6151-3892-0, FAX 49-6151-33164. Ed., R&P Margit Selka. Circ: 11,000. **U.S. subscr. to:** Western Hemisphere Publishing Corp. TEL 503-640-3736, FAX 503-640-2748.

668.4 DEU ISSN 0930-7451
KUNSTSTOFF INFORMATION. Text in German. 1971. w. EUR 470 (effective 2011). adv. **Document type:** *Magazine, Trade.*
—**CCC.**
Published by: Kunststoff Information Verlagsgesellschaft mbH, Saalburgstr 157, Bad Homburg, 61350, Germany. TEL 49-6172-960610, FAX 49-6172-960699, info@kiweb.de.

668.4 DEU ISSN 1431-0554
KUNSTSTOFF-MAGAZIN. Text in German. 1962. 12/yr. EUR 92; EUR 16 newsstand/cover (effective 2010). adv. **Document type:** *Magazine, Trade.*
Former titles: Kunststoff-Magazin-Prodoc (0941-8520); Prodoc-Kunststoff-Magazin (0936-6113); Prodoc-Kunststoff-Technik (0170-0820)
Published by: Hoppenstedt Publishing GmbH, Havelstr 9, Darmstadt, 64295, Germany. TEL 49-6151-3800, FAX 49-6151-380360, info@hoppenstedt.de, http://www.hoppenstedt.de. Ed. Meinolf Droege. Adv. contact Heike Heckmann. Circ: 17,857 (controlled).

668.4 DEU ISSN 0172-6374
TP1101 CODEN: KUNSDY
KUNSTSTOFFBERATER. Text in German. 1955. m. EUR 130.50 domestic; EUR 133.50 foreign (effective 2010). adv. bk.rev. illus.; mkt. index. reprints avail. **Document type:** *Magazine, Trade.*
Former titles (until 1979): Kunststoffberater, -Rundschau, -Technik (0340-8442); (until 1975): Kunststoffberater (0023-5520); Which incorporated (1954-1974): Kunststoff Rundschau (0023-5555); (1962-1974): Kunststofftechnik (0023-5601); Which was formerly (until 1968): Kunststoff und Gummi (0375-9296)
Related titles: Microform ed.: (from PQC).
Indexed: A22, CIN, CISA, ChemAb, ChemTitl, IPackAb, Inspec, PST, R18, SCOPUS, TM.
—BLDSC (5130.940000), CASDDS, IE, Infotrieve, Ingenta, INIST, Linda Hall. **CCC.**
Published by: Giesel Verlag GmbH (Subsidiary of: Schluetersche Verlagsgesellschaft mbH und Co. KG), Rehkamp 3, Isernhagen, 30916, Germany. TEL 49-511-73040, FAX 49-511-7304157, giesel@giesel.de. Ed. Joachim Roenisch. Adv. contact Gero Trinkaus. Circ: 5,965 (paid and controlled).

668.4 DEU ISSN 0023-5563
CODEN: KUNSAV
KUNSTSTOFFE; Werkstoffe, Verarbeitung, Anwendung. Text in German. 1911. m. EUR 294 combined subscription (print & online eds.); EUR 24.80 newsstand/cover (effective 2011). adv. bk.rev. charts; illus.; mkt.; pat.; tr.lit. index. **Document type:** *Journal, Trade.*

P

Incorporates (1939-1943): Kunststoff-Technik und Kunststoff-Anwendung (0368-6965); Which was formed by the merger of (1933-1939): Kunststoff-Verarbeitung (0932-2396); (1937-1939): Oesterreichische Kunststoff-Rundschau (0369-7185); (1931-1939): Kunstharze und Andere Plastische Massen (0932-240X); Which was formerly (until 1938): Plastische Massen in Wissenschaft und Technik (0370-0739)
Related titles: Microform ed.: (from PMC); Online - full text ed.; ◆ English ed.: Kunststoffe International. ISSN 1862-4243.
Indexed: A22, CBNB, CEABA, CIN, CISA, ChemAb, ChemTitl, KES, PST, R18, RefZh, SCOPUS, TM, WSCA.
—CASDDS, IE, Infotrieve, Ingenta, INIST, Linda Hall. **CCC.**
Published by: Carl Hanser Verlag GmbH & Co. KG, Kolbergerstr 22, Munich, 81679, Germany. TEL 49-89-998300, FAX 49-89-984809, info@hanser.de. Ed. Gerhard Gotzmann. Adv. contact Heike Herchenroether-Rosenstein. Circ: 13,638 (paid and controlled).

668.4 DEU ISSN 0075-7292
KUNSTSTOFFE IM LEBENSMITTELVERKEHR. Text in German. 1962. 3 base vols. plus irreg. updates. EUR 128 base vol(s).; EUR 88 updates (effective 2009). **Document type:** *Bulletin, Trade.*
Published by: (Germany. Bundesinstitut fuer Gesundheitlichen Verbraucherschutz und Veterinaermedizin), Carl Heymanns Verlag KG (Subsidiary of: Wolters Kluwer Deutschland GmbH), Luxemburger Str 449, Cologne, 50939, Germany. TEL 49-221-943730, FAX 49-221-94373901, marketing@heymanns.com, http://www.heymanns.com.

668.4 DEU ISSN 1862-4243
TP1101 CODEN: KUPEE3
KUNSTSTOFFE INTERNATIONAL; magazine for plastics. Text in English. 1994. m. EUR 358; EUR 24.80 newsstand/cover (effective 2011). adv. **Document type:** *Magazine, Trade.*
Formerly (until 2006): Kunststoffe - Plast Europe (0945-0084); Which was formed by the merger of (199?-1994): Kunststoffe - German Plastics (0723-0192); (1992-1994): Plast Europe (0941-3596); Which was formerly (1989-1991): Kunststoffe Europe (0938-9849)
Related titles: ◆ German ed.: Kunststoffe. ISSN 0023-5563.
Indexed: A20, A22, A28, APA, ASCA, B03, BrCerAb, C&ISA, CA/WCA, CIA, CerAb, CivEngAb, CorrAb, E&CAJ, E11, EEA, EMA, ESPM, EngInd, EnvEAb, H15, IPackAb, ISMEC, Inspec, M&TEA, M09, MBF, METADEX, R18, SCOPUS, SolStAb, T04, WAA.
—IE, Infotrieve, Ingenta, INIST, Linda Hall. **CCC.**
Published by: Carl Hanser Verlag GmbH & Co. KG, Kolbergerstr 22, Munich, 81679, Germany. TEL 49-89-998300, FAX 49-89-984809, info@hanser.de. Ed. Gerhard Gotzmann. Adv. contact Heike Herchenroether-Rosenstein.

678.5 DEU ISSN 0175-6753
KUNSTSTOFFVERARBEITUNG DEUTSCHLAND. Text in German. 19??. a. EUR 12 (effective 2007). adv. **Document type:** *Directory, Trade.*
Published by: Kuhn Fachverlag GmbH & Co. KG, Bert-Brecht-Str 15-19, Villingen-Schwenningen, 78054, Germany. TEL 49-7720-3940, FAX 49-7720-394175, kataloge@kuhnverlag.de. Ed. Steffi Findeisen. Adv. contact Siegfried Girrbach. B&W page EUR 2,270, color page EUR 2,885. Circ: 5,778 (paid and controlled).

668.4 CHE ISSN 1664-3933
▼ **KUNSTSTOFFXTRA.** Text in German. 2011. 10/yr. CHF 38 (effective 2011). adv. **Document type:** *Magazine, Trade.*
Published by: SIGWERB GmbH, Unter Altstadt 10, Zug, 6301, Switzerland. TEL 41-41-7116111, info@sigwerb.com, http://www.sigwerb.com. Ed. Marianne Flury. Adv. contact Joerg Signer. Circ: 6,000 (paid).

LIQUID CRYSTALS; an international journal in the field of anisotropic fluids. *see* CHEMISTRY—Crystallography

668.4 669 USA
M C GILL DOORWAY MAGAZINE. Text in English. q.
Published by: M C Gill Corporation, 4056 Easy St, El Monte, CA 91731-1087. TEL 626-443-4022, FAX 626-350-5880, info@mcgillcorp.com.

668.4 ITA ISSN 0394-3453
MACPLAS; rivista mensile per l'industria delle materie plastiche e della gomma. Text in Italian. 1976. m. (10/yr.). EUR 50 domestic (effective 2009). **Document type:** *Magazine, Trade.* **Description:** Covers the plastics and rubber industries.
Related titles: Online - full text ed.; ◆ Russian ed.: Macplas International (Russian Edition); ◆ Italian ed.: Macplas International (Spanish Edition); ◆ Italian ed.: Macplas International (English Edition). ISSN 1826-9591.
Indexed: A28, APA, BrCerAb, C&ISA, CA/WCA, CBNB, CIA, CerAb, CivEngAb, CorrAb, E&CAJ, E11, EEA, EMA, ESPM, EnvEAb, H15, M&TEA, M09, MBF, METADEX, R18, RefZh, SolStAb, T04, WAA.
—BLDSC (5330.393700), Linda Hall.
Published by: Promaplast Srl, Centro Commerciale Milanofiori, Palazzo F3, Assago, MI 20090, Italy. TEL 39-02-8228371, FAX 39-02-57512490, macplas@macplas.it, http://www.macplas.it. Circ: 11,500.

668.4 ITA ISSN 1826-9591
MACPLAS INTERNATIONAL (ENGLISH EDITION); technical magazine for the plastics and rubber industry. Text in Italian. 1986. q. EUR 50 foreign (effective 2009). back issues avail. **Document type:** *Magazine, Trade.*
Related titles: ◆ Italian ed.: Macplas. ISSN 0394-3453; ◆ Italian ed.: Macplas International (Spanish Edition); ◆ Russian ed.: Macplas International (Russian Edition).
—BLDSC (5330.393750).
Published by: Promaplast Srl, Centro Commerciale Milanofiori, Palazzo F3, Assago, MI 20090, Italy. TEL 39-02-8228371, FAX 39-02-57512490, macplas@macplas.it, http://www.macplas.it. Circ: 21,000.

668.4 ITA
MACPLAS INTERNATIONAL (RUSSIAN EDITION). Text in Russian. s-a. EUR 15 foreign (effective 2009). **Document type:** *Magazine, Trade.* **Description:** Covers the plastics and rubber industries.
Related titles: ◆ Italian ed.: Macplas. ISSN 0394-3453; ◆ Italian ed.: Macplas International (Spanish Edition); ◆ Italian ed.: Macplas International (English Edition). ISSN 1826-9591.
Published by: Promaplast Srl, Centro Commerciale Milanofiori, Palazzo F3, Assago, MI 20090, Italy. TEL 39-02-8228371, FAX 39-02-57512490, macplas@macplas.it, http://www.macplas.it.

668.4 ITA
MACPLAS INTERNATIONAL (SPANISH EDITION); revista tecnica para la industria de materias plasticas y del caucho. Text in Italian. s-a. EUR 15 foreign (effective 2009). **Document type:** *Magazine, Trade.*
Related titles: ◆ Italian ed.: Macplas. ISSN 0394-3453; ◆ Russian ed.: Macplas International (Russian Edition); ◆ Italian ed.: Macplas International (English Edition). ISSN 1826-9591.
Published by: Promaplast Srl, Centro Commerciale Milanofiori, Palazzo F3, Assago, MI 20090, Italy. TEL 39-02-8228371, FAX 39-02-57512490, macplas@macplas.it, http://www.macplas.it. Circ: 6,000.

668.4 MYS ISSN 1823-7789
➤ **MALAYSIAN POLYMER JOURNAL.** Text in English. 2006. s-a. free. **Document type:** *Journal, Academic/Scholarly.*
Media: Online - full text.
Published by: Plastics and Rubber Institute Malaysia, 20 Jalan U5 / 28, Mah Sing Integrated Industrial Park, Shah Alam, Selangor Darul Ehsan 40150, Malaysia. primy@prim.org.my, http://www.prim.org.my/. Ed. Azman Hassan.

668.4 ROM ISSN 0025-5289
TP1101 CODEN: MPLAAM
➤ **MATERIALE PLASTICE.** Key Title: Revista Materiale Plastice. Text in Romanian; Summaries in English, German. 1964. q. adv. bk.rev. abstr.; bibl.; charts; illus.; pat.; stat. index. 70 p./no.; back issues avail. **Document type:** *Journal, Academic/Scholarly.*
Indexed: A22, A28, APA, ASCA, BrCerAb, C&ISA, CA/WCA, CIA, CISA, CerAb, ChemAb, ChemTitl, CivEngAb, CorrAb, E&CAJ, E11, EEA, EMA, H15, M&TEA, M09, MBF, METADEX, MSCI, R18, SCI, SCOPUS, SolStAb, T04, W07, WAA.
—CASDDS, Ingenta, INIST, Linda Hall.
Published by: Syscom 18 s.r.l., Calea Plevnei 139B, Bucharest, 77131, Romania. http://www.bch.ro. Ed., Adv. contact Carmen Mihaela Ioan. Circ: 1,000.

670.941 GBR ISSN 1752-7473
MATERIALS K T N FOCUS. (Knowledge Trasnfer Network) Text in English. 2006 (Apr.). q. **Document type:** *Magazine, Trade.*
Published by: (Institute of Materials, Minerals and Mining), Materials Knowledge Transfer Network, The Institute of Materials, Minerals and Mining, 1 Carlton House Ter, London, SW1Y 5DB, United Kingdom. materials.ktn@iom3.org, http://amf.globalwatchonline.com/.

MATERIALS TECHNOLOGY; advanced performance materials. *see* METALLURGY

668.4 ITA ISSN 0025-5459
TP1101 CODEN: MPELAK
MATERIE PLASTICHE ED ELASTOMERI. Text mainly in Italian; Summaries in English. 1934. m. (11/yr.). Website rev. abstr.; bibl.; charts; illus.; pat.; stat. **Document type:** *Magazine, Trade.*
Related titles: CD-ROM ed.
Indexed: A22, ChemAb, R18.
—BLDSC (5399.010000), IE, Infotrieve, Ingenta, INIST, Linda Hall.
Published by: O.Ve.S.T. Srl, Via Simone D'Orsenigo 22, Milan, MI 20135, Italy. TEL 39-02-5469174, FAX 39-02-55185263, redampe@ovest.it. Ed. Carlo Latorre. Pub. Ugo Carutti. Circ: 6,000.

METALLIZED PLASTICS; fundamental and applied aspects. *see* CHEMISTRY—Electrochemistry

MICROSPHERES, MICROCAPSULES & LIPOSOMES. *see* PHARMACY AND PHARMACOLOGY

668.4 745.5 AUS ISSN 1445-0143
MODELART AUSTRALIA. Text in English. 1988. bi-m. AUD 6.95 newsstand/cover (effective 2009). back issues avail. **Document type:** *Magazine, Trade.* **Description:** Contains a mix of modelling & reference material and reviews covering all modelling genres, reference and aftermarket products, with a small section devoted to diecast modelling.
Formerly (until 2001): Plastics Modeller (1031-9824)
Published by: ModelArt Australia, PO Box 4045, Ringwood, VIC 3134, Australia. TEL 61-3-98122955. Ed. Frank Morgan.

668.4 CAN
MODERN MATERIALS. Text in English. s-a. free with subscr. to Construction Specifier. **Document type:** *Magazine, Trade.* **Description:** Dedicated to providing the facts regarding plastics and plastics-based building materials and to proving that they are sustainable, energy-efficient and can be successfully incorporated into green design.
Related titles: ◆ Supplement to: The Construction Specifier. ISSN 0010-6925.
Indexed: APA, C&ISA, CIA, CorrAb, E&CAJ, EEA, SolStAb, WAA.
Published by: (American Plastics Council USA), Kenilworth Media Inc., 15 Wertheim Ct, Ste 710, Richmond Hill, ON L4B 3H7, Canada. TEL 905-771-7333, 800-409-8688, FAX 905-771-7336, production@kenilworth.com, http://www.kenilworth.com.

668.4 USA ISSN 1554-8589
TP986.A1
MODERN PLASTICS WORLDWIDE; setting the standards in plastics distribution. Abbreviated title: M P W. Text in English. 2005 (Jan.). m. USD 59 domestic; USD 110 in Canada; USD 150 elsewhere; free to qualified personnel (effective 2008). adv. back issues avail. **Document type:** *Magazine, Consumer.* **Description:** Provides information on the plastics industry from both a global perspective and a strategic viewpoint.
Formed by the merger of (1934-2004): Modern Plastics (0026-8275); Which was formerly (until 1934): Plastic Products (0096-9141); (1971-2004): Modern Plastics International (0026-8283)
Related titles: Online - full text ed.
Indexed: A05, A22, A28, APA, AS&TA, AS&TI, B02, B04, B15, B17, B18, BrCerAb, C&ISA, C10, C13, CA/WCA, CIA, CerAb, CivEngAb, CorrAb, E&CAJ, E11, EEA, EMA, ESPM, EngInd, EnvEAb, G04, G06, G07, G08, H15, I05, M&TEA, M09, MBF, METADEX, P48, PQC, SCOPUS, SolStAb, T02, T04, WAA.
—BLDSC (5892.280000), IE, Ingenta, INIST, Linda Hall. **CCC.**
Published by: Canon Communications LLC (Subsidiary of: Apprise Media LLC), 11444 W Olympic Blvd, Ste 900, Los Angeles, CA 90064. TEL 310-445-4200, FAX 310-445-4299, info@cancom.com, http://www.cancom.com. Eds. Tony Deligio, Matt Defosse. adv.: B&W page USD 8,590, color page USD 9,380; trim 7.875 x 10.75. Circ: 61,240.

660.2 USA
TP1101
MODERN PLASTICS WORLDWIDE WORLD ENCYCLOPEDIA, WITH BUYER'S GUIDE. (Special Oct. issue of: Modern Plastics) Text in English. 1925. a. USD 57; included with subscr. to Modern Plastics. adv. illus. **Document type:** *Handbook/Manual/Guide, Trade.*
Former titles (until 2004): Modern Plastics World Encyclopedia (1539-4344); (until 2000): Modern Plastics Encyclopedia & Buyer's Guide; (until 1993): Modern Plastics Encyclopedia (0085-3518); (until 1965): Modern Plastics Encyclopedia Issue; (until 1953): Modern Plastics Encyclopedia and Engineer's Handbook; (until 1949): Modern Plastics Encyclopedia; (until 1945): Plastics Catalog; (until 1941): Modern Plastics Catalog
—Infotrieve, INIST. **CCC.**
Published by: Canon Communications LLC (Subsidiary of: Apprise Media LLC), 11444 W Olympic Blvd, Ste 900, Los Angeles, CA 90064. TEL 310-445-4200, FAX 310-445-4299, info@cancom.com, http://www.cancom.com. adv.: B&W page USD 7,290, color page USD 10,110; trim 11.13 x 8.38. Circ: 48,700.

668.4 HUN ISSN 0027-2914
CODEN: MUGUAO
MUANYAG ES GUMI/PLASTICS AND RUBBER. Text in Hungarian; Summaries in English, French, German, Russian. 1964. m. adv. bk.rev. bibl.; charts; illus.; mkt. index. 40 p./no.; **Document type:** *Journal, Academic/Scholarly.* **Description:** Covers testing methods, apparatus of rubbers, plastics, composite materials, processing and functional characteristics.
Indexed: A22, CIN, ChemAb, ChemTitl, HBB, R18, SCOPUS.
—BLDSC (5980.910000), CASDDS, IE, Ingenta, INIST, Linda Hall.
Published by: Gepipari Tudomanyos Egyesulet/Scientific Society of Mechanical Engineering, Fo utca 68, PF 337, Budapest, 1027, Hungary. TEL 36-1-2020656, FAX 36-1-2020252, mail.gte@mtesz.hu, http://www.gte.mtesz.hu. Eds. Gyula Toth, Levante Macskasi. Circ: 1,200. **Co-sponsor:** Magyar Kemikusok Egyesulete/Hungarian Chemical Society.

668.4 ESP ISSN 1887-8067
MUNDO PLAST; revista profesional del plastico y sus tecnologias. Text in Spanish. 2005. q. EUR 75 domestic; EUR 135 foreign (effective 2009). back issues avail. **Document type:** *Magazine, Trade.*
Published by: E T D Prensa Profesional, SA, Sicilia 95, Atico, Barcelona, 08013, Spain. TEL 34-93-5569500, FAX 34-93-5569560, http://www.etd.es. Ed. Javier Gomex.

668.4 FIN ISSN 0788-8430
MUOVI - PLAST. Text in Finnish. 1958. 8/yr. EUR 80 domestic; EUR 95 foreign (effective 2005). adv. bk.rev. **Document type:** *Bulletin, Trade.*
Formerly (until 1989): Muoviyhdistys Tiedottaa (0357-2196)
Published by: Muoviyhdistys ry/Finnish Plastics Association, Paelkaeneentic 18, Helsinki, 00510, Finland. TEL 358-9-868-9910, FAX 358-9-868-99115. Ed. Hannele Heikkila. Adv. contact Paivi Ritolammi. page EUR 1,650; 185 x 185.26. Circ: 1,800.

668.4 USA
N P E ADVISOR. Text in English. bi-m. back issues avail. **Document type:** *Magazine, Consumer.*
Media: E-mail.
Published by: Canon Communications LLC (Subsidiary of: Apprise Media LLC), 11444 W Olympic Blvd, Ste 900, Los Angeles, CA 90064. TEL 310-445-4200, FAX 310-445-4299, info@cancom.com, http://www.cancom.com. Ed. Jeff Sloan TEL 719-647-9772.

668.4 630 USA ISSN 1073-1768
NATIONAL AGRICULTURAL PLASTICS CONGRESS. PROCEEDINGS. Text in English. 1960. irreg., latest vol.28, 1999. price varies. **Document type:** *Proceedings.* **Description:** Papers presented at Congress on university research on effect of agricultural plastics on crop production.
Formerly: National Agricultural Plastics Association. Proceedings
Published by: American Society for Plasticulture, 526 Brittany Dr, State College, PA 16803. TEL 814-238-7045, FAX 814-238-7051. Ed., Pub., R&P, Adv. contact Patricia E Heuser. Circ: 350.

668.4 JPN
NEW MATERIALS DEVELOPED IN JAPAN (YEAR). Text in Japanese. 1984. irreg., latest 1991. USD 1,250. **Description:** Includes information on 379 new materials developed in Japan from April 1987 to March 1991.
Published by: Toray Research Center Inc., 3-1-8 Nihonbashimuro-Machi, Chuo-ku, Tokyo, 103-0022, Japan. TEL 81-3-3245-5895, FAX 81-3-3245-5789, TELEX J22623 TRC JA.

668.3 JPN ISSN 0916-4812
TP967 CODEN: NSEGE7
NIHON SETCHAKU GAKKAISHI/JOUNAL OF ADHESION. Text in English, Japanese. 1965. m. free to members. adv. bk.rev. abstr.; charts; illus.; pat. Index. **Document type:** *Journal, Academic/Scholarly.*
Formerly (until 1990): Nihon Setchaku Kyokaishi (0001-8201)
Indexed: A22, INIS AtomInd, JTA, RefZh.
—BLDSC (4676.300000), CASDDS, IE, Ingenta, Linda Hall. **CCC.**
Published by: Nihon Setchaku Gakkai/Adhesion Society of Japan, Koa Nipponbashi 203, 4-2-20 Nipponbashi, Naniwa-ku, Osaka-shi, 556-0005, Japan. TEL 81-6-66347561, FAX 81-6-66347563, adhesion@mist.ocn.ne.jp.

668.4 ARG ISSN 0325-0407
NOTICIERO DEL PLASTICO. Text in Spanish. 1959. m. ARS 150 (effective 1998). adv. bk.rev. bibl.; stat. back issues avail. **Description:** Covers plastics and rubber, machines, technology, design, analysis of markets, tests, events and reports.
Published by: Today S.A., Talcahuano, 342 Pb 4, Buenos Aires, 1013, Argentina. TEL 54-114-3754458, FAX 54-114-3754458. Ed. Graciela Pancotto. Circ: 5,000.

668.4 AUT
TP1101 CODEN: OKZSAV
OESTERREICHISCHE KUNSTSTOFF ZEITSCHRIFT. Text in German. 1970. bi-m. EUR 55.30 domestic; EUR 66.50 foreign (effective 2005). adv. bk.rev. illus.; pat.; stat. **Document type:** *Journal, Trade.*
Formerly: Oesterreichische Kunststoff Zeitung (0029-926X)
Indexed: A22, CIN, ChemAb, ChemTitl, RefZh.
—BLDSC (6307.850000), CASDDS, IE, Ingenta.

Published by: (Gesellschaft zur Foerderung der Kunststofftechnik), Verlag Lorenz, Ebendorferstr 10, Vienna, W 1010, Austria. TEL 43-1-40566950, FAX 43-1-4068693, office@verlag-lorenz.at. Ed. Robert Hillisch. Adv. contact Elfriede Wernicke. B&W page EUR 1,880, color page EUR 3,230; trim 184 x 265. Circ: 2,500.

668.4 USA
OXYCHEM NEWSBRIEFS. Text in English. 1930. q. free. adv.
Former titles: Durez Molder Newsbriefs; Durez Molder (0012-7264)
Published by: Occidental Chemical Corp., Durez Division, 528 Walck Rd, North Tonawanda, NY 14120. TEL 716-696-6000. Circ: 6,000.

668.4 USA ISSN 1094-656X
P E L PLASTICS UPDATE. Text in English. 1994. bi-m. looseleaf. USD 160 domestic; USD 185 foreign (effective 2001). adv. abstr.; pat. index. 5 p./no. 1 cols./p.; back issues avail. **Document type:** *Newsletter, Trade.* **Description:** Highlights progress in polymer and plastics technology, including catalysis, biopolymers, smart-functional polymers, alloys and blends, nanotechnology, polymer modifications and new ventures and alliances.
Related titles: E-mail ed.; Fax ed.; Online - full text ed.
Published by: P E L Associates, 1084 Shennecossett Rd, University of Connecticut, Avery Point, Groton, CT 06340. TEL 860-448-6522, FAX 860-448-6522. Ed., R&P, Adv. contact Morton L Wallach. Circ: 540.

668.4 USA
P M & F ILLUSTRATED BUYING GUIDE. (Plastics Machining & Fabricating) Text in English. a. **Document type:** *Directory, Trade.* **Description:** Lists products and services offered by manufacturers and distributors of molders, materials, fabricating equipment and other secondary processing needs.
Published by: Vance Publishing Corp., 400 Knightsbridge Pkwy, Lincolnshire, IL 60069. TEL 847-634-2600, FAX 847-634-4379, info@vancepublishing.com, http://www.vancepublishing.com.

P M S E PREPRINTS. (Polymeric Materials Science and Engineering) *see* CHEMISTRY—Organic Chemistry

668.4 USA
P M - U S A THE GREEN SHEET. Text in English. 1972. m. USD 35 domestic; USD 50 in Canada & Mexico; USD 100 elsewhere (effective 2000); USD 5 newsstand/cover. adv. **Document type:** *Newsletter.* **Description:** For the plastics, packaging and rubber processing industries.
Published by: Marketing Handbooks, Inc., 7094 Skyline Dr, Delray Beach, FL 33446-2212. TEL 561-498-7660, FAX 561-495-5278. Pub. Leon R Noe. Adv. contact Holly M Pastor. B&W page USD 1,600; trim 10 x 7.25. Circ: 8,000 (paid).

668.4 MEX
PANORAMA PLASTICO; la revista mexicana del plastico. Text in Spanish. 1984. m. MXN 84,000, USD 95. bk.rev. back issues avail. **Description:** Provides technical information on the plastics industry in Mexico.
Published by: Editorial Corso S.A. de C.V., INSURGENTES SUR 594-502, Col Del Valle, Mexico City, DF 03100, Mexico. TEL 669-30-87, FAX 523-22-03. Ed. Carlos Moreno. Circ: 10,000.

PAPER, FILM AND FOIL CONVERTER. *see* PACKAGING

THE PLACE. *see* PAPER AND PULP

668.4 ITA ISSN 0391-7401
CODEN: PLATDW
PLAST; rivista delle materie plastiche. Text in Italian; Summaries in English. 1970. 11/yr. EUR 49 domestic; EUR 78 foreign (effective 2009). adv. bk.rev. abstr.; bibl.; charts; illus.; pat.; stat. **Document type:** *Magazine, Trade.*
Indexed: A28, APA, BrCerAb, C&ISA, CA/WCA, CIA, CerAb, ChemAb, CivEngAb, CorrAb, E&CAJ, E11, EEA, EMA, H15, M&TEA, M09, MBF, METADEX, SolStAb, T04, WAA.
—CASDDS, Linda Hall.
Published by: Reed Business Information Spa (Subsidiary of: Reed Business Information International), Viale Giulio Richard 1, Milan, 20143, Italy. TEL 39-02-818301, FAX 39-02-81830406, info@reedbusiness.it, http://www.reedbusiness.it. Circ: 8,000.

668.4 ESP ISSN 1131-7515
PLAST 21. Text in Spanish. 1991. 9/yr. EUR 84 domestic; EUR 109 in Europe; EUR 175 elsewhere (effective 2009). **Document type:** *Magazine, Consumer.*
Related titles: Online - full text ed.
Indexed: R18.
—BLDSC (6528.795500).
Published by: Ediciones Tecnicas Izaro S.A., Mazustegui, 21, 3a planta, Bilbao, Vizcaya 48006, Spain. TEL 34-94-4487110, FAX 34-94-4162743, izaro@izaro.com, http://www.izaro.com/izaro_2005/index.php.

668.4 DNK ISSN 0106-1720
CODEN: PLPSD2
PLAST PANORAMA SCANDINAVIA. Text in Danish. 1950. m. DKK 856 (effective 2010). adv. **Document type:** *Magazine, Trade.* **Description:** Provides information about plastic raw materials, products and production methods for the industries processing and using plastics in Scandinavia.
Formerly (until 1979): Plastic (0032-1044)
Related titles: Online - full text ed.: 2007.
Indexed: IPackAb.
—CASDDS.
Published by: (Plastindustrien i Danmark/Association of Danish Plastics Industries), TechMedia A/S, Naverland 35, Glostrup, 2600, Denmark. TEL 45-43-242628, FAX 45-43-242626, info@techmedia.dk. Ed. Jan Cederberg TEL 45-43242601. Adv. contact Anne-Mette Broedsgaard TEL 45-43-242677. B&W page DKK 21,800, color page DKK 26,300; 260 x 175. Circ: 3,289 (controlled). **Co-sponsor:** Plast-Industriens Arbejdsgiverforening/Plastic Industry's Employers' Association.

668.4 SWE
PLASTER. Text in Swedish. 1969. biennial. SEK 160 (effective 2001). **Document type:** *Journal, Trade.*
Published by: Plast- och Kemibranscherna, Box 5501, Stockholm, 114 85, Sweden. FAX 46-8-411-45-26, info@plast-kemi.se, http://www.plast-kemi.se.

668.4 678 SWE ISSN 1653-557X
PLASTFORUM. Text in Swedish. 1999. 11/yr. SEK 924 domestic print ed.; SEK 1,155 domestic print & online eds.; SEK 1,124 foreign print ed.; SEK 1,355 foreign print & online eds.; SEK 693 online ed. (effective 2007). adv. **Document type:** *Magazine, Trade.*
Formerly (until 2003): Plastforum Nordica (1404-8469); Which was formed by the merger of (1982-1999): Plast Nordica (0281-0328); Which incorporates (1986-1991): Gumminytt Nordica (0282-9975); (1970-1999): Plastforum (1104-1501); Which was formerly (until 1992): Plastforum Scandinavia (0347-8262); (until 1977): Plastforum (0048-4369)
Related titles: Online - full text ed.
Indexed: A28, APA, BrCerAb, C&ISA, CA/WCA, CIA, CerAb, CivEngAb, CorrAb, E&CAJ, E11, EEA, EMA, H15, M&TEA, M09, MBF, METADEX, SolStAb, T04, WAA.
—Linda Hall.
Published by: Mentor Online AB, Landskronawaegen 1, PO Box 601, Helsingborg, 25106, Sweden. info@mentoronline.se, http://www.mentoronline.se. Ed. Peter Schulz TEL 46-42-4901901. Adv. contacts Agneta Gullberg TEL 46-42-1901955, Beth Holmkvist. color page SEK 28,100; trim 191 x 251. Circ: 4,600 (paid and controlled).

668.4 NOR ISSN 0809-5469
PLASTFORUM. Text in Norwegian. 1997. 11/yr. NOK 350 (effective 2003). adv.
Related titles: Online - full text ed.
Published by: Mentor Online AS (Subsidiary of: Mentor Online AB), Brugata 14, PO Box 9231, Groenland, Oslo, 0134, Norway. TEL 47-23-163430, FAX 47-23-163431. Ed. Asle Isakson TEL 47-23-163439. Adv. contact Erik Sigurdsson TEL 47-23-163434. B&W page NOK 11,300, color page NOK 14,900; 177 x 257. Circ: 3,200.

PLASTICHEM. *see* ENGINEERING—Chemical Engineering

668.4 RUS ISSN 0554-2901
CODEN: PLMSAI
PLASTICHESKIE MASSY/JOURNAL OF THE PLASTIC COMPOUNDS. Text in Russian. 1959. m. USD 189 foreign (effective 2005). **Document type:** *Journal, Trade.* **Description:** Covers production processes in the manufacture of plastics.
Indexed: C33, ChemAb, ChemTitl, R18, SCOPUS.
—BLDSC (0129.660000), CASDDS, East View, INIST. **CCC.**
Address: ul 8 Marta, 13-82, Moscow, 125319, Russian Federation. Ed. V V Kovriga. Circ: 900. **Dist. by:** East View Information Services, 10601 Wayzata Blvd, Minneapolis, MN 55305. TEL 952-252-1201, 800-477-1005, FAX 952-252-1202, info@eastview.com, http://www.eastview.com.

668.4 BRA ISSN 0102-1931
HD9661.B72 CODEN: PLMOEA
PLASTICO MODERNO. Text in Portuguese. 1971. m. USD 250 (effective 2000). adv. bk.rev. charts; illus. back issues avail. **Document type:** *Trade.* **Description:** Deals with the Brazilian plastics industry, its producers, manufacturers and customers. Also covers the rubber industry, new materials and processing, technology and application.
Related titles: Online - full text ed.
Indexed: B03, CBNB.
Published by: Editora Q D Ltda., Rua Conselheiro Brotero, 589 Cj 11-1o Andar, B Funda, Sao Paulo, SP 01154-001, Brazil. TEL 55-11-826-6899, FAX 55-11-825-8192. Eds. Denisard Gerila da Silva Pinto, Emanuel Fairbanks. Pub. Denisard Gerola da Silva Pinto. Adv. contact Rogerio Barbato. B&W page USD 3,290, color page USD 5,300. Circ: 12,000.

668.4 BRA ISSN 0032-1133
CODEN: PLRVBJ
PLASTICOS EM REVISTA. Text in Portuguese. 1962. m. BRL 45, USD 300. adv. bk.rev. abstr.; charts; illus.; mkt.; stat.; tr.lit. **Document type:** *Consumer.* **Description:** For the plastics products and raw materials industry.
Related titles: Online - full text ed.
Indexed: B03, C01, CBNB, ChemAb, PST.
—CASDDS, Linda Hall.
Published by: Editora Definicao Ltda., Rua Piaui, 1164, Casas 7 e 8, Higienopolis, Sao Paulo, SP 01241-000, Brazil. TEL 55-11-36678124, FAX 55-11-36660496. Ed., Pub. Helio Helman. Adv. contact Beatriz Demello Helman. B&W page USD 2,669, color page USD 4,922; 280 x 210. Circ: 10,000.

668.4 COL ISSN 0120-8624
PLASTICOS EN COLOMBIA. Text in Spanish. 1957. a. USD 65. adv.
Formerly (until 1968): Acoplasticos
Published by: Asociacion Colombiana de Industrias Plasticas Acoplasticos, Calle 69 No. 5-33, Bogota, CUND, Colombia.

668.4 ESP ISSN 0303-4011
CODEN: PLUVBY
PLASTICOS UNIVERSALES. Text in Spanish. 1957. 9/yr. EUR 86.21 domestic; EUR 190 foreign (effective 2007). adv. charts; illus.; mkt.; pat.; tr.lit. index.
Formerly (until 1974): Kunststoffe - Plasticos (0023-558X)
Indexed: ChemAb, IPackAb.
—CCC.
Published by: Nova Agora S.L., Amadeu Vives, 20-22, Molins De Rei, Barcelona 08750, Spain. TEL 34-93-6802027, FAX 34-93-6802031, http://www.interempresas.net. Circ: 4,000.

660 USA ISSN 0192-1789
PLASTICS. Text in English. 1974. bi-m. USD 15 to qualified personnel. adv. bk.rev.
Formerly: Western Plastics
Indexed: AIAP.
Published by: Western Plastics News Inc., 1704 Colorado Ave, Santa Monica, CA 90404-3410. TEL 213-829-4876. Ed. Aida Pavletich. Circ: 20,000.

688.4 GBR ISSN 1464-391X
TP1142
PLASTICS, ADDITIVES AND COMPOUNDING. Text in English. 1999. bi-m. EUR 570 in Europe to institutions; JPY 75,400 in Japan to institutions; USD 638 elsewhere to institutions (effective 2010). adv. back issues avail.; reprints avail. **Document type:** *Journal, Academic/Scholarly.* **Description:** Contains information on technical additives and pigments and their incorporation into compounds and masterbatches.
Related titles: Online - full text ed.: ISSN 1873-2275 (from IngentaConnect).
Indexed: A01, A03, A08, A26, CA, CPEI, EngInd, I05, R18, RefZh, S01, SCOPUS, T02.
—BLDSC (6531.250000), IE, Infotrieve, Ingenta. **CCC.**
Published by: Elsevier Advanced Technology (Subsidiary of: Elsevier Science & Technology), The Blvd, Langford Ln, Kidlington, Oxon OX5 1GB, United Kingdom. TEL 44-1865-843434, FAX 44-1865-843970, eatsales@elsevier.co.uk, http://www.elsevier.com. Ed. Mark Holmes TEL 44-1865-843441. Adv. contact Mark Sherman TEL 44-1865-843208.

668.4 USA ISSN 1530-2393
PLASTICS ADVISOR. Text in English. 2000 (Sep.). bi-w. back issues avail. **Document type:** *Newsletter, Trade.* **Description:** Covers plastics and competitive materials and provides a concise presentation of need to know information.
Related titles: Online - full text ed.: ISSN 1530-2407; Special ed(s).: Plastics Advisor. Sourceguide.
—Linda Hall.
Published by: Technical Insights (Subsidiary of: Frost & Sullivan), 7550 IH 10 W, Ste 400, San Antonio, TX 78229. TEL 210-348-1000, 877-463-7678, FAX 888-690-3329, myfrost@frost.com, http://www.frost.com/prod/servlet/ti-home.pag.

660 JPN ISSN 0551-0503
HD9661.J3 CODEN: PUEJDH
PLASTICS AGE/PURASUCHIKKUSU EJI. Text in Japanese; Summaries in English. 1954. m. JPY 21,000. adv. bk.rev. stat. Supplement avail. **Document type:** *Academic/Scholarly.*
Indexed: A28, APA, BrCerAb, C&ISA, CA/WCA, CIA, CIN, CerAb, ChemAb, ChemTitl, CivEngAb, CorrAb, E&CAJ, E11, EEA, EMA, ESPM, EnvEAb, H15, M&TEA, M09, MBF, METADEX, SolStAb, T04, WAA.
—BLDSC (6531.300000), CASDDS, IE, Ingenta, Linda Hall.
Published by: Plastics Age Co. Ltd./Purasuchikkuse Eji K. K., Okochi Bldg, 1-10-6 Kaji-cho, Chiyoda-ku, Tokyo, 101-0044, Japan. Ed. Takahiro Asayama. Pub. Eiichi Asayama. Adv. contact K Kenji. Circ: 27,000.

668.4 JPN
PLASTICS AGE ENCYCLOPEDIA. Text in English. irreg. JPY 6,300 newsstand/cover (effective 2005). **Document type:** *Monographic series, Trade.*
Published by: Plastics Age Co. Ltd./Purasuchikkuse Eji K. K., Okochi Bldg, 1-10-6 Kaji-cho, Chiyoda-ku, Tokyo, 101-0044, Japan. TEL 86-6-65325484.

668.4 678.2 GBR ISSN 1360-1245
PLASTICS AND RUBBER ASIA. Abbreviated title: P R A. Text in English. 1985. 8/yr. GBP 150, USD 305; free to qualified personnel (effective 2010). adv. bk.rev. back issues avail. **Document type:** *Magazine, Trade.* **Description:** Presents technical information for the processors of plastics and rubber in the Pacific Rim area.
Formerly (until 1995): Polymers and Rubber Asia (0268-9812)
Related titles: Online - full text ed.: free (effective 2010); ◆ Supplement(s): Injection Moulding Asia. ISSN 1462-0278; Rubber Journal Asia.
Indexed: B03, B11, CBNB, PROMT, R18.
—BLDSC (6531.453300).
Published by: Airports Publishing Network, The Stables, Willow Ln, Paddock Wood, Kent TN12 6PF, United Kingdom. TEL 44-1892-839202, FAX 44-1892-839210. Pub. Tim Ornellas TEL 44-1892-839209. adv.: B&W page USD 4,500, color page USD 6,200; trim 210 x 276. Circ: 14,079.

668.4 678.2 GBR ISSN 1356-7152
HD9661.A1
PLASTICS & RUBBER WEEKLY. Abbreviated title: P R W. Text in English. 1964. bi-w. GBP 85 domestic; GBP 110 in Europe; GBP 130 elsewhere; free domestic to qualified personnel (effective 2010). adv. illus.; mkt.; pat.; stat.; tr.mk. reprints avail. **Document type:** *Magazine, Trade.* **Description:** Contains articles relevant to the plastics and rubber industries.
Formerly (until 1989): Plastics and Rubber Weekly (0032-1168); Which superseded in part (in 1964): Rubber & Plastics Weekly (0370-6745); Which was formerly (until 1961): Rubber Journal and International Plastics (0370-5854); (until 1957): Rubber Journal (0035-9505); (until 1955): The India Rubber Journal (0367-9985); (until 1911): India-Rubber and Gutta-Percha and Electrical Trades Journal
Related titles: Microfilm ed.: (from PQC); Online - full text ed.
Indexed: A28, APA, BrCerAb, C&ISA, CA/WCA, CBNB, CIA, CerAb, ChemAb, CivEngAb, CorrAb, E&CAJ, E11, EEA, EMA, ESPM, EnvEAb, H15, IPackAb, M&TEA, M09, MBF, METADEX, PROMT, R18, SolStAb, T04, WAA, WSCA, WasteInfo.
—BLDSC (6531.460000), CIS, INIST, Linda Hall. **CCC.**
Published by: Crain Communications, Ltd., Carolyn House, 4th Fl, Ste 1, 26 Dingwall Rd, Croydon, CR0 9XF, United Kingdom. TEL 44-20-82539600, http://www.crain.co.uk. Ed. David Eldridge TEL 44-20-82539610. Adv. contact Matt Barber TEL 44-20-82539628. page GBP 4,600, page EUR 6,000, page USD 8,300; trim 248 x 342.

668.4 HKG ISSN 1024-462X
PLASTICS BULLETIN. Text in Chinese. 1978. bi-m. HKD 170; HKD 30 newsstand/cover. adv. **Document type:** *Bulletin.* **Description:** Provides up-to-date information to designers, engineers, technical management and approved authorities in industrial and scientific establishments concerned with the plastics industry.
Published by: Hong Kong Productivity Council, HKPC Bldg, 78 Tat Chee Ave, Kowloon, Hong Kong. TEL 852-2788-5950, FAX 852-2788-5959. Ed. Vincent Shin. adv.: B&W page HKD 3,400, color page HKD 5,800. Circ: 5,000.

668.4 USA
PLASTICS COMPOUNDING REDBOOK; for resign producers, formulators, and compounders. Text in English. 1981. a. adv. charts; illus. 200 p./no.; back issues avail.; reprints avail. **Document type:** *Directory, Trade.* **Description:** Contains everything compounders, formulators and resin producers need for locating suppliers of compounding ingredients, equipment and services vital to the compounding function.
Published by: Advanstar Communications, Inc., 6200 Canoga Ave, 2nd Fl, Woodland Hills, CA 91367. TEL 818-593-5000, FAX 818-593-5020, info@advanstar.com, http://www.advanstar.com. Pub. Jill Trupo. R&P Maureen Cannon TEL 440-891-2742. Adv. contact Matt Simoni TEL 440-891-3104.

668.4 USA
PLASTICS CONFERENCE PROCEEDINGS (YEAR). Text in English. 1976. a. USD 375 (effective 2005). back issues avail. **Document type:** *Proceedings.*
Formerly: Conference on Contingency Planning for Plastics. Proceedings

P

Related titles: Microfiche ed.; Microfilm ed.
Published by: Business Communications Co., Inc., 40 Washington St, Ste 110, Wellesley, MA 02481. TEL 781-489-7301, FAX 781-489-7308, sales@bccresearch.com, http://www.bccresearch.com. Ed. Louis Naturman.

668.4 USA
THE PLASTICS DISTRIBUTOR & FABRICATOR MAGAZINE. Text in English. 1980. bi-m. USD 50 out of North America. adv. bk.rev. back issues avail. **Document type:** *Magazine, Trade.* **Description:** For plastic distributors, fabricators and equipment manufacturers.
Formerly: Plastics Distributor
Related titles: CD-ROM ed.; Diskette ed.; Online - full text ed.
Published by: P M D Publishing Inc., 4535 W. Fullerton Ave., Chicago, IL 60639-1933. TEL 773-235-3800, FAX 773-235-7204. Ed., Pub., R&P Harry Greenwald. Adv. contact Brenda Kolar. B&W page USD 2,475, color page USD 2,875; trim 11 x 8.5. Circ: 28,000 (controlled).

668.4 USA ISSN 0091-9578
TP1101 CODEN: PLEGBB
PLASTICS ENGINEERING. Text in English. 1944. m. GBP 133 in United Kingdom to institutions; EUR 169 in Europe to institutions; USD 161 in United States to institutions; USD 261 elsewhere to institutions (effective 2012). adv. bk.rev. charts; illus.; pat.; stat. index. back issues avail.; reprint service avail. from PSC. **Document type:** *Magazine, Trade.* **Description:** Publishes articles on chemistry, manufacture, molding, extrusion, design, testing, and other phases of the plastics industry including machinery operations.
Former titles (until 1973): S P E Journal (0036-1844); (until 1949): S P E News; (until 1946): S P E News Bulletin
Related titles: Microfilm ed.: (from PQC); Online - full text ed.: ISSN 1941-9635.
Indexed: A05, A15, A22, A23, A24, A26, A28, ABIPC, ABIn, APA, AS&TA, AS&TI, ASCA, B04, B13, BrCerAb, C&ISA, C10, C24, CA, CA/WCA, CIA, CIN, CISA, CPEI, CerAb, ChemAb, ChemTitl, CivEngAb, CorrAb, CurCont, CurPA, E&CAJ, E08, E11, EEA, EMA, ESPM, EngInd, EnvEAb, G06, G07, G08, H15, I05, IPackAb, ISMEC, Inspec, M&TEA, M09, MBF, METADEX, MSCI, P10, P26, P48, P51, P52, P53, P54, PQC, PST, R18, RefZh, S06, S09, S10, SCI, SCOPUS, SolStAb, T02, T04, W07, WAA.
—BLDSC (6532.310000), CASDDS, IE, Infotrieve, Ingenta, INIST, Linda Hall. **CCC.**
Published by: (Society of Plastics Engineers, Inc.), Wiley-Blackwell Publishing, Inc. (Subsidiary of: Wiley-Blackwell Publishing Ltd.), 111 River St, Hoboken, NJ 07030. TEL 201-748-6000, FAX 201-748-6088, info@wiley.com, http://www.wiley.com/. Adv. contact Maria Russo TEL 203-405-1847.

668.4 USA ISSN 1040-2527
CODEN: PLENEZ
➤ **PLASTICS ENGINEERING SERIES.** Text in English. 1981. irreg., latest 2008. price varies. back issues avail. **Document type:** *Monographic series, Academic/Scholarly.*
Indexed: ChemAb, ChemTitl.
—BLDSC (6532.314000), CASDDS, IE, Ingenta. **CCC.**
Published by: C R C Press, LLC (Subsidiary of: Taylor & Francis Group), 6000 Broken Sound Pky, NW, Ste 300, Boca Raton, FL 33487. TEL 800-272-7737, FAX 800-374-3401, orders@crcpress.com.

668.4 USA
PLASTICS FABRICATING & FORMING. Text in English. 19??. bi-m. **Document type:** *Magazine, Trade.*
Published by: Key Communications, Inc., PO Box 569, Garrisonville, VA 22463. TEL 540-720-5584, FAX 540-720-5687, http://www.key-com.com/. **Subscr. to:** CirTec, 4 1/2 W Wilson St, Ste C6, Batavia, IL 60510. FAX 630-482-3051.

668.4 BEL
PLASTICS HIGH PERFORMANCE PACKAGING. Variant title: Society of Plastics Engineers. International Conference. Text in English. a., latest 1994, 15th, Duesseldorf. price varies. **Document type:** *Proceedings.*
Formerly (until 1994): High Performance Plastics Packaging
Published by: Society of Plastics Engineers, European Member Bureau, Bistkapellei 44, Antwerp, 2180, Belgium. TEL 32-3-5417755, FAX 32-3-5418425, spe.europe@ping.be. Ed. Yetty Pauwels.

668.4 USA
PLASTICS HOTLINE; the weekly marketplace for plastics processing equipment materials, suppliers and business services. Text in English. 1983. w. free to qualified personnel (print or online ed.) (effective 2009). adv. back issues avail. **Document type:** *Magazine, Trade.* **Description:** Provides information on current new and reconditioned plastics machinery, equipment and materials for sale.
Related titles: Online - full text ed.
Published by: Industry Marketing Solutions, 809 Central Ave, 2nd Fl, PO Box 893, Fort Dodge, IA 50501. TEL 515-574-2248, 888-247-2007, FAX 515-574-2237, http://www.industrymarketingsolutions.com/. Pub. Steve Scanlan. adv.: B&W page USD 638, color page USD 758; trim 7.625 x 10.75. Circ: 156,000 (controlled).

668.4 CAN ISSN 1198-225X
PLASTICS IN CANADA. Text in English. 1994. bi-m. adv. **Document type:** *Magazine, Trade.* **Description:** Presents a timely mix of news, technical developments, and market information for Canadian moulders, extruders and other plastics processors, as well as mouldmakers and end-users of plastic products.
Related titles: Online - full text ed.
Indexed: A15, ABIn, C03, CBCABus, P52, PQC.
—CCC.
Published by: Business Information Group, 80 Valleybrook Dr., Toronto, ON M3B 2S9, Canada. TEL 416-442-5600, FAX 416-510-5140, orders@businessinformationgroup.ca, http://www.businessinformationgroup.ca. Ed. Erika Beauchesne TEL 416-442-5600 ext 3261. Pub. Tim Dimopoulos TEL 416-442-5600 ext 5100.

338.4 CAN
PLASTICS IN CANADA BUYERS' GUIDE. Text in English. a. **Document type:** *Directory, Trade.* **Description:** Provides a comprehensive source to find suppliers of any plastics related equipment, material, or services in Canada.
Published by: Business Information Group, 80 Valleybrook Dr., Toronto, ON M3B 2S9, Canada. TEL 416-442-5600, FAX 416-510-5140, orders@businessinformationgroup.ca, http://www.businessinformationgroup.ca.

PLASTICS INDUSTRY DIRECTORY. *see* BUSINESS AND ECONOMICS—Trade And Industrial Directories

668.4 DEU ISSN 0944-1395
PLASTICS INFORMATION EUROPE. Text in English. 1977. fortn. EUR 329 in Europe; EUR 340 elsewhere (effective 2009). **Document type:** *Magazine, Trade.*
Formerly (until 1993): Plastics Industry Europe (0268-8247)
—CCC.
Published by: Kunststoff Information Verlagsgesellschaft mbH, Saalburgstr 157, Bad Homburg, 61350, Germany. TEL 49-6172-960610, FAX 49-6172-960699. Eds. Dede Williams, Ulrike Mau.

668.4 USA ISSN 1527-277X
PLASTICS MACHINING & FABRICATING. Text in English. 19??. bi-m. **Document type:** *Handbook/Manual/Guide, Trade.*
Related titles: Online - full text ed.
Published by: Vance Publishing Corp., 800 Liberty Dr., Libertyville, IL 60048. info@vancepublishing.com, http://www.vancepublishing.com.

668.4 USA
PLASTICS MOLDING & FABRICATING (ONLINE). Abbreviated title: P M & F. Text in English. 19??. a. adv. back issues avail. **Document type:** *Magazine, Trade.*
Formerly: Plastics Molding & Fabricating (Print)
Media: Online - full text.
Published by: Onsrud Cutter LP, 800 Liberty Dr, Libertyville, IL 60048. TEL 847-362-1560, FAX 847-362-5028, info@onsrud.com, https://www.onsrud.com.

668.4 IND ISSN 0971-3689
PLASTICS NEWS. Text in English. 1971. m. INR 750; INR 75 newsstand/cover (effective 2011). adv. bk.rev. back issues avail. **Document type:** *Newsletter, Trade.* **Description:** Contains news and the latest developments in the Indian plastics industry.
Related titles: Online - full text ed.: free.
Indexed: IPackAb.
—CIS.
Published by: All India Plastics Manufacturers Association, A-52, Rd No 1, M I D C, Marol, Andheri (E), Mumbai, Maharashtra 400 093, India. TEL 91-22-28217324, FAX 91-22-28216390, office@aipma.net. Ed. Raju Desai.

678 USA ISSN 1042-802X
HD9661.A1
PLASTICS NEWS. Abbreviated title: P N. Text in English. 1989. w. USD 84 combined subscription domestic (print &online eds.); USD 134 combined subscription in Canada (print &online eds.); USD 182 combined subscription in Mexico (print &online eds.); USD 292 combined subscription elsewhere (print &online eds.) (effective 2009). adv. charts; illus.; mkt.; stat.; tr.lit. back issues avail.; reprints avail. **Document type:** *Newspaper, Trade.* **Description:** Covers financial moves, plant closings, acquisitions, process developments, new machinery, and price indexing.
Related titles: Online - full text ed.: PlasticsNews.com. USD 99 (effective 2009).
Indexed: A09, A10, A22, A28, APA, B01, B02, B03, B06, B07, B08, B09, B11, B15, B17, B18, BrCerAb, C&ISA, C12, CA/WCA, CBNB, CIA, CWI, CerAb, CivEngAb, CorrAb, E&CAJ, E11, EEA, EMA, ESPM, EnvEAb, G02, G04, H15, I05, M&TEA, M01, M02, M09, MBF, METADEX, P34, PROMT, R18, S22, SolStAb, T02, T04, V02, V03, V04, WAA.
—BLDSC (6535.695000), Linda Hall. **CCC.**
Published by: Crain Communications, Inc., 1725 Merrimen Rd, Ste 300, Akron, OH 44313. TEL 330-836-9180, FAX 330-836-2831, info@crain.com, http://www.crain.com. Eds. Don Loepp TEL 330-865-6154, Robert Grace TEL 330-865-6151. Adv. contact Charla DeVoe TEL 330-865-6135. color page USD 15,760; bleed 11.25 x 14.75. Circ: 60,009.

678 USA
PLASTICS NEWS CHINA E-WEEKLY. Text in English. 19??. w. free (effective 2009). **Document type:** *Newsletter, Trade.*
Media: Online - full text.
Published by: Crain Communications, Inc., 1725 Merrimen Rd, Ste 300, Akron, OH 44313. TEL 330-836-9180, FAX 330-836-2322, info@crain.com, http://www.crain.com.

668.4 AUS ISSN 1328-7451
PLASTICS NEWS INTERNATIONAL. Abbreviated title: P N I. Text in English. 1950. m. AUD 93.50 combined subscription domestic (print & online eds.); USD 89 combined subscription foreign (print & online eds.) (effective 2008). adv. bk.rev.; software rev.; Website rev. back issues avail. **Document type:** *Magazine, Trade.* **Description:** Provides information to plastics industry about developments of plastics resins and their applications, including the machinery and equipment offered for sale to plastics processors.
Incorporates (in 2000): Plastics South East Asia Pacific; Former titles (until May 1989): Plastics News (0048-4377); (until 1965): P I A News; Plastics Newsletter; Plastics Institute of Australia. Monthly Newsletter
Related titles: Online - full text ed.; Supplement(s): Plastics South East Asia Pacific.
Indexed: ABIX, APA, ARI, C&ISA, CorrAb, E&CAJ, EEA, R18, SolStAb, WAA.
—BLDSC (6535.800000), IE.
Published by: Editors Desk Pty. Ltd., 2002 Summit Bldg, 163 City Rd, Southbank, VIC 3006, Australia. TEL 61-3-96459887, FAX 61-3-96459882, publisher@plasticsnews.net. Ed. Leonora Bor. Pub., Adv. contact John F McGough. color page USD 2,990; bleed 218 x 305. Circ: 2,100 (paid).

668.4 HKG
PLASTICS NEWSLETTER. Text in Chinese, English. m.
Formerly (until no.41, 1997): Plastics Technology
Indexed: R18.
Published by: Hong Kong Plastics Technology Centre Ltd. (HKPTC), U509, The Hong Kong Polytechnic University, Hung Hom, Kowloon, Hong Kong. TEL 852-2766-5577, FAX 852-2766-0131. Ed. Dick Wong.

PLASTICS RECYCLING UPDATE. *see* ENVIRONMENTAL STUDIES—Waste Management

668.4 678.2 GBR ISSN 1465-8011
TP1101 CODEN: PRUCFN
➤ **PLASTICS, RUBBER AND COMPOSITES**; macromolecular engineering. Text in English. 1981. 10/yr. GBP 1,188 combined subscription to institutions (print & online eds.); USD 1,900 combined subscription in United States to institutions (print & online eds.) (effective 2012). adv. bk.rev. illus. index. 50 p./no. 2 cols./p.; back issues avail.; reprint service avail. from PSC. **Document type:** *Journal, Academic/Scholarly.* **Description:** Provides an international forum for the presentation of science and technology involved in the plastics, rubber and composite industries.
Former titles (until 1999): Plastics, Rubber & Composites Processing and Applications (0959-8111); (until 1991): Plastics and Rubber Processing and Applications (0144-6045); Which was formed by the 1981 merger of: Plastics and Rubber. Processing (0307-9422); Plastics and Rubber. Materials and Applications (0307-9414)
Related titles: Microform ed.: (from PQC); Online - full text ed.: ISSN 1743-2898. GBP 1,073 to institutions; USD 1,718 in United States to institutions (effective 2012) (from IngentaConnect).
Indexed: A01, A03, A08, A10, A22, A28, APA, ASCA, BrCerAb, C&ISA, C33, CA, CA/WCA, CEA, CIA, CIN, CPEI, CerAb, ChemAb, ChemTitl, CivEngAb, CorrAb, CurCR, CurCont, CurPA, E&CAJ, E11, EEA, EMA, ESPM, EngInd, EnvEAb, FS&TA, H15, HRIS, ISMEC, Inspec, M&TEA, M09, MBF, METADEX, MSCI, R16, R18, SCI, SCOPUS, SolStAb, T02, T04, TCEA, TM, V03, W07, WAA.
—BLDSC (6537.186000), AskIEEE, CASDDS, IE, Infotrieve, Ingenta, INIST, Linda Hall. **CCC.**
Published by: (Institute of Materials, Minerals and Mining), Maney Publishing, Ste 1C, Joseph's Well, Hanover Walk, Leeds, W Yorks LS3 1AB, United Kingdom. TEL 44-113-2432800, FAX 44-113-3868178, maney@maney.co.uk, http://www.maney.co.uk. Ed. P D Coates. **Subscr. in N America to:** Maney Publishing, 875 Massachusetts Ave, 7th Fl, Cambridge, MA 02139. TEL 866-297-5154, FAX 617-354-6875, maney@maneyusa.com.

668.4 ZAF ISSN 0048-4385
PLASTICS SOUTHERN AFRICA. Abbreviated title: P S A. Text in English. 1971. m. ZAR 134.52; ZAR 172 in Africa; ZAR 196 elsewhere. adv. bk.rev. illus.; tr.lit. **Document type:** *Journal, Trade.* **Description:** Technical journal covering the plastics industry.
Indexed: ISAP.
Published by: (Plastics Institute of South Africa), George Warman Publications (Pty.) Ltd., Rondebosch, PO Box 705, Cape Town, 7701, South Africa. info@gwarmanpublications.co.za, http://www.gwarmanpublications.co.za. Ed. Martin Wells. Circ: 1,900.

668.4 ZAF
PLASTICS SOUTHERN AFRICA BUYERS GUIDE. Text in English. 1990. a. ZAR 110. **Document type:** *Directory.* **Description:** Guide for buyers of machinery for the plastics industry.
Published by: George Warman Publications (Pty.) Ltd., Rondebosch, PO Box 705, Cape Town, 7701, South Africa. info@gwarmanpublications.co.za, http://www.gwarmanpublications.co.za. Ed. Abdul Rawoot.

668.4 USA ISSN 0032-1257
TP1101 CODEN: PLTEAB
PLASTICS TECHNOLOGY. Abbreviated title: P T. Text in English. 1955. m. USD 89 domestic; USD 99 in Canada; USD 200 elsewhere; free to qualified personnel (effective 2008). adv. bk.rev. abstr.; charts; illus.; pat.; tr.lit. index. back issues avail.; reprints avail. **Document type:** *Magazine, Trade.* **Description:** Contains reports on technological innovations and developments in the plastics processing market and reaches more than 47,000 processors who are dependent on these reports for applying new technology, evaluating products and practical manufacturing.
Related titles: Online - full text ed.; ◆ Chinese ed.: Xiandai Suliao. ISSN 1674-5930; ◆ Spanish ed.: Tecnologia del Plastico. ISSN 0120-7644.
Indexed: A01, A03, A05, A08, A09, A10, A15, A22, A23, A24, A26, A28, ABIn, APA, AS&TA, AS&TI, B01, B02, B04, B06, B07, B08, B09, B13, B15, B17, B18, BRD, BrCerAb, C&ISA, C10, C12, CA, CA/WCA, CIA, CIN, CPEI, CerAb, ChemAb, ChemTitl, CivEngAb, CorrAb, E&CAJ, E11, EEA, EMA, ESPM, EngInd, EnvEAb, G04, G06, G07, G08, H15, I05, IPackAb, M&TEA, M01, M02, M09, MBF, METADEX, P26, P48, P51, P52, P54, PQC, PST, R18, S22, SCOPUS, SolStAb, T02, T04, V02, V03, V04, W03, W05, WAA.
—BLDSC (6537.300000), CASDDS, IE, Infotrieve, Ingenta, INIST, Linda Hall. **CCC.**
Published by: Gardner Publications, Inc., 6915 Valley Ave, Cincinnati, OH 45244. TEL 513-527-8800, 800-950-8020, FAX 513-527-8801, skline2@gardnerweb.com, http://www.gardnerweb.com. Eds. Jan H Schut, Matthew H Naitove, Mikell Knights. Pub. James J Callari TEL 646-827-4848 ext 710. adv.: color page USD 10,390, B&W page USD 8,765; trim 8 x 10.75. Circ: 46,951 (paid).

668.4 USA ISSN 1949-4394
PLASTICS WORLD INSIGHT. Abbreviated title: P W I. Text in English. 2008. m. USD 99.95 to individuals; USD 12.95 per issue to individuals (effective 2009). back issues avail. **Document type:** *Newsletter, Trade.* **Description:** Designed to keep professionals in the plastics industry abreast of key technical developments, business strategies and marketing initiatives in plastics and competitive materials that impact the sales and usage of plastics.
Media: Online - full content.
Published by: Momentum Press, LLC, 28 S First Ave, Highland Park, NJ 08904. TEL 732-828-0616, FAX 732-828-0616. Ed. Donald V Rosato. Pub. Joel Stein.

668.4 630 FRA ISSN 0257-9022
➤ **PLASTICULTURE**; les plastiques dans l'agriculture - plastics in agriculture and horticulture - los plasticos en la agricultura - Kunststoffe im Landbau. Text in English, French, Spanish. 1969. q. EUR 31; EUR 67 combined subscription print & online eds. (effective 2005). bk.rev. charts; illus. **Document type:** *Journal, Academic/Scholarly.* **Description:** Covers new plastics materials and products for applications in agriculture and horticulture, agricultural techniques based partially or wholly on the use of plastics.
Related titles: Online - full text ed.
Indexed: A22.
—BLDSC (6537.550000), IE, Ingenta, INIST. **CCC.**

Published by: Comite International des Plastiques en Agriculture/ International Committee for Plastics in Agriculture, 65 rue de Prony, Paris, Cedex 17 75854, France. TEL 33-1-44011649, FAX 33-1-44011655, cpacipa@club-internet.fr, http://www.cipa-cidapa.com. Ed. Pierre Bordes. Adv. contact Elizabeth Noel. Circ: 1,000. **Dist. in US by:** American Society for Plasticulture, 526 Brittany Dr, State College, PA 16803. TEL 814-238-7051, 814-238-7045.

668.4 678.4 SRB ISSN 0351-8787
CODEN: PLGUDV

PLASTIKA I GUMA. Text in Serbo-Croatian; Summaries in English. 1982. q. USD 50. adv. bk.rev.
Indexed: ChemAb, ChemTitl.
—CASDDS.
Published by: Savez Hemijskih Inzenjera Srbije/Association of the Chemical Engineers of Serbia, Kneza Milosa 9/I, Belgrade, 11000. FAX 381-11-643558, shi@yubc.net, http://www.ache.org.rs. Ed. Milenko Trbovic. Circ: 1,000.

668.4 GBR ISSN 1355-4859

PLASTIQUARIAN. Text in English. 1988. s-a. free to members (effective 2009). bk.rev. cum.index. back issues avail. **Document type:** *Journal, Academic/Scholarly.*
Published by: Plastics Historical Society, c/o The Institute of Materials, Minerals and Mining, 1 Carlton House Terr, London, SW1Y 5DB, United Kingdom. memb.sec@plastiquarian.com. Ed. Deborah Jaffe.

668.4 FRA ISSN 1776-1395

PLASTIQUES & CAOUTCHOUCS MAGAZINE. Text in French. 2005. m. **Document type:** *Magazine, Trade.*
Formed by the merger of (1924-2005): Caoutchoucs et Plastiques (1154-1105); Which was formerly (until 1989): Revue Generale du Caoutchouc et des Plastiques (0035-3175); (1924-1963): Revue Generale du Caoutchouc (0370-503X); (1943-2005): Plastiques et Elastomeres Magazine (1282-9277); Which was formerly (until 1999): Plastiques Modernes et Elastomeres (0032-1303); (until 1967): Industrie des Plastiques Modernes et Elastomeres (0367-9756); (1949-1964): Industrie des Plastiques Modernes (0367-8180); Which superseded in part (in 1949): Industries des Plastiques (0367-9748); Which was formerly (1943-1944): Plastiques (0551-0597)
—Linda Hall.
Published by: Editions Techniques pour l'Automobile et l'Industrie (E T A I), 48-50 Rue Benoit Malon, Gentilly, 94250, France. TEL 33-1-56794292, http://www.groupe-etai.com. Ed. Albane Canto TEL 33-1-41984075.

668.4 ITA ISSN 1824-8411
CODEN: INPLDK

PLASTIX. Text in Italian. 1978. 9/yr. EUR 60 domestic; EUR 120 in Europe; EUR 140 elsewhere (effective 2011). adv. **Document type:** *Magazine, Trade.* **Description:** Essays for those in the plastics field.
Formerly (until 2004): Interplastics (0392-3800)
Related titles: Online - full text ed.
Published by: Tecniche Nuove SpA, Via Eritrea 21, Milan, MI 201, Italy. TEL 39-02-390901, FAX 39-02-7570364, info@tecnichenuove.com. Ed. Nicoletta Boniardi.

668.4 GBR

PLASTRIBUTION NEWS. Text in English. s-a. **Document type:** *Newsletter, Trade.*
Published by: Plastribution Ltd, 81 Market St, Ashby de la Zouch, Leicester, LE65 1AH, United Kingdom. TEL 44-1530-560560, marketing@plastribution.co.uk, http://www.plastribution.co.uk.

668.4 DEU ISSN 0032-1338
TP986.A1 CODEN: PLARAN

PLASTVERARBEITER. Text in German. 1949. m. EUR 204.80 domestic; EUR 214.80 foreign; EUR 19 per issue (effective 2010). adv. bk.rev. illus. index. **Document type:** *Magazine, Trade.* **Description:** For plastics processors and users, machinery and appliance constructors, and raw material manufacturers.
Incorporates (1957-1964): Kunststoffmarkt (0368-7074)
Indexed: A&ATA, A22, A28, APA, BrCerAb, C&ISA, CA/WCA, CEABA, CIA, CIN, CISA, CerAb, ChemAb, ChemTitl, CivEngAb, CorrAb, E&CAJ, E11, EEA, EMA, H15, IPackAb, M&TEA, M09, MBF, METADEX, PST, R18, SolStAb, T04, TM, WAA.
—BLDSC (6537.750000), CASDDS, IE, Infotrieve, Ingenta, INIST, Linda Hall. **CCC.**
Published by: Huethig GmbH & Co. KG, Postfach 102869, Heidelberg, 69018, Germany. TEL 49-6221-4890, FAX 49-6221-489279, aboservice@huethig.de, http://www.huethig.de. Ed. Susanne Zinckgraf. Adv. contact Ludger Aulich. Circ: 13,300 (controlled).

668.4 USA ISSN 1935-8563
HD9650.3

PLUNKETT'S CHEMICALS, COATINGS & PLASTICS INDUSTRY ALMANAC. Variant title: Chemicals, Coatings & Plastics Industry Almanac. Text in English. 2005. a. USD 399.99 combined subscription (print, online & CD-ROM eds.); USD 299.99 combined subscription (print & CD-ROM eds.) (effective 2009). **Document type:** *Directory, Trade.* **Description:** Contains profiles of 400 leading companies of the chemicals, coatings and plastics industry.
Related titles: CD-ROM ed.; Online - full text ed.: USD 299.99 (effective 2009).
Published by: Plunkett Research, Ltd, PO Drawer 541737, Houston, TX 77254. TEL 713-932-0000, FAX 713-932-7080, customersupport@plunkettresearch.com. Ed. Jack W Plunkett.

668.4 678.2 HRV ISSN 0351-1871
TP1101 CODEN: PLMRDI

POLIMERI; casopis za plastiku i gumu. Text in Croatian. 1980. bi-m. adv. bk.rev. **Document type:** *Journal, Academic/Scholarly.* **Description:** Covers the latest developments in the plastics and rubber field, as well as the relevant equipment.
Related titles: Online - full text ed.: ISSN 1846-0828. free (effective 2011).
Indexed: A01, A22, C&ISA, CPEI, ChemAb, ChemTitl, E&CAJ, EngInd, R18, RefZh, SCOPUS, SolStAb, T02.
—BLDSC (6543.380600), CASDDS, IE, Ingenta, INIST, Linda Hall.
Published by: Drustvo za Plastiku i Gumu, Ivana Lucica 5, pp 119, Zagreb, 10001, Croatia. TEL 385-1-3095822, 385-1-6150081, FAX 385-1-3095822, 385-1-6150081, TELEX 22167. Ed. Barbara Vidosa. Pub. Stanislav Jurjasevic. R&P Igor Catic. Adv. contact Marija-Blanka Despotovic.

668.42 BRA ISSN 0104-1428
QD380 CODEN: PCTEFL

POLIMEROS; ciencia y tecnologia. Text in Portuguese. 1991. q. BRL 50 (effective 2005). back issues avail. **Document type:** *Journal, Trade.*
Related titles: Online - full text ed.: free (effective 2011).
Indexed: CPEI, EngInd, R18, RefZh, SCI, SCOPUS, W07.
—BLDSC (6543.396000), IE, Ingenta.
Published by: Associacao Brasileira de Polimeros, Rua Geminiano Costa No 355, Sao Carlos SP, 13560-970, Brazil. TEL 55-16-2743949, abpol@linkway.com.br, http://www.abpol.com.br. Ed. Antonio Aprigio Curvelo.

668.4 USA ISSN 0272-8397
TA418.9.C6 CODEN: PCOMDI

➤ **POLYMER COMPOSITES.** Text in English. 1980. m. GBP 1,062 in United Kingdom to institutions; EUR 1,343 in Europe to institutions; USD 1,954 in United States to institutions; USD 2,080 elsewhere to institutions; GBP 1,222 combined subscription in United Kingdom to institutions (print & online eds.); EUR 1,545 combined subscription in Europe to institutions (print & online eds.); USD 2,248 combined subscription in United States to institutions (print & online eds.); USD 2,374 combined subscription elsewhere to institutions (print & online eds.) (effective 2012). adv. charts; illus. index. back issues avail.; reprint service avail. from PSC. **Document type:** *Journal, Academic/Scholarly.* **Description:** Serves the fields of reinforced plastics and ploymer composites-including research, production, processing and applications.
Related titles: Online - full text ed.: ISSN 1548-0569. GBP 998 in United Kingdom to institutions; EUR 1,262 in Europe to institutions; USD 1,954 elsewhere to institutions (effective 2012).
Indexed: A22, A28, APA, ASCA, BrCerAb, C&ISA, C24, C33, CA/WCA, CIA, CIN, CPEI, Cadscan, CerAb, ChemAb, ChemTitl, CivEngAb, CorrAb, CurCR, CurCont, E&CAJ, E11, EEA, EMA, ESPM, EngInd, EnvEAb, H15, ISR, Inspec, LeadAb, M&TEA, M09, MBF, METADEX, MSCI, P26, P48, P52, P54, PQC, R16, R18, SCI, SCOPUS, SolStAb, T04, TM, W07, WAA, Zincscan.
—BLDSC (6547.704300), AskIEEE, CASDDS, IE, Infotrieve, Ingenta, INIST, Linda Hall. **CCC.**
Published by: (Society of Plastics Engineers, Inc.), John Wiley & Sons, Inc., 111 River St, Hoboken, NJ 07030. TEL 201-748-6000, FAX 201-748-6088, info@wiley.com, http://www.wiley.com/WileyCDA/. Eds. Alan J Lesser TEL 413-577-1316, Robert A Weiss.

668.4 660 GBR ISSN 1365-196X

POLYMER CURING TECHNOLOGIES. Text in English. 1979. bi-m. GBP 355 to non-members (print or online ed.); GBP 265 to members (print or online ed.); GBP 445 combined subscription to non-members (print & online eds.); GBP 335 combined subscription to members (print & online eds.) (effective 2009). **Document type:** *Journal, Trade.* **Description:** Covers curing types, radiation cure, physical properties, test methods, cure studies, resin types and curing catalysts.
Formerly (until 1996): Recent Advances in Crosslinking and Curing (0144-6266)
Related titles: E-mail ed.; Online - full text ed.
—CCC.
Published by: P R A Coatings Technology Centre, 14 Castle Mews, High St, Hampton, Mddlx. TW12 2NP, United Kingdom. TEL 44-20-84870800, FAX 44-20-84870801, publications@pra-world.com. Ed. Mircea Manea.

POLYMER DEGRADATION AND STABILITY. *see* CHEMISTRY—Organic Chemistry

POLYMER FRIENDS FOR RUBBER, PLASTICS AND FIBER/PORIMA NO TOMO. *see* RUBBER

668.42 GBR ISSN 0959-8103
TP1101 CODEN: PLYIEI

➤ **POLYMER INTERNATIONAL.** Text in English. 1969. m. GBP 1,677 in United Kingdom to institutions; EUR 2,120 in Europe to institutions; USD 3,286 elsewhere to institutions; GBP 1,930 combined subscription in United Kingdom to institutions (print & online eds.); EUR 2,438 combined subscription in Europe to institutions (print & online eds.); USD 3,779 combined subscription elsewhere to institutions (print & online eds.) (effective 2012). adv. bk.rev. charts; illus. index. back issues avail.; reprint service avail. from PSC. **Document type:** *Journal, Academic/Scholarly.* **Description:** Reports original research and advances in all branches of macromolecular science and technology, including polymer chemistry and physics, biopolymers and industrial polymer science.
Formerly (until 1991): British Polymer Journal (0007-1641)
Related titles: Microform ed.: (from PQC); Online - full text ed.: ISSN 1097-0126. 1996. GBP 1,677 in United Kingdom to institutions; EUR 2,120 in Europe to institutions; USD 3,286 elsewhere to institutions (effective 2012) (from IngentaConnect).
Indexed: A22, A28, A36, A37, APA, ASCA, B&BAb, B19, B21, BA, BioEngAb, BrCerAb, BrTechI, C&ISA, C24, C25, C33, CA/WCA, CABA, CCI, CEA, CEABA, CIA, CIN, CPEI, CerAb, ChemAb, ChemTitl, CivEngAb, CorrAb, CurCR, CurCont, CurPA, E&CAJ, E11, E12, EEA, EMA, ESPM, EngInd, EnvEAb, F08, F11, FCA, FLUIDEX, GH, H15, H16, I11, ISMEC, ISR, Inspec, M&TEA, M09, MBF, METADEX, MSCI, P30, PGrRegA, R16, R18, RefZh, S13, S16, SCI, SCOPUS, SolStAb, SoyAb, T01, T02, T04, TCEA, TM, TTI, W07, WAA, WSCA, WTA.
—CASDDS, IE, Infotrieve, Ingenta, INIST, Linda Hall. **CCC.**
Published by: (Society of Chemical Industry), John Wiley & Sons Ltd. (Subsidiary of: John Wiley & Sons, Inc.), 1-7 Oldlands Way, PO Box 808, Bognor Regis, West Sussex PO21 9FF, United Kingdom. customer@wiley.co.uk, http://eu.wiley.com/WileyCDA/. Ed. K E Geckeler. **Subscr. in the Americas to:** John Wiley & Sons, Inc., 111 River St, Hoboken, NJ 07030. TEL 201-748-6645, subinfo@wiley.com; **Subscr. to:** 1-7 Oldlands Way, PO Box 809, Bognor Regis, West Sussex PO21 9FG, United Kingdom.

668.4 GBR

POLYMER PRICE PROFILE. Text in English. 19??. q. GBP 30; free to members (effective 2010). **Document type:** *Newsletter, Trade.* **Description:** Compiles bulk buy prices for 11 grades of bulk polymers and 9 grades of bulk technical polymers throughout Europe.
Published by: British Plastics Federation, 5 - 6 Bath Pl, Rivington St, London, EC2A 3JE, United Kingdom. TEL 44-171-457-5000, FAX 44-171-457-5045, imcllwee@bpf.co.uk.

668.4 547 GBR ISSN 0142-9418
TA455.P58 CODEN: POTEDZ

➤ **POLYMER TESTING.** Text in English. 1980. 8/yr. EUR 1,762 in Europe to institutions; JPY 233,500 in Japan to institutions; USD 1,967 elsewhere to institutions (effective 2012). adv. bk.rev. illus.; abstr. index. back issues avail. **Document type:** *Journal, Academic/Scholarly.* **Description:** Provides a forum for developments in the testing of polymers and polymeric products.
Related titles: Microform ed.: (from PQC); Online - full text ed.: ISSN 1873-2348 (from IngentaConnect, ScienceDirect).
Indexed: A01, A03, A08, A22, A26, A28, APA, ASCA, B21, BrCerAb, C&ISA, C24, C33, CA, CA/WCA, CCI, CIA, CIN, CPEI, CerAb, ChemAb, ChemTitl, CivEngAb, CorrAb, CurCR, CurCont, E&CAJ, E11, EEA, EMA, ESPM, EngInd, EnvEAb, H&SSA, H15, I05, ISR, Inspec, M&TEA, M09, MBF, METADEX, MSCI, P30, R16, R18, RefZh, S01, SCI, SCOPUS, SolStAb, T01, T02, T04, TM, TTI, W07, WAA.
—BLDSC (6547.740500), AskIEEE, CASDDS, IE, Infotrieve, Ingenta, INIST, Linda Hall. **CCC.**
Published by: Elsevier Ltd (Subsidiary of: Elsevier Science & Technology), The Blvd, Langford Ln, Kidlington, Oxford, OX5 1GB, United Kingdom. TEL 44-1865-843000, FAX 44-1865-843010, journalscustomerserviceemea@elsevier.com. Ed. R Brown. **Subscr. to:** Elsevier BV, Radarweg 29, PO Box 211, Amsterdam 1000 AE, Netherlands. TEL 31-20-4853757, FAX 31-20-4853432, http://www.elsevier.nl.

668.4 GBR ISSN 0967-3911
TA418.9.C6 CODEN: PPOCEC

➤ **POLYMERS AND POLYMER COMPOSITES.** Text in English. 1988. 9/yr. GBP 600, USD 982.20, EUR 665.40 (effective 2010). bk.rev. abstr.; bibl.; charts; illus.; stat. a.index. 2 cols./p.; back issues avail.; reprints avail. **Document type:** *Journal, Academic/Scholarly.* **Description:** Designed for engineers, scientists and designers working with polymeric organic matrix composite materials, particularly those needing original papers for research, material specification, sales or end-use purposes.
Incorporates (1988-1996): Engineering Plastics (0952-6900); Formerly (until 1993): Composite Polymers (0952-6919)
Related titles: Online - full text ed.: ISSN 1478-2391.
Indexed: A22, A26, A28, APA, ASCA, ApMecR, BrCerAb, C&ISA, C24, C33, CA, CA/WCA, CCI, CIA, CIN, CPEI, CerAb, ChemAb, ChemTitl, CivEngAb, CorrAb, CurCont, E&CAJ, E11, EEA, EMA, ESPM, EngInd, EnvEAb, GeoRef, H15, I05, ISR, M&TEA, M09, MBF, METADEX, MSCI, P10, P26, P48, P52, P53, P54, PQC, R18, S10, SCI, SCOPUS, SolStAb, T02, T04, TM, W07, WAA.
—BLDSC (6547.742310), CASDDS, IE, Infotrieve, Ingenta, INIST, Linda Hall. **CCC.**
Published by: iSmithers, Shawbury, Shrewsbury, Shrops SY4 4NR, United Kingdom. TEL 44-1939-250383, FAX 44-1939-251118, info@ismithers.net. Ed. P Koot.

668.4 540 GBR ISSN 1042-7147
TP1080 CODEN: PADTE5

➤ **POLYMERS FOR ADVANCED TECHNOLOGIES.** Text in English. 1990. m. GBP 2,381 in United Kingdom to institutions; EUR 3,010 in Europe to institutions; USD 4,665 elsewhere to institutions; GBP 2,739 combined subscription in United Kingdom to institutions (print & online eds.); EUR 3,462 combined subscription in Europe to institutions (print & online eds.); USD 5,365 combined subscription elsewhere to institutions (print & online eds.) (effective 2012). adv. back issues avail.; reprint service avail. from PSC. **Document type:** *Journal, Academic/Scholarly.* **Description:** Focuses on the interest of scientists and engineers from academia and industry participating in new areas of polymer research and development related to advanced technologies.
Related titles: Microform ed.: (from PQC); Online - full text ed.: ISSN 1099-1581. GBP 2,381 in United Kingdom to institutions; EUR 3,010 in Europe to institutions; USD 4,665 elsewhere to institutions (effective 2012).
Indexed: A22, A28, APA, ASCA, BrCerAb, C&ISA, C24, C33, CA/WCA, CCI, CIA, CIN, CPEI, CerAb, ChemAb, ChemTitl, CivEngAb, CorrAb, CurCont, E&CAJ, E11, EEA, EMA, ESPM, EngInd, EnvEAb, FLUIDEX, H15, ISR, Inspec, M&TEA, M09, MBF, METADEX, MSCI, P30, R18, RefZh, SCI, SCOPUS, SolStAb, T01, T02, T04, TM, TTI, W07, WAA, WTA.
—CASDDS, IE, Infotrieve, Ingenta, INIST, Linda Hall. **CCC.**
Published by: John Wiley & Sons Ltd. (Subsidiary of: John Wiley & Sons, Inc.), 1-7 Oldlands Way, PO Box 808, Bognor Regis, West Sussex PO21 9FF, United Kingdom. TEL 44-1865-778315, FAX 44-1243-843232, cs-journals@wiley.com, http://eu.wiley.com/WileyCDA/. Ed. Menachem Lewin. **Subscr. in the Americas to:** John Wiley & Sons, Inc., 111 River St, Hoboken, NJ 07030. TEL 201-748-6645, 800-225-5945, subinfo@wiley.com; **Subscr. to:** 1-7 Oldlands Way, PO Box 809, Bognor Regis, West Sussex PO21 9FG, United Kingdom. TEL 44-1865-778054, cs-agency@wiley.com.

668.4 GBR ISSN 2041-2479

▼ **POLYMERS FROM RENEWABLE RESOURCES.** Text in English. 2010. q. GBP 420, USD 668.89, EUR 480.06 combined subscription (print & online eds.) (effective 2010). **Document type:** *Journal, Trade.* **Description:** Focuses on the development of renewable polymers and their application in the production of industrial, consumer, and medical products.
Related titles: Online - full text ed.: ISSN 2045-1377.
Indexed: A26, E08, P02, P10, P48, P52, P53, P54, P56, PQC.
Published by: iSmithers, Shawbury, Shrewsbury, Shrops SY4 4NR, United Kingdom. TEL 44-1939-250383, FAX 44-1939-251118, info@ismithers.net. Ed. Sigbritt Karlsson.

POLYTECHNICAL UNIVERSITY OF BUCHAREST. SCIENTIFIC BULLETIN. SERIES B: CHEMISTRY AND MATERIALS SCIENCE. *see* CHEMISTRY

668.4 IND ISSN 0971-0078
CODEN: PPPAEB

POPULAR PLASTICS & PACKAGING. Text in English. 1955. m. INR 600 (effective 2011). adv. bk.rev. abstr.; charts; illus. reprints avail.
Former titles (until 1989): Popular Plastics (0253-7303); (until 1981): Popular Plastics and Rubber (0253-7311); (until 1979): Popular Plastics (0032-4604)
Related titles: Microfilm ed.: (from PQC).
Indexed: A28, APA, B01, B07, BrCerAb, C&ISA, CA/WCA, CIA, CerAb, ChemAb, CivEngAb, CorrAb, E&CAJ, E11, EEA, EMA, H15, IPackAb, M&TEA, M09, MBF, METADEX, R18, SolStAb, T04, WAA.

P

—BLDSC (6550.810000), CASDDS, IE, Ingenta, INIST, Linda Hall.
Published by: Colour Publications Pvt. Ltd., Dhuruwadi 126-A, A.V. Nagveka Marg, Prabhadevi, Mumbai, Maharashtra 400 025, India. TEL 91-22-24306319, FAX 91-22-24300601, paintindia.2010@gmail.com, http://www.paintindia.in. Circ: 10,375.

POWDER INJECTION MOULDING INTERNATIONAL. *see* METALLURGY

PROGRESS IN RUBBER, PLASTICS AND RECYCLING TECHNOLOGY. *see* ENGINEERING—Chemical Engineering

668.4 JPN ISSN 0289-4556
PURASUCHIKKU SEIKEI GIJUTSU/PLASTIC MOLDING TECHNOLOGY. Text in Japanese. 1984. m. JPY 1,000 per issue.
Published by: Shiguma Shuppan/Sigma Publishing Co., Ltd., 15-8-602 Sakuragaoka-cho, Shibuya-ku, Tokyo, 150-0031, Japan. TEL 81-3-3477-0336, FAX 81-3-3477-2710. Ed. Minoru Takahashi.

668.4 660 GBR ISSN 0966-9698
RADNEWS. Text in English. 1992. q. GBP 235 to non-members (print or online ed.); GBP 195 to members (print or online ed.); GBP 294 combined subscription to non-members (print & online eds.); GBP 244 combined subscription to members (print & online eds.) (effective 2009). adv. **Document type:** *Bulletin, Trade.* **Description:** Provides information on the radiation curing industry.
Related titles: E-mail ed.; Online - full text ed.; Supplement(s): Radnews Supplement. ISSN 0967-0939.
Indexed: WSCA.
—CCC.
Published by: P R A Coatings Technology Centre, 14 Castle Mews, High St, Hampton, Mddlx. TW12 2NP, United Kingdom. TEL 44-20-84870800, FAX 44-20-84870801, publications@pra-world.com. Ed. Richard Kennedy TEL 44-20-84870835.

668.4 614 USA ISSN 1065-1896
REGULATORY UPDATE; government legislation and regulations related to plastics industry. Text in English. 1983. m. USD 95 domestic; USD 105 foreign (effective 2000). back issues avail. **Document type:** *Newsletter, Trade.* **Description:** Covers regulatory (Federal Register) and legislative updates in public health and safety and environmental developments affecting the plastics industry.
Related titles: Diskette ed.; Online - full text ed.: USD 49.95 (effective 2000).
Published by: Lewis B. Weisfeld, Ed. & Pub., 1 Franklin Town Blvd, Ste 1204, Philadelphia, PA 19103. TEL 215-567-7235, FAX 215-567-7235. Ed., Pub., R&P Lewis B Weisfeld.

668.4 GBR ISSN 0034-3617
TA455.P55
REINFORCED PLASTICS. Text in English. 1956. 11/yr. EUR 405 in Europe to institutions; JPY 53,900 in Japan to institutions; USD 454 elsewhere to institutions (effective 2012). adv. bk.rev. charts; illus.; tr.lit. index. back issues avail.; reprints avail. **Document type:** *Journal, Trade.* **Description:** Provides information for those involved in the polymer-based composites industry.
Related titles: Online - full text ed.: ISSN 1873-1694 (from IngentaConnect, ScienceDirect).
Indexed: A01, A03, A08, A22, A26, A28, APA, BMT, BrCerAb, C&ISA, CA, CA/WCA, CBNB, CEABA, CIA, CerAb, ChemAb, CivEngAb, CorrAb, E&CAJ, E11, EEA, EMA, ESPM, EngInd, EnvEAb, FLUIDEX, H15, I05, IPackAb, Inspec, M&TEA, M09, MBF, METADEX, OceAb, R18, S01, SCOPUS, SolStAb, T01, T02, T04, TM, TTI, WAA, WTA.
—BLDSC (7351.200000), IE, Infotrieve, Ingenta, INIST, Linda Hall. **CCC.**
Published by: Elsevier Advanced Technology (Subsidiary of: Elsevier Science & Technology), The Blvd, Langford Ln, Kidlington, Oxon OX5 1GB, United Kingdom. TEL 44-1865-843434, FAX 44-1865-843970, eatsales@elsevier.co.uk, http://www.elsevier.com. Ed. Amanda Jacob TEL 44-1865-843638. Pub. Laurence Zipson TEL 44-1865-843685. Adv. contact Mark Sherman TEL 44-1865-843208. **Subscr. to:** Elsevier BV, Radarweg 29, PO Box 211, Amsterdam 1000 AE, Netherlands. TEL 31-20-4853757, FAX 31-20-4853432, JournalsCustomerServiceEMEA@elsevier.com, http://www.elsevier.nl.

668.4 PRT
REVIMOLD. Text in Portuguese. 200?. q. EUR 28.65 (effective 2011). **Document type:** *Newsletter, Trade.*
Related titles: Online - full text ed.: EUR 17.64 (effective 2011).
Published by: Oditecnica, Apartado 30, Odivelas, 2676-901, Portugal. http://www.oditecnica.wordpress.com.

668.4 PRT ISSN 1647-8142
REVIPLAST. Text in Portuguese. 1997. q. EUR 28.65 (effective 2011). **Document type:** *Magazine, Trade.*
Related titles: Online - full text ed.: EUR 17.64 (effective 2011).
Published by: (Associacao Portuguesa da Industria de Plasticos (A P I P)), Oditecnica, Apartado 30, Odivelas, 2676-901, Portugal. http://www.oditecnica.wordpress.com.

668.4 ESP ISSN 0034-8708
TP986.A1 CODEN: RPMOAM
REVISTA DE PLASTICOS MODERNOS. Text in Spanish. 1950. m. EUR 60 domestic; EUR 85 foreign (effective 2009). adv. bk.rev. charts; illus.; pat. back issues avail. **Document type:** *Magazine, Trade.*
Formerly (until 1962): Revista de Plasticos (0370-4513)
Related titles: Online - full text ed.
Indexed: A&ATA, A22, CBNB, CIN, ChemAb, ChemTitl, IECT, R18, RefZh, WSCA.
—BLDSC (7869.810000), CASDDS, IE, Infotrieve, Ingenta, INIST, Linda Hall. **CCC.**
Published by: Instituto de Estudios Documentales sobre Ciencia y Tecnologia (I E D C Y T), Ciencia y Tecnologia, Joaquin Costa 22, Madrid, 28002, Spain. TEL 34-91-5635482, FAX 34-91-5642644, http://www.cindoc.csic.es. Circ: 5,000.

RUBBER & PLASTICS NEWS; the rubber industry's international newspaper. *see* RUBBER

668.4 USA
RUBBER & PLASTICS NEWS II (ONLINE). Text in English. 1979. 25/yr. incl. with subscr. to Rubber & Plastics News. **Document type:** *Newspaper, Trade.*
Media: Online - full text. **Related titles:** E-mail ed.
Published by: Crain Communications, Inc., 1725 Merrimen Rd, Ste 300, Akron, OH 44313. TEL 330-836-9180, FAX 330-836-2831, info@crain.com, http://www.crain.com.

RUBBER, FIBRES, PLASTICS INTERNATIONAL. *see* RUBBER

RUBBER RESEARCH INSTITUTE OF SRI LANKA. JOURNAL. *see* RUBBER

RUBBER SOUTHERN AFRICA. *see* RUBBER

668.9 USA ISSN 1093-2984
RUSSIAN POLYMER NEWS. Text in English. 1996. q. free to members. **Description:** Covers the scientific and technical achievements obtained by the specialists in Russia and other countries of the former Soviet Unioin in the area of rubber technology and plastics processing.
—BLDSC (8052.816700), IE, Ingenta.
Published by: AM-RUSS Rubber and Plastics Consulting, PO Box 32, Fair Lawn, NJ 07410. amrusrubb@aol.com, http://members.aol.com/amrusrubb/Amruss2.htm. Ed. G I Brodsky.

668.0029 USA
S P I MEMBERSHIP DIRECTORY AND BUYER'S GUIDE. (Society of the Plastics Industry) Text in English. 1937. a. USD 270 to non-members; USD 90 to members. back issues avail. **Document type:** *Directory.* **Description:** Lists 2,000 SPI member companies and their products and services.
Published by: Society of the Plastics Industry, 1801 K St, NW, Ste 600K, Washington, DC 20006. TEL 202-974-5293, FAX 202-296-7539. Ed., R&P Diana D Wright. Circ: 3,000.

SCRAP PLASTICS MARKETS DIRECTORY. *see* BUSINESS AND ECONOMICS—Trade And Industrial Directories

668.4 JPN ISSN 0915-4027
CODEN: SIKAE4
SEIKEI KAKOU/JAPAN SOCIETY OF POLYMER PROCESSING. JOURNAL. Text in Japanese. 1989. m. JPY 10,000 membership (effective 2004). **Document type:** *Journal, Academic/Scholarly.* **Description:** Contains articles such as technical notes, special lecture, technical reports, topics on products and technologies, and original papers.
Indexed: ChemAb, ChemTitl.
—BLDSC (8219.724000), CASDDS, IE, Ingenta. **CCC.**
Published by: Purasuchikku Seikei Kako Gakkai/Japan Society of Polymer Processing, c/o Mr. Hidetoshi In-nami, 8-5, O-saki 5, Shinagawa-ku, Tokyo, 141-0032, Japan. TEL 81-3-54363822, FAX 81-3-37799698, plakakou@sepia.ocn.ne.jp.

668.4 USA
SOCIETY OF PLASTICS ENGINEERS. ANNUAL TECHNICAL CONFERENCE (ANTEC). PROCEEDINGS. Variant title: A N T E C Conference Proceedings. Text in English. 19??. a. **Document type:** *Proceedings, Trade.* **Description:** Provides information about plastics industry.
Former titles (until 1983): Society of Plastics Engineers. Annual Technical Conference and Exhibition (0733-4192); (until 1981): Society of Plastics Engineers. Annual Technical Conference (0272-5223); (until 1970): Society of Plastics Engineers. Technical Papers (0583-9580); (until 1956): Papers Presented at Annual National Technical Conference
Related titles: CD-ROM ed.: USD 250 per issue (effective 2010); Online - full text ed.: ISSN 1539-2252.
Indexed: A22, CIN, ChemAb, ChemTitl, TM.
—Ingenta, Linda Hall. **CCC.**
Published by: Society of Plastics Engineers, Inc., 13 Church Hill Rd, Newtown, CT 06470. TEL 203-775-0471, FAX 203-775-8490, info@4spe.org.

668.4 USA
SOCIETY OF THE PLASTICS INDUSTRY. REINFORCED PLASTICS COMPOSITES INSTITUTE. ANNUAL TECHNICAL CONFERENCE. PREPRINT. Text in English. 1946. a. USD 165 to non-members; USD 110 to members. **Document type:** *Proceedings.*
Formerly: Society of the Plastics Industry. Reinforced Plastics Composites Institute. Annual Technical Conference. Proceedings
Indexed: ChemAb.
Published by: Society of the Plastics Industry, Inc., Composites Institute, 1801 K St, N W, Ste 600K, Washington, DC 20006-1300. TEL 202-974-5200. Circ: 3,000.

STUDIES IN POLYMER SCIENCE. *see* CHEMISTRY

668.4 CHN ISSN 1001-9456
TP1101 CODEN: SULIEF
SULIAO/PLASTICS. Text in Chinese. 1972. bi-m. CNY 108; CNY 18 per issue (effective 2009). **Document type:** *Magazine, Trade.*
Related titles: Online - full text ed.
—BLDSC (6530.980000).
Published by: Beijing Suliao Yanjiusuo, 47, Jiugulou Dajie, Beijing, 100009, China. TEL 86-10-84022529, FAX 86-10-84022529, http://www.slyjs.com.cn/.

668.4 CHN ISSN 1005-3360
TP1101
SULIAO KEJI/PLASTICS SCIENCE AND TECHNOLOGY. Text in Chinese. 1973. bi-m. USD 74.40 (effective 2009). **Document type:** *Journal, Academic/Scholarly.*
Related titles: Online - full text ed.
Indexed: A28, APA, BrCerAb, C&ISA, CA/WCA, CIA, CerAb, CivEngAb, CorrAb, E&CAJ, E11, EEA, EMA, ESPM, EnvEAb, H15, M&TEA, M09, MBF, METADEX, RefZh, SolStAb, T04, WAA.
—BLDSC (8516.608000), East View.
Published by: Dalian Suliao Yanjiusuo/Dalian Plastics Research Institute, 11, Zhoujia St., Dalian, 116033, China. http://www.dsy-cn.com/.

668.4 CHN ISSN 1672-6294
SULIAO ZHUJI/PLASTIC ADDITIVES. Text in Chinese. 1997. bi-m. USD 31.20 (effective 2009). **Document type:** *Magazine, Trade.*
Related titles: Online - full text ed.
—BLDSC (8516.609000).
Published by: Nanjing shi Huaxue Gongye Yanjiu Shejiyuan/Nanjing Institute of Chemical Industrial Research and Design, 119, Diaoyuta, Nanjing, Jiangsu 210006, China. TEL 86-25-86626096, FAX 86-25-86620386.

668.4 CHN
SUOLIAO/PLASTICS. Text in Chinese, English. bi-m.
Published by: Beijing Plastics Research Institute, 47 Jiu Gu Lou St, Beijing, 100009, China. TELEX 22470 BFTCC CN. Ed. Zhao Yiming. **Dist. overseas by:** China International Book Trading Corp, 35 Chegongzhuang Xilu, Haidian District, PO Box 399, Beijing 100044, China. TEL 86-10-68412045, FAX 86-10-68412023, cibtc@mail.cibtc.com.cn, http://www.cibtc.com.cn/.

674.8 USA ISSN 1538-6252
SURFACING SOLUTIONS. Text in English. 1996. bi-m. USD 48; USD 68 in Canada & Mexico; USD 99 elsewhere. illus. **Document type:** *Journal, Trade.*
Formerly (until 2002): Laminating Design & Technology (1088-2421)
—Linda Hall.
Published by: Cygnus Business Media, Inc., 1233 Janesville Ave, PO Box 803, Fort Atkinson, WI 53538. TEL 920-563-6388, FAX 920-563-1702, http://www.cygnusb2b.com.

SUXING GONGCHENG XUEBAO/JOURNAL OF PLASTICITY ENGINEERING. *see* ENGINEERING—Chemical Engineering

668.4 678.2 SRB ISSN 1450-6734
SVET POLIMERA/WORLD OF POLYMERS. Text in Serbian; Contents page in English, Serbian. 1998. 5/yr. USD 60 foreign (effective 2007). **Document type:** *Magazine, Trade.*
—BLDSC (8573.506000).
Published by: Drustvo Inzenjera Plasticara i Gumara/Society of Plastics and Rubber Engineers, P Fah 23, Belgrade. TEL 381-11-3230455, ipg_am@ptt.yu. Ed. Vojislav Bogdanovic.

668.4 CHE ISSN 1662-0739
TP986.A1 CODEN: KUSYEA
SWISSPLASTICS; Das Schweizer Magazin fuer die Kunststoffindustrie. Text in German. 1953. 10/yr. CHF 96 (effective 2007). adv. bk.rev. illus. index. **Document type:** *Magazine, Trade.*
Former titles (until 2007): Kunststoffe - Synthetics (1021-0601); (until 1992): Kunststoffe - Plastics (0023-5598); Which incorporated (1970-1990): Synthetic (0378-4827); Which incorporated (1969-1974): Kunststoff in der Praxis (0023-5547)
Indexed: CIN, ChemAb, ChemTitl, IPackAb, KES, R18.
—BLDSC (8577.165000), CASDDS, IE, Infotrieve, Ingenta, INIST.
Published by: Vogt-Schild AG, Zuchwilerstr 21, Solothurn, 4501, Switzerland. TEL 41-32-6247111, FAX 41-32-6247444, http://www.vsonline.ch. Ed. Marianne Flury. Adv. contact Joerg Signer. B&W page CHF 2,340, color page CHF 3,440; trim 260 x 185. Circ: 7,300.

TECHNICAL TEXTILES INTERNATIONAL. *see* TEXTILE INDUSTRIES AND FABRICS

668.4 USA ISSN 0120-7644
TECNOLOGIA DEL PLASTICO. Text in Spanish. 1985. bi-m. adv. tr.lit. back issues avail. **Document type:** *Magazine, Consumer.*
Related titles: Online - full text ed.; ◆ English ed.: Plastics Technology. ISSN 0032-1257; ◆ Chinese ed.: Xiandai Suliao. ISSN 1674-5930.
Published by: B 2 B Portales, Inc (Subsidiary of: Carvajal International, Inc.), 6505 Blue Lagoon Dr, Ste 430, Miami, FL 33126. TEL 305-448-6875, FAX 305-448-9942, contactenos@b2bportales.com, http://www.b2bportales.com. Ed. Natalia Ortega.

TI02 WORLDWIDE UPDATE. *see* CHEMISTRY—Inorganic Chemistry

628 338 USA
TOWNSEND PROFILE. Text in English. q. **Document type:** *Newsletter, Trade.*
Indexed: C&ISA, E&CAJ.
Published by: Philip Townsend Associates, PO Box 90327, Houston, TX 77290-0327. TEL 281-873-8733, info@ptai.org.

UMFORMTECHNIK. *see* METALLURGY

UNION DES SYNDICATS DES PME DU CAOUTCHOUC ET DE LA PLASTURGIE. *see* RUBBER

668.4 GBR ISSN 1754-1352
TP1180.P8
URETHANES TECHNOLOGY INTERNATIONAL. Variant title: Utech. Text in English. 1882. bi-m. GBP 75; GBP 114 combined subscription (print & online eds.) (effective 2010). adv. bk.rev. back issues avail.; reprints avail. **Document type:** *Magazine, Trade.* **Description:** Covers reports to commercial and technical developments in the polyurethane industry worldwide.
Formerly (until 2007): Urethanes Technology (0265-637X); Which superseded in part (in 1984): European Rubber Journal (0266-4151); Which was formerly (until 1982): European Rubber Journal and Urethanes Today (0260-5317); (until 1981): European Rubber Journal (0305-2222); (until 1973): Rubber Journal (0035-9505); (until 1964): Rubber and Plastics Weekly; (until 1961): Rubber Journal and International Plastics; (until 1957): Rubber Journal; (until 1955): The India Rubber Journal (0367-9985); (until 1911): India-Rubber and Gutta-Percha and Electrical Trades Journal
Related titles: Online - full text ed.: GBP 98 (effective 2010); Chinese ed.: Urethanes Technology - Mandarin Edition; Supplement(s): Global Polyurethane Directory and Buyer's Guide.
Indexed: A22, A28, APA, B01, B03, B06, B07, B09, BrCerAb, C&ISA, CA/WCA, CIA, CWI, CerAb, CivEngAb, CorrAb, E&CAJ, E11, EEA, EMA, ESPM, EngInd, EnvEAb, H15, I05, M&TEA, M09, MBF, METADEX, PROMT, R18, RefZh, SCOPUS, SolStAb, T02, T04, WAA.
—BLDSC (9124.148750), IE, Infotrieve, Ingenta, INIST, Linda Hall. **CCC.**
Published by: Crain Communications, Ltd., 3rd Fl, 21 St Thomas St, London, SE1 9RY, United Kingdom. TEL 44-20-74571400, FAX 44-20-74571440, http://www.crain.co.uk. Ed. Liz White TEL 44-20-74571405. Adv. contact Paul Mitchell TEL 44-20-74571431. B&W page EUR 2,450, color page EUR 4,006; trim 208 x 284. Circ: 6,380. **Subscr. to:** The Coach House, Turners Dr, Thatcham, Berkshire RG1 4QB, United Kingdom. TEL 44-1635-879382, FAX 44-1635-868594.

668.4 GBR
▼ **URETHANES TECHNOLOGY INTERNATIONAL NORTH AMERICA.** Text in English. 2009. q. adv. **Document type:** *Magazine, Trade.*
Published by: Crain Communications, Ltd., 3rd Fl, 21 St Thomas St, London, SE1 9RY, United Kingdom. TEL 44-20-74571400, FAX 44-20-74571440, http://www.crain.co.uk. Ed. David Reed. Pub. Paul Mitchell TEL 44-20-74571431. adv.: B&W page USD 6,600; trim 276 x 368.

WHO'S WHO IN WORLD PETROCHEMICALS AND PLASTICS. *see* BUSINESS AND ECONOMICS—Trade And Industrial Directories

668.4 CHN ISSN 1674-5930
XIANDAI SULIAO. Text in Chinese. 2003. m. free. **Document type:** *Magazine, Trade.*
Related titles: Online - full text ed.; ◆ English ed.: Plastics Technology. ISSN 0032-1257; ◆ Spanish ed.: Tecnologia del Plastico. ISSN 0120-7644.

Published by: Deguo Fuge Gongye Meiti Jituan/Vogel Media Group (Subsidiary of: Vogel Business Media GmbH & Co.KG), 11/F, 1, Baiyue Lu, Xicheng-qu, Beijing, 100045, China. **Co-sponsor:** Gardner Publications, Inc.

668.4 678.2 CHN ISSN 1009-797X
XIANGSU JISHU YU ZHUANGBEI/CHINA RUBBER / PLASTICS TECHNOLOGY & EQUIPMENT. Text in Chinese. 1975. m. USD 74.40 (effective 2009). **Document type:** *Journal, Academic/Scholarly.*
Related titles: Online - full text ed.
—East View.
Published by: Beijing Xiangjiao Gongye Yanjiu Shejiyuan/Beijing Research and Design Institute of Rubber Industry, Fushi Lu Jia #19, Beijing, 100039, China. http://www.china-rp.com.cn/.

XIANWEI FUHE CAILIAO/FIBER COMPOSITES. *see* ENGINEERING—Chemical Engineering

668.4 CHN ISSN 1009-5640
ZHONGGUO XIANGJIAO/CHINA RUBBER. Text in Chinese. 1985. bi-m. USD 86.40 (effective 2009). **Document type:** *Journal, Academic/Scholarly.*
—East View.
Published by: Zhongguo Xiangjiao Gongye Xiehui, Zhiqiangyuan Jia #22 Lou, Beijing, 100088, China. TEL 86-10-62263523, FAX 86-10-62261173.

PLASTICS—Abstracting, Bibliographies, Statistics

668.4 USA ISSN 0734-869X CODEN: CAFPEU
C A SELECTS. FIBER - REINFORCED PLASTICS. Text in English. s-w. USD 385 to non-members; USD 115 to members; USD 575 combined subscription to individuals (print & online eds.) (effective 2011). **Document type:** *Abstract/Index.* **Description:** Covers properties, processing, use of thermoplastics and thermosetting resins reinforced by natural or synthetic fibers.
Related titles: Online - full text ed.: USD 380 to non-members; USD 114 to members (effective 2011).
Published by: Chemical Abstracts Service (Subsidiary of: American Chemical Society), 2540 Olentangy River Rd, Columbus, OH 43210-0012. TEL 614-447-3600, FAX 614-447-3713, help@cas.com, http://caselects.cas.org. **Subscr. to:** PO Box 3012, Columbus, OH 43210. TEL 800-753-4227, FAX 614-447-3751.

668.4 USA ISSN 0734-8673 CODEN: CANPE2
C A SELECTS. NEW PLASTICS. Text in English. s-w. USD 385 to non-members; USD 115 to members; USD 575 combined subscription to individuals (print & online eds.) (effective 2011). **Document type:** *Abstract/Index.* **Description:** Covers newly synthesized or newly reported thermoplastic and thermosetting resins.
Related titles: Online - full text ed.: USD 380 to non-members; USD 114 to members (effective 2011).
Published by: Chemical Abstracts Service (Subsidiary of: American Chemical Society), 2540 Olentangy River Rd, Columbus, OH 43210-0012. TEL 614-447-3600, FAX 614-447-3713, help@cas.com, http://caselects.cas.org. **Subscr. to:** PO Box 3012, Columbus, OH 43210. TEL 800-753-4227, FAX 614-447-3751.

668.4 USA ISSN 0195-511X CODEN: CSPFD5
C A SELECTS. PLASTIC FILMS. Text in English. s-w. USD 385 to non-members; USD 115 to members; USD 575 combined subscription to individuals (print & online eds.) (effective 2011). **Document type:** *Abstract/Index.* **Description:** Covers manufacture, properties, fabrication, and applications of polymeric films.
Related titles: Online - full text ed.: USD 380 to non-members; USD 114 to members (effective 2011).
Published by: Chemical Abstracts Service (Subsidiary of: American Chemical Society), 2540 Olentangy River Rd, Columbus, OH 43210-0012. TEL 614-447-3600, FAX 614-447-3713, help@cas.com, http://caselects.cas.org. **Subscr. to:** PO Box 3012, Columbus, OH 43210. TEL 800-753-4227, FAX 614-447-3751.

668.4 USA ISSN 0734-8681 CODEN: CAADE3
C A SELECTS. PLASTICS ADDITIVES. Text in English. s-w. USD 385 to non-members; USD 115 to members; USD 575 combined subscription to individuals (print & online eds.) (effective 2011). **Document type:** *Abstract/Index.* **Description:** Covers materials added to thermoplastic and thermosetting resins to modify properties; plasticizers, inert and reinforcing fillers, pigments, heat and light stabilizers, antioxidants, blowing agents.
Related titles: Online - full text ed.: USD 380 to non-members; USD 114 to members (effective 2011).
Published by: Chemical Abstracts Service (Subsidiary of: American Chemical Society), 2540 Olentangy River Rd, Columbus, OH 43210-0012. TEL 614-447-3600, FAX 614-447-3713, help@cas.com, http://caselects.cas.org. **Subscr. to:** PO Box 3012, Columbus, OH 43210. TEL 800-753-4227, FAX 614-447-3751.

668.4 USA ISSN 0275-7125 CODEN: CPFUDD
C A SELECTS. PLASTICS FABRICATION & USES. Text in English. s-w. USD 385 to non-members; USD 115 to members; USD 575 combined subscription to individuals (print & online eds.) (effective 2011). **Document type:** *Abstract/Index.* **Description:** Covers processes of chemical or chemical engineering interest for fabricating polymers or compositions containing them.
Related titles: Online - full text ed.: USD 380 to non-members; USD 114 to members (effective 2011).
Published by: Chemical Abstracts Service (Subsidiary of: American Chemical Society), 2540 Olentangy River Rd, Columbus, OH 43210-0012. TEL 614-447-3600, FAX 614-447-3713, help@cas.com, http://caselects.cas.org. **Subscr. to:** PO Box 3012, Columbus, OH 43210. TEL 800-753-4227, FAX 614-447-3751.

668.4 USA ISSN 0275-7133 CODEN: CSPPDZ
C A SELECTS. PLASTICS MANUFACTURE & PROCESSING. Text in English. s-w. USD 385 to non-members; USD 115 to members; USD 575 combined subscription to individuals (print & online eds.) (effective 2011). **Document type:** *Abstract/Index.* **Description:** Covers manufacture, testing, compounding, and processing of polymeric materials for use as resins or unsupported films; natural resins of industrial interest; additives for plastics and resins, crosslinking agents, plasticizers, fillers, foaming agents, pigments.
Related titles: Online - full text ed.: USD 380 to non-members; USD 114 to members (effective 2011).
Published by: Chemical Abstracts Service (Subsidiary of: American Chemical Society), 2540 Olentangy River Rd, Columbus, OH 43210-0012. TEL 614-447-3600, FAX 614-447-3713, help@cas.com, http://caselects.cas.org. **Subscr. to:** PO Box 3012, Columbus, OH 43210. TEL 800-753-4227, FAX 614-447-3751.

668.4 338 USA ISSN 1555-6433
COMPOSITES INDUSTRY ABSTRACTS. Text in English. 1996. base vol. plus m. updates. **Document type:** *Database, Abstract/Index.* **Description:** Focuses on polymers and ceramics reinforced with fibers, honeycombs, whiskers and laminates. This database, centralizing information on composite materials, is a subset of the Engineered Materials Abstracts database. Sources covered include over 3,000 periodicals, conference proceedings, technical reports, trade journal/newsletter items, patents, books, and press releases.
Media: Online - full text.
Published by: (A S M International), ProQuest LLC (Bethesda) (Subsidiary of: Cambridge Information Group), 789 E Eisenhower Pky, Ann Arbor, MI 48103. TEL 734-761-4700, FAX 734-997-4222, info@proquest.com.

KEY ABSTRACTS - ADVANCED MATERIALS. *see* PHYSICS—Abstracting, Bibliographies, Statistics

R A P R A ABSTRACTS. (Rubber and Plastics Research Association) *see* RUBBER—Abstracting, Bibliographies, Statistics

668.4 678.2 GBR ISSN 0889-3144
TA455.P58 CODEN: RRVREQ
R A P R A REVIEW REPORTS; expert overviews covering the science and technology of rubbers and plastics. (Rubber and Plastics Research Association) Text in English. 1987. m. price varies. back issues avail. **Document type:** *Monographic series.* **Description:** Covers recent advances within specific fields of plastics, rubber and composite materials technology.
Related titles: Online - full text ed.: ISSN 1478-4149.
Indexed: A22, CIN, ChemAb, ChemTitl, R18.
—BLDSC (7291.760000), CASDDS, IE, Infotrieve, Ingenta, INIST, Linda Hall. **CCC.**
Published by: iSmithers, Shawbury, Shrewsbury, Shrops SY4 4NR, United Kingdom. TEL 44-1939-250383, FAX 44-1939-251118, info@ismithers.net.

RAPRA ABSTRACTS - CD-ROM. *see* RUBBER—Abstracting, Bibliographies, Statistics

RAPRA ABSTRACTS DATABASE. *see* RUBBER—Abstracting, Bibliographies, Statistics

668.4 GBR
RAPRA ABSTRACTS. PLASTICS MATERIALS. Text in English. 19??. bi-m. price varies. **Document type:** *Abstract/Index.*
Media: CD-ROM.
Published by: iSmithers, Shawbury, Shrewsbury, Shrops SY4 4NR, United Kingdom. TEL 44-1939-250383, FAX 44-1939-251118, info@ismithers.net, http://www.ismithers.net.

REFERATIVNYI ZHURNAL. TEKHNOLOGIYA POLIMERNYKH MATERYALOV: PLASTMASSY, IONOOBMENNYE MATERYALY; vypusk svodnogo toma. *see* CHEMISTRY—Abstracting, Bibliographies, Statistics

POETRY

see LITERATURE—Poetry

POLITICAL SCIENCE

see also LITERARY AND POLITICAL REVIEWS ; POLITICAL SCIENCE—Civil Rights ; POLITICAL SCIENCE—International Relations ; PUBLIC ADMINISTRATION

320 340 USA
A B A WASHINGTON SUMMARY (ONLINE). Text in English. w. free to members (effective 2010). **Document type:** *Newsletter, Government.* **Description:** Provides up-to-date information on congressional and executive branch activity with regard to legislative issues of interest to the organized bar.
Media: Online - full text.
Published by: American Bar Association, Governmental Affairs Office, 740 15th St, Washington, DC 20005. TEL 202-662-1000, FAX 202-662-1762, http://www.abanet.org/legadv. Ed. Jacklyn Schay TEL 202-662-1016.

322.4 CAN ISSN 1710-209X
HN1
A BABORD; revue sociale et politique. Text in French. 2003. 5/yr. CAD 35 domestic to individuals; CAD 50 domestic to institutions; CAD 65, EUR 43 foreign (effective 2007). **Document type:** *Journal, Consumer.*
Published by: A Babord, 5819 de Lorimier, Montreal, PQ H2G 2N8, Canada. TEL 514-523-6928, info@ababord.org, http://www.ababord.org.

320.531 ITA ISSN 1970-8343
A C L I OGGI. (Associazioni Cristiane Lavoratori Italiani) Text in Italian. 1963. w. **Document type:** *Newsletter, Consumer.*
Published by: Associazioni Cristiane Lavoratori Italiani (A C L I), Via Giuseppe Marcora 18-20, Rome, 00153, Italy. TEL 39-06-58401, FAX 39-06-5840202, acli@acli.it, http://www.acli.it.

324.2736 USA
A D A NEWS AND NOTES. Text in English. 1989. w. (when Congress in session). looseleaf. USD 20 (effective 2000). back issues avail. **Document type:** *Newsletter, Government.* **Description:** Reports on congressional action.
Related titles: E-mail ed.; Online - full text ed.
Published by: Americans for Democratic Action, 1625 K St N W, Ste 210, Washington, DC 20006. TEL 202-785-5980, FAX 202-785-5969. Ed., R&P Mike Alpern. Circ: 3,000 (paid).

320 DEU ISSN 0930-8199
A F B INFO. Text in English, German. 1986. 2/yr. free (effective 2008). Website rev. bibl. back issues avail. **Document type:** *Magazine, Consumer.* **Description:** Contains news about peace research related topics.
Published by: Arbeitsstelle Friedensforschung Bonn/Peace Research Information Unit Bonn, Beethovenallee 4, Bonn, 53173, Germany. TEL 49-228-356032, FAX 49-228-3670339, afb@priub.org. Ed., R&P Regine Mehl. Circ: 3,000.

320.51 USA ISSN 0893-293X
A L F NEWS. NEWSLETTER. Text in English. 1976. q. USD 10 (effective 2000). bk.rev. **Document type:** *Newsletter.* **Description:** Discusses the women's movement, the contemporary political scene, individual rights aimed at feminists and women in general.
Related titles: Online - full text ed.
Published by: Association of Libertarian Feminists, Box 20252, London Terrace Post Office, New York, NY 10011. TEL 212-924-4345, FAX 212-924-4345. Ed., R&P Joan Kennedy Taylor. Circ: 300.

320 USA
A P S A DIRECTORY OF POLITICAL SCIENCE DEPARTMENT CHAIRPERSONS (ONLINE). Text in English. 1972. a., latest 2002-2003. USD 50 per issue to non-members; USD 30 per issue to members (effective 2010). 60 p./no.; **Document type:** *Directory, Trade.* **Description:** Contains names and addresses of chairpersons of undergraduate political science degree-granting departments at four-year institutions.
Former titles (until 2000): A P S A Directory of Political Science Department Chairpersons (Print); (until 199?): A P S A Directory of Department Chairpersons (0196-5255); (until 197?): A P S A Directory of Department Chairmen (0092-8658)
Media: Online - full text.
Published by: American Political Science Association, 1527 New Hampshire Ave, NW, Washington, DC 20036. TEL 202-483-2512, FAX 202-483-2657, apsa@apsanet.org.

P

378.025 USA
A P S A DIRECTORY OF POLITICAL SCIENCE FACULTY (YEAR). Variant title: A P S A Directory of Political Science Faculty and Programs. Text in English. 2004. triennial. USD 75 per issue to non-members; USD 50 per issue to members (print or online ed.) (effective 2010). **Document type:** *Directory, Trade.* **Description:** Provides departmental mailing addresses and contact information, along with an indication of the highest degree offered and availability of a Pi Sigma Alpha chapter.
Formed by the merger of (1984-2004): Directory of Undergraduate Political Science Faculty (0884-5859); (1994-2004): Graduate Faculty and Programs in Political Science (1065-6049); Which was formerly (1972-1994): Guide to Graduate Study in Political Science (0091-9632)
Related titles: Online - full text ed.
Published by: American Political Science Association, 1527 New Hampshire Ave, NW, Washington, DC 20036. TEL 202-483-2512, FAX 202-483-2657, apsa@apsanet.org.

320 USA ISSN 1087-3872
JA28
A P S A SURVEY OF POLITICAL SCIENCE DEPARTMENTS. Text in English. 1971. a. USD 20 per issue (effective 2010). stat. **Document type:** *Monographic series.* **Description:** Provides practical advice from political scientists and publishers.
Formerly (until 1992): A P S A Departmental Services Program. Survey of Departments (0094-7954)
Indexed: SRI.
Published by: American Political Science Association, 1527 New Hampshire Ave, NW, Washington, DC 20036. TEL 202-483-2512, FAX 202-483-2657, apsa@apsanet.org.

320 297 CYP
A P S DIPLOMAT REDRAWING THE ISLAMIC MAP. Text in English. m. **Document type:** *Newsletter.*
Published by: Arab Press Service, PO Box 23896, Nicosia, Cyprus. TEL 357-2-350265, FAX 357-2-351778, apsnews@spidernet.com.cy.

320 AUS ISSN 1443-3605
DU80
➤ **A Q (BALMAIN).** (Australian Quarterly) Text in English. 1929. bi-m. AUD 85 membership (effective 2008). adv. bk.rev. illus. index, cum.index: 1954-1963, 1964-1968, 1969-1978. 40 p./no.; back issues avail.; reprints avail. **Document type:** *Journal, Academic/Scholarly.* **Description:** Publishes original manuscripts dealing with economic, political, social, philosophical, historical and scientific matters which have a bearing on the contemporary Australian scene.
Formerly (until 1997): Australian Quarterly (0005-0091)
Related titles: Online - full text ed.
Indexed: A01, A02, A03, A08, A11, A26, ABCPolSci, AEI, AESIS, AusPAIS, BAS, E08, G08, GdIns, GeoRef, HistAb, I05, I13, IBR, IBZ, M01, M02, MEA&I, MLA-IB, P06, P30, P42, PAIS, PCI, PSA, RASB, S09, SCOPUS, SociolAb, T02, WBA, WMB.
—BLDSC (1581.852700), IE, Ingenta. **CCC.**
Published by: Australian Institute of Political Science, Missenden Rd, PO Box M145, Balmain, NSW 2050, Australia. TEL 61-2-93510819, FAX 61-2-93510758, info@aips.net.au. Ed. Jim Morris. R&P Famena Khaya. Circ: 900.

335.83 ITA
HX821
A - RIVISTA. Text in Italian. 1971. m. bk.rev. illus. 52 p./no.; back issues avail. **Document type:** *Journal, Academic/Scholarly.* **Description:** Features articles that cover political events and ideas concerning the anarchist movement worldwide.
Formerly (until 199?): A - Rivista Anarchica (0044-5592)
Related titles: Online - full text ed.
Published by: Editrice A, Casella Postale 17120, Milan, MI 20170, Italy. TEL 39-02-2896627, FAX 39-02-28001271, arivista@tin.it. Circ: 4,500.

A S E A N BRIEFING. *see* BUSINESS AND ECONOMICS—Economic Situation And Conditions

A S E A S: AUSTRIAN JOURNAL OF SOUTH-EAST ASIAN STUDIES. *see* ASIAN STUDIES

320 ITA ISSN 2038-1662
A S T R I D. RASSEGNA. (Associazione per gli Studi e le Ricerche sulla Riforma delle Istituzioni Democratiche) Text in Multiple languages. 2005. bi-w. **Document type:** *Magazine, Trade.*
Media: Online - full text.
Published by: Fondazione per l'Analisi, gli Studi e le Ricerche sulla Riforma delle Istituzioni Democratiche e sull'Innovazione nelle Amministrazioni Pubbliche (A S T R I D), Corso Vittorio Emanuele II, 142, Rome, 00186, Italy. TEL 39-06-6810261.

320 USA
A W O L MAGAZINE. Text in English. irreg. **Document type:** *Magazine, Consumer.* **Description:** Covers urban social issues, counter-military topics, police brutality, and conscientious objectors' views; includes photos, art works, music, prose & poetry, and a CD.
Published by: A W O L Magazine, 1515 Cherry St, Philadelphia, PA 19102. **Dist. by:** A K Press, Inc. info@akpress.org, http://www.akpress.org/.

ABRAHAM LINCOLN ASSOCIATION. JOURNAL. *see* HISTORY

ACADEMIA BRASILEIRA DE CIENCIAS MORAIS E POLITICAS. REVISTA. *see* PHILOSOPHY

320 VEN ISSN 0798-1457
ACADEMIA DE CIENCIAS POLITICAS Y SOCIALES. BOLETIN. Text in Spanish. 1937. a. bibl. **Document type:** *Bulletin, Trade.*
Published by: Academia de Ciencias Politicas y Sociales, Palacio de las Academias, Avenida Universidad, Bolsa a San Francisco, Caracas, 1010, Venezuela. TEL 58-0212-4828845, FAX 58-0212-4832674, acienpoli@cantv.net, http://www.acienpol.com.

320 ARG
ACADEMIA NACIONAL DE CIENCIAS MORALES Y POLITICAS. ANALES. Text in Spanish. 1972. a.
Published by: Academia Nacional de Ciencias Morales y Politicas, Avda. Alvear 1711, P B, Buenos Aires, 1014, Argentina.

324.2469 PRT ISSN 0871-102X
HX9.P8
ACCAO SOCIALISTA. Text in Portuguese. 1976. w.
Published by: Partido Socialista, Largo do Rato, 2, Lisbon, 1200, Portugal. TEL 01-3464375. Ed. Jose Manuel Vilaca.

320 BRA ISSN 1677-8855
ACHEGAS.NET. Text in Portuguese. 2002. m. free (effective 2006). back issues avail. **Document type:** *Magazine.*
Media: Online - full text.
Address: Rua Senados Euzabio, 03-702, Rio de Janeiro, 22250-080, Brazil. TEL 55-21-25520418, FAX 55-21-25264384, revista@achegas.net. Ed. Alvizio Alves Filho.

320 910.02 CAN ISSN 1492-9732
H1
➤ **ACME;** an international e-journal for critical geographies. Text in English, French, German. 2002. s-a. free (effective 2011). adv. back issues avail. **Document type:** *Journal, Academic/Scholarly.* **Description:** Provides a forum for the publication of critical and radical work about space in the social sciences - including anarchist, anti-racist, environmentalist, feminist, Marxist, postcolonial, poststructuralist, queer, situationist and socialist perspectives.
Media: Online - full text.
Indexed: A01, A39, C27, C29, D03, D04, E13, IBSS, LeftInd, R14, S14, S15, S18, SCOPUS, T02.
—CCC.
Published by: University of British Columbia - Okanagan, 3333 University Way, Kelowna, BC V1V 1V7, Canada. TEL 250-807-8000, FAX 250-807-8001.

320 ITA ISSN 1826-8870
L'ACROPOLI. Text in Italian. 2000. bi-m. **Document type:** *Magazine, Consumer.*
Published by: Rubbettino Editore, Viale Rosario Rubbettino 10, Soveria Mannelli, CZ 88049, Italy. TEL 39-0968-662034, FAX 39-0968-662055, segreteria@rubettino.it, http://www.rubbettino.it. Ed. Giuseppe Galasso.

ACTA FACULTATIS POLITICO-JURIDICAE UNIVERSITATIS SCIENTIARUM BUDAPESTIENSIS DE ROLANDO EOTVOS NOMINATAE. *see* LAW

320 GBR ISSN 0001-6810
JA26
➤ **ACTA POLITICA;** international journal of political science. Abbreviated title: A P. Text in English. 1965. q. USD 688 in North America to institutions; GBP 370 elsewhere to institutions (effective 2012). adv. bk.rev. charts. back issues avail.; reprint service avail. from PSC. **Document type:** *Journal, Academic/Scholarly.* **Description:** Brings out work reflecting research and developments of both a theoretical and empirical nature in all sub-areas of the discipline, including Dutch and comparative politics, international relations, political theory, public administration, and political communication.
Related titles: Online - full text ed.: ISSN 1741-1416 (from IngentaConnect).
Indexed: A22, ABCPolSci, CA, E01, EI, HistAb, I13, IBSS, M07, MEA&I, P10, P42, P45, P46, P47, P48, P53, P54, PCI, PQC, PSA, S02, S03, S11, SCOPUS, SOPODA, SSA, SSCI, SociolAb, T02, W07.
—BLDSC (0658.700000), IE, Infotrieve, Ingenta. **CCC.**
Published by: (Nederlandse Kring voor Wetenschap der Politiek/Dutch Political Science Association NLD), Palgrave Macmillan Ltd. (Subsidiary of: Macmillan Publishers Ltd.), Houndmills, Basingstoke, Hants RG21 6XS, United Kingdom. TEL 44-1256-329242, FAX 44-1256-479476, orders@palgrave.com, http://www.palgrave.com. Eds. Ingrid van Biezen, Kees Aarts. **Subscr. to:** Subscription Department, Brunel Rd, Houndmills, Basingstoke, Hants RG21 2XS, United Kingdom. TEL 44-1256-357893, FAX 44-1256-812358, subscriptions@palgrave.com.

320 FIN ISSN 0355-323X
➤ **ACTA UNIVERSITATIS OULUENSIS. SERIES E. SCIENTIAE RERUM SOCIALIUM.** Text in Multiple languages. 1979. irreg. back issues avail. **Document type:** *Monographic series, Academic/Scholarly.*
Related titles: Online - full text ed.: ISSN 1796-2242.
Published by: Oulun Yliopisto, Julkaisupalvelut/University of Oulu. Publications Committee, Pentti Kaiteran Katu 1, PO Box 8000, Oulu, 90014, Finland. TEL 358-8-5531011, FAX 358-8-5534112, university.of.oulu@oulu.fi, http://www.oulu.fi. Eds. Eila Estola, Olli Vuolteenaho TEL 358-8-5375302. R&P Olli Vuolteenaho TEL 358-8-5375302.

➤ **ACTA UNIVERSITATIS SZEGEDIENSIS. ACTA IURIDICA ET POLITICA.** *see* LAW

320 POL ISSN 0867-7409
ACTA UNIVERSITATIS WRATISLAVIENSIS. POLITOLOGIA. Text in Polish; Summaries in English, German. 1991. irreg., latest vol.31, 2000. price varies. **Document type:** *Monographic series, Academic/Scholarly.*
Indexed: RASB.
Published by: (Uniwersytet Wroclawski), Wydawnictwo Uniwersytetu Wroclawskiego Sp. z o.o., pl Uniwersytecki 15, Wroclaw, 50137, Poland. TEL 48-71-3752809, FAX 48-71-3752735, marketing@wuwr.com.pl, http://www.wuwr.com.pl. Ed. Andrzej W Jablonski. Circ: 300.

320 FRA ISSN 1765-2022
ACTEURS PUBLICS. Text in French. 1988. m. (10/yr). EUR 65 (effective 2009). back issues avail. **Document type:** *Magazine, Consumer.* **Description:** Contains information about political news and elected officials.
Former titles (until 2004): Profession Politique. L'Actualite des Nominations, Elections et Mouvements (1277-0302); (until 1997): Profession Politique (0992-5163)
Published by: Societe d'Edition Publique, 26 Rue Marceau, Issy-les-Moulineaux, 92130, France. TEL 33-1-46292930, FAX 33-1-47362052, http://www.acteurspublics.com. Circ: 15,000.

320.5 FRA
L'ACTION FRANCAISE 2000. Text in French. 1908. w. adv. bk.rev. **Document type:** *Newspaper.*
Former titles (until 1993): L' Action Francaise (1166-3286); (until 1992): Aspects de la France (0223-5773); (until 1951): Aspects de la France et du Monde (0995-9688); (until 1947): L' Action Francaise (0995-9599)
Published by: S N I E P, 10 rue Croix des Petits Champs, Paris, 75001, France. TEL 1-40-399206. Ed. Pierre Pujo.

322.4 CAN ISSN 0001-7469
F1027
➤ **ACTION NATIONALE.** Text in English. 1917. 10/yr. CAD 42 domestic; USD 70 foreign (effective 1999 - 2000). adv. bk.rev. index. **Document type:** *Journal, Academic/Scholarly.* **Description:** Includes cultural, social and political texts.
Related titles: CD-ROM ed.
Indexed: AmH&L, C03, CBCARef, CBPI, CPerI, FR, I05, IBSS, MLA-IB, P48, PCI, PQC, PdeR, RASB.
Published by: Ligue d'Action Nationale, 425 Blvd de Maisonneuve Ouest, bureau 1002, Montreal, PQ H3A 3G5, Canada. TEL 514-845-8533, FAX 514-845-8529, http://www.repere.qc.ca. Ed., Adv. contact Robert Laplante. Circ: 2,000.

320.9 BEN ISSN 0044-6106
ACTION POPULAIRE. Text in French. 1964. 3/w. XOF 2,160, USD 25.
Address: c/o Julian Aza, Ed., BP 215, Cotonou, Benin.

322.4 CHE ISSN 0001-7507
ACTION SOCIALE. Text in French. s-m. CHF 12.
Published by: Organisations Chretiennes-Sociales, Rue de l Abbe Bovet 6, Fribourg, 1700, Switzerland.

320 USA ISSN 1074-2360
ACTIVE VOICE; of the people, by the people, for the people. Text in English. 1988. m. USD 10; USD 12 in Canada & Mexico; USD 25 elsewhere. adv. **Document type:** *Newspaper.*
Published by: Active Communication Inc., PO Box 394, Berea, OH 44017. TEL 216-243-2189, FAX 216-362-6553. Ed., Pub., R&P Ron McEntee. adv.: page USD 600.

320 ARG ISSN 0327-6058
F2849.2
ACTUALIZACION POLITICA. Text in Spanish. 1991. m.?. **Description:** Provides political, economic, cultural and social analysis and information.
Published by: Fundacion Integracion Americana, Avda. Callao, 420 6o A, Buenos Aires, 1022, Argentina. TEL 54-114-491182. Ed. Mario A Balzan.

320.5322 FRA ISSN 0994-4524
HX5
➤ **ACTUEL MARX.** Text in French; Abstracts in English. 1987. s-a. EUR 67 foreign to institutions (effective 2012). **Document type:** *Journal, Academic/Scholarly.* **Description:** Covers the philosophical, economic, historical, social science and literary aspects of Marxism.
Related titles: Online - full content ed.: ISSN 1969-6728. 200?; ◆ Spanish ed.: Actuel Marx Intervenciones. ISSN 0718-0179.
Indexed: A22, FR, IBSS, PCI, SCOPUS.
—IE, Infotrieve, INIST. **CCC.**
Published by: Presses Universitaires de France, 6 Avenue Reille, Paris, 75685, France. TEL 33-1-58103161, FAX 33-1-45897530, revues@puf.com, http://www.puf.com. Ed. Emmanuel Renault.

320.5322 FRA ISSN 1158-5900
ACTUEL MARX CONFRONTATION. Text in French. 1991. irreg. **Document type:** *Monographic series, Academic/Scholarly.*
Related titles: Series: Actuel Marx Confrontation. Serie Sociologie. ISSN 1761-8134. 2002; Actuel Marx Confrontation. Serie Politique. ISSN 1637-0376. 2002; Actuel Marx Confrontation. Serie Droit. ISSN 1630-0599. 2001; Actuel Marx Confrontation. Serie Histoire. ISSN 1622-7239. 2000; Actuel Marx Confrontation. Serie Economie. ISSN 1624-2661. 2000; Actuel Marx Confrontation. Serie Philosophie. ISSN 1296-5669. 2000.
—CCC.
Published by: Presses Universitaires de France, 6 Avenue Reille, Paris, 75685, France. TEL 33-1-58103161, FAX 33-1-45897530, revues@puf.com.

321 CHL ISSN 0718-0179
ACTUEL MARX INTERVENCIONES. Text in Spanish. 2003. s-a. **Document type:** *Journal, Trade.*
Related titles: ◆ French ed.: Actuel Marx. ISSN 0994-4524.
Published by: LOM Ediciones, Concha y Toro 23, Santiago, Chile. TEL 56-2-6885273, lom@lom.cl, http://www.lom.cl/. Ed. Maria Emilia Tijoux.

320 USA
ADJUDICATOR. Text in English. q. free. **Document type:** *Newsletter.*
Published by: Industrial Commission of Ohio, 30 W. Spring St, 5th Fl, Columbus, OH 43266. TEL 614-644-8361, FAX 614-728-4795.

ADMINISTRATION & SOCIETY. *see* PUBLIC ADMINISTRATION

320 ESP ISSN 1697-0403
AFKAR IDEAS. Text in Spanish. 2003. q. EUR 20 domestic; EUR 26 foreign (effective 2009). **Document type:** *Magazine, Consumer.*
Published by: (Instituto Europeo del Mediterrano/Institut Europeu de la Mediterrania), Estudios de Politica Exterior S.A., Nunez de Balboa 49, 5o Piso, Madrid, 28001, Spain.

320 GBR ISSN 0044-6483
DT1
AFRICA CONFIDENTIAL. Text in English. 1960. fortn. (25/yr.). GBP 723 combined subscription domestic (print & online eds.); USD 1,265 combined subscription foreign (print & online eds.) (effective 2009). illus. Index. back issues avail.; reprints avail. **Document type:** *Newspaper, Consumer.* **Description:** Covers political and economic analysis of African countries, dealing with critical subjects of the day.
Formerly (until 1967): Africa
Related titles: Online - full text ed.: ISSN 1467-6338. GBP 632 domestic; USD 1,106 foreign (effective 2009).
Indexed: A01, A03, A08, A22, A26, CA, CCME, E01, I05, KES, M10, P34, PAIS, RASB, S02, S03, T02.
—BLDSC (0732.153000), IE, Infotrieve, Ingenta. **CCC.**
Published by: Asempa Ltd., 73 Farringdon Rd, London, ECIM 3JQ, United Kingdom. TEL 44-20-78313511, FAX 44-20-78316778. Ed. Patrick Smith. **Subscr. to:** Vine House, Fair Green, Reach, Cambridge CB25 0JD, United Kingdom. TEL 44-1638-743633, FAX 44-1638-743988, subscriptions@africa-confidential.com.

AFRICA INSIGHT. *see* HISTORY—History Of Africa

AFRICA INSTITUTE. OCCASIONAL PUBLICATIONS. *see* HISTORY—History Of Africa

AFRICA MONITOR. NORTH AFRICA. *see* BUSINESS AND ECONOMICS—Economic Situation And Conditions

AFRICA MONITOR. SOUTHERN AFRICA. *see* BUSINESS AND ECONOMICS—Economic Situation And Conditions

AFRICA MONITOR. WEST AFRICA. *see* BUSINESS AND ECONOMICS—Economic Situation And Conditions

320 USA ISSN 1075-2536
DT1
AFRICA NEWS ONLINE. Text in English. 1973. s-m. free. adv. bk.rev. illus. s-a. index. back issues avail.; reprints avail. **Document type:** *Newspaper.* **Description:** Covers American politics, the economy, culture, sports, technology and health issues from more than sixty sources, including readings from African newspapers and agencies.
Formerly: Africa News (0191-6521)
Media: Online - full text. **Related titles:** Microform ed.: (from PQC).
Indexed: A22, A26, AltPI, E08, HRIR, I08, P02, P10, P48, P53, P54, PQC, RASB, S09.
—CIS. **CCC.**
Published by: Africa News Service, Inc., PO Box 3851, Durham, NC 27702. TEL 919-286-0747, FAX 919-286-2614. Ed. Tamela Hultman. R&P Bertie Howard.

AFRICA POLICY JOURNAL. *see* BUSINESS AND ECONOMICS

320.9 IND ISSN 0001-9828
DT1
AFRICA QUARTERLY; a journal of African affairs. Text in English. 1961. q. adv. bk.rev. illus. index. reprints avail. **Document type:** *Journal, Academic/Scholarly.* **Description:** Provides information on African affairs and India's relations with the African nations.
Related titles: Microform ed.: (from PQC).
Indexed: A22, ABCPolSci, ASD, CCA, DIP, HistAb, IBR, IBSS, IBZ, MEA&I, MLA-IB, P06, P30, PerIslam, RASB.
—BLDSC (0732.170000), IE, Infotrieve, Ingenta.
Published by: Indian Council for Cultural Relations, Azad Bhavan, Indraprastha Estate, New Delhi, 110 002, India. TEL 91-11-23379158, FAX 91-11-23379056, pdpub@iccrindia.org.

960.3 GBR ISSN 1744-2532
DT1
AFRICA RENAISSANCE. Text in English. 2004. q. GBP 100 to individuals; GBP 250 to institutions (effective 2009). back issues avail. **Document type:** *Journal, Academic/Scholarly.*
Related titles: Online - full text ed.: GBP 80 to individuals; GBP 200 to institutions (effective 2009).
Published by: Adonis & Abbey Publishers Ltd., PO Box 43418, London, SE11 4XZ, United Kingdom. TEL 44-20-77938803. Ed. Dr. Jideofor Adibe.

320.96 JPN ISSN 0911-5552
DT1
AFRICA REPORT. Text in Japanese. 1985. 2/yr. JPY 1,770 (effective 2003). bk.rev. bibl. **Document type:** *Academic/Scholarly.* **Description:** Includes papers, field reports, and book information with a regional focus on Africa.
Published by: Institute of Developing Economies/Ajia Keizai Kenkyusho, 3-2-2 Wakaba, Mihana-ku, Chiba-shi, Chiba 261-8545, Japan. TEL 81-43-2999536, FAX 84-43-2999724. Circ: 250.

916 320 FRA ISSN 1950-4810
HC800.A1
THE AFRICA REPORT (PARIS). Text in English. 2005. bi-m. EUR 29 domestic; EUR 35 in Europe; EUR 35 in North America; EUR 39 elsewhere (effective 2009). **Document type:** *Magazine, Consumer.*
Indexed: CABA, R12, TAR, W11.
Published by: Groupe Jeune Afrique, 57 bis, Rue d'Auteuil, Paris, 75016, France. TEL 33-1-44301960, FAX 33-1-44301930, http://www.groupeja.com.

320 GBR ISSN 0001-9844
AFRICA RESEARCH BULLETIN. POLITICAL, SOCIAL AND CULTURAL SERIES. Text in English. 1964. m. GBP 967 in United Kingdom to institutions; EUR 1,228 in Europe to institutions; USD 1,834 in the Americas to institutions; USD 2,142 elsewhere to institutions; GBP 1,112 combined subscription in United Kingdom to institutions (print & online eds.); EUR 1,412 combined subscription in Europe to institutions (print & online eds.); USD 2,110 combined subscription in the Americas to institutions (print & online eds.); USD 2,463 combined subscription elsewhere to institutions (print & online eds.) (effective 2012). illus. Index. back issues avail.; reprints avail. **Document type:** *Journal, Academic/Scholarly.* **Description:** Provides impartial summaries and extensive reports on political and economic developments throughout Africa.
Former titles (until 1992): Africa Research Bulletin. Political Series; (until 1985): Africa Research Bulletin. Political, Social, and Cultural Series; (until Mar.1965): Africa Research Bulletin. Africa, Political, Social, and Cultural Series; (until Feb.1965): Africa Research Bulletin. Africa, Political, Social, and Cultural
Related titles: Online - full text ed.: ISSN 1467-825X. GBP 967 in United Kingdom to institutions; EUR 1,228 in Europe to institutions; USD 1,834 in the Americas to institutions; USD 2,142 elsewhere to institutions (effective 2012) (from IngentaConnect).
Indexed: A01, A03, A08, A22, A26, CA, CCA, E01, M10, P02, P10, P34, P42, P47, P48, P53, P54, PAIS, PQC, RASB, S02, S03, S11, T02.
—IE, Infotrieve, Ingenta. **CCC.**
Published by: Wiley-Blackwell Publishing Ltd. (Subsidiary of: John Wiley & Sons, Inc.), 9600 Garsington Rd, Oxford, OX4 2DQ, United Kingdom. TEL 44-1865-776868, FAX 44-1865-714591, customerservices@blackwellpublishing.com, http://www.wiley.com/WileyCDA/. Eds. Veronica Hoskins TEL 44-1363-775207, Virginia Baily TEL 44-13-92214290.

320.9 GBR ISSN 0065-3896
DT351
AFRICA SOUTH OF THE SAHARA (YEAR). Text in English. 1971. a. USD 760 per issue (effective 2009). illus. Index. reprints avail. **Document type:** *Directory, Academic/Scholarly.* **Description:** Follows a general introduction, with essays on African affairs and a section covering regional organizations. Includes separate chapters on each of the countries. Supplies the latest facts and figures and directory material.
Indexed: IBR, IBZ, P30.
—BLDSC (0732.188000), Infotrieve. **CCC.**
Published by: (Europa Publications Ltd.), Routledge (Subsidiary of: Taylor & Francis Group), 2 Park Sq, Milton Park, Abingdon, Oxon OX14 4RN, United Kingdom. TEL 44-20-70176000, FAX 44-20-70176699, orders@taylorandfrancis.com. **Dist. by:** Current Pacific Ltd., 7 La Roche Pl, Northcote, PO Box 36-536, Auckland 0627, New Zealand.

320.9 USA ISSN 0001-9887
➤ **AFRICA TODAY.** Text in English. 1954. q. USD 196.50 combined subscription (print & online eds.) (effective 2012). adv. bk.rev. bibl.; illus. index. back issues avail.; reprint service avail. from PSC. **Document type:** *Journal, Academic/Scholarly.* **Description:** Examines issues affecting contemporary Africa, with emphasis on politics and economics.
Related titles: Microform ed.: (from PQC); Online - full text ed.: ISSN 1527-1978. USD 130.50 (effective 2012).
Indexed: A01, A02, A03, A08, A20, A22, A25, A26, A36, A38, ABCPolSci, ASCA, ASD, AbAn, AcaI, B04, BA, BRD, CA, CABA, CBRI, CCA, CERDIC, DIP, E01, E08, E12, ESPM, F08, F12, FamI, G08, G09, GEOBASE, GH, H09, HPNRM, HRIR, HistAb, I05, I07, I08, IBR, IBSS, IBZ, IIBP, L&LBA, LT, M01, M02, M08, M10, MEA&I, MLA, MLA-IB, P02, P06, P10, P13, P27, P30, P34, P42, P45, P46, P48, P53, P54, PAIS, PCI, PQC, PRA, PSA, PerIslam, PlantSci, PollutAb, R12, RILM, RRTA, RefugAb, S02, S03, S05, S08, S09, S13, S16, S23, SCOPUS, SSAI, SSAb, SSI, SSciA, SociolAb, T02, T05, TAR, W03, W05, W09, W11.
—BLDSC (0732.190000), IE, Infotrieve, Ingenta. **CCC.**
Published by: Indiana University Press, 601 N Morton St, Bloomington, IN 47404. TEL 812-855-9449, 800-842-6796, FAX 812-855-8507, journals@indiana.edu, http://iupjournals.org. Eds. Eileen Julien, Maria Grosz-Ngate, Patrick McNaughton, Samuel Obeng. Circ: 1,300 (paid).

320.96 330.96 GBR ISSN 1744-0734
DT1
AFRICA WEEK; networking intelligence. Text in English. 2004. w. GBP 30 domestic; GBP 40 in Europe; USD 65 in US & Canada; GBP 65 elsewhere; GBP 63 combined subscription domestic (print & online eds.); GBP 65 combined subscription in Europe (print & online eds.); USD 100 combined subscription in US & Canada (print & online eds.); GBP 75 combined subscription elsewhere (print & online eds.) (effective 2009). back issues avail. **Document type:** *Magazine, Consumer.* **Description:** Covers African affairs and issues. Aims to enhance knowledge in Africa and about Africa.
Related titles: Online - full text ed.: ISSN 1744-0742.
Published by: Trans Africa Publishing Company Limited, PO Box 50010, London, SE6 2WJ, United Kingdom. TEL 44-208-2851675, FAX 44-870-4292026, info@africaweekmagazine.com. Ed. Desmond Davies.

AFRICA YEARBOOK; politics, economy and society south of the Sahara. *see* ANTHROPOLOGY

320 GBR ISSN 0001-9909
DT1
➤ **AFRICAN AFFAIRS.** Text in English. 1901. q. GBP 272 in United Kingdom to institutions; EUR 408 in Europe to institutions; USD 543 in US & Canada to institutions; GBP 272 elsewhere to institutions; GBP 296 combined subscription in United Kingdom to institutions (print & online eds.); EUR 445 combined subscription in Europe to institutions (print & online eds.); USD 593 combined subscription in US & Canada to institutions (print & online eds.); GBP 296 combined subscription elsewhere to institutions (print & online eds.) (effective 2012). adv. bk.rev. bibl.; illus. index. 168 p./no.; back issues avail.; reprint service avail. from PSC. **Document type:** *Journal, Academic/Scholarly.* **Description:** Publishes articles on recent political, social, and economic developments in sub-Saharan countries.
Former titles (until 1944): Royal African Society. Journal (0368-4016); (until 1935): Journal of the African Society (1753-4577)
Related titles: Microform ed.; Online - full text ed.: ISSN 1468-2621. 2000. GBP 247 in United Kingdom to institutions; EUR 371 in Europe to institutions; USD 494 in US & Canada to institutions; GBP 247 elsewhere to institutions (effective 2012) (from IngentaConnect).
Indexed: A01, A02, A03, A08, A20, A22, A25, A26, A36, ABCPolSci, AICP, ARDT, ASCA, ASD, AbAn, AmH&L, AmHI, B04, BRD, BrHumI, C25, CA, CABA, CCA, CurCont, DIP, E01, E08, E12, ESPM, FR, G08, GEOBASE, GH, GeoRef, H07, H08, H09, H10, HAb, HistAb, HumInd, I05, I08, I11, I13, IBR, IBSS, IBZ, IIBP, ILD, LT, LeftInd, M10, MLA-IB, MaizeAb, N02, P02, P06, P10, P30, P34, P42, P45, P48, P53, P54, PAIS, PCI, PQC, PRA, PSA, R12, RA&MP, RASB, RILM, RRTA, RefSour, RefugAb, S02, S03, S05, S08, S09, S13, S16, S23, SCOPUS, SOPODA, SSA, SSCI, SSciA, SociolAb, T02, T05, TAR, W03, W07, W11.
—BLDSC (0732.300000), IE, Infotrieve, Ingenta. **CCC.**
Published by: (Royal African Society), Oxford University Press, Great Clarendon St, Oxford, OX2 6DP, United Kingdom. TEL 44-1865-556767, FAX 44-1865-556646, enquiry@oup.co.uk, http://www.oxfordjournals.org. Eds. Rita Abrahamsen, Sara Rich Dorman, Tim Kelsall. Adv. contact Linda Hann TEL 44-1344-779945. B&W page GBP 290, B&W page USD 520; 118 x 198. Circ: 2,350.

320.96 ZAF ISSN 1024-3194
AFRICAN AGENDA. Text in English. 1995. m. ZAR 55; USD 30 in Africa; GBP 35 in Europe; USD 70 in North America; USD 100 elsewhere. adv. illus. **Description:** Covers national, regional and international development issues and trends affecting the African continent.
Published by: (Third World Network), Africa South & East Publications Trust, PO Box 94154, Yeoville, Johannesberg 2198, South Africa. TEL 27-11-4871596, FAX 27-11-648-0907. Ed. Gwen Ansell.

320.532 ZAF ISSN 0001-9976
HX3
AFRICAN COMMUNIST. Text in English. 1959. q. ZAR 35, USD 30. adv. bk.rev. stat.; illus. cum.index: 1959-1988. reprints avail. **Description:** Serves as a forum for Marxist-Leninist thought by the South African Communist Party.
Related titles: Microform ed.: (from PQC); Online - full content ed.: ISSN 1560-7887. 1995.
Indexed: A22, ASD, CCA, IBR, IBZ, ISAP, LeftInd, MLA-IB, PCI, RASB.
—BLDSC (0732.390000), IE, Infotrieve, Ingenta.
Published by: South African Communist Party, PO Box 1027, Johannesburg, 2000, South Africa. TEL 27-11-3393633, FAX 27-11-3394244, sacp1@wn.apc.org, http://www.arc.org.za. Circ: 10,000.

AFRICAN IDENTITIES; journal of economics, culture and society. *see* ETHNIC INTERESTS

320 ZAF ISSN 1027-0353
JQ1871.A1
AFRICAN JOURNAL OF POLITICAL SCIENCE. Text in English, Arabic. 1985. s-a. USD 20 domestic; USD 25 foreign (effective 2004). back issues avail. **Document type:** *Journal, Academic/Scholarly.* **Description:** Provides a platform for African perspectives on issues of politics, economy and society in Africa.
Formerly (until 1996): African Journal of Political Economy (1017-4974)
Related titles: Online - full text ed.
Indexed: I13, IIBP.
—BLDSC (0732.554000).
Published by: African Association of Political Science, The Tramshed, PO Box 13995, Pretoria, 0126, South Africa. TEL 27-12-3261724, FAX 27-12-3261726, program@aaps.org.za. Ed. S. Rugumamu.

320 327 NGA ISSN 1996-0832
JA26
AFRICAN JOURNAL OF POLITICAL SCIENCE AND INTERNATIONAL RELATIONS. Variant title: A J P S I R. Text in English. 2007. m. free (effective 2007). **Document type:** *Journal, Academic/Scholarly.*
Media: Online - full text.
Indexed: P42, PSA.
Published by: Academic Journals, PO Box 73023, Victoria Island, Lagos, Nigeria. service@academicjournals.org. Ed. Dr. Mojubaolu Olufunke Okome.

320 GBR ISSN 2040-333X
▼ **AFRICAN LEADERSHIP REVIEW**; journal of governance, leadership and development in Africa. Text in English. 2009. s-a. GBP 100 combined subscription domestic to individuals (print & online eds.); GBP 160 combined subscription foreign to individuals (print & online eds.); GBP 350 combined subscription domestic to institutions (print & online eds.); GBP 565 combined subscription foreign to institutions (print & online eds.) (effective 2010). adv. back issues avail. **Document type:** *Journal, Trade.* **Description:** Addresses the challenges of leadership on the African continent vis-a-vis African development.
Related titles: Online - full text ed.: ISSN 2040-3348. GBP 60 domestic to individuals; GBP 100 foreign to individuals; GBP 260 domestic to institutions; GBP 395 foreign to institutions (effective 2010).
Published by: White Media UK Ltd., PO Box 3116, Glasgow, G60 9BH, United Kingdom. TEL 44-141-5488035, info@whitemediauk.com, http://www.whitemediauk.com. Ed. Oluyemi Borisade.

320.9 TZA ISSN 0856-0056
AFRICAN REVIEW; a journal of African politics, development and international affairs. Text in English. 1971. s-a. adv. bk.rev. back issues avail. **Document type:** *Journal, Academic/Scholarly.*
Formerly: African Political Review (0002-0117)
Indexed: ABCPolSci, ASD, IBR, IBZ, IIBP, P06, P30, PAIS, PCI, PLESA, RASB.
—Ingenta.
Published by: University of Dar es Salaam, Department of Political Science, PO Box 35042, Dar Es Salaam, Tanzania. TEL 255-51-43130, FAX 255-51-43395. Ed. Charles Gasarasi. Circ: 1,000.

320 330.9 300 USA ISSN 1939-2206
AFRICAN SECURITY. Text in English. 2008. s-a. GBP 226 combined subscription in United Kingdom to institutions (print & online eds.); EUR 292, USD 448 combined subscription to institutions (print & online eds.) (effective 2012). reprint service avail. from PSC. **Document type:** *Journal, Academic/Scholarly.* **Description:** Investigates competing analytical approaches to understanding real world security issues in Africa, including the myriad issues relating to conflict and security within and between African nations with theoretical challenges drawn from the perspectives of other disciplines, such as anthropology, development studies, environmental studies, and economics.
Related titles: Online - full text ed.: ISSN 1939-2214. GBP 203 in United Kingdom to institutions; EUR 263, USD 404 to institutions (effective 2012).
Indexed: I02, IBSS, P42, PAIS, PSA, T02.
—IE. **CCC.**
Published by: Routledge (Subsidiary of: Taylor & Francis Group), 325 Chestnut St, Ste 800, Philadelphia, PA 19106. TEL 215-625-8900, 800-354-1420, FAX 215-625-8914, journals@routledge.com, http://www.routledge.com. Eds. Gladys Mokhawa, Ian Taylor, James J. Hentz.

AFRICAN STUDIES. *see* ANTHROPOLOGY

320 960 USA ISSN 2155-7829
JQ1873.5.P65
➤ **AFRICANA (BOSTON).** Text in English. 2007. s-a. **Document type:** *Journal, Academic/Scholarly.* **Description:** Provides practical, theoretical and critical perspectives on Africa, Africans, and the African Diaspora.
Related titles: Online - full text ed.: ISSN 2155-7837.
Published by: Boston University, African Studies Center, 270 Bay State Rd, Boston, MA 02215. FAX 617-353-4975, ascpub@bu.edu, http://www.bu.edu/africa/index.html, http://www.bu.edu/africa.

320 ZAF ISSN 0304-615X
DT763
➤ **AFRICANUS**; journal of development alternatives. Text in English. 1971. s-a. ZAR 50 domestic to individuals; USD 15 foreign to individuals; ZAR 70 domestic to institutions; USD 40 foreign to institutions (effective 2006). bk.rev. abstr.; bibl.; charts; illus.; stat. back issues avail. **Document type:** *Journal, Academic/Scholarly.* **Description:** Publishes articles, research reports, reviews and bibliographies on subjects relating to development theory and practice in the Third World.
Related titles: Microfiche ed.; Online - full text ed.
Indexed: ASD, AbAn, CA, CCA, DIP, ESPM, IBR, IBZ, IIBP, ISAP, P42, PSA, S02, S03, SCOPUS, SSciA, SociolAb, T02.
Published by: (University of South Africa), UniSA Press, PO Box 392, Pretoria, 0003, South Africa. TEL 27-12-4292953, FAX 27-12-4293449, unisa-press@unisa.ac.za, http://www.unisa.ac.za/press. Ed. I M M du Plessis. R&P Phoebe van der Walt TEL 27-12-429-3051. Circ: 1,000.

320.96 DEU ISSN 0935-3534
AFRIKA JAHRBUCH. Text in German. 1988. a. **Document type:** *Journal, Academic/Scholarly.*
Indexed: ASD, DIP, IBR, IBZ.
Published by: V S - Verlag fuer Sozialwissenschaften (Subsidiary of: Springer Fachmedien Wiesbaden GmbH), Abraham-Lincoln-Str 46, Wiesbaden, 65189, Germany. TEL 49-611-78780, FAX 49-611-7878400, springerfachmedien-wiesbaden@springer.com, http://www.vs-verlag.de.

P

320 DEU ISSN 0002-0397
DT1
➤ **AFRIKA SPECTRUM**; Zeitschrift fuer gegenwartsbezogene Afrikaforschung. Text in English, French, German; Summaries in English, French, German. 1966. 3/yr. EUR 60; EUR 22 per issue (effective 2009). adv. bk.rev. bibl.; charts. index. 150 p./no.; back issues avail. **Document type:** *Journal, Academic/Scholarly.* **Description:** Focuses on the social sciences dealing with Africa and aims to promote a deeper understanding of African peoples and cultures.
Related titles: Online - full text ed.: free (effective 2011).
Indexed: A20, A22, ASD, CA, CCA, DIP, ESPM, FR, I13, IBR, IBSS, IBZ, IIBP, ILD, KES, M10, MLA-IB, P06, P34, P42, PAIS, PCI, PRA, PSA, PerIslam, RASB, REE&TA, S02, S03, SCOPUS, SSCI, SSciA, SociolAb, T02, W07.
—BLDSC (0735.268000), IE, Infotrieve, Ingenta, INIST.
Published by: G I G A Institute of African Affairs, Neuer Jungfernstieg 21, Hamburg, 20354, Germany. TEL 49-40-42825523, FAX 49-40-42825511, iaa@giga-hamburg.de, http://www.duei.de/iak. Eds. Andreas Mehler, Henning Melber. Circ: 500.

320.52 ZAF ISSN 1994-9340
DIE AFRIKANER. Text in Afrikaans. 1969. w. looseleaf. ZAR 250 (effective 2007). back issues avail. **Description:** Covers political and business issues from a right-wing perspective.
Published by: (Herstigte Nasionale Party), Strydpers BPK, Posbus 1888, Pretoria, 0001, South Africa. TEL 27-12-3358523. Ed. Dr. J L Basson. Circ: 10,000.

320.9 FRA ISSN 1779-0042
DT1
AFRIQUE ASIE. Text in French. 1969. m. EUR 28 domestic to individuals; EUR 30 to individuals in Maghreb; EUR 44 in Europe to individuals; EUR 44 in Africa to individuals CFA; EUR 76 elsewhere to individuals (effective 2008). adv. **Document type:** *Magazine, Consumer.* **Description:** Covers the politics, culture and economy of Africa and the Middle East.
Former titles (until 2005): Le Nouvel Afrique Asie (1141-9946); (until 1987): Afrique-Asie (0302-6485); (until 1972): Africasia (1141-9954)
Indexed: CCA, M10, MLA-IB, PAIS, RASB.
Published by: Afriam, 3 rue de l'Atlas, Paris, 75019, France. Circ: 100,000.

320.57
AGAINST SLEEP AND NIGHTMARE. Text in English. irreg. USD 2 newsstand/cover (effective 2002). **Document type:** *Magazine, Consumer.* **Description:** Contains essays on work, alienation, organization and other ultra-leftist views.
Related titles: Online - full text ed.
Address: PO Box 3305, Oakland, CA 94609. **Dist. by:** A K Press, Inc., 674-A 23rd St, Oakland, CA 94612. TEL 510-208-1700, FAX 510-208-1701, info@akpress.org, http://www.akpress.org/.

320.531 USA ISSN 0739-4853
HX1
➤ **AGAINST THE CURRENT.** Text in English. 1979; N.S. 1986. bi-m. USD 25 (effective 2011). adv. bk.rev. illus. First five volumes. 48 p./no. 3 cols./p.; back issues avail.; reprints avail. **Document type:** *Magazine, Trade.* **Description:** Contains discussions of movements for social and political change, and commentary from a socialist and feminist viewpoint with special emphasis on labor.
Supersedes: Changes (Detroit) (0746-5335); Formerly (until 1984): Changes Socialist Monthly
Related titles: Microform ed.: N.S. (from PQC); Online - full text ed.: ISSN 2162-2876.

Indexed: A01, APW, AltPI, ChPerI, DIP, IBR, IBZ, LeftInd, MLA-IB, P34, RASB.
—BLDSC (0735.826000), IE, Ingenta.
Published by: Center for Changes, 7012 Michigan Ave, Detroit, MI 48210. TEL 313-841-0160, info@solidarity-us.org.

320.9 BOL ISSN 0252-8444
AGENCIA DE NOTICIAS FIDES. NOTAS. Text in Spanish. 1972. w. USD 200. **Document type:** *Newsletter.* **Description:** Political and economic analysis of Bolivia.
Published by: Agencia de Noticias Fides, Casilla 5782, La Paz, Bolivia. TEL 591-2-365152, FAX 591-2-365153, TELEX 3236 FIDES BV. Ed. Jose Gramunt. Circ: 1,200.

321 PER ISSN 1609-9915
AGENCIAPERU.COM. Text in Spanish. 1998. d.
Media: Online - full text.
Published by: AgenciaPeru.com, Jr. Diez Canseco 276 Depto. "L" Miraflores, Lima, Peru. TEL 51-1-7105635, FAX 51-1-4454425, info@agenciaperu.com, http://www.agenciaperu.com/. Ed. Marcos Sifuentes.

320.609416 GBR ISSN 1752-4466
AGENDA N I; informing Northern Ireland's decision makers. (Northern Ireland) Text in English. 2006. m. GBP 29.95 (effective 2009). adv. back issues avail. **Document type:** *Magazine, Trade.* **Description:** Contains in-depth of public policy issues.
Related titles: Online - full text ed.
Published by: B M F Publishing, Davidson House, Glenavy Rd Business Park, Moira, Co. Down BT67 0LT, United Kingdom. TEL 44-28-92619933, FAX 44-28-92619951, info@agendani.com.

320.982 ARG ISSN 0328-3623
AGORA; cuaderno de estudios politicos. Text in Spanish. 1993. s-a. USD 20 domestic to individuals; USD 24 in Latin America to individuals; USD 25 domestic to institutions; USD 35 in Latin America to institutions.
Published by: Grupo Universitario de Estudios Politicos, Defensa, 1111 1o A, Buenos Aires, Buenos Aires 1065, Argentina. TEL 54-114-8013606, FAX 54-114-8116501. Eds. Andres Clerici, Sebastian Mazzuca.

320.57 CAN
AHIMSA. Text in English. q. USD 8; USD 2 newsstand/cover (effective 2001). **Document type:** *Newspaper, Consumer.* **Description:** Covers the anarchopacifists movements and includes global & local news, editorials, historical essays, and contacts.
Address: Affinity Place, Argenta, BC V0G 1B0, Canada. http://members.nbci.com/ahimsazine/index.html.

320.532 CUB ISSN 0864-1641
AHORA. Text in Spanish. 1962. w. back issues avail.
Related titles: Online - full text ed.: ISSN 1607-6389. 2000.
Published by: Partido Comunista de Cuba, Comite Provincial Holguin, Apdo. de Correos 316, Holguin, 80100, Cuba. TEL 53-24-423013, FAX 53-24-422460, ahoraweb@ahora.cu, http://www.ahora.cu/. Ed. Jorge Luis Cruz Bermudes.

320 ZAF
AIDA PARKER NEWSLETTER. Text in English. 1983. m. ZAR 100, USD 80 (effective 2001). bk.rev. 16 p./no.; back issues avail. **Document type:** *Newsletter.* **Description:** Analysis and perspectives on Southern African affairs.
Published by: Aida Parker Newsletter Pty. Ltd., PO Box 91059, Auckland Park, Johannesburg 2006, South Africa. TEL 27-11-726-6856, FAX 27-11-726-5537. Ed. Aida Parker. Circ: 2,500.

320 FRA ISSN 2107-3910
▼ **L'AIGUILLON BOUILLADISSIEN.** Text in French. 2009. q. **Document type:** *Consumer.*
Published by: L' Aiguillon Bouilladissien, 1 Bd Fortis-Capuano, La Bouilladisse, 13720, France.

AJIKEN TOPIC REPORT. *see* BUSINESS AND ECONOMICS

AKTIEF. *see* LITERARY AND POLITICAL REVIEWS

320 DEU ISSN 0939-3099
AKTUELLE OSTINFORMATIONEN. Text in German. 1969. s-a. bk.rev. **Document type:** *Newspaper, Consumer.*
Indexed: IBR, IBZ.
Published by: Gesamteuropaeisches Studienwerk e.V., Suedfeldstr 2-4, Vlotho, 32602, Germany. TEL 49-5733-91380, FAX 49-5733-913847, info@gesw.de, http://www.gesw.de. Circ: 2,000.

329.14 SWE ISSN 1403-7505
AKTUELLT I POLITIKEN; socialdemokraternas nyhetstidning. Text in Swedish. 1953. 49/yr. SEK 398 (effective 2011). adv. illus. **Document type:** *Newspaper, Consumer.*
Former titles (until 1995): Nyhetstidningen A i P (1103-0399); (until 1992): Aktuellt i Politiken (0345-0635); (until 1972): Aktuellt Politik och Samhaelle (0002-3884)
Related titles: Online - full text ed.
Indexed: RASB.
Published by: (Sveriges Socialdemokratiska Arbetareparti/Swedish Social Democratic Labour Party), A i P Media Produktion AB (Subsidiary of: Sveriges Socialdemokratiska Arbetareparti/Swedish Social Democratic Labour Party), Sveavaegen 68, Stockholm, 10560, Sweden. TEL 46-8-7002600, FAX 46-8-4116542, http://www.aip.sap.se. Ed. Fredrik Kornebaeck. Adv. contact Joergen Rosengren.

956.9442 GBR ISSN 1463-3930
DS109.32.M38
AL-AQSA. Cover title: Al-Aqsa Journal. Variant title: Aqsa. Text in English. 1998. s-a. GBP 5 (effective 2009). back issues avail. **Document type:** *Journal, Academic/Scholarly.* **Description:** Covers history, politics, architecture, religion, international law and human rights violations.
Related titles: Online - full text ed.: free (effective 2009).
Published by: Friends of Al-Aqsa, PO Box 5127, Leicester, LE2 0WU, United Kingdom. TEL 44-116-2125441, FAX 44-116-2537575, info@aqsa.orf.uk. Ed. Ismail Patel.

320 VEN
ALARMA. Text in Spanish. 1977. fortn.
Address: Torre de la Prensa, Plaza del Panteon, Apdo 2976, Caracas, DF 1010-A, Venezuela. Ed. Jose Campos Suarez. Circ: 65,150.

328.798 USA ISSN 1072-8058
ALASKA LEGISLATIVE DIGEST. Text in English. 1971. w. (Jan.-Jun.). USD 295 (effective 2000). **Document type:** *Newspaper.* **Description:** Provides analytical and interpretive coverage of Alaska legislative session, interim activity and administrative action.
Published by: Information & Research Service, 3037 South Circle, Anchorage, AK 99507. TEL 907-349-7711, FAX 907-522-1761. Pub. Mike Bradner.

328.798 USA ISSN 0095-3865
HJ11
ALASKA. LEGISLATURE. BUDGET AND AUDIT COMMITTEE. ANNUAL REPORT. Text in English. 1965. a. free. **Document type:** *Government.*
Published by: Legislative Budget and Audit Committee, PO Box W, Juneau, AK 99811. Circ: 200.

320 USA ISSN 1932-7986
➤ **ALBANIAN JOURNAL OF POLITICS.** Abbreviated title: A J P. Text in English. 2005. a. back issues avail. **Document type:** *Journal, Academic/Scholarly.* **Description:** Aims to provide a publication venue for members of ALPSA, as well as a forum for the academic study of Albanian politics and society.
Related titles: Online - full text ed.: ISSN 1932-7978.
Indexed: CA, P42, T02.
—BLDSC (0786.567030).
Published by: (Albanian Political Science Association), Globic Press, PO Box 788, Chapel Hill, NC 27514. TEL 919-809-6841, books@globic.us, http://press.globic.us. Eds. Ada Huibregtse, Fatmir Haskaj.

320 USA ISSN 1052-1054
ALBERT EINSTEIN INSTITUTION. MONOGRAPH SERIES. Variant title: Albert Einstein Institution Monograph Series. Text in English. 1990. irreg., latest vol.8, 2002. price varies. back issues avail. **Document type:** *Monographic series, Academic/Scholarly.* **Description:** Explores the power and potential of nonviolent action in conflict and defense.
Indexed: LID&ISL.
Published by: Albert Einstein Institution, PO Box 455, East Boston, MA 02128. TEL 617-247-4882, FAX 617-247-4035, einstein@igc.org.

320 AUS ISSN 1837-7432
▼ **ALFRED DEAKIN RESEARCH INSTITUTE. WORKING PAPER.** Text in English. 2010. irreg., latest vol.17. back issues avail. **Document type:** *Monographic series, Trade.* **Description:** Promotes research that integrates knowledge generated from a broad range of disciplines in ways that address problems of local, national and international importance.
Related titles: Online - full text ed.: ISSN 1837-7440. free (effective 2011).
Published by: Alfred Deakin Research Institute, Geelong Waterfront Campus, Deakin University, Geelong, VIC 3217, Australia. TEL 61-3-52272691, FAX 61-3-52278650, director-adri@deakin.edu.au. Ed. Kristina Murphy.

324.2738 USA
ALICE REPORTS. Text in English. 1972. m. USD 30. **Document type:** *Newsletter.*
Published by: Alice B. Toklas Lesbian & Gay Democratic Club, PO Box 422698, San Francisco, CA 94142-2698. TEL 415-522-3809. Circ: 800.

320 USA ISSN 1040-2055
ALL THE WAY; the fighting journal of the nationalist movement. Text in English. 1987. m. USD 12 domestic; USD 32 foreign; USD 1 newsstand/cover (effective 2001). bk.rev.; music rev.; tel.rev.; video rev. illus. back issues avail. **Description:** Contains news, current events and American political issues from a nationalist perspective.
Related titles: Diskette ed.; E-mail ed.; Online - full text ed.
Published by: Nationalist Movement, PO Box 2000, Learned, MS 39154. TEL 601-885-2288. Ed., R&P Richard Barrett.

ALLAM- ES JOGTUDOMANY/POLITICAL SCIENCE AND JURISPRUDENCE. *see* LAW

324.241 GBR ISSN 0002-6085
ALLIANCE NEWS. Text in English. 1971. bi-m. free membership. bk.rev. charts; illus. **Document type:** *Magazine, Consumer.*
Formerly: Alliance (0044-734X)
Published by: Alliance Party of Northern Ireland, 88 University St, Belfast, N Ireland BT7 1HE, United Kingdom. TEL 44-28-90324274, FAX 44-28-90333147, alliance@allianceparty.org, http://www.allianceparty.org. Circ: 3,000.

320 CUB ISSN 0864-0572
ALMA MATER. Text in Spanish. 1922. m. **Document type:** *Magazine, Consumer.*
Related titles: Online - full text ed.: ISSN 1681-9977.
Published by: Casa Editora Abril, Prado 535 esq a Tte Rey, Havan, 10200, Cuba. http://www.editoraabril.cu. Ed. Marta Leida Cruz Sanchez.

320.973 USA ISSN 0362-076X
JK1012
ALMANAC OF AMERICAN POLITICS. Text in English. 1972. biennial. USD 79.95 combined subscription (print & online eds.) (effective 2009). back issues avail.; reprints avail. **Document type:** *Directory, Trade.* **Description:** Provides comprehensive information on every senator, representative and governor, as well as the people and politics of their states and districts.
Related titles: Online - full text ed.
—CCC.
Published by: National Journal Group, Inc., The Watergate 600 New Hampshire Ave, NW, Washington, DC 20037. TEL 800-356-4838, 800-613-6701, FAX 202-266-7240, service@nationaljournal.com. Ed. Charles Mahtesian.

328 USA ISSN 1047-0999
JK1083
ALMANAC OF THE UNELECTED; staff of the U.S. Congress (Year). Text in English. 1988. a. USD 275 (effective 2000). **Document type:** *Directory.*
Related titles: Online - full text ed.
Published by: Bernan Associates, Bernan, 4611-F Assembly Dr., Lanham, MD 20706-4391. bpress@bernan.com, http://www.bernan.com. Ed. Steve Piacente. Pub. Jeffrey B Trammell. R&P Gary Ositchih.

328.75 USA ISSN 0276-9980
JK3968
THE ALMANAC OF VIRGINIA POLITICS. Text in English. 1977. biennial. USD 37.50 per issue (effective 2006). 290 p./no.;
Related titles: Supplement(s): The Almanac of Virginia Politics. Supplement. ISSN 0276-9999. 1978.
Published by: Kendall - Hunt Publishing Co., 4050 Westmark Dr, Dubuque, IA 52002. TEL 563-589-1000, 800-228-0810, FAX 563-589-1046, orders@kendallhunt.com, http://www.kendallhunt.com.

324.2 UKR
AL'TERNATIVA. Text in Ukrainian. w. USD 220 in United States.
Published by: Sots.-Demokratychnya Partiya Ukrainy, Kiev, Ukraine. TEL 380-44-216-1260. **Dist. by:** East View Information Services, 10601 Wayzata Blvd, Minneapolis, MN 55305. TEL 952-252-1201, 800-477-1005, FAX 952-252-1202, info@eastview.com, http://www.eastview.com.

321.8 SEN ISSN 0850-0622
JF60
ALTERNATIVE DEMOCRATIQUE; dans le Tiers Monde. Text in French. s-a.
Published by: Centre d'Etudes et de Recherches sur la Democratie Pluraliste dans le Tiers Monde, Av Bourguiba, Villa 2565, BP 12092, Dakar - Colobane, Senegal. TEL 221-24-47-81, FAX 221-25-29-36.

320 FRA ISSN 1157-8661
ALTERNATIVE LIBERTAIRE. Text in French. 1991. m. EUR 20 (effective 2008). back issues avail. **Document type:** *Magazine, Consumer.*
Related titles: Online - full text ed.: 2006.
Indexed: AltPI.
Address: 92 Rue d'Aubervilliers, Paris, 75019, France. TEL 33-8-70231936, contacts@alternativelibertaire.org.

320 FRA ISSN 1953-1222
ALTERNATIVE TIBETAINE. Text in French. 2006. a. **Document type:** *Newspaper, Consumer.*
Address: 38 Rue Baussenque, Marseille, 13002, France. redaction@alternative-tibetaine.org.

320 USA
ALTERNATIVE TIMES. Text in English. 1990. m. USD 12. adv. **Document type:** *Newspaper.*
Published by: Timeless Publications, PO Box 7134, Tyler, TX 75711-7134. TEL 214-597-7973. Ed. James Dixon. Circ: 3,000.

320 FRA ISSN 1634-6386
ALTERNATIVES INTERNATIONALES. Text in French. 2002. bi-m. EUR 38.50 combined subscription print & online eds. (effective 2011). back issues avail. **Document type:** *Magazine, Consumer.*
Related titles: Online - full text ed.: ISSN 2108-6575. 200?.
Indexed: IBSS.
Published by: Alternatives Economiques, 28 rue du Sentier, Paris, 75002, France. TEL 33-1-44882890, FAX 33-1-40284358, http://www.alternatives-economiques.fr.

320 BOL
ALTOS ESTUDIOS. Text in Spanish. 1989. a. BOB 10. bk.rev. **Document type:** *Bulletin.* **Description:** Promotes the works, studies and projects of the schools graduates.
Published by: Centro de Diplomados en Altos Estudios Nacionales, Casilla 5899, Ave. Mcal Santa Cruz, 1364 Edif. "La Primera" piso 13 Bloque, La Paz, Bolivia. TEL 358459. Ed. Hugo A Castrillo Mercado. Circ: 1,400.

320 ZAF ISSN 1995-8854
JQ1981
AMANDLA!. Text in English. 2007. m. ZAR 400 domestic; USD 75 in Africa; EUR 65 in Europe; GBP 45 in United Kingdom; GBP 85 in North America (effective 2007). **Document type:** *Magazine, Consumer.* **Description:** Provides coverage and analysis of current political developments, economic policy issues, and social processes, events and struggles from a radical left perspective.
Related titles: Online - full text ed.: ISSN 1995-8862.
Published by: Amandla Publishers, PO Box 13349, Mowbray, Cape Town, 7705, South Africa. FAX 27-21-6853087, info@amandlapublishers.com, http://www.amandlapublishers.com.

AMERICA AT THE POLLS. *see* LITERARY AND POLITICAL REVIEWS

320 USA ISSN 1932-8125
THE AMERICAN (ONLINE). Text in English. 2006. bi-m. adv. **Document type:** *Magazine, Trade.*
Media: Online - full text. **Related titles:** Microfiche ed.: (from NBI).
—CCC.
Published by: American Enterprise Institute for Public Policy Research, 1150 17th St NW, Washington, DC 20036. TEL 202-862-5800, FAX 202-862-7177, http://www.aei.org/. Ed. Nick Schulz. Pub. Arthur C Brooks.

320 USA ISSN 0002-7162
H1 CODEN: AAYPA
➤ **AMERICAN ACADEMY OF POLITICAL AND SOCIAL SCIENCE. ANNALS.** Text in English. 1889. bi-m. USD 810, GBP 476 to institutions; USD 827, GBP 486 combined subscription to institutions (print & online eds.) (effective 2012). adv. bk.rev. charts; illus. cum.index every 5 yrs. back issues avail.; reprint service avail. from PSC. **Document type:** *Journal, Academic/Scholarly.* **Description:** Provides an interdisciplinary discussion of problems and policy issues affecting America and the world community.
Related titles: Microfiche ed.: (from IDC); Microfilm ed.: (from PMC, PQC); Online - full text ed.: ISSN 1552-3349. USD 744, GBP 437 to institutions (effective 2012).
Indexed: A20, A21, A22, A23, A24, A25, A26, ABCPolSci, ABS&EES, ASCA, Acal, AgeL, AmH&L, B04, B05, B13, BAS, BEL&L, BRD, BrArAb, C28, CA, CBRI, CJPI, Chicano, CompR, CurCont, DIP, E01, E06, E08, EAA, ESPM, EconLit, F09, FR, FutSurv, G05, G06, G07, G08, G10, GSS&RPL, H09, HEA, HRA, HistAb, I02, I03, I05, I13, I14, IBR, IBSS, IBZ, ILD, JEL, KES, L09, LeftInd, M06, MEA&I, MLA-IB, MagInd, P02, P03, P06, P10, P27, P30, P34, P42, P48, P53, P54, PAIS, PCI, PQC, PRA, PSA, PersLit, PsycInfo, PsycholAb, R04, RASB, RI-1, RI-2, RILM, RiskAb, S02, S03, S05, S08, S09, S11, SCOPUS, SFSA, SOPODA, SPAA, SRRA, SSA, SSAI, SSAb, SSCI, SSI, SSciA, SUSA, SociolAb, T02, V&AA, W03, W07, W09.
—BLDSC (1018.800000), CIS, IE, Infotrieve, Ingenta, INIST. **CCC.**

Published by: (American Academy of Political and Social Science), Sage Publications, Inc., 2455 Teller Rd, Thousand Oaks, CA 91320. TEL 800-818-7243, FAX 800-583-2665, info@sagepub.com, http://www.sagepub.com. Ed. Emily Wood. **Subscr. overseas to:** Sage Publications Ltd., 1 Oliver's Yard, 55 City Rd, London EC1Y 1SP, United Kingdom. TEL 44-207-3248701, FAX 44-207-3248733, subscription@sagepub.co.uk.

328 USA ISSN 0569-2245
AMERICAN ASSEMBLY. REPORT. Text in English. 1951. 2/yr. free. **Document type:** *Proceedings.*
Supersedes in part: American Assembly (Background Papers and Final Report) (0065-6976)
Indexed: IIS.
Published by: American Assembly, Columbia University, 475 Riverside Dr, New York, NY 10115-0456. TEL 212-870-3500, FAX 212-870-3555. Ed., R&P David Mortimer. Circ: 25,000.

AMERICAN COMMUNIST HISTORY. *see* HISTORY—History Of North And South America

320 USA ISSN 1540-966X
JC573.2.U6
THE AMERICAN CONSERVATIVE. Text in English. 2002 (Oct.). 24/yr. USD 29.95; USD 3 newsstand/cover (effective 2002).
Indexed: A01, A26, APW, B04, CA, G06, G07, I05, M02, P05, P34, P45, P48, PQC, R03, RGAb, RGPR, S23, T02, W03, W05.
Published by: American Conservative LLC, 1300 Wilson Blvd., Ste. 120, Arlington, VA 22209. TEL 703-875-7600, FAX 703-875-3350.

327.2 USA ISSN 1094-8120
E183.7
AMERICAN DIPLOMACY. Text in English. 1996. q. free (effective 2011). bk.rev. back issues avail. **Document type:** *Journal, Academic/Scholarly.* **Description:** Includes commentary, analysis and research on American foreign policy and its practice.
Media: Online - full text.
Indexed: A26, A39, C27, C29, CA, D03, D04, E13, I05, P42, PAIS, R14, S14, S15, S18, T02.
Address: PO Box 5084, Chapel Hill, NC 27514. TEL 919-542-4414, hmattox@mindspring.com. Ed. William P Kiehl.

320 USA ISSN 0748-626X
H62.5.U5
AMERICAN ENTERPRISE INSTITUTE FOR PUBLIC POLICY RESEARCH. ANNUAL REPORT. Text in English. 19??. a. **Document type:** *Journal, Trade.*
Formerly: American Enterprise Institute for Public Policy Research
Related titles: Online - full text ed.: free (effective 2010).
—CCC.
Published by: American Enterprise Institute for Public Policy Research, 1150 17th St NW, Washington, DC 20036. TEL 202-862-5800, FAX 202-862-7176.

320 USA ISSN 1556-5777
E895
THE AMERICAN INTEREST. Text in English. 2005 (Fall). bi-m. USD 39 domestic; USD 53 in Canada; USD 72 elsewhere; USD 49 combined subscription domestic (print & online eds.); USD 63 combined subscription in Canada (print & online eds.); USD 82 combined subscription elsewhere (print & online eds.) (effective 2010). adv. back issues avail. **Document type:** *Magazine, Academic/Scholarly.* **Description:** Analyzes America's global position, covering topics such as America's conduct in terms of strategic aspects, economics, cultural and historical. Also inlcudes topics such as American foreign policy and the influence of American power on the rest of the world.
Related titles: Online - full text ed.: USD 19 domestic (effective 2010).
Indexed: A01, ABS&EES, P27, P34, P42, P45, P48, P54, PAIS, PQC.
—CCC.
Published by: The American Interest, PO Box 15115, N Hollywood, CA 91615. TEL 818-487-2033, 800-362-8433, FAX 818-487-4550. Ed. Adam Garfinkle. Pub. Charles Davidson. Adv. contact Damir Marusic TEL 202-223-4408 ext 111.

320 USA ISSN 0092-5853
JA1
➤ **AMERICAN JOURNAL OF POLITICAL SCIENCE.** Abbreviated title: A J P S. Text in English. 1950. q. GBP 447 in United Kingdom to institutions; EUR 566 in Europe to institutions; USD 574 in the Americas to institutions; USD 875 elsewhere to institutions; GBP 514 combined subscription in United Kingdom to institutions (print & online eds.); EUR 652 combined subscription in Europe to institutions (print & online eds.); USD 660 combined subscription in the Americas to institutions (print & online eds.); USD 1,047 combined subscription elsewhere to institutions (print & online eds.) (effective 2012). charts; stat.; illus. index. back issues avail.; reprint service avail. from PSC. **Document type:** *Journal, Academic/Scholarly.* **Description:** Presents academic research in American politics and international methodology.
Formerly (until 1973): Midwest Journal of Political Science (0026-3397)
Related titles: Microform ed.: (from PQC); Online - full text ed.: ISSN 1540-5907. GBP 447 in United Kingdom to institutions; EUR 566 in Europe to institutions; USD 574 in the Americas to institutions; USD 875 elsewhere to institutions (effective 2012) (from IngentaConnect).
Indexed: A01, A02, A03, A08, A12, A20, A22, A25, A26, ABCPolSci, ABIn, ABS&EES, AC&P, ASCA, AmH&L, B01, B04, B06, B07, B09, BAS, BRD, CA, CIS, CurCont, DIP, E01, E08, ESPM, G08, H09, HistAb, I05, I13, IBR, IBSS, IBZ, IPARL, MEA&I, P02, P06, P10, P13, P27, P30, P34, P42, P48, P51, P53, P54, PAIS, PCI, PQC, PRA, PSA, PSI, PhilInd, RASB, RiskAb, S02, S03, S05, S08, S09, S11, S21, SCOPUS, SOPODA, SPAA, SRRA, SSA, SSAI, SSAb, SSCI, SSI, SociolAb, T02, W03, W04, W07.
—BLDSC (0834.300000), IE, Infotrieve, Ingenta. **CCC.**
Published by: (Midwest Political Science Association), Wiley-Blackwell Publishing, Inc. (Subsidiary of: Wiley-Blackwell Publishing Ltd.), 111 River St, Hoboken, NJ 07030. TEL 201-748-6000, FAX 201-748-6088, info@wiley.com, http://www.wiley.com/WileyCDA/. Ed. Rick K Wilson. Adv. contact Kristin McCarthy TEL 201-748-7683.

320 GBR ISSN 0003-0554
JA1
➤ **AMERICAN POLITICAL SCIENCE REVIEW**; the leading journal of political science research. Abbreviated title: A P S R. Text in English. 1906. q. GBP 436, USD 816 combined subscription to institutions (print & online eds.) (effective 2010). adv. charts; illus. index, cum.index. back issues avail.; reprint service avail. from PSC. **Document type:** *Journal, Academic/Scholarly.* **Description:** Contains scholarly articles in political science.
Incorporates (1904-1914): American Political Science Association. Proceedings (1520-8605)
Related titles: Microform ed.: (from MIM, PMC, PQC); Online - full text ed.: ISSN 1537-5943. GBP 400, USD 740 to institutions (effective 2010).
Indexed: A01, A02, A03, A08, A12, A20, A22, A25, A26, ABCPolSci, ABIn, ABRCLP, ABS&EES, AC&P, ASCA, Acal, AmH&L, B01, B04, B06, B07, B09, BAS, BEL&L, BRD, CA, CBRI, CERDIC, CIS, ChPerI, Chicano, CurCont, DIP, E01, E06, E07, E08, ESPM, EconLit, FR, FamI, FutSurv, G05, G06, G07, G08, G10, H09, H10, HistAb, I03, I05, I13, I14, IBR, IBSS, IBZ, Inspec, JEL, L09, MEA&I, MLA-IB, P02, P06, P10, P13, P18, P27, P30, P34, P42, P45, P48, P51, P53, P54, PAA&I, PAIS, PCI, PQC, PRA, PSA, PersLit, R04, RASB, RefSour, RiskAb, S02, S03, S05, S08, S09, S11, SCOPUS, SPAA, SRRA, SSAI, SSAb, SSCI, SSI, SWR&A, SociolAb, T02, V02, W03, W05, W07.
—BLDSC (0851.500000), IE, Infotrieve, Ingenta, INIST. **CCC.**
Published by: (American Political Science Association USA), Cambridge University Press, The Edinburgh Bldg, Shaftesbury Rd, Cambridge, CB2 8RU, United Kingdom. TEL 44-1223-312393, FAX 44-1223-315052, journals@cambridge.org, http://www.cambridge.org/uk. Ed. Joseph Riser. adv.: B&W page USD 1,090, B&W page GBP 680; 7.1875 x 9.75. Circ: 16,000. **Subscr. to:** Cambridge University Press, 32 Ave of the Americas, New York, NY 10013. TEL 212-337-5000, FAX 212-691-3239.

320 USA ISSN 2161-1580
▼ **AMERICAN POLITICAL THOUGHT**; a journal of ideas, institutions, and culture. Text in English. forthcoming 2011. s-a. USD 25 combined subscription to institutions (print & online eds.) (effective 2012). **Document type:** *Journal, Academic/Scholarly.*
Related titles: Online - full text ed.: ISSN 2161-1599. forthcoming.
Published by: (Jack Miller Center for Teaching American Founding Principles and History), University of Chicago Press, 1427 E 60th St, Chicago, IL 60637. TEL 877-705-1878, FAX 877-705-1879, custserv@press.uchicago.edu, http://www.press.uchicago.edu. Ed. Michael Zuckert.

320.9 USA ISSN 1532-673X
JK1
➤ **AMERICAN POLITICS RESEARCH.** Abbreviated title: A P R. Text in English. 1973. bi-m. USD 1,096, GBP 645 to institutions; USD 1,118, GBP 658 combined subscription to institutions (print & online eds.) (effective 2012). adv. bk.rev. charts; illus. index. back issues avail.; reprint service avail. from PSC. **Document type:** *Journal, Academic/Scholarly.* **Description:** Promotes basic research in all areas of American political behavior, including urban, state, and national policies, as well as pressing social problems requiring political solutions.
Formerly (until 2001): American Politics Quarterly (0044-7803)
Related titles: Online - full text ed.: ISSN 1552-3373. USD 1,006, GBP 592 to institutions (effective 2012).
Indexed: A01, A02, A03, A08, A20, A22, A26, ABCPolSci, ASCA, AmH&L, B07, BRD, CA, CMM, CommAb, CurCont, E01, E02, E03, E07, E08, ERI, ESPM, EdA, EdI, G08, H04, I05, I13, IBR, IBSS, IBZ, MEA&I, P02, P04, P06, P10, P13, P27, P30, P34, P42, P48, P53, P54, PAIS, PCI, PQC, PRA, PSA, RASB, RiskAb, S02, S03, S09, S11, S21, SCOPUS, SPAA, SRRA, SSA, SSAI, SSAb, SSCI, SSI, SociolAb, T02, V02, W03, W07.
—BLDSC (0851.610000), IE, Infotrieve, Ingenta. **CCC.**
Published by: Sage Publications, Inc., 2455 Teller Rd, Thousand Oaks, CA 91320. TEL 800-818-7243, FAX 800-583-2665, info@sagepub.com, http://www.sagepub.com. Ed. Brian J Gaines. **Subscr. outside the Americas to:** Sage Publications Ltd., 1 Oliver's Yard, 55 City Rd, London EC1Y 1SP, United Kingdom. TEL 44-20-73248701, FAX 44-20-73248733, subscription@sagepub.co.uk.

320.51 USA ISSN 1049-7285
E838 CODEN: APROEY
THE AMERICAN PROSPECT; literal intelligence. Text in English. 1990. 10/yr. USD 19.95 (effective 2010). adv. film rev.; tel.rev.; bk.rev. back issues avail. **Document type:** *Magazine, Consumer.* **Description:** Provides political and cultural news and commentary for those who lead the liberal community.
Related titles: Microform ed.: (from PQC); Online - full text ed.: USD 14.95 (effective 2010).
Indexed: A01, A12, A22, A25, A26, ABIn, ABS&EES, APW, ASIP, AltPI, B04, B07, BRD, CA, E08, EconLit, G05, G06, G07, G08, G10, I05, I06, I07, JEL, LeftInd, M06, P02, P05, P10, P27, P30, P34, P42, P48, P51, P53, P54, PAIS, PQC, RI-1, RI-2, S02, S03, S08, S09, S11, S23, SCOPUS, SOPODA, SSAI, SSAb, SSI, SWR&A, SociolAb, T02, W01, W02, W03, W05, W09.
—BLDSC (0853.330000), CIS, IE, Ingenta. **CCC.**
Published by: The American Prospect, Inc., 2000 L St N W, Ste 717, Washington, DC 20036. TEL 202-776-0730, FAX 202-776-0740. Pub. George W Slowik Jr.

AMERICAN REVIEW. *see* HISTORY—History Of North And South America

THE AMERICAN REVIEW OF POLITICAL ECONOMY. *see* BUSINESS AND ECONOMICS—Economic Systems And Theories, Economic History

320 USA
➤ **AMERICAN REVIEW OF POLITICS.** Text in English. 1980. q. bk.rev. **Document type:** *Journal, Academic/Scholarly.* **Description:** Contains articles focussed on American politics and the American political process.
Former titles (until 1993): Midsouth Political Science Journal (1051-5054); (until 1988): Arkansas Political Science Journal
Indexed: CA, DIP, IBR, IBZ, P42, PAIS, PSA, SCOPUS, SociolAb, T02.
Published by: University of Arkansas, Center for the Study of Representation, 439 Old Main, Fayetteville, AR 72701.

➤ **AMERICAN SOCIAL AND POLITICAL MOVEMENTS.** *see* SOCIOLOGY

320.9 USA ISSN 0003-1593
JA1
AMERICA'S FUTURE. Text in English. 1959. m. USD 15 (effective 2001); free to public and school libraries. bk.rev. index. back issues avail. **Document type:** *Newsletter.* **Description:** Brings political, economic, and cultural commentary, emphasizing the benefits of free enterprise and constitutional government.
Related titles: Microfilm ed.; Online - full text ed.
Published by: America's Future, Inc., 7800 Bonhomme Ave., St. Louis, MO 63105. TEL 314-725-6003, FAX 314-721-3373. Ed. F R Duplantier. Pub. James L Tyson. Circ: 8,000.

320 FRA ISSN 1954-2542
AMICUS CURIAE. Text in French. 2004. irreg. **Document type:** *Newsletter.* **Description:** Features ideas from an independent political think tank that addresses political issues of the day including economic, tax, social programs, education.
Related titles: Online - full text ed.: free.
Published by: Institut Montaigne, 38 Rue Jean Mermoz, Paris, 75008, France. TEL 33-1-58183929, FAX 33-1-58183928, info@institutmontaigne.org.

320.52 CYP
AMMOCHOSTOS. Text in Greek. w. **Description:** Presents a right-wing political review reflecting the voice of Famagusta refugees.
Address: 44 Egnatias, Plati, Eylenya, Nicosia, Cyprus. TEL 357-2-352918. Ed. Niko Falas. Circ: 2,800.

AMMUDIM; bulletin of the religious kibbutzim. *see* BUSINESS AND ECONOMICS—Cooperatives

059.89 GRC ISSN 1105-7858
AMUNA KAI DIPLOMATIA. Text in Greek. 1990. m. adv. **Document type:** *Magazine, Consumer.* **Description:** Contains articles and analyses on the latest military, nautical and aeronautical news in Greece and worldwide, as well as reports on political and foreign affairs issues.
Published by: Daphne Communications S.A., 26-28 G Averof Str, Athens, 14232, Greece. TEL 30-210-2594100, FAX 30-210-2586740, info@daphne.gr, http://www.daphne.gr. Circ: 2,700 (paid).

320 ARG ISSN 0327-0297
JA5
ANALES DE CIENCIAS POLITICAS Y SOCIALES. Text in Spanish. 1950. s-a. free or exchange basis. adv. bk.rev. charts; stat. **Document type:** *Bulletin.*
Formerly (until 1987): Boletin de Ciencias Politicas y Sociales (0045-2394)
Indexed: C01, PAIS.
Published by: Universidad Nacional de Cuyo, Facultad de Ciencias Politicas y Sociales, Biblioteca, Casilla de Correos 217, Mendoza, 5500, Argentina. TEL 54-61-234393, FAX 54-61-381347. Ed. Isaac Francisco Gutierrez. Adv. contact Carlos Finochio.

320 PER ISSN 0252-8851
ANALISIS; cuadernos de investigacion. Text in Spanish. 1977. 2/yr. PEN 750, USD 12 to individuals; USD 20 to institutions. adv. bk.rev.
Indexed: C01, IBR, IBZ.
Address: Correo Santa Beatriz, Apdo Postal 11093, Lince, Lima 14, Peru. Ed. Ernesto Yepes. Circ: 5,000.

320.972 MEX
ANALISIS DEL TIEMPO. Text in Spanish. 1994. m. MXN 15 newsstand/cover. back issues avail.
Published by: Fundacion Analisis del Tiempo, A.C., Donato Guerra No 294 B, Tlaquepaque, Jalisco, Mexico. TEL 52-36-657-1472, FAX 52-36-657-2500. Ed. Crescenciano Fonseca-Gonzalez. Circ: 3,000.

320 028.1 COL ISSN 0121-4705
➤ **ANALISIS POLITICO**; revista de estudios politicos y relaciones internacionales. Text in Spanish. 1987 (Aug.). 3/yr. COP 33,000 domestic to individual members; USD 32 foreign to individual members (effective 2010). bk.rev. bibl.; abstr. Index. 130 p./no.; back issues avail. **Document type:** *Journal, Academic/Scholarly.* **Description:** Has an interdisciplinary approach to issues such as governance, society, democracy and foreign affairs.
Related titles: CD-ROM ed.: COP 15,000 domestic; USD 15 foreign (effective 2004); Online - full text ed.: free (effective 2011) (from SciELO).
Indexed: CA, H21, I13, IBR, IBZ, P08, P09, P42, PCI, PSA, S02, S03, SCOPUS, SOPODA, SSA, SociolAb, T02.
Published by: Universidad Nacional de Colombia, Instituto de Estudios Politicos y Relaciones Internacionales, Edificio Manuel Ancizar, Of 3032, Bogota, Colombia. Ed. Julie Massal.

320 MEX
ANALISIS XXI; una vision independiente hacia el futuro. Text in Spanish. 1998. m. MXN 200 domestic; USD 40 in North America; USD 55 in Europe; USD 75 elsewhere (effective 2000). back issues avail. **Document type:** *Academic/Scholarly.* **Description:** Includes in-depth articles on Mexican domistic politics.
Published by: Analisis XXI Editores, S.A. de C.V., Manual M. Ponce No 142-A, Col. Guadalope Inn, Mexico, DF 01020, Mexico. TEL 52-5-662-0564, FAX 52-5-662-0382, analisisxx1@infosel.net.mx. Ed. Guillermo Knochenhauer y Muller. Adv. contact Alejandro Zendejas. Circ: 1,500.

320 DEU ISSN 0941-4762
ANALYSEN ZUM WANDEL POLITISCH-OEKONOMISCHER SYSTEME. Text in German. 1992. irreg., latest vol.14, 2001. price varies. **Document type:** *Monographic series, Academic/Scholarly.*
Published by: Peter Lang GmbH (Subsidiary of: Peter Lang Publishing Group), Eschborner Landstr 42-50, Frankfurt Am Main, 60489, Germany. TEL 49-69-7807050, FAX 49-69-78070550, zentrale.frankfurt@peterlang.com. Eds. Dieter Grosser, Stephan Bierling.

320.5 AUS ISSN 1838-5966
▼ **THE ANALYST.** Text in English. 2010. m. free (effective 2011). **Document type:** *Journal, Academic/Scholarly.* **Description:** Devoted to champion the work of emerging voices, established practitioners and theorists of all persuasions.
Media: Online - full text.
Published by: Micah Group Pty Ltd.

320 FRA ISSN 2107-4429
ANALYTICA IRANICA. Text in French, English. 2005. s-a. **Document type:** *Journal, Academic/Scholarly.*
Formerly (until 2010): Journal d'Iran (1774-444X)

P

Published by: Editions Europerse, 2 Rue des Favorites, Paris, 75015, France. TEL 33-1-45313821, directeur@analyticairanica.com, http://www.analyticairanica.com/index.htm.

320.57 GBR ISSN 0967-3393
HX821
➤ **ANARCHIST STUDIES.** Text in English. 1993. s-a. GBP 52 to institutions (effective 2009). adv. 96 p./no.; back issues avail. **Document type:** *Journal, Academic/Scholarly.* **Description:** Features articles concerned with all aspects of anarchist research and theory, with the primary focus on contemporary developments in anarchism.
Indexed: A26, AltPI, B04, BrHumI, CA, I05, IBSS, LeftInd, MLA-IB, P42, PSA, PhilInd, S02, S03, SCOPUS, SOPODA, SSA, SSAI, SSAb, SSI, SociolAb, T02, W03, W05.
—**CCC.**
Published by: Lawrence & Wishart Ltd, 99a Wallis Rd, London, E9 5LN, United Kingdom. TEL 44-20-85332506, FAX 44-20-85337369, info@lwbooks.co.uk. Ed. Ruth Kinna. Adv. contact Sally Davison. page GBP 250; 120 x 195.

335.83 100 USA
ANARCHIST YELLOW PAGES. Text in English. 1997. a. USD 2 newsstand/cover. **Document type:** *Directory.* **Description:** Contains worldwide listings of anarchist, syndicalist, autonomous, libertarian socialist and anti-fascist groups and "liberated spaces".
Related titles: Diskette ed.
Published by: Nihil Press, 339 Lafayette St, 202, New York, NY 10012. Ed. Felix Frost. **Dist. by:** A K Press, Inc., 674-A 23rd St, Oakland, CA 94612. TEL 510-208-1700, FAX 510-208-1701, info@akpress.org, http://www.akpress.org/.

ANARCHO-SYNDICALIST REVIEW; anarchosyndicalist ideas and discussion. *see* BUSINESS AND ECONOMICS—Labor And Industrial Relations

331.87 354.97 FRA ISSN 1959-5093
ANARCHOSYNDICALISME. Text in French. 19??. bi-m. **Document type:** *Magazine.*
Former titles (until 2007): Combat SyndicalisteToulouse (1293-7185); (until 1994): Centre de Documentation et d'Etudes Sociales. La Lettre - Toulouse (1166-3502)
Related titles: Online - full text ed.: free.
Published by: Confederation Nationale du Travail - Association Internationale des Travailleurs (C N T - A I T), 7 Rue Saint Remesy, Toulouse, 31000, France.

320.57 USA ISSN 1044-1387
HX821
ANARCHY; a journal of desire armed. Text in English. 1980. s-a. USD 20 for 2 yrs. domestic to individuals; USD 36 for 2 yrs. foreign to individuals; USD 24 for 2 yrs. domestic to institutions; USD 48 for 2 yrs. foreign to institutions (effective 2008). bk.rev. illus. back issues avail.; reprints avail. **Document type:** *Magazine, Consumer.* **Description:** Presents an anti-authoritarian point ofview; critical of ideology, religion, nationalism, militarism and all political hierarchy.
Indexed: AltPI.
Published by: C A L Press, PO Box 3448, Berkeley, CA 94703. http://www.calpress.org. Eds. Jason McQuinn, John Henry Nolette, L D Hobson, Lawrence Jarach, Leona Benten. Circ: 6,000 (paid); 500 (controlled).

328 BEL ISSN 0066-1589
ANCIENS PAYS ET ASSEMBLEES D'ETATS. 1950. irreg., latest vol.102. price varies. **Document type:** *Monographic series.*
Published by: (International Committee of Historical Sciences, Commission for the History of State Assemblies), U. G. A., Stijn Streuvelslaan 73, Heule-Kortrijk, B-8501, Belgium. TEL 32-56-363200, FAX 32-56-356096. Ed. Cauchies. Pub. Patrick Vanssche.

320 338.4791 GBR ISSN 2045-4236
ANGLO-MALAGASY SOCIETY. NEWSLETTER. Text in English. 1978. q. free to members (effective 2010). **Document type:** *Newsletter, Trade.* **Description:** Covers the latest news and developments in Madagascar, with sections on politics, economic and social affairs, tourism, minerals, wildlife and bilateral relations.
Published by: Anglo-Malagasy Society, c/o Stuart M Edgill, 6 Bidborough Ridge, Bidborough, Tunbridge Wells, Kent, TN4 0UP, United Kingdom. TEL 44-1892-546149. Ed. Julian Cooke.

320 CHN ISSN 1674-8638
ANHUI XINGZHENG XUEYUAN XUEBAO/ANHUI ADMINISTRATION INSTITUTE. JOURNAL. Text in Chinese. 1985. q. **Document type:** *Journal, Academic/Scholarly.*
Former titles (until 2010): Xiangzhen Jingji Yanjiu/Rural Economy Study (1004-9940); (until 1999): Xiangzhen Jingji/Rural Economy
Related titles: Online - full text ed.
Published by: Anhui Xingzheng Xueyuan/Anhui Administration Institute, 115, Wangjiang Dong Lu, Hefei, 230059, China. TEL 86-551-3454849, FAX 86-551-3442879, http://www.ahsa.edu.cn/.

320 TUR ISSN 0378-2921
ANKARA UNIVERSITESI. SIYASAL BILGILER FAKULTESI DERGISI. Text in Turkish. 1943. 3/yr. **Document type:** *Journal, Academic/Scholarly.*
Related titles: Online - full text ed.: free (effective 2009).
Indexed: MLA-IB.
Published by: Ankara Universitesi, Siyasal Bilgiler Fakultesi, Yayin Kurulu, Cebeci, Ankara, 06590, Turkey. TEL 90-312-3197720, FAX 90-312-3197736, tarlakaz@politics.ankara.edu.tr. Ed. Melek Firat.

320 POL ISSN 2081-3333
ANNALES UNIVERSITATES PAEDAGOGICAE CRACOVIENSIS. STUDIA POLITOLOGICA. Text in Polish. 2002. irreg., latest vol.4, 2010. price varies. **Document type:** *Monographic series, Academic/Scholarly.*
Formerly (until 2010): Annales Academiae Paedagogicae Cracoviensis. Studia Politologica (1644-7921)
Published by: (Uniwersytet Pedagogiczny im. Komisji Edukacji Narodowej w Krakowie), Wydawnictwo Naukowe Uniwersytetu Pedagogicznego im. Komisji Edukacji Narodowej w Krakowie, ul Podchorazych 2, Krakow, 30084, Poland. TEL 48-12-6626383, redakcja@wydawnictwoup.pl, http://www.wydawnictwoap.pl. Ed. Wladyslaw Wic.

320 POL ISSN 1428-9512
JA26
➤ **ANNALES UNIVERSITATIS MARIAE CURIE-SKLODOWSKA. SECTIO K. POLITOLOGIA.** Text in Polish; Summaries in English. 1994. a. price varies. **Document type:** *Journal, Academic/Scholarly.*
Published by: (Uniwersytet Marii Curie-Sklodowskiej w Lublinie, Wydzial Politologii), Wydawnictwo Uniwersytetu Marii Curie-Sklodowskiej w Lublinie, Pl Marii Curie-Sklodowskiej 5, Lublin, 20031, Poland. TEL 48-81-5375304, press@ramzes.umcs.lublin.pl, http://www.press.umcs.lublin.pl. Ed. Dr. Jan Jakymek.

320.9 SEN ISSN 0066-2364
ANNEE POLITIQUE AFRICAINE. Text in French. 1964. a. XOF 17.50. **Document type:** *Magazine, Consumer.*
Formed by the 1981 merger of: Annee Politique Africaine; Economie Africaine
Published by: Societe Africaine d'Edition, 16 bis rue de Thiong, BP 1877, Dakar, Senegal.

320.9 CHE ISSN 0066-2372
HC397
ANNEE POLITIQUE SUISSE/SCHWEIZERISCHE POLITIK. Text in French, German. 1965. a. CHF 45 (effective 2001). index. **Document type:** *Journal, Academic/Scholarly.* **Description:** Complete review and analysis of all political events and developments in Swiss politics.
Published by: Universitaet Bern, Institut fuer Politikwissenschaft/ Universite de Berne, Institut de Science Politique, Lerchenweg 36, Bern 9, 3000, Switzerland. TEL 41-31-6318331, FAX 41-31-6318590, hirter@ipw.unibe.ch, http://www.cx.unibe.ch/ipw. Ed. Hans Hirter. Circ: 1,500.

320.9 USA ISSN 0891-3390
JK1
➤ **ANNUAL EDITIONS: AMERICAN GOVERNMENT.** Text in English. 1971. a. USD 22.25 per issue (effective 2010). illus. back issues avail. **Document type:** *Journal, Academic/Scholarly.*
Formerly (until 1981): Annual Editions: Readings in American Government (0090-547X)
Related titles: Online - full text ed.
Published by: McGraw-Hill, Contemporary Learning Series (Subsidiary of: McGraw-Hill Companies, Inc.), 1221 Ave of the Americas, New York, NY 10020. TEL 212-904-2000, FAX 212-512-2000, customer.service@mcgraw-hill.com, http://www.mhhe.com/cls/.

320 USA ISSN 0741-7233
JF37
➤ **ANNUAL EDITIONS: COMPARATIVE POLITICS.** Text in English. 1983. a. USD 22.25 per issue (effective 2010). illus. back issues avail. **Document type:** *Journal, Academic/Scholarly.*
Related titles: Online - full text ed.
Published by: McGraw-Hill, Contemporary Learning Series (Subsidiary of: McGraw-Hill Companies, Inc.), 1221 Ave of the Americas, New York, NY 10020. TEL 212-904-2000, FAX 212-512-2000, customer.service@mcgraw-hill.com, http://www.mhhe.com/cls/.

320 USA ISSN 1093-7021
JK2403
➤ **ANNUAL EDITIONS: STATE & LOCAL GOVERNMENT.** Text in English. 1978. a. USD 22.25 per issue (effective 2010). **Document type:** *Journal, Academic/Scholarly.*
Related titles: Online - full text ed.
Published by: McGraw-Hill, Contemporary Learning Series (Subsidiary of: McGraw-Hill Companies, Inc.), 1221 Ave of the Americas, New York, NY 10020. TEL 212-904-2000, FAX 212-512-2000, customer.service@mcgraw-hill.com, http://www.mhhe.com/cls/.

320 USA ISSN 0266-6170
D2
THE ANNUAL REGISTER (YEAR); a record of world events. Text in English. 1758. a. USD 250 per vol. in North America; GBP 170 per vol. elsewhere (effective 2011). maps; stat.; tr.lit. Index. back issues avail.; reprints avail. **Document type:** *Journal, Academic/Scholarly.* **Description:** Provides comprehensive coverage of events in countries worldwide, from national elections and international incidents to economic trends and major disasters.
Formerly (until 1964): Annual Register of World Events (0066-4057)
Related titles: CD-ROM ed.; Microform ed.: (from PMC); Online - full content ed.
—BLDSC (1094.200000). **CCC.**
Published by: ProQuest LLC (Bethesda) (Subsidiary of: Cambridge Information Group), 7200 Wisconsin Ave, Ste 715, Bethesda, MD 20814. TEL 301-961-6798, 800-843-7751, FAX 301-961-6799, service@csa.com, http://www.csa.com. Eds. D S Lewis, W Slater.

320 USA ISSN 1094-2939
JA1
ANNUAL REVIEW OF POLITICAL SCIENCE. Text in English. 1986-1990 (vol.3); resumed 1997. a. USD 251 combined subscription per issue to institutions (print & online eds.); USD 209 per issue to institutions (print or online ed.) (effective 2012). bibl.; charts; abstr. index, cum.index. back issues avail.; reprints avail. **Document type:** *Journal, Academic/Scholarly.* **Description:** Synthesizes and filters primary research to identify the principal contributions in the field of political science.
Related titles: Microfilm ed.: (from PQC); Online - full text ed.: ISSN 1545-1577.
Indexed: A01, A02, A03, A08, A20, A22, A26, B01, B06, B07, B09, CA, CurCont, DIP, E08, I05, I13, IBR, IBSS, IBZ, P34, P42, PAIS, PSA, S02, S03, SCOPUS, SSA, SSCI, SociolAb, T02, W07.
—BLDSC (1528.130000), IE, Ingenta. **CCC.**
Published by: Annual Reviews, PO Box 10139, Palo Alto, CA 94303. TEL 650-493-4400, FAX 650-424-0910, 800-523-8635, service@annualreviews.org. Ed. Margaret Levi TEL 206-543-7947.

ANNUAL THIRD WORLD CONFERENCE PROCEEDINGS. *see* HISTORY

320 ARG
ANOCERO. Text in Spanish. 1985. w.
Published by: Editorial Ano Cero, Libertad 936 5-D, Buenos Aires, 1012, Argentina.

320 NZL ISSN 1173-5716
JA51
➤ **ANTEPODIUM.** Text in English. 1995. irreg. free (effective 2011). **Document type:** *Journal, Academic/Scholarly.* **Description:** Dedicated to scholarly research on the politico-strategic, politico-economic and politico-cultural dimensions of world affairs.
Media: Online - full content.
Indexed: A39, C27, C29, D03, D04, E13, P42, R14, S14, S15, S18, T02.
—**CCC.**
Published by: Victoria University of Wellington, School of Political Science and International Relations (Subsidiary of: Victoria University of Wellington), PO Box 600, Wellington, New Zealand. Ed. Xavier Forde.

320 GRC
➤ **ANTI**; independent fortnightly political review. Text in English. 1972. fortn. USD 140 in United States; EUR 140 in Europe (effective 2002). adv. bk.rev.; dance rev.; film rev.; music rev.; play rev.; rec.rev.; tel.rev.; Website rev. index. 68 p./no.; back issues avail. **Document type:** *Magazine, Academic/Scholarly.*
Related titles: E-mail ed.; Fax ed.; Online - full content ed.
Address: 60 Dimocharous St, Athens, 115 21, Greece. TEL 30-010-723-2713, FAX 30-010-722-6107. Ed. Olga Fakotopoulou. Pub. Christos G Papontsakis. Adv. contact Tassia Roumpou TEL 30-010-7232713. Circ: 30,000.

320.54 DEU ISSN 0863-2936
ANTIFA; Magazin fuer antifaschistische Politik und Kultur. Text in German. 1975. bi-m. EUR 12; EUR 2 per issue (effective 2010). **Document type:** *Magazine, Consumer.* **Description:** Contains articles and features on opposing fascism in politics and culture.
Formerly (until 1990): Antifaschistische Widerstandskaempfer (0232-6418)
Published by: Vereinigung der Verfolgten des Naziregimes, Bund der Antifaschistinnen und Antifaschisten e.V., Franz-Mehring-Platz 1, Berlin, 10243, Germany. TEL 49-30-29784175, FAX 49-30-29784179, http://www.vvn-bda.de. Ed. Regina Girod.

320 CAN
ANTIFA FORUM. Text in English. irreg. **Document type:** *Magazine, Consumer.* **Description:** Publishes information on fascism in North America.
Published by: Anti-Fascist Forum, PO Box 6326, Stn A, Toronto, ON M5W 1P7, Canada. aff@burn.ucsd.edu. **Dist. by:** A K Press, Inc., 674-A 23rd St, Oakland, CA 94612. TEL 510-208-1700, FAX 510-208-1701, info@akpress.org, http://www.akpress.org/.

320 MEX
ANUARIO POLITICO DE AMERICA LATINA. Text in Spanish. 1974. a.
Published by: Universidad Nacional Autonoma de Mexico, Facultad de Ciencias Politicas y Sociales, Ciudad Universitaria, Mexico, D.F., 04510, Mexico. TEL 52-55-56229470, http://www.politicas.unam.mx/.

320.57 CAN
ANY TIME NOW; social anarchist and decentralist zine. Text in English. 1989. q. CAD 4 (effective 2001). **Description:** Provides information, news and discussion from and about activists in the social anarchist movement.
Address: Box 174, Montreal, PQ H3K 3B9, Canada. dimar@direct.ca, redlionpress@hotmail.com. Eds. Dick Martin, Larry Gambone.

320 NLD ISSN 1879-8152
▼ **APERCUS DES POLITIQUES ET PRATIQUES.** Text in French. 2010. bi-m.
Related titles: Online - full text ed.: ISSN 1879-8160; ◆ Translation of: Policy and Management Insights. ISSN 1879-6745.
Published by: European Centre for Development Policy Management/ Centre Europeen de Gestion de Politiques de Developpement, Onze Lieve Vrouweplein 21, Maastricht, 6211 HE, Netherlands. TEL 31-43-3502900, FAX 31-43-3502902, info@ecdpm.org.

320 330 ARG ISSN 0328-6401
APERTURA. Text in Spanish. 1983. m. USD 77 (effective 2002).
Description: Major monthly business magazine. Thanks to an agreement with McGraw-Hill, it includes selections from Business Week.
Published by: Editorial Mind Opener S.A., Av de Mayo 605, 3er Piso, Buenos Aires, 1514, Argentina. TEL 54-11-4331-6505, FAX 54-11-4331-5208. Ed. Marcelo Longobardi.

320 CRI
APORTES. Text in Spanish. 1980. m. CRC 550, USD 45. adv. bk.rev.; film rev.; play rev. illus. cum.index 1980-1988. back issues avail.
Published by: Editorial Aportes para la Educacion, S.A., Apdo. 103, Fecosa, San Jose 1009, Costa Rica. TEL 21-13-20. Ed. Melvin Jimenez. Circ: 2,600.

320 ESP ISSN 1578-4487
APPLIED ECONOMETRICS AND INTERNATIONAL DEVELOPMENT. Text in English. 2001. 4/yr. EUR 80 combined subscription print & online eds. (effective 2008). **Document type:** *Journal, Academic/Scholarly.* **Description:** Focuses on international development analysis based on econometric modelling, and economic history.
Related titles: Online - full text ed.: EUR 120 (effective 2008).
Indexed: EconLit, IBSS, JEL, SCOPUS.
Published by: Asociacion Euro-Americana de Estudios del Desarrollo Economico/Euro-American Association of Economic Development Studies, Ave. Burgo Nacionales s/n, Santiago de Compostela, 15704, Spain. TEL 34-981-563100, FAX 34-981-563676, http://www.usc.es/~economet/eaa.htm. Ed. Maria-Carmen Guisan.

320.9 FRA ISSN 0003-7176
APRES - DEMAIN. Text in French. 1957. q. EUR 34 domestic to individuals; EUR 51 foreign to individuals; EUR 26 domestic to students (effective 2010). adv. bk.rev. abstr.; bibl. index, cum.index. back issues avail. **Document type:** *Journal, Academic/Scholarly.* **Description:** For those who want to understand and those who must explain the world's political, economic and social problems.
Indexed: A22, FR, IBSS, P30, PAIS.
—BLDSC (1581.600000), IE, Infotrieve, Ingenta.
Published by: Fondation Seligmann, Apres-demain, BP 458-07, Paris, Cedex 07 75327, France. fondation-seligmann@orange.fr. Circ: 8,000.

AQUACULTURE, AQUARIUM, CONSERVATION & LEGISLATION. *see* FISH AND FISHERIES

AQUI. *see* SOCIOLOGY

320 USA ISSN 1942-5805
ARAB REFORM BULLETIN. Text in English. 2003. m. **Document type:** *Bulletin, Academic/Scholarly.* **Description:** Provides analysis from experts, resource guides and synopses from news sources about political reform in the Middle East.
Media: Online - full text. **Related titles:** Arabic ed.
Indexed: LeftInd.

Published by: Carnegie Endowment for International Peace, 1779 Massachusetts Ave, NW, Washington, DC 20036. TEL 202-939-2230, FAX 202-483-4430, info@CarnegieEndowment.org, http://www.carnegieendowment.org/. Ed. Michele Dunne.

320 IND
ARASIYAL THARASU. Text in Tamil. w. INR 3 per issue (effective 2011). **Document type:** *Magazine, Consumer.*
Address: 14, Shet Colony, Chennai, Tamil Nadu 600 008, India. Ed. A Shyam.

320.5322 DEU ISSN 0943-402X
ARBEITERSTIMME; Zeitschrift fuer marxistische Theorie und Praxis. Text in German. 1971. q. EUR 13 (effective 2010). adv. bk.rev. back issues avail. **Document type:** *Journal, Academic/Scholarly.*
Related titles: Microfilm ed.: (from PQC).
Published by: Gruppe Arbeiterstimme, Postfach 910307, Nuernberg, 90261, Germany. redaktion@arbeiterstimme.org, http://www.arbeiterstimme.org. Ed. Thomas Gradl. Circ: 2,000.

320.3 311.11 SWE ISSN 0345-0961
ARBETAREN; veckotidning foer frihetlig politik, ekonomi och kultur. Text in Swedish. 1922 (vol.69). w. SEK 352 (effective 2011). adv. bk.rev. charts; illus. **Document type:** *Newspaper, Consumer.* **Description:** Publishes news on politics, economy, culture and union affairs.
Formerly (until 1958): Dagstidningen Arbetaren
Related titles: Microform ed.; Online - full text ed.: 1997.
Published by: Sveriges Arbetares Centralorganisation, PO Box 6507, Stockholm, 11383, Sweden. TEL 46-8-160890, http://www.sac.se. Ed. Daniel Wiklander TEL 46-8-52245660. Circ: 3,200 (controlled).

320.9 DEU ISSN 0003-8865
D410
ARCHIV DER GEGENWART; die weltweite Dokumentation fuer Politik und Wirtschaft. Text in German. 1931. m. abstr.; charts; stat. index. reprints avail. **Document type:** *Directory.* **Description:** Detailed information on current world politics and economics; record of world events based on a variety of international sources.
Related titles: CD-ROM ed.
Indexed: RASB.
Published by: Siegler & Co. Verlag fuer Zeitarchive GmbH, Einsteinstr 10, Sankt Augustin, 53757, Germany. TEL 49-2241-3164-0, FAX 49-2241-316436. Ed. Juergen Hermann. Circ: 1,200.

328 FRA
ARCHIVES PARLEMENTAIRES DE 1787 A 1860. Text in French. irreg. price varies. adv. bk.rev. index. **Document type:** *Academic/Scholarly.*
Related titles: Microfiche ed.: (from BHP).
Published by: Centre National de la Recherche Scientifique, Campus Gerard-Megie, 3 Rue Michel-Ange, Paris, 75794, France. TEL 33-1-44964000, FAX 33-1-44965390, http://www.cnrseditions.fr. Circ: 1,500 (controlled).

320 MNG
ARDYN TOR/PEOPLE'S STATE. Text in Mongol. 1950. bi-m.
Published by: People's Great Hural, Ulan Bator, Mongolia.

320.531 SWE ISSN 1652-0556
ARENA. Text in Swedish. 1993. 6/yr. SEK 395 domestic; SEK 699 in Europe; SEK 819 elsewhere (effective 2010). adv. **Document type:** *Magazine, Consumer.*
Formerly (until 2003): Politikens, Kulturens och Ideernas Arena (1104-4209)
Related titles: Online - full text ed.
Published by: Arenagruppen, Drottninggatan 83, Stockholm, 11160, Sweden. TEL 46-8-7891160, FAX 46-8-4114242, http://www.arenagruppen.se. Ed. Olav Fumarola Unsgaard.

320 AUS ISSN 1320-6567
HM891
➤ **ARENA JOURNAL.** Text in English. 1963. s-a. AUD 60 domestic to libraries; AUD 74 foreign to libraries; AUD 51 combined subscription includes Arena Magazine (effective 2008). back issues avail.; reprint service avail. from PSC. **Document type:** *Journal, Academic/Scholarly.* **Description:** Covers theoretically and ethically concerned discussions on the prospects for co-operation within contemporary life.
Supersedes in part (in 1993): Arena (0004-0932)
Related titles: CD-ROM ed.; Online - full text ed.
Indexed: A26, AEI, AltPI, AusPAIS, CA, E08, G08, I05, IBSS, LeftInd, P42, PSA, S02, S03, S09, SCOPUS, SociolAb, T02.
—BLDSC (1664.071000), IE, Ingenta. **CCC.**
Published by: Arena Printing and Publications Pty. Ltd., PO Box 18, Carlton North, VIC 3054, Australia. TEL 61-3-94160232, FAX 61-3-94160684. Eds. John Hinkson TEL 61-3-94160232, Simon Cooper.

320.531 AUS ISSN 1039-1010
HX3.A74
ARENA MAGAZINE. Text in English. 1963. bi-m. AUD 36 domestic; AUD 64 foreign; AUD 47 domestic membership; AUD 75 foreign membership; AUD 88 domestic to libraries; AUD 116 foreign to libraries (effective 2008). adv. bk.rev.; film rev.; play rev. reprint service avail. from PSC. **Document type:** *Magazine, Academic/Scholarly.* **Description:** Provides left-wing political, social and cultural commentary.
Formerly (until 1992): Arena (0004-0932)
Related titles: CD-ROM ed.; Online - full text ed.
Indexed: A26, AEI, AltPI, AusPAIS, B14, BRI, CA, CBRI, E08, G08, I05, IBSS, LeftInd, PerIslam, RASB, S09, SCOPUS, T02.
—Ingenta. **CCC.**
Published by: Arena Printing and Publications Pty. Ltd., PO Box 18, Carlton North, VIC 3054, Australia. TEL 61-3-94165166. Eds. Christopher Scanlon, Matthew Ryan. Circ: 900.

ARGENTINA BUSINESS FORECAST REPORT. see BUSINESS AND ECONOMICS—Economic Situation And Conditions

ARGENTINE LETTER. see BUSINESS AND ECONOMICS—Economic Situation And Conditions

ARIZONA CAPITOL TIMES. see PUBLIC ADMINISTRATION

ARMED FORCES AND SOCIETY; an interdisciplinary journal on military institutions, civil-military relations, arms control and peacekeeping, and conflict management. see MILITARY

320 NPL
ARPAN WEEKLY. Text in Nepali, English. 1964. w. USD 50 (effective 2003). adv. bk.rev.; dance rev.; music rev.; play rev.; software rev.; tel.rev.; video rev. abstr.; bibl.; charts; illus.; maps; mkt.; pat.; stat.; tr.lit.; tr.mk. 8 p./no. 4 cols./p.; back issues avail.; reprints avail. **Document type:** *Newspaper, Consumer.* **Description:** Covers politics, social affairs, sports, business, and tourism.
Formerly: Arpan
Related titles: CD-ROM ed.; Microform ed.; Online - full text ed.
Published by: Nepal Economic and Commerce Research Centre, 7/358, Kohity Bahal, P O Box 285, Kathmandu, Nepal. TEL 977-1-4220531, FAX 977-1-4279544, manju_sakya@hotmail.com. Ed., Pub., R&P Manju Ratna Sakya. Adv. contact Mr. Rabindra Man Prajapati. Circ: 20,000.

ARQUIVO EDGARD LEUENROTH. CADERNOS. see SOCIAL SCIENCES: COMPREHENSIVE WORKS

320.57 USA
ARSENAL (CHICAGO); a magazine Of anarchist strategy And culture. Text in English. irreg. USD 4 (effective 2002). **Document type:** *Magazine, Consumer.*
Published by: Arsenal, 1573 N Milwaukee Ave #420, Chicago, IL 60622. **Dist. by:** A K Press, Inc., 674-A 23rd St, Oakland, CA 94612. TEL 510-208-1700, FAX 510-208-1701, info@akpress.org, http://www.akpress.org/.

320.972 MEX
ASAMBLEA; organo de difusion de la Asamblea Legislativa. Text in Spanish. bi-m.
Published by: Asamblea Legislative del Distrito Federal, Venustiano Carranza 49, Col Centro, Mexico, D.F. 06018, Mexico. TEL 52-5-521-0499, FAX 52-5-510-9694. Ed. Daniel Gonzalez Martin.

320 USA ISSN 1934-385X
JQ26
ASIA IN FOCUS. Text in English. 2005. bi-w. **Document type:** *Newsletter, Consumer.* **Description:** Analyzes security, politics, and related social and economic issues that impact the region.
Media: Online - full text.
Indexed: A16, P51.
Published by: Asia America Initiative, 1523 16th St., NW, Washington, DC 20036. TEL 202-232-7020, FAX 202-232-7023, admin@asiaamerica.org, http://www.asiaamerica.org/index.html.

ASIA MONITOR. CHINA & NORTH EAST ASIA. see BUSINESS AND ECONOMICS—Economic Situation And Conditions

ASIA MONITOR. SOUTH ASIA. see BUSINESS AND ECONOMICS—Economic Situation And Conditions

ASIA MONITOR. SOUTH EAST ASIA. see BUSINESS AND ECONOMICS—Economic Situation And Conditions

ASIA PACIFIC BULLETIN. see BUSINESS AND ECONOMICS

ASIA PACIFIC FOUNDATION OF CANADA. APSUMMIT SERIES. see BUSINESS AND ECONOMICS

ASIA PACIFIC FOUNDATION OF CANADA. EVENT REPORTS. see BUSINESS AND ECONOMICS

ASIA PACIFIC FOUNDATION OF CANADA. IMPACT REPORTS. see BUSINESS AND ECONOMICS

ASIA PACIFIC FOUNDATION OF CANADA. ROUNDTABLE WORKSHOP REPORTS. see BUSINESS AND ECONOMICS

ASIA PACIFIC FOUNDATION OF CANADA. SURVEYS. see BUSINESS AND ECONOMICS

659.2 AUS ISSN 1440-4389
➤ **ASIA PACIFIC PUBLIC RELATIONS JOURNAL.** Abbreviated title: A P P R J. Text in English. 1999. s-a. AUD 35 to individuals; AUD 95 to institutions (effective 2008). back issues avail. **Document type:** *Journal, Academic/Scholarly.* **Description:** Aims to explore emerging public relations trends within social, political and economic contexts, theoretical frameworks and education at a local, national and international level.
Related titles: Online - full text ed.: free (effective 2008).
—BLDSC (1742.261308).
Published by: Deakin University, School of Communication and Creative Arts, Melbourne Campus, 221 Burwood Hwy, Burwood, VIC 3125, Australia. TEL 61-3-92517353, FAX 61-3-92517635, arts-head-scca@deakin.edu.au, http://www.deakin.edu.au/arts-ed/scca/. Ed. Mark Sheehan TEL 61-3-52272424.

320 330 HKG
ASIA TIMES. Text in English. 1995. d. **Document type:** *Newspaper, Consumer.*
Media: Online - full content. **Related titles:** Chinese ed.: Yazhou Shibao.
Address: Unit B, 16/F, Li Dong Bldg, No. 9 Li Yuen St E, Central, Hong Kong. TEL 852-2367-3715, FAX 852-2316-7647.

320.951 HKG ISSN 1029-1903
ASIAN AFFAIRS. Text in English. 1997. q. HKD 780 domestic; EUR 110 in Europe; USD 100 elsewhere; USD 75 to Universities & Think Tanks (effective 2003). adv. **Document type:** *Journal, Academic/Scholarly.* **Description:** Publishes exclusive interviews and contributions from Asian leaders to provide a strategic perspective of Asian politics and economics.
Related titles: ◆ Online - full text ed.: Asian Affairs Online. ISSN 1607-0631.
—Infotrieve.
Published by: Larkincil International Ltd, 15 Fl Supreme Commercial Bldg, 368 King's Rd, North Point, Hong Kong. TEL 852-2980-2240, FAX 852-2980-2824. adv.: page USD 3,500.

320.951 HKG ISSN 1607-0631
ASIAN AFFAIRS ONLINE. Text in English. bi-m.
Media: Online - full text. **Related titles:** ◆ Print ed.: Asian Affairs. ISSN 1029-1903.
Published by: Larkincil International Ltd, 15 Fl Supreme Commercial Bldg, 368 King's Rd, North Point, Hong Kong. TEL 852-2980-2240, FAX 852-2980-2824.

ASIAN ECONOMIES/AJIA KEIZAI. see BUSINESS AND ECONOMICS—International Development And Assistance

320.95 GBR ISSN 0218-5377
JQ21.A1
➤ **ASIAN JOURNAL OF POLITICAL SCIENCE.** Abbreviated title: A J P S. Text in English. 1993. 3/yr. GBP 252 combined subscription in United Kingdom to institutions (print & online eds.); EUR 334, USD 419 combined subscription to institutions (print & online eds.) (effective 2012). adv. bk.rev. illus.; abstr.; bibl. 160 p./no.; back issues avail.; reprint service avail. from PSC. **Document type:** *Journal, Academic/Scholarly.* **Description:** Publishes articles in the four sub-fields of political theory, comparative politics, international relations and public administration.
Related titles: Online - full text ed.: ISSN 1750-7812. GBP 227 in United Kingdom to institutions; EUR 301, USD 378 to institutions (effective 2012) (from IngentaConnect).
Indexed: A01, A02, A03, A08, A22, APEL, BAS, CA, DIP, E01, IBR, IBSS, IBZ, P34, P42, PAIS, PSA, S02, S03, SCOPUS, SociolAb, T02.
—BLDSC (1742.568000), IE, Ingenta. **CCC.**
Published by: (National University Of Singapore, Department of Political Science SGP), Routledge (Subsidiary of: Taylor & Francis Group), 4 Park Sq, Milton Park, Abingdon, Oxon OX14 4RN, United Kingdom. TEL 44-20-70176000, FAX 44-20-70176336, subscriptions@tandf.co.uk, http://www.routledge.com. Eds. M Shamsul Haque, Terry Nardin. Adv. contact Linda Hann TEL 44-1344-779945. Circ: 250. **Subscr. to:** Taylor & Francis Ltd., Journals Customer Service, Sheepen Pl, Colchester, Essex CO3 3LP, United Kingdom. TEL 44-20-70175544, FAX 44-20-70175198.

➤ **ASIAN OUTLOOK.** see BUSINESS AND ECONOMICS

➤ **ASIAN PACIFIC JOURNAL OF PUBLIC ADMINISTRATION/YA TAI GONG GONG XING ZHENG XUE.** see PUBLIC ADMINISTRATION

320 USA ISSN 0258-9184
DS1
➤ **ASIAN PERSPECTIVE.** Text in English. 1977. q. USD 120 domestic to institutions; USD 138 foreign to institutions (effective 2011). adv. bk.rev. illus. cum.index. back issues avail.; reprints avail. **Document type:** *Journal, Academic/Scholarly.*
Related titles: Online - full text ed.
Indexed: A12, A17, A22, ABIn, APEL, B16, BAS, CA, EI, EIP, I13, IBSS, LID&ISL, P10, P27, P30, P34, P42, P45, P46, P48, P51, P53, P54, PAIS, PCI, PQC, PSA, PerIslam, RASB, S02, S03, SCOPUS, SSA, SSCI, SociolAb, T02, W07.
—BLDSC (1742.708000), IE, Ingenta.
Published by: (Portland State University, Mark O. Hatfield School of Government, Kyungnam University, Institute for Far Eastern Studies/Gyeongnam Daehag'gyo, Geugdong Munje Yeon'guso KOR), Lynne Rienner Publishers, 1800 30th St, Ste 314, Boulder, CO 80301. TEL 303-444-6684, FAX 303-444-0824. Ed. Melvin Gurtov. Pub. Jae Kyu Park. Circ: 2,300.

320 USA
ASIAN POLITICAL NEWS. Text in English. w. **Document type:** *Newspaper, Consumer.*
Media: Online - full content.
Published by: Kyodo News International, Inc., 50 Rockefeller Plaza, Ste 803, New York, NY 10020. TEL 212-397-3723, FAX 212-397-3721, kni@kyodonews.com, http://www.kyodonews.com/.

320.9 USA ISSN 0004-4687
DS1
➤ **ASIAN SURVEY**; a bimonthly review of contemporary Asian affairs. Text in English. 1932. bi-m. USD 400 combined subscription to institutions (print & online eds.) (effective 2012). adv. bibl.; illus. Index. 208 p./no.; back issues avail.; reprint service avail. from PSC. **Document type:** *Journal, Academic/Scholarly.* **Description:** Provides detailed commentary on political, economic, and social developments in Asia.
Supersedes (in 1961): Far Eastern Survey (0362-8949); Which was formerly (until 1935): Institute of Pacific Relations. American Council. Memorandum (1536-0385)
Related titles: Microform ed.: (from PQC); Online - full text ed.: ISSN 1533-838X. USD 315 to institutions (effective 2012).
Indexed: A01, A02, A03, A08, A20, A21, A22, A25, A26, ABCPolSci, ABS&EES, APEL, ASCA, AbAn, Acal, AmH&L, B04, BAS, BRD, C12, CA, CABA, CurCont, DIP, E01, E08, E12, EI, ENW, FR, G05, G06, G07, G08, GEOBASE, H09, H10, HistAb, I05, I08, I13, I14, IBR, IBSS, IBZ, ILD, KES, M01, M02, M10, MEA&I, MLA-IB, P02, P06, P10, P13, P14, P27, P30, P34, P42, P45, P48, P53, P54, PAA&I, PAIS, PCI, PQC, PRA, PSA, PerIslam, R05, R12, RASB, RI-1, RI-2, S02, S03, S05, S08, S09, S13, S16, SCOPUS, SPAA, SPPI, SSAI, SSAb, SSCI, SSI, SociolAb, T02, TAR, W03, W07, W11.
—BLDSC (1742.750000), IE, Infotrieve, Ingenta. **CCC.**
Published by: (University of California, Berkeley), University of California Press, Journals Division, 2000 Ctr St, Ste 303, Berkeley, CA 94704. TEL 510-643-7154, 877-262-4226, FAX 510-642-9917, customerservice@ucpressjournals.com. Ed. Lowell Dittmer. Adv. contact Jennifer Rogers TEL 510-642-6188. **Subscr. to:** 149 5th Ave, 8th Fl, New York, NY 10010. participation@jstor.org.

956 LBN ISSN 0004-5012
ASSAYAD. Text in Arabic. 1943. w. LBP 100,000 domestic; USD 250 in US & Canada; USD 150 in Europe (effective 2000). adv. **Document type:** *Consumer.*
Published by: Dar As-Sayad S.A.L., C/o Said Freiha, Hazmieh, P O Box 1038, Beirut, Lebanon. TEL 961-5-456373, FAX 961-5-452700, contactpr@csi.com, alanwar@alanwar.com, http://www.alanwar.com. Ed. Issam Freiha. Adv. contact Said Freiha. color page USD 5,500; bleed 236 x 308. Circ: 89,775.

ASSOCIATION OF COLLEGE AND RESEARCH LIBRARIES. LAW AND POLITICAL SCIENCE SECTION. NEWS. see LAW

320.9 SEN
ASSOCIATION SENEGALAISE POUR L'ETUDE DU QUATERNAIRE AFRICAIN. BULLETIN DE LIAISON. Text in English, French. 1964. q. membership. bk.rev. index, cum.index.
Formerly: Association Senegalaise pour l'Etude du Quaternaire de l'Ouest African. Bulletin de Liaison (0044-9725)
Indexed: SpeleolAb.
—INIST.
Published by: Association Senegalaise pour l'Etude du Quaternaire Africain, Laboratoire de Geologie, Faculte des Sciences, Dakar - Fann, Senegal. Circ: 700.

ATENCION. see HISTORY—History Of North And South America

ATOPIA: PHILOSOPHY, POLITICAL THEORY, AESTHETICS. see PHILOSOPHY

P

320.532 305 GBR
AUFHEBEN; revolutionary perspectives. Text in English. 1992. a., latest no.12, 2004. GBP 9 domestic for 3 issues; GBP 11 in Europe for 3 issues; GBP 13 elsewhere for 3 issues (effective 2009). bk.rev. back issues avail. **Document type:** *Journal, Trade.* **Description:** Discusses politics from a Marxist perspective as well as Marxist theory.
Related titles: Online - full text ed.
Indexed: AltPI, LeftInd.
Address: PO Box 2536, Rottingdean, Brighton BN2 6LK, United Kingdom. Ed. Tim Ahern.

322.4 FRA ISSN 0339-9958
DT1
AUJOURD'HUI L'AFRIQUE. Text in French. 1975. 4/yr. EUR 25 domestic; EUR 33 foreign (effective 2008). adv. bk.rev. **Document type:** *Magazine, Consumer.*
Formerly: Association Francaise d'Amitie et de Solidarite avec les Peuples d'Afrique. Bulletin d'Information (0335-0290)
Indexed: RASB.
Published by: Association Francaise d'Amitie et de Solidarite avec les Peuples d'Afrique, 13 Rue Pierre et Marie Curie, Bagnolet, 93170, France. TEL 33-1-49930760, FAX 33-1-49930831. Ed. Francis Arzalier. Adv. contact Pierre Kaldor.

328 DEU ISSN 0479-611X
AUS POLITIK UND ZEITGESCHICHTE. Text in German. 1951. w. **Document type:** *Newspaper, Academic/Scholarly.*
Related titles: ◆ Supplement(s): Das Parlament. ISSN 0031-2258.
Indexed: BAS, DIP, I13, IBR, IBZ, P30, PRA, RASB.
—**CCC.**
Published by: Bundeszentrale fuer Politische Bildung, Adenauerallee 86, Bonn, 53113, Germany. TEL 49-1888-5150, FAX 49-1888-515113, info@bpb.de. Ed. Klaus W. Wippermann.

328.764 USA ISSN 1063-0368
AUSTIN REPORT. Text in English. 1947. w. USD 28. **Description:** Covers Texas legislative and political activity.
Published by: Report Publications, Inc., PO Box 12368, Austin, TX 78711. TEL 512-478-5663. Ed. Bill Kidd. Circ: 1,150.

AUSTRALASIAN JOURNAL OF BUSINESS AND SOCIAL INQUIRY. *see* BUSINESS AND ECONOMICS

320.532 AUS ISSN 0311-3264
AUSTRALASIAN SPARTACIST. Text in English. 1973. q. AUD 5 domestic; AUD 7 foreign (effective 2009). bk.rev. 12 p./no.; back issues avail. **Document type:** *Newspaper, Consumer.* **Description:** Marxist newspaper of the Spartacist League Australia.
Formerly (until 1973): Spartacist Leaflets (0311-5798)
Indexed: LeftInd.
Published by: (International Communist League, Central Committee of the Spartacist League of Australia), Spartacist A N Z Publishing Co., GPO Box 3473, Sydney, NSW 2001, Australia. TEL 61-2-92812181, spartacist@exemail.com.au.

320.9 AUS ISSN 1833-4229
THE AUSTRALIAN CONSTITUTIONAL DEFENDER. Text in English. 2006. m. **Document type:** *Journal, Academic/Scholarly.*
Published by: Australians For Constitutional Monarchy, GPO Box 9841, Sydney, NSW 2001, Australia. TEL 61-2-9251-2500, FAX 61-2-9251-9833, http://www.norepublic.com.au.

320 AUS ISSN 1448-210X
AUSTRALIAN FABIAN NEWS. Text in English. 1961. q. free to members. bk.rev. **Document type:** *Newsletter, Consumer.*
Former titles (until 2002): Fabian Newsletter (1444-7274); (until 1995): Fabian News; (until 1994): Fabian Newsletter
Related titles: Online - full text ed.: free to members (effective 2008).
Published by: Australian Fabian Society, PO Box 2707, Melbourne, VIC 3001, Australia. TEL 61-2-96622596, national@fabian.org.au, http://www.fabian.org.au. Circ: 1,500.

320 AUS ISSN 1036-1146
JQ3995.A1
➤ **AUSTRALIAN JOURNAL OF POLITICAL SCIENCE.** Abbreviated title: A J P S. Text in English. 1956. q. GBP 462 combined subscription in United Kingdom to institutions (print & online eds.); EUR 608, AUD 812, USD 764 combined subscription to institutions (print & online eds.) (effective 2012). adv. bk.rev. bibl.; charts; stat. back issues avail.; reprint service avail. from PSC. **Document type:** *Journal, Academic/Scholarly.* **Description:** Publishes articles of high quality at the cutting edge of the discipline, characterized by conceptual clarity, methodological rigour, substantive interest, theoretical coherence, broad appeal, originality and insight.
Former titles (until 1990): Politics (0032-3268); (until 1966): A P S A News (0515-0000)
Related titles: Microfilm ed.: (from PQC); Online - full text ed.: ISSN 1363-030X. GBP 416 in United Kingdom to institutions; EUR 548, AUD 731, USD 688 to institutions (effective 2012) (from IngentaConnect).
Indexed: A01, A02, A03, A08, A11, A20, A22, A26, ABCPolSci, AEI, ASCA, AmH&L, AusPAIS, B14, BRI, CA, CurCont, DIP, E01, E08, G08, HistAb, I05, I13, IBR, IBSS, IBZ, P02, P06, P10, P30, P34, P42, P45, P48, P53, P54, PCI, PQC, PSA, RASB, S02, S03, S09, S11, SCOPUS, SPPI, SSA, SSCI, SociolAb, T02, W04, W07, WBA, WMB.
—IE, Infotrieve, Ingenta. **CCC.**
Published by: (Australasian Political Studies Association (Canberra)), Routledge (Subsidiary of: Taylor & Francis Group), Level 2, 11 Queens Rd, Melbourne, VIC 3004, Australia. TEL 61-03-90098134, FAX 61-03-98668822, http://www.informaworld.com. Circ: 800. **Subscr. to:** Taylor & Francis Ltd., Journals Customer Service, Sheepen Pl, Colchester, Essex CO3 3LP, United Kingdom. TEL 44-20-70175544, FAX 44-20-70175198.

320.09 990 AUS ISSN 0004-9522
DU80
➤ **AUSTRALIAN JOURNAL OF POLITICS AND HISTORY.** Abbreviated title: A J P H. Text in English. 1955. q. GBP 245 in United Kingdom to institutions; EUR 311 in Europe to institutions; USD 350 in the Americas to institutions; USD 477 elsewhere to institutions; GBP 282 combined subscription in United Kingdom to institutions (print & online eds.); EUR 358 combined subscription in Europe to institutions (print & online eds.); USD 403 combined subscription in the Americas to institutions (print & online eds.); USD 550 combined subscription elsewhere to institutions (print & online eds.) (effective 2012). adv. bk.rev. charts; tr.lit.; illus. Index. back issues avail.; reprint service avail. from PSC. **Document type:** *Journal, Academic/Scholarly.* **Description:** Contains articles in the fields of international politics, Australian foreign policy, and Australia's relations with the countries of the Asia-Pacific region.
Related titles: Online - full text ed.: ISSN 1467-8497. GBP 245 in United Kingdom to institutions; EUR 311 in Europe to institutions; USD 350 in the Americas to institutions; USD 477 elsewhere to institutions (effective 2012) (from IngentaConnect).
Indexed: A01, A02, A03, A08, A11, A20, A22, A26, ABCPolSci, APEL, ASCA, AmH&L, ArtHuCI, AusPAIS, BAS, CA, CurCont, DIP, E01, E08, EI, G08, Gdlns, H05, H14, HistAb, I05, I13, IBR, IBSS, IBZ, INZP, MEA&I, MLA-IB, P06, P10, P30, P34, P42, P48, P53, P54, PCI, PQC, PRA, PSA, RASB, S02, S03, S09, S11, S23, SCOPUS, SPPI, SSA, SociolAb, T02, W07.
—BLDSC (1811.150000), IE, Infotrieve, Ingenta. **CCC.**
Published by: (University of Queensland), Wiley-Blackwell Publishing Asia (Subsidiary of: Wiley-Blackwell Publishing Ltd.), 155 Cremorne St, Richmond, VIC 3121, Australia. TEL 61-3-92743100, FAX 61-3-92743101, melbourne@wiley.com, http://www.wiley.com/WileyCDA/. Eds. Andrew Bonnell, Ian Ward. Adv. contact Yasemin Caglar TEL 61-3-92743165. Circ: 750.

320.5322 AUS ISSN 0310-8252
AUSTRALIAN MARXIST REVIEW. Abbreviated title: A M R. Text in English. 1972. q. AUD 16 domestic (effective 2008). bibl. back issues avail. **Document type:** *Journal, Trade.*
Formerly (until 1971): Socialist Theory and Practice
Related titles: Online - full text ed.
Indexed: LeftInd.
Published by: Communist Party of Australia, 74 Buckingham St, Surry Hills, NSW 2010, Australia. TEL 61-2-96998844, FAX 61-2-96999833, cpa@cpa.org.au. Ed. Eddie Clynes.

320.5322 AUS ISSN 1324-0749
AUSTRALIAN OPTIONS; discussions for social justice and political change. Text in English. 1995. q. AUD 20 (effective 2011). **Document type:** *Magazine, Consumer.* **Description:** Includes articles on political affairs and social change.
Media: Online - full text.
Published by: Australian Options Publishing, PO Box 431, Goodwood, SA 5034, Australia. Ed. Greg Ogle.

320 AUS ISSN 1834-2736
AUSTRALIAN PROSPECT. Text in English. 2004. 3/yr. **Document type:** *Journal, Consumer.* **Description:** A forum for the development of policies and thinking about Australia's future.
Media: Online - full text.
Address: PO Box 29, Barrengarry, NSW, Australia. TEL 61-2-4465-1665, FAX 61-2-4465-2305, editor@australianprospect.com.au, http://www.australianprospect.com.au.

320 330.9 AUS ISSN 1832-1526
➤ **AUSTRALIAN REVIEW OF PUBLIC AFFAIRS.** Text in English. 2000. a. free (effective 2011). back issues avail. **Document type:** *Journal, Academic/Scholarly.* **Description:** It aims at reflecting upon and evaluating the design and redesign of Australia's public policies and institutions and its relations and responsibilities in the broader world community.
Formerly (until 2004): The Drawing Board (1443-8607)
Media: Online - full text.
Indexed: A11, A39, AusPAIS, C27, C29, D03, D04, E13, ERO, P42, R14, S14, S15, S18, T02.
—**CCC.**
Published by: University of Sydney, Faculty of Economics and Business, Level 2, Merewether Bldg (H69), Sydney, NSW 2006, Australia. TEL 61-2-90365356, FAX 61-2-93514567, http://www.econ.usyd.edu.au/. Ed. Gabrielle Meagher.

320.531 320.971 CAN
L'AUT'JOURNAL. Text in French. 1984. m. CAD 30 (effective 2001). **Document type:** *Newspaper, Consumer.* **Description:** Covers political issues with a perspective from the left.
Related titles: Online - full content ed.
Published by: Editions du Renouveau Quebecois, 3575 bd. St-Laurent, bureau 117, Montreal, PQ H2X 2T7, Canada. TEL 514-843-5236, FAX 514-849-0637, autjour@microtec.net.

320.84 BOL ISSN 1029-4341
AUTODETERMINACION. Text in Spanish. 1994. q.
Published by: Centro de Informacion para el Desarrollo, Casilla 13801, La Paz, Bolivia. Eds. Jean Paul Guevara, Seemin Qayum.

AUTONOMIE LOCALI E SERVIZI SOCIALI; vademecum a schede. *see* SOCIAL SERVICES AND WELFARE

324.2 FRA ISSN 1950-4624
L'AUTRE PARIS. Text in French. 2006. q. EUR 10 (effective 2007). **Document type:** *Magazine, Consumer.*
Published by: Association Departementale des Elus Communistes et Republicains de Paris, ADECR 75, Groupe Communiste, Hotel de Ville, Paris, 75196 RP, France. TEL 33-1-42765768, FAX 33-1-42766239, info@elusparis.pcf.fr, http://www.elusparis.pcf.fr.

324.27285 NIC
AVANCE. Text in Spanish. 1972. w.
Published by: Partido Comunista de Nicaragua, Cuidad Jardin 0-30, Apdo. 4231, Managua Jr, Nicaragua. TEL 2-43750. Circ: 20,000.

320.972 MEX
AVANTE; periodismo de analisis. Text in Spanish. 1992. bi-m. adv.
Published by: Editora Comunicacion, Paseo Sierra Vista No 67, Residencial Sierra Vista, Hermosillo, Sonora, 83148, Mexico. TEL 52-62-112-190, FAX 52-62-110-870. Ed. Lorena Myrna Galvez.

324.2469 PRT ISSN 0870-1865
AVANTE. Text in Portuguese. 1931. w. **Document type:** *Magazine, Consumer.* **Description:** Official publication of the Portuguese Communist Party.
Published by: Communist Party, Rua Soeiro Pereira Gomes, 1699, Lisbon, 1699, Portugal. TEL 01-769725. Ed. A Dias Lourenco da Silva.

320 ARG
AVISPA; revista mensual de politica y cultura. Text in Spanish. 1994. m. (10/yr.). ARS 4 per issue; USD 5 per issue foreign. adv.
Published by: Centro de Estudios Union para la Nueva Mayoria, Estados Unidos 943, Buenos Aires, 1101, Argentina. FAX 54-114-3003077. Ed. Carolina Barros. Pub. Rosendo Fraga. R&P Julio Burdman TEL 54-1-3004061. Adv. contact Alejandro Colle. Circ: 1,950.

320 LBN
AZTAG SHAPATORIAG-TROSHAG. Text in Armenian. 1969. w. USD 24.
Published by: Ste. Aztag S.A.R.L., Salim Bustany St., Beirut, Lebanon. Ed. Sarkis Zeitlian. **Dist. in U.S. by:** Haig Gakavian, 9417 Curren Rd, Silver Spring, MD 20901.

320 DEU
B D V NACHRICHTEN. (Bund der Vertriebenen) Text in German. 1952. q. EUR 25 (effective 2009). bk.rev. **Document type:** *Magazine, Consumer.*
Former titles (until 1965): Bund der Vertriebenen. Mitteilungsblatt; (until 1959): Bund der Vertriebenen Deutschen. Mitteilungsblatt; (until 1958): Bund der Vertriebenen Deutschen. Mitgliederdienst
Published by: Bund der Vertriebenen, Landesverband Baden-Wuerttemberg e.V., Schlossstr 92, Stuttgart, 70176, Germany. TEL 49-711-625277, FAX 49-711-610162, zentrale@bdv-bw.de. Ed. Ulrich Klein.

320.5 USA
B E A R S; in moral and political philosophy. (Brown Electronic Article Review Service) Text in English. irreg. bk.rev.
Media: Online - full text.
Published by: Brown University Library, Friends of the Library, PO Box A, Providence, RI 02912. TEL 401-863-1000, james_dreier@brown.edu, david_estlund@brown.edu. Eds. David Estlund, James Dreier.

320 NLD ISSN 1389-0069
JA26
B EN M. (Beleid en Maatschappij) Text in Dutch. 1973. 4/yr. EUR 98 to individuals; EUR 227 to institutions (effective 2008). adv. Supplement avail. **Document type:** *Academic/Scholarly.*
Formerly (until 1998): Beleid en Maatschappij (0165-1625)
Related titles: Online - full text ed.: ISSN 1875-712X. EUR 79 to individuals; EUR 209 to institutions (effective 2008).
Indexed: A22, ELLIS, KES.
—IE, Infotrieve.
Published by: Boom Uitgevers Amsterdam, Prinsengracht 747-751, Amsterdam, 1017 JX, Netherlands. TEL 31-20-6226107, FAX 31-20-6253327, info@uitgeverijboom.nl, http://www.uitgeverijboom.nl. Circ: 1,000.

320.5 USA
BAD SUBJECTS; political education for everyday life. Text in English. 1992. 6/yr. **Description:** Covers issues in pop culture, current events, economics, politics, and multiculturalism.
Related titles: Online - full text ed.: ISSN 1094-0715.
Indexed: CA, LeftInd.
Published by: Bad Subjects Production Team, 322 Wheeler Hall, University of California, Berkeley, CA 94720.

320 340 001.3 CHN ISSN 1673-3118
BAICHENG SHIFAN XUEYUAN XUEBAO/BAICHENG NORMAL COLLEGE. JOURNAL. Text in Chinese. 2003. bi-m. **Document type:** *Journal, Academic/Scholarly.*
Formerly: Baicheng Shifan Gaodeng Zhuanke Xuexiao Xuebao
Published by: Baicheng Shifan Xueyuan/Baicheng Normal College, 9, Zhongxing Dong Dalu, Baicheng, 137000, China. TEL 86-436-3251604, http://www.bcsfxy.com/.

BAINIANCHAO/HUNDRED YEAR TIDE. *see* HISTORY—History Of Asia

320.6 USA ISSN 1941-6466
E839.5
BAKER INSTITUTE POLICY REPORT. Text in English. 19??. irreg., latest vol.43, 2010. back issues avail. **Document type:** *Monographic series, Academic/Scholarly.*
Formerly (until 2006): Baker Institute Study (1933-4583)
Related titles: Online - full text ed.: free (effective 2011).
Published by: Rice University, James A. Baker III Institute for Public Policy, Baker Hall, Ste 120, 6100 Main St, Houston, TX 77005. TEL 713-348-4683, FAX 713-348-5993, bipp@rice.edu.

320 FRA ISSN 1279-7952
BALKANOLOGIE; revue d'etudes pluridisciplinaires. Text in French. 1991. s-a. **Document type:** *Journal, Academic/Scholarly.*
Formerly (until 1991): Homo Balkanicus (1162-1257)
Related titles: Online - full text ed.: free (effective 2011).
Indexed: I13, IBSS.
Published by: Association Francaise d'Etudes sur les Balkans, Maison des Sciences de l'Homme, Bureau 108, 54 Boulevard Raspail, Paris, 75006, France. contact@afebalk.org.

320 DEU ISSN 0005-4526
AP30
BALTISCHE BRIEFE. Text in German. 1948. m. EUR 5.10 newsstand/cover (effective 2006). adv. bk.rev. bibl.; illus. **Document type:** *Journal, Academic/Scholarly.*
Indexed: RASB.
Published by: Verlag Baltische Briefe Wolf J. von Kleist GmbH, Deefkamp 13, Grosshansdorf, 22927, Germany. TEL 49-4102-61112, FAX 49-4102-65388. adv.: B&W page EUR 1,771, color page EUR 3,364.90. Circ: 4,200 (paid and controlled).

320.532 ITA ISSN 1122-519X
BANDIERA ROSSA. Text in Italian. 1951. m. **Document type:** *Magazine, Consumer.*
Published by: Associazione Politico-Culturale Quarta Internazionale, Via Benedetto Varchi, 3, Milan, MI 20158, Italy. TEL 39-2-3760027, FAX 39-2-39320935.

320 BGD
BANGLADESH POLITICAL STUDIES. Text in English, Bengali. 1978. a. BDT 50, USD 10. adv. bk.rev.

Published by: University of Chittagong, Department of Political Science, Chittagong, Bangladesh. TEL 414393. Ed. Muhammad A Hakim. Circ: 1,000.

328.72981 BRB ISSN 0377-144X
J137
BARBADOS. LEGISLATURE. HOUSE OF ASSEMBLY. MINUTES OF PROCEEDINGS. Text in English. w. **Document type:** *Government.*
Published by: Legislature, House of Assembly, Bridgetown, Barbados.

328.72981 BRB ISSN 0377-1458
J137
BARBADOS. LEGISLATURE. SENATE. MINUTES OF PROCEEDINGS. Text in English. w. **Document type:** *Government.*
Published by: Legislature, Senate, Bridgetown, Barbados.

320 USA ISSN 1553-3700
D861
BARDPOLITIK. Text in English. 2002 (Spr). s-a. free (effective 2005). **Document type:** *Journal, Academic/Scholarly.*
Media: Online - full content.
Published by: Bard College, Globalization and International Affairs Program, 410 W 58th St, New York, NY 10019. TEL 212-333-7575, FAX 212-397-3055, bgia@bard.edu.

320.57 322.4 FRA ISSN 1954-4049
BARRICATA. Text in French. 1999. irreg. EUR 10 (effective 2008). back issues avail. **Document type:** *Magazine, Consumer.*
Published by: Barricata - R A S H Paris-Banlieue, c/o Crash Disques, 21 ter Rue Voltaire, Paris, 75011, France.

320 CHE ISSN 1664-6681
▼ **BASEL PAPERS ON POLITICAL TRANSFORMATIONS.** Text in English. 2011. irreg. price varies. **Document type:** *Monographic series, Academic/Scholarly.*
Related titles: Online - full text ed.: ISSN 1664-669X. 2011.
Published by: Universitaet Basel, Ethnologisches Seminar, Muensterplatz 19, Basel, 4051, Switzerland. TEL 41-61-2672738, ethnologie@unibas.ch, http://www.unibas-ethno.ch.

320 RUS
BASHKORTOSTAN. Text in Bashkir. 260/yr. USD 439 in the Americas (effective 2000).
Indexed: RASB.
Address: Ul. 50 letiya Oktyabrya, 13, 5 etazh, Ufa, 450079, Russian Federation. TEL 3472-227266, FAX 3472-234992, bashkor@basginform.ru. Ed. F Khisamov. **Dist. by:** East View Information Services, 10601 Wayzata Blvd, Minneapolis, MN 55305. TEL 952-252-1201, 800-477-1005, FAX 952-252-1202, info@eastview.com, http://www.eastview.com.

320 ESP
AS302.O84
EL BASILISCO (ONLINE); revista de materialismo filosofico. Text in Spanish. 1978. q. free (effective 2010). **Document type:** *Magazine, Consumer.*
Formerly: El Basilisco (Print) (0210-0088)
Media: Online - full text.
Indexed: BibInd, MLA-IB, P09, PCI, PhilInd, RILM, SOPODA, SociolAb.
—**CCC.**
Published by: El Basilisco, Avenida de Galicia 31, Oviedo, 33005, Spain.

306.2 DEU ISSN 2191-7582
➤ **BEHEMOTH**; a journal on civilisation. Text in English. 2008. 3/yr. EUR 154 combined subscription to institutions (print & online eds.) (effective 2012). **Document type:** *Journal, Academic/Scholarly.* **Description:** Focuses on the general problem of fading and/or failing statecraft and the consequences resulting out of it.
Media: Online - full text. **Related titles:** Online - full text ed.: ISSN 1866-2447.
Published by: Walter de Gruyter GmbH & Co. KG, Genthiner Str 13, Berlin, 10785, Germany. TEL 49-30-260050, FAX 49-30-26005251, info@degruyter.com, http://www.degruyter.de.

320.531 951 CHN ISSN 1008-1798
BEIJING DANGSHI. Text in Chinese. 1982. bi-m. CNY 5 per issue (effective 2010). back issues avail. **Document type:** *Magazine, Government.*
Formerly (until 1999): Beijing Dangshi Yanjiu
Related titles: Online - full text ed.
Published by: Zhong-Gong Beijing Shi-Wei Dangshi Yanjiushi, 6, Chegongzhuang Dajie, Xicheng-qu, Beijing, 100044, China. TEL 86-10-68007470, http://www.bjdj.gov.cn.

320.532 CHN ISSN 1008-1208
BEIJING GUANCHA/BEIJING OBSERVATION. Text in Chinese. 1986. m. USD 43.20 (effective 2009). **Document type:** *Journal, Academic/Scholarly.*
Formerly (until 1998): Beijing Zheng-Xie (1006-4419)
—East View.
Published by: Zhongguo Renmin Zhengzhi Xieshang Huiyi Beijing Shi Weiyuanhui/Chinese People's Political Consultative Conference Beijing Committee, 13, Jianguomen Nei Dajie, Beijing, 100005, China. TEL 86-10-65190512, FAX 86-10-65262668, http://www.bjzx.gov.cn/. **Dist. by:** China International Book Trading Corp, 35 Chegongzhuang Xilu, Haidian District, PO Box 399, Beijing 100044, China. TEL 86-10-68412045, FAX 86-10-68412023, cibtc@mail.cibtc.com.cn, http://www.cibtc.com.cn.

320 CHN ISSN 1008-4002
BEIJING QINGNIAN ZHENGZHI XUEYUAN XUEBAO/BEIJING YOUTH POLITICS COLLEGE. JOURNAL. Text in Chinese. 1999. q. USD 16.40 (effective 2009). **Document type:** *Journal, Academic/Scholarly.*
Related titles: Online - full text ed.
—East View.
Published by: Beijing Qingnian Zhengzhi Xueyuan, 1, Wangjing Zhonghuan Nan Lu, Beijing, 100102, China. TEL 86-10-64722087.

320 CHN ISSN 1672-9285
BEIJING ZHENG-FA ZHIYE XUEYUAN XUEBAO/BEIJING COLLEGE OF POLITICAL SCIENCE AND LAW. JOURNAL. Text in Chinese. 1987. q. **Document type:** *Journal, Academic/Scholarly.*
Former titles (until 2004): Beijing Shi Zhengfa Guanli Ganbu Xueyuan Xuebao/Beijing Management College of Politics and Law Journal (1008-7273); (until 1999): Fayuan
Related titles: Online - full text ed.
Published by: Beijing Zheng-Fa Zhiye Xueyuan/Beijing College of Political Science and Law, Chaoyang-qu Yangzha, Beijing, 100024, China. TEL 86-10-65750411, FAX 86-10-65754999, http://www.bcpl.cn/.

320.532 CHN ISSN 1002-7998
BEIJING ZHIBU SHENGHUO. Text in Chinese. 1958-1966; resumed 1980. m. **Document type:** *Magazine, Government.* **Description:** Covers the Beijing communist party news, events, policies, laws, regulations, and party philosophy.
Supersedes in part: Zhibu Shenghuo (1003-6032)
Published by: (Zhongguo Gongchadang Beijing Shi Weiyuanhui), Beijing Zhibu Shenghuo Zazhishe, 14, Xin Jie Kouwai Dajie Jia, Sheyue Dasha 7/F, Beijing, 100088, China.

320 DEU ISSN 0722-0189
BEITRAEGE ZUR FEMINISTISCHEN THEORIE UND PRAXIS. Text in German. 1978. 3/yr. EUR 43; EUR 15 newsstand/cover (effective 2009). **Document type:** *Journal, Academic/Scholarly.*
Indexed: A22, DIP, IBR, IBZ, MLA-IB, PAIS.
—**CCC.**
Published by: Beitraege Redaktion, Niederichstr 6, Cologne, 50668, Germany. TEL 49-221-138490, FAX 49-221-1390194.

320 DEU ISSN 0942-3060
BEITRAEGE ZUR GESCHICHTE DER ARBEITERBEWEGUNG. Text in German. 1959. 3/yr. EUR 40 domestic; EUR 48 foreign; EUR 12 newsstand/cover (effective 2011). bk.rev. bibl. index. reprints avail. **Document type:** *Journal, Academic/Scholarly.* **Description:** Contains information on the German and international history of labor, labor political parties, trade unions and other labor organizations.
Former titles (until 1992): B Z G (0942-3079); (until 1990): Beitraege zur Geschichte der Arbeiterbewegung (0005-8068); (until 1969): Beitraege zur Geschichte der Deutschen Arbeiterbewegung (0323-7672)
Indexed: A20, AmH&L, ArtHuCI, CA, CurCont, DIP, HistAb, IBR, IBZ, P30, PCI, PRA, RASB, SCOPUS, T02, W07.
—BLDSC (1883.900000), IE, Infotrieve, Ingenta. **CCC.**
Published by: Trafo Verlag, Finkenstr 8, Berlin, 12621, Germany. TEL 49-30-61299418, FAX 49-30-61299421, info@trafoberlin.de. Ed. Dr. Herbert Mayer. Pub., R&P, Adv. contact Dr. Wolfgang Weist.

BEITRAEGE ZUR GESCHICHTE DER NATIONALSOZIALISTISCHEN VERFOLGUNG IN NORDDEUTSCHLAND. *see* HISTORY—History Of Europe

328 DEU ISSN 0522-6643
DD117
BEITRAEGE ZUR GESCHICHTE DES PARLEMENTARISMUS UND DER POLITISCHEN PARTEIEN. Text in German. 1952. irreg., latest vol.154, 2009. price varies. **Document type:** *Monographic series, Academic/Scholarly.*
Indexed: RASB.
Published by: Droste Verlag GmbH, Martin Luther Platz 26, Duesseldorf, 40212, Germany. TEL 49-211-8605220, FAX 49-211-3230098, vertrieb@drosteverlag.de, http://www.drosteverlag.de.

320 DEU ISSN 0170-8384
BEITRAEGE ZUR POLITIKWISSENSCHAFT (FRANKFURT AM MAIN). Text in German. 1975. irreg., latest vol.93, 2008. price varies. **Document type:** *Monographic series, Academic/Scholarly.*
Published by: Peter Lang GmbH (Subsidiary of: Peter Lang Publishing Group), Eschborner Landstr 42-50, Frankfurt Am Main, 60489, Germany. TEL 49-69-7807050, FAX 49-69-78070550, zentrale.frankfurt@peterlang.com.

320 DEU
BEITRAEGE ZUR POLITIKWISSENSCHAFT (MUNICH). Text in German. 2002. irreg., latest vol.11, 2009. price varies. **Document type:** *Monographic series, Academic/Scholarly.*
Published by: Herbert Utz Verlag GmbH, Adalbertstr 57, Munich, 80799, Germany. TEL 49-89-27779100, FAX 49-89-27779101, utz@utzverlag.com.

320 DEU ISSN 0582-0421
BEITRAEGE ZUR POLITISCHEN WISSENSCHAFT. Text in German. 1967. irreg., latest vol.161, 2010. price varies. **Document type:** *Monographic series, Academic/Scholarly.*
Published by: Duncker und Humblot GmbH, Carl-Heinrich-Becker-Weg 9, Berlin, 12165, Germany. TEL 49-30-7900060, FAX 49-30-79000631, info@duncker-humblot.de.

320 BLZ
BELIZE TIMES. Text in English. 1956. w. **Document type:** *Newspaper.*
Related titles: Print ed.: ISSN 1563-8057. 1999.
Published by: People's United Party, 3 Queen St, PO Box 506, Belize City, Belize. TEL 2-45757. Ed. Amalia Mai. Circ: 5,000.

320.9 NGA
BENDEL STATE GAZETTE. Text in English. 1964. w. NGN 9.50, USD 11. charts; stat. **Document type:** *Government.*
Formerly: Midwestern Nigeria Gazette (0026-3494)
Published by: Ministry of Home Affairs and Information, Printing and Stationery Division, PMB 1099, Benin City, Bendel State, Nigeria. Circ: 4,500.

BERG FRENCH STUDIES SERIES. *see* LITERATURE

321.8 DEU ISSN 0945-8573
BERLINER SCHRIFTEN ZUR DEMOKRATIEFORSCHUNG. Text in German. 1994. irreg., latest vol.5, 1997. price varies. **Document type:** *Monographic series, Academic/Scholarly.*
Published by: Peter Lang GmbH (Subsidiary of: Peter Lang Publishing Group), Eschborner Landstr 42-50, Frankfurt Am Main, 60489, Germany. TEL 49-69-7807050, FAX 49-69-78070550, zentrale.frankfurt@peterlang.com. Ed. Gert-Joachim Glaessner.

320.53 DEU ISSN 0933-6516
BERLINER SCHRIFTEN ZUR POLITIK UND GESELLSCHAFT IM SOZIALISMUS UND KOMMUNISMUS. Text in German. 1988. irreg., latest vol.9, 1996. price varies. **Document type:** *Monographic series, Academic/Scholarly.*
Published by: Peter Lang GmbH (Subsidiary of: Peter Lang Publishing Group), Eschborner Landstr 42-50, Frankfurt Am Main, 60489, Germany. TEL 49-69-7807050, FAX 49-69-78070550, zentrale.frankfurt@peterlang.com.

320 USA ISSN 1930-3092
E839.5
THE BEST POLITICAL CARTOONS OF THE YEAR. Text in English. 200?. a. USD 11.69 per issue; USD 15.54 combined subscription per issue (print & online eds.) (effective 2011). back issues avail. **Document type:** *Consumer.*
Related titles: Online - full text ed.: USD 9.89 per issue (effective 2011).
Published by: (Cagle Cartoons, Inc.), Que Publishing Corporation, 800 E 96th St, Indianapolis, IN 46240. TEL 800-571-5840, information@quepublishing.com.

320 CAN ISSN 1920-8561
BEYOND THE HILL. Text in English. 2004. q. free (effective 2010). **Document type:** *Magazine, Trade.*
Related titles: Online - full text ed.
Published by: Canadian Association of Former Parliamentarians, 131 Queen St, House of Commons, PO Box 1, Ottawa, ON K1A 0A6, Canada. TEL 888-567-4764, FAX 613-947-1764, exparl@parl.gc.ca.

320 ITA ISSN 0006-1654
BIBLIOTECA DELLA LIBERTA. Abbreviated title: B d L. Text in Italian. 1964. 5/yr. adv. bk.rev.; film rev.; play rev. bibl.; illus. index. **Document type:** *Monographic series, Academic/Scholarly.*
Related titles: Online - full text ed.: ISSN 2035-5866.
Indexed: I13.
Published by: Centro di Ricerca e Documentazione Luigi Einaudi, Via Ponza 4, Turin, 10121, Italy. TEL 39-011-5591611, FAX 39-011-5591691, segreteria@centroeinaudi.it. Circ: 7,000.

324.2 ESP ISSN 1699-0897
BIBLIOTECA POPULAR CARLISTA. Text in Spanish. 2000. irreg. **Document type:** *Monographic series, Academic/Scholarly.*
Published by: (Partido Carlista), Magalia Ediciones, Apartado de Correos 10185, Madrid, 28080, Spain. TEL 34-91-6692039.

320.9 POL ISSN 0138-094X
BIBLIOTEKA POLONIJNA/POLONIA LIBRARY. Text in Polish. 1960. irreg., latest 2001. price varies. **Document type:** *Monographic series, Academic/Scholarly.*
Formerly (until 1977): Problemy Polonii Zagranicznej (0079-5798)
Published by: Polska Akademia Nauk, Komitet Badania Polonii, Uniwersytet Jagiellonski, Instytut Studiow Polonijnych, ul Jodlowa 13, Krakow, 30252, Poland. TEL 48-12-4297110, FAX 48-12-4299351. Ed. Wladyslaw Miodunka.

320.9 FRA ISSN 1956-5372
BIBLIOTHEQUE GEOPOLITIQUE. Text in French. 2007. irreg. price varies. **Document type:** *Monographic series, Academic/Scholarly.*
Published by: Editions Eres, 33 Av. Marcel Dassault, Toulouse, 31500, France. TEL 33-5-61751576, FAX 33-5-61735289, eres@edition-eres.com.

BILANS POLITIQUES ECONOMIQUES ET SOCIAUX HEBDOMADAIRES. *see* BUSINESS AND ECONOMICS

BILL STATUS SHEET. *see* PUBLIC ADMINISTRATION

BINGTUAN DANGXIAO XUEBAO/PARTY SCHOOL OF X P C C OF C.P.C. JOURNAL. *see* SOCIAL SCIENCES: COMPREHENSIVE WORKS

LES BIOGRAPHIES.COM. L'ASSEMBLEE NATIONALE. *see* BIOGRAPHY

320.52 USA
THE BLACK AND BLUE. Text in English. 1996. irreg. **Description:** Dedicated to fighting the corporatization of the university and the rightwing onslaught in society-at-large.
Media: Online - full text.
Published by: University of Pensylvania, 221 Church St, 2, Philadelphia, PA 19106-4514. Ed. Matthew Ruben.

328 USA ISSN 0895-1780
KF49
BLACK CONGRESSIONAL MONITOR; legislative initiatives of Senator Barack Obama and the 42 other African Americans in the 110th Congress. Variant title: B C Monitor. Text in English. 1986 (Oct.). s-m. USD 60 domestic; USD 75 foreign (effective 2008). adv. bk.rev. back issues avail. **Document type:** *Newsletter, Trade.* **Description:** Contains unedited report of US Federal Government policies, programs, other initiative of particular interest/benefit to African Americans, e.g., available grant awards, scholarships/fellowships, contract/subcontract opportunities, public meetings and notices, public policy documents and other publications, and legislative initiative of African Americans in Congress.
Related titles: Online - full text ed.
Published by: Len Mor Publications, PO Box 75035, Washington, DC 20013. TEL 202-488-8879, FAX 202-554-3116, lenora.moragne@verizon.net. Ed., Pub., R&P Lenora Moragne.

THE BLACK SCHOLAR; journal of black studies and research. *see* ETHNIC INTERESTS

320.994 AUS ISSN 1833-508X
THE BLADE. Text in English. 2006. q.
Published by: The Blade, 4/1 Aaron Pl, Wahroonga, NSW 2076, Australia. TEL 61-2-82148916. Ed. Ross Blade.

320 DEU ISSN 1435-9146
BLICKPUNKT BUNDESTAG. Text in German. 1998. 8/yr. EUR 16 (effective 2008). **Document type:** *Magazine, Trade.*
Formed by the merger of (1971-1998): Woche im Bundestag (1438-1990); (1987-1998): Bundestag-Report (0933-2731); Which was formerly (1980-1987): Bundestag-Report zur Aktuellen Parlamentarischen Diskussion (0176-5000)
—**CCC.**
Published by: Media Consulta Deutschland GmbH, Hildeboldplatz 15-17, Cologne, 50672, Germany. TEL 49-221-35000, FAX 49-221-3500350, mc@media-consulta.com, http://www.media-consulta.com.

320 NLD ISSN 2210-4194
BLIK OPENER. Text in Dutch. 2008. bi-m.
Published by: (Socialistische Partij, Tweede Kamerfractie), ROOD, Jong in de S P, Vijverhofstraat 65, Rotterdam, 3032 SC, Netherlands. TEL 31-10-2435557, FAX 31-10-2435566, rood@sp.nl.

320 USA
BLU MAGAZINE. Text in English. bi-m. USD 29.95 domestic; USD 45 in Canada; USD 60 elsewhere; USD 5 newsstand/cover (effective 2001). **Document type:** *Magazine, Consumer.* **Description:** Serves as the survival guide to politics for the new generation of youth and activists.
Related titles: CD-ROM ed.
Address: PO Box 903, Rifton, NY 12471. TEL 914-658-3317, FAX 800-778-7461. Circ: 10,000.

P

320 USA ISSN 1527-439X
JK2311
BLUEPRINT (WASHINGTON, D.C.); ideas for a new century. Text in English. 6/yr. USD 25 domestic; USD 75 foreign; USD 5 newsstand/cover (effective 2005).
Related titles: Online - full text ed.
Indexed: A01, A03, A08, P34, P42, PAIS, T02.
Published by: Democratic Leadership Council, 600 Pennsylvania Ave., S E, Ste 400, Washington, DC 20003. TEL 800-546-0027, blueprint@dlc.org. Ed. Chuck Alston.

320.5 SWE ISSN 0345-1631
BOHUS LAENS FOLKBLAD. Text in Swedish. 1947. bi-m. SEK 100; SEK 10 newsstand/cover (effective 2005). 4 p./no.; **Document type:** *Bulletin, Consumer.*
Published by: Frisinnade Unions-Partiet, Dr Resmarks Vaeg, Bua 6186, Elloes, 44080, Sweden. TEL 46-304-50160. Ed., Pub. Sven A Lundehaell.

320.531 FRA ISSN 0395-4269
LE BOLCHEVIK. Text in French. 1976. q. **Document type:** *Newspaper, Consumer.* **Description:** Newspaper of the Ligue trotskyste de France.
Published by: Ligue Trotskyste de France, BP 135-10, Paris Cedex 10, 75463, France.

320.531 USA
BOLCHEVIQUE. Text in Spanish. 1980. m. USD 20.
Published by: October Publications, 3309 1/2 Mission St, Ste 135, San Francisco, CA 94110. TEL 415-695-0340. Circ: 2,500.

320 MEX ISSN 0186-0461
BOLETIN DE POLITICA INFORMATICA. Text in Spanish. 1982. m. free or exchange basis.
Published by: Instituto Nacional de Estadistica, Geografia e Informatica, Secretaria de Programacion y Presupuesto, Prol. Heroe de Nacozari 2301 Sur, Puerta 11, Acceso, Aguascalientes, 20270, Mexico. TEL 52-4-918-1948, FAX 52-4-918-0739. Circ: 700.

324.6 CRI ISSN 1020-0940
BOLETIN ELECTORAL LATINOAMERICANO. Text in Spanish. 1989. s-a. USD 15. back issues avail. **Document type:** *Bulletin.* **Description:** Analyzes the electoral processes in the region. Contains official results.
Published by: Instituto Interamericano de Derechos Humanos, Apartado Postal 10081, San Jose, 1000, Costa Rica. TEL 506-234-04-04, FAX 506-234-09-55. Ed. Daniel Zovatto. Circ: 1,000.

320 ITA ISSN 1591-4305
JA18
BOLLETTINO SISTEMATICO DI FILOSOFIA POLITICA; online journal of political philosophy. Text in Multiple languages. 1998. w. free (effective 2011). **Document type:** *Journal, Academic/Scholarly.*
Formerly (until 1999): Bollettino di Filosofia Politica (Online Edition) (1128-7861)
Media: Online - full text.
Published by: Universita degli Studi di Pisa, Dipartimento di Scienze Politiche e Sociali, Via Serafini 3 A, Pisa, 56126, Italy. TEL 39-050-2212472, FAX 39-050-2212400.

320.5322 ITA ISSN 0392-3886
IL BOLSCEVICO. Text in Italian. 1969. w. EUR 60 domestic; EUR 100 foreign (effective 2009). 12 p./no.; back issues avail. **Document type:** *Newspaper, Consumer.* **Description:** Covers the Italian Marxist-Leninist party.
Related titles: Online - full text ed.
Published by: Editoriale il Girasole, C.P. 477, Florence, FI 50100, Italy. Ed. Monica Martenghi.

328 USA ISSN 0068-0125
JK2403
THE BOOK OF THE STATES. Text in English. 1935. a. USD 99 per issue (paperback ed.); USD 125 per issue (hardcover ed.) (effective 2009). abstr.; charts; stat. index. back issues avail.; reprints avail. **Document type:** *Directory, Academic/Scholarly.* **Description:** Provides a comprehensive reference on all state governments with information on reorganization, management, productivity, and efficiency efforts.
Related titles: Microfiche ed.: (from PMC, PQC, WSH); Online - full text ed.
Indexed: SRI.
—**CCC.**
Published by: Council of State Governments, 2760 Research Park Dr, PO Box 11910, Lexington, KY 40578. TEL 859-244-8000, 800-800-1910, FAX 859-244-8001, info@csg.org.

320.5 305.8 USA
BORDERLINES (MINNEAPOLIS). Text in English. 1995. irreg., latest vol.30, 2007. price varies. bk.rev. illus. back issues avail. **Document type:** *Monographic series, Academic/Scholarly.* **Description:** Aims to encourage a dialogue among scholars from a range of disciplines including, on the one hand, international relations and comparative politics and, on the other, cultural studies, feminist theory, literary theory, and cultural anthropology.
Published by: University of Minnesota Press, Ste 290, 111 Third Ave S, Minneapolis, MN 55401. TEL 612-627-1970, FAX 612-627-1980, ump@umn.edu. Eds. David Campbell, Michael J Shapiro. **Dist. by:** c/o Chicago Distribution Center, 11030 S Langley Ave, Chicago, IL 60628. TEL 800-621-2736; Plymbridge Distributors Ltd, Estover Rd, Plymouth, Devon PL6 7PY, United Kingdom. TEL 44-1752-202-301, FAX 44-1752-202-331.

320.52 GBR
THE BOW GROUP. POLICY PAPERS. Text in English. 19??. irreg.
Published by: The Bow Group, CAN Mezzanine, 32-36 Loman St, Southwark, London, SE1 0EH, United Kingdom. TEL 44-207-9227718, FAX 44-207-4316668, office@bowgroup.org.

320 IRL
BRANCHLINES. Text in English. 1978. 6/yr. free. adv. bk.rev. illus. **Document type:** *Newsletter.*
Former titles (until 1995): Fine Gael News; (until 1984): New Democrat (0790-1267); (until 1983): National Democrat
Published by: Fine Gael Party, Fine Gael Press Rooms, Leinster House, Dublin, 2, Ireland. TEL 353-1-6789030, FAX 353-1-6785806. Ed. Niall O Muilleoir. Circ: 17,000 (controlled).

BRAZIL BUSINESS FORECAST REPORT. *see* BUSINESS AND ECONOMICS—Economic Situation And Conditions

BRAZIL WATCH. *see* BUSINESS AND ECONOMICS—Economic Situation And Conditions

320 BRA ISSN 1981-3821
JA26
BRAZILIAN POLITICAL SCIENCE REVIEW. Text in English. 2007. s-a. free (effective 2011). **Document type:** *Journal, Academic/Scholarly.*
Media: Online - full text.
Published by: Associacao Brasileira de Ciencia Politica, Rua da Matriz 82, Botafogo, Rio de Janeiro, Brazil. TEL 55-21-25378020, FAX 55-21-22867146.

320.5 USA ISSN 1073-2519
HQ75
BREAKTHROUGH (SAN FRANCISCO). Text in English. 1977. 3/yr. USD 10 to individuals; USD 15 to institutions. bk.rev. illus. back issues avail. **Description:** Provides original articles, interviews and selected reprints analyzing international and domestic issues of concern to the left and progressive movements.
Indexed: AltPI.
Published by: (Prairie Fire Organizing Committee), John Brown Education Fund, PO Box 14422, San Francisco, CA 94114. Circ: 3,500.

320 CAN ISSN 0703-8968
BRIARPATCH. Text in English. 1973. 8/yr. CAD 28.95 domestic to individuals; CAD 48.98 foreign to individuals; CAD 38.98 domestic to institutions; CAD 58.98 foreign to institutions; CAD 4.95 per issue (effective 2008). adv. bk.rev.; music rev.; video rev. illus. back issues avail.; reprints avail. **Document type:** *Magazine, Consumer.* **Description:** Covers issues related to labor, the environment, peace, native people, and provincial and national politics, from a leftist perspective.
Related titles: Microfiche ed.: (from MML); Microform ed.: (from MML); Online - full text ed.
Indexed: A26, AltPI, C03, C05, CBCARef, CBPI, CPerI, G08, I05, I06, I07, LeftInd, MLA-IB, P48, PQC, S23, W09.
—CIS.
Published by: Briarpatch, Inc., 2138 McIntyre St, Regina, SK S4P 2R7, Canada. TEL 306-525-2949, FAX 306-565-3430, http://www.cmpa.ca. Ed. David Oswald Mitchell. adv.: B&W page USD 350; trim 11 x 8.5. Circ: 2,300 (paid).

320 330.9 GBR
THE BRITAIN-RUSSIA & BRITISH-EAST WEST CENTRES. NEWSLETTER. Text in English. 1962. 3/yr. membership. bk.rev. back issues avail. **Document type:** *Newsletter.* **Description:** Covers topics on Russia and the other former Soviet republics, except Estonia, Latvia, and Lithuania.
Former titles (until 2000): The British East - West Journal (1353-1786); (until 1994): Britain - Russia (0969-9813); (until 1991): Britain - U S S R (0140-0967); (until 1966): Great Britain - U S S R Association. Bulletin (0140-0959)
—BLDSC (2299.148000).
Published by: Britain - Russia Centre, British East - West Centre, c/o RBCC, 11 Belgrave Rd, London, SW1V 1RB, United Kingdom. TEL 44-20-79316455, FAX 44-20-72339736, mail@bewc.org, http://www.bewc.org/. Circ: 1,600.

BRITISH COLUMBIA. LEGISLATIVE ASSEMBLY. DEBATES (HANSARD DAILY). *see* PUBLIC ADMINISTRATION

BRITISH COLUMBIA. LEGISLATIVE ASSEMBLY. DEBATES (HANSARD PAPERBOUND). *see* PUBLIC ADMINISTRATION

BRITISH COLUMBIA. LEGISLATIVE ASSEMBLY. JOURNALS. *see* PUBLIC ADMINISTRATION

BRITISH COLUMBIA. LEGISLATIVE ASSEMBLY. THIRD READING BILLS. *see* PUBLIC ADMINISTRATION

320 GBR ISSN 0007-1234
JA8
➤ **BRITISH JOURNAL OF POLITICAL SCIENCE.** Text in English. 1971. q. GBP 275, USD 475 to institutions; GBP 290, USD 490 combined subscription to institutions (print & online eds.) (effective 2012). adv. charts; illus. index. back issues avail.; reprint service avail. from PSC. **Document type:** *Journal, Academic/Scholarly.* **Description:** Covers developments across a wide range of countries and specialisms.
Related titles: Microform ed.: (from PQC); Online - full text ed.: ISSN 1469-2112. GBP 255, USD 440 to institutions (effective 2012).
Indexed: A01, A02, A03, A08, A12, A20, A22, A26, ABCPolSci, ABIn, ASCA, AmH&L, B01, B04, B06, B07, B09, BAS, BRD, CA, CurCont, DIP, E01, E08, ELLIS, ESPM, FR, G06, G07, G08, H09, HistAb, I05, I07, I13, IBR, IBSS, IBZ, MEA&I, P02, P10, P27, P30, P34, P42, P45, P47, P48, P51, P53, P54, PAA&I, PAIS, PCI, PQC, PRA, PSA, RASB, RiskAb, S02, S03, S05, S09, S11, S23, SCOPUS, SOPODA, SPAA, SSA, SSAI, SSAb, SSCI, SSI, SociolAb, T02, W03, W07.
—BLDSC (2319.600000), IE, Infotrieve, Ingenta, INIST. **CCC.**
Published by: Cambridge University Press, The Edinburgh Bldg, Shaftesbury Rd, Cambridge, CB2 8RU, United Kingdom. TEL 44-1223-312393, FAX 44-1223-315052, journals@cambridge.org, http://www.cambridge.org/uk. Eds. Albert Weale, David Sanders, Sarah Birch. R&P Linda Nicol TEL 44-1223-325702. Adv. contact Rebecca Roberts TEL 44-1223-325083. page GBP 470, page USD 895. Circ: 1,350. **Subscr. to:** Cambridge University Press, 32 Ave of the Americas, New York, NY 10013. TEL 212-337-5000, FAX 212-691-3239, journals_subscriptions@cup.org.

320 GBR ISSN 1369-1481
DA589.7
➤ **THE BRITISH JOURNAL OF POLITICS AND INTERNATIONAL RELATIONS.** Abbreviated title: B J P I R. Text in English. 1999. q. GBP 349 combined subscription in United Kingdom to institutions (print & online eds.); EUR 444 combined subscription in Europe to institutions (print & online eds.); USD 635 combined subscription in the Americas to institutions (print & online eds.); USD 683 combined subscription elsewhere to institutions (print & online eds.) (effective 2012). adv. back issues avail.; reprint service avail. from PSC. **Document type:** *Journal, Academic/Scholarly.* **Description:** Provides an outlet for theoretically informed analysis of British politics, including the role of Britain in European and world politics.
Related titles: Online - full text ed.: ISSN 1467-856X. GBP 315 in United Kingdom to institutions; EUR 400 in Europe to institutions; USD 571 in the Americas to institutions; USD 615 elsewhere to institutions (effective 2012) (from IngentaConnect).
Indexed: A01, A02, A03, A08, A20, A22, A26, CA, CurCont, E01, ESPM, GEOBASE, I08, IBSS, P02, P10, P34, P42, P48, P53, P54, PQC, PSA, RiskAb, S02, S03, S11, SCOPUS, SSA, SSCI, SSciA, SociolAb, T02, W07.
—BLDSC (2319.800000), IE, Infotrieve, Ingenta. **CCC.**
Published by: (Political Studies Association), Wiley-Blackwell Publishing Ltd. (Subsidiary of: John Wiley & Sons, Inc.), 9600 Garsington Rd, Oxford, OX4 2DQ, United Kingdom. TEL 44-1865-776868, FAX 44-1865-714591, customerservices@blackwellpublishing.com, http://www.wiley.com/. Adv. contact Craig Pickett TEL 44-1865-476267. B&W page GBP 445, B&W page USD 823; 125 x 200. Circ: 2,650.

320 GBR ISSN 1746-918X
JA8
➤ **BRITISH POLITICS.** Abbreviated title: B P. Text in English. 2006. q. USD 838 in North America to institutions; GBP 451 elsewhere to institutions (effective 2012). adv. back issues avail.; reprint service avail. from PSC. **Document type:** *Journal, Academic/Scholarly.* **Description:** Aims to promote a holistic understanding of British politics by encouraging a closer integration between theoretical and empirical research, between historical and contemporary analyses, and by fostering a conception of British politics as a broad and multi-disciplinary field of study.
Related titles: Online - full text ed.: ISSN 1746-9198 (from IngentaConnect).
Indexed: A12, A13, A17, A22, A26, ABIn, CA, CurCont, E01, G08, I05, P10, P42, P45, P48, P51, P53, P54, PQC, PSA, SCOPUS, SSCI, SociolAb, T02, W07.
—BLDSC (2339.155000), IE. **CCC.**
Published by: Palgrave Macmillan Ltd. (Subsidiary of: Macmillan Publishers Ltd.), Houndmills, Basingstoke, Hants RG21 6XS, United Kingdom. TEL 44-1256-329242, FAX 44-1256-479476, orders@palgrave.com, http://www.palgrave.com. **Subscr. to:** Subscription Department, Brunel Rd, Houndmills, Basingstoke, Hants RG21 2XS, United Kingdom. TEL 44-1256-357893, FAX 44-1256-812358, subscriptions@palgrave.com.

320 USA ISSN 1467-1441
BRITISH POLITICS AND SOCIETY. Text in English. 1999. irreg. **Document type:** *Monographic series, Academic/Scholarly.* **Description:** Features monographs on cross-disciplinary issues in British politics, including history, culture, sociology and media studies.
Related titles: Online - full text ed.: ISSN 2154-4972.
Published by: C R C Press, LLC (Subsidiary of: Taylor & Francis Group), 6000 Broken Sound Pky, NW, Ste 300, Boca Raton, FL 33487. TEL 561-994-0555, FAX 561-989-9732, journals@crcpress.com, http://www.crcpress.com.

320 USA
BROADSIDE (WASHINGTON). Text in English. 1980. bi-m. USD 18. adv. bk.rev. **Document type:** *Newspaper.* **Description:** Dedicated to informing and mobilizing young conservatives on college campuses.
Former titles (until 1994): College Republican; C R Report
Published by: College Republican National Committee, 600 Pennsylvania Ave, S E, Ste 215, Washington, DC 20003-4316. TEL 888-765-3564, FAX 202-608-1429, info@crnc.org, http://www.crnc.org. Ed. Bill Spadea. Adv. contact Paul S Teller. Circ: 25,000.

320 SWE ISSN 0007-2141
BRODERSKAP. Variant title: Nya Broderskap. Text in Swedish. 1928. 52/yr. SEK 399 (effective 2003). adv. **Description:** Weekly with emphasis on state and religion.
Related titles: Audio cassette/tape ed.: 1928.
Indexed: RASB.
Published by: Broderskapsroerelsen, Kungholmsgatan 8, PO Box 70411, Stockholm, 10725, Sweden. TEL 46-8-54555330, FAX 46-8-7917722. Ed. Jan Lindvall. Adv. contact Boerje Svendlund TEL 46-019-12 67 90. B&W page SEK 14,000, color page SEK 18,900; 254 x 360.

THE BROOKLYN RAIL; critical perspectives on arts, politics and culture. *see* ART

DIE BRUECKE (SAARBRUECKEN); Forum fuer antirassistische Politik und Kultur. *see* ETHNIC INTERESTS

320.54095694 USA
B'TNUA. Text in English. 1970. s-a. free to members (effective 2006). **Document type:** *Magazine, Consumer.* **Description:** Forum for discussing relevant Zionist issues and internal Habonim Dror Labor Camp Zionist Youth issues and events.
Formerly: Bagolah (0005-3929)
Related titles: Microfilm ed.: 1970 (from AJP); Online - full text ed.
Published by: Habonim Dror North America, 114 West 26th St, Ste 1004, New York, NY 10001. TEL 212-255-1796, FAX 212-929-3459, mazkir@habonimdror.org. Circ: 2,500 (controlled).

320 DEU ISSN 0007-3121
DER BUERGER IM STAAT. Text in German. 1951. q. EUR 12.80 (effective 2008). bk.rev. abstr.; bibl.; stat. index. reprints avail. **Document type:** *Magazine, Trade.*
Indexed: IBR, IBZ, PRA.
Published by: Landeszentrale fuer Politische Bildung, Stafflenbergstr 38, Stuttgart, 70184, Germany. Circ: 36,000.

320 DEU
BUKO KAMPAGNE STOPPT DEN RUESTUNGSEXPORT. RUNDBRIEF. Text in German. 1984. irreg. illus. **Document type:** *Newsletter.*
Published by: IntKom - Verein fuer Internationalismus und Kommunikation e.V., Bernhardstr 12, Bremen, 28203, Germany. http://www.outofthisworld.de/intkom/impress.htm.

320 FRA ISSN 1774-492X
BULLETIN DE LIAISON CLEOPHAS; "rien de ce qui est solidaire ne nous est etranger". Text in French. 200?. q. **Document type:** *Bulletin, Trade.*
Published by: Centre de Liaison et de Formation pour Auteurs de Solidarite, 1 rue de Segure, Pau, 64000, France.

321.8 FRA ISSN 0221-7090
BULLETIN DES ELUS LOCAUX. Text in French. 1979. m. EUR 46 (effective 2008). adv. back issues avail. **Document type:** *Magazine, Consumer.*
Published by: Association Nationale pour la Democratie Locale, 55 Rue La Boetie, Paris, 75008, France. TEL 33-1-40766118, FAX 33-1-40766115, contact@andl.fr. Ed. Liliane Ricalens. Circ: 40,000.

322.4 BEL ISSN 1784-3847
LE BULLETIN DES MILITANTS. Text in French. 2007. q. **Document type:** *Bulletin.* **Description:** Aims to defend democratic values, social justice, solidarity, worker participation and equal rights.

Published by: Groupement National des Cadres, 19 Rue Pletinckx, Bruxelles, 1000, Belgium. TEL 32-2-5088770, FAX 32-2-5088828, cne.bruxelles@acv-csc.be, http://www.cne-gnc.be.

320 ITA ISSN 0407-8438
D1060
BULLETIN EUROPEEN. Text in Italian, French. 1950. m. free. **Document type:** *Bulletin, Consumer.* **Description:** Examines political, international relations, and social issues of concerning Europe.
Related titles: French ed.: 1950. free.
Indexed: RASB.
Published by: (Fondation Europeenne Dragan/Fondazione Europea Dragan), Edizioni Nagard Srl, Via Larga 9, Milan, 20122, Italy. TEL 39-02-58371400, FAX 39-02-58304790, http://www.fondazionedragan.it/it/2.5.htm.

320 GBR ISSN 1759-3077
▼ **BULLETIN OF ITALIAN POLITICS.** Text in English. 2009. irreg. **Document type:** *Journal, Academic/Scholarly.*
Related titles: Online - full text ed.: free (effective 2011).
Published by: University of Glasgow, 16 University Gardens, Rm 301, University of Glasgow, Glasgow, G12 8QL, United Kingdom. Eds. James L Newell, Maurizio Carbone.

320 FRA ISSN 0766-5849
BULLETIN QUOTIDIEN; quotidien d'information documentation et prospective. Text in French. d. EUR 4,650; EUR 25 per issue (effective 2009). **Document type:** *Newsletter.*
Indexed: RASB.
—CCC.
Published by: Societe Generale de Presse, 13 Avenue de l'Opera, Paris Cedex 01, 75001, France. TEL 33-1-40151789, FAX 33-1-40151715, http://www.sgpresse.fr.

320.071 DEU ISSN 0435-7604
JN3966
BUNDESZENTRALE FUER POLITISCHE BILDUNG. SCHRIFTENREIHE. Text in German. 1953. irreg., latest vol.758, 2009. price varies. **Document type:** *Monographic series, Academic/Scholarly.*
Published by: Bundeszentrale fuer Politische Bildung, Adenauerallee 86, Bonn, 53113, Germany. TEL 49-1888-5150, FAX 49-1888-515113, info@bpb.de.

BUSINESS AND POLITICS (ONLINE). *see* BUSINESS AND ECONOMICS

BUSQUEDA. *see* BUSINESS AND ECONOMICS—Economic Situation And Conditions

320 KAZ
BYULLETEN' NORMATIVNYKH AKTOV TSENTRAL'NYKH ISPOLNITEL'NYKH I INYKH GOSUDARSTVENNYKH ORGANOV RESPUBLIKI KAZAKHSTAN/BULLETIN OF REGULATORY DOCUMENTS OF CENTRAL EXECUTIVE AND OTHER GOVERNMENT AGENCIES OF THE REPUBLIC OF KAZAKHSTAN. Text in Kazakh, Russian. 1999. 8/yr. USD 499 in North America (effective 2011).
Indexed: RASB.
Published by: President Administration Office of Kazakhstan, Akorda Bldg, Astana, Kazakstan. TEL 7-7172-745667, http://www.akorda.kz/en/the_administration_of_the_president. **Dist. by:** East View Information Services, 10601 Wayzata Blvd, Minneapolis, MN 55305. TEL 952-252-1201, 800-477-1005, FAX 952-252-1202, info@eastview.com, http://www.eastview.com.

320 NLD ISSN 1871-6733
C D A.NL. (Christen Democratisch Appel) Text in Dutch. 2005. bi-m. EUR 19.95 membership (effective 2009). **Document type:** *Journal, Trade.*
Formed by the merger of (1993-2005): Vrouw en Politiek (1383-9888); (2000-2005): C D A Krant (1567-7370); Which was formerly (1984-2000): Appel (1389-7349); (1999-2005): C D A Magazine (1566-7383); Which was formerly (1989-1999): C D Actueel (0924-2260); (1986-1989): C D A Actueel (0920-3559); (1980-1986): C D Actueel (0168-2091)
—IE.
Published by: Christen Democratisch Appel (CDA), Buitenom 18, Postbus 30453, The Hague, 2500 GL, Netherlands. TEL 31-70-3424888, FAX 31-70-3643417, cda@cda.nl, http://www.cda.nl.

324.2 BEL
C D - INFO. Text in Dutch, English, French, German, Hungarian, Italian, Polish, Russian, Spanish. 1964. 4/yr. **Document type:** *Newsletter.*
Former titles: Christian Democrat International. Information Bulletin; Christian Democratic World Union. Information Bulletin; (until 1972): International Christian Democratic Study and Documentation Center. Bulletin International (0538-5520)
Published by: Christian Democrat International, Rue de la Victoire 16, Bte 1, Brussels, 1060, Belgium. TEL 32-2-537-13-22, FAX 32-2-537-93-48.

320 DEU
C D U GERLINGEN INFORM. (Christlich-Demokratische Union) Text in German. 1983. s-a. **Document type:** *Bulletin, Consumer.* **Description:** Contains contributions on political subjects of local or regional interest such as educational programs, social activities, development of urban infrastructure, and public transportation.
Published by: (Christlich-Demokratische Union (C D U)), C D U Gerlingen, Max-Eyth-Str 6/2, Gerlingen, 70839, Germany. TEL 49-7156-435534, info@cdu-gerlingen.de. Circ: 250.

C E A S CADERNOS. (Centro de Estudos e Acao Social) *see* SOCIOLOGY

▼ **C E E - FORUM LEGAL THEORY YEARBOOK.** (Central & Eastern European) *see* LAW

320 HUN ISSN 1992-3147
C E U POLITICAL SCIENCE JOURNAL. (Central European University) Text in English. 2006. q. **Document type:** *Journal, Academic/Scholarly.* **Description:** Seeks to promote scholarly research in Political Science and related fields.
Related titles: Online - full text ed.: ISSN 1818-7668. free (effective 2011).
Published by: Central European University Press, Oktober 6 utca 14, Budapest, 1051, Hungary. TEL 36-1-3273000, FAX 36-1-3273183, ceupress@ceu.hu, http://www.ceupress.com.

320 CUB ISSN 0864-2478
CODEN: ALNUE4
C I A C SINTESIS INFORMATIVA. Text in Spanish. 1978. q. free. **Description:** Promotes materials on peace issues and against military build-up.
Related titles: Diskette ed.
Published by: Centro Informativo para las Americas y el Caribe/W P C Information Center for the Americas and the Caribbean, Linea No. 556,, Vedado, La Habana, Cuba. TEL 537-32-0506, FAX 537-33-3860. Ed. Livia M Reyes Ramirez.

320.57 CHE
C I R A BULLETIN. Text in English, French, German, Italian, Spanish. 1957. s-a. CHF 20. bk.rev. bibl. **Document type:** *Bibliography.*
Published by: Centre International de Recherches sur l'Anarchisme, Av de Beaumont 24, Lausanne, 1012, Switzerland. Circ: 1,000.

320 297.071 QAT ISSN 2072-750X
C I R S BRIEF. (Center for International and Regional Studies) Text in English. 2008. irreg. **Document type:** *Newsletter, Academic/Scholarly.*
Related titles: Online - full text ed.: ISSN 2072-7518.
Published by: Georgetown University School of Foreign Service in Qatar, Center for International and Regional Studies, PO Box 23689, Doha, Qatar. TEL 974-457-8400, CirsResearch@georgetown.edu.

C I R S NEWSLETTER. (Center for International and Regional Studies) *see* EDUCATION

320 AUS ISSN 1832-0384
C I S CLASSICS. (Centre for Independent Studies) Text in English. 2005. biennial. **Document type:** *Monographic series, Academic/Scholarly.*
Published by: The Centre for Independent Studies Ltd., PO Box 92, St Leonards, NSW 1590, Australia. TEL 61-2-94384377, FAX 61-2-94397310, office@cis.org.au, http://www.cis.org.au.

320.6 370 AUS ISSN 0158-1260
C I S POLICY MONOGRAPHS. (Centre for Independent Studies) Abbreviated title: P M. Text in English. 1979. irreg., latest vol.88, 2008. free to members (effective 2008). back issues avail. **Document type:** *Monographic series, Academic/Scholarly.*
Related titles: Online - full text ed.: free (effective 2008).
Indexed: A01, A03, A08, A11.
—BLDSC (3267.639100).
Published by: The Centre for Independent Studies Ltd., PO Box 92, St Leonards, NSW 1590, Australia. TEL 61-2-94384377, FAX 61-2-94397310, office@cis.org.au.

320 ZAF
C O D E S R I A BOOK SERIES. Text in English. irreg. **Document type:** *Monographic series.*
Published by: (Council for the Development of Economic and Social Research in Africa), Skotaville Publishers, PO Box 32483, Braamfontein, Johannesburg 2017, South Africa. **Dist. outside Africa by:** African Books Collective Ltd., The Jam Factory, 27 Park End St, Oxford, Oxon OX1 1HU, United Kingdom. TEL 0865-726686, FAX 0865-793298.

328 USA ISSN 1944-5520
JK1
C Q ALMANAC. (Congressional Quarterly) Text in English. 1948. a., latest 2007. USD 475 per issue (effective 2008). **Document type:** *Handbook/Manual/Guide, Trade.* **Description:** Key bills and amendments explained; laws passed; roll-call votes cast by every member.
Former titles (until 2007): Congressional Quarterly Almanac Plus (1935-8334); (until 2001): Congressional Quarterly Almanac (0095-6007); Which superseded in part (1945-1947): Congressional Quarterly
Related titles: Online - full text ed.
Indexed: A22.
—BLDSC (3415.955500). **CCC.**
Published by: C Q Press, Inc. (Subsidiary of: Sage Publications, Inc.), 2300 N St, NW, Ste 800, Washington, DC 20037. TEL 202-729-1900, 866-427-7737, FAX 800-380-3810, customerservice@cqpress.com. Ed., Pub. Robert W Merry.

320.9 USA ISSN 1941-6768
C Q GLOBAL RESEARCHER; exploring international perspectives. (Congressional Quarterly) Text in English. 2007. m. back issues avail. **Document type:** *Magazine, Consumer.* **Description:** Provides coverage of global affairs from a multitude of international viewpoints.
Media: Online - full content.
Published by: C Q Press, Inc. (Subsidiary of: Sage Publications, Inc.), 2300 N St, NW, Ste 800, Washington, DC 20037. TEL 202-729-1900, 866-427-7737, FAX 202-419-8749, 800-380-3810, customerservice@cqpress.com.

328 USA
C Q HOUSE ACTION REPORTS. Text in English. irreg. USD 6,150 (effective 2009). **Description:** Provides summaries and analyses of every bill up for consideration on the House floor.
Media: Online - full text.
Published by: Congressional Quarterly, Inc., 1255, 22nd St, N.W., Washington, DC 20037. TEL 202-419-8500, 800-432-2250, FAX 202-419-8760, customerservice@cq.com, http://corporate.cq.com. Ed. Michael Riley. Pub. Keith A White.

320.9 USA ISSN 1056-2036
H35 CODEN: CQREEX
C Q RESEARCHER. (Congressional Quarterly) Text in English. 1923. 44/yr. USD 578 (effective 2008). bk.rev. charts. index. back issues avail.; reprints avail. **Document type:** *Magazine, Trade.* **Description:** Designed for people who need a place to begin research on current topics.
Former titles (until 1991): Congressional Quarterly's Editorial Research Reports (1057-0926); (until 1987): Editorial Research Reports (0013-0958)
Related titles: Online - full text ed.: ISSN 1942-5635.
Indexed: A01, A02, A03, A08, A22, A25, A26, AMHA, Acal, C05, CPerl, E08, G05, G06, G07, G08, I02, I05, M01, M02, M04, M06, MASUSE, MEA&I, MagInd, NPPA, P02, P06, P10, P13, P30, P34, P42, P53, P54, PAIS, PQC, R06, RASB, S08, S09, S11, T02, TOM.
—BLDSC (3486.410000), Ingenta. **CCC.**
Published by: C Q Press, Inc. (Subsidiary of: Sage Publications, Inc.), 2300 N St, NW, Ste 800, Washington, DC 20037. TEL 202-729-1900, 866-427-7737, FAX 800-380-3810, customerservice@cqpress.com. Eds. Kenneth Jost, Marcia Clemmitt, Peter Katel. Circ: 5,000 (paid).

320 USA
C Q RESEARCHER BOUND VOLUME. (Congressional Quarterly) Text in English. a. USD 330 (effective 2008). indes. back issues avail.; reprints avail. **Description:** Contains reports that cover various topics including war in Iraq, consumer debt, universal healthcare, urban schools and national ID cards.
Formerly: E R R Bound Volume
Related titles: Online - full text ed.
Published by: C Q Press, Inc. (Subsidiary of: Sage Publications, Inc.), 2300 N St, NW, Ste 800, Washington, DC 20037. TEL 202-729-1900, FAX 800-380-3810, customerservice@cqpress.com.

328 USA ISSN 1931-4108
KF4935.A15
C Q TODAY. (Congressional Quarterly) Text in English. d. USD 3,319 (effective 2009). **Document type:** *Newsletter, Consumer.* **Description:** Covers forward-looking articles on all-important activities scheduled for that day plus a comprehensive wrap-up of all the previous day's Hill news.
Formerly (until 2004): C Q Daily Monitor
Related titles: Online - full text ed.: USD 2,074 PDF format (effective 2004).
Indexed: G06, G07, G08, I05.
—CCC.
Published by: Congressional Quarterly, Inc., 1255, 22nd St, N.W., Washington, DC 20037. TEL 202-419-8500, 800-432-2250, FAX 202-419-8760, customerservice@cq.com. Ed. Michael Riley.

328 USA ISSN 1521-5997
JK1
C Q WEEKLY. (Congressional Quarterly) Text in English. 1945. w. (48/yr.). USD 2,729 (effective 2009). adv. charts; illus. index every 90 days and a. Supplement avail.; reprints avail. **Document type:** *Newsletter, Government.* **Description:** Provides detailed reports on all major legislative action, the president's legislative proposals, statements and major speeches and analyses of the Supreme Court's decisions. Includes coverage of political and lobbying activities.
Formerly (until vol.56, no.15, 1998): Congressional Quarterly Weekly Report (0010-5910)
Related titles: Online - full text ed.: ISSN 1942-5643.
Indexed: A01, A02, A03, A08, A11, A22, A25, A26, ABS&EES, Acal, B01, B04, B06, B07, B08, B09, BLI, BRD, C05, C12, CPerl, Chicano, E08, G05, G06, G07, G08, I02, I05, I07, IPARL, L01, L02, L03, M01, M02, M05, M06, MASUSE, MEA&I, MagInd, NPPA, P02, P06, P10, P13, P27, P30, P34, P47, P48, P53, P54, PAIS, PQC, R02, RASB, S08, S09, S11, SSAI, SSAb, SSI, T02, U01, W01, W02, W03, WBA, WMB.
—BLDSC (3415.958000), IE, Infotrieve, Ingenta. **CCC.**
Published by: Congressional Quarterly, Inc., 1255, 22nd St, N.W., Washington, DC 20037. TEL 202-419-8500, 800-432-2250, FAX 202-419-8760, customerservice@cq.com. Circ: 11,000.

320 USA ISSN 1527-8913
JK1012
C Q'S POLITICS IN AMERICA. (Congressional Quarterly) Variant title: Politics in America. Text in English. 1981. biennial, latest 110th ed. USD 85 per issue (paperback ed.); USD 125 per issue (cloth ed.) (effective 2008). back issues avail. **Description:** Provides in great detail authoritative information on the members of the 110th Congress.
Former titles (until 2000): Congressional Quarterly's Politics in America (1064-6809); (until 1990): Politics in America
Related titles: Online - full text ed.: USD 150 (effective 2006).
—CCC.
Published by: C Q Press, Inc. (Subsidiary of: Sage Publications, Inc.), 2300 N St, NW, Ste 800, Washington, DC 20037. TEL 202-729-1900, 866-427-7737, FAX 800-380-3810, customerservice@cqpress.com. Eds. Jackie Koszczuk, Martha Angle.

328 USA ISSN 1536-4666
JK2495
C S G STATE DIRECTORY. DIRECTORY II, LEGISLATIVE LEADERSHIP, COMMITTEES & STAFF. Variant title: C S G Directory II. Text in English. 1979. a., latest 2002. USD 65 per issue (effective 2009). **Document type:** *Directory, Trade.* **Description:** Contains a Lists all legislative leadership positions, all committee chairs, key staff and legislative research staff.
Former titles (until 1998): Legislative Leadership Directory II; (until 1996): State Legislative Leadership, Committees and Staff (0195-6639); (until 1979): Principal Legislative Staff Offices; Which was formed by the merger of (19??-1979): Roster of Legislative Service Agencies; (1960-1979): Permanent Legislative Service Agencies
Related titles: CD-ROM ed.; Diskette ed.
—CCC.
Published by: Council of State Governments, 2760 Research Park Dr, PO Box 11910, Lexington, KY 40578. TEL 859-244-8000, 800-800-1910, FAX 859-244-8001, info@csg.org, http://www.csg.org/.

C S S P CONGRESSIONAL SOURCEBOOK. *see* PUBLIC ADMINISTRATION

320.5 CAN ISSN 1190-9153
JA1
➤ **C THEORY.** Text in English. 1993. w. adv. bk.rev.; film rev. index. back issues avail. **Document type:** *Journal, Academic/Scholarly.* **Description:** Internationally oriented, focusing on theory, technology and culture from a critical and feminist perspective.
Supersedes (1977-1991): Canadian Journal of Political and Social Theory (0380-9420)
Media: Online - full content. **Related titles:** Microform ed.: (from PQC); Online - full text ed.
Indexed: A26, ABCPolSci, AltPI, C03, CBCARef, CBPI, CPerl, CWPI, E08, G08, I05, LeftInd, P48, PAIS, PQC, RILM, S09, SOPODA, SocioIAb.
—Ingenta. **CCC.**
Address: Concordia University, 1455 de Maisonneuve West, Montreal, PQ H3G 1M8, Canada. TEL 514-282-9298. Ed. Marilouise Kroker. Circ: 10,000.

320.6 NLD ISSN 1572-3267
C V B RAPPORTEN. (Centrum voor Beleidsstatistiek) Text in Dutch. 2003. irreg.
Published by: Centraal Bureau voor de Statistiek, Prinses Beatrixlaan 428, PO Box 4000, Voorburg, 2270 JM, Netherlands. TEL 31-70-3373800, FAX 31-70-3877429, infoserv@cbs.nl, http://www.cbs.nl.

P

320.944 FRA ISSN 1951-6134
C6NECESSAIRE. Text in French. 2006. s-a. free. back issues avail. **Document type:** *Newsletter, Consumer.*
Media: Online - full text.
Published by: C 6 R, 4-6 Pl. de Valois, Paris, 75001, France. contactparis@c6r.org.

CADERNOS DE POS-GRADUACAO EM DIREITO POLITICO E ECONOMICO. *see* LAW

320 BRA ISSN 1983-4500
JZ9
CADERNOS DE RELACOES INTERNACIONAIS. Text in Portuguese. 2008. s-a. free (effective 2011). **Document type:** *Journal, Academic/Scholarly.*
Media: Online - full text.
Published by: Pontificia Universidade Catolica do Rio de Janeiro, Rua Marques de Sao Vicente, 225,, 22 453, ZC-20, Rio De Janeiro, RJ 22451041, Brazil.

CADERNOS DE SOCIOLOGIA E POLITICA. *see* SOCIOLOGY

320 BRA ISSN 0101-7993
HC59.7
CADERNOS DO TERCEIRO MUNDO. Text in Portuguese. 1974. bi-m. BRL 54; USD 110 foreign; BRL 5.50 newsstand/cover. adv. bk.rev. charts; illus.
Related titles: Spanish ed.: Cuadernos del Tercer Mundo.
Indexed: RASB.
Published by: Editora Terceiro Mundo Ltda., Rua da Gloria, 122 105-106, Gloria, Rio De Janeiro, RJ 20241-180, Brazil. FAX 55-21-2528455. Ed., R&P Beatriz Bissio TEL 55-21-2217511. Adv. contact Euler Sathler. page USD 4,500; trim 270 x 205. Circ: 20,000.

CAHIER DES SCIENCES MORALES ET POLITIQUES. *see* PHILOSOPHY

CAHIERS AFRICAINS/AFRIKA STUDIES. *see* HISTORY—History Of Africa

320 FRA ISSN 1761-8630
LES CAHIERS DE CRITIQUE COMMUNISTE. Text in French. 2003. irreg. back issues avail. **Document type:** *Monographic series, Consumer.*
Published by: Editions Syllepse, 69 rue des Rigoles, Paris, 75020, France. TEL 33-1-44620889.

320 FRA ISSN 0007-9839
LES CAHIERS DE LA RECONCILIATION. Text in French. 1926. q. EUR 24 domestic; EUR 26 in Europe; CHF 42 in Switzerland (effective 2009). bk.rev.
Indexed: CERDIC.
Published by: Mouvement International de la Reconciliation, 68 rue de Babylone, Paris, 75007, France. TEL 33-1-45538405, FAX 33-1-45538405, mirfr@club-internet.fr, http://www.multimania.com/mirfr. Eds. Christian Baccuet, Christian Renoux. Pub. Francois Jourdan. Circ: 1,800.

320 FRA ISSN 1775-1519
LES CAHIERS DE L'AS DE TREFLE. Text in French. 2005. irreg. **Document type:** *Monographic series, Consumer.*
Published by: Editions de Paris, 13 rue Saint-Honore, Versailles, 78000, France.

320 300 FRA ISSN 0764-9878
DS41
CAHIERS D'ETUDES SUR LA MEDITERRANEE ORIENTALE ET LE MONDE TURCO-IRANIEN. Abbreviated title: C E M O T I. Text in French. 1984. s-a. EUR 30 domestic to individuals; EUR 35 foreign to individuals; EUR 40 domestic to institutions; EUR 50 foreign to institutions (effective 2005).
Formerly (until 1985): Equipe de Recherche sur la Turquie (0767-2365)
Indexed: CA, DIP, FR, I13, I14, IBR, IBSS, IBZ, M10, MLA-IB, P30, PSA, S02, S03, SCOPUS, SociolAb, T02.
—INIST.
Published by: (Fondation Nationale des Sciences Politiques), Association Francaise pour l'Etude de la Mediterranee Orientale et du Monde Turco-Iranien, 56 Rue Jacob, Paris, 75006, France. TEL 33-1-58717056, FAX 33-1-58717090.

320.5322 FRA ISSN 1271-6669
CAHIERS D'HISTOIRE (PARIS); revue d'histoire critique. Text in French. 1966. q. adv. bk.rev. **Document type:** *Academic/Scholarly.*
Former titles: Institut de Recherches Marxistes. Cahiers d'Histoire (0246-9731); Institut Maurice Thorez. Cahiers d'Histoire (0020-2363)
Indexed: A22, CA, HistAb, I13, P30, P42, RASB, T02.
—BLDSC (2948.975500), IE, Ingenta. **CCC.**
Published by: S E P I R M - Espaces Marx, 6 ave. Mathurin Moreau, Cedex 19, Paris, 75167, France. TEL 33-1-43364524. Ed. Anne Jollet. Adv. contact Joel Biard. Circ: 3,000.

CAHIERS DU MONDE RUSSE; Empire Russe, Union Sovietique, etats independants. *see* HISTORY—History Of Europe

320 920 FRA ISSN 1969-6809
CAHIERS JAURES. Text in French. 200?. q. EUR 25 domestic to individuals; EUR 30 foreign to individuals; EUR 35 to institutions (effective 2009). **Document type:** *Journal, Academic/Scholarly.*
Published by: Societe d'Etudes Jauresiennes, Alain Chatriot, CRH-AHMOC, 10 rue Monsieur le Prince, Paris, 75006, France.

320.531 BEL ISSN 0591-0633
CAHIERS MARXISTES. Text in French. 1969. 5/yr. EUR 30 domestic; EUR 35 in the European Union; EUR 40 elsewhere; EUR 8 per issue (effective 2004). adv. bk.rev. back issues avail.
Indexed: AltPI, FR, IBSS, RASB.
Published by: (Universite Libre de Bruxelles, Groupe de Recherche Marx et les Sciences Sociales de l'Institut de Sociologie), F R E E Gazette, Avenue Derache, 94, Bte 6, Bruxelles, 1050, Belgium. FAX 32-2-650-4921. Circ: 2,000.

320 FRA ISSN 0068-5194
CAHIERS NEPALAIS. Text in French. 1969. irreg. price varies. adv. bk.rev. index. **Document type:** *Academic/Scholarly.*
Indexed: SpeleolAb.
Published by: Centre National de la Recherche Scientifique, Campus Gerard-Megie, 3 Rue Michel-Ange, Paris, 75794, France. Circ: 1,500 (controlled).

320 COD ISSN 0304-2707
HC591.C6
CAHIERS ZAIROIS D'ETUDES POLITIQUES ET SOCIALES. Text in French. 1973. q. bibl.
Indexed: PAIS.
Published by: Universite de Lubumbashi, Faculte des Sciences Socials, Politiques et Administratives, BP 1825, Lubumbashi, Congo, Dem. Republic.

320.531 GBR ISSN 0262-723X
CALDER VOICE; Calderdale's socialist journal. Text in English. 1977. m. GBP 1.80. illus.
Published by: Independent Labour Publications, c/o A. Graham, 4 Upper Gaukroger, Sowerby New Rd, Sowerby Bridge, W Yorks, United Kingdom.

320 700 USA
CALIFORNIA CONVERSATIONS. Text in English. irreg. **Document type:** *Magazine, Consumer.* **Description:** Contains articles, news and interviews mainly on politics but also arts, sports, and lifestyles.
Media: Online - full content.
Published by: Aaron Read & Associates, LLC., 1415 L St, Ste 1100, Sacramento, CA 95814. TEL 916-448-3444.

320.9794 USA ISSN 0279-0246
THE CALIFORNIA EYE. Text in English. irreg. USD 195 (effective 2000). **Document type:** *Newsletter.* **Description:** Covers news and issues in California politics and government.
Published by: The Political Animal Co., 1100 Montecito Dr, Los Angeles, CA 90031-1637. TEL 323-276-9224, FAX 323-417-4964. Ed., Pub., R&P Bill Homer.

320 USA ISSN 1944-4370
▼➤ **CALIFORNIA JOURNAL OF POLITICS AND POLICY.** Text in English. 2009. a. USD 275 per issue to institutions; USD 825 per issue to corporations (effective 2011). **Document type:** *Journal, Academic/Scholarly.* **Description:** Contains research and commentary on state and local government politics and policies in California and in relation to national and international developments.
Media: Online - full text.
Indexed: ESPM, PAIS, PSA, SSciA.
—**CCC.**
Published by: Berkeley Electronic Press, 2809 Telegraph Ave, Ste 202, Berkeley, CA 94705. TEL 510-665-1200, FAX 510-665-1201, info@bepress.com. Eds. Jack Citrin, James Wilson.

320 USA ISSN 0195-6175
CALIFORNIA POLITICAL WEEK. Variant title: Calpeek. Text in English. 1979. 42/yr. USD 95; USD 175 for 2 yrs. (effective 2007). adv. **Document type:** *Newsletter, Consumer.* **Description:** Covers California and western U.S. state and local government and political developments and trends.
Published by: California Political Week, Inc., PO Box 1468, Beverly Hills, CA 90213. TEL 310-659-0205, FAX 310-657-4340. Ed., Pub. Dick Rosengarten. Circ: 3,000 (paid and controlled).

320.6 USA ISSN 1051-032X
CALIFORNIA SERIES ON SOCIAL CHOICE & POLITICAL ECONOMY. Text in English. 1981. irreg., latest vol.25, 1996. price varies. back issues avail. **Document type:** *Monographic series.* **Description:** Discusses a wide variety of sociopolitical issues.
—BLDSC (3015.288000). **CCC.**
Published by: University of California Press, Book Series, 2120 Berkeley Way, Berkeley, CA 94704. TEL 510-642-4247, FAX 510-643-7127, foundation@ucpress.edu. **Subscr. to:** California - Princeton Fulfillment Services, Inc., 1445 Lower Ferry Rd, Ewing, NJ 08618. TEL 609-883-1759, 800-777-4726, FAX 800-999-1958, orders@cpfsinc.com.

321.8 PER
CAMBIO Y DESARROLLO; revista del pensamiento social and democratico. Text in Spanish. 1991. s-a.
Published by: Instituto de Investigaciones, Ave. Dos De Mayo, 1890, San Isidro, Lima 27, Peru. TEL 417955, FAX 429411. Ed. Jose Manuel Mejia.

321.8 ARG
CAMBIOS. Text in Spanish. 2000. q. back issues avail.
Media: Online - full text. **Related titles:** ◆ English ed.: Changes.
Published by: Fundacion para el Cambio Democratico, Talcahuano 768, Piso 1o, Buenos Aires, Argentina. TEL 54-114-8167555, fundacion@cambiodemocratico.org, http://www.cambiodemocratico.org.

320 GBR ISSN 1752-1378
HM548
➤ **CAMBRIDGE JOURNAL OF REGIONS, ECONOMY AND SOCIETY.** Text in English. 2008 (Apr.). 3/yr. GBP 183 in United Kingdom to institutions; EUR 274 in Europe to institutions; USD 365 in US & Canada to institutions; GBP 183 elsewhere to institutions; GBP 199 combined subscription in United Kingdom to institutions (print & online eds.); EUR 299 combined subscription in Europe to institutions (print & online eds.); USD 398 combined subscription in US & Canada to institutions (print & online eds.); GBP 199 combined subscription elsewhere to institutions (print & online eds.) (effective 2012). back issues avail.; reprint service avail. from PSC. **Document type:** *Journal, Academic/Scholarly.* **Description:** Publishes multi-disciplinary international research on the regional dimensions of contemporary socio-economic-political change.
Related titles: Online - full text ed.: ISSN 1752-1386. 2008. GBP 166 in United Kingdom to institutions; EUR 249 in Europe to institutions; USD 332 in US & Canada to institutions; GBP 166 elsewhere to institutions (effective 2012) (from IngentaConnect).
Indexed: EconLit, P42, SCOPUS, SSciA, T02.
—IE. **CCC.**
Published by: (Cambridge Political Economy Society), Oxford University Press, Great Clarendon St, Oxford, OX2 6DP, United Kingdom. TEL 44-1865-556767, FAX 44-1865-556646, enquiry@oup.co.uk, http://www.oxfordjournals.org. Adv. contact Linda Hann TEL 44-1344-779945.

320 ITA ISSN 2037-8203
CAMERA DEI DEPUTATI. COLLANA FONDAZIONE. I GRANDI DIBATTITI. Text in Italian. 2006. irreg. **Document type:** *Monographic series, Academic/Scholarly.*
Published by: (Fondazione Camera dei Deputati), Laterza Editori, Via di Villa Sacchetti 17, Rome, 00197, Italy. TEL 39-06-3218393, FAX 39-06-3223853, http://www.laterza.it.

320 ITA ISSN 2037-8211
CAMERA DEI DEPUTATI. COLLANA FONDAZIONE. STUDI DELLA FONDAZIONE. Text in Italian. 2006. irreg. **Document type:** *Monographic series, Academic/Scholarly.*
Published by: (Fondazione Camera dei Deputati), Laterza Editori, Via di Villa Sacchetti 17, Rome, 00197, Italy. TEL 39-06-3218393, FAX 39-06-3223853, http://www.laterza.it.

320 ITA ISSN 2037-819X
CAMERA DEI DEPUTATI. COLLANA FONDAZIONE. VOCI DAL PARLAMENTO. Text in Italian. 2006. irreg. **Document type:** *Monographic series, Academic/Scholarly.*
Published by: (Fondazione Camera dei Deputati), Laterza Editori, Via di Villa Sacchetti 17, Rome, 00197, Italy. TEL 39-06-3218393, FAX 39-06-3223853, http://www.laterza.it.

321.8 USA ISSN 1938-3584
DT578
CAMEROON JOURNAL ON DEMOCRACY AND HUMAN RIGHTS. Abbreviated title: C J D H R. Text in English, French. 2007. s-a. free (effective 2010). back issues avail. **Document type:** *Journal, Academic/Scholarly.* **Description:** Aims to promote research and scholarship among Cameroonians and non-Cameroonians interested in issues pertinent to the establishment of a functional and sustainable democracy in Cameroon. Topics covered include social justice, public accountability, economic development, and good governance.
Media: Online - full text.
Published by: Progressive Initiative for Cameroon, 6229 Springhill Ct, #302, Greenbelt, MD 20770. TEL 301-938-5221, FAX 240-595-6203, info@picam.org, http://www.picam.org.

320 URY
CAMINOS. Text in Spanish. 1991. m.?. UYP 2,500 per issue.
Address: Pando, 2694, Montevideo, 11819, Uruguay. Ed. Omar Rovira.

324.78 USA ISSN 0884-8351
KF4920.Z95
CAMPAIGN FINANCE LAW; a summary of state campaign finance laws with quick reference charts. Text in English. 1981. biennial. USD 57 domestic; USD 71.25 foreign (effective 2000). **Document type:** *Government.*
Published by: (U.S. Library of Congress, Congressional Research Service, American Law Division), National Clearing House on Education Administration, c/o Superintendent of Documents, Box 371954, Pittsburgh, PA 15250. **Dist. by:** U.S. Government Printing Office, Superintendent of Documents, PO Box 371954, Pittsburgh, PA 15250. TEL 202-512-1800, FAX 202-512-2250, orders@gpo.gov, http://www.access.gpo.gov.

324.6 USA ISSN 1936-2528
JK1991
CAMPAIGN GUIDE FOR CONGRESSIONAL CANDIDATES AND COMMITTEES. Text in English. 1978. irreg., latest 2008. free (effective 2011). back issues avail. **Document type:** *Handbook/Manual/Guide, Government.* **Description:** Helps House and Senate candidate committees to comply with the federal campaign finance laws.
Related titles: Online - full text ed.
Published by: Federal Election Commission, 999 E St NW, Washington, DC 20463. TEL 202-694-1100, 800-424-9530, FAX 202-219-8504, info@fec.gov.

320 USA
CAMPAIGN GUIDE FOR NONCONNECTED COMMITTEES. Text in English. 19??. irreg., latest 2008. free (effective 2011). **Document type:** *Handbook/Manual/Guide, Government.* **Description:** Helps independent political committees to comply with federal election campaign finance laws.
Related titles: Online - full text ed.
Published by: Federal Election Commission, 999 E St NW, Washington, DC 20463. TEL 202-694-1100, 800-424-9530, FAX 202-219-8504, info@fec.gov.

324.6 USA ISSN 1936-2536
JK1991
CAMPAIGN GUIDE FOR POLITICAL PARTY COMMITTEES. Text in English. 198?. irreg., latest 2009. free (effective 2011). back issues avail. **Document type:** *Handbook/Manual/Guide, Government.* **Description:** Helps political party committees to comply with federal election campaign finance laws.
Formerly (until 198?): Campaign Guide for Party Committees
Published by: Federal Election Commission, 999 E St NW, Washington, DC 20463. TEL 202-694-1100, 800-424-9530, FAX 202-219-8504, info@fec.gov.

324.72 USA ISSN 2160-603X
JK1976
CAMPAIGNS & ELECTIONS. Text in English. 1980. m. USD 49.95 in US & Canada; USD 64.94 elsewhere (effective 2011). adv. bk.rev. charts; illus.; stat. back issues avail.; reprints avail. **Document type:** *Magazine, Trade.* **Description:** For political professionals; includes news, views and how-to's for modern campaigns.
Former titles (until 2010): Politics (1945-3191); (until 2008): Campaigns and Elections (0197-0771); Which incorporated (1971-1999): Politeia (0096-3135); (1991-1993): Campaign (1061-964X); Which was formerly (until 1991): Campaign Magazine (1054-0075); (until 1990): Campaign Industry News
Related titles: Microform ed.: (from PQC); Online - full text ed.: USD 19.99 (effective 2011).
Indexed: A01, A02, A03, A08, A22, A25, A26, C12, CA, E08, G05, G06, G07, G08, I05, I06, I07, M01, M02, MASUSE, P02, P05, P10, P34, P42, PAIS, PCI, PQC, RASB, S08, S09, S23, SCOPUS, T02.
—BLDSC (6543.936575), CIS, IE, Infotrieve, Ingenta. **CCC.**
Published by: Political World Communications, Inc., 666 Plainsboro Rd, Bldg 300, Plainsboro, NJ 08536. TEL 609-716-7777, FAX 609-716-4747. Ed. Costas Panagopoulos. Pub. James O'Brien TEL 703-778-4021.

CANADA ASIA COMMENTARY. *see* BUSINESS AND ECONOMICS

CANADA ASIA REVIEW. *see* BUSINESS AND ECONOMICS

324 CAN ISSN 0700-1568
JL193
CANADA. CHIEF ELECTORAL OFFICER. REPORT. Text in English, French. 1922. irreg. **Description:** Contains highlights in the administration of recent elections and includes preliminary voting results.
Published by: Elections Canada, 257 Slater St, Ottawa, ON K1A OM6, Canada. TEL 613-993-2975, 800-463-6868, FAX 888-524-1444, http://www.elections.ca/.

320.971 CAN ISSN 1203-9268
J103.N15
CANADA. GOVERNOR GENERAL. SPEECH FROM THE THRONE TO OPEN THE SESSION OF PARLIAMENT. Text in English, French. 1994. irreg.
Related titles: Online - full text ed.: ISSN 1493-3551.
Published by: (Governor General of Canada), Government of Canada, Privy Council Office/Gouvernement du Canada. Bureau du Conseil Prive, 85 Sparks St, Room 1000, Ottawa, ON K1A 0A3, Canada. TEL 613-957-5153, FAX 613-957-5043, info@pco-bcp.gc.ca, http://www.pco-bcp.gc.ca.

324.4 CAN ISSN 1184-0471
CANADA. LOBBYISTS REGISTRATION BRANCH. LOBBYISTS REGISTRATION ACT ANNUAL REPORT. Text in English, French. 1990. a.
Related titles: Online - full text ed.: ISSN 1700-5876. 1995.
Published by: Industry Canada, Lobbyists Registration Branch, 66 Slater St, 22nd Flr, Ottawa, ON K1A 0C9, Canada. http://strategis.ic.gc.cag.

324.65 CAN ISSN 1483-7293
CA1BT31-4 58
CANADA. OFFICE OF THE CHIEF ELECTORAL OFFICER. PERFORMANCE REPORT. Text in English, French. 1997. a.
Related titles: Online - full text ed.: ISSN 1490-5426.
Published by: (Elections Canada), Treasury Board of Canada Secretariat, Corporate Communications/Secretariat du Conseil du Tresor du Canada, West Tower, Rm P-135, 300 Laurier Ave W, Ottawa, ON K1A 0R5, Canada. TEL 613-995-2855, FAX 613-996-0518, services-publications@tbs-sct.gc.ca, http://www.tbs-sct.gc.ca.

323.67 CAN ISSN 1193-0675
CANADA. PASSPORT OFFICE. ANNUAL REPORT. Text in English. 1991. a.
Published by: External Affairs and International Trade Canada, Foreign Policy Communications Division, 125 Sussex Dr, Ottawa, ON K1A 0G2, Canada. TEL 613-992-9280.

320 CAN ISSN 0846-9547
E92
CANADA. SPECIAL COMMITTEE ON INDIAN SELF-GOVERNMENT. PROCEEDINGS. MINUTES. Text in English. 1982. irreg.?.
Former titles: Canada. Special Committee on Indian Self-Government. Proceedings and Evidence. Minutes (0826-3051); Canada. Standing Committee on Indian Affairs and Northern Development. Sub-Committee on Indian Self-Government. Proceedings and Evidence. Minutes (0826-3043)
Published by: Canadian Publications Centre, Supply and Services Canada, Hull, PQ K1A 0S9, Canada.

328 CAN ISSN 0827-0708
JL27
➤ **CANADA: THE STATE OF THE FEDERATION.** Text in English, French. 1985. a. CAD 25. back issues avail. **Document type:** *Monographic series, Academic/Scholarly.* **Description:** Studies fiscal federalism, constitutional reform, federal-provincial relations, the global economy, comparative federalism.
Former titles (until 1984): Year in Review: Intergovernmental Relations in Canada (0825-1207); (until 1980): Intergovernmental Relations in Canada: the Year in Review (0226-9341); (until 1978): Federal Year in Review (0706-1234)
Indexed: CA, ICLPL, P42, PSA, T02.
—CCC.
Published by: Institute of Intergovernmental Relations, Queen s University, Kingston, ON K7L 3N6, Canada. TEL 613-533-2080, FAX 613-533-6868, http://qsilver.queensu.ca/iigr/. Ed. Harvey Lazar. R&P M Kennedy. Circ: 800.

325.21 CAN
CANADA'S REFUGEE PROTECTION SYSTEM. Text in English. 1989. irreg. **Document type:** *Government.*
Former titles: Canada's Refugee Status Determination System (1189-3729); (until 1989): Canada's New Refugee Status Determination System (1189-3710)
Related titles: Online - full content ed.: ISSN 1713-515X; French ed.
Published by: Library of Parliament, Parliamentary Research Branch, Information Service, Ottawa, ON K1A 0A9, Canada.

320 CAN ISSN 0008-3402
AP5
CANADIAN DIMENSION; for people who want to change the world. Abbreviated title: C D. Text in English. 1963. bi-m. CAD 29.99 domestic to individuals; CAD 39.99 in United States to individuals; CAD 49.99 elsewhere to individuals; CAD 39.99 domestic to institutions; CAD 49.99 in United States to institutions; CAD 59.99 elsewhere to institutions (effective 2008). adv. bk.rev. illus. index. reprints avail. **Document type:** *Magazine, Consumer.* **Description:** Provides activists with a forum to debate issues, share information, recount victories, and evaluate strategies for social change.
Related titles: Microfiche ed.: (from MML, PQC); Microform ed.: (from MML); Online - full text ed.
Indexed: A01, A02, A03, A08, A22, A26, APW, AltPI, AmH&L, BAS, C03, C04, C05, C12, CBCARef, CBPI, CPerI, CWPI, E08, G05, G06, G07, G08, H05, HistAb, I05, I06, I07, I08, LeftInd, M01, M02, MEA&I, MagInd, P02, P10, P30, P34, P45, P48, P53, P54, PQC, PRA, PerIslam, RASB, S09, S23, T02.
—CIS. **CCC.**
Published by: Dimension Publishing Inc., 91 Albert St, Rm 2 B, Winnipeg, MB R3B 1G5, Canada. TEL 204-957-1519, 800-737-7051, FAX 204-943-4617. Ed., Pub. Cy Gonick. Circ: 3,200.

320 GBR ISSN 0008-4239
JA4
➤ **CANADIAN JOURNAL OF POLITICAL SCIENCE/REVUE CANADIENNE DE SCIENCE POLITIQUE.** Abbreviated title: C J P S. Text in English, French. 1968. q. GBP 89, USD 142 combined subscription to institutions (print & online eds.) (effective 2012). adv. bk.rev. illus. index. back issues avail.; reprint service avail. from PSC. **Document type:** *Journal, Academic/Scholarly.* **Description:** Crosses the range of subfields in political science. Presents articles, notes, commentaries and book reviews in French and in English.
Supersedes in part (in 1967): Canadian Journal of Economics and Political Science (0315-4890); Which was formerly (until 1935): Contributions to Canada Economics (0383-6258)
Related titles: Microfiche ed.: (from MML); Microform ed.: (from MML); Online - full text ed.: ISSN 1744-9324. GBP 77, USD 123 to institutions (effective 2012).
Indexed: A01, A02, A03, A08, A20, A22, A25, A26, ABCPolSci, ABS&EES, ASCA, AmH&L, B04, BAS, BRD, C03, CA, CBCARef, CBPI, CPerI, CWPI, CurCont, DIP, E01, E08, ESPM, G08, G10, H09, H10, I05, I13, IBR, IBSS, IBZ, ICLPL, M01, M02, MEA&I, P02, P06, P10, P27, P30, P34, P42, P45, P47, P48, P53, P54, PAIS, PCI, PQC, PRA, PSA, PdeR, PhilInd, RASB, RiskAb, S02, S03, S05, S08, S09, S11, SCOPUS, SOPODA, SRRA, SSA, SSAI, SSAb, SSCI, SSI, SociolAb, T02, W03, W07, W09.
—BLDSC (3034.600000), IE, Infotrieve, Ingenta. **CCC.**
Published by: (Canadian Political Science Association/Societe Quebecoise de Science Politique CAN), Cambridge University Press, The Edinburgh Bldg, Shaftesbury Rd, Cambridge, CB2 8RU, United Kingdom. TEL 44-1223-312393, FAX 44-1223-315052, journals@cambridge.org, http://www.cambridge.org/uk. Eds. Andre Lecours, Csaba Nikolenyi, Dimitri Karmis. adv.: page GBP 305, page USD 580. Circ: 2,200 (paid). **Subscr. to:** Cambridge University Press, 32 Ave of the Americas, New York, NY 10013. TEL 212-337-5000, FAX 212-691-3239, journals_subscriptions@cup.org

328 CAN ISSN 0315-6168
CANADIAN PARLIAMENTARY GUIDE (YEAR)/GUIDE PARLEMENTAIRE CANADIEN. Text in English, French. 1862. a., latest 2005. USD 184 per issue (effective 2009). stat. **Document type:** *Government.* **Description:** Contains general, biographical and electoral information for members of the House of Commons, Senate, Privy Council and each of the provincial and territorial legislatures.
Former titles (until 1901): Parliamentary Guide (0315-6176); (until 1897): Canadian Parliamentary Companion (0315-6184); (until 1881): Canadian Parliamentary Companion and Annual Register (0315-6192); (until 1876): Canadian Parliamentary Companion (0315-6206)
Related titles: Microform ed.: (from MML); Online - full text ed.
Indexed: CPerI.
Published by: Grey House Publishing Canada, Inc., 555 Richmond St W, Ste 301, Toronto, ON M5V 3B1, Canada. TEL 416-644-6479, 866-433-4739, FAX 416-644-1904, info@greyhouse.ca.

CANADIAN PARLIAMENTARY HANDBOOK. *see* PUBLIC ADMINISTRATION

328.73 CAN ISSN 0229-2548
JL148
CANADIAN PARLIAMENTARY REVIEW. Text in English. 1978. q. CAD 20 (effective 2000). adv. bk.rev. **Document type:** *Newsletter, Government.*
Related titles: Online - full text ed.; French ed.: ISSN 0229-2556.
Indexed: A22, A26, AmH&L, C03, C04, C05, CBCARef, CBPI, CPerI, G08, I05, P42, P45, P48, PAIS, PQC.
—CIS. **CCC.**
Published by: Commonwealth Parliamentary Association, Canadian Region, Confederation Bldg, House of Parliament, P O Box 950, Ottawa, ON K1A 0A6, Canada. TEL 613-996-1662, FAX 613-943-0307. Ed., R&P Gary Levy. Circ: 3,500.

320 CAN ISSN 1911-4125
JA84.C3
➤ **CANADIAN POLITICAL SCIENCE REVIEW;** a new journal of political science. Text in English. 2007. irreg. free (effective 2011). **Document type:** *Journal, Academic/Scholarly.* **Description:** Aims to stimulate the intellectual development of political science within the Canadian political science community and the international community of scholars in the field.
Media: Online - full text.
Indexed: A39, C04, C27, C29, CA, D03, D04, E13, P42, PSA, R14, S14, S15, S18, T02.
Address: c/o Tracy Summerville, Department of Political Science, University of Northern British Columbia, Prince George, BC, Canada. Ed. Tracy Summerville.

➤ **CANADIAN REVIEW OF AMERICAN STUDIES.** *see* HISTORY—History Of North And South America

➤ **CANADIAN SPEECHES.** *see* BUSINESS AND ECONOMICS

➤ **CANBERRA PAPERS ON STRATEGY AND DEFENCE.** *see* MILITARY

➤ **CAPITAL AND CLASS.** *see* BUSINESS AND ECONOMICS—Economic Systems And Theories, Economic History

324 USA ISSN 1089-4500
CAPITAL EYE. Text in English. 2002. irreg. free (effective 2007). **Document type:** *Newsletter, Consumer.* **Description:** Explores the impact of money on politics, elections and the political process, primarily at the federal level.
Related titles: Online - full text ed.: ISSN 1936-3230.
Published by: Center for Responsive Politics, 1101 14th St NW, Ste 1030, Washington, DC 20005. TEL 202-857-0044, FAX 202-857-7809, info@crp.org, http://www.opensecrets.org. Ed. Massie Ritsch.

320 USA ISSN 0898-6916
F192.3
CAPITAL SOURCE. Text in English. 1986. irreg. USD 39.95 per issue (print & online eds.) (effective 2009). **Document type:** *Directory, Consumer.* **Description:** Lists over 7,000 government officials, trade associations, interest groups, political consultants, lobbyists, news media, and more.
Related titles: Online - full text ed.; ◆ Supplement to: National Journal. ISSN 0360-4217.
—BLDSC (3050.669230).
Published by: National Journal Group, Inc., The Watergate 600 New Hampshire Ave, NW, Washington, DC 20037. TEL 202-739-8400, FAX 202-833-8069, orders@nationaljournal.com, http://www.nationaljournal.com. Adv. contact Alisha Johnson TEL 202-266-7312.

320 BHS
CAPITALISM MAGAZINE; in defense of individual rights. Text in English. d. free. adv. **Description:** Covers news events from a pro-capitalist, laissez-faire, pro-individual rights perspective.
Media: Online - full content.
Address: PO Box F44518, Freeport, Bahamas. letters@capitalismmagazine.com, http://www.capitalismmagazine.com. Pub. Mark Da Cunha.

333.72 GBR ISSN 1045-5752
HD75.6 CODEN: CNSOED
➤ **CAPITALISM, NATURE, SOCIALISM;** a journal of socialist ecology. Abbreviated title: C N S. Text in English. 1988. q. GBP 248 combined subscription in United Kingdom to institutions (print & online eds.); EUR 329, USD 413 combined subscription to institutions (print & online eds.) (effective 2012). adv. back issues avail.; reprint service avail. from PSC. **Document type:** *Journal, Academic/Scholarly.* **Description:** Contains articles on international red-green theories and politics including the dialectics of human and natural history, labor and land, workplace struggles and community struggles, economics and ecology, and the politics of ecology and ecology of politics.
Related titles: Online - full text ed.: ISSN 1548-3290. GBP 223 in United Kingdom to institutions; EUR 295, USD 371 to institutions (effective 2012) (from IngentaConnect).
Indexed: A22, ABS&EES, AbAn, AltPI, B16, CA, ChPerI, DIP, E01, E04, E05, EnvAb, EnvInd, GEOBASE, IBR, IBSS, IBZ, LeftInd, P10, P13, P34, P42, P45, P46, P48, P52, P53, P54, P56, PQC, PSA, PerIslam, RI-1, RI-2, S02, S03, S10, SCOPUS, SOPODA, SSA, SociolAb, T02.
—BLDSC (3050.669720), IE, Infotrieve, Ingenta. **CCC.**
Published by: Routledge (Subsidiary of: Taylor & Francis Group), 4 Park Sq, Milton Park, Abingdon, Oxon OX14 4RN, United Kingdom. TEL 44-20-70176000, FAX 44-20-70176336, subscriptions@tandf.co.uk, http://www.routledge.com. Ed. Joel Kovel. Adv. contact Linda Hann TEL 44-1344-779945. Circ: 1,000. **Subscr. to:** Taylor & Francis Ltd., Journals Customer Service, Sheepen Pl, Colchester, Essex CO3 3LP, United Kingdom. TEL 44-20-70175544, FAX 44-20-70175198.

320.789 USA
CAPITOL GOVERNMENT REPORTS WEEKLY. Text in English. 1948. w. USD 245 (effective 2000). **Document type:** *Newsletter.* **Description:** Reports on New Mexico government and politics.
Published by: Capitol Government Reports, PO Box 602, Santa Fe, NM 87504-0602. TEL 505-988-9835, FAX 505-988-9835. Ed., R&P Jack Flynn. Pub. Rene Parker.

CAPITOL IDEAS. *see* PUBLIC ADMINISTRATION

320.972 MEX
CARTA DE NEXOS. Text in Spanish. 1995. 51/yr. MXN 6,000 domestic; USD 600 foreign (effective 2001). back issues avail. **Document type:** *Newsletter, Consumer.* **Description:** Contains analyses and opinion on Mexican internal politics, Mexican foreign politics, and economics.
Related titles: E-mail ed.
Published by: Nexos Sociedad Ciencia y Literatura S.A. de C.V., Mazatlan 119, Col Condesa, Del Cuahutemoc, Mexico City, DF 06140, Mexico. TEL 52-5-553-1374, FAX 52-5-211-5886. Ed., R&P Andres Hofmann. Pub. Hector Aguilar Camin. Circ: 687 (paid).

CARTA LOCAL; boletin informativo. *see* PUBLIC ADMINISTRATION

CARTHAGE; Tunisian quarterly review. *see* HISTORY—History Of Africa

CASOPIS MATICE MORAVSKE. *see* HISTORY—History Of Europe

CATHOLIC CAMPAIGN FOR AMERICA. CAMPAIGN UPDATE. *see* RELIGIONS AND THEOLOGY—Roman Catholic

320.6 USA ISSN 1936-038X
CATO. HANDBOOK ON POLICY. Text in English. 1995. biennial, latest 2009, 7th ed. USD 24.95 per issue (effective 2010). back issues avail. **Document type:** *Handbook/Manual/Guide, Academic/Scholarly.*
Formerly (until 2005): The Cato Handbook for Congress
Related titles: Online - full text ed.: USD 14 per issue (effective 2010).
Published by: Cato Institute, 1000 Massachusetts Ave, NW, Washington, DC 20001. TEL 202-842-0200, FAX 202-842-3490, subscriptions@cato.org.

320.6 USA ISSN 1061-7280
H97
CATO INSTITUTE. BRIEFING PAPERS. Text in English. 19??. irreg., latest vol.118, 2010. price varies. back issues avail. **Document type:** *Monographic series, Academic/Scholarly.*
—CCC.
Published by: Cato Institute, 1000 Massachusetts Ave, NW, Washington, DC 20001. TEL 202-842-0200, FAX 202-842-3490, subscriptions@cato.org.

320.6 USA ISSN 0273-3072
H1
➤ **THE CATO JOURNAL;** an interdisciplinary journal of public policy analysis. Text in English. 1981. 3/yr. USD 22 to individuals; USD 50 to institutions (effective 2011). adv. bk.rev. illus. back issues avail.; reprints avail. **Document type:** *Journal, Academic/Scholarly.* **Description:** Features articles dedicated to public policy analysis.
Related titles: Online - full text ed.: ISSN 1943-3468. free (effective 2011).
Indexed: A01, A02, A03, A08, A12, A13, A17, A20, A22, A25, A26, A39, ABCPolSci, ABIn, ABS&EES, ASCA, AmH&L, B01, B02, B04, B06, B07, B08, B09, B15, B17, B18, BAS, BRD, C12, C27, C29, CA, CLI, D03, D04, E08, E13, EconLit, EnvAb, G04, G08, HistAb, I05, I13, IBSS, JEL, M01, M02, P02, P10, P13, P27, P30, P34, P42, P45, P48, P51, P53, P54, PAIS, PQC, PSA, R14, RASB, S02, S03, S08, S09, S11, S14, S15, S18, SCOPUS, SSAI, SSAb, SSI, SociolAb, T02, W03, W04, W05.
—BLDSC (3093.272000), IE, Infotrieve, Ingenta. **CCC.**
Published by: Cato Institute, 1000 Massachusetts Ave, NW, Washington, DC 20001. TEL 202-842-0200, FAX 202-842-3490, subscriptions@cato.org. Ed. James A Dorn TEL 202-789-5200. Pub. Edward H Crane. Adv. contact Heidi Minora TEL 202-789-5266. B&W page USD 180.

➤ **EL CATOBLEPAS;** revista critica del presente. *see* PHILOSOPHY

320.51 USA
CATO'S LETTER; a quarterly message on liberty. Text in English. 2002. q. free to members (effective 2010). **Document type:** *Newsletter, Consumer.* **Description:** Addresses the traditional American ideas of individual liberty, limited government, free markets and peace.
Published by: Cato Institute, 1000 Massachusetts Ave, NW, Washington, DC 20001. TEL 202-842-0200, FAX 202-842-3490, subscriptions@cato.org.

320 GEO ISSN 1027-8540
DK511.C1
CAUCASIAN REGIONAL STUDIES. Text in English, Russian. 1996. q. **Description:** Publishes contributions on collective security, inter-state relations, ethnic conflicts, democratization, civil society, and economics.
Indexed: PAIS.

P

Published by: International Association for Caucasian Regional Studies, David Agmashenebeli Ave, 89/24, 5th Flr, Tbilisi, 380008, Georgia. iacrs@iacrs.org.ge, sfjones@mhc.mtholyoke.edu.

320 DEU ISSN 1865-6773
DK509
➤ **CAUCASIAN REVIEW OF INTERNATIONAL AFFAIRS.** Text in English; Text occasionally in Russian. 2006. q. free (effective 2011). **Document type:** *Journal, Academic/Scholarly.*
Formerly (until 200?): Caucasian Journal of European Affairs
Media: Online - full text.
Indexed: A26, E08, I05, M10, P02, P10, P42, P45, P48, P53, P54, PQC, PSA, T02.
Published by: Caucasian Review of International Affairs (C R I A) Ed: Nasimi Aghayev.

➤ **CAUSE COMMUNE**; Revue Citoyenne d'Actualite Reflechie. *see* HUMANITIES: COMPREHENSIVE WORKS

328 CYM ISSN 0300-4740
CAYMAN ISLANDS. LEGISLATIVE ASSEMBLY. MINUTES. Text in English. 1966. irreg. price varies. **Document type:** *Government.*
Media: Duplicated (not offset).
Published by: Legislative Assembly, PO Box 890, Grand Cayman, Cayman Isl.

320 USA
CENTENNIAL BIOGRAPHICAL DIRECTORY OF MEMBERS. Text in English. 1945. irreg., latest 2001. USD 65 combined subscription per issue to members (print & CD-ROM eds.); USD 95 per issue to non-members; USD 50 per issue to members (print or CD-ROM ed.) (effective 2010). stat. Index. **Document type:** *Directory, Trade.* **Description:** Contains names, addresses, emails, phone number, URL, institutional affiliations, highest degrees, fields of specialization, employment history, professional honors, and publications of over 13,000 APSA members.
Former titles (until 1968): American Political Science Association. Biographical Directory; (until 1953): American Political Science Association. Directory
Related titles: CD-ROM ed.; Supplement(s): Trennial Directory of Members.
Published by: American Political Science Association, 1527 New Hampshire Ave, NW, Washington, DC 20036. TEL 202-483-2512, FAX 202-483-2657, apsa@apsanet.org.

CENTER FOR EUROPEAN STUDIES WORKING PAPER SERIES. *see* HISTORY—History Of Europe

320.6 USA
CENTER FOR LAW IN THE PUBLIC INTEREST. NEWSLETTER. Text in English. 1971. q. free to members. bk.rev. **Document type:** *Newsletter.* **Description:** Conducts high impact litigation on a broad range of important issues: civil rights, free speech, affordable housing, the homeless, fair elections, environmental protection, land use, corporate and governmental accountability.
Formerly: Public Interest Briefs
Related titles: Online - full text ed.
Published by: Center for Law in the Public Interest, 1055 Wilshire Blvd, Ste 1660, Los Angeles, CA 90017. TEL 213-977-1035, FAX 213-977-5457, info@clipi.org, http://www.clipi.org. Ed. Marian Samuels. Circ: 2,000.

320 USA
CENTER FOR THE STUDY OF THE PRESIDENCY. ANNUAL REPORT. Text in English. a. reprints avail. **Document type:** *Corporate.*
Published by: Center for the Study of the Presidency, 1020 Nineteenth St, NW, Ste 250, Washington, DC 20036. TEL 212-249-1200, FAX 212-628-9503.

320 USA
CENTER FOR THE STUDY OF THE PRESIDENCY. PROCEEDINGS. Text in English. 1971. irreg., latest vol.6, 1989. membership. reprints avail. **Document type:** *Monographic series.*
Related titles: Microform ed.: (from PQC).
Indexed: AMB.
Published by: Center for the Study of the Presidency, 1020 Nineteenth St, NW, Ste 250, Washington, DC 20036. TEL 212-249-1200, FAX 212-628-9503. Ed. R Gordon Hoxie. Circ: 11,000.

320 301 ITA ISSN 2239-7434
▼ **CENTER OF STUDIES ON POLITICS AND SOCIETY. WORKING PAPERS SERIES.** Text in English. 2011. **Document type:** *Monographic series, Academic/Scholarly.*
Media: Online - full text.
Published by: Universita degli Studi del Salento, Coordinamento S I B A, Viale Gallipoli 49, Lecce, 73100, Italy. TEL 39-083-2291111, http://siba2.unile.it.

321.8 POL ISSN 1232-7999
DJK51
CENTERS FOR PLURALISM NEWSLETTER. Text in English. 1992. q. USD 30; free in Eastern Europe (effective 2005). **Document type:** *Newsletter.* **Description:** Provides information on the activities, programs, publications and conferences of non-governmental organizations in Central and Eastern Europe and the former Soviet Union.
Related titles: Russian ed.
Published by: Institute for Democracy in Eastern Europe, Warsaw Center for Pluralism, ul Marszalkowska 10/16, Warsaw, 00626, Poland. TEL 48-22-6271845, idee@idee.ngo.pl, http://www.idee.ngo.pl. Circ: 1,500. **Co-sponsor:** National Endowment for Democracy.

320.6 NLD ISSN 1877-3028
▼ **CENTRAAL BUREAU VOOR DE STATISTIEK. CENTRUM VOOR BELEIDSSTATISTIEK. PAPERS.** Text in Dutch. 2009. irreg. free (effective 2011). **Document type:** *Monographic series, Trade.*
Media: Online - full text.
Published by: (Centraal Bureau voor de Statistiek, Centrum voor Beleidsstatistiek), Centraal Bureau voor de Statistiek, Henri Faasdreef 312, The Hague, 2492 JP, Netherlands. TEL 31-70-3373800, FAX 31-70-3375994, infoserv@cbs.nl.

320.54095694 ZWE ISSN 0008-9184
CENTRAL AFRICAN ZIONIST DIGEST. Text in English. 1958. m. free. illus.
Published by: Central African Zionist Organisation, PO Box 1162, Bulawayo, Zimbabwe. Ed. Barney Katz.

CENTRAL AMERICA - MEXICO REPORT. *see* RELIGIONS AND THEOLOGY

320.9 GTM ISSN 0254-2471
HC141.A1
CENTRAL AMERICA REPORT. Text in English. 1974. w. USD 225 in the Americas; USD 247 in Europe; USD 264 elsewhere (effective 2000). back issues avail. **Document type:** *Bulletin, Consumer.* **Description:** Contains information and analysis on the economic and political events in Belize, Guatemala, El Salvador, Honduras, Nicaragua, Costa Rica and Panama.
Indexed: HRIR, RASB.
Published by: Inforpress Centroamericana, 11 Ave. 16-60, Apdo. 2823, Guatemala City Zona, Guatemala. TEL 502-2510604, FAX 502-2514362. **Subscr. to:** Inforpress Centroamericana, Section 23, Box 52 7270, Miami, FL 33152-7270.

322.44 GBR
CENTRAL AMERICA REPORT. Text in English. 2/yr. free to members (effective 2009). bk.rev. 16 p./no. 4 cols./p.; back issues avail. **Document type:** *Magazine, Trade.* **Description:** Contains news and political analysis from Central America. Includes information on solidarity work.
Former titles (until 1997): Nicaragua Update (1360-0303); (until 1994): Nicaragua Today (0269-4832)
Published by: Nicaragua Solidarity Campaign, 86, Durham Rd, London, N7 7DT, United Kingdom. TEL 44-20-75614836, nsc@nicaraguasc.org.

320 GBR ISSN 1470-5699
HC244.A1
CENTRAL AND SOUTH EASTERN EUROPE; Europa regional surveys of the world. Text in English. 2000 (Sept.). a. USD 700 per issue (effective 2009). bibl.; stat. reprints avail. **Document type:** *Report, Trade.* **Description:** Outlines the economic, political and social background to the countries & territories of Central & South Eastern Europe, covering topics relating to the region as a whole as well as provides more indepth statistics and directory details on each country.
Supersedes in part (in 1999): Eastern Europe and the Commonwealth of Independent States (0962-1040); Which was formerly (until 1991): Eastern Europe and the U S S R
—CCC.
Published by: Routledge (Subsidiary of: Taylor & Francis Group), 2 Park Sq, Milton Park, Abingdon, Oxon OX14 4RN, United Kingdom. TEL 44-20-70176000, FAX 44-20-70176699, orders@taylorandfrancis.com. **Dist. by:** Current Pacific Ltd., 7 La Roche Pl, Northcote, PO Box 36-536, Auckland 0627, New Zealand.

320 SWE ISSN 1404-6091
DS327
➤ **CENTRAL ASIA AND THE CAUCASUS.** Text in English. 2000. bi-m. EUR 130 to individuals; EUR 180 to institutions; EUR 30 per issue (effective 2010). **Document type:** *Journal, Academic/Scholarly.*
Related titles: Online - full text ed.; ◆ Russian ed.: Tsentral'naya Aziya i Kavkaz. ISSN 1403-7068.
Indexed: CA, T02.
Published by: C A & C C Press AB, Hubertusstigen 9, Lulea, 97455, Sweden. TEL 46-70-2321655. Ed. Murad Esenov TEL 46-70-2321655.

320 USA
CENTRAL ASIA-CAUCASUS ANALYST. Text in English. 19??. bi-w. back issues avail. **Document type:** *Journal, Trade.* **Description:** Features analytical articles on Georgia's constitutional reforms, BP's new investment in Azerbaijan, threats to NATO supply lines in Afghanistan, and mining in Kazakhstan.
Related titles: Online - full text ed.: free (effective 2010).
Indexed: LeftInd.
Published by: Johns Hopkins University, Central Asia-Caucasus Institute, Silk Road Studies Program, 1619 Massachusetts Ave, NW, Washington, DC 20036. TEL 202-663-5642. Ed. Suante E Cornell.

320 GBR ISSN 0263-4937
DS327 CODEN: CASUF9
➤ **CENTRAL ASIAN SURVEY.** Text in English. 1982. q. GBP 721 combined subscription in United Kingdom to institutions (print & online eds.); EUR 1,040, USD 1,306 combined subscription to institutions (print & online eds.) (effective 2012). adv. bk.rev. illus. Index. back issues avail.; reprint service avail. from PSC. **Document type:** *Journal, Academic/Scholarly.* **Description:** Publishes research in the history, politics, cultures and economics of the Turkic peoples of the central Asian region (from western Anatolia to western China, including the republics of former Soviet central Asia) sharing a common ethnic, cultural, linguistic and religious heritage.
Related titles: Online - full text ed.: ISSN 1465-3354. GBP 649 in United Kingdom to institutions; EUR 936, USD 1,175 to institutions (effective 2012) (from IngentaConnect).
Indexed: A01, A03, A08, A22, AICP, AMR, APEL, AmHI, B21, CA, DIP, E01, E17, ESPM, FR, GEOBASE, H07, HistAb, I08, I13, I14, IBR, IBSS, IBZ, LeftInd, M10, MLA-IB, P10, P14, P30, P34, P42, P48, P53, P54, PAIS, PCI, PQC, PSA, PerIslam, RASB, S02, S03, S21, SCOPUS, SOPODA, SSA, SSciA, SociolAb, T02, W04.
—IE, Infotrieve, Ingenta. **CCC.**
Published by: (Society for Central Asian Studies), Routledge (Subsidiary of: Taylor & Francis Group), 4 Park Sq, Milton Park, Abingdon, Oxon OX14 4RN, United Kingdom. TEL 44-20-70176000, FAX 44-20-70176336, subscriptions@tandf.co.uk, http://www.routledge.com. Ed. Deniz Kandiyoti TEL 44-20-78984488. Adv. contact Linda Hann TEL 44-1344-779945. **Subscr. in N. America to:** Taylor & Francis Inc., Customer Services Dept, 325 Chestnut St, 8th Fl, Philadelphia, PA 19106. TEL 215-625-8900, 800-354-1420, FAX 215-625-2940, customerservice@taylorandfrancis.com; **Subscr. to:** Taylor & Francis Ltd., Journals Customer Service, Sheepen Pl, Colchester, Essex CO3 3LP, United Kingdom. TEL 44-20-70175544, FAX 44-20-70175198, tf.enquiries@tfinforma.com.

320 CZE ISSN 1802-4866
H96
➤ **CENTRAL EUROPEAN JOURNAL OF PUBLIC POLICY.** Text in English. 2007. s-a. free (effective 2011). bk.rev. abstr.; bibl.; charts; illus.; maps; stat. back issues avail. **Document type:** *Journal, Academic/Scholarly.* **Description:** Aims to cover a wide variety of public policy including: civil society, social services and healthcare, environmental protection, education, labour market, immigration, security, public financing and budgeting, administrative reform, performance measurements and governance.
Media: Online - full text.
Indexed: CA, H05, T02.
Published by: Univerzita Karlova v Praze, Fakulta Socialnih Ved, Centrum pro Socialni a Ekonomicke Strategie/Charles University in Prague, Faculty of Social Sciences, Center for Social and Economic Strategies, Celetna 20, Prague, 11636, Czech Republic. TEL 420-2-24491493, FAX 420-2-24227950, ceses@fsv.cuni.cz, http://www.ceses.cuni.cz. Ed. Martin Nekola. Pub. Martin Potucek.

320 HUN ISSN 1586-4197
JN96.A1
CENTRAL EUROPEAN POLITICAL SCIENCE REVIEW. Text in English. 2000. q. **Document type:** *Journal, Academic/Scholarly.*
Related titles: Online - full text ed.: ISSN 1586-7897.
Indexed: IBSS.
—BLDSC (3106.138340), IE, Ingenta.
Published by: (Central European Political Science Foundation), Magyar Tudomanyos Akademia, Szazadveg Politikai Iskola/Hungarian Academy of Sciences, Institute for Political Science, Benczur 33, Budapest, 1068, Hungary. szazad@bsp.mtapti.hu. Ed. Janos Simon.

320 GBR
CENTRE ON REGULATION AND COMPETITION. WORKING PAPERS. Text in English. 2001 (June). irreg., latest vol.128, 2006. back issues avail. **Document type:** *Monographic series, Academic/Scholarly.* **Description:** Contains relevant topics in regulation and competition.
Related titles: Online - full text ed.: free (effective 2009).
Published by: Centre on Regulation and Competition at I D P M, School of Environment and Development, The University of Manchester, Harold Hankins Bldg, Precinct Centre, Oxford Rd, Manchester, M13 9QH, United Kingdom. TEL 44-161-2752798, FAX 44-161-2750808, crc@manchester.ac.uk.

320 PRI
CENTRO DE ESTUDIOS DE LA REALIDAD PUERTORRIQUENA. CUADERNOS. Text in Spanish. 1982 (no.5). irreg.
Published by: (Centro de Estudios de la Realidad Puertorriquena USA), Ediciones Huracan, Inc., Avda. Gonzalez 1003, Santa Rica, Rio Piedras, 00925, Puerto Rico.

CENTRO DE ESTUDIOS PUBLICOS. DOCUMENTO DE TRABAJO. *see* BUSINESS AND ECONOMICS—Economic Situation And Conditions

320 ITA ISSN 2038-0623
CENTRO STUDI SUL FEDERALISMO. RESEARCH PAPERS. Text in Multiple languages. 2002. irreg. **Document type:** *Monographic series, Academic/Scholarly.*
Media: Online - full text.
Published by: Centro Studi sul Federalismo, Via Real Collegio 30, Moncalieri, TO 10024, Italy. TEL 39-011-6705024, FAX 39-011-6705081, info@csfederalismo.it, http://www.csfederalismo.it.

320 860 CRI
CENTROAMERICA INTERNACIONAL. Text in Spanish. 1992. irreg.
Published by: Centro Cultural de Espana en Costa Rica, Barrio Escalante, de la Iglesia Santa Teresa, 200 E y 200 N, San Jose, 150-1000, Costa Rica.

320.6 USA ISSN 1539-1418
AS25
THE CENTURY FOUNDATION. ANNUAL REPORT. Text in English. a. free (effective 2004).
Formerly (until 1997): Twentieth Century Fund. Annual Report (0363-3047)
Related titles: Online - full content ed.
Published by: The Century Foundation, 41 E 70th St, New York, NY 10021. TEL 212-535-4441, FAX 212-535-7534, info@tcf.org, http://www.tcf.org.

▼ **CERF POLITIQUE, DEMOCRATIE OU TOTALITARISME.** *see* HISTORY—History Of Europe

CHAIN REACTION. *see* ENVIRONMENTAL STUDIES

CHALCEDON REPORT. *see* RELIGIONS AND THEOLOGY

320.532 USA ISSN 0009-1049
CHALLENGE (NEW YORK); the Revolutionary Communist newspaper. Text in English, Spanish. 1964. w. USD 15 to individuals; USD 35 to institutions (effective 2005). illus. **Document type:** *Newspaper.*
Related titles: Microform ed.: (from PQC); French ed.: Defi; Supplement(s): Desafio.
Indexed: BPIA, FutSurv.
Published by: Progressive Labor Party, 808, Brooklyn, NY 11202-0808. TEL 212-255-3959. Ed. Louis Castro. Circ: 10,000.

CHANGBAI XUEKAN/CHANGBAI JOURNAL. *see* SOCIAL SCIENCES: COMPREHENSIVE WORKS

321.8 ARG
CHANGES. Text in English. 2000. q. back issues avail.
Media: Online - full text. **Related titles:** ◆ Spanish ed.: Cambios.
Published by: Fundacion para el Cambio Democratico, Talcahuano 768, Piso 1o, Buenos Aires, Argentina. TEL 54-114-8167555, fundacion@cambiodemocratico.org, http://www.cambiodemocratico.org.

320.532 CHN ISSN 1005-3980
CHANGJIANG LUNTAN/YANGTZE TRIBUNE. Text in Chinese. 1993. bi-m. USD 24.60 (effective 2009). **Document type:** *Journal, Academic/Scholarly.*
Related titles: Online - full text ed.
Published by: Zhonggong Wuhan-shi Weidangxiao, Jianghan-qu, 100, Dangxiao Lu, Wuhan, 430023, China. TEL 86-27-85618039, FAX 86-27-85618076, http://www.whdx.gov.cn/. **Dist. by:** China International Book Trading Corp, 35 Chegongzhuang Xilu, Haidian District, PO Box 399, Beijing 100044, China. TEL 86-10-68412045, FAX 86-10-68412023, cibtc@mail.cibtc.com.cn, http://www.cibtc.com.cn.

324.2 GBR ISSN 0968-7866
➤ **CHARTIST**; for democratic socialism. Text in English. 1970. bi-m. GBP 15 domestic to individuals; GBP 20 foreign to individuals; GBP 25 domestic to institutions; GBP 35 foreign to institutions; GBP 2 newsstand/cover (effective 2009). adv. tel.rev.; Website rev.; bk.rev. 32 p./no. 3 cols./p.; **Document type:** *Magazine, Academic/Scholarly.* **Description:** Provides political analysis and debate with a focus on UK politics and the British Labor Party but including international and wider issues, plus a review section.
Indexed: AltPI, CA, LeftInd, T02.
Published by: Chartist Publications, PO Box 52751, London, SE4 1WB, United Kingdom. news@chartistmagazine.org.uk. Ed. Mike Davis. R&P, Adv. contact John Sunderland.

327.1745 NLD ISSN 1728-3892
JZ5830
CHEMICAL DISARMAMENT. Text in English. 2002. q. **Document type:** *Journal, Academic/Scholarly.*
Formerly (until 2003): O P C W Synthesis (1029-4376)
Related titles: Online - full content ed.: ISSN 1728-3906.
Published by: Organisation for the Prohibition of Chemical Weapons, Johan de Wittlaan 32, The Hague, 2517 JR, Netherlands. TEL 31-70-4163300, FAX 31-70-3063535, http://www.opcw.org/index.html.

320 CHN ISSN 1673-2774
CHENGSHI DANGBAO YANJIU. Text in Chinese. 2001. bi-m. **Document type:** *Magazine, Consumer.*
Related titles: Online - full text ed.
Published by: Wuxi Ribao Baoye Jituan, 1, Xueqian Donglu, Xinwen Dasha, Wuxi, Jiangsu 214002, China. TEL 86-510-82729912.

320.532 CHN
CHENGSHIDANGBAO YANJIU. Text in Chinese. 2001. q. **Document type:** *Academic/Scholarly.*
Published by: Wuxi Ribao Baoye Jituan, 1, Xueqian Donglu, Xinwen Dasha, Wuxi, Jiangsu 214002, China. TEL 86-510-2757557 ext 218, wxrb@wxrb.com.

CHICAGO JEWISH STAR. *see* RELIGIONS AND THEOLOGY—Judaic

320.6 USA ISSN 1093-8990
H96
CHICAGO POLICY REVIEW. Text in English. 1996. s-a. USD 10; USD 5 to students (effective 2010). adv. bk.rev. **Document type:** *Journal, Academic/Scholarly.*
Indexed: CA, P30, P42, PAIS, PSA, S02, S03, SCOPUS, SSA, SociolAb, T02.
Published by: University of Chicago, Irving B Harris Graduate School of Public Policy Studies, 1155 E 60th St, Chicago, IL 60637. TEL 773-702-8400, harrisschool@uchicago.edu. Ed. Andrew Post.

324 CAN ISSN 0846-6351
CA1SE1-5
CHIEF ELECTORAL OFFICER OF CANADA. REPORT. Text in English, French. 1979. irreg.
Formerly (until 1986): Chief Electoral Officer of Canada. Statutory Report (0225-9486)
Published by: Elections Canada, 257 Slater St, Ottawa, ON K1A OM6, Canada. TEL 613-993-2975, 800-463-6868, FAX 888-524-1444, http://www.elections.ca/.

CHILE BUSINESS FORECAST REPORT. *see* BUSINESS AND ECONOMICS—Economic Situation And Conditions

320 USA ISSN 1653-4212
DS701
THE CHINA AND EURASIA FORUM QUARTERLY. Text in English. 2005. q. USD 100 to individuals; USD 200 to institutions (effective 2010). **Document type:** *Journal, Academic/Scholarly.* **Description:** Devoted to analysis of the current issues facing China and Eurasia.
Related titles: Online - full text ed.: free (effective 2011).
Indexed: A39, C27, C29, CA, D03, D04, E13, I14, IBSS, R14, S14, S15, S18, T02.
—BLDSC (3180.081000).
Published by: Johns Hopkins University, Central Asia-Caucasus Institute, Silk Road Studies Program, 1619 Massachusetts Ave, NW, Washington, DC 20036. TEL 202-663-7723, FAX 202-663-7785, caci2@jhu.edu, http://www.silkroadstudies.org/new/. Ed. Niklas Swanstrom.

THE CHINA BUSINESS FORECAST REPORT. *see* BUSINESS AND ECONOMICS—Economic Situation And Conditions

320 DEU
DS777.545
CHINA DATA SUPPLEMENT; PR China - Hong Kong SAR - Macau SAR - Taiwan. Text in English. 1976. bi-m. free (effective 2009). bibl.; stat. back issues avail. **Document type:** *Journal, Academic/Scholarly.* **Description:** Offers information on any change within the political leadership of the People's Republic of China from provincial level upwards, of Hong Kong, Macau and Taiwan.
Former titles (until 2006): China Aktuell. Data Supplement (Print) (1867-8904); (until 2004): China Monthly Data (0943-7533); (until 1993): P R C Official Activities and Monthly Bibliography
Media: Online - full text. **Related titles:** ◆ Supplement(s): Journal of Current Chinese Affairs. ISSN 1868-1026.
—CCC.
Published by: G I G A Institut fuer Asien-Studien, Rothenbaumchaussee 32, Hamburg, 20148, Germany. TEL 49-40-4288740, FAX 49-40-4107945, ias@giga-hamburg.de, http://www.giga-hamburg.de/english/ias.

THE CHINA JOURNAL. *see* ASIAN STUDIES

320.951 USA ISSN 1542-4197
CHINA LEADERSHIP MONITOR. Text in English. 2002 (Winter). q. **Description:** Informs the American foreign policy community about current trends in China's leadership politics and in its foreign and domestic policies.
Related titles: Online - full text ed.: ISSN 1542-4200. free (effective 2010).
Indexed: P42, PSA.
Published by: Hoover Institution, 434 Galvez Mall, Stanford University, Stanford, CA 94305. TEL 650-723-1754, FAX 650-723-8611, schieron@stanford.edu. Ed. Alice Miller.

CHINA NEWS ANALYSIS. *see* GENERAL INTEREST PERIODICALS—China

CHINESE LAW AND GOVERNMENT; a journal of translations. *see* LAW

320 USA ISSN 1557-3176
DS779.35
CHINESE PUBLIC AFFAIRS QUARTERLY. Text in English. 2004. q. free to members (effective 2010). back issues avail. **Document type:** *Journal, Academic/Scholarly.*
Media: Online - full text.
Published by: China Institute for Public Affairs, 1470 First Ave. Apt 6J, New York, NY 10021. membership@chinaipa.org, http://chinaipa.org.

320.532 CHN ISSN 1674-0297
CHONGQING JIAOTONG DAXUE XUEBAO (SHEHUI KEXUE BAN)/CHONGQING JIAOTONG UNIVERSITY. JOURNAL (SOCIAL SCIENCES EDITION). Text in Chinese. 2001. bi-m. CNY 10 newsstand/cover (effective 2009). **Document type:** *Journal, Academic/Scholarly.*
Formerly (until 2006): Chongqing Jiaotong Xueyuan Xuebao (Shehui Kexue Ban) (1009-9794)
Related titles: Online - full text ed.
Published by: Chongqing Jiaotong Daxue/Chongqing Jiaotong University, 66, Xuefu Ave., Nan'an District, Chongqing, 400074, China. FAX 86-23-62652474, 86-23-62652104, http://www.cqjtu.edu.cn/index.html.

320.531 CHN ISSN 1008-6269
CHONGQING SHEHUI ZHUYI XUEYUAN XUEBAO/CHONGQING INSTITUTE OF SOCIALISM. JOURNAL. Text in Chinese. 1999. bi-m. **Document type:** *Journal, Academic/Scholarly.*
Related titles: Online - full text ed.: (from WanFang Data Corp.).
Published by: Chongqing Shehui Zhuyi Xueyuan, 140, Tushan Lu, Nanan-qu, Chongqing, 400064, China. TEL 86-23-62876761, FAX 86-23-62874725, cqsy.org@163.com.

320 NLD ISSN 0167-9155
JN5981
CHRISTEN DEMOCRATISCHE VERKENNINGEN. Text in Dutch. 1971. q. EUR 54.50 to individuals; EUR 79.50 to institutions; EUR 29.50 to students (effective 2008). adv. bk.rev. index. **Document type:** *Academic/Scholarly.*
Supersedes: Politiek Perspectief (0166-8196); Which was formerly: Politiek (0032-3330)
—IE, Infotrieve.
Published by: C D A Wetenschappelijk Instituut, Buitenom 18, Postbus 30453, The Hague, 2500 GL, Netherlands. TEL 31-70-3424870, FAX 31-70-3926004, http://www.wi.cda.nl. Eds. J Prij, M ten Hooven.

322.1 GBR ISSN 0009-5648
HX51
CHRISTIAN SOCIALIST. Text in English. 1960. q. GBP 2. adv. bk.rev. **Document type:** *Newsletter.* **Description:** Forum for debate between Christians of all denominations on issues of peace and social justice.
Formerly: C S M News
Related titles: Microfilm ed.: (from PQC).
Published by: Christian Socialist Movement, 133 Shepherdess Walk, London, N1 7QA, United Kingdom. TEL 44-71-253-6301. Circ: 1,300.

328 CHE ISSN 0302-2498
JF501
CHRONICLE OF PARLIAMENTARY ELECTIONS. Text in English, French. 1966. a. CHF 35 (effective 2001). **Document type:** *Bulletin, Academic/Scholarly.* **Description:** Contains separate chapters on national legislative elections held throughout the world during the previous year. Includes information on the electoral system, the background and outcome of the elections, and statistics on the results of the poll and new members of Parliament.
Related titles: French ed.
—BLDSC (3186.280000).
Published by: Inter-Parliamentary Union, 5, chemin du Pommier, Case postale 330, Geneva, 1218, Switzerland. TEL 41-22-9194150, FAX 41-22-9194160, TELEX 414217-IPU-CH AND 9194160, postbox@mail.ipu.org, http://www.ipu.org.

CHRONIQUE JUDICIAIRE D'HAITI; revue juridique et culturelle Haitienne. *see* LAW

172.2 CAN ISSN 1914-7600
CHUMIR ETHICS FORUM; sheldon chumir foundation for ethics in leadership. Text in English. 2001. q. free to qualified personnel (effective 2011). back issues avail. **Document type:** *Newsletter, Trade.*
Related titles: Online - full text ed.: ISSN 1924-7915. free (effective 2011).
Published by: Sheldon Chumir Foundation, 1202 Centre St S, Ste 970, Calgary, AB T2G 5A5, Canada. TEL 403-244-6666, FAX 403-244-5596, info@chumirethicsfoundation.ca.

320.532 TWN ISSN 1015-9355
CHUNG KUNG YEN CHIU/STUDIES ON CHINESE COMMUNISM. Key Title: Zhonggong Yanjiu. Text in Chinese; Contents page in English. 1967. m. TWD 1,000, USD 35. index. **Document type:** *Academic/Scholarly.*
Formerly: Fei Ch'ing Yen Chiu (0014-9667)
Published by: Institute for the Study of Chinese Communist Problems, P.O. Box 351, Taipei, Taiwan. TEL 7089780, FAX 3259915. Ed. Wang Han Ming. Pub. Hu Cha Chi. R&P Sun Ke Chao. Circ: 1,800.

320 KOR ISSN 1012-3563
DS777.75
CHUNG-SSO YON'GU/SINO-SOVIET AFFAIRS. Text in English, Korean. 1980. q. membership. **Document type:** *Journal, Academic/Scholarly.*
Formed by the merger of (1975-19??): Chungguk Munje/Chinese Affairs; (1979-19??): Soryon Yongu/Korean Journal of Soviet Studies
Related titles: Online - full text ed.
Published by: Hanyang Taehakkyo Chung-sso Yon'guso/Hanyang University, Asia Pacific Research Center, 17, Haengdangdong, Seongdonggu, Seoul, 133-791, Korea, S. TEL 82-2-22201494, FAX 82-2-22953607, aprc@hanyang.ac.kr, http://aprc.hanyang.ac.kr/.

320.532 CHN ISSN 1672-5794
CHUNQIU. Text in Chinese. 1993. bi-m. (q. until 1995). CNY 5 per issue (effective 2009). **Document type:** *Magazine, Government.*
Published by: Zhongguo Renmin Zhengzhi Xieshang Huiyi, Shandong Sheng Weiyuanhui/Shangdong Committee of Chinese Political Consultative Conference, 73, Quancheng Lu, Ji'nan, Shandong 250011, China. TEL 86-531-86082749, szx@sdzx.gov.cn, http://www.sdzx.gov.cn/.

322.1 IRL ISSN 0332-3625
CHURCH & STATE; a magazine of Irish secularist opinion. Text in English. 1973. q. EUR 10 (effective 2005). adv. bk.rev. **Document type:** *Magazine, Consumer.* **Description:** Aims to assist in the growth of a powerful secular and liberal opinion in Ireland.
Address: P.O. Box 159, Cork, Ireland. Ed. Angela Clifford. Pub., Adv. contact Patrick Maloney. **Dist. by:** Athol Books, PO Box 6589, London N7 6SG, United Kingdom.

CHURCH & STATE. *see* RELIGIONS AND THEOLOGY

CIEN DIAS. *see* SOCIAL SCIENCES: COMPREHENSIVE WORKS

320.532 CUB ISSN 0864-0467
CINCO DE SEPTIEMBRE. Text in Spanish. w.
Related titles: Online - full text ed.: ISSN 1605-2277.
Published by: Partido Comunista de Cuba, Comite Provincial en Cienfuegos, Calle 63 y Circunvalacion, 2do. Piso, Cienfuegos, 55500, Cuba. TEL 53-22636, FAX 53-21906, cip219@cip.etecsa.cu, http://www.5septiembre.cu/.

320 FRA ISSN 0756-3205
CITE; revue de la nouvelle citoyennete. Text in French. 1982. 4/yr. EUR 28 (effective 2009). back issues avail.
Indexed: IBSS.
Published by: Societe Nationale Presse Francaise, 17 rue des Petits Champs, Paris, 75001, France. TEL 33-1-42974257, revuecite@altern.org. Ed. Bertrand Renouvin. Circ: 3,000.

CITES. *see* PHILOSOPHY

324.273 USA ISSN 0887-3186
CITIZENS INFORMER. Text in English. 1971. q. USD 19.95; USD 2 newsstand/cover (effective 2004). adv. bk.rev. 36 p./no. 4 cols./p.; back issues avail. **Document type:** *Newspaper.* **Description:** Discusses government policy, civil rights, and ethnic interests from a conservative perspective.
Published by: Tri-State Informer, Inc., PO Box 221683, St. Louis, MO 63122. TEL 314-940-8474, FAX 636-916-4322. Ed. Samuel Francis. R&P Gordon Lee Baum. Adv. contact Lewis S Doherty IV.

323.6 GBR ISSN 1748-8923
CITIZENSHIP NEWS. Text in English. 2002. q. back issues avail. **Document type:** *Magazine, Consumer.*
Related titles: Online - full text ed.: ISSN 1748-8931. free (effective 2009).
Published by: Learning and Skills Development Agency, Fifth Fl, Holborn Ctr, 120 Holborn, London, EC1N 2AD, United Kingdom. TEL 44-20-74925000, FAX 44-20-74925001, enquiries@lsnlearning.org.uk, http://www.lsnlearning.org.uk. Ed. Tim Morris.

CITIZENSHIP, SOCIAL AND ECONOMICS EDUCATION (ONLINE). *see* EDUCATION

320 GBR ISSN 1362-1025
JF801 CODEN: CISDFE
➤ **CITIZENSHIP STUDIES.** Text in English. 1997. bi-m. GBP 734 combined subscription in United Kingdom to institutions (print & online eds.); EUR 966, AUD 1,579, USD 1,212 combined subscription to institutions (print & online eds.) (effective 2012). adv. back issues avail.; reprint service avail. from PSC. **Document type:** *Journal, Academic/Scholarly.* **Description:** Publishes internationally recognized scholarly work on contemporary issues in citizenship, human rights and democratic processes from an interdisciplinary perspective covering the fields of politics, sociology, history, philosophy and cultural studies.
Related titles: Online - full text ed.: ISSN 1469-3593. GBP 660 in United Kingdom to institutions; EUR 869, AUD 1,421, USD 1,091 to institutions (effective 2012) (from IngentaConnect).
Indexed: A01, A03, A08, A20, A22, AEI, B29, CA, CurCont, DIP, E01, E03, ESPM, GEOBASE, HPNRM, I02, I13, IBR, IBSS, IBZ, P34, P42, PSA, R02, S02, S03, SCOPUS, SOPODA, SSA, SSCI, SSciA, SociolAb, T02, W07.
—IE, Infotrieve, Ingenta. **CCC.**
Published by: Routledge (Subsidiary of: Taylor & Francis Group), 4 Park Sq, Milton Park, Abingdon, Oxon OX14 4RN, United Kingdom. TEL 44-20-70176000, FAX 44-20-70176336, subscriptions@tandf.co.uk, http://www.routledge.com. Ed. Bryan S Turner TEL 65-6516-5205. Adv. contact Linda Hann TEL 44-1344-779945. **Subscr. in N America to:** Taylor & Francis Inc., Customer Services Dept, 325 Chestnut St, 8th Fl, Philadelphia, PA 19106. TEL 215-625-8900, 800-354-1420, FAX 215-625-2940, customerservice@taylorandfrancis.com; **Subscr. to:** Taylor & Francis Ltd., Journals Customer Service, Sheepen Pl, Colchester, Essex CO3 3LP, United Kingdom. TEL 44-20-70175544, FAX 44-20-70175198, tf.enquiries@tfinforma.com.

320 ITA
CITTA D'UTOPIA. Text in Italian. 1992. bi-m. **Document type:** *Magazine, Consumer.*
Published by: Rubbettino Editore, Viale Rosario Rubbettino 10, Soveria Mannelli, CZ 88049, Italy. TEL 39-0968-662034, FAX 39-0968-662055, segreteria@rubbettino.it, http://www.rubbettino.it.

320 ITA ISSN 1970-0873
IL CITTADINO. Text in Italian. 1890. d. EUR 210 (effective 2009). **Document type:** *Newspaper, Consumer.*
Related titles: Online - full text ed.
Published by: Editoriale Laudense Srl, Via Paolo Gorini 34, Lodi, 26900, Italy.

320.352 GBR ISSN 1740-3952
CITY MAYORS; running the world's cities. Text in English. 2003. m. free (effective 2009). adv. **Document type:** *Directory, Consumer.* **Description:** Aims to promote strong cities and good local government and it examines how city mayors, and others who govern metropolitan areas, develop innovative solutions to long-standing urban problems such as housing, transport, education and employment, but also how they meet the latest environmental, technological, social and security challenges, which affect the well-being of their citizens.
Media: Online - full content.
Address: London, SW1, United Kingdom. TEL 44-20-76300615. Ed., Pub. Tann vom Hove.

CIVILIAN CONGRESS; includes a directory of persons holding executive branch-military office in Congress contrary to constitutional prohibition (Art.1, Sec.6, Cl.2) of concurrent office-holding. *see* LAW

320 NLD ISSN 0030-3283
AP15
CIVIS MUNDI; journal of political philosophy and culture. Text in Dutch. 1962. q. EUR 25 domestic to individuals; EUR 27 in Belgium to individuals; EUR 29 foreign to individuals; EUR 32 to institutions; EUR 23 to students (effective 2008). adv. bk.rev. bibl. index. 60 p./no. 2 cols./p.; back issues avail. **Document type:** *Academic/Scholarly.* **Description:** Covers political philosophy and cultural problems.
Formerly: Oost-West
Indexed: A22, KES.
—IE, Infotrieve.

P

Published by: (Stichting Civis Mundi), Uitgeverij Damon, Postbus 2014, Budel, 6020 AA, Netherlands. TEL 31-495-499319, FAX 31-495-499889, info@damon.nl, http://www.damon.nl. Ed. S W Couwenberg TEL 31-10-4182580.

320 ITA ISSN 0009-8191
H7
CIVITAS; periodico di studi politici. Text in Italian; Summaries in English, French, German, Serbo-Croatian, Spanish. 1919-1995; resumed 2004 (New series). m. adv. bk.rev. charts; stat. index. **Document type:** *Journal, Academic/Scholarly.*
Indexed: CA, HistAb, MLA-IB, P42, PAIS, RASB, T02.
Published by: Rubbettino Editore, Viale Rosario Rubbettino 10, Soveria Mannelli, CZ 88049, Italy. TEL 39-0968-662034, FAX 39-0968-662055, segreteria@rubettino.it, http://www.rubbettino.it. Circ: 8,580.

324.2 SWE ISSN 1652-5728
CIVITAS. Text in Swedish. 1992. q. **Document type:** *Journal.*
Formerly (until 2004): Kristdemokratisk Debatt (1103-1522)
Published by: Civitas - Stiftelsen Kristdemokratiska Ideinstitutet, PO Box 3137, Stockholm, 10362, Sweden. TEL 46-8-58710400, FAX 46-8-58710429. Eds. Lars F. Eklund, Marcus Svensson.

320.532 SWE ISSN 0345-2085
HX9.S9
CLARTE. Text in Swedish. 1924. q. SEK 150 domestic; SEK 190 elsewhere (effective 2004). **Document type:** *Consumer.* **Description:** Publishes analysis and debate on social, scientific and cultural questions.
Published by: Svenska Clartefoerbundet, Bondegatan 69, Stockholm, 11634, Sweden. TEL 46-8-886819. Ed. Olle Josephson TEL 46-8-886819. Pub. Mikael Nyberg.

320 ESP ISSN 1699-0528
CLASICOS DEL PENSAMIENTO POLITICO. Text in Spanish. 2002. irreg. EUR 11 (effective 2009). back issues avail. **Document type:** *Monographic series, Academic/Scholarly.*
Published by: Editorial Biblioteca Nueva, C. Almagro 38, Madrid, 28010, Spain. TEL 34-91-3100436, FAX 34-91-2198235, editorial@bibliotecanueva.es, http://www.bibliotecanueva.es/.

320 CHE ISSN 0069-4533
CLASSIQUES DE LA PENSEE POLITIQUE. Text in French. 1965. irreg., latest vol.23, 2010. price varies. **Document type:** *Monographic series, Academic/Scholarly.*
—CCC.
Published by: Librairie Droz S.A., 11 rue Firmin-Massot, Geneva 12, 1211, Switzerland. TEL 41-22-3466666, FAX 41-22-3472391, droz@droz.org, http://www.droz.org. Circ: 1,000.

320 CUB ISSN 0864-1404
CLAVE. Text in Spanish. 1986. q. USD 7 in North America; USD 8 in Europe; USD 9 elsewhere.
Indexed: IIMP.
Published by: Instituto Cubano de la Musica, C Linea No 365 Esq A G, Vedado, Havana, 10400, Cuba. TEL 53-7-8320828, FAX 53-7-8333716, clave@cubarte.cult.cu. Ed. Laura Vilar Alvarez.

320 ARG
CLAVES PARA INTERPRETAR LOS HECHOS. Text in Spanish. 1984. m.
Published by: Editorial Claves, Riombamba 212, Buenos Aires, Argentina. Ed. Juan Carlos Cerutti.

322.1 NLD ISSN 2212-2486
CLEARFACTS. Text in Dutch. 1977. q. **Document type:** *Newsletter, Consumer.*
Former titles (until 2011): Klare Wijn (1877-1017); (until 2008): Schenkt Klare Wijn (1382-8185); (until 1979): Zuid-Afrika Belicht (1382-8193)
Published by: Stichting Geen Kerkgeld voor Geweld, Postbus 1177, Nijkerk, 3860 BD, Netherlands. TEL 31-33-2465497, http://www.gkvg.org.

320 CZE ISSN 1801-8785
CLOVEK. Text in Czech. 2006. irreg. free. **Document type:** *Journal, Academic/Scholarly.*
Media: Online - full content.
Published by: Univerzita Karlova v Praze, Filozoficka Fakulta, Ustav Politologie, U Krize 8, Prague, 15800, Czech Republic. TEL 420-2-51080210, upol@ff.cuni.cz, http://upol.ff.cuni.cz.

320 GBR ISSN 2046-0287
CLUN CHRONICLE AND NEWCASTLE NOTES. Text in English. 1999. m. GBP 20 (effective 2011). adv. back issues avail. **Document type:** *Magazine, Consumer.* **Description:** Covers news, information, events about the community of Newcastle.
Formerly (until 2004): Clun Courier
Published by: The Clun Chronicle, c/o Donald Pickard, 11 Chruch St, Clun Craven Arms, Clun, SY7 8JW, United Kingdom. TEL 44-1588-649737. Eds. Joan Kerry, John Garside. Adv. contact John Childliw TEL 44-1588-640827.

324.2 GBR ISSN 0959-3926
JN1129.C8
CO-OP COMMONWEAL. Text in English. 1965. 3/yr. GBP 0.50; GBP 0.50 newsstand/cover (effective 2000). adv. bk.rev. charts; illus.; stat. **Document type:** *Newspaper.* **Description:** Contains news of the Co-operative Party and all its sectors of cooperative movement.
Former titles (until 1995): Co-operators' Platform (0956-4640); (until 1989): Platform (London) (0032-1370)
Published by: Co-operative Party, 1st Fl, 77 Weston St, London, SE1 3SD, United Kingdom. TEL 44-20-7357-0230, FAX 44-20-7407-4476. Ed., R&P Jean Whitehead. Adv. contact Tim Pearce. Circ: 24,000.

320 NLD ISSN 2210-4186
CODE ROOD. Text in Dutch. 2007. 3/yr. **Document type:** *Newspaper, Consumer.*
Published by: ROOD, Jong in de S P, Vijverhofstraat 65, Rotterdam, 3032 SC, Netherlands. TEL 31-10-2435557, FAX 31-10-2435566, rood@sp.nl.

COGISCOPE. *see* LAW—International Law

COGITATIONS ON LAW AND GOVERNMENT. *see* LAW

320 ESP ISSN 2013-2638
COL-LECCION PAPERS DE RELACIONS GOVERN-PARLAMENT. Text in Catalan. 2008. a. **Document type:** *Monographic series, Academic/Scholarly.*
Related titles: Online - full text ed.: ISSN 2013-7710. 2008.
Published by: Generalitat de Catalunya, Departament d'Interior, Relacions Institucionals i Participacio. Institut d'Estudis Autonomics/Catalan Government. Ministry of Home Affairs, Institutional Relations and Participation. Institut d' Estudis Autonomics, Baixada de Sant Miquel, 8, Barcelona, 08002, Spain. TEL 34-93-3429800, FAX 34-93-3429801, http://www.gencat.cat/iea.

320 BRA
COLECCAO CAMINHOS BRASILEIROS. Text in Portuguese. irreg.
Published by: Edicoes Tempo Brasileiro Ltda, Rua Gago Coutinho, 61, Laranjeiras, Rio De Janeiro, RJ 22221-070, Brazil. Ed. Carlos Chagas Filho.

320 BRA
COLECCAO TENDENCIAS. Text in Portuguese. irreg., latest vol.3, 1982.
Published by: Edicoes Graal Ltda., Rua Hermenegildo de Barros, 31-A, Gloria, S Teresa, Rio De Janeiro, RJ 20241-040, Brazil.

320 ARG ISSN 0328-7998
COLECCION. Text in Spanish. 1995. q. USD 10 per issue (effective 2005). **Document type:** *Journal, Academic/Scholarly.*
Indexed: CA, F04, T02.
Published by: (Pontificia Universidad Catolica Argentina, Instituto de Ciencias Politicas y Relaciones Internacionales), Pontificia Universidad Catolica Argentina, E D U C A, Av Alicia M de Justo 1400, Buenos Aires, C1107AFD, Argentina. educa@uca.edu.ar, http://www.uca.edu.ar/educa.htm. Ed. Enrique Aguilar.

COLECCION DE ECONOMIA Y POLITICA. *see* BUSINESS AND ECONOMICS

COLECCION DE HISTORIA ECONOMICA Y SOCIAL. *see* HISTORY

320 SLV
➤ **COLECCION DEBATE.** Text in Spanish. 1983. irreg. price varies. bk.rev. **Document type:** *Academic/Scholarly.*
Published by: (Universidad Centroamericana Jose Simeon Canas, U C A Editores), U C A Editores, Autopista Sur, Jardines de Guadalupe, Apdo. Postal 01-575, San Salvador, El Salvador. TEL 503-273-3556, FAX 503-273-3556. Ed. Rodolfo Cardenal. Pub. Carolina Elizabeth Cordova. Circ: 1,300.

320.7 ESP ISSN 1989-8150
COLECCION EDUCACION CRITICA. Text in Spanish. 1994. irreg. **Document type:** *Monographic series, Academic/Scholarly.*
Published by: Instituto de Estudios Politicos para America Latina y Africa, C Hermanos Garcia Noblejas, 41 8o, Madrid, 28037, Spain. TEL 34-91-4084112, FAX 34-91-4087047, iepala@iepala.es, http://www.iepala.es/.

320 DOM
COLECCION ESTUDIOS POLITICOS. Text in Spanish. irreg.
Published by: Publicaciones O N A P, Edif. de Oficinas Gubernamentales, Av. Mexico esq. Leopoldo Navarro, Santo Domingo, Dominican Republic. Circ: 750.

320 ARG ISSN 1851-5940
COLECCION RAZON POLITICA. Text in Spanish. 1997. a. **Document type:** *Monographic series, Academic/Scholarly.*
Published by: Ediciones del Signo, Julian Alvarez 2844 1o A, Buenos Aires, 1425, Argentina. TEL 54-11-48044147, FAX 54-11-51764168, info@edicionesdelsiglo.com.ar, http://www.edicionesdelsiglo.com.ar/.

320 ESP ISSN 2171-7699
▼ **COLECCION TESTIMONIOS.** Text in Spanish. 2010. irreg. **Document type:** *Monographic series, Academic/Scholarly.*
Published by: Fundacion Transicion Espanola, Calle Juan de Mena, 25 1o. B, Madrid, 28014, Spain. TEL 34-91-5212985, info@transicion.org, http://transicion.org/.

320.5322 ESP ISSN 1698-6393
COLECCION TESTIMONIOS REVOLUCIONARIOS. Key Title: Testimonios Revolucionarios. Text in Spanish. 1998. irreg. EUR 16.22 domestic; EUR 21 foreign (effective 2009). back issues avail. **Document type:** *Monographic series, Academic/Scholarly.*
Published by: Ediciones Curso, Via Laietana, 40 Pral 1-B, Barcelona, 08003, Spain. TEL 34-93-3103612, FAX 34-93-3101962, http://www.edicionescurso.com/, edcurso@edicionescurso.com. Ed. Bea Miro.

320 USA
THE COLLECTED WORKS OF JACQUES MARITAIN. Text in English. 1995. irreg., latest 2007. price varies. back issues avail. **Document type:** *Monographic series, Academic/Scholarly.*
Published by: University of Notre Dame Press, 310 Flanner Hall, Notre Dame, IN 46556. TEL 574-631-6346, FAX 574-631-8148, undpress.1@nd.edu. **Dist. overseas by:** Eurospan Group, c/o Turpin Distribution Pegasus Dr, Stratton Business Park, Biggleswade, Bedfordshire SG18 8TQ, United Kingdom. TEL 44-1767-604972, FAX 44-1767-601640, eurospan@turpin-distribution.com, http://www.eurospangroup.com; **Dist. by:** c/o Chicago Distribution Ctr, 11030 S Langley Ave, Chicago, IL 60628. TEL 773-702-7000, 800-621-2736, FAX 773-702-7212, 800-621-8476.

320 912 FRA ISSN 1272-0151
COLLECTION ATLAS - MONDE. Variant title: Atlas Monde. Text in French. 1996. irreg. **Document type:** *Monographic series.*
Published by: Editions Autrement, 77 Rue du Faubourg St Antoine, Paris, 75011, France. TEL 33-1-44738000, FAX 33-1-44730012, contact@autrement.com.

327.1 FRA ISSN 1775-6561
COLLECTION CHAOS INTERNATIONAL. Text in French. 2005. irreg. **Document type:** *Monographic series, Consumer.*
Published by: L' Harmattan, 5 Rue de l'Ecole Polytechnique, Paris, 75005, France. TEL 33-1-43257651, FAX 33-1-43258203.

320 FRA ISSN 1159-7240
COLLECTION CURSUS. SCIENCE POLITIQUE. Variant title: Cursus. Science Politique. Text in French. 1992. irreg. price varies. **Document type:** *Monographic series, Academic/Scholarly.*
Published by: Armand Colin, 21 Rue du Montparnasse, Paris, 75283 Cedex 06, France. TEL 33-1-44395447, FAX 33-1-44394343, infos@armand-colin.fr.

320 CAN ISSN 1912-5763
COLLECTION INTERVENTIONS. Text in French. 1998. irreg. price varies. **Document type:** *Monographic series, Consumer.*
Published by: Editions Nota Bene, 1230 Boul. Rene-Levesque Ouest, Quebec, PQ G1S 1W2, Canada. TEL 418-682-3535, FAX 418-656-7701, nbe@videotron.ca.

COLLECTION L'AFRIQUE POLITIQUE. *see* HISTORY—History Of Africa

COLLECTION LES CAHIERS D'ECONOMIE POLITIQUE. *see* BUSINESS AND ECONOMICS—Economic Systems And Theories, Economic History

COLLECTION LUSOTOPIE. *see* HUMANITIES: COMPREHENSIVE WORKS

320 900 FRA ISSN 1637-0929
COLLECTION TROPIQUES. Text in French. 2002. irreg. back issues avail. **Document type:** *Monographic series.*
Published by: Editions Karthala, 22-24 Boulevard Arago, Paris, 75013, France. TEL 33-1-43311559, FAX 33-1-45352705, karthala@orange.fr, http://www.karthala.com.

320.531 USA ISSN 1094-1584
COLLECTIVE ACTION NOTES. Text in English. 1994. irreg. **Document type:** *Magazine, Consumer.*
Indexed: AltPI.
Address: PO Box 39521, Baltimore, MD 21212.

320.52 USA ISSN 2150-9778
▼ **THE COLLEGIATE CONSERVATIVE.** Text and summaries in English. 2010 (Jan.). s-a. free (effective 2010). **Document type:** *Journal, Academic/Scholarly.* **Description:** Features essays on conservatism for college students.
Media: Online - full content.
Published by: Pax Americana Institute, 6666 Odana Rd, PMB 518, Madison, WI 53719. TEL 608-393-0798, execdirector@paxamerica.org.

320 ITA ISSN 1970-3945
COLLOQUI SULLA REPUBBLICA. Text in Italian. 2003. irreg. **Document type:** *Monographic series, Consumer.*
Published by: Salerno Editrice, Via Valadier 52, Rome, 00193, Italy. TEL 39-06-3608201, FAX 39-06-3223132, info@salernoeditrice.it, http://www.salernoeditrice.it.

COLOMBIA BUSINESS FORECAST REPORT. *see* BUSINESS AND ECONOMICS—Economic Situation And Conditions

320 COL ISSN 0121-5612
F2279
➤ **COLOMBIA INTERNACIONAL.** Text in Spanish; Text occasionally in English, Portuguese. 1986. s-a. **Document type:** *Journal, Academic/Scholarly.*
Related titles: Online - full text ed.: ISSN 1900-6004. 2005. free (effective 2011) (from SciELO).
Indexed: A01, A26, C01, CA, F03, F04, H21, I04, I05, IBSS, P08, P10, P42, P45, PAIS, PQC, PSA, SCOPUS, SociolAb, T02.
Published by: (Universidad de los Andes, Facultad de Ciencias Sociales/Universidad de los Andes, Social Sciences Faculty), Universidad de los Andes, Departamento de Ciencia Politica/Universidad de los Andes, Department of Political Science, Carrera 1 Este 18a, Bogota, 10, Colombia. Ed. Felipe Botero. Circ: 300. **Dist. by:** Siglo del Hombre Editores, Cra. 32 No.25-46/50, Bogota, D.C., Colombia. TEL 57-1-3377700, FAX 57-1-3377665, http://www.siglodelhombre.com; Libreria Universidad de los Andes, Cra. 1 No. 19-27 Ed AU106, Bogota, D. C., Colombia. libreria@uniandes.edu.co, http://libreria.uniandes.edu.co/.

320 USA ISSN 1098-3503
E184.A1
COLORLINES; race culture action. Text in English. 1982. bi-m. USD 16 domestic to individuals; USD 20 in Canada & Mexico to individuals; USD 24 elsewhere to individuals; USD 32 domestic to institutions (effective 2003). adv. bk.rev.; film rev.; play rev. illus. reprints avail. **Document type:** *Magazine, Consumer.* **Description:** Examines the issues affecting minority communities and their conditions, including local activism, labor organizing, and environmental racism.
Former titles (until 1998): Third Force (1067-3237); (until 1993): Minority Trendsletter
Related titles: Online - full text ed.
Indexed: APW, AltPI, CWI, ChPerI, Chicano, ENW, G05, G06, G07, G08, I05, I07, IIBP, LeftInd, P27, P46, P48, P54, PAIS, PQC, SCOPUS.
—CIS.
Published by: ColorLines Magazine, 4096 Piedmont Ave, PMB 319, Oakland, CA 94611-5221. TEL 510-653-3415, FAX 510-653-3427, http://www.arc.org/C_Lines/index.html. Ed. Jahahara Armstrong. Pub., R&P, Adv. contact John Anner. B&W page USD 1,025; bleed 8.875 x 11.374. Circ: 30,000.

320 895.1 USA
COLUMBIA EAST ASIAN REVIEW. Text in English. q.
Published by: Columbia University, Weatherhead East Asian Institute, 401 Alfred Lerner Hall, Mail Code #2602, 2920 Broadway, New York, NY 10027.

320.9 PAK ISSN 0010-2121
COMBAT; an independent news weekly. Text in English. 1969. w. PKR 24. adv.
Address: 81-82 Farid Chambers, Abdullah Haroon Rd., Karachi 3, Pakistan. Ed. Yunus Said.

324.7 USA ISSN 1936-0029
JK1991
COMBINED FEDERAL/STATE DISCLOSURE AND ELECTION DIRECTORY. Text in English. 1987. a. free (effective 2011). back issues avail. **Document type:** *Directory, Government.* **Description:** Features to locate and identify organizations and individuals at the state and national level who have a responsibility to disclose information on money in politics.
Formerly (until 1998): Combined Federal/State Disclosure Directory
Related titles: Online - full text ed.
Published by: Federal Election Commission, 999 E St NW, Washington, DC 20463. TEL 202-694-1100, 800-424-9530, FAX 202-219-8504, info@fec.gov.

COMISION ECONOMICA PARA AMERICA LATINA Y EL CARIBE. SERIE REFORMAS DE POLITICA PUBLICA. *see* BUSINESS AND ECONOMICS—Economic Situation And Conditions

322.4 COL
COMITE DE ACCION INTERAMERICANA DE COLOMBIA. BOLETIN. Text in Spanish. irreg.
Published by: Comite de Accion Interamericana de Colombia, Carrera 7, 32-33, Of. 1601, Apartado Aereo 10598, Bogota, CUND, Colombia.

COMMITTEE TO RESTORE THE CONSTITUTION. BULLETIN. *see* LAW

320.9 CAN ISSN 0010-3357
COMMONWEALTH; official journal of the Saskatchewan N D P / C C F. (New Democratic Party / Co-operative Commonwealth Federation) Text in English. 1938. 5/yr. free to members; CAD 15 domestic; CAD 19 in United States; CAD 26 elsewhere (effective 2004). adv. bk.rev. illus. **Document type:** *Newspaper, Consumer.* **Description:** News on democratic socialist politics in Saskatchewan and across Canada.
Incorporates (1936-1952): People's Weekly (0847-6780); Formerly (until 1946): The Saskatchewan Commonwealth
Related titles: Microfilm ed.
Indexed: RASB, SPPI.
—CCC.
Published by: New Democratic Party, 1122 Saskatchewan Dr, Regina, SK S4P 0C4, Canada. TEL 306-525-8321, FAX 306-569-1363, sask.npp@sk.sympatico.ca, http://www3.sk.sympatico.ca/sasknpp. Ed. Don Black. Circ: 10,000.

320.532 FRA ISSN 0751-3496
HX5
COMMUNISME; revue d'histoire, de sociologie et de science politique. Text in French; Summaries in English, French. 1982. 3/yr. bk.rev.
Indexed: FR, I02, I13, IBSS, P42, RASB, T02.
—INIST.
Published by: Editions l'Age d'Homme, 5 rue Ferou, Paris, 75006, France. TEL 33-1-55427979, FAX 33-1-40517102. Ed. Stephane Courtois. Circ: 700. **Dist. by:** Editions Les Belles Lettres, 25 Rue du General Leclerc, Kremlin Bicetre 94270, France. TEL 33-1-45151970, FAX 33-1-45151980.

320.532 GBR ISSN 0967-067X
HX1
➤ **COMMUNIST AND POST-COMMUNIST STUDIES.** Text in English. 1962. 4/yr. EUR 489 in Europe to institutions; JPY 64,900 in Japan to institutions; USD 547 elsewhere to institutions (effective 2012). adv. bk.rev. illus. index, cum.index: vols.1-10 (1968-1977). back issues avail.; reprints avail. **Document type:** *Journal, Academic/Scholarly.* **Description:** Provides research, probes the origins of the malaise, and evaluates the reforms and likelihood of their success.
Former titles (until 1993): Studies in Comparative Communism (0039-3592); (until 1968): Communist Affairs (0588-8174)
Related titles: Microform ed.: (from PQC); Online - full text ed.: ISSN 1873-6920 (from IngentaConnect, ScienceDirect).
Indexed: A01, A02, A03, A08, A20, A22, A26, ABCPolSci, ABS&EES, ASCA, B04, BAS, BRD, CA, CurCont, DIP, E08, G08, H09, HistAb, I05, I08, I13, I14, IBR, IBSS, IBZ, LeftInd, M10, MEA&I, MLA-IB, P02, P06, P10, P13, P27, P30, P34, P42, P47, P48, P53, P54, PAIS, PCI, PQC, PRA, PSA, RASB, S02, S03, S05, S09, SCOPUS, SSAI, SSAb, SSCI, SSI, SociolAb, T02, W01, W02, W03, W07.
—BLDSC (3363.547700), IE, Infotrieve, Ingenta. **CCC.**
Published by: Pergamon (Subsidiary of: Elsevier Science & Technology), The Blvd, Langford Ln, East Park, Kidlington, Oxford OX5 1GB, United Kingdom. TEL 44-1865-843000, FAX 44-1865-843010, JournalsCustomerServiceEMEA@elsevier.com. Eds. Andrzej Korbonski, Luba Fajfer, Lucy Kerner. **Subscr. to:** Elsevier BV, Radarweg 29, PO Box 211, Amsterdam 1000 AE, Netherlands. TEL 31-20-4853757, FAX 31-20-4853432, http://www.elsevier.nl.

320.532 CAN ISSN 1719-8984
COMMUNIST PARTY OF CANADA. Text in English, French. irreg. **Document type:** *Consumer.*
Media: Online - full text.
Address: 290A Danforth Ave., Toronto, ON M4K 1N6, Canada. TEL 416-469-2446, FAX 416-469-4063, info@cpc-pcc.ca, http://www.communist-party.ca.

320.532 GBR ISSN 1474-9246
COMMUNIST REVIEW; theoretical & discussion journal. Text in English. 1986. q. GBP 12 domestic; GBP 14 in Europe; GBP 16 elsewhere; GBP 3 per issue (effective 2009). back issues avail. **Document type:** *Journal, Academic/Scholarly.* **Description:** Contains theoretical and discussion book review of communist party.
Formerly (until 1988): Communist Campaign Review (0950-2416)
Related titles: Microfilm ed.: (from WMP).
Published by: Communist Party of Britain, Ruskin House, 23 Coombe Rd, Croydon, London, CR0 1BD, United Kingdom. TEL 44-20-86861659, office@communist-party.org.uk. Ed. Martin Levy.

320 AUS ISSN 1832-5157
COMMUNITY GOVERNANCE. Text in English. 2005. q. free (effective 2008). **Document type:** *Newsletter, Academic/Scholarly.*
Media: Online - full text.
Published by: Australian National University, Centre for Aboriginal Economic Policy Research, Hanna Neumann Bldg, # 21, Canberra, ACT 0200, Australia. TEL 61-2-61250587, FAX 61-2-61259730, publications.caepr@anu.edu.au, http://www.anu.edu.au/caepr/index.php. Eds. Janet Hunt TEL 61-2-61258209, Stephanie Garling.

320.3 USA ISSN 0010-4140
JA3
➤ **COMPARATIVE POLITICAL STUDIES.** Text in English. 1968. m. USD 1,300, GBP 765 combined subscription to institutions (print & online eds.); USD 1,274, GBP 750 to institutions (effective 2011). adv. bk.rev. bibl.; charts; stat.; illus. index. back issues avail.; reprint service avail. from PSC. **Document type:** *Journal, Academic/Scholarly.* **Description:** Publishes theoretical and empirical research articles by scholars engaged in comparative, cross-national studies.
Related titles: Microform ed.: (from PQC); Online - full text ed.: ISSN 1552-3829. USD 1,170, GBP 689 to institutions (effective 2011).
Indexed: A01, A02, A03, A08, A20, A22, A26, ABCPolSci, ABS&EES, AC&P, ASCA, AmH&L, B04, B07, BAS, BRD, CA, CIS, CMM, CurCont, DIP, E01, E08, ESPM, G08, H04, H09, HistAb, I05, I13, I14, IBR, IBSS, IBZ, LeftInd, MEA&I, P02, P06, P10, P27, P30, P34, P42, P47, P48, P53, P54, PAA&I, PAIS, PCI, PQC, PRA, PSA, PerIslam, RASB, RiskAb, S02, S03, S05, S09, S11, S21, SCOPUS, SPAA, SSA, SSAI, SSAb, SSCI, SSI, SociolAb, T02, V02, W01, W02, W03, W07.
—BLDSC (3363.795000), IE, Infotrieve, Ingenta, INIST. **CCC.**
Published by: Sage Publications, Inc., 2455 Teller Rd, Thousand Oaks, CA 91320. TEL 805-499-9774, 800-818-7243, FAX 805-499-0871, 800-583-2665, info@sagepub.com. Ed. James A Caporaso. adv.: color page USD 775, B&W page USD 385; 4.5 x 7.5. Circ: 850 (paid). **Subscr. outside the Americas to:** Sage Publications Ltd., 1 Oliver's Yard, 55 City Rd, London EC1Y 1SP, United Kingdom. TEL 44-20-73248701, FAX 44-20-73248733, subscription@sagepub.co.uk.

320.3 USA ISSN 0010-4159
JA3
➤ **COMPARATIVE POLITICS.** Text in English. 1968. q. USD 39 domestic to individuals; USD 52 foreign to individuals; USD 78 domestic to institutions; USD 91 foreign to institutions; USD 131 combined subscription domestic to institutions (print & online eds.); USD 144 combined subscription foreign to institutions (print & online eds.); USD 13 per issue to individuals; USD 22 per issue to institutions (effective 2009). bk.rev. charts; illus. index. 128 p./no.; back issues avail.; reprints avail. **Document type:** *Journal, Academic/Scholarly.* **Description:** Provides new ideas and research findings to social scientists, scholars, and students.
Related titles: Microform ed.: (from MIM, PQC); Online - full text ed.: ISSN 2151-6227 (from IngentaConnect).
Indexed: A01, A02, A03, A08, A20, A22, A25, A26, ABCPolSci, ABS&EES, AcaI, AmH&L, B04, BAS, BRD, CA, CurCont, DIP, E08, FR, G08, H09, HistAb, I05, I13, I14, IBR, IBSS, IBZ, MEA&I, P02, P06, P10, P13, P27, P30, P34, P42, P47, P48, P53, P54, PAA&I, PAIS, PCI, PQC, PRA, PSA, RASB, S02, S03, S05, S08, S09, S11, SCOPUS, SPAA, SSAI, SSAb, SSCI, SSI, SociolAb, T02, W03, W07.
—BLDSC (3363.797000), IE, Infotrieve, Ingenta, INIST.
Published by: City University of New York, Political Science Program, 365 Fifth Ave, New York, NY 10016. TEL 212-817-8686, FAX 212-817-1645, politicalscience@gc.cuny.edu, comppol@gc.cuny.edu, http://web.gc.cuny.edu/dept/polit/. Eds. Irving Leonard Markovitz, Kenneth P Erickson. **Subscr. to:** Boyd Printing Co., 5 Sand Creek Rd, Albany, NY 12205. TEL 518-436-9686 ext 134, 800-877-2693, FAX 518-436-7433, info@boydprinting.com, http://www.boydprinting.com.

320 USA ISSN 1047-1006
JK2403
COMPARATIVE STATE POLITICS. Text in English. 1988 (vol.9). bi-m. USD 12.50. bk.rev. index. **Description:** Covers political events nationwide, focusing on state governments. Analyzes election results, and provides highlights of legislative works.
Formerly (until 1989): Comparative State Politics Newsletter (0273-1347)
Indexed: PAIS.
—Ingenta.
Published by: Illinois Legislative Studies Center, University of Illinois, 1 University Plaza, Springfield, IL 62703. http://www.uis.edu. Ed. David H Everson. Circ: 375.

320 USA ISSN 0149-5933
JX1 CODEN: COSTDY
➤ **COMPARATIVE STRATEGY**; an international journal. Text in English. 1978. 5/yr. GBP 384 combined subscription in United Kingdom to institutions (print & online eds.); EUR 508, USD 635 combined subscription to institutions (print & online eds.) (effective 2012). adv. bk.rev. abstr. Index. reprint service avail. from PSC. **Document type:** *Journal, Academic/Scholarly.* **Description:** Focuses on American strategic thought and the influence of history and ideas on the strategic interactions between the West and the former Soviet Union.
Related titles: Online - full text ed.: ISSN 1521-0448. GBP 345 in United Kingdom to institutions; EUR 457, USD 572 to institutions (effective 2012) (from IngentaConnect).
Indexed: A01, A02, A03, A08, A20, A22, A26, ABS&EES, AMB, B01, B04, B06, B07, B09, BAS, BRD, CA, DIP, E01, E08, G08, I02, I05, I13, I14, IBR, IBSS, IBZ, LID&ISL, M05, M06, P02, P10, P27, P34, P42, P47, P48, P53, P54, PAIS, PCI, PQC, PRA, PSA, R02, RASB, S02, S03, S09, S11, SCOPUS, SSAI, SSAb, SSCI, SSI, SociolAb, T02, W01, W02, W03.
—IE, Infotrieve, Ingenta. **CCC.**
Published by: (National Institute for Public Policy), Taylor & Francis Inc. (Subsidiary of: Taylor & Francis Group), 325 Chestnut St, Ste 800, Philadelphia, PA 19106. TEL 215-625-2940, 800-354-1420, orders@taylorandfrancis.com, http://www.taylorandfrancis.com. Ed. Keith B Payne. Adv. contact Linda Hann TEL 44-1344-779945.

➤ **COMPETITION & CHANGE**; the journal of global business and political economy. *see* BUSINESS AND ECONOMICS

320 ARG
COMPROMISO POLITICO Y SOCIAL. Text in Spanish. 1984. m.
Published by: Ediciones Compromiso, Mendez de Andes 33-35, Buenos Aires, 1405, Argentina. Ed. Miguel Angel Marcos.

COMSTOCK'S BUSINESS - CALIFORNIA'S CAPITOL REGION. *see* BUSINESS AND ECONOMICS

COMUNI D'EUROPA. *see* PUBLIC ADMINISTRATION—Municipal Government

COMUNICAZIONE POLITICA. *see* COMMUNICATIONS

320 SWE ISSN 0283-2925
COMUNIDAD. Text in Spanish. 1977. q. SEK 130, USD 25. bk.rev. back issues avail.
Published by: Centrum foer Kooperativa Studier och Verkamhetet, Fack 15128, Stockholm, 10465, Sweden. FAX 46-8-6445985. Ed. Ruben G Prieto. Circ: 2,500.

320.532 ITA ISSN 0393-6740
HX7
COMUNISMO. Text in Italian. 1979. s-a. EUR 10 domestic; EUR 12 foreign (effective 2009). 70 p./no.; back issues avail. **Document type:** *Magazine, Consumer.*
Related titles: Online - full text ed.
Published by: (Partito Comunista Internazionale), Edizioni Il Partito Comunista, Casella Postale 1157, Florence, FI 50121, Italy. http://www.perso.wanadoo.fr/italian.left/.

320.5 141 USA
CONCEPTS IN SOCIAL THOUGHT SERIES. Text in English. 1988. irreg., latest 1999, 2nd ed. price varies. back issues avail. **Document type:** *Monographic series, Academic/Scholarly.* **Description:** Provides useful overviews and offers historical, comparative, and theoretical analyses of important concepts in political science, sociology, and history.
Published by: University of Minnesota Press, Ste 290, 111 Third Ave S, Minneapolis, MN 55401. TEL 612-627-1970, FAX 612-627-1980, ump@umn.edu. Ed. Frank Parkin. **Dist. by:** c/o Chicago Distribution Center, 11030 S Langley Ave, Chicago, IL 60628. TEL 800-621-2736; Plymbridge Distributors Ltd, Estover Rd, Plymouth, Devon PL6 7PY, United Kingdom. TEL 44-1752-202-301, FAX 44-1752-202-331.

320 GTM
CONCERTACION. Text in Spanish. m.
Published by: Presidencia de la Republica de Guatemala, Secretaria de Relaciones Publicas, Guatemala City, Guatemala.

320 ARG
CONCIENCIA NACIONAL. Text in Spanish. 1991. m.?. ARS 15,000 per issue.
Address: Corrientes 1250, 6o B, Buenos Aires, 1043, Argentina. TEL 54-114-351861. Ed. Alberto Guerberof.

320.57 USA
CONDITION RED QUARTERLY; A zine of the A B C F's Tactical Defense Caucus. Text in English. q. **Document type:** *Magazine, Consumer.* **Description:** Contains information on survivalist warfare skills and political debates on the practice of armed self-defense; includes reviews, theory, history, and reports.
Published by: Anarchist Black Cross Federation, PO Box 350392, Jacksonville, FL 32235-0392 . **Dist. by:** A K Press, Inc., 674-A 23rd St, Oakland, CA 94612. TEL 510-208-1700, FAX 510-208-1701, info@akpress.org, http://www.akpress.org/.

321.8 SWE ISSN 1653-5561
CONDITIONS OF DEMOCRACY. Text in Swedish. 2006. irreg., latest vol.2, 2006. SEK 180 (effective 2006). back issues avail. **Document type:** *Monographic series, Academic/Scholarly.*
Published by: Oerebro Universitet, Universitetsbiblioteket/University of Oerebro. University Library, Fakultetsgatan 1, Oerebro, 70182, Sweden. TEL 46-19-303240, FAX 46-19-331217, biblioteket@ub.oru.se. Ed. Joanna Jansdotter.

320 MEX ISSN 1870-3569
JZ9
CONFINES DE RELACIONS INTERNACIONALES Y CIENCIA POLITICA. Text in Spanish. 2005. s-a. USD 14 domestic; USD 25 in United States; USD 31 elsewhere (effective 2007). back issues avail. **Document type:** *Journal, Academic/Scholarly.*
Related titles: Online - full text ed.: free (effective 2011).
Indexed: A01, C01, CA, F03, F04, P42, PSA, S02, S03, SSAI, SSAb, SSI, SociolAb, T02, W03, W05.
—IE.
Published by: Instituto Tecnologico y de Estudios Superiores de Monterrey, Departamento de Relaciones Internacionales y Ciencia Politica, Ave Eugenio Garza Sada, 2501, Monterrey, Nuevo Leon, 64849, Mexico. confinex.mty@itesm.mx. Ed. Ignacio Irazuzta.

320 ARG
CONFRONTACION; de ideas para una nueva sociedad. Text in Spanish. 1986. q.
Address: Belgrano 1787, Piso 2, Buenos Aires, 1093, Argentina. TEL 54-114-454756. Ed. Julian Lemoine.

320.94 FRA ISSN 1955-7337
CONFRONTATIONS EUROPE. LA REVUE. Text in French. 2007. q. EUR 28 (effective 2009). back issues avail. **Document type:** *Journal.*
Published by: Confrontations Europe, 227 Bd Saint-Germain, Paris, 75007, France. TEL 33-1-43173283, FAX 33-1-45561886.

320 ITA ISSN 0391-2396
CONFRONTO; rivista di opinione politica, economica e sociale. Text in Italian. 1976. s-a. **Document type:** *Magazine, Consumer.*
Published by: Associazione Confronto, Scali d'Azeglio 20, Leghorn, 57123, Italy. TEL 39-0586-897088, FAX 39-0586-200530.

CONG BAO/OFFICIAL GAZETTE. *see* PUBLIC ADMINISTRATION

320.9 COD
DT1
CONGO-AFRIQUE; economie, culture, vie sociale. Text in French. 1961. m. XAF 5,000, USD 60. adv. bk.rev. bibl. Index. **Document type:** *Journal, Academic/Scholarly.*
Former titles: Zaire-Afrique (0251-298X); (until 1971): Congo-Afrique (0010-5767)
Indexed: ASD, BibLing, CCA, CERDIC, HistAb, IBR, IBZ, P30.
Published by: Centre d'Etudes pour l'Action Sociale, 9 av. Pere Boka, BP 3375, Kinshasa-Gombe, Congo, Dem. Republic. Eds. Francis Kikassa Mwanalessa, Rene Beeckmans. Adv. contact Francis Kikassa Mwanalessa. Circ: 4,500.

CONGRESS. *see* PUBLIC ADMINISTRATION

328 USA ISSN 1047-1324
KF49
CONGRESS AND THE NATION. Text in English. 1965. every 4 yrs. USD 300 per issue (effective 2008). back issues avail.; reprints avail. **Description:** Covers summary of Reagan's first term and important congressional decisions between 1981 and 1984. Description of legislative issues summarize key activities for each year.
Related titles: Online - full text ed.
Published by: C Q Press, Inc. (Subsidiary of: Sage Publications, Inc.), 2300 N St, NW, Ste 800, Washington, DC 20037. TEL 202-729-1900, 866-427-7737, FAX 800-380-3810, customerservice@cqpress.com.

328.73 973 320 USA ISSN 0734-3469
JK1041
➤ **CONGRESS & THE PRESIDENCY**; a journal of capital studies. Text in English. 1972. 3/yr. GBP 108 combined subscription in United Kingdom to institutions (print & online eds.); EUR 156, USD 196 combined subscription to institutions (print & online eds.) (effective 2012). adv. bk.rev. abstr.; bibl.; illus. back issues avail.; reprint service avail. from PSC. **Document type:** *Journal, Academic/Scholarly.* **Description:** Covers political science and history featuring articles on Congress, the President, the interaction between the two institutions, and national policy-making.
Former titles (until 1982): Congressional Studies (0194-4053); (until 1979): Capitol Studies (0045-5687)
Related titles: Online - full text ed.: ISSN 1944-1053. GBP 98 in United Kingdom to institutions; EUR 140, USD 176 to institutions (effective 2012).
Indexed: A01, A02, A03, A08, A20, A22, A25, A26, ABCPolSci, AIAP, AmH&L, C12, CA, CMM, E08, G08, I02, I05, I13, M01, M02, MASUSE, P02, P06, P10, P34, P42, P45, P47, P48, P53, P54, PAIS, PCI, PQC, R02, RASB, S08, S09, S11, T02, W04.
—BLDSC (3415.828000), IE, Infotrieve, Ingenta. **CCC.**
Published by: (American University, Center for Congressional and Presidential Studies), Routledge (Subsidiary of: Taylor & Francis Group), 270 Madison Ave, New York, NY 10016. TEL 212-216-7800, FAX 212-244-1563, orders@taylorandfrancis.com, http://www.routledge.com. Eds. Brian F Schaffner, Charles E Walcott. Adv. contact Linda Hann TEL 44-1344-779945. **Subscr. to:** Congress & the Presidency.

P

328 USA ISSN 0010-5899
JK1
CONGRESSIONAL DIGEST; a pro & con monthly. Text in English. 1921. m. (except June/July & Aug./Sep.). USD 84; USD 12 newsstand/cover (effective 2011). illus. index, cum.index: 1921-2000. 32 p./no. 2 cols./p.; reprints avail. **Document type:** *Journal, Academic/Scholarly.* **Description:** Features the major issues and controversies in the Congress, pro and con.
Formerly (until 1922): The Capitol Eye
Related titles: Microform ed.; Online - full text ed.: ISSN 1944-7566.
Indexed: A01, A02, A03, A08, A22, A23, A24, A25, A26, AMHA, ARG, Acal, B04, B07, B13, BRD, C12, CA, E08, EnerRev, G05, G06, G07, G08, H05, H09, I02, I05, I07, M01, M02, M05, M06, MASUSE, MEA&I, MagInd, P02, P05, P06, P10, P13, P27, P34, P47, P48, P53, P54, PAIS, PMR, PQC, PRA, PSI, R02, R03, R04, R06, RASB, RGAb, RGPR, S02, S03, S05, S08, S09, S11, SCOPUS, SSAI, SSAb, SSI, T02, TOM, W01, W02, W03.
—BLDSC (3415.950000), IE, Infotrieve, Ingenta.
Published by: Congressional Digest Corp., PO Box 240, Boyds, MD 20841-0240. TEL 301-916-1800, 800-637-9915, FAX 240-599-7679, info@congressionaldigest.com, http://www.pro-and-con.org. Ed. Sarah Orrick. Pub. Page Robinson Thomas.

320 USA
CONGRESSIONAL NEWS BRIEFING. Text in English. d. 30 p./no.; **Document type:** *Newsletter, Trade.* **Description:** Provides information on national and local news media's coverage of Congress and its members.
Media: Online - full content.
Published by: Bulletin News Network, Inc., 7915 Jones Branch, Ste 6200, McLean, VA 22102. TEL 703-749-0040, FAX 703-749-0060, frontdesk@bulletinnews.com.

328 USA ISSN 0363-7239
KF35 CODEN: CGLRB3
CONGRESSIONAL RECORD; proceedings and debates of the Congress. Text in English. 1774. d. USD 503 domestic; USD 704.20 foreign (effective 2010). illus. Index. back issues avail.; reprints avail. **Document type:** *Proceedings, Government.* **Description:** Covers the proceedings and debates of the United States Congress.
Former titles (until 1873): Congressional Globe; (until 1833): Register of Debates in Congress; (until 1824): United States. Congress. Debates and Proceedings; (until 1789): United States. Continental Congress. Journal
Related titles: CD-ROM ed.: ISSN 1068-5448. 1873; Online - full text ed.: 1873; Special ed(s).: U.S. Congressional Record (Permanent Edition). ISSN 0883-1947. 1873.
Indexed: L09, P06, P30, RASB.
—CASDDS.
Published by: (U.S. Congress), U.S. Government Printing Office, 732 N Capitol St, NW, Washington, DC 20401. TEL 866-512-1800, FAX 202-512-2104. **Subscr. to:** U.S. Government Printing Office, Superintendent of Documents, PO Box 371954, Pittsburgh, PA 15250. TEL 202-512-1800, FAX 202-512-2250, orders@gpo.gov, http://www.access.gpo.gov, http://www.gpoaccess.gov.

328.73 USA
CONGRESSIONAL RESEARCH SERVICE. SELECTED REPORTS. Text in English. irreg. free. **Document type:** *Government.*
Media: Online - full text.
Published by: U.S. Senate, Congressional Research Service, The Library of Congress, 101 Independence Ave, S E, Washington, DC 20540-7500. TEL 202-224-3121.

320 USA ISSN 0191-1473
JK1
CONGRESSIONAL ROLL CALL (YEAR); a chronology and analysis of votes in the House and Senate. Text in English. 1972. a. USD 45 per issue (effective 2008). charts. 348 p./no.; back issues avail.; reprints avail. **Description:** Provides an objective member-by-member survey and analysis of every roll call vote taken in the house and senate during 2007 with summaries of the bills.
Related titles: Online - full text ed.
Published by: C Q Press, Inc. (Subsidiary of: Sage Publications, Inc.), 2300 N St, NW, Ste 800, Washington, DC 20037. TEL 202-729-1900, FAX 800-380-3810, customerservice@cqpress.com.

328.73 USA ISSN 0589-3178
JK1012
CONGRESSIONAL STAFF DIRECTORY. Text in English. 1959. 3/yr. USD 473 (effective 2009). index. back issues avail. **Document type:** *Directory, Trade.* **Description:** Guides to locate key decision-makers and support staff that work behind the scenes on important legislative issues.
Related titles: CD-ROM ed.; Online - full text ed.
Published by: C Q Press, Inc. (Subsidiary of: Sage Publications, Inc.), 2300 N St, NW, Ste 800, Washington, DC 20037. TEL 202-729-1900, 866-427-7737, FAX 800-380-3810, customerservice@cqpress.com, http://www.cqpress.com. Ed. Joel Treese.

320 USA
➤ **CONGRESSIONAL STUDIES SERIES.** Text in English. 1998. irreg., latest vol.6, 2008. price varies. back issues avail. **Document type:** *Monographic series, Academic/Scholarly.* **Description:** Examine any aspect of Congress, such as influential acts and legislation, lobbying and constituency issues.
Published by: University of Oklahoma Press, 2800 Venture Dr, Norman, OK 73069. TEL 405-325-2000, 800-627-7377, FAX 405-364-5798, 800-735-0476, presscs@ou.edu.

320 USA
CONNECTIONS (DAYTON). Text in English. 1961. a. free (effective 2010). 35 p./no.; back issues avail. **Document type:** *Newsletter, Trade.*
Former titles: Kettering Report (0743-8478); (until 1982): Charles F. Kettering Foundation. Annual Report (0069-2735); (until 1970): Charles F. Kettering Foundation. Report
Related titles: Online - full text ed.: free (effective 2010).
Published by: Charles F. Kettering Foundation, 200 Commons Rd, Dayton, OH 45459. TEL 937-434-7300, 800-221-3657. Ed. Randall Nielsen.

320 CAN ISSN 0845-874X
CONNEXIONS DIGEST; a social change sourcebook. Text in English. 1976. q. CAD 15.50 (effective 1999). adv. bk.rev. abstr.; bibl.; illus. index. back issues avail. **Document type:** *Handbook/Manual/Guide, Trade.* **Description:** Acts as a networking medium, improving the exchange of ideas, strategies and resources among grass roots groups in Canada.
Formerly (until 1989): Connexions (0708-9422)
Indexed: HRIR.
Published by: Connexions Information Sharing Services, P O Box 158, Sta D, Toronto, ON M6P 3J8, Canada. TEL 416-537-3949. Ed. Ulli Diemer. Circ: 1,200.

322.4 HND
CONSEJO CENTRAL EJECUTIVO DEL PARTIDO LIBERAL DE HONDURAS. MEMORIA. Text in Spanish. irreg.
Published by: Partido Liberal, Consejo Central Ejecutivo, Tegucigalpa DC, Honduras.

320.52 USA ISSN 0888-7403
CONSERVATIVE CHRONICLE. Text in English. 1975. w. USD 45; USD 80 foreign (effective 1999). adv. **Document type:** *Newspaper.* **Description:** Reprints syndicated columns.
Formerly (until 1986): Hampton's Weekly Conservative Chronicle (0888-1359)
Published by: Hampton Publishing Company, PO Box 29, Hampton, IA 50441-0029. TEL 515-456-2585, FAX 515-456-2587. Ed., Pub., R&P, Adv. contact Joseph P Roth. Circ: 28,601 (paid). **Subscr. to:** PO Box 11297, Des Moines, IA 50309.

320.52 USA
THE CONSERVATIVE VOICE. Text in English. d. **Document type:** *Newsletter, Consumer.*
Media: Online - full text.
Published by: The Conservative Voice newsletter@theconservativevoice.com.

329.18 NLD ISSN 1874-0529
CONSORTIUM DE LEVENSBOOM. Text in Multiple languages. 200?. bi-m.
Address: Postbus 122, Arnhem, 6800 AC, Netherlands. tonningen@telenet.be.

320 USA ISSN 0270-532X
THE CONSTANTIAN. Text in English. 1970. 4/yr. USD 12 to non-members; USD 15 foreign to non-members (effective 1999). adv. bk.rev. charts; illus.; stat. **Document type:** *Newsletter.* **Description:** Features articles and essays on current and historical topics regarding royalty and monarchy throughout the world, biographical sketches, analysis, genealogical information, and reports on current developments and trends.
Published by: Constantian Society, PO Box 534, Shrewsbury, MA 01545. monarchy@put.com. Ed. Louis Epstein. Circ: 550.

321.8 GBR ISSN 1351-0487
H1 CODEN: CNSTES
➤ **CONSTELLATIONS**; an international journal of critical and democratic theory. Text in English. 1965. q. GBP 555 in United Kingdom to institutions; EUR 705 in Europe to institutions; USD 1,060 in the Americas to institutions; USD 1,339 elsewhere to institutions; GBP 639 combined subscription in United Kingdom to institutions (print & online eds.); EUR 811 combined subscription in Europe to institutions (print & online eds.); USD 1,219 combined subscription in the Americas to institutions (print & online eds.); USD 1,541 combined subscription elsewhere to institutions (print & online eds.) (effective 2012). adv. bk.rev. illus. back issues avail.; reprint service avail. from PSC. **Document type:** *Journal, Academic/Scholarly.* **Description:** Aims to publish the best of contemporary critical and democratic theory.
Former titles (until 1994): Praxis International (0260-8448); (until 1981): Praxis
Related titles: Microfilm ed.: (from PQC); Online - full text ed.: ISSN 1467-8675. GBP 555 in United Kingdom to institutions; EUR 705 in Europe to institutions; USD 1,060 in the Americas to institutions; USD 1,339 elsewhere to institutions (effective 2012) (from IngentaConnect).
Indexed: A01, A03, A08, A22, A26, AltPI, CA, E01, FR, IPB, LeftInd, MLA-IB, P02, P10, P30, P34, P42, P48, P53, P54, PCI, PQC, PSA, PhilInd, RASB, S02, S03, S10, SCOPUS, SOPODA, SSA, SociolAb, T02.
—BLDSC (3420.346000), IE, Infotrieve, Ingenta, INIST. **CCC.**
Published by: Wiley-Blackwell Publishing Ltd. (Subsidiary of: John Wiley & Sons, Inc.), 9600 Garsington Rd, Oxford, OX4 2DQ, United Kingdom. TEL 44-1865-776868, FAX 44-1865-714591, customerservices@blackwellpublishing.com, http://www.wiley.com/WileyCDA/. Eds. Andrew Arato TEL 212-229-8920, Nadia Urbinati TEL 212-854-3977. Adv. contact Craig Pickett TEL 44-1865-476267.

➤ **CONSTITUTIONAL POLITICAL ECONOMY.** *see* LAW—Constitutional Law

321.8 USA ISSN 1933-9402
CONSTITUTIONALISM AND DEMOCRACY. Text in English. 1993. irreg., latest 2010. price varies. **Document type:** *Monographic series, Academic/Scholarly.* **Description:** Focuses on constitutional politics, legal culture, and the historical relationship between democratic government and the social and economic forces that shape it.
Published by: University of Virginia Press, PO Box 400318, Charlottesville, VA 22904. TEL 800-831-3406, FAX 877-288-6400, upressva@virginia.edu. Eds. Gregg Ivers, Kevin T McGuire.

320 FRA ISSN 1775-7290
CONSTRUIRE LES ALTERNATIVES. Text in French. 2005. irreg. back issues avail. **Document type:** *Monographic series, Consumer.*
Published by: Editions Syllepse, 69 rue des Rigoles, Paris, 75020, France. TEL 33-1-44620889.

CONTEMPORARY BRITISH HISTORY. *see* HISTORY—History Of Europe

CONTEMPORARY ISSUES IN ASIA AND THE PACIFIC. *see* ASIAN STUDIES

320.956 JPN ISSN 0912-8107
➤ **THE CONTEMPORARY MIDDLE EAST/GENDAI NO CHUTO.** Text in Japanese. 1986. 2/yr. JPY 3,030 (effective 2003). bk.rev. bibl. **Document type:** *Academic/Scholarly.* **Description:** Includes papers, field reports, and book information with a regional focus on the Middle East.
Published by: Institute of Developing Economies/Ajia Keizai Kenkyusho, 3-2-2 Wakaba, Mihana-ku, Chiba-shi, Chiba 261-8545, Japan. TEL 81-43-2999536, FAX 84-43-2999724. Circ: 200.

172.2 GBR ISSN 1470-8914
JA1
➤ **CONTEMPORARY POLITICAL THEORY.** Abbreviated title: C P T. Text in English. 2002 (Mar.). q. USD 970 in North America to institutions; GBP 522 elsewhere to institutions (effective 2012). adv. bk.rev. abstr. back issues avail.; reprint service avail. from PSC. **Document type:** *Journal, Academic/Scholarly.* **Description:** Aims to publish contributions to contemporary theory encompassing a wide range of approaches, all international in scope.
Related titles: Online - full text ed.: ISSN 1476-9336 (from IngentaConnect).
Indexed: A12, A13, A20, A22, ABIn, CA, CurCont, E01, G09, IBSS, P02, P10, P27, P42, P45, P48, P51, P53, P54, PAIS, PQC, PSA, PhilInd, S02, S03, S11, SCOPUS, SSCI, SociolAb, T02, W07.
—BLDSC (3425.208400), IE, Ingenta. **CCC.**
Published by: Palgrave Macmillan Ltd. (Subsidiary of: Macmillan Publishers Ltd.), Houndmills, Basingstoke, Hants RG21 6XS, United Kingdom. TEL 44-1256-329242, FAX 44-1256-479476, orders@palgrave.com, http://www.palgrave.com. Eds. Samuel A Chambers, Terrell Carver. **Subscr. to:** Subscription Department, Brunel Rd, Houndmills, Basingstoke, Hants RG21 2XS, United Kingdom. TEL 44-1256-357893, FAX 44-1256-812358, subscriptions@palgrave.com.

320 GBR ISSN 1356-9775
JA8
➤ **CONTEMPORARY POLITICS.** Text in English. 1995. q. GBP 467 combined subscription in United Kingdom to institutions (print & online eds.); EUR 617, USD 777 combined subscription to institutions (print & online eds.) (effective 2012). adv. back issues avail.; reprint service avail. from PSC. **Document type:** *Journal, Academic/Scholarly.* **Description:** Publishes analysis and articulation of contemporary issues, controversies and theoretical debates relating to politics defined broadly—including social, economic, developmental, environmental and gender issues.
Related titles: Online - full text ed.: ISSN 1469-3631. GBP 420 in United Kingdom to institutions; EUR 555, USD 699 to institutions (effective 2012) (from IngentaConnect).
Indexed: A01, A03, A08, A22, B21, CA, DIP, E01, E17, ESPM, I13, IBR, IBSS, IBZ, P34, P42, PSA, RiskAb, S02, S03, SCOPUS, SSA, SociolAb, T02.
—IE, Infotrieve, Ingenta. **CCC.**
Published by: Routledge (Subsidiary of: Taylor & Francis Group), 4 Park Sq, Milton Park, Abingdon, Oxon OX14 4RN, United Kingdom. TEL 44-20-70176000, FAX 44-20-70176336, subscriptions@tandf.co.uk, http://www.routledge.com. Eds. David Evans, Paul Crawshaw. Adv. contact Linda Hann TEL 44-1344-779945. **Subscr. to:** Taylor & Francis Ltd., Journals Customer Service, Sheepen Pl, Colchester, Essex CO3 3LP, United Kingdom. TEL 44-20-70175544, FAX 44-20-70175198.

320 GBR ISSN 0958-4935
DS331
➤ **CONTEMPORARY SOUTH ASIA.** Text in English. 1992. q. GBP 820 combined subscription in United Kingdom to institutions (print & online eds.); EUR 1,108, USD 1,392 combined subscription to institutions (print & online eds.) (effective 2012). adv. back issues avail.; reprint service avail. from PSC. **Document type:** *Journal, Academic/Scholarly.* **Description:** Presents research and analysis of contemporary policy issues, as well as historical articles on southeastern Asia.
Related titles: Microfiche ed.; Online - full text ed.: ISSN 1469-364X. GBP 738 in United Kingdom to institutions; EUR 997, USD 1,252 to institutions (effective 2012) (from IngentaConnect).
Indexed: A01, A02, A03, A08, A22, B21, BAS, C12, CA, DIP, E01, E17, ESPM, GEOBASE, HistAb, I08, I13, I14, IBR, IBSS, IBZ, M02, M10, P02, P10, P34, P42, P45, P48, P53, P54, PAIS, PQC, PSA, PerIslam, RASB, RiskAb, S02, S03, SCOPUS, SSciA, SociolAb, T02, WBA, WMB.
—BLDSC (3425.305300), IE, Infotrieve, Ingenta. **CCC.**
Published by: Routledge (Subsidiary of: Taylor & Francis Group), 4 Park Sq, Milton Park, Abingdon, Oxon OX14 4RN, United Kingdom. TEL 44-20-70176000, FAX 44-20-70176336, subscriptions@tandf.co.uk, http://www.routledge.com. Ed. John Zavos. Adv. contact Linda Hann TEL 44-1344-779945. **Subscr. in N. America to:** Taylor & Francis Inc., Customer Services Dept, 325 Chestnut St, 8th Fl, Philadelphia, PA 19106. TEL 215-625-8900, 800-354-1420, FAX 215-625-2940, customerservice@taylorandfrancis.com; **Subscr. to:** Taylor & Francis Ltd., Journals Customer Service, Sheepen Pl, Colchester, Essex CO3 3LP, United Kingdom. TEL 44-20-70175544, FAX 44-20-70175198.

320 SGP ISSN 0129-797X
DS520
➤ **CONTEMPORARY SOUTHEAST ASIA**; a journal of international and strategic affairs. Text in English. 1979. 3/yr. (Apr., Aug. & Dec.). SGD 76 to individuals in Singapore, Malaysia & Brunei; USD 49 to individuals in Asia, Japan, Australia & New Zealand; USD 59 elsewhere to individuals; SGD 119 to institutions in Singapore, Malaysia & Brunei; USD 77 to institutions in Asia, Japan, Australia & New Zealand; USD 94 elsewhere to institutions (effective 2011). adv. bk.rev. bibl.; illus. cum.index. 200 p./no.; back issues avail.; reprint service avail. from SCH. **Document type:** *Journal, Academic/Scholarly.* **Description:** Specializes in the politics, international relations, and security-related issues of Southeast Asia and its wider geostrategic environment.
Related titles: Microform ed.: (from PQC); Online - full text ed.
Indexed: A01, A02, A03, A08, A11, A22, A25, A26, APEL, AmH&L, BAS, CA, DIP, E01, E08, EI, ESPM, G05, G06, G07, G08, HistAb, I02, I05, I07, I08, I13, IBR, IBSS, IBZ, M05, M06, MEA&I, P02, P10, P14, P27, P30, P34, P42, P45, P47, P48, P51, P53, P54, PAIS, PCI, PQC, PRA, PSA, PerIslam, RASB, RiskAb, S02, S03, S08, S09, S23, SPAA, SSA, SociolAb, T02, WBA, WMB.
—BLDSC (3425.305500), IE, Infotrieve, Ingenta.
Published by: Institute of Southeast Asian Studies, 30 Heng Mui Keng Terrace, Pasir Panjang, Singapore, 119614, Singapore. FAX 65-67756259, pubsunit@iseas.edu.sg, http://www.iseas.edu.sg/. Ed. Ian Storey.

➤ **CONTENTION.** *see* HANDICAPPED—Visually Impaired

320 NLD ISSN 1878-8378
CONTEXT. Text in Dutch. 4/yr. free (effective 2008). **Document type:** *Magazine, Consumer.*
Published by: BMC, Postbus 490, Amersfoort, 3800 AL, Netherlands. TEL 31-33-4965200, bmc@bmc.nl.

320 USA
CONTINUING INQUIRY. Text in English. 1976. m. USD 24. bk.rev.
Published by: Penn Jones Publications, Inc., Rt. 6, Box 356, Watahachie, TX 75165. Ed. Penn Jones. Circ: 300.

321.8 SWE ISSN 0347-6472
CONTRA; oberoende borgerlig tidskrift. Text in Swedish. 1975. bi-m. SEK 145 (effective 2004). adv. bk.rev. **Document type:** *Magazine.* **Description:** Devoted to freedom and human rights, free market economy and Western democratic ideals.
Formerly (until 1975, vol.4): Progressiv Information
Related titles: Online - full text ed.: ISSN 1402-4330. 1996.
Published by: Stiftelsen Contra, PO Box 8052, Stockholm, 10420, Sweden. TEL 46-8-7200145, FAX 46-8-7200195, redax@contra.nu, http://www/contra.nu. Ed. Tommy Hansson. Pub., R&P Carl G. Holm. Circ: 2,500.

320.5322 ITA ISSN 1126-716X
LA CONTRADDIZIONE; bimestrale di marxismo. Text in Italian. 1987. bi-m. bk.rev. cum.index. back issues avail. **Document type:** *Magazine, Consumer.* **Description:** Forum on Marxism that looks at theoretical problems in the structure of economics, society and history, from an analytical rather than an ideological point of view.
Related titles: Diskette ed.
Published by: Contaddizione, Casella Postale 11-188, Montesacro (Rome), 00141, Italy. TEL 39-06-87190070. Circ: 550.

320 BEL ISSN 0770-8521
CONTRADICTIONS. Text in French. 1972. q.
Indexed: CJA, IBSS, P30, P34, PAIS, S02, S03, SociolAb, T02.
Published by: A.S.B.L. Contradictions, 6 rue Warichet, Walhain, B-1457, Belgium. Ed. Baudouin Piret.

320.972 USA
THE CONTRERAS REPORT. Text in English. w. free. **Document type:** *Newsletter.* **Description:** Presents articles on NAFTA, Mexican politics and government, and the role and place of Hispanics in America and how they view the issues of the day.
Media: E-mail.
Published by: Contreras Report sdraoul@aol.com, http://impian.dokkyomed.ac.jp/ml-open/new-list/1997-a/077. Ed. Raoul Lowery Contreras.

CONTRIBUTIONS TO POLITICAL ECONOMY. *see* BUSINESS AND ECONOMICS—Economic Situation And Conditions

CONTRIBUTIONS TO THE HISTORY OF CONCEPTS. *see* HISTORY

320 COL ISSN 0120-4165
F2279
CONTROVERSIA. Text in Spanish. 1972. irreg. COP 35,000 (effective 2002). stat. **Document type:** *Academic/Scholarly.*
Formerly (until 1975): Anali C I A S
Related titles: Microfiche ed.
Published by: Centro de Investigacion y Educacion Popular (Cinep), Carrera 5 No.33A-08, Bogota, Colombia. TEL 57-1-2858977, info@cinep.org.co, http://www.cinep.org.co. Ed. Alejandro Angulo. Circ: 2,000.

CONTROVERSIA. *see* EDUCATION—Teaching Methods And Curriculum

320.6 USA
HD9502.A2M348
CONTROVERSIAL ISSUES IN PUBLIC POLICY SERIES. Text in English. irreg., latest 1992. price varies. **Document type:** *Monographic series, Academic/Scholarly.*
Published by: Sage Publications, Inc., Books (Subsidiary of: Sage Publications, Inc.), 2455 Teller Rd, Thousand Oaks, CA 91320. TEL 805-499-0721, 800-818-7243, FAX 805-499-0871, journals@sagepub.com. Eds. Dennis Palumbo, Rita Mae Kelly.

CONVERGENCIA; revista de ciencias sociales. *see* PUBLIC ADMINISTRATION

320 USA
COOK POLITICAL REPORT (ONLINE EDITION). Text in English. 1984. m. USD 295 (effective 2005). **Document type:** *Newsletter, Consumer.* **Description:** Presents a non-partisan analysis of congressional, gubernatorial and presidential elections as well as political trends.
Former titles (until 2004): Cook Political Report (Print Edition); National Political Review
Media: Online - full content.
Published by: Cook Political Report, The Watergate, 600 New Hampshire Ave, NW, Washington, DC 20037. TEL 202-739-8525. Ed. Charles E Cook Jr. Circ: 800.

327.17 FRA ISSN 1629-7830
COOPERATION INTERNATIONALE. Text in French. 2001. irreg. **Document type:** *Monographic series.*
Published by: Editions Karthala, 22-24 Boulevard Arago, Paris, 75013, France. TEL 33-1-43311559, FAX 33-1-45352705, karthala@orange.fr, http://www.karthala.com.

CORNELL JOURNAL OF LAW AND PUBLIC POLICY. *see* LAW

321.8 GBR
CORNER HOUSE. BRIEFING PAPERS. Text in English. 1997. irreg., latest vol.40, 2009. free (effective 2009). bk.rev. **Document type:** *Monographic series, Trade.* **Description:** Covers a range of social and environmental justice issues.
Media: Online - full text. **Related titles:** E-mail ed.: free; Print ed.
Published by: Corner House, Station Rd, Sturminster Newton, Dorset DT10 1YJ, United Kingdom. TEL 44-1258-473795, FAX 44-1258-473748, enquiries@thecornerhouse.org.uk.

CORPORATE KENYA. *see* BUSINESS AND ECONOMICS—Economic Situation And Conditions

CORPORATE NIGERIA. *see* BUSINESS AND ECONOMICS—Economic Situation And Conditions

321.94 USA
CORPORATE STATEMENT; the organ of the United Fascist Union. Text in English. 1994. q. looseleaf. free to members; USD 120 (effective 2001). adv. bk.rev.; tel.rev.; video rev. bibl. **Document type:** *Newsletter.* **Description:** Covers fascist propaganda, new age occultism, ancient civilizations, and economics.
Related titles: Online - full text ed.
Published by: United Fascist Union, PO Box 26020, Wilmington, DE 19899-6020. TEL 410-620-9717. Ed. Daniel Riccico. Pub., R&P Jack Grimes. Adv. contact Sally Parker. Circ: 666.

CORPORATE TANZANIA. *see* BUSINESS AND ECONOMICS—Economic Situation And Conditions

CORPORATE U A E. (United Arab Emirates) *see* BUSINESS AND ECONOMICS—Economic Situation And Conditions

322.44 GBR ISSN 1470-5842
CORPORATE WATCH. Variant title: Corporate Watch Newsletter. Text in English. 1996. bi-m. GBP 8 domestic to individuals; GBP 12 foreign to individuals; GBP 25 to non-profit organizations; GBP 5,000 to corporations; GBP 1 per issue (effective 2009). bk.rev. bibl.; illus.; maps. 8 p./no. 3 cols./p.; back issues avail. **Document type:** *Newsletter, Trade.* **Description:** Aims to expose the mechanisms by which corporations function and the detrimental effects they have on society and the environment as an inevitable result of their current legal structure.
Related titles: Online - full text ed.: free (effective 2009).
Indexed: LeftInd.
Address: c/o Freedom Press, Angel Alley, 84b Whitechapel High St, London, E1 7QX, United Kingdom. TEL 44-207-4260005, contact@corporatewatch.org. **Subscr. to:** Office 14, Unit 6, Wilmer Industrial Estate, Wilmer Pl, London N16 0LW, United Kingdom.

COUNTERPUNCH; tells the facts, names the names. *see* JOURNALISM

320 USA ISSN 0196-2809
G1
COUNTRIES OF THE WORLD AND THEIR LEADERS YEARBOOK. Text in English. 1980. a. USD 367 (effective 2009). illus.; maps; stat. Supplement avail.; back issues avail. **Document type:** *Directory, Trade.* **Description:** Provides an annual reference on countries worldwide with a guide to their leadership.
Formerly (until 1980): Countries of the World
Related titles: Online - full text ed.
Indexed: CPerI.
—BLDSC (3481.520000).
Published by: Gale (Subsidiary of: Cengage Learning), 27500 Drake Rd, Farmington Hills, MI 48331. TEL 248-699-4253, 800-877-4253, FAX 877-363-4253, gale.customerservice@cengage.com, http://gale.cengage.com. Ed. Frank E Bair.

320.967 USA
HC800.A1
COUNTRY FORECAST. AFRICA. Text in English. 1994. m. USD 1,035; USD 560 per issue (effective 2007). charts; stat. **Document type:** *Report, Trade.* **Description:** Focuses on the key factors affecting Sub-Saharan Africa's political and economic outlook and its business environment over the next five years.
Formerly: Country Forecast. Sub-Saharan Africa (1356-4013)
Related titles: Online - full text ed.: E I U Country Forecasts: Middle East-Africa.
Published by: Economist Intelligence Unit Ltd. (Subsidiary of: Economist Intelligence Unit Ltd.), 111 W 57th St, New York, NY 10019. TEL 212-554-0600, FAX 212-586-1181, newyork@eiu.com, http://www.eiu.com.

320.965 USA
COUNTRY FORECAST. ALGERIA. Text in English. 199?. m. USD 1,140 (print or online ed.); USD 605 per issue (print or online ed.) (effective 2008). charts; stat. back issues avail. **Document type:** *Report, Trade.* **Description:** Focuses on the key factors affecting Algeria's political and economic outlook and its business environment over the next five years.
Formerly (until 1992): Global Forecasting Service. Algeria (0966-8969)
Related titles: Online - full text ed.: E I U Country Forecasts: Middle East-Africa.
Published by: Economist Intelligence Unit Ltd. (Subsidiary of: Economist Intelligence Unit Ltd.), 111 W 57th St, New York, NY 10019. TEL 212-554-0600, FAX 212-586-1181, newyork@eiu.com, http://www.eiu.com.

320.982 USA
COUNTRY FORECAST. ARGENTINA. Text in English. 199?. m. USD 1,140 (print or online ed.); USD 605 per issue (print or online ed.) (effective 2008). charts; stat. back issues avail. **Document type:** *Report, Trade.* **Description:** Provides information about political, policy and economic forecast for each country.
Formerly (until 1992): Global Forecasting Service. Argentina (0966-8977)
Related titles: Online - full text ed.: ISSN 2047-4563.
Published by: Economist Intelligence Unit Ltd. (Subsidiary of: Economist Intelligence Unit Ltd.), 111 W 57th St, New York, NY 10019. TEL 212-554-0600, FAX 212-586-1181, newyork@eiu.com, http://www.eiu.com.

320 USA
COUNTRY FORECAST. ASIA. Text in English. 1977. m. USD 1,035; USD 560 per issue (effective 2007). charts; stat. back issues avail. **Document type:** *Report, Trade.* **Description:** Focuses on the key factors affecting the region's political and economic outlook and its business environment over the next five years.
Supersedes in part: Country Forecast. Asia and Australasia Regional Overview (1368-4825); Which was formerly: Business International Forecasting. Asia - Pacific; (until 1992): Global Forecasting Service. Asia - Pacific (0966-8713); Asia - Pacific Forecasting Study
Related titles: Online - full text ed.: E I U Country Forecasts: Asia-Pacific. 1994.
Published by: Economist Intelligence Unit Ltd. (Subsidiary of: Economist Intelligence Unit Ltd.), 111 W 57th St, New York, NY 10019. TEL 212-554-0600, FAX 212-586-1181, newyork@eiu.com, http://www.eiu.com.

320.994 USA
COUNTRY FORECAST. AUSTRALIA. Text in English. 199?. q. USD 1,140; USD 605 per issue (effective 2008). charts; stat. back issues avail. **Document type:** *Report, Trade.* **Description:** Focuses on the key factors affecting Australia's political and economic outlook and its business environment over the next five years.
Formerly (until 1992): Global Forecasting Service. Australia (0966-8942)
Related titles: Online - full text ed.: E I U Country Forecasts: Asia-Pacific. 1994.
Indexed: A15, ABIn, P45, P48, P51, PQC.
Published by: Economist Intelligence Unit Ltd. (Subsidiary of: Economist Intelligence Unit Ltd.), 111 W 57th St, New York, NY 10019. TEL 212-554-0600, FAX 212-586-1181, newyork@eiu.com, http://www.eiu.com.

320.9436 USA
COUNTRY FORECAST. AUSTRIA. Text in English. 199?. a. USD 1,140 (print or online ed.); USD 605 per issue (print or online ed.) (effective 2008). charts; stat. back issues avail. **Document type:** *Report, Trade.* **Description:** Focuses on the key factors affecting Austria's political and economic outlook and its business environment over the next five years.
Formerly (until 1992): Global Forecasting Service. Austria (0966-8950)
Related titles: Online - full text ed.: E I U Country Forecasts: Western Europe.
Indexed: A15, ABIn, P45, P48, P51, PQC.
Published by: Economist Intelligence Unit Ltd. (Subsidiary of: Economist Intelligence Unit Ltd.), 111 W 57th St, New York, NY 10019. TEL 212-554-0600, FAX 212-586-1181, newyork@eiu.com, http://www.eiu.com.

320.9493 USA ISSN 0966-9353
HC311
COUNTRY FORECAST. BELGIUM. Text in English. 199?. a. USD 1,140 (print or online ed.); USD 605 per issue (print or online ed.) (effective 2008). charts; stat. back issues avail. **Document type:** *Report, Trade.* **Description:** Focuses on the key factors affecting Belgium's political and economic outlook and its business environment over the next five years.
Formerly (until 1992): Global Forecasting Service. Belgium
Related titles: Online - full text ed.: E I U Country Forecasts: Western Europe.
Indexed: A15, ABIn, P45, P48, P51, PQC.
Published by: Economist Intelligence Unit Ltd. (Subsidiary of: Economist Intelligence Unit Ltd.), 111 W 57th St, New York, NY 10019. TEL 212-554-0600, FAX 212-586-1181, newyork@eiu.com, http://www.eiu.com.

320.981 USA ISSN 0966-9361
COUNTRY FORECAST. BRAZIL. Text in English. 199?. m. USD 1,140 (print or online ed.); USD 605 per issue (print or online ed.) (effective 2008). charts; stat. back issues avail. **Document type:** *Report, Trade.* **Description:** Provides information about political, policy and economic forecast for each country.
Formerly (until 1992): Global Forecasting Service. Brazil
Related titles: Online - full text ed.: ISSN 2047-4563.
Indexed: A15, ABIn, P45, P48, P51, PQC.
Published by: Economist Intelligence Unit Ltd. (Subsidiary of: Economist Intelligence Unit Ltd.), 111 W 57th St, New York, NY 10019. TEL 212-554-0600, FAX 212-586-1181, newyork@eiu.com, http://www.eiu.com.

P

320.9499 USA ISSN 0966-937X
HC403.A1
COUNTRY FORECAST. BULGARIA. Text in English. 1992. m. USD 1,140 (print or online ed.); USD 605 per issue (print or online ed.) (effective 2008). charts; stat. back issues avail. **Document type:** *Report, Trade.* **Description:** Focuses on the key factors affecting Bulgaria's political and economic outlook and its business environment over the next five years.
Formerly (until 1993): Global Forecasting Service. Bulgaria
Related titles: Online - full text ed.: E I U Country Forecasts: Eastern Europe.
Published by: Economist Intelligence Unit Ltd. (Subsidiary of: Economist Intelligence Unit Ltd.), 111 W 57th St, New York, NY 10019. TEL 212-554-0600, FAX 212-586-1181, newyork@eiu.com, http://www.eiu.com.

320.971 USA ISSN 0966-9329
HC111
COUNTRY FORECAST. CANADA. Text in English. 1990. m. USD 1,140 (print or online ed.); USD 605 per issue (print or online ed.) (effective 2008). charts; stat. back issues avail. **Document type:** *Report, Trade.* **Description:** Focuses on the key factors affecting Canada's political and economic outlook and its business environment over the next five years.
Formerly (until 199?): Global Forecasting Service. Canada
Related titles: Online - full text ed.: ISSN 2047-4563.
Indexed: A15, ABIn, P45, P48, P51, PQC.
Published by: Economist Intelligence Unit Ltd. (Subsidiary of: Economist Intelligence Unit Ltd.), 111 W 57th St, New York, NY 10019. TEL 212-554-0600, FAX 212-586-1181, newyork@eiu.com, http://www.eiu.com.

320.983 USA ISSN 0966-9310
HC191
COUNTRY FORECAST. CHILE. Text in English. 199?. m. USD 1,140 per issue (print or online ed.); USD 605 per issue (print or online ed.) (effective 2008). charts; stat. back issues avail. **Document type:** *Report, Trade.* **Description:** Provides information about political, policy and economic forecast for each country.
Formerly (until 1992): Global Forecasting Service. Chile
Related titles: Online - full text ed.: ISSN 2047-4563.
Indexed: A15, ABIn, P45, P48, P51, PQC.
Published by: Economist Intelligence Unit Ltd. (Subsidiary of: Economist Intelligence Unit Ltd.), 111 W 57th St, New York, NY 10019. TEL 212-554-0600, FAX 212-586-1181, newyork@eiu.com, http://www.eiu.com.

320.951 USA ISSN 0966-9493
HC460.5.A1
COUNTRY FORECAST. CHINA. Text in English. 1992. a. USD 1,140 (print or online ed.); USD 605 per issue (print or online ed.) (effective 2008). charts; stat. back issues avail. **Document type:** *Report, Trade.* **Description:** Focuses on the key factors affecting China's political and economic outlook and its business environment over the next five years.
Formerly (until 1993): Global Forecasting Service. China
Related titles: Online - full text ed.: E I U Country Forecasts: Asia-Pacific. 1994.
Indexed: A15, ABIn, P45, P48, P51, PQC.
—CCC.
Published by: Economist Intelligence Unit Ltd. (Subsidiary of: Economist Intelligence Unit Ltd.), 111 W 57th St, New York, NY 10019. TEL 212-554-0600, FAX 212-586-1181, newyork@eiu.com, http://www.eiu.com.

320.9861 USA ISSN 0966-9337
HC196
COUNTRY FORECAST. COLOMBIA. Text in English. 199?. m. USD 1,140 (print or online ed.); USD 605 per issue (print or online ed.) (effective 2008). charts; stat. back issues avail. **Document type:** *Report, Trade.* **Description:** Provides information about political, policy and economic forecast for each country.
Formerly (until 1992): Global Forecasting Service. Colombia
Related titles: Online - full text ed.: ISSN 2047-4563.
—CCC.
Published by: Economist Intelligence Unit Ltd. (Subsidiary of: Economist Intelligence Unit Ltd.), 111 W 57th St, New York, NY 10019. TEL 212-554-0600, FAX 212-586-1181, newyork@eiu.com, http://www.eiu.com.

320.94371 USA ISSN 1351-8712
HC270.2
COUNTRY FORECAST. CZECH REPUBLIC. Text in English. 1992. m. USD 1,140 (print or online ed.); USD 605 per issue (print or online ed.) (effective 2008). charts; stat. back issues avail. **Document type:** *Report, Trade.* **Description:** Focuses on the key factors affecting the Czech Republic's political and economic outlook and its business environment over the next five years.
Formerly (until 1993): Global Forecasting Service. Czech Republic; Which superseded in part: Global Forecasting Service. Czechoslovakia (0966-9345)
Related titles: Online - full text ed.: E I U Country Forecasts: Eastern Europe.
Published by: Economist Intelligence Unit Ltd. (Subsidiary of: Economist Intelligence Unit Ltd.), 111 W 57th St, New York, NY 10019. TEL 212-554-0600, FAX 212-586-1181, newyork@eiu.com, http://www.eiu.com.

320.9489 USA ISSN 0966-9485
HC351
COUNTRY FORECAST. DENMARK. Text in English. 199?. a. USD 1,040 (print or online ed.); USD 605 per issue (print or online ed.) (effective 2008). charts; stat. back issues avail. **Document type:** *Report, Trade.* **Description:** Focuses on the key factors affecting Denmark's political and economic outlook and its business environment over the next five years.
Formerly (until 1992): Global Forecasting Service. Denmark
Related titles: Online - full text ed.: E I U Country Forecasts: Western Europe.
Indexed: A15, ABIn, P48, P51, PQC.
Published by: Economist Intelligence Unit Ltd. (Subsidiary of: Economist Intelligence Unit Ltd.), 111 W 57th St, New York, NY 10019. TEL 212-554-0600, FAX 212-586-1181, newyork@eiu.com, http://www.eiu.com.

320.947 USA
COUNTRY FORECAST. EASTERN EUROPE. Text in English. 199?. m. USD 1,140 (print or online ed.); USD 605 per issue (print or online ed.) (effective 2008). charts; stat. back issues avail. **Document type:** *Report, Trade.* **Description:** Focuses on the key factors affecting the covered areas' political and economic outlooks and their business environments over the next five years.
Formerly: Country Forecast. Eastern Europe and the Former Soviet Union (1356-4005)
Related titles: Online - full text ed.: E I U Country Forecasts: Eastern Europe.
—CCC.
Published by: Economist Intelligence Unit Ltd. (Subsidiary of: Economist Intelligence Unit Ltd.), 111 W 57th St, New York, NY 10019. TEL 212-554-0600, FAX 212-586-1181, newyork@eiu.com, http://www.eiu.com.

320.9866 USA
COUNTRY FORECAST. ECUADOR. Text in English. 199?. m. USD 1,140 (print or online ed.); USD 605 per issue (print or online ed.) (effective 2008). charts; stat. back issues avail. **Document type:** *Report, Trade.* **Description:** Focuses on the key factors affecting Ecuador's political and economic outlook and its business environment over the next five years.
Formerly (until 1992): Global Forecasting Service. Ecuador (0966-9515)
Related titles: Online - full text ed.: ISSN 2047-4563.
Indexed: A15, ABIn, P45, P48, P51, PQC.
Published by: Economist Intelligence Unit Ltd. (Subsidiary of: Economist Intelligence Unit Ltd.), 111 W 57th St, New York, NY 10019. TEL 212-554-0600, FAX 212-586-1181, newyork@eiu.com, http://www.eiu.com.

320.962 USA
COUNTRY FORECAST. EGYPT. Text in English. 199?. m. USD 1,140 (print or online ed.); USD 605 per issue (print or online ed.) (effective 2008). back issues avail. **Document type:** *Report, Trade.* **Description:** Focuses on the key factors affecting Egypt's political and economic outlook and its business environment over the next five years.
Formerly (until 1992): Global Forecasting Service. Egypt (0966-9507)
Related titles: Online - full text ed.: E I U Country Forecasts: Middle East-Africa.
Indexed: A15, ABIn, P45, P48, P51, PQC.
Published by: Economist Intelligence Unit Ltd. (Subsidiary of: Economist Intelligence Unit Ltd.), 111 W 57th St, New York, NY 10019. TEL 212-554-0600, FAX 212-586-1181, newyork@eiu.com, http://www.eiu.com.

320.94 USA ISSN 1357-7670
COUNTRY FORECAST. EUROPE. Text in English. 199?. m. USD 1,035; USD 560 per issue (effective 2007). charts; stat. **Document type:** *Report, Trade.* **Description:** Focuses on the key factors affecting the region's political and economic outlook and its business environment over the next five years.
Formerly (until 1992): Global Forecasting Service. Europe
Related titles: CD-ROM ed.; Online - full text ed.
Indexed: A15, ABIn, P45, P48, P51, PQC.
Published by: Economist Intelligence Unit Ltd. (Subsidiary of: Economist Intelligence Unit Ltd.), 111 W 57th St, New York, NY 10019. TEL 212-554-0600, FAX 212-586-1181, newyork@eiu.com, http://www.eiu.com.

320.94897 USA
COUNTRY FORECAST. FINLAND. Text in English. 1992. m. USD 1,140 (print or online ed.); USD 605 per issue (print or online ed.) (effective 2008). charts; stat. back issues avail. **Document type:** *Report, Trade.* **Description:** Focuses on the key factors affecting Finland's political and economic outlook and its business environment over the next five years.
Formerly (until 1993): Global Forecasting Service. Finland (0966-9523)
Related titles: Online - full text ed.: E I U Country Forecasts: Western Europe.
Published by: Economist Intelligence Unit Ltd. (Subsidiary of: Economist Intelligence Unit Ltd.), 111 W 57th St, New York, NY 10019. TEL 212-554-0600, FAX 212-586-1181, newyork@eiu.com, http://www.eiu.com.

320.944 USA
COUNTRY FORECAST. FRANCE. Text in English. 1992. m. USD 1,140 (print or online ed.); USD 605 per issue (print or online ed.) (effective 2008). charts; stat. back issues avail. **Document type:** *Report, Trade.* **Description:** Focuses on the key factors affecting France's political and economic outlook and its business environment over the next five years.
Formerly (until 1993): Global Forecasting Service. France (0966-9531)
Related titles: Online - full text ed.: E I U Country Forecasts: Western Europe.
Indexed: A15, ABIn, P45, P48, P51, PQC.
—CCC.
Published by: Economist Intelligence Unit Ltd. (Subsidiary of: Economist Intelligence Unit Ltd.), 111 W 57th St, New York, NY 10019. TEL 212-554-0600, FAX 212-586-1181, newyork@eiu.com, http://www.eiu.com.

320.943 USA
HC281
COUNTRY FORECAST. GERMANY. Text in English. 1992. m. USD 1,140 (print or online ed.); USD 605 per issue (print or online ed.) (effective 2008). charts; stat. back issues avail. **Document type:** *Report, Trade.* **Description:** Focuses on the key factors affecting Germany's political and economic outlook and its business environment over the next five years.
Formerly (until 1993): Global Forecasting Service. Germany (0966-9388)
Related titles: CD-ROM ed.; Online - full text ed.
Indexed: A15, ABIn, P45, P48, P51, PQC.
—BLDSC (3481.690110).
Published by: Economist Intelligence Unit Ltd. (Subsidiary of: Economist Intelligence Unit Ltd.), 111 W 57th St, New York, NY 10019. TEL 212-554-0600, FAX 212-586-1181, newyork@eiu.com, http://www.eiu.com.

320.9 USA
HC10
COUNTRY FORECAST. GLOBAL OUTLOOK. Text in English. m. USD 1,035; USD 560 per issue (effective 2007); included with subscr. to Country Forecasts. charts; stat. **Document type:** *Report, Trade.*
Related titles: CD-ROM ed.; Online - full text ed.
Published by: Economist Intelligence Unit Ltd. (Subsidiary of: Economist Intelligence Unit Ltd.), 111 W 57th St, New York, NY 10019. TEL 212-554-0600, FAX 212-586-1181, newyork@eiu.com, http://www.eiu.com.

320.9495 USA
COUNTRY FORECAST. GREECE. Text in English. 1992. m. USD 1,140 (print or online ed.); USD 605 per issue (print or online ed.) (effective 2008). charts; stat. back issues avail. **Document type:** *Report, Trade.* **Description:** Focuses on the key factors affecting Greece's political and economic outlook and its business environment over the next five years.
Formerly (until 1993): Global Forecasting Service. Greece (0966-954X)
Related titles: Online - full text ed.: E I U Country Forecasts: Western Europe.
Indexed: A15, ABIn, P45, P48, P51, PQC.
Published by: Economist Intelligence Unit Ltd. (Subsidiary of: Economist Intelligence Unit Ltd.), 111 W 57th St, New York, NY 10019. TEL 212-554-0600, FAX 212-586-1181, newyork@eiu.com, http://www.eiu.com.

320.95125 USA ISSN 0966-8748
HC470.3.A1
COUNTRY FORECAST. HONG KONG. Text in English. 1992. a. USD 1,140 (print or online ed.); USD 605 per issue (print or online ed.) (effective 2008). charts; stat. back issues avail. **Document type:** *Report, Trade.* **Description:** Focuses on the key factors affecting Hong Kong's political and economic outlook and its business environment over the next five years.
Formerly (until 1993): Global Forecasting Service. Hong Kong
Related titles: Online - full text ed.: E I U Country Forecasts: Asia-Pacific. 1994.
Published by: Economist Intelligence Unit Ltd. (Subsidiary of: Economist Intelligence Unit Ltd.), 111 W 57th St, New York, NY 10019. TEL 212-554-0600, FAX 212-586-1181, newyork@eiu.com, http://www.eiu.com.

320.9439 USA
COUNTRY FORECAST. HUNGARY. Text in English. 1992. m. USD 1,140 (print or online ed.); USD 605 per issue (print or online ed.) (effective 2008). charts; stat. back issues avail. **Document type:** *Report, Trade.* **Description:** Focuses on the key factors affecting Hungary's political and economic outlook and its business environment over the next five years.
Formerly (until 1993): Global Forecasting Service. Hungary (0966-8810)
Related titles: Online - full text ed.: E I U Country Forecasts: Eastern Europe.
Published by: Economist Intelligence Unit Ltd. (Subsidiary of: Economist Intelligence Unit Ltd.), 111 W 57th St, New York, NY 10019. TEL 212-554-0600, FAX 212-586-1181, newyork@eiu.com, http://www.eiu.com.

320.954 USA ISSN 0966-8829
HC431
COUNTRY FORECAST. INDIA. Text in English. 1992. a. USD 1,140 (print or online ed.); USD 605 per issue (print or online ed.) (effective 2008). charts; stat. back issues avail. **Document type:** *Report, Trade.* **Description:** Focuses on the key factors affecting India's political and economic outlook and its business environment over the next five years.
Formerly (until 1993): Global Forecasting Service. India
Related titles: Online - full text ed.: E I U Country Forecasts: Asia-Pacific. 1994.
Indexed: A15, ABIn, P45, P48, P51, PQC.
Published by: Economist Intelligence Unit Ltd. (Subsidiary of: Economist Intelligence Unit Ltd.), 111 W 57th St, New York, NY 10019. TEL 212-554-0600, FAX 212-586-1181, newyork@eiu.com, http://www.eiu.com.

320.9598 USA ISSN 0966-9426
HC446
COUNTRY FORECAST. INDONESIA. Text in English. 199?. a. USD 1,140 (print or online ed.); USD 605 per issue (print or online ed.) (effective 2008). charts; stat. back issues avail. **Document type:** *Report, Trade.* **Description:** Focuses on the key factors affecting Indonesia's political and economic outlook and its business environment over the next five years.
Formerly (until 1992): Global Forecasting Service. Indonesia
Related titles: Online - full text ed.: E I U Country Forecasts: Asia-Pacific. 1994.
Indexed: A15, ABIn, P45, P48, P51, PQC.
Published by: Economist Intelligence Unit Ltd. (Subsidiary of: Economist Intelligence Unit Ltd.), 111 W 57th St, New York, NY 10019. TEL 212-554-0600, FAX 212-586-1181, newyork@eiu.com, http://www.eiu.com.

320.955 USA
COUNTRY FORECAST. IRAN. Text in English. 199?. m. USD 1,140 (print or online ed.); USD 605 per issue (print or online ed.) (effective 2008). charts; stat. back issues avail. **Document type:** *Report, Trade.* **Description:** Focuses on the key factors affecting Iran's political and economic outlook and its business environment over the next five years.
Formerly (until 1992): Global Forecasting Service. Iran (0966-9566)
Related titles: Online - full text ed.: E I U Country Forecasts: Middle East-Africa.
Indexed: A15, ABIn, P48, P51, PQC.
Published by: Economist Intelligence Unit Ltd. (Subsidiary of: Economist Intelligence Unit Ltd.), 111 W 57th St, New York, NY 10019. TEL 212-554-0600, FAX 212-586-1181, newyork@eiu.com, http://www.eiu.com.

320.9567 USA
COUNTRY FORECAST. IRAQ. Text in English. 199?. m. USD 1,140 (print or online ed.); USD 605 per issue (print or online ed.) (effective 2008). charts; stat. back issues avail. **Document type:** *Report, Trade.* **Description:** Focuses on the key factors affecting Iraq's political and economic outlook and its business environment over the next five years.
Formerly (until 1992): Global Forecasting Service. Iraq (0966-9434)
Related titles: Online - full text ed.: E I U Country Forecasts: Middle East-Africa.
Published by: Economist Intelligence Unit Ltd. (Subsidiary of: Economist Intelligence Unit Ltd.), 111 W 57th St, New York, NY 10019. TEL 212-554-0600, FAX 212-586-1181, newyork@eiu.com, http://www.eiu.com.

320.9417 USA
COUNTRY FORECAST. IRELAND. Text in English. 1992. m. USD 1,140 (print or online ed.); USD 605 per issue (print or online ed.) (effective 2008). charts; stat. back issues avail. **Document type:** *Report, Trade.* **Description:** Focuses on the key factors affecting Ireland's political and economic outlook and its business environment over the next five years.
Formerly (until 1993): Global Forecasting Service. Ireland (0966-8837)
Related titles: Online - full text ed.: E I U Country Forecasts: Western Europe.
Published by: Economist Intelligence Unit Ltd. (Subsidiary of: Economist Intelligence Unit Ltd.), 111 W 57th St, New York, NY 10019. TEL 212-554-0600, FAX 212-586-1181, newyork@eiu.com, http://www.eiu.com.

320.95694 USA ISSN 1361-9047
HC415.25.A1
COUNTRY FORECAST. ISRAEL. Text in English. 1990. a. USD 1,140 (print or online ed.); USD 605 per issue (print or online ed.) (effective 2008). charts; stat. back issues avail. **Document type:** *Report, Trade.* **Description:** Focuses on the key factors affecting Israel's political and economic outlook and its business environment over the next five years.
Related titles: Online - full text ed.: E I U Country Forecasts: Middle East-Africa.
Published by: Economist Intelligence Unit Ltd. (Subsidiary of: Economist Intelligence Unit Ltd.), 111 W 57th St, New York, NY 10019. TEL 212-554-0600, FAX 212-586-1181, newyork@eiu.com, http://www.eiu.com.

320.945 USA
COUNTRY FORECAST. ITALY. Text in English. 199?. m. USD 1,140 (print or online ed.); USD 605 per issue (print or online ed.) (effective 2008). charts; stat. back issues avail. **Document type:** *Report, Trade.* **Description:** Focuses on the key factors affecting Italy's political and economic outlook and its business environment over the next five years.
Formerly (until 1992): Global Forecasting Service. Italy (0966-8845)
Related titles: Online - full text ed.: E I U Country Forecasts: Western Europe.
Indexed: A15, ABIn, P45, P48, P51, PQC.
Published by: Economist Intelligence Unit Ltd. (Subsidiary of: Economist Intelligence Unit Ltd.), 111 W 57th St, New York, NY 10019. TEL 212-554-0600, FAX 212-586-1181, newyork@eiu.com, http://www.eiu.com.

320.952 USA ISSN 0966-8853
COUNTRY FORECAST. JAPAN. Text in English. 1992. a. USD 1,140 (print or online ed.); USD 605 per issue (print or online ed.) (effective 2008). charts; stat. back issues avail. **Document type:** *Report, Trade.* **Description:** Focuses on the key factors affecting Japan's political and economic outlook and its business environment over the next five years.
Formerly (until 1993): Global Forecasting Service. Japan
Related titles: Online - full text ed.: E I U Country Forecasts: Asia-Pacific. 1994.
Published by: Economist Intelligence Unit Ltd. (Subsidiary of: Economist Intelligence Unit Ltd.), 111 W 57th St, New York, NY 10019. TEL 212-554-0600, FAX 212-586-1181, newyork@eiu.com, http://www.eiu.com.

320.98 USA ISSN 0966-9396
HC121
COUNTRY FORECAST. LATIN AMERICA. Text in English. 199?. m. USD 1,140 (print or online ed.); USD 605 per issue (print or online ed.) (effective 2008). charts; stat. back issues avail. **Document type:** *Report, Trade.* **Description:** Focuses on the key factors affecting the region's political and economic outlook and its business environment over the next five years.
Formerly (until 1992): Global Forecasting Service. Latin America
Related titles: Online - full text ed.: ISSN 2047-4563.
Published by: Economist Intelligence Unit Ltd. (Subsidiary of: Economist Intelligence Unit Ltd.), 111 W 57th St, New York, NY 10019. TEL 212-554-0600, FAX 212-586-1181, newyork@eiu.com, http://www.eiu.com.

320.9595 338 USA
COUNTRY FORECAST. MALAYSIA. Text in English. 199?. a. USD 1,140 (print or online ed.); USD 605 per issue (print or online ed.) (effective 2008). charts; stat. back issues avail. **Document type:** *Report, Trade.* **Description:** Focuses on the key factors affecting Malaysia's political and economic outlook and its business environment over the next five years.
Formerly (until 1992): Global Forecasting Service. Malaysia (0966-9442)
Related titles: Online - full text ed.: E I U Country Forecasts: Asia-Pacific. 1994.
Published by: Economist Intelligence Unit Ltd. (Subsidiary of: Economist Intelligence Unit Ltd.), 111 W 57th St, New York, NY 10019. TEL 212-554-0600, FAX 212-586-1181, newyork@eiu.com, http://www.eiu.com.

320.972 USA
COUNTRY FORECAST. MEXICO. Text in English. 199?. m. USD 1,140 (print or online ed.); USD 605 per issue (print or online ed.) (effective 2008). charts; stat. back issues avail. **Document type:** *Report, Trade.* **Description:** Focuses on the key factors affecting Mexico's political and economic outlook and its business environment over the next five years.
Formerly (until 1992): Global Forecasting Service. Mexico (0966-9469)
Related titles: Online - full text ed.: ISSN 2047-4563.
Indexed: A15, ABIn, P45, P48, P51, PQC.
Published by: Economist Intelligence Unit Ltd. (Subsidiary of: Economist Intelligence Unit Ltd.), 111 W 57th St, New York, NY 10019. TEL 212-554-0600, FAX 212-586-1181, newyork@eiu.com, http://www.eiu.com.

320 330.9 USA
COUNTRY FORECAST. MIDDLE EAST. Text in English. m. USD 1,140 (print or online ed.); USD 605 per issue (print or online ed.) (effective 2008). charts; stat. back issues avail. **Document type:** *Journal, Trade.* **Description:** Focuses on the key factors affecting the region's political and economic outlook and its business environment over the next five years.
Supersedes in part: Country Forecast. Middle East and North Africa (1351-8739); Which was formerly: Country Forecast. Middle East and Africa; (until 1992): Global Forecasting Service. Middle East and Africa
Related titles: Online - full text ed.: E I U Country Forecasts: Middle East-Africa.
—CCC.
Published by: Economist Intelligence Unit Ltd. (Subsidiary of: Economist Intelligence Unit Ltd.), 111 W 57th St, New York, NY 10019. TEL 212-554-0600, FAX 212-586-1181, newyork@eiu.com, http://www.eiu.com.

320.9492 USA
COUNTRY FORECAST. NETHERLANDS. Text in English. 1992. m. USD 1,140 (print or online ed.); USD 605 per issue (print or online ed.) (effective 2008). charts; stat. back issues avail. **Document type:** *Report, Trade.* **Description:** Focuses on the key factors affecting the Netherlands' political and economic outlook and its business environment over the next five years.
Formerly (until 1993): Global Forecasting Service. Netherlands (0966-8861)
Related titles: Online - full text ed.: E I U Country Forecasts: Western Europe.
Indexed: A15, ABIn, P45, P48, P51, PQC.
Published by: Economist Intelligence Unit Ltd. (Subsidiary of: Economist Intelligence Unit Ltd.), 111 W 57th St, New York, NY 10019. TEL 212-554-0600, FAX 212-586-1181, newyork@eiu.com, http://www.eiu.com.

320.993 338 USA ISSN 1351-8704
HC661
COUNTRY FORECAST. NEW ZEALAND. Text in English. 1993. a. USD 1,140 (print or online ed.); USD 605 per issue (print or online ed.) (effective 2008). charts; stat. back issues avail. **Document type:** *Report, Trade.* **Description:** Focuses on the key factors affecting New Zealand's political and economic outlook and its business environment over the next five years.
Formerly (until 1992): Global Forecasting Service. New Zealand
Related titles: Online - full text ed.: E I U Country Forecasts: Asia-Pacific. 1994.
Published by: Economist Intelligence Unit Ltd. (Subsidiary of: Economist Intelligence Unit Ltd.), 111 W 57th St, New York, NY 10019. TEL 212-554-0600, FAX 212-586-1181, newyork@eiu.com, http://www.eiu.com.

320.9669 USA
COUNTRY FORECAST. NIGERIA. Text in English. 199?. m. USD 1,140 (print or online ed.); USD 605 per issue (print or online ed.) (effective 2008). charts; stat. back issues avail. **Document type:** *Report, Trade.* **Description:** Focuses on the key factors affecting Nigeria's political and economic outlook and its business environment over the next five years.
Formerly (until 1992): Global Forecasting Service. Nigeria (0966-887X)
Related titles: Online - full text ed.: E I U Country Forecasts: Middle East-Africa.
Indexed: A15, ABIn, P45, P48, P51, PQC.
Published by: Economist Intelligence Unit Ltd. (Subsidiary of: Economist Intelligence Unit Ltd.), 111 W 57th St, New York, NY 10019. TEL 212-554-0600, FAX 212-586-1181, newyork@eiu.com, http://www.eiu.com.

320.9481 USA
COUNTRY FORECAST. NORWAY. Text in English. 1992. m. USD 1,140 (print or online ed.); USD 605 per issue (print or online ed.) (effective 2008). charts; stat. back issues avail. **Document type:** *Report, Trade.* **Description:** Focuses on the key factors affecting Norway's political and economic outlook and its business environment over the next five years.
Formerly (until 1993): Global Forecasting Service. Norway (0966-9450)
Related titles: Online - full text ed.: E I U Country Forecasts: Western Europe.
Indexed: A15, ABIn, P45, P48, P51, PQC.
Published by: Economist Intelligence Unit Ltd. (Subsidiary of: Economist Intelligence Unit Ltd.), 111 W 57th St, New York, NY 10019. TEL 212-554-0600, FAX 212-586-1181, newyork@eiu.com, http://www.eiu.com.

320.95491 338 USA
COUNTRY FORECAST. PAKISTAN. Text in English. 199?. a. USD 1,140 (print or online ed.); USD 605 per issue (print or online ed.) (effective 2008). charts; stat. back issues avail. **Document type:** *Report, Trade.* **Description:** Focuses on the key factors affecting Pakistan's political and economic outlook and its business environment over the next five years.
Formerly (until 1992): Global Forecasting Service. Pakistan (0966-8888)
Related titles: Online - full text ed.: E I U Country Forecasts: Asia-Pacific. 1994.
Indexed: A15, ABIn, P45, P48, P51, PQC.
Published by: Economist Intelligence Unit Ltd. (Subsidiary of: Economist Intelligence Unit Ltd.), 111 W 57th St, New York, NY 10019. TEL 212-554-0600, FAX 212-586-1181, newyork@eiu.com, http://www.eiu.com.

320.985 USA
COUNTRY FORECAST. PERU. Text in English. 199?. m. USD 1,140 (print or online ed.); USD 605 per issue (print or online ed.) (effective 2008). charts; stat. back issues avail. **Document type:** *Report, Trade.* **Description:** Focuses on the key factors affecting Peru's political and economic outlook and its business environment over the next five years.
Formerly (until 1992): Global Forecasting Service. Peru (0966-9477)
Related titles: Online - full text ed.: ISSN 2047-4563.
Indexed: A15, ABIn, P45, P48, P51, PQC.
—CCC.
Published by: Economist Intelligence Unit Ltd. (Subsidiary of: Economist Intelligence Unit Ltd.), 111 W 57th St, New York, NY 10019. TEL 212-554-0600, FAX 212-586-1181, newyork@eiu.com, http://www.eiu.com.

320.9599 USA
COUNTRY FORECAST. PHILIPPINES. Text in English. 199?. a. USD 1,140 (print or online ed.); USD 605 per issue (print or online ed.) (effective 2008). charts; stat. back issues avail. **Document type:** *Report, Trade.* **Description:** Focuses on the key factors affecting the Philippines's political and economic outlook and its business environment over the next five years.
Formerly (until 1992): Global Forecasting Service. Philippines (0966-8896)
Related titles: Online - full text ed.: E I U Country Forecasts: Asia-Pacific. 1994.
Indexed: A15, ABIn, P45, P48, P51, PQC.
Published by: Economist Intelligence Unit Ltd. (Subsidiary of: Economist Intelligence Unit Ltd.), 111 W 57th St, New York, NY 10019. TEL 212-554-0600, FAX 212-586-1181, newyork@eiu.com, http://www.eiu.com.

320.9438 USA
COUNTRY FORECAST. POLAND. Text in English. 1992. m. USD 1,140 (print or online ed.); USD 605 per issue (print or online ed.) (effective 2008). charts; stat. back issues avail. **Document type:** *Report, Trade.* **Description:** Focuses on the key factors affecting Poland's political and economic outlook and its business environment over the next five years.
Formerly (until 1993): Global Forecasting Service. Poland (0966-890X)
Related titles: Online - full text ed.: E I U Country Forecasts: Eastern Europe.
Indexed: A15, ABIn, P48, P51, PQC.
Published by: Economist Intelligence Unit Ltd. (Subsidiary of: Economist Intelligence Unit Ltd.), 111 W 57th St, New York, NY 10019. TEL 212-554-0600, FAX 212-586-1181, newyork@eiu.com, http://www.eiu.com.

320.9469 USA
COUNTRY FORECAST. PORTUGAL. Text in English. 1992. m. USD 1,140 (print or online ed.); USD 605 per issue (print or online ed.) (effective 2008). charts; stat. back issues avail. **Document type:** *Report, Trade.* **Description:** Focuses on the key factors affecting Portugal's political and economic outlook and its business environment over the next five years.
Formerly (until 1993): Global Forecasting Service. Portugal (0966-8721)
Related titles: Online - full text ed.: E I U Country Forecasts: Western Europe.
Published by: Economist Intelligence Unit Ltd. (Subsidiary of: Economist Intelligence Unit Ltd.), 111 W 57th St, New York, NY 10019. TEL 212-554-0600, FAX 212-586-1181, newyork@eiu.com, http://www.eiu.com.

320.9498 USA
COUNTRY FORECAST. ROMANIA. Text in English. 1992. m. USD 1,140 (print or online ed.); USD 605 per issue (print or online ed.) (effective 2008). charts; stat. back issues avail. **Document type:** *Report, Trade.* **Description:** Focuses on the key factors affecting Romania's political and economic outlook and its business environment over the next five years.
Formerly (until 1993): Global Forecasting Service. Romania (0966-8918)
Related titles: Online - full text ed.: E I U Country Forecasts: Eastern Europe.
Published by: Economist Intelligence Unit Ltd. (Subsidiary of: Economist Intelligence Unit Ltd.), 111 W 57th St, New York, NY 10019. TEL 212-554-0600, FAX 212-586-1181, newyork@eiu.com, http://www.eiu.com.

320.947 USA ISSN 1351-8720
HC340.12.A1
COUNTRY FORECAST. RUSSIA. Text in English. 1993. m. USD 1,140 (print or online ed.); USD 605 per issue (print or online ed.) (effective 2008). charts; stat. back issues avail. **Document type:** *Report, Trade.* **Description:** Focuses on the key factors affecting Russia's political and economic outlook and its business environment over the next five years.
Related titles: Online - full text ed.: E I U Country Forecasts: Eastern Europe.
Indexed: A15, ABIn, P45, P48, P51, PQC.
—CCC.
Published by: Economist Intelligence Unit Ltd. (Subsidiary of: Economist Intelligence Unit Ltd.), 111 W 57th St, New York, NY 10019. TEL 212-554-0600, FAX 212-586-1181, newyork@eiu.com, http://www.eiu.com.

320.9538 USA
HC415.33.A1
COUNTRY FORECAST. SAUDI ARABIA. Text in English. 199?. m. USD 1,140 (print or online ed.); USD 605 per issue (print or online ed.) (effective 2008). charts; stat. back issues avail. **Document type:** *Report, Trade.* **Description:** Focuses on the key factors affecting Saudi Arabia's political and economic outlook and its business environment over the next five years.
Formerly (until 1992): Global Forecasting Service. Saudi Arabia (0966-873X)
Related titles: Online - full text ed.: E I U Country Forecasts: Middle East-Africa.
Indexed: A15, ABIn, P45, P48, P51, PQC.
Published by: Economist Intelligence Unit Ltd. (Subsidiary of: Economist Intelligence Unit Ltd.), 111 W 57th St, New York, NY 10019. TEL 212-554-0600, FAX 212-586-1181, newyork@eiu.com, http://www.eiu.com.

320.95957 USA
COUNTRY FORECAST. SINGAPORE. Text in English. 199?. a. USD 1,140 (print or online ed.); USD 605 per issue (print or online ed.) (effective 2008). charts; stat. back issues avail. **Document type:** *Report, Trade.* **Description:** Focuses on the key factors affecting Singapore's political and economic outlook and its business environment over the next five years.
Formerly (until 1992): Global Forecasting Service. Singapore (0966-8926)
Related titles: Online - full text ed.: E I U Country Forecasts: Asia-Pacific. 1994.
Published by: Economist Intelligence Unit Ltd. (Subsidiary of: Economist Intelligence Unit Ltd.), 111 W 57th St, New York, NY 10019. TEL 212-554-0600, FAX 212-586-1181, newyork@eiu.com, http://www.eiu.com.

P

320.94373 USA ISSN 1359-8201
HC270.3.A1
COUNTRY FORECAST. SLOVAKIA. Key Title: Slovakia (Economist Intelligence Unit). Text in English. 1995. a. USD 1,140 (print or online ed.); USD 605 per issue (print or online ed.) (effective 2008). charts; stat. back issues avail. **Document type:** *Report, Trade.* **Description:** Focuses on the key factors affecting Slovakia's political and economic outlook and its business environment over the next five years.
Supersedes in part: Global Forecasting Service. Czechoslovakia (0966-9345)
Related titles: Online - full text ed.: E I U Country Forecasts: Eastern Europe.
Published by: Economist Intelligence Unit Ltd. (Subsidiary of: Economist Intelligence Unit Ltd.), 111 W 57th St, New York, NY 10019. TEL 212-554-0600, FAX 212-586-1181, newyork@eiu.com, http://www.eiu.com.

320.968 USA
COUNTRY FORECAST. SOUTH AFRICA. Text in English. 199?. m. USD 1,140 (print or online ed.); USD 605 per issue (print or online ed.) (effective 2008). charts; stat. back issues avail. **Document type:** *Report, Trade.* **Description:** Focuses on the key factors affecting South Africa's political and economic outlook and its business environment over the next five years.
Formerly (until 1992): Global Forecasting Service. South Africa (0966-8683)
Related titles: Online - full text ed.: E I U Country Forecasts: Middle East-Africa.
Indexed: A15, ABIn, P45, P48, P51, PQC.
Published by: Economist Intelligence Unit Ltd. (Subsidiary of: Economist Intelligence Unit Ltd.), 111 W 57th St, New York, NY 10019. TEL 212-554-0600, FAX 212-586-1181, newyork@eiu.com, http://www.eiu.com.

320.95195 USA
COUNTRY FORECAST. SOUTH KOREA. Text in English. 199?. a. USD 1,140 (print or online ed.); USD 605 per issue (print or online ed.) (effective 2008). charts; stat. back issues avail. **Document type:** *Report, Trade.* **Description:** Focuses on the key factors affecting South Korea's political and economic outlook and its business environment over the next five years.
Formerly (until 1992): Global Forecasting Service. South Korea (0966-8675)
Related titles: Online - full text ed.: E I U Country Forecasts: Asia-Pacific. 1994.
Indexed: A15, ABIn, P45, P48, P51, PQC.
Published by: Economist Intelligence Unit Ltd. (Subsidiary of: Economist Intelligence Unit Ltd.), 111 W 57th St, New York, NY 10019. TEL 212-554-0600, FAX 212-586-1181, newyork@eiu.com, http://www.eiu.com.

320.946 USA
COUNTRY FORECAST. SPAIN. Text in English. 199?. m. USD 1,140 (print or online ed.); USD 605 per issue (print or online ed.) (effective 2008). charts; stat. back issues avail. **Document type:** *Report, Trade.* **Description:** Focuses on the key factors affecting Spain's political and economic outlook and its business environment over the next five years.
Formerly (until 1992): Global Forecasting Service. Spain (0966-8659)
Related titles: Online - full text ed.: E I U Country Forecasts: Western Europe.
Indexed: A15, ABIn, P45, P48, P51, PQC.

Published by: Economist Intelligence Unit Ltd. (Subsidiary of: Economist Intelligence Unit Ltd.), 111 W 57th St, New York, NY 10019. TEL 212-554-0600, FAX 212-586-1181, newyork@eiu.com, http://www.eiu.com.

320.95493 USA
COUNTRY FORECAST. SRI LANKA. Text in English. 199?. a. USD 1,140 (print or online ed.); USD 605 per issue (print or online ed.) (effective 2008). charts; stat. back issues avail. **Document type:** *Report, Trade.* **Description:** Focuses on the key factors affecting Sri Lanka's political and economic outlook and its business environment over the next five years.
Formerly (until 1992): Global Forecasting Service. Sri Lanka (0966-8691)
Related titles: Online - full text ed.: E I U Country Forecasts: Asia-Pacific. 1994.
Published by: Economist Intelligence Unit Ltd. (Subsidiary of: Economist Intelligence Unit Ltd.), 111 W 57th St, New York, NY 10019. TEL 212-554-0600, FAX 212-586-1181, newyork@eiu.com, http://www.eiu.com.

320.9485 USA
COUNTRY FORECAST. SWEDEN. Text in English. 1992. m. USD 1,140 (print or online ed.); USD 605 per issue (print or online ed.) (effective 2008). charts; stat. back issues avail. **Document type:** *Report, Trade.* **Description:** Focuses on the key factors affecting Sweden's political and economic outlook and its business environment over the next five years.
Formerly (until 1993): Global Forecasting Service. Sweden (0966-8667)
Related titles: Online - full text ed.: E I U Country Forecasts: Western Europe.
Published by: Economist Intelligence Unit Ltd. (Subsidiary of: Economist Intelligence Unit Ltd.), 111 W 57th St, New York, NY 10019. TEL 212-554-0600, FAX 212-586-1181, newyork@eiu.com, http://www.eiu.com.

320.9494 USA
COUNTRY FORECAST. SWITZERLAND. Text in English. 199?. m. USD 1,140 (print or online ed.); USD 605 per issue (print or online ed.) (effective 2008). charts; stat. back issues avail. **Document type:** *Report, Trade.* **Description:** Focuses on the key factors affecting Switzerland's political and economic outlook and its business environment over the next five years.
Formerly (until 1992): Global Forecasting Service. Switzerland (0966-8934)
Related titles: Online - full text ed.: E I U Country Forecasts: Western Europe.
Published by: Economist Intelligence Unit Ltd. (Subsidiary of: Economist Intelligence Unit Ltd.), 111 W 57th St, New York, NY 10019. TEL 212-554-0600, FAX 212-586-1181, newyork@eiu.com, http://www.eiu.com.

320.951249 USA
COUNTRY FORECAST. TAIWAN. Text in English. 199?. a. USD 1,140 (print or online ed.); USD 605 per issue (print or online ed.) (effective 2008). charts; stat. back issues avail. **Document type:** *Report, Trade.* **Description:** Focuses on the key factors affecting Taiwan's political and economic outlook and its business environment over the next five years.
Formerly (until 1992): Global Forecasting Service. Taiwan (0966-8640)
Related titles: Online - full text ed.: E I U Country Forecasts: Asia-Pacific. 1994.
Published by: Economist Intelligence Unit Ltd. (Subsidiary of: Economist Intelligence Unit Ltd.), 111 W 57th St, New York, NY 10019. TEL 212-554-0600, FAX 212-586-1181, newyork@eiu.com, http://www.eiu.com.

320.9593 USA
COUNTRY FORECAST. THAILAND. Text in English. 199?. a. USD 1,140 (print or online ed.); USD 605 per issue (print or online ed.) (effective 2008). charts; stat. back issues avail. **Document type:** *Report, Trade.* **Description:** Focuses on the key factors affecting Thailand's political and economic outlook and its business environment over the next five years.
Formerly (until 1992): Global Forecasting Service. Thailand (0966-8624)
Related titles: Online - full text ed.: E I U Country Forecasts: Asia-Pacific. 1994.
Indexed: A15, ABIn, P45, P48, P51, PQC.
Published by: Economist Intelligence Unit Ltd. (Subsidiary of: Economist Intelligence Unit Ltd.), 111 W 57th St, New York, NY 10019. TEL 212-554-0600, FAX 212-586-1181, newyork@eiu.com, http://www.eiu.com.

320.9561 USA
COUNTRY FORECAST. TURKEY. Text in English. 1992. m. USD 1,140 (print or online ed.); USD 605 per issue (print or online ed.) (effective 2008). charts; stat. back issues avail. **Document type:** *Report, Trade.* **Description:** Focuses on the key factors affecting Turkey's political and economic outlook and its business environment over the next five years.
Formerly (until 1993): Global Forecasting Service. Turkey (0966-8632)
Related titles: Online - full text ed.: E I U Country Forecasts: Western Europe.
Indexed: A15, ABIn, P45, P48, P51, PQC.
—CCC.
Published by: Economist Intelligence Unit Ltd. (Subsidiary of: Economist Intelligence Unit Ltd.), 111 W 57th St, New York, NY 10019. TEL 212-554-0600, FAX 212-586-1181, newyork@eiu.com, http://www.eiu.com.

320.941 USA
COUNTRY FORECAST. UNITED KINGDOM. Text in English. 1992. m. USD 1,140 (print or online ed.); USD 605 per issue (print or online ed.) (effective 2008). charts; stat. back issues avail. **Document type:** *Report, Trade.* **Description:** Focuses on the key factors affecting the United Kingdom's political and economic outlook and its business environment over the next five years.
Formerly (until 1993): Global Forecasting Service. United Kingdom
Related titles: Online - full text ed.: E I U Country Forecasts: Western Europe.
Published by: Economist Intelligence Unit Ltd. (Subsidiary of: Economist Intelligence Unit Ltd.), 111 W 57th St, New York, NY 10019. TEL 212-554-0600, FAX 212-586-1181, newyork@eiu.com, http://www.eiu.com.

320.9394 USA ISSN 1358-6661
COUNTRY FORECAST. UNITED STATES OF AMERICA. Text in English. m. USD 1,140 (print or online ed.); USD 605 per issue (print or online ed.) (effective 2008). charts; stat. back issues avail. **Document type:** *Report, Trade.* **Description:** Focuses on the key factors affecting the US political and economic outlook and its business environment over the next five years.
Formerly (until 1994): United States (Economist Intelligence Unit) (0966-9299)
Related titles: Online - full text ed.: ISSN 2047-4563.
Indexed: A15, ABIn, P45, P48, P51, PQC.
—CCC.
Published by: Economist Intelligence Unit Ltd. (Subsidiary of: Economist Intelligence Unit Ltd.), 111 W 57th St, New York, NY 10019. TEL 212-554-0600, FAX 212-586-1181, newyork@eiu.com, http://www.eiu.com.

320.987 USA
COUNTRY FORECAST. VENEZUELA. Text in English. 199?. m. USD 1,140 (print or online ed.); USD 605 per issue (print or online ed.) (effective 2008). charts; stat. back issues avail. **Document type:** *Report, Trade.* **Description:** Focuses on the key factors affecting Venezuela's political and economic outlook and its business environment over the next five years.
Formerly (until 1992): Global Forecasting Service. Venezuela (0966-9574)
Related titles: Online - full text ed.: ISSN 2047-4563.
Indexed: A15, ABIn, P45, P48, P51, PQC.
Published by: Economist Intelligence Unit Ltd. (Subsidiary of: Economist Intelligence Unit Ltd.), 111 W 57th St, New York, NY 10019. TEL 212-554-0600, FAX 212-586-1181, newyork@eiu.com, http://www.eiu.com.

320.9597 USA ISSN 1359-8198
HC444.A1
COUNTRY FORECAST. VIETNAM. Text in English. 1995. a. USD 1,140 (print or online ed.); USD 605 per issue (print or online ed.) (effective 2008). charts; stat. back issues avail. **Document type:** *Report, Trade.* **Description:** Focuses on the key factors affecting Vietnam's political and economic outlook and its business environment over the next five years.
Related titles: Online - full text ed.: E I U Country Forecasts: Asia-Pacific. 1994.
Published by: Economist Intelligence Unit Ltd. (Subsidiary of: Economist Intelligence Unit Ltd.), 111 W 57th St, New York, NY 10019. TEL 212-554-0600, FAX 212-586-1181, newyork@eiu.com, http://www.eiu.com.

320 330.9 USA
COUNTRY FORECAST. WORLD. Text in English. m. USD 1,035; USD 560 per issue (effective 2007). illus.; stat. **Document type:** *Report, Trade.*
Related titles: Online - full text ed.
Published by: Economist Intelligence Unit Ltd. (Subsidiary of: Economist Intelligence Unit Ltd.), 111 W 57th St, New York, NY 10019. TEL 212-554-0600, FAX 212-586-1181, newyork@eiu.com, http://www.eiu.com.

COUNTRY REPORT. AFGHANISTAN; analysis of economic and political trends every quarter. *see* BUSINESS AND ECONOMICS—Economic Situation And Conditions

COUNTRY REPORT. ALBANIA; analysis of economic and political trends every quarter. *see* BUSINESS AND ECONOMICS—Economic Situation And Conditions

COUNTRY REPORT. ALGERIA; analysis of economic and political trends every quarter. *see* BUSINESS AND ECONOMICS—Economic Situation And Conditions

COUNTRY REPORT. ANGOLA; analysis of economic and political trends every quarter. *see* BUSINESS AND ECONOMICS—Economic Situation And Conditions

COUNTRY REPORT. ARGENTINA; analysis of economic and political trends every quarter. *see* BUSINESS AND ECONOMICS—Economic Situation And Conditions

COUNTRY REPORT. ARMENIA; analysis of economic and political trends every quarter. *see* BUSINESS AND ECONOMICS—Economic Situation And Conditions

COUNTRY REPORT. ARUBA; analysis of economic and political trends every quarter. *see* BUSINESS AND ECONOMICS—Economic Situation And Conditions

COUNTRY REPORT. AUSTRALIA; analysis of economic and political trends every quarter. *see* BUSINESS AND ECONOMICS—Economic Situation And Conditions

COUNTRY REPORT. AUSTRIA; analysis of economic and political trends every quarter. *see* BUSINESS AND ECONOMICS—Economic Situation And Conditions

COUNTRY REPORT. AZERBAIJAN; analysis of economic and political trends every quarter. *see* BUSINESS AND ECONOMICS—Economic Situation And Conditions

COUNTRY REPORT. BAHAMAS; analysis of economic and political trends every quarter. *see* BUSINESS AND ECONOMICS—Economic Situation And Conditions

COUNTRY REPORT. BAHRAIN; analysis of economic and political trends every quarter. *see* BUSINESS AND ECONOMICS—Economic Situation And Conditions

COUNTRY REPORT. BANGLADESH; analysis of economic and political trends every quarter. *see* BUSINESS AND ECONOMICS—Economic Situation And Conditions

COUNTRY REPORT. BARBADOS; analysis of economic and political trends every quarter. *see* BUSINESS AND ECONOMICS—Economic Situation And Conditions

COUNTRY REPORT. BELARUS; analysis of economic and political trends every quarter. *see* BUSINESS AND ECONOMICS—Economic Situation And Conditions

COUNTRY REPORT. BELGIUM; analysis of economic and political trends every quarter. *see* BUSINESS AND ECONOMICS—Economic Situation And Conditions

COUNTRY REPORT. BELIZE; analysis of economic and political trends every quarter. *see* BUSINESS AND ECONOMICS—Economic Situation And Conditions

COUNTRY REPORT. BENIN. *see* BUSINESS AND ECONOMICS—Economic Situation And Conditions

COUNTRY REPORT. BERMUDA; analysis of economic and political trends every quarter. *see* BUSINESS AND ECONOMICS—Economic Situation And Conditions

COUNTRY REPORT. BOLIVIA; analysis of economic and political trends every quarter. *see* BUSINESS AND ECONOMICS—Economic Situation And Conditions

COUNTRY REPORT. BOSNIA-HERCEGOVINA; analysis of economic and political trends every quarter. *see* BUSINESS AND ECONOMICS—Economic Situation And Conditions

COUNTRY REPORT. BRAZIL; analysis of economic and political trends every quarter. *see* BUSINESS AND ECONOMICS—Economic Situation And Conditions

COUNTRY REPORT. BRITISH VIRGIN ISLANDS. *see* BUSINESS AND ECONOMICS—Economic Situation And Conditions

COUNTRY REPORT. BRUNEI; analysis of economic and political trends every quarter. *see* BUSINESS AND ECONOMICS—Economic Situation And Conditions

COUNTRY REPORT. BULGARIA; analysis of economic and political trends every quarter. *see* BUSINESS AND ECONOMICS—Economic Situation And Conditions

COUNTRY REPORT. BURKINA FASO; analysis of economic and political trends every quarter. *see* BUSINESS AND ECONOMICS—Economic Situation And Conditions

COUNTRY REPORT. BURUNDI. *see* BUSINESS AND ECONOMICS—Economic Situation And Conditions

COUNTRY REPORT. CAMBODIA; analysis of economic and political trends every quarter. *see* BUSINESS AND ECONOMICS—Economic Situation And Conditions

COUNTRY REPORT. CAMEROON. *see* BUSINESS AND ECONOMICS—Economic Situation And Conditions

COUNTRY REPORT. CANADA; analysis of economic and political trends every quarter. *see* BUSINESS AND ECONOMICS—Economic Situation And Conditions

COUNTRY REPORT. CAPE VERDE; analysis of economic and political trends every quarter. *see* BUSINESS AND ECONOMICS—Economic Situation And Conditions

COUNTRY REPORT. CAYMAN ISLANDS. *see* BUSINESS AND ECONOMICS—Economic Situation And Conditions

COUNTRY REPORT. CENTRAL AFRICAN REPUBLIC; analysis of economic and political trends every quarter. *see* BUSINESS AND ECONOMICS—Economic Situation And Conditions

COUNTRY REPORT. CHAD; analysis of economic and political trends every quarter. *see* BUSINESS AND ECONOMICS—Economic Situation And Conditions

COUNTRY REPORT. CHAD, CENTRAL AFRICAN REPUBLIC; analysis of economic and political trends every quarter. *see* BUSINESS AND ECONOMICS—Economic Situation And Conditions

COUNTRY REPORT. CHILE; analysis of economic and political trends every quarter. *see* BUSINESS AND ECONOMICS—Economic Situation And Conditions

COUNTRY REPORT. CHINA; analysis of economic and political trends every quarter. *see* BUSINESS AND ECONOMICS—Economic Situation And Conditions

COUNTRY REPORT. COLOMBIA; analysis of economic and political trends every quarter. *see* BUSINESS AND ECONOMICS—Economic Situation And Conditions

COUNTRY REPORT. COMOROS; analysis of economic and political trends every quarter. *see* BUSINESS AND ECONOMICS—Economic Situation And Conditions

COUNTRY REPORT. CONGO (BRAZZAVILLE); analysis of economic and political trends every quarter. *see* BUSINESS AND ECONOMICS—Economic Situation And Conditions

COUNTRY REPORT. COSTA RICA. *see* BUSINESS AND ECONOMICS—Economic Situation And Conditions

COUNTRY REPORT. COTE D'IVOIRE; analysis of economic and political trends every quarter. *see* BUSINESS AND ECONOMICS—Economic Situation And Conditions

COUNTRY REPORT. CROATIA; analysis of economic and political trends every quarter. *see* BUSINESS AND ECONOMICS—Economic Situation And Conditions

COUNTRY REPORT. CUBA; analysis of economic and political trends every quarter. *see* BUSINESS AND ECONOMICS—Economic Situation And Conditions

COUNTRY REPORT. CURACAO. *see* BUSINESS AND ECONOMICS—Economic Situation And Conditions

COUNTRY REPORT. CYPRUS; analysis of economic and political trends every quarter. *see* BUSINESS AND ECONOMICS—Economic Situation And Conditions

COUNTRY REPORT. CZECH REPUBLIC; analysis of economic and political trends every quarter. *see* BUSINESS AND ECONOMICS—Economic Situation And Conditions

COUNTRY REPORT. DEMOCRATIC REPUBLIC OF CONGO; analysis of economic and political trends every quarter. *see* BUSINESS AND ECONOMICS—Economic Situation And Conditions

COUNTRY REPORT. DENMARK; analysis of economic and political trends every quarter. *see* BUSINESS AND ECONOMICS—Economic Situation And Conditions

COUNTRY REPORT. DJIBOUTI; analysis of economic and political trends every quarter. *see* BUSINESS AND ECONOMICS—Economic Situation And Conditions

COUNTRY REPORT. DOMINICAN REPUBLIC; analysis of economic and political trends every quarter. *see* BUSINESS AND ECONOMICS—Economic Situation And Conditions

COUNTRY REPORT. ECUADOR; analysis of economic and political trends every quarter. *see* BUSINESS AND ECONOMICS—Economic Situation And Conditions

COUNTRY REPORT. EGYPT; analysis of economic and political trends every quarter. *see* BUSINESS AND ECONOMICS—Economic Situation And Conditions

COUNTRY REPORT. EL SALVADOR; analysis of economic and political trends every quarter. *see* BUSINESS AND ECONOMICS—Economic Situation And Conditions

COUNTRY REPORT. EQUATORIAL GUINEA; analysis of economic and political trends every quarter. *see* BUSINESS AND ECONOMICS—Economic Situation And Conditions

COUNTRY REPORT. ERITREA; analysis of economic and political trends every quarter. *see* BUSINESS AND ECONOMICS—Economic Situation And Conditions

COUNTRY REPORT. ESTONIA; analysis of economic and political trends every quarter. *see* BUSINESS AND ECONOMICS—Economic Situation And Conditions

COUNTRY REPORT. ETHIOPIA. *see* BUSINESS AND ECONOMICS—Economic Situation And Conditions

COUNTRY REPORT. EUROPEAN UNION. *see* BUSINESS AND ECONOMICS—Economic Situation And Conditions

COUNTRY REPORT. FIJI; analysis of economic and political trends every quarter. *see* BUSINESS AND ECONOMICS—Economic Situation And Conditions

COUNTRY REPORT. FINLAND; analysis of economic and political trends every quarter. *see* BUSINESS AND ECONOMICS—Economic Situation And Conditions

COUNTRY REPORT. FRANCE; analysis of economic and political trends every quarter. *see* BUSINESS AND ECONOMICS—Economic Situation And Conditions

COUNTRY REPORT. GABON; analysis of economic and political trends every quarter. *see* BUSINESS AND ECONOMICS—Economic Situation And Conditions

COUNTRY REPORT. GEORGIA; analysis of economic and political trends every quarter. *see* BUSINESS AND ECONOMICS—Economic Situation And Conditions

COUNTRY REPORT. GERMANY; analysis of economic and political trends every quarter. *see* BUSINESS AND ECONOMICS—Economic Situation And Conditions

COUNTRY REPORT. GHANA. *see* BUSINESS AND ECONOMICS—Economic Situation And Conditions

COUNTRY REPORT. GREECE; analysis of economic and political trends every quarter. *see* BUSINESS AND ECONOMICS—Economic Situation And Conditions

COUNTRY REPORT. GUATEMALA; analysis of economic and political trends every quarter. *see* BUSINESS AND ECONOMICS—Economic Situation And Conditions

COUNTRY REPORT. GUINEA; analysis of economic and political trends every quarter. *see* BUSINESS AND ECONOMICS—Economic Situation And Conditions

COUNTRY REPORT. GUINEA-BISSAU; analysis of economic and political trends every quarter. *see* BUSINESS AND ECONOMICS—Economic Situation And Conditions

COUNTRY REPORT. GUYANA. *see* BUSINESS AND ECONOMICS—Economic Situation And Conditions

COUNTRY REPORT. HAITI; analysis of economic and political trends every quarter. *see* BUSINESS AND ECONOMICS—Economic Situation And Conditions

COUNTRY REPORT. HONDURAS; analysis of economic and political trends every quarter. *see* BUSINESS AND ECONOMICS—Economic Situation And Conditions

COUNTRY REPORT. HONG KONG; analysis of economic and political trends every quarter. *see* BUSINESS AND ECONOMICS—Economic Situation And Conditions

COUNTRY REPORT. HUNGARY; analysis of economic and political trends every quarter. *see* BUSINESS AND ECONOMICS—Economic Situation And Conditions

COUNTRY REPORT. ICELAND; analysis of economic and political trends every quarter. *see* BUSINESS AND ECONOMICS—Economic Situation And Conditions

COUNTRY REPORT. INDIA. *see* BUSINESS AND ECONOMICS—Economic Situation And Conditions

COUNTRY REPORT. INDONESIA; analysis of economic and political trends every quarter. *see* BUSINESS AND ECONOMICS—Economic Situation And Conditions

COUNTRY REPORT. IRAN; analysis of economic and political trends every quarter. *see* BUSINESS AND ECONOMICS—Economic Situation And Conditions

COUNTRY REPORT. IRAQ; analysis of economic and political trends every quarter. *see* BUSINESS AND ECONOMICS—Economic Situation And Conditions

COUNTRY REPORT. IRELAND; analysis of economic and political trends every quarter. *see* BUSINESS AND ECONOMICS—Economic Situation And Conditions

COUNTRY REPORT. ISRAEL; analysis of economic and political trends every quarter. *see* BUSINESS AND ECONOMICS—Economic Situation And Conditions

COUNTRY REPORT. ITALY; analysis of economic and political trends every quarter. *see* BUSINESS AND ECONOMICS—Economic Situation And Conditions

COUNTRY REPORT. JAMAICA; analysis of economic and political trends every quarter. *see* BUSINESS AND ECONOMICS—Economic Situation And Conditions

COUNTRY REPORT. JAPAN; analysis of economic and political trends every quarter. *see* BUSINESS AND ECONOMICS—Economic Situation And Conditions

COUNTRY REPORT. JORDAN; analysis of economic and political trends every quarter. *see* BUSINESS AND ECONOMICS—Economic Situation And Conditions

COUNTRY REPORT. KAZAKHSTAN. *see* BUSINESS AND ECONOMICS—Economic Situation And Conditions

COUNTRY REPORT. KENYA; analysis of economic and political trends every quarter. *see* BUSINESS AND ECONOMICS—Economic Situation And Conditions

COUNTRY REPORT. KUWAIT; analysis of economic and political trends every quarter. *see* BUSINESS AND ECONOMICS—Economic Situation And Conditions

COUNTRY REPORT. KYRGYZ REPUBLIC; analysis of economic and political trends every quarter. *see* BUSINESS AND ECONOMICS—Economic Situation And Conditions

COUNTRY REPORT. LAOS; analysis of economic and political trends every quarter. *see* BUSINESS AND ECONOMICS—Economic Situation And Conditions

COUNTRY REPORT. LATVIA; analysis of economic and political trends every quarter. *see* BUSINESS AND ECONOMICS—Economic Situation And Conditions

COUNTRY REPORT. LEBANON; analysis of economic and political trends every quarter. *see* BUSINESS AND ECONOMICS—Economic Situation And Conditions

COUNTRY REPORT. LESOTHO, SWAZILAND; analysis of economic and political trends every quarter. *see* BUSINESS AND ECONOMICS—Economic Situation And Conditions

COUNTRY REPORT. LIBERIA; analysis of economic and political trends every quarter. *see* BUSINESS AND ECONOMICS—Economic Situation And Conditions

COUNTRY REPORT. LIBYA; analysis of economic and political trends every quarter. *see* BUSINESS AND ECONOMICS—Economic Situation And Conditions

COUNTRY REPORT. LITHUANIA; analysis of economic and political trends every quarter. *see* BUSINESS AND ECONOMICS—Economic Situation And Conditions

COUNTRY REPORT. LUXEMBOURG; analysis of economic and political trends every quarter. *see* BUSINESS AND ECONOMICS—Economic Situation And Conditions

COUNTRY REPORT. MACAU; analysis of economic and political trends every quarter. *see* BUSINESS AND ECONOMICS—Economic Situation And Conditions

COUNTRY REPORT. MACEDONIA; analysis of economic and political trends every quarter. *see* BUSINESS AND ECONOMICS—Economic Situation And Conditions

COUNTRY REPORT. MADAGASCAR; analysis of economic and political trends every quarter. *see* BUSINESS AND ECONOMICS—Economic Situation And Conditions

COUNTRY REPORT. MALAWI; analysis of economic and political trends every quarter. *see* BUSINESS AND ECONOMICS—Economic Situation And Conditions

COUNTRY REPORT. MALAYSIA; analysis of economic and political trends every quarter. *see* BUSINESS AND ECONOMICS—Economic Situation And Conditions

COUNTRY REPORT. MALI; analysis of economic and political trends every quarter. *see* BUSINESS AND ECONOMICS—Economic Situation And Conditions

COUNTRY REPORT. MALTA; analysis of economic and political trends every quarter. *see* BUSINESS AND ECONOMICS—Economic Situation And Conditions

COUNTRY REPORT. MAURITANIA, THE GAMBIA; analysis of economic and political trends every quarter. *see* BUSINESS AND ECONOMICS—Economic Situation And Conditions

COUNTRY REPORT. MAURITIUS; analysis of economic and political trends every quarter. *see* BUSINESS AND ECONOMICS—Economic Situation And Conditions

COUNTRY REPORT. MEXICO; analysis of economic and political trends every quarter. *see* BUSINESS AND ECONOMICS—Economic Situation And Conditions

COUNTRY REPORT. MOLDOVA; analysis of economic and political trends every quarter. *see* BUSINESS AND ECONOMICS—Economic Situation And Conditions

COUNTRY REPORT. MONGOLIA; analysis of economic and political trends every quarter. *see* BUSINESS AND ECONOMICS—Economic Situation And Conditions

COUNTRY REPORT. MOROCCO; analysis of economic and political trends every quarter. *see* BUSINESS AND ECONOMICS—Economic Situation And Conditions

COUNTRY REPORT. MOZAMBIQUE. *see* BUSINESS AND ECONOMICS—Economic Situation And Conditions

COUNTRY REPORT. MYANMAR; analysis of economic and political trends every quarter. *see* BUSINESS AND ECONOMICS—Economic Situation And Conditions

COUNTRY REPORT. NAMIBIA; analysis of economic and political trends every quarter. *see* BUSINESS AND ECONOMICS—Economic Situation And Conditions

COUNTRY REPORT. NEPAL, MONGOLIA, BHUTAN; analysis of economic and political trends every quarter. *see* BUSINESS AND ECONOMICS—Economic Situation And Conditions

COUNTRY REPORT. NETHERLANDS; analysis of economic and political trends every quarter. *see* BUSINESS AND ECONOMICS—Economic Situation And Conditions

COUNTRY REPORT. NEW CALEDONIA; analysis of economic and political trends every quarter. *see* BUSINESS AND ECONOMICS—Economic Situation And Conditions

COUNTRY REPORT. NEW ZEALAND; analysis of economic and political trends every quarter. *see* BUSINESS AND ECONOMICS—Economic Situation And Conditions

COUNTRY REPORT. NICARAGUA; analysis of economic and political trends every quarter. *see* BUSINESS AND ECONOMICS—Economic Situation And Conditions

COUNTRY REPORT. NIGER; analysis of economic and political trends every quarter. *see* BUSINESS AND ECONOMICS—Economic Situation And Conditions

COUNTRY REPORT. NIGERIA; analysis of economic and political trends every quarter. *see* BUSINESS AND ECONOMICS—Economic Situation And Conditions

COUNTRY REPORT. NORTH KOREA; analysis of economic and political trends every quarter. *see* BUSINESS AND ECONOMICS—Economic Situation And Conditions

COUNTRY REPORT. NORWAY; analysis of economic and political trends every quarter. *see* BUSINESS AND ECONOMICS—Economic Situation And Conditions

COUNTRY REPORT. OMAN. *see* BUSINESS AND ECONOMICS—Economic Situation And Conditions

COUNTRY REPORT. ORGANISATION OF EASTERN CARIBBEAN STATES. *see* BUSINESS AND ECONOMICS—Economic Situation And Conditions

COUNTRY REPORT. PAKISTAN; analysis of economic and political trends every quarter. *see* BUSINESS AND ECONOMICS—Economic Situation And Conditions

COUNTRY REPORT. PANAMA; analysis of economic and political trends every quarter. *see* BUSINESS AND ECONOMICS—Economic Situation And Conditions

COUNTRY REPORT. PAPUA NEW GUINEA, TIMOR-LESTE; analysis of economic and political trends every quarter. *see* BUSINESS AND ECONOMICS—Economic Situation And Conditions

COUNTRY REPORT. PARAGUAY; analysis of economic and political trends every quarter. *see* BUSINESS AND ECONOMICS—Economic Situation And Conditions

COUNTRY REPORT. PHILIPPINES; analysis of economic and political trends every quarter. *see* BUSINESS AND ECONOMICS—Economic Situation And Conditions

COUNTRY REPORT. POLAND; analysis of economic and political trends every quarter. *see* BUSINESS AND ECONOMICS—Economic Situation And Conditions

COUNTRY REPORT. PORTUGAL; analysis of economic and political trends every quarter. *see* BUSINESS AND ECONOMICS—Economic Situation And Conditions

COUNTRY REPORT. PUERTO RICO; analysis of economic and political trends every quarter. *see* BUSINESS AND ECONOMICS—Economic Situation And Conditions

COUNTRY REPORT. QATAR; analysis of economic and political trends every quarter. *see* BUSINESS AND ECONOMICS—Economic Situation And Conditions

COUNTRY REPORT. ROMANIA; analysis of economic and political trends every quarter. *see* BUSINESS AND ECONOMICS—Economic Situation And Conditions

COUNTRY REPORT. RUSSIA. *see* BUSINESS AND ECONOMICS—Economic Situation And Conditions

COUNTRY REPORT. RWANDA; analysis of economic and political trends every quarter. *see* BUSINESS AND ECONOMICS—Economic Situation And Conditions

COUNTRY REPORT. SAMOA; analysis of economic and political trends every quarter. *see* BUSINESS AND ECONOMICS—Economic Situation And Conditions

COUNTRY REPORT. SAO TOME AND PRINCIPE; analysis of economic and political trends every quarter. *see* BUSINESS AND ECONOMICS—Economic Situation And Conditions

COUNTRY REPORT. SAUDI ARABIA; analysis of economic and political trends every quarter. *see* BUSINESS AND ECONOMICS—Economic Situation And Conditions

COUNTRY REPORT. SENEGAL; analysis of economic and political trends every quarter. *see* BUSINESS AND ECONOMICS—Economic Situation And Conditions

COUNTRY REPORT. SEYCHELLES; analysis of economic and political trends every quarter. *see* BUSINESS AND ECONOMICS—Economic Situation And Conditions

COUNTRY REPORT. SIERRA LEONE; analysis of economic and political trends every quarter. *see* BUSINESS AND ECONOMICS—Economic Situation And Conditions

COUNTRY REPORT. SINGAPORE; analysis of economic and political trends every quarter. *see* BUSINESS AND ECONOMICS—Economic Situation And Conditions

COUNTRY REPORT. SLOVAKIA; analysis of economic and political trends every quarter. *see* BUSINESS AND ECONOMICS—Economic Situation And Conditions

COUNTRY REPORT. SLOVENIA; analysis of economic and political trends every quarter. *see* BUSINESS AND ECONOMICS—Economic Situation And Conditions

COUNTRY REPORT. SOLOMON ISLANDS; analysis of economic and political trends every quarter. *see* BUSINESS AND ECONOMICS—Economic Situation And Conditions

COUNTRY REPORT. SOMALIA; analysis of economic and political trends every quarter. *see* BUSINESS AND ECONOMICS—Economic Situation And Conditions

COUNTRY REPORT. SOUTH AFRICA; analysis of economic and political trends every quarter. *see* BUSINESS AND ECONOMICS—Economic Situation And Conditions

COUNTRY REPORT. SOUTH KOREA; analysis of economic and political trends every quarter. *see* BUSINESS AND ECONOMICS—Economic Situation And Conditions

COUNTRY REPORT. SPAIN; analysis of economic and political trends every quarter. *see* BUSINESS AND ECONOMICS—Economic Situation And Conditions

COUNTRY REPORT. SRI LANKA; analysis of economic and political trends every quarter. *see* BUSINESS AND ECONOMICS—Economic Situation And Conditions

COUNTRY REPORT. ST MAARTEN; analysis of economic and political trends every quarter. *see* BUSINESS AND ECONOMICS—Economic Situation And Conditions

COUNTRY REPORT. SUDAN; analysis of economic and political trends every quarter. *see* BUSINESS AND ECONOMICS—Economic Situation And Conditions

COUNTRY REPORT. SURINAME; analysis of economic and political trends every quarter. *see* BUSINESS AND ECONOMICS—Economic Situation And Conditions

COUNTRY REPORT. SWAZILAND; analysis of economic and political trends every quarter. *see* BUSINESS AND ECONOMICS—Economic Situation And Conditions

COUNTRY REVIEW. MACEDONIA. *see* BUSINESS AND ECONOMICS—Economic Situation And Conditions

COUNTRY REVIEW. MADAGASCAR. *see* BUSINESS AND ECONOMICS—Economic Situation And Conditions

COUNTRY REVIEW. MALAWI. *see* BUSINESS AND ECONOMICS—Economic Situation And Conditions

COUNTRY REVIEW. MALAYSIA. *see* BUSINESS AND ECONOMICS—Economic Situation And Conditions

COUNTRY REVIEW. MALDIVES. *see* BUSINESS AND ECONOMICS—Economic Situation And Conditions

COUNTRY REVIEW. MALI. *see* BUSINESS AND ECONOMICS—Economic Situation And Conditions

COUNTRY REVIEW. MALTA. *see* BUSINESS AND ECONOMICS—Economic Situation And Conditions

COUNTRY REVIEW. MARSHALL ISLANDS. *see* BUSINESS AND ECONOMICS—Economic Situation And Conditions

COUNTRY REVIEW. MAURITANIA. *see* BUSINESS AND ECONOMICS—Economic Situation And Conditions

COUNTRY REVIEW. MAURITIUS. *see* BUSINESS AND ECONOMICS—Economic Situation And Conditions

COUNTRY REVIEW. MEXICO. *see* BUSINESS AND ECONOMICS—Economic Situation And Conditions

COUNTRY REVIEW. MICRONESIA. *see* BUSINESS AND ECONOMICS—Economic Situation And Conditions

COUNTRY REVIEW. MOLDOVA. *see* BUSINESS AND ECONOMICS—Economic Situation And Conditions

COUNTRY REVIEW. MONACO. *see* BUSINESS AND ECONOMICS—Economic Situation And Conditions

COUNTRY REVIEW. MONGOLIA. *see* BUSINESS AND ECONOMICS—Economic Situation And Conditions

COUNTRY REVIEW. MOROCCO. *see* BUSINESS AND ECONOMICS—Economic Situation And Conditions

COUNTRY REVIEW. MOZAMBIQUE. *see* BUSINESS AND ECONOMICS—Economic Situation And Conditions

COUNTRY REVIEW. NAMIBIA. *see* BUSINESS AND ECONOMICS—Economic Situation And Conditions

COUNTRY REVIEW. NAURU. *see* BUSINESS AND ECONOMICS—Economic Situation And Conditions

COUNTRY REVIEW. NEPAL. *see* BUSINESS AND ECONOMICS—Economic Situation And Conditions

COUNTRY REVIEW. NETHERLANDS. *see* BUSINESS AND ECONOMICS—Economic Situation And Conditions

COUNTRY REVIEW. NEW ZEALAND. *see* BUSINESS AND ECONOMICS—Economic Situation And Conditions

COUNTRY REVIEW. NICARAGUA. *see* BUSINESS AND ECONOMICS—Economic Situation And Conditions

COUNTRY REVIEW. NIGER. *see* BUSINESS AND ECONOMICS—Economic Situation And Conditions

COUNTRY REVIEW. NIGERIA. *see* BUSINESS AND ECONOMICS—Economic Situation And Conditions

COUNTRY REVIEW. NORTH KOREA. *see* BUSINESS AND ECONOMICS—Economic Situation And Conditions

COUNTRY REVIEW. NORWAY. *see* BUSINESS AND ECONOMICS—Economic Situation And Conditions

COUNTRY REVIEW. OMAN. *see* BUSINESS AND ECONOMICS—Economic Situation And Conditions

COUNTRY REVIEW. PAKISTAN. *see* BUSINESS AND ECONOMICS—Economic Situation And Conditions

COUNTRY REVIEW. PALAU. *see* BUSINESS AND ECONOMICS—Economic Situation And Conditions

COUNTRY REVIEW. PANAMA. *see* BUSINESS AND ECONOMICS—Economic Situation And Conditions

COUNTRY REVIEW. PAPUA NEW GUINEA. *see* BUSINESS AND ECONOMICS—Economic Situation And Conditions

COUNTRY REVIEW. PARAGUAY. *see* BUSINESS AND ECONOMICS—Economic Situation And Conditions

COUNTRY REVIEW. PERU. *see* BUSINESS AND ECONOMICS—Economic Situation And Conditions

COUNTRY REVIEW. PHILIPPINES. *see* BUSINESS AND ECONOMICS—Economic Situation And Conditions

COUNTRY REVIEW. POLAND. *see* BUSINESS AND ECONOMICS—Economic Situation And Conditions

COUNTRY REVIEW. PORTUGAL. *see* BUSINESS AND ECONOMICS—Economic Situation And Conditions

COUNTRY REVIEW. QATAR. *see* BUSINESS AND ECONOMICS—Economic Situation And Conditions

COUNTRY REVIEW. ROMANIA. *see* BUSINESS AND ECONOMICS—Economic Situation And Conditions

COUNTRY REVIEW. RUSSIA. *see* BUSINESS AND ECONOMICS—Economic Situation And Conditions

COUNTRY REVIEW. RWANDA. *see* BUSINESS AND ECONOMICS—Economic Situation And Conditions

COUNTRY REVIEW. SAIN VICENT AND THE GRENADINES. *see* BUSINESS AND ECONOMICS—Economic Situation And Conditions

COUNTRY REVIEW. SAINT KITTS NEVIS. *see* BUSINESS AND ECONOMICS—Economic Situation And Conditions

COUNTRY REVIEW. SAINT LUCIA. *see* BUSINESS AND ECONOMICS—Economic Situation And Conditions

COUNTRY REVIEW. SAMOA. *see* BUSINESS AND ECONOMICS—Economic Situation And Conditions

COUNTRY REVIEW. SAN MARINO. *see* BUSINESS AND ECONOMICS—Economic Situation And Conditions

COUNTRY REVIEW. SAO TOME & PRINCIPE. *see* BUSINESS AND ECONOMICS—Economic Situation And Conditions

COUNTRY REVIEW. SAUDI ARABIA. *see* BUSINESS AND ECONOMICS—Economic Situation And Conditions

COUNTRY REVIEW. SENEGAL. *see* BUSINESS AND ECONOMICS—Economic Situation And Conditions

COUNTRY REVIEW. SERBIA. *see* BUSINESS AND ECONOMICS—Economic Situation And Conditions

COUNTRY REVIEW. SEYCHELLES. *see* BUSINESS AND ECONOMICS—Economic Situation And Conditions

COUNTRY REVIEW. SIERRA LEONE. *see* BUSINESS AND ECONOMICS—Economic Situation And Conditions

COUNTRY REVIEW. SINGAPORE. *see* BUSINESS AND ECONOMICS—Production Of Goods And Services

COUNTRY REVIEW. SLOVAKIA. *see* BUSINESS AND ECONOMICS—Economic Situation And Conditions

COUNTRY REVIEW. SLOVENIA. *see* BUSINESS AND ECONOMICS—Economic Situation And Conditions

COUNTRY REVIEW. SOLOMON ISLANDS. *see* BUSINESS AND ECONOMICS—Economic Situation And Conditions

COUNTRY REVIEW. SOMALIA. *see* BUSINESS AND ECONOMICS—Economic Situation And Conditions

COUNTRY REVIEW. SOUTH AFRICA. *see* BUSINESS AND ECONOMICS—Economic Situation And Conditions

COUNTRY REVIEW. SOUTH KOREA. *see* BUSINESS AND ECONOMICS—Economic Situation And Conditions

COUNTRY REVIEW. SPAIN. *see* BUSINESS AND ECONOMICS—Economic Situation And Conditions

COUNTRY REVIEW. SRI LANKA. *see* BUSINESS AND ECONOMICS—Economic Situation And Conditions

COUNTRY REVIEW. SUDAN. *see* BUSINESS AND ECONOMICS—Economic Situation And Conditions

COUNTRY REVIEW. SURINAME. *see* BUSINESS AND ECONOMICS—Economic Situation And Conditions

COUNTRY REVIEW. SWAZILAND. *see* BUSINESS AND ECONOMICS—Economic Situation And Conditions

COUNTRY REVIEW. SWEDEN. *see* BUSINESS AND ECONOMICS—Economic Situation And Conditions

COUNTRY REVIEW. SWITZERLAND. *see* BUSINESS AND ECONOMICS—Economic Situation And Conditions

COUNTRY REVIEW. SYRIA. *see* BUSINESS AND ECONOMICS—Economic Situation And Conditions

COUNTRY REVIEW. TAJIKISTAN. *see* BUSINESS AND ECONOMICS—Economic Situation And Conditions

COUNTRY REVIEW. TANZANIA. *see* BUSINESS AND ECONOMICS—Economic Situation And Conditions

COUNTRY REVIEW. THAILAND. *see* BUSINESS AND ECONOMICS—Economic Situation And Conditions

COUNTRY REVIEW. TOGO. *see* BUSINESS AND ECONOMICS—Economic Situation And Conditions

COUNTRY REVIEW. TONGA. *see* BUSINESS AND ECONOMICS—Economic Situation And Conditions

COUNTRY REVIEW. TRINIDAD AND TOBAGO. *see* BUSINESS AND ECONOMICS—Economic Situation And Conditions

COUNTRY REVIEW. TUNISIA. *see* BUSINESS AND ECONOMICS—Economic Situation And Conditions

COUNTRY REVIEW. TURKEY. *see* BUSINESS AND ECONOMICS—Economic Situation And Conditions

COUNTRY REVIEW. TURKMENISTAN. *see* BUSINESS AND ECONOMICS—Economic Situation And Conditions

COUNTRY REVIEW. TUVALU. *see* BUSINESS AND ECONOMICS—Economic Situation And Conditions

COUNTRY REVIEW. UGANDA. *see* BUSINESS AND ECONOMICS—Economic Situation And Conditions

COUNTRY REVIEW. UKRAINE. *see* BUSINESS AND ECONOMICS—Economic Situation And Conditions

COUNTRY REVIEW. UNITED ARAB EMIRATES. *see* BUSINESS AND ECONOMICS—Economic Situation And Conditions

COUNTRY REVIEW. UNITED KINGDOM. *see* BUSINESS AND ECONOMICS—Economic Situation And Conditions

COUNTRY REVIEW. UNITED STATES. *see* BUSINESS AND ECONOMICS—Economic Situation And Conditions

COUNTRY REVIEW. URUGUAY. *see* BUSINESS AND ECONOMICS—Economic Situation And Conditions

COUNTRY REVIEW. UZBEKISTAN. *see* BUSINESS AND ECONOMICS—Economic Situation And Conditions

COUNTRY REVIEW. VANUATU. *see* BUSINESS AND ECONOMICS—Economic Situation And Conditions

COUNTRY REVIEW. VENEZUELA. *see* BUSINESS AND ECONOMICS—Economic Situation And Conditions

COUNTRY REVIEW. VIETNAM. *see* BUSINESS AND ECONOMICS—Economic Situation And Conditions

COUNTRY REVIEW. YEMEN. *see* BUSINESS AND ECONOMICS—Economic Situation And Conditions

COUNTRY REVIEW. ZAMBIA. *see* BUSINESS AND ECONOMICS—Economic Situation And Conditions

COUNTRY REVIEW. ZIMBABWE. *see* BUSINESS AND ECONOMICS—Economic Situation And Conditions

COUNTRY VIEWSWIRE. *see* BUSINESS AND ECONOMICS—Economic Situation And Conditions

320.9 VNM ISSN 0045-8902
DS557.A7

COURRIER DU VIETNAM. Text in French. 1964. m. USD 10.70. adv. bk.rev. charts; illus. **Document type:** *Newspaper.*
Related titles: ◆ English ed.: Vietnam Courier. ISSN 0866-8140; Russian ed.
Indexed: RASB.
Published by: Vietnam News Agency, 79 Ly Thuong Kiet, Hanoi, Viet Nam. TEL 84-4-9334587, FAX 84-4-8258363, vnnews@vnagency.com.vn, http://www.vnagency.com.vn/. Ed., R&P Nguyen Tuong.

320 BEL ISSN 0008-9664

COURRIER HEBDOMADAIRE. Text in French. 1959. w. (40/yr.). EUR 235 (effective 2010). **Document type:** *Magazine, Consumer.*
Related titles: Online - full text ed.: ISSN 1782-141X; Dutch ed.: Weekberichten. ISSN 0776-9458.
Indexed: ELLIS, ILD, RASB.
Published by: Centre de Recherche et d'Information Socio-Politiques (C R I S P), 1A Place Quetelet, Brussels, 1210, Belgium. TEL 32-2-2110180, FAX 32-2-2197934, http://www.crisp.be.

CRACKING THE A P U.S. GOVERNMENT AND POLITICS EXAM. (Advanced Placement, United States) *see* EDUCATION—Higher Education

320.52 336 FRA ISSN 1772-340X

LE CRI DU CONTRIBUABLE; trop de depenses publiques, c'est trop d'impots. Text in French. 2004. bi-m. (22/yr). EUR 41.80 (effective 2009). **Document type:** *Newsletter, Consumer.*
Related titles: Supplement(s): Les Dossiers du Contribuable. ISSN 2116-0260. 2009.
Published by: Contribuables Associes, 42 Rue des Jeuneurs, Paris, Cedex 02 75077, France. TEL 33-1-42211624, FAX 33-1-42332935, http://www.contribuables.org.

320 CUB

CRITERIOS; teoria literaria, estetica y cultural. Text in Spanish. q. USD 4 in North America; USD 12 in South America; USD 17 in Europe.
Indexed: RASB.
Published by: (Cuba. Ministerio de Cultura), Ediciones Cubanas, Obispo 527, Havana, Cuba.

320 ITA ISSN 1825-4977

CRITICA LIBERALE. Text in Italian. 1968. m. EUR 30 domestic; EUR 60 foreign (effective 2009). bk.rev. **Document type:** *Journal, Consumer.*
Published by: Edizioni Dedalo, Viale Luigi Jacobini 5, Bari, BA 70123, Italy. TEL 39-080-5311413, FAX 39-080-5311414, info@edizionidedalo.it, http://www.edizionidedalo.it. Ed. Enzo Marzo.

320.5322 ITA ISSN 0011-152X

CRITICA MARXISTA/MARXIST CRITICISM. Text in Italian. 1963. bi-m. EUR 40 domestic; EUR 80 foreign (effective 2008). bibl.; charts. index. **Document type:** *Journal, Academic/Scholarly.*
Related titles: Online - full text ed.
Indexed: A22, IBR, IBSS, IBZ, MLA-IB, RASB.
—IE, Infotrieve.
Published by: Editori Riuniti, c/o The Media Factory, Via Tuscolana 4, Rome, 00182, Italy. TEL 39-06-70614211, FAX 39-06-70613928, http://www.editoririuniti.it. Circ: 12,000.

320.972 MEX

CRITICA PERIODISMO EN SONORA. Text in Spanish. 1999. m. MXN 15 newsstand/cover (effective 2000).
Published by: Editorial El Autentico, Revolucion No 14, Entre San Luis Potosi y Zacatecas, Hermosillo, Sonora, Mexico. TEL 52-62-145-600, critica@correoweb.com. Ed. Gaspar Navarro Ruiz.

320.531 ITA ISSN 0011-1538
HX7

CRITICA SOCIALE; rivista del socialismo fondata da Filippo Turati. Text in Italian. 1891. m. adv. bk.rev. **Document type:** *Magazine, Consumer.*
Related titles: Online - full text ed.
Indexed: RASB.
Published by: Societa Editrice dell Critica Sociale s.r.l., Via Confalonieri 38, Milan, 20124, Italy.

320 ZAF ISSN 1726-8494

CRITICAL DIALOGUE; public participation in review. Text in English. 2003. q. **Document type:** *Journal, Academic/Scholarly.*
Published by: Centre for Public Participation, Forest Pods Intuthuko Junction, Suite 801, 750 Francois Rd, Durban, 4001, South Africa. TEL 27-31-2619001, FAX 27-31-2619059, info@cpp.org.za, http://www.cpp.org.za. Ed. Imraan Buccus.

320 USA ISSN 1940-3186

CRITICAL ISSUES IN JUSTICE AND POLITICS; discussing the present - Influencing the future. Abbreviated title: C I J P. Text in English. 2008 (Mar.). 3/yr. USD 3.99 per issue (effective 2011). **Document type:** *Journal, Academic/Scholarly.*
Media: Online - full text. **Related titles:** Print ed.: USD 10.59 per issue (effective 2011).
Published by: Southern Utah University, Department of Political Science & Criminal Justice, 351 W University Blvd, GC 406, Cedar City, UT 84720. TEL 435-586-5429, FAX 435-586-1925, levy@suu.edu.

320.05 GBR ISSN 1946-0171
JS3001

➤ **CRITICAL POLICY STUDIES.** Text in English. 1974. q. GBP 231 combined subscription in United Kingdom to institutions (print & online eds.); EUR 333, USD 415 combined subscription to institutions (print & online eds.) (effective 2012). reprint service avail. from PSC. **Document type:** *Journal, Academic/Scholarly.* **Description:** Offers an innovative forum for researchers, policy-makers and practitioners to challenge mainstream approaches to policy analysis and democratic governance.
Former titles (until 2009): Critical Policy Analysis (1750-8762); (until 2007): Local Governance (1464-0899); (until 1998): Local Government Policy Making (0264-2050); (until 1981): Corporate Planning Journal; (until 1979): Corporate Planning (0305-3695)
Related titles: Online - full text ed.: ISSN 1946-018X. GBP 208 in United Kingdom to institutions; EUR 300, USD 373 to institutions (effective 2012).
Indexed: A22, CA, H05, P42, PAIS, T02.
—BLDSC (3487.458200), IE. **CCC.**
Published by: Routledge (Subsidiary of: Taylor & Francis Group), 4 Park Sq, Milton Park, Abingdon, Oxon OX14 4RN, United Kingdom. TEL 44-20-70176000, FAX 44-20-70176336, info@routledge.co.uk, http://www.routledge.com. Eds. Frank Fischer, Steven Griggs.

➤ **CRITICAL SOCIAL POLICY**; a journal of theory and practice in social welfare. *see* SOCIAL SERVICES AND WELFARE

320.531 GBR ISSN 0301-7605
DK246
➤ **CRITIQUE**; a journal of socialist theory. Text in English. 1973. q. GBP 352 combined subscription in United Kingdom to institutions (print & online eds.); EUR 423, USD 529 combined subscription to institutions (print & online eds.) (effective 2012). adv. bk.rev. cum.index: vols.1-6, 7-12, 13-21. back issues avail.; reprint service avail. from PSC. **Document type:** *Journal, Academic/Scholarly.* **Description:** Marxist theory, political economy, and history of socialism. Purpose: to develop above subjects. Audience: scholars, students and workers.
Related titles: Online - full text ed.: ISSN 1748-8605. GBP 316 in United Kingdom to institutions; EUR 381, USD 476 to institutions (effective 2012) (from IngentaConnect).
Indexed: A22, AltPI, CA, DIP, E01, HistAb, IBR, IBZ, Inspec, LeftInd, P42, PCI, RASB, S02, S03, SCOPUS, SociolAb, T02.
—IE, Ingenta. **CCC.**
Published by: Routledge (Subsidiary of: Taylor & Francis Group), 4 Park Sq, Milton Park, Abingdon, Oxon OX14 4RN, United Kingdom. TEL 44-20-70176000, FAX 44-20-70176336, subscriptions@tandf.co.uk, http://www.routledge.com. Ed. Hillel Ticktin TEL 44-1555-840242. Adv. contact Linda Hann TEL 44-1344-779945. B&W page USD 75; trim 5.66 x 8.32. Circ: 1,000. **Subscr. to:** Taylor & Francis Ltd., Journals Customer Service, Sheepen Pl, Colchester, Essex CO3 3LP, United Kingdom. TEL 44-20-70175544, FAX 44-20-70175198.

320 ARG
CRONICA DOCUMENTAL DE LAS MALVINAS. Text in Spanish. w.
Published by: Editorial Redaccion S.A., Bme. Mitre 1970, 2o piso, Buenos Aires, Argentina. Eds. Emiliana Lopez Saavedra, Hugo Gambini.

CROWN & KORU; supporting the monarchy of New Zealand. *see* PUBLIC ADMINISTRATION

320.5 MEX ISSN 0011-2208
CRUZADO; si lo leyo en el cruzado es veridico. Text in Spanish. 1961. s-w. MXN 500, USD 24. **Document type:** *Newspaper.*
Published by: Roberto Murillo Rocha, Ed. & Pub., Priv. de Lerdo de Tejada 2B, Apdo. Postal 233, Uruapan, MICHOACAN 60000, Mexico. TEL 3-44-88, FAX 3-52-93. adv.: page MXN 2,000. Circ: 5,000.

320 ARG
CUADERNOS DE ESTUDIOS LATINOAMERICANOS. Text in Spanish. 1974 (no.2). irreg.
Published by: Universidad Nacional del Nordeste, Instituto de Letras, Resistencia, Chaco 3500, Argentina. Ed. Alfredo Veirave.

320.9 CUB ISSN 1016-9504
JL951.A1
CUADERNOS DE NUESTRA AMERICA. Text in Spanish. s-a. USD 12 in the Americas; USD 14 in Europe; USD 16 elsewhere.
Indexed: IBR, IBSS, IBZ, RASB.
Published by: (Centro de Estudios sobre America) Ediciones Cubanas, Obispo 527, Havana, Cuba. TEL 32-5556-60.

320 ESP ISSN 1696-8441
DP63.9
CUADERNOS DE PENSAMIENTO POLITICO. Text in Spanish. 2003. q. back issues avail. **Document type:** *Journal, Academic/Scholarly.*
Published by: Fundacion para el Analisis y los Estudios Sociales (F A E S), C Maria de Molina 40 6a. Planta, Madrid, 28006, Spain. TEL 34-91-5766857, fundaes@fundaes.org, http://www.fundaes.org.

CUADERNOS DEL C E D L A. *see* HISTORY—History Of North And South America

320 CUB ISSN 1013-6207
CUBA. MINISTERIO DE CULTURA. CARTELERA. Text in English, Spanish. 1982. w. **Description:** Publishes articles on the cultural offerings, national customs, and anecdotal aspects of Havana. Includes a directory of attractions.
Published by: Ministerio de Cultura, Instituto Cubano del Libro, Calle 15, no. 602, esquina a C, Vedado, Plaza, La Habana, Cuba. FAX 333732. Ed. Virgilio Calvo Menendez.

CUBAN STUDIES/ESTUDIOS CUBANOS; scholarly multidisciplinary annual book publication devoted entirely to Cuba. *see* HISTORY—History Of North And South America

321.8 PER
CUESTION DE ESTADO. Text in Spanish. 1992. bi-m.
Published by: Instituto Democracia y Socialismo, Jiron Junin, 249, Magdalena, Lima 17, Peru. TEL 51-14-625137, FAX 51-14-618710.

320 VEN ISSN 0798-1406
JL3881
➤ **CUESTIONES POLITICAS.** Text in Spanish; Abstracts in Spanish, English. 1985. s-a. VEB 80 domestic; USD 45 in Latin America; USD 50 elsewhere (effective 2011). bibl.; abstr. **Document type:** *Journal, Academic/Scholarly.* **Description:** Publishes original works and research results in the areas of political science and civil rights.
Indexed: H21, I13, IBSS, P08.
Published by: Universidad del Zulia, Facultad de Ciencias Juridicas, Apdo Postal 10432, Maracaibo, Venezuela. TEL 58-261-596677, FAX 58-261-7986313, luisediaz@interlink.net.ve.

320 ARG
CULTURA NACIONAL; revista bimestrale de politica y ciencias sociales. Text in Spanish. bi-m.
Address: Cnel. Zelaya 1438, Lanus Oeste, Buenos Aires, Argentina. Ed. Eduardo Varela.

CULTURAL CRITIQUE (MINNEAPOLIS, 1985); an international journal of cultural studies. *see* ANTHROPOLOGY

CULTURAL POLICY. *see* POLITICAL SCIENCE—International Relations

350 USA ISSN 1743-2197
JA75.7
➤ **CULTURAL POLITICS.** Text in English. 2005 (Mar.). 3/yr. USD 40 to individuals; USD 282 to institutions; USD 300 combined subscription to institutions (print & online eds.); USD 94 per issue to institutions (effective 2012). adv. back issues avail.; reprint service avail. from PSC. **Document type:** *Journal, Academic/Scholarly.* **Description:** Explores the global character and effects of contemporary culture and politics. Analyses the linkages between cultural identities, agencies and actors, political issues and conflicts, and global media.
Related titles: Online - full text ed.: ISSN 1751-7435. USD 268 to institutions (effective 2012) (from IngentaConnect).
Indexed: A26, B04, BRD, BrHumI, CA, I05, IBR, IBSS, IBZ, MLA-IB, P42, PSA, S02, S03, SCOPUS, SSAI, SSAb, SSI, SociolAb, T02, W01, W02, W03, W05.
—BLDSC (3491.668258), IE, Ingenta. **CCC.**
Published by: Duke University Press, 905 W Main St, Ste 18 B, Durham, NC 27701. TEL 919-688-5134, 888-651-0122, FAX 919-688-2615, 888-651-0124, subscriptions@dukeupress.edu.

350 USA
CULTURAL POLITICS SERIES. Text in English. 1989. irreg., latest vol.19, 2002. price varies. back issues avail. **Document type:** *Monographic series, Academic/Scholarly.* **Description:** Aims to debates the political direction of current cultural theory and practice by combining contemporary analysis with a more traditional sense of historical and socio-economic evaluation.
Published by: University of Minnesota Press, Ste 290, 111 Third Ave S, Minneapolis, MN 55401. TEL 612-627-1970, FAX 612-627-1980, ump@umn.edu. **Dist. by:** c/o Chicago Distribution Center, 11030 S Langley Ave, Chicago, IL 60628. TEL 800-621-2736; Plymbridge Distributors Ltd, Estover Rd, Plymouth, Devon PL6 7PY, United Kingdom. TEL 44-1752-202-301, FAX 44-1752-202-331.

CULTURAL SURVIVAL VOICES (ONLINE). *see* ETHNIC INTERESTS

CULTURE MAGAZINE. *see* ART

CULTURE WARS MAGAZINE. *see* RELIGIONS AND THEOLOGY—Roman Catholic

320 ARG
CUMPA. Text in Spanish. 1986. s-m.
Published by: Hechos S.A., Florida, 716 3, Buenos Aires, 1005, Argentina. TEL 54-114-3928529.

320 PAK
CURRENT. Text in English. 1975. w. PKR 65. illus.
Indexed: GSS&RPL.
Address: Sheika Bldg., Faiz Mohd Fatehali Rd., P O Box 789, Karachi, Pakistan. Ed. M T Bokhari.

CURRENT (WASHINGTON, 1960); required reading recommended by leading opinion makers. *see* EDUCATION

320 330.9 USA ISSN 1098-4070
DT31
➤ **CURRENT POLITICS AND ECONOMICS OF AFRICA.** Text in English. 2008 (Mar.). q. USD 400 to institutions; USD 600 combined subscription to institutions (print & online eds.) (effective 2012). **Document type:** *Journal, Academic/Scholarly.*
Related titles: Online - full text ed.: USD 400 to institutions (effective 2012).
Published by: Nova Science Publishers, Inc., 400 Oser Ave, Ste 1600, Hauppauge, NY 11788. TEL 631-231-7269, FAX 631-231-8175, main@novapublishers.com. Ed. Frank Columbus.

320.95 USA
HC462.9
➤ **CURRENT POLITICS AND ECONOMICS OF ASIA.** Text in English. 1991. q. USD 715 to institutions; USD 1,072 combined subscription to institutions (print & online eds.) (effective 2012). **Document type:** *Journal, Academic/Scholarly.* **Description:** Deals with Asia, its political dynamics, economic policies, institutions and its future.
Formerly (until 2010): Current Politics and Economics of Asia and China; Which incorporated (1995-2006): Current Politics and Economics of China (1098-4151); Which was formerly: Current Politics and Economics of Asia (1537-8055); Which was formed by the 1997 merger of: Bulletin of Asian - Pacific Economic and Pacific Issues; (1991-1997): Current Politics and Economics of Japan (1056-7593)
Related titles: Online - full text ed.: USD 715 to institutions (effective 2012).
Indexed: BAS.
Published by: Nova Science Publishers, Inc., 400 Oser Ave, Ste 1600, Hauppauge, NY 11788. TEL 631-231-7269, FAX 631-231-8175, main@novapublishers.com. Ed. Felix Chin.

320 USA ISSN 1057-2309
D2009
➤ **CURRENT POLITICS AND ECONOMICS OF EUROPE.** Text in English. 1990. q. USD 715 to institutions (effective 2012). **Document type:** *Journal, Academic/Scholarly.* **Description:** Focuses on the momentous changes in Europe, spanning the entire spectrum of contemporary politics and economics.
Related titles: Online - full text ed.
Indexed: B01, CA, IBSS, T02.
Published by: Nova Science Publishers, Inc., 400 Oser Ave, Ste 1600, Hauppauge, NY 11788. TEL 631-231-7269, FAX 631-231-8175, main@novapublishers.com. Ed. Frank Columbus.

320 330.9 USA ISSN 1935-2549
F1401
CURRENT POLITICS AND ECONOMICS OF SOUTH AND CENTRAL AMERICA. Text in English. 2007. q. USD 400 to institutions; USD 600 combined subscription to institutions (print & online eds.) (effective 2012). **Document type:** *Journal, Academic/Scholarly.* **Description:** Deals with South and Central America, its political dynamics, economic policies, institutions and its future.
Related titles: Online - full text ed.: 2007. USD 400 to institutions (effective 2012).
Published by: Nova Science Publishers, Inc., 400 Oser Ave, Ste 1600, Hauppauge, NY 11788. TEL 631-231-7269, FAX 631-231-8175, main@novapublishers.com. Ed. Frank Columbus.

320 330.9 USA ISSN 1937-5492
DK509
CURRENT POLITICS AND ECONOMICS OF THE CAUCASUS REGION. Text in English. 2007 (Sep.). q. USD 295 to institutions; USD 442 combined subscription to institutions (print & online eds.) (effective 2012). **Document type:** *Journal, Academic/Scholarly.*
Related titles: Online - full text ed.: USD 295 (effective 2012).
Published by: Nova Science Publishers, Inc., 400 Oser Ave, Ste 1600, Hauppauge, NY 11788. TEL 631-231-7269, FAX 631-231-8175, main@novapublishers.com. Ed. Frank Columbus.

320 330.9 USA ISSN 1939-5809
CURRENT POLITICS AND ECONOMICS OF THE MIDDLE EAST. Text in English. 2008. q. USD 250 to institutions; USD 375 combined subscription to institutions (print & online eds.) (effective 2012). **Document type:** *Journal, Academic/Scholarly.*
Related titles: Online - full text ed.: USD 250 to institutions (effective 2012).
Published by: Nova Science Publishers, Inc., 400 Oser Ave, Ste 1600, Hauppauge, NY 11788. TEL 631-231-7269, FAX 631-231-8175, main@novapublishers.com. Ed. Frank Columbus.

320.973 USA
CURRENT POLITICS AND ECONOMICS OF THE UNITED STATES, CANADA AND MEXICO. Text in English. 1993. 9/yr. USD 715 to institutions; USD 1,072 combined subscription to institutions (print & online eds.) (effective 2012). **Document type:** *Journal, Academic/Scholarly.*
Formerly (until 2006): Current Politics and Economics of the United States (1098-4143)
Related titles: Online - full text ed.: USD 715 to institutions (effective 2012).
Published by: Nova Science Publishers, Inc., 400 Oser Ave, Ste 1600, Hauppauge, NY 11788. TEL 631-231-7269, FAX 631-231-8175, main@novapublishers.com. Ed. Frank Columbus.

320 USA
CURRENT POPULATION REPORTS. POPULATION CHARACTERISTICS. VOTING AND REGISTRATION IN THE ELECTION. Text in English. a. **Document type:** *Government.*
Related titles: Online - full content ed.
Published by: U.S. Census Bureau. Population Division (Subsidiary of: U.S. Department of Commerce), 4600 Silver Hill Rd., Washington, DC 20233. TEL 866-758-1060.

CURRENT TRENDS IN ISLAMIST IDEOLOGY. *see* RELIGIONS AND THEOLOGY—Islamic

320.9 GBR
CYMRU. Text in English, Welsh. 1997. q. GBP 10 (effective 1998). adv. bk.rev. illus. **Document type:** *Newspaper.* **Description:** Contains critical and radical political articles, historical articles, and general information about the Plaid Cymru political party.
Formed by the merger of (1932-1997): Welsh Nation (0043-2458); (1925-1997): Y Ddraig Goch
Related titles: Microfilm ed.: (from WMP).
Published by: Plaid Cymru, National Office, 18 Park Grove, Cardiff, CF1 3BN, United Kingdom. TEL 44-1222-646000, FAX 44-1222-646001. Ed. Anna Brychan. Adv. contacts Geraint Day TEL 29-2064-6000, Nigel Bevan. Circ: 11,000.

322 DEU
DT36
D A S P - REIHE. Text in German. 1985. irreg., latest vol.143, 2008. price varies. **Document type:** *Monographic series, Academic/Scholarly.*
Formerly (until 1995): D A S P - Hefte (0935-5480)
Indexed: MLA-IB, PAIS.
Published by: Deutsche Gesellschaft fuer die Afrikanischen Staaten Portugiesischer Sprache, Baadenberger Str 40, Cologne, 50825, Germany. FAX 49-221-552425, info@dasp.eu.com.

D D R STUDIEN/EAST GERMAN STUDIES. *see* HISTORY

320 DNK ISSN 0905-5525
D S U'EREN. (Danmarks Socialdemokratiske Ungdom) Text in Danish. 1990. 4/yr. DKK 200 (effective 2008). adv. bk.rev. illus. **Document type:** *Bulletin, Consumer.* **Description:** Focuses on Danish and international politics as seen through the eyes of young Danish Social Democrats.
Formed by the merger of (1970-1990): Roedt og Rimeligt (0902-3550); Which was formerly (until 1986): S O C (0108-6081); (1987-1990): 5 Minutter (0904-6356)
Published by: Danmarks Socialdemokratiske Ungdom, Danasvej 7, Frederiksberg, 1910, Denmark. TEL 45-72-300880, FAX 45-72-300899, dsu@dsu.net, http://www.dsu.net. Ed. Niels Peter Boegballe.

320 VNM ISSN 1022-8829
DAI DOAN KET/GREAT UNITY. Text in Vietnamese. 1977. w.
Published by: Viet-Nam Fatherland Front, 66 Ba Trieu, Hanoi, Viet Nam. TEL 62420. Ed. Nguyen Ngoc Thach.

321 USA ISSN 1946-6986
J80
DAILY COMPILATION OF PRESIDENTIAL DOCUMENTS. Text in English. 1965. w. USD 133 domestic; USD 186.20 foreign (effective 2005). illus. index. back issues avail.; reprints avail. **Document type:** *Government.* **Description:** Makes available to the public transcripts of the President's news conferences, messages to Congress, public speeches and statements, and other presidential materials released by the White House.
Formerly (until 2009): Weekly Compilation of Presidential Documents (0511-4187)
Media: Online - full text. **Related titles:** Microfiche ed.: (from WSH); Online - full text ed.
Indexed: A01, A02, A03, A08, A22, A25, A26, C12, ChPerI, Chicano, E08, G05, G06, G07, G08, I02, I05, I07, M01, M02, M05, M06, MASUSE, P02, P05, P06, P34, PAIS, PQC, PRA, R02, RASB, S08, S09.
Published by: National Archives and Records Administration, U.S. Office of the Federal Register, 8601 Adelphi Rd, College Park, MD 20740. TEL 202-741-6000, FAX 202-741-6012, http://www.federalregister.gov. Circ: 7,000. **Subscr. to:** U.S. Government Printing Office, Superintendent of Documents, PO Box 371954, Pittsburgh, PA 15250. TEL 202-512-1800, FAX 202-512-2250, orders@gpo.gov, http://www.access.gpo.gov.

DAILY LEGISLATIVE REPORT (BATON ROUGE). *see* PUBLIC ADMINISTRATION

DAILY LEGISLATIVE REPORT (JACKSON). *see* PUBLIC ADMINISTRATION

DAILY LEGISLATIVE REPORT (SPRINGFIELD). *see* PUBLIC ADMINISTRATION

DAILY LEGISLATIVE REPORTER. *see* PUBLIC ADMINISTRATION

DAITO BUNKA COMPARATIVE LAW AND POLITICAL SCIENCE REVIEW. *see* LAW

320.532 CHN ISSN 1006-5458
JQ1519.A5
DANG DE JIANSHE. Text in Chinese. 1982. m. **Document type:** *Magazine, Government.*
Related titles: Online - full text ed.
Published by: (Zhong-Gong Gansu Sheng-Wei), Dang De Jianshe Zazhishe, 1648, Nanchang Lu, Lanzhou, 730030, China. TEL 86-931-8288536, FAX 86-931-8729085.

320.532 CHN ISSN 1002-2597
DANG DE SHENGHUO (HA'ERBIN). Text in Chinese. 1959. m. **Document type:** *Magazine, Government.*
Supersedes in part: Zhibu Shenghuo (1003-6032)
Related titles: Online - full text ed.

Published by: Dang De Shenghuo Zazhishe, 8, Ashenhe Lu, Ha'erbin, 150001, China. TEL 86-451-53633001, FAX 86-451-53642328.

320.532 CHN ISSN 1003-7497
DANG DE SHENGHUO (NANJING). Text in Chinese. 1965. m. **Document type:** *Magazine, Government.*
Supersedes in part: Zhibu Shenghuo (1003-6032)
Published by: Dang De Shenghuo Zazhishe, 16, Beijing Xi Lu, Nanjing, 210008, China. TEL 86-25-83249405.

320.532 CHN ISSN 1003-9570
DANG DE SHENGHUO (ZHENGZHOU). Text in English. m. **Document type:** *Magazine, Government.*
Supersedes in part: Zhibu Shenghuo (1003-6032)
Published by: (Zhong-Gong Henan Sheng-Wei), Dang De Shenghuo Zazhishe, 6, Jinshui Lu, Zhengzhou, 450003, China. TEL 86-371-65629080.

320.532 CHN ISSN 1002-9702
DANG JIAN/PARTY CONSTRUCTION. Text in Chinese. 1988. m. CNY 16.80 (effective 1994). adv. bk.rev. **Document type:** *Government.*
Related titles: Online - full text ed.
Published by: (China, People's Republic. Xuanchuan Bu/Ministry of Propaganda), Dang Jian Zazhishe, 5, Xichangan Jie, Xicheng-qu, Beijing, 100806, China. TEL 301-7964. Ed. Song Shizhong. Adv. contact Hu Pengguang.

320.532 CHN ISSN 1002-6045
DANG-JIAN YANJIU/C P C CONSTRUCTION STUDIES. Text in Chinese. 1989. m. **Document type:** *Journal, Academic/Scholarly.*
Published by: Zhong-Gong Zhongyang Zuzhibu, Dang-Jian Yanjiu Zazhishe, 80, Xichangan Lu, Beijing, 100815, China. TEL 86-10-58586930.

320.532 CHN ISSN 1007-3566
DANGDAI DANGYUAN/MODERN PARTY MEMBER. Text in Chinese. 1982. m. **Document type:** *Magazine, Government.*
Former titles (until 1990): Chongqing Zhibu Shenghuo; (until 1988): Zhibu Shenghuo
Published by: Zhongguo Gongchandang Chongqing Shi Weiyuanhui, 1, Zaozilan Yacun, Chongqing, 400015, China. TEL 86-23-63865241, FAX 86-23-63857051.

320.531 CHN ISSN 1001-5574
DANGDAI SHIJIE SHEHUIZHUYI WENTI/ISSUES OF CONTEMPORARY WORLD SOCIALISM. Text in Chinese. 1986. q. USD 16.40 (effective 2009). **Document type:** *Journal, Academic/Scholarly.*
Related titles: Online - full text ed.
—East View.
Address: Shangdong Daxue, 27, Danan Lu, no. 5, Hongjialou, Jinan, 250100, China.

320.532 CHN ISSN 1006-8031
DANGSHI BOCAI. Text in Chinese. 1988. m. USD 36 (effective 2009). **Document type:** *Journal, Academic/Scholarly.*
Related titles: Online - full text ed.
Address: 265, Heping Xilu, Shijiazhuang, 050071, China. TEL 86-311-7041637, FAX 86-311-7824874.

335.4 CHN ISSN 1005-1686
JQ1519.A5
DANGSHI BOLAN/GENERAL REVIEW OF THE COMMUNIST PARTY OF CHINA. Text in Chinese. 1992. m. USD 28.80 (effective 2009). **Document type:** *Journal, Academic/Scholarly.* **Description:** Contains information on Chinese communism, information about key party leaders, the history of the political movement, and the modern China.
Related titles: Online - full text ed.
—East View.
Published by: Dangshi Bolan Zazhishe, Shengwei Dayuan, Zhengzhou, 450003, China. TEL 86-371-65903334, FAX 86-371-65904173.

320.532 900 800 CHN ISSN 1004-8707
JQ1519.A5
DANGSHI TIANDI/STORIES FROM C P C HISTORY. Text in Chinese. 1992. m. USD 36 (effective 2009). **Document type:** *Journal, Academic/Scholarly.*
Related titles: Online - full content ed.; Online - full text ed.
Published by: Zhonggong Hubeisheng Weidangshi Yanjiushi, Shuiguohushengwei Dayuang, Wuhan, 430071, China. TEL 86-27-87232724.

320.532 CHN ISSN 1003-708X
JQ1519.A5
DANGSHI YANJIU YU JIAOXUE/PARTY HISTORY RESEARCH & TEACHING. Text in Chinese. 1979. bi-m. **Document type:** *Journal, Academic/Scholarly.*
Former titles (until 1987): Dangshi Ziliao yu Yanjiu; (until 1982): Dangshi Yanjiu Cankao Ziliao
Published by: Zhong-Gong Fujian Sheng-Wei Dangxiao, 61, Liuhe Lu, Fuzhou, 350001, China. TEL 86-591-83792054, FAX 86-591-83792054, http://www.fjdx.gov.cn/.

320.532 951 CHN ISSN 1005-9482
DANGSHI ZONGLAN/SCAN OF THE C P C HISTORY. Text in Chinese. 1981. m. USD 36 (effective 2009). **Document type:** *Journal, Academic/Scholarly.*
Formerly: Anhui Dangshi Yanjiu (1004-2067)
Related titles: Online - full text ed.
—East View.
Address: 57, Changjiang Zhong Lu, Hefei, 230001, China. TEL 86-551-2606693, FAX 86-551-2608236. **Dist. by:** China International Book Trading Corp, 35 Chegongzhuang Xilu, Haidian District, PO Box 399, Beijing 100044, China. TEL 86-10-68412045, FAX 86-10-68412023, cibtc@mail.cibtc.com.cn, http://www.cibtc.com.cn.

320.532 CHN ISSN 1007-3388
DANGYUAN WENZHAI. Text in Chinese. 1985. m. **Document type:** *Magazine, Government.*
Published by: Zhongguo Gongchandang Chongqing Shi Weiyuanhui, 1, Zaozilan Yacun, Chongqing, 400015, China. TEL 86-23-63865053, FAX 86-23-63852616.

320.532 CHN ISSN 1672-8734
DANGZHIBU GONGZUO ZHIDAO. Text in Chinese. 1990. m. **Document type:** *Journal, Academic/Scholarly.*
Address: 3-A-28C, Chaoyang Lu Shilipu Jia, Beijing, 100025, China.

320.532 CHN ISSN 1673-2561
DANGZHIBU SHUJI. Text in Chinese. s-m. CNY 96 (effective 2009). **Document type:** *Government.* **Description:** Contains 2 editions: 1st-Half Month Edition covers the current work of the party, and 2nd-Half Month Edition covers political education and party views on specific subjects.
Related titles: Online - full text ed.
Published by: Dangzhibu Shuji Zazhishe, 45, Heping Nan Dajie, Shenyang, 110006, China. TEL 86-24-23218742, FAX 86-24-23862253, reader@zhxf.cn.

320 CHN ISSN 1005-6807
DAODE YU WENMING/MORALITY AND CIVILIZATION. Text in Chinese. 1982. bi-m. **Document type:** *Journal, Academic/Scholarly.*
Formerly: Lunlixue yu Jingshen Wenming
Related titles: Online - full text ed.
Published by: Tianjin Shi Shehui Kexueyuan, 7, Yingshuidao, Nankai-qu, Tianjin, 300191, China. TEL 86-22-23075325. Ed. Li Qi. **Dist. by:** China International Book Trading Corp, 35 Chegongzhuang Xilu, Haidian District, PO Box 399, Beijing 100044, China. TEL 86-10-68412045, FAX 86-10-68412023, cibtc@mail.cibtc.com.cn, http://www.cibtc.com.cn.

320.6 GBR ISSN 0958-6067
DAVID HUME PAPER. Text in English. 1985. irreg. **Document type:** *Monographic series, Academic/Scholarly.*
Formerly (until 1988): Hume Paper (0955-3177)
—CCC.
Published by: David Hume Institute, 25 Buccleuch Place, Edinburgh, EH8 9LN, United Kingdom. Hume.Institute@ed.ac.uk, http://www.davidhumeinstitute.com.

320.57 USA
THE DAWN; a monthly advocate for constructive anarchism. Text in English. m. USD 10 domestic; GBP 15 in United Kingdom (effective 2005).
Published by: The Dawn Group, P O Box 24715, Oakland, CA 94623. ed@the-dawn.org, http://www.the-dawn.org.

320 351.753 USA ISSN 1546-4296
JK2716
DCWATCH. (District of Columbia) Text in English. 1997 (Aug.). irreg. free (effective 2004). **Description:** Covers Washington, DC, local city politics and public affairs.
Media: Online - full content.
Address: 1327 Girard St, N W, Washington, DC 20009-4915.

DE L'AUTRE COTE. *see* ETHNIC INTERESTS

320 NLD ISSN 1877-0304
DEBAT. Text in Dutch. 1988. 5/yr. EUR 16 (effective 2011). **Document type:** *Journal, Academic/Scholarly.*
Published by: Studievereniging voor Politicologen in Leiden, Wassenaarseweg 52, Leiden, 2333 AK, Netherlands. TEL 31-71-5273872, spil@fsw.leidenuniv.nl.

320.6 AUS ISSN 1835-7873
DEBATE; debating tomorrow's public policy. Text in English. 2007. q. AUD 38; AUD 9.95 per issue (print or online ed.) (effective 2011). adv. back issues avail. **Document type:** *Magazine, Trade.* **Description:** Focuses on exposing, comparing and critically analysing public policy issues or party policy positions.
Related titles: Online - full text ed.: ISSN 1835-7881. AUD 32 (effective 2011).
Published by: Fine Line Design & Publishing Pty Ltd., Unit 1, Ground Fl Rowland House, 10 Thesiger Ct, Deakin, ACT 2600, Australia. TEL 61-2-61623336, FAX 61-2-61623337, http://www.finelinedesign.net.au.

320 ARG ISSN 1668-1789
EL DEBATE POLITICO. Text in Spanish. 2003. s-a. ARS 19 to individuals; ARS 25 to institutions (effective 2010). **Document type:** *Journal, Academic/Scholarly.*
Published by: Fondo de Cultura Economica de Argentina, El Salvador, 5665, Buenos Aires, 1414, Argentina. TEL 54-11-52389300, FAX 54-11-43751373, fondo@fce.com.ar, http://www.fce.com.ar.

DEBATES I E S A. *see* SOCIAL SCIENCES: COMPREHENSIVE WORKS

320.531 GUF ISSN 0751-9044
DEBOUT GUYANE. Text in French. 1956. m. GNF 20.
Published by: Parti Socialiste Guyanais, Cite Cesaire, Cayenne, 97300, French Guiana. TEL 594-305904, FAX 594-305597. Circ: 1,500.

320.5 303.4 FRA ISSN 1767-0187
LA DECROISSANCE. Text in French. 2004. m. EUR 19 domestic; EUR 25 in the European Union; EUR 28 elsewhere (effective 2009). **Document type:** *Magazine, Consumer.*
Published by: Casseurs de Pub, 11 Place Croix-Paquet, Lyon, 69001, France. TEL 33-4-72000982, redaction@ladecroissance.net.

320 USA ISSN 1947-4962
▼ **DEFINING IDEAS.** Text in English. 2009 (Fall). q. USD 25 (effective 2009). **Document type:** *Journal, Academic/Scholarly.* **Description:** Outreach and information from the Hoover Institute.
Related titles: Online - full text ed.: ISSN 1947-4970. 2009.
Published by: Hoover Institution on War, Revolution and Peace, Stanford, CA 94305-6010. TEL 650-723-1754, FAX 650-723-1687, lmaune@stanford.edu, http://www.hoover.org.

320.5 UKR ISSN 0135-566X
DELOVAYA ZHIZN'. Text in Russian. 1990. m. USD 155 (effective 2000). adv. **Document type:** *Journal.* **Description:** Covers politics, taxes, legislation, economics, bank activity, enterprise affairs, business leaders.
Published by: Vostochno-Ukrain'skaya Akademiya Biznesa, Ul Artema 43, Kharkov, 61002, Ukraine. TEL 380-572-437057, 380-572-142388, FAX 380-572-142388, acadof@online.kharkov.ua. Circ: 5,000. **Dist. by:** East View Information Services, 10601 Wayzata Blvd, Minneapolis, MN 55305. TEL 952-252-1201, 800-477-1005, FAX 952-252-1202, info@eastview.com, http://www.eastview.com.

320.5 RUS ISSN 0869-4729
JN6598.V7
DELOVAYA ZHIZN'. Text in Russian. 1919. m. USD 292 foreign (effective 2005). adv. bk.rev. bibl. **Document type:** *Magazine, Consumer.*
Formerly (until 1991): Partiinaya Zhizn' (0132-0734)
Indexed: CDSP, RASB.
Address: Miusskaya pl 6, Moscow, 125267, Russian Federation. Ed. V Churilov. adv.: B&W page USD 1,000, color page USD 1,500. Circ: 20,000 (paid and controlled). **Dist. by:** East View Information Services, 10601 Wayzata Blvd, Minneapolis, MN 55305. TEL 952-252-1201, 800-477-1005, FAX 952-252-1202, info@eastview.com, http://www.eastview.com.

320.532 CUB ISSN 0864-1269
LA DEMAJAGUA. Text in Spanish. 1977. w.
Related titles: Online - full text ed.: ISSN 1681-9942.
Published by: Partido Comunista de Cuba, Comite Provincial Granma, Amado Estevez y Calle 10, Granma, Cuba. TEL 537-424221, FAX 537-425889, ibrsc@yahoo.es. Ed. Ibrahim Sanchez Carrillo.

320.51 NLD ISSN 0925-4390
DEMO; liberal-democratic magazine. Text in Dutch. 1984. q. adv. bk.rev. illus.; stat. **Document type:** *Bulletin.*
Related titles: Online - full text ed.
Published by: Jonge Democraten/Young Democrats, Postbus 660, The Hague, 2501 CR, Netherlands. FAX 31-70-3641917, info@jongedemocraten.nl, http://www.jongedemocraten.nl. Ed. Thijs Kleinpaste. Circ: 2,750.

324.2 NLD ISSN 0167-0034
DEMOCRAAT. Text in Dutch. 1967. 3/yr. free (effective 2010). adv. 4 p./no. 3 cols./p.; **Document type:** *Magazine, Consumer.* **Description:** Contains articles on various political subjects, interviews with Dutch politicians, party news and agenda, and political columns.
Incorporates: D 66 Nieuwsbrief (0922-6796)
Related titles: Online - full text ed.
—IE, Infotrieve.
Published by: Democraten 66, Postbus 660, The Hague, 2501 CR, Netherlands. TEL 31-70-3566066, info@d66.nl. Circ: 15,000.

321.8 SLV
DEMOCRACIA. Text in Spanish. 199?. m.?. illus. **Document type:** *Academic/Scholarly.*
Published by: Instituto Salvadoreno de Estudios Politicos, 1a Calle Poniente No. 3549, Col. Escalon,, Apdo. Postal 2687, San Salvador, El Salvador. TEL 98-1908.

321.8 BRA
DEMOCRACIA NA TERRA. Text in Portuguese. bi-m. BRL 5,000, USD 30 to individuals; BRL 8,500, USD 60 to institutions. **Document type:** *Bulletin.*
Supersedes (in 1991): C N R A Informa
Published by: Instituto Brasileiro de Analises Sociais e Economicas, Rua Vicente de Sousa 29, Botafogo, RJ 22251-070, Brazil. TEL 286-6161. **Co-sponsor:** Campanha Nacional pela Reforma Agraria.

320.51 USA ISSN 1931-8693
JK1
DEMOCRACY (WASHINGTON, D.C.); a journal of ideas. Text in English. 2006. q. USD 24 domestic; USD 34 in Canada; USD 50 elsewhere (effective 2008). adv. **Document type:** *Magazine, Consumer.*
Related titles: Online - full text ed.: ISSN 1931-8707.
Indexed: CA, P10, P27, P42, P45, P48, P54, PAIS, PQC, PSA, S02, S03, SociolAb, T02.
Published by: Democracy, a Journal of Ideas, Inc., 2120 L St, NW, Ste 305, Washington, DC 20037. TEL 202-263-4382, 888-238-0048, dajoi@democracyjournal.org, http://www.democracyjournal.org/index.php. Eds. Andrei Cherny, Kenneth Baer.

321.8 USA ISSN 1741-9166
UA10.5
DEMOCRACY AND SECURITY. Text in English. 2005. 3/yr. GBP 277 combined subscription in United Kingdom to institutions (print & online eds.); EUR 368, USD 462 combined subscription to institutions (print & online eds.) (effective 2012). adv. reprint service avail. from PSC. **Document type:** *Journal, Academic/Scholarly.* **Description:** Publishes theoretical and empirical articles on the concepts and functions of democracy and security, with a focus on the diverse perspectives of national and internal security challenges and policies, and policy analysis.
Related titles: Online - full text ed.: ISSN 1555-5860. GBP 249 in United Kingdom to institutions; EUR 332, USD 416 to institutions (effective 2012) (from IngentaConnect).
Indexed: A22, CA, E01, ESPM, I02, IBSS, P42, PAIS, PSA, RiskAb, SSciA, T02.
—IE, Ingenta. **CCC.**
Published by: Taylor & Francis Inc. (Subsidiary of: Taylor & Francis Group), 325 Chestnut St, Ste 800, Philadelphia, PA 19106. TEL 215-625-2940, 800-354-1420, orders@taylorandfrancis.com, http://www.taylorandfrancis.com. Eds. Gabriel Ben-Dor, Leonard Weinberg.

DEMOCRACY AND THE NEWS. *see* JOURNALISM

321.8 USA
DEMOCRACY IN THE WORLD. Text in English. 1986. irreg., latest 1988. price varies. **Document type:** *Monographic series.*
Published by: Praeger Publishers (Subsidiary of: Greenwood Publishing Group Inc.), 88 Post Rd W, Westport, CT 06881. TEL 800-368-6868, tech.support@greenwood.com, http://www.greenwood.com.

321.8 USA ISSN 1938-6931
DEMOCRACY STUDIES WEEKLY. Text in English. 2007 (Aug.). q. USD 9.98 to students 1-9 students; USD 4.99 to students 10 or more students (effective 2010 - 2011). **Document type:** *Newsletter, Consumer.*
Published by: American Legacy Publishing, 1922 W 200 N, Lindon, UT 84042. TEL 866-311-8734, FAX 866-531-5589, service@studiesweekly.com. Ed. Nicole Hefner. Pub. Edward Rickers.

324.2468 ZAF
DEMOCRAT. Text in Afrikaans, English. 1971. 5/yr. free to members. adv. bk.rev. illus. **Document type:** *Newsletter.*
Former titles (until Mar. 1989): Progress; Newsline; Deurbraak (0033-0582); Which was formed by the merger of: Party's Afrikaans Magazine; (1967-1970): Progress
Published by: Democratic Party/Demokratiese Party, 501 Ruskin House, 2 Roeland St, Cape Town, 8001, South Africa. TEL 27-21-451431, FAX 27-21-4615276. Circ: 60,000.

320 USA ISSN 0164-3207
HX1 CODEN: ADPHDK
DEMOCRATIC LEFT. Text in English. 1972. bi-m. USD 35 membership (effective 2005). adv. bk.rev. bibl.; illus. back issues avail.; reprints avail. **Document type:** *Newsletter.* **Description:** Features organizational affairs. Views of rank-and-file activists are also heard in this effective alliance of grassroots and national organizers.
Formerly: Newsletter of the Democratic Left
Related titles: Microform ed.; Online - full text ed.
Indexed: APW, AltPI, P45.
Published by: Democratic Socialists of America, 180 Varick St, 12th Fl, New York, NY 10014-4606. TEL 212-727-8610, campd227@pachell.net. Ed. Kathy Quinn. Circ: 12,000.

321.8 SDN
DEMOCRATIC REPUBLIC OF THE SUDAN GAZETTE. LEGISLATIVE SUPPLEMENT. Variant title: Democratic Republic of the Sudan Gazette. Special Legislative Supplement. Text in English. irreg.
Related titles: Arabic ed.: Mulhaq at-Tashri Lil-Jaridah ar-Rasmiyah li-Jumhuriyat as-Sudan ad-Dimuqratiyah.
Published by: Attorney General, Attorney General's Chambers, P O Box 302, Khartoum, Sudan.

321.8 ZAF
DEMOKRATIA. Text in Afrikaans, English. 1989. every 6 wks. free to qualified personnel. **Document type:** *Newsletter.*
Published by: Democratic Party/Demokratiese Party, 501 Ruskin House, 2 Roeland St, Cape Town, 8001, South Africa. TEL 27-21-451431, FAX 27-21-4615276. Circ: 4,000.

320 700 100 BGR ISSN 1310-2311
DR51
DEMOKRATICHESKI PREGLED. Text in Bulgarian. 1993. q. USD 52 foreign; BGL 5 newsstand/cover domestic (effective 2002). **Document type:** *Magazine, Consumer.* **Description:** Tries to cover the interdisciplinary diversity of contemporary liberal political and cultural studies, presenting current world debates (on minorities and communities, turn-of-the century collectivistic emotions, views of and on liberalism) and challenging them in a Bulgarian cultural context by having Bulgarian and foreign authors in dialogue with each other.
Published by: Grazhdanin/Citizen, 24 Ekzarh Lossif St, Sofia, 1000, Bulgaria. TEL 359-2-9877302 359-2-, FAX 359-2-9877567, csociety@mbox.cit.bg, http://www.dem-pr.hit.bg. Ed. Mikhail Nedelchev. **Dist. by:** Sofia Books, ul Silivria 16, Sofia 1404, Bulgaria. TEL 359-2-9586257, info@sofiabooks-bg.com, http://www.sofiabooks-bg.com.

321.8 DEU ISSN 1613-7930
DEMOKRATIE UND DEMOKRATISIERUNGSPROZESSE. Text in German. 2004. irreg., latest vol.7, 2009. price varies. **Document type:** *Monographic series, Academic/Scholarly.*
Published by: Verlag Dr. Kovac, Leverkusenstr 13, Hamburg, 22761, Germany. TEL 49-40-3988800, FAX 49-40-39888055, info@verlagdrkovac.de.

DEMOKRATIE UND GESCHICHTE. *see* HISTORY—History Of Europe

320.943 AUT
DEMOKRATISCHE BEWEGUNGEN IN MITTELDEUTSCHLAND. Text in German. irreg., latest vol.9, 2003. price varies. **Document type:** *Monographic series, Academic/Scholarly.*
Published by: Boehlau Verlag GmbH & Co.KG., Wiesingerstr 1, Vienna, W 1010, Austria. TEL 43-1-3302427, FAX 43-1-3302432, boehlau@boehlau.at, http://www.boehlau.at.

321.8 USA ISSN 1074-6846
JN6501
➤ **DEMOKRATIZATSIYA**; the journal of post-soviet democratization. Text in English. 1992. q. USD 148 to institutions; USD 60 combined subscription to individuals (print & online eds.); USD 177 combined subscription to institutions (print & online eds.) (effective 2010). adv. back issues avail.; reprint service avail. from PSC. **Document type:** *Journal, Academic/Scholarly.* **Description:** Covers the historical and current transformation in the Soviet Union and its successor states.
Related titles: Online - full text ed.: ISSN 1940-4603. USD 57 to individuals; USD 148 to institutions (effective 2010).
Indexed: A01, A03, A08, A26, ABS&EES, APW, B04, BRD, CA, E08, G06, G07, G08, GEOBASE, I05, I13, P10, P13, P34, P42, P45, P47, P48, P53, P54, PAIS, PQC, PSA, S02, S03, S09, S11, SCOPUS, SSAI, SSAb, SSI, SociolAb, T02, W01, W02, W03, W05.
—BLDSC (3550.623700), IE, Ingenta. **CCC.**
Published by: (Helen Dwight Reid Educational Foundation), Heldref Publications, c/o Taylor & Francis, 325 Chestnut St, Ste 800, Philadelphia, PA 19106. TEL 215-625-8900, heldref@subscriptionoffice.com, http://www.heldref.org. **Subscr. to:** Allen Press Inc., PO Box 1897, Lawrence, KS 66044; **Subscr. to:** PO Box 830350, Birmingham, AL 35283. TEL 866-802-7059, FAX 205-995-1588.

320 BGR
DEMOKRATSIA. Text in Bulgarian. d. **Document type:** *Newspaper.*
Published by: Union of Democratic Forces, 134 Rakovski St., Sofia, Bulgaria. TEL 359-2-9818035, pr@sds.bg.

320 300 GBR
DEMOS COLLECTION. Text in English. 1994. biennial. GBP 100 (effective 2000); includes monographs. **Document type:** *Journal, Academic/Scholarly.*
Formerly (until no. 11): Demos Quarterly (1361-1275)
—BLDSC (3550.630250), IE, Ingenta. **CCC.**
Published by: Demos, The Mezzanine, Elizabeth House, 39 York Rd, London, SE1 7NQ, United Kingdom. TEL 44-20-7401-5330, FAX 44-20-7401-5331, http://www.demos.co.uk. R&P Lindsay Nash. **Dist. by:** Central Books, 99 Wallis Rd, London E9 5LN, United Kingdom. TEL 44-20-8986-5488, FAX 44-20-8533-5821.

320 300 GBR
DEMOS. PUBLICATIONS. Text in English. 1993. irreg. GBP 35 to individuals; GBP 175 to institutions (effective 2001). **Document type:** *Monographic series, Academic/Scholarly.* **Description:** Seeks radical solutions to long-term problems.
Formerly (until 1999): Demos. Papers
Published by: Demos, The Mezzanine, Elizabeth House, 39 York Rd, London, SE1 7NQ, United Kingdom. TEL 44-20-7401-5330, FAX 44-20-7401-5331, http://www.demos.co.uk. Ed. Tom Bentley. R&P Lindsay Nash. **Dist. by:** Central Books, 99 Wallis Rd, London E9 5LN, United Kingdom. TEL 44-20-8986-5488, FAX 44-20-8533-5821.

I DEPUTATI E SENATORI DEL PARLAMENTO REPUBBLICANO. ANNUARIO. *see* PUBLIC ADMINISTRATION

320 FRA ISSN 1950-0378
DES PAROLES EN ACTES. Text in French. 2006. irreg. back issues avail. **Document type:** *Monographic series, Consumer.*
Published by: Editions Syllepse, 69 rue des Rigoles, Paris, 75020, France. TEL 33-1-44620889.

320.531 FRA ISSN 1952-2452
DES POINGS ET DES ROSES. Text in French. 2006. irreg. back issues avail. **Document type:** *Monographic series.*
Published by: (Office Universitaire de Recherche Socialiste (OURS)), L' Harmattan, 5 Rue de l'Ecole Polytechnique, Paris, 75005, France. TEL 33-1-43257651, FAX 33-1-43258203.

320 ARG ISSN 1666-5007
DEUS MORTALIS. Text in Spanish. 2002. a. ARS 15 (effective 2010). back issues avail. **Document type:** *Monographic series, Academic/Scholarly.*
Published by: Dotti Publicaciones, Guemes 776, Buenos Aires, 1641, Argentina. TEL 54-11-48135463, FAX 54-11-47734474, jorgedotti@uolsinectis.com.ar. Circ: 500.

320.51 DEU ISSN 0934-3040
DEUTSCHE STIMME; Monatszeitung fuer Politik und Kultur. Text in German. 1976. m. EUR 28 domestic; EUR 35 foreign (effective 2009). adv. bk.rev. **Document type:** *Newspaper, Consumer.*
Published by: Deutsche Stimme Verlagsgesellschaft mbH, Mannheimer Str 4, Riesa, 01591, Germany. TEL 49-3525-52920, FAX 49-3525-529222. Ed. Karl Richter. Adv. contact Karin Haase. Circ: 25,000 (paid and controlled).

320 DEU ISSN 0723-4295
DEUTSCHE UMSCHAU. Text in German. 1954. m. EUR 16; EUR 1.50 newsstand/cover (effective 2009). adv. bk.rev. illus.; stat. **Document type:** *Magazine, Consumer.*
Formerly: Heimatwacht
Published by: Bund der Vertriebene e.V., Bismarckstr 90, Duesseldorf, 40210, Germany. TEL 49-211-350361, FAX 49-211-369676, info@bdv-nrw.de, http://www.bdv-nrw.de. Ed. Markus Patzke. adv.: B&W page EUR 2,500. Circ: 28,000 (paid and controlled).

DEVELOPING ECONOMIES. *see* BUSINESS AND ECONOMICS—International Development And Assistance

320 USA ISSN 1086-7937
THE DEWEESE REPORT. Text in English. 1994-2000; resumed. m. USD 57 (effective 2007). 8 p./no.; **Document type:** *Newsletter, Trade.*
Contact Owner: American Policy Center, 70 Main St., Ste 23, Warrenton, VA 20186. TEL 540-341-8911, FAX 540-341-8917, apc@americanpolicy.org. Circ: 40,000.

DIALECTICAL ANTHROPOLOGY; an independent international journal in the critical tradition committed to the transformation of our society and the humane union of theory and practice. *see* ANTHROPOLOGY

320.9 RUS ISSN 0236-0942
DK266.A2 CODEN: DIALEQ
DIALOG. Text in Russian. 1990. m. USD 95 (effective 1998).
Formed by the merger of (1956-1990): Agitator (0320-7161); Politicheskoe Obrazovanie (0235-327X); Formerly: Politicheskoe Samoobrazovanie (0132-070X)
Related titles: Microfiche ed.; Online - full text ed.
Indexed: CDSP, RASB.
Address: Miusskaya pr 6, Moscow, 125267, Russian Federation. TEL 7-095-9723913. Ed. N Y Klepach. **Dist. by:** M K - Periodica, ul Gilyarovskogo 39, Moscow 129110, Russian Federation. TEL 7-095-2845008, FAX 7-095-2813798, info@periodicals.ru, http://www.mkniga.ru; **Dist. in U.S. by:** Victor Kamkin Inc., 220 Girard St, Ste 1, Gaithersburg, MD 20877. kamkin@kamkin.com.

DIALOGO SOCIAL. *see* SOCIOLOGY

321 CHL ISSN 0718-4581
DIALOGOS DE POLITICAS PUBLICAS. Text in Spanish. 2007. a. **Document type:** *Monographic series, Academic/Scholarly.*
Media: Online - full text.
Published by: Facultad Latinoamericana de Ciencias Sociales (F L A C S O), Chile, Av Dag Hammerskjold 3269, Vitacura, Santiago de Chile, Chile. TEL 56-2-2900200, FAX 56-2-2900263, publicaciones@flacso.cl.

324.2 GAB
DIALOGUE. Text in French. 1969. m.
Published by: Parti Democratique Gabonais, BP 213, Libreville, Gabon. Ed. Eloie Chambrien. Circ: 3,000.

320 ITA ISSN 1827-5575
DIBATTITI STORICI IN PARLAMENTO. Text in Italian. 2003. irreg. price varies. **Document type:** *Monographic series, Academic/Scholarly.*
Published by: Societa Editrice Il Mulino, Strada Maggiore 37, Bologna, 40125, Italy. TEL 39-051-256011, FAX 39-051-256034, riviste@mulino.it, http://www.mulino.it.

320 GBR
A DICTIONARY OF MODERN POLITICS. (Vol.2 is out of print. Vol.3 is due for publication in Spring 2002.) Text in English. 1985. irreg., latest 2002, 3rd ed. USD 265 per issue (effective 2009). reprints avail. **Document type:** *Monographic series, Trade.* **Description:** Provides a comprehensive guide to the ideology and terminology of the world of politics.
Published by: Routledge (Subsidiary of: Taylor & Francis Group), 2 Park Sq, Milton Park, Abingdon, Oxon OX14 4RN, United Kingdom. TEL 44-20-70176000, FAX 44-20-70176699, orders@taylorandfrancis.com.

320 CAN ISSN 1910-0884
DICTIONNAIRE SOCIETAS CRITICUS. Text in French. 2006. irreg. **Document type:** *Consumer.*
Media: Online - full text.
Published by: Michel Handfield delinkanintellectuel@hotmail.com, http://www.netrover.com/%7Estratji/dictio.htm. Ed. Michel Handfield.

320 DEU ISSN 0932-6162
DIESSEITS; Zeitschrift fur Aufklaerung und Humanismus. Text in German. 1959. q. EUR 12; EUR 4 newsstand/cover (effective 2006). bk.rev. back issues avail. **Document type:** *Magazine, Consumer.*
Formerly (until 1987): Stimme des Freidenkers (0721-1988)
Published by: Humanistischer Verband Deutschlands, Wallstr 61-65, Berlin, 10179, Germany. TEL 49-30-61390441, hvd-berlin@humanismus.de. Circ: 8,000.

320 DEU
DIKTATUREN UND IHRE UEBERWINDUNG IM 20. UND 21. JAHRHUNDERT. Text in German. 2008. irreg., latest vol.5, 2010. price varies. **Document type:** *Monographic series, Academic/Scholarly.*
Published by: Wallstein Verlag GmbH, Geiststr 11, Goettingen, 37073, Germany. TEL 49-551-548980, FAX 49-551-5489833, info@wallstein-verlag.de, http://www.wallstein-verlag.de.

320 USA ISSN 2161-7260
THE DIPLOMATIC COURIER; a global affairs magazine. Abbreviated title: D C. Text in English. 2006. q. USD 24.95 domestic to individuals; USD 49.95 to individuals in Africa, Europe, Middle East; USD 39.95 to individuals in Canada, South, Central America; USD 59.95 to individuals in Asia, Australia; USD 175 to institutions; USD 6.99 per issue (effective 2011). adv. back issues avail. **Document type:** *Magazine, Trade.*
Related titles: Online - full text ed.: ISSN 2161-7287. free (effective 2011).
Published by: Medauras Global, Llc., 1660 L St, NW, Ste 501, Washington, DC 20036. TEL 978-317-3844, FAX 202-659-5234, info@medauras.com, http://www.medauras.com/. Ed. Ana Carcani Rold.

320 RUS ISSN 0869-4869
DIPLOMATICHESKII VESTNIK. Text in Russian. 1987. m. USD 175 in the Americas (effective 2000).
Formerly (until 1990): Vestnik Ministerstva Inostrannyh del S S S R (0234-0038)
Related titles: Microfiche ed.: (from EVP).
Indexed: RASB.
Published by: Mezhdunarodnye Otnosheniya, Pr-t Vernadskogo 76, Moscow, 117454, Russian Federation. TEL 7-095-4349552, FAX 7-095-2002204.

320 DEU ISSN 1861-8162
DIPLOMICA. Text in German. 2003. irreg., latest vol.30, 2006. price varies. **Document type:** *Monographic series, Academic/Scholarly.*
Published by: Tectum Wissenschaftsverlag Marburg, Biegenstr 4, Marburg, 35037, Germany. TEL 49-6421-481523, FAX 49-6421-43470, email@tectum-verlag.de. Ed. Bjoern Bedey.

320 LBN ISSN 0417-5190
DS41
➤ **DIRASAT ARABIYAT/ARAB STUDIES**; majallat fikriyat iqtisdiyat ijtimaiyat. Text in Arabic. 1964. bi-m. USD 75. adv. bk.rev. **Document type:** *Journal, Academic/Scholarly.*
Indexed: M10, PerIslam.
Address: Dar at-Tali'at, P O Box 111813, Beirut, Lebanon. TEL 961-1-314659, FAX 961-1-309470, TELEX INTCO 20376 LE. Ed. Bashir Daouk. Circ: 6,500.

320.57 GBR ISSN 0261-8753
DIRECT ACTION. Text in English. 1981. q. GBP 5 domestic; GBP 10 in Europe; GBP 15 elsewhere (effective 2009). **Document type:** *Magazine, Consumer.* **Description:** Covers varies political-economics issues related to anarcho-syndicalist movement.
Related titles: Online - full text ed.: free (effective 2009).
Published by: Solidarity Federation, South West D.O, PO Box 29, Manchester, M15 5HW, United Kingdom. TEL 44-7-984675281, solfed@solfed.org.uk, http://www.solfed.org.uk/.

320.5322 CUB ISSN 0046-0338
DIRECT FROM CUBA. Text in English. 1969. s-m. USD 108. illus. reprints avail.
Related titles: Microform ed.: (from PQC).
Published by: Prensa Latina Agencia Informativa Latinoamericana, Calle 23 No. 201,, Vedado, La Habana, Cuba. Circ: (controlled).

DIRECTORIO DEL GOBIERNO. *see* PUBLIC ADMINISTRATION

320.9 BGR
DIRECTORY OF KEY BULGARIAN GOVERNMENT AND PARTY OFFICIALS. Text in Bulgarian. a. BGL 42. Supplement avail. **Description:** Includes state agencies, institutions, organizations.
Published by: Bulgarska Telegrafna Agentsia/Bulgarian Telegraph Agency, Tsarigradsko shose 49, Sofia, 1040, Bulgaria. TEL 359-2-9881719.

DIRECTORY OF WISCONSIN LEGISLATIVE AND CONGRESSIONAL DISTRICTS. *see* PUBLIC ADMINISTRATION

322.4 FRA ISSN 0294-8281
HD28
DIRIGEANT; magazine trimestriel du centre des jeunes dirigeants d'entreprise. Text in French. 1968. q. EUR 54 (effective 2009). adv. bk.rev. illus. **Document type:** *Magazine, Trade.*
Indexed: RASB.
Published by: Centre des Jeunes Dirigeants d'Entreprise, 19 Av. George V, Paris, 75008, France. TEL 33-1-53239250, FAX 33-1-40701566, http://www.cjd.net. Ed. Jean Marie Gorse. Circ: 5,000.

306.2 NLD ISSN 1569-9463
DISCOURSE APPROACHES TO POLITICS, SOCIETY AND CULTURE. Text in English. 2002. irreg., latest vol.43, 2011. price varies. **Document type:** *Monographic series, Academic/Scholarly.* **Description:** Investigates political, social and cultural processes from a linguistic/discourse-analytic point of view.
Published by: John Benjamins Publishing Co., PO Box 36224, Amsterdam, 1020 ME, Netherlands. TEL 31-20-6304747, FAX 31-20-6739773, customer.services@benjamins.nl. Eds. Greg Myers, Ruth Wodak.

320 ITA ISSN 0416-0371
LA DISCUSSIONE. Text in Italian. 1953. w. **Document type:** *Magazine, Consumer.*
Related titles: Online - full text ed.: ISSN 1722-3741. 2001.
Indexed: RASB.
Published by: Editrice Europa Oggi Srl, Via del Tritone 87, Rome, 00187, Italy. TEL 39-06-45496800. Ed. Marco Maddalena.

320 DEU ISSN 1865-6846
➤ **DISKURS**; politikwissenschaftliche und geschichtsphilosophische Interventionen. Text in German. 2005. 2/yr. EUR 40; EUR 24 newsstand/cover (effective 2010). **Document type:** *Journal, Academic/Scholarly.*
Published by: Meine Verlag OHG, Werner-Heisenberg-Str 3, Magdeburg, 39106, Germany. TEL 49-391-5446964, FAX 49-1803-62222910031, post@meine-verlag.de, http://www.meine-verlag.de.

320 GBR
DISPATCHES. Text in English. 2008. q. GBP 52.50 domestic; GBP 55.50 in Western Europe; USD 75 in United States; USD 82.50 in Canada; USD 84 in Latin America; GBP 58.50 elsewhere (effective 2009). back issues avail. **Document type:** *Magazine, Consumer.* **Description:** Addresses critical global issues.
Address: PO Box 2068, Bushey, WD23 3ZF, United Kingdom. TEL 44-20-89509117, info@rethink-dispatches.com. Eds. Gary Knight, Mort Rosenblum. Pub. Simba Gill.

320 DEU ISSN 0948-2407
DISPUT. Text in German. 1973. fortn. **Document type:** *Bulletin.*
Former titles (until 1992): Disput Was und Wie (0863-596X); (until 1990): Links Was und Wie (0863-5951); (until 1990): Was und Wie (0232-5772)
Published by: Parteivorstand der P D S, Kleine Alexanderstr 28, Berlin, 10178, Germany. TEL 49-30-24009657, FAX 49-30-24009400. Eds. Erwin Mueller, Georg Fehst.

320 AUS ISSN 1443-2102
DISSENT. Text in English. 1999. 3/yr. AUD 22 domestic; AUD 34.60 in Asia & the Pacific; AUD 40.45 elsewhere; AUD 7.70 per issue (effective 2009). back issues avail.; reprints avail. **Document type:** *Magazine, Trade.* **Description:** Discusses public affairs that include social and economic policy, education, politics, science and the environment, cultural matters, media and the arts.
Indexed: A11, AEI, AusPAIS, ERO, P42.
Published by: Dissent Publications Pty. Ltd., PO Box 26, Deakin West, ACT 2600, Australia. Eds. Kenneth Davidson, Lesley Vick.

320.9 USA ISSN 0012-3846
HX1
DISSENT (NEW YORK). Text in English. 1954. q. USD 25 to individuals; USD 53 to institutions; USD 18 to students (effective 2011). adv. bk.rev. illus. cum.index every 2 yrs. 128 p./no.; back issues avail.; reprints avail. **Document type:** *Magazine, Consumer.* **Description:** Contains features and articles about politics in the US, social and cultural commentary, and detailed coverage of European politics.
Related titles: Microform ed.: (from PQC); Online - full text ed.: ISSN 1946-0910. USD 17 to individuals (effective 2011).
Indexed: A01, A02, A03, A08, A20, A22, A25, A26, ABCPolSci, ABS&EES, APW, ASCA, AcaI, AltPI, AmH&L, AmHI, B04, B14, BAS, BRD, BRI, CA, CBRI, CurCont, DIP, E01, E02, E03, E07, E08, ERI, ESPM, EdA, EdI, FamI, FutSurv, G08, H07, H09, HPNRM, HRA, HistAb, I05, I13, IBR, IBZ, LeftInd, M01, M02, M06, M10, MLA-IB, P02, P04, P05, P06, P07, P10, P13, P27, P30, P34, P42, P45, P46, P47, P48, P53, P54, PAIS, PCI, PQC, PRA, PSA, PerIslam, RASB, RILM, S02, S03, S05, S08, S09, S11, SCOPUS, SOPODA, SSA, SSAI, SSAb, SSCI, SSI, SSciA, SWR&A, SociolAb, T02, W03, W05, W07.
—BLDSC (3598.900000), IE, Infotrieve, Ingenta. **CCC.**
Published by: Foundation for the Study of Independent Social Ideas, Inc., 310 Riverside Dr, Ste 2008, New York, NY 10025. Eds. Michael Kazin, Michael Walzer. Circ: 9,000.

320 301 DNK ISSN 1600-910X
HN1
➤ **DISTINKTION**; tidsskrift for samfundsteori. Text in English. 2000. s-a. GBP 155 combined subscription in United Kingdom to institutions (print & online eds.); EUR 140, USD 248 combined subscription to institutions (print & online eds.) (effective 2012). back issues avail. **Document type:** *Journal, Academic/Scholarly.* **Description:** Scandinavian journal of social theory.
Related titles: Online - full text ed.: GBP 139 in United Kingdom to institutions; EUR 127, USD 223 to institutions (effective 2012).
Indexed: CA, P42, PSA, S02, S03, SCOPUS, SociolAb, T02.
—BLDSC (3602.660410).
Published by: Aarhus Universitet, Institut for Statskundskab/University of Aarhus, Department of Political Science, Bygning 1331, Aarhus C, 8000, Denmark. TEL 46-89-421323, FAX 46-89-421330, http://www.ps.au.dk. Ed. Per Mouritsen. **Dist. by:** Aarhus Universitetsforlag. http://www.unipress.dk.

320 RUS
DNEVNIK ZASEDANII GOSUDARSTVENNOI DUMY. PRILOZHENIE K BYULLETENYU GOSUDARSTVENNAYA DUMA. Text in Russian. 1994. q. USD 95 in the Americas (effective 2000).
Published by: Gosudarstvennaya Duma, Okhotnyi ryad 1, Moscow, 103001, Russian Federation. TEL 7-095-2927999.

320 ESP ISSN 1698-2894
DOCUMENTOS DE TRABAJO POLITICA Y GESTION. Text in Spanish. 2004. a. back issues avail. **Document type:** *Monographic series, Academic/Scholarly.*
Related titles: Online - full text ed.: ISSN 1698-482X. 2004.
Published by: Univesidad Carlos III de Madrid, Departamento de Ciencia Politica y Sociologia, Campus de Getafe C. Madrid 126, Madrid, 28903, Spain. TEL 34-91-6245821, FAX 34-91-6249574, http://www.uc3m.es/uc3m/dpto/CPS/dpcps.html.

328 FRA ISSN 1621-3939
JN2301
DOCUMENTS ET INFORMATIONS PARLEMENTAIRES; revue hebdomadaire d'information et de documentation sur la vie politique et parlementaire en France. Text in French. w. EUR 714.70 domestic; EUR 744 foreign (effective 2009).
Published by: Societe Generale de Presse, 13 Avenue de l'Opera, Paris Cedex 01, 75001, France. TEL 33-1-40151789, FAX 33-1-40151715, http://www.sgpresse.fr.

328 GBR ISSN 0070-7007
JN500
DOD'S PARLIAMENTARY COMPANION. Text in English. 1832. a. GBP 255 per issue domestic; GBP 295 per issue in Europe; GBP 298 per issue elsewhere (effective 2010). adv. bk.rev. Index. back issues avail. **Document type:** *Directory, Trade.* **Description:** Provides complete guide to who's who in UK politics and government. Includes over 7,000 contacts and information.
Former titles (until 1865): Parliamentary Companion; (until 1847): Parliamentary Pocket Companion
Related titles: CD-ROM ed.
—BLDSC (3614.300000). **CCC.**
Published by: Dod's Parliamentary Communications Ltd., Westminster Tower, 3rd Fl, 3 Albert Embankment, London, SE1 7SP, United Kingdom. TEL 44-20-70917500, FAX 44-20-70917505, uk@dods.co.uk.

320 PAK ISSN 0012-4907
DOGAR'S GENERAL KNOWLEDGE DIGEST. Variant title: General Knowledge Digest. Text in English. 1970 (vol.4). m. PKR 70.
Published by: Dogar Bros., Santnagar, Lahore, Pakistan. Ed. Haji Wali Muhammad Dogar.

320 DEU ISSN 0070-7031
DD257.4
➤ **DOKUMENTE ZUR DEUTSCHLANDPOLITIK.** Text in German. 1961. irreg., latest vol.2, no.4, 2002. price varies. reprints avail. **Document type:** *Monographic series, Academic/Scholarly.*
Related titles: ◆ Supplement(s): Dokumente zur Deutschlandpolitik. Beihefte. ISSN 0341-3276.
Published by: Oldenbourg Wissenschaftsverlag GmbH, Rosenheimer Str 145, Munich, 81671, Germany. TEL 49-89-450510, FAX 49-89-45051333, orders@oldenbourg.de, http://www.oldenbourg.de.

320 DEU ISSN 0341-3276
➤ **DOKUMENTE ZUR DEUTSCHLANDPOLITIK. BEIHEFTE.** Text in German. 1975. irreg. price varies. **Document type:** *Monographic series, Academic/Scholarly.*
Related titles: ◆ Supplement to: Dokumente zur Deutschlandpolitik. ISSN 0070-7031.
—CCC.
Published by: Oldenbourg Wissenschaftsverlag GmbH, Rosenheimer Str 145, Munich, 81671, Germany. TEL 49-89-450510, FAX 49-89-45051333, orders@oldenbourg.de, http://www.oldenbourg.de.

➤ **DOMINI. LE ISTITUZIONI GIURIDICHE E POLITICHE.** *see* LAW

320 DMA
DOMINICA OFFICIAL GAZETTE. Text in English. 1877. w. XEC 50 domestic; USD 40 foreign (effective 2000). adv. **Document type:** *Government.*
Related titles: Microfilm ed.: (from PQC).
Published by: (Dominica. House of Assembly), Government Printery, Roseau, Dominica. TEL 767-448-8960, pmoffice@cwdom.dm. Ed. Ambrose L Blanc. Circ: 600.

320 AUT ISSN 0012-5415
DB443
DER DONAURAUM. Text in German. 1956. q. EUR 34.50; EUR 9.60 newsstand/cover (effective 2011). adv. bk.rev. bibl. **Document type:** *Journal, Academic/Scholarly.* **Description:** Provides results of research work in the fields of culture, economy, history, politics and law in Central Europe and the Danubian region.
Indexed: CERDIC, DIP, HistAb, I13, IBR, IBZ, MLA-IB, P30, RASB.
Published by: (Institut fuer den Donauraum und Mitteleuropa), Boehlau Verlag GmbH & Co.KG., Wiesingerstr 1, Vienna, W 1010, Austria. TEL 43-1-3302427, FAX 43-1-3302432, boehlau@boehlau.at, http://www.boehlau.at. Circ: 1,000.

322.4 NLD ISSN 1877-8186
DOORBRAAK. Text in Dutch. 1997. bi-m. EUR 25; EUR 3 newsstand/cover (effective 2011).
Formerly (until 2009): De Fabel van de Illegaal (1566-158X)
Published by: Stichting Gebladerte, Musschenbroekstraat 19, Leiden, 2316 AW, Netherlands. TEL 31-71-5127619, FAX 31-71-5134907, http://www.gebladerte.nl/.

172.2 DEU ISSN 1613-7256
DORTMUNDER POLITISCH-PHILOSOPHISCHE DISKURSE. Text in German. 2004. irreg., latest vol.8, 2010. price varies. **Document type:** *Monographic series, Academic/Scholarly.*
Published by: Projekt Verlag GbR, Oskar-Hoffmann-Str 25, Bochum, 44789, Germany. TEL 49-234-3251570, FAX 49-234-3251571, lektorat@projektverlag.de.

327.1 FRA ISSN 1962-3542
DOSSIERS SECRETS D'ETATS. Text in French. 2008. q. **Document type:** *Magazine, Consumer.*
Published by: Export Press, 91 Rue de Turenne, Paris, 75003, France. TEL 33-1-40291451, FAX 33-1-42720743, dir@exportpress.com, http://www.exportpress.com.

320.51 USA ISSN 1932-6319
JK275
DOUBLETHINK. Text in English. 1995. q. **Document type:** *Magazine, Consumer.*
Related titles: Online - full text ed.: ISSN 1932-6327. 200?.
Published by: America's Future Foundation, 1001 Connecticut Ave. NW, Ste 1250, Washington, DC 20036. TEL 202-331-2261, info@americasfuture.org, http://www.americasfuture.org/index.php.

322.4 FRA ISSN 2107-5077
▼ **DROITE LIGNE.** Text in French. 2010. 11/yr. EUR 38 (effective 2010).
Address: 231 Rue Saint-Honore, Paris, 75001, France. TEL 33-6-48785101, contact@droite-ligne.com, http://droite-ligne.com. Ed. Yvan Benedetti.

320.531 USA ISSN 0741-0263
DYNAMIC. Text in English. 1983. q. USD 15 (effective 2006). adv. bk.rev. **Document type:** *Magazine, Consumer.* **Description:** Covers current events, student rights, culture, international affairs from a leftist perspective.
Formerly (until May 1983): Young Worker
Indexed: RASB.
Published by: Young Communist League USA, 235 W 23rd St, Ste 245, New York, NY 10011. Circ: 30,000.

320 ROM ISSN 2067-9211
▼ **E I R P PROCEEDINGS.** (European Integration Realities and Perspectives) Text in English, French. 2009. irreg. free (effective 2011). **Document type:** *Journal, Academic/Scholarly.*
Media: Online - full text.
Published by: Universitatea "Danubius" Galati/Danubius University of Galati, B-dul Galati nr. 3, Galati, 800654, Romania. TEL 40-749-084355.

E I U COUNTRY REPORTS ON DISC: WESTERN EUROPE. *see* BUSINESS AND ECONOMICS—Economic Situation And Conditions

320.711 USA ISSN 1541-8057
JA1
E P R. (Emory Political Review) Text in English. 2002 (Spring). s-a.
Published by: Emory Political Review, Emory University, Boisfeuillet Jones Center, Atlanta, GA 30322. Ed. Mitchell S. Kominsky.

320.1 GBR ISSN 0960-071X
E P R U PAPERS. (European Policy Research Unit) Text in English. 1987. irreg. GBP 2.95 per issue (effective 2009). back issues avail. **Document type:** *Monographic series, Consumer.*
Formerly (until 1991): Manchester Papers in Politics (0952-7087)
Published by: European Policy Research Unit, University of Manchester, Oxford Rd, Manchester, M113 9PL, United Kingdom. TEL 44-161-2754883, FAX 44-161-2754925.

320 GBR ISSN 2043-8877
E-POL. Text in English. 2008. 3/yr. GBP 40 to individuals; GBP 100 to institutions (effective 2010). back issues avail. **Document type:** *Journal, Academic/Scholarly.* **Description:** Provides a political education forum with a regular and scholarly look at ongoing political events.
Media: Online - full text.
—CCC.
Published by: Political Education Forum, Ltd., Old Hall Ln, Manchester, Lancashire M13 0XT, United Kingdom. TEL 44-7765-641297, info@politicaleducationforum.com. Ed. Richard Kelly.

320 DEU
E-POLITIK.DE; Politik, Gesellschaft & Politikwissenschaft. Text in German. 1999. d. **Document type:** *Magazine, Trade.*
Media: Online - full text.
Address: c/o Christian Heise, Prinzessinnenstr 19/20, Berlin, 10969, Germany. TEL 49-30-53014673. Ed. Christian Miess.

320 ITA ISSN 1028-3633
E U I PAPERS IN POLITICAL AND SOCIAL SCIENCES. Text in English. 1990 (no.90-1). irreg. **Document type:** *Monographic series, Academic/Scholarly.*
Published by: European University Institute, Via dei Roccettini 9, San Domenico di Fiesole, FI 50014, Italy. TEL 39-055-4685266, forinfo@iue.it, http://www.iue.it.

320 330.9 ITA
E U I REVIEW. (European University Institute) Text in English, French. 1997. 3/yr. **Document type:** *Journal, Academic/Scholarly.*
Related titles: Online - full text ed.
Published by: European University Institute, Via dei Roccettini 9, San Domenico di Fiesole, FI 50014, Italy. TEL 39-055-4685266, forinfo@iue.it.

E U MAGAZIN. (Europaeische Union) *see* BUSINESS AND ECONOMICS—Economic Situation And Conditions

320 UGA
EAST AFRICA ANALYSIS; economic - political updates in East Africa. Text in English. 1992. fortn. USD 105 to individuals; USD 130 to institutions. bk.rev. **Document type:** *Newspaper.* **Description:** Provides a forum for the popular discussion of economic and political issues in Uganda, Kenya, and Tanzania.
Address: PO Box 9948, Kampala, Uganda. FAX 256-41-245580. Eds. Gerald Mwaita, John Kateeba. Circ: 25,000 (paid).

EAST ASIAN REVIEW. *see* ASIAN STUDIES

320 USA ISSN 1934-6379
EAST BAY QUARTERLY. Variant title: E B Q. Text in English. 2008. q. **Document type:** *Magazine, Consumer.*
Related titles: Online - full text ed.: ISSN 1934-6387.
Published by: Unlimited Publishing, 582 Market St #1112, San Francisco, CA 94104. Pub. Danny O Snow.

320 USA ISSN 0888-3254
JN96.A2
➤ **EAST EUROPEAN POLITICS & SOCIETIES.** Abbreviated title: E E P S. Text in English. 1987. q. USD 390, GBP 229 combined subscription to institutions (print & online eds.); USD 382, GBP 224 to institutions (effective 2011). adv. illus. back issues avail.; reprint service avail. from PSC. **Document type:** *Journal, Academic/Scholarly.* **Description:** Examines the social, political, and economic issues in Eastern Europe.
Related titles: Microform ed.: (from PQC); Online - full text ed.: ISSN 1533-8371. USD 351, GBP 206 to institutions (effective 2011).
Indexed: A01, A02, A03, A08, A20, A22, A26, ABCPolSci, ABS&EES, B04, BRD, CA, CurCont, E01, E08, ESPM, G08, HistAb, I05, I08, I13, I14, IBSS, MLA-IB, P02, P10, P27, P30, P34, P42, P47, P48, P53, P54, PAIS, PCI, PQC, PSA, PerIslam, RiskAb, S02, S03, S09, SCOPUS, SSAI, SSAb, SSCI, SSI, SociolAb, T02, W03, W07.
—BLDSC (3646.317000), IE, Infotrieve, Ingenta. **CCC.**
Published by: (American Council of Learned Societies), Sage Publications, Inc., 2455 Teller Rd, Thousand Oaks, CA 91320. TEL 805-499-9774, 800-818-7243, FAX 805-499-0871, 800-583-2665, info@sagepub.com. Eds. Irena Grudzinska-Gross, Ivo Banac. Circ: 1,200.

947 GBR ISSN 1470-5702
HC244.A1
EASTERN EUROPE, RUSSIA AND CENTRAL ASIA (YEAR). Text in English. 2000 (Nov.). a., latest 2009, Nov. USD 750 per vol. (effective 2010). **Document type:** *Journal, Academic/Scholarly.* **Description:** Contains extensive coverage of the political, economic and social affairs of the region.
Supersedes in part (in 2000): Eastern Europe and the Commonwealth of Independent States (Year) (0962-1040)
—CCC.
Published by: (Europa Publications Ltd.), Routledge (Subsidiary of: Taylor & Francis Group), 2 Park Sq, Milton Park, Abingdon, Oxon OX14 4RN, United Kingdom. TEL 44-20-70176000, FAX 44-20-70176699, orders@taylorandfrancis.com, http://www.routledge.com.

320.947 GBR ISSN 1368-6909
EASTERN EUROPEAN NEWSLETTER. Text in English. 2 base vols. plus updates 6/yr. included with subscr. to Doing Business in Europe. **Document type:** *Newsletter, Trade.* **Description:** Provides an overview of the year's political and economic developments in Serbia and Montenegro.
Incorporates (1992-1997): Doing Business in Eastern Europe (0941-2115); Formerly (until 199?): Eastern European Newsletter - Briefing. Serbia - Montenegro
Related titles: ◆ Supplement to: Doing Business in Europe.
Published by: (Eastern Europe Newsletter Ltd.), Sweet & Maxwell Ltd. (Subsidiary of: Thomson Reuters Corp.), 100 Avenue Rd, London, NW3 3PF, United Kingdom.

320.531 USA
ECO SOCIALIST REVIEW. Text in English. 1986. q. USD 10. adv. back issues avail. **Document type:** *Newsletter.* **Description:** To network green leftists and socialists, and to develop the intellectual and strategic agenda for eco-socialists.
Indexed: LeftInd.

Published by: Chicago Democratic Socialists of America, 1608 N Milwaukee, Ste 403, Chicago, IL 60647. TEL 773-384-0327, FAX 773-702-0090, http://www.chicagodsa.org. Ed. J Hughes. Adv. contact J. Hughes. Circ: 800.

ECOLOGIA POLITICA. *see* ENVIRONMENTAL STUDIES

320 363.7 FRA ISSN 1775-1616
ECOLOGIE ET POLITIQUE. Text in French. 2005. irreg. back issues avail. **Document type:** *Monographic series, Consumer.*
Indexed: MLA-IB.
Published by: Editions Syllepse, 69 rue des Rigoles, Paris, 75020, France. TEL 33-1-44620889.

THE ECOLOGIST (ONLINE). *see* ENVIRONMENTAL STUDIES

ECONOMIC AFFAIRS. *see* BUSINESS AND ECONOMICS

320.9 GBR ISSN 0143-831X
HD5650
➤ **ECONOMIC AND INDUSTRIAL DEMOCRACY**; an international journal. Abbreviated title: E I D. Text in English. 1980. q. USD 1,018, GBP 550 combined subscription to institutions (print & online eds.); USD 998, GBP 539 to institutions (effective 2011). adv. bk.rev. back issues avail.; reprint service avail. from PSC. **Document type:** *Journal, Academic/Scholarly.* **Description:** Covers all aspects of industrial democracy, from the practical problems of democratic management to wide-ranging social, political and economic analysis.
Related titles: Online - full text ed.: ISSN 1461-7099. USD 916, GBP 495 to institutions (effective 2011).
Indexed: A12, A13, A17, A20, A22, A26, ABIn, ADPA, ASCA, B01, B06, B07, B08, B09, BAS, BPIA, BusI, CA, CPM, CurCont, DIP, E01, E03, E07, ERI, ESPM, EconLit, FR, G08, H04, HRA, I13, IBR, IBSS, IBZ, ILD, JEL, ManagCont, P04, P42, P48, P51, P53, P54, PAIS, PCI, PMA, PQC, PRA, PSA, RiskAb, S02, S03, SCOPUS, SOPODA, SSA, SSCI, SociolAb, T02, V02, W07, WorkRelAb.
—BLDSC (3651.466000), IE, Infotrieve, Ingenta. **CCC.**
Published by: (Uppsala Universitet, Ekonomisk-Historisk Institutionen/ University of Uppsala, Department of Economic History SWE), Sage Publications Ltd. (Subsidiary of: Sage Publications, Inc.), 1 Oliver's Yard, 55 City Rd, London, EC1Y 1SP, United Kingdom. TEL 44-20-73248500, FAX 44-20-73248600, info@sagepub.co.uk, http://www.uk.sagepub.com/home.nav. Eds. Jan Ottosson, Lars Magnusson. **Subscr. in the Americas to:** Sage Publications, Inc., 2455 Teller Rd, Thousand Oaks, CA 91320. TEL 805-499-9774, FAX 805-499-0871, journals@sagepub.com.

➤ **ECONOMIC & POLITICAL WEEKLY.** *see* BUSINESS AND ECONOMICS

320 GBR ISSN 1350-1070
ECONOMIC INTELLIGENCE REVIEW. Text in English. 1993. bi-m. USD 475 (effective 2009). **Document type:** *Journal, Academic/Scholarly.* **Description:** Global economic, financial and investment review covering geopolitics, currencies, economies, stock markets, and precious metals, gold, for corporate, financial sector and private investors worldwide.
Formerly (until 1993): World Economic Review (0965-223X)
Published by: World Reports Ltd., 108 Horseferry Rd, London, SW1P 2EF, United Kingdom. TEL 44-20-72223836, FAX 44-20-72330185, subs@worldreports.org. Ed. Christopher Story.

ECONOMICS & POLITICS. *see* BUSINESS AND ECONOMICS—Economic Systems And Theories, Economic History

320.5322 FRA ISSN 0424-3218
HB3
ECONOMIE ET POLITIQUE; revue Marxiste d'economie. Text in French. 1954. bi-m. bibl. **Document type:** *Magazine, Consumer.*
Indexed: A22, FR, IBSS, PAIS.
—IE, Infotrieve.
Address: 2 Pl. du Colonel Fabien, Paris, 75019, France. TEL 33-1-40401347, FAX 33-1-40401395, ecopo@club-internet.fr. Ed. Denis Recoquillon. Pub. Jean Louis Raach.

L'ECONOMIE POLITIQUE. *see* BUSINESS AND ECONOMICS—Economic Systems And Theories, Economic History

ECONOMY AND SOCIETY. *see* SOCIAL SCIENCES: COMPREHENSIVE WORKS

320 ARG ISSN 0326-7180
ECOS DE A L A D I. Text in Spanish. 1982. m.
Published by: Asociacion Latinoamericana de Integracion, Cangallo 1515, 10 Piso, Buenos Aires, Argentina.

320 ECU ISSN 1012-1498
HD1531.E2
➤ **ECUADOR DEBATE.** Text in Spanish. 1982. 3/yr. ECS 110 domestic; USD 30 foreign (effective 2003). adv. bk.rev. **Document type:** *Academic/Scholarly.* **Description:** Each issue offers a discussion of current political issues, a central theme concerning a major structural problem, an agrarian section and analyses of social issues.
Indexed: C01, CA, P09, P42, PCI, PSA, S02, S03, SCOPUS, SociolAb, T02.
Published by: Centro Andino de Accion Popular, Apartado 17-15-173B, Quito, Pichincha, Ecuador. TEL 593-2-522763, FAX 593-2-568452, caapl@caap.org.ec. Ed., R&P Francisco Rhon Davila. Adv. contact Nelson Catagna. Circ: 1,500 (controlled).

320 DEU
▼ **EDITION POLITIK.** Text in German. 2010. irreg., latest vol.3, 2011. price varies. **Document type:** *Monographic series, Academic/ Scholarly.*
Published by: Transcript, Muehlenstr 47, Bielefeld, 33607, Germany. TEL 49-521-63454, FAX 49-521-61040, live@transcript-verlag.de.

320 AUT
EDITION POLITISCHE KOMMUNIKATION. Text in German. 2006. irreg., latest vol.2, 2008. price varies. **Document type:** *Monographic series, Academic/Scholarly.*
Published by: Boehlau Verlag GmbH & Co.KG., Wiesingerstr 1, Vienna, W 1010, Austria. TEL 43-1-3302427, FAX 43-1-3302432, boehlau@boehlau.at.

EDUCATION AND URBAN SOCIETY; an independent quarterly journal of social research. *see* EDUCATION

EGE AKADEMIK BAKIS/EGE ACADEMIC REVIEW. *see* BUSINESS AND ECONOMICS

EGOV. *see* COMPUTERS—Electronic Data Processing

320 EGY ISSN 1110-5097
DT43
➤ **EGYPTE - MONDE ARABE.** Text in English, French. 1990; N.S. 1999. 2/yr. adv. bk.rev. **Document type:** *Journal, Academic/Scholarly.* **Description:** Covers politics, the social and human sciences in Egypt and the Middle East.
Formed by the merger of (1981-1990): Revue de la Presse Egyptienne (0752-4412); (1984-1990): Centre de Documentation d'Etudes Juridiques, Economiques et Sociales. Bulletin (1110-0117)
Indexed: FLP, FR, I14, MLA-IB, P30, PAIS, RILM.
—BLDSC (3664.223000).
Published by: Centre d'Etudes et de Documentation Economique, Juridique et Sociale, 14 Sharia Gameyet al-Nisr, Mohandessin, Cairo, Egypt. publications@cedej.org.eg. Ed. Jean-Noel Ferrie TEL 202-392-8711. Circ: 1,000.

320 AUT ISSN 2075-9517
▼ **EJOURNAL OF EDEMOCRACY AND OPEN GOVERNMENT.** Text in English, German. 2009. s-a. free (effective 2011). **Document type:** *Journal, Academic/Scholarly.*
Media: Online - full text.
Published by: Donau-Universitaet Krems, Center for E-Government, Dr Karl Dorrek Strasse 30, Krems, 3500, Austria. Ed. Judith Schlossboeck.

320 FIN ISSN 1455-1233
ELAVA HELSINKI. Text in Finnish. 1995. q. adv. back issues avail. **Document type:** *Newsletter, Consumer.*
Related titles: Online - full text ed.: ISSN 1795-746X.
Published by: Helsingin Kokoomus ry, Johanneksentie 6 A, Helsinki, 00120, Finland. TEL 358-207-488488, FAX 358-9-6943214, http://www.helsinginkokoomus.fi. Ed. Tuomo Valve TEL 358-207-488517. adv.: page EUR 2,000; 255 x 350.

320.51 DEU
ELDE. Text in German. bi-m. adv. **Document type:** *Magazine, Consumer.*
Published by: Liberal Verlag GmbH, Reinhardtstr 16, Berlin, 10117, Germany. TEL 49-30-27572871, FAX 49-30-27572880, christian.renatus@liberalverlag.de, http://www.liberalverlag.de. Pub. Christian Renatus. Adv. contact Maren Schoening. B&W page EUR 14,500, color page EUR 16,100; trim 180 x 252. Circ: 105,000 (controlled).

324.6 PER ISSN 1994-5272
ELECCIONES. Text in Spanish. 2002. a. **Document type:** *Journal, Academic/Scholarly.*
Related titles: Online - full text ed.: ISSN 1995-6290.
Published by: Oficina Nacional de Procesos Electorales (O N P E), Jr. Washington 1894, Lima 1, Peru. TEL 51-14-170630, publicaciones@onpe.gob.pe, http://www.onpe.gob.pe/. Ed. Teresa Watanabe Varas. Circ: 600.

324 USA ISSN 0145-8124
KF4886.A45
ELECTION ADMINISTRATION REPORTS. Text in English. 1971. s-m. USD 197 (effective 2007). bk.rev. back issues avail. **Document type:** *Newsletter, Trade.* **Description:** Covers all developments in election law and administration, voter registration, voting machines and devices, and judicial decisions affecting elections.
Formerly (until 1976): Electionews
Address: 5620 33rd St, N W, Washington, DC 20015. TEL 202-244-5844, FAX 202-362-2304. Ed., R&P Richard G Smolka. **Subscr. to:** EBSCO Information Services, PO Box 830409, Birmingham, AL 35283. TEL 205-995-1567, 800-633-4931, FAX 205-995-1588.

342.07 USA
ELECTION AND RELATED LAWS AND RULES AND REGULATIONS OF NORTH CAROLINA. Text in English. 1996. a., latest 1999. USD 35 (effective 2008). 647 p./no.; Supplement avail. **Document type:** *Handbook/Manual/Guide, Trade.* **Description:** Contains information about election and related laws and rules and regulations of North Carolina.
Published by: Michie Company (Subsidiary of: LexisNexis North America), 701 E Water St, Charlottesville, VA 22902. TEL 434-972-7600, 800-446-3410, FAX 434-972-7677, customer.support@lexisnexis.com, http://www.michie.com.

324.6 ZAF
ELECTION TALK. Text in English. 1997. q. ZAR 200, USD 50 (effective 1999). bk.rev. back issues avail. **Document type:** *Newsletter.* **Description:** Includes information on elections and democracy in South Africa, southern Africa, and Africa in general.
Related titles: Online - full text ed.
Published by: Electoral Institute of South Africa, PO Box 740, Auckland Park, Johannesburg 2006, South Africa. TEL 27-11-4825495, FAX 27-11-4826163. Ed. Lesley Hudson. Circ: 1,000.

324.6 CAN ISSN 1704-8389
JL298
ELECTIONS MANITOBA. ANNUAL REPORT. Text in English. 1981. a.
Former titles (until 1999): Annual Report Including Conduct of the .. Provincial General Election (1497-830X); (until 1998): Chief Electoral Officer on the Elections Finances Act. Annual Report (1193-977X); (until 1990): Elections Finances Act. Annual Report (0848-5550); (until 1984): Elections Commission. Annual Report (0715-8092)
Published by: Elections Manitoba, 200 Vaughan St, Winnipeg, MB R3C 1T5, Canada. TEL 204-945-3225, FAX 204-945-6011, election@elections.mb.ca, http://www.electionsmanitoba.ca.

324.6 CAN ISSN 1488-3538
CA1SE2-1
ELECTORAL INSIGHT. Text in Multiple languages. 1999. s-a. back issues avail.
Related titles: Print ed.: ISSN 1488-3546. 1999.
Indexed: C03, CBCARef, P48, PQC.
Published by: Elections Canada, 257 Slater St, Ottawa, ON K1A OM6, Canada. TEL 613-993-2975, FAX 888-524-1444.

324.63 GBR ISSN 0261-3794
JF1001
➤ **ELECTORAL STUDIES.** Text in English. 1982. 4/yr. EUR 928 in Europe to institutions; JPY 123,100 in Japan to institutions; USD 1,037 elsewhere to institutions (effective 2012). adv. bk.rev. illus. index. back issues avail.; reprints avail. **Document type:** *Journal, Academic/Scholarly.* **Description:** Focuses on the behavior of voters, the effect of electoral systems, and the rules pertaining to elections. Aimed at historians, sociologists, political scientists, economists, geographers, lawyers, game theorists, and statisticians.
Related titles: Microform ed.: (from PQC); Online - full text ed.: ISSN 1873-6890 (from IngentaConnect, ScienceDirect).
Indexed: A01, A03, A08, A20, A22, A26, ABCPolSci, ASCA, CA, CommAb, CurCont, ESPM, GEOBASE, HistAb, I05, I13, IBSS, P34, P42, PAIS, PCI, PSA, RiskAb, SCOPUS, SSCI, SociolAb, T02, W07.
—BLDSC (3670.890000), IE, Infotrieve, Ingenta. **CCC.**
Published by: Pergamon (Subsidiary of: Elsevier Science & Technology), The Blvd, Langford Ln, East Park, Kidlington, Oxford OX5 1GB, United Kingdom. TEL 44-1865-843000, FAX 44-1865-843010, JournalsCustomerServiceEMEA@elsevier.com. Eds. Elinor Scarbrough, Geoffrey Evans TEL 44-1865-278613, Dr. Harold D Clarke TEL 972-883-4891. **Subscr. to:** Elsevier BV, Radarweg 29, PO Box 211, Amsterdam 1000 AE, Netherlands. TEL 31-20-4853757, FAX 31-20-4853432, http://www.elsevier.nl.

320 GBR ISSN 1479-439X
JF1525.A8
➤ **ELECTRONIC JOURNAL OF E-GOVERNMENT.** Abbreviated title: E J E G. Text in English. 2003. s-a. free (effective 2011). back issues avail. **Document type:** *Journal, Academic/Scholarly.* **Description:** Features articles and papers that contribute to the development of both the study and practice of all aspects of e-Government and web-enabling technology in the public sector.
Media: Online - full content.
Indexed: A39, C27, C29, CA, D03, D04, E13, P42, P45, P52, R14, S14, S15, S18, T02.
Published by: Academic Conferences Ltd., Curtis Farm, Kidmore End, Nr Reading, RG4 9AY, United Kingdom. TEL 44-1189-724148, FAX 44-1189-724691. Ed. Frank Bannister.

320.5 DEU ISSN 0177-2430
ELEMENTE DER METAPOLITIK ZUR EUROPAEISCHEN NEUGEBURT. Text in German. 1986. a. (plus 2 special issues). EUR 20.50 (effective 2003). adv. back issues avail. **Document type:** *Journal, Academic/Scholarly.*
Formerly (until 1990): Elemente zur Metapolitik (0178-7659)
Published by: Thule-Seminar e.V., Postfach 410347, Kassel, 34065, Germany. FAX 49-561-405129. Ed. Pierre Krebs. adv.: B&W page EUR 300; trim 167 x 210. Circ: 5,000.

EMERGING EUROPE MONITOR. CENTRAL EUROPE & BALTIC STATES. *see* BUSINESS AND ECONOMICS—Economic Situation And Conditions

EMERGING EUROPE MONITOR. RUSSIA & C I S. *see* BUSINESS AND ECONOMICS—Economic Situation And Conditions

EMERGING EUROPE MONITOR. SOUTH EAST EUROPE. *see* BUSINESS AND ECONOMICS—Economic Situation And Conditions

EMERGING LEBANON. *see* BUSINESS AND ECONOMICS—Economic Situation And Conditions

THE EMIRATES OCCASIONAL PAPERS. *see* HISTORY—History Of The Near East

320.6 USA ISSN 0747-0711
JK3401
EMPIRE STATE REPORT; the magazine of politics and policy for New York State. Variant title: E.S.R. Magazine. Empire State Report Magazine. Text in English. 1974. 10/yr. USD 19.95 domestic; USD 75 foreign (effective 2011). bk.rev. bibl. 40 p./no. 3 cols./p.; back issues avail.; reprints avail. **Document type:** *Magazine, Consumer.* **Description:** Devoted to government politics and business of government of New York State. Features articles on significant current and projected issues, political profiles of key people in and around the state government.
Former titles (until 1989): Changing Faces (0885-7067); (until 1985): Empire State Report Weekly (0745-8622); (until 1983): Empire State Report (0363-7190); (until 1979): Empire (0164-3630); (until 1978): Empire State Report (0196-8580)
Related titles: Microfilm ed.: 1982.
Indexed: A22, P06, P30, PAIS.
Published by: Empire State Report Inc (Subsidiary of: CINN Worldwide Inc), PO Box 9001, Mt Vernon, NY 10552-9001. Pub. Stephen H Acunto. Circ: 15,600 (paid and controlled).

322.1 323.47 NLD ISSN 1877-881X
▼ **EMPIRICAL RESEARCH IN RELIGION AND HUMAN RIGHTS.** Text in English. 2010. irreg. **Document type:** *Monographic series, Academic/Scholarly.*
Published by: Brill, PO Box 9000, Leiden, 2300 PA, Netherlands. TEL 31-71-5353500, FAX 31-71-5317532, cs@brill.nl.

324.27285 NIC
EN MARCHA. Text in Spanish. m. NIC 2.
Published by: Partido Conservador Democrata de Nicaragua, CINE Carr., 2, Apdo 725, Managua, Nicaragua.

320 ARG ISSN 1666-3535
ENCUENTRO (BUENOS AIRES). Text in Spanish. 2001. m. **Document type:** *Magazine, Trade.*
Published by: Asociacion Encuentro para la Esperanza, A.C., Gallo, 102, Buenos Aires, 1172, Argentina. TEL 54-11-43707112, FAX 54-11-49619138, http://www.eeac.org.ar/encuentro.htm. Ed. Alberto Agustin Coto.

320 305.896 USA ISSN 1529-2924
JA1
ENDARCH; journal of Black political research. Text in English. 2000. s-a. **Document type:** *Journal, Academic/Scholarly.*
Related titles: Online - full text ed.
Published by: Clark Atlanta University, Department of Political Science, 223 James P. Brawley Dr. SW, Atlanta, GA 30314. TEL 404-880-8718, FAX 404-880-8717, polisci@cau.edu, http://www.cau.edu/ default.html.

ENGLISH CHURCHMAN & ST. JAMES'S CHRONICLE. *see* RELIGIONS AND THEOLOGY—Protestant

320 FRA ISSN 1953-1605
ENJEUX MEDITERRANEE. Text in French; Abstracts in English, Arabic. 2006. q. EUR 6.50 newsstand/cover (effective 2008). **Document type:** *Magazine.*
Published by: Areion Publishing, Chateau de Valmousse, Departementale 572, Lambesc, 13410, France. TEL 33-4-42921738, FAX 33-4-42924872. Circ: 35,000.

ENLIGHTENMENT AND DISSENT. *see* HISTORY

ENTELEQUIA; revista interdisciplinar. *see* SOCIAL SCIENCES: COMPREHENSIVE WORKS

320 MEX
ENTORNO. Text in Spanish. m. **Document type:** *Journal, Academic/Scholarly.*
Published by: Confederacion Patronal de la Republica Mexicana, Insurgentes Sur 950 1er piso Col. del Valle,, Mexico DF, c.p. 03100, Mexico. TEL 52-5682-5466, FAX 52-5536-1698, http://www.coparmex.org.mx/.

320.943 DEU
DIE ENTSCHEIDUNG (MONSCHAU). Text in German. 1953. 10/yr. adv. **Document type:** *Magazine, Consumer.*
Published by: (Bundesvorstand Junge Union Deutschland), Weiss Verlag GmbH & Co. KG, Industriestr 7, Monschau, 52153, Germany. TEL 49-2472-982114, FAX 49-2472-9827714. Eds. Sidney Pfannstiel, Stefan Ewert. adv.: B&W page EUR 1,900, color page EUR 2,889.66. Circ: 12,000 (controlled).

324.247 RUS
EPOKHA. Text in Russian. 1989. w.?. **Document type:** *Newspaper.*
Formerly (until 1990): E S D E K
Published by: Sotsial Demokraticheskaya Partiya R.S.F.S.R., Pr Suslova 36, korp 7, kv 25, St Petersburg, 198215, Russian Federation. TEL 255-84-95. Ed. Vadim Lifshitz.

320 RUS
ERA ROSSII; vserossiiskaya obshchestvenno-politicheskaya gazeta. Text in Russian. 1994. 24/yr. USD 150 in the Americas (effective 2000).
Published by: Narodnaya Natsional'naya Partiya, B Kondrtat'evskii per 4, kor 3, kv 4, Moscow, 123056, Russian Federation. TEL 7-095-2544026. **Dist. by:** East View Information Services, 10601 Wayzata Blvd, Minneapolis, MN 55305. TEL 952-252-1201, 800-477-1005, FAX 952-252-1202, info@eastview.com, http://www.eastview.com.

ERAS. *see* HISTORY

320.532 CUB ISSN 0864-1277
ESCAMBRAY. Text in Spanish. 1979. w. back issues avail.
Related titles: Online - full text ed.: ISSN 1605-9050. 2000.
Published by: Partido Comunista de Cuba, Comite Provincial Sancti, Adolfo del Castillo, 10, Sancti Spiritus, Cuba. TEL 53-23003, cip220@cip.etecsa.cu, http://www.escambray.islagrande.cu/. Ed. Juan A Borrego.

320 ARG ISSN 0329-8728
ESCENARIOS ALTERNATIVOS. Text in Spanish. 1997. 3/yr. **Document type:** *Journal, Academic/Scholarly.*
Published by: Fundacion de Estudios para el Desarrollo Social, Ave de Mayo, 2370, Piso 8 Ofic. 210, Buenos Aires, 1085, Argentina. TEL 54-11-43815458, FAX 54-11-47724390. Ed. Jesus Rodriguez. Circ: 1,500.

320.531 HUN ISSN 0865-0810
HM7
ESELY. Text in Hungarian. 1989. bi-m.
Published by: Hilscher Reszo Szocialpolitikai Alapitvany, Ludovika ter 2, Budapest, 1083, Hungary.

320 FRA ISSN 1958-5500
JC319
➤ **L'ESPACE POLITIQUE.** Text in French. 2007. q. free (effective 2011). **Document type:** *Journal, Academic/Scholarly.*
Media: Online - full text.
Published by: Comite National Francais de Geographie. Commission de Geographie Politique et Geopolitique, c/o Mme Emmanuelle Chaveneau, 191 rue St Jacques, Paris, 75005, France. echaveneau@yahoo.fr.

320.9728 CRI
ESPACIOS; revista centroamericana de cultura politica. Text in Spanish. q.
Indexed: AIAP.
Published by: Facultad Latinoamericana de Ciencias Sociales, Programa Costa Rica, Apartado Postal 11747, San Jose, 1000, Costa Rica. TEL 506-2346890, FAX 506-2256779. Ed. Sebastian Vaquerano. Pub. Rafael Menjivar Larin.

320 MEX ISSN 1665-8140
F1236
ESPACIOS PUBLICOS. Text in Spanish. 1998. s-a. **Document type:** *Journal, Academic/Scholarly.*
Related titles: Online - full text ed.: free (effective 2011).
Indexed: C01.
Published by: Universidad Autnoma del Estado de Mexico, Facultad de Ciencias Politicas, Cerro de Coatepec s-n, Toluca, Edo. de Mexico, 50100, Mexico. TEL 52-722-2150494, FAX 52-722-2131607, espapubs@politicas.uamex.mx, http://www.politicas.uaemex.mx/. Ed. Leobardo Ruiz Alanis.

320 MEX
ESPARTACO. Text in Spanish. 1989. q. MXN 15 domestic; USD 4 foreign (effective 2003). **Document type:** *Newspaper, Consumer.*
Description: Publication of the Grupo Espartaquista de Mexico.
Related titles: ◆ English ed.: Spartacist. ISSN 0038-6596.
Published by: Grupo Espartaquista de Mexico, c/o Roberto garcia, Admon Palacio Postal 1, Apartado Postal 1251, Mexico DF, 06002, Mexico.

320.1 MEX ISSN 1665-0565
H8.S7
ESPIRAL; estudios sobre estado y sociedad. Text in Spanish. 1994. 3/yr. MXN 325 domestic; USD 40 in North America; USD 60 elsewhere (effective 2006). back issues avail. **Document type:** *Journal, Academic/Scholarly.*
Related titles: Online - full text ed.: free (effective 2011).
Indexed: A01, C01, CA, F03, F04, H21, P08, P42, PSA, S02, S03, SCOPUS, SSA, SociolAb, T02.
Published by: Universidad de Guadalajara, Centro Universitario de Ciencias Sociales y Humanidades, Depto de Letras, Centro Universitario de Ciencias Sociales y Humanidades, Universidad de Guadalajara, Jalisco, JAL 44210, Mexico. TEL 52-3-8237505, FAX 52-3-8237631.

320.531 CHE ISSN 0014-0732
L'ESPOIR DU MONDE. Text in French. 1908. q. CHF 20 (effective 2007). bk.rev. **Document type:** *Bulletin, Consumer.*
Formerly (until 1967): Le Socialiste Chretien (1421-7627); Which incorporated (1908-1946): L' Espoir du Monde (1421-7635)
Published by: Socialistes Chretiens de Langue Francaise, Ste Helene 26, Neuchatel, 2000, Switzerland.

320 DEU
ESPRESSO (HOFHEIM AM TAUNUS). Text in German. 1985. q. adv. bk.rev.; film rev.; play rev. back issues avail. **Document type:** *Bulletin, Consumer.*
Published by: Junge Union Main-Taunus, Hattersheimerstr 46, Hofheim Am Taunus, 65719, Germany. info@ju-main-taunus.de, http://www.ju-main-taunus.de. Ed. Marc Bockholt. Circ: 1,200.

320.5 GBR ISSN 1369-006X
ESSEX PAPERS IN POLITICS AND GOVERNMENT. Text in English. 1984. irreg., latest vol.161, 2004. price varies. back issues avail. **Document type:** *Monographic series, Academic/Scholarly.*
Related titles: Online - full text ed.: free (effective 2009).
—CCC.
Published by: University of Essex, Department of Government, Wivenhoe Park, Colchester, Essex CO4 3SQ, United Kingdom. TEL 44-1206-872741, FAX 44-1206-873234.

320.5 GBR ISSN 1367-2088
ESSEX PAPERS IN POLITICS AND GOVERNMENT. SUB-SERIES IN IDEOLOGY AND DISCOURSE ANALYSIS (ONLINE). Text in English. 1992. irreg., latest vol.22, 2005. free (effective 2009). back issues avail. **Document type:** *Monographic series, Academic/Scholarly.*
Formerly (until 2004): Essex Papers in Politics and Government. Sub-Series in Ideology and Discourse Analysis (Print)
Media: Online - full text.
Published by: University of Essex, Department of Government, Wivenhoe Park, Colchester, Essex CO4 3SQ, United Kingdom. TEL 44-1206-872741, FAX 44-1206-873234.

ESTHETIQUE & POLITIQUE. *see* PHILOSOPHY

320 PER ISSN 0014-1429
HC161
ESTUDIOS ANDINOS (LIMA). Text in Spanish. 1970. 3/yr. bk.rev. bibl. **Document type:** *Journal, Academic/Scholarly.*
Indexed: H21, L09, P08.
Published by: Universidad del Pacifico, Ave Salaverry 2020, Jesus Maria, Lima, 11, Peru. TEL 51-1-2190100, http://www.up.edu.pe.

320 CHL ISSN 0716-1468
ESTUDIOS NORTEAMERICANOS. Text in Spanish. 1984. q. CLP 1,000, USD 10.
Related titles: Online - full text ed.
Indexed: C01.
Published by: Universidad de Chile, Instituto de Asuntos Publicos, Santa Lucia 240, Santiago, Chile. TEL 56-2-9771502, FAX 56-2-6648536, dp_cpoli@uchile.cl, http://www.cien-politica.uchile.cl. Ed. Hernan Rodriquez Fisse.

320 MEX ISSN 0185-1616
JA5 CODEN: ESPOFM
ESTUDIOS POLITICOS. Text in Spanish; Summaries in English, Spanish. 1975. 3/yr. MXN 300 domestic; USD 110 foreign (effective 2004).
Description: Examines political issues, both actual and theoretical, in Mexico and abroad.
Indexed: C01, CA, DIP, HistAb, I04, I05, I13, IBR, IBSS, IBZ, P09, P42, PAIS, PCI, PSA, SCOPUS, SOPODA, SociolAb, T02.
Published by: (Coordinacion de Ciencias Politicas y Coordinacion de Administracion Publica), Universidad Nacional Autonoma de Mexico, Facultad de Ciencias Politicas y Sociales, Circuito Cultural Mario de la Cueva, Edif C 2o piso, Ciudad Universitaria, Mexico City, DF 04510, Mexico. TEL 52-5-6229402, FAX 52-5-6668334, http://sociolan.politicas.unam.mx/. Ed. Margarita Flores Santiago. Circ: 1,000.

327.861 COL ISSN 0121-5167
JA5
ESTUDIOS POLITICOS. Text in Spanish. 1992. s-a. COP 28,000 domestic; USD 55 foreign (effective 2010). adv. abstr. **Document type:** *Journal, Academic/Scholarly.*
Related titles: Online - full text ed.: (from SciELO).
Indexed: C01, CA, IBSS, P42, PSA, SociolAb, T02.
Published by: Universidad de Antioquia, Instituto de Estudios Politicos, Calle 67, no 53-108, Bl 14, Of 209, Apartado Postal 1226, Medellin, Colombia. TEL 57-4-2105690, FAX 57-4-2105960, espol@quimbaya.udea.edu.co, http://www.quimbaya.udea.edu.co/~iep. Pub. Deicy Patricia Hurtado Galeano. Circ: 750.

320 CHL ISSN 0717-6392
F3082
ESTUDIOS POLITICOS MILITARES. Text in Spanish. 2001. s-a. **Document type:** *Journal, Academic/Scholarly.*
Published by: Universidad Arcis, Centro de Estudios Estrategicos, Carlos Gutierrez - Huerfano, 1721, Santiago, Chile. TEL 56-2-3866942, admin@cee-chile.org, http://www.cee-chile.org/quienes/quienes.htm. Ed. Juan Domingo Silva.

320 GTM ISSN 0254-1696
H8.S7
ESTUDIOS SOCIALES. Text in Spanish. s-a. back issues avail. **Document type:** *Monographic series, Academic/Scholarly.*
Indexed: P09, PCI.
Published by: Universidad Rafael Landivar, Instituto de Ciencias Politicas y Sociales, Campus Central Vista Hermosa III, Zona 16, Guatemala, Guatemala. TEL 502-2-2797979.

320 PRT ISSN 0014-1623
➤ **ESTUDOS POLITICOS E SOCIAIS.** Text in English, French, Portuguese. 1963. q. USD 3.60. adv. bk.rev. bibl.; charts; illus. index. **Document type:** *Journal, Academic/Scholarly.*
Indexed: CA, P42, PSA, S02, S03, SociolAb, T02.
Published by: Instituto Superior de Ciencias Sociais e Politicas, Rua Junqueira, 86, Lisbon, 1399, Portugal. TEL 351-1-3637121, FAX 351-1-3642081. Ed. Prof Adriano Moreira. Adv. contact Acacio Almeida Santos. Circ: 1,500 (paid).

320 SWE ISSN 1654-4951
➤ **ETHICS & GLOBAL POLITICS.** Text in English. 2008. q. **Document type:** *Journal, Academic/Scholarly.*
Related titles: Online - full text ed.: ISSN 1654-6369. free (effective 2011).
Indexed: A39, C27, C29, CA, CurCont, D03, D04, E13, P42, PSA, PhilInd, R14, S14, S15, S18, SCOPUS, SSA, SSCI, SociolAb, T02, W07.
Published by: Co-Action Publishing, Ripvaegen 7, Jaerfaella, 17564, Sweden. TEL 46-18-4951150, FAX 46-18-4951138, info@co-action.net, http://www.co-action.net.

320 USA
ETHICS AND PUBLIC POLICY CENTER NEWSLETTER. Text in English. 1982. q. per issue contribution. **Document type:** *Newsletter.*
Description: Reports on activities of the Center, a non-partisan organization that conducts a program of research, writing, publications, and conferences to encourage debate on domestic and foreign policy issues among religious, academic, political, and other leaders. Special interest in positions of religious bodies on public policy questions.
Published by: Ethics and Public Policy Center, 1015 15th St, N W, Ste 900, Washington, DC 20005. TEL 202-682-1200, FAX 202-408-0632, Ethics@eppc.org, http://www.eppc.org/. Ed. Jacqui Stark. Circ: 15,000.

ETHIK UND POLITISCHE PHILOSOPHIE. *see* PHILOSOPHY

ETHIKON SERIES IN COMPARATIVE ETHICS. *see* PHILOSOPHY

THE ETHIOPIA BUSINESS FORECAST REPORT ANNUAL. *see* BUSINESS AND ECONOMICS

320 GBR ISSN 1744-9057
GN496
➤ **ETHNOPOLITICS.** Text in English. 2001. q. GBP 300 combined subscription in United Kingdom to institutions (print & online eds.); EUR 396, USD 498 combined subscription to institutions (print & online eds.) (effective 2012). adv. back issues avail.; reprint service avail. from PSC. **Document type:** *Journal, Academic/Scholarly.*
Description: Covers the field of ethnopolitics with methodological approaches covering mainly the disciplines of political science and international relations and taking primarily a contemporary, current affairs perspective.
Formerly (until 2005): Global Review of Ethnopolitics (1471-8804)
Related titles: Online - full text ed.: ISSN 1744-9065. GBP 269 in United Kingdom to institutions; EUR 357, USD 448 to institutions (effective 2012).
Indexed: A01, A22, B21, CA, E01, E17, ESPM, HistAb, P34, P42, PSA, SCOPUS, SociolAb, T02.
—IE, Ingenta. **CCC.**
Published by: (Specialist Group on Ethnopolitics), Routledge (Subsidiary of: Taylor & Francis Group), 4 Park Sq, Milton Park, Abingdon, Oxon OX14 4RN, United Kingdom. TEL 44-20-70176000, FAX 44-20-70176336, subscriptions@tandf.co.uk, http://www.routledge.com. Eds. Karl Cordell TEL 44-1752-233279, Stefan Wolff TEL 44-115-9514878. Adv. contact Linda Hann TEL 44-1344-779945. **Subscr. to:** Taylor & Francis Ltd., Journals Customer Service, Sheepen Pl, Colchester, Essex CO3 3LP, United Kingdom. TEL 44-20-70175544, FAX 44-20-70175198.

324.272976 GLP ISSN 0755-2947
CODEN: ATREEW
ETINCELLE. Text in French. w.
Address: 119 rue Vatable, Pointe-a-Pitre, 97110, Guadeloupe. TELEX 919419. Ed. Raymond Baron. Circ: 5,000.

320 IRN ISSN 1017-4141
ETTELA'AT-E SIYASSI EQTESADI; mahnameh siyassi ve eqtesadi. Text in Persian, Modern; Contents page in English. 1987. bi-m. GBP 36 in the Middle East; GBP 50 in Japan; GBP 41 in Europe; GBP 50 in North America (effective 2003). bk.rev. illus. **Document type:** *Academic/Scholarly.* **Description:** Publishes analytical and critical articles addressing Iranian domestic policies and issues, and international political and economic developments.
Published by: Ettela'at Publications, Mirdamad Blvd., Naft-e Jonubi St., Ettala'at Bldg., Tehran, 1549951199, Iran. TEL 98-21-29999, FAX 98-21-2258022, ettelaat@ettalaat.com, http://www.ettelaat.com. Ed. Mahdi Besharat. Circ: 50,000.

320 FRA ISSN 2109-375X
▼ **ETUDES & DEBATS.** Text in French. 2010. irreg.
Published by: Fondation pour la Recherche Strategique, 27 rue Damesme, Paris, 75013, France. TEL 33-01-43137777, FAX 33-01-43137778, webmaster@frstrategie.org, http://www.frstrategie.org.

320 FRA ISSN 1297-8450
LES ETUDES DU CERI. (Centre d'Etudes et de Recherches Internationales) Text in French. 1995. 10/yr. EUR 350 (effective 2011). back issues avail. **Document type:** *Journal, Academic/Scholarly.*
Related titles: Online - full text ed.: free.
Indexed: IBSS.
Published by: Sciences Po, Centre d'Etudes et de Recherches Internationales, 56 Rue Jacob, Paris, 75006, France. TEL 33-1-58717000, FAX 33-1-58717090, info@ceri-sciences-po.org, http://www.ceri-sciencespo.com.

▼ **ETUDES RICOEURIENNES/ RICOEUR STUDIES.** *see* PHILOSOPHY

320.9 VNM ISSN 0531-206X
ETUDES VIETNAMIENNES. Text in French. 1964. q. USD 15.70 domestic; USD 30.30 in Asia; USD 31.32 in Europe; USD 32.52 in Africa; USD 33 in United States (effective 2002). charts; illus. **Document type:** *Academic/Scholarly.*
Related titles: ◆ English ed.: Vietnamese Studies. ISSN 0085-7823.
Indexed: BAS.
Published by: Gioi Publishers/Foreign Languages Publishing House, 46 Tran Hung Dao, Hanoi, Viet Nam. TEL 84-4-8253841, FAX 84-4-8269578. Ed. Tan Doan Lam.

320 COD ISSN 0301-9209
DT658
ETUDES ZAIROISES. Text in French. 1961. q. bibl.
Supersedes: Etudes Congolaises (0425-4805)
Indexed: MLA-IB, P30.
Published by: Institut National d'Etudes Politiques, BP 2307, Kinshasa, Congo, Dem. Republic.

EUROPA ETHNICA. *see* ETHNIC INTERESTS

320 ITA ISSN 1974-2711
EUROPAE. Text in Italian. 2008. 3/yr. EUR 20 (effective 2010). **Document type:** *Journal, Consumer.*
Published by: Rubbettino Editore, Viale Rosario Rubbettino 10, Soveria Mannelli, CZ 88049, Italy. TEL 39-0968-662034, FAX 39-0968-662055, segreteria@rubbettino.it, http://www.rubbettino.it.

P

320 DEU ISSN 0721-3654
EUROPAEISCHE HOCHSCHULSCHRIFTEN. REIHE 31: POLITIKWISSENSCHAFT/EUROPEAN UNIVERSITY STUDIES. SERIES 31: POLITICAL SCIENCES. Text in German. 1974. irreg., latest vol.583, 2010. price varies. **Document type:** *Monographic series, Academic/Scholarly.*
Published by: Peter Lang GmbH (Subsidiary of: Peter Lang Publishing Group), Eschborner Landstr 42-50, Frankfurt Am Main, 60489, Germany. TEL 49-69-7807050, FAX 49-69-78070550, zentrale.frankfurt@peterlang.com, http://www.peterlang.com.

EUROPE - ASIA STUDIES. *see* BUSINESS AND ECONOMICS

320.51 LUX
EUROPEAN COMMISSION. BACKGROUND BRIEFING. Text in English. irreg.
Published by: European Commission, Office for Official Publications of the European Union, 2 Rue Mercier, Luxembourg, L-2985, Luxembourg. TEL 352-29291, info@publications.europa.eu, http://publications.europa.eu.

341.2422 333.79 BEL ISSN 0376-5482
T177.E9
EUROPEAN COMMISSION. JOINT RESEARCH CENTER. ANNUAL REPORT. Text in English. a. free. **Document type:** *Corporate.*
Formerly (until 1995): Joint Nuclear Research Center, Ispra, Italy. Annual Report
Related titles: Online - full content ed.: J R C Annual Report. ISSN 1684-0917.
Published by: European Commission, Directorate General - Joint Research Center, Public Relations Unit, SDME 10/78, Brussels, B-1049, Belgium. TEL 32-2-2957624, FAX 32-2-2996322, jrc-info@cec.eu.int.

321.8 SWE ISSN 1652-5345
EUROPEAN DEMOCRACY SERIES. Text in English. 2004. irreg., latest vol.1, 2004. SEK 180 per issue (effective 2006). **Document type:** *Monographic series, Academic/Scholarly.*
Published by: Oerebro Universitet, Universitetsbiblioteket/University of Oerebro. University Library, Fakultetsgatan 1, Oerebro, 70182, Sweden. TEL 46-19-303240, FAX 46-19-331217, biblioteket@ub.oru.se. Ed. Joanna Jansdotter.

320 ITA ISSN 1827-8361
JN26
EUROPEAN DIVERSITY AND AUTONOMY PAPERS. Abbreviated title: E D A P. Text in Italian, English, German, French, Spanish. 2004. irreg. free (effective 2011). **Document type:** *Journal, Academic/Scholarly.* **Description:** Aims to contribute to the theoretical development and empirical exploration of various approaches to the growing reality of diversity embedded within the European Union.
Media: Online - full text.
Indexed: CA, P42, T02.
Published by: Accademia Europea Bolzano (E U R A C)/European Academy Bolzano, Viale Druso 1, Bolzano, Italy. TEL 39-0471-055055, FAX 39-0471-055059.

320.3 370 GBR ISSN 1468-9049
EUROPEAN ESSAY. Text in English. 2000. bi-m. back issues avail. **Document type:** *Monographic series, Academic/Scholarly.* **Description:** Aims to enlightening the debate on good governance.
Related titles: Online - full text ed.: free (effective 2009).
Published by: Federal Trust for Education and Research, 31 Jewry St, London, EC3N 2EY, United Kingdom. TEL 44-20-73203045, info@fedtrust.co.uk.

320 GBR ISSN 1351-6620
JN15
THE EUROPEAN JOURNAL. Text in English. 1993. 10/yr. GBP 30 domestic; GBP 34 in Europe; GBP 38 elsewhere (effective 2009). adv. back issues avail. **Document type:** *Monographic series, Academic/Scholarly.* **Description:** Addresses the economic and political concerns of the European Community and encourages debate among politicians and other policy-makers, journalists, academics, trade unionists, and businessmen.
Indexed: RASB.
—BLDSC (3829.721950), IE, Ingenta.
Published by: European Foundation, 83 Victoria St, London, SW1H 0HW, United Kingdom. TEL 44-20-31787038. Ed. James McConalogue.

THE EUROPEAN JOURNAL OF DEVELOPMENT RESEARCH. *see* BUSINESS AND ECONOMICS—International Development And Assistance

EUROPEAN JOURNAL OF ECONOMIC AND POLITICAL STUDIES. *see* BUSINESS AND ECONOMICS

320.9 NLD ISSN 0176-2680
HB1
➤ **EUROPEAN JOURNAL OF POLITICAL ECONOMY/ EUROPAEISCHE ZEITSCHRIFT FUER POLITISCHE OEKONOMIE.** Text in English. 1985. 4/yr. EUR 851 in Europe to institutions; JPY 112,800 in Japan to institutions; USD 951 elsewhere to institutions (effective 2012). adv. bk.rev. abstr. index. back issues avail.; reprints avail. **Document type:** *Journal, Academic/Scholarly.* **Description:** Devoted to the study of classical and neoclassical political economy, public choice and collective decision making, law and economics, and economic history.
Related titles: Microform ed.: (from PQC); Online - full text ed.: ISSN 1873-5703 (from IngentaConnect, ScienceDirect).
Indexed: A01, A03, A08, A22, A26, B01, B06, B07, B09, CA, ESPM, EconLit, I05, I13, IBR, IBSS, IBZ, JEL, P34, P42, PSA, RiskAb, S02, S03, SCOPUS, SOPODA, SSA, SSCI, SociolAb, T02, W07.
—BLDSC (3829.736500), IE, Infotrieve, Ingenta. **CCC.**
Published by: Elsevier BV, North-Holland (Subsidiary of: Elsevier Science & Technology), Sara Burgerhartstraat 25, Amsterdam, 1055 KV, Netherlands. TEL 31-20-4853911, FAX 31-20-4852457, JournalsCustomerServiceEMEA@elsevier.com. Eds. A L Hillman, H W Ursprung, J de Haan. **Subscr. to:** Elsevier BV, Radarweg 29, PO Box 211, Amsterdam 1000 AE, Netherlands. TEL 31-20-4853757, FAX 31-20-4853432.

320 GBR ISSN 0304-4130
CODEN: EJPRDY
➤ **EUROPEAN JOURNAL OF POLITICAL RESEARCH.** Abbreviated title: E J P R. Text in English. 1973. 8/yr. GBP 649 in United Kingdom to institutions; EUR 824 in Europe to institutions; USD 1,180 in the Americas to institutions; USD 1,271 elsewhere to institutions; GBP 747 combined subscription in United Kingdom to institutions (print & online eds.); EUR 948 combined subscription in Europe to institutions (print & online eds.); USD 1,357 combined subscription in the Americas to institutions (print & online eds.); USD 1,462 combined subscription elsewhere to institutions (print & online eds.) (effective 2012). adv. illus. index. back issues avail.; reprint service avail. from PSC. **Document type:** *Journal, Academic/Scholarly.* **Description:** Provides short research notes outlining ongoing research in more specific areas of research.
Related titles: Microform ed.: (from PQC); Online - full text ed.: ISSN 1475-6765. GBP 649 in United Kingdom to institutions; EUR 824 in Europe to institutions; USD 1,180 in the Americas to institutions; USD 1,271 elsewhere to institutions (effective 2012) (from IngentaConnect).
Indexed: A01, A02, A03, A08, A20, A22, A26, ABCPolSci, AC&P, ASCA, CA, CurCont, DIP, E01, ESPM, FR, I13, IBR, IBSS, IBZ, MEA&I, P02, P27, P30, P34, P42, P48, P54, PCI, PQC, PRA, PSA, PhilInd, RiskAb, S02, S03, S21, SCOPUS, SD, SOPODA, SSA, SSCI, SociolAb, T02, W07.
—BLDSC (3829.737000), IE, Infotrieve, Ingenta, INIST. **CCC.**
Published by: (European Consortium for Political Research), Wiley-Blackwell Publishing Ltd. (Subsidiary of: John Wiley & Sons, Inc.), 9600 Garsington Rd, Oxford, OX4 2DQ, United Kingdom. TEL 44-1865-776868, FAX 44-1865-714591, customerservices@blackwellpublishing.com. Eds. Kris Deschouwer, Richard S Katz. Adv. contact Craig Pickett TEL 44-1865-476267. B&W page GBP 445, B&W page USD 445.008; 120 x 200. Circ: 900.

320 GBR ISSN 1474-8851
JA8
➤ **EUROPEAN JOURNAL OF POLITICAL THEORY.** Text in English. 2002 (Jul.). q. USD 766, GBP 414 combined subscription to institutions (print & online eds.); USD 751, GBP 406 to institutions (effective 2011). adv. bk.rev. back issues avail.; reprint service avail. from PSC. **Document type:** *Journal, Academic/Scholarly.* **Description:** Will provide a much needed and long awaited research forum for political theory in a European context. Broad in scope and international in readership, this new journal will publish the very best articles in political thought and theory from top international scholars from Europe and beyond.
Related titles: Online - full text ed.: ISSN 1741-2730. USD 689, GBP 373 to institutions (effective 2011).
Indexed: A22, CA, DIP, E01, IBR, IBSS, IBZ, P42, PRA, PSA, SCOPUS, SociolAb, T02.
—BLDSC (3829.737300), IE, Ingenta. **CCC.**
Published by: Sage Publications Ltd. (Subsidiary of: Sage Publications, Inc.), 1 Oliver's Yard, 55 City Rd, London, EC1Y 1SP, United Kingdom. TEL 44-20-73248500, FAX 44-20-73248600, info@sagepub.co.uk, http://www.uk.sagepub.com/home.nav. Ed. Richard North. adv.: B&W page GBP 350; 130 x 205. **Subscr. in the Americas to:** Sage Publications, Inc., 2455 Teller Rd, Thousand Oaks, CA 91320. TEL 805-499-9774, FAX 805-499-0871, journals@sagepub.com.

➤ **EUROPEAN MONOGRAPHS.** *see* LAW—International Law

328.3 LUX ISSN 0423-7846
JN32
EUROPEAN PARLIAMENT. BULLETIN. Text in English. w. Supplement avail. **Document type:** *Bulletin.*
Indexed: RASB.
Published by: European Parliament, Secretariat, B.P. 1601, Luxembourg, L-2929, Luxembourg. FAX 352-43-70-09.

328 351 LUX
EUROPEAN PARLIAMENT. GROUP OF THE EUROPEAN PEOPLE'S PARTY. CHRISTIAN DEMOCRAT GROUP. REPORT ON THE ACTIVITIES. Text in English. 1994. a. charts; stat. **Document type:** *Corporate.* **Description:** Offers an in-depth chronology and analysis of the activities of the European Union European People's Party, Christian Democrat Group.
Published by: European Parliament, European People's Party, Secretariat, Luxembourg, 2929, Luxembourg. FAX 352-6-437009, http://www.europarl.eu.int/ppe.

328.4 LUX ISSN 0250-7781
EUROPEAN PARLIAMENT'S OFFICIAL HANDBOOK. Text in English. 1980. a. (plus s-a. updates). **Document type:** *Directory, Government.*
Related titles: Danish ed.: suspended; Dutch ed.: suspended; Italian ed.: suspended; German ed.: suspended; French ed.: suspended.
Indexed: RASB.
Published by: European Parliament, Secretariat, B.P. 1601, Luxembourg, L-2929, Luxembourg. FAX 352-43-70-09.

320.6 GBR
EUROPEAN POLICY RESEARCH PAPERS. Text in English. 1989. irreg., latest vol.68, 2009. free (effective 2009). back issues avail. **Document type:** *Monographic series, Academic/Scholarly.* **Description:** Papers for academics and policy-makers on public policy in Europe.
Formerly (until 199?): Regional and Industrial Policy Research Papers (Print)
Media: Online - full text.
Published by: University of Strathclyde, European Policies Research Centre, 40 George St, Glasgow, G1 1QE, United Kingdom. TEL 44-141-5483672, FAX 44-141-5484898, eprc@strath.ac.uk.

320 GBR ISSN 1680-4333
JA8
➤ **EUROPEAN POLITICAL SCIENCE.** Text in English. 2001. q. USD 561 in North America to institutions; EUR 421 in Europe to institutions; GBP 295 elsewhere to institutions (effective 2011). adv. back issues avail.; reprint service avail. from PSC. **Document type:** *Journal, Academic/Scholarly.* **Description:** Devoted to publishing contributions by and for the political science community.
Related titles: Online - full text ed.: ISSN 1682-0983 (from IngentaConnect).
Indexed: A01, A02, A03, A08, A22, A26, CA, E01, E08, I05, IBSS, P10, P27, P42, P45, P48, P54, PQC, PSA, S09, SCOPUS, SSCI, SociolAb, T02, W07.
—BLDSC (3829.788700), IE, Ingenta. **CCC.**
Published by: (European Consortium for Political Research), Palgrave Macmillan Ltd. (Subsidiary of: Macmillan Publishers Ltd.), Houndmills, Basingstoke, Hants RG21 6XS, United Kingdom. TEL 44-1256-329242, FAX 44-1256-479476, orders@palgrave.com, http://www.palgrave.com. Eds. Luis de Sousa, Martin Bull. Pub. Guy Edwards. Circ: 2,700. **Subscr. to:** Subscription Department, Brunel Rd, Houndmills, Basingstoke, Hants RG21 2XS, United Kingdom. TEL 44-1256-357893, FAX 44-1256-328339, subscriptions@palgrave.com.

320 GBR ISSN 1755-7739
JA88.E9
▼ ➤ **EUROPEAN POLITICAL SCIENCE REVIEW.** Abbreviated title: E P S R. Text in English. 2009. 3/yr. GBP 305, USD 535 to institutions; GBP 305, USD 530 combined subscription to institutions (print & online eds.) (effective 2012). adv. back issues avail. **Document type:** *Journal, Academic/Scholarly.* **Description:** Features original research from leading political scientists around the world as well as the work of the best young scholars in the discipline.
Related titles: Online - full text ed.: ISSN 1755-7747. GBP 255, USD 445 to institutions (effective 2012).
Indexed: P27, P45, P48, P54, PQC.
—**CCC.**
Published by: (European Consortium for Political Research), Cambridge University Press, The Edinburgh Bldg, Shaftesbury Rd, Cambridge, CB2 8RU, United Kingdom. TEL 44-1223-312393, FAX 44-1223-315052, information@cambridge.org. Ed. B Guy Peters. Adv. contact Rebecca Roberts TEL 44-1223-325083. B&W page GBP 465, B&W page USD 885. **Subscr. to:** Cambridge University Press, 100 Brook Hill Dr, W Nyack, NY 10994. TEL 845-353-7500, 800-872-7423, FAX 845-353-4141, subscriptions_newyork@cambridge.org.

320 ITA ISSN 2036-945X
EUROPEAN PROGRESS. Variant title: European Progress. Collana di Studi Europei. Text in Italian. 2005. irreg. **Document type:** *Monographic series, Academic/Scholarly.*
Published by: Casa Editrice C L U E B, Via Marsala 31, Bologna, BO 40126, Italy. TEL 39-051-220736, FAX 39-051-237758, clueb@clueb.com, http://www.clueb.eu/home.html.

320 GBR ISSN 2042-6844
➤ **EUROPEAN SOCIAL AND POLITICAL RESEARCH.** Abbreviated title: E S P R. Text in English. 1995. a. free (effective 2010). bibl.; charts; illus.; maps. 1 cols./p.; back issues avail. **Document type:** *Journal, Academic/Scholarly.* **Description:** Contains articles written by ESPS undergraduates, based on their course projects and provides a unique opportunity for some of our students to publish their work.
Formerly (until 2009): Modern European Research (Print) (1361-2689)
Media: Online - full text. **Related titles:** E-mail ed.
Indexed: CA, P42, S02, S03, SociolAb, T02.
—BLDSC (5886.446300).
Published by: University College London, European Social and Political Studies, Foster Ct, N Side, Ground Fl, London, WC1E 6BT, United Kingdom. TEL 44-20-76793707, FAX 44-20-76793226, esps-admin@ucl.ac.uk. Ed. Philippe Marliere TEL 44-20-76794424.

320 GBR ISSN 1362-0541
EUROPEAN UNION POLICY PAPERS. Text in English. 1996. irreg. GBP 2.95 per issue (effective 2009). back issues avail. **Document type:** *Monographic series, Academic/Scholarly.* **Description:** Aims to promote discussion and debate on issues pertaining to the future of European integration.
Published by: (Edinburgh University, Europa Institute), University of Manchester, European Policy Research Unit, Oxford Rd, Manchester, M13 9PL, United Kingdom. TEL 44-161-3066000.

EUROPEAN UNIVERSITY INSTITUTE. ROBERT SCHUMAN CENTRE FOR ADVANCED STUDIES. WORKING PAPERS. *see* LAW

320 BEL ISSN 1782-0642
EUROPE'S WORLD; the only Europe-wide policy journal. Text in English. 2005. 3/yr. EUR 33 domestic; EUR 38 in Europe; EUR 41 elsewhere (effective 2010). adv. **Document type:** *Journal, Academic/Scholarly.*
Related titles: Online - full text ed.: ISSN 1784-9713. free.
Address: La Bibliotheque Solvay, 137, rue Belliard, Brussels, 1040, Belgium. TEL 32-2-7387592, FAX 32-2-7391592, info@europesworld.org.

EVANGELICAL REVIEW OF SOCIETY AND POLITICS. *see* RELIGIONS AND THEOLOGY—Other Denominations And Sects

324 CZE ISSN 1801-6545
➤ **EVROPSKA VOLEBNI STUDIA/EUROPEAN ELECTORAL STUDIES.** Text in Czech, English, Slovak. 2006. 2/yr. **Document type:** *Journal, Academic/Scholarly.* **Description:** Covers all aspects of elections, electoral systems, electoral geography, campaigns, and methods of electoral research.
Related titles: Online - full text ed.: free (effective 2011).
Indexed: CA, P42, T02.
Published by: Masarykova Univerzita, Institut pro Srovnavaci Politologicky Vyzkum/Masaryk University, Institute for Comparative Political Research, Jostova 10, Brno, 60200, Czech Republic. TEL 420-549-494235, FAX 420-549-491920, ispo@fss.muni.cz. Ed. Jakub Sedo.

➤ **EVROPSKE NOVINY.** *see* BUSINESS AND ECONOMICS

321.8 MEX
EXAMEN; una publicacion por la democracia. Text in Spanish. 1972. m. MXN 60,000; USD 65 foreign. adv. bk.rev. bibl.; illus.; stat.
Formerly (until 1989): Linea
Related titles: Online - full text ed.: ISSN 1607-1247. 2000.
Published by: Partido Revolucionario Institucional, Insurgentes Norte No.59, Mexico, Col Buenavista, Mexico City, DF 06350, Mexico. TEL 535-82-31, FAX 525-566-8417. Circ: 15,000.

EXCARCERATE. *see* LAW—Criminal Law

320 USA ISSN 0273-6314
HF1410
EXECUTIVE INTELLIGENCE REVIEW. Short title: E I R. Text in English. 1974. w. USD 396 in North America; USD 490 elsewhere; USD 10 newsstand/cover (effective 2005). bk.rev.; Website rev. 80 p./no.; back issues avail. **Document type:** *Magazine, Consumer.* **Description:** Review of economics, science, politics and culture.
Related titles: Online - full text ed.: E I R Online. USD 360 (effective 2005).
Indexed: P30, Perlslam, RefZh.
—BLDSC (3836.219500), IE, Infotrieve, Ingenta.

Published by: E I R News Service, 317 Pennsylvania Ave., SE., 3rd Fl, PO Box 17390, Washington, DC 20041. TEL 202-544-7022, FAX 202-771-3099. Ed. Lyndon H Larouche Jr. R&P Susan Welsh TEL 703-777-9451 ext. 541. Adv. contact Lonnie Wolfe. Circ: 14,000.

320.51 323 SWE ISSN 1400-9846
HN580.R3
EXPO; demokratisk tidskrift. Text in Swedish. 1995-1997. 4/yr. SEK 290; SEK 75 per issue (effective 2010). adv. bk.rev. back issues avail. **Document type:** *Magazine, Consumer.*
Incorporates (1987-2002): Svartvitt (0284-7191)
Related titles: Online - full text ed.: ISSN 1402-4535. 1996.
Published by: Stiftelsen Expo, PO Box 8165, Stockholm, 10420, Sweden. TEL 46-8-6526004, FAX 46-8-6526005. Ed. Daniel Poohl. Circ: 1,800 (controlled).

320.531 DEU ISSN 0343-5121
HD6691
EXPRESS (OFFENBACH); Zeitung fuer sozialistische Betriebs- und Gewerkschaftsarbeit. Text in German. 1972. 10/yr. EUR 35; EUR 3.50 newsstand/cover (effective 2008). adv. bk.rev. illus. **Document type:** *Newspaper, Trade.*
Formed by the merger of (19??-1972): Sozialistische Betriebskorrespondenz (0343-513X); (1963-1972): Express International (0341-7867); Which incorporated (195?-1966): Sozialistische Politik (0340-9597)
Published by: Arbeitsgemeinschaft zur Foerderung der Politischen Bildung e.V., Niddastr 64, Frankfurt am Main, 60329, Germany. TEL 49-69-679984.

320 USA ISSN 1071-4340
EXTENSIONS. Text in English. 1982. s-a. free (effective 2010). bk.rev. **Document type:** *Journal, Academic/Scholarly.* **Description:** Provides analysis and commentary on the U.S. Congress and on representative government in general.
Published by: University of Oklahoma, Carl Albert Center, 630 Parrington Oval, Rm 101, Norman, OK 73019. TEL 405-325-6372, FAX 405-325-6419, csrosenthal@ou.edu.

EXTRA!. *see* JOURNALISM

320 GBR ISSN 1473-4362
EYE SPY. Text in English. 1996. 8/yr. GBP 27.50 domestic; USD 49.99 in United States; CAD 60 in Canada; GBP 30 elsewhere; GBP 3.95 per issue domestic; USD 7 per issue in United States; GBP 3.99 per issue elsewhere (effective 2009). adv. back issues avail. **Document type:** *Magazine, Consumer.* **Description:** Covers international intelligence gathering and counter intelligence, featuring photos and articles on global incidents, military technology, and historical conspiracies.
Formerly (until 2001): Unopened Files (1364-8446)
Published by: Eye Spy Publishing Ltd, PO Box 10, Skipton, North Yorkshire BD23 5US, United Kingdom. TEL 44-1756-770199. Ed. Mark Birdsall.

320 RUS
EZHENEDEL'NYI BYULLETEN' ZAKONODATEL'NYKH I VEDOMSTVENNYKH AKTOV. Text in Russian. 1998. w. USD 488 in the Americas (effective 2000).
Published by: Agentstvo Informbank, Ul T Frunze 8-5, k 35-36, Moscow, 119021, Russian Federation. TEL 7-095-2450213, FAX 7-095-2453509. **Dist. by:** East View Information Services, 10601 Wayzata Blvd, Minneapolis, MN 55305. TEL 952-252-1201, 800-477-1005, FAX 952-252-1202, info@eastview.com, http://www.eastview.com.

324.2 DNK ISSN 1902-1321
F!; S F Magasin. (Socialistisk Folkeparti) Text in Danish. 1977. bi-m. DKK 240 membership (effective 2009). **Document type:** *Magazine, Consumer.*
Former titles (until 2006): Folkesocialisten (0106-0635); Which incorporates (1985-1990): Faglig Kontakt (0901-9251); (until 1978): S F Medlemsblad (0106-0309)
Related titles: Online - full text ed.: ISSN 1902-133X. 2006.
Published by: Socialistisk Folkeparti/Socialist People's Party, Christiansborg, Copenhagen K, 1240, Denmark. TEL 45-33-374444, FAX 45-33-327248, sf@sf.dk. Eds. Rosa Juel Nordentoft, Turid Leirvoll. Circ: 18,000.

320 USA ISSN 0532-7091
F C L NEWSLETTER. Text in English. 1952. 10/yr. USD 20 (effective 2000). **Document type:** *Newsletter.* **Description:** Informs readers of state legislation and related matters regarding social issues, including criminal justice, human services, and peace.
Indexed: ChPerI.
Published by: Friends Committee on Legislation of California, 717 K St., Ste. 500, Sacramento, CA 95814-3408. TEL 916-443-3734, http://www.webcom.com/peace/. Ed. Ken Larsen. Circ: 3,000.

322.1 USA ISSN 0014-5734
F C N L WASHINGTON NEWSLETTER. Text in English. 1943. m. (11/yr.). free to donors. 8 p./no. 2 cols./p.; reprints avail. **Document type:** *Newsletter.* **Description:** Public policy and issues of interest to Quakers and others.
Related titles: Audio cassette/tape ed.; Microform ed.: (from PQC); Online - full text ed.
Indexed: APW, HRIR, P06.
Published by: Friends Committee on National Legislation, 245 Second St, N E, Washington, DC 20002. TEL 202-547-6000, FAX 202-547-6019. Ed. Florence Kimball. Circ: 10,000.

F E E. ENSAIOS. (Fundacao de Economia e Estatistica) *see* BUSINESS AND ECONOMICS—Economic Systems And Theories, Economic History

F G V. BOLETIM CENARIOS. (Fundacao Getulio Vargas) *see* BUSINESS AND ECONOMICS—Economic Situation And Conditions

320.5322 ESP ISSN 1133-0562
HX13.A3
F I M. PAPELES. (Fundacion de Investigaciones Marxistas) Text in Spanish. 1980. s-a. back issues avail. **Document type:** *Magazine, Consumer.* **Description:** Contributes to the debate on options, proposals and projects which at this century's end are proposing a reformulation of the ideas of the Left.
Published by: Fundacion de Investigaciones Marxistas, C. Alameda 5, Madrid, 28014, Spain. TEL 34-91-4201388, FAX 34-91-4202004, info@fim.og.es, http://www.fim.org.es/. Ed. Juan Trias. **Dist. by:** Asociacion de Revistas Culturales de Espana, C Covarruvias 9 2o. Derecha, Madrid 28010, Spain. TEL 34-91-3086066, FAX 34-91-3199267, info@arce.es, http://www.arce.es/.

320 GBR ISSN 1746-1146
HX11
FABIAN IDEAS. Variant title: Ideas Pamphlets. Text in English. 1884. irreg. free to members (effective 2009). back issues avail.; reprints avail. **Document type:** *Monographic series, Academic/Scholarly.*
Former titles (until 2000): Fabian Pamphlet (1469-0136); (until 1996): Fabian Tracts (0307-7535)
Indexed: PCI.
—IE. **CCC.**
Published by: Fabian Society, 11 Dartmouth St, London, SW1H 9BN, United Kingdom. TEL 44-20-72274900, info@fabians.org.uk. Ed. Tom Hampson.

320.531 GBR ISSN 1356-1812
HX3
FABIAN REVIEW. Text in English. 1891. q. GBP 4.95 per issue to non-members; free to members (effective 2009). adv. bk.rev. back issues avail.; reprint service avail. from PSC. **Document type:** *Journal, Academic/Scholarly.* **Description:** Explores issues that pertain to Britain's Labour movement.
Formerly (until 1991): Fabian News (0014-6196)
Indexed: RASB.
—IE, Infotrieve.
Published by: Fabian Society, 11 Dartmouth St, London, SW1H 9BN, United Kingdom. TEL 44-20-72274900, info@fabians.org.uk. Ed. Tom Hampson.

FACTA UNIVERSITATIS. SERIES LAW AND POLITICS. *see* LAW

320 ESP ISSN 1139-4633
LA FACTORIA; la revista catalana de pensamiento social. Text in Spanish. 1996. 3/yr. free (effective 2009). back issues avail. **Document type:** *Magazine, Consumer.*
Related titles: Online - full text ed.: ISSN 1139-5699. 1998.
Published by: Factoria, La Rectoria Colomers, Girona, 17144, Spain. TEL 34-934-145955, tu.revista@revistalafactoria.eu, http://www.lafactoria.com/. Ed. Carlos Navales. **Dist. by:** Asociacion de Revistas Culturales de Espana, C Covarruvias 9 2o. Derecha, Madrid 28010, Spain. TEL 34-91-3086066, FAX 34-91-3199267, info@arce.es, http://www.arce.es/.

320 BRA
FACULDADE DE FILOSOFIA, CIENCIAS E LETRAS DE ARARAQUARA. CADEIRA DE POLITICA. BOLETIM. Text in Portuguese. 1968. m. bk.rev. bibl.
Published by: Faculdade de Filosofia Ciencias e Letras de Araraquara, Praca Santos Dumont, Centro, Caixa Postal 174, Araraquara, SP 14801-970, Brazil.

320 PER
FAENA. Text in Spanish. q. PEN 200.
Published by: Instituto de Promocion y Educacion Popular, Apartado 16, Ancash, Chimbote, Peru. Ed. Roberto Lopez Linares.

FANFUBAI DAOKAN. *see* LAW

320 GBR ISSN 0071-3791
DS1
FAR EAST AND AUSTRALASIA (YEAR). Text in English. 1969. a. USD 760 per issue (effective 2009). reprints avail. **Document type:** *Journal, Academic/Scholarly.* **Description:** Contains information on the region as a whole followed by separate chapters on each of the countries and territories; these include general and statistical surveys, and directories of the government, diplomatic corps, political parties, communications, finance, trade and industry, tourism, and nuclear energy.
—BLDSC (3865.785000). **CCC.**
Published by: (Europa Publications Ltd.), Routledge (Subsidiary of: Taylor & Francis Group), 2 Park Sq, Milton Park, Abingdon, Oxon OX14 4RN, United Kingdom. TEL 44-20-70176000, FAX 44-20-70176699, orders@taylorandfrancis.com. **Dist. by:** Current Pacific Ltd., 7 La Roche Pl, Northcote, PO Box 36-536, Auckland 0627, New Zealand.

320.5 NLD ISSN 2211-6249
▼ ➤ **FASCISM.** Text in English. forthcoming 2012. s-a. EUR 150, USD 210 combined subscription to institutions (print & online eds.) (effective 2012). **Document type:** *Journal, Academic/Scholarly.*
Related titles: Online - full text ed.: ISSN 2211-6257. forthcoming 2012. free (effective 2012).
Published by: Brill, PO Box 9000, Leiden, 2300 PA, Netherlands. TEL 31-71-5353500, FAX 31-71-5317532, cs@brill.nl. Ed. Madelon de Keizer.

320 300 USA ISSN 1930-014X
HM851
➤ **FAST CAPITALISM.** Text in English. 2005. s-a. free (effective 2011). back issues avail. **Document type:** *Journal, Academic/Scholarly.* **Description:** Publishes scholarship and essays about the impact of rapid information and communication technologies on self, society and culture in the 21st century.
Media: Online - full text.
Indexed: A39, C27, C29, D03, D04, E13, R14, S14, S15, S18.
Address: aggerfastcap@uta.edu. Ed. Ben Agger.

324.23 USA
FEDERAL ELECTION COMMISSION. CAMPAIGN GUIDE. CORPORATIONS AND LABOR ORGANIZATIONS. Text in English. 19??. irreg., latest 2007. free (effective 2011). **Document type:** *Handbook/Manual/Guide, Government.* **Description:** Helps segregated funds, political action committees, labor organizations and corporations comply with federal campaign finance law.
Formerly (until 2001): Campaign Guide for Corporations and Labor Organizations
Related titles: Online - full text ed.
Published by: Federal Election Commission, 999 E St NW, Washington, DC 20463. TEL 202-694-1100, 800-424-9530, FAX 202-219-8504, info@fec.gov.

324.6 USA ISSN 0145-8566
KF4885.A15
FEDERAL ELECTION COMMISSION. RECORD. Text in English. 1975. m. looseleaf. free (effective 2011). stat.; charts. index. back issues avail. **Document type:** *Newsletter, Government.* **Description:** Reports on all F.E.C. actions. Includes summaries of advisory opinions, litigation and compliance, and provides data on reporting requirements.
Related titles: Microfilm ed.; Online - full text ed.
Indexed: IUSGP.
—Ingenta.
Published by: Federal Election Commission, 999 E St NW, Washington, DC 20463. TEL 202-694-1100, 800-424-9530, FAX 202-219-8504, info@fec.gov. Ed. Myles G Martin.

324.9 USA ISSN 8756-4890
JK1967
FEDERAL ELECTIONS. Text in English. 1982. biennial. free (effective 2011). back issues avail. **Document type:** *Handbook/Manual/Guide, Government.*
Related titles: Online - full text ed.
Published by: Federal Election Commission, 999 E St NW, Washington, DC 20463. TEL 202-694-1100, 800-424-9530, FAX 202-219-8504, info@fec.gov.

320 CAN
➤ **FEDERAL GOVERNANCE**; a graduate journal of theory and politics. Text in English. 2002 (Oct.). irreg. bk.rev. back issues avail. **Document type:** *Journal, Academic/Scholarly.* **Description:** Publishes graduate student essays on topics relating to federalism and multi-level governance.
Media: Online - full content.
Address: c/o Institute of Intergovernmental Relations, Room 301, School of Policy Studies, Queen's University, Kingston, ON K7L 3N6, Canada. TEL 613-533-2080, FAX 613-533-6868, federalgovernance@cnfs.queensu.ca. Ed. Michael Kocsis.

320 973 USA ISSN 1943-8036
JK325
➤ **FEDERAL HISTORY.** Text in English. 2008 (Dec.). a. free (effective 2010). **Document type:** *Journal, Academic/Scholarly.* **Description:** Seeks to promote scholarship on the history and workings of the federal government and of the developmental relationships between American society and the U.S. military or U.S. government, 1776 to the present.
Media: Online - full text.
Indexed: T02.
Published by: Society for History in the Federal Government, PO Box 14139, Washington, DC 20044. benjamin.guterman@nara.gov. Eds. Benjamin Guterman, Terrance Rucker.

328 USA ISSN 0195-749X
KF5406.A15
FEDERAL REGULATORY DIRECTORY. Abbreviated title: F R E D. Text in English. biennial, latest 13th ed. USD 165 per issue (effective 2008). 881 p./no.; reprints avail. **Document type:** *Directory.* **Description:** Describes more than 100 federal regulatory bodies, including the laws and regulations they enforce. Includes names, addresses and phone numbers of key personnel; organization charts; appendix with texts of major regulatory laws.
Related titles: Online - full text ed.
—**CCC.**
Published by: C Q Press, Inc. (Subsidiary of: Sage Publications, Inc.), 2300 N St, NW, Ste 800, Washington, DC 20037. TEL 202-729-1900, 866-427-7737, FAX 800-380-3810, customerservice@cqpress.com.

FEDERAL STAFF DIRECTORY. *see* PUBLIC ADMINISTRATION

FEDERAL YELLOW BOOK; who's who in the federal departments and agencies. *see* PUBLIC ADMINISTRATION

320 USA ISSN 0194-2840
JC355
FEDERALISM REPORT. Text in English. 1971. q. membership. adv. bk.rev. back issues avail. **Document type:** *Newsletter.* **Description:** Provides reports on research, publications, and conference activities of the Center for the Study of Federalism.
Former titles: C S F Notebook; C F S Notebook
Published by: Temple University, Center for the Study of Federalism, 1616 Walnut St, Rm 507, Philadelphia, PA 19103. TEL 215-787-1480, FAX 215-787-7784. Ed. Daniel J Elazar. Pub., Adv. contact Kimberly J Robinson. Circ: 1,700.

320 BEL ISSN 1374-3864
FEDERALISME - REGIONALISME. Text in Multiple languages. 1998. s-a. **Document type:** *Journal, Academic/Scholarly.*
Related titles: Online - full text ed.: free (effective 2011).
Published by: Universite de Liege, Boulevard du Rectorat 7, Liege, 4000, Belgium. http://www.ulg.ac.be. Ed. Pierre Verjans.

324.251 CHN
FENDOU/STRUGGLE. Text in Chinese. m. CNY 1 per issue. illus. **Document type:** *Magazine, Consumer.*
Published by: (Zhongguo Gongchandang/Chinese Communist Party, Heilongjiang Sheng-Wei/Heilongjiang Provincial Committee), Fendou Zazhishe, 62 Huayuan Jie, Nangang-qu, Harbin, Heilongjiang 150001, China. TEL 37784.

320 GBR ISSN 0143-5426
HX3
FIGHT RACISM! FIGHT IMPERIALISM!. Text in English. 1979. bi-m. GBP 7.50 domestic to individuals; GBP 11 in Europe to individuals; GBP 12.50 elsewhere to individuals; GBP 15 domestic to institutions; GBP 22 in Europe to institutions; GBP 25 elsewhere to institutions (effective 2010). adv. bk.rev. back issues avail. **Document type:** *Newspaper, Consumer.* **Description:** Focuses on building an independent working class movement in Britain, linking that with support for anti-imperialist movements in Ireland, Turkey and Kurdistan from a communist perspective.
Indexed: LeftInd, RASB.
—BLDSC (3925.490200).
Published by: (Revolutionary Communist Group (RCG)), Larkin Publications, BCM Box 5909, London, WC1N 3XX, United Kingdom. TEL 44-20-78371688, office@rcgfrfi.plus.com. Circ: 7,000.

320 BRA ISSN 0103-1880
FILOSOFIA POLITICA. Text in Portuguese. 1985. 2/yr.
Published by: L & P M Editores Ltda., Rua Comendador Coruja 314, Loja 09, Porto Alegre, RGS 90220-180, Brazil. TEL 55-51-32255777, http://www.lpm.com.br.

320 ITA ISSN 0394-7297
JA18
FILOSOFIA POLITICA. Text in Italian. 1987. 3/yr. EUR 105 combined subscription domestic to institutions print & online eds.); EUR 140.50 combined subscription foreign to institutions (print & online eds.) (effective 2009). adv. index. back issues avail. **Document type:** *Journal, Academic/Scholarly.*
Related titles: Online - full text ed.
Indexed: DIP, IBR, IBZ, PCI, PhilInd.

P

Published by: Societa Editrice Il Mulino, Strada Maggiore 37, Bologna, 40125, Italy. TEL 39-051-256011, FAX 39-051-256034, riviste@mulino.it. Ed. Carlo Galli. Circ: 1,000.

FILOZOFIJA I DRUSTVO. *see* PHILOSOPHY

FIN DE SIGLO. *see* GENERAL INTEREST PERIODICALS—Argentina

FINANCIAL TIMES (FRANKFURT EDITION). *see* BUSINESS AND ECONOMICS—Banking And Finance

FINANCIAL TIMES (LONDON, 1888). *see* BUSINESS AND ECONOMICS—Banking And Finance

FINANCIAL TIMES (NORTH AMERICAN EDITION). *see* BUSINESS AND ECONOMICS—Banking And Finance

320 FIN ISSN 0785-1928
FINNISH POLITICAL SCIENCE ASSOCIATION. BOOKS. Text in English. 1983. irreg. price varies. back issues avail. **Document type:** *Monographic series, Academic/Scholarly.*
Published by: Valtiotieteellinen Yhdistyks/Finnish Political Science Association, c/o Department of Political Science, University of Helsinki, PO Box 35, Helsinki, 00014, Finland.

322.4 USA ISSN 0015-2722
FIRING LINE. Text in English. 1952. m. USD 7 (effective 2001). index. **Document type:** *Newsletter.*
Published by: American Legion, National Americanism Commission, PO Box 1055, Indianapolis, IN 46204. TEL 317-630-1212. Circ: 3,000.

FIRST OF THE YEAR. *see* ETHNIC INTERESTS

320 USA
FIRSTLINE MIDWEST. Text in English. 1994. 10/yr. USD 25; USD 75 including Stateline Midwest. **Document type:** *Magazine, Consumer.* **Description:** Reports quickly on single issues getting significant attention in the Midwest. Has examined topics such as rural health care, assisted suicide, and the future of tobacco taxes.
Published by: Council of State Governments, Midwestern Office, 641 E Butterfield Rd, 401, Lombard, IL 60148-5651. TEL 630-810-0210, 800-800-1910, FAX 630-810-0145. Ed. Paul Cohan.

FLINDERS JOURNAL OF HISTORY AND POLITICS. *see* HISTORY—History Of Australasia And Other Areas

320 USA ISSN 1549-1323
JA1
➤ **FLORIDA POLITICAL CHRONICLE.** Text in English. 1988. a. **Document type:** *Journal, Academic/Scholarly.* **Description:** Focuses on the politics of Florida and political science research for political scientists and interested parties.
Formerly (until 2004): Political Chronicle (1042-3885)
Published by: Florida Political Science Association, c/o J. Edwin Benton, Department of Government and International Affairs, SOC 107, University of South Florida, 4202 Fowler Ave, Tampa, FL 33620. http://fpsanet.web.officelive.com.

321.7 ZAF ISSN 1680-9882
FOCUS (HOUGHTON). Text in English. 2001. q.
Related titles: Online - full text ed.: ISSN 1996-1189.
Published by: Helen Suzman Foundation, Postnet Suite 130, Private X2600, Houghton, 2041, South Africa. TEL 27-11-6460150, FAX 27-11-6460160, info@hsf.org.za, http://www.hsf.org.za.

320.96 DEU ISSN 0947-9368
FOCUS AFRIKA; I A K Diskussionsbeitraege. Text in German. 1994. irreg., latest vol.19. price varies. back issues avail.; reprints avail. **Document type:** *Monographic series, Academic/Scholarly.*
Published by: G I G A Institute of African Affairs, Neuer Jungfernstieg 21, Hamburg, 20354, Germany. TEL 49-40-42834-523, FAX 49-40-42834-511, iaa@giga-hamburg.de, http://www.rrz.uni-hamburg.de/iak. Eds. Andreas Mehler, Armin Osmanovic.

FOERSVAR I NUTID. *see* MILITARY

320 NOR ISSN 0805-5300
FOLKETS FRAMTID. Text in Norwegian. 1946. w. NOK 490 (effective 2004). bk.rev. 24 p./no.; **Document type:** *Newspaper.*
Related titles: Online - full text ed.
Published by: (Kristelig Folkeparti), Folkets Framtid A/S, PO Box 453, Sentrum, Oslo, 0104, Norway. TEL 47-23-102820, FAX 47-23-102828. Eds. Ole Andreas Husoey, Odd Hagen.

320 ITA ISSN 1122-3960
FONDAZIONE GUARASCI. BOLLETTINO. Text in Italian. 1986. m. **Document type:** *Magazine, Consumer.* **Description:** Forum covering regional social and political issues.
Published by: Fondazione Guarasci, Via Adige 31 L, Cosenza, CS 87100, Italy. http://www.fondazioneguarasci.com. Ed. Franco Bartucci.

320.531 ITA ISSN 1972-2818
FONDAZIONE ISTITUTO GRAMSCI. ANNALI. Text in Italian. 1991. a. **Document type:** *Journal, Academic/Scholarly.*
Published by: (Fondazione Istituto Gramsci), Editori Riuniti, c/o The Media Factory, Via Tuscolana 4, Rome, 00182, Italy. TEL 39-06-70614211, FAX 39-06-70613928, http://www.editoririuniti.it.

320 ITA ISSN 1122-4312
FONDAZIONE LUIGI FIRPO. STUDI E TESTI. Text in Italian. 1992. irreg., latest vol.17, 2001. price varies. **Document type:** *Monographic series, Academic/Scholarly.* **Description:** Features studies gathered by the Centro di Studi sul Pensiero Politico (Center for the Study of Political Thought).
Published by: Casa Editrice Leo S. Olschki, Viuzzo del Pozzetto 8, Florence, 50126, Italy. TEL 39-055-6530684, FAX 39-055-6530214, celso@olschki.it, http://www.olschki.it.

320 ITA ISSN 1828-4493
FONDAZIONE MARIANO RUMOR. ANNALI. Text in Italian. 2005. a. **Document type:** *Magazine, Consumer.*
Published by: (Fondazione Mariano Rumor), Editrice Veneta, Via Ozanam 8, Vicenza, 36100, Italy. TEL 39-0444-567526, FAX 39-0444-564901, http://www.editriceveneta.com.

320 ITA ISSN 1826-8854
FONDAZIONE UGO LA MALFA. ANNALI. Text in Italian. 1986. a. **Document type:** *Journal, Academic/Scholarly.*
Formerly (until 2001): Istituto Ugo La Malfa. Annali (0394-1752)
Published by: Fondazione Ugo La Malfa, Via S Anna 13, Rome, 00186, Italy. TEL 39-06-68300795, FAX 39-06-68211476, info@fulm.org, http://www.fulm.org.

320 USA
FOOD FIRST NEWS & VIEWS. Text in English. 1978. 4/yr. looseleaf. bk.rev. 4 p./no. 2 cols./p.; back issues avail.; reprints avail. **Document type:** *Newsletter, Trade.* **Description:** Provides alternative analysis of the root causes of hunger and environmental degredation. Issues include foreign aid, organic farming, structural adjustment impact on the poor, alternatives to the Third World development, and more.
Formerly (until 1991): Food First News (0749-9825)
Published by: Institute for Food & Development Policy, 398 60th St, Oakland, CA 94618-1212. TEL 510-654-4400, FAX 510-654-4551. Ed. Sal Glynn. Pub. Peter Rosset. R&P Martha Fernandez TEL 510-654-4400. Circ: 9,000.

320 USA
FOOD NOT BOMBS MENU. Text in English. 1980. m. USD 2 newsstand/cover (effective 2005). **Document type:** *Newsletter.* **Description:** Provides an overview of the Food Not Bombs movement on food distribution and anti-war protest.
Published by: Food Not Bombs, PO Box 744, Tucson, AZ 85702-0744. TEL 800-884-1136, http://www.foodnotbombs.net/secondindex.html. Ed. Keith McHenry.

FORME DELL'UTOPIA. *see* LITERATURE

320.92 USA ISSN 1070-0374
THE FORMER PRESIDENTS QUARTERLY; a focus on our current retired presidents of the United States. Text in English. 1993. q. USD 12 (effective 2006). bk.rev. back issues avail. **Document type:** *Newsletter, Consumer.* **Description:** Reports on the activities of retired US presidents, including notable speeches, overseas travel, articles and books they have written or agreed to write.
Published by: R H L Enterprises, PO Box 6443, Fullerton, CA 92834. TEL 714-738-4386. Ed., Pub., R&P Robert H Lewandoski. Circ: 100 (paid and free).

320 CAN ISSN 1203-9241
HX3
FORMER "STATE SOCIALIST" WORLD. Text in English. 1996. a.
—CCC.
Published by: Black Rose Books Ltd., Succ. Place du Parc, CP 1258, Montreal, PQ H2W 2R3, Canada. http://www.blackrosebooks.net.

FORO INTERNO. *see* SOCIAL SCIENCES: COMPREHENSIVE WORKS

320 ARG ISSN 0327-9456
JL951.A1
FORO POLITICO. Text in Spanish. 1990. s-a.
Indexed: PSA.
Published by: Universidad del Museo Social Argentino, Instituto de Ciencias Politicas, Avda. Corrientes, 1723, Buenos Aires, 1042, Argentina. TEL 54-114-406924.

FORSCHUNGSINSTITUT FUER POLITISCH-HISTORISCHE STUDIEN - DR. WILFRIED-HASLAUER-BIBLIOTHEK. SCHRIFTENREIHE. *see* HISTORY—History Of Europe

324.6 ISL ISSN 1017-6675
HA149.A4
FORSETAKJOER/PRESIDENTIAL ELECTIONS. Text in Icelandic. 1952. irreg. USD 15 (effective 2001). back issues avail. **Document type:** *Government.*
Published by: Hagstofa Islands/Statistics Iceland, Borgartuni 12 A, Reykjavik, 150, Iceland. TEL 354-560-9800, FAX 354-562-8865, hagstofa@hag.stjr.is, http://www.statice.is/stat/e-mail.htm. Ed. Gudni Baldursson.

320 USA ISSN 1540-8884
JK1
THE FORUM; a journal of applied research in contemporary politics. Text in English. 2002 (July). q. USD 150 to institutions; USD 450 to corporations (effective 2011). back issues avail. **Document type:** *Journal, Academic/Scholarly.* **Description:** Provides a forum for professionally informed commentary on issues in contemporary American politics.
Media: Online - full text.
Indexed: A01, A22, A26, AmH&L, CA, CurCont, E01, E07, E08, G05, G06, G07, G08, I05, I07, IBSS, LRI, P34, P42, PAIS, PSA, S09, SSCI, T02, W07.
—CCC.
Published by: Berkeley Electronic Press, 2809 Telegraph Ave, Ste 202, Berkeley, CA 94705. TEL 510-665-1200, FAX 510-665-1201, info@bepress.com. Ed. Byron E Shafer.

FORUM (VALPARAISO). *see* LAW

320 IDN ISSN 0215-8280
DS644.4
FORUM KEADILAN/MAJALAH HUKUM DAN DEMOKRASI. Text in Indonesian. 1992. bi-w. IDR 5,900 per issue. **Document type:** *Academic/Scholarly.* **Description:** Publishes articles on law and democracy.
Published by: P.T. Keadilan, Kebayoran Center No. 12a-14, Jl. Kabayoran Baru - Velbak, Jakarta Selatan, 12240, Indonesia. TEL 62-21-751-0734, FAX 62-21-720-6620, TELEX 62797-IA. Ed. Karni Ilyas. adv.: B&W page IDR 4,500,000, color page IDR 9,750,000; trim 275 x 210. Circ: 140,000.

320.51 DEU
FORUM LIBERAL (ONLINE); liberale Zeitung. Text in German. 1972. 8/yr. free. bk.rev. back issues avail. **Document type:** *Newspaper, Consumer.*
Formerly (until 2004): Forum Liberal (Print)
Media: Online - full content.
Published by: Wirtschafts- und Sozialpolitik Verlag, An Zirkus 5, Berlin, 10117, Germany. Eds. Christophe Hilbring, Lorenz Becker. Circ: 50,000.

320.943 DEU
FORUM NEUE LAENDER. Text in German. 1997. q. adv. **Document type:** *Magazine, Trade.*
Published by: Union Betriebs GmbH, Egermannstr 2, Rheinbach, 53359, Germany. TEL 49-2226-8020, FAX 49-2226-802111, info@ubg-medienzentrum.de, http://www.ubg-medienzentrum.de. Ed. Michael Schaefer. adv.: B&W page EUR 2,350, color page EUR 4,050. Circ: 8,194 (controlled).

320 DEU
FORUM RECHT; das rechtspolitische magazin fuer uni und soziale bewegungen. Text in German. irreg.
Media: Online - full content.
Published by: Forum Recht Vertrieb, c/o Marcus Lippe, Boddinstr. 44, Berlin, 12053, Germany. TEL 49-30-56824615, vertrieb@forum-recht-online.de.

FORUM SOZIALPOLITIK. *see* SOCIAL SCIENCES: COMPREHENSIVE WORKS

320.5 SWE ISSN 0345-3618
FOSTERLAENDSK ENAD UNGDOM; organ foer Frisinnade Unions-Partiets ungfylking, Nordisk Ungdom. Text in Swedish. 1957. q.
Published by: Frisinnade Unions-Partiet, Dr Resmarks Vaeg, Bua 6186, Elloes, 44080, Sweden.

320 CAN ISSN 1719-3796
FOUNDATION FOR THE STUDY OF PROCESSES OF GOVERNMENT IN CANADA. ANNUAL REPORT. Text in English. a., latest 2005. **Document type:** *Report, Consumer.*
Related titles: French ed.: Fondation pour l'Etude des Processus de Gouvernement au Canada. Rapport Annuel.
Published by: The Foundation for the Study of Processes of Government in Canada/Fondation pour l'Etude des Processus de Gouvernement au Canada, 81 Metcalfe St, Ste 800, Ottawa, ON, Canada. TEL 613-233-4086, FAX 613-233-2351, foundation@forum.ca.

FOURTH WORLD REVIEW; for small nations, small communities, small farms, small shops, small industries, small banks, small fisheries & the inalienable sovereignty of the human spirit. *see* LITERARY AND POLITICAL REVIEWS

FRAAN RIKSDAG & DEPARTEMENT; rakt og relevant om politiken i Sverige och E U. *see* PUBLIC ADMINISTRATION

328.44 FRA ISSN 1952-448X
J341
FRANCE. ASSEMBLEE NATIONALE. BULLETIN. BILAN DE SESSION. Text in French. 1972. w. free. **Document type:** *Proceedings, Government.*
Supersedes in part (in 200?): France. Parlement. Assemblee Nationale. Bulletin (0755-2793)
Media: Online - full text.
Indexed: RASB.
Published by: Assemblee Nationale, 126 rue de l'Universite, Paris, 75355, France. TEL 33-1-40636000, FAX 33-1-45557523, http://www.assemblee-nationale.fr/europe. Circ: 6,700.

320.9 FRA ISSN 0046-4910
FRANCE FORUM. Text in French. 1957. 4/yr. adv. bk.rev.; film rev. illus. **Document type:** *Journal, Academic/Scholarly.*
Indexed: IBSS, PAIS.
—CCC.
Address: 133 bis Rue de l'Universite, Paris, 75007, France. TEL 33-1-45551010, FAX 33-1-45518953, france-forum@orange.fr. Ed. Rene Plantade. Circ: 3,500.

FRANCE MAGAZINE. *see* LITERARY AND POLITICAL REVIEWS

FRANK. *see* PUBLIC ADMINISTRATION

324.26668 CIV
FRATERNITE - HEBDO. Text in French. w.
Published by: Parti Democratique de la Cote d'Ivoire, Blvd. du General de Gaulle, 01 BP 1212, Abidjan, Ivory Coast. TEL 21-29-15. Ed. Guy Pierre Nouama.

324.26668 CIV
FRATERNITE MATIN. Text in French. 1964. d. **Document type:** *Newspaper.* **Description:** Official journal of record for government activities.
Related titles: Online - full text ed.
Published by: Societe Nouvelle de Presse et d'Edition de Cote d'Ivoire (SNPECI), Blvd. du General de Gaulle, 01 BP 1807, Abidjan, Ivory Coast. TEL 225-370666, FAX 225-372545, TELEX 24115, http://www.africaonline.co.ci. Ed. Dan Moussa. Circ: 45,000.

320 DEU ISSN 0016-0202
FRAU UND POLITIK. Text in German. 1954. 6/yr. adv. bk.rev. charts; illus.; stat. index. **Document type:** *Magazine, Consumer.* **Description:** Contains articles on the past and present involvement of women in the political process.
Published by: (Christlich-Demokratische Union (CDU), Frauen-Union), Union-Betriebs-Gesellschaft mbH, Friedrich-Ebert-Allee 73-75, Bonn, 53113, Germany. TEL 49-228-5307-0, FAX 49-228-5307118. Ed. Kristel Bendig. Circ: 2,700.

320 CAN
FREE WORLD PRESS; pressing for a free world. Text in English. irreg. **Document type:** *Newsletter.* **Description:** Includes articles and news on liberty, freedom and responsibility and solutions to Canada's everyday political problems.
Media: Online - full text.
Address: 5334 Yonge St, Ste 1010, Willowdale, ON M2N 6V1, Canada. Ed. Paul Coulbeck.

320 301 DEU ISSN 1434-419X
FREIE UNIVERSITAET BERLIN. OSTEUROPA-INSTITUT. ARBEITSPAPIERE. BEREICH POLITIK UND GESELLSCHAFT. Text in German. 1997. irreg., latest vol.69, 2009. price varies. **Document type:** *Journal, Academic/Scholarly.*
Published by: Freie Universitaet Berlin, Osteuropa-Institut, Garystr 55, Berlin, 14195, Germany. TEL 49-30-83853380, FAX 49-30-83853788, oei@zedat.fu-berlin.de, http://www.oei.fu-berlin.de. Ed. Klaus Segbers.

335.007 DEU ISSN 0067-589X
FREIE UNIVERSITAET BERLIN. OSTEUROPA-INSTITUT. ERZIEHUNGSWISSENSCHAFTLICHE VEROEFFENTLICHUNGEN. Text in German. 1964. irreg., latest vol.22, 1994. price varies. **Document type:** *Monographic series, Academic/Scholarly.*
Published by: (Freie Universitaet Berlin, Osteuropa-Institut, Freie Universitaet Berlin), Harrassowitz Verlag, Kreuzberger Ring 7b-d, Wiesbaden, 65205, Germany. TEL 49-611-5300, FAX 49-611-530560. Ed. Siegfried Baske Oskar Anweiler. R&P Michael Langfeld. Adv. contact Robert Gietz.

320 301 DEU ISSN 1436-2430
FREIE UNIVERSITAET BERLIN. OSTEUROPA-INSTITUT. INTERDISZIPLINAERE ARBEITSPAPIERE. Text in German. 1998. irreg., latest vol.3, 2005. price varies. **Document type:** *Journal, Academic/Scholarly.*
Published by: Freie Universitaet Berlin, Osteuropa-Institut, Garystr 55, Berlin, 14195, Germany. TEL 49-30-83853380, FAX 49-30-83853788, oei@zedat.fu-berlin.de.

FREIE UNIVERSITAET BERLIN. OSTEUROPA-INSTITUT. PHILOSOPHISCHE UND SOZIOLOGISCHE VEROEFFENTLICHUNGEN. see PHILOSOPHY

320 AUT
FREIHEITLICHER PRESSEDIENST. Text in German. 1953. s-w. looseleaf. **Document type:** *Bulletin.*
Published by: Die Freiheitlichen, Parlament, Vienna, W 1017, Austria. TEL 43-1-5123535, FAX 43-1-5123277. Circ: 180.

320 CHE
FREISINN. Text in German. 1979. 10/yr. CHF 20. adv. back issues avail. **Document type:** *Newspaper.*
Published by: Freisinnig-Demokratische Partei der Schweiz, Neuengasse 20, Postfach 6136, Bern, 3001, Switzerland. TEL 41-31-3203535, FAX 41-31-3121951. Ed. Guido Schommer.

320 GBR ISSN 1476-3419
JN2451
➤ **FRENCH POLITICS**; a journal of contemporary and comparative French politics, policy and society. Abbreviated title: F P. Text in English. 2003. q. USD 812 in North America to institutions; GBP 436 elsewhere to institutions (effective 2011). adv. bk.rev. abstr. 144 p./no.; back issues avail.; reprint service avail. from PSC. **Document type:** *Journal, Academic/Scholarly.* **Description:** Focuses on the role of political institutions, political behavior, public policy, political economy, international relations, public administration and public law as they relate to France.
Related titles: Online - full text ed.: ISSN 1476-3427. 2003 (from IngentaConnect).
Indexed: A12, A13, A22, ABIn, CA, DIP, E01, I08, IBR, IBSS, IBZ, M08, P02, P10, P42, P45, P48, P51, P53, P54, PAIS, PQC, PSA, S11, SCOPUS, SociolAb, T02.
—BLDSC (4034.404000), IE, Ingenta. **CCC.**
Published by: Palgrave Macmillan Ltd. (Subsidiary of: Macmillan Publishers Ltd.), Houndmills, Basingstoke, Hants RG21 6XS, United Kingdom. TEL 44-1256-329242, FAX 44-1256-479476, orders@palgrave.com, http://www.palgrave.com. Eds. Andrew Appleton, Robert Elgie. Pub. Guy Edwards. Circ: 250. **Subscr. to:** Subscription Department, Brunel Rd, Houndmills, Basingstoke, Hants RG21 2XS, United Kingdom. TEL 44-1256-357893, FAX 44-1256-328339, subscriptions@palgrave.com.

320.9 USA ISSN 1537-6370
DC417 CODEN: FPSOFR
➤ **FRENCH POLITICS, CULTURE & SOCIETY.** Abbreviated title: F P C & S. Text in English, French. 19??. 3/yr. GBP 120 combined subscription in United Kingdom to institutions (print & online eds.); EUR 155 combined subscription in Europe to institutions (print & online eds.); USD 196 combined subscription elsewhere to institutions (print & online eds.) (effective 2011). adv. bk.rev. back issues avail.; reprint service avail. from PSC. **Document type:** *Journal, Academic/Scholarly.* **Description:** Provides current information on developments in contemporary France.
Former titles (until 1999): French Politics & Society (0882-1267); (until 1984): Conference Group on French Politics and Society. Newsletter
Related titles: Online - full text ed.: ISSN 1558-5271. GBP 108 in United Kingdom to institutions; EUR 140 in Europe to institutions; USD 177 elsewhere to institutions (effective 2011) (from IngentaConnect).
Indexed: A01, A03, A08, A26, B04, CA, E08, G08, HistAb, I05, I07, I13, IBSS, L05, L06, MLA-IB, P10, P27, P42, P45, P48, P54, PCI, PQC, PSA, S02, S03, S09, S23, SCOPUS, SOPODA, SSA, SSAI, SSAb, SSI, SociolAb, T02, W03, W05.
—BLDSC (4034.407000), IE, Ingenta. **CCC.**
Published by: (Harvard University, Minda de Gunzburg Center for European Studies, New York University, Institute of French Studies), Berghahn Books Inc., 150 Broadway, Ste 812, New York, NY 10038. TEL 212-222-6007, FAX 212-222-6004, http://www.berghahnbooks.com. Ed. Herrick Chapman. **Dist. in Europe by:** Turpin Distribution Services Ltd., Pegasus Dr, Stratton Business Park, Biggleswade, Bedfordshire SG18 8QB, United Kingdom. TEL 44-1767-604951, FAX 44-1767-601640, berghahnjournalsuk@turpin-distribution.com, http://www.turpin-distribution.com/; **Dist. outside of Europe by:** Turpin Distribution Services Ltd., The Bleachery, 143 W St, New Milford, CT 06776. TEL 860-350-0041, FAX 860-350-0039, berghahnjournalsus@turpin-distribution.com.

➤ **FREUNDSCHAFT/FRIENDSHIP**; democratic monthly. see ETHNIC INTERESTS

324.2 DEU ISSN 0179-7131
FRIEDENSFORUM; Rundbrief der Friedensbewegung. Text in German. 1983. bi-m. EUR 18; EUR 3 newsstand/cover (effective 2005). adv. **Document type:** *Bulletin, Consumer.*
Published by: Foerderverein Frieden, Romerstr 88, Bonn, 53111, Germany. TEL 49-228-692904, FAX 49-228-692906, friekoop@bonn.comlink.org, http://www.friedenskooperative.de. Eds. Christine Schweitzer, Martin Singe. Circ: 3,500 (paid and controlled).

320 SWE ISSN 0345-3693
FRIHETSFACKLAN; frihet - sanning - raettvisa. Text in Swedish. 1965. m. SEK 10 newsstand/cover (effective 2001). illus. **Document type:** *Newsletter.*
Published by: Frisinnade Unions-Partiet, Dr Resmarks Vaeg, Bua 6186, Elloes, 44080, Sweden. Ed. Sven A Lundehaell.

320.5 SWE ISSN 0345-3723
FRISINNAD TIDSKRIFT. Text in Swedish. 1936. 10/yr. (2 dbl. vols.). SEK 150 (effective 2003). adv. bk.rev. **Document type:** *Magazine.* **Description:** Politically independent journal; seeks to interpret situations from a socially liberal and Christian viewpoint.
Former titles (until 1938): Frisinnad Tidskrift, Vaest Sverige; (until 1936): Vaest-Sverige
Published by: Stiftelsen Frisinnad Tidskrift/Liberal Journal Association, Gaasmyregatan 7, Vaesteraas, 72215, Sweden. TEL 46-21-142804. Ed. Birgitta Nilsson. **Subscr. to:** c/o Kerstin Sandborg, Groenagatan 62, Joenkoeping 55336, Sweden.

320 DNK ISSN 0901-6813
FRIT NORDEN. Text in Danish. 1973. irreg. (3-4/yr). DKK 200; DKK 100 to students (effective 2009). bk.rev. **Document type:** *Magazine, Consumer.*
Related titles: Online - full text ed.: 1998.
Address: c/o Jesper Morville, Christianshvilevej 3, Charlottenlund, 2920, Denmark. TEL 45-39-633537, http://www.fritnorden.dk.

320 SWE ISSN 1404-2614
FRONESIS. Text in Swedish; Text occasionally in English. 1998. q. SEK 300 domestic; SEK 400 in Europe; SEK 450 elsewhere (effective 2010). back issues avail. **Document type:** *Magazine, Consumer.* **Description:** Aims to be an arena for a radical dialogue about the future, engaging both the traditional labor movement, new social movements, as well as academic scholars and students.
Published by: Tidskriftfoereningen Fronesis, St. Gertrudsgatan 4 C, PO Box 4319, Malmoe, 20314, Sweden. TEL 46-40-232001, info@fronesis.nu, http://www.fronesis.nu. Ed. Magnus Wennerhag.

320.9 IND ISSN 0016-2094
➤ **FRONTIER.** Text in English. 1968. w. INR 200 domestic; INR 750 in Nepal & Bangladesh; USD 50 elsewhere (effective 2011). bk.rev.; film rev. 16 p./no. 3 cols./p.; back issues avail. **Document type:** *Journal, Academic/Scholarly.* **Description:** Analysis of the social and political events.
Indexed: RASB.
Published by: Germinal Publications Pvt. Ltd., 61 Mott Ln, Kolkata, West Bengal 700 013, India. TEL 91-33-22653202. Ed. Timir Basu.

320 384 USA ISSN 1525-9730
FRONTIERS IN POLITICAL COMMUNICATION. Text in English. 2002. irreg., latest vol.18, 2010. price varies. **Document type:** *Monographic series, Academic/Scholarly.*
Published by: Peter Lang Publishing, Inc. (Subsidiary of: Peter Lang Publishing Group), 29 Broadway, New York, NY 10006. TEL 212-647-7700, 800-770-5264, FAX 212-647-7707, customerservice@plang.com, http://www.peterlangusa.com. Eds. Bruce Gronbeck, Lynda Lee Kaid.

320.52 USA
FRONTPAGE MAGAZINE. Text in English. w. free. adv. **Description:** Covers political news from a conservative perspective.
Media: Online - full content.
Published by: Center for the Study of Popular Culture, PO Box 67398, Los Angeles, CA 90067. TEL 310-843-3699, FAX 310-843-3692, http://www.frontpagemag.com. Ed. David Horowitz.

320 USA
FRONTRUNNER. Text in English. d. 60 p./no.; **Document type:** *Newsletter, Trade.* **Description:** Provides information on national media's coverage of policy and politics.
Media: Online - full content. **Related titles:** Print ed.: Washington Morning Update.
Published by: Bulletin News Network, Inc., 7915 Jones Branch, Ste 6200, McLean, VA 22102. TEL 703-749-0040, FAX 703-749-0060, frontdesk@bulletinnews.com.

FUCHSBRIEFE. see BUSINESS AND ECONOMICS

320 CHN ISSN 0427-7112
FUDAO YUAN/INSTRUCTOR. Text in Chinese. 1954. m. USD 32.40 (effective 2009). **Document type:** *Journal, Academic/Scholarly.*
—East View.
Published by: Gongqingtuan Zhongyang, 10, Qianmen Dong Dajie, Beijing, 100051, China. TEL 86-10-85212084.

320 CHN ISSN 1002-364X
FUJIAN ZHIBU SHENGHUO. Text in Chinese. 1961. q. **Document type:** *Journal, Academic/Scholarly.*
Formerly (until 2000): Zhibu Shenghuo
Published by: Fujian Zhibu Shenghuo Zazhishe, Fuyu Lu Fuyu Xiao-qu 17F, Fuzhou, 350002, China.

320 ESP ISSN 1138-4514
H53
FUNDACIO RAFAEL CAMPALANS. PAPERS DE LA FUNDACIO. Text in Catalan, Spanish. 1989. m. back issues avail. **Document type:** *Monographic series, Consumer.*
Published by: Fundacio Rafael Campalans, Trafalgar, 12 entresol 1a, Barcelona, 08010, Spain. TEL 34-93-3195412, FAX 34-93-3199844, fundacio@fcampalans.cat.

320 ARG
FUNDACION ECUMENICA DE CUYO. BOLETIN DE DOCUMENTACION. Text in Spanish. 1979. bi-m. ARS 70, USD 10.
Published by: Fundacion Ecumenica de Cuyo, Pedernera 1291, Guaymallen, Mendoza, Argentina. Ed. Maria Teresa Brachetta. **Subscr. to:** Libros Dialogo, 9 De Julio, 718, Mendoza 5500, Argentina.

FUSE MAGAZINE; a magazine about issues of art and culture. see ART

306.2 USA ISSN 1930-7004
FUTUROS. Text in Spanish. 2003. q. back issues avail. **Document type:** *Magazine, Consumer.*
Media: Online - full text. **Related titles:** CD-ROM ed.: ISSN 1930-6997.
Published by: American Friends Service Committee, Inc., 1501 Cherry St, Philadelphia, PA 19102. TEL 215-241-7000, FAX 215-241-7275, afscinfo@afsc.org, http://www.afsc.org.

G A N P A C BRIEF. see ETHNIC INTERESTS

323.4 378 FRA ISSN 1951-5952
G E R M E. (Groupe d'Etudes et de Recherche sur les Mouvements Etudiants) Text in French. 2006. irreg. back issues avail. **Document type:** *Monographic series, Consumer.*
Published by: (Groupe d'Etudes et de Recherche sur les Mouvements Etudiants), Editions Syllepse, 69 rue des Rigoles, Paris, 75020, France. TEL 33-1-44620889.

GACETA LABORAL. see LAW

320 CHN ISSN 1007-788X
K7
GANSU ZHENG-FA XUEYUAN XUEBAO/GANSU POLITICAL SCIENCE AND LAW INSTITUTE. JOURNAL. Text in Chinese. 1986. bi-m. USD 40.20 (effective 2009). **Document type:** *Journal, Academic/Scholarly.*
Related titles: Online - full text ed.
Published by: Gansu Zheng-Fa Xueyuan, 6, Anning Xi Lu, Lanzhou, 730070, China. TEL 86-931-7601471.

GARIBALDI (ONLINE). see LITERARY AND POLITICAL REVIEWS

320 USA ISSN 0745-6468
HN90.P8
GARTH ANALYSIS; research by Penn & Schoen Associates. Text in English. 1982. bi-m. USD 295. stat.
Related titles: Microform ed.: (from PQC).
Published by: Penn and Schoen Associates, Inc., 245 E 92nd St, New York, NY 10028. TEL 212-534-4000. Ed. Jeffrey Toobin. Circ: 200.

GAY VOTE. see HOMOSEXUALITY

320 NLD ISSN 1566-161X
GEBLADERTE-REEKS. Text in Dutch. 1997. irreg., latest vol.32, 2009. EUR 3 per issue (effective 2010).
Published by: Stichting Gebladerte, Musschenbroekstraat 19, Leiden, 2316 AW, Netherlands. TEL 31-71-5127619, FAX 31-71-5134907, http://www.gebladerte.nl/.

320.5322 DEU ISSN 0941-5831
GEGENSTANDPUNKT; politische Vierteljahreszeitschrift. Text in German. 1992. q. EUR 60; EUR 15 newsstand/cover (effective 2010). **Document type:** *Journal, Trade.*
Indexed: IBR, IBZ.
Published by: Gegenstandpunkt Verlag, Kirchenstr 88, Munich, 81675, Germany. TEL 49-89-2721604, FAX 49-89-2721605.

321.8 JPN
GEKKAN SHAKAIMINSHU. Text in Japanese. m. JPY 620 per issue. illus.
Formerly: Gekkan Shakaito (0435-1754)
Published by: Social Democratic of Japan/Nihon Shakaito, 1-8-1 Nagata-cho, Chiyoda-ku, Tokyo, 1000014, Japan. TEL 81-3-3580-1171, FAX 81-3-3580-0691.

GENDER REPORT CARD. see SOCIOLOGY

GENERAL REPORT ON THE ACTIVITIES OF THE EUROPEAN UNION. see GENERAL INTEREST PERIODICALS—Europe

GENTE SUR; un nuevo periodismo. see BUSINESS AND ECONOMICS—Economic Situation And Conditions

320 USA
GEORGIA BEAT. Text in English. 1986. 22/yr. USD 90 (effective 1999). **Description:** Inside report of people and politics of Georgia.
Published by: Joe Sports Associates, Inc., 21 Finch Trail, Atlanta, GA 30308. TEL 404-873-3728, FAX 404-874-8512. Ed. Joe Sports. Circ: 1,000.

324.6 USA
GEORGIA RECALL ACT OF 1989. Text in English. irreg., latest 2001. USD 10 per issue (effective 2008). 26 p./no.; Supplement avail. **Document type:** *Monographic series, Trade.* **Description:** Contains newly passed laws on recalling elections from the 2001 regular General Session and the 2001 Special Session. Updated as required to keep current with legislation.
Published by: Michie Company (Subsidiary of: LexisNexis North America), 701 E Water St, Charlottesville, VA 22902. TEL 434-972-7600, 800-446-3410, FAX 434-972-7677, customer.support@lexisnexis.com, http://www.michie.com.

GEORGIA STUDIES WEEKLY. DEMOCRACY. see EDUCATION

320.9 USA ISSN 1045-0300
DD1
➤ **GERMAN POLITICS AND SOCIETY.** Text in English. 1983. q. GBP 140 combined subscription in United Kingdom to institutions (print & online eds.); EUR 188 combined subscription in Europe to institutions (print & online eds.); USD 235 combined subscription elsewhere to institutions (print & online eds.) (effective 2011). adv. bk.rev. back issues avail.; reprint service avail. from PSC. **Document type:** *Journal, Academic/Scholarly.* **Description:** Focuses on political and economic transitions in Germany from the combined perspectives of the social sciences, history, and cultural studies.
Formerly (until 1986): German Studies Newsletter (0882-7079)
Related titles: Online - full text ed.: ISSN 1558-5441. GBP 126 in United Kingdom to institutions; EUR 169 in Europe to institutions; USD 212 elsewhere to institutions (effective 2011) (from IngentaConnect).
Indexed: A01, A03, A08, A26, B04, BrHumI, CA, E08, G08, HistAb, I05, IBR, IBZ, MLA-IB, P10, P27, P34, P42, P45, P48, P53, P54, PAIS, PCI, PQC, PSA, S02, S03, S09, S11, SCOPUS, SSAI, SSAb, SSI, SociolAb, T02, V&AA, W03, W05.
—BLDSC (4162.150700), IE, Ingenta. **CCC.**
Published by: (Harvard University, Minda de Gunzburg Center for European Studies), Berghahn Books Inc., 150 Broadway, Ste 812, New York, NY 10038. TEL 212-222-6007, FAX 212-222-6004, journals@berghahnbooks.com, http://www.berghahnbooks.com. Ed. Jeffrey J Anderson. **Dist. in Europe by:** Turpin Distribution Services Ltd., Pegasus Dr, Stratton Business Park, Biggleswade, Bedfordshire SG18 8QB, United Kingdom. TEL 44-1767-604951, FAX 44-1767-601640, berghahnjournalsuk@turpin-distribution.com, http://www.turpin-distribution.com/; **Dist. outside of Europe by:** Turpin Distribution Services Ltd., The Bleachery, 143 W St, New Milford, CT 06776. TEL 860-350-0041, FAX 860-350-0039, berghahnjournalsus@turpin-distribution.com. **Co-sponsor:** Georgetown University. Center for German & European Studies.

➤ **GERMAN STUDIES REVIEW.** see HISTORY—History Of Europe

➤ **GERMAN STUDIES SERIES.** see BUSINESS AND ECONOMICS

320 BRA ISSN 2175-5604
▼ **GERMINAL**; marxismo e educao em debate. Text in Portuguese. 2009. 3/yr. free (effective 2011). **Document type:** *Journal, Academic/Scholarly.*
Media: Online - full text.
Published by: Universidade Estadual de Londrina, Caixa Postal 6001, Londrina, PR 86051-990, Brazil. TEL 55-43-33714000, FAX 55-43-33284440. Ed. Elza Margarida de Mendonca Peixoto.

GESCHICHTE FUER HEUTE. see EDUCATION—Teaching Methods And Curriculum

GESCHICHTE UND POLITIK IN SACHSEN. see HISTORY—History Of Europe

320 900 DEU ISSN 1433-8831
GESCHICHTLICHE GRUNDLAGEN DER POLITIK. Text in German. 1998. irreg. price varies. **Document type:** *Monographic series, Academic/Scholarly.*
Published by: Peter Lang GmbH (Subsidiary of: Peter Lang Publishing Group), Eschborner Landstr 42-50, Frankfurt Am Main, 60489, Germany. TEL 49-69-7807050, FAX 49-69-78070550, zentrale.frankfurt@peterlang.com.

320 AUT ISSN 0016-9099
HN401
GESELLSCHAFT UND POLITIK; Zeitschrift fuer soziales und wirtschafliches Engagement. Text in German. 1965. q. EUR 17; EUR 5 newsstand/cover (effective 2005). adv. bk.rev. charts; stat. **Document type:** *Journal, Academic/Scholarly.*
Indexed: RASB.

P

Published by: Dr. Karl Kummer-Institut - Institut fuer Sozialreform, Sozial- und Wirtschaftspolitik, Ebendorferstrasse 6-4, Vienna, W 1010, Austria. TEL 43-1-4052674, FAX 43-1-405267499, office@kummer-institut.at, http://www.kummer-institut.at. Ed. Josef Steurer. Circ: 1,500.

320 DEU ISSN 0016-9102
GESELLSCHAFTSPOLITISCHE KOMMENTARE. Text in German. 1954. s-m. looseleaf. bk.rev. index. **Document type:** *Newsletter, Consumer.*
—CCC.
Published by: Verlag Gesellschaftspolitische Kommentare, Rheinweg 104, Bonn, 53129, Germany. TEL 49-228-5389013, FAX 49-228-5389016, leo.schutze@t-online.de. Ed., Pub. Leo Schuetze. Circ: 5,500. **Subscr. to:** Postfach 1017, Schoenecken 54614, Germany. TEL 49-6553-92110, FAX 49-6553-92113.

320 MEX ISSN 1405-1079
JA5 CODEN: GPPUF7
➤ **GESTION Y POLITICA PUBLICA.** Text in Spanish. 1992. s-a. MXN 360, USD 65 for 2 yrs. to individuals; MXN 380, USD 150 for 2 yrs. to institutions (effective 2009). bk.rev. illus. reprints avail. **Document type:** *Journal, Academic/Scholarly.* **Description:** Publishes original articles in political science dealing with Mexico, comparative studies, and analyses on theoretical propositions.
Related titles: Online - full text ed.: 2000. free (effective 2011).
Indexed: A01, A26, B01, B07, C01, CA, F03, F04, FR, GEOBASE, H21, I04, I05, I13, P08, P42, PAIS, PSA, S02, S03, SOPODA, SSCI, SociolAb, T02, W07.
Published by: Centro de Investigacion y Docencia Economicas, Carretera Mexico-Toluca Km. 16.5, Apdo. Postal 116-114, Mexico City, DF 01130, Mexico. TEL 52-5-7279800, FAX 52-5-7279875, nacif@dis1.cide.mx, http://www.cide.mx.

320 GHA
THE GHANA DIGEST. Text in English. 1973-199?; resumed 1996. m. illus. **Document type:** *Government.* **Description:** Contains U.N., O.A.U., and other agency reports.
Published by: Information Services Department, PO Box 745, Accra, Ghana. TEL 233-21-228011. Circ: 12,000.

320.9 USA ISSN 0016-9579
GHANA NEWS. Text in English. 1970. m. free. illus. **Document type:** *Newsletter.*
Published by: Embassy of Ghana, Information Section, 3512 International Dr, N W, Washington, DC 20003-3035. TEL 202-686-4520. Ed. Kimgsley Owusu Afriyie. Circ: 8,000.

306.2 340 ITA ISSN 2036-5993
GIUSTIZIA INSIEME. Text in Italian. 2008. 3/yr. **Document type:** *Journal, Academic/Scholarly.*
Published by: Aracne Editrice, Via Raffaele Garofalo 133 A/B, Rome, 00173, Italy. info@aracneeditrice.it, http://store.aracneeditrice.com.

320.531 DEU ISSN 1434-5617
GLEICHHEIT; Zeitschrift fuer sozialistische Politik und Kultur. Text in German. 1986. bi-m. EUR 17.50; EUR 3 newsstand/cover (effective 2005). adv. bk.rev. back issues avail. **Document type:** *Magazine, Consumer.*
Formerly (until 1997): Vierte Internationale (0259-5818)
Indexed: IBR, IBZ.
Published by: Partei fuer Soziale Gleichheit, Postfach 040144, Berlin, 10061, Germany. TEL 49-30-30872786, FAX 49-30-30872620, psg@gleichheit.de, http://www.gleichheit.de.

320 GBR ISSN 2043-7897
▼ ➤ **GLOBAL DISCOURSE**; a developmental journal of research in politics and international relations. Text in English. 2010. s-a. free (effective 2010). **Document type:** *Journal, Academic/Scholarly.* **Description:** Aims to provide a critical, developmental forum for postgraduates and young academics.
Media: Online - full text.
Published by: M. Johnson, Ed. & Pub., 40-42 Great N Rd, Newcastle University, Newcastle Upon Tyne, NE1 7RU, United Kingdom. Eds. Mark Edward, Matthew Johnson.

320 GBR ISSN 1226-508X
CB251
➤ **GLOBAL ECONOMIC REVIEW.** Text in English. 1973. q. GBP 269 combined subscription in United Kingdom to institutions (print & online eds.); EUR 356, USD 449 combined subscription to institutions (print & online eds.) (effective 2012). adv. bk.rev. abstr.; bibl.; charts; stat. back issues avail.; reprint service avail. from PSC. **Document type:** *Journal, Academic/Scholarly.* **Description:** Publishes articles on global issues including regional studies on Northeast Asia, international political economy, business and relations, globalization, government-business relations, and changes of international technology and world economy.
Formerly (until 1997): Journal of East and West Studies (1229-4098)
Related titles: Online - full text ed.: ISSN 1744-3873. GBP 242 in United Kingdom to institutions; EUR 320, USD 405 to institutions (effective 2012) (from IngentaConnect).
Indexed: A22, B01, B07, BAS, CA, E01, ESPM, EconLit, IBSS, JEL, P06, P34, P42, PAIS, PSA, RASB, RiskAb, S02, S03, SCOPUS, SSCI, SociolAb, T02, W07.
—BLDSC (4195.392200), IE, Ingenta. **CCC.**
Published by: (Yonsei University, Institute of East and West Studies KOR), Routledge (Subsidiary of: Taylor & Francis Group), 4 Park Sq, Milton Park, Abingdon, Oxon OX14 4RN, United Kingdom. TEL 44-20-70176000, FAX 44-20-70176336, subscriptions@tandf.co.uk, http://www.routledge.com. Ed., Pub. Kap Young Jeong TEL 82-2-21233506. Adv. contact Linda Hann TEL 44-1344-779945. Circ: 1,000. **Subscr. to:** Taylor & Francis Ltd., Journals Customer Service, Sheepen Pl, Colchester, Essex CO3 3LP, United Kingdom. TEL 44-20-70175544, FAX 44-20-70175198.

320 USA
GLOBAL INFORMATION NETWORK. Text in English, Spanish. d. back issues avail. **Document type:** *Newsletter, Consumer.* **Description:** Supplys wide ranging coverage of the Third World - news, analysis, features, breaking stories, and blanket coverage - to print, broadcast and web media in the US.
Media: E-mail.
Indexed: P54.
Published by: Inter Press Service, 592 14th St N W, Washington, DC 20045. TEL 212-662-7160, FAX 212-662-7164, ipswas@igc.apc.org.

320 CAN ISSN 1499-7754
GLOBAL OUTLOOK (SHANTY BAY). Text in English. 2002. q. CAD 91.10 (effective 2006). **Document type:** *Magazine, Academic/Scholarly.*
Indexed: AltPI, PAIS.
Published by: Global Outlook, PO Box 222, Oro, ON L0L 2X0, Canada. TEL 705-720-6500, 888-713-8500, FAX 705-728-6500, 888-713-8883, info@globaloutlook.ca.

320 GBR ISSN 1758-5880
▼ **GLOBAL POLICY.** Text in English. 2010. 3/yr. GBP 166 in United Kingdom to institutions; EUR 210 in Europe to institutions; USD 332 elsewhere to institutions (effective 2012). **Document type:** *Journal, Trade.* **Description:** Focuses on problems of global policy; topics range from intellectual property to international climate policy, resource management of the Arctic, international law.
Related titles: Online - full text ed.: ISSN 1758-5899. GBP 166 in United Kingdom to institutions; EUR 210 in Europe to institutions; USD 332 elsewhere to institutions (effective 2012).
Indexed: A22, E01.
—CCC.
Published by: (London School of Economics & Political Science), Wiley-Blackwell Publishing Ltd. (Subsidiary of: John Wiley & Sons, Inc.), The Atrium, Southern Gate, Chichester, West Sussex PO19 8SQ, United Kingdom. TEL 44-1243-779777, FAX 44-1243-775878, customer@wiley.co.uk, http://www.wiley.com/WileyCDA/. Eds. David Held, Eva-Maria Nag, Patrick Dunleavy.

GLOBALIZATION AND HEALTH. *see* PUBLIC HEALTH AND SAFETY

320 SWE ISSN 0346-5942
GOETEBORG STUDIES IN POLITICS. Text in Multiple languages. 1958. irreg. price varies.
Formerly (until 1974): Studier i Politik - Studies in Politics (0081-7422)
Published by: (Goeteborgs Universitet, Statsvetenskapliga Institutionen), Goeteborgs Universitet, PO Box 100, Goeteborg, 40530, Sweden. TEL 46-31-7771000, FAX 46-31-7771064. Ed. Bo Rothstein.

321.8 DEU ISSN 2191-3951
JN3971.A1
▼ **GOETTINGER INSTITUT FUER DEMOKRATIEFORSCHUNG. JAHRBUCH.** Text in German. 2010. irreg. price varies. **Document type:** *Monographic series, Academic/Scholarly.*
Published by: (Goettinger Institut fuer Demokratieforschung), Ibidem Verlag, Melchiorstr 15, Stuttgart, 70439, Germany. TEL 49-711-9807954, FAX 49-711-9807952, ibidem@ibidem-verlag.de, http://www.ibidem-verlag.de.

321.8 DEU ISSN 2190-2305
▼ **GOETTINGER JUNGE FORSCHUNG**; Schriftenreihe des Goettinger Instituts fuer Demokratieforschung. Text in German. 2010. irreg., latest vol.3, 2010. price varies. **Document type:** *Monographic series, Academic/Scholarly.*
Published by: Ibidem Verlag, Melchiorstr 15, Stuttgart, 70439, Germany. TEL 49-711-9807954, FAX 49-711-9807952, ibidem@ibidem-verlag.de, http://www.ibidem-verlag.de.

320 IND ISSN 0436-1326
GOKHALE INSTITUTE MIMEOGRAPH SERIES. Text in English. 1968. irreg., latest vol.52, 2002. back issues avail. **Document type:** *Monographic series, Academic/Scholarly.*
Published by: Gokhale Institute of Politics and Economics, BMCC Rd, Deccan Gymkhana, Pune, 411004, India. TEL 91-20-25650287, FAX 91-20-25652579, gokhaleinstitute@gipe.ac.in.

320 IND
GOKHALE INSTITUTE. STUDIES. Variant title: G I P E Studies. Text in English. 1931. irreg., latest vol.73, 2008. price varies. back issues avail. **Document type:** *Monographic series, Academic/Scholarly.*
Formerly (until 1961): Gokhale Institute of Politics and Economics. Publications (0072-4912)
Published by: Gokhale Institute of Politics and Economics, BMCC Rd, Deccan Gymkhana, Pune, 411004, India. TEL 91-20-25650287, FAX 91-20-25652579, gokhaleinstitute@gipe.ac.in.

320 UKR
GOLOS KRYMA. Text in Russian. w. USD 286 in North America (effective 2000).
Published by: Redaktsiya Golos Kryma, Ul Semashko 8, Simferopol', 333000, Ukraine. TEL 25-81-01. **Dist. by:** East View Information Services, 10601 Wayzata Blvd, Minneapolis, MN 55305. TEL 952-252-1201, 800-477-1005, FAX 952-252-1202, info@eastview.com, http://www.eastview.com.

320 USA ISSN 2160-262X
▼ **THE GOOD AMERICAN POST**; free markets, new media. Text in English. 2009. bi-m. USD 39.95 (effective 2011). adv. back issues avail. **Document type:** *Newspaper, Trade.* **Description:** Promotes non-biased information on governance, the economy, and sustainability.
Related titles: Online - full text ed.: ISSN 2160-2638.
Published by: 91 Image, Inc, PO Box 2, Trinidad, CO 81082. TEL 888-317-9990. Circ: 3,000.

GOOD GOVERNMENT; a journal of political, social & economic comment. *see* BUSINESS AND ECONOMICS—Economic Systems And Theories, Economic History

320 USA ISSN 1089-0017
HB1
THE GOOD SOCIETY. Variant title: The Good Society - P E G S. Text in English. 1991. s-a. USD 137 combined subscription to institutions (print & online eds.) (effective 2012). adv. back issues avail.; reprint service avail. from PSC. **Document type:** *Journal, Academic/Scholarly.* **Description:** Aims to promote inquiry into institutional designs for a good society.
Formerly (until 1995): The P E G S Newsletter (2157-2968)
Related titles: Online - full text ed.: ISSN 1538-9731. USD 98 to institutions (effective 2012).
Indexed: A01, A03, A08, A22, AmHI, BRD, CA, E01, E04, E05, H07, H08, HAb, HumInd, P34, P42, S02, S03, SCOPUS, T02, W03, W05.
—CCC.
Published by: (P E G S), Pennsylvania State University Press, 820 N University Dr, University Support Bldg 1, Ste C, University Park, PA 16802. TEL 814-865-1327, 800-326-9180, FAX 814-863-1408, info@psupress.org, http://www.psupress.org. Eds. Stephen L. Elkin, Kendra Boileau. Adv. contact Brian Beer TEL 814-863-5992. **Dist. by:** The Johns Hopkins University Press, PO Box 19966, Baltimore, MD 21211. TEL 410-516-6987, 800-548-1784, FAX 410-516-3866, jrnlcirc@press.jhu.edu, https://www.press.jhu.edu/.

320 USA ISSN 0952-1895
JA1.A1
➤ **GOVERNANCE**; an international journal of policy, administration, and institutions. Text in English. 1987. q. GBP 567 in United Kingdom to institutions; EUR 718 in Europe to institutions; USD 737 in the Americas to institutions; USD 1,108 elsewhere to institutions; GBP 652 combined subscription in United Kingdom to institutions (print & online eds.); EUR 826 combined subscription in Europe to institutions (print & online eds.); USD 848 combined subscription in the Americas to institutions (print & online eds.); USD 1,275 combined subscription elsewhere to institutions (print & online eds.) (effective 2012). adv. reprint service avail. from PSC. **Document type:** *Journal, Academic/Scholarly.* **Description:** Provides a forum for work in the field of international executive politics, primarily from a comparative perspective.
Related titles: Online - full text ed.: ISSN 1468-0491. GBP 567 in United Kingdom to institutions; EUR 718 in Europe to institutions; USD 737 in the Americas to institutions; USD 1,108 elsewhere to institutions (effective 2012) (from IngentaConnect).
Indexed: A01, A03, A08, A12, A17, A22, A26, ABIn, ASCA, B01, B06, B07, B09, CA, CurCont, E01, ESPM, FR, I13, IBSS, P30, P34, P42, P48, P51, P53, P54, PAIS, PQC, PRA, PSA, RiskAb, S02, S03, SCOPUS, SPAA, SSCI, SociolAb, T02, W07.
—BLDSC (4203.819600), IE, Infotrieve, Ingenta. **CCC.**
Published by: Wiley-Blackwell Publishing, Inc. (Subsidiary of: Wiley-Blackwell Publishing Ltd.), Commerce Pl, 350 Main St, Malden, MA 02148. TEL 781-388-8206, FAX 781-388-8232, info@wiley.com, http://www.wiley.com/WileyCDA/. Eds. Alasdair Roberts, Robert Henry Cox. adv.: B&W page USD 400; trim 6 x 9. Circ: 567 (paid).

320 100 ITA ISSN 1974-4935
GOVERNARE LA PAURA. Text in Multiple languages. 2008. irreg. **Document type:** *Journal, Academic/Scholarly.*
Media: Online - full text.
Published by: Universita degli Studi di Bologna, Dipartimento di Politica, Istituzioni, Storia, Via Zamboni 33, Bologna, 40126, Italy. http://www.dpis.unibo.it/PoliticaIstituzioniStoria/default.htm. Ed. Maria Laura Lanzillo.

320 GBR ISSN 0017-257X
JA8
➤ **GOVERNMENT AND OPPOSITION**; an international journal of comparative politics. Text in English. 1965. q. GBP 165 in United Kingdom to institutions; EUR 208 in Europe to institutions; USD 294 in the Americas to institutions; USD 321 elsewhere to institutions; GBP 190 combined subscription in United Kingdom to institutions (print & online eds.); EUR 240 combined subscription in Europe to institutions (print & online eds.); USD 337 combined subscription in the Americas to institutions (print & online eds.); USD 369 combined subscription elsewhere to institutions (print & online eds.) (effective 2012). adv. bk.rev. abstr.; illus. cum.index: vols.1-5, 6-10. back issues avail.; reprint service avail. from PSC. **Document type:** *Journal, Academic/Scholarly.* **Description:** Focuses on articles identifying and reflecting on the longer-term significance of events and developments such as the increasing importance of the European Union, processes of democratisation and the challenges of global interdependence.
Related titles: Online - full text ed.: ISSN 1477-7053. GBP 165 in United Kingdom to institutions; EUR 208 in Europe to institutions; USD 294 in the Americas to institutions; USD 321 elsewhere to institutions (effective 2012) (from IngentaConnect).
Indexed: A01, A02, A03, A08, A20, A22, A26, ABCPolSci, ASCA, AmHI, B04, BAS, BRD, BrHumI, C12, CA, CommAb, CurCont, DIP, E01, E08, ELLIS, ESPM, G08, H07, H09, HistAb, I02, I05, I13, IBR, IBSS, IBZ, LeftInd, M05, M06, MEA&I, P02, P06, P10, P27, P34, P42, P47, P48, P53, P54, PAA&I, PAIS, PCI, PQC, PSA, PerIslam, R02, RASB, RiskAb, S02, S03, S05, S09, S11, SCOPUS, SOPODA, SSA, SSAI, SSAb, SSCI, SSI, SSciA, SociolAb, T02, W03, W07.
—BLDSC (4203.900000), IE, Infotrieve, Ingenta. **CCC.**
Published by: (Government Opposition Ltd.), Wiley-Blackwell Publishing Ltd. (Subsidiary of: John Wiley & Sons, Inc.), 9600 Garsington Rd, Oxford, OX4 2DQ, United Kingdom. TEL 44-1865-776868, FAX 44-1865-714591, customerservices@blackwellpublishing.com. Eds. Helen Thompson TEL 44-1223-767264, Paul Heywood TEL 44-1159-514869. Adv. contact Craig Pickett TEL 44-1865-476267.

320 USA
GOVERNORS' BULLETIN. Text in English. 1967. bi-w. USD 50. **Document type:** *Bulletin.* **Description:** Features latest information on Governors' initiatives and policies, giving readers an insider's perspective on opportunities and problems faced by state governors.
Former titles: Governors' Weekly Bulletin (0888-8647); Capital Ideas; Governors' Bulletin
Published by: National Governors' Association, 444 N Capitol St, Washington, DC 20001. TEL 202-624-5330. Ed. Gary Enos. Circ: 3,400.

321 FRA ISSN 1775-111X
LES GRANDS HOMMES D'ETAT; une galerie de portraits qui vaut une lecon d'histoire. Text in French. 2005. irreg. **Document type:** *Monographic series, Consumer.*
Published by: Bayard Presse, 3-5 rue Bayard, Paris, 75393 Cedex 08, France. TEL 33-1-44356060, FAX 33-1-44356161, http://www.bayardpresse.com.

324.2 CUB ISSN 1028-088X
GRANMA INTERNACIONAL (GERMAN EDITION). Text in German. 1966. m. USD 12 (effective 2008). **Document type:** *Newspaper, Consumer.*
Related titles: Online - full text ed.: ISSN 1563-8324. 1999; ◆ Spanish ed.: Granma Internacional (Portuguese Edition). ISSN 0864-4632; ◆ Spanish ed.: Granma Internacional (Spanish Edition). ISSN 0864-4616; ◆ Spanish ed.: Granma International (English Edition). ISSN 0864-4624; ◆ Spanish ed.: Granma International (French Edition). ISSN 0864-4640.

Published by: Comite Central del Partido Comunista de Cuba/Central Committee of the Communist Party of Cuba, Plaza de la Revolucion J. Marti, Ave. General Suarez y Territorial, Apdo. Postal 6260, Havana, 100699, Cuba. TEL 53-7-816265, FAX 53-7-335176, redac@granmai.get.cma.net. Ed. Gabriel Molina Franchossi.

320.532 CUB ISSN 0864-4632
GRANMA INTERNACIONAL (PORTUGUESE EDITION). Text in Spanish. 1984. w. USD 40.
Related titles: Online - full text ed.: ISSN 1563-8316. 1999; ◆ German ed.: Granma Internacional (German Edition). ISSN 1028-088X; ◆ Spanish ed.: Granma Internacional (Spanish Edition). ISSN 0864-4616; ◆ Spanish ed.: Granma International (English Edition). ISSN 0864-4624; ◆ Spanish ed.: Granma International (French Edition). ISSN 0864-4640.
Published by: Comite Central del Partido Comunista de Cuba/Central Committee of the Communist Party of Cuba, Plaza de la Revolucion J. Marti, Ave. General Suarez y Territorial, Apdo. Postal 6260, Havana, 100699, Cuba. TEL 53-7-816265, FAX 53-7-335176. Ed. Gabriel Molina Franchossi. Circ: 5,000.

320.532 CUB ISSN 0864-4616
GRANMA INTERNACIONAL (SPANISH EDITION); resumen semanal. Text in Spanish. 1966. w. USD 40.
Related titles: Online - full text ed.: ISSN 1563-8286. 1999; ◆ German ed.: Granma Internacional (German Edition). ISSN 1028-088X; ◆ Spanish ed.: Granma Internacional (Portuguese Edition). ISSN 0864-4632; ◆ Spanish ed.: Granma International (English Edition). ISSN 0864-4624; ◆ Spanish ed.: Granma International (French Edition). ISSN 0864-4640.
Published by: Comite Central del Partido Comunista de Cuba/Central Committee of the Communist Party of Cuba, Plaza de la Revolucion J. Marti, Ave. General Suarez y Territorial, Apdo. Postal 6260, Havana, 100699, Cuba. TEL 53-7-816265, FAX 53-7-335176. Ed. Gabriel Molina Franchossi. Circ: 25,000.

324.2 CUB ISSN 0864-4624
GRANMA INTERNATIONAL (ENGLISH EDITION); weekly review. Text in Spanish. 1966. w. USD 40 (effective 2008). adv. bk.rev. charts; illus. **Document type:** *Newspaper, Consumer.*
Related titles: Microfilm ed.: (from PQC); Microform ed.: (from PQC); Online - full text ed.: ISSN 1563-8294. 1999; ◆ Spanish ed.: Granma Internacional (Portuguese Edition). ISSN 0864-4632; ◆ Spanish ed.: Granma Internacional (Spanish Edition). ISSN 0864-4616; ◆ German ed.: Granma Internacional (German Edition). ISSN 1028-088X; ◆ Spanish ed.: Granma International (French Edition). ISSN 0864-4640.
Indexed: RASB.
Published by: Comite Central del Partido Comunista de Cuba/Central Committee of the Communist Party of Cuba, Plaza de la Revolucion J. Marti, Ave. General Suarez y Territorial, Apdo. Postal 6260, Havana, 100699, Cuba. TEL 53-7-816265, FAX 53-7-335176, redac@granmai.get.cma.net. Ed. Gabriel Molina Franchossi. Circ: 23,000.

320.532 CUB ISSN 0864-4640
F1751
GRANMA INTERNATIONAL (FRENCH EDITION); resume hebdomadaire. Text in Spanish. 1966. w. USD 40.
Related titles: Online - full text ed.: ISSN 1563-8308. 1999; ◆ German ed.: Granma Internacional (German Edition). ISSN 1028-088X; ◆ Spanish ed.: Granma Internacional (Portuguese Edition). ISSN 0864-4632; ◆ Spanish ed.: Granma International (English Edition). ISSN 0864-4624; ◆ Spanish ed.: Granma Internacional (Spanish Edition). ISSN 0864-4616.
Published by: Comite Central del Partido Comunista de Cuba/Central Committee of the Communist Party of Cuba, Plaza de la Revolucion J. Marti, Ave. General Suarez y Territorial, Apdo. Postal 6260, Havana, 100699, Cuba. TEL 53-7-816265, FAX 53-7-335176. Ed. Gabriel Molina Franchossi. Circ: 10,000.

320.5 USA
GRASS ROOTS CAMPAIGNING. Text in English. 1979. m. looseleaf. USD 36 (effective 1999). bk.rev. back issues avail. **Document type:** *Newsletter.* **Description:** Covers political campaign techniques, philosophy, and psychology.
Published by: Campaign Consultants, PO Box 7281, Little Rock, AR 72217. TEL 501-225-3996. Ed. Jerry L Russell. Circ: 510.

320 RUS ISSN 0869-5881
GRAZHDANSKAYA ZASHCHITA. Text in Russian. 1956. m. USD 110 in North America (effective 2000).
Indexed: RefZh.
—East View.
Published by: Ministerstvo Rossiiskoi Federatsii po Delam Grazhdanskoi Oborony, Chrezvychainym Situatsiyam i Likvidatsii Posledstvii Stikhiinykh Bedstvii, Ul Vatutina 1, Moscow, 121357, Russian Federation. TEL 7-095-4499716, FAX 7-095-4499714. **Dist. by:** East View Information Services, 10601 Wayzata Blvd, Minneapolis, MN 55305. TEL 952-252-1201, 800-477-1005, FAX 952-252-1202, info@eastview.com, http://www.eastview.com.

GREAT BRITAIN. HOUSE OF COMMONS. PARLIAMENTARY DEBATES. WEEKLY HANSARD. *see* PUBLIC ADMINISTRATION

328.42 GBR ISSN 0309-8834
J301
GREAT BRITAIN. HOUSE OF LORDS. PARLIAMENTARY DEBATES. Key Title: Parliamentary Debates, Hansard. House of Lords Official Report. Text in English. 1892. d. GBP 525; GBP 3.50 per issue (effective 2010). index. **Document type:** *Government.* **Description:** Covers written answers to questions put by members to various ministers and government departments.
Formerly (until 1944): Parliamentary Debates, Official Report. House of Lords (0309-9024); Which superseded in part (in 1909): Parliamentary Debates. Authorised Edition (0309-9032)
Related titles: CD-ROM ed.; Microfiche ed.: (from BHP); (from PQC); Alternate Frequency ed(s).: ISSN 0261-8311. w.
Indexed: IMMAb.
Published by: (Great Britain. House of Lords), The Stationery Office, St Crispins, Duke St, Norwich, NR3 1PD, United Kingdom. TEL 44-1603-622211, customer.services@tso.co.uk, http://www.tso.co.uk.

335.83 GBR ISSN 0957-5170
GREEN ANARCHIST; global anarcho-primitivist 'zine. Text in English. 1984. q. GBP 5 domestic; GBP 7.50 foreign (effective 2004). adv. bk.rev.; film rev.; music rev.; rec.rev.; video rev. illus. 20 p./no. 5 cols./p.; **Document type:** *Newspaper, Consumer.*
Address: BCM 1715, London, London WC1N 3XX, United Kingdom. Ed. John Connor. Circ: 1,000.

320 AUS ISSN 1036-126X
HX821
GREEN LEFT WEEKLY. Abbreviated title: G L W. Text in English. 1970. w. AUD 83 domestic; AUD 148.50 in Asia & the Pacific; AUD 198 elsewhere (effective 2009). adv. bk.rev.; dance rev.; film rev.; music rev.; play rev.; tel.rev.; video rev. charts; illus.; stat. 28 p./no. 5 cols./p.; back issues avail. **Document type:** *Newspaper, Consumer.* **Description:** Covers current affairs from a left, green and progressive perspective.
Formerly (until 1991): Direct Action (0815-9238)
Related titles: CD-ROM ed.: AUD 10 newsstand/cover (effective 2002); Online - full text ed.
Indexed: AltPI, G02, G10, LeftInd, W09.
—CCC.
Published by: Green Left Publishing Association, PO Box 394, Broadway, NSW 2007, Australia. TEL 61-2-96901220, 800-634-206, subscriptions@greenleft.org.au. adv.: page AUD 750. Circ: 6,000.

346.044 USA
GREEN POLITICS. Text in English. 1993. q. USD 25 to members (effective 2000). **Document type:** *Newspaper, Consumer.* **Description:** Prints news articles, announcements, organizing articles, letters and related pieces on the Green Party and allied environmental and social justice movements.
Published by: Green Party U S A, PO Box 1134, Lawrence, MA 01842-2134. TEL 978-682-4353. Circ: 10,000.

324.2 USA ISSN 1544-1253
GREEN SEATTLE. Text in English. 1997. q.
Published by: Green Party of Seattle, P. O. Box 95515, Seattle, WA 98145. TEL 206-524-3377, info@seattlegreens.org, http://www.seattlegreens.org. Ed. Lansing Scott.

THE GREEN VOICE. *see* ENVIRONMENTAL STUDIES

GREEN WORLD. *see* ENVIRONMENTAL STUDIES

GREY ROOM. *see* ARCHITECTURE

320.5 SWE ISSN 1652-1196
GROENT. Text in Swedish. 1988. 5/yr. **Description:** Political news and analysis of "green" ideas.
Formerly (until 2003): Groensaken (1100-0872)
Published by: Miljoepartiet De Groena, PO Box 1244, Lund, 22105, Sweden. TEL 46-46-162240, FAX 46-46-162259, info@mp.se, http://www.mp.se.

324.2 DEU
GRUENE BLAETTER. Text in German. 1981. 4/yr. **Document type:** *Magazine, Consumer.*
Published by: Buendnis 90 - Die Gruenen Baden-Wuerttemberg, Forststr 93, Stuttgart, 70176, Germany. TEL 49-711-993590, FAX 49-711-9935999, landesverband@gruene-bw.de.

320.53 AUT ISSN 1814-3156
GRUNDRISSE; Zeitschrift fuer linke Theorie & Debatte. Text in German. 2002. 4/yr. EUR 20 (effective 2011). **Document type:** *Journal, Academic/Scholarly.*
Related titles: Online - full text ed.: ISSN 1814-3164. 2002.
Published by: Partei Grundrisse, Antonigasse 100/8, Vienna, 1180, Austria.

320 GLP ISSN 0757-7907
GUADELOUPE 2000 MAGAZINE. Text in French. 1970. fortn.
Formerly (until 1982): Guadeloupe 2000 (0757-7893)
Address: Residence Massabielle, Pointe-a-Pitre, 97110, Guadeloupe. Ed. Edouard Boulogne. Circ: 4,000.

320.532 CHN ISSN 1008-4533
GUANGDONG XINGZHENG XUEYUAN XUEBAO. Text in Chinese. 1989. bi-m. USD 24.60 (effective 2009). **Document type:** *Journal, Academic/Scholarly.*
Related titles: Online - full text ed.
—East View.
Published by: Guangdong Xingzheng Xueyuan/Guangdong Institute of Public Administration, 3, Jianshe Dama Lu, Guangzhou, 510050, China. TEL 86-20-83122361. **Dist. by:** China International Book Trading Corp, 35 Chegongzhuang Xilu, Haidian District, PO Box 399, Beijing 100044, China. TEL 86-10-68412045, FAX 86-10-68412023, cibtc@mail.cibtc.com.cn, http://www.cibtc.com.cn.

324.78 USA ISSN 1059-6224
KF4568.A15
THE GUARDIAN (LOS ANGELES). Text in English. 1980. q. USD 60 to non-members; USD 25 to members (effective 1999). bk.rev. abstr.; bibl.; stat. back issues avail. **Document type:** *Newsletter.* **Description:** Reports on campaign finance, conflict of interest and lobbying issues, legislation and litigation.
Former titles: C O G E L Guardian (1071-6734); C O G E L Newsletter
Related titles: Online - full text ed.
Published by: Council on Governmental Ethics Laws, c/o Center for Governmental Studies, 10951 W Pico Blvd, Ste 120, Los Angeles, CA 90064. TEL 310-470-6590, FAX 310-475-3752. Ed. Robert M Stern. R&P Bob Stern. Circ: 400.

320.531 AUS ISSN 1325-295X
THE GUARDIAN (SURRY HILLS); the worker's weekly. Text in English. 19??. w. AUD 88 domestic; AUD 1.50 per issue (effective 2008). back issues avail. **Document type:** *Newspaper, Trade.*
Formerly: Socialist
Indexed: RASB.
Published by: Communist Party of Australia, 74 Buckingham St, Surry Hills, NSW 2010, Australia. TEL 61-2-96998844, FAX 61-2-96999833, cpa@cpa.org.au.

GUIA DEL MUNDO; el mundo visto desde el sur. *see* ENCYCLOPEDIAS AND GENERAL ALMANACS

320.4 ESP ISSN 1988-7779
GUIAS PARA ENSENANZAS MEDIAS. EDUCACION PARA LA CIUDADANIA. Text in Spanish. 2007. m. **Document type:** *Monographic series, Academic/Scholarly.*
Media: Online - full text.
Published by: Wolters Kluwer Espana - Educacion (Subsidiary of: Wolters Kluwer N.V.), C Collado Mediano 9, Las Rozas, Madrid, 28230, Spain. TEL 34-902-250510, FAX 34-902-250515, cleintes@wkeducacion.es, http://www.wkeducacion.es/index.asp. Ed. Joaquin Gairin.

320.5 USA ISSN 0894-4547
HX81
GUIDE TO THE AMERICAN LEFT. Text in English. 1979. a. USD 19.95 (effective 2000). bibl. **Document type:** *Directory.* **Description:** Lists 1,400 left-wing organizations and serials.
Former titles: Directory of the American Left (0733-9623); (until 1970): Guide to the American Left (0017-5315)
Published by: Laird Wilcox, Ed. & Pub., PO Box 2047, Olathe, KS 66061. TEL 913-829-0609, FAX 913-829-0609. Circ: 700.

320.5322 CHN ISSN 1001-3202
GUOJI GONGCHANZHUYI YUNDONG/INTERNATIONAL COMMUNIST MOVEMENT. Text in Chinese. 1978. q. USD 29 (effective 2009). 64 p./no.; **Document type:** *Journal, Academic/Scholarly.* **Description:** Covers the development and history of international Communist movement.
Published by: Zhongguo Renmin Daxue Shubao Ziliao Zhongxin/Renmin University of China, Information Center for Social Sciences, Dongcheng-qu, 3, Zhangzizhong Lu, Beijing, 100007, China. TEL 86-10-64039458, 86-10-84043003, center@zlzx.org, http://www.zlzx.org/. **Dist. in US by:** China Publications Service, PO Box 49614, Chicago, IL 60649. TEL 312-288-3291, FAX 312-288-8570; **Dist. by:** China International Book Trading Corp, 35 Chegongzhuang Xilu, Haidian District, PO Box 399, Beijing 100044, China. TEL 86-10-68412045, FAX 86-10-68412023, cibtc@mail.cibtc.com.cn, http://www.cibtc.com.cn.

320 GUY
GUYANA INFORMATION BULLETIN. Text in English. 1964. m. free.
Former titles (until 1979): Overseas Mirror; (until 1978): Guyana Information Bulletin (0017-5862)
Indexed: HRIR.
Published by: People's Progressive Party, Freedom House, Robb St 41, Georgetown, Guyana. Ed. Janet Jagan. Circ: 1,000.

H S R C CENTRE FOR CONSTITUTIONAL ANALYSIS. *see* LAW

320.54095694 ISR
HA-KONGRES HA-TSIYONI. HAHLATOT/WORLD ZIONIST ORGANIZATION. ZIONIST CONGRESS. Text in Hebrew. 1926. irreg. **Document type:** *Proceedings.*
Published by: World Zionist Organization, P O Box 92, Jerusalem, Israel. TEL 972-2-527156, FAX 972-2-533542.

320.532 CHN ISSN 1008-8520
HAERBIN SHI-WEI DANGXIAO XUEBAO/HARBIN COMMITTEE SCHOOL OF THE C C P. JOURNAL. Text in Chinese. 1999. bi-m. USD 21.60 (effective 2009). **Document type:** *Journal, Academic/Scholarly.*
Related titles: Online - full text ed.
—East View.
Published by: Zhong-Gong Haerbin Shi-Wei Dangxiao/Harbin Committee School of the C C P, 29, Yanxing Lu, Harbin, 150080, China. TEL 86-451-86345174, FAX 86-451-86326646. **Dist. by:** China International Book Trading Corp, 35 Chegongzhuang Xilu, Haidian District, PO Box 399, Beijing 100044, China. TEL 86-10-68412045, FAX 86-10-68412023, cibtc@mail.cibtc.com.cn, http://www.cibtc.com.cn.

320 PAK
HALAT O AFKAR. Text in Urdu. w. adv.
Published by: Independent Newspapers Corp. Pvt. Ltd., Printing House, I.I. Chundrigar Rd., P O Box 32, Karachi, (Sindh) 74200, Pakistan. FAX 92-21-2636066, subscription@akhbar-e-jehan.com. Ed., Pub. Mir Shakil-ur-Rahman. R&P Shahrukh Hasan TEL 92-21-2629523. Adv. contact Sarmad Ali.

320 DEU ISSN 0440-1670
DT1
HAMBURGER BEITRAEGE ZUR AFRIKA-KUNDE. Text in German. 1965. irreg., latest vol.64. 250 p./no.; back issues avail.; reprints avail. **Document type:** *Monographic series, Academic/Scholarly.* **Description:** Contemporary problems and developments in Africa.
Published by: G I G A Institute of African Affairs, Neuer Jungfernstieg 21, Hamburg, 20354, Germany. TEL 49-40-42834-523, FAX 49-40-42834-511, iaa@giga-hamburg.de, http://www.rrz.uni-hamburg.de/iak. Circ: 250.

320 SGP
HAMMER. Text in English. 1972. 10/yr. SGD 10 (effective 2010). illus. **Document type:** *Magazine, Consumer.*
Related titles: Online - full content ed.
Published by: The Workers' Party of Singapore, 216-G Syed Alwi Rd #02-03, Singapore, 207799, Singapore. TEL 65-6-2984765, FAX 65-6-4544404, http://www.wp.org.sg/wordpress/index.php.

324.2 NLD ISSN 1571-4365
HANDSCHRIFT. Text in Dutch. N.S. 2000. 7/yr. EUR 25 (effective 2008). adv. bk.rev. index.
Formed by the 2000 merger of: Ons Burgerschap (0167-028X); Which was formerly (1948-1975): Ons Politeuma (0030-2740); R P F-Signaal (1388-2651); Which was formerly (1975-1997): Nieuw Nederland (0166-8048)
Published by: ChristenUnie, Postbus 439, Amersfoort, 3800 AK, Netherlands. TEL 31-33-4226969, FAX 31-33-4226968, bureau@christenunie.nl. Eds. Jacolien Viveen, Shahied Badoella. Circ: 26,000.

HANNAH-ARENDT-INSTITUT FUER TOTALITARISMUSFORSCHUNG. BERICHTE UND STUDIEN. *see* HISTORY—History Of Europe

320 DEU ISSN 1611-1192
HANNAH-ARENDT-STUDIEN; Schriftenreihe des Hannah-Arendt-Zentrums der Carl-von-Ossietzky-Universitaet Oldenburg. Text in German. 2003. irreg., latest vol.5, 2009. price varies. **Document type:** *Monographic series, Academic/Scholarly.*
Published by: Peter Lang GmbH (Subsidiary of: Peter Lang Publishing Group), Eschborner Landstr 42-50, Frankfurt Am Main, 60489, Germany. TEL 49-69-7807050, FAX 49-69-78070550, zentrale.frankfurt@peterlang.com, http://www.peterlang.com. Ed. Antonia Grunenberg.

AL HAQQ/DROIT. *see* LAW

320 MYS ISSN 0127-4147
AL-HARAKAH; parti Islam se-Malaysia. Text in Malay. 1973. 2/w. MYR 0.70 per issue. adv. bk.rev. **Description:** Provides news about the Islamic Party of Malaysia.
Formerly (until 1987): Berita Pas

P

Published by: Islamic Party of Malaysia, 28 A Jalan Pahang Barat, Kuala Lumpur, Pahang 53000, Malaysia. TEL 603-4213343, FAX 603-4212422. Circ: 50,000 (controlled).

320 338.91 FRA ISSN 1956-6824
L'HARMATTAN BURKINA FASO. Variant title: Burkina Faso. Text in French. 2007. irreg. back issues avail. **Document type:** *Monographic series, Academic/Scholarly.*
Published by: L' Harmattan, 5 Rue de l'Ecole Polytechnique, Paris, 75005, France. TEL 33-1-43257651, FAX 33-1-43258203.

320 USA ISSN 1522-1113
DS1
HARVARD ASIA PACIFIC REVIEW. Text in English. 1996. s-a. USD 20 domestic; USD 40 foreign (effective 2007). adv. bk.rev. 64 p./no.; back issues avail. **Document type:** *Magazine, Consumer.*
Related titles: Online - full text ed.
Indexed: A01, BAS, CA, P10, P14, P48, P53, P54, PQC, T02.
Published by: Harvard University, Dept. of East Asian Languages and Civilizations, 9 Kirkland Pl, Cambridge, MA 02138. TEL 617-495-3437, FAX 617-495-1620, http://www.hcs.harvard.edu/~hapr. Ed. Angela Tseng. Pub., R&P Stephan Bosshart. Adv. contact Ju-lie Lee. B&W page USD 750, color page USD 1,000. Circ: 10,000.

HARVARD CHINA REVIEW. *see* BUSINESS AND ECONOMICS

HARVARD EAST ASIAN MONOGRAPHS. *see* HISTORY—History Of Asia

HARVARD JOURNAL OF HISPANIC POLICY. *see* ETHNIC INTERESTS

HARVARD JOURNAL OF LAW AND PUBLIC POLICY. *see* LAW

HARVARD KENNEDY SCHOOL REVIEW. *see* PUBLIC ADMINISTRATION

320 USA ISSN 0090-1032
JK1
HARVARD POLITICAL REVIEW. Abbreviated title: H P R. Text in English. 1969. q. USD 25; free to students (effective 2011). adv. bk.rev. illus. 40 p./no. 2 cols./p.; back issues avail. **Document type:** *Magazine, Consumer.*
Indexed: PAIS.
—IE.
Published by: Institute of Politics, Student Advisory Committee, 79 John F Kennedy St, Cambridge, MA 02138. pmbok@fas.harvard.edu, http://www.iop.harvard.edu/About-Us/Student-Advisory-Committee. Ed. Max Novendstern. Pub. Katherine Lee.

328.969 USA
HAWAII. LEGISLATIVE AUDITOR. SPECIAL REPORTS. Text in English. 1965. irreg. (3-5/yr.). free. charts; stat.
Published by: Office of the Auditor, State Capitol, Honolulu, HI 96813. TEL 808-548-2450.

328.969 USA ISSN 0073-1277
KFH20
HAWAII. LEGISLATIVE REFERENCE BUREAU. REPORT. Variant title: Legislative Reference Bureau. Session Reports. Text in English. 1950. a. back issues avail. **Document type:** *Handbook/Manual/ Guide, Government.*
Related titles: Online - full text ed.: free (effective 2011).
Published by: Legislative Reference Bureau, State Capitol, Rm 005, Honolulu, HI 96813. TEL 808-587-0690, FAX 808-587-0699, lrb@capitol.hawaii.gov.

320 AUS ISSN 1832-2573
HEADLINES. Text in English. 2005. s-a. **Document type:** *Bulletin, Consumer.*
Published by: The Bob Hawke Prime Ministerial Centre, GPO Box 2471, Adelaide, SA 5001, Australia. TEL 61-8-8302-0371, FAX 61-8-8302-0420, hawke.centre@unisa.edu.au, http://www.unisa.edu.au/hawkecentre/default.asp.

320 IRL
HEADS OF STATE AND CHIEF EXECUTIVES' AWARD. Text in English. 1980. a. USD 350. adv. bk.rev. **Document type:** *Bulletin.*
Description: Lists prominent politicians and chief executives who distinguished themselves and contributed to the cause of humanity and world at large.
Published by: Royal University, Ltd., 6 Lower Hatch St., Dublin, 2, Ireland. FAX 353-1-6686632.

320 USA ISSN 1931-3489
HEATH HAUSSAMEN ON NEW MEXICO POLITICS. Text in English. 2006. w. **Document type:** *Newsletter, Consumer.*
Media: Online - full text.
Published by: Haussamen Publications heath@haussamen.com, http://haussamen.blogspot.com.

320 296 ISR ISSN 1565-6640
BM645.P64
➤ **HEBRAIC POLITICAL STUDIES.** Text in English. 2005. q. USD 54 to individuals; USD 102 to institutions; USD 29 to students (effective 2009). **Document type:** *Journal, Academic/Scholarly.* **Description:** Presents scholarly articles in the fields of political science, philosophy, history, law, and religious studies that explore the political concepts of the Hebrew Bible and rabbinic literature, the significance of reflections on the Hebrew Bible and Judaic sources in the history of ideas, and the role of Jewish sources in the history of the West. The journal aims to evaluate the place of the Jewish textual tradition, alongside the traditions of Greece and Rome, in political history and the history of political thought.
Indexed: P42, PSA.
—BLDSC (4282.223000), IE.
Published by: The Shalem Center, 13 Yehoshua Bin-Nun St, P O Box 8787, Jerusalem, Israel. TEL 972-2-5605555, FAX 972-2-5605556, shalem@shalem.org.il, http://www.shalem.org.il. Eds. Arthur Eyffinger, Gordon Schochet.

324.2 FRA ISSN 1763-5853
L'HERITAGE. Text in French. 2004. q. EUR 16; EUR 31 in Europe; EUR 32 in Africa; EUR 33 elsewhere (effective 2008). **Document type:** *Magazine, Consumer.*
Published by: A S M A, B P 80308, Paris, Cedex 15 75723, France.

320 USA
THE HERITAGE MEMBERS NEWSLETTER. Text in English. 1973. m. voluntary donation. **Document type:** *Newsletter, Consumer.*
Formerly: The Heritage Foundation
Published by: The Heritage Foundation, 214 Massachusetts Ave NE, Washington, DC 20002-4999. TEL 202-546-4400, FAX 202-546-8328, info@heritage.org, http://www.heritage.org.

320 ARG
HERRAMIENTA. Text in Spanish. 1996. 3/yr. ARS 110 domestic; USD 65 in Latin America; EUR 60 in Europe (effective 2010). back issues avail. **Document type:** *Journal, Academic/Scholarly.*
Related titles: Online - full text ed.: ISSN 1852-4710.
Published by: Ediciones Herramienta, Rivadavia, 3772 1o. B, Buenos Aires, 1204, Argentina. TEL 54-11-49824146, revista@herramienta.com.ar.

320.52 DEU
HESSEN KURIER. Text in German. q. adv. **Document type:** *Magazine, Trade.*
Published by: CDU Hessen, Alfred-Dregger-Haus, Frankfurter Str. 6, Wiesbaden, 65189, Germany. TEL 49-611-16650, FAX 49-611-1665440. adv.: B&W page EUR 6,990. Circ: 70,000 (paid and controlled).

320.51 USA ISSN 1069-7268
HETERODOXY; articles and animadversions on political correctness and other follies. Text in English. 1992. 10/yr. USD 25 domestic; USD 45 foreign (effective 2004). adv. bk.rev. illus. back issues avail.; reprints avail. **Document type:** *Newspaper.* **Description:** Reports on liberal and politically correct ideologies from a conservative point of view.
Published by: Center for the Study of Popular Culture, 4401 Wilshire Dr 4th Fl, Los Angeles, CA 90010. TEL 323-556-2550, info@cspc.org, http://www.cspc.org/. Ed. Peter Collier. R&P Bruce Donaldson. Adv. contact J P Duberg. Circ: 14,400 (paid).

THE HILL. *see* PUBLIC ADMINISTRATION

320.954 NPL ISSN 1012-9804
HC430.6.Z7
HIMAL SOUTH ASIAN. Text in Nepali. 1987. m. USD 8 domestic to individuals; USD 13 to individuals India & Southasia; USD 33 elsewhere to individuals; USD 12 domestic to institutions; USD 19 to institutions India & Southasia; USD 54 elsewhere to institutions (effective 2010). adv. music rev.; tel.rev.; bk.rev. abstr.; illus. index, cum.index on diskette. back issues avail. **Document type:** *Magazine, Consumer.* **Description:** Covers political, social and cultural issues and news pertaining to the Himalayan regions, including Nepal, Sikkim, Bhutan, India, Tibet and Tibetans in exile. Also covers recent publications on the region.
Related titles: Online - full content ed.: ISSN 1605-9255. 1996. free (effective 2010).
Indexed: AICP, BAS.
Published by: The Southasia Trust, Patan Dhoka, Lalitpur, G P O Box 24393, Kathmandu, Nepal. TEL 977-1-5547279, FAX 977-1-5552141, info@himalmag.com, subscription@himalmag.com, editorial@himalmag.com. adv.: B&W page USD 1,000, color page USD 1,200; trim 19.5 x 27. Circ: 10,000 (paid); 5,000 (controlled).

317.172 JPN ISSN 0386-3565
H8.J3
HIROSHIMA HEIWA KAGAKU/HIROSHIMA PEACE SCIENCE. Text in Japanese. 1977. a., latest vol.24, 2002. **Document type:** *Journal, Academic/Scholarly.*
—BLDSC (4315.625000).
Published by: Hiroshima Daigaku, Heiwa Kagaku Kenkyu Senta/ Hiroshima University, Institute for Peace Science, Higashisenda-machi 1-1-89, Naka-ku, Hiroshima 730-0053, Japan. TEL 81-82-5426975, FAX 81-82-5420585, heiwa@hiroshima-u.ac.jp, http://home.hiroshima-u.ac.jp/heiwa/index.html.

HISTORIA CONSTITUCIONAL. *see* LAW—Constitutional Law

320 ESP ISSN 0210-7716
D1
HISTORIA, INSTITUCIONES, DOCUMENTOS. Text in Greek, Latin, Spanish. 1974. a. **Document type:** *Journal, Academic/Scholarly.*
Related titles: Online - full text ed.
Indexed: P09, PCI.
Published by: (Universidad de Sevilla, Departamentos de Historia Medieval, Historia del Derecho, Paleografia y Diplomatica), Universidad de Sevilla, Secretariado de Publicaciones, Calle Porvenir 27, Sevilla, 41013, Spain. TEL 34-95-4487444, FAX 34-95-4487443, secpub10@us.es, http://www.us.es/publius/inicio.html.

HISTORIC DOCUMENTS OF (YEAR). *see* HISTORY—History Of North And South America

320.5322 NLD ISSN 1570-1522
HISTORICAL MATERIALISM BOOK SERIES. Text in English. 2003. irreg., latest vol.19, 2008. price varies. **Document type:** *Monographic series, Academic/Scholarly.*
Indexed: IZBG.
Published by: Brill, PO Box 9000, Leiden, 2300 PA, Netherlands. TEL 31-71-5353500, FAX 31-71-5317532, cs@brill.nl. Eds. Michael Kratke, Paul Blackledge, Sebastien Budgen.

HISTORICAL SOCIAL RESEARCH/HISTORISCHE SOZIALFORSCHUNG. *see* HISTORY—History Of Europe

DAS HISTORISCH-POLITISCHE BUCH; Ein Wegweiser durch das Schrifttum. *see* HISTORY

HISTORISCH-POLITISCHE MITTEILUNGEN; Archiv fuer Christlich-Demokratische Politik. *see* HISTORY

321.8 DEU
▼ **HISTORISCHE DEMOKRATIEFORSCHUNG.** Text in German. 2011. irreg., latest vol.3, 2011. price varies. **Document type:** *Monographic series, Academic/Scholarly.*
Published by: Boehlau Verlag GmbH & Cie, Ursulaplatz 1, Cologne, 50668, Germany. TEL 49-221-913900, FAX 49-221-9139011, vertrieb@boehlau.de, http://www.boehlau.de.

320.09 GBR ISSN 0143-781X
JA8
➤ **HISTORY OF POLITICAL THOUGHT.** Text in English. 1980. q. GBP 115, USD 230 combined subscription to institutions (print & online eds.) (effective 2009). bk.rev. bibl.; illus. Index. 192 p./no. 1 cols./p.; back issues avail.; reprints avail. **Document type:** *Journal, Academic/ Scholarly.* **Description:** Takes a multidisciplinary approach to the historical study of political ideas and associated methodological problems.
Related titles: Online - full text ed.: (from IngentaConnect).
Indexed: A20, A22, ABCPolSci, ASCA, AmH&L, ArtHuCI, CA, CurCont, DIP, E01, HistAb, I13, IBR, IBSS, IBZ, IPB, P30, P42, PCI, PSA, Perlslam, Philind, RASB, S02, S03, SCOPUS, SociolAb, T02, W07.
—BLDSC (4318.405000), IE, Infotrieve, Ingenta. **CCC.**

Published by: Imprint Academic, PO Box 200, Exeter, Devon EXS 5YX, United Kingdom. TEL 44-1392-851550, FAX 44-1392-851178. Pub. Mr. Keith Sutherland.

➤ **HISTORY WORKSHOP JOURNAL.** *see* HISTORY

➤ **HITOTSUBASHI JOURNAL OF LAW AND POLITICS.** *see* LAW

324.248104 NOR ISSN 1504-6494
HOEYREMAGASINET. Text in Norwegian. 1992. 10/yr. NOK 300 membership; NOK 150 to students (effective 2007). **Document type:** *Magazine, Consumer.*
Formerly (until 2007): Medarbeideren (0804-1415)
Published by: Hoeyres Hovedorganisasjon/Conservative Party of Norway, PO Box 1536, Vika, Oslo, 0117, Norway. TEL 47-22-829000, FAX 47-22-829080, politikk@hoyre.no, http://www.hoyre.no. Ed. Christian I Wangberg.

HOGAKU/JOURNAL OF LAW AND POLITICAL SCIENCE. *see* LAW

HOGAKU KENKYU/JOURNAL OF LAW, POLITICS, AND SOCIOLOGY. *see* LAW

HOGAKU ZASSHI/JOURNAL OF LAW AND POLITICS OF OSAKA CITY UNIVERSITY. *see* LAW

HOKOUK. *see* LAW

HOMOSEXUS. *see* HOMOSEXUALITY

320 306.2 USA ISSN 1947-0983
HONG KONG JOURNAL; the quarterly online journal about issues relating to Hong Kong and China. Abbreviated title: H K J. Text in English. 2006. q. free (effective 2009). back issues avail. **Document type:** *Journal, Consumer.* **Description:** Provides thoughtful writing about political, economic and social issues relating to Hong Kong and its neighborhood.
Media: Online - full content.
Published by: Carnegie Endowment for International Peace, 1779 Massachusetts Ave, NW, Washington, DC 20036. TEL 202-483-7600, FAX 202-483-1840, info@CarnegieEndowment.org, http://www.carnegieendowment.org/. Ed. Robert Keatley.

HONG KONG. LEGISLATIVE COUNCIL. PROCEEDINGS. *see* PUBLIC ADMINISTRATION

HONG KONG. LEGISLATIVE COUNCIL. PUBLIC WORKS SUB-COMMITTEE. REPORT. *see* PUBLIC ADMINISTRATION

320.6 USA ISSN 1088-5161
H96
➤ **HOOVER DIGEST**; research and opinion on public policy. Text in English. 1996. q. USD 25; USD 5 per issue (effective 2010). adv. back issues avail. **Document type:** *Journal, Academic/Scholarly.* **Description:** Offers informative writing on politics, economics, and history by the scholars and researchers of the Hoover Institution, the public policy research center at Stanford University.
Related titles: Online - full text ed.
Indexed: B04, BRD, PAIS, R03, RGAb, RGPR, W03, W05.
—BLDSC (4326.595600).
Published by: (Hoover Institution on War, Revolution and Peace), Hoover Institution, 434 Galvez Mall, Stanford University, Stanford, CA 94305. TEL 650-723-1754, FAX 650-723-8611, schieron@stanford.edu. Ed. Peter Robinson. **Subscr. to:** PO Box 37005, Chicago, IL 60615. TEL 773-753-3347, 877-705-1878, hoover@press.uchicago.edu.

320.6 USA ISSN 0091-6293
HOOVER INSTITUTION ON WAR, REVOLUTION AND PEACE. REPORT. Text in English. irreg.
Published by: Hoover Institution on War, Revolution and Peace, Stanford, CA 94305-6010. TEL 650-723-1754, FAX 650-723-1687, lmaune@stanford.edu, http://www.hoover.org.

320 PRT
HORIZONTE UNIVERSITARIO. Text in Portuguese. 1982 (no.30). irreg., latest vol.56, 1991. **Document type:** *Monographic series, Academic/ Scholarly.*
Published by: Livros Horizonte, Rua da Chagas 17, Lisbon, 1200-106, Portugal. TEL 351-213-466917, geral@livroshorizonte.pt, http://www.livroshorizonte.pt.

HOSEI RONSHU/JOURNAL OF LAW AND POLITICAL SCIENCE (NAGOYA). *see* LAW

320 AUS ISSN 1838-1537
▼ ➤ **HOT TOPICS FROM THE TROPICS.** Text in English. 2009. s-a. free (effective 2011). **Document type:** *Journal, Academic/Scholarly.* **Description:** Aims to provide an international forum for researchers based at or working in partnership with Charles Darwin University.
Media: Online - full text.
Published by: Charles Darwin University Press, Orange 10.1.01, Mail Box 6, Darwin, N.T. 0909, Australia. TEL 61-8-89466801, FAX 61-8-89466815, cdupress@cdu.edu.au, http://cdupress.cdu.edu.au.

320 USA ISSN 1946-3472
HOTLINE (WASHINGTON). Text in English. 1987. d. free to members (effective 2009). adv. back issues avail. **Document type:** *Newsletter, Consumer.* **Description:** Provides information on American politics, polling, and campaign developments with original reporting and coverage from over 2,500 media sources.
Media: Online - full content.
Indexed: P45.
—CCC.
Published by: National Journal Group, Inc., The Watergate 600 New Hampshire Ave, NW, Washington, DC 20037. TEL 202-739-8400, 800-613-6701, FAX 202-833-8069, service@nationaljournal.com. Eds. John Mercurio, Amy Walter. Adv. contact Arielle Elliott TEL 202-266-7288.

320 USA
HOW TO CONTACT WORLD LEADERS. Text in English. 1990. a., latest 2004. **Description:** Provides information on how to contact world leaders. Gives profiles of world leaders; information on names, titles, addresses, telephone, fax, e-mail, etc.
Former titles: World Leader Update (1065-335X); How to Write to World Leaders
Published by: MinRef Press, 3814 Winona Way, North Highlands, CA 95660. TEL 916-977-0122. Ed. Rick Lawler.

320.9 CAN ISSN 0702-3855
F1035.C7
HRVATSKI PUT/CROATIAN WAY. Text mainly in Croatian; Text occasionally in English. 1962. m. CAD 36. adv. bk.rev. illus.
Description: Covers world affairs and Croatian national culture and political activity throughout the world.
Formerly: Nas Put - Our Way (0027-8092)
Published by: Croatian-Canadian Society, 34 Southport St, Ste 88510, Toronto, ON M6S 3N0, Canada. TEL 416-979-5341, FAX 416-621-4819. Ed. Rudi Tomic. Circ: 3,000.

320 TWN
HSIEN CHENG SSU CH'AO. Text in Chinese. q. **Description:** Investigates systems of government and political theories, centering on the concept and reality of Constitutional rule. Includes translations.
Published by: (Kuo Min Ta Hui/National People's Council, Hsien Cheng Yen T'ao Wei Yuan Hui/Committee for the Discussion of Constitutional Government), Hsien Cheng Ssu Ch'ao Magazine House, No 1, Hsiushan St, Taipei, Taiwan. TEL 02-311-4066.

HUADONG ZHENG-FA XUEYUAN XUEBAO/EAST CHINA UNIVERSITY OF POLITICS AND LAW. JOURNAL. *see* LAW

320 DEU
HUMANE GESELLSCHAFT. Text in German. 1972. q. free to members (effective 2008). adv. bk.rev.; film rev.; play rev. bibl.; illus.; stat.
Document type: *Magazine, Consumer.*
Published by: Junge Union Baden-Wuerttemberg, Hasenbergstr 49B, Stuttgart, 70176, Germany. TEL 49-711-6690453, FAX 49-711-6690445, lgs@ju-bw.de. Ed. Ralf Stefan Huebner. Circ: 13,000 (controlled).

HUMANISTEN. *see* PHILOSOPHY

320.6 GBR ISSN 0955-3169
HUME OCCASIONAL PAPERS. Text in English. 198?. irreg., latest vol.83, 2009. price varies. back issues avail. **Document type:** *Monographic series, Academic/Scholarly.*
Related titles: Online - full text ed.: free (effective 2009).
—BLDSC (4336.610000), IE, Ingenta.
Published by: David Hume Institute, 26 Forth St, Edinburgh, EH1 3LH, United Kingdom. TEL 44-131-5503746, enquiries@davidhumeinstitute.com.

HUNGARIAN STUDIES REVIEW. *see* HISTORY—History Of Europe

HUNGARY BUSINESS FORECAST REPORT. *see* BUSINESS AND ECONOMICS—Economic Situation And Conditions

320 KOR ISSN 1229-4616
HYEONDAE BUGHAN YEON'GU/NORTH KOREAN STUDIES REVIEW. Text in Korean. 1998. 3/yr. **Document type:** *Journal, Academic/Scholarly.*
Published by: Kyungnam University, Institute for Far Eastern Studies/ Gyeongnam Daehag'gyo, Geugdong Munje Yeon'guso, 28-42 Samchung-dong, Chongro-Ku, Seoul, 110-230, Korea, S. TEL 82-2-37000700, FAX 82-2-37000707, ifes@kyungnam.ac.kr, http://ifes.kyungnam.ac.kr/ifes/ifes/eng/default.asp.

I C P S R BULLETIN (ONLINE). *see* SOCIAL SCIENCES: COMPREHENSIVE WORKS

I D E OCCASIONAL PAPERS SERIES. *see* BUSINESS AND ECONOMICS

I D E SPOT SURVEY. *see* BUSINESS AND ECONOMICS

I D E SYMPOSIUM PROCEEDINGS. *see* BUSINESS AND ECONOMICS

322.4 FRA ISSN 1959-5360
I D MAGAZINE. Text in French. 199?. irreg. EUR 16 domestic; EUR 16 in Belgium; EUR 30 in Europe; EUR 35 elsewhere (effective 2008).
Document type: *Magazine, Consumer.*
Formerly (until 2005): Jeune Resistance (1279-4759)
Published by: Bloc Identitaire, B P 13, Nice, Cedex 4 06301, France. contact@bloc-identitaire.com, http://www.bloc-identitaire.com.

I F M - S E I BULLETIN. *see* EDUCATION

I M F C REVIEW. (Institute of Marriage and Family Canada) *see* MATRIMONY

320 NLD
I M I S C O E RESEARCH. (International Migration, Integration and Social Cohesion in Europe) Text in English. irreg. price varies. **Document type:** *Monographic series, Academic/Scholarly.*
Published by: (International Migration, Integration and Social Cohesion in Europe (I M I S C O E)), Amsterdam University Press, Herengracht 221, Amsterdam, 1016 BG, Netherlands. TEL 31-20-4200050, FAX 31-20-4203214, info@aup.nl, http://www.aup.nl.

320 USA
I M P: THE MAGAZINE ON INFORMATION IMPACTS. Text in English. 10/yr. back issues avail. **Document type:** *Newsletter.*
Media: E-mail.
Published by: Center for Information Strategy and Policy, 1710 Saic Dr, McLean, VA 22102. TEL 703-676-4055. Ed. Amy Friedlander.

320.95491 PAK ISSN 1684-9787
JQ629.A1
➤ **I P R I JOURNAL.** Text in English. 2001. s-a. PKR 250 newsstand/ cover (effective 2007). **Document type:** *Journal, Academic/Scholarly.*
Related titles: Online - full text ed.: ISSN 1684-9809.
—BLDSC (4567.475350).
Published by: Islamabad Policy Research Institute, House no 2, St no 15, Main Margalla Rd F-7/2, Islamabad, Pakistan. TEL 92-51-92136802, FAX 92-51-9213683, ipripak@ipripak.org, http://www.ipripak.org. Ed. Rashid Ahmed Khan. Circ: 750 (paid).

320 365.34 SGP ISSN 0218-8953
I S E A S WORKING PAPERS SERIES: INTERNATIONAL POLITICS AND SECURITY ISSUES. Text in English. irreg. **Document type:** *Monographic series, Academic/Scholarly.*
Published by: Institute of Southeast Asian Studies, 30 Heng Mui Keng Terrace, Pasir Panjang, Singapore, 119614, Singapore. FAX 65-67756259, pubsunit@iseas.edu.sg, http://www.iseas.edu.sg/.

320 GBR ISSN 2044-2114
I, SCIENCE. Text in English. 2005. q. back issues avail. **Document type:** *Magazine, Academic/Scholarly.* **Description:** Covers scientific features, articles and news domestically and internationally.
Related titles: Online - full text ed.: ISSN 2044-2122. free (effective 2010).
Published by: (Imperial College of London), Felix Newspaper, Beit Quad, Prince Consort Rd, London, SW7 2BB, United Kingdom. TEL 44-20-75948072, felix@imperial.ac.uk, http://felixonline.co.uk. Ed. Adrian Giordani.

320.9485 SWE ISSN 1653-8307
I TJAENST FOER RIKSDAGEN. Text in Swedish. 2006. a. free.
Document type: *Government.*
Related titles: Online - full text ed.
Published by: Sveriges Riksdag, Informationsenheten/The Swedish Parliament. Information Department, Stockholm, 10012, Sweden. TEL 46-8-7864000, riksdagsinformation@riksdagen.se. **Dist. by:** Sveriges Riksdag, Tryckeriexpeditionen, Stockholm 10012, Sweden. TEL 46-8-7865810, FAX 46-8-7866176, ordermottagningen@riksdagen.se.

320.531 AUT
I U S Y NEWSLETTER. Text in German. 1971. irreg. free. bk.rev. illus.
Document type: *Newsletter.*
Former titles (until 1985): I U S Y Bulletin; I U S Y Survey (0019-0888)
Published by: International Union of Socialist Youth, Neustiftgasse 3, Vienna, W 1070, Austria. TEL 43-1-5231267, FAX 43-1-52695849, TELEX 75312469 SJOE. Ed. Alfredo Lazzeretti. Circ: 1,500.

320 CHE ISSN 0172-1275
I V W - SCHRIFTENREIHE. (Institut fuer Versicherungswirtschaft) Text in German. 1975. irreg., latest vol.6, 1981. price varies. **Document type:** *Monographic series, Academic/Scholarly.*
Formerly (until 1977): Schriftenreihe Risikopolitik
Published by: Peter Lang AG (Subsidiary of: Peter Lang Publishing Group), Hochfeldstr 32, Postfach 746, Bern 9, 3000, Switzerland. TEL 41-31-3061717, FAX 41-31-3061727, info@peterlang.com, http://www.peterlang.com.

I W K. (Internationale Wissenschaftliche Korrespondenz zur Geschichte der Deutschen Arbeiterbewegung) *see* LABOR UNIONS

IBYKUS; Zeitschrift fuer Poesie, Wissenschaft und Staatskunst. *see* LITERATURE—Poetry

320 RUS
ICHKERIYA. Text in Chechen. 1991. 24/yr. USD 499 in North America (effective 2000).
Published by: Redaktiya/Ichkeriya, Dadin Aibikin Uram 92, Groznyi, 364000, Russian Federation. Ed. G R Isaev. **Dist. by:** East View Information Services, 10601 Wayzata Blvd, Minneapolis, MN 55305. TEL 952-252-1201, 800-477-1005, FAX 952-252-1202, info@eastview.com, http://www.eastview.com.

324.248108 NOR ISSN 1890-0135
IDE (OSLO, 2006). Text in Norwegian. 2006. bi-m. adv. **Document type:** *Magazine, Consumer.* **Description:** Magazine for members of the political Kristelig Folkeparti in Norway.
Published by: Kristelig Folkeparti, Oevre Slottsgade 18-10, PO Box 478, Sentrum, Oslo, 0105, Norway. TEL 47-23-102800, FAX 47-23-102810, krf@krf.no, http://www.krf.no. Ed., Adv. contact Erik Lunde TEL 47-23-102856. page NOK 20,000. Circ: 40,500 (controlled and free).

IDEAS IN CONTEXT. *see* HUMANITIES: COMPREHENSIVE WORKS

IDEBATE. N. *see* EDUCATION—Teaching Methods And Curriculum

324.2 NLD ISSN 0927-2518
IDEE; tijdschrift voor het wetenschappelijk bureau van D66. Text in Dutch. 1980. 6/yr. EUR 35; EUR 20 to students (effective 2008).
Formerly (until 1991): Idee '66 (0167-2339)
—IE, Infotrieve.
Published by: Democraten 66, Postbus 660, The Hague, 2501 CR, Netherlands. TEL 31-70-3566066, FAX 31-70-3641917, info@d66.nl, http://www.d66.nl.

IDENTITET. *see* ETHNIC INTERESTS

IDENTITIES; global studies in culture and power. *see* ETHNIC INTERESTS

IDENTITY, CULTURE AND POLITICS/IDENTITE, CULTURE ET POLITIQUE; an Afro-Asian dialogue. *see* SOCIOLOGY

320 PER ISSN 1019-455X
IDEOLOGIA Y POLITICA. Text in Spanish. 1973. irreg., latest vol.12, 1999. price varies. back issues avail. **Document type:** *Monographic series, Academic/Scholarly.*
Published by: (Instituto de Estudios Peruanos), I E P Ediciones (Subsidiary of: Instituto de Estudios Peruanos), Horacio Urteaga 694, Jesus Maria, Lima, 11, Peru. TEL 51-14-3326194, FAX 51-14-3326173, libreria@iep.org.pe, http://iep.perucultural.org.pe.

320 USA ISSN 0738-9663
JK5701
ILLINOIS ISSUES. Text in English. 1975. m. (10/yr.). USD 35.95 domestic; USD 94.95 foreign (effective 2009). adv. bk.rev. illus. reprints avail. **Document type:** *Journal, Academic/Scholarly.* **Description:** Covers political and governmental issues affecting Illinois.
Indexed: PAIS, UAA.
—Ingenta.
Published by: University of Illinois at Springfield, PO Box 19243, Springfield, IL 62794-9243. TEL 217-206-6084, http://www.uis.edu. adv.: B&W page USD 998, color page USD 1,448. Circ: 6,500. **Subscr. to:** PO Box 251, Mt Morris, IL 61054.

324.6 USA ISSN 1041-1283
ILLINOIS VOTER. Text in English. 1920. q. USD 8 (effective 2000). adv. illus. back issues avail. **Document type:** *Newsletter.*
Published by: League of Women Voters of Illinois, 332 S Michigan Ave, Ste 1050, Chicago, IL 60604. TEL 312-939-5935, FAX 312-939-6887. Ed., Adv. contact Mary English. Pub., R&P Stacey Patricoski.

IMPACT; Asian magazine for human transformation. *see* SOCIAL SCIENCES: COMPREHENSIVE WORKS

320 DEU
▼ **IMPULSE (BERLIN).** Text in German. 2009. irreg. price varies. **Document type:** *Monographic series, Academic/Scholarly.*
Published by: Wissenschaftlicher Verlag Berlin, Koertestr 10, Berlin, 10967, Germany. TEL 49-30-89379899, FAX 49-30-6185021, verlag@wvberlin.de, http://www.wvberlin.de.

320.531 USA ISSN 0160-5992
AP2
IN THESE TIMES. Text in English. 1976. m. USD 24.95 domestic; USD 39.95 in Canada; USD 45.95 elsewhere (effective 2010). adv. bk.rev. illus. back issues avail.; reprints avail. **Document type:** *Magazine, Consumer.* **Description:** Features provocative essays, debates about US political future, humorous anecdotes and much more.
Related titles: Microfilm ed.: (from PQC); Online - full text ed.
Indexed: A22, APW, ASIP, AltPI, B04, ChPerI, Chicano, HRIR, LeftInd, MLA-IB, P45, PAIS, R03, RASB, RGAb, RGPR, W03, W05.
—CIS, Ingenta.
Published by: Institute for Public Affairs, 2040 N Milwaukee Ave, Chicago, IL 60647. TEL 773-772-0100, FAX 773-772-4180. Ed., Pub. Joel Bleifuss. Adv. contact Selena Kohel. color page USD 1,000; trim 8.125 x 10.625. **Subscr. to:** PO Box 1912, Mt. Morris, IL 61054. TEL 800-827-0270.

INCHIESTA. *see* SOCIAL SERVICES AND WELFARE

INCITE INFORMATION; inquiry and commentary. *see* JOURNALISM

320 ITA ISSN 1971-9612
INDAGINI E PROSPETTIVE. Text in Multiple languages. 1973. irreg., latest vol.25. price varies. **Document type:** *Monographic series, Academic/Scholarly.*
Published by: Angelo Longo Editore, Via Paolo Costa 33, Ravenna, 48121, Italy. TEL 39-0544-217026, FAX 39-0544-217554, longo@longo-editore.it, http://www.longo-editore.it.

320 AUS ISSN 1449-5961
THE INDEPENDENT AUSTRALIAN. Text in English. 2003. q. AUD 25 (effective 2009). back issues avail.; reprints avail. **Document type:** *Magazine, Consumer.* **Description:** Discusses politics based on independent views of people.
Published by: Independent Australian Publications Pty Ltd., PO Box 8, Essendon, VIC 3040, Australia. Ed. Peter A Wilkinson.

320 USA
INDEPENDENT POLITICS!. Text in English. q. USD 12 (effective 2008).
Document type: *Newspaper, Trade.* **Description:** Builds a unified, independent, progressive alternative to the corporate-controlled Democrat-Republican political and economic system.
Former titles (until 2006): Independent Politics News; Independent Progressive Politics News; Independent Political Action Bulletin; (until 1996): National Committee for Independent Political Action. Discussion Bulletin
Related titles: Online - full text ed.
Indexed: APW, AltPI.
Published by: Independent Progressive Politics Network, PO Box 1041, Bloomfield, NJ 07003-1041. TEL 973-338-5398, indpol@igc.org. Ed. Ted Glick. Circ: 2,000.

P

320 USA ISSN 1086-1653
H1 CODEN: IREVFP
➤ **THE INDEPENDENT REVIEW**; a journal of political economy. Text in English. 1996. q. USD 28.95 domestic to individuals; USD 41.95 in Canada & Mexico to individuals; USD 56.95 elsewhere to individuals; USD 84.95 domestic to institutions; USD 112.95 foreign to institutions (effective 2009). adv. bk.rev. illus. Index. 160 p./no.; back issues avail.; reprints avail. **Document type:** *Journal, Academic/Scholarly.*
Description: Interdisciplinary journal devoted to political economy broadly construed. Features pathbreaking, non-politicized articles and reviews in economics, law, history, political science, philosophy, sociology, and other fields.
Related titles: Online - full text ed.
Indexed: A01, A02, A03, A08, A12, A17, A20, A26, ABIn, APW, B01, B04, B06, B07, B09, B14, BRD, BRI, CA, CBRI, CurCont, E08, ESPM, EconLit, EnvAb, G08, GEOBASE, HRA, I05, I13, JEL, L03, M01, M02, P10, P34, P42, P45, P48, P51, P53, P54, PAIS, PQC, PRA, PSA, RiskAb, S02, S03, S09, SCOPUS, SOPODA, SPAA, SSAI, SSAb, SSCI, SSI, SociolAb, T02, W03, W05, W07.
—BLDSC (4375.897000), IE, Ingenta. **CCC.**
Published by: Independent Institute, 100 Swan Way, Oakland, CA 94621. TEL 510-632-1366, 800-927-8733, FAX 510-568-6040, info@independent.org. Ed. Robert Higgs. Pub. David J Theroux. adv.: page USD 775; 5.5 x 8.5. Circ: 4,000 (paid); 1,000 (controlled).

320 USA ISSN 1095-7308
HB95
INDEX OF ECONOMIC FREEDOM; the link between economic opportunity & prosperity. Text in English. 1995. a. USD 24.95 per issue (effective 2010). **Document type:** *Journal, Trade.* **Description:** Aims to measure the degree of economic freedom in the world's nations. Covers 10 different kinds of freedoms from property rights to entrepreneurship in 183 countries.
Related titles: Online - full text ed.: free (effective 2010).
—BLDSC (4377.835000).
Published by: The Heritage Foundation, 214 Massachusetts Ave NE, Washington, DC 20002-4999. TEL 202-546-4400, FAX 202-546-8328, info@heritage.org.

320 IND ISSN 0019-5510
JA26
➤ **INDIAN JOURNAL OF POLITICAL SCIENCE.** Abbreviated title: I J P S. Text in English. 1939. q. INR 800 domestic to individuals; USD 150 foreign to individuals; INR 1,200 domestic to institutions; USD 220 foreign to institutions; INR 400 domestic to members; USD 90 foreign to members; INR 250 per issue domestic to individuals; USD 40 per issue foreign to individuals; INR 300 per issue domestic to institutions; USD 60 per issue foreign to institutions; INR 150 per issue domestic to members; USD 30 per issue foreign to members (effective 2011). adv. bk.rev. bibl. back issues avail.; reprints avail. **Document type:** *Journal, Academic/Scholarly.* **Description:** Covers political theory, comparative politics, Indian politics, international relations.
Related titles: Microform ed.: (from PQC).
Indexed: ABCPolSci, BAS, CA, IBR, IBSS, IBZ, P06, P42, PAA&I, PSA, RASB, SCOPUS, SociolAb, T02.
—Ingenta.
Published by: Indian Political Science Association, C/o Dr.C.P.Barthwal, Dept of Public Administration, University of Lucknow, Lucknow, Uttar Pradesh, India. cbarthwal@yahoo.co.in, http://www.ijps.net/ipsa.html. Ed. Sanjeev Kumar Sharma TEL 91-121-2764455.

320 IND ISSN 0303-9951
JA26
INDIAN JOURNAL OF POLITICS. Text in English. 1967. q. INR 250 domestic to individuals; INR 1,000 domestic to institutions; USD 50 foreign (effective 2011). bk.rev. reprints avail. **Document type:** *Journal, Academic/Scholarly.*
Related titles: Microform ed.
Indexed: BAS, CA, I13, IIPL, P42, PSA, RASB, SCOPUS, T02.
—Ingenta. **CCC.**
Published by: Aligarh Muslim University, Administrative Block, Aligarh Muslim University, Aligarh, Uttar Pradesh 202 002, India. TEL 91-571-2703038, FAX 91-571-2702331. Ed. M Mahmood. **Subscr. to:** I N S I O Scientific Books & Periodicals, PO Box 7234, Indraprastha HPO, New Delhi 110 002, India. iihm@ap.nic.in, http://iihm.ap.nic.in/.

INDIANA LEGISLATIVE INSIGHT. *see* PUBLIC ADMINISTRATION

INDONESIA BUSINESS FORECAST REPORT. *see* BUSINESS AND ECONOMICS—Economic Situation And Conditions

INDONESIA LETTER. *see* BUSINESS AND ECONOMICS—Economic Situation And Conditions

320.9 IDN ISSN 0304-2170
DS611
INDONESIAN QUARTERLY. Text in English. 1972. 3/m. IDR 100,000 domestic; USD 100 in Asia & the Pacific; USD 125 in Europe; USD 150 in the Americas; USD 175 elsewhere (effective 2006). adv. bk.rev. bibl.; charts. **Document type:** *Journal, Academic/Scholarly.*
Description: A medium for Indonesian views on national, regional and global problems.
Indexed: A22, AMB, APEL, BAS, EI, I13, LID&ISL, P06, P30, PAIS, Perlslam, RASB, SCOPUS.
—BLDSC (4438.045000), IE, Infotrieve, Ingenta.
Published by: Centre for Strategic and International Studies, Jalan Tanah Abang III/27, Jakarta, 10160, Indonesia. TEL 62-21-3865532, FAX 62-21-3809641, csis@csis.or.id. Ed., R&P Vidhyandika Moeljarto. Circ: 3,000.

320.57 USA
THE INDYPENDENT. Text in English. m. **Document type:** *Newspaper, Consumer.* **Description:** Covers the news & events of the local & global anarchy movement.
Published by: The New York City - Independent Media Center, 34 E 29th St, 2nd Fl, New York, NY 10016-7918. TEL 212-684-8112, nycimc@indymedia.org, nyceditors@indymedia.org, http://nyc.indymedia.org/.

INFORMACION POLITICA Y ECONOMICA. *see* BUSINESS AND ECONOMICS—Economic Situation And Conditions

INFORMATION FUER ORMESHEIM. *see* PUBLIC ADMINISTRATION—Municipal Government

320 DEU ISSN 0046-9408
JA88.G3
INFORMATIONEN ZUR POLITISCHEN BILDUNG/INFORMATION FOR CIVIC EDUCATION. Text in German. 1952. q. free (effective 2009). bk.rev. **Document type:** *Journal, Academic/Scholarly.* **Description:** Devoted to the study and teaching of political science in Germany. Includes bibliography and list of educational materials.
Incorporates (1952-1963): Staatsbuergerliche Informationen (0561-7693)
Indexed: DIP, FR, IBR, IBZ, RASB, SpeleolAb.
—BLDSC (4496.478300). **CCC.**
Published by: Bundeszentrale fuer Politische Bildung, Adenauerallee 86, Bonn, 53113, Germany. TEL 49-1888-5150, FAX 49-1888-515113, info@bpb.de. Ed. Juergen Faulenbach. Circ: 950,000 (free).

324 AUT
INFORMATIONEN ZUR POLITISCHEN BILDUNG. Text in German. 2/yr. EUR 9.50 per issue (effective 2009). **Document type:** *Journal, Academic/Scholarly.*
Published by: (Forum Politische Bildung), StudienVerlag, Erlerstr 10, Innsbruck, 6020, Austria. TEL 43-512-395045, FAX 43-512-39504515, order@studienverlag.at.

320 DEU
INFORMATIONEN ZUR POLITISCHEN BILDUNG - AKTUELL. Text in German. irreg. free (effective 2009). **Document type:** *Magazine, Consumer.*
Published by: Bundeszentrale fuer Politische Bildung, Adenauerallee 86, Bonn, 53113, Germany. TEL 49-1888-5150, FAX 49-1888-515113, info@bpb.de.

328 FRA ISSN 0251-3617
JF8
INFORMATIONS CONSTITUTIONNELLES ET PARLEMENTAIRES. Text in English. 1948. s-a. adv. index.
Related titles: English ed.: Constitutional and Parliamentary Information. ISSN 0010-6623.
Indexed: RASB.
—IE.
Published by: (Union Interparlementaire/Inter-Parliamentary Union CHE), Association des Secretaires Generaux des Parlements/Association of Secretaries General of Parliaments, Assemble Nationale, 126 rue de l'Universite, Paris, 75355, France. TEL 33-1-40635568, FAX 33-1-40635240, asgp@assemblee-nationale.fr. Circ: 1,500.

320 AZE
INFORMATSIONNOE AGENTSTVO TURAN. POLITIKO-SOBYTIINYI BYULLETEN'. Text in Russian. 260/yr. USD 1,199 in United States.
Related titles: ◆ English ed.: Turan Information Agency. Daily Political - Eventual.
Published by: Turan Information Agency/Turna Informasiya Agentilyi, Khagani ul 33, Baku, 370000, Azerbaijan. TEL 994-12-984226. Ed. Mekhman Aliev. **Dist. by:** East View Information Services, 10601 Wayzata Blvd, Minneapolis, MN 55305. TEL 952-252-1201, 800-477-1005, FAX 952-252-1202, info@eastview.com, http://www.eastview.com.

INFORME LATINOAMERICANO. *see* BUSINESS AND ECONOMICS—Economic Situation And Conditions

320 PER
INFORMES. Text in Spanish. 1982 (no.8). irreg.
Published by: Instituto de Promocion y Educacion Popular, Apartado 16, Ancash, Chimbote, Peru.

320 ESP ISSN 1887-4037
INFORMES FRC. Text in Spanish, Catalan. 2007. q. **Document type:** *Bulletin, Consumer.*
Published by: Fundacio Rafael Campalans, Trafalgar, 12 entresol 1a, Barcelona, 08010, Spain. TEL 34-93-3195412, FAX 34-93-3199844, fundacio@fcampalans.cat.

320 GTM ISSN 0252-8754
HC141.A1
INFORPRESS CENTROAMERICANA. Text in Spanish. 1972. d. USD 451 in the Americas; USD 467 in Europe; USD 528 elsewhere (effective 2000). charts. back issues avail. **Document type:** *Newspaper, Consumer.* **Description:** Contains information and analysis on the economic and political events in Belize, Guatemala, El Salvador, Honduras, Nicaragua, Costa Rica and Panama.
Indexed: C01.
Address: 11 Ave. 16-60, Apdo. 2823, Guatemala City Zona, Guatemala. TEL 502-2510604, FAX 502-2514562. **Subscr. to:** Inforpress Centroamericana, Section 23, Box 52 7270, Miami, FL 33152-7270.

320.532 FRA ISSN 1962-5766
INITIATIVES. Text in French. 2000. m. **Document type:** *Newsletter.*
Published by: Groupe Communiste Republicain et Citoyen, 15 rue de Vaugirard, Paris, Cedex 06 75291, France. TEL 33-1-42342124, FAX 33-1-42343811.

320 USA ISSN 1938-7350
JA1
INITIUM; all things political. Text in English. 2007. a. **Document type:** *Journal, Academic/Scholarly.* **Description:** Features graduate and undergraduate writings on all aspects of political science.
Related titles: Online - full text ed.: ISSN 1939-0092.
Published by: University of Texas at San Antonio, Department of Political Science and Geography, 1 UTSA Circle, San Antonio, TX 78249. TEL 210-458-5600, FAX 210-458-4629, mansour.elkikhia@utsa.edu, http://colfa.utsa.edu/polisci/.

INKWEL. *see* WOMEN'S INTERESTS

320 CAN ISSN 1480-6339
INNOVATIONS (CALGARY); a journal of politics. Text in English. 1998. a. USD 15 to individuals; USD 35 to institutions; USD 10 to students (effective 2006). adv. **Document type:** *Journal, Academic/Scholarly.*
Indexed: C03, CBCARef, P48, PQC.
—**CCC.**
Published by: University of Calgary, Department of Political Science, 2500 University Dr, NW, Calgary, AB T2N 1N4, Canada. Eds. Anita Singh, Scott Fitzsimmons.

320 USA ISSN 1930-6857
INNOVATORS INSIGHTS. Text in English. 2004. bi-w. **Document type:** *Newsletter.*
Media: Online - full text.
Published by: Harvard University, John F. Kennedy School of Government. Ash Institute for Democratic Governance and Innovation, 79 John F. Kennedy St, Cambridge, MA 02138. TEL 617-495-0557, FAX 617-496-4602, innovations@harvard.edu, http://www.ashinstitute.harvard.edu/Ash/index.htm.

INSIDE ALABAMA POLITICS. *see* PUBLIC ADMINISTRATION

320 AUS ISSN 0046-9629
INSIDE CANBERRA. Text in English. 1948. w. AUD 450 combined subscription domestic print & email eds. (effective 2008). **Document type:** *Newsletter, Government.* **Description:** Brings you the latest facts, analysis and contacts from inside the Federal Government.
Related titles: E-mail ed.: AUD 375 (effective 2008).
Published by: Crown Content, Level 2, 141 Capel St, North Melbourne, VIC 3051, Australia. TEL 61-3-93299800, FAX 61-3-93299698, online@crowncontent.com.au, http://www.crowncontent.com.au. Ed. Max Berry.

320.958 GBR ISSN 1352-4100
INSIDE CENTRAL ASIA; a weekly roundup of media reports covered by B B C Monitoring. Text in English. 1994. w. GBP 450 domestic; GBP 472 in Europe; GBP 495 elsewhere (effective 2000). **Document type:** *Newspaper.* **Description:** Offers insight into the economic and political trends of central Asian republics.
Published by: B B C Monitoring, Caversham Park, Peppard Rd, Reading, Berks RG4 8TZ, United Kingdom. Ed. Mike Elliott. R&P Rosy Wolfe.

INSIDE MICHIGAN POLITICS. *see* PUBLIC ADMINISTRATION

320 ZAF
INSIG. Text in Afrikaans. m.
Published by: Media24 Ltd., Naspers Centre, 40 Heerengracht St, PO Box 1802, Cape Town, 8000, South Africa. TEL 27-21-4398252, FAX 27-21-4398277.

INSIGHT (WELLINGTON, 2004). *see* BUSINESS AND ECONOMICS—Domestic Commerce

INSTITUT DES HAUTES ETUDES DE L'AMERIQUE LATINE. COLLECTION DES TRAVAUX ET MEMOIRES. *see* HUMANITIES: COMPREHENSIVE WORKS

320.96 DEU ISSN 0945-3601
INSTITUT FUER AFRIKA-KUNDE. ARBEITEN. Text in German. 1974. irreg., latest vol.109. 250 p./no.; back issues avail.; reprints avail. **Document type:** *Monographic series, Academic/Scholarly.*
Published by: G I G A Institute of African Affairs, Neuer Jungfernstieg 21, Hamburg, 20354, Germany. TEL 49-40-42834-523, FAX 49-40-42834-511, iaa@giga-hamburg.de, http://www.rrz.uni-hamburg.de/iak. Circ: 250 (controlled).

321.02 AUT
INSTITUT FUER FOEDERALISMUS. BERICHTE. Text in German. 1975. irreg., latest vol.34, 2011. price varies. **Document type:** *Monographic series, Academic/Scholarly.*
Formerly: Institut fuer Foederalismusforschung. Berichte
Published by: (Institut fuer Foederalismus), Wilhelm Braumueller Universitaets-Verlagsbuchhandlung GmbH, Servitengasse 5, Vienna, 1090, Austria. TEL 43-1-3191159, FAX 43-1-3102805, office@braumueller.at.

321.02 AUT
INSTITUT FUER FOEDERALISMUS. SCHRIFTENREIHE. Text in German. 1976. irreg., latest vol.112, 2011. price varies. **Document type:** *Monographic series, Academic/Scholarly.*
Formerly: Institut fuer Foederalismusforschung. Schriftenreihe
Published by: (Institut fuer Foederalismus), Wilhelm Braumueller Universitaets-Verlagsbuchhandlung GmbH, Servitengasse 5, Vienna, 1090, Austria. TEL 43-1-3191159, FAX 43-1-3102805, office@braumueller.at. Ed. Peter Bussjaeger.

330.9 USA ISSN 0364-0779
HV95 CODEN: JISSDW
INSTITUTE FOR SOCIOECONOMIC STUDIES. JOURNAL. Key Title: Journal of the Institute for Socioeconomic Studies. Text in English. 1976. q. reprints avail.
Related titles: Microfiche ed.: (from PMC, WSH); Microfilm ed.: (from PMC, WSH).
Indexed: A12, A13, A17, ABIn, BAS, BPIA, FutSurv, HRA, MCR, MEA&I, P48, P51, P53, P54, PAIS, PQC.
Published by: Institute for Socioeconomic Studies, Airport Rd, White Plains, NY 10604. TEL 914-428-7400. Ed. B A Rittersporn Jr. Circ: 17,500.

320.6 NZL ISSN 1178-3656
INSTITUTE OF POLICY STUDIES. WORKING PAPER. Text in English. 2007. irreg.
Supersedes (1989-1994): I P S Working Paper (1170-7984)
Media: Online - full text.
Published by: Victoria University of Wellington, Institute of Policy Studies, PO Box 600, Wellington, New Zealand. TEL 64-4-4635307, FAX 64-4-4637413, ips@vuw.ac.nz.

320 ARG ISSN 0074-0063
INSTITUTO DE CIENCIA POLITICA RAFAEL BIELSA. ANUARIO. Text in Spanish. 1968. a. ARS 75, USD 8.
Published by: Instituto de Ciencia Politica Rafael Bielsa, Facultad de Ciencia Politica y Relaciones Internacionales, Cordoba 2020, Rosario, Argentina. Ed. Alberto Dominguez.

320 PER ISSN 1022-0372
INSTITUTO DE ESTUDIOS PERUANOS. DOCUMENTOS DE TRABAJO. SERIE DOCUMENTOS DE POLITICA. Key Title: Serie Documentos de Politica. Variant title: Documentos de Trabajo. Serie Documentos de Politica. Text in Spanish. 1985. irreg. price varies. back issues avail. **Document type:** *Monographic series, Academic/Scholarly.* **Description:** Publishes research into the politics of Peru.
Related titles: ◆ Series of: Instituto de Estudios Peruanos. Documentos de Trabajo. ISSN 1022-0356.
Published by: (Instituto de Estudios Peruanos), I E P Ediciones (Subsidiary of: Instituto de Estudios Peruanos), Horacio Urteaga 694, Jesus Maria, Lima, 11, Peru. TEL 51-14-3326194, FAX 51-14-3326173, libreria@iep.org.pe, http://iep.perucultural.org.pe.

INSTITUTO DE ESTUDIOS PERUANOS. DOCUMENTOS DE TRABAJO. SERIE SOCIOLOGIA, POLITICA. *see* SOCIOLOGY

320 PER
INSTITUTO PERUANO DE POLEMOLOGIA. Text in Spanish. 1986. s-a. free.
Address: Apartado Postal 2284, Lima, 1, Peru. ip_polemologia@latinmail.com. Ed. Luis Callegari Botteri. Circ: 2,000.

306.2 NLD ISSN 1871-9767
INSTITUUT VOOR PUBLIEK EN POLITIEK. NIEUWSBRIEF. Text in Dutch. 2005. q. free (effective 2009).
Published by: Instituut voor Publiek en Politiek, Prinsengracht 911-915, Amsterdam, 1017 KD, Netherlands. TEL 31-20-5217600, FAX 31-20-6383118, info@publiek-politiek.nl, http://www.publiek-politiek.nl. Ed. Sandra Boersma.

320 BRA ISSN 1807-1260
D861
➤ **INTELLECTOR.** Text in Portuguese, Spanish. 2004. s-a. free (effective 2011). **Document type:** *Journal, Academic/Scholarly.* **Description:** Analyses important contemporary issues from a Brazilian and Latin American point of view.
Media: Online - full text.
Indexed: C01.
Published by: Centro de Estudos em Geopolitica e Relacoes Internacionais (C E N E G R I)/Centre for Studies on Geopolitics and Foreign Affairs, Rua Mexico 168, Grupo 807, Rio de Janeiro, 20031-143, Brazil. TEL 55-21-22102128, FAX 55-21-22109149, contato@cenegri.org, http://www.cenegri.org.

328 CHE ISSN 0579-8337
INTER-PARLIAMENTARY UNION. SERIES: REPORTS AND DOCUMENTS. Text in Multiple languages. 1965. irreg., latest vol.39, 2001. price varies. **Document type:** *Monographic series, Trade.* **Description:** Presents discussions of political, social and economic issues of immediate interest and relevance to Swiss society.
Published by: Inter-Parliamentary Union, 5, chemin du Pommier, Case postale 330, Geneva, 1218, Switzerland. TEL 41-22-7333141, FAX 41-22-9194160, postbox@mail.ipu.org, http://www.ipu.org.

328 CHE
INTER-PARLIAMENTARY UNION. SUMMARY RECORDS OF THE INTER-PARLIAMENTARY CONFERENCES. Text in English, French. 1897. s-a. CHF 30 (effective 2005). **Document type:** *Proceedings, Trade.* **Description:** Summarizes the Interparliamentary Union's two annual statutory conferences.
Formerly: Inter-Parliamentary Union. Conference Proceedings (0074-1051)
Published by: Inter-Parliamentary Union, 5, chemin du Pommier, Case postale 330, Geneva, 1218, Switzerland. TEL 41-22-9194150, FAX 41-22-9194160, postbox@mail.ipu.org, http://www.ipu.org. Circ: 800.

320 USA ISSN 0074-1078
INTER-UNIVERSITY CONSORTIUM FOR POLITICAL AND SOCIAL RESEARCH. ANNUAL REPORT. Text in English. 1963. a. free. **Document type:** *Corporate.* **Description:** Report of finances, data collections released, major activities, funding, member organizations, council, and staff of computerized social science data archives.
Related titles: Online - full text ed.
Published by: Inter-University Consortium for Political and Social Research, PO Box 1248, Ann Arbor, MI 48106. TEL 734-998-9900, FAX 734-998-9889, http://www.icpsr.umich.edu.

INTERAMERICAN JOURNAL OF EDUCATION FOR DEMOCRACY/REVISTA INTERAMERICANA DE EDUCACION PARA LA DEMOCRACIA. *see* EDUCATION

INTERESSE; soziale Information. *see* SOCIAL SERVICES AND WELFARE

INTERNATIONAL COUNTRY RISK GUIDE. *see* BUSINESS AND ECONOMICS—Economic Situation And Conditions

INTERNATIONAL COUNTRY RISK GUIDE ANNUAL. VOL. 1, THE AMERICAS. *see* BUSINESS AND ECONOMICS—Economic Situation And Conditions

INTERNATIONAL COUNTRY RISK GUIDE ANNUAL. VOL. 2, EUROPE (EUROPEAN UNION). *see* BUSINESS AND ECONOMICS—Economic Situation And Conditions

INTERNATIONAL COUNTRY RISK GUIDE ANNUAL. VOL. 3, EUROPE (NON-EUROPEAN UNION). *see* BUSINESS AND ECONOMICS—Economic Situation And Conditions

INTERNATIONAL COUNTRY RISK GUIDE ANNUAL. VOL. 4, THE MIDDLE EAST & NORTH AFRICA. *see* BUSINESS AND ECONOMICS—Economic Situation And Conditions

INTERNATIONAL COUNTRY RISK GUIDE ANNUAL. VOL. 5, SUB-SAHARAN AFRICA. *see* BUSINESS AND ECONOMICS—Economic Situation And Conditions

INTERNATIONAL COUNTRY RISK GUIDE ANNUAL. VOL. 6, ASIA & THE PACIFIC. *see* BUSINESS AND ECONOMICS—Economic Situation And Conditions

INTERNATIONAL COUNTRY RISK GUIDE ANNUAL. VOL. 7, RISK RATINGS & STATISTICS. *see* BUSINESS AND ECONOMICS—Economic Situation And Conditions

320.082 GBR ISSN 1461-6742
HQ1190

➤ **INTERNATIONAL FEMINIST JOURNAL OF POLITICS.** Abbreviated title: I F J P. Text in English. 1999. q. GBP 435 combined subscription in United Kingdom to institutions (print & online eds.); EUR 574, USD 722 combined subscription to institutions (print & online eds.) (effective 2012). adv. bk.rev. back issues avail.; reprint service avail. from PSC. **Document type:** *Journal, Academic/Scholarly.* **Description:** Examines the relationships between gender and different political processes and social relations, and analyzes a variety of political issues and debates involving women, race and class in national and cross-national contexts.

Related titles: Online - full text ed.: ISSN 1468-4470. GBP 391 in United Kingdom to institutions; EUR 517, USD 650 to institutions (effective 2012) (from IngentaConnect).

Indexed: A01, A03, A08, A22, B21, CA, CurCont, DIP, E01, E17, ESPM, FemPer, I13, IBR, IBSS, IBZ, P34, P42, PRA, PSA, S02, S03, SCOPUS, SSCI, SociolAb, T02, W07, W09.

—IE, Infotrieve, Ingenta. **CCC.**

Published by: Routledge (Subsidiary of: Taylor & Francis Group), 4 Park Square, Milton Park, Abingdon, Oxon OX14 4RN, United Kingdom. subscriptions@tandf.co.uk, http://www.routledge.com. Ed. Teresia Teaiwa. Adv. contact Linda Hann TEL 44-1344-779945. **Subscr. to:** Taylor & Francis Ltd., Journals Customer Service, Sheepen Pl, Colchester, Essex CO3 3LP, United Kingdom. TEL 44-20-70175544, FAX 44-20-70175198.

320 ESP ISSN 1698-4153

INTERNATIONAL JOURNAL OF APPLIED ECONOMETRICS AND QUANTITATIVE STUDIES. Text in English. 4/yr. EUR 120 combined subscription print & online eds. (effective 2008). **Document type:** *Journal, Academic/Scholarly.*

Related titles: Online - full text ed.: ISSN 1988-0081. free (effective 2011).

Indexed: EconLit, JEL.

—CCC.

Published by: Asociacion Euro-Americana de Estudios del Desarrollo Economico/Euro-American Association of Economic Development Studies, Ave. Burgo Nacionales s/n, Santiago de Compostela, 15704, Spain. TEL 34-981-563100, FAX 34-981-563676, eccgs@usc.es, http://www.usc.es/~economet/eaa.htm. Ed. Maria-Carmen Guisan.

320 340 DEU ISSN 1864-1385
HM1126

➤ **INTERNATIONAL JOURNAL OF CONFLICT AND VIOLENCE/ JOURNAL OF CONFLICT AND VIOLENCE RESEARCH.** Text in English, German. 1999. s-a. free (effective 2011). **Document type:** *Journal, Academic/Scholarly.* **Description:** Provides a forum for the exchange of ideas on political science, history, law, psychology, political philosophy, ethnology, sociology, and educational science.

Formerly (until 2007): Journal fuer Konflikt- und Gewaltforschung (1438-9444)

Media: Online - full content.

Indexed: CA, CJA, CurCont, DIP, I13, IBR, IBZ, P30, P42, P48, P54, PSA, S02, S03, SCOPUS, SSCI, SociolAb, T02, W07.

—CCC.

Published by: Universitaet Bielefeld, Institut fuer Interdisziplinaere Konflikt- und Gewaltforschung/University of Bielefeld, Institute for Interdisciplinary Research on Conflict and Violence, Universitaetsstr 25, Bielefeld, 33615, Germany. TEL 49-521-1063163, FAX 49-521-1066415, ikg@uni-bielefeld.de, http://www.uni-bielefeld.de/ikg/. Eds. Douglas S Massey, Steven F Messner, Wilhelm Heitmeyer TEL 49-521-1063164.

320 004 USA ISSN 1947-9131
JA26

▼ ➤ **INTERNATIONAL JOURNAL OF E-POLITICS.** Text in English. 2010. q. USD 210 to individuals; USD 595 to institutions; USD 275 combined subscription to individuals (print & online eds.); USD 860 combined subscription to institutions (print & online eds.) (effective 2012). **Document type:** *Journal, Academic/Scholarly.* **Description:** Covers topics in e-politics including all forms of electronic media in government, political parties, organizations and labor unions.

Related titles: Online - full text ed.: ISSN 1947-914X. 2010. USD 140 to individuals; USD 595 to institutions (effective 2012).

Indexed: PAIS, PSA.

Published by: I G I Global, 701 E Chocolate Ave, Ste 200, Hershey, PA 17033. TEL 717-533-8845 ext 100, FAX 717-533-8661, cust@igi-global.com, http://www.igi-pub.com. Ed. Celia Romm Livermore.

320 351 658 GBR ISSN 1742-4224

➤ **INTERNATIONAL JOURNAL OF ELECTRONIC DEMOCRACY.** Abbreviated title: I J E D. Text in English. 2008 (Nov.). 4/yr. EUR 494 to institutions (print or online ed.); EUR 672 combined subscription to institutions (print & online eds.) (effective 2012). back issues avail. **Document type:** *Journal, Academic/Scholarly.* **Description:** Designed to help policy makers, academics, researchers, and professionals working in the field of political management, public administration, political science, and information technology to disseminate information and to learn from each other's work.

Related titles: Online - full text ed.: ISSN 1742-4232 (from IngentaConnect).

Indexed: A26, E08.

—IE. **CCC.**

Published by: Inderscience Publishers, PO Box 735, Olney, Bucks MK46 5WB, United Kingdom. TEL 44-1234-240519, FAX 44-1234-240515, editorial@inderscience.com. Eds. Dr. Miltiadis Lytras, Dr. Patricia Ordonez de Pablos. **Subscr. to:** World Trade Centre Bldg, 29 Rte de Pre-Bois, Case Postale 856, Geneva 15 1215, Switzerland. subs@inderscience.com.

172.2 USA ISSN 1556-4444
JA79

➤ **INTERNATIONAL JOURNAL OF ETHICS.** Text in English. 2001. q. USD 340 to institutions (effective 2012). bk.rev. **Document type:** *Journal, Academic/Scholarly.* **Description:** Provides a forum for diverse interests and attitudes in all matters relating to politics and ethics, including their possible intersections.

Formerly (until 2004): International Journal of Politics and Ethics (1535-4776)

Related titles: Online - full text ed.: ISSN 1937-433X.

Indexed: A26, AmHI, CA, E08, G08, H07, I05, PhilInd, S09, T02.

Published by: (Center for International Politics and Ethics), Nova Science Publishers, Inc., 400 Oser Ave, Ste 1600, Hauppauge, NY 11788. TEL 631-231-7269, FAX 631-231-8175, main@novapublishers.com. Ed. Frank Columbus.

320 SVN ISSN 1855-3362

INTERNATIONAL JOURNAL OF EURO - MEDITERRANEAN STUDIES/ MEDNARODNA REVIJA ZA EVRO - MEDTERANSKE STUDIJE/ REVUE INTERNATIONALE D'ETUDES EURO - MEDITERRANEENNES. Text in Slovenian, English, French. 2008. q. **Document type:** *Journal, Academic/Scholarly.*

Related titles: Online - full text ed.: free (effective 2011).

Published by: Evro - Sredozemska Univerza / Emuni Univerza, Soncna Pot 20, Portoroz, 6320, Slovenia. TEL 386-59-250050, FAX 386-59-250054, http://www.emuni.si.

INTERNATIONAL JOURNAL OF GAME THEORY. *see* MATHEMATICS

320 USA ISSN 1941-2266

INTERNATIONAL JOURNAL OF GANDHI STUDIES. Text in English. 2008 (Dec.). a. **Document type:** *Journal, Academic/Scholarly.* **Description:** Committed to publishing scholarship on well-established topics in Gandhi Studies, to fostering new work in neglected areas, and to stimulating alternative perspectives on a wide range of issues.

Related titles: Online - full text ed.: ISSN 1941-2274.

Published by: James Madison University, Mahatma Gandhi Center for Global Nonviolence, MSC 2604, Cardinal House, 200 Cardinal Dr, Harrisonburg, VA 22807. TEL 540-568-6394, FAX 540-568-7251, GandhiCenter@jmu.edu. Ed. Sushil Mittal.

321.8 GBR ISSN 1753-240X
GE195

THE INTERNATIONAL JOURNAL OF INCLUSIVE DEMOCRACY. Text in English. 2000. q. free (effective 2011). **Document type:** *Journal, Academic/Scholarly.* **Description:** Provides an international forum for the new conception of inclusive democracy.

Formerly (until 2004): Democracy & Nature (Online) (1469-3720)

Media: Online - full text (from IngentaConnect).

Indexed: A39, AltPI, C27, C29, CA, D03, D04, E13, LeftInd, P42, PSA, R14, S14, S15, S18, T02.

—CCC.

Published by: Inclusive Democracy editors@inclusivedemocracy.org. Ed. Takis Fotopoulos.

INTERNATIONAL JOURNAL OF MEDIA AND CULTURAL POLITICS. *see* COMMUNICATIONS

320 TWN ISSN 1085-7494
JX1904.5 CODEN: IPSTF7

➤ **INTERNATIONAL JOURNAL OF PEACE STUDIES.** Text in English. 1996. s-a. adv. back issues avail. **Document type:** *Journal, Academic/Scholarly.* **Description:** Contains articles on conceptual ideas on aspects of world peace; examines the role of the UN in terms of security and development, disarmament, and non-offensive defense. Other issues include: sustainable development; basic human needs, an alternative world order; human rights; discourse on peace and social order; ecological protection; feminist interpretations of security; post-modernist critique of a nation-state system, and peace education.

Related titles: Online - full text ed.

Indexed: A26, CA, E08, G06, G07, G08, I05, P42, PAIS, PRA, PSA, S02, S03, S09, SCOPUS, SSA, SociolAb, T02.

—BLDSC (4542.449800), IE, Ingenta.

Published by: (World United Formosans for Independence, Formosa College), Grassroots Publishing Co., PO Box 26-447, Taipei, 106, Taiwan. TEL 886-2-27060962, FAX 886-2-27077965, ohio3106@ms8.hinet.net. Ed. Ho Won Jeong. R&P Cheng Fing Shih. Adv. contact Cheng Feng Shih. **Co-sponsor:** International Peace Research Association, Human Marginalization in the Global Political Economy Study Commission.

320 USA ISSN 0891-1916
JA1.A1

➤ **INTERNATIONAL JOURNAL OF POLITICAL ECONOMY;** a journal of translations. Abbreviated title: I J P E. Text in English. 19??. q. USD 1,134 combined subscription domestic to institutions (print & online eds.); USD 1,254 combined subscription foreign to institutions (print & online eds.) (effective 2012). adv. index. back issues avail.; reprint service avail. from PSC. **Document type:** *Journal, Academic/Scholarly.* **Description:** Publishes English translations of scholarly work from around the world on the themes of critical political economy: the conditions of economic growth; the role of finance; governmental intervention in the market economy; and theories of modernization and democratization. Each issue is devoted to a topic of basic theory or of empirical research.

Former titles (until 1987): International Journal of Politics (0012-8783); (until 1971): Eastern European Studies in Law and Government

Related titles: Online - full text ed.: ISSN 1558-0970. 2004 (Mar.). USD 1,025 to institutions (effective 2012).

Indexed: A12, A17, A20, A22, ABIn, B01, B06, B07, B08, B09, CA, E01, EconLit, HistAb, IBR, IBZ, MEA&I, P30, P34, P42, P48, P51, P53, P54, PAIS, PCI, PQC, RASB, S02, S03, SCOPUS, SSciA, T02.

—BLDSC (4542.470900), IE, Infotrieve, Ingenta. **CCC.**

Published by: M.E. Sharpe, Inc., 80 Business Park Dr, Armonk, NY 10504. TEL 914-273-1800, 800-541-6563, FAX 914-273-2106, custserv@mesharpe.com. Ed. Mario Seccareccia. Adv. contact Barbara Ladd TEL 914-273-1800.

➤ **INTERNATIONAL JOURNAL OF PRESS / POLITICS.** *see* JOURNALISM

320 GBR ISSN 0954-2892
HM261 CODEN: IJPOE2

➤ **INTERNATIONAL JOURNAL OF PUBLIC OPINION RESEARCH.** Text in English. 1989. q. GBP 270 in United Kingdom to institutions; EUR 403 in Europe to institutions; USD 525 in US & Canada to institutions; GBP 270 elsewhere to institutions; GBP 294 combined subscription in United Kingdom to institutions (print & online eds.); EUR 439 combined subscription in Europe to institutions (print & online eds.); USD 572 combined subscription in US & Canada to institutions (print & online eds.); GBP 294 combined subscription elsewhere to institutions (print & online eds.) (effective 2012). adv. bk.rev. illus. back issues avail.; reprint service avail. from PSC. **Document type:** *Journal, Academic/Scholarly.* **Description:** Provides a source of informed analysis and comment in the field of public opinion research. Covers matters of interest to both the professional and academic community.

Related titles: Online - full text ed.: ISSN 1471-6909. 2001. GBP 245 in United Kingdom to institutions; EUR 366 in Europe to institutions; USD 477 in US & Canada to institutions; GBP 245 elsewhere to institutions (effective 2012) (from IngentaConnect).

Indexed: A01, A02, A03, A08, A20, A22, A25, A26, ASCA, B01, B06, B07, B09, CA, CMM, CommAb, CurCont, E-psyche, E01, E08, FS&TA, G08, I05, I13, IBSS, MResA, P02, P03, P10, P25, P34, P42, P45, P46, P47, P48, P53, P54, PAIS, PCI, PQC, PSA, PsycInfo, PsycholAb, S02, S03, S08, S09, S11, SCOPUS, SOPODA, SSA, SSCI, SociolAb, T02, W07.

—BLDSC (4542.509100), IE, Infotrieve, Ingenta. **CCC.**

Published by: (World Association for Public Opinion Research USA), Oxford University Press, Great Clarendon St, Oxford, OX2 6DP, United Kingdom. TEL 44-1865-556767, FAX 44-1865-556646, enquiry@oup.co.uk, http://www.oxfordjournals.org. Eds. Michael W Traugott, Wolfgang Donsbach.

▼ ➤ **INTERNATIONAL JOURNAL OF SPORT POLICY.** *see* SPORTS AND GAMES

320 NLD ISSN 1875-0281
HD1286

INTERNATIONAL JOURNAL OF THE COMMONS. Text in English. 2007. irreg. free (effective 2011). **Document type:** *Journal, Academic/ Scholarly.*

Media: Online - full text.

Indexed: A39, C27, C29, CA, D03, D04, E13, G02, R14, S14, S15, S18, T02.

Published by: Igitur, Utrecht Publishing & Archiving Services, Postbus 80124, Utrecht, 3508 TC, Netherlands. TEL 31-30-2536635, FAX 31-30-2536959, info@igitur.uu.nl, http://www.igitur.uu.nl.

INTERNATIONAL PERSPECTIVES ON EUROPE. *see* SOCIOLOGY

320 CAN

INTERNATIONAL POLITICAL SCIENCE ASSOCIATION. WORLD CONGRESS. Text in English. 1951. triennial (Papers of XVIII World Congress, Quebec, 2000). price varies. abstr. back issues avail. **Document type:** *Proceedings, Academic/Scholarly.*

Formerly: International Political Science Association. World Conference. Proceedings (0074-7467)

Related titles: Microfiche ed.

Published by: Association Internationale de Science Politique - International Political Science Association (A I S P - I P S A), 1590 Ave Docteur-Penfield, Bureau 331, Montreal, PQ H3G 1C5, Canada. TEL 514-848-8717, FAX 514-848-4095, info@ipsa.org, http://www.ipsa.org.

INTERNATIONAL POLITICAL SOCIOLOGY. *see* SOCIOLOGY

320.6 GBR ISSN 1748-5207

➤ **INTERNATIONAL PUBLIC POLICY REVIEW.** Text in English. 2005. s-a. free (effective 2009). **Document type:** *Journal, Academic/ Scholarly.* **Description:** Aims to serve as a tool for students, academics and policymakers by providing a look into the ideas, actors, and mechanisms that shape our world.

Media: Online - full content.

Published by: University of London, School of Public Policy, The Rubin Bldg, 29/30 Tavistock Sq, London, WC1H 9QU, United Kingdom. TEL 44-20-76794999, FAX 44-20-76794969, spp@ucl.ac.uk, http://www.ucl.ac.uk/spp/.

320.6 GBR ISSN 1051-4694
H96

INTERNATIONAL REVIEW OF COMPARATIVE PUBLIC POLICY. Text in English. 1989. irreg., latest vol.13, 2002. price varies. back issues avail. **Document type:** *Monographic series, Academic/Scholarly.* **Description:** Dedicated to publishing original, scholarly articles that systematically analyze international public policy issues.

—CCC.

P

Published by: Emerald Group Publishing Ltd., Howard House, Wagon Ln, Bingley, W Yorks BD16 1WA, United Kingdom. TEL 44-1274-777700, FAX 44-1274-785201, emerald@emeraldinsight.com. Ed. S G Witter. **Dist. by:** Turpin Distribution Services Ltd., Pegasus Dr, Stratton Business Park, Biggleswade, Bedfordshire SG18 8QB, United Kingdom. TEL 44-1767-604951, FAX 44-1767-601640, custserv@turpin-distribution.com, http://www.turpin-distribution.com/.

320.531 GBR ISSN 0020-8736
HX3
INTERNATIONAL SOCIALISM; a quarterly journal of Socialist theory. Text in English. 1960. q. GBP 22 domestic to individuals; GBP 24 in Europe to individuals; GBP 26 elsewhere to individuals; GBP 125 to institutions (effective 2010). back issues avail. **Document type:** *Journal, Academic/Scholarly.* **Description:** Contains articles and reviews on international socialism.
Related titles: Online - full text ed.: ISSN 1754-4653. free (effective 2011).
Indexed: A39, AltPI, C27, C29, CA, D03, D04, E13, IBR, IBZ, P42, R14, S14, S15, S18, T02.
—BLDSC (4549.525000), IE.
Published by: Socialist Workers Party (Britain), PO Box 42184, London, SW8 2WD, United Kingdom. TEL 44-20-78191177, http://www.swp.org.uk/. Ed. Alex Callinicos.

320.531 USA ISSN 1097-315X
HX1
INTERNATIONAL SOCIALIST REVIEW. Text in English. 1997. bi-m. USD 29 domestic to individuals; USD 35 in Canada & Mexico to individuals; USD 60 domestic to institutions; USD 120 foreign to institutions; USD 7 per issue domestic; USD 12 per issue foreign (effective 2010). **Document type:** *Journal, Academic/Scholarly.* **Description:** Provides information about revolutionary Marxism.
Indexed: AltPI.
Published by: International Socialist Organization, PO Box 16085, Chicago, IL 60616. TEL 773-583-5069, FAX 773-583-6144, contact@internationalsocialist.org, http://www.internationalsocialist.org. Ed. Ahmed Shawki. **Co-publisher:** Center for Economic Research and Social Chang.

320 DEU ISSN 0934-7461
INTERNATIONAL STUDIES IN POLITICAL SOCIALIZATION AND POLITICAL EDUCATION. Text in English. 1988. irreg., latest vol.9, 2000. price varies. **Document type:** *Monographic series, Academic/Scholarly.*
Published by: Galda und Leuchter GmbH, Franz-Schubert-Str 61, Glienicke, 16548, Germany. TEL 49-33056-88090, FAX 49-33056-80157, contact@galda.com, http://www.galda.com.

INTERNATIONAL YEAR BOOK AND STATESMEN'S WHO'S WHO. *see* BIOGRAPHY

320 DEU ISSN 0933-9884
INTERNATIONALE DIREKTINVESTIONEN. Text in German. 1975. irreg. price varies. **Document type:** *Monographic series, Academic/Scholarly.*
Related titles: ◆ Series of: H W W A - Report. ISSN 0179-2253.
Published by: H W W A - Hamburgisches Welt-Wirtschafts-Archiv, Neuer Jungfernstieg 21, Hamburg, 20347, Germany. TEL 49-40-428340, FAX 49-40-42834451, hwwa@hwwa.de, http://www.hwwa.de.

INTERNATIONALE FORSCHUNGSSTELLE DEMOKRATISCHE BEWEGUNGEN IN MITTELEUROPA VON 1770-1850. SCHRIFTENREIHE. *see* HISTORY—History Of Europe

320.531 SWE ISSN 0345-5467
INTERNATIONALEN. Text in Swedish. 1971. w. SEK 490 (effective 2002).
Formerly (until 1974): Mullvaden
Published by: Socialistiska Partiet, PO Box 6087, Stockholm, 10232, Sweden. TEL 46-8-31-08-58, FAX 46-8-441-45-75.

320.531 USA
INTERNATIONALISM. Text in English. q. **Document type:** *Newsletter, Trade.*
Indexed: LeftInd.
Published by: International Communist Current, 320 7th Ave, Ste 211, Brooklyn, NY 11215. http://en.internationalism.org. Circ: 5,000.

322.42 SWE ISSN 0283-2372
INTERNATIONELL REVOLUTION. Text in Swedish. 1980. bi-m. SEK 100 domestic; EUR 13 in Europe; EUR 14 elsewhere (effective 2000). bk.rev. **Document type:** *Newspaper, Consumer.*
Address: Fack 21106, Stockholm, 10031, Sweden. Ed. Anders Person.

320 USA
JA26
➤ **INTERPRETATION (FLUSHING, ONLINE)**; a journal of political philosophy. Text in English. 1970. 3/yr. free (effective 2011). bk.rev. back issues avail. **Document type:** *Journal, Academic/Scholarly.* **Description:** Contains articles which are interpretations of literary works, theological works, and writings on jurisprudence with an important bearing on political philosophy.
Formerly (until 2010): Interpretation (Print) (0020-9635)
Media: Online - full text.
Indexed: A01, A02, A03, A08, A20, A22, ArtHuCI, CA, CERDIC, CurCont, FR, GSS&RPL, IBR, IBZ, IPB, MEA&I, MLA, MLA-IB, OTA, P42, PSA, PhilInd, RASB, RI-1, SCOPUS, T02, W07.
—BLDSC (4557.347200), IE, Infotrieve, Ingenta, INIST.
Published by: Interpretation, Inc., Queens College, King Hall, Room 101, Flushing, NY 11367. TEL 718-997-5542, FAX 718-997-5565. Ed. Hilail Gildin.

320 FRA ISSN 0715-3570
INTERVENTIONS ECONOMIQUES/PAPERS IN POLITICAL ECONOMY. Variant title: Interventions Economiques pour une Alternative Sociale. Text in English, French. 197?. 3/yr. **Document type:** *Journal, Academic/Scholarly.*
Formerly (until 1981): Interventions Critiques en Economie Politique (0715-3589)
Related titles: Online - full text ed.: ISSN 1710-7377. free (effective 2011).
Published by: Revues.org, 3 Place Victor Hugo, Case no 86, Marseille, 13331, France. TEL 33-4-13550355, FAX 33-4-13550341, http://www.revues.org.

INTERVIR; online journal of education, technology and politics. *see* EDUCATION

320.532 CUB ISSN 0864-1110
INVASOR. Text in Spanish. 1979. w. back issues avail.
Related titles: Online - full text ed.: Invasor Digital. ISSN 1605-9042. 2000.
Published by: Partido Comunista de Cuba, Comite Provincial Ciego de Avila, Ave. de los Deportes, s-n, Ciego de Alva, Cuba. invasor@esica.co.cu, http://www.invasor.islagrande.cu/. Ed. Armando Santana Martinez.

320 AUS ISSN 1832-2794
INVESTIGATE. Text in English. 2000. m. **Document type:** *Magazine, Consumer.*
Indexed: A26, G06, G07, G08, I05.
Published by: Investigate Publishing Pty. Ltd., PO Box 602, Bondi Junction, Sydney, NSW 1355, Australia.

IOWA LEGISLATIVE NEWS SERVICE BULLETIN. *see* PUBLIC ADMINISTRATION

320 330.9 USA ISSN 1079-8846
CODEN: TBNAAB
THE IRAN BRIEF; policy, trade & strategic affairs. Text in English. 1994. m. USD 250, USD 1,100 to individuals (effective 2002). **Description:** An investigative tool for business executives, government, and the media.
Related titles: Online - full text ed.
—CIS.
Published by: The Middle East Data Project, Inc., 7831 Woodmont Ave, Ste 395, Bethesda, MD 20814. TEL 301-946-2918, FAX 301-942-5341, medp@erols.com.

THE IRAN BUSINESS FORECAST REPORT. *see* BUSINESS AND ECONOMICS—Economic Situation And Conditions

320 LKA
IRANAMA. Text in Singhalese. 1964. w.
Address: 5 Gunasena Mawatha, Colombo, 12, Sri Lanka. TEL 1-23864.

320.9 GBR
IRELAND AGENDA. Text in English. 1980. 3/yr. GBP 5 domestic; GBP 10 foreign. adv. bk.rev. illus. **Document type:** *Newsletter.* **Description:** News and opinion within British labor movement on Ireland.
Formerly: Labour and Ireland (0260-6615)
Published by: Labour Committee on Ireland, c/o L.C.I. BM, Box 5355, London, WC1N 3XX, United Kingdom. TEL 44-181-525-1653, FAX 44-181-525-1654, 100544.3665@compuserve.com. Ed. Kate Foley. Circ: 1,000.

IRISH JOURNAL OF LAW AND POLITICS. *see* LAW

320 IRL
IRISH POLITICAL REVIEW - NORTHERN STAR. Text in English. 1996. m. EUR 25 (effective 2005). adv. bk.rev. back issues avail. **Document type:** *Magazine, Consumer.* **Description:** Covers current affairs and political commentary and analysis in Ireland, Northern Ireland and the rest of the world.
Formed by the merger of (1986-1996): Irish Political Review (0790-7672); (1988-1996): Northern Star (0954-5891)
Related titles: Online - full text ed.: EUR 15 (effective 2005).
Indexed: LeftInd.
Published by: Reform Society, 2 Corrig Rd., Dalkey, Co. Dublin, Ireland. Circ: 1,000.

320 GBR ISSN 0790-7184
JN1400
➤ **IRISH POLITICAL STUDIES.** Abbreviated title: I P S. Text and summaries in English. 1986. q. GBP 238 combined subscription in United Kingdom to institutions (print & online eds.); EUR 312, USD 393 combined subscription to institutions (print & online eds.) (effective 2012). adv. bk.rev. Index. back issues avail.; reprint service avail. from PSC. **Document type:** *Journal, Academic/Scholarly.* **Description:** Contains articles and information on or related to, Irish politics, including extensive data section and bibliography.
Related titles: Online - full text ed.: ISSN 1743-9078. GBP 214 in United Kingdom to institutions; EUR 281, USD 354 to institutions (effective 2012) (from IngentaConnect).
Indexed: A01, A22, BibInd, CA, CurCont, E01, ESPM, HistAb, I13, IBSS, P34, P42, PSA, RiskAb, SCOPUS, SSCI, T02, W07.
—IE, Ingenta. **CCC.**
Published by: (Political Studies Association of Ireland IRL), Routledge (Subsidiary of: Taylor & Francis Group), 4 Park Sq, Milton Park, Abingdon, Oxon OX14 4RN, United Kingdom. TEL 44-20-70176000, FAX 44-20-70176336, subscriptions@tandf.co.uk, http://www.routledge.com. Adv. contact Linda Hann TEL 44-1344-779945. Circ: 500. **Subscr. to:** Taylor & Francis Ltd., Journals Customer Service, Sheepen Pl, Colchester, Essex CO3 3LP, United Kingdom. TEL 44-20-70175544, FAX 44-20-70175198.

➤ **THE IRISH REVIEW.** *see* ETHNIC INTERESTS

➤ **IRISH VOICE.** *see* ETHNIC INTERESTS

320 USA ISSN 1932-4952
IRREVERENT MAGAZINE. Text in English. 1993. irreg. **Document type:** *Magazine, Consumer.* **Description:** A political humor and satire magazine.
Media: Online - full text.
Published by: Irreverent Publishing, LLC http://www.irrmag.com.

320.557 USA ISSN 1553-2070
HV6431
ISLAMIC EXTREMISM NEWSWATCH. Abbreviated title: I E N. Text in English. irreg. **Document type:** *Newsletter.*
Published by: Jewish Institute for National Security Affairs, 1779 Massachusetts Ave NW, Ste 515, Washington, DC 20036. TEL 202-667-3900, FAX 202-667-0601, info@jinsa.org, http://www.jinsa.org. Ed. Zohar Neuman.

320 910.02 CAN ISSN 1715-2593
GB471
➤ **ISLAND STUDIES JOURNAL.** Text in English. 2006. 2/yr. free (effective 2011). back issues avail. **Document type:** *Journal, Academic/Scholarly.* **Description:** Publishes original scholarly articles, review essays and book reviews that focus on the critical study of islands and island affairs.
Media: Online - full text.
Indexed: A01, A39, C27, C29, CA, D03, D04, E13, R14, S13, S14, S15, S16, S18, SociolAb, T02.
—CCC.
Published by: University of Prince Edward Island, Institute of Island Studies, 550 University Ave, Charlottetown, PE C1A 4P3, Canada. TEL 902-566-0386, FAX 902-566-0756, iis@upei.ca, http://www.upei.ca/~iis/about.htm. Ed., Pub., R&P Godfrey Baldacchino.

320 DNK ISSN 0021-194X
ISRAEL. Text in Danish. 1948. 3/yr. DKK 100 (effective 2009). adv. bk.rev. illus. **Document type:** *Magazine, Consumer.* **Description:** Covers events in Israel and the Middle East as well as events of interest to Jews elsewhere.
Related titles: ◆ Includes: Magbit Nyt. ISSN 1397-4505; ◆ Supplement(s): Magbit Nyt. ISSN 1397-4505.
Published by: (Det Mosaiske Trossamfund. Det Joediske Samfund i Danmark/Jewish Denmark. The Jewish Community in Denmark), Dansk Zionist Forbund, Ny Kongensgade 6, Copenhagen K, 1472, Denmark. TEL 45-33-930093, office@zionist.dk. Ed. Otto Ruehl. Adv. contact Erik Overgaard. **Co-sponsor:** Danish-Israeli Society.

ISRAEL HORIZONS. *see* POLITICAL SCIENCE—International Relations

320 ISR ISSN 0334-0309
ISRAEL. KNESSET. DIVREI HA-KNESSET. Text in Hebrew. 1948. 3/w. **Document type:** *Government.*
Formerly (until 1949): Protokol Ha-Diyyunim shel Yeshivot Mo'etset Ha-M'dina Ha-Z'manit
Related titles: Online - full text ed.
Published by: Knesset, Jerusalem, Israel. Ed. Gideon Greif.

ISRAEL STUDIES. *see* SOCIAL SCIENCES: COMPREHENSIVE WORKS

320 401 USA ISSN 1941-7209
P302.77
➤ **ISSUES IN POLITICAL DISCOURSE ANALYSIS.** Text in English. 2006. q. USD 345 to institutions; USD 517 combined subscription to institutions (print & online eds.) (effective 2012). **Document type:** *Journal, Academic/Scholarly.* **Description:** Focuses on the analysis of language (possibly in conjunction with other semiotic systems) in course the of our lives as citizens of established politics of various scopes.
Related titles: Online - full text ed.: USD 345 to institutions (effective 2012).
Published by: Nova Science Publishers, Inc., 400 Oser Ave, Ste 1600, Hauppauge, NY 11788. TEL 631-231-7269, FAX 631-231-8175, main@novapublishers.com. Ed. Samuel Obeng.

320 330 USA
➤ **ISSUES IN POLITICAL ECONOMY**; undergraduate student research in Economics. Text in English. 19??. a. back issues avail. **Document type:** *Journal, Academic/Scholarly.*
Media: Online - full text.
Address: c/o Steven Greenlaw, Professor and Chair of Economics, Mary Washington College, Fredericksburg, VA 22401 . http://www.elon.edu/ipe/. Ed. Andrew Godburn.

320.5 ITA ISSN 1128-9279
ISTITUTO GRAMSCI EMILIA-ROMAGNA. ANNALI. Text in Italian. 1992. a. **Document type:** *Journal, Academic/Scholarly.*
Related titles: Online - full text ed.: ISSN 1828-2423. 2000.
Published by: (Fondazione Istituto Gramsci Emilia-Romagna), Casa Editrice C L U E B, Via Marsala 31, Bologna, BO 40126, Italy. TEL 39-051-220736, FAX 39-051-237758, clueb@clueb.com, http://www.clueb.eu/home.html.

320.6 CAN ISSN 1492-0611
JL86 P64I68
ISUMA; Canadian journal of policy research. Text in Multiple languages. 2000. s-a. **Document type:** *Journal.*
Indexed: C03, CBCARef, PQC.
—CCC.
Published by: (Universite de Montreal, Secretariat de la Recherche sur les Politiques), Presses de l'Universite de Montreal, 3535, chemin Queen-Mary, Bureau 206, Montreal, PQ H3V 1H8, Canada. TEL 514-343-6933, FAX 514-343-2232, pum@umontreal.ca, http://www.pum.umontreal.ca.

ITALIA CONTEMPORANEA. *see* HISTORY—History Of Europe

ITALIAN POLITICS. *see* BUSINESS AND ECONOMICS

320 ISR ISSN 0579-2770
JQ1825.P325
IYYUNIM B'VIQORET HA-MEDINA. Text in Hebrew. 1960. a., latest no.61, 2007. bk.rev. **Document type:** *Government.*
Published by: State Comptroller and Ombudsman, P O Box 1081, Jerusalem, 91010, Israel. TEL 972-2-666-5000, FAX 972-2-666-5204, http://www.mevaker.gov.il/serve/default.asp. Ed. B Geist. Circ: 1,000.

320.532 ESP ISSN 1699-1818
IZAR GORRI. Text in Multiple languages. 2001. m. **Document type:** *Newsletter, Consumer.*
Related titles: Online - full text ed.: ISSN 1699-2784. 2001.
Published by: Juventudes Comunistas de Euskadi, C Ronda, 24 1o B, Bilbao, Bizkaia 41003, Spain. TEL 34-94-4161833, http://www.gazkom.org/.

321 CHL ISSN 0718-5049
IZQUIERDAS. Text in Spanish. 2007. s-a. **Document type:** *Journal, Academic/Scholarly.*
Published by: Universidad de Santiago de Chile, Instituto de Estudios Avanzados, Roman Diaz 89, Providencia, Santiago, Chile. TEL 56-2-7181360, FAX 56-2-7181358, revistaidea@usach.cl, http://web.usach.cl/revistaidea/index.html. Ed. Manuel Loyola.

IZVESTIYA NA DARZHAVNITE ARKHIVI/JOURNAL OF THE STATE ARCHIVES. *see* HISTORY—History Of Europe

320 ZAF
IZWI LABASEBENZI SERIES. Text in English. irreg. **Document type:** *Monographic series.*
Published by: Skotaville Publishers, PO Box 32483, Braamfontein, Johannesburg 2017, South Africa. **Dist. outside Africa by:** African Books Collective Ltd., The Jam Factory, 27 Park End St, Oxford, Oxon OX1 1HU, United Kingdom. TEL 0865-726686, FAX 0865-793298.

320 337.142 GBR
J C M S ANNUAL REVIEW OF THE EUROPEAN UNION IN ..; annual review. Text in English. 1992. a. GBP 17.99, EUR 21.60 per issue (effective 2009). back issues avail. **Document type:** *Monographic series, Academic/Scholarly.* **Description:** Covers the key developments in the European Union, its member states and acceding and/or applicant countries. Contains key analytical articles on political, economic and legal issues in the EU, together with a keynote articles.

Former titles (until 2005): The European Union (1747-5244); (until 1993): European Community: Annual Review of Activities (1351-9131)
Related titles: ◆ Supplement to: Journal of Common Market Studies. ISSN 0021-9886.
Published by: (University Association for Contemporary European Studies (U A C E S)), Wiley-Blackwell Publishing Ltd. (Subsidiary of: John Wiley & Sons, Inc.), 9600 Garsington Rd, Oxford, OX4 2DQ, United Kingdom. TEL 44-1865-776868, FAX 44-1865-714591, customerservices@blackwellpublishing.com, http://www.wiley.com/.

320 DEU ISSN 0721-5436
HC241.2
JAHRBUCH DER EUROPAEISCHEN INTEGRATION. Text in German. 1981. a. EUR 49 (effective 2009). **Document type:** *Journal, Academic/Scholarly.*
Indexed: DIP, IBR, IBZ, PRA.
Published by: Institut fuer Europaeische Politik e.V., Bundesallee 23, Berlin, 10717, Germany. TEL 49-30-8891340, FAX 49-30-88913499, info@iep-berlin.de.

JAHRBUCH DES OESTERREICHISCHEN PARLAMENTS; Daten - Fakten - Analysen. *see* PUBLIC ADMINISTRATION

320 900 DEU ISSN 2191-2289
▼ **JAHRBUCH FUER POLITIK UND GESCHICHTE.** Text in German. 2010. a. EUR 48 (effective 2012). **Document type:** *Journal, Academic/Scholarly.*
Published by: Franz Steiner Verlag GmbH, Birkenwaldstr 44, Stuttgart, 70191, Germany. TEL 49-711-25820, FAX 49-711-2582290, service@steiner-verlag.de. Eds. Claudia Froehlich, Harald Schmid, Horst-Alfred Heinrich.

JAM RAG. *see* MUSIC

323.1 CAN ISSN 0838-8814
JAMES BAY AND NORTHERN QUEBEC AGREEMENT. ANNUAL REPORT. Text in Multiple languages. 1985. a.
Formerly (until 1986): James Bay and Northern Quebec Agreement, Northeastern Quebec Agreement, "Crest-Inuit-Naskapis". Anuual Reports (0838-8806)
Published by: Indian and Northern Affairs Canada/Affaires Indiennes et du Nord Canada, Terrasses de la Chaudiere, 10 Wellington St, N Tower, Rm 1210, Gatineau, PQ K1A 0H4, Canada. TEL 800-567-9604, infopubs@ainc-inac.gc.ca, http://www.ainc-inac.gc.ca.

320 LKA
JANAKAVI. Text in Singhalese. fortn.
Address: 47 Jayantha Weerasekera Mawatha, Colombo, 10, Sri Lanka. Ed. Karunaratne Amerasinghe.

320 GBR ISSN 0969-4234
DS35.3
JANE'S ISLAMIC AFFAIRS ANALYST. Text in English. 10/yr. GBP 310 (effective 2010). illus. **Document type:** *Newsletter, Trade.* **Description:** Reports on political, economic, and strategic developments throughout the Islamic world.
Related titles: CD-ROM ed.: EUR 820 (effective 2010); Online - full text ed.: EUR 1,145 (effective 2010).
Indexed: M10.
—CCC.
Published by: (Intelligence International Ltd.), I H S Jane's (Subsidiary of: I H S), Sentinel House, 163 Brighton Rd, Coulsdon, Surrey CR5 2YH, United Kingdom. TEL 44-20-87003700, FAX 44-20-87003751, info@janes.co.uk, http://www.janes.com. Ed. Alex Vatanka. **Dist. by:** 1340 Braddock Pl, Ste 300, Alexandria, VA 22314-1651. TEL 703-683-3700, 800-824-0768, FAX 703-836-0297, 800-836-0297, info@janes.com; Jane's Information Group Australia, PO Box 3502, Rozelle, NSW 2039, Australia. TEL 61-2-8587-7900, FAX 61-2-8587-7901, info@janes.thomson.com.au; Jane's Information Group Asia, 60 Albert St, #15-01 Albert Complex, Singapore 189969, Singapore. TEL 65-331-6280, FAX 65-336-9921, info@janes.com.sg.

JAPAN. *see* ASIAN STUDIES

JAPAN JOURNAL (ENGLISH EDITION). *see* BUSINESS AND ECONOMICS—International Development And Assistance

320 330 USA
JAPAN POLICY AND POLITICS. Text in English. w. **Document type:** *Journal, Trade.*
Media: Online - full content.
Published by: Kyodo News International, Inc., 50 Rockefeller Plaza, Ste 803, New York, NY 10020. TEL 212-397-3723, FAX 212-397-3721, kni@kyodonews.com, http://www.kyodonews.com/.

320.9 USA ISSN 1051-1776
JAPAN POLITICAL RESEARCH; an annual review. Text in English. 1969. a. USD 7; USD 8 foreign (effective 2000). bk.rev. bibl. back issues avail. **Document type:** *Newsletter.*
Formerly (until 1990): Newsletter of Research on Japanese Politics (0160-1164)
Published by: Brigham Young University, Political Science Department, 730 SWKT, Provo, UT 84602. TEL 801-378-5133, FAX 801-378-5730. Ed. Ray Christensen. Circ: 200.

JAPAN SPOTLIGHT: ECONOMY, CULTURE & HISTORY. *see* BUSINESS AND ECONOMICS

320 GBR ISSN 1468-1099
JA8
JAPANESE JOURNAL OF POLITICAL SCIENCE. Text in English. 2000. 3/yr. GBP 155, USD 274 to institutions; GBP 178, USD 295 combined subscription to institutions (print & online eds.) (effective 2012). adv. bk.rev. back issues avail.; reprint service avail. from PSC. **Document type:** *Journal, Academic/Scholarly.* **Description:** Features articles that have a conceptual thrust, including political theory, comparative politics, political behavior, political institutions, public policy, and international relations.
Related titles: Online - full text ed.: ISSN 1474-0060. GBP 150, USD 248 to institutions (effective 2012).
Indexed: A22, CA, E01, ESPM, I13, IBSS, P10, P27, P42, P45, P48, P54, PQC, PSA, RiskAb, SCOPUS, SSCI, T02, W07.
—BLDSC (4658.115000), IE, Infotrieve. **CCC.**
Published by: Cambridge University Press, The Edinburgh Bldg, Shaftesbury Rd, Cambridge, CB2 8RU, United Kingdom. TEL 44-1223-312393, FAX 44-1223-315052, journals@cambridge.org, http://www.cambridge.org/uk. Eds. Ikuo Kabashima, Junko Kato. **Subscr. to:** Cambridge University Press, 32 Ave of the Americas, New York, NY 10013. TEL 212-337-5000, FAX 212-691-3239, journals_subscriptions@cup.org.

JAPANESE STUDIES. *see* SOCIOLOGY

JEBAT; Malaysian journal of history, politics and strategic studies. *see* HISTORY—History Of Asia

320 DEU ISSN 0949-3247
JEDERMENSCH; Zeitung fuer soziale Dreigliederung, Umweltfragen, neue Lebensformen. Text in German. 1958. q. EUR 13; EUR 2.50 newsstand/cover (effective 2006).
Former titles: Jedefrau und Jedermann; Jedermann
Published by: Jedermensch Verlag, Dorfstr 25, Wasserburg, 88142, Germany. TEL 49-8382-89056. Ed. Dieter Koschek. Circ: 500.

320 FRA ISSN 2105-0988
▼ **JEUNE REPUBLIQUE.** Text in French. 2009. 3/yr. **Document type:** *Consumer.*
Media: Online - full text.
Address: 92 Rue de Rennes, Paris, 75006, France. contact@jeunerepublique.fr, http://jeunerepublique.fr/wp.

JEWISH CURRENTS. *see* ETHNIC INTERESTS

320 ISR ISSN 0792-335X
DS140 CODEN: JPRVEI
JEWISH POLITICAL STUDIES REVIEW. Text in English. 1989. 2/yr. USD 26 to individuals; USD 40 to institutions; USD 20 to students (effective 2009). **Document type:** *Journal, Academic/Scholarly.* **Description:** Studies Jewish political institutions and behavior, Jewish political thought and Jewish public affairs.
Related titles: Online - full text ed.
Indexed: CA, I02, I14, IJP, J01, M10, P02, P10, P27, P42, P45, P48, P53, P54, PAIS, PCI, PQC, PSA, PerIslam, S02, S03, S11, SCOPUS, SociolAb, T02.
—BLDSC (4668.367300), IE.
Published by: (Jerusalem Center for Public Affairs/Ha-Merkaz Ha-Yerushalmi Le'inyene Tsibbur Umedina), Jerusalem Center for Public Affairs, Institute for Global Jewish Affairs/Ha-Makhon L'Nos'im Y'hudiyyim K'lal-'Olamiyyim (Subsidiary of: Jerusalem Center for Public Affairs/Ha-Merkaz Ha-Yerushalmi Le'inyene Tsibbur Umedina), Beit Milken, 13 Tel Hai St, Jerusalem, 92107, Israel. TEL 972-2-5619281, FAX 972-2-5619112, jcpa@netvision.net.il, http://www.jcpa.org/JCPA/indexph.asp.

JEWISH PRESS (BROOKLYN). *see* RELIGIONS AND THEOLOGY—Judaic

322.1 USA ISSN 0047-200X
JEWISH RADICAL. Text in English. 1969. 3/yr. USD 5 to individuals; USD 10 to institutions.
Related titles: Microfilm ed.: (from AJP).
Published by: Radical Jewish Union, 300 Eshleman Hall, University of Calif, Berkeley, CA 94720. TEL 415-642-6000. Circ: 6,000.

JIANGHUAI - WENZHAI. *see* PUBLIC ADMINISTRATION

320.532 CHN ISSN 1673-3347
JIEFANGJUN LILUN XUEXI. Text in Chinese. 2001. m. **Document type:** *Government.*
Formerly (until 2006): Deng Xiaoping Lilun Xuexi yu Yanjiu (1672-1772)
Published by: Guofang Daxue Zhongguo Tese Shehui Zhuyi Liluan Tixi Yanjiu Zhongxin, 3, Hongshankou Jia, Beijing, 100091, China. TEL 86-10-66769565.

JIHOCESKY SBORNIK HISTORICKY. *see* HISTORY—History Of Europe

320.6 USA ISSN 1946-9519
JOHN F KENNEDY SCHOOL OF GOVERNMENT. IMPACT. Text in English. 2008. q. **Document type:** *Newsletter, Academic/Scholarly.* **Description:** Aims to bring Harvard Kennedy School's groundbreaking research to a non-academic audience of decision makers and practitioners.
Published by: John F Kennedy School of Government, Office of Communications and Public Affairs, 124 Mt Auburn St, Ste 2110, Cambridge, MA 02138. TEL 617-495-1115, FAX 617-495-5424, http://www.hks.harvard.edu/news-events/contact. Ed. Robert O'Neill.

320 USA ISSN 1933-687X
JOHN F. KENNEDY SCHOOL OF GOVERNMENT. RESEARCH REPORT. Text in English. 19??. irreg. **Document type:** *Monographic series, Academic/Scholarly.* **Description:** Provides updated Harvard Kennedy School faculty publication citations, including books, edited volumes, academic journal articles, magazine and newspaper articles, op-eds, public testimony, research reports and working papers.
Former titles (until 1997): John F. Kennedy School of Government. Faculty Research Abstracts (1066-0410); (until 1991): John F. Kennedy School of Government. Research Report (1041-6315); (until 1979): John F. Kennedy School of Government. Research
Published by: Harvard University, John F. Kennedy School of Government, 79 John F Kennedy St, PO Box 142, Cambridge, MA 02138. TEL 617-496-0668, FAX 617-496-8753, http://www.hks.harvard.edu/.

JOHNS HOPKINS UNIVERSITY STUDIES IN HISTORICAL AND POLITICAL SCIENCE. *see* HISTORY

320 ARG ISSN 1852-7078
▼ **JORNADAS DE HISTORIA DE LAS IZQUIERDAS.** Text in Spanish. 2009. biennial. **Document type:** *Monographic series.*
Media: Online - full text.
Published by: Centro de Investigacion y Documentacion de la Cultura de Izquierdas en la Argentina, Fray Luis Beltran 125, Buenos Aires, 1406, Argentina. TEL 54-11-46318893, informes@cedinci.org, http://www.cendici.org/.

320 AUS
JOURNAL FOR STUDENTS OF V C E POLITICAL STUDIES. Text in English. 1973. irreg. **Document type:** *Journal, Academic/Scholarly.*
Former titles (until 1995): V C E Political Studies Papers; (until 1994): Journal for Students of V C E Political and International Studies; (until 1991): Journal for Students of Year 12 Politics; (until 1987): Journal for Students of H S C Politics; (until 1983): Journal of H S C Politics; (until 1976): Journal of Social Studies (0311-4058)
Published by: Social Education Victoria Inc., 150 Palmerston St, Carlton, VIC 3053, Australia. TEL 61-3-93494957, FAX 61-3-93492050, admin@sev.asn.au, http://www.sev.asn.au.

320.53 USA ISSN 1930-1189
HN49.R33
JOURNAL FOR THE STUDY OF RADICALISM. Text in English. 2006. s-a. USD 42 (effective 2011). adv. bk.rev. reprint service avail. from PSC. **Document type:** *Journal, Academic/Scholarly.* **Description:** Explores the meanings and influences of radical social movements within historical and cultural contexts.
Related titles: Online - full text ed.: ISSN 1930-1197.
Indexed: A22, APW, AltPI, AmH&L, AmHI, CA, E01, H07, HistAb, LeftInd, P45, S02, S03, SSAI, SSAb, SSI, SociolAb, T02, W03, W05.
—BLDSC (5066.927570), IE. **CCC.**
Published by: Michigan State University Press, 1405 S Harrison Rd, Manly Miles Bldg, Ste 25, East Lansing, MI 48823. TEL 517-355-9543, FAX 517-432-2611, msupress@msu.edu, http://www.msupress.msu.edu. Eds. Ann Larabee, Arthur Versluis.

320 ZAF ISSN 1609-4700
JQ1879.A5
JOURNAL OF AFRICAN ELECTIONS. Text in English. 2001. s-a.
Indexed: ISAP.
Published by: Electoral Institute of Southern Africa, P O Box 740, Johannesburg, Auckland Pk. 2006, South Africa. TEL 27-11-4825495, FAX 27-11-4826163, jkalley@eisa.org.za, http://www.eisa.org.za.

JOURNAL OF BALKAN AND NEAR EASTERN STUDIES. *see* HISTORY—History Of Europe

THE JOURNAL OF BORDERLAND STUDIES. *see* GEOGRAPHY

320 NLD ISSN 1080-6954
JA26
➤ **JOURNAL OF CHINESE POLITICAL SCIENCE.** Text in English. 1995. q. EUR 302, USD 412 combined subscription to institutions (print & online eds.) (effective 2012). bk.rev. reprint service avail. from PSC. **Document type:** *Journal, Academic/Scholarly.*
Related titles: Online - full text ed.: ISSN 1874-6357 (from IngentaConnect).
Indexed: A01, A03, A08, A22, A26, CA, E01, H12, HistAb, I05, I13, P10, P34, P42, P45, P48, PAIS, PQC, PSA, SCOPUS, SociolAb, T02.
—IE. **CCC.**
Published by: (Association of Chinese Political Studies USA), Springer Netherlands (Subsidiary of: Springer Science+Business Media), Van Godewijckstraat 30, Dordrecht, 3311 GX, Netherlands. TEL 31-78-6576050, FAX 31-78-6576474, http://www.springer.com. Ed. Sujian Guo.

➤ **JOURNAL OF CHURCH AND STATE.** *see* RELIGIONS AND THEOLOGY

301 320 GBR ISSN 1744-8689
JOURNAL OF CIVIL SOCIETY. Abbreviated title: J C S. Text in English. 2005 (May). 3/yr. GBP 357 combined subscription in United Kingdom to institutions (print & online eds.); EUR 472, USD 595 combined subscription to institutions (print & online eds.) (effective 2012). adv. back issues avail.; reprint service avail. from PSC. **Document type:** *Journal, Academic/Scholarly.* **Description:** Seeks to improve the theoretical understanding and empirical knowledge of civil society, its nature, patterns and composition, history, developments and economic and political systems.
Related titles: Online - full text ed.: ISSN 1744-8697. GBP 321 in United Kingdom to institutions; EUR 425, USD 536 to institutions (effective 2012) (from IngentaConnect).
Indexed: A01, A22, CA, E01, IBSS, P42, S02, S03, T02.
—IE, Ingenta. **CCC.**
Published by: Routledge (Subsidiary of: Taylor & Francis Group), 4 Park Sq, Milton Park, Abingdon, Oxon OX14 4RN, United Kingdom. TEL 44-20-70176000, FAX 44-20-70176336, subscriptions@tandf.co.uk, http://www.routledge.com. Ed. Helmut K Anheier TEL 310-825-2318. Adv. contact Linda Hann TEL 44-1344-779945. **Subscr. to:** Taylor & Francis Ltd., Journals Customer Service, Sheepen Pl, Colchester, Essex CO3 3LP, United Kingdom. TEL 44-20-70175544, FAX 44-20-70175198.

320 GBR ISSN 0021-9886
HC241
➤ **JOURNAL OF COMMON MARKET STUDIES.** Text in English. 1962. 5/yr. GBP 762 in United Kingdom to institutions; EUR 966 in Europe to institutions; USD 1,537 in the Americas to institutions; USD 1,795 elsewhere to institutions; GBP 876 combined subscription in United Kingdom to institutions (print & online eds.); EUR 1,111 combined subscription in Europe to institutions (print & online eds.); USD 1,769 combined subscription in the Americas to institutions (print & online eds.); USD 2,064 combined subscription elsewhere to institutions (print & online eds.) (effective 2012). adv. bk.rev. illus. Index. back issues avail.; reprints avail. **Document type:** *Journal, Academic/Scholarly.* **Description:** Aims to achieve a disciplinary balance between political science, economics and international relations, including the various sub disciplines such as international political economy.
Related titles: Microfilm ed.: (from WSH); Online - full text ed.: ISSN 1468-5965. GBP 762 in United Kingdom to institutions; EUR 966 in Europe to institutions; USD 1,537 in the Americas to institutions; USD 1,795 elsewhere to institutions (effective 2012) (from IngentaConnect); ◆ Supplement(s): J C M S Annual Review of the European Union in ..
Indexed: A12, A13, A14, A17, A20, A22, A23, A25, A26, ABCPolSci, ABIn, APEL, ASCA, B01, B02, B06, B07, B08, B09, B11, B13, B15, B16, B17, B18, BAS, BPI, BPIA, BRD, BrHumI, BusI, C12, CA, CABA, CLI, CPM, CREJ, CurCont, DIP, E01, E08, E10, E12, ELJI, ELLIS, ESPM, EconLit, G04, G05, G06, G07, G08, GH, H09, HistAb, I05, I13, IBR, IBSS, IBZ, ILD, JEL, KES, LJI, LT, M&MA, ManagCont, N02, P02, P06, P10, P30, P34, P42, P48, P51, P53, P54, PAIS, PCI, PQC, PSA, R12, RASB, RRTA, RiskAb, S02, S03, S05, S08, S09, S13, S16, SCIMP, SCOPUS, SSCI, SociolAb, T&II, T02, TAR, W01, W02, W03, W07, W11, WBA.
—BLDSC (4961.200000), IE, Infotrieve, Ingenta. **CCC.**
Published by: (University Association for Contemporary European Studies (U A C E S)), Wiley-Blackwell Publishing Ltd. (Subsidiary of: John Wiley & Sons, Inc.), 9600 Garsington Rd, Oxford, OX4 2DQ, United Kingdom. TEL 44-1865-776868, FAX 44-1865-714591, customerservices@blackwellpublishing.com. Eds. Daniel Wincott, Jim Rollo. Adv. contact Craig Pickett TEL 44-1865-476267.

➤ **THE JOURNAL OF COMPARATIVE ASIAN DEVELOPMENT.** *see* BUSINESS AND ECONOMICS—International Development And Assistance

P

320 SVN ISSN 1337-7477
JOURNAL OF COMPARATIVE POLITICS. Text in English. 2008. s-a. **Document type:** *Journal, Academic/Scholarly.*
Related titles: Online - full text ed.: ISSN 1338-1385. free (effective 2011).
Indexed: IBSS.
Published by: Univerza v Ljubljani, Fakulteta za Druzbene Vede/University of Ljubljana, Faculty of Social Sciences, Kerdeljeva Poscad 5, Ljubljana, 1000, Slovenia. TEL 386-1-5805100, FAX 386-1-5805101, fdv.faculty@fdv.uni-lj.si, http://www.fdv.uni-lj.si. Ed. Miro Hacek.

320 ESP ISSN 2013-8857
▼ **JOURNAL OF CONFLICTOLOGY.** Text in English. 2010. s-a. free (effective 2011). **Document type:** *Journal, Academic/Scholarly.*
Media: Online - full text.
Published by: Universitat Oberta de Catalunya, Av Tibidabo 39-43, Barcelona, 08035, Spain. TEL 34-902-372373, FAX 34-93-2110126, http://www.uoc.edu.

328 IND ISSN 0022-0043
JQ201
JOURNAL OF CONSTITUTIONAL & PARLIAMENTARY STUDIES. Text in English. 1967. q. free to members (effective 2011). reprints avail. **Document type:** *Journal, Academic/Scholarly.*
Related titles: Microfilm ed.: (from PQC).
Indexed: ABCPolSci, I13, IIPL, PAA&I.
Published by: Institute of Constitutional and Parliamentary Studies, 18-21 Vithalbhai Patel House, Rafi Marg, New Delhi, 110 001, India. TEL 91-11-23710405, icpsnewdelhi@gmail.com. Circ: 1,000.

940.5 GBR ISSN 1478-2790
JOURNAL OF CONTEMPORARY EUROPEAN STUDIES (ONLINE EDITION). Text in English. 3/m. GBP 428 in United Kingdom to institutions; EUR 577, USD 725 to institutions (effective 2012). **Document type:** *Journal, Academic/Scholarly.*
Formerly (until 2003): Journal of European Area Studies (Online Edition) (1469-946X)
Media: Online - full text (from IngentaConnect). **Related titles:** ◆ Print ed.: Journal of Contemporary European Studies (Print Edition). ISSN 1478-2804.
—BLDSC (4965.228100), Ingenta. **CCC.**
Published by: Routledge (Subsidiary of: Taylor & Francis Group), 4 Park Sq, Milton Park, Abingdon, Oxon OX14 4RN, United Kingdom. TEL 44-20-7017-6000, FAX 44-20-7017-6336, info@routledge.co.uk, http://www.routledge.com/journals/.

940.5 GBR ISSN 1478-2804
➤ **JOURNAL OF CONTEMPORARY EUROPEAN STUDIES (PRINT EDITION).** Text in English. 1980. 3/yr. GBP 476 combined subscription in United Kingdom to institutions (print & online eds.); EUR 642, USD 805 combined subscription to institutions (print & online eds.) (effective 2012). adv. bk.rev. back issues avail.; reprint service avail. from PSC. **Document type:** *Journal, Academic/Scholarly.* **Description:** Provides a forum for interdisciplinary debate about the theory and practice of area studies.
Former titles (until 2003): Journal of European Area Studies (Print Edition) (1460-8464); (until 1999): Journal of Area Studies (0261-3530)
Related titles: ◆ Online - full text ed.: Journal of Contemporary European Studies (Online Edition). ISSN 1478-2790.
Indexed: A01, A02, A03, A08, A22, ABCPolSci, AmHI, B01, B06, B07, B09, B21, CA, DIP, E01, E17, ESPM, H07, HistAb, I02, IBR, IBZ, MLA-IB, P34, P42, PSA, R02, S02, S03, SCOPUS, SociolAb, T02.
—BLDSC (4965.228100), IE, Infotrieve, Ingenta. **CCC.**
Published by: (Portsmouth Polytechnic, School of Languages and Area Studies, Research and Seminars Committee), Routledge (Subsidiary of: Taylor & Francis Group), 4 Park Sq, Milton Park, Abingdon, Oxon OX14 4RN, United Kingdom. TEL 44-20-70176000, FAX 44-20-70176336, subscriptions@tandf.co.uk, http://www.routledge.com. Eds. Brian Jenkins, Jeremy Leaman. Adv. contact Linda Hann TEL 44-1344-779945. Circ: 400. **Subscr. to:** Taylor & Francis Ltd., Journals Customer Service, Sheepen Pl, Colchester, Essex CO3 3LP, United Kingdom. TEL 44-20-70175544, FAX 44-20-70175198.

320 IND ISSN 0971-4731
JOURNAL OF CONTEMPORARY THOUGHT. Text in English. 1991. a. INR 200 domestic to individuals; USD 20 foreign to individuals; INR 400 domestic to institutions; USD 30 foreign to institutions (effective 2008). **Document type:** *Journal, Academic/Scholarly.*
Published by: M.S. University of Baroda, Forum on Contemporary Theory, Baroda, Gujarat 390 002, India. TEL 91-265-2794396, FAX 91-265-2792508.

320 GBR ISSN 2040-8498
▼ ➤ **JOURNAL OF CRITICAL GLOBALISATION STUDIES.** Text in English. 2009. irreg. free (effective 2011). **Document type:** *Journal, Academic/Scholarly.*
Media: Online - full text.
Published by: University of London, Royal Holloway, Department of Politics and International Relations, Royal Holloway, Egham, Surrey TW20 0EX, United Kingdom. TEL 44-1784-443149, FAX 44-1784-434375, Lisa.Dacunha@rhul.ac.uk, http://www.rhul.ac.uk/politics-and-IR/.

320 DEU ISSN 1868-1026
DS701
➤ **JOURNAL OF CURRENT CHINESE AFFAIRS.** Text in English, German. 1972. bi-m. EUR 82 (effective 2009). adv. bibl.; stat. back issues avail.; reprints avail. **Document type:** *Journal, Academic/Scholarly.* **Description:** Publishes original research on current issues in China in a format and style that is accessible across disciplines and to professionals with an interest in the region.
Formerly (until 2008): China Aktuell (0341-6631)
Related titles: Online - full text ed.: ISSN 1868-4874. free (effective 2011); ◆ Supplement to: China Data Supplement.
Indexed: A22, BAS, IBR, IBZ, KES, P30, P42, PAIS, RASB, SociolAb.
—IE, Infotrieve.
Published by: G I G A Institut fuer Asien-Studien, Rothenbaumchaussee 32, Hamburg, 20148, Germany. TEL 49-40-4288740, FAX 49-40-4107945, ias@giga-hamburg.de, http://www.giga-hamburg.de/english/ias. Eds. Flemming Christiansen, Heike Holbig, Karsten Giese. Circ: 1,000.

320 DEU ISSN 1868-1034
DS520
JOURNAL OF CURRENT SOUTHEAST ASIAN AFFAIRS. Text in German. bi-m. EUR 82; EUR 40 to students; EUR 25 newsstand/cover (effective 2010). adv. bibl.; stat. back issues avail.; reprints avail. **Document type:** *Journal, Academic/Scholarly.*
Formerly (until 2008): Suedostasien Aktuell (0722-8821)
Related titles: Online - full text ed.: free (effective 2011).
Indexed: BAS, CA, DIP, IBR, IBZ, P42, PAIS, PSA, SSA, T02.
Published by: G I G A Institut fuer Asien-Studien, Rothenbaumchaussee 32, Hamburg, 20148, Germany. TEL 49-40-4288740, FAX 49-40-4107945, ias@giga-hamburg.de, http://www.giga-hamburg.de/english/ias.

320 MYS ISSN 2180-284X
▼ **JOURNAL OF DEFENCE AND SECURITY.** Text in English. 2010. s-a. **Document type:** *Journal, Academic/Scholarly.* **Description:** Publishes original papers and reviews covering all aspects of defence and security. It will be a platform to promote awareness on the capabilities and requirements of modern defence & security technologies and policies, covering topics in the areas of, but not limited to: Evolution of military information & communication systems, smart weapons, modern vehicle & aerospace engineering challenges, intelligence, surveillance & reconnaissance, biological & chemical terrorism countermeasures, personnel protection & performance, military medicine, emergent naval technology, and defense & security strategic management.
Published by: Malaysian Institute of Defence and Security, Wisma Pertahanan Jalan Padang Tembak, Kuala Lumpur, Selangor 50634, Malaysia. TEL 603-20714561, FAX 603-26938371, midas@mod.gov.my. Ed. Shohaimi Abdullah.

321.8 USA ISSN 1045-5736
JF1051
➤ **JOURNAL OF DEMOCRACY.** Text in English. 1990. q. USD 150 to institutions; USD 210 combined subscription to institutions (print & online eds.); USD 45 per issue to institutions (effective 2012). adv. bk.rev. illus. Index. 192 p./no.; back issues avail.; reprint service avail. from PSC. **Document type:** *Journal, Academic/Scholarly.* **Description:** Provides a forum for scholarly analysis and competing democratic viewpoints. Features a unique blend of scholarly analysis, reports from democratic activists, updates on news and elections, and reviews of important recent books.
Related titles: Online - full text ed.: ISSN 1086-3214. 1996. USD 155 to institutions (effective 2012).
Indexed: A01, A02, A03, A08, A20, A22, A26, ABCPolSci, ABS&EES, ASCA, B04, BRD, CA, CCME, CurCont, DIP, E01, E08, G08, HRIR, I05, I13, IBR, IBSS, IBZ, M10, P02, P10, P27, P34, P42, P45, P47, P48, P53, P54, PAIS, PCI, PQC, PSA, PerIslam, PhilInd, S02, S03, S09, S11, SCOPUS, SSA, SSAI, SSAb, SSCI, SSI, SociolAb, T02, W01, W02, W03, W07.
—BLDSC (4968.250000), IE, Infotrieve, Ingenta. **CCC.**
Published by: (National Endowment for Democracy), The Johns Hopkins University Press, 2715 N Charles St, Baltimore, MD 21218. TEL 410-516-6900, FAX 410-516-6968. Eds. Larry Diamond, Marc F Plattner. **Subscr. to:** PO Box 19966, Baltimore, MD 21211. TEL 410-516-6987, 800-548-1784, FAX 410-516-3866, jrnlcirc@press.jhu.edu.

321.8 AUS ISSN 1838-8795
▼ ➤ **JOURNAL OF DEMOCRATIC THEORY.** Text in English. 2011. q. free (effective 2011). **Document type:** *Journal, Academic/Scholarly.* **Description:** Publishes articles that deal with the political theory of democracy, democratization, styles of democracy, democratic governance, and democratic systems.
Media: Online - full text.
Published by: Mitigating Endemic Democratic Problems http://www.med-p.org. Ed. Jean-Paul Gagnon.

➤ **THE JOURNAL OF DEVELOPMENT STUDIES.** *see* BUSINESS AND ECONOMICS—International Development And Assistance

➤ **THE JOURNAL OF ECONOMIC INEQUALITY.** *see* BUSINESS AND ECONOMICS—Economic Situation And Conditions

324.6 GBR ISSN 1745-7289
JF1001
➤ **JOURNAL OF ELECTIONS, PUBLIC OPINION, AND PARTIES.** Abbreviated title: J E P O P. Text in English. 1991. q. GBP 306 combined subscription in United Kingdom to institutions (print & online eds.); EUR 407, USD 510 combined subscription to institutions (print & online eds.) (effective 2012). adv. back issues avail.; reprint service avail. from PSC. **Document type:** *Journal, Academic/Scholarly.* **Description:** Presents a review of the latest research on parties, elections and voting behavior in the United Kingdom.
Former titles (until 2006): British Elections & Parties Review (1368-9886); (until 1997): British Elections and Parties Yearbook (0968-2481)
Related titles: Online - full text ed.: ISSN 1745-7297. GBP 276 in United Kingdom to institutions; EUR 366, USD 459 to institutions (effective 2012).
Indexed: A01, A22, CA, E01, I13, IBSS, P34, P42, PAIS, PSA, SCOPUS, SociolAb, T02.
—BLDSC (2299.320000), IE, Ingenta. **CCC.**
Published by: (Political Studies Association, Elections, Public Opinion and Parties), Routledge (Subsidiary of: Taylor & Francis Group), 4 Park Sq, Milton Park, Abingdon, Oxon OX14 4RN, United Kingdom. TEL 44-20-70176000, FAX 44-20-70176336, subscriptions@tandf.co.uk, http://www.routledge.com. Eds. Christopher Wlezien TEL 215-204-7747, Justin Fisher TEL 44-1895-266309. Adv. contact Linda Hann TEL 44-1344-779945. **Subscr. to:** Taylor & Francis Ltd., Journals Customer Service, Sheepen Pl, Colchester, Essex CO3 3LP, United Kingdom. TEL 44-20-70175544, FAX 44-20-70175198.

320.6 GBR ISSN 1350-1763
JN26 CODEN: JEPPFG
➤ **JOURNAL OF EUROPEAN PUBLIC POLICY.** Abbreviated title: J E P P. Text in English. 1994. 8/yr. GBP 750 combined subscription in United Kingdom to institutions (print & online eds.); EUR 992, USD 1,245 combined subscription to institutions (print & online eds.) (effective 2012). adv. back issues avail.; reprint service avail. from PSC. **Document type:** *Journal, Academic/Scholarly.* **Description:** Provides a comprehensive source of analytical articles in the field of European public policy.
Related titles: Online - full text ed.: ISSN 1466-4429. GBP 675 in United Kingdom to institutions; EUR 893, USD 1,120 to institutions (effective 2012) (from IngentaConnect).
Indexed: A01, A02, A03, A08, A20, A22, AmHI, B01, B06, B07, B09, BrHumI, CA, CurCont, DIP, E01, ESPM, FamI, H07, I13, IBR, IBSS, IBZ, P34, P42, PAIS, PSA, S02, S03, SCOPUS, SOPODA, SPAA, SSA, SSCI, SSciA, SociolAb, T02, W07.
—IE, Infotrieve, Ingenta. **CCC.**
Published by: Routledge (Subsidiary of: Taylor & Francis Group), 4 Park Sq, Milton Park, Abingdon, Oxon OX14 4RN, United Kingdom. TEL 44-20-70176000, FAX 44-20-70176336, subscriptions@tandf.co.uk, http://www.routledge.com. Ed. Jeremy Richardson TEL 44-1865-278625. Adv. contact Linda Hann TEL 44-1344-779945. **Subscr. to:** Taylor & Francis Ltd., Journals Customer Service, Sheepen Pl, Colchester, Essex CO3 3LP, United Kingdom. TEL 44-20-70175544, FAX 44-20-70175198, tf.enquiries@tfinforma.com.

320 IND ISSN 0970-9908
DS481.G3
JOURNAL OF GANDHIAN STUDIES. Text in English. 1973. q. bk.rev. bibl. **Document type:** *Journal, Academic/Scholarly.* **Description:** Encourages objective study of Gandhi's non-violent methods.
Indexed: IBR, IBZ.
Published by: Institute of Gandhian Thought and Peace Studies, University of Allahabad, Gandhi Bhawan, Allahabad, Uttar Pradesh 211 002, India.

320 TUR ISSN 1307-9778
JOURNAL OF GAZI ACADEMIC VIEW. Text in Turkish. 2007. irreg. free (effective 2011). **Document type:** *Journal, Academic/Scholarly.*
Media: Online - full text.
Indexed: A01, CA, T02.
Published by: Gazi Universitesi, Gazi University Rectorate, Teknikokullar, Ankara, 06500, Turkey. TEL 90-312-2126840, FAX 90-312-2213202, fkilic@gazi.edu.tr, http://www.gazi.edu.tr.

341.778 GBR ISSN 1462-3528
HV6322.7
➤ **JOURNAL OF GENOCIDE RESEARCH.** Text in English. 1999. q. GBP 367 combined subscription in United Kingdom to institutions (print & online eds.); EUR 488, USD 613 combined subscription to institutions (print & online eds.) (effective 2012). adv. back issues avail.; reprint service avail. from PSC. **Document type:** *Journal, Academic/Scholarly.* **Description:** Aims to promote an interdisciplinary and comparative approach to the study of genocide.
Related titles: Online - full text ed.: ISSN 1469-9494. GBP 331 in United Kingdom to institutions; EUR 439, USD 551 to institutions (effective 2012) (from IngentaConnect).
Indexed: A01, A03, A08, A22, AmH&L, CA, DIP, E01, HistAb, I02, I13, IBR, IBSS, IBZ, M10, P30, P42, PSA, S02, S03, SCOPUS, SSA, SociolAb, T02, V&AA.
—IE, Infotrieve, Ingenta. **CCC.**
Published by: (International Network of Genocide Scholars), Routledge (Subsidiary of: Taylor & Francis Group), 4 Park Sq, Milton Park, Abingdon, Oxon OX14 4RN, United Kingdom. TEL 44-20-70176000, FAX 44-20-70176336, subscriptions@tandf.co.uk, http://www.routledge.com. Eds. Dominik J Schaller TEL 41-31-6315478, Henry R Huttenbach TEL 212-650-7384. Adv. contact Linda Hann TEL 44-1344-779945. **Subscr. to:** Taylor & Francis Ltd., Journals Customer Service, Sheepen Pl, Colchester, Essex CO3 3LP, United Kingdom. TEL 44-20-70175544, FAX 44-20-70175198.

➤ **JOURNAL OF GLOBAL INITIATIVES.** *see* SOCIAL SCIENCES: COMPREHENSIVE WORKS

➤ **JOURNAL OF HEALTH POLITICS, POLICY AND LAW.** *see* MEDICAL SCIENCES

306.2 AUS ISSN 1835-3800
➤ **JOURNAL OF HUMAN SECURITY.** Text in English. 2005. s-a. **Document type:** *Journal, Academic/Scholarly.* **Description:** Provides a forum for reseach in human security issues, including ethnic conflict, terrorism, human rights, population health, human ecology, sustainable economics, and others.
Formerly (until 2007): Australasian Journal of Human Security (Print) (1176-8614)
Media: Online - full text.
Indexed: A26, CA, I02, I05, P45, P48, P51, P53, P54, PQC, S02, S03, SCOPUS, SSAI, SSAb, SSI, T02, W01, W02, W03, W05.
Published by: RMIT Publishing, Level 3, Swanston St, Melbourne, VIC, Australia. TEL 61-03-99258100, FAX 61-03-99258134, info@rmitpublishing.com.au. Ed. Sabina W Lautensach.

320 304.6 ROM ISSN 1843-5610
JV6006
JOURNAL OF IDENTITY AND MIGRATION STUDIES. Text in English. 2007. s-a. free (effective 2011). **Document type:** *Journal, Academic/Scholarly.*
Media: Online - full text.
Indexed: P42, T02.
Published by: Universitatea din Oradea, Faculty of Political Science and Communication Science/University of Oradea, Faculty of Political Science and Communication Science, Research Centre on Identity and Migration Studies, Str Traian Blajovici 2, Oradea, 410238, Romania.

320 DEU ISSN 0932-4569
H5
➤ **JOURNAL OF INSTITUTIONAL AND THEORETICAL ECONOMICS.** Text in English. 1844. q. EUR 179 to individuals; EUR 329 to institutions (effective 2012). adv. bk.rev. charts; illus. index. reprint service avail. from SCH. **Document type:** *Journal, Academic/Scholarly.* **Description:** Covers political economy and modern institutional economics.
Formerly (until 1986): Zeitschrift fuer die Gesamte Staatswissenschaft (0044-2550)
Related titles: Online - full text ed.: ISSN 1614-0559 (from IngentaConnect).
Indexed: A12, A17, A20, A22, A26, ABIn, ASCA, B02, B11, B15, B17, B18, BAS, CA, CREJ, CurCont, DIP, ELLIS, EconLit, FLP, G04, G08, I05, I13, IBR, IBSS, IBZ, JEL, KES, P06, P30, P42, P48, P51, P53, P54, PAIS, PCI, PQC, PRA, RASB, S02, S03, SCIMP, SCOPUS, SSCI, T02, W07.
—BLDSC (5007.506000), IE, Infotrieve, Ingenta. **CCC.**

Published by: Mohr Siebeck GmbH & Co. KG, Wilhelmstr 18, Tuebingen, 72074, Germany. TEL 49-7071-9230, FAX 49-7071-51104, info@mohr.de. Ed. Yvan Lengwiler. Adv. contact Tilman Gaebler. Circ: 1,070 (paid and controlled).

➤ **JOURNAL OF INTERCULTURAL STUDIES.** *see* ETHNIC INTERESTS

➤ **JOURNAL OF INTERNATIONAL CRIMINAL JUSTICE.** *see* CRIMINOLOGY AND LAW ENFORCEMENT

320 300 GBR ISSN 1755-0882
JA79

➤ **JOURNAL OF INTERNATIONAL POLITICAL THEORY.** Abbreviated title: J I P T. Text in English. 2005. s-a. GBP 105 domestic to institutions; USD 205 in North America to institutions; GBP 113 elsewhere to institutions; GBP 131 combined subscription domestic to institutions (print & online eds.); USD 257 combined subscription in North America to institutions (print & online eds.); GBP 141 combined subscription elsewhere to institutions (print & online eds.) (effective 2012). back issues avail.; reprints avail. **Document type:** *Journal, Academic/Scholarly.* **Description:** Focuses both on major theoretical debates such as power, justice, multiculturalism, sovereignty, liberty, nationalism and globalization, as well as on major policy issues such as democratization, human rights, terrorism, war and peace, economic development and environmental protection.
Formerly (until 2008): Politics and Ethics Review (1743-453X)
Related titles: Online - full text ed.: ISSN 1755-1722. USD 172 in North America to institutions; GBP 95 elsewhere to institutions (effective 2012).
Indexed: CA, P42, PSA, PhilInd, T02.
—BLDSC (5007.683500), IE, Ingenta. **CCC.**
Published by: Edinburgh University Press, 22 George Sq, Edinburgh, Scotland EH8 9LF, United Kingdom. TEL 44-131-6504218, FAX 44-131-6503286, journals@eup.ed.ac.uk. Ed. Patrick Hayden. Adv. contact Ruth Allison TEL 44-131-6504220.

➤ **THE JOURNAL OF ISRAELI HISTORY;** politics, society, culture. *see* HISTORY—History Of The Near East

➤ **JOURNAL OF LANGUAGE & POLITICS.** *see* LINGUISTICS

➤ **JOURNAL OF LATIN AMERICAN STUDIES.** *see* HISTORY—History Of North And South America

➤ **JOURNAL OF LAW AND POLITICS.** *see* LAW

➤ **JOURNAL OF LAW AND POLITICS/HO-SEI KENKYU.** *see* LAW

320 GBR ISSN 0022-278X
DT1

➤ **JOURNAL OF MODERN AFRICAN STUDIES.** Text in English. 1963. q. GBP 239, USD 422 to institutions; GBP 250, USD 438 combined subscription to institutions (print & online eds.) (effective 2012). adv. bk.rev. bibl.; illus. index. back issues avail.; reprint service avail. from PSC. **Document type:** *Journal, Academic/Scholarly.* **Description:** Covers the politics, economics and related aspects of contemporary Africa.
Related titles: Microform ed.: (from PQC); Online - full text ed.: ISSN 1469-7777. GBP 225, USD 388 to institutions (effective 2012).
Indexed: A01, A02, A03, A08, A12, A20, A22, A25, A26, A34, ABCPolSci, ABIn, ASCA, ASD, AbAn, AcaI, AmHI, B04, BA, BAS, BRD, BrHumI, C25, CA, CABA, CCA, CERDIC, CREJ, CurCont, DIP, E01, E08, E12, ESPM, F08, F12, FR, FamI, G08, G11, GEOBASE, GH, H07, H09, H10, H16, HRIR, HistAb, I05, I08, I11, I13, I14, IBR, IBSS, IBZ, IIBP, ILD, L09, LT, LeftInd, M01, M02, M10, MEA&I, MLA, MLA-IB, MaizeAb, N02, NumL, O01, P02, P06, P10, P13, P27, P30, P34, P38, P42, P45, P48, P51, P53, P54, PAIS, PCI, PQC, PRA, PSA, R11, R12, RASB, RRTA, RiskAb, S02, S03, S05, S08, S09, S13, S16, SCOPUS, SOPODA, SPAA, SSA, SSAI, SSAb, SSCI, SSI, SociolAb, T02, T05, TAR, W03, W07, W11.
—BLDSC (5020.600000), IE, Infotrieve, Ingenta. **CCC.**
Published by: Cambridge University Press, The Edinburgh Bldg, Shaftesbury Rd, Cambridge, CB2 8RU, United Kingdom. TEL 44-1223-312393, FAX 44-1223-315052, journals@cambridge.org, http://www.cambridge.org/uk. Ed. Christopher Clapham. R&P Linda Nicol TEL 44-1223-325702. Adv. contact Rebecca Roberts TEL 44-1223-325083. page GBP 470, page USD 895. Circ: 1,600. **Subscr. to:** Cambridge University Press, 32 Ave of the Americas, New York, NY 10013. TEL 212-337-5000, FAX 212-691-3239, journals_subscriptions@cup.org.

➤ **JOURNAL OF PAN AFRICAN STUDIES (ONLINE).** *see* SOCIOLOGY

➤ **JOURNAL OF POLICY ANALYSIS AND MANAGEMENT.** *see* PUBLIC ADMINISTRATION

320.6 GBR ISSN 0898-0306
H96 CODEN: JPHIEV

➤ **JOURNAL OF POLICY HISTORY.** Text in English. 1989. q. GBP 65, USD 122 to institutions; GBP 73, USD 136 combined subscription to institutions (print & online eds.) (effective 2012). adv. bk.rev. back issues avail. **Document type:** *Journal, Academic/Scholarly.* **Description:** Encourages interdisciplinary research into the origins and development of public policy in the U.S.A. and in other countries as well.
Related titles: Microform ed.: (from PQC); Online - full text ed.: ISSN 1528-4190. 2000. GBP 56, USD 109 to institutions (effective 2012).
Indexed: A01, A03, A08, A22, AmH&L, B04, BRD, CA, DIP, E01, HistAb, IBR, IBZ, P10, P30, P34, P42, P45, P48, PAIS, PCI, PQC, PSA, S02, S03, SCOPUS, SOPODA, SSA, SSAI, SSAb, SSI, SociolAb, T02, W01, W02, W03, W05.
—IE, Infotrieve, Ingenta. **CCC.**
Published by: Cambridge University Press, The Edinburgh Bldg, Shaftesbury Rd, Cambridge, CB2 8RU, United Kingdom. TEL 44-1223-326070, FAX 44-1223-325150, journals@cambridge.org. Eds. Edward C Page, Richard Rose. adv.: page USD 225; 5.5 x 7.5. Circ: 366 (paid).

320.6 USA ISSN 0161-8938
H1 CODEN: JPMOD5

➤ **JOURNAL OF POLICY MODELING.** Text in English. 1979. bi-m. EUR 843 in Europe to institutions; JPY 112,200 in Japan to institutions; USD 945 elsewhere to institutions (effective 2012). adv. back issues avail.; reprints avail. **Document type:** *Journal, Academic/Scholarly.* **Description:** Addresses questions of import to the world community as a whole, and it focuses upon the economic, social, and political interdependencies between national and regional systems.
Related titles: Microform ed.: (from PQC); Online - full text ed.: ISSN 1873-8060 (from IngentaConnect, ScienceDirect).
Indexed: A01, A02, A03, A08, A12, A13, A17, A22, A26, ABIn, ASCA, B01, B02, B06, B07, B08, B09, B11, B17, B18, BPIA, BusI, CA, CREJ, CurCont, E08, EconLit, FamI, FutSurv, G04, G06, G07, G08, I05, I13, IBR, IBSS, IBZ, JEL, P10, P34, P42, P48, P51, P53, P54, PAIS, PCI, PQC, RASB, S02, S03, S09, S11, SCOPUS, SOPODA, SSCI, SociolAb, T&II, T02, W07.
—BLDSC (5040.843000), IE, Infotrieve, Ingenta. **CCC.**
Published by: (Society for Policy Modeling), Elsevier Inc. (Subsidiary of: Elsevier Science & Technology), 1600 John F Kennedy Blvd, Philadelphia, PA 19103. TEL 215-239-3900, FAX 215-238-7883, JournalCustomerService-usa@elsevier.com, http://www.elsevier.com. Eds. Dominick Salvatore, Antonio Maria Costa. Adv. contact Janine Castle TEL 44-1865-843844.

➤ **JOURNAL OF POLITICAL ECONOMY.** *see* BUSINESS AND ECONOMICS

320.5 GBR ISSN 1356-9317
JA8

JOURNAL OF POLITICAL IDEOLOGIES. Text in English. 1996. 3/yr. GBP 324 combined subscription in United Kingdom to institutions (print & online eds.); EUR 428, USD 541 combined subscription to institutions (print & online eds.) (effective 2012). adv. back issues avail.; reprint service avail. from PSC. **Document type:** *Journal, Academic/Scholarly.* **Description:** Dedicated to the analysis of political ideology both in its theoretical and conceptual aspects, and with reference to the nature and roles of concrete ideological manifestations.
Related titles: Online - full text ed.: ISSN 1469-9613. GBP 292 in United Kingdom to institutions; EUR 386, USD 487 to institutions (effective 2012) (from IngentaConnect).
Indexed: A01, A02, A03, A08, A22, B21, CA, DIP, E01, E17, ESPM, GEOBASE, I13, IBR, IBSS, IBZ, P02, P10, P42, P45, P47, P48, P53, P54, PQC, PSA, S02, S03, S11, SCOPUS, SociolAb, T02.
—IE, Infotrieve, Ingenta. **CCC.**
Published by: Routledge (Subsidiary of: Taylor & Francis Group), 4 Park Sq, Milton Park, Abingdon, Oxon OX14 4RN, United Kingdom. TEL 44-20-70176000, FAX 44-20-70176336, subscriptions@tandf.co.uk, http://www.routledge.com. Ed. Michael Freeden TEL 44-1865-270977. Adv. contact Linda Hann TEL 44-1344-779945. **Subscr. to:** Taylor & Francis Ltd., Journals Customer Service, Sheepen Pl, Colchester, Essex CO3 3LP, United Kingdom. TEL 44-20-70175544, FAX 44-20-70175198.

320 USA ISSN 1537-7857
CODEN: JIHOAU

➤ **JOURNAL OF POLITICAL MARKETING;** political campaigns in the new millennium. Text in English. 2002 (Spr.). q. GBP 404 combined subscription in United Kingdom to institutions (print & online eds.); EUR 522, USD 529 combined subscription to institutions (print & online eds.) (effective 2012). adv. reprint service avail. from PSC. **Document type:** *Journal, Academic/Scholarly.* **Description:** Designed for politicians and candidates at every level of office as well as political party officials, political consultants, and educators in these and related fields.
Related titles: Online - full text ed.: ISSN 1537-7865. 2002. GBP 363 in United Kingdom to institutions; EUR 470, USD 476 to institutions (effective 2012).
Indexed: A01, A03, A22, AmH&L, B01, B07, B09, CA, DIP, E01, ESPM, HistAb, IBR, IBZ, M02, P34, P42, PAIS, PRA, PSA, RiskAb, SCOPUS, SociolAb, T02, TM.
—BLDSC (5040.884000), IE, Ingenta. **CCC.**
Published by: Routledge (Subsidiary of: Taylor & Francis Group), 325 Chestnut St, Ste 800, Philadelphia, PA 19106. TEL 215-625-8900, 800-354-1420, FAX 215-625-8914, journals@routledge.com, http://www.routledge.com. Ed. Bruce I Newman. adv.: B&W page USD 315, color page USD 55,000; trim 4.375 x 7.125. Circ: 11 (paid).

➤ **JOURNAL OF POLITICAL PHILOSOPHY.** *see* PHILOSOPHY

320 USA ISSN 0098-4612
JA1

➤ **JOURNAL OF POLITICAL SCIENCE.** Text in English. 1969. a. free to members (effective 2010). bk.rev. **Document type:** *Journal, Academic/Scholarly.* **Description:** Covers issues related to political science; occasional special topic such as "Metropolitan politics.".
Formerly (until 1973): South Carolina Journal of Political Science (0587-0577)
Indexed: ABCPolSci, AmH&L, CA, HistAb, P06, P30, P42, PSA, SCOPUS, T02.
Published by: (South Carolina Political Science Association), University of South Carolina, Department of Political Science, 817 Henderson St, Columbia, SC 29208. TEL 803-777-3109, FAX 803-777-8255, Poli@sc.edu, http://www.cas.sc.edu/POLI/. Ed. Don Sabia TEL 803-777-4547.

320 PAK

➤ **JOURNAL OF POLITICAL SCIENCE.** Text in English. 1971. a. PKR 200, USD 7. adv. bk.rev. bibl.; charts; stat. **Document type:** *Journal, Academic/Scholarly.*
Formerly: Journal of History and Political Science
Indexed: ABCPolSci, BAS.
Published by: Government College, Department of Political Science, No.C-40, G O R III, Shadman, Lahore, Pakistan. Ed. A K Rai. Circ: 300.

320.9 NPL

➤ **JOURNAL OF POLITICAL SCIENCE.** Text in Nepali. 1979. s-a. **Document type:** *Journal, Academic/Scholarly.* **Description:** Publishes papers on political science issues in Nepal.
Formerly: Nepalese Journal of Political Science
Related titles: Online - full text ed.
Published by: Tribhuvan University, Department of Political Science and Sociology, Prithwi Narayan Campus, Pokhara, Nepal. Ed. Tara Nath Baral.

320 USA ISSN 1551-2169
JA86

➤ **JOURNAL OF POLITICAL SCIENCE EDUCATION.** Text in English. 2005 (Jan.-Apr.). q. GBP 343 combined subscription in United Kingdom to institutions (print & online eds.); EUR 457, USD 573 combined subscription to institutions (print & online eds.) (effective 2012). adv. reprint service avail. from PSC. **Document type:** *Journal, Academic/Scholarly.* **Description:** Covers topics regarding pedagogical scholarship and the scholarship of teaching and learning; discussion of assessment issues; and reviews of both textbooks and relevant teaching technologies of use to political scientists.
Related titles: Online - full text ed.: ISSN 1551-2177. GBP 310 in United Kingdom to institutions; EUR 412, USD 516 to institutions (effective 2012) (from IngentaConnect).
Indexed: A22, CA, E01, E03, ERI, ERIC, FamI, P42, PSA, SociolAb, T02.
—BLDSC (5040.889500), IE, Ingenta. **CCC.**
Published by: (American Political Science Association), Taylor & Francis Inc. (Subsidiary of: Taylor & Francis Group), 325 Chestnut St, Ste 800, Philadelphia, PA 19106. TEL 215-625-2940, 800-354-1420, orders@taylorandfrancis.com, http://www.taylorandfrancis.com. Eds. John Ishiyama, Marijke Breuning. Adv. contact Linda Hann TEL 44-1344-779945.

320 PAK ISSN 1994-1080
JA88.P18

JOURNAL OF POLITICAL STUDIES. Text in English. 2000. s-a. USD 20; USD 10 newsstand/cover (effective 2007). **Document type:** *Journal, Academic/Scholarly.* **Description:** Contains review articles and policy papers on themes of contemporary domestic, regional and international political issues.
Indexed: A26, I05, P02, P10, P45, P48, P53, P54, PQC, PSA.
Published by: University of the Punjab, Department of Political Science, Quaid-i-Azam Campus, Lahore, Pakistan. TEL 92-42-9231229, FAX 92-42-5838263, chairperson@polsc.pu.edu.pk, http://www.pu.edu.pk/departments/default.asp?deptid=14. Ed., R&P Umbreen Javaid. Circ: 200 (paid and controlled).

320 IND ISSN 0047-2700
JQ201

JOURNAL OF POLITICAL STUDIES. Text in English. 19??. s-a. INR 200 domestic; USD 20 foreign (effective 2011). bk.rev. bibl. **Document type:** *Journal, Academic/Scholarly.*
Related titles: Microfilm ed.
Indexed: BAS.
Published by: D.A.V. College, Post-Graduate Department of Political Science, Mahatma Hans Raj Marg, Dayanand Nagar, Jalandhar, Punjab 144 008, India. TEL 91-181-2255641, FAX 91-181-2203120. Eds. B B Sharma, Satish Tandon.

320 GBR ISSN 0022-3816
JA1

➤ **THE JOURNAL OF POLITICS.** Text in English. 1933. q. GBP 240, USD 342 combined subscription to institutions (print & online eds.) (effective 2012). adv. bk.rev. bibl.; charts; illus. index. back issues avail.; reprint service avail. from PSC. **Document type:** *Journal, Academic/Scholarly.* **Description:** Covers American, comparative, and international political science. Includes various methodological approaches.
Supersedes (in 1939): Southern Political Science Association. Annual Session. Proceedings
Related titles: Microform ed.: (from PQC); Online - full text ed.: ISSN 1468-2508. GBP 221, USD 316 to institutions (effective 2012) (from IngentaConnect).
Indexed: A01, A02, A03, A08, A20, A22, A25, A26, ABCPolSci, ABS&EES, ASCA, AcaI, AmH&L, B01, B04, B06, B07, B09, BAS, BRD, CA, CBRI, ChPerI, Chicano, CurCont, DIP, E01, E08, ESPM, G08, G10, H09, H10, HistAb, I05, I13, I14, IBR, IBZ, IPARL, MLA-IB, P02, P03, P06, P10, P13, P27, P30, P34, P42, P47, P48, P53, P54, PAIS, PCI, PQC, PRA, PSA, PersLit, PhilInd, PsycInfo, PsycholAb, RASB, RiskAb, S02, S03, S05, S08, S09, S11, S21, SCOPUS, SOPODA, SRRA, SSA, SSAI, SSAb, SSCI, SSI, SociolAb, T02, W03, W04, W07, W09.
—BLDSC (5040.900000), IE, Infotrieve, Ingenta. **CCC.**
Published by: (Southern Political Science Association USA), Cambridge University Press, The Edinburgh Bldg, Shaftesbury Rd, Cambridge, CB2 8RU, United Kingdom. TEL 44-1223-312393, FAX 44-1223-315052, journals@cambridge.org, http://www.cambridge.org/uk. Eds. Jan E Leighley, William Mishler. Adv. contact Rebecca Roberts TEL 44-1223-325083. B&W page GBP 245, B&W page USD 470.

320 340 CAN ISSN 1913-9047

➤ **JOURNAL OF POLITICS AND LAW.** Text in English. 2008. q. CAD 20 (effective 2009). software rev. abstr.; bibl. Index. back issues avail. **Document type:** *Journal, Academic/Scholarly.* **Description:** Aims to encourage and publish research in the field of politics and law.
Related titles: Online - full text ed.: ISSN 1913-9055. 2008. free (effective 2011).
Indexed: A26, CPerI, I05, P10, P42, P48, P51, P53, P54, PQC, T02.
Published by: Canadian Center of Science and Education, 4915 Bathurst St, Unit 209-309, Toronto, ON M2R 1X9, Canada. TEL 416-208-4027, FAX 416-208-4028, info@ccsenet.org. Ed. Wenwu Zhao. Circ: 200 (paid and controlled). **Subscr. to:** JournalBuy.com, Rm. 666, 118 Chongqing S. Rd., Qingdao 266032, China. TEL 86-532-86069259, FAX 86-532-95105198 ext 81082, order@journalbuy.com, http://www.journalbuy.com/.

➤ **JOURNAL OF PROGRESSIVE HUMAN SERVICES;** successor to catalyst: a socialist journal of the social services. *see* SOCIAL SERVICES AND WELFARE

➤ **JOURNAL OF PUBLIC ADMINISTRATION AND POLICY RESEARCH.** *see* PUBLIC ADMINISTRATION

321.8 USA ISSN 1937-2841
JF799

➤ **JOURNAL OF PUBLIC DELIBERATION.** Abbreviated title: J P D. Text in English. 2005. a. free (effective 2011). **Document type:** *Journal, Academic/Scholarly.* **Description:** Designed mainly for academic researchers and field practitioners who require high quality theory, information and analysis of deliberative democracy phenomena. Synthesizes the research, opinion, projects, experiments and experiences of academics and practitioners in the field of deliberative democracy.
Media: Online - full text.
Indexed: A01, CA, P34, P42, SCOPUS, T02.
Published by: Auburn University, Department of Political Science, 7080 Haley Ctr, Auburn University, Auburn, AL 36849. farnejb@auburn.edu. Ed. Dr. Ted Becker.

➤ **JOURNAL OF PUNJAB STUDIES.** *see* SOCIAL SCIENCES: COMPREHENSIVE WORKS

320.6 305.8 USA ISSN 1540-8450
E184.A1

THE JOURNAL OF RACE AND POLICY. Text in English. 2005 (Spr.-Sum.). a. **Document type:** *Journal, Academic/Scholarly.*
Related titles: Online - full text ed.
Indexed: CA, IIBP, P45, S02, S03, SSAI, SSAb, SSI, T02, W03, W05.

Published by: Old Dominion University, Institute for the Study of Race and Ethnicity, Batten Arts & Letters, #2023, Norfolk, VA 23529. TEL 757-683-5586, FAX 757-683-6171, msumter@odu.edu. Ed. Michael L. Clemons.

306.2 IND ISSN 0973-3426
➤ **JOURNAL OF SOCIAL AND ECONOMIC POLICY.** Abbreviated title: J S E P. Text in English. 2005. s-a. INR 3,000, USD 95 to institutions (effective 2011). **Document type:** *Journal, Academic/Scholarly.* **Description:** Provides a forum for debate and deliberations of academics, social and economic policy makers.
Indexed: JEL.
Published by: Serials Publications, 4830/24, Ansari Rd, Darya Ganj, New Delhi, 110 002, India. TEL 91-11-23245225, FAX 91-11-23272135, serialspublications.india@gmail.com. Ed. N Narayana.

320.6 CAN ISSN 1481-5842
H61
➤ **JOURNAL OF SOCIAL AND POLITICAL THOUGHT.** Abbreviated title: J-SPOT. Text in English. 1999. irreg. **Document type:** *Journal, Academic/Scholarly.* **Description:** Focuses on a wide range of intersections between theory, politics, culture, and social justice.
Media: Online - full text.
Published by: York University, Graduate Programme in Social and Political Thought, S714 Ross Bldg., 4700 Keele St., Toronto, ON M3J 1P3, Canada.

320 USA ISSN 0278-839X
H1
➤ **JOURNAL OF SOCIAL, POLITICAL AND ECONOMIC STUDIES.** Abbreviated title: J S P E S. Text in English. 1976. q. USD 112 domestic to institutions; USD 128 foreign to institutions; USD 162 combined subscription domestic to institutions (print & online eds.); USD 178 combined subscription foreign to institutions (print & online eds.) (effective 2010). bk.rev. index. 128 p./no. 1 cols./p.; back issues avail. **Document type:** *Journal, Academic/Scholarly.* **Description:** An academic level publication providing in-depth data relating to contemporary events and issues of international interest and significance.
Formerly (until 1981): Journal of Social and Political Studies (0193-5941); Which superseded in part (in 1977): Journal of Social and Political Affairs (0362-580X)
Related titles: Online - full text ed.: USD 128 to institutions (effective 2010).
Indexed: A12, A20, A22, A26, ABCPolSci, ABIn, ABS&EES, AmH&L, B04, BAS, BRD, CA, CCME, ChPerI, DIP, E08, EIA, EnerInd, G08, HistAb, I05, I13, IBR, IBZ, MEA&I, MLA-IB, MagInd, P02, P10, P27, P30, P45, P46, P47, P48, P51, P53, P54, PAIS, PCI, PQC, PSA, RASB, S02, S03, S09, S11, SCOPUS, SOPODA, SSA, SSAI, SSAb, SSI, SociolAb, T02, V&AA, W03, W05.
—BLDSC (5064.790000), IE, Infotrieve, Ingenta, Linda Hall.
Published by: Council for Social and Economic Studies, 1133 13th St NW, Washington, DC 20005. TEL 202-371-2700, FAX 202-371-1523, socecon@aol.com. Ed. Roger Pearson.

320 USA ISSN 0895-724X
JOURNAL OF SOCIAL, POLITICAL AND ECONOMIC STUDIES MONOGRAPH SERIES. Text in English. 1976. irreg. back issues avail.; reprints avail. **Document type:** *Monographic series, Academic/Scholarly.* **Description:** Deals with contemporary issues of national and world interest in historical perspectives. Emphasis is on data rather than theory.
Related titles: Online - full text ed.: USD 128 to institutions (effective 2010).
Published by: Council for Social and Economic Studies, 1133 13th St NW, Washington, DC 20005. TEL 202-371-2700, FAX 202-371-1523, socecon@aol.com. Ed. Roger Pearson.

JOURNAL OF SOUTHEAST ASIAN STUDIES. *see* HISTORY—History Of Asia

320.5 GBR ISSN 0951-6298
JA1.A1 CODEN: JTPOEF
➤ **JOURNAL OF THEORETICAL POLITICS.** Abbreviated title: J T P. Text in English. 1989. q. GBP 583, USD 1,079 to institutions; GBP 595, USD 1,101 combined subscription to institutions (print & online eds.) (effective 2012). bk.rev. charts; illus. Index. back issues avail.; reprint service avail. from PSC. **Document type:** *Journal, Academic/Scholarly.* **Description:** An international journal fostering the development of theory in the study of political processes.
Related titles: Online - full text ed.: ISSN 1460-3667. GBP 536, USD 991 to institutions (effective 2012).
Indexed: A01, A03, A08, A20, A22, ABCPolSci, ASCA, B07, BibInd, CA, CurCont, E01, H04, IBR, IBSS, IBZ, P02, P10, P30, P34, P42, P47, P48, P53, P54, PCI, PQC, PRA, PSA, PerIslam, RASB, S02, S03, S11, SCOPUS, SOPODA, SPAA, SSA, SSCI, SociolAb, T02, V02, W07.
—BLDSC (5069.075600), IE, Infotrieve, Ingenta. **CCC.**
Published by: Sage Publications Ltd. (Subsidiary of: Sage Publications, Inc.), 1 Oliver's Yard, 55 City Rd, London, EC1Y 1SP, United Kingdom. TEL 44-20-73248500, FAX 44-20-73248600, info@sagepub.co.uk, http://www.uk.sagepub.com/home.nav. Eds. James R Rogers, Keith Dowding.

320.082 USA ISSN 1554-477X
HQ1236
➤ **JOURNAL OF WOMEN, POLITICS & POLICY**; a quarterly journal of research & policy studies. Text in English. 1980. q. GBP 454 combined subscription in United Kingdom to institutions (print & online eds.); EUR 592, USD 587 combined subscription to institutions (print & online eds.) (effective 2012). adv. bk.rev. charts; illus. 120 p./no. 1 cols./p.; back issues avail.; reprints avail. **Document type:** *Journal, Academic/Scholarly.* **Description:** Emphasizes women's places in the political spectrum, including the areas of political philosophy, international relations, American politics and comparative politics.
Formerly (until 2005): Women & Politics (0195-7732)
Related titles: Microfiche ed.: (from PQC); Microform ed.; Online - full text ed.: ISSN 1554-4788. GBP 409 in United Kingdom to institutions; EUR 532, USD 528 to institutions (effective 2012).
Indexed: A01, A02, A03, A08, A20, A22, A26, ABCPolSci, ABS&EES, AmH&L, B04, BRD, CA, CWI, ChPerI, Chicano, CurCont, DIP, E01, E08, FamI, FemPer, G08, GW, HistAb, I05, I13, IBR, IBSS, IBZ, M01, M02, P02, P10, P27, P30, P34, P42, P48, P53, P54, PAIS, PCI, PQC, PSA, PerIslam, S02, S03, S09, S21, SCOPUS, SOPODA, SSAI, SSAb, SSCI, SSI, SWR&A, SociolAb, T02, UAA, W03, W06, W07, W09, WSA.
—BLDSC (5072.633900), IE, Infotrieve, Ingenta. **CCC.**

Published by: Routledge (Subsidiary of: Taylor & Francis Group), 325 Chestnut St, Ste 800, Philadelphia, PA 19106. TEL 215-625-8900, 800-354-1420, FAX 215-625-8914, journals@routledge.com, http://www.routledge.com. Eds. Carol Hardy-Fanta, Heidi Hartmann. adv.: B&W page USD 315, color page USD 550; trim 4.375 x 7.125. Circ: 566 (paid).

320 FRA ISSN 1773-2719
JOURNAL POLIQUE. Text in French. 2005. m. EUR 25 domestic; EUR 35 foreign (effective 2009). **Document type:** *Newsletter, Consumer.*
Published by: Journal Politique, s/c Le Perroquet, B P 84, Paris, Cedex 10 75462, France. http://orgapoli.net.

351 330 CHN ISSN 1002-8129
HD30.23
JUECE YU XINXI/DECISION & INFORMATION. Text in Chinese. 1984. s-m. back issues avail. **Document type:** *Magazine, Consumer.* **Description:** The first issue of the month is the business edition and the second issue is the politics edition.
Published by: (Wuhan Juece Xinxi Yanjiu Kaifa Zhongxin), Juece yu Xinxi Zazhishe, Wuchang Shuiguohu, 10-3, Huming Lu, 3/F, Wuhan, 430071, China. TEL 86-27-87232260. **Co-sponsors:** Zhongguo Guoji Gonggong Guanxi Xiehui/China International Public Relations Association; Hubei Ruankexue Yanjiuso; Zhongguo Diqu Kaifa Cujinhui.

324 DEU ISSN 0939-8635
➤ **JUGENDPOLITIK.** Text in German. 1975. q. EUR 12; EUR 4 newsstand/cover (effective 2010). bk.rev. **Document type:** *Journal, Academic/Scholarly.* **Description:** Publication of interest to youth, youth leaders, politicians, and those concerned with youth issues. Covers politics, education, international youth relations, youth societies, and political youth parties.
Indexed: DIP, IBR, IBZ.
Published by: Deutscher Bundesjugendring, Muehlendamm 3, Berlin, 10178, Germany. TEL 49-30-40040412, FAX 49-30-40040422, info@dbjr.de, http://www.dbjr.de.

320 USA
JULIAN J. ROTHBAUM DISTINGUISHED LECTURE SERIES. Text in English. 1987. irreg., latest vol.11, 2009. price varies. back issues avail. **Document type:** *Monographic series, Academic/Scholarly.* **Description:** Examines the decline of the political center within America's party system.
Published by: University of Oklahoma Press, 2800 Venture Dr, Norman, OK 73069. TEL 405-325-2000, 800-627-7377, FAX 405-364-5798, 800-735-0476, kbenson@ou.edu.

JULUKA. *see* TRAVEL AND TOURISM

JUNDUI DANGDE SHENGHUO. *see* MILITARY

320 DEU
JUNG UND LIBERAL. Text in German. q. adv. **Document type:** *Magazine, Consumer.*
Published by: Junge Liberale, Ackerstr 3b, Berlin, 10115, Germany. TEL 49-30-28388791, FAX 49-30-28388799, info@julis.de. Ed. Jan Krawitz. Circ: 8,000.

320.51 DEU
JUNGE LIBERALE BAYERN. FORUM. Text in German. 1983. q. adv. **Document type:** *Bulletin.*
Published by: Junge Liberale Bayern e.V., Agnesstr 47, Munich, 80798, Germany. TEL 089-12600960, FAX 089-1294149. Circ: 1,000.

JUNGES FORUM. *see* HISTORY—History Of Europe

JURIDICAL REVIEW; the law journal of Scottish universities. *see* LAW

▼ **JURISPRUDENCE**; an international journal of legal and political thought. *see* LAW

JURISPRUDENCIJA/JURISPRUDENCE. *see* LAW

320 GBR ISSN 1475-0309
K S L. (Kate Sharpley Library) Variant title: Bulletin of the Kate Sharpley Library. Text in English. 1992. q. GBP 5, USD 10 domestic to individuals; EUR 15 in Europe to individuals; GBP 20, USD 40 to institutions (effective 2009). bk.rev. **Document type:** *Bulletin, Bibliography.* **Description:** Focuses on various aspects of anarchist bibliography and history.
Related titles: Online - full text ed.
Address: BM Hurricane, London, WCIN 3XX, United Kingdom.

KAILASH; an interdisciplinary journal of Himalayan studies. *see* HISTORY—History Of Asia

KANSAI UNIVERSITY REVIEW OF LAW AND POLITICS. *see* LAW

328 USA ISSN 0270-4331
KFK20
KANSAS. LEGISLATIVE RESEARCH DEPARTMENT. REPORT ON KANSAS LEGISLATIVE INTERIM STUDIES. Text in English. 1971. a. free.
Published by: Legislative Research Department, 300 S W 10th Ave, Room 545-N, Topeka, KS 66612-1504. TEL 785-296-3181. Circ: (controlled).

320 FIN ISSN 1795-4126
KANSSALAINEN. Text in Finnish. 2004. s-a. free. **Document type:** *Magazine, Government.*
Related titles: Online - full text ed.: ISSN 1795-4134.
Published by: Oikeusministerio, Kansalaisvaikuttamisen Politiikkaohjelma/Ministry of Justice. Citizen Participation Policy Programme, PO Box 25, Government, Helsinki, 00023, Finland. TEL 358-9-16003, FAX 358-9-16067730, om-tiedet@om.fi. Ed. Maria Wakeham.

323.11994 305.8994 NZL ISSN 1173-6011
TE KARAKA. Variant title: Ngai Tahu Magazine. Text in English. 1995. 3/yr. **Document type:** *Magazine, Consumer.* **Description:** Offers insight into the contemporary world of Ngai Tahu, issues that affect the iwi, and in turn affect New Zealand. It serves to inform, record, debate and inspire. It reflects what is happening within the tribe from its South Island base to wherever Ngai Tahu people may be.
Related titles: Online - full text ed.: ISSN 1177-7222.
Indexed: A11, RILM, T02.
Published by: Ngai Tahu Communications Ltd., PO Box 13 469, Christchurch, New Zealand. TEL 64-3-3664344, FAX 64-3-3713901, info@ngaitahu.iwi.nz, http://ngaitahu.iwi.nz. Ed. Phil Tuihataroa.

320.5322 ZAF
KEEP LEFT!. Text in English. 1998. m. ZAR 30, GBP 20 (effective 2000); ZAR 2 newsstand/cover. illus. 20 p./no. 3 cols./p.; **Document type:** *Newsletter.* **Description:** Classical Marxist analysis of local and international events.
Published by: Communist Young Lions Network, PO Box 93428, Yeoville, Johannesburg 2143, South Africa. TEL 27-11-487-2812, FAX 27-11-487-2812, keepleft@ananzi.co.za. Ed. Claire C Ceruti.

324.6 USA
KENTUCKY DIRECTORY OF BLACK ELECTED OFFICIALS. Text in English. 1970. quadrennial. free. reprints avail.
Published by: Kentucky Commission on Human Rights, 332 W Broadway, 7th Fl, Louisville, KY 40202. TEL 502-595-4024, FAX 502-595-4801. Circ: 2,000.

320 IND
KERALASABDAM. Text in Malayalam. 1972. w. INR 530; INR 12 per issue (effective 2011). adv. **Document type:** *Magazine, Consumer.*
Address: R. Krishnaswamy Memorial Bldg, Lekshminada, Kollam, Kerala 691 013, India. TEL 91-474-2750777, FAX 91-474-2740710.

320.5322 GBR ISSN 1369-9725
KEY WORDS; a journal of cultural materialism. Text in English. 1998. irreg., latest no.7, 2009. back issues avail. **Document type:** *Journal, Academic/Scholarly.* **Description:** Contains articles which analyzes arts, media, and politics in the contemporary global era based on the work of Raymond Williams.
Related titles: Online - full text ed.
Indexed: MLA-IB.
Published by: Raymond Williams Society, c/o J. Birkett, Department of French Studies, University of Birmingham, Edgbaston, Birmingham B15 2TT, United Kingdom. postmaster@raymondwilliams.co.uk, http://www.raymondwilliams.co.uk/.

320 EGY ISSN 2090-0589
KHAMASIN; reflections on the social and political. Text in English. 2006. s-a. **Document type:** *Journal, Academic/Scholarly.*
Media: Online - full text.
Published by: American University in Cairo, Department of Political Science, PO Box 74, New Cairo, 11835, Egypt. TEL 20-2-26151906, http://www.aucegypt.edu/academics/dept/pols/Pages/default.aspx.

320.57 CAN ISSN 0823-6526
KICK IT OVER; a social anarchist/anti-authoritarian quarterly. Text in English. 1981. q. CAD 14 domestic to individuals; USD 14 foreign to individuals; CAD 18 domestic to institutions; USD 18 foreign to institutions; CAD 3 newsstand/cover (effective 2001). adv. bk.rev.; film rev.; rec.rev. illus. back issues avail.; reprints avail. **Document type:** *Journal, Consumer.* **Description:** Explores political, social and personal issues from an anarchist, feminist and ecological perspective.
Indexed: AltPI, C03, CBCARef, PQC.
Published by: Kick it Over Collective, P O Box 5811, Stn A, Toronto, ON M5W 1P2, Canada. TEL 519-822-3110, FAX 519-822-7089, kio@tao.ca. Ed., R&P Bob Melcombe. Circ: 2,000. **Dist. by:** Doormouse distribution, 4 Davis Ave, Toronto, ON, Canada.

320 DEU ISSN 0932-4224
KIELER SCHRIFTEN ZUR POLITISCHEN WISSENSCHAFT. Text in German. 1987. irreg., latest vol.19, 2007. price varies. **Document type:** *Monographic series, Academic/Scholarly.*
—**CCC.**
Published by: Peter Lang GmbH (Subsidiary of: Peter Lang Publishing Group), Eschborner Landstr 42-50, Frankfurt Am Main, 60489, Germany. TEL 49-69-7807050, FAX 49-69-78070550, zentrale.frankfurt@peterlang.com. Ed. Joachim Krause.

320.5 SWE ISSN 0345-6188
KLASSKAMPEN. Text in Swedish. 1970. irreg. (4-5/yr.). SEK 240 to members (effective 1991).
Published by: K P M L, Box 31187, Goeteborg, 40032, Sweden.

324 NLD ISSN 1879-940X
▼ **DE KLEINE GIDS VERKIEZINGEN.** Text in Dutch. 2009. a. EUR 13.94 (effective 2010).
Published by: Kluwer B.V. (Subsidiary of: Wolters Kluwer N.V.), Postbus 23, Deventer, 7400 GA, Netherlands. TEL 31-570-673449, FAX 31-570-691555, info@kluwer.nl, http://www.kluwer.nl.

320 RUS
KLUB REALISTY. Text in Russian. 1995. 8/yr. USD 125 in North America (effective 2000).
Indexed: RASB.
Published by: Politicheskii Klub Realisty, Ul Elizarovoi d 6 str 3, Moscow, 103064, Russian Federation. TEL 7-095-9177188, FAX 7-095-9175021. Ed. G A Cherneiko. **Dist. by:** East View Information Services, 10601 Wayzata Blvd, Minneapolis, MN 55305. TEL 952-252-1201, 800-477-1005, FAX 952-252-1202, info@eastview.com, http://www.eastview.com.

320 GBR ISSN 1757-7675
KNOWLEDGE POLITICS QUARTERLY. Text in English. 2007. s-a. back issues avail. **Document type:** *Journal, Academic/Scholarly.* **Description:** Features original articles by established scholars, graduate students and non-academic practitioners.
Media: Online - full text.
Indexed: A39, C27, C29, D03, D04, E13, R14, S14, S15, S18.
Published by: Knowledge Politics

KOBLENZER GEOGRAPHISCHES KOLLOQUIUM. *see* GEOGRAPHY

320 DNK ISSN 0906-1444
KOEBENHAVNS UNIVERSITET. INSTITUT FOR STATSVIDENSKAB. ARBEJDSPAPIR. Text in Danish, English. 1975. irreg., latest 2009. back issues avail. **Document type:** *Monographic series, Academic/Scholarly.*
Former titles (until 1990): Koebenhavns Universitet. Institut for Samfundsfag og Forvaltning. Arbejdspapir (0901-022X); (until 1984): Koebenhavns Universitet.Institur for Samfundsfag. Arbejdspapir (0109-5412)
Related titles: Online - full text ed.: 2003.
Published by: Koebenhavns Universitet, Institut for Statskundskab/ Copenhagen University, Institute of Political Studies, Oester Farimagsgade 5, Copenhagen K, 1353, Denmark. TEL 45-33-323366, FAX 45-35-323399, ps@ifs.ku.dk, http://www.polsci.ku.dk.

320 DEU ISSN 0075-6539
KOELNER SCHRIFTEN ZUR POLITISCHEN WISSENSCHAFT. Text in German. 1964. irreg., latest vol.5, 1975. price varies. **Document type:** *Monographic series, Academic/Scholarly.*

Published by: (Forschungsinstitut fuer Politische Wissenschaft und Europaeische Fragen), Duncker und Humblot GmbH, Carl-Heinrich-Becker-Weg 9, Berlin, 12165, Germany. TEL 49-30-7900060, FAX 49-30-79000631, verlag@duncker-humblot.de, http://www.duncker-humblot.de.

320 300 JPN ISSN 0023-2793
K11
KOKKA GAKKAI ZASSHI/ASSOCIATION OF POLITICAL AND SOCIAL SCIENCES. JOURNAL. Text in Japanese. 1887. bi-m. **Document type:** *Journal, Academic/Scholarly.*
Indexed: HistAb.
—Ingenta.
Published by: (Kokka Gakkai Jimusho/Association of Political and Social Sciences), Yuhikaku Publishing Co. Ltd., 2-17, Kanda Jimbo-cho, Chiyoda-ku, Tokyo, 101-0051, Japan. TEL 81-3-32641312, FAX 81-3-32645030, ygc@ygc-yuhi.co.jp, http://www.yuhikaku.co.jp/.

320.9 JPN ISSN 0454-1723
K11
KOKUGAKUIN UNIVERSITY. FACULTY OF LAW AND POLITICS. JOURNAL/KOKUGAKUIN HOGAKU. Text in Japanese. 1963. q. JPY 3,000. **Document type:** *Academic/Scholarly.*
Indexed: S02, S03.
—BLDSC (5101.776000).
Published by: Kokugakuin University, Faculty of Law and Politics, 4-10-28 Higashi, Shibuya-ku, Tokyo, 150-0011, Japan. TEL 03-5466-0304, FAX 03-5466-0757. Ed. Osamu Niikura.

320 365.34 355 JPN
UA845
➤ **KOKUSAI ANZEN HOSHO/JOURNAL OF INTERNATIONAL SECURITY.** Text in Japanese; Abstracts in English. 1973. q. JPY 4,000 (effective 2003). bk.rev. 120 p./no.; **Document type:** *Journal, Academic/Scholarly.* **Description:** Contains research on national security issues, military strategy, and international peacekeeping.
Former titles: Kokusai Anzen Hoshou (1346-7573); (until 2001): Shin Boei Ronshu (0286-9241)
—BLDSC (5101.784960).
Published by: (Kokusai Anzen Hosho Gakkai/Japan Association for International Security), Naigai Publishers, Ltd., Takaban 3-6-1, Meguro, Tokyo, 152-004, Japan. TEL 81-3-37120142, FAX 81-3-37123130. Ed. Seiichiro Takagi. R&P Tomorori Yoshizaki. Circ: 2,200.

320 330 UKR
KOMMENTARII. Text in Russian. 5/w. 40 p./no.; **Document type:** *Journal, Consumer.* **Description:** Keeps readers abreast of political and economic developments in the Ukraine, including news on related legislation and finance.
Published by: Ekspressinform, Ul Bozhenko 15, korp 7, k 309, Kiev, Ukraine. TEL 380-44-2615406, 380-44-2278952, FAX 380-44-2278952. Ed. Leonid Gusak.

320.943 DEU ISSN 0177-9184
KOMMUNALPOLITISCHE BLAETTER. Text in German. 1949. m. EUR 70.80; EUR 6.50 newsstand/cover (effective 2007). adv. **Document type:** *Magazine, Trade.*
Published by: Union Betriebs GmbH, Egermannstr 2, Rheinbach, 53359, Germany. TEL 49-2226-8020, FAX 49-2226-802111, info@ubg-medienzentrum.de, http://www.ubg-medienzentrum.de. Ed. Gaby Grabowski. adv.: B&W page EUR 1,990, color page EUR 3,780. Circ: 5,462 (paid and controlled).

342.43 DEU ISSN 2190-9695
▼ **KOMMUNALPRAXIS WAHLEN**; Fachzeitschrift fuer Wahlen und Abstimmungen. Text in German. 2010. 2/yr. EUR 49; EUR 28.50 newsstand/cover (effective 2011). **Document type:** *Journal, Trade.*
Published by: Carl Link Verlag (Subsidiary of: Wolters Kluwer Deutschland GmbH), Adolf-Kolping-Str 10, Kronach, 96317, Germany. TEL 49-9261-9694000, FAX 49-9261-9694111, info@wolters-kluwer.de, http://www.carllink.de.

320.532 DEU ISSN 0723-7669
DD260
KOMMUNE; Forum fuer Politik - Oekonomie - Kultur. Text in German. 1981. bi-m. EUR 55 domestic; EUR 60 foreign; EUR 10 newsstand/cover (effective 2008). adv. bk.rev. **Document type:** *Magazine, Consumer.*
Formerly (until 1983): Kommunistische Volkszeitung (0720-8898); Which was formed by the merger of (1976-1981): Kommunistische Volkszeitung. Ausgabe Mitte (0344-466X); (1976-1981): Kommunistische Volkszeitung. Ausgabe fuer die Bezirke Kassel/Nordhessen, Giessen/Sieg-Lahn, Frankfurt/Suedhessen und Mainz/Rheinhessen-Taunus (0721-7609); (1976-1981): Kommunistische Volkszeitung. Ausgabe Nord (0721-7617); All 3 superseded in part (1973-1976): Kommunistische Volkszeitung (0721-7625)
Indexed: DIP, IBR, IBZ, RASB.
Published by: Kuehl Verwaltung GmbH & Co. Verlags KG, Kasseler Str 1A, Frankfurt Am Main, 60486, Germany. TEL 49-69-79209781, FAX 49-69-79209783. Ed. Michael Ackermann. Circ: 4,000.

320.532 RUS
KOMMUNIST. Text in Russian. bi-m. USD 95 in United States.
Indexed: LID&ISL.
Published by: Kooperativ Tematik, Ul Kosmodem yanskikh 10-12, Moscow, 125130, Russian Federation. TEL 7-095-1592112. Ed. V V Burdyukov. **Dist. by:** East View Information Services, 10601 Wayzata Blvd, Minneapolis, MN 55305. TEL 952-252-1201, 800-477-1005, FAX 952-252-1202, info@eastview.com, http://www.eastview.com.

320.532 RUS
KOMMUNISTICHESKAYA PERSPEKTIVA. Text in Russian. irreg. USD 65 in United States.
Published by: Rossiiskaya Partiya Kommunistov, Ul Marshala Sokolovskogo 3, Moscow, 123060, Russian Federation. TEL 7-095-1947570. Ed. Glagoleva O N.

320 AUS
KONSTRUKTO. Text in English. 1996. every 2 mos. **Description:** Contains political satire and editorial.
Media: Online - full text.
Address: andypc@dove.mtx.net.au.

322.2 DNK ISSN 1902-2832
KONTRAST; globalisering, faglige rettigheder, solidaritet, udvikling, international handel. Text in Danish. 2007. s-a. free. **Document type:** *Magazine, Consumer.* **Description:** News, analysis and reports on global problems as seen from the wage-earner's perspective.
Related titles: Online - full text ed.: ISSN 1902-2859.
Published by: Landsorganisationen i Danmark/Danish Confederation of Trade Unions, Islands Brygge 32 D, Copenhagen S, 2300, Denmark. TEL 45-35-246000, FAX 45-35-246300, lo@lo.dk. Ed. Harald Bjoersting.

320.53 DEU ISSN 1867-3163
KONTROVERS; Beitraege zur politischen Bildung. Text in German. 2006. irreg. **Document type:** *Monographic series, Academic/Scholarly.*
Published by: Rosa-Luxemburg-Stiftung, Franz-Mehring Platz 1, Berlin, 10243, Germany. TEL 49-30-443100, FAX 49-30-44310222, info@rosalux.de, http://www.rosalux.de.

320 KOR ISSN 2005-2162
KOREA. Text in English. 2005. m. **Document type:** *Magazine, Consumer.*
Formerly (until 2008): Korea Policy Review (1739-7308)
Related titles: Online - full text ed.
Published by: The Korean Culture and Information Service (K O I S), 3-4 Fl., Fnc, Kolon Corp., 15, Hyojaro, Jongno-gu, Seoul, 110-040, Korea, S. TEL 82-2-3981-961, FAX 82-2-3981-882, http://www.korea.net/.

320.531 PRK ISSN 0454-4072
DS930
KOREA TODAY. Text in English. m. USD 60. charts; illus. reprints avail.
Related titles: Arabic ed.; Chinese ed.; Spanish ed.; Russian ed.; French ed.
Indexed: BAS, GeoRef, RASB, SpeleolAb.
Published by: Foreign Languages Publishing House, Pyongyang, Korea, N. TELEX 37018 EPB KP. Ed. Nam Suk Hahn. **Dist. by:** Korean Publications Exchange Association, Export Section, P.O. Box 222, Pyongyang, Korea, S. FAX 8502-814632.

320 USA
KOREAN RESEARCH BULLETIN. Text in English. 1976 (vol.6). s-a. free.
Indexed: BAS.
Published by: Korean Research Council, 1565 Miramar Ave, Seaside, CA 93955. Ed. Sae Woon Chang.

320.531 DEU ISSN 0944-6575
KRISIS; beitraege zur kritik der warengesellschaft. Text in German. 1980. irreg., latest vol.30, 2006. EUR 10 (effective 2006). adv. back issues avail. **Document type:** *Academic/Scholarly.*
Former titles (until 1990): Marxistische Kritik (0178-7691); (until 1986): Neue Stroemung (0720-5252)
Indexed: IPB.
Published by: (Foerderverein und Redaktion Krisis e.V.), Unrast e.V., Postfach 8020, Muenster, 48043, Germany. TEL 49-251-666293, FAX 49-251-666120, kontakt@unrast-verlag.de, http://www.unrast-verlag.de. Circ: 900 (paid).

320 DEU ISSN 1865-3103
KRITIK UND REFLEXION; interdisziplinaere Beitraege zur kritischen Gesellschaftstheorie. Text in German. 2007. irreg., latest vol.9, 2009. price varies. **Document type:** *Monographic series, Academic/Scholarly.*
Published by: Verlag Dr. Kovac, Leverkusenstr 13, Hamburg, 22761, Germany. TEL 49-40-3988800, FAX 49-40-39888055, info@verlagdrkovac.de. Ed. Gerhard Stapelfeldt.

KRONIKA WARSZAWY. see HISTORY—History Of Europe

320 RUS
KUBANSKIE NOVOSTI. Text in Russian. 260/yr. USD 399 in United States.
Address: Ul Kalinina 339, Krasnodar, 350681, Russian Federation. TEL 8612-57-60-27. Ed. P Pridius. **Dist. by:** East View Information Services, 10601 Wayzata Blvd, Minneapolis, MN 55305. TEL 952-252-1201, 800-477-1005, FAX 952-252-1202, info@eastview.com, http://www.eastview.com.

320 KOR
KUKHOEBO/NATIONAL ASSEMBLY REVIEW. Text in Korean. 1949. m. free. charts; illus.; stat. **Document type:** *Magazine, Trade.* **Description:** Provides current information on the National Assembly.
Former titles (until 1964): Ch'oego Hoeui Po; (until 1961): Minuiwon Po; (until 1961): Kukhoebo (0027-8580)
Published by: Kukhoe Tosogwan/National Assembly Library of Korea, Youngdeungpo-gu,Yoido-dong 1, Seoul, 150-703, Korea, S. TEL 82-2-7882001, http://www.nanet.go.kr/. Ed. Man Seop. Circ: 5,500 (controlled).

322.4 DEU ISSN 0723-8088
AP30
KULTURREVOLUTION; Zeitschrift fuer angewandte Diskurstheorie. Text in German. 1982. 2/yr. EUR 17.50; EUR 10 newsstand/cover (effective 2010). **Document type:** *Bulletin.*
Indexed: DIP, IBR, IBZ, MLA-IB.
Published by: Klartext Verlag GmbH, Hesslerstr 37, Essen, 45329, Germany. TEL 49-201-8620631, FAX 49-201-8620622, info@klartext-verlag.de, http://www.klartext-verlag.de. Ed. Juergen Link.

KURIER (LIESBORN); der christlichen Mitte. see RELIGIONS AND THEOLOGY

KURSIV; Journal fuer politische Bildung. see EDUCATION—Teaching Methods And Curriculum

320 BWA ISSN 0023-5733
DT790
KUTLWANO/MUTUAL UNDERSTANDING. Text in English. 1962. a., latest vol.39. BWP 100 (effective 2001). adv. music rev. charts; illus. **Document type:** *Magazine, Government.* **Description:** Features development issues in the country.
Indexed: RASB.
Published by: Botswana, Department of Information and Broadcasting, Private Bag 0060, Gaborone, Botswana. TEL 267-3653000, FAX 267-301675, ib.publicity@gov.bw, http://www.gov.bw. Ed. Russ Molosiwa. Adv. contact Thomas Lesego. B&W page BWP 650, color page BWP 1,300. Circ: 40,000 (controlled).

320 RUS
KVORUM; ezhenedel'naya parliamentskaya obshchestvenno-politicheskaya gazeta. Text in Russian, English. 1998. w.
Related titles: Online - full text ed.
Published by: Gosudarstvennaya Duma Rossiiskoi Federatsii, Okhotnyi riad 1, Moscow, 103001, Russian Federation. **Co-sponsor:** Moscow Press Laboratory.

KYIVS'KYI NATSIONAL'NYI UNIVERSYTET IMENI TARASA SHEVCHENKA. VISNYK. FILOSOFIYA, POLITOLOHIYA. see PHILOSOPHY

320 GBR ISSN 1470-1952
HX3
L M. (Living Marxism) Text in English. 1988. m. GBP 27.50 in United Kingdom; GBP 35 in Europe; GBP 45 rest of world; GBP 2.95 newsstand/cover; USD 6 newsstand/cover in United States; EUR 4.50 newsstand/cover (effective 2000). adv. bk.rev.; film rev.; play rev. **Document type:** *Bulletin.* **Description:** Provides news and current-affairs commentary and analysis, along with regular features on social issues, science, arts, and culture.
Formerly (until 1997): Living Marxism (0955-2448)
Related titles: Microfilm ed.
Indexed: AltPI.
—CCC.
Published by: Informinc Ltd., Signet House, 49-51 Farringdon Rd, London, EC1M 3JB, United Kingdom. TEL 44-20-7269-9220, FAX 44-20-7269-9235. Ed. Mick Hume. Pubs. Claire Fox, Helene Guldberg. R&P Claire Fox. Adv. contact Helene Guldberg. B&W page GBP 1,050, color page GBP 1,250. Circ: 10,000. **Dist. by:** Comag, Tavistock Rd, W Drayton, Middlesex UB7 7QE, United Kingdom. TEL 44-1895-433600, FAX 44-189-543-3606.

320 ITA ISSN 2036-1246
L P F WORKING PAPERS. (Laboratorio di Politica Comparata e Filosofia Pubblica) Text in Multiple languages. 2008. irreg. **Document type:** *Monographic series, Academic/Scholarly.*
Media: Online - full text.
Published by: Centro di Ricerca e Documentazione Luigi Einaudi, Via Ponza 4, Turin, 10121, Italy. TEL 39-011-5591611, FAX 39-011-5591691, segreteria@centroeinauidi.it.

324.2 USA ISSN 1529-563X
HD8076
LABOR PARTY PRESS. Text in English. 1996 (Sum.). bi-m. USD 20 to individual members. **Document type:** *Newspaper.*
Indexed: AltPI.
Address: PO Box 53177, Washington, DC 20009. TEL 202-234-5190, FAX 202-234-5266, lp@thelaborparty.org, http://www.thelaborparty.org. Ed. Laura McClure.

320.5322 AUS ISSN 1329-3745
LABOR REVIEW. Text in English. 1946-1984; N.S. 1987. q. AUD 10; AUD 20 foreign. bk.rev. **Description:** Includes articles on politics, economics and history from a Marxist viewpoint.
Formerly (until 1993): Labor College Review (0159-1908)
Published by: Victorian Labor College, Trades Hall, PO Box 39, Carlton South, VIC 3053, Australia.

LABOUR & TRADE UNION REVIEW. see LABOR UNIONS

324.2 IRL ISSN 0790-1712
LABOUR COMMENT (CORK). Text in English. 1968. m. adv. bk.rev. back issues avail. **Document type:** *Magazine, Consumer.*
Former titles (until 1984): Socialist Comment (0790-1909); Communist Comment
Indexed: RASB.
Published by: Labour Comment (Cork) Ireland, c/o Shandon Street Post Office, Cork, Ireland. FAX 353-21-506360. Pub., Adv. contact Patrick N Maloney. Circ: 1,000. **Co-publisher:** Athol Books. **Co-sponsor:** Brotherhood of Irish Compositors.

320 GBR
LABOUR REVIEW. Text in English. 1996. irreg.
Media: Online - full content.
Address: http://www.cix.co.uk/~ecotrend/LR/Review.

322.4 GBR ISSN 0309-3689
LABOUR STUDENT. Text in English. 1980. 3/yr. GBP 3. adv. bk.rev. illus.
Formerly: Socialist Youth (0260-7336)
—CCC.
Published by: Labour Students, 150 Walnorth Rd, London, SE17 1JT, United Kingdom. Circ: 12,000.

LABSI WORKING PAPER. see BUSINESS AND ECONOMICS—Economic Systems And Theories, Economic History

320 USA
LAISSEZ FAIRE BOOKS. FREE MARKET CATALOG. Text in English. 1973. m. free (effective 2000). adv. bk.rev. tr.lit. **Document type:** *Catalog.*
Former titles: Laissez Faire Free Market Catalog; Laissez Faire Libertarian Catalog
Published by: Laissez Faire Books, 938 Howard St, San Francisco, CA 94103. TEL 415-541-9780, FAX 415-541-0597, http://Laisezfaire.org. Ed. Jim Powell. Pub. Andrea Rich. Adv. contact Dave Brooks. Circ: 50,000.

320 ESP ISSN 1579-2803
LAMUSA DIGITAL. Text in Spanish. 2002. 3/yr. **Document type:** *Journal, Academic/Scholarly.*
Media: Online - full text. **Related titles:** Print ed.: Lamusa. ISSN 1695-7229.
Published by: Universidad de Castilla-La Mancha, Facultad de Humanidades de Albacete, Edif Benjamin Palencia, Campus Universitario s/n, Albacete, 02071, Spain. TEL 34-976-599200.

THE LANE REPORT; Kentucky's business news source. see BUSINESS AND ECONOMICS

320 USA
LANGUAGE AND IDEOLOGY. Text in English. 1991. irreg. price varies. **Document type:** *Monographic series.*
Published by: Praeger Publishers (Subsidiary of: Greenwood Publishing Group Inc.), 88 Post Rd W, Westport, CT 06881. TEL 800-368-6868, tech.support@greenwood.com, http://www.greenwood.com. Ed. Donaldo Macedo.

LATIN AMERICA MONITOR. ANDEAN GROUP. see BUSINESS AND ECONOMICS—Economic Situation And Conditions

LATIN AMERICA MONITOR. BRAZIL. see BUSINESS AND ECONOMICS—Economic Situation And Conditions

LATIN AMERICA MONITOR. CARIBBEAN. see BUSINESS AND ECONOMICS—Economic Situation And Conditions

P

LATIN AMERICA MONITOR. CENTRAL AMERICA. *see* BUSINESS AND ECONOMICS—Economic Situation And Conditions

LATIN AMERICA MONITOR. MEXICO. *see* BUSINESS AND ECONOMICS—Economic Situation And Conditions

LATIN AMERICA MONITOR. SOUTHERN CONE. *see* BUSINESS AND ECONOMICS—Economic Situation And Conditions

320.98 JPN ISSN 0910-3317
HC121
➤ **LATIN AMERICA REPORT.** Text in Japanese. 1984. q. JPY 1,980 (effective 2003). bk.rev. bibl. **Document type:** *Academic/Scholarly.* **Description:** Includes papers, field reports, and book information with a regional focus on Latin America.
Published by: Institute of Developing Economies/Ajia Keizai Kenkyusho, 3-2-2 Wakaba, Mihana-ku, Chiba-shi, Chiba 261-8545, Japan. TEL 81-43-2999536, FAX 84-43-2999724. Circ: 250.

➤ **LATIN AMERICAN PERSPECTIVES**; a journal on capitalism and socialism. *see* SOCIAL SCIENCES: COMPREHENSIVE WORKS

320.98 USA ISSN 1097-4997
F1401
LATIN AMERICAN POLITICAL YEARBOOK. Text in English. 1997. irreg., latest vol.6, 2003. USD 59.95 per issue (effective 2010). back issues avail. **Document type:** *Monographic series, Academic/Scholarly.* **Description:** Provides comprehensive single source of information on changes in government, electoral processes, revolutionary movements and key personalities for Mexico, Cuba, the Caribbean and South America.
Published by: Transaction Publishers, 35 Berrue Cir, Piscataway, NJ 08854. TEL 732-445-2280, FAX 732-445-3138, trans@transactionpub.com, http://www.transactionpub.com.

LATIN AMERICAN REGIONAL REPORT. BRAZIL AND SOUTHERN CONE. *see* BUSINESS AND ECONOMICS—Economic Situation And Conditions

LATIN AMERICAN REGIONAL REPORTS - ANDEAN GROUP. *see* BUSINESS AND ECONOMICS—Economic Situation And Conditions

LATIN AMERICAN REGIONAL REPORTS. CARIBBEAN & CENTRAL AMERICA REPORT. *see* BUSINESS AND ECONOMICS—Economic Situation And Conditions

320.3 ECU ISSN 1390-4248
JA5
➤ **LATIN AMERICAN REVIEW OF COMPARATIVE POLITICS.** Text in Spanish. 2008. 2/yr. USD 80 to individuals; USD 140 to institutions (effective 2008). adv. **Document type:** *Journal, Academic/Scholarly.* **Description:** Addresses broad aspects of Latin American politics as well as worldwide works on comparative politics in areas such as constitutionalism, institutions, electoral studies, legislative studies, political parties, and governance.
Related titles: Online - full text ed.
Indexed: P42, PSA, S02, S03, SSAI, SSAb, SSI, T02, W03, W05.
Published by: Centro Latinoamericano de Estudios Politicos/Latin American Center for Political Studies, Av 12 de octubre N24-562 y Cordero, Edif World Trade Ctr, Torre B, Mezanine, Of No 05-B, Quito, Ecuador. TEL 583-2-2566985, FAX 583-2-2566985. Eds. Felipe Cisneros, Sebastian Mantilla. R&P, Adv. contact Sebastian Mantilla. page USD 1,200. Circ: 400 (paid).

➤ **LATIN AMERICAN WEEKLY REPORT.** *see* BUSINESS AND ECONOMICS—Economic Situation And Conditions

➤ **THE LATIN AMERICANIST.** *see* HISTORY

320.531 NLD ISSN 1389-1847
LAVA. Text in Dutch. 1974. 5/yr. EUR 15 to non-members (effective 2009). adv. bk.rev. illus.; stat.
Formed by the 1999 merger of: Clinch (0929-5100); Which was formerly (until Mar. 1993): Linksaf (0167-093X); Supersedes: Opinie (0030-3771); Which was formerly: Kapitalist; Paraat; (1983-1998): Aktief (1383-7885)
Published by: Jonge Socialisten in de Partij van de Arbeid, Postbus 1310, Amsterdam, 1000 BH, Netherlands. TEL 31-20-5512131, FAX 31-20-5512250, js@js.nl, http://www.js.nl. Ed. Pepijn van den Brink TEL 31-06-51631137.

LAW & POLICY. *see* LAW

LAW AND POLITICS BOOK REVIEW. *see* LAW

THE LEADERSHIP QUARTERLY. *see* BUSINESS AND ECONOMICS—Management

LEAGUE OF WOMEN VOTERS OF GEORGIA. LEGISLATIVE NEWSLETTER. *see* LAW

LEARNING FOR DEMOCRACY; an international journal of thought and practice. *see* EDUCATION

320 ISR ISSN 1565-0103
LEBNS FRAGN. Text in Yiddish. 1951. bi-m. ILS 60 domestic; USD 25 in North America; EUR 25 in Europe; USD 30 in South Africa; USD 30 in Australia (effective 2008). bk.rev.; play rev. 28 p./no. 2 cols./p.; **Document type:** *Newspaper, Consumer.*
Published by: Brith Haavoda - Arbeter Ring, 48 Kalisher St, Tel Aviv, 65165, Israel. Ed. Yitzhak Luden. Circ: 2,500.

320 PER ISSN 1026-2679
LECTURAS CONTEMPORANEAS. Text in Spanish. 1995. irreg. price varies. **Document type:** *Monographic series, Academic/Scholarly.*
Published by: I E P Ediciones (Subsidiary of: Instituto de Estudios Peruanos), Horacio Urteaga 694, Jesus Maria, Lima, 11, Peru. TEL 51-14-3326194, FAX 51-14-3326173, libreria@iep.org.pe, http://iep.perucultural.org.pe.

320 NLD
LEEFBAAR NIEUWS. Text in Dutch. 2007. irreg.
Published by: Fractie Leefbaar Rotterdam, Postbus 8734, Rotterdam, 3009 AS, Netherlands. TEL 31-10-4173945, FAX 31-10-4173950, leefbaarrotterdam@stadhuis.rotterdam.nl, http://www.leefbaarrotterdam.nl. Circ: 269,000.

THE LEFT GUIDE; a guide to liberal, progressive, and left-of-center organizations. *see* BUSINESS AND ECONOMICS—Trade And Industrial Directories

322.4 USA
K1
THE LEGAL REFORMER. Text in English. 1979. s-a. USD 20 to members (effective 2000). bk.rev. **Document type:** *Newsletter.*
Formerly (until vol.8, no.4, 1988): Americans for Legal Reform (0739-6813)
Published by: (Organization of Americans for Legal Reform), HALT, Inc., 1612 K St, N W, Ste 510, Washington, DC 20006-2802. TEL 202-347-9600, 888-367-4258, FAX 202-347-9606. Ed., R&P Theresa Meehan Rudy. Circ: 50,000.

320.531 CUB
LEGALIDAD SOCIALISTA. Text in Spanish. q. USD 15 in the Americas; USD 16 in Europe; USD 18 elsewhere.
Published by: (Cuba. Fiscalia General de la Republica), Ediciones Cubanas, Obispo 527, Havana, Cuba.

LEGISBRIEFS. *see* PUBLIC ADMINISTRATION

LEGISCON STATEHOUSE REPORT. *see* PUBLIC ADMINISTRATION

328.1 USA
LEGISLATIVE COVERAGE & ANALYSIS. Text in English. d. (during legislative session). USD 795 (effective 2000).
Related titles: Online - full text ed.: USD 895 (effective 2000).
Published by: Capitol Government Reports, PO Box 602, Santa Fe, NM 87504-0602. TEL 505-988-9835, FAX 505-988-9835.

328 USA ISSN 1064-203X
THE LEGISLATIVE GAZETTE. Text in English. 1978. w. (except July-Aug.). USD 99 (effective 2005). adv. bk.rev. **Document type:** *Newspaper, Consumer.* **Description:** Covers New York legislative and related state government activity.
Related titles: Microform ed.
Published by: Research Foundation of State University of New York, Empire State Plaza, Room 106, Concourse Level, PO Box 7329, Albany, NY 12224. TEL 518-473-9739, FAX 518-486-7394, gvadney@legislativegazette.com. Ed., R&P Glenn C Doty TEL 518-486-6513. Pub. Alan Chartock. Adv. contact Glenn Vadney. B&W page USD 1,798.23; 10 x 16. Circ: 1,800 (controlled).

320 USA ISSN 0362-9805
JF501
➤ **LEGISLATIVE STUDIES QUARTERLY.** Abbreviated title: L S Q. Text in English. 1976. q. GBP 290 combined subscription in United Kingdom to institutions (print & online eds.); EUR 334 combined subscription in Europe to institutions (print & online eds.); USD 390 combined subscription in the Americas to institutions (print & online eds.); USD 411 combined subscription elsewhere to institutions (print & online eds.) (effective 2012). bk.rev. bibl.; charts; illus. cum index: 1976-2004. 150 p./no.; back issues avail.; reprint service avail. from PSC. **Document type:** *Journal, Academic/Scholarly.* **Description:** Aims to disseminate scholarly work on parliaments and legislatures, their relations to other political institutions, their functions in the political system, and the activities of their members both within the institution and outside.
Related titles: Microform ed.: (from PQC); Online - full text ed.: ISSN 1939-9162. GBP 265 in United Kingdom to institutions; EUR 306 in Europe to institutions; USD 355 in the Americas to institutions; USD 376 elsewhere to institutions (effective 2012) (from IngentaConnect).
Indexed: A01, A20, A22, ABCPolSci, ABS&EES, ASCA, B01, B06, B07, B09, CA, CurCont, E04, E05, I13, IBR, IBSS, IBZ, P34, P42, PAA&I, PAIS, PRA, PSA, RASB, S02, S03, SCOPUS, SPAA, SSCI, SociolAb, T02, W07.
—BLDSC (5181.461000), IE, Infotrieve, Ingenta. **CCC.**
Published by: (University of Iowa, Comparative Legislative Research Center), John Wiley & Sons, Inc., 111 River St, Hoboken, NJ 07030. TEL 201-748-6000, 800-825-7550, FAX 201-748-5915, info@wiley.com, http://www.wiley.com/WileyCDA/. Eds. David T Canon, John M Carey.

328 USA
LEGISLATIVE UPDATE (DALLAS); opinion ballot, national poll & voting records. Text in English. 1958. m. USD 125 membership (effective 2000). adv. **Document type:** *Newsletter.* **Description:** Contains excerpts from congressmen's speeches, opinion polls and letters to the editor on major national issues including SDI, abortion, gun control, taxation and government spending. Includes a ballot on state issues to be sent to representatives in Congress & governors.
Related titles: Fax ed.: USD 40 (effective 1999).
Published by: National "Write Your Congressman" Inc., 9696 Skillman, Ste 170, Dallas, TX 75243. TEL 214-342-0299, FAX 214-324-2455. Ed. Charles M Huston. Adv. contact Randy Ford. Circ: 75,000 (paid).

LE LETTRE A; la lettre de tous les pouvoirs. *see* BUSINESS AND ECONOMICS—Economic Situation And Conditions

320.9 FRA ISSN 1951-1329
LA LETTRE EUROPEENNE. Text in French. 2005. q. **Document type:** *Bulletin, Government.*
Published by: Assemblee Nationale, 126 rue de l'Universite, Paris, 75355, France. TEL 33-1-40636000, FAX 33-1-45557523, http://www.assemblee-nationale.fr/europe.

320 NLD ISSN 1872-0862
LIBER. Text in Dutch. 2000. 8/yr. adv.
Formerly (until 2006): Politiek! (1567-8598); Which incorporated (1948-2000): Vrijheid en Democratie (0166-8498)
Published by: Volkspartij voor Vrijheid en Democratie, Postbus 30836, The Hague, 2500 GV, Netherlands. TEL 31-70-3613061, FAX 31-70-3608276, info@vvd.nl, http://www.vvd.nl.

320 NOR ISSN 1504-7431
LIBERAL; venstres medlemsmagasin. Text in Norwegian. 1988. s-m. back issues avail. **Document type:** *Magazine, Consumer.*
Former titles (until 2007): Liberal.no (1502-2900); (until 2000): Liberalt Forum (0805-6862); (until 1994): Liberalt Perspektiv (0805-6854)
Related titles: Online - full text ed.: ISSN 1504-744X.
Published by: Venstre/The Liberal Party of Norway, Moellergate 16, Oslo, 0179, Norway. TEL 47-22-404350, FAX 47-22-404351, venstre@venstre.no. Eds. Frode Fjeldstad, Terje Breivik. Circ: 9,700.

320.51 DEU ISSN 0459-1992
JN3971.A1
LIBERAL. Text in German. 1959. q. EUR 43; EUR 12.50 newsstand/cover (effective 2007). adv. bk.rev. index. back issues avail.; reprints avail. **Document type:** *Magazine, Consumer.*
Indexed: DIP, IBR, IBZ, PAIS, RASB.
Published by: (Friedrich-Naumann-Stiftung ZAF), Liberal Verlag GmbH, Reinhardtstr 16, Berlin, 10117, Germany. TEL 49-30-27572871, FAX 49-30-27572880, christian.renatus@liberalverlag.de, http://www.liberalverlag.de. Ed. Barthold Witte. Adv. contact Christian Renatus. page EUR 1,534; trim 218 x 145.

320.531 SWE ISSN 0024-1814
LIBERAL DEBATT; den liberala idetidskriften. Text in Swedish. 1948. q. adv. bk.rev. abstr.
Former titles (until 1985): Frihetlig Socialistisk Tidskrift (0345-3685); (until 1972): Liberal Debatt
Published by: Stiftelsen Liberal Debatt, PO Box 10113, Stockholm, 10055, Sweden. Ed. Karin Ekdahl. Pub. Thorbjoern Pettersson. Circ: 1,500.

LIBERAL DEMOCRACY NEPAL BULLETIN. *see* HISTORY—History Of Asia

320.51 GBR
LIBERAL DEMOCRAT NEWS. Variant title: L D N. Text in English. 1946. w. GBP 30 (effective 2010). adv. bk.rev. illus. back issues avail. **Document type:** *Newspaper, Consumer.* **Description:** Reports on current affairs, social issues, and internal Party news.
Formerly (until 1989): Social and Liberal Democrats News (0954-5735); Which was formed by the merger of (1982-1988): Social Democrat (0024-1849); Liberal News (0264-8938)
—BLDSC (5186.565000). **CCC.**
Published by: Liberal Democrats, 4 Cowley St, London, SW1P 3NB, United Kingdom. TEL 44-20-72227999, info@libdems.org.uk, http://www.libdems.org.uk/. Circ: 11,000.

320.51 IND ISSN 0973-0273
LIBERAL DIGEST. Text in English. 2004. irreg., latest 2004. **Document type:** *Monographic series, Trade.*
Published by: Friedrich-Naumann-Foundation, USO House, 6 Special Institutional Area, New Delhi, 110 067, India. TEL 91-11-26862064, FAX 91-11-26862042, india@fnst.org.

320.5105 GBR ISSN 1754-1964
LIBERAL MATTERS. Text in English. 1992. q. back issues avail. **Document type:** *Magazine, Consumer.* **Description:** Contains articles by leading international figures and by rank and file liberals.
Former titles (until 2006): Liberal Aerogramme (1475-4770); (until 2001): London Aerogramme (0968-1884)
Published by: Liberal International, 1 Whitehall Pl, London, SW1A 2HD, United Kingdom. TEL 44-20-78395905, FAX 44-20-79252685, all@liberal-international.org. Ed. Emil Kirjas.

324.2 SWE ISSN 2000-396X
LIBERAL UNGDOM. Text in Swedish. 1934. q. adv. bk.rev. illus. **Document type:** *Magazine, Consumer.*
Former titles (until 2009): Liebling (1651-8950); (until 2003): Liberal Ungdom (0024-1857); (until 1961): Frisinnad Ungdom
Related titles: Online - full text ed.
Published by: Liberala Ungdomsfoerbundet/Youth Organization of the Swedish Liberal Party, Stora Nygatan 2 A, PO Box 2253, Stockholm, 10316, Sweden. TEL 46-8-41024200, FAX 46-8-50911660, luf@liberal.se. Ed. Linda Nordlund.

324.2 DNK ISSN 1602-1878
DL101
LIBERALT OVERBLIK. Text in Danish. 1970. 5/yr. DKK 250 membership (effective 2010). **Document type:** *Magazine, Consumer.* **Description:** Membership magazine for the Danish political Party "Venstre".
Formerly (until 2002): Liberal (0047-4460); Which incorporated (1988-2000): Venstre Her og Nu (1603-7413)
Related titles: Online - full text ed.
Published by: Venstres Landsorganisation, Soelleroedvej 30, Holte, 2840, Denmark. TEL 45-45-802233, FAX 45-45-803830, venstre@venstre.dk. Eds. Charlotte Wognsen, Jens Skipper Rasmussen. Circ: 56,000.

320.510715 USA ISSN 1046-5065
THE LIBERATOR (CARTERSVILLE). Text in English. 1985. q. USD 15 (effective 1999). bk.rev. back issues avail. **Document type:** *Newsletter, Trade.* **Description:** Teaches communication skills and provides outreach programs to libertarians.
Related titles: Online - full text ed.
Published by: Advocates for Self-Government, Inc., 5 S. Public Sq., Ste. 304, Cartersville, GA 30120-3348. TEL 800-932-1776, FAX 770-386-8373. Ed. James W Harris. R&P, Adv. contact Sharon Harris TEL 770-381-8372.

320 CRI
LIBERTAD. Text in Spanish. 1962. w.
Published by: Partido del Pueblo Costarricense, Calle 4 Avda. 8 y 10, Apdo 10138, San Jose, 1000, Costa Rica. TEL 506-225-9024, FAX 506-253-2628. Ed. Jose A Zuniga. Circ: 10,000.

320.51 GBR ISSN 0953-7791
LIBERTARIAN ALLIANCE. ATHEIST NOTES. Text in English. 1989. irreg., latest 2004. back issues avail. **Document type:** *Monographic series, Trade.*
Related titles: Online - full text ed.: ISSN 2042-2520. free (effective 2009).
Published by: Libertarian Alliance, 2 Lansdowne Row, Ste 35, London, W1J 6HL, United Kingdom. TEL 44-7956-472199. Ed. Nigel Meek.

320.51 GBR ISSN 0267-677X
LIBERTARIAN ALLIANCE. CULTURAL NOTES. Text in English. 1983. irreg., latest 2006. bk.rev.; film rev. bibl. back issues avail. **Document type:** *Monographic series, Trade.*
Related titles: Online - full text ed.: ISSN 2042-2539. free (effective 2009).
Published by: Libertarian Alliance, 2 Lansdowne Row, Ste 35, London, W1J 6HL, United Kingdom. TEL 44-7956-472199. Ed. Nigel Meek.

320.51 GBR ISSN 0953-7783
LIBERTARIAN ALLIANCE. PAMPHLETS. Text in English. 1980. irreg., latest 2002. back issues avail. **Document type:** *Monographic series, Trade.*
Related titles: Online - full text ed.: ISSN 2042-2598. free (effective 2009).
—**CCC.**
Published by: Libertarian Alliance, 2 Lansdowne Row, Ste 35, London, W1J 6HL, United Kingdom. TEL 44-7956-472199. Ed. Nigel Meek.

320.51 GBR ISSN 0267-7156
LIBERTARIAN ALLIANCE. PERSONAL PERSPECTIVES. Text in English. 1984. irreg., latest 2008. bk.rev.; film rev. bibl. back issues avail. **Document type:** *Monographic series, Trade.*
Related titles: Online - full text ed.: ISSN 2042-275X. free (effective 2009).
Published by: Libertarian Alliance, 2 Lansdowne Row, Ste 35, London, W1J 6HL, United Kingdom. TEL 44-7956-472199. Ed. Nigel Meek.

320.51 GBR ISSN 0267-7059
LIBERTARIAN ALLIANCE. POLITICAL NOTES. Text in English. 1979. irreg., latest 2009. bk.rev.; film rev. bibl. back issues avail. **Document type:** *Monographic series, Trade.*
Related titles: Online - full text ed.: ISSN 2042-2776. free (effective 2009).
Published by: Libertarian Alliance, 2 Lansdowne Row, Ste 35, London, W1J 6HL, United Kingdom. TEL 44-7956-472199. Ed. Nigel Meek.

320.51 GBR ISSN 0267-7067
LIBERTARIAN ALLIANCE. SCIENTIFIC NOTES. Text in English. 1985. irreg., latest 2007. bk.rev.; film rev. bibl. back issues avail. **Document type:** *Monographic series, Trade.*
Related titles: Online - full text ed.: ISSN 2040-5774. free (effective 2009).
Published by: Libertarian Alliance, 2 Lansdowne Row, Ste 35, London, W1J 6HL, United Kingdom. TEL 44-7956-472199. Ed. Nigel Meek.

320.51 GBR ISSN 0267-7180
LIBERTARIAN ALLIANCE. STUDY GUIDES. Text in English. 1985. irreg., latest 1998. back issues avail. **Document type:** *Monographic series, Trade.*
Related titles: Online - full text ed.: ISSN 2042-2814. free (effective 2009).
Published by: Libertarian Alliance, 2 Lansdowne Row, Ste 35, London, W1J 6HL, United Kingdom. TEL 44-7956-472199. Ed. Nigel Meek.

320.51 GBR ISSN 0268-2923
LIBERTARIAN ALLIANCE. TACTICAL NOTES. Text in English. 1985. irreg., latest 2008. bk.rev.; film rev. bibl. back issues avail. **Document type:** *Monographic series, Trade.*
Related titles: Online - full text ed.: ISSN 2042-2822. free (effective 2009).
Published by: Libertarian Alliance, 2 Lansdowne Row, Ste 35, London, W1J 6HL, United Kingdom. TEL 44-7956-472199. Ed. Nigel Meek.

320.51 GBR ISSN 0959-566X
LIBERTARIAN HERITAGE. Text in English. 1990. irreg., latest 2008. back issues avail. **Document type:** *Monographic series, Trade.*
Related titles: Online - full text ed.: ISSN 2042-2733. free (effective 2009).
Published by: Libertarian Alliance, 2 Lansdowne Row, Ste 35, London, W1J 6HL, United Kingdom. TEL 44-7956-472199. Ed. Nigel Meek.

320.51 USA ISSN 1947-6949
JC571
➤ **LIBERTARIAN PAPERS.** Text in English. 1977. irreg. free (effective 2011). bk.rev. back issues avail. **Document type:** *Journal, Academic/Scholarly.* **Description:** Publishes scholarly papers on libertarian topics, including review essays, lectures and essays.
Formerly (until 2009): Journal of Libertarian Studies (1947-6957)
Media: Online - full text.
Indexed: A26, CA, G08, I05, P42, T02.
Published by: Ludwig von Mises Institute, 518 W Magnolia Ave, Auburn, AL 36832. TEL 334-321-2100, FAX 334-321-2119, contact@mises.org, http://www.mises.org. Ed. Stephan Kinsella.

320.51 USA ISSN 8755-139X
JK2391.L9 CODEN: AAGNE7
LIBERTARIAN PARTY NEWS. Text in English. 1972. m. USD 25. adv. bk.rev. **Document type:** *Newspaper.*
Published by: Libertarian National Committee, 2600 Virginia Ave, NW, Ste 200, Washington, DC 20037. TEL 800-Elect-Us, admin@lpstuff.com, http://www.lp.org. Circ: 18,000.

LIBERTAS. *see* COLLEGE AND ALUMNI

320.51 USA
JK1759
LIBERTAS. Text in English. 1942. m. free (effective 2005). bk.rev. reprints avail. **Document type:** *Newsletter, Consumer.* **Description:** Deals with national and international issues and with youth, from a generally conservative and patriotic perspective.
Former titles: Looking Ahead (Oklahoma City); (until 1995): National Program Letter (0027-9943); Harding College Letter
Related titles: Microform ed.: (from PQC).
Published by: Oklahoma Christian University, American Citizenship Center, 2501 E. Memorial Rd., Oklahoma City, OK 73111. TEL 405-425-5040, FAX 405-425-5113. Ed. Pendleton Woods. Circ: 5,000 (free).

LIBERTY (PORT TOWNSEND). *see* LITERARY AND POLITICAL REVIEWS

320 USA ISSN 2156-681X
JC423
▼ **LIBERTY INK JOURNAL.** Text in English. 2010. m. USD 17.76 (effective 2010). **Document type:** *Journal, Consumer.* **Description:** Provides analysis of current events and legislative activities at all levels of government, always illuminated by the principles upon which this nation was founded.
Related titles: Online - full text ed.: ISSN 2156-6828. free (effective 2010).
Published by: Stephanie Anderson, Fran Telarico & Ken Clark Eds. & Pubs., 1708 Carriage Rd, Fort Collins, CO 80525. TEL 307-286-4776. Ed. Stephanie Anderson. Pub. Ken Clark.

321.8 USA ISSN 1932-1732
JC423
LIBERTY TREE. Text in English. 2005. q. **Document type:** *Journal, Consumer.*
Indexed: MLA-IB.
Published by: Liberty Tree Foundation for the Democratic Revolution, PO Box 260217, Madison, WI 53726-0217. TEL 608-257-1606, http://www.libertytreefdr.org/index.php.

320 CAN ISSN 1925-0770
▼ **LIBRUS.** Text in English. 2010. q. adv. **Document type:** *Magazine, Consumer.* **Description:** Features articles on political science and international affairs.
Published by: Imprint Publications, Waterloo, Student Life Ctr, Rm 1116, University of Waterloo, Waterloo, ON N2L 3G1, Canada. TEL 519-888-4048, FAX 519-884-7800, editor@imprint.uwaterloo.ca, http://theimprint.ca.

320 LIE ISSN 0259-4137
DB153
LIECHTENSTEIN POLITISCHE SCHRIFTEN. Text in German. 1972. irreg., latest vol.41, 2006. price varies. **Document type:** *Monographic series, Academic/Scholarly.*
Published by: Verlag der Liechtensteinischen Akademischen Gesellschaft, Bildgass 52, Postfach 829, Schaan, 9494, Liechtenstein. TEL 423-2323028, FAX 423-2331449, info@verlag-lag.li, http://www.verlag-lag.li. Circ: 520.

320 300 340 USA ISSN 1536-173X
THE LIGHTHOUSE. Text in English. 1999. w. free (effective 2010). bk.rev. abstr.; bibl. back issues avail.; reprints avail. **Document type:** *Newsletter, Academic/Scholarly.* **Description:** Provides updates of the Institute's current research, publications, events and media programs, plus comment on current issues.
Media: E-mail. **Related titles:** Online - full text ed.
Indexed: SCOPUS.
—CCC.
Published by: Independent Institute, 100 Swan Way, Oakland, CA 94621. TEL 510-632-1366, FAX 510-568-6040, info@independent.org. Ed. Carl P Close. Pub. David J Theroux.

320.531 CHN ISSN 1002-7408
LILUN DAOKAN/JOURNAL OF SOCIALIST THEORY GUIDE. Text in Chinese. 1979. m. **Document type:** *Journal, Academic/Scholarly.*
Former titles (until 1988): Lilun Xuekan; (until 1985): Lilun Jiaokan
Related titles: Online - full text ed.
Published by: Zhong-Gong Shaanxi Sheng-Wei Dangxiao, 119, Xiaozhai Xi Lu, Xi'an, 710061, China. TEL 86-29-85378162, FAX 86-29-85377162.

320.532 CHN ISSN 1007-1962
LILUN QIANYAN/THEORY FRONT. Text in Chinese. 1996. s-a. USD 72 (effective 2009). **Document type:** *Journal, Academic/Scholarly.*
Related titles: Online - full text ed.
—East View.
Published by: Zhong-Gong Zhongyang Dangxiao, Deng Xiaoping Yanjiu Zhongxin, 100, Dayouzhuang, Beijing, 100091, China. **Dist. by:** China International Book Trading Corp, 35 Chegongzhuang Xilu, Haidian District, PO Box 399, Beijing 100044, China. TEL 86-10-68412045, FAX 86-10-68412023, cibtc@mail.cibtc.com.cn, http://www.cibtc.com.cn.

320 USA ISSN 1065-0377
JC573.2.U6
THE LIMBAUGH LETTER. Text in English. 1992. m. USD 29.95; USD 2.95 newsstand/cover (effective 2006). bk.rev. charts; illus.; stat. back issues avail. **Document type:** *Newsletter.*
Published by: E F M Publishing, Inc., 366 Madison Ave., 7th Fl, New York, NY 10017. TEL 800-829-5386. Ed. Rush Limbaugh. Circ: 198,000 (paid).

322.4 USA
LIMIT. Text in English. 1974. m. USD 5. adv. bk.rev.
Published by: Libertarian Republican Alliance, 1149 E 32nd St, Brooklyn, NY 11210. Ed. Elliott Capon. Circ: 500.

320 305.8924 NLD ISSN 2210-7150
LINK. Text in Dutch. 198?. s-a. **Document type:** *Newsletter, Consumer.*
Published by: Stichting C.O.M.E., Engweg 31, Driebergen, 3972 JC, Netherlands. TEL 31-343-520994.

320.531 AUS
LINKS (ONLINE); international journal of socialist renewal. Text in English. 1994. 3/yr. free (effective 2009). bk.rev. 128 p./no.; back issues avail. **Document type:** *Journal, Academic/Scholarly.* **Description:** Rejects the Stalinist distortion of the socialist project; promotes feminism and ecology; and facilitates open and constructive debate in the international left.
Formerly: Links (Print) (1321-795X)
Media: Online - full text.
Indexed: AltPI, LeftInd.
Published by: New Course Publications, PO Box 515, Broadway, NSW 2007, Australia. TEL 61-2-96901210, FAX 61-2-96901381.

320 USA
LIP MAGAZINE. Text in English. 1996. q. USD 16; USD 4.95 newsstand/cover domestic; USD 6.95 newsstand/cover in Canada (effective 2005). **Document type:** *Magazine, Consumer.*
Indexed: APW.
Address: P O Box 3478, Oakland, CA 94609. info@lipmagazine.org. Ed. Brian Awehali.

320 LTU ISSN 1392-9321
JA26
LITHUANIAN POLITICAL SCIENCE YEARBOOK. Text in English, Lithuanian. 2000. a. **Document type:** *Yearbook, Academic/Scholarly.*
Indexed: IBSS, P42, T02.
Published by: Vilniaus Universitetas, Tarptautiniu Santykiu ir Politicos Mokslu/University of Vilnius, Institute of International Relations and Political Science, Vokieciu St 10, Vilnius, 01130, Lithuania. TEL 370-5-2514130, FAX 370-5-2514134, tspmi@tspmi.vu.lt.

LITIGATION UNDER THE FEDERAL OPEN GOVERNMENT LAWS. *see* LAW

320 CAN ISSN 1910-2895
LIU INSTITUTE NEWSLETTER. Text in English. 2004. m. **Document type:** *Newsletter, Academic/Scholarly.*
Media: Online - full text.
Published by: University of British Columbia, Liu Institute for Global Issues (Subsidiary of: University of British Columbia), 6476 NW Marine Dr, Vancouver, BC V6T 1Z2, Canada. FAX 604-822-6966, liu.institute@ubc.ca, http://www.ligi.ubc.ca.

320.5 GBR ISSN 0047-4827
LIVERPOOL NEWSLETTER. Text in English. 1960. m. GBP 5 domestic; GBP 6 in Europe; GBP 9 elsewhere (effective 2009). adv. bk.rev.; film rev.; music rev.; video rev.; Website rev. **Document type:** *Newsletter.* **Description:** Long-standing journal in support of the economic and sociological philosophy of distributism - the advocacy of co-operative and widespread property ownership.
—CCC.
Published by: Third Way Publications Ltd., Rm 407, 12 S Bridge, Edinburg, EH1 1DD, United Kingdom. info@thirdway.eu.

320.5 USA
LIVING FREE; a personal journal of self liberation. Text in English. 1979. bi-m. USD 12 domestic; USD 15 overseas; USD 2 sample (effective 2000). adv. bk.rev. back issues avail. **Document type:** *Newsletter.* **Description:** Survivalists, homesteaders and anarchists discuss self-reliant living.
Related titles: Microfiche ed.
Indexed: RASB.
Address: Box 29, Hiler Branch, Buffalo, NY 14223. Ed., Pub., Adv. contact Jim Stumm. Circ: 200 (paid).

320 CHE ISSN 1663-0165
▼ **LIVING REVIEWS IN DEMOCRACY.** Text in English. 2009. a. free (effective 2011). **Document type:** *Journal, Academic/Scholarly.*
Media: Online - full text.
Indexed: A01, A03, CA, P42.
Published by: Center for Comparative and International Studies, Seilergraben 49, SEI G12, Zurich, 8092, Switzerland. TEL 41-44-6328062. Ed. Frank Schimmelfennig.

320 FRA ISSN 1951-5774
LE LIVRE CITOYEN. Text in French. 2006. irreg. back issues avail. **Document type:** *Monographic series, Consumer.*
Published by: Gulf Stream Editeur, Impasse du Forgeron, CP 910, Saint-Herblain, 44806, France. TEL 33-2-40480668, FAX 33-2-40487469, contact@gulfstream.fr, ttp://www.gulfstream.fr.

324.294 AUS ISSN 0156-8701
LOBBY; the A C T Labor journal. Variant title: Ausralian Capital Territory Labor Journal. A L P Lobby(Australian Labor Party). Text in English. 1978. irreg. AUD 10 to non-members. adv. bk.rev. back issues avail. **Document type:** *Journal, Trade.*
Former titles: Australian Labor Party. A.C.T. Branch. Magazine; Australian Labor Party. A.C.T. Branch. Newsletter
Published by: Australian Labor Party, Australian Capital Territory Branch, 21 Torrens St, Braddon, ACT 2612, Australia. TEL 61-2-62474066, FAX 61-2-62473865, info@act.alp.org.au. Ed. John Hannoush. Circ: 1,500.

320 GBR ISSN 0960-619X
LOCAL AND CENTRAL GOVERNMENT RELATIONS RESEARCH PROGRAMME. Text in English. 1989. irreg., latest vol.3. **Document type:** *Report, Academic/Scholarly.*
Related titles: Online - full text ed.: free (effective 2011).
Published by: Policy Studies Institute, 50 Hanson St, London, W1W 6UP, United Kingdom. TEL 44-20-79117500, FAX 44-20-79117501, psi-admin@psi.org.uk.

LOGIQUES SOCIALES. SERIE SOCIOLOGIE POLITIQUE. *see* SOCIOLOGY

322.4 DEU
LOKALES; Stadtzeitung fuer Babenhausen. Text in German. 1981. irreg. free (effective 2009). **Document type:** *Newspaper, Consumer.*
Published by: Buendnis 90 - Die Gruenen, Am Falkenhorst 8, Babenhausen, 64832, Germany. TEL 49-1212-511434052, FAX 49-1212-511434052, ov@gruene-babenhausen.de, http://www.gruene-babenhausen.de. Circ: 7,000.

328 IND ISSN 0024-595X
LOKTANTRA SAMIKSHA. Text in Hindi. 1969. q. free to members (effective 2011). **Document type:** *Journal, Trade.*
Published by: Institute of Constitutional and Parliamentary Studies, 18-21 Vithalbhai Patel House, Rafi Marg, New Delhi, 110 001, India. TEL 91-11-23710405, icpsnewdelhi@gmail.com.

320.531 USA ISSN 1067-6155
LONE STAR SOCIALIST; voice of the Socialist Party of Texas. Text mainly in English; Text occasionally in Spanish. 1979. irreg. (approx. 2/yr.). USD 8 (effective 2002). adv. bk.rev. 8 p./no. 2 cols./p.; back issues avail. **Document type:** *Newsletter.* **Description:** Aims to provide a forum for news and discussion of radical politics. Emphasizes labor news, reviews, and radical economic analysis. Includes articles on issues such as prisons and corporate boycotts.
Related titles: Online - full text ed.
Published by: Socialist Party of Texas, PO Box 2640, Austin, TX 78768-2640. http://www.sp-usa.org/linestar/. Ed. Matt Parker. Adv. contact Steve Rossignol. page USD 100. Circ: 600.

320 HKG
LOOK MAGAZINE. Text in Chinese. 1958. m. USD 20. bk.rev.
Formerly: Look Fortnightly (0024-6387)
Indexed: MagInd, RASB.
Published by: Chih Luen Press, B1, Carnarvon Mansion, 10th Fl, 12 Carnarvon Rd, Kowloon, Hong Kong. Ed. Smarlo Ma.

320.532 ITA ISSN 1970-6278
LOTTA COMUNISTA. Text in Italian. 1965. m. **Document type:** *Magazine, Consumer.*
Published by: Edizioni Lotta Comunista, Viale Sarca 76, Milan, 20125, Italy. TEL 39-02-6434579, FAX 39-02-26825868, info@edizionilottacomunista.com, http://www.edizionilottacomunista.com.

LOTUS. *see* PHILOSOPHY

320 BRA ISSN 0102-6445
LUA NOVA; cultura e politica. Text in Portuguese. 1984. 3/yr. USD 60 to individuals; USD 90 to institutions. **Document type:** *Academic/Scholarly.* **Description:** Provides theoretical studies, research, and contemporary debates in political science and sociology.
Related titles: Online - full text ed.: free (effective 2011).
Indexed: BibInd, C01, CA, IBR, IBSS, IBZ, P42, PSA, RASB, S02, S03, SCOPUS, SociolAb, T02.
Published by: CEDEC, Rua Airosa Galvao, 64, A Branca, Sao Paulo, SP 05002-070, Brazil. TEL 55-11-871-2966, FAX 55-11-871-2123. Ed. Gabriel Cohn. Circ: 2,000.

320 USA ISSN 1092-3667
LUMPEN MAGAZINE. Text in English. 1993. q. (m. until 2002). USD 30; USD 39 in Canada; USD 60 elsewhere; USD 3, CAD 3.95 newsstand/cover (effective 2005). adv. bk.rev. illus. reprints avail. **Document type:** *Magazine, Consumer.* **Description:** Covers progressive politics and underground culture.
Related titles: Online - full text ed.
Indexed: AltPI.
Published by: Lumpen Media Group, 960 W 31st St, Chicago, IL 60608. TEL 312-829-0022, lumpen@lumpen.com. Adv. contact Ed Marszewski. page USD 800; 7.25 x 10. Circ: 22,500 (controlled).

320 BRA ISSN 1415-854X
HX9.P65
LUTAS SOCIAIS. Text in Portuguese. 1996. s-a. **Document type:** *Journal, Academic/Scholarly.*
Indexed: PSA, T02.
Published by: Pontificia Universidade Catolica de Sao Paulo, Programa de Estudos Pos-Graduados em Ciencias Sociais, NEILS, Rua Ministro de Godoi 969, 4o Andar, Sala 4E20, Perdizes, Sao Paulo, SP, Brazil. neils@pucsp.br. Ed. Renata Goncalves.

P

324.2663 SEN
LUTTE. Text in French. 1977. q.
Published by: Parti Africain de l'Independance, BP 820, Dakar, Senegal. Ed. Bara Goudiaby. Circ: 1,000.

320 FRA ISSN 0024-7650
LUTTE OUVRIERE. Text in French. 1968. w. **Document type:** *Newspaper, Consumer.*
Related titles: Online - full text ed.
Address: BP 233, Paris, Cedex 18 75865, France. TEL 33-01-44830377, FAX 33-01-44839673. Circ: 17,000.

320.5 GBR ISSN 1749-9747
M A N C E P T WORKING PAPER SERIES. Text in English. 1997. irreg., latest 2007. free (effective 2009). back issues avail. **Document type:** *Monographic series, Academic/Scholarly.*
Formerly (until 2004): University of Manchester. Manchester Centre for Political Theory. Working Paper Series (Print) (1367-2010)
Media: Online - full text.
Published by: University of Manchester, Manchester Centre for Political Thought, Oxford Rd, Manchester, Lancs M13 9PL, United Kingdom. TEL 44-161-3066000.

320 MAR ISSN 0851-0229
DT325
M A P ACTUALITE; daily national and international political news bulletin. Text in French. 1977. d. MAD 2,779, USD 173.89 (effective 1998).
Published by: Maghreb Arabe Presse, 122 Avenue Allal Ben Abdellah, B P 1049, Rabat, 10000, Morocco. TEL 212-7-764083, FAX 212-7-767097. Ed. Abdeljalil Fenjiro. Circ: 1,000.

324.6 USA
M I R S LEGISLATIVE REPORT. Text in English. 1961. d. USD 1,260 (effective 1997). **Document type:** *Newsletter, Government.* **Description:** Summarizes news regarding Michigan elections, politics, legislative and state government issues. Includes bill status information, committee and meeting schedules, and other related information and services.
Published by: Michigan Information and Research Service, Inc., 318 W Ottawa, Box 19303, Lansing, MI 48901-9303. TEL 517-482-2125, FAX 517-374-0949. Ed., R&P John T Reurink.

320 USA ISSN 0076-1729
M L SEIDMAN MEMORIAL TOWN HALL LECTURE SERIES. Text in English. 1967. a. USD 5. **Document type:** *Monographic series.*
Published by: Rhodes College, 2000 N Pkwy, Memphis, TN 38112. TEL 901-726-3818. Ed. Daniel L Cullen. Circ: 600 (controlled).

320 USA ISSN 0464-1973
M O P S A NEWSLETTER. Text in English. 1957. a. USD 10 (effective 1997). bibl. **Document type:** *Newsletter.*
Published by: Missouri Political Science Association, c/o George Connor, Sect -Treas, Dept of Political Science, Southwest Missouri State University, Springfield, MO 65804. TEL 417-836-6956. Circ: 80 (controlled).

320 FRA ISSN 0243-6450
JA11
M O T S; les langages du politique. (Mots, Ordinateurs, Textes, Societes) Text in French; Summaries in English, French, Spanish. 1980. q. EUR 46 domestic to individuals; EUR 49 foreign to individuals; EUR 60 domestic to institutions; EUR 63 foreign to institutions; EUR 34 domestic to students; EUR 37 foreign to students (effective 2009). adv. bk.rev. abstr.; bibl. **Document type:** *Journal, Academic/ Scholarly.*
Formerly: Travaux de Lexicometrie et Lexicologie Politique (0294-796X)
Related titles: Online - full text ed.: ISSN 1960-6001.
Indexed: A22, FR, IBSS, MLA-IB.
—BLDSC (5978.718300), IE, Infotrieve, INIST. **CCC.**
Published by: E N S Editions, 15 Pavis Rene Descartes, B P 7000, Lyon, Cedex 07 69342, France. TEL 33-4-37376022, FAX 33-4-37376096, ENS-Editions@ens-lsh.fr, http://www.ens-lsh.fr/editions. Adv. contact Chrystel Pons. Circ: 800.

320.54095694 USA ISSN 0017-6850
HA-MAAPIL. Text in English. 1962. m. membership. **Description:** University students' progressive Zionist journal.
Media: Duplicated (not offset).
Published by: Habonim Dror North America, 114 West 26th St, Ste 1004, New York, NY 10001. http://www.habonimdror.org. Ed. Charles Boxbaum. Circ: 1,650.

MAATSCHAPPIJ & POLITIEK; vakblad voor maatschappijleer. *see* EDUCATION

MACEDONIAN TRIBUNE. *see* CLUBS

320.082 ARG ISSN 0327-1129
MADRES DE PLAZA DE MAYO. Text in Spanish. 1984. m. USD 72 (effective 1998). **Description:** Covers all activities of the association of mothers: cultural events, speeches, and educational topics.
Published by: Asociacion Madres de Plaza de Mayo, Hipolito Yrigoyen 1442, Buenos Aires, 1089, Argentina. TEL 54-114-3836430, FAX 54-114-9540381, madres@madres.org. Circ: 5,000 (paid).

320 FRA ISSN 1762-3162
DT181
MAGHREB MACHREK. Key Title: Monde Arabe. Text in French. 1964. q. EUR 75 domestic; EUR 85 foreign (effective 2009). bk.rev. bibl. cum.index. **Document type:** *Journal, Academic/Scholarly.*
Former titles (until 2002): Monde Arabe Maghreb - Machrek (1241-5294); (until 1992): Maghreb, Machrek, Monde Arabe (0336-6324); (until 1973): Maghreb (0024-9890)
Related titles: Microfiche ed.
Indexed: A20, A22, ASD, CA, CCA, CCME, FR, HistAb, I02, I13, I14, IBR, IBSS, IBZ, ISR, LeftInd, M10, P30, P42, PAIS, RASB, SCOPUS, SSCI, T02, W07.
—BLDSC (5334.753500), IE, Infotrieve, Ingenta, INIST.
Published by: (Fondation Nationale des Politiques et Direction de la Documentation), Choiseul Editions, 28 Rue Etienne Marcel, Paris, 75002, France. TEL 33-1-53340993, FAX 33-1-53340994, http://choiseul-editions.com. Ed. Jean-Francois Daguzan. Circ: 2,000.

THE MAGHREB REVIEW. *see* HISTORY—History Of Africa

320.6 USA ISSN 1059-3535
MAJOR CONCEPTS IN POLITICS AND POLITICAL THEORY. Text in English. 1992. irreg., latest vol.27, 2009. price varies. back issues avail. **Document type:** *Monographic series, Academic/Scholarly.* **Description:** Focuses on major concepts in politics and political theory in prominent traditions, periods, and thinkers.
—BLDSC (5353.604315), IE, Ingenta.
Published by: Peter Lang Publishing, Inc. (Subsidiary of: Peter Lang Publishing Group), 29 Broadway, New York, NY 10006. TEL 212-647-7706, 212-647-7700, 800-770-5264, FAX 212-647-7707, customerservice@plang.com. Ed. Garrett Ward Sheldon.

320.5322 CHN ISSN 1674-4470
B3305.M74
MAKESI LIENING ZHUYI YANJIU/RESEARCH ON MARXISM-LENINISM. Text in Chinese. 1987. m. CNY 120; CNY 10 per issue (effective 2011). 80 p./no.; **Document type:** *Journal, Academic/ Scholarly.* **Description:** Contains reprints of researches on Marxism and Leninism.
Formerly (until 2009): Makesi Zhuyi, Liening Zhuyi Yanjiu/Marxism-Leninism Research (1001-2699)
Published by: Zhongguo Renmin Daxue Shubao Ziliao Zhongxin/Renmin University of China, Information Center for Social Sciences, 59, Zhongguancun Dajie, Haidian-qu, Beijing, 100872, China. TEL 86-10-84043003, FAX 86-10-64015080, center@zlzx.org. **Dist. in US by:** China Publications Service, PO Box 49614, Chicago, IL 60649. TEL 312-288-3291, FAX 312-288-8570; **Dist. by:** China International Book Trading Corp, 35 Chegongzhuang Xilu, Haidian District, PO Box 399, Beijing 100044, China. TEL 86-10-68412045, FAX 86-10-68412023, cibtc@mail.cibtc.com.cn, http://www.cibtc.com.cn.

320.5322 CHN ISSN 1006-5199
MAKESI ZHUYI YANJIU/STUDIES ON MARXISM. Key Title: Marx Zhuyi Yanjiu. Text in Chinese. 1983. bi-m. USD 85.20 (effective 2009). **Document type:** *Journal, Academic/Scholarly.*
Related titles: Online - full text ed.
—East View.
Published by: Zhongguo Shehui Kexueyuan, Malie Yanjiusuo, 5, Jianguomennei Dajie, 13-ceng, Beijing, 100732, China. TEL 86-10-65138265, FAX 86-10-65245820. **Dist. by:** China International Book Trading Corp, 35 Chegongzhuang Xilu, Haidian District, PO Box 399, Beijing 100044, China. TEL 86-10-68412045, FAX 86-10-68412023, cibtc@mail.cibtc.com.cn, http://www.cibtc.com.cn.

320.5322 CHN ISSN 1004-5961
MAKESI ZHUYI YU XIANSHI/MARXISM & REALITY. Key Title: Marx Zhuyi yu Xianshi. Text in Chinese. 1990. bi-m. USD 53.40 (effective 2009). **Document type:** *Journal, Academic/Scholarly.*
Related titles: Online - full text ed.
—East View.
Published by: Zhongyang Bianyiju/Central Compliation & Translation Bureau, Xicheng-qu, 26, Xixiejie, Beijing, 100032, China. TEL 86-10-66509601, FAX 86-10-66173568, http://www.cctb.net/. **Dist. by:** China International Book Trading Corp, 35 Chegongzhuang Xilu, Haidian District, PO Box 399, Beijing 100044, China. TEL 86-10-68412045, FAX 86-10-68412023, cibtc@mail.cibtc.com.cn, http://www.cibtc.com.cn.

320.531 LKA
MAKSVADAYA. Text in Singhalese. 1970. irreg. adv. bk.rev.
Published by: Nava Sama Samaja Party, 17 Barracks Lane, Colombo, 2, Sri Lanka. Ed. Vickamabahu Karanarathne. Circ: 500.

320 MWI ISSN 0076-3225
MALAWI. MINISTRY OF LOCAL GOVERNMENT. ANNUAL REPORT. Text in English. a. **Document type:** *Government.*
Published by: (Malawi. Ministry of Local Government), Government Printer, PO Box 37, Zomba, Malawi.

THE MALAYSIA BUSINESS FORECAST REPORT. *see* BUSINESS AND ECONOMICS—Economic Situation And Conditions

320.9 MYS ISSN 0047-5629
DS591
MALAYSIAN DIGEST. Text in English. 1969. m. free. charts; illus. **Description:** Discusses current political, economic, social and cultural affairs.
Indexed: RASB.
Published by: Ministry of Foreign Affairs/Kementerian Luar Negeri, Jalan Wisma Putra, Kuala Lumpur, Malaysia. TEL 03-2488088. Ed. Sulochana K Indran. Circ: 25,000.

322.42 MNG
MANAY INDER/OUR PLATFORM. Text in Mongol. 1990. m.
Formerly: Namyn Am'dral
Indexed: RASB.
Published by: Mongolian People's Revolutionary Party, Ulan Bator, Mongolia.

320 FRA ISSN 1241-6290
JZ11
MANIERE DE VOIR. Text in French. 1987. bi-m. EUR 35 domestic (effective 2011); EUR 39 in the European Union; EUR 45.90 in US & Canada; EUR 50 in Asia & the Pacific; EUR 41.30 elsewhere (effective 2008). back issues avail. **Document type:** *Magazine, Consumer.*
Formerly (until 1992): Le Monde Diplomatique. Maniere de Voir (0987-8610)
Related titles: Online - full text ed.: ISSN 2108-677X. 200?. EUR 34 (effective 2011); ◆ Spanish ed.: El Punto de Vista de Le Monde Diplomatique. ISSN 1699-0080.
Indexed: IBSS.
Published by: Monde Diplomatique S A, 1 Av. Stephen Pichon, Paris, 75013, France. TEL 33-1-53949601, FAX 33-1-53949626, secretariat@monde-diplomatique.fr.

320 USA
MANTOOTH REPORT. Text in English. 1979. m. USD 20. adv. bk.rev. back issues avail. **Document type:** *Newspaper.* **Description:** Contains political and economic news of the real world and the new world order.
Address: RR 1 Box 387, Salem, IN 47167. TEL 812-883-2435, FAX 812-883-2435. Ed. Don Mantooth. Circ: 2,000.

320.53230951 CHN ISSN 1005-8273
DS778.M3
MAO ZEDONG DENG XIAOPING LILUN YANJIU/STUDIES ON MAO ZEDONG AND DENG XIAOPING THEORIES. Text in Chinese. 1980. m. USD 62.40 (effective 2009). adv. bk.rev. **Document type:** *Journal, Academic/Scholarly.* **Description:** Introduces and reviews main contemporary philosophy.
Formerly (until Apr. 1994): Mao Zedong Zhexue Sixiang Yanjiu/Studies in Mao Zedong's Philosophical Thought
Related titles: Online - full text ed.
—East View.
Published by: Shanghai Shehui Kexueyuan, Zhexue Yanjiusuo, 1610, Zhongshan Xilu, 1608-shi, Shanghai, 200235, China. TEL 86-21-64274736, FAX 86-21-64280796. **Dist. by:** China International Book Trading Corp, 35 Chegongzhuang Xilu, Haidian District, PO Box 399, Beijing 100044, China. TEL 86-10-68412045, FAX 86-10-68412023, cibtc@mail.cibtc.com.cn, http://www.cibtc.com.cn.

320.532 CHN ISSN 1009-7570
MAO ZEDONG SIXIANG/MAO ZEDONG THOUGHTS. Text in Chinese. 1987. bi-m. USD 32.50 (effective 2009). 80 p./no.; **Document type:** *Journal, Academic/Scholarly.* **Description:** Contains reprints of biographies and other articles on Chinese communist leaders. Focuses on Mao Zedong thoughts and theories.
Formerly: Maozedong Sixiang Yanjiu (1001-2702)
Related titles: ◆ Alternate Frequency ed(s).: Mao Zedong Sixiang (Nian Kan). a.
Published by: Zhongguo Renmin Daxue Shubao Ziliao Zhongxin/Renmin University of China, Information Center for Social Sciences, Dongcheng-qu, 3, Zhangzizhong Lu, Beijing, 100007, China. TEL 86-10-64039458, 86-10-84043003, FAX 86-10-64015080, center@zlzx.org, http://www.zlzx.org/. **Dist. in US by:** China Publications Service, PO Box 49614, Chicago, IL 60649. TEL 312-288-3291, FAX 312-288-8570; **Dist. by:** China International Book Trading Corp, 35 Chegongzhuang Xilu, Haidian District, PO Box 399, Beijing 100044, China. TEL 86-10-68412045, FAX 86-10-68412023, cibtc@mail.cibtc.com.cn, http://www.cibtc.com.cn.

320.532 CHN
MAO ZEDONG SIXIANG (NIAN KAN)/MAO ZEDONG THOUGHT (ANNUAL EDITION). Text in Chinese. a. CNY 49, USD 17.80 (effective 2004). **Document type:** *Journal, Academic/Scholarly.*
Related titles: ◆ Alternate Frequency ed(s).: Mao Zedong Sixiang. ISSN 1009-7570. bi-m.
Published by: Zhongguo Renmin Daxue Shubao Ziliao Zhongxin/Renmin University of China, Information Center for Social Sciences, Dongcheng-qu, 3, Zhangzizhong Lu, Beijing, 100007, China. TEL 86-10-84043003, 86-10-64039458, FAX 86-10-64015080, center@zlzx.org, http://www.zlzx.org/. **Dist. by:** China International Book Trading Corp, 35 Chegongzhuang Xilu, Haidian District, PO Box 399, Beijing 100044, China. TEL 86-10-68412045, FAX 86-10-68412023, cibtc@mail.cibtc.com.cn, http://www.cibtc.com.cn/.

320.53230951 CHN ISSN 1001-8999
DS778.M3
MAO ZEDONG SIXIANG YANJIU/STUDY OF MAO ZEDONG THOUGHT. Text in Chinese. 1983. bi-m. USD 31.20 (effective 2009). **Document type:** *Journal, Academic/Scholarly.*
Related titles: Online - full text ed.
Published by: Sichuan Sheng Shehui Kexueyuan/Sichuan Academy of Social Science, Qingyang Gong, Chengdu, Sichuan 610072, China. **Dist. by:** China International Book Trading Corp, 35 Chegongzhuang Xilu, Haidian District, PO Box 399, Beijing 100044, China. TEL 86-10-68412045, FAX 86-10-68412023, cibtc@mail.cibtc.com.cn, http://www.cibtc.com.cn.

MARKET INDICATORS AND FORECASTS. *see* BUSINESS AND ECONOMICS—Economic Situation And Conditions

320.531 DEU
MARKTGEFLUESTER. Text in German. 1986. irreg. (1-2/yr.).
Published by: Sozialdemokratische Partei Deutschlands (SPD), Ortsvereine im Markt Maroldsweisach, Meininger Str 4, Maroldsweisach, 96126, Germany. TEL 09532-325.

320 GBR ISSN 0969-1154
MARX MEMORIAL LIBRARY. BULLETIN. Text in English. 1957. irreg. (2-3/yr.). free to members (effective 2009). bk.rev. back issues avail. **Document type:** *Bulletin, Academic/Scholarly.* **Description:** Contains information regarding lectures, news and recent additions at the library, articles of interest, and resumes of lectures.
Formerly (until 1982): Marx Memorial Library. Quarterly Bulletin (0025-410X)
Indexed: RASB.
Published by: Marx Memorial Library, 37a Clerkenwell Green, London, EC1R 0DU, United Kingdom. TEL 44-207-2531485, FAX 44-207-2516039, http://www.marx-memorial-library.org.

320.5322 ITA
MARXISMO OGGI; rivista quadrimestrale di cultura politica. Text in Italian. 1987. 3/yr. adv. **Document type:** *Magazine, Consumer.*
Published by: Associazione Culturale Marxista, Via Spallanzani 6, Milan, MI 20129, Italy. TEL 39-02-29513473, FAX 39-02-29405405, ass.cultmarx@libero.it, http://www.assculturamarxista.org.

320 AUS ISSN 1836-6597
➤ **MARXIST INTERVENTIONS.** Text in English. 2000. a. free (effective 2011). **Document type:** *Journal, Academic/Scholarly.*
Media: Online - full text.
Published by: Australian National University, College of Arts and Social Sciences, Canberra, ACT 0200, Australia. TEL 61-2-61252898, FAX 61-2-61250743, http://cass.anu.edu.au. Eds. Rick Kuhn, Tom O'Lincoln.

320.5322 DEU ISSN 0542-7770
HX6
MARXISTISCHE BLAETTER. Text in German. 1963. bi-m. EUR 42.50; EUR 27.50 to students; EUR 7.50 newsstand/cover (effective 2005). adv. bk.rev. index. back issues avail. **Document type:** *Academic/ Scholarly.*
Indexed: A22, DIP, IBR, IBZ, PAIS, PRA, RASB.
—IE, Infotrieve. **CCC.**
Published by: Neue Impulse Verlag GmbH, Hoffnungstr 18, Essen, 45127, Germany. TEL 49-201-2486482, FAX 49-201-2486484, neueimpulse@aol.com, http://www.dkp-online.de/niv/.

328.752 USA
MARYLAND. HOUSE OF DELEGATES. JOURNAL OF PROCEEDINGS. REGULAR SESSION. Text in English. 1826. a. free (effective 2011). back issues avail. **Document type:** *Government.*
Related titles: Online - full text ed.
Published by: Department of Legislative Services, Legislative Sales, Legislative Services Bldg, 90 State Cir, Annapolis, MD 21401. TEL 410-946-5400, libr@mlis.state.md.us, http://dls.state.md.us.

MARYLAND REGISTER. *see* PUBLIC ADMINISTRATION

THE MARYLAND REPORT. *see* PUBLIC ADMINISTRATION

MARYLAND REPORT'S GUIDEBOOK TO MARYLAND LEGISLATORS. *see* PUBLIC ADMINISTRATION

328.752 USA
MARYLAND. SENATE. JOURNAL OF PROCEEDINGS. REGULAR SESSION. Text in English. 1826. a. free (effective 2011). back issues avail. **Document type:** *Government.*
Related titles: Online - full text ed.
Published by: Department of Legislative Services, Legislative Sales, Legislative Services Bldg, 90 State Cir, Annapolis, MD 21401. TEL 410-946-5400, libr@mlis.state.md.us, http://dls.state.md.us.

320.51 ESP ISSN 2171-6919
▼ **MAS PLURAL.** Text in Spanish. 2010. bi-m. **Document type:** *Bulletin, Consumer.*
Related titles: Online - full text ed.: ISSN 2171-7427. 2010.
Published by: Accion Plural, Calle Nueve, No. 7 Piso 1o. Puerta 218, El Escorial, Madrid, 28280, Spain.

324.6 USA ISSN 1057-4549
MASSACHUSETTS VOTER. Text in English. 1972. 5/yr. USD 12.50 (effective 2001). **Document type:** *Newsletter.*
Former titles (until 1990): Voter (0899-4935); State House Reporter
Published by: League of Women Voters of Massachusetts, 133 Portland St, Boston, MA 02114-1730. TEL 617-523-2999, FAX 617-248-0881, http://www.ma.lwv.org. Ed. Alix Driscoll. Circ: 6,000.

320.57 USA
THE MATCH; an anarchist journal. Text in English. 1969. q. USD 10 (effective 2000). bk.rev.
Published by: Fred Woodworth, Ed. & Pub., PO Box 3012, Tucson, AZ 85702. Circ: 1,750.

320.9 URY
MATE AMARGO. Text in Spanish. 1986. 2/yr.
Published by: Movimiento de Liberacion Nacional, Bartolome Mitre, 1431-Of 203, Montevideo, 11004, Uruguay. TEL 91 56 08. Ed. Emundo Canalda. Circ: 22,500.

320 ITA ISSN 2039-1439
MATERIALI DI DISCUSSIONE. Text in Multiple languages. 1985. irreg. **Document type:** *Journal, Academic/Scholarly.*
Related titles: Online - full text ed.: ISSN 2039-1447.
Published by: Universita degli Studi di Modena e Reggio Emilia, Dipartimento di Economia Politica, Viale Berengario 51, Modena, 41121, Italy. TEL 39-059-2056942, FAX 39-059-2056947, http://www.dep.unimore.it/dipartimento.asp.

MATERIAUX POUR L'HISTOIRE DE NOTRE TEMPS. *see* HISTORY—History Of Europe

324.25493 LKA
MAVBIMA. Text in Singhalese. w. LKR 0.35 per issue.
Published by: Ceylon Communist Party, 91 Cotta Rd., Colombo, 8, Sri Lanka.

320.95694 ISR
JQ1830.A1
➤ **M'DINA VAHEVRA/STATE AND SOCIETY.** Text in Hebrew; Abstracts in English. 2002. 3/yr. ILS 85; ILS 35 newsstand/cover (effective 2002). **Document type:** *Journal, Academic/Scholarly.* **Description:** Provides interdisciplinary coverage of political and social issues pertaining to Israeli society.
Published by: University of Haifa, Department of Political Science, Mt. Carmel, Haifa, 31905, Israel. TEL 972-4-8240500, FAX 972-4-8257785, poliweb@poli.haifa.ac.il.

320.531 SWE ISSN 0025-665X
MEDBORGAREN. Text in Swedish. 1914. 8/yr. SEK 300 (effective 2001). adv. bk.rev. abstr.; charts; illus. **Document type:** *Magazine, Consumer.*
Formerly (until vol.2, 1920): Allmaenna Valmansfoerbundets Maanadsblad
Related titles: Audio cassette/tape ed.
Published by: Moderata Samlingspartiet/Swedish Moderate Party, Box 1243, Stockholm, 11182, Sweden. TEL 46-8-676-80-00, FAX 46-8-21-61-23, http://www.moderat.se/. Ed. Cecilia Brinck. Adv. contact Hans Birger Ekstroem. color page SEK 24,900; trim 190 x 275. Circ: 70,100.

MEDIA MONITOR (WASHINGTON). *see* SOCIOLOGY

MEDIANOMICS. *see* JOURNALISM

320.5322 USA ISSN 1075-041X
PN80
MEDIATIONS. Text in English. 1976. s-a. **Document type:** *Journal, Academic/Scholarly.*
Related titles: Online - full text ed.: ISSN 1942-2458. free (effective 2011).
Indexed: AmHI, CA, H07, L06, MLA-IB, T02.
Published by: Marxist Literary Group, Department of English, University of Illinois at Chicago, 607 S Morgan St, IL 60607. http://mlg.eserver.org.

MEDIAWATCH. *see* JOURNALISM

320 AUS ISSN 0085-3224
➤ **MELBOURNE JOURNAL OF POLITICS.** Abbreviated title: M J P. Text in English. 1968. a., latest vol.34, 2008. AUD 20 per issue domestic; AUD 35 per issue foreign (effective 2009). bk.rev. back issues avail. **Document type:** *Journal, Academic/Scholarly.* **Description:** Covers all the fields associated with political science, including political theory, public policy, international relations, European studies, post-colonial studies, political science and sociology.
Related titles: Online - full text ed.: free (effective 2009).
Indexed: A26, AusPAIS, CA, E08, G06, G07, G08, I05, IBR, IBZ, P42, PAIS, PCI, PSA, S09, SCOPUS, SociolAb, T02.
—Ingenta.
Published by: University of Melbourne, School of Social and Political Sciences, Rm 203, Level 2, 234, Queensberry St, Carlton, VIC 3053, Australia. TEL 61-3-83449485, ssps-enquiries@unimelb.edu.au. Ed. David Walker.

320.531 MEX ISSN 0186-1395
HD8111
MEMORIA; revista mensual de politica y cultura. Text in Spanish. 1988. m. MXN 20 (effective 2002). back issues avail.
Related titles: Online - full text ed.: ISSN 1563-7522.
Published by: Centro de Estudios del Movimiento Obrero y Socialista, Pallares y Portillo No. 99, Col. Parque San Andres, Mexico, D.F., 04040, Mexico. TEL 52-5-5496117, FAX 52-5-5490253, cemos@servidor.unam.mx. Eds. Elvira Concheiro Borquez, Modonesi Massimo.

320 ARG ISSN 1853-0435
▼ **MENTE PUBLICA.** Text in Spanish. 2010. q. **Document type:** *Journal, Academic/Scholarly.*
Published by: Fundacion Apertura, Nicaragua, 5669 Piso 5, Depto B, Buenos Aires, C1414BWE, Argentina. TEL 54-11-35350140, http://www.fundacionapertura.org.ar/.

320.6 USA ISSN 1943-6777
MERCATUS POLICY SERIES: COUNTRY BRIEF. Text in English. 2005. irreg., latest no.3, 2009. **Document type:** *Monographic series, Academic/Scholarly.*
Related titles: Online - full text ed.: ISSN 1943-6785. free (effective 2010).
Published by: George Mason University, Mercatus Center, 3301 N Fairfax Dr, Ste 450, Arlington, VA 22201. TEL 703-993-4930, 800-815-5711, FAX 703-993-4935, mercatus@gmu.edu, http://www.mercatus.org.

320.6 USA ISSN 1944-4591
MERCATUS POLICY SERIES: POLICY COMMENT. Text in English. 2005. irreg., latest no.25, 2009. **Document type:** *Monographic series, Academic/Scholarly.*
Related titles: Online - full text ed.: ISSN 1944-4605. free (effective 2010).
Published by: George Mason University, Mercatus Center, 3301 N Fairfax Dr, Ste 450, Arlington, VA 22201. TEL 703-993-4930, 800-815-5711, FAX 703-993-4935, mercatus@gmu.edu, http://www.mercatus.org.

320.6 USA ISSN 1943-6793
MERCATUS POLICY SERIES: POLICY PRIMER. Text in English. 2005. irreg., latest no.10, 2009. **Document type:** *Monographic series, Academic/Scholarly.*
Related titles: Online - full text ed.: ISSN 1943-6807. free (effective 2010).
Published by: George Mason University, Mercatus Center, 3301 N Fairfax Dr, Ste 450, Arlington, VA 22201. TEL 703-993-4930, 800-815-5711, FAX 703-993-4935, mercatus@gmu.edu, http://www.mercatus.org.

320.6 USA ISSN 1943-6750
MERCATUS POLICY SERIES: POLICY RESOURCE. Text in English. 2005. irreg., latest no.6, 2009. **Document type:** *Monographic series, Academic/Scholarly.*
Related titles: Online - full text ed.: ISSN 1943-6769. free (effective 2010).
Published by: George Mason University, Mercatus Center, 3301 N Fairfax Dr, Ste 450, Arlington, VA 22201. TEL 703-993-4930, 800-815-5711, FAX 703-993-4935, mercatus@gmu.edu, http://www.mercatus.org.

320 ITA ISSN 1594-5472
HC301
MERIDIONE, SUD E NORD NEL MONDO. Text in Italian. 1954. bi-m. EUR 89.50 domestic to institutions; EUR 122.50 foreign (effective 2010). bk.rev. charts; illus. index. **Document type:** *Magazine, Consumer.*
Formerly (until 2000): Nord e Sud (0029-1188)
Indexed: I13, IBR, IBZ, MLA-IB, RASB.
Published by: Edizioni Scientifiche Italiane SpA, Via Chiatamone 7, Naples, NA 80121, Italy. TEL 39-081-7645443, FAX 39-081-7646477, info@edizioniesi.it, http://www.edizioniesi.it. Ed. Guido D'Agostino.

MESOAMERICA. *see* GENERAL INTEREST PERIODICALS—Costa Rica

320 MEX ISSN 1405-4558
JA5 CODEN: MAPOFI
➤ **METAPOLITICA**; revista trimestral de teoria y ciencia de la politica. Text in Spanish; Summaries in English. 1997. bi-m. MXN 650 domestic; USD 70 in North America; USD 90 in South America and Europe; USD 110 elsewhere and Europe (effective 2004). adv. bk.rev. **Document type:** *Academic/Scholarly.* **Description:** Covers political sciences, history and philosophy.
Related titles: Online - full text ed.: ISSN 1605-0576. 1997.
Indexed: A01, C01, CA, DIP, F03, F04, I13, IBR, IBZ, P42, PAIS, PSA, R15, S02, S03, SCOPUS, SOPODA, SSA, SociolAb, T02.
Published by: Centro de Estudios de Politica Comparada A.C., Augusto Rodin No.398, Col. Insurgentes Extremadura, Mexico City, DF 03740, Mexico. TEL 52-5-6333873, FAX 52-5-6333859. Ed., R&P Cesar Cansino. Adv. contact Sergio Ortiz Leroux.

➤ **MEXICO & N A F T A REPORT.** (North American Free Trade Agreement) *see* BUSINESS AND ECONOMICS—Economic Situation And Conditions

➤ **MEXICO BUSINESS FORECAST REPORT.** *see* BUSINESS AND ECONOMICS—Economic Situation And Conditions

320 USA ISSN 0733-4486
JA1
MICHIGAN JOURNAL OF POLITICAL SCIENCE. Text in English. 1981. s-a. USD 15 (effective 2011). bk.rev. **Document type:** *Journal, Academic/Scholarly.* **Description:** Covers all aspects of political science including, but not limited to, political theory, methodology, world politics, comparative politics, American government, public policy, economics, sociology and political economy. All papers written by graduate and undergraduate students.
Related titles: Online - full text ed.
Indexed: CA, P27, P42, P45, P48, P54, PQC, SCOPUS, T02.
Published by: University of Michigan, Michigan Journal of Political Science, 5700 Haven Hall, 505 S State St, Ann Arbor, MI 48109.

320 ARG ISSN 1852-5881
▼ **MICROPOLITICAS.** Text in Spanish. 2009. bi-m. **Document type:** *Magazine.*
Address: Rio de Janeiro 1240, Rosario, Santa Fe, 2000, Argentina. TEL 54-341-4381008. Ed. Ana Sargues.

320.9 GBR ISSN 0076-8502
DS49
MIDDLE EAST AND NORTH AFRICA (YEAR). Text in English. 1948. a. USD 760 per issue (effective 2009). reprints avail. **Document type:** *Directory, Academic/Scholarly.* **Description:** Covers economic, social, cultural, and political affairs.
Formerly (until 1965): The Middle East
Indexed: RASB.
—BLDSC (5761.350000), IE, Ingenta. **CCC.**
Published by: (Europa Publications Ltd.), Routledge (Subsidiary of: Taylor & Francis Group), 2 Park Sq, Milton Park, Abingdon, Oxon OX14 4RN, United Kingdom. TEL 44-20-70176000, FAX 44-20-70176699, orders@taylorandfrancis.com. **Dist. by:** Current Pacific Ltd., 7 La Roche Pl, Northcote, PO Box 36-536, Auckland 0627, New Zealand.

320 GBR ISSN 0047-7249
DS63.1
MIDDLE EAST INTERNATIONAL. Text in English. 1971. 25/yr. USD 120 in North America to individuals; GBP 85 in United Kingdom to individuals; GBP 110 elsewhere to individuals; USD 170 in North America to institutions; GBP 120 in United Kingdom to institutions; GBP 135 elsewhere to institutions (effective 2005). adv. bk.rev. reprints avail. **Document type:** *Journal, Academic/Scholarly.* **Description:** Political and social developments in the Middle East and Arab world.
Related titles: Microform ed.: (from PQC); Online - full text ed.
Indexed: A22, AltPI, CCME, M10, MEA&I, PAIS, PCI, PerIslam, RASB, SCOPUS.
—BLDSC (5761.378000), IE, Infotrieve, Ingenta.
Published by: Middle East International (Publishers) Ltd., 1 Gough Square, London, EC4A 3DE, United Kingdom. TEL 44-207-832-1330, FAX 44-207-832-1339. Ed. Steven Sherman. R&P, Adv. contact Al Staats TEL 202-232-8354. Circ: 10,000.

MIDDLE EAST JOURNAL OF CULTURE AND COMMUNICATION. *see* ASIAN STUDIES

MIDDLE EAST MONITOR. EAST MED; analysis, data & forecasts on every country across the region. *see* BUSINESS AND ECONOMICS—Economic Situation And Conditions

MIDDLE EAST MONITOR. THE GULF; analysis, data & forecasts on every country across the region. *see* BUSINESS AND ECONOMICS—Economic Situation And Conditions

MIDDLE EAST QUARTERLY. *see* POLITICAL SCIENCE—International Relations

320 USA
MIDWEST POLITICAL CONSULTANT. Text in English. 1987. m. USD 50 (effective 2000). adv. bk.rev. **Document type:** *Newsletter.* **Description:** Focuses on politics and political campaigning.
Published by: Christian Schock and Associates, 1079 Paradise Acres, Galesburg, IL 61401. TEL 309-343-3006. Ed., Pub., R&P, Adv. contact Christian Schock TEL 309-343-3006.

P

320 USA ISSN 0887-378X
HV97.M6 CODEN: MIQUES
➤ **THE MILBANK QUARTERLY**; a journal of public health and health care policy . Text in English. 1923. q. GBP 173 in United Kingdom to institutions; EUR 219 in Europe to institutions; USD 236 in the Americas to institutions; USD 337 elsewhere to institutions; GBP 200 combined subscription in United Kingdom to institutions (print & online eds.); EUR 252 combined subscription in Europe to institutions (print & online eds.); USD 272 combined subscription in the Americas to institutions (print & online eds.); USD 387 combined subscription elsewhere to institutions (print & online eds.) (effective 2012). charts; illus.; stat. Index. back issues avail.; reprint service avail. from PSC. **Document type:** *Journal, Academic/Scholarly.* **Description:** Contains scholarly articles on research and policy analysis in health care focusing on economic, social, demographic, ethical and philosophical aspects.
Former titles (until 1986): Health and Society (0160-1997); (until 1973): Milbank Memorial Fund Quarterly (0026-3745); (until 1934): Milbank Memorial Fund Quarterly Bulletin (0276-5187)
Related titles: Microfiche ed.; Microform ed.: (from PQC); Online - full text ed.: ISSN 1468-0009. GBP 173 in United Kingdom to institutions; EUR 219 in Europe to institutions; USD 236 in the Americas to institutions; USD 337 elsewhere to institutions (effective 2012) (from IngentaConnect).
Indexed: A01, A02, A03, A08, A20, A22, A23, A25, A26, AHCMS, ASCA, ASG, ASSIA, AcaI, AgeL, B01, B02, B04, B06, B07, B08, B09, B13, B15, B17, B18, B21, BAS, BPI, BPIA, BRD, C06, C07, C12, CA, CLFP, ChemAb, CurCont, E-psyche, E01, E08, EMBASE, ESPM, ExcerpMed, FR, FamI, FutSurv, G04, G06, G07, G08, H01, H05, H11, H12, H13, HRA, HlthInd, HospLI, I05, IBSS, IPI, ISR, IndMed, L03, MCR, MEA&I, MEDLINE, P02, P03, P06, P10, P13, P20, P21, P27, P30, P34, P42, P43, P48, P50, P52, P53, P54, P56, PAIS, PCI, PQC, PSA, PsycInfo, PsycholAb, RiskAb, S02, S03, S08, S09, SCI, SCOPUS, SOPODA, SSA, SSAI, SSAb, SSCI, SSI, SWR&A, SociolAb, T&II, T02, THA, W01, W02, W03, W07.
—BLDSC (5766.040000), GNLM, IE, Infotrieve, Ingenta, INIST. **CCC.**
Published by: (Milbank Memorial Fund), Wiley-Blackwell Publishing, Inc. (Subsidiary of: Wiley-Blackwell Publishing Ltd.), 111 River St, Hoboken, NJ 07030. TEL 201-748-6000, FAX 201-748-6088, info@wiley.com, http://www.wiley.com/WileyCDA/. Ed. Bradford H Gray. Adv. contact Kristin McCarthy TEL 201-748-7683.

320.531 USA ISSN 0026-3885
MILITANT; a socialist newsweekly published in the interests of the working people. Text in English, Spanish. 1928. w. USD 35 domestic (effective 2000). adv. bk.rev. back issues avail.; reprints avail. **Document type:** *Newspaper, Consumer.* **Description:** Covers developments in the labor movement, women's rights issues and Black and Latino issues. Coverage is international.
Incorporates (1977-2005): Perspectiva Mundial (0164-3169); Formerly (until 1941): Socialist Appeal; Which superseded in part: Intercontinental Press
Related titles: Microform ed.: (from PQC).
Indexed: Chicano, M10.
Published by: 408 Printing & Publishing Co., 306 W. 37th St., 10th Fl., New York, NY 10018. TEL 212-244-4899, FAX 212-244-4947. Ed. Argiris Malapanis. Circ: 6,000.

MILJOEMAGASINET. *see* ENVIRONMENTAL STUDIES

324.248906 363.7 DNK ISSN 0900-3746
MILJOEPOLITIK. Text in Danish. 1982. bi-m. free to libraries. adv. bk.rev. illus. **Document type:** *Magazine, Consumer.*
Published by: Danmarks Miljoeparti, Ryesgade 124 A, Copenhagen OE, 2100, Denmark. leif.eigil@larsen.tdcadsl.dk.

320 PAK
MILLAT. Text in Urdu. 1978. w. PKR 4.
Published by: Islamabad Publications (Private) Ltd., Hameed Chambers 9, Islamabad, 44000, Pakistan.

320.5322 FRA ISSN 1778-4662
MILLE MARXISMES. Text in French. 2005. **Document type:** *Monographic series.*
Published by: Editions Syllepse, 69 rue des Rigoles, Paris, 75020, France. TEL 33-1-44620889.

320 USA
MILLER CENTER OF PUBLIC AFFAIRS. PAPERS. Text in English. 19??. irreg. price varies. back issues avail. **Document type:** *Monographic series, Academic/Scholarly.* **Description:** Discusses a wide variety of public affairs issues affecting the US presidency.
Related titles: Online - full text ed.
Published by: University of Virginia, Miller Center of Public Affairs, 2201 Old Ivy Rd, PO Box 400406, Charlottesville, VA 22904. TEL 434-924-7236, FAX 434-982-2739, rmo6r@virginia.edu.

320 USA ISSN 1051-3094
JA88.U6
MILLER CENTER REPORT. Text in English. 1986. q. free (effective 2010). back issues avail. **Document type:** *Report, Academic/Scholarly.* **Description:** Reports on the day-to-day activities of the Miller Center, with accounts of forthcoming speakers, functions, and publications.
Related titles: Online - full text ed.
Published by: University of Virginia, Miller Center of Public Affairs, 2201 Old Ivy Rd, PO Box 400406, Charlottesville, VA 22904. TEL 434-924-7236, FAX 434-982-2739, rmo6r@virginia.edu.

320.6 301 351 USA ISSN 1941-5672
HN1
MILLER-MCCUNE; turning research into solutions. Text in English. 2008 (Apr.). bi-m. USD 29.94; USD 4.99 newsstand/cover (effective 2008). adv. bk.rev.; software rev.; video rev. illus.; stat.; maps; charts. back issues avail. **Document type:** *Magazine, Consumer.* **Description:** Explores academic and research-based solutions to current social issues in topics including politics, social problems, science and economics.
Related titles: Online - full content ed.
Indexed: CA, CMM, G08, I05.
Published by: Miller-McCune Center for Research, Media and Public Policy, 804 Anacapa St, Santa Barbara, CA 93101. TEL 805-899-8620, FAX 805-899-8141, TheEditor@miller-mccune.com, http://www.miller-mccune.com. Eds. Michael Todd, John Mecklin. Pub. Sara Miller-McCune. Adv. contact Geane de Lima. B&W page USD 5,197; trim 8.125 x 10.875. Circ: 92,000 (paid and controlled).

MILLS CAPITOL OBSERVER. *see* PUBLIC ADMINISTRATION

306.2 DEU ISSN 1618-288X
MINDERHEITEN UND MINDERHEITENPOLITIK IN EUROPA. Text in German. 2002. irreg., latest vol.6, 2004. price varies. **Document type:** *Monographic series, Academic/Scholarly.*
Published by: Peter Lang GmbH (Subsidiary of: Peter Lang Publishing Group), Eschborner Landstr 42-50, Frankfurt Am Main, 60489, Germany. TEL 49-69-7807050, FAX 49-69-78070550, zentrale.frankfurt@peterlang.com. Ed. Albert Reiterer.

MINDFIELD MAGAZINE. *see* LITERARY AND POLITICAL REVIEWS

320 ZAF ISSN 1816-7748
MINDSHIFT. Text in English. 2005. bi-m. ZAR 191.52 domestic; ZAR 341.70 foreign (effective 2006). **Document type:** *Journal, Academic/Scholarly.* **Description:** Covers the socio-economic issues in modern South Africa.
Published by: (University of Cape Town, Graduate School of Business), Ince (Pty) Ltd., PO Box 1749, Cape Town, South Africa. TEL 27-21-4407400, FAX 27-21-4487619, ince@ince.co.za, http://www.ince.co.za. Ed. Monica Graaff.

320.9 USA ISSN 0026-4474
MINDSZENTY REPORT. Text in English. 1958. m. USD 20 (effective 2007). bk.rev. **Document type:** *Newsletter, Consumer.*
Formerly: Release (St. Louis)
Related titles: Microform ed.: (from PQC).
Published by: Cardinal Mindszenty Foundation, Inc., PO Box 11321, St. Louis, MO 63105. TEL 314-727-6279, FAX 314-727-5897, info@mindszenty.org, http://www.mindszenty.org. Pub. Eleanor Schlafly. Circ: 8,000 (paid and controlled).

320 305 ITA
MINERVA; laboratorio di cultura e politica. Text in Italian. 1983. m. EUR 65 (effective 2009). adv. bk.rev. illus.; tr.lit. back issues avail. **Document type:** *Magazine, Consumer.* **Description:** Deals with culture, politics, and the economy.
Related titles: CD-ROM ed.; E-mail ed.; Online - full text ed.
Published by: Minerva Edizioni, Via Pacinotti 13, Rome, 00135, Italy. TEL 39-06-6892972. Circ: 30,000.

320 RUS
MINISTERSTVO OBRAZOVANIYA I NAUKI ROSSIISKOI FEDERATSII. BYULLETEN'. VYSSHEE I SREDNEE PROFESSIONAL'NOE OBRAZOVANIE. Text in Russian. 1992. m. USD 125 in the Americas (effective 2000).
Former titles (until 2004): Ministerstvo Obrazovaniya Rossiiskoi Federatsii. Byulleten'; (until 1999): Ministerstvo Obshchego i Professional'nogo Obrazovaniya R F. Byulleten'; (until 1997): Gosudarstvennyi Komitet R F po Vysshemu Obrazovaniyu. Byulleten'; (until 1993): Ministerstvo Nauki, Vysshei Shkoly i Tekhnicheskoi Politiki R F. Komitet po Vysshei Shkole. Byulleten'
Indexed: RASB.
Published by: Ministerstvo Obrazovaniya i Nauki Rossiiskoi Federatsii/ Ministry of Education and Science of the Russian Federation, ul Kedrova 8, korp 2, Moscow, 117804, Russian Federation. TEL 7-495-6295327, FAX 7-495-6294173, press@mon.gov.ru, http://mon.gov.ru.

MINNESOTA LAW & POLITICS. *see* LAW

328.776 USA
MINNESOTA RULES. SUPPLEMENT. Text in English. 1984. biennial. **Document type:** *Government.*
Published by: Office of Revisor of Statutes, 700 State Office Bldg, 100 Rev. Dr. Martin Luther King Jr. Blvd, St. Paul, MN 55155. TEL 651-296-2868, 800-627-3529, FAX 651-296-0569, revisor@revisor.mn.gov.

MINORITY SUPPLIER NEWS. *see* BUSINESS AND ECONOMICS—Small Business

321.8 CHN ISSN 1003-1936
DS779.26
MINZHU/DEMOCRACY. Text in Chinese. 1989. m. USD 21.60 (effective 2009). adv. bk.rev. **Description:** Covers politics, education, science and cultural issues.
Published by: Minjin Zhongyang Weiyuanhui, No 98 Gulou Xin'anli, Beijing, 100009, China. TEL 4035673. Ed. Mao Qibin.

321.8 CHN ISSN 1003-1723
MINZHU YU FAZHI/DEMOCRACY AND LEGAL SYSTEM. Text in Chinese. 1979. s-m. USD 60 (effective 2009). **Document type:** *Journal, Academic/Scholarly.*
—East View.
Published by: Zhongguo Faxuehui/China law Society, 63, Beingmahutong, Beijing, 100034, China. TEL 86-10-66186234, FAX 86-10-66135938. **Dist. by:** China International Book Trading Corp, 35 Chegongzhuang Xilu, Haidian District, PO Box 399, Beijing 100044, China. TEL 86-10-68412045, FAX 86-10-68412023, cibtc@mail.cibtc.com.cn, http://www.cibtc.com.cn.

321.8 CHN
MINZHU YU FAZHI SHIBAO/DEMOCRACY AND LAW. Text in Chinese. 1985. w. **Document type:** *Newspaper, Government.*
Published by: Zhongguo Faxuehui/China law Society, 63, Beingmahutong, Beijing, 100034, China. http://www.chinalawsociety.com/. **Dist. by:** China International Book Trading Corp, 35 Chegongzhuang Xilu, Haidian District, PO Box 399, Beijing 100044, China. TEL 86-10-68412045, FAX 86-10-68412023, cibtc@mail.cibtc.com.cn, http://www.cibtc.com.cn.

321.8 CHN ISSN 1003-0026
MINZHU YU KEXUE/DEMOCRACY AND SCIENCE. Text in Chinese. bi-m. USD 21.60 (effective 2009).
Related titles: Online - full text ed.
—East View.
Published by: Jiusan Xueshe Zhongyang Weiyuanhui, No 4 Banshang Hutong, Xisi, Beijing, 100034, China. TEL 6011627. Ed. Li Fengming.

320.532 CHN ISSN 1007-8592
DS730
MINZU LUNTAN/NATIONALITIES FORUM. Text in Chinese. 1983. m. USD 43.20 (effective 2009). **Document type:** *Journal, Academic/Scholarly.*
Related titles: Online - full text ed.
Published by: Minzu Luntan Zazhishe, 505, Caie Bei Lu, Changsha, 410008, China. TEL 86-731-2356663, FAX 86-731-4319212.

320 ESP ISSN 1695-8993
LA MIRADA LIMPIA; o la existencia del otro. Text in Spanish. 2001. bi-m. EUR 7.20 newsstand/cover (effective 2008). 98 p./no.; **Document type:** *Magazine, Academic/Scholarly.*
Published by: 129 Producciones, S.L., Cruz de la Rauda, 1, Granada, Andalucia 18010, Spain. TEL 34-958-20411, miradalimpia@inicia.es. Ed. Jose Heredia Maya. **Dist. by:** Asociacion de Revistas Culturales de Espana, C Covarruvias 9 2o. Derecha, Madrid 28010, Spain. TEL 34-91-3086066, FAX 34-91-3199267, info@arce.es, http://www.arce.es/.

320.531 300 CHN ISSN 1674-2354
MISHU/SECRETARY. Text in Chinese. 1983. m. CNY 63.60; CNY 5.30 per issue (effective 2011). **Document type:** *Journal, Academic/Scholarly.*
Related titles: Online - full text ed.
—BLDSC (5828.621670).
Published by: Shanghai Daxue/Shanghai University, 99, Shangda Lu, PO Box 128, Shanghai, 200444, China. TEL 86-21-66135686, FAX 86-21-66135686.

324.6 USA
MISSOURI ANNUAL CAMPAIGN FINANCE REPORT. Text in English. 1979. a. free. **Document type:** *Government.*
Published by: Missouri Ethics Commission, PO Box 1254, Jefferson City, MO 65102. TEL 573-751-3077, FAX 573-751-2020. Circ: 1,000.

MOBILIZATION; an international journal. *see* SOCIOLOGY

320.5 SWE
MODERAT DEBATT. Text in Swedish. 1934. bi-m. SEK 100, USD 5. adv. bk.rev. **Document type:** *Academic/Scholarly.*
Former titles (until 1996): Debatt; (until 1969): Ung Hoeger (0026-7449); (until 1947): Ungsvensk Loesen
Published by: Moderata Ungdomsfoerbundet/Young Conservatives, Fack 1243, Stockholm, 11182, Sweden. FAX 46-8-20-34-49. Ed. Karin Isberg. Adv. contact Christina Mourad. Circ: 30,000.

MODERN ASIAN STUDIES. *see* ASIAN STUDIES

MODERN GERMAN STUDIES. *see* SOCIOLOGY

MODERN ITALY. *see* HISTORY—History Of Europe

MODERN JUDAISM; a journal of Jewish ideas and experience. *see* ETHNIC INTERESTS

320 USA ISSN 1941-9732
MODERN REPUBLIC. Text in English. 2008. m. free (effective 2009). **Document type:** *Magazine, Consumer.* **Description:** Covers news on political science, current events and culture.
Media: Online - full text.
Published by: Cyber Publishing, JAF Station, PO Box 911, New York, NY 10116. TEL 646-239-1598, 866-217-2120, info@cyberpublishing.org, http://cyberpublishing.xbuild.com.

MODERNE GESCHICHTE UND POLITIK. *see* HISTORY—History Of Europe

320.57 CAN ISSN 1920-809X
THE MOLOTOV RAG; Toronto's anarchist quarterly. Text in English. 2008. q. USD 5 per issue (effective 2010). **Document type:** *Magazine, Consumer.*
Published by: The Molotov Rag Magazine, 588 Bloor St, W, Toronto, ON M6G 1K4, Canada. Ed. Ben Hackman.

324.2663 SEN
MOMSAREEW. Text in French. 1958. m.
Published by: Parti Africain de l'Independance, BP 820, Dakar, Senegal. Ed. Malamine Badji. Circ: 2,000.

321.6 GBR
MONARCHY. Text in English. 1948. q. GBP 20, USD 40 (effective 2001). adv. bk.rev. bibl.; illus. **Document type:** *Newsletter.*
Former titles (until 1993): Monarchist League Newsletter; Monarchist Newsletter; Monarchist (0047-7834)
Published by: Monarchist League, International Headquarters, BM Monarchist, London, WC1N 3XX, United Kingdom. FAX 44-1892-835899. Ed. Nick Law. R&P Donald Foreman. Adv. contact Denis Walker. B&W page GBP 90. Circ: 3,000.

321.6 CAN ISSN 0319-4019
MONARCHY CANADA. Text in English. 1970. q. USD 20; USD 25 foreign. adv. bk.rev. charts; illus. **Description:** Looks at the monarchy from a Canadian perspective and at Canada from a monarchist one. Offers current and historical articles on constitutional, social and political affairs, as well as personality profiles and reviews of books and the arts.
Formerly: Canadian Monarchist
Published by: Fealty Enterprises, 3050 Yonge St, Ste 206B, Toronto, ON M4N 2K4, Canada. TEL 416-482-4157, FAX 416-482-4909. Ed. Arthur Bousfield. Circ: 8,000.

MONASH UNIVERSITY. CENTRE OF SOUTHEAST ASIAN STUDIES. MONASH PAPERS ON SOUTHEAST ASIA; a series of monographs from the Centre of Southeast Asian Studies. *see* HISTORY—History Of Asia

320.951 FRA ISSN 1767-3755
HC427.95
MONDE CHINOIS. Text in French. 2004. q. EUR 85 domestic; EUR 95 foreign (effective 2009). **Document type:** *Journal, Academic/Scholarly.* **Description:** Focuses on the political and cultural evolution of China.
Indexed: IBSS.
Published by: Choiseul Editions, 28 Rue Etienne Marcel, Paris, 75002, France. TEL 33-1-53340993, FAX 33-1-53340994, http://choiseul-editions.com. Ed. Pascal Lorot.

320.9 FRA ISSN 1775-7266
MONDE IMPARFAIT. Text in French. 2004. irreg. back issues avail. **Document type:** *Monographic series, Consumer.*
Published by: Editions Duboiris, 67 rue Saint Jacques, Paris, 75005, France. contact@editionsduboiris.com.

335.83 FRA ISSN 0026-9433
LE MONDE LIBERTAIRE; federation anarchiste weekly. Text in French. 1954. w. (45/yr). EUR 61 domestic; EUR 61 DOM-TOM; EUR 77 elsewhere (effective 2009). adv. bk.rev.; film rev.; tel.rev. bibl. **Document type:** *Newspaper, Consumer.*
Published by: Federation Anarchiste, 145 rue Amelot, Paris, 75011, France. TEL 33-1-48053408, FAX 33-1-49299859, http://www.federation-anarchiste.org/. Ed. A Deuriendt. Adv. contact Andre Devriendt. Circ: 17,500.

324.245 ITA ISSN 0392-1115
HX7
MONDOPERAIO. Text in Italian. 1948. m. adv. bk.rev.; film rev.; play rev. **Document type:** *Magazine, Consumer.* **Description:** This is the official organ of the Partito Socialista Italiano and was founded in 1948 by Pietro Nenni.
Formerly (until 1973): Mondo Operaio (1121-2330)
Indexed: ELLIS, MLA-IB, RASB.
Published by: (Partito Socialista Italiano), Mondo Operaio Edizioni Avanti SpA, Via Tomacelli, 146, Rome, RM 00186, Italy. Circ: 15,000.

MONETARY DIGEST. *see* BUSINESS AND ECONOMICS—Investments

320.9 CAN ISSN 1718-780X
LE MONITEUR DU M A E P. (Mecanisme Africain d'Evaluation par les Pairs) Text in French. 2006. 3/yr. **Document type:** *Newsletter, Trade.*
Published by: Partenariat Afrique Canada, 323, rue Chapel, Ottawa, ON K1N 7Z2, Canada. TEL 613-237-6768, FAX 613-237-6530, info@pacweb.org, http://www.pacweb.org/f/index.php?option=com_frontpage&Itemid=1.

320.531 USA ISSN 0027-0520
HX1
➤ **MONTHLY REVIEW.** Abbreviated title: M R. Text in English. 1949. m. USD 39 in US & Canada to individuals; USD 47 elsewhere to individuals; USD 5 per issue (effective 2010). adv. bk.rev. illus. index. back issues avail.; reprints avail. **Document type:** *Journal, Academic/Scholarly.* **Description:** Uses Marxist thought to critique contemporary conditions.
Related titles: Microform ed.: (from PQC); Online - full text ed.
Indexed: A01, A02, A03, A08, A20, A22, A25, A26, ABS&EES, APW, AcaI, AltPI, AmH&L, B02, B04, B15, B17, B18, BAS, BRD, BusI, C04, C12, CA, CurCont, DIP, E08, FR, G04, G05, G06, G07, G08, H09, HistAb, I05, I07, IBR, IBZ, LeftInd, M01, M02, MEA&I, MLA-IB, MagInd, P02, P05, P06, P10, P13, P27, P30, P34, P42, P45, P46, P47, P48, P53, P54, PAA&I, PAIS, PCI, PQC, PSA, RASB, S02, S03, S05, S08, S09, S11, S23, SCOPUS, SOPODA, SSA, SSAI, SSAb, SSCI, SSI, SociolAb, T&II, T02, W03, W05, W07.
—BLDSC (5947.800000), IE, Infotrieve, Ingenta. **CCC.**
Published by: Monthly Review Foundation, 146 W 29th St, #6W, New York, NY 10001. TEL 212-691-2555, 800-670-9499, FAX 212-727-3676. Ed. John Bellamy Foster.

➤ **MOSKOVSKII GOSUDARSTVENNYI OBLASTNOI UNIVERSITET. VESTNIK. SERIYA ISTORIYA I POLITICHESKIE NAUKI.** *see* HISTORY

320 RUS ISSN 0868-4871
➤ **MOSKOVSKII GOSUDARSTVENNYI UNIVERSITET. VESTNIK. SERIYA 12: POLITICHESKIE NAUKI.** Variant title: Vestnik Moskovskogo Universiteta. Seriya 12. Politicheskie Nauki. Text in Russian. 1971. bi-m. USD 186 in North America; USD 269 combined subscription in North America (print & online eds.) (effective 2011). **Document type:** *Journal, Academic/Scholarly.*
Formerly (until 1990): Moskovskii Universitet. Vestnik. Seriya 13: Teoriya Nauchnogo Kommunizma (0320-8087)
Related titles: Online - full text ed.
Indexed: RASB.
—East View.
Published by: (Moskovskii Gosudarstvennyi Universitet im. M.V. Lomonosova, Fakul'tet Politologii), Izdatel'stvo Moskovskogo Gosudarstvennogo Universiteta im. M. V. Lomonosova/Publishing House of Moscow State University, B Nikitskaya 5/7, Moscow, 103009, Russian Federation. TEL 7-095-2295091, FAX 7-095-2036671, kd_mgu@rambler.ru, http://www.msu.ru/depts/MSUPubl. Ed. Andrey Shutov. **Dist. by:** East View Information Services, 10601 Wayzata Blvd, Minneapolis, MN 55305. TEL 952-252-1201, 800-477-1005, FAX 952-252-1202, info@eastview.com, http://www.eastview.com.

➤ **MOTMAELE;** medlemsblad for Norsk maalungdom. *see* LINGUISTICS

➤ **MOTU WORKING PAPER.** *see* BUSINESS AND ECONOMICS

320 DEU
MUENSTERANER FORUM ZUR POLITISCHEN BILDUNG. Text in German. 2000. irreg., latest vol.3, 2003. price varies. **Document type:** *Monographic series, Academic/Scholarly.*
Published by: (Forschungsstelle fuer Didaktik der Politikwissenschaft), Waxmann Verlag GmbH, Steinfurter Str 555, Muenster, 48159, Germany. TEL 49-251-265040, FAX 49-251-2650426, info@waxmann.com.

MUGAK. *see* ETHNIC INTERESTS

320 IND
MUJAHANA. Text in Hindi. 19??. w. INR 100; INR 2 per issue (effective 2011). **Document type:** *Magazine, Consumer.*
Address: Manav Raksha Sangh Rd, 77 Khera Khurd, New Delhi, 110 082, India.

320.972 MEX
MUJERES AVANTE/WOMEN ON FORWARD. Text in English. q. MXN 110 domestic; USD 15 foreign (effective 2000).
Published by: Editora Comunicacion, Paseo Sierra Vista No 67, Residencial Sierra Vista, Hermosillo, Sonora, 83148, Mexico. TEL 52-62-112-190, FAX 52-62-110-870. Ed. Lorena Myrna Galvez.

320.971 327.71 CAN ISSN 1911-7744
LE MULTILATERAL; la revue pour mieux comprendre la politique internationale du Canada. Text in French. 2007. bi-m. CAD 25 domestic to individuals; CAD 40 domestic to institutions; CAD 30 in United States to individuals; CAD 45 in United States to institutions; CAD 45 elsewhere to individuals; CAD 60 elsewhere to institutions (effective 2007). back issues avail. **Document type:** *Newsletter, Consumer.*
Published by: Le Multilateral, 13 Rue des Narcisses, Gatineau, PQ J9A 1T2, Canada. TEL 819-439-8033, info@lemultilateral.ca, http://lemultilateral.ca.

MULTITUDES; revue politique, artistique et philosophique. *see* PHILOSOPHY

320 FRA ISSN 1958-9743
MULTITUDES-IDEES. Text in French. 2007. irreg. **Document type:** *Monographic series.*
Published by: (Association Multitudes), Editions Amsterdam, 31 Rue Paul Fort, Paris, 75014, France. TEL 33-1-45412333, FAX 33-8-26699502, info@editionsamsterdam.fr, http://www.editionsamsterdam.fr. **Dist. by:** Editions Les Belles Lettres, 25 Rue du General Leclerc, Kremlin Bicetre 94270, France. TEL 33-1-45151970, FAX 33-1-45151980.

320 RUS
MUNITSIPAL'NAYA VLAST'. Text in Russian. 1998. m. USD 135 in North America (effective 2000).
Address: Ul Smol'naya 14, Moscow, 125493, Russian Federation. TEL 7-095-4568431. Ed. Yu Zarechkin. **Dist. by:** East View Information Services, 10601 Wayzata Blvd, Minneapolis, MN 55305. TEL 952-252-1201, 800-477-1005, FAX 952-252-1202, info@eastview.com, http://www.eastview.com.

MUSIC AND POLITICS. *see* MUSIC

320 PAK ISSN 0464-0756
MUSLIM WORLD; weekly review of the Motamar. Text in English. 1963. w. PKR 60, USD 30. adv. charts.
Related titles: Online - full text ed.; ◆ Supplement(s): World Muslim Conference. Proceedings. ISSN 0084-2052.
Indexed: AMR.
Published by: World Muslim Congress/Motamar al-Alam al-Islami, P O Box 5030, Karachi, 74000, Pakistan. FAX 92-21-466878, http://www.motamaralalamalislami.org. Ed. Inamullah Khan.

MUZEUM JIHOVYCHODNI MORAVY. ACTA MUSEALIA. *see* HISTORY—History Of Europe

N A C R C BULLETIN. *see* PUBLIC ADMINISTRATION

341.37 BEL ISSN 1608-7569
N A T O REVIEW (ONLINE). (North Atlantic Treaty Organization) Text in English. 1998. q. free (effective 2010). back issues avail. **Document type:** *Journal, Academic/Scholarly.*
Media: Online - full text. **Related titles:** French ed.: Revue de l'O T A N (Online). ISSN 1608-7607. 199?; Lithuanian ed.: N A T O Apzvalga. 2004; Dutch ed.: N A V O Kroniek (Online). ISSN 1608-7593; Spanish ed.: Revista de la O T A N (Online). ISSN 1608-7690. 1998; Danish ed.: N A T O Nyt (Online). ISSN 1608-7585. 1998; Greek ed.: Deltio N A T O (Online). ISSN 1608-7623. 1999; Portuguese ed.: Noticias da O T A N (Online). ISSN 1608-7682. 1999; Turkish ed.: N A T O Dergisi (Online). 2003; Icelandic ed.: N A T O Frettir (Online). ISSN 1608-764X. 1998; Czech ed.: N A T O Review (Czech Edition, Online). ISSN 1608-7577. 1999; Italian ed.: Rivista della N A T O (Online). ISSN 1608-7658. 1998; Bulgarian ed.: N A T O Pregled. 2004; Russian ed.: N A T O Vestnik (Online). ISSN 1608-7704. 1998; Lithuanian ed.: N A T O Revu. ISSN 1608-7712. 2004; Latvian ed.: N A T O Vestnesis. 2004; Slovak ed.: Prehla'd N A T O. 2004; Slovenian ed.: Revija N A T O. 2004; Estonian ed.: N A T O Teataja. 2004; Romanian ed.: Revista N A T O. 2004; Hungarian ed.: N A T O Tukor (Online). ISSN 1608-7631. 1999; Polish ed.: Przeglad N A T O (Online). ISSN 1608-7674. 2000; Norwegian ed.: N A T O Nytt (Online). ISSN 1608-7666. 2000; German ed.: N A T O Brief (Online). ISSN 1608-7615. 1998.
Published by: North Atlantic Treaty Organization (N A T O), Office of Information and Press, Blvd Leopold III, Brussels, 1110, Belgium. TEL 32-2-7075009, FAX 32-2-7074579, natodoc@hq.nato.int. Ed. Christopher Bennett.

N C B A REPORTS. *see* BUSINESS AND ECONOMICS—Public Finance, Taxation

320 AUT
N F Z - NEUE FREIE ZEITUNG. Text in German. 1973. w. EUR 30.60 domestic; EUR 73 foreign; EUR 0.80 newsstand/cover (effective 2004). adv. bk.rev. illus. **Document type:** *Newspaper, Consumer.*
Supersedes: Neue Front: Zeitung der Freiheitlichen
Published by: Die Freiheitlichen, Theobaldgasse 19-4, Vienna, W 1060, Austria. TEL 43-1-5123535311, FAX 43-1-5123535412, verwaltung.nfz@fpoe.at. Ed. Walter Howadt.

320 MEX ISSN 0027-7509
NACION; organo de accion nacional. Text in Spanish. 1941. fortn. MXN 60,000, USD 45. adv. charts; illus.
Related titles: Online - full text ed.: ISSN 1607-1115. 1998.
Indexed: B03.
Published by: Estudios y Publicaciones Economicas y Sociales S.A., CERRADA DE EUGENIA 25, Col Del Valle, Delegacion Benito Juarez, Apartado Postal 32 470, Mexico City, DF 03100, Mexico. TEL 536-18-31, FAX 525-687-2922. Circ: 15,000 (controlled).

NANZAN UNIVERSITY. CENTRE FOR LATIN AMERICAN STUDIES. WORKING PAPER. *see* HISTORY—History Of North And South America

320 PAK
NAQIB-I MILLAT. Text in Urdu. 1978 (vol.2). w. PKR 3.
Published by: Maulvi Hidayatullah, Kucha Chen Teliyan, Bazar Wachchuwali, Shah Alam Market, Lahore, Pakistan.

320 IND
NATION AND THE WORLD. Text in English. 1991. fortn. INR 325, USD 75, GBP 50 (effective 2011). adv. bk.rev. back issues avail. **Description:** Covers the trends in politics, economy, business, science, medicine, environment and art.
Published by: Indian Publications Ltd., Talimabad, Sangam Vihar, New Delhi, 110 062, India. TEL 91-11-4620808, FAX 91-11-4622614. Ed. Saiyid Hamid.

320 USA ISSN 2150-6469
E839.5
▼ **NATIONAL AFFAIRS.** Text in English. 2009. q. USD 27.99 (effective 2010). illus. **Document type:** *Journal, Consumer.* **Description:** Features essays about domestic policy, political economy, society, culture, and political thought.
Related titles: Online - full text ed.
Indexed: A01.
Published by: National Affairs, Inc., 1015 15th St NW, Ste 900, Washington, DC 20005. TEL 202-289-4175, mclyne@nationalaffairs.com.

NATIONAL DIRECTORY OF CORPORATE PUBLIC AFFAIRS. *see* BUSINESS AND ECONOMICS—Trade And Industrial Directories

320 AUS ISSN 1030-6641
JQ4021
NATIONAL GUIDE TO GOVERNMENT. Text in English. 1986. 3/yr. (Apr., Aug. & Dec.). AUD 479 domestic; AUD 435.45 foreign; AUD 749 combined subscription domestic (print & online eds.); AUD 680.91 combined subscription foreign (print & online eds.) (effective 2008). **Document type:** *Directory, Trade.*
Formerly (until 1988): National Guide to Government and the Bureaucracy
Related titles: Online - full text ed.: AUD 529 domestic; AUD 480.91 foreign (effective 2008).
Published by: Crown Content, Level 2, 141 Capel St, North Melbourne, VIC 3051, Australia. TEL 61-3-93299800, FAX 61-3-93299698, online@crowncontent.com.au. Eds. Amy O'Halloran, Mr. Scott O'Halloran. Pub. Michael Wilkinson. Circ: 1,400.

320 GBR ISSN 1460-8944
JC311
➤ **NATIONAL IDENTITIES.** Text in English. 1999. q. GBP 319 combined subscription in United Kingdom to institutions (print & online eds.); EUR 422, USD 529 combined subscription to institutions (print & online eds.) (effective 2012). adv. back issues avail.; reprint service avail. from PSC. **Document type:** *Journal, Academic/Scholarly.* **Description:** Explores the formation and expression of national identity from antiquity to the present day.
Related titles: Online - full text ed.: ISSN 1469-9907. GBP 287 in United Kingdom to institutions; EUR 380, USD 476 to institutions (effective 2012) (from IngentaConnect).
Indexed: A01, A03, A08, A22, AmH&L, B21, BrHumI, CA, E01, E17, ESPM, HistAb, IBSS, P42, PSA, S02, S03, SCOPUS, SSA, SSciA, SociolAb, T02.
—IE, Infotrieve, Ingenta. **CCC.**
Published by: Routledge (Subsidiary of: Taylor & Francis Group), 4 Park Sq, Milton Park, Abingdon, Oxon OX14 4RN, United Kingdom. TEL 44-20-70176000, FAX 44-20-70176336, subscriptions@tandf.co.uk, http://www.routledge.com. Adv. contact Linda Hann TEL 44-1344-779945. **Subscr. in N America to:** Taylor & Francis Inc., Customer Services Dept, 325 Chestnut St, 8th Fl, Philadelphia, PA 19106. TEL 215-625-8900, 800-354-1420, FAX 215-625-2940, customerservice@taylorandfrancis.com; **Subscr. to:** Taylor & Francis Ltd., Journals Customer Service, Sheepen Pl, Colchester, Essex CO3 3LP, United Kingdom. TEL 44-20-70175544, FAX 44-20-70175198.

320 USA ISSN 0360-4217
JK1
NATIONAL JOURNAL; the weekly on politics and government. Text in English. 1969. w. adv. bk.rev. charts; illus. s-a. index. back issues avail.; reprints avail. **Document type:** *Journal, Trade.* **Description:** Provides nonpartisan analysis of politics, policy and government.
Former titles (until 1975): National Journal Reports (0091-3685); (until 1973): National Journal (0027-9560)
Related titles: Microfilm ed.: (from PQC); Online - full text ed.: ISSN 1943-4553. USD 25 per day (effective 2005); ◆ Supplement(s): Capital Source. ISSN 0898-6916.
Indexed: A01, A03, A08, A22, A25, A26, A33, ABS&EES, AgeL, B02, B07, B15, B17, B18, BAS, BLI, C05, C12, CADCAM, CPerI, E08, EIA, EnerInd, EnvAb, G04, G06, G07, G08, I05, I07, IPARL, M01, M02, M06, MASUSE, MCR, P02, P05, P06, P10, P30, P34, P45, P47, P48, P53, P54, PAIS, PQC, PersLit, RASB, S02, S03, S08, S09, S11, SCOPUS, SWR&A, T02, TelAb, Telegen.
—BLDSC (6026.150000), IE, Infotrieve, Ingenta. **CCC.**
Published by: National Journal Group, Inc., The Watergate 600 New Hampshire Ave, NW, Washington, DC 20037. TEL 202-739-8400, 800-613-6701, FAX 202-833-8069, service@nationaljournal.com. Ed. Ron Fournier. Adv. contact Victoria Monroe. Circ: 11,381 (paid).

328 USA ISSN 2158-3862
JK1
NATIONAL JOURNAL DAILY. Variant title: National Journal's Congress Daily. Text in English. 1991. d. back issues avail. **Document type:** *Newsletter, Consumer.* **Description:** Provides the latest news and scheduling information from Capitol Hill.
Formerly (until 2010): National Journal's Congress Daily (2153-7410)
Related titles: E-mail ed.; Fax ed.; Online - full text ed.: ISSN 2158-3870.
Published by: National Journal Group, Inc., The Watergate 600 New Hampshire Ave, NW, Washington, DC 20037. TEL 202-739-8400, FAX 202-833-8069, subscriptions@nationaljournal.com. Ed. Jason Dick.

320 AUS
NATIONAL LEADER. Text in English. 1948. q. adv. **Document type:** *Newsletter.* **Description:** Discusses matters affecting rural and metropolitan electorates.
Former titles (until 2008): National News; (until 2003): National Leader (0811-3300); (until 1982): New South Wales Countryman
—Ingenta.
Published by: National Party of Australia - N.S.W., 5th Fl., 30 Carrington St, Sydney, NSW 2000, Australia. npansw@ozemail.com.au, http://www.ozemail.com.au/~npansw. Circ: 30,000.

320 USA ISSN 0896-629X
JK1 CODEN: NPSREL
➤ **NATIONAL POLITICAL SCIENCE REVIEW.** Abbreviated title: N P S R. Text in English. 1989. a. back issues avail. **Document type:** *Journal, Academic/Scholarly.* **Description:** Examines the theoretical and empirical aspects of politics and policies that gives groups an advantage or disadvantage by reasons of race, ethnicity, sex, and other factors.
Related titles: Online - full text ed.
Indexed: AmH&L, CA, HistAb, IIBP, P42, PCI, PSA, S02, S03, SCOPUS, SOPODA, SociolAb, T02.
—**CCC.**
Published by: (National Conference of Black Political Scientists), Transaction Publishers, 35 Berrue Cir, Piscataway, NJ 08854. TEL 732-445-2280, FAX 732-445-3138, trans@transactionpub.com, http://www.transactionpub.com. Eds. David Covin, Michael Mitchell TEL 480-964-3902.

320.52 USA ISSN 0028-0038
AP2
NATIONAL REVIEW. Abbreviated title: N R. Text in English. 1955. bi-w. USD 29.50 domestic; USD 51 foreign; USD 5 per issue (effective 2009). adv. bk.rev. illus. Index. back issues avail.; reprints avail. **Document type:** *Magazine, Consumer.* **Description:** Discusses national and international issues from a conservative viewpoint.
Related titles: Audio cassette/tape ed.; Online - full text ed.: USD 21.95 (effective 2009).
Indexed: A01, A02, A03, A08, A21, A22, A25, A26, A33, ABS&EES, ARG, Acal, B04, B05, B07, B14, BAS, BRD, BRI, C05, C12, CA, CBRI, CLFP, CPerI, CWI, Chicano, E08, F01, F02, FutSurv, G05, G06, G07, G08, I02, I05, I07, L03, M01, M02, M05, M06, MASUSE, MEA&I, MLA-IB, MRD, MagInd, P02, P05, P06, P10, P13, P30, P34, P47, P48, P53, P54, PCI, PMR, PQC, PRA, PSI, PersLit, R02, R03, R04, R06, RASB, RGAb, RGPR, RI-1, RI-2, S02, S03, S08, S09, S11, S23, SWR&A, T02, TOM, W03, W05.
—BLDSC (6031.050000), CIS, IE, Infotrieve, Ingenta. **CCC.**
Published by: National Review, Inc., 215 Lexington Ave, 4th Fl, New York, NY 10016. TEL 212-679-7330, FAX 212-849-2835, nronline@nationalreview.com. Ed. Rich Lowry. Adv. contact Scott Budd. B&W page USD 8,640, color page USD 12,100; bleed 8.125 x 10.75. Circ: 160,000.

320 USA
NATIONAL VANGUARD; toward a new consciousness, a new order, a new people. Text in English. 1978. bi-m. USD 18 domestic; USD 26 in Canada; USD 36 elsewhere (effective 2004). bk.rev.; film rev.; tel.rev. back issues avail. **Document type:** *Monographic series, Consumer.*
Published by: (National Alliance), National Vanguard Books, PO Box 330, Hillsboro, WV 24946. TEL 304-653-4707, FAX 304-653-4690, http://natvan.com.

324.24 USA ISSN 0028-0372
E740
NATIONAL VOTER. Text in English. 1951. 4/yr. free to members. adv. bk.rev. index. **Document type:** *Newsletter, Consumer.* **Description:** Nonpartisan articles on public policy and campaign issues of interest to the American electorate.
Related titles: Microfilm ed.: (from PQC); Online - full text ed.
Indexed: A22, A26, CWI, E08, G05, G06, G07, G08, I05, I07, PAIS, S09, S23.
—CIS.
Published by: League of Women Voters of the U S, 1730 M St N W, 10th fl, Washington, DC 20036. TEL 202-429-1965, 202-263-2334, FAX 202-429-0854, 202-429-4343, http://www.lwv.org. Ed. Meg S Dusken. Pub. Monica Sullivan. adv.: B&W page USD 3,465; trim 10.88 x 8.38. Circ: 110,000 (paid).

320.54 GBR ISSN 1662-9116
▼ ➤ **NATIONALISMS ACROSS THE GLOBE.** Text in English. 2009. irreg. price varies. **Document type:** *Monographic series, Academic/Scholarly.* **Description:** Contains interdisciplinary research involving nationalism and ethnicity.
Published by: Peter Lang Ltd. (Subsidiary of: Peter Lang Publishing Group), Evenlode Ct, Main Rd, Long Hanborough, Oxfordshire OX29 8SZ, United Kingdom. TEL 44-1993-880088, FAX 44-1993-882040, info@peterlang.com. Eds. Krzysztof Jasculowski, Tomasz Kamusella.

320.54 GBR ISSN 1354-5078
JC311 CODEN: NANAFB
➤ **NATIONS AND NATIONALISM.** Abbreviated title: N A N. Text in English. 1995. q. GBP 333 domestic to institutions; EUR 423 in Europe to institutions; USD 555 in the Americas to institutions; USD 653 elsewhere to institutions; GBP 366 combined subscription domestic to institutions (print & online eds.); EUR 465 combined subscription in Europe to institutions (print & online eds.); USD 612 combined subscription in the Americas to institutions (print & online eds.); USD 717 combined subscription elsewhere to institutions (print & online eds.) (effective 2009); subscr. includes Studies in Ethnicity and Nationalism. adv. bk.rev. back issues avail.; reprint service avail. from PSC. **Document type:** *Journal, Academic/Scholarly.* **Description:** Responds to the growing interest in the study of nationalism and nationalist movements throughout the world.
Related titles: Online - full text ed.: ISSN 1469-8129. 1999. GBP 333 domestic to institutions; EUR 423 in Europe to institutions; USD 555 in the Americas to institutions; USD 653 elsewhere to institutions (effective 2009) (from IngentaConnect).
Indexed: A01, A03, A08, A20, A22, A26, AICP, BibInd, CA, CCME, CurCont, E01, GEOBASE, I02, I13, IBSS, P02, P10, P34, P42, P47, P48, P53, P54, PQC, PSA, S02, S03, S11, SCOPUS, SOPODA, SSA, SSCI, SociolAb, T02, W07.
—BLDSC (6033.595000), IE, Infotrieve, Ingenta. **CCC.**

Published by: (Association for the Study of Ethnicity and Nationalism), Wiley-Blackwell Publishing Ltd. (Subsidiary of: John Wiley & Sons, Inc.), 9600 Garsington Rd, Oxford, OX4 2DQ, United Kingdom. TEL 44-1865-776868, FAX 44-1865-714591, customerservices@blackwellpublishing.com. Ed. Anthony D Smith. Adv. contact Craig Pickett TEL 44-1865-476267.

320 POL ISSN 0137-141X
NAUKI POLITYCZNE. Text in Polish. 1974. irreg., latest vol.22, 2008. price varies. **Document type:** *Monographic series, Academic/Scholarly.* **Description:** Contains current research results on one author in the field of political science including Ph.D. works and other monographs.
Published by: (Uniwersytet im. Adama Mickiewicza w Poznaniu/Adam Mickiewicz University), Wydawnictwo Naukowe Uniwersytetu im. Adama Mickiewicza/Adam Mickiewicz University Press, ul Fredry 10, Poznan, 61701, Poland. TEL 48-61-8294646, FAX 48-61-8294647, press@amu.edu.pl, http://press.amu.edu.pl. Ed. Katarzyna Zodz-Kuznia.

324.2 LKA
NAVA SAMA SAMAJA BULLETINE. Text in English. 1985. irreg. adv. bk.rev.
Published by: Nava Sama Samaja Party, 17 Barracks Lane, Colombo, 2, Sri Lanka. Ed. Vickamabahu Karanarathne.

NEIMENGGU TONGZHAN LILUN YANJIU/INNER MONGOLIA THEORY RESEARCH OF UNITED FRONT. *see* SOCIAL SCIENCES: COMPREHENSIVE WORKS

NEPAL - ANTIQUARY; journal of social-historical research and digest. *see* ASIAN STUDIES

320 LKA ISSN 1391-2380
DS331
NETHRA. Text in English. bi-m. USD 10 per issue (effective 2000). **Document type:** *Journal, Consumer.*
Formerly: The Thatched Patio
Published by: International Centre for Ethnic Studies, 2 Kynsey Terrace, Colombo, 8, Sri Lanka. TEL 94-8-698048, FAX 94-8-698048, ices@slt.lk. Eds. Regi Siriwarden, K M De Silva. R&P P Thambiraja. Adv. contact K M De Silva.

320.531 AUT ISSN 0028-3061
NEUE ALTERNATIVE; sozialistische Zeitschrift fuer Kultur, Wirtschaft, Politik. Text in German. 1965. m. adv. bk.rev. illus. **Document type:** *Magazine, Consumer.*
Published by: Verband Sozialistischer StudentInnen Oesterreichs, Amtshausgasse 4, Vienna, W 1050, Austria. TEL 43-1-5268986, FAX 43-1-5268989, vsstoe@vsstoe.at, http://www.vsstoe.at. Circ: 12,000.

320.5 DEU ISSN 0177-6738
H5
DIE NEUE GESELLSCHAFT - FRANKFURTER HEFTE. Text in German. 1985. 10/yr. EUR 50.60; EUR 5.50 newsstand/cover (effective 2010). adv. bk.rev. index. reprints avail. **Document type:** *Journal, Academic/Scholarly.*
Formed by the merger of (1954-1985): Neue Gesellschaft (0028-3177); (1946-1985): Frankfurter Hefte (0015-9999)
Indexed: A22, AmH&L, BAS, CERDIC, DIP, IBR, IBSS, IBZ, MLA-IB, P30, PAIS, PCI, PRA, RASB.
—IE, Infotrieve. **CCC.**
Published by: (Friedrich-Ebert-Stiftung), Verlag J.H.W. Dietz Nachf. GmbH, Dreizehnmorgenweg 24, Bonn, 53175, Germany. TEL 49-228-238083, FAX 49-228-234104, info@dietz-verlag.de, http://www.dietz-verlag.de. Ed. Thomas Meyer. adv.: page EUR 820. Circ: 6,500 (paid and controlled).

320 DEU ISSN 0934-9200
HV6022.G3
NEUE KRIMINALPOLITIK. Text in German. 1989. q. EUR 87 (effective 2011). adv. reprint service avail. from SCH. **Document type:** *Journal, Academic/Scholarly.*
Indexed: DIP, IBR, IBZ.
Published by: Nomos Verlagsgesellschaft mbH und Co. KG, Waldseestr 3-5, Baden-Baden, 76530, Germany. TEL 49-7221-21040, FAX 49-7221-210427, marketing@nomos.de, nomos@nomos.de, http://www.nomos.de. Ed. Monika Frommel. Adv. contact Bettina Roos. Circ: 1,200 (paid and controlled).

320.9 DEU ISSN 0028-3320
H5
NEUE POLITISCHE LITERATUR; Berichte ueber das internationale Schrifttum. Text in German. 1952. 3/yr. EUR 51 domestic; CHF 66 in Switzerland; EUR 47 in Europe; GBP 42, USD 66; EUR 35 domestic to students; CHF 46 in Switzerland to students; EUR 33 in Europe to students; GBP 29, USD 46 to students (effective 2011). bk.rev. bibl. index. back issues avail.; reprints avail. **Document type:** *Journal, Academic/Scholarly.*
Formerly (until 1956): Politische Literatur (0477-2776)
Indexed: A22, AmH&L, CA, DIP, HistAb, IBR, IBSS, IBZ, P30, P42, PAIS, PCI, PRA, RASB, T02.
—IE, Infotrieve. **CCC.**
Published by: Peter Lang GmbH (Subsidiary of: Peter Lang Publishing Group), Eschborner Landstr 42-50, Frankfurt Am Main, 60489, Germany. TEL 49-69-7807050, FAX 49-69-78070550, zentrale.frankfurt@peterlang.com, http://www.peterlang.com. Ed. Ute Scheider. Circ: 1,000.

320.531 DEU
HN1 CODEN: FNSBE7
NEUE SOZIALE BEWEGUNGEN. Text in German. 1988. q. EUR 42 to individuals; EUR 54 to libraries; EUR 30 to students; EUR 16 per issue (effective 2011). adv. abstr. 90 p./no.; back issues avail. **Document type:** *Journal, Academic/Scholarly.*
Formerly (until 1994): Forschungsjournal Neue Soziale Bewegungen (0933-9361)
Indexed: CA, DIP, FR, I13, IBR, IBSS, IBZ, P30, P42, PSA, S02, S03, SOPODA, SSA, SociolAb, T02.
—BLDSC (4011.805000). **CCC.**
Published by: Lucius und Lucius Verlagsgesellschaft mbH, Gerokstr 51, Stuttgart, 70184, Germany. TEL 49-711-242060, FAX 49-711-242088, lucius@luciusverlag.com. Eds. Ansgar Klein, Hans-Josef Legrand, Thomas Leif. Circ: 800. **Dist. by:** Brockhaus Commission, Kreidlerstr 9, Kornwestheim 70806, Germany. TEL 49-7154-13270, FAX 49-7154-132713, info@brocom.de.

320 AUT
DAS NEUE WORT. Text in German. 1972. m. bk.rev. **Document type:** *Newsletter, Consumer.* **Description:** Newsletter of Socialist analysis and opinion.
Published by: Volkssozialistische Bewegung Oesterreichs, Apfelgasse 1-7, Vienna, W 1040, Austria. Ed. Alfred von Warton. Circ: 1,000.

320 DEU
NEUIGKEIDNBLAEDDLE. Text in German. 1982. q. free. back issues avail.
Published by: Sozialdemokratische Partei Deutschlands (SPD), Ortsverein Gartenstadt-Theuerbruennlein-Eselhoehe, Kornmarkt 17, Schweinfurt, 97421, Germany. TEL 049-9721-21429. Circ: 2,200.

328.793 USA
HJ11
NEVADA. OFFICE OF LEGISLATIVE AUDITOR. BIENNIAL REPORT. Text in English. 1974. biennial. free. stat. **Document type:** *Government.*
Formerly: Nevada. Office of Fiscal Analyst. Annual Report (0092-6841)
Related titles: Series of: Nevada. Legislative Counsel Bureau. Bulletin.
Published by: Office of Legislative Auditor, 401 S Carson St, Carson City, NV 89701. TEL 702-687-6815. R&P Gary Crews.

326.8092 USA
NEW ABOLITIONIST NEWS; abolish the white race - by any means necessary. Text in English. q. USD 20 to individuals; USD 40 to institutions (effective 2000). **Document type:** *Newsletter.* **Description:** Discusses issues on the topic of race. Calls for the abolition of the white race.
Published by: (D C New Abolitionists), New Abolitionists, Inc., PO Box 499, Dorchester, MA 02122. TEL 781-255-5964, newabolition@hotmail.com, http://www.newabolition.org.

320.532 IND ISSN 0047-9500
AP8
NEW AGE. Variant title: New Age Weekly. Text in English. 1952; N.S. 1964. w. INR 250; INR 5 per issue (effective 2011). bk.rev.; film rev.; play rev. charts; illus. back issues avail. **Document type:** *Newspaper, Consumer.*
Related titles: Online - full text ed.: free (effective 2011).
Indexed: CBRI, RASB.
Published by: Communist Party of India, Ajoy Bhavan, 15, Indrajit Gupta Marg, New Delhi, 110 002, India. TEL 91-11-23235546, FAX 91-11-23235543, nationalcouncil@communistparty.in, http://www.communistparty.in/. **Subscr. to:** I N S I O Scientific Books & Periodicals, PO Box 7234, Indraprastha HPO, New Delhi 110 002, India.

320 USA ISSN 0885-6540
THE NEW AMERICAN (APPLETON). Text in English. 1985. bi-w. USD 39 domestic; USD 48 in Canada; USD 66 elsewhere; USD 49 combined subscription (print & online eds.) (effective 2010). adv. bk.rev.; film rev.; video rev. illus. 48 p./no.; back issues avail.; reprints avail. **Document type:** *Magazine, Consumer.* **Description:** Provides constitutional conservatives and economic libertarians with significant articles that focus on political science, social opinion and economic theory, while rejecting an accidental view of history and exposing the behind-the-scenes forces shaping American politics and culture.
Formed by the merger of (1958-1985): American Opinion (0003-0236); Which was formed by the 1958 merger of: One Man's Opinion; Hubert Kregeloh Comments; (1965-1985): Review of the News (0034-6802); Which was formerly (until 1965): Correction, Please!; Review of the News incorporated (1956-1971): The Dan Smoot Report; Which was formerly (until 1956): Dan Smoot Speaks
Related titles: Microform ed.: (from PQC); Online - full text ed.: USD 34 (effective 2010).
Indexed: A01, A22, A26, G05, G06, G07, G08, G09, GSS&RPL, H09, I05, I07, M06, MASUSE, MLA-IB, P02, P05, P06, P10, P34, P48, P53, P54, PQC, S05, S23.
—Ingenta.
Published by: American Opinion Publishing Inc., PO Box 8040, Appleton, WI 54912. Ed. Gary Benoit. Pub. John F McManus. Adv. contact Julie DuFrane.

NEW ARABIAN STUDIES. *see* HISTORY—History Of The Near East

178 USA ISSN 1543-1215
BJ59
THE NEW ATLANTIS; a journal of technology & society. Text in English. 2003 (Spring). q. USD 20 domestic; USD 30 foreign (effective 2003). adv. **Document type:** *Journal, Academic/Scholarly.* **Description:** Aims to clarify the nation's moral and political understanding of all areas of technology from stem cells to hydrogen cells to weapons of mass destruction.
Related titles: Online - full text ed.: ISSN 1555-5569.
Indexed: A01, A03, A10, P30, PAIS, SCOPUS, V03.
Published by: Ethics and Public Policy Center, 1015 15th St, N W, Ste 900, Washington, DC 20005. TEL 202-682-1200, FAX 202-408-0632, Ethics@eppc.org, http://www.eppc.org/. Ed. Eric Cohen. Adv. contact Adam Keiper. **Subscr. to:** The New Atlantis, Subscription Services, PO Box 3000, Denville, NJ 07834-3000. TEL 866-440-6916.

320 MKD ISSN 1409-9454
JN97.A1
NEW BALKAN POLITICS. Text in Multiple languages. 2000. irreg. **Document type:** *Journal, Academic/Scholarly.*
Related titles: Online - full text ed.: ISSN 1409-8709. free (effective 2011).
Indexed: CA, P42, S02, S03, SCOPUS, T02.
Address: c/o Mirjana Maleska, South East European University, "Ilindenska" pn, Tetovo, 1200, Macedonia. TEL 389-44-356000. Ed. Mirjana Maleska.

320 NLD ISSN 1875-0184
▼ ➤ **NEW DIRECTIONS IN DIPLOMATIC HISTORY.** Text in English. 2009. irreg. **Document type:** *Monographic series, Academic/Scholarly.*
Published by: Martinus Nijhoff (Subsidiary of: Brill), PO Box 9000, Leiden, 2300 PA, Netherlands. TEL 31-71-5353500, FAX 31-71-5317532, marketing@brill.nl. Eds. Jeremy Black, John Charmley, Thomas Otte.

320 USA ISSN 1550-1604
JA1
➤ **THE NEW ENGLAND JOURNAL OF POLITICAL SCIENCE.** Text in English. 2005. s-a. free (effective 2011). back issues avail. **Document type:** *Journal, Academic/Scholarly.* **Description:** Contains academic research articles in general interest political science as well as focuses on the six New England States such as Connecticut, Maine, Massachusetts, New Hampshire, Rhode Island, and Vermont plus Canada.
Media: Online - full text.
Indexed: CA, P42, PSA, T02.
Published by: New England Political Science Association, c/o Northeastern University, Boston, MA 02115. http://www.northeastern.edu/nepsa/index.php. Ed. Mark Brewer.

➤ **NEW EUROPE**; the European weekly. *see* BUSINESS AND ECONOMICS—Economic Situation And Conditions

320 301 USA
➤ **NEW FORUM BOOKS.** Text in English. 1999. irreg., latest 2007. price varies. back issues avail. **Document type:** *Monographic series, Academic/Scholarly.* **Description:** Covers current sociopolitical topics and issues.
Published by: Princeton University Press, 41 William St, Princeton, NJ 08540. TEL 609-258-4900, 800-777-4726, FAX 609-258-6305, cpriday@pupress.co.uk. Ed. Robert P George. **Subscr. addr. in US:** California - Princeton Fulfillment Services, Inc., 1445 Lower Ferry Rd, Ewing, NJ 08618. TEL 609-883-1759, 800-777-4726, FAX 609-883-7413, 800-999-1958, orders@cpfsinc.com. **Dist. addr. in Canada:** University Press Group.; **Dist. addt. in UK:** John Wiley & Sons Ltd.

320 330 ZAF ISSN 1814-2621
NEW FRONTIERS. Variant title: C D E New Frontiers. Text in English. 2003. irreg., latest vol.4, 2005. price varies. **Document type:** *Monographic series.*
Published by: Centre for Development and Enterprise, PO Box 1936, Johannesburg, 2000, South Africa. TEL 27-11-4825140, FAX 27-11-4825089, info@cde.org.za, http://www.cde.org.za.

320.531 USA
NEW GROUND. Text in English. 1987. bi-m. USD 10 (effective 2000). adv. film rev.; music rev.; play rev.; software rev.; video rev.; dance rev.; Website rev. charts; illus. 16 p./no.; back issues avail. **Document type:** *Newsletter.*
Related titles: Diskette ed.
Published by: Chicago Democratic Socialists of America, 1608 N Milwaukee, Ste 403, Chicago, IL 60647. TEL 773-384-0327, FAX 773-702-0090, http://www.chicagodsa.org. Adv. contact Robert Roman. Circ: 800.

363.7 GBR ISSN 0266-7835
NEW GROUND. Text in English. 1983. q. adv. bk.rev. charts; illus.; stat. back issues avail. **Document type:** *Journal, Academic/Scholarly.* **Description:** Covers environmental issues from a socialist point of view and provides theoretical articles on green socialism.
Related titles: Online - full text ed.
Indexed: ISAP.
Published by: Socialist Environment and Resources Association, 2nd Fl, 1 London Bridge, Downstream Bldg, London, SE1 9BG, United Kingdom. TEL 44-207-0221985, enquiries@sera.org.uk. Ed. Melanie Smallman.

320.5322 NGA ISSN 0794-439X
NEW HORIZON; Nigeria's Marxist monthly. Text in English. 1975. m. NGN 48, USD 24.
Published by: I F & W O G Enterprises, PO Box 2165, Mushin, Lagos, Nigeria. Ed. Ikpe Etokudo. Circ: 25,000.

320.5322 USA ISSN 0737-3724
HX1
NEW INTERNATIONAL; a magazine of Marxist politics and theory. Text in English. 1983. irreg. price varies. bk.rev. back issues avail. **Document type:** *Newsletter.*
Related titles: Online - full text ed.; Spanish ed.: Nueva Internacional. ISSN 1056-8921. 1983; French ed.: Nouvelle Internationale. ISSN 0827-0929. 1983.
Published by: 408 Printing & Publishing Co., 410 West St, New York, NY 10014. TEL 212-929-3486, FAX 212-924-6040. Circ: 2,500.

NEW LABOR FORUM; a journal of ideas, analysis and debate. *see* LABOR UNIONS

NEW LEFT REVIEW. *see* LITERARY AND POLITICAL REVIEWS

NEW LEFT REVIEW (SPANISH EDITION). *see* LITERARY AND POLITICAL REVIEWS

320.51 USA
NEW LIBERTARIAN; the journal of record of the libertarian movement. Text in English. 1971. bi-m. USD 30. adv. bk.rev. **Description:** Covers news of the movement and analysis of the world.
Former titles: New Libertarian Weekly; New Libertarian Notes
Related titles: Microfiche ed.
Published by: New Libertarian Company of Free Traders, 3151 Airway Ave., Ste. A1, Costa Mesa, CA 92626-4620. TEL 310-289-4126, FAX 310-839-0975, info@newlibertarian.com. Ed. Samuel Edward Konkin III. adv.: B&W page USD 300, color page USD 1,000; trim 10.75 x 8.25. Circ: 2,000 (paid).

NEW METRO NEWS. *see* ETHNIC INTERESTS

322.4 TZA
NEW OUTLOOK TANZANIA. Variant title: New Outlook. Text in English. 1976. m. TZS 90, USD 30.
Address: PO Box 165, Dar Es Salaam, Tanzania. Ed. Joe Kamuzora.

320 CZE ISSN 1804-6290
HB1.A1
➤ **NEW PERSPECTIVES ON POLITICAL ECONOMY.** Text in Czech, English. 2005. s-a. free (effective 2011). **Document type:** *Journal, Academic/Scholarly.* **Description:** Aims to resurrect the tradition of Austrian economics- and liberty-oriented thinking that thrived in central Europe at the beginning of the 20th century.
Related titles: Online - full text ed.: ISSN 1801-0938. free (effective 2011).
Indexed: CA, P42, T02.
Published by: Liberalni Institut, Spalena 51, Prague, 110 00, Czech Republic. Eds. Dan Stastny, Josef Sima.

321.8 USA ISSN 0893-7850
E839.5

➤ **NEW PERSPECTIVES QUARTERLY**; a journal of social and political thought. Short title: N P Q. Text in English. 1963. q. GBP 347 in United Kingdom to institutions; EUR 440 in Europe to institutions; USD 434 in the Americas to institutions; USD 679 elsewhere to institutions; GBP 400 combined subscription in United Kingdom to institutions (print & online eds.); EUR 507 combined subscription in Europe to institutions (print & online eds.); USD 500 combined subscription in the Americas to institutions (print & online eds.); USD 781 combined subscription elsewhere to institutions (print & online eds.) (effective 2012). adv. bk.rev. illus.; abstr. back issues avail.; reprint service avail. from PSC. **Document type:** *Journal, Academic/Scholarly.* **Description:** Examines social and political thought on economics, environment, politics, culture, and the critical issues of our common future.
Formerly (until 1986): Center for the Study of Democratic Institutions. Center Magazine (0008-9125); (until 1967): Center for the Study of Democratic Institutions. Center Diary (0577-0165)
Related titles: Microform ed.: (from PQC); Online - full text ed.: ISSN 1540-5842. GBP 347 in United Kingdom to institutions; EUR 440 in Europe to institutions; USD 434 in the Americas to institutions; USD 679 elsewhere to institutions (effective 2012).
Indexed: A01, A02, A03, A08, A20, A22, A25, A26, ABS&EES, Acal, B01, B04, B06, B07, B09, BAS, BRD, CA, DIP, E01, E08, G05, G06, G07, G08, H09, I05, I07, I13, IBR, IBZ, L09, LeftInd, M01, M02, M10, MASUSE, MagInd, P02, P06, P10, P13, P30, P34, P42, P47, P48, P53, P54, PAIS, PQC, PRA, PSA, PSI, Perlslam, R03, R04, RGAb, RGPR, S02, S03, S05, S08, S09, S11, SSAI, SSAb, SSI, SociolAb, T02, W03, W05.
—BLDSC (6084.924200), IE, Infotrieve, Ingenta. **CCC.**
Published by: (Center for the Study of Democratic Institutions), Wiley-Blackwell Publishing, Inc. (Subsidiary of: Wiley-Blackwell Publishing Ltd.), 111 River St, Hoboken, NJ 07030. TEL 201-748-6000, FAX 201-748-6088, info@wiley.com, http://www.wiley.com/WileyCDA/. Ed. Nathan Gardels TEL 310-474-0011. Adv. contact Kristin McCarthy TEL 201-748-7683.

➤ **NEW POLITICAL ECONOMY (NEW YORK).** *see* BUSINESS AND ECONOMICS

320 GBR ISSN 0739-3148
JA1

➤ **NEW POLITICAL SCIENCE**; a journal of politics & culture . Text in English. 1972. q. GBP 306 combined subscription in United Kingdom to institutions (print & online eds.); EUR 382, USD 477 combined subscription to institutions (print & online eds.) (effective 2012). adv. bk.rev. illus. Index. back issues avail.; reprint service avail. from PSC. **Document type:** *Journal, Academic/Scholarly.* **Description:** Discusses political science scholarship from a radical perspective.
Related titles: Online - full text ed.: ISSN 1469-9931. GBP 276 in United Kingdom to institutions; EUR 343, USD 430 to institutions (effective 2012) (from IngentaConnect).
Indexed: A01, A03, A08, A22, ABS&EES, AltPI, B21, CA, DIP, E01, E17, ESPM, I13, IBR, IBSS, IBZ, LeftInd, P34, P42, PAIS, PSA, S02, S03, SCOPUS, SOPODA, SSA, SociolAb, T02.
—IE, Infotrieve, Ingenta. **CCC.**
Published by: (Caucus for a New Political Science USA), Routledge (Subsidiary of: Taylor & Francis Group), 4 Park Sq, Milton Park, Abingdon, Oxon OX14 4RN, United Kingdom. TEL 44-20-70176000, FAX 44-20-70176336, subscriptions@tandf.co.uk, http://www.routledge.com. Eds. Joseph Peschek, Mark S Mattern, Nancy S Love. **Subscr. to:** Taylor & Francis Ltd., Journals Customer Service, Sheepen Pl, Colchester, Essex CO3 3LP, United Kingdom. TEL 44-20-70175544, FAX 44-20-70175198.

320 ITA ISSN 1825-7445
NEW POLITICS. Text in Italian. 2005. m. **Document type:** *Magazine, Consumer.*
Published by: Edizioni Riformiste, Piazza Barberini 52, Rome, 00187, Italy. TEL 39-06-427481, info@ilriformista.it, http://www.ilriformista.it.

320.531 USA ISSN 0028-6494
HX1 CODEN: NEPOEM
NEW POLITICS; a journal of socialist thought. Abbreviated title: N P. Text in English. 1961-1978; N.S. 1986. s-a. USD 24 for 2 yrs. domestic to individuals; USD 40 for 2 yrs. foreign to individuals; USD 50 for 2 yrs. domestic to institutions; USD 60 for 2 yrs. foreign to institutions; USD 7 per issue domestic; USD 9 per issue in Canada (effective 2010). adv. bk.rev. bibl.; illus. index. back issues avail.; reprints avail. **Document type:** *Journal, Consumer.* **Description:** Features coverage of labor issues, social movements, electoral politics, intellectual history, and the prospects for democratic and radical renewal in different parts of the world, along with interviews, book reviews, the popular "Words and Pictures" feature, and film criticism by Kurt Jacobsen.
Related titles: Microform ed.: N.S. (from PQC); Online - full text ed.
Indexed: A22, ABS&EES, APW, AltPI, I13, IBSS, LeftInd, M02, P05, P06, P34, P42, P45, PAIS, PCI, PSA, S02, S03, SCOPUS, SOPODA, SPAA, SSA, SociolAb, T02.
—BLDSC (6085.800000), IE, Ingenta.
Published by: New Politics Associates, Inc., 155 W 72nd St, Rm 402, New York, NY 10023. Eds. Betty Reid Mandell, Marvin Mandell.

320.943 CZE ISSN 1211-8303
DB2238.7
THE NEW PRESENCE; the Prague journal of Central European affairs. Text in English. 1996. q. CZK 380 domestic; EUR 15 in Europe; USD 22 elsewhere (effective 2009). adv. music rev.; bk.rev.; film rev. back issues avail.; reprints avail. **Document type:** *Magazine, Consumer.* **Description:** Covers Central European affairs.
Related titles: Online - full text ed.; ◆ Czech ed.: Pritomnost. ISSN 1213-0133.
Indexed: A01, A03, A08, CA, G08, I02, I05, P02, P10, P27, P34, P42, P45, P48, P53, P54, PQC, R02, S02, S03, S11, T02.
Published by: Martin Jan Stransky Foundation, Narodni tr 11, Prague, 11000, Czech Republic. TEL 42-2-22075600, FAX 42-2-22075605, info@vydavatelstvimjs.cz, http://www.nova-pritomnost.cz. Eds. Ivan Maly, Martin Riegl. Pub. Martin Jan Stransky.

320 CAN ISSN 1715-6718
HX3

➤ **NEW PROPOSALS: JOURNAL OF MARXISM AND INTERDISCIPLINARY INQUIRY.** Text in English, French. 2007. s-a. free (effective 2011). **Document type:** *Journal, Academic/Scholarly.* **Description:** Dedicated to the radical transformation of the contemporary world order.
Media: Online - full text.
Published by: New Proposals Publishing Society, Dept of Anthropology, University of British Columbia, 6303 NW Marine Dr, Vancouver, BC V6T 1Z1, Canada. TEL 604-822-2240. Ed. Charles Menzies.

320.531 BEL ISSN 1783-8940
THE NEW SOCIAL EUROPE. Text in Multiple languages. 2007. irreg. **Document type:** *Journal.*
Related titles: CD-ROM ed.: ISSN 1783-8967; Online - full text ed.: ISSN 1783-8959.
Published by: Parti Socialiste Europeen/Party of European Socialists, 98 Rue du Trone, Bruxelles, 1050, Belgium. TEL 32-2-5489080, FAX 32-2-2301766, info@pes.org, http://www.pes.org.

320.531 303.3 CAN
NEW SOCIALIST; ideas for radical change. Text in English. bi-m. CAD 25 domestic; CAD 30 foreign; CAD 4.95 newsstand/cover domestic (effective 2005). **Document type:** *Magazine, Consumer.*
Related titles: Online - full content ed.
Address: 253 College St, PO Box 167, Toronto, ON M5T 1R5, Canada. TEL 416-955-1581, http://www.web.net/~newsoc. Eds. Harold Lavender, Nick Scanlan, Sebastian Lamb, Todd Gordon, Tony Tracy. Pub., R&P, Adv. contact Tony Tracy. Circ: 200 (paid).

NEW SOUTH AFRICAN OUTLOOK; an ecumencial magazine for thinkers and decision makers. *see* RELIGIONS AND THEOLOGY

320.6 360 USA
NEW STUDIES IN SOCIAL POLICY. Text in English. 1999. irreg., latest 2001. USD 29.95, GBP 26.95, CAD 30.95 per issue (effective 2010). back issues avail. **Document type:** *Monographic series, Academic/Scholarly.*
Published by: Transaction Publishers, 35 Berrue Cir, Piscataway, NJ 08854. TEL 732-445-2280, FAX 732-445-3138, trans@transactionpub.com, http://www.transactionpub.com.

320 371.051 USA ISSN 1947-2633
H96
NEW VOICES IN PUBLIC POLICY. Text in English. 2007. s-a. free (effective 2009). back issues avail. **Document type:** *Journal, Academic/Scholarly.* **Description:** Acts as a forum for insightful and innovative works in the public policy arena that highlight the diversity of ideas and range of study undertaken by the SPP student body.
Media: Online - full content.
Published by: George Mason University, School of Public Policy, 3401 Fairfax Dr, Arlington, VA 22201. TEL 703-993-3762, FAX 703-993-4876, spp@gmu.edu, http://policy.gmu.edu.

320.9 USA ISSN 0895-8505
NEW WEST NOTES. Text in English. 1987. m. USD 150. **Description:** Reports on national political and economic issues from a California perspective.
Formerly: Larkspur Report
Address: PO Box 221364, Sacramento, CA 95822. TEL 916-395-0709. Ed. Bill Bradley.

320 GUY ISSN 0028-7008
NEW WORLD. Text in English. 1963. fortn. adv. bk.rev. illus.
Media: Duplicated (not offset).
Published by: New World Associates, King St 215, Georgetown, Guyana. Ed. David De Caires. Circ: 800.

320 USA
NEW YORK PEARL. Text in English. q. **Document type:** *Newsletter.*
Formerly: Pearl Newsletter
Published by: Committee for Public Education and Religious Liberty, 165 E 56 St, New York, NY 10022. TEL 212-223-8012. Ed. Vivian Lindermayer.

328.747 USA ISSN 0196-4623
JK3430
NEW YORK RED BOOK. Text in English. 1892. a. USD 125 combined subscription per issue (print & online eds.) (effective 2011). **Document type:** *Trade.*
Related titles: Online - full text ed.: USD 100 per issue (effective 2011).
Published by: New York Legal Publishing Corp., 136 Railroad Ave Ext, Albany, NY 12205. TEL 518-459-1100, 800-541-2681, FAX 518-459-9718, nylp@nycap.rr.com.

324 NZL ISSN 1177-956X
NEW ZEALAND. ELECTORAL COMMISSION, TE KAITIAKI TAKI KOWHIRI. ANNUAL REPORT. Text in English. 1997. a.
Formerly (until 2004): Electoral Commission. Report (1174-3727)
Related titles: Online - full text ed.: ISSN 1177-9551.
Published by: Electoral Commission/Te Kaitiaki Taki Kowhiri, Level 9, 180 Molesworth St, PO Box 3220, Wellington, New Zealand. TEL 64-4-4950030, FAX 64-4-4950031, http://www.elections.org.nz.

NEW ZEALAND SLAVONIC JOURNAL. *see* HUMANITIES: COMPREHENSIVE WORKS

320.9 USA ISSN 0028-8969
HX1
NEWS & LETTERS. Text in English. 1955. 10/yr. USD 5 (effective 1999). bk.rev.; film rev. illus. back issues avail.; reprints avail. **Document type:** *Newspaper.* **Description:** Journal of labor, civil rights, women's liberation, and anti-war struggles nationally and internationally with an emphasis on Marxist-Humanist theory.
Related titles: Microfilm ed.: (from PQC).
Indexed: AltPI, M10, Perlslam, W09.
Address: 36 S Wabash, Rm 1440, Chicago, IL 60603. TEL 312-236-0799, nandl@igc.apc.org. Ed. Jim Mills. R&P Olga Domanski. Circ: 6,000 (paid).

320.532 USA
NEWS BEHIND THE NEWS; an independent research report. Text in English. 1979-1991 (Oct.); resumed. w. USD 400 (effective 2006). **Document type:** *Newsletter.* **Description:** Reports on communist mind warfare operations against the U.S.
Address: 5909 E 26th St, Tulsa, OK 74114. TEL 918-836-4431. Ed. Julian Williams. Circ: 150. **Subscr. to:** I N S I O Scientific Books & Periodicals, PO Box 7234, Indraprastha HPO, New Delhi 110 002, India. iihm@ap.nic.in, http://iihm.ap.nic.in/.

320.9 USA
NEWS FROM GREECE. Text in English. 1974. 11/yr. free. illus. **Document type:** *Government.*
Formerly: Greece
Published by: Embassy of Greece, Press and Information Office, 2211 Massachusetts Ave, N W, Washington, DC 20008. TEL 202-332-2727, FAX 202-265-4931. Ed. Achilles Paparseuos. Circ: 3,000.

322.4 USA ISSN 1064-1556
BR115.J8
NEWS NOTES; a bi-monthly newsletter of information on international justice and peace issues. Text in English. 1975. bi-m. USD 12 (effective 2001). 26 p./no.; back issues avail. **Document type:** *Newsletter.* **Description:** Covers international justice and peace issues.
Related titles: Online - full text ed.
Indexed: HRIR.
Published by: Maryknoll Office for Global Concerns, 401 Michigan Ave, N E, PO Box 29132, Washington, DC 20017-0132. TEL 202-832-1780, FAX 202-832-5195, hphillips@mksisters.org, http://home.maryknoll.org/. Ed. Marie Dennis. Circ: 2,000 (paid and controlled).

320 USA ISSN 1546-5497
NEWSMAX. Text in English. 2000. m. USD 39.95; USD 5.95 newsstand/cover (effective 2011). adv. cum.index 2000-2001. back issues avail. **Document type:** *Magazine, Consumer.*
Former titles (until 2003): NewsMax.com (1536-0482); (until 2001): Newsmax.com vortex (1531-6955)
Published by: NewsMax Media, Inc., 560 Village Blvd, Ste 120, West Palm Beach, FL 33409. TEL 561-686-1165, FAX 561-686-3350.

320 AUS ISSN 1838-2649
▼ **THE NEXT STRATEGY.** Text in English. 2010. m. AUD 71.40 domestic; AUD 95.20 in New Zealand; AUD 125 elsewhere (effective 2011). back issues avail. **Document type:** *Magazine, Consumer.* **Description:** Aims to educate the Australian people in the fields of politics, religion, history, law and education etc.
Published by: The Next Strategy, PO Box 7, Meeniyan, VIC 3956, Australia. TEL 61-3-56647506, FAX 61-3-56640141.

328 VNM
NGUOI DAI BIEU NHAN DAN/PEOPLE'S DEPUTY. Text in Vietnamese. 1988. bi-m. **Description:** Disseminates resolutions of the National Assembly and Council of State.
Address: 35 Ngo Quyen, Hanoi, Viet Nam. TEL 52861. Ed. Nguyen Ngoc Tho.

320 NER ISSN 0545-9532
NIGER: FRATERNITE - TRAVAIL - PROGRES. Text in French. w. illus.
Published by: Ministere de l'Information, BP 368, Niamey, Niger. Ed. Sahidou Alou.

320 NGA
NIGERIAN JOURNAL OF POLICY AND STRATEGY. Text in English. s-a. **Document type:** *Journal, Academic/Scholarly.*
Published by: National Institute for Policy and Strategic Studies, Private Mail Bag 2024, Bukuru, Nigeria. TEL 234-73-280730, FAX 234-73-280740, dg@nipss-ng.org, http://www.nipss-ng.org.

320.5 SWE ISSN 1100-763X
NISSE HULT. Variant title: N H. Ung och Groen. Text in Swedish. 1987. q. SEK 100 to individuals; SEK 300 to institutions (effective 2004).
Former titles: Ung och Groen; New Zine
Published by: (Miljoepartiet De Groenas Ungdomsfoerbund), Groen Ungdom, PO Box 1244, Lund, 22105, Sweden. TEL 46-46-162255, FAX 46-46-162259, gu@mp.se. Ed. Lasse Nilsson. Circ: 1,500.

324.998 GRL ISSN 0904-1567
NIVIARSIAQ. Text in Danish, Eskimo. 1975. m. USD 50 (effective 1998). **Document type:** *Newsletter.*
Former titles (until 1987): Siumut (0105-5968); (until 1977): Sujumut (0105-5372)
Related titles: ◆ Supplement(s): A G. ISSN 0904-2458.
Published by: Siumut, PO Box 357, Nuuk, 3900, Greenland. TEL 299-22077, FAX 299-22319. Ed. J Waever Johansen. Circ: 1,200.

320.531 LKA ISSN 1391-1031
NIYAMUWA. Text in Singhalese. 1994. m. LKR 15 (effective 2008). **Document type:** *Newspaper, Consumer.*
Related titles: Online - full text ed.
Published by: Janatha Vimukthi Peramuna/People's Liberation Front, 149-6 Devanam Piyatissa Mawatha, Colombo, 10, Sri Lanka. jvp_sl@usa.net, http://www.geocities.com/jvpsite.

320 ARG ISSN 0327-5248
K14
NO HAY DERECHO. Text in Spanish. 1990. bi-m.
Address: Libertador, 2640, Olivos, Buenos Aires 1636, Argentina. Eds. Alejandro Rua, Martin Clemente.

055.1 320 ITA ISSN 0029-0920
NOIDONNE. Text in Italian. 1944. m. EUR 25 (effective 2008). bk.rev.; film rev.; play rev. illus.; tr.lit. index. **Document type:** *Magazine, Consumer.*
Related titles: Supplement(s): Leggendaria. ISSN 1825-523X. 1987.
Indexed: RASB.
Published by: Cooperativa Libera Stampa, Piazza Istria 2, Rome, 00198, Italy.

320 USA ISSN 0078-0979
NOMOS; yearbook of the American Society for Political and Legal Philosophy. Text in English. 1958. irreg., latest vol.49, 2008. price varies. back issues avail. **Document type:** *Monographic series, Academic/Scholarly.*
Indexed: AICP, DIP, I13, IBR, IBZ, PhilInd, SCOPUS.
Published by: (American Society for Political and Legal Philosophy), New York University Press, 838 Broadway, 3rd Fl, New York, NY 10003. TEL 212-998-2575, 800-996-6987, FAX 212-995-3833, information@nyupress.org. Eds. James Fleming, Melissa S Williams.

NOMOS; revista do curso de mestrado em direito da ufc. *see* LAW

320 ITA ISSN 1970-612X
NON SOLO OCCIDENTE. Text in Multiple languages. 1995. irreg. **Document type:** *Magazine, Consumer.*
Published by: L' Harmattan Italia, Via degli Artisti 15, Turin, 10124, Italy. harmattan.italia@agora.it, http://www.editions-harmattan.fr/harmattan/harmattan_italia.htm.

NONGCUN QINGNIAN/RURAL YOUTH. *see* CHILDREN AND YOUTH—For

320 DNK ISSN 0903-7004
NORD. Variant title: Nordiska Ministerraadet. Skriftserie. Text in Danish. 1983. irreg. price varies. **Document type:** *Monographic series, Government.*
Indexed: ASFA, B21, MLA-IB.
—**CCC.**

Published by: Nordisk Ministerraad/Nordic Council of Ministers, Store Strandstraede 18, Copenhagen K, 1255, Denmark. TEL 45-33-960200, FAX 45-33-960202, nmr@norden.org, http://www.norden.org.

320 ITA ISSN 1827-1219
NORDESTEUROPA.IT; mensile di confronto fra le culture riformiste del Nordest. Text in Italian. 2005. m. **Document type:** *Magazine, Consumer.*
Related titles: Online - full text ed.: ISSN 1827-1227.
Published by: Nordesteuropa Editore, Via del Borromeo 16, Padua, 35137, Italy. TEL 39-049-8757589, info@nordesteuropa.it.

320 DEU ISSN 1863-639X
NORDEUROPA FORUM (ONLINE); periodical for politics, economics and culture. Text in German, English. 1991. s-a. free (effective 2011). adv. **Document type:** *Journal, Academic/Scholarly.* **Description:** Provides a forum for socio-cultural observations of North Europe.
Formerly (until 2005): Nordeuropa Forum (Print) (0940-5585)
Media: Online - full text.
Indexed: DIP, IBR, IBZ.
Published by: Humboldt-Universitaet zu Berlin, Nordeuropa-Institut, Unter den Linden 6, Berlin, 10099, Germany. TEL 49-30-20939625, FAX 49-30-20935325, marzena.debska-buddenhagen@rz.hu-berlin.de, http://www.ni.hu-berlin.de.

320.948 SWE
NORDIC NEWS NETWORK; international newsletter. Text in English, Swedish. 1994. q. free. charts; illus.; stat. **Document type:** *Newsletter, Consumer.* **Description:** Nordic News Network is an independent non-profit organization whose purpose is to provide accurate reports and analysis of significant developments in the Nordic region. Includes analysis of the world press coverage of the Nordic region.
Formerly (until 2001): Swedish Example (Print Edition) (1104-9197)
Media: Online - full text.
Address: PO Box 1181, Lidingoe, 18123, Sweden. TEL 46-8-731-92-00, FAX 46-8-731-92-00. Ed. Al Burke.

320.948 306.09 FRA ISSN 1761-7677
DL87
NORDIQUES. Text in French. 2003. 3/yr. EUR 65 domestic; EUR 79 foreign (effective 2009). **Document type:** *Journal, Academic/Scholarly.*
Indexed: FR, IBSS.
Published by: Choiseul Editions, 28 Rue Etienne Marcel, Paris, 75002, France. TEL 33-1-53340993, FAX 33-1-53340994, http://choiseul-editions.com. Ed. Nathalie Blanc-Noel.

320.57 USA ISSN 2158-6659
THE NOR'EASTER. Text in English. 2008. q. **Document type:** *Journal, Trade.* **Description:** Aims to provide an outlet for anarchist related news and events while simultaneously introducing non-anarchists to anarchism and plugging them into the movement.
Related titles: Online - full text ed.: ISSN 2158-6667.
Published by: Northeast Anarchist Network, Syracuse, NY 13210.

NORK QUARTERLY. *see* PUBLIC ADMINISTRATION

320 NOR ISSN 0801-1745
JA26 CODEN: OPDTEV
NORSK STATSVITENSKAPELIG TIDSSKRIFT/NORWEGIAN POLITICAL SCIENCE JOURNAL. Text in Norwegian; Summaries in English. 1985. q. NOK 500 to individuals; NOK 860 to institutions; NOK 270 to students (effective 2010). bk.rev. index. back issues avail. **Document type:** *Journal, Academic/Scholarly.* **Description:** Publishes articles on and analyses of politics, public administration, political behavior and international politics.
Formerly (until 1985): Statsviteren (0800-6245)
Related titles: Online - full text ed.: ISSN 1504-2936. NOK 960 (effective 2010).
Indexed: I13.
Published by: (Norwegian Association for Political Science), Universitetsforlaget AS/Scandinavian University Press (Subsidiary of: Aschehoug & Co.), Sehesteds Gate 3, P O Box 508, Sentrum, Oslo, 0105, Norway. TEL 47-24-147500, FAX 47-24-147501, post@universitetsforlaget.no. Eds. Bjorn Hoyland, Havard Hegre. Circ: 700.

320 USA
NORTH CAROLINA INSIGHT. Text in English. 1978. s-a. USD 40 (effective 2011). adv. **Document type:** *Magazine, Consumer.* **Description:** Focuses on public policy issues and problems affecting North Carolina state and local government.
Published by: North Carolina Center for Public Policy Research, Inc., 5 W Hargett St, Ste 701, Raleigh, NC 27602. TEL 919-832-2839, FAX 919-832-2847, http://www.nando.net/insider/nccppr. Ed. Mebane Rash. Circ: 1,000 (paid).

320.9 USA ISSN 1040-8614
NORTHERN IRELAND NEWS SERVICE; NINS NewsBreak. Text in English. 1985. w. USD 44. back issues avail. **Document type:** *Bulletin.* **Description:** Covers the Irish republican, nationalist and loyalist news sources and spokespersons, as well as the British and Irish governments' Northern Ireland offices. Covers Anglo-Irish relations, public demonstrations, street and border disputes, business openings and closings, application of MacBride Principles, employment and unemployment, and the churches.
Related titles: Online - full text ed.
Address: PO Box 57, Albany, NY 12211-0057. TEL 518-329-3003. Ed. Rev. Francis G McCloskey. Circ: 266.

320.531 CAN ISSN 1200-3387
NORTHSTAR COMPASS. Text in English. 1992. m. **Description:** Devoted to international cooperation in building socialism and solidarity in a world at peace.
Indexed: LeftInd.
Published by: Council of Canadian Friends of Soviet People, 280 Queen St W, Toronto, ON M5F 2A1, Canada. TEL 416-977-5819, FAX 416-593-0781. Ed., R&P Michael Lucas.

320 USA
NORTHWESTLETTER; the pacific northwest's inside source on government and politics from Washington D.C. Text in English. 1981. m. USD 167 (effective 2002). bk.rev. charts; illus.; maps; stat. back issues avail.; reprints avail. **Document type:** *Newsletter, Newspaper-distributed.* **Description:** Focuses on politics and issues of Pacific Northwest - Idaho, Oregon and Washington - in the nation's capitol.
Formerly (until 1995): Steve Forrester's Northwest Letter from Washington D.C. (0890-9776)
Related titles: E-mail ed.: USD 157 (effective 2002); Fax ed.: USD 177 (effective 2001).
Address: PO Box 2361, Washington, DC 20013. TEL 202-546-2547, FAX 202-546-2734. Ed., Pub., R&P, Adv. contact Larry Swisher.

320.532 CUB
NOSOTROS. Text in Spanish. bi-m. USD 24 in South America; USD 26 in North America; USD 30 elsewhere.
Published by: Union de Jovenes Comunistas, Obispo No. 527, Apdo. 605, Havana, Cuba.

320.9 SEN ISSN 0029-3954
NOTES AFRICAINES. Text in French. 1939. q. charts; illus.; maps. cum.index: 1939-1948, 1949-1963, 1964-1976.
Indexed: AICP, ASD, GeoRef, MLA-IB, RILM, SpeleolAb.
—Linda Hall.
Published by: Institut Fondamental d'Afrique Noire/Cheikh Anta Diop, BP 206, Dakar, Senegal. Ed. Abdoulaye Bara Diop. Circ: 1,500.

363.7 329.24087 FRA ISSN 1779-0433
LES NOTES DE SINOPLE. Text in French. 2004. irreg., latest 2009. **Document type:** *Newsletter.* **Description:** Contains information on studies and actions taken by the French Green Party to the European Parliament.
Published by: Sinople, 288 Bd St Germain, Paris, 75007, France. TEL 33-1-47537676, contact@verts-europe-sinople.net, http://verts-europe-sinople.net.

NOTICE DE GESTION DES POLITIQUES DE DEVELOPPEMENT. *see* BUSINESS AND ECONOMICS—International Development And Assistance

980 330.9 USA
F1401
NOTISUR; South American political and economic affairs. Text in English. 198?. w. (Fri.). USD 30 to individuals; USD 750 to institutions (effective 2010); Institutional subscr. includes NotiCen, NotiSur & SourceMex. back issues avail. **Document type:** *Bulletin, Academic/Scholarly.* **Description:** Covers political and economic developments in South America.
Former titles (until 1996): Chronicle of Latin American Economic Affairs; (until 1993): Central America Update (1054-8882)
Media: Online - full text. **Related titles:** CD-ROM ed.; E-mail ed.
Published by: Latin America Database, The University of New Mexico, Albuquerque, NM 87131. TEL 505-277-0111, info@ladb.unm.edu.

NOUS HORITZONS. *see* SOCIAL SCIENCES: COMPREHENSIVE WORKS

320 MUS
NOUVEAU MILITANT. Text in French. w.
Former titles: Peuple; Militant
Published by: Mouvement Militant Mauricien, 21 rue Poudriere, Port Louis, Mauritius.

320 CIV ISSN 1018-7480
NOUVEL HORIZON. Text in French. 1990. w.
Published by: Front Populaire Ivoirien, Abidjan, Ivory Coast. Circ: 15,000.

320 FRA ISSN 0764-7565
JC599.E92
LA NOUVELLE ALTERNATIVE; politique et societe a l'Est. Text in French. 1979. bi-m. EUR 50 in the European Union to individuals; EUR 55 elsewhere to individuals; EUR 70 in the European Union to institutions; EUR 106 elsewhere to institutions (effective 2006). back issues avail. **Document type:** *Journal, Consumer.*
Formerly (until 1985): L' Alternative (0240-1568)
Indexed: IBSS, PAIS, PCI.
Published by: Association des Amis et Lecteurs de La Nouvelle Alternative, 41 Rue Bobillot, Paris, 75013, France. TEL 33-1-45815472. Ed. Francois Maspero.

320 RWA
LA NOUVELLE RELEVE. Text in French. 1976. m. USD 27. adv. bk.rev. illus. reprints avail. **Document type:** *Newspaper.* **Description:** Covers politics, economics and culture.
Formerly: La Releve (1013-6371); Incorporates: Rwanda-Carrefour d'Afrique (0036-0481)
Indexed: RASB.
Published by: Office Rwandais d'Information, BP 83, Kigali, Rwanda. TEL 250-575735, FAX 250-576539. Ed. Christophe Mfizi. Circ: 1,000.

NOUVELLES PRATIQUES SOCIALES. *see* SOCIAL SERVICES AND WELFARE

NOUVELLES UNIVERSITAIRES EUROPEENNES/EUROPEAN UNIVERSITY NEWS. *see* EDUCATION

NOW AND THEN. *see* PUBLIC ADMINISTRATION

320.5 SWE ISSN 0281-4285
NU; det liberala nyhetsmagasinet. Text in Swedish. 1983. w. SEK 350 (effective 2001). adv. **Description:** Discusses politics, specially in Sweden.
Address: PO Box 6508, Stockholm, 11383, Sweden. TEL 08-674-16-70, FAX 08-612-40-65, nu_redaktionen@liberal.se. Ed. Jan Froeman. R&P Christina Andersson. Adv. contact Eva Bosved TEL 46-8-509-11677. Circ: 7,400 (paid).

324.2 USA ISSN 0883-9875
NUCLEAR RESISTER; a chronicle of hope. Text in English. 1980. 6/yr. USD 15 domestic; USD 20 in Canada; USD 25 elsewhere (effective 2005). bk.rev. stat.; illus. 8 p./no.; back issues avail.; reprints avail. **Document type:** *Newsletter, Consumer.* **Description:** Dedicated to jailed and imprisoned anti-nuclear and anti-war activists in the United States and Canada. Provides comprehensive reporting on arrests and jailings of the civilly disobedient, while encouraging support for those behind bars.
Formerly (until 1982): National No-Nukes Prison Support Collective. Newsletter
Related titles: Microfiche ed.: (from PQC); Online - full text ed.
Indexed: APW.
Published by: National No-Nukes Prison Support Collective, PO Box 43383, Tucson, AZ 85733. TEL 520-323-8697, nukeresister@igc.org, http://www.nonviolence.org/nukeresister. Ed. Jack Cohen Joppa. Pub. Felice Cohen Joppa. Circ: 1,000.

320 VEN ISSN 0251-3552
F1401
NUEVA SOCIEDAD; democracia y politica en America Latina. Text in Spanish. 1972. bi-m. adv. bk.rev. index. **Document type:** *Journal, Academic/Scholarly.* **Description:** Covers political, economic and cultural reviews of Latin America. Includes topics such as international relations, trade unions and various social movements.
Related titles: CD-ROM ed.; Online - full text ed.: free (effective 2011).
Indexed: A22, C01, DIP, FR, H21, IBR, IBZ, P08, P42, PAIS, PSA, RASB, SocioIAb.
—IE, Infotrieve. **CCC.**
Published by: Editorial Nueva Sociedad Ltda., Chacao, Apdo 61712, Caracas, DF 1060-A, Venezuela. TEL 58-2-2651849, FAX 58-2-2673397, megonzal@ccs.internet.ve, http://www.internet.ve/nuso. Ed., R&P Sergio Chejfec. Pub. Heidulf Schmidt. Circ: 7,500.

NY SOLIDARITET; internationell tidning foer politik, ekonomi, vetenskap och kultur. *see* GENERAL INTEREST PERIODICALS—Sweden

320.51 SWE ISSN 1100-6447
NYLIBERALEN; foer kapitalism och individuell frihet. Variant title: Tidskriften Nyliberalen. Text in Swedish. 1989. q. SEK 150 (effective 2004). back issues avail. **Description:** Ideological and philosophical debate about liberalism.
Published by: Frihetsfronten, PO Box 620, Stockholm, 11479, Sweden. info@frihetsfronten.se, http://www.frihetsfronten.se. Ed. Erik Lakomaa TEL 46-707-415129. R&P, Adv. contact Henrik Bejke TEL 46-8-345647.

320.5 SWE ISSN 1404-7853
NYSVENSK TIDENDE. Text in Swedish. 1932-1992; resumed 1999. q. SEK 50.
Formerly (until 1992): Vaegen Framaat (0346-4849)
Published by: Nysvenska Roerelsen, PO Box 503, Malmoe, 20125, Sweden.

320 NOR ISSN 0800-336X
JA26
NYTT NORSK TIDSSKRIFT. Text in Norwegian. 1984. q. NOK 425 to individuals; NOK 795 to institutions; NOK 305 to students (effective 2010). adv. bk.rev. index. **Document type:** *Journal, Academic/Scholarly.* **Description:** Focuses on politics, scientific research, and culture.
Related titles: Online - full text ed.: ISSN 1504-3053. NOK 895 (effective 2010).
Published by: Universitetsforlaget AS/Scandinavian University Press (Subsidiary of: Aschehoug & Co.), Sehesteds Gate 3, P O Box 508, Sentrum, Oslo, 0105, Norway. TEL 47-24-147500, FAX 47-24-147501, post@universitetsforlaget.no, http://www.universitetsforlaget.no. Ed. Cathrine Holst.

O E C D GOVERNANCE ILIBRARY. (Organisation for Economic Cooperation and Development) *see* BUSINESS AND ECONOMICS

O E C D ILIBRARY: GOUVERNANCE. (Organisation for Economic Cooperation and Development) *see* BUSINESS AND ECONOMICS

327.1745 NLD ISSN 1607-503X
O P C W ANNUAL REPORT. Text in English. 199?. a. **Document type:** *Report, Academic/Scholarly.*
Related titles: Online - full content ed.
Published by: Organisation for the Prohibition of Chemical Weapons, Johan de Wittlaan 32, The Hague, 2517 JR, Netherlands. TEL 31-70-4163300, FAX 31-70-3063535, http://www.opcw.org/index.html.

O P I ISSUES NOTES. *see* SOCIAL SERVICES AND WELFARE

O P I POLICY BRIEFS. *see* SOCIAL SERVICES AND WELFARE

320 CAN ISSN 1910-1112
O P / POSITION. Text in English. 2006. irreg., latest vol.1, 2006. **Document type:** *Monographic series, Academic/Scholarly.* **Description:** Poses hard questions about often-difficult issues and the directions in which Canadian society should be heading.
Published by: University of Calgary Press, 2500 University Dr NW, Calgary, AB T2N 1N4, Canada. TEL 403-220-7578, FAX 403-282-0085, ucpmail@ucalgary.ca. Eds. Bart Beaty, Rebecca Sullivan.

OAK BROOK COLLEGE JOURNAL OF LAW AND GOVERNMENT POLICY. *see* LAW

320 FRA ISSN 2106-5187
▼ **OBSERVATOIRE D'ETUDES GEOPOLITIQUES. BULLETIN D'INFORMATION.** Text in French. 2009. bi-m. **Document type:** *Bulletin.*
Published by: Observatoire d'Etudes Geopolitiques, 14 Av d'Eylau, Paris, 75016, France. TEL 33-1-77726427, FAX 33-1-77726429, etudesgeo@yahoo.com, http://www.etudes-geopolitiques.com.

OBSERVATORIO DE POLITICAS, EJECUCION Y RESULTADOS DE LA ADMINISTRACION PUBLICA. *see* PUBLIC ADMINISTRATION

OBSHCHESTVO I PRAVO/SOCIETY AND LAW. *see* LAW

320 RUS ISSN 2071-9701
OBSHCHESTVO: POLITIKA, EKONOMIKA, PRAVO/SOCIETY: POLITICS, ECONOMICS, LAW. Text in Russian; Summaries in Russian, English. 2007. q. bk.rev. back issues avail. **Document type:** *Journal, Academic/Scholarly.*
Related titles: Online - full text ed.: ISSN 2223-6392.
Indexed: RefZh.
Published by: Izdatel'skii Dom HORS, ul Yankovskogo 156, Krasnodar, Russian Federation. TEL 7-861-2901335, dom-hors@mail.ru. Eds. Kirill V Vishnevetskii, Victoria L Kharseeva.

320 GBR ISSN 0968-4476
OCCASIONAL PAPERS IN POLITICS AND INTERNATIONAL RELATIONS. Text in English. irreg.
Published by: Nottingham Trent University, Department of Economics and Politics, Burton Street, Nottingham, NG1 4BU, United Kingdom. TEL 44-115-8485506, FAX 44-115-8486829, politics@ntu.ac.uk. Ed. Dr. Lawrence Wilde.

OCCUPATION IN EUROPE SERIES. *see* HISTORY—History Of Europe

320.531 HKG
OCTOBER REVIEW/SHIH YUEH P'ING LUN. Text mainly in Chinese; Contents page in English. bi-m. HKD 12. illus. **Description:** Covers world news, events, and politics from a socialist perspective.
Address: GPO Box 10144, Hong Kong, Hong Kong. TEL 3-862780.

320 AUT ISSN 1615-5548
JA14
➤ **OE Z P - OESTERREICHISCHE ZEITSCHRIFT FUER POLITIKWISSENSCHAFT.** Text in English, German. 1972. q. EUR 52; EUR 15 per issue (effective 2011). adv. **Document type:** *Journal, Academic/Scholarly.* **Description:** Contains studies on all aspects of political science with a special emphasis on Austrian politics.
Formerly (until 1999): Oesterreichische Zeitschrift fuer Politikwissenschaft (0378-5149)
Indexed: A20, CA, DIP, I13, IBR, IBSS, IBZ, P34, P42, PAIS, PCI, PRA, PSA, RASB, S02, S03, SCOPUS, SSCI, SociolAb, T02, W07.
—BLDSC (6323.000000), IE, Ingenta.
Published by: (Oesterreichische Gesellschaft fuer Politikwissenschaft, Institut fuer Staats- und Politikwissenschaft), Facultas Verlags- und Buchhandels AG, Berggasse 5, Vienna, W 1090, Austria. TEL 43-1-3105356, FAX 43-1-3197050, office@facultas.at, http://facultas.wuv.at. Ed. Dr. Marcel Fink.

➤ **DIE OEFFENTLICHE VERWALTUNG**; Zeitschrift fuer oeffentliches Recht und Verwaltungswissenschaft. *see* LAW

306.2 DEU ISSN 1862-3417
OEFFENTLICHKEIT UND POLITISCHE KOMMUNIKATION. Text in German. 2006. irreg. **Document type:** *Monographic series, Academic/Scholarly.*
Media: Online - full content.
Address: c/o Barbara Pfetsch, Fruwirthstr 47, Stuttgart, 70593, Germany. TEL 49-711-4592628, FAX 49-711-4593739. Ed. Barbara Pfetsch.

OEKOLOGIEPOLITIK. *see* CONSERVATION

320 SWE ISSN 1650-1632
OEREBRO STUDIES IN POLITICAL SCIENCE. Text in English, Swedish. 2000. irreg., latest vol.15, 2006. SEK 180 per issue (effective 2006). back issues avail. **Document type:** *Monographic series, Academic/Scholarly.*
Published by: Oerebro Universitet, Universitetsbiblioteket/University of Oerebro. University Library, Fakultetsgatan 1, Oerebro, 70182, Sweden. TEL 46-19-303240, FAX 46-19-331217, biblioteket@ub.oru.se. Ed. Joanna Jansdotter.

OESTERREICHISCHE GESELLSCHAFT FUER EUROPAFORSCHUNG. SCHRIFTENREIHE. *see* LAW

320.9 AUT ISSN 0029-9308
DB99.1
OESTERREICHISCHE MONATSHEFTE; Zeitschrift fuer Politik. Text in German. 1945. m. adv. bk.rev. charts; illus.; stat. index. **Document type:** *Magazine, Consumer.* **Description:** Publication of the Bundespartei covering Austrian and foreign politics, economics, and ecology. Includes list of events.
Indexed: PAIS, RASB.
—BLDSC (6307.967000).
Published by: Oesterreichische Volkspartei, Bundesparteileitung, Lichtenfelsgasse 7, Vienna, W 1010, Austria. TEL 43-1-401260, FAX 43-1-40126109, email@oevp.at, http://www.oevp.at. Ed. Gerhard Wiflinger. Circ: 3,000.

320 AUT ISSN 0170-0847
JN2012.3
OESTERREICHISCHES JAHRBUCH FUER POLITIK. Text in German. 1978. a. EUR 49.80 (effective 2010). **Document type:** *Journal, Academic/Scholarly.*
Indexed: ABCPolSci, DIP, IBR, IBZ, RASB.
Published by: Boehlau Verlag GmbH & Co.KG., Wiesingerstr 1, Vienna, W 1010, Austria. TEL 43-1-3302427, FAX 43-1-3302432, boehlau@boehlau.at.

320.5322 SWE ISSN 0348-5447
OFFENSIV; marxistiska tidningen foer arbetarroerelsen. Text in Swedish. 1973. bi-m. SEK 100.
Address: Fack 374, Farsta, 12303, Sweden.

320 RUS
OFITSYAL'NYE DOKUMENTY ORGANOV GOSUDARSTVENNOI VLASTI ROSSIISKOI FEDERATSII. BIBLIOGRAFICHESKII UKAZATEL'. Text in Russian. 1997. bi-m. USD 110 in North America (effective 2000).
Published by: Gosudarstvennaya Duma Rossiiskoi Federatsii, Okhotnyi riad 1, Moscow, 103001, Russian Federation. **Dist. by:** East View Information Services, 10601 Wayzata Blvd, Minneapolis, MN 55305. TEL 952-252-1201, 800-477-1005, FAX 952-252-1202, info@eastview.com, http://www.eastview.com.

320 RUS
OFITSYAL'NYE DOKUMENTY ORGANOV VLASTI SUB'EKTOV ROSSIISKOI FEDERATSII. BIBLIOGRAFICHESKII UKAZATEL'. Text in Russian. 1997. bi-m. USD 79 in North America (effective 2000).
Indexed: RASB.
Published by: Gosudarstvennaya Duma Rossiiskoi Federatsii, Okhotnyi riad 1, Moscow, 103001, Russian Federation. **Dist. by:** East View Information Services, 10601 Wayzata Blvd, Minneapolis, MN 55305. TEL 952-252-1201, 800-477-1005, FAX 952-252-1202, info@eastview.com, http://www.eastview.com.

OJKUMENA; regional researches. *see* SOCIOLOGY

328.766 USA
OKLAHOMA AGENCIES, BOARDS AND COMMISSIONS. Text in English. 1953. a. free (effective 2011). **Document type:** *Directory, Trade.* **Description:** Contact directory of state government agencies, entities and personnel.
Former titles (until 2005): A B C; (until 1996): Oklahoma State Agencies, Boards, Commissions, Courts, Institutions, Legislature and Officers; (until 19??): Officers and Members of Oklahoma State Offices and Boards, Commissions, Courts, and the Legislature
Related titles: Online - full text ed.
Published by: (Oklahoma. Public Information Office), Oklahoma Department of Libraries, 200 NE 18th St, Oklahoma City, OK 73105. TEL 405-521-2502, 800-522-8116, FAX 405-525-7804.

320 USA ISSN 0030-1795
OKLAHOMA OBSERVER. Text in English. 1969. s-m. USD 30 (effective 2000). adv. bk.rev.; film rev. 20 p./no.; reprints avail. **Document type:** *Newspaper, Consumer.* **Description:** Offers commentary on politics, government, education, and social issues.
Related titles: Microform ed.: (from PQC).
Indexed: ASIP.
Published by: Troy Enterprises, Co., 500 N E 39 Terr, Box 53371, Oklahoma City, OK 73152. TEL 405-525-5582. Ed. Frosty Troy. Pub., Adv. contact Helen B Troy. B&W page USD 419; 14 x 10.5. Circ: 8,000 (paid).

320 USA
OLD TROUT. Text in English. bi-m. USD 9.95, USD 19.95 domestic (effective 2006). **Document type:** *Magazine, Consumer.*
Published by: Old Trout Media Group, LLC, PO Box 1636, Lafayette, CA 94549.

OLYMPE; feministische Arbeitshefte zur Politik. *see* WOMEN'S STUDIES

320 AUS ISSN 1442-8458
ON LINE OPINION; Australia's e-journal of social and political debate. Abbreviated title: O L O. Text in English. 1999. d. free (effective 2009). back issues avail. **Document type:** *Journal, Trade.* **Description:** Provides a forum for public social and political debate about current Australian issues.
Media: Online - full content.
Indexed: AusPAIS.
Published by: Internet Thinking Pty Ltd., PO Box 1365, Fortitude Valley, QLD 4006, Australia. TEL 61-7-32521470, FAX 61-7-32529818, tech@internet-thinking.com.au, http://www.internet-thinking.com.au. Eds. Susan Prior, Graham Young. Pub. Graham Young.

330 USA
ON TAP (BOSTON). Text in English. s-a. **Document type:** *Newsletter.*
Published by: The Electronic Policy Network at the American Prospect, 5 Broadway St, PO Box 383080, Boston, MA 02109. TEL 617-570-8030, tap@epn.org.

ON THE LINE (NEW YORK). *see* BUSINESS AND ECONOMICS—Labor And Industrial Relations

051 USA
ONPOLITICS. Text in English. 2000. d. **Document type:** *Newsletter, Consumer.* **Description:** Provides a daily digest of the day's political news and links to stories and updates from Congressional Quarterly and the Associated Press.
Media: E-mail.
Published by: Washington Post Co., 1150 15th St, N W, Washington, DC 20071. TEL 202-334-4293, FAX 202-334-5059.

320 GBR ISSN 1476-5888
OPEN DEMOCRACY; free thinking for the world. Text in English. 2001. w. free; donations welcomed. adv. **Document type:** *Magazine, Consumer.* **Description:** Online global magazine of politics and culture. It publishes clarifying debates which help people make up their own minds.
Media: Online - full content.
Indexed: LeftInd.
Published by: OpenDemocracy, PO Box 49799, London, WC1X 8XA, United Kingdom. TEL 44-20-71930676. Ed. Tony Curzon Price. Pub. Julian Stern.

320 NLD ISSN 1874-9496
JA1
➤ **THE OPEN POLITICAL SCIENCE JOURNAL.** Text in English. 2008. irreg. free (effective 2011). **Document type:** *Journal, Academic/Scholarly.*
Media: Online - full text.
Indexed: A39, C27, C29, D03, D04, E13, ESPM, P42, R14, RiskAb, S14, S15, S18.
Published by: Bentham Open (Subsidiary of: Bentham Science Publishers Ltd.), PO Box 294, Bussum, AG 1400, Netherlands. TEL 31-35-6923800, FAX 31-35-6980150, subscriptions@bentham.org. Ed. Heikki Paloheimo.

➤ **OPEN SECRETS**; all the truth that's fit to release. *see* HISTORY—History Of North And South America

320.101 BRA ISSN 0104-6276
HM261
OPINIAO PUBLICA. Text in Portuguese. 1993. s-a. BRL 12.50 (effective 2004). **Description:** Provides a forum for ideas, theses and reflections on theory, methodology, and analysis of public opinion.
Related titles: Online - full text ed.: ISSN 1807-0191. 2002. free (effective 2011).
Indexed: C01, CA, H21, IBSS, P08, P42, PSA, S02, S03, SCOPUS, SSA, SociolAb, T02.
Published by: Universidade Estadual de Campinas, Centro de Estudos de Opiniao Publica, Caixa Postal 6110, Campinas, SP 13081-970, Brazil. TEL 55-19-37887093, FAX 55-19-32894309, cesop@unicamp.br. Ed. Rachel Meneguello.

320 MUS ISSN 1694-0466
OPINION EXPRESS. Text in English. 2005. m. **Document type:** *Magazine, Consumer.*
Published by: Opinion Express Mass Communication Ltd, 32, Doyen Ave, Quatre Bornes, Mauritius. Ed., Pub. Rajiv Agnihotri.

321.094 CRI
OPINION POPULAR. Text in Spanish. 198?. m. USD 5.
Indexed: HRIR.
Published by: Movimiento Nacional Revolucionario de El Salvador, Apdo. 230, San Pedro De Montes De Oca, San Jose, 2050, Costa Rica.

OPPORTUNITY IN AMERICA; a series on economic and social mobility. *see* SOCIOLOGY

ORD & BILD/WORDS AND PICTURES. *see* LITERARY AND POLITICAL REVIEWS

324.4 DEU
OSNABRUECKER BEITRAEGE ZUR PARTEIENFORSCHUNG. Text in German. 2003. irreg., latest vol.4, 2009. price varies. **Document type:** *Monographic series, Academic/Scholarly.*
Published by: V & R Unipress GmbH (Subsidiary of: Vandenhoeck und Ruprecht), Robert-Bosch-Breite 6, Goettingen, 37079, Germany. TEL 49-551-5084303, FAX 49-551-5084333, info@vr-unipress.de, http://www.v-r.de/en/publisher/unipress.

OSNABRUECKER JAHRBUCH FRIEDEN UND WISSENSCHAFT. *see* SCIENCES: COMPREHENSIVE WORKS

320 DEU ISSN 0030-6428
DR1 CODEN: OSURAP
➤ **OSTEUROPA**; Zeitschrift fuer Gegenwartsfragen des Ostens. Text in German. 1950. m. EUR 84; EUR 10 newsstand/cover (effective 2010). adv. bk.rev. bibl.; charts. index. reprint service avail. from SCH. **Document type:** *Journal, Academic/Scholarly.*
Related titles: ◆ Supplement(s): Osteuropa-Archiv. ISSN 0179-485X.
Indexed: A20, A22, ABCPolSci, ASCA, BAS, CA, CERDIC, CurCont, DIP, HistAb, I13, IBR, IBSS, IBZ, KES, MLA-IB, P30, P34, P42, PAIS, PCI, PRA, PSA, RASB, RILM, S02, S03, SCIMP, SSCI, SociolAb, T02, W07.
—BLDSC (6312.190000), IE, Infotrieve, Ingenta. **CCC.**
Published by: (Deutsche Gesellschaft fuer Osteuropakunde), B W V - Berliner Wissenschafts Verlag GmbH, Markgrafenstr 12-14, Berlin, 10969, Germany. TEL 49-30-8417700, FAX 49-30-84177021, bwv@bwv-verlag.de, http://www.bwv-verlag.de. Ed. Manfred Sapper. Circ: 2,100 (paid and controlled).

320 DEU ISSN 0179-485X
OSTEUROPA-ARCHIV. Text in German. 1949. m. **Document type:** *Journal, Academic/Scholarly.*
Formerly (until 1969): Ost-Probleme (0472-2027)
Related titles: ◆ Supplement to: Osteuropa. ISSN 0030-6428.
Indexed: MLA-IB, PRA.
Published by: B W V - Berliner Wissenschafts Verlag GmbH, Markgrafenstr 12-14, Berlin, 10969, Germany. TEL 49-30-8417700, FAX 49-30-84177021, bwv@bwv-verlag.de, http://www.bwv-verlag.de.

OTTAWA UPDATE. *see* PUBLIC ADMINISTRATION

320 ATG
OUTLET. Text in English. 1975. w. XEC 224 in Antigua; XEC 280 in the Caribbean; USD 120 in United States; USD 120 in United Kingdom; USD 127 in Europe (effective 2000). adv. **Document type:** *Newspaper.*
Published by: (Antigua Caribbean Liberation Movement), Outlet Publishers, Mckinnons, PO Box 493, St. John"s, Antigua. TEL 268-462-4453. Ed. Tim Hector. Adv. contact Donna Cornelius Benn. page USD 410; 14 x 10.5. Circ: 5,500.

320.5322 301 BRA ISSN 1516-6333
HX9.P65
➤ **OUTUBRO.** Text in Portuguese. 1998. s-a. BRL 50 for 2 yrs. domestic to individual members; BRL 100 for 2 yrs. foreign to individual members; BRL 100 for 2 yrs. domestic to institutional members; BRL 200 for 2 yrs. foreign to institutional members (effective 2003). bk.rev. back issues avail. **Document type:** *Journal, Academic/Scholarly.*
Indexed: C01, CA, MLA-IB, P42, PSA, S02, S03, SociolAb, T02.
Published by: Instituto de Estudos Socialistas, R. Caconde 536, Sao Paulo, SP 111, Brazil. albianchi@terra.com.br. Ed. Mr. Alvaro Bianchi. Pub. Mr. Expedito Correa. Circ: 1,000 (paid); 250.

320 GBR
OVERSEAS DEVELOPMENT GROUP. HUMANITARIAN PRACTICE NETWORK PAPERS. Text in English. 1994. irreg., latest no.66, 2009, Jun. GBP 4 per issue (effective 2009). back issues avail. **Document type:** *Monographic series, Trade.* **Description:** Provides information, analysis and specialist resources for practitioners and policy makers.
Related titles: Online - full text ed.: free (effective 2009).
Published by: Overseas Development Institute, Humanitarian Policy Group, 111 Westminster Bridge Rd, London, SE1 7JD, United Kingdom. odi@gn.apc.org, http://www.odi.org.uk/. Ed. Matthew Foley.

OVERVIEW. *see* BUSINESS AND ECONOMICS—Economic Situation And Conditions

352.14 USA ISSN 0030-7807
JK4701
P A R ANALYSIS. (Public Affairs Research) Text in English. 1951. irreg. charts; stat. **Document type:** *Newsletter.*
Formerly: P.A.R. News Analysis
Indexed: P06, PAIS.
Published by: Public Affairs Research Council of Louisiana, Inc., 4664 Jamestown Ave., Ste. 300, PO Box 14776, Baton Rouge, LA 70898-4776. staff@la-par.org, http://www.la-par.org/. Ed. Richard Omdal. Circ: 4,500.

320.9 USA ISSN 1949-0283
P A S WORKING PAPERS. (Program of African Studies) Text in English. 1996. irreg., latest no.16, 2009. USD 5 per issue (effective 2009). back issues avail. **Document type:** *Monographic series, Academic/Scholarly.* **Description:** Showcases writings in African studies by Northwestern faculty, graduate students, and advanced undergraduates, as well as work by PAS visiting scholars and resident research fellows.
Related titles: Online - full text ed.: ISSN 1949-0291. free (effective 2009).
Published by: Northwestern University, Program of African Studies, 620 Library Pl, Evanston, IL 60208. TEL 847-491-7323, FAX 847-491-3739, african-studies@northwestern.edu.

320 DEU
P & A. (Preiswert & Attraktiv) Text in German. 1977. q.
Published by: P & A Schuelerzeitung am Gymnasium Pegnitz, Wilhelm von Humboldt Str 7, Pegnitz, 91257, Germany. Circ: 600.

320.52 CAN
P.C. TALK. Text in English. 2/yr. CAD 5 to members (effective 1997). adv. **Document type:** *Newsletter.*
Former titles: P.C. Action (Year); Progressive Conservative Association of Alberta. Progress Bulletin
Published by: (Progressive Conservative Association of Alberta), University of Alberta, Faculty of Law, The Hon. W.A. Stevenson House, Edmonton, AB T6G 2H5, Canada. Ed., Adv. contact Brian Stecyk. Pub., R&P Marilyn Haley. Circ: 80,000.

303.484 322.4 FRA ISSN 1957-0031
LE P I A F. (Pour une Information Alternative, Forcement!) Text in French. 2006. m. EUR 12 (effective 2009). back issues avail. **Document type:** *Newsletter, Consumer.*
Related titles: Online - full text ed.: free.
Published by: Pour une Information Alternative Forcement (P I A F), 3 Rue d'Orchampt, Paris, 75018, France. contact@le-piaf.org, http://www.le-piaf.org.

320 NLD ISSN 1871-143X
P M. (Post Meridiem) Text in Dutch. 2002. bi-w. EUR 149 (effective 2010). adv.
Formerly (until 2005): P.M.denHaag (1571-9154)
Indexed: T02.
Published by: Sdu Uitgevers bv, Postbus 20025, The Hague, 2500 EA, Netherlands. TEL 31-70-3789911, FAX 31-70-3854321, sdu@sdu.nl, http://www.sdu.nl/. Ed. Cindy Castricum TEL 31-70-3780721. Pubs. Esther van Doesburg, Heleen Hupkens. Adv. contact Asha Narain. page EUR 3,340; 190 x 268.

P

THE P R S GROUP. COUNTRY REPORTS: ALGERIA. (Political Risk Services) *see* BUSINESS AND ECONOMICS—Economic Situation And Conditions

THE P R S GROUP. COUNTRY REPORTS: ANGOLA. (Political Risk Services) *see* BUSINESS AND ECONOMICS—Economic Situation And Conditions

THE P R S GROUP. COUNTRY REPORTS: ARGENTINA. (Political Risk Services) *see* BUSINESS AND ECONOMICS—Economic Situation And Conditions

THE P R S GROUP. COUNTRY REPORTS: AUSTRALIA. (Political Risk Services) *see* BUSINESS AND ECONOMICS—Economic Situation And Conditions

THE P R S GROUP. COUNTRY REPORTS: AUSTRIA. (Political Risk Services) *see* BUSINESS AND ECONOMICS—Economic Situation And Conditions

THE P R S GROUP. COUNTRY REPORTS: AZERBAIJAN. (Political Risk Services) *see* BUSINESS AND ECONOMICS—Economic Situation And Conditions

THE P R S GROUP. COUNTRY REPORTS: BANGLADESH. (Political Risk Services) *see* BUSINESS AND ECONOMICS—Economic Situation And Conditions

THE P R S GROUP. COUNTRY REPORTS: BELGIUM. (Political Risk Services) *see* BUSINESS AND ECONOMICS—Economic Situation And Conditions

THE P R S GROUP. COUNTRY REPORTS: BOLIVIA. (Political Risk Services) *see* BUSINESS AND ECONOMICS—Economic Situation And Conditions

THE P R S GROUP. COUNTRY REPORTS: BOTSWANA. (Political Risk Services) *see* BUSINESS AND ECONOMICS—Economic Situation And Conditions

THE P R S GROUP. COUNTRY REPORTS: BRAZIL. (Political Risk Services) *see* BUSINESS AND ECONOMICS—Economic Situation And Conditions

THE P R S GROUP. COUNTRY REPORTS: BULGARIA. (Political Risk Services) *see* BUSINESS AND ECONOMICS—Economic Situation And Conditions

THE P R S GROUP. COUNTRY REPORTS: CAMEROON. (Political Risk Services) *see* BUSINESS AND ECONOMICS—Economic Situation And Conditions

THE P R S GROUP. COUNTRY REPORTS: CANADA. (Political Risk Services) *see* BUSINESS AND ECONOMICS—Economic Situation And Conditions

THE P R S GROUP. COUNTRY REPORTS: CHILE. (Political Risk Services) *see* BUSINESS AND ECONOMICS—Economic Situation And Conditions

THE P R S GROUP. COUNTRY REPORTS: CHINA. (Political Risk Services) *see* BUSINESS AND ECONOMICS—Economic Situation And Conditions

THE P R S GROUP. COUNTRY REPORTS: COLOMBIA. (Political Risk Services) *see* BUSINESS AND ECONOMICS—Economic Situation And Conditions

THE P R S GROUP. COUNTRY REPORTS: CONGO (BRAZZAVILLE). (Political Risk Services) *see* BUSINESS AND ECONOMICS—Economic Situation And Conditions

THE P R S GROUP. COUNTRY REPORTS: CONGO (KINSHASA). (Political Risk Services) *see* BUSINESS AND ECONOMICS—Economic Situation And Conditions

THE P R S GROUP. COUNTRY REPORTS: COSTA RICA. (Political Risk Services) *see* BUSINESS AND ECONOMICS—Economic Situation And Conditions

THE P R S GROUP. COUNTRY REPORTS: COTE D'IVOIRE. (Political Risk Services) *see* BUSINESS AND ECONOMICS—Economic Situation And Conditions

THE P R S GROUP. COUNTRY REPORTS: CUBA. (Political Risk Services) *see* BUSINESS AND ECONOMICS—Economic Situation And Conditions

THE P R S GROUP. COUNTRY REPORTS: CZECH REPUBLIC. (Political Risk Services) *see* BUSINESS AND ECONOMICS—Economic Situation And Conditions

THE P R S GROUP. COUNTRY REPORTS: DENMARK. (Political Risk Services) *see* BUSINESS AND ECONOMICS—Economic Situation And Conditions

THE P R S GROUP. COUNTRY REPORTS: DOMINICAN REPUBLIC. (Political Risk Services) *see* BUSINESS AND ECONOMICS—Economic Situation And Conditions

THE P R S GROUP. COUNTRY REPORTS: ECUADOR. (Political Risk Services) *see* BUSINESS AND ECONOMICS—Economic Situation And Conditions

THE P R S GROUP. COUNTRY REPORTS: EGYPT. (Political Risk Services) *see* BUSINESS AND ECONOMICS—Economic Situation And Conditions

THE P R S GROUP. COUNTRY REPORTS: EL SALVADOR. (Political Risk Services) *see* BUSINESS AND ECONOMICS—Economic Situation And Conditions

THE P R S GROUP. COUNTRY REPORTS: FINLAND. (Political Risk Services) *see* BUSINESS AND ECONOMICS—Economic Situation And Conditions

THE P R S GROUP. COUNTRY REPORTS: FRANCE. (Political Risk Services) *see* BUSINESS AND ECONOMICS—Economic Situation And Conditions

THE P R S GROUP. COUNTRY REPORTS: GABON. (Political Risk Services) *see* BUSINESS AND ECONOMICS—Economic Situation And Conditions

THE P R S GROUP. COUNTRY REPORTS: GERMANY. (Political Risk Services) *see* BUSINESS AND ECONOMICS—Economic Situation And Conditions

THE P R S GROUP. COUNTRY REPORTS: GHANA. (Political Risk Services) *see* BUSINESS AND ECONOMICS—Economic Situation And Conditions

THE P R S GROUP. COUNTRY REPORTS: GREECE. (Political Risk Services) *see* BUSINESS AND ECONOMICS—Economic Situation And Conditions

THE P R S GROUP. COUNTRY REPORTS: GUATEMALA. (Political Risk Services) *see* BUSINESS AND ECONOMICS—Economic Situation And Conditions

THE P R S GROUP. COUNTRY REPORTS: GUINEA. (Political Risk Services) *see* BUSINESS AND ECONOMICS—Economic Situation And Conditions

THE P R S GROUP. COUNTRY REPORTS: GUYANA. (Political Risk Services) *see* BUSINESS AND ECONOMICS—Economic Situation And Conditions

THE P R S GROUP. COUNTRY REPORTS: HAITI. (Political Risk Services) *see* BUSINESS AND ECONOMICS—Economic Situation And Conditions

THE P R S GROUP. COUNTRY REPORTS: HONDURAS. (Political Risk Services) *see* BUSINESS AND ECONOMICS—Economic Situation And Conditions

THE P R S GROUP. COUNTRY REPORTS: HONG KONG. (Political Risk Services) *see* BUSINESS AND ECONOMICS—Economic Situation And Conditions

THE P R S GROUP. COUNTRY REPORTS: HUNGARY. (Political Risk Services) *see* BUSINESS AND ECONOMICS—Economic Situation And Conditions

THE P R S GROUP. COUNTRY REPORTS: INDIA. (Political Risk Services) *see* BUSINESS AND ECONOMICS—Economic Situation And Conditions

THE P R S GROUP. COUNTRY REPORTS: INDONESIA. (Political Risk Services) *see* BUSINESS AND ECONOMICS—Economic Situation And Conditions

THE P R S GROUP. COUNTRY REPORTS: IRAN. (Political Risk Services) *see* BUSINESS AND ECONOMICS—Economic Situation And Conditions

THE P R S GROUP. COUNTRY REPORTS: IRAQ. (Political Risk Services) *see* BUSINESS AND ECONOMICS—Economic Situation And Conditions

THE P R S GROUP. COUNTRY REPORTS: IRELAND. (Political Risk Services) *see* BUSINESS AND ECONOMICS—Economic Situation And Conditions

THE P R S GROUP. COUNTRY REPORTS: ISRAEL. (Political Risk Services) *see* BUSINESS AND ECONOMICS—Economic Situation And Conditions

THE P R S GROUP. COUNTRY REPORTS: ITALY. (Political Risk Services) *see* BUSINESS AND ECONOMICS—Economic Situation And Conditions

THE P R S GROUP. COUNTRY REPORTS: JAMAICA. (Political Risk Services) *see* BUSINESS AND ECONOMICS—Economic Situation And Conditions

THE P R S GROUP. COUNTRY REPORTS: JAPAN. (Political Risk Services) *see* BUSINESS AND ECONOMICS—Economic Situation And Conditions

THE P R S GROUP. COUNTRY REPORTS: KAZAKSTAN. (Political Risk Services) *see* BUSINESS AND ECONOMICS—Economic Situation And Conditions

THE P R S GROUP. COUNTRY REPORTS: KENYA. (Political Risk Services) *see* BUSINESS AND ECONOMICS—Economic Situation And Conditions

THE P R S GROUP. COUNTRY REPORTS: KUWAIT. (Political Risk Services) *see* BUSINESS AND ECONOMICS—Economic Situation And Conditions

THE P R S GROUP. COUNTRY REPORTS: KYRGYZSTAN. (Political Risk Services) *see* BUSINESS AND ECONOMICS—Economic Situation And Conditions

THE P R S GROUP. COUNTRY REPORTS: LIBYA. (Political Risk Services) *see* BUSINESS AND ECONOMICS—Economic Situation And Conditions

THE P R S GROUP. COUNTRY REPORTS: LITHUANIA. (Political Risk Services) *see* BUSINESS AND ECONOMICS—Economic Situation And Conditions

THE P R S GROUP. COUNTRY REPORTS: MALAYSIA. (Political Risk Services) *see* BUSINESS AND ECONOMICS—Economic Situation And Conditions

THE P R S GROUP. COUNTRY REPORTS: MEXICO. (Political Risk Services) *see* BUSINESS AND ECONOMICS—Economic Situation And Conditions

THE P R S GROUP. COUNTRY REPORTS: MOROCCO. (Political Risk Services) *see* BUSINESS AND ECONOMICS—Economic Situation And Conditions

THE P R S GROUP. COUNTRY REPORTS: MYANMAR. (Political Risk Services) *see* BUSINESS AND ECONOMICS—Economic Situation And Conditions

THE P R S GROUP. COUNTRY REPORTS: NETHERLANDS. (Political Risk Services) *see* BUSINESS AND ECONOMICS—Economic Situation And Conditions

THE P R S GROUP. COUNTRY REPORTS: NEW ZEALAND. (Political Risk Services) *see* BUSINESS AND ECONOMICS—Economic Situation And Conditions

THE P R S GROUP. COUNTRY REPORTS: NICARAGUA. (Political Risk Services) *see* BUSINESS AND ECONOMICS—Economic Situation And Conditions

THE P R S GROUP. COUNTRY REPORTS: NIGERIA. (Political Risk Services) *see* BUSINESS AND ECONOMICS—Economic Situation And Conditions

THE P R S GROUP. COUNTRY REPORTS: NORWAY. (Political Risk Services) *see* BUSINESS AND ECONOMICS—Economic Situation And Conditions

THE P R S GROUP. COUNTRY REPORTS: OMAN. (Political Risk Services) *see* BUSINESS AND ECONOMICS—Economic Situation And Conditions

THE P R S GROUP. COUNTRY REPORTS: PAKISTAN. (Political Risk Services) *see* BUSINESS AND ECONOMICS—Economic Situation And Conditions

THE P R S GROUP. COUNTRY REPORTS: PANAMA. (Political Risk Services) *see* BUSINESS AND ECONOMICS—Economic Situation And Conditions

THE P R S GROUP. COUNTRY REPORTS: PAPUA NEW GUINEA. (Political Risk Services) *see* BUSINESS AND ECONOMICS—Economic Situation And Conditions

THE P R S GROUP. COUNTRY REPORTS: PARAGUAY. (Political Risk Services) *see* BUSINESS AND ECONOMICS—Economic Situation And Conditions

THE P R S GROUP. COUNTRY REPORTS: PERU. (Political Risk Services) *see* BUSINESS AND ECONOMICS—Economic Situation And Conditions

THE P R S GROUP. COUNTRY REPORTS: PHILIPPINES. (Political Risk Services) *see* BUSINESS AND ECONOMICS—Economic Situation And Conditions

THE P R S GROUP. COUNTRY REPORTS: POLAND. (Political Risk Services) *see* BUSINESS AND ECONOMICS—Economic Situation And Conditions

THE P R S GROUP. COUNTRY REPORTS: PORTUGAL. (Political Risk Services) *see* BUSINESS AND ECONOMICS—Economic Situation And Conditions

THE P R S GROUP. COUNTRY REPORTS: PUERTO RICO. (Political Risk Services) *see* BUSINESS AND ECONOMICS—Economic Situation And Conditions

THE P R S GROUP. COUNTRY REPORTS: QATAR. (Political Risk Services) *see* BUSINESS AND ECONOMICS—Economic Situation And Conditions

THE P R S GROUP. COUNTRY REPORTS: ROMANIA. (Political Risk Services) *see* BUSINESS AND ECONOMICS—Economic Situation And Conditions

THE P R S GROUP. COUNTRY REPORTS: RUSSIA. (Political Risk Services) *see* BUSINESS AND ECONOMICS—Economic Situation And Conditions

THE P R S GROUP. COUNTRY REPORTS: SAUDI ARABIA. (Political Risk Services) *see* BUSINESS AND ECONOMICS—Economic Situation And Conditions

THE P R S GROUP. COUNTRY REPORTS: SINGAPORE. (Political Risk Services) *see* BUSINESS AND ECONOMICS—Economic Situation And Conditions

THE P R S GROUP. COUNTRY REPORTS: SLOVAK REPUBLIC. (Political Risk Services) *see* BUSINESS AND ECONOMICS—Economic Situation And Conditions

THE P R S GROUP. COUNTRY REPORTS: SOUTH AFRICA. (Political Risk Services) *see* BUSINESS AND ECONOMICS—Economic Situation And Conditions

THE P R S GROUP. COUNTRY REPORTS: SOUTH KOREA. (Political Risk Services) *see* BUSINESS AND ECONOMICS—Economic Situation And Conditions

THE P R S GROUP. COUNTRY REPORTS: SPAIN. (Political Risk Services) *see* BUSINESS AND ECONOMICS—Economic Situation And Conditions

THE P R S GROUP. COUNTRY REPORTS: SRI LANKA. (Political Risk Services) *see* BUSINESS AND ECONOMICS—Economic Situation And Conditions

THE P R S GROUP. COUNTRY REPORTS: SUDAN. (Political Risk Services) *see* BUSINESS AND ECONOMICS—Economic Situation And Conditions

THE P R S GROUP. COUNTRY REPORTS: SURINAME. (Political Risk Services) *see* BUSINESS AND ECONOMICS—Economic Situation And Conditions

THE P R S GROUP. COUNTRY REPORTS: SWEDEN. (Political Risk Services) *see* BUSINESS AND ECONOMICS—Economic Situation And Conditions

THE P R S GROUP. COUNTRY REPORTS: SWITZERLAND. (Political Risk Services) *see* BUSINESS AND ECONOMICS—Economic Situation And Conditions

THE P R S GROUP. COUNTRY REPORTS: SYRIA. (Political Risk Services) *see* BUSINESS AND ECONOMICS—Economic Situation And Conditions

THE P R S GROUP. COUNTRY REPORTS: TAIWAN. (Political Risk Services) *see* BUSINESS AND ECONOMICS—Economic Situation And Conditions

THE P R S GROUP. COUNTRY REPORTS: THAILAND. (Political Risk Services) *see* BUSINESS AND ECONOMICS—Economic Situation And Conditions

THE P R S GROUP. COUNTRY REPORTS: TRINIDAD & TOBAGO. (Political Risk Services) *see* BUSINESS AND ECONOMICS—Economic Situation And Conditions

THE P R S GROUP. COUNTRY REPORTS: TUNISIA. (Political Risk Services) *see* BUSINESS AND ECONOMICS—Economic Situation And Conditions

THE P R S GROUP. COUNTRY REPORTS: TURKEY. (Political Risk Services) *see* BUSINESS AND ECONOMICS—Economic Situation And Conditions

THE P R S GROUP. COUNTRY REPORTS: TURKMENISTAN. (Political Risk Services) *see* BUSINESS AND ECONOMICS—Economic Situation And Conditions

THE P R S GROUP. COUNTRY REPORTS: UKRAINE. (Political Risk Services) *see* BUSINESS AND ECONOMICS—Economic Situation And Conditions

THE P R S GROUP. COUNTRY REPORTS: UNITED ARAB EMIRATES. (Political Risk Services) *see* BUSINESS AND ECONOMICS—Economic Situation And Conditions

THE P R S GROUP. COUNTRY REPORTS: UNITED KINGDOM. (Political Risk Services) *see* BUSINESS AND ECONOMICS—Economic Situation And Conditions

THE P R S GROUP. COUNTRY REPORTS: UNITED STATES. (Political Risk Services) *see* BUSINESS AND ECONOMICS—Economic Situation And Conditions

THE P R S GROUP. COUNTRY REPORTS: URUGUAY. (Political Risk Services) *see* BUSINESS AND ECONOMICS—Economic Situation And Conditions

THE P R S GROUP. COUNTRY REPORTS: UZBEKISTAN. (Political Risk Services) *see* BUSINESS AND ECONOMICS—Economic Situation And Conditions

THE P R S GROUP. COUNTRY REPORTS: VENEZUELA. (Political Risk Services) *see* BUSINESS AND ECONOMICS—Economic Situation And Conditions

THE P R S GROUP. COUNTRY REPORTS: VIETNAM. (Political Risk Services) *see* BUSINESS AND ECONOMICS—Economic Situation And Conditions

THE P R S GROUP. COUNTRY REPORTS: WORLD SERVICE. (Political Risk Services) *see* BUSINESS AND ECONOMICS—Economic Situation And Conditions

THE P R S GROUP. COUNTRY REPORTS: YEMEN. (Political Risk Services) *see* BUSINESS AND ECONOMICS—Economic Situation And Conditions

THE P R S GROUP. COUNTRY REPORTS: ZAMBIA. (Political Risk Services) *see* BUSINESS AND ECONOMICS—Economic Situation And Conditions

THE P R S GROUP. COUNTRY REPORTS: ZIMBABWE. (Political Risk Services) *see* BUSINESS AND ECONOMICS—Economic Situation And Conditions

320 GBR
P S A AND B I S A DIRECTORY. (Political Studies Association / British International Studies Association) Text in English. 19??. a. free to members (effective 2010). **Document type:** *Directory, Trade.*
Formerly (until 1999): P S A Directory
Published by: Political Studies Association, National Office, Department of Politics, University of Newcastle, Newcastle-upon-Tyne, NE1 7RU, United Kingdom. TEL 44-191-2228021, FAX 44-191-2223499, psa@ncl.ac.uk, http://www.psa.ac.uk/. **Co-sponsor:** British International Studies Association.

320 GBR
THE P S A MEDIA REGISTER OF EXPERTS. Text in English. 1998. biennial. free to members (effective 2010). bibl. **Document type:** *Journal, Academic/Scholarly.* **Description:** Promotes the study of politics.
Related titles: Online - full text ed.: free (effective 2010).
Published by: Political Studies Association, National Office, Department of Politics, University of Newcastle, Newcastle-upon-Tyne, NE1 7RU, United Kingdom. TEL 44-191-2228021, FAX 44-191-2223499, psa@ncl.ac.uk.

320 GBR ISSN 0955-6281
P S A NEWS. Text in English. 1975. q. free to members (effective 2010). adv. bk.rev. back issues avail. **Document type:** *Newsletter, Trade.* **Description:** Contains articles, news, listings of current and forthcoming politcal studies events and conferences.
Formerly (until 1988): Political Studies Association of the United Kingdom. Newsletter (0144-7440)
Related titles: Online - full text ed.: free (effective 2010).
Indexed: SOPODA.
Published by: Political Studies Association, National Office, Department of Politics, University of Newcastle, Newcastle-upon-Tyne, NE1 7RU, United Kingdom. TEL 44-191-2228021, FAX 44-191-2223499, psa@ncl.ac.uk.

320 GBR ISSN 1049-0965
JA28
➤ **P S: POLITICAL SCIENCE & POLITICS.** Variant title: Political Science & Politics. Text in English. 1968. q. GBP 436, USD 816 combined subscription to institutions (print & online eds.) (effective 2010). adv. charts; stat.; illus. Index. back issues avail.; reprint service avail. from PSC. **Document type:** *Journal, Academic/Scholarly.* **Description:** Includes articles of contemporary political analysis, and features news of the profession and its members.
Incorporates (1974-1990): Political Science Teacher (0896-0828); Formerly (until 1988): P S (Washington, DC) (0030-8269); Which superseded in part (in 1968): American Political Science Review (0003-0554)
Related titles: Microform ed.: (from PQC); Online - full text ed.: ISSN 1537-5935. GBP 400, USD 740 to institutions (effective 2010).
Indexed: A20, A22, A26, ABCPolSci, ABS&EES, ASCA, AmH&L, B04, BRD, CA, ChPerl, Chicano, CurCont, E01, E07, E08, ESPM, G08, H09, I05, I13, IBR, IBZ, P02, P06, P10, P13, P18, P27, P30, P42, P45, P47, P48, P53, P54, PAIS, PCI, PQC, PSA, PersLit, RASB, RiskAb, S02, S03, S05, S09, S11, SCOPUS, SSAI, SSAb, SSCI, SSI, SWR&A, SociolAb, T02, W01, W02, W03, W05, W07.
—BLDSC (6945.711000), IE, Infotrieve, Ingenta. **CCC.**
Published by: (American Political Science Association USA), Cambridge University Press, The Edinburgh Bldg, Shaftesbury Rd, Cambridge, CB2 8RU, United Kingdom. TEL 44-1223-312393, FAX 44-1223-315052, journals@cambridge.org, http://www.cambridge.org/uk. Ed. Robert Hauck. R&P Linda Nicol TEL 44-1223-325702. Adv. contact Rebecca Roberts TEL 44-1223-325083. page GBP 455, page USD 840. Circ: 16,000. **Subscr. to:** Cambridge University Press, 32 Ave of the Americas, New York, NY 10013. TEL 212-337-5000, FAX 212-691-3239, journals_subscriptions@cup.org

➤ **P.T. MAGAZIN**; fuer Wirtschaft, Politik und Kultur. *see* BUSINESS AND ECONOMICS

320.6 USA ISSN 1933-1223
PACIFIC ISLANDS POLICY. Text in English. 2006. irreg., latest vol.6, 2010. USD 10 per issue (effective 2010). back issues avail. **Document type:** *Monographic series, Academic/Scholarly.* **Description:** Examines issues, problems, and opportunities that are relevant to the Pacific Islands region.
Related titles: Online - full text ed.: ISSN 1933-172X. free (effective 2010).
Indexed: A01, CA, P34, P42, T02.
Published by: East-West Center, 1601 EW Rd, Honolulu, HI 96848. TEL 808-944-7111, FAX 808-944-7376, ewcbooks@eastwestcenter.org. Eds. Gerard A Finin, Robert C Kiste TEL 808-944-7745.

320 AUS ISSN 1832-3952
THE PAGE REVIEW. Text in English. 2005. s-a. bk.rev. **Document type:** *Magazine, Consumer.* **Description:** Deals with politics and policy.
Published by: The Page Research Centre Limited, PO Box 5971, Wagga Wagga, NSW 2650, Australia. pagemail@page.org.au, http://www.page.org.au.

PAKISTAN. NATIONAL ASSEMBLY. DEBATES. OFFICIAL REPORT. *see* PUBLIC ADMINISTRATION

320 956 ISR ISSN 0793-1395
DS119.7
➤ **PALESTINE - ISRAEL JOURNAL OF POLITICS, ECONOMICS AND CULTURE.** Text in English. 1994. q. ILS 100 domestic to individuals; EUR 45 in Europe to individuals; USD 60 elsewhere to individuals; ILS 120 domestic to institutions; EUR 55 in Europe to institutions; USD 75 elsewhere to institutions; ILS 80 domestic to senior citizens; EUR 35 in Europe to senior citizens; USD 50 elsewhere to senior citizens (effective 2009). adv. bk.rev. Index. 128 p./no.; back issues avail. **Document type:** *Journal, Academic/Scholarly.* **Description:** Aims to shed light on and analyze freely and critically the issues dividing Israelis and Palestinians.
Related titles: Online - full text ed.
Indexed: A01, A02, A03, A08, APW, AltPI, B01, B06, B07, B09, CA, CCME, ENW, I02, I14, IBSS, IJP, J01, LeftInd, M10, P34, P45, PAIS, R02, S02, S03, T02.
Address: 4 El Hariri St., Jerusalem, Israel. TEL 972-2-6282115, FAX 972-2-6273388. Eds. Daniel Bar-Tal, Ziad Abu Zayyad. R&P Zahra Khalidi. Adv. contact Karen Pacht.

➤ **PALOMAR**; rivista di cultura e politica. *see* HUMANITIES: COMPREHENSIVE WORKS

➤ **PAMIATKY A MUZEA**; revue pre kulturne dedicstvo. *see* HISTORY—History Of Europe

➤ **PAMIETNIKARSTWO POLSKIE.** *see* HISTORY—History Of Europe

324.27287 PAN
PANAMA. TRIBUNAL ELECTORAL. MEMORIA. Text in Spanish. irreg.
Published by: Tribunal Electoral, Panama City, Panama.

320.532 CHN ISSN 1001-5647
PANDENG/ASCENT. Text in Chinese. 1982. bi-m. **Document type:** *Magazine, Consumer.*
Related titles: Tibetan ed.: Pandeng (Zangwen Ban). ISSN 1005-2089. CNY 20 domestic; USD 5.20 in Hong Kong, Macau & Taiwan; USD 10 elsewhere (effective 2007).
Published by: Zhong Gong Qinghai Sheng Weidangxiao, 2, Huanghe Lu, Xining, 810001, China. TEL 86-971-4396460, FAX 86-971-6123556.

320 GTM ISSN 1018-1822
F1439.5
PANORAMA CENTROAMERICANO. PENSAMIENTO Y ACCION. Text in Spanish. 1986. q.
Published by: Instituto Centroamericano de Estudios Politicos, 8a Calle 0-32, Zona 9, Apdo. Postal 611-A, Guatemala City, 01009, Guatemala. TEL 502-360-3615, 502-334-5214, FAX 502-332-3743, comunicaciones@incep.org, http://www.incep.org.

320 GTM ISSN 1017-8902
PANORAMA CENTROAMERICANO. REPORTE POLITICO. Text in Spanish. m. **Description:** Summarizes the political, economic and social factors occurring in the region, as well as other factors affecting other countries or regions as a whole.
Published by: Instituto Centroamericano de Estudios Politicos, 8a Calle 0-32, Zona 9, Apdo. Postal 611-A, Guatemala City, 01009, Guatemala. TEL 502-334-5214, 502-360-3615, FAX 502-332-3743, comunicaciones@incep.org.

320 GTM ISSN 1018-1814
PANORAMA CENTROAMERICANO. TEMAS Y DOCUMENTOS DE DEBATES. Text in Spanish. 1986. irreg. **Description:** Compilation of studies, analyses and documents covering the social reality, politics, economics, and culture in Central America.
Published by: Instituto Centroamericano de Estudios Politicos, 8a Calle 0-32, Zona 9, Apdo. Postal 611-A, Guatemala City, 01009, Guatemala. TEL 502-360-3615, 502-334-5214, FAX 502-332-3743, comunicaciones@incep.org.

PANSTWO I PRAWO. *see* LAW

320 COL ISSN 0122-4409
JA5
PAPEL POLITICO. Text in Spanish. 1995. s-a. back issues avail. **Document type:** *Journal, Academic/Scholarly.*
Related titles: Online - full text ed.: ISSN 2145-0617. 2009 (from SciELO).
Indexed: A01, C01, CA, F03, F04, P42, T02.
Published by: Pontificia Universidad Javeriana, Facultad de Ciencias Politicas y Relaciones Internacionales, Cra. 7 No. 46-62, Bogota, Colombia. TEL 57-1-3208320 ext. 2483, http://www.javeriana.edu.co/Facultades/politicas/inicio.htm. Ed. Claudia Dangond.

320 330.9 ESP ISSN 1576-6500
PAPELES DEL ESTE; transiciones postcomunistas. Text in Spanish, English. 2000. s-a. **Document type:** *Journal, Academic/Scholarly.*
Media: Online - full text.
Indexed: I04, I05.
Published by: (Universidad Complutense de Madrid, Facultad de Ciencias Economicas y Empresariales), Universidad Complutense de Madrid, Servicio de Publicaciones, C/ Obispo Trejo 2, Ciudad Universitaria, Madrid, 28040, Spain. TEL 34-91-3941127, FAX 34-91-3941126, servicio.publicaciones@rect.ucm.es, http://www.ucm.es/publicaciones.

320 GBR ISSN 1755-6740
PAPERS IN THE POLITICS OF GLOBAL COMPETITIVENESS. Text in English. 2006 (Nov.). irreg. free (effective 2009). back issues avail. **Document type:** *Monographic series, Academic/Scholarly.*
Media: Online - full content.
Published by: (Manchester Metropolitan University, Global Competitiveness Research Group), Manchester Metropolitan University, Institute for Global Studies, All Saints Building, All Saints, Manchester, M15 6BH, United Kingdom. TEL 44-161-2472000, FAX 44-161-2476390, enquiries@mmu.ac.uk, http://www.sociology.mmu.ac.uk/igs/.

PARAMETERS (CARLISLE). *see* MILITARY

320 USA
PARANOIA; the conspiracy reader. Text in English. 1992. q. USD 20; USD 5 newsstand/cover. adv. bk.rev. back issues avail. **Document type:** *Magazine, Consumer.* **Description:** Includes hard to find and controversial conspiracy theories and writing for a mainstream audience.
Published by: Paranoia Publishing, PO Box 1041, Providence, RI 02901. TEL 401-467-2830. Ed. Al Hidell. Pubs. Al Hidell, Joan d'Arc. Circ: 5,000 (paid).

328 DEU ISSN 0031-2258
DAS PARLAMENT. Text in German. 1951. 38/yr. EUR 34.90 (effective 2009). adv. bk.rev. index. **Document type:** *Newspaper, Government.*
Related titles: Microfiche ed.: (from PQC); Microfilm ed.: (from ALP, PQC); ◆ Supplement to: Aus Politik und Zeitgeschichte. ISSN 0479-611X.
Indexed: RASB.
Published by: Deutscher Bundestag, Platz der Republik 1, Berlin, 11011, Germany. TEL 49-30-22730515, FAX 49-30-22736524, mail@bundestag.de, http://www.bundestag.de. Ed. Saskia Leuenberger. adv.: B&W page EUR 2,990, color page EUR 5,430; trim 360 x 527. Circ: 61,069 (controlled).

PARLAMENTO DE NAVARRA. BOLETIN. *see* PUBLIC ADMINISTRATION

PARLAMENTO DE NAVARRA. DIARIO DE SESIONES. *see* PUBLIC ADMINISTRATION

320 FRA ISSN 1768-6520
JF501
➤ **PARLEMENTS**; revue d'histoire politique. Text in French. 2004. s-a. EUR 45 domestic to individuals; EUR 50 foreign to individuals; EUR 50 domestic to institutions; EUR 55 foreign to institutions (effective 2008). bk.rev. abstr. back issues avail. **Document type:** *Journal, Academic/Scholarly.* **Description:** Deals with contemporary political history in France and throughout the world.
Media: Large Type.
Indexed: CA, IBSS, P42, PSA, T02.
Published by: (Comite d'Histoire Parlementaire et Politique), L' Harmattan, 5 Rue de l'Ecole Polytechnique, Paris, 75005, France. TEL 33-1-43257651, FAX 33-1-43258203, diffusion.harmattan@wanadoo.fr, http://www.editions-harmattan.fr. Ed. Jean Garrigues. Pub., Adv. contact Sonny Perseil. Circ: 200 (paid).

328 ISR
PARLIAMENT. Text in Hebrew, English. 1987. q. free (effective 2008). bk.rev. **Document type:** *Journal, Trade.*
Formerly (until 1993): Israeli Democracy (print)
Media: Online - full text. **Related titles:** Hebrew ed.
Published by: Israel Democracy Institute, P O Box 4702, Jerusalem, 91040, Israel. FAX 972-2-5635319, sandraf@idi.org.il. Ed. Sandra Fine. Circ: 1,000.

328 GBR ISSN 1372-7966
JN26
THE PARLIAMENT MAGAZINE; politics, policy and people. Text in English. 1997. fortn. GBP 120 (effective 2009). adv. back issues avail. **Document type:** *Magazine, Trade.* **Description:** Deals with the European Parliament and its business.
Related titles: Online - full text ed.: free.
—**CCC.**
Published by: Dod's Parliamentary Communications Ltd., Westminster Tower, 3rd Fl, 3 Albert Embankment, London, SE1 7SP, United Kingdom. TEL 44-20-70917500, FAX 44-20-70917505, uk@dods.co.uk, http://www.dods.co.uk. Ed. Catherine Stihler. Pub. Martin Beck. adv.: B&W page GBP 5,975, color page GBP 6,700; 210 x 270.

328 GBR ISSN 2043-8370
THE PARLIAMENT MAGAZINE'S REGIONAL REVIEW. Text in English. 2006. q. GBP 38, EUR 48 (effective 2010). adv. back issues avail. **Document type:** *Magazine, Trade.* **Description:** Deals with the European Parliament and its business.
Related titles: Online - full text ed.
Published by: Dod's Parliamentary Communications Ltd., Westminster Tower, 3rd Fl, 3 Albert Embankment, London, SE1 7SP, United Kingdom. TEL 44-20-70917500, FAX 44-20-70917505, uk@dods.co.uk, http://www.dods.co.uk. Ed. Martha Moss TEL 32-2-2850829. Adv. contact Nick Ragier TEL 44-20-70917668.

328 GBR ISSN 2043-8389
THE PARLIAMENT MAGAZINE'S RESEARCH REVIEW. Text in English. 2007. q. GBP 38, EUR 48 (effective 2010). adv. back issues avail. **Document type:** *Magazine, Trade.* **Description:** Deals with the European Parliament and its business.
Published by: Dod's Parliamentary Communications Ltd., Westminster Tower, 3rd Fl, 3 Albert Embankment, London, SE1 7SP, United Kingdom. TEL 44-20-70917500, FAX 44-20-70917505, uk@dods.co.uk, http://www.dods.co.uk. Ed. Francesca Ross TEL 32-2-2850842. Adv. contact Nick Ragier TEL 44-20-70917668.

328 GBR ISSN 0031-2282
JN101
THE PARLIAMENTARIAN. Text in English. 1920. q. free to members (effective 2009). adv. bk.rev. illus. index, cum.index: 1966-1980, 1981-1985, 1986-1990,1991-1995. back issues avail.; reprints avail. **Document type:** *Journal, Academic/Scholarly.* **Description:** Contains news of developments in other parliaments.
Former titles (until 1966): Journal of the Parliaments of the Commonwealth; (until 1949): Journal of the Parliaments of the Empire
Related titles: Microfilm ed.: (from PQC); Online - full text ed.
Indexed: A20, A22, ABCPolSci, AmHI, BAS, BrHumI, CA, H07, I13, MEA&I, P42, PAIS, SCOPUS, SPPI, T02.
—BLDSC (6406.830000), IE, Infotrieve, Ingenta. **CCC.**
Published by: Commonwealth Parliamentary Association, c o Secretariat, Ste 700, Westminster House, 7 Millbank, London, SW1P 3JA, United Kingdom. TEL 44-20-7799-1460, FAX 44-20-7222-6073, pirc@cpahq.org. Circ: 15,000.

P

328 GBR ISSN 0031-2290
JN101
➤ **PARLIAMENTARY AFFAIRS**; a journal of representative politics. Text in English. 1947. q. GBP 271 in United Kingdom to institutions; EUR 407 in Europe to institutions; USD 540 in US & Canada to institutions; GBP 271 elsewhere to institutions; GBP 295 combined subscription in United Kingdom to institutions (print & online eds.); EUR 444 combined subscription in Europe to institutions (print & online eds.); USD 589 combined subscription in US & Canada to institutions (print & online eds.); GBP 295 combined subscription elsewhere to institutions (print & online eds.) (effective 2012). adv. bk.rev. charts; illus. index, cum.index. 208 p./no.; back issues avail.; reprint service avail. from PSC. **Document type:** *Journal, Academic/Scholarly.* **Description:** Covers all aspects of government and politics directly or indirectly connected with Parliament and parliamentary systems in Britain and throughout the world.
Related titles: Microform ed.: (from PQC); Online - full text ed.: ISSN 1460-2482. GBP 246 in United Kingdom to institutions; EUR 370 in Europe to institutions; USD 491 in US & Canada to institutions; GBP 246 elsewhere to institutions (effective 2012) (from IngentaConnect).
Indexed: A01, A02, A03, A08, A20, A22, A26, ABCPolSci, AC&P, ASCA, AmH&L, AmHI, B04, BRD, BrHumI, CA, CurCont, DIP, E01, E08, ELJI, ELLIS, FamI, G08, H07, H09, HistAb, I05, I13, IBR, IBSS, IBZ, LJI, MEA&I, P02, P06, P10, P27, P30, P34, P42, P45, P47, P48, P53, P54, PAA&I, PAIS, PCI, PQC, PRA, PSA, RASB, S02, S03, S05, S09, S11, SCOPUS, SOPODA, SSA, SSAI, SSAb, SSCI, SSI, SociolAb, T02, W01, W02, W03, W05, W07, W09.
—BLDSC (6406.840000), IE, Infotrieve, Ingenta. **CCC.**
Published by: (Hansard Society for Parliamentary Government), Oxford University Press, Great Clarendon St, Oxford, OX2 6DP, United Kingdom. TEL 44-1865-556767, FAX 44-1865-556646, enquiry@oup.co.uk, http://www.oxfordjournals.org. Eds. Dr. Jocelyn Evans, Steven Fielding. Adv. contact Linda Hann TEL 44-1344-779945.

328 GBR
PARLIAMENTARY BULLETIN FOR LOCAL GOVERNMENT EXECUTIVES. Text in English. 1949. w. GBP 38.
Published by: Parliamentary and Common Market News Services, 19 Kingsdowne Rd, Surbiton, KT6 6JZ, United Kingdom.

PARLIAMENTARY DEBATES. *see* PUBLIC ADMINISTRATION

320 AUS ISSN 0813-541X
PARLIAMENTARY HANDBOOK OF THE COMMONWEALTH OF AUSTRALIA. Text in English. 1915. irreg., latest 1998. price varies. illus. **Document type:** *Directory, Government.*
Former titles: Australian Parliamentary Handbook; Parliamentary Handbook of the Commonwealth of Australia
Related titles: Online - full text ed.; ◆ Series of: Commonwealth of Australia. Parliament. Parliamentary Paper. ISSN 0727-4181.
—CCC.
Published by: (Australia. Parliament), AusInfo, Parliament House, Canberra Mc, ACT 2600, Australia. TEL 61-2-62777111, webmanager@aph.gov.au. Circ: 2,000.

328 USA ISSN 0048-2994
PARLIAMENTARY JOURNAL. Text in English. 1960. q. free to members (effective 2011). bk.rev. 40 p./no. 1 cols./p.; back issues avail.; reprints avail. **Document type:** *Journal, Academic/Scholarly.* **Description:** Articles on parliamentary procedure in organizations, including informal articles on homeowners associations and condos.
Related titles: Microform ed.: (from PQC).
Indexed: A22, MEA&I, SSAI, SSAb, SSI, W03, W05.
Published by: American Institute of Parliamentarians, 550M Ritchie Hwy, 271, Severna Park, MD 21146. TEL 888-664-0428, FAX 410-544-4640. Ed. Paul J Lamb.

328.71025 CAN ISSN 1198-3205
PARLIAMENTARY NAMES & NUMBERS; your guide to governments in Canada. Text in English. 1994. s-a. CAD 55 per issue (effective 2003). adv. **Document type:** *Directory.* **Description:** Includes contact names and numbers for federal and provincial government and senate, also cabinet and critic responsibilities, government agencies, Canadian embassies abroad and lobbyists.
Related titles: Online - full text ed.
Published by: Sources Publishing, 489 College St, Ste 305, Toronto M6G 1A5, ON M6G 1A5, Canada. TEL 416-964-7799, FAX 416-964-8763, sources@sources.com, http://www.sources.com. Ed., R&P Ulli Diemer. Pub. Barrie Zwicker. Adv. contact Michelle Hernandez. Circ: 1,500.

328 GBR
PARLIAMENTARY YEARBOOK. Text in English. 1979. a. adv. **Document type:** *Yearbook.* **Description:** Designed for the Parliamentarians and those who do business with the Palace of Westminster.
Former titles (until 2008): Parliamentary Yearbook & Diary (1369-9296); (until 1998): Parliamentary Yearbook
Related titles: Online - full text ed.
Published by: Blakes, Gadd House, Arcadia Ave, London, N3 2JU, United Kingdom. TEL 44-20-89564000, FAX 44-20-89564009, comms@blakemedia.org. Pub. David Blake. Circ: 5,500.

320.531 ITA ISSN 1122-5300
HX7
PAROLECHIAVE. Text in Italian. 1958. s-a. EUR 38.10 domestic; EUR 60.25 foreign (effective 2008). adv. bk.rev. bibl. index. back issues avail. **Document type:** *Monographic series, Academic/Scholarly.*
Formerly (until 1991): Problemi del Socialismo (0552-1807)
Related titles: Online - full text ed.: ISSN 1827-8965.
Indexed: A22, IBR, IBZ.
—IE.
Published by: (Fondazione Lelio e Lisli Basso Issoco), Carocci Editore, Via Sardegna 50, Rome, 00187, Italy. TEL 39-06-42818417, FAX 39-06-42747931, clienti@carocci.it, http://www.carocci.it. Ed. Claudio Pavone. Circ: 2,500.

320 ITA ISSN 1972-7623
PARTECIPAZIONE E CONFLITTO. Text in Multiple languages. 2008. 3/yr. EUR 70.50 combined subscription domestic to institutions (print & online eds.); EUR 109 combined subscription foreign to institutions (print & online eds.) (effective 2010). **Document type:** *Journal, Academic/Scholarly.*
Related titles: Online - full text ed.: ISSN 2035-6609.
Published by: Franco Angeli Edizioni, Viale Monza 106, Milan, 20127, Italy. TEL 39-02-2837141, FAX 39-02-26144793, redazioni@francoangeli.it, http://www.francoangeli.it.

320 CAN ISSN 0709-6941
JA27
PARTICIPATION. Text in English, French. 1977. 3/yr. adv. bk.rev. 40 p./no. 3 cols./p.; Supplement avail.; back issues avail. **Document type:** *Bulletin, Consumer.* **Description:** Covers academic interests.
Formerly: International Political Science Association. Circular (0074-7459)
—BLDSC (6407.230000). **CCC.**
Published by: Association Internationale de Science Politique - International Political Science Association (A I S P - I P S A), 1590 Ave Docteur-Penfield, Bureau 331, Montreal, PQ H3G 1C5, Canada. TEL 514-848-8717, FAX 514-848-4095, info@ipsa.org, http://www.ipsa.org. adv.: B&W page USD 400. Circ: 2,000.

324.2 ITA
IL PARTITO COMUNISTA; organo del Partito Comunista Internazionale. Text in Italian. 1974. m. USD 9 domestic; USD 11 foreign (effective 2009). 4 p./no. 5 cols./p.; **Document type:** *Newsletter, Consumer.*
Published by: (Partito Comunista Internazionale), Edizioni Il Partito Comunista, Casella Postale 1157, Florence, FI 50121, Italy. http://perso.wanadoo.fr/italian.left.

324.2 GBR ISSN 1354-0688
JF2051 CODEN: PAPOFH
➤ **PARTY POLITICS**; the international journal for the study of political parties and political organizations. Text in English. 1995. bi-m. USD 1,153, GBP 623 combined subscription to institutions (print & online eds.); USD 1,130, GBP 611 to institutions (effective 2011). adv. bk.rev. back issues avail.; reprint service avail. from PSC. **Document type:** *Journal, Academic/Scholarly.* **Description:** Provides a forum for discussion of the character and organization of political parties, and their role within their various national political systems.
Related titles: Online - full text ed.: ISSN 1460-3683. USD 1,038, GBP 561 to institutions (effective 2011).
Indexed: A01, A03, A08, A20, A22, ASCA, B07, BibInd, CA, CurCont, DIP, E01, ESPM, H04, I13, IBR, IBSS, IBZ, P02, P10, P34, P42, P47, P48, P53, P54, PAIS, PQC, PSA, RASB, RiskAb, S02, S03, S11, SCOPUS, SOPODA, SPAA, SSA, SSCI, SociolAb, T02, V02, W07.
—BLDSC (6407.791000), IE, Infotrieve, Ingenta. **CCC.**
Published by: (American Political Science Association, Political Organizations and Parties USA), Sage Publications Ltd. (Subsidiary of: Sage Publications, Inc.), 1 Oliver's Yard, 55 City Rd, London, EC1Y 1SP, United Kingdom. TEL 44-20-73248500, FAX 44-20-73248600, info@sagepub.co.uk, http://www.uk.sagepub.com/home.nav. Eds. David M Farrell, Kenneth Janda, Paul D Webb. adv.: B&W page GBP 400; 130 x 205. **Subscr. in the Americas to:** Sage Publications, Inc., 2455 Teller Rd, Thousand Oaks, CA 91320. TEL 805-499-9774, FAX 805-499-0871, journals@sagepub.com.

320 ESP ISSN 1575-2259
CB3
PASAJES. Text in Spanish. 1999. 3/yr. **Document type:** *Journal, Academic/Scholarly.* **Description:** Focuses on issues and problems in the field of political science, social sciences, humanities and other related issues.
Published by: Universitat de Valencia, Fundacion Canada Blanch, C El Batxiller 1, 1o, Valencia, Spain. **Dist. by:** Asociacion de Revistas Culturales de Espana, C Covarruvias 9 2o. Derecha, Madrid 28010, Spain. TEL 34-91-3086066, FAX 34-91-3199267, info@arce.es, http://www.arce.es/.

320 NZL ISSN 1177-9063
PASIFIKA INTERACTIONS PROJECT. WORKING PAPER. Text in English. 2006. irreg. **Document type:** *Monographic series, Academic/Scholarly.* **Description:** Cover a wide range of research and policy issues. Their aim is to inform and stimulate debate.
Media: Online - full text.
Published by: Victoria University of Wellington, Institute of Policy Studies, PO Box 600, Wellington, New Zealand. TEL 64-4-4635307, FAX 64-4-4637413, ips@vuw.ac.nz.

320 NLD ISSN 0928-2513
PASSAGE REEKS. Text in Dutch. 1992. irreg., latest vol.36, 2010. price varies. **Document type:** *Monographic series, Academic/Scholarly.*
Published by: Uitgeverij Verloren, Torenlaan 25, Hilversum, 1211 JA, Netherlands. TEL 31-35-6859856, FAX 31-35-6836557, info@verloren.nl, http://www.verloren.nl.

PASSATO E PRESENTE. *see* HISTORY—History Of Europe

320.9 CUB
PATRIA. Text in Spanish. m.
Published by: Antiguos Alumnos del Seminario Martiano, Fragua Martiana, Principe y Hospital, Havana, Cuba.

320 ARG ISSN 1853-0974
PATRIA GRANDE. Text in Spanish. 2007. bi-w. **Document type:** *Magazine, Consumer.*
Published by: Movimiento Libres del Sur, Humberto 1o. 542, Buenos Aires, Argentina. http://libresdelsur.org.ar/.

322.4 ITA ISSN 0031-3130
PATRIA INDIPENDENTE; periodico della Resistenza e degli ex-combattenti. Text in Italian. 1952. m. adv. bk.rev.; film rev. bibl.; illus. **Document type:** *Magazine, Consumer.*
Related titles: Online - full text ed.
Indexed: RASB.
Published by: Associazione Nazionale Partigiani d'Italia, Comitato Nazionale, Via Degli Scipioni 271, Rome, 00192, Italy. TEL 39-06-3211949, FAX 39-06-3218495, info@anpi.it, http://www.anpi.it. Circ: 20,000.

320 ARG
PATRIA Y PUEBLO. Text in Spanish. 1986. m. ARS 20.
Address: Juan Bautista Alberdi, 1878, Buenos Aires, 1406, Argentina. Ed. Carlos A D'Aprile.

320.5 USA
THE PATRIOT REVIEW. Text in English. irreg. (approx. bi-m.). USD 24 for 12 issues. adv. **Document type:** *Newspaper.* **Description:** Discusses tax resistance, extremist political theories and conspiracies.
Published by: Christian Patriot Association, PO Box 905, Sandy, OR 97055. TEL 503-668-4941.

320.531 FRA ISSN 2107-349X
▼ **LE PAVE.** Text in French. 2009. s-a. **Document type:** *Magazine, Consumer.*
Published by: Association La Rose au Poing de Boutigny-sur-Essonne et Environs, 39 Rue de Marchais, Boutigny-sur-Essonne, 91820, France. Ed. Pierre Gerard.

320 CRI ISSN 1659-3995
JZ5511.2
PEACE AND CONFLICT REVIEW. Text in English. 2006. irreg. free (effective 2011). **Document type:** *Journal, Academic/Scholarly.*
Media: Online - full text.
Published by: University for Peace/Universidad para la Paz, Apartado 138-6100, Ciudad Colon, Costa Rica. TEL 506-2205-9000, FAX 506-2249-1929, http://www.upeace.org.

320 USA ISSN 1554-8597
PEACE ECONOMICS, PEACE SCIENCE AND PUBLIC POLICY (ONLINE). Text in English. 1993. irreg. (2-4/yr). USD 300 to institutions; USD 900 to corporations (effective 2011). back issues avail. **Document type:** *Journal, Academic/Scholarly.* **Description:** Features articles in the context of broad, global issues as well as specific policies and case studies related to conflict resolution and analysis.
Media: Online - full text.
Indexed: B01, B07, CA, ESPM, I02, P34, P42, PAIS, PSA, R02, RiskAb, S02, S03, T02.
—CCC.
Published by: Berkeley Electronic Press, 2809 Telegraph Ave, Ste 202, Berkeley, CA 94705. TEL 510-665-1200, FAX 510-665-1201, info@bepress.com. Eds. Raul Caruso, Walter Israd.

320 USA ISSN 0748-0725
JX1901
PEACEWORK; peace and social justice magazine. Text in English. 1972. m. (11/yr.). USD 23 domestic; USD 25 in Canada & Mexico; USD 40 elsewhere; USD 14 to students (effective 2005). adv. bk.rev. **Document type:** *Newspaper.* **Description:** Promotes global thought and local action for nonviolent social change.
Related titles: Audio cassette/tape ed.; Microform ed.: (from PQC); Online - full text ed.
Indexed: APW, AltPI, P10, P28, P47, P48, P53, P54, PQC.
Published by: American Friends Service Committee, Inc., New England Regional Office, 2161 Massachusetts Ave, Cambridge, MA 02140. TEL 617-661-6130, FAX 617-354-2832. Ed., R&P Patricia Watson. Adv. contact Sara Burke. Circ: 2,500. **Audio cassette subscr. to:** Braille and Talking Book Library, Perkins School for the Blind, 175 N Beacon St, Watertown, MA 02172. TEL 617-924-3434.

320 CAN ISSN 1925-525X
▼ ➤ **PENINSULA**; a journal of relational politics. Text in English. 2011. irreg., latest vol.1, no.1, 2011. free (effective 2011). **Document type:** *Journal, Academic/Scholarly.* **Description:** Explains political theory open to a broad range of methodological, philosophical, and disciplinary perspectives.
Media: Online - full text.
Published by: University of Victoria, Department of Political Science, PO Box 3060, STN CSC, Victoria, BC V8W 3R4, Canada. FAX 250-721-7485, chairpol@uvic.ca, http://web.uvic.ca/polisci/. Eds. Anne-Marie Halle, Liam Mitchell, Sebastien Malette.

324.6 USA
PENNSYLVANIA. DEPARTMENT OF STATE. BUREAU OF ELECTIONS. ELECTION CALENDAR. Text in English. a.
Published by: Department of State, Bureau of Elections, 305 N Office Building, Harrisburg, PA 17120. TEL 717-787-5280.

PENSAMENTO PLURAL. *see* SOCIAL SCIENCES: COMPREHENSIVE WORKS

320 PER ISSN 1027-6769
➤ **PENSAMIENTO CONSTITUCIONAL.** Text in Spanish. 1994. a., latest vol.8, 2001. USD 30 (effective 2003). **Document type:** *Academic/Scholarly.*
Indexed: A01, A26, CA, F03, F04, I04, I05, P42, T02.
Published by: Pontificia Universidad Catolica del Peru, Avenuda Universitaria, Cdra 18 s/n, san Miguel, Lima, 32, Peru. feditor@pucp.edu.pe. Ed. Cesar Landa Arroyo.

➤ **PENSARES Y QUEHACERES**; revista de politicas de la filosofia. *see* PHILOSOPHY

320.5322 FRA ISSN 0031-4773
AP20
LA PENSEE (PARIS). Text in French; Summaries in English. 1939. q. adv. bk.rev. illus. cum.index. reprint service avail. from PSC. **Document type:** *Academic/Scholarly.*
Indexed: A20, A22, CERDIC, CurCont, FR, HistAb, I13, IBSS, MLA-IB, P30, PCI, RASB, RILM, SCOPUS, SSCI, W07.
—IE, Infotrieve, INIST. **CCC.**
Published by: Espaces Marx, 6 Av. Mathurin Moreau, Paris, Cedex 19 75167, France. TEL 33-1-42174510, FAX 33-1-45359204, Espaces_marx@internatif.org, http://www.espaces-marx.eu.org. Ed. Antoine Casanova. Circ: 5,000.

PENSIERO GIURIDICO E POLITICO. NUOVA SERIE. *see* LAW

320.5 ITA ISSN 0031-482X
IL PENSIERO MAZZINIANO. Text in Italian. 1946. m. bk.rev. illus. index. **Document type:** *Magazine, Consumer.*
Related titles: Supplement(s): L' Azione Mazziniana. ISSN 1971-5471.
Published by: Associazione Mazziniana Italiana, Via D Giovanni Verita 33, Modigliana, FC 47015, Italy.

320 ITA ISSN 0031-4846
JA18
IL PENSIERO POLITICO (FLORENCE); rivista di storia delle idee politiche e sociali. Text in Italian. 1968. 3/yr. EUR 130 combined subscription foreign to institutions (print & online eds.) (effective 2012). adv. bk.rev. bibl. reprints avail. **Document type:** *Journal, Academic/Scholarly.*
Related titles: Online - full text ed.: ISSN 2035-7958.
Indexed: A22, AmH&L, CA, DIP, HistAb, I13, IBR, IBSS, IBZ, MLA, MLA-IB, P30, P42, P45, P48, PCI, PQC, RASB, T02.
—BLDSC (6422.640000), IE, Infotrieve, Ingenta.
Published by: Casa Editrice Leo S. Olschki, Viuzzo del Pozzetto 8, Florence, 50126, Italy. TEL 39-055-6530684, FAX 39-055-6530214, celso@olschki.it, http://www.olschki.it. Ed. Vittor Ivo Comparato. Circ: 1,000.

320 ITA ISSN 1971-2375
IL PENSIERO POLITICO (ROME). Text in Italian. 1999. irreg. **Document type:** *Monographic series, Academic/Scholarly.*
Published by: Aracne Editrice, Via Raffaele Garofalo 133 A/B, Rome, 00173, Italy. info@aracneeditrice.it, http://store.aracneeditrice.com.

320 ITA ISSN 1122-0767
IL PENSIERO POLITICO. BIBLIOTECA. Text in Italian. 1969. irreg., latest vol.24, 1999. price varies. **Document type:** *Monographic series, Academic/Scholarly.*
Published by: Casa Editrice Leo S. Olschki, Viuzzo del Pozzetto 8, Florence, 50126, Italy. TEL 39-055-6530684, FAX 39-055-6530214, celso@olschki.it, http://www.olschki.it.

324.2 SYC ISSN 0031-4994
THE PEOPLE. Text in Creoles and Pidgins, English, French. m. USD 5.
Published by: Seychelles People's United Party (SPPF), Victoria St., PO Box 154, Victoria, Mahe, Seychelles. Ed. Jacques Hodoul. Circ: 1,000.

320.5322 USA ISSN 0199-350X
HX1
THE PEOPLE (MOUNTAIN VIEW). Text in English. 1891. bi-m. USD 5; USD 1 per issue (effective 2009). bk.rev. illus. reprints avail. **Document type:** *Newspaper.* **Description:** Marxist analysis and commentary about major socioeconomic developments affecting working people. Resource for labor, politics, economics, and history.
Formerly (until 1979): Weekly People (0043-1885)
Related titles: E-mail ed.; Microfilm ed.: (from PQC); Microform ed.: (from BHP, PQC); Online - full content ed.; Online - full text ed.: ISSN 1938-3495.
Indexed: A22.
Published by: Socialist Labor Party of America, PO Box 218, Mountain View, CA 94042-0218. TEL 408-280-7266, FAX 408-280-6964. Ed., R&P Robert Bills. Circ: 9,300.

320.092 GBR ISSN 0965-7517
PEOPLE IN POWER. Text in English. 1987. bi-m. looseleaf. GBP 365; GBP 50 per month (effective 2009). **Document type:** *Magazine, Trade.* **Description:** Describes the structure of the government and the legislature, details dates of the constitution and elections, lists government ministers, and provides details of embassies to and from the UK and USA for each country.
Related titles: CD-ROM ed.: ISSN 1475-5696; Diskette ed.; E-mail ed.; Online - full text ed.
Published by: C I R C A Ltd., 13-17 Sturton St, Cambridge, CB1 2SN, United Kingdom. TEL 44-1223-568017, FAX 44-1223-354643, info@circaworld.com, http://www.circaworld.com/. Ed. Catherine Jagger.

320 JPN ISSN 0031-5036
THE PEOPLE'S KOREA. Text in English, French, Spanish. 1961. every 2 wks. JPY 12,000, USD 100; USD 2 per issue. adv. bk.rev. charts; illus.; maps; stat. 8 p./no. 4 cols./p.; **Document type:** *Newspaper.* **Description:** Reports political, economic, and social news of North Korea. Also includes coverage of South Korea, issues relating to Koreans in Japan, and cultural events.
Related titles: Microform ed.: (from PQC); Online - full content ed.
Indexed: RASB.
Published by: Choson Shinbo Co., Inc., 2-4 Tsukudo Hachiman-cho, Shinjuku-ku, Tokyo, 162, Japan. TEL 81-3-3260-5881, FAX 83-3-3260-8583. Ed. Ri Sang Pal. Circ: 30,000.

320 USA ISSN 1081-4787
PEOPLE'S TRIBUNE. Text in English. 1974. m. USD 20 to individuals; USD 30 to institutions (effective 2000). bk.rev. illus. **Document type:** *Newspaper.* **Description:** Provides revolutionary commentary on the issues of the day.
Related titles: ◆ English ed.: Tribuno del Pueblo. ISSN 1081-5112.
Address: PO Box 3524, Chicago, IL 60654. TEL 312-486-3551. Ed., R&P Laura Garcia. Circ: 15,000.

322.4 SDN
PEOPLE'S VOICE. Text in English. irreg., latest vol.2, no.7, 1980.
Published by: Tigray People's Liberation Front, Foreign Relations Bureau, P O Box 8177, Khartoum, Sudan.

320.532 USA
PEOPLE'S WEEKLY WORLD (NEW YORK). Text in English. w.
Media: Online - full text.
Published by: Communist Party, U S A, 235 W 23rd St, 7th Fl, New York, NY 10011. TEL 212-989-4994.

320 USA
PEOPLE'S WORLD (NEW YORK). Text in English. 1986. w. (Sat.). adv. bk.rev.; film rev. illus. **Document type:** *Newspaper, Consumer.*
Former titles: People's Weekly World (1076-0091); (until 1990): People's Daily World (1052-2743); Which was formed by the merger of (1968-1986): Daily World (0011-5533); (19??-1986): People's World
Related titles: Online - full text ed.: free (effective 2011).
Indexed: APW, LeftInd, RASB.
Published by: Long View Publishing Co., 3339 S Halsted St, Chicago, IL 60608-6705. TEL 773-446-9920, FAX 773-446-9928, contact@peoplesworld.org. Eds. Joe Sims, Susan Webb, Terrie Albano. Circ: 25,000.

320 TUR ISSN 1300-8641
JZ6.5
PERCEPTIONS/JOURNAL OF INTERNATIONAL AFFAIRS; journal of international affairs. Text in English. 1996. q. **Document type:** *Journal, Academic/Scholarly.*
Related titles: Online - full text ed.: free (effective 2011).
Indexed: CA, LID&ISL, M10, P10, P42, P45, PAIS, PQC, PSA, SociolAb, T02.
Published by: Turkey. Republic of Turkey. Ministry of Foreign Affairs, Center for Strategic Research (SAM), Dr. Sadik Ahmet Cad. No.8 A Blok 12, Balgat, G O P, Ankara, 06100, Turkey. TEL 90-312-2922628, FAX 90-312-2922635, info@mfa.gov.tr, http://www.mfa.gov.tr/default.en.mfa. Ed. Bulent Aras.

320 ITA ISSN 1594-4557
PERCORSI DI CULTURA POLITICA. Variant title: Percorsi. Text in Italian. 2002. bi-m. **Document type:** *Magazine, Consumer.*
Published by: Editoriale Pantheon, Via Alatri 30, Rome, 00171, Italy.

PERIPHERIE; Zeitschrift fuer Politik und Oekonomie in der dritten Welt. *see* BUSINESS AND ECONOMICS—International Development And Assistance

320 FRA ISSN 0031-5478
PERMANENCES; organe de formation civique. Text in French. 1963. 10/yr. bk.rev. **Document type:** *Magazine, Consumer.*
Published by: (Office International Oeuvres Formation Civique), Ichtus - Au Service de la Cite, 49 rue des Renaudes, Paris, 75017, France. TEL 33-01-47637786, http://www.ichtus.fr.

320 330.9 CHL ISSN 0717-3768
PERSPECTIVAS EN POLITICA, ECONOMIA Y GESTION. Text in Spanish. 1997. s-a. CLP 10,000 domestic to individuals; USD 60 foreign to individuals; CLP 15 domestic to institutions; USD 90 foreign to institutions (effective 2004). **Document type:** *Journal, Academic/Scholarly.*
Related titles: Online - full text ed.
Indexed: A01, F03, F04, MLA-IB.
Published by: Universidad de Chile, Departamento de Ingenieria Industrial, Domeyko 2313, 2o piso, Santiago, Chile. TEL 56-2-6784026, leonorh@dii.uchile.cl, epolimen@dii.uchile.cl.

320.9 IND
PERSPECTIVE ON CURRENT AFFAIRS; empowering tomorrow's leaders. Text in English. 1976. s-a. INR 150 per issue (effective 2011). adv. bk.rev. illus. 380 p./no.; back issues avail. **Document type:** *Journal, Academic/Scholarly.* **Description:** Deals with current Indian and international political, economic and military affairs.
Published by: Natraj Publishers, 17 Rajpur Rd, Dehra Dun, Uttar Pradesh 248 001, India. TEL 91-135-2653382, FAX 91-135-2749914, editorial@natrajbooks.co.in.

320 ROM ISSN 1841-6098
▼ ➤ **PERSPECTIVES IN POLITICS.** Text in English, Romanian. 2010. s-a. ROL 40 domestic to institutions; USD 20 foreign to institutions (effective 2011). bk.rev. back issues avail. **Document type:** *Journal, Academic/Scholarly.* **Description:** Covers all aspects of political science and international relations.
Published by: Scoala Nationala de Studii Politice si Administrative/ National School of Political and Administrative Studies, 6-8, Povernei St., Bucharest, Romania. TEL 40-21-3180858, FAX 40-21-3180858, http://www.snspa.ro/. Ed. Andrei Taranu. Pub. Paul Dobrescu. R&P, Adv. contact Alexandru Gabor.

320.57 USA ISSN 1715-7552
PERSPECTIVES ON ANARCHIST THEORY. Text in English. 1997. s-a. **Document type:** *Journal, Academic/Scholarly.* **Description:** Aims to promote critical scholarship that explores social domination and reconstructive visions of a free society.
Indexed: APW.
Published by: Institute for Anarchist Studies, PO Box 15586, Washington, DC 20003. info@anarchiststudies.org. Eds. Lara Messersmith-Glavin, Maia Ramnath, Paul Messersmith-Glavin.

320 ITA ISSN 2036-5438
PERSPECTIVES ON FEDERALISM. Text in Multiple languages. 2008. irreg. **Document type:** *Journal, Academic/Scholarly.*
Media: Online - full text.
Published by: Centro Studi sul Federalismo, Via Real Collegio 30, Moncalieri, TO 10024, Italy. TEL 39-011-6705024, FAX 39-011-6705081, info@csfederalismo.it, http://www.csfederalismo.it.

320 USA ISSN 1045-7097
JA1
➤ **PERSPECTIVES ON POLITICAL SCIENCE.** Text in English. 1990. q. GBP 165 combined subscription in United Kingdom to institutions (print & online eds.); EUR 217, USD 271 combined subscription to institutions (print & online eds.) (effective 2012). adv. bk.rev. back issues avail.; reprint service avail. from PSC. **Document type:** *Journal, Academic/Scholarly.* **Description:** Covers contemporary politics and culture to the enduring questions.
Formed by the merger of (1972-1990): Perspective (0048-3494); (1973-1990): Teaching Political Science (0092-2013)
Related titles: CD-ROM ed.; Microform ed.; Online - full text ed.: ISSN 1930-5478. GBP 149 in United Kingdom to institutions; EUR 196, USD 244 to institutions (effective 2012).
Indexed: A01, A02, A03, A08, A20, A22, A26, ABCPolSci, ABS&EES, APW, AmH&L, B04, B14, BRD, BRI, CA, CBRI, DIP, E02, E03, E06, E07, E08, ERI, EdA, EdI, G08, GSS&RPL, HistAb, I02, I05, I07, I13, IBR, IBZ, M01, M02, M05, M06, P10, P18, P30, P34, P42, P45, P47, P48, P53, P54, PCI, PQC, PSA, PerIslam, R02, RASB, S02, S03, S09, S11, S23, SCOPUS, SociolAb, T02, W03, W04, W05.
—BLDSC (6428.149950), IE, Infotrieve, Ingenta. **CCC.**
Published by: (Helen Dwight Reid Educational Foundation), Routledge (Subsidiary of: Taylor & Francis Group), 325 Chestnut St, Ste 800, Philadelphia, PA 19106. TEL 215-625-8900, FAX 215-625-2940, journals@routledge.com, http://www.routledge.com. Ed. Peter Augustine Lawler.

320 GBR ISSN 1537-5927
JA1
PERSPECTIVES ON POLITICS. Text in English. 2003 (Mar.). q. GBP 436, USD 816 combined subscription to institutions (print & online eds.) (effective 2010). adv. back issues avail.; reprint service avail. from PSC. **Document type:** *Journal, Academic/Scholarly.* **Description:** Aims to connect research findings, conceptual innovations, or theoretical developments to real problems of politics.
Related titles: Online - full text ed.: ISSN 1541-0986. GBP 400, USD 740 to institutions (effective 2010).
Indexed: A22, ABS&EES, CA, CurCont, E01, IBR, IBSS, IBZ, P10, P42, P45, P48, P53, P54, PAIS, PQC, PSA, SCOPUS, SSCI, SociolAb, T02, W07.
—BLDSC (6428.149970), IE, Ingenta. **CCC.**
Published by: (American Political Science Association USA), Cambridge University Press, The Edinburgh Bldg, Shaftesbury Rd, Cambridge, CB2 8RU, United Kingdom. TEL 44-1223-312393, FAX 44-1223-315052, journals@cambridge.org, http://www.cambridge.org/uk. Ed. James d Johnson. R&P Linda Nicol TEL 44-1223-325702. Adv. contact Rebecca Roberts TEL 44-1223-325083. page GBP 590, page USD 950. Circ: 16,000. **Subscr. to:** Cambridge University Press, 32 Ave of the Americas, New York, NY 10013. TEL 212-337-5000, FAX 212-691-3239, journals_subscriptions@cup.org

320 USA
PERSPECTIVES ON SOUTHERN AFRICA. Text in English. 1971. irreg., latest vol.56, 2002. price varies. back issues avail. **Document type:** *Monographic series, Academic/Scholarly.* **Description:** Examines various aspects of the history, politics, culture, and sociology of South Africa.
Published by: University of California Press, Book Series, 2120 Berkeley Way, Berkeley, CA 94704. TEL 510-642-4247, FAX 510-643-7127, foundation@ucpress.edu. **Subscr. to:** California - Princeton Fulfillment Services, Inc., 1445 Lower Ferry Rd, Ewing, NJ 08618. TEL 609-883-1759, 800-777-4726, FAX 800-999-1958, orders@cpfsinc.com.

321.8 DEU ISSN 0939-3013
PERSPEKTIVEN D S; Zeitschrift fuer Gesellschaftsanalyse und Reformpolitik. (Demokratischen Sozialismus) Text in German. 1984. s-a. EUR 16.90; EUR 9.90 newsstand/cover (effective 2011). adv. bk.rev. back issues avail. **Document type:** *Journal, Academic/Scholarly.*
Formerly: P D S (0176-0750)
Indexed: DIP, IBR, IBZ, RASB.
Published by: (Hochschulinitiative Demokratischer Sozialismus), Schueren Verlag GmbH, Universitaetsstr 55, Marburg, 35037, Germany. TEL 49-6421-63084, FAX 49-6421-681190, info@schueren-verlag.de, http://www.schueren-verlag.de. Ed. Roland Popp.

PERU BUSINESS FORECAST REPORT. *see* BUSINESS AND ECONOMICS—Economic Situation And Conditions

320 USA ISSN 1940-6622
JK271
PETERSON'S MASTER A P U.S. GOVERNMENT & POLITICS. (Advanced Placement) Text in English. 2007. biennial. **Document type:** *Guide, Academic/Scholarly.*
Former titles (until 2005): Peterson's A P U.S. Government & Politics; (until 2004): Master the A P Government & Politics Tests
Published by: Peterson's Guides, Box 67005, Lawrenceville, NJ 08648-6105. TEL 609-896-1800, FAX 609-896-4531, custsvc@petersons.com, http://www.petersons.com.

PHILIPPINE JOURNAL OF DEVELOPMENT. *see* BUSINESS AND ECONOMICS

320.9 PHL ISSN 0115-4451
PHILIPPINE POLITICAL SCIENCE JOURNAL. Text in English. 1974. s-a. membership. **Document type:** *Journal, Academic/Scholarly.*
Indexed: BAS, IPP, RASB, SSCI, W07.
Published by: Philippine Political Science Association, Diliman, PO Box 205, UP Post Office, Quezon City, 1101, Philippines. http://www.philpolsci.net/. Circ: 300.

PHILIPPINES BUSNIESS FORECAST REPORT. *see* BUSINESS AND ECONOMICS—Economic Situation And Conditions

PHILIPPINES YEARBOOK OF THE FOOKIEN TIMES. *see* BUSINESS AND ECONOMICS—Banking And Finance

PHILOSOPHIE ET POLITIQUE. *see* PHILOSOPHY

320 USA ISSN 0048-3915
➤ **PHILOSOPHY AND PUBLIC AFFAIRS.** Text in English. 1971. q. GBP 136 in United Kingdom to institutions; EUR 173 in Europe to institutions; USD 181 in the Americas to institutions; USD 265 elsewhere to institutions; GBP 157 combined subscription in United Kingdom to institutions (print & online eds.); EUR 200 combined subscription in Europe to institutions (print & online eds.); USD 208 combined subscription in the Americas to institutions (print & online eds.); USD 306 combined subscription elsewhere to institutions (print & online eds.) (effective 2012). adv. illus. index. back issues avail.; reprint service avail. from PSC. **Document type:** *Monographic series, Academic/Scholarly.* **Description:** It contains philosophical discussions of substantive legal, social and political problems, as well as discussions of the more abstract questions to which these discussions give rise.
Related titles: Microform ed.: (from PQC); Online - full text ed.: ISSN 1088-4963. GBP 136 in United Kingdom to institutions; EUR 173 in Europe to institutions; USD 181 in the Americas to institutions; USD 265 elsewhere to institutions (effective 2012) (from IngentaConnect).
Indexed: A20, A21, A22, A25, A26, ABCPolSci, AC&P, ASCA, AmHI, B04, BRD, C12, CA, CJPI, CurCont, DIP, E01, E08, FR, FutSurv, G08, H07, H08, H09, H10, H14, HAb, HumInd, I05, I13, IBR, IBSS, IBZ, IPARL, IPB, LegCont, MEA&I, P02, P10, P13, P30, P34, P42, P48, P53, P54, PCI, PQC, PSA, PhilInd, R05, RASB, RI-1, RI-2, S02, S03, S08, S09, SCOPUS, SOPODA, SSA, SSCI, SociolAb, T02, W03, W07.
—BLDSC (6464.650000), IE, Infotrieve, Ingenta, INIST. **CCC.**
Published by: Wiley-Blackwell Publishing, Inc. (Subsidiary of: Wiley-Blackwell Publishing Ltd.), 111 River St, Hoboken, NJ 07030. TEL 201-748-6000, FAX 201-748-6088, info@wiley.com, http://www.wiley.com/WileyCDA/. Ed. Alan W Patten. Adv. contact Kristin McCarthy TEL 201-748-7683.

➤ **AN PHOBLACHT/REPUBLICAN NEWS.** *see* GENERAL INTEREST PERIODICALS—Ireland

320.9 PAK ISSN 0031-9651
PICTORIAL NEWS REVIEW. Text in English. 1970. m. PKR 300 domestic; USD 40 foreign; PKR 40 newsstand/cover domestic; USD 3 newsstand/cover foreign (effective 2000). adv. bk.rev. charts; illus. **Document type:** *Newspaper.* **Description:** Highlights political developments in Pakistan and abroad. Includes activities of the diplomatic and consular corps and features on other countries. For executives, parliamentarians, Pakistanis abroad, and foreigners in Pakistan.
Related titles: Microfilm ed.
Published by: Pictorial News Review Publications, Hajji Abdullah Haroon Rd., Victoria Chambers 1, Karachi, 74400, Pakistan. TEL 92-21-5682694, FAX 92-21-5845473, TELEX 23035 PCOKR PK 284. Ed., Pub. Mahmudul Aziz. R&P, Adv. contact Naveedul Aziz. Circ: 5,000.

PISTIL MAGAZINE. *see* WOMEN'S INTERESTS

PITTSBURGH INTERNATIONAL NEWS. *see* ETHNIC INTERESTS

320 BRA ISSN 0103-4138
HC186
PLANEJAMENTO E POLITICAS PUBLICAS. Text in Spanish. 1989. s-a.
Indexed: PAIS.
Published by: Instituto de Pesquisa Economica Aplicada, Av Presidente Antonio Carlos, 51 Andar 13, Centro, Rio De Janeiro, RJ 20020-010, Brazil.

327 303 FRA ISSN 1773-9241
PLANETE PAIX. Text in French. 1978. m. EUR 30 (effective 2010). back issues avail. **Document type:** *Magazine, Consumer.*

P

Former titles (until 2005): Combat pour la Paix, la Paix en Mouvement (1623-4170); (until 1996): La Paix en Mouvement, Combat pour la Paix (0994-1126); (until 1987): Combat pour la Paix (0184-0932); Which was formed by the merger of (1976-1978): Bulletin d'Information du Mouvement de la Paix (0395-3912); (1975-1978): Les Cahiers de Combat Pour la Paix (0335-9395); Which supersedes in part (in 1976): Le Combat Pour la Paix (0045-7450)
Related titles: Online - full text ed.: ISSN 2105-3049. 200?.
Published by: Le Mouvement de la Paix, Maison de la Paix, 9 Rue Dulcie September, Saint-Ouen, 93400, France. TEL 33-1-40120912, FAX 33-1-40115787, national@mvtpaix.org.

320.531 DEU
PLATFORMA SPARTAKUSOWCOW. Text in Polish. q. PLZ 6 (effective 2003). **Document type:** *Newspaper, Consumer.* **Description:** Publication of the Spartakowska Grupa Polski.
Published by: Spartak-Arbeiterpartei Deutschlands, SpAD c/o Verlag Avantgarde, Postfach 52355, Berlin, 10127, Germany.

320 CHL ISSN 0718-655X
PLEYADE. Text in Spanish. 2008. s-a. **Document type:** *Journal, Academic/Scholarly.*
Published by: Centro de Analisis de Investigacion Politica, Vaticano 3778, Los Condes, Santiago, 7550459, Chile. TEL 56-9-85942044, FAX 56-9-77770573, contacto@caip.cl, http://www.caip.cl/. Ed. Jose Parada Flores.

320 CAN ISSN 1499-321X
PLOUGHSHARES MONITOR. Text in English. 1977. q. CAD 25; USD 25 in United States; USD 30 elsewhere (effective 2002). bk.rev. **Description:** Provides information on disarmament, militarism, global security, Canadian military production and exports, regional conflicts and alternatives to Canadian security policies.
Former titles (until 2001): Monitor (1700-1536); (until 1998): Ploughshares Monitor (0703-1866)
Related titles: Online - full text ed.
Indexed: C03, CBCARef, CPerI, G06, G07, G08, HRIR, I02, I05, P42, P48, PQC, PRA.
Published by: Institute of Peace and Conflict Studies, Project Ploughshares, Conrad Grebel College, Waterloo, ON N2L 3G6, Canada. TEL 519-888-6541, FAX 519-885-0806. Ed. Ernie Regehr. Circ: 7,000.

POLAND BUSINESS FORECAST REPORT. *see* BUSINESS AND ECONOMICS—Economic Situation And Conditions

306.2 FRA ISSN 1262-1676
D2009
POLE SUD; revue de science politique de l'Europe Meridionale. Text in French. 1994. s-a. EUR 42 for 2 yrs. to individuals; EUR 46 for 2 yrs. to institutions; EUR 31 for 2 yrs. to students (effective 2003). **Document type:** *Journal, Academic/Scholarly.* **Description:** Political analyses on France and Europe with a particular emphasis on the relations between the Mediterranean regions and the rest of Europe.
Indexed: CA, DIP, FR, IBR, IBSS, IBZ, P42, PSA, SCOPUS, SociolAb, T02.
—INIST.
Published by: Centre Comparatif d'Etudes sur les Politiques Publiques et les Espaces Locaux (C E P E L), Faculte de Droit, 39 rue de l'Universite, Montpellier, cedex 1, France. TEL 33-4-67614654, 33-4-67615460, FAX 33-4-67615482, cepel@sc.univ-montp1.fr. Ed. Mohammad-Said Darviche. **Co-publisher:** Observatoire des Politiques Publiques en Europe du Sud (O P P E S).

POLEMIC; an independent journal of law and society. *see* LAW

POLEMICA; revista centroamericana de ciencias sociales. *see* SOCIAL SCIENCES: COMPREHENSIVE WORKS

320 CRI ISSN 1018-0664
POLEMICA. Text in Spanish. 1981. 3/yr.
Indexed: C01, HRIR, RASB.
Published by: Instituto Centroamericano de Documentacion e Investigaciones Sociales, Icadis, Apdo 174, Sabanilla, San Jose 2070, Costa Rica. **Subscr. to:** Secy. Gen. de FLASCO, c/o Secy. Gen. de FLASCO, Apartado Postal 5429, San Jose 1000, Costa Rica.

306.2 355 HRV ISSN 1331-5595
POLEMOS; casopis za interdisciplinarna istrazivanja rata i mira. Text in Serbo-Croatian. 1998. s-a. HRK 80 domestic; USD 25 foreign (effective 2004). **Document type:** *Journal, Academic/Scholarly.* **Description:** Covers various aspects of security studies, the study of war, and of the military in its sociological, psychological, anthropological, philosophical, economical, demographic, medical, political science, and military history perspectives.
Indexed: CA, P42, PSA, S02, S03, SCOPUS, SociolAb, T02.
Published by: (Sociolosko Drustvo Hrvatske/Croatian Sociological Association), Naklada Jesenski i Turk/Jesenski & Turk Publishing House, Sokolgradska 58, Zagreb, 10000, Croatia. TEL 385-1-3845048, FAX 385-1-3845049, naklada@jesenski-turk.hr, http://www.jesenski-turk.hr. Ed. Ozren Zunec.

320 340 ITA ISSN 2035-5262
POLEMOS. Text in Italian. 2007. s-a. **Document type:** *Journal, Consumer.*
Related titles: Online - full text ed.: ISSN 2036-4601.
Published by: G Giappichelli Editore, Via Po 21, Turin, Italy. TEL 39-011-8153111, FAX 39-011-8125100.

320 ITA ISSN 1724-4625
POLENA; rivista italiana di analisi elettorale. (POLitical and Electoral NAvigations) Text in Italian. 2004. 3/yr. EUR 41 domestic to individuals; EUR 51 domestic to institutions; EUR 61 foreign (effective 2008). **Document type:** *Magazine, Consumer.*
Related titles: Online - full text ed.: ISSN 1827-8930. 2004.
Published by: Carocci Editore, Via Sardegna 50, Rome, 00187, Italy. TEL 39-06-42818417, FAX 39-06-42747931, clienti@carocci.it, http://www.carocci.it.

320.6 USA ISSN 1069-8124
H96
POLICY ANALYSIS (WASHINGTON). Text in English. 1980. irreg., latest vol.644, 2010. price varies. back issues avail. **Document type:** *Monographic series, Academic/Scholarly.*
Related titles: Online - full text ed.: ISSN 1936-363X.
—CCC.
Published by: Cato Institute, 1000 Massachusetts Ave, NW, Washington, DC 20001. TEL 202-842-0200, FAX 202-842-3490, subscriptions@cato.org.

320.6 NLD ISSN 1879-6745
▼ **POLICY AND MANAGEMENT INSIGHTS.** Text in English. 2009. irreg., latest vol.2, 2011.
Formerly (until 2011): Policy and Practice Insights
Related titles: Online - full text ed.: ISSN 1879-6753; ◆ Portuguese Translation: Politicas e Gestao em Analise. ISSN 2211-4696; ◆ French Translation: Apercus des Politiques et Pratiques. ISSN 1879-8152.
Published by: European Centre for Development Policy Management/ Centre Europeen de Gestion de Politiques de Developpement, Onze Lieve Vrouweplein 21, Maastricht, 6211 HE, Netherlands. TEL 31-43-3502900, FAX 31-43-3502902, info@ecdpm.org, http://www.ecdpm.org.

320.6 GBR ISSN 0305-5736
JS40
➤ **POLICY AND POLITICS**; an international journal. Text in English; Abstracts in French, Spanish. 1972. q. GBP 423, EUR 560 combined subscription in Europe to institutions (print & online eds.); USD 741 combined subscription in the Americas to institutions (print & online eds.); GBP 452 combined subscription elsewhere to institutions (print & online eds.) (effective 2012). adv. bk.rev. abstr. back issues avail.; reprint service avail. from SCH. **Document type:** *Journal, Academic/ Scholarly.* **Description:** Provides insight into the origins, implementation and impact of public policy.
Related titles: Online - full text ed.: ISSN 1470-8442. EUR 504 in Europe to institutions; USD 629 in the Americas to institutions; GBP 359 worldwide to institutions (effective 2011) (from IngentaConnect).
Indexed: A20, A22, ABCPolSci, ASCA, AmHI, BrHumI, CA, CurCont, DIP, ELLIS, FamI, GEOBASE, H07, I13, IBR, IBSS, IBZ, MEA&I, P30, P34, P42, PAIS, PCI, PSA, S02, S03, S21, SCOPUS, SOPODA, SPAA, SSA, SSCI, SUSA, SWR&A, SociolAb, T02, W07.
—BLDSC (6543.322000), IE, Infotrieve, Ingenta. **CCC.**
Published by: (School for Policy Studies), The Policy Press, University of Bristol, 4th Fl, Beacon House, Queen's Rd, Bristol, BS8 1QU, United Kingdom. TEL 44-117-3314054, FAX 44-117-3314093, tpp-info@bristol.ac.uk, http://www.policypress.org.uk. Eds. Geetanjali Gangoli, Tony Fitzpatrick. **Subscr. to:** Portland Customer Services, Commerce Way, Colchester CO2 8HP, United Kingdom. TEL 44-1206-796351, FAX 44-1206-799331, sales@portland-services.com, http://www.portland-services.com.

320 NLD ISSN 1449-4035
DU117.17
➤ **POLICY & SOCIETY.** Text in English. 1981. s-a. EUR 188 in Europe to institutions; JPY 30,800 in Japan to institutions; USD 291 elsewhere to institutions (effective 2012). **Document type:** *Journal, Academic/ Scholarly.* **Description:** An interdisciplinary journal of comparative public policy, comparing domestic and international public policy and the social, political, and economic conditions and forces that shape them. The focus is on policy substance and process rather than on the methodologies of comparison.
Formerly (until 2003): Policy, Organisation and Society (1034-9952)
Related titles: Online - full text ed.: (from ScienceDirect).
Indexed: AusPAIS, CA, P42, PAIS, PCI, PSA, RiskAb, SCOPUS, SSciA, SociolAb, T02.
—IE. **CCC.**
Published by: (National University of Singapore SGP), Elsevier BV (Subsidiary of: Elsevier Science & Technology), Radarweg 29, PO Box 211, Amsterdam, 1000 AE, Netherlands. TEL 31-20-4853911, FAX 31-20-4852457, JournalsCustomerServiceEMEA@elsevier.com, http://www.elsevier.nl. Eds. D S L Jarvis, Giliberto Capano, M Ramesh. Circ: 82 (paid).

320.6 USA
➤ **POLICY FORUM.** Text in English. 1988. q. free (effective 2011). back issues avail. **Document type:** *Journal, Academic/Scholarly.* **Description:** Analysis of current policy issues.
Related titles: Online - full text ed.
Published by: University of Illinois at Urbana-Champaign, Institute of Government and Public Affairs, 1007 W Nevada St, Urbana, IL 61801. TEL 217-333-3340, 866-794-3340, FAX 217-244-4817, skoenema@vivc.edu.

➤ **POLICY MANAGEMENT BRIEF.** *see* BUSINESS AND ECONOMICS—International Development And Assistance

320.6 CAN ISSN 0226-5893
CODEN: POOPFB
POLICY OPTIONS. Text in English. 1979. 10/yr. CAD 47.60 domestic; CAD 67.60 in United States; CAD 87.60 elsewhere (effective 2011). adv. bk.rev. illus. back issues avail.; reprints avail. **Document type:** *Magazine, Consumer.* **Description:** Provides a forum for views on Canadian public policy.
Related titles: Online - full text ed.: ISSN 1910-9741. 1997. free (effective 2010); French ed.: Options Politiques. ISSN 1912-0052.
Indexed: C03, CBCARef, CBPI, CPerI, I05, P48, PAIS, PQC.
—BLDSC (6543.326650), IE, Ingenta. **CCC.**
Published by: Institute for Research on Public Policy/Institut de Recherches Politiques, 1470 Peel St, Ste 200, Montreal, PQ H3A 1T1, Canada. TEL 514-985-2461, FAX 514-985-2559, irrp@irrp.org. Ed. L Ian MacDonald. adv.: color page CAD 2,500; 7.125 x 9.5. Circ: 3,000.

320.6 NZL ISSN 1176-8797
POLICY QUARTERLY. Text in English. 1986. q. **Document type:** *Journal, Academic/Scholarly.*
Former titles (until 2005): I P S Policy Newsletter (1175-1975); (until 1998): Institute of Policy Studies. Newsletter (0113-4086)
Related titles: Online - full text ed.: ISSN 1176-4325. 2005. free.
Published by: Victoria University of Wellington, Institute of Policy Studies, PO Box 600, Wellington, New Zealand. TEL 64-4-4635307, FAX 64-4-4637413, ips@vuw.ac.nz. Ed. Jonathan Boston.

320 USA ISSN 1933-5296
POLICY REPORT (WASHINGTON, D.C.). Text in English. 1989. irreg. **Document type:** *Monographic series, Consumer.*
Published by: Progressive Policy Institute, 600 Pennsylvania Ave SE, Ste 400, Washington, DC 20003. TEL 202-547-0001, FAX 202-544-5014, http://www.ppionline.org.

320 CAN ISSN 1487-7090
POLICY RESEARCH INITIATIVE. HORIZONS. Text in English, French. 1998. irreg. **Document type:** *Journal, Academic/Scholarly.*
Related titles: Online - full text ed.: free (effective 2011).
Indexed: A39, C27, C29, D03, D04, E13, R14, S14, S15, S18.
—CCC.
Published by: Policy Research Initiative, 56 Sparks St, 1st Fl, Ottawa, ON K1P 5A9, Canada. TEL 613-947-1956, FAX 613-995-6006.

320 USA ISSN 0146-5945
H1
➤ **POLICY REVIEW.** Text in English. 1977. bi-m. USD 36; USD 6 per issue (effective 2010). adv. bk.rev. bibl.; charts; illus. index. back issues avail.; reprints avail. **Document type:** *Journal, Academic/ Scholarly.*
Related titles: Online - full text ed.
Indexed: A01, A02, A03, A08, A12, A20, A21, A22, A26, ABCPolSci, ABIn, ABS&EES, APW, ARG, ASCA, B01, B04, B07, BRD, C12, CA, CBRI, CCR, CurCont, E02, E03, E07, E08, ERI, EconLit, EdA, EdI, EnvAb, EnvInd, FamI, FutSurv, G08, H09, HRIR, I05, I07, I13, IPARL, IPP, ISAP, JEL, KES, L03, LID&ISL, M01, M02, M05, M06, MEA&I, MagInd, P02, P10, P13, P18, P30, P34, P42, P45, P47, P48, P51, P53, P54, PAIS, PCI, PQC, PSA, PerIslam, R03, R05, RASB, RGAb, RGPR, RI-1, RI-2, S02, S03, S05, S09, S11, S23, SCOPUS, SOPODA, SSAI, SSAb, SSCI, SSI, SociolAb, T02, UAA, W03, W05, W07.
—BLDSC (6543.327850), IE, Infotrieve, Ingenta.
Published by: Hoover Institution, 434 Galvez Mall, Stanford University, Stanford, CA 94305. TEL 650-723-1754, FAX 650-723-8611, schieron@stanford.edu. Ed. Tod Lindberg. Adv. contact Sharon Ragland TEL 202-466-3121. **Subscr. to:** PO Box 37005, Chicago, IL 60615. TEL 773-753-3347, 877-705-1878, hoover@press.uchicago.edu.

320 USA ISSN 0032-2687
H1
➤ **POLICY SCIENCES**; an international journal devoted to the improvement of policy making. Text in Dutch. 1970. q. EUR 716, USD 729 combined subscription to institutions (print & online eds.) (effective 2012). adv. bk.rev. illus. Index. back issues avail.; reprint service avail. from PSC. **Document type:** *Journal, Academic/ Scholarly.* **Description:** Features articles that examine the normative aspects of policy sciences; conceptual articles addressing concrete policy issues; articles on particularly controversial pieces of analysis; opposing perspectives, including critiques and rejoinders on articles already published.
Related titles: Microform ed.: (from PQC); Online - full text ed.: ISSN 1573-0891 (from IngentaConnect).
Indexed: A01, A02, A03, A08, A12, A13, A17, A20, A22, A26, ABCPolSci, ABIn, ASCA, B01, B06, B07, B08, B09, BibLing, C12, CA, CPM, CurCont, DIP, E01, E08, EAA, EI, EIA, EIP, ESPM, EconLit, EnerInd, FutSurv, G08, GEOBASE, HPNRM, I05, I13, IAOP, IBR, IBSS, IBZ, Inspec, JEL, MCR, MEA&I, P02, P10, P30, P34, P42, P45, P47, P48, P51, P53, P54, PAA&I, PAIS, PCI, PQC, PRA, PSA, RASB, RiskAb, S02, S03, S09, S11, SCIMP, SCOPUS, SOPODA, SPAA, SSA, SSCI, SSciA, SUSA, SociolAb, T02, UAA, W07.
—BLDSC (6543.328000), IE, Infotrieve, Ingenta, INIST. **CCC.**
Published by: Springer New York LLC (Subsidiary of: Springer Science+Business Media), 233 Spring St, New York, NY 10013. TEL 212-460-1500, FAX 212-460-1575, service-ny@springer.com. Ed. Toddl Steelman. **Subscr. to:** Journal Fulfillment, PO Box 2485, Secaucus, NJ 07096. TEL 201-348-4033, FAX 201-348-4505, journals-ny@springer.com.

320 GBR ISSN 0144-2872
H96
➤ **POLICY STUDIES.** Text in English. 1976. 5/yr. GBP 751 combined subscription in United Kingdom to institutions (print & online eds.); EUR 992, USD 1,242 combined subscription to institutions (print & online eds.) (effective 2012). adv. back issues avail.; reprint service avail. from PSC. **Document type:** *Journal, Academic/Scholarly.* **Description:** Focuses on the policy implications of research and the analysis of developments in social policy and professional practice.
Related titles: Online - full text ed.: ISSN 1470-1006. GBP 676 in United Kingdom to institutions; EUR 893, USD 1,118 to institutions (effective 2012) (from IngentaConnect).
Indexed: A01, A03, A08, A12, A17, A22, ABIn, B01, B06, B07, B08, B09, B21, CA, CJPI, CPM, CurCont, E01, E17, ESPM, EconLit, H05, I13, IBSS, ILD, JEL, KES, MEA&I, P34, P42, P48, P51, P53, P54, PAIS, PCI, PQC, PSA, S02, S03, SCOPUS, SSA, SSCI, SociolAb, T02, W07.
—IE, Infotrieve, Ingenta. **CCC.**
Published by: (Policy Studies Institute), Routledge (Subsidiary of: Taylor & Francis Group), 4 Park Sq, Milton Park, Abingdon, Oxon OX14 4RN, United Kingdom. TEL 44-20-70176000, FAX 44-20-70176336, subscriptions@tandf.co.uk, http://www.routledge.com. Ed. Dr. Mark Evans. Adv. contact Linda Hann TEL 44-1344-779945. **Subscr. to:** Taylor & Francis Ltd., Journals Customer Service, Sheepen Pl, Colchester, Essex CO3 3LP, United Kingdom. TEL 44-20-70175544, FAX 44-20-70175198, tf.enquiries@tfinforma.com.

320 USA ISSN 0190-292X
H1
➤ **POLICY STUDIES JOURNAL.** Text in English. 1972. q. GBP 1,071 in United Kingdom to institutions; EUR 1,361 in Europe to institutions; USD 1,457 in the Americas to institutions; USD 2,099 elsewhere to institutions; GBP 1,232 combined subscription in United Kingdom to institutions (print & online eds.); EUR 1,566 combined subscription in Europe to institutions (print & online eds.); USD 1,676 combined subscription in the Americas to institutions (print & online eds.); USD 2,414 combined subscription elsewhere to institutions (print & online eds.) (effective 2011). bk.rev. illus. Index. reprint service avail. from PSC. **Document type:** *Journal, Academic/Scholarly.* **Description:** Covers the application of political science and social science to important public policy problems.
Related titles: Microform ed.; Online - full text ed.: ISSN 1541-0072. GBP 1,071 in United Kingdom to institutions; EUR 1,361 in Europe to institutions; USD 1,457 in the Americas to institutions; USD 2,099 elsewhere to institutions (effective 2011) (from IngentaConnect).
Indexed: A01, A02, A03, A08, A12, A20, A22, A25, A26, A36, ABCPolSci, ABIn, ABS&EES, AC&P, ASCA, Agr, AmH&L, B01, B04, B06, B07, B09, BRD, CA, CABA, CBRI, CJA, CJPI, CurCont, DIP, E01, E08, E12, EAA, EI, ESPM, EconLit, EnvAb, F08, F12, FamI, FutSurv, G08, GEOBASE, GH, H05, HRA, HRIS, HistAb, I05, I11, I13, I14, IBR, IBZ, LT, M06, MEA&I, N02, P02, P06, P10, P13, P27, P30, P34, P42, P45, P47, P48, P51, P53, P54, PAA&I, PAIS, PCI, PQC, PRA, PSA, PersLit, RASB, RiskAb, S02, S03, S08, S09, S11, S13, S16, S21, S23, SCOPUS, SOPODA, SPAA, SSA, SSAI, SSAb, SSCI, SSI, SUSA, SociolAb, T02, TelAb, W01, W02, W03, W05, W07, W11.
—BLDSC (6543.329100), IE, Infotrieve, Ingenta. **CCC.**

Published by: (Policy Studies Organization), Wiley-Blackwell Publishing, Inc. (Subsidiary of: Wiley-Blackwell Publishing Ltd.), 111 River St, Hoboken, NJ 07030. TEL 201-748-6000, FAX 201-748-6088, info@wiley.com, http://www.wiley.com/WileyCDA/. Eds. Chris Weible, Peter deLeon. Adv. contact Kristin McCarthy TEL 201-748-7683.
Co-sponsor: American Political Science Association.

320 USA ISSN 1557-833X
POLICY TODAY; a principled approach to practical politics. Text in English. 2004. s-m. adv. **Document type:** *Magazine, Consumer.*
Media: Online - full text.
Published by: Qiosk.com Corp. http://www.policytoday.com/index.php. adv.: color page USD 3,500; 10.5 x 7.1.

320 MEX ISSN 1870-2333
HN111
POLIS; investigacion y analisis sociopolitico y psicosocial. Text in Spanish. 1990. s-a. MXN 100; MXN 50 newsstand/cover (effective 2010). back issues avail. **Document type:** *Journal, Academic/Scholarly.*
Related titles: Online - full text ed.
Indexed: C01.
Published by: Universidad Autonoma Metropolitana - Iztapalapa, Division de Ciencias Sociales y Humanidades. Departamento de Antropologia, Ave San Rafael Atlixco # 186, Col Vicentina, Del Iztapalapa, Mexico City, 09340, Mexico. TEL 52-55-7724-4760, cedit@xanum.uam.mx, http://www.iztapalapa.uam.mx/.

320 ITA ISSN 1120-9488
HN471 CODEN: POLBEL
POLIS; ricerche e studi su societa e politica in Italia. Text in Italian. 1987. 3/yr. EUR 49 domestic to individuals; EUR 85 foreign to individuals (effective 2006); EUR 96 combined subscription domestic to institutions (print & online eds.); EUR 139.50 combined subscription foreign to institutions (print & online eds.) (effective 2009). adv. back issues avail. **Document type:** *Journal, Academic/Scholarly.*
Related titles: Online - full text ed.
Indexed: CA, I13, IBR, IBZ, P42, PSA, S02, S03, SOPODA, SSA, SociolAb, T02.
—BLDSC (6543.503000).
Published by: (Istituto Carlo Cattaneo), Societa Editrice Il Mulino, Strada Maggiore 37, Bologna, 40125, Italy. TEL 39-051-256011, FAX 39-051-256034, riviste@mulino.it. Ed. Asher Colombo.

320.011 GBR ISSN 0142-257X
JC73
➤ **POLIS.** Variant title: Polis - The Journal of the Society for Greek Politics. Text in English. 19??. s-a. GBP 63, USD 126 combined subscription to institutions (print & online eds.) (effective 2009). bk.rev. abstr. back issues avail. **Document type:** *Journal, Academic/Scholarly.* **Description:** Publishes material of interest to those who study ancient Greek political thought,whether they do so as classicists, ancient historians, philosophers, political scientists or whatever. Covers political thinking at all levels, and thus the study of political institutions and practices, history, and literature are all included.
Formerly (until 1977): Political Studies Association. Study Group in Greek Political Thought. Newsletter
Related titles: Online - full text ed.: (from IngentaConnect).
Indexed: A20, A22, ArtHuCI, BrHumI, CA, E01, P42, PCI, T02, W07.
—BLDSC (6543.507000), IE, Ingenta. **CCC.**
Published by: Imprint Academic, PO Box 200, Exeter, Devon EXS 5YX, United Kingdom. TEL 44-1392-851550, FAX 44-1392-851178. Ed. Kyriakos Demetriou. Pub. Mr. Keith Sutherland.

322.42 RUS ISSN 1026-9487
POLIS; politicheskie issledovaniya. Text in Russian. 1971. bi-m. USD 95 in United States.
Formerly (until 1991): Rabochii Klass i Sovremennyi Mir (0321-2017)
Related titles: Online - full text ed.: ISSN 1684-0070.
Indexed: CA, I13, IBSS, P42, T02.
—East View.
Published by: Izdatel'skaya Gruppa Progress, Ul Entuziastov 15, k 48, Moscow, 111024, Russian Federation. TEL 7-095-2731438. **Dist. by:** East View Information Services, 10601 Wayzata Blvd, Minneapolis, MN 55305. TEL 952-252-1201, 800-477-1005, FAX 952-252-1202, info@eastview.com, http://www.eastview.com.

320 POL ISSN 0208-7375
HM7
POLISH POLITICAL SCIENCE. Text in English. 1967. a. price varies. **Document type:** *Yearbook, Academic/Scholarly.* **Description:** Basic problems of political theory, political organization and functioning of society.
Formerly (until 1981): Polish Round Table (0079-3000)
Indexed: I13, IBR, IBZ, RASB.
Published by: (Polskie Towarzystwo Nauk Politycznych), Wydawnictwo Adam Marszalek, ul Lubicka 44, Torun, 87100, Poland. TEL 48-56-6485070, FAX 48-56-6608160, info@marszalek.com.pl, http://www.marszalek.com.pl. Ed. Teresa Sasinska-Klas. Circ: 700.

POLIT; a journal of literature and politics. *see* LITERATURE

320 SGP ISSN 0217-7587
POLITEIA. Text in English. 1971. a. SGD 2.50. adv. bk.rev.
Formerly: University of Singapore Political Science Society. Journal
Indexed: ISAP.
Published by: National University of Singapore, Political Science Society, c/o Department of Political Science, Kent Ridge, Singapore, 0511, Singapore. Ed. Leong Sook Mei. Circ: 2,000.

320 ZAF ISSN 0256-8845
JA26
POLITEIA. Text in English. 1982. 3/yr. ZAR 90 domestic to individuals; USD 40 foreign to individuals; ZAR 120 domestic to institutions; USD 100 foreign to institutions (effective 2006). bk.rev. back issues avail.; reprint service avail. from PSC. **Document type:** *Journal, Academic/Scholarly.* **Description:** Articles on political science, public administration, municipal government and administration, international politics and strategic studies.
Related titles: Online - full text ed.
Indexed: ASD, CA, I13, IIBP, ISAP, P42, PCI, PSA, SCOPUS, SociolAb, T02.
Published by: (University of South Africa), UniSA Press, PO Box 392, Pretoria, 0003, South Africa. TEL 27-12-4292953, FAX 27-12-4293449, unisa-press@unisa.ac.za, http://www.unisa.ac.za/press. Ed. C J Auriacombe. Circ: 2,400.

320 VEN ISSN 0303-9757
JA5
➤ **POLITEIA.** Text in Spanish. 1972. s-a. VEB 60 domestic; USD 28 foreign (effective 2008). bk.rev. **Document type:** *Journal, Academic/Scholarly.* **Description:** Covers research and theories in the political sciences at the national and international levels.
Related titles: Online - full text ed.
Indexed: C01, ECI, H21, I13, P08.
Published by: (Instituto de Estudios Politicos), Universidad Central de Venezuela, Facultad de Ciencias Juridicas y Politicas, Ciudad Universitaria, Los Chaguaramos, Caracas, DF 1040, Venezuela. TEL 58-2-126052382, FAX 58-2-126052382, politeia_iep@yahoo.com, http://150.185.70.3:8080/FCJP_UCV/index.jsp. Ed. Geraldine Leon. Circ: 1,000 (paid and controlled).

320.5 RUS
POLITEKONOM. Text in Russian. q. USD 65 in United States.
Indexed: RASB.
Published by: Nekommercheskoe Partnerstvo Politekonom, Ul Novocheremushkinskaya 46, Moscow, 117036, Russian Federation. TEL 7-095-9784633, FAX 7-095-1202170. **Dist. by:** East View Information Services, 10601 Wayzata Blvd, Minneapolis, MN 55305. TEL 952-252-1201, 800-477-1005, FAX 952-252-1202, info@eastview.com, http://www.eastview.com.

631 CHE ISSN 1661-4771
POLITFOCUS AGRARPOLITIK. Text in German. 2004. bi-m. CHF 480 (effective 2007). **Document type:** *Journal, Trade.*
Published by: Ecopolitics GmbH, Schuetzengaesschen 5, Postfach 288, Bern 7, 3000, Switzerland. TEL 41-31-3133434, FAX 41-31-3133435, http://www.ecopolitics.ch.

371 CHE ISSN 1661-4801
POLITFOCUS BILDUNGSPOLITIK. Text in German. 2003. bi-m. CHF 480 (effective 2007). **Document type:** *Journal, Trade.*
Published by: Ecopolitics GmbH, Schuetzengaesschen 5, Postfach 288, Bern 7, 3000, Switzerland. TEL 41-31-3133434, FAX 41-31-3133435, http://www.ecopolitics.ch.

614 CHE ISSN 1661-481X
POLITFOCUS GESUNDHEITSPOLITIK. Text in German. 2003. bi-m. CHF 480 (effective 2007). **Document type:** *Journal, Trade.*
Published by: Ecopolitics GmbH, Schuetzengaesschen 5, Postfach 288, Bern 7, 3000, Switzerland. TEL 41-31-3133434, FAX 41-31-3133435, http://www.ecopolitics.ch.

361 CHE ISSN 1661-5549
POLITFOCUS SOZIALPOLITIK. Text in German. 2006. bi-m. CHF 480 (effective 2007). **Document type:** *Journal, Trade.*
Published by: Ecopolitics GmbH, Schuetzengaesschen 5, Postfach 288, Bern 7, 3000, Switzerland. TEL 41-31-3133434, FAX 41-31-3133435, http://www.ecopolitics.ch.

179.3 CHE ISSN 1661-4828
POLITFOCUS TIERSCHUTZPOLITIK. Text in German. 2003. bi-m. CHF 480 (effective 2007). **Document type:** *Journal, Trade.*
Published by: Ecopolitics GmbH, Schuetzengaesschen 5, Postfach 288, Bern 7, 3000, Switzerland. TEL 41-31-3133434, FAX 41-31-3133435, http://www.ecopolitics.ch.

502 CHE ISSN 1661-4836
POLITFOCUS UMWELTPOLITIK. Text in German. 2005. bi-m. CHF 480 (effective 2007). **Document type:** *Journal, Trade.*
Related titles: French ed.: Politfocus Politique Environmentale. ISSN 1661-5557. 2006.
Published by: Ecopolitics GmbH, Schuetzengaesschen 5, Postfach 288, Bern 7, 3000, Switzerland. TEL 41-31-3133434, FAX 41-31-3133435, http://www.ecopolitics.ch.

330 CHE ISSN 1661-5530
POLITFOCUS WIRTSCHAFTSPOLITIK. Text in German. 2006. bi-m. CHF 480 (effective 2007). **Document type:** *Journal, Trade.*
Published by: Ecopolitics GmbH, Schuetzengaesschen 5, Postfach 288, Bern 7, 3000, Switzerland. TEL 41-31-3133434, FAX 41-31-3133435, http://www.ecopolitics.ch.

320 DNK ISSN 0105-0710
JA26
➤ **POLITICA**; tidsskrift for politisk videnskab. Text in Danish; Text occasionally in English. 1968. 4/yr. DKK 300 to individuals; DKK 500 to institutions; DKK 225 to students (effective 2011). bk.rev. back issues avail. **Document type:** *Journal, Academic/Scholarly.*
Indexed: A22, CA, I13, IBSS, P42, PCI, T02.
—IE, Infotrieve.
Published by: (Aarhus Universitet, Institut for Statskundskab/University of Aarhus, Department of Political Science, Politica), Syddansk Universitetsforlag/University Press of Southern Denmark, Campusvej 55, Odense M, 5230, Denmark. TEL 45-66-157999, FAX 45-66-158126, press@forlag.sdu.dk, http://www.universitypress.dk. Ed. Anne Skorkjaer Binderkrantz. Circ: 500.

320 DEU ISSN 1435-6643
POLITICA; Schriftenreihe zur politischen Wissenschaft. Text in German. 1991. irreg., latest vol.78, 2010. price varies. **Document type:** *Monographic series, Academic/Scholarly.*
Published by: Verlag Dr. Kovac, Leverkusenstr 13, Hamburg, 22761, Germany. TEL 49-40-3988800, FAX 49-40-39888055, info@verlagdrkovac.de.

320 URY ISSN 0079-3027
POLITICA. Text in Spanish. irreg.
Published by: Editorial Arca, Colonia, 1263, Montevideo, 11107, Uruguay.

320 CHL ISSN 0716-1077
POLITICA. Text in Spanish. 1982. s-a. CLP 8,000 domestic; USD 50 foreign (effective 2010). bk.rev. back issues avail. **Document type:** *Journal, Academic/Scholarly.*
Related titles: Online - full text ed.
Indexed: IBR, IBZ, PAIS.
Published by: Universidad de Chile, Instituto de Asuntos Publicos, Santa Lucia 240, Santiago, Chile. TEL 56-2-9771502, FAX 56-2-6648536, dp_cpoli@uchile.cl, http://www.cien-politica.uchile.cl. Ed. Bernardino Bravo Lira. Circ: 300.

320 BRA
POLITICA. Text in Portuguese. 1976. q. BRL 50. bk.rev.
Published by: Fundacao Milton Campos para Pesquisas e Estudos Politicos, Camara dos Deputados, Edificio do Congresso Nacional, Brasilia, DF 70160, Brazil. Ed. Walter Costa Porto. Circ: 5,000.

320 ITA ISSN 1973-9028
POLITICA E STORIA. Text in Italian. 2002. irreg. **Document type:** *Monographic series, Academic/Scholarly.*
Published by: Universita degli Studi di Roma "La Sapienza", Dipartimento di Studi Politici, 5 Piazzale Aldo Moro, Rome, 00185, Italy. TEL 39-06-49911, http://www.uniroma1.it.

320 330 ARG ISSN 1851-6025
POLITICA, ECONOMIA Y SOCIEDAD. Text in Spanish. 1995. irreg.
Published by: Universidad Nacional de Quilmes, Avda. Rivadavia, 2358 Piso 6, Buenos Aires, 1034, Argentina. TEL 54-11-43657100, FAX 54-11-43657101, info@unq.edu.arg, http://www.unq.edu.ar/.

320 ROM ISSN 1453-4657
POLITICA EXTERNA/FOREIGN POLICY. Text in Romanian. 1996. q.
Published by: Societatea Academica din Romania/Romanian Academic Society, Str. Petofi Sandor 15, Bucuresti 1, Romania. FAX 401-222-18-68, sar@starnets.ro.

320 FRA ISSN 1143-4562
POLITICA HERMETICA. Text in French. 1987. a. adv. bk.rev. **Document type:** *Academic/Scholarly.*
Published by: Editions l'Age d'Homme, 5 rue Ferou, Paris, 75006, France. TEL 33-1-55427979, FAX 33-1-40517102, lagedhomme@orange.fr, http://www.lagedhomme.com. Ed. Jean Pierre Brach. Adv. contact Jean Pierre Laurant. **Dist. by:** Editions Les Belles Lettres, 25 Rue du General Leclerc, Kremlin Bicetre 94270, France. TEL 33-1-45151970, FAX 33-1-45151980.

320 BRA
POLITICA HOJE. Text in Portuguese. 1994. s-a. **Document type:** *Academic/Scholarly.*
Published by: Universidade Federal de Pernambuco, Mestrado em Ciencia Politica, Cidade Universitaria Varzea, Recife, PE 50740530, Brazil. TEL 55-81-2718283. Ed. Marcos Aurelio Guedes de Oliveira.

320.9 ITA ISSN 1120-950X
POLITICA IN ITALIA; i fatti dell'anno e le interpretazioni. Text in Italian. 1986. a. price varies. back issues avail. **Document type:** *Monographic series, Academic/Scholarly.*
Related titles: ◆ English ed.: Italian Politics. ISSN 1086-4946.
Published by: (Istituto Carlo Cattaneo), Societa Editrice Il Mulino, Strada Maggiore 37, Bologna, 40125, Italy. TEL 39-051-256011, FAX 39-051-256034, riviste@mulino.it, http://www.mulino.it. Ed. Gianfranco Baldini. Circ: 1,500.

324.2 ARG
POLITICA OBRERA. Text in Spanish. bi-m. USD 4. bk.rev.
Published by: Partido Obrero, Ayacucho, 444, Buenos Aires, 1026, Argentina. TEL 54-114-9533824, FAX 54-114-9537164. Circ: 5,000.

320.972 306 MEX ISSN 0188-7742
F1236
➤ **POLITICA Y CULTURA.** Text mainly in Spanish; Text in English; Abstracts in Spanish, English. 1992. s-a. MXN 150 domestic; USD 40 foreign (effective 2011). **Document type:** *Journal, Academic/Scholarly.*
Related titles: CD-ROM ed.; Online - full text ed.: 2001. free (effective 2011).
Indexed: A01, C01, CA, F04, H21, IBSS, P08, P42, PSA, S02, S03, SCOPUS, SociolAb, T02.
Published by: Universidad Autonoma Metropolitana - Xochimilco, Division de Ciencias Sociales y Humanidades, Calz del Hueso 1100, Col Villa Quietud, Mexico City, DF 04960, Mexico. TEL 52-55-54837110, FAX 52-55-55949100.

320 ARG ISSN 1669-5100
POLITICA Y GESTION. Text in Spanish. 2005. s-a. back issues avail. **Document type:** *Journal, Academic/Scholarly.*
Published by: Universidad Nacional de San Martin, Ave 25 de Mayo y Martin de Irigoyen, San Martin, Buenos Aires, Argentina. TEL 54-11-45807550. Ed. Marcelo Cavarozzi. Circ: 500.

320 ESP ISSN 1130-8001
➤ **POLITICA Y SOCIEDAD.** Text in Spanish, English. 1988. 3/yr. EUR 36 domestic to institutions; EUR 50 in Europe to institutions; EUR 56 elsewhere to institutions (effective 2011). back issues avail. **Document type:** *Journal, Academic/Scholarly.* **Description:** Interdisciplinary journal that covers social sciences, political sciences and democracy in Spain and Latin American countries.
Related titles: CD-ROM ed.: EUR 81 to individuals; EUR 108 to institutions (effective 2003); Online - full text ed.: ISSN 1988-3129. free (effective 2011).
Indexed: A26, CA, FR, H21, I04, I05, I13, P08, P10, P42, P45, P46, P48, PAIS, PQC, PSA, S02, S03, SCOPUS, SOPODA, SSA, SociolAb, T02.
—INIST.
Published by: (Universidad Complutense de Madrid, Facultad de Ciencias Politicas y Sociologia), Universidad Complutense de Madrid, Servicio de Publicaciones, C/ Obispo Trejo 2, Ciudad Universitaria, Madrid, 28040, Spain. TEL 34-91-3941127, FAX 34-91-3941126, servicio.publicaciones@rect.ucm.es, http://www.ucm.es/publicaciones. Ed. Laureano Perez Latorre.

320.532 USA
POLITICAL AFFAIRS (ONLINE); Marxist thought online. Variant title: P A. Text in English. m. free. **Document type:** *Journal, Academic/Scholarly.* **Description:** Covers the lasted world news and events from a Marxist perspective, including commentary and analysis.
Media: Online - full text.
Published by: (Communist Party, USA), Political Affairs, 235 W. 23rd St., New York, NY 10011. TEL 646-437-5341. Ed. Joel Wendland. Pub. Joe Sims.

320.5 GBR ISSN 1047-1987
JA73
➤ **POLITICAL ANALYSIS.** Text in English. 1974-1985; resumed 1989. q. GBP 287 in United Kingdom to institutions; EUR 429 in Europe to institutions; USD 429 in US & Canada to institutions; GBP 287 elsewhere to institutions; GBP 313 combined subscription in United Kingdom to institutions (print & online eds.); EUR 468 combined subscription in Europe to institutions (print & online eds.); USD 468 combined subscription in US & Canada to institutions (print & online eds.); GBP 313 combined subscription elsewhere to institutions (print & online eds.) (effective 2012). adv. bk.rev. back issues avail.; reprint service avail. from PSC. **Document type:** *Journal, Academic/Scholarly.* **Description:** Publishes scholarly articles on topics related to all areas of political science methodology.
Formerly (until 1985): Political Methodology (0162-2021)

P

Related titles: Online - full text ed.: ISSN 1476-4989. GBP 261 in United Kingdom to institutions; EUR 391 in Europe to institutions; USD 391 in US & Canada to institutions; GBP 261 elsewhere to institutions (effective 2012) (from IngentaConnect).
Indexed: A22, CA, CIS, CurCont, E01, ESPM, IBR, IBZ, P02, P10, P27, P30, P42, P45, P47, P48, P53, P54, PAIS, PQC, PSA, RiskAb, S11, SCOPUS, SSCI, SSciA, SociolAb, T02, W07.
—BLDSC (6543.870020), IE, Infotrieve, Ingenta. **CCC.**
Published by: (American Political Science Association, Methodology Section USA, The Society for Political Methodology USA), Oxford University Press, Great Clarendon St, Oxford, OX2 6DP, United Kingdom. TEL 44-1865-556767, FAX 44-1865-556646, enquiry@oup.co.uk, http://www.oxfordjournals.org. Ed. Christopher Zorn. Adv. contact Linda Hann TEL 44-1344-779945.

320.947 GBR
POLITICAL AND ECONOMIC DICTIONARY OF EASTERN EUROPE. Text in English. 2001. irreg., latest 2007, 2nd ed. USD 260 per issue (effective 2009). reprints avail. **Document type:** *Handbook/Manual/ Guide, Academic/Scholarly.* **Description:** Provides a comprehensive guide to the countries, regions, political parties, politicians, organizations, religions, and geographical features of Eastern Europe.
Published by: Routledge (Subsidiary of: Taylor & Francis Group), 2 Park Sq, Milton Park, Abingdon, Oxon OX14 4RN, United Kingdom. TEL 44-20-70176000, FAX 44-20-70176699, orders@taylorandfrancis.com.

POLITICAL AND LEGAL ANTHROPOLOGY REVIEW. *see* ANTHROPOLOGY

POLITICAL AND MILITARY SOCIOLOGY: AN ANNUAL REVIEW. *see* SOCIOLOGY

320 USA ISSN 1070-1753
E839.5
THE POLITICAL ANIMAL. Text in English. 1973. irreg. USD 195 (effective 2000). **Document type:** *Newsletter.* **Description:** Covers news and issues in national and Californian politics and government.
Former titles (until 1993): Joe Scott's The Political Animal (0747-5659); Political Animal (0195-9670)
Published by: The Political Animal Co., 1100 Montecito Dr, Los Angeles, CA 90031-1637. TEL 323-276-9224, FAX 323-417-4964. Ed., Pub., R&P Bill Homer.

320 USA ISSN 0190-9320
JA74.5
➤ **POLITICAL BEHAVIOR.** Text in English. 1979. q. EUR 775, USD 805 combined subscription to institutions (print & online eds.) (effective 2012). adv. abstr. index. back issues avail.; reprint service avail. from PSC. **Document type:** *Journal, Academic/Scholarly.* **Description:** Brings out research in the general fields of political behavior, institutions, processes, and policies.
Related titles: Microfilm ed.: (from PQC); Online - full text ed.: ISSN 1573-6687 (from IngentaConnect).
Indexed: A01, A03, A08, A20, A22, A26, ABCPolSci, BibInd, BibLing, CA, ChPerI, CurCont, E-psyche, E01, ESPM, I13, MEA&I, P03, P10, P34, P42, P43, P45, P48, P53, P54, PQC, PSA, PsycInfo, PsycholAb, RASB, RiskAb, S02, S03, S11, SCOPUS, SOPODA, SSA, SSCI, SociolAb, T02, W07.
—BLDSC (6543.873000), IE, Infotrieve, Ingenta. **CCC.**
Published by: Springer New York LLC (Subsidiary of: Springer Science+Business Media), 233 Spring St, New York, NY 10013. TEL 212-460-1500, FAX 212-460-1575, service-ny@springer.com, http://www.springer.com/. Eds. Jonathan M Hurwitz, Mark Peffley.

320 USA ISSN 1058-4609
JF1525.P8 CODEN: PLCMEM
➤ **POLITICAL COMMUNICATION**; an international journal. Text in English. 1980. q. GBP 357 combined subscription in United Kingdom to institutions (print & online eds.); EUR 474, USD 593 combined subscription to institutions (print & online eds.) (effective 2012). adv. bk.rev. abstr.; illus. back issues avail.; reprint service avail. from PSC. **Document type:** *Journal, Academic/Scholarly.* **Description:** Examines the roles of governmental, intergovernmental, and nongovernmental organizations as political communicators.
Formerly (until 1992): Political Communication and Persuasion (0195-7473)
Related titles: Online - full text ed.: ISSN 1091-7675. GBP 321 in United Kingdom to institutions; EUR 426, USD 534 to institutions (effective 2012) (from IngentaConnect).
Indexed: A01, A02, A03, A08, A20, A22, A26, ABCPolSci, ASCA, B04, BRD, CA, CMM, CommAb, CurCont, E01, E02, E03, E07, E08, ERI, EdA, EdI, FamI, G08, I05, I13, IBSS, LID&ISL, P02, P10, P27, P34, P42, P47, P48, P53, P54, PAIS, PCI, PQC, PRA, PSA, S02, S03, S09, S11, SCOPUS, SOPODA, SSA, SSAI, SSAb, SSCI, SSI, SociolAb, T02, W01, W02, W03, W07.
—IE, Infotrieve, Ingenta. **CCC.**
Published by: Taylor & Francis Inc. (Subsidiary of: Taylor & Francis Group), 325 Chestnut St, Ste 800, Philadelphia, PA 19106. TEL 215-625-8900, 800-354-1420, FAX 215-625-8914, orders@taylorandfrancis.com, http://www.taylorandfrancis.com. Ed. Shanto Iyenga. **Subscr. addr. in Europe:** Taylor & Francis Ltd., Journals Customer Service, Sheepen Pl, Colchester, Essex CO3 3LP, United Kingdom. TEL 44-20-70175544, FAX 44-20-70175198, subscriptions@tandf.co.uk. **Co-sponsor:** American Political Science Association.

➤ **POLITICAL ECONOMY RESEARCH CENTRE. OCCASIONAL PAPERS.** *see* BUSINESS AND ECONOMICS

➤ **POLITICAL ECONOMY RESEARCH CENTRE. POLICY PAPERS.** *see* BUSINESS AND ECONOMICS

➤ **POLITICAL ECONOMY RESEARCH CENTRE. WORKING PAPERS.** *see* BUSINESS AND ECONOMICS

320 USA ISSN 1948-2809
POLITICAL EQUINOX; clear views, balanced opinions, innovative plans. Text in English. 2007. m. free (effective 2009). back issues avail. **Document type:** *Magazine, Trade.*
Media: Online - full content.
Published by: Thrive44 Strategy Group, LLC. http://thrive44.com. Eds. Neil Kelty, Patrick McAlister.

324 CAN ISSN 1910-8672
POLITICAL FINANCING UNDER THE POLITICAL PROCESS FINANCING ACT. REPORT OF THE SUPERVISOR/FINANCEMENT POLITIQUE EN VERTU DE LA LOI SUR LE FINANCEMENT DE L'ACTIVITE POLITIQUE. RAPPORT DU CONTROLEUR. Text in English, French. 1979. a. **Document type:** *Report, Trade.*
Formerly (until 2002): Political Financing under the Political Process Financing Act. Annual Report of the Supervisor (0225-5839)
Published by: New Brunswick, Office of the Supervisor of Political Financing, PO Box 6000, Fredericton, NB E3B 5H1, Canada. TEL 506-453-2224, FAX 506-453-3868, OSPF-BCFP@gnb.ca, http://www.gnb.ca/legis/OSPF-BCFP/index-e.asp.

320.9 GBR ISSN 0962-6298
JC319
➤ **POLITICAL GEOGRAPHY.** Text in English. 1982. 8/yr. EUR 1,407 in Europe to institutions; JPY 186,700 in Japan to institutions; USD 1,574 elsewhere to institutions (effective 2012). adv. bk.rev. illus. index. reprints avail. **Document type:** *Journal, Academic/Scholarly.* **Description:** Contains information for students of political studies with an interest in the geographical or spatial aspects of their subject. Provides a central focus for developments in this subdiscipline.
Formerly (until 1992): Political Geography Quarterly (0260-9827)
Related titles: Microform ed.: (from PQC); Online - full text ed.: ISSN 1873-5096 (from IngentaConnect, ScienceDirect).
Indexed: A01, A03, A08, A20, A22, A26, ABCPolSci, ASCA, AmH&L, B04, B14, BRD, BRI, CA, CurCont, DIP, E04, E05, E08, EI, ESPM, FR, G08, GEOBASE, HistAb, I13, I14, IBR, IBSS, IBZ, M10, P30, P34, P42, PAIS, PCI, PSA, RASB, S02, S03, S09, SCOPUS, SSAI, SSAb, SSCI, SSI, SSciA, SociolAb, T02, W01, W02, W03, W07.
—BLDSC (6543.885950), IE, Infotrieve, Ingenta. **CCC.**
Published by: Pergamon (Subsidiary of: Elsevier Science & Technology), The Blvd, Langford Ln, East Park, Kidlington, Oxford OX5 1GB, United Kingdom. TEL 44-1865-843000, FAX 44-1865-843010, JournalsCustomerServiceEMEA@elsevier.com. Ed. John O'Loughlin. **Subscr. to:** Elsevier BV, Radarweg 29, PO Box 211, Amsterdam 1000 AE, Netherlands. TEL 31-20-4853757, FAX 31-20-4853432, http://www.elsevier.nl.

320.3 USA ISSN 1944-0456
JF37
POLITICAL HANDBOOK OF THE AMERICAS. Text in English. 2008. a. USD 135 per issue (effective 2009).
Published by: C Q Press, Inc. (Subsidiary of: Sage Publications, Inc.), 2300 N St, NW, Ste 800, Washington, DC 20037. TEL 202-729-1900, 866-427-7737, FAX 202-419-8749, 800-380-3810, customerservice@cqpress.com, http://www.cqpress.com.

320 USA ISSN 0193-175X
JF37
POLITICAL HANDBOOK OF THE WORLD. Text in English. 1928. a. USD 49.95. reprints avail.
Formerly: Political Handbook and Atlas of the World (0079-3035)
—BLDSC (6543.886000).
Published by: (State University of New York at Binghamton, Center for Social Analysis), McGraw-Hill Companies, Inc., 1221 Ave of the Americas, 43rd fl, New York, NY 10020. TEL 212-512-2000, FAX 212-426-7087, customer.service@mcgraw-hill.com, http://www.mcgraw-hill.com. Ed. Arthur S Banks. Circ: 7,000.

320 GBR ISSN 2041-9058
▼ **POLITICAL INSIGHT.** Text in English. 2010. 3/yr. GBP 29 in United Kingdom to institutions; EUR 34 in Europe to institutions; USD 48 elsewhere to institutions; GBP 32 combined subscription in United Kingdom to institutions (print & online eds.); EUR 39 combined subscription in Europe to institutions (print & online eds.); USD 53 combined subscription elsewhere to institutions (print & online eds.) (effective 2012). back issues avail. **Document type:** *Journal, Academic/Scholarly.* **Description:** Covers the research into politics and international studies, including articles on human rights, terrorism, recent innovations in policy-making across the advanced industrial world, the impact of globalization on politics and society, the changing nature of democracy, and more.
Related titles: Online - full text ed.: ISSN 2041-9066. GBP 29 in United Kingdom to institutions; EUR 34 in Europe to institutions; USD 48 elsewhere to institutions (effective 2012).
Indexed: A22, E01, P42, T02.
—IE. **CCC.**
Published by: (Political Studies Association), Wiley-Blackwell Publishing Ltd. (Subsidiary of: John Wiley & Sons, Inc.), 9600 Garsington Rd, Oxford, OX4 2DQ, United Kingdom. TEL 44-1865-776868, FAX 44-1865-714591, customer@wiley.co.uk, http://www.blackwell-compass.com. Ed. Peter Geoghegan.

320 AZE
POLITICAL MONITORING OF AZERBAIJAN. Text in English. m. **Description:** Chronicles and analyzes the past month's political events. Covers government bodies, election process, human rights, media, as well as features on political parties and leaders.
Related titles: Russian ed.: Analiticheskii Monitoring Azerbaidzhana.
Published by: Turan Information Agency/Turna Informasiya Agentiyi, Khagani ul 33, Baku, 370000, Azerbaijan. TEL 994-12-984226, 994-12-935967, FAX 994-12-983817, root@turan.baku.az, http://www.turaninfo.com.

324.2 GBR
POLITICAL PARTIES OF THE WORLD. Text in English. 1980. triennial. GBP 105, EUR 150 per issue (effective 2009). **Document type:** *Monographic series, Academic/Scholarly.*
Published by: John Harper Publishing Ltd., 27 Palace Gates Rd, London, N22 7BW, United Kingdom. TEL 44-20-88814774, jhpublish@aol.com. Ed. D J Sagar. **Dist. & Sales:** Turpin Distribution Services Ltd., Pegasus Dr, Stratton Business Park, Biggleswade, Bedfordshire SG18 8QB, United Kingdom. TEL 44-1767-604951, books@turpin-distribution.com, http://www.turpin-distribution.com/.

320.5 GBR ISSN 0198-8719
JA1
POLITICAL POWER AND SOCIAL THEORY. Text in English. 1980. irreg., latest vol.20, 2009. price varies. back issues avail. **Document type:** *Monographic series, Academic/Scholarly.* **Description:** Features on advancing interdisciplinary, critical understanding of the linkages between social relations, political power, and historical development.
Related titles: Online - full text ed.
Indexed: A22, ABS&EES, CA, I13, P42, PSA, S02, S03, SCOPUS, SOPODA, SSA, SociolAb, T02.
—BLDSC (6543.888000), IE, Ingenta. **CCC.**
Published by: Emerald Group Publishing Ltd., Howard House, Wagon Ln, Bingley, W Yorks BD16 1WA, United Kingdom. TEL 44-1274-777700, FAX 44-1274-785201, emerald@emeraldinsight.com. Eds. Diane E Davis, Julian Go. **Dist. by:** Turpin Distribution Services Ltd., Pegasus Dr, Stratton Business Park, Biggleswade, Bedfordshire SG18 8QB, United Kingdom. TEL 44-1767-604951, FAX 44-1767-601640, custserv@turpin-distribution.com, http://www.turpin-distribution.com/.

320 USA ISSN 0162-895X
JA74.5 CODEN: POPSEO
➤ **POLITICAL PSYCHOLOGY.** Text in English. 1979. bi-m. GBP 1,081 combined subscription in United Kingdom to institutions (print & online eds.); EUR 1,314 combined subscription in Europe to institutions (print & online eds.); USD 1,365 combined subscription in the Americas to institutions (print & online eds.); USD 2,116 combined subscription elsewhere to institutions (print & online eds.) (effective 2012). bk.rev. illus. back issues avail.; reprint service avail. from PSC. **Document type:** *Journal, Academic/Scholarly.* **Description:** Interdisciplinary journal dedicated to the analysis of the inter-relationships between psychological and political processes.
Related titles: Microfilm ed.: (from PQC); Online - full text ed.: ISSN 1467-9221. GBP 983 in United Kingdom to institutions; EUR 1,247 in Europe to institutions; USD 1,242 in the Americas to institutions; USD 1,924 elsewhere to institutions (effective 2012) (from IngentaConnect).
Indexed: A01, A03, A08, A12, A20, A22, A26, ABIn, ABS&EES, ASCA, B01, B06, B07, B09, BibInd, CA, CommAb, CurCont, E-psyche, E01, ESPM, I13, IBSS, IPsyAb, LeftInd, P02, P03, P10, P12, P30, P34, P42, P43, P48, P51, P53, P54, PCI, PQC, PRA, PSA, PsycInfo, PsycholAb, RASB, RiskAb, S02, S03, S11, SCOPUS, SPAA, SSCI, SociolAb, T02, W07.
—BLDSC (6543.888500), IE, Infotrieve, Ingenta, INIST. **CCC.**
Published by: (International Society of Political Psychology), Wiley-Blackwell Publishing, Inc. (Subsidiary of: Wiley-Blackwell Publishing Ltd.), 111 River St, Hoboken, NJ 07030. TEL 201-748-6000, FAX 201-748-6088, info@wiley.com, http://www.wiley.com/WileyCDA/. Adv. contact Kristin McCarthy TEL 201-748-7683.

320 USA ISSN 8756-9248
JK8701
POLITICAL PULSE. Text in English. 1985. fortn. USD 337 print or email ed. (effective 2007). **Document type:** *Newsletter.* **Description:** News of California politics and government.
Related titles: E-mail ed.
Published by: York Family Publishing, 926 J St, Ste 1214, Sacramento, CA 95814. TEL 916-446-2048. Ed., Pub. Anthony York. Circ: 600.

320 GBR ISSN 0032-3179
JA8
➤ **THE POLITICAL QUARTERLY.** Text in English. 1930. q. GBP 233 in United Kingdom to institutions; EUR 296 in Europe to institutions; USD 458 in the Americas to institutions; USD 539 elsewhere to institutions; GBP 256 combined subscription in United Kingdom to institutions (print & online eds.); EUR 326 combined subscription in Europe to institutions (print & online eds.); USD 504 combined subscription in the Americas to institutions (print & online eds.); USD 593 combined subscription elsewhere to institutions (print & online eds.) (effective 2012). adv. bk.rev. illus. index. Supplement avail.; back issues avail.; reprint service avail. from PSC. **Document type:** *Journal, Academic/Scholarly.* **Description:** Addresses current issues through serious and thought-provoking articles, written in clear jargon-free english.
Related titles: Microfilm ed.: (from PMC, RPI); Online - full text ed.: ISSN 1467-923X. 1997. GBP 222 in United Kingdom to institutions; EUR 281 in Europe to institutions; USD 435 in the Americas to institutions; USD 509 elsewhere to institutions (effective 2012) (from IngentaConnect).
Indexed: A01, A02, A03, A08, A20, A22, A25, A26, ABCPolSci, AIAP, ASCA, AmHI, B04, BAS, BRD, BrHumI, CA, CurCont, DIP, E01, E08, ESPM, G08, H07, H09, H10, HistAb, I05, I13, IBR, IBSS, IBZ, IPP, LID&ISL, MEA&I, MLA-IB, P02, P06, P10, P27, P30, P34, P42, P47, P48, P53, P54, PAA&I, PAIS, PCI, PQC, PRA, PSA, RASB, RiskAb, S02, S03, S05, S08, S09, S11, SCOPUS, SSA, SSAI, SSAb, SSCI, SSI, SociolAb, T02, W03, W07.
—BLDSC (6543.890000), IE, Infotrieve, Ingenta. **CCC.**
Published by: Wiley-Blackwell Publishing Ltd. (Subsidiary of: John Wiley & Sons, Inc.), 9600 Garsington Rd, Oxford, OX4 2DQ, United Kingdom. TEL 44-1865-776868, FAX 44-1865-714591, customerservices@blackwellpublishing.com. Eds. Andrew Gamble TEL 44-1223-767255, Tony Wright TEL 44-207-2195583. Adv. contact Craig Pickett TEL 44-1865-476267.

320 IRN ISSN 1735-9678
POLITICAL QUARTERLY. Text in Iranian. q. **Document type:** *Journal, Academic/Scholarly.*
Published by: University of Tehran, Faculty of Law and Political Science, Enghelab Ave, P O Box 14155-6448, Tehran, 6448, Iran. FAX 98-21-66494990, lawmag@ut.ac.ir, http://jpq.ut.ac.ir. Ed. Abd al-Rahman Alem.

320 USA ISSN 1051-4287
POLITICAL REPORT. Text in English. 1978. fortn. USD 197 (effective 1999). **Document type:** *Newsletter.* **Description:** Reports on congressional campaigns and elections and provides analysis on national political trends and developments.
Address: 50 F St, N W, Fl 7, Washington, DC 20001-1530. Ed., Pub. Stuart Rothenberg.

320 USA ISSN 1065-9129
JA1
➤ **POLITICAL RESEARCH QUARTERLY.** Text in English. 1948. q. USD 251, GBP 147 combined subscription to institutions (print & online eds.); USD 246, GBP 144 to institutions (effective 2011). adv. bk.rev. illus. index. back issues avail.; reprint service avail. from PSC. **Document type:** *Journal, Academic/Scholarly.* **Description:** Publishes original research in all areas of political science. Most issues also feature field essays integrating and summarizing current knowledge in particular research areas.
Formerly (until 1993): Western Political Quarterly (0043-4078)
Related titles: Online - full text ed.: ISSN 1938-274X. USD 226, GBP 132 to institutions (effective 2011).

Indexed: A01, A02, A03, A08, A20, A22, A25, A26, ABCPolSci, ABS&EES, ASCA, AcaI, AmH&L, B04, BAS, BRD, CA, CBRI, Chicano, CurCont, DIP, E01, E08, G08, H09, H10, HistAb, I05, I13, I14, IBR, IBSS, IBZ, IPARL, M01, M02, MEA&I, MLA-IB, P02, P06, P10, P13, P27, P30, P34, P42, P45, P47, P48, P53, P54, PAA&I, PAIS, PCI, PQC, PRA, PSA, PhilInd, RASB, S02, S03, S05, S08, S09, S11, SCOPUS, SD, SPAA, SSAI, SSAb, SSCI, SSI, SociolAb, T02, W03, W05, W07.
—BLDSC (6543.903000), IE, Infotrieve, Ingenta. **CCC.**
Published by: (University of Utah, Political Science Department, Western Political Science Association), Sage Publications, Inc., 2455 Teller Rd, Thousand Oaks, CA 91320. TEL 805-499-9774, 800-818-7243, FAX 805-499-0871, 800-583-2665, http://www.sagepub.com. Eds. Amy Mazur, Cornell Clayton. adv.: B&W page USD 100; trim 9 x 6. Circ: 2,300 (paid). **Subscr. outside the Americas to:** Sage Publications Ltd., 1 Oliver's Yard, 55 City Rd, London EC1Y 1SP, United Kingdom. TEL 44-20-73248701, FAX 44-20-73248733, subscription@sagepub.co.uk.

320.025 USA
JK2283
POLITICAL RESOURCE DIRECTORY (ONLINE). Text in English. 1989. a. adv. **Document type:** *Directory, Trade.* **Description:** Offers comprehensive information on political professional organizations. Acts as an official directory for the American Association of Political Consultants with information on products and services to politicaland corporate campaigns.
Formerly (until 2008): Political Resource Directory (Print) (0898-4271); Which incorporates (1989-199?): A A P C Directory (0897-4284)
Media: Online - full text. **Related titles:** CD-ROM ed.: USD 14.99 (effective 2009); E-mail ed.
Published by: (American Association of Political Consultants), Political Resources, Inc., PO Box 1403, Lake Worth, FL 33460. TEL 800-423-2677, FAX 561-533-0104, info@politicalresources.com. Ed., Pub. Carol Hess. Adv. contact Emily Hess. B&W page USD 2,500, color page USD 3,600; trim 11 x 8.5. Circ: 5,000.

POLITICAL RISK LETTER. *see* BUSINESS AND ECONOMICS—International Commerce

320 GBR ISSN 0032-3187
JA1
➤ **POLITICAL SCIENCE.** Text in English. 1948. s-a. USD 353, GBP 191 combined subscription to institutions (print & online eds.); USD 346, GBP 187 to institutions (effective 2011). adv. bk.rev. bibl.; charts; illus. cum.index every 2 yrs. back issues avail.; reprint service avail. from PSC. **Document type:** *Journal, Academic/Scholarly.*
Related titles: Online - full text ed.: ISSN 2041-0611. USD 318, GBP 172 to institutions (effective 2011).
Indexed: A20, A22, ABCPolSci, AmHI, BrHumI, CA, CurCont, E01, EI, H07, I13, IBSS, INZP, MEA&I, P06, P30, P34, P42, PAA&I, PCI, PSA, RASB, S02, S03, SCOPUS, SPPI, SSA, SSCI, SociolAb, T02, W07.
—BLDSC (6543.908000), IE, Ingenta. **CCC.**
Published by: (New Zealand Political Studies Association USA), Sage Publications Ltd. (Subsidiary of: Sage Publications, Inc.), 1 Oliver's Yard, 55 City Rd, London, EC1Y 1SP, United Kingdom. TEL 44-20-73248500, FAX 44-20-73248600, info@sagepub.co.uk, http://www.uk.sagepub.com/home.nav. Eds. Nigel Roberts, Stephen Levine. Circ: 600.

320 USA ISSN 0032-3195
H1
➤ **POLITICAL SCIENCE QUARTERLY**; the journal of public and international affairs. Text in English. 1886. q. USD 49 combined subscription domestic to individuals (print & online eds.); USD 60 combined subscription foreign to individuals (print & online eds.); USD 399 combined subscription domestic to institutions (print & online eds.); USD 410 combined subscription foreign to institutions (print & online eds.) (effective 2011). adv. bk.rev. index. 192 p./no. 1 cols./p.; back issues avail.; reprints avail. **Document type:** *Journal, Academic/Scholarly.* **Description:** Devoted to the study of contemporary and historical aspects of government, politics, and public affairs.
Related titles: Microfiche ed.: (from PMC, PQC); Microfilm ed.; Online - full text ed.: ISSN 1538-165X (from IngentaConnect).
Indexed: A01, A02, A03, A08, A12, A20, A22, A25, A26, ABCPolSci, ABIn, ABRCLP, ABS&EES, ASCA, AbAn, AcaI, AmH&L, B04, B05, B14, BAS, BRD, BRI, C12, CA, CBRI, CCME, CERDIC, ChPerI, CurCont, DIP, E08, EI, EconLit, FR, FamI, FutSurv, G05, G06, G07, G08, G10, H09, H10, HistAb, I02, I03, I05, I07, I13, IBR, IBSS, IBZ, IPARL, JEL, LID&ISL, M01, M02, M05, M06, MEA&I, MLA-IB, P02, P06, P10, P13, P27, P30, P34, P42, P45, P47, P48, P51, P53, P54, PAIS, PCI, PQC, PRA, PSA, PerIslam, R02, R04, RASB, RefugAb, S02, S03, S05, S08, S09, S11, S23, SCOPUS, SPAA, SRRA, SSA, SSAI, SSAb, SSCI, SSI, SWR&A, SociolAb, T02, W01, W02, W03, W04, W05, W07.
—BLDSC (6543.914000), IE, Infotrieve, Ingenta. **CCC.**
Published by: Academy of Political Science, 475 Riverside Dr, Ste 1274, New York, NY 10115-1274. TEL 212-870-2500, FAX 212-870-2202. Ed. Demetrios Caraley. R&P, Adv. contact Loren Morales TEL 212-870-3526. page USD 300; trim 6.75 x 10. Circ: 8,000 (paid).

320 IND ISSN 0554-5196
JA26
POLITICAL SCIENCE REVIEW. Text in English. 1962. q. bk.rev. bibl. index. back issues avail.; reprints avail. **Document type:** *Journal, Academic/Scholarly.*
Related titles: Microfilm ed.: (from PQC).
Indexed: ABCPolSci, BAS, IBR, IBZ, RASB.
Published by: University of Rajasthan, Department of Political Science, Bapunagar, Jaipur, Rajasthan 302 004, India. info@uniraj.ernet.in, http://www.uniraj.ac.in/.

320 USA ISSN 0091-3715
JA1
THE POLITICAL SCIENCE REVIEWER; an annual review of books. Text in English. 1971. a. USD 12 per issue domestic; USD 15 per issue foreign (effective 2010). adv. bk.rev. back issues avail. **Document type:** *Journal, Academic/Scholarly.* **Description:** Features articles on classic and contemporary studies in law and politics.
Related titles: Microform ed.: (from PQC); Online - full text ed.
Indexed: A01, A03, A08, A22, AmH&L, BRI, CA, CBRI, HistAb, I13, L03, P42, P45, PCI, PSA, PhilInd, RASB, SCOPUS, SociolAb, T02, W04.
—IE, Infotrieve. **CCC.**
Published by: The Intercollegiate Studies Institute Inc., 3901 Centerville Rd, Wilmington, DE 19807. TEL 302-652-4600, 800-526-7022, FAX 302-652-1760, info@isi.org. Ed. Bruce P Frohnen. Adv. contact Carol Houseal TEL 302-524-6167.

320 CHE ISSN 2076-3395
▼ ➤ **POLITICAL SCIENCES.** Text in English. forthcoming 2011. q. free (effective 2011). **Document type:** *Journal, Academic/Scholarly.*
Media: Online - full text.
Published by: M D P I AG, Postfach, Basel, 4005, Switzerland. TEL 41-61-6837734, FAX 41-61-3028918, http://www.mdpi.org/.

320 GBR ISSN 0032-3217
JA1
➤ **POLITICAL STUDIES.** Text in English. 1953. q. GBP 616 combined subscription domestic to institutions (print & online eds.); EUR 782 combined subscription in Europe to institutions (print & online eds.); USD 1,307 combined subscription in the Americas to institutions (print & online eds.); USD 1,408 combined subscription elsewhere to institutions (print & online eds.) (effective 2009); subscr. includes British Journal of Politics and Industrial Relations, Politics and Political Studies Review. adv. bk.rev. illus. index, cum.index every 10 yrs. back issues avail.; reprint service avail. from PSC. **Document type:** *Journal, Academic/Scholarly.* **Description:** Aims to develop the most promising new work available and to facilitate professional communication in political science.
Related titles: Microfilm ed.: (from PQC); Online - full text ed.: ISSN 1467-9248. GBP 555 domestic to institutions; EUR 705 in Europe to institutions; USD 1,177 in the Americas to institutions; USD 1,266 elsewhere to institutions (effective 2009) (from IngentaConnect).
Indexed: A01, A02, A03, A08, A20, A21, A22, A26, ABCPolSci, ASCA, AmH&L, AmHI, B04, BAS, BRD, BrHumI, CA, CurCont, DIP, E01, E08, ESPM, FamI, G08, G10, H07, H09, H10, HistAb, I05, I13, IBR, IBSS, IBZ, M10, MEA&I, MLA-IB, P02, P06, P10, P27, P30, P34, P42, P47, P48, P53, P54, PAA&I, PAIS, PCI, PQC, PRA, PSA, PhilInd, R05, RASB, RI-1, RI-2, RiskAb, S02, S03, S05, S09, S11, S21, SCOPUS, SOPODA, SPAA, SSA, SSAI, SSAb, SSCI, SSI, SociolAb, T02, W03, W04, W07, W09.
—BLDSC (6543.924000), IE, Infotrieve, Ingenta. **CCC.**
Published by: (Political Studies Association), Wiley-Blackwell Publishing Ltd. (Subsidiary of: John Wiley & Sons, Inc.), 9600 Garsington Rd, Oxford, OX4 2DQ, United Kingdom. TEL 44-1865-776868, FAX 44-1865-714591, customerservices@blackwellpublishing.com. Adv. contact Craig Pickett TEL 44-1865-476267.

320 GBR
POLITICAL STUDIES ASSOCIATION. YEARBOOK. Text in English. a.
Formerly: The P S A Yearbook
Published by: (Political Studies Association), Palgrave Macmillan Ltd. (Subsidiary of: Macmillan Publishers Ltd.), Houndmills, Basingstoke, Hants RG21 6XS, United Kingdom. TEL 44-1256-329242, FAX 44-1256-810526, subscriptions@palgrave.com, http://www.palgrave.com.

320 GBR ISSN 1478-9299
JA8
POLITICAL STUDIES REVIEW. Abbreviated title: P S R. Text in English. 2003. 3/yr. GBP 174 in United Kingdom to institutions; EUR 204 in Europe to institutions; USD 286 elsewhere to institutions; GBP 201 combined subscription in United Kingdom to institutions (print & online eds.); EUR 235 combined subscription in Europe to institutions (print & online eds.); USD 329 combined subscription elsewhere to institutions (print & online eds.) (effective 2012). adv. back issues avail.; reprint service avail. from PSC. **Document type:** *Journal, Academic/Scholarly.* **Description:** Contains reviews of political science books in English.
Related titles: Online - full text ed.: ISSN 1478-9302. GBP 174 in United Kingdom to institutions; EUR 204 in Europe to institutions; USD 286 elsewhere to institutions (effective 2012) (from IngentaConnect).
Indexed: A01, A03, A08, A22, A26, CA, CurCont, E01, ESPM, GEOBASE, P34, P42, RiskAb, S02, S03, SCOPUS, SSCI, T02, W07.
—BLDSC (6543.924650), IE, Ingenta. **CCC.**
Published by: (Political Studies Association), Wiley-Blackwell Publishing Ltd. (Subsidiary of: John Wiley & Sons, Inc.), 9600 Garsington Rd, Oxford, OX4 2DQ, United Kingdom. TEL 44-1865-776868, FAX 44-1865-714591, customerservices@blackwellpublishing.com, http://www.wiley.com/. Adv. contact Craig Pickett TEL 44-1865-476267. B&W page GBP 445, B&W page USD 823; 125 x 205. Circ: 2,500.

POLITICAL THEOLOGY. *see* RELIGIONS AND THEOLOGY

320 USA ISSN 0090-5917
JA1.A1
➤ **POLITICAL THEORY**; an international journal of political philosophy. Text in English. 1973. bi-m. USD 1,043, GBP 614 combined subscription to institutions (print & online eds.); USD 1,022, GBP 602 to institutions (effective 2011). bk.rev. bibl.; abstr.; illus. index. back issues avail.; reprint service avail. from PSC. **Document type:** *Journal, Academic/Scholarly.* **Description:** Provides a forum for the diverse orientations in the study of political ideas, including the history of political thought, modern theory, conceptual analysis, and polemic argumentation.
Related titles: Microfilm ed.: (from PQC); Online - full text ed.: ISSN 1552-7476. USD 939, GBP 553 to institutions (effective 2011).
Indexed: A01, A02, A03, A08, A20, A22, A25, A26, ABCPolSci, ABS&EES, ASCA, B04, B07, BRD, CA, CERDIC, CurCont, DIP, E01, E08, FR, G08, H04, HistAb, I05, I13, IBR, IBSS, IBZ, IPB, MEA&I, P02, P10, P13, P27, P30, P34, P42, P47, P48, P53, P54, PCI, PQC, PSA, PhilInd, RASB, S02, S03, S08, S09, S11, SCOPUS, SPAA, SSA, SSAI, SSAb, SSCI, SSI, SociolAb, T02, V02, W01, W02, W03, W07, W09.
—BLDSC (6543.926000), IE, Infotrieve, Ingenta, INIST. **CCC.**
Published by: Sage Publications, Inc., 2455 Teller Rd, Thousand Oaks, CA 91320. TEL 805-499-9774, 800-818-7243, FAX 805-499-0871, 800-583-2665, info@sagepub.com. Ed. Mary G Dietz. Circ: 1,478 (paid). **Subscr. overseas to:** Sage Publications Ltd., 1 Oliver's Yard, 55 City Rd, London EC1Y 1SP, United Kingdom. TEL 44-207-3248701, FAX 44-207-3248733, subscription@sagepub.co.uk.

320.5 UKR
POLITICAL THOUGHT. Text in Ukrainian. q. USD 95 in United States. **Document type:** *Academic/Scholarly.*
Related titles: Russian ed.; English ed.
Indexed: RASB.
Published by: Izdatel'stvo Politicheskaya Mysl', Ul Leontovicha 5, Kiev, Ukraine. TEL 380-44-225-0229. **Dist. by:** East View Information Services, 10601 Wayzata Blvd, Minneapolis, MN 55305. TEL 952-252-1201, 800-477-1005, FAX 952-252-1202, info@eastview.com, http://www.eastview.com.

POLITICAL VIOLENCE AGAINST AMERICANS. *see* CRIMINOLOGY AND LAW ENFORCEMENT

320 CHL ISSN 0716-7415
POLITICAL Y ESTRATEGIA. Text in Spanish. 1976. q. back issues avail. **Document type:** *Magazine, Consumer.*
Former titles (until 1989): Politica y Geoestrategia (0716-6508); (unitl 1982): Seguridad Nacional (0716-6516)
Related titles: Online - full text ed.
Published by: Academia Nacional de Estudios Politicos y Estrategicos, Eliodoro Yanez 2760, Providencia, Santiago, Chile. TEL 56-2-5981034, FAX 56-2-5981043, publicac@anepe.cl. Ed. Julio Soto Silva. Circ: 350.

POLITICALCIRCUS. *see* ETHNIC INTERESTS

320 ARG ISSN 1668-4885
POLITICAS DE LA MEMORIA. Text in Spanish. 1998. a. **Document type:** *Monographic series, Academic/Scholarly.*
Published by: Centro de Documentacion e Investigacion de la Cultura de Izquierdas en la Argentina, Fray Luis Beltran, 125, Buenos Aires, C1406BEC, Argentina. TEL 54-11-46318893, informes@cedinci.org, http://www.cedinci.org/. Ed. Laura Ehrlich. Circ: 1,000.

POLITICAS PUBLICAS. *see* PUBLIC ADMINISTRATION

320.5 RUS
POLITICHESKAYA NAUKA. Text in Russian. 1997. q. USD 100 in United States (effective 2004). **Document type:** *Journal, Academic/Scholarly.*
Published by: Rossiiskaya Akademiya Nauk, Institut Nauchnoi Informatsii po Obshchestvennym Naukam, Nakhimovskii pr-t 51/21, Moscow, 117997, Russian Federation. TEL 7-095-1288930, FAX 7-095-4202261, info@inion.ru, http://www.inion.ru. **Dist. by:** East View Information Services, 10601 Wayzata Blvd, Minneapolis, MN 55305. TEL 952-252-1201, 800-477-1005, FAX 952-252-1202, info@eastview.com, http://www.eastview.com.

320 658 RUS
POLITICHESKII MARKETING. Text in Russian. m.
Related titles: ◆ Supplement to: Prakticheskii Marketing.
Published by: B C I Marketing, ul Malaya Cherkizovskaya, dom 66, Moscow, 107392, Russian Federation. bcimarketing@mtu-net.ru, http://www.bci-marketing.aha.ru. Ed. Vladimir Boushev. Circ: 500.

320 HRV ISSN 0032-3241
JA26
POLITICKA MISAO/POLITICAL THOUGHT; casopis za politicke nauke. Text in Croatian; Summaries in English. 1964. q. USD 15 (effective 2000). bk.rev. abstr.; bibl. **Document type:** *Academic/Scholarly.*
Related titles: Online - full text ed.
Indexed: A01, A03, A08, A26, CA, DIP, HistAb, I13, IBR, IBSS, IBZ, P42, PAIS, PSA, RASB, S02, S03, SociolAb, T02.
Published by: Sveuciliste u Zagrebu, Fakultet Politickih Znanosti/ University of Zagreb, Department of Political Sciences, Lepusiceva 6, Zagreb, 10000, Croatia. TEL 385-1-4558022, FAX 385-1-412283. Ed. Davor Rodin. Adv. contact Liljana Milankovic. Circ: 1,200.

320 ITA ISSN 0032-325X
JA18
IL POLITICO; rivista italiana di scienze politiche. Text and summaries in English, French, Italian. 1928. 3/yr. adv. bk.rev. bibl.; illus. index. reprints avail. **Document type:** *Journal, Academic/Scholarly.* **Description:** Contains articles on current topics in international political science.
Formerly (until 1941): Annali di Scienze Politiche (0391-4682)
Indexed: A22, ABCPolSci, AmH&L, BAS, ELLIS, HistAb, I13, IBR, IBSS, IBZ, JEL, MEA&I, P06, PAIS, PCI, PSA, RASB, SCOPUS, SociolAb.
—IE, Ingenta.
Published by: (Universita degli Studi di Pavia, Istituto di Scienze Politiche), Rubbettino Editore, Viale Rosario Rubbettino 10, Soveria Mannelli, CZ 88049, Italy. TEL 39-0968-662034, FAX 39-0968-662055, segreteria@rubbettino.it, http://www.rubbettino.it.

320 USA
THE POLITICO (ARLINGTON). Text in English. 2007. 3/w. USD 200 domestic; USD 600 foreign (effective 2009); free in locations around Capitol Hill and Washington, D.C. adv. **Document type:** *Newspaper, Consumer.* **Description:** Covers the politics of Capitol Hill and of the presidential campaign, and the business of Washington lobbying and advocacy.
Published by: Capitol News Company, LLC, 1100 Wilson Blvd, Ste 601, Arlington, VA 22209. TEL 703-647-7999, FAX 703-647-8550. Ed. John F Harris. Pub. Robert Allbritton. adv.: B&W page USD 10,038, color page USD 11,410; trim 10 x 13.5.

320 USA
POLITICO (PHOENIX); the magazine for Latino politics and culture. Text in English. w. **Document type:** *Newsletter.* **Description:** Delivers news and analysis of political events and culture impacting the Latino community nationwide.
Media: Online - full content.
Published by: Politico, 1020 E Mountain Vista Dr, Phoenix, AZ 85048. TEL 480-460-7646, FAX 509-356-8263, politico1@aol.com, http://www.politicomagazine.com/. Ed., Pub. James E Garcia.

320 GBR ISSN 0140-9387
POLITICS (LONDON). Text in English. 1977. irreg. **Document type:** *Monographic series, Trade.*
—**CCC.**
Published by: Labour Party, 150 Walworth Rd, London, SE17 1JT, United Kingdom. FAX 44-171-701-6363, marketing@new.labour.org.uk, http://www.labour.org.uk.

P

320 GBR ISSN 0263-3957
JA8

➤ **POLITICS (OXFORD)**; cutting edge political science in short-article format. Text in English. 1980. 3/yr. GBP 204 combined subscription in United Kingdom to institutions (print & online eds.); EUR 259 combined subscription in Europe to institutions (print & online eds.); USD 497 combined subscription in the Americas to institutions (print & online eds.); USD 535 combined subscription elsewhere to institutions (print & online eds.) (effective 2012). adv. bk.rev. illus. Index. back issues avail.; reprint service avail. from PSC. **Document type:** *Journal, Academic/Scholarly.* **Description:** Aims to publish cutting-edge political analysis in an accessible format and style.
Related titles: Microform ed.: (from PQC); Online - full text ed.: ISSN 1467-9256. GBP 185 in United Kingdom to institutions; EUR 234 in Europe to institutions; USD 447 in the Americas to institutions; USD 481 elsewhere to institutions (effective 2012) (from IngentaConnect).
Indexed: A01, A03, A08, A22, A26, CA, E01, ESPM, GEOBASE, I13, IBR, IBSS, IBZ, LeftInd, P34, P42, PAIS, PCI, PSA, RiskAb, S02, S03, SCOPUS, SOPODA, SSA, SociolAb, T02.
—BLDSC (6543.937500), IE, Infotrieve, Ingenta. **CCC.**
Published by: (Political Studies Association), Wiley-Blackwell Publishing Ltd. (Subsidiary of: John Wiley & Sons, Inc.), 9600 Garsington Rd, Oxford, OX4 2DQ, United Kingdom. TEL 44-1865-776868, FAX 44-1865-714591, customerservices@blackwellpublishing.com, http://www.wiley.com/. Eds. Dr. Alasdair Young TEL 44-1413-304679, Dr. Jane Duckett TEL 44-1413-302871, Dr. Paul Graham TEL 44-1413-304982.

320.9 USA ISSN 2158-5741
DT30.5

POLITICS AND ECONOMICS OF AFRICA. Text in English. 2001. irreg., latest vol.9, 2011. price varies. back issues avail. **Document type:** *Monographic series, Academic/Scholarly.* **Description:** Contains series of papers which examines number of topics related to politics and economics and how they impact African nations, the United States and the global community.
Related titles: Online - full text ed.
Published by: Nova Science Publishers, Inc., 400 Oser Ave, Ste 1600, Hauppauge, NY 11788. TEL 631-231-7269, FAX 631-231-8175, journals@novapublishers.com.

320 305.4 GBR ISSN 1743-923X
HQ1075

POLITICS & GENDER. Text in English. 2005 (Mar.). q. GBP 156, USD 272 to institutions; GBP 167, USD 298 combined subscription to institutions (print & online eds.) (effective 2012). adv. bk.rev. back issues avail.; reprint service avail. from PSC. **Document type:** *Journal, Academic/Scholarly.* **Description:** Presents issues and approaches on gender and women in all fields of political science.
Related titles: Online - full text ed.: ISSN 1743-9248. GBP 142, USD 255 to institutions (effective 2012).
Indexed: A22, CA, CurCont, E01, ESPM, FemPer, G10, GW, IBSS, P10, P42, P45, PQC, PSA, RiskAb, S02, S03, SCOPUS, SSCI, SociolAb, T02, W07, W09.
—BLDSC (6543.941535), IE, Ingenta. **CCC.**
Published by: (American Political Science Association, Women and Politics Research Section USA), Cambridge University Press, The Edinburgh Bldg, Shaftesbury Rd, Cambridge, CB2 8RU, United Kingdom. TEL 44-1223-312393, FAX 44-1223-315052, journals@cambridge.org, http://www.cambridge.org/uk. Eds. Aili Mari Tripp, Kathleen Dolan. Adv. contact Rebecca Roberts TEL 44-1223-325083. **Subscr. to:** Cambridge University Press, 32 Ave of the Americas, New York, NY 10013. TEL 212-337-5000, FAX 212-691-3239, journals_subscriptions@cup.org.

320 USA ISSN 1944-2696

POLITICS & GOVERNMENT WEEK. Text in English. 2008. w. USD 2,295 in US & Canada; USD 2,495 elsewhere; USD 2,525 combined subscription in US & Canada (print & online eds.); USD 2,755 combined subscription elsewhere (print & online eds.) (effective 2011). back issues avail. **Document type:** *Newsletter, Trade.*
Related titles: E-mail ed.; Online - full text ed.: ISSN 1944-270X. USD 2,295 combined subscription (online & e-mail eds.) (effective 2011).
Indexed: P45, P47, P48, PQC.
Published by: NewsRx, 2727 Paces Ferry Rd SE, Ste 2-440, Atlanta, GA 30339. TEL 770-435-8286, 800-726-4550, FAX 770-435-6800, pressrelease@newsrx.com, http://www.newsrx.com. Pub., Adv. contact Susan Hasty TEL 770-507-7777.

320 USA ISSN 1555-5623
JA1

➤ **POLITICS & POLICY.** Text in English. 1973. bi-m. USD 1,246 combined subscription domestic to institutions (print & online eds.); GBP 916 combined subscription in United Kingdom to institutions (print & online eds.); EUR 1,163 combined subscription in Europe to institutions (print & online eds.); USD 1,795 combined subscription elsewhere to institutions (print & online eds.) (effective 2009); subscr. includes Policy Studies Journal and Review of Policy Research. adv. bk.rev. stat.; bibl.; charts. Index. back issues avail.; reprint service avail. from PSC. **Document type:** *Journal, Academic/Scholarly.* **Description:** Targets teaching political scientists.
Former titles (until 2001): Southeastern Political Review (0730-2177); (until 1981): G P S A Journal (0092-9395)
Related titles: Online - full text ed.: ISSN 1747-1346 (from IngentaConnect).
Indexed: A01, A22, A26, ABS&EES, CA, DIP, E01, ESPM, G08, I05, I13, I14, IBR, IBZ, P34, P42, PAIS, PRA, PSA, RiskAb, SCOPUS, SPAA, SociolAb, T02.
—BLDSC (6543.942500), IE, Ingenta. **CCC.**
Published by: (Policy Studies Organization), Wiley-Blackwell Publishing, Inc. (Subsidiary of: Wiley-Blackwell Publishing Ltd.), Commerce Pl, 350 Main St, Malden, MA 02148. TEL 781-388-8206, 800-835-6770, FAX 781-388-8232, info@wiley.com, http://www.wiley.com/WileyCDA/. Eds. David Mena Aleman, Emma R Norton. Circ: 425 (paid).

320 200 GBR ISSN 1755-0483

➤ **POLITICS AND RELIGION.** Text in English. 2008 (Apr.). 3/yr. GBP 119, USD 222 combined subscription to institutions (print & online eds.) (effective 2012). adv. back issues avail.; reprint service avail. from PSC. **Document type:** *Journal, Academic/Scholarly.* **Description:** Covers all aspects of the relationship between politics and religion around the world.
Related titles: Online - full text ed.: ISSN 1755-0491. GBP 112, USD 201 to institutions (effective 2012).
Indexed: A20, ArtHuCI, CurCont, P42, T02, W07.
—CCC.
Published by: (American Political Science Association USA), Cambridge University Press, The Edinburgh Bldg, Shaftesbury Rd, Cambridge, CB2 8RU, United Kingdom. TEL 44-1223-312393, FAX 44-1223-315052, journals@cambridge.org, http://www.cambridge.org/uk. Eds. Sabrina Petra Ramet, Ted G Jelen. Adv. contact Rebecca Roberts TEL 44-1223-325083. page GBP 260, page USD 495.

320 USA ISSN 0032-3292
H1 CODEN: PSOCEX

➤ **POLITICS AND SOCIETY.** Text in English. 1970. q. USD 838, GBP 493 combined subscription to institutions (print & online eds.); USD 821, GBP 483 to institutions (effective 2011). adv. bk.rev. abstr.; illus. Index. back issues avail.; reprint service avail. from PSC. **Document type:** *Journal, Academic/Scholarly.* **Description:** Analyzes politics, its social roots, and consequences. It publishes well-researched articles that raise questions about the way the world is organized politically, economically and socially.
Related titles: Microform ed.: (from PQC); Online - full text ed.: ISSN 1552-7514. USD 754, GBP 444 to institutions (effective 2011).
Indexed: A01, A02, A03, A08, A20, A22, A26, ABCPolSci, ABS&EES, ASCA, AltPI, AmH&L, B04, B07, BAS, BRD, CA, CJA, CurCont, DIP, E01, E08, EI, ESPM, FR, FamI, G08, H04, H09, HPNRM, HistAb, I05, I13, I14, IBR, IBSS, IBZ, LeftInd, MEA&I, P02, P10, P27, P30, P34, P42, P47, P48, P53, P54, PAIS, PCI, PQC, PRA, PSA, PerIslam, RASB, RiskAb, S02, S03, S05, S09, S11, SCOPUS, SOPODA, SPAA, SRRA, SSA, SSAI, SSAb, SSCI, SSI, SSciA, SociolAb, T02, V02, W03, W07.
—BLDSC (6543.944000), IE, Infotrieve, Ingenta, INIST. **CCC.**
Published by: Sage Publications, Inc., 2455 Teller Rd, Thousand Oaks, CA 91320. TEL 805-499-9774, 800-818-7243, FAX 805-499-0871, 800-583-2665, info@sagepub.com. Circ: 1,400. **Subscr. outside of N. America to:** Sage Publications Ltd., 1 Oliver's Yard, 55 City Rd, London EC1Y 1SP, United Kingdom. TEL 44-207-3248701, FAX 44-207-3248733, subscription@sagepub.co.uk.

320 973 USA

POLITICS AND SOCIETY IN TWENTIETH CENTURY AMERICA. Text in English. 2000. irreg., latest 2010. price varies. charts; illus. back issues avail. **Document type:** *Monographic series, Academic/Scholarly.* **Description:** Features works on the presidents, political institutions, reform movements, and other traditional topics in political history.
Published by: Princeton University Press, 41 William St, Princeton, NJ 08540. TEL 609-258-4900, 800-777-4726, FAX 609-258-6305, cpriday@pupress.co.uk. **Subscr. to:** California - Princeton Fulfillment Services, Inc., 1445 Lower Ferry Rd, Ewing, NJ 08618. TEL 609-883-1759, 800-777-4726, FAX 609-883-7413, 800-999-1958, orders@cpfsinc.com.

POLITICS AND THE ENVIRONMENT. *see* ENVIRONMENTAL STUDIES

320 USA ISSN 0730-9384
JA80

➤ **POLITICS AND THE LIFE SCIENCES.** Abbreviated title: P L S. Text in English. 1982. s-a. USD 150 to institutions (print or online ed.); USD 190 combined subscription to institutions (print & online eds.); free to members (effective 2011). bk.rev. bibl.; charts; illus. back issues avail. **Document type:** *Journal, Academic/Scholarly.* **Description:** Provides a forum for scholars interested in both the methods and the findings of research in the life sciences that relates to the study of politics and public policy.
Related titles: Online - full text ed.: ISSN 1471-5457 (from IngentaConnect).
Indexed: A01, A02, A03, A08, A20, A22, A25, A26, ABCPolSci, ASCA, B04, BRD, BiolDig, C23, CA, CLOSS, DIP, E08, EMBASE, ExcerpMed, FamI, G08, I05, I13, IBR, IBSS, IBZ, MEDLINE, MycolAb, P02, P10, P11, P15, P27, P30, P34, P42, P43, P47, P48, P52, P53, P54, P56, PCI, PQC, PSA, PerIslam, R10, Reac, S02, S03, S08, S09, S11, SCOPUS, SOPODA, SSA, SSAI, SSAb, SSI, SociolAb, T02, W03, W05.
—BLDSC (6543.941850), IE, Infotrieve, Ingenta, Linda Hall. **CCC.**
Published by: Association for Politics and the Life Sciences, Political Science Department, Utah State University, Logan, UT 84322-0725. sprinkle@umd.edu, http://www.msj.edu/APLS. Ed. Erik P Bucy.

320.1 USA ISSN 2151-4283
JA1

▼ ➤ **POLITICS, BUREAUCRACY, AND JUSTICE.** Abbreviated title: P B & J. Text in English. 2009. s-a. free (effective 2009). **Document type:** *Journal, Academic/Scholarly.* **Description:** Provides information about American politics, international affairs and theories of power and its use.
Related titles: Online - full text ed.: ISSN 2151-4313.
Indexed: P42, PSA, T02.
Published by: West Texas A&M University, Department of Political Science and Criminal Justice, c/o Business Office, Old Main, Rm 104, Canyon, TX 79016. TEL 806-651-3310, rlwelch@wtamu.edu, http://www.wtamu.edu/academics/political-science-criminal-justice.aspx. Ed. Jesse Jones.

320 USA

POLITICS IN LATIN AMERICA. Text in English. 1982. irreg., latest 1992. price varies. back issues avail. **Document type:** *Monographic series.*
Published by: Praeger Publishers (Subsidiary of: Greenwood Publishing Group Inc.), 88 Post Rd W, Westport, CT 06881. TEL 800-368-6868, tech.support@greenwood.com, http://www.greenwood.com.

320.9 USA ISSN 1536-4623

POLITICS IN MINNESOTA. Text in English. 1983. 22/yr. USD 56 (effective 2000). **Document type:** *Newsletter.* **Description:** Reports on Minnesota politics.
Related titles: Online - full text ed.
Published by: Political Communications, Inc., 293 Como Ave., 2nd Fl., Saint Paul, MN 55103-1842. TEL 651-293-0949, FAX 651-293-9056, Staff@politicsinminnesota.com, http://www.politicsinminnesota.com. Ed., Pub. Wyman Spano.

POLITICS, MEDIA, AND POPULAR CULTURE. *see* SOCIOLOGY

172.2 320 100 GBR ISSN 1470-594X
JA76

➤ **POLITICS, PHILOSOPHY & ECONOMICS.** Abbreviated title: P P E. Text in English. 2002 (Feb.). q. USD 781, GBP 422 combined subscription to institutions (print & online eds.); USD 765, GBP 414 to institutions (effective 2011). adv. back issues avail.; reprint service avail. from PSC. **Document type:** *Journal, Academic/Scholarly.* **Description:** Provides a forum for the interchange of methods and concepts among political scientists, philosophers and economists interested in the analysis and evaluation of political and economic institutions and practices. The journal brings moral, economic and political theory to bear on the analysis, justification and criticism of social institutions and public policies, addressing matters such as constitutional design, property rights, distributive justice, the welfare state, egalitarianism, morals of the market, democratic socialism, and the evolution of norms.
Related titles: Online - full text ed.: ISSN 1741-3060. USD 703, GBP 380 to institutions (effective 2011).
Indexed: A22, CA, CurCont, E01, ESPM, EconLit, IBSS, JEL, P03, P42, PSA, PhilInd, PsycInfo, PsycholAb, RiskAb, SCOPUS, SPAA, SSCI, SSciA, SociolAb, T02, W07.
—BLDSC (6543.949400), IE, Ingenta. **CCC.**
Published by: (The Murphy Institute of Political Economy USA), Sage Publications Ltd. (Subsidiary of: Sage Publications, Inc.), 1 Oliver's Yard, 55 City Rd, London, EC1Y 1SP, United Kingdom. TEL 44-20-73248500, FAX 44-20-73248600, info@sagepub.co.uk, http://www.uk.sagepub.com/home.nav. Eds. Fred B D'Agostino, Jonathan Riley, Thomas Christiano. adv.: B&W page GBP 350; 130 x 205. **Subscr. in the Americas to:** Sage Publications, Inc., 2455 Teller Rd, Thousand Oaks, CA 91320. TEL 805-499-9774, FAX 805-499-0871, journals@sagepub.com.

320 GBR ISSN 0959-8480
JA8

POLITICS REVIEW. Text in English. 1991. 4/yr. (Sept.-Apr.). GBP 26.95 domestic; GBP 33 in Europe; GBP 38 elsewhere (effective 2010). adv. **Document type:** *Magazine, Academic/Scholarly.*
Related titles: Online - full text ed.: free to qualified personnel (effective 2010).
Indexed: AmHI, BrHumI, DIP, G05, G06, G07, G08, H07, I05, I06, I07, IBR, IBZ, M06, P42, S23, SCOPUS, T02.
—BLDSC (6543.949650), IE, Ingenta. **CCC.**
Published by: Philip Allan Updates, Market Pl, Deddington, Banbury, Oxon OX15 0SE, United Kingdom. TEL 44-1869-338652, FAX 44-1869-337590, sales@philipallan.co.uk. Ed. Eric Magee. **Subscr. to:** Turpin Distribution, Pegasus Dr, Stratton Business Park, Biggleswade, Bedfordshire SG18 8TQ, United Kingdom. TEL 44-1767-604974, FAX 44-845-0095840, custserv@turpin-distribution.com.

320 BEL ISSN 0048-475X

POLITIEKE DOKUMENTATIE. Text in Dutch. 1969. q. adv. bk.rev. bibl. index every 3 yrs. reprints avail.
Published by: Instituut voor Everyone Vorming V.Z.M., Montoyerst. 1, Buite 20, Brussels, 1000, Belgium. FAX 32-2-428-5614. Ed. Yvo J D Peeters. Circ: 350.

324 USA

POLITIFAX NEW JERSEY; a weekly electronic newsletter for politics in New Jersey. Text in English. 46/yr. USD 369 (effective 2007). **Document type:** *Newsletter, Trade.*
Media: E-mail.
Published by: Newsletter Enterprises, L.L.C., 409 Washington St, Ste 101, Hoboken, NJ 07030. TEL 201-792-4204, FAX 201-393-5569. Ed., Pub. Nicholas Acocella.

320 FIN ISSN 0032-3365
JN6701.A1

POLITIIKKA. Text in Finnish, Swedish; Summaries in English. 1959. q. EUR 50 (effective 2004). adv. bk.rev. charts; illus. index. **Document type:** *Journal, Academic/Scholarly.*
Indexed: ABCPolSci, AmH&L, CA, HistAb, I13, IBSS, P42, PSA, RASB, SCOPUS, SociolAb, T02.
Published by: Valtiotieteellinen Yhdistyks/Finnish Political Science Association, c/o Department of Political Science, University of Helsinki, PO Box 35, Helsinki, 00014, Finland. Eds. Paul-Erik Korvela TEL 358-14-2603120, Kia Lindroos TEL 358-14-2603073. Circ: 1,400. **Subscr. to:** Kampus Kirja. TEL 358-14-603157, FAX 358-14-611143.

320 DNK ISSN 1604-0058

➤ **POLITIK.** Text in Danish. 1998. 4/yr. DKK 295 to individuals; DKK 495 to institutions; DKK 195 to students; DKK 99 online ed. (effective 2010). back issues avail. **Document type:** *Magazine, Academic/Scholarly.*
Formerly (until 2004): Politologiske Studier (1398-523X)
Related titles: Online - full text ed.
Indexed: CA, P42, PSA, SCOPUS, SociolAb, T02.
Published by: Koebenhavns Universitet, Institut for Statskundskab/Copenhagen University, Institute of Political Studies, Oester Farimagsgade 5, Copenhagen K, 1353, Denmark. TEL 45-33-323366, FAX 45-35-323399, http://www.polsci.ku.dk. Eds. Nicklas Freislebene Lund TEL 45-35-323567, Jens Hoff.

320 DEU ISSN 0342-5746

POLITIK - AKTUELL FUER DEN UNTERRICHT. Text in German. 1975. 40/yr. EUR 51.20 (effective 2006). bk.rev. **Document type:** *Newsletter.*
Published by: Madog Verlag GmbH, Postfach 101348, Kaarst, 41545, Germany. TEL 49-2131-64053, FAX 49-2131-63580, madogverlag@aol.com. Circ: 2,500.

320 DEU ISSN 1867-755X

POLITIK BEGREIFEN. Text in German. 2007. irreg., latest vol.13, 2010. price varies. **Document type:** *Monographic series, Academic/Scholarly.*
Published by: Tectum Wissenschaftsverlag Marburg, Biegenstr 4, Marburg, 35037, Germany. TEL 49-6421-481523, FAX 49-6421-43470, email@tectum-verlag.de. Eds. Annette Schmitt, Johannes Marx, Volker Kunz.

POLITIK, RET OG SAMFUND. *see* SOCIAL SCIENCES: COMPREHENSIVE WORKS

321.8 DEU ISSN 1613-706X

POLITIK UND DEMOKRATIE. Text in German. 2004. irreg., latest vol.18, 2010. price varies. **Document type:** *Monographic series, Academic/Scholarly.*

Published by: Peter Lang GmbH (Subsidiary of: Peter Lang Publishing Group), Eschborner Landstr 42-50, Frankfurt Am Main, 60489, Germany. TEL 49-69-7807050, FAX 49-69-78070550, zentrale.frankfurt@peterlang.com. Eds. Eva Kreisky, Helmut Kramer.

320 DEU ISSN 1432-0290
➤ **POLITIK UND GESELLSCHAFT. WUERZBURGER UNIVERSITAETSSCHRIFTEN.** Text in German. 1991. irreg., latest vol.9. price varies. **Document type:** *Monographic series, Academic/ Scholarly.*
Published by: Ergon Verlag, Keesburgstr 11, Wuerzburg, 97074, Germany. TEL 49-931-280084, FAX 49-931-282872, service@ergon-verlag.de.

327.43 DEU ISSN 1610-5060
POLITIK UND KOMMUNIKATION. Text in German. 2002. 8/yr. EUR 72 (effective 2010). adv. **Document type:** *Magazine, Trade.*
Published by: Helios Media GmbH, Friedrichstr 209, Berlin, 10969, Germany. TEL 49-30-848590, FAX 49-30-84859200, info@helios-media.com, http://www.helios-media.com. Ed. Sebastian Lange. Circ: 10,000 (controlled).

320.071 DEU ISSN 0344-3531
POLITIK UND UNTERRICHT; Zeitschrift fuer die Praxis der politischen Bildung. Text in German. 1975. q. EUR 12; EUR 3 newsstand/cover (effective 2011). adv. back issues avail. **Document type:** *Journal, Academic/Scholarly.* **Description:** Discusses political education in schools, lessons for social science, history and political science.
Published by: (Landeszentrale fuer Politische Bildung Baden-Wuerttemberg), Neckar Verlag GmbH, Postfach 1820, Villingen-Schwenningen, 78008, Germany. TEL 49-7721-89870, FAX 49-7721-898750, service@neckar-verlag.de, http://www.neckar-verlag.de. Adv. contact Uwe Stockburger. Circ: 19,000 (paid and controlled).

320 327 ISR
POLITIKA. Text in Hebrew. 1998. s-a. ILS 60; ILS 50 to students (effective 2008). **Document type:** *Journal, Academic/Scholarly.*
Published by: Hebrew University of Jerusalem, Leonard Davis Institute for International Relations, Jerusalem, 91905, Israel. TEL 972-2-588-5534, FAX 972-2-588-2339. Ed. Aryeh Katzovitz.

320 DEU ISSN 1868-1808
▼ **POLITIKA (BADEN-BADEN)**; Passauer Studien zur Politikwissenschaft. Text in German. 2009. irreg., latest vol.4, 2011. price varies. **Document type:** *Monographic series, Academic/ Scholarly.*
Published by: Nomos Verlagsgesellschaft mbH und Co. KG, Waldseestr 3-5, Baden-Baden, 76530, Germany. TEL 49-7221-21040, FAX 49-7221-210427, nomos@nomos.de, http://www.nomos.de. Eds. Barbara Zehnpfennig, Heinrich Oberreuter.

320 DEU ISSN 1867-1349
▼ **POLITIKA (TUEBINGEN).** Text in German. 2009. irreg., latest vol.4, 2011. price varies. **Document type:** *Monographic series, Academic/ Scholarly.*
Published by: Mohr Siebeck GmbH & Co. KG, Wilhelmstr 18, Tuebingen, 72074, Germany. TEL 49-7071-9230, FAX 49-7071-51104, info@mohr.de.

320 GRC ISSN 1105-9745
POLITIKA THEMATA. Text in Greek. 1973. w. adv. **Document type:** *Consumer.*
Published by: J. Chorn Ed. & Pub., 25 Ipsilantou, Athens, 106 75, Greece. TEL 30-1-721-8421, FAX 30-1-722-4353. Circ: 5,544.

320 HUN ISSN 1216-1438
JA26
POLITIKATUDOMANYI SZEMLE. Text in Hungarian. 1992. q.
Indexed: IBSS.
Published by: Magyar Tudomanyos Akademia, Politikai Tudomanyok Intezete/Hungarian Academy of Science, Institute for Political Sciences, Pf. 694/115, Budapest, 1399, Hungary. TEL 36-1-2246700, FAX 36-1-2246725, http://www.mtapti.hu/.

320 DEU ISSN 1864-2233
POLITIKDIDAKTISCHE FORSCHUNG. Text in German. 2007. irreg. price varies. **Document type:** *Monographic series, Academic/ Scholarly.*
Published by: Waxmann Verlag GmbH, Steinfurter Str 555, Muenster, 48159, Germany. TEL 49-251-265040, FAX 49-251-2650426, info@waxmann.com.

320 SVN ISSN 1583-3984
JA26
➤ **POLITIKON.** Text in English. 2001. q. **Document type:** *Journal, Academic/Scholarly.* **Description:** Publishes the work of students from across the fields of political science and international relations.
Media: Online - full text.
Indexed: CA, P42, T02.
Published by: International Association for Political Science Students (I A P S S), Kongresni Trg 12, Ljubljana, 1000, Slovenia. info@iapss.org, http://www.iapss.org.

320.9 GBR ISSN 0258-9346
JA26
➤ **POLITIKON**; South African journal of political science. Text and summaries in Afrikaans, English. 1974. 3/yr. GBP 341 combined subscription in United Kingdom to institutions (print & online eds.); EUR 453, USD 569 combined subscription to institutions (print & online eds.) (effective 2012). adv. bk.rev. back issues avail.; reprint service avail. from PSC. **Document type:** *Journal, Academic/ Scholarly.* **Description:** Advances the study of political science, international politics and related topics through scholarly discourse and dissemination of research results.
Related titles: Microfilm ed.: (from PQC); Online - full text ed.: ISSN 1470-1014. GBP 307 in United Kingdom to institutions; EUR 408, USD 512 to institutions (effective 2012) (from IngentaConnect).
Indexed: A01, A03, A08, A20, A22, ABCPolSci, ASD, BibInd, CA, DIP, E01, HistAb, IBR, IBSS, IBZ, IIBP, ISAP, P34, P42, PAIS, PCI, PSA, S02, S03, SCOPUS, SSA, SSCI, SociolAb, T02, W07.
—IE, Infotrieve, Ingenta. **CCC.**
Published by: (South African Association of Political Studies ZAF, Staatkundige Vereniging van Suid Afrika), Routledge (Subsidiary of: Taylor & Francis Group), 4 Park Sq, Milton Park, Abingdon, Oxon OX14 4RN, United Kingdom. TEL 44-20-70176000, FAX 44-20-70176336, subscriptions@tandf.co.uk, http://www.routledge.com. Ed. Dr. Meenal Shrivastava TEL 866-500-2924. Adv. contact Linda Hann TEL 44-1344-779945. **Subscr. to:** Taylor & Francis Ltd., Journals Customer Service, Sheepen Pl, Colchester, Essex CO3 3LP, United Kingdom. TEL 44-20-70175544, FAX 44-20-70175198.

320.9 DEU ISSN 1611-9193
POLITIKSZENE. Text in German. 2002. w. **Document type:** *Newsletter, Trade.*
Published by: Helios Media GmbH, Friedrichstr 209, Berlin, 10969, Germany. TEL 49-30-848590, FAX 49-30-84859200, info@helios-media.com, http://www.helios-media.com.

320 DEU ISSN 1862-6130
POLITIKWISSENSCHAFT. Text in German. 2005. irreg., latest vol.3, 2007. price varies. **Document type:** *Monographic series, Academic/ Scholarly.*
Published by: Frank und Timme GmbH, Wittelsbacherstr 27a, Berlin, 10707, Germany. TEL 49-30-88667911, FAX 49-30-86398731, info@frank-timme.de.

320.5 DEU ISSN 1863-9089
POLITIKWISSENSCHAFTLICHE THEORIE. Text in German. 2005. irreg., latest vol.5, 2009. price varies. **Document type:** *Monographic series, Academic/Scholarly.*
Published by: Ergon Verlag, Keesburgstr 11, Wuerzburg, 97074, Germany. TEL 49-931-280084, FAX 49-931-282872, service@ergon-verlag.de.

320.9 FRA ISSN 0244-7827
JQ1872
➤ **POLITIQUE AFRICAINE.** Text in French. 1981. q. EUR 75 domestic; EUR 85 in Europe; EUR 85 in Africa; EUR 95 elsewhere (effective 2009). adv. bk.rev. bibl.; illus. back issues avail.; reprints avail. **Document type:** *Journal, Academic/Scholarly.* **Description:** Provides analysis and political news of contemporary Africa.
Indexed: A22, ASD, BibLing, CA, FR, IBR, IBSS, IBZ, MLA-IB, P30, P42, PAIS, PCI, PSA, RASB, RILM, S02, S03, SCOPUS, SociolAb, T02.
—BLDSC (6544.093000), IE, Infotrieve, Ingenta, INIST. **CCC.**
Published by: (Association des Chercheurs de Politique Africaine), Editions Karthala, 22-24 Boulevard Arago, Paris, 75013, France. TEL 33-1-43311559, FAX 33-1-45352705, karthala@orange.fr, http://www.karthala.com. Ed. Richard Banegas. Pub. Georges Courade. Circ: 3,500.

320.973 FRA ISSN 1771-8848
JK1
POLITIQUE AMERICAINE. Text in French. 2005. 3/yr. EUR 58 domestic; EUR 79 foreign (effective 2009). **Document type:** *Journal, Academic/ Scholarly.* **Description:** Deals with contemporary political issues in the United States.
Indexed: IBSS.
Published by: Choiseul Editions, 28 Rue Etienne Marcel, Paris, 75002, France. TEL 33-1-53340993, FAX 33-1-53340994, http://choiseul-editions.com. Ed. Yannick Mireur.

306.2 338.2 NLD ISSN 1871-8833
POLITIQUE ECONOMIQUE ET SOCIALE. Cover title: Politique Economique et Sociale. Resume. Text in French. 2000. irreg. price varies.
Published by: Sociaal-Economische Raad, Postbus 90405, The Hague, 2509 LK, Netherlands. TEL 31-70-3499499, FAX 31-70-3832535, ser.info@ser.nl, http://www.ser.nl.

320 CAN ISSN 1203-9438
JA4 CODEN: POSOFS
➤ **POLITIQUE ET SOCIETES.** Text in French; Summaries in English, French. 1982. 3/yr. CAD 41 to institutions (effective 2008). adv. bk.rev. back issues avail. **Document type:** *Journal, Academic/Scholarly.*
Former titles: Revue Quebecoise de Science Politique (1189-9565); (until 1989): Politique (0711-608X)
Related titles: Online - full text ed.
Indexed: A26, AmH&L, CA, CPerI, DIP, FR, HistAb, I05, I13, IBR, IBSS, IBZ, P34, P42, PAIS, PSA, S02, S03, SCOPUS, SOPODA, SSA, SociolAb, T02.
—INIST. **CCC.**
Published by: Societe Quebecoise de Science Politique, Departement de Science Politique, Universite du Quebec a Montreal, C P 8888, Succ Centre ville, Montreal, PQ H3C 3P8, Canada. TEL 514-987-3000 ext 4582, FAX 514-987-4878, sqsp@er.uquam.ca, http://www.unites.uqam.ca/sqsp. Ed. Linda Cardinal. adv.: page CAD 200. Circ: 1,000.

➤ **POLITISCHE BILDUNG.** *see* EDUCATION—Teaching Methods And Curriculum

320 DEU
POLITISCHE DOKUMENTE. Text in German. 1972. irreg., latest vol.14, 1996. price varies. **Document type:** *Monographic series, Academic/ Scholarly.*
Published by: B W V - Berliner Wissenschafts Verlag GmbH, Markgrafenstr 12-14, Berlin, 10969, Germany. TEL 49-30-8417700, FAX 49-30-84177021, bwv@bwv-verlag.de, http://www.bwv-verlag.de.

320 DEU ISSN 1866-783X
▼ **POLITISCHE KULTURFORSCHUNG.** Text in German. 2009. irreg., latest vol.4, 2010. price varies. **Document type:** *Monographic series, Academic/Scholarly.*
Published by: Peter Lang GmbH (Subsidiary of: Peter Lang Publishing Group), Eschborner Landstr 42-50, Frankfurt Am Main, 60489, Germany. TEL 49-69-7807050, FAX 49-69-78070550, zentrale.frankfurt@peterlang.com. Ed. Samuel Salzborn.

320 DEU ISSN 0032-3446
H5
DIE POLITISCHE MEINUNG; Monatsschrift zu Fragen der Zeit. Text in German. 1956. m. EUR 50; EUR 6 newsstand/cover (effective 2007). adv. bk.rev. charts. **Document type:** *Magazine, Consumer.* **Description:** VIP's (political, cultural, and economical).
Indexed: DIP, IBR, IBZ, P30, PAIS, PRA, RASB.
—BLDSC (6544.115000). **CCC.**
Published by: Konrad-Adenauer-Stiftung e.V., Rathausallee 12, St. Augustin, 53757, Germany. TEL 49-2241-2462522, FAX 49-2241-2462591, zentrale@kas.de, http://www.kas.de. Ed., R&P Wolfgang Bergsdorf. Pub. Bernhard Vogel. adv.: page EUR 1,450. Circ: 5,700 (paid and controlled). **Subscr. to:** Verlag A. Fromm, Postfach 1948, Osnabrueck 49009, Germany. TEL 49-541-310334, FAX 49-541-310440.

320 CHE ISSN 0251-351X
POLITISCHE RUNDSCHAU/REVUE POLITIQUE; Zeitschrift fuer Kultur, Politik und Wirtschaft. Text in German, French. 1921. q. CHF 20. bk.rev. bibl.; stat. **Document type:** *Bulletin.*
Published by: Freisinnig-Demokratische Partei der Schweiz, Neuengasse 20, Postfach 6136, Bern, 3001, Switzerland. TEL 41-31-3203535, FAX 41-31-3121951. Ed. Guido Schommer.

320 DEU ISSN 0032-3462
H35
POLITISCHE STUDIEN. Text in German. 1950. bi-m. EUR 4.50 newsstand/cover (effective 2011). adv. bk.rev. charts. index. reprints avail. **Document type:** *Journal, Academic/Scholarly.*
Former titles (until 1954): Politische Bildung (0721-8869); (until 1951): Hochschule fuer Politische Wissenschaften. Schriftenreihe (0721-8850)
Related titles: Microform ed.: (from MIM, PQC).
Indexed: A20, A22, BAS, CA, CERDIC, DIP, I13, IBR, IBSS, IBZ, P06, P30, P42, PAIS, PCI, PRA, PSA, RASB, SociolAb, T02.
—BLDSC (6544.125000), IE, Infotrieve, Ingenta. **CCC.**
Published by: Hanns-Seidel-Stiftung e.V., Lazarettstr 33, Munich, 80636, Germany. TEL 49-89-12580, FAX 49-89-1258356, info@hss.de, http://www.hss.de. Circ: 4,000.

320 DEU ISSN 0032-3470
JA14
➤ **POLITISCHE VIERTELJAHRESSCHRIFT.** Abbreviated title: P V S. Text in German. 1960. q. EUR 259 combined subscription to institutions (print & online eds.) (effective 2011). adv. bk.rev. reprint service avail. from PSC. **Document type:** *Journal, Academic/ Scholarly.*
Incorporates (1979-1987): P V S-Literatur (0720-7182)
Related titles: Online - full text ed.: ISSN 1862-2860; Supplement(s): Politische Vierteljahresschrift. Sonderheft. ISSN 0720-4809. 1969.
Indexed: A20, A22, A26, ABCPolSci, ASCA, BibInd, CA, CurCont, DIP, E01, HistAb, I13, IBR, IBSS, IBZ, P10, P30, P34, P42, P45, P48, PAIS, PCI, PQC, PRA, PSA, RASB, S02, S03, SCOPUS, SSA, SSCI, SociolAb, T02, W07.
—IE, Infotrieve, Ingenta. **CCC.**
Published by: (Deutsche Vereinigung fuer Politische Wissenschaft), V S - Verlag fuer Sozialwissenschaften (Subsidiary of: Springer Fachmedien Wiesbaden GmbH), Abraham-Lincoln-Str 46, Wiesbaden, 65189, Germany. TEL 49-611-78780, FAX 49-611-7878400, springerfachmedien-wiesbaden@springer.com. Circ: 1,160 (paid).

320 BEL ISSN 0295-2319
JA11
POLITIX; revue de science sociale du politique. Text in French; Summaries in English, French. 1988. q. EUR 65 in France to individuals; EUR 65 in Belgium to individuals; EUR 69 elsewhere to individuals; EUR 115 in France to institutions; EUR 115 in Belgium to institutions; EUR 119 elsewhere to institutions (effective 2011). abstr. back issues avail. **Document type:** *Journal, Academic/Scholarly.* **Description:** Forum for political scientists, sociologists, historians, geographers, economists, and anthropologists.
Related titles: Online - full text ed.: ISSN 1953-8286.
Indexed: CA, FR, IBSS, P34, P42, PAIS, PSA, S02, S03, SCOPUS, SSCI, SociolAb, T02, W07.
—INIST. **CCC.**
Published by: De Boeck Universite (Subsidiary of: Editis), Fond Jean-Paques 4, Louvain-la-Neuve, 1348, Belgium. TEL 32-10-482511, FAX 32-10-482519, info@superieur.deboeck.com.

320 CZE ISSN 1211-0353
JA26
➤ **POLITOLOGICKA REVUE.** Text in Czech. 1995. s-a. CZK 100 (effective 2008). **Document type:** *Journal, Academic/Scholarly.*
Indexed: CA, I13, P42, T02.
Published by: Ceska Spolecnost pro Politicke Vedy, Nam. W. Churchilla 4, Prague, 13067, Czech Republic. cspv@vsers.cz. Ed. Vladimira Dvorakova.

320 CZE ISSN 1211-3247
DB2238.7
➤ **POLITOLOGICKY CASOPIS/CZECH JOURNAL OF POLITICAL SCIENCE.** Text in Czech. 1994. q. EUR 61 foreign (effective 2009). bk.rev. Index. **Document type:** *Journal, Academic/Scholarly.* **Description:** Covers political science, international relations and European studies.
Related titles: Online - full content ed.
Indexed: CA, IBSS, P42, PSA, SCOPUS, SociolAb, T02.
—**CCC.**
Published by: Masarykova Univerzita, Mezinarodni Politologicky Ustav/Masaryk University, International Institute of Political Science, Jostova 10, Brno, 60200, Czech Republic. TEL 420-549-498438, FAX 420-549-495769, iips@iips.cz, http://www.iips.cz. Ed. Vit Hlousek. Circ: 400 (controlled). **Dist. by:** Kubon & Sagner Buchexport - Import GmbH, Hessstr 39-41, Munich 80798, Germany. TEL 49-89-542180, FAX 49-89-54218218, postmaster@kubon-sagner.de, http://www.kubon-sagner.de.

320 LTU ISSN 1392-1681
DK505
POLITOLOGIJA. Text in Lithuanian. 1993. s-a. **Document type:** *Journal, Academic/Scholarly.*
Related titles: Online - full text ed.: free (effective 2011).
Indexed: CA, I13, P42, PSA, T02.
Published by: Vilniaus Universiteto Leidykla, Universiteto g 1, Vilnius, 2734, Lithuania. TEL 370-5-2687260, FAX 370-5-2123939, leidykla@leidykla.vu.lt, http://www.leidykla.vu.lt.

320 DEU
POLITOLOGISCHE STUDIEN. Text in German. 1973. irreg., latest vol.40, 1996. price varies. **Document type:** *Monographic series, Academic/ Scholarly.*

P

Published by: B W V - Berliner Wissenschafts Verlag GmbH, Markgrafenstr 12-14, Berlin, 10969, Germany. TEL 49-30-8417700, FAX 49-30-84177021, bwv@bwv-verlag.de, http://www.bwv-verlag.de.

320 GBR ISSN 0032-3497
JA3
➤ **POLITY.** Text in English. 1968. q. USD 238 in North America to institutions; GBP 147 elsewhere to institutions (effective 2011). adv. bk.rev. illus. index, cum.index every 3 vols. back issues avail.; reprint service avail. from PSC. **Document type:** *Journal, Academic/Scholarly.* **Description:** Aims to the publication of scholarship reflecting the variety of approaches to the study of politics.
Related titles: Microform ed.: (from PQC); Online - full text ed.: ISSN 1744-1684 (from IngentaConnect).
Indexed: A01, A02, A03, A08, A20, A22, A26, ABCPolSci, ABS&EES, ASCA, AmH&L, B04, BAS, BRD, CA, CurCont, E01, E08, EI, FutSurv, G08, HistAb, I05, I13, LeftInd, MEA&I, P02, P10, P27, P30, P34, P42, P45, P47, P48, P53, P54, PAIS, PCI, PQC, PRA, PSA, RASB, S02, S03, S09, S11, SCOPUS, SPAA, SSAI, SSAb, SSCI, SSI, SociolAb, T02, W03, W05, W07.
—BLDSC (6544.155000), IE, Infotrieve, Ingenta. **CCC.**
Published by: (Northeastern Political Science Association USA), Palgrave Macmillan Ltd. (Subsidiary of: Macmillan Publishers Ltd.), Houndmills, Basingstoke, Hants RG21 6XS, United Kingdom. TEL 44-1256-329242, FAX 44-1256-479476, orders@palgrave.com, http://www.palgrave.com. Eds. Cyrus Ernesto Zirakzadeh, Jeffrey Ladewig. Pub. Guy Edwards. Circ: 1,050. **Subscr. to:** Subscription Department, Brunel Rd, Houndmills, Basingstoke, Hants RG21 2XS, United Kingdom. TEL 44-1256-357893, FAX 44-1256-328339, subscriptions@palgrave.com.

➤ **POLSKA MYSL POLITYCZNA XIX I XX WIEKU.** *see* HISTORY—History Of Europe

320 BRA ISSN 0102-8529
D849
PONTIFICIA UNIVERSIDADE CATOLICA DE RIO DE JANEIRO. INSTITUTO DE RELACOES INTERNACIONAIS. CONTEXTO INTERNACIONAL. Text in Portuguese. 1985. s-a. **Document type:** *Journal, Academic/Scholarly.*
Related titles: Online - full text ed.: ISSN 1982-0240. free (effective 2011).
Indexed: C01, CA, I13, P42, PAIS, PSA, S02, S03, SCOPUS, SociolAb, T02.
Published by: Pontificia Universidade Catolica do Rio de Janeiro, Rua Marques de Sao Vicente, 225,, 22 453, ZC-20, Rio De Janeiro, RJ 22451041, Brazil. Ed. Sonia de Camargo.

306.2 781.64 USA
POP POLITICS.COM. Text in English. 2000. bi-m. free. adv. **Description:** It blends pop culture and politics and covers the connections between them.
Media: Online - full text.
Address: editor@poppolitics.com, http://www.poppolitics.com. Ed. Christine Cupaiuolo.

▼ **POPE CENTER SERIES FOR PROSPECTIVE AND CURRENT COLLEGE STUDENTS.** *see* EDUCATION—Higher Education

320 USA ISSN 1932-0612
POPULAR CULTURE AND POLITICS IN ASIA PACIFIC. Abbreviated title: P C P A. Text in English. 2005. irreg., latest 2008. price varies. back issues avail. **Document type:** *Monographic series.* **Description:** Features articles that employ a variety of approaches ranging from cultural studies and gender studies to national and group identity issues, adds nuances to and provides understanding of the complexity of life and transnational cultural formation in a rapidly changing Asia.
Published by: University of Illinois Press, 1325 S Oak St, Champaign, IL 61820. TEL 217-333-0950, FAX 217-244-8082, uipress@uillinois.edu. Ed. Poshek Fu.

320 USA ISSN 1529-241X
POPULAR POLITICS AND GOVERNANCE IN AMERICA. Text in English. 2002. irreg., latest vol.11, 2007. price varies. back issues avail. **Document type:** *Monographic series, Academic/Scholarly.* **Description:** Publishes scholarly and teaching materials about the processes of popular politics and the operations of governmental institutions at both the national and state levels.
Published by: Peter Lang Publishing, Inc. (Subsidiary of: Peter Lang Publishing Group), 29 Broadway, New York, NY 10006. TEL 212-647-7700, 800-770-5264, FAX 212-647-7707, customerservice@plang.com, http://www.peterlangusa.com. Ed. Steven Schier.

POROI; an interdisciplinary journal of rethorical analysis and invention. (Project on Rhetoric of Inquiry) *see* LINGUISTICS

▼ **PORT VITORIA.** *see* LITERATURE

324.2469 PRT
PORTUGAL SOCIALISTA. Text in Portuguese. 1967. q.
Indexed: RASB.
Published by: Partido Socialista, Largo do Rato, 2, Lisbon, 1200, Portugal. TEL 01-3464375. Ed. Antonio Reis. Circ: 5,000.

PORTUGUESE TIMES. *see* ETHNIC INTERESTS

320.531 DOM
POSICION SOCIALISTA. Text in Spanish. 3/yr.
Published by: Editora Nuevo Rumbo, Apdo Postal 2298, Santo Domingo, Dominican Republic.

320 AUT ISSN 2073-5782
▼ **POSITIONEN.** Text in German. 2009. irreg., latest vol.2, 2010. price varies. **Document type:** *Monographic series, Academic/Scholarly.*
Published by: Wilhelm Braumueller Universitaets-Verlagsbuchhandlung GmbH, Servitengasse 5, Vienna, 1090, Austria. TEL 43-1-3191159, FAX 43-1-3102805, office@braumueller.at. Eds. Barbara Blaha, Josef Weidenholzer.

322.4 USA ISSN 1065-0075
HC79.D4
POSITIVE ALTERNATIVES. Text in English. 1975. q. USD 35 to individuals; USD 3 newsstand/cover (effective 1999). bk.rev. **Document type:** *Newsletter.* **Description:** International newsletter on economic conversion, which promotes the orderly redirection of resources from the military economy to more socially useful and environmentally sustainable economic activity.
Formerly (until vol.15, no.3, 1990): Plowshare Press
Published by: Center for Economic Conversion, 222C View St, Ste C, Mountain View, CA 94041. TEL 650-968-8798, FAX 650-968-1126. Ed. Michael Closson. Circ: 7,500.

320 USA
POST-AMERIKAN. Text in English. 1972. 6/yr. USD 6 (effective 2000). adv. bk.rev.; film rev.; play rev. charts; illus. back issues avail. **Document type:** *Newspaper, Consumer.*
Related titles: Microfiche ed.
Address: PO Box 3452, Bloomington, IL 61701. TEL 309-828-4473. Ed. Sherrin Fitzer. Circ: 3,500.

POST-AUTISTIC ECONOMIC REVIEW. *see* BUSINESS AND ECONOMICS

POST-COMMUNIST ECONOMIES. *see* BUSINESS AND ECONOMICS—Economic Systems And Theories, Economic History

320 USA
POST-CONTEMPORARY INTERVENTIONS. Text in English. 1989. irreg. price varies. back issues avail. **Document type:** *Monographic series, Academic/Scholarly.*
Published by: Duke University Press, 905 W Main St, Ste 18 B, Durham, NC 27701. TEL 888-651-0122, FAX 888-651-0124, subscriptions@dukeupress.edu.

320.947 FRA ISSN 1958-9301
POST-SOVIET ARMIES NEWSLETTER. Text in English. 2006. d. **Document type:** *Newsletter.*
Published by: Centre d'Etudes et de Recherche sur les Societes et les Institutions Post-Sovietiques/Centre for Research and Study on Post-Soviet Societies and Institutions, 15 Rue Charlot, Paris, 75003, France. http://www.pipss.org.

POSTCOLONIAL STUDIES; culture, politics, economy. *see* HISTORY

321 ARG ISSN 1515-209X
POSTDATA. Text in Spanish. 1996. s-a. **Document type:** *Journal, Academic/Scholarly.*
Related titles: Online - full text ed.: ISSN 1851-9601. free (effective 2011) (from SciELO).
Published by: Grupo Interuniversitario Postdata, Ladines 2525 Piso D, Buenos Aires, 1419, Argentina. TEL 54-11-49021464. Ed. Martin D'Alessandro.

320 DEU ISSN 1618-7520
POTSDAMER ANALYSEN. Text in German. 2001. irreg. price varies. **Document type:** *Monographic series, Academic/Scholarly.*
Published by: Universitaetsverlag Potsdam, Am Neuen Palais 10, Potsdam, 14469, Germany. TEL 49-331-9774458, FAX 49-331-9774625, ubpub@uni-potsdam.de, http://info.ub.uni-potsdam.de/verlag.htm.

320 FRA ISSN 0152-0768
JA11
POUVOIRS. Text in French. 1977. q. bk.rev. bibl. reprint service avail. from SCH. **Document type:** *Magazine, Consumer.* **Description:** Covers the political aspects of the economy, social life and culture.
Indexed: A22, ABCPolSci, CA, ELLIS, FR, I13, IBSS, P42, PCI, PSA, RASB, SCOPUS, SociolAb, T02.
—BLDSC (6571.420000), IE, Infotrieve, Ingenta, INIST. **CCC.**
Published by: Editions du Seuil, 27 Rue Jacob, Paris, 75006, France. TEL 33-1-40465050, FAX 33-1-40464300, contact@seuil.com, http://www.seuil.com. Eds. Olivier Duhamel, Philippe Ardant. Circ: 9,000. **Subscr. to:** Altek Data, La Vigne aux Loups, 55 rue de Longjumeau, Chilly Mazarin Cedex 91388, France. TEL 33-1-69106465.

POUVOIRS LOCAUX. *see* PUBLIC ADMINISTRATION—Municipal Government

324.2469 PRT ISSN 0870-2144
POVO LIVRE. Text in Portuguese. 1974. w. EUR 30 domestic; EUR 40 in Europe; EUR 60 in Africa; EUR 100 elsewhere (effective 2005). back issues avail. **Document type:** *Newspaper, Consumer.*
Related titles: Online - full text ed.
Indexed: RASB.
Published by: Partido Social Democrata, Rua de Sao Caetano a Lapa 9, Lisbon, 1249-087, Portugal. TEL 251-21-3952140, http://www.psd.pt. Ed. Pacheco Pereira.

320 CAN
POWER (TORONTO). Text in English. 1975. m. USD 40. bk.rev. **Document type:** *Newsletter.* **Description:** Presents an alternative viewpoint that current interpretations of the Holocaust and its extent are incorrect.
Published by: Samisdat Publishers Ltd., 206 Carlton St, Toronto, ON M5A 2L1, Canada. TEL 416-922-9850, FAX 416-922-8614. Ed. Ernst Zuendel. Circ: 50,000.

320 FRA ISSN 1769-7069
JN6501
POWER INSTITUTIONS IN POST - SOVIET SOCIETIES; an electronic journal of social sciences. Variant title: The Journal of Power Institutions in Post-Soviet Societies. Text in Multiple languages. 2004. s-a. free (effective 2011). **Document type:** *Journal, Academic/Scholarly.* **Description:** Its main objective is to study changes and their underlying mechanisms in post-Soviet republics, through the analysis of the institutions that remain most hidden from the public eye: armies and power institutions.
Media: Online - full text.
Indexed: IBSS.
Published by: Centre d'Etudes et de Recherche sur les Societes et les Institutions Post-Sovietiques/Centre for Research and Study on Post-Soviet Societies and Institutions, 15 Rue Charlot, Paris, 75003, France. Ed. Elisabeth Sieca-Kozlowski.

320.532 RUS
POZITSIYA. Text in Russian. 1991. w.
Indexed: RASB.
Address: K Marksa pr-t 39, Omsk, 644056, Russian Federation. TEL 7-3812-319220, FAX 7-3812-310719. Ed. Galina Pochkaeva. Circ: 3,000.

321.07 USA
PRACTICAL ANARCHY. Text in English. 1991. q. looseleaf. USD 10 domestic; USD 12 in Canada & Mexico; USD 15 elsewhere (effective 2001). adv. bk.rev. bibl. back issues avail. **Document type:** *Newsletter.* **Description:** Provides a forum for readers interested in exploring the practical aspects of anarchy. Also covers cooperative housing, communal agriculture, Native American struggles, and women's interests.
Related titles: Online - full text ed.: 1991.
Address: PO Box 76930, Washington, DC 20013. editors@practicalanarchy.org, http://www.practicalanarchy.org/. Ed. Chuck Munson. Circ: 350.

320 USA ISSN 1062-5623
PRAEGER SERIES IN POLITICAL COMMUNICATION. Text in English. 1990. irreg., latest 1996. price varies. back issues avail. **Document type:** *Monographic series.*
Published by: Praeger Publishers (Subsidiary of: Greenwood Publishing Group Inc.), 88 Post Rd W, Westport, CT 06881. TEL 800-368-6868, tech.support@greenwood.com, http://www.greenwood.com. Ed. Robert Denton.

320 USA ISSN 1072-2882
PRAEGER SERIES IN POLITICAL ECONOMY. Text in English. 1988. irreg., latest 1998. price varies. back issues avail. **Document type:** *Monographic series.*
Published by: Praeger Publishers (Subsidiary of: Greenwood Publishing Group Inc.), 88 Post Rd W, Westport, CT 06881. TEL 800-368-6868, tech.support@greenwood.com, http://www.greenwood.com. Ed. Rodney Green.

320 USA ISSN 1062-0931
PRAEGER SERIES IN PRESIDENTIAL STUDIES. Text in English. 1992. irreg., latest 2003. price varies. back issues avail. **Document type:** *Monographic series.*
Published by: Information Age Publishing, Inc., PO Box 79049, Charlotte, NC 28271. TEL 704-752-9125, FAX 704-752-9113, infoage@infoagepub.com, http://www.infoagepub.com.

320 USA ISSN 1061-5261
PRAEGER SERIES IN TRANSFORMATIONAL POLITICS AND POLITICAL SCIENCE. Text in English. 1992. irreg., latest 2000. price varies. back issues avail. **Document type:** *Monographic series.*
Published by: Praeger Publishers (Subsidiary of: Greenwood Publishing Group Inc.), 88 Post Rd W, Westport, CT 06881. TEL 800-368-6868, tech.support@greenwood.com, http://www.greenwood.com. Ed. Theodore Becker.

320 USA ISSN 1936-7082
PRAIRIE FIRE; the progressive voice of the Great Plains. Text in English. 2007 (May). m. **Document type:** *Newspaper, Consumer.*
Published by: Prairie Fire Enterprises LLC, 7312 Sherman St, Lincoln, NE 68506. TEL 402-483-4100, FAX 402-483-4085, info@prairiefirenewspaper.com. Pub. W Don Nelson.

324.3 NOR ISSN 0801-6798
PRAKSIS. Text in Norwegian. 1923. irreg. adv. bk.rev. **Document type:** *Magazine, Consumer.*
Former titles (until 1986): Arbeiderrungdommen (0801-6801); (until 1974): Fritt Slag (0801-7255); (until 1951): Arbeiderungdommen (1892-2767); (until 1929): Den Roede Ungdom (1892-2759)
Published by: Arbeidernes Ungdomsfylking/Norwegian Labour Youth, PO Box 8863, Youngstorget, Oslo, 0028, Norway. TEL 47-22-396140, FAX 47-22-555592, auf@auf.no, http://www.auf.no.

320 PHL ISSN 0116-709X
DS686.614
PRAXIS; journal of political science. Text in English. 1987. a. PHP 90, USD 3.41. adv. bk.rev. **Document type:** *Journal, Academic/Scholarly.* **Description:** Publishes scholarly articles reflecting significant quantitative or qualitative research. Includes speeches, research reports, and "state of the art" papers.
Indexed: IPP, MLA-IB, SCOPUS.
Published by: De La Salle University, Political Science Department, 2401 Taft Ave, Manila, Philippines. TEL 63-2-524-4611, FAX 63-2-524-0361. Ed. Rizal G Buendia. Circ: 300.

PRAXIS POLITIK. *see* EDUCATION—Teaching Methods And Curriculum

320.071 DEU ISSN 1433-4755
PRAXIS POLITISCHE BILDUNG. Text in German. 1997. q. adv. **Document type:** *Journal, Academic/Scholarly.*
Indexed: DIP, IBR, IBZ.
Published by: Wochenschau Verlag, Adolf Damaschke Str 10, Schwalbach, 65824, Germany. TEL 49-6196-86065, FAX 49-6196-86060, info@wochenschau-verlag.de, http://www.wochenschau-verlag.de. Circ: 1,300 (paid and controlled).

321.92 ARG
PRENSA OBRERA; semanario del Partido Obrero. Text in Spanish. 1982. w. bk.rev. back issues avail. **Document type:** *Magazine, Consumer.* **Description:** Includes general news about the Party.
Related titles: Online - full text ed.
Published by: (Partido Obrero), Editorial Rumbos S.R.L., Ayacucho, 444, Buenos Aires, 1026, Argentina. TEL 54-114-9537164. Ed. Eduardo Salas. Circ: 16,000.

321.8 USA ISSN 0360-4918
JK501
➤ **PRESIDENTIAL STUDIES QUARTERLY.** Text in English. 1972. q. GBP 278 in United Kingdom to institutions; EUR 353 in Europe to institutions; USD 430 in the Americas to institutions; USD 546 elsewhere to institutions; GBP 321 combined subscription in United Kingdom to institutions (print & online eds.); EUR 406 combined subscription in Europe to institutions (print & online eds.); USD 494 combined subscription in the Americas to institutions (print & online eds.); USD 629 combined subscription elsewhere to institutions (print & online eds.) (effective 2012). bk.rev. bibl.; illus. Index. back issues avail.; reprint service avail. from PSC. **Document type:** *Journal, Academic/Scholarly.* **Description:** Offers articles, features, review essays, and book reviews covering the operations of the White House; presidential decision making; presidential relations with Congress, the courts, the bureaucracy, the public, and the press; and the president's involvement in public policy issues in both the domestic and international arenas.
Formerly (until 1974): Center House Bulletin (0098-809X)
Related titles: Microform ed.: (from PQC); Online - full text ed.: ISSN 1741-5705. GBP 278 in United Kingdom to institutions; EUR 353 in Europe to institutions; USD 430 in the Americas to institutions; USD 546 elsewhere to institutions (effective 2012) (from IngentaConnect).
Indexed: A01, A21, A22, A26, ABCPolSci, ABS&EES, AmH&L, B04, B14, BRD, BRI, CA, CBRI, CMM, DIP, E01, E08, ESPM, G08, I02, I05, I07, IBR, IBSS, IBZ, M06, MEA&I, P02, P06, P10, P13, P27, P30, P34, P42, P47, P48, P53, P54, PAIS, PQC, PRA, PSA, PerIslam, PersLit, RASB, RI-1, RI-2, RiskAb, S02, S03, S09, S11, S23, SPAA, SSAI, SSAb, SSI, T02, W03, W05.
—BLDSC (6609.880000), IE, Infotrieve, Ingenta. **CCC.**

Published by: (Center for the Study of the Presidency), Wiley-Blackwell Publishing, Inc. (Subsidiary of: Wiley-Blackwell Publishing Ltd.), 111 River St, Hoboken, NJ 07030. TEL 201-748-6000, FAX 201-748-6088, info@wiley.com, http://www.wiley.com/WileyCDA/. Ed. George C Edwards III. Adv. contact Kristin McCarthy TEL 201-748-7683.

324.2 DEU
PRESSEDIENST P D S. (Partei des Demokratischen Sozialismus) Text in German. w. EUR 57; EUR 1.20 newsstand/cover (effective 2005). **Document type:** *Newsletter.*
Published by: Partei des Demokratischen Sozialismus, Parteivorstand, Kleine Alexanderstr 28, Berlin, 10178, Germany. TEL 49-30-240090, FAX 40-30-2411046, parteivorstand@linkspartei.de, http://www.sozialisten.de.

320 RUS ISSN 0869-6462
HV9960.R9
PRESTUPLENIE I NAKAZANIE. Text in Russian. 1960. m. USD 147 in North America (effective 2000).
—East View.
Address: Ivanovskii pr 24, Moscow, 127434, Russian Federation. TEL 7-095-9766644. Ed. V V Shmatkov. **Dist. by:** East View Information Services, 10601 Wayzata Blvd, Minneapolis, MN 55305. TEL 952-252-1201, 800-477-1005, FAX 952-252-1202, info@eastview.com, http://www.eastview.com.

320 PER ISSN 1021-6480
PRETEXTOS. Text in Spanish. 1990. s-a. USD 20 per issue. adv. back issues avail. **Document type:** *Academic/Scholarly.*
Published by: Centro de Estudios y Promocion del Desarrollo (DESCO), Leon De La Fuente, 110, Magdalena Del Mar, Lima 17, Peru. TEL 51-1-2641316, FAX 51-1-2640128. Circ: 1,000.

320 RUS
PREZIDENTSKII KONTROL'. Text in Russian. bi-m. USD 99.95 in United States.
Indexed: RASB.
Published by: Izdanie Administratsii Prezidenta Rossiiskoi Federatsii, Novaya pl 14, Moscow, 103132, Russian Federation. TEL 7-095-2065420. Ed. I Yu Rybakov. **Dist. by:** East View Information Services, 10601 Wayzata Blvd, Minneapolis, MN 55305. TEL 952-252-1201, 800-477-1005, FAX 952-252-1202, info@eastview.com, http://www.eastview.com.

320 CAN
PRINCE EDWARD ISLAND. STAFFING & CLASSIFICATION BOARD. ANNUAL REPORT. Text in English. 1963. a. free. **Document type:** *Government.*
Formerly: Prince Edward Island. Civil Service Commission. Annual Report
Published by: Staffing and Classification Board, P O Box 2000, Charlottetown, PE C1A 7N8, Canada. TEL 902-368-4185, FAX 902-368-5544. Circ: 125.

320.9 973 USA ISSN 1549-1307
➤ **PRINCETON STUDIES IN AMERICAN POLITICS**; historical, international, and comparative perspectives. Text in English. 1993. irreg., latest 2009. price varies. charts; illus. back issues avail. **Document type:** *Monographic series, Academic/Scholarly.* **Description:** Examines sociopolitical issues and trends throughout US history.
—CCC.
Published by: Princeton University Press, 41 William St, Princeton, NJ 08540. TEL 609-258-4900, 800-777-4726, FAX 609-258-6305, cpriday@pupress.co.uk. Eds. Ira Katznelson, Martin Shefter, Theda Skocpol. **Subscr. addr. in US:** California - Princeton Fulfillment Services, Inc., 1445 Lower Ferry Rd, Ewing, NJ 08618. TEL 609-883-1759, 800-777-4726, FAX 609-883-7413, 800-999-1958, orders@cpfsinc.com. **Dist. addr. in Canada:** University Press Group.; **Dist. addr. in UK:** John Wiley & Sons Ltd.

➤ **PRINCETON STUDIES IN MUSLIM POLITICS.** *see* RELIGIONS AND THEOLOGY—Islamic

320.94 CZE ISSN 1213-0133
AP52
PRITOMNOST. Text in Czech. 1990. q. bk.rev.; dance rev.; film rev.; music rev. 66 p./no.; back issues avail.; reprints avail. **Document type:** *Consumer.* **Description:** Covers Central European affairs.
Former titles (until 2000): Nova Pritomnost (1211-3883); (until 1995): Pritomnost (0862-7614)
Related titles: Online - full text ed.; ◆ English ed.: The New Presence. ISSN 1211-8303.
Published by: Martin Jan Stransky Foundation, Narodni tr 11, Prague, 11000, Czech Republic. TEL 42-2-22075600, FAX 42-2-22075605, info@vydavatelstvimjs.cz, http://www.new-presence.cz. Eds. Ivan Maly, Martin Riegl. Pub. Martin Jan Stransky.

320 USA
PRIVATIZATION WATCH. Text in English. 1976. m. adv. back issues avail. **Document type:** *Magazine, Consumer.* **Description:** Covers news in the area of the privatization of government services.
Formerly (until 1988): Fiscal Watchdog
Published by: Reason Foundation, 3415 S Sepulveda Blvd, Ste 400, Los Angeles, CA 90034. TEL 310-391-2245, FAX 310-391-4395, chris.mitchell@reason.org, http://reason.org/. Ed. Leonard Gilroy TEL 310-391-2245. Adv. contact Mike Alissi TEL 203-407-0114.

320 CHE
PRO UND KONTRA. Text in German. 1982. irreg. CHF 8. back issues avail. **Document type:** *Bulletin.*
Published by: Schweizerische Arbeitsgemeinschaft fuer Demokratie, Postfach 387, Zurich, 8034, Switzerland. Circ: 3,000.

PROBLEMES D'AMERIQUE LATINE. *see* HISTORY—History Of North And South America

320.5 GBR ISSN 1365-7887
HX3
PROBLEMS OF CAPITALISM AND SOCIALISM. Text in English. 1974. 4/yr. GBP 20 domestic; GBP 25 foreign (effective 2003). bk.rev. back issues avail. **Document type:** *Journal, Academic/Scholarly.* **Description:** Review of events and ideas relevant to social organization.
Former titles: Problems of Communism and Capitalism; Problems of Communism
Indexed: ABCPolSci, AcaI, IUSGP, MEA&I.
Published by: Problems of Communism Committee, PO Box 339, Belfast, Co Antrim BT12 4GQ, United Kingdom. Ed. Jack Lane. Circ: 750. **Dist by:** Athol Books, PO Box 6589, London N7 6SG, United Kingdom.

320.532 USA ISSN 1075-8216
HX1
➤ **PROBLEMS OF POST-COMMUNISM.** Text in English. 1951-1992 (Jun.); resumed 1994. bi-m. USD 353 combined subscription domestic to institutions (print & online eds.); USD 413 combined subscription foreign to institutions (print & online eds.) (effective 2012). adv. bk.rev. illus. index. back issues avail.; reprint service avail. from PSC. **Document type:** *Journal, Academic/Scholarly.* **Description:** Provides analyses and significant information about contemporary affairs in the former Soviet Union and in China.
Formerly (until Jan.1995): Problems of Communism (0032-941X)
Related titles: Microform ed.: (from PQC); Online - full text ed.: ISSN 1557-783X. 2004 (Feb.). USD 319 to institutions (effective 2012).
Indexed: A01, A02, A03, A08, A20, A22, A25, A26, ABCPolSci, ABS&EES, B04, BAS, BRD, CA, CERDIC, CurCont, E01, E08, G08, H09, H10, HRIR, HistAb, I02, IBR, IBZ, IUSGP, KES, LID&ISL, M01, M02, M05, M10, MLA-IB, P02, P06, P10, P34, P42, P47, P48, P53, P54, PAIS, PCI, PQC, PRA, PSA, R02, RASB, S02, S03, S05, S08, S09, S11, SCOPUS, SSAI, SSAb, SSCI, SSI, SociolAb, T02, W03, W07.
—BLDSC (6617.898300), IE, Infotrieve, Ingenta. **CCC.**
Published by: (George Washington University), M.E. Sharpe, Inc., 80 Business Park Dr, Armonk, NY 10504. TEL 914-273-1800, 800-541-6563, FAX 914-273-2106, custserv@mesharpe.com. Ed. Robert T Huber. Adv. contact Barbara Ladd TEL 914-273-1800.

➤ **PROBLEMY DAL'NEGO VOSTOKA**; nauchnyi i obshchestvenno-politicheskii zhurnal. *see* HISTORY—History Of Europe

332.4 SLV ISSN 0259-9864
F1488.3
PROCESO; informativo semanal. Key Title: El Salvador Proceso. Text in Spanish. 1980. w. looseleaf. SVC 120 domestic; USD 35 in Central America; USD 60 in North America; USD 75 in Europe; USD 80 elsewhere (effective 2006). Index. back issues avail. **Document type:** *Magazine, Consumer.* **Description:** Analyzes the current political, economic, military, labor and human rights situation of El Salvador.
Related titles: Online - full text ed.
Indexed: C01.
Published by: (Centro de Informacion, Documentacion y Apoyo a la Investigacion), Universidad Centroamericana Jose Simeon Canas, U C A Editores, Apartado Postal 01-168, San Salvador, El Salvador. TEL 503-210-6600, FAX 503-210-6655, correo@www.uca.edu.sv. Circ: 1,200.

PROFANE EXISTENCE. *see* MUSIC

PROFESIONALES Y CUADROS. *see* BUSINESS AND ECONOMICS

320.092 USA ISSN 1080-7063
D839.5
PROFILES OF WORLDWIDE GOVERNMENT LEADERS. Text in English. 1993. a. USD 387 combined subscription (print & online eds.) (effective 2008). reprints avail. **Document type:** *Directory.* **Description:** Provides "snapshots" of decision makers in governments worldwide.
Related titles: CD-ROM ed.: 1993; Online - full text ed.
—CCC.
Published by: C Q Press, Inc. (Subsidiary of: Sage Publications, Inc.), 2300 N St, NW, Ste 800, Washington, DC 20037. TEL 202-729-1900, 866-427-7737, FAX 800-380-3810, customerservice@cqpress.com. Ed. Linda Dziobek.

PROGRAMA DE PROMOCION DE LA REFORMA EDUCATIVA EN AMERICA LATINA Y EL CARIBE. SERIE POLITICAS. *see* EDUCATION

320.532 ITA
IL PROGRAMMA COMUNISTA; organo del partito comunista internazionale. Text in Italian. 1952. m. bk.rev. 8 p./no. 6 cols./p.; **Document type:** *Newspaper, Consumer.* **Description:** Promotes revolutionary communism in the tradition of the Italian communist left, for the rebirth of the international communist movement.
Related titles: Online - full text ed.
Published by: (Partito Comunista Internazionale), Il Programma Comunista, Casella Postale 962, Milan, MI 20101, Italy.

320.5 USA ISSN 0033-0736
AP2
THE PROGRESSIVE (MADISON). Text in English. 1909. m. USD 14.97 domestic (print or online ed.) (effective 2010). adv. bk.rev.; film rev. illus. index. back issues avail.; reprints avail. **Document type:** *Magazine, Consumer.* **Description:** Covers investigative reporting, analysis, and commentary on political, economic and social issues, culture, and the arts.
Supersedes (in 1929): La Follette's Magazine; Which was formerly (until 1914): La Follette's Weekly; (until 1913): La Follette's Weekly Magazine
Related titles: Microform ed.: (from PQC); Online - full text ed.
Indexed: A01, A02, A03, A08, A11, A22, A25, A26, ABS&EES, AcaI, AltPI, B04, B14, BAS, BRD, BRI, C05, C12, CA, CBRI, CPerI, CWI, ChPerI, Chicano, E04, E05, E08, FutSurv, G05, G06, G07, G08, HRA, I05, I07, IPARL, LeftInd, M01, M02, M05, M06, M10, MASUSE, MEA&I, MLA-IB, MRD, MagInd, P02, P05, P06, P10, P13, P30, P34, P45, P47, P48, P53, P54, PMR, PQC, PRA, PerIslam, R03, R04, R06, RASB, RGAb, RGPR, S08, S09, S11, S23, T02, W03, W05, W09.
—BLDSC (6924.640000), CIS, IE, Infotrieve, Ingenta. **CCC.**
Published by: The Progressive, Inc., 409 E Main St, Madison, WI 53703. Adv. contact Erika Baer TEL 608-257-4626. B&W page USD 2,500, color page USD 2,900; trim 8.375 x 10.875.

320 USA ISSN 1096-5971
JK2372
PROGRESSIVE POPULIST; a journal from the heartland. Text in English. 1995. bi-m. USD 29.95 domestic to individuals; USD 60 in Europe to individuals; USD 70 in Asia to individuals; USD 2 newsstand/cover (effective 2000). adv. bk.rev.; music rev.; tel.rev. back issues avail. **Document type:** *Newspaper.* **Description:** Reports from the heartland on issues of interest to workers rogressive values.
Media: Online - full text. **Related titles:** E-mail ed.
Indexed: AltPI, LeftInd, M10.
Published by: Ampersand Publishing Co., PO Box 487, Storm Lake, IA 50588. TEL 712-732-4991, FAX 712-732-4331, mmir35701@aol.com. Ed., R&P James Cullen TEL 512-447-0455. Pub., Adv. contact John Cullen. B&W page USD 625. Circ: 3,000 (paid); 2,000 (controlled).

320 USA
PROJECT; ruling class conspiracy analysis for investors & political activists. Text in English. 1974. m. looseleaf. USD 30. adv. bk.rev. back issues avail. **Description:** Tests theory that Vatican and Neo-British Empire are in covert battle for world hegemony.
Formerly (until 1984): Conspiracy Digest
Published by: (A-albionic Society), A-albionic Research, PO Box 20273, Ferndale, MI 48220. Ed. Lloyd Miller. Circ: 1,000.

PROJECT ON GOBAL MIGRATION AND TRANSNATIONAL POLITICS. *see* POPULATION STUDIES

321.92 SWE ISSN 0345-9578
PROLETAEREN. Text in Swedish. 1970. w. SEK 450 (effective 2001). **Document type:** *Newspaper, Consumer.*
Published by: K P M L, Box 31187, Goeteborg, 40032, Sweden. TEL 46-31-242615, FAX 46-31-244464. Ed. Jan Kihlman.

321.92 USA ISSN 0894-0754
HX1
PROLETARIAN REVOLUTION. Text in English, German, Spanish, Russian. 1976. 3/yr. USD 7 for 2 yrs. domestic; USD 15 for 2 yrs. foreign (effective 2008). back issues avail.
Formerly: Socialist Voice
Published by: (League for the Revolutionary Party), Socialist Voice Publishing Co., PO Box 1936, Murray Hill Sta, New York, NY 10156. Circ: 1,000.

321.8 PRY
PROPUESTAS DEMOCRATICAS; para la sociedad y el estado del Paraguay del siglo XXI. Text in Spanish. 1994. q. **Document type:** *Academic/Scholarly.*
Published by: Universidad Nacional de Asuncion, Facultad de Ciencias Economicas, Administrativas y Contables, Gonzales Rioboo 680 - C Chaco Borea, Asuncion, Paraguay. FAX 595-21-610381, http://www.una.py. Ed. Jose Luis Simon G.

320 FRA ISSN 2106-9875
PROSPECTIVE RHONE - ALPES - MEDITERRANEE. Text in French. 1986. w. **Document type:** *Newsletter, Consumer.*
Former titles (until 2010): Prospective Rhone-Alpes (1155-3405); (until 1990): La Lettre Politique Rhone-Alpes (0989-1870)
Published by: Informations Recherches et Etudes Sociales, 2 Place de la Bourse, Lyon, 69002, France. TEL 33-4-78372599, FAX 33-4-78375792, http://www.informations-politiques.com. Ed. Bernard Lachaise.

PROSPETTIVA PERSONA; trimestrale di cultura etica e politica. *see* PHILOSOPHY

320 VEN ISSN 1317-9535
JL3800
➤ **PROVINCIA**; revista venezolana de estudios territoriales. Text in Spanish. 2001. s-a. free (effective 2011). **Document type:** *Journal, Academic/Scholarly.* **Description:** Covers investigations and work about state and municipal government.
Media: Online - full text.
Indexed: A01, A26, CA, F03, F04, I04, I05, P42, PSA, SociolAb, T02.
Published by: Universidad de Los Andes, Facultad de Ciencias Juridicas, Politicas y Criminologicas, Centro Iberoamericano de Estudios Provinciales y Locales, Av Las Americas, Edif de Post5grados, Piso 3, Of 02-10, Merida, 5101, Venezuela. TEL 58-274-2402067.

328.71 CAN ISSN 0835-0329
KE72
PROVINCIAL LEGISLATIVE RECORD. Text in English. 1983. m. looseleaf. CAD 540 (effective 2008). index. **Document type:** *Journal, Trade.* **Description:** Complete reporting of the status of legislation for the Canadian provinces and territories, including all proclamations.
Formerly: Provincial Pulse Newsletter (0714-7015)
Published by: C C H Canadian Ltd. (Subsidiary of: Wolters Kluwer N.V.), 90 Sheppard Ave E, Ste 300, North York, ON M2N 6X1, Canada. TEL 416-224-2248, 800-268-4522, FAX 416-224-2243, 800-461-4131, cservice@cch.ca.

PSYCHOLOGY, PUBLIC POLICY, AND LAW. *see* PSYCHOLOGY

PSYCHOTHERAPY AND POLITICS INTERNATIONAL. *see* MEDICAL SCIENCES—Psychiatry And Neurology

320.531 FRA ISSN 2105-7362
LE P'TIT CASTELROUSSIN. Text in French. 1995. m. **Document type:** *Newspaper, Consumer.*
Formerly (until 2009): Liaisons - Section du Parti Socialiste de Chateauroux (1267-1096)
Published by: Parti Socialiste Section Andre Parpais de Chateauroux, 70 Av Charles de Gaulle, Chateauroux, France.

PUBLIC ADMINISTRATION AND DEVELOPMENT; the international journal of management research and practice. *see* BUSINESS AND ECONOMICS—International Development And Assistance

320 USA ISSN 0555-5914
JK6501
PUBLIC AFFAIRS. Text in English. 1960. irreg. (approx. 3/yr.). free. charts; illus. **Document type:** *Monographic series.* **Description:** Each issue focuses on a different public policy issue.
Indexed: P06, PAIS.
Published by: University of South Dakota, Governmental Research Bureau, 414 E. Clark St., Dakota Hall 233, Vermillion, SD 57069. TEL 605-677-5708, FAX 605-677-8808, william.Anderson@usd.edu, http://www.usd.edu/grb/. Circ: 1,800.

320.9 USA ISSN 0033-3417
JK8701
PUBLIC AFFAIRS REPORT. Text in English. 1960. bi-m. free. charts; stat. back issues avail.; reprints avail. **Document type:** *Magazine, Consumer.*
Indexed: EnvAb, GeoRef, MCR, P06, P30, PAIS, SpeleolAb.
—CCC.
Published by: University of California, Berkeley, Institute of Governmental Studies, 109 Moses Hall #2370, Berkeley, CA 94720-2370. TEL 510-642-1474, FAX 510-642-3020. Ed. Gerald Lubenow. Circ: 6,000.

PUBLIC CHOICE. *see* BUSINESS AND ECONOMICS

P

320.9 USA ISSN 1094-8759
THE PUBLIC EYE (SOMERVILLE). Text in English. 1977-1988; resumed 1992. 3/yr. USD 29 to individuals; USD 29 to non-profit organizations; USD 39 to institutions (effective 2000). bk.rev. bibl. **Document type:** *Newsletter.* **Description:** Monitors the political activities and publications of the American right-wing, and provides in-depth analysis of right-wing political activism and emerging trends.
Formerly (until 1992): The Public Eye (Washington, D.C.) (0271-6569)
Related titles: Microfilm ed.; Online - full text ed.
Indexed: APW, HRIR.
Published by: Political Research Associates, 1310 Broadway, Ste 201, Somerville, MA 02144-1731. TEL 617-666-5300, FAX 617-666-6622, pra@igc.org, http://www.publiceye.org/. Ed. Judith Glaubman.

PUBLIC INTEGRITY. *see* PUBLIC ADMINISTRATION

320.6 USA ISSN 1948-3511
H96
▼ ➤ **PUBLIC KNOWLEDGE JOURNAL.** Abbreviated title: P K J. Text in English. 2009. s-a. free (effective 2011). back issues avail. **Document type:** *Journal, Academic/Scholarly.* **Description:** Contains scholarly refereed articles, as well as book reviews, essays, interviews, and other works utilizing a variety of media.
Media: Online - full text.
Published by: (Virginia Polytechnic Institute and State University, National Capital Region), Public Knowledge Journal Ed. Kimberly Carlson.

320.6 GBR ISSN 1467-5064
PUBLIC MANAGEMENT AND POLICY ASSOCIATION. REVIEW. Abbreviated title: P M P A Review. Text in English. 1994. q. free to members (effective 2010). back issues avail. **Document type:** *Newsletter, Trade.* **Description:** Contains articles and news about British public sector management and government.
Formerly (until 1998): Public Finance Foundation. Review (1357-0781); Supersedes: Chartered Institute of Public Finance and Accountancy. Public Finance Foundation. Privatisation Series
Related titles: Online - full text ed.
—**CCC.**
Published by: (Public Management and Policy Association), Chartered Institute of Public Finance and Accountancy, 3 Robert St, London, WC2N 6RL, United Kingdom. TEL 44-20-75435600, FAX 44-20-75435700, info@cipfa.org.uk.

320.9 GBR ISSN 0033-362X
HM261.A1 CODEN: POPQAE
➤ **PUBLIC OPINION QUARTERLY.** Abbreviated title: P O Q. Text in English. 1937. q. (plus special issue). GBP 162 in United Kingdom to institutions; EUR 243 in Europe to institutions; USD 243 in US & Canada to institutions; GBP 162 elsewhere to institutions; GBP 176 combined subscription in United Kingdom to institutions (print & online eds.); EUR 265 combined subscription in Europe to institutions (print & online eds.); USD 265 combined subscription in US & Canada to institutions (print & online eds.); GBP 176 combined subscription elsewhere to institutions (print & online eds.) (effective 2012). adv. bk.rev. charts; illus. index, cum.index: vols.1-46. back issues avail.; reprint service avail. from PSC. **Document type:** *Journal, Academic/Scholarly.* **Description:** Devoted to research in public opinion. Covers survey methods, communication, and propaganda.
Related titles: Microform ed.: (from CIS, PQC); Online - full text ed.: ISSN 1537-5331. GBP 147 in United Kingdom to institutions; EUR 221 in Europe to institutions; USD 221 in US & Canada to institutions; GBP 147 elsewhere to institutions (effective 2012) (from IngentaConnect).
Indexed: A01, A02, A03, A08, A12, A13, A14, A17, A20, A22, A25, A26, ABCPolSci, ABIn, ABS&EES, AC&P, ASCA, AcaI, AmH&L, B01, B04, B06, B07, B08, B09, B14, BAS, BRD, BRI, BusI, CA, CBRI, CIS, CMM, CPM, Chicano, CommAb, CurCont, DIP, E-psyche, E01, E07, E08, FR, FamI, G05, G06, G07, G08, G10, H09, H10, HistAb, I05, I13, IBR, IBSS, IBZ, IPARL, L09, M06, MEA&I, MLA-IB, MResA, MagInd, NRN, P02, P03, P06, P07, P10, P13, P25, P27, P30, P34, P42, P45, P46, P47, P48, P51, P53, P54, PAIS, PCI, PQC, PRA, PSA, PsycInfo, PsycholAb, RASB, S02, S03, S05, S08, S09, S11, S23, SCOPUS, SOPODA, SPAA, SRI, SRRA, SSA, SSAI, SSAb, SSCI, SSI, SociolAb, T02, W03, W07, W09.
—BLDSC (6967.850000), IE, Infotrieve, Ingenta, INIST. **CCC.**
Published by: (American Association for Public Opinion Research USA), Oxford University Press, Great Clarendon St, Oxford, OX2 6DP, United Kingdom. TEL 44-1865-556767, FAX 44-1865-556646, enquiry@oup.co.uk, http://www.oxfordjournals.org. Eds. James N Druckman, Nancy A Mathiowetz. Adv. contact Linda Hann TEL 44-1344-779945.

320 USA
PUBLIC OPINION REPORT. Text in English. 1988. q. free. **Document type:** *Newsletter.* **Description:** Reports of public opinion surveys in Rhode Island.
Published by: (Public Opinion Laboratory), Brown University, A. Alfred Taubman Center for Public Policy and American Institutions, PO Box 1977, Providence, RI 02912. TEL 401-863-1163. Ed. Darrell West. R&P Darrell M West. Circ: 800.

320 AUS ISSN 1833-2110
PUBLIC POLICY. Text in English. 2006. 3/yr.
Indexed: AusPAIS.
Published by: Curtin University of Technology, John Curtin Institute of Public Policy, GPO Box U1987, Perth, W.A. 6845, Australia. TEL 61-8-9266-1111, FAX 61-8-9266-3658, jcipp@curtin.edu.au, http://www.jcipp.curtin.edu.au/index.html.

PUBLIC POLICY AND POLITICS. *see* PUBLIC ADMINISTRATION

320.6 USA ISSN 1540-1499
PUBLIC POLICY & PRACTICE; an electronic journal devoted to governance and public policy in south carolina. Text in English. 2001 (Oct.). q.
Media: Online - full content.
Indexed: PAIS.
Published by: University of South Carolina, Institute for Public Service and Policy Research, 937 Assembly St., Rm. 1416, Columbia, SC 29208. TEL 803-777-0453. Ed. Richard Young.

320.6 AUT
PUBLIC POLICY AND SOCIAL WELFARE. Text in English. 3/yr. price varies. **Document type:** *Monographic series, Academic/Scholarly.*
Published by: European Centre for Social Welfare Policy and Research, Berggasse 17, Vienna, W 1090, Austria. TEL 43-1-3194505-27, FAX 43-1-3194505-19, stamatiou@euro.centre.org, http://www.euro.centre.org. Ed. Bernd Marin. R&P Willem Stamatiou. **Subscr. to:** Ashgate Publishing Ltd, Gower House, Croft Rd, Aldershot, Hants GU11 3HR, United Kingdom; **U.S. subscr. to:** Ashgate Publishing Co.

320 USA ISSN 1933-6640
PUBLIC POLICY INSTITUTE OF CALIFORNIA. RESEARCH BRIEF. Text in English. 1996. irreg. **Document type:** *Monographic series, Academic/Scholarly.*
Related titles: Online - full text ed.: ISSN 1933-6659. free (effective 2010).
Published by: Public Policy Institute of California, 500 Washington St, Ste 600, San Francisco, CA 94111. TEL 415-291-4400, FAX 415-291-4401, http://www.ppic.org/main/home.asp.

PUBLICATIONES UNIVERSITATIS MISKOLCIENSIS. SERIES JURIDICA ET POLITICA. *see* LAW

320.1 GBR ISSN 0048-5950
JK1
➤ **PUBLIUS**; the journal of federalism. Text in English. 1971. q. GBP 257 in United Kingdom to institutions; EUR 385 in Europe to institutions; USD 385 in US & Canada to institutions; GBP 257 elsewhere to institutions; GBP 281 combined subscription in United Kingdom to institutions (print & online eds.); EUR 421 combined subscription in Europe to institutions (print & online eds.); USD 421 combined subscription in US & Canada to institutions (print & online eds.); GBP 281 combined subscription elsewhere to institutions (print & online eds.) (effective 2012). adv. bk.rev. bibl.; charts; stat.; illus. index. back issues avail.; reprint service avail. from PSC. **Document type:** *Journal, Academic/Scholarly.* **Description:** Devoted to federalism. It is required reading for scholars of many disciplines who want the latest developments, trends, and empirical and theoretical work on federalism and intergovernmental relations.
Related titles: Microform ed.: (from PQC); Online - full text ed.: ISSN 1747-7107. GBP 234 in United Kingdom to institutions; EUR 351 in Europe to institutions; USD 351 in US & Canada to institutions; GBP 234 elsewhere to institutions (effective 2012) (from IngentaConnect).
Indexed: A01, A02, A03, A08, A20, A22, A25, A26, ABCPolSci, ABS&EES, ASCA, AmH&L, B04, BRD, CA, CurCont, DIP, E01, E08, G08, HistAb, I05, I07, I13, IBR, IBSS, IBZ, IPARL, M06, MEA&I, P02, P06, P10, P27, P30, P34, P42, P45, P48, P53, P54, PAIS, PCI, PQC, PRA, PSA, RASB, S02, S03, S08, S09, S11, S23, SCOPUS, SOPODA, SPAA, SSA, SSAI, SSAb, SSCI, SSI, SUSA, SociolAb, T02, W03, W05, W07.
—BLDSC (7156.095000), IE, Infotrieve, Ingenta. **CCC.**
Published by: Oxford University Press, Great Clarendon St, Oxford, OX2 6DP, United Kingdom. TEL 44-1865-556767, FAX 44-1865-556646, enquiry@oup.co.uk, http://www.oxfordjournals.org. Ed. Carol S Weissert TEL 850-645-2940. Adv. contact Linda Hann TEL 44-1344-779945.

➤ **PULP FICTIONS.** *see* LAW—Constitutional Law

320 BOL
PUNTO DE VISTA; revista de opinion y analisis. Text in Spanish. 1994. m.
Address: Casilla 2317, Calle Tumusla, 77, Santa Cruz, Bolivia. TEL 591-33-324321, FAX 591-33-333830. Ed. Gustavo Parada Vaca.

320 ESP ISSN 1699-0080
AP60
EL PUNTO DE VISTA DE LE MONDE DIPLOMATIQUE. Text in Spanish. 2004. bi-m. back issues avail. **Document type:** *Magazine, Consumer.*
Related titles: ◆ French ed.: Maniere de Voir. ISSN 1241-6290; ◆ Supplement to: Le Monde Diplomatique en Espanol. ISSN 1888-6434.
Published by: Ediciones Cybermonde S.L., C/ Aparisi i Guijarro 5, Pta 2, Valencia, 46003, Spain. TEL 34-902-212150, FAX 34-902-212160, admon@mundiplo.com.

320 MEX ISSN 0188-1094
PUNTO FINAL INTERNACIONAL. Text in Spanish. m. MXN 80, USD 60.
Published by: Centro Latinoamericano de Comunicaciones, San Lorenzo 173, Interior 101, Colonia del Valle, Mexico.

320 PRK
THE PYONGYANG TIMES. Text in English. w. USD 60. **Document type:** *Newspaper.*
Related titles: Spanish ed.; French ed.
Indexed: RASB.
Published by: Pyongyang Times, Sochon-dong, Sosong District, Pyongyang, Korea, N. TELEX 37018 EPB KP. **Dist. by:** Korean Publications Exchange Association, Export Section, P.O. Box 222, Pyongyang, Korea, S. FAX 850-2-3814632.

320.531 ITA ISSN 1592-5277
HD8473
Q A S. QUADERNI DI AZIONE SOCIALE. Variant title: I Quaderni di Azione Sociale. Text in Italian. 1947. bi-m. price varies. adv. bk.rev. **Document type:** *Monographic series, Academic/Scholarly.*
Former titles (until 1984): Quaderni di Azione Sociale (0033-4901); (until 1949): Informazioni Sindacali (1592-5269)
Indexed: P30, PAIS, RASB.
Published by: Associazioni Cristiane Lavoratori Italiani (A C L I), Via Giuseppe Marcora 18-20, Rome, 00153, Italy. TEL 39-06-58401, FAX 39-06-5840202, acli@acli.it, http://www.acli.it. Circ: 2,500.

Q C R QUADERNI DEL CIRCOLO ROSSELLI. *see* CLUBS

320.5 USA ISSN 0738-9752
B823.3
➤ **Q J I.** (Quarterly Journal of Ideology) Text in English. 1976. q. USD 10 to individuals; USD 20 to institutions (effective 2010). adv. bk.rev. back issues avail. **Document type:** *Journal, Academic/Scholarly.* **Description:** Brings out philosophical and theoretical papers analyzing ideological issues in sociology, economics, history, political science and other fields, with a multidisciplinary perspective.
Related titles: Online - full text ed.
Indexed: Chicano, LeftInd, MLA-IB, SCOPUS, SOPODA, SociolAb.
—Ingenta.
Published by: Louisiana State University, Shreveport, 1 University Pl, Shreveport, LA 71115. TEL 318-797-5000. Ed. Edward C Polson.

320 SWE
Q O G WORKING PAPER SERIES. (Quality of Government) Text in English, Swedish. 2005. irreg. free (effective 2011). **Document type:** *Journal, Academic/Scholarly.* **Description:** It aims at conducting and promoting research on the causes, consequences and nature of "good governance", that is, trustworthy, reliable, impartial, not corrupt and competent government.
Media: Online - full text.
Published by: Goeteborgs Universitet, Quality of Government Institut, Spraengkullsgatan 19, Goeteborg, SE-405 30, Sweden. TEL 46-31-7731307, FAX 46-31-7734599.

320 EGY ISSN 1687-6504
HN786
QADAYA WA-'ARA'/ARTICLES BULLETIN. Text in Arabic. 2007. m. **Document type:** *Bulletin, Government.*
Related titles: Online - full text ed.: ISSN 1687-8949.
Published by: Egypt, The Cabinet. Information and Decision Support Center (I D S C), 1 Magless El Sha'ab St, Cairo, Egypt. TEL 202-2792-9292, FAX 202-2792-9222, info@idsc.net.eg, http://www.idsc.gov.eg/default.aspx, http://www.eip.gov.eg/Default.aspx.

320 KAZ
QAZAQSTAN RESPUBLIKASYNYNG KHALYQARALYQ SHARTTARY BIULLETENI/BULLETIN OF INTERNATIONAL TREATIES OF THE REPUBLIC OF KAZAKHSTAN/BYULLETEN' MEZHDUNARODNYKH DOGOVOROV, SOGLASHENII I OTDEL'NYKH ZAKONODATEL'NYKH AKTOV RESPUBLIKI KAZAKHSTAN. Text in Russian, Kazakh. bi-m. USD 222 in North America (effective 2011). **Document type:** *Bulletin, Government.*
Published by: President Administration Office of Kazakhstan, Akorda Bldg, Astana, Kazakhstan. TEL 7-7172-745667. **Dist. by:** East View Information Services, 10601 Wayzata Blvd, Minneapolis, MN 55305. TEL 952-252-1201, 800-477-1005, FAX 952-252-1202, info@eastview.com, http://www.eastview.com.

324.251 CHN ISSN 1001-8239
QIU ZHI/SEEK KNOWLEDGE. Text in Chinese. 1984. m. USD 36 (effective 2009). adv. **Document type:** *Government.*
—East View.
Published by: (Zhongguo Gongchandang/Chinese Communist Party, Tianjin Shi-Wei Dangxiao/Tianjin City Committee Party School), Qiu Zhi Bianjibu, 4 Yuliang Dao, Nankai-qu, Xinjiang 300191, China. TEL 86-22-23362087. Ed. Chang Qiu Rong. Circ: 30,000. **Dist. by:** China Publications Foreign Trade Corp., Tianjin Branch, 27 Hubei Lu, Tianjin, China.

320.5 CHN ISSN 1002-4980
AP95.C4
QIUSHI/SEEKING TRUTH. Text in Chinese. 1958. s-m. CNY 5.80 per issue (effective 2011). back issues avail. **Document type:** *Journal, Academic/Scholarly.* **Description:** Covers various aspects of Chinese socialism, including Marxism-Leninism studies, Mao Zedong and Deng Xiaoping research.
Formerly (until 1988): Hongqi (0441-4381)
Related titles: Online - full text ed.; ◆ English ed.: Qiushi (English Edition). ISSN 1674-7569; ◆ Partial Tibetan translation(s): Qiushi Wenxuan (Zangwen). ISSN 1006-5881; ◆ Qiushi Wenxuan (Weiwen). ISSN 1006-5857; ◆ Qiushi Wenxuan (Hawen). ISSN 1006-589X.
—East View.
Published by: Qiushi Zazhishe, 83, Beiheyan Dajiejia, Dongcheng-qu, Beijing, 100727, China. TEL 86-10-64037005, FAX 86-10-64051668. **Dist. by:** China International Book Trading Corp, 35 Chegongzhuang Xilu, Haidian District, PO Box 399, Beijing 100044, China. TEL 86-10-68412045, FAX 86-10-68412023, cibtc@mail.cibtc.com.cn, http://www.cibtc.com.cn.

320.532 CHN ISSN 1674-7569
▼ **QIUSHI (ENGLISH EDITION)**; organ of the Central Committee of the Communist Party of China. Text in English. 2009. q.
Related titles: ◆ Chinese ed.: Qiushi. ISSN 1002-4980.
Published by: Qiushi Zazhishe, 83, Beiheyan Dajiejia, Dongcheng-qu, Beijing, 100727, China. TEL 86-10-64037005, FAX 86-10-64051668. **Dist. by:** China International Book Trading Corp, 35 Chegongzhuang Xilu, Haidian District, PO Box 399, Beijing 100044, China. TEL 86-10-68412045, FAX 86-10-68412023, cibtc@mail.cibtc.com.cn, http://www.cibtc.com.cn.

320.531 CHN ISSN 1006-589X
QIUSHI WENXUAN (HAWEN). Text in Kazakh. 1988. m. USD 25.20 (effective 2009). **Document type:** *Journal, Academic/Scholarly.*
Related titles: ◆ Partial translation of: Qiushi. ISSN 1002-4980.
—East View.
Published by: Minzu Chubanshe/Ethnic Publishing House, 14, Heping Li Bei Jie, Beijing, 100013, China. TEL 86-10-64212794, http://www.e56.com.cn/.

320.531 CHN ISSN 1006-5857
QIUSHI WENXUAN (WEIWEN)/SELECTED ARTICLES FROM SEEKING TRUTH (IN UIGHUR). Text in Uigur. 1988. m. **Document type:** *Journal, Academic/Scholarly.*
Related titles: ◆ Partial translation of: Qiushi. ISSN 1002-4980.
—East View.
Published by: Minzu Chubanshe/Ethnic Publishing House, 14, Heping Li Bei Jie, Beijing, 100013, China. TEL 86-10-64212794, http://www.e56.com.cn/.

320.531 CHN ISSN 1006-5881
QIUSHI WENXUAN (ZANGWEN)/SELECTED ARTICLES FROM SEEKING TRUTH (IN TIBETAN). Text in Tibetan. 1988. m.
Related titles: ◆ Partial translation of: Qiushi. ISSN 1002-4980.
—East View.
Published by: Minzu Chubanshe/Ethnic Publishing House, 14, Heping Li Bei Jie, Beijing, 100013, China. TEL 86-10-64212794, http://www.e56.com.cn/.

320 ITA ISSN 2038-9884
I QUADERNI. Text in Multiple languages. 2006. s-a. free. **Document type:** *Magazine, Consumer.*
Media: Online - full text.
Published by: Centro Studi Difesa Civile, Via della Cellulosa 112, Rome, 00166, Italy. roma@pacedifesa.org, http://www.pacedifesa.org.

320 ITA ISSN 1826-8846
JN26
QUADERNI EUROPEI. Key Title: 2004 Quaderni Europei. Abbreviated title: 2004 Q E. Text in Italian. 2001. 3/yr. **Document type:** *Magazine, Consumer.*

Published by: Rubbettino Editore, Viale Rosario Rubbettino 10, Soveria Mannelli, CZ 88049, Italy. TEL 39-0968-662034, FAX 39-0968-662055, segreteria@rubettino.it, http://www.rubbettino.it.

QUADERNI FIORENTINI PER LA STORIA DEL PENSIERO GIURIDICO MODERNO. *see* LAW

320 ITA ISSN 2038-4211
QUADERNI FORUM. Text in Italian. 1987. 3/yr. EUR 30 (effective 2011). **Document type:** *Journal, Academic/Scholarly.*
Published by: (Forum per i Problemi della Pace e della Guerra), Edizioni E T S, Piazza Carrara 16-19, Pisa, Italy. TEL 39-050-29544, FAX 39-050-20158, info@edizioniets.it, http://www.edizioniets.it. Ed. Rodolfo Ragionieri.

QUALE STATO. *see* BUSINESS AND ECONOMICS—Labor And Industrial Relations

QUALE SVILUPPO. *see* HISTORY—History Of North And South America

320 USA ISSN 2153-6767
JA71
QUALITATIVE & MULTI-METHOD RESEARCH. Text in English. 2003 (Spr.). bi-m. **Document type:** *Newsletter, Trade.*
Formerly (until 2008): Qualitative Methods (1544-8045)
Related titles: Online - full text ed.: ISSN 2153-6783.
—CCC.
Published by: American Political Science Association, 1527 New Hampshire Ave, NW, Washington, DC 20036. TEL 202-483-2512, FAX 202-483-2657, apsa@apsanet.org, http://www.apsanet.org. Ed. John Gerring.

320 USA ISSN 1554-0626
JA1
➤ **QUARTERLY JOURNAL OF POLITICAL SCIENCE.** Text in English. 2006. q. USD 400 in the Americas (print or online ed.); EUR 400 elsewhere (print or online ed.); USD 470 combined subscription in the Americas (print & online eds.); EUR 470 combined subscription elsewhere (print & online eds.) (effective 2012). back issues avail.; reprints avail. **Document type:** *Journal, Academic/Scholarly.* **Description:** Contains research on any and all aspects of private, local, national, comparative, or international politics, while focusing on positive political theories, empirical tests of those theories, and the measurement of causal relationships.
Related titles: Online - full text ed.: ISSN 1554-0634. 2006. USD 400 in the Americas; EUR 400 elsewhere (effective 2012).
Indexed: A26, CA, CurCont, E10, EconLit, I05, JEL, P30, P42, PSA, SCOPUS, SSCI, T02, W07.
—BLDSC (7195.540000), IE. **CCC.**
Published by: Now Publishers Inc., PO Box 1024, Hanover, MA 02339. TEL 781-871-0245, FAX 781-871-6172, sales@nowpublishers.com, http://www.nowpublishers.com. Eds. Keith Krehbiel, Nolan McCarty. Pub. Zac Rolnik TEL 781-871-0245.

320 CAN ISSN 0824-2348
THE QUEBECER. Text in English. 1982. q. CAD 10. adv. bk.rev. **Document type:** *Newsletter.*
Related titles: French ed.: Quebecer (French Edition). ISSN 0824-1783.
Published by: Alliance Quebec, 630 Rene Levesque Blvd, Ste 930, Montreal, PQ H3B 1S6, Canada. TEL 514-875-2771, FAX 514-875-7507. Ed., R&P Rob Bull. Adv. contact Ted Cash. Circ: 15,000.

320 PER ISSN 0250-9806
F3448.2
QUEHACER; realidad nacional - problemas y alternativas. Text in Spanish. 1979. bi-m. USD 60 in North America; USD 80 elsewhere (effective 2000). adv. back issues avail.
Related titles: Online - full text ed.: ISSN 1605-3435. 1995.
Indexed: A26, I04, I05, IBR, IBZ, MLA-IB, PAIS.
Published by: Centro de Estudios y Promocion del Desarrollo (DESCO), Leon De La Fuente, 110, Magdalena Del Mar, Lima 17, Peru. TEL 51-1-2641316, FAX 51-1-2640128. Ed. Juan Larco Guichard. Pub. Eduardo Ballon. Circ: 5,000.

320 DEU ISSN 0931-0495
JN3671
QUELLEN ZUR GESCHICHTE DES PARLAMENTARISMUS UND DER POLITISCHEN PARTEIEN. DRITTE REIHE: DIE WEIMARER REPUBLIK. Text in German. 1970. irreg., latest vol.10, 2001. price varies. **Document type:** *Monographic series, Academic/Scholarly.*
Published by: Droste Verlag GmbH, Martin Luther Platz 26, Duesseldorf, 40212, Germany. TEL 49-211-8605220, FAX 49-211-3230098, vertrieb@drosteverlag.de, http://www.drosteverlag.de.

320 DEU ISSN 0481-3650
JN3925
QUELLEN ZUR GESCHICHTE DES PARLAMENTARISMUS UND DER POLITISCHEN PARTEIEN. ERSTE REIHE: VON DER KONSTITUTIONELLEN MONARCHIE ZUR PARLAMENTARISCHEN REPUBLIK. Text in German. 1959. irreg. price varies. **Document type:** *Monographic series, Academic/Scholarly.*
Published by: Droste Verlag GmbH, Martin Luther Platz 26, Duesseldorf, 40212, Germany. TEL 49-211-8605220, FAX 49-211-3230098, vertrieb@drosteverlag.de, http://www.drosteverlag.de.

320 943 DEU ISSN 0931-0614
JN3971.A71
QUELLEN ZUR GESCHICHTE DES PARLAMENTARISMUS UND DER POLITISCHEN PARTEIEN. VIERTE REIHE: DEUTSCHLAND SEIT 1945. Text in German. 1984. irreg. price varies. **Document type:** *Monographic series, Academic/Scholarly.*
Published by: Droste Verlag GmbH, Martin Luther Platz 26, Duesseldorf, 40212, Germany. TEL 49-211-8605220, FAX 49-211-3230098, vertrieb@drosteverlag.de, http://www.drosteverlag.de.

320 943 DEU ISSN 0931-0274
JN3203
QUELLEN ZUR GESCHICHTE DES PARLAMENTARISMUS UND DER POLITISCHEN PARTEIEN. ZWEITE REIHE: MILITAER UND POLITIK. Text in German. 1970. irreg. **Document type:** *Monographic series, Academic/Scholarly.*
Published by: Droste Verlag GmbH, Martin Luther Platz 26, Duesseldorf, 40212, Germany. TEL 49-211-8605220, FAX 49-211-3230098, vertrieb@drosteverlag.de, http://www.drosteverlag.de.

320.9 ITA ISSN 1121-3353
QUESTE ISTITUZIONI; cronache del sistema politico. Text in Italian. 1973. q. adv. bk.rev. illus. **Document type:** *Monographic series.* **Description:** Covers problems related to the public policy of the central government and the local administration in Italy, European integration, the relationship between Church and State, territorial management, non-profit sector, and institutions and new computer technologies.
Related titles: Online - full text ed.: ISSN 1974-4846. 2007.
Indexed: IBR, IBZ.
Address: Via Ovidio 20, Rome, 00193, Italy. TEL 39-06-68136085, FAX 39-06-68134167, quesire@quesire.it. Ed. Sergio Ristuccia.

305.8 FRA ISSN 1778-333X
QUESTIONS AUTOCHTONES. Text in French. 2005. **Document type:** *Monographic series.*
Published by: L' Harmattan, 5 Rue de l'Ecole Polytechnique, Paris, 75005, France. TEL 33-1-43257651, FAX 33-1-43258203.

320 327 FRA ISSN 1634-0671
QUESTIONS DE RECHERCHE. Text in French. 1991. irreg. free. back issues avail. **Document type:** *Journal, Academic/Scholarly.*
Formerly (until 1999): Cahiers du CERI (1159-3733)
Media: Online - full text.
Indexed: FR.
Published by: Sciences Po, Centre d'Etudes et de Recherches Internationales, 56 Rue Jacob, Paris, 75006, France. TEL 33-1-58717000, FAX 33-1-58717090, info@ceri-sciences-po.org, http://www.ceri-sciencespo.com.

323.4 361 FRA ISSN 1951-0829
QUESTIONS SOCIAL. Text in French. 2006. q. back issues avail. **Document type:** *Bulletin, Trade.*
Former titles (until 2006): Syndicat National Unitaire des Assistants Sociaux de la Fonction Publique. S N U A S F P (1632-7985); (until 2000): Syndicat National Unitaire des Assistants Sociaux de l'Education Nationale. S N U A S E N (1247-4207)
Published by: Syndicat National Unitaire des Assistants Sociaux de la Fonction Publique (S N U A S - F P), 3-5 Rue de Metz, Paris, 75010, France.

QUINNIPIAC LAW REVIEW. *see* LAW

320.5322 USA ISSN 0033-6629
QUIXOTE; the anti-capitalist renegade post- and future Marxist wordslingers collective. Text in English. 1965. m. USD 20. adv. bk.rev.; film rev.; play rev.
Formerly: Quickoats
Media: Duplicated (not offset).
Published by: (Post- and Future Marxist Renegade Collective), Quixote Press, Inc., 2407 Watts St, Houston, TX 77030-1829. TEL 713-667-6639. Eds. Melissa Bondy, Morris Edelson. Circ: 200.

320 ESP ISSN 1575-4227
JL966
QUORUM; revista de pensamiento iberoamericano. Text in Spanish. 2001. 3/yr. EUR 27.04 domestic; USD 26 foreign (effective 2003). 182 p./no.; **Document type:** *Journal, Academic/Scholarly.* **Description:** Aims at renovating American studies on government and public institutions, private companies, political parties, social organizations, and political sciences.
Related titles: Online - full text ed.: free (effective 2011).
Published by: Universidad de Alcala de Henares, Servicio de Publicaciones, Colegio Mayor de San Ildefonso, Plaza San Diego, Alcala de Henares, Madrid, Spain. suscripcion.public@uah.es, http://www.uah.es/servi/publicaciones. Eds. Arsenio Lope Huerta, Josefa Toro. **Dist. by:** Asociacion de Revistas Culturales de Espana, C Covarruvias 9 2o. Derecha, Madrid 28010, Spain. TEL 34-91-3086066, FAX 34-91-3199267, info@arce.es, http://www.arce.es/.

QUORUM REPORT (ONLINE). *see* PUBLIC ADMINISTRATION

320 IND
R B R R KALE MEMORIAL LECTURES. Text in English. 1937. a. price varies. back issues avail. **Document type:** *Monographic series, Academic/Scholarly.*
Published by: Gokhale Institute of Politics and Economics, BMCC Rd, Deccan Gymkhana, Pune, 411004, India. TEL 91-20-25650287, FAX 91-20-25652579, gokhaleinstitute@gipe.ac.in.

320 NOR ISSN 1504-7253
R E C O N REPORT. (Reconstituting Democracy in Europe) Text in English. 2007. irreg. **Document type:** *Monographic series, Academic/Scholarly.*
Related titles: Online - full text ed.: ISSN 1504-7261; ◆ Issued with: Universitetet i Oslo. ARENA - Centre for European Studies. Report. ISSN 0807-3139.
Published by: Universitetet i Oslo, ARENA - Senter for Europaforskning/ University of Oslo, ARENA - Centre for European Studies, PO Box 1143, Blindern, Oslo, 0318, Norway. TEL 47-22-858700, FAX 47-22-858710, arena@arena.uio.no, http://www.arena.uio.no.

320 AUS ISSN 0815-7251
➤ **R I M A: REVIEW OF INDONESIAN AND MALAYSIAN AFFAIRS**; a semi-annual survey of political, economic, social and cultural aspects of Indonesia and Malaysia. Text in English. 1967. s-a. (Jun. & Dec.). bk.rev. illus. 120 p./no.; back issues avail. **Document type:** *Journal, Academic/Scholarly.* **Description:** A survey of political, economic, social and cultural aspects of Indonesia and Malaysia.
Formerly (until 1982): Review of Indonesian and Malayan Affairs (0034-6594)
Indexed: A11, AICP, APEL, AusPAIS, BAS, BibLing, CA, EI, FR, I13, IBR, IBZ, MLA, MLA-IB, P27, P42, P45, P46, P48, P54, PQC, PSA, RASB, S02, S03, SCOPUS, SociolAb, T02.
—Ingenta, INIST. **CCC.**
Published by: Association for the Publication of Indonesian and Malaysian Studies, Inc., GPO Box 1820, Canberra, ACT 1820, Australia. TEL 61-2-62516446. Eds. Campbell Macknight, Paul Tickell. R&P Campbell Macknight. Circ: 400.

320 301 ESP ISSN 1577-239X
JA26
R I P S. REVISTA DE INVESTIGACIONES POLITICAS Y SOCIOLOGICAS. Text in Multiple languages. 1999. s-a. **Document type:** *Journal, Academic/Scholarly.*
Related titles: Online - full text ed.: free (effective 2011).
Indexed: F04, T02.
—CCC.
Published by: Universidade de Santiago de Compostela, Servizo de Publicacions e Intercambio Cientifico, Campus Universitario Sur, Santiago de Compostela, 15782, Spain. TEL 34-981-593500, FAX 34-981-593963, spublic@usc.es, http://www.usc.es/spubl. Circ: 500 (paid).

320.531 371.33 USA ISSN 0191-4847
L11
➤ **RADICAL TEACHER**; a socialist and feminist journal on the theory and practice of teaching. Text in English. 1975. 3/yr. USD 83 combined subscription to institutions (print & online eds.) (effective 2012). adv. bk.rev. illus. back issues avail.; reprints avail. **Document type:** *Journal, Academic/Scholarly.* **Description:** Focuses on critical teaching practice, the political economy of education, and institutional struggles.
Related titles: Online - full text ed.: ISSN 1941-0832. USD 78 to institutions (effective 2012).
Indexed: A01, A02, A03, A08, A22, A26, APW, AltPI, B04, BRD, CA, CWI, E01, E02, E03, E07, E08, ERI, EdA, EdI, G08, I05, LeftInd, MLA, MLA-IB, P04, S09, SCOPUS, SOPODA, SociolAb, T02, W03, W05.
—BLDSC (7228.099100), CIS, IE, Ingenta. **CCC.**
Published by: (Center for Critical Education), University of Illinois Press, 1325 S Oak St, Champaign, IL 61820. TEL 217-333-0950, 866-244-0626, FAX 217-244-8082, journals@uillinois.edu, http://www.press.uillinois.edu. Adv. contact Jeff McArdle TEL 217-244-0381.

324.2 DNK ISSN 0107-279X
RADIKAL POLITIK. Text in Danish. 1972. bi-m. DKK 200 membership (effective 2009). adv. bk.rev. **Document type:** *Magazine, Consumer.*
Formerly (until 1981): Fremsyn (0107-2803)
Related titles: Online - full text ed.: 2007.
Published by: Det Radikale Venstre/Danish Social-Liberal Party, Christiansborg, Copenhagen K, 1240, Denmark. TEL 45-33-374747, FAX 45-33-137251, radikale@radikale.dk. Ed. Soeren Hoejlund Carlsen TEL 45-22-992850. Adv. contact Rene Vestergaard TEL 45-98-510030. Circ: 10,000.

320 FRA ISSN 1291-1941
JA11
RAISONS POLITIQUES; etudes de pensee politique. Text in French. 1998. q. EUR 51 domestic to individuals; EUR 61.50 foreign to individuals; EUR 67 domestic to institutions; EUR 81 foreign to institutions; EUR 44 domestic to students (effective 2009). back issues avail. **Document type:** *Journal, Academic/Scholarly.*
Related titles: Online - full text ed.: ISSN 1950-6708. 2006.
Indexed: CA, I13, IBR, IBSS, IBZ, MLA-IB, P42, PSA, S02, S03, SCOPUS, SociolAb, T02.
—IE.
Published by: Presses de Sciences Po, 117 Boulevard Saint Germain, Paris, 75006, France. TEL 33-1-45498331, FAX 33-1-45498334, info@presses.sciences-po.fr, http://www.sciences-po.fr.

P

320 053.1 DEU ISSN 0004-7899
RAN (COLOGNE); das junge Magazin der Gewerkschaften. Text in German. 1948. m. EUR 24.60 domestic; EUR 27.60 foreign; EUR 2.05 newsstand/cover (effective 2010). adv. bk.rev. illus. **Document type:** *Magazine, Consumer.*
Formerly (until 1970): Aufwaerts (0172-0791)
—CCC.
Published by: (Deutscher Gewerkschaftsbund), Ran Verlag GmbH, Amsterdamer Str 228, Cologne, 50735, Germany. TEL 49-221-973280, FAX 49-221-9732828, info@ranverlag.de, http://www.ranverlag.de. Ed. Katja Brittig.

320 USA ISSN 1557-2897
RAND REVIEW. Text in English. 1977. 3/yr. free. charts; illus. 32 p./no.; **Document type:** *Magazine, Consumer.* **Description:** Reports on Rand Corporation's research programs on matters affecting the nation's security and domestic welfare.
Formerly (until Fall 1998): Rand Research Review (0740-9281)
Related titles: Online - full content ed.
Indexed: PAIS.
—BLDSC (7254.410850). **CCC.**
Published by: Rand Corporation, Publications Department, 1776 Main St, PO Box 2138, Santa Monica, CA 90407-2138. TEL 310-451-7002, 877-584-8642, FAX 412-802-4981, order@rand.org. Ed. John Godges. Circ: 14,000.

332 ROM
RAPORT ASUPRA GUVERNARII/POLICY WARNING REPORT. Text in Romanian. irreg.
Published by: Societatea Academica din Romania/Romanian Academic Society, Str. Petofi Sandor 15, Bucuresti 1, Romania. FAX 401-222-18-68, sar@starnets.ro.

320 ITA ISSN 1128-2185
RAPPORTI SOCIALI. Text in English, French, Italian. 1983. q. **Document type:** *Bulletin.*
Related titles: CD-ROM ed.
Published by: Edizioni Rapporti Sociali, Via Tanaro 7, Milan, MI 20128, Italy. carcmi@micronet.it, http://www.carc.it. Ed. Giuseppe Maj.

324.2 NZL ISSN 2230-3065
RAU MATA. Text in English. 19??. m. back issues avail. **Document type:** *Newsletter, Trade.*
Formerly (until 2001): Northern News
Related titles: Online - full text ed.: ISSN 1178-7333. free (effective 2011).
Published by: Green Party of Aotearoa New Zealand, Level 2, 17 Garrett St, Te Aro, PO Box 11-652, Wellington, 6142, New Zealand. TEL 64-4-8015102, FAX 64-4-8015104, greenparty@greens.org.nz. Ed. David Cooke.

RAZON ESPANOLA. *see* PHILOSOPHY

321 ARG ISSN 1515-1913
HX9.S7
RAZON Y REVOLUCION. Text in Spanish. 1995. s-a. **Document type:** *Newsletter, Consumer.*
Media: Online - full text.
Published by: Razon y Revolucion Organizacion Cultural ryrweb@razonyrevolucion.org. Ed. Eduardo Sartelli. Circ: 1,000.

320 ESP ISSN 0210-4121
REAL ACADEMIA DE CIENCIAS MORALES Y POLITICAS. ANALES. Text in Spanish. 1934. a. **Document type:** *Monographic series, Academic/Scholarly.*

Formerly (until 1949): Academia de Ciencias Morales y Politicas. Anales (1138-4360)
Related titles: ◆ Supplement(s): Real Academia de Ciencias Politicas y Morales. Publicaciones. ISSN 0400-2938.
Indexed: CA, PSA, SCOPUS, SociolAb.
Published by: Real Academia de Ciencias Morales y Politicas (R A C M Y P), Plaza de la Villa 3, Madrid, 28005, Spain. TEL 34-91-7581505, FAX 34-91-7481975, secretaria.racmyp@inside.es, http://www.racmyp.es.

320 ESP ISSN 0400-2938
REAL ACADEMIA DE CIENCIAS POLITICAS Y MORALES. PUBLICACIONES. Text in Spanish. 1860. irreg. **Document type:** *Academic/Scholarly.*
Related titles: ◆ Supplement to: Real Academia de Ciencias Morales y Politicas. Anales. ISSN 0210-4121.
Published by: Real Academia de Ciencias Morales y Politicas (R A C M Y P), Plaza de la Villa 3, Madrid, 28005, Spain. TEL 34-91-7581505, FAX 34-91-7481975, secretaria.racmyp@inside.es, http://www.racmyp.es.

320 GAB ISSN 0486-106X
L81
REALITES GABONAISES. Text in French. 1960. irreg. (3-4/yr.). XOF 1,000, USD 44.12. illus.
Indexed: CCA.
Published by: Institut Pedagogique National, BP 813, Libreville, Gabon. Ed. M A Bouanga.

320.5 POL ISSN 1426-2924
REALIZM - NOWY USTROJ SPOLECZNO-POLITYCZNY; miesiecznik IV Rzeczypospolitej. Text in Polish. 1996. m. PLZ 3.40 newsstand/cover. **Description:** Presents ideas on political and economic systems for future Poland.
Published by: Faktor Sp. z o.o., ul Ksiecia Wladyslawa Opolskiego 3 a, Kety, 32650, Poland. TEL 48-33-453888. Ed. Jozef Gaweda. Circ: 7,000.

REASON; free minds and free markets. *see* LITERARY AND POLITICAL REVIEWS

320.5315 FRA ISSN 0294-3069
RECHERCHES INTERNATIONALES. Text in French. 1957. q. adv. bk.rev. cum.index.
Former titles: Institut des Recherches Marxistes. Recherches Internationales; (until 1981): Recherches Internationales a la Lumiere du Marxisme (0486-1345); Supersedes: Recherches Sovietiques
Indexed: IBSS, RASB.
—IE, Infotrieve.
Published by: Espaces Marx, 6 Av. Mathurin Moreau, Paris, Cedex 19 75167, France. Circ: 2,500.

320 DEU ISSN 0949-1953
RECHT UND WAHRHEIT; Stimme des parteiunabhaengigen freien Deutschen. Text in German. 1983. bi-m. **Document type:** *Bulletin, Consumer.*
Address: Hohensteinstr 29, Wolfsburg, 38440, Germany. TEL 49-5361-22576, FAX 49-5361-23596. Ed., Pub. Georg Albert Bosse.

RECHTSPHILOSOPHISCHE HEFTE; Beitraege zur Rechtswissenschaft, Philosophie und Politik. *see* PHILOSOPHY

RECHTSPOLITISCHES SYMPOSIUM. *see* LAW

RECHTSPRAAK NOTARIAAT. *see* PUBLIC ADMINISTRATION

RECHTSWISSENSCHAFT UND SOZIALPOLITIK. *see* LAW

RECLAIMING QUARTERLY. *see* ENVIRONMENTAL STUDIES

320.57 AUS
RED AND BLACK. Text in English. 1964. irreg. (1-2/yr.). bk.rev. back issues avail. **Document type:** *Newsletter.* **Description:** Features anarchism, libertarianism and feminism.
Address: PO Box 12, Quaama, NSW 2550, Australia.

330.1 GBR ISSN 1353-7024
AP4
RED PEPPER; raising the political temperature. Text in English. 1993. bi-m. GBP 29 domestic to individuals; GBP 35 in Europe to individuals; GBP 40 elsewhere to individuals; GBP 50 domestic to institutions; GBP 60 foreign to institutions; GBP 4 per issue domestic; GBP 3.95 newsstand/cover (effective 2009). adv. illus. back issues avail. **Document type:** *Magazine, Consumer.*
Formerly (until 1994): Red, Green & Radical (0964-4954)
Related titles: Online - full text ed.: GBP 10 (effective 2009).
Indexed: AltPI, LeftInd.
—IE.
Published by: Socialist Newspaper (Publications) Ltd., 1b Waterlow Rd, London, N19 5NJ, United Kingdom. TEL 44-20-72817024, FAX 44-20-72639345. Eds. Hilary Wainwright, James O'Nions, Michael Calderbank.

322.42 AUS ISSN 1320-6435
RED POLITICS; a journal for the discussion of revolutionary ideas. Text in English. 1993. irreg.
Media: Online - full text.
Published by: R P Publishing, 2-77 Holden St, Fitzroy, VIC 3065, Australia.

320.531 LKA ISSN 1391-1023
RED POWER. Text in English. 1995. m. LKR 15 newsstand/cover (effective 2008). **Document type:** *Newspaper, Consumer.*
Related titles: Online - full text ed.; Supplement(s): Voice for the Voiceless.
Published by: Janatha Vimukthi Peramuna/People's Liberation Front, 149-6 Devanam Piyatissa Mawatha, Colombo, 10, Sri Lanka. jvp_sl@usa.net, http://www.geocities.com/jvpsite.

321 COL ISSN 0124-0781
JL2801
REFLEXION POLITICA. Text in Spanish. 1999. s-a. back issues avail. **Document type:** *Journal, Academic/Scholarly.*
Indexed: C01, F04, H21, P08, T02.
Published by: Universidad Autonoma de Bucaramanga, Instituto de Estudios Politicos, Calle 48 No. 39-234, Bucaramanga, Colombia. TEL 57-7-6436111, reflepol@unab.edu.co, http://caribdis.unab.edu.co/portal/page?_pageid=233,1&_dad=portal&_schema=PORTAL. Ed. Alfonso Gomez Gomez.

320.531 BEL ISSN 1371-676X
HX5
REFLEXIONS. Text in French. 1954. m. adv. bk.rev.; film rev. abstr.
Formerly (until 1995): Socialisme (0037-8127)
Indexed: A20, ASCA, P30, PAIS, RASB.
Published by: Institut Emile Vandervelde, Bd de l'Empereur 13, Brussels, 1000, Belgium. TEL 32-2-548-3213, iev@ps.be. Ed. Philippe Lallemand. Circ: 2,000.

320.51 GBR ISSN 1353-0461
JN1129.L45
THE REFORMER; the journal of liberal democrat policy and strategy. Text in English. 1993. q. GBP 16; GBP 20 foreign (effective 1999 - 2000). adv. bk.rev. **Document type:** *Bulletin.* **Description:** Forum for the development, debate and critique of Liberal Democrat policy and strategy.
Published by: Reformer Publications Ltd., 3 De Laune St, London, SE17 3UU, United Kingdom. TEL 44-171-582-6120, FAX 44-171-564-0582. Ed. James Gurling. R&P, Adv. contact Clive Parry. Circ: 800 (paid).

320.9 CAN ISSN 0384-9120
DS119.8.C2
REGARDS SUR ISRAEL. Text in French. 1973. m. free. adv. bk.rev. illus.
Published by: Canada Israel Committee, 1310 Avenue Green, Ste 710, Montreal, PQ H3Z 2B2, Canada. TEL 514-934-0771. Ed. Michel M Solomon. Circ: 4,000.

320 PAK ISSN 0254-7988
DS331
REGIONAL STUDIES. Text in English. 1983. q. **Document type:** *Journal, Academic/Scholarly.*
Indexed: I13.
—BLDSC (7336.731000), IE, Ingenta.
Published by: Institute of Regional Studies, No.12, Street no.84, G-6/4, Attaturk Ave, Islamabad, Pakistan. TEL 92-51-9203974, FAX 92-51-9204055, irspak@comsats.net.pk, http://www.irs.org.pk.

323.17 BEL ISSN 1379-4507
REGIONALISME ET FEDERALISME/REGIONALISM AND FEDERALISM. Text in French. 2003. irreg., latest vol.15, 2009. price varies. **Document type:** *Monographic series, Academic/Scholarly.*
—BLDSC (7336.794500).
Published by: P I E - Peter Lang SA, 1 avenue Maurice, 6e etage, Brussels, 1050, Belgium. TEL 32-2-3477236, FAX 32-2-3477237, pie@peterlang.com, http://www.peterlang.net. Ed. Michael Keating.

320 GBR ISSN 0264-522X
JN297.R44
THE REGIONALIST. Text in English. 1982. irreg. GBP 1.50 to individuals; GBP 7.50 to institutions. bk.rev. **Document type:** *Bulletin.*
Media: Duplicated (not offset).
Indexed: SCOPUS.
Published by: Regionalist, c/o David Robins, Ed, 16 Adolphus St West, Seaham Harbour, Durham, United Kingdom. TEL 44-191-581-6689. Circ: 500.

342.07 USA
REGISTRATION AND ELECTION LAWS OF MARYLAND. Text in English. latest 2007, base vol. plus irreg. updates. looseleaf. USD 40 per issue (effective 2008). index. Supplement avail. **Document type:** *Handbook/Manual/Guide, Trade.* **Description:** Features information about registration and election laws of Maryland.
Formerly: Maryland Registration and Election Laws
Published by: Michie Company (Subsidiary of: LexisNexis North America), 701 E Water St, Charlottesville, VA 22902. TEL 434-972-7600, 800-446-3410, FAX 434-972-7677, customer.support@lexisnexis.com, http://www.michie.com.

320 USA ISSN 0147-0590
K18 CODEN: REGUD4
REGULATION (WASHINGTON, 1977). Text in English. 1977. q. USD 20 to individuals; USD 40 to institutions (effective 2010). adv. illus. back issues avail.; reprints avail. **Document type:** *Journal, Academic/Scholarly.* **Description:** Features items on economics, law and politics of government regulation. Reviews recent scholarship.
Related titles: Online - full text ed.: ISSN 1931-0668.
Indexed: A12, A13, A17, A22, A26, ABIn, B01, B02, B06, B07, B08, B09, B15, B17, B18, BLI, BPIA, BusI, C12, CA, E08, EconLit, G04, G06, G07, G08, H01, I05, JEL, M06, MCR, P30, P34, P45, P47, P48, P51, P53, P54, PAIS, PQC, RASB, S09, T&II, T02.
—BLDSC (7345.670000), IE, Infotrieve, Ingenta. **CCC.**
Published by: Cato Institute, 1000 Massachusetts Ave, NW, Washington, DC 20001. TEL 202-842-0200, FAX 202-842-3490, subscriptions@cato.org. Ed. Peter van Doren. Pub. Edward H Crane.

320 DEU
REIHE POLITIKWISSENSCHAFTEN. Text in German. 1983. irreg., latest vol.82, 2007. price varies. **Document type:** *Monographic series, Academic/Scholarly.*
Published by: Herbert Utz Verlag GmbH, Adalbertstr 57, Munich, 80799, Germany. TEL 49-89-27779100, FAX 49-89-27779101, utz@utzverlag.com.

320 AUT
REIHE POLITISCHE BILDUNG. Text in German. 2000. irreg., latest vol.8, 2010. price varies. **Document type:** *Monographic series, Academic/Scholarly.*
Published by: (Institut fuer Foederalismus), Wilhelm Braumueller Universitaets-Verlagsbuchhandlung GmbH, Servitengasse 5, Vienna, 1090, Austria. TEL 43-1-3191159, FAX 43-1-3102805, office@braumueller.at.

RELIGION IN THE NEWS. *see* JOURNALISM

322.1 USA ISSN 1934-290X
RELIGION, POLITICS, AND PUBLIC LIFE. Text in English. 2007 (Mar.). irreg., latest 2008. price varies. back issues avail. **Document type:** *Monographic series, Academic/Scholarly.*
Published by: Praeger Publishers (Subsidiary of: Greenwood Publishing Group Inc.), 88 Post Rd W, Westport, CT 06881. TEL 800-368-6868, info@greenwood.com, http://www.greenwood.com.

RELIGION - POLITIK - GESELLSCHAFT IN DER SCHWEIZ. *see* RELIGIONS AND THEOLOGY

322.1 USA ISSN 0278-7784
HX536
➤ **RELIGIOUS SOCIALISM.** Abbreviated title: R S. Text in English. 1977. s-a. free to members (effective 2010). bk.rev.; music rev. illus. back issues avail. **Document type:** *Journal, Academic/Scholarly.* **Description:** Dedicated to people of faith and socialism in North America.
Published by: Democratic Socialists of America, Religion & Socialism Commission, 536 W 111th St, # 37, New York, NY 10025. http://www.dsausa.org.

320.5 GBR ISSN 0968-252X
HD8381
RENEWAL (LONDON); the journal of labour politics. Text in English. 1993. q. GBP 65 domestic to institutions; GBP 75 foreign to institutions (effective 2009). bk.rev. 96 p./no.; back issues avail. **Document type:** *Journal, Academic/Scholarly.* **Description:** Features material on economic policy, public services, democratic agenda, cultural strategy, and other issues that are geared towards renewing the Labour Party.
Indexed: A26, CA, I05, IBSS, P10, P42, P45, P48, P53, P54, PAIS, PQC, PSA, S11, SociolAb, T02.
—BLDSC (7364.193200), IE, Ingenta.
Published by: Lawrence & Wishart Ltd, 99a Wallis Rd, London, E9 5LN, United Kingdom. TEL 44-20-85332506, FAX 44-20-85337369, info@lwbooks.co.uk, http://www.lwbooks.co.uk. Ed. Martin McIvor.

320 MEX ISSN 0188-5650
RENGLON. Text in Spanish. 1986. q. MXN 2,500. bk.rev.
Indexed: C01.
Published by: Editorial Terra Firme, PRIV DE LA PROVIDENCIA 38, San Jeronimo Lidice, Mexico City, DF 10200, Mexico. Ed. Ulises Canchola Gutierrez. Circ: 2,000.

RENMIN ZHENGXIE BAO/JOURNAL OF THE C P P C C. *see* PUBLIC ADMINISTRATION

324.2663 SEN
RENOVATEUR. Text in French. m.
Published by: Parti Democratique Senegalais - Renovation, BP 12172, Dakar, Senegal.

328.764 REU
REPERTOIRE DES TEXTES LEGISLATIFS ET REGLEMENTAIRES ET DES REPONSES AUX QUESTIONS ECRITES CONCERNANT LA REUNION. Text in French. 1975. a.
Published by: Centre Universitaire de la Reunion, Centre d'Etudes Administratives, 24, 26 av. de la Victoire, Saint-denis, Reunion. Circ: 150.

THE REPORT. ALGERIA. *see* BUSINESS AND ECONOMICS—Production Of Goods And Services

THE REPORT. BAHRAIN. *see* BUSINESS AND ECONOMICS—Economic Situation And Conditions

THE REPORT. BULGARIA. *see* BUSINESS AND ECONOMICS—Economic Situation And Conditions

THE REPORT. EGYPT. *see* BUSINESS AND ECONOMICS—Economic Situation And Conditions

324.64 USA
REPORT FROM STATE CIRCLE. Text in English. 1968. 7/yr. USD 25 to non-members (effective 2007). back issues avail. **Document type:** *Newsletter.*
Formerly (until 1985): Legislative News Service
Published by: League of Women Voters of Maryland, 106-B South St, Annapolis, MD 21401. TEL 410-269-0232, info@lwvmd.org, http://www.lwvmd.org. Ed., R&P Becky Goode. Circ: 300.

REPORT FROM THE CAPITAL. *see* RELIGIONS AND THEOLOGY—Protestant

▼ **THE REPORT. GABON.** *see* BUSINESS AND ECONOMICS—Economic Situation And Conditions

THE REPORT. INDONESIA. *see* BUSINESS AND ECONOMICS—Economic Situation And Conditions

THE REPORT. JORDAN. *see* BUSINESS AND ECONOMICS—Economic Situation And Conditions

THE REPORT. MOROCCO. *see* BUSINESS AND ECONOMICS—Economic Situation And Conditions

▼ **THE REPORT. NIGERIA.** *see* BUSINESS AND ECONOMICS—Economic Situation And Conditions

THE REPORT. OMAN. *see* BUSINESS AND ECONOMICS—Economic Situation And Conditions

320.9 GBR ISSN 0034-4737
D410
REPORT ON WORLD AFFAIRS. Text in English. 1919. q. GBP 5, USD 14. reprints avail.
Formerly: Report on Foreign Affairs
Related titles: Microform ed.: (from MIM, PQC).
Published by: Fitzken Publishers, 3 Alma Sq, London, NW8 6QD, United Kingdom.

THE REPORT. QATAR. *see* BUSINESS AND ECONOMICS—Economic Situation And Conditions

THE REPORT. RAS AL-KHAIMAH. *see* BUSINESS AND ECONOMICS—Economic Situation And Conditions

THE REPORT. ROMANIA. *see* BUSINESS AND ECONOMICS—Economic Situation And Conditions

THE REPORT. SHARJAH. *see* BUSINESS AND ECONOMICS—Economic Situation And Conditions

THE REPORT. SYRIA. *see* BUSINESS AND ECONOMICS—Economic Situation And Conditions

THE REPORT. TUNISIA. *see* BUSINESS AND ECONOMICS—Economic Situation And Conditions

THE REPORT. TURKEY. *see* BUSINESS AND ECONOMICS—Economic Situation And Conditions

THE REPORT. UKRAINE. *see* BUSINESS AND ECONOMICS

REPORTAGE. *see* JOURNALISM

623.4 PER
REPORTE ELECTORAL. Text in Spanish. 2003. irreg. **Document type:** *Bulletin.*
Media: Online - full content.
Published by: Oficina Nacional de Procesos Electorales, Gerencia de Informacion y Educacion Electoral, Jr. Washington 1894, Lima 1, Peru. TEL 000OficNacProEle, publicaciones@onpe.gob.pe, http://www.onpe.gob.pe/.

321.8 324 GBR ISSN 0034-4893
JF1001
➤ **REPRESENTATION**; journal of representative democracy. Text in English. N.S. 1908. q. GBP 274 combined subscription in United Kingdom to institutions (print & online eds.); EUR 362, USD 456 combined subscription to institutions (print & online eds.) (effective 2012). adv. bk.rev. charts; maps; stat. 80 p./no.; back issues avail.; reprint service avail. from PSC. **Document type:** *Journal, Academic/Scholarly.* **Description:** Provides a Records, comments, and analyzes elections and voting systems and their place inside the democratic body politic.
Formerly (1908-1927): Representation: The Journal of the Proportional Representation Society
Related titles: Online - full text ed.: ISSN 1749-4001. GBP 246 in United Kingdom to institutions; EUR 326, USD 410 to institutions (effective 2012) (from IngentaConnect).
Indexed: A01, A22, AmHI, B21, CA, E01, E17, ESPM, P34, P42, PSA, T02.
—IE, Ingenta. **CCC.**
Published by: (Electoral Reform Society), Routledge (Subsidiary of: Taylor & Francis Group), 4 Park Sq, Milton Park, Abingdon, Oxon OX14 4RN, United Kingdom. TEL 44-20-70176000, FAX 44-20-70176336, subscriptions@tandf.co.uk, http://www.routledge.com. Eds. Andrew Russell, Steve de Wijze. Adv. contact Linda Hann TEL 44-1344-779945. **Subscr. to:** Taylor & Francis Ltd., Journals Customer Service, Sheepen Pl, Colchester, Essex CO3 3LP, United Kingdom. TEL 44-20-70175544, FAX 44-20-70175198, tf.enquiries@tfinforma.com.

324.2734 USA ISSN 0363-9290
JK1967
REPUBLICAN ALMANAC. Text in English. biennial. USD 60. illus. **Description:** Provides statistical data and information on federal, state, county elections on a state-by-state basis.
Published by: (Computer Services Division), Republican National Committee, 310 First St, S E, Washington, DC 20003. FAX 202-863-8851, http://www.gop.com/. Ed. Clark H Bensen.

324.274704 GBR ISSN 0144-7548
REPUBLICAN ENGLISHMAN. Text in English. 1979. irreg. bk.rev.
Published by: Republican Party of England, 44 Water St, Accrington, Lancs BB5 6QZ, United Kingdom. Ed. Thomas Smith. Circ: 50.

324.2734 USA
THE REPUBLICAN WOMAN. Text in English. 1972. q. USD 15. bk.rev. illus. **Document type:** *Newsletter.*
Former titles (until Oct.-Nov. 1987): New Challenge (Washington); Challenge (Washington) (0045-6233)
Published by: National Federation of Republican Women, 124 N Alfred St, Alexandria, VA 22314. TEL 703-548-9688, FAX 703-548-9836. Ed. Frederick Ver Hulst. Circ: 130,000.

320 DEU
DER REPUBLIKANER; offizielles Organ der Bundespartei. Text in German. 1984. bi-m. **Document type:** *Journal, Consumer.*
Published by: (Bundespartei Der Republikaner), R E P - Verlags GmbH Berlin, Berliner Str 128, Berlin, 13187, Germany. TEL 49-1805-737000, FAX 49-1805-737111, verlag@der-republikaner.de.

321.8 NLD ISSN 1574-1834
DE REPUBLIKEIN. Text in Dutch. 2005. q. EUR 39.50; EUR 10.90 newsstand/cover (effective 2009). **Document type:** *Magazine, Consumer.*
Published by: (Stichting De Republikein), Uitgeverij Bas Lubberhuizen, Singel 389, Amsterdam, 1012 WN, Netherlands. TEL 31-20-6184132, FAX 31-20-6753213, info@lubberhuizen.nl, http://www.lubberhuizen.nl/.

320 BEL ISSN 0486-4700
JA1.A1
➤ **RES PUBLICA**; Belgian journal of political science. Text in Dutch, English, French; Summaries in English. 1959. 4/yr. EUR 35 in Europe to individuals; EUR 80 in Europe to institutions (effective 2005). adv. reprints avail. **Document type:** *Journal, Academic/Scholarly.* **Description:** Belgian journal of political science.
Related titles: Online - full text ed.
Indexed: A22, ABCPolSci, CA, I13, IBR, IBSS, IBZ, IBibSS, MLA, P42, PCI, PSA, RASB, S02, S03, SOPODA, SSA, SociolAb, T02.
—IE, Infotrieve. **CCC.**
Published by: (Politologisch Instituut), Uitgeverij Acco, Brusselsestraat 153, Leuven, 3000, Belgium. TEL 32-16-628000, FAX 32-16-628001, uitgeverij@acco.be, http://www.acco.be. Ed. Stefaan Fiers TEL 32-16-323246. adv.: B&W page EUR 500; 14 x 22. Circ: 1,000.

➤ **RESEARCH IN ORGANIZATIONAL BEHAVIOR.** *see* PSYCHOLOGY

➤ **RESEARCH IN POLITICAL ECONOMY.** *see* BUSINESS AND ECONOMICS—Economic Systems And Theories, Economic History

➤ **RESEARCH IN POLITICAL SOCIOLOGY.** *see* SOCIOLOGY

306.2 GBR ISSN 0885-212X
JA76
RESEARCH IN POLITICS AND SOCIETY. Text in English. 1985. irreg., latest vol.7, 2000. price varies. **Document type:** *Monographic series, Academic/Scholarly.* **Description:** Examines the interrelations of politics and society culled from an international and interdisciplinary community of scholars.
Related titles: Online - full text ed.
Indexed: CA, P42, S02, S03, SCOPUS, T02.
—BLDSC (7755.077400). **CCC.**
Published by: Emerald Group Publishing Ltd., Howard House, Wagon Ln, Bingley, W Yorks BD16 1WA, United Kingdom. TEL 44-1274-777700, FAX 44-1274-785201, emerald@emeraldinsight.com. Eds. Allen Whitt, Gwen Moore. **Dist. by:** Turpin Distribution Services Ltd., Pegasus Dr, Stratton Business Park, Biggleswade, Bedfordshire SG18 8QB, United Kingdom. TEL 44-1767-604951, FAX 44-1767-601640, custserv@turpin-distribution.com, http://www.turpin-distribution.com/.

320.6 GBR ISSN 0732-1317
H97
RESEARCH IN PUBLIC POLICY ANALYSIS AND MANAGEMENT. Text in English. 1981. a. price varies. back issues avail. **Document type:** *Monographic series, Academic/Scholarly.* **Description:** Presents papers that deal with important methodological and theoretical issues in the policy sciences, with substantive research in policy-related disciplines and applied research on issues in public policy analysis and public management.
Related titles: Online - full text ed.: ISSN 1875-5135.
Indexed: SCOPUS.
—BLDSC (7755.745000). **CCC.**
Published by: (Association for Public Policy Analysis and Management USA), Emerald Group Publishing Ltd., Howard House, Wagon Ln, Bingley, W Yorks BD16 1WA, United Kingdom. TEL 44-1274-777700, FAX 44-1274-785201, emerald@emeraldinsight.com. Ed. Lawrence R Jones. **Dist. by:** Turpin Distribution Services Ltd., Pegasus Dr, Stratton Business Park, Biggleswade, Bedfordshire SG18 8QB, United Kingdom. TEL 44-1767-604951, FAX 44-1767-601640, custserv@turpin-distribution.com, http://www.turpin-distribution.com/.

RESEARCH IN SOCIAL PROBLEMS AND PUBLIC POLICY. *see* SOCIOLOGY

320 300 GBR
➤ **RESEARCH JOURNAL OF INTERNATIONAL STUDIES.** Text in English. 2006. q. free (effective 2011). **Document type:** *Journal, Academic/Scholarly.* **Description:** Covers the variety of intellectual traditions included under the heading of international studies.
Media: Online - full text.
Published by: EuroJournals, 115 Ashby Rd., Leicestershire, LE153AB, United Kingdom. editor@eurojournals.com. Ed. Adrian M Steinberg.

320 USA ISSN 1544-466X
Q180.U5
RESEARCH U S A. Text in English. 2003 (Apr.). bi-w. (22x/yr.).
Related titles: Online - full text ed.: ISSN 1544-449X.
Published by: Research Research USA, National Press Bldg. Ste. 499, 529 14th St., NW, Washington, DC 20045. TEL 202-662-7090, FAX 202-783-4525, infousa@researchresearch.com, http://www.researchresearch.com. Ed. Rebecca Trager. Pub. William Brown. Adv. contact Penelope Walker.

RESEAUX - CIEPHUM; revue interdisciplinaire de philosophie morale et politique. *see* PHILOSOPHY

320 USA
RESPONSE TO TERRORISM. Text in English. 19??. w. back issues avail. **Document type:** *Newsletter, Trade.* **Description:** Covers all aspects of homeland security, with updated information from states throughout the country.
Published by: State Capitals Newsletters, PO Box 7376, Alexandria, VA 22307. TEL 703-768-9600, FAX 703-768-9690, newsletters@statecapitals.com.

320 PER ISSN 0250-9792
RESUMEN SEMANAL. Variant title: D E S C O Resumen Semanal. Text in Spanish. 1978. w. (50/yr.). USD 150. adv.
Published by: Centro de Estudios y Promocion del Desarrollo (DESCO), Leon De La Fuente, 110, Magdalena Del Mar, Lima 17, Peru. TEL 51-1-2641316, FAX 51-1-2640128. Circ: 3,000.

320.5 GBR ISSN 0034-5970
JX1901
RESURGENCE; an international magazine for ecological and spiritual thinking. Text in English. 1966. bi-m. GBP 4.95 per issue to non-members; free to members (effective 2009). adv. bk.rev. index. back issues avail. **Document type:** *Magazine, Consumer.* **Description:** Designed to promote ecological sustainability, social justice and spiritual values.
Incorporates (1972-1984): Undercurrents (0306-2392)
Related titles: Online - full text ed.: GBP 4 per issue (effective 2009).
Indexed: E04, E05, FutSurv.
—BLDSC (7785.410000), IE, Ingenta. **CCC.**
Published by: Kingfisher Print and Design Ltd, Ford House, Hartland, Bideford, Devon EX39 6EE, United Kingdom. TEL 44-1237-441293, info@kingfisherprint.co.uk, http://www.kingfisherprint.co.uk. Adv. contact Gwyd Batten. B&W page GBP 960, color page GBP 1,104; 188 x 276.

320.5322 GBR ISSN 0893-5696
HX1
➤ **RETHINKING MARXISM**; a journal of economics, culture and society. Text in English. 1988. q. GBP 268 combined subscription in United Kingdom to institutions (print & online eds.); EUR 356, USD 449 combined subscription to institutions (print & online eds.) (effective 2012). adv. bk.rev. back issues avail.; reprint service avail. from PSC. **Document type:** *Journal, Academic/Scholarly.* **Description:** Examines developments for racial and societal change, from a wide range of political and cultural perspectives.
Related titles: Microform ed.: (from PQC); Online - full text ed.: ISSN 1475-8059. GBP 241 in United Kingdom to institutions; EUR 320, USD 405 to institutions (effective 2012) (from IngentaConnect).
Indexed: A01, A22, AltPI, CA, DIP, E01, IBR, IBSS, IBZ, LeftInd, MLA-IB, P34, P42, P48, PQC, PSA, Perlslam, RASB, RILM, S02, S03, SCOPUS, SOPODA, SSA, SociolAb, T02.
—BLDSC (7785.509800), IE, Infotrieve, Ingenta. **CCC.**
Published by: (Association for Economic and Social Analysis USA), Routledge (Subsidiary of: Taylor & Francis Group), 4 Park Sq, Milton Park, Abingdon, Oxon OX14 4RN, United Kingdom. TEL 44-20-70176000, FAX 44-20-70176336, subscriptions@tandf.co.uk, http://www.routledge.com. Adv. contact Linda Hann TEL 44-1344-779945. **Subscr. to:** Taylor & Francis Ltd., Journals Customer Service, Sheepen Pl, Colchester, Essex CO3 3LP, United Kingdom. TEL 44-20-70175544, FAX 44-20-70175198, tf.enquiries@tfinforma.com.

320 100 USA ISSN 1752-2056
➤ **REVIEW JOURNAL OF POLITICAL PHILOSOPHY.** Text in English. 200?. a. USD 89.99, GBP 59.99 (effective 2009). **Document type:** *Journal, Academic/Scholarly.* **Description:** Expresses the over-arching goals to advance the conversation of moral and political philosophy by providing an outlet for analytic and continential philosophy alike-an outlet open historical exploration as well as contemporary debate.
Indexed: AmHI, H07, PhilInd, T02.
Published by: Hartwick College, One Hartwick Dr, Oneonta, NY 13820. TEL 607-431-4000. Ed. Jeremy Wisnewski.

➤ **REVIEW OF CENTRAL AND EAST EUROPEAN LAW.** *see* LAW

➤ **REVIEW OF MIDDLE EAST STUDIES.** *see* SOCIAL SCIENCES: COMPREHENSIVE WORKS

320 USA ISSN 1541-132X
H97
➤ **THE REVIEW OF POLICY RESEARCH.** Abbreviated title: R P R. Text in English. 1981. bi-m. USD 1,336 in the Americas (print or online ed.); GBP 982 in United Kingdom (print or online ed.); EUR 1,248 in Europe (print or online ed.); USD 1,925 elsewhere (print or online ed.); USD 1,471 combined subscription in the Americas (print & online eds.); GBP 1,081 combined subscription in United Kingdom (print & online eds.); EUR 1,373 combined subscription in Europe (print & online eds.); USD 2,119 combined subscription elsewhere (print & online eds.) (effective 2010); subscr. includes Policy Studies Journal. adv. back issues avail.; reprint service avail. from PSC. **Document type:** *Journal, Academic/Scholarly.* **Description:** Covers the application of political and social science to important public policy problems.
Formerly (until 2002): Policy Studies Review (0278-4416)
Related titles: Microfiche ed.: (from PQC); Microfilm ed.: (from PQC); Online - full text ed.: ISSN 1541-1338 (from IngentaConnect).
Indexed: A01, A03, A08, A22, A26, A35, A36, ABCPolSci, AgBio, AmH&L, B01, B04, B06, B07, B09, BRD, CA, CABA, CJA, CurCont, DIP, E01, E08, E12, EI, EIA, ESPM, EnvAb, FamI, FutSurv, G08, GEOBASE, GH, H05, HRIS, HistAb, I05, I14, IBR, IBZ, LT, N02, P02, P10, P27, P30, P32, P34, P42, P47, P48, P53, P54, PAA&I, PAIS, PQC, PSA, PersLit, RiskAb, S02, S03, S09, S11, S13, S16, SCOPUS, SOPODA, SPAA, SSA, SSAI, SSAb, SSCI, SSI, SociolAb, T02, W01, W02, W03, W05, W07, W11.
—BLDSC (7794.107500), IE, Infotrieve, Ingenta. **CCC.**
Published by: (Policy Studies Organization), Wiley-Blackwell Publishing, Inc. (Subsidiary of: Wiley-Blackwell Publishing Ltd.), 111 River St, Hoboken, NJ 07030. TEL 201-748-6000, FAX 201-748-6088, info@wiley.com. Ed. Christopher Gore. Adv. contact Kristin McCarthy TEL 201-748-7683.

320 GBR ISSN 0953-8259
HB1 CODEN: RPECEI
➤ **REVIEW OF POLITICAL ECONOMY.** Text in English. 1989. q. GBP 612 combined subscription in United Kingdom to institutions (print & online eds.); EUR 843, USD 1,058 combined subscription to institutions (print & online eds.) (effective 2012). adv. bk.rev. illus. Index. back issues avail.; reprint service avail. from PSC. **Document type:** *Journal, Academic/Scholarly.* **Description:** Publishes both theoretical and empirical research, and is also open to submissions in methodology, economic history and the history of economic thought that cast light on issues of contemporary relevance in political economy.
Related titles: Online - full text ed.: ISSN 1465-3982. GBP 551 in United Kingdom to institutions; EUR 758, USD 952 to institutions (effective 2012) (from IngentaConnect).
Indexed: A12, A17, A22, ABIn, B01, B06, B07, B08, B09, B16, B21, C12, CA, DIP, E01, E17, ESPM, EconLit, IBR, IBSS, IBZ, JEL, P10, P13, P42, P45, P48, P51, P53, P54, PAIS, PQC, PSA, S02, S03, SCOPUS, SSA, SociolAb, T02.
—IE, Infotrieve, Ingenta. **CCC.**
Published by: Routledge (Subsidiary of: Taylor & Francis Group), 4 Park Sq, Milton Park, Abingdon, Oxon OX14 4RN, United Kingdom. TEL 44-20-70176000, FAX 44-20-70176336, subscriptions@tandf.co.uk, http://www.routledge.com. Eds. Gary Mongiovi TEL 718-990-7380, Steve Pressman TEL 732-571-3658. Adv. contact Linda Hann TEL 44-1344-779945. **Subscr. to:** Taylor & Francis Ltd., Journals Customer Service, Sheepen Pl, Colchester, Essex CO3 3LP, United Kingdom. TEL 44-20-70175544, FAX 44-20-70175198, tf.enquiries@tfinforma.com.

320 GBR ISSN 0034-6705
JA1
➤ **THE REVIEW OF POLITICS.** Text in English. 1939. q. GBP 73, USD 134 to institutions; GBP 81, USD 139 combined subscription to institutions (print & online eds.) (effective 2012). adv. bk.rev. illus.; abstr. index. back issues avail.; reprint service avail. from PSC. **Document type:** *Journal, Academic/Scholarly.* **Description:** Publishes primarily philosophical and historical studies of politics, especially those concentrating on political theory and American political thought.
Related titles: Microform ed.: (from PMC, PQC); Online - full text ed.: ISSN 1748-6858. GBP 68, USD 124 to institutions (effective 2012).
Indexed: A01, A02, A03, A06, A08, A20, A22, A25, A26, ABCPolSci, ABS&EES, Acal, AmH&L, B04, BAS, BRD, C12, CA, CBRI, CPL, DIP, E01, E08, ESPM, FR, G08, H09, H10, HistAb, I05, I13, IBR, IBSS, IBZ, L03, M01, M02, MASUSE, MEA&I, MLA-IB, P02, P06, P10, P13, P27, P30, P34, P42, P45, P47, P48, P53, P54, PAIS, PCI, PQC, PRA, PSA, Perlslam, PhilInd, RASB, RiskAb, S02, S03, S05, S08, S09, S11, SCOPUS, SPAA, SSAI, SSAb, SSI, SociolAb, T02, W03, W04, W05.
—BLDSC (7794.120000), IE, Infotrieve, Ingenta, INIST. **CCC.**
Published by: (University of Notre Dame, Review of Politics USA), Cambridge University Press, The Edinburgh Bldg, Shaftesbury Rd, Cambridge, CB2 8RU, United Kingdom. TEL 44-1223-312393, FAX 44-1223-315052, journals@cambridge.org, http://www.cambridge.org/uk. Ed. Catherine H Zuckert. R&P Linda Nicol TEL 44-1223-325702. Adv. contact Rebecca Roberts TEL 44-1223-325083. page GBP 175, page USD 330. Circ: 1,400.

320 SRB
REVIJA RADA. Text in Serbo-Croatian. 1971. m.
Indexed: CISA.
Published by: Zastita Press, Jelene Cetkovic 3, Belgrade, 11000. Ed. Veroljub Micic.

320 ARG ISSN 0329-3092
JA5
REVISTA ARGENTINA DE CIENCIA POLITICA. Text in Spanish. 1997. s-a. bk.rev. **Document type:** *Magazine, Consumer.*
Published by: (Asociacion Argentina de Ciencia Politica), Eudeba, Ave. Rivadavia 1573, Buenos Aires, 1033, Argentina. TEL 54-11-43838025, FAX 54-11-43832202, eudeba@eudeba.com.ar, http://www.eudeb.com.ar/. Ed. Victor Palacios.

320 ARG
REVISTA ARGENTINA DE ESTUDIOS POLITICOS. Text in Spanish. 1945. 3/yr. bk.rev. bibl.
Indexed: RASB.
Published by: Instituto Argentino de Estudios Politicos, Mansilla 2698, Buenos Aires, Argentina.

P

320 BRA ISSN 0103-3352
F2538.3
REVISTA BRASILEIRA DE CIENCIA POLITICA. Text in Portuguese. 1989. q. **Document type:** *Journal, Academic/Scholarly.*
Indexed: C01, PAIS.
Published by: Universidade de Brasilia, Departamento de Ciencia Politica e Relacoes Internacionais, Campus Universitario, Asa Norte, Brasilia, 04359, Brazil.

320 BRA ISSN 0034-7191
JA5
REVISTA BRASILEIRA DE ESTUDOS POLITICOS. Text in Portuguese. 1956. 2/yr. BRL 30 per issue domestic; USD 25 foreign (effective 2006). bk.rev. bibl. cum.index. **Document type:** *Journal, Academic/Scholarly.* **Description:** Aims to promote cultural, political and legal exchanges among law students and professors throughout the world.
Indexed: ABCPolSci, C01, CA, DIP, FR, H21, HistAb, IBR, IBZ, MLA-IB, P08, P42, PAIS, PSA, RASB, SCOPUS, SociolAb, T02.
—INIST.
Published by: Universidade Federal de Minas Gerais, Imprensa Universitaria, Av Joao Pinheiro 100, 11 andar, sala 1107, Belo Horizonte, Minas Gerais 30130-180, Brazil. TEL 55-31-32174628, FAX 55-31-32174628. Ed. Silma Mendes Berti. Circ: 1,500 (paid).

320 URY
REVISTA COMPANERO. Text in Spanish. 1991. bi-m. UYP 2,000 per issue.
Published by: Impresa Editorial Espacio s.r.l., Daniel Fernandez Crespo, 2242, Montevideo, 11813, Uruguay. TEL 94-2518. Ed. Hugo Cores.

320.5322 ESP ISSN 1989-2217
REVISTA DE CRITICA LITERARIA MARXISTA. Text in Spanish. 2008. s-a. back issues avail. **Document type:** *Journal, Academic/Scholarly.*
Published by: Fundacion de Investigaciones Marxistas, C. Alameda 5, Madrid, 28014, Spain. TEL 34-91-4201388, FAX 34-91-4202004, info@fim.og.es, http://www.fim.org.es/.

320 ESP ISSN 1138-4026
K19
REVISTA DE DERECHO COMUNITARIO EUROPEO. Text in Spanish. 1974. 3/yr. EUR 49 (effective 2007). bibl. back issues avail. **Document type:** *Journal, Academic/Scholarly.*
Formerly (until 1997): Revista de Instituciones Europeas (0210-0924)
Related titles: Optical Disk - DVD ed.: ISSN 1885-6578. 2005.
Indexed: A22, ELLIS, FR, I13, IBR, IBZ, P30, PAIS, SSCI, W07.
—IE.
Published by: Centro de Estudios Politicos y Constitucionales, Plaza de la Marina Espanola 9, Madrid, 28071, Spain. TEL 34-91-5401950, FAX 34-91-5419574, public@cepc.es. Ed. Alejandro del Valle Galvez. R&P Julian Sanchez Garcia.

324.6 CRI ISSN 1659-2069
REVISTA DE DERECHO ELECTORAL. Text in Spanish. 2006. s-a. back issues avail. **Document type:** *Journal, Academic/Scholarly.*
Media: Online - full text.
Published by: Tribunal Supremo de Elecciones, Apdo Postal 2163, San Jose, Costa Rica. TEL 506-287-5555, bibliotecatse@tse.go.vr. Ed. Luis Antonio Sobrado Gonzalez.

320 ESP ISSN 0211-979X
K19
REVISTA DE DERECHO POLITICO. Text in Spanish. 1979. 3/yr. **Document type:** *Journal, Academic/Scholarly.*
Formerly (until 1980): Departamento de Derecho Politico. Revista (0210-7562)
Indexed: F04, IBR, IBZ, PAIS.
Published by: Universidad Nacional de Educacion a Distancia (U N E D), Departamento de Derecho Politico, C. Bravo Murillo, 38, Madrid, 28040, Spain. TEL 34-91-3986111, FAX 34-91-3986044.

REVISTA DE DERECHO Y CIENCIAS POLITICAS. *see* LAW

320 BRA
REVISTA DE DIREITO CONSTITUCIONAL E CIENCIA POLITICA. Text in Portuguese. q.
Published by: Instituto Brasileiro de Direito Constitucional, Rua da Consolacao 3064, Conj 121, bloco C, 12 andar, Sao Paulo, 01416-000, Brazil.

REVISTA DE DIREITO INTERNACIONAL. *see* LAW

320.9 BRA ISSN 0101-3157
HC186
➤ **REVISTA DE ECONOMIA POLITICA/BRAZILIAN JOURNAL OF POLITICAL ECONOMY.** Text in English, Portuguese. 1981. q. BRL 90 domestic to individuals; USD 65 foreign to individuals; BRL 170 domestic to institutions; USD 150 foreign to institutions (effective 2005). adv. bk.rev. back issues avail. **Document type:** *Journal, Academic/Scholarly.*
Related titles: CD-ROM ed.; Online - full text ed.: 2005. free (effective 2011).
Indexed: A01, C01, CA, EconLit, F03, F04, H21, IBR, IBZ, JEL, P08, P42, PAIS, PCI, PSA, RASB, SCOPUS, SociolAb, T02.
Published by: Centro de Economia Politica, Rua Araripina 106, Cidade Jardim, Sao Paulo, 05603-030, Brazil. TEL 55-11-37443196, FAX 55-11-37446137, ceciliaheise@uol.com.br, http://www.rep.org.br. Ed. Luiz C Bresser Pereira. R&P, Adv. contact Luiz Carlos Bresser Pereira. Circ: 1,500.

320.94 CUB
REVISTA DE ESTUDIOS EUROPEOS. Text in Spanish. 1987. 4/yr. USD 22 in South America; USD 24 in North America; USD 28 elsewhere. adv.
Indexed: RASB.
Published by: (Centro de Estudios Europeos), Ediciones Cubanas, Obispo 527, Havana, Cuba. Ed. Jose Eloy Valdes. **U.S. Dist.:** Publications Exchanges Inc., 8306 Mills Dr, Ste 241, Miami, FL 33183. TEL 800-375-2822.

320 ESP ISSN 0048-7694
H8
REVISTA DE ESTUDIOS POLITICOS. Text in Spanish. 1940. q. EUR 53 (effective 2007). bk.rev. bibl. back issues avail. **Document type:** *Journal, Academic/Scholarly.*
Related titles: Online - full text ed.: ISSN 1989-0613. 1941; Optical Disk - DVD ed.: ISSN 1885-6675. 2005.
Indexed: A22, ABCPolSci, CA, CERDIC, HistAb, I13, IBR, IBZ, JEL, MLA-IB, P09, P42, PAIS, PCI, PSA, RASB, SCOPUS, SSCI, SociolAb, T02, W07.
—BLDSC (7854.510000), IE, Infotrieve. **CCC.**
Published by: Centro de Estudios Politicos y Constitucionales, Plaza de la Marina Espanola 9, Madrid, 28071, Spain. TEL 34-91-5401950, FAX 34-91-5419574, public@cepc.es. Ed. Pedro de Vega Garcia. R&P Julian Sanchez Garcia. Circ: 1,000.

REVISTA DE HISTORIA ECONOMICA. *see* BUSINESS AND ECONOMICS—Economic Situation And Conditions

REVISTA DE INTERNET, DERECHO Y POLITICA/REVISTA D'INTERNET, DRET I POLITICA. *see* LAW

REVISTA DE SERVICIOS SOCIALES Y POLITICA SOCIAL. *see* SOCIOLOGY

REVISTA DE SOCIOLOGIA E POLITICA. *see* SOCIOLOGY

320 ROM ISSN 1584-224X
REVISTA DE STINTE POLITICE. Text in Romanian, English, French. 2004. q. **Document type:** *Journal, Academic/Scholarly.*
Related titles: Online - full text ed.: free (effective 2011).
Indexed: A26, I04, I05, P02, P10, P42, P45, P48, P53, P54, PQC, S11, T02.
Published by: Universitatea din Craiova/University of Craiova, Str A.I. Cuza 13, Craiova, 200585, Romania. TEL 40-251-414398, FAX 40-251-411688, relint@central.ucv.ro, http://www.ucv.ro.

320 BRA ISSN 1982-5269
REVISTA DEBATES. Text in Portuguese. 2007. s-a. free (effective 2011). **Document type:** *Journal, Academic/Scholarly.*
Media: Online - full text.
Published by: Universidade Federal do Rio Grande do Sul, Instituto de Filosofia e Ciencias Humanas, Av Bento Gocalves 9500, Porto Alegre, RS 91509-900, Brazil. TEL 55-51-33166647, FAX 55-51-33166638.

321.8 BRA
JL2400
REVISTA DEMOCRACIA. Text in Portuguese. 1985. m. USD 80 to individuals; USD 85 to institutions. charts; illus.; stat. index.
Formerly: Politicas Governamentais (0104-1436)
Published by: Instituto Brasileiro de Analises Sociais e Economicas, Rua Vicente de Sousa 29, Botafogo, RJ 22251-070, Brazil. TEL 55-21-286-6161, FAX 286-0541. Ed. Nilo Sergio Gomes. Circ: 3,500.

320 BRA ISSN 0104-9178
REVISTA DO MERCOSUL/REVISTA DEL MERCOSUR; revista mensal bilingue de integracao latino-americana. Text in Portuguese, Spanish. 1992. m. BRL 54 domestic; USD 110 foreign; BRL 5.50 newsstand/cover. adv. **Document type:** *Consumer.* **Description:** Publishes articles focusing on the process of developing Mercosul, the common market of Brazil, Argentina, Paraguay and Uruguay.
Published by: Editora Terceiro Mundo Ltda., Rua da Gloria, 122 105-106, Gloria, Rio De Janeiro, RJ 20241-180, Brazil. FAX 55-21-2528455. Ed. Antonio Carlos Cunha. R&P Beatriz Bissio TEL 55-21-2217511. Adv. contact Euler Sathler. page USD 3,500. Circ: 8,000.

320 ESP ISSN 1575-6548
JA26
REVISTA ESPANOLA DE CIENCIA POLITICA. Text in Spanish. 1999. s-a. EUR 25 to individuals; EUR 30 to institutions (effective 2008). **Document type:** *Journal, Academic/Scholarly.*
Related titles: Online - full text ed.
Indexed: A01, CA, F03, F04, I13, P42, PSA, SociolAb, T02.
Published by: Asociacion Espanola de Ciencia Politica y de la Administracion, Montalban, 8, Madrid, 28014, Spain. TEL 34-91-5232741, recp@eacpa.es. Ed. Ramon Maiz.

320 DOM ISSN 0259-1049
REVISTA ESTUDIOS DOMINICANOS. Text in Spanish. 1984. 3/yr. USD 8.
Published by: (Instituto de Estudios Dominicanos), Liberia America, C. Ciriaco Ramirez 49, 3 Piso, Apdo. Postal 20693, Santo Domingo, Dominican Republic. Circ: 300.

321.09 ESP ISSN 2174-0135
▼ **REVISTA EUROPEA DE HISTORIA DE LAS IDEAS POLITICAS Y DE LAS INSTITUCIONES PUBLICAS.** Text in Spanish. 2011. s-a. **Document type:** *Journal, Academic/Scholarly.*
Media: Online - full text.
Published by: Universidad de Malaga, Ave Cervantes, 2, Malaga, 29071, Spain. TEL 34-952-131000, informacion@uma.es, http://www.uma.es/. Ed. Juan Carlos Martinez Coll.

▼ **REVISTA F I D E S.** (Revista de Filosofia do Diretito, do Estado e da Sociedade) *see* LAW

320 ESP ISSN 1139-0883
F1751
REVISTA HISPANO CUBANA. Text in Spanish. 1997. 3/yr. EUR 24 domestic; EUR 60 foreign (effective 2009). 240 p./no.; back issues avail. **Document type:** *Magazine, Consumer.* **Description:** Covers articles, short notes and reviews on democracy and human rights.
Formerly (until 1998): Fundacion Hispano Cubana. Boletin Informativo (1139-1227)
Related titles: CD-ROM ed.: EUR 12 domestic; EUR 18 foreign (effective 2009); Online - full text ed.
Indexed: MLA-IB.
Published by: Fundacion Hispano Cubana, C Orfilla 8, 1o. A, Madrid, 28010, Spain. TEL 34-91-3196313, FAX 34-91-3197008, http://www.hispanocubana.org/. **Dist. by:** Asociacion de Revistas Culturales de Espana, C Covarruvias 9 2o. Derecha, Madrid 28010, Spain. TEL 34-91-3086066, FAX 34-91-3199267, info@arce.es, http://www.arce.es/.

REVISTA INTERNACIONAL DE FILOSOFIA POLITICA. *see* PHILOSOPHY

320 ESP ISSN 1885-589X
REVISTA INTERNACIONAL DE PENSAMIENTO POLITICO/INTERNATIONAL JOURNAL OF POLITICAL THOUGHT. Text in Multiple languages. 2006. s-a. EUR 50 (effective 2009). back issues avail. **Document type:** *Journal, Academic/Scholarly.*
Published by: Fundacion Tercer Milenio, Avda Cardenal Bueno Monreal s/n, Edif ATS, Bo - Local A, Seville, 41013, Spain. TEL 34-95-4622727, FAX 34-95-4623435, correo@iiimilenio.org, http://www.iiimilenio.org. Ed. Francisco Rubiales.

320.9 COL ISSN 0120-3088
REVISTA JAVERIANA. Text in Spanish. 1934. m. (Feb.-Nov.). COP 28,500, USD 50 (effective 1995). adv. bk.rev. bibl. index. **Description:** Studies important current themes of national and international interest in Latin America.
Related titles: Microform ed.: (from PQC).
Indexed: A21, H21, IBR, IBZ, P08, P09, PCI, RI-1, RILM.
Published by: Compania de Jesus de Colombia, Carrera 23, 39-69, Apartado Aereo 24773, Bogota, CUND, Colombia. Ed. Javier Sanin. Circ: 8,000.

320 MEX ISSN 0185-1918
JA5
REVISTA MEXICANA DE CIENCIAS POLITICAS Y SOCIALES. Text in Spanish; Summaries in English, Spanish. 1955. 3/yr. adv. bk.rev. bibl.; charts. index. **Document type:** *Journal, Academic/Scholarly.* **Description:** Offers theoretical perspectives and contemporary questions on various political and societal issues.
Former titles (until 1975): Revista Mexicana de Ciencia Politica (0034-9976); (until 1968): Ciencias Politicas y Sociales (0185-8084)
Related titles: Online - full text ed.: free (effective 2011).
Indexed: A22, ABCPolSci, C01, CA, DIP, FR, H21, HistAb, I13, IBR, IBZ, P08, P09, P30, P42, PAIS, PCI, PSA, RASB, S02, S03, SOPODA, SSA, SociolAb, T02.
—IE, INIST.
Published by: Universidad Nacional Autonoma de Mexico, Facultad de Ciencias Politicas y Sociales, Circuito Cultural Mario de la Cueva, Edif C 2o piso, Ciudad Universitaria, Mexico City, DF 04510, Mexico. Ed. Judit Bokser Misses.

320 PRT ISSN 1647-4090
▼ **REVISTA PORTUGUESA DE CIENCIA POLITICA.** Text in Portuguese. 2009. s-a. **Document type:** *Journal, Academic/Scholarly.*
Published by: Universidade Nova de Lisboa, Faculdade de Ciencias Sociais e Humanas, Avenida de Berna 26, Lisbon, 1069-061, Portugal. http://www.cham.fcsh.unl.pt.

321 SLV ISSN 1605-1939
REVISTA PROBIDAD. Text in Spanish. 1993. bi-m.
Related titles: Online - full text ed.: ISSN 1605-1920. 1999.
Address: Res. Quetzaltcoalt 1-B, Antiguo Cuscatlan, San Salvador, El Salvador. TEL 503-2431951, contacto@probidad.org, http://www.prodibad.org.sv. Ed. Jaime Lopez.

320 ROM ISSN 1582-456X
JA84.R6
REVISTA ROMANA DE STIINTE POLITICE/ROMANIAN JOURNAL OF POLITICAL SCIENCE. Text in Romanian. 2001. s-a.
Related titles: Online - full text ed.
Indexed: A01, A03, A08, A26, CA, I05, P42, SSCI, T02, W07.
Published by: Societatea Academica din Romania/Romanian Academic Society, Str. Petofi Sandor 15, Bucuresti 1, Romania. FAX 401-222-18-68, sar@starnets.ro. Ed. Alina Mungiu-Pippidi.

320 ARG ISSN 1666-7883
F2801
➤ **REVISTA S A A P.** (Sociedad Argentina de Analisis Politico) Text in Spanish; Summaries in English, Spanish. 2002. s-a. (until 2009). ARS 200 domestic; USD 100 foreign; ARS 30 per issue domestic; USD 15 per issue foreign (effective 2011). bk.rev. abstr.; bibl.; charts; illus.; stat. back issues avail. **Document type:** *Magazine, Consumer.* **Description:** Publishes articles of current and controversial subjects, concepts and/or methodological matters on Argentine and worldwide political issues.
Indexed: PSA.
Published by: Sociedad Argentina de Analisis Politico, Castex 3217, 1er Piso, Buenos Aires, 1425, Argentina. TEL 54-11-48066019, FAX 54-11-48066019, contacto@saap.org.ar, http://www.saap.org.ar. Ed. Martin D'Alessandro. R&P Guido Moscoso. Adv. contact Gustavo Dufour. Circ: 1,000.

320.531 ARG ISSN 1852-4346
▼ **REVISTA SOCIALISTA.** Text in Spanish. 2009. s-a. **Document type:** *Magazine, Consumer.*
Published by: Editorial la Vanguardia, Hipolito Yrigoyen 1516 Piso 5 Pto O, Buenos Aires, 1089AAB, Argentina.

320 BRA ISSN 1982-3290
➤ **REVISTA TERCEIRO SETOR.** Text in Portuguese. 2007. a. free. **Document type:** *Journal, Academic/Scholarly.* **Description:** Contains articles that covers various 3rd world issues.
Media: Online - full text.
Published by: Universidade Guarulhos, Praca Tereza Cristina, 229 - Centro, Guarulhos, Sao Paulo 07011-040, Brazil. http://www.ung.br/. Eds. Edson Roberto Berbel, Julio Cesar Freschi, Mariana Ramalhaes Feitosa.

320 DOM ISSN 1015-440X
REVISTA U N I B E DE CIENCIA Y CULTURA. (Universidad Iberoamericana) Text in Spanish. 1989. 3/yr. **Document type:** *Journal, Academic/Scholarly.*
Published by: Universdidad Iberoamericana, Avenida Francia 129, Gazcue, Santo Domingo, Dominican Republic. TEL 809-689-4111, FAX 809-689-9384, http://www.unibe.edu.do.

320 URY ISSN 0797-9789
JA5
REVISTA URUGUAYA DE CIENCIA POLITICA. Text in Spanish. 1987. irreg. **Document type:** *Journal, Academic/Scholarly.*
Formerly (until 1990): Revista de Ciencia Politica (0797-0498)
Related titles: Online - full text ed.
Indexed: CA, F04, LID&ISL, P42, T02.
Published by: Fundacion de Cultura Universitaria, 25 de Mayo 568, Montevideo, 11003, Uruguay. TEL 598-2-9161152, FAX 598-2-9152549, fcuventa@multi.com.uy, http://www.fcu.com.uy.

320 VEN ISSN 0798-9881
JL3881
REVISTA VENEZOLANA DE CIENCIA POLITICA. Text in Spanish. 1987. a. **Document type:** *Journal, Academic/Scholarly.*
Indexed: A26, I04, I05, I13.
Published by: Universidad de Los Andes, Facultad de Ciencias Juridicas, Politicas y Criminologicas, Av Las Americas, Sector La Liria, Merida, 5110, Venezuela. TEL 58-274-2402652, FAX 58-274-2402651.

320.532 USA ISSN 1557-413X
REVOLUTION (CHICAGO). Text in English. 1979. 39/yr. USD 40 (effective 2006). bk.rev. charts; illus.; stat.; tr.lit. index. back issues avail. **Document type:** *Newspaper.*
Formerly (until May 2005): Revolutionary Worker (0193-3485)
Related titles: Online - full text ed.: ISSN 1557-6728; Supplement to: Obrero Revolucionario. ISSN 0193-354X. 197?.

Published by: (Revolutionary Communist Party), R C P Publications, Inc., Merchandise Mart, PO Box 3486, Chicago, IL 60654. TEL 312-663-5920. Circ: 50,000.

322.42 DZA ISSN 0484-8365
REVOLUTION ET TRAVAIL. Text in French. m. subscr. on per issue basis; some issues may not be avail. due to supply.
Related titles: Arabic ed.
Indexed: RASB.
Published by: Union General des Travailleurs Algeriens Ed. Lakhdari Mohamed Lakhdar.

REVUE BURKINABE DE DROIT. *see* LAW

320 FRA ISSN 0035-2578
REVUE DU DROIT PUBLIC ET DE LA SCIENCE POLITIQUE EN FRANCE ET A L'ETRANGER. Text in French. 1894. bi-m. EUR 123 domestic; EUR 133 foreign (effective 2009). bk.rev. abstr.; bibl. index, cum.index: 1951-1964. reprint service avail. from SCH. **Document type:** *Journal, Academic/Scholarly.*
Related titles: Online - full text ed.: ISSN 1963-1790.
Indexed: A22, FLP, FR, I13, IBR, IBSS, IBZ, PAIS, PCI, RASB.
—BLDSC (7898.550000), IE, Infotrieve, Ingenta, INIST. **CCC.**
Published by: (Librairie Generale de Droit et de Jurisprudence), Lextenso, 33 Rue du Mail, Paris, Cedex 02 75081, France. TEL 33-1-56541600, FAX 33-1-56541649, http://www.lextenso.fr. Circ: 3,800.

320 FRA ISSN 0035-2950
JA11
REVUE FRANCAISE DE SCIENCE POLITIQUE. Text in French; Summaries in English, French. 1951. bi-m. EUR 73 domestic to individuals; EUR 81 foreign to individuals; EUR 130 domestic to institutions; EUR 140 foreign to institutions (effective 2009); EUR 52 domestic to students (effective 2006). bk.rev. abstr.; bibl. index. reprints avail. **Document type:** *Journal, Academic/Scholarly.* **Description:** Scientific presentation of research, ideas and methodological criticism of politics.
Related titles: Online - full text ed.: ISSN 1950-6686.
Indexed: A20, A22, ABCPolSci, BAS, BibInd, CA, DIP, EI, FR, HistAb, I13, IBR, IBSS, IBZ, ILD, P30, P34, P42, PAIS, PCI, PRA, PSA, PdeR, RASB, S02, S03, SCOPUS, SociolAb, T02.
—BLDSC (7904.420000), IE, Infotrieve, Ingenta, INIST. **CCC.**
Published by: (Fondation Nationale des Sciences Politiques), Presses de Sciences Po, 117 Boulevard Saint Germain, Paris, 75006, France. TEL 33-1-45498331, FAX 33-1-45498334, info@presses.sciences-po.fr, http://www.sciences-po.fr. Ed. Jean Luc Parodi. Circ: 3,000. **Co-sponsor:** Association Francaise de Science Politique.

320.09 FRA ISSN 1266-7862
JA11
REVUE FRANCAISE D'HISTOIRE DES IDEES POLITIQUES. Text in French. 1995. s-a. EUR 35 (effective 2009). bk.rev. bibl. **Document type:** *Academic/Scholarly.*
Indexed: FR, IBSS.
—INIST.
Published by: Picard Editeur, 82 rue Bonaparte, Paris, 75006, France. TEL 33-1-43267978, FAX 33-1-43264264. Ed. Guillaume Bacot.

320 CAN ISSN 1912-0362
REVUE GOUVERNANCE. Text in French. 2004. s-a. **Document type:** *Journal, Academic/Scholarly.*
Media: Online - full text. **Related titles:** English ed.: ISSN 1912-0370.
Published by: (University of Ottawa, School of Political Studies), The Summit Group, 100-263 Holmwood Ave, Ottawa, ON K1S 2P8, Canada. TEL 613-688-0763, 800-575-1146, FAX 613-688-0767, http://www.summitconnects.com/index.htm.

328 FRA ISSN 0035-385X
H3
REVUE POLITIQUE ET PARLEMENTAIRE. Text in French. 1894. q. EUR 24 per issue (effective 2009). adv. bk.rev. charts; illus.; stat. index. reprint service avail. from SCH. **Document type:** *Journal.* **Description:** Discusses domestic politics and the role of France in Europe and in the world.
Related titles: Microform ed.
Indexed: A22, CA, ELLIS, FR, I13, IBSS, MLA-IB, P42, PAIS, PRA, PSA, RASB, SCOPUS, T02.
—BLDSC (7942.550000), IE, Infotrieve, Ingenta, INIST. **CCC.**
Address: 3 rue Bellini, Puteaux, 92800, France. TEL 33-1-46981374, FAX 33-1-47730148, joc.picard@wanadoo.fr. Ed. Mario Guastoni. Pub. Bertrand Cluzel. Circ: 5,500.

327 960.3 FRA ISSN 1951-1841
LA REVUE POUR L'INTELLIGENCE DU MONDE. Key Title: La Revue. Text in French. 2003. bi-m. EUR 45 (effective 2009). **Document type:** *Magazine, Consumer.*
Formerly (until 2004): La Revue de l'Intelligence (1763-3400)
Published by: Groupe Jeune Afrique, 57 bis, Rue d'Auteuil, Paris, 75016, France. TEL 33-1-44301960, FAX 33-1-44301930, http://www.groupeja.com.

320.531 FRA ISSN 1294-2529
HX5
LA REVUE SOCIALISTE. Text in French. 1885. q. EUR 10 per issue (effective 2009). adv. bk.rev. index. **Document type:** *Magazine, Consumer.*
Former titles (until 1999): L' Hebdo des Socialistes (1278-6772); (until 1996): Vendredi (0995-0583); Which incorporated (1885-1993): Vendredi Idees (1241-798X); Which was formerly (until 1992): N R S La Nouvelle Revue Socialiste (0222-4275); (until 1978): La Nouvelle Revue Socialiste (0222-4283); (until 1974): Revue Socialiste (0035-4139)
Indexed: BAS, IBSS, PCI.
Published by: Parti Socialiste, 10 rue de Solferino, Paris, 75333, France. TEL 33-1-45567700, FAX 33-1-47051578, http://www.parti-socialiste.fr.

320 USA ISSN 1558-4291
JK1967
THE RHODES COOK LETTER (ONLINE). Text in English. 2000. bi-m. USD 115 to institutions; USD 345 to corporations (effective 2011). back issues avail. **Document type:** *Newsletter, Consumer.* **Description:** Provides a distinctive analysis of the American political scene - with texts, maps and a variety of other colorful graphics that seek to put current elections into a broader historical context.
Formerly: The Rhodes Cook Letter (Print) (1552-8189)
Media: Online - full text.
Indexed: A01, CA, P34, P42, PAIS, SCOPUS, T02.
—CCC.
Published by: Berkeley Electronic Press, 2809 Telegraph Ave, Ste 202, Berkeley, CA 94705. TEL 510-665-1200, FAX 510-665-1201, info@bepress.com.

THE RIGHT GUIDE; a guide to conservative, free-market, and traditional organizations. *see* BUSINESS AND ECONOMICS—Trade And Industrial Directories

328 SWE ISSN 1402-8239
JN7934
RIKSDAGENS LEDAMOETER. Text in Swedish. 1995. a. free. **Document type:** *Government.* **Description:** Information on members of the Swedish Parliament.
Former titles (until 1995): Riksdagen (0280-0365); Which was formed by the merger of (1971-1980): Foerteckning oever Riksdagens Ledamoeter (0349-604X); (1971-1980): Foerteckning oever Ersaettare foer Riksdagens Ledamoeter (0349-5736)
Published by: Sveriges Riksdag, Informationsenheten/The Swedish Parliament. Information Department, Stockholm, 10012, Sweden. TEL 46-8-7864000, riksdagsinformation@riksdagen.se, http://www.riksdagen.se. Circ: 10,000. **Dist. by:** Sveriges Riksdag, Tryckeriexpeditionen, Stockholm 10012, Sweden.

320.5 USA ISSN 0094-7865
JK2351
RIPON QUARTERLY. Text in English. 1962. q. membership. adv. bk.rev. illus. cum.index. reprints avail. **Document type:** *Newsletter.*
Incorporates (1965-1997): Ripon Forum (0035-5526); Formerly (1962-1980): Ripon Society Newsletter
Related titles: Microfilm ed.: (from PQC).
Indexed: A22, ABS&EES, P06, P30, P42, PQC.
—Ingenta.
Published by: Ripon Society, 1300 L St NW, Ste. 900, Washington, DC 20005-4182. TEL 202-546-1292. Ed., R&P Mike Gill. Circ: 10,000.

320 IND
RISING SUN. Text in English. 1971. w. bk.rev. illus. **Document type:** *Magazine, Consumer.*
Address: 52-A Kodam Bakkam High Rd, Chennai, Tamil Nadu 600 034, India.

324.2734 USA ISSN 1072-5687
JK1
RISING TIDE. Text in English. 1993. q. USD 12. **Document type:** *Magazine, Consumer.* **Description:** Serves as a forum for the Republican Party's principles and agenda.
Published by: Republican National Committee, 310 First St, S E, Washington, DC 20003. info@gop.com. Ed. Chuck Greener.

320 ITA ISSN 2037-495X
▼ **RIVISTA DI POLITICA.** Text in Italian. 2010. q. **Document type:** *Magazine, Consumer.*
Published by: Rubbettino Editore, Viale Rosario Rubbettino 10, Soveria Mannelli, CZ 88049, Italy. TEL 39-0968-662034, FAX 39-0968-662055, segreteria@rubettino.it, http://www.rubbettino.it.

320 ITA ISSN 1120-4036
RIVISTA DI STUDI POLITICI. Text in Italian. 1989. q. EUR 40 domestic; EUR 80 foreign (effective 2009). adv. bk.rev. **Document type:** *Journal, Academic/Scholarly.*
Published by: (Istituto di Studi Politici San Pio V), Editrice A P E S, Piazza Navona, 93, Rome, RM 00186, Italy. http://www.editriceapes.it.

320 ITA ISSN 1971-1921
RIVISTA ITALIANA DI CONFLITTOLOGIA. Text in Italian. 2007. 3/yr. EUR 30 (effective 2008). **Document type:** *Magazine, Consumer.*
Related titles: Online - full text ed.: ISSN 1971-1913.
Published by: Associazione Italiana di Confittologia, Via R Ruffilli s/n, Benevento, 82100, Italy. info@confittologia.it, http://www.confittologia.it.

320 ITA ISSN 1722-1137
RIVISTA ITALIANA DI POLITICHE PUBBLICHE. Text in Italian. 2002. 3/yr. EUR 94 combined subscription domestic to institutions (print & online eds.); EUR 144.50 combined subscription foreign to institutions (print & online eds.) (effective 2009). **Document type:** *Journal, Academic/Scholarly.*
Related titles: Online - full text ed.
Indexed: IBSS, PSA.
Published by: (Universita degli Studi di Bologna, Dipartimento di Organizzazione e Sistema Politico), Societa Editrice Il Mulino, Strada Maggiore 37, Bologna, 40125, Italy. TEL 39-051-256011, FAX 39-051-256034, riviste@mulino.it. Ed. Giorgio Freddi.

320 ITA ISSN 0048-8402
JA18
RIVISTA ITALIANA DI SCIENZA POLITICA. Text in Italian; Summaries in English. 1971. 3/yr. EUR 97.50 combined subscription domestic to institutions (print & online eds.); EUR 147.50 combined subscription foreign to institutions (print & online eds.) (effective 2009). bk.rev. bibl. index. back issues avail. **Document type:** *Journal, Academic/Scholarly.*
Related titles: Online - full text ed.
Indexed: A20, A22, ABCPolSci, CA, FR, HistAb, I13, IBSS, P42, PAIS, PCI, PSA, RASB, SCOPUS, SociolAb, T02.
—IE, Infotrieve, INIST.
Published by: Societa Editrice Il Mulino, Strada Maggiore 37, Bologna, 40125, Italy. TEL 39-051-256011, FAX 39-051-256034, riviste@mulino.it. Ed. Sergio Fabbrini. Circ: 1,700.

RIVISTA STORICA DELL'ANARCHISMO. QUADERNI. *see* HISTORY

324.27109 CAN ISSN 0047-6110
ROAD OF THE PARTY. Text in English. 1970. irreg. CAD 20. charts; illus.
Formerly (until 1980): Mass Line
Published by: Communist Party of Canada (Marxist - Leninist), Central Committee, P O Box 666, Sta C, Montreal, PQ, Canada. TEL 416-252-3658. Ed. Hardial S Bains. **Dist. by:** National Publications Centre.

320.531 GBR ISSN 0483-2027
ROBOTNIK. Text in Polish; Summaries in English. 1975 (vol.81). q. bk.rev.
Published by: Polish Socialist Party in Exile, 84 Fordhook Ave, London, W. 5, United Kingdom. Ed. Leszek Talko. Circ: 2,000.

324.2595 MYS ISSN 0048-8461
ROCKET. Text in English. 1971 (vol.6). bi-m. MYR 3.20. bk.rev. charts; illus.
Published by: Democratic Action Party of Malaysia, 77 Jalan, 20-9 Paramount Garden, Petaling Jaya, Selangor, Malaysia. FAX 04-361909. Circ: 35,000.

320 POL
ROCZNIK STRATEGICZNY. Text in Polish. a. price varies. **Document type:** *Monographic series, Academic/Scholarly.*
Published by: Wydawnictwo Naukowe Scholar, Krakowskie Przedmiescie 62, Warsaw, 00322, Poland. TEL 48-22-6357404 ext 218, FAX 48-22-8289391, info@scholar.com.pl, http://www.scholar.com.pl.

320.5 SWE ISSN 0280-6010
ROED PRESS. Text in Swedish. 1972. 5/yr. SEK 100 (effective 2004).
Former titles (until 1982): Stormklockan (0349-957X); (until 1977, vol.10): K U - Stormklockan (0345-6714)
Published by: Ung Vaenster, Kungsgatan 84, PO Box 12660, Stockholm, 11293, Sweden. TEL 46-8-6543100, FAX 46-8-6508557, info@ungvanster.se, http://www.ungvanster.se/rodpress. Ed. Tove Fraurud.

324.248507 SWE
ROEDA RUMMET; Socialistiska Partiets teoretiska tidskrift. Text in Swedish. 1969. q. SEK 175 (effective 2000). **Document type:** *Bulletin, Consumer.*
Formerly: Fjaerde Internationalen (0345-3375)
Published by: Socialistiska Partiet, PO Box 6087, Stockholm, 10232, Sweden. TEL 46-31-24-15-13, FAX 46-31-24-91-55, rodarummet@hotmail.com, http://www.internationalen.se/roda_rummet. Ed. Bjoern Roennblad.

324.2 NOR ISSN 1504-4777
ROEDT!; marxistisk tidsskrift. Text in Norwegian. 1972. q. NOK 240 (effective 2011). bk.rev. back issues avail. **Document type:** *Magazine, Consumer.*
Formerly (until 2005): Roede Fane (0332-7892)
Related titles: Online - full text ed.: ISSN 1504-4785. 199?.
Published by: Arbeidernes Kommunistparti, Osterhaus Gate 27, Oslo, 0183, Norway. TEL 47-22-989060, FAX 47-22-989055, akp@akp.no. Ed. Erik Ness.

328 USA ISSN 0035-788X
ROLL CALL. Text in English. 1955. d. (Mon.-Thu.). USD 380 subscr - mailed; USD 3.75 newsstand/cover (effective 2005). adv. **Document type:** *Newspaper, Trade.*
Related titles: Online - full text ed.: 1955.
Indexed: P34, P48, PQC, SWR&A.
—CIS. **CCC.**
Published by: Roll Call, Inc (Subsidiary of: The Economist Newspaper Ltd.), 50 F St, NW, 7th Fl, Washington, DC 20001-1530. TEL 202-824-6800, 800-289-9331, FAX 202-824-0475, letters@rollcall.com. Ed. Charlie Mitchell. Pub. Laurie Battaglia. adv.: color page USD 8,650, B&W page USD 7,650. Circ: 17,866 (controlled and free).

320 ROM
ROMANIAN ACADEMIC SOCIETY. CRISIS PAPERS COLLECTION. Text in English. irreg.
Published by: Societatea Academica din Romania/Romanian Academic Society, Str. Petofi Sandor 15, Bucuresti 1, Romania. FAX 401-222-18-68, sar@starnets.ro.

320 ROM
ROMANIAN ACADEMIC SOCIETY. WORKING PAPERS COLLECTION. Text in English. irreg.
Published by: Societatea Academica din Romania/Romanian Academic Society, Str. Petofi Sandor 15, Bucuresti 1, Romania. FAX 401-222-18-68, sar@starnets.ro.

320 301 ROM
ROMANIAN JOURNAL OF SOCIETY AND POLITICS. Text in English. 2001. s-a. **Document type:** *Journal, Academic/Scholarly.*
Published by: Civic Education Project, Bd Unirii 76, Bucharest, Romania.

320.531 NLD ISSN 1574-2733
ROOD. Text in Dutch. 2001. bi-m.
Formerly (until 2004): Pro en Contra (1570-5188); Which was formed by the merger of (1996-2000): Pro Binnenhof (1570-517X); (1991-2001): PRO (0928-396X); Which was formerly (until 1992): Rood (0926-888X)
Published by: Partij van de Arbeid, Herengracht 54, Amsterdam, 1015 BN, Netherlands. TEL 31-20-5512155, FAX 31-20-5512250, http://www.pvda.nl. Circ: 55,000.

320.53 DEU ISSN 1864-6794
ROSALUX. Text in German. 2007. q. **Document type:** *Journal, Trade.*
Published by: Rosa-Luxemburg-Stiftung, Franz-Mehring Platz 1, Berlin, 10243, Germany. TEL 49-30-443100, FAX 49-30-44310222, info@rosalux.de, http://www.rosalux.de.

320 RUS
ROSSIISKAYA FEDERATSIYA. GAZETA. Text in Russian. 48/yr. USD 145 in United States. **Document type:** *Newspaper, Consumer.*
Address: Balaklavskii pr-d 28, Moscow, 113452, Russian Federation. TEL 7-095-3186691. **Dist. by:** East View Information Services, 10601 Wayzata Blvd, Minneapolis, MN 55305. TEL 952-252-1201, 800-477-1005, FAX 952-252-1202, info@eastview.com, http://www.eastview.com.

320 RUS
DK510.763
ROSSIISKAYA FEDERATSIYA SEGODNYA. Text in Russian. 1957. 24/yr. USD 145. bibl.; illus. back issues avail.
Former titles (until 1998): Rossiiskaya Federatsiya; Narodnyi Deputat (0236-0918); (until 1990): Sovety Narodnykh Deputatov (0201-5250); (until 1977): Sovety Deputatov Trudyashchikhsya (0132-1374)
Related titles: Microfiche ed.: (from EVP).
Indexed: RASB.
—East View.
Published by: Russia, Ul Chekhova 3-10, Moscow, 103800, Russian Federation. TEL 7-095-2994055, FAX 7-095-200-3080. Ed. M I Piskotin. Circ: 50,000. **Dist. by:** East View Information Services, 10601 Wayzata Blvd, Minneapolis, MN 55305. TEL 952-252-1201, 800-477-1005, FAX 952-252-1202, info@eastview.com, http://www.eastview.com.

320 RUS
ROSSIISKII SOTSYAL'NO-POLITICHESKII VESTNIK. Text in Russian. bi-m. USD 99.95 in United States.

P

Published by: Assotsiatsiya Sotsioekonomika, Ul Krasikova 32, Moscow, 117218, Russian Federation. TEL 7-095-3324488. **Dist. by:** East View Information Services, 10601 Wayzata Blvd, Minneapolis, MN 55305. TEL 952-252-1201, 800-477-1005, FAX 952-252-1202, info@eastview.com, http://www.eastview.com.

324.22 RUS ISSN 1606-1543
ROSSIISKIYE POLITICHESKIYE PORTRETY. Text in Russian. 1999. w. free (effective 2004). **Document type:** *Consumer.*
Media: Online - full text.
Published by: Al'yans Midiya, Bolotnaya ul 12, str 3, Moscow, 115035, Russian Federation. TEL 7-095-2345380, FAX 7-095-2345363, allmedia@allmedia.ru, http://allmedia.ru, http:// www.businesspress.ru.

322.1 RUS
ROSSIYA I MUSUL'MANSKII MIR; biulleten' informativno-analiticheskoi informatsii. Text in Russian. 1992. m. USD 275 in United States (effective 2004). **Document type:** *Journal, Academic/Scholarly.* **Description:** Designed to help businessmen, diplomats, political writers, journalists and specialists in social sciences to answer questions like what is the political role of Islam in Transcaucasia, Central Asia, and other Moslem enclaves inside Russia, etc.
Related titles: ◆ English Translation: Russia and the Moslem World.
Indexed: RASB.
Published by: Rossiiskaya Akademiya Nauk, Institut Nauchnoi Informatsii po Obshchestvennym Naukam, Nakhimovskii pr-t 51/21, Moscow, 117997, Russian Federation. TEL 7-095-1288930, FAX 7-095-4202261, info@inion.ru, http://www.inion.ru. **Dist. by:** East View Information Services, 10601 Wayzata Blvd, Minneapolis, MN 55305. TEL 952-252-1201, 800-477-1005, FAX 952-252-1202, info@eastview.com, http://www.eastview.com.

324 RUS ISSN 1606-1500
ROSSIYA VYBIRAYET. Text in Russian. 1999. w. free (effective 2004). **Document type:** *Consumer.*
Media: Online - full text.
Published by: Al'yans Midiya, Bolotnaya ul 12, str 3, Moscow, 115035, Russian Federation. TEL 7-095-2345380, FAX 7-095-2345363, allmedia@allmedia.ru, http://www.businesspress.ru, http:// allmedia.ru.

320 USA ISSN 1053-9530
ROSTER & GOVERNMENT GUIDE. Variant title: California Journal Roster & Government Guide. Text in English. a. USD 3.50 (effective 2004). adv.
Published by: Information for Public Affairs, Inc., 2101 K St, Sacramento, CA 95816. TEL 916-444-2840, FAX 916-446-5369, pubs@californiajournal.org, http://www.californiajournal.org. Circ: 75,000.

320.532 DEU ISSN 0936-1421
ROTE FAHNE; Wochenzeitung der M L P D. Text in German. 1970. w. bk.rev. illus. **Document type:** *Newspaper.*
Published by: (Marxistisch-Leninistische Partei Deutschland), Neuer Weg Verlag & Druck GmbH, Kaninenberghoehe 2, Essen, 45136, Germany. TEL 49-201-25915, FAX 49-201-268577.

320.531 CHE ISSN 1421-8763
ROTE REVUE; Zeitschrift fuer Politik, Wirtschaft und Kultur. Text in German. 1915. 4/yr. CHF 40; CHF 12 newsstand/cover (effective 2008). adv. bk.rev. index. **Document type:** *Magazine, Trade.*
Former titles (until 1989): Rote Revue - Profil (0253-5009); (until 1980): Profil (0555-3482); (until 1967): Rote Revue (0035-8428); (until 1921): Neues Leben (1421-8755)
Indexed: RASB.
Published by: Sozialdemokratische Partei der Schweiz, Spitalgasse 34, Bern, 3001, Switzerland. TEL 41-31-3296969, sekretariat@sp-ps.ch, http://www.sp-ps.ch. Circ: 3,000.

320.532 DEU ISSN 0939-2947
ROTER MORGEN. Text in German. 1967. fortn. looseleaf. EUR 16 per month; EUR 10 per month to students (effective 2010). back issues avail. **Document type:** *Newspaper.*
Related titles: Online - full text ed.
Published by: (Kommunistische Partei Deutschlands), Zeitungsverlag Roter Morgen, Postfach 900753, Frankfurt am Main, 60447, Germany. TEL 49-69-97071025, info@kpd-online.info. Circ: 900.

320 USA ISSN 2150-1181
▼ **THE ROTUNDA (MIDLAND)**; the journal of national politics. Text in English. 2009 (Nov.). q. USD 120 to individuals; USD 1,200 to libraries (effective 2009). **Document type:** *Journal, Consumer.* **Description:** Features essays on national politics for conservatives.
Related titles: Online - full text ed.: ISSN 2150-119X. 2009 (Nov.). USD 55 (effective 2009).
Published by: Sterling, Hoffman & Co., PO Box 1074, Midland, MI 48641. TEL 206-203-1614, mail@sterlinghoffmanco.com.

ROUTLEDGE FRONTIERS OF POLITICAL ECONOMY. *see* BUSINESS AND ECONOMICS

320 GBR
ROUTLEDGE STUDIES IN GOVERNANCE AND PUBLIC POLICY. Text in English. 1998 (Aug.). irreg., latest 2009. price varies. back issues avail. **Document type:** *Monographic series, Academic/Scholarly.* **Description:** Provides detailed analysis of the exercise of power in institutional contexts and within the public sector.
Published by: Routledge (Subsidiary of: Taylor & Francis Group), 4 Park Sq, Milton Park, Abingdon, Oxon OX14 4RN, United Kingdom. TEL 44-20-70176000, FAX 44-20-70176336, subscriptions@tandf.co.uk.

320.5 GBR
ROUTLEDGE STUDIES IN SOCIAL AND POLITICAL THOUGHT. Text in English. 1996. irreg., latest 2009. price varies. back issues avail. **Document type:** *Monographic series, Academic/Scholarly.* **Description:** Addresses theoretical subjects of both historical and contemporary relevance, the series has broad appeal across the social sciences.
Published by: Routledge (Subsidiary of: Taylor & Francis Group), 4 Park Sq, Milton Park, Abingdon, Oxon OX14 4RN, United Kingdom. TEL 44-20-70176000, FAX 44-20-70176336, subscriptions@tandf.co.uk.

RUSSIA BUSINESS FORECAST REPORT. *see* BUSINESS AND ECONOMICS—Economic Situation And Conditions

320.53 USA
JN6598.K4
RUSSIA, CHINA, AND EURASIA: SOCIAL, HISTORICAL AND CULTURAL ISSUES. Text in English. 1990. bi-m. USD 1,045 to institutions; USD 1,567 combined subscription to institutions (print & online eds.) (effective 2012). **Document type:** *Journal, Academic/Scholarly.* **Description:** Deals with the sometimes explosive political history of Russia, ending with the Gorbachev resignation. Coverage includes the Soviet period as well as earlier periods.
Formerly (until 2010): Political History and Culture of Russia, China and Eurasia; Which incorporated (2008-2009): Political History and Culture of China (1939-5957); (until 200?): Political History and Culture of Russia (1931-910X); (until 1997): Political History of Russia (1080-7748); (until 1994): Political Archives of Russia (1069-093X); (until 1991): Political Archives of the Soviet Union (1049-7714)
Related titles: Online - full text ed.: USD 1,045 to institutions (effective 2012).
Indexed: ABS&EES.
—IE, Ingenta.
Published by: Nova Science Publishers, Inc., 400 Oser Ave, Ste 1600, Hauppauge, NY 11788. TEL 631-231-7269, FAX 631-231-8175, main@novapublishers.com. Ed. Frank Columbus.

320.947 FRA ISSN 1771-3900
RUSSIA INTELLIGENCE; politics and business inside Russia. Text in French. 2004. s-m. EUR 770 (effective 2009). **Document type:** *Newsletter, Consumer.*
Related titles: Online - full text ed.: EUR 880 (effective 2007); English Translation:.
Published by: Eurasian Intelligence, 115 Rue Saint-Dominique, Paris, 75007, France.

320 RUS
RUSSIAN DIPLOMATIC COURIER. Text in English. w. USD 199.95 in United States.
Indexed: RASB.
Address: Zubovskii bulv 4, Moscow, 119021, Russian Federation. TEL 7-095-2015735, FAX 7-095-2013440. **Dist. by:** East View Information Services, 10601 Wayzata Blvd, Minneapolis, MN 55305. TEL 952-252-1201, 800-477-1005, FAX 952-252-1202, info@eastview.com, http://www.eastview.com.

RUSSIAN POLITICS AND LAW. *see* LAW

320.9 USA ISSN 1061-1428
AS261
➤ **RUSSIAN SOCIAL SCIENCE REVIEW.** Abbreviated title: R S S. Text in English. 1959. bi-m. USD 410 combined subscription domestic to institutions (print & online eds.); USD 494 combined subscription foreign to institutions (print & online eds.) (effective 2012). adv. illus. index. back issues avail.; reprint service avail. from PSC. **Document type:** *Journal, Academic/Scholarly.* **Description:** Presents works by experts and scholars who live in the former Soviet Union. Essays and studies are from a broad range of fields including sociology, economics, education, literary criticism, history, anthropology, psychology, and political science.
Formerly (until 1992): Soviet Review (0038-5794); Which superseded (in 1960): Soviet Highlights (0561-2403)
Related titles: Microform ed.: (from PQC); Online - full text ed.: ISSN 1557-7848. 2004 (Feb.). USD 373 to institutions (effective 2012).
Indexed: A01, A02, A03, A08, A12, A22, A26, ABIn, ABS&EES, B04, BRD, C12, CA, E-psyche, E01, E08, G08, H09, H10, I05, I08, L09, M01, M02, MEA&I, MLA-IB, P02, P06, P10, P13, P27, P30, P34, P42, P47, P53, P54, PAIS, PCI, PQC, PSA, S02, S03, S05, S09, SSAI, SSAb, SSI, SociolAb, T02, W03, W05.
—BLDSC (8052.920000), IE, Infotrieve, Ingenta. **CCC.**
Published by: M.E. Sharpe, Inc., 80 Business Park Dr, Armonk, NY 10504. TEL 914-273-1800, 800-541-6563, FAX 914-273-2106, custserv@mesharpe.com. Ed. Patricia A Kolb. Adv. contact Barbara Ladd TEL 914-273-1800.

321 SWE ISSN 1404-5052
S C O R E RAPPORTSERIE. (Stockholm Center for Organizational Research) Text in English, Swedish. 1996. irreg. **Document type:** *Monographic series, Academic/Scholarly.*
Related titles: Online - full text ed.: S C O R E Arbetsrapporter. ISSN 1653-7505.
Published by: Stockholms Centrum foer Forskning om Offentlig Sektor/Stockholm Center for Organizational Research, Kraftriket Hus 7A, Roslagvaegen 101, Stockholm, 10691, Sweden. TEL 46-8-6747412, FAX 46-8-164908.

320.531 DEU ISSN 0170-4613
HX6
S P W. (Sozialistische Politik und Wirtschaft) Variant title: Zeitschrift fuer Sozialistische Politik und Wirtschaft. Text in German. 1978. bi-m. EUR 34 domestic; EUR 37 foreign (effective 2006). bk.rev. back issues avail. **Document type:** *Bulletin, Consumer.*
Indexed: DIP, IBR, IBZ.
Published by: S P W Verlag GmbH, Postfach 120333, Dortmund, 44293, Germany. TEL 49-231-402410, FAX 49-231-402416, spw-verlag@spw.de, http://www.spw.de. Circ: 2,000.

321.8 USA ISSN 1930-4331
S U N Y SERIES IN AMERICAN CONSTITUTIONALISM. (State University of New York) Text in English. 1997. irreg., latest 2010. price varies. back issues avail. **Document type:** *Monographic series, Academic/Scholarly.*
Published by: State University of New York Press, 22 Corporate Woods Blvd, 3rd Fl, Albany, NY 12211. TEL 518-472-5000, 866-430-7869, FAX 518-472-5038, info@sunypress.edu.

320 ITA ISSN 1970-2442
SAGGI. POLITICA. Text in Italian. 1998. irreg. **Document type:** *Monographic series, Academic/Scholarly.*
Published by: Editori Riuniti, c/o The Media Factory, Via Tuscolana 4, Rome, 00182, Italy. TEL 39-06-70614211, FAX 39-06-70613928, http://www.editoririuniti.it.

SALISBURY REVIEW; a quarterly magazine of conservative thought. *see* LITERARY AND POLITICAL REVIEWS

320 362 ITA ISSN 1723-9427
SALUTE E SOCIETA. Text in Italian. 2002. 3/yr. EUR 71 combined subscription domestic to institutions (print & online eds.); EUR 93 combined subscription foreign to institutions (print & online eds.) (effective 2009). **Document type:** *Journal, Academic/Scholarly.*
Related titles: Online - full text ed.: ISSN 1972-4845.
Published by: Franco Angeli Edizioni, Viale Monza 106, Milan, 20127, Italy. TEL 39-02-2837141, FAX 39-02-26144793, redazioni@francoangeli.it, http://www.francoangeli.it.

320 AUT
SALZBURGER JAHRBUCH FUER POLITIK. Text in German. 1989. biennial. EUR 23.80 per vol. (effective 2011). **Document type:** *Journal, Academic/Scholarly.*
Published by: Boehlau Verlag GmbH & Co.KG., Wiesingerstr 1, Vienna, W 1010, Austria. TEL 43-1-3302427, FAX 43-1-3302432, boehlau@boehlau.at, http://www.boehlau.at.

320 RUS
➤ **SAMARSKII GOSUDARSTVENNYI UNIVERSITET. VESTNIK. GUMANITARNAYA SERIYA. POLITOLOGIYA.** Text in Russian. 2003. bi-m. **Document type:** *Journal, Academic/Scholarly.*
Published by: Izdatel'stvo Samarskii Universitet/Publishing House of Samara State University, ul Akademika Pavlova 1, k 209, Samara, 443011, Russian Federation. TEL 7-846-3345406, FAX 7-846-3345406, university-press@ssu.samara.ru, http://publisher.samsu.ru.

320 330 NLD ISSN 1875-0109
SAMENGEVAT. Variant title: Regiomagazine SamenGevat. Text in Dutch. 200?. q.
Published by: Holland Rijnland, Postbus 558, Leiden, 2300 AN, Netherlands. TEL 31-71-5239090, FAX 31-71-5239099, secretariaat@hollandrijnland.net.

SAMFUNNSOEKONOMEN. *see* BUSINESS AND ECONOMICS

324.281072 NOR ISSN 1503-6855
SAMMEN. Text in Norwegian. 1979. bk.rev. bibl. **Document type:** *Magazine, Consumer.*
Former titles (until 2003): Medlemskontakt (1503-6901); (until 1999): Aktuelt Perspektiv (0332-7426); Which was formed by the merger of (1964-1978): Sosialistisk Perspektiv (0049-1330); (1959-1978): Arbeiderkvinnen (0806-2528); (1952-1978): Tillitsmannen (0332-866X)
Related titles: Online - full text ed.: ISSN 1891-8042. 2009.
Indexed: RASB.
Published by: Det Norske Arbeiderparti/Norwegian Labour Party, PO Box 8824, Youngstorget, Oslo, 0028, Norway. TEL 47-24-144000, FAX 47-24-144001, post@arbeiderpartiet.no, http:// www.arbeiderpartiet.no. Ed. Marte Ingul. Circ: 52,000.

320 CHE
ST. GALLER STUDIEN ZUR POLITIKWISSENSCHAFT. Text in German. 1975. irreg., latest vol.27, 2002. price varies. **Document type:** *Monographic series, Academic/Scholarly.*
Published by: Paul Haupt AG, Falkenplatz 14, Bern, 3001, Switzerland. TEL 41-31-3012425, FAX 41-31-3014669, verlag@haupt.ch, http://www.haupt.ch.

SANT SIPAHI. *see* RELIGIONS AND THEOLOGY—Other Denominations And Sects

320 USA ISSN 1932-9628
THE SANTA CRUZ COMIC NEWS. Text in English. 19??. m. **Document type:** *Magazine, Consumer.*
Published by: The Santa Cruz Comic News, PO Box 1335, Santa Cruz, CA 95061. TEL 831-466-3269, office@thecomicnews.com, http://thecomicnews.com.

320 GBR
SAPIENTIA (ABERDEEN). Text in English. q.
Media: Online - full content.
Published by: (Political Studies Association Graduate Network), University of Aberdeen, Department of Politics and International Relations, Edward Wright Bldg, Aberdeen, AB24 3QY, United Kingdom. TEL 44-1224-272714, FAX 44-1224-272552.

SAPIO. *see* BUSINESS AND ECONOMICS

320.9 BGD
SAPTAHIKA THIKANA. Variant title: Thikana. Text in Bengali. 1976. w. BDT 0.50 per issue. **Description:** Covers political news and views.
Published by: Abul Hossain Mir, Ed. & Pub., Press Club Bhavan, Mujib Sarak, Jessore, Bangladesh.

320.944 322.4 FRA ISSN 1960-100X
LE SARKOPHAGE; contre tous les Sarkozysmes. Text in French. 2007. bi-m. EUR 12 (effective 2008). back issues avail. **Document type:** *Newsletter, Consumer.* **Description:** Analyzes the current political situation in France while promoting anti-Sarkosy sentiments.
Published by: Les Temps Mauvais, 161 Chemin de Champgravier, Saint Georges de Reneins, 69830, France.

SAUDI ARABIA BUSINESS FORECAST REPORT. *see* BUSINESS AND ECONOMICS—Economic Situation And Conditions

320 FRA ISSN 1958-7856
DC425
SAVOIR - AGIR. LA REVUE. Text in French. 2007. q. EUR 50 domestic; EUR 60 foreign (effective 2009). **Document type:** *Journal, Academic/Scholarly.*
Related titles: Online - full text ed.: ISSN 1958-5535.
Published by: (Raisons d'Agir), Editions du Croquant, Broissieux, Bellecombe-en-Bauges, 73340, France. TEL 33-6-89213525, info@editionsducroquant.org. **Dist. by:** Editions Les Belles Lettres, 25 Rue du General Leclerc, Kremlin Bicetre 94270, France. TEL 33-1-45151970, FAX 33-1-45151980.

320 KAZ
SAYASAT - POLITIKA; sobytya, problemy, analiz, prognozy. Text in Russian. m. USD 225 in United States (effective 2000).
Indexed: RASB.
Address: c/o Institute of Development, Almaty, Kazakstan. TEL 3272-621678. **Dist. by:** East View Information Services, 10601 Wayzata Blvd, Minneapolis, MN 55305. TEL 952-252-1201, 800-477-1005, FAX 952-252-1202, info@eastview.com, http:// www.eastview.com.

320 GBR ISSN 0080-6757
JN7001
➤ **SCANDINAVIAN POLITICAL STUDIES.** Abbreviated title: S P S. Text in English. 1966; N.S. 1978. q. GBP 236 in United Kingdom to institutions; EUR 298 in Europe to institutions; USD 397 in the Americas to institutions; USD 462 elsewhere to institutions; GBP 271 combined subscription in United Kingdom to institutions (print & online eds.); EUR 343 combined subscription in Europe to institutions (print & online eds.); USD 456 combined subscription in the Americas to institutions (print & online eds.); USD 530 combined subscription elsewhere to institutions (print & online eds.) (effective 2012). adv. bk.rev. bibl.; illus. index. back issues avail.; reprint service avail. from PSC. **Document type:** *Journal, Academic/Scholarly.* **Description:** Presents political studies on Scandinavia to an international forum of political scientists and sociologists.
Supersedes (1968-1977): Scandinavian Political Studies Yearbook
Related titles: Microform ed.: N.S. (from PQC); Online - full text ed.: ISSN 1467-9477. N.S. GBP 236 in United Kingdom to institutions; EUR 298 in Europe to institutions; USD 397 in the Americas to institutions; USD 462 elsewhere to institutions (effective 2012) (from IngentaConnect).
Indexed: A01, A03, A08, A22, A26, ABCPolSci, ASCA, CA, CurCont, DIP, E01, E04, E05, ESPM, FR, HistAb, I13, IBR, IBSS, IBZ, P34, P42, PCI, PSA, RASB, RiskAb, S02, S03, SCOPUS, SOPODA, SSA, SSCI, SociolAb, T02, W07.
—BLDSC (8087.572000), IE, Infotrieve, Ingenta, INIST. **CCC.**
Published by: (Nordic Political Science Association), Wiley-Blackwell Publishing Ltd. (Subsidiary of: John Wiley & Sons, Inc.), 9600 Garsington Rd, Oxford, OX4 2DQ, United Kingdom. TEL 44-1865-776868, FAX 44-1865-714591, customerservices@blackwellpublishing.com. Eds. Christoffer Green-Pedersen TEL 45-8-9421297, Karina Kosiara-Pedersen TEL 45-3-5323416, Peter Munk Christiansen TEL 45-8-9421276.

320.531 AUT
SCHLAGLICHT. Text in German. 1978. m. looseleaf. bk.rev. back issues avail. **Document type:** *Newsletter, Consumer.*
Formerly: Der Volkssozialist
Published by: Volkssozialisten Oesterreichs, Apfelgasse 1-7, Vienna, W 1040, Austria. TEL 43-1-5034204. Ed. Karl Pfann. Circ: 500 (paid).

324 DEU ISSN 1438-4299
SCHNITTPUNKTE VON FORSCHUNG UND POLITIK. Text in German. 1999. irreg., latest vol.9, 2007. price varies. **Document type:** *Monographic series, Academic/Scholarly.*
Published by: (Gesellschaft fuer Programmforschung), Waxmann Verlag GmbH, Steinfurter Str 555, Muenster, 48159, Germany. TEL 49-251-265040, FAX 49-251-2650426, info@waxmann.com. Ed. Dieter Schimanke.

320.5 DEU ISSN 1434-3835
SCHRAEGSTRICH; Zeitschrift fuer buendnisgruene Politik. Text in German. 1994. q. EUR 11.90 (effective 2007). adv. **Document type:** *Magazine, Consumer.*
Published by: (Buendnis 90 - Die Gruenen), Kompakt Medienbuero, Hessische Str. 10, Berlin, 10115, Germany. TEL 49-30-28094110, FAX 49-30-28094111, info@kompakt-medien.de. Adv. contact Michael Blum. B&W page EUR 2,975, color page EUR 4,500. Circ: 48,000 (controlled).

320 DEU
▼ **SCHRIFTEN ZUR POLITISCHEN KOMMUNIKATION.** Text in German. 2009. irreg., latest vol.6, 2010. price varies. **Document type:** *Monographic series, Academic/Scholarly.*
Published by: V & R Unipress GmbH (Subsidiary of: Vandenhoeck und Ruprecht), Robert-Bosch-Breite 6, Goettingen, 37079, Germany. TEL 49-551-5084303, FAX 49-551-5084333, info@vr-unipress.de, http://www.v-r.de/en/publisher/unipress.

320 DEU ISSN 1611-1494
SCHRIFTEN ZUR POLITISCHEN THEORIE. Text in German. 2003. irreg., latest vol.9, 2009. price varies. **Document type:** *Monographic series, Academic/Scholarly.*
Published by: Verlag Dr. Kovac, Leverkusenstr 13, Hamburg, 22761, Germany. TEL 49-40-3988800, FAX 49-40-39888055, info@verlagdrkovac.de.

320 DEU
SCHRIFTENREIHE POLITIKWISSENSCHAFT. Text in German. 1997. irreg., latest vol.16, 2009. price varies. **Document type:** *Monographic series, Academic/Scholarly.*
Published by: Verlag Dr. Koester, Rungestr 22-24, Berlin, 10179, Germany. TEL 49-30-76403224, FAX 49-30-76403227, verlag-koester@t-online.de, http://www.verlag-koester.de.

320 AUT ISSN 1814-5582
SCHRIFTENREIHE ZUM OEFFENTLICHEN RECHT UND ZU DEN POLITISCHEN WISSENSCHAFTEN. Text in German. 1976. irreg., latest vol.10, 2009. price varies. **Document type:** *Monographic series, Academic/Scholarly.*
Formerly (until 1998): Oesterreichische Schriftenreihe fuer Rechts- und Politikwissenschaft
Published by: Wilhelm Braumueller Universitaets-Verlagsbuchhandlung GmbH, Servitengasse 5, Vienna, 1090, Austria. TEL 43-1-3191159, FAX 43-1-3102805, office@braumueller.at. Ed. Karl Korinek.

320.5322 USA
THE SCHWARZ REPORT. Text in English. 1960. m. USD 15 (effective 2001). bk.rev. back issues avail. **Document type:** *Newsletter.* **Description:** Speaks out against Communism and the atheism it fosters worldwide.
Formerly (until 1998): Christian Anti-Communism Crusade. Newsletter (0195-9387)
Related titles: Microform ed.: (from PQC); Online - full text ed.
Published by: (Summit Ministries), Imperial Press, 928 Osage Ave, Box 129, Manitou Springs, CO 80829. TEL 719-685-9103, 719-685-9043, FAX 719-685-9330, info@summit.org, cacc@summit.org, http://www.schwarzreport.org. Eds. David A Noebel TEL 719-685-9043, Michael Bauman. Circ: 25,000.

324.2 DEU ISSN 0722-8988
SCHWARZER FADEN; Vierteljahresschrift fuer Lust und Freiheit. Text in German. 1980. q. EUR 16 (effective 2001). adv. bk.rev.; film rev.; play rev.; music rev.; video rev. bibl.; illus. cum.index. back issues avail. **Document type:** *Magazine, Consumer.*
Published by: Trotzdem Verlagsgenossenschaft eG, Postfach 1159, Grafenau, 71117, Germany. TEL 49-7033-44273, FAX 49-7033-45264, trotzdemusf@t-online.de. Ed., Pub. Wolfgang Haug. Adv. contact Dieter Schmidt. Circ: 3,000.

320 GBR ISSN 1424-7755
JA14
➤ **SCHWEIZERISCHE ZEITSCHRIFT FUER POLITIKWISSENSCHAFT/ REVUE SUISSE DE SCIENCE POLITIQUE/SWISS POLITICAL SCIENCE REVIEW.** Text in English, French, German. 1961. q. GBP 212 in United Kingdom to institutions; EUR 249 in Europe to institutions; USD 357 elsewhere to institutions; GBP 234 combined subscription in United Kingdom to institutions (print & online eds.); EUR 273 combined subscription in Europe to institutions (print & online eds.); USD 393 combined subscription elsewhere to institutions (print & online eds.) (effective 2012). reprint service avail. from PSC. **Document type:** *Journal, Academic/Scholarly.*
Former titles (until 1999): Schweizerische Zeitschrift fur Politische Wissenschaft (1420-3529); (until 1995): S V P W Jahrbuch (1420-4177); (until 1986): Annuaire Suisse de Science Politique (0066-3727); (until 1965): Association Suisse de Science Politique. Annuaire (1420-4215)
Related titles: Online - full text ed.: ISSN 1662-6370. GBP 212 in United Kingdom to institutions; EUR 249 in Europe to institutions; USD 357 elsewhere to institutions (effective 2012).
Indexed: ABCPolSci, CA, DIP, EconLit, HistAb, I13, IBR, IBZ, JEL, P42, PAIS, PSA, SCOPUS, SSCI, SociolAb, T02, W07.
—BLDSC (8425.050515), IE, Ingenta. **CCC.**
Published by: (Swiss Political Science Association CHE), John Wiley & Sons Ltd. (Subsidiary of: John Wiley & Sons, Inc.), 9600 Garsington Rd, Oxford, OX4 2DQ, United Kingdom. TEL 44-1865-776868, FAX 44-1865-714591, cs-journals@wiley.com, http://onlinelibrary.wiley.com/.

320.6 GBR ISSN 0302-3427
Q179.9
➤ **SCIENCE AND PUBLIC POLICY.** Abbreviated title: S P P. Text in English. 1967. 10/yr. EUR 589 combined subscription in the European Union to institutions (print & online eds.); USD 662 combined subscription in North America to institutions (print & online eds.); GBP 278, USD 473 combined subscription in developing nations to institutions (print & online eds.); GBP 385 combined subscription elsewhere to institutions (print & online eds.); EUR 60 combined subscription per issue in the European Union to institutions (print & online eds.); USD 68 combined subscription per issue to institutions in developing nations & North America (print & online eds.); GBP 39 combined subscription per issue to institutions in developing nations & elsewhere (print & online eds.) (effective 2011). bk.rev. bibl.; charts; illus.; abstr. index. 76 p./no. 2 cols./p.; back issues avail.; reprints avail. **Document type:** *Journal, Academic/ Scholarly.* **Description:** Explores on how science and technology affect public policy.
Former titles (until 1974): Science Policy (0048-9700); (until 1972): Science Policy News
Related titles: Online - full text ed.: ISSN 1471-5430. EUR 515 in the European Union to institutions; USD 578 in North America to institutions; USD 413, GBP 242 in developing nations to institutions; GBP 336 elsewhere to institutions (effective 2011) (from IngentaConnect).
Indexed: A01, A03, A08, A22, APEL, CA, CLOSS, CMM, CurCont, DIP, E15, EIA, ERA, EnerInd, EnerRev, EnvAb, EnvInd, F&EA, FR, GEOBASE, GeoRef, HECAB, IBR, IBSS, IBZ, P30, P34, P42, PAIS, PSA, R17, RASB, S02, S03, S19, SCOPUS, SOPODA, SSCI, SociolAb, SpeleolAb, T02, V05, W07.
—BLDSC (8134.179000), IE, Infotrieve, Ingenta. **CCC.**
Published by: Beech Tree Publishing, 10 Watford Close, Guildford, Surrey GU1 2EP, United Kingdom. TEL 44-1483-824871, FAX 44-1483-567497, page@scipol.co.uk. Eds. Caroline S Wagner, Nicholas Vonortas, Susana Borras. **Dist. by:** Turpin Distribution Services Ltd., Pegasus Dr, Stratton Business Park, Biggleswade, Bedfordshire SG18 8QB, United Kingdom. TEL 44-1767-604951, FAX 44-1767-601640, custserv@turpin-distribution.com, http://www.turpin-distribution.com/.

320.5322 USA ISSN 0036-8237
H1
➤ **SCIENCE & SOCIETY;** a journal of marxist thought and analysis. Text in English. 1937. q. USD 45 combined subscription domestic to individuals (print & online eds.); USD 70 combined subscription foreign to individuals (print & online eds.); USD 315 combined subscription domestic to institutions (print & online eds.); USD 340 combined subscription foreign to institutions (print & online eds.) (effective 2011). adv. bk.rev. illus. index, cum.index every 25 yrs. 128 p./no.; back issues avail.; reprints avail. **Document type:** *Journal, Academic/Scholarly.* **Description:** Examines new ideas in economic and social thought.
Related titles: Microform ed.: (from MIM, PQC); Online - full text ed.: ISSN 1943-2801.
Indexed: A01, A02, A03, A06, A08, A12, A20, A22, A25, A26, ABCPolSci, ABIn, ABS&EES, ASCA, AcaI, AltPI, AmH&L, B04, B14, BRD, BRI, BrHumI, CA, CBRI, CurCont, DIP, E01, E08, EIA, EconLit, EnerInd, FR, G08, G10, H09, H10, HistAb, I05, I13, IBR, IBSS, IBZ, ILD, IPARL, JEL, LeftInd, M01, M02, MEA&I, MLA-IB, P02, P06, P10, P13, P26, P27, P30, P34, P42, P45, P46, P48, P51, P53, P54, PAA&I, PAIS, PCI, PQC, PRA, PSA, PerIslam, RASB, RI-1, RI-2, S02, S03, S05, S08, S09, S11, SCOPUS, SOPODA, SPPI, SSA, SSAI, SSAb, SSCI, SSI, SociolAb, T02, W01, W02, W03, W07, W09.
—BLDSC (8134.190000), IE, Infotrieve, Ingenta, INIST. **CCC.**
Published by: Guilford Publications, Inc., 72 Spring St, 4th Fl, New York, NY 10012. TEL 800-365-7006, FAX 212-966-6708, info@guilford.com. Ed. David Laibman. R&P Kathy Kuehl. Adv. contact Marian Robinson. Circ: 1,400 (paid).

➤ **SCIENCE AS CULTURE.** *see* SCIENCES: COMPREHENSIVE WORKS

320 ITA ISSN 2039-1749
▼ **SCIENZA E PACE.** Text in Multiple languages. 2010. q.
Published by: Universita degli Studi di Pisa, Centro Interdisciplinare di Scienze per la Pace, Via Gioberti 39, Pisa, 56124, Italy. TEL 39-050-2211200, FAX 39-050-2211206.

320 GBR ISSN 0036-9071
SCOTS INDEPENDENT. Text in English. 1926. w. GBP 24 domestic; GBP 33 foreign (effective 2009). adv. bk.rev.; play rev. stat. back issues avail. **Document type:** *Newspaper, Consumer.*
Related titles: Online - full text ed.
Indexed: RASB.
Published by: Scots Independent (Newspapers) Ltd., 51 Cowane St, Stirling, Scotland FK8 1JW, United Kingdom. Ed. Jim Lynch.

320 GBR ISSN 0966-0356
JN1187
➤ **SCOTTISH AFFAIRS.** Text in English. 1977. q. GBP 27.50 to individuals; GBP 45 to institutions (effective 2009). bk.rev. bibl.; stat. back issues avail. **Document type:** *Journal, Academic/Scholarly.* **Description:** Forum for comment and debate on Scottish politics, society and current affairs.
Formerly (until 1992): Scottish Government Yearbook (0141-0482)
—BLDSC (8205.989600), IE, Ingenta. **CCC.**
Address: Chisholm House, High School Yards, Edinburgh, Scotland EH1 1LZ, United Kingdom. TEL 44-131-6502456, l.adams@ed.ac.uk. Ed. Lindsay Paterson.

320.5 SWE ISSN 1103-4009
SD-KURIREN. Text in Swedish. 1988. q. SEK 150; SEK 40 per issue (effective 2002). **Document type:** *Newsletter, Consumer.*
Formerly (until 1991): Sverige-kurriren (0284-6861); Incorporates (1984-1986): Patrioten (0282-1559)
Published by: (Sverigedemokraterna), SD-Kuriren, PO Box 1194, Lund, 22105, Sweden. TEL 46-046-37 02 84, FAX 46-046-40 07 315. Ed. Richard Jomshof TEL 46-073-62 60 661.

320 GBR ISSN 0262-4591
SEARCHLIGHT (ILFORD). Text in English. 1975. m. GBP 25.50 domestic to individuals; GBP 34 domestic to institutions; GBP 38 in Europe; GBP 45.50 elsewhere; GBP 3 per issue domestic; GBP 3.75 per issue foreign (effective 2009). bk.rev. illus. index. 36 p./no.; back issues avail. **Document type:** *Bulletin.* **Description:** Provides coverage of contemporary fascism and neo-Nazi organizations in Britain, Europe, the U.S. and occasionally elsewhere.
Incorporates (1977-1979): C A R F (0140-735X); Formerly (until 1977): Searchlight on the Struggle Against Racism and Fascism
—CCC.
Published by: Searchlight Magazine Ltd., PO Box 1576, Ilford, IG5 0NG, United Kingdom. TEL 44-20-76818660, FAX 44-20-76818650.

320.96 FRA ISSN 1778-5359
SECRETS D'ETATS. Text in French. 2004. back issues avail. **Document type:** *Monographic series.*
Published by: Editions Duboiris, 67 rue Saint Jacques, Paris, 75005, France. contact@editionsduboiris.com.

P

320.531 AUS ISSN 1449-2822
SEEING RED. Text in English. 2004. q. AUD 90 combined subscription subscription includes Green Left Weekly; free to members (effective 2009). back issues avail. **Document type:** *Magazine, Consumer.* **Description:** Covers social, political and cultural dissent information.
Published by: Socialist Alliance, PO Box A2323, Sydney South, NSW 1235, Australia. TEL 61-2-96902508, FAX 61-2-96901381, national_office@socialist-alliance.org, http://www.socialist-alliance.org.

324.205 LKA ISSN 1391-1015
SEENUWA. Text in Singhalese. 1994. m. LKR 15 (effective 2008). **Document type:** *Newspaper, Consumer.*
Related titles: Online - full text ed.
Published by: Janatha Vimukthi Peramuna/People's Liberation Front, 149-6 Devanam Piyatissa Mawatha, Colombo, 10, Sri Lanka. jvp_sl@usa.net, http://www.geocities.com/jvpsite.

320 JPN ISSN 0919-4851
SEISAKU KAGAKU/POLICY SCIENCE. Text in English. 1993. q. JPY 1,500 newsstand/cover (effective 2005).
—BLDSC (8219.782000).
Published by: Ritsumeikan Daigaku Seisaku Kagakukai/Policy Science Association of Ritsumeikan University, 56-1 Toji-in Kitamachi, Kita-ku, Kyoto, 603-8577, Japan. TEL 81-75-4651111, FAX 81-75-4657853, http://www.ps.ritsumei.ac.jp/assoc/policy_science/.

320 JPN ISSN 0582-4532
AP95.J2
SEKAI/WORLD. Text in Japanese. 1946. m. JPY 9,360 (effective 2005). **Document type:** *Journal, Academic/Scholarly.*
Indexed: RASB.
Published by: Iwanami Shoten, Publishers, 2-5-5 Hitotsubashi, Chiyoda-ku, Tokyo, 101-0003, Japan. TEL 81-3-52104000. Circ: 100,000. **Dist. overseas by:** Japan Publications Trading Co., Ltd., Book Export II Dept, PO Box 5030, Tokyo International, Tokyo 101-3191, Japan. TEL 81-3-32923753, FAX 81-3-32920410, infoserials@jptco.co.jp, http://www.jptco.co.jp.

320 USA ISSN 0745-7170
HF1019
SELF-RELIANT. Text in English. 1982. 10/yr. USD 12.
Formerly (until 1983): Traders' Journal (0744-7558)
Published by: F J L Publishing Co., 817 Stark Circle, Yardley, PA 19067-4313. Ed. Frank Lyons.

320.532 CUB
SEMANARIO INFANTIL PIONERO. Text in Spanish. w. USD 50 in North America; USD 72 in South America; USD 82 in Europe; USD 85 elsewhere. illus.
Published by: (Union de Jovenes Comunistas, Organizacion de Pioneros "Jose Marti"), Ediciones Cubanas, Obispo 527, Havana, Cuba. TEL 32-5556-60. Ed. Pedro Gonzalez. Circ: 210,000.

320 IND ISSN 0971-6742
SEMINAR (NEW DELHI); the monthly symposium. Text in English. 1959. m. INR 400 domestic; INR 1,600 in South Asia; USD 80, GBP 50, EUR 63 elsewhere (effective 2011). **Document type:** *Journal, Academic/Scholarly.* **Description:** Focuses on national and international problems.
Related titles: Online - full text ed.: free (effective 2011).
Indexed: I13.
Published by: Seminar Publications, F-46 Malhotra Bldg, Janpath, New Delhi, 110 001, India. TEL 91-11-23316534, FAX 91-11-23346445. Ed. Tejbir Singh. Pub. Malvika Singh.

SEMINARIA PA'LANTE. *see* LITERARY AND POLITICAL REVIEWS

320.531 LKA
SEN SHAKTHI. Text in Singhalese. m. **Document type:** *Newspaper, Consumer.*
Related titles: Online - full text ed.

Published by: Janatha Vimukthi Peramuna/People's Liberation Front, 149-6 Devanam Piyatissa Mawatha, Colombo, 10, Sri Lanka. jvp_sl@usa.net, http://www.geocities.com/jvpsite.

320.531 FRA ISSN 2106-3567
▼ **SENATEURS SOCIALISTES D'ILLE-ET-VILAINE.** Text in French. 2009. s-a. **Document type:** *Newspaper, Consumer.*
Published by: Edmond Herve, Senateur d'Ille-et-Vilaine, 21, Quai Lamennais, Rennes, 35000, France. TEL 33-2-99782710, FAX 33-2-99351896, eherve-senat@orange.fr, http://senateurs-socialistes35.fr.

321.8 JPN ISSN 1348-8783
SENKYO GAKKAI KIYOU/REVIEW OF ELECTORAL STUDIES. Text in Japanese. 2003. s-a. **Document type:** *Journal, Academic/Scholarly.*
Related titles: Online - full text ed.
Published by: Hokuju Shuppan Nihon Senkyo Gakkai/Japanese Association of Electoral Studies, University of Tokyo, 7-3-1 Hongo, Bunkyo-ku, Tokyo, 113-0033, Japan. yasuno@tamacc.chuo-u.ac.jp.

321.8 JPN ISSN 0912-3512
JQ1692
SENKYO KENKYU/JAPANESE JOURNAL OF ELECTORAL STUDIES. Text in Japanese. 1986. a. price varies. **Document type:** *Journal, Academic/Scholarly.*
Related titles: Online - full text ed.
Published by: Hokuju Shuppan Nihon Senkyo Gakkai/Japanese Association of Electoral Studies, University of Tokyo, 7-3-1 Hongo, Bunkyo-ku, Tokyo, 113-0033, Japan. yasuno@tamacc.chuo-u.ac.jp.

320.51 PER ISSN 2078-8894
SERIE DEMOCRACIA. Text in Spanish. 2001. a. back issues avail. **Document type:** *Monographic series, Academic/Scholarly.*
Published by: Comision Andina de Juristas, Los Sauces, 285, Lima, Peru. TEL 51-1-4407907, FAX 51-1-2027179, myauyo@cajpe.org.pe, http://www.cajpe.org.pe/index.html.

320 FRA ISSN 0586-9889
SERIE VIE LOCALE. Text in French. 1969. irreg. price varies.
—CCC.
Published by: (Institut d'Etudes Politiques de Bordeaux, Centre d'Etude et de Recherche sur la Vie Locale), Editions A. Pedone, 13 rue Soufflot, Paris, 75005, France. TEL 33-1-43540597, FAX 33-1-46340760.

304.8 ITA ISSN 0037-2803
SERVIZIO MIGRANTI. Text in Italian. 1965. bi-m. adv. bk.rev. stat. index. **Document type:** *Bulletin, Consumer.*
Formerly: Ufficio Centrale per l'Emigrazione Italiana, Bollettino
Related titles: ◆ Supplement(s): Migranti-Press. ISSN 0391-5492.
Published by: Fondazione Migrantes, Via Aurelia 468, Rome, RM 00165, Italy. TEL 39-06-66398452, FAX 39-06-66398492, http://www.chiesacattolica.it/cci_new/UfficiCEI/. Circ: 2,700.

328 USA ISSN 1941-1510
JK1083
SETTING COURSE; a congressional management guide. Text in English. 1984. biennial. USD 20 per issue; USD 15 per issue to qualified personnel (effective 2008).
Published by: Congressional Management Foundation, 513 Capitol Court NE, Ste 300, Washington, DC 20002. TEL 202-546-0100, FAX 202-547-0936, http://www.cmfweb.org.

▼ **SETTLER COLONIAL STUDIES.** *see* SOCIOLOGY

320 ROM ISSN 1221-6720
SFERA POLITICII. Text in Romanian. 1992. m. **Document type:** *Journal, Academic/Scholarly.*
Related titles: Online - full text ed.: free (effective 2011).
Published by: Fundatia Societatea Civila redactia@sferapoliticii.ro. Ed. Alexandru Radu.

324.251 JPN
SHAKAI SHIMPO. Text in Japanese. s-w. JPY 800. **Document type:** *Newspaper.*
Published by: Social Democratic of Japan/Nihon Shakaito, 1-8-1 Nagata-cho, Chiyoda-ku, Tokyo, 1000014, Japan. TEL 81-3-3580-1171, FAX 81-3-3580-0691.

320.532 951 CHN ISSN 1009-928X
SHANGHAI DANGSHI YU DANGJIAN/SHANGHAI STUDIES ON C C P HISTORY AND CONSTRUCTION. Text in Chinese. 1982. m. USD 36 (effective 2009). **Document type:** *Journal, Academic/Scholarly.*
Formerly (until 2000): Shanghai Dangshi Yanjiu
Related titles: Online - full text ed.
—East View.
Published by: Zhong-Gong Shanghai Shi- Wei-Dangshi Yanjiushi, 141, Kangping Lu, Shanghai, 200030, China. **Dist. by:** China International Book Trading Corp, 35 Chegongzhuang Xilu, Haidian District, PO Box 399, Beijing 100044, China. TEL 86-10-68412045, FAX 86-10-68412023, cibtc@mail.cibtc.com.cn, http://www.cibtc.com.cn.

SHANGHAI XINGZHENG XUEYUAN XUEBAO/SHANGHAI ADMINISTRATION INSTITUTE. JOURNAL. *see* SOCIAL SCIENCES: COMPREHENSIVE WORKS

320 340 CHN ISSN 1674-9502
SHANGHAI ZHENG-FA XUEYUAN XUEBAO. FAZHI LUNCONG/ SHANGHAI UNIVERSITY OF POLITICAL SCIENCE & LAW. JOURNAL. THE RULE OF LAW FORUM. Text in Chinese. 1987 (Internal publication until 1989). bi-m. **Document type:** *Journal, Academic/Scholarly.*
Former titles (until 2002): Shanghai Shi Zheng-Fa Guanli Ganbu Xueyuan Xuebao/Law Journal of Shanghai Administrative Cadre Institute of Politics & Law (1008-4525); (until 1998): Fazhi Luncong/ Law Forum
Published by: Shanghai Zheng-Fa Xueyuan/Shanghai University of Political Science & Law, 7989, Waiqingsong Lu, Shanghai, 201701, China. TEL 86-21-39225058, FAX 86-21-39225268, http://www.shupl.edu.cn.

SHEHUI ZHUYI JINGJI LILUN YU SHIJIAN/SOCIALIST ECONOMIC THEORY AND PRACTICE. *see* BUSINESS AND ECONOMICS

320.531 CHN ISSN 1009-7554
SHEHUI ZHUYI LUNCONG/COLLECTED ESSAYS ON SOCIALISM. Text in Chinese. m. USD 79 (effective 2009). 144 p./no.; **Description:** Contains articles and researches on the formation, development, history and present situation of socialist system.
Formerly (until 2000): Shehuizhuyi Yanjiu (Beijing) (1005-4227)
Published by: Zhongguo Renmin Daxue Shubao Ziliao Zhongxin/Renmin University of China, Information Center for Social Sciences, Dongcheng-qu, 3, Zhangzizhong Lu, Beijing, 100007, China. TEL 86-10-64039458, FAX 86-10-64015080, center@zlzx.org, http://www.zlzx.org/. **Dist. in US by:** China Publications Service, PO Box 49614, Chicago, IL 60649. TEL 312-288-3291, FAX 312-288-8570.

320.531 CHN ISSN 1001-4527
HX9.C5
SHEHUIZHUYI YANJIU (WUHAN)/STUDIES ON SOCIALISM. Text in Chinese. 1978. bi-m. USD 37.20 (effective 2009). adv. abstr.; bibl. 96 p./no.; reprints avail. **Document type:** *Journal, Academic/Scholarly.* **Description:** Contains academic research on Chinese and world socialism development.
Formerly (until 1985): Kexueshehuizhuyi Yanjiu
Related titles: Online - full text ed.
Indexed: RASB.
—East View.
Published by: Kexue Shehuizhuyi Yanjiusuo, Wuhan, Hubei 430070, China. TEL 86-27-87673305, FAX 86-27-87673306. Ed. Sinian Yu. Adv. contact Lingling Hu TEL 86-27-87675612. page USD 500; 210 x 295. Circ: 5,000 (paid); 200 (controlled).

SHIMANE LAW REVIEW. *see* LAW

320.532 JPN ISSN 1344-7904
HX9.J3
➤ **SHINSEIKI/COMMUNIST.** Variant title: Japan Revolutionary Communist League. Journal. New Century. Text in English, Japanese. 1959. bi-m. JPY 9,060 domestic; JPY 8,640 foreign; JPY 1,260 newsstand/cover foreign (effective 2003). adv. bk.rev. 200 p./no.; back issues avail. **Document type:** *Journal, Academic/Scholarly.* **Description:** Analyzes world situations, including crises of global warfare, financial turbulence, and environmental devastation. Contains views on bourgeois ideologies, bankrupt Stalinism and social democracy. Presents a guide for the new century from revolutionary Marxism, including theoretical works in economics, philosophy, theory of state, and revolution.
Formerly (until 1999): Kyosanshugisha (1342-9868)
Published by: (Nihon Kakumeiteki Kyosan Shugisha Domei - Kakumeiteki Marukusu Shugiha/Japan Revolutionary Communist League - Revolutionary Marxist Faction), Kaihohsha, 525-3 Waseda-Tsurumaki-cho, Shinjuku-ku, Tokyo, 162-0041, Japan. TEL 81-3-3207-1261, FAX 81-3-5273-2351, info@jrcl.org, http://www.jrcl.org. Ed., Pub., R&P, Adv. contact Yoshida Masao. Circ: 7,000 (paid). **Dist. by:** Akane Books, 525 Waseda-Tsurumaki-cho, Tokyo 162-0041, Japan. TEL 81-3-5292-1210, FAX 81-3-5292-1218, info@akanebooks.com, http://www.akanebooks.com.

320 CHN ISSN 1003-4641
SHISHI QIUSHI/SEEK TRUTH FROM FACTS. Text in Chinese. 1978. bi-m. USD 18 (effective 2009). **Document type:** *Journal, Academic/ Scholarly.*
Related titles: Online - full text ed.
—East View.
Published by: Shishi Qiushi Zazhishe, 65, Jianguo Lu, Urumqi, Xinjiang 830002, China. TEL 86-991-2658224, FAX 86-991-2658465. **Dist. by:** China International Book Trading Corp, 35 Chegongzhuang Xilu, Haidian District, PO Box 399, Beijing 100044, China. TEL 86-10-68412045, FAX 86-10-68412023, cibtc@mail.cibtc.com.cn, http://www.cibtc.com.cn.

320 CHN
SHISHI ZILIAO SHOUCE. Text in Chinese. 19??. bi-m. CNY 30; CNY 5.50 newsstand/cover (effective 2010). **Document type:** *Magazine, Consumer.* **Description:** Covers current events in China and the region.
Published by: Banyuetan Zazhishe, Shijingshan-qu, 8, Jingyuan Lu, Beijing, 100043, China. TEL 86-10-63074102.

SHVUT; studies in Russian and East European Jewish history and culture. *see* ETHNIC INTERESTS

SI XING YUEKAN. *see* SOCIAL SCIENCES: COMPREHENSIVE WORKS

320.9 PAK
SIND JOURNAL OF POLITICAL SCIENCE AND MODERN HISTORY; an international publication. Text in English. 1975. s-a. PKR 25, USD 10. adv.
Published by: University of Sind, Department of Political Science & Modern History, Jamshoro, Sind, Pakistan. **Subscr. in U.S., Canada, and other Western countries to:** Edinboro State College, Office of International Education, Box 318, Edinboro, PA 16412. **Co-sponsor:** Edinboro State College, Department of History.

SINGAPORE PERSPECTIVES. *see* SOCIAL SCIENCES: COMPREHENSIVE WORKS

SINTESE. *see* PHILOSOPHY

320 ITA ISSN 1828-5155
SINTESI (MILAN); quaderni del dottorato di storia dell'industria dell'Universita di Salerno. Text in Italian. 1997. s-a. **Document type:** *Monographic series, Academic/Scholarly.*
Published by: (Universita degli Studi di Salerno, Dipartimento di Scienze Storiche e Sociali), Franco Angeli Edizioni, Viale Monza 106, Milan, 20127, Italy. TEL 39-02-2837141, FAX 39-02-26144793, redazioni@francoangeli.it, http://www.francoangeli.it.

320.532 CHN ISSN 1002-9907
JQ1519.A5
SIXIANG ZHENGZHI GONGZUO YANJIU/STUDY IN IDEOLOGY AND POLITICS. Text in Chinese. m. USD 49.20 (effective 2009). **Document type:** *Academic/Scholarly.*
Related titles: Online - full text ed.
—East View.
Published by: Zhongguo Zhigong Sixiang Zhengzhi Gongzuo Yanjiuhui, c/o Dong Yuan, 9 Xihuangchenggen Nanjie, Dongcheng-qu, Beijing, 100032, China. TEL 66-6982. Ed. Yang Wenshang.

320.5 LBN
SIYASSA WA-STRATEGIA/POLITICS AND STRATEGY/POLITIQUE ET STRATEGIE. Text in Arabic. 1981. 3/m. USD 1,500 (effective 2001). index. **Document type:** *Consumer.* **Description:** Covers regional political, economic, and strategic issues affecting the Arab world.
Published by: Dar Naaman lith-Thaqafah, P O Box 567, Jounieh, Lebanon. TEL 961-9-935096, FAX 961-9-935096. Ed. Naji Naaman.

320.5 SWE ISSN 1101-9522
SKAANEKURIREN. Text in Swedish. 1989. q. SEK 50 to members (effective 1990).
Published by: Skaanepartiet, Malmgatan 16, Malmo, 21132, Sweden.

SLOVAK PRESS DIGEST. *see* ETHNIC INTERESTS

SLOVANSKE STUDIE. *see* HISTORY—History Of Europe

320.9 CZE ISSN 0037-6922
SLOVANSKY PREHLED/SLAVIC SURVEY. Text in Czech; Summaries in English, German. 1898. q. CZK 200 (effective 2010). bk.rev. abstr.; illus. index, cum.index. 120 p./no.; **Document type:** *Journal, Academic/Scholarly.* **Description:** Scholarly articles on the history and culture of the central, southeast and east European nations, their mutual relations and their relations to the West.
Indexed: AmH&L, BibLing, CA, HistAb, IBSS, P30, RASB, T02.
Published by: Akademie Ved Ceske Republiky, Historicky Ustav, Prosecka 76, Prague 9, 19000, Czech Republic. mikulec@hiu.cas.cz. Eds. Ladislav Hldaky, Dr. Radomir Vlcek. Circ: 1,750.

SLOVENSKA ARCHIVISTIKA. *see* HISTORY—History Of Europe

324.2 CAN ISSN 0037-6957
SLOVENSKA DRZAVA; for a free Slovenia. Text in Slovenian; Summaries in English, Slovenian. 1949. m. CAD 12. adv. bk.rev.; play rev. bibl.; illus.
Published by: Slovenian National Federation of Canada, 79 Watson Ave, Toronto, ON M6S 4E2, Canada. TEL 416-767-8999. Circ: 3,560.

320 USA ISSN 0194-2735
HT123
THE SMALL CITY AND REGIONAL COMMUNITY. Text in English. 1978. biennial. USD 30 per vol. (effective 2005). **Description:** Conference proceedings.
Published by: University of Wisconsin at Stevens Point, Center for the Small City, Collins Classroom Center, Stevens Point, WI 54481. http://www.uwsp.edu/polisci/smallcity/center.html.

306.2 338.2 NLD ISSN 1571-2249
SOCIAAL - ECONOMISCH BELEID. Text in Dutch. 2002. quadrennial.
Related titles: English ed.: Social and Economic Policy. ISSN 1871-885X.
Published by: Sociaal-Economische Raad, Postbus 90405, The Hague, 2509 LK, Netherlands. TEL 31-70-3499499, FAX 31-70-3832535, ser.info@ser.nl, http://www.ser.nl.

SOCIAL ALTERNATIVES. *see* SOCIOLOGY

THE SOCIAL CONTRACT. *see* SOCIOLOGY

320.9 AUS ISSN 0037-7694
THE SOCIAL CREDITER. Text in English. 1933. bi-m. bk.rev. index 1960-1995. **Document type:** *Bulletin, Academic/Scholarly.* **Description:** Political, economic and social analysis and commentary on global and national issues.
Incorporates (in 1953): The Australian Social Crediter for Political and Economic Realism
Published by: Social Credit School of Studies, Social Credit Secretariat, 209 Palm Lake Resort, Deception Bay, QLD 4508, Australia. TEL 61-7-33859794, FAX 61-7-33859794, socred@ecn.net.au, http://www.ecn.net.au/~socred/. Circ: 800 (paid).

321.8 GBR ISSN 2046-9810
SOCIAL EUROPE JOURNAL. Abbreviated title: S E J. Text in English. 2005. q. free (effective 2011). **Document type:** *Journal, Trade.*
Media: Online - full text.
Published by: Social Europe Ltd.

320.531 USA
➤ **SOCIAL MOVEMENTS, PROTEST, AND CONTENTION SERIES.** Text in English. 1994. irreg., latest vol.35, 2010. price varies. back issues avail. **Document type:** *Monographic series, Academic/ Scholarly.* **Description:** Aims to take an interdisciplinary look at social movements and other protests through the ages and throughout the world.
Published by: University of Minnesota Press, Ste 290, 111 Third Ave S, Minneapolis, MN 55401. TEL 612-627-1970, FAX 612-627-1980, ump@umn.edu. Ed. Bert Klandermans. **Dist. by:** c/o Chicago Distribution Center, 11030 S Langley Ave, Chicago, IL 60628. TEL 800-621-2736; Plymbridge Distributors Ltd, Estover Rd, Plymouth, Devon PL6 7PY, United Kingdom. TEL 44-1752-202-301, FAX 44-1752-202-331.

320.6 360 NZL ISSN 1172-4382
HN930.5
➤ **SOCIAL POLICY JOURNAL OF NEW ZEALAND**; te puna whakaaro. Text in English. 1993. every 3 yrs. free (effective 2008). **Document type:** *Journal, Academic/Scholarly.*
Related titles: Online - full content ed.; Online - full text ed.: ISSN 1177-9837.
Indexed: A01, A02, A03, A08, A11, A26, CA, E08, G06, G07, G08, H05, I05, INZP, P34, P42, PAIS, PSA, S02, S03, S09, SCOPUS, SSA, SSCI, SociolAb, T02, W07.
—BLDSC (8318.132400), IE, Ingenta.
Published by: (Ministry of Social Development), Social Policy Agency, Department of Social Welfare, Private Bag 21, Wellington, New Zealand. TEL 64-4-4710321, FAX 64-4-4724543. Ed. Marlene Levin.

➤ **SOCIAL, POLITICAL & LEGAL PHILOSOPHY.** *see* PHILOSOPHY

➤ **SOCIAL RESEARCH**; an international quarterly of the social sciences. *see* SOCIAL SCIENCES: COMPREHENSIVE WORKS

320.5 GBR ISSN 0885-4300
HX1
SOCIALISM AND DEMOCRACY. Text in English. 1985. 3/yr. GBP 305 combined subscription in United Kingdom to institutions (print & online eds.); EUR 366, USD 460 combined subscription to institutions (print & online eds.) (effective 2012). adv. bk.rev. back issues avail.; reprint service avail. from PSC. **Document type:** *Journal, Academic/ Scholarly.* **Description:** Provides a worlds of scholarship and activism, theory and practice, to examine in depth the core issues and popular movements of our time.
Related titles: Microform ed.: 1985 (from PQC); Online - full text ed.: ISSN 1745-2635. GBP 275 in United Kingdom to institutions; EUR 330, USD 414 to institutions (effective 2012).
Indexed: A01, A02, A03, A08, A22, A25, A26, ABS&EES, APW, AltPI, CA, DIP, E01, E08, G08, HistAb, I02, I05, I13, IBR, IBSS, IBZ, LeftInd, P02, P34, P42, PAIS, PCI, PSA, R02, S02, S03, S08, S09, SCOPUS, SSA, SociolAb, T02.
—IE, Ingenta. **CCC.**

Published by: (The Research Group on Socialism and Democracy USA), Routledge (Subsidiary of: Taylor & Francis Group), 4 Park Sq, Milton Park, Abingdon, Oxon OX14 4RN, United Kingdom. TEL 44-20-70176000, FAX 44-20-70176336, subscriptions@tandf.co.uk, http://www.routledge.com. Adv. contact Linda Hann TEL 44-1344-779945. **Subscr. to:** Taylor & Francis Ltd., Journals Customer Service, Sheepen Pl, Colchester, Essex CO3 3LP, United Kingdom. TEL 44-20-70175544, FAX 44-20-70175198, tf.enquiries@tfinforma.com.

320.51 USA ISSN 1930-3017
HX1
SOCIALISM AND LIBERATION. Text in English. 2004. m. USD 30 (effective 2007). **Document type:** *Magazine, Consumer.*
Published by: Party for Socialism and Liberation, 3181 Mission St. #29, San Francisco, CA 94110. TEL 415-821-6171, sf@socialismandliberation.org, http://www.pslweb.org/site/PageServer.

320 NLD ISSN 0037-8135
HX8
SOCIALISME EN DEMOCRATIE. Cover title: S en D. Text in Dutch. 1916. 10/yr. EUR 77.50 domestic to individuals; EUR 142.50 foreign to individuals; EUR 142.50 domestic to institutions; EUR 149 foreign to institutions; EUR 37.50 to students (effective 2009).
Formerly (until 1939): De Socialistische Gids (2210-5166)
Indexed: PCI, RASB.
—IE, Infotrieve.
Published by: (Wiardi Beckman Stichting), Boom Uitgevers Amsterdam, Prinsengracht 747-751, Amsterdam, 1017 JX, Netherlands. TEL 31-20-6226107, FAX 31-20-6253327, info@uitgeverijboom.nl, http://www.uitgeverijboom.nl. Ed. Mare Faber.

320.531 PRT
SOCIALISMO & POLITICA. Text in Portuguese. 3/yr.
Address: c/o F. Marcelo Curto, Av. da Republica, 36, Lado A 3rd Fl. Esq., Lisbon, 1000, Portugal. Ed. Herdeiros de Jose Trigo de Morais.

320.531 PER ISSN 0252-8827
JL3401
➤ **SOCIALISMO Y PARTICIPACION.** Text in Spanish. 1977. q. USD 65; USD 70 foreign. adv. bk.rev. charts; stat. cum.index: 1977-1979. **Document type:** *Academic/Scholarly.* **Description:** Dedicated to the study and analysis of the economic, social, political and cultural reality of Peru. Also looks at the rest of Latin America and the Third World.
Indexed: CA, IBR, IBZ, P42, PSA, RASB, S02, S03, SCOPUS, SociolAb, T02.
Published by: (Centro de Estudios para el Desarrollo y la Participacion (CEDEP)), Ediciones Socialismo y Participacion, Ave. Jose Faustino Sanchez Carrion 790-798,, Magdalena Del Mar, Lima 17, Peru. TEL 51-1-4602855, FAX 51-1-4616446. Ed., R&P, Adv. contact Hector Bejar Rivera. Circ: 1,500.

320.531 USA ISSN 0884-6154
HX1
SOCIALIST. Text in English. 1972. m. USD 8. adv. bk.rev.; film rev. illus. reprints avail. **Description:** Provides news and editorials of interest to democratic socialists.
Formerly: Socialist Tribune
Indexed: LeftInd.
Published by: Socialist Party, U S A, 339 Lafayette St, Ste 303, New York, NY 10012. socialistparty@sp-usa.org. Ed. Charles Curtiss. Circ: 2,000.

320.531 NLD ISSN 1566-0125
DE SOCIALIST. Text in Dutch. m. (10/yr.). EUR 15 (effective 2011). **Document type:** *Newspaper, Consumer.*
Related titles: Online - full text ed.: ISSN 1874-7922.
Published by: Internationale Socialisten, Postbus 92025, Amsterdam, 1090 AA, Netherlands. info@socialisme.nu.

320.531 USA ISSN 0037-8194
SOCIALIST FORUM. Text in English. 1969. s-a. USD 10; USD 15 foreign (effective 1998). bk.rev. bibl.; illus. **Document type:** *Bulletin.* **Description:** Informs readers of the activities, political direction and strategy and debates of the Democratic Socialists of America.
Related titles: Microform ed.: (from PQC).
Published by: Institute for Democratic Socialism, 180 Varick St, 12th Fl, New York, NY 10014-4606. TEL 212-962-0390. Ed. Michael Lighty. Circ: 1,000.

SOCIALIST HISTORY WORKING PAPERS. *see* HISTORY

SOCIALIST LAWYER. *see* LAW

320.531 LKA
SOCIALIST NATION. Text in English. w. LKR 3.75 per issue. **Description:** Focuses on Trotskyism.
Published by: Lanka Sama Samaja Party, 42 Jayakantha Lane, Colombo, 5, Sri Lanka.

320.531 GBR ISSN 0081-0606
HX15
SOCIALIST REGISTER. Text in English. 1964. a. GBP 50 per vol.; GBP 40 combined subscription per vol. to individuals (print & online eds.); GBP 155 combined subscription per vol. to institutions (print & online eds.) (effective 2010). bk.rev. back issues avail. **Document type:** *Monographic series, Academic/Scholarly.* **Description:** Examines both the concept and the reality of class. Contributions explore work and pay, women and men in the work-force, migrant and city workers, and the new distance working. Includes regional experiences throughout the world.
Related titles: Online - full text ed.: GBP 25 to individuals; GBP 120 to institutions (effective 2010).
Indexed: A22, AltPI, I13, LeftInd, P42, PSA, RASB, SociolAb.
—BLDSC (8318.248500), IE, Ingenta. **CCC.**
Published by: Merlin Press Ltd., 99b Wallis Rd, London, E9 5LN, United Kingdom. info@merlinpress.co.uk, http://www.merlinpress.co.uk. Eds. Greg Albo, Leo Panitch, Vivek Chibber. **Dist. in Europe by:** Central Books.

320.531 GBR
SOCIALIST REVIEW. Text in English. 1978. m. GBP 30 domestic; GBP 39 in Europe; GBP 46 elsewhere; GBP 2.50 per issue in Afghanistan (effective 2010). adv. bk.rev.; film rev.; music rev.; tel.rev.; video rev. 36 p./no.; back issues avail.; reprint service avail. from PSC. **Document type:** *Magazine, Consumer.* **Description:** Contains articles and reviews on socialism.
(until 1984): Socialist Review (0141-2442)
Related titles: Microfilm ed.: (from BHP); Online - full text ed.: free (effective 2010).
Indexed: ASCA, AcaI, DIP, IBR, IBZ, RASB.
—Ingenta.
Published by: Socialist Workers Party (Britain), PO Box 42184, London, SW8 2WD, United Kingdom. TEL 44-20-78191176, letters@socialistreview.org.uk, http://www.swp.org.uk/. Ed. Judith Orr.

320.531 GBR ISSN 0037-8259
HX3
SOCIALIST STANDARD. Text in English. 1904. m. GBP 15 domestic; GBP 20 in Europe; GBP 25 elsewhere; GBP 1.50 newsstand/cover (effective 2009). bk.rev. illus. index. back issues avail. **Document type:** *Bulletin, Trade.* **Description:** Presents the case for a world society based on common ownership and democratic control of productive resources.
Related titles: Microfilm ed.: (from RPI); Online - full text ed.: free (effective 2009).
Indexed: RASB.
—CCC.
Published by: Socialist Party of Great Britain, 52 Clapham High St, London, SW4 7UN, United Kingdom. TEL 44-20-76223811, FAX 44-20-77203665, spgb@worldsocialism.org, http://www.worldsocialism.org/spgb.

320.531 GBR
SOCIALIST STUDIES; analysis of capitalist system from a Marxist viewpoint. Text in English. 1991. 4/yr. GBP 3.70 domestic; GBP 4.90 in Europe; GBP 7 elsewhere (effective 2010). **Document type:** *Journal, Academic/Scholarly.* **Description:** Analyzes the capitalist system and democracy from a Marxist viewpoint.
Indexed: AltPI.
—BLDSC (8318.248975).
Published by: Socialist Studies (Group), PO Box 46338, London, SW17 9US, United Kingdom.

320.531 USA ISSN 1535-5438
SOCIALIST VIEWPOINT; news and analysis for working people. Text in English. 2001. m. USD 24 (effective 2006). **Document type:** *Magazine, Consumer.*
Indexed: AltPI, LeftInd.
Address: 1380 Valencia, San Francisco, CA 94110. http://www.socialistviewpoint.org/index.html.

320.531 GBR ISSN 1475-9705
SOCIALIST WORKER; a revolutionary anti-capitalist paper in Britain. Text in English. 1968. w. GBP 60 domestic; GBP 75 in Europe; GBP 95 elsewhere (effective 2010). back issues avail. **Document type:** *Newspaper, Consumer.* **Description:** Contains the latest news, political demonstrations and analysis.
Related titles: Online - full text ed.: free (effective 2010).
Indexed: LeftInd.
Published by: Socialist Workers Party (Britain), PO Box 42184, London, SW8 2WD, United Kingdom. TEL 44-20-78191180, FAX 44-20-78191179, reports@socialistworker.co.uk, circ@socialistworker.co.uk, http://www.swp.org.uk/.

320.531 USA ISSN 0885-1468
THE SOCIALIST WORKER. Text in English. 1977. m. USD 50 domestic to institutions; USD 40 in Canada & Mexico to institutions (effective 2010). **Document type:** *Newspaper, Consumer.* **Description:** Provides socialist news, analysis and commentary.
Related titles: Online - full text ed.: free (effective 2010).
Published by: International Socialist Organization, PO Box 16085, Chicago, IL 60616. TEL 773-583-5069, FAX 773-583-6144, contact@internationalsocialist.org, http://www.internationalsocialist.org.

320.531 CAN ISSN 0836-7094
SOCIALIST WORKER. Text in English. 1975. 24/yr. CAD 20 domestic to individuals; USD 30 in United States to individuals; USD 40 overseas to individuals; CAD 30 domestic to institutions; USD 40 overseas to institutions; CAD 2 newsstand/cover (effective 2000). adv. bk.rev. **Description:** Marxist analysis of Canadian, American and international social and political issues. Anti-Stalinist and non-dogmatic.
Published by: International Socialist, P O Box 339, Sta E, Toronto, ON M6H 4E3, Canada. TEL 416-972-6391, FAX 416-972-6319, sworker@web.net, http://webhome.idirect.com/~sworker/intro.html. Ed., R&P Paul Kellog. Adv. contact A Bakan. Circ: 2,000.

331 320.531 IRL ISSN 1649-6655
SOCIALIST WORKER. Text in English. 1971. fortn.
Formerly (until 1986): The Worker (1649-6647)
Published by: Socialist Workers Party in Ireland, PO Box 1648, Dublin, 8, Ireland. TEL 353-1-8722682, FAX 353-1-8723838, info@swp.ie.

320.531 NIC
EL SOCIALISTA. Text in Spanish. fortn.
Published by: Partido Revolucionario de los Trabajadores, Apartado SV 68, Managua, Nicaragua. Ed. Bonifacio Miranda Bengoechea.

320.531 NLD ISSN 2211-629X
SOCIALISTISCH ALTERNATIEF. Text in Dutch. 1976. 5/yr. EUR 15 (effective 2011). **Document type:** *Newspaper, Consumer.*
Former titles (until 2010): Offensief (0169-7714); (until 1981): Voorwaarts (Amsterdam) (0166-154X); (until 1977): Inter (0169-5029)
Published by: Comite voor een Arbeiders Internationale, Postbus 11561, Amsterdam, 1001 GN, Netherlands. TEL 31-84-8310656, info@socialisten.net, http://www.socialisten.net. Ed. Ecfje Schrevel.

320.531 SWE ISSN 0346-1491
HX9.S9
SOCIALISTISK DEBATT. Text in Swedish. 1967-1969; resumed 1971. 4/yr. SEK 200; SEK 100 to students (effective 2005). adv. bk.rev. **Document type:** *Magazine, Consumer.* **Description:** Covers many different aspects of political science, history and culture.
Incorporates (1976-1979): Arbete och Kultur (0349-3784)
Indexed: RASB.
Published by: Centrum foer Marxistika Samhaellsstudier, PO Box 126 60, Stockholm, 11293, Sweden. TEL 46-8-6517004, cms@cmsmarx.org, http://www.cmsmarx.org.

320.532 DNK ISSN 0108-1861
SOCIALISTISK INFORMATION. Text in Danish. 1977. q. DKK 200 (effective 2009). bk.rev. illus. back issues avail. **Document type:** *Magazine, Consumer.*
Former titles (until 1982): R S - Information (0108-5980); (until 1979): Internationale Informationer (0106-4274); (1972-1973): Folkets Avis
Related titles: Online - full text ed.
Published by: Socialistisk Arbejderparti/Socialist Workers' Party, Studiestraede 24, 3, Copenhagen K, 1455, Denmark. TEL 45-33-337948, FAX 45-33-330317, sap@sap-fi.dk.

320 330 BRA ISSN 1415-1979
HC186
SOCIEDADE BRASILEIRA DE ECONOMIA POLITICA. REVISTA. Text in Portuguese. 1997. s-a. **Document type:** *Journal, Academic/Scholarly.*
Published by: Sociedade Brasileira de Economia Politica, Av Prof Luciano Gualberto 908, Ed FEA II, Sala 214, Cidade Universitaria, Sao Paulo, 05508-900, Brazil. sep@sep.org.br, http://www.sep.org.br.

320 ITA
SOCIETA E CONFLITTO; rivista semestrale di storia e cultura politica. Text in Italian. 1988. s-a. Supplement avail. **Document type:** *Magazine, Consumer.*
Published by: Associazione Culturale Relazioni, Via G Matteotti, 127, Mercogliano, AV 83013, Italy. TEL 39-825-789242. Ed. Antonello Petrillo.

320 ROM ISSN 1843-1348
SOCIETATE SI POLITICA. Text in Romanian, English. 2007. s-a. **Document type:** *Journal, Academic/Scholarly.*
Related titles: Online - full text ed.: ISSN 2067-7812. free (effective 2011).
Published by: Universitatea de Vest "Vasile Goldis"/"Vasile Goldis" University Press, B dul Revolutiei 94-96, Arad, 310025, Romania. http://uvvg.ro/editura/. Ed. Martian Iovan.

320 CAN ISSN 0832-008X
SOCIETE QUEBECOISE DE SCIENCE POLITIQUE. BULLETIN/ CANADIAN POLITICAL SCIENCE ASSOCIATION. BULLETIN. Cover title: Bulletin S Q S P. Text in French. 1973. irreg. **Document type:** *Bulletin.*
Published by: Societe Quebecoise de Science Politique, Departement de Science Politique, Universite du Quebec a Montreal, C P 8888, Succ Centre ville, Montreal, PQ H3C 3P8, Canada. TEL 514-987-3000 ext 4582, FAX 514-987-4878, sqsp@er.uquam.ca, http://www.unites.uqam.ca/sqsp.

SOCIETE SAINT-JEAN-BAPTISTE DE MONTREAL. INFORMATION NATIONALE. *see* SOCIOLOGY

SOCIETY AND POLITICS IN AFRICA. *see* SOCIOLOGY

SOCIETY FOR HISTORY IN THE FEDERAL GOVERNMENT. OCCASIONAL PAPERS. *see* HISTORY—History Of North And South America

SOCIOLOGIE ET SOCIETES. *see* SOCIOLOGY

320 BGR
SOFIA NEWS; weekly for politics, economics, culture, tourism and sport. Text in English. 1969. w. looseleaf. USD 20. charts; illus.
Related titles: French ed.; Russian ed.; German ed.
Published by: Sofia Press Agency, 29 Slavianska ul, Sofia, 1040, Bulgaria. Circ: 30,000. **Dist. by:** Hemus, 6 Rouski Blvd., Sofia 1000, Bulgaria.

320 BGR ISSN 0861-8526
JA26
SOFIISKI UNIVERSITET SV. KLIMENT OHRIDSKI. FILOSOFSKI FAKULTET. KNIGA POLITICHESKI NAUKI. Text in Bulgarian. 1975. a., latest vol.85, 1994. BGL 2.36 (effective 2001).
Former titles (until 1988): Sofiiskii Universitet Sv. Kliment Ohridski. Filosofski Fakultet. Katedra po Nauchen Komunizm. Godishnik (0204-9619); (until 1979): Sofiiski Universitet. Filosofskii Fakultet. Godishnik (1310-5248)
Published by: (Sofiiski Universitet Sv. Kliment Ohridski, Filosofski Fakultet), Sofiiski Universitet Sv. Kliment Ohridski, Universitetsko Izdatelstvo/Sofia University St. Kliment Ohridski University Press, Akad G Bonchev 6, Sofia, 1113, Bulgaria. TEL 359-2-9792914. Circ: 550.

322 DNK ISSN 1396-6545
SOLIDARITET. Text in Danish. 1996. q. DKK 80 (effective 2010). **Document type:** *Magazine, Consumer.*
Related titles: Online - full text ed.: ISSN 1601-7773.
Published by: Venstresocialisterne, Solidaritetshuset, Griffenfeldsgade 41, Copenhagen N, 2200, Denmark. TEL 45-24-221923, http://www.venstresocialisterne.dk.

322.4 RUS
SOLIDARNOST'. Text in Russian. s-m. USD 165 in United States.
Indexed: RASB.
Address: Protopopovskii per 25, Moscow, 129010, Russian Federation. TEL 7-095-2883700, FAX 7-095-2883700. Ed. A K Isaev. **Dist. by:** East View Information Services, 10601 Wayzata Blvd, Minneapolis, MN 55305. TEL 952-252-1201, 800-477-1005, FAX 952-252-1202, info@eastview.com, http://www.eastview.com.

320 TWN ISSN 1019-8636
JA26
SOOCHOW JOURNAL OF POLITICAL SCIENCE/DONGWU ZHENGZHI XUEBAO. Text in Chinese, English. 1977. s-a. USD 20 per issue. reprints avail. **Document type:** *Journal, Academic/Scholarly.*
Supersedes in part (in 1992): Soochow Journal of Political Science and Sociology (0259-3785); Which was formerly: Soochow Journal of Social and Political Sciences
Indexed: BAS.
Published by: Soochow University, Wai Shuang Hsi, Shih Lin, Taipei, Taiwan. FAX 886-02-8812317.

324.2663 SEN
SOPI ONLINE. Text in French. 1988. w.
Former titles: Sopi (Print); Le Democrat
Media: Online - full text.
Published by: Parti Democratique Senegalais, 5 bd Dial Diop, Dakar, Senegal. Ed. Cheikh Koureyssi Ba.

324.24965 ALB
SOT. Text in Albanian; Summaries in English. 1991. m.?.
Published by: Partia Socialiste e Shqiperise/Socialist Party of Albania, Bulevardi Deshmoret e Kombit, Tirana, Albania. TEL 355-42-27409, FAX 355-42-27417.

P

328.73 USA ISSN 0730-1154
KF165
SOURCE BOOK OF AMERICAN STATE LEGISLATION. Text in English. 1976. irreg. **Description:** Compendium of model state legislation, with analysis in the areas of: tax and fiscal policy, education, health care, energy, environment, labor, housing, welfare, civil justice, criminal justice, substance abuse, agriculture, telecommunications, transportation, and insurance.
Published by: American Legislative Exchange Council, 910 17th St, N W, 5th Fl, Washington, DC 20006. TEL 202-466-3800, FAX 202-466-3801. Ed. Noel Card. Circ: 7,500.

SOURCEMEX. *see* BUSINESS AND ECONOMICS—Economic Situation And Conditions

SOUTH; the business and politics of Atlanta. *see* BUSINESS AND ECONOMICS

SOUTH AFRICA BUSINESS FORECAST REPORT. *see* BUSINESS AND ECONOMICS—Economic Situation And Conditions

SOUTH AFRICA FOUNDATION REVIEW. *see* BUSINESS AND ECONOMICS—Economic Situation And Conditions

320 ZAF ISSN 0038-2515
SOUTH AFRICAN OBSERVER; a journal for realists. Text in English. 1955. m. ZAR 20, USD 18. bk.rev.
Indexed: ASD.
Published by: S.E.D. Brown, Ed. & Pub., Box 2401, Pretoria, South Africa. TEL 012-322-2950, FAX 012-322-0215. Circ: 6,000.

320 GBR ISSN 0268-0661
F1401
SOUTH AMERICA, CENTRAL AMERICA AND THE CARIBBEAN (YEAR). Text in English. 1985. a. USD 760 per issue (effective 2009). bibl.; stat. reprints avail. **Document type:** *Directory, Academic/Scholarly.* **Description:** Contains essays on important aspects of economic and political life in Latin America and a general essay on the Caribbean. Provides up-to-date statistical surveys on each of the major countries and a directory of essential names and addresses.
—CCC.
Published by: (Europa Publications Ltd.), Routledge (Subsidiary of: Taylor & Francis Group), 2 Park Sq, Milton Park, Abingdon, Oxon OX14 4RN, United Kingdom. TEL 44-20-70176000, FAX 44-20-70176699, orders@taylorandfrancis.com. **Dist. by:** Current Pacific Ltd., 7 La Roche Pl, Northcote, PO Box 36-536, Auckland 0627, New Zealand.

SOUTH ASIAN STUDIES. *see* SOCIAL SCIENCES: COMPREHENSIVE WORKS

320 GBR ISSN 0967-828X
DS520
➤ **SOUTH EAST ASIA RESEARCH.** Text in English. 1993. 3/yr. EUR 256 combined subscription in Europe to institutions (print & online eds.); USD 269 combined subscription in United States to institutions (print & online eds.); GBP 174 combined subscription to institutions in the UK & elsewhere (print & online eds.) (effective 2012). bk.rev. abstr. back issues avail.; reprints avail. **Document type:** *Journal, Academic/Scholarly.* **Description:** Contains research papers on Southeast Asia studies, focusing on political, social, cultural, and legal issues.
Related titles: Online - full text ed.: ISSN 2043-6874. 2000 (from IngentaConnect).
Indexed: A01, A03, A08, A20, A22, APEL, ArtHuCI, BAS, CA, CABA, CurCont, F08, F12, GEOBASE, GH, HistAb, I13, IBSS, LT, N02, P42, PSA, PerIslam, R12, RASB, RRTA, S02, S03, SCOPUS, SociolAb, T02, T05, TAR, W07, W11.
—BLDSC (8351.453000), IE, Ingenta. **CCC.**
Published by: (University of London, School of Oriental and African Studies), I P Publishing Ltd., 258 Belsize Rd, London, NW6 4BT, United Kingdom. TEL 44-20-73161870, FAX 44-20-76249994, JEdmondson@ippublishing.com. Ed. Dr. Rachel Harrison. **Dist. by:** Turpin Distribution Services Ltd., Pegasus Dr, Stratton Business Park, Biggleswade, Bedfordshire SG18 8QB, United Kingdom. TEL 44-1767-604957, FAX 44-1767-601640, subscriptions@turpin-distribution.com, http://www.turpin-distribution.com/.

320 SGP ISSN 0377-5437
DS502
SOUTHEAST ASIAN AFFAIRS. Text in English. 1974. a., latest 2003. price varies. reprint service avail. from SCH. **Document type:** *Monographic series, Academic/Scholarly.* **Description:** Reviews major political, economic and social issues of each country in Southeast Asia.
Formerly: Institute of Southeast Asian Studies. Annual Review
Related titles: Online - full text ed.
Indexed: A01, A03, A08, A22, BAS, CA, E01, I02, I13, IBR, IBSS, IBZ, M05, P10, P14, P27, P34, P42, P45, P48, P53, P54, PCI, PQC, PSA, PerIslam, R02, S02, S03, SCOPUS, SociolAb, T02.
—BLDSC (8352.292000), IE, Ingenta.
Published by: Institute of Southeast Asian Studies, 30 Heng Mui Keng Terrace, Pasir Panjang, Singapore, 119614, Singapore. FAX 65-67756259, pubsunit@iseas.edu.sg. Ed. Daljit Singh. R&P Mrs. Triena Ong TEL 65-6870-2449.

320.96 GBR ISSN 0966-8802
DT1001
SOUTHERN AFRICA MONTHLY REGIONAL BULLETIN. Text in English. 1992. m. USD 525 combined subscription print & online eds. (effective 2007). **Document type:** *Newsletter, Trade.* **Description:** Economic and political analysis of southern African countries based on network of local correspondents.
Related titles: Online - full content ed.: USD 425 (effective 2007).
—CCC.
Published by: SouthScan Ltd., PO Box 724, London, N16 5RZ, United Kingdom. southscan@allafrica.com, http://southscan.gn.apc.org/.

320 USA ISSN 0739-3938
SOUTHERN POLITICAL REPORT. Text in English. 1978. fortn. USD 157. back issues avail. **Description:** Focuses on the politics and politicians of the 13 Southern states.
Related titles: E-mail ed.
Address: PO Box 15507, Washington, DC 20003-5507. TEL 202-547-8098, FAX 888-584-9953. Ed., Pub. Hastings Wyman. Circ: 350 (paid).

320.9 GBR ISSN 0952-7524
DT1001
SOUTHSCAN; a bulletin of African affairs. Text in English. 1986. bi-w. USD 300 combined subscription to individuals (print & online eds.); USD 695 combined subscription to institutions (print & online eds.) (effective 2009). bk.rev. **Document type:** *Newsletter.* **Description:** News and analysis of current situation in South Africa and region.
Related titles: Online - full text ed.: ISSN 1741-3281. USD 200 to individuals; USD 595 to institutions (effective 2009).
—CIS.
Published by: SouthScan Ltd., PO Box 724, London, N16 5RZ, United Kingdom. southscan@allafrica.com, http://southscan.gn.apc.org/.

324.2 RUS
SOVETSKAYA PRAVDA. Text in Russian. s-a. USD 95 in United States.
Indexed: RASB.
Address: Ul Planernaya 12, kv 131, Moscow, 123481, Russian Federation. TEL 7-095-1592112, FAX 7-095-2307398. Ed. M V Kholin. **Dist. by:** East View Information Services, 10601 Wayzata Blvd, Minneapolis, MN 55305. TEL 952-252-1201, 800-477-1005, FAX 952-252-1202, info@eastview.com, http://www.eastview.com.

320.531 GBR ISSN 0049-1713
DK274
SOVIET ANALYST; an intelligence commentary. Text in English. 1972. 10/yr. USD 475 (effective 2009). back issues avail. **Document type:** *Newsletter, Trade.* **Description:** Analyzes geopolitical developments relevant to Soviet deception strategy and the world Leninist revolution being prosecuted by Russia in collaboration with China.
Indexed: RASB.
—CCC.
Published by: World Reports Ltd., 108 Horseferry Rd, London, SW1P 2EF, United Kingdom. TEL 44-20-72223836, FAX 44-20-72330185, subs@worldreports.org, http://www.worldreports.org. Ed. Christopher Story.

320.532 947 DEU ISSN 1614-3515
SOVIET AND POST-SOVIET POLITICS AND SOCIETY. Text in English, German, Russian. 2004. irreg., latest vol.100, 2010. price varies. **Document type:** *Monographic series, Academic/Scholarly.*
Published by: Ibidem Verlag, Melchiorstr 15, Stuttgart, 70439, Germany. TEL 49-711-9807954, FAX 49-711-9807952, ibidem@ibidem-verlag.de, http://www.ibidem-verlag.de.

306.2 338.2 NLD ISSN 1871-8841
SOZIAL- UND WIRTSCHAFTSPOLITIK. Cover title: Sozial- und Wirtschaftspolitik. Zusammenfassung. Text in German. 2001. irreg.
Published by: Sociaal-Economische Raad, Postbus 90405, The Hague, 2509 LK, Netherlands. TEL 31-70-3499499, FAX 31-70-3832535, ser.info@ser.nl, http://www.ser.nl.

SOZIALISTISCHE ERZIEHUNG; Zeitschrift fuer Erziehung, Bildung, Kultur. *see* EDUCATION

320.531 AUT ISSN 0038-6162
DER SOZIALISTISCHE KAEMPFER. Text in German. 1949. bi-m. adv. bk.rev. charts; illus. **Document type:** *Magazine, Consumer.*
Published by: Bund Sozialistischer Freiheitskaempfer, Opfer des Faschismus und Aktiver Antifaschisten, Loewelstr 18, Vienna, 1014, Austria. TEL 43-1-53427277, FAX 43-1-53427258, kaempfer@spoe.at. Circ: 5,000.

320.531 DEU ISSN 0932-8750
SOZIALISTISCHE ZEITUNG. Text in German. 1968. fortn. EUR 50 (effective 2006). bk.rev. charts; illus. index. 16 p./no. 5 cols./p.; **Document type:** *Newspaper.*
Formerly (until 1986): Was Tun (0043-0404)
Published by: (Vereinigung fuer Sozialistische Politik), S O Z Verlag, Dasselstr 75-77, Cologne, 50674, Germany. TEL 49-221-9231196, FAX 49-221-9231197.

320.531 DEU ISSN 0341-1117
SOZIALPOLITISCHE INFORMATIONEN. Text in German. 1967. 4/yr. free (effective 2009). stat. 8 p./no. 3 cols./p.; **Document type:** *Newsletter, Trade.*
Published by: Bundesminister fuer Arbeit und Soziales, Wilhelmstr 49, Berlin, 11017, Germany. TEL 49-30-185270, FAX 49-30-185271830, spi@bma.bund.de, http://www.bma.bund.de. Ed. Rolf Fischer. Pub. Susanne Gasde.

320.51 AUT
SOZIALWISSENSCHAFTLICHE SCHRIFTENREIHE. Text in German. 1981-1988; N.S. 2006. irreg., latest vol.33, 2010. price varies. **Document type:** *Monographic series, Academic/Scholarly.*
Formerly (until 1988): Institut fuer Politische Grundlagenforschung. Sozialwissenschaftliche Schriftenreihe
Published by: Internationales Institut fuer Liberale Politik Wien, Custozzagasse 8/2, Vienna, 1030, Austria. FAX 43-1-5120405, office@iilp.at.

320 GBR ISSN 1356-2576
JC319
➤ **SPACE AND POLITY.** Text in English. 1997. 3/yr. GBP 346 combined subscription in United Kingdom to institutions (print & online eds.); EUR 459, USD 574 combined subscription to institutions (print & online eds.) (effective 2012). adv. bk.rev. illus. back issues avail.; reprint service avail. from PSC. **Document type:** *Journal, Academic/Scholarly.* **Description:** Provides a forum aimed particularly at bringing together social scientists currently working in a variety of disciplines, including geography, political science, sociology, economics, anthropology and development studies and who have a common interest in the relationships between space, place and politics in less developed as well as the advanced economies.
Related titles: Online - full text ed.: ISSN 1470-1235. GBP 312 in United Kingdom to institutions; EUR 413, USD 517 to institutions (effective 2012) (from IngentaConnect).
Indexed: A01, A03, A08, A22, B21, CA, DIP, E01, E17, ESPM, GEOBASE, I13, IBR, IBSS, IBZ, P34, P42, P47, PAIS, PQC, PSA, S02, S03, S21, SCOPUS, SociolAb, T02.
—IE, Infotrieve, Ingenta. **CCC.**
Published by: Routledge (Subsidiary of: Taylor & Francis Group), 4 Park Sq, Milton Park, Abingdon, Oxon OX14 4RN, United Kingdom. TEL 44-20-70176000, FAX 44-20-70176336, subscriptions@tandf.co.uk, http://www.routledge.com. Ed. Ronan Paddison TEL 44-141-3304788. Adv. contact Linda Hann TEL 44-1344-779945. **Subscr. to:** Taylor & Francis Ltd., Journals Customer Service, Sheepen Pl, Colchester, Essex CO3 3LP, United Kingdom. TEL 44-20-70175544, FAX 44-20-70175198.

320.531 NLD ISSN 1574-986X
SPANNING. Text in Dutch. 1999. m. EUR 25 to non-members; EUR 12 to members (effective 2010).
Published by: (Socialistische Partij Rotterdam), Socialistische Partij, Wetenschappelijk Bureau, Vijverhofstr 65, Rotterdam, 3032 SC, Netherlands. TEL 31-10-2435559, FAX 31-10-2435566, onderzoek@sp.nl, http://www.sp.nl/onderzoek. Eds. Diederik Olders, Sjaak van der Velden.

320 NZL ISSN 1177-0724
THE SPARK. Text in English. 1991. m. free to members. **Document type:** *Magazine, Trade.*
Related titles: Online - full text ed.
Published by: Revolutionary Workers League, Dominion Rd, PO Box 10 282, Auckland, New Zealand. wpnz@clear.net.nz, http://www.workersparty.org.nz.

320.531 USA ISSN 0038-6596
HX1
SPARTACIST. Text in English. 1964. irreg. USD 1.50 per issue. charts; illus.; maps. back issues avail. **Document type:** *Magazine, Consumer.*
Related titles: ◆ Spanish ed.: Espartaco; ◆ Supplement to: Workers Vanguard. ISSN 0276-0746.
Indexed: LeftInd.
Published by: (Spartacist League), Spartacist Publishing Co., PO Box 1377, New York, NY 10116. TEL 212-732-7861, vanguard@tirc.net, http://www.icl-fi.org.

320.531 JPN
SPARTACIST (JAPANESE EDITION). Text in Japanese. JPY 500 for 2 yrs. domestic; JPY 1,000 for 2 yrs. foreign (effective 2003). **Document type:** *Newspaper, Consumer.* **Description:** Publication of the Spartacist Group Japan.
Published by: Spartacist Group Japan, Akabane Yubinkyoku, Kita-ku, PO Box 49, Tokyo, 115, Japan.

320.5322 CAN ISSN 0229-5415
SPARTACIST CANADA. Text in English. 1975. q. CAD 3 (effective 2003). back issues avail. **Document type:** *Newspaper, Consumer.* **Description:** English language newspaper of the Trotskyist League/Ligue trotskyste.
Published by: (Trotskyist League of Canada), Spartacist Canada Publishing Association, P O Box 6867, Sta A, Toronto, ON M5W 1X6, Canada. TEL 416-593-4138, FAX 416-593-1529. Ed. Peter Stegner.

320.5322 IRL
SPARTACIST IRELAND. Text in English. q. EUR 4 domestic; EUR 7 in Europe; EUR 10 elsewhere (effective 2003). **Document type:** *Newspaper, Consumer.* **Description:** Marxist publication of the Spartacist Group Ireland.
Published by: Spartacist Group Ireland, Dublin Spartacist Group, PO Box 2944, Dublin, 1, Ireland.

320.5322 ZAF
SPARTACIST SOUTH AFRICA. Text in English. q. ZAR 10 domestic; USD 4 foreign (effective 2003). **Document type:** *Newspaper, Consumer.* **Description:** Marxist publication of Spartacist South Africa.
Address: PostNet Suite 248, Private Bag X2226, Johannesburg, 2000, South Africa.

320 ITA
SPARTACO. Text in Italian. 1980. q. EUR 6 in Europe; EUR 8 elsewhere (effective 2009). **Document type:** *Newspaper, Consumer.* **Description:** Publication of the Lega trotskista d'Italia.
Published by: Lega Trotskysta d'Italia, c/o Walter Fidacaro, CP 1591, Milan, 20101, Italy.

320.531 DEU ISSN 0173-7430
SPARTAKIST. Text in German. 1974. q. EUR 4 (effective 2003). **Document type:** *Newspaper, Consumer.* **Description:** Newspaper of the Spartakist-Arbeiterpartei Deutschlands.
Formerly (until 1980): Kommunistische Korrespondenz (0173-5748)
Published by: Spartak-Arbeiterpartei Deutschlands, SpAD c/o Verlag Avantgarde, Postfach 52355, Berlin, 10127, Germany.

320 CAN ISSN 0383-9370
SPEAK UP!. Text in English. 1973. q. bk.rev. illus. back issues avail. **Document type:** *Newsletter.* **Description:** Activist view against racist conditions, racial segregation, discrimination and against all forms of slavery, peonage, prostitution and child labour. All current information on CCRE.
Published by: (Christians Concerned for Racial Equality), Bible Holiness Movement, P O Box 223, Sta A, Vancouver, BC V6C 2M3, Canada. TEL 250-492-3376. Ed. Wesley H Wakefield. Circ: 1,500 (controlled).

320.5 DEU ISSN 1436-8099
SPEKTRUM POLITIKWISSENSCHAFT. Text in German. 1997. irreg., latest vol.40, 2009. price varies. **Document type:** *Monographic series, Academic/Scholarly.*
Published by: Ergon Verlag, Keesburgstr 11, Wuerzburg, 97074, Germany. TEL 49-931-280084, FAX 49-931-282872, service@ergon-verlag.de, http://www.ergon-verlag.de.

SPIKE. *see* LITERARY AND POLITICAL REVIEWS

320 GRC
SPOTLIGHT. Text in Greek. m.
Published by: (Institute of Political Studies), George Nicolopoulos Ed. & Pub., 13 Kerkyras St, Athens, 163 42, Greece.

320 USA ISSN 0584-9365
DT1
SPOTLIGHT ON AFRICA. Text in English. 1966. bi-m. USD 10. bk.rev. **Document type:** *Newsletter.*
Published by: American-African Affairs Association, 10315 Georgetown Pike., # RB, Great Falls, VA 22066-2415. TEL 202-223-5110. Ed. J A Parker. Circ: 1,500.

320 DEU
SPRETI-STUDIEN. Text in German. 2008. irreg. price varies. **Document type:** *Monographic series, Academic/Scholarly.*
Published by: Herbert Utz Verlag GmbH, Adalbertstr 57, Munich, 80799, Germany. TEL 49-89-27779100, FAX 49-89-27779101, utz@utzverlag.com. Ed. Hans-Michael Koerner.

320 DEU ISSN 0038-884X
K23
DER STAAT; Zeitschrift fuer Staatslehre und Verfassungsgeschichte. Text in German. 1962. q. EUR 108 combined subscription to individuals (print & online eds.); EUR 176 combined subscription to institutions (print & online eds.); EUR 36 newsstand/cover (effective 2012). adv. bk.rev. index. **Document type:** *Journal, Academic/Scholarly.*
Related titles: Online - full text ed.: ISSN 1865-5203. 2008; ◆ Supplement(s): Der Staat. Beiheft. ISSN 0720-6828.
Indexed: A22, CA, CERDIC, DIP, FLP, HistAb, I13, IBR, IBSS, IBZ, P42, PAIS, PCI, PSA, RASB, SCOPUS, T02.
—BLDSC (8425.530000), IE, Infotrieve, Ingenta. **CCC.**
Published by: Duncker und Humblot GmbH, Carl-Heinrich-Becker-Weg 9, Berlin, 12165, Germany. TEL 49-30-7900060, FAX 49-30-79000631, info@duncker-humblot.de. Ed. Christoph Moellers. Circ: 780 (paid and controlled).

320 DEU ISSN 0720-6828
DER STAAT. BEIHEFT. Text in German. 1975. irreg., latest vol.17, 2006. price varies. **Document type:** *Monographic series, Academic/Scholarly.*
Related titles: ◆ Supplement to: Der Staat. ISSN 0038-884X.
Published by: Duncker und Humblot GmbH, Carl-Heinrich-Becker-Weg 9, Berlin, 12165, Germany. TEL 49-30-7900060, FAX 49-30-79000631, info@duncker-humblot.de.

320.6 NLD ISSN 1872-0021
STAAT VAN DE BELEIDSINFORMATIE. Text in Dutch. 2004. a.
Published by: (Algemene Rekenkamer, Tweede Kamer de Staten-Generaal), Sdu Uitgevers bv, Postbus 20025, The Hague, 2500 EA, Netherlands. TEL 31-70-3789911, FAX 31-70-3854321, sdu@sdu.nl, http://www.sdu.nl/.

320 DEU ISSN 1439-1082
STAATLICHKEIT IM WANDEL. Text in German. 1999. irreg., latest vol.7, 2008. price varies. **Document type:** *Monographic series, Academic/Scholarly.*
Published by: Galda und Leuchter GmbH, Franz-Schubert-Str 61, Glienicke, 16548, Germany. TEL 49-33056-88090, FAX 49-33056-80157, contact@galda.com, http://www.galda.com.

324.2 DEU
STACHLIGE ARGUMENTE. Text in German. 1985. 10/yr. EUR 20 (effective 2009). adv. bk.rev. back issues avail. **Document type:** *Magazine, Consumer.* **Description:** Presents discussion of topics concerning the issues and politics of the Green Party in Berlin.
Published by: Buendnis 90 - Die Gruenen Berlin, Kommandantenstr 80, Berlin, 10117, Germany. TEL 49-30-6150050, info@gruene-berlin.de, http://www.gruene-berlin.de. Circ: 4,000 (controlled).

320.531 DEU
STAFFEL AKTUELL; Buergerinformation der SPD. Text in German. 1984. q. **Document type:** *Newspaper.*
Published by: Sozialdemokratische Partei Deutschlands (SPD), Ortsbezirk Staffel, c/o Frank Schmidt, Ed, Koblenzer Str 23A, Limburg, 65556, Germany. TEL 06431-26545.

320 GBR ISSN 1367-9759
THE STAKEHOLDER; public values in public service. Text in English. 1997. bi-m. GBP 39; GBP 45 foreign. adv. bk.rev. charts. back issues avail. **Description:** Contains advice on standards and values in public life for governors, managers, academics and others in public service.
Published by: Stakeholder Consultancy Ltd., 9 Pickwick Rd, London, SE21 7JN, United Kingdom. TEL 44-171-738-7565, FAX 44-171-274-8794. Ed., R&P, Adv. contact Christopher Price. B&W page GBP 300, color page GBP 750; trim 210 x 210. Circ: 1,200.

STANFORD LAWYER. *see* LAW

320.5322 LKA
STATE; a Marxist quarterly. Text in English. 1975. q.
Published by: Lanka Sama Samaja Party, 42 Jayakantha Lane, Colombo, 5, Sri Lanka.

STATE & LOCAL GOVERNMENT (WASHINGTON); guide to current issues and activities. *see* PUBLIC ADMINISTRATION

STATE CAPITOLS REPORT; the weekly briefing on news from the 50 states. *see* PUBLIC ADMINISTRATION

STATE HOUSE WATCH. *see* PUBLIC ADMINISTRATION

320.1 344.03 GBR ISSN 1354-5957
➤ **STATE, LAW AND SOCIETY.** Text in English. 1994. irreg., latest 1994. price varies. **Document type:** *Monographic series, Academic/Scholarly.* **Description:** Concerned with recent comparative work in the field of legal and political history, but it also makes available in translation some of the classics of this tradition.
Published by: Berg Publishers (Subsidiary of: Oxford International Publishers Ltd.), 1st Fl Angel Ct, 81 St Clements St, Oxford, Berks OX4 1AW, United Kingdom. TEL 44-1865-245104, FAX 44-1865-791165, enquiry@bergpublishers.com. Ed. Andrew Altman.

328 USA ISSN 0735-8733
KF85
STATE LEGISLATIVE REPORT (DENVER). Text in English. 1980. irreg., latest no.1. price varies. **Document type:** *Report, Trade.* **Description:** Reports on issues of current interest to state legislatures in the areas of natural resources and the environment, legislative management, health, education and fiscal issues.
Indexed: EnvAb.
—**CCC.**
Published by: National Conference of State Legislatures, 7700 E First Pl, Denver, CO 80230. TEL 303-364-7700, FAX 303-364-7800, ncslnet-admin@ncsl.org, http://www.ncsl.org/.

STATE LEGISLATIVE SOURCEBOOK; a resource guide to legislative information in the fifty states. *see* PUBLIC ADMINISTRATION

328 USA ISSN 0147-6041
JK2403
STATE LEGISLATURES. Text in English. 1975. m. (10/yr.). USD 49 domestic; USD 55 in Canada (effective 2009). adv. charts; illus. index. 45 p./no. 3 cols./p.; reprints avail. **Document type:** *Magazine, Trade.* **Description:** Presents articles on state tax reform, education, child welfare, criminal justice, health care and other public policy issues.
Related titles: Online - full text ed.
Indexed: A01, A02, A03, A08, A22, A25, A26, Acal, CA, E03, E07, E08, EMBASE, ERI, ExcerpMed, G06, G07, G08, I05, I07, M02, M06, MASUSE, MEDLINE, P02, P04, P10, P13, P30, P34, P42, P45, P48, P53, P54, PAIS, PQC, S08, S09, S11, S23, SCOPUS, SPAA, T02.
—CIS. **CCC.**
Published by: National Conference of State Legislatures, 7700 E First Pl, Denver, CO 80230. TEL 303-364-7700, FAX 303-364-7800, http://www.ncsl.org/. Ed. Edward Smith. Circ: 18,200.

320.6 USA ISSN 1946-4185
STATE OF THE FUTURE. Text in English. 1997. a. USD 49.95 combined subscription per issue (print & CD-ROM eds.) (effective 2010). back issues avail. **Document type:** *Report, Trade.*
Related titles: CD-ROM ed.
Published by: The Millennium Project, 4421 Garrison St, NW, Washington, DC 20016. TEL 202-686-5179, FAX 202-686-5179, millennium-project@igc.org.

320 USA ISSN 1532-4400
➤ **STATE POLITICS & POLICY QUARTERLY.** Abbreviated title: S P P Q. Text in English. 2000. q. USD 270, GBP 156 to institutions; USD 270, GBP 159 combined subscription to institutions (print & online eds.) (effective 2011). adv. abstr. 128 p./no.; back issues avail.; reprint service avail. from PSC. **Document type:** *Journal, Academic/Scholarly.* **Description:** Features studies that develop general hypothesis using the methodological advantage of the states.
Related titles: Online - full text ed.: ISSN 1946-1607. USD 243, GBP 143 to institutions (effective 2011).
Indexed: A01, A03, A08, AmH&L, CA, CurCont, I02, IBSS, P02, P10, P13, P34, P42, P45, P48, P53, P54, PAIS, PQC, PSA, R02, S02, S03, S11, SCOPUS, SPAA, SSCI, SociolAb, T02, W07.
—BLDSC (8438.274000), IE, Ingenta. **CCC.**
Published by: (University of Illinois At Springfield, Legislative Studies Center), Sage Publications, Inc., 2455 Teller Rd, Thousand Oaks, CA 91320. TEL 800-818-7243, FAX 805-499-0871, 800-583-2665, info@sagepub.com, http://www.sagepub.com. Ed. Thomas Carsey.

320 USA
STATELINE MIDWEST. Text in English. 1981. m. USD 60; free to qualified personnel (effective 2009). back issues avail. **Document type:** *Newsletter, Trade.* **Description:** Provides in-depth articles covering issues of importance to Midwestern lawmakers.
Formerly (until 1999): Midwesterner
Published by: Council of State Governments, 701 E 22nd St, Ste 110, Lombard, IL 60148. TEL 630-925-1922, FAX 630-925-1930, csgm@csg.org, http://www.csg.org/.

324.971 CAN ISSN 0227-9207
JL439.A15
STATEMENT OF VOTES - GENERAL ELECTION AND BY-ELECTION. Text in English. irreg.
Published by: (British Columbia Chief Electoral Officer), Queen's Printer for British Columbia, PO BOX 9452 STN PROV GOVT, Victoria, BC V8W9V7, Canada.

320 USA
STATES NEWS SERVICE. Text in English. irreg. **Document type:** *Newspaper, Consumer.*
Media: Online - full content.
Address: 1331 Pennsylvania Ave, NW, Ste 232, Washington, DC 20004. TEL 202-628-3100. Ed. Leland Schwartz.

320 NGA
STATESMAN. Text in English. 1973. a. NGN 1, USD 3.40. adv. bk.rev. bibl. **Document type:** *Journal, Academic/Scholarly.*
Published by: Political Science Student Association, University of Ibadan, Department of Political Science, Ibadan, Oyo, Nigeria. Circ: 500.

320.6 NLD ISSN 1877-3036
▼ **STATISTICS NETHERLANDS. CENTRE FOR POLICY RELATED STATISTICS. PAPERS.** Text in English. 2009. irreg. free (effective 2011). **Document type:** *Monographic series, Trade.*
Media: Online - full text.
Published by: (Centraal Bureau voor de Statistiek, Centrum voor Beleidsstatistiek), Centraal Bureau voor de Statistiek, Henri Faasdreef 312, The Hague, 2492 JP, Netherlands. TEL 31-70-3373800, FAX 31-70-3375994, infoserv@cbs.nl.

320 ITA ISSN 0392-9701
HF19
STATO E MERCATO. Text in Italian. 1981. 3/yr. EUR 100 combined subscription domestic to institutions (print & online eds.); EUR 147.50 combined subscription foreign to institutions (print & online eds.) (effective 2009). index. back issues avail. **Document type:** *Journal, Academic/Scholarly.*
Related titles: Online - full text ed.
Indexed: A22, CA, I13, IBR, IBZ, P42, PAIS, PSA, S02, S03, SociolAb, T02.
—BLDSC (8457.800000), IE, Infotrieve.
Published by: Societa Editrice Il Mulino, Strada Maggiore 37, Bologna, 40125, Italy. TEL 39-051-256011, FAX 39-051-256034, riviste@mulino.it. Ed. Lorenzo Bordogna. Circ: 1,500.

320 SWE ISSN 0039-0747
H8
➤ **STATSVETENSKAPLIG TIDSKRIFT**; ny foeljd. Text mainly in Swedish, Danish, Norwegian; Text occasionally in English; Abstracts in English. 1897. q. SEK 360; SEK 95 per issue (effective 2007). adv. bk.rev. charts. cum index: 1944-1977, 1978-1997. back issues avail. **Document type:** *Magazine, Academic/Scholarly.*
Formerly (until 1964): Statsvetenskaplig Tidskrift foer Politik, Statistik, Ekonomi
Indexed: ABCPolSci, CA, DIP, HistAb, I13, IBR, IBSS, IBZ, P42, PCI, PSA, RASB, SCOPUS, SociolAb, T02.
Published by: Fahlbeckska Stiftelsen, PO Box 52, Lund, 22100, Sweden. TEL 46-46-2221071, FAX 46-46-2224006. Eds. Bengt Lundell, Mats Sjoelin. Adv. contact Bengt Lundell.

320 SWE ISSN 0346-7538
➤ **STATSVETENSKAPLIGA FOERENINGEN I UPPSALA. SKRIFTER/ UPPSALA POLITICAL SCIENCE ASSOCIATION. PUBLICATIONS.** Text in Multiple languages. 1933. irreg. price varies. back issues avail. **Document type:** *Monographic series, Academic/Scholarly.*
Related titles: ◆ Series of: Acta Universitatis Upsaliensis. ISSN 0346-5462.
—BLDSC (7107.861000).
Published by: Statsvetenskapliga Foereningen i Uppsala/Uppsala Political Science Association, Statsvetenskapliga Institutionen, PO Box 514, Uppsala, 75420, Sweden. asa.viksten@statsvet.uu.se. Ed. Leif Lewin TEL 46-18-4713412. **Dist. by:** Indiana University, Humanities Press; Almqvist & Wiksell International; Uppsala Universitet, Universitetsbiblioteket, Box 510, Uppsala 75120, Sweden.

320 AUT
STEIRISCHE NACHRICHTEN; freiheitliche Zeitung fuer die Steiermark. Text in German. 1962. m. looseleaf. software rev. bibl.; tr.lit. back issues avail. **Document type:** *Newsletter, Consumer.*
Related titles: Diskette ed.
Published by: Freiheitliche Partei Landesgruppe Steiermark, Griesplatz 10-2, Graz, St 8020, Austria. TEL 43-316-70720, FAX 43-316-7072219, lgst@fpoe-stmk.at, http://www.fpoe-stmk.at. Ed. Hubert Feichter.

320 SWE ISSN 0346-6620
➤ **STOCKHOLM STUDIES IN POLITICS.** Text in Swedish, English; Summaries in English. 1971. irreg., latest vol.107, 2004. price varies. **Document type:** *Monographic series, Academic/Scholarly.* **Description:** Doctoral dissertations in political science.
—BLDSC (8465.700000).
Published by: Stockholms Universitet, Statsvetenskapliga Institutionen/ Stockholm University, Department of Political Science, Universitetsvaegen 10 F, Stockholm, 10691, Sweden. TEL 46-8-162000, FAX 46-8-152529, http://statsvet.su.se. R&P Lena Helldner. Circ: 300.

324.2 SWE ISSN 1402-8069
STOCKHOLMSTIDNINGEN. Text in Swedish. 1993. 50/yr. SEK 410; SEK 49 per issue (effective 2011). adv. **Document type:** *Magazine, Consumer.*
Related titles: Online - full text ed.
Published by: A i P Media Produktion AB (Subsidiary of: Sveriges Socialdemokratiska Arbetareparti/Swedish Social Democratic Labour Party), Sveavaegen 68, Stockholm, 10560, Sweden. TEL 46-8-7002600, FAX 46-8-4116542, aip@sap.se, http://www.aip.sap.se. Ed. Ylva Saefvelin. Circ: 4,000.

320 ITA ISSN 1971-1255
STORIA DELLE DOTTRINE POLITICHE. SAGGI E RICERCHE. Text in Italian. 2000. m. **Document type:** *Magazine, Consumer.*
Published by: (Universita degli Studi di Milano, Facolta di Giurisprudenza), Casa Editrice Dott. A. Giuffre (Subsidiary of: LexisNexis Europe and Africa), Via Busto Arsizio, 40, Milan, MI 20151, Italy. TEL 39-02-380891, FAX 39-02-38009582, giuffre@giuffre.it, http://www.giuffre.it.

320 900 ITA ISSN 2036-3907
➤ **STORIA E POLITICA (NUOVA SERIE).** Text in Italian. 1962-1984; resumed 2009. 3/yr. EUR 80 combined subscription domestic (print & online eds.); EUR 100 combined subscription foreign (print & online eds.) (effective 2010). bk.rev. bibl. index. **Document type:** *Journal, Academic/Scholarly.*
Formerly (until 1984): Storia e Politica (0039-1905)
Related titles: Online - full text ed.: ISSN 2037-0520. 2009.
Indexed: ABCPolSci, BAS, HistAb, MLA, MLA-IB, RASB.
Published by: Universita degli Studi di Palermo, Facolta di Scienze Politiche, Via Maqueda 324, Palermo, 90134, Italy. http://www.unipa.it/scienzepolitiche/.

➤ **STORIA E TEORIA POLITICA.** *see* HISTORY

➤ **STRATEGIC ASIA.** *see* BUSINESS AND ECONOMICS

320 ISR ISSN 0793-8942
STRATEGIC ASSESSMENT. Text in English. 1998. q. **Document type:** *Journal, Academic/Scholarly.*
Related titles: Online - full text ed.: free (effective 2011).
Indexed: PAIS.
Published by: Institute for National Security Studies, 40 Haim Levanon St, Tel Aviv, 61398, Israel. TEL 972-3-6400400, FAX 972-3-7447590, info@inss.org.il.

320 GBR ISSN 1356-7888
U162
STRATEGIC COMMENTS. Text in English. 1995. 10/yr. GBP 195 in United Kingdom to institutions; EUR 287 to institutions; USD 341 in North America to institutions; USD 360 elsewhere to institutions (effective 2012). adv. back issues avail. **Document type:** *Journal, Academic/Scholarly.* **Description:** Contains five articles in each issue, Strategic Comments briefing papers offer succinct and cogent insights of consistent authority to its core readership of policy-makers, journalists, business executives and foreign affairs analysts.
Media: Online - full content.
Indexed: A22, CA, E01, I02, LID&ISL, R02, T02.
—IE. **CCC.**
Published by: (International Institute for Strategic Studies), Routledge (Subsidiary of: Taylor & Francis Group), 4 Park Sq, Milton Park, Abingdon, Oxon OX14 4RN, United Kingdom. TEL 44-20-70176000, FAX 44-20-70176336, subscriptions@tandf.co.uk, http://www.routledge.com. Eds. Adam Ward, Alexander Nicoll TEL 44-20-73797676. Adv. contact Linda Hann TEL 44-1344-779945. **Subscr. in N America to:** Taylor & Francis Inc., Customer Services Dept, 325 Chestnut St, 8th Fl, Philadelphia, PA 19106. TEL 215-625-8900, 800-354-1420, FAX 215-625-2940, customerservice@taylorandfrancis.com; **Subscr. outside N America to:** Taylor & Francis Ltd., Journals Customer Service, Sheepen Pl, Colchester, Essex CO3 3LP, United Kingdom. TEL 44-20-70175544, FAX 44-20-70175198, tf.enquiries@tfinforma.com.

STRATEGIQUE. *see* MILITARY

320.3 CZE ISSN 1212-7817
DB2000
➤ **STREDOEVROPSKE POLITICKE STUDIE/CENTRAL EUROPEAN POLITICAL STUDIES REVIEW.** Text in Czech, Slovak, English. 1999. 3/yr. free. **Document type:** *Journal, Academic/Scholarly.* **Description:** Contains research and texts on comparative politics, European studies, and foreign and security policies.
Media: Online - full content.
Published by: Masarykova Univerzita, Mezinarodni Politologicky Ustav/Masarykovy University, International Institute of Political Science, Jostova 10, Brno, 60200, Czech Republic. TEL 420-549-498438, FAX 420-549-495769, iips@iips.cz, http://www.iips.cz. Eds. Jan Holzer, Vera Stojarova.

➤ **STRUGGLE**; a magazine of proletarian revolutionary literature. *see* LITERARY AND POLITICAL REVIEWS

➤ **STUDI PARLAMENTARI E DI POLITICA COSTITUZIONALE.** *see* LAW

P

320 POL ISSN 1230-3135
JA26
STUDIA POLITYCZNE. Text in Polish; Summaries in English. 1992. irreg., latest vol.12. USD 15 per issue foreign (effective 2003). adv. bk.rev. abstr. 250 p./no. 1 cols./p.; back issues avail. **Document type:** *Academic/Scholarly.* **Description:** Covers political science, sociology, international relations, modern history of Poland and Central-Eastern Europe.
Indexed: RASB.
Published by: Polska Akademia Nauk, Instytut Studiow Politycznych/ Polish Academy of Sciences, Institute of Political Studies, ul Polna 18-20, Warsaw, 00625, Poland. TEL 48-22-8255221, FAX 48-22-8252146, http://www.isppan.waw.pl. Ed. Wojciech Roszkowski. R&P Ryszard Zelichowski. Adv. contact Jozef Dawid. Circ: 500. **Dist. by:** Ars Polona, Obroncow 25, Warsaw 03933, Poland. TEL 48-22-5098609, FAX 48-22-5098610, arspolona@arspolona.com.pl, http://www.arspolona.com.pl.

320 ROM ISSN 1224-8711
➤ **STUDIA UNIVERSITATIS BABES-BOLYAI. POLITICA.** Text in English. 1970. a. exchange basis. abstr.; charts; illus. index. **Document type:** *Journal, Academic/Scholarly.*
Supersedes in part (in 1996): Studia Universitatis "Babes-Bolyai". Sociologia - Politica (1221-8197); Which was formerly (until 1975): Studia Universitatis "Babes-Bolyai". Series Sociologica (1221-812X)
Related titles: Online - full text ed.: ISSN 2065-9423.
Indexed: CA, IBSS, T02.
Published by: Universitatea "Babes-Bolyai", Studia/Babes-Bolyai University, Studia, 51 Hasdeu Str, Cluj-Napoca, 400371, Romania. TEL 40-264-405352, FAX 40-264-591906, office@studia.ubbcluj.ro, http://www.studia.ubbcluj.ro. Ed. Gabriel Badescu. **Dist by:** "Lucian Blaga" Central University Library, International Exchange Department, Clinicilor st no 2, Cluj-Napoca 400371, Romania. TEL 40-264-597092, FAX 40-264-597633, iancu@bcucluj.ro.

320 DEU
▼ **STUDIEN DES GOETTINGER INSTITUTS FUER DEMOKRATIEFORSCHUNG ZUR GESCHICHTE POLITISCHER UND GESELLSCHAFTLICHER KONTROVERSEN.** Text in German. 2011. irreg., latest vol.3, 2011. price varies. **Document type:** *Monographic series, Academic/Scholarly.*
Published by: (Goettinger Institut fuer Demokratieforschung), Transcript, Muehlenstr 47, Bielefeld, 33607, Germany. TEL 49-521-63454, FAX 49-521-61040, live@transcript-verlag.de.

320.52 DEU ISSN 1439-3743
STUDIEN UND TEXTE ZUR ERFORSCHUNG DER KONSERVATISMUS. Text in German. 2000. irreg., latest vol.6, 2005. price varies. **Document type:** *Monographic series, Academic/ Scholarly.*
Published by: (Foerderstiftung Konservative Bildung und Forschung), Duncker und Humblot GmbH, Carl-Heinrich-Becker-Weg 9, Berlin, 12165, Germany. TEL 49-30-7900060, FAX 49-30-79000631, info@duncker-humblot.de.

STUDIEN VON ZEITFRAGEN (ONLINE EDITION); Nonkonforme Beitraege zu Fragen der Zeit. *see* HISTORY

STUDIEN ZU POLITIK UND VERWALTUNG. *see* LAW

320 AUT ISSN 1814-5604
STUDIEN ZUR POLITISCHEN WIRKLICHKEIT. Text in German. 1989. irreg., latest vol.25, 2010. price varies. **Document type:** *Monographic series, Academic/Scholarly.*
Published by: Wilhelm Braumueller Universitaets-Verlagsbuchhandlung GmbH, Servitengasse 5, Vienna, 1090, Austria. TEL 43-1-3191159, FAX 43-1-3102805, office@braumueller.at. Ed. Anton Pelinka.

322.4 DEU ISSN 1611-1826
STUDIEN ZUR UMWELTPOLITIK. Text in German. 2003. irreg., latest vol.10, 2007. price varies. **Document type:** *Monographic series, Academic/Scholarly.*
Published by: Verlag Dr. Kovac, Leverkusenstr 13, Hamburg, 22761, Germany. TEL 49-40-3988800, FAX 49-40-39888055, info@verlagdrkovac.de.

320 GBR ISSN 0898-588X
E183 CODEN: SAPDFH
➤ **STUDIES IN AMERICAN POLITICAL DEVELOPMENT.** Abbreviated title: S A P D. Text in English. 1986. s-a. GBP 140, USD 243 to institutions; GBP 148, USD 257 combined subscription to institutions (print & online eds.) (effective 2012). adv. bk.rev. back issues avail.; reprint service avail. from PSC. **Document type:** *Journal, Academic/ Scholarly.* **Description:** Covers American political change and institutional development from a historical perspective.
Related titles: Online - full text ed.: ISSN 1469-8692. GBP 125, USD 220 to institutions (effective 2012).
Indexed: A20, A22, ASCA, AmH&L, CA, CurCont, E01, I13, IBSS, P02, P10, P42, P45, P47, P48, P53, P54, PAIS, PCI, PQC, PSA, RASB, S02, S03, S11, SCOPUS, SOPODA, SSA, SSCI, SociolAb, T02, W07.
—BLDSC (8489.086500), IE, Infotrieve, Ingenta. **CCC.**
Published by: Cambridge University Press, The Edinburgh Bldg, Shaftesbury Rd, Cambridge, CB2 8RU, United Kingdom. TEL 44-1223-312393, FAX 44-1223-315052, journals@cambridge.org, http://www.cambridge.org/uk. Eds. Daniel Carpenter, Elisabeth Clemens, Scott James. adv.: page GBP 445, page USD 845. Circ: 400. **Subscr. to:** Cambridge University Press, 32 Ave of the Americas, New York, NY 10013. TEL 212-337-5000, FAX 212-691-3239, journals_subscriptions@cup.org.

➤ **STUDIES IN CHURCH AND STATE.** *see* RELIGIONS AND THEOLOGY

321.8 USA ISSN 1541-6542
STUDIES IN DEMOCRATIZATION. Text in English. 2002 (Fall). s-a.
Media: Online - full content.
Published by: Northeastern University, Center for the Study of Democracy, 303 Meserve Hall, 360 Huntington Ave., Boston, MA 02115. TEL 617-373-2877, FAX 617-373-7527.

320.94 NLD ISSN 0925-9392
B809.8 CODEN: SEETE3
➤ **STUDIES IN EAST EUROPEAN THOUGHT.** Text in English, French, German. 1961. q. EUR 588, USD 627 combined subscription to institutions (print & online eds.) (effective 2012). adv. bk.rev. bibl.; illus. index. back issues avail.; reprint service avail. from PSC. **Document type:** *Journal, Academic/Scholarly.* **Description:** Provides a forum for writings on philosophy, philosophers and schools of philosophy connected with East and central Europe, including Russia, the Ukraine and the Baltic nations.
Formerly (until 1992): Studies in Soviet Thought (0039-3797)
Related titles: Microform ed.: (from PQC); Online - full text ed.: ISSN 1573-0948 (from IngentaConnect).
Indexed: A01, A03, A08, A20, A22, A26, ABCPolSci, ABS&EES, ASCA, AmHI, ArtHuCI, B04, BAS, BRD, BibInd, BibLing, CA, CurCont, DIP, E01, FR, H07, H08, HAb, HistAb, HumInd, I05, I13, IBR, IBSS, IBZ, IPB, P02, P10, P30, P42, P45, P48, P53, P54, PCI, PQC, PSA, PhilInd, RASB, S02, S03, S11, SCOPUS, SSCI, SociolAb, T02, W03, W05, W07.
—BLDSC (8490.413600), IE, Infotrieve, Ingenta, INIST. **CCC.**
Published by: Springer Netherlands (Subsidiary of: Springer Science+Business Media), Van Godewijckstraat 30, Dordrecht, 3311 GX, Netherlands. TEL 31-78-6576050, FAX 31-78-6576474, http://www.springer.com. Ed. Edward M Swiderski. **Co-sponsors:** Munich University, Seminar for Political Theory; Fribourg University, Institute of East European Studies.

320 IND
STUDIES IN ELECTORAL POLITICS IN THE INDIAN STATES. Text in English. 19??. irreg. charts; stat.
Published by: Manohar Book Service, Panna Bhawan, Ansari Rd., 2 Daryaganj, New Delhi, 110 006, India.

320 GBR ISSN 1473-8481
JC311
➤ **STUDIES IN ETHNICITY AND NATIONALISM.** Abbreviated title: S E N. Text in English. 1991. s-a. free to members (effective 2009). back issues avail.; reprint service avail. from PSC. **Document type:** *Journal, Academic/Scholarly.* **Description:** Contains information on publications, conferences, public lectures and courses in the areas of ethnicity and nationalism, both in the UK and abroad. It also includes short articles on current events.
Formerly (until 2001): A S E N Bulletin (1353-8004)
Related titles: Online - full text ed.: ISSN 1754-9469.
Indexed: A01, A22, CA, E01, T02.
—BLDSC (8490.531180), IE, Ingenta. **CCC.**
Published by: Association for the Study of Ethnicity and Nationalism, London School of Economics, Houghton St, London, WC2A 2AE, United Kingdom. TEL 44-20-79556801, FAX 44-20-79556218, ASEN@lse.ac.uk. Ed. Victor Teo.

320 341 USA ISSN 1094-6209
STUDIES IN EUROPEAN UNION (NEW YORK). Text in English. 2000. irreg., latest vol.2, 2003. price varies. **Document type:** *Monographic series, Academic/Scholarly.* **Description:** Explore the practical and institutional aspects of the ongoing process as well as to elucidate the anthropological, sociological and cultural issues which pose a challenge to or, on the contrary, may be helping the process of achieving a continental identity.
Published by: Peter Lang Publishing, Inc. (Subsidiary of: Peter Lang Publishing Group), 29 Broadway, New York, NY 10006. TEL 212-647-7700, 800-770-5264, FAX 212-647-7707, customerservice@plang.com, http://www.peterlangusa.com. Ed. Margherita Repetto-Alaia.

320 USA ISSN 0081-7996
STUDIES IN HISTORICAL AND POLITICAL SCIENCE. EXTRA VOLUMES. Text in English. irreg., latest vol.15, 1968.
Published by: (Johns Hopkins University), Bergman Publishers, Inc., 224 W 20th St, New York, NY 10011. TEL 212-685-9074.

STUDIES IN LAW AND POLITICS. *see* LAW

320 CAN ISSN 0707-8552
➤ **STUDIES IN POLITICAL ECONOMY;** a socialist review. Text in English. 1979. 3/yr. USD 40 to individuals; USD 100 to institutions; USD 20 to students (effective 2005). bk.rev. back issues avail.; reprints avail. **Document type:** *Journal, Academic/Scholarly.* **Description:** Scholarly journal providing detailed analyses of current issues and informed commentary on topics in Canadian and international political economy.
Related titles: Online - full text ed.
Indexed: A22, A26, APEL, AltPI, AmH&L, B01, B07, BAS, C03, CA, CBCARef, CBPI, CPerI, E08, G08, I13, IBR, IBSS, IBZ, LeftInd, P34, P42, P48, PAIS, PQC, PSA, S02, S03, S09, SCOPUS, SOPODA, SSA, SociolAb, T02.
—BLDSC (8491.223720), IE, Infotrieve, Ingenta. **CCC.**
Published by: Association d'Economie Politique, SR 303, Carleton University, 1125 Colonel By Dr, Ottawa, ON K1S 5B6, Canada. TEL 613-520-2600 x 6625. Circ: 1,000.

320.6 GBR ISSN 0140-8240
H96
STUDIES IN PUBLIC POLICY. Text in English. 1977. irreg., latest no.462. price varies. back issues avail. **Document type:** *Monographic series, Academic/Scholarly.* **Description:** Publishes topical analysis of Barometer data and related studies by social scientists from all over Europe and the United States.
Related titles: Online - full text ed.
—IE, Ingenta. **CCC.**
Published by: University of Aberdeen, Centre for the Study of Public Policy, Edward Wright Bldg, Aberdeen, AB24 3QY, United Kingdom. TEL 44-1224-272000, cspp@abdn.ac.uk.

STUDIES IN RELIGION, POLITICS, AND PUBLIC LIFE. *see* RELIGIONS AND THEOLOGY

322.1 NLD ISSN 1871-7829
STUDIES IN RELIGION, SECULAR BELIEFS AND HUMAN RIGHTS. Text in English. 2006. irreg., latest vol.7, 2008. price varies. **Document type:** *Monographic series, Academic/Scholarly.*
Indexed: IZBG.
Published by: Martinus Nijhoff (Subsidiary of: Brill), PO Box 9000, Leiden, 2300 PA, Netherlands. TEL 31-71-5353500, FAX 31-71-5317532, marketing@brill.nl.

STUDIES IN SOCIAL JUSTICE. *see* SOCIOLOGY

320.5 NLD ISSN 1873-6548
▼ **STUDIES IN THE HISTORY OF POLITICAL THOUGHT.** Text in English. 2009. irreg., latest vol.4, 2010. price varies. **Document type:** *Monographic series, Academic/Scholarly.*
Published by: Brill, PO Box 9000, Leiden, 2300 PA, Netherlands. TEL 31-71-5353500, FAX 31-71-5317532, cs@brill.nl. Eds. Jorn Leonhard, Terence Ball, Wyger Velema.

STUDIES IN THE HISTORY OF RELIGIOUS AND POLITICAL PLURALISM. *see* RELIGIONS AND THEOLOGY

320 EST ISSN 1736-874X
▼ **STUDIES OF TRANSITION STATES AND SOCIETIES.** Text in English. 2009. s-a. **Document type:** *Journal, Academic/Scholarly.*
Related titles: Online - full text ed.: ISSN 1736-8758. free (effective 2011).
Indexed: P45.
Published by: (Tallinna Ulikool, Institute of International and Social Studies), Tallinna Ulikool, Institute of Political Science and Government, Narva mnt 25, Tallin, 10120, Estonia. TEL 372-6409101, FAX 372-6409116, http://www.tlu.ee/?LangID=2&CatID=2832 http://www.tlu.ee/?LangID=2&CatID=2832.

320 NLD
STUDIES OVER POLITIEKE VERNIEUWING. Text in Dutch. irreg. price varies. **Document type:** *Monographic series.*
Published by: Amsterdam University Press, Herengracht 221, Amsterdam, 1016 BG, Netherlands. TEL 31-20-4200050, FAX 31-20-4203214, info@aup.nl, http://www.aup.nl. Eds. Ido de Haan, Tsjalling Swierstra.

SUDAN STUDIES SERIES. *see* SOCIAL SCIENCES: COMPREHENSIVE WORKS

320 DEU ISSN 0722-480X
H5
➤ **SUEDOST-EUROPA;** Zeitschrift fuer Gegenwartsforschung. Text in German. 1952. 4/yr. EUR 54.80 to non-members; EUR 29.80 to members; EUR 24.80 newsstand/cover (effective 2011). bibl.; charts; stat. index. reprints avail. **Document type:** *Journal, Academic/ Scholarly.*
Formerly (until 1982): Wissenschaftlicher Dienst Suedosteuropa (0043-695X)
Indexed: A22, CA, DIP, I13, IBR, IBZ, MLA-IB, P30, P42, PAIS, PSA, RASB, T02.
—BLDSC (8509.285000), IE, Infotrieve, Ingenta. **CCC.**
Published by: (Suedost-Institut), Oldenbourg Wissenschaftsverlag GmbH, Rosenheimer Str 145, Munich, 81671, Germany. TEL 49-89-450510, FAX 49-89-45051204, orders@oldenbourg.de, http://www.oldenbourg.de. Ed. Marie-Janine Calic.

➤ **SURMACH.** *see* MILITARY

320.07 CHN ISSN 1672-0237
LC315.C6
SUZHI JIAOYU DACANKAO/POLITICAL EDUCATION. Text in Chinese. 1990 (no.103). m. CNY 4.50 per issue (effective 2009). **Document type:** *Journal, Academic/Scholarly.* **Description:** Contains articles and papers on political education in China, as well as other economic and political issues.
Formerly: Zhengzhi Jiaoyu (1006-1649)
Published by: (Guojia Jiaoyu Weiyuanhui/State Education Commission), Shanghai Jiaoyu Chubanshe/Shanghai Educational Publishing House, 123 Yongfu Rd, Shanghai, 200031, China. TEL 86-21-64373159. Ed. Chen He. Circ: 23,000.

320.5 SWE ISSN 1101-7597
SVEAMAAL; frispraakig nationell tidning foer debatt och information. Text in Swedish. 1991. 10/yr. SEK 150 (effective 1991).
Address: Fack 20085, Stockholm, 10460, Sweden.

324.6 ISL ISSN 1021-5646
SVEITARSTJORNARKOSNINGAR/LOCAL GOVERNMENT ELECTIONS. Text in Icelandic. 1993. irreg. USD 15 (effective 2001). back issues avail. **Document type:** *Government.*
Published by: Hagstofa Islands/Statistics Iceland, Borgartuni 12 A, Reykjavik, 150, Iceland. TEL 354-560-9800, FAX 354-562-3312, hagstofa@hag.stjr.is, http://www.statice.is/stat/e-mail.htm. Ed. Gudni Baldursson.

320.5 SWE ISSN 0346-2161
SVENSK LINJE. Text in Swedish. 1942. 4/yr. SEK 150 (effective 2001). **Document type:** *Magazine, Consumer.*
Published by: Fria Moderata Studentfoerbundet, Box 2294, Stockholm, 10317, Sweden. TEL 46-8-791-50-05, FAX 46-8-791-50-02, http://www.moderat.se. Ed. Joakim Nilsson. Adv. contact Staffan Ingvarsson.

320.5 SWE ISSN 0346-2366
SVENSKA NYHETER. Text in Swedish. 1970-1984; resumed 1988. q.
Published by: (Presstjaenst), Frisinnade Unions-Partiet, Dr Resmarks Vaeg, Bua 6186, Elloes, 44080, Sweden.

320.9485 SWE ISSN 1651-6249
SVERIGES RIKSDAG. SVERIGES RIKSDAG. Text in Swedish. 2003. quadrennial, latest 2008. **Document type:** *Government.* **Description:** A general presentation of the Swedish parliament, its functions and work.
Related titles: French ed.: Sverigs Riksdag. Le Parlement Suedois. ISSN 1651-6281; German ed.: Sveriges Riksdag. Der Schwedische Reichstag. ISSN 1651-629X; English ed.: Sveriges Riksdag. The Swedish Parliament. ISSN 1651-6273; Spanish ed.: Sveriges Riksdag. Parlamento de Suecia. ISSN 1651-6303; Finnish ed.: Sveriges Riksdag. Valtiopaivien Viestintayksikko. ISSN 1651-7911; Russian ed.: Sveriges Riksdag. Svedskij Parlament. ISSN 1651-6311.
Published by: Sveriges Riksdag, Informationsenheten/The Swedish Parliament. Information Department, Stockholm, 10012, Sweden. TEL 46-8-7864000, riksdagsinformation@riksdagen.se, http://www.riksdagen.se.

320.9 AUS ISSN 1035-7068
CODEN: SYPAF6
➤ **THE SYDNEY PAPERS.** Text in English. 1989. s-a. AUD 33 to non-members; free to members (effective 2009). back issues avail. **Document type:** *Journal, Academic/Scholarly.*
Related titles: Online - full text ed.
Indexed: AusPAIS.
—Ingenta.

Published by: Sydney Institute, 41 Philip St, Sydney, NSW 2000, Australia. TEL 61-2-92523366, FAX 61-2-92523360, mail@sydneyins.org.au, http://www.sydneyins.org.auge. Ed. Anne Henderson.

➤ **SYNTHESIS - REGENERATION**; a magazine of green social thought. *see* ENVIRONMENTAL STUDIES

320 ARG ISSN 1666-0714
JL2001

T. D. TEMAS Y DEBATES. Text in Spanish. 1996. s-a. **Document type:** *Journal, Academic/Scholarly.*
Published by: Universidad Nacional de Rosario, Facultad de Ciencias Politicas y Relaciones Internacionales, Riomba y Berutti C.U.R., Rosario, 2000, Argentina. TEL 54-341-4808520, academica@fcpolit.unr.edu.ar, http://fcpolit.unr.edu.ar/. Ed. Adriana Chiroleu.

T I P R O TARGET NEWSLETTER. *see* PUBLIC ADMINISTRATION

320 330 NLD ISSN 1875-8797

➤ **T P E DIGITAAL.** (Tijdschrift Politieke Ekonomie) Text in Dutch. 1977. q. free (effective 2011). **Document type:** *Journal, Academic/Scholarly.*
Formerly (until 2007): Tijdschrift voor Politieke Ekonomie (0165-442X)
Media: Online - full text.
Indexed: FR.
—IE.
Published by: Stichting TPEdigitaal, Amstelveenseweg 1056, Amsterdam, 1081 JV, Netherlands. Eds. M W Hofkes, M de Graaf, W H J Hassink.

320 TZA ISSN 0049-2817
JQ2945.A1

TAAMULI; a political science forum. Text in English. 1970. s-a. TZS 25. adv. bk.rev. **Document type:** *Journal, Academic/Scholarly.*
Related titles: Microform ed.: (from PQC).
Indexed: ASD, CCA, HistAb, IBR, IBZ.
Published by: University of Dar es Salaam, Department of Political Science, PO Box 35042, Dar Es Salaam, Tanzania. TEL 255-51-43130, FAX 255-51-43395. Ed. Samule Mushi. Circ: 1,000.

TAIWAN YANJIU/TAIWAN STUDY. *see* SOCIAL SCIENCES: COMPREHENSIVE WORKS

320 USA
JK271

TAKING SIDES: CLASHING VIEWS ON POLITICAL ISSUES. Text in English. irreg., latest 2003, 13th ed. (rev. ed.). USD 33.44 per vol. (effective 2010). illus. **Document type:** *Monographic series, Academic/Scholarly.*
Formerly (until 2007): Taking Sides: Clashing Views on Controversial Political Issues (1080-580X)
Related titles: Online - full text ed.: ISSN 2153-2850. 2010. USD 4 per issue (effective 2010).
Published by: McGraw-Hill, Contemporary Learning Series (Subsidiary of: McGraw-Hill Companies, Inc.), 2460 Kerper Blvd, Dubuque, IA 52001. TEL 800-243-6532, customer.service@mcgraw-hill.com, http://www.dushkin.com. Eds. George McKenna, Stanley Feingold. Pub. David Dean. R&P Cheryl Greenleaf.

320 AUT

TANGENTE. Text in German. bi-m. EUR 10 membership (effective 2005). adv. **Document type:** *Magazine, Consumer.*
Published by: Ring Freiheitlicher Jugend, Stuckgasse 9, Vienna, W 1070, Austria. TEL 43-1-4080748, FAX 43-1-408074820, info@rfj.at, http://www.rfj.at. Circ: 6,000.

320 TZA

➤ **TANZANIA PUBLISHING HOUSE. INAUGURAL LECTURE SERIES.** Text in English. irreg. **Document type:** *Monographic series, Academic/Scholarly.*
Published by: Tanzania Publishing House Limited, Samora Machel Ave 47, PO Box 2138, Dar es Salaam, Tanzania. TEL 255-51-32164. Ed. Primus Isidor Karugendo. R&P Josephat Litereko TEL 255-51-32165. **Dist. outside Africa by:** African Books Collective Ltd., The Jam Factory, 27 Park End St, Oxford, Oxon OX1 1HU, United Kingdom. TEL 44-1865-726686, FAX 44-1865-793298.

320.532 VNM

TAP CHI CONG SAN/COMMUNIST REVIEW. Text in Vietnamese. 1955. m.
Formerly: Hoc Tap
Indexed: RASB.
Address: 1 Nguyen Thuong Hien, Hanoi, Viet Nam. TEL 52061. Ed. Ha Xuan Truong. Circ: 55,000.

321.8 ISR

TARBUT DEMOQRATIT/DEMOCRATIC CULTURE. Text in Hebrew, English. 1999. irreg., latest vol.12, 2009. USD 18 per issue (effective 2011). **Document type:** *Journal, Academic/Scholarly.* **Description:** An exploration of questions relating to the texture of democratic life in the State of Israel.
Published by: Bar-Ilan University Press (Subsidiary of: Bar-Ilan University), Journals, Ramat-Gan, 52900, Israel. TEL 972-3-531-8111, FAX 972-3-535-3446, press@mail.biu.ac.il, http://www.biu.ac.il/Press. Ed. Avi Sagi.

TARJETA; analisis y debate parlamentario. *see* PUBLIC ADMINISTRATION

323.6 371.102 GBR ISSN 1474-9335

TEACHING CITIZENSHIP. Text in English. 2001. 3/yr. free to members (effective 2010). **Document type:** *Journal, Academic/Scholarly.*
Related titles: Online - full text ed.
—IE.
Published by: (Association for Citizenship Teaching), Questions Publishing Company Ltd., 1st Fl, Leonard House, 321 Bradford St, Digbeth, Birmingham, Warks B1 3ET, United Kingdom. TEL 44-121-6667878, FAX 44-121-6667879, rchima@qiis.co.uk, http://www.education-quest.com/. Ed. Roy Honeybone.

TEACHING TEXTS IN LAW AND POLITICS. *see* LAW

TECHNISCHE UNIVERSITAET DRESDEN. HANNAH-ARENDT-INSTITUT FUER TOTALITARISMUSFORSCHUNG. SCHRIFTEN. *see* HISTORY—History Of Europe

TELOS; revista iberamericana de estudios utilitaristas. *see* PHILOSOPHY

320 ESP ISSN 1989-8118

TEMAS DE POLITICA Y SOCIOLOGIA. Text in Spanish. 2000. irreg. **Document type:** *Monographic series, Academic/Scholarly.*
Published by: Universitat Pompeu Fabra, Placa de la Merce 10-12, Barcelona, 08002, Spain. TEL 34-93-5422000, FAX 34-93-5422002, http://www.upf.edu.

320 ESP ISSN 1134-6574
DP1

TEMAS PARA EL DEBATE. Text in Spanish. 1994. m. EUR 40 domestic; EUR 85 in Europe; EUR 115 elsewhere (effective 2009). adv. 80 p./no.; **Document type:** *Magazine, Consumer.*
Published by: Fundacion Sistema, Fuencarral 127, 1o, Madrid, 28010, Spain. TEL 34-91-4487319, FAX 34-91-4487339, info@fundacionsistema.com. **Dist. by:** Asociacion de Revistas Culturales de Espana, C Covarruvias 9 2o. Derecha, Madrid 28010, Spain. TEL 34-91-3086066, FAX 34-91-3199267, info@arce.es, http://www.arce.es/.

TEME; casopis za drustvene nauke. *see* SOCIOLOGY

320 ESP ISSN 1579-6582

TEMPO EXTERIOR; revista de analise e estudios internacionais. Text in Gallegan. 1997. 3/yr. back issues avail. **Document type:** *Journal, Academic/Scholarly.*
Related titles: Online - full text ed.: free (effective 2011).
Published by: Instituto Galego de Analise e Documentacion Internacional (I G A D I), Av Joselin 7, Portal 3-4B, Baiona, Pontevedra 36300, Spain. info@igadi.org.

TENNESSEE JOURNAL OF LAW & POLICY. *see* LAW

320.5 ITA ISSN 0394-1248
JA18

TEORIA POLITICA. Text in Italian. 1983. 3/yr. EUR 74.50 combined subscription domestic to institutions; EUR 104 combined subscription foreign to institutions (effective 2009). **Document type:** *Journal, Academic/Scholarly.*
Related titles: Online - full text ed.: ISSN 1972-5477.
Indexed: DIP, I13, IBR, IBZ.
Published by: Franco Angeli Edizioni, Viale Monza 106, Milan, 20127, Italy. TEL 39-02-2837141, FAX 39-02-26144793, redazioni@francoangeli.it, http://www.francoangeli.it.

320 FRA ISSN 0040-3814

LA TERRE; l'hebdomadaire pour que vivre le monde rural. Text in French. 1937. 25/yr. EUR 40 (effective 2010). adv. bk.rev.; film rev.; play rev. illus.; stat. **Document type:** *Newspaper.*
Indexed: RASB.
Published by: (Parti Communiste Francais), La Terre, 164 rue Ambroise Croizat, Saint Denis, 93207, France. TEL 33-1-49227250, FAX 33-1-49227380, laterre@laterre.fr. Ed. Denis Recoquillon. Circ: 197,000.

320 GBR ISSN 1947-2277

▼ ➤ **TERRITORIAL POLITICS.** Text in English. forthcoming 2011 (Mar.). q. **Document type:** *Journal, Academic/Scholarly.*
Related titles: Online - full text ed.: ISSN 1947-2285. forthcoming 2011 (Mar.).
Published by: Taylor & Francis Ltd. (Subsidiary of: Taylor & Francis Group), 4 Park Sq, Milton Park, Abingdon, Oxfordshire OX14 4RN, United Kingdom. TEL 44-20-70176000, FAX 44-20-70176336, info@tandf.co.uk, http://www.tandf.co.uk/journals.

320.947 GBR ISSN 1465-461X
JN6699.A88

THE TERRITORIES OF THE RUSSIAN FEDERATION. Text in English. 1999. a. USD 310 per issue (effective 2009). reprints avail. **Document type:** *Directory, Academic/Scholarly.* **Description:** Presents maps, analysis and statistics on the 89 constituent units of the Russian Federation.
Published by: (Europa Publications Ltd.), Routledge (Subsidiary of: Taylor & Francis Group), 2 Park Sq, Milton Park, Abingdon, Oxon OX14 4RN, United Kingdom. TEL 44-20-70176000, FAX 44-20-70176699, orders@taylorandfrancis.com. **Dist. by:** Current Pacific Ltd., 7 La Roche Pl, Northcote, PO Box 36-536, Auckland 0627, New Zealand.

TESINSKO; vlastivedny casopis. *see* HISTORY—History Of Europe

TEXAS REVIEW OF LAW & POLITICS. *see* LAW

TEXAS WEEKLY. *see* PUBLIC ADMINISTRATION

TEXTE ZUR RECHTSPOLITIK. *see* LAW

321.8 DEU

THEMA IM UNTERRICHT. Text in German. irreg. free (effective 2009). **Document type:** *Monographic series, Academic/Scholarly.*
Published by: Bundeszentrale fuer Politische Bildung, Adenauerallee 86, Bonn, 53113, Germany. TEL 49-1888-5150, FAX 49-1888-515113, info@bpb.de.

321.8 DEU

THEMENBLAETTER IM UNTERRICHT. Text in German. 2000. irreg., latest vol.75, 2008. free (effective 2009). **Document type:** *Monographic series, Academic/Scholarly.*
Published by: Bundeszentrale fuer Politische Bildung, Adenauerallee 86, Bonn, 53113, Germany. TEL 49-1888-5150, FAX 49-1888-515113, info@bpb.de, http://www.bpb.de.

320.6 USA

THEODORE M. HESBURGH LECTURES ON ETHICS AND PUBLIC POLICY. Text in English. 1995. irreg., latest 1997. price varies. **Document type:** *Monographic series, Academic/Scholarly.*
Published by: University of Notre Dame Press, 310 Flanner Hall, Notre Dame, IN 46556. TEL 574-631-6346, FAX 574-631-8148, undpress.1@nd.edu. **Dist. by:** c/o Chicago Distribution Ctr, 11030 S Langley Ave, Chicago, IL 60628. TEL 773-702-7000, 800-621-2736, FAX 773-702-7212, 800-621-8476; Eurospan Group, c/o Turpin Distribution Pegasus Dr, Stratton Business Park, Biggleswade, Bedfordshire SG18 8TQ, United Kingdom. TEL 44-1767-604972, FAX 44-1767-601640, eurospan@turpin-distribution.com, http://www.eurospangroup.com.

320.011 USA ISSN 1092-311X
JA1

THEORY & EVENT; an online journal of political theory. Text in English. 1997. q. USD 95 to institutions (effective 2011). back issues avail. **Document type:** *Journal, Academic/Scholarly.* **Description:** Brings out political thought in the humanities and the social sciences, featuring essays and other forms of writing and representation which address the power of sovereignty, territory and government.
Media: Online - full text.
Indexed: A01, A03, A08, A22, CA, E01, LeftInd, MLA-IB, P10, P42, P45, P48, P53, P54, PQC, S11, T02.
—CCC.
Published by: The Johns Hopkins University Press, 2715 N Charles St, Baltimore, MD 21218. TEL 410-516-6900, FAX 410-516-6968, bjs@press.jhu.edu. Ed. Jodi Dean. Pub. William M Breichner. **Subscr. to:** PO Box 19966, Baltimore, MD 21211. TEL 410-516-6987, 800-548-1784, FAX 410-516-3866, jrnlcirc@press.jhu.edu.

320.6 GBR ISSN 0725-5136
H61

➤ **THESIS ELEVEN**; critical theory and historical sociology. Text in English. 1980. q. USD 930, GBP 502 combined subscription to institutions (print & online eds.); USD 911, GBP 492 to institutions (effective 2011). adv. bk.rev. illus. cum.index. back issues avail.; reprint service avail. from PSC. **Document type:** *Journal, Academic/Scholarly.* **Description:** Encourages the development of social theory across the social sciences and liberal arts. It brings together articles on place, region or problems in the world today, encouraging civilizational analysis and work on alternative modernities from fascism and communism to Japan and Southeast Asia.
Related titles: Microform ed.: (from PQC); Online - full text ed.: ISSN 1461-7455. USD 837, GBP 452 to institutions (effective 2011).
Indexed: A01, A03, A08, A22, AltPI, AusPAIS, B07, CA, DIP, E01, H04, I13, IBR, IBSS, IBZ, IBibSS, IPB, LeftInd, P02, P10, P42, P48, P53, P54, PQC, PSA, PerIslam, S02, S03, S11, SCOPUS, SOPODA, SSA, SociolAb, T02, V02.
—BLDSC (8820.095000), IE, Infotrieve, Ingenta. **CCC.**
Published by: Sage Publications Ltd. (Subsidiary of: Sage Publications, Inc.), 1 Oliver's Yard, 55 City Rd, London, EC1Y 1SP, United Kingdom. TEL 44-20-73248500, FAX 44-20-73248600, info@sagepub.co.uk, http://www.uk.sagepub.com/home.nav. adv.: B&W page GBP 400; 130 x 205. **Subscr. in the Americas to:** Sage Publications, Inc., 2455 Teller Rd, Thousand Oaks, CA 91320. TEL 805-499-9774, FAX 805-499-0871, journals@sagepub.com.

320.6025 USA ISSN 1063-3340
H96

THINK TANK DIRECTORY; guide to nonprofit public policy research organizations. Text in English. 1996. irreg., latest 2006, Aug.; 2nd ed. USD 125 (effective 2006). **Document type:** *Directory, Government.* **Description:** Includes name, address, tel and fax, e-mail, website, chief executive officer, mission statement, board members, budget categories, and areas of research interest for over 1500 think tanks.
Published by: Government Research Service, PO Box 2067, Topeka, KS 66601-2067. TEL 785-232-7720, FAX 785-232-1615.

P

322.4 GBR ISSN 0959-5031

THIRD WAY (LONDON); voice of the radical centre. Text in English. 1990. q. GBP 15 domestic; GBP 18 in Europe; GBP 20 elsewhere (effective 2009). bk.rev.; film rev.; video rev.; Website rev. illus. **Document type:** *Magazine, Consumer.* **Description:** A voice of opposition to all forms of authoritarianism, promoting popular democracy and co-operative economics.
Former titles (until 19??): Third Way - Beyond Capitalism and Communism; (until 1990): Third Way
—CCC.
Published by: Third Way Publications Ltd., Rm 407, 12 S Bridge, Edinburg, EH1 1DD, United Kingdom. info@thirdway.eu, http://www.thirdway.eu.

320 USA ISSN 0317-0659
HC59.7

THIRD WORLD FORUM. Text in English. 1975. q. USD 30 (effective 1999). adv. bk.rev. illus. back issues avail. **Document type:** *Bulletin.* **Description:** Covers political changes, building democracy, development and trade. Includes interviews with Third World VIPs.
Indexed: HRIR.
Published by: Association on Third World Affairs, Inc., 1717 K St NW, Ste. 600, Washington, DC 20036-5346. TEL 202-331-8455, FAX 202-785-3605. Ed., Adv. contact Lu Anne Feik. R&P Lorna Hahn. Circ: 2,500.

320 CAN ISSN 1491-2678
L11

THIS MAGAZINE. Text in English. 1966. 6/yr. USD 26.66 domestic; USD 40 foreign (effective 2010). adv. bk.rev. illus. Index. back issues avail.; reprints avail. **Document type:** *Magazine, Consumer.* **Description:** Presents critical, intelligent writing about culture, politics and the arts in Canada.
Former titles (until 1998): This Magazine - Education, Culture, Politics (0381-3746); (until 1973): This Magazine is About Schools (0040-6228)
Related titles: Microfiche ed.: (from MML); Microfilm ed.: (from MML, PQC); Online - full text ed.
Indexed: A22, A26, APC, AltPI, C03, CBCARef, CBPI, CPerI, E08, G08, I05, LeftInd, MEA&I, NPI, P48, PQC, S09.
—CIS, Ingenta. **CCC.**
Published by: Red Maple Foundation, 396-401 Richmond St W, Toronto, ON M5V 3A8, Canada. TEL 416-979-9429, FAX 416-979-1143. Ed. Graham F Scott TEL 416-979-8400. Pub. Lisa Whittington-Hill TEL 416-979-9429. Adv. contact Olivia Tsang TEL 647-430-5888. Circ: 5,000.

328.73 USA

THIS WEEK IN WASHINGTON (ONLINE). Abbreviated title: T W I W. Text in English. 1980. w. (45/yr.). USD 220 to non-members; USD 200 to members (effective 2009). back issues avail. **Document type:** *Newsletter, Trade.* **Description:** Contains updates on legislative action, federal legislation, and personnel changes.
Formerly (until 200?): This Week in Washington (Print) (0743-2437)
Media: Online - full text.
Indexed: A01, P34.
Published by: American Public Human Services Association, 1133 19th St, NW, Ste 400, Washington, DC 20036. TEL 202-682-0100, FAX 202-289-6555, MemberServicesHelpDesk@aphsa.org.

320.5 GBR ISSN 1476-3966

THOMAS PAINE SOCIETY. BULLETIN AND JOURNAL OF RADICAL HISTORY. Variant title: Journal of Radical History. Text in English. 2001. a. GBP 15 domestic to members; EUR 35 in Europe to members; USD 35 elsewhere to members; GBP 5 to non-members (effective 2010). adv. bk.rev. bibl.; illus. back issues avail. **Document type:** *Journal, Academic/Scholarly.* **Description:** Provides information on the life and times of Thomas Paine and his relevance in many respects to today's world, and to make his great life and works better known.

Formed by the merger of (1983-2001): Journal of Radical History (0265-3648); (1990-2001): T P S Bulletin (0965-1411); Which was formerly (1965-1990): Thomas Paine Society. Bulletin (0049-3813)
Indexed: AES, RASB.
Published by: Thomas Paine Society, c/o Barbara Jacobson, Secretary, 19 Charles Rowan House, Margery St, London, WC1X 0EH, United Kingdom. TEL 44-20-78331395, postmaster@thomaspainesocietyuk.org.uk, http://www.thomaspainesocietyuk.org.uk/. Ed. R W Morrell. Circ: 250.

320 IND
THUGLUK. Text in Tamil. 19??. w. **Document type:** *Magazine, Trade.*
Related titles: Online - full text ed.: INR 900 (effective 2011).
Address: 46, Greenways Rd, Chennai, 600 028, India. Ed., Pub. Cho Ramaswamy.

324.2 GUY ISSN 0040-6635
JL689.A8
THUNDER. Text in English. 1950. q. GYD 300. bk.rev.
Published by: People's Progressive Party, Freedom House, Robb St 41, Georgetown, Guyana. Ed. Ralph Ramkarran. Circ: 7,000.

320.531 CHN ISSN 1672-4089
TIANJIN SHI SHEHUI ZHUYI XUEYUAN XUEBAO/TIANJIN INSTITUTE OF SOCIALISM. JOURNAL. Text in Chinese. 2003. q. CNY 5 newsstand/cover (effective 2006). **Document type:** *Journal, Academic/Scholarly.*
Related titles: Online - full text ed.
Published by: Tianjin Shi Shehui Zhuyi Xueyuan, 340, Anshan Xi Dao, Tianjin, 300193, China. TEL 86-22-27381295.

320 IND ISSN 0040-6708
DS785.A1
TIBETAN REVIEW. Text in English. 1968. m. INR 90 domestic; INR 240 in Nepal and Bhutan; INR 950, USD 25, EUR 25, GBP 15 elsewhere; INR 8 per issue (effective 2011). bk.rev. illus. index. 32 p./no. 3 cols./p.; reprints avail. **Document type:** *Magazine, Consumer.* **Description:** Covers news from Tibet, Tibetans in exile, interviews, social, cultural and political commentary, and aspects of Tibetan religion, history, medicine and arts and crafts.
Formerly: Voice of Tibet
Indexed: A01, AmHI, BAS, CA, DIP, H07, HRIR, IBR, IBZ, P34, RASB, T02.
Address: c/o Tibetan SOS Youth Hostel, Sector 14 Ext, Rohini, New Delhi, 110 085, India. TEL 91-11-27860828, FAX 91-11-27569702.

320 SWE ISSN 0040-6759
HX8
TIDEN; socialdemokratisk ide-och debattidskrift. Text in Swedish. 1908. 6/yr. SEK 288; SEK 49 per issue (effective 2011). adv. bk.rev. illus. index. back issues avail. **Document type:** *Magazine, Consumer.* **Description:** Contains social democratic debates and ideas.
Related titles: Online - full text ed.: 1930.
Indexed: MLA-IB, PCI, RASB.
Published by: (Sveriges Socialdemokratiska Arbetareparti/Swedish Social Democratic Labour Party), A i P Media Produktion AB (Subsidiary of: Sveriges Socialdemokratiska Arbetareparti/Swedish Social Democratic Labour Party), Sveavaegen 68, Stockholm, 10560, Sweden. TEL 46-8-7002600, FAX 46-8-4116542, aip@sap.se, http://www.aip.sap.se. Ed. Bo Bernhardsson TEL 46-70-5661196. Adv. contact Joergen Rosengren.

320.52 SWE ISSN 1651-4521
TIDNINGEN C. Text in Swedish. 1980. 4/yr. SEK 100 (effective 2002). adv. **Document type:** *Newspaper, Consumer.*
Formerly (until 2002): Focus (0349-7623); Formed by the merger of (1952-1980): Svensk Politik (0346-220X); (1959-1980): Budkavle till Sveriges Kvinnor (0345-1194)
Related titles: Audio cassette/tape ed.
Indexed: Perlslam, RASB.
Published by: Centerpartiets Riksorganisation, PO Box 2200, Stockholm, 10315, Sweden. TEL 46-8-617-38-00, FAX 46-8-617-38-10. Ed. Eva-Karin Lind. adv.: B&W page SEK 28,500, color page SEK 35,150; trim 250 x 370.

320.5 SWE ISSN 1402-2710
TIDSKRIFT FOER POLITISK FILOSOFI. Text in Swedish. 1997. 3/yr. SEK 150 domestic; SEK 250 elsewhere (effective 2010). back issues avail. **Document type:** *Journal, Academic/Scholarly.* **Description:** Political science as an interdisciplinary field covered partly by economics, law, political science and ethics.
Published by: (Stiftelsen Bokfoerlaget Thales, Stockholms Universitet, Filosofiska Institutionen), Thales (Subsidiary of: Stiftelsen Bokfoerlaget Thales), PO Box 50034, Stockholm, 10405, Sweden. TEL 46-8-7596410, FAX 46-8-152226, info@bokforlagetthales.se. Eds. Magnus Jedenheim-Edling, Jens Johansson.

320 SWE ISSN 0040-6988
TIDSKRIFTEN HEIMDAL. Text in Swedish. 1962. q. SEK 150 membership (effective 2011). adv. bk.rev. illus. **Document type:** *Magazine, Consumer.*
Former titles (until vol.5, 1965): Heimdals Hornstoetar; (until vol.7, 1964): Hornstoetar
Published by: Foereningen Heimdal, c/o Daniel Bergstroem, St. Larsgatan 6, Uppsala, 75002, Sweden. http://www.heimdal.nu. Ed. Robert Vickstroem.

320 FIN ISSN 0782-0674
TIEDEPOLITIIKKA. Text in Finnish. 1976. q. EUR 30 (effective 2005). back issues avail. **Document type:** *Journal, Academic/Scholarly.*
Related titles: Online - full text ed.
Published by: Edistyksellinen Tiedeliitto, Hietaniemenkatu 10 D 3, PO Box 344, Helsinki, 00101, Finland. TEL 358-9-652101, FAX 358-9-662503, tiedeliitto@netlife.fi, http://www.saunalahti.fi/~nl03449/index.htm. Ed. Katriina Jaervinen.

320.532 VNM
TIEN PHONG/VANGUARD. Text in Vietnamese. 1953. w. USD 110 (effective 1992).
Published by: Ho Chi Minh Communist Youth Union, 15 Ho Xuan Huong, Hanoi, Viet Nam. TEL 64031. Ed. Duong Xuan Nam. Circ: 110,000.

324.247 RUS
TIKHVIISKAYA PLOSHCHAD'. Text in Russian. 1990. 6/yr.
Published by: Irkutskaya Organizatsiya Demokraticheskii Soyuz, Mikroraion Pervomaiskii, d 42, kv 80, Irkutsk, 664058, Russian Federation. Ed. Irina Shishkina. Circ: 3,000.

328 GBR ISSN 0082-4399
TIMES GUIDE TO THE HOUSE OF COMMONS; complete survey of Parliament after a General Election. Text in English. 1880. irreg., latest 1997, May. GBP 25 (effective 2000). index. **Document type:** *Directory.*
Published by: Times Books Ltd., Flat 77, 85 Fulham Palace Rd, London, W6 8JA, United Kingdom. TEL 44-181-741-7070, FAX 44-181-307-4440. Ed. Alan Wood. Circ: 7,500.

TO MATSAKONI. *see* SOCIOLOGY

320.52 NLD ISSN 1871-160X
TOCQUEVILLE REEKS. Text in Dutch. 2003. irreg., latest vol.8, 2005. **Document type:** *Monographic series.*
Published by: Edmund Burke Stichting, Postbus 10498, The Hague, 2501 HL, Netherlands. TEL 31-70-3925180, FAX 31-70-3651809.

TOLEDO JOURNAL OF GREAT LAKES' LAW, SCIENCE & POLICY. *see* LAW

TOMAS RIVERA POLICY INSTITUTE. POLICY BRIEF. *see* ETHNIC INTERESTS

TOMPAINE.COMMON SENSE; a journal of opinion. *see* LITERARY AND POLITICAL REVIEWS

TOPICS IN REGULATORY ECONOMICS AND POLICY. *see* BUSINESS AND ECONOMICS—International Development And Assistance

TORIYN MEDEELEL/STATE INFORMATION. *see* PUBLIC ADMINISTRATION

320 ESP ISSN 1136-4343
DP1
TORRE DE LOS LUJANES. Text in Spanish. 1986. irreg.
Formerly (until 1989): Real Sociedad Economica Matritense de Amigos del Pais. Boletin (1136-4408)
Indexed: PhilInd.
—CCC.
Published by: Real Sociedad Economica Matritense de Amigos del Pais, Plaza de la Villa, 2, Madrid, 28005, Spain. TEL 34-91-5418139, http://www.economicamatritense.com/.

TOTALITARISMUS UND DEMOKRATIE. *see* HISTORY—History Of Europe

TOUCHSTONE (CHICAGO); a journal of mere christianity. *see* RELIGIONS AND THEOLOGY—Roman Catholic

320.531 RUS
TOVARISHCH. Text in Russian. 1991. 8/yr. USD 90 foreign (effective 2003). **Document type:** *Newspaper.*
Published by: Gruppa Segodnya, Novyi Arbat 19, k 2211, Moscow, 121090, Russian Federation. TEL 7-095-2510503, FAX 7-095-2038345. Circ: 5,000. **Dist. by:** M K - Periodica, ul Gilyarovskogo 39, Moscow 129110, Russian Federation. TEL 7-095-2845008, FAX 7-095-2813798, info@periodicals.ru, http://www.mkniga.ru; East View Information Services, 10601 Wayzata Blvd, Minneapolis, MN 55305. TEL 952-252-1201, 800-477-1005, FAX 952-252-1202, info@eastview.com, http://www.eastview.com.

320.531 UKR
TOVARYSH. Text in Ukrainian. w. USD 220 in United States.
Published by: Sotsyalisticheskaya Partiya Ukrainy, Ul Klovskii Spusk 14a, Kiev, Ukraine. TEL 290-38-03. **Dist. by:** East View Information Services, 10601 Wayzata Blvd, Minneapolis, MN 55305. TEL 952-252-1201, 800-477-1005, FAX 952-252-1202, info@eastview.com, http://www.eastview.com.

324 USA ISSN 1937-8882
E902
TOWNHALL. Text in English. 2008 (Jan.). m. USD 39.95 (effective 2008). **Document type:** *Magazine, Consumer.* **Description:** Connects the community of America's engaged conservatives through insightful reporting, informed commentary and in-depth information about the blogosphere, talk radio, and television news.
Related titles: Online - full text ed.
Published by: C C M Communications, 104 Woodmont Blvd, Ste 300, Nashville, TN 37205. TEL 615-386-3011, 615-312-4231, FAX 615-312-4277. Ed. Chuck DeFeo. Adv. contact Eric Getzinger TEL 703-247-1237.

320 ESP ISSN 2172-3435
TRABE ATLANTICA. Text in Spanish. 2005. a. **Document type:** *Monographic series, Academic/Scholarly.*
Published by: Ediciones Trabe, C Forncalada, 10 2u A, Asturias, Oviedo 33002, Spain. TEL 34-985-208206, ediciones@trabe.org, http://www.trabe.org/.

TRAMITE PARLAMENTARIO. *see* PUBLIC ADMINISTRATION

330.993005 NZL ISSN 1171-2961
TRANS TASMAN. Variant title: The Trans Tasman Political Letter. Text in English. 1968. w. NZD 597 (effective 2008). back issues avail. **Document type:** *Newsletter.*
Published by: Trans Tasman Media Ltd., PO Box 2197, Christchurch, 8015, New Zealand. TEL 64-3-3653891, FAX 64-3-3653894, jmurray@transtasman.co.nz, http://www.transtasman.co.nz. Circ: 1,000 (paid).

320 ROM ISSN 1583-6592
TRANSCARPATHICA; germanistisches jahrbuch rumaenien. Text in German. 2003. a. **Document type:** *Journal, Academic/Scholarly.*
Published by: Societatea Germanistilor din Romania (S G R)/Gesellscahft der Germanitsen Rumaeniens (G G R), Str Pitar Mos 7-11, Bucharest, 010451, Romania. http://www.ggr.ro.

320.5322 FRA ISSN 2102-0663
TRANSFORM !. Text in French. 200?. s-a. EUR 18 (effective 2009). **Document type:** *Journal, Academic/Scholarly.*
Published by: Espaces Marx, 6 Av. Mathurin Moreau, Paris, Cedex 19 75167, France. TEL 33-1-42174510, FAX 33-1-45359204, Espaces_marx@internatif.org, http://www.espaces-marx.eu.org.

320 339 NLD ISSN 1871-3408
TRANSNATIONAL INSTITUTE. BRIEFING SERIES. Key Title: T N I Briefing Series. Text in English. 2001. irreg., latest 2006.
Published by: Transnational Institute, PO Box 14656, Amsterdam, 1001 LD, Netherlands. TEL 31-20-6626608, FAX 31-20-6757176, tni@tni.org, http://www.tni.org.

320 ITA ISSN 0394-1418
JA18
TRASGRESSIONI; rivista quadrimestrale di cultura politica. Text in Italian. 1986. 3/yr. EUR 18 domestic; EUR 23 foreign (effective 2008). 128 p./no.; back issues avail. **Document type:** *Journal, Academic/Scholarly.* **Description:** Reviews political culture. Aims to contribute to the reconstruction of the European thought in a communitarian, anti-utilitarian direction.
Indexed: PAIS.
Published by: Cooperativa Culturale "La Roccia di Erec", Casella Postale 1292, Florence, FI 50122, Italy. TEL 39-55-2340714. Ed. Marco Tarchi. Circ: 1,000 (paid).

320.531 ESP ISSN 1886-1083
TRASVERSALES. Text in Spanish. 1989. bi-m.
Formerly (until 2005): Iniciativa Socialista (1130-829X)
Related titles: Online - full text ed.
Indexed: AltPI, CA, P42, PAIS, S02, S03, SociolAb, T02.
Published by: Iniciativa Socialista, Apdo. 6088, Madrid, 28080, Spain. insoc@inisoc.org, http://www.inisoc.org/.

324.2 MUS
TRAVAILLEUR. Text in English, French. 1968. fortn. MUR 26, USD 6. adv. bk.rev. bibl.; illus.
Published by: Mauritius People's Progressive Party, PO Box 545, Port Louis, Mauritius. Ed. Teekaran Sibsurun. Circ: 15,000.

TRAYECTORIAS; revista de ciencias sociales de la Universidad Autonoma de Nuevo Leon. *see* SOCIAL SCIENCES: COMPREHENSIVE WORKS

320.531 ARG ISSN 1851-5045
HV6322.3.A7
30,000 REVOLUCIONES. Text in Spanish. 2007. s-a.
Published by: Universidad Popular Madres de Plazo de Mayo, Hipolito Yrigoyen 1584, Buenos Aires, 1089, Argentina. TEL 54-11-43830577, FAX 54-11-49540381, madres@madres.org, http://www.madres.org/index.asp.

320.532 CUB ISSN 0864-1609
TRIBUNA DE LA HABANA; el periodico de la capital de Cuba. Text in Spanish. 1980. w.
Related titles: Online - full text ed.: ISSN 1563-8332.
Published by: Partido Comunista de Cuba, Comite Provincial Ciudad de la Habana, Territorial y General Suarez, Plaza de la Revolucion, Havana, Cuba. TEL 53-78-818021. Ed. Angel Rodriguez Alvarez.

320.5322 COL
TRIBUNA ROJA. Text in Spanish. 1971. q.
Published by: Pro-Maoist Communist Party (MOIR), Apartado Aereo 19042, Bogota, CUND, Colombia. TEL 57-1-243-0371. Ed. Carlos Naranjo. Circ: 300,000.

TRIBUNE; voice of the left. *see* LABOR UNIONS

320 USA ISSN 1081-5112
TRIBUNO DEL PUEBLO. Text in English, Spanish. 1975. m. USD 10 to individuals; USD 15 to institutions. **Document type:** *Newspaper.* **Description:** Provides revolutionary commentary on the issues of the day.
Related titles: ◆ English ed.: People's Tribune. ISSN 1081-4787.
Published by: Tribuno del Peublo, PO Box 3524, Chicago, IL 60654. TEL 312-486-3551. Ed. Richard Monje.

320 SRB ISSN 0041-302X
TRINAESTI MAJ; casopis saveznog sekretarijata za unutresnje poslove. Text in Serbo-Croatian. 1948. bi-m. YUN 40.
Published by: Savezni Sekretarijat za Unutresnje Poslove, Kneza Milosa 92, Postanski Fah 870, Belgrade. Ed. Radoman Zarkovic.

320.531 AUT ISSN 0041-3356
TROTZDEM; das sozialistische Jugendmagazin. Text in German. 1948. 4/yr. adv. bk.rev.; film rev. illus. **Document type:** *Magazine, Consumer.*
Published by: Sozialistische Jugend Oesterreichs/Socialist Youth of Austria, Amtshausgasse 4, Vienna, W 1050, Austria. TEL 43-1-5234123, FAX 43-1-523412385, office@sjoe.at, http://www.sjoe.at. Ed. M Winkler. Circ: 40,000.

320.531 CHE
TROUBLES. Text in French. 1992. irreg. CHF 80. **Document type:** *Bulletin.*
Published by: Commission Socialiste de Solidarite Internationale, Case Postale 343, Geneva 4, 1211, Switzerland. TEL 41-77-582842, FAX 41-77-582842. Circ: 1,000 (paid).

TSENTR EKOLOGICHESKOI POLITIKI ROSSII. BYULLETEN'. *see* CONSERVATION

320 SWE ISSN 1403-7068
➤ **TSENTRAL'NAYA AZIYA I KAVKAZ.** Text in Russian. 1995. bi-m. EUR 130 to individuals; EUR 180 to institutions; EUR 30 per issue (effective 2010). back issues avail. **Document type:** *Journal, Academic/Scholarly.*
Formerly (until 1998): Tsentral'naya Aziya (1402-6627)
Related titles: Online - full text ed.; ◆ English ed.: Central Asia and the Caucasus. ISSN 1404-6091.
Published by: C A & C C Press AB, Hubertusstigen 9, Lulea, 97455, Sweden. TEL 46-70-2321655. Ed. Murad Esenov TEL 46-70-2321655.

324.6 RUS
TSENTRAL'NAYA IZBIRATEL'NAYA KOMISSIYA ROSSIISKOI FEDERATSII. VESTNIK. Text in Russian. m.
Related titles: Microfiche ed.: (from EVP).
Indexed: RASB.
Published by: Vestnik Tsentral'noi Izbiratel'noi Komissii Rossiiskoi Federatsii, Ul Il'inka 10, Moscow, 103012, Russian Federation. TEL 7-095-2069910. **Dist. by:** East View Information Services, 10601 Wayzata Blvd, Minneapolis, MN 55305. TEL 952-252-1201, 800-477-1005, FAX 952-252-1202, info@eastview.com, http://www.eastview.com.

320.5 CHN
TUANJIE BAO/UNITY. Text in Chinese. 3/w. CNY 40.08. **Document type:** *Newspaper, Government.* **Description:** Official newspaper of Kuomintang.
Published by: Tuanjie Baoshe, 84 Donghuangchenggen Nanjie, Beijing, 100006, China. TEL 86-10-5250360. Ed. Yan Tianjia. **Dist. overseas by:** China International Book Trading Corp, 35 Chegongzhuang Xilu, Haidian District, PO Box 399, Beijing 100044, China.

TUMULTES. *see* SOCIOLOGY

320 TUR ISSN 1308-8041
▼ ➤ **TURAN STRATEJIK ARASTIRMALARI MERKEZI**; uluslararasi bilimsel hakemli mevsimlik dergi. Variant title: Turan S A M. Text in Turkish; Text occasionally in Azerbaijani, English. 2009. q. TRY 200 domestic; USD 200 foreign (effective 2011). abstr.; bibl.; illus.; maps; pat.; stat.; tr.mk.; tr.lit. Index. back issues avail.; reprints avail. **Document type:** *Journal, Academic/Scholarly.*
Related titles: CD-ROM ed.; E-mail ed.; Online - full text ed.: ISSN 1309-4033.
Published by: Hakimiyet Gazetesi Matbbasi, Bosna Hersek Mah. Kermes sok. Ahmet Yesevi sit 1/9, Selcuklu, Konya 42250, Turkey. TEL 90-531-8121361, FAX 90-332-2413539. Ed. Elnur Hasan Mikail. Pub. Ali Caglayan. Circ: 100.

➤ **TURKEY BUSINESS FORECAST REPORT.** *see* BUSINESS AND ECONOMICS—Economic Situation And Conditions

320 TUR ISSN 2146-1988
▼ ➤ **TURKISH JOURNAL OF POLITICS.** Text in English. 2010. q. free. bk.rev. abstr.; bibl. back issues avail. **Document type:** *Journal, Academic/Scholarly.* **Description:** Publishes analytical/theoretical articles in the fields of international relations, comparative politics and political science.
Media: Online - full text.
Published by: Fatih University, Social Sciences Institute, 34500, Buyukcekmece, Istanbul, Turkey. TEL 90-212-8663300, FAX 90-212-8663342, http://sbe.fatih.edu.tr/. Ed. Ihsan Yilmaz.

320 TUR ISSN 0544-1943
DR401
TURKISH YEARBOOK OF INTERNATIONAL RELATIONS/ MILLETLERARASI MUNASEBETLER TURK YILLIGI. Text in English. a. bk.rev. abstr.; bibl.; charts; maps. back issues avail.; reprints avail. **Document type:** *Yearbook, Academic/Scholarly.*
Indexed: CA, I13, IBSS, P42, PAIS, PSA, T02.
Published by: Ankara Universitesi, Faculty of Political Sciences, Department of International Affairs, Research Centre for Int. Political and Economic Relations, Ankara, 06100, Turkey. TEL 90-312-3197720, FAX 90-312-3197736, uzgel@politics.ankara.edu.tr, http://www.ankara.edu.tr/political.

323.11924 USA ISSN 1082-6491
E184.A1
TURNING THE TIDE; journal of anti-racist action, research and education. Text in English. 1987. bi-m. USD 16 in North America; USD 26 elsewhere (effective 2005). adv. bk.rev. illus. quarterly index. 24 p./no. 4 cols./p.; back issues avail.; reprints avail. **Document type:** *Newspaper, Consumer.* **Description:** Covers the fight against racism, sexism, and colonialism. Targets youthful activists.
Related titles: Online - full text ed.
Indexed: APW, AltPI, P45.
Published by: Anti-Racist Action L. A., PO Box 1055, Culver City, CA 90232-1055. TEL 310-495-0299, antiracistaction_la@yahoo.com, http://www.antiracist.org. Ed., Pub., R&P, Adv. contact Michael Novick. Circ: 9,000.

320 DEU ISSN 0564-9021
H5
TUTZINGER STUDIEN; Texte und Dokumente zur politischen Bildung. Text in German. 1971-1981; N.S. 1985. irreg. bk.rev. bibl. **Document type:** *Monographic series, Academic/Scholarly.*
Published by: Evangelische Akademie Tutzing, Schlossstr 2-4, Tutzing, 82327, Germany. TEL 49-8158-2510, FAX 49-8158-251137, http://www.ev-akademie-tutzing.de, info@ev-akademie-tutzing.de. Ed. Axel Schwanebeck.

324.2 SWE ISSN 0281-2657
TVAERDRAG. Text in Swedish. 1983. 6/yr. SEK 100 (effective 2011). adv. bibl.; illus. back issues avail. **Document type:** *Magazine, Consumer.* **Description:** Presents articles on political and daily issues of concern to a general readership.
Supersedes: P Information
Published by: Sveriges Socialdemokratiska Ungdomsfoerbund/Swedish Social Democratic Youth League, PO Box 11544, Stockholm, 10061, Sweden. TEL 46-8-7144800, FAX 46-8-7149508, info@ssu.se, http://www.ssu.se. Ed. Daniel Suhonen.

TWENTIETH-CENTURY CHINA. *see* HISTORY—History Of Asia

320.532 GBR ISSN 1758-6437
HX40
▼ ➤ **TWENTIETH CENTURY COMMUNISM**; a journal of international history. Variant title: 20th Century Communism. Text in English. 2009. a. ((May)). GBP 40 to institutions (effective 2009). back issues avail. **Document type:** *Journal, Academic/Scholarly.* **Description:** Provides an international forum for the latest research on the subject and an entry-point into key developments and debates not immediately accessible to English-language historians.
Related titles: Online - full text ed.: (from IngentaConnect).
Indexed: A26, AmH&L, HistAb, I05, S23, T02.
Published by: Lawrence & Wishart Ltd, 99a Wallis Rd, London, E9 5LN, United Kingdom. TEL 44-20-85332506, FAX 44-20-85337369, info@lwbooks.co.uk. Eds. Kevin Morgan, Matthew Worley, Richard Cross.

➤ **TYGODNIK SOLIDARNOSC/SOLIDARITY WEEKLY.** *see* BUSINESS AND ECONOMICS—Economic Situation And Conditions

➤ **THE U A E BUSINESS FORECAST REPORT.** (United Arab Emirates) *see* BUSINESS AND ECONOMICS—Economic Situation And Conditions

320.943 DEU
U I D. (Union in Deutschland) Text in German. fortn. EUR 32; EUR 1 newsstand/cover (effective 2005). **Document type:** *Magazine, Consumer.* **Description:** Provides coverage of events and happenings affecting the Christian Democratic Union political party in Germany.
Indexed: RASB.
Published by: Union Betriebs GmbH, Egermannstr 2, Rheinbach, 53359, Germany. TEL 49-2226-8020, FAX 49-2226-802111, info@ubg-medienzentrum.de, http://www.ubg-medienzentrum.de.

U R P E NEWSLETTER. *see* BUSINESS AND ECONOMICS

320 GBR ISSN 0956-0904
E838
THE U S A AND CANADA (YEAR). Text in English. 1989. triennial. USD 760 per issue (effective 2009). reprints avail. **Document type:** *Directory, Academic/Scholarly.* **Description:** Provides a detailed analytical survey of these neighboring North American nations and of their constituent states, provinces, and territories.
Published by: (Europa Publications Ltd.), Routledge (Subsidiary of: Taylor & Francis Group), 2 Park Sq, Milton Park, Abingdon, Oxon OX14 4RN, United Kingdom. TEL 44-20-70176000, FAX 44-20-70176699, orders@taylorandfrancis.com.

328.73 USA ISSN 0160-9890
JK1011 CODEN: CODIDS
U.S. CONGRESS. CONGRESSIONAL DIRECTORY. (Avail. in 2 eds.: paperbound; clothbound) Text in English. a. USD 30 for paperback ed; USD 43 for clothbound ed. **Document type:** *Directory, Government.*
Related titles: Microform ed.: (from PQC); Online - full text ed.
Published by: U.S. Congress, Office of the Congressional Directory, Rm SH 818, Hart Office Bldg, Washington, DC 20510-6650. TEL 202-224-5241, FAX 202-224-1176. Ed., R&P Kathryn McConnell TEL 202-512-1710. Circ: 100,000. **Subscr. to:** U.S. Government Printing Office, Superintendent of Documents, PO Box 371954, Pittsburgh, PA 15250. TEL 202-512-1800, FAX 202-512-2250, orders@gpo.gov, http://www.access.gpo.gov. **Dist. by:** Bernan Associates, Bernan, 4611-F Assembly Dr., Lanham, MD 20706-4391. TEL 301-459-7666, 301-459-0056.

324.6 USA ISSN 0145-7284
KF4886
U.S. FEDERAL ELECTION COMMISSION. ANNUAL REPORT. Text in English. 1975. a. free. charts; illus.; stat. back issues avail. **Document type:** *Government.* **Description:** Summarizes legal issues and describes F.E.C. programs, internal operations and efforts to administer federal election law.
Related titles: Microfilm ed.; Online - full text ed.
Published by: U.S. Federal Election Commission, 999 E St, N W, Washington, DC 20463. TEL 202-694-1100, 800-424-9530. Ed. Greg Scott. Circ: 1,800.

U.S. NEWS & WORLD REPORT (ONLINE). *see* GENERAL INTEREST PERIODICALS—United States

320 USA ISSN 1931-6534
JK274
U.S. POLICY & POLITICS. Text in English. 200?. irreg. **Document type:** *Monographic series, Consumer.*
Published by: National Student Leadership Conference, 111 W Jackson Blvd, 7th Flr, Chicago, IL 60604. TEL 800-994-6752, FAX 312-765-0081, info@nslcleaders.org, http://www.nslcleaders.org/index.html.

320 USA
UGANDA NEWSLETTER. Text in English. 1968. m. free.
Published by: Embassy of the Republic of Uganda, 5909 16th St, N W, Washington, DC 20011. TEL 202-726-7100. Circ: 3,000.

320 HUN ISSN 1215-1386
UJ MAGYARORSZAG; national edition. Text in Hungarian. 1991. d. HUF 3,480, USD 310 (effective 1998). adv. bk.rev. **Document type:** *Newspaper.* **Description:** Includes articles on politics, culture and science.
Related titles: Regional ed(s).: Uj Magyarorszag (Budapest Edition). ISSN 1215-0185.
Published by: Publica Rt., Blaha Lujza ter 3, PO Box 1410, Budapest, 1085, Hungary. TEL 266-5009, FAX 266-2288. Ed. Laszlo Fabian. Circ: 60,000.

320 CAN ISSN 1923-029X
UKRAINE ANALYST; strategic intelligence on Ukraine's politics and economics. Text in English. 2008. bi-m. USD 100 to individuals; USD 200 to institutions (effective 2010). back issues avail. **Document type:** *Journal, Trade.* **Description:** Devoted to current politics, international affairs, energy, business and trade in Ukraine.
Related titles: Online - full text ed.
Published by: Kuzio Associates, 22 Salisbury Ave, Toronto, ON M4X 1C2, Canada. http://www.taraskuzio.net/ka.html. Ed. Taras Kuzio.

320 AUT
UKRAINISCHE FREIE UNIVERSITAET. STUDIEN ZU NATIONALITATENFRAGEN. Text in German. irreg.
Published by: Ukrainische Freie Universitat, Pienzenauerstr 15, Munchen, 81679, Austria.

320 GBR ISSN 1740-2611
ULSTER NATION; a third way for Ulster. Text in English. 1988. bi-m. GBP 7.50 domestic; EUR 15 in Europe; USD 22 in North America (effective 2009). music rev.; video rev.; Website rev.; bk.rev. illus. **Document type:** *Bulletin.* **Description:** Promotes the identity and culture of the Ulster nation and advocates political independence for Northern Ireland.
Published by: Third Way Publications Ltd., First Fl, 316 Shankill Rd, Belfast, BT13 3AB, United Kingdom. info@thirdway.eu, http://www.thirdway.eu.

320.532 ZAF
UMBSEBENZI; voice of the South African Communist Party. Text in English. 1996. m. ZAR 10,000; USD 15 foreign. **Document type:** *Newsletter.*
Media: Online - full text.
Published by: South African Communist Party, PO Box 1027, Johannesburg, 2000, South Africa. http://www.arc.org.za. Ed. Dale T McKinely.

320 SWE ISSN 1654-2398
UMEAA WORKING PAPERS IN PEACE AND CONFLICT STUDIES. Text in English. 2007. irreg., latest vol.6, 2007. back issues avail. **Document type:** *Monographic series, Academic/Scholarly.*
Media: Online - full content.
Published by: Umeaa Universitet, Statsvetenskapliga Institutionen/ University of Umeaa. Department of Political Science, Samhaellsvetarhuset, Umeaa, 90187, Sweden. TEL 46-90-7865000, FAX 46-90-7866681. Ed. Ramses Amer.

320 SWE ISSN 1654-238X
UMEAA WORKING PAPERS IN POLITICAL SCIENCE. Text in English. 2007. irreg., latest vol.2, 2007. back issues avail. **Document type:** *Monographic series, Academic/Scholarly.*
Media: Online - full content.
Published by: Umeaa Universitet, Statsvetenskapliga Institutionen/ University of Umeaa. Department of Political Science, Samhaellsvetarhuset, Umeaa, 90187, Sweden. TEL 46-90-7865000, FAX 46-90-7866681. Ed. Torbjoern Bergman.

320.9 AUT ISSN 1015-8529
UMFELD; Osterreichische Unabhangige Zeitung. Text in German. 1983. q. EUR 10 domestic; EUR 15 foreign (effective 2003). adv. bk.rev. maps; stat. 40 p./no. 3 cols./p.; **Document type:** *Newspaper, Consumer.*
Formerly: Gruene Demokraten
Published by: Die Gruenen Demokraten, Schulgasse 46, Vienna, 1180, Austria. TEL 43-1-4780170, FAX 43-1-4780170. Ed. Guenter Ofner. Circ: 2,200.

320.532 ZAF ISSN 0814-0693
HX450.5
UMSEBENZI. Text in English. 1985. 6/yr. ZAR 0.50 newsstand/cover. **Description:** News journal of the South African Communist Party.
Indexed: LeftInd.
Published by: (South African Communist Party), Inkululeko Publications, PO Box 1027, Johannesburg, 2000, South Africa. TEL 27-11-339-3644, FAX 27-11-339-6880. Circ: 30,000.

320 CAN ISSN 1712-0934
UNDERCURRENT. Text in English, French. 2004. irreg. free (effective 2011). **Document type:** *Journal, Academic/Scholarly.*
Media: Online - full text.
Indexed: A01, A39, C27, C29, CA, D03, D04, E13, R14, S14, S15, S18, T02. Ed. Paige Morrow.

320 USA ISSN 1556-8512
UNDERSTANDING OUR GOVERNMENT. Variant title: Understanding Our Government. Text in English. 2006. irreg., latest 2006. price varies. back issues avail. **Document type:** *Monographic series, Consumer.*
Related titles: Online - full text ed.
Published by: Greenwood Publishing Group Inc. (Subsidiary of: A B C - C L I O), 88 Post Rd W, PO Box 5007, Westport, CT 06881. TEL 203-226-3571, 800-225-5800, FAX 877-231-6980, info@greenwoodpublishing.com.

320.52 SWE ISSN 1402-3229
UNG CENTER & POLITISK TIDSKRIFT. Text in Swedish. 1996. 5/yr. SEK 160 (effective 2004). adv.
Formed by the merger of (1941-1996): Politisk Tidskrift (0032-3489); (1921-1996): Ung Center (0346-3508); Which was formerly (until 1964): S L U - Bladet; (until 1927): By och Bygd
Related titles: Audio cassette/tape ed.
Published by: Centerpartiets Ungdomsfoerbund, Stora Nygatan 4, PO Box 2200, Stockholm, 10315, Sweden. TEL 46-8-6173800, FAX 46-8-6173810, cuf@centerpartiet.se, http://www.cuf.se. Ed. Dan Pettersson.

320 DEU ISSN 0946-6878
UNION. Text in German. 1948. q. EUR 10; EUR 2.50 newsstand/cover (effective 2009). adv. bk.rev. **Document type:** *Magazine, Consumer.*
Former titles (until 1990): Deutsches Monatsblatt. Ausgabe A (0721-233X); (until 196?): Deutsches Monatsblatt (0721-3697)
Related titles: Regional ed(s).: Union. Ausgabe Schleswig-Holstein. ISSN 0946-6886. 1954; Union. Ausgabe Brandenburg. ISSN 0946-6894. 199?; Union. Ausgabe Baden-Wuerttemberg. ISSN 0946-6908. 19??; Union. Ausgabe Niedersachsen. ISSN 0946-6916. 195?; Union. Ausgabe Bremen. ISSN 0946-6924. 195?; Union. Ausgabe Hessen. ISSN 0946-6932. 1954; Union. Ausgabe Thueringen. ISSN 0946-7041. 199?; Union. Ausgabe Nordrhein-Westfalen. ISSN 0946-6959. 19??; Union. Ausgabe Saar. ISSN 0946-6967. 19??; Union. Ausgabe Hamburg. ISSN 0946-6975. 19??; Union. Ausgabe Mecklenburg-Vorpommern. ISSN 0946-6991. 199?; Union. Ausgabe Sachsen. ISSN 0946-7025. 199?; Union. Ausgabe Sachsen-Anhalt. ISSN 0946-7033. 199?; Union. Ausgabe Berlin. ISSN 0946-6940. 1954.
Published by: (Christlich-Demokratische Union (CDU)), BurdaYukom Publishing GmbH (Subsidiary of: Hubert Burda Media Holding GmbH & Co. KG), Konrad-Zuse-Platz 11, Munich, 81829, Germany. TEL 49-89-306200, FAX 49-89-30620100, info@burdayukom.de, http://www.yukom.de. adv.: color page EUR 21,500. Circ: 520,000 (controlled).

UNION DEMOCRACY REVIEW. *see* LABOR UNIONS

320.972 MEX
LA UNION POLITICA. Text in Spanish. 1993. d. MXN 7,000; USD 70 foreign. adv. back issues avail. **Document type:** *Newspaper, Consumer.*
Published by: Union Politica, Ave. VICENTE GUERRERO 77, Col Tezontepec, Cuernavaca, MOR 62250, Mexico. Circ: 10,000.

324.245 ITA ISSN 0391-7002
L'UNITA. Text in Italian. 1924. d. adv. bk.rev.; film rev.; play rev. bibl.; charts; illus.; tr.lit. **Document type:** *Newspaper, Consumer.*
Related titles: Microfilm ed.; Online - full text ed.
Indexed: RASB.
Published by: Nuova Iniziativa Editoriale SpA, Via dei Due Macelli 23/13, Rome, 00187, Italy. TEL 39-06-699961, FAX 39-06-69996217, unitaedi@unita.it. Eds. Claudio Petruccioli, Luca Pavolini. Circ: 137,000.

322.4 CAN ISSN 1718-1178
UNITE. Text in French. 1992. m. **Document type:** *Magazine, Consumer.*
Published by: Conseil Central du Montreal Metropolitain (C S N), 1601 Av. de Lorimier, Montreal, PQ H2K 4M5, Canada. TEL 514-598-2021, FAX 514-598-2020, http://www.ccmm-csn.qc.ca.

320 MYS
UNITED MALAYS NATIONAL ORGANISATION. ANNUAL REPORT. Text in English. 1949. a. free to party delegates. **Document type:** *Corporate.*
Formerly: United Malays National Organisation. Penvata
Published by: United Malays National Organisation, Tingkat 38 Menara Dato Oun, Jalan Tun Ismail, Kuala Lumpur, 50480, Malaysia. TEL 60-3-2939511. Circ: 3,000.

320 USA
UNITED NATIONS PUBLICATIONS. Text in English. 1982. bi-m. free. **Document type:** *Bulletin.*
Formerly: New United Nations Publications (0108-1829)
Indexed: RASB.

P

Address: 2 United Nations Plaza, Rm DC2-853, New York, NY 10017. TEL 212-963-8302, 800-253-9646, FAX 212-963-3489, publications@un.org, unpubli@unog.ch, https://unp.un.org.

THE UNITED STATES GOVERNMENT INTERNET DIRECTORY. *see* PUBLIC ADMINISTRATION

320.9 USA ISSN 0092-1904
JK421
UNITED STATES GOVERNMENT MANUAL. Text in English. 1935. a. USD 29 per issue domestic; USD 40.60 per issue foreign (effective 2009). back issues avail. **Document type:** *Directory, Government.* **Description:** Provides information on the agencies of the legislative, judicial, and executive branches.
Former titles (until 1974): United States Government Organization Manual (0083-1174); (until 1949): United States Government Manual (0892-9149)
Related titles: Diskette ed.; Microfilm ed.: (from BHP); Microform ed.: (from BHP, PQC); Online - full text ed.: free (effective 2009).
—BLDSC (9099.295000), CASDDS, Linda Hall.
Published by: National Archives and Records Administration, U.S. Office of the Federal Register, 8601 Adelphi Rd, College Park, MD 20740. TEL 202-741-6000, FAX 202-741-6012, fedreg.info@nara.gov, http://www.federalregister.gov. **Dist. by:** Bernan Associates, Bernan, 4611-F Assembly Dr., Lanham, MD 20706-4391.

320 USA ISSN 1932-412X
JZ5524.U55
UNITED STATES INSTITUTE OF PEACE. SPECIAL REPORT. Text in English. 199?. irreg. **Document type:** *Report, Trade.*
Published by: United States Institute of Peace, 1200 17th St NW, Washington, DC 20036. TEL 202-457-1700, FAX 202-429-6063.

320.5 NZL ISSN 1176-9327
UNITY. Text in English. 1939. 11/yr. illus. **Document type:** *Journal, Academic/Scholarly.* **Description:** Deals with Communism in the country.
Former titles (until 2005): Socialist Worker Monthly Review (1176-0559); (until 2002): Socialist Worker; (until 1995): Workers Voice (1171-2953); (until 1991): People's Voice (0048-3354); (until 1989): New Zealand People's Voice; (until 1967): People's Voice; Which incorporated (1941-1943): In Print; Which incorporated: Unity
Indexed: RASB.
—CCC.
Published by: Socialist Worker, PO Box 13-685, Auckland, New Zealand. TEL 64-9-6343984, socialist-worker@pl.net.

UNIVERSAL JUSTICE. *see* LAW

320.97287 PAN
UNIVERSIDAD DE PANAMA. FACULTAD DE DERECHO Y CIENCIAS POLITICAS. CUADERNOS. Text in Spanish. 1960. irreg.
Published by: Universidad de Panama, Facultad de Derecho y Ciencias Politicas, c/o Oficina de Informacion y Publicaciones, Panama City, Panama.

UNIVERSIDAD PONTIFICIA BOLIVARIANA. FACULTAD DE DERECHO Y CIENCIAS POLITICAS. REVISTA. *see* LAW

320 DEU ISSN 1867-7614
UNIVERSITAET DUISBURG-ESSEN. INSTITUT FUER POLITIKWISSENSCHAFT. SCHRIFTENREIHE. Variant title: Schriftenreihe des Instituts fuer Politikwissenschaft der Universitaet Duisburg-Essen. Text in German. 2007. irreg., latest vol.3, 2010. price varies. **Document type:** *Monographic series, Academic/Scholarly.*
Published by: (Universitaet Duisburg-Essen, Institut fuer Politikwissenschaft), Tectum Wissenschaftsverlag Marburg, Biegenstr 4, Marburg, 35037, Germany. TEL 49-6421-481523, FAX 49-6421-43470, email@tectum-verlag.de.

321.8 NOR ISSN 1504-6907
➤ **UNIVERSITETET I OSLO. ARENA - CENTRE FOR EUROPEAN STUDIES. RECON ONLINE WORKING PAPER.** (Advanced Research on the Europeanisation of the Nation State. Reconstituting Democracy in Europe) Text in English. 2007. irreg., latest vol.17, 2007. back issues avail. **Document type:** *Monographic series, Academic/Scholarly.*
Media: Online - full content.
Indexed: P42.
Published by: Universitetet i Oslo, ARENA - Senter for Europaforskning/ University of Oslo, ARENA - Centre for European Studies, PO Box 1143, Blindern, Oslo, 0318, Norway. TEL 47-22-858700, FAX 47-22-858710, arena@arena.uio.no, http://www.arena.uio.no. Ed. Erik O Eriksen.

320.6 GBR
UNIVERSITY OF BIRMINGHAM. SCHOOL OF PUBLIC POLICY. OCCASIONAL PAPERS. Text in English. 1995. irreg. price varies. **Document type:** *Monographic series.*
Published by: University of Birmingham, School of Public Policy, University Of Birmingham, Edgbaston, Birmingham, Worcs B15 2TT, United Kingdom. TEL 0121-4146210, FAX 0121-4147051.

UNIVERSITY OF DENVER JOURNAL. *see* COLLEGE AND ALUMNI

320 GBR ISSN 1363-7177
UNIVERSITY OF LEICESTER DISCUSSION PAPERS IN POLITICS. Text in English. 1991. irreg. **Document type:** *Monographic series, Academic/Scholarly.*
Published by: University of Leicester, Department of Politics and International Relations, University Rd, Leicester, Leics LE1 7RH, United Kingdom. TEL 44-116-2522702, FAX 44-116-2525082, politics@le.ac.uk, http://www.le.ac.uk/po/.

UNIVERSITY OF PETROSANI. SOCIAL SCIENCES. ANNALS. *see* SOCIAL SCIENCES: COMPREHENSIVE WORKS

320 AUS ISSN 1446-3814
UNIVERSITY OF SYDNEY. SCHOOL OF ECONOMICS AND POLITICAL SCIENCE. WORKING PAPERS. DISCIPLINE OF POLITICAL ECONOMY. Text in English. 2000. irreg. price varies. **Document type:** *Journal, Academic/Scholarly.*
Supersedes in part (in 2000): University of Sydney. Department of Economics. Working Papers in Economics (1446-392X)
Media: Online - full content.
Published by: University of Sydney, Faculty of Economics and Business, Level 2, Merewether Bldg (H69), Sydney, NSW 2006, Australia. TEL 61-2-90365356, FAX 61-2-93514567, f.stilwell@econ.usyd.edu.au, http://www.econ.usyd.edu.au/. R&P Kerrie Legge TEL 61-2-9351-6625.

320 USA ISSN 0196-0369
UNIVERSITY OF TEXAS, AUSTIN. LYNDON B. JOHNSON SCHOOL OF PUBLIC AFFAIRS. POLICY RESEARCH PROJECT REPORT SERIES. Text in English. 1971. irreg. charts; stat. back issues avail. **Document type:** *Monographic series, Academic/Scholarly.*
Former titles (until 197?): University of Texas at Austin. Lyndon B. Johnson School of Public Affairs. Policy Research Project Report; University of Texas at Austin. Lyndon B. Johnson School of Public Affairs. Seminar Research Report
Published by: University of Texas at Austin, Lyndon B. Johnson School of Public Affairs, PO Box Y, Austin, TX 78713. TEL 512-471-3200, lbjdeansoffice@austin.utexas.edu, http://www.utexas.edu/lbj/.

UNIVERSITY OF TOKUSHIMA. SOCIAL SCIENCE RESEARCH. *see* SOCIAL SCIENCES: COMPREHENSIVE WORKS

320 GBR
UNIVERSITY OF YORK. DEPARTMENT OF POLITICS. WORKING PAPER. Text in English. 1994. irreg., latest vol.23, 2006. GBP 6.50 per issue (effective 2009). back issues avail. **Document type:** *Monographic series, Academic/Scholarly.* **Description:** Contains working papers that reflects the broader research concerns of the department.
Published by: University of York, Department of Politics, Derwent College, Heslington, York, N W Yorks YO10 5DD, United Kingdom. TEL 44-1904 433542, FAX 44-1904-433563, politics@york.ac.uk. Ed. Mark Beeson TEL 44-1904-433556.

320.972 MEX
UNIVERSO DEL BUHO. Text in Spanish. 2000. m.
Address: Fuegp 610, Col Jardines del Pedregal, Del Alvaro Obregon, Mexico, D.F. 01090, Mexico. TEL 52-5-568-4504, buhocult@hotmail.com. Ed. Rene Aviles Fabila. Circ: 10,000.

UNIWERSYTET SLASKI W KATOWICACH. PRACE NAUKOWE. Z PROBLEMATYKI PRAWA PRACY I POLITYKI SOCJALNEJ. *see* LAW

320 DEU
UNSER DORFBLAETTCHEN. Text in German. 1984. 7/yr. **Document type:** *Newsletter.*
Published by: S P D Ortsverein Erkeln, Gelle Breite 2, Brakel, 33034, Germany. TEL 49-5272-8290, FAX 49-5272-355923. Ed. Manfred Kuhlewind. Circ: 300.

320 DEU
UNSERE STADT. Text in German. 1975. 3/yr. free. adv. **Document type:** *Bulletin.*
Published by: S P D Stadtverband Landau, Karl Sauer Str 8, Landau In Der Pfalz, 76829, Germany. TEL 49-6341-32565. Ed. Elisabeth Morawietz.

UNTERRICHT WIRTSCHAFT UND POLITIK. *see* EDUCATION—Teaching Methods And Curriculum

320 CAN ISSN 1718-0872
UPPING THE ANTI; a journal of theory and action. Text in English. 2005. 3/yr. **Document type:** *Journal, Consumer.*
Indexed: AltPI, LeftInd.
Published by: Autonomy & Solidarity Network, PO Box 10571, Toronto, ON M6H 4H9, Canada. http://auto_sol.tao.ca.

320 USA ISSN 1067-9065
URBAN AFFAIRS (NEWARK). Text in English. 1971. 5/yr. **Document type:** *Newsletter, Consumer.*
Formerly (until 1991): Urban Affairs Association Communication
Published by: Urban Affairs Association, 298 Graham Hall, University of Delaware, Newark, DE 19716.

320.532 ESP ISSN 1133-567X
JN8395.C6
UTOPIAS - NUESTRA BANDERA. Text in Spanish. 1937. q. EUR 24 domestic; EUR 30 in Europe and the Americas; EUR 48 elsewhere (effective 2010). 160 p./no.; **Document type:** *Magazine, Consumer.* **Description:** Contributes to the renovation of the ideas of socialism and social progress.
Supersedes (in 1993): Nuestra Bandera (0210-458X)
Indexed: RASB.
Published by: Partido Comunista de Espana, C Olimpo 35, Madrid, 28043, Spain. TEL 34-91-3004696, FAX 34-91-3611774. Ed. Pedro Marset. **Dist. by:** Asociacion de Revistas Culturales de Espana, C Covarruvias 9 2o. Derecha, Madrid 28010, Spain. TEL 34-91-3086066, FAX 34-91-3199267, info@arce.es, http://www.arce.es/.

302 DEU ISSN 1860-8957
UTOPIE UND ALTERNATIVE. Text in German. 2005. irreg., latest vol.3, 2008. price varies. **Document type:** *Monographic series, Academic/ Scholarly.*
Published by: Verlag Dr. Kovac, Leverkusenstr 13, Hamburg, 22761, Germany. TEL 49-40-3988800, FAX 49-40-39888055, info@verlagdrkovac.de. Ed. Andreas Heyer.

320.5 SWE ISSN 0346-3788
UTSIKT. Text in Swedish. 1935. irreg. (4-5/yr.). SEK 100 (effective 1990). adv. bk.rev. illus.
Former titles (until 1956): Folkpartiet; (until 1937): Folkpartiet i Riksdagen och Riket
Published by: Folkpartiet/Swedish Liberal Party, Fack 6508, Stockholm, 11383, Sweden. FAX 08-349591. Ed. Anette Britalk. Circ: 65,000.

322.4 NOR ISSN 1503-8386
UTVEIER. Text in Norwegian; Text occasionally in English. 2004. q. NOK 100 to individuals; NOK 200 to institutions (effective 2006). back issues avail. **Document type:** *Magazine, Consumer.*
Related titles: Online - full text ed.: ISSN 0809-8956. 2004.
Published by: Attac Norge, Solidaritetshuset, Osterhausgate 27, Oslo, 0183, Norway. TEL 47-22-989304, FAX 47-22-989301, attac@attac.no. Ed. Marte Nilsen.

320 UZB
UZBEKISTON RESPUBLIKASI KHIKUMATINING KARORLARY TUPLAMI. Text in Russian. m. USD 235 in United States (effective 2000).
Published by: President's Administration, Ul Turaba Tula 51, Tashkent, 700000, Uzbekistan. TEL 139-82-73. **Dist. by:** East View Information Services, 10601 Wayzata Blvd, Minneapolis, MN 55305. TEL 952-252-1201, 800-477-1005, FAX 952-252-1202, info@eastview.com, http://www.eastview.com.

320 SWE ISSN 1101-9182
VAENSTERPRESS. Text in Swedish. 1972. 16/yr. SEK 150 (effective 2001). 12 p./no.; **Document type:** *Newspaper.*
Former titles (until 1991): Nytt fraan Vensterpartiet; (until 1990, vol.5): V P K - Information
Published by: Vaensterpartiet, Kungsgatan 84, Stockholm, 11227, Sweden. TEL 46-8-617-69-75, FAX 46-8-653-23-85. Ed. Boerje Graaf. Circ: 12,000.

320 LAO
VALASAN PATHET LAO. Text in Laotian. q. illus.
Address: 80 rue Sethathirath, BP 989, Vientiane, Laos. TEL 2405. Circ: 2,000.

320 LTU ISSN 1392-4559
KKJ5007
VALSTYBES ZINIOS. Text in Lithuanian. 96/yr. USD 445 in United States.
Address: Gedimino 53, Vilnius, 2000, Lithuania. TEL 370-2-622927. Ed. Z Dautartas. **Dist. by:** East View Information Services, 10601 Wayzata Blvd, Minneapolis, MN 55305. TEL 952-252-1201, 800-477-1005, FAX 952-252-1202, info@eastview.com, http:// www.eastview.com.

321.51 GBR ISSN 0950-5229
VANGUARD. Text in English. 1987. q. GBP 12 domestic for 8 nos.; GBP 15 in Europe for 8 nos.; GBP 21 elsewhere for 8 nos. adv. bk.rev. back issues avail. **Document type:** *Bulletin.*
Indexed: CPerI, G08.
Published by: (National Democrats), Vanguard Publications, PO Box 2269, London, E6 3RF, United Kingdom. TEL 44-181-471-6872, FAX 44-181-592-3009. Ed. Stephen Ebbs. Adv. contact Ian Anderson. Circ: 8,000.

320 BRA
VANGUARDA. Text in Portuguese. 1993. bi-m. BRL 2,400.
Published by: Editora Vanguarda, Rua Rocha Miranda 99-201, Usini Rio De Janeiro, RJ 20530-000, Brazil. Ed. Hector Duarte Filho.

320.532 CUB ISSN 0864-098X
VANGUARDIA. Text in Spanish. 1962. w. back issues avail.
Related titles: Online - full text ed.: Vanguardia Web. ISSN 1607-5900. 2000.
Published by: Partido Comunista de Cuba, Comite Provincial Villa Clara, C. Cespedes No. 5, entre Placido y Maceo, Santa Clara, Villa Clara, 50100, Cuba. TEL 53-42-204545, FAX 53-42-206224, cip218@cip.etecsa.cu, http://www.vanguardia.cubaweb.cu/. Ed. Rayma Elena Hernandez.

320 NPL
VASHUDHA. Text in English. m. **Description:** Covers social, political and economic affairs.
Published by: T.L. Shrestha, Ed. & Pub., Makhan, Kathmandu, Nepal.

320 RUS
VEDOMOSTI FEDERAL'NOGO SOBRANIYA ROSSIISKOI FEDERATSII. Text in Russian. 36/yr. USD 269.95 in United States.
Indexed: RASB.
Published by: Gosudarstvennaya Duma, Okhotnyi ryad 1, Moscow, 103001, Russian Federation. TEL 7-095-2927999. **Dist. by:** East View Information Services, 10601 Wayzata Blvd, Minneapolis, MN 55305. TEL 952-252-1201, 800-477-1005, FAX 952-252-1202, info@eastview.com, http://www.eastview.com.

320 LTU
VEDOMOSTI LITOVSKOI RESPUBLIKI. Text in Russian. 36/yr. USD 339 in United States.
Published by: Izdatel'stvo Valstybes Zinios, Gedimino 53, Vilnius, 2000, Lithuania. TEL 3702-22-61-92, FAX 3702-22-62-06. Ed. Z Dautartas. **Dist. by:** East View Information Services, 10601 Wayzata Blvd, Minneapolis, MN 55305. TEL 952-252-1201, 800-477-1005, FAX 952-252-1202, info@eastview.com, http://www.eastview.com.

320 TKM ISSN 0206-0388
VEDOMOSTI MEDZHLISA TURKMENISTANA. Text in Russian. q. USD 159 in United States.
Indexed: RASB.
Published by: President Administration, Ashgabat, 744000, Turkmenistan. **Dist. by:** East View Information Services, 10601 Wayzata Blvd, Minneapolis, MN 55305. TEL 952-252-1201, 800-477-1005, FAX 952-252-1202, info@eastview.com, http:// www.eastview.com.

320 RUS
VEDOMOSTI MOSKOVSKOI DUMY. Text in Russian. bi-m. USD 75 in United States.
Indexed: RASB.
Published by: Moskovskaya Gorodskaya Duma, Ul Petrovka 22, Moscow, 101498, Russian Federation. TEL 7-095-9281244. **Dist. by:** East View Information Services, 10601 Wayzata Blvd, Minneapolis, MN 55305. TEL 952-252-1201, 800-477-1005, FAX 952-252-1202, info@eastview.com, http://www.eastview.com.

320 RUS
VEDOMOSTI VERKHOVNOGO SOVETA TATARSTANA. Text in Russian. m. USD 149 in United States.
Indexed: RASB.
Address: Ul N Ershova 31-b, Kazan, 420045, Russian Federation. **Dist. by:** East View Information Services, 10601 Wayzata Blvd, Minneapolis, MN 55305. TEL 952-252-1201, 800-477-1005, FAX 952-252-1202, info@eastview.com, http://www.eastview.com.

320 330 VEN
VENEZUELA ANALITICA. Text in Spanish. 1996. m. **Description:** Covers politics, economics, international relations, culture and other topics for people interested in Latin America and Venezuela.
Media: Online - full text.
Published by: Venezuela Analitica Editores, Ave Francisco de Miranda Piso 10, Oficina 10-C, Caracas, Venezuela. editorva@analitica.com, http://www.analitica.com/. Ed. Emilio Figueredo.

VENEZUELA BUSINESS FORECAST REPORT. *see* BUSINESS AND ECONOMICS—Economic Situation And Conditions

320 DEU
VERBAND DEUTSCHER ARCHIVARINNEN UND ARCHIVARE. FACHGRUPPE 6. MITTEILUNGEN. Text in German. 1977. a. **Document type:** *Journal, Academic/Scholarly.*
Former titles: Verein Deutscher Archivare. Fachgruppe 6. Mitteilungen (0944-4513); (until 1991): Parlaments- und Parteistiftungsarchivare Berichten (0933-6958)

Published by: Verband Deutscher Archivarinnen und Archivare. Fachgruppe 6: Archive der Parlamente, Politischen Parteien, Stiftungen und Verbaende, c/o Guenter Buchstab, Rathausallee 12, Sankt Augustin, 53757, Germany. TEL 49-2241-246210, FAX 49-2241-246669, guenter.buchstab@kas.de, http://www.vda.archiv.net. Ed. Guenter Buchstab. Circ: 400.

320 NOR ISSN 1503-4879
VERDENSMAGASINET X; tidsskrift for solidaritetsbevegelsen. Text in Norwegian. 1992. bi-m. NOK 240 in Scandinavia to individuals; NOK 270 elsewhere to individuals; NOK 300 to institutions; NOK 180 to students (effective 2003). adv.
Formerly (until 2002): 3. Verden Magasinet X (0803-723X); Which was formed by the merger of (1979-1992): Latin-Amerika Idag (0800-5516); (1978-1992): Afrika-informasjon (0332-6241); (1986-1992): Perspektiv (0801-6224); Incorporated (1983-1992): U-nytt (0805-7621)
Related titles: Online - full text ed.
Address: c/o Solidarity House, Osterhausgate 27, Oslo, 0183, Norway. TEL 47-22-989330, FAX 47-22-989301. Ed. Aksel Bolle. adv.: B&W page NOK 6,500, color page NOK 8,060; 205 x 295. Circ: 4,000. **Co-publishers:** Fellesraadet for Afrika/The Norwegian Council for Africa; Utviklingsfondet/The Development Fund; Studenternes og Akademikernes Internasjonale Hjelpefond; Latin-Amerika Grupperne i Norge.

320 DEU ISSN 0083-5676
VERFASSUNG UND VERFASSUNGSWIRKLICHKEIT. Text in German. 1966. irreg., latest vol.12, 1978. price varies. adv. bk.rev. reprints avail. **Document type:** *Monographic series, Academic/Scholarly.*
Published by: Duncker und Humblot GmbH, Carl-Heinrich-Becker-Weg 9, Berlin, 12165, Germany. TEL 49-30-7900060, FAX 49-30-79000631, verlag@duncker-humblot.de. Ed. Werner Kaltefleiter.

320 AUT ISSN 1814-5671
VERGLEICHENDE GESELLSCHAFTSGESCHICHTE UND POLITISCHE IDEENGESCHICHTE. Text in German. 1980. irreg., latest vol.21, 2008. price varies. **Document type:** *Monographic series, Academic/Scholarly.*
Formerly (until 1991): Vergleichende Gesellschaftsgeschichte und Politische Ideengeschichte der Neuzeit (1812-8084)
Published by: Wilhelm Braumueller Universitaets-Verlagsbuchhandlung GmbH, Servitengasse 5, Vienna, 1090, Austria. TEL 43-1-3191159, FAX 43-1-3102805, office@braumueller.at. Eds. Anton Pelinka, Helmut Reinalter.

320 MEX ISSN 0188-8242
P94.6 CODEN: VERSFV
VERSION; estudios de comunicacion y politica. Text in Spanish. 1991. a. back issues avail. **Document type:** *Monographic series, Academic/Scholarly.*
Indexed: C01, SociolAb.
Published by: Universidad Autonoma Metropolitana - Xochimilco, Departamento de Educacion y Comunicacion, Calzada del Hueso, 1100, Col. Villa Quietud, Mexico, D.F., 04961, Mexico. TEL 52-55-57235444, version@cueyatl.uam.mx, http://www.xoc.uam.mx/uam/divisiones/csh/decweb/.

320 ITA ISSN 1972-2583
VERSO SUD. Text in Italian. 2007. m. **Document type:** *Magazine, Consumer.*
Published by: Fondazione Marincola Politi, Via Verdi 5, Soverato, CZ, Italy. TEL 39-0967-530182, http://www.fondazionemarincolapoliti.it.

VERTIGO; la revue electronique en sciences de l'environnement. *see* ENVIRONMENTAL STUDIES

VI MAENSKOR. *see* WOMEN'S INTERESTS

320 TWN ISSN 0582-9860
AP95.C4
VICTORIOUS. Key Title: Shengli zhi Guang. Text mainly in Chinese; Text occasionally in English. 1953. m. TWD 600; USD 67 in Hong Kong; USD 75 in Asia & the Pacific; USD 83 elsewhere. adv. bk.rev. illus.
Formerly (until 1984): Torch of Victory
Published by: New China Publication Service/Hsin Chung-kuo Ch'u Pan She, 7F, 3 Hsinyi Rd Sec 1, Taipei, Taiwan. TEL 866-2-396-9856. Ed. Kao Chuan Hsi. Circ: 30,000.

321 ESP ISSN 1133-5637
VIENTO SUR. Text in Spanish. 1992. bi-m. **Document type:** *Magazine, Consumer.*
Indexed: PhilInd.
Address: Embajadores, 24 1o. Izq., Madrid, 28012, Spain. http://nodo50.org/viento_sur.

VIETNAM BUSINESS FORECAST REPORT. *see* BUSINESS AND ECONOMICS—Economic Situation And Conditions

VIETNAM'S URGENT ISSUES. *see* SOCIAL SERVICES AND WELFARE

320.6 AUS ISSN 1838-9066
▼ ➤ **VIEWPOINT**; perspectives on public policy. Text in English. 2009. 3/yr. AUD 40.75; AUD 12.50 per issue (effective 2011). adv. back issues avail. **Document type:** *Magazine, Consumer.* **Description:** Aims to inform and influence policy makers on issues to be discussed.
Related titles: Online - full text ed.
Published by: Australian Christian Lobby, 4 Campion St, Deakin, ACT 2600, Australia. TEL 61-2-62590431, FAX 61-2-62590462, natoffice@acl.org.au, http://australianchristianlobby.org.au/. Ed., Adv. contact Paul O'Rourke.

320.9 GBR ISSN 0042-5834
VIEWPOINT (LONDON, 1965). Text in English. 1965. q. bk.rev. illus. **Document type:** *Bulletin.* **Description:** Political review with particular emphasis on corporatism, freemasonry, and subversion of the social order.
Published by: Delane Press, 157 Vicarage Rd, London, E10 5DU, United Kingdom. defence@smartgroups.com. Ed., Pub. Ronald King. Circ: (controlled).

320 USA ISSN 1936-1491
VIEWPOINT ON PUBLIC ISSUES. Text in English. 200?. d. free (effective 2007). **Document type:** *Newsletter, Consumer.*
Related titles: Online - full text ed.: ISSN 1936-1505.
Published by: Buckeye Institute for Public Policy Solutions, 88 E Broad St, Ste 1120, Columbus, OH 43215. TEL 614-224-4422, FAX 614-224-4644, buckeye@buckeyeinstitute.org, http://www.buckeyeinstitute.org.

320.51 USA
VIRGINIA LIBERTY. Text in English. 1985. bi-m. USD 25 (effective 2000). adv. bk.rev.; film rev.; music rev.; tel.rev.; video rev. 8 p./no.; back issues avail. **Document type:** *Newsletter, Consumer.* **Description:** Publishes news and commentary of interest to libertarians in and around Virginia.
Published by: Libertarian Party of Virginia, PO Box 28263, Richmond, VA 23228-0263. TEL 703-715-6230. Ed. Stew Engle. Adv. contact Marc Montoni. Circ: 1,200.

320.6 USA ISSN 2150-3206
VIRGINIA POLICY REVIEW. Text in English. 2008. 3/yr. free (effective 2009). back issues avail. **Document type:** *Magazine, Trade.* **Description:** Features information on public policy for the University of Virginia.
Related titles: Online - full text ed.: ISSN 2150-3214. free (effective 2009).
Published by: The Virginia Policy Review, 2 E Lawn, Charlottesville, VA 22903. Ed. Xiao Wang.

320 USA ISSN 1056-6368
E185.5
VITAL ISSUES; the journal of African American speeches. Variant title: Journal of African American Speeches. Text in English. 1950-1984; N.S. 1991. q. USD 49 (effective 2010). adv. bibl.; charts; illus. index. reprints avail. **Document type:** *Journal, Academic/Scholarly.* **Description:** Provides from all disciplines, this publication exposes the breadth of Black rhetoric. Including dozens of addresses from a wide spectrum of persons, events, and topics, this publication fills an enormous gap by compiling the words of African American leaders. Resource for leaders, policy makers, youth, researchers, and the general audience.
Indexed: IIBP.
Published by: The Bethune - DuBois Institute, 8630 Featon St, Ste 925, Silver Spring, MD 20910. TEL 301-562-8300, FAX 301-562-8303, info@bethune-dubois.org, http://www.bethune-dubois.org. Eds. A Peter Bailey, Teta V Banks. Circ: 5,000.

VIZIER. *see* RELIGIONS AND THEOLOGY

320 RUS
VLAST'. Text in Russian. m. USD 129.95 in United States.
Indexed: RASB.
Address: Gogolevskii bulv 10, str 1, Moscow, 121019, Russian Federation. TEL 7-095-2029331, FAX 7-095-2029331. Ed. V D Dzodziev. **Dist. by:** East View Information Services, 10601 Wayzata Blvd, Minneapolis, MN 55305. TEL 952-252-1201, 800-477-1005, FAX 952-252-1202, info@eastview.com, http://www.eastview.com.

VLASTIVEDNE MUZEUM V OLOMOUCI. ZPRAVY. *see* HISTORY—History Of Europe

324.2 ITA
LA VOCE DELLE VOCI. Text in Italian. m. EUR 30 (effective 2009). **Document type:** *Newsletter, Consumer.* **Description:** Covers politics for political leaders.
Formerly (until 2007): La Voce della Campania (0390-4628)
Related titles: Online - full text ed.
Published by: La Voce della Campania, Via San Romualdo 10, Naples, NA 80131, Italy. TEL 39-081-5875497.

VOCE DELL'EMIGRANTE; periodico sulle problematiche dell'emigrazione ed immigrazione. *see* SOCIAL SERVICES AND WELFARE

320 ITA ISSN 1970-3414
LA VOCE DEMOCRATICA. Text in Italian. 2007. fortn. EUR 20 (effective 2008). **Document type:** *Magazine, Consumer.*
Published by: Editoriale La Voce Democratica, Via Merulana 139, Rome, 00185, Italy. TEL 39-06-77205514.

VOELKERRECHT UND POLITIK. *see* LAW—International Law

320 RUS
VOL'NAYA KUBAN'. Text in Russian. 260/yr.
Address: Ul Shaumyana 106, Krasnodar, 350681, Russian Federation. TEL 8612-55-35-56, FAX 8612-55-39-75. Ed. V A Lameikin. **Dist. by:** East View Information Services, 10601 Wayzata Blvd, Minneapolis, MN 55305. TEL 952-252-1201, 800-477-1005, FAX 952-252-1202, info@eastview.com, http://www.eastview.com.

320 RUS
VOORUZHENIE. POLITIKA. KONVERSIYA. Text in Russian. q.
Indexed: RASB.
Address: 1-ya Myasnikovskaya ul 3, Moscow, 107564, Russian Federation. TEL 7-095-1698310, FAX 7-095-1697280. Ed. V V Panov. **Dist. by:** East View Information Services, 10601 Wayzata Blvd, Minneapolis, MN 55305. TEL 952-252-1201, 800-477-1005, FAX 952-252-1202, info@eastview.com, http://www.eastview.com.

320.532 NLD
VOORWAARTS! (ONLINE). Text in Dutch. 2001. m.
Formerly (until 2006): Voorwaarts! (Print) (1572-5456)
Media: Online - full text.
Published by: Communistische Jongeren Beweging, Haarlemmerweg 177, Amsterdam, 1051 LB, Netherlands. TEL 31-6-26396078, info@cjb.nu.

320 DEU ISSN 0507-4150
VORGAENGE; Zeitschrift fuer Buergerrechte und Gesellschaftspolitik. Text in German. 1962. q. EUR 43; EUR 28 to students; EUR 14 newsstand/cover (effective 2010). adv. bibl. reprint service avail. from SCH. **Document type:** *Journal, Academic/Scholarly.*
Indexed: CERDIC, DIP, FR, IBR, IBSS, IBZ, P30, PAIS. —INIST.
Published by: B W V - Berliner Wissenschafts Verlag GmbH, Markgrafenstr 12-14, Berlin, 10969, Germany. TEL 49-30-8417700, FAX 49-30-84177021, bwv@bwv-verlag.de, http://www.bwv-verlag.de. Ed. Dieter Rulff.

320 NLD ISSN 1878-4909
VORM GEVEN AAN INHOUD. Text in Dutch. 2007. irreg., latest vol.13, 2010. **Document type:** *Monographic series, Academic/Scholarly.*
Published by: Nederlandse School voor Openbaar Bestuur, Lange Voorhout 17, The Hague, 2514 EB, Netherlands. TEL 31-70-3024910, FAX 31-70-3024911, info@nsob.nl.

VORONEZHSKII GOSUDARSTVENNYI UNIVERSITET. VESTNIK. SERIYA: ISTORIYA, POLITOLOGIYA, SOTSIOLOGIYA. *see* HISTORY

320.5 193 DEU ISSN 0947-6261
VORSCHEIN. Text in German. 1993. a. EUR 22 (effective 2009). **Document type:** *Monographic series, Academic/Scholarly.*
Published by: Ernst-Bloch-Assoziation, c/o Doris Zeilinger, Fenitzerstr 35, Nuernberg, 90489, Germany. TEL 49-911-286089, FAX 49-911-5974266, postmaster@ernst-bloch.net, http://www.ernst-bloch.net.

320 DEU ISSN 1860-613X
VORWAERTS (REGIONALAUSGABE HESSEN-SUED); Parteilich, Politisch, Initiativ. Text in German. 1876. 10/yr. EUR 22 (effective 2009). adv. bk.rev. illus. **Document type:** *Magazine, Consumer.*
Supersedes in part (1956-1995): Der Sozialdemokrat (0038-6030); (1955-1995): Vorwaerts (0042-8949); Which incorporated (1982-1989): SM. Sozialdemokrat-Magazin (0724-5785); Which was formerly (1974-1982): Sozialdemokrat-Magazin (0724-5777); (1973-1974): Einblick (Bonn) (0724-5793)
Related titles: Regional ed(s).: Vorwaerts (Regionalausgabe Saarland-Rundschau). ISSN 1860-6121; Vorwaerts (Regionalausgabe Nordrhein-Westfalen). ISSN 1860-6113.
Indexed: RASB.
Published by: Berliner Vorwaerts Verlagsgesellschaft mbH, Stresemannstr 30, Berlin, 10963, Germany. TEL 49-30-25594100, FAX 49-30-25594192, verlag@vorwaerts.de. Ed. Susanne Dohrn. Adv. contact Michael Blum. B&W page EUR 15,300, color page EUR 18,000; trim 226 x 317. Circ: 483,663 (paid and controlled).

320 USA
VOTE AND SURVEY; magazine of political, social and economic issues. Text in English. 1986. m. bk.rev. **Document type:** *Magazine, Consumer.*
Published by: Gibbs Publishing Company, 15421 N E Tenth Ave, North Miami Beach, FL 33162. TEL 828-586-2229, gibbsic@aol.com. Ed. James Calvin Gibbs.

324 USA
VOTER. Text in English. 1920. 4/yr. adv. **Document type:** *Newsletter.*
Published by: League of Women Voters of New York State, 62 Grand St, Albany, NY 12207-1403. http://www.lwvny.org/index.html. Circ: 10,000.

324 USA ISSN 0734-4414
JK1873
VOTING ASSISTANCE GUIDE. Abbreviated title: V A G. Text in English. 1973. biennial. free to qualified personnel (effective 2009). **Document type:** *Government.* **Description:** Primary source of information for citizens covered by the Uniformed and Overseas Citizens Absentee Voting Act (UOCAVA) regarding the procedures for registering to vote, requesting a ballot, and voting in their state or territory of legal residence.
Related titles: CD-ROM ed.; Online - full text ed.: ISSN 1946-6765.
Published by: Department of Defense, Federal Voting Assistance Program, 1155 Defense Pentagon, Washington, DC 20301. TEL 703-588-1584, 800-438-8683.

324 USA
VOTING PRACTICES IN THE UNITED NATIONS. Text in English. 1991. a.
Published by: U.S. Department of State. Bureau of International Organization Affairs, 2201 C Street NW, Washington, DC 20520. TEL 202-647-4000, http://www.state.gov/p/io/.

324.6 USA
VOTING RECORD: SENATE NATIONAL SECURITY INDEX. Text in English. 1982. a. free. **Document type:** *Newsletter.*
Formerly: Council for a Livable World. Newsletter
Related titles: Online - full text ed.
Published by: Council for a Livable World, 110 Maryland Ave, N E, Washington, DC 20002. TEL 202-543-4100. Ed. John D Isaacs.

320 ITA ISSN 0391-3155
VUOTO, SCIENZA E TECNOLOGIA. Key Title: Vuoto. Text in Italian. 1968. q. adv. illus. back issues avail. **Document type:** *Magazine, Trade.* **Description:** Examines all aspects of vacuum science and technology through research articles, technical notes, conference reports, and reviews from the Associazione Italiana del Vuoto and other organizations.
Indexed: A22, Inspec, RASB. —Ingenta, Linda Hall.
Published by: Associazione Italiana del Vuoto, c/o FAST, Piazzale R. Morandi 2, Milan, 20121, Italy. segreteria@aiv.it, http://www.aiv.it. Circ: 1,500.

W F D Y NEWS. *see* CHILDREN AND YOUTH—For

320 NLD
W R R RAPPORTEN. Text in Dutch. irreg. price varies. **Document type:** *Monographic series, Academic/Scholarly.*
Published by: (Wetenschappelijke Raad voor het Regeringsbeleid), Amsterdam University Press, Herengracht 221, Amsterdam, 1016 BG, Netherlands. TEL 31-20-4200050, FAX 31-20-4203214, info@aup.nl, http://www.aup.nl.

320 NLD ISSN 1572-1159
W R R VERKENNINGEN. Text in Dutch. 2003. irreg. price varies. **Document type:** *Monographic series, Academic/Scholarly.*
Formed by the merger of (1983-2003): Wetenschappelijke Raad voor het Regeringsbeleid. Werkdocumenten (0169-6637); (1975-2003): Wetenschappelijke Raad voor het Regeringsbeleid. Voorstudies en Achtergronden (0169-6688)
Published by: (Wetenschappelijke Raad voor het Regeringsbeleid), Amsterdam University Press, Herengracht 221, Amsterdam, 1016 BG, Netherlands. TEL 31-20-4200050, FAX 31-20-4203214, info@aup.nl, http://www.aup.nl.

W Z B - MITTEILUNGEN. *see* SOCIAL SCIENCES: COMPREHENSIVE WORKS

WAGNER LATIN AMERICAN NEWSLETTER. *see* HISTORY—History Of North And South America

320.531 AUT ISSN 0042-9996
DIE WAHRHEIT; Betriebszeitung der Voest-Alpine. Text in German. 1950. m. adv. bk.rev.; play rev. charts; illus.; stat. **Document type:** *Newspaper, Consumer.*
Published by: Sozialistische Partei Oesterreichs, Bezirksorganisation Linz-Stadt, Landstr 36-II, Linz, O 4020, Austria. TEL 43-732-772620, FAX 43-732-771785, spoe.linz@linzpartei.at, http://www.linzpartei.at. Circ: 16,000. **Co-sponsor:** Betriebsektion Voest Alpine.

P

320 GBR
THE WALES YEARBOOK (YEAR); the annual reference book of public affairs in Wales. Text in English. 1990. a. GBP 75 per issue (effective 2010). **Document type:** *Yearbook, Trade.* **Description:** Lists addresses, telephone and fax numbers, email and website addresses with over 5,000 named contacts, completely revised each year.
Published by: Francis Balsom Associates Ltd., 4 the Science Park, Aberstwyth, Wales SY23 3AH, United Kingdom. TEL 44-1970-636403, FAX 44-1970-636414, aber@fbagroup.co.uk, http://www.fbagroup.co.uk/.

320 JPN ISSN 0511-196X
JA26
WASEDA POLITICAL STUDIES. Text in English. 1957. a. free.
Indexed: BAS, CA, I13, P42, PAIS, PSA, T02.
Published by: Waseda University, Graduate School of Political Science, 1-6-1 Nishi-Waseda, Shinjuku-ku, Tokyo, 169, Japan. TEL 03-3203-4141.

320.9 JPN ISSN 0287-7007
JA26
WASEDA SEIJI KEIZAIGAKU ZASSHI/WASEDA JOURNAL OF POLITICAL SCIENCE AND ECONOMICS. Text in Japanese. 1925. bi-m. bk.rev.
Indexed: RASB.
—BLDSC (9263.080000), Ingenta.
Published by: Waseda Daigaku, Seiji Keizai Gakkai/Waseda University, Society of Political Science and Economics, 6-1 Nishi-Waseda 1-chome, Shinjuku-ku, Tokyo, 160-0000, Japan. Ed. Seiichi Iwakura. Circ: 3,000.

328.797 USA ISSN 0091-8253
JK9230
WASHINGTON (STATE) LEGISLATURE. PICTORIAL DIRECTORY. Key Title: Pictorial Directory - Washington State Legislature. Text in English. 1909. irreg. (during legislative session). free. illus. **Document type:** *Directory, Government.*
Published by: Legislature, P O Box 40482, Olympia, WA 98504-0482. TEL 360-786-7550, FAX 360-786-7520. Circ: 19,000.

▼ **WASHINGTON COLLEGE STUDIES IN RELIGION, POLITICS AND CULTURE.** *see* RELIGIONS AND THEOLOGY

320.025 USA ISSN 0887-8064
F192.3
WASHINGTON INFORMATION DIRECTORY (YEAR). Abbreviated title: W I D. Text in English. 1976. a. USD 130 per issue (effective 2008). back issues avail.; reprints avail. **Document type:** *Directory, Government.* **Description:** Organizes thousands of names, addresses, and phone numbers for the federal government and the many private groups in its orbit. Includes name and subject indexes; organized by area of activity.
Related titles: Online - full text ed.: USD 140 single-user (effective 2005).
—CCC.
Published by: C Q Press, Inc. (Subsidiary of: Sage Publications, Inc.), 2300 N St, NW, Ste 800, Washington, DC 20037. TEL 202-729-1900, 866-427-7737, FAX 800-380-3810, customerservice@cqpress.com, http://www.cqpress.com.

320.9 USA
WASHINGTON INSTITUTE FOR NEAR EAST POLICY. POLICY CONFERENCE. PROCEEDINGS. Text in English. 1985. s-a. **Document type:** *Proceedings.*
Formerly: Washington Institute for Near East Policy. Policy Forum. Proceedings (1053-3230)
Published by: The Washington Institute for Near East Policy, 1828 L St, N W, Ste 1050, Washington, DC 20036. Ed. Robert Satloff. R&P John Wilner TEL 202-452-0650.

320.9 USA
WASHINGTON INSTITUTE FOR NEAR EAST POLICY. POLICY FOCUS. Text in English. 1985. irreg. USD 9.95 newsstand/cover (effective 2004).
Published by: The Washington Institute for Near East Policy, 1828 L St, N W, Ste 1050, Washington, DC 20036. TEL 202-452-0650, FAX 202-223-5364, info@washingtoninstitute.org. Ed. Robert Satloff.

320.9 USA
WASHINGTON INSTITUTE FOR NEAR EAST POLICY. POLICY PAPERS. Text in English. irreg., latest vol.44, 1996. USD 120; USD 180 foreign. adv. **Document type:** *Monographic series.*
Published by: The Washington Institute for Near East Policy, 1828 L St, N W, Ste 1050, Washington, DC 20036. Ed. Robert Satloff. R&P, Adv. contact John Wilner TEL 202-452-0650.

WASHINGTON LAW & POLITICS. *see* LAW

328 USA ISSN 0043-0633
E838
THE WASHINGTON MONTHLY. Text in English. 1969. 6/yr. USD 29.95 domestic; USD 39.95 foreign (effective 2009). adv. bk.rev. illus. back issues avail.; reprints avail. **Document type:** *Magazine, Consumer.* **Description:** Covers politics and government for journalists, government workers, business people, and educators with articles about the White House, Congress, and other current affairs.
Related titles: Microform ed.: (from PQC); Online - full text ed.
Indexed: A01, A02, A03, A08, A12, A21, A22, A25, A26, ABIn, ABS&EES, Acal, AmH&L, B01, B02, B04, B06, B07, B08, B09, B15, B17, B18, BRD, C12, CBRI, CCR, E07, E08, FutSurv, G04, G05, G06, G07, G08, H09, HRA, I02, I05, I07, L09, M01, M02, M05, M06, MASUSE, MEA&I, MagInd, P02, P05, P06, P07, P10, P13, P30, P34, P47, P48, P51, P53, P54, PAIS, PQC, PerIslam, PersLit, R02, R03, R04, RASB, RGAb, RGPR, RI-1, RI-2, RehabLit, S05, S08, S09, S11, S22, S23, SPAA, T02, W03, W05.
—BLDSC (9263.170000), IE, Infotrieve, Ingenta.
Published by: Washington Monthly LLC, 5471 Wisconsin Ave, Ste 300, Chevy Chase, MD 20815. TEL 240-497-0321, FAX 240-497-0322. Ed. Paul Glastris. Pub. Diane Straus Tucker. Adv. contact Carl Iseli. Circ: 33,000.

320 USA ISSN 0748-6359
DU30
THE WASHINGTON PACIFIC REPORT; the insider's newsletter highlighting the latest developments of interest involving the insular Pacific. Text in English. 1982. s-m. USD 164 domestic; USD 189 foreign (effective 2005). 6 p./no. 2 cols./p.; back issues avail. **Document type:** *Newsletter.* **Description:** Covers current events in the Pacific islands and offers analysis of political topics, especially U.S. government actions that affect these nations and territories.
Published by: Washington Pacific Publications, Inc., PO Box 26142, Alexandria, VA 22313-6142. TEL 703-519-7757, FAX 703-548-0633, piwowpr@erols.comom. Ed., Pub., R&P Fred Radewagen TEL 703-519-7757.

WASHINGTON PUBLIC AFFAIRS DIGEST. *see* PUBLIC ADMINISTRATION

WASHINGTON REPRESENTATIVES. *see* PUBLIC ADMINISTRATION

WASHINGTON SEMESTERS AND INTERNSHIPS; promoting civic and cultural education in the nation's capital. *see* EDUCATION

320 USA ISSN 0887-428X
E839.5
WASHINGTON SPECTATOR. Text in English. 1976. s-m. USD 15 domestic membership; USD 31 in Canada & Mexico membership; USD 37 elsewhere membership; USD 12 to senior citizens; USD 12 to students (effective 2000). bk.rev. back issues avail.; reprints avail. **Document type:** *Newsletter.* **Description:** Provides information on major news developments, including political, social and economic issues.
Formerly: Washington Spectator - Between the Lines (0145-160X); Formed by the 1976 merger of: Washington Spectator (0162-3133); Between the Lines (0006-0305)
Related titles: Microform ed.: (from PQC).
Indexed: A22.
Published by: Public Concern Foundation, Inc., PO Box 20065, London Terrace Sta, New York, NY 10011. TEL 212-741-2365, FAX 212-366-6585. Ed. Benjamin A Franklin. Pub. Phillip Frazer. R&P Ben Franklin. Circ: 60,000 (paid).

320 NGA ISSN 0795-896X
WEEKLY PROBES. Text in English. 1988. w. NGN 52, USD 40.
Published by: Crier Communications Ltd., PO Box 681, Surulere, Lagos State, Nigeria. TEL 234-1-921198. Ed. Bosun Adewunmi. Circ: 50,000.

WEEKLY REVIEW. *see* PUBLIC ADMINISTRATION

324.2734 USA ISSN 1083-3013
E839.5
THE WEEKLY STANDARD. Text in English. 1995. 48/yr. USD 54 domestic; USD 124.96 in Canada; USD 139.96 in Mexico; USD 214.96 elsewhere; USD 3.95 newsstand/cover (effective 2007). adv. bk.rev. illus. reprints avail. **Document type:** *Magazine, Consumer.* **Description:** Provides a forum for conservative perspectives on political issues.
Related titles: Online - full text ed.
Indexed: A26, B04, B05, BRD, CCR, G05, G06, G07, G08, I05, M02, P02, P10, P34, P42, P48, P53, P54, PAIS, PQC, R03, RGAb, RGPR, S11, T02, W03.
—CIS.
Published by: The Weekly Standard (Subsidiary of: News America Inc.), 1150 17th St, NW, Ste 505, Washington, DC 20036. TEL 202-293-4900, FAX 202-293-4901. Ed. William Kristol. Pub. Terry Eastland. adv.: color page USD 10,400. Circ: 80,395 (paid and controlled).

320 AUT
DIE WEISSE ROSE; analytische Schriften - Zeitschrift gegen den Zeitgeist. Text in German. 1988. q. adv. bk.rev. **Document type:** *Journal, Academic/Scholarly.*
Published by: Weisse Rose, Postfach 192, Vienna, W 1060, Austria. TEL 43-1-5964175. Ed. Albert Pethoe.

320.6 GBR ISSN 1471-9681
WELSH GOVERNANCE CENTRE. WORKING PAPER. Text in English. irreg. GBP 4 domestic; GBP 5.50 foreign (effective 2002).
Published by: Welsh Governance Centre, Cardiff University, P.O. Box 908, Cardiff, CF10 3YQ, United Kingdom. TEL 44-029-20874885, FAX 44-029-20874885, welshgovernance@Cardiff.ac.uk, http://www.cf.ac.uk/euros/welsh-governance.

WENHUA ZONGHENG/BEIJING CULTURAL REVIEW. *see* SOCIAL SCIENCES: COMPREHENSIVE WORKS

324.2 DEU
WENTORFER COURIER. Text in German. 1974. q. looseleaf. back issues avail.
Published by: Sozialdemokratische Partei Deutschlands, Orstverein Wentorf bei Hamburg, Sandweg 22, Wentorf, 21465, Germany. TEL 040-7201143. Circ: 3,500.

WEST AFRICA REVIEW. *see* HISTORY—History Of Africa

WEST AFRICAN JOURNAL OF SOCIOLOGY AND POLITICAL SCIENCE. *see* SOCIOLOGY

WEST BENGAL. *see* PUBLIC ADMINISTRATION

WEST COAST LEAF. *see* DRUG ABUSE AND ALCOHOLISM

WEST COAST LIBERTARIAN. *see* LITERARY AND POLITICAL REVIEWS

328.754 USA
WEST VIRGINIA. LEGISLATURE. COMMISSION ON SPECIAL INVESTIGATIONS. REPORT TO THE WEST VIRGINIA LEGISLATURE. Text in English. 1981. a. free. **Document type:** *Government.* **Description:** Summarizes cases and identifies commission members and staff.
Formerly: West Virginia. Legislature. Purchasing Practices and Procedures Commission. Report to the West Virginia Legislature.
Published by: Legislature, 1 Players Club Dr, Ste 501, Charleston, WV 25311-1626. TEL 304-558-2345, FAX 304-558-3325. Ed., R&P Gary W Slater. Circ: 300.

320.9 GBR ISSN 0953-6906
HC240.A1
WESTERN EUROPE (YEAR). Text in English. 1988. triennial. USD 760 per issue (effective 2009). bibl.; charts; stat. reprints avail. **Document type:** *Directory, Academic/Scholarly.* **Description:** Covers recent history and politics, economy, geography, social affairs, media and communications, transport, and tourism.
—BLDSC (9300.717800).
Published by: (Europa Publications Ltd.), Routledge (Subsidiary of: Taylor & Francis Group), 2 Park Sq, Milton Park, Abingdon, Oxon OX14 4RN, United Kingdom. TEL 44-20-70176000, FAX 44-20-70176699, orders@taylorandfrancis.com. **Dist. by:** Current Pacific Ltd., 7 La Roche Pl, Northcote, PO Box 36-536, Auckland 0627, New Zealand.

320 USA
WESTERN LEGISLATURE. Text in English. bi-m. USD 25 (effective 2001). **Document type:** *Newsletter, Government.* **Description:** Covers current state legislative issues and actions in the West.
Formerly: States West
Published by: Council of State Governments, Western Office, 121 Second St 4th Fl, San Francisco, CA 94105. TEL 415-974-6422, FAX 415-974-1747, http://www.csguest.org. Ed. Mary Lou Cooper.

320 IRL
WESTERN POLICIES. Text in English. 1985. a. looseleaf. USD 100. adv. bk.rev. **Document type:** *Journal, Academic/Scholarly.* **Description:** Provides a forum for objective analysis of various issues that confront the Western nations due to their policies.
Formerly: N A T O - Warsaw and Strategies (0749-0674)
Published by: Royal University, Ltd., 6 Lower Hatch St., Dublin, 2, Ireland. FAX 353-1-6686632. Ed. C V Ramasastry.

328 GBR ISSN 1355-9753
WESTMINSTER CONFIDENTIAL. Text in English. 1955. 40/yr. GBP 50 (effective 1999). **Document type:** *Newsletter.*
Published by: Parliamentary Profile Services Ltd., 34 Somali Rd, London, NW2 3RL, United Kingdom. TEL 44-171-222-5884, FAX 44-171-222-5889. Ed., R&P Andrew Roth. Circ: 150.

324.2 DEU
WEYHER WECKER. Text in German. 1985. s-a. **Document type:** *Bulletin.*
Published by: Sozialdemokratische Partei Deutschlands (SPD), c/o R. von Larcher, Boettcherei 210, Weyhe, 28844, Germany. Circ: 7,000.

WHAT IS ASIA SERIES/AJIA O MIRUME SERIES. *see* BUSINESS AND ECONOMICS—International Development And Assistance

WHEELER REPORT. *see* PUBLIC ADMINISTRATION

320 USA
WHITE HOUSE BULLETIN. Text in English. d. **Document type:** *Bulletin, Trade.* **Description:** Covers the latest developments in the White House.
Media: Online - full content. **Related titles:** E-mail ed.; Fax ed.
Published by: Bulletin News Network, Inc., 7915 Jones Branch, Ste 6200, McLean, VA 22102. TEL 703-749-0040, FAX 703-749-0060, frontdesk@bulletinnews.com.

WHITE HOUSE HISTORY. *see* HISTORY—History Of North And South America

WHITE HOUSE STUDIES (HAUPPAUGE). *see* HISTORY—History Of North And South America

WHITE HOUSE WEEKLY. *see* PUBLIC ADMINISTRATION

WHO'S WHO IN AMERICAN POLITICS. *see* BIOGRAPHY

320 DEU ISSN 1437-9015
WIENER VORLESUNGEN: FORSCHUNGEN. Text in German. 2000. irreg., latest vol.3, 2008. price varies. **Document type:** *Monographic series, Academic/Scholarly.*
Published by: Peter Lang GmbH (Subsidiary of: Peter Lang Publishing Group), Eschborner Landstr 42-50, Frankfurt Am Main, 60489, Germany. TEL 49-69-7807050, FAX 49-69-78070550, zentrale.frankfurt@peterlang.com, http://www.peterlang.com.

WIENZEILE; Supranationales Magazin fuer Literatur, Kunst und Politik. *see* ART

322.4 USA
WIN MAGAZINE. Text in English. m. free.
Media: Online - full text.
Indexed: NPI.
Address: 301 E79th St, 12A, New York, NY 10021. TEL 646-349-2763, FAX 646-349-2763, editor@winmagazine.org, http://www.winmagazine.org. Ed. Judith Colp Rubin.

324.2 DEU
WINDESHEIMER RUNDSCHAU. Text in German. 1982. s-a. free.
Published by: Sozialdemokratische Partei Deutschlands (SPD), Ortsverein Windesheim, Waldstr 13, Windesheim, 55452, Germany. TEL 06707-564. Circ: 750.

WIRTSCHAFTS- UND VERWALTUNGSRECHTLICHE STUDIEN. *see* LAW

WIRTSCHAFTSUNIVERSITAET WIEN. FORSCHUNGSINSTITUT FUER EUROPA-FRAGEN. SCHRIFTENREIHE/RESEARCH INSTITUTE FOR EUROPEAN AFFAIRS. PUBLICATION SERIES. *see* LAW

324.6 USA
WISCONSIN. STATE ELECTIONS BOARD. BIENNIAL REPORT. Text in English. 1975. biennial. USD 20. adv. **Document type:** *Government.* **Description:** Lists political financial activity for two-year periods in Wisconsin.
Published by: State Elections Board, 132 E Wilson St, 2nd Fl, Ste 200, Madison, WI 53702. TEL 608-266-8005, FAX 608-267-0500. Ed., Adv. contact Mary Scheer. R&P Kevin Kennedy. Circ: 100.

WISSENSCHAFTLICHE ABHANDLUNGEN UND REDEN ZUR PHILOSOPHIE, POLITIK UND GEISTESGESCHICHTE. *see* PHILOSOPHY

320 DEU ISSN 1861-7840
WISSENSCHAFTLICHE BEITRAEGE AUS DEM TECTUM-VERLAG. REIHE POLITIKWISSENSCHAFTEN. Text in German. 1999. irreg., latest vol.30, 2010. price varies. **Document type:** *Monographic series, Academic/Scholarly.*
Published by: Tectum Wissenschaftsverlag Marburg, Biegenstr 4, Marburg, 35037, Germany. TEL 49-6421-481523, FAX 49-6421-43470, email@tectum-verlag.de.

THE WITNESS. *see* RELIGIONS AND THEOLOGY—Protestant

320.082 305.8 USA ISSN 1937-6510
WOMEN AND MINORITIES IN POLITICS. Text in English. 2007 (Dec.). irreg., latest 2010. price varies. back issues avail. **Document type:** *Monographic series, Academic/Scholarly.* **Description:** Covers information on global comparison of women's campaigns for executive office.
Published by: Praeger Publishers (Subsidiary of: Greenwood Publishing Group Inc.), 88 Post Rd W, Westport, CT 06881. TEL 800-368-6868, tech.support@greenwood.com. Ed. Melody Rose.

320.082 USA
WOMEN AND POLITICS (WESTPORT). Text in English. 1985. irreg., latest 1987. price varies. back issues avail. **Document type:** *Monographic series.*
Indexed: SWR&A.

Published by: Praeger Publishers (Subsidiary of: Greenwood Publishing Group Inc.), 88 Post Rd W, Westport, CT 06881. TEL 800-368-6868, tech.support@greenwood.com, http://www.greenwood.com.

WOMEN FOR PEACE AND WOMEN'S INTERNATIONAL LEAGUE FOR PEACE & FREEDOM. NEWSLETTER. *see* WOMEN'S INTERESTS

WOMEN'S ENVIRONMENT AND DEVELOPMENT ORGANIZATION NEWS & VIEWS. *see* WOMEN'S INTERESTS

320.5322 GBR ISSN 0267-8721
HX3
WORKERS HAMMER. Text in English. 1978. a. GBP 3 domestic; GBP 5 in Europe (effective 2003). **Document type:** *Newspaper, Consumer.* **Description:** Marxist newspaper of the Spartacist League, Britain.
Formerly (until 1984): Spartacist Britain (0141-6960)
Published by: Spartacist Publications, PO Box 1041, London, NW5 3EU, United Kingdom.

WORKERS NEWS. *see* LABOR UNIONS

320 USA ISSN 0276-0746
HX1
WORKERS VANGUARD. Text in English. 1970. bi-w. USD 10 domestic; USD 25 foreign (effective 2003); includes subscr. to Spartacist, Black History and the Class Struggle. bibl.; illus.; charts. **Document type:** *Newspaper, Consumer.*
Formerly: Workers Action
Related titles: ◆ Supplement(s): Spartacist. ISSN 0038-6596.
Indexed: LeftInd.
Published by: (Spartacist League), Spartacist Publishing Co., PO Box 1377, New York, NY 10116. TEL 212-732-7861, vanguard@tirc.net, http://www.icl-fi.org. Ed. Len Meyers.

320.531 USA ISSN 0043-809X
WORKERS WORLD. Text in English. 1959. w. USD 25 in North America to individuals; USD 35 elsewhere to individuals; USD 35 to institutions (effective 2001). bk.rev. 12 p./no. 4 cols./p.; **Document type:** *Newspaper.*
Related titles: Microform ed.: (from PQC).
Indexed: LeftInd, W09.
Published by: (Workers World Party), W W Publishers Inc., 55 W 17th St, 5th Fl, New York, NY 10011. TEL 212-627-2994, FAX 212-675-7869. Ed. Deirdre Griswold. R&P John Catalinotto. Circ: 3,400.

320.531 USA
WORKING CLASS OPPOSITION/OPOSICION OBRERA. Text in English, Spanish. 1981. m. USD 20. bk.rev. illus. **Description:** Covers political events throughout the world from a socialist and communist perspective.
Published by: (Internationalist Workers Party (Fourth International)), October Publications, 3309 1/2 Mission St, Ste 135, San Francisco, CA 94110. TEL 415-695-0340. Eds. Claudia Mejia, Ted Baker. Circ: 3,500. **Co-sponsor:** International Workers League.

324.6 AUT ISSN 1992-6014
WORKING PAPER SERIES ON ELECTRONIC VOTING AND PARTICIPATION. Text in English. 2006. irreg. **Document type:** *Monographic series, Academic/Scholarly.*
Related titles: Online - full text ed.: ISSN 1992-6022.
Published by: Competence Center for Electronic Participation and Electronic Voting, Liechtensteinstr 143-3, Vienna, 1090, Austria. TEL 43-1-9581645, FAX 43-1-3193955, office@e-voting.cc, http://www.e-voting.cc.

324.2 NLD ISSN 2211-1034
▼ **WORKING PAPER SERIES ON THE LEGAL REGULATION OF POLITICAL PARTIES.** Variant title: The Legal Regulation of Political Parties in Post-War Europe. Text in English. 2009. irreg., latest vol.6, 2010. **Document type:** *Monographic series, Academic/Scholarly.*
Media: Online - full text.
Published by: (Universiteit Leiden, Institute of Political Sciences), Universiteit Leiden, PO Box 9500, Leiden, 2300 RA, Netherlands. TEL 31-71-5278026, FAX 31-71-5273118, http://www.leiden.edu.

320 NLD ISSN 1569-3546
WORKING PAPERS POLITICAL SCIENCE. Text in English. 2002. irreg., latest vol.26, 2007. **Document type:** *Monographic series, Academic/Scholarly.*
Published by: Vrije Universiteit Amsterdam, Department of Political Science, De Boelelaan 1081, Amsterdam, 1081 HV, Netherlands. TEL 31-20-5986852, FAX 31-20-5986820, http://www.fsw.vu.nl.

322.1 USA ISSN 1949-2308
WORKING PEOPLE'S ADVOCATE. Abbreviated title: W P A. Text in English. 2004. w. back issues avail. **Document type:** *Newspaper, Consumer.*
Related titles: Online - full text ed.: ISSN 1949-2316. free (effective 2009).
Published by: (Workers Party in America), United Communist Press Association, PO Box 14999, Detroit, MI 48214. editor@ucpa.us, http://www.ucpa.us. Ed. Henry Miles.

WORLD BANK COUNTRY STUDY. *see* BUSINESS AND ECONOMICS—International Development And Assistance

WORLD BANK REGIONAL AND SECTORAL STUDIES. *see* BUSINESS AND ECONOMICS—International Development And Assistance

WORLD BUSINESS REVIEW. *see* BUSINESS AND ECONOMICS—International Commerce

328 CHE ISSN 1013-0365
JF501
WORLD DIRECTORY OF PARLIAMENTS. Text in English, French. a. free. **Document type:** *Directory, Trade.* **Description:** Presents a reference book providing information on the basic characteristics of each of the world's national parliaments; the addresses of parliment members and data on telecommunications.
Published by: Inter-Parliamentary Union, 5, chemin du Pommier, Case postale 330, Geneva, 1218, Switzerland. TEL 41-22-9194150, FAX 41-22-9194160, postbox@mail.ipu.org, http://www.ipu.org.

320.9 IND ISSN 2231-0185
▼ **WORLD FOCUS (NEW DELHI).** Text in Hindi. 2011. m. INR 550 domestic; USD 100 foreign (effective 2011). **Document type:** *Magazine, Consumer.*
Related titles: Online - full text ed.
Published by: World Focus, B-49, Ground Fl, Joshi Colony, IP Extn, New Delhi, 110 092, India. TEL 91-11-22246905, cnfworldfocus@gmail.com, info@cnfworldfocus.org. Ed. G Kishore Babu.

321.8 ZAF ISSN 1991-1092
WORLD JOURNAL OF DEMOCRACY AND TRANSFORMATION. Text in English. 2006. q. USD 120 in Africa to individuals; USD 180 elsewhere to individuals; USD 350 in Africa to institutions; USD 450 elsewhere to institutions; USD 85 in Africa to students; USD 100 elsewhere to students (effective 2007). **Document type:** *Journal, Academic/Scholarly.* **Description:** Aims to engage activistss and intellectuals in critical discussions of the problems and prospects from democracy and transformation around the world.
Published by: (World Research Organization), Isis Press, PO Box 1919, Cape Town, 8000, South Africa. TEL 27-21-4471574, FAX 27-86-6219999, orders@unwro.org, http://www.unwro.org/isispress.html.

320 ZAF ISSN 1990-8709
➤ **WORLD JOURNAL OF DIVERSITY AND NATIONS.** Text in English. 2006. q. USD 120 in Africa to individuals; USD 180 elsewhere to individuals; USD 350 in Africa to institutions; USD 450 elsewhere to institutions; USD 85 in Africa to students; USD 100 elsewhere to students (effective 2007). **Document type:** *Journal, Academic/Scholarly.* **Description:** Examines the realities of difference and diversity today, touching upon the topics of difference, diversity, globalization, commerce and personality.
Published by: (World Research Organization), Isis Press, PO Box 1919, Cape Town, 8000, South Africa. TEL 27-21-4471574, FAX 27-86-6219999, orders@unwro.org, http://www.unwro.org/isispress.html.

320 ZAF ISSN 1991-1149
WORLD JOURNAL OF GOVERNMENTAL STUDIES. Text in English. 2006. q. USD 120 in Africa to individuals; USD 180 elsewhere to individuals; USD 350 in Africa to institutions; USD 450 elsewhere to institutions; USD 85 in Africa to students; USD 100 elsewhere to students (effective 2007). **Document type:** *Journal, Academic/Scholarly.* **Description:** Focuses on the study of politics, administration and management of local affairs.
Published by: (World Research Organization), Isis Press, PO Box 1919, Cape Town, 8000, South Africa. TEL 27-21-4471574, FAX 27-86-6219999, orders@unwro.org, http://www.unwro.org/isispress.html.

324 307.1 362.1 ZAF ISSN 1991-1319
➤ **WORLD JOURNAL OF PLANNING AND DEVELOPMENT.** Text in English. 2006. q. USD 120 in Africa to individuals; USD 180 elsewhere to individuals; USD 350 in Africa to institutions; USD 450 elsewhere to institutions; USD 85 in Africa to students; USD 100 elsewhere to students (effective 2007). **Document type:** *Journal, Academic/Scholarly.* **Description:** Links the interests of those working in economic, social and political history, historical geography, and historical sociology with those in the applied fields of public health, housing construction, architecture, and town planning.
Published by: (World Research Organization), Isis Press, PO Box 1919, Cape Town, 8000, South Africa. TEL 27-21-4471574, FAX 27-86-6219999, orders@unwro.org, http://www.unwro.org/isispress.html.

320 ZAF ISSN 1991-1327
➤ **WORLD JOURNAL OF POLITICAL STUDIES.** Text in English. 2006. q. USD 120 in Africa to individuals; USD 180 elsewhere to individuals; USD 350 in Africa to institutions; USD 450 elsewhere to institutions; USD 85 in Africa to students; USD 100 elsewhere to students (effective 2007). **Document type:** *Journal, Academic/Scholarly.* **Description:** Examines various dimensions of politics and governance in the world, primarily comparative politics, international relations, political theory, and public administration, with specific reference to Asian regions and countries.
Published by: (World Research Organization), Isis Press, PO Box 1919, Cape Town, 8000, South Africa. TEL 27-21-4471574, FAX 27-86-6219999, orders@unwro.org, http://www.unwro.org/isispress.html.

320.6 ZAF ISSN 1819-8597
WORLD JOURNAL OF PUBLIC POLICY. Text in English. 2006. q. USD 120 in Africa to individuals; USD 180 elsewhere to individuals; USD 350 in Africa to institutions; USD 450 elsewhere to institutions; USD 85 in Africa to students; USD 100 elsewhere to students (effective 2007). **Document type:** *Journal, Academic/Scholarly.* **Description:** Provides analysis of developments in the organizational, administrative, and policy sciences as they apply to government and governance.
Published by: (World Research Organization), Isis Press, PO Box 1919, Cape Town, 8000, South Africa. TEL 27-21-4471574, FAX 27-86-6219999, orders@unwro.org, http://www.unwro.org/isispress.html.

WORLD OF INFORMATION BUSINESS INTELLIGENCE REPORTS. ALBANIA. *see* BUSINESS AND ECONOMICS—Economic Situation And Conditions

WORLD OF INFORMATION BUSINESS INTELLIGENCE REPORTS. AMERICAN SAMOA. *see* BUSINESS AND ECONOMICS—Economic Situation And Conditions

WORLD OF INFORMATION BUSINESS INTELLIGENCE REPORTS. ANGOLA. *see* BUSINESS AND ECONOMICS—Economic Situation And Conditions

WORLD OF INFORMATION BUSINESS INTELLIGENCE REPORTS. ANGUILLA. *see* BUSINESS AND ECONOMICS—Economic Situation And Conditions

WORLD OF INFORMATION BUSINESS INTELLIGENCE REPORTS. ANTIGUA AND BARBUDA. *see* BUSINESS AND ECONOMICS—Economic Situation And Conditions

WORLD OF INFORMATION BUSINESS INTELLIGENCE REPORTS. ARGENTINA. *see* BUSINESS AND ECONOMICS—Economic Situation And Conditions

WORLD OF INFORMATION BUSINESS INTELLIGENCE REPORTS. ARMENIA. *see* BUSINESS AND ECONOMICS—Economic Situation And Conditions

WORLD OF INFORMATION BUSINESS INTELLIGENCE REPORTS. ARUBA. *see* BUSINESS AND ECONOMICS—Economic Situation And Conditions

WORLD OF INFORMATION BUSINESS INTELLIGENCE REPORTS. ASCENSION ISLAND. *see* BUSINESS AND ECONOMICS—Economic Situation And Conditions

WORLD OF INFORMATION BUSINESS INTELLIGENCE REPORTS. AUSTRALIA. *see* BUSINESS AND ECONOMICS—Economic Situation And Conditions

WORLD OF INFORMATION BUSINESS INTELLIGENCE REPORTS. AUSTRIA. *see* BUSINESS AND ECONOMICS—Economic Situation And Conditions

WORLD OF INFORMATION BUSINESS INTELLIGENCE REPORTS. AZERBAIJAN. *see* BUSINESS AND ECONOMICS—Economic Situation And Conditions

WORLD OF INFORMATION BUSINESS INTELLIGENCE REPORTS. BAHAMAS. *see* BUSINESS AND ECONOMICS—Economic Situation And Conditions

WORLD OF INFORMATION BUSINESS INTELLIGENCE REPORTS. BAHRAIN. *see* BUSINESS AND ECONOMICS—Economic Situation And Conditions

WORLD OF INFORMATION BUSINESS INTELLIGENCE REPORTS. BANGLADESH. *see* BUSINESS AND ECONOMICS—Economic Situation And Conditions

WORLD OF INFORMATION BUSINESS INTELLIGENCE REPORTS. BARBADOS. *see* BUSINESS AND ECONOMICS—Economic Situation And Conditions

WORLD OF INFORMATION BUSINESS INTELLIGENCE REPORTS. BELARUS. *see* BUSINESS AND ECONOMICS—Economic Situation And Conditions

WORLD OF INFORMATION BUSINESS INTELLIGENCE REPORTS. BELGIUM. *see* BUSINESS AND ECONOMICS—Economic Situation And Conditions

WORLD OF INFORMATION BUSINESS INTELLIGENCE REPORTS. BELIZE. *see* BUSINESS AND ECONOMICS—Economic Situation And Conditions

WORLD OF INFORMATION BUSINESS INTELLIGENCE REPORTS. BENIN. *see* BUSINESS AND ECONOMICS—Economic Situation And Conditions

WORLD OF INFORMATION BUSINESS INTELLIGENCE REPORTS. BERMUDA. *see* BUSINESS AND ECONOMICS—Economic Situation And Conditions

WORLD OF INFORMATION BUSINESS INTELLIGENCE REPORTS. BHUTAN. *see* BUSINESS AND ECONOMICS—Economic Situation And Conditions

WORLD OF INFORMATION BUSINESS INTELLIGENCE REPORTS. BOLIVIA. *see* BUSINESS AND ECONOMICS—Economic Situation And Conditions

WORLD OF INFORMATION BUSINESS INTELLIGENCE REPORTS. BOSNIA & HERCEGOVINA. *see* BUSINESS AND ECONOMICS—Economic Situation And Conditions

WORLD OF INFORMATION BUSINESS INTELLIGENCE REPORTS. BOTSWANA. *see* BUSINESS AND ECONOMICS—Economic Situation And Conditions

WORLD OF INFORMATION BUSINESS INTELLIGENCE REPORTS. BRAZIL. *see* BUSINESS AND ECONOMICS—Economic Situation And Conditions

WORLD OF INFORMATION BUSINESS INTELLIGENCE REPORTS. BRITISH VIRGIN ISLANDS. *see* BUSINESS AND ECONOMICS—Economic Situation And Conditions

WORLD OF INFORMATION BUSINESS INTELLIGENCE REPORTS. BRUNEI. *see* BUSINESS AND ECONOMICS—Economic Situation And Conditions

WORLD OF INFORMATION BUSINESS INTELLIGENCE REPORTS. BURKINA FASO. *see* BUSINESS AND ECONOMICS—Economic Situation And Conditions

WORLD OF INFORMATION BUSINESS INTELLIGENCE REPORTS. BURUNDI. *see* BUSINESS AND ECONOMICS—Economic Situation And Conditions

WORLD OF INFORMATION BUSINESS INTELLIGENCE REPORTS. CAMBODIA. *see* BUSINESS AND ECONOMICS—Economic Situation And Conditions

WORLD OF INFORMATION BUSINESS INTELLIGENCE REPORTS. CAMEROON. *see* BUSINESS AND ECONOMICS—Economic Situation And Conditions

WORLD OF INFORMATION BUSINESS INTELLIGENCE REPORTS. CANADA. *see* BUSINESS AND ECONOMICS—Economic Situation And Conditions

WORLD OF INFORMATION BUSINESS INTELLIGENCE REPORTS. CAPE VERDE. *see* BUSINESS AND ECONOMICS—Economic Situation And Conditions

WORLD OF INFORMATION BUSINESS INTELLIGENCE REPORTS. CAYMAN ISLANDS. *see* BUSINESS AND ECONOMICS—Economic Situation And Conditions

WORLD OF INFORMATION BUSINESS INTELLIGENCE REPORTS. CENTRAL AFRICAN REPUBLIC. *see* BUSINESS AND ECONOMICS—Economic Situation And Conditions

WORLD OF INFORMATION BUSINESS INTELLIGENCE REPORTS. CHAD. *see* BUSINESS AND ECONOMICS—Economic Situation And Conditions

WORLD OF INFORMATION BUSINESS INTELLIGENCE REPORTS. CHILE. *see* BUSINESS AND ECONOMICS—Economic Situation And Conditions

WORLD OF INFORMATION BUSINESS INTELLIGENCE REPORTS. CHINA. *see* BUSINESS AND ECONOMICS—Economic Situation And Conditions

WORLD OF INFORMATION BUSINESS INTELLIGENCE REPORTS. COLOMBIA. *see* BUSINESS AND ECONOMICS—Economic Situation And Conditions

WORLD OF INFORMATION BUSINESS INTELLIGENCE REPORTS. COMOROS. *see* BUSINESS AND ECONOMICS—Economic Situation And Conditions

WORLD OF INFORMATION BUSINESS INTELLIGENCE REPORTS. CONGO. *see* BUSINESS AND ECONOMICS—Economic Situation And Conditions

WORLD OF INFORMATION BUSINESS INTELLIGENCE REPORTS. COOK ISLANDS. *see* BUSINESS AND ECONOMICS—Economic Situation And Conditions

WORLD OF INFORMATION BUSINESS INTELLIGENCE REPORTS. COSTA RICA. *see* BUSINESS AND ECONOMICS—Economic Situation And Conditions

P

WORLD OF INFORMATION BUSINESS INTELLIGENCE REPORTS. COTE D'IVOIRE. *see* BUSINESS AND ECONOMICS—Economic Situation And Conditions

WORLD OF INFORMATION BUSINESS INTELLIGENCE REPORTS. CROATIA. *see* BUSINESS AND ECONOMICS—Economic Situation And Conditions

WORLD OF INFORMATION BUSINESS INTELLIGENCE REPORTS. CUBA. *see* BUSINESS AND ECONOMICS—Economic Situation And Conditions

WORLD OF INFORMATION BUSINESS INTELLIGENCE REPORTS. CYPRUS. *see* BUSINESS AND ECONOMICS—Economic Situation And Conditions

WORLD OF INFORMATION BUSINESS INTELLIGENCE REPORTS. DENMARK. *see* BUSINESS AND ECONOMICS—Economic Situation And Conditions

WORLD OF INFORMATION BUSINESS INTELLIGENCE REPORTS. DJIBOUTI. *see* BUSINESS AND ECONOMICS—Economic Situation And Conditions

WORLD OF INFORMATION BUSINESS INTELLIGENCE REPORTS. DOMINICA. *see* BUSINESS AND ECONOMICS—Economic Situation And Conditions

WORLD OF INFORMATION BUSINESS INTELLIGENCE REPORTS. DOMINICAN REPUBLIC. *see* BUSINESS AND ECONOMICS—Economic Situation And Conditions

WORLD OF INFORMATION BUSINESS INTELLIGENCE REPORTS. EASTER ISLAND. *see* BUSINESS AND ECONOMICS—Economic Situation And Conditions

WORLD OF INFORMATION BUSINESS INTELLIGENCE REPORTS. ECUADOR. *see* BUSINESS AND ECONOMICS—Economic Situation And Conditions

WORLD OF INFORMATION BUSINESS INTELLIGENCE REPORTS. EGYPT. *see* BUSINESS AND ECONOMICS—Economic Situation And Conditions

WORLD OF INFORMATION BUSINESS INTELLIGENCE REPORTS. EL SALVADOR. *see* BUSINESS AND ECONOMICS—Economic Situation And Conditions

WORLD OF INFORMATION BUSINESS INTELLIGENCE REPORTS. EQUATORIAL GUINEA. *see* BUSINESS AND ECONOMICS—Economic Situation And Conditions

WORLD OF INFORMATION BUSINESS INTELLIGENCE REPORTS. ERITREA. *see* BUSINESS AND ECONOMICS—Economic Situation And Conditions

WORLD OF INFORMATION BUSINESS INTELLIGENCE REPORTS. ESTONIA. *see* BUSINESS AND ECONOMICS—Economic Situation And Conditions

WORLD OF INFORMATION BUSINESS INTELLIGENCE REPORTS. ETHIOPIA. *see* BUSINESS AND ECONOMICS—Economic Situation And Conditions

WORLD OF INFORMATION BUSINESS INTELLIGENCE REPORTS. FALKLAND ISLANDS/ISLAS MALVINAS. *see* BUSINESS AND ECONOMICS—Economic Situation And Conditions

WORLD OF INFORMATION BUSINESS INTELLIGENCE REPORTS. FAROE ISLANDS. *see* BUSINESS AND ECONOMICS—Economic Situation And Conditions

WORLD OF INFORMATION BUSINESS INTELLIGENCE REPORTS. FEDERATED STATES OF MICRONESIA. *see* BUSINESS AND ECONOMICS—Economic Situation And Conditions

WORLD OF INFORMATION BUSINESS INTELLIGENCE REPORTS. FIJI. *see* BUSINESS AND ECONOMICS—Economic Situation And Conditions

WORLD OF INFORMATION BUSINESS INTELLIGENCE REPORTS. FINLAND. *see* BUSINESS AND ECONOMICS—Economic Situation And Conditions

WORLD OF INFORMATION BUSINESS INTELLIGENCE REPORTS. FRANCE. *see* BUSINESS AND ECONOMICS—Economic Situation And Conditions

WORLD OF INFORMATION BUSINESS INTELLIGENCE REPORTS. FRENCH GUIANA. *see* BUSINESS AND ECONOMICS—Economic Situation And Conditions

WORLD OF INFORMATION BUSINESS INTELLIGENCE REPORTS. FRENCH POLYNESIA. *see* BUSINESS AND ECONOMICS—Economic Situation And Conditions

WORLD OF INFORMATION BUSINESS INTELLIGENCE REPORTS. GABON. *see* BUSINESS AND ECONOMICS—Economic Situation And Conditions

WORLD OF INFORMATION BUSINESS INTELLIGENCE REPORTS. GEORGIA. *see* BUSINESS AND ECONOMICS—Economic Situation And Conditions

WORLD OF INFORMATION BUSINESS INTELLIGENCE REPORTS. GERMANY. *see* BUSINESS AND ECONOMICS—Economic Situation And Conditions

WORLD OF INFORMATION BUSINESS INTELLIGENCE REPORTS. GHANA. *see* BUSINESS AND ECONOMICS—Economic Situation And Conditions

WORLD OF INFORMATION BUSINESS INTELLIGENCE REPORTS. GIBRALTAR. *see* BUSINESS AND ECONOMICS—Economic Situation And Conditions

WORLD OF INFORMATION BUSINESS INTELLIGENCE REPORTS. GREECE. *see* BUSINESS AND ECONOMICS—Economic Situation And Conditions

WORLD OF INFORMATION BUSINESS INTELLIGENCE REPORTS. GREENLAND. *see* BUSINESS AND ECONOMICS—Economic Situation And Conditions

WORLD OF INFORMATION BUSINESS INTELLIGENCE REPORTS. GRENADA. *see* BUSINESS AND ECONOMICS—Economic Situation And Conditions

WORLD OF INFORMATION BUSINESS INTELLIGENCE REPORTS. GUADELOUPE. *see* BUSINESS AND ECONOMICS—Economic Situation And Conditions

WORLD OF INFORMATION BUSINESS INTELLIGENCE REPORTS. GUAM. *see* BUSINESS AND ECONOMICS—Economic Situation And Conditions

WORLD OF INFORMATION BUSINESS INTELLIGENCE REPORTS. GUATEMALA. *see* BUSINESS AND ECONOMICS—Economic Situation And Conditions

WORLD OF INFORMATION BUSINESS INTELLIGENCE REPORTS. GUINEA. *see* BUSINESS AND ECONOMICS—Economic Situation And Conditions

WORLD OF INFORMATION BUSINESS INTELLIGENCE REPORTS. GUINEA-BISSAU. *see* BUSINESS AND ECONOMICS—Economic Situation And Conditions

WORLD OF INFORMATION BUSINESS INTELLIGENCE REPORTS. GUYANA. *see* BUSINESS AND ECONOMICS—Economic Situation And Conditions

WORLD OF INFORMATION BUSINESS INTELLIGENCE REPORTS. HAITI. *see* BUSINESS AND ECONOMICS—Economic Situation And Conditions

WORLD OF INFORMATION BUSINESS INTELLIGENCE REPORTS. HONDURAS. *see* BUSINESS AND ECONOMICS—Economic Situation And Conditions

WORLD OF INFORMATION BUSINESS INTELLIGENCE REPORTS. HONG KONG. *see* BUSINESS AND ECONOMICS—Economic Situation And Conditions

WORLD OF INFORMATION BUSINESS INTELLIGENCE REPORTS. ICELAND. *see* BUSINESS AND ECONOMICS—Economic Situation And Conditions

WORLD OF INFORMATION BUSINESS INTELLIGENCE REPORTS. INDIA. *see* BUSINESS AND ECONOMICS—Economic Situation And Conditions

WORLD OF INFORMATION BUSINESS INTELLIGENCE REPORTS. INDONESIA. *see* BUSINESS AND ECONOMICS—Economic Situation And Conditions

WORLD OF INFORMATION BUSINESS INTELLIGENCE REPORTS. IRAN. *see* BUSINESS AND ECONOMICS—Economic Situation And Conditions

WORLD OF INFORMATION BUSINESS INTELLIGENCE REPORTS. IRAQ. *see* BUSINESS AND ECONOMICS—Economic Situation And Conditions

WORLD OF INFORMATION BUSINESS INTELLIGENCE REPORTS. IRELAND. *see* BUSINESS AND ECONOMICS—Economic Situation And Conditions

WORLD OF INFORMATION BUSINESS INTELLIGENCE REPORTS. ISRAEL. *see* BUSINESS AND ECONOMICS—Economic Situation And Conditions

WORLD OF INFORMATION BUSINESS INTELLIGENCE REPORTS. ITALY. *see* BUSINESS AND ECONOMICS—Economic Situation And Conditions

WORLD OF INFORMATION BUSINESS INTELLIGENCE REPORTS. JAMAICA. *see* BUSINESS AND ECONOMICS—Economic Situation And Conditions

WORLD OF INFORMATION BUSINESS INTELLIGENCE REPORTS. JAPAN. *see* BUSINESS AND ECONOMICS—Economic Situation And Conditions

WORLD OF INFORMATION BUSINESS INTELLIGENCE REPORTS. JORDAN. *see* BUSINESS AND ECONOMICS—Economic Situation And Conditions

WORLD OF INFORMATION BUSINESS INTELLIGENCE REPORTS. KAZAKHSTAN. *see* BUSINESS AND ECONOMICS—Economic Situation And Conditions

WORLD OF INFORMATION BUSINESS INTELLIGENCE REPORTS. KENYA. *see* BUSINESS AND ECONOMICS—Economic Situation And Conditions

WORLD OF INFORMATION BUSINESS INTELLIGENCE REPORTS. KIRIBATI. *see* BUSINESS AND ECONOMICS—Economic Situation And Conditions

WORLD OF INFORMATION BUSINESS INTELLIGENCE REPORTS. KOREA. *see* BUSINESS AND ECONOMICS—Economic Situation And Conditions

WORLD OF INFORMATION BUSINESS INTELLIGENCE REPORTS. KUWAIT. *see* BUSINESS AND ECONOMICS—Economic Situation And Conditions

WORLD OF INFORMATION BUSINESS INTELLIGENCE REPORTS. KYRGHYZSTAN. *see* BUSINESS AND ECONOMICS—Economic Situation And Conditions

WORLD OF INFORMATION BUSINESS INTELLIGENCE REPORTS. LAOS. *see* BUSINESS AND ECONOMICS—Economic Situation And Conditions

WORLD OF INFORMATION BUSINESS INTELLIGENCE REPORTS. LATVIA. *see* BUSINESS AND ECONOMICS—Economic Situation And Conditions

WORLD OF INFORMATION BUSINESS INTELLIGENCE REPORTS. LEBANON. *see* BUSINESS AND ECONOMICS—Economic Situation And Conditions

WORLD OF INFORMATION BUSINESS INTELLIGENCE REPORTS. LESOTHO. *see* BUSINESS AND ECONOMICS—Economic Situation And Conditions

WORLD OF INFORMATION BUSINESS INTELLIGENCE REPORTS. LIBERIA. *see* BUSINESS AND ECONOMICS—Economic Situation And Conditions

WORLD OF INFORMATION BUSINESS INTELLIGENCE REPORTS. LIBYA. *see* BUSINESS AND ECONOMICS—Economic Situation And Conditions

WORLD OF INFORMATION BUSINESS INTELLIGENCE REPORTS. LIECHTENSTEIN. *see* BUSINESS AND ECONOMICS—Economic Situation And Conditions

WORLD OF INFORMATION BUSINESS INTELLIGENCE REPORTS. LITHUANIA. *see* BUSINESS AND ECONOMICS—Economic Situation And Conditions

WORLD OF INFORMATION BUSINESS INTELLIGENCE REPORTS. LUXEMBOURG. *see* BUSINESS AND ECONOMICS—Economic Situation And Conditions

WORLD OF INFORMATION BUSINESS INTELLIGENCE REPORTS. MACAO. *see* BUSINESS AND ECONOMICS—Economic Situation And Conditions

WORLD OF INFORMATION BUSINESS INTELLIGENCE REPORTS. MADAGASCAR. *see* BUSINESS AND ECONOMICS—Economic Situation And Conditions

WORLD OF INFORMATION BUSINESS INTELLIGENCE REPORTS. MALAWI. *see* BUSINESS AND ECONOMICS—Economic Situation And Conditions

WORLD OF INFORMATION BUSINESS INTELLIGENCE REPORTS. MALAYSIA. *see* BUSINESS AND ECONOMICS—Economic Situation And Conditions

WORLD OF INFORMATION BUSINESS INTELLIGENCE REPORTS. MALDIVES. *see* BUSINESS AND ECONOMICS—Economic Situation And Conditions

WORLD OF INFORMATION BUSINESS INTELLIGENCE REPORTS. MALI. *see* BUSINESS AND ECONOMICS—Economic Situation And Conditions

WORLD OF INFORMATION BUSINESS INTELLIGENCE REPORTS. MALTA. *see* BUSINESS AND ECONOMICS—Economic Situation And Conditions

WORLD OF INFORMATION BUSINESS INTELLIGENCE REPORTS. MARSHALL ISLANDS. *see* BUSINESS AND ECONOMICS—Economic Situation And Conditions

WORLD OF INFORMATION BUSINESS INTELLIGENCE REPORTS. MARTINIQUE. *see* BUSINESS AND ECONOMICS—Economic Situation And Conditions

WORLD OF INFORMATION BUSINESS INTELLIGENCE REPORTS. MAURITANIA. *see* BUSINESS AND ECONOMICS—Economic Situation And Conditions

WORLD OF INFORMATION BUSINESS INTELLIGENCE REPORTS. MAURITIUS. *see* BUSINESS AND ECONOMICS—Economic Situation And Conditions

WORLD OF INFORMATION BUSINESS INTELLIGENCE REPORTS. MEXICO. *see* BUSINESS AND ECONOMICS—Economic Situation And Conditions

WORLD OF INFORMATION BUSINESS INTELLIGENCE REPORTS. MOLDOVA. *see* BUSINESS AND ECONOMICS—Economic Situation And Conditions

WORLD OF INFORMATION BUSINESS INTELLIGENCE REPORTS. MONACO. *see* BUSINESS AND ECONOMICS—Economic Situation And Conditions

WORLD OF INFORMATION BUSINESS INTELLIGENCE REPORTS. MONGOLIA. *see* BUSINESS AND ECONOMICS—Economic Situation And Conditions

WORLD OF INFORMATION BUSINESS INTELLIGENCE REPORTS. MONTSERRAT. *see* BUSINESS AND ECONOMICS—Economic Situation And Conditions

WORLD OF INFORMATION BUSINESS INTELLIGENCE REPORTS. MOROCCO. *see* BUSINESS AND ECONOMICS—Economic Situation And Conditions

WORLD OF INFORMATION BUSINESS INTELLIGENCE REPORTS. MOZAMBIQUE. *see* BUSINESS AND ECONOMICS—Economic Situation And Conditions

WORLD OF INFORMATION BUSINESS INTELLIGENCE REPORTS. MYANMAR. *see* BUSINESS AND ECONOMICS—Economic Situation And Conditions

WORLD OF INFORMATION BUSINESS INTELLIGENCE REPORTS. NAMIBIA. *see* BUSINESS AND ECONOMICS—Economic Situation And Conditions

WORLD OF INFORMATION BUSINESS INTELLIGENCE REPORTS. NAURU. *see* BUSINESS AND ECONOMICS—Economic Situation And Conditions

WORLD OF INFORMATION BUSINESS INTELLIGENCE REPORTS. NEPAL. *see* BUSINESS AND ECONOMICS—Economic Situation And Conditions

WORLD OF INFORMATION BUSINESS INTELLIGENCE REPORTS. NETHERLANDS. *see* BUSINESS AND ECONOMICS—Economic Situation And Conditions

WORLD OF INFORMATION BUSINESS INTELLIGENCE REPORTS. NEW CALEDONIA. *see* BUSINESS AND ECONOMICS—Economic Situation And Conditions

WORLD OF INFORMATION BUSINESS INTELLIGENCE REPORTS. NEW ZEALAND. *see* BUSINESS AND ECONOMICS—Economic Situation And Conditions

WORLD OF INFORMATION BUSINESS INTELLIGENCE REPORTS. NICARAGUA. *see* BUSINESS AND ECONOMICS—Economic Situation And Conditions

WORLD OF INFORMATION BUSINESS INTELLIGENCE REPORTS. NIGER. *see* BUSINESS AND ECONOMICS—Economic Situation And Conditions

WORLD OF INFORMATION BUSINESS INTELLIGENCE REPORTS. NIGERIA. *see* BUSINESS AND ECONOMICS—Economic Situation And Conditions

WORLD OF INFORMATION BUSINESS INTELLIGENCE REPORTS. NIUE. *see* BUSINESS AND ECONOMICS—Economic Situation And Conditions

WORLD OF INFORMATION BUSINESS INTELLIGENCE REPORTS. NORFOLK ISLAND. *see* BUSINESS AND ECONOMICS—Economic Situation And Conditions

WORLD OF INFORMATION BUSINESS INTELLIGENCE REPORTS. NORTH KOREA. *see* BUSINESS AND ECONOMICS—Economic Situation And Conditions

WORLD OF INFORMATION BUSINESS INTELLIGENCE REPORTS. NORWAY. *see* BUSINESS AND ECONOMICS—Economic Situation And Conditions

WORLD OF INFORMATION BUSINESS INTELLIGENCE REPORTS. OMAN. *see* BUSINESS AND ECONOMICS—Economic Situation And Conditions

WORLD OF INFORMATION BUSINESS INTELLIGENCE REPORTS. PAKISTAN. *see* BUSINESS AND ECONOMICS—Economic Situation And Conditions

WORLD OF INFORMATION BUSINESS INTELLIGENCE REPORTS. PALESTINE. *see* BUSINESS AND ECONOMICS—Economic Situation And Conditions

WORLD OF INFORMATION BUSINESS INTELLIGENCE REPORTS. PANAMA. *see* BUSINESS AND ECONOMICS—Economic Situation And Conditions

WORLD OF INFORMATION BUSINESS INTELLIGENCE REPORTS. PAPUA NEW GUINEA. *see* BUSINESS AND ECONOMICS—Economic Situation And Conditions

WORLD OF INFORMATION BUSINESS INTELLIGENCE REPORTS. PARAGUAY. *see* BUSINESS AND ECONOMICS—Economic Situation And Conditions

WORLD OF INFORMATION BUSINESS INTELLIGENCE REPORTS. PERU. *see* BUSINESS AND ECONOMICS—Economic Situation And Conditions

WORLD OF INFORMATION BUSINESS INTELLIGENCE REPORTS. PHILIPPINES. *see* BUSINESS AND ECONOMICS—Economic Situation And Conditions

WORLD OF INFORMATION BUSINESS INTELLIGENCE REPORTS. PITCAIRN ISLAND. *see* BUSINESS AND ECONOMICS—Economic Situation And Conditions

WORLD OF INFORMATION BUSINESS INTELLIGENCE REPORTS. PORTUGAL. *see* BUSINESS AND ECONOMICS—Economic Situation And Conditions

WORLD OF INFORMATION BUSINESS INTELLIGENCE REPORTS. PUERTO RICO. *see* BUSINESS AND ECONOMICS—Economic Situation And Conditions

WORLD OF INFORMATION BUSINESS INTELLIGENCE REPORTS. QATAR. *see* BUSINESS AND ECONOMICS—Economic Situation And Conditions

WORLD OF INFORMATION BUSINESS INTELLIGENCE REPORTS. REUNION. *see* BUSINESS AND ECONOMICS—Economic Situation And Conditions

WORLD OF INFORMATION BUSINESS INTELLIGENCE REPORTS. RUSSIA. *see* BUSINESS AND ECONOMICS—Economic Situation And Conditions

WORLD OF INFORMATION BUSINESS INTELLIGENCE REPORTS. RWANDA. *see* BUSINESS AND ECONOMICS—Economic Situation And Conditions

WORLD OF INFORMATION BUSINESS INTELLIGENCE REPORTS. SAMOA. *see* BUSINESS AND ECONOMICS—Economic Situation And Conditions

WORLD OF INFORMATION BUSINESS INTELLIGENCE REPORTS. SAN MARINO. *see* BUSINESS AND ECONOMICS—Economic Situation And Conditions

WORLD OF INFORMATION BUSINESS INTELLIGENCE REPORTS. SAO TOME AND PRINCIPE. *see* BUSINESS AND ECONOMICS—Economic Situation And Conditions

WORLD OF INFORMATION BUSINESS INTELLIGENCE REPORTS. SAUDI ARABIA. *see* BUSINESS AND ECONOMICS—Economic Situation And Conditions

WORLD OF INFORMATION BUSINESS INTELLIGENCE REPORTS. SENEGAL. *see* BUSINESS AND ECONOMICS—Economic Situation And Conditions

WORLD OF INFORMATION BUSINESS INTELLIGENCE REPORTS. SERBIA. *see* BUSINESS AND ECONOMICS—Economic Situation And Conditions

WORLD OF INFORMATION BUSINESS INTELLIGENCE REPORTS. SERBIA AND MONTENEGRO. *see* BUSINESS AND ECONOMICS—Economic Situation And Conditions

WORLD OF INFORMATION BUSINESS INTELLIGENCE REPORTS. SEYCHELLES. *see* BUSINESS AND ECONOMICS—Economic Situation And Conditions

WORLD OF INFORMATION BUSINESS INTELLIGENCE REPORTS. SIERRA LEONE. *see* BUSINESS AND ECONOMICS—Economic Situation And Conditions

WORLD OF INFORMATION BUSINESS INTELLIGENCE REPORTS. SINGAPORE. *see* BUSINESS AND ECONOMICS—Economic Situation And Conditions

WORLD OF INFORMATION BUSINESS INTELLIGENCE REPORTS. SLOVAKIA. *see* BUSINESS AND ECONOMICS—Economic Situation And Conditions

WORLD OF INFORMATION BUSINESS INTELLIGENCE REPORTS. SLOVENIA. *see* BUSINESS AND ECONOMICS—Economic Situation And Conditions

WORLD OF INFORMATION BUSINESS INTELLIGENCE REPORTS. SOLOMON ISLANDS. *see* BUSINESS AND ECONOMICS—Economic Situation And Conditions

WORLD OF INFORMATION BUSINESS INTELLIGENCE REPORTS. SOMALIA. *see* BUSINESS AND ECONOMICS—Economic Situation And Conditions

WORLD OF INFORMATION BUSINESS INTELLIGENCE REPORTS. SOUTH AFRICA. *see* BUSINESS AND ECONOMICS—Economic Situation And Conditions

WORLD OF INFORMATION BUSINESS INTELLIGENCE REPORTS. SOUTH GEORGIA. *see* BUSINESS AND ECONOMICS—Economic Situation And Conditions

WORLD OF INFORMATION BUSINESS INTELLIGENCE REPORTS. SPAIN. *see* BUSINESS AND ECONOMICS—Economic Situation And Conditions

WORLD OF INFORMATION BUSINESS INTELLIGENCE REPORTS. SRI LANKA. *see* BUSINESS AND ECONOMICS—Economic Situation And Conditions

WORLD OF INFORMATION BUSINESS INTELLIGENCE REPORTS. ST HELENA. *see* BUSINESS AND ECONOMICS—Economic Situation And Conditions

WORLD OF INFORMATION BUSINESS INTELLIGENCE REPORTS. ST KITTS AND NEVIS. *see* BUSINESS AND ECONOMICS—Economic Situation And Conditions

WORLD OF INFORMATION BUSINESS INTELLIGENCE REPORTS. ST LUCIA. *see* BUSINESS AND ECONOMICS—Economic Situation And Conditions

WORLD OF INFORMATION BUSINESS INTELLIGENCE REPORTS. ST VINCENT AND THE GRENADINES. *see* BUSINESS AND ECONOMICS—Economic Situation And Conditions

WORLD OF INFORMATION BUSINESS INTELLIGENCE REPORTS. SUDAN. *see* BUSINESS AND ECONOMICS—Economic Situation And Conditions

WORLD OF INFORMATION BUSINESS INTELLIGENCE REPORTS. SURINAME. *see* BUSINESS AND ECONOMICS—Economic Situation And Conditions

WORLD OF INFORMATION BUSINESS INTELLIGENCE REPORTS. SWAZILAND. *see* BUSINESS AND ECONOMICS—Economic Situation And Conditions

WORLD OF INFORMATION BUSINESS INTELLIGENCE REPORTS. SWEDEN. *see* BUSINESS AND ECONOMICS—Economic Situation And Conditions

WORLD OF INFORMATION BUSINESS INTELLIGENCE REPORTS. SWITZERLAND. *see* BUSINESS AND ECONOMICS—Economic Situation And Conditions

WORLD OF INFORMATION BUSINESS INTELLIGENCE REPORTS. SYRIA. *see* BUSINESS AND ECONOMICS—Economic Situation And Conditions

WORLD OF INFORMATION BUSINESS INTELLIGENCE REPORTS. TAIWAN. *see* BUSINESS AND ECONOMICS—Economic Situation And Conditions

WORLD OF INFORMATION BUSINESS INTELLIGENCE REPORTS. TAJIKISTAN. *see* BUSINESS AND ECONOMICS—Economic Situation And Conditions

WORLD OF INFORMATION BUSINESS INTELLIGENCE REPORTS. TANZANIA. *see* BUSINESS AND ECONOMICS—Economic Situation And Conditions

WORLD OF INFORMATION BUSINESS INTELLIGENCE REPORTS. TERRES AUSTRALES. *see* BUSINESS AND ECONOMICS—Economic Situation And Conditions

WORLD OF INFORMATION BUSINESS INTELLIGENCE REPORTS. THAILAND. *see* BUSINESS AND ECONOMICS—Economic Situation And Conditions

WORLD OF INFORMATION BUSINESS INTELLIGENCE REPORTS. THE GAMBIA. *see* BUSINESS AND ECONOMICS—Economic Situation And Conditions

WORLD OF INFORMATION BUSINESS INTELLIGENCE REPORTS. THE NETHERLANDS ANTILLES. *see* BUSINESS AND ECONOMICS—Economic Situation And Conditions

WORLD OF INFORMATION BUSINESS INTELLIGENCE REPORTS. TIMOR-LESTE. *see* BUSINESS AND ECONOMICS—Economic Situation And Conditions

WORLD OF INFORMATION BUSINESS INTELLIGENCE REPORTS. TOGO. *see* BUSINESS AND ECONOMICS—Economic Situation And Conditions

WORLD OF INFORMATION BUSINESS INTELLIGENCE REPORTS. TOKELAU. *see* BUSINESS AND ECONOMICS—Economic Situation And Conditions

WORLD OF INFORMATION BUSINESS INTELLIGENCE REPORTS. TONGA. *see* BUSINESS AND ECONOMICS—Economic Situation And Conditions

WORLD OF INFORMATION BUSINESS INTELLIGENCE REPORTS. TUNISIA. *see* BUSINESS AND ECONOMICS—Economic Situation And Conditions

WORLD OF INFORMATION BUSINESS INTELLIGENCE REPORTS. TURKEY. *see* BUSINESS AND ECONOMICS—Economic Situation And Conditions

WORLD OF INFORMATION BUSINESS INTELLIGENCE REPORTS. TURKMENISTAN. *see* BUSINESS AND ECONOMICS—Economic Situation And Conditions

WORLD OF INFORMATION BUSINESS INTELLIGENCE REPORTS. TURKS AND CAICOS ISLANDS. *see* BUSINESS AND ECONOMICS—Economic Situation And Conditions

WORLD OF INFORMATION BUSINESS INTELLIGENCE REPORTS. TUVALU. *see* BUSINESS AND ECONOMICS—Economic Situation And Conditions

WORLD OF INFORMATION BUSINESS INTELLIGENCE REPORTS. UGANDA. *see* BUSINESS AND ECONOMICS—Economic Situation And Conditions

WORLD OF INFORMATION BUSINESS INTELLIGENCE REPORTS. UKRAINE. *see* BUSINESS AND ECONOMICS—Economic Situation And Conditions

WORLD OF INFORMATION BUSINESS INTELLIGENCE REPORTS. UNITED ARAB EMIRATES. *see* BUSINESS AND ECONOMICS—Economic Situation And Conditions

WORLD OF INFORMATION BUSINESS INTELLIGENCE REPORTS. UNITED KINGDOM. *see* BUSINESS AND ECONOMICS—Economic Situation And Conditions

WORLD OF INFORMATION BUSINESS INTELLIGENCE REPORTS. UNITED STATES. *see* BUSINESS AND ECONOMICS—Economic Situation And Conditions

WORLD OF INFORMATION BUSINESS INTELLIGENCE REPORTS. URUGUAY. *see* BUSINESS AND ECONOMICS—Economic Situation And Conditions

WORLD OF INFORMATION BUSINESS INTELLIGENCE REPORTS. US VIRGIN ISLANDS. *see* BUSINESS AND ECONOMICS—Economic Situation And Conditions

WORLD OF INFORMATION BUSINESS INTELLIGENCE REPORTS. UZBEKISTAN. *see* BUSINESS AND ECONOMICS—Economic Situation And Conditions

WORLD OF INFORMATION BUSINESS INTELLIGENCE REPORTS. VANUATU. *see* BUSINESS AND ECONOMICS—Economic Situation And Conditions

WORLD OF INFORMATION BUSINESS INTELLIGENCE REPORTS. VATICAN CITY. *see* BUSINESS AND ECONOMICS—Economic Situation And Conditions

WORLD OF INFORMATION BUSINESS INTELLIGENCE REPORTS. VENEZUELA. *see* BUSINESS AND ECONOMICS—Economic Situation And Conditions

WORLD OF INFORMATION BUSINESS INTELLIGENCE REPORTS. VIETNAM. *see* BUSINESS AND ECONOMICS—Economic Situation And Conditions

WORLD OF INFORMATION BUSINESS INTELLIGENCE REPORTS. WALLIS AND FUTUNA. *see* BUSINESS AND ECONOMICS—Economic Situation And Conditions

WORLD OF INFORMATION BUSINESS INTELLIGENCE REPORTS. YEMEN. *see* BUSINESS AND ECONOMICS—Economic Situation And Conditions

WORLD OF INFORMATION BUSINESS INTELLIGENCE REPORTS. ZAMBIA. *see* BUSINESS AND ECONOMICS—Economic Situation And Conditions

WORLD OF INFORMATION BUSINESS INTELLIGENCE REPORTS. ZIMBABWE. *see* BUSINESS AND ECONOMICS—Economic Situation And Conditions

328 CHE
JX1930

THE WORLD OF PARLIAMENTS; a quarterly review of the Inter-Parliamentary Union. Text in English, French. 1921. s-a. CHF 20 (effective 2001). adv. bk.rev. **Document type:** *Newsletter, Trade.*
Description: Constitutes an official organ of the Inter-Parliamentary Union, contains detailed information on all IPU conferences, meetings and events, articles on the work of the various programs of the IPU.
Formerly (until 2001): Inter-Parliamentary Bulletin (0020-5079)
Related titles: French ed.
Indexed: MEA&I, P06, PAIS, RASB.
Published by: Inter-Parliamentary Union, 5, chemin du Pommier, Case postale 330, Geneva, 1218, Switzerland. TEL 41-22-9194160, FAX 41-22-9194160, postbox@mail.ipu.org, http://www.ipu.org. Circ: 1,700.

P

320.9 TWN
DS1

WORLD OUTLOOK. Text in Chinese. 1954. bi-m. USD 15. adv. bk.rev. illus.
Former titles (until 1991): Asian Outlook (0004-4628); Free China and Asia
Indexed: APEL, BAS, HRIR, P06, PAIS, RehabLit.
—Ingenta.
Published by: World League for Freedom and Democracy, Taipei, 3Fl, 333 Tun Hua South Rd, Sec 2, Taipei, 106, Taiwan. wlfd@wlfd.org, http://www.wlfd.org/. Circ: 20,000.

320 USA ISSN 2158-6713

▼ **WORLD PEACE.** Text in English. 2009. 8/yr. USD 20; free to qualified personnel (effective 2011). **Document type:** *Newsletter, Trade.*
Description: Contains a national proposal and a survey.
Published by: On the Rainbow Publishing, On The Rainbow Training Center, PO Box 4131, Brookings, OR 97415. TEL 541-412-7000.

320 USA ISSN 1935-6226

WORLD POLITICAL SCIENCE REVIEW. Abbreviated title: W P S R. Text in English. 200?. a. USD 275 per issue to institutions; USD 825 per issue to corporations (effective 2011). back issues avail. **Document type:** *Journal, Academic/Scholarly.* **Description:** Features prize-winning articles by non-English language political scientists from around the world (translated into English).
Formerly (until 2005): Encounters (1715-0647)
Media: Online - full text.
Indexed: P42, PSA, SCOPUS.
—CCC.
Published by: Berkeley Electronic Press, 2809 Telegraph Ave, Ste 202, Berkeley, CA 94705. TEL 510-665-1200, FAX 510-665-1201, info@bepress.com. Eds. M Ramesh, Michael Howlett.

320 USA ISSN 1944-6284

WORLD POLITICS REVIEW. Text in English. 2008 (Dec.). bi-m. USD 99 (effective 2009). **Document type:** *Magazine, Consumer.*
Media: Online - full text.
Indexed: I02.
—CCC.
Address: 1776 I St NW, 9th Fl, Washington, DC 20016. info@worldpoliticsreview.com, http://worldpoliticsreview.com. Ed. Hampton Stephens.

320 320.531 USA ISSN 2152-6826
JZ1251

WORLD SOCIALIST WEB SITE PERSPECTIVES. Text in English. 1998. m. USD 85; USD 7 per issue (effective 2010). **Document type:** *Journal, Academic/Scholarly.* **Description:** Deals with political statements.
Former titles (until 2010): World Socialist Web Site Review (1443-1912); (until 1999): wsws.org Monthly Review (1441-0133)
Published by: (International Committee of the Fourth International), Mehring Books, PO Box 48377, Oak Park, MI 48237. TEL 248-967-2924, FAX 248-967-3023, sales@mehring.com.

320.531 GBR ISSN 0269-9141
HX3
A WORLD TO WIN. Text in English. 1985. s-a. GBP 8 domestic to individuals for 4 issues; except Canada; USD 24 in North America to individuals for 4 issues; USD 30 in Canada to individuals for 4 issues; INR 80 to individuals for 4 issues; in South Asia; USD 40 in North America to institutions for 4 issues; except Canada; USD 45 in Canada to institutions for 4 issues (effective 2010). adv. bk.rev. back issues avail. **Document type:** *Journal, Academic/Scholarly.*
Description: Presents the views of, and reports on the activity of, the parties and organizations united in the Revolutionary Internationalist Movement. RIM groups together many of the leading Maoist groups from around the world. It includes parties from five continents, including the countries of Nepal, Bangladesh, Sri Lanka, Peru, Colombia, the USA, Tunisia, Afghanistan, Iran, Turkey, Italy and candidate participant groups from other counties.
Related titles: Persian, Modern ed.; Spanish ed.; Turkish ed.; French ed.; Bengali ed.; German ed.; Hindi ed.
Indexed: CA, LeftInd, T02.
—BLDSC (9360.260000).
Published by: A World to Win, 27 Old Gloucester St, London, WC1N 3XX, United Kingdom. FAX 44-20- 78319489. Ed. Don Horne. Pub. K Muralidharan. Adv. contact Lili Adams. Circ: 5,000. **Subscr. in N America to:** Revolution Books, 9 W 19th St, New York, NY 10011. TEL 212-645-1952.

WORLD TODAY SERIES: AFRICA. *see* HISTORY—History Of Africa

WORLD TODAY SERIES: CANADA. *see* HISTORY—History Of North And South America

WORLD TODAY SERIES: EAST AND SOUTHEAST ASIA. *see* HISTORY—History Of Asia

WORLD TODAY SERIES: LATIN AMERICA. *see* HISTORY—History Of North And South America

WORLD TODAY SERIES: NORDIC, CENTRAL AND SOUTHEASTERN EUROPE. *see* HISTORY—History Of Europe

WORLD TODAY SERIES: WESTERN EUROPE. *see* HISTORY—History Of Europe

320 741.5 USA
WORLD WAR THREE ILLUSTRATED. Text in English. 1980. irreg.
Description: Includes graphic arts, poetry. Addresses militarism, homophobia and racism.
Published by: World War Three, PO Box 20777, Tompkins Sq Sta, New York, NY 10009.

WORLD YOUTH/JEUNESSE DU MONDE/JUVENTUD DEL MUNDO; international youth magazine. *see* CHILDREN AND YOUTH—For

320 USA ISSN 1527-6503
G1
WORLDMARK YEARBOOK. Text in English. 2001. irreg. (in 2 vols.), latest 2001. USD 295, GBP 185.85 (effective 2004). **Document type:** *Yearbook, Academic/Scholarly.* **Description:** Provides authoritative, detailed and comprehensive coverage of recent social, political and economic events worldwide.
Related titles: Online - full content ed.
Published by: Gale (Subsidiary of: Cengage Learning), 27500 Drake Rd, Farmington Hills, MI 48331. TEL 248-699-4253, 800-877-4253, FAX 877-363-4253, gale.customerservice@cengage.com, http:// gale.cengage.com.

WORLDWIDE DIRECTORY OF DEFENSE AUTHORITIES. *see* MILITARY

320 SEN
XARELI. Text in French. forth.
Published by: And Jef - Mouvement Revolutionnaire pour la Democratie Nouvelle, BP 12136, Dakar, Senegal. TEL 22-54-63. Circ: 7,000.

320 CHN ISSN 1000-4513
HM141
XIANDAI LINGDAO/MODERN LEADERSHIP. Text in Chinese. 1986. m. USD 42 (effective 2009). adv. bk.rev. **Document type:** *Journal, Academic/Scholarly.* **Description:** Explores the science and the art of leadership in China.
—East View.
Published by: Xiandai Lingdao Zazhishe, 345, Xinhua Rd., no.2 Bldg., Shanghai, 200052, China. TEL 86-21-62804449, FAX 86-21-62804898. Adv. contact Hengxin Chen. B&W page CNY 5,000. Circ: 40,000. **Dist. by:** China International Book Trading Corp, 35 Chegongzhuang Xilu, Haidian District, PO Box 399, Beijing 100044, China. TEL 86-10-68412045, FAX 86-10-68412023, cibtc@mail.cibtc.com.cn, http://www.cibtc.com.cn.

320 TWN ISSN 1026-0811
XIN TAIWAN/NEW TAIWAN WEEKLY. Text in Chinese. 1996. w. TWD 4,200 (effective 2007). **Document type:** *Magazine, Consumer.*
Address: Mingsheng East Rd., Sect.3, no.69, 4/F, Taipei, Taiwan. TEL 886-2-25176200.

320.532 CHN ISSN 1006-0138
HC427.92
XINSHIYE/EXPANDING HORIZONS. Text in Chinese. 1993. bi-m. USD 24.60 (effective 2009). **Document type:** *Academic/Scholarly.*
Related titles: Online - full text ed.
—East View.
Published by: Beijing Weidangxiao, Xicheng-qu, 6, Chegongzhuang Dajie, no.1 Luo, 1-Ceng, Beijing, 100044, China. TEL 86-10-68007100, bjdjyjh@email.bac.edu.cn, http://www.bjdj.gov.cn/. **Dist. by:** China International Book Trading Corp, 35 Chegongzhuang Xilu, Haidian District, PO Box 399, Beijing 100044, China. TEL 86-10-68412045, FAX 86-10-68412023, cibtc@mail.cibtc.com.cn, http://www.cibtc.com.cn.

320 CHN ISSN 1673-2669
XIZANG FAZHAN LUNTAN/THEORETICAL PLATFORM OF TIBETAN DEVELOPEMENT. Text in Chinese. 1985. bi-m. **Document type:** *Journal, Academic/Scholarly.*
Formerly (until 2000): Xizang Dangxiao
Related titles: Online - full text ed.
Published by: Xizang Zizhiqu Xingzheng Xueyuan, 9, Luding Bei Lu, Lhasa, 850000, China. TEL 86-891-6850460, http:// www.xzqwdx.gov.cn/. **Co-sponsor:** Xizang Zizhiqu Weidangxiao.

320.5 NLD ISSN 1574-6585
XPRES. Text in Dutch. 1969. q.
Formerly (until 1995): XminY Bulletin (0165-7593)
Published by: XminY Solidariteitsfonds, De Wittenstraat 43-45, Amsterdam, 1052 AL, Netherlands. TEL 31-20-6279661, FAX 31-20-6228229, info@xminy.nl, http://www.x-y.org.

320 CHN
XUANCHUAN SHOUCE/PROPAGANDA HANDBOOK. Text in Chinese. 1984. s-m. CNY 2 newsstand/cover (effective 2004). **Document type:** *Government.*
Related titles: Online - full content ed.
Published by: Beijing Ribao Baoye Jituan/Beijing Daily Newspaper Group, Zhaoyang-qu, 21, Hepingli Xi Jia, Beijing, 100013, China. TEL 86-10-84275511 ext 2042. Ed. Wang Minying. **Dist. by:** China International Book Trading Corp, 35 Chegongzhuang Xilu, Haidian District, PO Box 399, Beijing 100044, China. TEL 86-10-68412045, FAX 86-10-68412023, cibtc@mail.cibtc.com.cn, http:// www.cibtc.com.cn.

320.532 CHN ISSN 2095-0888
XUEXI HUOYE WENXUAN. Text in Chinese. 2001. 3/yr. **Document type:** *Journal, Government.*
Published by: Dang Jian Zazhishe, 5, Xichangan Jie, Xicheng-qu, Beijing, 100806, China.

324.2 CHN
XUEXI YU YANJIU/REFERENCE MATERIALS FOR STUDY AND RESEARCH. Variant title: Learn and Study. Text in Chinese. 1981. m. CNY 69, USD 28.80 (effective 2005). **Document type:** *Journal, Academic/Scholarly.*
Published by: (Zhonggong Beijing Shiwei), Xuexi yu Janjiu Zazhishe, 6, Chegongzhuang Dajie, Beijing, 100044, China. TEL 86-10-63093184, FAX 86-10-63096278. Ed. Tao Yifan. **Dist. by:** China International Book Trading Corp, 35 Chegongzhuang Xilu, Haidian District, PO Box 399, Beijing 100044, China.

320.532 CHN ISSN 1007-5968
XUEXIAO DANGJIAN YU SIXIANG JIAOYU. Text in Chinese. 1983. m. CNY 96 (effective 2009). **Description:** Covers Chinese Communist education, thoughts, ideas, and studies.
Formerly (until 1996): Xuexiao Sixiang Jiaoyu (1002-8056)
Related titles: Online - full text ed.
Published by: Hubei Jiaoyu Baokanshe, 58, Luoyu Lu, Hongshan-qu, Wuhan, 430079, China. TEL 86-27-87870401.

320 CHN
YAN - ZHAO XIANGYIN. Text in Chinese. bi-m.
Published by: Hebei Sheng Zhengzhi Xieshang Weiyuanhui, 34, Weiming Jie, Shijiazhuang, Hebei 050051, China. TEL 23477. Ed. Wang Xin.

YEARBOOK OF ASIAN AFFAIRS/ASIA DOKO-NENPO. *see* BUSINESS AND ECONOMICS

YELLOW SHEET REPORT. *see* PUBLIC ADMINISTRATION

320 GBR ISSN 0513-5982
HX11
YOUNG FABIAN PAMPHLET. Text in English. 1961. irreg. GBP 5 per issue (effective 2009). adv. charts; stat. back issues avail.; reprints avail. **Document type:** *Monographic series, Academic/Scholarly.*
Formerly (until 1962): Young Fabian Publication
Published by: Fabian Society, 11 Dartmouth St, London, SW1H 9BN, United Kingdom. TEL 44-20-72274900, info@fabians.org.uk, http://www.fabians.org.uk. Ed. Tom Hampson.

YOUTH & SOCIETY. *see* CHILDREN AND YOUTH—About

320 NLD ISSN 1876-1127
DT746
Z A M AFRICA MAGAZINE. Text in Dutch. 1977. q. EUR 25 domestic; EUR 32.50 in Europe; EUR 35 elsewhere; EUR 6.95 newsstand/ cover (effective 2009). adv. bk.rev.; dance rev.; film rev.; music rev. illus.; charts. 48 p./no.; back issues avail. **Document type:** *Magazine, Consumer.* **Description:** Covers politics, society, culture, daily life, travelling in Southern Africa.
Former titles (until 2008): Zuidelijk Afrika (1386-4297); (until 1997): Amandla (0166-0373); Which was formed by the merger of (1967-1977): Angola Bulletin (0044-8281); (1973-1977): B O A Bulletin (1385-6898); (1969-1977): Kairos Berichten (1385-6901)
Related titles: Online - full text ed.: ISSN 1876-1135.
Published by: Stichting ZAM-net, Postbus 16711, Amsterdam, 1001 RE, Netherlands. TEL 31-20-5318497, FAX 31-20-5318498. Ed. Bart Luirink. Circ: 12,500.

320 DEU ISSN 1864-6638
Z E F WORKING PAPERS SERIES. (Zentrum fuer Entwicklungsforschung) Text in English, German. 2005. free (effective 2011). **Document type:** *Monographic series, Academic/Scholarly.*
Media: Online - full text.
Published by: Universitaet Bonn, Zentrum fuer Entwicklungsforschung, Walter-Flex Str 3, Bonn, 53113, Germany.

320 USA ISSN 1056-5507
HN51
Z MAGAZINE. Text in English. 1987. m. USD 33 domestic (effective 2010). bk.rev.; film rev. illus. back issues avail.; reprints avail. **Document type:** *Magazine, Academic/Scholarly.* **Description:** Provides critical thinking on political, cultural, social, and economic life in the US. Discusses racial, gender, class and political dimensions of personal life.
Formerly (until 1989): Zeta Magazine (0896-1328)
Related titles: Online - full text ed.
Indexed: ABS&EES, AltPI, G10, M10, MLA-IB, P30, PAIS, SCOPUS, W09.
—IE, Ingenta.
Published by: (Institute for Social and Cultural Communications), ZCommunications, 18 Millfield St, Woods Hole, MA 02543. TEL 508-548-9063, FAX 508-457-0626, eric.sargent@zmag.org. Eds. Eric Sargent, Lydia Sargent.

320 RUS
ZAVTRA ROSSII. Text in Russian. w. USD 299 in United States.
Address: Ul Svetlanskaya 72, Vladivostok, 690091, Russian Federation. TEL 7-4232-222859, FAX 7-4232-222859. Ed. M Solov'enko. **Dist. by:** East View Information Services, 10601 Wayzata Blvd, Minneapolis, MN 55305. TEL 952-252-1201, 800-477-1005, FAX 952-252-1202, info@eastview.com, http://www.eastview.com.

320.51 POL ISSN 0137-3242
AP54
ZDANIE. Text in Polish. 1978. q. PLZ 3 newsstand/cover. bk.rev. back issues avail. **Description:** Socio-political magazine with leftist orientation.
Indexed: RASB.
Published by: (Stowarzyszenie "Kuznica"), Oficyna Cracovia, Ul Czyzynska 21A, Krakow, 31571, Poland. TEL 48-12-4115492, FAX 48-12-4120321, cracovia@drukarnie.com.pl. Ed. Adam Komorowski. Circ: 1,000 (controlled).

ZEITGESCHICHTE, KOMMUNISMUS, STALINISMUS. *see* HISTORY—History Of Europe

320.5 DEU ISSN 0948-9878
ZEITSCHRIFT DES FORSCHUNGSVERBUNDES S E D - STAAT. Text in German. 1995. s-a. EUR 8.40 per issue (effective 2010). **Document type:** *Monographic series, Academic/Scholarly.*
Published by: Freie Universitaet Berlin, Forschungsverbundes S E D - Staat, Koserstr 21, Berlin, 14195, Germany. TEL 49-30-83852091, FAX 49-30-83855141, apt@zedat.fu-berlin.de. Ed. Jochen Staadt.

ZEITSCHRIFT FUER IDEENGESCHICHTE. *see* PHILOSOPHY

320 DEU ISSN 0340-1758
JN3971.A7
➤ **ZEITSCHRIFT FUER PARLAMENTSFRAGEN.** Text in German. 1970. q. EUR 52 (effective 2011). adv. bk.rev. bibl. reprint service avail. from SCH. **Document type:** *Journal, Academic/Scholarly.*
Indexed: A22, A26, CA, DIP, E01, I13, IBR, IBSS, IBZ, P42, PCI, PRA, PSA, SCOPUS, SociolAb, T02.
—BLDSC (9476.500000), IE, Infotrieve, Ingenta. **CCC.**
Published by: (Deutsche Vereinigung fuer Parlamentsfragen), Nomos Verlagsgesellschaft mbH und Co. KG, Waldseestr 3-5, Baden-Baden, 76530, Germany. TEL 49-7221-21040, FAX 49-7221-210427, nomos@nomos.de, http://www.nomos.de. Ed. Suzanne Schuettemeyer. Circ: 2,200 (paid).

320 DEU ISSN 0044-3360
JA14
ZEITSCHRIFT FUER POLITIK. Text in German. 1907; N.S. 1954. q. EUR 95 (effective 2011). adv. bk.rev. bibl. index. reprint service avail. from SCH. **Document type:** *Journal, Academic/Scholarly.*
Indexed: A22, ABCPolSci, BAS, CA, DIP, HistAb, I13, IBR, IBSS, IBZ, P30, P42, PAIS, PCI, PRA, PSA, RASB, SociolAb, T02.
—BLDSC (9484.300000), IE, Infotrieve, Ingenta.
Published by: (Hochschule fuer Politik), Nomos Verlagsgesellschaft mbH und Co. KG, Waldseestr 3-5, Baden-Baden, 76530, Germany. TEL 49-7221-21040, FAX 49-7221-210427, nomos@nomos.de, http://www.nomos.de. Ed. Andreas Vierecke. Circ: 1,200 (paid and controlled).

320 DEU ISSN 1865-4789
ZEITSCHRIFT FUER POLITIKBERATUNG. Text in German. 2008. q. EUR 348 combined subscription to institutions (print & online eds.) (effective 2011). adv. reprint service avail. from PSC. **Document type:** *Journal, Academic/Scholarly.*
Related titles: Online - full text ed.: ISSN 1865-4797. 2008.
Indexed: A22, A26, E01, E08, SCOPUS.
—IE. **CCC.**
Published by: V S - Verlag fuer Sozialwissenschaften (Subsidiary of: Springer Fachmedien Wiesbaden GmbH), Abraham-Lincoln-Str 46, Wiesbaden, 65189, Germany. TEL 49-611-78780, FAX 49-611-7878400, springerfachmedien-wiesbaden@springer.com, http:// www.vs-verlag.de. Circ: 420 (paid).

320 DEU ISSN 1869-3016
▼ **ZEITSCHRIFT FUER POLITISCHE THEORIE.** Text in German. 2010. 2/yr. EUR 39.90; EUR 34 to students (effective 2010). **Document type:** *Journal, Academic/Scholarly.*
Published by: Verlag Barbara Budrich, Stauffenbergstr 7, Leverkusen, 51379, Germany. TEL 49-2171-344594, FAX 49-2171-344693, info@budrich-verlag.de, http://www.budrich-verlag.de.

320.531 DEU ISSN 0514-2776
HN1
➤ **ZEITSCHRIFT FUER SOZIALREFORM.** Text in German. 1954. 4/yr. EUR 130 to individuals; EUR 153 to institutions; EUR 60 to students; EUR 52 newsstand/cover (effective 2011). adv. back issues avail. **Document type:** *Journal, Academic/Scholarly.*
Indexed: A22, C28, CA, IBR, IBZ, P30, P42, PAIS, S02, S03, T02.
—IE, Infotrieve. **CCC.**
Published by: Lucius und Lucius Verlagsgesellschaft mbH, Gerokstr 51, Stuttgart, 70184, Germany. TEL 49-711-242060, FAX 49-711-242088, lucius@luciusverlag.com. Circ: 450 (paid and controlled).

320.3 DEU ISSN 1865-2646
ZEITSCHRIFT FUER VERGLEICHENDE POLITIKWISSENSCHAFT. Text in German, English. 2008. 2/yr. EUR 325.23, USD 400 combined subscription to institutions (print & online eds.) (effective 2012). adv. reprint service avail. from PSC. **Document type:** *Journal, Academic/ Scholarly.*
Related titles: Online - full text ed.: ISSN 1865-2654. 2008.
Indexed: A22, A26, E01, E08, P45, P54, PQC, SCOPUS.
—IE. **CCC.**
Published by: V S - Verlag fuer Sozialwissenschaften (Subsidiary of: Springer Fachmedien Wiesbaden GmbH), Abraham-Lincoln-Str 46, Wiesbaden, 65189, Germany. TEL 49-611-78780, FAX 49-611-7878400, springerfachmedien-wiesbaden@springer.com, http:// www.vs-verlag.de. Circ: 410 (paid).

ZEITSCHRIFT MARXISTISCHE ERNEUERUNG. *see* SOCIAL SCIENCES: COMPREHENSIVE WORKS

320.972 MEX ISSN 1605-0363
ZETA. Text in Spanish. 1999. w.
Media: Online - full text. **Related titles:** Print ed.
Address: TEL 52-664-221213. Adv. contact Aurora Yanez Uribe.

320 GBR ISSN 2045-0222
▼ **ZETTER'S POLITICAL COMPANION.** Abbreviated title: Z P C. Variant title: Zetter's Parliamentary Companion. Text in English. 2010. q. GBP 65; GBP 20 per issue (effective 2011). adv. **Document type:** *Directory, Consumer.* **Description:** Contains information about political parties, the European Union, and the devolved parliaments and assemblies.
Published by: Zetter's Political Services Ltd., 6 Radcliffe Rd, London, N21 2SE, United Kingdom. TEL 44-20-83640009.

320.532 CHN ISSN 1673-5463
ZHENG-GONG YANJIU DONGTAI. Text in Chinese. 1998. s-m. CNY 8.80 per issue (effective 2010). **Document type:** *Journal, Academic/ Scholarly.*
Published by: (Zhongguo Sixiang Zhengzhi Gongzuo Yanjiuhui/Chinese Society of Ideological and Political Work), Zheng-gong Yanjiu Dongtai Zazhishe, 17, Chunshu Yuan, Beijing, 100052, China. TEL 86-10-63109746, FAX 86-10-63109743.

ZHENGFA LUNTAN/POLITICAL SCIENCE & LAW TRIBUNE; Zhongguo Zhengfa Daxue xuebao. *see* LAW

▼ **ZHENGZHI JINGJIXUE PINGLUN/CHINA REVIEW OF POLITICAL ECONOMY.** *see* BUSINESS AND ECONOMICS

ZHENGZHI YU FALU/POLITICAL SCIENCE AND LAW. *see* LAW

320 CHN ISSN 1005-4405
ZHENGZHIXUE/POLITICS. Text in Chinese. bi-m. USD 63.80 (effective 2009). 80 p./no.; **Document type:** *Journal, Academic/Scholarly.*
Published by: Zhongguo Renmin Daxue Shubao Ziliao Zhongxin/Renmin University of China, Information Center for Social Sciences, Dongcheng-qu, 3, Zhangzizhong Lu, Beijing, 100007, China. TEL 86-10-64039458, FAX 86-10-64015080, center@zlzx.org, http://www.zlzx.org/. **Dist. in US by:** China Publications Service, PO Box 49614, Chicago, IL 60649. TEL 312-288-3291, FAX 312-288-8570; **Dist. by:** China International Book Trading Corp, 35 Chegongzhuang Xilu, Haidian District, PO Box 399, Beijing 100044, China. TEL 86-10-68412045, FAX 86-10-68412023, cibtc@mail.cibtc.com.cn, http://www.cibtc.com.cn.

324 CHN ISSN 1000-3355
JA26
ZHENGZHIXUE YANJIU/POLITICAL SCIENCE RESEARCH. Text in Chinese. 1985. bi-m. USD 53.40 (effective 2009).
Related titles: Online - full text ed.
Indexed: RASB.
—East View.
Published by: (Zhongguo Shehui Kexueyuan/Chinese Academy of Social Sciences, Zhengzhixue Yanjiusuo/Institute of Political Science), Zhongguo Shehui Kexueyuan Chubanshe, Gulou Xidajie A 158, Beijing, China.

320 RUS
ZHIVOI MIR. Text in Russian. m. USD 85 in United States.
Published by: Elita Publisher, A-ya 8, Moscow, 125252, Russian Federation. TEL 7-095-9438660, FAX 7-095-9435289. Ed. E Turina. **Dist. by:** East View Information Services, 10601 Wayzata Blvd, Minneapolis, MN 55305. TEL 952-252-1201, 800-477-1005, FAX 952-252-1202, info@eastview.com, http://www.eastview.com.

320 RUS
ZHIZN' NATSIONAL'NOSTEI. Text in Russian. bi-m.
Indexed: RASB.
Address: Ul Babushkina 16, Moscow, 129344, Russian Federation. TEL 7-095-1251921. **Dist. by:** East View Information Services, 10601 Wayzata Blvd, Minneapolis, MN 55305. TEL 952-252-1201, 800-477-1005, FAX 952-252-1202, info@eastview.com, http://www.eastview.com.

320.532 CHN ISSN 1671-6175
ZHONG-GONG YILI ZHOU-WEI DANGXIAO XUEBAO/YILI PREFECTURE COMMUNIST PARTY INSTITUTE. JOURNAL. Text in Chinese. 1989. bi-m. USD 12 (effective 2009). **Document type:** *Journal, Academic/Scholarly.*
Related titles: Online - full text ed.; Kazakh ed.: CNY 20 domestic; USD 5.20 in Hong Kong, Macau & Taiwan; USD 10 elsewhere (effective 2007).
—East View.
Published by: Zhong-Gong Yili Zhou-Wei Dangxiao/Yili Prefecture Communist Party Institute, 154, Xinhua Xi Lu, Yining, Xinjiang 835000, China. TEL 86-999-8320039, FAX 86-999-8324573. **Dist. by:** China International Book Trading Corp, 35 Chegongzhuang Xilu, Haidian District, PO Box 399, Beijing 100044, China. TEL 86-10-68412045, FAX 86-10-68412023, cibtc@mail.cibtc.com.cn, http://www.cibtc.com.cn.

320.532 CHN
ZHONGGONG DANGSHI/HISTORY OF THE CHINESE COMMUNIST PARTY. Text in Chinese. s-m.
Published by: Zhongguo Zhonggong Dangshi Xuehui, Zhongyang Dangxiao Nanyuan Nei, PO Box 1924, Beijing, 100091, China. TEL 2581534. Ed. Wang Zhixin.

ZHONGGONG DANGSHI YANJIU/STUDY OF C.P.C. HISTORY. *see* HISTORY—History Of Asia

320.531 CHN ISSN 1006-0391
ZHONGGUO DANGZHENG GANBU LUNTAN/CHINESE CADRES TRIBUNE. Text in Chinese. 1988. m. USD 49.20 (effective 2009). 48 p./no.; **Document type:** *Journal, Academic/Scholarly.* **Description:** Covers Chinese socialism theories and new developments of Chinese Communist Party government.
Formerly: Dangxiao Luntan (1002-4816)
Related titles: Online - full text ed.
—East View.
Published by: Zhonggong Zhongyang Dangxiao, 100 Dayouzhuang, Haidian-qu, Beijing, 100091, China. TEL 86-10-62805370, FAX 86-10-62805368. **Dist. by:** China International Book Trading Corp, 35 Chegongzhuang Xilu, Haidian District, PO Box 399, Beijing 100044, China.

ZHONGGUO GAIGE/CHINA'S REFORM. *see* BUSINESS AND ECONOMICS

303.484 CHN
ZHONGGUO GAIGE BAO/CHINA REFORM NEWS. Text in Chinese. 6/w. USD 130.80 (effective 2009). **Document type:** *Newspaper, Government.*
Published by: Zhonghua Renmin Gongheguo Guojia/National Development and Reform Commission, 38, Yuetan Nan Lu, Beijing, 100824, China. ndrc@ndrc.gov.cn, http://www.ndrc.gov.cn/. **Dist. by:** China International Book Trading Corp, 35 Chegongzhuang Xilu, Haidian District, PO Box 399, Beijing 100044, China. TEL 86-10-68412045, FAX 86-10-68412023, cibtc@mail.cibtc.com.cn, http://www.cibtc.com.cn.

324.251 CHN ISSN 1001-3180
JQ1519.A5
ZHONGGUO GONGCHANDANG/COMMUNIST PARTY OF CHINA. Text in Chinese. 1978. m. USD 127.50 (effective 2009). 160 p./no.; **Document type:** *Journal, Academic/Scholarly.* **Description:** Covers major Chinese Communist Party conference proceedings as well as speeches by prominent Communist leaders. Also covers the party's activities.
Indexed: RASB.
Published by: Zhongguo Renmin Daxue Shubao Ziliao Zhongxin/Renmin University of China, Information Center for Social Sciences, Dongcheng-qu, 3, Zhangzizhong Lu, Beijing, 100007, China. TEL 86-10-64039458, FAX 86-10-64015080, center@zlzx.org, http://www.zlzx.org/. **Dist. in US by:** China Publications Service, PO Box 49614, Chicago, IL 60649. TEL 312-288-3291, FAX 312-288-8570.

320 CHN ISSN 1002-4441
HV416
ZHONGGUO MINZHENG/CHINA CIVIL AFFAIRS. Text in Chinese. 1969. m. USD 49.20 (effective 2009). **Document type:** *Journal, Academic/ Scholarly.*
Related titles: Online - full text ed.
Published by: Minzheng Bu, Zhengci Yanjiu Zhongxin, 147, Beiheyan Dajie, Beijing, 100721, China. TEL 86-10-85203791, FAX 86-10-65142203.

320.532 CHN ISSN 1674-4195
DS778.T39
ZHONGGUO TESE SHEHUI ZHUYI LILUN/THEORIES OF SOCIALISM WITH CHINESE CHARACTERISTICS. Text in Chinese. 1996. m. CNY 144; CNY 12 per issue (effective 2011). 72 p./no.; **Document type:** *Journal, Academic/Scholarly.* **Description:** Contains reprints of researches and studies on Deng Xiaoping thoughts and theories.
Former titles (until 2009): Deng Xiaoping lilun San'ge Daibiao Zhongyao Sixiang/Deng Xiaoping Theory & Important Thoughts of Three Represents (1673-0631); (until 2004): Deng Xiaoping Lilun/Deng Xiaoping Theories (1009-7562); (until 2001): Deng Xiaoping Sixiang Yanjiu/Researches in Deng Xiaoping's Theories (1007-6700); (until 1997): Dengxiaoping Sixiang Yanjiu (1007-0494)
Published by: Zhongguo Renmin Daxue Shubao Ziliao Zhongxin/Renmin University of China, Information Center for Social Sciences, 59, Zhongguancun Dajie, Haidian-qu, Beijing, 100872, China. TEL 86-10-84043003, FAX 86-10-64015080, center@zlzx.org. **Dist. in US by:** China Publications Service, PO Box 49614, Chicago, IL 60649. TEL 312-288-3291, FAX 312-288-8570; **Dist. outside of China by:** China International Book Trading Corp, 35 Chegongzhuang Xilu, Haidian District, PO Box 399, Beijing 100044, China. TEL 86-10-68412045, FAX 86-10-68412023, cibtc@mail.cibtc.com.cn, http://www.cibtc.com.cn.

320.951 CHN ISSN 1001-3067
DS779.15
ZHONGGUO ZHENGZHI/POLITICS OF CHINA. Text in Chinese. 1978. m. USD 79 (effective 2009). 128 p./no.; **Document type:** *Journal, Academic/Scholarly.*
Published by: Zhongguo Renmin Daxue Shubao Ziliao Zhongxin/Renmin University of China, Information Center for Social Sciences, Dongcheng-qu, 3, Zhangzizhong Lu, Beijing, 100007, China. TEL 86-10-64039458, FAX 86-10-64015080, center@zlzx.org, http://www.zlzx.org/. **Dist. in US by:** China Publications Service, PO Box 49614, Chicago, IL 60649. TEL 312-288-3291, FAX 312-288-8570.

ZHONGXUE ZHENGZHI JI QITA GEKE JIAOXUE/TEACHING AND LEARNING OF POLITICS AND OTHER SUBJECTS IN MIDDLE SCHOOL. *see* EDUCATION

320 POL ISSN 0137-9399
ZIELONY SZTANDAR. Text in Polish. 1931. w. USD 150 (effective 2002). Website rev. 26 p./no.; back issues avail. **Document type:** *Magazine.*
Related titles: E-mail ed.; Fax ed.; Supplement(s): Zielony Sztandar. Dodatek Ilustrowany. ISSN 0239-2666.
Published by: Polskie Stronnictwo Ludowe (PSL)/Polish People's Party, Ul Grzybowska 4, Warsaw, 00-131, Poland. TEL 48-22-207554, biuronkw@nkw.psl.org.pl. Ed. Jolanta Ball. Circ: 195,800.

324.2 DEU
DIE ZIGARRE. Text in German. 1970. s-a.
Published by: Sozialdemokratische Partei Deutschlands (SPD), Ortsverein Hatzenbuehl, c/o Dieter Boehm, Schubertstr 7, Hatzenbuehl, 76770, Germany. TEL 07275-4803.

ZIGUANGGE/PURPLE LIGHT PAVILION. *see* BUSINESS AND ECONOMICS—Economic Situation And Conditions

320 DEU ISSN 1868-3002
▼ **ZIVILGESELLSCHAFTLICHE VERSTAENDIGUNGSPROZESSE VOM 19. JAHRHUNDERT BIS ZUR GEGENWART**; Deutschland und die Niederlande im Vergleich. Text in German. 2009. irreg., latest vol.6, 2011. price varies. **Document type:** *Monographic series, Academic/Scholarly.*
Published by: Waxmann Verlag GmbH, Steinfurter Str 555, Muenster, 48159, Germany. TEL 49-251-265040, FAX 49-251-2650426, info@waxmann.com.

324.25694 ISR
ZO HA-DEREKH. Text in Hebrew. 1965. w. USD 144; USD 123 in Europe.
Related titles: Online - full text ed.
Published by: Communist Party of Israel, P O Box 26205, Tel-Aviv, Israel. TEL 972-3-6293944, FAX 972-3-6297263, http://www.maki.org.il. Ed. Tamar Gozansky.

320.972 MEX ISSN 1607-1123
ZONA LIBRE; periodismo sin frontera. Text in Spanish. 1999. m. MXN 168 (effective 2001).
Media: Online - full text. **Related titles:** Print ed.
Published by: High Tech Editores, S.A. de C.V., Ave Tres No 51, Col San Pedro de los Pinos, Mexico, D.F. 03800, Mexico. TEL 52-5-278-8110, FAX 52-5-272-1640, htech@htech.com.mx. Ed. Martin Enrique Mendivil. Circ: 6,000.

321.8 CHE
ZUERCHER FREISINN. Text in German. 10/yr. **Document type:** *Bulletin.*
Published by: (Freisinnig-Demokratischen Partei), Kretz AG, General Wille-Str 147, Postfach, Feldmeilen, 8706, Switzerland. TEL 41-1-9237656, FAX 41-1-9237657, info@kretzag.ch. Circ: 19,000 (controlled).

320.9 NLD ISSN 0044-5428
DT751
ZUID-AFRIKA. Short title: Z - A. Text in Dutch. 1924. 10/yr. EUR 35; EUR 25 to students (effective 2009). adv. bk.rev. abstr.; bibl.; illus. index. **Document type:** *Magazine, Consumer.* **Description:** Covers political developments in South Africa, with commentary from a Dutch point of view.
Published by: De Nederlands - Zuid - Afrikaanse Vereniging/The Dutch South African Association, Keizersgracht 141, Amsterdam, 1015 CK, Netherlands. TEL 31-20-624-9318, FAX 31-20-638-2596, info@zuidafrikahuis.nl. Circ: 1,400.

322.4 DEU ISSN 0044-5487
ZUM NACHDENKEN. Text in German. 1963. irreg., latest vol.35, 1992. free. adv.
Published by: Hessische Landeszentrale fuer Politische Bildung, Rheinbahnstr 2, Wiesbaden, 65185, Germany. FAX 0611-3682653. Ed. Herbert Lilge. Circ: 7,000.

320.5 POL ISSN 1230-9605
IV RZECZPOSPOLITA - POLSKA JAKA BEDZIE; miesiecznik IV Rzeczypospolitej. Variant title: Czwarta Rzeczpospolita. Text in Polish. 1991. m. PLZ 2.50 newsstand/cover. back issues avail. **Description:** Presents thoughts on political and moral revival of the Polish society.
Published by: Faktor Sp. z o.o., ul Ksiecia Wladyslawa Opolskiego 3 a, Kety, 32650, Poland. TEL 48-33-453888. Ed. Jozej Gaweda. Circ: 8,000.

320 FRA ISSN 1961-1935
▼ **25 QUESTIONS DECISIVES.** Text in French. 2009. irreg., latest 2011. **Document type:** *Monographic series, Consumer.*
Published by: Armand Colin, 21 Rue du Montparnasse, Paris, 75283 Cedex 06, France. TEL 33-1-44395447, FAX 33-1-44394343, infos@armand-colin.fr.

POLITICAL SCIENCE—Abstracting, Bibliographies, Statistics

016.32 DNK ISSN 0107-4628
A B AS BIBLIOGRAFISKE SERIE. (Arbejderbevaegelsens Bibliotek og Arkiv) Text in Danish. 1973. irreg. price varies. back issues avail. **Document type:** *Bibliography.* **Description:** Presents bibliographies of the Danish labor movement, its publishing houses, and foreign-language material on the Danish labor movement.
Published by: Arbejdermuseet og Arbejderbevaegelsens Bibliotek og Arkiv/Workers' Museum & the Labour Movement's Library and Archives, Roemersgade 22, Copenhagen K, 1362, Denmark. TEL 45-33-932575, FAX 45-33-145258, am@arbejdermuseet.dk, http://www.aba.dk. Ed. Gerd Callesen.

016.96 016.3276 USA ISSN 0011-3255
Z3501
➤ **A CURRENT BIBLIOGRAPHY ON AFRICAN AFFAIRS.** Text in English. 1968. q. USD 435 to institutions (effective 2011). bk.rev. bibl.; illus. author index. back issues avail.; reprints avail. **Document type:** *Journal, Bibliography.* **Description:** Focuses on study and research in the field of African studies and related subjects.
Indexed: A21, ASD, BibInd, BibLing, CCA, CERDIC, HistAb, IBR, IBZ, MLA, MLA-IB, RI-1, RI-2.
—IE, Infotrieve. **CCC.**
Published by: Baywood Publishing Co., Inc., 26 Austin Ave, PO Box 337, Amityville, NY 11701. TEL 631-691-1270, 800-638-7819, FAX 631-691-1770, Baywood@baywood.com. Ed. Roger W Moeller.

➤ **AFRICAN STUDIES.** *see* HISTORY—Abstracting, Bibliographies, Statistics

016.32053 USA
ALTERNATIVE PRESS INDEX. Text in English. base vol. plus q. updates. **Document type:** *Database, Abstract/Index.*
Media: Online - full text. **Related titles:** CD-ROM ed.: ISSN 1093-331X; Online - full text ed.: Alternative Press Index Archive; ◆ Print ed.: Alternative Press Index (Print). ISSN 0002-662X.
Published by: Alternative Press Center, Inc, PO Box 47739, Chicago, MD 60647. TEL 312-451-8133, FAX 773-772-4180, altpress@altpress.org, http://www.altpress.org.

016.32053 USA ISSN 0002-662X
AI3
ALTERNATIVE PRESS INDEX (PRINT); access to movements, news, policy, theory. Text in English. 1969. s-a. USD 75 to individuals; USD 425 to institutions (effective 2007). back issues avail.; reprints avail. **Document type:** *Abstract/Index.* **Description:** Indexes popular and scholarly periodicals of the alternative (progressive) press.
Related titles: CD-ROM ed.: ISSN 1093-331X; ◆ Online - full text ed.: Alternative Press Index; Alternative Press Index Archive.
Published by: Alternative Press Center, Inc, PO Box 47739, Chicago, MD 60647. TEL 312-451-8133, altpress@altpress.org. Eds. Charles D'Adamo, Les Wade. R&P Chuck D'Adamo. Circ: 650 (paid).

324.6 ISL ISSN 1017-6667
ALTHINGISKOSNINGAR/ELECTIONS TO THE ALTHING. Text in English, Icelandic. 1882. irreg. USD 15 (effective 2001). back issues avail. **Document type:** *Monographic series, Government.*
Published by: Hagstofa Islands/Statistics Iceland, Borgartuni 12 A, Reykjavik, 150, Iceland. TEL 354-560-9800, FAX 354-562-8865, hagstofa@hag.stjr.is, http://www.statice.is/stat/e-mail.htm. Ed. Gudni Baldursson.

324.6021 USA ISSN 0065-678X
JK1967
AMERICA VOTES; election returns by state. Text in English. 1956. biennial, latest 2007, 27th edition. USD 195 per issue (effective 2008). back issues avail.; reprints avail. **Description:** Contents include most recent election results for senator, representative and governor by ward, county, town and congressional district; most recent state-by-state primary results; state-by-state presidential election totals since 1920; and presidential primary totals since 1972.
Related titles: Online - full text ed.
Indexed: SRI.
Published by: C Q Press, Inc. (Subsidiary of: Sage Publications, Inc.), 2300 N St, NW, Ste 800, Washington, DC 20037. TEL 202-729-1900, 866-427-7737, FAX 800-380-3810, customerservice@cqpress.com. Eds. Alice V McGillivray, Richard M Scammon.

016.32095 SGP ISSN 0004-4520
DS1
ASIAN ALMANAC; weekly abstracts of Asian affairs. Text in English. 1963. w. looseleaf. SGD 300, USD 150. index. back issues avail.
Address: P.O. Box 2737, Singapore, 9047, Singapore. Ed. Vedagiri T Sambandan. Circ: 600.

323.4021 AUS
AUSTRALIA. BUREAU OF STATISTICS. AUSTRALIAN INDIGENOUS STATISTICS CATALOGUE ON FLOPPY DISK. Text in English. 1995. irreg., latest 1996. **Document type:** *Government.* **Description:** Contains information dealing with Aboriginal and Torres Strait Islander people, families, dwellings and communities.
Media: Diskette.
Published by: Australian Bureau of Statistics, Locked Bag 10, Belconnen, ACT 2616, Australia. TEL 61-2-92684909, 61-2-62527037, 300-135-070, FAX 61-2-62528103, client.services@abs.gov.au.

016.32 AUT ISSN 1563-3799
AUSTRIAN POLITICIANS, PARTIES AND MAYORS INDEX/ OESTERREICHISCHER POLITIKER-, PARTEIEN- UND BUERGERMEISTERINDEX. Text in English, German. a. EUR 75, USD 94 (effective 2001). **Document type:** *Directory, Trade.*
Published by: Indexdatenverlag Wien, Frimmelgasse 41, Vienna, W 1190, Austria. TEL 43-1-3701577, FAX 43-1-3704659, redaktion@indexverlag.at. Ed. Alexander Trobinger. Pub., R&P Peter Hoffer. Circ: 1,800 (paid).

016.328 DEU ISSN 0523-2775
BIBLIOGRAPHIEN ZUR GESCHICHTE DES PARLAMENTARISMUS UND DER POLITISCHEN PARTEIEN. Text in German. 1953. irreg., latest vol.8, 1986. price varies. **Document type:** *Monographic series, Academic/Scholarly.*
Published by: Droste Verlag GmbH, Martin Luther Platz 26, Duesseldorf, 40212, Germany. TEL 49-211-8605220, FAX 49-211-3230098, vertrieb@drosteverlag.de, http://www.drosteverlag.de.

016.328 USA ISSN 1056-5515
BIBLIOGRAPHIES OF BRITISH STATESMEN. Text in English. 1988. irreg., latest 1998. price varies. back issues avail. **Document type:** *Monographic series, Bibliography.*
Published by: Greenwood Publishing Group Inc. (Subsidiary of: A B C - C L I O), 88 Post Rd W, PO Box 5007, Westport, CT 06881. TEL 203-226-3571, 800-225-5800, FAX 877-231-6980, sales@greenwood.com. Ed. Gregory Palmer.

016.32 USA ISSN 1061-6500
BIBLIOGRAPHIES OF THE PRESIDENTS OF THE UNITED STATES. Text in English. 1988. irreg., latest 2005. price varies. back issues avail. **Document type:** *Monographic series, Bibliography.*
Published by: Greenwood Publishing Group Inc. (Subsidiary of: A B C - C L I O), 88 Post Rd W, PO Box 5007, Westport, CT 06881. TEL 203-226-3571, 800-225-5800, FAX 877-231-6980, sales@greenwood.com. Eds. Carol Bondhus Fitzgerald, Mary McElligott Ellen.

016.32 USA ISSN 1056-5523
BIBLIOGRAPHIES OF WORLD LEADERS. Text in English. 1989. irreg., latest 2000. price varies. back issues avail. **Document type:** *Monographic series, Bibliography.*
Related titles: Online - full text ed.
Published by: Greenwood Publishing Group Inc. (Subsidiary of: A B C - C L I O), 88 Post Rd W, PO Box 5007, Westport, CT 06881. TEL 203-226-3571, 800-225-5800, FAX 877-231-6980, sales@greenwood.com. Ed. Philip Dwyer.

C S A POLITICAL SCIENCE & GOVERNMENT; a guide to periodical literature. (Cambridge Scientific Abstracts) *see* PUBLIC ADMINISTRATION—Abstracting, Bibliographies, Statistics

016.32 USA
C S A WORLDWIDE POLITICAL SCIENCE ABSTRACTS. (Cambridge Scientific Abstracts) Text in English. 2000. base vol. plus m. updates. illus. back issues avail.; reprints avail. **Document type:** *Database, Abstract/Index.* **Description:** Covers all aspects of political science and related fields, including international relations, law and public administration/policy.
Formed by the 2000 merger of: A B C Pol Sci (Online); (1984-2000): Political Science Abstracts (Online); Which superseded (in 1997): Political Science Abstracts. Annual Supplement (Print) (0731-8022); (1967-1980): Political Science, Government, and Public Policy Series. Annual Supplement (0364-5908)
Media: Online - full text. **Related titles:** ◆ Print ed.: C S A Political Science & Government. ISSN 1542-9040.
Published by: ProQuest LLC (Bethesda) (Subsidiary of: Cambridge Information Group), 789 E Eisenhower Pky, Ann Arbor, MI 48103. TEL 734-761-4700, FAX 734-997-4222, info@proquest.com.

320.021 USA
(YEAR) CENSUS OF POPULATION AND HOUSING. Text in English. 1961. decennial, latest 2000. price varies. **Document type:** *Government.*
Formerly (until 2000): Census of Population and Housing: Population and Housing Characteristics for Congressional Districts
Related titles: Online - full text ed.
Published by: U.S. Census Bureau. Population Division (Subsidiary of: U.S. Department of Commerce), 4600 Silver Hill Rd., Washington, DC 20233. TEL 866-758-1060, http://www.census.gov/population/www/.

016.328 USA
CONGRESSIONAL RECORD SCANNER. Text in English. 180/yr. looseleaf. USD 2,100 (effective 2009). **Document type:** *Abstract/ Index.* **Description:** Abstracts of each day's Congressional Record.
Media: Online - full text.
Published by: Congressional Quarterly, Inc., 1255, 22nd St, N.W., Washington, DC 20037. TEL 202-419-8500, 800-432-2250, FAX 202-419-8760, customerservice@cq.com. Ed. Michael Riley. Pub. Keith A White.

016.32 FRA
COUNCIL OF EUROPE. DOCUMENTATION SECTION. BIBLIO BULLETIN. SERIES: POLITICAL, ECONOMIC AND SOCIAL AFFAIRS. Text in French. 1972. m. free. **Document type:** *Bibliography.* **Description:** Index of periodical articles on international relations, politics, economic and social affairs.
Former titles: Council of Europe. Central Library. Biblio Bulletin. Series: Political and Social Affairs; Council of Europe. Documentation Section and Library. Bibliographical Bulletin. Series: Political, Economic and Social Affairs; Council of Europe. Documentation Section and Library. Bibliographical Bulletin. Series: Political and Economic Affairs
Published by: Council of Europe/Conseil de l'Europe, Avenue de l'Europe, Strasbourg, 67075, France. TEL 33-3-88412581, FAX 33-3-88413910, publishing@coe.int, http://www.coe.int. Circ: 300. **Dist. in U.S. by:** Manhattan Publishing Co., 468 Albany Post Rd, Croton On Hudson, NY 10520. TEL 914-271-5856.

016.32 USA ISSN 1074-0007
CODEN: PATIEI
CURRENT DIGEST OF THE POST-SOVIET PRESS. QUARTERLY INDEX. Text in English. 1949. q. USD 165 to institutions (effective 2009). **Document type:** *Abstract/Index.*
Formerly (until 1992): Current Digest of the Soviet Press. Quarterly Index
Related titles: Microfilm ed.
—CCC.
Published by: East View Information Services, 10601 Wayzata Blvd, Minneapolis, MN 55305. TEL 952-252-1201, 800-477-1005, FAX 952-252-1202, info@eastview.com, http://www.eastview.com/.

016.32747 USA ISSN 2159-3612
D839
CURRENT DIGEST OF THE RUSSIAN PRESS. Text in English. 1949. w. USD 1,889 to institutions; USD 1,997 combined subscription to institutions (print & online eds.) (effective 2011). abstr.; charts; illus. q. index, a. cum.index. back issues avail.; reprints avail. **Document type:** *Journal, Academic/Scholarly.* **Description:** Translations or abstracts of materials selected from a wide variety of Russian-language periodicals. Covers political reform, public health, privatization, foreign policy and international affairs, and other social, cultural and legal issues.
Former titles (until 2011): Current Digest of the Post-Soviet Press (1067-7542); (until 1992): Current Digest of the Soviet Press (0011-3425); Which incorporated (1968-1970): Current Abstracts of the Soviet Press (0011-3166)
Related titles: Microfilm ed.: USD 325 per vol. (effective 2003); Online - full text ed.: ISSN 2159-3639. USD 1,851 to institutions (effective 2011).
Indexed: A01, A02, A03, A08, A22, A25, A26, BAS, CA, E08, G08, I05, I08, M01, M02, MLA-IB, P02, P06, P10, P30, P34, P48, P53, P54, PAIS, PQC, PRA, S08, S09, SCOPUS, T02.
—BLDSC (3496.345000), IE, Infotrieve, Ingenta. **CCC.**
Published by: East View Information Services, 10601 Wayzata Blvd, Minneapolis, MN 55305. TEL 952-252-1201, 800-477-1005, FAX 952-252-1202, info@eastview.com, http://www.eastview.com/.

016.327 USA
Z1223.Z9
DECLASSIFIED DOCUMENTS REFERENCE SYSTEM. Text in English. 1975. 6/yr. back issues avail. **Document type:** *Catalog, Abstract/ Index.* **Description:** Includes information regarding United States' post-World War II international relations from the Cold War through the Vietnam era. Provides a comprehensive compilation of documents microfilmed, abstracted, and indexed as they are released by government agencies or obtained from the National Archives and Presidential Libraries.
Former titles (until 1998): Declassified Documents Catalog (Print) (1046-4239); (until 1986): Declassified Documents Quarterly Catalog (0099-0957)
Media: Online - full text. **Related titles:** Microfiche ed.: (from RPI).
Published by: Primary Source Media (Subsidiary of: Gale), 12 Lunar Dr, Woodbridge, CT 06525-2398. TEL 203-397-2600, 800-444-0799, FAX 203-397-3893, gale.sales@cengage.com.

016.328 BRA
DEPUTADOS BRASILEIROS: REPERTORIO BIOGRAFICO. Text in Portuguese. 1966. every 4 yrs. **Document type:** *Government.* **Description:** Lists biographical data of elected deputies in each legislative period, including personal and professional information.
Published by: Camara dos Deputados, Coordenacao de Publicacoes, Brasilia, DF, Brazil. TEL 55-61-3186865, FAX 55-61-3182190, publicacoes@cedi.camara.gov.br. Ed., R&P Nelda Mendonca Raulino. Circ: 4,000.

320.021 EGY ISSN 0013-239X
HC531
L'EGYPTE CONTEMPORAINE. Text in Arabic, French. 1909. q. USD 12, EGP 225. bk.rev. bibl. cum.index: 1910-1959. **Document type:** *Journal, Academic/Scholarly.*
Indexed: ASD, IBR, IBZ, ILD, M10, P06, P30, PAIS.
Published by: Egyptian Society of Political Economy, Statistics and Legislation/Societe Egyptienne d'Economie Politique, de Statistique et de Legislation, 16 Sharia Ramses, P O Box 732, Cairo, Egypt. TEL 202-2574-3491, FAX 202-3575-0797. Ed. Dr. Mustafa Kamel El-Sa'id. Circ: 1,500.

314 320 FIN ISSN 1457-0904
FINLAND. TILASTOKESKUS. EDUSKUNTAVAALIT/FINLAND. STATISTICS FINLAND. PARLIAMENTARY ELECTIONS/FINLAND. STATISTIKCENTRALEN. RIKSDAGSVALET. (Section XXIX A of Official Statistics of Finland) Text in Finnish, Swedish, English. 1909. irreg. EUR 65 (effective 2008). **Document type:** *Government.*
Former titles (until 1999): Finland. Tilastokeskus. Kansanedustajain Vaalit (0789-7960); (until 1987): Finland. Suomen Virallinen Tilasto. 29 A, Vaalitilasto (0355-2209); Which superseded in part (in 1931): Finland. Suomen Virallinen Tilasto. 29, Vaalitilasto (0430-5531)
Related titles: Online - full text ed.; ◆ Series of: Finland. Tilastokeskus. Suomen Virallinen Tilasto. ISSN 1795-5165.
Published by: Tilastokeskus/Statistics Finland, Tyopajakatu 13, Statistics Finland, Helsinki, 00022, Finland. TEL 358-9-17341, FAX 358-9-17342279.

320.021 FIN ISSN 1239-7415
JN36
FINLAND. TILASTOKESKUS. EUROPARLAMENTTIVAALIT/FINLAND. STATISTICS FINLAND. ELECTIONS FOR THE EUROPEAN PARLIAMENT/FINLAND. STATISTIKCENTRALEN. VALET TILL EUROPAPARLAMENTET. Text in English, Finnish, Swedish. 1997. irreg. **Document type:** *Government.*
Related titles: Online - full text ed.; ◆ Series of: Finland. Tilastokeskus. Suomen Virallinen Tilasto. ISSN 1795-5165.
Published by: Tilastokeskus/Statistics Finland, Tyopajakatu 13, Statistics Finland, Helsinki, 00022, Finland. TEL 358-9-17341, FAX 358-9-17342279.

320.021 FIN ISSN 1239-7407
FINLAND. TILASTOKESKUS. EUROPARLAMENTTIVAALIT, ENNAKKOTILASTO/FINLAND. STATISTICS FINLAND. ELECTIONS FOR THE EUROPEAN PARLIAMENT/FINLAND. STATISTIKCENTRALEN. VALET TILL EUROPAPARLAMENTET. Text in English, Finnish, Swedish. 1996. irreg. **Document type:** *Government.*
Published by: Tilastokeskus/Statistics Finland, Tyopajakatu 13, Statistics Finland, Helsinki, 00022, Finland. TEL 358-9-17341, FAX 358-9-17342279, http://www.stat.fi.

320.021 FIN ISSN 0788-9178
FINLAND. TILASTOKESKUS. KANSANEDUSTAJAIN VAALIT, ENNAKKOTILASTO/FINLAND. STATISTIKCENTRALEN. RIKSDAGSVALET, FOERHANDSSTATISTIK. Text in Finnish, Swedish. 1991. irreg. **Document type:** *Government.*
Related titles: Online - full text ed.; ◆ Series of: Finland. Tilastokeskus. Suomen Virallinen Tilasto. ISSN 1795-5165.
Published by: Tilastokeskus/Statistics Finland, Tyopajakatu 13, Statistics Finland, Helsinki, 00022, Finland. TEL 358-9-17341, FAX 358-9-17342279.

320.021 FIN ISSN 1235-9777
FINLAND. TILASTOKESKUS. KUNNALLISVAALIT, ENNAKKOTILASTO. Text in English, Finnish, Swedish. 1992. irreg. **Document type:** *Government.*
Related titles: Online - full text ed.; ◆ Series of: Finland. Tilastokeskus. Suomen Virallinen Tilasto. ISSN 1795-5165.
Published by: Tilastokeskus/Statistics Finland, Tyopajakatu 13, Statistics Finland, Helsinki, 00022, Finland. TEL 358-9-17341, FAX 358-9-17342279.

320.021 FIN ISSN 1237-6779
FINLAND. TILASTOKESKUS. PRESIDENTIN VAALIT/FFINLAND. STATISTIKCENTRALEN. PRESIDENTVALET/FINLAND. STATISTICS FINLAND. PRESIDENTIAL ELECTION. Text in English, Finnish, Swedish. 1988. irreg. **Document type:** *Government.*
Related titles: Online - full text ed.; ◆ Series of: Finland. Tilastokeskus. Suomen Virallinen Tilasto. ISSN 1795-5165.
Published by: Tilastokeskus/Statistics Finland, Tyopajakatu 13, Statistics Finland, Helsinki, 00022, Finland. TEL 358-9-17341, FAX 358-9-17342279.

016.32052 USA ISSN 8756-0216
HS2321
GUIDE TO THE AMERICAN RIGHT; directory and bibliography. Text in English. 1978. a. USD 19.95 (effective 2000). bibl. **Document type:** *Directory, Bibliography.* **Description:** Lists 1,500 right-wing organizations and serials.
Formerly: Directory of the American Right
Published by: Laird Wilcox, Ed. & Pub., PO Box 2047, Olathe, KS 66061. TEL 913-829-0609, FAX 913-829-0609. Circ: 1,800.

016.3234 USA ISSN 0098-0579
KF4741
HUMAN RIGHTS ORGANIZATIONS & PERIODICALS DIRECTORY. Text in English. 1973. biennial. USD 100 per issue to individuals; USD 175 per issue to institutions (effective 2010). bibl. **Document type:** *Directory, Trade.* **Description:** Descriptions of over 1200 U.S. local and national organizations that focus on human rights.
Published by: Meiklejohn Civil Liberties Institute, PO Box 673, Berkeley, CA 94701. TEL 510-848-0599, FAX 510-848-6008, http://mcli.org. Circ: 2,000.

016.32 IND ISSN 0250-9660
JA26
I C S S R JOURNAL OF ABSTRACTS AND REVIEWS: POLITICAL SCIENCE. Text in English. 1973. s-a. bk.rev. bibl.; abstr. index. back issues avail. **Document type:** *Journal, Abstract/Index.* **Description:** Abstracts of articles in political science published in Indian journals, book reviews and list of reviews published in political science journals.
Published by: Indian Council of Social Science Research, JNU Institutional Area, Aruna Asaf Ali Marg, New Delhi, 110 067, India. TEL 91-11-26741849, FAX 91-11-26741836, info@icssr.org.

016.32 USA ISSN 0191-1058
Z1223.5.I3
ILLINOIS. STATE LIBRARY, SPRINGFIELD. PUBLICATIONS OF THE STATE OF ILLINOIS. Text in English. a. free. **Document type:** *Bibliography.*
Related titles: Microform ed.
Published by: Illinois State Library, 300 S Second St, Springfield, IL 62701. TEL 217-785-5600, www.cyberdriveillinois.com/library/isl/depos/pubsofil.txt.

016.32 SEN
INDEX OF AFRICAN SOCIAL SCIENCE PERIODICAL ARTICLES. Text in French. 1993. irreg. GBP 19.95, USD 35 foreign (effective 2000). **Document type:** *Journal, Abstract/Index.*
Published by: Council for the Development of Social Science Research in Africa, Avenue Cheikh, Anta Diop x Canal IV, BP 3304, Dakar, Senegal. TEL 221-825-9822, FAX 221-824-1289, TELEX 61339 CODES SG24, codesria@ssonatel.senet.net. **Dist. outside Africa by:** African Books Collective Ltd., The Jam Factory, 27 Park End St, Oxford, Oxon OX1 1HU, United Kingdom. TEL 44-1865-726686, FAX 44-1865-793298.

016.628 USA ISSN 1354-6597
J301
INDEX TO HOUSE OF COMMONS PARLIAMENTARY PAPERS. Text in English. 1992. m. **Document type:** *Abstract/Index.*
Related titles: CD-ROM ed.
Published by: ProQuest (Subsidiary of: Cambridge Information Group), 789 E Eisenhower Pky, PO Box 1346, Ann Arbor, MI 48106. TEL 734-761-4700, 800-521-0600, FAX 734-997-4040, 888-241-5612, info@proquest.com, http://www.proquest.com.

016.327 USA ISSN 1065-1365
Z6482
INDEX TO UNITED NATIONS DOCUMENTS AND PUBLICATIONS. Text in English. 1946. q. (plus a. cumulation). price varies. index. **Document type:** *Abstract/Index.* **Description:** Contains documents for researchers, academics, and graduate and undergraduate students.
Former titles: United Nations Documents and Publications. Checklist; United Nations Documents (0191-8087); Readex Microprint Publications (0079-984X)
Media: CD-ROM. **Related titles:** Online - full text ed.: Access U N.

Published by: Newsbank, Inc., 5801 Pelican Bay Blvd., Ste. 600, Naples, FL 34108. TEL 802-875-2910, 800-762-8182, FAX 239-263-3004, sales@newsbank.com, http://www.newsbank.com. Circ: 6,975.

016.32 GBR ISSN 0085-2058
Z7163
INTERNATIONAL BIBLIOGRAPHY OF POLITICAL SCIENCE/ BIBLIOGRAPHIE INTERNATIONALE DE SCIENCE POLITIQUE. Text in English; Prefatory materials in French. 1953. a., latest vol.51, 2002. USD 495 per issue (effective 2009). adv. back issues avail. **Document type:** *Bibliography.* **Description:** Focuses on all aspects of political science including international, national and comparative politics, political theory and political philosophy.
Incorporates (1931-1989): London Bibliography of the Social Sciences (0076-051X)
Related titles: ◆ Online - full text ed.: International Bibliography of the Social Sciences; ◆ Print ed.: International Bibliography of the Social Sciences. Anthropology; ◆ International Bibliography of the Social Sciences. Economics. ISSN 0085-204X; ◆ International Bibliography of the Social Sciences. Sociology. ISSN 0085-2066.
Published by: (British Library of Political and Economic Science), Routledge (Subsidiary of: Taylor & Francis Group), 4 Park Sq, Milton Park, Abingdon, Oxon OX14 4RN, United Kingdom. TEL 44-20-70176000, FAX 44-20-70176336, subscriptions@tandf.co.uk, http://www.routledge.com.

016.327 GBR ISSN 0020-8345
JA36
INTERNATIONAL POLITICAL SCIENCE ABSTRACTS/ DOCUMENTATION POLITIQUE INTERNATIONALE. Text in Multiple languages; Abstracts in English, French. 1951. bi-m. GBP 455, USD 841 to institutions; GBP 464, USD 858 combined subscription to institutions (print & online eds.) (effective 2012). adv. abstr. index. 160 p./no.; back issues avail.; reprints avail. **Document type:** *Journal, Abstract/Index.* **Description:** Abstracts of political science articles in periodicals and yearbooks worldwide.
Related titles: CD-ROM ed.: 1994. USD 1,359 (effective 2003); Online - full text ed.: International Political Science Abstracts Database; ISSN 1751-9292. GBP 418, USD 772 to institutions (effective 2012).
Indexed: A22, E01, RASB.
—BLDSC (4544.960000), IE. **CCC.**
Published by: (Association Internationale de Science Politique - International Political Science Association (A I S P - I P S A) CAN), Sage Publications Ltd. (Subsidiary of: Sage Publications, Inc.), 1 Oliver's Yard, 55 City Rd, London, EC1Y 1SP, United Kingdom. TEL 44-20-73248500, FAX 44-20-73248600, info@sagepub.co.uk, http://www.uk.sagepub.com/home.nav. Ed. Paul Godt.

016.32 IRN ISSN 1026-7182
IRANIAN GOVERNMENT REPORTS/GUZARISHHA-YI DAWLATI-I IRAN. Text in Persian, Modern; Summaries in English. 1995. q. USD 97 foreign (effective 2003). 140 p./no. 2 cols./p.; back issues avail. **Document type:** *Government.* **Description:** Contains Iranian Government reports.
Related titles: CD-ROM ed.; Diskette ed.
Published by: Iranian Information & Documentation Center (IRANDOC), 1188 Enqelab Ave., P O Box 13185-1371, Tehran, Iran. TEL 98-21-6494955, FAX 98-21-6462254, journal@irandoc.ac.ir, http://www.irandoc.ac.ir. Ed. M Jayaher Kalam. Pub. Hussein Gharibi. **Co-sponsor:** Ministry of Culture and Higher Education.

016.327 USA ISSN 0950-6128
D410
KEESING'S RECORD OF WORLD EVENTS. Text in English. 1931. m. USD 422 (effective 2005). charts. q. index. **Document type:** *Directory, Consumer.* **Description:** Contains a distillation of political, economic, and social events in concise reports from every country in the world.
Formerly: Keesing's Contemporary Archives (0022-9679)
Related titles: CD-ROM ed.; Microfiche ed.: (from RPI); Online - full text ed.
Indexed: A22, RASB, RefugAb.
—BLDSC (5088.350500), IE, Infotrieve. **CCC.**
Published by: Keesing's Worldwide, LLC (Subsidiary of: C Q Press, Inc.), 4905 Del Ray Ave., Ste. 405, Bethesda, MD 20814-2557. TEL 800-332-3535, info@keesings.com, http://www.keesings.com. Ed. Stephen Lewis.

LANCASTER INDEX TO DEFENCE & INTERNATIONAL SECURITY LITERATURE. *see* MILITARY—Abstracting, Bibliographies, Statistics

016.32 USA
Z7164.S67
LEFT INDEX (ONLINE). Text in English. 1990. base vol. plus irreg. updates. reprints avail. **Document type:** *Database, Abstract/Index.* **Description:** Provides a subject author index to the contents of periodicals with a leftist perspective.
Media: Online - full text. **Related titles:** CD-ROM ed.: USD 198 to individuals; USD 235 in developing nations to individuals; USD 330 to institutions single user; USD 495 to institutions 2-5 concurrent users; USD 660 to institutions 6-10 concurrent users; USD 825 to institutions unlimited concurrent users (effective 2005).
Indexed: RASB.
Published by: N I S C, Inc. (Subsidiary of: EBSCO Publishing), Wyman Towers, 3100 St Paul St, Baltimore, MD 21218. TEL 410-243-0797, FAX 410-243-0982, sales@nisc.com, http://www.nisc.com.

MILITARY & GOVERNMENT COLLECTION. *see* MILITARY—Abstracting, Bibliographies, Statistics

016.32 USA
THE NEW YORK TIMES INDEX HIGHLIGHTS. Text in English. 1977. q. free to New York Times Index subscribers. **Document type:** *Abstract/Index.*
Published by: (New York Times Company), ProQuest (Subsidiary of: Cambridge Information Group), 789 E Eisenhower Pky, PO Box 1346, Ann Arbor, MI 48106. TEL 734-761-4700, 800-521-0600, FAX 734-997-4040, 888-241-5612, info@proquest.com.

016.327 CAN ISSN 0383-2848
NORMAN PATERSON SCHOOL OF INTERNATIONAL AFFAIRS. BIBLIOGRAPHY SERIES. Text in English. 1975. irreg. (1-2/yr). CAD 6 per issue. **Document type:** *Bibliography.*
Published by: Norman Paterson School of International Affairs, Carleton University, 1125 Colonel By Dr, Ottawa, ON K1S 5B6, Canada. TEL 613-520-2600, FAX 613-520-2889. Ed. Vivian Cummins. Circ: 600.

320.021 ARG
NOTAS SOBRE POLITICA ESTADISTICA EN EL MUNDO. Text in Spanish. m. ARS 1, USD 3 per issue (effective 1999). **Document type:** *Government.* **Description:** Presents aspects of official statistics from different countries.
Published by: Instituto Nacional de Estadistica y Censos, Presidente Julio A Roca 615, Buenos Aires, 1067, Argentina. TEL 54-114-3499662, FAX 54-114-3499621.

016.32 USA
P A I S ARCHIVE. Text in English. base vol. plus irreg. updates. **Document type:** *Database, Abstract/Index.*
Media: Online - full text. **Related titles:** ◆ Print ed.: P A I S International in Print (Monthly). ISSN 1051-4015.
Published by: ProQuest LLC (Bethesda) (Subsidiary of: Cambridge Information Group), 7200 Wisconsin Ave, Ste 715, Bethesda, MD 20814. TEL 301-961-6700, FAX 301-961-6720, service@csa.com, http://www.csa.com.

016.32 USA
P A I S INTERNATIONAL. (Public Affairs Information Service) Text in English. 1994. m. back issues avail. **Document type:** *Database, Abstract/Index.*
Media: Online - full text. **Related titles:** ◆ Print ed.: P A I S International in Print (Monthly). ISSN 1051-4015.
Published by: ProQuest LLC (Bethesda) (Subsidiary of: Cambridge Information Group), 789 E Eisenhower Pky, Ann Arbor, MI 48103. TEL 734-761-4700, FAX 734-997-4222, journals@csa.com.

016.32 USA ISSN 1076-2094
Z7164.E2 CODEN: DGAPEO
P A I S INTERNATIONAL IN PRINT (ANNUAL). (Public Affairs Information Service) Text in English. 1915. a. (plus 3/yr cumulation). USD 150 per vol. (effective 2011). illus. reprint service avail. from PSC. **Document type:** *Abstract/Index.* **Description:** Publishes bibliographic indexes with abstracts to the public policy literature in journal articles, books, and government documents on business, economics, health and medicine, agriculture, environment, international relations, government, political science and other social sciences.
Former titles (until 1991): P A I S Bulletin (0898-2201); (until 1985): Public Affairs Information Service Bulletin (0033-3409); (until 1967): Public Affairs Information Service. Bulletin (0731-0110)
Related titles: ◆ Cumulative ed. of: P A I S International in Print (Monthly). ISSN 1051-4015.
Indexed: PopulInd, RASB.
Published by: ProQuest LLC (Bethesda) (Subsidiary of: Cambridge Information Group), 7200 Wisconsin Ave, Ste 715, Bethesda, MD 20814. TEL 301-961-6798, 800-843-7751, FAX 301-961-6799, journals@csa.com. Eds. Chris Adcock, Sandra Stanton, Sonia V Diaz.

016.32 USA ISSN 1051-4015
Z7164.E2
P A I S INTERNATIONAL IN PRINT (MONTHLY). (Public Affairs Information Service) Text in English. 1971. m. (exc. Dec.). USD 1,165 combined subscription (includes a. cum. ed. & a. index on CD-ROM) (effective 2011). **Document type:** *Abstract/Index.* **Description:** Contains citations to journal articles, books, government documents, statistical directories, grey literature, research reports, conference reports, publications of international agencies, microfiche, Internet material, etc.
Former titles (until 1990): P A I S Foreign Language Index (0896-792X); (until 1984): Foreign Language Index (0048-5810)
Related titles: ◆ Online - full text ed.: P A I S International; ◆ P A I S Archive; ◆ Cumulative ed(s).: P A I S International in Print (Annual). ISSN 1076-2094.
Published by: ProQuest LLC (Bethesda) (Subsidiary of: Cambridge Information Group), 7200 Wisconsin Ave, Ste 715, Bethesda, MD 20814. TEL 301-961-6798, 800-843-7751, FAX 301-961-6799, journals@csa.com.

016.327172 USA
PEACE RESEARCH ABSTRACTS. Text in English. 200?. base vol. plus s-m. updates. **Document type:** *Database, Abstract/Index.* **Description:** Includes bibliographic records covering essential areas related to peace research, including conflict resolution, international affairs, peace psychology, and other areas of key relevance to the discipline.
Media: Online - full text.
Published by: EBSCO Publishing (Subsidiary of: EBSCO Industries, Inc.), 10 Estes St, PO Box 682, Ipswich, MA 01938. TEL 978-356-6500, 800-653-2726, FAX 978-356-6565, information@ebscohost.com.

016.32 USA
▼ **POLITICAL SCIENCE COMPLETE.** Text in English. 2009. base vol. plus m. updates. **Document type:** *Database, Abstract/Index.* **Description:** Provides indexing and abstracts for over 2,900 titles.
Media: Online - full text.
Published by: EBSCO Publishing (Subsidiary of: EBSCO Industries, Inc.), 10 Estes St, PO Box 682, Ipswich, MA 01938. TEL 978-356-6500, 800-653-2726, information@ebscohost.com.

016.32 UKR
POLITYKA. POLITYCHNI NAUKY. Text in Ukrainian. 1997. m. USD 207 foreign (effective 2005). 36 p./no.; **Document type:** *Bibliography.* **Description:** Abstracts of books and articles on politics.
Related titles: Online - full text ed.
Published by: Knyzhkova Palata Ukrainy imeni Ivana Fedorova/Ivan Fedorov Book Chamber of Ukraine, Pr Gagarina 27, Kyiv, 02094, Ukraine. TEL 380-44-5520134, ukrbook@ukr.net, http://www.ukrbook.net. **Dist. by:** East View Information Services, 10601 Wayzata Blvd, Minneapolis, MN 55305. TEL 952-252-1201, 800-477-1005, FAX 952-252-1202, info@eastview.com, http://www.eastview.com.

320.021 USA ISSN 0887-171X
HN90.P8
POLLING REPORT. Text in English. 1985. fortn. (w. in fall of even numbered yrs.). USD 195; USD 78 to students. bk.rev. **Document type:** *Newsletter.* **Description:** Reports results of public opinion surveys on political, public affairs and business issues. Provides analytical articles by pollsters, academics and other opinion experts.
Related titles: Online - full text ed.
Indexed: SCOPUS.
Published by: Polling Report, Inc., PO Box 42580, Washington, DC 20015-0580. TEL 202-237-2000, FAX 202-237-2001. Ed., Pub., R&P Thomas H Silver. Circ: 1,000.

PROQUEST MILITARY COLLECTION. *see* MILITARY—Abstracting, Bibliographies, Statistics

016.32 USA
PROQUEST POLITICAL SCIENCE. Text in English. 2008. base vol. plus updates. **Document type:** *Database, Abstract/Index.* **Description:** Covers the literature of political science and international relations, including such topics as comparative politics, political economy, international development, environmental policy, and hundreds of related topics.
Media: Online - full text.
Published by: ProQuest (Subsidiary of: Cambridge Information Group), 789 E Eisenhower Pky, PO Box 1346, Ann Arbor, MI 48106. TEL 734-761-4700, 800-521-0600, FAX 734-997-4040, 888-241-5612, info@proquest.com.

320.021 USA
RATINGS OF CONGRESS. Text in English. 1971. a. back issues avail. **Document type:** *Directory.* **Description:** Provides a numerical annual and cumulative score for US representatives and senators, measuring their ideological leanings based on actual votes cast on a variety of issues.
Related titles: Online - full text ed.
Published by: American Conservative Union, 1007 Cameron St, Alexandria, VA 22314. TEL 703-836-8602, FAX 703-836-8606.

016.32 LUX ISSN 1024-011X
RECENT PUBLICATIONS ON THE EUROPEAN UNION RECEIVED BY THE LIBRARY/NEUERSCHEINUNGEN UEBER DIE EUROPAEISCHE UNION EINGEGANGEN IN DER BIBLIOTHEK/ NYE PUBLIKATIONER OM DEN EUROPAEISKE UNION MODTAGET AF BIBLIOTEKET/PUBBLICAZIONI RECENTI SULL'UNIONE EUROPEA RECEVUTE DALLA BIBLIOTECA/ PUBLICACIONES RECIENTES SOBRE LA UNION EUROPEA RECIBIDAS POR LA BIBLIOTECA/PUBLICATIONS RECENTES SUR L'UNION EUROPEENNE RECUES PAR LA BIBLIOTHEQUE. Text in English. bi-m.
Formerly: Recent Publications on the European Communities Received by the Library (0257-1080)
Published by: European Commission, Office for Official Publications of the European Union, 2 Rue Mercier, Luxembourg, L-2985, Luxembourg. FAX 352-29291.

016.32 LUX ISSN 0256-3096
Z7165.E8
S C A D BULLETIN. (Systeme Communautaire d'Acces a la Documentation) Text in Danish, Dutch, English, French, German, Italian, Portuguese, Spanish. 1977. w. USD 400. **Document type:** *Bibliography.* **Description:** Analytical bulletin mentioning the bibliographic references of the main Community acts.
Formerly (until 1985): Commission of the European Communities. Documentation Bulletin (0378-441X)
Related titles: Online - full text ed.
Published by: European Commission, Office for Official Publications of the European Union, 2 Rue Mercier, Luxembourg, L-2985, Luxembourg. info@publications.europa.eu, http://europa.eu. **Dist. in U.S. by:** Bernan Associates, Bernan, 4611-F Assembly Dr., Lanham, MD 20706-4391. TEL 301-459-0056, 800-274-4447.

320.021 GTM
SECRETARIA PERMANENTE DEL TRATADO GENERAL DE INTEGRACION ECONOMICA CENTROAMERICANA. BOLETIN ESTADISTICO. Text in Spanish. 1976 (Mar., no.31). q. USD 10; USD 15 foreign. charts; stat.
Formerly (until 1993): Integracion en Cifras (0252-8746)
Published by: Secretaria Permanente del Tratado General de Integracion Economica Centroamericana, 4a Avda. 10-25, ZONA, 14, PO Box 1237, Guatemala City, 01901, Guatemala. TEL 502-3682151, FAX 502-3681071, TELEX 6203 SIECA GU. Ed. Eduardo Bolanos.

320.021 USA ISSN 0081-4601
ML156.4.P6
THE STATESMAN'S YEAR-BOOK (YEAR); the politics, cultures and economies of the world. Text in English. 1864. a. USD 265 (effective 2009). index. back issues avail. **Document type:** *Yearbook, Academic/Scholarly.* **Description:** Essential political and economical guide to all the counrties of the world.
Indexed: RASB.
—BLDSC (8442.500000). **CCC.**
Published by: St. Martin's Press, LLC (Subsidiary of: Holtzbrink Publishers), 175 Fifth Ave, New York, NY 10010. TEL 646-307-5151, press.inquiries@macmillanusa.com, http://us.macmillan.com/SMP.aspx. Ed. Barry Turner. Circ: 35,000.

320.021 USA ISSN 0081-4687
HA935
STATISTICAL ABSTRACT OF LATIN AMERICA. Text in English. 1956. a., latest vol.38, 2002. USD 325 (effective 2004). stat.; maps. 1100 p./no.; back issues avail. **Document type:** *Abstract/Index.* **Description:** Includes the latest data available on the 20 major Latin American republics; statistics are gathered from nearly 250 sources.
Indexed: RASB, SRI.
Published by: University of California, Los Angeles, Latin American Center, 10343 Bunche Hall, Box 951447, Los Angeles, CA 90095-1447. TEL 310-825-7547, FAX 310-206-6859. Ed. James W Wilkie. R&P Colleen H Trujillo TEL 310-825-7547.

320.021 TUR
TURKEY. TURKIYE ISTATISTIK KURUMU. MILLETVEKILI GENEL SECIMI IL VE ILCE SONUCLARI (YEAR)/TURKEY. TURKISH STATISTICAL INSTITUTE. GENERAL ELECTION OF REPRESENTATIVES; PROVINCE AND DISTRICT RESULTS (YEAR). Text in English, Turkish. 1962. irreg. (election year), latest 2007. TRY 10 per issue domestic; USD 20 per issue foreign (effective 2009). **Document type:** *Government.* **Description:** Covers data on the results of general election of representatives held on the period of time from 1991 to 2007 by province and district.
Related titles: CD-ROM ed.: TRY 5 per issue domestic; USD 10 per issue foreign (effective 2009).

P

Published by: T.C. Basbakanlik, Turkiye Istatistik Kurumu/Prime Ministry Republic of Turkey, Turkish Statistical Institute, Yucetepe Mah. Necatibey Cad No.114, Cankaya, Ankara, 06100, Turkey. TEL 90-312-4100410, FAX 90-312-4175886, bilgi@tuik.gov.tr, ulka.unsal@tuik.gov.tr, http://www.tuik.gov.tr.

320.021 TUR
TURKEY. TURKIYE ISTATISTIK KURUMU. MILLETVEKILI GENERL SECIMLERI (YEAR)/TURKEY. TURKISH STATISTICAL INSTITUTE. THE GENERAL ELECTIONS (YEAR). Text in English, Turkish. 1962. irreg., latest 1923. TRY 20 per issue domestic; USD 20 per issue foreign (effective 2009). **Document type:** *Government.*
Related titles: CD-ROM ed.: TRY 10 per issue domestic; USD 10 per issue foreign (effective 2009).
Published by: T.C. Basbakanlik, Turkiye Istatistik Kurumu/Prime Ministry Republic of Turkey, Turkish Statistical Institute, Yucetepe Mah. Necatibey Cad No.114, Cankaya, Ankara, 06100, Turkey. TEL 90-312-4100410, FAX 90-312-4175886, bilgi@tuik.gov.tr, ulka.unsal@tuik.gov.tr, http://www.tuik.gov.tr.

341.13 USA ISSN 0082-8084
Z7161
UNITED NATIONS. ECONOMIC AND SOCIAL COUNCIL. INDEX TO PROCEEDINGS. Text in English. 1946. irreg., latest 2007. price varies. back issues avail.; reprints avail. **Document type:** *Proceedings, Bibliography.* **Description:** Contains indices to the activities of each session, as well as information on organizational matters such as members.
Related titles: Chinese ed.: ISSN 0252-547X.
Published by: (United Nations, Economic and Social Council), United Nations Publications, 2 United Nations Plaza, Rm DC2-853, New York, NY 10017. TEL 212-963-8302, 800-253-9646, FAX 212-963-3489, publications@un.org, https://unp.un.org.

341.13 USA ISSN 0082-8157
JX1977
UNITED NATIONS. GENERAL ASSEMBLY. INDEX TO PROCEEDINGS. Text in English. 1946. a. price varies. back issues avail.; reprints avail. **Document type:** *Proceedings, Abstract/Index.* **Description:** Contains proceedings of the general assembly is a bibliographic guide to the proceedings and documentation of the general assembly.
Formerly: Resolutions of the General Assembly of the United Nations (0082-8211)
Related titles: Arabic ed.: Fihris a'mal al-gam'iyyat al-'ammatt - al-Umam al-Muttahidat. ISSN 0251-7655; French ed.: Nations Unies. Assemblee Generale. Index des Actes. ISSN 0258-3682; Chinese ed.: Biaoti suoyin dahui huiyi jilu, Lianheguo. ISSN 0251-7647.
—CCC.
Published by: (United Nations General Assembly), United Nations Publications, 2 United Nations Plaza, Rm DC2-853, New York, NY 10017. TEL 212-963-8302, 800-253-9646, FAX 212-963-3489, publications@un.org, https://unp.un.org.

341.13 USA ISSN 0082-8408
JX1977
UNITED NATIONS. SECURITY COUNCIL. INDEX TO PROCEEDINGS. Text in English. 1946. a., latest 2007. price varies. back issues avail.; reprints avail. **Document type:** *Proceedings, Abstract/Index.* **Description:** Contains records by subject and by country, including names of speakers and voting records of member states, reports, resolutions and documents of the council.
Related titles: Chinese ed.: Anquan Lishihui Huiyi Biaoti Suoyin, Lianheguo. ISSN 0251-3994; Arabic ed.: Fihris a'mal maglis al-amn, Al-Umam al-Muttahidat. ISSN 1014-8833; French ed.: Index des actes du Conseil de securite, Nations Unies. ISSN 1014-8019.
Published by: (United Nations Security Council), United Nations Publications, 2 United Nations Plaza, Rm DC2-853, New York, NY 10017. TEL 212-963-8302, 800-253-9646, FAX 212-963-3489, publications@un.org, https://unp.un.org.

016.34126 USA ISSN 0082-8491
UNITED NATIONS. TRUSTEESHIP COUNCIL. INDEX TO PROCEEDINGS. Text in English. 1953. a. USD 4. reprints avail. **Document type:** *Abstract/Index.*
Related titles: Microfiche ed.
Published by: (United Nations Trustee Council), United Nations Publications, 2 United Nations Plaza, Rm DC2-853, New York, NY 10017. TEL 212-963-8302, 800-253-9646, FAX 212-963-3489, publications@un.org, https://unp.un.org.

WASHINGTON (STATE). EMPLOYMENT SECURITY DEPARTMENT. AFFIRMATIVE ACTION INFORMATION. *see* BUSINESS AND ECONOMICS—Abstracting, Bibliographies, Statistics

016.32 CHN
ZHENGZHI LILUN WENZHI KA/POLITICAL THEORIES ABSTRACTS ON CARDS. Text in Chinese. q. CNY 5, USD 2.40 per issue (effective 2003). **Document type:** *Abstract/Index.*
Published by: Zhongguo Renmin Daxue Shubao Ziliao Zhongxin/Renmin University of China, Information Center for Social Sciences, Dongcheng-qu, 3, Zhangzizhong Lu, Beijing, 100007, China. TEL 86-10-64039458, FAX 86-10-64015080, center@zlzx.org, http://www.zlzx.org/. **Dist. in the US by:** China Publications Service, PO Box 49614, Chicago, IL 60649. TEL 312-288-3291, FAX 312-288-8570; **Dist. outside of China by:** China International Book Trading Corp, 35 Chegongzhuang Xilu, Haidian District, PO Box 399, Beijing 100044, China. TEL 86-10-68412045, FAX 86-10-68412023, cibtc@mail.cibtc.com.cn, http://www.cibtc.com.cn/.

POLITICAL SCIENCE—Civil Rights

323.9 USA ISSN 0896-8217
HF5549.5.A34
A A A A NEWS. Text in English. q. free to members. adv. bk.rev. **Document type:** *Newsletter.*
Published by: American Association for Affirmative Action, 888 16th St, NW, Ste 800, Washington, DC 20006. TEL 202-349-9855 ext 1857, 800-252-8952, FAX 202-355-1399, ExecAdminAsst@affirmativeaction.org, http://www.affirmativeaction.org. Ed., Adv. contact Joyce Pratt. Circ: 1,500.

323.4 CAN
A A R WORLDWATCH. Text in English. 1997. m. free. back issues avail. **Document type:** *Newsletter.* **Description:** Summarizes racist and anti-racist activities reported in the Canadian and international press.
Related titles: E-mail ed.
Published by: Artists Against Racism, PO Box 54511, Toronto, ON M5M 4N5, Canada. TEL 416-410-5631, aar@direct.com, http://www.vrx.net/aar.

323.4 USA
A C L U CYBER-LIBERTIES UPDATE. (American Civil Liberties Union) Text in English. 1995. bi-w. **Document type:** *Newsletter.*
Media: Online - full content. **Related titles:** E-mail ed.
Published by: American Civil Liberties Union, 132 W. 43rd St., New York, NY 10036. http://www.aclu.org.

323.4 USA
A C L U NEWS. Text in English. 1936. 6/yr. USD 20 to members (effective 2000). bk.rev. **Document type:** *Newsletter.*
Indexed: ChPerI.
Published by: American Civil Liberties Union of Northern California, 1663 Mission, Ste 460, San Francisco, CA 94103. TEL 415-621-2493, FAX 415-255-1478. Ed., R&P Elaine Elinson. Pub. Dorothy Ehrlich. Circ: 30,000.

A D C TIMES. *see* ETHNIC INTERESTS

323.4 USA ISSN 1061-5202
DS146.U6
A D L ON THE FRONTLINE. Text in English. 1943. bi-m. illus. reprints avail. **Document type:** *Newsletter, Consumer.* **Description:** Discusses incidents of anti-Semitism and other forms of bigotry in the US and around the world. Provides materials for teaching ways to recognize and combat bigotry and racism in schools and universities.
Formerly (until 1991): A D L Bulletin (0001-0936)
Related titles: Microform ed.: (from PQC); Online - full text ed.
Indexed: A22, ENW, HRIR, IJP, P45.
Published by: Anti-Defamation League, 823 United Nations Plz, New York, NY 10017. TEL 212-885-7700, FAX 212-867-0779, http://www.adl.org.

323 342.085 NLD ISSN 1384-282X
KQC572.A15
A F L A QUARTERLY. Text in Dutch. 1996. q. **Document type:** *Journal.* **Description:** Provides information for human rights and legal developments relating to Africa.
Published by: Africa Legal Aid, Anna Paulownastr 103, The Hague, 2518 BC, Netherlands. TEL 31-703-452842, FAX 31-703-454968, nl.afla@africalegalaid.org, http://www.africalegalaid.org.

323.4 ZAF
A F R A NEWS. Text in English. N.S. 1988. bi-m. back issues avail. **Document type:** *Newsletter.* **Description:** Aims to publicize rural removals and farm worker conditions, and encourage rural African development in Natal, South Africa.
Former titles (until no.20, 1993): A F R A Newsletter; (until 1988): A F R A Report
Published by: Association for Rural Advancement, PO Box 2517, Pietermaritzburg, KwaZulu-Natal 3200, South Africa. TEL 0331-57607, FAX 0331-455106. Circ: 900.

323.4 ZAF
A F R A SPECIAL REPORTS. Text in English. 1980. irreg. looseleaf. back issues avail.
Published by: Association for Rural Advancement, PO Box 2517, Pietermaritzburg, KwaZulu-Natal 3200, South Africa. TEL 0331-57607, FAX 0331-455106. Ed. Marie Dyer. Circ: 1,400.

323.4 AUS ISSN 1833-8631
A I R. (Australia/Israel Review) Text in English. 1976. m. AUD 54 to non-members; AUD 35 to members; AUD 43 to students (effective 2008). adv. bk.rev. back issues avail. **Document type:** *Newsletter, Consumer.* **Description:** Covers developments in the Middle East affecting Israel, and public policy issues of concern to the Australian Jewish community.
Former titles (until 2006): Australia, Israel and Jewish Affairs Council. The Review (1442-3693); (until 1999): Australia/Israel Review (0313-9727); (until 1996): Review; (until 1988): Australia/Israel Review
Published by: Australia, Israel and Jewish Affairs Council, Level 1, 22 Albert Rd, South Melbourne, VIC 3205, Australia. TEL 61-3-96816660, FAX 61-3-96816650, aijac@aijac.org.au. Ed. Dr. Tzvi Fleischer. Circ: 5,000 (paid).

323 AUS ISSN 1838-742X
▼ **A M H R C REVIEW.** Text in English. 2009. q. free (effective 2011). back issues avail. **Document type:** *Report, Trade.*
Related titles: Online - full text ed.: ISSN 1838-7438. free (effective 2011).
Published by: Australian Macedonian Human Rights Committee, Ste 106, Level 1, 55 Flemington Rd, North Melbourne, VIC 3051, Australia. TEL 61-3-93298960, info@macedonianhr.org.au.

323.4 CAN
A R A RESEARCH BULLETIN. Text in English. irreg. **Document type:** *Bulletin, Consumer.*
Published by: Anti-Racist Action, 414 Mont Royal Est, #8, Montreal, PQ H2J 1W1, Canada. http://www.antiracistaction.ca/. **Dist. by:** A K Press, Inc., 674-A 23rd St, Oakland, CA 94612. TEL 510-208-1700, FAX 510-208-1701, info@akpress.org, http://www.akpress.org/.

323.43 USA
A U L FORUM. Text in English. q. membership. **Document type:** *Newsletter.*
Related titles: Online - full content ed.
Published by: Americans United for Life, 310 S Peoria St, Ste 300, Chicago, IL 60607-3534. TEL 312-492-7234, FAX 312-492-7235, information@unitedforlife.org, http://www.unitedforlife.org.

323 NOR ISSN 1504-5145
AARBOK OM MENNESKERETTIGHETER I NORGE. Text in Norwegian. 2004. a. back issues avail. **Document type:** *Report, Consumer.* **Description:** Report on present human rights in Norway.
Related titles: Online - full text ed.: ISSN 1504-5153.
Published by: Universitetet i Oslo, Norsk Senter for Menneskerettigheter/University of Oslo, Centre for Human Rights, PO Box 6706, St Olavs Plass, Oslo, 0130, Norway. TEL 47-22-842001, FAX 47-22-842002, info@nchr.uio.no.

ACCESS CURRENTS. *see* HANDICAPPED—Physically Impaired

323.445 USA ISSN 0364-7625
JK468.S4
ACCESS REPORTS; freedom of information. Text in English. 1975. bi-w. looseleaf. USD 350 (effective 2001). abstr.; charts; stat. q. index. back issues avail. **Document type:** *Newsletter.*
Published by: Access Reports, Inc., 1624 Dogwood Ln, Lynchburg, VA 24503. TEL 804-384-5334, FAX 804-384-8272. Ed., R&P Harry A Hammitt.

323 EST ISSN 1736-3918
ACTA SOCIETATIS MARTENSIS. Text in Estonian. 2006. a. **Document type:** *Journal, Academic/Scholarly.*
Related titles: Online - full text ed.: ISSN 1736-3926. free (effective 2011).
Published by: Martensi Selts/The Martens Society, Kaarli pst 3, Tallinn, 10119, Estonia. info@martens.ee.

ACTION NOW!/A L'ACTION. *see* WOMEN'S INTERESTS

323.4 DEU ISSN 0930-3251
ACTIONS FOR THREATENED PEOPLE. Text in German. 1986. irreg. **Document type:** *Monographic series, Academic/Scholarly.*
Published by: Gesellschaft fuer Bedrohte Voelker, Gemeinnuetziger Verein e.V./Society for Threatened Peoples, Postfach 2024, Goettingen, 37010, Germany. TEL 49-551-4990611, FAX 49-551-58028, info@gfbv.de, http://www.gfbv.de.

323.4 CAN ISSN 1201-7892
JC571
THE ACTIVIST. Text in English. 1995. bi-m. CAD 35 (effective 2006). back issues avail. **Document type:** *Newsletter.* **Description:** Contains news, feature and action-oriented material setting out Amnesty International's concerns regarding human rights violations around the world.
Published by: Amnesty International, Canadian Section (English Speaking), 214 Montreal Rd, Ste 401, Vanier, ON K1L 1A4, Canada. TEL 613-744-7667, 800-266-3789, FAX 613-746-2411, info@amnesty.ca. R&P Ann Simpson. Circ: 9,000.

323.4 GEO
ADAMIANIS UPLEBEBI. Text in English. q. **Description:** Monitors human rights and basic freedoms in Georgia and elsewhere in the Caucasus.
Address: Tsabadze St 3-32, Tbilisi, 380012, Georgia. TEL 995-32-348651, FAX 995-32-001153, adupl@mmc.net.ge. Ed. Levan Urushadze.

ADVOKAT; casopis za pravnu praksu, teoriju i probleme ljudskih prava. *see* LAW—Civil Law

323.4 ITA
AESSE - AZIONE SOCIALE; il mensile dell'A C L I. Text in Italian. 1985. m. **Document type:** *Magazine, Consumer.*
Published by: Associazioni Cristiane Lavoratori Italiani (A C L I), Via Giuseppe Marcora 18-20, Rome, 00153, Italy. TEL 39-06-58401, FAX 39-06-5840202, acli@acli.it, http://www.acli.it.

AFRICA RENAISSANCE. *see* POLITICAL SCIENCE

AFRICAN-AMERICAN GRADUATES OF KENTUCKY DIRECTORY. *see* EDUCATION—Higher Education

323.4 ZAF ISSN 1609-073X
K1
➤ **AFRICAN HUMAN RIGHTS LAW JOURNAL.** Text in English. 2001. s-a. ZAR 710 domestic; ZAR 848 foreign (effective 2011). reprint service avail. from WSH. **Document type:** *Journal, Academic/Scholarly.*
Related titles: Online - full text ed.: ISSN 1996-2096.
Indexed: IBSS, ISAP.
—BLDSC (0732.501000), IE, Ingenta. **CCC.**
Published by: Juta & Company Ltd., Juta Law, PO Box 14373, Lansdowne, 7779, South Africa. TEL 27-21-7633500, FAX 27-11-8838169, cserv@juta.co.za, http://www.juta.co.za.

➤ **AFRICAN JOURNAL OF LEGAL STUDIES.** *see* LAW

323.42 USA
AGE DISCRIMINATION. Text in English. 1981. latest 2nd ed., 3 base vols. plus a. updates. looseleaf. USD 432 (effective 2008). 3420 p./no.; Supplement avail. **Document type:** *Monographic series, Trade.* **Description:** Annotates more than 3,200 cases and hundreds of statutory and regulatory provisions.
Published by: Thomson West (Subsidiary of: Thomson Reuters Corp.), 610 Opperman Dr, Eagan, MN 55123. TEL 651-687-7000, 800-344-5008, FAX 651-687-6674, west.support@thomson.com. Ed. Howard C Eglit.

AGENDA; empowering women for gender equity. *see* WOMEN'S STUDIES

AHAVA KIDS. *see* CHILDREN AND YOUTH—About

AIDS POLICY AND LAW; biweekly newsletter on legislation, regulation and litigation. (Acquired Immune Deficiency Syndrome) *see* LAW

AIM MAGAZINE (CHICAGO). *see* ETHNIC INTERESTS

ALAWI NEWS. *see* LAW

323.4 DEU
ALL-EUROPEAN HUMAN RIGHTS YEARBOOK. Text in German. 1991. a. **Document type:** *Academic/Scholarly.*
Published by: N.P. Engel Verlag, Gutenbergstr 29, Kehl, 77694, Germany. TEL 49-7851-2463, FAX 49-7851-4234. **US subscr. to:** N.P. Engel. TEL 703-920-3126, FAX 703-920-3127.

ALTERMONDES; revue trimestrielle de solidarite internationale. *see* BUSINESS AND ECONOMICS—International Development And Assistance

305.42 USA ISSN 1532-6861
HQ767.5.U5
AMERICAN FEMINIST. Text in English. 1973. q. USD 25 membership (effective 2005). adv. bk.rev. **Document type:** *Newsletter, Consumer.* **Description:** Devoted to the philosophy of Pro Life feminism, which holds that abortion is detrimental to women and undermines the moral foundation of feminism. Reports current legislative issues.
Formerly (until 1994): Sisterlife Journal (1062-6204)
Related titles: Online - full text ed.
Indexed: CWI.
Published by: Feminists for Life of America, Inc., 733 15th St, N W, Ste 1100, Washington, DC 20005. TEL 202-737-3352, FAX 202-737-0414, http://www.serve.com/fem4life. Ed. Erin Sullivan. Circ: 6,000.

AMERICANS WITH DISABILITIES ACT; law and regulations. *see* LAW

AMERICANS WITH DISABILITIES ACT TECHNICAL ASSISTANCE MANUAL: TITLE I. *see* SOCIAL SERVICES AND WELFARE

AMERICANS WITH DISABILITIES ACT TECHNICAL ASSISTANCE MANUAL: TITLE II. *see* SOCIAL SERVICES AND WELFARE

AMERICANS WITH DISABILITIES ACT TECHNICAL ASSISTANCE MANUAL: TITLE III. *see* SOCIAL SERVICES AND WELFARE

365.450 GBR ISSN 0264-3278
JC571
AMNESTY. Text in English. 1983. bi-m. free to members (effective 2009). **Document type:** *Magazine, Consumer.* **Description:** Contains news, campaign and activity updates, special features and human rights stories from around the world to show you how your money helps.
—CCC.
Published by: Amnesty International U K, 17-25 New Inn Yard, London, EC2A 3EA, United Kingdom. TEL 44-20-70331500, FAX 44-20-70331503, sct@amnesty.org.uk.

323.4 NLD ISSN 1569-0393
AMNESTY.NL. Text in Dutch. 1992. 3/yr. **Document type:** *Bulletin, Consumer.* **Description:** Provides an overview of current concerns, action suggestions, and developments in the field of human rights.
Former titles (until 2011): Amnesty.nl (1569-0393); (until 2001): Globaal (0927-3824)
Published by: Amnesty International, Dutch Section, Postbus 1968, Amsterdam, 1000 BZ, Netherlands. TEL 31-20-6264436, FAX 31-20-6240889. Circ: 245,000.

364.65 SWE ISSN 0284-7108
AMNESTY PRESS. Text in Swedish. 1969. 5/yr. SEK 160 (effective 2008). **Document type:** *Magazine, Consumer.*
Formerly (until 1988): Amnestybulletinen (0345-0848)
Related titles: Audio cassette/tape ed.
Published by: Amnesty International, Svenska Sektionen, Alsnoegatan 11, PO Box 4719, Stockholm, 11692, Sweden. TEL 46-8-7290200, FAX 46-8-7290201, info@amnesty.se, http://net19.amnesty.se.

323.4 CAN ISSN 1480-3445
ANNOTATED BRITISH COLUMBIA HUMAN RIGHTS CODE. Text in English. 1998. base vol. plus s-a. updates. looseleaf. CAD 105 per vol. (effective 2005). charts. **Document type:** *Handbook/Manual/ Guide, Trade.* **Description:** Presents the British Columbia Human Rights Code with annotations and expert commentary, along with commentary on relevant caselaw and legislation.
Published by: Canada Law Book Inc., 240 Edward St, Aurora, ON L4G 3S9, Canada. TEL 905-841-6472, 800-263-3269, FAX 905-841-5085, b.loney@canadalawbook.ca, http://www.canadalawbook.ca. Ed. W Anita Braha. R&P Nancy Nesbitt.

323 GBR ISSN 1362-0258
ANTI-SLAVERY REPORTER. Text in English. 1825. q. free to members (effective 2009). adv. bk.rev. **Document type:** *Magazine, Consumer.* **Description:** Features new developments in the fight to end slavery.
Formerly (until 1833): Anti-Slavery Monthly Reporter (1356-1804)
Related titles: Microform ed.: (from PQC); Online - full text ed.
Indexed: AICP.
Published by: Anti-Slavery International, The Stableyard, Broomgrove Rd, London, SW9 9TL, United Kingdom. TEL 44-20-75018920, FAX 44-20-77384110, info@antislavery.org. Ed. Beth Herzfeld TEL 44-20-75018934.

323.11924 GBR
DS145
ANTISEMITISM AND XENOPHOBIA TODAY. Abbreviated title: A X T. Text in English. 1992. a. back issues avail. **Document type:** *Magazine, Academic/Scholarly.* **Description:** Monitors anti-Semitism throughout the world and identifies trouble spots. Assesses each country's history of anti-Semitism; anti-Semitic parties and organizations; anti-Semitism in mainstream political, cultural, and religious life; denial of the Holocaust; opinion polls; anti-Semitism in the media; legal matters; and efforts to combat anti-Semitism.
Formerly (until 1997): Antisemitism World Report (Year) (Print) (1350-0996)
Media: Online - full text.
Published by: Institute for Jewish Policy Research, 7-8 Market Pl, London, W1W 8AG, United Kingdom. TEL 44-20-74361553, FAX 44-20-74367262, jpr@jpr.org.uk, http://www.jpr.org.uk.

ANUARIO DE ACCION HUMANITARIA Y DERECHOS HUMANOS. *see* LAW—Civil Law

323 ESP ISSN 0212-0364
ANUARIO DE DERECHOS HUMANOS. Text in Spanish. 1982. a. **Document type:** *Journal, Academic/Scholarly.*
Published by: (Universidad Complutense de Madrid, Instituto de Derechos Humanos), Universidad Complutense de Madrid, Servicio de Publicaciones, C/ Obispo Trejo 2, Ciudad Universitaria, Madrid, 28040, Spain. TEL 34-91-3941127, FAX 34-91-3941126, servicio.publicaciones@rect.ucm.es, http://www.ucm.es/ publicaciones.

323 CAN ISSN 1483-2852
APPLIED RESEARCH BULLETIN. Text in Multiple languages. 1995. s-a.
Related titles: Online - full text ed.: ISSN 1493-5546.
Published by: Human Resources Development Canada, Applied Research Branch, 165 Hotel de Ville St, Phase II, 7th Fl, Hull, PQ K1A OJ2, Canada. FAX 819-953-8868, http://www.hrsdc.gc.ca.

323.4 USA
THE ASIA PACIFIC ADVOCATE. Text in English. 1995. q. looseleaf. USD 25 (effective 2001). bk.rev. bibl.; charts; illus. **Document type:** *Newsletter.* **Description:** Supports justice and world peace throughout Asia and the Pacific through monitoring of countries and issues, policy analysis, advocacy, constituency and public education, support of people-to-people relationships, and resourcing networks.
Former titles (until 1996): Philippine Witness; A P C Focus
Indexed: IPP.
Published by: Asia Pacific Center for Justice and Peace, 110 Maryland Ave, N E, Ste 504, Box 70, Washington, DC 20002. TEL 202-543-1094, FAX 202-546-5103. R&P M Young. Circ: 2,000.

342.085 NLD ISSN 1388-1906
KM572.A15 CODEN: AJHRAF
➤ **ASIA - PACIFIC JOURNAL ON HUMAN RIGHTS AND THE LAW.** Text in English. 1999. s-a. EUR 248, USD 347 to institutions; EUR 270, USD 378 combined subscription to institutions (print & online eds.) (effective 2012). bk.rev. Index. back issues avail.; reprint service avail. from PSC,WSH. **Document type:** *Journal, Academic/Scholarly.* **Description:** Examines issues in human rights law in Southeast Asia.
Related titles: Online - full text ed.: ISSN 1571-8158. EUR 225, USD 315 to institutions (effective 2012) (from IngentaConnect).
Indexed: A01, A03, A08, A22, A26, B07, CA, CJA, E01, G08, I05, I13, I14, IZBG, L03, LRI, P34, P42, PSA, S02, S03, SCOPUS, SociolAb, T02.
—BLDSC (1742.260692), IE, Infotrieve, Ingenta. **CCC.**
Published by: Martinus Nijhoff (Subsidiary of: Brill), PO Box 9000, Leiden, 2300 PA, Netherlands. TEL 31-71-5353500, FAX 31-71-5317532, marketing@brill.nl. **Dist. by:** Turpin Distribution Services Ltd., Pegasus Dr, Stratton Business Park, Biggleswade, Bedfordshire SG18 8QB, United Kingdom. TEL 44-1767-604800, FAX 44-1767-601640, custserv@turpin-distribution.com, http://www.turpin-distribution.com/.

➤ **ASIAN AMERICAN POLICY REVIEW.** *see* ETHNIC INTERESTS

323 AUS ISSN 1832-0910
JC599.A78
ASIARIGHTS JOURNAL; journal of human rights, media and society in Asia and the Pacific. Text in English. 2004. bi-m. free (effective 2010). back issues avail. **Document type:** *Journal, Academic/Scholarly.* **Description:** Aims to promote informed debate within the Asia-Pacific region about the human rights implications of current national security policies.
Media: Online - full text.
Published by: Australian National University, Division of Pacific and Asian History, Research School of Pacific & Asian Studies, Coombs Bldg # 9, Canberra, ACT 0200, Australia. TEL 61-2-61253106, FAX 61-2-61255525, divadmin.pah@anu.edu.au, http://rspas.anu.edu.au/ pah/. Eds. Julia Yonetani, Tessa Morris-Suzuki.

ASUNTOS INDIGENAS. *see* ANTHROPOLOGY

323.4 USA
AUDIT OF ANTI-SEMITIC INCIDENTS. Text in English. 19??. a. back issues avail. **Document type:** *Bulletin, Trade.* **Description:** Discusses ADL's efforts to publicize and combat acts of hate and bigotry in all areas of society.
Related titles: Online - full content ed.
Published by: Anti-Defamation League, 823 United Nations Plz, New York, NY 10017. TEL 212-885-7700, FAX 212-867-0779.

AUSTRALIA. BUREAU OF STATISTICS. AUSTRALIAN INDIGENOUS STATISTICS CATALOGUE ON FLOPPY DISK. *see* POLITICAL SCIENCE—Abstracting, Bibliographies, Statistics

323.352 AUS ISSN 1320-7091
AUSTRALIAN CHILDREN'S RIGHTS NEWS. Abbreviated title: A C R N. Text in English. 1993. s-a. back issues avail. **Document type:** *Newsletter, Consumer.*
Related titles: Online - full text ed.: ISSN 1448-451X.
Published by: Defence for Children International Australia, c/o - NCYLC, The Law Bldg, University of New South Wales, Sydney, NSW 2052, Australia. TEL 61-2-93859588, FAX 61-2-93859589, info@dci-au.org.

342.085 AUS ISSN 1835-0186
KU519.I64
➤ **AUSTRALIAN INDIGENOUS LAW REVIEW.** Abbreviated title: A I L R. Text in English. 1996. q. AUD 220 (effective 2009). back issues avail. **Document type:** *Journal, Academic/Scholarly.* **Description:** Examines and discusses issues concerning law relating to indigenous peoples in Australia and throughout the world.
Formerly (until 2006): Australian Indigenous Law Reporter (1323-7756)
Related titles: Online - full text ed.
—IE, Ingenta.
Published by: University of New South Wales, Indigenous Law Centre, The Law Bldg, Bldg F8, Union Rd, UNSW Kensington Campus, Sydney, NSW 2052, Australia. TEL 61-2-93852252, FAX 61-2-93851266, ilb@unsw.edu.au. Ed. Dylan Lino TEL 61-2-93859636. **Co-sponsor:** University of New South Wales, Faculty of Law.

323.4 AUS ISSN 1323-238X
K1
AUSTRALIAN JOURNAL OF HUMAN RIGHTS. Abbreviated title: A J H R. Text in English. 1994. s-a. AUD 154 (effective 2008). bk.rev. **Document type:** *Journal, Academic/Scholarly.* **Description:** Publishes articles, reviews, commentary, and case notes relating to human rights.
Related titles: Online - full text ed.
Indexed: A22, AusPAIS.
—IE, Ingenta.
Published by: (University Of New South Wales, Human Rights Centre), LexisNexis Butterworths (Subsidiary of: LexisNexis Asia Pacific), Level 9, Tower 2, 475-495 Victoria Ave, Locked Bag 2222, Chatswood Delivery Ctr, Chatswood, NSW 2067, Australia. TEL 61-2-94222174, FAX 61-2-94222405, customer.relations@lexisnexis.com.au.

323.4 PSE ISSN 1995-9818
'AWRAQ 'AMAL MARKAZ BADIL LIL-NIQASH. Text in Arabic. 2000. irreg.
Related titles: Online - full text ed.: ISSN 1995-9826; ♦ English ed.: Information & Discussion Brief. ISSN 1994-0777.
Published by: Badil Resource Center for Palestinian Residency & Refugee Rights, PO Box 728, Bethlehem, Palestine. TEL 972-2-2777086, FAX 972-2-2747346, info@badil.org, http://www.badil.org/ index.html.

B M C INTERNATIONAL HEALTH AND HUMAN RIGHTS. (BioMed Central) *see* PUBLIC HEALTH AND SAFETY

323.4 PSE ISSN 1728-1660
BADIL RESOURCE CENTER FOR PALESTINIAN RESIDENCY & REFUGEE RIGHTS. WORKING PAPERS. Text in English, Arabic. 2003. irreg., latest no.10, 2005. **Document type:** *Monographic series.*
Published by: Badil Resource Center for Palestinian Residency & Refugee Rights, PO Box 728, Bethlehem, Palestine. TEL 972-2-2777086, FAX 972-2-2747346, info@badil.org, http://www.badil.org/ index.html.

323.4 AUS ISSN 1441-4872
BALANCING THE ACT. Text in English. 1997. 3/yr. free (effective 2008). back issues avail. **Document type:** *Newsletter, Consumer.* **Description:** Provides news, questions and answers, statistics, reports of tribunal outcomes, case studies and other articles and stories related to discrimination and human rights issues.
Formerly (until 1997): Under One Sun (1038-3751)
Related titles: Online - full content ed.
Published by: Anti-Discrimination Commission, Queensland, PO Box 2122, Milton, QLD 4064, Australia. TEL info@adcq.qld.gov.au, 61-7-32470922, 300-130-680, FAX 61-7-32470960.

323.4 USA ISSN 1043-6898
KF4885.A15
BALLOT ACCESS NEWS. Text in English. 1985. m. USD 14 (effective 2005). bk.rev. 8 p./no.; back issues avail. **Document type:** *Newsletter, Consumer.* **Description:** Focuses on the rights of voters to support minor political parties and describes the progress being made against restrictive ballot access laws. Covers First Amendment rights of all parties (major and minor).
Related titles: Online - full content ed.
Published by: Coalition for Free and Open Elections, PO Box 470296, San Francisco, CA 94147. TEL 415-922-9779, FAX 415-441-4268. Ed., Pub., R&P, Adv. contact Richard Winger. Circ: 880 (paid).

305 323 USA ISSN 2152-6788
▼ **BECAUSE**; women's lives are worth saving. Text in English. 2009. s-a. free to qualified personnel (effective 2010). **Document type:** *Magazine, Consumer.* **Description:** Includes articles on reproductive health care, the perception of abortion as a human right.
Related titles: Online - full text ed.
Published by: I P A S, PO Box 5027, Chapel Hill, NC 27514. TEL 919-967-7052, 800-334-8446, FAX 919-929-0258, info@ipas.org. Ed. Jennifer Daw Holloway.

323 USA ISSN 1074-469X
DS779.26
BEIJING SPRING. Text in Chinese. 19??. m. adv. bk.rev. back issues avail. **Document type:** *Journal, Academic/Scholarly.* **Description:** Studies the political and social changes, human rights, and democratic reforms in China.
Formerly (until 1993): Beijing Zhi Chun
Related titles: Diskette ed.
Published by: Beijing Spring, Inc, PO Box 520709, Flushing, NY 11352. TEL 718-661-9977, FAX 718-661-9922.

320 DEU
▼ **BELTER DIALOGE**; Impulse zu Zivilcourage und Widerstand. Text in German. 2009. irreg. price varies. **Document type:** *Monographic series, Academic/Scholarly.*
Published by: Leipziger Universitaetsverlag GmbH, Oststr 41, Leipzig, 04317, Germany. TEL 49-341-9900440, FAX 49-341-9900440, info@univerlag-leipzig.de.

323.4 FRA ISSN 1772-2543
BEMDEZ. Text in French, Breton. 2006. irreg. **Document type:** *Monographic series, Consumer.*
Address: 6 Rue de la Tannerie, Vannes, 56000, France. TEL 33-6-11514315.

323 USA ISSN 0160-7731
KF4742
BILL OF RIGHTS IN ACTION. Short title: B R I A. Text in English. 1971. q. free (effective 2006). bk.rev. back issues avail.; reprints avail. **Document type:** *Newsletter, Trade.* **Description:** Contains educational materials for grades 7-12.
Formerly: Bill of Rights Newsletter (0006-2502)
Related titles: Microform ed.: (from PQC); Online - full text ed.: ISSN 1534-9799.
Published by: Constitutional Rights Foundation, 601 S Kingsley Dr, Los Angeles, CA 90005. TEL 213-487-5590, FAX 213-386-0459, crf@crf-usa.org, http://www.crf-usa.org. Ed. Marshall Croddy. R&P Andrew Costly. Circ: 40,000.

051 USA
BILLWATCH. Text in English. 1995. w.
Media: Online - full content.
Published by: Voters Communications, 233 Court St, Brooklyn, NY 11201. http://www.vtw.org.

323.4 004.678 NLD ISSN 1569-1160
BITS OF FREEDOM NIEUWSBRIEF. Text in Dutch. 2001. bi-w. **Document type:** *Newsletter, Trade.*
Media: Online - full text.
Published by: Stichting Bits of Freedom, Postbus 10746, Amsterdam, 1001 ES, Netherlands. info@bof.nl, http://www.bof.nl.

323.4 PER
BLANCO Y NEGRO. Text in Spanish. 1993. bi-m.
Published by: Instituto Democracia y Trabajo, Jr. Parra del Riego 903, El Tambo, Apdo. 270, Huancayo, Junin, Peru. TEL 51-64-223473. Ed. Hugo Reynoso Ayvar.

323.4 USA ISSN 0895-5786
HN30
BLUEPRINT FOR SOCIAL JUSTICE. Text in English. 1948. 10/yr. free (effective 2010). back issues avail. **Document type:** *Journal, Academic/Scholarly.* **Description:** Offers reflections on local, national, and global issues of peace, social, and environmental justice.
Published by: Twomey Center for Peace through Justice, 6363 St Charles Ave, Campus Box 24, New Orleans, LA 70118. TEL 504-864-7433, FAX 504-864-7438, quant@loyno.edu. Ed. Alvaro B Alcazar TEL 504-864-7868.

BRAILLE MONITOR; voice of the nation's blind. *see* HANDICAPPED—Visually Impaired

323.4 USA
BRAT; because your school paper sucks. Text in English. 1996. q. USD 8; USD 2 newsstand/cover (effective 1999). adv. bk.rev. back issues avail. **Document type:** *Bulletin.* **Description:** Promotes social awareness about and among youth, encourages community-based activism, and supports independent, progressive cultures.
Published by: BRAT Media, PO Box 4964, Louisville, KY 40204. TEL 502-459-4492. Ed., Pub., R&P Liz Palmer. Adv. contact Jamie Miller. B&W page USD 200, color page USD 350; trim 10 x 7.

323.4 CAN
KEB458.A72
BRITISH COLUMBIA. HUMAN RIGHTS COMMISSION. ANNUAL REPORT. Text in English. a. free. **Document type:** *Government.*
Formerly: British Columbia. Council of Human Rights. Annual Report (0830-0437)
Published by: BC Human Rights Commission, Parliament Bldgs, Victoria, BC V8V 1X4, Canada. TEL 604-387-3710, FAX 604-387-3643.

P

323.4 CAN ISSN 1198-5909
KEB505.62.A13
BRITISH COLUMBIA. OFFICE OF THE INFORMATION & PRIVACY COMMISSIONER. ANNUAL REPORT. Text in English. 1994. a.
Published by: Office of the Information & Privacy Commissioner, British Columbia, Box 9038, Stn. Prov. Gov't, Victoria, BC V8W 9A4, Canada. TEL 250-387-5629, FAX 250-387-1696, info@oipc.bc.ca.

323.4 CAN ISSN 1198-6182
BRITISH COLUMBIA. OFFICE OF THE INFORMATION AND PRIVACY COMMISSIONER. ORDER. Text in English. 1994. irreg.
Published by: Office of the Information & Privacy Commissioner, British Columbia, Box 9038, Stn. Prov. Gov't, Victoria, BC V8W 9A4, Canada. TEL 250-387-5629, FAX 250-387-1696, info@oipc.bc.ca, http://www.oipcbc.org.

323 NLD ISSN 1568-1297
THE BRITISH INSTITUTE OF HUMAN RIGHTS LIBRARY. Text in English. 2000. irreg., latest vol.2, 2002. price varies. **Document type:** *Monographic series.*
Indexed: IZBG.
Published by: (British Institute of Human Rights GBR), Martinus Nijhoff (Subsidiary of: Brill), PO Box 9000, Leiden, 2300 PA, Netherlands. TEL 31-71-5353500, FAX 31-71-5317532, marketing@brill.nl.

BUERGERRECHTE & POLIZEI. *see* CRIMINOLOGY AND LAW ENFORCEMENT

BUFFALO HUMAN RIGHTS LAW REVIEW. *see* LAW

323.4 CAN ISSN 0847-9798
JC571A44
BULLETIN AGIR. Text in French. 1979. q. CAD 30; CAD 35 foreign. **Document type:** *Bulletin.* **Description:** Updates the human rights situation around the world and highlights the activities of the French branch.
Published by: Amnistie Internationale, Section Canadienne Francophone, 6250 bd Monk, Montreal, PQ H4E 3H7, Canada. TEL 514-766-9766, FAX 514-766-2088. Ed. Anne Ste Marie. Pub. Michel Frenette. Circ: 35,000.

323 FRA ISSN 1608-960X
BULLETIN D'INFORMATION SUR LES DROITS DE L'HOMME. Text in French. 19??. 3/yr. **Document type:** *Bulletin, Academic/Scholarly.*
Formerly (until 1997): Council of Europe. Feuille d'Information (0259-1391)
Related titles: Online - full content ed.: ISSN 1608-7380; ◆ English ed.: Human Rights Information Bulletin. ISSN 1608-9618.
Published by: Council of Europe/Conseil de l'Europe, Avenue de l'Europe, Strasbourg, 67075, France. TEL 33-3-88412033, FAX 33-3-88412745, publishing@coe.int, http://www.coe.int.

323.4 305.89607 USA
BUNCHE RESEARCH REPORT. (Center for African American Studies) Text in English. 2002 (Jun.). s-a. back issues avail. **Document type:** *Report, Academic/Scholarly.*
Formerly (until 2003): The C A A S Research Report (1540-1065)
Related titles: Online - full text ed.
Indexed: IIBP, P45.
Published by: University of California, Los Angeles, Ralph J. Bunche Center for African American Studies, 160 Haines Hall, PO Box 951545, Los Angeles, CA 90095. TEL 310-825-7403, FAX 310-825-5019, http://www.bunche.ucla.edu.

C A A UPDATE. *see* ETHNIC INTERESTS

C A B NEWS. (Citizens Advice Bureaux) *see* LAW

C C C O ACTION ALERT. *see* MILITARY

323.4 PRY
C I P A E. ESTUDIOS. Text in Spanish. irreg., latest vol.40.
Published by: Comite de Iglesias para Ayudas de Emergencia, GENERAL DIAZ, 429, Asuncion, Paraguay.

323.4 USA ISSN 0300-743X
E185.5
C O R E MAGAZINE. Text in English. 1973 (vol.3). q. USD 10. adv. bk.rev.; film rev. charts; illus.
Published by: (Congress of Racial Equality), C O R E Publications, 30 Cooper Sq, 9, New York, NY 10003-7151. TEL 212-598-4000, FAX 212-982-0184. Ed. George Holmes. Adv. contact Kwazi Akyeampong. Circ: 50,000.

C W A SECTOR NEWS. *see* LABOR UNIONS

CAHIERS DE L'AVENIR DE LA BRETAGNE. *see* HISTORY

CAHIERS DU FEMINISME. *see* WOMEN'S STUDIES

CAN NEWS. *see* RELIGIONS AND THEOLOGY

CANADA. INFORMATION COMMISSIONER. ANNUAL REPORT. *see* LAW—International Law

323 CAN ISSN 0226-2177
KE4381.A45
CANADIAN HUMAN RIGHTS REPORTER. Text in English, French. 1980. m. CAD 250 domestic; CAD 295 foreign (effective 2004). **Document type:** *Journal, Academic/Scholarly.* **Description:** Publishes decisions of boards of inquiry, tribunals and courts from all jurisdictions, as well as the decisions on appeals which flow from them.
Related titles: ◆ Supplement(s): Revised Consolidated Index. ISSN 1910-2844.
Published by: Canadian Human Rights Reporter, Inc., 1662 W 75th Ave, Vancouver, BC V6P 6G2, Canada. TEL 604-266-5322, FAX 604-266-4475.

CANADIAN HUMAN RIGHTS TRIBUNAL. ANNUAL REPORT. *see* PUBLIC ADMINISTRATION

CANADIAN JOURNAL OF QUANTUUM ECONOMICS; the journal of academic research and current affairs on quality-of-life issues. *see* SOCIAL SCIENCES: COMPREHENSIVE WORKS

CANADIAN ONLINE JOURNAL OF QUEER STUDIES IN EDUCATION/ JOURNAL CANADIEN POUR LES ETUDES QUEER EN EDUCATION. *see* EDUCATION

342.085 USA ISSN 1948-6936
CARRYING THE TORCH (INDIANAPOLIS). Text in English. 19??. s-a. free to members (effective 2009). illus. 30 p./no.; back issues avail. **Document type:** *Magazine, Trade.*
Former titles (until 2000): The Advocate; (until 1984): I C L U and You; (until 1970): I C L U News (0441-8549)
Related titles: Online - full text ed.
Indexed: CLI.
Published by: Indiana Civil Liberties Union, 1031 E Washington St, Indianapolis, IN 46202. TEL 317-635-4059, gholmes@aclu-in.org, http://www.iclu.org.

323.4 CAN ISSN 0824-2062
THE CATALYST (TORONTO). Text in English. 1978. bi-m. CAD 15 domestic to non-members (effective 2004). bk.rev. illus. **Document type:** *Newsletter.* **Description:** Provides a catalyst for Christian political action and reviews CPJ activities.
Former titles: Committee for Justice and Liberty. Newsletter (0705-2103); C J L Foundation. Newsletter
Indexed: APW, P45, PQC, Telegen.
—CCC.
Published by: Citizens for Public Justice, 229 College St. Ste 311, Toronto, ON M5T 1R4, Canada. TEL 416-979-2443, FAX 416-979-2458, cpj@cpj.ca. Ed., R&P Murray MacAdam. Circ: 4,000.

323.4 AUS ISSN 1324-6879
CATHOLIC SOCIAL JUSTICE SERIES. Text in English. 1984. irreg., latest vol.61. AUD 30 (effective 2008); includes Justice Trends. back issues avail. **Document type:** *Monographic series, Academic/Scholarly.* **Description:** Provides information for discussion and reflection on social justice and human rights issues.
Former titles (until Sep.1995): A C S J C Occasional Papers (Australian Catholic Social Justice Council) (1032-2205); (until 1988): C C J P Occasional Papers (Catholic Commission for Justice and Peace) (0813-5436)
Published by: Australian Catholic Social Justice Council, 24-32 O'Riordan St, PO Box 7246, Alexandria, NSW 2015, Australia. TEL 61-2-83063499, FAX 61-2-83063498, admin@acsjc.org.au. Eds. David Brennan, Mark Zucker.

323.34 USA
CATT'S CLAWS. Text in English. 1994. 3/w. **Document type:** *Newsletter.* **Description:** Covers issues related to women's rights.
Media: Online - full text.
Address: PO Box 6185, Hot Springs, AR 71902. TEL 501-624-1566, istuber@direclynx.net, istuber@undelete.org. Ed., R&P Irene Stuber. Circ: 25,000.

323.445 GBR ISSN 0967-8514
JC591
CENSORSHIP NEWS. Text in English. 1991. irreg. GBP 1, USD 2 per issue (effective 2000). back issues avail. **Document type:** *Monographic series, Academic/Scholarly.* **Description:** Reports government attempts throughout the world to suppress freedom of the press.
—BLDSC (3102.735000).
Published by: International Centre Against Censorship, Lancaster House, 33 Islington High St, London, N1 9LH, United Kingdom. TEL 44-171-278-9292, FAX 44-171-713-1356. R&P Joyce Pooley.

344.0531 USA ISSN 0749-6001
Z658.U6
CENSORSHIP NEWS. Text in English. 1975. q. free. bk.rev. 4 p./no.; back issues avail. **Document type:** *Newsletter.* **Description:** Covers current school book censorship controversies, including threats to the free flow of information, obscenity laws, sexual expression, creationism and school textbooks.
Related titles: Online - full text ed.
Published by: National Coalition Against Censorship, 275 Seventh Ave, 15th Fl, New York, NY 10001. TEL 212-807-6222, FAX 212-807-6245, ncac@ncac.org. Ed., R&P Justin Goldberg TEL 212-807-6222 ext. 13. Circ: 31,000 (paid and controlled).

CHARTER OF RIGHTS AND FREEDOMS: EQUALITY RIGHTS. *see* LAW—Constitutional Law

▼ **CHILD POLICY FORUM OF NEW YORK. PROCEEDINGS.** *see* CHILDREN AND YOUTH—About

CHILD SUPPORT HANDBOOK. *see* LAW—Family And Matrimonial Law

323 CAN ISSN 1028-7531
CHILDREN'S RIGHTS. Text in English. 1997. irreg.
Related titles: Online - full text ed.: ISSN 1028-8767; French ed.: Droit de l'Enfant. ISSN 1028-8759.
Published by: International Bureau for Children's Rights/Bureau International des Droits des Enfants, 1185 Saint-Mathieu, Montreal, PQ H3H 2P7, Canada. TEL 514-932-7656, FAX 514-932-9453, info@ibcr.org, http://www.ibcr.org.

323.4 USA ISSN 1068-4166
JC599.C6
➤ **CHINA RIGHTS FORUM**; the journal of human rights in China. Abbreviated title: C R F. Text in English, Chinese. 1990. q. bk.rev. bibl.; illus.; charts. back issues avail. **Document type:** *Journal, Academic/Scholarly.* **Description:** Provides space for the voices of Chinese dissidents, scholars, artists, writers and activists promoting democratic reform, labor rights, freedom of expression, and the rights of religious and ethnic minorities and disadvantaged groups.
Formerly (until 1993): Human Rights Tribune (1057-0748)
Indexed: BAS, HRIR, PAIS, PerIslam, SociolAb.
—Ingenta.
Published by: Human Rights in China, 350 Fifth Ave, Ste 3311, New York, NY 10118. TEL 212-239-4495, FAX 212-239-2561, hrichina@hrichina.org.

323 USA ISSN 0735-8237
DS779.20
CHINA SPRING. Key Title: Zhongguo zhi Chun. Text in Chinese. 1982. m. USD 28 to individuals; USD 60 to institutions. adv. bk.rev. back issues avail. **Description:** Covers human rights, economics, and the politics of China.
Published by: China Spring Research, Inc., 74-14 Woodside Ave., Elmhurst, NY 11373. TEL 718-429-6777, FAX 718-476-1602. Circ: 6,000. **Subscr. to:** PO Box 701400, Trainsmeadow Sta, Flushing, NY 11370-9998.

CHR. MICHELSEN INSTITUTE. REPORT. *see* SOCIAL SCIENCES: COMPREHENSIVE WORKS

CHR. MICHELSEN INSTITUTE. WORKING PAPER. *see* SOCIAL SCIENCES: COMPREHENSIVE WORKS

CHRISTIANS IN CRISIS. *see* RELIGIONS AND THEOLOGY

323.4 FRA ISSN 2116-9535
LE CH'TITOYEN. Text in French. 2000. q. **Document type:** *Consumer.*
Published by: Mouvement Contre le Racisme et pour l'Amitie entre les Peuples, Federation Regionale du Nord-Pas-de-Calais, BP 1261, Lille, 59014, France. mrap.nordpdc@wanadoo.fr, http://www.mrap.fr.

323.042 GBR
THE CITIZEN. Text in English. 1995. q. (plus w. updates). GBP 5 in the European Union. adv. bk.rev. **Document type:** *Newsletter.* **Description:** Deals with a wide range of Scottish, UK, European and international issues, particularly relating to the environment, peace, the Labour Party, trade unions, economics, government, democracy and human rights.
Related titles: Online - full text ed.
Published by: Citizen, 25 Church St, Inverkeithing, Fife KY11 1LG, United Kingdom. Ed., Pub., R&P, Adv. contact Dave Smith. Circ: 2,000.

CIVIL LIBERTIES ALERT. *see* MEETINGS AND CONGRESSES

CIVIL LIBERTIES REPORTER. *see* LAW—Civil Law

323 AUS ISSN 1326-8333
➤ **CIVIL LIBERTY.** Text in English. 1964. q. AUD 60 to institutions; free to members (effective 2008). adv. bk.rev. illus. **Document type:** *Journal, Academic/Scholarly.*
Formerly (until 1967): Council for Civil Liberties. Newsletter
Related titles: Online - full text ed.: free to members (effective 2008).
Published by: New South Wales Council for Civil Liberties, PO Box 201, Glebe, NSW 2037, Australia. TEL 61-2-96607582, FAX 61-2-95664162, office@nswccl.org.au. Ed. Jeremy Adair.

323.4 GBR ISSN 1358-4030
JC599.G7
CIVIL LIBERTY AGENDA. Text in English. 1976. q. GBP 7; GBP 8.50 foreign. adv. bk.rev. **Document type:** *Newsletter.* **Description:** Examines human rights and rights abuses in the U.K.
Former titles (until 1991): Civil Liberty (0267-5153); (until 1985): Rights (0308-8227)
Indexed: HRIR.
Published by: National Council for Civil Liberties, 21 Tabard St, London, SE1 4LA, United Kingdom. TEL 44-171-403-3888, FAX 44-171-407-5354. Ed. Kate Wilkinson. Adv. contact Sam Watson. Circ: 8,000.

323.4 USA
CIVIL RIGHTS ACTIONS. Text in English. 1983. 7 base vols. plus irreg. updates. looseleaf. USD 1,581 base vol(s). (effective 2008). Supplement avail. **Document type:** *Journal, Trade.* **Description:** Discusses various aspects of civil rights and provides case-critical information, from statutes that Congress enacted in the late 1950s to the latest developments in civil rights legislation.
Related titles: CD-ROM ed.: USD 1,625 (effective 2008).
Published by: Matthew Bender & Co., Inc. (Subsidiary of: LexisNexis North America), 1275 Broadway, Albany, NY 12204. TEL 518-487-3000, 800-424-4200, FAX 518-487-3083, international@bender.com, http://bender.lexisnexis.com. Eds. John Sobieski, Joseph Cook.

CIVIL RIGHTS AND CIVIL LIBERTIES LITIGATION: THE LAW OF SECTION 1983. *see* LAW—Civil Law

CIVIL RIGHTS MONITOR. *see* LAW—Civil Law

323.4 340 USA ISSN 0732-5738
CIVIL RIGHTS RESEARCH REVIEW. Text in English. 1972. q. USD 10. bk.rev.
Formerly (until 1981): Clearinghouse for Civil Rights Research (0887-9524)
Indexed: PAIS.
Published by: Catholic University of America School of Law, Center for National Policy Review, Washington, DC 20064. TEL 202-832-8525. Ed. Diana M Pearce. Circ: 1,100.

COALITION FOR PRISONERS' RIGHTS NEWSLETTER. *see* CRIMINOLOGY AND LAW ENFORCEMENT

323.4 MEX
COMISION ESTATAL DE DERECHOS HUMANOS, NUEVO LEON. REVISTA. Text in Spanish. q.
Published by: Comision Estatal de Derechos Humanos, CORPUS CHRISTI 2313, Lomas de San Francisco, Monterrey, NL 64710, Mexico.

323.4 PRY
COMITE DE IGLESIAS PARA AYUDAS DE EMERGENCIA. CUADERNOS. Text in Spanish. 1987. irreg., latest vol.11, 1991.
Published by: Comite de Iglesias para Ayudas de Emergencia, GENERAL DIAZ, 429, Asuncion, Paraguay.

323.4 PRY
COMITE DE IGLESIAS PARA AYUDAS DE EMERGENCIA. NOTAS TRIMESTRALES. Text in Spanish. 1991 (no.20). q. PYG 40,000 to individuals; PYG 50,000 to institutions.
Indexed: HRIR.
Published by: Comite de Iglesias para Ayudas de Emergencia, Gral Diaz e. 14 de Mayo y Alberdi, Asuncion, Paraguay. TEL 595-21-495161.

323.4 FRA
COMITE SOLIDARITE PHILIPPINES. BULLETIN. Text in French. q.
Published by: Comite Solidarite Philippines, 68 rue de Babylone, Paris, 75007, France.

323 NLD ISSN 1574-8626
A COMMENTARY ON THE UNITED NATIONS CONVENTION ON THE RIGHTS OF THE CHILD. Text in English. 2005. irreg., latest vol.43, 2006. price varies. **Document type:** *Monographic series.*
Indexed: IZBG.
Published by: Martinus Nijhoff (Subsidiary of: Brill), PO Box 9000, Leiden, 2300 PA, Netherlands. TEL 31-71-5353500, FAX 31-71-5317532, marketing@brill.nl. Eds. A Alen, E Verhellen, J Vande Lanotte.

323.4 CAN ISSN 1706-9297
COMMISSION DES DROITS DE LA PERSONNE ET DES DROITS DE LA JEUNESSE. RAPPORT D'ACTIVITES ET DE GESTION, QUEBEC. Text in French. 1996. a. **Document type:** *Government.*
Formerly (until 2001): Commission des Droits de la Personne et des Droits de la Jeunesse. Rapport Annuel, Quebec (1487-0290); Which was formed by the merger of (1976-1996): Commission des Droits de la Personne du Quebec. Rapport Annuel (0703-1343); (1977-1996): Commission de Protection des Droits de la Jeunesse. Rapport Annuel, Quebec (1193-7092); Which was formerly (until 1991): Commission de Protection des Droits de la Jeunesse. Rapport

d'Activite, Quebec (1193-7084); (until 1990): Comite de la Protection de la Jeunesse. Rapport d'Activites (0829-8505); (until 1984): Comite de la Protection de la Jeunesse. Rapport Annuel (0829-8491); (until 1983): Comite de la Protection de la Jeunesse. Rapport d'Activites (0711-0251); (until 1981): Comite de la Protection de la Jeunesse. Rapport Annuel (0226-3262); (until 1979): Comite popur la Protection de la Jeunesse. Rapport d'Activites (0703-2242)
Published by: Commission des Droits de la Personne et des Droits de la Jeunesse, 360, Street Saint-Jacques, 2nd fl, Montreal, PQ H2Y 1P5, Canada. TEL 514-873-5146, 800-361-6477, FAX 514-873-6032, http://www.cdpdj.qc.ca/fr/accueil.asp?noeud1=0&noeud2=0&cle=0.

323 FRA
COMMISSIONER FOR HUMAN RIGHTS. ANNUAL REPORT TO THE COMMITTEE OF MINISTERS AND THE PARLIAMENTARY ASSEMBLY. Text in English. 1999. a. **Document type:** *Report, Consumer.*
Related titles: Print ed.
Published by: Council of Europe/Conseil de l'Europe, Avenue de l'Europe, Strasbourg, 67075, France. TEL 33-3-88412033, FAX 33-3-88412745, publishing@coe.int, http://www.coe.int.

323.4 GBR ISSN 1363-7169
K3239.23
COMMONWEALTH HUMAN RIGHTS LAW DIGEST. Text in English. 1995. s-a. GBP 45, USD 90 (effective 2009). back issues avail. **Document type:** *Bulletin.* **Description:** Focuses exclusively on human rights cases from Commonwealth jurisdictions.
Published by: Interights, Lancaster House, 33 Islington High St, London, N1 9LH, United Kingdom. TEL 44-20-72783230, FAX 44-20-72784334, ir@interights.org.

323.4 USA
COMMUNICATOR (DES MOINES). Text in English. 1975. s-a. illus. back issues avail. **Document type:** *Newsletter, Government.* **Description:** News of agency's work, civil rights events in Iowa, and articles on civil rights issues.
Formerly (until 1980): Challenger
Media: Online - full content.
Published by: Iowa Civil Rights Commission, 211 E Maple St, 2nd Fl, Des Moines, IA 50309-1858. TEL 515-281-4121, FAX 515-242-5840. Ed. Dawn Peterson. Circ: 6,000.

323 336.2 CAN ISSN 1196-9970
CONSCIENCE CANADA. Text in English. 1979. 3/yr. CAD 10 (effective 2007). **Document type:** *Newsletter.* **Description:** Contains Canadian and international news on peace tax, conscientious objection, non-violence, and other human rights issues.
Former titles (until 1995): Conscience Canada Newsletter (0823-8669); (until 1984): Taxes for Peace, Not War (0229-5377)
Related titles: Online - full content ed.
Published by: Conscience Canada Inc., 901-70 Mill St, Toronto, ON M5A 4R1, Canada. TEL 416-203-1402, consciencecanada@shaw.ca. Circ: 1,000.

323 GBR ISSN 1474-8789
CONSCIENCE UPDATE. Text in English. 1978. q. free to members (effective 2009). back issues avail. **Document type:** *Newsletter, Consumer.* **Description:** Campaigns for the legal right for those who have a conscientious objection to war to have the military part of their taxes spent on peacebuilding initiatives.
Former titles (until 2000): Conscience (1364-9477); (until 1996): Peace Tax Campaign. Newsletter (0264-8253)
Published by: The Peace Tax Campaign, Archway Resource Ctr, 1B Waterlou Rd, London, N19 5NJ, United Kingdom. TEL 44-20-75611061, FAX 44-20-72816508, info@conscienceonline.org.uk.

305.4 323.4 CAN ISSN 1706-9750
CONSEIL DU STATUT DE LA FEMME. RAPPORT ANNUEL DE GESTION QUEBEC. Text in French. 1974. a.
Formerly (until 2001): Conseil du Statut de la Femme. Rapport Annuel Quebec (0705-6435)
Published by: Conseil du Statut de la Femme, 8 rue Cook, 3e Etage, Bur 300, Quebec, PQ G1R 5J7, Canada. TEL 418-643-4326, FAX 418-643-8926, gazette@csf.gouv.qc.ca, http://www.csf.gouv.qc.ca/fr/accueil.

327.17 323 FRA ISSN 1958-4210
CONTENTIEUX DES REFUGIES (ANNUAL). Text in French. 1993. a. **Document type:** *Government.*
Published by: France. Commission des Recours des Refugies, 35 Rue Cuvier, Montreuil sous Bois, Cedex 93558, France. TEL 33-1-48184000, http://www.commission-refugies.fr.

327 323 FRA ISSN 1958-4229
CONTENTIEUX DES REFUGIES (QUARTERLY). Text in French. 1998. q. **Document type:** *Government.*
Published by: France. Commission des Recours des Refugies, 35 Rue Cuvier, Montreuil sous Bois, Cedex 93558, France. TEL 33-1-48184000, http://www.commission-refugies.fr.

323 USA
THE COPSWATCH REPORT; ..the media parasite. (in Real Player streaming audio format; some archives in text format) Text in English. irreg. **Document type:** *Report, Consumer.* **Description:** Provides information on the law, civil rights, and police issues.
Media: Online - full content.
Published by: Spectral Mindustries specmind@culturejam.com, http://www.specmind.com/.

323.4 GBR
COUNCIL OF EUROPE. EUROPEAN COMMITTEE FOR THE PREVENTION OF TORTURE. YEARBOOK. Text in English, French. a. GBP 90, USD 160. **Document type:** *Yearbook, Academic/Scholarly.*
Published by: (Council of Europe/Conseil de l'Europe FRA), University of Nottingham, Department of Law, University Park, Nottingham, Notts NG7 2RD, United Kingdom. TEL 44-115-9515700, FAX 44-115-9515696, law-enquiries@nottingham.ac.uk. **Dist. in N. America by:** Gaunt, Inc., Gaunt Bldg, 3011 Gulf Dr, Holmes Beach, FL 34217. TEL 941-778-5211, 941-778-5252, 800-942-8683, info@gaunt.com, http://www.gaunt.com.

342.085 GBR ISSN 1369-9865
KJC9769.A7
COUNCIL OF EUROPE. EUROPEAN CONVENTION FOR THE PREVENTION OF TORTURE AND INHUMAN OR DEGRADING TREATMENT OR PUNISHMENT. YEARBOOK. Text in English. 1997. a. price varies. **Description:** Contains primary materials relating to the European convention for the prevention of torture.
Published by: (Council of Europe/Conseil de l'Europe FRA), University of Nottingham, Human Rights Law Center, University Park, Nottingham, Notts NG7 2RD, United Kingdom. TEL 44-115-8466309, FAX 44-115-8466579, HRLC@nottingham.ac.uk. Ed. David Harris. **Dist. in N. America by:** Gaunt, Inc.

323.4 FRA ISSN 0377-2748
COUNCIL OF EUROPE. STANDING COMMITTEE ON THE EUROPEAN CONVENTION ON ESTABLISHMENT (INDIVIDUALS). PERIODICAL REPORT. Text in French. 1971. irreg.
Published by: Council of Europe/Conseil de l'Europe, Avenue de l'Europe, Strasbourg, 67075, France. TEL 33-3-88412581, FAX 33-3-88413910, publishing@coe.int, http://www.coe.int. **Dist. in U.S. by:** Manhattan Publishing Co., 468 Albany Post Rd, Croton On Hudson, NY 10520.

323.4 USA ISSN 0198-9669
JC571
COUNTRY REPORTS ON HUMAN RIGHTS PRACTICES FOR (YEAR). Variant title: Human Rights Country Reports. Text in English. 1979. a. USD 61; USD 76.25 foreign. **Document type:** *Government.* **Description:** Monitors the human rights situation in U.N. member nations.
Indexed: A26, CWI, I05.
Published by: U.S. State Department, Bureau of Public Affairs, Public Information, Washington, DC 20520-6810. TEL 202-647-6575. **Orders to:** U.S. Government Printing Office, Superintendent of Documents. **Co-sponsors:** U.S. House of Representatives, Committee on International Relations; U.S. Senate, Committee on Foreign Relations.

COUR INTERNATIONALE DE JUSTICE. ACTES ET DOCUMENTS/ INTERNATIONAL COURT OF JUSTICE. ACTS AND DOCUMENTS. *see* LAW—International Law

COUR INTERNATIONALE DE JUSTICE. BIBLIOGRAPHIE/ INTERNATIONAL COURT OF JUSTICE. BIBLIOGRAPHY. *see* LAW—Abstracting, Bibliographies, Statistics

COYOTE. *see* NATIVE AMERICAN STUDIES

THE CRISIS. *see* ETHNIC INTERESTS

CRITICAL ASIAN STUDIES. *see* POLITICAL SCIENCE—International Relations

323.4 NLD ISSN 1388-1345
CROSS THE LINES (ENGLISH EDITION); newsletter of I F O R Women Peacemakers Program. Text in English. 1997. 3/yr. EUR 10 (effective 2009). Website rev. 4 p./no.; back issues avail. **Document type:** *Newsletter.*
Supersedes in part (in 1998): Cross the Lines (Multiple Languages Edition) (1386-6583)
Related titles: E-mail ed.; Spanish ed.: Cruzar las Fronteras. ISSN 1388-1361; French ed.: Franchir les Lignes. ISSN 1388-1353.
Published by: International Fellowship of Reconciliation, Spoorstraat 38, Alkmaar, 1815 BK, Netherlands. TEL 31-72-5123014, FAX 31-72-5151102, office@ifor.org. Ed. Jose de Vries.

CRYPTORIGHTS JOURNAL; the security quarterly for human rights & journalism. *see* COMPUTERS—Computer Security

323.4 USA ISSN 1045-4098
JC599.C85
CUBA: POLITICAL EXECUTIONS AND HUMAN RIGHTS. Text in English. a.
Published by: Cuban Committee for Human Rights, Georgetown University, PO Box 2160, Hoya Sta, Washington, DC 20054.

CULTURAL SURVIVAL QUARTERLY; world report on the rights of indigenous peoples and ethnic minorities. *see* ETHNIC INTERESTS

323 322.4 FRA ISSN 1962-6096
CULTURE DE NON-VIOLENCE. Text in French. 2004. irreg. **Document type:** *Monographic series.*
Published by: Centre de Ressources sur la Non-Violence, 11 Allee de Guerande, Colomiers, 31770, France. TEL 33-5-61786680, crnv.midi-pyrenees@wanadoo.fr, http://www.non-violence-mp.org/centrededoc.htm.

323.4 MEX ISSN 2007-1280
D H MAGAZINE. (Derechos Humanos) Text in Spanish. 2008. m. **Document type:** *Magazine, Trade.*
Published by: Comision de Derechos Humanos del Estado de Mexico, Dr. Nicolas San Juan No. 113, Esq. Vaquerias Col. Cuauhtemoc, Toluca, Estado de Mexico 50010, Mexico. TEL 52-722-2360560, uipe@codhem,org,mx, http;//www.codhem,org.mx/.

323.4 364.6 USA
D P I C REPORTS. (Death Penalty Information Center) Text in English. 1991. irreg. (approx 1-2/yr). free (effective 2010). bibl.; charts; illus.; stat. back issues avail. **Document type:** *Monographic series, Academic/Scholarly.* **Description:** Examines critical issues and trends in capital punishment of concern to persons who question the basic fairness of the death penalty on both practical and moral grounds.
Media: Online - full text. **Related titles:** Print ed.: price varies.
Published by: Death Penalty Information Center, 1015 18th St, NW, 704, Washington, DC 20036. TEL 202-289-2275, FAX 202-289-7336, dpic@deathpenltyinfo.org.

DALILI. *see* ETHNIC INTERESTS

323.4 USA ISSN 1087-4593
DARK NIGHT: FIELD NOTES; a journal of human liberation. Text in English. 1995. q. USD 18 domestic; USD 25 in Canada & Mexico; USD 38 elsewhere; USD 10 to senior citizens (effective 2001). illus. **Document type:** *Magazine, Consumer.* **Description:** Focused on indigeneous liberation issues world wide. It is intended as a way for those deeply involved in the struggle for freedom to share their thoughts and experiences from the field from the battle lines of that struggle.
Related titles: Online - full text ed.
Indexed: APW, AltPI.
Published by: Dark Night Press, P O Box 3629, Chicago, IL 60690-3629. TEL 207-839-5794, darknight@igc.apc.org. Ed. Faith Attaguile.

323 GBR
DATA PROTECTION QUARTERLY. Text in English. q. GBP 170 (effective 2008). **Document type:** *Newsletter, Trade.* **Description:** Contains news and analysis on data protection, privacy and relevant developments under Human Rights legislation.
Former titles (until 2007): Data Protection & Privacy Practice; (until 1999): Data Protection News
—BLDSC (3535.197850).
Published by: Pinsent Masons LLP, 30 Aylesbury St, London, EC1R 0ER, United Kingdom. TEL 44-20-74904000, FAX 44-20-74902545, http://www.pinsentmasons.com.

323.4 364.6 USA
DEATH PENALTY IN (YEAR): YEAR END REPORT. Text in English. 19??. a. free (effective 2010). bibl.; charts; illus.; stat. back issues avail. **Document type:** *Report, Trade.* **Description:** Examines issues and trends in capital punishment in the US, with state-by-state comparisons. Questions the justice and fairness of the US judicial system regarding the death penalty.
Media: Online - full text.
Published by: Death Penalty Information Center, 1015 18th St, NW, 704, Washington, DC 20036. TEL 202-289-2275, FAX 202-289-7336, dpic@deathpenltyinfo.org.

DEATH ROW U.S.A. REPORTER. *see* CRIMINOLOGY AND LAW ENFORCEMENT

DEBT ADVICE HANDBOOK. *see* SOCIAL SERVICES AND WELFARE

323 362.2 FRA ISSN 1963-2487
LE DECHAINE. Text in French. 2008. q. **Document type:** *Newsletter, Consumer.*
Published by: Commission des Citoyens pour les Droits de l'Homme (C C D H), B P 10076, Paris, Cedex 12 75561, France.

323.4 NGA ISSN 1465-0142
JQ2998.A1
➤ **DEMOCRACY & DEVELOPMENT**; journal of West African affairs. Text in English. 1998. q. USD 48, EUR 52 to individuals; USD 112, EUR 124 to institutions (effective 2007). **Document type:** *Journal, Academic/Scholarly.* **Description:** Devoted to reporting and explaining democratic developments in the sub-region.
Published by: Centre for Democracy & Development, Ikeja, PO Box 15700, Lagos, Nigeria. TEL 234-1-4730705, cdd@cdd.org.uk, http://www.cdd.org.uk. Ed. J K Fayemi.

323.4 CAN ISSN 0045-9909
THE DEMOCRATIC COMMITMENT. Text in English. 1967. s-a. free to members (effective 2011). bk.rev. back issues avail. **Document type:** *Newsletter, Trade.* **Description:** Contains updates on BCCLA work and analysis.
Related titles: Online - full text ed.: ISSN 1924-7192.
Published by: British Columbia Civil Liberties Association, 550 - 1188 W Georgia St, Vancouver, BC V6E 4A2, Canada. TEL 604-687-2919, FAX 604-687-3045, info@bccla.org.

DEMOCRAZIA, DIRITTI, COSTITUZIONI. *see* LAW—Constitutional Law

323.4 ESP ISSN 1133-3812
DERECHOS HUMANOS. Text in Spanish. q. USD 30 domestic (effective 2007). **Document type:** *Journal, Academic/Scholarly.* **Description:** Centers on the defense of human rights and freedoms worldwide.
Indexed: HRIR.
Published by: Asociacion Pro-Derechos Humanos de Espana, Jose Ortega y Gasset, 77 2o, Madrid, 28006, Spain. TEL 34-91-4022312, FAX 34-91-4024466. Ed. Jose Antonio Perez. Circ: 5,000.

DIARIO DE LAS CHICAS. *see* WOMEN'S STUDIES

323.03 GBR
A DICTIONARY OF HUMAN RIGHTS. Text in English. 1997. irreg., latest vol.1, 1997. **Document type:** *Monographic series, Consumer.* **Description:** Provides explanations of the terminology, issues, organizations and laws surrounding the subject of human rights.
Published by: Europa Publications Ltd. (Subsidiary of: Taylor & Francis Group), 11 New Fetter Ln, London, EC4P 4EE, United Kingdom. TEL 44-20-78224300, FAX 44-20-78422249, sales.europa@tandf.co.uk.

323 VAT ISSN 1970-2558
I DIRITTI DEI POPOLI OGGI; una carta internazionale. Text in Multiple languages. 1998. irreg. **Document type:** *Monographic series, Academic/Scholarly.*
Published by: Pontificia Universita Lateranense/Pontificia Universitas Lateranensis, Piazza S. Giovanni in Laterano 4, Vatican City, 00120, Vatican City.

344 USA ISSN 1086-1335
KF4244.P58
DISABILITY COMPLIANCE FOR HIGHER EDUCATION. Abbreviated title: D C H E. Text in English. 1995. m. GBP 1,409 in United Kingdom to institutions; EUR 2,175 in Europe to institutions; USD 2,677 in United States to institutions; USD 2,725 in Canada & Mexico to institutions; USD 2,743 elsewhere to institutions; GBP 1,621 combined subscription in United Kingdom to institutions (print & online eds.); EUR 2,501 combined subscription in Europe to institutions (print & online eds.); USD 3,084 combined subscription in United States to institutions (print & online eds.); USD 3,132 combined subscription in Canada & Mexico to institutions (print & online eds.); USD 3,150 combined subscription elsewhere to institutions (print & online eds.) (effective 2012). **Document type:** *Newsletter, Trade.* **Description:** Combines legal interpretation with practical implementation ideas to help accommodate students and staff with disabilities, while fulfilling the legal obligations.
Related titles: Online - full text ed.: ISSN 1943-8001. GBP 1,369 in United Kingdom to institutions; EUR 2,112 in Europe to institutions; USD 2,677 elsewhere to institutions (effective 2012).
Indexed: E03.
—CIS. **CCC.**
Published by: John Wiley & Sons, Inc., 111 River St, Hoboken, NJ 07030. TEL 201-748-6000, FAX 201-748-5915, http://www.wiley.com/WileyCDA/.

DISABILITY RIGHTS HANDBOOK. *see* SOCIAL SERVICES AND WELFARE

323 CAN ISSN 1922-2327
DISCOVER CANADA; the rights and responsibilities of citizenship. Text in English. 19??. a. free (effective 2010). **Document type:** *Magazine, Consumer.*
Formerly (until 2009): Look at Canada (1498-5861)
Related titles: Online - full text ed.: free (effective 2010).

P

Published by: Citizenship and Immigration Canada, 180 Kent St, 6th Fl, Ottawa, ON K1A 1L1, Canada. TEL 888-776-8584, FAX 613-998-1527, Multi-Canada@cic.gc.ca.

DISCRIMINATION ALERT. *see* BUSINESS AND ECONOMICS—Labor And Industrial Relations

DOCUMENTACAO E DIREITO COMPARADO. *see* LAW—Civil Law

DOOR OF HOPE MAGAZINE. *see* RELIGIONS AND THEOLOGY—Protestant

323.4 BEL ISSN 0012-5474
DOORBRAAK. Text in Dutch. 1962. m. EUR 16.50 domestic; EUR 25 foreign (effective 2005). adv. bk.rev. illus.
Published by: Vlaamse Dienstencentrum vzw., Passendalestraat 1A, Berchem, 2600, Belgium. TEL 32-3-366-1850, FAX 32-3-366-6045, http://www.vvb.org. Ed. Jan Van de Casteele.

323.4 RUS
DOS'E NA TSENZURU. Text in Russian. 1997. s-a. USD 75 in the Americas (effective 2000).
Published by: Fond Zashchity Glasnosti, Tishinskaya pl., 8, kv.17, Moscow, 123056, Russian Federation. TEL 7-095-2541570.

323 FRA ISSN 1765-2510
➤ **DROITS FONDAMENTAUX.** Text in French. 2001. a. **Document type:** *Journal, Academic/Scholarly.*
Media: Online - full text.
Published by: Centre de Recherche sur les Droits de l'Homme et le Droit Humanitaire, CRDH, Universite Pantheon-Assas, 12 Place Pantheon, Paris, 75005, France. http://www.droits-fondamentaux.org.

➤ **DRUG WAR CHRONICLE.** *see* PHARMACY AND PHARMACOLOGY

323.4 USA ISSN 1090-1043
K4
DUKE JOURNAL OF GENDER LAW & POLICY. Text in English. 1994. s-a. USD 22 domestic; USD 27 foreign (effective 2009). bk.rev. back issues avail.; reprint service avail. from WSH. **Document type:** *Journal, Academic/Scholarly.* **Description:** Discusses of gender, sexuality, race, and class in the context of law and public policy.
Related titles: Online - full text ed.: free (effective 2011).
Indexed: A26, A39, C27, C29, CA, CLI, CWI, D03, D04, E08, E13, FamI, G08, G10, GW, I05, LRI, P30, P34, P48, PQC, R14, S02, S03, S09, S14, S15, S18, T02, W09.
—CIS, Ingenta. **CCC.**
Published by: Duke University, School of Law, Science Dr & Toverview Rd, PO Box 90372, Durham, NC 27708. TEL 919-613-7223, 919-613-7101, FAX 919-681-8460, publications@law.duke.edu. Ed. Amelia Hairston-Porter.

323.4 USA
DYKES, DISABILITY & STUFF. Text in English. q. USD 20 to individuals; USD 50 to institutions. **Description:** Discusses racism, especially in the disability civil rights movement and in the lesbian community.
Related titles: Audio cassette/tape ed.; Braille ed.
Address: PO Box 8773, Madison, WI 53714. adv.: page USD 200; trim 11 x 8.5.

DZIENNIK POLSKI I DZIENNIK ZOLNIERZA/POLISH DAILY AND THE SOLDIERS DAILY. *see* ETHNIC INTERESTS

E C H O NEWS. (European Community Humanitarian Office) *see* BUSINESS AND ECONOMICS—International Development And Assistance

E-QUALITY. *see* RELIGIONS AND THEOLOGY

323.4 ZAF ISSN 1684-260X
E S R REVIEW. (Economic and Social Rights) Text in English. 1998. 3/yr.
Related titles: Online - full text ed.
Published by: University of Pretoria, Centre for Human Rights, Pretoria, 0002, South Africa. TEL 27-12-420-3034, FAX 27-12-362-5125, http://www.up.ac.za/chr. Ed. Sandra Liebenberg.

341.48 321.8 KEN ISSN 1682-900X
EAST AFRICAN JOURNAL OF HUMAN RIGHTS AND DEMOCRACY. Text in English. 2004. q. (Mar., Jun., Sep. & Dec.). **Document type:** *Journal, Academic/Scholarly.*
Related titles: Online - full text ed.: ISSN 1817-4264.
Published by: East African Human Rights Institute, Ambassador Court A6, Milimani Rd, PO Box 11391-00100, Nairobi, Kenya. TEL 254-20-2730158, FAX 254-20-2730159, eafricajournal@email.com.

323.4 340 UGA ISSN 1021-8858
K5
➤ **EAST AFRICAN JOURNAL OF PEACE AND HUMAN RIGHTS.** Text in English. 1993. s-a. USD 45 in North America & Europe to individuals; USD 50 in North America & Europe to institutions (effective 2007). bk.rev. illus. reprints avail. **Document type:** *Journal, Academic/Scholarly.* **Description:** Seeks to explore and amplify African concerns about the related questions of peace and human rights.
Indexed: ASD, FLP, IIBP.
—BLDSC (3644.670000), IE, Ingenta.
Published by: Human Rights and Peace Centre, Makerere University, Faculty of Law, PO Box 7062, Kampala, Uganda. TEL 256-41-532954, FAX 256-41-543110, dasiimwe@huripec.ac.ug, http://www1.umn.edu. Ed. James Katlikawe.

342.085 USA ISSN 1382-7987
K5
EAST EUROPEAN HUMAN RIGHTS REVIEW. Text in English. 1995. s-a. USD 154 per vol. domestic; USD 178 per vol. foreign (effective 2008). 150 p./no. 1 cols./p.; back issues avail. **Document type:** *Journal, Trade.* **Description:** Seeks not only to provide those interested with information but also to make a contribution to the improvement of human rights protection.
—BLDSC (3646.305550), IE, Ingenta.
Published by: Bookworld Publications/B W P - Bookcenter, PO Box 951361, Lake Mary, FL 32795. TEL 407-417-2470, FAX 407-321-7730, info@bwp-bookcenter.com. Ed. Leszek Leszczynski. Pub. Anton van de Plas.

323.4 USA
P95.8
EFFECTOR ONLINE NEWSLETTER. Text in English. 1991. irreg. (1-4/mo.). free (effective 2010). **Document type:** *Newsletter, Trade.* **Description:** Works in the public interest to protect privacy, free expression, and access to public resources and information in new media.
Former titles (until 2002): EFFector (1534-2697); (until 1997): EFFector Online (1062-9424); (until 1991): E F F News
Media: Online - full text.
Published by: Electronic Frontier Foundation, 454 Shotwell St., San Francisco, CA 94110. TEL 415-436-9333, FAX 415-436-9993, information@eff.org. Ed. Stanton McCandlish.

323.4 GBR ISSN 0962-7979
ELECTORAL REFORM SOCIETY NEWS. Text in English. 1990. w. back issues avail. **Document type:** *Newspaper.* **Description:** Covers latest news about the Electoral Reform Society.
Published by: Electoral Reform Society, Thomas Hare House, 6 Chancel St, London, SE1 0UU, United Kingdom. TEL 44-20-79281622, FAX 44-20-74017789.

▼ **EMPIRICAL RESEARCH IN RELIGION AND HUMAN RIGHTS.** *see* POLITICAL SCIENCE

331 USA ISSN 1530-8839
EMPLOYMENT IN THE MAINSTREAM. Text in English. 1975. q. USD 25 domestic; USD 40 in Canada & Mexico; USD 50 elsewhere (effective 2001). adv. bk.rev. back issues avail.; reprints avail. **Document type:** *Report, Trade.* **Description:** Reports on the practical and legal issues of bringing persons with disabilities into the workplace.
Formerly (until 1995): In the Mainstream (0888-9724)
Media: Online - full content.
Published by: Mainstream, Inc., 4795 Meadow Wood Ln., # 1163E, Chantilly, VA 20151-2222. TEL 301-891-8777, FAX 301-891-8778. Ed., R&P, Adv. contact Fritz Rumpel. Pub. Karen Morgret. online banner USD 300. Circ: 1,300 (paid).

ENLACE (WASHINGTON, 1975); politica y derechos humanos en las Americas. *see* POLITICAL SCIENCE—International Relations

323.4 GBR ISSN 0140-9468
EQUAL OPPORTUNITIES COMMISSION. ANNUAL REPORT. Text in English. 1977. a.
Related titles: Online - full text ed.
Published by: Equal Opportunities Commission, Arndale House, Arndale Centre, Manchester, M4 3EQ, United Kingdom. TEL 44-161-8339244, FAX 44-161-8388312, info@eoc.org.uk.

EQUAL RIGHTS. *see* WOMEN'S INTERESTS

EQUALITY, DIVERSITY AND INCLUSION. *see* WOMEN'S STUDIES

EQUALITY N O W!. (National Organization for Women) *see* WOMEN'S INTERESTS

EQUALITY NEWS. *see* ETHNIC INTERESTS

323.4 CAN
EQUALITY TODAY!. Text in English. irreg. **Document type:** *Bulletin.*
Media: Online - full text.
Published by: Young People's Press, 110 Eglinton Ave W, Ste 200, Toronto, ON M4R 1A3, Canada. TEL 416-484-4570, FAX 416-484-4570. Ed. Michael Hoechsmann.

323 CAN ISSN 1912-032X
EQUITAS INFO. Text in French. 1994. 3/yr. **Document type:** *Newsletter, Consumer.*
Former titles (until 2006): Info F C D P (1700-103X); Which superseded in part (in 2000): Parole aux Droits (1201-3641); Which was formerly (until 1994): Droits de la Personne (1491-4719); (until 199?): Droits Humains (1491-4700); (until 198?): Human Rights (0711-2122); (until 1975): Canadian Human Rights Foundation. Newsletter (0711-2114)
Related titles: ◆ English ed.: Equitas Info (English Edition). ISSN 1924-4983.
Published by: Equitas, 666 Sherbrooke W, Ste 1100, Montreal, PQ H3A 1E7, Canada. TEL 514-954-0382, FAX 514-954-0659, info@equitas.org, http://www.equitas.org.

323.4 CAN ISSN 1924-4983
EQUITAS INFO (ENGLISH EDITION). Text in English. 1975. s-a. back issues avail. **Document type:** *Magazine, Consumer.* **Description:** Provides a platform to explore issues in human rights education and to talk about partners in all corners of the world who do extraordinary work for the promotion and protection of human rights and social justice.
Former titles (until 2009): Equitas News (1912-0338); (until 2006): C H R F News (1700-1048); Which superseded in part (in 2001): Parole aux Droits (1201-3641); Which was formerly (until 1994): Droits de la Personne (1491-4719); (until 199?): Droits Humains (1491-4700); (until 1988): Human Rights (0711-2122); (until 1976): Canadian Human Rights Foundation. Newsletter (0711-2114)
Related titles: Online - full text ed.; ◆ French ed.: Equitas Info. ISSN 1912-032X.
Published by: Equitas, 666 Sherbrooke W, Ste 1100, Montreal, PQ H3A 1E7, Canada. TEL 514-954-0382, FAX 514-954-0659, info@equitas.org.

ESPACO JURIDICO. *see* LAW

323 GBR ISSN 1756-1957
JC571
➤ **ESSEX HUMAN RIGHTS REVIEW.** Text in English. 2004. s-a. free (effective 2009). **Document type:** *Journal, Academic/Scholarly.* **Description:** Addresses contemporary human rights issues.
Related titles: Online - full text ed.: free (effective 2011).
Indexed: SSciA.
Published by: University of Essex, Human Rights Centre, Colchester, Essex CO4 3SQ, United Kingdom. TEL 44-1206-872558, FAX 44-1206-873627, hrc@essex.ac.uk, http://www2.essex.ac.uk/human_rights_centre/. Ed. Anne Slowgrove.

323 BGR ISSN 1311-0276
DR64
ETNO REPORTER. Text in Bulgarian. 1998. bi-m. BGL 3.50 newsstand/cover (effective 2002). **Description:** Focuses on ethnic minorities, covers the various aspects of their everyday life. Primarily targeted at the majority and at state institutions. Publishes authors from various ethnic groups in Bulgaria and abroad.
Related titles: English ed.: Ethno Reporter. USD 3.50 newsstand/cover (effective 2002).
Published by: Inter Ethnic Initiative for Human Rights Foundation, Graf Ignatiev St. 9A, Sofia, 1000, Bulgaria. TEL 359-2-9801716, FAX 359-2-9800108, inetin@cblink.net. Ed. Kalina Bozeva.

323.4 GBR ISSN 1756-1272
EURASYLUM'S MONTHLY POLICY INTERVIEWS. Text in English. 2004. m. free (effective 2009). back issues avail. **Document type:** *Magazine, Trade.* **Description:** Contains a short interview of a leading player in international migration and asylum affairs, within a range of policy, academic and practitioners' areas of expertise.
Media: Online - full text.
Published by: Eurasylum Ltd., Carpenter Ct, 1 Maple Rd, Bramhall, Stockport, Cheshire SK7 2DH, United Kingdom. info@eurasylum.org.

323.4 AUT ISSN 1865-1089
EUROPAEISCHES JOURNAL FUER MINDERHEITENFRAGEN. Text in German. 2008. q. EUR 236, USD 313 combined subscription to institutions (print & online eds.) (effective 2012). adv. reprint service avail. from PSC. **Document type:** *Journal, Academic/Scholarly.*
Related titles: Online - full text ed.: ISSN 1865-1097. 2008 (from IngentaConnect).
Indexed: A22, A26, E01, E08, P45.
—IE. **CCC.**
Published by: Springer Wien (Subsidiary of: Springer Science+Business Media), Sachsenplatz 4-6, Vienna, W 1201, Austria. TEL 43-1-33024150, FAX 43-1-3302426, journals@springer.at, http://www.springer.at. Adv. contact Irene Hofmann. B&W page EUR 1,290; 155 x 235. Circ: 1,000 (paid). **Subscr. to:** Springer Distribution Center, Kundenservice Zeitschriften, Haberstr 7, Heidelberg 69126, Germany. TEL 49-6221-3454303, FAX 49-6221-3454229, subscriptions@springer.com.

323.4 NLD ISSN 0071-2701
EUROPEAN CONVENTION ON HUMAN RIGHTS. YEARBOOK/ CONVENTION EUROPEENNE DES DROITS DE L'HOMME. ANNUAIRE. Text in Dutch. 1959-1964; resumed 1965. a., latest vol.49, 2007, for the year 2006. price varies. **Document type:** *Yearbook.*
Indexed: RefugAb.
Published by: (Council of Europe/Conseil de l'Europe FRA), Martinus Nijhoff (Subsidiary of: Brill), PO Box 9000, Leiden, 2300 PA, Netherlands. TEL 31-71-5353500, FAX 31-71-5317532, marketing@brill.nl, http://www.brill.nl/.

341.481026 FRA ISSN 1682-7449
EUROPEAN COURT OF HUMAN RIGHTS. REPORTS OF JUDGEMENTS AND DECISIONS/COUR EUROPEENNE DES DROITS DE L'HOMME. RECUEIL DES ARRETS ET DECISIONS. Text in English, French. 1961. irreg. price varies. **Document type:** *Proceedings, Trade.*
Formerly (until 1996): European Court of Human Rights. Publications. Series A: Judgements and Decisions (0073-3903)
Published by: European Court of Human Rights, Council of Europe, Strasbourg-Cedex, 67075, France. TEL 33-3-88412018, FAX 33-3-88412730, http://www.echr.coe.int/ECHR/homepage_en.

323.4 SWE ISSN 0281-5206
EUROPEAN HUMAN RIGHTS. Text in Arabic, Danish, English, French, German, Japanese, Norwegian, Polish, Russian, Swedish, Spanish; Summaries in English. 1983. irreg. bk.rev. back issues avail. **Document type:** *Bulletin.*
Address: Marknadsvaegen 289, Taby, 18334, Sweden. TEL 47-08-768-13-98210. Ed. Ditlieb Felderer. Circ: 360,000.

EUROPEAN HUMAN RIGHTS LAW REVIEW. *see* LAW—Civil Law

323 GBR ISSN 0260-4868
KJC5132.A53
EUROPEAN HUMAN RIGHTS REPORTS. Text in English. 1979. m. GBP 889, EUR 1,172, USD 1,528 (effective 2012). **Document type:** *Journal, Trade.* **Description:** Provides full text judgments and all separate opinions of key cases decided in the European Court of Human Rights.
—BLDSC (3829.718500). **CCC.**
Published by: Sweet & Maxwell Ltd. (Subsidiary of: Thomson Reuters Corp.), 100 Avenue Rd, London, NW3 3PF, United Kingdom. TEL 44-20-73937000, FAX 44-20-74491144, sweetandmaxwell.customer.services@thomson.com. Eds. Nicholas Grief, Tim Eicke. **Subscr. to:** PO Box 1000, Andover SP10 9AF, United Kingdom. TEL 44-20-73938051, sweetandmaxwell.international.queries@thomson.com.

EUROPEAN RACE BULLETIN; a digest on the rise of racism and fascism in Europe. *see* ETHNIC INTERESTS

EVERYONE'S BACKYARD; the journal of the grassroots environmental movement. *see* ENVIRONMENTAL STUDIES—Waste Management

EXILFORSCHUNG; ein internationales Jahrbuch. *see* SOCIOLOGY

EXPO; demokratisk tidskrift. *see* POLITICAL SCIENCE

EXPONENT II; a quarterly newspaper concerning Mormon women, published by Mormon women, and of interest to Mormon women and others. *see* WOMEN'S INTERESTS

F O I A UPDATE. (Freedom of Information Act) *see* JOURNALISM

323.4 USA
FACTS & TRENDS. Text in English. 1992. s-a. **Document type:** *Newsletter.* **Description:** Provides an overview of research projects and reports.
Published by: (Institute for Civil Justice), Rand Corporation, 1700 Main St, Box 2138, Santa Monica, CA 90406-2138. Ed., R&P Beth Giddens TEL 310-393-0411.

FATHERS' JOURNAL. *see* MEN'S STUDIES

FEDERAL E E O ADVISOR. *see* LAW

THE FEDERAL LOBBYISTS. *see* LAW

FEMMES D'ICI. *see* WOMEN'S INTERESTS

FINANCIAL PRIVACY REPORT. *see* BUSINESS AND ECONOMICS—Banking And Finance

323.4 USA ISSN 0363-0447
KF4742
FIRST PRINCIPLES. Text in English. 1975. 4/yr. USD 15. bk.rev. **Document type:** *Newsletter.* **Description:** Articles and commentaries by experts on the relationship between national security and civil liberties.
Indexed: HRIR, IPARL.
Published by: (Center for National Security Studies, Washington Legislative Office), American Civil Liberties Union (Washington, DC), 915 15th St NW, Washington, DC 20005-2302. TEL 202-544-1681, FAX 202-546-0738. Ed. Gary Stern. Circ: 3,500.

FJAERDE VAERLDEN. *see* ETHNIC INTERESTS

323 CAN
FLIPSIDE ALTERNATIVE DAILY. Text in English. d. **Document type:** *Newspaper.* **Description:** Independent voice committed to human and civil rights, global and environmental sustainability, democracy and equality.
Published by: University of Windsor, Communication Studies Department, c/o Dr James Winter, 401 Sunset Ave, Windsor, ON N9B 3P4, Canada. Pub. James Winter.

323.4 USA ISSN 0740-0195
E185.5
FOCUS (WASHINGTON, D.C. 1986). Text in English. 1972. bi-m. USD 15 (effective 2010). charts; stat. cum.index: 1972-1985. back issues avail. **Document type:** *Magazine, Trade.* **Description:** Provides coverage of national issues to a leadership audience.
Related titles: Online - full text ed.
Indexed: IIBP, IJP, PAIS, SRI.
Published by: Joint Center for Political and Economic Studies, Inc., 1090 Vermont Ave, NW, Ste 1100, Washington, DC 20005. TEL 202-789-3500, FAX 202-789-6390, general@jointcenter.org. Ed. David Ruffin.

323 CAN
FOR THE RECORD (YEAR): THE UN HUMAN RIGHTS SYSTEM. Text in English, French. 1997. a. USD 100 (effective 2000). **Description:** Summarizes the work of the United Nations on human rights issues and developments for the last year.
Related titles: CD-ROM ed.
Published by: Human Rights Internet, 8 York St, Ste 302, Ottawa, ON K1N 5S6, Canada. TEL 613-789-7407, FAX 613-789-7414, hri@hri.ca. Adv. contact Vernon Lang.

FORUM; infarmacyjna-kulturny byuleten. *see* SOCIOLOGY

323.47 NOR ISSN 1504-2855
FORUM 18 NEWS SERVICE. Text in English. 2003. irreg. **Document type:** *Newsletter, Consumer.* **Description:** Ity is a Christian initiative independent of any one church or religious group. Its editorial objective is to present the truth of a situation, both implicitly and explicitly.
Media: Online - full content.
Address: PO Box 6663, Rodeloekka, Oslo, 0502, Norway.

FORWARD. *see* SOCIAL SCIENCES: COMPREHENSIVE WORKS

323.4 USA ISSN 0882-3723
FOURTH WORLD JOURNAL. Text in English. 198?. 3/yr. USD 15 (effective 2010). bk.rev. back issues avail. **Document type:** *Journal, Academic/Scholarly.* **Description:** Brings together news and different points of view, especially those of the very poor themselves, on topics related to extreme poverty.
Related titles: Online - full text ed.: ISSN 1090-5251.
Indexed: HRIR.
Published by: Fourth World Movement, 7600 Willow Hill Dr, Landover, MD 20785. TEL 301-336-9489, nationalcenter@4thworldmovement.org.

323.4 DEU ISSN 0015-928X
FRAGEN DER FREIHEIT; Schriftenreihe fuer Ordnungsfragen der Wirtschaft des Staates und des kulturellen Lebens. Text in German. 1957. q. EUR 25 (effective 2002). bk.rev. 64 p./no. 2 cols./p.; **Document type:** *Journal, Academic/Scholarly.*
Indexed: RASB.
Published by: Seminar fuer freiheitliche Ordnung e.V., Badstr 35, Boll, 73087, Germany. TEL 49-7164-3573, info@sffo.de, http://www.sffo.de. Pub., R&P Fritz Andres. Circ: 1,500.

323.443 USA
FREE SPEECH. Text in English. 1995. m. USD 40; USD 4 newsstand/cover (effective 2004). back issues avail. **Document type:** *Magazine, Consumer.* **Description:** For supporters of American Dissident Voices radio program.
Published by: National Vanguard Books, PO Box 330, Hillsboro, WV 24946. TEL 304-653-4707, FAX 304-653-4690, http://natvan.com. Ed. Alexander Wells.

323.4 GBR ISSN 0016-0504
HX821
FREEDOM; anarchist fortnightly. Text in English. 1886. fortn. GBP 20 in UK & Ireland; GBP 29 elsewhere (effective 2009). bk.rev. 3 cols./p.; back issues avail. **Document type:** *Newspaper, Consumer.* **Description:** Focuses on political science from an anarchist perspective.
Related titles: Microform ed.: (from RPI).
Published by: Freedom Press, 84b, Whitechapel High St, London, E1 7QX, United Kingdom. shop@freedompress.org.uk.

322.4 KOR ISSN 1028-8341
FREEDOM DIGEST. Text in English. 1967. q. USD 20. adv. bk.rev. abstr.; charts; illus.; stat. **Document type:** *Journal, Academic/Scholarly.* **Description:** Covers political philosophy: problems of communism and democracy and human rights.
Formerly (until 1982): W A C L Bulletin (World Anti-Communist League) (0042-9449)
Published by: (World League for Freedom and Democracy), World Freedom Center Press, World Freedom Center, Changchung-dong San 5-19, Chung-gu, Seoul, Korea, S. TEL 02-235-0823, FAX 02-236-7059, TELEX TOWER-K28246. Ed. Dr. Woo Jae Seung. Adv. contact Sun Kyong Kang. Circ: 2,000.

323.4 IND ISSN 0016-0547
FREEDOM FIRST; journal of liberal ideas. Text in English. 1952. m. INR 200 domestic; USD 20 foreign (effective 2011). bk.rev. reprints avail. **Document type:** *Journal, Academic/Scholarly.*
Related titles: Microfilm ed.: (from PQC).
Published by: Indian Committee for Cultural Freedom, 3rd Fl, Army & Navy Bldg, 148 Mahatma Gandhi Rd, Mumbai, Maharashtra 400 001, India. TEL 91-22-22843416, FAX 91-22-22843416, freedom@vsnl.com. Ed., R&P, Adv. contact S V Raju.

323.4 USA ISSN 0732-6610
JC571
FREEDOM IN THE WORLD (YEAR); the annual survey of political rights and civil liberties. Text in English. 1978. a., latest 2004. USD 49.95, GBP 31.95, EUR 34.95 per issue (effective 2010). 752 p./no.; back issues avail. **Document type:** *Monographic series, Trade.*
Related titles: Online - full text ed.
Indexed: HRIR.
—BLDSC (4033.361000).
Published by: (Freedom House), Rowman & Littlefield Publishers, Inc., 4501 Forbes Blvd, Ste 200, Lanham, MD 20706. TEL 301-459-3366, 800-462-6420, FAX 301-429-5748, 800-338-4550, custserv@rowman.com.

323.4 USA ISSN 0898-9265
FREEDOM MONITOR. Variant title: Freedom House Monitor. Text in English. 1985. 2/yr. membership. back issues avail. **Document type:** *Newsletter.*
Published by: Freedom House, 120 Wall St, 26th Fl, New York, NY 10005. TEL 212-514-8040, FAX 212-514-8055, fh@freedomhouse.org, http://www.freedomhouse.org. Ed. Michael Goldfarb. Circ: 3,000.

323.4 USA
FREEDOM NETWORK NEWS. Text in English. 1986. bi-m. USD 35 (effective 2007). bk.rev. **Document type:** *Newsletter.* **Description:** Dedicated to building a free and peaceful world, respect for individual rights and liberties and an open and competitive economic system based on voluntary exchange and free trade.
Incorporates (in 1989): Individual Liberty; Which was formerly: S I L News (0036-1550)
Published by: International Society for Individual Liberty, 836B Southampton Rd, #299, Benicia, CA 94510-1907. TEL 707-746-8796, FAX 707-746-8797, info@isil.org. Ed. Vincent H Miller. Circ: 3,500 (paid).

323.443 GBR
FREEDOM OF EXPRESSION IN HONG KONG: ANNUAL REPORT. Text in English. a. GBP 3.99, USD 5 (effective 2000). **Document type:** *Bulletin.* **Description:** Reports on government efforts to suppress freedom of the press in Hong Kong.
Published by: International Centre Against Censorship, Lancaster House, 33 Islington High St, London, N1 9LH, United Kingdom. TEL 44-171-278-9292, FAX 44-171-713-1356. **Co-sponsor:** Hong Kong Journalists Association.

FREEDOM OF INFORMATION AND PROTECTION OF PRIVACY ACT. ANNUAL REPORT. *see* LAW

323.4 GBR
FREEDOM ORGANISATION FOR THE RIGHT TO ENJOY SMOKING TOBACCO. Variant title: F O R E S T. Text in English. 1980. bi-m. GBP 10, USD 20 (effective 1999). adv. bk.rev. **Document type:** *Magazine, Consumer.* **Description:** Aims to defend the liberty of the adult consumer of tobacco products. Promotes ways in which smokers can be accomodated. Speaks out against legislation restricting the rights of adult smokers in the U.K. and worldwide.
Formerly (until 2001): Free Choice (0965-2051)
Media: Online - full text.
Published by: Freedom Organisation for the Right to Enjoy Smoking Tobacco (F O R E S T), 33 Margaret St, 6th Fl, London, W1G 0JD, United Kingdom. TEL 44-7071-766537. Ed. Simon Clark. R&P Jennifer Starkey. Adv. contact Juliette Wallbridge. Circ: 5,000.

323.47 GBR ISSN 0957-3070
FREEDOM TODAY. Text in English. 1976. bi-m. free to members (effective 2009). adv. bk.rev. back issues avail. **Document type:** *Bulletin.*
Formerly (until 1988): Free Nation (0309-3980)
Published by: Freedom Association Ltd., PO Box 3394, Faringdon, Oxfordshire SN7 7FN, United Kingdom. TEL 44-7985-550356. Ed., Adv. contact Simon Richards. Circ: 4,000.

323.4 USA ISSN 1559-1638
AP2
THE FREEMAN; ideas on liberty. Text in English. 1946. m. (10/yr.). USD 39 domestic; USD 54 in Canada; USD 64 elsewhere; USD 10 per academic year to students; USD 4 newsstand/cover (effective 2005). bk.rev. illus. index. back issues avail.; reprints avail. **Document type:** *Magazine, Consumer.*
Former titles (until Dec. 2003): Ideas on Liberty (1542-0698); (until 1999): Freeman (0016-0652); (until 1950): Plain Talk (0190-4140); Incorporates (1955-1955): Ideas on Liberty (0445-2259)
Related titles: Microform ed.: (from PQC); Online - full text ed.
Indexed: A22, AmH&L, IFP, MLA-IB, P05, P06, P10, P30, P45, P48, P53, P54, PAIS, PCI, PQC, S11, T02.
—IE, Ingenta.
Published by: Foundation for Economic Education, Inc., 30 S. Broadway, Irvington-on-Hudson, NY 10533. TEL 914-591-7230, FAX 914-591-8910, fee@fee.org. Ed. Sheldon Richman. Pub. Richard Exeling. R&P Beth A Hoffman TEL 732-356-5714. Circ: 8,000 (controlled).

323.4 GBR ISSN 1749-4095
FREEMEN OF ENGLAND & WALES JOURNAL. Variant title: F E W Journal. Text in English. 1970. q. **Document type:** *Journal, Consumer.*
Formerly (until 2003): Freeman of England & Wales. Newsletter (1465-8755)
Published by: Freemen of England & Wales, 23 Stanmore Hill, Stanmore, Middlesex HA7 3DS, United Kingdom. TEL 44-20-89546222, empacon@lineone.net, http://www.freemen-few.org.uk/.

323.4 DEU ISSN 0016-0911
DIE FREIHEITSGLOCKE/BELL OF FREEDOM. Text in German. 1950. 11/yr. bk.rev. index. **Document type:** *Magazine, Consumer.*
Published by: Gemeinschaft Ehemaliger Politischer Haeftlinge (VOS), Stresemannsstr 90, Berlin, 10963, Germany. TEL 49-30-26552380, FAX 49-30-26552382, VOS-Berlin@t-online.de, http://www.vos-fg.de. Ed. Alexander Richter. Circ: 4,800 (controlled).

323.4 SWE ISSN 0016-142X
FRIHET. Variant title: Tidningen Frihet. Text in Swedish. 1917. 8/yr. SEK 98 (effective 2011). adv. bk.rev.; play rev. illus. index. **Document type:** *Magazine, Consumer.* **Description:** For young people interested in politics. Deals with cultural trends and social phenomena with emphasis on young people's point of view.
Related titles: Audio cassette/tape ed.
Indexed: RASB.
Published by: (Sveriges Socialdemokratiska Ungdomsfoerbund/Swedish Social Democratic Youth League), Frihets Media Ekonomisk Foerening, PO Box 11544, Stockholm, 10061, Sweden. TEL 46-8-7144800, FAX 46-8-7149508, info@frihet.se, http://www.frihet.se. Ed. Daniel Mathisen. Adv. contact Lennart Sundberg. Circ: 10,100 (controlled).

FUEL RIGHTS HANDBOOK. *see* SOCIAL SERVICES AND WELFARE

G L A A D DISPATCH. *see* HOMOSEXUALITY

G L B AMES NEWSLETTER. (Gays, Lesbians and Bisexuals) *see* HOMOSEXUALITY

338.91 USA
G P I D FORUM. (Gendered Perspectives on International Development) Text in English. 1984. irreg., latest vol.27, 2005. back issues avail. **Document type:** *Monographic series, Academic/Scholarly.* **Description:** Features short reports that describe research projects and development programs and review current policy issues.
Formerly (until 200?): W I D Forum (0888-7772)
Published by: Michigan State University, Center for Gender in Global Context, 206 International Ctr, Michigan State University, East Lansing, MI 48824. TEL 517-353-5040, FAX 517-432-4845, gencen@msu.edu.

323.4 305.4 PHL
GABRIELA WOMEN'S UPDATE. Text in English. q. illus. **Document type:** *Newsletter.* **Description:** Features articles, news, artwork and photographs concerning Filipino women from all GABRIELA member organizations.
Published by: GABRIELA National Women's Coalition, PO Box 4386, Manila, 1800, Philippines.

323.4 NOR ISSN 1504-4262
GALDU CALA. Text in Norwegian. 2004. irreg. **Document type:** *Monographic series, Consumer.*
Related titles: Ed.: ISSN 1504-4289; English ed.: ISSN 1504-4270.
Published by: Kompetansesenteret for Urfolks Rettigheder/Resourse Centre for the Rights of Indigenous Peoples, Bredbuktnesveien 50, Kautokeino, 9520, Norway. TEL 47-78-488010, FAX 47-78-488020, galdu2004@galdu.org, http://www.galdu.org.

323.4 ITA ISSN 1828-4965
GARANTE PER LA PROTEZIONE DEI DATI PERSONALI. BOLLETTINO. Text in Italian. 1997. m. **Document type:** *Bulletin, Government.*
Formerly (until 2002): Cittadini e Societa dell'Informazione (1128-8280)
Published by: Presidenza del Consiglio dei Ministri, Dipartimento per l'Informazione e l'Editoria, Via Po 14, Rome, 00198, Italy. http://www.governo.it/die/.

GARDA RACIAL AND INTERCULTURAL NEWSLETTER. *see* POLITICAL SCIENCE—International Relations

GENDER NEWSLETTER. *see* BUSINESS AND ECONOMICS—International Development And Assistance

P

323.4 USA
GENDERED PERSPECTIVES ON INTERNATIONAL DEVELOPMENT. RESOURCE BULLETIN. Variant title: The G P I D Bulletin. Text in English. 19??. 3/yr. back issues avail. **Document type:** *Bulletin, Academic/Scholarly.* **Description:** Provides information on new publications, video resources, scholarships, conferences, and web sites for researchers, development practitioners, and policy-makers.
Former titles (until 2009): W I D Bulletin (1077-145X); (until 198?): W I D Newsletter
Related titles: Online - full text ed.: free (effective 2010).
Published by: Michigan State University, Center for Gender in Global Context, 206 International Ctr, Michigan State University, East Lansing, MI 48824. TEL 517-353-5040, FAX 517-432-4845, gencen@msu.edu. Ed. Galena Ostipow.

327 ESP ISSN 2013-1976
GENERALITAT DE CATALUNYA. OFICINA DE PROMOCIO DE LA PAU I DELS DRETS HUMANS. BOLETIN. Text in Spanish, Catalan. 2008. m. back issues avail. **Document type:** *Bulletin, Consumer.*
Related titles: Print ed.: ISSN 2013-2050. 2008.
Published by: Generalitat de Catalunya, Oficina de Promocio de la Pau i dels Drets Humans, Via Laietana, 69, Barcelona, 08003, Spain. TEL 34-93-484-000, FAX 34-93-484-0423, interior@gencat.cat, http://www.gencat.cat/dirip.

340 USA ISSN 1946-3154
▼ **GEORGETOWN JOURNAL OF LAW & MODERN CRITICAL RACE PERSPECTIVES.** Abbreviated title: M C R P. Text in English. 2009. s-a. USD 30; USD 15 per issue (effective 2010). **Document type:** *Journal, Academic/Scholarly.* **Description:** Provides a forum for scholarship by academics, students and practitioners who are committed to racial justice and to provide a editorial experience for students who have the same goal.
Indexed: LRI.
Published by: Georgetown University Law Center, 600 New Jersey Ave, NW, Washington, DC 20001. TEL 202-661-6514, FAX 202-662-9491. Eds. Christina J Bostick, Paloma E Hill.

323.4 USA
GEORGIA CIVIL RIGHTS REPORT. Text in English. q. USD 15 (effective 2000). **Document type:** *Newsletter.*
Published by: Center for Democratic Renewal and Education, Inc., PO Box 50469, Atlanta, GA 30302. TEL 404-221-0025, FAX 404-221-0045.

323.4 DEU ISSN 0179-6682
GESELLSCHAFT FUER BEDROHTE VOELKER. ARBEITSBERICHT. Text in German. 19??. irreg. **Document type:** *Monographic series, Academic/Scholarly.*
Published by: Gesellschaft fuer Bedrohte Voelker, Gemeinnuetziger Verein e.V./Society for Threatened Peoples, Postfach 2024, Goettingen, 37010, Germany. TEL 49-551-4990611, FAX 49-551-58028, info@gfbv.de, http://www.gfbv.de.

323.442 CHE ISSN 0259-0379
BV741
GEWISSEN UND FREIHEIT. Text in German. 1973. s-a.
Related titles: Ed.: Conscience et Liberte. ISSN 0259-0360. 1948; N.S. CHF 43 domestic; CHF 46 foreign (effective 2001).
Published by: International Association for the Defense of Religious Liberty/Association Internationale pour la Defense de la Liberte Religieuse, Schosshaldenstr 17, Bern, 3006, Switzerland.

GLAUBE IN DER 2. WELT; Zeitschrift fuer Religionsfreiheit und Menschenrechte. *see* RELIGIONS AND THEOLOGY

342.085 NLD ISSN 1384-6523
GLOBAL HUMAN RIGHTS LAW COLLECTION. Text in Dutch. 4 base vols. plus a. updates. EUR 100 (effective 2009). Supplement avail. **Document type:** *Journal, Academic/Scholarly.* **Description:** Presents UN human rights texts, including Islamic human rights law.

Published by: Global Law Association, PO Box 9001, Tilburg, 5000 HA, Netherlands. TEL 31-13-5821366, FAX 31-13-5821367, info@wolfpublishers.nl. Eds. P A van Laar, W van der Wolf, C Tofan. **Dist. in N. America by:** Gaunt, Inc., Gaunt Bldg, 3011 Gulf Dr, Holmes Beach, FL 34217. TEL 941-778-5211, FAX 941-778-5252, info@gaunt.com, http://www.gaunt.com.

323.44 ZAF
GLOBAL INFORMATION SOCIETY WATCH. Text in English. 2007. a.
Document type: *Journal, Trade.*
Published by: Association for Progressive Communications, PO Box 29755, Melville, 2109, South Africa. TEL 27-11-7261692, FAX 27-11-7261692, info@apc.org, http://www.apc.org.

342.085 NLD ISSN 1384-6256
K7
GLOBAL JOURNAL ON HUMAN RIGHTS LAW. Text in English. 1996. s-a. USD 140 (effective 2009). bk.rev. bibl. back issues avail. **Document type:** *Journal, Academic/Scholarly.* **Description:** Presents basic documents and legal articles in the areas of human rights and international law. Presents background information on relevant UN conferences and an extensive bibliography and index.
—Ingenta.
Published by: Global Law Association, PO Box 9001, Tilburg, 5000 HA, Netherlands. TEL 31-13-5821366, FAX 31-13-5821367, info@wolfpublishers.nl, http://www.globallaw.org. Ed. C Tofan. **Dist. in N. America by:** Gaunt, Inc., Gaunt Bldg, 3011 Gulf Dr, Holmes Beach, FL 34217. TEL 941-778-5211, FAX 941-778-5252, info@gaunt.com, http://www.gaunt.com.

GLOBAL WAR CRIMES TRIBUNAL COLLECTION. *see* LAW—International Law

DIE GLOCKE VOM ETTERSBERG. *see* HISTORY—History Of Europe

323.4 USA ISSN 1079-7858
KF299.M56
GOAL IX. Variant title: Goal 9. Text in English. 1992. q. **Document type:** *Newsletter.* **Description:** Covers ABA initiatives, federal policies and programming of importance to minority lawyers.
Related titles: Online - full content ed.
Published by: American Bar Association, Commission on Racial and Ethnic Diversity in the Profession, 321 N Clark St, Chicago, IL 60610. minorites@abanet.org. Ed. Robert C. Mussehl.

GOTHIX; a lifestyle magazine. *see* LITERATURE—Science Fiction, Fantasy, Horror

GRAUER PANTHER. *see* GERONTOLOGY AND GERIATRICS

323.4 GBR ISSN 1470-8302
KDC758.A13
GREEN'S SCOTTISH HUMAN RIGHTS JOURNAL. Variant title: Scottish Human Rights Journal. Text in English. 2000. q. GBP 267, EUR 352, USD 459 (effective 2012). back issues avail. **Document type:** *Journal, Academic/Scholarly.* **Description:** Focusing on all areas of legal practice.
Published by: Sweet & Maxwell Ltd. (Subsidiary of: Thomson Reuters Corp.), 100 Avenue Rd, London, NW3 3PF, United Kingdom. TEL 44-20-73937000, FAX 44-20-74491144, sweetandmaxwell.customer.services@thomson.com. **Subscr. to:** PO Box 1000, Andover SP10 9AF, United Kingdom. TEL 44-20-73938051, sweetandmaxwell.international.queries@thomson.com.

323 GBR
GREENS SCOTTISH HUMAN RIGHTS SERVICE. Text in English. 2000. base vol. plus updates 2/yr. looseleaf. GBP 414 base vol(s). domestic; EUR 547 base vol(s). in Europe; USD 712 base vol(s). elsewhere (effective 2011). **Document type:** *Handbook/Manual/ Guide, Trade.* **Description:** Draws together all Acts and sections of Acts, that have been created or amended through the European Convention on Human Rights, while case digests bring together all the relevant case law from Scotland, the UK, Strasbourg and Commonwealth jurisdictions.
Published by: Sweet & Maxwell Ltd. (Subsidiary of: Thomson Reuters Corp.), 100 Avenue Rd, London, NW3 3PF, United Kingdom. TEL 44-20-73937000, FAX 44-20-74491144, sweetandmaxwell.customer.services@thomson.com. Eds. Alan Miller, Lord Reed. **Subscr. to:** PO Box 1000, Andover SP10 9AF, United Kingdom. TEL 44-20-73938051, sweetandmaxwell.international.queries@thomson.com.

323.4 USA
GREENSBORO JUSTICE FUND NEWSLETTER. Text in English. 1980. s-a. back issues avail. **Document type:** *Newsletter, Consumer.*
Former titles: Greensboro Civil Rights Fund Newsletter; Greensboro Justice Fund Newsletter
Published by: Greensboro Justice Fund, PO Box 1594, Northampton, MA 01061. TEL 413-322-9730, ruthtrujillo@cpmcast.net, http://www.gjf.org. Circ: 15,000.

GROUNDWORK; a forum for the grassroots. *see* ENVIRONMENTAL STUDIES

THE GUIDE (BOSTON); gay travel, entertainment, politics and sex. *see* HOMOSEXUALITY

GUILD REPORTER. *see* LABOR UNIONS

323.143 NOR ISSN 1504-7571
H L-SENTERET. SKRIFTSERIE. Text in Multiple languages. 2007. irreg. price varies. **Document type:** *Monographic series.*
Published by: H L-Senteret/Center for Studies of Holocaust and Religious Minorities, PO Box 1168, Blindern, Oslo, 0318, Norway. TEL 47-22-842100, FAX 47-22-842101, post@hlsenteret.no.

323.4 USA ISSN 0896-243X
HARMONY (SAN FRANCISCO); voices for a just future. Text in English. 1987. bi-m. USD 12 domestic; GBP 10 in United Kingdom; USD 16 elsewhere. adv. bk.rev. **Document type:** *Magazine, Consumer.* **Description:** Covers ethics and the reverence for life. Opposes the death penalty, war, abortion, euthanasia, racism, and economic injustice.
Published by: Sea Fog Press, Inc., PO Box 210056, San Francisco, CA 94121-0056. TEL 415-221-8527. Ed., Pub. Rose Evans. Circ: 1,170.

347 USA ISSN 2153-2389
▼ **HARVARD CIVIL RIGHTS - CIVIL LIBERTIES AMICUS.** Text in English. 2009. m. free (effective 2010). back issues avail. **Document type:** *Journal, Academic/Scholarly.* **Description:** Aims to supplement and enhance CR-CL's regular content by providing a platform for internet-based civil rights and civil liberties scholarship.
Media: Online - full text. **Related titles:** ◆ Supplement to: Harvard Civil Rights - Civil Liberties Law Review. ISSN 0017-8039.
—CCC.
Published by: Harvard Law School Student Journals, Hastings Hall, 1541 Massachusetts Ave, Cambridge, MA 02138. TEL 617-495-3100, http://www.law.harvard.edu.

HARVARD CIVIL RIGHTS - CIVIL LIBERTIES LAW REVIEW. *see* LAW—Civil Law

323.4 USA ISSN 1057-5057
K8
HARVARD HUMAN RIGHTS JOURNAL. Text in English. 1988. a. USD 30 domestic; USD 35 foreign (effective 2011). back issues avail.; reprint service avail. from WSH. **Document type:** *Journal, Academic/ Scholarly.* **Description:** Features articles on international and domestic human rights issues.
Formerly (until 1990): Harvard Human Rights Yearbook (1047-0174)
Related titles: Microfiche ed.: (from WSH); Microform ed.: (from WSH); Online - full text ed.: ISSN 1943-5088. free (effective 2011).
Indexed: A01, A22, A26, A39, BAS, BRD, C27, C29, CA, CLI, D03, D04, E13, FamI, G08, HRIR, I01, I05, ILP, LRI, P30, P34, P42, PAIS, R14, S14, S15, S18, T02, W03, W05.
—BLDSC (4267.183000), CIS, IE, Infotrieve, Ingenta. **CCC.**
Published by: Harvard University, Law School, 1563 Massachusetts Ave, Cambridge, MA 02138. TEL 617-495-3100, http://www.law.harvard.edu/. Eds. Anne Siders, Neha Sheth.

HARVARD JOURNAL ON RACIAL & ETHNIC JUSTICE. *see* LAW—Civil Law

HATE CRIME STATISTICS (ONLINE). *see* CRIMINOLOGY AND LAW ENFORCEMENT—Abstracting, Bibliographies, Statistics

323.4 FRA ISSN 1957-5912
HAUTE AUTORITE DE LUTTE CONTRE LES DISCRIMINATIONS ET POUR L'EGALITE. RAPPORT ANNUEL. Text in French. 2006. a. **Document type:** *Journal.*
Related titles: Online - full text ed.: ISSN 1954-3921. free; English ed.
Published by: Haute Autorite de Lutte Contre les Discriminations et pour l'Egalite (H A L D E), 11 Rue Saint Georges, Paris, 75009, France. TEL 33-1-55316100.

HEALTH AND HUMAN RIGHTS; an international journal. *see* PUBLIC HEALTH AND SAFETY

HEALTH AND HUMAN RIGHTS PUBLICATION SERIES. *see* PUBLIC HEALTH AND SAFETY

HER YONUYLE DERNEKLER. *see* SOCIAL SCIENCES: COMPREHENSIVE WORKS

HERTHA. *see* WOMEN'S INTERESTS

HIDDEN CHILD. *see* RELIGIONS AND THEOLOGY—Judaic

HIV POLICY WATCH. (Human Immunodeficiency Virus) *see* PUBLIC HEALTH AND SAFETY

323.4 FRA ISSN 0180-8524
HOMMES ET LIBERTES. Variant title: Hommes & Libertes. Text in French. 1961. q. EUR 20 domestic; EUR 25 in the European Union; EUR 30 elsewhere (effective 2010). back issues avail. **Document type:** *Journal, Academic/Scholarly.* **Description:** Covers issues in civil liberties worldwide.
Formerly (until 1977): Ligue des Droits de l'Homme. Bulletin National (0180-8516)
Related titles: Online - full text ed.: ISSN 1777-5590. 1997.
Indexed: IBSS.
Published by: Ligue des Droits de l'Homme, 138 rue Marcadet, Paris, 75018, France. TEL 33-1-56555100, FAX 33-1-42555121. Ed. Bernard Wallon. Pub. Henri Leclerc.

323.4 CAN ISSN 1924-8350
HOW TO OBTAIN PROOF OF CANADIAN CITIZENSHIP. Text in English. 200?. irreg. free (effective 2011). **Document type:** *Handbook/ Manual/Guide, Government.*
Related titles: Online - full text ed.
Published by: Citizenship and Immigration Canada, 180 Kent St, 6th Fl, Ottawa, ON K1A 1L1, Canada. TEL 888-776-8584, FAX 613-998-1527, Multi-Canada@cic.gc.ca.

323.47 362 NLD ISSN 1878-4747
HULP MAGAZINE. Text in Dutch. 2007. bi-m. free (effective 2011). **Document type:** *Magazine, Consumer.*
Published by: Stichting Hulp Vervolgde Christenen, Dorpsweg 85, Hoogblokland, 4221 LJ, Netherlands. TEL 31-183-563628, FAX 31-183-565481, info@stichtinghvc.nl, http://www.stichtinghvc.nl.

HUMAN RESOURCES MANAGEMENT - EQUAL EMPLOYMENT OPPORTUNITY. *see* BUSINESS AND ECONOMICS—Labor And Industrial Relations

323.4 CHE ISSN 1020-6507
HUMAN RIGHTS. Text in Multiple languages. 1997. q. USD 17; free to members (effective 2007). **Document type:** *Journal, Academic/ Scholarly.*
Published by: (American Bar Association, Section of Individual Rights and Responsibilities USA), United Nations, High Commissioner for Human Rights, 8-14 Ave de la Paix, Geneva, 10 1210, Switzerland. TEL 41-22-9179000, http://www.unhchr.ch.

323.4 USA ISSN 0046-8185
K8
HUMAN RIGHTS (CHICAGO). Text in English. 1970. q. USD 25 to institutions; free to members (effective 2009). adv. bk.rev. bibl.; illus. Index. back issues avail.; reprint service avail. from WSH. **Document type:** *Magazine, Trade.* **Description:** Features articles on freedom of speech, student journalists, privacy, gender and race equality and health rights.
Incorporates (in 1978): Section of Individual Rights and Responsibilities Newsletter (0572-3590); (1967-1969): American Bar Association. Section of Individual Rights and Responsibilities. Edited Proceedings
Related titles: Microfiche ed.: (from WSH); Microfilm ed.: (from WSH); Microform ed.: (from WSH); Online - full text ed.
Indexed: A01, A02, A03, A08, A20, A22, A25, A26, B04, B07, BRD, CA, CLI, DIP, E08, ENW, FamI, G08, H09, HRIR, I01, I03, I05, IBR, IBZ, ILP, L03, L10, LRI, M01, M02, P02, P05, P10, P13, P30, P34, P45, P48, P53, P54, PAIS, PQC, RASB, S02, S03, S05, S08, S09, S11, SSAI, SSAb, SSI, T02, W03.
—BLDSC (4336.437000), IE, Ingenta. **CCC.**
Published by: (Individual Rights and Responsibilities Section), American Bar Association, 321 N Clark St, Chicago, IL 60610. TEL 312-988-6018, 800-285-2221, FAX 312-988-6234, service@abanet.org. Eds. Angela Gwizdala, Deborah Flores, Stephen J Wermiel. Circ: 7,000.

HUMAN RIGHTS & CHARTER LAW. *see* LAW

HUMAN RIGHTS & GLOBALIZATION LAW REVIEW. *see* LAW

323.4 USA ISSN 1533-0834
HUMAN RIGHTS & HUMAN WELFARE; an international review of books and other publications. Abbreviated title: H R H W. Text in English. 1999. q. free (effective 2011). **Document type:** *Journal, Academic/ Scholarly.* **Description:** Features thematic review essays, book notes, topical research digests, a monthly roundtable forum, as well as hosts working papers.
Formerly (until 2001): Global Justice (1527-8085)
Media: Online - full text.
Indexed: A26, A39, C27, C29, CA, D03, D04, E13, I05, R14, S02, S03, S14, S15, S18, T02.
Published by: University of Denver, Center on Rights Development, Josef Korbel School of International Studies, 2201 S Gaylord St, Denver, CO 80208. TEL 303-871-4610, FAX 303-871-2124, ducord@du.edu, http://www.du.edu/korbel/cord.

323 341 BEL ISSN 1783-7014
K8
➤ **HUMAN RIGHTS AND INTERNATIONAL LEGAL DISCOURSE.** Text in English. 2006. s-a. EUR 79; EUR 58 in developing nations; EUR 57 to students (effective 2008). **Document type:** *Journal, Academic/ Scholarly.* **Description:** Covers human rights law on international legal discourse, focusing on the interaction of human rights law with specific domains of international law, including international development law, international environmental law, international criminal law, international labour law, and international trade law.
Related titles: Online - full text ed.
—BLDSC (4336.438615), IE.
Published by: Intersentia N.V., Groenstraat 31, Mortsel, 2640, Belgium. TEL 32-3-6801550, FAX 32-3-6587121, mail@intersentia.be, http://www.intersentia.be.

323.094105 GBR ISSN 1468-3997
HUMAN RIGHTS & U K PRACTICE. Text in English. 1999. bi-m. **Document type:** *Journal, Trade.* **Description:** Provides a UK-wide survey of the impact of Human Rights decisions on practice and procedure, with the Human Rights Act affecting decisions in every court, tribunal or committee.
—CCC.
Published by: XPL Publishing, 99 Hatfield Rd, St Albans, Herts AL1 4EG, United Kingdom. TEL 44-870-1432569, FAX 44-845-4566385, info@xplpublishing.com, http://www.xplpublishing.com.

323.4 USA
HUMAN RIGHTS BULLETIN (NEW YORK). Text in English. 1945. s-a. USD 35; USD 40 foreign; includes International League for Human Rights. Annual Report. **Document type:** *Bulletin.*
Formerly: Rights of Man
Indexed: HRIR.
Published by: International League for Human Rights, 823 United Nations Plz., New York, NY 10017-3518. TEL 212-684-1221, FAX 212-684-1696. Ed. Charles H Norchi. Circ: 3,600.

323 GBR ISSN 1368-132X
HUMAN RIGHTS CENTRE. OCCASIONAL PAPERS. Text in English. 1996 (Dec). irreg., latest no.9, 2001, June. price varies. **Document type:** *Monographic series, Trade.*
Related titles: Online - full text ed.
Published by: Queen's University Belfast, Human Rights Centre, School of Law, 28 University Sq, Belfast, BT7 1NN, United Kingdom. TEL 44-28-90273472, FAX 44-28-90273376, d.p.coyle@qub.ac.uk.

323.4 CAN
HUMAN RIGHTS CODE OF BRITISH COLUMBIA. Text in English. 1976. irreg. free. **Document type:** *Government.*
Formerly: Human Rights Act of British Columbia
Published by: BC Human Rights Commission, Parliament Bldgs, Victoria, BC V8V 1X4, Canada. TEL 604-387-3710, FAX 604-387-3643.

323 NZL
HUMAN RIGHTS COMMISSION. REPORT. Text in English. a. **Document type:** *Government.*
Formerly (until 1995): Human Rights Commission and Race Relations Conciliator. Report (0112-4676); Which was formed by the merger of (1973-1979): Race Relations Conciliator. Report (0110-294X); (1980-1983): Human Rights Commission. Report (0111-3607); Which was formerly (until 1979): Human Rights Commission. Annual Report (0110-8727)
Published by: Human Rights Commission/Te Kahui Tika Tangata, PO Box 6751, Wellesley Street, Auckland, 1141, New Zealand. TEL 800-496-877, FAX 64-9-3773593, infoline@hrc.co.nz, http://www.hrc.co.nz.

323 USA ISSN 1540-0123
JC571
HUMAN RIGHTS DIALOGUE; an international forum for debating human rights. Text in English. 1994. s-a. USD 5 per issue (effective 2003).
Related titles: Online - full text ed.: ISSN 1540-0166.
Published by: Carnegie Council on Ethics and International Affairs, 170 E. 64th St., New York, NY 10021-7496. TEL 212-838-4120, FAX 212-752-2432, info@cceia.org.

323 CAN ISSN 1492-0719
KE4381.A48
HUMAN RIGHTS DIGEST. Text in English. 2000. 8/yr. CAD 180 (effective 2004). **Description:** Provides summaries and digests of recent tribunal and court human rights decisions from all jurisdictions in Canada.
Related titles: Online - full text ed.
Published by: Canadian Human Rights Reporter, Inc., 1662 W 75th Ave, Vancouver, BC V6P 6G2, Canada. TEL 604-266-5322, FAX 604-266-4475, http://www.cdn-hr-reporter.ca/index.htm.

323 NLD ISSN 2210-7975
▼ **HUMAN RIGHTS DOCUMENTS ONLINE.** Text in English. 2010. base vol. plus a. updates. EUR 7,930, USD 10,780 (effective 2010). **Document type:** *Database, Academic/Scholarly.*
Media: Online - full text.
Published by: Brill, PO Box 9000, Leiden, 2300 PA, Netherlands. TEL 31-71-5353500, FAX 31-71-5317532, cs@brill.nl, http://www.brill.nl.

323.4 CHE ISSN 1014-5567
K3240.4
HUMAN RIGHTS FACT SHEET. Text in English. irreg., latest vol.25. **Document type:** *Monographic series, Academic/Scholarly.* **Description:** Intends to assist in better understanding basic human rights, what the United Nations is doing to promote and protect them and the international machinery available to help realize those rights.
Published by: Office of the United Nations High Commissioner for Human Rights, 8-14 avenue de la Paix, Geneva 10, 1211, Switzerland. TEL 022-7346011, FAX 022-7339879, TELEX 289696.

323.4 PHL ISSN 0117-5521
KPM2095.A13
HUMAN RIGHTS FORUM. Text in English. 1991. s-a. PHP 300, USD 30; USD 60 foreign. adv. **Document type:** *Journal, Consumer.* **Description:** Covers human rights issues and trends in the Philippines and Asia-Pacific. Includes results of theoretical studies and field research on human rights (civil, political, economic, social and cultural rights).
Indexed: BAS, IPP.
Published by: Philippine Human Rights Information Center, Rm. 508 FMSG Bldg, No. 9 Balete Dr., Quezon City, 1112, Philippines. TEL 632-721-3482, FAX 632-721-7814. Ed. Lorna Kalaw Tirol. R&P Rosalinda M Galang. Adv. contact Ellen Apostol. page USD 40. Circ: 1,000.

HUMAN RIGHTS IN DEVELOPMENT. *see* LAW—Civil Law

323 FRA ISSN 1608-9618
KJC5132.A13
HUMAN RIGHTS INFORMATION BULLETIN. Text in English. 1978. 3/yr. free. **Document type:** *Bulletin, Academic/Scholarly.*
Related titles: Online - full content ed.: ISSN 1608-7372; ◆ French ed.: Bulletin d'Information sur les Droits de l'Homme. ISSN 1608-960X.
Published by: Council of Europe/Conseil de l'Europe, Avenue de l'Europe, Strasbourg, 67075, France. TEL 33-3-88412033, FAX 33-3-88412745, publishing@coe.int.

HUMAN RIGHTS LAW IN PERSPECTIVE. *see* LAW—Civil Law

HUMAN RIGHTS LAW JOURNAL. *see* LAW—Constitutional Law

323.4 GBR ISSN 1470-1669
KD4080.A38
HUMAN RIGHTS LAW REPORTS - UK CASES. Text in English. 2000. bi-m. GBP 395, EUR 521, USD 679 (effective 2012). **Document type:** *Report, Trade.* **Description:** Focuses entirely on the application of the Human Rights Act 1998 and the ECHR in the UK.
Published by: Sweet & Maxwell Ltd. (Subsidiary of: Thomson Reuters Corp.), 100 Avenue Rd, London, NW3 3PF, United Kingdom. TEL 44-20-73937000, FAX 44-20-74491144, sweetandmaxwell.customer.services@thomson.com. Eds. Merris Amos, Richard Gordon, Tim Ward. **Subscr. to:** PO Box 1000, Andover SP10 9AF, United Kingdom. TEL 44-20-73938051, sweetandmaxwell.international.queries@thomson.com.

323 GBR ISSN 1461-7781
K8
HUMAN RIGHTS LAW REVIEW. Text in English. 19??. q. GBP 199 in United Kingdom to institutions; EUR 298 in Europe to institutions; USD 396 in US & Canada to institutions; GBP 199 elsewhere to institutions; GBP 217 combined subscription in United Kingdom to institutions (print & online eds.); EUR 325 combined subscription in Europe to institutions (print & online eds.); USD 432 combined subscription in US & Canada to institutions (print & online eds.); GBP 217 combined subscription elsewhere to institutions (print & online eds.) (effective 2012). adv. back issues avail.; reprint service avail. from PSC,WSH. **Document type:** *Journal, Academic/Scholarly.* **Description:** Promotes knowledge, awareness and debate of human rights law and policy.
Formerly (until 1994): Student Human Rights Law Centre. Newsletter
Related titles: Online - full text ed.: ISSN 1744-1021. GBP 181 in United Kingdom to institutions; EUR 271 in Europe to institutions; USD 360 in US & Canada to institutions; GBP 181 elsewhere to institutions (effective 2012) (from IngentaConnect).
Indexed: A22, B04, BRD, CJA, CJPI, E01, I01, ILP, P27, P42, P48, P54, PQC, SCOPUS, T02, W03, W05.
—BLDSC (4336.440550), IE. **CCC.**
Published by: Oxford University Press, Great Clarendon St, Oxford, OX2 6DP, United Kingdom. TEL 44-1865-556767, FAX 44-1865-556646, enquiry@oup.co.uk, http://www.oxfordjournals.org. Ed. David Harris.

323.4 GBR
HUMAN RIGHTS PRACTICE. Text in English. 2000. base vol. plus updates 2/yr. looseleaf. GBP 416 base vol(s). domestic; EUR 550 base vol(s). in Europe; USD 715 base vol(s). elsewhere (effective 2011). **Document type:** *Handbook/Manual/Guide, Trade.* **Description:** Provides encyclopedic coverage on all aspects of the European Convention of Human Rights and the Human Rights Act 1998.
Published by: Sweet & Maxwell Ltd. (Subsidiary of: Thomson Reuters Corp.), 100 Avenue Rd, London, NW3 3PF, United Kingdom. TEL 44-20-73937000, FAX 44-20-74491144, sweetandmaxwell.customer.services@thomson.com. Ed. Jessica Simor. **Subscr. to:** PO Box 1000, Andover SP10 9AF, United Kingdom. TEL 44-20-73938051, sweetandmaxwell.international.queries@thomson.com.

323 USA ISSN 0275-0392
JC571
➤ **HUMAN RIGHTS QUARTERLY**; a comparative and international journal of the social sciences, humanities and law. Abbreviated title: H R Q. Text in English. 1979. q. USD 195 to institutions; USD 273 combined subscription to institutions (print & online eds.); USD 59 per issue to institutions (effective 2012). adv. bk.rev. illus.; abstr. Index. 232 p./no.; back issues avail.; reprint service avail. from PSC,WSH. **Document type:** *Journal, Academic/Scholarly.* **Description:** Presents current work in rights research and policy analysis, and philosophical essays probing the fundamental nature of human rights as defined by the Universal Declaration of Human Rights.
Formerly (until 1981): Universal Human Rights (0163-2647)
Related titles: Microfiche ed.: (from IDC, WSH); Microform ed.: (from PQC); Online - full text ed.: ISSN 1085-794X. 1995. USD 205 to institutions (effective 2012).
Indexed: A01, A02, A03, A08, A20, A21, A22, A25, A26, ABCPolSci, ABRCLP, ABS&EES, ASCA, B04, BAS, BPIA, BRD, CA, CCME, CJA, CLI, CurCont, DIP, E01, E08, ESPM, FLP, FR, FamI, G06, G07, G08, G10, GEOBASE, HPNRM, HRIR, HistAb, I05, I13, IBR, IBSS, IBZ, ILD, LRI, LegCont, M01, M02, M10, MLA-IB, P02, P10, P27, P30, P34, P42, P45, P47, P48, P53, P54, PAIS, PCI, PQC, PRA, PSA, PerIslam, PhilInd, RI-1, RI-2, RefugAb, RiskAb, S02, S03, S08, S09, S11, SCOPUS, SOPODA, SSA, SSAI, SSAb, SSCI, SSI, SSciA, SociolAb, T02, W03, W07, W09.
—BLDSC (4336.441500), IE, Infotrieve, Ingenta, INIST. **CCC.**
Published by: The Johns Hopkins University Press, 2715 N Charles St, Baltimore, MD 21218. TEL 410-516-6900, FAX 410-516-6968. Ed. Bert B Lockwood Jr. TEL 513-556-0068. Pub. William M Breichner. **Subscr. to:** PO Box 19966, Baltimore, MD 21211. TEL 410-516-6987, 800-548-1784, FAX 410-516-3866, jrnlcirc@press.jhu.edu.

➤ **HUMAN RIGHTS REPORTS OF NEW ZEALAND.** *see* LAW—Constitutional Law

323.4 NLD ISSN 1524-8879
JC571
HUMAN RIGHTS REVIEW. Text in English. 1999. q. EUR 362, USD 496 combined subscription to institutions (print & online eds.) (effective 2012). adv. bk.rev. reprint service avail. from PSC. **Document type:** *Journal, Academic/Scholarly.* **Description:** Aims to integrate social scientific information and historical perspective, while extending the autonomous and critical functions in the study of human rights.
Related titles: Online - full text ed.: ISSN 1874-6306.
Indexed: A01, A03, A08, A22, A26, APW, B07, CA, E01, E08, G05, G06, G07, G08, I02, I05, I07, IBR, IBSS, IBZ, L03, P10, P34, P42, P45, P48, P53, P54, PQC, PSA, PhilInd, S02, S03, S09, SCOPUS, SociolAb, T02.
—IE, Ingenta. **CCC.**
Published by: Springer Netherlands (Subsidiary of: Springer Science+Business Media), Van Godewijckstraat 30, Dordrecht, 3311 GX, Netherlands. TEL 31-78-6576050, FAX 31-78-6576474, http://www.springer.com. Ed. Gary B Herbert.

323.4 USA ISSN 1014-5680
HUMAN RIGHTS. STUDY SERIES. Text in English. 1989. irreg.
Related titles: Spanish ed.: Derechos Humanos. Serie de Estudios. ISSN 1014-5699; Russian ed.: Prava Cheloveka. Seriya Issledovanii. ISSN 1014-5737; French ed.: Droits de l'Homme. Serie d' Etudes. ISSN 1014-5702.
Published by: United Nations, Centre for Human Rights, United Nations Building, New York, NY 10017.

323.4 CAN
HUMAN RIGHTS TRIBUNAL DECISIONS. Text in English. irreg. (36-65/yr.). free on website (effective 2002). **Document type:** *Government.*
Formerly: Human Rights Council Decisions
Published by: Human Rights Tribunal, 401 800 Hornby, Vancouver, BC V6Z 2C5, Canada. TEL 604-775-2000, FAX 604-775-2020. **Subscr. to:** Crown Publications Inc. TEL 250-386-4636, FAX 250-386-0221.

323.4 CAN ISSN 1192-3822
HUMAN RIGHTS TRIBUNE (ONLINE)/TRIBUNE DES DROITS HUMAINS. Text in English, French. 1992. 3/yr. free. adv.
Formerly (until 2005): Human Rights Tribune (Print) (1188-6226)
Media: Online - full text.
Indexed: A26, ABS&EES, APW, AltPI, C03, CBCARef, CPerI, G08, PQC.
—IE, Infotrieve, Ingenta. **CCC.**
Published by: Human Rights Internet, 8 York St, Ste 302, Ottawa, ON K1N 5S6, Canada. TEL 613-789-7407, FAX 613-789-7414, hri@hri.ca. R&P Laurie S Wiseberg. Adv. contact Vernon Lang.

323.4 USA ISSN 1054-948X
JC571
HUMAN RIGHTS WATCH WORLD REPORT. Text in English. 1990. a. USD 30 per issue (effective 2011). **Document type:** *Report, Consumer.* **Description:** Contains the survey of human rights situation in more than 75 countries.
Formed by the merger of (1980-1989): Administration's Record On Human Rights In; (1987-1989): Human Rights Watch. Annual Report (1041-8954)
Related titles: Online - full text ed.: free (effective 2009).
Indexed: CWI.
—CCC.
Published by: Human Rights Watch, 350 Fifth Ave, 34th Fl, New York, NY 10118. TEL 212-290-4700, FAX 212-736-1300, hrwdc@hrw.org. Ed. Kenneth Roth.

HUMAN SERVE CAMPAIGN NEWSLETTER. *see* SOCIAL SERVICES AND WELFARE

323.4 ESP ISSN 1132-7294
HUMANA IURA. Text in Spanish. 1991. a. EUR 78.13 (effective 2009). **Document type:** *Journal, Academic/Scholarly.*
Related titles: ◆ Supplement to: Persona y Derecho. ISSN 0211-4526.
—CCC.
Published by: (Universidad de Navarra, Facultad de Derecho), Universidad de Navarra, Servicio de Publicaciones, Campus Universitario, Pamplona, 31009, Spain. http://www.unav.es/publicaciones/.

323 USA ISSN 2151-4364
▼ ➤ **HUMANITY (HANOVER).** Text in English. 2010 (Oct.). s-a. USD 85 combined subscription to institutions (print & online eds.) (effective 2011). **Document type:** *Journal, Academic/Scholarly.* **Description:** Dedicated to publishing original research and reflection on human rights, humanitarianism, and development in the modern and contemporary world.
Related titles: Online - full text ed.: ISSN 2151-4372. 2010 (Oct.). USD 76 (effective 2011).
Indexed: A22.
—CCC.
Published by: University of Pennsylvania Press, 3905 Spruce St, Philadelphia, PA 19104. TEL 215-898-6261, FAX 215-898-0404, custserv@pobox.upenn.edu, http://www.pennpress.org. Ed. Samuel Moyn.

323.4 MNG
HUNIY ERH/HUMAN RIGHTS. Text in Mongol. m. **Document type:** *Newsletter.*
Published by: Voluntary Committee for Defence of Human Rights, PO Box 107, Ulan Bator, Mongolia. Ed. N Tsevegmid. Circ: 3,000.

HYPERBOREAN. *see* PHILOSOPHY

323.4 JAM
I J C H R NEWS LETTER. (Independent Jamaica Council for Human Rights) Text in English. 1974. q. USD 20. bk.rev. **Document type:** *Newspaper, Newspaper-distributed.*
Related titles: E-mail ed.
Indexed: HRIR.
Published by: Independent Jamaica Council for Human Rights Limited, 131 Tower St., Kingston, Jamaica. TEL 876-922-5012, FAX 876-967-1204. Ed. Lloyd G Barnett. Circ: 2,000.

I L G A BULLETIN. *see* HOMOSEXUALITY

I W G I A DOCUMENT; documentation of oppression of ethnic groups in various countries. *see* ANTHROPOLOGY

I W G I A DOCUMENTO. (International Work Group for Indigenous Affairs) *see* ANTHROPOLOGY

IFACTION. *see* LIBRARY AND INFORMATION SCIENCES

IMAGES (NEW YORK); the GLAAD newsletter of images & representations in the media. *see* HOMOSEXUALITY

IMMIGRATION NEWSLETTER. *see* LAW—International Law

IMPACT! (SEATTLE). *see* BUSINESS AND ECONOMICS—International Development And Assistance

323 SWE ISSN 2000-3757
▼ **INDEPENDENT WORLD REPORT.** Text in English. 2009. 4/yr. GBP 75 (effective 2010). illus. **Document type:** *Magazine, Consumer.* **Description:** Covers global briefing on human rights, international politics, peace and justice. The examined issue includes articles about witch hunting in Africa, the Catholic Church child abuse scandal in Germany, land mines, rights of homosexuals, and Myanmar.
Related titles: Online - full text ed.: free (effective 2010).
Address: P O Box 1128, Orebro, 70111, Sweden. TEL 46-19-7679005, iwr@independentworldreport.com. Ed., Pub. Tasneem Khalil.

INDEX ON CENSORSHIP; for free expression. *see* LITERARY AND POLITICAL REVIEWS

323.4 340 IND ISSN 0973-0818
K3236.3
➤ **INDIAN JOURNAL OF HUMAN RIGHTS AND THE LAW.** Text in English. 2004. s-a. INR 3,000, USD 80 to institutions (effective 2011). **Document type:** *Journal, Academic/Scholarly.*
Published by: Serials Publications, 4830/24, Ansari Rd, Darya Ganj, New Delhi, 110 002, India. TEL 91-11-23245225, FAX 91-11-23272135, serialspublications.india@gmail.com. Ed. Y Gurappa Naidu.

➤ **INDIGENOUS AFFAIRS.** *see* ANTHROPOLOGY

➤ **INDIGENOUS PEOPLES' JOURNAL OF LAW CULTURE & RESISTANCE.** *see* LAW

➤ **INDIGENOUS WORLD/MUNDO INDIGENA.** *see* ANTHROPOLOGY

323.4 GBR
INDONESIA HUMAN RIGHTS CAMPAIGN. OCCASIONAL REPORTS. Text in English, Indonesian. irreg. **Document type:** *Monographic series, Consumer.* **Description:** Covers diverse topics related to human rights in Indonesia. Includes source documents in the original and translations into English.
Published by: Indonesia Human Rights Campaign, 111 Northwood Rd, Thornton Heath, Surrey CR7 8HW, United Kingdom. TEL 44-181-771-2904, FAX 44-181-653-0322.

323.4 PSE ISSN 1994-0777
INFORMATION & DISCUSSION BRIEF. Text in English. 2000. irreg. **Document type:** *Monographic series, Consumer.*
Related titles: Online - full text ed.: ISSN 1994-0785; ◆ Arabic ed.: 'Awraq 'Amal Markaz Badil Lil-Niqash. ISSN 1995-9818.
Published by: Badil Resource Center for Palestinian Residency & Refugee Rights, PO Box 728, Bethlehem, Palestine. TEL 972-2-2777086, FAX 972-2-2747346, info@badil.org, http://www.badil.org/index.html.

INFORMATION FOR SOCIAL CHANGE. *see* LIBRARY AND INFORMATION SCIENCES

344.7304197 USA ISSN 1532-2726
R726
INFORMATION PLUS REFERENCE SERIES. DEATH AND DYING; who decides?. Text in English. 1992. biennial. USD 49 per issue (effective 2008). back issues avail. **Document type:** *Monographic series, Academic/Scholarly.* **Description:** Provides a compilation of current and historical statistics, with analysis, on aspects of one contemporary social issue.
Related titles: Online - full content ed.; ◆ Series: Information Plus Reference Series.
Published by: Gale (Subsidiary of: Cengage Learning), 27500 Drake Rd, Farmington Hills, MI 48331. TEL 248-699-4253, 800-347-4253, FAX 800-414-5043, gale.customerservice@cengage.com, http://www.galegroup.com.

323.1 USA ISSN 1532-1185
E184.A1
INFORMATION PLUS REFERENCE SERIES. MINORITIES; race and ethnicity in America. Text in English. 1980. biennial. USD 49 per issue (effective 2008). **Document type:** *Monographic series, Academic/Scholarly.*
Related titles: Online - full text ed.; ◆ Series of: Information Plus Reference Series.
Published by: Gale (Subsidiary of: Cengage Learning), 27500 Drake Rd, Farmington Hills, MI 48331. TEL 248-699-4253, 800-877-4253, FAX 877-363-4253, gale.customerservice@cengage.com, http://www.galegroup.com.

323.4 VEN ISSN 0798-2879
JC599.V4
INFORME ANUAL SOBRE LA SITUACION DE LOS DERECHOS HUMANOS EN VENEZUELA. Text in Spanish. 1988. a. VEB 8 domestic; USD 10 in the Americas; USD 12 elsewhere (effective 2009). **Description:** Covers human rights in Venezuela.
Published by: Programa Venezolano de Educacion - Accion en Derechos Humanos (Provea), Blvd. Panteon Puente de Trinidad, Edif. Centro Plaza Las Mercedes, P.B. Local 6, Caracas, Venezuela. TEL 58-212-860-6669, FAX 58-212-862-5333, publicaciones@derechos.org.ve, http://www.derechos.org.ve/. Circ: 1,500.

P

323 ARG ISSN 0329-7888
INFORME ANUAL SOBRE LA SITUACION DE LOS DERECHOS HUMANOS EN LA ARGENTINA. Text in Spanish. 1997. a.
Document type: *Journal, Academic/Scholarly.*
Published by: Centro de Estudios Legales y Sociales/Center for Legal and Social Studies, Rodriguez Pena, Piedras 547, Piso 1, Buenos Aires, C1070AAK, Argentina. cels@cels.org.ar, http://www.cels.org.ar.

INSIGHT INTO DIVERSITY. *see* OCCUPATIONS AND CAREERS

INSTITUT POUR L'EGALITE DES FEMMES ET DES HOMMES. RAPPORT D'ACTIVITES. *see* WOMEN'S INTERESTS

323.4 USA ISSN 1041-4940
KF8700.A16
INSTITUTE FOR CIVIL JUSTICE. ANNUAL REPORT. Text in English. 1988. a. **Document type:** *Corporate.*
Published by: (Institute for Civil Justice), Rand Corporation, 1700 Main St, Box 2138, Santa Monica, CA 90406-2138. Ed., R&P Beth Giddens TEL 310-393-0411.

INSTITUTE FOR WOMEN'S POLICY RESEARCH. CONFERENCE PROCEEDINGS. *see* WOMEN'S STUDIES

323.4 CRI
INSTITUTO INTERAMERICANO DE DERECHOS HUMANOS. BOLETIN. Text in Spanish. 1985. q. **Document type:** *Newsletter.*
Description: Contains information on the main activities of the Institute's programs and projects and on the activities of the Interamerican Court of Human Rights.
Related titles: English ed.: Interamerican Institute of Human Rights. Newsletter.
Published by: Instituto Interamericano de Derechos Humanos, Apartado Postal 10081, San Jose, 1000, Costa Rica. TEL 506-234-04-04, FAX 506-234-09-55. Ed. Natalia Dobles Trejos. Circ: 1,000.

323.4 CRI
INSTITUTO INTERAMERICANO DE DERECHOS HUMANOS. BOLETIN DOCUMENTAL. Text in Spanish. irreg., latest vol.6, 1992. USD 4.
Document type: *Monographic series.*
Published by: Instituto Interamericano de Derechos Humanos, Apartado Postal 10081, San Jose, 1000, Costa Rica. TEL 506-234-04-04, FAX 506-234-09-55.

323.4 CRI ISSN 1015-5074
INSTITUTO INTERAMERICANO DE DERECHOS HUMANOS. REVISTA. Text in English, Spanish. 1985. s-a. USD 30. back issues avail. **Document type:** *Journal, Academic/Scholarly.* **Description:** Covers the main achievements and events concerning human rights in the inter-american system.
Published by: Instituto Interamericano de Derechos Humanos, Apartado Postal 10081, San Jose, 1000, Costa Rica. TEL 506-234-04-04, FAX 506-234-09-55. Ed. Daniel Zovatto. Circ: 1,300.

INTELLECTUAL FREEDOM MANUAL. *see* LIBRARY AND INFORMATION SCIENCES

323.4 USA
INTELLIGENCE REPORT. Text in English. 1981. q. free to qualified personnel (effective 2010). maps; illus.; charts; stat. back issues avail. **Document type:** *Magazine, Trade.* **Description:** Presents law-enforcement officials and other interested persons with the results of SPLC's ongoing research into the influence of militia, patriot, white-supremacist, skinhead, and neo-Nazi groups in the US, with an aim toward preventing and combatting intolerance.
Supersedes (in 1997): Klanwatch Intelligence Report (1084-0028)
Related titles: Online - full text ed.
—CCC.
Published by: Southern Poverty Law Center, Intelligence Project, 400 Washington Ave, Montgomery, AL 36104. TEL 334-956-8200.

323 USA
INTER-AMERICAN COMMISSION ON HUMAN RIGHTS. ANNUAL REPORT. Text in English, Spanish. 19??. a., latest 2000. back issues avail. **Document type:** *Yearbook.*
Related titles: CD-ROM ed.
Published by: Inter-American Commission on Human Rights, 1889 F St, N W, Ste 820E, Washington, DC 20006. TEL 202-458-6002, FAX 202-458-3992, cidhoea@oas.org.

323.44 USA
INTER AMERICAN PRESS ASSOCIATION. FREEDOM OF THE PRESS ANNUAL REPORT. Text in English. a. membership. **Document type:** *Proceedings.*
Formerly: Inter American Press Association. Committee on Freedom on the Press. Report (0579-6695)
Published by: Inter American Press Association, 1801 S W 3d Ave, 8th Fl, Miami, FL 33129. TEL 305-634-2465, FAX 305-635-2272, info@sipiapa.org. Ed. Ricardo Trotti.

INTERCULTURAL HUMAN RIGHTS LAW REVIEW. *see* LAW

323 USA ISSN 1933-0049
➤ **INTERDISCIPLINARY JOURNAL OF HUMAN RIGHTS LAW.** Abbreviated title: I J H R L. Text in English. 2006. a. USD 40 per issue to individuals; USD 200 per issue to institutions (effective 2010). back issues avail. **Document type:** *Journal, Academic/Scholarly.* **Description:** Covers political, philosophical, and legal questions related to international human rights.
Related titles: Online - full text ed.
Indexed: A26, CA, E08, I01, I05, ILP, LRI, P42, S09, T02, W03, W05.
Published by: Council for American Students in International Negotiations, PO Box 1617, New York, NY 10163. ted@americanstudents.us. Eds. Bernhard Kuschnik, Carla de Ycaza.

360 323 GBR ISSN 0268-3709
K9
INTERIGHTS BULLETIN. Text in English. 1985. q. GBP 36 to individuals; GBP 48 to institutions; GBP 24 to students (effective 2009). back issues avail. **Document type:** *Bulletin, Trade.* **Description:** Presents articles on issues of international human rights law, news and comment on developments as well as reviews of new publications.
Related titles: Online - full text ed.
—BLDSC (4533.531500).
Published by: The International Centre for the Legal Protection of Human Rights, Lancaster House, 33 Islington High St, London, N1 9LH, United Kingdom. TEL 44-20-72783230, FAX 44-20-72784334, ir@interights.org.

323.352 NLD ISSN 0259-3696
HQ789 CODEN: ICRMFQ
INTERNATIONAL CHILDREN'S RIGHTS MONITOR. Text in English. 1983. 3/yr. EUR 145, USD 145 to institutions (effective 2003). bk.rev. **Document type:** *Magazine, Consumer.* **Description:** Attempts to foster awareness about, and efforts in favor of, children and their rights throughout the world, by informing its readers about the needs and initiatives in this area.
Related titles: ◆ French ed.: Tribune Internationale des Droits de l'Enfant. ISSN 0259-370X.
Indexed: A22, E01, HRIR, RefugAb, T02.
—IE, Infotrieve, Ingenta.
Published by: (Defence for Children International CHE), Brill, PO Box 9000, Leiden, 2300 PA, Netherlands. TEL 31-71-5353500, FAX 31-71-5317532, cs@brill.nl, http://www.brill.nl. Circ: 6,500.

323 344.01 CAN ISSN 0839-4407
F1035.A1
INTERNATIONAL CONVENTION ON THE ELIMINATION OF ALL FORMS OF RACIAL DISCRIMINATION. REPORT OF CANADA. Text in English. 1971. biennial. free (effective 2004).
Incorporates (1971-1988): Convention Internationale sur l'Elimination de Toutes les Formes de Discrimination Raciale. Rapport du Canada (0839-4415)
—CCC.
Published by: Canadian Heritage, Human Rights Program (Subsidiary of: Canadian Heritage/Patrimoine Canadien), 25 Eddy St, 11th Flr, Box 25-11-S, Gatineau, PQ K1A 0M5, Canada. TEL 819-997-0055, 866-811-0055, rights-droits@pch.gc.ca, http://www.pch.gc.ca/progs/pdp-hrp/index_e.cfm.

INTERNATIONAL COURT OF JUSTICE. PLEADINGS, ORAL ARGUMENTS, DOCUMENTS/COUR INTERNATIONALE DE JUSTICE. MEMOIRES, PLAIDOIRIES ET DOCUMENTS. *see* LAW—International Law

INTERNATIONAL DIALOGUE ON MIGRATION. *see* POPULATION STUDIES

323.4 CHE
INTERNATIONAL DOCUMENTATION ON MACEDONIA. Text in English, French. 1979. irreg., latest vol.13, 1982. CHF 120, USD 60. bibl.; charts; illus. index. back issues avail.
Address: Case Postale 37, Chambesy, 1292, Switzerland. Ed. Theodore D Dimitrov.

323 AUT
INTERNATIONAL HELSINKI FEDERATION FOR HUMAN RIGHTS. ANNUAL REPORT. Text in English. a. 450 p./no. 2 cols./p.; back issues avail. **Document type:** *Journal, Academic/Scholarly.* **Description:** Seeks to promote compliance of the states participating in the OSCE with the human rights provision to which they committed themselves in the Helsinki Final Act and its follow-up documents, as well as with relevant international law.
Related titles: Online - full text ed.
Published by: International Helsinki Federation for Human Rights, Wickenburggasse 14-7, Vienna, 1080, Austria. TEL 43-1-4088822, FAX 43-1-408882250, office@ihf-hr.org. Ed. Paula Tscherne-Lempiaeinen.

323.4 GBR ISSN 1351-542X
K3239.23
INTERNATIONAL HUMAN RIGHTS REPORTS. Abbreviated title: I H R R. Text in English. 1994. q. price varies. reprints avail. **Document type:** *Monographic series, Academic/Scholarly.* **Description:** Aims to provide access to a range of international documents relating to human rights required by academics, students, practitioners and others.
Related titles: Online - full text ed.
Indexed: A22.
—IE. **CCC.**
Published by: University of Nottingham, Department of Law, University Park, Nottingham, Notts NG7 2RD, United Kingdom. TEL 44-115-9515700, FAX 44-115-9515696, law-enquiries@nottingham.ac.uk.

323 USA ISSN 1541-7409
INTERNATIONAL HUMANITARIAN AFFAIRS. Text in English. 2003. irreg., latest 2007. price varies. back issues avail. **Document type:** *Monographic series, Academic/Scholarly.*
—BLDSC (4540.794000).
Published by: (Center for International Health and Cooperation), Fordham University Press, 2546 Belmont Ave, University Box L, Bronx, NY 10458. TEL 718-817-4795, FAX 718-817-4785, fnachbaur@fordham.edu. Eds. Kevin M Cahill, Helen Tartar.

323.352 NLD ISSN 0927-5568
K9 CODEN: ICRIED
➤ **THE INTERNATIONAL JOURNAL OF CHILDREN'S RIGHTS.** Text in English. 1993. q. EUR 433, USD 607 to institutions; EUR 473, USD 662 combined subscription to institutions (print & online eds.) (effective 2012). reprint service avail. from PSC,WSH. **Document type:** *Journal, Academic/Scholarly.* **Description:** Covers critical scholarship and practical policy development in all fields relating to children's rights, including law, sociology, social work, health, education and psychiatry.
Related titles: Online - full text ed.: ISSN 1571-8182. EUR 394, USD 552 to institutions (effective 2012) (from IngentaConnect).
Indexed: A01, A02, A03, A08, A22, A26, C28, CA, CJA, E01, F09, FLP, Faml, IBR, IBSS, IBZ, IZBG, L03, LRI, P34, RASB, S02, S03, SCOPUS, T02.
—BLDSC (4542.165500), IE, Infotrieve, Ingenta. **CCC.**
Published by: Martinus Nijhoff (Subsidiary of: Brill), PO Box 9000, Leiden, 2300 PA, Netherlands. TEL 31-71-5353500, FAX 31-71-5317532, marketing@brill.nl. Ed. Michael Freeman. **Dist. by:** Turpin Distribution Services Ltd., Pegasus Dr, Stratton Business Park, Biggleswade, Bedfordshire SG18 8QB, United Kingdom. TEL 44-1767-604800, FAX 44-1767-601640, custserv@turpin-distribution.com, http://www.turpin-distribution.com/.

342.085 GBR ISSN 1358-2291
K9 CODEN: IJDLF2
➤ **INTERNATIONAL JOURNAL OF DISCRIMINATION AND THE LAW.** Text in English. 1995. 4/yr. (in 1 vol., 4 nos./vol.). GBP 179, USD 335 (effective 2010). bk.rev. abstr.; bibl. back issues avail. **Document type:** *Journal, Academic/Scholarly.* **Description:** Encompasses a wide range of areas of discrimination, including racism and sex discrimination, religious discrimination, the treatment of asylum seekers and refugees, issues of immigration and nationality, discrimination on physical disability, fair housing, equal opportunity employment, and bias on sexual orientation.
Indexed: CA, CJA, DIP, E-psyche, IBR, IBZ, P03, P42, PAIS, PSA, PsycInfo, PsycholAb, S02, S03, S21, SCOPUS, SOPODA, SSA, SociolAb, T02.
—BLDSC (4542.186000), IE, Ingenta.
Published by: Sage Publications Ltd. (Subsidiary of: Sage Publications, Inc.), 1 Oliver's Yard, 55 City Rd, London, EC1Y 1SP, United Kingdom. TEL 44-20-73248500, FAX 44-20-73248600, info@sagepub.co.uk, http://www.uk.sagepub.com/home.nav.

323.4 GBR ISSN 1364-2987
JC571 CODEN: IJHRF6
➤ **THE INTERNATIONAL JOURNAL OF HUMAN RIGHTS.** Text in English. 1997. 5/yr. GBP 662 combined subscription in United Kingdom to institutions (print & online eds.); EUR 875, USD 1,100 combined subscription to institutions (print & online eds.) (effective 2012). adv. bk.rev. index. back issues avail.; reprint service avail. from PSC. **Document type:** *Journal, Academic/Scholarly.* **Description:** Covers human rights issues, particularly relating to race; religion, gender; children; class; refugees and immigration as well as transnational organized crime, and human rights and the law.
Related titles: Online - full text ed.: ISSN 1744-053X. GBP 596 in United Kingdom to institutions; EUR 787, USD 990 to institutions (effective 2012) (from IngentaConnect).
Indexed: A01, A02, A03, A08, A22, CA, CCME, CJA, DIP, E01, ESPM, FLP, I13, IBR, IBZ, P34, P42, P47, PAIS, PQC, PRA, PSA, PhilInd, RiskAb, S02, S03, SCOPUS, SSciA, SociolAb, T02, V&AA.
—IE, Ingenta. **CCC.**
Published by: Routledge (Subsidiary of: Taylor & Francis Group), 4 Park Sq, Milton Park, Abingdon, Oxon OX14 4RN, United Kingdom. TEL 44-20-70176000, FAX 44-20-70176336, subscriptions@tandf.co.uk, http://www.routledge.com. Ed. Frank Barnaby TEL 44-1264-860423. Adv. contact Linda Hann TEL 44-1344-779945. **Subscr. to:** Taylor & Francis Ltd., Journals Customer Service, Sheepen Pl, Colchester, Essex CO3 3LP, United Kingdom. TEL 44-20-70175544, FAX 44-20-70175198.

➤ **INTERNATIONAL JOURNAL OF PUBLIC HEALTH AND HUMAN RIGHTS.** *see* PUBLIC HEALTH AND SAFETY

▼ ➤ **INTERNATIONAL JOURNAL OF TRANSITIONS AND INNOVATION SYSTEMS.** *see* COMPUTERS—Automation

305.8 NLD ISSN 1385-4879
JF1061 CODEN: IGRREY
➤ **INTERNATIONAL JOURNAL ON MINORITY AND GROUP RIGHTS.** Text in English. 1993. q. EUR 394, USD 552 to institutions; EUR 430, USD 602 combined subscription to institutions (print & online eds.) (effective 2012). bk.rev. back issues avail.; reprint service avail. from PSC,WSH. **Document type:** *Journal, Academic/Scholarly.* **Description:** Discusses legal, political and social issues arising from the presence of identifiable groups within society, examining groups distinguishable because of racial, ethnic, linguistic, cultural or religious factors.
Formerly: International Journal on Group Rights (0927-5908)
Related titles: Online - full text ed.: ISSN 1571-8115. EUR 358, USD 502 to institutions (effective 2012) (from IngentaConnect).
Indexed: A01, A03, A08, A22, A26, B07, CA, E01, GEOBASE, I02, I13, IBR, IBSS, IBZ, IZBG, L03, LRI, P34, P42, PAIS, PRA, PSA, R02, RASB, S02, S03, SCOPUS, SociolAb, T02.
—BLDSC (4542.364500), IE, Infotrieve, Ingenta. **CCC.**
Published by: Martinus Nijhoff (Subsidiary of: Brill), PO Box 9000, Leiden, 2300 PA, Netherlands. TEL 31-71-5353500, FAX 31-71-5317532, marketing@brill.nl. Ed. Gudmundur Alfredsson. **Dist. by:** Turpin Distribution Services Ltd., Pegasus Dr, Stratton Business Park, Biggleswade, Bedfordshire SG18 8QB, United Kingdom. TEL 44-1767-604800, FAX 44-1767-601640, custserv@turpin-distribution.com, http://www.turpin-distribution.com/.

323.4 USA
INTERNATIONAL P.E.N. WRITERS-IN-EXILE CENTER'S NEWSLETTER. Text in English. 1965. q. looseleaf. free to qualified personnel. bk.rev. back issues avail. **Document type:** *Newsletter.* **Description:** Provides an update about international prisoners and a list of their publications. Also includes international news.
Published by: International P.E.N., Writers in Exile Center, 42 Derby Ave, Orange, CT 06477. TEL 203-397-1479, FAX 203-397-5439, gyorgyey@aol.com. Ed. Clara Gyorgyey. Circ: 150 (controlled).

255 NLD
INTERNATIONAL RECONCILIATION. Text in English. 1977-2001 (June); resumed 2005. 4/yr. adv. bk.rev. back issues avail. **Document type:** *Magazine, Consumer.* **Description:** Covers peace and justice issues, religious response to social issues, nonviolence training and education, and the relevance of nonviolent methods of social change and conflict resolution.
Former titles (until 2005): R I; (until 1994): Reconciliation International (1381-7450); (until 1985): I F O R Report (0167-174X)
Indexed: AltPI, PerIslam.
Published by: International Fellowship of Reconciliation, Spoorstraat 38, Alkmaar, 1815 BK, Netherlands. TEL 31-72-5123014, FAX 31-72-5151102, office@ifor.org.

323.4 NLD ISSN 0924-4751
➤ **INTERNATIONAL STUDIES IN HUMAN RIGHTS.** Text in English. 1982. irreg., latest vol.102, 2009. price varies. **Document type:** *Monographic series, Academic/Scholarly.* **Description:** Presents legal and political aspects of process and organization in the field of human rights.
Indexed: IZBG.
—BLDSC (4549.787500), IE, Ingenta. **CCC.**
Published by: Martinus Nijhoff (Subsidiary of: Brill), PO Box 9000, Leiden, 2300 PA, Netherlands. TEL 31-71-5353500, FAX 31-71-5317532, marketing@brill.nl.

342.085 USA ISSN 1570-7520
K3242.A15
INTERNATIONAL YEARBOOK OF MINORITY ISSUES. Text in English. 2002. a. USD 107 per issue domestic; USD 119 per issue foreign (effective 2008). **Document type:** *Yearbook, Trade.* **Description:** Provides an overview of new legal and policy measures related to these developments.
Published by: Bookworld Publications/B W P - Bookcenter, PO Box 951361, Lake Mary, FL 32795. TEL 407-417-2470, FAX 407-321-7730, info@bwp-bookcenter.com.

INTERNET LAW & REGULATION. *see* LAW—Computer Applications

323 USA
IOWA CIVIL RIGHTS COMMISSION. ANNUAL REPORT. Text in English. 1975 (no.8). a. free. **Document type:** *Government.*
Published by: Iowa Civil Rights Commission, 211 E Maple St, 2nd Fl, Des Moines, IA 50309-1858. TEL 515-281-4121, FAX 515-242-5840. Ed. Carol Anne Leach. Circ: 1,000.

323.4 USA
IOWA CIVIL RIGHTS COMMISSION. CASE REPORTS. Text in English. 1977. a. free. **Document type:** *Proceedings, Government.* **Description:** Decisions from the Hearings, Iowa District Court of Appeals and Iowa Supreme Court on Commission cases.
Published by: Iowa Civil Rights Commission, 211 E Maple St, 2nd Fl, Des Moines, IA 50309-1858. TEL 515-281-4121, FAX 515-242-5840. Ed. Carol Anne Leach. Circ: 1,000.

323 IRL ISSN 1393-7804
IRELAND. DEPARTMENT OF FOREIGN AFFAIRS. INTERNATIONAL COVENANT ON CIVIL AND POLITICAL RIGHTS. Text in English. 1993. irreg.
Published by: Ireland. Department of Foreign Affairs/An Roinn Gnothai eachtracha, 80 St Stephen's Green, Dublin, 2, Ireland. TEL 353-1-4780822.

323.4 070 THA ISSN 1513-4881
DS530.65
IRRAWADDY. Text in English. 1992. 8/yr. USD 30 to individuals in Southeast Asia; USD 40 elsewhere to individuals; USD 55 to institutions in Southeast Asia; USD 75 elsewhere to institutions (effective 2007). adv. back issues avail. **Document type:** *Magazine, Consumer.* **Description:** Seeks to promote press freedom and access to unbiased information, particularly in Burma and the rest of Southeast Asia. Contains articles on business, arts, news and other related information.
Related titles: Online - full content ed.
Published by: Irrawaddy Publishing Group, PO Box 242, Chiang Mai University Post Office, Chiang Mai, 50200, Thailand. information@irrawaddy.org, http://www.irrawaddy.org/index.html. Ed. Aung Zaw. adv.: B&W page USD 135, color page USD 220.

323.4 ISR ISSN 0792-7029
ISRAEL EQUALITY MONITOR/MEDA' 'AL SHIVYON. Text in English, Hebrew. 1991. irreg. ILS 175 domestic; USD 40 foreign (effective 2002). back issues avail. **Document type:** *Journal, Consumer.*
Published by: Adva Center, P.O. Box 36529, Tel Aviv, 61364, Israel. TEL 972-3-5608871, FAX 972-3-5602205, advaninfo@netvision.net.il. Pub. Barbara Swirski. Circ: 1,500 (paid).

323 NLD ISSN 0333-5925
K3236.3
ISRAEL YEARBOOK ON HUMAN RIGHTS. Text in English. 1971. a., latest vol.39, 2009. price varies. bk.rev. cum.index: vols.1-20 in vol.21. back issues avail.; reprints avail. **Document type:** *Yearbook, Academic/Scholarly.* **Description:** Publishes studies by distinguished scholars on issues pertaining to human rights in peace and war, with particular emphasis on problems relevant to Israel and the Jewish people.
Indexed: A22, ABCPolSci, CCME, FLP, HRIR, IBSS, IZBG, PCI.
—BLDSC (4583.960000), IE, Ingenta.
Published by: (Tel Aviv University ISR), Martinus Nijhoff (Subsidiary of: Brill), PO Box 9000, Leiden, 2300 PA, Netherlands. TEL 31-71-5353500, FAX 31-71-5317532, marketing@brill.nl. Eds. Fania Domb, Yoram Dinstein.

323.4 CRI ISSN 1023-6813
KG574.A52
IUDICUM ET VITA; jurisprudencia nacional de America Latina en Derechos Humanos. Text in Spanish. 1994. q. **Document type:** *Academic/Scholarly.*
Published by: Instituto Interamericano de Derechos Humanos, Apartado Postal 10081, San Jose, 1000, Costa Rica. Ed. Jaime Ordonez.

323 NLD ISSN 2211-2200
JAARBOEK MINDERHEDEN. Text in Dutch. 1993. a. EUR 37.74 (effective 2011).
Former titles (until 2010): Jaarboek Multiculturele Samenleving in Ontwikkeling (1875-8916); (until 2007): Jaarboek Minderheden (0929-8908)
Published by: Sdu Uitgevers bv, Postbus 20025, The Hague, 2500 EA, Netherlands. TEL 31-70-3789911, FAX 31-70-3854321, sdu@sdu.nl, http://www.sdu.nl/.

323 325 NLD ISSN 1872-1354
JAARRAPPORT INTEGRATIE. Text in Dutch. 2004. biennial. price varies.
Formed by the 2004 merger of (2000-2002): Integratiemonitor (1571-3458); (1993-2003): Rapportage Minderheden (1380-0485); (1995-2004): Allochtonen in Nederland (1383-7311); Which was formerly (1987-1995): Minderheden in Nederland (0926-6518)
Related titles: Online - full text ed.
Published by: (Netherlands. Centraal Bureau voor de Statistiek), Sociaal en Cultureel Planbureau/Social and Cultural Planning Office, Postbus 16164, The Hague, 2500 BD, Netherlands. TEL 31-70-3407000, FAX 31-70-3407044, info@scp.nl, http://www.scp.nl. **Co-publisher:** Centraal Bureau voor de Statistiek.

JACKSONVILLE FREE PRESS. *see* ETHNIC INTERESTS

323 AUT
JAHRBUCH MENSCHENRECHTE. Text in German. 1998. a. EUR 24.90 (effective 2010). **Document type:** *Journal, Academic/Scholarly.*
Published by: Boehlau Verlag GmbH & Co.KG., Wiesingerstr 1, Vienna, W 1010, Austria. TEL 43-1-3302427, FAX 43-1-3302432, boehlau@boehlau.at, http://www.boehlau.at.

JEUNESSE DU QUART MONDE/FOURTH WORLD YOUTH JOURNAL. *see* CHILDREN AND YOUTH—For

323.4 ISR ISSN 1565-4907
DS101
➤ **JEWS IN RUSSIA AND EASTERN EUROPE.** Text in English. 1985; N.S. 1993. 3/yr. bk.rev. back issues avail. **Document type:** *Journal, Academic/Scholarly.* **Description:** Includes articles, reviews, documents and testimony concerning Jews and Jewish topics in the former Soviet Union and Eastern Europe.
Former titles (until 2003): Jews in Eastern Europe (0793-4041); (until 1993): Jews and Jewish Topics in the Soviet Union and Eastern Europe (0334-6641); (until 1989): Jews and Jewish Topics in Soviet and East European Publications (0334-6242)
Indexed: IJP, PCI.
Published by: (Hebrew University of Jerusalem, The Avraham Harman Institute of Contemporary Jewry), Hebrew University of Jerusalem, The Leonid Nevzlin Research Center for Russian and East European Jewry, Givat Ram, Jerusalem, 91904, Israel. TEL 972-2-6584271, FAX 972-2-666804. Eds. Yisrael Elliot Cohen, Mordechai Altschuler. Circ: 500.

323.4 BRA
JORNAL DA F U N A I. Text in Portuguese. 1986. m. free. illus.
Published by: Fundacao Nacional do Indio, Assessoria de Comunicacao Social, SEP Quadra 702/902 projecao A, Edificio Lex, Brasilia, DF CEP 70390-025, Brazil. TEL 55-61-3133500, http://www.funai.gov.br/.

364.6 323 FRA ISSN 1958-1327
JOURNAL DE L'ABOLITION. Text in French. 2001. s-a.
Published by: Ensemble Contre la Peine de Mort, 197-199 Av. Pierre Brossolette, Montrouge, 92120, France. TEL 33-1-57212273, FAX 33-1-57212274, http://www.abolition.fr.

323.4 USA
▼ ➤ **JOURNAL FOR HUMAN ADVANCEMENT.** Text in English. 2010 (Feb.). s-a. **Document type:** *Journal, Academic/Scholarly.* **Description:** Includes research, case studies, theoretical discussions, and scientific and artistic works that deal with any themes in human rights.
Related titles: CD-ROM ed.: ISSN 2152-2766. 2010 (Feb.); Online - full text ed.: 2010 (Feb.).
Published by: Goodis Center for Research and Reform, 30 Campus Rd, Annandale-Hudson, NY 12504-9800 . TEL 717-495-4300, admin@robertgoodis.org.

➤ **JOURNAL OF BEST PRACTICES IN HEALTH PROFESSIONS DIVERSITY;** research, education & policy. *see* HEALTH FACILITIES AND ADMINISTRATION

323 GBR ISSN 1475-4835
JC571
➤ **JOURNAL OF HUMAN RIGHTS.** Text in English. 2002. q. GBP 303 combined subscription in United Kingdom to institutions (print & online eds.); EUR 396, USD 498 combined subscription to institutions (print & online eds.) (effective 2012). adv. back issues avail.; reprint service avail. from PSC. **Document type:** *Journal, Academic/Scholarly.* **Description:** Seeks to broaden the study of human rights by fostering the critical re-examination of existing approaches to human rights, as well as to develop new perspectives on the theory and practice of human rights.
Related titles: Online - full text ed.: ISSN 1475-4843. GBP 272 in United Kingdom to institutions; EUR 357, USD 448 to institutions (effective 2012) (from IngentaConnect).
Indexed: A01, A02, A03, A08, A22, CA, CurCont, E01, I02, IBSS, LeftInd, MLA-IB, P34, P42, PSA, R02, S02, S03, SSCI, T02, V&AA, W07.
—IE, Infotrieve, Ingenta. **CCC.**
Published by: Routledge (Subsidiary of: Taylor & Francis Group), 4 Park Sq, Milton Park, Abingdon, Oxon OX14 4RN, United Kingdom. TEL 44-20-70176000, FAX 44-20-70176336, subscriptions@tandf.co.uk, http://www.routledge.com. Ed. Richard P Hiskes. Adv. contact Linda Hann TEL 44-1344-779945. **Subscr. to:** Taylor & Francis Ltd., Journals Customer Service, Sheepen Pl, Colchester, Essex CO3 3LP, United Kingdom. TEL 44-20-70175544, FAX 44-20-70175198.

323 GBR ISSN 1757-9619
K10
▼ ➤ **JOURNAL OF HUMAN RIGHTS PRACTICE.** Text in English. 2009 (Jun). 3/yr. GBP 176 in United Kingdom to institutions; EUR 264 in Europe to institutions; USD 351 in US & Canada to institutions; GBP 176 elsewhere to institutions; GBP 192 combined subscription in United Kingdom to institutions (print & online eds.); EUR 288 combined subscription in Europe to institutions (print & online eds.); USD 383 combined subscription in US & Canada to institutions (print & online eds.); GBP 192 combined subscription elsewhere to institutions (print & online eds.) (effective 2012). **Document type:** *Journal, Academic/Scholarly.* **Description:** Aims to capture learning and communicate the lessons of practice across professional and geographical boundaries, within and beyond the human rights mainstream, and to provide a platform for international and local practitioners world-wide.
Related titles: Online - full text ed.: ISSN 1757-9627. GBP 160 in United Kingdom to institutions; EUR 240 in Europe to institutions; USD 319 in US & Canada to institutions; GBP 160 elsewhere to institutions (effective 2012).
Indexed: P42, SCOPUS, T02.
—IE. **CCC.**
Published by: Oxford University Press, Great Clarendon St, Oxford, OX2 6DP, United Kingdom. TEL 44-1865-556767, FAX 44-1865-556646, enquiry@oup.co.uk, http://www.oxfordjournals.org. Eds. Brian Phillips, Paul Gready.

323 USA ISSN 0047-2492
CODEN: ELUKEJ
JOURNAL OF INTERGROUP RELATIONS. Text in English. 1958-1966; N.S. 1971. s-a. USD 18 domestic to individuals; USD 22 foreign to individuals; USD 20 domestic to institutions; USD 25 foreign to institutions (effective 2005). adv. bk.rev. reprints avail. **Document type:** *Journal, Academic/Scholarly.*
Related titles: Microfilm ed.: N.S. (from PQC).
Indexed: A21, A22, AmH&L, CA, ChPerI, E03, ERI, MLA-IB, P06, RI-1, S02, S03, T02.
—BLDSC (5007.548500), IE, Ingenta.
Published by: International Association of Official Human Rights Agencies (IAOHRA), 444 N. Capitol St., NW, Ste. 536, Washington, DC 20001. TEL 202-624-5410, FAX 202- 624-8185, iaohra@sso.org, http://www.iachra.org/. Ed. Jerrold Levinsky. Circ: 800.

JOURNAL OF LAW AND SOCIETY. *see* LAW

342.085 IND ISSN 2229-3663
JOURNAL OF MINORITIES RIGHTS. Text in English. 2008 (Apr.). s-a.
Published by: A.K.K. New Law Academy, 2390 - K. B. Hidayatullah Rd, New Modikhana, Pune, Maharastra 411 001, India. TEL 91-20-26442068, FAX 91-20-26447257, akkhanlaw@mcesociety.org.

JOURNAL OF SEXUAL LIBERTY. *see* LAW—Civil Law

JOURNAL OF SOUTH ASIA WOMEN STUDIES. *see* WOMEN'S STUDIES

323.4 DEU ISSN 1438-4701
JULI-MAGAZIN. Text in German. 1984. q. adv. bk.rev. bibl.; stat. back issues avail.
Published by: Junge Liberale NRW e.V., Sternstr 44, Duesseldorf, 40479, Germany. TEL 49-211-4925185, FAX 49-211-490028, nrw@julis.de, http://julis-nrw.de. Ed. Thorsten Palicki. Circ: 3,000.

JURISPRUDENTIE VOOR GEMEENTEN. *see* LAW

JUSTICE. *see* LAW—Constitutional Law

341.48 GBR
JUSTICE - BULLETIN (ONLINE). Text in English. 1993. 3/yr. free (effective 2009). back issues avail. **Document type:** *Bulletin, Trade.*
Formerly (until 2006): Justice - Bulletin (Print) (1467-4890); Which incorporated (1997-1998): Justice in Europe (1465-5349)
Media: Online - full text.
—**CCC.**
Published by: Justice, 59 Carter Ln, London, EC4V 5AQ, United Kingdom. TEL 44-20-73295100, FAX 44-20-73295055, admin@justice.org.uk.

323 GBR ISSN 1743-2472
K10
JUSTICE JOURNAL. Text in English. 2004 (Spring). s-a. GBP 60 domestic to non-members; USD 120, EUR 120 foreign to non-members; GBP 54 domestic to members; USD 108, EUR 108 foreign to members (effective 2009). back issues avail. **Document type:** *Journal, Academic/Scholarly.* **Description:** Aims to promote debate on topical issues relating to human rights and the rule of law.
—BLDSC (5075.629875). **CCC.**
Published by: Justice, 59 Carter Ln, London, EC4V 5AQ, United Kingdom. TEL 44-20-73295100, FAX 44-20-73295055, admin@justice.org.uk.

323.4 GBR
THE JUSTICE SERIES - PUTTING RIGHTS INTO PRACTICE. Text in English. 2000. irreg., latest vol.5, 2003. price varies. back issues avail. **Document type:** *Monographic series, Academic/Scholarly.* **Description:** Promotes awareness of the impact of the Human Rights Act 1998, and the interaction between it and different areas of the law.
Published by: Hart Publishing Ltd., 16c Worchester Pl, Oxford, OX1 2JW, United Kingdom. TEL 44-1865-517530, FAX 44-1865-510710, mail@hartpub.co.uk. Eds. Anne Owers, Jonathan Cooper.

P

323.4 AUS ISSN 0157-6011
JUSTICE TRENDS. Text in English. 1978. q. AUD 30 (effective 2008); includes Catholic Social Justice Series. **Document type:** *Journal, Academic/Scholarly.* **Description:** Provides information about the social justice developments in Australia and around the world.
Indexed: HRIR.
Published by: Australian Catholic Social Justice Council, 24-32 O'Riordan St, PO Box 7246, Alexandria, NSW 2015, Australia. TEL 61-2-83063499, FAX 61-2-83063498, admin@acsjc.org.au. Ed. David Brennan. Circ: 8,000.

323.4 USA
KO'AGA RON-E'ETA. Text in English. 1996. q. free. **Description:** Contents include articles, books and conference proceedings on human rights and humanitarian issues, directed to an audience of academics, lawyers, human rights professionals and activists.
Media: Online - full text.
Published by: Derechos Human Rights, 3205 San Mateo St, 1, Richmond, CA 94804. TEL 510-528-7794. Eds. Gregorio Dionis, Margarita Lacabe. **Co-sponsor:** Equipo Nizkor.

323.4 NZL
▼ **KOKIRI NGATAHI PANUI.** Text in English. 2010. irreg., latest no.2. free (effective 2010). **Document type:** *Government.*
Media: Online - full text.
Published by: Office of Treaty Settlements, Level 3, The Vogel Centre, 19 Aitken St, Wellington, 6011, New Zealand. TEL 64-4-4949800, FAX 64-4-4949801, reception.OTS@justice.govt.nz, http://www.ots.govt.nz.

323.4 951.9 KOR
KOREA INSTITUTE FOR NATIONAL UNIFICATION. WHITE PAPER ON HUMAN RIGHTS IN NORTH KOREA. Text in Korean, English. 1997. a. KRW 10,000, USD 10 per issue (effective 2009). **Document type:** *Journal, Academic/Scholarly.*
Published by: Korea Institute for National Unification, 535-353 Suyu 6-dong, Gangbuk-gu, Seoul, 142-728, Korea, S. TEL 82-2-900433, 82-2-9012528, FAX 82-2-9012546.

324.2 SWE ISSN 0284-9941
KRISTDEMOKRATEN. Text in Swedish. 1965. w. SEK 545 (effective 2004). adv. bk.rev.; film rev.; music rev.; play rev.; rec.rev.; Website rev. illus. 5 cols./p.; **Document type:** *Newspaper, Consumer.*
Incorporates (1977-2004): Ny Framtid (0347-8750); Formerly (until vol.9, 1988): Samhaellsgemenskap (0036-3782)
Related titles: Online - full text ed.
Published by: (Kristdemokratiska Partiet), Samhaellsgemenskaps Foerlags AB, Saltmaetargatan 8, P O Box 3127, Stockholm, 10362, Sweden. TEL 46-8-58710400, FAX 46-8-58710429. Ed. Henrik G Ehrenberg TEL 46-8-58710410. Adv. contact Sickan Palm TEL 46-8-58710422. page SEK 20,000; trim 375 x 255. Circ: 7,900 (controlled).

323.4 DEU ISSN 0023-4834
K11
KRITISCHE JUSTIZ. Text in German. 1968. q. EUR 69 (effective 2011). adv. bk.rev. index. reprint service avail. from SCH. **Document type:** *Journal, Academic/Scholarly.*
Indexed: A22, AC&P, AIAP, CA, DIP, I13, IBR, IBZ, P42, PSA, SociolAb, T02.
—IE, Infotrieve. **CCC.**

Published by: Nomos Verlagsgesellschaft mbH und Co. KG, Waldseestr 3-5, Baden-Baden, 76530, Germany. TEL 49-7221-21040, FAX 49-7221-210427, marketing@nomos.de, nomos@nomos.de, http://www.nomos.de. Ed. Rainer Erd. Adv. contact Bettina Roos. Circ: 2,200 (paid and controlled).

LES KURDES. *see* ANTHROPOLOGY

KVINNOR & FUNDAMENTALISM. *see* WOMEN'S INTERESTS

LAMBDA UPDATE. *see* HOMOSEXUALITY

LAND RIGHTS NEWS. *see* LAW

323.4 CAN ISSN 1922-8856
THE LANDOWNER. Text in English. 2006. bi-m. CAD 25 (effective 2010). adv. back issues avail. **Document type:** *Magazine, Consumer.* **Description:** Dedicated to promoting rural causes and bringing awareness to many of the issues that rural people are facing.
Published by: The Landowner, 6588 Fallowfield Rd, Stittsville, Ottawa, ON K2S 1B8, Canada. TEL 613-831-2668, FAX 613-831-2064, marlene@dilkie.com.

323 150 USA ISSN 1947-508X
▼ ➤ **LANDSCAPES OF VIOLENCE**; an interdisciplinary journal devoted to the study of violence, conflict, and trauma. Text in English. 2010. irreg. free (effective 2009). **Document type:** *Journal, Academic/Scholarly.* **Description:** Interdisciplinary research on theoretical and empirical issues around the study of violence, conflict, trauma, warfare, and human rights.
Media: Online - full text.
Published by: University of Massachusetts Amherst, Libraries, 154 Hicks Way, Amherst, MA 01003-9275. TEL 413-545-6846, mbanach@library.umass.edu, http://www.library.umass.edu/.

342.085 USA ISSN 1938-2545
➤ **LAW & ETHICS OF HUMAN RIGHTS.** Abbreviated title: L E H R. Text in English. 2008. a. USD 300 per issue to institutions; USD 900 per issue to corporations (effective 2011). **Document type:** *Journal, Academic/Scholarly.* **Description:** Focuses on contemporary human rights issues that raise major legal and moral questions for ethicists, legal scholars and policy-makers.
Media: Online - full text.
—**CCC.**
Published by: Berkeley Electronic Press, 2809 Telegraph Ave, Ste 202, Berkeley, CA 94705. TEL 510-665-1200, FAX 510-665-1201, info@bepress.com. Eds. Eyal Benvenisti, Stephen Macedo, Moshe Cohen-Eliya.

➤ **LAW & INEQUALITY**; a journal of theory and practice. *see* LAW

306.766 USA ISSN 1062-0680
K12
LAW & SEXUALITY. Text in English. 1991. a. USD 18 domestic to individuals; USD 20 domestic to institutions; USD 25 foreign; USD 12 to students (effective 2009). bk.rev. illus. 311 p./no.; back issues avail.; reprint service avail. from WSH. **Document type:** *Journal, Academic/Scholarly.* **Description:** Examines legal issues affecting gays and lesbians, including sexual discrimination and sexual harassment.
Related titles: Microfiche ed.: (from WSH); Microform ed.: (from WSH); Online - full text ed.
Indexed: A26, CA, CLI, FamI, G08, G10, I01, I05, ILP, L01, L02, LRI, RI-1, RI-2, S02, S03, T02.
—CIS.
Published by: Tulane University, School of Law, John Giffen Weinmann Hall, 6329 Freret St, New Orleans, LA 70118. TEL 504-865-5835, FAX 504-862-8878, avanpelt@tulane.edu. Ed. Jeffrey S Malfatti.

THE LAW HANDBOOK; your practical guide to the law in Victoria. *see* CONSUMER EDUCATION AND PROTECTION

342.085 NLD ISSN 1574-9398
LEGISLATING AGAINST DISCRIMINATION. Text in English. 2005. irreg., latest vol.1, 2005. **Document type:** *Monographic series.*
Indexed: IZBG.
Published by: Brill, PO Box 9000, Leiden, 2300 PA, Netherlands. TEL 31-71-5353500, FAX 31-71-5317532, cs@brill.nl, http://www.brill.nl.

LESBIAN CONNECTION. *see* HOMOSEXUALITY

LESOTHO LAW JOURNAL; a journal of law and development. *see* LAW

323.4 FRA ISSN 1957-519X
LA LETTRE DE NITASSINAN. Text in French. 1998. q. back issues avail. **Document type:** *Newsletter.*
Published by: Comite de Solidarite avec les Indiens des Ameriques, 21ter Rue Voltaire, Paris, 75011, France. TEL 33-1-43730580, FAX 33-1-43721577, info@csia-nitassinan.org.

LA LETTRE DES OBSERVATOIRES. *see* LAW—Civil Law

323.4 GBR ISSN 0024-1873
LIBERATION. Text in English. 1958. bi-m. free membership. adv. bk.rev. bibl. 16 p./no.; back issues avail. **Document type:** *Journal, Academic/Scholarly.* **Description:** Articles about struggles to achieve freedom from oppression and exploitation.
Formerly (until 1966): Colonial Freedom News (0531-108X)
—BLDSC (5186.679500). **CCC.**
Address: 9 Arkwright Rd, Hampstead, London, NW3 6AB, United Kingdom. TEL 44-20-7435-4547, liberation@btinternet.com. Ed. George Anthony. Adv. contact Maggie Bowden. Circ: 1,000.

323 ITA ISSN 2037-464X
▼ **LIBERTA CIVILI.** Text in Italian. 2010. bi-m. **Document type:** *Magazine, Consumer.*
Related titles: Online - full text ed.: ISSN 2037-6944.
Published by: Franco Angeli Edizioni, Viale Monza 106, Milan, 20127, Italy. TEL 39-02-2837141, FAX 39-02-26144793, redazioni@francoangeli.it, http://www.francoangeli.it.

323.4 USA ISSN 1048-4922
LIBERTYTREE; for your life, liberty, and prosperity. Text in English. 1990. s-a. bk.rev. 8 p./no. 3 cols./p.; **Document type:** *Journal, Trade.* **Description:** Focuses on the history, public policy and pursuit of liberty.
Related titles: Online - full text ed.
Published by: Independent Institute, 100 Swan Way, Oakland, CA 94621. TEL 510-632-1366, 800-927-8733, FAX 510-568-6040, info@independent.org, http://www.independent.org.

323.4 BEL
LIBRE. Text in French. 1974. q. EUR 12.40 domestic; EUR 17.35 foreign (effective 2002). back issues avail. **Document type:** *Newsletter, Trade.* **Description:** Contains articles on human rights, structure and functioning of the state, ethical problems, social and economic sectors. Includes relations of activities, announcements, articles of other publications.
Published by: Parti Feministe Humaniste, Av des Phalenes 35, Bte 14, Ixelles-Brussels, Brussels 1050, Belgium. TEL 32-2-648-8738, FAX 32-2-376-8863. Ed., R&P Renee Fosseprez. Circ: 150.

323.4 AUT
LIGA. Text in German. 1946. q. EUR 16; EUR 5 newsstand/cover (effective 2005). adv. bk.rev. charts; illus. cum.index. **Document type:** *Magazine, Consumer.*
Formerly: Das Menschenrecht (0025-9616)
Indexed: PAIS.
Published by: Oesterreichische Liga fuer Menschenrechte, Hermanngasse 9, Vienna, W 1070, Austria. TEL 43-1-5236317, FAX 43-1-52363174, http://www.liga.or.at. Ed. F J Bister. Circ: 3,000.

LOVER; tijdschrift over feminisme, cultuur, en wetenschap. *see* WOMEN'S STUDIES

M A L D E F NEWSLETTER. *see* ETHNIC INTERESTS

MA'DANG: JOURNAL OF CONTEXTUAL THEOLOGY IN EAST ASIA. *see* RELIGIONS AND THEOLOGY

323.4 DEU ISSN 0025-0511
DD256.3
DIE MAHNUNG. Text in German. 1953. m. EUR 24 (effective 2009). adv. bk.rev. **Document type:** *Magazine, Consumer.*
Published by: Bund der Verfolgten des Naziregimes Berlin e.V., Stauffenbergstr 13-14, Berlin, 10785, Germany. TEL 49-30-26995025, info@bvnberlin.de.

323.4 PSE ISSN 1726-7277
HV640.5.P36
AL-MAJDAL. Text in English. 1999. q. **Document type:** *Magazine, Consumer.*
Related titles: Online - full text ed.: ISSN 1726-7757.
Indexed: CA, I02, J01, LeftInd, M10, T02.
Published by: Badil Resource Center for Palestinian Residency & Refugee Rights, PO Box 728, Bethlehem, Palestine. TEL 972-2-2777086, FAX 972-2-2747346, info@badil.org, http://www.badil.org/index.html.

940.2 323.4 USA
THE MAKING OF MODERN FREEDOM. Text in English. 1992. irreg., latest 2003. price varies. back issues avail. **Document type:** *Monographic series, Academic/Scholarly.* **Description:** Explores the sociopolitical concept of freedom, as expressed in freedom of religion, freedom of speech and assembly, freedom of the individual from arbitrary and capricious authority over persons or property, freedom to produce and exchange goods and services, and freedom to take part in the political process that shapes people's destiny.
Published by: Stanford University Press (Subsidiary of: Stanford University), 1450 Page Mill Rd, Palo Alto, CA 94304. TEL 650-723-9434, FAX 650-725-3457, info@www.sup.org. Ed. R W Davis. **In Europe:** Cambridge University Press, The Edinburgh Bldg, Shaftesbury Rd, Cambridge CB2 8RU, United Kingdom. TEL 44-1223-312393, FAX 44-1223-315052, information@cambridge.org, http://www.cambridge.org/uk; **In the Americas:** Cambridge University Press Distribution Center, 100 Brookhill Dr, West Nyack, NY 10994. TEL 845-353-7500, FAX 845-353-4141, http://www.cambridge.org.

323.4 CAN ISSN 0383-5588
JC599.C2
MANITOBA. HUMAN RIGHTS COMMISSION. ANNUAL REPORT. Text in English. 1974. a. free. illus. **Document type:** *Government.*
Published by: Human Rights Commission, 7th Fl, 175 Hargrave St, Winnipeg, MB R3C 3R8, Canada. TEL 204-945-3007. Circ: 1,000.

323.4 USA
MARTIN LUTHER KING, JR. CENTER FOR NON-VIOLENT SOCIAL CHANGE NEWSLETTER. Text in English. 1973. irreg. donations. illus. **Document type:** *Newsletter.*
Formerly: Martin Luther King, Jr. Center for Social Change Newsletter
Published by: Martin Luther King, Jr. Center for Non-Violent Social Change, 449 Auburn Ave, N E, Atlanta, GA 30312. TEL 404-524-1956. Ed. Hilda R Tompkins. Circ: 30,000.

MARYKNOLL MAGAZINE. *see* RELIGIONS AND THEOLOGY—Roman Catholic

MARYKNOLL STUDY GUIDE. *see* RELIGIONS AND THEOLOGY—Roman Catholic

323.4 ARG ISSN 1852-2726
MATERIAL DEL PROGRAMA DE ESTUDIOS EN DERECHOS HUMANOS Y GLOBALIZACION. Text in Spanish. 2008. 3/yr. **Document type:** *Monographic series, Academic/Scholarly.*
Published by: Universidad del Salvador, Instituto de Investigacion en Ciencias Sociales, Hipolito Yrigoyen, 2441, Buenos Aires, C1089AAV, Argentina. http://www.salvador.edu.ar/csoc/idicso/home.htm.

323.4 ZAF ISSN 0025-6188
JQ1998.A4
MAYIBUYE. Text in English. N.S. 1975. 11/yr. ZAR 33 in Southern Africa; ZAR 165 elsewhere. adv. bk.rev. **Document type:** *Newspaper.* **Description:** Discusses political and social change in South Africa.
Related titles: Online - full text ed.: N.S.
Indexed: RASB.
Published by: African National Congress, PO Box 61884, Marshalltown, 2107, South Africa. TEL 27-11-3307277, FAX 27-11-3338870. Ed. Donovan Cloete. Pub. Cyril Ramaphosa. R&P Steyn Speed. Adv. contact Nazly Dangor. Circ: 20,000.

323 NLD ISSN 1871-6024
MEANDER BERICHTEN. Text in Dutch. 1996. q.
Formerly (until 2005): Meander Magazine (1385-1241)
Published by: Stichting Meander, Postbus 570, Alphen aan den Rijn, 2400 AN, Netherlands. TEL 31-172-495141, FAX 31-172-424017, meander@stmeander.nl, http://www.stmeander.nl. Ed. Trix van der Kamp. Circ: 1,600.

323 MLT ISSN 1027-4375
K13
➤ **MEDITERRANEAN JOURNAL OF HUMAN RIGHTS.** Text in English. 1997. s-a. **Document type:** *Journal, Academic/Scholarly.*
—BLDSC (5534.734700), IE, Ingenta.
Published by: University of Malta, Foundation for International Studies, Old University Bldg, St Paul St, Valletta, VLT 07, Malta. TEL 356-21231975, FAX 356-21230538, http://www.um.edu.my/intoff/fis.htmlg.

▼ ➤ **MEDIZIN UND MENSCHENRECHTE/MEDICINE AND HUMAN RIGHTS.** *see* MEDICAL SCIENCES

323.4 DEU ISSN 0171-5976
K3236.3
MENSCHENRECHTE; Dokumente - Schicksale - Informationen. Text in German. 1976. 4/yr. EUR 13.30; EUR 2.50 newsstand/cover (effective 2010). bk.rev. back issues avail. **Document type:** *Bulletin.*
Incorporates (1987-1990): Menschenrechte in der Welt (0934-1978)
Published by: Internationale Gesellschaft fuer Menschenrechte, Borsigallee 9, Frankfurt Am Main, 60388, Germany. TEL 49-69-4201080, FAX 49-69-42010833, info@igfm.de.

323 DEU ISSN 1434-2820
MENSCHENRECHTSMAGAZIN. Text in German. 1996. 2/yr. EUR 20 (effective 2009). **Document type:** *Journal, Academic/Scholarly.*
Published by: (Universitaet Potsdam, MenschenRechtsZentrum), Universitaetsverlag Potsdam, Am Neuen Palais 10, Potsdam, 14469, Germany. TEL 49-331-9774458, FAX 49-331-9774625, ubpub@uni-potsdam.de, http://info.ub.uni-potsdam.de/verlag.htm. Ed. Norman Weiss.

LA MER GELEE; revue franco-allemande, creation et critique. *see* LITERATURE

323 USA
MICHIGAN. CIVIL RIGHTS COMMISSION. ANNUAL REPORT. Text in English. 1964. a. free. **Document type:** *Government.* **Description:** Activities and accomplishments of the Michigan Civil Rights Commission. Describes the Commission's and Department's on-going efforts to obtain access and protection for individuals who have been denied equal opportunity in areas of jurisdiction.
Former titles (until 1972): Civil Rights in Michigan; (until 1970): Michigan. Civil Rights Commission. Report (0076-7875)
Published by: Department of Civil Rights, 201 N Washington Sq, Ste 700, Lansing, MI 48913. TEL 517-373-0089. Ed., R&P Rachel L Nusser. Circ: 1,000.

323.4 USA ISSN 0047-7087
MICHIGAN CIVIL RIGHTS COMMISSION NEWSLETTER. Text in English. 1971. q. free. charts; illus.; stat. **Document type:** *Newsletter.* **Description:** Activities and accomplishments of the Michigan Civil Rights Commission.
Published by: Department of Civil Rights, 201 N Washington Sq, Ste 700, Lansing, MI 48913. TEL 517-373-0089. Ed., R&P Rachel L Nusser. Circ: 7,000.

MIND FREEDOM JOURNAL; human rights in mental health. *see* MEDICAL SCIENCES—Psychiatry And Neurology

323 USA
JC599.U52
MINNESOTA DEPARTMENT OF HUMAN RIGHTS. BIENNIAL REPORT. Text in English. biennial. free. **Document type:** *Government.*
Former titles (until 1975): Minnesota. Department of Human Rights. Annual Report (0076-9118); (until 1968): Minnesota. State Commission Against Discrimination. Annual Report
Published by: Minnesota Department of Human Rights, 190 E 5th St, Ste 700, St. Paul, MN 55101. TEL 651-296-5663, 800-657-3704, FAX 651-296-1283, complaintinfo@therightsplace.net, http://www.humanrights.state.mn.us. Circ: 1,000.

323 327 GBR
MINORITY RIGHTS GROUP INTERNATIONAL. REPORT. Text in English. 1970. irreg. bibl.; illus.; stat.; maps. back issues avail. **Document type:** *Monographic series, Consumer.* **Description:** Investigates the plights of minority and majority groups suffering discrimination and prejudice - and works to alert and educate public opinion.
Formerly (until 19??): Minority Rights Group. Report (0305-6252)
Related titles: Online - full text ed.: free (effective 2009).
Indexed: HRIR, ILD, RefugAb, SCOPUS.
—**CCC.**
Published by: Minority Rights Group International, 54 Commercial St, London, E1 6LT, United Kingdom. TEL 44-20-74224200, FAX 44-20-74224201, minority.rights@mrgmail.org.

MIRA-SENTERET. TEMAHEFTE. *see* WOMEN'S INTERESTS

323.4 USA
MONITOR (ATLANTA). Text in English. 3/yr. USD 35 domestic membership; USD 75 domestic to institutions; USD 40 domestic to libraries; USD 45 foreign (effective 2000). **Document type:** *Newsletter.* **Description:** Opposes hate group violence and recruiting.
Published by: Center for Democratic Renewal and Education, Inc., PO Box 50469, Atlanta, GA 30302. TEL 404-221-0025, FAX 404-221-0045.

MORGONBRIS; s-kvinnors tidning. *see* WOMEN'S INTERESTS

323.4 RUS
MOSCOW RESEARCH CENTRE FOR HUMAN RIGHTS. MONTHLY INFORMATION NEWSLETTER. Text in English. m. USD 99.95 in United States.
Published by: Moscow Research Centre for Human Rights, Luchnikov per 4, Moscow, 101000, Russian Federation. TEL 7-095-2060923. **Dist. by:** East View Information Services, 10601 Wayzata Blvd, Minneapolis, MN 55305. TEL 952-252-1201, 800-477-1005, FAX 952-252-1202, info@eastview.com, http://www.eastview.com.

MULTICULTURAL PERSPECTIVES. *see* EDUCATION—Teaching Methods And Curriculum

EL MUNDO INDIGENA. *see* ANTHROPOLOGY

305.89915 AUS ISSN 1837-6460
▼ **MURASU.** Text in English. 2009. m. free (effective 2010). back issues avail. **Document type:** *Newsletter, Trade.*
Media: Online - full text.
Published by: Australian Tamil Congress, PO Box 22, Como, W.A. 6952, Australia. TEL 300-660-629.

323 297 USA ISSN 1554-4419
JC599
➤ **MUSLIM WORLD JOURNAL OF HUMAN RIGHTS.** Text in English. 2004 (Oct.). a. USD 225 per issue to institutions; USD 675 per issue to corporations (effective 2011). back issues avail. **Document type:** *Journal, Academic/Scholarly.* **Description:** Provides a medium for debate on various aspects of the question of human rights as it relates to the muslim world.
Media: Online - full text.
Indexed: A26, CA, ESPM, I02, I14, IBSS, LRI, LeftInd, M10, PAIS, S02, S03, SCOPUS, SSciA, T02.
—CCC.
Published by: Berkeley Electronic Press, 2809 Telegraph Ave, Ste 202, Berkeley, CA 94705. TEL 510-665-1200, FAX 510-665-1201, info@bepress.com. Eds. Mahmood Monshipouri, Mashood Baderin, Shadi Mokhtari.

323.4 FIN
MY LIFE DEPENDS ON YOU. Text in Finnish. 1981. a. free. bk.rev. **Document type:** *Bulletin.* **Description:** Examines electrical brain manipulation and the issue of human experimentation.
Published by: Martti Koski Ed. & Pub., Kanervakummuntie 5, Rusko, 21290, Finland. TEL 921-788482. Circ: 5,000.

N A A F A NEWSLETTER. *see* NUTRITION AND DIETETICS

THE N A P A L C REVIEW. (National Asian Pacific American Legal Consortium) *see* ETHNIC INTERESTS

324.3 USA
N C O M D R NEWS. Text in English. 1983. a. USD 5 per issue. bk.rev. **Document type:** *Newsletter.*
Published by: National Clearinghouse on Marital & Date Rape, 2325 Oak St, Berkeley, CA 94708. TEL 510-529-1582. Circ: 500.

323 331 IRL
N E S F NEWS. Text in English. q. free. **Document type:** *Newsletter, Trade.*
Formerly: National Economic and Social Forum. Newsletter
Media: Online - full content.
Published by: National Economic and Social Forum, 16 Parnell Sq, Dublin, 1, Ireland. TEL 353-1-8146361, FAX 353-1-8146301, secretariat@nesf.ie.

323.4 USA ISSN 0746-0201
N.Y. CIVIL LIBERTIES. Text in English. 1953. s-a. membership. bk.rev. reprints avail. **Document type:** *Newsletter.*
Formerly: Civil Liberties in New York (0009-7926)
Related titles: Microform ed.: (from PQC).
Published by: New York Civil Liberties Union, 125 Broad St, 17th Fl, New York, NY 10004-2400. TEL 212-344-3005, FAX 212-344-3318. Ed. Norman Siegel. Circ: 25,000.

323.4 SVN ISSN 0353-5347
AP58.S55
NASA SLOVENIJA. Text in Slovenian. 1978. m. Supplement avail. **Document type:** *Magazine, Consumer.*
Formerly (until 1989): Nas Delavec (1318-1351)
Address: Tavcarjeva ulica 5, Ljubljana, Slovenia.

323.4 CAN ISSN 1719-8518
NATIONAL DAY OF HEALING AND RECONCILIATION. Text in English. irreg. **Document type:** *Newsletter, Consumer.*
Related titles: French ed.: Journee Nationale de la Guerison et de la Reconciliation. ISSN 1719-8526.
Published by: National Day of Healing and Reconciliation National Campaign Office, c/o Native Counselling Services of Alberta, 10975 - 124 St, Edmonton, AB T5M 0H9, Canada. TEL 780-447-9342, FAX 780-428-0187, info@ndhr.ca, http://www.ndhr.ca/index.php.

NATIONAL GAY AND LESBIAN TASK FORCE. TASK FORCE REPORTS. *see* HOMOSEXUALITY

NATIONAL LAWYERS GUILD DISORIENTATION HANDBOOK; law for the people. *see* LAW

NATIONAL LAWYERS GUILD. GUILD NOTES. *see* LAW—Constitutional Law

NATIONAL LAWYERS GUILD REFERRAL DIRECTORY. *see* LAW

NATIONAL LAWYERS GUILD REVIEW. *see* LAW—Civil Law

NATIONAL N O W TIMES. *see* WOMEN'S INTERESTS

NATIONAL PRISON PROJECT JOURNAL. *see* CRIMINOLOGY AND LAW ENFORCEMENT

323.4 USA ISSN 2160-1003
▼ **NATIONAL SECURITY LAW BRIEF.** Text in English. 2010. s-a. **Document type:** *Journal, Trade.* **Description:** Covers traditional security issues such as counterterrorism, intelligence collection, and nuclear proliferation, and examines legal matters related to soft power and cybersecurity.
Related titles: Online - full text ed.: ISSN 2160-102X.
Published by: American University, Washington College of Law, 4801 Massachusetts Ave, N W, Ste 610, Washington, DC 20016. http://www.wcl.american.edu. Eds. Mora Namdar, Sean Shank.

200.8 USA
THE NATIONALIST OBSERVER. Text in English. m. USD 20 (effective 2001).
Published by: The Nationalist Observer, PO Box 152603, San Diego, CA 92195. AxCurtis@aol.com, http://www.whiteracist.com/.

NETHERLANDS QUARTERLY OF HUMAN RIGHTS. *see* LAW—Civil Law

NETWORK CONNECTION; national Catholic social justice lobby. *see* RELIGIONS AND THEOLOGY—Roman Catholic

323.40715 USA
NETWORK NEWS (SHERMAN). Text in English. 1966. s-a. USD 35 membership (effective 2000). back issues avail. **Document type:** *Newsletter.*
Formerly: Newsletter for Soulmates
Published by: Center for Nonviolent Communication, PO Box 2662, Sherman, TX 75091-2662. TEL 903-893-3886, FAX 903-893-2935. Ed. Rita Herzog. Circ: 25,000.

323.4 USA
NEW PARTY. Text in English. 1978. a. **Description:** Advocates the nationalization of health insurance and the abolishment of the death penalty and military conscription.
Published by: Sophia Circle, 8319 Fulham Ct, Richmond, VA 23227-1712. TEL 804-266-7400. Ed. Jerome Gorman.

323.4 USA
NEW YORK (STATE). DIVISION OF HUMAN RIGHTS. ANNUAL REPORT. Text in English. 1946. a. free.
Former titles: State of Human Rights in New York; New York (State). Division of Human Rights. Annual Report
Published by: Division of Human Rights, 55 W 125th St, New York, NY 10027. TEL 212-870-8400, FAX 212-870-8552. Circ: 3,000.

323.4 CAN
THE NEWSLETTER ON CIVIL LIBERTIES. Text in English. irreg. USD 2. **Document type:** *Newsletter.* **Description:** Monitors censorship activities and civil liberties infringements in Canada.
Related titles: Online - full text ed.
Published by: Newsletter on Civil Liberties, P O BOX 888, Sta F, Toronto, ON M4Y 2N9, Canada. Ed. Toshiya Kuwabara.

NEWSLETTER ON INTELLECTUAL FREEDOM. *see* LIBRARY AND INFORMATION SCIENCES

323.4 USA
NEWSWATCH. Text in English. 1975 (no.69). bi-m. USD 100 (effective 2007). **Document type:** *Newsletter.*
Former titles: Newsbreak (New York); National Conference on Soviet Jewry. Press Service; National Conference on Soviet Jewry. News Bulletin
Related titles: Online - full content ed.
Indexed: HRIR.
Published by: National Conference on Soviet Jewry, Soviet Jewry Research Bureau, 2020 K St, NW, Ste 7800, Washington, DC 20006. TEL 202-898-2500, FAX 202-898-0822, ncsj@ncsj.org, http://www.ncsj.org. Ed. Deborah Hart Strober. Circ: 1,500.

NICARAGUA MONITOR. *see* BUSINESS AND ECONOMICS—International Development And Assistance

323.4 POL ISSN 1428-0884
D725.5
NIGDY WIECEJ/NEVER AGAIN. Text in Polish. 1994. q. USD 25 in United States (effective 2007). **Document type:** *Magazine, Consumer.*
Published by: Stowarzyszenie Nigdy Wiecej, PO Box 6, Warsaw 4, 03700, Poland. TEL 48-22-507166196, FAX 48-22-601360835, http://www.nigdywiecej.prh.pl. Ed. Marcin Kornak. Circ: 3,000.

NIGHTSPOTS; club and events coverage for the LGBT community. *see* HOMOSEXUALITY

323.4 USA
NOCASTRO.COM. Text in English. m. free. **Document type:** *Newsletter.* **Description:** Informs readers about the political situation in Cuba, especially concerning human rights violations under the Castro regime.

323.4 DEU ISSN 1435-2206
NORD OE R. Text in German. 1998. 11/yr. EUR 173 (effective 2011). adv. reprint service avail. from SCH. **Document type:** *Journal, Academic/Scholarly.* **Description:** Reports on public rights in the counties of northern Germany.
Published by: Nomos Verlagsgesellschaft mbH und Co. KG, Waldseestr 3-5, Baden-Baden, 76530, Germany. TEL 49-7221-21040, FAX 49-7221-210427, marketing@nomos.de, nomos@nomos.de, http://www.nomos.de. Ed. Ulrich Ramsauer. Adv. contact Bettina Roos. Circ: 900 (paid and controlled).

323.4 NOR ISSN 1891-8131
JC585
NORDIC JOURNAL ON HUMAN RIGHTS. Variant title: N J H R. Text in English. 1983. q. NOK 415 to individuals; NOK 625 to institutions; NOK 229 to students (effective 2011). adv. bk.rev. back issues avail. **Document type:** *Journal, Academic/Scholarly.*
Former titles (until 2010): Nordisk Tidsskrift for Menneskerettigheter (1503-6480); (until 2003): Mennesker og Rettigheter (0800-0735)
Related titles: Online - full text ed.: ISSN 1891-814X. 2004. NOK 695 (effective 2010).
—CCC.
Published by: (Universitetet i Oslo, Norsk Senter for Menneskerettigheter/University of Oslo, Centre for Human Rights), Universitetsforlaget AS/Scandinavian University Press (Subsidiary of: Aschehoug & Co.), Sehesteds Gate 3, P O Box 508, Sentrum, Oslo, 0105, Norway. TEL 47-24-147500, FAX 47-24-147501, post@universitetsforlaget.no, http://www.universitetsforlaget.no. Eds. J Stigen, Baard A Andreasson. Adv. contact Lars Mauselhagen.

323 USA ISSN 1549-828X
JC571
NORTHWESTERN JOURNAL OF INTERNATIONAL HUMAN RIGHTS. Variant title: Northwestern University Journal of International Human Rights. Text in English. 2003 (Fall). s-a. free (effective 2011). back issues avail.; reprint service avail. from WSH. **Document type:** *Journal, Academic/Scholarly.* **Description:** Provides dynamic forum for the discussion of human rights issues and international human rights law.
Media: Online - full text.
Indexed: A01, A39, C04, C27, C29, CA, D03, D04, E13, P05, R14, S14, S15, S18, T02.
—CIS.
Published by: Northwestern University, School of Law, 375 E Chicago Ave, Chicago, IL 60611. TEL 312-503-3100, FAX 312-503-9230, admissions@law.northwestern.edu. Ed. Heather Scheiwe.

ON GUARD. *see* MILITARY

ONE COUNTRY; the earth is but one country, and mankind its citizens. *see* ENVIRONMENTAL STUDIES

323.44 CAN ISSN 1486-2174
ONE PEOPLE NEWSLETTER. Text in English. 1998. irreg. free. bk.rev.; dance rev.; film rev.; music rev.; play rev. illus. **Document type:** *Newsletter.* **Description:** Reports on civic activities and actions artists of all types are undertaking to bring an end to racism.
Published by: Artists Against Racism, PO Box 54511, Toronto, ON M5M 4N5, Canada. TEL 416-410-5631.

323.4 CAN ISSN 0702-0538
JC599.C2
ONTARIO. HUMAN RIGHTS COMMISSION. ANNUAL REPORT. Text in English, French. 1962. a. free.
Published by: Human Rights Commission, 400 University Ave, Toronto, ON M7A 2R9, Canada. TEL 416-314-4528, FAX 416-314-4533. Circ: 10,000.

OPEN FORUM (LOS ANGELES). *see* LAW

342.0853 GBR ISSN 1745-8293
K3255.A15
➤ **OPEN GOVERNMENT**; a journal on freedom of information. Text in English. 2005. a. free (effective 2011). back issues avail. **Document type:** *Journal, Academic/Scholarly.* **Description:** Covers research and communications related to Freedom of Information (FOI) legislation from the perspective of academics, practioners and FOI users.
Media: Online - full text.
Indexed: A39, C27, C29, CA, D03, D04, E13, IBSS, L04, L13, LISTA, P42, R14, S14, S15, S18, T02.
—CCC.
Published by: (Open Society Institute USA), Liverpool John Moores University, Faculty of Business & Law, John Foster Bldg, 80-98 Mount Pleasant, Liverpool, L3 5UZ, United Kingdom. TEL 44-151-2313976, FAX 44-151-2313908, http://www.ljmu.ac.uk/BLW/index.htm. Ed. Marc-Aurele Racicot.

323.4 CAN ISSN 1920-3381
THE ORATOR. Text in English. 2008. q. free (effective 2010). back issues avail. **Document type:** *Newsletter, Government.* **Description:** Helps the Ministry of Aboriginal Relations connect with diverse group of stakeholders, aboriginal communities and organizations and industry associations.
Related titles: Online - full text ed.: ISSN 1920-339X.
Published by: Alberta Aboriginal Relations, Rm 203, Legislature Bldg, 10800-97 Ave NW, Edmonton, AB T5K 2B6, Canada. TEL 780-422-4144, 800-232-7215, FAX 780-644-8389, deb.broughton@gov.ab.ca.

323.4 USA
OUR STRUGGLE/NUESTRA LUCHA. Text in English, Spanish. 1981. irreg. (4-5/yr.), latest vol.20. looseleaf. USD 15 (effective 2004). bk.rev. 8 p./no. 2 cols./p.; back issues avail. **Document type:** *Newsletter.* **Description:** Conveys common concerns of the Latino rights movement and democratic socialism. Demands economic democracy, equality and self-determination in Latin America and in the barrios of the US.
Published by: Democratic Socialists of America, 2827 Cantania Way, Sacramento, CA 95826. TEL 916-361-9072, campd227@pachell.net, http://www.dsusa.org. Ed. Duane Campbell. Circ: 250.

323.4 GBR ISSN 0260-6402
K3242.A13
OUTSIDER. Text in English. 1978. s-a. Included with subscr. to Minority Rights Group International. Reports. **Document type:** *Newsletter.*
Formerly: Minority Rights Group. Newsletter
Published by: Minority Rights Group International, 379 Brixton Rd, London, SW9 7DE, United Kingdom. TEL 44-20-7978-9498, FAX 44-20-7738-6265, minority.rights@mrgmail.org, http://www.minorityrights.org/.

306.7663 CAN
OUTWORDS. Text in English. 1975. 3/yr. CAD 40 to members (effective 2005). **Document type:** *Newsletter, Consumer.* **Description:** Provides information on lesbian, gay and bisexual rights and projects of the coalition.
Former titles: C L G R O Newsletter; C G R O Newsletter
Published by: Coalition for Lesbian and Gay Rights in Ontario, Sta A, P O Box 822, Toronto, ON M5W 1G3, Canada. TEL 416-405-8253. Circ: 500.

323.4 USA ISSN 1054-1675
JC571
P H R RECORD. Text in English. 1986. q. USD 50 membership (effective 2007). bk.rev. **Document type:** *Newsletter.*
Related titles: Microform ed.
Published by: Physicians for Human Rights, 2 Arrow St, Ste 301, # 301, Cambridge, MA 02138-5102. TEL 617-301-4200, FAX 617-301-4250, phrusa@phrusa.org, http://www.phrusa.org. Eds. Barbara Ayotte, Susannah Sirkin. R&P Barbara Ayotte. Circ: 5,000 (controlled).

323 USA ISSN 1543-575X
HN51
P R ACCESS. (Political Research) Text in English. 2002. s-a. **Document type:** *Newsletter.*
Indexed: APW, P45.
Published by: Political Research Associates, 1310 Broadway, Ste 201, Somerville, MA 02144-1731. TEL 617-666-5300, FAX 617-666-6622, pra@igc.org.

323 ITA ISSN 0394-7440
PACE, DIRITTI DELL'UOMO, DIRITTI DEI POPOLI. Text in Italian. 1986. 3/yr. **Document type:** *Journal, Academic/Scholarly.*
Related titles: Supplement(s): Bollettino Archivio Pace Diritti Umani. ISSN 1590-8011. 1991.
Published by: Universita degli Studi di Padova, Centro Diritti Umani, Rio Novo 3494 A, Dorsoduro, Venice, 30123, Italy. TEL 39-041-2791621, FAX 39-041-2791624.

323 ITA ISSN 1827-4056
PACE DIRITTI UMANI/PEACE HUMAN RIGHTS. Text in Italian. 1986. 3/yr. **Document type:** *Journal, Academic/Scholarly.*
Published by: Universita degli Studi di Padova, Centro Diritti Umani, Rio Novo 3494 A, Dorsoduro, Venice, 30123, Italy. TEL 39-041-2791621, FAX 39-041-2791624.

323 NZL ISSN 1178-1912
PACIFIC HUMAN RIGHTS ISSUES SERIES. Text in English. 2007. irreg.
Related titles: Online - full text ed.: ISSN 1178-1920.
Published by: Human Rights Commission/Te Kahui Tika Tangata, PO Box 6751, Wellesley Street, Auckland, 1141, New Zealand. TEL 800-496-877, FAX 64-9-3773593, infoline@hrc.co.nz. **Co-sponsor:** Pacific Islands Forum.

323 GBR
PAPERS IN THE THEORY AND PRACTICE OF HUMAN RIGHTS. Text in English. 19??. irreg., latest vol.38, 2007. price varies. back issues avail. **Document type:** *Monographic series, Academic/Scholarly.* **Description:** Provides articles concerning issues of human rights, including weapons control, wars, discrimination, etc. Also covers conferences, seminars, and reports of the same issues.
Related titles: Online - full text ed.: free (effective 2009).
—BLDSC (6400.461000).
Published by: University of Essex, Human Rights Centre, Colchester, Essex CO4 3SQ, United Kingdom. TEL 44-1206-872558, FAX 44-1206-873627, hrc@essex.ac.uk.

P

323.4 PRY
PARAGUAY NOTICIAS. Text in Spanish. 1982. m. USD 48. **Description:** Covers politics, human rights, indian matters, and trade unions in Paraguay.
Address: ESPANA, 596, Asuncion, Paraguay. TEL 24-845. Ed. Rafaela Guanes.

323.4 USA ISSN 1065-254X
PEACE TAX FUND NEWSLETTER. Text in English. 1970. q. USD 25 to non-members. back issues avail. **Document type:** *Newsletter.* **Description:** Covers the status of legislation establishing conscientious objection to military taxes.
Published by: National Campaign for a Peace Tax Fund, 2121 Decatur Pl, N W, Washington, DC 20008. TEL 202-483-3751, FAX 202-986-0667. Ed. Tom Kierans. Circ: 5,000.

PELNYM GLOSEM; periodyk feministyczny. *see* WOMEN'S INTERESTS

323.47 070 NLD ISSN 2211-9191
▼ **PERSVRIJHEIDSMONITOR NEDERLAND.** Text in Dutch. 2010. a. EUR 9.95 (effective 2011).
Published by: (Stichting Persvrijheidsfonds), Uitgeverij A M B, Postbus 7, Diemen, 1110 AA, Netherlands. TEL 31-20-6904144, info.amb@xs4all.nl, http://www.amb-press.nl.

323.4 DEU ISSN 0720-5058
JC312
POGROM. Text in German. 1970. bi-m. EUR 25; EUR 4.60 newsstand/cover (effective 2005). adv. bk.rev. illus. **Document type:** *Journal, Academic/Scholarly.*
Indexed: AICP, DIP, FR, HRIR, IBR, IBZ.
—INIST. **CCC.**
Published by: Gesellschaft fuer Bedrohte Voelker, Gemeinnuetziger Verein e.V./Society for Threatened Peoples, Postfach 2024, Goettingen, 37010, Germany. TEL 49-551-4990611, FAX 49-551-58028, info@gfbv.de, http://www.gfbv.de. Eds. Andreas Selmeci, Yvonne Bangert. R&P, Adv. contact Guenther Schierloh TEL 49-551-4990626. Circ: 5,000.

323 USA
POINT BLANK. Text in English. 1971. m. USD 15 domestic membership; USD 25 foreign membership (effective 2000). adv. bk.rev. **Document type:** *Newsletter.* **Description:** Information on federal and state firearms rights and related legislation.
Published by: Citizens Committee for the Right to Keep and Bear Arms, 12500 N E 10th Pl, Bellevue, WA 98005. TEL 425-454-4911, FAX 425-451-3959. Ed. John M Snyder. Pub., R&P, Adv. contact Alan Gottlieb. Circ: 150,000 (paid and controlled).

POLICE MISCONDUCT AND CIVIL RIGHTS LAW REPORT. *see* CRIMINOLOGY AND LAW ENFORCEMENT

POST HOLOCAUST AND ANTI-SEMITISM. *see* HISTORY

323.4 USA
POST-SOVIET JEWRY REPORT. Text in English. 1975. irreg. (2-3/yr.). looseleaf. USD 36 (effective 2001). back issues avail. **Document type:** *Newsletter.* **Description:** Updates readers on situation of Jews in former Soviet Union and on organization's effort to help.
Formerly: Soviet Jewry Report
Published by: Action for Post-Soviet Jewry, Inc., 24 Crescent St, Ste 306, Waltham, MA 02453-4089. TEL 781-893-2331, FAX 781-647-9474, actionpsj@aol.com, http://www.actionpsj.org. Ed., R&P Judy Patkin.

341.23 DEU ISSN 1617-4704
POTSDAMER U N O - KONFERENZEN. Text in German. 2000. irreg., latest vol.7, 2006. price varies. **Document type:** *Monographic series, Academic/Scholarly.*
Published by: Universitaetsverlag Potsdam, Am Neuen Palais 10, Potsdam, 14469, Germany. TEL 49-331-9774458, FAX 49-331-9774625, ubpub@uni-potsdam.de, http://info.ub.uni-potsdam.de/verlag.htm.

PRISONERS AND THE LAW. *see* CRIMINOLOGY AND LAW ENFORCEMENT

PRISONERS' ASSISTANCE DIRECTORY. *see* CRIMINOLOGY AND LAW ENFORCEMENT

PRIVACY AND HUMAN RIGHTS; an international survey of privacy laws and developments. *see* LAW

PRIVACY LAW AND PRACTICE. *see* LAW

PRIVACY LAW SOURCEBOOK; united states law, international law, and recent developments. *see* LAW

323.4 USA ISSN 1063-7222
KF1262.A15
PRIVACY TIMES. Text in English. 1981. fortn. USD 350 (effective 2009). **Document type:** *Newsletter, Trade.* **Description:** Designed for professionals and attorneys who need to follow the legislation, court rulings and industry developments concerning information privacy.
Address: PO Box 302, Cabin John, MD 20818. TEL 301-229-7002, FAX 301-229-8011. Ed., Pub. Evan Hendricks.

PRO-LIFE ACTION NEWS. *see* BIRTH CONTROL

323.4 USA
PRO-LIFE REPORTER. Text in English. 1973. q. USD 10 (effective 1999). bk.rev. bibl.; illus. **Document type:** *Newsletter.*
Published by: United States Coalition for Life, PO Box 315, Export, PA 15632. Pub. Randy Engel. Circ: 2,750.

323.4 USA ISSN 0032-9177
PROBE (SANTA BARBARA). Text in English. 1968. irreg. donations. adv. bk.rev. illus.
Formerly: Argo
Address: PO Box 13390 UCSB, Santa Barbara, CA 93107. Ed. Perry Adams. Circ: 15,000.

323.4 CHE ISSN 1020-1688
PROFESSIONAL TRAINING SERIES. Text in English. 1993. irreg., latest vol.5, 1997.
—BLDSC (6864.222300).
Published by: Office of the United Nations High Commissioner for Human Rights, 8-14 avenue de la Paix, Geneva 10, 1211, Switzerland. TEL 44-22-7346011, FAX 44-22-7339879.

323.4 USA ISSN 1537-2103
HF5549.5.M5
PROFILES IN DIVERSITY JOURNAL. Abbreviated title: P D J. Text in English. 1999. bi-m. USD 49.95 (effective 2010). adv. back issues avail. **Document type:** *Journal, Academic/Scholarly.*
Related titles: Online - full text ed.: USD 6.95 per issue to institutions (effective 2010).
Indexed: B01, B07.
Published by: Rector, Inc, 1991 Crocker Rd, Gemini Towers 1, Cleveland, OH 44145. TEL 440-892-0444, 800-573-2867, FAX 440-892-0737. Adv. contact Damian Johnson. Circ: 43,500.

PUBLIC ACCOMMODATIONS UNDER THE AMERICANS WITH DISABILITIES ACT; compliance and litigation manual. *see* LAW

323 USA ISSN 1541-5473
PUERTO RICO REPORT; from Washington. Text in English. 1989. 11/yr. USD 225 (effective 2002).
Formerly (until 1993): Target Washington (1047-6180)
Published by: E P I N Publishing, PO Box 21001, Washington, DC 20009. TEL 202-726-7923, 800-682-9507, FAX 202-726-7967. Ed., Pub. James McDonough.

323 FRA ISSN 1957-5017
LE QUAI D'EN FACE. Text in French. 2007. q. EUR 16 (effective 2007). **Document type:** *Journal.*
Published by: Droit et Soin Contre les Violences, 90 bis Rue de Fougeres, Rennes, 35700, France. TEL 33-6-21400724, droitetsoin@free.fr.

R C D A NEWSLETTER. (Religion in Communist Dominated Areas) *see* RELIGIONS AND THEOLOGY

323.4 GBR
R S P WORKING PAPER. (Refugee Studies Programme) Text in English. 1998. irreg., latest vol.52, 2009. GBP 5 per issue domestic; GBP 7 per issue foreign (effective 2009). back issues avail. **Document type:** *Monographic series, Academic/Scholarly.*
Related titles: Online - full text ed.: free (effective 2009).
Published by: University of Oxford, Refugee Studies Centre, Oxford Department of International Development, 3 Mansfield Rd, Oxford, OX1 3TB, United Kingdom. TEL 44-1865-281720, FAX 44-1865-281730, paul.ryder@qeh.ox.ac.uk.

323.4 340 USA ISSN 2153-3687
▼ ➤ **RACE AND JUSTICE.** Text in English. forthcoming 2011 (Jan.). q. USD 500, GBP 249 to institutions (effective 2011). **Document type:** *Journal, Academic/Scholarly.*
—IE. **CCC.**
Published by: (American Society of Criminology, Division on People of Color and Crime), Sage Publications, Inc., 2455 Teller Rd, Thousand Oaks, CA 91320. info@sagepub.com, http://www.sagepub.com/. Ed. Shaun L. Gabbidon.

353.4 GBR ISSN 1750-7049
RACE EQUALITY DIGEST. Text in English. 2002. irreg., latest no.19, 2006, May. **Document type:** *Monographic series, Academic/Scholarly.*
Related titles: Online - full text ed.: ISSN 1750-7057. free (PDF).
Published by: Race Equality West Midlands, iBiC, Unit 10 Holt Court, Jennens Rd, Ashton Science Park, Birmingham, B7 4EJ, United Kingdom. TEL 44-121-2503859, 44-121-2503543, FAX 44-121-2503522, rewm@rewm.org.uk.

323 USA
RACE TRAITOR; journal of the new abolitionism. Text in English. 1993. irreg., latest vol.14, 2001, Summer. USD 20 to individuals 4 issues.; USD 40 to institutions 4 issues; USD 6 per issue (effective 2005). adv. bk.rev.; film rev. back issues avail. **Document type:** *Magazine, Trade.* **Description:** Espouses the abolition of the white race as a social category: "Treason to whiteness is loyalty to humanity." Examines social and civil rights issues regarding white supremacy and white privilege.
Published by: New Abolitionists, Inc., PO Box 499, Dorchester, MA 02122. TEL 781-255-5964, http://www.newabolition.org. Eds. Beth Henson, John Garvey, Noel Ignatiev. adv.: page USD 100; trim 8.5 x 5.5. Circ: 2,000.

RAGGED EDGE (ONLINE). *see* HANDICAPPED—Visually Impaired

323.4 NLD ISSN 1384-6442
➤ **THE RAOUL WALLENBERG INSTITUTE HUMAN RIGHTS GUIDES.** Text in English. 1995. irreg., latest vol.2, 1998. price varies. **Document type:** *Monographic series, Academic/Scholarly.* **Description:** Provides important tools for individuals and institutions involved in the field of human rights and humanitarian law.
Indexed: IZBG.
Published by: (Raoul Wallenberg Institute), Brill, PO Box 9000, Leiden, 2300 PA, Netherlands. TEL 31-71-5353500, FAX 31-71-5317532, cs@brill.nl, http://www.brill.nl. **Dist. in N. America by:** Brill, PO Box 605, Herndon, VA 20172-0605. TEL 703-661-1585, 800-337-9255, FAX 703-661-1501, cs@brillusa.com; **Dist. by:** Turpin Distribution Services Ltd., Pegasus Dr, Stratton Business Park, Biggleswade, Bedfordshire SG18 8QB, United Kingdom. TEL 44-1767-604954, FAX 44-1767-601640, custserv@turpin-distribution.com, http://www.turpin-distribution.com/.

323 NLD ISSN 1878-5115
THE RAOUL WALLENBERG INSTITUTE PROFESSIONAL GUIDES TO HUMAN RIGHTS. Text in English. 2006. irreg., latest vol.8, 2008. price varies. **Document type:** *Monographic series, Academic/Scholarly.*
Published by: (Raoul Wallenberg Institute), Martinus Nijhoff (Subsidiary of: Brill), PO Box 9000, Leiden, 2300 PA, Netherlands. TEL 31-71-5353500, FAX 31-71-5317532, marketing@brill.nl. Ed. Leif Holmstroem.

323.4 NOR ISSN 0802-3786
REBELL (OSLO. TRYKT UTG.); roed ungdoms blad. Text in Norwegian. 1969. bi-m. NOK 110; NOK 200 foreign (effective 2000). adv. bk.rev.; music rev.; video rev. **Document type:** *Consumer.* **Description:** Puts forth articles on revolutionary working class politics, anti-racism, and womens' liberation for a youthful audience.
Formerly: Rute 80 (0802-3816)
Related titles: Online - full text ed.: Oslo.Online. ISSN 0807-1918.
Published by: Roed Ungdom, Osterhaus Gate 27, Oslo, 0183, Norway. TEL 47-22-989070, FAX 47-22-989055. Ed., R&P Eivind Volder Rutle. adv.: B&W page NOK 2,000, color page NOK 3,000; trim 210 x 297.

323.4 GTM
REENCUENTRO/REUNION. Text in English, Spanish. irreg. back issues avail. **Description:** Deals with such matters as civil rights, land issues, refugees, displaced persons, as well as topics of overarching importance to the national context, such as international cooperation and the peace process.
Media: Online - full text.
Published by: Coordinacion de Organizaciones No Gubernamentales y Cooperativas/Coordination of Nongovernmental Organizations and Cooperatives, 2 Calle 16-50, Mixco Zona, Guatemala. TEL 502-591-4638, FAX 502-593-4779. Ed. Jim Gronau.

323.4 VEN
REFERENCIAS. Text in Spanish. 1988. m. VEB 60 domestic; USD 25 in the Americas; USD 40 elsewhere (effective 2009). **Document type:** *Bulletin.* **Description:** Covers human rights in Venezuela.
Published by: Programa Venezolano de Educacion - Accion en Derechos Humanos (Provea), Blvd. Panteon Puente de Trinidad, Edif. Centro Plaza Las Mercedes, P.B. Local 6, Caracas, Venezuela. TEL 58-212-860-6669, FAX 58-212-862-5333, publicaciones@derechos.org.ve, http://www.derechos.org.ve/. Circ: 1,000.

323.4 NIC
REFLEXION. Text in Spanish. 1992. bi-m.
Published by: Asociacion Nicaraguense Pro-Derechos Humanos, Bo. Bolonia Emb. Alemana, 2c. Abajo 1c. al Lago, Apartado Postal 669, Managua, Nicaragua. TEL 505-2-668062, FAX 505-2-661352.

REGIO (BUDAPEST, 1990); kisebbseg, politika, tarsadalom. *see* POLITICAL SCIENCE—International Relations

REGIO (BUDAPEST, 1994); minorities, politics, society. *see* POLITICAL SCIENCE—International Relations

RELIGION AND HUMAN RIGHTS; an international journal. *see* RELIGIONS AND THEOLOGY

323 CHN ISSN 1009-6442
RENQUAN. Text in Chinese. 2002. bi-m. USD 37.20 (effective 2009). **Document type:** *Journal, Academic/Scholarly.*
Related titles: Online - full text ed.; English ed.: ISSN 1671-4016.
—East View.
Published by: Zhongguo Renquan Yanjiuhui, Lianhuachi Dong Lu Bei Xiaomachang #6, 26/F, Beijing, 100038, China. TEL 86-10-65592387, FAX 86-10-65592354, http://www.humanrights.cn/.

323 USA
REPORT ON THE HUMAN RIGHTS SITUATION IN PERU. Text in English, Spanish. 1993. irreg., latest 2000. back issues avail. **Document type:** *Report.*
Related titles: Online - full text ed.: free (effective 2011).
Published by: Inter-American Commission on Human Rights, 1889 F St, N W, Ste 820E, Washington, DC 20006. TEL 202-458-6002, FAX 202-458-3992, cidhoea@oas.org.

323 USA
REPORT ON THE SITUATION OF HUMAN RIGHTS IN PARAGUAY. Text in English, Spanish. 1978. irreg., latest 2001. back issues avail. **Document type:** *Report.*
Related titles: Online - full text ed.: free (effective 2011).
Published by: Inter-American Commission on Human Rights, 1889 F St, N W, Ste 820E, Washington, DC 20006. TEL 202-458-6002, FAX 202-458-3992, cidhoea@oas.org.

323 USA
REPORT ON THE SITUATION ON HUMAN RIGHTS IN THE REPUBLIC OF GUATEMALA. Text in Spanish, English. 1981. irreg., latest 2003. back issues avail. **Document type:** *Report.*
Related titles: CD-ROM ed.
Published by: Inter-American Commission on Human Rights, 1889 F St, N W, Ste 820E, Washington, DC 20006. TEL 202-458-6002, FAX 202-458-3992, cidhoea@oas.org. **Subscr. to:** General Secretariat, Organization of American States, Office of Publications, Washington, DC 20006.

323.4 USA ISSN 0897-2613
JC328.3
RESIST NEWSLETTER. Text in English. 1967. m. (10/yr.). USD 20 (effective 2005). bk.rev. back issues avail. **Document type:** *Newsletter, Consumer.* **Description:** Articles on topics of interest to all those concerned with peace and social justice. Covers AIDS, reproductive rights, homelessness, environmental movements, lesbian and gay organizing, Middle East and Third World organizing efforts.
Indexed: P34, T02.
Published by: Resist, Inc., 259 Elm St., Ste. 201, Somerville, MA 02144-2950. TEL 617-623-5110. Ed. Carol Schachet. Circ: 5,000 (paid and controlled).

323.04 SWE ISSN 1654-7063
RESISTANCE STUDIES MAGAZINE. Text in English. 2008. q. free (effective 2011). **Document type:** *Journal, Academic/Scholarly.*
Media: Online - full text.
Indexed: A39, C27, C29, D03, D04, E13, R14, S14, S15, S18.
Published by: Goeteborgs Universitet, Resistance Studies Network, c/o School of Global Studies, University of Gothenburg, PO Box 700, Goeteborg, 40530, Sweden. TEL 45-31-7860000. Ed. Christopher Kullenberg.

▼ **REVISTA DE DERECHOS HUMANOS.** *see* LAW

323 ESP ISSN 1699-1524
REVISTA EUROPEA DE DERECHOS FUNDAMENTALES. Text in Multiple languages. 2003. s-a. **Document type:** *Journal, Academic/Scholarly.*
Published by: Fundacion Profesor Manuel Broseta, Pl Comte de Carlet 3, Valencia, 46003, Spain. TEL 34-96-3922317, FAX 34-96-3920014, gerente@fundacionbroseta.org, http://www.fundacionbroseta.net.

REVISTA MARYKNOLL. *see* RELIGIONS AND THEOLOGY—Roman Catholic

REVUE DE DROIT DU TRAVAIL. *see* BUSINESS AND ECONOMICS—Labor And Industrial Relations

323 FRA ISSN 2107-450X
LA REVUE DU 68. Text in French. 198?. q. **Document type:** *Magazine, Consumer.*
Formerly (until 2007): Terre des Hommes France. Delegations du Haut-Rhin et du Bas-Rhin (0768-8512)
Published by: Terre des Hommes France, 18 Rue de la Republique, Guebwiller, 68190, France. TEL 33-3-89621092.

323.4 BEL ISSN 0777-3579
➤ **REVUE TRIMESTRIELLE DES DROITS DE L'HOMME.** Text in French. 1990. q. EUR 120 (effective 2005). adv. bk.rev. bibl. index. **Document type:** *Journal, Academic/Scholarly.* **Description:** Reviews laws pertaining to human rights and civil liberties.

Former titles (until 1990): Revue des Droits de l'Homme (0035-1989); (until 1969): Droits de l'Homme (0991-885X)
Indexed: A22, FLP, HRIR, IBSS, P06.
—IE, Infotrieve. **CCC.**
Published by: Bruylant, Rue de la Regence 67, Bruxelles, 1000, Belgium. TEL 32-2-512-9845, FAX 32-2-511-7202, http://www.bruylant.be. Circ: 500.

➤ **LA REVUE UNIVERSELLE DES DROITS DE L'HOMME.** *see* LAW—Constitutional Law

342.085 GBR ISSN 2045-4325
▼ **RIGHT OF PUBLICITY.** Variant title: Getting the Deal Through. Right of Publicity. Text in English. 2011. a. USD 400 per issue (effective 2011). **Document type:** *Trade.* **Description:** Provides international analysis in key areas of law and policy for corporate counsel, cross-border legal practitioners and business people.
Published by: Law Business Research Ltd., 87 Lancaster Rd, London, W11 1QQ, United Kingdom. TEL 44-20-79081188, FAX 44-20-72296910, customerservice@globalarbitrationreview.com.

323.4 CAN ISSN 1187-3272
RIGHTS AND LIBERTIES. Text in English. 1978. q. membership. bk.rev. back issues avail. **Document type:** *Newsletter.*
Formerly: M A R L Newsletter
Published by: Manitoba Association for Rights and Liberties, 507-294 Portage Ave, Winnipeg, MB R3C 0B9, Canada. TEL 204-947-0213, FAX 204-946-0403. Ed. Donald A Bailey. Circ: 300.

323 AUS ISSN 1837-5146
▼ **RIGHTS YARN UP.** Text in English. 2009. bi-m. free (effective 2010). back issues avail. **Document type:** *Newsletter, Government.*
Related titles: Online - full text ed.: ISSN 1837-5197. free (effective 2010).
Published by: Victorian Equal Opportunity & Human Rights Commission, Level 3, 380 Lonsdale St, Melbourne, VIC 3000, Australia. TEL 61-1-300891848, FAX 61-1-300891858, information@veohrc.vic.gov.au.

RISE UP. *see* ETHNIC INTERESTS

323.4 GBR ISSN 2045-404X
▼ **RUNNYMEDE BULLETIN.** Text in English. 2010. q. free (effective 2010). back issues avail. **Document type:** *Bulletin, Consumer.* **Description:** Contains reporting events relating to the UK's development as a multi-ethnic society, surveying and evaluating media coverage of race and ethnicity etc.
Media: Online - full text.
Published by: Runnymede Trust, 7 Plough Yard, Shoreditch, London, EC2A 3LP, United Kingdom. TEL 44-20-73779222, FAX 44-20-73776622, info@runnymedetrust.org. Ed. Nina Kelly.

S O C M SENTINEL. *see* ENVIRONMENTAL STUDIES

323.4 USA
S P L C REPORT. (Southern Poverty Law Center) Text in English. 1971. q. bk.rev. illus. back issues avail. **Document type:** *Newsletter, Consumer.* **Description:** Contains reports on the center's programs aimed at combating all forms of racial, religious, and social intolerance; providing legal assistance for the poor; and promoting racial harmony in the classroom.
Former titles (until 1992): Law Report; (until 1987): Klanwatch Law Report
Related titles: Online - full text ed.: free (effective 2009).
Published by: Southern Poverty Law Center, 400 Washington Ave, Montgomery, AL 36104. TEL 334-264-0286, FAX 334-264-3121.

323.4 USA ISSN 0891-608X
S P S C LETTER. Text in English. 1979. q. USD 5; donation. bk.rev. charts.
Indexed: HRIR.
Published by: Saharan People's Support Committee, 217 E Lehr, Ada, OH 45810. TEL 419-634-3666. Ed. Anne Lippert. Circ: 750.

323.4 USA
SAHARAN PEOPLE'S SUPPORT COMMITTEE. MONOGRAPH SERIES. Text in English. irreg. **Document type:** *Monographic series.*
Published by: Saharan People's Support Committee, 217 E Lehr, Ada, OH 45810. TEL 419-634-3666.

323 CHL
SANTIAGO TIMES. Text in English. 1990. d. USD 120 to individuals (effective 2011). adv. **Document type:** *Newspaper, Consumer.* **Description:** Summarizes Chilean news, with special emphasis on trade, environment, human rights, and mining issues.
Formerly: C H I P News (0717-1773)
Media: Online - full text. **Related titles:** Online - full text ed.
Published by: Chile Information Project, Avenida Santa Maria 227 of. 11, Recoleta, Santiago, Chile. TEL 56-2-737-5649, FAX 56-2-735-9044, info@chipsites.com, http://www.chipsites.com. Ed., Pub. Steve Anderson. Adv. contact Jen Foster.

323.044 USA ISSN 1061-7167
HV7240
SBORNIK/DOCUMENTS. Text in English, Russian. 1990. a. USD 5 (effective 2000). adv. bk.rev. back issues avail. **Document type:** *Bulletin.* **Description:** Prevention of unlaw repressions.
Indexed: AICP.
Published by: American Society of Former Soviet Political Prisoners, Inc., PO Box 8637, New York, NY 10116-4655. TEL 718-934-5079. Ed., Adv. contact Mikhail Malinin. R&P Sergey N Nikiforov.

SCHIEDSAMTSZEITUNG. *see* LAW

323 BEL
SCHOOL OF HUMAN RIGHTS RESEARCH SERIES. Text in English. 199?. irreg., latest vol.23, 2007. price varies. **Document type:** *Monographic series, Academic/Scholarly.*
Published by: (School of Human Rights Research NLD), Intersentia N.V., Groenstraat 31, Mortsel, 2640, Belgium. TEL 32-3-6801550, FAX 32-3-6587121, mail@intersentia.be, http://www.intersentia.be.

323.4 USA
SCIENCE AND HUMAN RIGHTS NEWSLETTER. Text in English. 1978. m. bk.rev. back issues avail. **Document type:** *Newsletter, Trade.*
Former titles (until 2007): Report on Science and Human Rights (0895-5999); (until 1987): Clearinghouse Report on Science and Human Rights (0734-4171)
Indexed: HRIR.
Published by: (Science and Human Rights Program), American Association for the Advancement of Science, 1200 New York Ave, NW, Washington, DC 20005. TEL 202-326-6600, FAX 202-289-4950, http://www.aaas.org. Circ: 3,000.

SCREAMING HYENA (ONLINE). *see* HOMOSEXUALITY

342.085 USA ISSN 1933-2734
SCROLL & SWORD; the journal & newsletter of the Civil Affairs Association. Text in English. 1949. bi-m. free to members (effective 2007). bk.rev. illus. **Document type:** *Newsletter, Trade.*
Former titles (until 2002): Civil Affairs Journal & Newsletter (0045-7035); (until 19??): Military Government Journal and Newsletter (0026-3990)
Related titles: Online - full content ed.: free.
Published by: Civil Affairs Association, 10130 Hyla Brook Rd, Columbia, MD 21044-1705. http://www.civilaffairsassoc.org. Circ: 2,600.

323.4 340 USA ISSN 1544-1245
K23
➤ **SEATTLE JOURNAL FOR SOCIAL JUSTICE.** Text in English. 2002. s-a. USD 25 to individuals; USD 40 to institutions (effective 2009). back issues avail.; reprint service avail. from WSH. **Document type:** *Journal, Academic/Scholarly.* **Description:** Publishes writings that reflect theoretical, literary and hands-on approaches toward achieving social justice.
Related titles: Online - full text ed.
—CIS.
Published by: Seattle University, School of Law, 901 12th Ave,, PO Box 222000, Seattle, WA 98122. TEL 206-398-4998, FAX 206-398-4272, lawhelp@seattleu.edu. Ed. Mary Beth Leepe.

323.4 NLD ISSN 1874-7337
JC599.E9 CODEN: HMEOAL
➤ **SECURITY AND HUMAN RIGHTS.** Text in English. 1990. q. EUR 184, USD 256 to institutions; EUR 200, USD 280 combined subscription to institutions (print & online eds.) (effective 2012). adv. bk.rev. back issues avail.; reprint service avail. from PSC,WSH. **Document type:** *Journal, Academic/Scholarly.* **Description:** Covers co-operation and security in Europe and human rights issues in OSCE area.
Formerly (until 2007): Helsinki Monitor (0925-0972)
Related titles: Online - full text ed.: ISSN 1875-0230. EUR 167, USD 233 to institutions (effective 2012) (from IngentaConnect).
Indexed: A01, A03, A08, A22, CA, E01, GEOBASE, IZBG, M10, P34, P42, PAIS, PRA, PSA, S02, S03, SCOPUS, T02.
—BLDSC (8217.148500), IE, Infotrieve, Ingenta. **CCC.**
Published by: (Netherlands Helsinki Committee, International Helsinki Federation for Human Rights AUT), Martinus Nijhoff (Subsidiary of: Brill), PO Box 9000, Leiden, 2300 PA, Netherlands. TEL 31-71-5353500, FAX 31-71-5317532, marketing@brill.nl, http://www.nijhoff.nl. Ed. Arie Bloed. Circ: 450. **Dist. by:** Turpin Distribution Services Ltd., Pegasus Dr, Stratton Business Park, Biggleswade, Bedfordshire SG18 8QB, United Kingdom. TEL 44-1767-604800, FAX 44-1767-601640, custserv@turpin-distribution.com, http://www.turpin-distribution.com/.

323.4 ESP ISSN 1135-7118
JC571
SEMINARIO PERMANENTE SOBRE DERECHOS HUMANOS. ANUARIO. Text in Spanish. 1995. a. **Document type:** *Proceedings, Academic/Scholarly.*
Published by: Universidad de Jean, Seminario Permanente sobre Derechos Humanos, Virgen de la Cabeza, 2-4, Jean, Andalucia 23071, Spain. TEL 34-953-212336, FAX 34-953-212343. Ed. Angustias Moreno Lopez.

323.1197 CAN ISSN 0846-9261
SENATE OF CANADA. STANDING SENATE COMMITTEE ON ABORIGINAL PEOPLES. PROCEEDINGS. Text in English, French. 1990. irreg.
Published by: (Senate of Canada, Standing Committee on Aboriginal Peoples), Supply and Services Canada, Printing and Publishing, 270 Albert St, Ottawa, ON K1A 0S9, Canada.

323 CAN ISSN 1700-1315
KE4381.A22
SENATE OF CANADA. STANDING SENATE COMMITTEE ON HUMAN RIGHTS. PROCEEDINGS/SENAT DU CANADA. DELIBERATIONS DU COMITE SENATORIAL PERMANENT DES DROITS DE LA PERSONNE. Text in English, French. 2001. irreg.
Related titles: Online - full text ed.: ISSN 1700-1323.
Published by: Senate of Canada, Standing Committee on Human Rights, Parliament of Canada, Ottawa, ON K1A 0A9, Canada. TEL 613-992-4793, 866-599-4999, info@parl.gc.ca, http://www.parl.gc.ca.

SETTLEMENTS INFORMATION NETWORK AFRICA NEWSLETTER. *see* HOUSING AND URBAN PLANNING

323.4 ARG
SIN ANESTESIA. Text in Spanish. m.?.
Published by: Asociacion Sin Anestesia Oyentes por la Libre Expresion, Of. 1, Campana, 889, Castelar, Buenos Aires 1712, Argentina. Ed. Luis Alperin.

SOCIAL IDENTITIES; journal for the study of race, nation and culture. *see* ETHNIC INTERESTS

323 FRA ISSN 1638-9840
SOLIDARITE GUATEMALA. Text in French. 1979. bi-m. **Document type:** *Newsletter.* **Description:** Follows Guatemalan news to permit an understanding of the political and social evolution going on there.
Former titles (until 2002): Lettre a l'Adherent (1277-5169); (until 1996): Solidarite Guatemala (0755-0332)
Published by: Collectif Guatemala, 21 ter Rue Voltaire, Paris, 75011, France. collectifguatemala1@libertysurf.fr.

323.4 ZAF
SOUTH AFRICAN HUMAN RIGHTS COMMISSION. MONTHLY REPORT. Short title: H R C Monthly Report. Text in English. 1993. m. free. **Document type:** *Newsletter.*
Formerly (until Feb. 1994): Monthly Repression Report (1021-4119); Which was formed by the merger of (1990-1993): Area Repression Report (1017-6144); (1988-1993): Human Rights Update (1017-6160)
Indexed: PerIslam.
Published by: South African Human Rights Commission, Private Bag 2700, Houghton, 2041, South Africa. TEL 27-11-4848300, sahrcinfo@sahrc.org.za.

323.4 ZAF ISSN 1354-3903
SOUTH AFRICAN HUMAN RIGHTS YEARBOOK. Text in English. 1972. a. ZAR 85 (effective 2000). adv. bk.rev. back issues avail.; reprint service avail. from WSH. **Document type:** *Yearbook, Academic/Scholarly.* **Description:** Covers constitutional and political developments, education, elections, health, environmental rights, labour, womens rights and other issues. Focuses on the shift from the general absence of human rights to the extension of those rights and other long-awaited developments.
Former titles (until 1991): South African Human Rights and Labour Law Yearbook (1354-389X); (until 1989): Natal University Law and Society Review; Natal University Law Review
Related titles: Online - full text ed.
Indexed: ASD, FLP, ISAP.
Published by: Centre for Socio-Legal Studies, University of Natal, Durban, KwaZulu-Natal 4001, South Africa. TEL 27-31-2601291, FAX 27-31-2601540, degrandprei@mtb.und.ac.za, http://www.csls.org.za. Ed. Ronald Louw. Circ: 700.

323.4 ZAF ISSN 1019-2514
DT763
SOUTH AFRICAN INSTITUTE OF RACE RELATIONS. FAST FACTS. Text in English. 1991. m. charts; stat. back issues avail.; reprints avail. **Document type:** *Journal, Academic/Scholarly.*
Related titles: E-mail ed.
Indexed: ASD.
Published by: South African Institute of Race Relations, PO Box 31044, Braamfontein, Johannesburg 2017, South Africa. TEL 27-11-403-3600, FAX 27-11-3392061, sairr@sairr.org.za, http://www.sairr.org.za/sairr. Ed. J S Kane Berman.

SOUTH AFRICAN INSTITUTE OF RACE RELATIONS. SPECIAL REPORTS. *see* ETHNIC INTERESTS

323.4 ZAF ISSN 0258-7203
K23
SOUTH AFRICAN JOURNAL ON HUMAN RIGHTS. Text in English. 1985. 3/yr. ZAR 890 domestic; ZAR 936 foreign (effective 2011). adv. bk.rev. index. back issues avail.; reprint service avail. from WSH. **Document type:** *Journal, Academic/Scholarly.* **Description:** Contains articles focusing on human rights and the South African constitution.
Related titles: Online - full text ed.: ISSN 1996-2126.
Indexed: A22, ASD, FLP, HRIR, I13, IBSS, IIBP, ISAP, P30, SSCI, W07.
—BLDSC (8338.869000), IE, Infotrieve, Ingenta. **CCC.**
Published by: (University of the Witwatersrand, Centre for Applied Legal Studies), Juta & Company Ltd., Juta Law, PO Box 14373, Lansdowne, 7779, South Africa. TEL 27-21-7633500, FAX 27-11-8838169, cserv@juta.co.za, http://www.juta.co.za. **Dist. in N. America by:** Gaunt, Inc., Gaunt Bldg, 3011 Gulf Dr, Holmes Beach, FL 34217. TEL 941-778-5252, 941-778-5211.

P

305.895 PAK
SOUTH ASIAN MINORITY AFFAIRS. Text in English. 1992. irreg. (approx. s-a.). PKR 60, USD 30 (effective 2001). back issues avail. **Document type:** *Monographic series, Academic/Scholarly.* **Description:** Promotes respect for human rights and freedom, particularly those guaranteed to minorities under international law and the treaties of the UN.
Published by: Centre for South Asian Studies, University of the Punjab, Quaid-i-Azam Campus, Lahore, 54590, Pakistan. TEL 92-42-5864014, FAX 92-42-5867206. Ed. Rafique Ahmad. R&P Sarfaraz Hussain Mirza.

323 AUS ISSN 1837-5480
SOUTH AUSTRALIA. OFFICE OF THE PUBLIC ADVOCATE. ANNUAL REPORT. Text in English. 1995. a. free (effective 2010). back issues avail. **Document type:** *Report, Government.* **Description:** Promotes and protects the rights of people with mental incapacity in South Australia.
Related titles: Online - full text ed.: ISSN 1837-5499. 1995. free (effective 2010).
Published by: South Australia Central, Office of the Public Advocate, PO Box 213, Prospect, SA 5082, Australia. TEL 61-8-83428200, 61-1-800-066-969, FAX 61-8-83428250.

323.4 USA ISSN 0193-2446
JC599.U5
SOUTHERN CHANGES. Text in English. 1978. q. USD 30 to individuals; USD 75 to institutions (effective 2010). bk.rev.; film rev. index. back issues avail.; reprints avail. **Document type:** *Journal, Academic/Scholarly.* **Description:** Reports on regional politics, civil, worker's and women's rights, literature and the arts. Provides a forum for opinion about issues affecting the South.
Former titles: New South; South Today; Southern Voices
Related titles: Microform ed.: (from PQC).
Indexed: A22.
—Ingenta.
Published by: Southern Regional Council, Inc., 1201 W Peachtree St, NE, Ste 2000, Atlanta, GA 30309. TEL 404-522-8764, FAX 404-522-8791, info@southerncouncil.org. Adv. contact Deborah Jennings TEL 404-522-8764.

SOUTHERN COMMUNITIES. *see* HOUSING AND URBAN PLANNING

SOUTHERN WOMEN: THE INTERSECTION OF RACE, CLASS AND GENDER. *see* WOMEN'S STUDIES

SPARTACUS INTERNATIONAL GAY GUIDE. *see* HOMOSEXUALITY

SPEAK OUT/KHULUMANI/TAURAI. *see* WOMEN'S STUDIES

323.4 USA ISSN 0191-6270
THE SPOTLIGHT (WASHINGTON). Text in English. 1975. w. USD 59 (effective 2000). adv. bk.rev. **Document type:** *Newspaper.*
Supersedes: Liberty Lowdown; Former titles: National Spotlight; Liberty Letter (0024-2098)
Related titles: Microform ed.: (from PQC).
Indexed: A22, RASB.
Published by: Cordite Fidelity Inc., 300 Independence Ave S E, Washington, DC 20003. TEL 202-544-1794. Ed. Chris Petherick. Adv. contact Sharon DeWitt. Circ: 100,000 (paid).

323 USA ISSN 0148-6985
E185.5
STATE OF BLACK AMERICA. Text in English. 1975. a. USD 20.10 (effective 2010). **Document type:** *Journal, Academic/Scholarly.* **Description:** Contains records of trends and events in black America. Features educators, public officials, and community leaders analyze recent developments in economics, education, housing, legislation, politics, and race relations as they affect and are affected by Afro-Americans.
Indexed: IIBP, P30, P45, SRI, SRRA.
—Ingenta. **CCC.**
Published by: National Urban League, 120 Wall St, New York, NY 10005. TEL 212-558-5300, FAX 212-344-5332, info@nul.org, http://www.nul.org.

STATE OF CALIFORNIA COMMISSION ON THE STATUS OF WOMEN. *see* WOMEN'S STUDIES

323 GBR ISSN 0961-7280
JC599.E9
STATEWATCH; monitoring the state and civil liberties in Europe. Text in English. 1991. bi-m. GBP 15 to individuals; GBP 30 to institutions (effective 2009). **Document type:** *Bulletin, Trade.* **Description:** Covers the civil liberties issues in the United Kingdom and across Europe.
Related titles: Online - full text ed.: ISSN 1756-851X. GBP 10 (effective 2009).
—BLDSC (8442.600000). **CCC.**
Address: PO Box 1516, London, N16 0EW, United Kingdom. TEL 44-20-88021882, FAX 44-20-88801727, office@statewatch.org, http://www.statewatch.org/.

341.242 GBR ISSN 1745-0276
STATEWATCH EUROPEAN MONITOR (ONLINE). Text in English. 1998. s-a. GBP 20 to individuals; GBP 50 to institutions (effective 2008). **Document type:** *Bulletin, Trade.*
Formerly (until Feb. 2003): Statewatch European Monitor (Print) (1463-5232)
Media: Online - full text.
—**CCC.**
Published by: Statewatch, PO Box 1516, London, N16 0EW, United Kingdom. TEL 44-20-88021882, FAX 44-20-88801727, office@statewatch.org.

323.4 NLD ISSN 2210-5174
▼ ➤ **STIGMA RESEARCH AND ACTION.** Text in English. 2011. (in 1 vol., 2 nos./vol.). free (effective 2011). back issues avail. **Document type:** *Journal, Academic/Scholarly.*
Media: Online - full text.
Published by: Vrije Universiteit Amsterdam. University Library e-Publishing, De Boelelaan 1103, Amsterdam, 1081 HV, Netherlands. http://www.ubvu.vu.nl/en/e-publishing. Ed. Heather Stuart.

➤ **STOPPA RASISMEN.** *see* ETHNIC INTERESTS

323 NZL ISSN 1177-2077
STOUT RESEARCH CENTRE FOR NEW ZEALAND STUDIES. TREATY OF WAITANGI RESEARCH UNIT. OCCASIONAL PAPERS SERIES. Text in English. 2000. irreg., latest vol.8, 2002. NZD 25 per issue (effective 2008). **Document type:** *Monographic series, Academic/Scholarly.*
Formerly (until 2002): Stout Research Centre. Treaty of Waitangi Research Unit. Occasional Papers Series (1175-4591)
Published by: Stout Research Centre for New Zealand Studies, Treaty of Waitangi Research Unit, PO Box 600, Wellington, 6015, New Zealand. stout-towru@vuw.ac.nz.

323.4 DEU ISSN 0175-4467
HQ1627
STREIT; feministische Rechtszeitschrift. Text in German. 1983. q. EUR 39; EUR 8.20 newsstand/cover (effective 2010). bk.rev. index. back issues avail. **Document type:** *Journal, Trade.* **Description:** Discusses legal issues from a feminist perspective.
Indexed: DIP, IBR, IBZ.
Published by: (Verein Frauen Streiten fuer Ihr Recht), Fachhochschulverlag - Der Verlag fuer Angewandte Wissenschaften e.K., Kleiststr 10, Frankfurt, 60318, Germany. TEL 49-69-15332820, FAX 49-69-15332840, kontakt@fhverlag.de, http://www.fhverlag.de. Circ: 1,600.

323 DEU ISSN 1435-9154
K3236.5
STUDIEN ZU GRUND- UND MENSCHENRECHTEN. Text in German. 1998. irreg., latest vol.14, 2007. price varies. **Document type:** *Monographic series, Academic/Scholarly.*
Published by: Universitaetsverlag Potsdam, Am Neuen Palais 10, Potsdam, 14469, Germany. TEL 49-331-9774458, FAX 49-331-9774625, ubpub@uni-potsdam.de, http://info.ub.uni-potsdam.de/verlag.htm.

▼ **STUDIES IN INTERCULTURAL HUMAN RIGHTS.** *see* LAW—Constitutional Law

323 BRA ISSN 1806-6445
JC571
➤ **SUR - REVISTA INTERNACIONAL DE DIREITOS HUMANOS/SUR - INTERNATIONAL JOURNAL ON HUMAN RIGHTS.** Text in Portuguese, English, Spanish. 2004. s-a. free (effective 2011). bk.rev. bibl.; abstr. back issues avail. **Document type:** *Journal, Academic/Scholarly.* **Description:** Aims at studying and defending human rights and social justice.
Media: Online - full text.
Indexed: CA, IBSS, P42, PSA, S02, S03, SociolAb, T02.
—BLDSC (8547.680300), IE.
Published by: Sur - Rede Universitaria de Direitos Humanos, Rua Pamplona 1197, Casa 4, Sao Paulo, 01405-030, Brazil. TEL 55-11-38847440, FAX 55-11-38841122. Ed. Pedro Paulo Poppovic. R&P Daniela Ikawa. Circ: 3,200 (controlled).

323.4 PSE ISSN 1728-1679
HV640.5.P36
SURVEY OF PALESTINIAN REFUGEES AND INTERNALLY DISPLACED PERSONS. Text in English, Arabic. 2003. irreg., latest 2007.
Published by: Badil Resource Center for Palestinian Residency & Refugee Rights, PO Box 728, Bethlehem, Palestine. TEL 972-2-2777086, FAX 972-2-2747346, info@badil.org, http://www.badil.org/index.html.

SURVIVAL (YEAR). *see* ETHNIC INTERESTS

T G H INFO. (Triangle Generation Humanitaire) *see* SOCIAL SERVICES AND WELFARE

630.968 323.4 ZAF
T R A C ANNUAL REPORT. (Transvaal Rural Action Committee) Text in English. 1993. a. ZAR 15. **Document type:** *Corporate.* **Description:** Reviews the organization's work on behalf of civil rights in agriculture and mining, as well as environmental sustainability and women's issues.
Published by: T R A C, PO Box 62535, Marshalltown, Johannesburg 2107, South Africa. TEL 27-11-833-1060, FAX 27-11-834-8385. Ed., R&P Stuart Marr. Circ: 500.

323.4 USA ISSN 1027-3999
JC599.T28
TAIWAN COMMUNIQUE. Text in English. 1980. bi-m. USD 25 (effective 2000). **Document type:** *Newsletter.* **Description:** Supports the establishment of a free and democratic political system in Taiwan and the recognition of Taiwan as an independent nation.
Indexed: HRIR.
Published by: International Committee for Human Rights in Taiwan, PO Box 15182, Chevy Chase, MD 20825. TEL 202-274-2726, FAX 301-468-9126. Ed. Gerrit van der Wees. Circ: 3,300.

323.4 GBR ISSN 1356-1154
TAPOL. Text in English. 1973. bi-m. GBP 18 to individuals; GBP 25 to institutions; GBP 9 to students. bk.rev. **Document type:** *Bulletin.*
Related titles: Microform ed.
Indexed: BAS, HRIR, RASB.
Published by: Indonesia Human Rights Campaign, 111 Northwood Rd, Thornton Heath, Surrey CR7 8HW, United Kingdom. TEL 44-181-771-2904, FAX 44-181-653-0322. Eds. C Budiardjo, S L Liem. Circ: 1,500.

TEACHING FOR SOCIAL JUSTICE SERIES. *see* EDUCATION

TEACHING TOLERANCE. *see* EDUCATION—Teaching Methods And Curriculum

TEXAS JOURNAL ON CIVIL LIBERTIES AND CIVIL RIGHTS. *see* LAW—Civil Law

THIS WEEK IN TEXAS. *see* HOMOSEXUALITY

320.56 USA
THULE. Text in English. irreg. **Description:** Contains white supremacist literature written by and for prisoners.
Address: PO Box 4542, Portland, OR 97208.

323.44 SWE ISSN 2000-5733
TIDSKRIFT FOER FOLKETS RAETTIGHETER (ONLINE). Text in Swedish; Summaries in English. 1977-1988; resumed 1993. q. bk.rev. **Document type:** *Magazine, Consumer.* **Description:** Focuses on issues of law, particularly freedom of the press and international law for the layman.
Former titles (until 2009): Tidskrift foer Folkets Raettigheter (Print) (0348-5803); (until 1977): FiB - Juristbladet
Media: Online - full text.
Published by: F i B-Juristerna, c/o Lars-Gunnar Liljestrand, Osbyringen 2, Spaangaa, 16373, Sweden. TEL 46-8-246004.

323.44 USA ISSN 1063-4134
D839
TOWARD FREEDOM; a progressive perspective on world events. Text in English. 1952. 8/yr. USD 25 domestic; USD 32 foreign (effective 2005). adv. bk.rev. maps. index. back issues avail. **Document type:** *Newsletter, Consumer.* **Description:** Offers international news, analysis and advocacy with a progressive perspective on world events, politics and culture.
Related titles: E-mail ed.: USD 12 (effective 2001); Online - full text ed.
Indexed: APW, AltPI.
Published by: Toward Freedom, Inc., PO Box 468, Burlington, VT 05402. TEL 802-657-3733, office@towardfreedom.com. Ed., R&P Greg Guma. Pub. Robin Lloyd. Circ: 4,500.

TRANSITIONS (MINNEAPOLIS). *see* MEN'S STUDIES

323.352 CHE ISSN 0259-370X
TRIBUNE INTERNATIONALE DES DROITS DE L'ENFANT. Text in French. 1984. q. **Document type:** *Magazine, Consumer.*
Related titles: ◆ English ed.: International Children's Rights Monitor. ISSN 0259-3696.
Published by: Defence for Children International, 1 Rue de Varembe, Case Postale 88, Geneva 20, 1211, Switzerland. TEL 41-22-7340558, FAX 41-22-7401145, administrator@dci-is.org, http://www.dci-is.org.

323.4 USA
THE TUNNEL. Text in Chinese. 1997. irreg.?. **Description:** Includes articles about the Chinese government, civil rights, and Tiananmen Square protest.
Media: Online - full text.
Published by: Tunnel voice@earthling.net, tunnel@earthling.net.

323.4 TUR ISSN 1300-1809
JC599.T87
➤ **TURKISH YEARBOOK OF HUMAN RIGHTS.** Text in English, French, German. 1979. a. USD 15 (effective 2001). back issues avail. **Document type:** *Journal, Academic/Scholarly.*
Indexed: ILD.
Published by: Institute of Public Administration for Turkey and Middle East, 1 Nolu Cadde No. 8, Yucetepe, Ankara, 06100, Turkey. TEL 90-312-2296170, FAX 91-312-2313881, todaie@todaie.gov.tr. Ed. Gencay Saylan. Circ: 1,500.

323 GBR ISSN 1469-168X
U K HUMAN RIGHTS REPORTS. (United Kingdom) Text in English. 2000. bi-m. GBP 240 (effective 2010). adv. back issues avail. **Document type:** *Report, Trade.* **Description:** Contains authoritative reporting on all important UK cases with significant human rights elements. All areas of law are covered, providing a one-source reference, saving you valuable research time and alerting you to all the important cases including those outside your specialist area.
Related titles: Online - full text ed.
Published by: Jordan Publishing Ltd., 21 St Thomas St, Bristol, BS1 6JS, United Kingdom. TEL 44-117-9230600, FAX 44-117-9250486, customerservice@jordanpublishing.co.uk. Eds. Hugh Southey, Mr. Justice Fulford. Adv. contact Sue Reynolds TEL 44-117-9181230.

323 USA ISSN 0082-9641
KF4755
U.S. COMMISSION ON CIVIL RIGHTS. CLEARINGHOUSE PUBLICATIONS. Text in English. 1965. irreg., latest 2003. free (effective 2011). back issues avail. **Document type:** *Monographic series, Government.* **Description:** Explores and discusses matters that may come under the jurisdiction of the Civil Rights Act of 1964.
—BLDSC (3278.538500).
Published by: U.S. Commission on Civil Rights, 624 Ninth St, NW, Rm 600, Washington, DC 20425. TEL 202-376-8128, publications@usccr.gov.

323.4 USA
U.S. COMMISSION ON CIVIL RIGHTS. CONSULTATIONS AND CONFERENCES. Text in English. 19??. irreg., latest 2000. free (effective 2011). back issues avail. **Document type:** *Monographic series, Government.* **Description:** Presents the results from commission conferences and roundtable discussions.
Published by: U.S. Commission on Civil Rights, 624 Ninth St, NW, Rm 600, Washington, DC 20425. TEL 202-376-8128, publications@usccr.gov.

323.4 USA
U.S. COMMISSION ON CIVIL RIGHTS. HEARINGS. Text in English. 197?. irreg., latest 1998. free (effective 2011). back issues avail. **Document type:** *Monographic series, Government.* **Description:** Presents results of hearings held before the commission.
Published by: U.S. Commission on Civil Rights, 624 Ninth St, NW, Rm 600, Washington, DC 20425. TEL 202-376-8128, publications@usccr.gov.

323.4 USA
U.S. COMMISSION ON CIVIL RIGHTS. STAFF REPORTS. Text in English. 197?. irreg., latest 2002. free (effective 2011). back issues avail. **Document type:** *Monographic series, Government.* **Description:** Discusses important civil rights issues in the U.S.
Published by: U.S. Commission on Civil Rights, 624 Ninth St, NW, Rm 600, Washington, DC 20425. TEL 202-376-8128, publications@usccr.gov.

323.4 USA
U.S. COMMISSION ON CIVIL RIGHTS. STATE ADVISORY COMMITTEE REPORTS. ALABAMA. Text in English. 19??. irreg., latest 1996. free (effective 2011). back issues avail. **Document type:** *Monographic series, Government.*
Published by: U.S. Commission on Civil Rights, 624 Ninth St, NW, Rm 600, Washington, DC 20425. TEL 202-376-8128, publications@usccr.gov.

323.4 USA
U.S. COMMISSION ON CIVIL RIGHTS. STATE ADVISORY COMMITTEE REPORTS. ALASKA. Text in English. 19??. irreg., latest 2002. free (effective 2011). back issues avail. **Document type:** *Monographic series, Government.*
Published by: U.S. Commission on Civil Rights, 624 Ninth St, NW, Rm 600, Washington, DC 20425. TEL 202-376-8128, publications@usccr.gov.

323.4 USA
U.S. COMMISSION ON CIVIL RIGHTS. STATE ADVISORY COMMITTEE REPORTS. ARIZONA. Text in English. 19??. irreg., latest 2002. free (effective 2011). back issues avail. **Document type:** *Monographic series, Government.*
Published by: U.S. Commission on Civil Rights, 624 Ninth St, NW, Rm 600, Washington, DC 20425. TEL 202-376-8128, publications@usccr.gov.

323.4 USA
U.S. COMMISSION ON CIVIL RIGHTS. STATE ADVISORY COMMITTEE REPORTS. ARKANSAS. Text in English. 19??. irreg., latest 2001. free (effective 2011). back issues avail. **Document type:** *Monographic series, Government.*
Published by: U.S. Commission on Civil Rights, 624 Ninth St, NW, Rm 600, Washington, DC 20425. TEL 202-376-8128, publications@usccr.gov.

323.4 USA
U.S. COMMISSION ON CIVIL RIGHTS. STATE ADVISORY COMMITTEE REPORTS. CALIFORNIA. Text in English. 19??. irreg., latest 2000. free (effective 2011). back issues avail. **Document type:** *Monographic series, Government.*
Published by: U.S. Commission on Civil Rights, 624 Ninth St, NW, Rm 600, Washington, DC 20425. TEL 202-376-8128, publications@usccr.gov.

323.4 USA
U.S. COMMISSION ON CIVIL RIGHTS. STATE ADVISORY COMMITTEE REPORTS. COLORADO. Text in English. 19??. irreg., latest 2003. free (effective 2011). back issues avail. **Document type:** *Monographic series, Government.*
Published by: U.S. Commission on Civil Rights, 624 Ninth St, NW, Rm 600, Washington, DC 20425. TEL 202-376-8128, publications@usccr.gov.

323.4 USA
U.S. COMMISSION ON CIVIL RIGHTS. STATE ADVISORY COMMITTEE REPORTS. CONNECTICUT. Text in English. 19??. irreg., latest 1994. free (effective 2011). back issues avail. **Document type:** *Monographic series, Government.*
Published by: U.S. Commission on Civil Rights, 624 Ninth St, NW, Rm 600, Washington, DC 20425. TEL 202-376-8128, publications@usccr.gov.

323.4 USA
U.S. COMMISSION ON CIVIL RIGHTS. STATE ADVISORY COMMITTEE REPORTS. DELAWARE. Text in English. 19??. irreg., latest 2001. free (effective 2011). back issues avail. **Document type:** *Monographic series, Government.*
Published by: U.S. Commission on Civil Rights, 624 Ninth St, NW, Rm 600, Washington, DC 20425. TEL 202-376-8128, publications@usccr.gov.

323.4 USA
U.S. COMMISSION ON CIVIL RIGHTS. STATE ADVISORY COMMITTEE REPORTS. DISTRICT OF COLUMBIA. Text in English. 19??. irreg., latest 1998. free (effective 2011). back issues avail. **Document type:** *Monographic series, Government.*
Published by: U.S. Commission on Civil Rights, 624 Ninth St, NW, Rm 600, Washington, DC 20425. TEL 202-376-8128, publications@usccr.gov.

323.4 USA
U.S. COMMISSION ON CIVIL RIGHTS. STATE ADVISORY COMMITTEE REPORTS. FLORIDA. Text in English. 19??. irreg., latest 1996. free (effective 2011). back issues avail. **Document type:** *Monographic series, Government.*
Published by: U.S. Commission on Civil Rights, 624 Ninth St, NW, Rm 600, Washington, DC 20425. TEL 202-376-8128, publications@usccr.gov.

323.4 USA
U.S. COMMISSION ON CIVIL RIGHTS. STATE ADVISORY COMMITTEE REPORTS. GEORGIA. Text in English. 19??. irreg., latest 1989. free (effective 2011). back issues avail. **Document type:** *Monographic series, Government.*
Published by: U.S. Commission on Civil Rights, 624 Ninth St, NW, Rm 600, Washington, DC 20425. TEL 202-376-8128, publications@usccr.gov.

323.4 USA
U.S. COMMISSION ON CIVIL RIGHTS. STATE ADVISORY COMMITTEE REPORTS. HAWAII. Text in English. 19??. irreg., latest 2001. free (effective 2011). back issues avail. **Document type:** *Monographic series, Government.*
Published by: U.S. Commission on Civil Rights, 624 Ninth St, NW, Rm 600, Washington, DC 20425. TEL 202-376-8128, publications@usccr.gov.

323.4 USA
U.S. COMMISSION ON CIVIL RIGHTS. STATE ADVISORY COMMITTEE REPORTS. IDAHO. Text in English. 19??. irreg., latest 1992. free (effective 2011). back issues avail. **Document type:** *Monographic series, Government.*
Published by: U.S. Commission on Civil Rights, 624 Ninth St, NW, Rm 600, Washington, DC 20425. TEL 202-376-8128, publications@usccr.gov.

323.4 USA
U.S. COMMISSION ON CIVIL RIGHTS. STATE ADVISORY COMMITTEE REPORTS. ILLINOIS. Text in English. 19??. irreg., latest 2003. free (effective 2011). back issues avail. **Document type:** *Monographic series, Government.*
Published by: U.S. Commission on Civil Rights, 624 Ninth St, NW, Rm 600, Washington, DC 20425. TEL 202-376-8128, publications@usccr.gov.

323.4 USA
U.S. COMMISSION ON CIVIL RIGHTS. STATE ADVISORY COMMITTEE REPORTS. INDIANA. Text in English. 19??. irreg., latest 2002. free (effective 2011). back issues avail. **Document type:** *Monographic series, Government.*
Published by: U.S. Commission on Civil Rights, 624 Ninth St, NW, Rm 600, Washington, DC 20425. TEL 202-376-8128, publications@usccr.gov.

323.4 USA
U.S. COMMISSION ON CIVIL RIGHTS. STATE ADVISORY COMMITTEE REPORTS. IOWA. Text in English. 19??. irreg., latest 2002. free (effective 2011). back issues avail. **Document type:** *Monographic series, Government.*
Published by: U.S. Commission on Civil Rights, 624 Ninth St, NW, Rm 600, Washington, DC 20425. TEL 202-376-8128, publications@usccr.gov.

323.4 USA
U.S. COMMISSION ON CIVIL RIGHTS. STATE ADVISORY COMMITTEE REPORTS. JOINT REPORTS. Text in English. 198?. irreg., latest 2003. free (effective 2011). back issues avail. **Document type:** *Monographic series, Government.*
Published by: U.S. Commission on Civil Rights, 624 Ninth St, NW, Rm 600, Washington, DC 20425. TEL 202-376-8128, publications@usccr.gov.

323.4 USA
U.S. COMMISSION ON CIVIL RIGHTS. STATE ADVISORY COMMITTEE REPORTS. KANSAS. Text in English. 19??. irreg., latest 1998. free (effective 2011). back issues avail. **Document type:** *Monographic series, Government.*
Published by: U.S. Commission on Civil Rights, 624 Ninth St, NW, Rm 600, Washington, DC 20425. TEL 202-376-8128, publications@usccr.gov.

323.4 USA
U.S. COMMISSION ON CIVIL RIGHTS. STATE ADVISORY COMMITTEE REPORTS. KENTUCKY. Text in English. 19??. irreg., latest 1997. free (effective 2011). back issues avail. **Document type:** *Monographic series, Government.*
Published by: U.S. Commission on Civil Rights, 624 Ninth St, NW, Rm 600, Washington, DC 20425. TEL 202-376-8128, publications@usccr.gov.

323.4 USA
U.S. COMMISSION ON CIVIL RIGHTS. STATE ADVISORY COMMITTEE REPORTS. LOUISIANA. Text in English. 19??. irreg., latest 1996. free (effective 2011). back issues avail. **Document type:** *Monographic series, Government.*
Published by: U.S. Commission on Civil Rights, 624 Ninth St, NW, Rm 600, Washington, DC 20425. TEL 202-376-8128, publications@usccr.gov.

323.4 USA
U.S. COMMISSION ON CIVIL RIGHTS. STATE ADVISORY COMMITTEE REPORTS. MAINE. Text in English. 19??. irreg., latest 2001. free (effective 2011). back issues avail. **Document type:** *Monographic series, Government.*
Published by: U.S. Commission on Civil Rights, 624 Ninth St, NW, Rm 600, Washington, DC 20425. TEL 202-376-8128, publications@usccr.gov.

323.4 USA
U.S. COMMISSION ON CIVIL RIGHTS. STATE ADVISORY COMMITTEE REPORTS. MASSACHUSETTS. Text in English. 19??. irreg., latest 1992. free (effective 2011). back issues avail. **Document type:** *Monographic series, Government.*
Published by: U.S. Commission on Civil Rights, 624 Ninth St, NW, Rm 600, Washington, DC 20425. TEL 202-376-8128, publications@usccr.gov.

323.4 USA
U.S. COMMISSION ON CIVIL RIGHTS. STATE ADVISORY COMMITTEE REPORTS. MICHIGAN. Text in English. 19??. irreg., latest 2001. free (effective 2011). back issues avail. **Document type:** *Monographic series, Government.*
Published by: U.S. Commission on Civil Rights, 624 Ninth St, NW, Rm 600, Washington, DC 20425. TEL 202-376-8128, publications@usccr.gov.

323.4 USA
U.S. COMMISSION ON CIVIL RIGHTS. STATE ADVISORY COMMITTEE REPORTS. MINNESOTA. Text in English. 19??. irreg., latest 2003. free (effective 2011). back issues avail. **Document type:** *Monographic series, Government.*
Published by: U.S. Commission on Civil Rights, 624 Ninth St, NW, Rm 600, Washington, DC 20425. TEL 202-376-8128, publications@usccr.gov.

323.4 USA
U.S. COMMISSION ON CIVIL RIGHTS. STATE ADVISORY COMMITTEE REPORTS. MISSOURI. Text in English. 19??. irreg., latest 1999. free (effective 2011). back issues avail. **Document type:** *Monographic series, Government.*
Published by: U.S. Commission on Civil Rights, 624 Ninth St, NW, Rm 600, Washington, DC 20425. TEL 202-376-8128, publications@usccr.gov.

323.4 USA
U.S. COMMISSION ON CIVIL RIGHTS. STATE ADVISORY COMMITTEE REPORTS. MONTANA. Text in English. 19??. irreg., latest 2001. free (effective 2011). back issues avail. **Document type:** *Monographic series, Government.*
Published by: U.S. Commission on Civil Rights, 624 Ninth St, NW, Rm 600, Washington, DC 20425. TEL 202-376-8128, publications@usccr.gov.

323.4 USA
U.S. COMMISSION ON CIVIL RIGHTS. STATE ADVISORY COMMITTEE REPORTS. NEBRASKA. Text in English. 19??. irreg., latest 1994. free (effective 2011). back issues avail. **Document type:** *Monographic series, Government.*
Published by: U.S. Commission on Civil Rights, 624 Ninth St, NW, Rm 600, Washington, DC 20425. TEL 202-376-8128, publications@usccr.gov.

323.4 USA
U.S. COMMISSION ON CIVIL RIGHTS. STATE ADVISORY COMMITTEE REPORTS. NEVADA. Text in English. 19??. irreg., latest 1999. free (effective 2011). back issues avail. **Document type:** *Monographic series, Government.*
Published by: U.S. Commission on Civil Rights, 624 Ninth St, NW, Rm 600, Washington, DC 20425. TEL 202-376-8128, publications@usccr.gov.

323.4 USA
U.S. COMMISSION ON CIVIL RIGHTS. STATE ADVISORY COMMITTEE REPORTS. NEW HAMPSHIRE. Text in English. 19??. irreg., latest 1982. free (effective 2011). back issues avail. **Document type:** *Monographic series, Government.*
Published by: U.S. Commission on Civil Rights, 624 Ninth St, NW, Rm 600, Washington, DC 20425. TEL 202-376-8128, publications@usccr.gov.

323.4 USA
U.S. COMMISSION ON CIVIL RIGHTS. STATE ADVISORY COMMITTEE REPORTS. NEW JERSEY. Text in English. 19??. irreg., latest 1990. free (effective 2011). back issues avail. **Document type:** *Monographic series, Government.*
Published by: U.S. Commission on Civil Rights, 624 Ninth St, NW, Rm 600, Washington, DC 20425. TEL 202-376-8128, publications@usccr.gov.

323.4 USA
U.S. COMMISSION ON CIVIL RIGHTS. STATE ADVISORY COMMITTEE REPORTS. NEW MEXICO. Text in English. 19??. irreg., latest 1989. free (effective 2011). **Document type:** *Monographic series, Government.*
Published by: U.S. Commission on Civil Rights, 624 Ninth St, NW, Rm 600, Washington, DC 20425. TEL 202-376-8128, publications@usccr.gov.

323.4 USA
U.S. COMMISSION ON CIVIL RIGHTS. STATE ADVISORY COMMITTEE REPORTS. NEW YORK. Text in English. 19??. irreg., latest 1999. free. back issues avail. **Document type:** *Monographic series, Government.*
Published by: U.S. Commission on Civil Rights, 624 Ninth St, NW, Rm 600, Washington, DC 20425. TEL 202-376-8128, publications@usccr.gov.

323.4 USA
U.S. COMMISSION ON CIVIL RIGHTS. STATE ADVISORY COMMITTEE REPORTS. NORTH CAROLINA. Text in English. 19??. irreg., latest 1996. free (effective 2011). back issues avail. **Document type:** *Monographic series, Government.*
Published by: U.S. Commission on Civil Rights, 624 Ninth St, NW, Rm 600, Washington, DC 20425. TEL 202-376-8128, publications@usccr.gov.

323.4 USA
U.S. COMMISSION ON CIVIL RIGHTS. STATE ADVISORY COMMITTEE REPORTS. NORTH DAKOTA. Text in English. 19??. irreg., latest 1999. free (effective 2011). back issues avail. **Document type:** *Monographic series, Government.*
Published by: U.S. Commission on Civil Rights, 624 Ninth St, NW, Rm 600, Washington, DC 20425. TEL 202-376-8128, publications@usccr.gov.

323.4 USA
U.S. COMMISSION ON CIVIL RIGHTS. STATE ADVISORY COMMITTEE REPORTS. OHIO. Text in English. 19??. irreg., latest 2002. free (effective 2011). back issues avail. **Document type:** *Monographic series, Government.*
Published by: U.S. Commission on Civil Rights, 624 Ninth St, NW, Rm 600, Washington, DC 20425. TEL 202-376-8128, publications@usccr.gov.

323.4 USA
U.S. COMMISSION ON CIVIL RIGHTS. STATE ADVISORY COMMITTEE REPORTS. OKLAHOMA. Text in English. 19??. irreg., latest 2000. free (effective 2011). back issues avail. **Document type:** *Monographic series, Government.*
Published by: U.S. Commission on Civil Rights, 624 Ninth St, NW, Rm 600, Washington, DC 20425. TEL 202-376-8128, publications@usccr.gov.

323.4 USA
U.S. COMMISSION ON CIVIL RIGHTS. STATE ADVISORY COMMITTEE REPORTS. PENNSYLVANIA. Text in English. 19??. irreg., latest 2002. free (effective 2011). back issues avail. **Document type:** *Monographic series, Government.*
Published by: U.S. Commission on Civil Rights, 624 Ninth St, NW, Rm 600, Washington, DC 20425. TEL 202-376-8128, publications@usccr.gov.

323.4 USA
U.S. COMMISSION ON CIVIL RIGHTS. STATE ADVISORY COMMITTEE REPORTS. RHODE ISLAND. Text in English. 19??. irreg., latest 2000. free (effective 2011). back issues avail. **Document type:** *Monographic series, Government.*
Published by: U.S. Commission on Civil Rights, 624 Ninth St, NW, Rm 600, Washington, DC 20425. TEL 202-376-8128, publications@usccr.gov.

323.4 USA
U.S. COMMISSION ON CIVIL RIGHTS. STATE ADVISORY COMMITTEE REPORTS. SOUTH CAROLINA. Text in English. 19??. irreg., latest 1996. free (effective 2011). back issues avail. **Document type:** *Monographic series, Government.*
Published by: U.S. Commission on Civil Rights, 624 Ninth St, NW, Rm 600, Washington, DC 20425. TEL 202-376-8128, publications@usccr.gov.

323.4 USA
U.S. COMMISSION ON CIVIL RIGHTS. STATE ADVISORY COMMITTEE REPORTS. SOUTH DAKOTA. Text in English. 19??. irreg., latest 2000. free (effective 2011). back issues avail. **Document type:** *Monographic series, Government.*
Published by: U.S. Commission on Civil Rights, 624 Ninth St, NW, Rm 600, Washington, DC 20425. TEL 202-376-8128, publications@usccr.gov.

323.4 USA
U.S. COMMISSION ON CIVIL RIGHTS. STATE ADVISORY COMMITTEE REPORTS. TENNESSEE. Text in English. 19??. irreg., latest 1996. free (effective 2011). back issues avail. **Document type:** *Monographic series, Government.*
Published by: U.S. Commission on Civil Rights, 624 Ninth St, NW, Rm 600, Washington, DC 20425. TEL 202-376-8128, publications@usccr.gov.

323.4 USA
U.S. COMMISSION ON CIVIL RIGHTS. STATE ADVISORY COMMITTEE REPORTS. TEXAS. Text in English. 19??. irreg., latest 1990. free (effective 2011). back issues avail. **Document type:** *Monographic series, Government.*
Published by: U.S. Commission on Civil Rights, 624 Ninth St, NW, Rm 600, Washington, DC 20425. TEL 202-376-8128, publications@usccr.gov.

323.4 USA
U.S. COMMISSION ON CIVIL RIGHTS. STATE ADVISORY COMMITTEE REPORTS. UTAH. Text in English. 19??. irreg., latest 1990. free (effective 2011). **Document type:** *Monographic series, Government.*
Published by: U.S. Commission on Civil Rights, 624 Ninth St, NW, Rm 600, Washington, DC 20425. TEL 202-376-8128, publications@usccr.gov.

323.4 USA
U.S. COMMISSION ON CIVIL RIGHTS. STATE ADVISORY COMMITTEE REPORTS. VERMONT. Text in English. 19??. irreg., latest 2003. free (effective 2011). back issues avail. **Document type:** *Monographic series, Government.*
Published by: U.S. Commission on Civil Rights, 624 Ninth St, NW, Rm 600, Washington, DC 20425. TEL 202-376-8128, publications@usccr.gov.

323.4 USA
U.S. COMMISSION ON CIVIL RIGHTS. STATE ADVISORY COMMITTEE REPORTS. VIRGINIA. Text in English. 19??. irreg., latest 2000. free (effective 2011). back issues avail. **Document type:** *Monographic series, Government.*
Published by: U.S. Commission on Civil Rights, 624 Ninth St, NW, Rm 600, Washington, DC 20425. TEL 202-376-8128, publications@usccr.gov.

323.4 USA
U.S. COMMISSION ON CIVIL RIGHTS. STATE ADVISORY COMMITTEE REPORTS. WASHINGTON. Text in English. 19??. irreg., latest 1997. free (effective 2011). back issues avail. **Document type:** *Monographic series, Government.*
Published by: U.S. Commission on Civil Rights, 624 Ninth St, NW, Rm 600, Washington, DC 20425. TEL 202-376-8128, publications@usccr.gov.

323.4 USA
U.S. COMMISSION ON CIVIL RIGHTS. STATE ADVISORY COMMITTEE REPORTS. WEST VIRGINIA. Text in English. 19??. irreg., latest 2004. free (effective 2011). back issues avail. **Document type:** *Monographic series, Government.*
Published by: U.S. Commission on Civil Rights, 624 Ninth St, NW, Rm 600, Washington, DC 20425. TEL 202-376-8128, publications@usccr.gov.

323.4 USA
U.S. COMMISSION ON CIVIL RIGHTS. STATE ADVISORY COMMITTEE REPORTS. WISCONSIN. Text in English. 19??. irreg., latest 2002. free (effective 2011). back issues avail. **Document type:** *Monographic series, Government.*
Published by: U.S. Commission on Civil Rights, 624 Ninth St, NW, Rm 600, Washington, DC 20425. TEL 202-376-8128, publications@usccr.gov.

323.4 USA
U.S. COMMISSION ON CIVIL RIGHTS. STATE ADVISORY COMMITTEE REPORTS. WYOMING. Text in English. 19??. irreg., latest 1988. free (effective 2011). back issues avail. **Document type:** *Monographic series, Government.*

P

Published by: U.S. Commission on Civil Rights, 624 Ninth St, NW, Rm 600, Washington, DC 20425. TEL 202-376-8128, publications@usccr.gov.

323.4 USA
U.S. COMMISSION ON CIVIL RIGHTS. STATUTORY AND INTERIM REPORTS. Text in English. 197?. irreg., latest 2003. free (effective 2011). back issues avail. **Document type:** *Monographic series, Government.* **Description:** Presents the results of studies and surveys, investigations of civil rights complaints, and appraisals of federal laws and policies undertaken by the commission. Deals with issues of long-term interest.
Published by: U.S. Commission on Civil Rights, 624 Ninth St, NW, Rm 600, Washington, DC 20425. TEL 202-376-8128, publications@usccr.gov.

U.S. DEPARTMENT OF THE INTERIOR. INTERIOR BOARD OF INDIAN APPEALS. *see* PUBLIC ADMINISTRATION

U.S. EQUAL EMPLOYMENT OPPORTUNITY COMMISSION. ANNUAL REPORT. *see* BUSINESS AND ECONOMICS—Labor And Industrial Relations

323.4 CHE ISSN 1020-3508
UNITED NATIONS. HUMAN RIGHTS COMMITTEE. OFFICIAL RECORDS. Text in English. 1985. a.
Formerly (until 1992): United Nations. Human Rights Committee. Yearbook (0256-9639)
—**CCC.**
Published by: United Nations, High Commissioner for Human Rights, 8-14 Ave de la Paix, Geneva, 10 1210, Switzerland. TEL 41-22-9179000, http://www.unhchr.ch.

323 NLD ISSN 1569-5174
THE UNIVERSAL DECLARATION OF HUMAN RIGHTS. Variant title: U D H R. Text in English. 2001. irreg., latest vol.2, 2007. price varies. **Document type:** *Monographic series.*
Published by: Martinus Nijhoff (Subsidiary of: Brill), PO Box 9000, Leiden, 2300 PA, Netherlands. TEL 31-71-5353500, FAX 31-71-5317532, marketing@brill.nl.

323.4 DEU
UNIVERSITAET POTSDAM. MENSCHENRECHTS-ZENTRUM. SCHRIFTEN. Text in German. 1995. irreg., latest vol.32, 2009. price varies. **Document type:** *Monographic series, Academic/Scholarly.*
Published by: (Universitaet Potsdam, MenschenRechtsZentrum), B W V - Berliner Wissenschafts Verlag GmbH, Markgrafenstr 12-14, Berlin, 10969, Germany. TEL 49-30-8417700, FAX 49-30-84177021, bwv@bwv-verlag.de, http://www.bwv-verlag.de.

323 DEU ISSN 1860-5958
UNIVERSITAET POTSDAM. MENSCHENRECHTSZENTRUM. JAHRESBERICHT. Text in German. 1994. a. **Document type:** *Journal, Academic/Scholarly.*
Published by: (Universitaet Potsdam, MenschenRechtsZentrum), Universitaetsverlag Potsdam, Am Neuen Palais 10, Potsdam, 14469, Germany. TEL 49-331-9774458, FAX 49-331-9774625, ubpub@uni-potsdam.de, http://info.ub.uni-potsdam.de/verlag.htm.

323.4 CAN ISSN 0826-7766
UNIVERSITE D'OTTAWA. CENTRE DE RECHERCHE ET D'ENSEIGNEMENT SUR LES DROITS DE LA PERSONNE. DROITS DE LA PERSONNE/HUMAN RIGHTS RESEARCH AND EDUCATION BULLETIN; bulletin de recherche et d'enseignement. Variant title: Bulletin d'Information sur la Recherche et l'Enseignement des Droits de la Personne. Text in English, French. 1984. q. CAD 13 (effective 2004).
Published by: University of Ottawa, Centre de Recherche et d'Enseignement sur les Droits de la Personne, 57 Louis Pasteur, Ottawa, ON K1N 6N5, Canada. TEL 613-562-5775, FAX 613-562-5125, hrrec@uottawa.ca.

323 NLD ISSN 1879-7156
▼ **UNIVERSITY FOR HUMANISTICS. PROMOTING PLURALISM KNOWLEDGE PROGRAMME. PLURALISM WORKING PAPER.** Variant title: Pluralism Working Paper Series. Text in English. 2009. irreg., latest vol.6, 2010. **Document type:** *Monographic series, Academic/Scholarly.*
Related titles: Online - full text ed.: ISSN 1879-7172.
Published by: (Kosmopolis Institute, Humanistisch Instituut voor Ontwikkelingssamenwerking/Humanist Institute for Development Cooperation), University for Humanistics, Promoting Pluralism Knowledge Programme, PO Box 797, Utrecht, 3500 AT, Netherlands. TEL 31-30-2390100, FAX 31-30-2340738, info@uvh.nl, http://www.uvh.nl.

URBAN DIRECTIONS. *see* HOUSING AND URBAN PLANNING

URBAN FAMILY; the magazine of hope and progress. *see* ETHNIC INTERESTS

323.4 DEU ISSN 0943-1985
V I A MAGAZIN; Fachzeitschrift fuer Praktiker. Text in German. 1986. s-a. EUR 2.05 newsstand/cover (effective 2006). **Document type:** *Bulletin.*
Published by: Verband der Initiativgruppen in der Auslaenderarbeit e.V., Hochemmericher Str 71, Duisburg, 47226, Germany. TEL 49-2065-53346, FAX 49-2065-53561, via@via-bund.de. Circ: 800.

323 SWE
VAAR TRYGGHET; vaara sociala raettigheter. Text in Swedish. 1964. a. SEK 50 (effective 1997). **Document type:** *Consumer.*
Published by: Folksam, Stockholm, 10660, Sweden. Ed. Bo Beckman.

323.4 USA ISSN 2158-7280
VANGUARD. Text in English. 2005. w. **Document type:** *Journal, Trade.*
Media: Online - full text.
Published by: Vanguardians, PO Box 11202, Glendale, CA 91226. http://www.vanguardians.org.

323.4 GTM
VERDAD Y VIDA. Text in Spanish. 1994. q. GTQ 32; USD 12 foreign.
Published by: Oficina de Derechos Humanos del Arzobispado de Guatemala, 7a Avda. 7-21, ZONA, 1, Apartado Postal 723, Guatemala City, 01001, Guatemala.

323.4 AUS ISSN 1836-1447
VICTORIAN EQUAL OPPORTUNITY & HUMAN RIGHTS COMMISSION. ANNUAL REPORT. Text in English. 1978. a. free (effective 2009). **Document type:** *Government.*
Former titles (until 2007): Victoria. Equal Opportunity Commission. Annual Report (1324-8499); Which superseded (in 1993): Victoria. Office of the Commissioner for Equal Opportunity. Annual Report (1036-9538); Which was formerly (until 1989): Victoria. Equal Opportunity Board. Report of the Equal Opportunity Board and the Commissioner for Equal Opportunity; (until 1986): Victoria. Equal Opportunity Board. Report; (until 1980): Victoria. Equal Opportunity Board. Annual Report (0156-9996)
Published by: Victorian Equal Opportunity & Human Rights Commission, Level 3, 380 Lonsdale St, Melbourne, VIC 3000, Australia. TEL 61-3-92817111, 800-134-142, FAX 61-3-92817171, information@veohrc.vic.gov.au. Circ: 500.

323.4 AUS
VICTORIAN EQUAL OPPORTUNITY & HUMAN RIGHTS COMMISSION. BULLETIN. Text in English. 1991. irreg. (1-4/yr.). free (effective 2009). charts; stat.; tr.lit. back issues avail. **Document type:** *Bulletin, Government.* **Description:** Provides news and views on Equal Opportunity Commission activities and equal opportunity issues for equal opportunity and discrimination professionals.
Former titles (until 2006): E Q (1445-646X); (until 2001): Equal Opportunity. Bulletin (1324-4450)
Media: Online - full content.
Published by: Victorian Equal Opportunity & Human Rights Commission, Level 3, 380 Lonsdale St, Melbourne, VIC 3000, Australia. TEL 61-3-92817111, 800-134-142, FAX 61-3-92817171, information@veohrc.vic.gov.au. Circ: 3,000 (controlled).

VIOLENCE AGAINST WOMEN; an international and interdisciplinary journal. *see* SOCIOLOGY

VOICE MALE. *see* MEN'S INTERESTS

323.4 USA
VOICE OF REASON. Text in English. 1981. q. USD 20; USD 25 foreign (effective 1999). bk.rev. back issues avail. **Document type:** *Newsletter.* **Description:** Covers church and state relations and civil liberties issues.
Related titles: Fax ed.
Published by: Americans for Religious Liberty, PO Box 6656, Silver Spring, MD 20916. TEL 301-598-2447, FAX 301-438-8424. Ed., R&P Edd Doerr. Circ: 3,500; 3,000 (paid).

VOICE OF THE BLACK COMMUNITY. *see* ETHNIC INTERESTS

VOICES FROM THE EARTH. *see* ENVIRONMENTAL STUDIES

323 USA
VOLUNTARYIST. Text in English. 1982. q. USD 20 for 6 mos. domestic; USD 25 for 6 mos. foreign (effective 2001). adv. bk.rev. 8 p./no. 2 cols./p.; back issues avail. **Document type:** *Newsletter.* **Description:** Advocates a non-state, pro free-market, anti-electoral and nonviolent position on social change.
Indexed: PQC.
Published by: Voluntaryists, PO Box 275, Gramling, SC 29348. TEL 864-472-2750, http://members.aol.com/vlntryst. Ed. Carl Watner. Circ: 300.

323.4 SLV
VOZ/VOICE; information and analysis bulletin. Text in English. 1992. m. **Description:** Provides reports and analysis on occurrences in El Salvador.
Published by: Comision de Derechos Humanos No Gubernamental/Non-governmental Human Rights Commission of El Salvador, Urb. La Esperanza, Pasaje 1, No. 119, San Salvador, El Salvador.

VREDES MAGAZINE. *see* MILITARY

323.4 RUS ISSN 0868-9520
VYZOV. Text in Russian. 1990. 6/yr.
Published by: Permskii Gorispolkom, Upravlenie Vnutrennikh Del, Ul Druzhby 34, Perm, 614600, Russian Federation. TEL 48-39-24, FAX 32-52-19. Ed. D E Krasik. Circ: 50,000 (controlled).

323.4 USA
W C P S QUARTERLY. Text in English. 1982. q. USD 25 to individuals; USD 30 to institutional members (effective 2000). bk.rev. **Document type:** *Newsletter.* **Description:** Presents information on WCPS events, networking, job openings, communications.
Published by: Women's Caucus for Political Science, c/o Ronnee Schreiber, Treasurer, SDSU Department of Political Science, 5500 Campanile Drive, San Diego, CA 92182. harrisonb@mail.montclair.edu, http://www.cas.sc.edu/poli/caucus/main.html. Ed. Brigid A Harrison. Circ: 1,075 (paid).

W D L NEWS. *see* BUSINESS AND ECONOMICS—Labor And Industrial Relations

W I N NEWS; all the news that is fit to print by, for, about women. *see* WOMEN'S STUDIES

323.4 296 NLD ISSN 1874-0944
WAFFEL. Variant title: J O K Verenigingsblad. Verenigingsblad Waffel. Text in Dutch. 199?. q. adv.
Published by: Vereniging Joodse OorlogsKinderen, Postbus 297, Purmerend, 1440 AG, Netherlands. TEL 31-299-644498, FAX 31-299-647661, info@j-o-k.nl, http://www.j-o-k.nl. Ed. Rob Bonn.

323 USA ISSN 0749-1050
WASHINGTON INQUIRER. Text in English. 1981. w. USD 33. adv. bk.rev. **Document type:** *Newspaper.* **Description:** Publishes international news about human freedoms from governmental tyranny, US strategic and military matters.
Published by: Council for the Defense of Freedom, 4455 Connecticut Ave, N W, Washington, DC 20009. TEL 202-364-2339. Ed., Adv. contact Arthur D Randall. Circ: 6,000.

323.4 USA
THE WEEK IN RIGHTS. Text in English. w. free. **Document type:** *Newsletter, Consumer.* **Description:** Highlights the impact of the Human Rights Watch work around the world.
Formerly (until 2010): Impact (New York)
Media: Online - full text.
Published by: Human Rights Watch, 350 Fifth Ave, 34th Fl, New York, NY 10118. TEL 212-290-4700, FAX 212-736-1300, hrwdc@hrw.org.

WELFARE BENEFITS AND TAX CREDITS HANDBOOK. *see* SOCIAL SERVICES AND WELFARE

WELFARE RIGHTS BULLETIN. *see* SOCIAL SERVICES AND WELFARE

323 USA ISSN 0083-8594
JC599.U52
WEST VIRGINIA. HUMAN RIGHTS COMMISSION. REPORT. Text in English. 1961. a. free. **Document type:** *Government.*
Published by: Human Rights Commission, 1321 Plaza E, Ste 108, Charleston, WV 25301-1400. TEL 304-558-2616, FAX 304-558-0085, wvhrc@wvhrc.state.wv.us, http://www.state.wv.us/wvhrc. Ed. Norman Lindell. Circ: 1,000.

323.448 USA
WIRETAPPING & EAVESDROPPING. Text in English. 19??. 2 base vols. plus a. updates. looseleaf. USD 592 base vol(s). (effective 2010). **Document type:** *Journal, Trade.* **Description:** Contains coverage of criminal and civil statutes, penalties, and remedies. Includes chapters addressing computer evidence covering Internet technology, the Fourth Amendment and computers, and federal and state computer legislation.
Published by: Thomson West (Subsidiary of: Thomson Reuters Corp.), 610 Opperman Dr, Eagan, MN 55123. TEL 651-687-7000, 800-344-5008, west.customer.service@thomson.com. Eds. Anne T McKenna, Clifford S Fishman.

323.34 USA ISSN 1933-7485
KF478
WOMEN AND THE LAW. Text in English. 1984. a. USD 652 per issue (effective 2010). **Document type:** *Journal, Trade.* **Description:** Provides coverage of the major areas surrounding women's legal protection. Legal issues are examined through a practice-oriented approach, covering current law, analysis, procedure, litigation advice, and strategy.
Published by: Thomson West (Subsidiary of: Thomson Reuters Corp.), 610 Opperman Dr, Eagan, MN 55123. TEL 651-687-7000, 800-344-5008, west.customer.service@thomson.com.

323.34 USA
WOMEN IN THE WORLD. Text in English. 1990. m. free. **Document type:** *Newsletter, Consumer.*
Formerly (until 200?): Human Rights Watch Women's Rights Project
Media: Online - full text.
Published by: Human Rights Watch, 350 Fifth Ave, 34th Fl, New York, NY 10118. TEL 212-290-4700, FAX 212-736-1300, hrwdc@hrw.org.

323.34 USA
WOMEN'S WATCH; reporting on law and policy change in accordance with the principles of the Convention on the Elimination of All Forms of Discrimination Against Women. Text in English. m. USD 20.
Indexed: CWI.
Published by: International Women's Rights Action Watch, Women, Public Policy and Development Program, Humphrey Institute of Public Affairs, University of Minnesota, 301 19th Ave S, Minneapolis, MN 55455.

323.4 NLD ISSN 0165-4241
WORDT VERVOLGD. Text in Dutch. 1968. m. (10/yr.). EUR 30; EUR 3.75 newsstand/cover (effective 2008). adv. **Document type:** *Newsletter, Consumer.* **Description:** Provides background to current concerns and developments in the human rights field and within the organization.
Published by: Amnesty International, Dutch Section, Postbus 1968, Amsterdam, 1000 BZ, Netherlands. TEL 31-20-6264436, FAX 31-20-6240889. Eds. Arend Hulshof, Monique van Ravenstein. Pub. Ali Remmelts. adv.: color page EUR 3,250; bleed 210 x 297. Circ: 30,000 (paid).

WORKERS SOLIDARITY; newsletter of the Workers Solidarity Alliance. *see* BUSINESS AND ECONOMICS—Labor And Industrial Relations

YALE HUMAN RIGHTS AND DEVELOPMENT LAW JOURNAL. *see* LAW

YEARBOOK OF WOMEN'S RIGHTS. *see* WOMEN'S STUDIES

ZEICHEN. *see* RELIGIONS AND THEOLOGY—Protestant

323.4 DEU ISSN 0342-5851
ZEITLUPE. Text in German. 1975. irreg. free (effective 2008). back issues avail. **Document type:** *Magazine, Consumer.*
Published by: Bundeszentrale fuer Politische Bildung, Adenauerallee 86, Bonn, 53113, Germany. TEL 49-1888-5150, FAX 49-1888-515113, info@bpb.de, http://www.bpb.de. Ed. Hanne Wurzel. Circ: 500,000.

323.4 DEU ISSN 0721-5746
K30
ZEITSCHRIFT FUER AUSLAENDERRECHT UND AUSLAENDERPOLITIK. Short title: Z A R. Text in German. 1981. 10/yr. EUR 154 (effective 2011). adv. reprint service avail. from SCH. **Document type:** *Journal, Academic/Scholarly.*
Indexed: DIP, ELLIS, IBR, IBZ, RefugAb.
—BLDSC (9426.775000), IE, Ingenta. **CCC.**
Published by: Nomos Verlagsgesellschaft mbH und Co. KG, Waldseestr 3-5, Baden-Baden, 76530, Germany. TEL 49-7221-21040, FAX 49-7221-210427, marketing@nomos.de, nomos@nomos.de, http://www.nomos.de. Ed. Winfried Kluth. Adv. contact Bettina Roos. Circ: 1,600 (paid and controlled).

323 342.6891 ZWE ISSN 1562-5958
K30
ZIMBABWE HUMAN RIGHTS BULLETIN. Text in English. 1999. s-a. ZWD 20 domestic; USD 40 in Africa; USD 50 elsewhere (effective 2007).
Published by: Zimbabwe Lawyers for Human Rights, 6th Flr Beverley Court, Corner Nelson Mandela Ave and Fourth St, Box CY 1393, Causeway, Harare, Zimbabwe. TEL 263-4-251468, 263-4-705370, FAX 263-4-723789, zlhr@icon.co.zw, http://www.zlhr.org.zw.

323.4 DEU ISSN 1430-5968
ZIVIL; Zeitschrift fuer Frieden und Gewaltfreiheit. Text in German. 1970. 5/yr. EUR 13.50 (effective 2009). adv. bk.rev. back issues avail. **Document type:** *Magazine, Consumer.*
Formerly (until 1996): Was Uns Betrifft (0936-6520)
Published by: Evangelische Arbeitsgemeinschaft zur Betreuung der Kriegsdienstverweigerer (EAK), Endenicher Str 41, Bonn, 53115, Germany. TEL 49-228-249990, FAX 49-228-2499920, office@eak-online.de, http://www.eak-online.de. Ed. Werner Schulz. adv.: page EUR 2,560; trim 194 x 265. Circ: 35,000 (paid and controlled).

POLITICAL SCIENCE—International Relations

see also LAW—International Law

341.72 AUT ISSN 1993-4939
A C I P S S NEWSLETTER. Text in English, German. 2007. w. **Document type:** *Newsletter, Trade.*
Media: Online - full content.
Published by: Austrian Center for Intelligence, Propaganda and Security Studies, Heinrichstr 26/IV, Graz, 8010, Austria. TEL 43-316-3802350, FAX 43-316-3809730, office@acipss.org. Ed. Verena Klug.

327 USA ISSN 0743-8834
A C O A ACTION NEWS. Text in English. irreg. free. bibl.; tr.lit.
Published by: American Committee on Africa, 50 Broad St, Ste 711, New York, NY 10040. TEL 212-785-1024, FAX 212-785-1078. Ed. Richard Knight.

A CURRENT BIBLIOGRAPHY ON AFRICAN AFFAIRS. *see* POLITICAL SCIENCE—Abstracting, Bibliographies, Statistics

327.1 USA ISSN 1941-4501
E840
A F P C COUNCIL REVIEW; an update for friends of the American Foreign Policy Council. Text in English. q.
Published by: American Foreign Policy Council, 509 C St, NE, Washington, DC 20002. TEL 202-543-1006, FAX 202-543-1007, afpc@afpc.org, http://www.afpc.org.

327 AUS ISSN 1838-5842
A I I A POLICY COMMENTARY. (Australian Institute of International Affairs) Text in English. 2006. s-a. back issues avail. **Document type:** *Trade.*
Related titles: Online - full text ed.: ISSN 1838-5850. free (effective 2011).
Published by: Australian Institute of International Affairs, Stephen House, 32 Thesiger Ct, Deakin, ACT 2600, Australia. TEL 61-2-62822133, FAX 61-2-62852334, ceo@aiia.asn.au. Ed. Shirley Scott.

325.21 USA ISSN 1066-3584
HC415.25.A1
A N E R A NEWSLETTER. (American Near East Refugee Aid) Text in English. 1969. q. free. bk.rev. illus. **Document type:** *Newsletter.* **Description:** Contains information about ANERA activities: economic development and relief in the West Bank, Gaza Strip and Lebanon.
Indexed: HRIR.
Published by: American Near East Refugee Aid, Inc., 1522 K St, N W, 202, Washington, DC 20005. TEL 202-347-2558, FAX 202-682-1637. Ed., Pub., R&P Doris Warrell. Circ: 15,000.

327.172 NGA
A P R I JOURNAL. Text in English. 1986. bi-m. NGN 48, USD 40. bk.rev. stat. cum.index. back issues avail. **Document type:** *Journal, Academic/Scholarly.* **Description:** Carries and analyzes information on current peace research issues, i.e., environment, violence, conflict, disarmament, and foreign debt.
Formerly: A P R I Newsletter
Published by: African Peace Research Institute, Falomo, PO Box 51757, Ikoyi, Lagos State, Nigeria. TEL 234-433437. Ed. Temitope Oguntayo. Circ: 250.

320 CYP
A P S DIPLOMAT RECORDER. Text in English. w. **Document type:** *Journal, Trade.*
Media: Online - full content.
Published by: Arab Press Service, PO Box 23896, Nicosia, Cyprus. TEL 357-2-350265, FAX 357-2-351778, apsnews@spidernet.com.cy.

A P S NEWS SERVICE. *see* ENERGY

320 CYP
A P S STRATEGIC BALANCE IN THE MIDDLE EAST. Text in English. m. **Document type:** *Journal, Trade.*
Media: Online - full content.
Published by: Arab Press Service, PO Box 23896, Nicosia, Cyprus. TEL 357-2-350265, FAX 357-2-351778, apsnews@spidernet.com.cy.

325.21 DEU ISSN 0001-2947
HV640
A W R BULLETIN; quarterly on refugee problems. Text in English, French, German, Italian. 1963. q. EUR 49; EUR 18 newsstand/cover (effective 2010). adv. bk.rev. index. **Document type:** *Magazine, Trade.*
Indexed: DIP, HRIR, IBR, IBSS, IBZ, P30, RefugAb.
Published by: (Association for the Study of the World Refugee Problem AUT), B W V - Berliner Wissenschafts Verlag GmbH, Markgrafenstr 12-14, Berlin, 10969, Germany. TEL 49-30-8417700, FAX 49-30-84177021, bwv@bwv-verlag.de, http://www.bwv-verlag.de. Ed. Sibylle Wollenschlaeger. Circ: 600 (controlled).

327.12 CHL ISSN 0718-5235
AAINTELIGENCIA. Text in Spanish. 2007. bi-m.
Media: Online - full text.
Published by: Aainteligencia Editores contacto@aainteligencia.cl, http://www.aainteligencia.cl/index.html. Ed. Andrea Lodeiro.

ABRAHAM LINCOLN ABROAD. *see* HISTORY—History Of North And South America

327 BOL
ACADEMIA DIPLOMATICA BOLIVIANA. REVISTA ANUAL. Text in Spanish. 1991. a. **Document type:** *Academic/Scholarly.*
Published by: Ministerio de Relaciones Exteriores y Culto, Academia Diplomatica Boliviana, Plaza Murillo esq. Junin, La Paz, Bolivia. TEL 366269.

327 ITA ISSN 1825-3679
D410
ACQUE & TERRE. Text in English, Italian. 1990. bi-m. EUR 26 domestic; EUR 50 foreign (effective 2007). adv. **Document type:** *Magazine, Consumer.* **Description:** Reviews international politics with a special emphasis on the dialetics of integration and disintigration in the contemporary world and on North-South relations and connected cultural, political and economic issues.
Related titles: Supplement(s): Marco Polo Magazine. ISSN 1825-3687. 1998.
Published by: Marco Polo Institute, Via Daniele Manin 4, Mestre, 30174, Italy. Ed. Nereo Laroni. Circ: 10,000.

327.714 GBR ISSN 1366-1523
THE ACRONYM. Variant title: Redbooks. Text in English. 1996. irreg., latest vol.13. free (effective 2009). back issues avail. **Document type:** *Monographic series, Academic/Scholarly.*
Related titles: Online - full text ed.
Published by: Acronym Institute, 24 Colvestone Cres, London, E8 2LH, United Kingdom. TEL 44-20-75038857, FAX 44-20-75038857, acronym@gn.apc.org.

ACTA UNIVERSITATIS WRATISLAVIENSIS. NIEMCOZNAWSTWO. *see* HISTORY—History Of Europe

327 DNK ISSN 1903-4954
ACTION MAGAZINE. Text in Danish. 2004. q. **Document type:** *Magazine, Consumer.*
Former titles (until 2008): Indflydelse (1902-5610); (until 2007): Magasinet (1901-6115); (until 2006): M S Bladet (1603-7707)
Related titles: Online - full text ed.
Published by: Mellemfolkeligt Samvirke/Danish Association for International Co-operation, Faelledvej 12, Copenhagen N, 2200, Denmark. TEL 45-77-310000, FAX 45-77-310101, ms@ms.dk. Eds. Henriette Winther, Vibeke Vinther. Circ: 9,500.

327.172 USA
JZ5584.U6
ACTION REPORT. Text in English. 1961. 4/yr. looseleaf. bk.rev. charts; illus. reprints avail. **Document type:** *Newsletter.*
Former titles: Peace Action (0813-7307); (until 1993): SANE - Freeze News; (until 1990): SANE World - Freeze Focus (0036-4304)
Related titles: Microfilm ed.: (from PQC).
Indexed: PRA.
Published by: Peace Action, 1100 Wayne Ave., Ste. 1020, Silver Spring, MD 20910-5643. TEL 202-862-9740, FAX 202-862-9762, paprog@igc.apc.org, http://www.webcom.com/peaceact/.

327.17 341.21 FRA ISSN 1772-8436
L'ACTUALITE DES NATIONS UNIES. Text in French. 2004. q. **Document type:** *Newsletter, Government.*
Published by: Association Francaise pour les Nations Unies, 1 Av de Tourville, Paris, 75007, France. TEL 33-1-45557173, FAX 33-1-45561988. Ed. Philippe Lafosse.

341.72 GBR ISSN 1944-5571
➤ **ADELPHI SERIES.** Text in English. 1963. 8/yr. GBP 525 combined subscription in United Kingdom to institutions (print & online eds.); EUR 777 combined subscription to institutions (print & online eds.); USD 924 combined subscription in North America to institutions (print & online eds.); USD 974 combined subscription elsewhere to institutions (print & online eds.) (effective 2012). adv. bibl.; charts; stat. 96 p./no.; back issues avail.; reprint service avail. from PSC. **Document type:** *Journal, Academic/Scholarly.* **Description:** Contains monographs analyzing current and future problems of international security concerns.
Formerly (until 2009): The Adelphi Papers (0567-932X)
Related titles: Microform ed.: (from PQC); Online - full text ed.: ISSN 1944-558X. GBP 473 in United Kingdom to institutions; EUR 699 to institutions; USD 832 in North America to institutions; USD 876 elsewhere to institutions (effective 2012) (from IngentaConnect).
Indexed: A22, AMB, CA, E01, I02, LID&ISL, P10, P34, P42, P47, P48, P53, P54, PAIS, PCI, PQC, PSA, R02, RASB, S11, SCOPUS, SociolAb, T02.
—BLDSC (0680.400000), IE, Infotrieve, Ingenta. **CCC.**
Published by: (International Institute for Strategic Studies), Routledge (Subsidiary of: Taylor & Francis Group), 4 Park Sq, Milton Park, Abingdon, Oxon OX14 4RN, United Kingdom. TEL 44-20-70176000, FAX 44-20-70176336, subscriptions@tandf.co.uk, http://www.routledge.com. Ed. Tim Huxley. Adv. contact Linda Hann TEL 44-1344-779945. **Subscr. to:** Taylor & Francis Ltd., Journals Customer Service, Sheepen Pl, Colchester, Essex CO3 3LP, United Kingdom. TEL 44-20-70175544, FAX 44-20-70175198, tf.enquiries@tfinforma.com.

327.17 USA ISSN 0886-778X
HC800.A1
ADVANCE (WASHINGTON). Text in English. 1987. a.
—Ingenta.
Published by: African Development Foundation, 1400 I St NW 10th Fl, Washington, DC 20005-2248. TEL 202-673-3916, FAX 202-673-8819, http://www.adf.gov/.

327.172 USA
ADVOCATE (PANHANDLE). Text in English. 1986. q. USD 5 (effective 2000). adv. bk.rev. back issues avail. **Document type:** *Newsletter.* **Description:** Anti-nuclear and anti-war activist news and views. Aims to create an environment for peace through peaceful means, to assert that peace can exist only where there is justice, and to develop an ecological model for nonviolent social change.
Published by: Peace Farm, Mavis Belisle, HC 2 Box 25, Panhandle, TX 79068. belislem@igc.apc.org. Ed., Pub., R&P Mavis Belisle. Circ: 450 (paid); 400 (controlled).

327 ITA ISSN 0001-964X
D839
AFFARI ESTERI. Text in Italian. 1969. q. adv. bk.rev. bibl. **Document type:** *Magazine, Consumer.*
Indexed: ELLIS, HistAb, I13, IBR, IBZ, PAIS, PCI, RASB.
Published by: Associazione Italiana per gli Studi di Politica Estera, Largo della Fontanella di Borghese 19, Rome, 00186, Italy. TEL 39-06-6878926, FAX 39-06-6833015.

AFFARI SOCIALI INTERNAZIONALI. *see* SOCIOLOGY

AFGHANISTAN - NYTT. *see* HISTORY—History Of Asia

AFRICA; rivista trimestrale di studi e documentazione. *see* HISTORY—History Of Africa

AFRICA. *see* HISTORY—History Of Africa

327.6 USA ISSN 0748-4356
DT38
AFRICA INSIDER; a twice monthly report on US-African affairs from Washington, DC. Text in English. 1984. fortn. USD 37.50 domestic to individuals; USD 67.50 foreign to individuals; USD 75 domestic to institutions; USD 175 foreign to institutions (effective 1999). bk.rev. tr.lit. back issues avail. **Document type:** *Newsletter.* **Description:** Covers political and foreign affairs analysis in relations between Africa and the United States.
Published by: Matthews Associates, 113 North Washington St 115, Rockville, MD 20850. TEL 301-738-2181, FAX 301-738-2423. Ed. Dan Matthews.

AFRICA REVIEW. *see* BUSINESS AND ECONOMICS—Economic Situation And Conditions

327 IND ISSN 0974-4053
▼ **AFRICA REVIEW.** Text in English. 2009. s-a. INR 950 domestic (print or online ed.); USD 105 foreign (print or online ed.); INR 1,800 combined subscription domestic (print & online eds.); USD 200 combined subscription foreign (print & online eds.) (effective 2010). **Document type:** *Journal, Academic/Scholarly.* **Description:** Covers theoretical and historical enquiries related to African affairs.
Related titles: Online - full text ed.
Published by: M D Publications Pvt Ltd, 11 Darya Ganj, New Delhi, 110 002, India. TEL 91-11-41563325, FAX 91-11-23275542, contact@mdppl.com. Ed. Rajen Harshe.

327.172 USA ISSN 2156-695X
▼ **AFRICAN CONFLICT AND PEACEBUILDING REVIEW.** Text in English. 2011. s-a. USD 111.30 combined subscription to institutions (print & online eds.) (effective 2012). **Document type:** *Journal, Academic/Scholarly.* **Description:** Provides an interdisciplinary forum for creative and rigorous studies of conflict and peace in Africa.
Related titles: Online - full text ed.: ISSN 2156-7263. 2011. USD 71.50 to institutions (effective 2012).
Published by: Indiana University Press, 601 N Morton St, Bloomington, IN 47404. TEL 812-855-8817, FAX 812-855-7931, iupress@indiana.edu, http://iupress.indiana.edu.

327 SEN ISSN 0850-7902
JZ6.5
➤ **AFRICAN JOURNAL OF INTERNATIONAL AFFAIRS**; revue africaine des affaires internationaux. Text in English, French. 1998. s-a. USD 15 domestic to individuals; USD 30 foreign to individuals; USD 20 domestic to institutions; USD 40 foreign to institutions (effective 2004). adv. bk.rev. bibl.; charts; illus.; maps. back issues avail. **Document type:** *Journal, Academic/Scholarly.* **Description:** Analyzes contemporary issues in international affairs in relation to global developments as they affect Africa. Welcomes contributions in English and French from both African scholars and scholars working on Africa.
Related titles: Online - full text ed.
Indexed: IBSS, IIBP.
Published by: Council for the Development of Social Science Research in Africa, Avenue Cheikh, Anta Diop x Canal IV, BP 3304, Dakar, Senegal. TEL 221-825-9822, FAX 221-824-1289, codesria@sentoo.sn, http://www.codesria.org. Ed. Adebayo Olukoshi.

P

327 NGA ISSN 1117-272X
AFRICAN JOURNAL OF INTERNATIONAL AFFAIRS & DEVELOPMENT. Text in English. 1995. s-a. USD 15 domestic to individuals; USD 25 foreign to individuals; USD 20 domestic to institutions; USD 40 foreign to institutions (effective 2004). bk.rev. **Document type:** *Journal, Academic/Scholarly.* **Description:** Publishes articles on the legal, political, diplomatic, economic, environmental, sociocultural, and military issues at the core of Africa's foreign relations and world affairs.
Related titles: CD-ROM ed.; Microfilm ed.: (from PQC); Online - full text ed.
Indexed: CA, P42, S02, S03, T02.
—BLDSC (0732.522800), IE, Ingenta.
Published by: (Obafemi Awolowo University), College Press Publishers Lts., c/o Dr. Jide Owoeye, PO Box 30678, Ibadan, Oyo, Nigeria. TEL 234-02-8101963, FAX 234-02-8104165, collegepresspublishers@yahoo.com. Ed., Pub. Jide Owoeye.

AFRICAN JOURNAL OF POLITICAL SCIENCE AND INTERNATIONAL RELATIONS. *see* POLITICAL SCIENCE

327.172 ZAF ISSN 1562-6997
HM1126
AFRICAN JOURNAL ON CONFLICT RESOLUTION. Text in English. 1999. s-a. free (effective 2006). back issues avail. **Document type:** *Journal, Academic/Scholarly.* **Description:** Aims at promoting African ideas and thought patterns in the field of conflict resolution.
Related titles: Online - full text ed.: free (effective 2011).
Indexed: IIBP, ISAP.
Published by: A C C O R D, Bag X018, Umhlanga Rocks, 4320, South Africa. TEL 27-31-502-3408, FAX 27-31-502-4160, info@accord.org.za. Ed. Jannie Malan.

AFRIKA SUED. *see* BUSINESS AND ECONOMICS—International Development And Assistance

320 BEL ISSN 1017-0952
DT1
AFRIQUE 2000. Text in French. 1990. q.
Indexed: P30, RILM.
Published by: Institut Panafricain de Relations Internationales, Rue Cesar Franck 34, Bruxelles, 1050, Belgium. TEL 32-2-42562573, FAX 32-2-42563693. Ed. Emmanuel Wonyu.

327 FRA ISSN 0002-0478
DT348
AFRIQUE CONTEMPORAINE; Afrique et developpement. Text in French. 1962. q. EUR 65 domestic; EUR 65 in Belgium; EUR 75 elsewhere (effective 2011). adv. bk.rev. bibl.; charts; stat.; illus. Index. back issues avail.; reprints avail. **Document type:** *Journal, Academic/Scholarly.* **Description:** Looks at important political, economic, social and cultural events in sub-Saharan Africa, Madagascar and the Indian Ocean islands.
Related titles: Microfiche ed.; Online - full text ed.: ISSN 1782-138X.
Indexed: A22, ASD, BibInd, BibLing, CCA, FR, I13, IBR, IBSS, IBZ, MLA-IB, P30, PAIS, PdeR, RASB, SCOPUS.
—BLDSC (0735.320000), IE, Infotrieve, Ingenta, INIST. **CCC.**
Published by: Agence Francaise de Developpement, 5 Rue Roland-Barthes, Paris, 75598 cedex 12, France. Circ: 2,000. **Subscr. to:** De Boeck Universite, Fond Jean-Paques 4, Louvain-la-Neuve 1348, Belgium. TEL 32-10-482570, abo@deboeckservices.com.

328 PER ISSN 1027-6750
JZ9
AGENDA INTERNACIONAL. Text in Spanish. 1994. s-a.
Indexed: A01, A26, F03, F04, I04, I05.
Published by: Pontificia Universidad Catolica del Peru, Fondo Editorial, Ave. Universitaria Cdra. 18, s-n, Urb. Pando, San Miguel, Lima, 32, Peru. TEL 51-14-4602870, FAX 51-14-4600872, feditor@pucp.edu.pe, http://www.pucp.edu.pe/~fedit/index.html.

327 FIN ISSN 1795-9101
AGENDA MAGAZINE. Text in English. 2005. bi-m. **Document type:** *Magazine, Consumer.* **Description:** Features the diplomatic life, Finnish politics, culture, practical information for those who have their first experience of Finland.
Related titles: Online - full text ed.
Published by: Denisa Udroiu, PO Box 123, Helsinki, 00531, Finland. TEL 358-45-6385302, denisa.udroiu@agendafin.com.

327 BEL ISSN 0002-080X
AGENOR. Text in English. 1967. q. adv. illus. back issues avail.
Related titles: Microfilm ed.: (from RPI).
Indexed: MEA&I.
Published by: Agenor Societe Cooperative, Rue Toulouse 22, Brussels, 1040, Belgium. FAX 32-2-230-5957. Circ: 1,000.

AHFAD JOURNAL; women and change. *see* WOMEN'S STUDIES

327 POL
➤ **AKADEMIA DYPLOMATYCZNA. ZBIOR DOKUMENTOW.** Text in Polish, English. 1936. q. USD 44 to individuals; USD 70 to institutions (effective 2004). cum.index: 1945-1954, 1955-1964. **Document type:** *Journal, Academic/Scholarly.*
Former titles: Polska Fundacja Spraw Miedzynarodowych. Zbior Dokumentow; (until 1996): Polski Instytut Spraw Miedzynarodowych. Zbior Dokumentow (0044-1929)
Indexed: RASB.
Published by: Akademia Dyplomatyczna/Diplomatic Academy, ul Tyniecka 15/17, Warsaw, 02630, Poland. TEL 48-22-5239086, FAX 48-22-5239027, aleksandra.zieliniecd@msz.gov.pl, http://www.sprawymiedzynarodowe.pl. Ed. Jerzy Menkes. Circ: 400.

327 RUS ISSN 0235-5620
AKTUAL'NYE PROBLEMY EVROPY. Text in Russian. 1996. q. USD 105 in United States (effective 2004). **Document type:** *Journal, Academic/Scholarly.*
Indexed: RASB, RefZh.
Published by: Rossiiskaya Akademiya Nauk, Institut Nauchnoi Informatsii po Obshchestvennym Naukam, Nakhimovskii pr-t 51/21, Moscow, 117997, Russian Federation. TEL 7-095-1288930, FAX 7-095-4202261, info@inion.ru, http://www.inion.ru. **Dist. by:** East View Information Services, 10601 Wayzata Blvd, Minneapolis, MN 55305. TEL 952-252-1201, 800-477-1005, FAX 952-252-1202, info@eastview.com, http://www.eastview.com.

327 DEU
AKTUELLE MATERIALIEN ZUR INTERNATIONALEN POLITIK. Text in German. 1983. irreg., latest vol.78, 2010. price varies. **Document type:** *Monographic series, Academic/Scholarly.*
Published by: Nomos Verlagsgesellschaft mbH und Co. KG, Waldseestr 3-5, Baden-Baden, 76530, Germany. TEL 49-7221-21040, FAX 49-7221-210427, nomos@nomos.de, http://www.nomos.de.

327 GBR ISSN 0950-8473
AL DIA. Text in Spanish. 1987. m. GBP 158, USD 220 (effective 2001). back issues avail. **Document type:** *Newsletter.*
Published by: Intelligence Research Ltd. (Subsidiary of: Lettres (U.K.) Ltd.), 61 Old St, London, EC1V 9HW, United Kingdom. TEL 44-20-7251-0012, FAX 44-20-7253-8193, info@latinnews.com, http://www.latinnews.com. Ed. Miguel Angel Diaz. R&P Alex McHallam TEL 44-20-7251-0012.

327 USA
AL-HEWAR MAGAZINE. Text in English, Arabic. 1989. q. USD 20 domestic; USD 30 in Canada; USD 40 elsewhere (effective 2001). adv. **Description:** Aims to be a voice for intellectual opinions related to the Middle East and Arabic and Islamic issues.
Related titles: Online - full text ed.
Published by: Al-Hewar Center, Box 2104, Vienna, VA 22180. TEL 703-281-8277, FAX 703-854-9864, alhewar@alhewar.com. adv.: page USD 300; 7.5 x 10.

ALBANIAN DAILY NEWS. *see* BUSINESS AND ECONOMICS—Economic Situation And Conditions

327 IND ISSN 0002-5585
ALL-INDIA ANGLO-INDIAN ASSOCIATION. REVIEW. Text in English. 1968 (vol.39). m. bk.rev. charts; illus. **Document type:** *Newsletter, Trade.*
Published by: All India Anglo-Indian Association, N-74, Bombay Life Bldg, Connaught Circus, New Delhi, 110 001, India. TEL 91-11-23312502, angloindia@vsnl.net.

327.172 ROM
ALLIANCE FOR PEACE IN RUMANIA. INFORMATION BULLETIN. Text in English. 1962. q. free. charts; illus. **Description:** Discusses economic progress, industry, agricultural development, security, disarmament and human rights.
Formerly (until vol.3, 1989): National Committee for the Defence of Peace in the Socialist Republic of Rumania. Information Bulletin (0547-5090)
Published by: Alliance for Peace in Rumania, Str. Biserica Amzei 29, Bucharest, 70172, Romania. TEL 118948.

ALTERNATIVE TRADING NEWS. *see* BUSINESS AND ECONOMICS—International Development And Assistance

327 USA ISSN 0304-3754
HC59.7
➤ **ALTERNATIVES**; global, local, political. Text in English. 1974. q. USD 414, GBP 243 to institutions; USD 422, GBP 248 combined subscription to institutions (print & online eds.) (effective 2012). adv. illus.; abstr. Index. back issues avail.; reprints avail. **Document type:** *Journal, Academic/Scholarly.* **Description:** Explores the possibilities of new forms of political practice and identity under increasing global conditions.
Related titles: Microfiche ed.: (from PQC, WSH); Microfilm ed.: (from PQC, WSH); Online - full text ed.: USD 380, GBP 223 to institutions (effective 2012).
Indexed: A01, A02, A03, A08, A20, A22, A26, ABCPolSci, APW, AltPI, AmHI, CA, CLI, CurCont, DIP, E08, EnvAb, EnvInd, FR, FutSurv, G08, H07, I02, I05, I13, IBR, IBSS, IBZ, LeftInd, M02, MLA-IB, MagInd, P02, P10, P34, P42, P45, PAIS, PCI, PQC, PRA, PSA, R02, RefZh, RefugAb, S02, S03, S09, SCOPUS, SOPODA, SSA, SSCI, SociolAb, T02, W07, WBA, WMB.
—BLDSC (0803.670000), IE, Infotrieve, Ingenta. **CCC.**
Published by: (World Order Models Project, Centre for the Study of Developing Societies, International Peace Research Institute, Meigaku), Sage Publications, Inc., 2455 Teller Rd, Thousand Oaks, CA 91320. TEL 800-818-7243, FAX 800-583-2665, info@sagepub.com, http://www.sagepub.com. Ed. R B J Walker.

327 TUR ISSN 2146-0809
JZ6.5
ALTERNATIVES; Turkish journal of international relations. Text in English. 2002. q. **Document type:** *Journal, Academic/Scholarly.* **Description:** Aims to publish scholarly research on international political, social, economic and legal issues.
Related titles: Online - full text ed.: ISSN 1303-5525. free (effective 2011).
Indexed: A01, A02, A03, A08, CA, I02, M10, P34, PAIS, PSA, R02, S02, S03, SCOPUS, SociolAb, T02.
Published by: Fatih University, Department of International Relations, c/o Bulent Aras, Ed., Buyukcekmece, Istanbul, 34500, Turkey. TEL 90-212-8663300, FAX 90-212-8663337, info@fatih.edu.tr, http://ir.fatih.edu.tr. Ed., Pub. Bulent Aras.

327 ROM ISSN 1841-1487
➤ **AMERICAN, BRITISH AND CANADIAN STUDIES.** Summaries in English; Text in English, French. 1999. s-a. EUR 50 combined subscription (print & online eds.); free to qualified personnel (effective 2009). bk.rev.; film rev.; play rev.; tel.rev.; video rev. illus.; maps. Index. back issues avail.; reprints avail. **Document type:** *Journal, Academic/Scholarly.* **Description:** Sets out to explore the intersections of culture, technology and the human sciences in the age of electronic information. It publishes work by scholars of any nationality on Anglophone studies, comparative literary and cultural studies, postcolonial theory, social and political science, anthropology, area studies, multimedia and digital arts, and related subjects with particular focus on articles addressing influential crosscurrents in English studies. ABC also publishes book reviews and review essays, interviews, conference reports, notes and comments.
Related titles: Online - full text ed.: ISSN 1841-964X.
Indexed: L06.
Published by: Academic Anglophone Society of Romania, Lucian Blaga University, Sibiu, Bulevardul Victoriei 5-7,, Sibiu, 550 024, Romania. TEL 40-269-216062 ext 225, 218, FAX 40-269-217887. Ed. Adriana Neagu. Adv. contact Alexandra Mitrea.

327.73 USA ISSN 1080-3920
E840
AMERICAN FOREIGN POLICY INTERESTS. Text in English. 1977. bi-m. GBP 240 combined subscription in United Kingdom to institutions (print & online eds.); EUR 318, USD 399 combined subscription to institutions (print & online eds.) (effective 2012). adv. bibl. back issues avail.; reprint service avail. from PSC. **Document type:** *Journal, Academic/Scholarly.* **Description:** Aims to publish thought-provoking pieces on these and other matters focusing on American interests in a shifting political and economic environment, including preserving and strengthening open-society countries; improving America's relations with the developing world; advancing human rights; curbing nuclear proliferation and extending arms control agreements; and promoting an open and global world economy.
Former titles (until 1994): American Foreign Policy Newsletter (0738-3169); (until 1982): National Committee on American Foreign Policy. Newsletter
Related titles: Online - full text ed.: ISSN 1533-2128. GBP 216 in United Kingdom to institutions; EUR 286, USD 360 to institutions (effective 2012) (from IngentaConnect).
Indexed: A01, A03, A08, A22, CA, E01, ESPM, I02, P34, P42, P47, PAIS, PQC, PSA, R02, RiskAb, SCOPUS, T02.
—BLDSC (0815.287000), IE, Infotrieve, Ingenta. **CCC.**
Published by: (National Committee on American Foreign Policy), Taylor & Francis Inc. (Subsidiary of: Taylor & Francis Group), 325 Chestnut St, Ste 800, Philadelphia, PA 19106. TEL 215-625-2940, 800-354-1420, orders@taylorandfrancis.com, http://www.taylorandfrancis.com. Ed. Dr. George D Schwab. Adv. contact Linda Hann TEL 44-1344-779945. Circ: 1,500.

AMERICAS (ENGLISH EDITION). *see* HUMANITIES: COMPREHENSIVE WORKS

327 USA ISSN 1936-797X
JL951.A1
AMERICAS QUARTERLY; the policy journal for our hemisphere. Text in English. 2006. q. USD 29.95 (print or online ed.); USD 48 combined subscription (print & online eds.) (effective 2010). adv. back issues avail. **Document type:** *Magazine, Trade.*
Related titles: Online - full text ed.
Indexed: H21, I08, P02, P05, P08, P10, P45, P48, P53, P54, PQC.
Published by: Americas Society, 680 Park Ave, New York, NY 10065. TEL 212-249-8950, 800-733-2388, FAX 212-249-1880, aqinfo@as-coa.org, http://www.as-coa.org. Ed. Christopher Sabatini. Pub. Susan Segal. Circ: 14,000.

AMERICAS REVIEW. *see* BUSINESS AND ECONOMICS—Economic Situation And Conditions

327 CAN ISSN 1195-7166
AMERICAS UPDATE. Text in English. 1979. q. looseleaf. CAD 25 domestic to individuals; CAD 31 foreign to individuals; CAD 40 domestic to institutions; CAD 46 foreign to institutions; CAD 15 to students; CAD 4.50 newsstand/cover (effective 2000). adv. bk.rev. back issues avail. **Document type:** *Bulletin, Consumer.* **Description:** Provides analysis of events in Latin America and the Caribbean; highlights Canada's relations to the region.
Formerly: Central America Update (0823-7689)
Indexed: C03, CBCARef, HRIR, PQC.
—CCC.
Address: 427 Bloor St W, Toronto, ON M5S 1X7, Canada. TEL 416-967-5562, FAX 416-922-8587, amupdate@web.net. Ed. Fiona Connelly. R&P, Adv. contact Carolyn Bassett. Circ: 1,000.

327.17 DEU
AMERIKA - NAHOST - EUROPA; regionalhistorische Komparatistik: Politik, Wirtschaft, Militaer und Kultur. Text in German. 2002. irreg., latest vol.9, 2006. price varies. **Document type:** *Monographic series, Academic/Scholarly.*
Published by: Trafo Verlag, Finkenstr 8, Berlin, 12621, Germany. TEL 49-30-61299418, FAX 49-30-61299421, info@trafoberlin.de, http://www.trafoberlin.de.

364.65 341 DNK ISSN 0906-4184
AMNESTY. Text in Danish. 1967. q. DKK 180 membership (effective 2008). back issues avail. **Document type:** *Magazine, Consumer.*
Former titles (until 1991): Amnesty Nyt (0109-632X); (until 1971): Amnesty International. Dansk Afdeling (1395-590X)
Related titles: Online - full text ed.
Published by: Amnesty International i Danmark, Gammeltorv 8, Copenhagen K, 1457, Denmark. TEL 45-33-456565, FAX 45-33-456566, amnesty@amnesty.dk.

364.65 NLD ISSN 1570-6192
AMNESTY IN ACTIE. Text in Dutch. 2000. m.
Published by: Amnesty International, Dutch Section, Postbus 1968, Amsterdam, 1000 BZ, Netherlands. TEL 31-20-6264436, FAX 31-20-6240889. Eds. Lotte van der Ploeg, Simone Appelman.

364.65 USA ISSN 1932-5053
HV6254
AMNESTY INTERNATIONAL. Text in English. 1966. q. free to members (effective 2009). bk.rev. illus. 16 p./no. 4 cols./p.; back issues avail. **Document type:** *Magazine, Consumer.* **Description:** Discusses Amnesty International's work on behalf of political prisoners worldwide and covers important conferences and other issues of interest to members.
Former titles (until 2004): Amnesty Now (1932-5045); (until 2000): Amnesty Action (0003-1933)
Related titles: Online - full text ed.: ISSN 1936-3699.
Indexed: APW, CJPI, HRIR, LeftInd, M10, PQC, W09.
Published by: Amnesty International U S A, 5 Penn Plz, 14th Fl, New York, NY 10001. TEL 212-807-8400, FAX 212-627-1451, aimember@aiusa.org.

364.65 FRA
AMNESTY INTERNATIONAL RAPPORT ANNUEL. Text in French. 1980. a. **Document type:** *Consumer.*
Related titles: ◆ English ed.: Amnesty International Report. ISSN 0309-068X; Spanish ed.: Amnistia Internacional Informe. 1980; Arabic ed.: 1987.
Published by: Amnesty International, French section, 4 rue de Pierre Lifting, Paris Cedex 11, 75553, France.

364.65 GBR ISSN 0309-068X
JC571
AMNESTY INTERNATIONAL REPORT. Text in English. 1962. a. GBP 25 per issue (effective 2009). maps. 312 p./no.; back issues avail. **Document type:** *Yearbook, Corporate.* **Description:** Documents human rights abuses including prisoners of conscience, political detention without trial, torture, disappearances, and executions in numerous countries around the world.
Formerly (until 1976): Amnesty International Annual Report (0569-9495)
Related titles: Microfiche ed.: (from IDC); Online - full text ed.: ISSN 1564-2119. 1997; ◆ French ed.: Amnesty International Rapport Annuel; Spanish ed.: Amnistia Internacional Informe. 1980; Arabic ed.: 1987; German Translation: Amnesty International Report (Deutsche Edition). ISSN 1866-9794; French Translation: Amnesty International Rapport. ISSN 0252-8312.
Indexed: HRIR, RefugAb.
—BLDSC (0859.395000). **CCC.**
Published by: Amnesty International U K, 17-25 New Inn Yard, London, EC2A 3EA, United Kingdom. TEL 44-20-70331500, FAX 44-20-70331503, sct@amnesty.org.uk.

327 NLD ISSN 1873-3042
AMSTERDAM STUDIES. Text in Dutch, English, Hungarian. 2006. irreg. **Description:** Provides a forum for analyses on political, economic and cultural developments in Europe.
Media: Online - full text.
Published by: Stichting European Committee Human Rights Hungarians Central Europe, Postbus 2492, 's-Hertogenbosch, 5202 CL, Netherlands. TEL 31-87-8724745, FAX 31-87-8304217, info@hungarian-human-rights.eu, http://www.hungarian-human-rights.eu. Ed. Laszlo Maracz.

327 PER ISSN 1021-6340
ANALISIS INTERNACIONAL. Text in Spanish. 1993. q.
Indexed: PAIS.
Published by: Pontificia Universidad Catolica del Peru, Instituto de Estudios Internacionales, Plaza Francia 1164, Lima, 1, Peru. TEL 51-1-3307380, FAX 51-1-3312498, idei@pucp.edu.pe, http://www.pucp.edu.pe/invest/idei.

327 AZE
ANALITIK BAXIS/ANALYTICAL VIEW. Text in Azerbaijani. s-a. back issues avail. **Document type:** *Journal, Academic/Scholarly.*
Published by: Center for Strategic Studies under the President of the Republic of Azerbaijan/Azerbaycan Respublikasinin Prezidenti yaninda Strateji Arasdirmalar Merkezi (S A M), M. Ibrahimov str. 8, Baku, 1005, Azerbaijan. TEL 994-12-5968239, FAX 994-12-4373458, info@sam.gov.az.

327 DEU
ANALYSEN ZUR KULTUR UND GESELLSCHAFT IM OESTLICHEN EUROPA. Text in German. 1992. irreg., latest vol.21, 2009. price varies. **Document type:** *Monographic series, Academic/Scholarly.*
Formerly (until 1999): Veroeffentlichungen zur Kultur und Gesellschaft im Oestlichen Europa
Published by: (Universitaet Bremen, Forschungsstelle Osteuropa/ Bremen University, Research Centre for East European Studies), Lit Verlag, Grevener Str/Fresnostr 2, Muenster, 48159, Germany. TEL 49-251-235091, FAX 49-251-231972, lit@lit-verlag.de.

327 355 DEU ISSN 1864-256X
ANALYSEN ZUR SICHERHEITSPOLITIK/GERMAN STRATEGIC STUDIES. Text in German. 2007. irreg., latest vol.5, 2009. price varies. **Document type:** *Monographic series, Academic/Scholarly.*
Published by: Peter Lang GmbH (Subsidiary of: Peter Lang Publishing Group), Eschborner Landstr 42-50, Frankfurt Am Main, 60489, Germany. TEL 49-69-7807050, FAX 49-69-78070550, zentrale.frankfurt@peterlang.com.

327 NLD ISSN 1385-7304
ANDER NIEUWS. Text in Dutch. 1997. bi-m. EUR 15 (effective 2009). illus. **Document type:** *Newsletter.* **Description:** News and reports of events concerning moral rearmament.
Former titles (until 1997): Nieuw Wereld Nieuws (0028-9876); (until 1962): M R A Morele Herbewapening
Published by: Initiatives of Change Nederland, Amaliastraat 10, The Hague, 2514 JC, Netherlands. TEL 31-70-3643591, FAX 31-70-3617209.

327 306 GBR ISSN 1354-3709
ANGLO-RUSSIAN AFFINITIES. Text in English. 1993. irreg. price varies. **Document type:** *Monographic series, Academic/Scholarly.* **Description:** Seeks to reflect more than four centuries of rich contacts between Russia and Great Britain. Provides a fresh insight into the multi-faceted relationship Russia has had with England and will raise new questions on mutual influences that are currently evolving.
Published by: Berg Publishers (Subsidiary of: Oxford International Publishers Ltd.), 1st Fl Angel Ct, 81 St Clements St, Oxford, Berks OX4 1AW, United Kingdom. TEL 44-1865-245104, FAX 44-1865-791165, enquiry@bergpublishers.com. Eds. Anthony Cross, Geraldine Billingham.

327 GBR
ANGOLA MONITOR. Text in English. 1995. q. free (effective 2009). back issues avail. **Document type:** *Newsletter, Consumer.* **Description:** Follows the progress of peace, stability, development and human rights in the country as it struggles to overcome the legacy of nearly 3 decades of war.
Formerly (until 2009): Angola Peace Monitor
Media: Online - full content.
Published by: A C T S A, 231 Vauxhall Bridge Rd, London, SW1V 1EH, United Kingdom. info@actsa.org.

327.2 FRA ISSN 0066-295X
JX1793
ANNUAIRE DIPLOMATIQUE ET CONSULAIRE DE LA REPUBLIQUE FRANCAISE. Text in French. 1858. a. **Document type:** *Directory, Government.*
Former titles (until 1877): Annuaire Diplomatique de la Republique Francaise (1245-9364); (until 1870): Annuaire Diplomatique de l'Empire Francais (1245-9356)
Published by: France. Ministere des Affaires Etrangeres, 37 Quai d'Orsay, Paris, 75007, France. http://www.diplomatie.gouv.fr.

327 USA ISSN 0198-0300
D839
➤ **ANNUAL EDITIONS: WORLD POLITICS.** Text in English. 1977. a. USD 22.25 per issue (effective 2010). illus. back issues avail. **Document type:** *Journal, Academic/Scholarly.*
Related titles: Online - full text ed.
—CCC.
Published by: McGraw-Hill, Contemporary Learning Series (Subsidiary of: McGraw-Hill Companies, Inc.), 1221 Ave of the Americas, New York, NY 10020. TEL 212-904-2000, FAX 212-512-2000, customer.service@mcgraw-hill.com, http://www.mhhe.com/cls/.

327.172 USA ISSN 1932-5819
JZ6374
ANNUAL REVIEW OF GLOBAL PEACE OPERATIONS. Text in English. 2006. a. USD 27.50 per issue (effective 2010). back issues avail. **Document type:** *Journal, Academic/Scholarly.*
—CCC.
Published by: Lynne Rienner Publishers, 1800 30th St, Ste 314, Boulder, CO 80301. TEL 303-444-6684, FAX 303-444-0824.

327 USA ISSN 0066-4340
JX1977.A1
ANNUAL REVIEW OF UNITED NATIONS AFFAIRS. Abbreviated title: A R U N A. Text in English. 1949. a. USD 120, GBP 80 per issue (effective 2010). back issues avail.; reprints avail. **Document type:** *Monographic series, Academic/Scholarly.* **Description:** Designed for researchers needing a document collection that highlights the work of the United Nations' six principal organs each year.
Published by: Oceana Publications, Inc. (Subsidiary of: Oxford University Press), 75 Main St, Dobbs Ferry, NY 10522. TEL 914-693-8100, FAX 914-693-0402, orders@oceanalaw.com, http://www.oceanalaw.com. **Dist. by:** Oxford University Press, 198 Madison Ave, New York, NY 10016. TEL 212-726-6000, 800-334-4249 ext 6469, FAX 212-726-6476, oxfordonline@oup.com, http://www.us.oup.com.

327 ESP ISSN 1699-8111
HC411
ANUARIO ASIA - PACIFICO. Text in Spanish. 2005. a. EUR 59 (effective 2009). back issues avail. **Document type:** *Yearbook, Consumer.*
Published by: Fundacio C I D O B, C. Elisabets, 12, Barcelona, 08001, Spain. TEL 34-93-3026495, FAX 34-93-3022118, publicaciones@cibod.org, http://www.cibod.org.

328 ESP ISSN 1139-7225
ANUARIO IBEROAMERICANO. Text in Spanish. 1963. a.
Related titles: ◆ Online - full text ed.: Anuario Iberoamericano (Online). ISSN 2174-1050.
Published by: Real Instituto El Cano de Estudios Internacionales y Estrategicos, C. Principe de Vergara, 51, Madrid, 28006, Spain. TEL 34-91-7816770, FAX 34-91-4262157, info@rielcano.org, http://www.realinstitutoelcano.org/.

328 ESP ISSN 2174-1050
ANUARIO IBEROAMERICANO (ONLINE). Text in Spanish. 1963. a. **Document type:** *Journal, Academic/Scholarly.*
Media: Online - full text. **Related titles:** ◆ Print ed.: Anuario Iberoamericano. ISSN 1139-7225.
Published by: (Real Instituto El Cano de Estudios Internacionales y Estrategicos, Instituto de Cultura Hispanica), Ediciones Piramide, Calle Juan Ignacio Luca de Tena 15, Madrid, 28027, Spain. TEL 34-91-3938989, FAX 34-91-7423662, piramide@anaya.es, http://www.edicionespiramide.es.

327 ESP ISSN 1133-2743
DP85.8
ANUARIO INTERNACIONAL C I D O B. (Centre d'Informacio i Documentacio Internacionals a Barcelona) Text in Spanish. 1990. a. EUR 59 (effective 2009). back issues avail. **Document type:** *Yearbook, Consumer.*
Related titles: Online - full text ed.
Indexed: A01, CA, F03, F04, I13, M02, R15, T02.
Published by: Fundacio C I D O B, C. Elisabets, 12, Barcelona, 08001, Spain. TEL 34-93-3026495, FAX 34-93-3022118, publicaciones@cibod.org, http://www.cibod.org.

327 TWN ISSN 1816-3114
AOZHOU YANJIU/TAIWANESE JOURNAL OF AUSTRALIAN STUDIES. Text in Chinese. 2000. a. TWD 300 newsstand/cover (effective 2005). **Document type:** *Journal, Academic/Scholarly.*
Published by: National Chengchi University, Center for Australian Studies, 64,Chih Nan Rd., Sec.2, Taipei, 11623, Taiwan. TEL 886-2-9393091 ext 50903, FAX 886-2-9390173, liu7249@nccu.edu.tw, http://www.ocia.nccu.edu.tw/Australia/. Ed. To-hai Liou.

327 PRT ISSN 1647-9122
APONTAMENTOS EUROPA - AMERICA. Text in Portuguese. 1987. irreg. **Document type:** *Magazine, Consumer.*
Published by: Publicacoes Europa - America, Rua Francisco Lyon de Castro 2, Mem Martins, 2725-354, Portugal. TEL 351-21-9267700, FAX 351-21-9267771, secretariado@europa-america.pt, http://www.europa-america.pt.

327 MEX
APORTES (COLIMA). Text in Spanish. 2000. s-a. MXN 120 domestic; USD 12 foreign (effective 2006). back issues avail. **Document type:** *Journal, Academic/Scholarly.*
Indexed: CA.
Published by: Universidad de Colima, Centro Universitario de Estudios e Investigaciones sobre la Cuenca del Pacifico, Ave Gonzalo de Sandoval, 444, Col La Oriental, Colima, Colima, 28045, Mexico. TEL 52-312-316131, FAX 52-312-316100, ce-apec@cgic.ucol.mx. Ed. Juan Gonzalez Garcia. Circ: 500.

ARAB AMERICAN ALMANAC. *see* ETHNIC INTERESTS

327 GBR ISSN 0196-3538
DS63.1
ARAB - ASIAN AFFAIRS; strategy and geopolitics. Text in English. 1975. 10/yr. USD 375 (effective 2009). back issues avail. **Document type:** *Newsletter.* **Description:** Covers geostrategic developments in the Middle East.
Formerly (until 1980): Afro-Asian Affairs (0163-819X)
Published by: World Reports Ltd., 108 Horseferry Rd, London, SW1P 2EF, United Kingdom. TEL 44-20-72223836, FAX 44-20-72330185, subs@worldreports.org. Ed. Christopher Story.

327 305.8927 USA ISSN 1936-8984
DS63.1
ARAB INSIGHT. Text in English. 2007 (May). q. USD 75 in US & Canada to individuals; USD 85 elsewhere to individuals; USD 100 in US & Canada to institutions; USD 110 elsewhere to institutions (effective 2010). back issues avail. **Document type:** *Journal, Academic/Scholarly.* **Description:** Focuses on the changing political and sociocultural trends of the Arab world.
Related titles: Online - full text ed.: ISSN 1936-8992. 2007 (May).
Indexed: PAIS.
Published by: World Security Institute, 1779 Massachusetts Ave, NW, Washington, DC 20036. TEL 202-332-0900, FAX 202-462-4559, info@worldsecurityinstitute.org.

327 KEN
ARAB WORLD. Text in English, Swahili. 1972. bi-m. illus.
Formerly: Voice of Egypt
Published by: League of Arab States, Uchumi House 10th Fl., PO Box 30770, Nairobi, Kenya.

327 LBN
THE ARAB WORLD. Text in English. 1985. s-m. USD 1,500 (effective 2001). illus. index. **Document type:** *Journal, Consumer.* **Description:** Covers political and economic developments in the Arab world.
Published by: Dar Naaman lith-Thaqafah, P O Box 567, Jounieh, Lebanon. TEL 961-9-935096, FAX 961-9-935096. Ed. Naji Naaman.

ARCHES QUARTERLY. *see* RELIGIONS AND THEOLOGY—Islamic

327 SYR
ARD. Text in Arabic. 1973. fortn. illus.
Published by: Al-Ard Institute of Palestine Studies/Muassasat al-Ard Lil-Dirasat al-Filastiniyah, P O Box 3392, Damascus, Syria.

327 HRV ISSN 0402-9283
ARENA; informativni drustveno politicki ilustrirani tjednik. Text in Croatian. 1959. w. USD 197. **Document type:** *Magazine, Consumer.*
Indexed: EI, RASB.
Published by: Arena d.d., Slavonska Avenija 4, Zagreb, 10000, Croatia. TEL 385-1-6162062, FAX 385-1-6162062.

355 ARG ISSN 0325-0792
ARGENTINA. ESCUELA DE DEFENSA NACIONAL. REVISTA. Text in Spanish. 1973. s-a. Exchange Basis. adv. charts; illus. index. **Document type:** *Government.* **Description:** Articles cover politics, foreign affairs, national defense and geopolitics.
Formerly (until 1974): Argentina. Escuela Nacional de Guerra. Revista (0325-0784)
Related titles: Online - full text ed.
Indexed: AMB.
Published by: Escuela de Defensa Nacional, Maipu, 262, Buenos Aires, 1084, Argentina. TEL 54-114-3261318, FAX 54-114-3253510, http://www.mindef.gov.ar/edn.htm. Ed. Col Eugenio Diaz Jausoro. Circ: 1,600.

327.82 ARG
ARGENTINA. MINISTERIO DE RELACIONES EXTERIORES Y CULTO. REVISTA. Text in Spanish. 1974. q. free.
Published by: Ministerio de Relaciones Exteriores y Culto, Buenos Aires, Argentina.

ARGENTINA WEEKLY FAX BULLETIN. *see* BUSINESS AND ECONOMICS—Economic Situation And Conditions

ARMENIAN INTERNATIONAL MAGAZINE. *see* ETHNIC INTERESTS

227.174 USA ISSN 0195-4741
UF503
ARMS CONTROL IMPACT STATEMENTS. Text in English. 1976. irreg. **Document type:** *Government.*
Published by: U.S. Government Printing Office, 732 N Capitol St, NW, Washington, DC 20401. TEL 202-512-1800, 866-512-1800, FAX 202-512-2104, ContactCenter@gpo.gov, http://www.gpo.gov.

ARMS CONTROL TODAY; the source on nonproliferation and global security. *see* LAW—International Law

327.174 CAN ISSN 0828-3664
ARMS CONTROL VERIFICATION STUDIES. Text in English. irreg. **Document type:** *Government.*
Indexed: LID&ISL.
Published by: Department of Foreign Affairs and International Trade, 125 Sussex Dr, Ottawa, ON K1A 0G2, Canada. TEL 613-944-4000, 800-267-8376, FAX 613-996-9709, enqserv@dfait-maeci.gc.ca.

327 330 AUS ISSN 1449-2946
➤ **AROUND THE GLOBE.** Text in English. 2004. 3/yr. bk.rev. illus. back issues avail.; reprints avail. **Document type:** *Journal, Academic/Scholarly.* **Description:** Covers global movements in their diverse economic, social, political and cultural dimensions.
—CCC.
Published by: Monash University, Monash Institute for the Study of Global Movements, Bldg 6, Clayton Campus, Monash University, Monash, VIC 3800, Australia. TEL 61-3-99051595, FAX 61-3-99052955, globalmovements@education.monash.edu.au. Circ: 2,500 (paid). **Dist. by:** Postscript Printing and Publishing, 212 Bolton St., Eltham, VIC 3095, Australia. postscript@optusnet.com.au.

➤ **ASIA - AFRICA FORUM.** *see* ETHNIC INTERESTS

➤ **ASIA & PACIFIC REVIEW**; the business and economic report. *see* BUSINESS AND ECONOMICS—Economic Situation And Conditions

327 NZL ISSN 1177-0031
ASIA NEW ZEALAND FOUNDATION. OUTLOOK. Text in English. 2005. s-a. **Document type:** *Journal, Academic/Scholarly.* **Description:** Designed to bring together researchers and policy makers through engagement on specific New Zealand-Asia related issues.
Related titles: Online - full text ed.: ISSN 1177-7893. free.
Published by: Asia New Zealand Foundation, Level 7, 36 Customhouse Quay, PO Box 10 144, Wellington, 6143, New Zealand. TEL 64-4-4712320, FAX 64-4-4712330, asianz@asianz.org.nz. Ed. Dr. Andrew Butcher.

382.09930505 NZL ISSN 1177-9586
ASIA NEW ZEALAND FOUNDATION. REVIEW (ONLINE). Variant title: Erview. Text in English. 1999. q. free (effective 2009). back issues avail. **Document type:** *Journal, Trade.*
Media: Online - full text.
Published by: Asia New Zealand Foundation, Level 7, 36 Customhouse Quay, PO Box 10 144, Wellington, 6143, New Zealand. TEL 64-4-4712320, FAX 64-4-4712330, asianz@asianz.org.nz. Ed. Dr. Andrew Butcher.

952.13 USA ISSN 1557-4660
DS821
➤ **THE ASIA - PACIFIC JOURNAL : JAPAN FOCUS.** Key Title: Japan Focus. Text in English, Japanese. 2002. w. free (effective 2011). back issues avail. **Document type:** *Journal, Academic/Scholarly.* **Description:** Offers regional and global perspectives on contemporary issues and conflicts within the Asia Pacific region from researchers, journalists, policy analysts and writers.
Media: Online - full text.
Indexed: CA, M10.
Published by: Japan Focus info.japanfocus@gmail.com.

327 MYS
ASIA - PACIFIC MILITARY BALANCE. Text in English. irreg., latest 1998-1999. MYR 50 domestic; USD 15 in other ASEAN countries; USD 25 in US & Europe; USD 20 elsewhere (effective 2000).
Published by: A D P R Consult (M) Sdn. Bhd., 19th Fl, SIME Bank Bldg, No.4 Jalan Sultan Sulaiman, Kuala Lumpur, 50000, Malaysia. TEL 603-22731355, 603-22735315, FAX 603-22735318, info@adprconsult.com, http://www.adprconsult.com/.

327 GBR ISSN 1343-9006
DS501
➤ **ASIA - PACIFIC REVIEW.** Text in English. 1994. s-a. GBP 216 combined subscription in United Kingdom to institutions (print & online eds.); EUR 288, USD 360 combined subscription to institutions (print & online eds.) (effective 2012). adv. illus. Index. back issues avail.; reprint service avail. from PSC. **Document type:** *Journal, Academic/Scholarly.* **Description:** Analyzes global political, economic, security, energy, and environmental issues, with specific emphasis on the Asia-Pacific region.
Related titles: Online - full text ed.: ISSN 1469-2937. GBP 194 in United Kingdom to institutions; EUR 259, USD 323 to institutions (effective 2012) (from IngentaConnect).
Indexed: A01, A03, A08, A22, B21, BAS, CA, DIP, E01, E17, ESPM, I13, I14, IBR, IBSS, IBZ, IPP, P34, P42, PSA, RiskAb, S02, S03, SCOPUS, SociolAb, T02.
—BLDSC (1742.261520), IE, Infotrieve, Ingenta. **CCC.**
Published by: (Institute for International Policy Studies (IIPS) JPN), Routledge (Subsidiary of: Taylor & Francis Group), 4 Park Sq, Milton Park, Abingdon, Oxon OX14 4RN, United Kingdom. TEL 44-20-70176000, FAX 44-20-70176336, subscriptions@tandf.co.uk, http://www.routledge.com. Ed. Terri Nii. Adv. contact Linda Hann TEL 44-1344-779945. **Subscr. to:** Taylor & Francis Ltd., Journals Customer Service, Sheepen Pl, Colchester, Essex CO3 3LP, United Kingdom. TEL 44-20-70175544, FAX 44-20-70175198.

327.1 950 USA ISSN 1559-0968
DS1
➤ **ASIA POLICY.** Text in English. 2006 (Jan.). s-a. USD 35 in North America to individuals; USD 65 elsewhere to individuals; USD 95 in North America to institutions; USD 125 elsewhere to institutions (effective 2010). back issues avail. **Document type:** *Magazine, Consumer.*
Related titles: Online - full text ed.: ISSN 1559-2960. USD 19.95 (effective 2010).
Indexed: A22.
Published by: National Bureau of Asian Research, 4518 University Way N E, Ste 300, Seattle, WA 98105-4530. TEL 206-632-7370, FAX 206-632-7487, nbr@nbr.org. Ed. Andrew Marble.

327 USA ISSN 0092-7678
DS33.4.U6
➤ **ASIAN AFFAIRS: AN AMERICAN REVIEW.** Key Title: Asian Affairs (New York). Text in English. 1965. q. GBP 132 combined subscription in United Kingdom to institutions (print & online eds.); EUR 175, USD 219 combined subscription to institutions (print & online eds.) (effective 2012). adv. bk.rev. illus.; charts. Index. 60 p./no.; back issues avail.; reprint service avail. from PSC. **Document type:** *Journal, Academic/Scholarly.* **Description:** Focuses on U.S. policy in Asia, as well as on the domestic politics, economics, and international relations of the Asian countries.
Former titles (until 1973): Southeast Asian Perspectives (0042-577X); (until 1971): Vietnam Perspectives (0506-9823)
Related titles: CD-ROM ed.; Microform ed.; Online - full text ed.: ISSN 1940-1590. GBP 119 in United Kingdom to institutions; EUR 157, USD 198 to institutions (effective 2012).

P

Indexed: A01, A02, A03, A08, A22, A26, ABCPolSci, ABS&EES, B04, BAS, BRD, C12, CA, DIP, E01, E08, ENW, G08, HistAb, I02, I05, I07, I08, I13, IBR, IBZ, M01, M02, M10, MASUSE, MEA&I, P02, P06, P10, P14, P34, P42, P45, P47, P48, P53, P54, PAIS, PCI, PQC, PSA, PerIslam, R02, RASB, S02, S03, S05, S09, S23, SCOPUS, SSAI, SSAb, SSI, SociolAb, T02, W03, W05.
—BLDSC (1742.270500), IE, Ingenta. **CCC.**
Published by: (American-Asian Educational Exchange, Inc.), Routledge (Subsidiary of: Taylor & Francis Group), 325 Chestnut St, Ste 800, Philadelphia, PA 19106. TEL 215-625-8900, FAX 215-625-2940, journals@routledge.com, http://www.routledge.com. **Co-sponsor:** Helen Dwight Reid Educational Foundation.

327.117 AUS ISSN 1838-8574
▼ **ASIAN CONFLICT REPORTS.** Text in English. 2009. bi-m. free (effective 2011). back issues avail. **Document type:** *Report, Trade.*
Media: Online - full text.
Published by: Council for Asian Transnational Threats Research, c/o Macquarie University, North Ryde, NSW 2109, Australia. cziemke@ida.org.

ASIAN DEFENCE AND DIPLOMACY. *see* MILITARY

ASIAN PERSPECTIVE. *see* POLITICAL SCIENCE

330 USA ISSN 1943-0779
DS33.3
▼ ➤ **ASIAN POLITICS AND POLICY.** Text in English. 2009. q. USD 1,471 combined subscription in the Americas to institutions (print & online eds.); GBP 1,081 combined subscription in United Kingdom to institutions (print & online eds.); EUR 1,373 combined subscription in Europe to institutions (print & online eds.); USD 2,119 combined subscription elsewhere to institutions (print & online eds.); USD 1,336 in the Americas to institutions (print or online ed.); GBP 982 in United Kingdom to institutions (print or online ed.); EUR 1,248 in Europe to institutions (print or online ed.); USD 1,925 elsewhere to institutions (print or online ed.) (effective 2010). adv. **Document type:** *Journal, Academic/Scholarly.* **Description:** Covers issues related to the domestic and international affairs of Asia.
Related titles: Online - full text ed.: ISSN 1943-0787. 2009.
Indexed: A22, A26, CA, E01, E08, I05, P42, PAIS, PSA, T02.
—BLDSC (1742.717500), IE. **CCC.**
Published by: (Policy Studies Organization), Wiley-Blackwell Publishing, Inc. (Subsidiary of: Wiley-Blackwell Publishing Ltd.), Commerce Pl, 350 Main St, Malden, MA 02148. TEL 781-388-8206, 800-835-6770, FAX 781-388-8232, info@wiley.com, http://www.wiley.com/WileyCDA/. Ed. David Zhigong. Adv. contact Kristin McCarthy TEL 201-748-7683.

327 USA ISSN 1944-8732
JZ1403
ASSOCIATION FOR DIPLOMATIC STUDIES AND TRAINING. NEWSLETTER. Text in English. irreg. **Document type:** *Newsletter.*
Related titles: Online - full text ed.
Published by: Association for Diplomatic Studies and Training, c/o Bentley, 2814 N Underwood St, Arlington, VA 22213. TEL 703-302-6990, FAX 703-302-6799, admin@adst.org, http://www.adst.org.

ASTROPOLITICS; the international journal of space politics and policy. *see* ASTRONOMY

327.117 ESP
➤ **ATHENA INTELLIGENCE JOURNAL.** Text in English, Spanish. 2006. q. free (effective 2010). back issues avail. **Document type:** *Journal, Academic/Scholarly.* **Description:** Focuses on theoretical and empirical studies on insurgency and terrorism.
Formerly (until Oct. 2007): Athena Occasional Papers (1988-5237)
Media: Online - full text.
Indexed: CA, I02, P42, PAIS, T02.
Published by: Athena Intelligence, C/Rector Lopez Argueta, Granada, 18001, Spain. contact@athenaintelligence.org, http://www.athenaintelligence.org. Ed., Adv. contact Javier Jordan Enamorado.

327 IND ISSN 0973-306X
D861
ATLANTIC JOURNAL OF WORLD AFFAIRS. Text in English. 2005. q. INR 250 per issue (effective 2011). back issues avail. **Document type:** *Journal, Academic/Scholarly.* **Description:** Contains information about world affairs.
Published by: Atlantic Publishers & Distributors, 7/22, Ansari Rd, Darya Ganj, New Delhi, 110002, India. TEL 91-11-40775252, 91-11-23285873, info@atlanticbooks.com. Ed. Dr. K R Gupta TEL 91-11-40775300.

327 NLD ISSN 0167-1847
UA646
ATLANTISCH PERSPECTIEF. Text in Dutch. 1963. 8/yr. EUR 25; EUR 20 to students (effective 2010). adv. bk.rev. **Document type:** *Journal, Academic/Scholarly.* **Description:** Covers issues related to international security.
Formerly (until 1979): Atlantische Tijdingen (0067-0235); Incorporates (1980-1991): Atlantisch Nieuws (0167-1898)
Indexed: KES.
Published by: Stichting Atlantische Commissie, Bezuidenhoutseweg 237a-239a, The Hague, 2594 AM, Netherlands. TEL 31-70-3639495, FAX 31-70-3646309, info@atlcom.nl. Ed. David den Dunnen.

327 AUS ISSN 0519-5950
D839.3
AUSTRALIA. DEPARTMENT OF FOREIGN AFFAIRS AND TRADE. SELECT DOCUMENTS ON INTERNATIONAL AFFAIRS. Text in English. 1954. a. price varies. **Document type:** *Government.* **Description:** Contains the texts of new multilateral treaties of importance to Australia.
Incorporates: Australia. Department of Foreign Affairs. International Treaties and Conventions (0084-7135)
Published by: Department of Foreign Affairs and Trade, Treaties Secretariat, R.G. Casey Bldg., John McEwen Cresc., Barton, ACT 0221, Australia. TEL 61-2-62611111, FAX 61-2-62613111, http://www.dfat.gov.au. **Subscr. to:** Australian Government. Information Management Office, Sales and Distribution, PO Box 84, Canberra, ACT 2600, Australia.

327.940 AUS ISSN 1321-1080
AUSTRALIA-INDIA COUNCIL. ANNUAL REPORT. Text in English. 1993. a. **Document type:** *Journal, Trade.*
—CCC.
Published by: Department of Foreign Affairs and Trade, Australia-India Council, PO Box 5363, Kingston, ACT 2604, Australia. TEL 61-2-62613833, FAX 61-2-61123833, ausindia.council@dfat.gov.au, http://www.dfat.gov.au/aic/index.html.

327 AUS ISSN 1836-1803
▼ ➤ **AUSTRALIAN AND NEW ZEALAND JOURNAL OF EUROPEAN STUDIES.** Text in English. 2009 (Jun.). s-a. free to qualified personnel (effective 2009). bk.rev. abstr. back issues avail. **Document type:** *Journal, Academic/Scholarly.* **Description:** Covers contemporary European issues and studies.
Published by: Contemporary European Studies Association of Australia, PO Box 2125, Hawthorn, VIC 3122, Australia. cesaa@cesaa.org.au, http://www.cesaa.org.au/. **Co-publisher:** European Union Studies Association of New Zealand.

327.172 AUS ISSN 1833-9603
➤ **THE AUSTRALIAN CENTRE FOR PEACE AND CONFLICT STUDIES. OCCASIONAL PAPERS SERIES.** Variant title: A C P A C S Occasional Paper Series. Text in English. 2006. irreg., latest vol.12, 2008. back issues avail. **Document type:** *Monographic series, Academic/Scholarly.*
Related titles: Online - full text ed.: ISSN 1833-9611.
Published by: University of Queensland, Australian Centre for Peace and Conflict Studies, Social Sciences Temporary Bldg 31B, Level 2, Room 205, Brisbane, QLD 4072, Australia. TEL 61-7-33651763, FAX 61-7-33468796, acpacs@uq.edu.au, http://www.uq.edu.au/acpacs.

327.94 AUS ISSN 1035-7718
DU80
➤ **AUSTRALIAN JOURNAL OF INTERNATIONAL AFFAIRS.** Abbreviated title: A J I A. Text in English. 1947. q. GBP 406 combined subscription in United Kingdom to institutions (print & online eds.); EUR 537, AUD 610, USD 672 combined subscription to institutions (print & online eds.) (effective 2012). adv. bk.rev. charts; illus. Index. back issues avail.; reprint service avail. from PSC. **Document type:** *Journal, Academic/Scholarly.* **Description:** Aims to publish high quality scholarly research on international political, social, economic and legal issues within the Asia-Pacific region.
Formerly (until 1990): Australian Outlook (0004-9913)
Related titles: Microfilm ed.; Online - full text ed.: ISSN 1465-332X. GBP 365 in United Kingdom to institutions; EUR 483, AUD 549, USD 604 to institutions (effective 2012) (from IngentaConnect).
Indexed: A01, A02, A03, A08, A11, A20, A22, ABCPolSci, AMB, APEL, ASCA, AmH&L, AmHI, AusPAIS, BAS, BrHumI, C12, CA, CurCont, DIP, E01, EI, ESPM, GEOBASE, GdIns, H07, HistAb, I08, I13, IBR, IBSS, IBZ, LeftInd, MEA&I, P02, P06, P10, P30, P34, P42, P45, P47, P48, P53, P54, PAIS, PCI, PQC, PSA, PerIslam, RASB, RiskAb, S02, S03, SCOPUS, SPPI, SSCI, SSciA, SociolAb, T02, W04, W07, WBA, WMB.
—IE, Infotrieve, Ingenta. **CCC.**
Published by: (Australian Institute of International Affairs), Routledge (Subsidiary of: Taylor & Francis Group), Level 2, 11 Queens Rd, Melbourne, VIC 3004, Australia. TEL 61-03-90098134, FAX 61-03-98668822, http://www.informaworld.com. Circ: 2,600. **Subscr. in N. America to:** Taylor & Francis Inc., Customer Services Dept, 325 Chestnut St, 8th Fl, Philadelphia, PA 19106. TEL 215-625-8900, 800-354-1420, FAX 215-625-2940, customerservice@taylorandfrancis.com; **Subscr. to:** Taylor & Francis Ltd., Journals Customer Service, Sheepen Pl, Colchester, Essex CO3 3LP, United Kingdom. TEL 44-20-70175544, FAX 44-20-70175198, tf.enquiries@tfinforma.com.

327.172 AUS ISSN 1833-993X
➤ **AUSTRALIAN JOURNAL OF PEACE STUDIES.** Text in English. 2006. a. free (effective 2009). back issues avail. **Document type:** *Journal, Academic/Scholarly.* **Description:** Covers a broad range of peace issues, particularly with a focus on the Asia-Pacific region.
Media: Online - full text.
Indexed: S02, S03.
Published by: Peace Organisation of Australia, Inc., 87 Smith St, Thornbury, VIC 3071, Australia. TEL 61-4-967233, peace@poa.org.au, http://www.poa.org.au. Eds. Aron Paul, Tim Wright.

354.9 AUS ISSN 0815-4562
J905
AUSTRALIAN SECURITY INTELLIGENCE ORGANIZATION. ANNUAL REPORT TO PARLIAMENT. Text in English. 1984. a. **Document type:** *Journal, Trade.*
Formerly (until 1985): Australian Security Intelligence Organization. Annual Report (0813-6408)
—CCC.
Published by: Australian Security Intelligence Organization, GPO Box 2176, Canberra, ACT 2601, Australia. TEL 61-2-62496299, http://www.asio.gov.au.

327 USA ISSN 0005-0520
DB1
AUSTRIAN INFORMATION. Text in English. 1947. m. free. bk.rev. illus. **Document type:** *Newsletter.*
Related titles: Microform ed.: (from PQC); Online - full text ed.
Indexed: P06.
Published by: Austrian Press and Information Service, 3524 International Ct, N W, Washington, DC 20008-3035. TEL 202-895-6775, FAX 202-895-6772, TELEX 440010. Ed. Martin Eichtinger. Circ: 18,000.

AYIN L'TZION. *see* ETHNIC INTERESTS

327 AZE ISSN 2071-5900
▼ ➤ **AZERBAIJAN FOCUS;** journal of international affairs. Text in English. 2009. s-a. back issues avail. **Document type:** *Journal, Academic/Scholarly.* **Description:** Covers Azerbaijan's international relations, including foreign policy, energy strategy, etc.
Related titles: Online - full text ed.: free (effective 2011).
Published by: Center for Strategic Studies under the President of the Republic of Azerbaijan/Azerbaycan Respublikasinin Prezidenti yaninda Strateji Arasdirmalar Merkezi (S A M), M. Ibrahimov str. 8, Baku, 1005, Azerbaijan. TEL 994-12-5968239, FAX 994-12-4373458, info@sam.gov.az. Circ: 400.

327.4754 USA ISSN 1075-086X
DK690
AZERBAIJAN INTERNATIONAL. Text in Azerbaijani, English. 1993. q. USD 36 domestic; USD 40 in Canada; USD 50 elsewhere (effective 2005). adv. illus. back issues avail. **Document type:** *Magazine, Consumer.* **Description:** Introduces Western audiences to a wide range of topics about Azerbaijan, including current affairs, international relations, and its culture.
Related titles: Online - full text ed.
Indexed: ENW, LeftInd, M10.
Address: PO Box 5217, Sherman Oaks, CA 91413. TEL 818-785-0077, FAX 818-997-7337. Ed. Betty A Blair. Pub., Adv. contact Pirouz Khanlou. R&P Judith Scott. Circ: 7,000.

327 RUS ISSN 0005-2574
➤ **AZIYA I AFRIKA SEGODNYA/ASIA AND AFRICA TODAY.** Text in Russian. 1947. m. USD 298 foreign (effective 2010). index. **Document type:** *Journal, Academic/Scholarly.*
Indexed: AmH&L, CCA, EI, HistAb, P30.
—CCC.
Published by: (Rossiiskaya Akademiya Nauk, Institut Vostokovedeniya), Izdatel'stvo Nauka, Profsoyuznaya ul 90, Moscow, 117864, Russian Federation. TEL 7-095-3347151, FAX 7-095-4202220, secret@naukaran.ru, http://www.naukaran.ru. **Dist. by:** East View Information Services, 10601 Wayzata Blvd, Minneapolis, MN 55305. TEL 952-252-1201, 800-477-1005, FAX 952-252-1202, info@eastview.com, http://www.eastview.com. **Co-sponsor:** Rossiiskaya Akademiya Nauk, Institut Afriki.

341.72 GBR
B A S I C NOTES. Text in English. 1995. irreg., latest 2007. free to members (effective 2010). back issues avail. **Document type:** *Newsletter, Trade.*
Published by: British American Security Information Council, The Grayston Centre, 2nd Fl, 28 Charles Sq, London, N1 6HT, United Kingdom. TEL 44-20-73244680, FAX 44-20-73244681, basicuk@basicint.org.

341.72 GBR ISSN 1353-0402
B A S I C PAPERS; occasional papers on international security issues. Text in English. 1995 (no.10). irreg., latest vol.57, 2008. **Document type:** *Bulletin.*
Related titles: Online - full text ed.
Published by: British American Security Information Council, The Grayston Centre, 2nd Fl, 28 Charles Sq, London, N1 6HT, United Kingdom. TEL 44-20-73244680, FAX 44-20-73244681, basicuk@basicint.org.

341.72 GBR ISSN 0966-9175
B A S I C REPORTS; newsletter on international security policy. Text in English. 1989. irreg. (every 6-8 wks). GBP 30, USD 50; GBP 3, USD 5 per issue (effective 2010). back issues avail. **Document type:** *Newsletter, Trade.*
Formerly (until 1991): B A S I C Reports on European Arms Control (0966-3266)
—CCC.
Published by: British American Security Information Council, The Grayston Centre, 2nd Fl, 28 Charles Sq, London, N1 6HT, United Kingdom. TEL 44-20-73244680, FAX 44-20-73244681.

341.72 GBR
B A S I C RESEARCH REPORTS. Text in English. 19??. irreg., latest vol.2, 2007. GBP 100, USD 150; GBP 7, USD 10 per issue (effective 2010). back issues avail. **Document type:** *Bulletin.*
Related titles: Online - full text ed.: free (effective 2010).
Published by: British American Security Information Council, The Grayston Centre, 2nd Fl, 28 Charles Sq, London, N1 6HT, United Kingdom. TEL 44-20-73244680, FAX 44-20-73244681, basicuk@basicint.org.

B C VOICE. *see* WOMEN'S INTERESTS

327 DEU
B I C C BRIEF. Text in English; Summaries in English, German. 1995. irreg., latest vol.37, 2008. free (effective 2009). back issues avail. **Document type:** *Monographic series, Academic/Scholarly.* **Description:** Explores various aspects of converting military resources to civilian use.
Related titles: Online - full text ed.
Published by: Bonn International Center for Conversion, An der Elisabethkirche 25, Bonn, 53113, Germany. TEL 49-228-911960, FAX 49-228-241215, bicc@bicc.de.

327 DEU
B I C C BULLETIN. Text in German. 1996. q. free (effective 2009). back issues avail. **Document type:** *Newsletter, Academic/Scholarly.* **Description:** Examines various issues concerning the conversion of military resources to civilian use and for civilian benefit.
Published by: Bonn International Center for Conversion, An der Elisabethkirche 25, Bonn, 53113, Germany. TEL 49-228-911960, FAX 49-228-241215, bicc@bicc.de.

327 DEU
B I C C PAPER. Text in English; Summaries in German. 1995. irreg., latest vol.53, 2006. free (effective 2009). back issues avail. **Document type:** *Monographic series, Academic/Scholarly.* **Description:** Reports on the conversion of military resources to civilian use in various contexts.
Published by: Bonn International Center for Conversion, An der Elisabethkirche 25, Bonn, 53113, Germany. TEL 49-228-911960, FAX 49-228-241215, bicc@bicc.de.

327 DEU ISSN 0947-7330
B I C C REPORT. Text in English; Summaries in English, German. 1995. irreg., latest vol.14, 2000. free (effective 2009). back issues avail. **Document type:** *Monographic series, Academic/Scholarly.* **Description:** Presents research on all aspects of converting military resources to civilian use and benefit.
Published by: Bonn International Center for Conversion, An der Elisabethkirche 25, Bonn, 53113, Germany. TEL 49-228-911960, FAX 49-228-241215, bicc@bicc.de.

327 LBN
BACKGROUND REPORTS. Text in Arabic. 3/m. adv.
Published by: Dar As-Sayad S.A.L., C/o Said Freiha, Hazmieh, P O Box 1038, Beirut, Lebanon. TEL 961-5-456373, FAX 961-5-452700, contactpr@csi.com, alanwar@alanwar.com, http://www.alanwar.com. Ed. Hassan El Khoury. Adv. contact Said Freiha.

327 GBR ISSN 0969-6040
BAILRIGG MEMORANDA. Text in English. 1992. irreg., latest 39. price varies. back issues avail. **Document type:** *Monographic series, Academic/Scholarly.*
Related titles: Online - full text ed.: free (effective 2009).
Indexed: LID&ISL.
Published by: University of Lancaster, Centre for Defence & International Security Studies, PO Box 801, Lancaster, LA1 9DX, United Kingdom. TEL 44-1524-221585, FAX 44-1524-221585, info@cdiss.org, http://www.cdiss.org/.

341.72 GBR ISSN 0969-6032
BAILRIGG PAPERS ON INTERNATIONAL SECURITY. Text in English. 1980. irreg., latest vol.31. price varies. **Document type:** *Monographic series, Academic/Scholarly.* **Description:** Provides information about defence and international security.
Related titles: Online - full text ed.
Indexed: LID&ISL.
Published by: University of Lancaster, Centre for Defence & International Security Studies, PO Box 801, Lancaster, LA1 9DX, United Kingdom. TEL 44-1524-221585, FAX 44-1524-221585, info@cdiss.org, http://www.cdiss.org/. Ed. Martin Edmonds.

327 USA
BALTIC CHRONOLOGY. Text in English. 1986. m. USD 40. back issues avail. **Document type:** *Newsletter.* **Description:** Summarizes important events in Lithuania, Latvia, and Estonia from various government, scholarly, and news sources.
Published by: United Baltic Appeal (U B A - B A T U N), 115 W 183rd St, Bronx, NY 10453. TEL 718-367-8802, FAX 718-562-7434. Eds. Janis Riekstins, Raimonds Kerno. Circ: 1,000 (paid).

341.734 EST ISSN 1736-1834
DK502.75
BALTIC HORIZONS. Text in English. 1990. q. EUR 3.19 per issue (effective 2011). **Document type:** *Journal, Academic/Scholarly.* **Description:** Analyses, documents and forecasts on current development in Estonia, Latvia and Lithuania.
Formerly (until 2004): Monthly Survey of Baltic and Post-Soviet Politics (1406-6165)
Related titles: ◆ Series of: EuroUniversity. Series. International Relations. ISSN 1406-4812.
Published by: Euroakadeemia, Mustamae tee 4, Tallinn, 10621, Estonia. TEL 372-6-115801, FAX 372-6-115811, euro@euroakadeemia.ee. Circ: 300.

327 BGD ISSN 1010-9536
BANGLADESH INSTITUTE OF INTERNATIONAL AND STRATEGIC STUDIES JOURNAL. Variant title: B I I S S Journal. Text in English. 1980. q. BDT 300, USD 40 (effective 2005). **Document type:** *Journal, Academic/Scholarly.* **Description:** Covers international affairs, security and development issues in national, regional and global perspective.
Indexed: I13.
Published by: Bangladesh Institute of International and Strategic Studies, 1/46 Old Elephant Rd., Eskaton, Dhaka, 1000, Bangladesh. TEL 880-2-8315808, FAX 880-2-8312625, info@biiss.org.

327 BGD
BANGLADESH. MINISTRY OF FOREIGN AFFAIRS. LIST OF THE DIPLOMATIC CORPS AND OTHER FOREIGN REPRESENTATIVES. Text in English. irreg. BDT 5.75. **Document type:** *Government.*
Published by: Ministry of Foreign Affairs, Dhaka, Bangladesh.

327 USA ISSN 0067-4419
JX1977.A37
BASIC FACTS ABOUT THE UNITED NATIONS. Text in English. 1947. irreg. USD 15 per issue (effective 2008). back issues avail. **Document type:** *Monographic series, Consumer.* **Description:** Provides information about the work of the organization in such areas as peace, development, human rights, humanitarian assistance, disarmament and international law.
Related titles: Online - full text ed.: USD 12 per issue (effective 2008).
—**CCC.**
Published by: United Nations Publications, 2 United Nations Plaza, Rm DC2-853, New York, NY 10017. TEL 212-963-8302, 800-253-9646, FAX 212-963-3489, publications@un.org, https://unp.un.org.

327 TUR ISSN 1303-9555
BASIC FACTS AND FIGURES ON O I C MEMBER COUNTRIES (YEAR). (Organisation of the Islamic Conference) Text in English. 2001. a. **Document type:** *Journal, Trade.*
Related titles: Online - full text ed.: free (effective 2009).
Published by: (Organisation of the Islamic Conference), Statistical Economic and Social Research and Training Centre for Islamic Countries, Attar Sokak, No: 4, Gaziosmanpasa, Ankara, 06700, Turkey. TEL 90-312-4686172, FAX 90-312-4673458, oicankara@sesrtcic.org.

327 DEU
BEGEGNUNG UND AUSTAUSCH MIT FRANZOSEN. Text in German. 1973. a. free (effective 2009). **Document type:** *Journal, Trade.*
Published by: Deutsch-Franzoesisches Jugendwerk, Molkenmarkt 1, Berlin, 10179, Germany. TEL 49-30-2887570, FAX 49-30-28875788, info@dfjw.org.

327.117 GBR ISSN 1943-4472
▼ **BEHAVIORAL SCIENCES OF TERRORISM AND POLITICAL AGGRESSION.** Text in English. 2009. 3/yr. GBP 230 combined subscription in United Kingdom to institutions (print & online eds.); EUR 344, USD 459 combined subscription to institutions (print & online eds.) (effective 2012). **Document type:** *Journal, Academic/Scholarly.* **Description:** Aims to address the complex causation and effects of terrorist activity by bringing together timely, consistently scientifically and theoretically sound, papers addressing terrorism from a behavioral science perspective, (encompassing biological, evolutionary, developmental, ecological, personality, social, military, and neuroscience approaches to psychology).
Annouced as: Interdisciplinary Research on Terrorism and Political Violence
Related titles: Online - full text ed.: ISSN 1943-4480. 2009. GBP 207 in United Kingdom to institutions; EUR 310, USD 413 to institutions (effective 2012).
Indexed: CA, I02, P46, P48, P54, PQC, T02.
—IE. **CCC.**
Published by: (Society for Terrorism Research USA), Taylor & Francis Ltd. (Subsidiary of: Taylor & Francis Group), 4 Park Sq, Milton Park, Abingdon, Oxfordshire OX14 4RN, United Kingdom. TEL 44-1235-828600, FAX 44-1235-829000, info@tandf.co.uk. Eds. Daniel Antonius, Dr. Samuel J Sinclair.

327 CAN ISSN 0005-7983
BEHIND THE HEADLINES. Text in English. 1940. q. CAD 19.95 domestic; USD 19.95 foreign; CAD 4.95 newsstand/cover (effective 2000). bk.rev. illus. Index. reprints avail. **Description:** Presents a news magazine on current international affairs for the general reader.
Related titles: Microfilm ed.: (from PQC); Online - full text ed.
Indexed: A22, A26, ABS&EES, BRD, C03, CA, CBCARef, CBPI, CPerI, G05, G06, G07, G08, I05, I06, I07, M02, P48, PQC, PRA, R03, RASB, RGAb, RGPR, S23, T02, W03, W05.
—CIS, IE, Infotrieve.
Published by: Canadian Institute of International Affairs, 205 Richmond St West, Ste 302, Toronto, ON M5V 1V3, Canada. TEL 416-487-6830, FAX 416-487-6831, copeland@ciia.org, http://www.ciia.org. R&P Michelle McAlear. Circ: 1,800.

327 CHN ISSN 1003-6539
BEIJING DI-ER WAIGUOYU XUEYUAN XUEBAO/BEIJING INTERNATIONAL STUDIES UNIVERSITY. JOURNAL. Text in Chinese. 1979. bi-m. USD 49.20 (effective 2009). **Document type:** *Journal, Academic/Scholarly.*
Related titles: Online - full text ed.
Published by: Beijing Di-2 Waiguoyu Xueyuan/Beijing International Studies University, 1, Dingfuzhuang Nan Li, Beijing, 100024, China. http://www.bisu.edu.cn/.

327 DEU
BEITRAEGE ZUR FRIEDENSFORSCHUNG UND SICHERHEITSPOLITIK. Text in German. 2001. irreg., latest vol.29, 2008. price varies. **Document type:** *Monographic series, Academic/Scholarly.*
Published by: Verlag Dr. Koester, Rungestr 22-24, Berlin, 10179, Germany. TEL 49-30-76403224, FAX 49-30-76403227, verlag-koester@t-online.de.

327 DEU ISSN 0175-6087
BEITRAEGE ZUR SOZIALFORSCHUNG. Text in German. 1982. irreg., latest vol.10, 2005. price varies. **Document type:** *Monographic series, Academic/Scholarly.*
Published by: Duncker und Humblot GmbH, Carl-Heinrich-Becker-Weg 9, Berlin, 12165, Germany. TEL 49-30-7900060, FAX 49-30-79000631, info@duncker-humblot.de.

327 DEU ISSN 1431-0341
BERLINER EUROPA-STUDIEN. Text in German. 1994. irreg., latest vol.8, 2000. price varies. **Document type:** *Monographic series, Academic/Scholarly.*
Published by: Verlag Dr. Koester, Rungestr 22-24, Berlin, 10179, Germany. TEL 49-30-76403224, FAX 49-30-76403227, verlag-koester@t-online.de. Ed. Volker Nessler.

327 DEU
BEWAFFNETE KONFLIKTE NACH DEM ENDE DES OST-WEST-KONFLIKTES. Text in German. 1996. irreg., latest vol.20, 2007. price varies. **Document type:** *Monographic series, Academic/Scholarly.*
Published by: Verlag Dr. Koester, Rungestr 22-24, Berlin, 10179, Germany. TEL 49-30-76403224, FAX 49-30-76403227, verlag-koester@t-online.de.

BEYOND BOUNDARIES: CANADIAN DEFENCE AND STRATEGIC STUDIES. *see* MILITARY

341.72 RUS ISSN 1607-7334
JZ6009.R8
BEZOPASNOST' EVRAZII. Text in Russian. 2000. q. USD 199 foreign (effective 2004). **Document type:** *Magazine.* **Description:** A private nonprofit magazine about security of private individuals, national and collective security and modern civilization.
Indexed: RefZh.
—East View.
Published by: Redaktsiya Zhurnala Bezopasnost' Evrazii, ul Akademika Pilyugina, 14, korp 2, k 861, Moscow, 117393, Russian Federation. TEL 7-095-1327615. Ed. G M Sergeev. **Dist. by:** East View Information Services, 10601 Wayzata Blvd, Minneapolis, MN 55305. TEL 952-252-1201, 800-477-1005, FAX 952-252-1202, info@eastview.com, http://www.eastview.com.

BIO-DIPLOMACY AND INTERNATIONAL COOPERATION. *see* ENVIRONMENTAL STUDIES

LES BIOGRAPHIES.COM. CORPS DIPLOMATIQUE ET CONSULAIRE, CONSEILLERS ET ATTACHES COMMERCIAUX ET FINANCIERS. *see* BIOGRAPHY

BIOTERRORISM AND PUBLIC HEALTH; an internet resource guide. *see* PUBLIC HEALTH AND SAFETY

341.734 362.1 USA ISSN 1547-8602
BIOTERRORISM WEEK. Text in English. 2002. w. USD 2,295 in US & Canada; USD 2,495 elsewhere; USD 2,525 combined subscription in US & Canada (print & online eds.); USD 2,755 combined subscription elsewhere (print & online eds.) (effective 2008). back issues avail. **Document type:** *Newsletter, Trade.* **Description:** This report gathers the latest discussion and research about the possibilities of biological terrorism and warfare and includes drug development, bacterial and viral research, governmental regulations, funding, and technology.
Formerly (until 2003): Bioterrorism.Info (1537-7717)
Related titles: E-mail ed.; Online - full text ed.: Bioterrorism Week (Online). ISSN 1547-8599. USD 2,295 combined subscription (online & email eds.); single user (effective 2008).
Indexed: A26, G08, H12, I05, M06, P15, P19, P20, P21, P47, P48, P50, P52, P54, P56, PQC.
—CIS.
Published by: NewsRx, 2727 Paces Ferry Rd SE, Ste 2-440, Atlanta, GA 30339. TEL 770-435-8286, 800-726-4550, FAX 770-435-6800, pressrelease@newsrx.com. Ed. Carol Kohn. Pub. Susan Hasty TEL 770-507-7777.

BLACK WORLD TIME. *see* ETHNIC INTERESTS

327 DEU ISSN 0006-4416
D839
BLAETTER FUER DEUTSCHE UND INTERNATIONALE POLITIK. Text in German. 1956. m. EUR 75.60; EUR 9 newsstand/cover (effective 2009). adv. bk.rev. bibl.; stat. index. 128 p./no.; back issues avail.; reprints avail. **Document type:** *Journal, Academic/Scholarly.*
Related titles: Online - full text ed.
Indexed: A22, BAS, DIP, ELLIS, I13, IBR, IBZ, P30, PAIS, PCI, PRA, RASB.
—Infotrieve. **CCC.**
Published by: Blaetter Verlagsgesellschaft mbH, Torstr 178, Berlin, 10115, Germany. TEL 49-30-30883640, FAX 49-30-30883645, info@blaetter.de. Eds. Annett Maengel, Daniel Leisegang. Pub. Annett Maengel. Adv. contact Daniel Leisegang. B&W page EUR 925; trim 118 x 295. Circ: 7,700 (paid and controlled).

THE BLUE BERET (ONLINE). *see* LAW—International Law

327 DEU ISSN 0944-467X
BLUE PRINT; journal of culture and science. Text in German, English, French. 1997. irreg. **Document type:** *Journal, Consumer.*
Media: Online - full text.
Address: Postfach 165, Petershausen, 85236, Germany. wiesner@lexpress.net, http://members.aol.com/bluemagzin/newblue.html. Ed. Dr. Wolfgang Wiesner.

327 GRC
BLUELINE; Greek and Mediterranean report. Text in English. m. Supplement avail.
Indexed: AmHI.
Published by: (Institute of Political Studies), Dimitris Dimopolous, 28 Pericleous St, Nea Halkidona, Athens 143 43, Greece.

327.26 ESP ISSN 1989-8495
BOLETIN ECOS. Text in Spanish. 2008. bi-m. back issues avail. **Document type:** *Bulletin, Consumer.*
Media: Online - full text.
Published by: Fundacion Hogar del Empleado, Centro de Investigacion para la Paz, Duque de Sesto, 40, Madrid, 28009, Spain. TEL 34-91-5763299, FAX 34-91-5774726, http://www.fuhemes/.

327 DEU
BONN INTERNATIONAL CENTER FOR CONVERSION. JAHRESBERICHT. Cover title: Conversion Survey. Text in English; Summaries in German. 1996. a. back issues avail. **Document type:** *Journal, Trade.* **Description:** Discusses issues concerning the converting of military resources to civilian use and benefit.
Formerly (until 2005): B I C C Yearbook. Conversion Survey (1463-8436)
Published by: Bonn International Center for Conversion, An der Elisabethkirche 25, Bonn, 53113, Germany. TEL 49-228-911960, FAX 49-228-241215, bicc@bicc.de.

327 DEU ISSN 1869-7186
▼ **BONNER STUDIEN ZUM GLOBALEN WANDEL.** Text in German. 2009. irreg., latest vol.7, 2010. price varies. **Document type:** *Monographic series, Academic/Scholarly.*
Published by: Tectum Wissenschaftsverlag Marburg, Biegenstr 4, Marburg, 35037, Germany. TEL 49-6421-481523, FAX 49-6421-43470, email@tectum-verlag.de. Ed. Wolfram Hilz.

327 DEU
BRAUNAUER RUNDBRIEF. Text in German. 1946. bi-m. EUR 20 (effective 2009). adv. bk.rev. back issues avail. **Document type:** *Newsletter, Consumer.* **Description:** Contains news and information concerning exiles from Eastern Bohemia.
Published by: Heimatkreis Braunau - Sudetenland, Paradeplatz 2, Forchheim, 91301, Germany. info@heimatkreis-braunau.de.

BRAZIL WATCH FAX BULLETIN. *see* BUSINESS AND ECONOMICS—Economic Situation And Conditions

327 USA
BREAKING THE SIEGE. Text in English. 1989. bi-m. USD 20; USD 30 foreign. **Document type:** *Newsletter.*
Indexed: Perlslam.
Published by: Middle East Justice Network, PO Box 495, Boston, MA 02112. TEL 617-542-5056, FAX 617-861-3783.

327 USA ISSN 1080-3009
BREAKTHROUGH NEWS. Text in English. 1982. 3/yr. USD 25 (effective 2000 - 2001). bk.rev. **Document type:** *Newsletter, Consumer.* **Description:** Covers world peace and security, ecological responsibility, human rights, and cooperative economic development.
Formerly (until 199?): Breakthrough (0889-3942)
Published by: Global Education Associates, 475 Riverside Dr, Ste 1848, New York, NY 10115. TEL 212-870-3290, FAX 212-870-2729. Ed. Melissa Merkling. R&P Sharon Fritsch. Circ: 3,500.

THE BRITISH JOURNAL OF POLITICS AND INTERNATIONAL RELATIONS. *see* POLITICAL SCIENCE

327 FRA
BULITAN-I KHABAR-I KURDISTAN. Text in Persian, Modern. 1990 (no.245). irreg.
Published by: (Hizb-i Dimukrat-i Kurdistan-i Iran/Democratic Party of the Iranian Kurdistan), Association Franco-Kurde, B.P. 102, Paris, Cedex 13 75623, France.

327 GBR ISSN 2044-4109
▼ **BULLETIN OF FRANCOPHONE POSTCOLONIAL STUDIES.** Text in English. 2010. s-a. free to members (effective 2011). back issues avail. **Document type:** *Bulletin, Trade.*
Media: Online - full text. **Related titles:** Print ed.: ISSN 2044-5512.
Published by: Society of Francophone Postcolonial Studies, c/o David Murphy, School of Languages, Cultures and Religions, University of Stirling, Stirling, FK9 4LA, United Kingdom. TEL 44-1786-467535, FAX 44-1786-466088, d.f.murphy@stir.ac.uk.

327.1747 USA ISSN 1938-3282
BULLETIN OF THE ATOMIC SCIENTISTS (ONLINE). Text in English. 1945. bi-m. USD 217, GBP 128 to institutions (effective 2011). back issues avail. **Document type:** *Bulletin, Trade.* **Description:** Helps redefine international security in terms that embrace economic, environmental, cultural, and military issues.
Media: Online - full text.
—Linda Hall. **CCC.**
Published by: Educational Foundation for Nuclear Science, 77 W Washington St, Ste 2120, Chicago, IL 60602. TEL 312-364-9710, FAX 312-364-9715. Ed. Josh Schollmeyer TEL 312-364-9710 ext 16. Pub. Kennette Benedict TEL 312-364-9710 ext 12. **Subscr. to:** Sage Publications, Inc., 2455 Teller Rd, Thousand Oaks, CA 91320. TEL 805-499-9774, FAX 805-499-0871, journals@sagepub.com.

327 CHE ISSN 1024-0608
JX1563
BULLETIN ZUR SCHWEIZERISCHEN SICHERHEITSPOLITIK. Variant title: Bulletin sur la Politique de Securite Suisse. Text in Multiple languages. 1991. a.

P

Indexed: PAIS.
Published by: Forschungsstelle fuer Sicherheitspolitik und Konfliktanalyse, ETH Zentrum SEI, Seilergraben 45-49, Zurich, 8092, Switzerland. TEL 41-1-6324025, FAX 41-1-6321941, postmaster@sipo.gess.ethz.ch, http://www.fsk.ethz.ch.

327 DEU
AP30
BUNDESPOLIZEI. Text in German. 1951. 5/yr. adv. bk.rev. **Document type:** *Magazine, Trade.*
Former titles (until 2005): B G S (0302-9468); (until 1974): Parole (0031-238X)
—CCC.
Published by: (Germany. Bundesministerium des Innern), A. Bernecker Verlag, Unter dem Schoeneberg 1, Melsungen, 34212, Germany. TEL 49-5661-7310, FAX 49-5661-731111, info@bernecker.de, http://www.bernecke.de. Ed. Conrad Fischer. adv.: page EUR 2,900; trim 185 x 270. Circ: 16,200.

327 JPN ISSN 0917-7566
DS805
BY THE WAY; bridging the US - Japan perception gap. Text in Japanese, English. 1991. bi-m. USD 33. adv. bk.rev. **Document type:** *Journal, Academic/Scholarly.* **Description:** Provides an insight into Japan and the issues it now faces, with a special focus on its relationship with the United States.
—Ingenta.
Published by: Raifu-sha Co. Ltd., 2-1-8 Sarugaku-cho, Chiyoda-ku, Tokyo, 101-0064, Japan. TEL 81-3-3294-0579, FAX 81-3-3294-0530. Ed. Yonnosake Tanaka. Pub. Naosuke Konuro. R&P, Adv. contact Masato Ohishi. Circ: 30,000. **Subscr. in US to:** By the Way, Inc, Box 10671, Seattle, WA 98110-9910. TEL 800-400-4836, FAX 206-842-4235.

327.17 GBR
C A A B U BRIEFINGS. Text in English. irreg., latest no.87, 2006. **Document type:** *Monographic series, Academic/Scholarly.* **Description:** Covers political issues concerning the Arab world.
Published by: Council for the Advancement of Arab-British Understanding, 1 Gough Sq, London, EC4A 3DE, United Kingdom. TEL 44-20-78321321, FAX 44-20-78321329, caabu@caabu.org, http://www.caabu.org/about/index.html.

327.172 GBR
C A A T NEWS. Text in English. 1974. q. GBP 1 per issue; free donation (effective 2009). bk.rev. back issues avail. **Document type:** *Magazine, Trade.* **Description:** Provides news, views, features and updates on campaigns and events.
Formerly (until 2000): C A A T Newsletter (0142-7113)
Related titles: Online - full text ed.: free (effective 2009).
Published by: Campaign Against Arms Trade, 11 Goodwin St, London, N4 3HQ, United Kingdom. TEL 44-20-7281-0297, FAX 44-20-7281-4369, enquiries@caat.org.uk. Ed. Melanie Jarman.

C C I A BACKGROUND INFORMATION. (Commission of the Churches on International Affairs) *see* RELIGIONS AND THEOLOGY

327.73 BEL ISSN 1783-6883
C E P E S S. CAHIERS. (Centre d'Etudes Politiques, Economiques et Sociales) Text in French. 1985. s-a. **Document type:** *Journal, Academic/Scholarly.*
Formerly (until 2006): La Revue Politique (0773-0535)
Related titles: Online - full text ed.: ISSN 1783-6891.
—CCC.
Published by: Centre d'Etudes Politiques, Economiques et Sociales, Rue des Deux Eglises, 41, Bruxelles, 1000, Belgium. TEL 32-2-2380111, FAX 32-2-2380129, cepess@lecdh.be, http://www.cepess.be.

327 BEL ISSN 0962-3876
C E P S PAPERS. Text in English. 1983. irreg., latest vol.71, 1996. adv. back issues avail. **Document type:** *Monographic series, Academic/Scholarly.* **Description:** Provides in-depth analysis of timely topics relating to E.U. policies.
Indexed: ELLIS.
Published by: Centre for European Policy Studies, Pl du Congres 1, Brussels, 1000, Belgium. TEL 32-2-229-3911, FAX 32-2-219-4151, info@ceps.be, http://www.ceps.be/Default.php. Ed. Anne Harrington. Adv. contact Dominic Gilmore.

327 BEL
C E P S WORKING DOCUMENTS. Text in English. 1983. irreg., latest vol.121, 1998. EUR 12 per issue (effective 2005). adv. back issues avail. **Document type:** *Monographic series, Trade.*
Formed by the merger of: C E P S Working Documents (Economic); C E P S Working Documents (Political)
Published by: Centre for European Policy Studies, Pl du Congres 1, Brussels, 1000, Belgium. TEL 32-2-229-3911, FAX 32-2-219-4151, info@ceps.be, http://www.ceps.be/Default.php. Ed., R&P Anne Harrington. Adv. contact Dominic Gilmore.

327 ESP ISSN 1133-6595
C I D O B D'AFERS INTERNATIONALS. (Centre d'Informacio i Documentacio Internacionals a Barcelona) Text in Spanish, Catalan; Abstracts in English. 1982. 4/yr. EUR 14 (effective 2009). adv. **Document type:** *Journal, Academic/Scholarly.* **Description:** Seeks to offer the reader an in-depth analysis of international relations and cooperation.
Formerly (until 1985): Afers Internacionals (0212-1786)
Related titles: Online - full text ed.: ISSN 2013-035X.
Indexed: A01, CA, F03, F04, I13, I14, P09, P34, P42, PCI, RASB, T02.
Published by: Fundacio C I D O B, C. Elisabets, 12, Barcelona, 08001, Spain. TEL 34-93-3026495, FAX 34-93-3022118, publicaciones@cibod.org, http://www.cibod.org. Ed. Josep Ribera. R&P, Adv. contact Elisabet Mane. **Dist. by:** Asociacion de Revistas Culturales de Espana, C Covarruvias 9 2o. Derecha, Madrid 28010, Spain. TEL 34-91-3086066, FAX 34-91-3199267, info@arce.es, http://www.arce.es/.

327 CAN ISSN 1204-2277
C I S S BULLETIN. Text in English. q. CAD 20 to non-members. bk.rev. **Description:** Contains information for members, including current events and upcoming public lectures and seminars.
Published by: Canadian Institute of Strategic Studies, 10 Adelaide St E, Suite 400, Toronto, ON M5C 1J3, Canada. TEL 416-322-8128, FAX 416-322-8129, info@ciss.ca.

341.72 CAN
C I S S MONOGRAPHS. (Centre for International and Security Studies) Text in English. 1982. irreg. price varies. **Document type:** *Monographic series, Academic/Scholarly.* **Description:** Based on research projects, conferences, and specialized work by outside experts. Consists of longer studies or collections of essays edited under the auspices of the Centre.
Indexed: LID&ISL.
Published by: York Centre for International and Security Studies, 375 York Lanes, York University, 4700 Keele St, Toronto, ON M3J 1P3, Canada. TEL 416-736-5156, FAX 416-736-5752, yciss@yorku.ca, http://www.yorku.ca/yciss.

341.72 CAN
C I S S WORKING PAPERS. (Centre for International and Security Studies) Text in English. irreg. price varies. **Document type:** *Journal, Academic/Scholarly.* **Description:** Explore topical themes that reflect work being undertaken at the Centre.
Published by: York Centre for International and Security Studies, 375 York Lanes, York University, 4700 Keele St, Toronto, ON M3J 1P3, Canada. TEL 416-736-5156, FAX 416-736-5752, yciss@yorku.ca, http://www.yorku.ca/yciss.

327 FIN ISSN 1796-9379
C M C FINLAND. (Crisis Management Centre Finland) Text in Finnish. 2007. s-a. **Document type:** *Magazine, Consumer.*
Related titles: Online - full text ed.
Published by: Kriisinhallintakeskus/Crisis Management Centre Finland, Hulkontie 83, PO Box 1325, Kuopio, 70821, Finland. TEL 358-17-307111, FAX 358-17-307210, cmcfinland@cmcfinland.fi.

327.1 NOR ISSN 0809-6732
C M I BRIEF. (Chr. Michelsen Institute) Text in English. 2002. irreg. back issues avail. **Document type:** *Monographic series.*
Formerly (until 2005): C M I Policy Brief (1503-3228)
Related titles: Online - full text ed.: ISSN 0809-6740.
Published by: Chr. Michelsen Institute, PO Box 6033 Postterminalen, Bergen, 5892, Norway. TEL 47-55-574000, FAX 47-55-574166, cmi@cmi.no.

327 LUX
C O M DOCUMENTS. Text in Danish, Dutch, English, French, German, Greek, Italian, Portuguese, Spanish. 1983. s-m. USD 2,680.
Related titles: Microfiche ed.
Published by: European Commission, Office for Official Publications of the European Union, 2 Rue Mercier, Luxembourg, L-2985, Luxembourg. **Dist. in the U.S. by:** Bernan Associates, Bernan, 4611-F Assembly Dr., Lanham, MD 20706-4391. TEL 301-459-0056, 800-274-4447.

327.17 CAN ISSN 1496-6387
C O P A MAGAZINE (FRENCH EDITION). (Confederation Parlementaire des Ameriques) Text in French. 2001. s-a. **Document type:** *Magazine, Consumer.* **Description:** It aims to foster dialogue on issues related to inter-American cooperation and hemispheric integration and respecting the projects and mechanisms stemming from the Summits of the Heads of State and Government of the Americas.
Related titles: English ed.: C O P A Magazine (English Edition). ISSN 1496-6360; Spanish ed.: C O P A Magazine (Spanish Edition). ISSN 1496-6344; Portuguese ed.: C O P A Magazine (Portuguese Edition). ISSN 1496-6328.
Published by: Confederation Parlementaire des Ameriques/ Parliamentary Confederation of the Americas, 1020 Rue des Parlementaires, 6e Etage, Quebec, PQ G1A 1A3, Canada. TEL 418-644-2888, FAX 418-643-1865, copa@assnat.qc.ca, http://www.copa.qc.ca.

327.172 USA ISSN 0194-0856
C P P A X NEWSLETTER. Text in English. 1962. 5/yr. USD 10 (effective 1999). **Document type:** *Newsletter.* **Description:** Covers reform-oriented topics in Massachusetts such as world peace, social justice, economic democracy, and open government.
Published by: Citizens for Participation in Political Action, 25 West St, 4th Fl, Boston, MA 02111. TEL 617-426-3040. Ed. Betsy Smith. Circ: 5,000.

327 GBR
C S D PERSPECTIVES. Text in English. 19??. irreg., latest 2002. price varies. **Document type:** *Monographic series, Academic/Scholarly.*
Related titles: Online - full text ed.: free (effective 2009).
Published by: University of Westminster, Centre for the Study of Democracy, 100 Park Village E, London, NW1 3SR, United Kingdom. http://www.wmin.ac.uk/sshl/page-3160.

CAG UNIVERSITY JOURNAL OF SOCIAL SCIENCES. *see* BUSINESS AND ECONOMICS

341 FRA ISSN 1017-7574
CAHIERS DE CHAILLOT. Text in French. 1991. m. **Document type:** *Monographic series, Trade.*
Related titles: Online - full text ed.: ISSN 1683-4925; ◆ English ed.: Chaillot Papers. ISSN 1017-7566.
Indexed: I13, IBSS.
Published by: European Union Institute for Security Studies, 43 Ave du President Wilson, Paris, 75775 Cedex 16, France. TEL 33-1-56891930, FAX 33-1-56891931, institute@iss-eu.org, http://www.iss-eu.org.

327 GBR ISSN 0955-7571
JZ6.5
➤ **CAMBRIDGE REVIEW OF INTERNATIONAL AFFAIRS.** Text in English. 1986. q. GBP 372 combined subscription in United Kingdom to institutions (print & online eds.); EUR 489, USD 614 combined subscription to institutions (print & online eds.) (effective 2012). adv. back issues avail.; reprint service avail. from PSC. **Document type:** *Journal, Academic/Scholarly.* **Description:** Aims to foster discussion about developing issues and theoretical approaches in the study of international relations.
Related titles: Online - full text ed.: ISSN 1474-449X. GBP 335 in United Kingdom to institutions; EUR 440, USD 552 to institutions (effective 2012) (from IngentaConnect).
Indexed: A01, A03, A08, A20, A22, B21, CA, CurCont, DIP, E01, E17, ESPM, I02, IBR, IBSS, IBZ, LID&ISL, P34, P42, P47, PAIS, PQC, PSA, R02, RiskAb, S02, S03, SCOPUS, SSCI, SociolAb, T02, W07.
—IE, Infotrieve, Ingenta. **CCC.**
Published by: Routledge (Subsidiary of: Taylor & Francis Group), 4 Park Sq, Milton Park, Abingdon, Oxon OX14 4RN, United Kingdom. TEL 44-20-70176000, FAX 44-20-70176336, subscriptions@tandf.co.uk, http://www.routledge.com. Ed. Josef Ansorge. Adv. contact Linda Hann TEL 44-1344-779945. **Subscr. to:** Taylor & Francis Ltd., Journals Customer Service, Sheepen Pl, Colchester, Essex CO3 3LP, United Kingdom. TEL 44-20-70175544, FAX 44-20-70175198.

327 GBR ISSN 0959-6844
CAMBRIDGE STUDIES IN INTERNATIONAL RELATIONS. Text in English. 1988. irreg., latest vol.112, 2009. price varies. adv. back issues avail.; reprints avail. **Document type:** *Monographic series, Academic/Scholarly.* **Description:** Aims to publish the best new scholarship in international studies from Europe, North America and the rest of the world.
—BLDSC (3015.993700), IE, Ingenta.
Published by: Cambridge University Press, The Edinburgh Bldg, Shaftesbury Rd, Cambridge, CB2 8RU, United Kingdom. TEL 44-1223-312393, FAX 44-1223-315052, journals@cambridge.org, http://www.cambridge.org/uk. Eds. Lene Hansen, Martha Finnemore, Robert Keohane. R&P Linda Nicol TEL 44-1223-325702.

327 CAN ISSN 0832-0683
F1034.2
CANADA AMONG NATIONS. Text in English. a. CAD 24.95. **Description:** Provides a review of world events and Canadian foreign policy.
Related titles: Online - full text ed.
Indexed: I13, P42.
—CIS. **CCC.**
Published by: McGill-Queens's University Press, 3430 McTavish St, Montreal, PQ H3A 1X9, Canada. TEL 514-398-3750, FAX 514-398-4333, mqup@mqup.mcgill.ca, orderbook@cupserv.org. **Dist. by:** CUP Services, PO Box 6525, Ithaca, NY 14851-6525. TEL 607-277-2211, FAX 607-277-6292, 800-688-2877, orderbook@cupserv.org.

327 CAN ISSN 1491-4573
F1034.2
CANADA WORLD VIEW. Text in English. 1998. q. free (effective 2005). **Description:** Provides an overview of Canada's perspective on foreign policy issues and highlights the government's international initiatives and contributions.
Related titles: Online - full text ed.: ISSN 1492-5168.
Published by: Canada, Department of Foreign Affairs and International Trade, 125 Sussex Dr, Ottawa, ON K1A OG2, Canada. TEL 613-944-4000, FAX 613-992-7114, FAX 613-992-5791, 613-996-9709, enqserv@dfait-maeci.gc.ca.

327 USA ISSN 1047-1073
CANADIAN - AMERICAN PUBLIC POLICY. Text in English. 1990. q. USD 21 domestic; USD 26 foreign (effective 2000). adv. **Document type:** *Monographic series.* **Description:** Focuses on contemporary issues in United States-Canada relations.
Related titles: Online - full text ed.
Indexed: A26, C03, CA, CBCARef, CPerI, E08, G06, G07, G08, I05, P42, P45, P47, P48, PQC, S09, T02.
Published by: (University of Maine), Canadian - American Center, University of Maine, 154 College Ave, Orono, ME 04473-1591. TEL 207-581-4220, FAX 207-581-4223. Ed., R&P Robert H Babcock. Circ: 300 (paid).

327 CAN ISSN 0317-5693
AS4.U825
CANADIAN COMMISSION FOR UNESCO. OCCASIONAL PAPER. Text and summaries in English, French. 1971. a. free.
Published by: UNESCO, Canadian Commission/Commission Canadienne pour l'UNESCO, 350 Albert St, 7th Fl, PO Box 1047, Ottawa, ON K1P 5V8, Canada. TEL 613-566-4414, FAX 613-566-4405. Circ: 4,000.

CANADIAN COMMISSION FOR UNESCO. SECRETARY GENERAL'S LETTER/COMMISSION CANADIENNE POUR L'UNESCO. LETTRE DU SECRETAIRE GENERAL. *see* EDUCATION

327.71 CAN ISSN 1192-6422
F1029
➤ **CANADIAN FOREIGN POLICY/POLITIQUE ETRANGERE DU CANADA.** Text in English. 1992. 3/yr. GBP 217 combined subscription in United Kingdom to institutions (print & online eds.); EUR 287, USD 359 combined subscription to institutions (print & online eds.) (effective 2012). adv. reprint service avail. from PSC. **Document type:** *Journal, Academic/Scholarly.* **Description:** Provides a Canadian perspective on foreign policy issues.
Related titles: Online - full text ed.: ISSN 2157-0817. GBP 196 in United Kingdom to institutions; EUR 258, USD 323 to institutions (effective 2012).
Indexed: A26, C03, C04, CA, CBCARef, CPerI, E08, G08, P02, P10, P27, P42, P45, P47, P48, P53, P54, PAIS, PQC, PSA, S09, S11, SCOPUS, SSAI, SSAb, SSI, T02, W03, W05.
—CCC.
Published by: Carleton University, Dunton Tower, Rm 2109, 1125 Colonel By Dr, Ottawa, ON K1S 5B6, Canada. TEL 613-520-6696, FAX 613-520-3981.

327.12 CAN ISSN 1192-277X
CANADIAN SECURITY INTELLIGENCE SERVICE. ANALYSIS AND PRODUCTION BRANCH. COMMENTARY. Text in English. 1990. irreg., latest 2003, iss. 86. **Document type:** *Government.*
—CCC.
Published by: Canadian Security Intelligence Service, PO Box 9732, Sta T, Ottawa, ON K1G 4G4, Canada. TEL 613-993-9620.

327.12 CAN ISSN 1494-1376
CA1JS73-2
CANADIAN SECURITY INTELLIGENCE SERVICE. PERSPECTIVES. Text in English, French. 1999. irreg., latest vol.11, 2002.
Related titles: Online - full text ed.: ISSN 1495-6926.
Published by: Canadian Security Intelligence Service, PO Box 9732, Sta T, Ottawa, ON K1G 4G4, Canada. TEL 613-993-9620.

327.12 CAN ISSN 1189-4415
CA1JS71-2
CANADIAN SECURITY INTELLIGENCE SERVICE. PUBLIC REPORT. Text in English, French. 1991. a. **Description:** Discusses Canada's security environment and national security.
Related titles: Online - full text ed.: ISSN 1495-0138.
Published by: Canadian Security Intelligence Service, PO Box 9732, Sta T, Ottawa, ON K1G 4G4, Canada. TEL 613-993-9620.

CANADO-AMERICAIN. *see* ETHNIC INTERESTS

CARDOZO JOURNAL OF CONFLICT RESOLUTION. *see* SOCIAL SCIENCES: COMPREHENSIVE WORKS

327 USA ISSN 0894-0223
F2155
CARIBBEAN NEWSLETTER. Text in English. 1980. q. USD 15 domestic to individuals; USD 18 foreign to individuals; USD 17 to institutions (effective 2001). bk.rev.; film rev. illus.; tr.lit. 8 p./no.; back issues avail. **Document type:** *Newsletter.* **Description:** Covers political, economic and social conditions in the English-speaking Caribbean.
Formerly: Friends for Jamaica Newsletter
Related titles: Microfiche ed.
Indexed: HRIR.
Published by: Friends for Jamaica Collective, PO Box 20392, Park West Sta, New York, NY 10025. Ed. Doris Kitson. Circ: 500.

327 USA ISSN 0271-6577
CARIBBEAN STUDIES NEWSLETTER. Text in English. 1974. q. USD 30. adv. back issues avail. **Document type:** *Newsletter.* **Description:** News of academic and general interest on Caribbean politics and government, teaching and research.
Indexed: C32, CA, T02.
Published by: (Caribbean Studies Association), City College of New York, Department of Political Science, Convent Ave & 138th St, New York, NY 10031. TEL 212-690-5470. Ed. J A Braveboy Wagner. Circ: 1,000.

327 GBR ISSN 0257-7860
CARN; a link between celtic nations. Text in English. 19??. q. GBP 13.50 domestic to non-members includes Isle of Man and Channel Islands; EUR 23 in Europe to non-members; USD 30 in United States to non-members; GBP 20 elsewhere to non-members; free to members (effective 2009). bk.rev. **Document type:** *Magazine, Consumer.* **Description:** Cover a broad range of topics from current affairs, political reporting and news on the Celtic nationalist movements to the Celtic languages, wider cultural matters and the related campaigns of the league across the political, language and rights issues.
Formerly (until 1973): Celtic League Annual; Formed by the merger of (19??-1973): Celtic News (0008-8773); (19??-1973): Breton News (0006-9671)
Published by: Celtic League, c/o Flo Kenna, 72 Compton St, London, EC1V 0BN, United Kingdom. Ed. Patricia Bridson.

327 USA
CARNEGIE COUNCIL NEWSLETTER. Text in English. 1984. q. free. **Document type:** *Newsletter.* **Description:** Contains information regarding Carnegie Council activities.
Published by: Carnegie Council on Ethics and International Affairs, Merrill House, 170 E 64th St, New York, NY 10021-7478. TEL 212-838-4120, FAX 212-752-2432.

327.84 BOL
CARTA DEL PERU. Text in Spanish. 1972. m. free. adv. charts; illus. **Document type:** *Bulletin.* **Description:** Includes articles on Peruvian economic, political and cultural issues, Peru-Bolivia relations, Peruvian foreign policy, history and tourism.
Formerly: Peru
Published by: Embajada del Peru en Bolivia, Calle Fernando Guachalla Cdra. 3, Sopocachi, La Paz, Bolivia. TEL 591-2-376773, FAX 591-2-367640. R&P, Adv. contact Elmer Schialer. Circ: 1,100.

327.172 AUS
CATHOLICS IN COALITION FOR JUSTICE AND PEACE NATIONAL NEWSLETTER. Text in English. 1988. q. free (effective 2008). adv. bk.rev. 18 p./no.; back issues avail. **Document type:** *Newsletter, Consumer.* **Description:** Covers a range of justice issues.
Formerly (until 1989): Catholics in Coalition for Justice and Peace. News Update
Published by: Catholics in Coalition for Justice and Peace, 33 Tavistock St, Croydon Park, NSW 2133, Australia. ccjp@bigpond.com, http://www.ccjpoz.org. Circ: 450.

327 FRA ISSN 1262-1218
CAUSES COMMUNES; le journal de la Cimade. Text in French. 1939. q. EUR 20 for 18 mos. (effective 2009). **Document type:** *Magazine, Consumer.* **Description:** Supports work among refugees and migrant workers in France, with an emphasis on the defense of human rights. Internationally, this organization works in partnership with local organizations supporting their projects in such fields as human rights, health and agriculture.
Formerly (until 1995): Cimade Information
Published by: Cimade - Service Oecumenique d'Entraide, 64 Rue Clisson, Paris, 75013, France. TEL 33-1-44186050, FAX 33-1-45560859, direction@cimade.org. Ed. Alain Bosc. Pub. Jean Marc Dupeux. Circ: 2,500.

327 CHE
CAUX INFORMATION; Informationsdienst Moralische Aufruestung. Text in German. 1949. bi-m. CHF 32 domestic; CHF 38 foreign (effective 2001). bk.rev. charts; illus. **Document type:** *Magazine, Consumer.* **Description:** Offers ideas about resolution of conflicts through personal, social and economic change.
Address: Postfach 4419, Luzern, 6002, Switzerland. TEL 41-41-3112213, FAX 41-41-3112214. Ed. Marianne Spreng. R&P Verena Gautschi. Circ: 1,400.

327 USA ISSN 1558-8947
CENTER FOR GLOBAL STUDIES REVIEW. Text in English. 2004 (Fall). q.
Formerly (until Fall 2005): Center for Global Studies Bulletin (1930-1480)
Related titles: Online - full text ed.: ISSN 1558-8955.
Published by: George Mason University, Center for Global Studies, 4400 University Dr MS 1B9, Fairfax, VA 22030-4444. TEL 703-993-4625, FAX 703-993-9430, cgs@gmu.edu.

327.172 USA
CENTER FOR PEACE AND CONFLICT STUDIES - DETROIT COUNCIL FOR WORLD AFFAIRS. NEWSLETTER. Text in English. 1965. 3/yr. membership. bibl. 4 p./no.; **Document type:** *Newsletter, Consumer.* **Description:** News and articles on the peacemaking process.
Formerly: Center for Teaching about Peace and War. Newsletter (0008-9133)
Published by: Wayne State University, Center for Peace and Conflict Studies, 656 W. Kirby, 2320 F/AB, Detroit, MI 48202. TEL 313-577-3453, FAX 313-577-8269, http://www.pcs.wayne.edu. Circ: 1,000.
Co-sponsor: Detroit Council for World Affairs.

327.172 USA
CENTER FOR PEACE AND CONFLICT STUDIES. PROGRAM ON MEDIATING THEORY AND DEMOCRATIC SYSTEMS. WORKING PAPERS. Text in English. 1981. irreg., latest 2002. price varies. back issues avail. **Document type:** *Monographic series, Academic/Scholarly.* **Description:** Articles on the peacemaking process.
Formerly: Center for Peace and Conflict Studies. Occasional Papers (0732-0078)
Published by: Wayne State University, Center for Peace and Conflict Studies, Program on Mediating Theory and Democratic Systems, 656 W Kirby, 2320 FAB, Detroit, MI 48202. TEL 313-577-3453, FAX 313-577-8269, ab3440@wayne.edu, http://www.clas.wayne.edu/pcs/.

CENTRAL AND INNER ASIAN STUDIES. *see* HISTORY—History Of Asia

327.47 ROM ISSN 1224-3809
DAW1044
CENTRAL EUROPEAN ISSUES. ROMANIAN FOREIGN AFFAIRS REVIEW. Text in English. 1995. q. USD 70 (effective 2000). adv. **Document type:** *Journal, Academic/Scholarly.*
Published by: Info-Team Ltd., Sos. Kiseleff 47, Bucharest, Romania. TEL 40-1-222-7162. Ed., R&P Ionel Nicu Sava. Pub., Adv. contact Sorin Encutescu.

327 CZE ISSN 1802-548X
JZ6.5
CENTRAL EUROPEAN JOURNAL OF INTERNATIONAL & SECURITY STUDIES. Text in English. 2007. s-a. **Document type:** *Journal, Academic/Scholarly.*
Related titles: Online - full text ed.: free (effective 2011).
Published by: Metropolitni Univerzita Praha, Dubeczka 900/10, Prague, 100 31, Czech Republic. http://www.mup.cz.

327.12 USA
CENTRAL INTELLIGENCE AGENCY. MONOGRAPHS. ALL COMMUNIST COUNTRIES REPORTS. Abbreviated title: Central Intelligence Agency. Monographs. All Communist Country Reports. Text in English. 19??. irreg., latest 2010. price varies. back issues avail. **Document type:** *Monographic series, Government.* **Description:** Presents the political, economic, statistical, and military conditions.
Related titles: ◆ Series of: Central Intelligence Agency. Monographs.
Published by: (Central Intelligence Agency), U.S. Department of Commerce, National Technical Information Service, 5301 Shawnee Rd, Alexandria, VA 22312. TEL 703-605-6000, 800-553-6847, info@ntis.gov.

327.12 USA
CENTRAL INTELLIGENCE AGENCY. MONOGRAPHS. CHINA REPORTS. Text in English. 19??. irreg., latest 2010. price varies. back issues avail. **Document type:** *Monographic series, Government.* **Description:** Covers the political, economic, statistical, and military conditions.
Related titles: ◆ Series of: Central Intelligence Agency. Monographs.
Published by: (Central Intelligence Agency), U.S. Department of Commerce, National Technical Information Service, 5301 Shawnee Rd, Alexandria, VA 22312. TEL 703-605-6000, 800-553-6847, info@ntis.gov.

327.12 USA
CENTRAL INTELLIGENCE AGENCY. MONOGRAPHS. COMMONWEALTH OF INDEPENDENT STATES REPORT. Text in English. 19??. irreg., latest 2010. back issues avail. **Document type:** *Monographic series, Government.* **Description:** Details the political, economic, statistical, and military conditions.
Formerly (until 1992): Central Intelligence Agency. Monographs. U.S.S.R. Reports
Related titles: ◆ Series of: Central Intelligence Agency. Monographs.
Published by: (Central Intelligence Agency), U.S. Department of Commerce, National Technical Information Service, 5301 Shawnee Rd, Alexandria, VA 22312. TEL 703-605-6000, 800-553-6847, info@ntis.gov.

327.73 BEL ISSN 0771-0097
CENTRE D'ETUDES POLITIQUES, ECONOMIQUES ET SOCIALES. DOCUMENTS. Text in French. 1962. bi-m. **Document type:** *Journal, Academic/Scholarly.*
Indexed: PAIS.
Published by: Centre d'Etudes Politiques, Economiques et Sociales, Rue des Deux Eglises, 41, Bruxelles, 1000, Belgium. TEL 32-2-2380111, FAX 32-2-2380129, cepess@lecdh.be, http://www.cepess.be.

327 BEL
CENTRE FOR EUROPEAN POLICY STUDIES. NEWSLETTER. Text in English. m. free. back issues avail. **Document type:** *Newsletter.*
Published by: Centre for European Policy Studies, Pl du Congres 1, Brussels, 1000, Belgium. TEL 32-2-2293911, FAX 32-2-2194151. R&P Dominic Gilmore.

341 FRA ISSN 1017-7566
CHAILLOT PAPERS. Text in English. 1991. m. **Document type:** *Monographic series, Academic/Scholarly.*
Related titles: Online - full text ed.: ISSN 1683-4917; ◆ French ed.: Cahiers de Chaillot. ISSN 1017-7574.
Indexed: I13, LID&ISL.
—BLDSC (3128.734100). **CCC.**
Published by: European Union Institute for Security Studies, 43 Ave du President Wilson, Paris, 75775 Cedex 16, France. TEL 33-1-56891930, FAX 33-1-56891931, institute@iss-eu.org, http://www.iss-eu.org. Ed. Antonio Missiroli.

327 CAN ISSN 1718-8148
CHAIRE DE RECHERCHE DU CANADA EN MONDIALISATION, CITOYENNETE ET DEMOCRATIE. BULLETIN. Text in French. 2003. s-a. **Document type:** *Newsletter, Academic/Scholarly.*
Published by: Universite du Quebec a Montreal, Chaire de Recherche du Canada en Mondialisation, Citoyennete et Democratie, CP 8888, succursale Centre-Ville, Montreal, PQ H3C 3P8, Canada. TEL 514-987-3000 ext 3366, FAX 514-987-7870, chaire.mcd@uqam.ca, http://www.chaire-mcd.ca.

351 BEL ISSN 1377-476X
CHAIRE GLAVERBEL D'ETUDES EUROPEENNES. ACTES. Text in French. 2001. irreg., latest vol.6, 2006. price varies. **Document type:** *Monographic series, Academic/Scholarly.*
Published by: P I E - Peter Lang SA, 1 avenue Maurice, 6e etage, Brussels, 1050, Belgium. TEL 32-2-3477236, FAX 32-2-3477237, pie@peterlang.com, http://www.peterlang.net. Ed. Michel Dumoulin.

327 ISR ISSN 0792-4143
DS119.7
➤ **CHALLENGE/'ETGAR**; a magazine covering the Israeli-Palestinian conflict. Text in English. 1990. bi-m. ILS 75 domestic; EUR 30 in Europe; GBP 20 in United Kingdom; USD 35 in United States (effective 2008). adv. bk.rev. illus.; maps; stat. cum.index: 1990-1994. 24 p./no.; back issues avail. **Document type:** *Magazine, Academic/Scholarly.* **Description:** Covers news and events in Israel, the former Occupied Territories and the Palestinian autonomous regions, with emphasis on human rights and efforts to secure a just peace. Advocates a two-state settlement to the conflict between Israel and the Palestinians.
Related titles: Online - full text ed.
Indexed: AltPI, P10, P47, P48, P53, P54, PQC.
Published by: Challenge for Peace and Progress, PO Box 35252, Tel Aviv, 61351, Israel. TEL 972-3-5373268, FAX 972-3-6839148, oda@netvision.net.il. Ed. Roni Ben-Efrat. Pub. Shimon Tzabar. Adv. contact Orit Soudri. Circ: 1,000 (paid).

327.172 SWE ISSN 2000-558X
CHALLENGES FORUM REPORT. Variant title: International Forum for the Challenges of Peace Operations. Annual Report. Text in English. 2008. a. **Document type:** *Consumer.*
Related titles: Online - full text ed.
Published by: International Forum for the Challenges of Peace Operations, c/o Folke Bernadotte Academy, Drottning Kristinas Vaeg 37, Stockholm, 10251, Sweden. TEL 46-612-82200, FAX 46-612-82021, info@challengesforum.org.

327 CHE ISSN 1017-2874
CHANGER. Text in French. 1964. bi-m. CHF 30 domestic; EUR 18 foreign (effective 1999). adv. bk.rev. **Document type:** *Bulletin.*
Former titles: Changer - Tribune de Caux; (until 1979): Tribune de Caux; Which incorporates: Courrier d'Information-Rearmement Moral (0011-0523)
Published by: Caux Edition S.A., Rue du Panorama, Caux, 1824, Switzerland. FAX 41-21-9629355. Ed. Frederic Chavanne. Circ: 1,500.

327 GBR ISSN 0731-8812
HF1410
CHATHAM HOUSE ANNUAL REVIEW. Text in English. 1981. a. **Document type:** *Journal, Academic/Scholarly.*
Formerly (until 2005): Chatham House. Annual Report
Related titles: Online - full text ed.: free (effective 2009).
—**CCC.**
Published by: Royal Institute of International Affairs, Chatham House, 10 St James's Sq, London, SW1Y 4LE, United Kingdom. TEL 44-20-79575700, FAX 44-20-79575710, contact@riia.org, http://www.riia.org.

P

327 GBR ISSN 0143-5795
CHATHAM HOUSE PAPERS. Text in English. 1979; N.S. 2003. irreg. price varies. back issues avail.; reprints avail. **Document type:** *Monographic series, Academic/Scholarly.* **Description:** Provides authoritative, informed, and impartial comment for international affairs.
Indexed: IMMAb.
—**CCC.**
Published by: (Royal Institute of International Affairs), Wiley-Blackwell Publishing Ltd. (Subsidiary of: John Wiley & Sons, Inc.), 9600 Garsington Rd, Oxford, OX4 2DQ, United Kingdom. TEL 44-1865-776868, FAX 44-1865-714591, customerservices@blackwellpublishing.com, http://www.wiley.com/.

CHICAGO JOURNAL OF INTERNATIONAL LAW. *see* LAW—International Law

327 USA
CHIEFS OF STATE AND CABINET MEMBERS OF FOREIGN GOVERNMENTS (ONLINE). Text in English. 19??. m. free (effective 2011). back issues avail.; reprints avail. **Document type:** *Directory, Government.* **Description:** Lists chiefs of state and cabinet members from over 150 governments.
Formerly (until 2003): Chiefs of State and Cabinet Members of Foreign Governments (Print) (0162-2951)
Media: Online - full text. **Related titles:** Microfiche ed.: (from CIS).
Indexed: AmStI.
Published by: (Central Intelligence Agency), U.S. Department of Commerce, National Technical Information Service, 5301 Shawnee Rd, Alexandria, VA 22312. TEL 703-605-6000, 800-553-6847, info@ntis.gov, http://www.ntis.gov.

CHILDREN AND WAR NEWSLETTER; a newsletter for adults. *see* CHILDREN AND YOUTH—About

327 GBR
CHILEAN NEWS. Text in English. 1942. s-a. free to members (effective 2009). bk.rev. bibl.; illus. **Document type:** *Bulletin, Trade.* **Description:** Covers activities of the society.
Published by: Anglo-Chilean Society, 12 Devonshire St, London, W1N 2DS, United Kingdom. TEL 44-20-75801271, FAX 44-20-75805901, info@anglochileansociety.org. Ed. Georgina Roberts.

327 CHN
CHINA AND AFRICA. Text in English. m.
Related titles: French ed.
Published by: Ministry of Culture, Foreign Language Bureau/Wenhua-bu, Waiwen-ju, 23 Baiwanzhuang Lu, Fuwai, Beijing, 100037, China. TEL 8315599. Ed. Zhang Lifang.

327.51 CHN
CHINA & THE WORLD; Beijing Review foreign affairs series. Text in English. 1982. m.?.
Published by: Beijing Review Publishing Co., 24 Baiwanzhuang Rd, Beijing, 100037, China. Ed. Zhou Guo. **Dist. by:** China Publications Center (Guoji Shudian), P.O. Box 399, Beijing, China.

327 GBR
CHINA EYE. Text in English. 1965. q. free to members (effective 2009). adv. bk.rev. index. back issues avail. **Document type:** *Journal, Academic/Scholarly.* **Description:** Provides detailed insight into current events in China and covers current affairs and reviews.
Former titles (until 200?): China in Focus (1366-5235); (until 1996): China Now (0045-6764); (until 1970): S A C U News (0583-8908)
Indexed: BAS, RASB.

Published by: Society for Anglo-Chinese Understanding Ltd., 16 Portland St, Cheltenham, Gloucs GL52 2PB, United Kingdom. TEL 44-1253-894582, cif@sacu.org.

327 CAN ISSN 1911-0758
CHINA FOCUS. Text in English, Chinese. 2006. bi-m. **Document type:** *Journal, Consumer.*
Published by: Canada - China Cultual Art Media Alliance Ltd., 201-6151 Westminster Hwy., Richmond, BC V7C 4V4, Canada. TEL 604-231-1661, FAX 604-231-1665, info@cccam.ca.

327 CHN ISSN 1673-3258
CHINA INTERNATIONAL STUDIES. Text in English. 2005. bi-m. **Document type:** *Journal, Academic/Scholarly.*
—BLDSC (9512.734730).
Published by: Zhongguo Guoji Wenti Yanjiusuo/China Institute of International Studies, 3, Taijichangtoutiao, Beijing, 100005, China. TEL 86-10-85119558, FAX 86-10-65284305, http://www.ciis.org.cn/. Ed. Zhengang Ma.

327 HKG ISSN 2070-3449
➤ **CHINA PERSPECTIVES.** Text in English. 1995. q. HKD 400 to individuals in Hong Kong & Macao; EUR 60 in Europe to individuals; USD 80 elsewhere to individuals; HKD 600 to institutions in Hong Kong & Macao; EUR 90 in Europe to institutions; USD 120 elsewhere to institutions; free to qualified personnel (effective 2009). bk.rev. illus.; maps. Index. back issues avail. **Document type:** *Journal, Academic/Scholarly.*
Related titles: Online - full text ed.: ISSN 1996-4617; ◆ French ed.: Perspectives Chinoises. ISSN 1021-9013.
Indexed: A01, PSA, T02.
Published by: Centre d'Etudes Francais sur la Chine Contemporaine/ French Centre for Research on Contemporary China, Rm. 304, Yu Yuet Lai Bldg., 43-55 Wyndham St., Central, Hong Kong. TEL 852-28151728, FAX 852-28153211, cefc@cefc.com.hk. Ed. Sebastien Billioud. Pub. Jean Francois Huchet. R&P, Adv. contact Gwendoline Debethune. Circ: 400 (paid and controlled).

327 IND ISSN 0009-4455
DS777.55
➤ **CHINA REPORT**; a journal of East Asian studies. Text in English. 1964. q. USD 408, GBP 221 to institutions; USD 416, GBP 225 combined subscription to institutions (print & online eds.) (effective 2011). adv. bk.rev. stat.; illus. index. back issues avail.; reprint service avail. from PSC. **Document type:** *Journal, Academic/Scholarly.* **Description:** Encourages the increased understanding of contemporary China and its East Asian neighbors, their cultures and ways of development, and their impact on India and other South Asian countries.
Related titles: Microfilm ed.: (from PQC); Online - full text ed.: ISSN 0973-063X. USD 374, GBP 203 to institutions (effective 2011).
Indexed: A22, AmH&L, BAS, CA, E01, ESPM, GEOBASE, HistAb, I13, IBSS, KES, MLA-IB, P30, P42, PAIS, PCI, PRA, PSA, RASB, RiskAb, S02, S03, SCOPUS, SOPODA, SSA, SSciA, SociolAb, T02.
—BLDSC (3180.233000), IE, Infotrieve, Ingenta. **CCC.**
Published by: (Centre for the Study of Developing Societies), Sage Publications India Pvt. Ltd. (Subsidiary of: Sage Publications, Inc.), M-32 Market, Greater Kailash-I, PO Box 4215, New Delhi, 110 048, India. TEL 91-11-6444958, FAX 91-11-6472426, journalsubs@sagepub.in, http://www.indiasage.com/. Ed. Alka Acharya. adv.: page USD 75. Circ: 700. **Subscr. in Europe, Middle East, Africa & Australasia to:** Sage Publications Ltd., 1 Oliver's Yard, 55 City Rd, London EC1Y 1SP, United Kingdom. TEL 44-207-3248701, FAX 44-207-3248733, subscription@sagepub.co.uk; **Subscr. in the Americas to:** Sage Publications, Inc., 2455 Teller Rd, Thousand Oaks, CA 91320. TEL 805-499-9774, FAX 805-499-0871, journals@sagepub.com; **Subscr. to:** I N S I O Scientific Books & Periodicals, PO Box 7234, Indraprastha HPO, New Delhi 110 002, India. iihm@ap.nic.in, http://iihm.ap.nic.in/.

➤ **CHINA SECURITY.** *see* CIVIL DEFENSE

327 USA ISSN 1551-9589
DS779.35
CHINASCOPE. Text in English. 2004. bi-m. USD 95 combined subscription domestic (print & online eds.); USD 105 combined subscription in Canada (print & online eds.); USD 115 combined subscription elsewhere (print & online eds.) (effective 2010). **Document type:** *Journal, Academic/Scholarly.*
Related titles: Online - full text ed.: USD 75 (effective 2010).
Indexed: A01, CA, P34, T02.
Published by: Global Communications Association, Inc., 2020 Pennsylvania Ave, #330, Washington, DC 20006. TEL 202-573-2087, FAX 202-315-0630, info@gcommassociates.com, http://gcommassociates.com.

327 GBR ISSN 1750-8916
DS740.4
➤ **CHINESE JOURNAL OF INTERNATIONAL POLITICS.** Text in English. 2006 (Jun.). q. GBP 239 in United Kingdom to institutions; EUR 359 in Europe to institutions; USD 454 in US & Canada to institutions; GBP 239 elsewhere to institutions; GBP 260 combined subscription in United Kingdom to institutions (print & online eds.); EUR 391 combined subscription in Europe to institutions (print & online eds.); USD 496 combined subscription in US & Canada to institutions (print & online eds.); GBP 260 combined subscription elsewhere to institutions (print & online eds.) (effective 2012). back issues avail.; reprint service avail. from PSC. **Document type:** *Journal, Academic/Scholarly.* **Description:** Aims to advance the systematic and rigorous study of international relations.
Related titles: Online - full text ed.: ISSN 1750-8924. GBP 217 in United Kingdom to institutions; EUR 326 in Europe to institutions; USD 413 in US & Canada to institutions; GBP 217 elsewhere to institutions (effective 2012) (from IngentaConnect); ◆ Translation of: Guoji Zhengzhi Kexue.
Indexed: A22, E01, P42, SCOPUS, T02.
—IE. **CCC.**
Published by: (Qinghua Daxue, Guoji Wenti Yanjiusuo/Tsinghua University, Institute of International Studies CHN), Oxford University Press, Great Clarendon St, Oxford, OX2 6DP, United Kingdom. TEL 44-1865-556767, FAX 44-1865-556646, enquiry@oup.co.uk, http://www.oxfordjournals.org. Eds. Chen Qi, Sun Xuefeng, Yan Xuetong.

364.65 FRA
LA CHRONIQUE D'AMNESTY INTERNATIONAL. Text in French. m. EUR 36 to individuals; EUR 20 to students (effective 2008). **Document type:** *Magazine, Consumer.*
Related titles: Online - full text ed.: free.
Published by: Amnesty International, French section, 76 Bd de la Villette, Paris, Cedex 19 75940, France. TEL 33-1-53386521.

372.2 USA ISSN 1025-8523
CHRONIQUE O N U. Text in French. 1952. q. USD 20 in Africa; USD 30 in Australia, New Zealand, Japan & Europe; USD 25 in North America; USD 30 elsewhere (effective 2010).
Former titles (until 1990): Chronique des Nations Unies (1013-5235); (until 1982): Chronique Mensuelle (0251-1843); (until 1964): Revue des Nations Unies (1013-5227)
Related titles: ◆ English ed.: U N Chronicle. ISSN 0251-7329; Spanish ed.: Cronica de las Naciones Unidas. ISSN 0254-8410.
Indexed: RASB.
—CCC.
Published by: United Nations, Department of Public Information, United Nations Building, L-172, New York, NY 10017. TEL 212-963-8262, FAX 917-367-6075.

327 GBR ISSN 1369-8249
➤ **CIVIL WARS.** Text in English. 1998. q. GBP 290 combined subscription in United Kingdom to institutions (print & online eds.); EUR 385, USD 482 combined subscription to institutions (print & online eds.) (effective 2012). adv. illus. Index. back issues avail.; reprint service avail. from PSC. **Document type:** *Journal, Academic/Scholarly.* **Description:** Includes pieces on key topics such as why state building can degenerate into civil war, how ethnic conflict turns into civil war, the ethics of intervention and the resource implications of such conflicts but also welcomes historical work on conflicts such as the US, Spanish or Chinese civil wars.
Related titles: Online - full text ed.: ISSN 1743-968X. GBP 261 in United Kingdom to institutions; EUR 346, USD 434 to institutions (effective 2012) (from IngentaConnect).
Indexed: A01, A03, A08, A22, AmH&L, B21, CA, E01, E17, ESPM, H05, HistAb, I02, I13, IBSS, LID&ISL, M05, P34, P42, PSA, RiskAb, S02, S03, SCOPUS, SociolAb, T02.
—BLDSC (3273.930750), IE, Ingenta. **CCC.**
Published by: Routledge (Subsidiary of: Taylor & Francis Group), 4 Park Sq, Milton Park, Abingdon, Oxon OX14 4RN, United Kingdom. TEL 44-20-70176000, FAX 44-20-70176336, subscriptions@tandf.co.uk, http://www.routledge.com. Eds. Alice Hills TEL 44-113-3432822, Clive Jones. Adv. contact Linda Hann TEL 44-1344-779945. page GBP 195, page USD 285; trim 110 x 178. **Subscr. to:** Taylor & Francis Ltd., Journals Customer Service, Sheepen Pl, Colchester, Essex CO3 3LP, United Kingdom. TEL 44-20-70175544, FAX 44-20-70175198.

➤ **CIVIS MUNDI**; journal of political philosophy and culture. *see* POLITICAL SCIENCE

327.12 GBR ISSN 1363-0164
CLASSICS OF ESPIONAGE SERIES. Text in English. 1996. irreg. price varies. **Document type:** *Monographic series, Academic/Scholarly.* **Description:** A reprint series of five books designed to recover lost and long forgotten texts that have been influential in the history and popular culture of modern espionage.
Published by: Routledge (Subsidiary of: Taylor & Francis Group), 4 Park Sq, Milton Park, Abingdon, Oxon OX14 4RN, United Kingdom. TEL 44-20-70176000, FAX 44-20-70176336, http://www.routledge.com/journals/.

327 SWE ISSN 1654-7489
CLAUDE AKE MEMORIAL PAPERS. Text in English. 2007. irreg., latest vol.2, 2008. **Document type:** *Monographic series, Academic/Scholarly.*
Related titles: Online - full text ed.
Published by: Uppsala Universitet, Institutionen foer Freds- och Konfliktforskning/University of Uppsala, Department of Peace and Conflict Research, Gamla Torget 3, PO Box 514, Uppsala, 75120, Sweden. TEL 46-18-4710000, FAX 46-18-695102, info@pcr.uu.se. **Co-publisher:** Nordiska Afrikainstitutet/The Nordic Africa Institute.

COLD WAR HISTORY. *see* HISTORY

COLD WAR INTERNATIONAL HISTORY PROJECT. BULLETIN. *see* HISTORY

327 BEL ISSN 1780-9665
COLLEGE OF EUROPE STUDIES/CAHIERS DU COLLEGE D'EUROPE. Text in English, French. 2004. irreg., latest vol.10, 2010. price varies. **Document type:** *Monographic series, Academic/Scholarly.*
—BLDSC (3311.066250).
Published by: P I E - Peter Lang SA, 1 avenue Maurice, 6e etage, Brussels, 1050, Belgium. TEL 32-2-3477236, FAX 32-2-3477237, pie@peterlang.com, http://www.peterlang.net.

327 NGA
COLLEGE PRESS. ANNUAL LECTURE SERIES; African journal of international affairs $. Text in English. 1995. a. USD 5 (effective 2003). adv. bk.rev. back issues avail. **Document type:** *Journal, Academic/Scholarly.*
Published by: College Press, 5 Baale Akintayo Rd, Jericho GRA, PO Box 30678, Ibadan, Oyo State, Nigeria. collegepresspublishers@yahoo.com. Eds. Hassan Saliu, Jim Adisa, Jide Owoeye.

352.14 BEL
COLLEGIUM. Text in French, English. 1998. 3/yr.
Published by: College of Europe, Dijver 11, Brugge, B-8000, Belgium. Ed. Dr. Marc Vuijlsteke.

327 LUX ISSN 0254-1475
HC336.27
COMMISSION OF THE EUROPEAN COMMUNITIES. DOCUMENTS. Text in English. 1983. w.
Related titles: Danish ed.: Kommissionen for de Europaeiske Faelleskaber. Dokumenter. ISSN 0254-1459; German ed.: Kommision der Europaischen Gemeinschaften. Dokumente. ISSN 0254-1467; Greek ed.: Epitrope ton Europaikon Koinoteton. Eggrafa. ISSN 0254-1483; French ed.: Commission des Communautes Europeennes. Documents. ISSN 0254-1491; Swedish ed.: Europeiska Gemenskapernas Kommission. Dokument. ISSN 1024-4506. 1995; Ed.: Commissie van de Europese Gemeenschappen. Dokumenten. ISSN 0254-1513; Spanish ed.: Comision de las Comunidades Europeas. Documentos. ISSN 0257-9545. 1986; Portuguese ed.: Comissao de las Comunidades Europeias. Documentos. ISSN 0257-9553. 1986; Finnish ed.: Euroopan Yhteisojen Komissio. Asiakirjat. ISSN 1024-4492. 1995; Italian ed.: Commissione delle Comunita Europee. Documenti. ISSN 0254-1505.
Indexed: R18.
Published by: European Commission, Office for Official Publications of the European Union, 2 Rue Mercier, Luxembourg, L-2985, Luxembourg. FAX 352-29291.

COMMON DEFENSE QUARTERLY. *see* MILITARY

327 GBR ISSN 1466-2043
JN248
➤ **COMMONWEALTH AND COMPARATIVE POLITICS.** Text in English. 1961. q. GBP 505 combined subscription in United Kingdom to institutions (print & online eds.); EUR 667, USD 838 combined subscription to institutions (print & online eds.) (effective 2012). adv. bk.rev. illus. index. back issues avail.; reprint service avail. from PSC. **Document type:** *Journal, Academic/Scholarly.* **Description:** Features articles on the comparative politics of Commonwealth countries.
Former titles (until 1998): The Journal of Commonwealth & Comparative Politics (0306-3631); (until 1974): Journal of Commonwealth Political Studies (0021-9908)
Related titles: CD-ROM ed.; Microfilm ed.: (from PQC); Online - full text ed.: ISSN 1743-9094. GBP 454 in United Kingdom to institutions; EUR 600, USD 754 to institutions (effective 2012) (from IngentaConnect).
Indexed: A01, A03, A08, A20, A22, A26, ABCPolSci, APEL, ASCA, ASD, AmHI, B21, BAS, BrHumI, CA, CABA, DIP, E01, E08, E17, ESPM, G08, GEOBASE, GH, H07, HistAb, I05, I13, IBR, IBSS, IBZ, LT, MEA&I, MLA-IB, P06, P30, P34, P42, PCI, PSA, R12, RASB, RRTA, S02, S03, S09, S13, S16, SCOPUS, SOPODA, SPAA, SPPI, SSA, SociolAb, T02, TAR, W11.
—IE, Infotrieve, Ingenta. **CCC.**
Published by: Routledge (Subsidiary of: Taylor & Francis Group), 4 Park Sq, Milton Park, Abingdon, Oxon OX14 4RN, United Kingdom. TEL 44-20-70176000, FAX 44-20-70176336, subscriptions@tandf.co.uk, http://www.routledge.com. Eds. James Chiriyankandath TEL 44-20-73201016, Roger Charlton TEL 44-141-3313161. Adv. contact Linda Hann TEL 44-1344-779945. B&W page GBP 195, B&W page USD 285; trim 110 x 178. **Subscr. to:** Taylor & Francis Ltd., Journals Customer Service, Sheepen Pl, Colchester, Essex CO3 3LP, United Kingdom. TEL 44-20-70175544, FAX 44-20-70175198.

➤ **COMMONWEALTH TOPIC.** *see* GEOGRAPHY

327 USA ISSN 1930-5370
DS501
COMPARATIVE CONNECTIONS; a quarterly e-journal on East Asian Bilateral Relations. Text in English. 1999. q. back issues avail. **Document type:** *Journal, Academic/Scholarly.* **Description:** Aims to inform and interpret the significant issues driving political, economic and security affairs of the United States adn East Asian relations by an ongoing analysis of events in each key bilateral relationship.
Related titles: Online - full text ed.: ISSN 1930-5389. free (effective 2010).
Indexed: CA, P42, S02, S03, SociolAb, T02.
Published by: Pacific Forum C S I S, 1001 Bishop St, Pauahi Tower, Ste 1150, Honolulu, HI 96813. TEL 808-521-6745, pacificforum@pacforum.org, http://csis.org/program/pacific-forum-csis. Eds. Brad Glosserman, Carl Baker.

327 GBR ISSN 1472-4790
D2009
➤ **COMPARATIVE EUROPEAN POLITICS.** Abbreviated title: C E P. Text in English. 2003. 5/yr. USD 1,006 in North America to institutions; GBP 541 elsewhere to institutions (effective 2012). adv. back issues avail.; reprint service avail. from PSC. **Document type:** *Journal, Academic/Scholarly.* **Description:** Provides an international and interdisciplinary forum for research, theory and debate.
Related titles: Online - full text ed.: ISSN 1740-388X (from IngentaConnect).
Indexed: A12, A13, A22, ABIn, CA, CurCont, E01, I08, IBSS, M08, P02, P10, P42, P45, P47, P48, P51, P53, P54, PAIS, PQC, PSA, S11, SCOPUS, SSCI, SociolAb, T02, W07.
—BLDSC (3363.780620), IE, Ingenta. **CCC.**
Published by: Palgrave Macmillan Ltd. (Subsidiary of: Macmillan Publishers Ltd.), Houndmills, Basingstoke, Hants RG21 6XS, United Kingdom. TEL 44-1256-329242, FAX 44-1256-479476, orders@palgrave.com, http://www.palgrave.com. Eds. Ben Rosamond, Colin Hay, Martin A Schain. **Subscr. to:** Subscription Department, Brunel Rd, Houndmills, Basingstoke, Hants RG21 2XS, United Kingdom. TEL 44-1256-357893, FAX 44-1256-812358, subscriptions@palgrave.com.

➤ **COMPARATIVE LAW REVIEW.** *see* LAW

327 ITA ISSN 0010-5066
JX1903
LA COMUNITA INTERNAZIONALE. Text in English, French, Italian. 1946. q. EUR 75 domestic; EUR 200 foreign; free to members (effective 2009). adv. bk.rev. index. **Document type:** *Magazine, Consumer.*
Indexed: A22, ABCPolSci, DoGi, ELLIS, FLP, I13, IBR, IBSS, IBZ, P06, PAIS, PCI, SCOPUS.
—BLDSC (3399.200000), IE, Infotrieve.
Published by: (Societa Italiana per l'Organizzazione Internazionale), Editoriale Scientifica s.r.l., Via San Biagio dei Librai 39, Naples, NA 80138, Italy. TEL 39-081-5800459, FAX 39-081-4971006, es@editorialescientificasrl.it, http://www.editorialescientificasrl.it. Ed. Luigi Ferrari Bravo.

CONFIDENTIAL A-I-R LETTER. (Air Incident Research) *see* CRIMINOLOGY AND LAW ENFORCEMENT

327.172 GBR ISSN 0738-8942
JX1291
➤ **CONFLICT MANAGEMENT AND PEACE SCIENCE.** Abbreviated title: C M P S. Text in English. 1973. 5/yr. USD 478, GBP 259 combined subscription to institutions (print & online eds.); USD 468, GBP 254 to institutions (effective 2011). bk.rev. illus. 150 p./no. 1 cols./p.; back issues avail.; reprint service avail. from PSC. **Document type:** *Journal, Academic/Scholarly.* **Description:** Features original and review articles focused on the scientific study of conflict and peace.
Formerly (until 1980): Journal of Peace Science (0094-3738)
Related titles: Online - full text ed.: ISSN 1549-9219. USD 430, GBP 233 to institutions (effective 2011) (from IngentaConnect).
Indexed: A20, A22, ABCPolSci, ASCA, CA, CMCI, CurCont, E01, ESPM, EconLit, I02, IBSS, JEL, MEA&I, P06, P34, P42, PAIS, PCI, PRA, PSA, RiskAb, S02, S03, SCOPUS, SSCI, SociolAb, T02, W07.
—BLDSC (3410.654000), IE, Infotrieve, Ingenta. **CCC.**
Published by: (Peace Science Society (International) USA), Sage Publications Ltd. (Subsidiary of: Sage Publications, Inc.), 1 Oliver's Yard, 55 City Rd, London, EC1Y 1SP, United Kingdom. TEL 44-20-73248500, FAX 44-20-73248600, info@sagepub.co.uk, http://www.uk.sagepub.com/home.nav. Ed. Glen Palmer.

327 USA ISSN 1946-0236
HD42
➤ **CONFLICT RESOLUTION & NEGOTIATION JOURNAL.** Text in English. 2006. q. USD 285 domestic; USD 320 foreign; USD 80 per issue domestic; USD 92 per issue foreign (effective 2010). back issues avail. **Document type:** *Journal, Academic/Scholarly.*
Published by: Franklin Publishing Company, 2723 Steamboat Cir, Arlington, TX 76006. TEL 817-548-1124, FAX 817-369-2689. Pub. Dr. Ludwig Otto.

327 CAN ISSN 1910-6629
CONFLICT RESOLUTION TODAY. Text in English. 1989. irreg., latest 2006, July. **Document type:** *Magazine, Consumer.*
Former titles (until 2006): The New Interaction (1717-0435); (until 2005): Interaction (1497-0449)
Published by: Conflict Resolution Network Canada, Institute of Peace and Conflict Studies, Conrad Grebel University College, University of Waterloo, Waterloo, ON N2L 3G6, Canada. TEL 519-885-0880, 877-885-0440, FAX 519-885-0806, crnetwork@crnetwork.ca.

322.5 GBR ISSN 1467-8802
JZ5588
➤ **CONFLICT, SECURITY & DEVELOPMENT.** Variant title: Journal of Conflict, Security and Development. Text in English. 2001. q. GBP 416 combined subscription in United Kingdom to institutions (print & online eds.); EUR 552, USD 695 combined subscription to institutions (print & online eds.) (effective 2012). adv. back issues avail.; reprint service avail. from PSC. **Document type:** *Journal, Academic/Scholarly.* **Description:** Presents analysis of economic and political changes taking place at the global level and their impact on developing and transitional countries.
Related titles: Online - full text ed.: ISSN 1478-1174. GBP 374 in United Kingdom to institutions; EUR 497, USD 625 to institutions (effective 2012) (from IngentaConnect).
Indexed: A22, B21, CA, E01, E17, ESPM, I02, P42, P47, PAIS, PQC, PRA, PSA, R02, RiskAb, S02, S03, SCOPUS, SSciA, T02, V&AA.
—IE, Ingenta. **CCC.**
Published by: (University of London King's College, Centre for Defence Studies), Routledge (Subsidiary of: Taylor & Francis Group), 4 Park Sq, Milton Park, Abingdon, Oxon OX14 4RN, United Kingdom. TEL 44-20-70176000, FAX 44-20-70176336, subscriptions@tandf.co.uk, http://www.routledge.com. Ed. Catherine Carney. Adv. contact Linda Hann TEL 44-1344-779945. **Subscr. to:** Taylor & Francis Ltd., Journals Customer Service, Sheepen Pl, Colchester, Essex CO3 3LP, United Kingdom. TEL 44-20-70175544, FAX 44-20-70175198.

▼ ➤ **CONFLICTINZICHT.** *see* SOCIAL SCIENCES: COMPREHENSIVE WORKS

327 FRA ISSN 1148-2664
DE100
➤ **CONFLUENCES MEDITERRANEE.** Variant title: Confluences en Mediterranee. Text in French. 1991. s-a. EUR 52 domestic; EUR 56 foreign (effective 2008). **Document type:** *Journal, Academic/Scholarly.* **Description:** Studies political and cultural questions of concern to the peoples and societies of the Mediterranean basin.
Indexed: CA, CCME, IBR, IBSS, IBZ, T02.
—IE.
Published by: L' Harmattan, 5 Rue de l'Ecole Polytechnique, Paris, 75005, France. TEL 33-1-43257651, FAX 33-1-43258203, http://www.editions-harmattan.fr.

327 ARG ISSN 0327-7852
CONO SUR. Text in Spanish. 1989. irreg.
Indexed: RASB.
Published by: Instituto Latinoamericano de Cooperacion Tecnologica y Relaciones Internacionales, Casilla 825, Guemes, 865 Piso 1 O, Comodoro Rivadavia, Chubut 9000, Argentina. Ed. Emilio Said Jose.

327 GBR ISSN 1755-0912
DS36
CONTEMPORARY ARAB AFFAIRS. Text in English. 2008. q. GBP 344 combined subscription in United Kingdom to institutions (print & online eds.); EUR 537, USD 673 combined subscription to institutions (print & online eds.) (effective 2012). adv. back issues avail.; reprint service avail. from PSC. **Document type:** *Journal, Academic/Scholarly.* **Description:** Publishes work by specialists, policy experts and scholars from the region itself and the international community.
Related titles: Online - full text ed.: ISSN 1755-0920. 2008. GBP 310 in United Kingdom to institutions; EUR 483, USD 605 to institutions (effective 2012).
Indexed: A22, CA, E01, I02, P42, T02.
—IE. **CCC.**
Published by: (Centre for Arab Unity Studies/Markaz Dirasat al-Wahdah al-Arabiyyah LBN), Routledge (Subsidiary of: Taylor & Francis Group), 4 Park Sq, Milton Park, Abingdon, Oxon OX14 4RN, United Kingdom. TEL 44-20-70176000, FAX 44-20-70176336, subscriptions@tandf.co.uk, http://www.routledge.com/journals/. Ed. Khair El-Din Haseeb. Adv. contact Linda Hann TEL 44-1344-779945. **Subscr. to:** Taylor & Francis Ltd., Journals Customer Service, Sheepen Pl, Colchester, Essex CO3 3LP, United Kingdom. TEL 44-20-70175544, FAX 44-20-70175198.

327 CHN ISSN 1003-3408
D849
CONTEMPORARY INTERNATIONAL RELATIONS. Text in English. 1991. m. USD 79.80 (effective 2009). adv. **Document type:** *Journal, Academic/Scholarly.* **Description:** Contains analyses by prominent Chinese scholars on various issues of contemporary international relations.
Related titles: ◆ Chinese ed.: Xiandai Guoji Guanxi. ISSN 1000-6192.
Indexed: RASB.
—East View, IE.
Published by: Xiandai Guoji Guanxi Yanjiusuo/China Institute of Contemporary International Relations, No A-2 Wanshousi, Haidian, Beijing, 100081, China. TEL 86-10-6841-8640, FAX 86-10-6841-8641. Ed. Liu Liping. Adv. contact Tang Lan. Circ: 500.

341.72 GBR ISSN 1352-3260
JX1974 CODEN: CNSPEG
➤ **CONTEMPORARY SECURITY POLICY.** Abbreviated title: C S P. Text in English. 1980. 3/yr. GBP 335 combined subscription in United Kingdom to institutions (print & online eds.); EUR 444, USD 554 combined subscription to institutions (print & online eds.) (effective 2012). adv. bk.rev. index. back issues avail.; reprint service avail. from PSC. **Document type:** *Journal, Academic/Scholarly.* **Description:** Covers the gamut of security agreements and security in the post-cold war world, including issues of arms control and disarmament.
Formerly (until 1994): Arms Control (0144-0381)
Related titles: Microfilm ed.: (from PQC); Online - full text ed.: ISSN 1743-8764. GBP 302 in United Kingdom to institutions; EUR 399, USD 499 to institutions (effective 2012) (from IngentaConnect).
Indexed: A22, ABCPolSci, AMB, AmHI, BrHumI, CA, DIP, E01, ESPM, H07, I02, I13, IBR, IBSS, IBZ, IBibSS, IPI, LID&ISL, P34, P42, P47, PAIS, PCI, PQC, PSA, R02, RASB, RiskAb, S02, S03, SCOPUS, SOPODA, SSA, SociolAb, T02.
—BLDSC (3425.302600), IE, Infotrieve, Ingenta. **CCC.**
Published by: Routledge (Subsidiary of: Taylor & Francis Group), 4 Park Sq, Milton Park, Abingdon, Oxon OX14 4RN, United Kingdom. TEL 44-20-70176000, FAX 44-20-70176336, subscriptions@tandf.co.uk, http://www.routledge.com. Eds. Aaron Karp TEL 757-683-5700, Regina Karp TEL 757-683-5702. Adv. contact Linda Hann TEL 44-1344-779945. B&W page GBP 195, B&W page USD 285; trim 110 x 178. **Subscr. to:** Taylor & Francis Ltd., Journals Customer Service, Sheepen Pl, Colchester, Essex CO3 3LP, United Kingdom. TEL 44-20-70175544, FAX 44-20-70175198.

327 GBR
CONTEMPORARY STRATEGIC ISSUES IN THE ARAB GULF. Text in English. irreg., latest vol.18, 1991. **Document type:** *Monographic series, Academic/Scholarly.*
Published by: Gulf Centre for Strategic Studies, 5 Charterhouse Bldgs, 3rd & 4th Fls, Goswell Rd, London, EC1M 7AN, United Kingdom. TEL 44-171-253-3805, FAX 44-171-253-3809, TELEX 267519 GULFRC G. Ed. Omar Al Hassan.

327.172 NLD ISSN 1574-1583
CONTROVERSIES. Text in English. 2005. irreg., latest vol.10, 2011. price varies. **Document type:** *Monographic series, Academic/Scholarly.* **Description:** Provides studies in the theory of controversy or its aspects, studies of the history of controversy forms and their evolution, and case studies of particular historical or current controversies in any field or period.
—BLDSC (3463.115320).
Published by: John Benjamins Publishing Co., PO Box 36224, Amsterdam, 1020 ME, Netherlands. TEL 31-20-6304747, FAX 31-20-6739773, customer.services@benjamins.nl. Ed. Marcelo Dascal.

327.17 DEU ISSN 1436-4433
CONTROVERSIES FROM THE PROMISED LAND. Text in English. 1999. irreg., latest vol.2, 2002. price varies. **Document type:** *Monographic series, Academic/Scholarly.*
Published by: Peter Lang GmbH (Subsidiary of: Peter Lang Publishing Group), Eschborner Landstr 42-50, Frankfurt Am Main, 60489, Germany. TEL 49-69-7807050, FAX 49-69-78070550, zentrale.frankfurt@peterlang.com. Ed. Wolfgang Freund.

327 FRA ISSN 0293-3292
CONVERGENCES. Text in French. m. EUR 10 (effective 2008). **Document type:** *Magazine, Consumer.*
Formerly: Defense
Published by: Secours Populaire Francais, 9-11 rue Froissart, Paris, 75140, France. TEL 33-1-44782100, FAX 33-1-42747101. Ed. Anne-Marie Cousin. Pub. Bernard Fillatre. Circ: 210,000.

327.48 GBR ISSN 0010-8367
DL55 CODEN: COCFEF
➤ **COOPERATION AND CONFLICT.** Text in English. 1965. q. USD 713, GBP 386 combined subscription to institutions (print & online eds.); USD 699, GBP 378 to institutions (effective 2011). adv. bk.rev. charts; illus. index. back issues avail.; reprint service avail. from PSC. **Document type:** *Journal, Academic/Scholarly.* **Description:** Reflects the vitality and diversity of contemporary Scandinavian international relations research, and addresses critical issues in the scholarly search for a better grasp on the complexities of world affairs.
Related titles: Microform ed.: (from PQC); Online - full text ed.: ISSN 1460-3691. USD 642, GBP 347 to institutions (effective 2011).
Indexed: A01, A03, A08, A20, A22, ABCPolSci, AMB, B01, B06, B07, B09, CA, CurCont, DIP, E-psyche, E01, ESPM, FR, H04, HistAb, I02, I13, I14, IBR, IBSS, IBZ, MEA&I, P06, P30, P34, P42, PAIS, PCI, PRA, PSA, PerIslam, R02, RASB, RiskAb, S02, S03, SCOPUS, SOPODA, SPAA, SSA, SSCI, SociolAb, T02, V02, W07.
—BLDSC (3464.120000), IE, Infotrieve, Ingenta. **CCC.**
Published by: (Nordic International Studies Association FIN), Sage Publications Ltd. (Subsidiary of: Sage Publications, Inc.), 1 Oliver's Yard, 55 City Rd, London, EC1Y 1SP, United Kingdom. TEL 44-20-73248500, FAX 44-20-73248600, info@sagepub.co.uk, http://www.uk.sagepub.com/home.nav. Eds. Frank Moller, Tarja Vayrynen. **Subscr. in the Americas to:** Sage Publications, Inc., 2455 Teller Rd, Thousand Oaks, CA 91320. TEL 805-499-9774, FAX 805-499-0871, journals@sagepub.com.

➤ **COOPERATION SOUTH.** *see* SOCIOLOGY

353.13263 351 DNK ISSN 0908-200X
THE COPENHAGEN DIPLOMATIC LIST. Text in English. 1960. s-a. **Document type:** *Directory, Government.*
Former titles (until 1992): Corps Diplomatique (0902-2732); (until 1967): Corps Diplomatique a Copenhague (0902-2724)
Related titles: Online - full text ed.: ISSN 1901-4015. 200?.
—BLDSC (3472.098000).
Published by: Udenrigsministeriet/Ministry of Foreign Affairs of Denmark, Asiatisk Plads 2, Copenhagen K, 1448, Denmark. TEL 45-33-920000, FAX 45-32-540533, um@um.dk.

327 GBR ISSN 1369-2178
CORBISHLEY MEMORIAL LECTURE. Variant title: Thomas Corbishley Lectures. Text in English. 1977. a. GBP 2.50 per issue (effective 2009). back issues avail. **Document type:** *Monographic series.*
—BLDSC (3470.343800).
Published by: Wyndham Place Charlemagne Trust, Copper Beeches, Gough Rd, Fleet, Hants, GU51 4LJ, United Kingdom. TEL 44-1252-612527, FAX 44-1252-612527, judykeep@yahoo.co.uk, http://www.wpct.co.uk.

327 USA ISSN 2156-0528
JZ6.5
➤ **CORNELL INTERNATIONAL AFFAIRS REVIEW.** Text in English. 2007. s-a. **Document type:** *Journal, Academic/Scholarly.* **Description:** Provides a nonpartisan undergraduate society and forum dedicated to the study of international relations in an increasingly globalized world.
Related titles: Online - full text ed.: ISSN 2156-0536.
Published by: Cornell University, 245 Goldwin Smith Hall, Ithaca, NY 14850. TEL 607-254-2473, FAX 607-254-2415, traces@cornell.edu, http://www.cornell.edu.

327 CHL
COSAS. Text in Spanish. 1976. fortn. CLP 49,500 (effective 2007). adv. **Document type:** *Magazine, Consumer.*
Address: Almirante Pastene, 329, Providencia, Santiago, Chile. TEL 56-2-3645100, FAX 56-2-2358331. Ed. Monica Comandari Kaiser. R&P Christian Plaetner-Moher. Adv. contact Matias Pfingsthorn. color page USD 5,500; trim 330 x 240. Circ: 25,000.

THE COTE D'IVOIRE BUSINESS FORECAST REPORT. *see* BUSINESS AND ECONOMICS

327 FRA
COUNCIL OF EUROPE. COMMITTEE OF INDEPENDENT EXPERTS ON THE EUROPEAN SOCIAL CHARTER. CONCLUSIONS. Text in English. 1970. biennial. price varies.
Related titles: French ed.
Published by: Council of Europe/Conseil de l'Europe, Avenue de l'Europe, Strasbourg, 67075, France. TEL 33-3-88412581, FAX 33-3-88413910, publishing@coe.int, http://www.coe.int. **Dist. in U.S. by:** Manhattan Publishing Co., 468 Albany Post Rd, Croton On Hudson, NY 10520.

327 AUS ISSN 1832-9705
COUNCIL ON AUSTRALIA LATIN AMERICA RELATIONS. ANNUAL REPORT. Text in English. 2002. a. back issues avail. **Document type:** *Report, Trade.*
Related titles: Online - full text ed.: free (effective 2009).
Published by: Council on Australia Latin America Relations, COALAR Secretariat, Department of Foreign Affairs & Trade, John McEwen Crescent, Barton, ACT 0221, Australia. TEL 61-2-62613334, FAX 61-2-62613629, latin.desk@dfat.gov.au, http://www.dfat.gov.au/coalar/index.html.

327.2 USA ISSN 0192-236X
JX27.C6
COUNCIL ON FOREIGN RELATIONS. ANNUAL REPORT. Text in English. 19??. a. free (effective 2009). **Document type:** *Corporate.*
Incorporates (19??-197?): Council on Foreign Relations. President's Report (0093-4615); Formerly (until 1953): Report of the Executive Director
Related titles: Microfilm ed.: (from PMC); Online - full text ed.
—**CCC.**
Published by: Council on Foreign Relations, Inc., The Harold Pratt House, 58 E 68th St, New York, NY 10065. TEL 212-434-9400, FAX 212-434-9800, corporate@cfr.org. Eds. James F Hoge Jr., James F Hoge Jr. Pub. David Kellogg.

COUNCIL ON HEMISPHERIC AFFAIRS NEWS AND ANALYSIS. *see* BUSINESS AND ECONOMICS—International Development And Assistance

COUNTER TERRORISM CHRONICLE. *see* CIVIL DEFENSE

327 GBR
COUNTRY RISK DAILY REPORT. Text in English. 1994. d. USD 760, GBP 460, AUD 1,200 (effective 2010). **Document type:** *Report, Trade.* **Description:** Contains contextual analysis of recent and impending events in international security.
Former titles (until 200?): Intelligence Watch Report (1524-3885); (until 199?): I W R Daily Update (1088-0569)
Media: Online - full text. **Related titles:** CD-ROM ed.: GBP 350, USD 585, AUD 915 (effective 2010).
—**CCC.**
Published by: I H S Jane's (Subsidiary of: I H S), Sentinel House, 163 Brighton Rd, Coulsdon, Surrey CR5 2YH, United Kingdom. TEL 44-20-87003700, FAX 44-20-87003751, info@janes.co.uk, http://www.janes.com.

327.1 USA ISSN 1044-5900
COURIER (MUSCATINE); provoking thought and encouraging dialogue about the world. Text in English. 1989. q. free to qualified personnel (effective 2009). back issues avail. **Document type:** *Magazine, Trade.* **Description:** Provides thought on world affairs by giving readers insight into issues driving foundation programming.
Related titles: E-mail ed.: free (effective 2009); Online - full text ed.: ISSN 1948-3112. free (effective 2009).
Indexed: PAIS.
Published by: The Stanley Foundation, 209 Iowa Ave, Muscatine, IA 52761. TEL 563-264-1500, FAX 563-264-0864, info@stanleyfoundation.org. Ed. Keith Porter.

COVERT INTELLIGENCE LETTER. *see* MILITARY

327 GBR ISSN 1749-1800
CRISIS STATES WORKING PAPERS. SERIES NO.2 (ONLINE). Text in English. 2001; N.S. 2005. irreg. free (effective 2009). back issues avail. **Document type:** *Monographic series, Academic/Scholarly.* **Description:** Covers the current phase of Crisis States research centre's work from 2006 onwards.
Formerly (until 2005): Crisis States Programme Working Papers (1740-5815)

P

Media: Online - full text. **Related titles:** ◆ Print ed.: Crisis States Working Papers. Series No.2 (Print). ISSN 1749-1797.
Published by: London School of Economics and Political Science, Crisis States Research Centre, Houghton St, Rm U610, London, WC2A 2AE, United Kingdom. TEL 44-20-78494631, FAX 44-20-79556421, csp@lse.ac.uk.

327 GBR ISSN 1749-1797
CRISIS STATES WORKING PAPERS. SERIES NO.2 (PRINT). Text in English. 2001; N.S. 2005. irreg. free (effective 2009). back issues avail. **Document type:** *Monographic series, Academic/Scholarly.* **Description:** Covers the current phase of Crisis States research centre's work from 2006 onwards.
Formerly (until 2005): Crisis States Programme Working Papers. (1740-5807)
Related titles: ◆ Online - full text ed.: Crisis States Working Papers. Series No.2 (Online). ISSN 1749-1800; ◆ Spanish ed.: Programa Crisis de los Estados Documentos de Trabajo. ISSN 1740-5823.
Published by: London School of Economics and Political Science, Crisis States Research Centre, Houghton St, Rm U610, London, WC2A 2AE, United Kingdom. TEL 44-20-78494631, FAX 44-20-79556421, csp@lse.ac.uk.

327 GBR ISSN 1467-2715
DS1
➤ **CRITICAL ASIAN STUDIES.** Abbreviated title: C A S. Text in English. 1968. q. GBP 196 combined subscription in United Kingdom to institutions (print & online eds.); EUR 250, USD 313 combined subscription to institutions (print & online eds.) (effective 2012). adv. bk.rev. bibl.; charts; illus. Index. 84 p./no.; back issues avail.; reprint service avail. from PSC. **Document type:** *Journal, Academic/Scholarly.* **Description:** Publishes scholarly articles and other materials that challenge the accepted formulas for understanding the Asia and Pacific regions, the world, and ourselves.
Former titles (until 2000): Bulletin of Concerned Asian Scholars (0007-4810); (until 1969): C C A S Newsletter (0898-7785)
Related titles: Microform ed.: (from PQC); Online - full text ed.: ISSN 1472-6033. GBP 176 in United Kingdom to institutions; EUR 225, USD 282 to institutions (effective 2012) (from IngentaConnect).
Indexed: A01, A03, A08, A20, A22, APEL, ASCA, AltPI, BAS, CA, CurCont, DIP, E01, EI, ESPM, FR, GEOBASE, HRIR, HistAb, I02, IBR, IBSS, IBZ, ILD, LeftInd, M10, MEA&I, MLA-IB, P30, P34, P42, PAIS, PSA, PerIslam, R02, S02, S03, SCOPUS, SPPI, SSCI, SSciA, SociolAb, T02, W07.
—BLDSC (3487.450230), IE, Infotrieve, Ingenta. **CCC.**
Published by: (Bulletin of Concerned Asian Scholars, Inc USA), Routledge (Subsidiary of: Taylor & Francis Group), 4 Park Sq, Milton Park, Abingdon, Oxon OX14 4RN, United Kingdom. TEL 44-20-70176000, FAX 44-20-70176336, subscriptions@tandf.co.uk, http://www.routledge.com/journals/. Adv. contact Linda Hann TEL 44-1344-779945. Circ: 1,000 (paid); 300 (controlled). **Subscr. outside N. America to:** Taylor & Francis Ltd., Journals Customer Service, Sheepen Pl, Colchester, Essex CO3 3LP, United Kingdom. TEL 44-20-70175544, FAX 44-20-70175198, tf.enquiries@tfinforma.com.

327.17 SWE ISSN 1654-4250
CRITICAL CURRENTS. Text in English. 2007. irreg. free. **Document type:** *Monographic series, Academic/Scholarly.*
Related titles: Online - full text ed.
Published by: Dag Hammarskjoeld Foundation, Dag Hammarskjoeld Centre, Oevre Slottsgatan 2, Uppsala, 75310, Sweden. TEL 46-18-4101000, FAX 46-18-122072, secretariat@dhf.uu.se.

327 NLD ISSN 1877-2110
▼ **CRITICAL GLOBAL STUDIES.** Text in English. 2010. irreg., latest vol.3, 2011. EUR 99, USD 141 per vol. (effective 2010). **Document type:** *Monographic series, Academic/Scholarly.*
Published by: Brill, PO Box 9000, Leiden, 2300 PA, Netherlands. TEL 31-71-5353500, FAX 31-71-5317532, cs@brill.nl, http://www.brill.nl. Ed. Richard A Dello Buono.

320.6 100 GBR ISSN 1369-8230
JA8
➤ **CRITICAL REVIEW OF INTERNATIONAL SOCIAL AND POLITICAL PHILOSOPHY.** Abbreviated title: C R I S P P. Text in English. 1998. q. GBP 423 combined subscription in United Kingdom to institutions (print & online eds.); EUR 560, USD 703 combined subscription to institutions (print & online eds.) (effective 2012). adv. bk.rev. back issues avail.; reprint service avail. from PSC. **Document type:** *Journal, Academic/Scholarly.* **Description:** Serves as a transdisciplinary journal concerned with the overlap between theory and practice. Focuses on major individual thinkers and major theories with special regard to their practical policy implications. For academics and practitioners with an interest in the tie between philosophical reflection and public policy.
Related titles: Online - full text ed.: ISSN 1743-8772. GBP 381 in United Kingdom to institutions; EUR 503, USD 632 to institutions (effective 2012) (from IngentaConnect).
Indexed: A22, B21, CA, E01, E17, ESPM, I13, P34, P42, P47, PQC, PSA, PhilInd, S02, S03, SCOPUS, SSA, SociolAb, T02.
—IE, Ingenta. **CCC.**
Published by: Routledge (Subsidiary of: Taylor & Francis Group), 4 Park Sq, Milton Park, Abingdon, Oxon OX14 4RN, United Kingdom. TEL 44-20-70176000, FAX 44-20-70176336, subscriptions@tandf.co.uk, http://www.routledge.com. Adv. contact Linda Hann TEL 44-1344-779945. page GBP 195, page USD 285; trim 110 x 178. **Subscr. to:** Taylor & Francis Ltd., Journals Customer Service, Sheepen Pl, Colchester, Essex CO3 3LP, United Kingdom. TEL 44-20-70175544, FAX 44-20-70175198.

327.117 GBR ISSN 1753-9153
HV6431
➤ **CRITICAL STUDIES ON TERRORISM.** Text in English. 2008. 3/yr. GBP 216 combined subscription in United Kingdom to institutions (print & online eds.); EUR 335, USD 420 combined subscription to institutions (print & online eds.) (effective 2012). adv. reprint service avail. from PSC. **Document type:** *Journal, Academic/Scholarly.* **Description:** Covers all aspects of terrorism, counter-terrorism and state terror.
Related titles: Online - full text ed.: ISSN 1753-9161. GBP 194 in United Kingdom to institutions; EUR 302, USD 379 to institutions (effective 2012).
Indexed: A22, C04, CA, E01, I02, P05, T02.
—IE. **CCC.**
Published by: Routledge (Subsidiary of: Taylor & Francis Group), 4 Park Sq, Milton Park, Abingdon, Oxon OX14 4RN, United Kingdom. TEL 44-20-70176000, FAX 44-20-70176336, subscriptions@tandf.co.uk, http://www.routledge.com/journals/. Eds. George Kassimeris, Piers Robinson. Adv. contact Linda Hann TEL 44-1344-779945. **Subscr. to:** Taylor & Francis Ltd., Journals Customer Service, Sheepen Pl, Colchester, Essex CO3 3LP, United Kingdom. TEL 44-20-70175544, FAX 44-20-70175198.

327 FRA ISSN 1290-7839
JZ11
CRITIQUE INTERNATIONALE. Text in French. 1998. q. EUR 55 domestic to individuals; EUR 63 foreign to individuals; EUR 76 domestic to institutions; EUR 93 foreign to institutions (effective 2009); EUR 46.50 domestic to students (effective 2007). back issues avail. **Document type:** *Journal, Academic/Scholarly.*
Related titles: Online - full text ed.: ISSN 1777-554X.
Indexed: CA, FR, I13, I14, IBR, IBSS, IBZ, P42, PSA, SCOPUS, SociolAb, T02.
—INIST.
Published by: Presses de Sciences Po, 117 Boulevard Saint Germain, Paris, 75006, France. TEL 33-1-45498331, FAX 33-1-45498334, info@presses.sciences-po.fr, http://www.sciences-po.fr.

327.4972 HRV ISSN 1331-1182
JZ6.5
➤ **CROATIAN INTERNATIONAL RELATIONS REVIEW.** Text in English. 1995. q. EUR 30 foreign (effective 2005). adv. bk.rev. **Document type:** *Journal, Academic/Scholarly.* **Description:** Publishes research on the Croatian international position.
Related titles: Online - full text ed.
Indexed: CA, I13, IBR, IBZ, P42, PAIS, PSA, RASB, SCOPUS, SociolAb, T02.
Published by: Institut za Medunarodne Odnose/Institute for International Relations, Ljudevita Farkasa Vukotinovica 2, PO Box 303, Zagreb, 10000, Croatia. TEL 385-1-4877460, FAX 385-1-4828361, ured@irmo.hr. Ed., R&P Mladen Stanicic. Adv. contact Andrea Ruk. Circ: 2,000.

➤ **CROSSROADS.** *see* BUSINESS AND ECONOMICS

327 ARG ISSN 0326-7806
CUADERNOS DE POLITICA EXTERIOR ARGENTINA. Text in Spanish. 1985. q. **Document type:** *Journal, Academic/Scholarly.*
Published by: Universidad Nacional de Rosario, Centro de Estudios en Relaciones Internacionales, San Juan 4290, Rosario, Santa Fe, S2000CGK, Argentina. cerir@unr.edu.ar, http://www.cerir.com.ar/#. Circ: 500.

327 MEX ISSN 2007-1248
CUADERNOS FRONTERIZOS. Text in Spanish. 2005. q. **Document type:** *Journal, Academic/Scholarly.*
Published by: Universidad Autonoma de Ciudad Juarez, Instituto de Ciencias Sociales y Administracion, Ave Colegio Militar y Ave Universidad, Zona Chamizal, Ciudad Juarez, Chihuahua 32310, Mexico. ciisme@uacj.mx, http://www.uacj.mx/ICSA/.

327 VEN ISSN 1856-349X
➤ **CUADERNOS SOBRE RELACIONES INTERNACIONALES, REGIONALISMO Y DESARROLLO.** Text in Spanish; Summaries in English, Spanish. 2006 (Jun.). s-a. USD 20 in South America; USD 30 in Europe; USD 25 in United States (effective 2010). back issues avail. **Document type:** *Journal, Academic/Scholarly.* **Description:** Analyzes the links between regionalism, economic integration and development. The audience is most academic but the journal is also used by public servant at the Ministry of Economy and Ministry of Foreign Affairs.
Related titles: Online - full text ed.: free.
Published by: Universidad de los Andes, Centro de Estudios de Fronteras e Integracion, Grupo de Investigacion sobre Regionalismo, Integracion y Desarrollo, Avenidad Universidad, Sector Paramillo, Edf. Administrativo, 3 Piso, San Cristobal, Tachira 5001, Venezuela. TEL 58-276-3405051, FAX 58-276-3405149. Ed., R&P Jose Briceno Ruiz. Pub. Raquel Alvarez de Flores.

327 CUB ISSN 0011-2593
AP63
CUBA INTERNACIONAL. Text in Spanish. 1969. m. charts; illus. **Document type:** *Magazine, Consumer.*
Related titles: Online - full text ed.: ISSN 1681-9985; Russian ed.
Indexed: IBR, IBZ, RASB.
Published by: Ediciones Cubanas, Obispo 527, Havana, Cuba. TEL 53-7-631942, FAX 53-7-338943. Ed. Jesus Hernandez. Circ: 30,000.

327 USA
CUBA UPDATE (ONLINE). Text in English. 200?. bi-m. **Document type:** *Journal, Trade.*
Media: Online - full text.
Published by: Center for Cuban Studies, Inc., 231 W 29 St, 4th fl, New York, NY 10001. TEL 212-242-0559, FAX 212-242-1937, cubanartspace@gmail.com.

327 320 FRA ISSN 0252-0869
CULTURAL POLICY. Text in English. 1977. q. free. bk.rev. bibl.; stat. back issues avail.
Indexed: MLA-IB.
Published by: Council of Europe/Conseil de l'Europe, Avenue de l'Europe, Strasbourg, 67075, France. TEL 33-3-88412033, FAX 33-3-88412745, publishing@coe.int, http://www.coe.int. Ed. Sezen Germen.

327 AUS
CULTURE MANDALA (ONLINE). Text in English. a. free (effective 2008). **Document type:** *Journal, Academic/Scholarly.*
Media: Online - full text.
Published by: Bond University, Faculty of Humanities and Social Sciences, University Dr., Robina, QLD 4226, Australia. TEL 61-7-55952522, FAX 61-7-55952545, http://www.bond.edu.au. Eds. R James Ferguson, Rosita Dellios.

327 FRA ISSN 1157-996X
U240 CODEN: CCONEF
CULTURES & CONFLITS. Text in Multiple languages. 1991. q. EUR 54.90 domestic; EUR 61 foreign (effective 2008). **Document type:** *Journal, Academic/Scholarly.*
Related titles: Online - full text ed.: ISSN 1777-5345. 2002.
Indexed: CA, FR, IBR, IBSS, IBZ, P30, P42, PAIS, PSA, S02, S03, SCOPUS, SOPODA, SSA, SociolAb, T02.
—IE, INIST. **CCC.**
Published by: (Centre d'Etude des Conflits), L' Harmattan, 5 Rue de l'Ecole Polytechnique, Paris, 75005, France. TEL 33-1-43257651, FAX 33-1-43258203, http://www.editions-harmattan.fr. Ed. Didier Bigo.

CUMMINGS CENTER SERIES. *see* HISTORY—History Of Europe

CURRENT DECISIONS REPORTS. *see* MILITARY

CURRENT DIGEST OF THE RUSSIAN PRESS. *see* POLITICAL SCIENCE—Abstracting, Bibliographies, Statistics

327.09 USA ISSN 0011-3530
CURRENT HISTORY; a journal of contemporary world affairs. Text in English. 1914. 9/yr. USD 38 domestic (print or online ed.); USD 46 foreign; USD 48 combined subscription domestic (print & online eds.); USD 56 combined subscription foreign (print & online eds.) (effective 2009). adv. bk.rev. illus. index. back issues avail.; reprints avail. **Document type:** *Magazine, Trade.* **Description:** Provides a forum for leading scholars and specialists to analyze events and trends in every region of a rapidly changing world.
Formed by the merger of (1940-1941): Current History & Forum (1932-7064); (1937-1941): Events; Incorporates (1940-1941): Key to Contemporary Affairs; (1945-1950): Forum; Which was formerly (until 1945): Forum and Column Review; (until 1943): Column Review and Editorial Digest; (until 1939): Column Review
Related titles: Microfiche ed.: (from NBI, PQC); Online - full text ed.: ISSN 1944-785X.
Indexed: A01, A02, A03, A08, A20, A22, A25, A26, ABCPolSci, ABS&EES, APEL, ARG, ASCA, Acal, AmH&L, AmHI, B04, B05, BAS, BRD, C05, CA, CBPI, CBRI, CPerl, ChPerl, CurCont, DIP, E01, E08, G05, G06, G07, G08, GSS&RPL, H07, H08, HAb, HistAb, HumInd, I05, I07, IBR, IBSS, IBZ, LID&ISL, LeftInd, M01, M02, M06, MASUSE, MEA&I, MLA-IB, MagInd, P02, P06, P10, P13, P30, P34, P42, P45, P47, P48, P53, P54, PAIS, PCI, PMR, PQC, PRA, PSA, PerIslam, R03, R04, RASB, REE&TA, RGAb, RGPR, S08, S09, S11, SCOPUS, SSCI, SociolAb, T02, TOM, W03, W07.
—BLDSC (3497.500000), IE, Infotrieve, Ingenta.
Published by: Current History, Inc., 4225 Main St, Philadelphia, PA 19127. TEL 215-482-4464, FAX 800-293-3755. Ed. Alan Sorensen. Pub., Adv. contact Mark Redmond.

327 USA ISSN 0161-6641
JK1
CURRENT ISSUES (ALEXANDRIA); critical policy choices facing the nation and the world. Text in English. 1977. a. USD 50 per issue for 10 copies (effective 2011). charts; illus.; stat. index. **Document type:** *Journal, Academic/Scholarly.* **Description:** Covers ten foreign and ten domestic policy issues. Contains an introduction to the issue, key questions, background and history, current issues (what's happening now), and outlook (what to expect in the future).
Related titles: Online - full text ed.
Published by: Close Up Foundation, 44 Canal Ctr Plz, 6th Fl, Alexandria, VA 22314. TEL 703-706-3300, info@closeup.org.

327 USA ISSN 1524-1688
DK510.763
CURRENT POLITICS AND ECONOMICS OF RUSSIA, EASTERN AND CENTRAL EUROPE. Text in English. 1991. bi-m. USD 1,150 to institutions; USD 1,725 combined subscription to institutions (print & online eds.) (effective 2012). **Document type:** *Journal, Academic/Scholarly.* **Description:** Presents current information concerning the changing political situation in Russia, Eastern and Central Europe.
Formerly (until 1998): Current Politics and Economics of Russia (1061-9186); Which was formed by the merger of (1990-1991): Current Politics of the Soviet Union (1048-7387); Political and Economic Spectrum of the Soviet Union (1057-2295)
Related titles: Online - full text ed.: USD 1,150 to institutions (effective 2012).
—IE, Ingenta.
Published by: Nova Science Publishers, Inc., 400 Oser Ave, Ste 1600, Hauppauge, NY 11788. TEL 631-231-7269, FAX 631-231-8175, main@novapublishers.com. Pub. Frank Columbus.

327 PHL
CURRENTS. Text in English. 2/yr. USD 14 (effective 2001). **Description:** Covers contemporary developments in China, overseas Chinese, and Philippine-Chinese relations.
Formerly: China Currents (0117-1186)
Indexed: IPP.
Published by: Philippine - China Development Resource Center, 23 Madison St, New Manila, Quezon City, 1112, Philippines. TEL 63-2-722-8861, FAX 63-2-722-8861, devex@info.com.ph, pdrc@info.com.ph.

327.2 CYP ISSN 1015-2873
CYPRUS DIPLOMATIST. Text in English. 1989. bi-m.
Address: 16-18 Halkokondyli St, PO Box 660, Nicosia, Cyprus. TEL 357-2-366866. Ed. George Lantis. Circ: 2,000.

CZECH AND SLOVAK HISTORY NEWSLETTER. *see* ETHNIC INTERESTS

328 ESP ISSN 1132-6107
D C I D O B. (Centre d'Informacio i Documentacio Internacionals a Barcelona) Text in Catalan, Spanish. 1979. bi-m. 48 p./no.; **Document type:** *Monographic series, Consumer.* **Description:** Aims to become an instrument of information and reflection on international relations and cooperation for development.
Former titles (until 1988): Dossier - C I D O B (1132-6093); (until 1983): C I D O B - T M (1132-6085)
Related titles: Online - full text ed.: ISSN 2013-3413.
Published by: Fundacio C I D O B, C. Elisabets, 12, Barcelona, 08001, Spain. TEL 34-93-3026495, FAX 34-93-3022118, publicaciones@cibod.org, http://www.cibod.org.

327 DEU ISSN 1866-9190
D G A P AKTUELL. (Deutsche Gesellschaft fuer Auswaertige Politik) Text in German. 2008. irreg., latest vol.7, 2009. **Document type:** *Monographic series, Academic/Scholarly.*
Published by: Deutsche Gesellschaft fuer Auswaertige Politik e.V., Rauchstr 17/18, Berlin, 10787, Germany. TEL 49-30-2542310, FAX 49-30-25423116, info@dgap.org.

327 DEU ISSN 1611-7034
D G A P ANALYSE. (Deutsche Gesellschaft fuer Auswaertige Politik) Text in German. 2003. irreg., latest vol.8, 2009. price varies. **Document type:** *Monographic series, Academic/Scholarly.*

Published by: Deutsche Gesellschaft fuer Auswaertige Politik e.V., Rauchstr 17/18, Berlin, 10787, Germany. TEL 49-30-2542310, FAX 49-30-25423116, info@dgap.org.

327 DEU ISSN 1865-701X
D G A P ANALYSE FRANKREICH. (Deutsche Gesellschaft fuer Auswaertige Politik) Text in German. 2007. irreg. **Document type:** *Monographic series, Academic/Scholarly.*
Media: Online - full content.
Published by: Deutsche Gesellschaft fuer Auswaertige Politik e.V., Rauchstr 17/18, Berlin, 10787, Germany. TEL 49-30-2542310, FAX 49-30-25423116, info@dgap.org.

327 DEU ISSN 1866-9174
D G A P BERICHT. (Deutsche Gesellschaft fuer Auswaertige Politik) Text in German, English. 2006. irreg. **Document type:** *Monographic series, Academic/Scholarly.*
Related titles: Online - full text ed.: ISSN 1866-9182.
Published by: Deutsche Gesellschaft fuer Auswaertige Politik e.V., Rauchstr 17/18, Berlin, 10787, Germany. TEL 49-30-2542310, FAX 49-30-25423116, info@dgap.org.

327 DEU
D G A P - SCHRIFTEN ZUR INTERNATIONALEN POLITIK. (Deutsche Gesellschaft fuer Auswaertige Politik) Text in German. 2005. irreg., latest 2010. price varies. **Document type:** *Monographic series, Academic/Scholarly.*
Published by: (Deutsche Gesellschaft fuer Auswaertige Politik e.V.), Nomos Verlagsgesellschaft mbH und Co. KG, Waldseestr 3-5, Baden-Baden, 76530, Germany. TEL 49-7221-21040, FAX 49-7221-210427, nomos@nomos.de, http://www.nomos.de.

327 DEU ISSN 1864-3477
D G A P STANDPUNKT. Text in German, English. 2007. m. **Document type:** *Journal, Academic/Scholarly.*
Media: Online - full text.
Published by: Deutsche Gesellschaft fuer Auswaertige Politik e.V., Rauchstr 17/18, Berlin, 10787, Germany. TEL 49-30-2542310, FAX 49-30-25423116, info@dgap.org.

327.172 USA
D P F NEWS NOTES. Text in English. q. USD 10. **Document type:** *Newsletter.*
Published by: Disciples Peace Fellowship, PO Box 1986, Indianapolis, IN 46206-1986. TEL 317-635-3113, FAX 317-635-4426. Ed. Dalene Vasbinder. Circ: 2,200.

327 382 CHN ISSN 1006-4206
DANGDAI SHIJIE/CONTEMPORARY WORLD. Text in Chinese. 1989. m. USD 49.20 (effective 2009). **Document type:** *Magazine, Consumer.*
Formerly (until 1994): Zhengdang yu Dangdai Shijie/Parties & the Contemporary World (1004-7719)
Related titles: Online - full text ed.
—East View.
Published by: Zhonggong Zhongyang Duiwai Lianluobu, 4, Fuxin Lu, Beijing, 100860, China. TEL 86-10-83908406. **Dist. by:** China International Book Trading Corp, 35 Chegongzhuang Xilu, Haidian District, PO Box 399, Beijing 100044, China. TEL 86-10-68412045, FAX 86-10-68412023, cibtc@mail.cibtc.com.cn, http://www.cibtc.com.cn.

327 CHN ISSN 1005-6505
HX9.C5
DANGDAI SHIJIE YU SHEHUI ZHUYI/CONTEMPORARY WORLD AND SOCIALISM. Text in Chinese. 1989. bi-m. USD 48 (effective 2009). adv. bk.rev. **Document type:** *Journal, Academic/Scholarly.* **Description:** Studies the history, theories and practices of world socialism, as well as the present conditions and developments of international politics and economics.
Formerly (until vol.4, 1993): Guoji Gongyunshi Yanjiu/Studies of History of International Communist Movement (1003-3858)
Related titles: Online - full text ed.
—East View.
Published by: Zhongyang Malie Zuzuo Bianyi-ju, Shijie Shehui Zhuyi Yanjiusuo/Institute for World Socialism Studies, 36 Xixie Jie, Xidan, Beijing, 100032, China. TEL 86-10-66173601, FAX 86-10-66117537. Ed. Hu Wenjian. Adv. contact Chen Lin. Circ: 2,500.

327.489 DNK ISSN 1397-2480
DL159
DANISH FOREIGN POLICY YEARBOOK. Text in English; Summaries in Danish, English. 1979. a. free. adv. back issues avail. **Document type:** *Yearbook, Academic/Scholarly.* **Description:** Publishes research articles on Danish foreign policy written by specialists in the field.
Supersedes in part (in 1997): Dansk Udenrigspolitisk Aarbog (0107-0487)
Related titles: Online - full text ed.
Indexed: I13, P42.
Published by: Dansk Institut for Internationale Studier/Danish Institute for International Studies, Strandgade 56, Copenhagen K, 1401, Denmark. TEL 45-32-698787, FAX 45-32-698700, diis@diis.dk.

DANSK FLYGTNINGEHJAELP. *see* SOCIAL SERVICES AND WELFARE

DAYAN CENTER NEWS. *see* HISTORY—History Of The Near East

DAYAN CENTER PAPERS. *see* HISTORY—History Of The Near East

328 ESP
DE SUR A SUR; revista andaluza de solidad, paz y cooperacion. Text in Spanish. s-a. back issues avail. **Document type:** *Magazine, Consumer.*
Related titles: Online - full text ed.
Published by: Asociacion Andaluza por la Solidaridad y la Paz, Avenuda de Rabanales 19, Cordoba, 14007, Spain. TEL 34-957-437251, FAX 34-957-437377, aspa.cordoba@nodo50.org, http://www.nodo50.org/aspa.

DEADLINE. *see* JOURNALISM

DECLASSIFIED DOCUMENTS REFERENCE SYSTEM. *see* POLITICAL SCIENCE—Abstracting, Bibliographies, Statistics

DEFENCE AND SECURITY ANALYSIS. *see* MILITARY

DEFENCE STUDIES. *see* MILITARY

327 USA ISSN 0277-4933
UA10
DEFENSE & FOREIGN AFFAIRS STRATEGIC POLICY. Text in English. 1972. m. USD 139 (effective 2009). adv. bk.rev. back issues avail. **Document type:** *Journal, Trade.* **Description:** Contains reports of U.S. and Soviet policies, arms transfer and price tables and in-depth strategic analysis, power tables.
Formerly (until 1979): Defense & Foreign Affairs Digest (0740-2724)
Related titles: Online - full text ed.
Indexed: A22, AUNI, CA, DM&T, LID&ISL, M05, M07, P02, P10, P45, P47, P48, P53, P54, PAIS, PQC, RASB, T02.
—CIS, IE, Infotrieve, Ingenta.
Published by: The International Strategic Studies Association, PO Box 320608, Alexandria, VA 22320. TEL 703-548-1070, FAX 703-684-7476, GRCopley@StrategicStudies.org, http://www.strategicstudies.org/. **Subscr. to:** PO Box 20407, Alexandria, VA 22320.

DEFENSE & SECURITY. *see* MILITARY

DEFENSE FOREIGN AFFAIRS HANDBOOK; political, economic & defense data on every country in the world. *see* MILITARY

327 FRA ISSN 1957-9578
DEFENSE, STRATEGIE & RELATIONS INTERNATIONALES. Text in French. 2007. irreg. back issues avail. **Document type:** *Monographic series, Academic/Scholarly.*
Published by: L' Harmattan, 5 Rue de l'Ecole Polytechnique, Paris, 75005, France. TEL 33-1-43257651, FAX 33-1-43258203.

327 305.83 CHN ISSN 1005-4871
DEGUO YANJIU/DEUTSCHLAND-STUDIEN. Text in Chinese. 1986. q. **Document type:** *Journal, Academic/Scholarly.*
Formerly: Liangbang Deguo Yanjiu
Related titles: Online - full text ed.
Published by: Tongji Daxue, Deyizhi Lianbang Gongheguo Wenti Yanjiusuo/Institut fuer Studien zur Bundesrepublik Deutschland der Tongji Universitat, 1239, Siping Lu, 11/F, Tongji Daxue Tushuguan, Shanghai, 200092, China. TEL 86-21-65980918, FAX 86-21-65987800, http://www.tjdgyj.com/index.asp.

341.7 USA ISSN 1541-8812
THE DELEGATE. Text in English. 2002 (Fall). s-a. **Document type:** *Handbook/Manual/Guide, Government.*
Published by: United Nations Association of the United States of America & the Business Council for the United Nations, 801 Second Ave, New York, NY 10017. TEL 212-907-1300, FAX 212-682-9185, inquiries@un.org, http://www.unausa.org.

327 GBR ISSN 1351-0347
JC421
➤ **DEMOCRATIZATION.** Text in English. 1994. bi-m. GBP 541 combined subscription in United Kingdom to institutions (print & online eds.); EUR 713, USD 893 combined subscription to institutions (print & online eds.) (effective 2012). adv. bk.rev. index. back issues avail.; reprint service avail. from PSC. **Document type:** *Journal, Academic/Scholarly.* **Description:** Aims to promote a better understanding of the process of democratization, in North America, Australasia, the European Union, as well as in the developing world and in post-communist societies.
Related titles: Online - full text ed.: ISSN 1743-890X. GBP 487 in United Kingdom to institutions; EUR 642, USD 804 to institutions (effective 2012) (from IngentaConnect).
Indexed: A01, A03, A08, A22, CA, CCME, CurCont, E01, ESPM, HistAb, I13, I14, IBSS, IBibSS, LID&ISL, LeftInd, P34, P42, PSA, RiskAb, S02, S03, SCOPUS, SSCI, SociolAb, T02, W07.
—BLDSC (3550.572500), IE, Infotrieve, Ingenta. **CCC.**
Published by: Routledge (Subsidiary of: Taylor & Francis Group), 4 Park Sq, Milton Park, Abingdon, Oxon OX14 4RN, United Kingdom. TEL 44-20-70176000, FAX 44-20-70176336, subscriptions@tandf.co.uk, http://www.routledge.com. Eds. Gordon Crawford, Jeffrey Haynes TEL 44-20-73201153. Adv. contact Linda Hann TEL 44-1344-779945. **Subscr. to:** Taylor & Francis Ltd., Journals Customer Service, Sheepen Pl, Colchester, Essex CO3 3LP, United Kingdom. TEL 44-20-70175544, FAX 44-20-70175198.

➤ **DENVER JOURNAL OF INTERNATIONAL LAW AND POLICY.** *see* LAW—International Law

➤ **DEVELOPMENT (BASINGSTOKE).** *see* BUSINESS AND ECONOMICS—International Development And Assistance

➤ **DEVELOPMENT AND CHANGE.** *see* BUSINESS AND ECONOMICS—International Development And Assistance

➤ **DEVELOPMENT BUSINESS (NEW YORK, 1978).** *see* BUSINESS AND ECONOMICS—International Development And Assistance

➤ **DEVELOPMENT CONNECTIONS.** *see* BUSINESS AND ECONOMICS—International Development And Assistance

327.17 SWE ISSN 0345-2328
HD82
DEVELOPMENT DIALOGUE; a journal of international development cooperation. Text in English; Text occasionally in French, Spanish. 1972. biennial (1-2/yr). free (effective 2005). bk.rev. back issues avail. **Document type:** *Journal, Academic/Scholarly.* **Description:** The journal reflects the outcomes of the Foundation's seminars.
Related titles: Online - full text ed.
Indexed: APEL, ASD, BAS, CA, EI, GEOBASE, HRIR, IBR, IBSS, IBZ, MEA&I, P06, P30, P42, PRA, PSA, PerIslam, RASB, S02, S03, SCOPUS, SociolAb, T02.
—BLDSC (3579.019700), IE, Infotrieve, Ingenta.
Published by: Dag Hammarskjoeld Foundation, Dag Hammarskjoeld Centre, Oevre Slottsgatan 2, Uppsala, 75310, Sweden. TEL 46-18-4101000, FAX 46-18-122072. Ed., R&P Olle Nordberg TEL 46-18-127272. Circ: 10,000 (controlled and free).

327 CAN
DEVELOPMENT STUDIES WORKING PAPERS. Text in English. 1990. irreg. CAD 6. **Document type:** *Monographic series, Academic/Scholarly.*
Published by: Norman Paterson School of International Affairs, Carleton University, 1125 Colonel By Dr, Ottawa, ON K1S 5B6, Canada. TEL 613-520-2600, FAX 613-520-2889. Ed. Vivian Cummins.

327 DEU ISSN 0938-1422
DIALOG (BERLIN); Deutsch-Polnisches Magazin. Text in German. 1987. q. EUR 15.30 domestic; EUR 20.50 foreign (effective 2009). adv. **Document type:** *Magazine, Consumer.*
Related titles: Online - full text ed.
Published by: Deutsch-Polnische Gesellschaft - Bundesverband e.V., Schillerstr 59, Berlin, 10627, Germany. TEL 49-30-26551630, FAX 49-30-26551631. Ed. Basil Kerski. Circ: 8,000 (controlled).

327 AUT
DIALOGO; Austria-America Latina. Text in Portuguese, Spanish. 1982. a. free. adv. back issues avail. **Document type:** *Bulletin.*
Published by: Oesterreichisches Lateinamerika-Institut, Schlickgasse 1, Vienna, W 1090, Austria. TEL 43-1-3107465, FAX 43-1-310746821. Ed. Stefanie Reinberg. Circ: 3,000.

DIALOGUE (MONTEREY). *see* SOCIOLOGY

327 314.5 IND ISSN 0973-9572
DS432.5
DIASPORA STUDIES. Text in English. 2007. s-a. INR 950 domestic (print or online ed.); USD 105 foreign (print or online ed.); INR 1,800 combined subscription domestic (print & online eds.); USD 200 combined subscription foreign (print & online eds.) (effective 2010). adv. bk.rev. **Document type:** *Journal, Academic/Scholarly.* **Description:** Focuses on transnational alliances and diasporic networks.
Related titles: Online - full text ed.
Indexed: P10, P48, P53, P54, PQC.
Published by: (Organisation for Diaspora Initiatives), M D Publications Pvt Ltd, 11 Darya Ganj, New Delhi, 110 002, India. TEL 91-11-41563325, FAX 91-11-23275542, contact@mdppl.com. Ed. Ajay Dubey.

327.2 UAE
AL-DIBLOMASI/DIPLOMAT. Text in Arabic. 1980. q. per issue exchange basis. **Description:** Publishes studies and research in diplomatic affairs and international relations, as well as news of conferences, official reports and documents pertaining to international matters.
Published by: Ministry of Foreign Affairs, Department of Legal Affairs and Studies/Wizarat al-Kharijiyyah, Idarat al-Shu'un al-Qanuniyyah wal-Dirasat, P O Box 1, Abu Dhabi, United Arab Emirates. TEL 652200, FAX 668015, TELEX 22217 KHARJIYA EM. Circ: 500 (controlled).

DIGEST OF WORLD EVENTS. *see* HISTORY

327 EST
➤ **DIPLOMAATIA.** Text in Estonian. m. EUR 12.78; EUR 1.28 newsstand/cover (effective 2011). **Document type:** *Journal, Academic/Scholarly.*
Related titles: Online - full text ed.
Published by: (Rahvusvaheline Kaitseuuringute Keskus/International Center for Defence Studies), SA Kultuurileht, Voorimehe St 9, Tallinn, 10146, Estonia. TEL 372-6833110, FAX 372-6833111, info@kl.ee, http://www.kl.ee. Ed. Kadri Liik.

328 CHL ISSN 0716-193X
F3051
DIPLOMACIA. Text in Spanish. 1974. q. free (effective 2010). **Document type:** *Bulletin, Government.*
Indexed: IBR, IBZ.
Published by: Academia Diplomatica de Chile, Catedral No. 1183, Santiago, Chile. TEL 56-2-6794156, http://www.minrel.gov.cl/. Circ: 4,000.

327.2 KOR ISSN 1227-2671
DIPLOMACY; international magazine. Text in English. 1975. m. adv. reprints avail. **Document type:** *Magazine, Trade.* **Description:** Promotes diplomatic relations through non-governmental diplomacy.
Indexed: RASB.
Published by: Diplomacy Co., 9th FL. Samduk Bldg, 131 Da-dong, Choong-ku, Seoul, 100-180, Korea, S. TEL 82-2-7773370, FAX 82-2-7738862. Ed. Kim Suk Won. Circ: 30,000.

DIPLOMACY & STATECRAFT. *see* HISTORY

327 GBR ISSN 0951-032X
DIPLOMAT; the review of the diplomatic and consular world. Text in English. 1947. 10/yr. GBP 100 domestic; GBP 120 foreign (effective 2009). adv. bk.rev. illus.; stat. back issues avail. **Document type:** *Magazine, Trade.* **Description:** Contains articles of interest to businesspersons and persons in government service who need to maintain contact with the foreign diplomatic community in London.
Formerly (until 1987): Diplomatist (0012-3110)
Related titles: Supplement(s): Lady Diplomat. ISSN 0264-892X.
Published by: Envoy Media Ltd., 11 Grosvenor Cres, London, SW1X 7EE, United Kingdom. TEL 44-20-72456794, FAX 44-20-78232679. adv.: color page GBP 2,000; trim 210 x 297. Circ: 8,000.

327 PAK
DIPLOMAT. Text in English. 1972. m. PKR 75. adv. charts; illus.
Indexed: PerIslam.
Address: 442-2 Jauharabad, Karachi 38, Pakistan. Ed. Mohammed Ali Jilani.

327.7 CAN ISSN 1190-8343
DIPLOMAT & INTERNATIONAL CANADA. Text in English. m. CAD 35 (effective 2008). adv. **Document type:** *Journal, Academic/Scholarly.* **Description:** Devoted to covering international affairs from a Canadian perspective.
Formerly (until 1993): Diplomat Canada (0848-1814)
Published by: Sparrow House Enterprises Inc., PO Box 1173, Sta B, Ottawa, ON K1P 5R2, Canada. TEL 613- 231-8476. Ed. Jennifer Campbell. Pub., Adv. contact Neil Reynolds.

327.2 DEU
DIPLOMATEN SPIEGEL. Text in German. 1992. irreg. **Document type:** *Trade.*
Published by: ProPress Verlag GmbH, Am Buschhof 8, Bonn, 53227, Germany. TEL 49-228-970970, FAX 49-228-9709775, verlag@behoerdenspiegel.de, http://www.behoerdenspiegel.de.

327.2 GBR
DIPLOMATIC & CONSULAR YEAR BOOK. Text in English. 1974. a. free to qualified personnel (effective 2009). adv. bk.rev. **Document type:** *Yearbook.*
Related titles: Online - full text ed.
Published by: Blakes, Gadd House, Arcadia Ave, London, N3 2JU, United Kingdom. TEL 44-20-89564000, FAX 44-20-89564009, comms@blakemedia.org. Pub. David Blake. Circ: 5,000.

327.17 AUS ISSN 1832-4878
DIPLOMATIC BULLETIN. Text in English. 2005. s-a. free. adv. back issues avail. **Document type:** *Journal, Academic/Scholarly.* **Description:** Covers college activities and progress, and other articles of diplomatic interest.
Related titles: Online - full text ed.: free (effective 2008).

P

Published by: Australian National University, Asia-Pacific College of Diplomacy, Coombs Extension (Bldg 8), Canberra, ACT 0200, Australia. TEL 61-2-61257983, FAX 61-2-61257985, ExecutiveOfficer.APCD@anu.edu.au.

327.2 CAN ISSN 1910-667X
DIPLOMATIC, CONSULAR AND OTHER REPRESENTATIVES IN CANADA/CORPS DIPLOMATIQUE ET REPRESENTANTS CONSULAIRES ET AUTRES AU CANADA. Text in English. 1969. m. free (effective 2006). **Document type:** *Government.*
Former titles (until 2001): Diplomatic, Consular and other Representatives in Canada (Print Edition) (0825-6683); (until 1983): Diplomatic Corps and Consular and Other Representatives in Canada (0486-4514); Which was formed by the merger of (19??-1969): Representatives of Other Countries in Canada (0706-8433); Which was formerly: Canadian Representatives Abroad (0008-4921); (until 1968): Canadian Representatives Abroad and Representatives of Other Countries in Canada (0706-8425); (until 1949): Canadian Representatives Abroad and British Commonwealth and Foreign Representatives in Canada (0704-366X); (until 1947): Canadian Representatives Abroad and Representatives in Canada of the British Commonwealth and Foreign Governments (0704-3678); (until 1944): Representatives in Canada of the British Commonwealth and Foreign Governments; (19??-1969): Diplomatic Corps (0527-6837); Which was formerly (until 1955): Diplomatic and Consular Representatives in Ottawa (0318-5613); (until 1949): Diplomatic Corps, British Commonwealth High Commissioners and their Staffs, and Consular Representatives in Ottawa (0318-5621); (until 1947): Diplomatic List with Which is Included the List of British Commonwealth Representatives and of Consuls-General in Ottawa (0318-563X)
Media: Online - full text. **Related titles:** French ed.: Representants Diplomatiques, Consulaires et Autres au Canada. ISSN 1910-6688.
Published by: Department of Foreign Affairs and International Trade, 125 Sussex Dr, Ottawa, ON K1A 0G2, Canada. enqserv@dfait-maeci.gc.ca.

DIPLOMATIC HISTORY; the journal of the Society for Historians of American Foreign Relations. *see* HISTORY

327 NPL
DIPLOMATIC LIST AND LIST OF REPRESENTATIVES OF UNITED NATIONS AND ITS SPECIALIZED AGENCIES AND OTHER MISSIONS. Text in English. a.
Published by: Protocol Division, Ministry of Foreign Affairs, Kathmandu, Nepal.

327 NLD ISSN 1872-8863
➤ **DIPLOMATIC STUDIES.** Text in English. 2007. irreg., latest vol.7, 2011. price varies. **Document type:** *Monographic series, Academic/Scholarly.* **Description:** Covers diplomacy and its role in international relations.
Indexed: IZBG.
—BLDSC (3589.380500), IE.
Published by: Martinus Nijhoff (Subsidiary of: Brill), PO Box 9000, Leiden, 2300 PA, Netherlands. TEL 31-71-5353500, FAX 31-71-5317532, marketing@brill.nl. Ed. Jan Melissen.

327 USA ISSN 0363-8200
JX1977.A1
DIPLOMATIC WORLD BULLETIN AND DELEGATES WORLD BULLETIN; dedicated to serving the United Nations and the international community. Text in English. 1982 (vol.12). fortn. USD 45. adv. illus.; tr.lit.
Formerly: Delegates World Bulletin
Indexed: RASB.
Published by: Diplomatic World Bulletin Publications, Inc., 307 E 44th St, Ste A, New York, NY 10017. TEL 212-747-9500. Ed. Richard A Holman.

930 BEL ISSN 1377-8765
DIPLOMATIE ET HISTOIRE. Text in French. 2002. irreg., latest vol.19, 2010. price varies. **Document type:** *Monographic series, Academic/Scholarly.*
Published by: P I E - Peter Lang SA, 1 avenue Maurice, 6e etage, Brussels, 1050, Belgium. TEL 32-2-3477236, FAX 32-2-3477237, pie@peterlang.com, http://www.peterlang.net.

327 FRA ISSN 1778-3275
DIPLOMATIE ET STRATEGIE. Key Title: Collection Diplomatie et Strategie. Text in French. 2005. irreg. **Document type:** *Monographic series.*
Published by: L' Harmattan, 5 Rue de l'Ecole Polytechnique, Paris, 75005, France. TEL 33-1-43257651, FAX 33-1-43258203.

DIPLOMATISCHE AKADEMIE WIEN. FAVORITA PAPERS. *see* EDUCATION—Teaching Methods And Curriculum

DIPLOMATISCHE AKADEMIE WIEN. JAHRBUCH. *see* EDUCATION—Teaching Methods And Curriculum

327.2 DEU ISSN 0937-3128
DIPLOMATISCHE MISSIONEN, KONSULARISCHE VERTRETUNGEN. Text in German. 19??. base vol. plus m. updates. looseleaf. EUR 46.64 combined subscription (print & CD-ROM eds.) (effective 2009). **Document type:** *Directory, Trade.*
Related titles: CD-ROM ed.: EUR 38.75 (effective 2009).
Published by: Edition Empirica, Caesarstr 6-10, Cologne, 50968, Germany. TEL 49-221-97761280, FAX 49-221-97761289, http://www.edition-empirica.de.

327.2 AUT
DIPLOMATISCHER PRESSEDIENST/DIPLOMATIC PRESS SERVICE. Text in English, German. 1989. bi-m. EUR 55; EUR 8 newsstand/cover (effective 2004). bk.rev. 64 p./no. 3 cols./p.; back issues avail. **Document type:** *Magazine, Trade.*
Published by: Club Fur International Gedankenaustausch, Diplomatischer Pressedienst, Neustiftgasse 104, Vienna, W 1070, Austria. TEL 43-1-5268080, FAX 43-1-5261810. Ed. Eduard Knapp. R&P Kurt Lechner. Adv. contact Adolf Wurzer. Circ: 5,000 (controlled).

327 BHR
DIRASAT ISTIRATIJIYAH/JOURNAL OF STRATEGIC STUDIES. Text in Arabic; Abstracts in Arabic, English. 2000. q. **Document type:** *Journal, Academic/Scholarly.* **Description:** Contains studies, analytical articles, and interviews on political, economic, social, educational and scientific issues, religion, the dialogue of civilizations and their strategic dimensions.
Published by: Markaz al-Bahrayn Li-l-dirasat Wa-al-buhut/Bahrain Center for Studies and Research, PO Box 496, Manama, Bahrain. TEL 973-17-754757, FAX 973-17-754678, Info@bcsr.gov.bh.

327.174 CHE ISSN 1020-7287
JZ5588
DISARMAMENT FORUM/FORUM DU DESARMEMENT. Text in English, French. 1988. q. free. adv. bk.rev. bibl. cum.index: 1988-1998. 150 p./no.; back issues avail. **Document type:** *Journal, Academic/Scholarly.* **Description:** Each issue focuses on a specific subject in the field of disarmament and international security, such as small arms, specific treaties, peacekeeping and human security.
Supersedes (in 1999): U N I D I R Newsletter (1012-4934)
Related titles: Online - full text ed.
Indexed: DIP, IBR, IBZ, PAIS, PRA, RASB.
—CCC.
Published by: United Nations Institute for Disarmament Research, Palais des Nations, Geneva 10, 1211, Switzerland. FAX 41-22-9170176, dforum@unog.ch, http://www.unidir.org. Ed., R&P Kerstin Vignard TEL 41-22-9171582. Circ: 4,000.

327.174 USA ISSN 0259-3629
JX1974
DISARMAMENT TIMES. Text in English. 1978. 6/yr. USD 15 in North America; USD 20 elsewhere. bk.rev. **Document type:** *Newspaper.*
Indexed: PRA.
Published by: Non-Governmental Organizations Committee on Disarmament, 777 United Nations Plaza, New York, NY 10017. TEL 212-687-5340, FAX 212-687-1643. Ed. Bhaskar Menon. Circ: 5,000.

327 USA ISSN 1942-1133
DISCOURSE (MEDFORD). Text in English. 2008. 3/yr. **Document type:** *Journal, Academic/Scholarly.* **Description:** Provides an inclusive platform for reasoned discussion and prescriptive analysis of issues of both international and domestic concern, while also including poetry, fiction, art and photography to illuminate the human condition.
Related titles: Online - full text ed.: free (effective 2010).
Published by: Tufts University, Institute for Global Leadership, 96 Packard Ave, Medford, MA 02115. TEL 617-627-3314, FAX 617-627-3940.

327.1 341.72 CAN
THE DISPATCH. Text in English. q. **Document type:** *Newsletter.*
Related titles: Online - full text ed.
Published by: Canadian Defence and Foreign Affairs Institute, PO Box 2204, Station M, Calgary, AB T2P 2M4, Canada. TEL 403-231-7624, FAX 403-231-7647, contact@cdfai.org.

327 ITA ISSN 1593-2176
DOC TOSCANA. Text in Italian. 2001. q. EUR 25 domestic; EUR 30 foreign (effective 2010). **Document type:** *Magazine, Consumer.*
Related titles: Online - full text ed.: ISSN 1972-5663.
Published by: Edizioni Polistampa, Via Livorno 8-32, Florence, FI 50142, Italy. TEL 39-055-737871, FAX 39-055-229430, info@polistampa.com, http://www.polistampa.com. Ed. Riccardo Monni.

351.88 BEL ISSN 1377-8773
JZ683
DOCUMENTS DIPLOMATIQUES FRANCAIS. Text in French. 2002. irreg., latest vol.34, 2010. price varies. **Document type:** *Monographic series, Academic/Scholarly.*
Published by: P I E - Peter Lang SA, 1 avenue Maurice, 6e etage, Brussels, 1050, Belgium. TEL 32-2-3477236, FAX 32-2-3477237, pie@peterlang.com, http://www.peterlang.net.

327 DEU
DOKUMENTATIONEN ZUR KULTUR UND GESELLSCHAFT IM OESTLICHEN EUROPA. Text in German. 1993. irreg., latest vol.9, 2000. price varies. **Document type:** *Monographic series, Academic/Scholarly.*
Published by: (Universitaet Bremen, Forschungsstelle Osteuropa/Bremen University, Research Centre for East European Studies), Edition Temmen, Hohenlohestr 21, Bremen, 28209, Germany. TEL 49-421-348430, FAX 49-421-348094, info@edition-temmen.de. Ed. Horst Temmen.

DOKUMENTE; Zeitschrift fuer den deutsch-franzoesischen Dialog. *see* GENERAL INTEREST PERIODICALS—Germany

327 USA ISSN 1053-5829
DONALD R. MORRIS NEWSLETTER; weekly news analysis and comment. Text in English. 1988. w. (50/yr.). looseleaf. USD 50 domestic; USD 82.50 foreign (effective 2000). back issues avail. **Document type:** *Newsletter.* **Description:** Offers insight into a wide range of current world events.
Published by: Trident Syndicate, Inc., PO Box 19909, Houston, TX 77224-1909. TEL 713-781-7094, 800-441-9837, FAX 713-668-8665. Ed. Donald R Morris. Pub., R&P Loran Sheffer TEL 713-781-2713. Circ: 420 (paid).

327 FRA ISSN 0335-5950
DOSSIERS NOIRS. Text in French. 1974. irreg. price varies. **Document type:** *Monographic series, Academic/Scholarly.*
Published by: L' Harmattan, 5 Rue de l'Ecole Polytechnique, Paris, 75005, France.

DRITTE WELT MATERIALIEN. *see* HISTORY

327 POL ISSN 0867-3608
DK4010
DZIS; przeglad spoleczny. Text in Polish. 1990. m. PLZ 48; USD 40 in United States. adv. bk.rev. back issues avail.
Indexed: AgrLib.
Published by: Kier Co. Ltd., Ul Poznanska 3 4 p, Warsaw, 00680, Poland. TEL 48-22-6210121, FAX 48-22-6251440. Circ: 5,000.

327 LUX
E C COMPETITION POLICY NEWSLETTER. (European Commission) Text in English. m. free (effective 2003).
Published by: European Commission, Office for Official Publications of the European Union, 2 Rue Mercier, Luxembourg, L-2985, Luxembourg. FAX 352-29291.

327.1 GBR ISSN 1474-1148
E F P U WORKING PAPERS. (European Foreign Policy Unit) Text in English. 2001. irreg. free (effective 2009). back issues avail. **Document type:** *Monographic series, Academic/Scholarly.*
Related titles: Online - full text ed.: ISSN 1474-113X. free (effective 2009).
Published by: London School of Economics and Political Science, International Relations Department, Houghton St, London, WC2A 2AE, United Kingdom. TEL 44-20-79557404, FAX 44-20-79557446, H.Parker@lse.ac.uk, http://www2.lse.ac.uk/internationalRelations/Home.aspx.

327 CAN ISSN 1488-240X
JZ6.6
E-MERGE; a student journal of international affairs. Text in English. irreg. bk.rev. **Document type:** *Journal, Academic/Scholarly.*
Media: Online - full content.
Published by: Carleton University, Norman Paterson School of International Affairs, 1125 Colonel By Dr, Ottawa, ON K1S 5B6, Canada. TEL 613-520-6655, FAX 613-520-2889, international_affairs@carleton.ca, http://www.carleton.ca/npsia/.

327 DNK ISSN 1602-1169
E U FAKTA. (Europaeiske Union) Text in Danish. 2000. irreg., latest vol.32, 2008. free. back issues avail. **Document type:** *Monographic series, Government.*
Formerly (until 2002): E U Nu!
Related titles: Online - full text ed.: ISSN 1903-2382. 2002.
Published by: Folketinget, EU-Oplysningen/Danish Parliament, EU-Information, Christiansborg, Copenhagen K, 1240, Denmark. TEL 45-33-373337, FAX 45-33-373330, euopl@folketinget.dk.

327 DEU ISSN 0721-2178
HC59.7
E & Z. (Entwicklung und Zusammenarbeit) Text in German. 1960. m. EUR 24 domestic; EUR 27 foreign (effective 2005). adv. bk.rev. **Document type:** *Magazine, Consumer.* **Description:** New trends and tendencies in the development debate and the German contribution to the development efforts.
Former titles (until 1972): Entwicklung und Zusammenarbeit (0013-9114); (until 1964): Deutsche Stiftung fuer Entwicklungslaender. Mitteilungen (0721-2194)
Indexed: A34, A35, A36, A38, AgBio, AgrForAb, BA, C25, CABA, DIP, E12, F08, F12, FCA, GH, GeoRef, H16, H17, I11, IBR, IBZ, LT, N02, OR, P32, P33, P40, PAIS, PGegResA, PHN&I, R12, RA&MP, RRTA, S12, S13, S16, T05, TAR, W11.
—CCC.
Published by: InWEnt - Internationale Weiterbildung und Entwicklung GmbH, Friedrich-Ebert-Allee 40, Bonn, 53113, Germany. TEL 49-228-44600, FAX 49-228-44601776, info@inwent.org. Ed. Hans Dembowski. Circ: 10,000.

327 338.91 BGR
EARLY WARNING: BULGARIA BEYOND THE FACTS (MONTHLY EDITION). Text in English. 2003. m. BGL 185 (effective 2003). **Document type:** *Magazine, Government.*
Related titles: Online - full content ed.: BGL 110 (effective 2003); Alternate Frequency ed(s).: a.
Published by: United Nations Development Programme Bulgaria, ATM Centre Tzarigradsko Shausse Blvd.,7th km, Sofia, 1784, Bulgaria. TEL 359-2-9696100, FAX 359-2-9743089, info@undp.bg, http://www.undp.bg/. **Subscr. to:** c/o M3 Communications Group, Inc., 34 Vladajska St, Sofia 1606, Bulgaria. **Co-publisher:** U.S. Agency for International Development.

EAST EUROPEAN JEWISH AFFAIRS. *see* HISTORY—History Of Europe

327 USA ISSN 1075-8569
CB251
EAST-WEST CENTER SPECIAL REPORTS. Text in English. 1993. irreg., latest vol.10, 2006. price varies. back issues avail. **Document type:** *Monographic series, Academic/Scholarly.* **Description:** Addresses topics relevant to current and emerging policy debates in the Asia Pacific region and the United States.
Related titles: Online - full text ed.: ISSN 1930-1456. free (effective 2010).
Indexed: A01, CA, T02.
Published by: East-West Center, 1601 EW Rd, Honolulu, HI 96848. TEL 808-944-7111, FAX 808-944-7376, ewcbooks@eastwestcenter.org. Ed. Elisa W Johnston.

EAST WEST REVIEW OF LABOR LAW & SOCIAL POLICY. *see* SOCIAL SERVICES AND WELFARE

327 DEU ISSN 2191-8864
▼ **EASTERN AND CENTRAL EUROPEAN STUDIES.** Text in English. forthcoming 2011. irreg. price varies. **Document type:** *Monographic series, Academic/Scholarly.*
Published by: Peter Lang GmbH (Subsidiary of: Peter Lang Publishing Group), Eschborner Landstr 42-50, Frankfurt Am Main, 60489, Germany. TEL 49-69-7807050, FAX 49-69-78070550, zentrale.frankfurt@peterlang.com. Eds. Alexandru Simon, Christian Gastgeber.

327 ROM ISSN 2068-651X
▼ ➤ **EASTERN JOURNAL OF EUROPEAN STUDIES.** Text in English. 2010 (Jun.). s-a. free. **Document type:** *Journal, Academic/Scholarly.* **Description:** Publishes theoretical studies, comparative studies, case studies, empirical analyses and reviews. Provides a forum for multidisciplinary and interdisciplinary dialogue between ideas, and a framework for theoretical and empirical analyses covering major areas of subjects in the European studies field: European history, politics, European economy and European policies, EU community law, European culture and society.
Related titles: Online - full text ed.: ISSN 2068-6633. free (effective 2011).
Indexed: A01.
Published by: Universitatea "Alexandru Ioan Cuza" din Iasi, Centrul de Studii Europene, Bulevardul Carol I, nr. 19, Iasi, 700507, Romania. TEL 40-232-201318, FAX 40-232-201318, cseadmin@uaic.ro, http://www.cse.uaic.ro/index.htm. Ed. Maria Birsan.

327 USA
EASTWEST INSTITUTE. ANNUAL REPORT. Text in Russian, English. 1981. a., latest 1999. free. bk.rev. **Document type:** *Yearbook.*
Former titles: Institute for East West Studies. Annual Report; Institute for East - West Security Studies. Annual Report
Published by: Institute for East West Studies, 700 Broadway, 2nd Fl, New York, NY 10003-9501. TEL 212-824-4160, FAX 212-824-4149, TELEX 760-8127 EWS, jews@iews.org. Ed. Elizabeth Belfer.

EDINBURGH STUDIES IN WORLD ETHICS. *see* PHILOSOPHY

327 USA ISSN 1948-4399
EJOURNAL USA. Text in English. 2007. m. free (effective 2009). back issues avail. **Document type:** *Journal, Government.*

Formed by the merger of (2004-2007): EjournalUSA. U.S. Foreign Policy Agenda (1942-311X); Which was formerly (until 2004): U.S. Foreign Policy Agenda; (2005-2007): EjournalUSA. Global Issues (1942-3098); Which was formerly (until 2005): Global issues; (2004-2007): EjournalUSA. U.S. Society & Values (1942-3101); Which was formerly (until 2004): U.S. Society & Values; (2004-2007): EjournalUSA. Economic Perspectives (1943-6378); Which was formerly (until 2004): Economic Perspectives; (2004-2007): EjournalUSA. Issues of Democracy; Which was formerly (until 2004): Issues of Democracy
Media: Online - full content. **Related titles:** Arabic Translation; French Translation; Spanish Translation; Russian Translation; Portuguese Translation:.
Published by: U.S. Department of State, Bureau of International Information Programs, 2201 C St NW, Washington, DC 20520. TEL 202-647-4000, 800-877-8339, http://www.state.gov/r/iip/. Ed. Richard W Huckaby.

327 CHN ISSN 1671-8461
ELUOSI ZHONGYA DONGOU YANJIU/RUSSIAN, CENTRAL ASIAN & EAST EUROPEAN STUDIES. Text in Chinese. 1981. m. USD 48 (effective 2009). **Document type:** *Journal, Academic/Scholarly.*
Formerly (until 2003): Dongou Zhongya Yanjiu (1005-1775)
Related titles: Online - full text ed.
—East View.
Published by: Zhongguo Shehui Kexueyuan, Eluosi Dongou Zhongya Yanjiusuo, 3, Zhangzizhong Lu, PO Box 1103, Beijing, 100007, China. TEL 86-10-64039120, FAX 86-10-64014008. **Dist. by:** China International Book Trading Corp, 35 Chegongzhuang Xilu, Haidian District, PO Box 399, Beijing 100044, China. TEL 86-10-68412045, FAX 86-10-68412023, cibtc@mail.cibtc.com.cn, http://www.cibtc.com.cn.

327 MEX
EMBAJADA DE LA FEDERACION DE RUSIA. BOLETIN INFORMATIVO. Text in Spanish. 1974 (vol.30). m. charts; illus.
Formerly: U R S S Embajada. Boletin de Informacion
Published by: Embajada de la Federacion de Rusia, Jose Vasconcelos 204, Col. Hipodromo Condesa, Mexico, D.F., 06140, Mexico. TEL 525-273-1305.

327 UAE ISSN 1682-1238
THE EMIRATES LECTURE SERIES. Text in English. 1997. irreg. AED 110, USD 30 to individuals; AED 220, USD 60 to institutions (effective 2003). **Document type:** *Monographic series.*
Related titles: Arabic ed.
Indexed: CA, I02, P10, P42, P45, P48, PQC, PSA, SCOPUS, T02.
Published by: Emirates Center for Strategic Studies and Research, PO Box 4567, Abu Dhabi, United Arab Emirates. TEL 971-2-6423776, FAX 971-2-6428844, pubdis@ecssr.ac.ae.

ENERGY AND ENVIRONMENTAL POLICY. *see* ENERGY

ENFANTS DU MONDE. *see* SOCIAL SERVICES AND WELFARE

327 USA
ENGLISH SPEAKING UNION TODAY. Text in English. 1953. 3/yr. membership. adv. **Document type:** *Newsletter.*
Former titles: English Speaking: The E-S U News; English-Speaking Union News (0013-8371)
Published by: English-Speaking Union of the United States, 16 E 69th St, New York, NY 10021. TEL 212-879-6800, FAX 212-772-2886. Ed. David Olyphant. Circ: 18,000.

327 FRA ISSN 1770-1643
ENJEUX DIPLOMATIQUES ET STRATEGIQUES. Text in French. 2004. a. EUR 29 newsstand/cover (effective 2008). **Document type:** *Journal, Government.*
Published by: Centre d'Etudes Diplomatiques et Strategiques (C E D S), 54 Av. Marceau, Paris, 75008, France. TEL 33-1-47205747, FAX 33-1-47205730.

327 BEL ISSN 1379-4205
G1
ENJEUX INTERNATIONAUX (BRUSSELS, 2003); revue de promotion humaine et chretienne en Afrique et dans le monde. Text in French. 2003. 3/yr. EUR 30 domestic; CHF 51 in Switzerland; EUR 35 in Europe; CAD 50 in Canada; EUR 40 elsewhere; EUR 25 domestic to students; CHF 44 in Switzerland to students; EUR 30 in Europe to students; CAD 40 in Canada to students; EUR 35 elsewhere to students (effective 2005). adv. bk.rev. abstr.; bibl.; charts; illus.; stat. **Document type:** *Journal, Academic/Scholarly.*
Formed by the merger of (1883-2003): Vivant Univers (0042-7527); Which was formerly (until 1969): Vivante Afrique (0771-1336); (until 1958): Grand Lacs (0771-128X); (until 1933): Missions d'Afrique des Peres Blancs (0771-1239); (1951-2003): Vivant Univers. Edition Suisse (1422-5883); Which was formerly (until 1969): Vivante Afrique (Fribourg) (1422-576X)
Indexed: FR, IBSS.
Published by: Enjeux Internationaux, 47, avenue des Myrtes, Bruxelles, 1080, Belgium. TEL 32-81-222891, FAX 32-81-241024. Ed. Anne-Marie Impe. Circ: 10,000.

327 USA ISSN 1059-6402
JC599.L3
ENLACE (WASHINGTON, 1975); politica y derechos humanos en las Americas. Text in Spanish. 1975. q. looseleaf. USD 35 (effective 2005). charts. index, cum.index. back issues avail. **Document type:** *Newsletter, Consumer.*
Supersedes (in 1991): Latin America Update (0738-601X)
Published by: Washington Office on Latin America, 1630 Connecticut Ave, N W, Ste 200, Washington, DC 20009-1053. TEL 202-797-2171, FAX 202-797-2172, wola@wola.org, http://www.wola.org. Ed. Kimberly Stanton. Circ: 2,000.

363.7 GBR ISSN 0964-4016
GE170
➤ **ENVIRONMENTAL POLITICS.** Text in English. 1992. bi-m. GBP 566 combined subscription in United Kingdom to institutions (print & online eds.); EUR 747, USD 934 combined subscription to institutions (print & online eds.) (effective 2012). adv. bk.rev. illus. index. back issues avail.; reprint service avail. from PSC. **Document type:** *Journal, Academic/Scholarly.* **Description:** Presents academic study of environmental politics with a focus on the industrialized countries.
Related titles: Microfiche ed.: (from PQC); Online - full text ed.: ISSN 1743-8934. GBP 510 in United Kingdom to institutions; EUR 672, USD 840 to institutions (effective 2012) (from IngentaConnect).
Indexed: A01, A02, A03, A08, A20, A22, A26, A34, A35, A38, AgBio, BRD, CA, CABA, CurCont, DIP, E01, E04, E05, E08, E11, E12, ESPM, EnvAb, EnvInd, F08, F11, F12, G02, G08, GEOBASE, HPNRM, I05, I11, I13, IBR, IBSS, IBZ, LID&ISL, N02, P02, P10, P26, P27, P30, P32, P34, P40, P42, P48, P52, P53, P54, P56, PAIS, PCI, PQC, PSA, PollutAb, R12, S02, S03, S09, S10, S13, S16, SCOPUS, SSA, SSAI, SSAb, SSCI, SSI, SSciA, SWRA, SociolAb, T02, T04, TAR, W03, W07, W10, W11, Z01.
—IE, Infotrieve, Ingenta. **CCC.**
Published by: Routledge (Subsidiary of: Taylor & Francis Group), 4 Park Sq, Milton Park, Abingdon, Oxon OX14 4RN, United Kingdom. TEL 44-20-70176000, FAX 44-20-70176336, subscriptions@tandf.co.uk, http://www.routledge.com. Eds. Christopher Rootes TEL 44-1227-823374, Neil Carter TEL 44-1904-433558. Adv. contact Linda Hann TEL 44-1344-779945. **Subscr. to:** Taylor & Francis Ltd., Journals Customer Service, Sheepen Pl, Colchester, Essex CO3 3LP, United Kingdom. TEL 44-20-70175544, FAX 44-20-70175198.

327 DEU ISSN 0939-7507
ERZIEHERBRIEF. Text in German. 1954. q. adv. bk.rev. bibl.; illus.; maps; stat. back issues avail. **Document type:** *Journal, Academic/Scholarly.* **Description:** Contains essays on history of Eastern Europe with an emphasis on the expulsion of Germans after 1945.
Formerly: Sudetendeutscher Erzieherbrief
Published by: Arbeitsgemeinschaft Sudetendeutscher Lehrer und Erzieher e.V., Mozartstr 2, Krailling, 82152, Germany. TEL 49-89-8571818. Pub. Ernst Korn. Circ: 1,250 (paid). **Co-sponsor:** Haus des Deutschen Ostens.

327.17 711.4 FRA ISSN 0183-0678
ESPACES TRANSFRONTALIERS. Text in French. 1997. irreg. **Document type:** *Newsletter.*
Related titles: German ed.: ISSN 1961-5914; English ed.: ISSN 1962-4573.
Published by: Mission Operationnelle Transfrontaliere, 38 Rue des Bordonnais, Paris, 75001, France. TEL 33-1-55805680, FAX 33-1-42335700, mot@mot.asso.fr.

ESPERANTIC STUDIES. *see* LINGUISTICS

327 950 USA ISSN 1088-8136
DS646.57
ESTAFETA; voice of the East Timor Action Network (US). Text in English. 1993. s-a. USD 15 domestic; USD 30 foreign (effective 2000). bk.rev. back issues avail. **Document type:** *Bulletin, Consumer.* **Description:** Covers developments in East Timor and US policy relating to East Timor, as well as activism in support of human rights and self-determination for East Timor.
Formerly: Network News
Published by: East Timor Action Network, PO Box 1182, White Plains, NY 10602. TEL 914-428-7299, FAX 914-428-7383. Eds. Ben Terrell, Charlie Scheiner. Circ: 10,000.

THE ESTIMATE; political and security intelligence analysis of the Islamic world and its neighbors. *see* MILITARY

327 330.9 600 ESP ISSN 1697-0764
ESTRATEGIA GLOBAL; revista bimestral de relaciones internacionales, economia, seguridad y defensa y tecnologia. Text in Spanish. 2003. bi-m. EUR 27 domestic; EUR 76 foreign (effective 2007). back issues avail. **Document type:** *Magazine, Consumer.*
Published by: Ares Europa, Angelita Cavero 13 3o. D, Madrid, 28027, Spain. TEL 34-91-7422487.

327 CHL ISSN 0716-0240
F1414.2
➤ **ESTUDIOS INTERNACIONALES.** Text in Spanish. 1967. q. CLP 23,000 domestic; USD 100 foreign (effective 2010). adv. bk.rev. index. **Document type:** *Journal, Academic/Scholarly.*
Indexed: A22, BibInd, C01, CA, H21, HistAb, IBR, IBSS, IBZ, JEL, P08, P42, PAIS, SociolAb, T02.
—IE, Infotrieve.
Published by: Universidad de Chile, Instituto de Estudios Internacionales, Casilla 14187 Suc. 21, 9, Condell, 249, Santiago, Chile. TEL 56-2-2745377, FAX 56-2-2740155, inesint@abello.dic.uchile.cl, http://www.ieiuchile.cl. Ed. Rose Cave. Circ: 500.

328 ESP ISSN 1575-7056
ESTUDIOS INTERNACIONALES DE LA COMPLUTENSE. Text in Spanish. 1999. quadrennial. back issues avail. **Document type:** *Journal, Academic/Scholarly.*
Published by: (Universidad Complutense de Madrid, Facultad de Ciencias de la Informacion), Universidad Complutense de Madrid, Servicio de Publicaciones, C/ Obispo Trejo 2, Ciudad Universitaria, Madrid, 28040, Spain. TEL 34-91-3941127, FAX 34-91-3941126, servicio.publicaciones@rect.ucm.es, http://www.ucm.es/publicaciones. Ed. Rafael Calduch.

L'ETAT DU MONDE (YEAR); annuaire economique et geopolitique mondial. *see* BUSINESS AND ECONOMICS—International Commerce

327 USA ISSN 0892-6794
JZ6.5
➤ **ETHICS & INTERNATIONAL AFFAIRS.** Text in English. 1987. q. GBP 239, USD 390 to institutions; GBP 250, USD 408 combined subscription to institutions (print & online eds.) (effective 2012). adv. back issues avail.; reprint service avail. from PSC. **Document type:** *Journal, Academic/Scholarly.* **Description:** Presents applications of ethics to international affairs from a variety of perspectives.
Related titles: Online - full text ed.: ISSN 1747-7093. GBP 226, USD 371 to institutions (effective 2012) (from IngentaConnect).
Indexed: A01, A03, A08, A22, A26, ABS&EES, BRD, CA, E01, E08, ESPM, G08, GSS&RPL, I02, I05, I13, IBSS, LID&ISL, P02, P05, P10, P27, P30, P34, P42, P45, P47, P48, P53, P54, PAIS, PCI, PQC, PSA, PerIslam, PhilInd, R02, RiskAb, S02, S03, S09, S11, SCOPUS, SSA, SSAb, SSI, SSciA, SociolAb, T02, W03, W05.
—BLDSC (3814.656700), IE, Ingenta. **CCC.**
Published by: (Carnegie Council on Ethics and International Affairs), Wiley-Blackwell Publishing, Inc. (Subsidiary of: Wiley-Blackwell Publishing Ltd.), Commerce Pl, 350 Main St, Malden, MA 02148. TEL 781-388-8206, 800-835-6770, FAX 781-388-8232, http://www.wiley.com/WileyCDA/. Eds. John Tessitore, Joel H Rosenthal. adv.: B&W page USD 300; trim 7 x 10. Circ: 534 (paid).

327 USA ISSN 1939-0203
THE ETHICS OF AMERICAN FOREIGN POLICY. Text in English. 2008. irreg., latest 2009. price varies. back issues avail. **Document type:** *Monographic series, Academic/Scholarly.*
Published by: Praeger Publishers (Subsidiary of: Greenwood Publishing Group Inc.), 88 Post Rd W, Westport, CT 06881. TEL 800-368-6868, tech.support@greenwood.com, http://www.greenwood.com. Eds. David Welch, Robert Patman.

327 300 DEU ISSN 0934-0343
ETHNIEN - REGIONEN - KONFLIKTE; Soziologische und politologische Untersuchungen. Text in German. 1988. irreg., latest vol.13, 2007. price varies. **Document type:** *Monographic series, Academic/Scholarly.*
Published by: Peter Lang GmbH (Subsidiary of: Peter Lang Publishing Group), Eschborner Landstr 42-50, Frankfurt Am Main, 60489, Germany. TEL 49-69-7807050, FAX 49-69-78070550, zentrale.frankfurt@peterlang.com. Ed. Abraham Ashkenasi.

327 CAN ISSN 0014-2123
D849
ETUDES INTERNATIONALES. Text in French. 1970. q. CAD 120 domestic to institutions; EUR 115 in the European Union to institutions; USD 120 elsewhere to institutions (effective 2011). adv. bk.rev. index, cum.index. **Document type:** *Journal, Academic/Scholarly.* **Description:** Publishes articles and reviews that cover important international political affairs.
Related titles: Online - full text ed.
Indexed: A20, A22, A26, ABCPolSci, ASD, AmH&L, BAS, C03, CA, CBCARef, CBPI, CPerI, DIP, FR, HistAb, I05, I13, IBR, IBSS, IBZ, LID&ISL, M10, P30, P42, P47, P48, PAIS, PCI, PQC, PRA, PSA, PdeR, PerIslam, SociolAb, T02.
—BLDSC (3820.720000), IE, Infotrieve, Ingenta.
Published by: Institut Quebecois des Hautes Etudes Internationales, Pavillon de Koninck, Universite Laval, Quebec, PQ G1V 0A6, Canada. TEL 418-656-2462, rei@hei.ulaval.ca, http://www.hei.ulaval.ca. Eds. Claude Basset, Louis Belanger, Pauline Curien.

EURASIAN STUDIES. *see* BUSINESS AND ECONOMICS

327 POL ISSN 1232-6070
EURAZJA. Text in Polish; Summaries in English. 1994. q. free. cum.index: 1994-1996. **Description:** Covers political, social and economic changes in the former Soviet Union.
Related titles: Diskette ed.
Published by: Osrodek Studiow Wschodnich/Centre for Eastern Studies, Ul Koszykowa 6 A, Warsaw, 00564, Poland. TEL 48-22-6253616, FAX 48-22-6223589.

327 USA ISSN 1538-7739
EURO-ATLANTIC INITIATIVES. Text in English. 2002. irreg. free (effective 2011). **Document type:** *Journal, Trade.* **Description:** Contains recommendations developed through conference discussions among US and European policy professionals to build and foster communities in the US and Europe committed to comprehensive Euro-Atlantic security.
Related titles: E-mail ed.; Online - full text ed.
Published by: The Stanley Foundation, 209 Iowa Ave, Muscatine, IA 52761. TEL 563-264-1500, FAX 563-264-0864, info@stanleyfoundation.org, http://www.stanleyfoundation.org/.

327 SVK ISSN 1336-8761
EURO-ATLANTIC QUARTERLY. Text in Slovak. 2006. q. **Document type:** *Journal, Academic/Scholarly.*
Published by: Euroatlanticke Centrum, Kuzmanyho 3, Banska Bystrica, 974 01, Slovakia. eac@eac.sk, http://www.eac.sk.

327 BEL ISSN 1021-4208
EURO-EAST. Text in English. 1992. 11/yr. EUR 625 (effective 2000). **Document type:** *Newsletter.* **Description:** Covers EU relations with Central and Eastern Europe.
Related titles: CD-ROM ed.: EUR 635 (effective 2000); Online - full text ed.; French ed.: Euro-Est. ISSN 1021-4216.
Indexed: A15, ABIn, B02, B03, B11, B15, B17, B18, G04, G06, G07, G08, I05, P23, P47, P53, P54, PQC.
—CIS. **CCC.**
Published by: Europe Information Service SA (E I S), Av Adolphe Lacomble 66-68, Brussels, 1030, Belgium. TEL 32-2-737-7709, FAX 32-2-732-6757, eis@eis.be, http://www.eis.be. Ed. Eric van Puyvelde. Pub. Eric Damiens.

EURO-GUIDE: YEARBOOK OF THE INSTITUTIONS OF THE EUROPEAN UNION AND OF THE OTHER EUROPEAN ORGANIZATIONS/ANNUAIRE DES INSTITUTIONS DE L'UNION EUROPEENNE ET DES AUTRES ORGANISATIONS EUROPEENNES. *see* PUBLIC ADMINISTRATION

327 ROM ISSN 1841-9259
➤ **EUROLIMES.** Text in English, French; Summaries in English. 2006. s-a. ROL 80, EUR 20 (effective 2011). abstr.; bibl.; charts; maps; illus.; stat. back issues avail. **Document type:** *Journal, Academic/Scholarly.* **Description:** Covers the research in European borders and borders policies, includes subfields such as conflict resolution, constitution drafting, and state building.
Related titles: Online - full text ed.
Indexed: A01, CA.
Published by: (Institute for Euroregional Studies Oradea/Institutului de Studii Euroregionale), Editura Universitatii din Oradea/University of Oradea Publishing House, Str Universitatii 1, Geotermal Bldg., 2nd Fl., Oradea, Jud.Bihor 410087, Romania. TEL 40-259-408642, editura@uoradea.ro, http://webhost.uoradea.ro/editura/. Ed., Pub. Neag Horea. Circ: 300.

327 FIN ISSN 1796-8542
EUROOPPALAINEN SUOMI. RAPORTTEJA. Text in Finnish. 2007. s-a. **Document type:** *Monographic series, Consumer.*
Related titles: Online - full text ed.
Published by: Eurooppalainen Suomi ry/The Europen Movement in Finland, Oikokatu 3, Helsinki, 00170, Finland. TEL 358-9-68115710, FAX 358-9-68115720, es@eurooppalainensuomi.fi.

327.025 GBR ISSN 1465-4628
JZ4838
EUROPA DIRECTORY OF INTERNATIONAL ORGANIZATIONS. Text in English. 1999. a. USD 460 per issue (effective 2009). reprints avail. **Document type:** *Directory, Academic/Scholarly.* **Description:** Research guide to over 1,700 international organizations around the world.

P

Published by: (Europa Publications Ltd.), Routledge (Subsidiary of: Taylor & Francis Group), 2 Park Sq, Milton Park, Abingdon, Oxon OX14 4RN, United Kingdom. orders@taylorandfrancis.com. **Dist. by:** Current Pacific Ltd., 7 La Roche Pl, Northcote, PO Box 36-536, Auckland 0627, New Zealand.

327 DEU ISSN 1433-7428
EUROPA KOMMUNAL. Text in German. 1981. bi-m. EUR 55; EUR 9 newsstand/cover (effective 2007). adv. **Document type:** *Magazine, Trade.*
Published by: Rat der Gemeinden und Regionen Europas, Deutsche Sektion, Lindenallee 13-17, Cologne, 50968, Germany. TEL 49-221-3771311, FAX 49-221-3771150, post@rgre.de. adv.: B&W page EUR 715.81, color page EUR 1,620.79. Circ: 5,200 (paid and controlled).

327 800 DEU ISSN 1862-6564
EUROPA REVUE. Text in French. 2006. irreg. **Document type:** *Journal, Trade.*
Published by: Sine Causa Verlag, Droysenstr 11, Berlin, 10629, Germany. TEL 49-30-74788767, sine-causa@arcor.de. Eds., Pubs. Herbert Neidhoefer, Selim Rauer.

EUROPAEISCHE GESUNDHEITSGESPRAECHE. *see* MEDICAL SCIENCES

327 AUT ISSN 0304-2782
JN12
EUROPAEISCHE RUNDSCHAU. Text in German. 1973. q. EUR 23; EUR 6.50 newsstand/cover (effective 2005). adv. bk.rev. bibl. reprint service avail. from SCH. **Document type:** *Magazine, Consumer.*
Indexed: A22, ELLIS, I13, IBR, IBZ, PAIS, PRA.
—BLDSC (3829.361000), IE, Ingenta.
Published by: Verein Europaeische Rundschau, Ebendorferstr 6/4, Vienna, 1010, Austria. TEL 43-1-4083400, FAX 43-1-408340011. Ed. Paul Lendvai. Circ: 2,750.

327 DEU ISSN 0071-2329
EUROPAEISCHE SCHRIFTEN. Text in German, English. 1963. irreg., latest vol.86, 2007. price varies. **Document type:** *Monographic series, Academic/Scholarly.*
Published by: (Institut fuer Europaeische Politik e.V.), Europa Union Verlag GmbH, Holtorfer Str 35, Bonn, 53229, Germany. TEL 49-228-729000, FAX 49-228-7290013, service@eu-verlag.de, http://www.europa-union-verlag.de. Ed. Mathias Jopp.

327 DEU ISSN 0721-3018
EUROPAEISCHES FORUM. Text in German. 1949. irreg., latest vol.15, 2005. price varies. bk.rev. **Document type:** *Monographic series, Academic/Scholarly.*
Formerly (until 1980): Informationsdienst des Deutschen Rates der Europaeischen Bewegung (0020-0549)
Published by: (Netzwerk Europaeische Bewegung Deutschland), Peter Lang GmbH (Subsidiary of: Peter Lang Publishing Group), Eschborner Landstr 42-50, Frankfurt Am Main, 60489, Germany. TEL 49-69-7807050, FAX 49-69-78070550, zentrale.frankfurt@peterlang.com, http://www.peterlang.com. Circ: 40,000.

327 AUT ISSN 0014-2727
EUROPASTIMME. Text in German. 1960. bi-m. EUR 0.58 newsstand/cover (effective 2005). bk.rev. illus.; stat. **Document type:** *Newspaper, Consumer.*
Published by: Europaeische Foederalistische Bewegung, Jahnweg 5, Feldbach, St 8330, Austria. TEL 43-3152-2497, FAX 43-3152-24974. Ed. Karl Menzinger. Circ: 10,000. **Co-sponsor:** Bund Europaeischer Jugend.

327 ITA ISSN 1721-3363
EUROPE AND THE BALKANS INTERNATIONAL NETWORK. Text in Italian, English. 1995. irreg., latest vol.13. price varies. **Document type:** *Monographic series, Academic/Scholarly.* **Description:** Contains studies on history and politics of East Europe.
Published by: (Universita degli Studi di Bologna, Network Europe and the Balkans), Angelo Longo Editore, Via Paolo Costa 33, Ravenna, 48121, Italy. TEL 39-0544-217026, FAX 39-0544-217554, longo@longo-editore.it, http://www.longo-editore.it.

327 BEL ISSN 0423-6386
EUROPE. BULLETIN QUOTIDIEN. Text in French. 1952. d. **Document type:** *Bulletin, Trade.*
Published by: Agence Europe S.A., 36 Rue de la Gare, Brussels, 1040, Belgium. TEL 32-2-7379494, FAX 32-2-7363700, info@agenceurope.com, http://www.agenceurope.com.

327 BEL ISSN 1784-0759
EUROPE. DIPLOMATIE & DEFENSE. Text in French. 1967. s-w. **Document type:** *Bulletin, Government.*
Formerly (until 2007): Nouvelles Atlantiques (1029-1105)
Published by: Agence Europe S.A., 36 Rue de la Gare, Brussels, 1040, Belgium. TEL 32-2-7379494, FAX 32-2-7363700, info@agenceurope.com.

327 BEL ISSN 1026-3012
EUROPE. DOCUMENTS. Text in Multiple languages. 1959. irreg. **Document type:** *Magazine, Trade.*
—BLDSC (3829.473000).
Published by: Agence Europe S.A., 36 Rue de la Gare, Brussels, 1040, Belgium. TEL 32-2-7379494, FAX 32-2-7363700, info@agenceurope.com, http://www.agenceurope.com.

327 FRA ISSN 1958-3672
EUROPE FEDERALE. Text in French. 200?. 3/yr. **Document type:** *Bulletin.*
Published by: Union pour l'Europe Federale, c/o Europe Direct, 13 Rue de l'Arbre Sec, Lyon, 69001, France.

327.1 BEL ISSN 1811-4148
EUROPE INFORMATION SOCIAL (ENGLISH EDITION). Text in English. 1991. m. EUR 690 (effective 2005). **Document type:** *Journal, Academic/Scholarly.* **Description:** Covers EU social policy, free movement of workers, social security, employment, workers' rights, pensions, and healthcare.
Formerly (until 2004): European Social Policy (1021-4143)
Related titles: CD-ROM ed.: EUR 635 (effective 2000); Online - full text ed.: ISSN 1811-9891; ◆ French ed.: Europe Information Social (French Edition). ISSN 1811-413X.
Indexed: A15, A26, ABIn, B02, B11, B15, B17, B18, E08, G04, G06, G07, G08, I05, P23, P47, P48, P51, P53, P54, PQC, S09.
—CIS. **CCC.**
Published by: Europe Information Service SA (E I S), Av Adolphe Lacomble 66-68, Brussels, 1030, Belgium. TEL 32-2-7377700, FAX 32-2-7326608, eis@eis.be, http://www.eis.be. Pub. Eric Damiens.

327 BEL ISSN 1811-413X
EUROPE INFORMATION SOCIAL (FRENCH EDITION). Text in French. 2004. m.
Formerly (until 2004): Lettre Sociale Europeenne (1021-4151)
Related titles: Online - full content ed.: ISSN 1811-9980; ◆ English ed.: Europe Information Social (English Edition). ISSN 1811-4148.
Published by: Europe Information Service SA (E I S), Av Adolphe Lacomble 66-68, Brussels, 1030, Belgium. TEL 32-2-7377700, FAX 32-2-7326608, eis@eis.be, http://www.eis.be.

EUROPE REVIEW (SAFFRON WALDEN). *see* BUSINESS AND ECONOMICS—Economic Situation And Conditions

327 USA ISSN 1527-8158
HC240.A1
EUROPEAN AFFAIRS. Text in English. 2000. q. USD 19.50 domestic; USD 20.75 in Canada; USD 54.50 elsewhere; USD 7.50 newsstand/cover (effective 2001). adv. bk.rev. back issues avail.; reprints avail. **Document type:** *Journal, Consumer.*
Related titles: CD-ROM ed.: ISSN 1527-8166.
Indexed: A26, I05, PAIS.
—BLDSC (3829.482971).
Published by: European Institute, 5225 Wisconsin Ave. NW, Ste. 200, Washington, DC 20015. TEL 202-895-1670, FAX 202-362-1088, ewebster@europeaninstitute.org, info@europeaninstitute.org, http://www.europeaninstitute.org. Ed. Reginald Dale. Pub. Jacqueline Grapin. R&P Maria Papathanassiou. Adv. contact Claire Le Goc. B&W page USD 2,000, color page USD 3,380; trim 7 x 10.

327 LUX
EUROPEAN COMMISSION. EUROPEAN UNION. BULLETIN. Variant title: Bulletin of the European Union. Text in English. 10/yr. **Document type:** *Bulletin, Government.*
Media: Online - full content. **Related titles:** CD-ROM ed.; Danish ed.: Bulletinen for Den Europaeiske Union; German ed.: Bulletin der Europaischen Union; Finnish ed.: Euroopan Unionin Tiedotteessa; Portuguese ed.: Boletim da Uniao Europeia; Dutch ed.: Bulletin van de Europese Unie; Italian ed.: Bollettino dell'Unione Europea; French ed.: Bulletin de l'Union Europeenne; Spanish ed.: Boletin de la Union Europea; Swedish ed.: Europeiska Unionens Bulletin.
Published by: European Commission, Office for Official Publications of the European Union, 2 Rue Mercier, Luxembourg, L-2985, Luxembourg. FAX 352-29291.

327 LUX ISSN 1029-354X
EUROPEAN COMMUNITIES. ASYLUM-SEEKERS. Text in English. 1996. q.
Published by: European Commission, Office for Official Publications of the European Union, 2 Rue Mercier, Luxembourg, L-2985, Luxembourg. TEL 352-29291, info@publications.europa.eu, http://europa.eu.

EUROPEAN COMMUNITIES. COST. *see* BUSINESS AND ECONOMICS—Public Finance, Taxation

EUROPEAN COMMUNITIES. ECONOMIC AND SOCIAL CONSULTATIVE ASSEMBLY. ANNUAL REPORT. *see* BUSINESS AND ECONOMICS

327 IRL ISSN 0791-8097
➤ **EUROPEAN DOCUMENT SERIES.** Text in English. 1993. q. EUR 19 per issue (effective 2005). bk.rev. bibl.; tr.lit. back issues avail. **Description:** Designed to highlight the texts of important speeches, papers and reports on European issues and themes.
Related titles: E-mail ed.; Fax ed.
Published by: Institute of European Affairs, Europe House, 8 North Great Georges St., Dublin, 1, Ireland. TEL 353-1-8746756, FAX 353-1-8786880, info@iiea.com, http://www.iiea.com. Ed. Tony Brown.

327 NLD ISSN 1384-6299
K5 CODEN: EFARCW
➤ **EUROPEAN FOREIGN AFFAIRS REVIEW.** Text in English. 1996. q. USD 502 to institutions; USD 616 combined subscription to institutions (print & online eds.) (effective 2011). back issues avail.; reprint service avail. from PSC. **Document type:** *Journal, Academic/Scholarly.* **Description:** Covers EU foreign policy interests and strategies.
Related titles: Online - full text ed.: ISSN 1875-8223. USD 465 to institutions (effective 2011).
Indexed: A01, A02, A03, A08, A22, A26, B01, B06, B07, B08, B09, CA, E01, E08, G08, I05, I13, IBSS, L03, P30, P34, P42, PSA, S09, S23, SCOPUS, T02.
—BLDSC (3829.715602), IE, Infotrieve, Ingenta. **CCC.**
Published by: Kluwer Law International (Subsidiary of: Aspen Publishers, Inc.), PO Box 316, Alphen aan den Rijn, 2400 AH, Netherlands. TEL 31-172-641500, FAX 31-172-641555, sales@kluwerlaw.com, http://www.kluwerlaw.com. Eds. Joerg Monar, Nanette Neuwahl.

327 ITA
D1058
EUROPEAN FOREIGN POLICY BULLETIN ONLINE. Text in English. a. **Document type:** *Bulletin.*
Formerly (until 1993): European Political Cooperation Documentation Bulletin (0259-2290)
Media: Online - full text.
Published by: European University Institute, Via dei Roccettini 9, San Domenico di Fiesole, FI 50014, Italy. TEL 39-055-4685266, forinfo@iue.it, http://www.iue.it.

327 GBR
EUROPEAN FOUNDATION. BRIEFING PAPER. Text in English. irreg. **Description:** Concerned with the politics and economics of the European Community.
—BLDSC (3829.715625).
Published by: European Foundation, 61 Pall Mall, London, SW1Y 5HZ, United Kingdom. TEL 44-20-7930-4193, FAX 44-20-7930-9706.

327 BEL ISSN 1021-4283
EUROPEAN INSIGHT. Text in English. 1982. 48/yr. EUR 460 (effective 2000). **Document type:** *Bulletin.* **Description:** Covers events in the EU in the preceding week.
Related titles: Online - full text ed.; French ed.: Lettre Europeenne. ISSN 1021-4291.
—CIS. **CCC.**
Published by: Europe Information Service SA (E I S), Av Adolphe Lacomble 66-68, Brussels, 1030, Belgium. TEL 32-2-737-7709, FAX 32-2-732-6757, eis@eis.be, http://www.eis.be. Pub. Eric Damiens.

327 AUT ISSN 1027-5193
JN15
➤ **EUROPEAN INTEGRATION ONLINE PAPERS.** Text in English. 1997. irreg. free (effective 2011).
Media: Online - full text.
Indexed: CA, IBSS, P10, P42, P45, P48, PQC, PSA, SCOPUS, SSCI, SociolAb, T02, W07.
Published by: European Communities Studies Association - Austria, c/o Research Institute for European Affairs, Althanstrasse 39-45, Vienna, A-1090, Austria. TEL 43-1-313364135, FAX 43-1-31336758, ecsa@wuw.at. Ed. Dr. Michael Nentwich.

327 BEL ISSN 0394-6444
D1050
THE EUROPEAN JOURNAL OF INTERNATIONAL AFFAIRS. Text in English. 1988. q. bk.rev. illus. **Document type:** *Journal, Academic/Scholarly.*
Related titles: Online - full text ed.
Indexed: P30, PAIS.
—Ingenta.
Published by: European Centre of International Affairs, Square de Meeus 38-4, Brussels, Belgium. TEL 32-2-4016120, FAX 32-2-4016119, info@european-centre.org, http://www.european-centre.org.

327 GBR ISSN 1354-0661
JX1
➤ **EUROPEAN JOURNAL OF INTERNATIONAL RELATIONS.** Abbreviated title: E J I R. Text in English. 1995. q. USD 1,212, GBP 655 combined subscription to institutions (print & online eds.); USD 1,188, GBP 642 to institutions (effective 2011). adv. illus. Index. back issues avail.; reprint service avail. from PSC. **Document type:** *Journal, Academic/Scholarly.* **Description:** Aims to stimulate and disseminate the latest research in international relations. Addresses methodological and epistemological questions as well as conceptual and empirical developments within the major sub-areas of the field.
Related titles: Online - full text ed.: ISSN 1460-3713. USD 1,091, GBP 590 to institutions (effective 2011).
Indexed: A01, A02, A03, A08, A12, A17, A20, A22, ABIn, B01, B06, B07, B09, CA, CurCont, DIP, E01, ESPM, EconLit, H04, I13, I14, IBR, IBSS, IBZ, JEL, P34, P42, P48, P51, P53, P54, PQC, PRA, PSA, RiskAb, S02, S03, SCOPUS, SPAA, SSA, SSCI, SociolAb, T02, V02, W07.
—BLDSC (3829.730920), IE, Infotrieve, Ingenta. **CCC.**
Published by: (Standing Group on International Relations), Sage Publications Ltd. (Subsidiary of: Sage Publications, Inc.), 1 Oliver's Yard, 55 City Rd, London, EC1Y 1SP, United Kingdom. TEL 44-20-73248500, FAX 44-20-73248600, info@sagepub.co.uk, http://www.uk.sagepub.com/home.nav. Ed. Colin Wight. adv.: B&W page GBP 400; 130 x 205. **Subscr. to:** Sage Publications, Inc., 2455 Teller Rd, Thousand Oaks, CA 91320. TEL 805-499-9774, FAX 805-499-0871, journals@sagepub.com.

327 GBR ISSN 0966-2839
UA646
➤ **EUROPEAN SECURITY.** Text in English. 1992. q. GBP 361 combined subscription in United Kingdom to institutions (print & online eds.); EUR 471, USD 592 combined subscription to institutions (print & online eds.) (effective 2012). adv. bk.rev. index. back issues avail.; reprint service avail. from PSC. **Document type:** *Journal, Academic/Scholarly.* **Description:** Publishes articles, essays, and reviews on the new architecture, concepts, institutions, problems, and prospects for European security in the wake of the end of the Cold War.
Related titles: Online - full text ed.: ISSN 1746-1545. GBP 324 in United Kingdom to institutions; EUR 424, USD 532 to institutions (effective 2012) (from IngentaConnect).
Indexed: A01, A22, AUNI, CA, E01, ESPM, I02, I13, IBSS, LID&ISL, M05, P02, P10, P34, P42, P47, P48, P53, P54, PCI, PQC, PSA, RiskAb, S02, S03, S11, SCOPUS, SociolAb, T02.
—IE, Infotrieve, Ingenta. **CCC.**
Published by: Routledge (Subsidiary of: Taylor & Francis Group), 4 Park Sq, Milton Park, Abingdon, Oxon OX14 4RN, United Kingdom. TEL 44-20-70176000, FAX 44-20-70176336, subscriptions@tandf.co.uk, http://www.routledge.com/journals/. Ed. Andrea Ellner TEL 44-118-3788501. Adv. contact Linda Hann TEL 44-1344-779945. **Subscr. to:** Taylor & Francis Ltd., Journals Customer Service, Sheepen Pl, Colchester, Essex CO3 3LP, United Kingdom. TEL 44-20-70175544, FAX 44-20-70175198.

327 NLD ISSN 1568-1858
D901
EUROPEAN STUDIES; a journal of European culture, history and politics. Text mainly in English; Text occasionally in French. 1988. irreg., latest vol.25, 2007. price varies. illus.; maps. back issues avail. **Document type:** *Monographic series, Academic/Scholarly.* **Description:** Interdisciplinary studies involving literature, history, law, and economics to assess topics within the field of European relations.
Formerly (until 2000): Yearbook of European Studies (0920-4792)
Related titles: Online - full text ed.: ISSN 1875-8150 (from IngentaConnect).
Indexed: A01, A03, A08, CA, MLA-IB, P02, P10, P42, P45, P48, P53, P54, PQC, T02.
—IE, Ingenta. **CCC.**
Published by: (Universiteit van Amsterdam, Afdeling Europeese Studies/University of Amsterdam, Department of European Studies), Editions Rodopi B.V., Tijnmuiden 7, Amsterdam, 1046 AK, Netherlands. TEL 31-20-6114821, FAX 31-20-4472979, orders-queries@rodopi.nl. Ed. Menno Spiering. **Dist in France by:** Nordeal, 30 rue de Verlinghem, BP 139, Lambersart 59832, France. TEL 33-3-20099060, FAX 33-3-20929495; **Dist in N America by:** Rodopi - USA, 295 North Michigan Avenue, Suite 1B, Kenilworth, NJ 07033. TEL 908-298-9071, 800-225-3998, FAX 908-298-9075.

327.03 GBR ISSN 1363-7045
THE EUROPEAN UNION ENCYCLOPEDIA AND DIRECTORY (YEAR). Text in English. 1991. irreg., latest 2008, 9th ed. USD 710 per issue (effective 2009). reprints avail. **Document type:** *Directory, Trade.* **Description:** Provides comprehensive details on the countries of the European Union, it's development from the creation of the single market in 1992 to the implementation of the Maastricht Treaty, and its continuing activities.

Formerly (until 1996): European Communities Encyclopedia and Directory (0962-1032)
—BLDSC (3830.351368).
Published by: (Europa Publications Ltd.), Routledge (Subsidiary of: Taylor & Francis Group), 2 Park Sq, Milton Park, Abingdon, Oxon OX14 4RN, United Kingdom. TEL 44-20-70176000, FAX 44-20-70176699, orders@taylorandfrancis.com.

327 365 FRA ISSN 1608-5000
EUROPEAN UNION INSTITUTE FOR SECURITY STUDIES. OCCASIONAL PAPERS/UNION DE L'EUROPE OCCIDENTALE. INSTITUT D'ETUDES DE SECURITE. PUBLICATIONS OCCASIONELLES. Text in Multiple languages. 1997. irreg.
Document type: *Monographic series, Trade.*
Related titles: Online - full text ed.: ISSN 1683-4976.
Indexed: LID&ISL.
—BLDSC (6217.250700).
Published by: European Union Institute for Security Studies, 43 Ave du President Wilson, Paris, 75775 Cedex 16, France. TEL 33-1-56891930, FAX 33-1-56891931, institute@iss-eu.org, http://www.iss-eu.org. Ed. Regine Serra.

327 LUX ISSN 1725-2423
KJE908 CODEN: OJEUBS
EUROPEAN UNION. OFFICIAL JOURNAL; the authoritative source of E U law. Text in English. 1973. d. m. index on diskette. **Document type:** *Government.*
Formerly (until Jan. 2003): European Communities. Official Journal. C: Information and Notices (0378-6986)
Related titles: ◆ CD-ROM ed.: European Union. Official Journal. L & C Series: Legislation and Information Notices (Quarterly Edition); Microfiche ed.: (from PQC); ◆ Spanish ed.: Diario Oficial de las Comunidades Europeas. C: Comunicaciones e Informaciones. ISSN 0257-7763; Danish ed.: De Europaiske Fallesskabers Tidende. C: Meddelelser og Oplysninger. ISSN 0378-7001. 1973; German ed.: Amtsblatt der Europaischen Gemeinschaften. C: Mitteilungen und Bekanntmachungen. ISSN 0376-9461. 1968; Greek ed.: Episeme Efemerida ton Europaikon Koinoteton. C. Anakoinoseis Kai Plerofories. ISSN 0250-815X. 1981; Portuguese ed.: Jornal Oficial das Comunidades Europeias. C: Comunicacoes e Informacoes. ISSN 0257-7771. 1986; Italian ed.: Gazzetta Ufficiale delle Comunita Europee. C. Comunicazioni ed Informazioni. ISSN 0378-701X. 1968; Finnish ed.: Euroopan Yhteisojen Virallinen Lehti. C: Tiedonantoja ja Ilmoituksia. ISSN 1024-302X; Swedish ed.: Europeiska Gemenskapernas Officiella Tidning. C: Oplysninger. ISSN 1024-3046. 1995; Dutch ed.: Publikatieblad van de Europese Gemeenschappen. C: Mededelingen en Bekendmakingen. ISSN 0378-7079. 1968; French ed.: Journal Officiel des Communautes Europeennes. C: Communications et Informations. ISSN 0378-7052; ◆ Special ed(s).: Justis CD-ROM Official Journal. C Series. ISSN 1351-8518; ◆ Supplement(s): European Union. Official Journal. L Series: Legislation; ◆ European Union. Official Journal. S Series: Tendering Procedures for Public Contracts. ISSN 0378-7273.
Indexed: A22, CBNB, ECI, ELLIS, F&EA, IPackAb, R18, WSCA.
—BLDSC (6239.837300), CASDDS, IE, Ingenta.
Published by: European Commission, Office for Official Publications of the European Union, 2 Rue Mercier, Luxembourg, L-2985, Luxembourg. TEL 352-29291, info@publications.europa.eu, http://publications.europa.eu. **Dist. in the U.S. by:** Bernan Associates, Bernan, 4611-F Assembly Dr., Lanham, MD 20706-4391. TEL 800-274-4447.

327 LUX
CODEN: OJELD3
EUROPEAN UNION. OFFICIAL JOURNAL. L SERIES: LEGISLATION. Text in English. 1973. d. EUR 700; EUR 70 per month (effective 2006). m. index on diskette. **Description:** Contains information on EU legislation, including regulations, directives, decisions, recommendations and opinions.
Formerly: Official Journal of the European Communities. L Series: Legislation (0378-6978)
Related titles: ◆ CD-ROM ed.: European Union. Official Journal. L & C Series: Legislation and Information Notices (Quarterly Edition); Microfiche ed.; French ed.: Journal Officiel des Communautes Europeennes. L: Legislation. ISSN 0378-7060. 1968; German ed.: Amtsblatt der Europaischen Gemeinschaften. L: Rechtsvorschriften. ISSN 0376-9453. 1952; Italian ed.: Gazzetta Ufficiale delle Comunita Europee. L: Legislazione. ISSN 0378-7028; Danish ed.: Europaeiske Faellesskabers Tidende. L: Retsforskrifter. ISSN 0378-6994. 1973; Dutch ed.: Publikatieblad van de Europese Gemeenschappen. L Serie: Wetgeving. ISSN 0378-7087. 1952; Greek ed.: Episeme Efemerida ton Europaikon Koinoteton. L: Nomothesia. ISSN 0250-8168. 1981; Finnish ed.: Euroopan Yhteisojen Virallinen Lehti. L: Lainsaadanto. ISSN 1024-3038; Spanish ed.: Diario Oficial de las Comunidades Europeas. L: Legislacion. ISSN 1012-9200. 1986; Portuguese ed.: Jornal Oficial das Comunidades Europeias. L: Legislacao. ISSN 1012-9219. 1986; Irish ed.: Iris Oifigiuil na gComhphobal Eorpach. L: Achtu. ISSN 0257-9537; Swedish ed.: Europeiska Gemenskapernas Officiella Tidning. L: Lagstiftning. ISSN 1024-3054. 1995; ◆ Supplement to: European Union. Official Journal. ISSN 1725-2423.
Indexed: A22, CBNB, Cadscan, ECI, ELLIS, IPackAb, LeadAb, M10, R18, RASB, Zincscan.
—CASDDS, Ingenta.
Published by: European Commission, Office for Official Publications of the European Union, 2 Rue Mercier, Luxembourg, L-2985, Luxembourg. TEL 352-29291, FAX 352-29291, info@publications.europa.eu, http://publications.europa.eu. **Dist. in the U.S. by:** Bernan Associates, Bernan, 4611-F Assembly Dr., Lanham, MD 20706-4391. TEL 301-459-2255, 800-274-4447, FAX 301-459-0056.

327.4 GBR ISSN 1465-1165
➤ **EUROPEAN UNION POLITICS.** Abbreviated title: E U P. Text in English. 2000. q. USD 787, GBP 425 combined subscription to institutions (print & online eds.); USD 771, GBP 417 to institutions (effective 2011). adv. bk.rev. back issues avail.; reprint service avail. from PSC. **Document type:** *Journal, Academic/Scholarly.*
Description: International journal which advances systematic research on the most important political processes and institutions of the European Union.
Related titles: Online - full text ed.: ISSN 1741-2757. USD 708, GBP 383 to institutions (effective 2011).
Indexed: A01, A03, A08, A22, CA, CurCont, E01, ESPM, I13, IBSS, P34, P42, PRA, PSA, RiskAb, S02, S03, SCOPUS, SPAA, SSCI, SociolAb, T02, W07.
—BLDSC (3830.351437), IE, Infotrieve, Ingenta. **CCC.**
Published by: Sage Publications Ltd. (Subsidiary of: Sage Publications, Inc.), 1 Oliver's Yard, 55 City Rd, London, EC1Y 1SP, United Kingdom. TEL 44-20-73248500, FAX 44-20-73248600, info@sagepub.co.uk, http://www.sagepub.co.uk, http://www.sagepub.com/home.nav. adv.: B&W page GBP 400; 130 x 205.

327 315 ITA ISSN 1606-8963
THE EUROPEAN UNION REVIEW. Text in English. 1996. 3/yr.
Document type: *Journal, Academic/Scholarly.*
Indexed: PAIS, SociolAb.
Published by: Universita degli Studi di Pavia, Centro Studi sulle Comunita Europee, Strada Nuova 65, Pavia, 27100, Italy. TEL 39-0382-304788, FAX 39-0382-23300, eur@unipv.it, http://www.unipv.it/cdepv. Ed. Silvia Bruzzi.

327 DEU ISSN 1781-6858
D1050
EUROPEAN VIEW. Text in English. 2005. s-a. EUR 185, USD 244 combined subscription to institutions (print & online eds.) (effective 2012). back issues avail.; reprint service avail. from PSC. **Document type:** *Journal, Academic/Scholarly.* **Description:** Covers contemporary European politics, focusing on one specific theme in each issue.
Related titles: Online - full content ed.: ISSN 1865-5831.
Indexed: A22, A26, E01, E08, P45, P46, P48, P51, P53, P54, PQC, S09, SCOPUS.
—IE. **CCC.**
Published by: (European People's Party, Centre for European Studies BEL), Springer (Subsidiary of: Springer Science+Business Media), Tiergartenstr 17, Heidelberg, 69121, Germany. TEL 49-6221-4870, FAX 49-6221-345229, orders-hd-individuals@springer.com. Ed. Tomi Huhtanen.

EUROPEAN YEARBOOK/ANNUAIRE EUROPEEN. *see* LAW—International Law

327 BEL ISSN 1021-4275
EUROPOLITIQUE (BRUXELLES). Text in French. 19??. irreg.
Related titles: ◆ English ed.: Europolitics; Supplement(s):.
Published by: Europe Information Service SA (E I S), Av Adolphe Lacomble 66-68, Brussels, 1030, Belgium. TEL 32-2-7377709, FAX 32-2-7326757, eis@eis.be, http://www.eis.be.

327 EST ISSN 1406-4812
EUROUNIVERSITY. SERIES. INTERNATIONAL RELATIONS. Text in Multiple languages. 1998. irreg. **Document type:** *Monographic series, Academic/Scholarly.*
Related titles: ◆ Series: Baltic Horizons. ISSN 1736-1834.
Published by: EuroUniversity, Faculty of International Relations, Mustamae tee 4, Tallinn, 10621, Estonia. TEL 372-2-6115801, FAX 372-2-6115811, euro@eurouniv.ee, http://www.eurouniv.ee.

327 USA ISSN 1063-6323
HF1532.92
EUROWATCH. Text in English. 1989. s-m. USD 914 combined subscription domestic (print & online eds.); USD 964 combined subscription foreign (print & online eds.) (effective 2008). adv. index. back issues avail. **Document type:** *Newsletter, Trade.* **Description:** Examines EU legal issues likely to impact business, such as recent judicial and legislative developments, trade, single market and currency issues, labor, tax and intellectual property issues.
Formerly (until 1991): 1992: The External Impact of European Unification (1043-4380)
Related titles: Online - full text ed.
—**CCC.**
Published by: WorldTrade Executive, Inc., 2250 Main St, Ste 100, PO Box 761, Concord, MA 01742. TEL 978-287-0301, FAX 978-287-0302, info@wtexec.com, http://www.wtexec.com. Pub. Gary A Brown.

327.17 POL ISSN 1643-0360
D2024
EVROPA. Text in Russian. 2001. q. EUR 104 foreign (effective 2006).
Document type: *Journal, Academic/Scholarly.*
Published by: Polski Instytut Spraw Miedzynarodowych/Polish Institute of International Affairs, ul Warecka 1a, skryt. poczt. nr 1010, Warsaw, 00950, Poland. TEL 48-22-5568000, FAX 48-22-5568099. Ed. Slavomir Debski. **Dist. by:** Ars Polona, Obroncow 25, Warsaw 03933, Poland. TEL 48-22-5098609, FAX 48-22-5098610, arspolona@arspolona.com.pl, http://www.arspolona.com.pl.

327 340 SRB ISSN 1451-3188
K5
EVROPSKO ZAKONODAVSTVO/EUROPEAN UNION LEGISLATION. Text in Serbian. 1998. q. **Document type:** *Journal, Academic/Scholarly.*
Formerly (until 2002): Pregled Evropskogo Zakonodavstva (1450-6815)
Published by: Institut za Medjunarodnu Politiku i Privredu/Institute of International Politics and Economics, Makedonska 25, Belgrade, 11000. TEL 381-11-3373838, FAX 381-11-3373835, iipe@diplomacy.bg.ac.yu. Ed. Blagoje Babic.

327 370.116 NLD ISSN 2210-9625
THE EXCHANGE. Text in English. 1996. irreg. (1-2/yr.).
Published by: The Atlantic & Pacific Exchange Program, Eendrachtsweg 21, Rotterdam, 3012 LB, Netherlands. TEL 31-10-4114588, FAX 31-10-4132543, exchange@apep.nl. Ed. Robin Doeswijk.

327 USA ISSN 8755-433X
H1
EXECUTIVE MEMORANDUM. Text in English. 1982. irreg., latest no.1029, 2008. looseleaf. back issues avail. **Document type:** *Monographic series, Trade.* **Description:** Promotes conservative public policies based on the principles of free enterprise, limited government, individual freedom, traditional American values, and a national defense.
Related titles: Online - full text ed.: free (effective 2010).
Published by: The Heritage Foundation, 214 Massachusetts Ave NE, Washington, DC 20002-4999. TEL 202-546-4400, FAX 202-546-8328, info@heritage.org.

327 ISR
EYE ON PALESTINE; monitoring Israeli colonizing activities in the Palestinian West Bank and Gaza. Text in English. m. **Document type:** *Journal, Consumer.*
Published by: Applied Research Institute - Jerusalem, Caritas Street, PO Box 860, Bethlehem, Israel. TEL 972-2-2741889, FAX 972-2-2776966, http://www.arij.org.

327 DNK ISSN 1901-645X
F N-FORBUNDET. NYHEDSBREV. Text in Danish. 1969. irreg. free. bk.rev. illus. **Document type:** *Newsletter, Consumer.*
Former titles (until 2006): F N Bladet (Print) (1395-2781); (until 1995): F N Orientering (0014-5998); Which was formed by the merger of (1964-1969): F N - Bladet (0906-3196); (1950-1969): Verden og Vi (0505-2521)
Media: E-mail.
Published by: F N - Forbundet/Danish United Nations Association, St Kongensgade 36-38, Copenhagen K, 1264, Denmark. TEL 45-33-464690, FAX 45-33-464649, fnforbundet@una.dk. Eds. Anni Herfort Andersen, Joergen Estrup.

327 FRA ISSN 0760-6443
FAIM, DEVELOPPEMENT MAGAZINE. Text in French. 1966. 9/yr. adv. bibl. **Document type:** *Magazine, Consumer.*
Published by: Comite Catholique contre la Faim et pour le Developpement, 4 rue Jean Lantier, Paris, 75001, France. TEL 33-1-44828000, FAX 33-1-44828144. Ed. Thierry Bresillon. Pub., Adv. contact Claude Baehrel. Circ: 60,000 (controlled).

THE FATE OF THE ARABIAN PENINSULA. *see* ENERGY

327.117 IND ISSN 0972-1290
HV6433.I4
FAULTLINES; writings on conflict & resolution. Text in English. 1999. q.
Document type: *Monographic series, Academic/Scholarly.*
Description: Focuses on various sources and aspects of existing and emerging conflict in the Indian subcontinent. Terrorism and low-intensity wars, communal, caste and other sectarian strife, political violence, organized crime, policing, the criminal justice system and human rights.
Related titles: Online - full text ed.: free (effective 2011).
—BLDSC (3897.794700), IE, Ingenta.
Published by: The Institute for Conflict Management, 11 Talkatora Rd, New Delhi, 110 001, India. TEL 91-11-371-5455, FAX 91-11-373-6471, icm@del3.vsnl.net.in. Ed., Pub. K P S Gill.

327 USA ISSN 0014-9810
JX1901
➤ **FELLOWSHIP.** Text in English. 1918. q. USD 40 in North America; USD 75 elsewhere; USD 6 per issue (effective 2010). adv. bk.rev.; film rev. illus. index. 36 p./no. 3 cols./p.; back issues avail.; reprints avail.
Document type: *Journal, Academic/Scholarly.* **Description:** Covers interfaith peacemaking and nonviolence, domestic and international issues.
Formerly (until 1935): The World Tomorrow (0364-8583)
Related titles: Microform ed.: (from PQC); Online - full text ed.
Indexed: A21, A22, APW, AltPI, HRIR, MRD, P06, P45, P47, P48, PQC, PRA, PerIslam, RI-1, RI-2, RehabLit.
Published by: Fellowship of Reconciliation, 521 N Broadway, PO Box 271, Nyack, NY 10960. TEL 845-358-4601, FAX 845-358-4924, for@forusa.org. Ed. Ethan Vesely-Flad.

➤ **FILMOTECA ULTRAMARINA PORTUGUESA. BOLETIM.** *see* HISTORY

327 FIN ISSN 0358-1489
FINLAND. ULKOASIAINMINISTERIO. JULKAISUJA/FINLAND. MINISTERIO DE LOS ASUNTOS EXTRANJEROS. PUBLICACIONES/FINLAND. MINISTRY FOR FOREIGN AFFAIRS. PUBLICATIONS/FINLAND. UTRIKESMINISTERIET. PUBLIKATIONER. Text in Multiple languages. 1980. irreg.
Document type: *Monographic series, Government.*
Related titles: ◆ Series: Finland. Ministry of Foreign Affairs. Helsinki Process. Publication Series. ISSN 1795-8628; ◆ Yhdistyneiden Kansakuntien Yleiskokous (Year). ISSN 0781-2442.
Published by: Ulkoasiainministerio/Ministry for Foreign Affairs of Finland, Merikasarmi, PO Box 176, Helsinki, 00161, Finland. TEL 358-9-16005, FAX 358-9-16055555, kirjaamo.um@formin.fi, http://formin.finland.fi/suomi.

327 FIN ISSN 1795-8059
FINNISH INSTITUTE OF INTERNATIONAL AFFAIRS. U P I BRIEFING PAPER. Text in English. 2005. irreg.
Media: Online - full content.
Published by: Ulkopoliittinen Instituutti/Finnish Institute of International Affairs, Mannerheimintie 15 A, Helsinki, 00260, Finland. TEL 358-9-4342070, FAX 358-9-43420769, ulkopolitiikka@upi-fiia.fi, http://www.upi-fiia.fi.

327 DEU
FINNLAND-INSTITUT IN DEUTSCHLAND. SCHRIFTENREIHE. Text in German. 1997. irreg., latest vol.10, 2008. price varies. **Document type:** *Monographic series, Academic/Scholarly.*
Published by: (Finnland-Institut in Deutschland), B W V - Berliner Wissenschafts Verlag GmbH, Markgrafenstr 12-14, Berlin, 10969, Germany. TEL 49-30-8417700, FAX 49-30-84177021, bwv@bwv-verlag.de, http://www.bwv-verlag.de.

327 USA ISSN 1046-1868
D839
➤ **FLETCHER FORUM OF WORLD AFFAIRS.** Text in English. 1975. s-a. USD 20 domestic to individuals; USD 40 foreign to individuals; USD 50 domestic to institutions; USD 70 foreign to institutions (effective 2010). adv. bk.rev. charts; illus. back issues avail.; reprint service avail. from WSH. **Document type:** *Journal, Academic/Scholarly.*
Description: Provides analysis of outstanding problems of international law, politics, economics, business, and diplomacy.
Formerly (until 1989): Fletcher Forum (0147-0981)
Related titles: Microfiche ed.: (from WSH); Microform ed.: (from WSH); Online - full text ed.
Indexed: A22, A26, ABCPolSci, ABS&EES, BAS, CA, CLI, G08, I05, I13, LRI, LegCont, P10, P30, P42, P45, P48, PAIS, PQC, PRA, PSA, PhilInd, RASB, SociolAb, T02.
—BLDSC (3950.532000), CIS, IE, Infotrieve, Ingenta.
Published by: The Fletcher School of Law and Diplomacy, Tufts University, 160 Packard Ave, Medford, MA 02155. TEL 617-627-3700, FAX 617-627-3712. Ed. Naureen Kabir.

327 340 USA
FLETCHER LEDGER. Text in English. 1999 (Oct.). 7/yr. free (effective 2008). **Description:** Documents events at Tufts Fletcher School of Law and Diplomacy.
Related titles: Online - full content ed.

P

Published by: The Fletcher School of Law and Diplomacy, Tufts University, 160 Packard Ave, Medford, MA 02155. TEL 617-623-3610, 617-627-5564, FAX 617-627-3979, forum@tufts.edu, http://www.tufts.edu. Ed. Carol Waters.

327 340 USA
FLETCHER NEWS. Text in English. 3/yr.
Related titles: Online - full content ed.
Published by: The Fletcher School of Law and Diplomacy, Tufts University, 160 Packard Ave, Medford, MA 02155. TEL 617-623-3610, 617-627-5564, FAX 617-627-3979, forum@tufts.edu, http://www.tufts.edu.

327 CHE ISSN 1014-1154
FLUCHTLINGE. Text in German. 1986. q.
Related titles: ◆ English ed.: Refugees. ISSN 0252-791X; ◆ French ed.: Refugies. ISSN 1014-0905; ◆ Spanish ed.: Refugiados. ISSN 1014-0891; ◆ Arabic ed.: Al Lagi'un. ISSN 1014-5370; ◆ Japanese ed.: Refyujizu. ISSN 1014-1162; ◆ Chinese ed.: Nanmin Zazhi. ISSN 1014-5389; ◆ Italian ed.: Rifugiati. ISSN 1014-0832.
Published by: United Nations High Commissioner for Refugees, Public Information Section, PO Box 2500, Geneva 2, 1211, Switzerland. TEL 41-22-739-81-11, FAX 41-22-739-84-49, http://www.unhcr.ch/.

341.734 AUT ISSN 1993-5293
FLUEQUAL - WORK IT! ARBEITSHEFTE. Text in German. 2007. irreg. **Document type:** *Monographic series, Academic/Scholarly.*
Published by: FluEqual - Salzburg Integriert Fluechtlinge, Lasserstr 17, Salzburg, 5020, Austria. TEL 43-662-908820, info@fluequal.at, http://www.fluequal.at.

341.734 AUT ISSN 1993-4580
FLURU. Text in German. 200?. q. **Document type:** *Newsletter, Trade.*
Related titles: Online - full text ed.: ISSN 1993-4599.
Published by: FluEqual - Salzburg Integriert Fluechtlinge, Lasserstr 17, Salzburg, 5020, Austria. TEL 43-662-908820, info@fluequal.at, http://www.fluequal.at.

327 NOR ISSN 1504-7369
FOCUS NORTH. Text in English. 2007. irreg. **Document type:** *Report, Consumer.* **Description:** Short fact sheets cover current issues on developments in The High North.
Related titles: Online - full text ed.: ISSN 1504-8128.
Published by: Den Norske Atlanterhavskomite/The Norwegian Atlantic Committee, Fridjof Nansens Plass 8, Oslo, 0160, Norway. TEL 47-22-403600, FAX 47-22-403610, post@dnak.org, http://www.dnak.org.

327.6 GBR ISSN 0959-9576
DT1
FOCUS ON AFRICA. Text in English. 1990. q. GBP 14 domestic to individuals; EUR 25 in Europe to individuals; USD 28 in Africa to individuals; USD 32 elsewhere to individuals; GBP 23 domestic to institutions; EUR 42 in Europe to institutions; USD 47 in Africa to institutions; USD 53 elsewhere to institutions; GBP 3.25 newsstand/cover (effective 2009). adv. bk.rev. illus. back issues avail.; reprints avail. **Document type:** *Magazine, Consumer.* **Description:** Covers political developments and news of Africa, and provides information on BBC African service programming.
Related titles: Online - full text ed.: GBP 6.50 (effective 2009).
Indexed: IIBP, MLA-IB.
Published by: (British Broadcasting Corporation (B B C)), B B C, African Service, Bush House, Strand, London, WC2B 4PH, United Kingdom. TEL 44-20-75572906, FAX 44-20-73790519, worldservice@bbc.co.uk. Eds. Nick Ericsson, Joseph Warungu.

327 USA
FOCUS ON IRAN. Text in English. 1995. m. USD 40 (effective 1999). **Description:** Dedicated to the Freedom and Liberty of Iranian People.
Media: Online - full text.
Published by: Azadegan Foundation, PO Box 40152, Washington, DC 20016. TEL 202-363-5985. Ed. Mehrdad Irani.

327 341.2422 DNK ISSN 1903-2080
FOKUSEUROPA. Variant title: Fokus Europa. Text in Danish. 1993. bi-w. bk.rev.; film rev. **Document type:** *Newsletter, Consumer.*
Media: Online - full text.
Published by: Den Danske Europabevaegelse/Danish European Movement, Bremerholm 6, Copenhagen K, 1069, Denmark. TEL 45-33-141141, FAX 45-33-155484, eubev@eubev.dk.

327.172 SWE ISSN 1652-7887
FOLKE BERNADOTTE ACADEMY. RESEARCH REPORT. Text in English. 2004. irreg. free. **Document type:** *Monographic series, Academic/Scholarly.*
Published by: Folke Bernadotteakademin/Folke Bernadotte Academy, Sandoevaegen 1, Sandoeverken, 87264, Sweden. TEL 46-612-82200, FAX 46-612-82021, info@folkebernadotteacademy.se, http://www.folkebernadotteacademy.se.

FOOD FIRST NEWS & VIEWS. *see* POLITICAL SCIENCE

327 USA ISSN 0015-7120
D410 CODEN: FRNAA3
FOREIGN AFFAIRS. Text in English. 1910. bi-m. USD 32 domestic; USD 44 in Canada; USD 67 elsewhere (effective 2009). adv. bk.rev. illus. Index. back issues avail.; reprint service avail. from WSH. **Document type:** *Magazine, Trade.* **Description:** Discusses international politics and economic thought.
Former titles (until 1922): The Journal of International Relations (0148-8937); (until 1919): The Journal of Race Development (1068-3380)
Related titles: CD-ROM ed.; Microfiche ed.: (from WSH); Microform ed.: (from PMC, PQC); Online - full text ed.; Spanish ed.: Spanish ed.: Foreign Affairs en Espanol. ISSN 1665-1707; Russian ed.
Indexed: A01, A02, A03, A08, A11, A12, A13, A17, A18, A20, A21, A22, A25, A26, ABCPolSci, ABIn, ABS&EES, AMB, APEL, ARG, Acal, AmH&L, B01, B02, B04, B05, B06, B07, B08, B09, B14, B15, B17, B18, BAS, BPIA, BRD, BRI, C04, C05, C12, CA, CBRI, CCME, CPerl, CREJ, ChPerl, CurCont, DIP, E08, EI, EconLit, FutSurv, G04, G05, G06, G07, G08, G10, H05, H09, H10, HRIR, HistAb, I02, I05, I07, I13, IBR, IBSS, IBZ, ILD, IPARL, JEL, KES, LID&ISL, M&MA, M01, M02, M05, M06, MASUSE, MEA&I, MLA-IB, MagInd, P02, P05, P06, P10, P13, P27, P30, P34, P42, P45, P47, P48, P51, P53, P54, PAIS, PCI, PQC, PRA, PSA, R02, R03, R04, R06, RASB, RGAb, RGPR, RI-1, RI-2, S02, S03, S05, S08, S09, S11, S23, SCOPUS, SSAI, SSAb, SSCI, SSI, SociolAb, T&II, T02, U01, V02, W01, W02, W03, W04, W05, W07, W09, WBA, WMB.
—BLDSC (3986.800000), CIS, IE, Infotrieve, Ingenta. **CCC.**
Published by: Council on Foreign Relations, Inc., PO Box 420235, Palm Coast, FL 32142. TEL 800-829-5539, FAX 386-246-3386, membership@cfr.org, http://www.cfr.org. Ed. James F Hoge Jr. Pub. David Kellogg. **Dist. in the UK by:** Comag.

327 NPL
FOREIGN AFFAIRS JOURNAL. Text in English. 1976. 3/yr. NPR 25.
Indexed: BAS.
Published by: Bhola Bikrum Rana, Ed. & Pub., 5-287 Lagon, Kathmandu, Nepal.

327.59 MYS ISSN 0126-690X
FOREIGN AFFAIRS MALAYSIA. Text in English. 1966. q. free. illus.
Indexed: AMB, RASB.
Published by: Ministry of Foreign Affairs/Kementerian Luar Negeri, Jalan Wisma Putra, Kuala Lumpur, Malaysia. Circ: 6,000.

327 IND ISSN 0536-9258
FOREIGN AFFAIRS RECORD. Text in English. 1955. m. index. back issues avail. **Document type:** *Report, Government.*
Published by: Ministry of External Affairs, 140 A Wing, Shastri Bhawan, New Delhi, 110 001, India. TEL 91-11-23389471, FAX 91-11-23385549, http://meaindia.nic.in/.

327.2 USA ISSN 0071-7320
JX1705
FOREIGN CONSULAR OFFICES IN THE UNITED STATES. Text in English. 1920. a. **Document type:** *Directory, Government.* **Description:** Provides a complete official listing of foreign consular offices in the U.S.
Formerly (until 1932): Foreign Consular Officers in the United States Corrected to December 30
Related titles: Online - full text ed.: free (effective 2011).
Published by: U.S. Department of State, 2201 C St NW, Washington, DC 20520. TEL 202-647-4000, 800-877-8339.

327 ROM ISSN 1844-2722
FOREIGN POLICY; Romania. Text in Romanian. 2007. bi-m. ROL 45 (effective 2011). adv. **Document type:** *Magazine, Trade.*
Related titles: Online - full text ed.: ISSN 2068-8164. 2007.
Published by: Adevarul Holding, Str Fabrica de Glucoza, nr 21, sector 2, Bucharest, Romania. TEL 40-21-4077632, FAX 40-21-4077602, redactie@adevarul.ro.

327.1 FRA ISSN 1957-5335
FOREIGN POLICY (FRENCH EDITION); geopolitique et economie internationale. Text in French. 2006. bi-m. EUR 44.50 (effective 2009). **Document type:** *Magazine, Consumer.*
Related titles: ◆ English ed.: Foreign Policy (Washington). ISSN 0015-7228; ◆ Spanish ed.: Foreign Policy (Spanish Edition). ISSN 1697-1515.
Published by: Foreign Policy France, 115 rue Saint-Dominique, Paris, 75007, France. Eds. Dimitri Friedman, Francois Roche.

327 ESP ISSN 1697-1515
E744
FOREIGN POLICY (SPANISH EDITION). Text in Spanish. 2004. bi-m. EUR 28 domestic; EUR 45 in Europe; EUR 65 elsewhere (effective 2009). **Document type:** *Journal, Academic/Scholarly.*
Related titles: Online - full text ed.: EUR 18 (effective 2009); ◆ English ed.: Foreign Policy (Washington). ISSN 0015-7228; ◆ French ed.: Foreign Policy (French Edition). ISSN 1957-5335.
Indexed: I14.
—**CCC.**
Published by: (Carnegie Endowment for International Peace USA), Fundacion para las Relaciones Internacionales y el Dialogo Exterior (F R I D E), Calle Goya 5-7, Pasaje 2o, Madrid, 28001, Spain. TEL 34-91-2444740, FAX 34-91-2444741, fride@fride.org, http://www.fride.org.

327 USA ISSN 0015-7228
E744
➤ **FOREIGN POLICY (WASHINGTON)**; the magazine of global politics, economics and ideas. Abbreviated title: F P. Text in English. 1971. bi-m. USD 19.95 domestic (print or online ed.) (effective 2010). bk.rev. illus. s-a. index. back issues avail.; reprints avail. **Document type:** *Journal, Academic/Scholarly.* **Description:** Features significant articles on political science and international relations.
Related titles: CD-ROM ed.; Microform ed.: (from PQC); Online - full text ed.: ISSN 1945-2276; ◆ French ed.: Foreign Policy (French Edition). ISSN 1957-5335; ◆ Spanish ed.: Foreign Policy (Spanish Edition). ISSN 1697-1515.
Indexed: A01, A02, A03, A08, A11, A12, A13, A17, A20, A22, A25, A26, ABCPolSci, ABIn, ABS&EES, AMB, Acal, AmH&L, B01, B02, B04, B06, B07, B08, B09, B15, B17, B18, BRD, C04, C05, C12, CA, CCME, CLI, CPerl, DIP, E08, FutSurv, G04, G05, G06, G07, G08, H09, HRIR, HistAb, I02, I05, I07, I13, IBR, IBSS, IBZ, LID&ISL, LeftInd, M01, M02, M05, M06, MAB, MASUSE, MagInd, P02, P05, P10, P13, P27, P30, P34, P42, P45, P47, P48, P51, P53, P54, PAIS, PCI, PMR, PQC, PRA, PSA, PerIslam, R02, R03, R04, RASB, RGAb, RGPR, S02, S03, S05, S08, S09, S11, S23, SCOPUS, SSAI, SSAb, SSI, SociolAb, T02, U01, W01, W02, W03, W05, WBA, WMB.
—BLDSC (3987.105000), IE, Infotrieve, Ingenta. **CCC.**
Published by: Slate Group, 1899 L St NW Ste 550, Washington, DC 20036. TEL 202-728-7300, FAX 202-728-7342, FP@ForeignPolicy.com. Ed. Moises Naim. Circ: 101,208.

327.1 USA ISSN 1743-8586
JZ6.5
➤ **FOREIGN POLICY ANALYSIS.** Text in English. 2005. 3/yr. USD 1,737 combined subscription in the Americas to institutions (print & online eds.); GBP 1,327 combined subscription in United Kingdom to institutions (print & online eds.); EUR 1,686 combined subscription in Europe to institutions (print & online eds.); USD 2,601 combined subscription elsewhere to institutions (print & online eds.); USD 1,579 in the Americas to institutions (print or online ed.); GBP 1,206 in United Kingdom to institutions (print or online ed.); EUR 1,532 in Europe to institutions (print or online ed.); USD 2,364 elsewhere to institutions (print or online ed.) (effective 2010). adv. reprint service avail. from PSC. **Document type:** *Journal, Academic/Scholarly.* **Description:** Publishes research into the processes, outcomes, and theories of foreign policy.
Related titles: Online - full text ed.: ISSN 1743-8594 (from IngentaConnect).
Indexed: A01, A22, A26, CA, CurCont, E01, ESPM, P34, P42, PAIS, PSA, RiskAb, SSCI, T02, W07.
—BLDSC (3987.105500), IE, Ingenta. **CCC.**
Published by: (International Studies Association), Wiley-Blackwell Publishing, Inc. (Subsidiary of: Wiley-Blackwell Publishing Ltd.), Commerce Pl, 350 Main St, Malden, MA 02148. TEL 781-388-8206, 800-835-6770, FAX 781-388-8232, info@wiley.com, http://www.wiley.com/WileyCDA/. Ed. A Cooper Drury. adv.: B&W page USD 475; trim 6.875 x 10. Circ: 3,422 (paid).

327 USA ISSN 0017-8780
E744
FOREIGN POLICY ASSOCIATION. HEADLINE SERIES. Text in English. 1935. irreg. price varies. adv. bibl.; charts; illus.; maps. back issues avail.; reprints avail. **Document type:** *Monographic series, Academic/Scholarly.* **Description:** Covers geographic areas or global issues for general readers and students in high schools or colleges.
Formerly (until 1943): Headline Books (0884-4402)
Related titles: Microfilm ed.: (from PQC); Online - full text ed.
Indexed: A22, BAS, E03, ERI, P02, P18, P45, P47, P48, P53, P54, P55, PQC, RASB, T02.
—BLDSC (4274.655000), IE, Ingenta.
Published by: Foreign Policy Association, 470 Park Ave S, New York, NY 10016-6819. TEL 212-481-8100, FAX 212-481-9275, info@fpa.org, http://www.fpa.org.

327.12 USA ISSN 1054-0083
E744
FOREIGN POLICY BRIEFING. Text in English. 1990. irreg., latest vol.90, 2010. price varies. back issues avail. **Document type:** *Monographic series, Academic/Scholarly.*
—**CCC.**
Published by: Cato Institute, 1000 Massachusetts Ave, NW, Washington, DC 20001. TEL 202-842-0200, FAX 202-842-3490, subscriptions@cato.org.

327 GBR ISSN 1052-7036
E840
➤ **FOREIGN POLICY BULLETIN**; the documentary record of United States foreign policy. Text in English. 1990-suspended; resumed 2002. q. GBP 183, USD 337 to institutions; GBP 199, USD 354 combined subscription to institutions (print & online eds.) (effective 2012). adv. bk.rev. index. back issues avail.; reprint service avail. from PSC. **Document type:** *Journal, Academic/Scholarly.* **Description:** Documents all major events in contemporary US foreign relations as they happen, including texts from Congress, as well as the Executive Branch and from other governments and international organizations. Lists Treaty Actions and new releases in the State Department's Foreign Relations of the United States series.
Related titles: Online - full text ed.: ISSN 1745-1302. GBP 166, USD 301 to institutions (effective 2012).
Indexed: A12, A13, A22, ABIn, ABS&EES, B16, E01, I08, P10, P45, P48, P51, P53, P54, PAIS, PQC, R04.
—IE, Ingenta. **CCC.**
Published by: Cambridge University Press, The Edinburgh Bldg, Shaftesbury Rd, Cambridge, CB2 8RU, United Kingdom. TEL 44-1223-326070, FAX 44-1223-315052, journals@cambridge.org, http://www.cambridge.org/uk. Ed. Jack Goldstone. Adv. contact Rebecca Roberts TEL 44-1223-325083.

327 USA ISSN 1524-1939
JZ6.5
FOREIGN POLICY IN FOCUS. Text in English. 1996. w. looseleaf. charts; illus.; stat. back issues avail. **Document type:** *Newsletter, Trade.* **Description:** Covers a variety of foreign policy issues for government officials, media activists and scholars. Encourages a more responsible US global affairs agenda.
Related titles: Online - full text ed.
Indexed: A25, A26, APW, AltPI, E08, G05, G06, G07, G08, I05, I07, LeftInd, M06, M10, P42, PAIS, S08, S09, S23.
—**CCC.**
Published by: (Institute for Policy Studies), International Relations Center, 1112 16th St NW, Ste 600, Washington, DC 20036. TEL 202-234-9382, irc@irc-online.org, http://www.irc-online.org/.

327.1 USA ISSN 0196-0334
FOREIGN POLICY RESEARCH INSTITUTE. MONOGRAPH SERIES. Text in English. 1964. irreg., latest 2009. **Document type:** *Monographic series, Academic/Scholarly.*
Formerly (until 1975): Foreign Policy Research Institute. Research Monograph Series
Related titles: Online - full text ed.: free (effective 2010).
Indexed: PRA.
—**CCC.**
Published by: Foreign Policy Research Institute, 1528 Walnut St, Ste 610, Philadelphia, PA 19102. TEL 215-732-3774, FAX 215-732-4401, fpri@fpri.org.

327 USA
FOREIGN POLICY REVIEW. Text in English. 1972. m. USD 20 domestic (effective 2005). adv. 4 p./no.; back issues avail. **Document type:** *Magazine, Consumer.*
Published by: W K Shearer, Pub. & Ed., 8158 Palm St, Lemon Grove, CA 91945. TEL 619-460-4484, FAX 619-698-2423. Ed., Pub. W K Shearer. adv.: page USD 200. Circ: 900 (paid and free).

327.73 USA ISSN 0071-7355
KZ233
FOREIGN RELATIONS OF THE UNITED STATES. Abbreviated title: F R U S. Text in English. 1861. irreg. back issues avail. **Document type:** *Monographic series, Academic/Scholarly.* **Description:** Presents the official documentary historical record of major U.S. foreign policy decisions and significant diplomatic activity.
Former titles (until 1932): Papers Relating to the Foreign Relations of the United States (1048-6445); (until 1870): Papers Relating to Foreign Affairs (1060-5428)
Related titles: Microform ed.: (from WSH); Online - full text ed.: free (effective 2010).
Indexed: A26, I05.
Published by: (Office of the Historian), U.S. Department of State, Bureau of Public Affairs, 2201 C St, NW, Washington, DC 20502. TEL 202-655-4000, http://www.state.gov/r/pa/. **Orders to:** U.S. Government Printing Office, Superintendent of Documents.

327.2 USA ISSN 1089-5833
E154.5
FOREIGN REPRESENTATIVES IN THE U.S. YELLOW BOOK; who's who in the U.S. offices of foreign corporations, foreign nations, the foreign press and intergovernmental organizations. Text in English. 1997. s-a. USD 355 (effective 2008). illus. **Document type:** *Directory, Trade.* **Description:** Contains over 19,000 executives and officials who manage the offices of the leading non-U.S. companies and organizations, that includes CEOs, legal representatives, ambassadors, attaches, managing directors, trade commissioners and international press offices.
Related titles: CD-ROM ed.; Online - full text ed.
—CCC.
Published by: Leadership Directories, Inc, 104 Fifth Ave, 2nd Fl, New York, NY 10011. TEL 212-627-4140, FAX 212-645-0931, info@leadershipdirectories.com. Ed. Seth Zupnik.

327 USA ISSN 0146-3543
JZ6.5
FOREIGN SERVICE JOURNAL. Text in English. 1919. m. USD 40 domestic; USD 58 foreign; USD 20 to students; USD 3.50 newsstand/cover (effective 2007). adv. bk.rev. illus. back issues avail.; reprints avail. **Document type:** *Journal, Consumer.* **Description:** Directed toward current and former US foreign service officers, located worldwide.
Former titles (until 1951): American Foreign Service Journal (0360-8425); (until 1924): American Consular Bulletin
Related titles: Microform ed.: (from PQC); Online - full text ed.
Indexed: A01, A22, ABS&EES, AmH&L, HistAb, L09, MEA&I, P06, P34, P42, PAIS, PRA, PersLit, T02.
—CCC.
Published by: American Foreign Service Association, 2101 E St, N W, Washington, DC 20037. TEL 202-338-4045, FAX 202-338-8244. Ed. Steven Alan Honley. R&P Mikkela Thompson TEL 202-944-5524. Adv. contact Ed Miltenberger TEL 202-338-4045 ext. 507. B&W page USD 1,315, color page USD 1,875; trim 7 x 9.25. Circ: 16,000 (paid).

327 MEX ISSN 0185-013X
D839
FORO INTERNACIONAL. Text in Spanish. 1960. 4/yr. MXN 75, USD 30 newsstand/cover per vol. (effective 2002). adv. bk.rev. bibl.; charts. index, cum.index. back issues avail.; reprints avail.
Indexed: A22, ABCPolSci, AmH&L, C01, CA, FR, H21, HistAb, I13, IBR, IBSS, IBZ, P08, P30, P42, PAIS, PSA, S02, S03, SociolAb, T02.
—BLDSC (4008.950000), IE, Infotrieve.
Published by: Colegio de Mexico, A.C., Departamento de Publicaciones, Camino al Ajusco 20, Col. Pedregal Santa Teresa, Mexico City, DF 10740, Mexico. TEL 52-5-4493077, FAX 52-5-4493083, emunos@colmex.mx, http://www.colmex.mx. Ed., R&P Francisco Gomez Rulz TEL 525-449-3080. Adv. contact Maria Cruz Mora. Circ: 2,000.

327.17 DEU ISSN 1860-370X
FORSCHUNGSPAPIERE "REGIERUNGSORGANISATION IN WESTEUROPA". Text in German. 2005. irreg., latest vol.2, 2006. price varies. **Document type:** *Monographic series, Academic/Scholarly.*
Related titles: Online - full text ed.: ISSN 1860-451X.
Published by: Universitaetsverlag Potsdam, Am Neuen Palais 10, Potsdam, 14469, Germany. TEL 49-331-9774458, FAX 49-331-9774625, ubpub@uni-potsdam.de, http://info.ub.uni-potsdam.de/verlag.htm.

FORUM FOR DEVELOPMENT STUDIES. *see* BUSINESS AND ECONOMICS—International Development And Assistance

327 DEU ISSN 1613-9070
FORUM PAZIFISMUS; Zeitschrift fuer Theorie und Praxis der Gewaltfreiheit. Text in German. 2004. q. EUR 20 (effective 2009). **Document type:** *Magazine, Consumer.*
Published by: Deutsche Friedensgesellschaft - Vereinigte Kriegsdienstgegnerinnen, Kasseler Str 1a, Frankfurt am Main, 60486, Germany. TEL 49-69-27298231, FAX 49-69-27298232, office@dfg-vk.de, http://www.dfg-vk.de.

327 FRA ISSN 0995-8622
FRANCE - ETATS-UNIS; journal des relations Franco-Americaines. Variant title: France - USA. Text in French. 1945. q. EUR 13. adv. bk.rev. illus.
Published by: Association France Etats Unis, 39 Boulevard Suchet, Paris, 75016, France. TEL 33-1-45278086. Ed., Adv. contact Emmanuelle J Vucher-Bondet. Circ: 5,000.

327 FRA ISSN 1773-0902
FRANCE. MINISTERE DES AFFAIRES ETRANGERES. LA POLITIQUE ETRANGERE DE LA FRANCE (CD-ROM). Text in French. 1966. s-a. bk.rev. bibl. index. **Document type:** *Magazine, Government.*
Formerly (until 2003): France. Ministere des Affaires Etrangeres. La Politique Etrangere de la France (Print) (0180-9563)
Media: CD-ROM. **Related titles:** Microfiche ed.
Indexed: ABCPolSci, AMB, EI, KES, PdeR, RASB.
Published by: France. Ministere des Affaires Etrangeres, 37 Quai d'Orsay, Paris, 75007, France. http://www.diplomatie.gouv.fr.

327 NLD ISSN 1878-7711
THE FRANKLIN DELANO ROOSEVELT FOUR FREEDOMS AWARDS. Text in English. 1984. biennial.
Published by: Roosevelt Study Center, PO Box 6001, Middelburg, 4330 LA, Netherlands. TEL 31-118-631590, FAX 31-118-631593, rsc@zeeland.nl.

327.172 SWE ISSN 0016-0288
FRED OCH FRIHET. Text in Swedish; Text occasionally in Danish, Norwegian. 1927. q. SEK 50 (effective 1991). bk.rev. illus. cum.index every 5 yrs.
Formerly (until vol.4, 1938): Internationella Kvinnofoerbundets foer Fred och Frihet Medlemsblad
Published by: Women's International League for Peace and Freedom, Swedish Section/Internationella Kvinnofoerbundet foer Fred och Frihet, Svenska Sektionen, Tjarhovsgatan 9, Stockholm, 11621, Sweden. TEL 46-8-702-98-10, FAX 46-8-702-19-73. Ed. Ingrid Segerstedt Wiberg. Circ: 1,750.

327.17 DNK ISSN 0902-9273
FRED OG FRIHED. Text in Danish. 1926. 3/yr. DKK 125; DKK 300 membership; DKK 210 to students (effective 2009). cum.index: 1985-1997. **Document type:** *Magazine, Consumer.*
Published by: Kvindernes Internationale Liga for Fred og Frihed/Women's International League for Peace and Freedom, Vesterbrogade 10, Copenhagen V, 1620, Denmark. TEL 45-33-231097, wilpf-dk@internet.dk, http://www.kvindefredsliga.dk.

327.172 SWE ISSN 1403-1442
FREDSTIDNINGEN PAX. Text in Swedish. 1972. 6/yr. SEK 125 to individuals; SEK 210 to institutions (effective 2004). adv. bk.rev. bibl.; illus. **Document type:** *Journal, Academic/Scholarly.* **Description:** Extensive peace magazine.
Formerly (until 1991): Pax (0048-3087); Which incorporated (1928-1975): Freden (0345-3650)
Related titles: Online - full text ed.
Published by: Svenska Freds- och Skiljedomsfoereningen/Swedish Peace and Arbitration Society, Svartensgatan 6, PO Box 4134, Stockholm, 10263, Sweden. TEL 46-8-7021830, FAX 46-8-7021846, info@svenska-freds.se. adv.: B&W page SEK 9,800, color page SEK 13,300; 210 x 303. Circ: 10,000.

DIE FRIEDENS-WARTE; Blaetter fuer internationale Verstaendigung und zwischenstaatliche Organisation. *see* LAW—International Law

327.36 DEU ISSN 0932-7983
JX1903
FRIEDENSGUTACHTEN. Text in German. 1987. a. EUR 12.90 (effective 2010). **Document type:** *Journal, Academic/Scholarly.*
Published by: (Hessische Stiftung Friedens- und Konfliktforschung), Lit Verlag, Grevener Str/Fresnostr 2, Muenster, 48159, Germany. TEL 49-251-235091, FAX 49-251-231972, lit@lit-verlag.de. **Co-sponsors:** Forschungsstaette der Evangelischen Studiengemeinschaft; Institut fuer Friedensforschung und Sicherheitspolitik an der Universitaet Hamburg.

327 BRA ISSN 1679-5377
➤ **FRONTEIRA.** Text in Portuguese. 2001. s-a. BRL 40 domestic; USD 20 foreign; BRL 25 newsstand/cover (effective 2007). back issues avail. **Document type:** *Journal, Academic/Scholarly.* **Description:** Aims to provide a permanent forum for debate over history, theory and practice of international relations, foreign policy and diplomacy, as well as issues that include law, economics and anthropology.
Indexed: CA, P42, PSA, S02, S03, SCOPUS, SociolAb, T02.
—CCC.
Published by: (Pontificia Universidade Catolica de Minas Gerais), Editora P U C Minas, Rua Padre Pedro Evangelista 377, Belo Horizonte, 30535-490, Brazil. TEL 55-31-33758189, FAX 55-31-33766498, editora@pucminas.br, http://www.pucminas.br/editora/. Ed. Eduardo Neves-Silva. Pub. Claudia Telles de Menezes Teixeira. R&P Cinda Aira. Circ: 100 (paid); 600 (controlled).

➤ **FRONTERA NORTE.** *see* POPULATION STUDIES

327 305.868 USA ISSN 1525-3260
F787
FRONTERA NORTE SUR (ONLINE). Abbreviated title: F N S. Text in English, Spanish. 1993. a. free (effective 2010). stat. back issues avail. **Document type:** *Report, Consumer.* **Description:** Provides on-line news coverage of the US-Mexico border.
Formerly (until 1996): Frontera Norte Sur (Print)
Media: Online - full text.
Published by: (New Mexico State University, Center for Latin American Studies), New Mexico State University, MSC 3AS, 775 College Dr, PO Box 30001, Las Cruces, NM 88003. TEL 505-646-6817, 866-678-2586, FAX 575-646-6123, alumni@nmsu.edu. Ed. Kent Paterson.

327.43 DEU
THE FUNNEL (ONLINE). Text in German. 2002. 3/yr. **Document type:** *Magazine, Consumer.* **Description:** Contains articles and features on current events in German-American relations.
Formerly (until 2006): The Funnel (Print)
Media: Online - full text.
Published by: German-American Fulbright Commission/Deutsch-Amerikanischen Fulbright Kommission, Oranienburger Str 13-14, Berlin, 10178, Germany. TEL 49-30-2844430, FAX 49-30-28444342, webmaster@fulbright.de.

G D I IMPULS; Vierteljahresschrift fuer Entscheidungstraeger in Wirtschaft und Gesellschaft. *see* BUSINESS AND ECONOMICS

327.6 DEU ISSN 1862-3603
G I G A FOCUS. AFRIKA. Text in German. 2002. m. **Document type:** *Journal, Academic/Scholarly.* **Description:** Contains analyses on topical political, economic or social events in Africa.
Formerly (until 2005): Afrika im Blickpunkt (Online Edition) (1619-9928)
Media: Online - full content.
Indexed: PAIS.
Published by: German Institute of Global and Area Studies, Neuer Jungfernstieg 21, Hamburg, 20354, Germany. TEL 49-40-42825593, FAX 49-40-42825547, info@giga-hamburg.de. Ed. Gero Erdmann.

327.5 DEU ISSN 1862-359X
G I G A FOCUS. ASIEN. Text in German. 2006. m. **Document type:** *Journal, Academic/Scholarly.*
Indexed: PAIS.
Published by: German Institute of Global and Area Studies, Neuer Jungfernstieg 21, Hamburg, 20354, Germany. TEL 49-40-42825593, FAX 49-40-42825547, info@giga-hamburg.de. Ed. Andreas Ufen.

327 DEU ISSN 1862-3581
G I G A FOCUS. GLOBAL. Text in German. 2006. m. **Document type:** *Journal, Academic/Scholarly.*
Media: Online - full content.
Indexed: PAIS.
Published by: German Institute of Global and Area Studies, Neuer Jungfernstieg 21, Hamburg, 20354, Germany. TEL 49-40-42825593, FAX 49-40-42825547, info@giga-hamburg.de. Ed. Andreas Mehler.

327.8 DEU ISSN 1862-3352
G I G A FOCUS. LATEINAMERIKA. Text in German. 1998. m. **Document type:** *Journal, Academic/Scholarly.*
Formerly (until 2006): Brennpunkt Lateinamerika (1437-6091)
Related titles: Online - full text ed.: ISSN 1862-3573. 1999.
Published by: German Institute of Global and Area Studies, Neuer Jungfernstieg 21, Hamburg, 20354, Germany. TEL 49-40-42825593, FAX 49-40-42825547, info@giga-hamburg.de. Ed. Michael Radseck.

327.56 DEU ISSN 1862-3611
G I G A FOCUS. NAHOST. Text in German. 2002. m. **Document type:** *Journal, Academic/Scholarly.*
Formerly (until 2006): D O I Focus (Online Edition) (1619-2737)
Indexed: PAIS.
Published by: German Institute of Global and Area Studies, Neuer Jungfernstieg 21, Hamburg, 20354, Germany. TEL 49-40-42825593, FAX 49-40-42825547, info@giga-hamburg.de. Ed. Henner Fuertig.

327 DEU
G I G A WORKING PAPERS. Text in English. 2005. irreg. (15-20/yr.). free. **Document type:** *Monographic series, Academic/Scholarly.* **Description:** Serves to disseminate research results prior to publication in order to encourage academic debate and the exchange of ideas.
Media: Online - full text.
Published by: German Institute of Global and Area Studies, Neuer Jungfernstieg 21, Hamburg, 20354, Germany. TEL 49-40-42825593, FAX 49-40-42825547, info@giga-hamburg.de. Ed. Martin Beck.

327 DNK ISSN 0908-2492
GAIA; tidsskrift for international solidaritet. Text in Danish. 1993. q. DKK 200 to individuals; DKK 400 to institutions (effective 2009). back issues avail. **Document type:** *Journal, Consumer.*
Related titles: Online - full text ed.: 1996.
Published by: Internationalt Forum, Griffenfeldtsgade 41, Copenhagen N, 2200, Denmark. TEL 45-35-371889, FAX 45-35-379079, info@internationaltforum.dk.

327 JPN ISSN 0915-1281
DS890.3
GAIKO FORAMU. Text in Japanese. 1988. m. JPY 780 (effective 2003). **Document type:** *Journal, Academic/Scholarly.*
Related titles: English ed.: Gaiko Forum. JPY 3,360 (effective 2003).
—BLDSC (4066.348910).
Published by: Toshi Shuppan Publishers, 1-5-8 Fujimi, Chiyodaku, Tokyo, 102-0071, Japan. TEL 81-3-32227541, FAX 81-3-32377347.

327.17 323 IRL
GARDA RACIAL AND INTERCULTURAL NEWSLETTER. Text in English. s-a.
Related titles: Online - full text ed.
Published by: Garda Racial and Intercultural Office, Community Relations Section, Harcourt Sq, Harcourt St, Dublin 2, Ireland. TEL 353-1-6663150, FAX 353-1-6663801, agecard@iol.ie.

327 BEL ISSN 0777-639X
LA GAZETTE DIPLOMATIQUE. Text in French. 1990. q. EUR 40 (effective 2007). **Document type:** *Magazine.*
Published by: (Club Diplomatique de Belgique), Dupedi, Rue de Stallestraat 70-82, Bruxelles, 1180, Belgium. TEL 32-2-3330700, FAX 32-2-3320598. Ed. Francoise Bouzin TEL 32-2-3330710.

327 DEU ISSN 0930-8571
GEHEIM. Text in German. 1985. 4/yr. adv. bk.rev. back issues avail. **Document type:** *Magazine, Consumer.*
Related titles: English ed.: Top Secret. ISSN 0935-3909.
Published by: Geheim Verlag, Postfach 270324, Cologne, 50509, Germany. TEL 49-221-2839995, FAX 49-221-2839997. Eds. Ingo Niebel, Michael Opperskalski. Circ: 3,500.

327.12 DEU
GEHEIME NACHRICHTENDIENSTE. Text in German. 2006. irreg., latest vol.5, 2010. price varies. **Document type:** *Monographic series, Academic/Scholarly.*
Published by: Verlag Dr. Koester, Rungestr 22-24, Berlin, 10179, Germany. TEL 49-30-76403224, FAX 49-30-76403227, verlag-koester@t-online.de.

327.172 FRA ISSN 1954-9229
GENEVA INTERNATIONAL PEACE RESEARCH INSTITUTE. CAHIERS. Key Title: Cahier du G I P R I. Text in French. 2004. s-a. back issues avail. **Document type:** *Journal.*
Published by: (Geneve. Institut International de Recherches sur la Paix CHE), L' Harmattan, 5 Rue de l'Ecole Polytechnique, Paris, 75005, France. TEL 33-1-43257651, FAX 33-1-43258203.

327.17 CHE ISSN 1422-2248
THE GENEVA POST QUARTERLY. Text in English. 2006. q. CHF 30 (effective 2007). **Document type:** *Magazine, Consumer.*
Published by: The Geneva Post Quarterly, PO Box 1544, Geneva 1, 1211, Switzerland. TEL 41-22-3103422, FAX 41-22-3114592. Ed., Pub. Jacques Werner.

327.172 CHE
GENEVA REPORTER. Text in English. q.
Published by: Quaker United Nations Office, 13 Ave du Mervelet, Geneva, 1209, Switzerland. TEL 41-22-7484800, FAX 41-22-7484819, quno@quno.ch, http://www.geneva.quno.info/.

GEOECONOMIE. *see* BUSINESS AND ECONOMICS—Economic Situation And Conditions

327 ESP ISSN 2172-3958
F3431
▼ ➤ **GEOPOLITICA(S)**; revista de estudios sobre espacio y poder. Text in Spanish, Portuguese. 2010. s-a. EUR 20 domestic; EUR 28 in Europe; EUR 32 elsewhere (effective 2011). **Document type:** *Journal, Academic/Scholarly.*
Related titles: Online - full text ed.
Published by: (Universidad Complutense de Madrid, Facultad de Ciencias Politicas y Sociologia), Universidad Complutense de Madrid, Servicio de Publicaciones, C/ Obispo Trejo 2, Ciudad Universitaria, Madrid, 28040, Spain. TEL 34-91-3941127, FAX 34-91-3941126, servicio.publicaciones@rect.ucm.es, http://www.ucm.es/publicaciones. Ed. Heriberto Cairo Carou.

327 GBR ISSN 1465-0045
JC319 CODEN: GEOPFC
➤ **GEOPOLITICS.** Text in English. 1996. q. GBP 378 combined subscription in United Kingdom to institutions (print & online eds.); EUR 500, USD 627 combined subscription to institutions (print & online eds.) (effective 2012). adv. bk.rev. index. back issues avail.; reprint service avail. from PSC. **Document type:** *Journal, Academic/Scholarly.* **Description:** Covers all aspects of the social sciences with particular emphasis on political geography, international relations, the territorial aspects of political science and international law.
Formerly (until 1998): Geopolitics and International Boundaries (1362-9379)
Related titles: Online - full text ed.: ISSN 1557-3028. GBP 340 in United Kingdom to institutions; EUR 450, USD 565 to institutions (effective 2012) (from IngentaConnect).
Indexed: A01, A03, A08, A20, A22, CA, CCME, CurCont, E01, ESPM, GEOBASE, GeoRef, I02, I13, IBSS, LeftInd, P34, P42, PAIS, PRA, PSA, R02, RiskAb, SCOPUS, SSCI, SociolAb, T02, W07.
—IE, Ingenta. **CCC.**

P

Published by: Routledge (Subsidiary of: Taylor & Francis Group), 4 Park Sq, Milton Park, Abingdon, Oxon OX14 4RN, United Kingdom. TEL 44-20-70176000, FAX 44-20-70176336, http://www.routledge.com. Eds. David Newman TEL 972-8-6477595, Simon Dalby. Adv. contact Linda Hann TEL 44-1344-779945. **Subscr. to:** Taylor & Francis Ltd., Journals Customer Service, Sheepen Pl, Colchester, Essex CO3 3LP, United Kingdom. TEL 44-20-70175544, FAX 44-20-70175198, subscriptions@tandf.co.uk.

327 900 USA ISSN 1948-9145
JC319
▼ **GEOPOLITICS, HISTORY, AND INTERNATIONAL RELATIONS.** Text in English. 2009. s-a. USD 10 per issue (effective 2009). **Document type:** *Journal, Academic/Scholarly.* **Description:** Academic journal on world politics and history.
Indexed: A39, C27, C29, CA, D03, D04, E13, P02, P10, P42, P45, P48, P52, P53, P54, PQC, R14, S14, S15, S18, T02.
Published by: Addleton Academic Publishers, 30-18 50th St, Woodside, NY 11377. TEL 718-626-6017, sales@addletonacademicpublishers.com, http://www.addletonacademicpublishers.com/.

327 665.5 CAN ISSN 0273-1371
HD9502.A1
GEOPOLITICS OF ENERGY. Text in English. m. CAD 500 domestic; CAD 220 domestic universities; USD 400 in United States; USD 175 in United States universities; USD 410 elsewhere; USD 185 elsewhere universities (effective 2005). **Document type:** *Journal, Academic/Scholarly.* **Description:** Provides insights and opinion from internationally recognized authorities on the political, economic and pricing factors affecting the trade of crude oil, natural gas, coal and other forms of energy around the world.
Indexed: GEOBASE, SCOPUS.
—IE, Infotrieve. **CCC.**
Published by: Canadian Energy Research Institute, #150, 3512 - 33rd St N W, Calgary, AB T2L 2A6, Canada. TEL 403-282-1231, FAX 403-284-4181, ceri@ceri.ca. Ed. Vincent A Lauerman.

327 FRA ISSN 0752-1693
D839
GEOPOLITIQUE (FRENCH EDITION). Text in French. 1983. q. EUR 33 domestic; EUR 45 foreign (effective 2005). adv. **Document type:** *Journal, Academic/Scholarly.*
Related titles: English ed.: Geopolitique (English Edition). ISSN 0894-6272.
Indexed: A22, FR, IBSS, PCI, SD.
—BLDSC (4158.197000), IE, Ingenta.
Published by: (Institut International de Geopolitique), Presses Universitaires de France, 6 Avenue Reille, Paris, 75685, France. TEL 33-1-58103161, FAX 33-1-45897530, revues@puf.com, http://www.puf.com. Ed., Pub. Marie France Garaud. Adv. contact Sophie Lannes. Circ: 25,000.

327 BEL ISSN 1780-5848
GEOPOLITIQUE ET RESOLUTION DES CONFLITS/GEOPOLITICS AND CONFLICT RESOLUTION. Text in French. 2004. irreg., latest vol.7, 2009. price varies. **Document type:** *Monographic series, Academic/Scholarly.*
Published by: P I E - Peter Lang SA, 1 avenue Maurice, 6e etage, Brussels, 1050, Belgium. TEL 32-2-3477236, FAX 32-2-3477237, pie@peterlang.com, http://www.peterlang.net.

327 USA ISSN 1526-0054
D839
GEORGETOWN JOURNAL OF INTERNATIONAL AFFAIRS. Text in English. 1998. s-a. USD 16 domestic to individuals; USD 18 in Canada to individuals; USD 24 elsewhere to individuals; USD 40 domestic to institutions; USD 42 in Canada to institutions; USD 48 elsewhere to institutions; USD 9.95 newsstand/cover (effective 2011). adv. reprint service avail. from WSH. **Document type:** *Journal, Academic/Scholarly.*
Related titles: Online - full text ed.
Indexed: A26, ABS&EES, CA, I05, I08, P02, P10, P42, P45, P47, P48, P53, P54, PAIS, PQC, SociolAb, T02.
Published by: Georgetown University, Edmund A. Walsh School of Foreign Service, 301 ICC, Washington, DC 20057. TEL 202-687-1461, FAX 202-687-1571, http://sfs.georgetown.edu. Ed. Michael B McKeon.

327 QAT ISSN 2072-5957
GEORGETOWN UNIVERSITY SCHOOL OF FOREIGN SERVICE IN QATAR, CENTER FOR INTERNATIONAL AND REGIONAL STUDIES. OCCASIONAL PAPER. Text in English. 2007. irreg. **Document type:** *Monographic series, Academic/Scholarly.*
Published by: Georgetown University School of Foreign Service in Qatar, Center for International and Regional Studies, PO Box 23689, Doha, Qatar. TEL 974-457-8400, CirsResearch@georgetown.edu.

327 URY ISSN 0250-7609
JC319
GEOSUR. Text in Spanish. 1979. bi-m. USD 142 (effective 2001). adv. bk.rev. Supplement avail. **Document type:** *Newspaper.*
Indexed: AMB.
Published by: Asociacion Sudamericana de Estudios Geopoliticos e Internacionales, Casilla de Correo 18112, Montevideo, 11400, Uruguay. TEL 598-2-6192953, FAX 598-2-9161923, bquaglio@adinet.com.uy. Ed. Bernardo Quagliotti de Bellis. Adv. contact Richard Gonzalez. Circ: 1,500 (controlled).

327 GBR ISSN 0964-4008
JN3201
➤ **GERMAN POLITICS.** Text in English. 1992. q. GBP 368 combined subscription in United Kingdom to institutions (print & online eds.); EUR 486, USD 610 combined subscription to institutions (print & online eds.) (effective 2012). adv. bk.rev. index. back issues avail.; reprint service avail. from PSC. **Document type:** *Journal, Academic/Scholarly.* **Description:** Provides an international forum for academic debate and political analysis on Germany, its changing role in European and world affairs, and its internal structure, including political economy, constitutional law, and social analysis.
Related titles: Online - full text ed.: ISSN 1743-8993. GBP 332 in United Kingdom to institutions; EUR 437, USD 549 to institutions (effective 2012) (from IngentaConnect).
Indexed: A01, A03, A08, A22, B21, CA, CurCont, DIP, E01, E17, ESPM, I13, IBR, IBSS, IBZ, LID&ISL, P30, P34, P42, PSA, S02, S03, SSCI, SociolAb, T02, W07.
—BLDSC (4162.150600), IE, Infotrieve, Ingenta. **CCC.**

Published by: (International Association for the Study of German Politics), Routledge (Subsidiary of: Taylor & Francis Group), 4 Park Sq, Milton Park, Abingdon, Oxon OX14 4RN, United Kingdom. TEL 44-20-70176000, FAX 44-20-70176336, subscriptions@tandf.co.uk, http://www.routledge.com. Eds. Stephen Padgett TEL 44-141-5482917 ext 2917, Thomas Saalfeld TEL 44-1227-824001. Adv. contact Linda Hann TEL 44-1344-779945. **Subscr. to:** Taylor & Francis Ltd., Journals Customer Service, Sheepen Pl, Colchester, Essex CO3 3LP, United Kingdom. TEL 44-20-70175544, FAX 44-20-70175198.

327.17 GBR ISSN 2042-3985
▼ **GLOBAL (CAMBRIDGE);** the international briefing. Text in English. 2009. q. GBP 6.50 per issue (effective 2011). adv. back issues avail. **Document type:** *Magazine, Trade.* **Description:** Aims to be a non-partisan guide through the highly contested and often complex discourse generated by the intensifying process of globalisation in the 21st century.
Related titles: Online - full text ed.: free (effective 2011).
Published by: (Great Britain. Commonwealth Secretariat), Nexus Strategic Partnerships Ltd., Alexander House, 1 Milton Rd, Cambridge, CB4 1UY, United Kingdom. TEL 44-1223-488814, FAX 44-1223-353130, info@nexuspartnerships.com, http://www.nexuspartnerships.com. Ed. Richard Synge. Pub. Smuts Beyers. Adv. contact Norma McCaskill.

327 382 ESP ISSN 1887-5076
GLOBAL AFFAIRS.ES. Text in English, Spanish. 2007. 3/yr. free. bibl.; charts; illus.; stat. **Document type:** *Journal, Academic/Scholarly.* **Description:** Contains articles directly related to political, social, economic and cultural events at international level with a wide variety of opinions.
Media: Online - full text. **Related titles:** E-mail ed.
Published by: Global Affairs eva.diez@globalaffairs.es. Pub., Adv. contact Eva Diez Ajenjo.

327 CAN ISSN 1920-6909
▼ **GLOBAL BRIEF.** Text in English. 2009. q. **Document type:** *Journal, Trade.*
Published by: Canadian International Council, 45 Willcocks St, Ste 210, Toronto, ON M5S 1C7, Canada. TEL 416-946-7209, FAX 416-946-7319, info@onlinecic.org. Ed., Pub. Irvin Studin.

327.12 GBR ISSN 1478-1166
GLOBAL CHANGE, PEACE & SECURITY (ONLINE). Text in English. 2000. 3/yr. GBP 375 in United Kingdom to institutions; EUR 500, AUD 446, USD 626 to institutions (effective 2012). adv. **Document type:** *Journal, Academic/Scholarly.*
Formerly (until 2003): Pacifica Review (Online) (1469-9974)
Media: Online - full text (from IngentaConnect). **Related titles:** ◆ Print ed.: Global Change, Peace & Security (Print). ISSN 1478-1158.
—BLDSC (4195.358370). **CCC.**
Published by: Routledge (Subsidiary of: Taylor & Francis Group), 4 Park Sq, Milton Park, Abingdon, Oxon OX14 4RN, United Kingdom. TEL 44-20-70176000, FAX 44-20-70176336, http://www.routledge.com.

327.172 GBR ISSN 1478-1158
JX1904.5
➤ **GLOBAL CHANGE, PEACE & SECURITY (PRINT).** Text in English. 1989. 3/yr. GBP 417 combined subscription in United Kingdom to institutions (print & online eds.); EUR 555, AUD 496, USD 696 combined subscription to institutions (print & online eds.) (effective 2012). adv. Index. back issues avail.; reprint service avail. from PSC. **Document type:** *Journal, Academic/Scholarly.* **Description:** Aims to establish connections between local, national, international, and transnational levels of organization, and between the cultural, economic, ecological and geopolitical dimensions of contemporary change.
Former titles (until 2003): Pacifica Review (Print) (1323-9104); (until 1994): Interdisciplinary Peace Research (1032-3856)
Related titles: ◆ Online - full text ed.: Global Change, Peace & Security (Online). ISSN 1478-1166.
Indexed: A22, ASFA, B21, CA, DIP, E01, E17, ESPM, G02, I02, I13, IBR, IBSS, IBZ, LID&ISL, P26, P42, P47, P54, PAIS, PQC, PRA, PSA, R02, RiskAb, S02, S03, SCOPUS, SOPODA, SSA, SSciA, SociolAb, T02.
—IE, Infotrieve, Ingenta. **CCC.**
Published by: (La Trobe University, Victoria, Australia, School of Social Sciences and the Centre for Dialogue AUS), Routledge (Subsidiary of: Taylor & Francis Group), 4 Park Sq, Milton Park, Abingdon, Oxon OX14 4RN, United Kingdom. TEL 44-20-70176000, FAX 44-20-70176336, subscriptions@tandf.co.uk, http://www.routledge.com. Ed. Stephen James. Adv. contact Linda Hann TEL 44-1344-779945. **Subscr. to:** Taylor & Francis Ltd., Journals Customer Service, Sheepen Pl, Colchester, Essex CO3 3LP, United Kingdom. TEL 44-20-70175544, FAX 44-20-70175198.

327 GBR
GLOBAL CIVIL SOCIETY (YEAR). Text in English. 2001. a. GBP 29.99 per vol. (effective 2009). back issues avail.; reprints avail. **Document type:** *Yearbook, Academic/Scholarly.* **Description:** Provides an indispensable guide to global civil society or civic participation and action around the world.
Published by: Sage Publications Ltd. (Subsidiary of: Sage Publications, Inc.), 1 Oliver's Yard, 55 City Rd, London, EC1Y 1SP, United Kingdom. TEL 44-20-73248500, FAX 44-20-73248600, info@sagepub.co.uk, http://www.uk.sagepub.com/home.nav. Ed. Ashwani Kumar.

327 GBR ISSN 1749-3161
JF1081
GLOBAL CORRUPTION REPORT. Abbreviated title: G C R. Text in English. 2001. a. USD 39.99 per issue (effective 2009). back issues avail. **Document type:** *Report, Trade.* **Description:** Examines a broad range of persistent and emerging corruption risks for business, assess the efficacy of existing remedies, and propose practical and innovative measures to strengthen and future-proof corporate integrity.
Related titles: Online - full text ed.
Published by: (Transparency International DEU), Pluto Publishing Ltd., 345 Archway Rd, London, N6 5AA, United Kingdom. TEL 44-20-83482724, FAX 44-20-83489133, pluto@plutobooks.com, http://www.plutobooks.com/. Eds. Dieter Zinnbauer, Rebecca Dobson.

327 GBR ISSN 1744-0572
HV6252
➤ **GLOBAL CRIME.** Text in English. 1995. q. GBP 314 combined subscription in United Kingdom to institutions (print & online eds.); EUR 413, USD 519 combined subscription to institutions (print & online eds.) (effective 2012). adv. bk.rev. index. back issues avail.; reprint service avail. from PSC. **Document type:** *Journal, Academic/Scholarly.* **Description:** Takes a multidisciplinary look at cross-border criminal activities, the transnational criminal organizations that engage in them, and the threat they pose to security and stability at both the national and international levels.
Formerly (until 2004): Transnational Organised Crime (1357-7387)
Related titles: Online - full text ed.: ISSN 1744-0580. GBP 283 in United Kingdom to institutions; EUR 371, USD 467 to institutions (effective 2012) (from IngentaConnect).
Indexed: A22, BrHumI, CA, CJA, CJPI, E01, ESPM, I02, I14, LID&ISL, P42, PQC, PSA, R02, RiskAb, S02, S03, SCOPUS, SociolAb, T02.
—IE, Ingenta. **CCC.**
Published by: Routledge (Subsidiary of: Taylor & Francis Group), 4 Park Sq, Milton Park, Abingdon, Oxon OX14 4RN, United Kingdom. TEL 44-20-70176000, FAX 44-20-70176336, subscriptions@tandf.co.uk, http://www.routledge.com. Ed. Federico Varese. Adv. contact Linda Hann TEL 44-1344-779945. **Subscr. to:** Taylor & Francis Ltd., Journals Customer Service, Sheepen Pl, Colchester, Essex CO3 3LP, United Kingdom. TEL 44-20-70175544, FAX 44-20-70175198.

➤ **GLOBAL DEVELOPMENT STUDIES.** *see* BUSINESS AND ECONOMICS—International Development And Assistance

327.092 CYP ISSN 1986-2601
HF1351
GLOBAL DIALOGUE (ONLINE). Text in English. s-a. **Document type:** *Magazine, Consumer.*
Formerly (until 2009): Global Dialogue (Print) (1450-0590)
Media: Online - full text.
Indexed: A12, A17, ABIn, CA, DIP, I13, IBR, IBSS, IBZ, MLA-IB, P10, P34, P45, P48, P51, P53, P54, PAIS, PQC, PSA, S02, S03, S11, SCOPUS, SociolAb, T02.
—BLDSC (4195.388500), IE, Ingenta.
Published by: Centre for World Dialogue, 39 Riga Fereou St, Ag Omologitae, P.O. Box 23992, Nicosia, CY-1687, Cyprus.

327.172 USA
GLOBAL DIRECTORY OF PEACE STUDIES & CONFLICT RESOLUTION PROGRAMS. Text in English. irreg. (every 4-5 yrs). USD 45. **Document type:** *Directory.*
Formerly: Directory of Peace Studies Programs
Published by: Consortium on Peace Research, Education and Development, c/o Institute for Conflict Analysis & Resolution, George Mason University, 4260 Chainbridge Rd, Ste 315, Fairfax, VA 22030-4444. TEL 703-993-2405, FAX 703-993-3070.

327.172 CAN ISSN 1719-9603
THE GLOBAL EDUCATOR. Text in English. 1986. irreg. CAD 46.55 to non-members; CAD 25 to members (effective 2008). **Document type:** *Newsletter.*
Former titles (until 2006): Pages (1200-4189); (until 1993): P A G E Journal (1184-2644); (until 1990): B.C. Peace and Global Educator (0849-9896); (until 1989): B.C. Peace Educator (0836-6330)
Published by: (B.C. Teachers for Peace and Global Education), British Columbia Teachers' Federation, 100-550 W 6th Ave, Vancouver, BC V5Z 4P2, Canada. TEL 604-871-2283, FAX 604-871-2291, http://www.bctf.ca. Ed. Gudrun Howard.

GLOBAL ENVIRONMENTAL POLITICS. *see* ENVIRONMENTAL STUDIES

327 USA ISSN 1075-2846
JZ6.5 CODEN: GLGOFI
➤ **GLOBAL GOVERNANCE;** a review of multilateralism and international organizations. Text in English. 1995. q. USD 140 combined subscription domestic to institutions (print & online eds.); USD 158 combined subscription foreign to institutions (print & online eds.) (effective 2011). adv. bibl.; charts; illus. Index. back issues avail.; reprint service avail. from WSH. **Document type:** *Journal, Academic/Scholarly.* **Description:** Provides a forum for practitioners and academics who want to explore the impact of international institutions and multilateral processes on economic development, peace and security, human rights, and preservation of the environment.
Related titles: Microfiche ed.: (from WSH); Microform ed.: (from WSH); Online - full text ed.: ISSN 1942-6720.
Indexed: A01, A02, A03, A08, A12, A20, A22, A26, ABIn, B01, B06, B07, B09, CA, CurCont, E04, E05, E08, G08, I02, I05, I08, I13, IBSS, L03, M05, M06, P10, P13, P34, P42, P45, P47, P48, P51, P53, P54, PAIS, PQC, PRA, PSA, S02, S03, S09, S11, SCOPUS, SOPODA, SPAA, SSA, SSCI, SociolAb, T02, W07.
—BLDSC (4195.415000), IE, Infotrieve, Ingenta. **CCC.**
Published by: Lynne Rienner Publishers, 1800 30th St, Ste 314, Boulder, CO 80301. TEL 303-444-6684, FAX 303-444-0824. Eds. Timothy D Sisk, Tom Farer. Circ: 1,500 (paid). **Co-sponsors:** United Nations University; Academic Council on the United Nations.

327 ZAF ISSN 1607-2375
GLOBAL INSIGHT. Text in English. 2000. irreg., latest vol.74, 2007. **Document type:** *Monographic series.*
Published by: Institute for Global Dialogue, PO Box 32571, Braamfontein, 2017, South Africa. TEL 27-11-3151299, FAX 27-11-3152149, info@igd.org.za, http://www.igd.org.za.

327 USA ISSN 1559-8047
JZ1318
GLOBAL ISSUES (WASHINGTON, D.C.); selections from C Q Researcher. Text in English. 2001. a. USD 36.95 (effective 2011). 439 p./no.; back issues avail.; reprints avail. **Document type:** *Monographic series, Academic/Scholarly.* **Description:** Offers an in-depth look at today's most pressing issues, ranging from the developing world and human rights to climate change and terrorism.
Published by: C Q Press, Inc. (Subsidiary of: Sage Publications, Inc.), 2300 N St, NW, Ste 800, Washington, DC 20037. TEL 202-729-1900, 866-427-7737, FAX 800-380-3810, customerservice@cqpress.com, http://www.cqpress.com.

341 CAN ISSN 1910-4332
GLOBAL JUSTICE REPORT. Text in English. 1973. q. CAD 25 domestic to individuals; CAD 30 foreign to individuals; CAD 40 to institutions (effective 2000). adv. bk.rev. illus. **Document type:** *Newsletter.*

Former titles (until 2006): Global Economic Justice Report (1706-9904); (until 2001): Economic Justice Report (0849-3391); (until 1989): GATT-Fly Report (0228-359X); (until 1979): Flying Together (0228-3603)
Related titles: Online - full text ed.
Indexed: C03, CBCARef, P47, P48, PQC.
—CIS.
Published by: Ecumenical Coalition for Economic Justice, 947 Queen St E, Ste 208, Toronto, ON M4M 1J9, Canada. TEL 416-462-1613, FAX 416-463-5569, ecej@accessv.com. R&P, Adv. contact Diana Gibbs. Circ: 1,000 (paid).

327.1 CAN ISSN 1914-1246
GLOBAL PARTNERSHIP PROGRAM/PROGRAMME DE PARTENARIAT MONDIAL. Text in English, French. 2005. a. **Document type:** *Government.*
Published by: Canada, Department of Foreign Affairs and International Trade, 125 Sussex Dr, Ottawa, ON K1A 0G2, Canada. TEL 613-944-4000, 800-267-8376, FAX 613-996-9709, enqserv@dfait-maeci.gc.ca, http://www.dfait-maeci.gc.ca.

327.172 CAN ISSN 1921-4022
▼ **GLOBAL PEACE STUDIES.** Text in English. 2009. irreg., latest vol.1, 2009. price varies. **Document type:** *Monographic series, Academic/Scholarly.* **Description:** Publishes works dealing with the discourses of war and peace, conflict and post-conflict studies, human rights and international development, human security and peacebuilding.
Related titles: Online - full text ed.: ISSN 1921-4030.
Published by: Athabasca University, 1 University Dr, Athabasca, AB T9S 3A3, Canada. TEL 780-675-6111, FAX 780-675-6437, http://www.athabascau.ca. Ed. George Melnyk.

327.172 NLD ISSN 1875-9858
▼ ➤ **GLOBAL RESPONSIBILITY TO PROTECT.** Text in English. 2009. q. EUR 257, USD 361 to institutions; EUR 281, USD 393 combined subscription to institutions (print & online eds.) (effective 2012). **Document type:** *Journal, Academic/Scholarly.* **Description:** Publishes the latest research on the R2P (Responsibility to Protect) principle, its development as a new norm in global politics, its operationalization through the work of governments, international and regional organizations and NGOs.
Related titles: Online - full text ed.: ISSN 1875-984X. EUR 234, USD 328 to institutions (effective 2012) (from IngentaConnect).
Indexed: A22, CA, E01, IZBG, P42, T02.
—CCC.
Published by: Martinus Nijhoff (Subsidiary of: Brill), PO Box 9000, Leiden, 2300 PA, Netherlands. TEL 31-71-5353500, FAX 31-71-5317532, marketing@brill.nl, http://www.nijhoff.nl. Ed. Alex J Bellamy.

▼ ➤ **GLOBAL SECURITY STUDIES.** *see* CRIMINOLOGY AND LAW ENFORCEMENT—Security

341.72 USA ISSN 1938-6168
GLOBAL SECURITY WATCH SERIES. Text in English. 2008 (Mar.). irreg., latest 2009. price varies. back issues avail. **Document type:** *Monographic series, Academic/Scholarly.* **Description:** Combining the expert analysis of social, political, and military affairs, titles in this series assess emerging security threats and concerns posed by nations such as the proliferation of nuclear weapons, promoting terrorist activities, drug and weapons trafficking, and other transnational crimes.
Published by: Greenwood Publishing Group Inc. (Subsidiary of: A B C - C L I O), 88 Post Rd W, PO Box 5007, Westport, CT 06881. TEL 203-226-3571, 800-225-5800, FAX 877-231-6980, sales@greenwood.com.

327 GBR ISSN 1360-0826
JX1
➤ **GLOBAL SOCIETY;** journal of interdisciplinary international relations. Text in English. 1986. q. GBP 511 combined subscription in United Kingdom to institutions (print & online eds.); EUR 674, USD 846 combined subscription to institutions (print & online eds.) (effective 2012). adv. illus. Index. back issues avail.; reprint service avail. from PSC. **Document type:** *Journal, Academic/Scholarly.* **Description:** Covers the new agenda in international relations and encourages innovative approaches to the study of international issues from a range of disciplines.
Formerly (until 1996): Paradigms (0951-9750)
Related titles: Online - full text ed.: ISSN 1469-798X. 2006. GBP 460 in United Kingdom to institutions; EUR 606, USD 761 to institutions (effective 2012) (from IngentaConnect).
Indexed: A01, A03, A08, A22, AmHI, BrHumI, CA, DIP, E01, GEOBASE, H07, I02, I13, I14, IBR, IBSS, IBZ, L03, M05, P34, P42, P47, P48, PAIS, PQC, PSA, R02, S02, S03, SCOPUS, SSA, SociolAb, T02.
—IE, Infotrieve, Ingenta. **CCC.**
Published by: Routledge (Subsidiary of: Taylor & Francis Group), 4 Park Sq, Milton Park, Abingdon, Oxon OX14 4RN, United Kingdom. TEL 44-20-70176000, FAX 44-20-70176336, subscriptions@tandf.co.uk, http://www.routledge.com. Ed. Florian Bieber. Adv. contact Linda Hann TEL 44-1344-779945. **Subscr. in N. America to:** Taylor & Francis Inc., Customer Services Dept, 325 Chestnut St, 8th Fl, Philadelphia, PA 19106. TEL 215-625-8900, 800-354-1420, FAX 215-625-2940, customerservice@taylorandfrancis.com; **Subscr. to:** Taylor & Francis Ltd., Journals Customer Service, Sheepen Pl, Colchester, Essex CO3 3LP, United Kingdom. TEL 44-20-70175544, FAX 44-20-70175198.

➤ **THE GLOBAL SOUTH.** *see* LITERARY AND POLITICAL REVIEWS

327 USA ISSN 1098-3880
DT1
GLOBAL STUDIES: AFRICA. Text in English. 1985. irreg., latest 2011, 13th ed. illus. back issues avail. **Document type:** *Catalog, Academic/Scholarly.* **Description:** Provides comprehensive background information and selected world press articles on the regions and countries of the world. Includes background essays and statistics for the countries of North Africa, Central Africa, East Africa, South Africa, and West Africa, with a regional essay showing the connection of North Africa to the rest of the continent.
Published by: McGraw-Hill, Contemporary Learning Series (Subsidiary of: McGraw-Hill Companies, Inc.), 1221 Ave of the Americas, New York, NY 10020. TEL 212-904-2000, FAX 212-512-2000, customer.service@mcgraw-hill.com, http://www.mhhe.com/cls/.

327 USA ISSN 1050-2025
DS701
GLOBAL STUDIES: CHINA. Text in English. 1984. irreg., latest 2010, 13th ed. illus. back issues avail. **Document type:** *Monographic series, Academic/Scholarly.* **Description:** Provides comprehensive background information and selected world press articles on the regions and countries of the world. Includes country reports and current statistics for the People's Republic of China, Taiwan, and Hong Kong, with essays discussing the region as a whole.
Published by: McGraw-Hill, Contemporary Learning Series (Subsidiary of: McGraw-Hill Companies, Inc.), 1221 Ave of the Americas, New York, NY 10020. TEL 212-904-2000, FAX 212-512-2000, customer.service@mcgraw-hill.com, http://www.mhhe.com/cls/.

327 USA ISSN 1943-8613
D1050
GLOBAL STUDIES: EUROPE. Text in English. 1989. irreg., latest 2009, 10th ed. illus. back issues avail. **Document type:** *Monographic series, Academic/Scholarly.* **Description:** Contains background essays on Western Europe and each of its countries. Each country report features detailed maps and statistics. A compilation of carefully selected articles from newspapers and magazines from around the world is reprinted in this volume, and an annotated list of World Wide Web sites guides students to additional resources.
Formerly (until 2002): Global Studies: Western Europe (1059-2334)
Published by: McGraw-Hill, Contemporary Learning Series (Subsidiary of: McGraw-Hill Companies, Inc.), 1221 Ave of the Americas, New York, NY 10020. TEL 212-904-2000, FAX 212-512-2000, customer.service@mcgraw-hill.com, http://www.mhhe.com/cls/.

327 USA ISSN 1059-5988
DS801
GLOBAL STUDIES: JAPAN AND THE PACIFIC RIM. Text in English. 1991. irreg., latest 2011, 10th ed. illus. back issues avail. **Document type:** *Monographic series, Academic/Scholarly.* **Description:** Provides comprehensive background information and selected world press articles on the regions and countries of the world. Includes country reports, current statistics, and background essays on the Pacific Rim, the Pacific Islands, and Japan.
Published by: McGraw-Hill, Contemporary Learning Series (Subsidiary of: McGraw-Hill Companies, Inc.), 1221 Ave of the Americas, New York, NY 10020. TEL 212-904-2000, FAX 212-512-2000, customer.service@mcgraw-hill.com, http://www.mhhe.com/cls/.

327 USA ISSN 1061-2831
F1401
GLOBAL STUDIES: LATIN AMERICA. Text in English. 1984. irreg., latest 2009, 13th ed. illus. **Document type:** *Monographic series, Academic/Scholarly.* **Description:** Provides comprehensive background information and selected world press articles on the regions and countries of the world. This edition includes introductory essays on Mexico, Central America, South America, and the Carribbean region, with concise reports and current statistics for each of the countries within these regions.
Published by: McGraw-Hill, Contemporary Learning Series (Subsidiary of: McGraw-Hill Companies, Inc.), 1221 Ave of the Americas, New York, NY 10020. TEL 212-904-2000, FAX 212-512-2000, customer.service@mcgraw-hill.com, http://www.mhhe.com/cls/.

327 USA ISSN 1056-6848
DS41
GLOBAL STUDIES: MIDDLE EAST. Text in English. 1986. irreg., latest 2011, 13th ed. illus. back issues avail. **Document type:** *Monographic series, Academic/Scholarly.* **Description:** Provides an introduction to the status and problems of the Middle East, through essays, statistics, current world press readings, and a listing of related World Wide Web sites.
Published by: McGraw-Hill, Contemporary Learning Series (Subsidiary of: McGraw-Hill Companies, Inc.), 1221 Ave of the Americas, New York, NY 10020. TEL 212-904-2000, FAX 212-512-2000, customer.service@mcgraw-hill.com, http://www.mhhe.com/cls/.

327 USA ISSN 1087-9064
DK1.5
GLOBAL STUDIES: RUSSIA, THE EURASIAN REPUBLICS, AND CENTRAL - EASTERN EUROPE. Text in English. 1986. irreg., latest 2008, 11th ed. illus. back issues avail. **Document type:** *Monographic series, Academic/Scholarly.* **Description:** Provides introductory essays, up-to-date background information, and current statistics on the region.
Former titles (until 1994): Global Studies: Commonwealth of Independent States and Central - Eastern Europe (1061-2823); (until 1992): Global Studies: Soviet Union and Eastern Europe (1052-7796)
Published by: McGraw-Hill, Contemporary Learning Series (Subsidiary of: McGraw-Hill Companies, Inc.), 1221 Ave of the Americas, New York, NY 10020. TEL 212-904-2000, FAX 212-512-2000, customer.service@mcgraw-hill.com, http://www.mhhe.com/cls/.

327 USA ISSN 1075-4644
GLOBAL SURVEY. Text in English. 1969. bi-m. USD 400 (effective 2001). charts; stat. back issues avail. **Document type:** *Newsletter, Consumer.* **Description:** Information on international, government, security and economic affairs.
Formerly: Defense Reference Reports
Published by: International Observer, 5624, Washington, DC 20016-1224. Ed., R&P J H Wagner. Pub. Joe H Wagner.

GLOBAL TERRORISM COLLECTION. *see* CRIMINOLOGY AND LAW ENFORCEMENT

GLOBAL WAR CRIMES TRIBUNAL COLLECTION. *see* LAW—International Law

GLOBALIZATION. *see* SOCIAL SCIENCES: COMPREHENSIVE WORKS

327 DEU ISSN 0721-0167
GLOBUS (SANKT AUGUSTIN). Text in German. 1969. 4/yr. EUR 2.25 newsstand/cover (effective 2005). adv. bk.rev. charts; illus.
Indexed: IBR, IBZ, SpeleolAb.
Published by: (Verein fuer Deutsche Kulturbeziehungen im Ausland eV), V D A Bundesgesellschaftsstelle, Koelnstr 76, Sankt Augustin, 53757, Germany. TEL 49-2241-21071, FAX 49-2241-29241, vda@vda-globus.de, http://www.vda-globus.de. Circ: 10,000.

327 GBR ISSN 0072-6397
GREAT BRITAIN. FOREIGN AND COMMONWEALTH OFFICE. TREATY SERIES. Text in English. 1892. irreg., latest 2004. price varies. reprints avail. **Document type:** *Government.*
—CCC.
Published by: The Stationery Office, St Crispins, Duke St, Norwich, NR3 1PD, United Kingdom. TEL 44-1603-622211, FAX 44-870-6005533, customer.services@tso.co.uk, http://www.tsoshop.co.uk/.

327.73 USA ISSN 0072-727X
E835
GREAT DECISIONS. Abbreviated title: G D. Text in English. 1955. s-a. USD 18 per issue (effective 2010). charts; illus.; maps. 104 p./no.; Supplement avail.; back issues avail.; reprints avail. **Document type:** *Journal, Academic/Scholarly.* **Description:** Contains annual briefing book, the Great Decisions television series on PBS, the National Opinion Ballot Report, thousands of discussion groups across the country and the GD online newsletter.
Related titles: Online - full text ed.: free (effective 2010).
Indexed: AMB, SRI.
Published by: Foreign Policy Association, 470 Park Ave S, New York, NY 10016-6819. TEL 212-481-8100, FAX 212-481-9275, info@fpa.org, http://www.fpa.org.

327.172 GBR
GREENPEACE NEWSLETTER. Text in English. 1971. q. bk.rev. **Document type:** *Newsletter, Academic/Scholarly.*
Media: Duplicated (not offset).
Published by: Greenpeace (London), 5 Caledonian Rd, London, N1, United Kingdom. Circ: 750.

327.519 KOR ISSN 1598-4818
D1
GUGJE JEONGCHI NONCHONG/KOREAN JOURNAL OF INTERNATIONAL RELATIONS. Text in Korean. 1963. q. membership. **Document type:** *Journal, Academic/Scholarly.*
Published by: Han'gug Gugje Jeongchi Haghoe/Korean Association Of International Studies, 467-4 Seokyo-Dong, Mapo-Gu, Seoul, 121-842, Korea, S. TEL 82-2-3250372, FAX 82-2-3250355, hkais@chol.com, http://www.kaisnet.or.kr/.

GUGJE JIYEOG YEON'GU/REVIEW OF INTERNATIONAL AND AREA STUDIES. *see* BUSINESS AND ECONOMICS—International Commerce

GUGJE SAHOE BOJANG DONGHYANG/INTERNATIONAL SOCIAL SECURITY TODAY. *see* SOCIAL SERVICES AND WELFARE

327 PRK
GUKJESAENGHWAL/INTERNATIONAL LIFE. Text in English, Korean. 1986. m. **Description:** Covers North Korea's foreign policy and international events.
Address: Pyongyang, Korea, N.

327 GBR ISSN 0953-5411
DS41
GULF STATES NEWSLETTER. Text in English. 1975. fortn. GBP 290 in United Kingdom; USD 585 overseas (effective 2000). bk.rev. **Document type:** *Newsletter.* **Description:** Covers political, economic and defense issues in the Gulf Region.
Indexed: PerIslam.
—CIS.
Published by: Middle East Newsletters, PO Box 124, Hastings, E Sussex TN34 1WP, United Kingdom. TEL 44-1342-712929, FAX 44-1342-712829, andrew.rathmell@kcl.ac.uk. Ed. Andrew Rathmell. Pub. John L Christie.

327 CHN ISSN 1005-4812
GUOJI GUANCHA/INTERNATIONAL REVIEW. Text in Chinese. 1993. bi-m. USD 24.60 (effective 2009). **Document type:** *Journal, Academic/Scholarly.*
Related titles: Online - full text ed.
—East View.
Published by: (Shanghai Waiguoyu Daxue), Shanghai Waiyu Jiaoyu Chubanshe/Shanghai Foreign Language Education Press, 558, Dalian Xilu, Hongkou-qu, Shanghai, 200083, China. TEL 86-21-65425300.

327 CHN ISSN 1004-3489
JZ6.5
GUOJI GUANXI XUEYUAN XUEBAO/JOURNAL OF UNIVERSITY OF INTERNATIONAL RELATIONS. Text in Chinese. 1983. bi-m. USD 31.20 (effective 2009). **Document type:** *Journal, Academic/Scholarly.*
Related titles: Online - full content ed.; Online - full text ed.
—East View.
Published by: Guoji Guanxi Xueyuan/Institute of International Relations, Haidian-qu, 12, Poshangcun, Shanghai, 100091, China. TEL 86-10-62861174.

327 CHN ISSN 1008-1755
GUOJI LUNTAN/INTERNATIONAL FORUM. Text in Chinese. 1995. bi-m. USD 24.60 (effective 2009). **Document type:** *Journal, Academic/Scholarly.*
—East View.
Published by: Beijing Waiguoyu Daxue, Guoji Wenti Yanjiusuo, 2, Xi San-Huan Bei Lu, 167 Xinxiang, Beijing, 100089, China. TEL 86-10-68916998, FAX 86-10-68916241.

327 TWN ISSN 1029-8010
GUOJI LUNTAN. Text in Chinese. 1998. 3/yr. back issues avail. **Document type:** *Journal, Academic/Scholarly.*
Related titles: Online - full text ed.
Published by: Nanhua Daxue, Ouzhou Yanjiuso/Nanhua University, Institute of European Studies, 32, Chung Keng Li, Dalin, Chiayi 62248, Taiwan. TEL 886-5-2721001 ext 2361, http://www.nhu.edu.tw/~europe/.

327 CHN ISSN 0452-8832
D849
GUOJI WENTI YANJIU/INTERNATIONAL STUDIES. Text in Chinese; Abstracts and contents page in English. 1959. bi-m. CNY 10 per issue (effective 2009). **Document type:** *Journal, Academic/Scholarly.*
Formerly: Journal of International Studies
Related titles: Online - full text ed.
—East View, Ingenta.
Published by: Zhongguo Guoji Wenti Yanjiusuo/China Institute of International Studies, 3, Taijichangtoutiao, Beijing, 100005, China. TEL 86-10-85119558, FAX 86-10-65284305. **Dist. by:** China International Book Trading Corp, 35 Chegongzhuang Xilu, Haidian District, PO Box 399, Beijing 100044, China.

327 CHN ISSN 0452-8778
GUOJI ZHANWANG/INTERNATIONAL PROSPECT. Text in Chinese. s-m.

Published by: Shanghai Guoji Wenti Yanjiusuo/Shanghai Research Institute of International Issues, No1, Alley 845, Julu Lu, Shanghai 200040, China. TEL 4334263.

327 CHN ISSN 1005-426X
D440
GUOJI ZHENGZHI/INTERNATIONAL POLITICS. Text in Chinese. 1978. m. USD 138.70 (effective 2009). 176 p./no.; **Document type:** *Journal, Academic/Scholarly.* **Description:** Covers theories on international politics and international relations. Also covers international organizations and their activities.
Formerly (until 1993): Waiguo Zhengzhi, Guoji Guanxi (1001-2877)
Indexed: RASB.
Published by: Zhongguo Renmin Daxue Shubao Ziliao Zhongxin/Renmin University of China, Information Center for Social Sciences, Dongcheng-qu, 3, Zhangzizhong Lu, Beijing, 100007, China. TEL 86-10-64039458, FAX 86-10-64015080, center@zlzx.org, http://www.zlzx.org/. **Dist. in US by:** China Publications Service, PO Box 49614, Chicago, IL 60649. TEL 312-288-3291, FAX 312-288-8570.

327 CHN
GUOJI ZHENGZHI KEXUE. Text in Chinese. 2005. q. CNY 15 newsstand/cover (effective 2006). **Document type:** *Journal, Academic/Scholarly.*
Related titles: ◆ English Translation: Chinese Journal of International Politics. ISSN 1750-8916.
Published by: (Qinghua Daxue, Guoji Wenti Yanjiusuo/Tsinghua University, Institute of International Studies), Beijing Daxue Chubanshe/Peking University Press, 205, Chengfu Lu, Haidian-qu, Beijing, 100871, China. TEL 86-10-62752024, fd@pup.pku.edu.cn, http://cbs.pku.edu.cn/.

327 CHN ISSN 1671-4709
GUOJI ZHENGZHI YANJIU. Text in Chinese. 1989. q. USD 32 (effective 2009). **Document type:** *Journal, Academic/Scholarly.*
Published by: Beijing Daxue, Guoji Guanxi Xueyuan/Peking University, School of International Studies, Beijing, 100871, China. TEL 86-10-62759984, FAX 86-10-62751639, http://www.sis.pku.edu.cn/web/.

327.0904 DEU
H E C E A S - AKTUELLE DEBATTE. (Heidelberger Centrum fuer Euro-Asiatische Studien) Text in German. 2005. irreg., latest vol.3, 2007. price varies. **Document type:** *Monographic series, Academic/Scholarly.*
Published by: (Heidelberger Centrum fuer Euro-Asiatische Studien e.V.), Dr. Ludwig Reichert Verlag, Tauernstr 11, Wiesbaden, 65199, Germany. TEL 49-611-461851, FAX 49-611-468613, info@reichert-verlag.de, http://www.reichert-verlag.de.

327 DEU
H S F K STANDPUNKTE - FRIEDENSFORSCHUNG AKTUELL. Text in English, German. 1981. q. free. back issues avail. **Document type:** *Journal, Academic/Scholarly.* **Description:** Reports on current topics of peace and foreign policy, as well as peace research and peace movements.
Formerly: Friedensforschung Aktuell (0930-830X)
Published by: Hessische Stiftung Friedens- und Konfliktforschung, Leimenrode 29, Frankfurt Am Main, 60322, Germany. TEL 49-69-9591040, FAX 49-69-558481. Ed. Eva von Hase-Mihalik. Circ: 4,000.

327 NLD ISSN 1871-1901
JZ11
THE HAGUE JOURNAL OF DIPLOMACY. Text in English. 2006 (Mar.). 4/yr. EUR 290, USD 407 to institutions; EUR 317, USD 444 combined subscription to institutions (print & online eds.) (effective 2012). reprint service avail. from PSC. **Document type:** *Journal, Academic/Scholarly.*
Related titles: Online - full text ed.: ISSN 1871-191X. EUR 264, USD 370 to institutions (effective 2012) (from IngentaConnect).
Indexed: A22, CA, E01, IBSS, IZBG, P42, PAIS, PSA, SCOPUS, T02.
—BLDSC (4238.160150), IE, Ingenta. **CCC.**
Published by: Martinus Nijhoff (Subsidiary of: Brill), PO Box 9000, Leiden, 2300 PA, Netherlands. TEL 31-71-5353500, FAX 31-71-5317532, marketing@brill.nl. Eds. Jan Melissen, Paul Sharp.

HAITI NEWS. *see* BUSINESS AND ECONOMICS—International Development And Assistance

327.172 NLD ISSN 1571-4934
HAMBURG STUDIES IN MULTILINGUALISM. Text in English. 2003. irreg., latest vol.12, 2011. price varies. **Document type:** *Monographic series, Academic/Scholarly.* **Description:** Publishes research from colloquia on linguistic aspects of multilingualism.
Published by: John Benjamins Publishing Co., PO Box 36224, Amsterdam, 1020 ME, Netherlands. TEL 31-20-6304747, FAX 31-20-6739773, customer.services@benjamins.nl. Eds. Barbara Haenel-Faulhaber, Christoph Gabriel, Kurt Braunmueller.

327 DEU ISSN 0936-0018
HAMBURGER BEITRAEGE ZUR FRIEDENSFORSCHUNG UND SICHERHEITSPOLITIK. Text in English, German. 1986. irreg., latest vol.151, 2008. price varies. adv. **Document type:** *Monographic series, Academic/Scholarly.* **Description:** Covers research in peace and national security. Each volume devoted to a single topic.
Indexed: PAIS.
Published by: Universitaet Hamburg, Institut fuer Friedensforschung und Sicherheitspolitik, Beim Schlump 83, Hamburg, 20144, Germany. TEL 49-40-8660770, FAX 49-40-8663615, ifsh@ifsh.de. Circ: 500.

327 DEU ISSN 0931-8399
HAMBURGER INFORMATIONEN ZUR FRIEDENSFORSCHUNG UND SICHERHEITSPOLITIK. Text in German. 1986. irreg. **Document type:** *Academic/Scholarly.*
Published by: Universitaet Hamburg, Institut fuer Friedensforschung und Sicherheitspolitik, Beim Schlump 83, Hamburg, 20144, Germany. ifsh@ifsh.de, http://www.ifsh.de.

341.72 USA ISSN 1550-9605
HAMPTON ROADS INTERNATIONAL SECURITY QUARTERLY. Abbreviated title: H R I S Q. Text in English. 2001 (Aug.). q. USD 59 (effective 2010). back issues avail. **Document type:** *Journal, Academic/Scholarly.* **Description:** Dedicated to international security and political issues effecting the cohesion and vital interests of the Atlantic community.
Related titles: Online - full text ed.: ISSN 1536-9609. USD 36 (effective 2010).
Indexed: M07, P10, PQC.
Published by: Transatlantic Euro-American Multimedia LLC, PO Box 6793, Portsmouth, VA 23703. service@teamultimedia.com.

327 FIN ISSN 1795-8830
HANASAARI AGENDA. Variant title: Agenda Hanaholmen. Text in Finnish, Swedish, English, German. 1995. s-a. back issues avail. **Document type:** *Magazine, Consumer.*
Formerly (until 2005): Hanasaari Meny (1238-0482)
Related titles: Online - full text ed.
Published by: Hanasaari/Swedish Finnish Cultural Centre, Espoo, 02100, Finland. TEL 358-9-435020, FAX 358-9-467291, hanasaari@hanaholmen.fi, http://www.hanaholmen.fi.

327 KOR ISSN 1225-3006
DS917.6
HAN'GUG GWA GUG'JE JEONG'CHI/KOREA AND WORLD POLITICS. Text in Korean. 1998. q. **Document type:** *Journal, Academic/Scholarly.*
Related titles: Online - full text ed.
Published by: Kyungnam University, Institute for Far Eastern Studies/Gyeongnam Daehag'gyo, Geugdong Munje Yeon'guso, 28-42 Samchung-dong, Chongro-Ku, Seoul, 110-230, Korea, S. TEL 82-2-37000700, FAX 82-2-37000707, ifes@kyungnam.ac.kr, http://ifes.kyungnam.ac.kr/ifes/ifes/eng/default.asp.

327 USA ISSN 1522-4147
DS1
HARVARD ASIA QUARTERLY. Abbreviated title: H A Q. Text in English. 1997. q. back issues avail. **Document type:** *Journal, Academic/Scholarly.* **Description:** Publishes articles, essays, and interviews from a broad range of disciplines, with especial emphasis given to contemporary politics.
Related titles: Online - full text ed.
Indexed: A01, CA, M10, T02.
—BLDSC (4265.721500), IE. **CCC.**
Published by: Harvard Asia Center, Ctr for Government & International Studies (CGIS), S Bldg, 1730 Cambridge St, Cambridge, MA 02138. arthur_kleinman@harvard.edu, http://www.fas.harvard.edu/~asiactr. **Subscr. to:** IvyMedia Corporation, 2285 Mass Ave, Ste 204, Cambridge, MA 02140 . TEL 617-354-2101, FAX 617-354-2109, http://www.ivymedia.com/.

327 USA ISSN 0739-1854
D839
HARVARD INTERNATIONAL REVIEW. Text in English. 1979. q. USD 20 domestic; USD 30 foreign (effective 2004). adv. bk.rev. back issues avail. **Document type:** *Journal, Consumer.* **Description:** Offers penetrating analyses of pressing issues in international affairs by today's most influential and insightful world leaders, scholars and professionals.
Related titles: Microform ed.: (from PQC); Online - full text ed.
Indexed: A01, A02, A03, A08, A11, A12, A17, A22, A26, ABIn, ABS&EES, B01, B02, B06, B07, B08, B09, B15, B17, B18, BAS, C05, C12, CA, CCR, CPerI, E08, G04, G06, G07, G08, I02, I05, I07, M01, M02, M05, M06, MASUSE, P10, P30, P34, P42, P45, P47, P48, P51, P53, P54, PAIS, PQC, PerIslam, R02, RASB, S02, S03, S09, S11, S23, SCOPUS, SociolAb, T02, WBA, WMB.
—BLDSC (4267.210000), IE, Infotrieve, Ingenta. **CCC.**
Published by: Harvard International Relations Council, Inc., PO Box 380226, Cambridge, MA 02238-0226. TEL 617-495-9607, FAX 617-496-4472. Eds. Genevieve Sheehan, Manik Suri. Circ: 15,000.

363.35 USA ISSN 2153-1358
▼ **HARVARD NATIONAL SECURITY JOURNAL.** Text in English. 2010 (June). irreg. **Document type:** *Journal, Academic/Scholarly.*
Media: Online - full text.
—**CCC.**
Published by: Harvard Law School, 1563 Massachusetts Ave, Cambridge, MA 02138. TEL 617-495-3100, hllr@law.harvard.edu, http://www.law.harvard.edu.

327 USA ISSN 0073-0734
JX1295.H45
HARVARD UNIVERSITY. CENTER FOR INTERNATIONAL AFFAIRS. ANNUAL REPORT. Text in English. 1961. a. free. reprints avail.
Published by: Harvard University, Center for International Affairs, 1737 Cambridge St, Cambridge, MA 02138. TEL 617-495-4420, FAX 617-495-8292. Ed. Pamela Slavsky. Circ: 3,000.

328 BRA ISSN 1809-1261
HEGEMONIA. Text in Portuguese. 2005. q. **Document type:** *Journal, Academic/Scholarly.*
Published by: Centro Universitario Uniero, Curso de Relacoes Internacionais, Trecho O Conj, 05, Ave das Nacoes Sul, Brasilia, 70200-001, Brazil. TEL 55-61-34455888.

327.172 JPN ISSN 0385-0749
JX1903
HEIWA KENKYU/PEACE STUDIES. Text in Japanese. 1976. a. JPY 3,200 (effective 1998). bk.rev.
Published by: (Nihon Heiwa Gakkai/Philosophy of Science Society, Japan), Waseda Daigaku Shuppanbu - Waseda University Press, 1-103 Totsuka-Machi, Shinjuku-ku, Tokyo, 1690071, Japan. TEL 81-3-3203-1551, FAX 81-3-3207-0406. Ed. Koji Terayama. Circ: 1,200.

HELLENIC JOURNAL. *see* ETHNIC INTERESTS

327 DEU
HELLMUTH-LOENING-ZENTRUM FUER STAATSWISSENSCHAFTEN JENA. SCHRIFTEN. Text in German. 1995. irreg., latest vol.18, 2009. price varies. **Document type:** *Monographic series, Academic/Scholarly.*
Published by: (Hellmuth-Loening-Zentrum fuer Staatswissenschaften Jena), B W V - Berliner Wissenschafts Verlag GmbH, Markgrafenstr 12-14, Berlin, 10969, Germany. TEL 49-30-8417700, FAX 49-30-84177021, bwv@bwv-verlag.de, http://www.bwv-verlag.de.

327 DEU
HESSISCHE STIFTUNG FRIEDENS- UND KONFLIKTFORSCHUNG. JAHRESBERICHT; Bericht ueber Organisation und laufende Forschung. Text in German. 1971. a. **Document type:** *Academic/Scholarly.* **Description:** Review of progress of the institute's research programs.
Formerly: Hessische Stiftung Friedens- und Konfliktforschung. Mitteilungen
Published by: Hessische Stiftung Friedens- und Konfliktforschung, Leimenrode 29, Frankfurt Am Main, 60322, Germany. TEL 49-69-9591040, FAX 49-69-558481. Ed. Eva von Hase-Mihalik. Circ: 180.

327 JPN
HIGHLIGHTING JAPAN. Text in English. m. **Document type:** *Magazine, Consumer.* **Description:** Covers Japanese politics, people, international contributions and communications, arts and culture, science and technology, lifestyles, and environment.
Media: Online - full content.
Published by: Government of Japan, Cabinet Office, 1-6-1 Nagatacho Chiyoda-ku, Tokyo, 100-8914, Japan.

327 JPN ISSN 1340-346X
HIKAKU BUNKA KENKYU/INSTITUTE OF COMPARATIVE STUDIES OF INTERNATIONAL CULTURES AND SOCIETIES. BULLETIN. Text in Japanese. 1987. s-a. **Document type:** *Bulletin, Academic/Scholarly.*
Formerly (until 1993): Kurume Daigaku Hikaku Bunka Kenkyujo Kiyo (0914-0034)
Published by: Kurume Daigaku, Hikaku Bunka Kenkyujo/Kurume University, Institute of Comparative Studies of International Cultures and Societies, 1635 Mii-machi, Kurume, Fukuoka 839-8502, Japan. morimoto_yoshiki@kurume-u.ac.jp, http://www.mii.kurume-u.ac.jp/~hikakubunka/.

327 JPN ISSN 1341-3546
JZ12
HIROSHIMA KOKUSAI KENKYU/HIROSHIMA JOURNAL OF INTERNATIONAL STUDIES. Text in Japanese. 1995. a.
—BLDSC (4315.606000).
Published by: Hiroshima Shiritsu Daigaku, Kokusai Gakubu/Hiroshima City University, Faculty of International Studies, 3-4-1 Ozuka-Higashi, Asa-Minami-ku, Hiroshima, 731-3194, Japan. TEL 81-82-8301500, FAX 81-82-8301656, http://www.hiroshima-cu.ac.jp/org/intl/.

327 NLD ISSN 1874-0294
➤ **HISTORY OF INTERNATIONAL RELATIONS, DIPLOMACY AND INTELLIGENCE.** Text in English. 2007. irreg., latest vol.5, 2008. price varies. **Document type:** *Monographic series, Academic/Scholarly.* **Description:** Addresses the field of international relations, including diplomacy, national security, economic conflict, and the role of individuals, as well as exploring the role of intelligence and intelligence agencies in shaping foreign relations.
Indexed: IZBG.
Published by: Martinus Nijhoff (Subsidiary of: Brill), PO Box 9000, Leiden, 2300 PA, Netherlands. TEL 31-71-5353500, FAX 31-71-5317532, marketing@brill.nl. Ed. Katherine Sibley.

327 USA ISSN 1934-631X
HOT SPOT HISTORIES. Text in English. 2008 (Feb.). irreg., latest 2010. USD 65, GBP 44.95 per issue (effective 2010). back issues avail. **Document type:** *Monographic series, Academic/Scholarly.* **Description:** Contains regionally organized topical chapters detail the who, what, why, when, and where of every significant conflict and extremist group in every region of the globe.
Published by: Greenwood Publishing Group Inc. (Subsidiary of: A B C - C L I O), PO Box 1911, Santa Barbara, CA 93116. TEL 800-368-6868, FAX 866-270-3856, customerservice@abc-clio.com, http://www.greenwood.com.

327.172 GBR ISSN 0957-0136
JX1905.5
HOUSMANS PEACE DIARY & WORLD PEACE DIRECTORY (YEAR). Variant title: Housmans Peace Diary with World Peace Directory. Text in English. 1954. a. GBP 8.95, EUR 13, USD 18 per issue (effective 2010). back issues avail. **Document type:** *Directory, Consumer.* **Description:** Provides up-to-date listings and information of 2,000 national and international organizations in more than 150 countries in the fields of peace campaigning, human rights, and environmental issues.
Former titles (until 1994): Housmans Peace Diary; (until 198?): Housmans World Peace Directory
Related titles: Diskette ed.
Published by: Housmans Bookshop Ltd., 5 Caledonian Rd, London, N1 9DX, United Kingdom. TEL 44-20-78374473, FAX 44-20-72780444, shop@housmans.com.

327 CHN ISSN 1002-7165
AP95.C4
HUANQIU/GLOBE. Text in Chinese. 1980. s-m. USD 86.40 (effective 2009). **Document type:** *Magazine, Consumer.*
Related titles: Online - full content ed.
—East View.
Published by: (Xinhua News Agency), Huanqiu Zazhishe, 57 Xuanwumen Xidajie, Beijing, 100803, China. TEL 86-10-63073510, FAX 86-10-63073516.

327 USA
AS30
HUDSON BRIEFING PAPER. Text in English. 19??. m. back issues avail. **Document type:** *Newsletter, Academic/Scholarly.*
Formerly: Hudson Institute Briefing Paper (1056-9391)
Related titles: Online - full text ed.: free (effective 2010).
Published by: Hudson Institute, 1015 15th St, NW, 6th Fl, Washington, DC 20005. TEL 202-974-2400, FAX 202-974-2410, info@hudson.org.

327 USA
Q180.U5
HUDSON INSTITUTE REPORT. Text in English. 1962. q. **Document type:** *Report, Academic/Scholarly.*
Formerly: Hudson Institute. Report to the Members (0073-3776)
Published by: Hudson Institute, 1015 15th St, NW, 6th Fl, Washington, DC 20005. TEL 202-974-2400, FAX 202-974-2410, info@hudson.org, http://www.hudson.org.

327 NOR ISSN 1890-176X
HVOR HENDER DET? (ONLINE). Text in Norwegian. 2000. 24/yr. **Document type:** *Consumer.*
Media: Online - full text.
Published by: Norsk Utenrikspolitisk Institutt/Norwegian Institute of International Affairs, C. J. Hambros Pl, PO Box 8159, Dep, Oslo, 0033, Norway. TEL 47-22-994000, FAX 47-22-362182, info@nupi.no, http://www.nupi.no. Ed. Ivar Windheim.

327 CHE ISSN 1013-1221
I C A NEWS. Text in English. 1987. 6/yr. CHF 25. **Document type:** *Newsletter, Consumer.*
Related titles: Online - full text ed.; French ed.; Spanish ed.; English ed.
Published by: International Co-Operative Alliance, 15 rte des Morillons, Grand Saconnex, 1218, Switzerland. TEL 41-22-9298888, FAX 41-22-7984122. Ed. Purushothaman Nair.

327.172 ESP ISSN 2013-5793
▼ ➤ **I C I P WORKING PAPERS.** Text in Catalan, English, Spanish. 2009. irreg. free. bibl. **Document type:** *Monographic series, Academic/Scholarly.* **Description:** Aims to participate in today's debates on peace, conflicts and security in the world, providing innovative perspectives and approaches.
Media: Online - full text.
Published by: Institut Catala Internacional per la Pau/International Catalan Institute for Peace, Gran Via de les Corts Catalanes, 658 baix, Barcelona, 08010, Spain. TEL 34-93-5544270, FAX 34-93-5544280, icip@gencat.cat, http://www.gencat.cat/icip/cat/icip_wp.html. Pub. Javier Alcalde.

327 IRL
I E A FINAL REPORTS. Text in English. 1992. irreg., latest vol.4, 1997. price varies. **Document type:** *Monographic series, Academic/Scholarly.*
Published by: Institute of European Affairs, Europe House, 8 North Great Georges St., Dublin, 1, Ireland. TEL 353-1-8746756, FAX 353-1-8786880, info@iiea.com, http://www.iiea.com.

327 IRL
I E A INTERIM REPORTS. Text in English. 1992. irreg., latest vol.3, 1995. price varies. **Document type:** *Monographic series, Academic/Scholarly.*
Published by: Institute of European Affairs, Europe House, 8 North Great Georges St., Dublin, 1, Ireland. TEL 353-1-8746756, FAX 353-1-8786880, info@iiea.com, http://www.iiea.com. Ed. Patrick Keatinge.

327 IRL
I E A NEWS. Text in English. q. **Document type:** *Newsletter.*
Published by: Institute of European Affairs, Europe House, 8 North Great Georges St., Dublin, 1, Ireland. TEL 353-1-8746756, FAX 353-1-8786880, info@iiea.com, http://www.iiea.com. Ed. Conall Quinn.

327 IRL
I E A SEMINAR PAPERS. Text in English. 1995. irreg., latest vol.2, 1996. price varies. **Document type:** *Monographic series, Academic/Scholarly.*
Published by: Institute of European Affairs, Europe House, 8 North Great Georges St., Dublin, 1, Ireland. TEL 353-1-8746756, FAX 353-1-8786880, info@iiea.com, http://www.iiea.com. Ed. Paul Gillespie.

327 IRL
I E A SEMINAR REPORTS. Text in English. 1995. irreg., latest vol.8, 1997. **Document type:** *Monographic series, Academic/Scholarly.*
Published by: Institute of European Affairs, Europe House, 8 North Great Georges St., Dublin, 1, Ireland. TEL 353-1-8746756, FAX 353-1-8786880, info@iiea.com, http://www.iiea.com. Ed. Joe Larragy.

327 NGA
I F R A DOCUMENTS IN SOCIAL SCIENCES AND HUMANITIES. Text in English. 1992. irreg., latest 1996. price varies. **Document type:** *Monographic series, Academic/Scholarly.* **Description:** Contains scholarly articles on various political and sociological issues affecting Nigeria and other African nations.
Formerly: C R E D U Documents in Social Sciences and Humanities
Published by: Institut Francais de Recherche en Afrique/French Institute for Research in Africa, Institute of African Studies, University of Ibadan, PO Box 21540, Ibadan, Oyo, Nigeria. TEL 234-2-8104077, FAX 234-2-8104077, ifra@skannet.com.

327 NGA
I F R A OCCASIONAL PUBLICATIONS. Text in English. 1992. irreg., latest vol.5, 1996. price varies. **Document type:** *Monographic series, Academic/Scholarly.* **Description:** Discusses democracy and other political and sociological topics pertaining to African nations.
Formerly: C R E D U Occasional Publications
Published by: Institut Francais de Recherche en Afrique/French Institute for Research in Africa, Institute of African Studies, University of Ibadan, PO Box 21540, Ibadan, Oyo, Nigeria. TEL 234-2-8104077, FAX 234-2-8104077, ifra@skannet.com.

327 JPN ISSN 0285-2608
DS801
I H J BULLETIN. Text in English. 1981. s-a. JPY 1,000, USD 10 (effective 2001). bk.rev. back issues avail. **Document type:** *Bulletin.*
Indexed: RASB.
Published by: International House of Japan Inc., 11-16 Roppongi 5-chome, Minato-ku, Tokyo, 106-0032, Japan. TEL 81-3-3470-3211, FAX 81-3-3470-3170, http://www.i-house.or.jp. Ed. Kato Mikio. R&P Haruna Ishizuka. Circ: 7,500.

327 AUT
I I P OCCASIONAL PAPER. Text in English, German. 1989. irreg. price varies. **Document type:** *Monographic series, Academic/Scholarly.*
Published by: International Institute for Peace, Moellwaldplatz 5, Vienna, W 1040, Austria. TEL 43-431-5046437, FAX 43-431-5053236, secretariat@iip.at, http://www.iip.at. Ed. Lev Voronkov. Circ: 200.

327 DEU ISSN 0256-4416
I N P R E K O R R. (Internationale Pressekorrespondenz) Text in German. 1971. bi-m. EUR 20 domestic; EUR 40 foreign (effective 2005). adv. bk.rev. index. back issues avail. **Document type:** *Newsletter.* **Description:** Presents issues of interest for working people, feminist movements, international solidarity groups, and those interested in socialist movements and Marxist theory.
Published by: (Vereinigtes Sekretariat der IV. Internationale), Neuer Kurs GmbH, Dasselstr 75-77, Cologne, 50674, Germany. TEL 49-221-9231196, FAX 49-221-9231197. Circ: 1,000.

327 FRA ISSN 2106-8410
▼ **I P E M E D NEWS.** (Institut de Prospective Economique du Monde Mediterraneen) Text in French. 2009. m. **Document type:** *Newsletter, Consumer.*
Published by: Institut de Prospective Economique du Monde Mediterraneen, 132 Bd du Montparnasse, Paris, 75014, France. TEL 33-1-56543838, FAX 33-1-40475884, ipemed@ipemedipemed.coop, http://www.ipemed.coop.

327.172 281.9 USA ISSN 2150-9638
▼ **I P S E C JOURNAL.** Variant title: IPSEC Journal. Text in English. 2010 (Dec.). a. USD 25 per issue (effective 2011). **Document type:** *Journal, Academic/Scholarly.* **Description:** For educators, policymakers, and religious leaders who explore and implement methods of peacemaking emerging from the traditions of Eastern Christianity.
Published by: Institute for Peace Studies in Eastern Christianity, 21 Oak Ridge Dr, Ayer, MA 01432. TEL 978-772-5349, simion@bc.edu, http://www2.bc.edu/~simion/ipsec/ipsec.html.

328 ESP ISSN 1025-9384
THE I P T S REPORT (ENGLISH EDITION). Text in English. 1996. m.
Related titles: ◆ German ed.: The I P T S Report (Geman Edition). ISSN 1025-9392; ◆ French ed.: The I P T S Report (French Edition). ISSN 1025-9406; ◆ Spanish ed.: The I P T S Report (Spanish Edition). ISSN 1026-0838.
Indexed: WasteInfo.
Published by: European Commission, Institute for Prospective Technological Studies, C. Inca Garcilaso, s-n, Sevilla, 41092, Spain. TEL 34-95-4488318, FAX 34-95-4488300, ipts@jrc.es, http://www.jrc.es/. Ed. J M Cadiou.

328 ESP ISSN 1025-9406
THE I P T S REPORT (FRENCH EDITION). Text in French. 1996. m. **Document type:** *Newsletter, Consumer.*
Related titles: ◆ English ed.: The I P T S Report (English Edition). ISSN 1025-9384; ◆ German ed.: The I P T S Report (Geman Edition). ISSN 1025-9392; ◆ Spanish ed.: The I P T S Report (Spanish Edition). ISSN 1026-0838.
Published by: European Commission, Institute for Prospective Technological Studies, C. Inca Garcilaso, s-n, Sevilla, 41092, Spain. TEL 34-95-4488318, FAX 34-95-4488300, ipts@jrc.es, http://www.jrc.es/. Ed. J M Cadiou.

328 ESP ISSN 1025-9392
THE I P T S REPORT (GEMAN EDITION). Text in German. 1996. m. **Document type:** *Newsletter, Consumer.*
Related titles: ◆ English ed.: The I P T S Report (English Edition). ISSN 1025-9384; ◆ Spanish ed.: The I P T S Report (Spanish Edition). ISSN 1026-0838; ◆ French ed.: The I P T S Report (French Edition). ISSN 1025-9406.
—CCC.
Published by: European Commission, Institute for Prospective Technological Studies, C. Inca Garcilaso, s-n, Sevilla, 41092, Spain. TEL 34-95-4488318, FAX 34-95-4488300, ipts@jrc.es, http://www.jrc.es/. Ed. J M Cadiou.

328 ESP ISSN 1026-0838
THE I P T S REPORT (SPANISH EDITION). Text in Spanish. 1995. m. **Document type:** *Newsletter, Consumer.*
Related titles: ◆ English ed.: The I P T S Report (English Edition). ISSN 1025-9384; ◆ German ed.: The I P T S Report (Geman Edition). ISSN 1025-9392; ◆ French ed.: The I P T S Report (French Edition). ISSN 1025-9406.
Published by: European Commission, Institute for Prospective Technological Studies, C. Inca Garcilaso, s-n, Sevilla, 41092, Spain. TEL 34-95-4488318, FAX 34-95-4488300, ipts@jrc.es, http://www.jrc.es/. Ed. J M Cadiou.

053.931 NLD
I S. (Internationale Samenwerking) Text in Dutch. 1969. m. free (effective 2008). **Document type:** *Magazine, Consumer.*
Formerly (until 1999): Internationale Samenwerking (0167-0158)
Published by: Nationale Commissie voor Internationale Samenwerking en Duurzame Ontwikkeling, Postbus 94020, Amsterdam, 1090 GA, Netherlands. TEL 31-20-5688755, FAX 31-20-5688787, info@ncdo.nl, http://www.ncdo.nl. Eds. Lonneke van Genugten, Hans Ariens.

327 PAK ISSN 2219-0562
▼ ➤ **I S S R A PAPERS.** (Institute of Strategic Studies Research and Analysis) Text in English. 2009. s-a. free to qualified personnel. bk.rev. **Document type:** *Journal, Academic/Scholarly.*
Published by: National Defence University Islamabad, Institute of Strategic Studies Research and Analysis, NDU Sector E-9, Islamabad, Pakistan. TEL 92-51-9260651, FAX 92-51-9260663. Ed. Lt.Col. Saif Ur Rehman. Pub. Abdul Rauf Iqbal.

327 NLD ISSN 1574-1311
JZ5588
➤ **I S Y P JOURNAL ON SCIENCE AND WORLD AFFAIRS.** (International Student Young Pugwash) Text in English. 2005. s-a. **Document type:** *Journal, Academic/Scholarly.* **Description:** Aims to serve as a forum for the discussion of the problems that our societies are confronted with, from the perspective of the world's youth.
Related titles: Online - full text ed.
Indexed: A01, A39, C27, C29, D03, D04, E13, R14, S14, S15, S18, T02.
Published by: (International Student Young Pugwash (I S Y P)), Het Spinhuis Publishers, Oudezijds Achterburgwal 185, Amsterdam, 1012 DK, Netherlands. TEL 31-20-5252711, FAX 31-20-5253010.

327 909 DNK ISSN 1901-9211
IBIS FOKUS; uddannelse skaber udvikling. Text in Danish. 1991. q. free. back issues avail. **Document type:** *Journal, Consumer.*
Formerly (until 2006): Zigzag (0906-2408); Which was formed by the merger of (1986-1991): Cikaden (0901-5418); (1980-1991): W U S Nyhedsbrev (0107-3710); Zigzag incorporated (1991-1992): Nyhedsbrev fra Ibis (0907-4872); Which was formerly (until 1991): W U S - Nyt (0906-3595)
Related titles: Online - full text ed.
Published by: IBIS, Noerrebrogade 68 B, Copenhagen N, 2200, Denmark. TEL 45-35-358788, FAX 45-35-350696, ibis@ibis.dk. Ed. Rene Jacobsen.

327 IRL ISSN 0791-590X
IMPLICATIONS FOR IRELAND. Text in English. 1991. irreg., latest vol.3, 1996. price varies. **Document type:** *Monographic series.*
Published by: Institute of European Affairs, Europe House, 8 North Great Georges St., Dublin, 1, Ireland. TEL 353-1-8746756, FAX 353-1-8786880, info@iiea.com, http://www.iiea.com.

327.172 ITA ISSN 1972-7429
IMPRONTE SOCIALI. Text in Italian. 2004. w. **Document type:** *Magazine, Consumer.*
Published by: Associazione Melagrana, Via Caudio, S Maria a Vico, CE 81028, Italy. http://www.melagrana.eu.

325.21 AUS
IN THE FIELD. Text in English. 1977. 3/yr. AUD 5. adv. bk.rev. back issues avail. **Document type:** *Newsletter, Consumer.* **Description:** Aims to help people affected by conflict and natural disaster, and to build human security.
Former titles (until 2003): Austcare News (1035-0519); Which incorporated (1984-198?): Austcare Refugee Bulletin (0815-5747); (1983-198?): Austcare Refugee Papers (0815-4341)
Related titles: Online - full text ed.: free (effective 2008).
Published by: Australians Care for Refugees (Austcare), 69-71 Parramatta Rd, Camperdown, Sydney, NSW 2050, Australia. TEL 61-2-95659111, FAX 61-2-95504509, info@austcare.org.au, http://www.austcare.com.au. Circ: 11,000.

355 RUS ISSN 1992-9242
JX1974.7
INDEKS BEZOPASNOSTI; Rossiiskii zhurnal o mezhdunarodnoi bezopasnosti. Text in Russian. 1994. 3/yr. USD 621 (effective 2009). **Document type:** *Journal, Academic/Scholarly.* **Description:** Discusses problems of weapons of mass destruction in Russia and the NIS; export controls, nuclear security, nuclear strategies and defense policies, chemical weapons, biological weapons, conventional arms.
Formerly (until 2007): Yadernyi Kontrol' (1026-9878)
Related titles: ◆ English ed.: Security Index. ISSN 1993-4270.
—East View.
Published by: P I R - Tsentr, 4-i Dobryninskii pereulok, dom 8, Moscow, 119049, Russian Federation. TEL 7-495-9871915, FAX 7-495-9871914, info@pircenter.org. Ed. Vladimir Orlov. **Dist. by:** East View Information Services, 10601 Wayzata Blvd, Minneapolis, MN 55305. TEL 952-252-1201, 800-477-1005, FAX 952-252-1202, info@eastview.com, http://www.eastview.com.

INDEX TO UNITED NATIONS DOCUMENTS AND PUBLICATIONS. *see* POLITICAL SCIENCE—Abstracting, Bibliographies, Statistics

327 IND ISSN 0376-9771
DS401
INDIA INTERNATIONAL CENTRE QUARTERLY. Variant title: I I C Quarterly. Text in English. 1974. 3/yr. INR 500, USD 45 to individuals; INR 750, USD 55 to institutions; INR 350, USD 35 to members (effective 2011). bk.rev. bibl. **Document type:** *Journal, Consumer.*
Indexed: BAS, I13, IndIndia, MLA-IB, PAA&I.
Published by: India International Centre, 40 Max Mueller Marg, New Delhi, 110 003, India. TEL 91-11-24619431, secretary.iic@nic.in. Ed. Ira Pande TEL 91-11-24698318.

327.54 IND ISSN 0974-9284
D410
INDIA QUARTERLY; a journal of international affairs. Text in English. 1945. q. USD 449, GBP 243 combined subscription to institutions (print & online eds.); USD 440, GBP 238 to institutions (effective 2011). adv. bk.rev. bibl.; illus. index. reprint service avail. from PSC. **Document type:** *Journal, Academic/Scholarly.*
Related titles: Online - full text ed.: ISSN 0975-2684. USD 404, GBP 219 to institutions (effective 2011).
Indexed: A01, A02, A03, A08, A22, ABCPolSci, AMB, AmH&L, BAS, CA, DIP, E01, HistAb, IBSS, MEA&I, P34, P42, PAA&I, PCI, PRA, PerIslam, RASB, T02.
—BLDSC (4391.300000), Infotrieve, Ingenta.
Published by: (Indian Council of World Affairs), Sage Publications India Pvt. Ltd. (Subsidiary of: Sage Publications, Inc.), M-32 Market, Greater Kailash-I, PO Box 4215, New Delhi, 110 048, India. TEL 91-11-6444958, FAX 91-11-6472426, sage@vsnl.com, http://www.indiasage.com/. Eds. Partha S Ghosh, Sudhir T Devare. Circ: 2,000.

327 GBR ISSN 1473-6489
DS401
➤ **INDIA REVIEW.** Text in English. 2002 (Jan). q. GBP 254 combined subscription in United Kingdom to institutions (print & online eds.); EUR 327, USD 412 combined subscription to institutions (print & online eds.) (effective 2012). adv. bk.rev. illus. annual. back issues avail.; reprint service avail. from PSC. **Document type:** *Journal, Academic/Scholarly.* **Description:** Publishes scholarly research on Indian politics, economics and society.
Related titles: Online - full text ed.: ISSN 1557-3036. GBP 229 in United Kingdom to institutions; EUR 294, USD 370 to institutions (effective 2012) (from IngentaConnect).
Indexed: A01, A03, A08, A22, AmH&L, B01, B06, B07, B09, CA, E01, ESPM, HistAb, IBSS, LID&ISL, P42, PSA, RiskAb, S02, S03, SCOPUS, SociolAb, T02.
—IE, Ingenta. **CCC.**
Published by: Routledge (Subsidiary of: Taylor & Francis Group), 4 Park Sq, Milton Park, Abingdon, Oxon OX14 4RN, United Kingdom. TEL 44-20-70176000, FAX 44-20-70176336, subscriptions@tandf.co.uk, http://www.routledge.com. Ed. Eswaran Sridharan TEL 91-11-24604126. Adv. contact Linda Hann TEL 44-1344-779945. **Subscr. to:** Taylor & Francis Ltd., Journals Customer Service, Sheepen Pl, Colchester, Essex CO3 3LP, United Kingdom. TEL 44-20-70175544, FAX 44-20-70175198.

327.54 IND ISSN 0970-6402
DS480.84
INDIAN JOURNAL OF ASIAN AFFAIRS. Text in English. 1988. s-a. bk.rev. **Document type:** *Journal, Academic/Scholarly.* **Description:** Analyzes contemporary and current Asian political, economic, social and military affairs.
Indexed: BAS.
—Ingenta.
Address: 4-87 Jawahar Nagar, Jaipur, Rajasthan 302 004, India. TEL 91-141-2652227.

327 FRA ISSN 0294-6475
DT365
INDIAN OCEAN NEWSLETTER. Text in English. 1981. s-m. (23/yr). looseleaf. EUR 720, USD 1,010 (effective 2009). adv. bk.rev. index. back issues avail. **Document type:** *Newsletter.* **Description:** Covers newsworthy, diplomatic, political and economic events from the 16 countries in the Horn of Africa, Eastern Africa, Southern Africa and the islands of the Indian Ocean.
Related titles: Online - full text ed.; ◆ French ed.: Lettre de l'Ocean Indien. ISSN 0294-6467.
Indexed: HRIR.
—CIS. **CCC.**
Published by: Indigo Publications, 142 rue Montmartre, Paris, 75002, France. TEL 33-1-44882610, FAX 33-1-44882615, http://www.indigo-net.com. Ed. Maurice Botbol. R&P Francis Glaser. Circ: 1,500.

327 DEU
INDIEN WIRTSCHAFTSNACHRICHTEN. Text in German. 1972. m. free. bk.rev. charts; illus.; stat. **Document type:** *Newsletter.*
Formerly: Indien (0046-9149)
Published by: Indische Botschaft, Adenauerallee 262-264, Bonn, 53113, Germany. TEL 49-228-5405146, FAX 49-228-5405153. Eds. Debnath Shaw, Tanmaya Lal. Circ: 5,500.

P

327 DEU ISSN 1867-9978
INDO-EUROPEAN STUDIES IN POLITICS AND SOCIETY. Text in German. 1976. irreg., latest vol.5, 2008. price varies. **Document type:** *Monographic series, Academic/Scholarly.*
Former titles (until 2008): Berliner Studien zur Internationalen Politik und Gesellschaft (1861-2407); (until 2005): Berliner Studien zur Internationalen Politik (0939-236X)
Published by: Weissensee Verlag e.K., Simplonstr 59, Berlin, 10245, Germany. TEL 49-30-29049192, FAX 49-30-27574315, mail@weissensee-verlag.de.

INDO-IRANICA. *see* LITERATURE

327 USA ISSN 1949-2375
▼ **INDO - U S TALKS.** Text in English. 2009. w. free (effective 2009).
Related titles: Online - full text ed.: ISSN 1949-2383.
Published by: Omkara Publication LLC, 70 Arizona Ave, Old Bridge, NJ 08857. TEL 718-757-2840, alpesh73@gmail.com.

327 USA
INDOCHINA DIGEST. Text in English. 1987. w. USD 35 domestic to individuals; USD 45 foreign to individuals; USD 350 domestic to corporations; USD 450 foreign to corporations. **Document type:** *Newsletter.* **Description:** Tracks developments in or related to Indochina, with emphasis on business, economics, and politics.
Published by: Indochina Project, 2001 S St N W, Ste 740, Washington, DC 20009. TEL 202-483-9222, FAX 202-483-9214. Circ: 1,500.

327 IDN ISSN 0046-9173
DS638
INDONESIAN REVIEW OF INTERNATIONAL AFFAIRS. Text in English. 1970. q. USD 1.50 per issue. adv.
Indexed: BAS, P06.
Published by: Indonesian Institute of International Affairs, 82 Jalan Tjikini Raya, Jakarta 4, Indonesia. Eds. A Subardjo Djovoadisuryo, S Suryodpuro. Circ: 60,000.

341 LUX ISSN 1025-7039
HT395.E82
INFOREGIO NEWS (ENGLISH EDITION). Text in English. 1995. irreg.
Related titles: French ed.: Inforegio News (French Edition). ISSN 1025-7020; German ed.: Inforegio News (German Edition). ISSN 1025-7047; Italian ed.: Inforegio News (Italian Edition). ISSN 1025-7055; Portuguese ed.: Inforegio News (Portuguese Edition). ISSN 1025-7063; Spanish ed.: Inforegio News (Spanish Edition). ISSN 1025-7128; Finnish ed.: Inforegio News (Finnish Edition). ISSN 1025-708X; Greek ed.: Inforegio News (Greek Edition). ISSN 1025-7098; Danish ed.: Inforegio News (Danish Edition). ISSN 1025-7101; Dutch ed.: Inforegio News (Dutch Edition). ISSN 1025-711X; Swedish ed.: Inforegio News (Swedish Edition). ISSN 1025-7071.
—BLDSC (4478.881200).
Published by: European Commission, Office for Official Publications of the European Union, 2 Rue Mercier, Luxembourg, L-2985, Luxembourg. FAX 352-29291, http://publications.europa.eu.

304.873 USA ISSN 1536-5263
JV6465
INFORMATION PLUS REFERENCE SERIES. IMMIGRATION AND ILLEGAL ALIENS; burden or blessing?. Text in English. 1981. biennial. USD 49 per issue (effective 2008). **Document type:** *Monographic series, Academic/Scholarly.*
Related titles: Online - full text ed.; ◆ Series of: Information Plus Reference Series.
Published by: Gale (Subsidiary of: Cengage Learning), 27500 Drake Rd, Farmington Hills, MI 48331. TEL 248-699-4253, 800-877-4253, FAX 877-363-4253, gale.customerservice@cengage.com, http://www.galegroup.com.

327 ESP ISSN 1135-7088
INFORME SEMANAL DE POLITICA EXTERIOR. Text in Spanish. 1995. w. EUR 160 (effective 2009). back issues avail. **Document type:** *Magazine, Trade.*
Related titles: Online - full text ed.
Published by: Estudios de Politica Exterior S.A., Nunez de Balboa 49, 5o Piso, Madrid, 28001, Spain. TEL 34-91-4312628, FAX 34-91-4354027, revista@politicaexterior.com. Ed. Dario Valcarcel.

328 ESP ISSN 1698-885X
INFORMES ELCANO. Text in Spanish. 2005. a. price varies. back issues avail. **Document type:** *Monographic series, Academic/Scholarly.*
Published by: Real Instituto El Cano de Estudios Internacionales y Estrategicos, C. Principe de Vergara, 51, Madrid, 28006, Spain. TEL 34-91-7816770, FAX 34-91-4262157, info@rielcano.org, http://www.realinstitutoelcano.org/.

327 GBR ISSN 1754-6869
INITIATIVE FOR POLICY DIALOGUE SERIES. Text in English. 200?. irreg., latest 2008. price varies. **Document type:** *Monographic series, Academic/Scholarly.*
Published by: Oxford University Press, Great Clarendon St, Oxford, OX2 6DP, United Kingdom. TEL 44-1865-556767, FAX 44-1865-556646, enquiry@oup.co.uk, http://www.oup-usa.org/catalogs/general/series/. Eds. Giovanni Dosi, Joseph E Stiglitz, Mario Cimoli.

327 AUS ISSN 1441-1954
INSIDE INDONESIA (ONLINE). Text in English. 1996. q. free (effective 2009). back issues avail. **Document type:** *Magazine, Consumer.* **Description:** Reports on Indonesian culture, politics, economy, human rights, social conditions, labor issues, civil society, independence movements, and the environment.
Media: Online - full text.
Published by: Indonesia Resources & Information Programme admin@insideindonesia.org.

327 IND ISSN 0975-0878
DT1
▼ **INSIGHT ON AFRICA.** Text in English. 2009. s-a. INR 950 domestic (print or online ed.); USD 105 foreign (print or online ed.); INR 1,800 combined subscription domestic (print & online eds.); USD 200 combined subscription foreign (print & online eds.) (effective 2010). **Document type:** *Journal, Academic/Scholarly.*
Related titles: Online - full text ed.
Indexed: P10, P48, P53, P54, PQC.
Published by: (African Studies Association of India (ASA)), M D Publications Pvt Ltd, 11 Darya Ganj, New Delhi, 110 002, India. TEL 91-11-41563325, FAX 91-11-23275542, contact@mdppl.com.

327.1 TUR ISSN 1302-177X
DR401
➤ **INSIGHT TURKEY.** Text in English. 1999. q. EUR 45 domestic to individuals; EUR 60 foreign to individuals; EUR 90 domestic to institutions; EUR 180 foreign to institutions (effective 2009). adv. **Document type:** *Journal, Academic/Scholarly.* **Description:** Covers a broad range of topics related to Turkish domestic and foreign policy, as well as its adjacent regions such as the Middle East, the Caucasus, the Balkans and Europe.
Related titles: Online - full text ed.: free (effective 2009).
Indexed: A01, A03, A12, A17, A26, ABIn, CA, E08, G05, G06, G07, G08, I05, IBR, IBSS, IBZ, M10, MLA-IB, P10, P42, P45, P48, P51, P53, P54, PAIS, PQC, PSA, S09, SCOPUS, SociolAb, T02.
Published by: Siyaset Ekonomi ve Toplum Arastirmalari Vakfi, Resit Galip Caddesi Hereke Sokak no 10, GOP - Cankaya, Ankara, 06700, Turkey. TEL 90-312-4056151, FAX 90-312-4056903, http://www.setav.org. Ed. Ihsan Dagi. R&P Tuba Nur Sonmez. adv.: page EUR 200. Circ: 2,000 (paid).

327 TWN ISSN 0256-5552
INSTITUT DE RELATIONS INTERNATIONALES. ETUDES ET DOCUMENTS. Text in French. 1980. q. **Document type:** *Journal, Academic/Scholarly.*
Indexed: PAIS.
Published by: National Chengchi University, Institute of International Relations, 64 Wanshou Road, Wenshan District, Taipei, 116, Taiwan. TEL 886-2-82377277, FAX 886-2-29378606, http://iir.nccu.edu.tw/.

327 FRA ISSN 1962-610X
DK510.764
INSTITUT FRANCAIS DES RELATIONS INTERNATIONALES. ETUDES. Text in French. 2007. irreg. **Document type:** *Monographic series, Academic/Scholarly.*
Published by: Institut Francais des Relations Internationales, 27 rue de la Procession, Paris, Cedex 15 75740, France. TEL 33-1-40616000, FAX 33-1-40616060, http://www.ifri.org.

327 FRA ISSN 1272-9914
INSTITUT FRANCAIS DES RELATIONS INTERNATIONALES. NOTES. Variant title: Notes de l'I F R I. Text in French. 1996. irreg. **Document type:** *Bulletin, Academic/Scholarly.*
Related titles: Online - full text ed.: ISSN 1954-3514.
Published by: Institut Francais des Relations Internationales, 27 rue de la Procession, Paris, Cedex 15 75740, France. TEL 33-1-40616000, FAX 33-1-40616060, http://www.ifri.org.

327 USA
INSTITUTE FOR FOREIGN POLICY ANALYSIS. CONFERENCE AND WORKSHOP REPORTS. Text in English. 1991. irreg., latest 2010. USD 1 per issue (effective 2010). **Document type:** *Report, Trade.* **Description:** Covers reports on conference and workshop conducted by Institute for Foreign Policy Analysis.
Related titles: Online - full text ed.: free (effective 2010).
Published by: Institute for Foreign Policy Analysis, Inc., 1725 DeSales St, NW, Ste 402, Washington, DC 20036. TEL 202-463-7942, FAX 202-785-2785, DCMail@ifpa.org.

327 USA
INSTITUTE FOR FOREIGN POLICY ANALYSIS. SPECIAL REPORTS AND MONOGRAPHS. Text in English. 1991. irreg. (3-4/yr.). latest 2010. **Document type:** *Monographic series, Academic/Scholarly.* **Description:** Covers topics of importance to the foreign affairs and security studies communities.
Related titles: Online - full text ed.: free (effective 2010).
Published by: Institute for Foreign Policy Analysis, Inc., 1725 DeSales St, NW, Ste 402, Washington, DC 20036. TEL 202-463-7942, FAX 202-785-2785, DCMail@ifpa.org.

327.12 ZAF ISSN 0257-1447
➤ **INSTITUTE FOR STRATEGIC STUDIES. BULLETIN/INSTITUUT VIR STRATEGIESE STUDIES. BULLETIN.** Key Title: I S S U P Bulletin. Text in English. 1979. irreg. (approx. 6/yr.). ZAR 70 domestic; USD 60 foreign; ZAR 4.50 per issue foreign (effective 2009). bk.rev. 10 p./no.; back issues avail. **Document type:** *Monographic series, Academic/Scholarly.*
Indexed: CA, PSA, T02.
Published by: University of Pretoria, Institute for Strategic Studies, The Editor, Strategic Review for Southern Africa, University of Pretoria, Pretoria, 0002, South Africa. wilma.martin@up.ac.za. Ed., R&P Mike Hough. Circ: 500.

➤ **INSTITUTE FOR THE STUDY OF GENOCIDE NEWSLETTER.** *see* SOCIOLOGY

327 IRL
INSTITUTE OF EUROPEAN AFFAIRS. OCCASIONAL PAPERS. Text in English. 1992. irreg., latest vol.7, 1995. price varies. **Document type:** *Monographic series.*
Published by: Institute of European Affairs, Europe House, 8 North Great Georges St., Dublin, 1, Ireland. TEL 353-1-8746756, FAX 353-1-8786880, info@iiea.com, http://www.iiea.com. Eds. Eamonn Gallagher, John Temple Lang.

327 BRA
INSTITUTO CULTURAL ITALO-BRASILEIRO. CADERNO. Text in Portuguese. 1972 (no.8). irreg. **Document type:** *Monographic series.*
Published by: Instituto Cultural Italo-Brasileiro, Rua Frei Caneca, 1071, Consolacao, Sao Paulo, SP 01307-003, Brazil.

INSTITUTS ZUR ERFORSCHUNG DER EUROPAEISCHEN ARBEITERBEWEGUNG. MITTEILUNGSBLATT. *see* LABOR UNIONS

327.4 DEU ISSN 0720-5120
JN15
INTEGRATION. Text in German. 1978. q. EUR 48 (effective 2011). adv. 70 p./no.; back issues avail.; reprint service avail. from SCH. **Document type:** *Journal, Academic/Scholarly.* **Description:** European integration in science and research.
Incorporates (in 1992): Europaeische Integration. Mitteilungen
Indexed: A22, CA, DIP, ELLIS, IBR, IBZ, P42, PSA, RASB, T02.
—BLDSC (4531.816290), IE, Ingenta. **CCC.**
Published by: (Institut fuer Europaeische Politik e.V.), Nomos Verlagsgesellschaft mbH und Co. KG, Waldseestr 3-5, Baden-Baden, 76530, Germany. TEL 49-7221-21040, FAX 49-7221-210427, nomos@nomos.de, http://www.nomos.de. Ed. Elfriede Regelsberger. Adv. contact Bettina Roos. Circ: 2,900 (paid).

327.12 GBR ISSN 0268-4527
JF1525.I6
➤ **INTELLIGENCE AND NATIONAL SECURITY.** Text in English. 1986. bi-m. GBP 616 combined subscription in United Kingdom to institutions (print & online eds.); EUR 808, USD 1,015 combined subscription to institutions (print & online eds.) (effective 2012). adv. bk.rev. index. back issues avail.; reprint service avail. from PSC. **Document type:** *Journal, Academic/Scholarly.* **Description:** Covers the history of intelligence and counterintelligence by the major powers.
Related titles: Microfilm ed.: (from PQC); Online - full text ed.: ISSN 1743-9019. GBP 554 in United Kingdom to institutions; EUR 727, USD 913 to institutions (effective 2012) (from IngentaConnect).
Indexed: A22, ABS&EES, AmH&L, AmHI, BAS, BrHumI, C&CSA, C10, CA, CCME, DIP, E01, ESPM, H07, HistAb, I02, I13, IBR, IBSS, IBZ, LID&ISL, LeftInd, P02, P10, P42, P47, P48, P53, P54, PCI, PQC, PSA, RASB, RiskAb, S02, S03, S11, SCOPUS, SOPODA, SociolAb, T02.
—IE, Infotrieve, Ingenta. **CCC.**
Published by: Routledge (Subsidiary of: Taylor & Francis Group), 4 Park Sq, Milton Park, Abingdon, Oxon OX14 4RN, United Kingdom. TEL 44-20-70176000, FAX 44-20-70176336, subscriptions@tandf.co.uk, http://www.routledge.com. Eds. Loch K Johnson TEL 706-542-6705, Peter Jackson TEL 44-1970-621771. Adv. contact Linda Hann TEL 44-1344-779945. **Subscr. to:** Taylor & Francis Ltd., Journals Customer Service, Sheepen Pl, Colchester, Essex CO3 3LP, United Kingdom. TEL 44-20-70175544, FAX 44-20-70175198.

327 FRA ISSN 1765-582X
INTELLIGENCE & STRATEGIE; la lettre professionelle d'actualite geostrategique. Text in French. 2004. m. (11/yr.). EUR 120 to individuals; EUR 240 to institutions (effective 2009). **Document type:** *Newsletter, Trade.*
Published by: Intelligence et Strategie, 5 Rue Claude Pouillet, Paris, 75017, France.

327 USA ISSN 0094-5072
THE INTERDEPENDENT. Text in English. 1974. q. free to members (effective 2011). adv. illus. **Document type:** *Newspaper, Government.* **Description:** Covers world affairs and features news and analysis of global issues shaping international politics not found in the mainstream media.
Supersedes (in 1974): United Nations Association. Vista (0042-711X); Which was formerly (until 1965): U N A News
Related titles: Online - full text ed.: free (effective 2011).
Indexed: HistAb, P06, PAIS, PRA.
Published by: United Nations Association of the United States of America & the Business Council for the United Nations, 801 Second Ave, New York, NY 10017. TEL 212-907-1300, FAX 212-682-9185, inquiries@un.org, http://www.unausa.org.

327 ITA ISSN 2039-8573
▼ ➤ **INTERDISCIPLINARY POLITICAL STUDIES.** Text in English. 2011. 3/yr. free (effective 2011). **Document type:** *Journal, Academic/Scholarly.*
Media: Online - full text.
Published by: (Universita degli Studi di Siena, Graduate School in Comparative and European Politics), Universita degli Studi di Trento, School of International Studies, Via Verdi 10, Trent, 38122, Italy. TEL 39-0461-283150, FAX 39-0461-283152. Eds. Nelli Babayan, Stefano Braghiroli.

327.17 DEU ISSN 0934-1668
INTERDISZIPLINAERE EUROPA STUDIEN. Text in German. 2000. irreg., latest vol.4, 2007. price varies. **Document type:** *Monographic series, Academic/Scholarly.*
Published by: Peter Lang GmbH (Subsidiary of: Peter Lang Publishing Group), Eschborner Landstr 42-50, Frankfurt Am Main, 60489, Germany. TEL 49-69-7807050, FAX 49-69-78070550, 49-69-78070550, zentrale.frankfurt@peterlang.com.

320 330 RUS
INTERFAX. RUSSIA & C I S DIPLOMATIC PANORAMA. (Commonwealth of Independent States) Text in English. d. price varies. **Document type:** *Bulletin, Trade.* **Description:** Provides news from the executive offices and governments in Russia, the CIS and the Baltic countries.
Formerly: Interfax. Diplomatic Panorama (1072-2688)
Related titles: Online - full text ed.; Russian ed.
Indexed: A15, P48, P51, R01.
Published by: Interfax Ltd., 1-ya Tverskaya-Yamskaya, dom 2, stroenie 1, Moscow, 127006, Russian Federation. TEL 7-095-2509840, FAX 7-095-2509727, info@interfax.ru, http://www.interfax.ru. **Dist. elsewhere by:** Interfax America, Inc., 3025 S Parker Rd, Ste 737, Aurora, CO 80014. TEL 303-368-1421, FAX 303-368-1458, http://www.interfax.com; **Dist. in Germany, Austria and Switzerland by:** Interfax Deutschland GmbH, 54, Taunusstrasse, Frankfurt 61476, Germany. TEL 49-6171-695750, FAX 49-6171-989995; **Dist. in Western Europe by:** Interfax Europe Ltd., 2-3 Philpot Lane, 3rd Fl, London EC3M 8AQ, United Kingdom. TEL 44-20-76210595, FAX 44-20-79294263.

327 NOR ISSN 0020-577X
D839
➤ **INTERNASJONAL POLITIKK.** Text in Norwegian; Summaries in English. 1937. q. NOK 400 to individuals; NOK 550 to institutions; NOK 270 to students (effective 2010). adv. bk.rev. charts; stat. cum.index. back issues avail.; reprints avail. **Document type:** *Journal, Academic/Scholarly.*
Related titles: Microform ed.: (from PQC); Online - full text ed.: ISSN 1891-1757. NOK 650 (effective 2010).
Indexed: A20, A22, ABCPolSci, AMB, ASCA, AmH&L, CA, CurCont, HistAb, I13, IBSS, P42, PAIS, PCI, PSA, PerIslam, RASB, SCOPUS, SSCI, SociolAb, T02, W07.
—BLDSC (4534.925000), IE, Ingenta. **CCC.**
Published by: (Norsk Utenrikspolitisk Institutt/Norwegian Institute of International Affairs), Universitetsforlaget AS/Scandinavian University Press (Subsidiary of: Aschehoug & Co.), Sehesteds Gate 3, P O Box 508, Sentrum, Oslo, 0105, Norway. TEL 47-24-147500, FAX 47-24-147501, post@universitetsforlaget.no, http://www.scup.no.

327 GBR ISSN 0960-1503
THE INTERNATIONAL (LONDON, 1990). Text in English. 1990. q. GBP 26 for 6 issues. adv. bk.rev. **Document type:** *Bulletin.*
Related titles: Microform ed.: (from PQC).

Published by: Workers International to Rebuild the Fourth International, PO Box 735, London, SW8 1YB, United Kingdom. TEL 0171-582-8882, FAX 0171-582-8834. Eds. Bob Archer, Bridget Leach. Adv. contact Jill Oxley. Circ: 500.

327 973.7 USA ISSN 1528-7211
E457
➤ **THE INTERNATIONAL ABRAHAM LINCOLN JOURNAL.** Text in English. 2000. a. bk.rev. charts; illus.; maps; tr.lit. 150 p./no.; back issues avail. **Document type:** *Journal, Academic/Scholarly.* **Description:** Focuses on the contemporary or "living Abraham Lincoln" abroad. The journal considers Lincoln's leadership style as one of the greatest gifts to the world of America's experiment with self-government, and the journal aims to preserve the historical legacy of Lincoln.
Published by: International Lincoln Center for American Studies, LSU in Shreveport, 323 Bronson Hall, 1 University Place, Bronsun Hall, Shreveport, LA 71115. TEL 318-797-5138, FAX 318-795-4203, lincoln@lsus.edu, http://www.lsus.edu/lincoln/Site/Home.html.

327 USA ISSN 0130-9641
D839
INTERNATIONAL AFFAIRS; a Russian journal of world politics, diplomacy and international relations. Text in English. 1955. bi-m. USD 571 to institutions; USD 628 combined subscription to institutions (print & online eds.) (effective 2009). adv. bk.rev. charts. Index. back issues avail. **Document type:** *Journal, Government.* **Description:** Contains studies and researches on foreign policy and international relations of Russia; issues of arms race and disarmament; the role of the UN; Russian economic and trade cooperation; and Russian political development.
Related titles: Microfiche ed.: (from EVP); Online - full text ed.: USD 66 to individuals; USD 571 to institutions (effective 2009); ◆ Translation of: Mezhdunarodnaya Zhizn'. ISSN 0130-9625.
Indexed: A01, A02, A03, A08, A22, ABCPolSci, APEL, AmH&L, CA, DIP, HistAb, I02, I08, IBR, IBSS, IBZ, LID&ISL, MAB, MEA&I, P02, P06, P10, P34, P42, P45, P47, P48, P53, P54, PAIS, PQC, PSA, R02, S02, S03, SCOPUS, T02.
—East View, IE, Infotrieve, Ingenta. **CCC.**
Published by: (Ministerstvo Inostrannykh Del Rossiiskoi Federatsii/ Ministry of Foreign Affairs of the Russian Federation RUS), East View Information Services, 10601 Wayzata Blvd, Minneapolis, MN 55305. TEL 952-252-1201, 800-477-1005, FAX 952-252-1202, info@eastview.com, http://www.eastview.com/. Ed. Armen Oganesyan. adv.: page USD 380; trim 5 x 8. Circ: 920 (paid and controlled).

327 GBR ISSN 0020-5850
JX1
➤ **INTERNATIONAL AFFAIRS (LONDON)**; promoting dialogue between academics and policy-makers. Text in English. 1922. bi-m. GBP 378 in United Kingdom to institutions; EUR 481 in Europe to institutions; USD 633 in the Americas to institutions; USD 741 elsewhere to institutions; GBP 434 combined subscription in United Kingdom to institutions (print & online eds.); EUR 553 combined subscription in Europe to institutions (print & online eds.); USD 729 combined subscription in the Americas to institutions (print & online eds.); USD 853 combined subscription elsewhere to institutions (print & online eds.) (effective 2012). adv. bk.rev. illus. index, cum.index. back issues avail.; reprint service avail. from PSC. **Document type:** *Journal, Academic/Scholarly.* **Description:** Provides comprehensive coverage of the latest publications in print and electronic media.
Former titles (until 1944): International Affairs Review Supplement (1473-8112); (until 1940): International Affairs (1473-8104); (until 1931): Royal Institute of International Affairs. Journal (1473-799X); (until 1926): British Institute of International Affairs. Journal (1473-7981)
Related titles: Microform ed.: (from PMC); Online - full text ed.: ISSN 1468-2346. GBP 378 in United Kingdom to institutions; EUR 481 in Europe to institutions; USD 633 in the Americas to institutions; USD 741 elsewhere to institutions (effective 2012) (from IngentaConnect).
Indexed: A01, A02, A03, A08, A20, A22, A25, A26, ABCPolSci, AMB, APEL, AcaI, AmH&L, AmHI, B01, B04, B06, B07, B09, B21, BAS, BRD, BrHumI, CA, CCME, CREJ, CurCont, DIP, E01, E08, E17, EI, ELLIS, ESPM, G06, G07, G08, GeoRef, H07, H09, H10, HistAb, I02, I05, I07, I13, IBR, IBSS, IBZ, KES, LID&ISL, LeftInd, M05, M06, M10, MEA&I, P02, P06, P10, P13, P27, P30, P34, P42, P47, P48, P53, P54, PAIS, PCI, PQC, PRA, PSA, PerIslam, R02, RiskAb, S02, S03, S05, S08, S09, S11, SCOPUS, SPAA, SSAI, SSAb, SSCI, SSI, SociolAb, T02, W03, W04, W07.
—BLDSC (4535.630000), IE, Infotrieve, Ingenta. **CCC.**
Published by: (Royal Institute of International Affairs), Wiley-Blackwell Publishing Ltd. (Subsidiary of: John Wiley & Sons, Inc.), 9600 Garsington Rd, Oxford, OX4 2DQ, United Kingdom. TEL 44-1865-776868, FAX 44-1865-714591, customerservices@blackwellpublishing.com. Ed. Caroline Soper TEL 44-20-79575724. Adv. contact Katy Taylor TEL 44-20-73143662.

➤ **INTERNATIONAL COMMITTEE OF THE RED CROSS. FORUM.** *see* SOCIAL SERVICES AND WELFARE

327 GBR ISSN 1741-4970
THE INTERNATIONAL COMPARATIVE LEGAL GUIDE TO: INTERNATIONAL ARBITRATION (YEAR). Text in English. 2003. a. **Document type:** *Handbook/Manual/Guide, Trade.*
Related titles: Online - full text ed.: free (effective 2009).
Published by: Global Legal Group Ltd., 59 Tanner St, London, SE1 3PL, United Kingdom. TEL 44-207-3670720, FAX 44-207-4075255, http://www.glgroup.co.uk. Pub. Richard Firth TEL 44-207-3670722.

327.1 USA ISSN 1542-0345
JZ6.5
INTERNATIONAL DEBATES; a pro & con monthly. Text in English. 2003. 9/yr. USD 47 (effective 2003). **Document type:** *Journal, Academic/ Scholarly.* **Description:** Features all the latest controversies, pro & con, in the United Nations and other international forums.
Related titles: Online - full text ed.: USD 295 (effective 2010); multi-user access is included as part of Congressional Digest Debates Online.
Indexed: A01, A02, A03, A08, CA, M02, MASUSE, P34, PAIS, T02.
Published by: Congressional Digest Corp., PO Box 240, Boyds, MD 20841-0240. TEL 301-916-1800, 800-637-9915, FAX 240-599-7679, info@congressionaldigest.com, http://www.congressionaldigest.com, http://www.pro-and-con.org. Pub. Page Robinson Thomas.

320 USA ISSN 2155-160X
▼ **INTERNATIONAL DIALOGUE.** Text in English. forthcoming 2011 (Nov.). a. free (effective 2010). **Document type:** *Journal, Academic/ Scholarly.* **Description:** A multidisciplinary journal of world affairs.
Media: Online - full text.
Published by: University of Nebraska at Omaha, Department of Philosophy and Religion, 60th & Dodge Streets, Omaha, NE 68182. TEL 402-554-2628, FAX 402-554-3296, religion@unomaha.edu, http://www.unomaha.edu/wwwphrel/.

327.2 TZA
INTERNATIONAL DIPLOMATIC REVIEW. Text in English. 1987. 2/yr.
Indexed: PLESA.
Published by: Centre for Foreign Relations, PO Box 2824, Dar Es Salaam, Tanzania.

THE INTERNATIONAL HISTORY REVIEW. *see* HISTORY

327 CAN ISSN 0829-321X
➤ **INTERNATIONAL INSIGHTS.** Text in English. 1985. s-a. **Document type:** *Journal, Academic/Scholarly.*
Published by: Dalhousie University, Department of Political Science, Centre for Foreign Policy Studies, Arts & Administration Bldg, Halifax, NS B3H 4H6, Canada. TEL 902-494-3769, FAX 902-494-3825, centre@dal.ca, http://centreforforeignpolicystudies.dal.ca.

327 USA ISSN 0305-0629
JZ6.5 CODEN: INIAAH
➤ **INTERNATIONAL INTERACTIONS**; empirical research in industrial relations. Text in English. 1974. q. GBP 1,150 combined subscription in United Kingdom to institutions (print & online eds.); EUR 1,266, USD 1,591 combined subscription to institutions (print & online eds.) (effective 2012). adv. bk.rev. abstr.; bibl.; charts; illus. index, cum.index. reprint service avail. from PSC. **Document type:** *Journal, Academic/Scholarly.* **Description:** Publishes original empirical, analytic and/or theoretical research in the general field of international relations. The journal has particular interest in research that focuses upon the broad range of relations and interactions among the actors in the global system.
Incorporates (1961-1974): War - Peace Report (0043-0277)
Related titles: Microform ed.; Online - full text ed.: ISSN 1547-7444. GBP 1,035 in United Kingdom to institutions; EUR 1,139, USD 1,432 to institutions (effective 2012) (from IngentaConnect).
Indexed: A01, A03, A08, A20, A22, ASCA, CA, CurCont, E01, FamI, H09, MEA&I, P06, P34, P42, P47, PAIS, PQC, PRA, PSA, RASB, S01, S05, SCOPUS, SSCI, SociolAb, T02, W07.
—IE, Infotrieve, Ingenta. **CCC.**
Published by: Taylor & Francis Inc. (Subsidiary of: Taylor & Francis Group), 325 Chestnut St, Ste 800, Philadelphia, PA 19106. TEL 215-625-2940, 800-354-1420, orders@taylorandfrancis.com, http://www.taylorandfrancis.com. Ed. Paul F Diehl. Adv. contact Linda Hann TEL 44-1344-779945.

327 SVK ISSN 1337-5482
INTERNATIONAL ISSUES & SLOVAK FOREIGN POLICY AFFAIRS. Text in English. 2006. q.
Formed by the merger of (1992-2005): Medzinarodne Otazky (1210-1583); (2000-2005): Slovak Foreign Policy Affairs (1335-6259)
Related titles: Online - full text ed.
Indexed: IBSS, P45, P48, PQC, PSA.
Published by: Slovenska Spolocnost pre Zahranicnu Politiku/Slovak Foreign Policy Association, Panenska 33, Bratislava, 81103, Slovakia. TEL 421-2-54433151, sfpa@sfpa.sk.

327 CAN ISSN 0020-7020
D839
➤ **INTERNATIONAL JOURNAL.** Text in English, French. 1946. q. CAD 46.01 domestic to individuals; USD 43 in United States to individuals; CAD 80.25 domestic to institutions; USD 75 in United States to institutions; CAD 26.95 domestic to students; USD 25 in United States to students; CAD 16 per issue domestic to individuals; CAD 20 per issue domestic to institutions; USD 16, USD 20 per issue in United States to individuals (effective 2004). bk.rev. index. back issues avail.; reprint service avail. from WSH. **Document type:** *Journal, Academic/Scholarly.* **Description:** Devoted to scholarly articles on post-1945 international affairs.
Related titles: Microfilm ed.: (from PQC); Online - full text ed.
Indexed: A20, A22, A26, ABCPolSci, ABS&EES, AMB, AmH&L, BAS, BusI, C03, CA, CBCARef, CBPI, CPerI, CurCont, DIP, E08, G08, HistAb, I05, I13, IBR, IBSS, IBZ, ILD, LID&ISL, M10, MAB, MEA&I, P06, P10, P30, P34, P42, P45, P48, PCI, PQC, PRA, PSA, RASB, S02, S03, S09, SCOPUS, SSCI, SociolAb, T02, W07.
—BLDSC (4541.450000), CIS, IE, Infotrieve, Ingenta. **CCC.**
Published by: Canadian Institute of International Affairs, 205 Richmond St West, Ste 302, Toronto, ON M5V 1V3, Canada. TEL 416-977-9000, 800-668-2442, FAX 416-977-7521, mailbox@ciia.org. Eds. Margaret MacMillan, Norman Hillmer. R&P Michelle McAlear. Circ: 1,500.

▼ ➤ **INTERNATIONAL JOURNAL OF BORDER SECURITY AND IMMIGRATION POLICY.** *see* LAW—Constitutional Law

▼ ➤ **INTERNATIONAL JOURNAL OF CHINA STUDIES.** *see* ETHNIC INTERESTS

327 SGP ISSN 2010-2690
▼ **INTERNATIONAL JOURNAL OF DEVELOPMENT AND CONFLICT.** Text in English. 2011. 3/yr. SGD 482 combined subscription domestic to institutions (print & online eds.); EUR 264 combined subscription in Europe to institutions (print & online eds.); USD 311 combined subscription elsewhere to institutions (print & online eds.) (effective 2012). **Document type:** *Journal, Academic/Scholarly.*
Related titles: Online - full text ed.: ISSN 2010-2704. SGD 438 domestic to institutions; EUR 240 in Europe to institutions; USD 283 elsewhere to institutions (effective 2012).
Published by: World Scientific Publishing Co. Pte. Ltd., 5 Toh Tuck Link, Singapore, 596224, Singapore. TEL 65-6466-5775, FAX 65-6467-7667, wspc@wspc.com.sg, http://www.worldscientific.com. **Subscr. to:** Farrer Rd, PO Box 128, Singapore 912805, Singapore. **Dist. by:** World Scientific Publishing Ltd., 57 Shelton St, London WC2H 9HE, United Kingdom. TEL 44-207-8360888, FAX 44-207-8362020, sales@wspc.co.uk.; World Scientific Publishing Co., Inc., 27 Warren St, Ste 401-402, Hackensack, NJ 07601. TEL 201-487-9655, 800-227-7562, FAX 201-487-9656, 888-977-2665.

327 GBR ISSN 1446-8956
➤ **INTERNATIONAL JOURNAL OF DEVELOPMENT ISSUES.** Text in English. 2002. 3/yr. EUR 209 combined subscription in Europe (print & online eds.); USD 299 combined subscription in the Americas (print & online eds.); GBP 149 combined subscription in the UK & elsewhere (print & online eds.); AUD 339 combined subscription in Australasia (print & online eds.) (effective 2012). reprint service avail. from PSC. **Document type:** *Journal, Academic/Scholarly.* **Description:** Covers the inter-disciplinary research in development issues, including critical analysis from multiple viewpoints.
Related titles: Online - full text ed.: (from IngentaConnect).
Indexed: CABA, EconLit, GH, JEL, LT, N02, R12, TAR, W11.
—BLDSC (4542.185025), IE. **CCC.**
Published by: (University of Sydney, Faculty of Economics and Business AUS), Emerald Group Publishing Ltd., Howard House, Wagon Ln, Bingley, W Yorks BD16 1WA, United Kingdom. TEL 44-1274-777700, information@emeraldinsight.com. Ed. Dilip Dutta.

327.12 USA ISSN 0885-0607
UB250
➤ **INTERNATIONAL JOURNAL OF INTELLIGENCE AND COUNTERINTELLIGENCE.** Text in English. 1986. q. GBP 232 combined subscription in United Kingdom to institutions (print & online eds.); EUR 309, USD 388 combined subscription to institutions (print & online eds.) (effective 2012). adv. illus. back issues avail.; reprint service avail. from PSC. **Document type:** *Journal, Academic/ Scholarly.* **Description:** Designed to serve as a medium for professionals and scholars to exchange opinions on issues and challenges encountered by both the government and business institutions in making contemporary intelligence-related decisions and policy.
Related titles: Online - full text ed.: ISSN 1521-0561. GBP 209 in United Kingdom to institutions; EUR 278, USD 349 to institutions (effective 2012) (from IngentaConnect).
Indexed: A22, AmH&L, CA, CJA, E01, ESPM, HistAb, I02, P26, P34, P42, P47, P54, PAIS, PCI, PQC, PSA, RiskAb, S02, S03, SCOPUS, T02.
—IE, Infotrieve, Ingenta. **CCC.**
Published by: Taylor & Francis Inc. (Subsidiary of: Taylor & Francis Group), 325 Chestnut St, Ste 800, Philadelphia, PA 19106. TEL 215-625-8900, 800-354-1420, FAX 215-625- 8914, orders@taylorandfrancis.com, http://www.taylorandfrancis.com. Ed. Richard R Valcourt. **Subscr. outside N. America to:** Taylor & Francis Ltd., Journals Customer Service, Sheepen Pl, Colchester, Essex CO3 3LP, United Kingdom. TEL 44-20-70175544, FAX 44-20-70175198, tf.enquiries@tfinforma.com.

327.17 170 363.35 USA ISSN 2151-2868
JF1525.I6
▼ ➤ **INTERNATIONAL JOURNAL OF INTELLIGENCE ETHICS.** Text in English. 2009. s-a. USD 60 to individuals; USD 90 to institutions (effective 2010). **Document type:** *Journal, Academic/Scholarly.* **Description:** Features research on the role of ethics in intelligence activities, from both a national security and law enforcement perspective.
Published by: (International Intelligence Ethics Association), Scarecrow Press, Inc. (Subsidiary of: Rowman & Littlefield Publishers, Inc.), 4501 Forbes Blvd, Ste 200, Lanham, MD 20706. TEL 301-459-3366, FAX 301-429-5748, custserv@rowman.com.

327.172 NGA
➤ **INTERNATIONAL JOURNAL OF PEACE AND DEVELOPMENT STUDIES.** Text in English. m. free (effective 2010). adv. **Document type:** *Journal, Academic/Scholarly.*
Media: Online - full text.
Published by: Academic Journals, PO Box 73023, Victoria Island, Lagos, Nigeria. service@academicjournals.org.

327 USA ISSN 0891-4486
JA76 CODEN: ICSOE2
➤ **INTERNATIONAL JOURNAL OF POLITICS, CULTURE, AND SOCIETY.** Text in English. 1984. q. EUR 967, USD 1,026 combined subscription to institutions (print & online eds.) (effective 2012). adv. bk.rev. illus. Index. back issues avail.; reprint service avail. from PSC. **Document type:** *Journal, Academic/Scholarly.* **Description:** Provides a forum for discussion, dialogue and debate on points of tension between state and civil society, between nations and global institutions.
Formerly (until 1987): State, Culture, and Society (0743-9245)
Related titles: Microfilm ed.: (from PQC); Online - full text ed.: ISSN 1573-3416 (from IngentaConnect).
Indexed: A01, A03, A08, A22, A26, AmH&L, BibLing, CA, E01, ESPM, HPNRM, I13, IBSS, P10, P27, P34, P42, P45, P46, P48, P53, P54, PAIS, PQC, PSA, RiskAb, S02, S03, S11, SOPODA, SPAA, SSA, SSciA, SWR&A, SociolAb, T02.
—BLDSC (4542.473000), IE, Infotrieve, Ingenta. **CCC.**
Published by: (Florida Atlantic University), Springer New York LLC (Subsidiary of: Springer Science+Business Media), 233 Spring St, New York, NY 10013. TEL 212-460-1500, FAX 212-460-1575, service-ny@springer.com. Eds. Elzbieta Matynia, Jeffrey Goldfarb, Vera Zolberg.

325.21 GBR ISSN 0953-8186
K9
➤ **INTERNATIONAL JOURNAL OF REFUGEE LAW.** Text in English. 1989. q. GBP 259 in United Kingdom to institutions; EUR 387 in Europe to institutions; USD 516 in US & Canada to institutions; GBP 259 elsewhere to institutions; GBP 282 combined subscription in United Kingdom to institutions (print & online eds.); EUR 422 combined subscription in Europe to institutions (print & online eds.); USD 563 combined subscription in US & Canada to institutions (print & online eds.); GBP 282 combined subscription elsewhere to institutions (print & online eds.) (effective 2012). adv. bk.rev. index. back issues avail.; reprint service avail. from PSC,WSH. **Document type:** *Journal, Academic/Scholarly.* **Description:** Aims to stimulate research and thinking on refugee law and its development.
Related titles: Online - full text ed.: ISSN 1464-3715. GBP 235 in United Kingdom to institutions; EUR 352 in Europe to institutions; USD 469 in US & Canada to institutions; GBP 235 elsewhere to institutions (effective 2012) (from IngentaConnect).
Indexed: A22, A26, B04, BRD, CA, CJPI, CLI, E01, ELJI, ESPM, FamI, G08, GEOBASE, HRIR, I01, I02, I05, ILP, L10, LJI, LRI, P10, P42, P45, P47, P48, P53, P54, PCI, PQC, PRA, PSA, PerIslam, R02, RefugAb, S02, S03, SCOPUS, SPAA, SSciA, SociolAb, T02, W03, W05.

P

—BLDSC (4542.525600), IE, Infotrieve, Ingenta. **CCC.**
Published by: Oxford University Press, Great Clarendon St, Oxford, OX2 6DP, United Kingdom. TEL 44-1865-556767, FAX 44-1865-556646, enquiry@oup.co.uk, http://www.oxfordjournals.org. Ed. Geoff Gilbert. Pub. Nina Curtis. R&P Fiona Bennett.

327 346 IND ISSN 0972-4907
K9
INTERNATIONAL JOURNAL OF REGULATION AND GOVERNANCE. Text in English. 2001. s-a. INR 2,100 combined subscription domestic (print & online eds.) (effective 2011); USD 140 combined subscription in North America (print & online eds.); EUR 122 combined subscription elsewhere (print & online eds.) (effective 2012). **Document type:** *Journal, Academic/Scholarly.* **Description:** Provides a forum for detailed and comprehensive investigation, analysis, and review of such sectors as energy, telecommunications, water, environment, and transport. Aimed at decision-makers, planners, consultants, corporate executives, and researchers.
Related titles: Online - full text ed.: ISSN 1875-8851. INR 1,400 domestic; USD 110 foreign (effective 2011).
Indexed: CA, CABA, E04, E05, E12, GEOBASE, PAIS, R12, S13, S16, SCOPUS, SSciA, T02, TAR, W11.
Published by: Tata Energy Research Institute, Darbari Seth Block, IHC Complex, Lodhi Rd, New Delhi, 110 003, India. TEL 91-11-24682100, FAX 91-11-24682144, mailbox@teri.res.in, http://www.teriin.org. Ed. Leena Srivastava. **Dist. by:** I O S Press, Nieuwe Hemweg 6B, Amsterdam 1013 BG, Netherlands. TEL 31-20-6883355, FAX 31-20-6203419.

327.117 USA ISSN 1932-7889
HV6431
INTERNATIONAL JOURNAL OF TERRORISM AND POLITICAL HOT SPOTS. Text in English. q. USD 450 to institutions (effective 2012). **Document type:** *Journal, Academic/Scholarly.* **Description:** Brings together the most important analysis of the new war of the 21st century. Topics covered include: bioterrorism, chemical terrorism, weapons of mass destruction, aviation security, cyberwarfare and agroterrorism.
Related titles: Online - full text ed.
Indexed: CA, I02, T02.
Published by: Nova Science Publishers, Inc., 400 Oser Ave, Ste 1600, Hauppauge, NY 11788. TEL 631-231-7269, FAX 631-231-8175, main@novapublishers.com.

327.172 USA ISSN 0742-3640
➤ **INTERNATIONAL JOURNAL ON WORLD PEACE.** Abbreviated title: I J W P. Text in English. 1984. q. USD 25 to individuals; USD 35 to libraries (effective 2010). bk.rev. illus. index. back issues avail.; reprints avail. **Document type:** *Journal, Academic/Scholarly.* **Description:** Discusses all aspects of world peace. Theory, practice, qualitative and quantitative, past, present and future. International debate is emphasized.
Related titles: Microform ed.: (from PQC); Online - full text ed.
Indexed: A01, A02, A03, A08, A20, A22, A26, CA, CWI, DIP, E08, G06, G07, G08, I02, I05, IBR, IBZ, KES, M06, P02, P10, P34, P42, P45, P47, P48, P53, P54, PAIS, PQC, PRA, PSA, Perlslam, PsycholAb, RASB, S02, S03, S09, S11, SOPODA, SSA, SWR&A, SociolAb, T02, WBA, WMB.
—BLDSC (4542.701900), IE, Infotrieve, Ingenta.
Published by: Professors World Peace Academy, 1925 Oakcrest Ave, Ste 7, Saint Paul, MN 55113. http://www.pwpa.org. Ed. Gordon L Anderson. **Subscr. to:** IJWP.

➤ **INTERNATIONAL LAW NEWS.** *see* LAW—International Law

➤ **INTERNATIONAL LAW REPORTS.** *see* LAW—International Law

➤ **INTERNATIONAL LEADS.** *see* LIBRARY AND INFORMATION SCIENCES

327 GBR
INTERNATIONAL LIBRARY OF WAR STUDIES. Text in English. 2004. irreg., latest 2009. price varies. back issues avail. **Document type:** *Monographic series, Academic/Scholarly.*
Published by: I B Tauris & Co. Ltd., 6 Salem Rd, London, W2 4BU, United Kingdom. TEL 44-20-72431225, FAX 44-20-72431226.

341 NLD ISSN 1382-340X
JZ6045 CODEN: INEGFK
➤ **INTERNATIONAL NEGOTIATION;** a journal of theory and practice. Text in English. 1996. 3/yr. EUR 339, USD 474 to institutions; EUR 369, USD 517 combined subscription to institutions (print & online eds.) (effective 2012). back issues avail.; reprint service avail. from PSC. **Document type:** *Journal, Academic/Scholarly.* **Description:** Addresses the processes of negotiation relating to political, security, environmental, ethnic, economic, business, legal, scientific and cultural issues and conflicts among nations, international and regional organisations, multinational corporations and other non-state parties.
Related titles: Microform ed.: (from PQC); Online - full text ed.: ISSN 1571-8069. EUR 308, USD 431 to institutions (effective 2012) (from IngentaConnect).
Indexed: A01, A03, A08, A12, A17, A22, ABIn, B01, B06, B07, B09, CA, E01, I13, IBSS, IZBG, P34, P42, P48, P51, P53, P54, PQC, PRA, PSA, S02, S03, SCOPUS, SociolAb, T02.
—BLDSC (4544.419000), IE, Infotrieve, Ingenta. **CCC.**
Published by: Martinus Nijhoff (Subsidiary of: Brill), PO Box 9000, Leiden, 2300 PA, Netherlands. TEL 31-71-5353500, FAX 31-71-5317532, marketing@brill.nl. Ed. Bertram I Spector. **Dist. by:** Turpin Distribution Services Ltd., Pegasus Dr, Stratton Business Park, Biggleswade, Bedfordshire SG18 8QB, United Kingdom. TEL 44-1767-604800, FAX 44-1767-601640, custserv@turpin-distribution.com, http://www.turpin-distribution.com/.

329 658 NLD ISSN 1871-3319
➤ **INTERNATIONAL NEGOTIATION SERIES.** Text in English. 2006. irreg., latest vol.6, 2008. price varies. **Document type:** *Monographic series, Academic/Scholarly.* **Description:** Explores negotiation from many perspectives, explores its theoretical foundations, and promotes its practical application.
Indexed: IZBG.
Published by: Martinus Nijhoff (Subsidiary of: Brill), PO Box 9000, Leiden, 2300 PA, Netherlands. TEL 31-71-5353500, FAX 31-71-5317532, marketing@brill.nl. Eds. Daniel Druckman, William Donohue.

327 USA ISSN 1061-0324
UA10
INTERNATIONAL OBSERVER. Text in English. 1992. m. USD 360 (effective 2007). bk.rev. 20 p./no. 2 cols./p.; back issues avail. **Document type:** *Newsletter, Consumer.* **Description:** Report on international affairs and political, government, security and economic developments in countries around the world. Special attention is given to government changes, elections, domestic conditions and political leaders.
Address: PO Box 5624, Washington, DC 20016. TEL 202-244-7050. Ed., Pub. Joe H Wagner.

327 USA ISSN 1554-2181
D860
INTERNATIONAL OBSERVER POLITICAL REPORT. Text in English. 2005 (Jan.). m.
Published by: International Observer, PO Box 5624, Washington, DC 20016. TEL 202-244-7050, FAX 202-244-5410, http://www.theinternationalobserver.com. Ed. J H Wagner.

327.06 340 GBR ISSN 0020-8183
CODEN: IOCMFZ
➤ **INTERNATIONAL ORGANIZATION.** Text in English. 1947. q. GBP 154, USD 257 to institutions; GBP 167, USD 273 combined subscription to institutions (print & online eds.) (effective 2012). adv. bk.rev. bibl.; charts; illus. index. 200 p./no.; back issues avail.; reprint service avail. from PSC. **Document type:** *Journal, Academic/Scholarly.* **Description:** Contains articles on various aspects of international and regional organizations, international politics and economics.
Related titles: Microform ed.: (from PQC); Online - full text ed.: ISSN 1531-5088. GBP 143, USD 228 to institutions (effective 2012).
Indexed: A12, A17, A20, A22, A26, ABIn, ABS&EES, ASCA, AmH&L, B01, B02, B04, B06, B07, B08, B09, B15, B17, B18, BAS, BRD, C12, CA, CLI, CurCont, DIP, E01, E08, ESPM, EconLit, FR, FutSurv, G04, G08, H09, HRIR, HistAb, I02, I03, I05, I13, IBR, IBSS, IBZ, IBibSS, ILD, IPARL, JEL, KES, LRI, M05, M06, M10, MEA&I, P02, P03, P06, P10, P13, P27, P30, P34, P42, P45, P47, P48, P51, P53, P54, PAIS, PCI, PQC, PRA, PSA, PsycInfo, PsycholAb, RASB, RiskAb, S02, S03, S05, S09, S11, SCIMP, SCOPUS, SOPODA, SSA, SSAI, SSAb, SSCI, SSI, SociolAb, T02, W03, W05, W07.
—BLDSC (4544.850000), IE, Infotrieve, Ingenta. **CCC.**
Published by: (Munk Centre for International Studies CAN), Cambridge University Press, The Edinburgh Bldg, Shaftesbury Rd, Cambridge, CB2 8RU, United Kingdom. TEL 44-1223-312393, FAX 44-1223-315052, journals@cambridge.org, http://www.cambridge.org/uk. Eds. Emanuel Adler, Louis W Pauly. **Subscr. in N. America to:** Cambridge University Press, 32 Ave of the Americas, New York, NY 10013. TEL 212-337-5000, FAX 212-691-3239, journals_subscriptions@cup.org.

327.172 CHE
JX1901
INTERNATIONAL PEACE UPDATE. Abbreviated title: I P U. Text in English. 1925. bi-m. CHF 20, USD 15 (effective 2001). adv. bk.rev. **Document type:** *Newsletter.* **Description:** Analyzes economic, social, political and military developments and trends with a focus on women.
Formerly (until 1995): Pax et Libertas (0031-3327)
Media: Duplicated (not offset). **Related titles:** Online - full text ed.
Indexed: CWI, G05, G07, PRA, Perlslam.
—CIS.
Published by: Women's International League for Peace and Freedom, 1 rue Varembe, Geneva 20, 1211, Switzerland. TEL 41-22-9197080, FAX 41-22-9197081, wilpf@iprolink.ch, http://www.wilpf.int.ch. Ed., R&P Barbara Lochbihler. Circ: 2,000.

327.172 GBR ISSN 1353-3312
JX1981.P7
➤ **INTERNATIONAL PEACEKEEPING.** Text in English. 1994. 5/yr. GBP 446 combined subscription in United Kingdom to institutions (print & online eds.); EUR 590, USD 739 combined subscription to institutions (print & online eds.) (effective 2012). adv. bk.rev. illus. index. back issues avail.; reprint service avail. from PSC. **Document type:** *Journal, Academic/Scholarly.* **Description:** Covers the history and practice of peacekeeping and reflects the principle that peacekeeping is essentially a political art in which military forces are the instruments of policy at an international level.
Related titles: Online - full text ed.: ISSN 1743-906X. GBP 401 in United Kingdom to institutions; EUR 530, USD 666 to institutions (effective 2012) (from IngentaConnect).
Indexed: A01, A03, A08, A22, AmH&L, CA, CCME, E01, ESPM, HistAb, I02, I13, IBSS, LID&ISL, M05, M10, P02, P10, P30, P34, P42, P47, P48, P53, P54, PAIS, PQC, PRA, PSA, RiskAb, S02, S03, S11, SCOPUS, SociolAb, T02, V&AA.
—IE, Ingenta. **CCC.**
Published by: Taylor & Francis Ltd. (Subsidiary of: Taylor & Francis Group), 4 Park Sq, Milton Park, Abingdon, Oxfordshire OX14 4RN, United Kingdom. Ed. Michael Pugh.

327 USA ISSN 0738-6508
JX1
INTERNATIONAL POLICY REPORT. Text in English, Spanish. 1975. irreg. looseleaf. USD 2.50 per issue (effective 2011). adv. back issues avail. **Document type:** *Report, Trade.* **Description:** Reports on US policy towards the Third World and its impact on human rights and human needs.
Related titles: Online - full text ed.: free (effective 2011).
Indexed: HRIR.
Published by: Center for International Policy, 1717 Massachusetts Ave NW, Suite 801, Washington, DC 20036. TEL 202-232-3317, FAX 202-232-3440, cip@ciponline.org.

327 USA ISSN 1088-7326
K9 CODEN: IPREFP
INTERNATIONAL POLICY REVIEW. Text in English. 199?. irreg.
Indexed: B07, CA, EconLit, JEL, SCOPUS, SociolAb, T02.
Published by: Concordia College, 901 S Eighth St, Moorhead, MN 56562. TEL 218-299-4000, FAX 218-299-3646.

327 USA ISSN 8755-8335
HF1410
INTERNATIONAL POLITICAL ECONOMY YEARBOOK. Text in English. 1985. a., latest vol.17. price varies. **Document type:** *Monographic series, Academic/Scholarly.*
Indexed: RASB.
—BLDSC (4544.958500). **CCC.**

Published by: Lynne Rienner Publishers, 1800 30th St, Ste 314, Boulder, CO 80301. TEL 303-444-6684, FAX 303-444-0824, http://www.rienner.com.

INTERNATIONAL POLITICAL SCIENCE ABSTRACTS/ DOCUMENTATION POLITIQUE INTERNATIONALE. *see* POLITICAL SCIENCE—Abstracting, Bibliographies, Statistics

327 GBR ISSN 0192-5121
JA1.A1
➤ **INTERNATIONAL POLITICAL SCIENCE REVIEW/REVUE INTERNATIONALE DE SCIENCE POLITIQUE.** Abbreviated title: I P S R - R I S P. Text in English, French. 1980. 5/yr. GBP 389, USD 705 to institutions; GBP 381, USD 719 combined subscription to institutions (print & online eds.) (effective 2012). abstr.; illus. index. back issues avail.; reprint service avail. from PSC. **Document type:** *Journal, Academic/Scholarly.* **Description:** Creates and disseminates rigorous political enquiry free of any subdisciplinary or other orthodoxy.
Related titles: Microfilm ed.: (from PMC, WSH); Microform ed.: (from PQC); Online - full text ed.: ISSN 1460-373X. GBP 350, USD 647 to institutions (effective 2012).
Indexed: A01, A02, A03, A08, A20, A22, A26, ABCPolSci, ASCA, B04, B07, BAS, BRD, CA, CurCont, DIP, E01, E08, ESPM, G08, I05, I13, I14, IBR, IBSS, IBZ, MEA&I, P02, P10, P27, P34, P42, P47, P48, P53, P54, PAA&I, PAIS, PCI, PQC, PRA, PSA, Perlslam, RASB, S02, S03, S09, S11, SCOPUS, SPAA, SSA, SSAI, SSAb, SSCI, SSI, SSciA, SociolAb, T02, W03, W07.
—BLDSC (4544.965200), IE, Infotrieve, Ingenta, INIST. **CCC.**
Published by: (Association Internationale de Science Politique - International Political Science Association (A I S P - I P S A) CAN), Sage Publications Ltd. (Subsidiary of: Sage Publications, Inc.), 1 Oliver's Yard, 55 City Rd, London, EC1Y 1SP, United Kingdom. TEL 44-20-73248500, FAX 44-20-73248600, info@sagepub.co.uk, http://www.uk.sagepub.com/home.nav. Eds. Mark Kesselman, Yvonne Galligan. **Subscr. in the Americas to:** Sage Publications, Inc., 2455 Teller Rd, Thousand Oaks, CA 91320. TEL 805-499-9774, FAX 805-499-0871, journals@sagepub.com.

327 GBR ISSN 1384-5748
H1 CODEN: INPOFV
➤ **INTERNATIONAL POLITICS.** Abbreviated title: I P. Text and summaries in English. 1963. bi-m. USD 971 in North America to institutions; GBP 521 elsewhere to institutions (effective 2011). adv. bk.rev. index. back issues avail.; reprint service avail. from PSC. **Document type:** *Journal, Academic/Scholarly.* **Description:** Dedicated to transnational issues and global problems.
Formerly (until 1996): Co-Existence (0587-5994)
Related titles: Microfiche ed.: (from WSH); Microform ed.: (from PQC); Online - full text ed.: ISSN 1740-3898 (from IngentaConnect).
Indexed: A20, A22, ABCPolSci, ABS&EES, AmH&L, BAS, CA, CurCont, DIP, E01, GEOBASE, HistAb, I13, IBR, IBSS, IBZ, IPARL, MEA&I, P02, P06, P10, P13, P27, P30, P34, P42, P45, P47, P48, P53, P54, PQC, PSA, RASB, S02, S03, S11, SCOPUS, SOPODA, SSA, SSCI, SociolAb, T02, W07.
—BLDSC (4544.965250), IE, Infotrieve, Ingenta. **CCC.**
Published by: Palgrave Macmillan Ltd. (Subsidiary of: Macmillan Publishers Ltd.), Houndmills, Basingstoke, Hants RG21 6XS, United Kingdom. TEL 44-1256-329242, FAX 44-1256-479476, orders@palgrave.com, http://www.palgrave.com. Ed. Michael Cox. Pub. Guy Edwards. Circ: 450. **Subscr. to:** Subscription Department, Brunel Rd, Houndmills, Basingstoke, Hants RG21 2XS, United Kingdom. TEL 44-1256-357893, FAX 44-1256-328339, subscriptions@palgrave.com.

327 GBR ISSN 1741-7996
INTERNATIONAL POLITICS OF THE MIDDLE EAST SERIES. Text in English. 1995. irreg., latest 1999. price varies. back issues avail. **Document type:** *Monographic series, Academic/Scholarly.* **Description:** Covers twentieth century Middle Eastern history and international relations between countries in the region.
—CCC.
Published by: Ithaca Press (Subsidiary of: Garnet Publishing), 8 Southern Ct, South St, Reading, Berks RG1 4QS, United Kingdom. TEL 44-118-9597847, FAX 44-118-9597356, http://www.ithacapress.co.uk. **Dist. in the US by:** Information Specialized Book Services Inc.

INTERNATIONAL PRACTITIONERS' WORKSHOP SERIES. *see* LAW—International Law

327 CAN ISSN 0269-0357
HM263 CODEN: IPRRET
➤ **INTERNATIONAL PUBLIC RELATIONS REVIEW.** Text in English. 1976. q. GBP 30 (effective 1998). adv. bk.rev. back issues avail. **Document type:** *Journal, Academic/Scholarly.* **Description:** Serves as a forum for discussing international public relations at the senior executive level, from a variety of perspectives. Examines the history, evolution and current state of the profession and analyzes current events from a public relations perspective.
Formerly (until 1986): I P R A Review (0142-7067)
Indexed: A22, ADPA, BPIA, IBR, IBZ.
—IE, Ingenta. **CCC.**
Published by: International Public Relations Association, Ste 1007, South Tower, 175 Bloor St E, Toronto, ON M4W 3R8, Canada. TEL 416-968-7311, FAX 416-968-6281, rargyle@argylecomm.com. Ed. Raymond Argyle. Circ: 1,300.

327 GBR ISSN 0047-1178
JZ6.5
➤ **INTERNATIONAL RELATIONS.** Abbreviated title: I R. Text in English. 1954. q. GBP 430, USD 796 to institutions; GBP 439, USD 812 combined subscription to institutions (print & online eds.) (effective 2012). bk.rev. back issues avail.; reprint service avail. from PSC. **Document type:** *Journal, Academic/Scholarly.* **Description:** Seeks to advance and promote the development of international relations in all its aspects and to carry out and instigate research and study in this field.
Related titles: Online - full text ed.: ISSN 1741-2862. GBP 395, USD 731 to institutions (effective 2012).
Indexed: A01, A03, A08, A22, ABCPolSci, B21, BAS, CA, CMM, CurCont, DIP, E01, ELJI, ESPM, HPNRM, I13, I14, IBR, IBSS, IBZ, LJI, LeftInd, MAB, P06, P34, P42, PAIS, PCI, PRA, PSA, RiskAb, S02, S03, SCOPUS, SSCI, SSciA, SociolAb, T02, VirolAbstr, W07.
—BLDSC (4545.820000), IE, Ingenta. **CCC.**

Published by: (David Davies Memorial Institute of International Studies), Sage Publications Ltd. (Subsidiary of: Sage Publications, Inc.), 1 Oliver's Yard, 55 City Rd, London, EC1Y 1SP, United Kingdom. TEL 44-20-73248500, FAX 44-20-73248600, info@sagepub.co.uk, http://www.uk.sagepub.com/home.nav. Eds. Ken Booth, Michael Foley. **Subscr. in the Americas to:** Sage Publications, Inc., 2455 Teller Rd, Thousand Oaks, CA 91320. TEL 805-499-9774, FAX 805-499-0871, journals@sagepub.com.

327.9 GBR ISSN 1470-482X
JZ6.5

➤ **INTERNATIONAL RELATIONS OF THE ASIA-PACIFIC.** Text in English. 2001. 3/yr. GBP 238 in United Kingdom to institutions; EUR 356 in Europe to institutions; USD 476 in US & Canada to institutions; GBP 238 elsewhere to institutions; GBP 259 combined subscription in United Kingdom to institutions (print & online eds.); EUR 389 combined subscription in Europe to institutions (print & online eds.); USD 520 combined subscription in US & Canada to institutions (print & online eds.); GBP 259 combined subscription elsewhere to institutions (print & online eds.) (effective 2012). adv. bk.rev. back issues avail.; reprint service avail. from PSC. **Document type:** *Journal, Academic/Scholarly.* **Description:** Aims to bring outstanding general scholarship in international relations to readers in the Asia-Pacific and to provide a dedicated outlet for scholars working on the international relations of the region. Focuses on the relations between countries with the region; the relations between it and the rest of the world; and general issues and theories bearing on one or more countries of the Asia-Pacific.
Related titles: Online - full text ed.: ISSN 1470-4838. 2001. GBP 216 in United Kingdom to institutions; EUR 324 in Europe to institutions; USD 433 in US & Canada to institutions; GBP 216 elsewhere to institutions (effective 2012) (from IngentaConnect).
Indexed: A01, A03, A08, A22, CA, E01, I08, I13, IBSS, P10, P42, P45, P47, P48, P53, P54, PQC, PSA, SCOPUS, SSCI, SociolAb, T02, W07.
—BLDSC (4545.820250), IE, Infotrieve, Ingenta. **CCC.**
Published by: (Japan Association of International Relations JPN), Oxford University Press, Great Clarendon St, Oxford, OX2 6DP, United Kingdom. TEL 44-1865-556767, FAX 44-1865-556646, enquiry@oup.co.uk, http://www.oxfordjournals.org. Eds. G John Ikenberry, Yoshihide Soeya TEL 81-3-5427-1640.

327.1029 GBR
INTERNATIONAL RELATIONS RESEARCH DIRECTORY. Text in English. 1995. irreg., latest 1995, 1st ed. USD 380 per issue (effective 2009). reprints avail. **Document type:** *Directory, Trade.* **Description:** Lists major research institutes worldwide concerned with international relations. Enumerates journals and periodicals in the field.
Published by: Routledge (Subsidiary of: Taylor & Francis Group), 2 Park Sq, Milton Park, Abingdon, Oxon OX14 4RN, United Kingdom. TEL 44-20-70176000, FAX 44-20-70176699, orders@taylorandfrancis.com.

327 USA ISSN 2151-738X
▼ ➤ **THE INTERNATIONAL RELATIONS REVIEW.** Text in English. 2009. q. free per issue (effective 2010). **Document type:** *Journal, Academic/Scholarly.* **Description:** Features essays on international relations published, written, and edited by the undergraduate students of Boston University.
Related titles: Online - full text ed.: ISSN 2151-7398. 2010.
Published by: Boston University, Center for International Relations, 154 Bay State Rd, Boston, MA 02215. TEL 617-358-0914, FAX 617-353-9290, bacevich@bu.edu, http://www.bu.edu/ir/cir.html.

327 NLD ISSN 1570-6451
INTERNATIONAL RELATIONS STUDIES SERIES. Text in English. 2006. irreg., latest vol.2, 2008. EUR 99, USD 139 per vol. (effective 2008). **Document type:** *Monographic series, Academic/Scholarly.*
Indexed: IZBG.
Published by: Martinus Nijhoff (Subsidiary of: Brill), PO Box 9000, Leiden, 2300 PA, Netherlands. TEL 31-71-5353500, FAX 31-71-5317532, marketing@brill.nl.

341.72 USA ISSN 0162-2889
JX1901
➤ **INTERNATIONAL SECURITY.** Abbreviated title: I S. Text in English. 1976. q. USD 257 combined subscription in US & Canada to institutions (print & online eds.); USD 64 per issue in US & Canada to institutions (effective 2012). adv. illus. back issues avail.; reprints avail. **Document type:** *Journal, Academic/Scholarly.* **Description:** Publishes essays on all aspects of the control and use of force from all political viewpoints. Articles cover contemporary policy issues, probing the historical and theoretical and questions behind them.
Related titles: Microform ed.: (from PQC); Online - full text ed.: ISSN 1531-4804. USD 221 in US & Canada to institutions (effective 2012).
Indexed: A01, A20, A22, A26, ABCPolSci, ABS&EES, AMB, ASCA, AUNI, AmH&L, BAS, BRD, CA, CurCont, DIP, DM&T, E01, E08, ESPM, FutSurv, G05, G06, G07, G08, HistAb, I02, I05, I13, I14, IBR, IBSS, IBZ, IPARL, LID&ISL, M05, M06, M07, MEA&I, P02, P06, P10, P27, P30, P42, P47, P48, P53, P54, PAIS, PCI, PQC, PRA, PSA, R02, RASB, RiskAb, S02, S03, S09, S11, SCOPUS, SSAI, SSAb, SSCI, SSI, SociolAb, T02, W03, W05, W07.
—BLDSC (4548.895500), IE, Infotrieve. **CCC.**
Published by: (Harvard University, Harvard University, John F. Kennedy School of Government. Belfer Center for Science and International Affairs. Program on Intrastate Conflict), M I T Press, 55 Hayward St, Cambridge, MA 02142. TEL 617-253-5646, FAX 617-258-6779, journals-info@mit.edu, http://mitpress.mit.edu. Eds. Owen R Cote, Sean M Lynn-Jones TEL 617-495-1463, Steven E Miller TEL 617-495-1411.

341.72 DEU ISSN 1610-529X
INTERNATIONAL SECURITY STUDIES. Text in English, German. 2003. irreg., latest vol.7, 2008. price varies. **Document type:** *Monographic series, Academic/Scholarly.*
Published by: Peter Lang GmbH (Subsidiary of: Peter Lang Publishing Group), Eschborner Landstr 42-50, Frankfurt Am Main, 60489, Germany. TEL 49-69-7807050, FAX 49-69-78070550, zentrale.frankfurt@peterlang.com. Ed. Andrea Riemer.

327 CAN ISSN 0823-1931
INTERNATIONAL SKYLINE. Text in English, French. 1965. q. CAD 650. bk.rev. bibl.
Related titles: Microfiche ed.
Published by: I.S.P. of Canada, 3738 39th Ave W, Vancouver, BC V6N 3A7, Canada. Ed. J Andrew de Lilio Rymsza. Circ: 21,000 (controlled).

327 GBR ISSN 0393-2729
D839
➤ **THE INTERNATIONAL SPECTATOR.** Text in English. 1966. q. GBP 300 combined subscription in United Kingdom to institutions (print & online eds.); EUR 395, USD 496 combined subscription to institutions (print & online eds.) (effective 2012). adv. back issues avail.; reprint service avail. from PSC. **Document type:** *Journal, Academic/Scholarly.* **Description:** Provides in-depth analysis and opinions on topical international issues from an Italian point of view.
Formerly (until 1983): Lo Spettatore Internazionale (English Edition) (0584-8776)
Related titles: Online - full text ed.: ISSN 1751-9721. 2007. GBP 269 in United Kingdom to institutions; EUR 356, USD 446 to institutions (effective 2012) (from IngentaConnect).
Indexed: A22, CA, CCME, E01, EI, I13, IBSS, P30, P34, P42, PAIS, PCI, PRA, PSA, SCOPUS, T02.
—BLDSC (4549.626500), IE, Infotrieve, Ingenta. **CCC.**
Published by: (Istituto Affari Internazionali ITA), Routledge (Subsidiary of: Taylor & Francis Group), 4 Park Sq, Milton Park, Abingdon, Oxon OX14 4RN, United Kingdom. TEL 44-20-70176000, FAX 44-20-70176336, subscriptions@tandf.co.uk, http://www.routledge.com. Adv. contact Linda Hann TEL 44-1344-779945. **Subscr. to:** Taylor & Francis Ltd., Journals Customer Service, Sheepen Pl, Colchester, Essex CO3 3LP, United Kingdom. TEL 44-20-70175544, FAX 44-20-70175198, tf.enquiries@tfinforma.com.

327 NLD ISSN 0924-4867
➤ **INTERNATIONAL STRAITS OF THE WORLD.** Text in English. 1978. irreg., latest vol.14, 2004. price varies. back issues avail. **Document type:** *Monographic series, Academic/Scholarly.*
Published by: Martinus Nijhoff (Subsidiary of: Brill), PO Box 9000, Leiden, 2300 PA, Netherlands. TEL 31-71-5353500, FAX 31-71-5317532, marketing@brill.nl. Ed. Gerard J Mangone.

327 IND ISSN 0020-8817
JZ6.5 CODEN: ITSDFL
➤ **INTERNATIONAL STUDIES.** Text in English. 1961. q. USD 507, GBP 273 to institutions; USD 517, GBP 279 combined subscription to institutions (print & online eds.) (effective 2012). bk.rev. bibl. index. back issues avail.; reprint service avail. from PSC. **Document type:** *Journal, Academic/Scholarly.* **Description:** Presents an Asian perspective on international affairs and area studies through original research articles that concentrate on issues and problems of contemporary relevance.
Formerly: International Studies Newsletter (0097-8965)
Related titles: Microform ed.: (from PQC); Online - full text ed.: ISSN 0973-0702. USD 465, GBP 251 to institutions (effective 2012).
Indexed: A22, AMB, APEL, B07, BAS, CA, E01, EI, ESPM, GEOBASE, HistAb, I13, IBSS, MEA&I, P06, P34, P42, PAIS, PRA, PSA, PerIslam, RASB, RiskAb, S02, S03, SCOPUS, SOPODA, SSA, SociolAb, T02.
—BLDSC (4549.750000), IE, Infotrieve, Ingenta. **CCC.**
Published by: (Jawaharlal Nehru University, School of International Studies), Sage Publications India Pvt. Ltd. (Subsidiary of: Sage Publications, Inc.), B-1/I-1 Mohan Cooperative Industrial Area, Mathura Rd, PO Box 7, New Delhi, 110 044, India. TEL 91-11-40539222, FAX 91-11-40539234, info@sagepub.in, http://www.sagepub.in. Ed. P Sahadevan. **Subscr. to:** Sage Publications Ltd., 1 Oliver's Yard, 55 City Rd, London EC1Y 1SP, United Kingdom. TEL 44-207-3248701, FAX 44-207-3248733, subscription@sagepub.co.uk; Sage Publications, Inc., 2455 Teller Rd, Thousand Oaks, CA 91320. TEL 805-499-9774, FAX 805-499-0871, journals@sagepub.com.

327 USA ISSN 1528-3577
JZ1234
➤ **INTERNATIONAL STUDIES PERSPECTIVES.** Text in English. 2000. q. USD 1,737 combined subscription in the Americas to institutions (print & online eds.); GBP 1,327 combined subscription in United Kingdom to institutions (print & online eds.); EUR 1,686 combined subscription in Europe to institutions (print & online eds.); USD 2,601 combined subscription elsewhere to institutions (print & online eds.); USD 1,579 in the Americas to institutions (print or online ed.); GBP 1,206 in United Kingdom to institutions (print or online ed.); EUR 1,532 in Europe to institutions (print or online ed.); USD 2,364 elsewhere to institutions (print or online ed.) (effective 2010); subscr. includes: Foreign Policy Analysis and International Political Sociology and International Studies Quarterly and International Studies Review. adv. reprint service avail. from PSC. **Document type:** *Journal, Academic/Scholarly.* **Description:** Publishes articles that bridge the interests of researchers, teachers, and practitioners working within any and all subfields of international studies.
Related titles: Online - full text ed.: ISSN 1528-3585 (from IngentaConnect).
Indexed: A01, A03, A08, A22, A26, CA, CurCont, E01, E09, ERA, ESPM, GEOBASE, I14, LID&ISL, LeftInd, P02, P10, P18, P34, P42, P48, P53, P54, PAIS, PQC, PRA, PSA, RiskAb, S02, S03, S11, S21, SCOPUS, SPAA, SSCI, SSciA, SociolAb, T02, W07.
—BLDSC (4549.794250), IE, Infotrieve, Ingenta. **CCC.**
Published by: (International Studies Association), Wiley-Blackwell Publishing, Inc. (Subsidiary of: Wiley-Blackwell Publishing Ltd.), Commerce Pl, 350 Main St, Malden, MA 02148. TEL 781-388-8206, FAX 781-388-8232, info@wiley.com, http://www.wiley.com/WileyCDA/. Ed. Douglas A Van Belle. adv.: B&W page USD 525; trim 6.875 x 10. Circ: 3,675 (paid).

327 USA ISSN 0020-8833
D839
➤ **INTERNATIONAL STUDIES QUARTERLY.** Text in English. 1957. q. USD 1,737 combined subscription in the Americas to institutions (print & online eds.); GBP 1,327 combined subscription in United Kingdom to institutions (print & online eds.) (effective 2011); EUR 1,686 combined subscription in Europe to institutions (print & online eds.) (effective 2012); USD 2,601 combined subscription elsewhere to institutions (print & online eds.) (effective 2011); subscr. includes: Foreign Policy Analysis, International Political Sociology, International Studies Perspectives and International Studies Review. adv. charts; illus. index. back issues avail.; reprint service avail. from PSC. **Document type:** *Journal, Academic/Scholarly.* **Description:** Presents theoretical and practical papers addressing the various political, economic, social, or cultural forces affecting more than one society and supporting diverse outlooks and practices.
Former titles (until 1967): Background (0361-5448); (until 1962): Background on World Politics (1533-6689)
Related titles: Microform ed.: (from PQC); Online - full text ed.: ISSN 1468-2478. 1997 (from IngentaConnect).
Indexed: A01, A02, A03, A08, A20, A22, A25, A26, ABCPolSci, ABS&EES, ASCA, AmH&L, AmHI, B04, BAS, BRD, BrHumI, CA, CIS, CurCont, DIP, E01, E08, ESPM, G08, GEOBASE, H07, H09, HistAb, I05, I13, IBR, IBSS, IBZ, LID&ISL, LeftInd, MEA&I, P02, P10, P27, P30, P34, P42, P47, P48, P53, P54, PAIS, PCI, PQC, PRA, PSA, RASB, RiskAb, S02, S03, S05, S08, S09, S11, S21, SCOPUS, SPAA, SSAI, SSAb, SSCI, SSI, SociolAb, T02, W01, W02, W03, W07.
—BLDSC (4549.800000), IE, Infotrieve, Ingenta. **CCC.**
Published by: (International Studies Association), Wiley-Blackwell Publishing, Inc. (Subsidiary of: Wiley-Blackwell Publishing Ltd.), 111 River St, Hoboken, NJ 07030. TEL 201-748-6000, FAX 201-748-6088, info@wiley.com, http://www.wiley.com/WileyCDA/. Adv. contact Kristin McCarthy TEL 201-748-7683. B&W page USD 620; trim 6.875 x 10. Circ: 4,154 (paid).

327 USA ISSN 1521-9488
D839
➤ **INTERNATIONAL STUDIES REVIEW.** Abbreviated title: I S R. Text in English. 1994. q. USD 1,579 in the Americas to institutions (print or online ed.); GBP 1,206 in United Kingdom to institutions (print or online ed.); EUR 1,532 in Europe to institutions (print or online ed.); USD 2,364 elsewhere to institutions (print or online ed.); USD 1,737 combined subscription in the Americas to institutions (print & online eds.); GBP 1,327 combined subscription in United Kingdom to institutions (print & online eds.); EUR 1,686 combined subscription in Europe to institutions (print & online eds.); USD 2,601 combined subscription elsewhere to institutions (print & online eds.) (effective 2010); subscr. includes International Studies Quarterly, Foreign Policy Analysis, International Studies Perspectives & International Political Sociology. adv. back issues avail.; reprint service avail. from PSC. **Document type:** *Journal, Academic/Scholarly.* **Description:** Enhances the understanding of the theory and practice of international relations in global and regional settings by publishing analyses of current scholarship, review essays and reviews.
Formerly (until 1999): Mershon International Studies Review (1079-1760)
Related titles: Online - full text ed.: ISSN 1468-2486 (from IngentaConnect).
Indexed: A01, A03, A08, A22, A26, CA, CurCont, E01, ESPM, GEOBASE, I02, IBSS, P02, P10, P34, P42, P48, P53, P54, PAIS, PQC, PRA, PSA, R02, RiskAb, S02, S03, S11, S21, SCOPUS, SSCI, SociolAb, T02, W07.
—BLDSC (4549.805000), IE, Infotrieve, Ingenta. **CCC.**
Published by: (International Studies Association), Wiley-Blackwell Publishing, Inc. (Subsidiary of: Wiley-Blackwell Publishing Ltd.), 111 River St, Hoboken, NJ 07030. TEL 201-748-6000, FAX 201-748-6088, info@wiley.com. Eds. Jennifer Sterling-Folker, Mark A Boyer.

327 KOR ISSN 1226-8240
D839
INTERNATIONAL STUDIES REVIEW. Text in English. 1997. s-a. KRW 42,500, USD 25 to individuals; KRW 85,000, USD 50 to institutions (effective 2008). **Document type:** *Journal, Academic/Scholarly.* **Description:** Contains articles with analysis of current and historical international issues and events in the fields of international business, international economics, international law, international relations, international political economy, political science and sociology.
Related titles: Online - full text ed.
Published by: Ewha Womans University, Institute for International Trade and Cooperation, #1201, International Education Bldg, 11-1 Daehyun-dong, Seodaemun-gu, Seoul, 120-750, Korea, S. TEL 82-2-3277-3628, FAX 82-2-32773627, gsis97@ewha.ac.kr, http://gsis.ewha.ac.kr/iitc/. Ed. Kye Woo Lee.

327 GBR ISSN 1752-9719
JZ6.5
▼ ➤ **INTERNATIONAL THEORY;** a journal of international politics, law and philosophy. Abbreviated title: I T. Text in English. 2009. 3/yr. GBP 145, USD 250 to institutions; GBP 150, USD 260 combined subscription to institutions (print & online eds.) (effective 2012). adv. back issues avail.; reprints avail. **Document type:** *Journal, Academic/Scholarly.* **Description:** Promotes theoretical scholarship about the positive, legal, and normative aspects of world politics respectively.
Related titles: Online - full text ed.: ISSN 1752-9727. GBP 130, USD 245 to institutions (effective 2012).
Indexed: P45, P48, PQC, PSA.
—**CCC.**
Published by: Cambridge University Press, The Edinburgh Bldg, Shaftesbury Rd, Cambridge, CB2 8RU, United Kingdom. TEL 44-1223-312393, FAX 44-1223-315052, information@cambridge.org, http://www.cambridge.org/uk. Eds. Alexander Wendt, Duncan Snidal. Adv. contact Rebecca Roberts TEL 44-1223-325083. **Subscr. to:** Cambridge University Press, 100 Brook Hill Dr, W Nyack, NY 10994. TEL 845-353-7500, 800-872-7423, FAX 845-353-4141, subscriptions_newyork@cambridge.org

327 USA ISSN 1932-2127
JZ6.5
INTERNATIONAL TOPICS. Text in English. 2005. bi-m. back issues avail. **Document type:** *Journal, Academic/Scholarly.* **Description:** Brings out articles written by graduate students nationwide in several fields including international studies, political science, international relations, philosophy, peace studies, and regional studies.
Published by: Old Dominion University, Graduate Program in International Studies, 620 Batten Arts & Letters, Norfolk, VA 23529. TEL 757-683-5700, FAX 757-683-5701, isgpd@odu.edu.

327 FRA ISSN 0294-2925
HX3
INTERNATIONAL VIEWPOINT. Text in English. 1982. m. (11/yr.). adv. bk.rev. charts; illus.; stat. index. 36 p./no.; back issues avail. **Document type:** *Magazine, Consumer.* **Description:** News and analysis under the auspices of the United Secretariat of the Fourth International. Likely to be of interest to activists in socialist, workers' and Third World solidarity movements.
Related titles: French ed.: Inprecor.
Indexed: AltPI, LeftInd, RASB.
Published by: Presse-Edition-Communication Internationale (P E C I), B.P. 85, Paris, Cedex 11 75522, France. TEL 33-1-43-79-29-61, FAX 33-1-43-79-29-61, inprecor@igc.apc.org. Ed., Pub., Adv. contact Jan Malewski. Circ: 1,500.

INTERNATIONAL WOMEN'S NEWS. *see* WOMEN'S INTERESTS

327 DEU ISSN 0936-5184
INTERNATIONALE BEZIEHUNGEN. Text in German. 1989. irreg., latest vol.6, 1997. price varies. **Document type:** *Monographic series, Academic/Scholarly.*
Published by: Franz Steiner Verlag GmbH, Birkenwaldstr 44, Stuttgart, 70191, Germany. TEL 49-711-25820, FAX 49-711-2582290, service@steiner-verlag.de, http://www.steiner-verlag.de. R&P Sabine Koerner.

327 DEU ISSN 0941-3669
INTERNATIONALE BEZIEHUNGEN (FRANKFURT AM MAIN). Text in German. 1993. irreg., latest vol.10, 2008. price varies. **Document type:** *Monographic series, Academic/Scholarly.*
Published by: Peter Lang GmbH (Subsidiary of: Peter Lang Publishing Group), Eschborner Landstr 42-50, Frankfurt Am Main, 60489, Germany. TEL 49-69-7807050, FAX 49-69-78070550, zentrale.frankfurt@peterlang.com, http://www.peterlang.com.

327 DEU
INTERNATIONALE BEZIEHUNGEN (GOETTINGEN). Text in German. 2006. irreg., latest vol.5, 2008. price varies. **Document type:** *Monographic series, Academic/Scholarly.*
Published by: V & R Unipress GmbH (Subsidiary of: Vandenhoeck und Ruprecht), Robert-Bosch-Breite 6, Goettingen, 37079, Germany. TEL 49-551-5084303, FAX 49-551-5084333, info@vr-unipress.de, http://www.v-r.de/en/publisher/unipress.

327 DEU ISSN 1430-175X
D839
INTERNATIONALE POLITIK. Text in German. 1946. q. EUR 118 domestic; EUR 126 in Europe; EUR 128 elsewhere; EUR 14.91 newsstand/cover (effective 2010). adv. bk.rev. bibl.; charts. index. cum.index: 1946-1965, 1966-1970, 1971-1975, 1976-1980, 1981-1985. reprints avail. **Document type:** *Magazine, Consumer.* **Description:** Features debate on fundamental questions of global politics.
Formerly (until 1995): Europa-Archiv (0014-2476)
Related titles: English ed.: Internationale Politik - Transatlantic Edition. ISSN 1439-8443. 2000. EUR 39.80, USD 39.80; EUR 9.95, USD 9.95 newsstand/cover (effective 2003).
Indexed: A20, A22, ABCPolSci, AMB, AmH&L, BAS, BibInd, CurCont, DIP, HistAb, I13, IBR, IBSS, IBZ, KES, M10, P30, P34, P42, PAIS, PCI, PRA, PSA, SCOPUS, SSCI, SociolAb, W07.
—BLDSC (4554.519510), IE, Infotrieve. **CCC.**
Published by: Deutsche Gesellschaft fuer Auswaertige Politik e.V., Rauchstr 17/18, Berlin, 10787, Germany. TEL 49-30-2542310, FAX 49-30-25423116, info@dgap.org, http://www.dgap.org. Ed. Sylke Tempel. Adv. contact Stefan Dauwe. page EUR 3,800; bleed 175 x 251. Circ: 6,000 (paid and free).

327 DEU ISSN 0945-2419
D839 CODEN: IPGEE3
INTERNATIONALE POLITIK UND GESELLSCHAFT. Text in German; Summaries in English, French. 1960. q. EUR 37; EUR 11 per issue (effective 2010). adv. bk.rev. abstr.; bibl. index. **Document type:** *Journal, Academic/Scholarly.*
Former titles (until 1993): Vierteljahresberichte - Probleme der Internationalen Zusammenarbeit (0936-451X); (until 1983): Vierteljahresberichte - Probleme der Entwicklungslaender (0015-7910); (until 1967): Ostblock und die Entwicklungslaender (0344-9513)
Related titles: Online - full text ed.
Indexed: ASD, BAS, BibInd, CA, DIP, I13, IBR, IBSS, IBZ, P06, P30, P34, P42, PAA&I, PAIS, PSA, RASB, S02, S03, SCOPUS, SOPODA, SSA, SociolAb, T02.
—BLDSC (4554.520500), IE, Ingenta. **CCC.**
Published by: (Friedrich-Ebert-Stiftung, Forschung Institut), Verlag J.H.W. Dietz Nachf. GmbH, Dreizehnmorgenweg 24, Bonn, 53175, Germany. TEL 49-228-238083, FAX 49-228-234104, info@dietz-verlag.de, http://www.dietz-verlag.de. adv.: B&W page EUR 500. Circ: 3,700 (paid).

327 DEU ISSN 0170-0162
➤ **INTERNATIONALE POLITIK UND SICHERHEIT.** Text in German. 1978. irreg., latest vol.54, 2003. price varies. **Document type:** *Monographic series, Academic/Scholarly.*
Published by: Nomos Verlagsgesellschaft mbH und Co. KG, Waldseestr 3-5, Baden-Baden, 76530, Germany. TEL 49-7221-2104-0, FAX 49-7221-210427, nomos@nomos.de, http://www.nomos.de. Ed. Albrecht Zunker.

327.1 DEU ISSN 1618-5706
INTERNATIONALE SICHERHEIT. Text in German. 2002. irreg., latest vol.8, 2008. price varies. **Document type:** *Monographic series, Academic/Scholarly.*
Published by: Peter Lang GmbH (Subsidiary of: Peter Lang Publishing Group), Eschborner Landstr 42-50, Frankfurt Am Main, 60489, Germany. TEL 49-69-7807050, FAX 49-69-78070550, zentrale.frankfurt@peterlang.com. Ed. Heinz Gaertner.

327.172 AUT
INTERNATIONALE SICHERHEIT UND KONFLIKTMANAGEMENT. Text in German. 2008. irreg., latest vol.6, 2010. price varies. **Document type:** *Monographic series, Academic/Scholarly.*
Published by: (Institut fuer Friedenssicherung und Konfliktmanagement), Boehlau Verlag GmbH & Co.KG., Wiesingerstr 1, Vienna, W 1010, Austria. TEL 43-1-3302427, FAX 43-1-3302432, boehlau@boehlau.at.

327 DEU ISSN 0934-9685
INTERNATIONALES HANDBUCH - LAENDER AKTUELL. Text in German. 1936. w. adv. **Document type:** *Newsletter, Consumer.*
Formerly: Internationales Handbuch (0020-949X)
Published by: Munzinger Archiv GmbH, Albersfelder Str 34, Ravensburg, 88213, Germany. TEL 49-751-769310, FAX 49-751-652424, box@munzinger.de, http://www.munzinger.de. Ed. Dr. Ludwig Munzinger. adv.: page EUR 600. Circ: 1,600 (controlled).

327 SWE ISSN 0020-952X
JX18
INTERNATIONELLA STUDIER. Text in Swedish. 1968. q. SEK 300; SEK 80 per issue (effective 2008). adv. bk.rev. charts. back issues avail. **Document type:** *Journal, Academic/Scholarly.*
Indexed: MLA-IB.
Published by: Utrikespolitiska Institutet/The Swedish Institute of International Affairs, Drottning Kristinas Vaeg 37, PO Box 27035, Stockholm, 10251, Sweden. TEL 46-8-51176800, FAX 46-8-51176899, info@ui.se. Ed. Ulla Nordloef Lagerkranz TEL 46-8-6960533.

327 USA
INTERNEWSLETTER AFRIQUE; la seule revue de presse Americaine en Francais sur l'Afrique. Text in French. 1977. s-m. looseleaf. USD 599 to individuals; USD 499 to libraries. adv. back issues avail.
Published by: Internews Media Services Inc., 1063 National, Washington, DC 20045-0001. TEL 202-347-4575, FAX 703-734-6956. Ed. Marie Benoite Allizon.

INTRIGUE. *see* CRIMINOLOGY AND LAW ENFORCEMENT—Security

327 IRN ISSN 1016-6130
D1
IRANIAN JOURNAL OF INTERNATIONAL AFFAIRS. Text in English. 1989. q. IRR 27,000, USD 40. bk.rev. **Document type:** *Journal, Academic/Scholarly.*
Indexed: CCME, I13, M10, PAIS, PerIslam.
—IE, Ingenta.
Published by: Institute for Political and International Studies, P O Box 19395-1793, Tehran, Iran. TEL 98-21-2571010, FAX 98-21-270964. Ed. Abbas Maleki. Circ: 7,500.

327 IRN ISSN 0378-990X
JX18
IRANIAN REVIEW OF INTERNATIONAL RELATIONS/REVUE IRANIENNE DES RELATIONS INTERNATIONALES. Text in French, English. 1974. q. IRR 250, USD 18. bk.rev. abstr.; bibl. **Document type:** *Journal, Academic/Scholarly.*
Formerly (until 1975): Relations Internationales (1016-1589)
Indexed: P06, PAIS.
Published by: University of Teheran, Center for International Studies, Englehab Ave., Tehran, 14174, Iran. Ed. Prof Habibi. Circ: 2,000.

327 955 NLD
IRANIAN STUDIES SERIES. Text in English. irreg., latest vol.2, 2008. price varies. **Document type:** *Monographic series, Academic/Scholarly.*
Published by: Rozenberg Publishers, Lindengracht 302 D&E, Amsterdam, 1015 KM, Netherlands. TEL 31-20-6255429, FAX 31-20-6203395, info@rozenbergps.com.

327 IRL ISSN 0332-1460
DA964.A2
IRISH STUDIES IN INTERNATIONAL AFFAIRS. Text in English. 1979. a. EUR 35 to individuals; EUR 100 to institutions; EUR 20 to students (effective 2007). back issues avail. **Document type:** *Journal, Academic/Scholarly.*
Related titles: Online - full text ed.: ISSN 2009-0072.
Indexed: IBSS, LID&ISL, P42, PSA, SSAI, SSAb, SSI, W03, W05.
—BLDSC (4574.830000), IE. **CCC.**
Published by: Royal Irish Academy, 19 Dawson St., Dublin, 2, Ireland. TEL 353-1-6762570, FAX 353-1-6762346, publications@ria.ie. Ed. Dr. John Doyle. **Dist. by:** International Specialized Book Services Inc., 920 NE 58th Ave Ste 300, Portland, OR 97213. TEL 503-287-3093, 800-944-6190, FAX 503-280-8832, sales@isbs.com.

327.172 PAK ISSN 1813-520X
ISLAMABAD PAPERS. Text in English. 2001. irreg., latest vol.5, 2004. price varies. **Document type:** *Monographic series, Academic/Scholarly.* **Description:** Contains papers on specific issues relating to various international and regional issues.
Published by: Institute of Strategic Studies, Sector F-5/2, Islamabad, Pakistan. TEL 92-51-9204423, FAX 92-51-9204658, strategy@isb.paknet.com.pk, http://www.issi.org.pk.

327 GBR ISSN 1353-7121
DS128.2 CODEN: ISAFFW
➤ **ISRAEL AFFAIRS.** Text in English. 1994. q. GBP 415 combined subscription in United Kingdom to institutions (print & online eds.); EUR 548, USD 687 combined subscription to institutions (print & online eds.) (effective 2012). adv. bk.rev. index. back issues avail.; reprint service avail. from PSC. **Document type:** *Journal, Academic/Scholarly.* **Description:** Covers Israeli history, politics, literature, art, strategic affairs, economics, the Arab-Israeli conflict, and Israel-diaspora relations.
Related titles: Online - full text ed.: ISSN 1743-9086. GBP 373 in United Kingdom to institutions; EUR 493, USD 619 to institutions (effective 2012) (from IngentaConnect).
Indexed: A01, A02, A03, A08, A22, CA, CCME, E01, ESPM, I02, I13, I14, IBSS, IJP, J01, M02, M10, P34, P42, P47, PAIS, PQC, PSA, R02, RiskAb, S02, S03, SCOPUS, SOPODA, SSA, SSCI, SociolAb, T02, W07.
—IE, Ingenta. **CCC.**
Published by: Routledge (Subsidiary of: Taylor & Francis Group), 4 Park Sq, Milton Park, Abingdon, Oxon OX14 4RN, United Kingdom. TEL 44-20-70176000, FAX 44-20-70176336, subscriptions@tandf.co.uk, http://www.routledge.com. Ed. Efraim Karsh TEL 44-20-78365454. Adv. contact Linda Hann TEL 44-1344-779945. **Subscr. to:** Taylor & Francis Ltd., Journals Customer Service, Sheepen Pl, Colchester, Essex CO3 3LP, United Kingdom. TEL 44-20-70175544, FAX 44-20-70175198.

➤ **ISRAEL AKTUEEL.** *see* ETHNIC INTERESTS

320.54095694 USA ISSN 0021-2083
DS101
ISRAEL HORIZONS. Text in English. 1952. q. USD 25 (effective 2010). bk.rev.; film rev. charts; illus. index. **Document type:** *Journal, Academic/Scholarly.* **Description:** Deals with the Israeli left and the peace camp in Israel, Israeli culture and life, and the world Jewish community.
Related titles: Online - full text ed.: USD 18 (effective 2010).
Indexed: HRIR, IJP, LeftInd, M10, MEA&I, P06, PAIS.
Published by: Meretz U S A, 114 W 26th St, Ste 1002, New York, NY 10001. TEL 212-242-4500, FAX 212-242-5718, mail@meretzusa.org.

327 DEU ISSN 0175-7024
DS63.1
ISRAEL UND PALAESTINA; Zeitschrift fuer Dialog. Text in German. 1984. q. EUR 10 newsstand/cover (effective 2009). adv. bk.rev. back issues avail. **Document type:** *Magazine, Consumer.*
Indexed: DIP, IBR, IBZ.
Published by: Deutsch-Israelischer Arbeitskreis fuer Frieden im Nahen Osten, Zeissstr 51, Hamburg, 22765, Germany. TEL 49-40-395573, info@diak.org. Circ: 500.

327 GBR ISSN 1368-4795
ISRAELI HISTORY, POLITICS AND SOCIETY. Text in English. 1997. irreg., latest 2008. price varies. back issues avail. **Document type:** *Monographic series, Academic/Scholarly.* **Description:** Provides a multidisciplinary examination of all aspects of Israeli history, politics and society and serves as a means of communication between the various communities interested in Israel.
Published by: Routledge (Subsidiary of: Taylor & Francis Group), 4 Park Sq, Milton Park, Abingdon, Oxon OX14 4RN, United Kingdom. TEL 44-20-70176000, FAX 44-20-70176336.

327 TWN ISSN 1013-2511
D839
➤ **ISSUES & STUDIES**; an international quarterly on China, Taiwan, and East Asian affairs. Text in English. 1964. q. (Mar., Jun., Sep & Dec.). adv. bk.rev. stat.; illus.; abstr.; charts; maps; bibl. Index. 250 p./no.; back issues avail.; reprints avail. **Document type:** *Journal, Academic/Scholarly.* **Description:** Highlights contemporary China studies and East Asian regional affairs.
Related titles: Microform ed.: (from PQC).
Indexed: A20, A22, A34, A35, A38, ABCPolSci, APEL, ASCA, AgBio, AmH&L, CA, CABA, CurCont, DIP, E12, GH, HistAb, I13, IBR, IBSS, IBZ, LT, P30, P32, P34, P40, P42, PAIS, PGegResA, PRA, PSA, R12, RRTA, S02, S03, S13, S16, SCOPUS, SSCI, SociolAb, T02, T05, TAR, W07, W11.
—BLDSC (4584.120000), IE, Infotrieve, Ingenta.
Published by: National Chengchi University, Institute of International Relations, 64 Wanshou Road, Wenshan District, Taipei, 116, Taiwan. TEL 886-2-82377277, FAX 886-2-29378606, iir@nccu.edu.tw. Circ: 550 (paid); 700 (controlled).

327 SGP
ISSUES IN SOUTHEAST ASIAN SECURITY. Text in English. 1984. irreg., latest vol.23, 2002. price varies. **Document type:** *Monographic series, Academic/Scholarly.* **Description:** International relations and strategic studies pertaining to the Asia-Pacific region.
Published by: Institute of Southeast Asian Studies, 30 Heng Mui Keng Terrace, Pasir Panjang, Singapore, 119614, Singapore. TEL 65-6870-2447, FAX 65-6775-6259, pubsunit@iseas.edu.sg, http://www.iseas.edu.sg/. Ed., R&P Mrs. Triena Ong TEL 65-6870-2449.

327 AUS ISSN 1443-0258
ITALY DOWN UNDER. Text in English. 2000. q. back issues avail. **Document type:** *Magazine, Consumer.* **Description:** Contains articles and features on Italian culture, arts, food and wine, and lifestyles.
Related titles: Online - full text ed.
Published by: Italy Down Under Pty Ltd., 478 William St, West Melbourne, VIC 3003, Australia. TEL 61-3-93281433, FAX 61-3-93281385, editor@italydownunder.com.au.

327 USA ISSN 0449-0754
E740.J6
J B S BULLETIN. (John Birch Society) Text in English. 1959. m. USD 48 membership (effective 2007). adv. bk.rev. back issues avail. **Document type:** *Bulletin.* **Description:** Reviews historical trends and current affairs. Recommends activities to restore the constitutional American system.
Related titles: E-mail ed.
Published by: John Birch Society, Inc., PO Box 8040, Appleton, WI 54912-8040. TEL 920-749-3780, FAX 920-749-5062, wmass@jbs.org. Ed. Thomas G Gow. Pub. John F McManus. Circ: 29,000 (paid); 1,000 (controlled).

327 341 IND ISSN 0973-5984
JADAVPUR JOURNAL OF INTERNATIONAL RELATIONS. Text in English. 1995. a. **Document type:** *Journal, Academic/Scholarly.*
Published by: Javadpur University, Department of International Relations, Kolkata, 700 032, India. hod@ir.jdvu.ac.in, http://jadavpur.academia.edu/Departments/Department_of_International_Relations.

327 DEU ISSN 1434-5153
D839
➤ **JAHRBUCH INTERNATIONALE POLITIK.** Text in German. 1958. irreg., latest vol.27, 2008. price varies. **Document type:** *Monographic series, Academic/Scholarly.*
Formerly (until 1996): Die Internationale Politik (0539-158X)
Indexed: RASB.
—CCC.
Published by: (Deutsche Gesellschaft fuer Auswaertige Politik e.V.), Oldenbourg Wissenschaftsverlag GmbH, Rosenheimer Str 145, Munich, 81671, Germany. TEL 49-89-450510, FAX 49-89-45051204, orders@oldenbourg.de, http://www.oldenbourg.de.

➤ **JAHRBUCH POLEN**; Jahrbuch der Deutschen Polen-Instituts Darmstadt. *see* LITERATURE

327 GBR ISSN 2040-8315
D410
▼ **JANE'S INTELLIGENCE WEEKLY.** Variant title: Intelligence Weekly. Text in English. 2009. 48/yr. GBP 275 domestic; GBP 280 in Europe; GBP 325 elsewhere (effective 2010). illus. **Document type:** *Journal, Trade.* **Description:** Provides authoritative and predictive analysis of security issues worldwide.
Formed by the merger of (1946-2009): Jane's Foreign Report (2040-2473); Which was formerly (until 1999): Foreign Report (0532-1328); (1938-2009): Jane's Intelligence Digest; Which was formerly: Intelligence Digest; Intelligence Digest Political and Strategic Review; Intelligence Digest World Report; Intelligence Digest (0020-4900); (until 198?): Intelligence Digest Weekly Review (0307-188X); (until 1975): Weekly Review (0043-1915)
Related titles: CD-ROM ed.: 2009; Online - full text ed.: 2009.
—CCC.
Published by: I H S Jane's (Subsidiary of: I H S), Sentinel House, 163 Brighton Rd, Coulsdon, Surrey CR5 2YH, United Kingdom. TEL 44-20-87003700, FAX 44-20-87003751, http://www.janes.com.

327.117 GBR ISSN 1367-0409
JANE'S TERRORISM & SECURITY MONITOR. Text in English. 1996. 10/yr. GBP 310 (effective 2010). illus. **Document type:** *Newsletter, Trade.* **Description:** Reports on global terrorism and security issues with regional security updates and risk assessment.

Related titles: CD-ROM ed.: GBP 820 (effective 2010); Online - full text ed.: GBP 1,145 (effective 2010).
—CCC.
Published by: I H S Jane's (Subsidiary of: I H S), Sentinel House, 163 Brighton Rd, Coulsdon, Surrey CR5 2YH, United Kingdom. TEL 44-20-87003700, FAX 44-20-87003751, info@janes.co.uk, http://www.janes.com. Ed. Jeremy Binnie. **Dist. in Asia by:** Jane's Information Group Asia, 60 Albert St, #15-01 Albert Complex, Singapore 189969, Singapore. TEL 65-331-6280, FAX 65-336-9921, info@janes.com.sg; **Dist. in Australia by:** Jane's Information Group Australia, PO Box 3502, Rozelle, NSW 2039, Australia. TEL 61-2-8587-7900, FAX 61-2-8587-7901, info@janes.thomson.com.au; **Dist. in the Americas by:** 1340 Braddock Pl, Ste 300, Alexandria, VA 22314-1651. TEL 703-683-3700, 800-824-0768, FAX 703-836-0297, 800-836-0297.

327.117 GBR ISSN 1524-3877
JANE'S TERRORISM WATCH REPORT. Text in English. 199?. d. GBP 460 (effective 2010). illus. **Document type:** *Report, Trade.*
Description: Tracks and monitors international terrorist groups and insurgency movements, intelligence communities, economic espionage and computer security issues with this comprehensive briefing.
Media: Online - full content. **Related titles:** CD-ROM ed.: GBP 350 (effective 2010).
Published by: I H S Jane's (Subsidiary of: I H S), Sentinel House, 163 Brighton Rd, Coulsdon, Surrey CR5 2YH, United Kingdom. TEL 44-20-87003700, FAX 44-20-87003751, info@janes.co.uk, http://www.janes.com.

327 GBR ISSN 0955-5803
DS801
➤ **JAPAN FORUM**; the international journal of Japanese studies. Text in English. 1989. 3/yr. GBP 518 combined subscription in United Kingdom to institutions (print & online eds.); EUR 680, USD 855 combined subscription to institutions (print & online eds.) (effective 2012). adv. bk.rev. illus. Index. back issues avail.; reprint service avail. from PSC. **Document type:** *Journal, Academic/Scholarly.*
Description: Provides scholarly articles on Japanese culture, both historical and contemporary.
Related titles: Online - full text ed.: ISSN 1469-932X. GBP 466 in United Kingdom to institutions; EUR 613, USD 770 to institutions (effective 2012) (from IngentaConnect).
Indexed: A01, A03, A08, A22, APEL, AmH&L, AmHI, B21, BAS, BrHumI, CA, DIP, E01, E17, ESPM, H07, HistAb, I13, IBR, IBSS, IBZ, MLA-IB, P42, PAIS, PSA, RASB, S02, S03, SCOPUS, SociolAb, T02.
—IE, Infotrieve, Ingenta. **CCC.**
Published by: (British Association for Japanese Studies), Routledge (Subsidiary of: Taylor & Francis Group), 4 Park Sq, Milton Park, Abingdon, Oxon OX14 4RN, United Kingdom. TEL 44-20-70176000, FAX 44-20-70176336, subscriptions@tandf.co.uk, http://www.routledge.com. Ed. Angus Lockyer TEL 44-20-78984626. Adv. contact Linda Hann TEL 44-1344-779945. Circ: 900. **Subscr. to:** Taylor & Francis Ltd., Journals Customer Service, Sheepen Pl, Colchester, Essex CO3 3LP, United Kingdom. TEL 44-20-70175544, FAX 44-20-70175198, tf.enquiries@tfinforma.com.

327 JPN ISSN 0915-4981
DS849.N4
JAPAN-NETHERLANDS INSTITUTE. JOURNAL. Text in English. 1989. irreg., latest vol.7, 2001.
Published by: Japan-Netherlands Institute/Nichi-Ran Gakkai, Kyobashi Plaza Bldg 3F, 25-3, Ginza 1-chome, Chuo-ku, Tokyo, 104-0061, Japan. TEL 81-3-35672123, FAX 81-3-35675658, http://www.jni.or.jp/.

327 JPN ISSN 0913-8773
D839
JAPAN REVIEW OF INTERNATIONAL AFFAIRS. Text in English. 1987. q. JPY 1,942 per issue (effective 2004). back issues avail. **Document type:** *Journal, Academic/Scholarly.* **Description:** Covers global and regional issues of current interest.
Indexed: APEL, BAS, PCI, RASB.
—IE, Ingenta.
Published by: Nihon Kokusai Mondai Kenkyujo/Japan Institute of International Affairs, Kasumigaseki Bldg 11F, 3-2-5 Kasumigaseki, Chiyoda-ku, Tokyo, 100-6011, Japan. TEL 81-3-35037801, FAX 81-3-35037186, jiiajoho@jiia.or.jp. Ed. Yukio Satoh. **Dist. overseas by:** Japan Publications Trading Co., Ltd., Book Export II Dept, PO Box 5030, Tokyo International, Tokyo 101-3191, Japan. TEL 81-3-32923753, FAX 81-3-32920410, infoserials@jptco.co.jp, http://www.jptco.co.jp.

327.52 GBR ISSN 0952-2050
JAPAN SOCIETY. PROCEEDINGS. Text in English. 1892. 2/yr. free membership (effective 2009). bk.rev. **Document type:** *Proceedings.*
Former titles (until 1985): Japan Society of London. Bulletin (0021-4701); (until 1950): Japan Society. Transactions and Proceedings (1359-1029)
Indexed: BAS.
—BLDSC (6742.206000).
Published by: Japan Society, Swire House, 59 Buckingham Gate, London, SW1E 6AJ, United Kingdom. TEL 44-20-78286330, FAX 44-20-78286331, info@japansociety.org.uk. Ed. R Douglas. Circ: 1,500.

327 JPN ISSN 0389-1186
DJK1
JAPANESE SLAVIC & EAST EUROPEAN STUDIES. Text in English, German, Russian; Summaries in English, Japanese. 1980. a. JPY 6,000 membership (effective 2006). **Document type:** *Journal, Academic/Scholarly.*
Indexed: BibLing, RASB.
Published by: Japanese Society for Slavic & East European Studies, Kyoto University, Graduate School of Letters, Department of Slavic Languages & Literatures, Kyoto, 606, Japan. TEL 81-75-7532781, FAX 81-75-7610692, http://wwwsoc.nii.ac.jp/jssees/.

365.34 327.117 USA ISSN 1934-9742
JEBSEN CENTER FOR COUNTER-TERRORISM STUDIES RESEARCH BRIEFING SERIES. Text in English. 2006. irreg., latest vol.3, no.1, 2008. **Document type:** *Monographic series, Academic/Scholarly.* **Description:** Includes brief pieces by leading counter-terrorism experts, with the aim of promoting dialogue and new thinking on current issues in terrorism studies.
Media: Online - full text.
Published by: Fletcher School of Law and Diplomacy, Jebsen Center for Counter-Terrorism Studies, 160 Packard Ave, Medford, MA 02155. TEL 617-627-4740, 617-627-3700, FAX 617-627-3712.

327. FRA ISSN 1950-1285
AP27
JEUNE AFRIQUE. Text in French. 1960. w. (44/yr). EUR 124 domestic; EUR 154 in Europe; EUR 174 in North Africa; EUR 214 in North America; EUR 224 elsewhere (effective 2009). adv. bk.rev. charts; illus. reprints avail. **Document type:** *Magazine, Consumer.*
Description: Features articles about events taking place in Africa and important figures of African descent.
Former titles (until 2006): L' Intelligent (1621-6032); (until 2000): Jeune Afrique (0021-6089)
Related titles: Microfilm ed.: (from PQC); Online - full text ed.: ISSN 1952-4366.
Indexed: A22, CCA, CCME, KES, M10, MLA-IB, P30, PAIS, PdeR, PerIslam, RASB, SCOPUS.
—BLDSC (4668.221000), IE, Ingenta. **CCC.**
Published by: Groupe Jeune Afrique, 57 bis, Rue d'Auteuil, Paris, 75016, France. TEL 33-1-44301960, FAX 33-1-44301930, redaction@jeuneafrique.com, http://www.groupeja.com. Ed. Bechir Ben Yahmed. Circ: 100,000.

327.172 PRK
JOKOOK TONGIL. Text in Korean. 1961. m.
Published by: Committee for the Peaceful Unification of Korea, Kangan 1 Dong, Youth Avenue, Sonkyo District, Pyongyang, Korea, N. Ed. Li Myong Gyu. Circ: 70,000.

327 JOR ISSN 2075-1850
JORDAN INSTITUTE OF DIPLOMACY. Text in English. 200?. irreg. **Document type:** *Monographic series, Academic/Scholarly.*
Published by: The Jordan Institute of Diplomacy, PO Box 850746, Amman, 11185, Jordan. TEL 9626-593-4400, FAX 9626-593-4408, http://www.id.gov.jo/index.asp.

327 JOR ISSN 1999-5628
DS62.8
JORDAN JOURNAL OF INTERNATIONAL AFFAIRS/MAJALLAT AL-URDUNN LI-L-SHU'WUN AL-DUWALIYYAT. Text in Arabic, English. 2007. s-a. **Document type:** *Journal, Academic/Scholarly.*
Published by: The Jordan Institute of Diplomacy, PO Box 850746, Amman, 11185, Jordan. TEL 9626-593-4400, FAX 9626-593-4408, id@id.gov.jo, http://www.id.gov.jo/index.asp. Ed. Abeer Qatanani.

327 ZAF ISSN 0258-2422
➤ **JOURNAL FOR CONTEMPORARY HISTORY/JOERNAAL VIR EIETYDSE GESKIEDENIS.** Text in English. 1976. s-a. USD 25 foreign (effective 2000). adv. abstr.; illus. back issues avail. **Document type:** *Journal, Academic/Scholarly.* **Description:** Publishes articles on contemporary South African and international political, constitutional and social history.
Formerly: Journal for Contemporary History and International Relations
Indexed: CA, ISAP, P42, PSA, S02, S03, SCOPUS, SociolAb, T02.
Published by: (University of the Free State/Universiteit van die Vrystaat, Department of History/Instituut vir Eietydse Geskiedenis), U O F S Printer (Subsidiary of: University of the Free State/Universiteit van die Vrystaat), PO Box 339, Bloemfontein, 9300, South Africa. FAX 27-51-448-3942. Ed., R&P Leo Barnard TEL 27-51-401-2330. adv.: B&W page USD 65. Circ: 500.

327.172 USA ISSN 1095-1962
K10
➤ **JOURNAL FOR THE STUDY OF PEACE AND CONFLICT.** Text in English. 19??. a. **Document type:** *Journal, Academic/Scholarly.*
Former titles (until 1998): Viewpoints on War, Peace, and Global Cooperation; (until 1993): Viewpoints
Related titles: Online - full text ed.: free (effective 2011).
Indexed: CA, P10, P42, PQC, PSA, PhilInd, S02, S03, SCOPUS, SociolAb, T02.
Published by: Wisconsin Institute for Peace and Conflict Studies, UWSP LRC, 900 Reserve St, Stevens Point, WI 54481. TEL 715-346-3383, wiinst@uwsp.edu, http://matcmadison.edu/multicul/peace.

➤ **JOURNAL FUER ENTWICKLUNGSPOLITIK.** see BUSINESS AND ECONOMICS—International Development And Assistance

327 RWA ISSN 1996-3157
JZ5584.A35
JOURNAL OF AFRICAN CONFLICTS AND PEACE STUDIES. Text in English. 2007. biennial.
Published by: National University of Rwanda, Center for Conflict Management, PO Box 56, Butare, Rwanda. TEL 250-530122, FAX 250-530121, infos@nur.ac.rw, http://www.nur.ac.rw.

327 USA ISSN 2155-1235
▼ ➤ **JOURNAL OF ASIA CONFLICT RESOLUTION.** Text in English. 2010 (Sept.). a. free (effective 2010). **Description:** Features student papers from the Asia Working Group and the Department of Conflict Analysis and Conflict Resolution at Nova Southeastern University.
Media: Online - full text.
Published by: Nova Southeastern University, Asia Working Group, 3625 College Ave, RH 2079, Davie, FL 33314. TEL 610-564-2165, asiaworkinggroup@gmail.com.

327 KOR ISSN 1229-9774
DS501
JOURNAL OF ASIA-PACIFIC AFFAIRS. Text in English. 1999. s-a. membership. **Document type:** *Journal, Academic/Scholarly.*
Description: Multidisciplinary scholarly journal focusing on the integration of the Asia-Pacific region, relations between Asia-Pacific nations, and developments within Asia-Pacific nations, particularly Korea, Japan, and the United States.
Related titles: Online - full text ed.
Published by: Hanyang Taehakkyo Chung-sso Yon'guso/Hanyang University, Asia Pacific Research Center, 17, Haengdangdong, Seongdonggu, Seoul, 133-791, Korea, S. TEL 82-2-22201494, FAX 82-2-22953607, aprc@hanyang.ac.kr, http://aprc.hanyang.ac.kr/.

327 USA ISSN 0886-5655
F787
➤ **JOURNAL OF BORDERLANDS STUDIES.** Text in English. 1986. 3/yr. GBP 208 combined subscription in United Kingdom to institutions (print & online eds.); EUR 275, USD 343 combined subscription to institutions (print & online eds.) (effective 2012). adv. bk.rev. cum.index: 1986-1990. back issues avail.; reprint service avail. from PSC. **Document type:** *Journal, Academic/Scholarly.* **Description:** Multidisciplinary journal focusing on international borders.
Related titles: Online - full text ed.: ISSN 2159-1229. GBP 187 in United Kingdom to institutions; EUR 248, USD 309 to institutions (effective 2012).
Indexed: A01, ChPerI, Chicano, H21, P08, RILM, T02.
—Ingenta. **CCC.**
Published by: Association for Borderlands Scholars, c/o Javier Duran, Department of Spanish & Portuguese, The University of Arizona, PO Box 1700, Tucson, AZ V8W 2Y2. TEL 520-621-3123, FAX 520-621-6104, duran@u.arizona.edu. Eds. Emmanuel Brunet-Jailly, Henk van Houtum, Martin van der Velde. Circ: 425. **Co-sponsor:** New Mexico State University.

327 USA ISSN 1520-3972
D839
➤ **JOURNAL OF COLD WAR STUDIES.** Abbreviated title: J C W S. Text in English. 1999. q. USD 242 combined subscription in US & Canada to institutions (print & online eds.); USD 61 in US & Canada to institutions (effective 2012). adv. back issues avail.; reprints avail. **Document type:** *Journal, Academic/Scholarly.* **Description:** Includes articles that use declassified materials and new memoirs to illuminate and raise questions about theoretical concerns of the Cold War.
Related titles: Online - full text ed.: ISSN 1531-3298. USD 208 in US & Canada to institutions (effective 2012).
Indexed: A01, A03, A08, A22, ABS&EES, AmH&L, CA, DIP, E01, GeoRef, HistAb, I02, I13, IBR, IBZ, M05, P10, P34, P42, P47, P48, P53, P54, PAIS, PQC, PRA, PSA, S11, SCOPUS, SociolAb, T02.
—BLDSC (4958.799420), IE, Infotrieve. **CCC.**
Published by: (Harvard Project on Cold War Studies), M I T Press, 55 Hayward St, Cambridge, MA 02142. TEL 617-253-2889, FAX 617-577-1545, journals-cs@mit.edu, http://mitpress.mit.edu. Ed. Mark Kramer.

327 GBR ISSN 1352-3279
HX3
➤ **JOURNAL OF COMMUNIST STUDIES AND TRANSITION POLITICS.** Text in English. 1977. q. GBP 387 combined subscription in United Kingdom to institutions (print & online eds.); EUR 512, USD 642 combined subscription to institutions (print & online eds.) (effective 2012). bk.rev. illus. index. back issues avail.; reprint service avail. from PSC. **Document type:** *Journal, Academic/Scholarly.*
Description: Covers the study of communism and its current transformation, following the effects of this upheaval on communist parties worldwide.
Former titles (until 1994): Journal of Communist Studies (0268-4535); (until 1985): Communist Affairs (0260-9819); (until 1982): Documents in Communist Affairs (0958-8329)
Related titles: Microform ed.: (from PQC); Online - full text ed.: ISSN 1743-9116. GBP 348 in United Kingdom to institutions; EUR 461, USD 577 to institutions (effective 2012) (from IngentaConnect).
Indexed: A01, A03, A08, A22, ABCPolSci, AmH&L, AmHI, B21, BrHumI, CA, DIP, E01, E17, ESPM, H07, HistAb, I02, I13, IBR, IBSS, IBZ, LID&ISL, P34, P42, P47, PCI, PQC, PSA, RASB, S02, S03, SCOPUS, SociolAb, T02.
—IE, Infotrieve, Ingenta. **CCC.**
Published by: Routledge (Subsidiary of: Taylor & Francis Group), 4 Park Sq, Milton Park, Abingdon, Oxon OX14 4RN, United Kingdom. TEL 44-20-70176000, FAX 44-20-70176336, info@routledge.co.uk, http://www.routledge.com. Adv. contact Linda Hann TEL 44-1344-779945.

➤ **JOURNAL OF CONFLICT RESOLUTION**; research on war and peace between and within nations. see SOCIAL SCIENCES: COMPREHENSIVE WORKS

947 USA ISSN 2155-5478
▼ **JOURNAL OF CONFLICT TRANSFORMATION (CAUCASUS EDITION).** Text in English. 2010. s-m. free (effective 2010). back issues avail. **Document type:** *Academic/Scholarly.* **Description:** Provides a forum for scholars, practitioners, policy analysts, starting researchers and bloggers to analyze as well as discuss the Nagorno-Karabakh conflict and issues related to it.
Media: Online - full text.
Published by: Imagine Center for Conflict Transformation chris@imaginedialogue.com, http://www.imaginedialogue.com.

327 GBR ISSN 1815-347X
D1050
➤ **JOURNAL OF CONTEMPORARY EUROPEAN RESEARCH.** Abbreviated title: J C E R. Text in English. 2005. s-a. free (effective 2011). back issues avail. **Document type:** *Journal, Academic/Scholarly.* **Description:** Aims to support PhD students and early career researchers by providing them with a forum to disseminate their work alongside established scholars and practitioners.
Media: Online - full text.
Indexed: A39, C27, C29, CA, D03, D04, E13, P42, R14, S14, S15, S18, T02.
Published by: University Association for Contemporary European Studies (U A C E S), School of Public Policy, University College London, 29-30 Tavistock Sq, London, WC1H 9QU, United Kingdom. TEL 44-20-76794975, FAX 44-20-76794973, admin@uaces.org, http://www.uaces.org. Eds. Christian Kaunert, Eammon Butler, Sarah Leonard.

➤ **JOURNAL OF COUNTERTERRORISM & HOMELAND SECURITY INTERNATIONAL.** see CRIMINOLOGY AND LAW ENFORCEMENT—Security

327 KOR ISSN 1010-1608
DS501
➤ **JOURNAL OF EAST ASIAN AFFAIRS.** Text in English. 1980-1983; resumed 19??. s-a. KRW 30,000 domestic; USD 30 foreign (effective 2011). **Document type:** *Journal, Academic/Scholarly.* **Description:** Contains articles on East Asia in the fields of international politics, economics, social, and security aspects of contemporary East Asian affairs.
Related titles: Online - full text ed.
Indexed: A22, ABCPolSci, APEL, BAS, CA, I13, IBSS, P30, P42, PAIS, PRA, PSA, RASB, SCOPUS, SociolAb, T02.
—BLDSC (4971.450000), IE, Infotrieve, Ingenta. **CCC.**
Published by: Institute for National Security Strategy, Instopia Bldg., 16th Fl, 467-23, Dogok-dong, Kangnam-gu, Seoul, Korea, S. TEL 82-2-25727090 ext 230. Ed. Kyusun Han. Pub. Sung Wook Nam. Circ: 2,000.

➤ **JOURNAL OF ENVIRONMENT & DEVELOPMENT**; a review of international policy. see ENVIRONMENTAL STUDIES

P

327 DEU ISSN 0947-9511
JN15

JOURNAL OF EUROPEAN INTEGRATION HISTORY/REVUE D'HISTOIRE DE L'INTEGRATION EUROPEENNE/ZEITSCHRIFT FUER GESCHICHTE DER EUROPAEISCHEN INTEGRATION. Text in English, French, German. 1995. s-a. EUR 72 (effective 2011). adv. reprint service avail. from SCH. **Document type:** *Journal, Academic/Scholarly.*
Indexed: A22, DIP, IBR, IBSS, IBZ.
—BLDSC (4979.606100), IE, Infotrieve, Ingenta. **CCC.**
Published by: (Groupe de Liaison des Professeurs d'Histoire Contemporaine), Nomos Verlagsgesellschaft mbH und Co. KG, Waldseestr 3-5, Baden-Baden, 76530, Germany. TEL 49-7221-21040, FAX 49-7221-210427, nomos@nomos.de, marketing@nomos.de, http://www.nomos.de. Ed. Charles Barthel. Adv. contact Bettina Roos. Circ: 900 (controlled).

327 GBR ISSN 0958-9287
HN371

➤ **JOURNAL OF EUROPEAN SOCIAL POLICY.** Abbreviated title: J E S P. Text in English. 1991. 5/yr. USD 1,030, GBP 557 combined subscription to institutions (print & online eds.); USD 1,009, GBP 546 to institutions (effective 2011). adv. bk.rev. back issues avail.; reprint service avail. from PSC. **Document type:** *Journal, Academic/Scholarly.* **Description:** Provides coverage of key European social policy issues, including aging and pensions, benefits, family policy, gender, health care, international organizations. migration, poverty, professional mobility, unemployment and the voluntary sector.
Related titles: Online - full text ed.: ISSN 1461-7269. USD 927, GBP 501 to institutions (effective 2011).
Indexed: A01, A03, A08, A20, A22, B07, C06, C07, C08, CA, CINAHL, CurCont, E01, FamI, GEOBASE, H04, I13, IBSS, P02, P10, P30, P34, P42, P47, P48, P53, P54, PAIS, PQC, PSA, S02, S03, S11, S21, SCOPUS, SPAA, SSA, SSCI, SociolAb, T02, V02, W07, WBA.
—BLDSC (4979.609000), IE, Infotrieve, Ingenta. **CCC.**
Published by: Sage Publications Ltd. (Subsidiary of: Sage Publications, Inc.), 1 Oliver's Yard, 55 City Rd, London, EC1Y 1SP, United Kingdom. TEL 44-20-73248500, FAX 44-20-73248600, info@sagepub.co.uk, http://www.uk.sagepub.com/home.nav. Eds. Jochen Clasen, Traute Meyer. adv.: B&W page GBP 400; 140 x 210. **Subscr. in the Americas to:** Sage Publications, Inc., 2455 Teller Rd, Thousand Oaks, CA 91320. TEL 805-499-9774, FAX 805-499-0871, journals@sagepub.com.

327 USA ISSN 1941-8760
JZ1318

JOURNAL OF GLOBAL CHANGE AND GOVERNANCE. Abbreviated title: J G C G. Text in English. 2007. q. back issues avail. **Document type:** *Journal, Academic/Scholarly.* **Description:** Provides a forum for the exchange of views on the relationships between the post-cold war realignment of great-powers, globalization, interstate politics, and the growing prominence of international institutions, transnational corporations, non-governmental organizations and social movements.
Media: Online - full text.
Indexed: CA, P42, T02.
Published by: Rutgers University, Division of Global Affairs, 123 Washington St, Ste 510, Ctr for Law and Justice, Newark, NJ 07102. TEL 973-353-5585, FAX 973-353-5074.

327.172 USA ISSN 2152-3908

▼ **THE JOURNAL OF GLOBAL DEVELOPMENT AND PEACE.** Text in English. 2009. s-a. free (effective 2010). **Document type:** *Journal, Academic/Scholarly.*
Media: Online - full text.
Published by: The International College of the University of Bridgeport, 126 Park Ave, Bridgeport, CT 06604. TEL 203-576-4552, 800-392-3582, intlcoll@bridgeport.edu, https://www.bridgeport.edu.

327 USA ISSN 1942-8189
AS30

➤ **JOURNAL OF GLOBAL INTELLIGENCE & POLICY.** Abbreviated title: J G I P. Text in English. 2008 (Jul.). s-a. USD 55; USD 90 combined subscription (print & CD-ROM eds.); USD 225 domestic to libraries; USD 255 foreign to libraries (effective 2009). **Document type:** *Journal, Academic/Scholarly.* **Description:** Provides intellectual analysis on global intelligence and administrative policies.
Related titles: CD-ROM ed.: ISSN 1942-8197. USD 45 (effective 2009); Online - full text ed.: ISSN 2150-6825.
Indexed: A01.
Published by: Intellectbase International Consortium, 1615 7th Ave N, Nashville, TN 37208. TEL 615-739-5124, FAX 615-739-5124, membership@intellectbase.org.

325.21 USA ISSN 1556-2948
HV4010

➤ **JOURNAL OF IMMIGRANT & REFUGEE STUDIES.** Text in English. 2002 (Spring). q. GBP 354 combined subscription in United Kingdom to institutions (print & online eds.); EUR 459, USD 466 combined subscription to institutions (print & online eds.) (effective 2012). adv. reprint service avail. from PSC. **Document type:** *Journal, Academic/Scholarly.* **Description:** Provides articles on global immigration issues including policy analysis, individual and societal experiences, acculturation behavior, and cross-cultural dialogues on theory, research, and practice.
Formerly (until 2006): Journal of Immigrant & Refugee Services (1536-2949)
Related titles: Online - full text ed.: ISSN 1556-2956. GBP 318 in United Kingdom to institutions; EUR 413, USD 419 to institutions (effective 2012).
Indexed: A01, A03, A22, A36, CA, CABA, DIP, E-psyche, E01, E03, ERI, ESPM, FamI, GEOBASE, GH, IBR, IBZ, M02, N02, N03, P30, P34, PAIS, PRA, R12, S02, S03, S21, SCOPUS, SSA, SSciA, SociolAb, T02, T05.
—BLDSC (5004.558600), IE, Ingenta. **CCC.**
Published by: Routledge (Subsidiary of: Taylor & Francis Group), 325 Chestnut St, Ste 800, Philadelphia, PA 19106. TEL 215-625-8900, 800-354-1420, FAX 215-625-8914, journals@routledge.com, http://www.routledge.com. Ed. Dr. Uma A Segal. adv.: B&W page USD 315, color page USD 550; trim 4.375 x 7.125. Circ: 53 (paid).

327 USA ISSN 0022-197X
JZ6.5

JOURNAL OF INTERNATIONAL AFFAIRS. Text in English. 1947. s-a. looseleaf. USD 29 domestic to individuals; USD 37 foreign to individuals; USD 66 domestic to institutions; USD 88 foreign to institutions (effective 2011). adv. bk.rev. cum.index every 5 yrs. back issues avail.; reprints avail. **Document type:** *Journal, Academic/Scholarly.* **Description:** Features analysis of international affairs issues.
Formerly (until 1952): Columbia Journal of International Affairs (1045-3466)
Related titles: Microform ed.: (from PQC); Online - full text ed.
Indexed: A01, A02, A03, A08, A12, A17, A20, A22, A25, A26, ABCPolSci, ABIn, ABS&EES, APEL, AmH&L, B01, B04, B06, B07, B08, B09, BAS, BRD, C12, CA, CLI, DIP, E08, FR, G05, G06, G07, G08, H09, H10, HistAb, I02, I05, I07, IBR, IBSS, IBZ, LID&ISL, LRI, M01, M02, M05, M06, M10, MEA&I, P02, P06, P10, P13, P27, P30, P34, P42, P45, P47, P48, P51, P53, P54, PAIS, PCI, PQC, PRA, PhilInd, R02, RASB, S02, S03, S05, S08, S09, S11, S23, SCOPUS, SSAI, SSAb, SSI, T02, W03, W05.
—BLDSC (5007.550000), IE, Infotrieve, Ingenta, INIST. **CCC.**
Published by: Columbia University, School of International & Public Affairs, International Affairs Bldg, 420 W 118th St, PO Box 4, New York, NY 10027. TEL 212-854-4775, FAX 212-662-0398, sipa_admission@columbia.edu, http://www.sipa.columbia.edu. Ed. Rikha Rani. Adv. contact Kris Clark.

JOURNAL OF INTERNATIONAL AND AREA STUDIES. *see* BUSINESS AND ECONOMICS—International Commerce

JOURNAL OF INTERNATIONAL DEVELOPMENT. *see* BUSINESS AND ECONOMICS—International Development And Assistance

▼ **JOURNAL OF INTERNATIONAL DISPUTE SETTLEMENT.** *see* LAW—International Law

327 USA ISSN 1947-5241
JA76

▼ **THE JOURNAL OF INTERNATIONAL GOVERNMENTAL SYSTEMS AND STRUCTURES.** Text in English. 2009. s-a. USD 50 to qualified personnel; USD 40 to students; USD 25 per issue (effective 2010). **Document type:** *Journal, Academic/Scholarly.* **Description:** Articles on international governmental systems and structures.
Published by: Policy Analysis Institute, PO Box 1517, Upland, CA 91786. TEL 909-593-3511 ext 4399, ltsaye@aol.com.

327 USA ISSN 1933-8198

JOURNAL OF INTERNATIONAL PEACE OPERATIONS. Text in English. 2004. bi-m. USD 30 domestic; USD 35 foreign (effective 2007). **Document type:** *Magazine, Consumer.* **Description:** Covers worldwide political, war, governmental and election events as they relate to contractors, NGOs and peacekeeping operations.
Formerly (until 2006): I P O A Quarterly (1933-818X)
Indexed: A01, APW, C04, CA, I02, P05, P45.
Published by: International Peace Operations Association, 1900 L St NW, Ste 320, Washington, DC 20036. TEL 202-464-0721, FAX 202-464-0726, http://ipoaonline.org/php. Ed. J J Messner. Pub. Douglas Brooks.

327.172 NLD ISSN 1875-4104
JX1981.P7 CODEN: IPEAEF

➤ **JOURNAL OF INTERNATIONAL PEACEKEEPING.** Text in English. 1994. q. EUR 257, USD 361 to institutions; EUR 281, USD 393 combined subscription to institutions (print & online eds.) (effective 2012). back issues avail.; reprint service avail. from PSC. **Document type:** *Journal, Academic/Scholarly.* **Description:** Reports and analyzes developments in international peacekeeping, with emphasis on legal and policy issues.
Formerly (until 2008): International Peacekeeping (1380-748X)
Related titles: Online - full text ed.: ISSN 1875-4112. EUR 234, USD 328 to institutions (effective 2012) (from IngentaConnect).
Indexed: A22, E01, I02, IZBG, P42, T02.
—IE, Infotrieve, Ingenta. **CCC.**
Published by: Martinus Nijhoff (Subsidiary of: Brill), PO Box 9000, Leiden, 2300 PA, Netherlands. TEL 31-71-5353500, FAX 31-71-5317532, marketing@brill.nl. Eds. Boris Kondoch, Harvey Langholtz. **Dist. in N. America by:** Brill, PO Box 605, Herndon, VA 20172-0605. TEL 703-661-1585, 800-337-9255, FAX 703-661-1501, cs@brillusa.com; **Dist. by:** Turpin Distribution Services Ltd., Pegasus Dr, Stratton Business Park, Biggleswade, Bedfordshire SG18 8QB, United Kingdom. TEL 44-1767-604954, FAX 44-1767-601640, custserv@turpin-distribution.com, http://www.turpin-distribution.com/.

327 USA ISSN 1937-1284
JZ6.5

THE JOURNAL OF INTERNATIONAL POLICY SOLUTIONS. Text in English. 2004. s-a. **Document type:** *Journal, Academic/Scholarly.* **Description:** Discusses solutions to international problems and encourages communication across institutional and international boundaries with a particular focus on Latin America and Asia-Pacific regions.
Related titles: Online - full text ed.: ISSN 1937-1292. free (effective 2010).
Published by: University of California, San Diego, Graduate School of International Relations & Pacific Studies, 9500 Gilman Dr, Mail Code 0519, La Jolla, CA 92093. TEL 858-534-2660, FAX 858-534-3939, irps-web@ucsd.edu. Ed. Abigail Aronofsky.

327 NGA ISSN 1597-3522

➤ **JOURNAL OF INTERNATIONAL POLITICS AND DEVELOPMENT.** Text in English. s-m. NGN 3,000, USD 36 to individuals; NGN 6,000, USD 100 to institutions (effective 2009). bk.rev. abstr.; bibl.; charts; stat. back issues avail. **Document type:** *Journal, Academic/Scholarly.*
Published by: Babcock University, Department of Political Science and Public Administration, Vice Chancellor's Office, Ilisan-Remo, Ogun State, PMB 21244, Ikeja, Lagos, Nigeria. TEL 234-803-7133-298, dijiaina@yahoo.com. Eds. Robert Dibie, Ayandiji Aina. **Co-publisher:** Indiana University Kokomo, School of Public and Environmental Affairs.

327 USA ISSN 2159-1741

JOURNAL OF INTERNATIONAL RELATIONS. Text in English. 1998. a. **Document type:** *Journal, Academic/Scholarly.* **Description:** Provides a unique opportunity for undergraduate students in the field of international studies to publish their work in a nationally distributed scholarly publication.
Published by: University of Pennsylvania, 3451 Walnut St, Philadelphia, PA 19104. TEL 215-898-5000, regist@pobox.upenn.edu, http://www.upenn.edu/.

327 GBR ISSN 1408-6980
HD72

➤ **JOURNAL OF INTERNATIONAL RELATIONS AND DEVELOPMENT.** Abbreviated title: J I R D. Text in English; Summaries in English, Slovenian. 1998. q. USD 582 in North America to institutions; GBP 306 elsewhere to institutions (effective 2011). adv. bk.rev. abstr. 110 p./no. 2 cols./p.; back issues avail.; reprints avail. **Document type:** *Journal, Academic/Scholarly.* **Description:** Concerns international political, economic and legal issues, as well as development issues.
Formed by the merger of (1994-1998): Journal of International Relations (1318-2862); (1991-1998): Development and International Cooperation (0354-1258); Which was formerly (1985-1991): Development and South-South Cooperation (0352-7670)
Related titles: Online - full text ed.: ISSN 1581-1980 (from IngentaConnect).
Indexed: A01, A03, A08, A22, B01, B06, B07, B09, CA, E01, GEOBASE, I13, IBSS, M07, P10, P34, P42, P45, P47, P48, P53, P54, PQC, PSA, PerIslam, S02, S03, S11, SCOPUS, SSCI, SociolAb, T02, W07.
—BLDSC (5007.685850), IE, Ingenta. **CCC.**
Published by: (Univerza v Ljubljani, Fakulteta za Druzbene Vede/University of Ljubljana, Faculty of Social Sciences SVN), Palgrave Macmillan Ltd. (Subsidiary of: Macmillan Publishers Ltd.), Houndmills, Basingstoke, Hants RG21 6XS, United Kingdom. TEL 44-1256-329242, FAX 44-1256-479476, orders@palgrave.com, http://www.palgrave.com. Ed. Patrick Thaddeus Jackson. Pub. Guy Edwards. Circ: 400. **Subscr. to:** Subscription Department, Brunel Rd, Houndmills, Basingstoke, Hants RG21 2XS, United Kingdom. TEL 44-1256-357893, FAX 44-1256-328339, subscriptions@palgrave.com.

327.17 341.5 GBR ISSN 1750-2977

JOURNAL OF INTERVENTION AND STATEBUILDING. Text in English. 2007 (Spring). 3/yr. GBP 305 combined subscription in United Kingdom to institutions (print & online eds.); EUR 402, USD 505 combined subscription to institutions (print & online eds.) (effective 2012). adv. back issues avail.; reprint service avail. from PSC. **Document type:** *Journal, Academic/Scholarly.* **Description:** Devoted to academic and practitioner analysis of international intervention with the purpose of strengthening state capacities.
Related titles: Online - full text ed.: ISSN 1750-2985. GBP 275 in United Kingdom to institutions; EUR 362, USD 454 to institutions (effective 2012).
Indexed: A22, CA, E01, I02, IBSS, P42, PAIS, PSA, T02.
—IE. **CCC.**
Published by: Routledge (Subsidiary of: Taylor & Francis Group), 4 Park Sq, Milton Park, Abingdon, Oxon OX14 4RN, United Kingdom. TEL 44-20-70176000, FAX 44-20-70176336, subscriptions@tandf.co.uk, http://www.routledge.com. Ed. David Chandler TEL 44-20-79115000 ext 7605. Adv. contact Linda Hann TEL 44-1344-779945. **Subscr. to:** Taylor & Francis Ltd., Journals Customer Service, Sheepen Pl, Colchester, Essex CO3 3LP, United Kingdom. TEL 44-20-70175544, FAX 44-20-70175198.

327 USA ISSN 1549-9502
E184.S75 CODEN: LSTJEZ

➤ **THE JOURNAL OF LATINO-LATIN AMERICAN STUDIES.** Abbreviated title: J O L L A S. Text in English. 1990. q. USD 60 to individuals; USD 70 to institutions; USD 50 to students (effective 2010). adv. bk.rev. **Document type:** *Journal, Academic/Scholarly.* **Description:** Dedicated to the multidisciplinary and transnational study of Latino and Latin American economic, social, political, and cultural matters in the US and across borders throughout the Americas.
Formerly (until 2003): Latino Studies Journal (1066-1344)
Related titles: Online - full text ed.
Indexed: A01, A02, A03, A08, A26, AmH&L, BibInd, CA, ChPerI, Chicano, E07, E08, G08, H21, I02, I05, P08, P27, P45, P46, P48, P54, PQC, S02, S03, S09, T02.
Published by: The Journal of Latino-Latin American Studies, 287-L Arts and Sciences Hall, University of Nebraska at Omaha, Omaha, NE 68182-0271. Ed., R&P Maria M Arbelaez.

341 GBR ISSN 1357-2334
JA8

➤ **THE JOURNAL OF LEGISLATIVE STUDIES.** Text in English. 1995. q. GBP 361 combined subscription in United Kingdom to institutions (print & online eds.); EUR 476, USD 599 combined subscription to institutions (print & online eds.) (effective 2012). adv. bk.rev. index. back issues avail.; reprint service avail. from PSC. **Document type:** *Journal, Academic/Scholarly.* **Description:** Covers all aspects of legislative research and development for scholars and researchers of legislative studies.
Related titles: Online - full text ed.: ISSN 1743-9337. GBP 324 in United Kingdom to institutions; EUR 428, USD 539 to institutions (effective 2012) (from IngentaConnect).
Indexed: A01, A22, B21, CA, E01, E17, ESPM, I13, IBSS, P34, P42, PSA, S02, S03, SCOPUS, SSA, SociolAb, T02.
—IE, Ingenta. **CCC.**
Published by: Routledge (Subsidiary of: Taylor & Francis Group), 4 Park Sq, Milton Park, Abingdon, Oxon OX14 4RN, United Kingdom. TEL 44-20-70176000, FAX 44-20-70176336, subscriptions@tandf.co.uk, http://www.routledge.com. Ed. Philip Norton TEL 44-1482-465863. Adv. contact Linda Hann TEL 44-1344-779945. **Subscr. to:** Taylor & Francis Ltd., Journals Customer Service, Sheepen Pl, Colchester, Essex CO3 3LP, United Kingdom. TEL 44-20-70175544, FAX 44-20-70175198.

➤ **JOURNAL OF MODERN EUROPEAN HISTORY/REVUE D'HISTOIRE EUROPEENNE CONTEMPORAINE/ZEITSCHRIFT FUER MODERNE EUROPAEISCHE GESCHICHTE.** *see* HISTORY—History Of Europe

➤ **THE JOURNAL OF NORTH AFRICAN STUDIES.** *see* HISTORY—History Of Africa

327.172 GBR ISSN 1740-0201
JZ5511.2

➤ **JOURNAL OF PEACE EDUCATION.** Text in English. 2004. s-a. GBP 262 combined subscription in United Kingdom to institutions (print & online eds.); EUR 350, USD 439 combined subscription to institutions (print & online eds.) (effective 2012). adv. back issues avail.; reprint service avail. from PSC. **Document type:** *Journal, Academic/Scholarly.* **Description:** Features articles that promote discussions on theories, research and practices in peace education in varied educational and cultural settings.

Related titles: Online - full text ed.: ISSN 1740-021X. GBP 236 in United Kingdom to institutions; EUR 315, USD 395 to institutions (effective 2012) (from IngentaConnect).

Indexed: A01, A22, CA, CPE, E01, E03, ERI, P42, S02, S03, T02.

—IE, Ingenta. **CCC.**

Published by: Routledge (Subsidiary of: Taylor & Francis Group), 4 Park Sq, Milton Park, Abingdon, Oxon OX14 4RN, United Kingdom. TEL 44-20-7017-6000, FAX 44-20-7017-6336, info@routledge.co.uk, http://www.routledge.com. Ed. Jeannie Lum. Adv. contact Linda Hann TEL 44-1344-779945. **Subscr. to:** Taylor & Francis Ltd., Journals Customer Service, Sheepen Pl, Colchester, Essex CO3 3LP, United Kingdom. TEL 44-20-70175544, FAX 44-20-70175198.

327.172 GBR ISSN 0022-3433
AS9

➤ **JOURNAL OF PEACE RESEARCH.** Abbreviated title: J P R. Text in English. 1964. bi-m. USD 1,412, GBP 763 combined subscription to institutions (print & online eds.); USD 1,384, GBP 748 to institutions (effective 2011). adv. bk.rev. charts; illus.; stat. index. back issues avail.; reprint service avail. from PSC. **Document type:** *Journal, Academic/Scholarly.* **Description:** Interdisciplinary and international quarterly publishing scholarly work in peace research concentrating on the causes of violence and conflict resolution.

Related titles: Microform ed.: (from PQC); Online - full text ed.: ISSN 1460-3578. USD 1,271, GBP 687 to institutions (effective 2011).

Indexed: A01, A02, A03, A08, A20, A22, A25, A26, ABCPolSci, AMB, ASCA, AmH&L, AmHI, B04, B07, B14, BRD, BRI, BrHumI, CA, CBRI, CMM, CurCont, DIP, E01, E08, ESPM, EconLit, FutSurv, G08, H04, H07, H09, HRIR, HistAb, I02, I05, I13, I14, IBR, IBSS, IBZ, ILD, JEL, LID&ISL, LeftInd, M10, MEA&I, P02, P06, P10, P27, P30, P34, P42, P47, P48, P53, P54, PAIS, PCI, PQC, PRA, PSA, PerIslam, R05, RASB, RiskAb, S02, S03, S05, S08, S09, S11, S21, SCOPUS, SOPODA, SPAA, SSA, SSAI, SSAb, SSCI, SSI, SSciA, SWR&A, SociolAb, T02, V&AA, V02, W03, W07.

—BLDSC (5030.100000), IE, Infotrieve, Ingenta. **CCC.**

Published by: (International Peace Research Institute, Oslo NOR), Sage Publications Ltd. (Subsidiary of: Sage Publications, Inc.), 1 Oliver's Yard, 55 City Rd, London, EC1Y 1SP, United Kingdom. TEL 44-20-73248500, FAX 44-20-73248600, info@sagepub.co.uk, http://www.uk.sagepub.com/home.nav. Ed. Nils Petter Gleditsch. adv.: B&W page GBP 400; 140 x 210. **Subscr. in the Americas to:** Sage Publications, Inc., 2455 Teller Rd, Thousand Oaks, CA 91320. TEL 805-499-9774, FAX 805-499-0871, journals@sagepub.com.

327.172 ZWE ISSN 1542-3166

JOURNAL OF PEACEBUILDING AND DEVELOPMENT. Text in English. 2003. 3/yr. ZWD 8,000 domestic to individuals; USD 50 to individuals USA, Canada, Europe, Australia, Japan; USD 30 to individuals Africa, India, Latin America, South East Asia; ZWD 15,000 domestic to institutions; USD 150 to institutions USA, Canada, Europe, Australia, Japan; USD 50 to institutions Africa, India, Latin America, South East Asia (effective 2005). **Document type:** *Journal, Academic/Scholarly.*

Related titles: Online - full text ed.: (from IngentaConnect).

Indexed: CA, CABA, E12, ESPM, IBSS, LT, N02, P42, PSA, R12, RRTA, RiskAb, S02, S03, S13, S16, SCOPUS, SociolAb, T02, TAR, W11.

—BLDSC (5030.130000). **CCC.**

Published by: South North Centre for Peacebuilding and Development, Highlands, PO Box HG358, Harare, Zimbabwe. TEL 263-4-746543, FAX 263-4-776519, jpd@africaonline.co.zw. Eds. Erin McCandless, Mohammed Abu-Nimer. **Subscr. outside Zimbabwe to:** American University, Center for Global Peace, 4400 Massachusetts Ave, NW, Washington, DC 20016-8123. TEL 202-885-1656, FAX 202-885-5989, jpd@american.edu. **Co-publisher:** American University, Center for Global Peace.

JOURNAL OF POLICING, INTELLIGENCE AND COUNTER TERRORISM. *see* CRIMINOLOGY AND LAW ENFORCEMENT

327 DEU ISSN 1866-802X
HC121

➤ **JOURNAL OF POLITICS IN LATIN AMERICA.** Text in English. 1984. 3/yr. EUR 29.70; EUR 13.30 per issue (effective 2009). back issues avail. **Document type:** *Journal, Academic/Scholarly.* **Description:** Covers Latin American Studies as well as for comparativists focusing on Latin America, including various research areas within the field of political science including parliamentary versus presidential governments, legislatures, electoral and party systems, judiciaries, public policy, political behavior, federalism, and related topics.

Former titles (until 2009): Lateinamerika Analysen (1619-1684); (until 2002): Lateinamerika (0176-2818)

Related titles: Online - full text ed.: free (effective 2011).

Indexed: CA, DIP, ESPM, H21, IBR, IBSS, IBZ, P08, P42, PAIS, PSA, S02, S03, SCOPUS, SociolAb, T02.

Published by: German Institute of Global and Area Studies (G I G A). Institute of Latin American Studies/Leibniz-Institut fuer Globale und Regionale Studien. Institut fuer Lateinamerika-Studien, Neuer Jungfernstieg 21, Hamburg, 20354, Germany. TEL 49-40-42825561, FAX 49-40-42825562, ilas@giga-hamburg.de, http://www.giga-hamburg.de/ilas/. Circ: 400 (paid and controlled).

325.21 GBR ISSN 0951-6328
HV640 CODEN: JRESEQ

➤ **JOURNAL OF REFUGEE STUDIES.** Text in English. 1988. q. GBP 257 in United Kingdom to institutions; EUR 386 in Europe to institutions; USD 514 in US & Canada to institutions; GBP 257 elsewhere to institutions; GBP 281 combined subscription in United Kingdom to institutions (print & online eds.); EUR 421 combined subscription in Europe to institutions (print & online eds.); USD 560 combined subscription in US & Canada to institutions (print & online eds.); GBP 281 combined subscription elsewhere to institutions (print & online eds.) (effective 2012). adv. bk.rev. back issues avail.; reprint service avail. from PSC,WSH. **Document type:** *Journal, Academic/Scholarly.* **Description:** Provides an academic exploration of the complex problems of forced migration and national and international responses. Includes anthropology, economics, health and education, international relations, law, politics, psychology and sociology.

Related titles: Online - full text ed.: ISSN 1471-6925. GBP 234 in United Kingdom to institutions; EUR 351 in Europe to institutions; USD 467 in US & Canada to institutions; GBP 234 elsewhere to institutions (effective 2012) (from IngentaConnect).

Indexed: A22, A36, BibInd, CA, CABA, CurCont, E01, E12, ESPM, GEOBASE, GH, HPNRM, HRIR, I02, I13, I14, IBSS, LT, M10, N02, N03, P10, P30, P34, P42, P46, P48, P53, P54, PAIS, PCI, PQC, PSA, PerIslam, R12, RA&MP, RefugAb, S02, S03, S11, S13, S16, SCOPUS, SOPODA, SSA, SSCI, SSciA, SociolAb, T02, T05, TAR, W07, W11.

—BLDSC (5048.550000), IE, Infotrieve, Ingenta. **CCC.**

Published by: (Refugee Studies Centre), Oxford University Press, Great Clarendon St, Oxford, OX2 6DP, United Kingdom. TEL 44-1865-556767, FAX 44-1865-556646, jnl.orders@oup.co.uk, http://www.oxfordjournals.org. Eds. Joanne van Selm, Richard Black. Pub. Nina Curtis. R&P Fiona Bennett. Adv. contact Linda Hann TEL 44-1344-779945. **U.S. subscr. to:** Oxford University Press, 2001 Evans Rd, Cary, NC 27513. TEL 919-677-0977 ext 5777, 800-852-7323, FAX 919-677-1714, jnlorders@oup-usa.org, http://www.us.oup.com.

➤ **THE JOURNAL OF SLAVIC MILITARY STUDIES.** *see* MILITARY

341.734 947 GBR ISSN 1468-3857
HC401.A1

➤ **JOURNAL OF SOUTHEAST EUROPEAN AND BLACK SEA STUDIES.** Abbreviated title: J S E E B S S. Text in English. 2001 (Jan). q. GBP 373 combined subscription in United Kingdom to institutions (print & online eds.); EUR 493, USD 622 combined subscription to institutions (print & online eds.) (effective 2012). adv. bk.rev. index. back issues avail.; reprint service avail. from PSC. **Document type:** *Journal, Academic/Scholarly.* **Description:** Covers the politics, political economy, international relations and modern history of south east Europe and the black sea area.

Related titles: Online - full text ed.: ISSN 1743-9639. GBP 336 in United Kingdom to institutions; EUR 444, USD 560 to institutions (effective 2012) (from IngentaConnect).

Indexed: A01, A03, A08, A22, AmHI, B21, CA, DIP, E01, E17, ESPM, H07, HistAb, I02, I13, I14, IBR, IBSS, IBZ, M10, P34, P42, PAIS, PSA, S02, S03, SCOPUS, SSCI, SociolAb, T02, W07.

—IE, Ingenta. **CCC.**

Published by: (The Hellenic Foundation for European and Foreign Policy GRC), Routledge (Subsidiary of: Taylor & Francis Group), 4 Park Sq, Milton Park, Abingdon, Oxon OX14 4RN, United Kingdom. TEL 44-20-70176000, FAX 44-20-70176336, subscriptions@tandf.co.uk, http://www.routledge.com. Adv. contact Linda Hann TEL 44-1344-779945. **Subscr. to:** Taylor & Francis Ltd., Journals Customer Service, Sheepen Pl, Colchester, Essex CO3 3LP, United Kingdom. TEL 44-20-70175544, FAX 44-20-70175198, tf.enquiries@tfinforma.com.

327 GBR ISSN 0140-2390
U162

➤ **THE JOURNAL OF STRATEGIC STUDIES.** Text in English. 1978. bi-m. GBP 572 combined subscription in United Kingdom to institutions (print & online eds.); EUR 759, USD 953 combined subscription to institutions (print & online eds.) (effective 2012). adv. bk.rev. illus. index. back issues avail.; reprint service avail. from PSC. **Document type:** *Journal, Academic/Scholarly.* **Description:** Covers both contemporary and historical issues in the field of strategic studies.

Related titles: Microfilm ed.: (from PQC); Online - full text ed.: ISSN 1743-937X. GBP 515 in United Kingdom to institutions; EUR 683, USD 857 to institutions (effective 2012) (from IngentaConnect).

Indexed: A01, A03, A08, A20, A22, AMB, ASCA, AmH&L, AmHI, BAS, BrHumI, CA, CurCont, DIP, E01, GEOBASE, H07, HistAb, I02, I13, IBR, IBSS, IBZ, LID&ISL, M05, P02, P10, P34, P42, P47, P48, P53, P54, PAIS, PCI, PQC, PRA, PSA, PsycholAb, R02, RASB, S02, S03, S11, SCOPUS, SOPODA, SSCI, SociolAb, T02, W07.

—IE, Infotrieve, Ingenta. **CCC.**

Published by: Routledge (Subsidiary of: Taylor & Francis Group), 4 Park Sq, Milton Park, Abingdon, Oxon OX14 4RN, United Kingdom. TEL 44-20-70176000, FAX 44-20-70176336, subscriptions@tandf.co.uk, http://www.routledge.com. Eds. Joe A Maiolo TEL 44-20-78482201, Thomas G Mahnken TEL 202-663-5947. Adv. contact Linda Hann TEL 44-1344-779945. **Subscr. to:** Taylor & Francis Ltd., Journals Customer Service, Sheepen Pl, Colchester, Essex CO3 3LP, United Kingdom. TEL 44-20-70175544, FAX 44-20-70175198.

370.72 USA ISSN 2155-1642

▼ **THE JOURNAL OF THE MARTIN SCHOOL OF INTERNATIONAL STUDIES.** Text in English. 2009. s-a. free (effective 2010). **Document type:** *Journal, Academic/Scholarly.* **Description:** Features student research in the Martin School.

Related titles: Online - full text ed.: ISSN 2155-1650.

Published by: University of Idaho, Martin School of International Studies, PO Box 443177, Moscow, ID 83844. TEL 208-885-6527, FAX 208-885-9464, martin@uidaho.edu.

JOURNAL OF THIRD WORLD STUDIES. *see* HISTORY

327 GBR ISSN 1479-4012

JOURNAL OF TRANSATLANTIC STUDIES. Text in English. 2003. q. GBP 259 combined subscription in United Kingdom to institutions (print & online eds.); EUR 406, USD 508 combined subscription to institutions (print & online eds.) (effective 2012). adv. back issues avail.; reprint service avail. from PSC. **Document type:** *Journal, Academic/Scholarly.* **Description:** Publishes articles with a focus on the transatlantic region as an area with a distinct character and a rich history.

Related titles: Online - full text ed.: ISSN 1754-1018. GBP 233 in United Kingdom to institutions; EUR 365, USD 457 to institutions (effective 2012).

Indexed: A01, A03, A08, A22, AmH&L, CA, E01, IBSS, T02.

—BLDSC (5069.792000), IE, Ingenta. **CCC.**

Published by: (Translantic Studies Association), Routledge (Subsidiary of: Taylor & Francis Group), 4 Park Sq, Milton Park, Abingdon, Oxon OX14 4RN, United Kingdom. TEL 44-20-70176000, FAX 44-20-70176336, subscriptions@tandf.co.uk, http://www.routledge.com. Ed. Alan P Dobson TEL 44-1382-384588. Adv. contact Linda Hann TEL 44-1344-779945. **Subscr. to:** Taylor & Francis Ltd., Journals Customer Service, Sheepen Pl, Colchester, Essex CO3 3LP, United Kingdom. TEL 44-20-70175544, FAX 44-20-70175198.

327 JPN ISSN 0453-0950

JOURNAL OF WORLD AFFAIRS/KAIGAI JIJO. Text in English, Japanese. m. JPY 3,600.

Published by: Takushohu University, Institute of World Studies, 4-14 Kohinata 3-chome, Bunkyo-ku, Tokyo, 112-0006, Japan. Ed. Muneyoshi Date.

327 GBR ISSN 2046-2514

▼ **JOURNAL OF WORLD DEVELOPMENT.** Text in English. 2010 (Apr.). q. free. adv. **Description:** Publishes theoretical and empirical scholarly papers and case studies relating to broad field of business, social sciences, science in general and related disciplines. Discusses new concepts, techniques, strategies, models, and trends that could be of particular importance to academics actively involved in teaching, consulting and executive training and practitioner.

Media: Online - full text.

Published by: Institute of Business Research, 156A, Plumstead Common Rd., London, SE18 2UL, United Kingdom. Ed., Pub. Syed A. Tarek. R&P Sofina Sunzida TEL 44-20-8854-3773.

JUSTPEACE; journal of Pax Christi. *see* RELIGIONS AND THEOLOGY

327 JPN ISSN 0287-0932
HG41

KAIGAI JIJO KENKYU/FOREIGN AFFAIRS STUDIES. Text in Japanese. 1973. s-a. **Document type:** *Journal, Academic/Scholarly.*

Indexed: RILM.

Published by: Kumamoto Gakuen Daigaku, Fuzoku Kaigai Jijou Kenkyuujo/Kumamoto Gakuen University, Institute of Foreign Affairs, 2-5-1 Oe Kumamoto, Kumamoto, 862-8680, Japan. TEL 81-96-3645161, FAX 81-96-3645201, kaigai@kumagaku.ac.jp, http://www3.kumagaku.ac.jp/institute/fa/index.html.

KALASCHNIKOW; das Politmagazin. *see* LITERARY AND POLITICAL REVIEWS

P

327 NLD ISSN 0925-5893

KAN ANDERS. Text in Dutch. 1978. q. EUR 13 (effective 2010). adv. bk.rev.; play rev. illus. 12 p./no. 3 cols./p.; back issues avail. **Document type:** *Journal, Consumer.*

Published by: P A I S, Vlamingstraat 82, Delft, 2611 LA, Netherlands. pais@worldmail.nl, http://www.vredesbeweging.nl. Ed. Gerard van Alkemade. Circ: 750 (controlled).

327 GBR ISSN 1754-8381

KASHMIR AFFAIRS. Text in English. 2007. q. free. **Document type:** *Journal, Academic/Scholarly.* **Description:** Aims to offer different view points and a balanced analysis on the affairs of the various regions of Kashmir, both in India and Pakistan.

Media: Online - full text.

Address: 16 Millway Gardens, Northholt, London, UB5 5DU, United Kingdom. Ed. Murtaza Shibli.

327.4 GBR

KEELE EUROPEAN RESEARCH CENTRE. WORKING PAPERS. Text in English. irreg. **Document type:** *Monographic series, Academic/Scholarly.*

Published by: Keele University, Keele European Research Centre, Keele, Staffs ST5 5BG, United Kingdom. TEL 44-1782-583452, FAX 44-1782-583592, r.ladrech@keele.ac.uk, http://www.keele.ac.uk/depts/spire/Research/kerc/kerc_home.htm.

KEESING'S RECORD OF WORLD EVENTS. *see* POLITICAL SCIENCE—Abstracting, Bibliographies, Statistics

327 KEN ISSN 0376-8465
JX1873.K42

KENYA. MINISTRY OF FOREIGN AFFAIRS. DIRECTORY OF DIPLOMATIC CORPS & INTERNATIONAL ORGANIZATIONS. Key Title: Directory of Diplomatic Corps and International Organizations. Text in English. a. KES 300. **Document type:** *Directory, Government.*

Formerly: Kenya. Ministry of Foreign Affairs. Diplomatic Directory

Published by: Ministry of Foreign Affairs., Protocol Department, Nairobi, Kenya. TEL 254-2-334433, FAX 254-2-335494. **Subscr. to:** Government Press, Haile Selaissie Ave., PO Box 30128, Nairobi, Kenya. TEL 254-2-334075.

327 DEU ISSN 0947-7993

KOELNER ARBEITEN ZUR INTERNATIONALEN POLITIK. Abbreviated title: K A I P(Koelner Arbeiten zur Internationalen Politik). Text in German. 1995. irreg., latest vol.14, 2002. price varies. **Document type:** *Monographic series, Academic/Scholarly.*

Published by: S H Verlag GmbH, Auerstr 17, Cologne, 50733, Germany. TEL 49-221-9561740, FAX 49-221-9561741, info@sh-verlag.de, http://www.sh-verlag.de.

327 JPN ISSN 1345-7861

KOKUSAI KANKEI KENKYU. Text in Japanese. 2000. q. **Document type:** *Journal, Academic/Scholarly.*

Formed by the merger of (1989-2000): Kokusai Kankei Kenkyu. Sogo-hen (0915-6844); (1989-1999): Kokusai Kankei Kenkyu. Kokusai Kankei-hen (0916-3646); (1989-1999): Kokusai Kankei Kenkyu. Kokusai Bunka-hen (0916-3654); All 3 titles superseded (in 1990): Kokusai Kankei Kenkyu (0389-2603)

Indexed: RILM.

Published by: Nihon Daigaku, Kokusai Kankei Kenkyujo, Kokusai Kankei Gakubu/Nihon University, College of International Relations, Institute of International Relations, 2-31-145, Bunkyo-cho, Mishima-shi, Shizuoka 411-8555, Japan. http://www.ir.nihon-u.ac.jp/.

327 JPN ISSN 0910-0156
H8.J3

KOKUSAI KENKYU/INTERNATIONAL STUDIES. Text in Japanese, Multiple languages. 1984. irreg. (approx. 1/yr.). per issue exchange basis.

Published by: Chubu University, Institute for International Studies/Chubu Daigaku, Kokusai Chiiki Kenkyujo, 1200 Matsumoto-cho, Kasugai-shi, Aichi-ken 487-0027, Japan. TEL 0568-51-1111.

327.17 JPN ISSN 0285-7928
HC60
KOKUSAI KYORYOKU/INTERNATIONAL COOPERATION. Text in Japanese. 1953. m. JPY 500 per issue. bk.rev.
Formerly: Kaigai Gijutsu Kyoryoku
Published by: Japan International Cooperation Agency/Kokusai Kyoryoku Jigyodan, 6-13F, Shinjuku Maynds Tower, 1-1, Yoyogi 2-chome, Shibuya-ku, Tokyo, 151-8558, Japan. TEL 81-3-5352-5311, http://www.jica.go.jp/. Ed. Kenzo Osima. Circ: 17,000.

327 JPN ISSN 0919-8636
H8.J3
KOKUSAI KYORYOKU RONSHU/JOURNAL OF INTERNATIONAL COOPERATION STUDIES. Text in Japanese. 1993. s-a. **Document type:** *Journal, Academic/Scholarly.*
—BLDSC (5101.786650).
Published by: Kobe Daigaku, Daigakuin, Kokusai Kyoryoku Kenkyuka./Kobe University, Graduate School of International Cooperation Studies, Rokkodai-cho, Nada, Kobe 657-8501, Japan. TEL 81-78-8011241, FAX 81-78-8011263, http://www.kobe-u.ac.jp/~gsics/indexj.html.

327 JPN ISSN 0452-3377
JX18
KOKUSAI MONDAI/INTERNATIONAL AFFAIRS. Text in Japanese. 1960. m. **Document type:** *Journal, Academic/Scholarly.*
Published by: Nihon Kokusai Mondai Kenkyujo/Japan Institute of International Affairs, Kasumigaseki Bldg 11F, 3-2-5 Kasumigaseki, Chiyoda-ku, Tokyo, 100-6011, Japan. TEL 81-3-35037801, FAX 81-3-35037186, jiiajoho@jiia.or.jp, http://www.jiia.or.jp/.

327 JPN ISSN 0916-2690
KOKUSAIGAKU REBYU/REVIEW OF INTERNATIONAL STUDIES. Text in Japanese. 1988. a. **Document type:** *Journal, Academic/Scholarly.*
Indexed: P30.
Published by: Obirin Daigaku, Kokusai Gakubu/Obirin University, School of International Studies, 3758 Tokiwa Machi, Machida-shi, Tokyo, 194-0294, Japan.

327 DEU ISSN 0944-6311
KONSTANZER SCHRIFTEN ZUR ENTWICKLUNGSPOLITIK. Text in German. 1993. irreg. price varies. **Document type:** *Monographic series, Academic/Scholarly.*
Published by: Hartung-Gorre Verlag, Konstanz, 78465, Germany. TEL 49-7533-97227, FAX 49-7533-97228, Hartung.Gorre@t-online.de, http://www.hartung-gorre.de.

327.519 KOR ISSN 0259-9686
KOREA & WORLD AFFAIRS. Text in English. 1977. q. USD 46; USD 12 per issue (effective 2009). bk.rev. illus. Index. reprints avail. **Document type:** *Journal, Academic/Scholarly.*
Indexed: APEL, AmH&L, CA, HistAb, I13, IBSS, P42, PAIS, PCI, PRA, PSA, SociolAb, T02.
—BLDSC (5113.448000), IE, Ingenta.
Published by: Research Center for Peace and Unification, CPO Box 6545, Seoul, 100-032, Korea, S. TEL 82-2-34531853, FAX 82-2-5539591, rcpu@hotmail.com, rcpuok@hanmail.net. Ed. Ok-Za Yoo. Pub. Hoon Dong.

327 DNK ISSN 0108-8467
KOREA BULLETIN. Text in Danish. 1971. 4/yr. DKK 240 membership (effective 2010). bk.rev. **Document type:** *Magazine, Consumer.* **Description:** Articles, news and essays concerning the economical, social, political and cultural development in North Korea.
Former titles (until 1983): Det Ny Korea (0106-1356); (until 1977): Chollima Korea
Related titles: Online - full text ed.: 2005.
Published by: Venskabsforeningen Danmark-Den Demokratiske Folkerepublik Korea, Tordenskjoldsgade 14, Copenhagen K, 1055, Denmark. TEL 45-33-141526, FAX 45-33-141566, dk-korea@inform.dk.

327 951.9 USA ISSN 1558-8467
DS901
KOREA POLICY REVIEW. Text in English. 2005. a. **Document type:** *Journal, Academic/Scholarly.* **Description:** Serves as a bridge for discussion, the exchange of ideas and the examination of policy issues contributing to Korea-United States relationship.
Related titles: Online - full text ed.: ISSN 1558-8475.
Published by: Harvard University, John F. Kennedy School of Government, 79 John F Kennedy St, PO Box 142, Cambridge, MA 02138. FAX 617-496-8753, cpl@ksg.harvard.edu, http://www.hks.harvard.edu/. Eds. Jong-Sung You, Justin Rhee.

327 951.95 USA ISSN 1548-176X
DS901
THE KOREA SOCIETY QUARTERLY. Text in English. 1992. q. USD 15 to non-members; free to members (effective 2004). **Document type:** *Magazine, Consumer.* **Description:** Provides information about the relationship between the United States and Korea, and on current events in Korea.
Formerly (until 2000): The U.S. - Korea Review (1072-382X)
Published by: The Korea Society, 950 3rd Ave. 8th Fl., New York, NY 10022. TEL 212-759-7525, FAX 212-759-7530, korea.ny@koreasociety.org, http://www.koreasociety.org. Ed. Frederick F. Carriere. Pub. Donald P. Gregg.

327.519 USA ISSN 0163-0229
DS922
KOREAN REVIEW. Text in English. 1978. bi-m. USD 10 to individuals; USD 15 to institutions.
Indexed: APEL, PAIS.
Address: PO Box 32, Knickerbocker Sta, New York, NY 10002. Ed. S J Noumoff.

327.172 FIN ISSN 1236-1372
KOSMOPOLIS. Text in Finnish. 1971. q. EUR 30 domestic; EUR 36 elsewhere; EUR 9 per issue (effective 2004). back issues avail. **Document type:** *Journal, Academic/Scholarly.*
Former titles (until 1993): Rauhantutkimus (0782-1751); (until 1985): Rauhaan Tutkien (0357-0207)
Indexed: IBSS.
Published by: Suomen Rauhantutkimusyhdistys/Finnish Peace Research Association, c/o Samu Pehkonen, Rauhan- ja Konfliktintutkimuskeskus, TAPRI, Tampereen Yliopisto, Tampere, 33014, Finland.

327.47 DEU ISSN 1867-0628
KULTURA; Russland-Kulturanalysen. Text in German, English. 2006. m. free. **Document type:** *Journal, Academic/Scholarly.* **Description:** Covers current events and trends in Russian culture.
Media: Online - full content.
Published by: Universitaet Bremen, Forschungsstelle Osteuropa/Bremen University, Research Centre for East European Studies, Klagenfurter Str 3, Bremen, 28359, Germany. TEL 49-421-2187891, FAX 49-421-2183269, publikationsreferat@osteuropa.uni-bremen.de, http://www.forschungsstelle.uni-bremen.de. Ed. Hartmute Trepper.

327 HUN ISSN 1587-9089
D839
KULUGYI SZEMLE/FOREIGN AFFAIRS. Text in Hungarian; Summaries in English. 1974. q. HUF 3,200 domestic (effective 2008). bk.rev. bibl. **Document type:** *Journal, Academic/Scholarly.*
Formerly (until 2001): Kulpolitika (0133-0616)
Related titles: English Translation: Foreign Policy Review. ISSN 1588-7855. 1997.
Indexed: RASB.
Published by: Magyar Kulugyi Intezet/Hungarian Institute of International Affairs, Berc utca 13-15, Budapest, 1125, Hungary. TEL 36-1-2795700, FAX 36-1-2795701, titkarsag@hiia.hu. Ed. Magyarics Tamas.

306.2 DEU ISSN 1439-0205
N72.P6
KUNST UND POLITIK. Text in German. 1999. irreg., latest vol.11, 2009. price varies. **Document type:** *Monographic series, Academic/Scholarly.*
Indexed: B24, IBR, IBZ.
Published by: V & R Unipress GmbH (Subsidiary of: Vandenhoeck und Ruprecht), Robert-Bosch-Breite 6, Goettingen, 37079, Germany. TEL 49-551-5084301, FAX 49-551-5084333, info@vr-unipress.de, http://www.v-r.de/en/publisher/unipress.

327 UKR ISSN 0236-3879
KUR'IER YUNESKO. Text in Ukrainian. m. USD 125 in United States.
Address: Ul Degtyarevskaya 38-44, Kiev, Ukraine. TEL 213-13-11, FAX 211-04-81. **Dist. by:** East View Information Services, 10601 Wayzata Blvd, Minneapolis, MN 55305. TEL 952-252-1201, 800-477-1005, FAX 952-252-1202, info@eastview.com, http://www.eastview.com.

327.1 SWE ISSN 0280-8447
KVINNOR FOER FRED. Text in Swedish. 1978. q. SEK 60 (effective 1993).
Published by: Kvinnor foer Fred (KFF), Tjarhovsgatan 9, Stockholm, 11621, Sweden.

327 UKR ISSN 1728-2292
➤ **KYIVS'KYI NATSIONAL'NYI UNIVERSYTET IMENI TARASA SHEVCHENKA. VISNYK. MIZHNARODNI VIDNOSYNY.** Text in Ukrainian. 1975. a. **Document type:** *Journal, Academic/Scholarly.*
Formerly (until 1993): Kievskii Universitet. Vestnik. Mezhdunarodnye Otnosheniya i Mezhdunarodnoe Pravo (0136-488X)
Related titles: Online - full text ed.; ◆ Series: Kyivs'kyi Natsional'nyi Universytet imeni Tarasa Shevchenka. Visnyk. Matematyka ta Mekhanika. ISSN 1684-1565; ◆ Kyivs'kyi Natsional'nyi Universytet imeni Tarasa Shevchenka. Visnyk. Yurydychni Nauky. ISSN 1728-2195; ◆ Kyivs'kyi Natsional'nyi Universytet imeni Tarasa Shevchenka. Visnyk. Khimiya. ISSN 1728-2209; ◆ Kyivs'kyi Natsional'nyi Universytet imeni Tarasa Shevchenka. Visnyk. Fizyka. ISSN 1728-2411; ◆ Kyivs'kyi Natsional'nyi Universytet imeni Tarasa Shevchenka. Visnyk. Biolohiya. ISSN 1728-2748; ◆ Kyivs'kyi Natsional'nyi Universytet imeni Tarasa Shevchenka. Visnyk. Ekonomika. ISSN 1728-2667; ◆ Kyivs'kyi Natsional'nyi Universytet imeni Tarasa Shevchenka. Visnyk. Istoriya. ISSN 1728-2640; ◆ Kyivs'kyi Natsional'nyi Universytet imeni Tarasa Shevchenka. Visnyk. Kibernetyka. ISSN 1728-2276; ◆ Kyivs'kyi Natsional'nyi Universytet imeni Tarasa Shevchenka. Visnyk. Problemy Rehulyatsii Fiziolohichnykh Funktsii. ISSN 1728-2624; ◆ Kyivs'kyi Natsional'nyi Universytet imeni Tarasa Shevchenka. Visnyk. Radiofizyka ta Elektronika. ISSN 1728-2306; ◆ Kyivs'kyi Natsional'nyi Universytet imeni Tarasa Shevchenka. Visnyk. Filosofiya, Politolohiya. ISSN 1728-2632; ◆ Kyivs'kyi Natsional'nyi Universytet imeni Tarasa Shevchenka. Visnyk. Introduktsiya ta Zberezhennya Roslynnogo Riznomanittya. ISSN 1728-2284; ◆ Kyivs'kyi Natsional'nyi Universytet imeni Tarasa Shevchenka. Visnyk. Ukrainoznavstvo. ISSN 1728-2330; ◆ Kyivs'kyi Natsional'nyi Universytet imeni Tarasa Shevchenka. Visnyk. Sotsiolohiya, Psykholohiya, Pedahohika. ISSN 1728-2322; ◆ Kyivs'kyi Natsional'nyi Universytet imeni Tarasa Shevchenka. Visnyk. Literaturoznavstvo, Movoznavstvo, Fol'klorystyka. ISSN 1728-2659; ◆ Kyivs'kyi Natsional'nyi Universytet imeni Tarasa Shevchenka. Visnyk. Astronomiya. ISSN 1728-273X; ◆ Kyivs'kyi Natsional'nyi Universytet imeni Tarasa Shevchenka. Visnyk. Seriya: Fizyko-Matematychni Nauky. ISSN 1812-5409; ◆ Kyivs'kyi Natsional'nyi Universytet imeni Tarasa Shevchenka. Visnyk. Heohrafiya. ISSN 1728-2721; ◆ Kyivs'kyi Natsional'nyi Universytet imeni Tarasa Shevchenka. Visnyk. Heolohiya. ISSN 1728-2713; ◆ Kyivs'kyi Natsional'nyi Universytet imeni Tarasa Shevchenka. Visnyk. Zhurnalistyka. ISSN 1728-2705; ◆ Kyivs'kyi Natsional'nyi Universytet imeni Tarasa Shevchenka. Visnyk. Inozemna Filolohiya. ISSN 1728-2683; ◆ Kyivs'kyi Natsional'nyi Universytet imeni Tarasa Shevchenka. Visnyk. Shidni Movy ta Literatury. ISSN 1728-242X; ◆ Kyivs'kyi Natsional'nyi Universytet imeni Tarasa Shevchenka. Visnyk. ISSN 1728-3817.
Published by: (Kyivs'kyi Natsional'nyi Universytet imeni Tarasa Shevchenka/National Taras Shevchenko University of Kyiv), Vydavnycho-Poligrafichnyi Tsentr Kyivs'kyi Universytet, bul'var Tarasa Shevchenko, 14, ofis 43, Kyiv, 01601, Ukraine. TEL 380-44-2393172, FAX 380-44-2393128. Ed. Leonid Hubers'kyi.

327 JPN ISSN 1340-9425
KYUSHU SANGYO DAIGAKU KOKUSAI BUNKA GAKUBU KIYO/KYUSHU SANGYO UNIVERSITY. FACULTY OF INTERNATIONAL STUDIES OF CULTURE. JOURNAL. Text in Japanese. 1964. a. **Document type:** *Journal, Academic/Scholarly.*
Formerly (until 1994): Kyushu Sangyo Daigaku Kyoyobu Kiyo/Kyushu Sangyo University. College of Liberal Arts. Bulletin (0286-780X)
Indexed: CCMJ, MSN, MathR, Z02.
Published by: Kyushu Sangyo Daigaku, Kokusai Bunka Gakubu/Kyushu Sangyo University, Faculty of International Studies of Culture, 2-3-1 Matsukadai, Higashi-ku, Fukuoka, 813-8503, Japan. http://www.ip.kyusan-u.ac.jp/gakubu/kokusai/kokusai_top.html.

327 CAN ISSN 0316-3393
F1401
L A W G LETTER. Text in English. 1967. irreg. bk.rev. illus. **Description:** Focuses on Canada's trade, aid and investment links to South and Central America and popular movements in the Americas.
Indexed: HRIR.
—CCC.
Published by: Latin American Working Group, 603 1/2 Parliament St, Toronto, ON M4X 1P9, Canada. TEL 416-966-4773, FAX 416-920-0604. Circ: 7,000.

327 GHA ISSN 0855-076X
D410
L E C I A BULLETIN. Text in English. 1991. a.
Published by: Legon Centre for International Affairs, Accra, Ghana.

327 GBR ISSN 1755-1390
L I S A JOURNAL. Text in English. 2007. q. GBP 5 domestic; GBP 10 foreign (effective 2009). back issues avail. **Document type:** *Journal, Academic/Scholarly.*
Related titles: Online - full text ed.
Published by: London Institute of South Asia, 3 Blacklands Dr, Hayes, Midds UB4 8EU, United Kingdom. TEL 44-20-87973729, http://www.lisauk.com.

327 FRA ISSN 1162-6208
DC1
LABEL FRANCE. Text in French. 1967. q. free. back issues avail. **Document type:** *Magazine, Government.* **Description:** Distributed by the French diplomatic service to foreign opinion formers throughout the world, with a print run of almost 200,000 copies in nine language editions.
Formerly (until 1991): France Informations (0015-959X)
Related titles: Online - full text ed.: ISSN 1140-6216; German ed.: ISSN 1168-5751; Russian ed.: ISSN 1252-6479; Portuguese ed.: ISSN 1296-6932; Japanese ed.: ISSN 1771-1177; English ed.: ISSN 1162-6216; Spanish ed.: ISSN 1162-6224.
Indexed: FR.
Published by: France. Ministere des Affaires Etrangeres, 37 Quai d'Orsay, Paris, 75007, France.

327 SWE ISSN 1101-0193
LAEGET I VAERLDEN. Text in Swedish. 1988. a., latest 2003. price varies. back issues avail. **Document type:** *Yearbook, Consumer.* **Description:** A "State of the World" yearly factbook from UN Sweden.
Published by: Svenska FN-Foerbundet/United Nations Association of Sweden, PO Box 15115, Stockholm, 10465, Sweden. TEL 46-8-4622540, FAX 46-8-6418876, info@fn.se, http://www.fn.se.

327 CHE ISSN 1014-5370
AL LAGI'UN. Text in Arabic. 1984. irreg.
Related titles: ◆ English ed.: Refugees. ISSN 0252-791X; ◆ French ed.: Refugies. ISSN 1014-0905; ◆ Spanish ed.: Refugiados. ISSN 1014-0891; ◆ Chinese ed.: Nanmin Zazhi. ISSN 1014-5389; ◆ Japanese ed.: Refyujizu. ISSN 1014-1162; ◆ German ed.: Fluchtlinge. ISSN 1014-1154; ◆ Italian ed.: Rifugiati. ISSN 1014-0832.
Published by: United Nations High Commissioner for Refugees, Public Information Section, PO Box 2500, Geneva 2, 1211, Switzerland. TEL 41-22-739-81-11, FAX 41-22-739-84-49, http://www.unhcr.ch/.

327.8 AUT ISSN 1028-9453
LATEINAMERIKA ANDERS PANORAMA. Text in German. 1976. m. adv. bk.rev. back issues avail. **Document type:** *Newsletter, Consumer.* **Description:** News and background information on Latin America.
Formerly (until 1993): Lateinamerika Anders Report
Published by: Informationsgruppe Lateinamerika, Waehringerstr 59, Vienna, W 1090, Austria. igla@compuserve.com. Eds. Hermann Klosius, Werner Hoertner. Circ: 1,000.

LATEINAMERIKA NACHRICHTEN. *see* BUSINESS AND ECONOMICS—International Development And Assistance

327 CHL ISSN 0718-8552
JZ9
▼ **LATIN AMERICAN JOURNAL OF INTERNATIONAL AFFAIRS/REVISTA DE ASUNTOS INTERNACIONALES.** Text in Multiple languages. 2009. 3/yr. free (effective 2011). **Document type:** *Journal, Academic/Scholarly.*
Media: Online - full text.
Published by: Escuela de Asuntos Internacionales http://www.asuntosinternacionales.com.

327 USA ISSN 1531-426X
F1401 CODEN: LAPSCG
➤ **LATIN AMERICAN POLITICS AND SOCIETY.** Text in English. 1959. q. GBP 290 in United Kingdom to institutions; EUR 367 in Europe to institutions; USD 505 in the Americas to institutions; USD 567 elsewhere to institutions; GBP 333 combined subscription in United Kingdom to institutions (print & online eds.); EUR 422 combined subscription in Europe to institutions (print & online eds.); USD 581 combined subscription in the Americas to institutions (print & online eds.); USD 652 combined subscription elsewhere to institutions (print & online eds.) (effective 2012). adv. bk.rev. charts; illus. index. back issues avail.; reprint service avail. from PSC. **Document type:** *Journal, Academic/Scholarly.* **Description:** Dedicated to challenging prevailing orthodoxies and promoting innovative perspectives on the states, societies, economies and international relations of the Americas in a globalizing world.
Former titles (until 2001): Journal of Interamerican Studies and World Affairs (0022-1937); (until 1970): Journal of Inter-American Studies (0885-3118)
Related titles: Microfilm ed.: (from PQC); Online - full text ed.: ISSN 1548-2456. GBP 290 in United Kingdom to institutions; EUR 367 in Europe to institutions; USD 505 in the Americas to institutions; USD 567 elsewhere to institutions (effective 2012) (from IngentaConnect).

Indexed: A01, A02, A03, A08, A12, A20, A22, A26, ABCPolSci, ABIn, ABS&EES, AMB, ASCA, AmH&L, B01, B04, B06, B07, B08, B09, BAS, BRD, C12, CA, CERDIC, CurCont, E01, E08, EconLit, G08, GEOBASE, H09, H21, HistAb, I02, I04, I05, I07, I13, IBR, IBSS, IBZ, JEL, M01, M02, M05, M06, MEA&I, MLA-IB, P02, P06, P08, P10, P13, P27, P30, P34, P42, P45, P47, P48, P51, P53, P54, PAIS, PCI, PQC, PRA, PSA, R02, RASB, S02, S03, S05, S09, S11, S23, SCOPUS, SSAI, SSAb, SSCI, SSI, SociolAb, T02, W03, W04, W05, W07, WBA, WMB.
—BLDSC (5160.092000), IE, Ingenta. **CCC.**
Published by: (University of Miami, Center for Latin-American Studies), Wiley-Blackwell Publishing, Inc. (Subsidiary of: Wiley-Blackwell Publishing Ltd.), 111 River St, Hoboken, NJ 07030. TEL 201-748-6000, FAX 201-748-6088, info@wiley.com, http://www.wiley.com/WileyCDA/. Ed. William C Smith. Adv. contact Kristin McCarthy TEL 201-748-7683.

➤ **THE LATIN AMERICAN TIMES.** *see* BUSINESS AND ECONOMICS—International Commerce

➤ **LAW OF THE SEA INSTITUTE. OCCASIONAL PAPER.** *see* LAW—Maritime Law

➤ **LEADERS.** *see* BUSINESS AND ECONOMICS—International Commerce

327.5692 LBN ISSN 1019-0740
DS80.95
LEBANON REPORT. Text in English. 1990. q. USD 20; USD 40 foreign. back issues avail. **Document type:** *Newsletter.* **Description:** Analyzes political, diplomatic, military and economic trends in Lebanon, and developments in the Middle East affecting the Lebanese situation.
Related titles: E-mail ed.
Indexed: PerIslam.
Published by: Lebanese Center for Policy Studies, Tayyar Bldg., Mkalles Sin al-Fil, Beirut, Lebanon. TEL 961-1-490561, FAX 961-1-601787, info@lcps-lebanon.org. Ed. Michael Bacos Young. **Subscr. outside Lebanon to:** LCPS, PO Box 1377, Highland Park, NJ 08904. TEL 732-937-6697, 732-220-0885.

327 GBR ISSN 2044-7892
▼ **LEEDS EAST ASIA PAPERS (ONLINE).** Abbreviated title: L E A P. Text in English. 2010. irreg., latest vol.1, 2010. free (effective 2010). **Document type:** *Monographic series, Academic/Scholarly.* **Description:** Covers East and South East Asia, and areas of interest from the arts, humanities and social sciences.
Media: Online - full text.
Published by: University of Leeds, Department of East Asian Studies, Michael Sadler Bldg, Woodhouse Ln, Leeds, LS2 9JT, United Kingdom. TEL 44-113-3433460, eastasian@leeds.ac.uk. Ed. Michael J G Parnwell TEL 44-113-3436334.

327.6885 LSO ISSN 0460-2099
LESOTHO. MINISTRY OF FOREIGN AFFAIRS. DIPLOMATIC AND CONSULAR LIST. Text in English. 1976. a. USD 1.
Published by: Ministry of Foreign Affairs, Maseru, Lesotho. Circ: 500.

327 FRA ISSN 0296-399X
LETTRE DU CONTINENT. Text in French. 1985. 23/yr. EUR 685 (effective 2009). adv. **Document type:** *Newsletter.* **Description:** Carries decisive information on French-speaking Africa.
Related titles: Online - full text ed.: ISSN 1624-611X.
—CIS.
Published by: Indigo Publications, 10 rue du Sentier, Paris, 75002, France. TEL 33-1-44882610, FAX 33-1-44882615. Ed. Maurice Botbol. R&P Antoine Glaser. Adv. contact Magali Oudard.

327 ITA ISSN 0024-1504
DS63.2.I8
LEVANTE. Text in Arabic, Italian. 1953. q. adv. bk.rev. bibl.; charts; illus.; stat. cum.index: 1953-1968. **Document type:** *Journal, Academic/Scholarly.* **Description:** Includes articles written on Italian-Arab relations, with emphasis on Arab culture.
Indexed: IBR, IBZ, M10.
Published by: Istituto Italiano per l'Africa e l'Oriente, Via Ulisse Aldrovandi 16, Rome, 00197, Italy. TEL 39-06-328551, FAX 39-06-3225348, biblio.dir@isiao.it, http://www.isiao.it. Ed. Salvatore Bono.

327 CHN ISSN 1006-5679
LIANG'AN GUANXI/RELATIONS ACROSS TAIWAN STRAITS. Text in Chinese. 1997. m. USD 62.40 (effective 2009). **Document type:** *Journal, Academic/Scholarly.*
Related titles: Online - full text ed.
—East View.
Published by: Liang'an Guanxi Zazhishe, 35, Fujia Dajie Jia, Beijing, 100037, China. TEL 86-10-68995642, FAX 86-10-68995564. **Dist. by:** China International Book Trading Corp, 35 Chegongzhuang Xilu, Haidian District, PO Box 399, Beijing 100044, China. TEL 86-10-68412045, FAX 86-10-68412023, cibtc@mail.cibtc.com.cn, http://www.cibtc.com.cn.

327 CHN ISSN 1003-2282
LIANHEGUO JISHI/UNITED NATIONS CHRONICLE. Text in Chinese. 1984. q.
Indexed: SPPI.
Published by: Zhongguo Duiwai Fanyi Chuban Gongsi/China Translation and Publishing Corporation, Wuhua Dasha 6F, 4 Chegongzhuang Dajie Jia, Xicheng-qu, Beijing, 100044, China. http://www.ctpc.com.cn. Ed. Zheng Yuzhi.

LIBERATION. *see* POLITICAL SCIENCE—Civil Rights

327 GBR ISSN 0267-6761
LIBERTARIAN ALLIANCE. FOREIGN POLICY PERSPECTIVES. Text in English. 1983. irreg., latest 2002. bk.rev.; film rev. bibl. back issues avail. **Document type:** *Monographic series, Trade.*
Related titles: Online - full text ed.: ISSN 2042-2563.
Published by: Libertarian Alliance, 2 Lansdowne Row, Ste 35, London, W1J 6HL, United Kingdom. TEL 44-7956-472199. Ed. Nigel Meek.

327 DEU ISSN 0944-8039
LIBERTAS OPTIMA RERUM. Text in German. 1984. irreg., latest vol.13, 1996. price varies. **Document type:** *Monographic series, Academic/Scholarly.*
Published by: Duncker und Humblot GmbH, Carl-Heinrich-Becker-Weg 9, Berlin, 12165, Germany. TEL 49-30-7900060, FAX 49-30-79000631, info@duncker-humblot.de.

LIBERTY AT BAY; issues impacting on freedom in our time. *see* BUSINESS AND ECONOMICS—Economic Situation And Conditions

327 GBR ISSN 1460-9649
THE LIBRARY OF LEGISLATIVE STUDIES. Text in English. 1996. irreg., latest 2009. price varies. back issues avail. **Document type:** *Monographic series, Academic/Scholarly.* **Description:** Comprises scholarly books including individual country studies as well as major comparative works that advance knowledge of legislatures and legislative processes.
Published by: Routledge (Subsidiary of: Taylor & Francis Group), 4 Park Sq, Milton Park, Abingdon, Oxon OX14 4RN, United Kingdom. TEL 44-20-70176000, FAX 44-20-70176336, subscriptions@tandf.co.uk, http://www.routledge.com.

LIETUVOS METINE STRATEGINE APZVALGA. *see* MILITARY

327 USA ISSN 0024-4007
DS119.7
LINK (NEW YORK, 1967). Text in English. 1967. bi-m. USD 40 voluntary contribution (effective 2005). bk.rev. abstr.; bibl.; illus. reprints avail. **Document type:** *Newsletter.*
Indexed: HECAB, HRIR, M10.
—Ingenta.
Published by: Americans for Middle East Understanding, Inc., 475 Riverside Dr, Rm 245, New York, NY 10115. TEL 212-870-2336, FAX 212-870-2050. Pub., R&P John Mahoney TEL 212-870-2053. Circ: 50,000.

LITHUANIAN ANNUAL STRATEGIC REVIEW/LIETUVOS METINE STRATEGINE APZVALGA. *see* MILITARY

327.1 LTU ISSN 1392-5504
DK505.68
LITHUANIAN FOREIGN POLICY REVIEW. Text in English, Russian. 1998. s-a. **Document type:** *Journal, Academic/Scholarly.* **Description:** Serve as a public forum in which the foreign policy makers and those implementing policy will are able to exchange views with Lithuanian and foreign academics specializing in the areas of foreign policy and diplomacy.
Related titles: Online - full text ed.: free (effective 2011).
Indexed: CA, IBSS, T02.
Published by: Vilniaus Universitetas, Tarptautiniu Santykiu ir Politicos Mokslu/University of Vilnius, Institute of International Relations and Political Science, Vokieciu St 10, Vilnius, 01130, Lithuania. TEL 370-5-2514130, FAX 370-5-2514134, tspmi@tspmi.vu.lt, http://www.tspmi.vu.lt. Ed. Tomas Janeliunas.

LITHUANIAN PAPERS. *see* ETHNIC INTERESTS

327 AUT ISSN 1813-856X
JN26
➤ **LIVING REVIEWS IN EUROPEAN GOVERNANCE.** Text in English. 2006. irreg. free (effective 2011). **Document type:** *Journal, Academic/Scholarly.* **Description:** Publishes reviews of research on core themes relating to European Governance.
Media: Online - full text.
Indexed: CA, P42, PSA, SCOPUS, T02.
Published by: European Community Studies Association, Althanstr 39-45, Vienna, 1090, Austria. TEL 43-1-313364135, FAX 43-1-31336758, ecsa@wu-wien.ac.at, http://www2.wu-wien.ac.at/ecsa/. Ed. Gerda Falkner. **Co-publisher:** New Modes of Governance Project.

327 PRT ISSN 1647-9572
LIVROS DE BOLSO EUROPA - AMERICA. Text in Portuguese. 1971. irreg. **Document type:** *Monographic series, Academic/Scholarly.*
Published by: Publicacoes Europa - America, Rua Francisco Lyon de Castro 2, Mem Martins, 2725-354, Portugal. TEL 351-21-9267700, FAX 351-21-9267771, secretariado@europa-america.pt, http://www.europa-america.pt.

327.12 GBR ISSN 2042-7182
▼ **LOBSTER (ONLINE);** politics, parapolitics, history. Text in English. 2009. s-a. free (effective 2010). back issues avail. **Document type:** *Magazine, Trade.* **Description:** Focuses on the impact of the intelligence and security services on contemporary history and politics, economics and economic politics, conspiracy theories and the contemporary conspiracist subculture.
Media: Online - full text. **Related titles:** CD-ROM ed.: ISSN 1755-9049.
Published by: Lobster, 214 Westbourne Ave, Hull, N Humberside HU5 3JB, United Kingdom. TEL 44-1482-447558. Ed. Robin Ramsay.

341.72 PRT ISSN 1647-1342
LUSIADA. POLITICA INTERNACIONAL E SEGURANCA. Text in Portuguese. 2008. a. **Document type:** *Journal, Academic/Scholarly.*
Published by: Universidade Lusiada de Lisboa, Rua da Junqueira 188-198, Lisbon, 1349-001, Portugal. TEL 351-213-611527, FAX 351-213-638307, editora@lis.ulusiada.pt, http://editora.lis.ulusiada.pt.

327 FRA ISSN 0295-5385
LUTTE DE CLASSE; pour la reconstruction de la quatrieme internationale. Text in French. 1956. m. (10/yr.). **Document type:** *Magazine, Consumer.*
Published by: Lutte Ouvriere, BP 233, Paris, Cedex 18 75865, France. TEL 33-01-44830377, FAX 33-01-44839673.

327 NLD
LUXEMBOURG INSTITUTE FOR EUROPEAN AND INTERNATIONAL STUDIES. Text in English. irreg., latest 2008. price varies. **Document type:** *Monographic series, Academic/Scholarly.*
Published by: (Luxembourg Institute for European and International Studies LUX), Rozenberg Publishers, Lindengracht 302 D&E, Amsterdam, 1015 KM, Netherlands. TEL 31-20-6255429, FAX 31-20-6203395, info@rozenbergps.com.

M E R I A JOURNAL. (Middle East Review of International Affairs) *see* ASIAN STUDIES

327 USA ISSN 1081-9649
MACALESTER INTERNATIONAL. Text in English. 1978. s-a. **Document type:** *Journal, Trade.*
Related titles: Online - full text ed.: ISSN 2158-3676.
Published by: Macalester College, 1600 Grand Ave, St. Paul, MN 55105. TEL 651-696-6000, communications@macalester.edu, http://www.macalester.edu/.

327 USA ISSN 1087-9404
DS126.5
THE MACCABEAN; political analysis and commentary on Israeli and Jewish affairs. Text in English. 1993. m. USD 45 in US & Canada; USD 50 in Europe and Israel. adv. **Document type:** *Newsletter.*
Related titles: Microfilm ed.: (from AJP); Online - full text ed.
Indexed: J01.
Published by: Freeman Center for Strategic Studies, PO Box 35661, Houston, TX 77235-5661. TEL 713-723-6016. Ed., R&P, Adv. contact Bernard Shapiro. page USD 200; trim 11 x 8.5. Circ: 1,000.

341.734 327.1 CAN
MACKENZIE PAPERS. Text in English. 1986. irreg. **Document type:** *Journal, Academic/Scholarly.*
Indexed: LID&ISL.
Published by: Mackenzie Institute, PO Box 338, Adelaide Station, Toronto, ON M5C 2J4, Canada. TEL 416-686-4063, mackenzieinstitute@bellnet.ca, http://www.mackenzieinstitute.com.

MADRE SPEAKS. *see* WOMEN'S INTERESTS

327 FRA ISSN 1150-4447
MAGHREB CONFIDENTIEL. Text in French. 1990. 46/yr. EUR 535 (effective 2009). adv. back issues avail. **Document type:** *Newsletter.* **Description:** Provides insight into the politics and economy of North African countries; Tunisia, Morocco, Algeria and Libya.
Related titles: Online - full text ed.: ISSN 1624-6128; ◆ English ed.: Maghreb Confidential. ISSN 1624-6136.
—CIS.
Published by: Indigo Publications, 142 rue Montmartre, Paris, 75002, France. TEL 33-1-44882610, FAX 33-1-44882615, info@indigo-net.com, http://www.indigo-net.com. Ed., R&P Maurice Botbol. Adv. contact Magali Oudard.

327 HUN ISSN 0541-9220
DB956
MAGYAR KULPOLITIKAI EVKONYV. Text in Hungarian. 1968. a. USD 7.20. **Document type:** *Government.*
Indexed: RASB.
Published by: Magyar Kulugyminiszterium, Doumentacios Foosztaly, Budapest, Hungary. **Dist. by:** Kultura, Fo utca 82, Budapest 1011, Hungary.

P

327 SAU ISSN 1319-304X
JX18
MAJALLAT AL-DIRASSAT AL-DIBLOMASIYAH/JOURNAL OF DIPLOMATIC STUDIES. Text in Arabic, English. 1984. a. **Description:** Includes political, legal, economical, geographical, social, and media studies related to regional and international issues.
Published by: Institute of Diplomatic Studies, Ministry of Foreign Affairs, P O Box 51988, Riyadh, 11553, Saudi Arabia. TEL 966-4018881, FAX 966-4018864. Ed. Mohammed Omar Madani.

327 IRQ ISSN 1819-5571
MAJALLAT MARKAZ AL-DIRASAT AL-FILASTINIYYAT/JOURNAL OF THE CENTER FOR PALESTINE STUDIES. Text in Arabic. 1967. q. **Document type:** *Journal, Academic/Scholarly.*
Published by: University of Baghdad, Center for Palestine Studies (Subsidiary of: Jami'at Baghdad/University of Baghdad), Jadriya Campus, Baghdad, Iraq. http://www.univofbaghdad.com/english_main/3.htm.

341.72 USA ISSN 1532-0359
THE MANAGEMENT OF SECURITY ASSISTANCE. Text in English. 1979. a. back issues avail. **Document type:** *Journal, Academic/Scholarly.* **Description:** Provides official guidance concerning new security assistance policies and procedural requirements, and includes the most recently enacted legislation governing security assistance activities.
Related titles: Online - full text ed.: D I S A M Journal. ISSN 1525-3236. 1999. free (effective 2010).
Indexed: A01, A03, A08, A26, G05, G06, G07, G08, I05, M06.
Published by: Defense Institute of Security Assistance Management, 2475 K St, Bldg 52, Wright-Patterson, OH 45433. TEL 937-255-2994, FAX 937-656-4685. Ed. Lonnie M Prater.

327 300 DEU ISSN 0542-6758
DK502.3
MARE BALTICUM. Text in German. 1965. a. EUR 8 (effective 2006). bk.rev. bibl.; charts; illus. index. back issues avail. **Document type:** *Academic/Scholarly.*
Published by: Ostsee-Akademie Travemuende, Europaweg 3, Luebeck, 23570, Germany. TEL 49-4502-8030, FAX 49-4502-803200, http://www.ostseeakademie.de. Circ: 3,000.

327.1 PAK
➤ **MARGALLA PAPERS.** Text in English. a. PKR 400, USD 50 (effective 2008). **Document type:** *Journal, Academic/Scholarly.*
Published by: National Defence University Islamabad, Institute of Strategic Studies Research and Analysis, NDU Sector E-9, Islamabad, Pakistan. TEL 92-51-9260651, FAX 92-51-9260663. Ed., R&P Hayatullah Khan Khattack. Circ: 1,000 (controlled).

327 TUR ISSN 1301-1359
➤ **MARMARA UNIVERSITESI AVRUPA TOPLULUGU ENSTITUSU AVRUPA ARASTIRMALARI DERGISI/MARMARA JOURNAL OF EUROPEAN STUDIES.** Text in English, Turkish. 1991. bi-m. adv. bk.rev. back issues avail. **Document type:** *Journal, Academic/Scholarly.* **Description:** Presents studies pertinent to European integration and the position of turkey in this context.
Published by: Marmara Universitesi, European Community Institute, Goztepe Kampusu, Kuyubasi, Istanbul, 81040, Turkey. TEL 90-216-3384196, FAX 90-216-3474543. Ed. Cengiz Okman. Pub. Haluk Kabaalighi. R&P Muzaffer Dartan. Adv. contact Esra Hatipoglu. B&W page USD 750, color page USD 1,000. Circ: 1,000.

327.17 DEU
MARSHALL CENTER PAPERS. Text in English. 2000. irreg., latest vol.7, 2005. price varies. **Document type:** *Monographic series, Academic/Scholarly.* **Description:** Aims to disseminate scholarly monographs that contribute George C. Marshall's ideal of ensuring that Europe and Eurasia are democratic, free, undivided and at peace in the 21st Century.
Indexed: LID&ISL.
Published by: George C. Marshall European Center for Security Studies, Gernackerstr 2, Garmisch-Partenkirchen, 82467, Germany. TEL 49-8821-7502469, FAX 49-8821-7502452, library@marshallcenter.org.

327 DEU ISSN 0948-7557
AP31
MATICES; Zeitschrift zu Lateinamerika, Spanien und Portugal. Text in German. 1994. q. EUR 21 to individuals; EUR 25 to institutions; EUR 20 to students (effective 2006). adv. **Document type:** *Magazine, Academic/Scholarly.* **Description:** Covers Latin America and the Iberian Peninsula, examining cultural, social, political, economic, and historical issues of the regions.
Published by: Projektgruppe Matices e.V., Melchiorstr 3, Cologne, 50670, Germany. matices@is-koeln.de.

327 CAN
MCNAUGHTON PAPERS; the Canadian journal of strategic studies. Text in English. 2/yr. CAD 15. adv. **Document type:** *Journal, Academic/Scholarly.*
Published by: Canadian Institute of Strategic Studies, 10 Adelaide St E, Suite 400, Toronto, ON M5C 1J3, Canada. TEL 416-322-8128, FAX 416-322-8129, info@ciss.ca. Ed. Alex Morrison. Adv. contact Mark Larsen.

327 ESP ISSN 1697-8897
MED.; anuario del Mediterraneo. Text in Spanish. 2004. a. EUR 50 (effective 2009). back issues avail. **Document type:** *Yearbook, Consumer.*
Related titles: French ed.: ISSN 1697-8927; English ed.: ISSN 1698-3068.
Published by: Fundacio C I D O B, C. Elisabets, 12, Barcelona, 08001, Spain. TEL 34-93-3026495, FAX 34-93-3022118, publicaciones@cibod.org, http://www.cibod.org.

MEDIA, WAR & CONFLICT. *see* JOURNALISM

MEDICINE, CONFLICT AND SURVIVAL. *see* MEDICAL SCIENCES

327 GBR ISSN 1362-9395
DE100
➤ **MEDITERRANEAN POLITICS.** Text in English. 1994; N.S. 1996. 3/yr. GBP 300 combined subscription in United Kingdom to institutions (print & online eds.); EUR 397, USD 498 combined subscription to institutions (print & online eds.) (effective 2012). adv. index. back issues avail.; reprint service avail. from PSC. **Document type:** *Journal, Academic/Scholarly.* **Description:** Covers political developments at the national and international levels in the mediterranean region.
Supersedes: Mediterranean Politics (Monographs) (1354-2982)
Related titles: Online - full text ed.: ISSN 1743-9418. GBP 269 in United Kingdom to institutions; EUR 358, USD 448 to institutions (effective 2012) (from IngentaConnect).
Indexed: A01, A03, A08, A22, CA, CCME, E01, ESPM, GEOBASE, I13, I14, IBSS, LeftInd, M10, P34, P42, PAIS, PSA, RiskAb, S02, S03, SCOPUS, SSCI, SociolAb, T02, W07.
—IE, Ingenta. **CCC.**
Published by: Routledge (Subsidiary of: Taylor & Francis Group), 4 Park Sq, Milton Park, Abingdon, Oxon OX14 4RN, United Kingdom. TEL 44-20-70176000, FAX 44-20-70176336, subscriptions@tandf.co.uk, http://www.routledge.com. Eds. Emma Murphy, Richard Gillespie TEL 44-151-7942890. Adv. contact Linda Hann TEL 44-1344-779945. **Subscr. to:** Taylor & Francis Ltd., Journals Customer Service, Sheepen Pl, Colchester, Essex CO3 3LP, United Kingdom. TEL 44-20-70175544, FAX 44-20-70175198.

327 USA ISSN 1047-4552
D839
➤ **MEDITERRANEAN QUARTERLY;** a journal of global issues. Text in English. 1989. q. USD 30 to individuals; USD 92 to institutions; USD 97 combined subscription to institutions (print & online eds.); USD 23 per issue to institutions (effective 2012). adv. back issues avail.; reprint service avail. from PSC. **Document type:** *Journal, Academic/Scholarly.* **Description:** Addresses the problems of the Mediterranean region and voices from around the world with depth about the effects of history, culture, politics, and economics on the Mediterranean and the world.
Related titles: Online - full text ed.: ISSN 1527-1935. 1999. USD 75 to institutions (effective 2011).
Indexed: A01, A03, A08, A22, ABS&EES, CA, CCME, E01, GEOBASE, IBSS, LeftInd, M10, P34, P42, PAIS, PCI, PSA, PerIslam, SCOPUS, SociolAb, T02.
—BLDSC (5534.743000), IE, Ingenta. **CCC.**
Published by: (Mediterranean Affairs, Inc.), Duke University Press, 905 W Main St, Ste 18 B, Durham, NC 27701. TEL 919-688-5134, 888-651-0122, FAX 919-688-2615, 888-651-0124, subscriptions@dukeupress.edu, http://www.dukeupress.edu. Ed. Nikolaus A Stavrou. Adv. contact Karen Goldstein TEL 919-687-3636.

327 SRB ISSN 0543-3657
D839
MEDJUNARODNA POLITIKA. Text in Serbian. 1950. m. EUR 60 domestic to individuals; EUR 80 foreign to individuals; EUR 80 domestic to institutions; EUR 100 foreign to institutions (effective 2007). bk.rev. index. reprints avail. **Document type:** *Journal, Academic/Scholarly.* **Description:** Focuses on foreign policy, military treaties and strategies, economic developments and disarmament.
Related titles: English ed.: Review of International Affairs. ISSN 0486-6096.
Indexed: CA, HRIR, I13, P06, P42, PAIS, PRA, RASB, T02.
Published by: Institut za Medjunarodnu Politiku i Privredu/Institute of International Politics and Economics, Makedonska 25, Belgrade, 11000. TEL 381-11-3373838, FAX 381-11-3373835, iipe@diplomacy.bg.ac.yu. Ed. Brana Markovic. Circ: 7,000.

327 SRB ISSN 0025-8555
D839
MEDJUNARODNI PROBLEMI/INTERNATIONAL PROBLEMS. Text and summaries in English, Serbo-Croatian. 1949. q. EUR 80 foreign (effective 2007). **Document type:** *Journal, Academic/Scholarly.*
Related titles: Online - full text ed.: free (effective 2011).
Indexed: ABCPolSci, HistAb, I13, PSA, RASB, SCOPUS.
Published by: Institut za Medjunarodnu Politiku i Privredu/Institute of International Politics and Economics, Makedonska 25, Belgrade, 11000. TEL 381-11-3373838, FAX 381-11-3373835, iipe@diplomacy.bg.ac.yu, http://www.diplomacy.bg.ac.yu. Ed. Brana Markovic.

327 BEL ISSN 0025-908X
DH403
MEMO FROM BELGIUM. Text in English. 1960. irreg. free. charts; illus.
Related titles: Dutch ed.; French ed.; Spanish ed.; Italian ed.; German ed.
Indexed: P06.
Published by: Ministere des Affaires Etrangeres, Rue Quatre Bras 2, Brussels, 1000, Belgium. Circ: 3,000.

327 330.9 BRA ISSN 1518-1219
JZ9
MERIDIANO 47; boletim de analise de conjuntura em relacoes internacionais. Variant title: Meridiano Quarenta e Sete. Text in Portuguese; Summaries in English. 2000. bi-m. free (effective 2011). bk.rev. back issues avail. **Document type:** *Journal, Academic/Scholarly.*
Media: Online - full text.
Indexed: A01, A26, CA, E08, F03, F04, I02, I04, I05, P42, PSA, S09, T02.
Published by: Instituto Brasileiro de Relacoes Internacionais, Caixa Postal 4400, Brasilia, DF 70919-970, Brazil. TEL 55-61-21929460, FAX 55-61-33072426, secretaria@ibri-rbpi.org, http://www.ibri-rbpi.org. Ed. Dr. Antonio Carlos Lessa.

327 ESP ISSN 1135-710X
MERIDIANO C E R I. (Centro Espanol de Relaciones Internacionales) Text in Spanish. 1995. bi-m. back issues avail. **Document type:** *Bulletin, Academic/Scholarly.*
Indexed: I13, PAIS.
Published by: Fundacion Jose Ortega y Gasset, Fortuny 53, Madrid, 28010, Spain. TEL 34-91-7004100, FAX 34-91-7003530, comunicacion@fog.es, http://www.ortegaygasset.edu/.

327 RUS ISSN 0130-9625
MEZHDUNARODNAYA ZHIZN'. Text in Russian. 1954. m. USD 230 (effective 2009). **Document type:** *Journal, Government.* **Description:** Covers problems of world politics, diplomacy and international relations.
Related titles: Online - full text ed.: USD 139 foreign to institutions (effective 2008); ◆ English Translation: International Affairs. ISSN 0130-9641.
Indexed: AmH&L, HistAb, LID&ISL, RASB, RefZh.
—BLDSC (0107.810000), East View.
Published by: (Ministerstvo Inostrannykh Del Rossiiskoi Federatsii/ Ministry of Foreign Affairs of the Russian Federation), Mezhdunarodnaya Zhizn', 14 Gorokhovskii per, Moscow, 103064, Russian Federation. TEL 7-498-2653781, FAX 7-495-2653771, inter_affairs@mid.ru. Ed. Boris Pyadyshev. **Dist. by:** East View Information Services, 10601 Wayzata Blvd, Minneapolis, MN 55305. TEL 952-252-1201, 800-477-1005, FAX 952-252-1202, info@eastview.com, http://www.eastview.com.

327 RUS
MEZHDUNARODNIK. Text in Russian. 1968. m. **Document type:** *Newspaper, Academic/Scholarly.*
Related titles: Online - full text ed.
Published by: Moskovskii Gosudarstvennyi Institut Mezhdunarodnykh Otnoshenii/Moscow State Institute of International Relations, prospekt Vernadskogo, 76, Moscow, 119454, Russian Federation. TEL 7-495-5046570. Ed. Stanislav Sazhin.

327 CZE ISSN 0543-7962
D839
MEZINARODNI POLITIKA. Text in Czech. 1956. m. CZK 490 domestic; CZK 49 per issue domestic; EUR 82.40 foreign (effective 2009). adv. bk.rev. charts; illus. index. 44 p./no. 3 cols./p.; **Document type:** *Journal, Academic/Scholarly.*
Related titles: Microfilm ed.: (from PQC).
Indexed: PRA.
Published by: Ustav Mezinarodnich Vztahu/Institute of International Relations, Nerudova 3, Prague, 11850, Czech Republic. TEL 420-25-1108111, FAX 420-25-1108222, umvedo@iir.cz. Ed. Robert Schuster. **Dist. by:** Kubon & Sagner Buchexport - Import GmbH, Hesstr 39-41, Munich 80798, Germany. TEL 49-89-542180, FAX 49-89-54218218, postmaster@kubon-sagner.de, http://www.kubon-sagner.de.

327 CZE ISSN 0323-1844
D839
➤ **MEZINARODNI VZTAHY.** Text in Czech. 1966. q. CZK 285 domestic; CZK 95 per issue domestic; EUR 61 foreign (effective 2009). bk.rev. bibl.; charts. 120 p./no. 1 cols./p.; **Document type:** *Journal, Academic/Scholarly.*
Related titles: Microform ed.: (from PQC).
Indexed: CA, I13, IBSS, P42, PCI, PSA, T02.
Published by: Ustav Mezinarodnich Vztahu/Institute of International Relations, Nerudova 3, Prague, 11850, Czech Republic. TEL 420-25-1108111, FAX 420-25-1108222, umvedo@iir.cz. Ed. Ondrej Cisar. **Dist. by:** Kubon & Sagner Buchexport - Import GmbH, Hessstr 39-41, Munich 80798, Germany. TEL 49-89-542180, FAX 49-89-54218218, postmaster@kubon-sagner.de, http://www.kubon-sagner.de.

327 GRC
➤ **MIDDLE EAST FORUM.** Text in Greek. 1996. 2/yr. USD 25 per issue to individuals; USD 50 per issue to institutions (effective 2001). adv. **Document type:** *Academic/Scholarly.*
Published by: Institute of Middle East Studies "Al Mamun" (IMSAM), c/o Prof. John Karkazis, Ed., Smirnis 1, Zografos, 157 72, Greece. TEL 30-1-6123631, FAX 30-1-6123631. Ed., Adv. contact Adel Zaghah. R&P John Karkazis. page USD 500.

327 USA
MIDDLE EAST INSTITUTE NEWSLETTER. Text in English. bi-m. USD 60 to members (effective 1999). bibl. **Document type:** *Newsletter.* **Description:** Covers events and activities at the Middle East Institute.
Published by: Middle East Institute, 1761 N St, NW, Washington, DC 20036. TEL 202-785-0191, FAX 202-331-8861. Ed. David Colvin. Circ: 1,750.

327.5692 USA
MIDDLE EAST INTELLIGENCE BULLETIN. Text in English. 1999. m. free. **Document type:** *Bulletin, Consumer.* **Description:** Contains detailed and informed analyses of political and strategic developments in Lebanon, Syria and the Middle East, dossiers on important political figures who influence these developments, and interviews with various sources.
Media: Online - full content.
Indexed: CA.
Published by: United States Committee for a Free Lebanon, 2013 Q St, NW, Washington, DC 20009. FAX 212-202-6166, info@freelebanon.org, http://www.freelebanon.org. Ed. Gary Gambill.

327 USA ISSN 0026-3141
DS1
➤ **MIDDLE EAST JOURNAL.** Abbreviated title: M E J. Text in English. 1947. q. USD 50 to individuals; free to members (effective 2010). adv. bk.rev. bibl.; charts; illus.; abstr. index, cum.index: 1947-1966, 1967-1977. back issues avail.; reprints avail. **Document type:** *Journal, Academic/Scholarly.* **Description:** Provides original and objective analysis, as well as source material, on the area from Morocco to Pakistan and including Central Asia.
Related titles: Microform ed.: (from PQC); Online - full text ed.: ISSN 1940-3461. free to members (effective 2010) (from IngentaConnect).
Indexed: A01, A02, A03, A08, A12, A20, A21, A22, A25, A26, ABCPolSci, ABIn, ABS&EES, AICP, ASCA, ASD, Acal, AmH&L, B04, B05, B14, BAS, BRD, BRI, BibLing, CA, CBRI, CCME, CurCont, DIP, E01, E08, ESPM, FR, G08, G10, GEOBASE, GSS&RPL, H09, H10, HPNRM, HistAb, I05, I07, I08, I13, I14, IBR, IBSS, IBZ, ILD, J01, JEL, KES, LeftInd, M01, M02, M10, MEA&I, MLA-IB, P02, P06, P10, P13, P27, P30, P34, P42, P45, P47, P48, P51, P53, P54, PAIS, PCI, PQC, PRA, PSA, PerIslam, PopulInd, RASB, RI-1, RI-2, RefSour, RiskAb, S02, S03, S05, S08, S09, S23, SCOPUS, SSAI, SSAb, SSCI, SSI, SSciA, SociolAb, T02, W03, W05, W07.
—BLDSC (5761.380000), IE, Infotrieve, Ingenta, INIST. **CCC.**
Published by: Middle East Institute, 1761 N St, NW, Washington, DC 20036. TEL 202-785-1141, FAX 202-331-8861, man-ed@mei.edu. Ed. Michael Collins Dunn. Adv. contact Adam Mendelson TEL 202-785-0191. page USD 1,000; trim 6.5 x 9.5.

327.56 USA
MIDDLE EAST MEDIA RESEARCH INSTITUTE. Abbreviated title: M E M R I. Text in English. 1998. d. free (effective 2010). back issues avail. **Document type:** *Newsletter, Consumer.* **Description:** Provides timely translations of Arabic, Farsi, and Hebrew media, as well as original analysis of political, ideological, intellectual, social, cultural, and religious trends in the Middle East.
Media: Online - full text.
Address: PO Box 27837, Washington, DC 20038. TEL 202-955-9070, FAX 202-955-9077.

327.56 USA ISSN 0026-315X
MIDDLE EAST MONITOR. Text in English. 1971. m. USD 130 domestic; USD 140 foreign (effective 2005). stat. back issues avail. **Document type:** *Newsletter.* **Description:** Reports middle east news events including foreign affairs, economics on Arbs, Iran and Israel.
Related titles: Fax ed.; Microfilm ed.
Indexed: PerIslam, SCOPUS.
Address: PO Box 236, Ridgewood, NJ 07451-0236. TEL 201-670-9623, FAX 808-545-1871. Ed., Pub. Amir N Ghazaii. R&P Amir Ghazaii.

327 USA ISSN 1061-1924
DS41
➤ **MIDDLE EAST POLICY.** Text in English. 1981. q. GBP 199 in United Kingdom to institutions; EUR 253 in Europe to institutions; USD 252 in the Americas to institutions; USD 388 elsewhere to institutions; GBP 229 combined subscription in United Kingdom to institutions (print & online eds.); EUR 291 combined subscription in Europe to institutions (print & online eds.); USD 290 combined subscription in the Americas to institutions (print & online eds.); USD 447 combined subscription elsewhere to institutions (print & online eds.) (effective 2012). adv. bk.rev. illus. cum.index: 1982-1993 in vol.46. back issues avail.; reprint service avail. from PSC. **Document type:** *Journal, Academic/Scholarly.* **Description:** Provides viewpoints on recent developments that affect U.S. - Middle East policy.
Formerly (until 1992): American Arab Affairs (0731-6763)
Related titles: Microform ed.; Online - full text ed.: ISSN 1475-4967. GBP 199 in United Kingdom to institutions; EUR 253 in Europe to institutions; USD 252 in the Americas to institutions; USD 388 elsewhere to institutions (effective 2012) (from IngentaConnect).
Indexed: A01, A02, A03, A08, A20, A22, A26, ABCPolSci, ASCA, B14, BRI, CA, CBRI, CCME, CurCont, DIP, E01, E08, ENW, ESPM, FamI, G06, G07, G08, HPNRM, HRIR, I02, I05, I07, I08, I13, I14, IBR, IBSS, IBZ, IPARL, LeftInd, M06, M10, MEA&I, P02, P10, P34, P42, P45, P47, P48, P53, P54, PAIS, PQC, PRA, PSA, PerIslam, R02, RiskAb, S02, S03, S09, S23, SCOPUS, SSCI, SSciA, SWRA, SociolAb, T02, W07.
—BLDSC (5761.400200), IE, Infotrieve, Ingenta. **CCC.**
Published by: (Middle East Policy Council), Wiley-Blackwell Publishing, Inc. (Subsidiary of: Wiley-Blackwell Publishing Ltd.), 111 River St, Hoboken, NJ 07030. TEL 201-748-6000, FAX 201-748-6088, info@wiley.com. Ed. Anne Joyce. Adv. contact Kristin McCarthy TEL 201-748-7683.

327 USA ISSN 0276-5632
DS63.2.U5
MIDDLE EAST POLICY SURVEY. Text in English. 1980. m. USD 150 (effective 2000). back issues avail. **Document type:** *Newsletter.* **Description:** Insider's guide to Middle East events, issues, and personalities.
Published by: Middle East Policy Group, 3405 Rodman St N W, Washington, DC 20008. TEL 202-363-3495, FAX 202-352-4513. Ed., R&P Richard Straus. Circ: 500.

327 USA ISSN 1073-9467
DS41 CODEN: MEQUFZ
MIDDLE EAST QUARTERLY. Text in English. 1994. q. USD 70 domestic (effective 2009). adv. bk.rev. charts; illus. back issues avail.; reprints avail. **Document type:** *Magazine, Consumer.* **Description:** Educates readers about Middle East trends and current events and seeks to construct a framework for a US policy in the region.
Related titles: Online - full content ed.; Online - full text ed.
Indexed: A01, A03, A08, A22, A26, B14, BRI, CA, CBRI, E08, G06, G07, G08, I02, I05, I07, I13, I14, IBSS, IJP, J01, JewAb, LeftInd, M10, P10, P34, P42, P45, P48, PAIS, PQC, PSA, R02, S02, S03, S09, S23, SCOPUS, SOPODA, SociolAb, T02.
—BLDSC (5761.400700), IE, Ingenta. **CCC.**
Published by: Middle East Forum, 1500 Walnut St, Ste 1050, Philadelphia, PA 19103-4624. TEL 215-546-5406, FAX 215-546-5409, mideastq@aol.com. Ed. Denis MacEoin. adv.: B&W page USD 325; trim 6.25 x 9.25. Circ: 2,100 (paid).

MIDDLE EAST REVIEW. *see* BUSINESS AND ECONOMICS—Economic Situation And Conditions

327.1 USA ISSN 1937-9242
DS41
MIDDLE EASTERN OUTLOOK. Text in English. 2007. bi-m. back issues avail. **Document type:** *Journal, Academic/Scholarly.*

Published by: American Enterprise Institute for Public Policy Research, 1150 17th St NW, Washington, DC 20036. TEL 202-862-5800, FAX 202-862-7177.

327.5694 USA
MIDEAST MONITOR. Text in English. 2006. bi-m. **Document type:** *Newsletter, Consumer.* **Description:** Devoted to specialized analysis of political developments, issues, and personalities shaping the Middle East today.
Media: Online - full content.
Address: 1250 24th St, N W, Ste 300, Washington, DC 20037. TEL 646-242-1101, epperly@mideastmonitor.org. Ed. Gary C Gambill.

327 ISR ISSN 0793-1050
MIDEAST SECURITY AND POLICY STUDIES/DIYYUNIM BEVITAHON LE'UMI. Text in English, Hebrew. 1991. 5/yr. **Document type:** *Monographic series, Academic/Scholarly.*
Published by: Bar-Ilan University, Begin-Sadat Center for Strategic Studies, 16 Chaim v'Elisha St., Tel Aviv, Israel. TEL 972-3-531-8959, FAX 972-3-535-9195, besa.center@mail.biu.ac.il, http://www.biu.ac.il/soc/besa/index.html.

MIGRANTENSTUDIES. *see* ETHNIC INTERESTS

MILITARY HISTORY AND POLICY. *see* MILITARY

MILITARY THOUGHT; a Russian journal of military theory and strategy. *see* MILITARY

327 GBR
MILLENIUM; journal of international studies. Text in English. 3/yr. bk.rev. **Document type:** *Journal, Academic/Scholarly.*
Published by: London School of Economics and Political Science, International Relations Department, Houghton St, London, WC2A 2AE, United Kingdom. TEL 44-20-79557404, FAX 44-20-79557446. Eds. Elisabetta Brighi, Harry Bauer.

327 GBR ISSN 0305-8298
JZ6.5 CODEN: MILLFB
➤ **MILLENNIUM**; journal of international studies. Text in English. 1971. 3/yr. USD 429, GBP 232 combined subscription to institutions (print & online eds.); USD 420, GBP 227 to institutions (effective 2011). bk.rev. index. back issues avail.; reprint service avail. from PSC. **Document type:** *Journal, Academic/Scholarly.* **Description:** Features the most innovative articles from the discipline of international studies, as well as social sciences with an international perspective.
Related titles: Microfilm ed.: (from PQC); Online - full text ed.: ISSN 1477-9021. 1999. USD 386, GBP 209 to institutions (effective 2011).
Indexed: A01, A20, A22, ABCPolSci, AICP, AMB, AmHI, BAS, BrHumI, CA, CurCont, E01, H07, HistAb, I13, I14, IBR, IBSS, IBZ, IITV, LID&ISL, M10, P06, P34, P42, PAIS, PCI, PSA, PerIslam, RASB, S02, S03, SCOPUS, SOPODA, SSA, SSCI, SociolAb, T02, W07.
—BLDSC (5773.945000), IE, Infotrieve, Ingenta. **CCC.**
Published by: (London School of Economics), Sage Publications Ltd. (Subsidiary of: Sage Publications, Inc.), 1 Oliver's Yard, 55 City Rd, London, EC1Y 1SP, United Kingdom. TEL 44-20-73248500, FAX 44-20-73248600, info@sagepub.co.uk, http://www.uk.sagepub.com/home.nav. Eds. Kevork Oskanian, Ramon Pacheco Pardo, Rebekka Friedman.

327 FRA ISSN 2106-9263
MINISTERE DES AFFAIRES ETRANGERES ET EUROPEENNES. LES BIOGRAPHIES.COM. Text in French. 2007. a. EUR 175 per issue (effective 2011). **Document type:** *Government.*
Formed by the merger of (200?-2007): Ministere des Affaires Etrangeres. Les Biographies.com. Tome I, Organigramme (1953-437X); (200?-2007): Ministere des Affaires Etrangeres. Les Biographies.com. Tome II, Biographies (1953-4388)
Published by: Societe Generale de Presse, 13 Avenue de l'Opera, Paris Cedex 01, 75001, France. TEL 33-1-40151789, FAX 33-1-40151715, contact@sna.asso.fr, http://www.sgpresse.fr.

327 SWE ISSN 1400-9412
MINOR FIELD STUDY. Text in English. 1994. irreg., latest vol.25, 2005. SEK 25 per issue (effective 2006). back issues avail. **Document type:** *Monographic series, Academic/Scholarly.*
Related titles: Online - full text ed.: 2004.
Published by: Uppsala Universitet, Institutionen foer Freds- och Konfliktforskning/University of Uppsala, Department of Peace and Conflict Research, Gamla Torget 3, PO Box 514, Uppsala, 75120, Sweden. TEL 46-18-4710000, FAX 46-18-695102, info@pcr.uu.se.

MINORITY RIGHTS GROUP INTERNATIONAL. REPORT. *see* POLITICAL SCIENCE—Civil Rights

MIROVAYA EKONOMIKA I MEZHDUNARODNYE OTNOSHENIYA. *see* BUSINESS AND ECONOMICS

327 NLD ISSN 0165-6546
DS611
MOESSON; het indisch maandblad. Text in Dutch. 1958. m. EUR 47.65 domestic; EUR 54.45 in Europe; EUR 58.99 elsewhere (effective 2010). adv. bk.rev. bibl.; charts; illus. 52 p./no.; back issues avail. **Document type:** *Magazine, Abstract/Index.*
Formerly (until 1978): Tong-Tong (0040-9189)
Indexed: BAS.
Published by: Tjalie Robinson B.V., Bergstraat 27, Amersfoort, 3811 NE, Netherlands. TEL 31-33-4611611, FAX 31-33-4655208. adv.: page EUR 1,045; trim 210 x 297. Circ: 10,000.

327 FRA ISSN 0026-9395
JZ11
LE MONDE DIPLOMATIQUE. Text in French. 1954. m. EUR 49 (effective 2011). adv. illus. index. back issues avail.; reprints avail. **Document type:** *Consumer.*
Related titles: Microfilm ed.: (from RPI); Online - full text ed.: ISSN 1950-6260. EUR 34 (effective 2011); ◆ Spanish ed.: Le Monde Diplomatique en Espanol. ISSN 1888-6434; ◆ French ed.: Le Monde Diplomatique. ISSN 0718-4344.
Indexed: A22, AltPI, CCME, ELLIS, FR, HRIR, ILD, M10, MLA-IB, PAIS, PdeR, RASB, RefugAb, SpeleolAb.
—IE, Infotrieve. **CCC.**
Published by: Monde Diplomatique S A, 1 Av. Stephen Pichon, Paris, 75013, France. TEL 33-1-53949601, FAX 33-1-53949626, secretariat@monde-diplomatique.fr. Adv. contact Nedjma Liassine TEL 33-1-57283867. Circ: 165,000.

327 CHL ISSN 0718-4344
LE MONDE DIPLOMATIQUE. Text in French. 2000. m. CLP 19,500 domestic; EUR 70 in Europe (effective 2007). **Document type:** *Newspaper, Consumer.*
Related titles: Online - full text ed.: ISSN 0718-4352. 2000; ◆ Spanish ed.: Le Monde Diplomatique en Espanol. ISSN 1888-6434; ◆ French ed.: Le Monde Diplomatique. ISSN 0026-9395.
Published by: Editorial Aun Creemos en los Suenos, San Antonio 434 Local 14, Santiago, Chile. TEL 56-2-6642050, FAX 56-2-6381723, chile@leondediplomatique.cl, http://www.editorialauncreemos.cl/catalog/. Ed. Victor Hugo De la Fuente. Circ: 300,000.

327 ESP ISSN 1888-6434
LE MONDE DIPLOMATIQUE EN ESPANOL. Text in Spanish. 1995. m. EUR 44 domestic; EUR 69 in Europe; EUR 74 elsewhere (effective 2009). back issues avail. **Document type:** *Newspaper, Consumer.*
Formerly (until 2008): Le Monde Diplomatique (1696-036X)
Related titles: ◆ French ed.: Le Monde Diplomatique. ISSN 0026-9395; ◆ French ed.: Le Monde Diplomatique. ISSN 0718-4344; ◆ Supplement(s): El Punto de Vista de Le Monde Diplomatique. ISSN 1699-0080.
Published by: Ediciones Cybermonde S.L., C/ Aparisi i Guijarro 5, Pta 2, Valencia, 46003, Spain. TEL 34-902-212150, FAX 34-902-212160, admon@mundiplo.com.

MONDES ET NATIONS. *see* SOCIAL SCIENCES: COMPREHENSIVE WORKS

MONDIAL/FEDERALISTE MONDIAL DU CANADA. *see* LAW—International Law

327 MNG ISSN 1023-3741
DS798.A2
MONGOLIAN JOURNAL OF INTERNATIONAL AFFAIRS. Text in English. 1994. a. USD 12.50 foreign (effective 2000). **Description:** Covers Mongolia's Asia Pacific policy and regional security strategy, security of small states in the 21st century, US-China relations in the Northeast Asia security context, Mongolia's economic development in the context of Northeast Asian economic cooperation, Northeast Asian economic cooperation and economic development of inner Mongolia: situation and prospects.
Published by: (Institute of International Studies), Mongolian Academy of Sciences, PO Box 48 17, Ulan Bator, Mongolia. Ed. Ts Batbayar.

327 BEL ISSN 1021-4224
MONTHLY REPORT ON EUROPE. Text in English. m. (11/yr.). EUR 610 (effective 2000). **Document type:** *Bulletin.* **Description:** Reviews of noteworthy institutional, legislative, monetary, business and political events and developments in the EU.
Related titles: French ed.: Rapport Mensuel sur l'Europe. ISSN 0259-7527.
Indexed: ELLIS.
Published by: Europe Information Service SA (E I S), Av Adolphe Lacomble 66-68, Brussels, 1030, Belgium. TEL 32-2-737-7709, FAX 32-2-732-6757, eis@eis.be, http://www.eis.be. Pub. Eric Damiens.

MONUMENTA GERMANIAE HISTORICA. DIPLOMATA. *see* HISTORY—History Of Europe

327.1 363.35 RUS
MOSCOW DEFENCE BRIEF; your professional guide inside. Text in English. 2004. q.
Published by: Center for Analysis of Strategies and Technologies, Leninskiy pr-kt 45, Ste 480, Moscow, 119334, Russian Federation. TEL 7-495-1351378, FAX 7-495-7750418, mdb@cast.ru, http://www.mdb.cast.ru. Ed. Ilya Nevorotov. Pub. Ruslan Pukhov.

MOSHE DAYAN CENTER. DATA AND ANALYSIS SERIES. *see* HISTORY—History Of The Near East

327 ISR
MOSHE DAYAN CENTER FOR MIDDLE EASTERN AND AFRICAN STUDIES. BULLETIN. Text in English. s-a. free (effective 2008). **Document type:** *Bulletin.*
Published by: Tel Aviv University, Moshe Dayan Center for Middle Eastern and African Studies, Ramat Aviv, PO Box 39040, Tel Aviv, 69978, Israel. TEL 972-3-6409646, FAX 972-3-6415802, dayancen@post.tau.ac.il.

327 RUS ISSN 2076-7404
▼ ➤ **MOSKOVSKII GOSUDARSTVENNYI UNIVERSITET. VESTNIK. SERIYA 25: MEZHDUNARODNYE OTNOSHENIYA I MIROVAYA POLITIKA.** Text in Russian. 2009. q. USD 162 in North America; USD 235 combined subscription in North America (print & online eds.) (effective 2011). **Document type:** *Journal, Academic/Scholarly.*
Related titles: Online - full text ed.
Published by: (Moskovskii Gosudarstvennyi Universitet im. M.V. Lomonosova, Fakul'tet Mirovoi Politiki), Izdatel'stvo Moskovskogo Gosudarstvennogo Universiteta im. M. V. Lomonosova/Publishing House of Moscow State University, B Nikitskaya 5/7, Moscow, 103009, Russian Federation. TEL 7-095-2295091, FAX 7-095-2036671, kd_mgu@rambler.ru, http://www.msu.ru/depts/MSUPubl. Ed. A A Kokoshin.

➤ **LE MULTILATERAL**; la revue pour mieux comprendre la politique internationale du Canada. *see* POLITICAL SCIENCE

658.1 BEL ISSN 1376-0912
MULTIPLE EUROPES. Text in English. 1994. irreg., latest vol.43, 2009. price varies. **Document type:** *Monographic series, Academic/Scholarly.*
Related titles: French ed.: Europe Plurielle. ISSN 1376-0904.
Published by: P I E - Peter Lang SA, 1 avenue Maurice, 6e etage, Brussels, 1050, Belgium. TEL 32-2-3477236, FAX 32-2-3477237, pie@peterlang.com, http://www.peterlang.net. Ed. Bo Strath.

327 CAN ISSN 1924-3316
MUNK MONITOR. Text in English. 2004. s-a. back issues avail. **Document type:** *Magazine, Trade.* **Description:** Provides a forum to extend and enhance the contribution of the Munk School of Global Affairs to public debate on important international issues and contribute to public education.
Formerly (until 2010): Munk Centre Monitor (1924-3308)
Related titles: Online - full text ed.: free (effective 2010).
Published by: Munk School of Global Affairs, 1 Devonshire Pl, Toronto, ON M5S 3K7, Canada. TEL 416-946-8900, munkschool@utoronto.ca, http://www.munkschool.utoronto.ca.

327.172 DEU ISSN 0027-5093
MUT. Text in German. 1965. m. EUR 111 (effective 2005). bk.rev. illus. **Document type:** *Bulletin.* **Description:** Non-political publication promoting unity, justice, freedom and world peace.
Published by: Mut-Verlag, Postfach 1, Asendorf, 27330, Germany. TEL 49-4253-566, FAX 49-4253-1603, vertrieb@mut-verlag.de, http://www.mut-verlag.de.

327 USA ISSN 1071-4839
F1401
➤ **N A C L A REPORT ON THE AMERICAS.** Text in English. 1967. bi-m. USD 36 domestic to individuals; USD 46 foreign to individuals; USD 60 domestic to institutions; USD 70 foreign to institutions (effective 2010). adv. bk.rev.; video rev. bibl.; illus.; abstr. 54 p./no.; back issues avail.; reprints avail. **Document type:** *Magazine, Trade.* **Description:** Provides critical analysis of political, social and economic trends in Latin America and the Caribbean including analysis of U.S.-Latin America relations, human rights developments, and historical and cultural issues.
Former titles (until 1993): Report on the Americas (1058-5397); (until 1991): N A C L A Report on the Americas (0149-1598); (until 1977): N A C L A's Latin America and Empire Report (0095-5930); (until 1971): N A C L A Newsletter (0048-0630)
Related titles: CD-ROM ed.; Microfilm ed.: (from PQC); Online - full text ed.: USD 28 (effective 2010).
Indexed: A01, A02, A03, A08, A22, A25, A26, AltPI, B04, BRD, C12, CA, E08, G06, G07, G08, H21, HRIR, I04, I05, I08, IBR, IBZ, IPARL, LeftInd, M01, M02, M06, P02, P06, P08, P10, P27, P34, P42, P45, P47, P48, P53, P54, PAIS, PQC, RASB, RILM, S02, S03, S08, S09, SCOPUS, SRRA, SSAI, SSAb, SSI, SociolAb, T02, W03, W05.
—BLDSC (6011.315600), IE, Infotrieve, Ingenta.
Published by: North American Congress on Latin America, Inc., 38 Greene St, 4th Fl, New York, NY 10013. TEL 646-613-1440, FAX 646-613-1443, nacla@nacla.org, http://www.nacla.org. Ed. Pablo Morales. Pub. Christy Thornton. Adv. contact Joao Da Silva TEL 646-613-1440 ext 203. Circ: 7,000.

➤ **N A T O DATA.** *see* MILITARY

341.06 BEL
N A T O FINAL COMMUNIQUES/O T A N COMMUNIQUES. (North Atlantic Treaty Organization) Text in English, French. 1970. a.
Published by: North Atlantic Treaty Organization (N A T O), Office of Information and Press, Blvd Leopold III, Brussels, 1110, Belgium. TEL 32-2-7075009, FAX 32-2-7074579.

P

341.37 BEL ISSN 1015-4892
N A T O HANDBOGEN. (North Atlantic Treaty Organization) Text in Danish. irreg. **Document type:** *Journal, Trade.*
Related titles: ◆ English ed.: N A T O Handbook. ISSN 0259-4331; ◆ French ed.: O T A N. Manuel; Multiple languages ed.
Published by: North Atlantic Treaty Organization (N A T O), Office of Information and Press, Blvd Leopold III, Brussels, 1110, Belgium.

341.37 BEL ISSN 0259-4331
JX1393
N A T O HANDBOOK. (North Atlantic Treaty Organization) Text in English. 1952. irreg., latest 1998. free.
Related titles: ◆ French ed.: O T A N. Manuel; ◆ Danish ed.: N A T O Handbogen. ISSN 1015-4892; Multiple languages ed.
—BLDSC (6033.660000).
Published by: (Office of Information and Press), North Atlantic Treaty Organization (N A T O), Office of Information and Press, Blvd Leopold III, Brussels, 1110, Belgium. TEL 32-2-7075009, FAX 32-2-7074579, TELEX 23-867.

327.17 004 NLD ISSN 1874-6268
N A T O SCIENCE FOR PEACE AND SECURITY SERIES. D: INFORMATION AND COMMUNICATION SECURITY. (North Atlantic Treaty Organization) Text in English. 2006. irreg., latest vol.28, 2010. price varies. **Document type:** *Monographic series, Academic/Scholarly.*
Formerly (until 2007): N A T O Security Through Science Series. D: Information and Communication Security (1574-5589)
Related titles: Online - full text ed.: ISSN 1879-8292.
Indexed: CCMJ, MSN, MathR.
Published by: I O S Press, Nieuwe Hemweg 6B, Amsterdam, 1013 BG, Netherlands. TEL 31-20-6883355, FAX 31-20-6870039, info@iospress.nl, http://www.iospress.nl.

327.1 303.4 NLD ISSN 1874-6276
N A T O SCIENCE FOR PEACE AND SECURITY SERIES. E: HUMAN AND SOCIETAL DYNAMICS. (North Atlantic Treaty Organization) Text in English. 2005. irreg., latest vol.76, 2010. price varies. **Document type:** *Monographic series, Academic/Scholarly.*
Formerly (until 2007): N A T O Security Through Science Series. E: Human and Societal Dynamics (1574-5597)
Related titles: Online - full text ed.: ISSN 1879-8268.
—BLDSC (6033.694250), IE.
Published by: I O S Press, Nieuwe Hemweg 6B, Amsterdam, 1013 BG, Netherlands. TEL 31-20-6883355, FAX 31-20-6870039, info@iospress.nl.

355 DEU ISSN 1566-9009
UA646
N A T O'S NATIONS AND PARTNERS FOR PEACE. (North Atlantic Treaty Organization) Text in German. 1955. 4/yr. EUR 75; EUR 23.50 newsstand/cover (effective 2008). adv. **Document type:** *Magazine, Trade.* **Description:** Contains articles on defense policies, technologies and economics.
Former titles (until 1999): N A T O's Sixteen Nations (0169-1821); N A T O's Fifteen Nations (0027-6065)
Related titles: Online - full text ed.
Indexed: A22, AMB, AUNI, BAS, DM&T, I02, LID&ISL, M05, M07, MEA&I, P02, P10, P47, P48, P53, P54, PAIS, PQC, PRA, RASB, T02.
—BLDSC (6033.700500), IE, Infotrieve, Ingenta. **CCC.**
Published by: Moench Verlagsgesellschaft mbH, Heilsbachstr 26, Bonn, 53123, Germany. TEL 49-228-64830, FAX 49-228-6483109, info@moench-group.com. Ed. Manfred Sadlowski. Adv. contact Ute Steuer. B&W page EUR 5,050, color page EUR 8,050; trim 7.31 x 10.63. Circ: 21,985 (paid and controlled).

327 USA
N B R ANALYSIS (ONLINE). Text in English. 1990. irreg. USD 8.95 per issue (effective 2010). **Document type:** *Monographic series, Academic/Scholarly.*
Media: Online - full text.

Published by: National Bureau of Asian Research, 1414 NE 42nd St, Ste 300, Seattle, WA 98105. TEL 206-632-7370, FAX 206-632-7487, nbr@nbr.org.

327 USA
N B R SPECIAL REPORT (ONLINE). Text in English. 2001. irreg., latest vol.23, 2010. USD 8.95 per issue (effective 2010). back issues avail. **Document type:** *Report, Trade.*
Media: Online - full text.
Published by: National Bureau of Asian Research, 1414 NE 42nd St, Ste 300, Seattle, WA 98105. TEL 206-632-7370, FAX 206-632-7487, nbr@nbr.org.

341.21 940 NZL ISSN 1178-5632
N C R E WORKING PAPER. (National Centre for Research on Europe) Text in English. 2007. irreg. **Document type:** *Monographic series, Academic/Scholarly.*
Media: Online - full text.
Published by: University of Canterbury, National Centre for Research on Europe, 2nd Level Geography Bldg, Private Bag 4800, Christchurch, New Zealand. TEL 64-3-3642348, FAX 64-3-3642634, ncre@canterbury.ac.nz.

327 300 PAK
➤ **N D U JOURNAL.** (National Defence University) Text in English. 1987. a. PKR 200, USD 25 (effective 2009). **Document type:** *Journal, Academic/Scholarly.*
Published by: National Defence University Islamabad, Institute of Strategic Studies Research and Analysis, NDU Sector E-9, Islamabad, Pakistan. TEL 92-51-9260651, FAX 92-51-9260663. Ed. Nayer Fardows. Circ: 1,000.

327 RUS
N G DIPKUR'YER. Text in Russian. s-m. **Document type:** *Magazine, Consumer.*
Related titles: Online - full content ed.; ◆ Supplement to: Nezavisimaya Gazeta. ISSN 1560-1005.
Published by: Nezavisimaya Gazeta, Myasnitskaya 13, Moscow, 101000, Russian Federation. TEL 7-095-9255543, info@ng.ru.

327 NOR ISSN 0809-7445
D839
N U P I NOTAT (ONLINE)/N U P I WORKING PAPER. Text in English. 1970. irreg., latest vol.786, 2011. back issues avail. **Document type:** *Monographic series, Academic/Scholarly.*
Formerly (until 2004): N U P I Notat (Print) (0800-0018)
Media: Online - full content.
Indexed: AMB.
Published by: Norsk Utenrikspolitisk Institutt/Norwegian Institute of International Affairs, C. J. Hambros Pl, PO Box 8159, Dep, Oslo, 0033, Norway. TEL 47-22-994000, FAX 47-22-362182, info@nupi.no.

327 NOR
N U P I RAPPORT (ONLINE)/N U P I REPORT. Text in English, Norwegian. 1970. irreg., latest 2011. price varies. back issues avail. **Document type:** *Monographic series, Academic/Scholarly.*
Former titles (until 2006): N U P I Rapport (Print) (0804-7235); (until 1994): N U P I Forskningsrapport (0803-8503); (until 1992): N U P I Rapport (0800-000X)
Media: Online - full text.
Published by: Norsk Utenrikspolitisk Institutt/Norwegian Institute of International Affairs, C. J. Hambros Pl, PO Box 8159, Dep, Oslo, 0033, Norway. TEL 47-22-994000, FAX 47-22-362182, info@nupi.no.

327.1 NZL ISSN 1177-8628
N Z A I REGIONAL ANALYSIS. (New Zealand Asia Institute) Text in English. 2006. irreg. **Document type:** *Monographic series.* **Description:** Addresses international policy issues that confront regional policy communities.
Related titles: Online - full text ed.: ISSN 1177-861X.
Published by: University of Auckland Business School, New Zealand Asia Institute, Private Bag 92019, Auckland, 1142, New Zealand. TEL 64-9-3737599 ext 86936, FAX 64-9-3082312, nzai@auckland.ac.nz.

NAJDA NEWSLETTER. *see* WOMEN'S INTERESTS

327 330 CHN ISSN 1004-0641
AP95.C4
NAN FENG CHUANG/SOUTH WIND THROUGH WINDOW. Text in Chinese. 1985. s-m. USD 106.60 (effective 2009). **Document type:** *Magazine, Consumer.* **Description:** Reflects the social life of Chinese people in the midst of economic development.
Related titles: Online - full text ed.
—East View.
Published by: Guangzhou Ribao Baoye Jituan/Guangzhou Daily Newspaper Group, 10, Renmin Zhonglu Tongle Lu, Guangzhou, 510121, China. TEL 86-20-81883088. Circ: 500,000. **Dist. overseas by:** China International Book Trading Corp, 35 Chegongzhuang Xilu, Haidian District, PO Box 399, Beijing 100044, China. TEL 86-10-68412045, FAX 86-10-68412023, cibtc@mail.cibtc.com.cn, http://www.cibtc.com.cn.

327 CHE ISSN 1014-5389
NANMIN ZAZHI. Text in Chinese. 1984. irreg.
Related titles: ◆ English ed.: Refugees. ISSN 0252-791X; ◆ French ed.: Refugies. ISSN 1014-0905; ◆ Spanish ed.: Refugiados. ISSN 1014-0891; ◆ Arabic ed.: Al Lagi'un. ISSN 1014-5370; ◆ Japanese ed.: Refyujizu. ISSN 1014-1162; ◆ German ed.: Fluchtlinge. ISSN 1014-1154; ◆ Italian ed.: Rifugiati. ISSN 1014-0832.
Published by: United Nations High Commissioner for Refugees, Public Information Section, PO Box 2500, Geneva 2, 1211, Switzerland. TEL 41-22-739-81-11, FAX 41-22-739-84-49, http://www.unhcr.ch/.

327 NOR
NANSEN NEWS. Text in English. s-a. **Document type:** *Journal, Academic/Scholarly.*
Related titles: Online - full text ed.
Published by: Fridtjof Nansen Institute, PO Box 326, Lysaker, 1326, Norway. TEL 47-67-111900, FAX 47-67-111910, post@fni.no.

327 USA ISSN 1542-3743
NATIONAL COMMITTEE ON U.S.-CHINA RELATIONS. NOTES FROM THE NATIONAL COMMITTEE. Text in English. 1969. 3/yr. bk.rev. charts. **Description:** Reports on committee activities and current trends in China.
Formerly: National Committee on U.S. China Relations. Highlights of Notes
Published by: National Committee on U.S.-China Relations, Inc., 71 W 23rd St, 19th FL, New York, NY 10010-4102. TEL 212-922-1385, FAX 212-557-8258, info@ncuscr.org, http://www.ncuscr.org. Circ: 3,000.

327.12 USA ISSN 1940-4042
NATIONAL INTELLIGENCE JOURNAL. Text in English. 1992. s-a. USD 60 domestic; USD 75 foreign (effective 2009). adv. bk.rev. **Document type:** *Journal, Academic/Scholarly.* **Description:** Provides a forum for analytic essays on topics of importance to defense intelligence and national security professionals and scholars.
Formerly (until 2009): Defense Intelligence Journal (1061-6845)
Indexed: A22, CA, I02, M05, PAIS, T02.
—IE.
Published by: National Intelligence Education Foundation, Inc., 901 Stuart St, Ste 205, Arlington, VA 22203. TEL 703-224-4672 ex. 26, info@niefoundation.org. Circ: 1,250.

327 USA ISSN 0884-9382
E840
THE NATIONAL INTEREST. Abbreviated title: T N I. Text in English. 1985. bi-m. USD 34 combined subscription in US & Canada (print & online eds.); USD 59 combined subscription elsewhere (print & online eds.) (effective 2010). adv. bk.rev. illus. back issues avail. **Document type:** *Magazine, Consumer.* **Description:** Covers American foreign policy and world politics, containing discussions on foreign policy, history, culture, economics, technology, philosophy and religion.
Related titles: Microform ed.: (from PQC); Online - full text ed.: ISSN 1938-1573. USD 20.80 (effective 2010).
Indexed: A01, A02, A03, A08, A22, A25, A26, ABS&EES, AmH&L, B04, BRD, C12, DIP, E08, G06, G07, G08, HistAb, I02, I05, I07, I13, IBR, IBSS, IBZ, IPARL, LID&ISL, M01, M02, P02, P05, P10, P27, P34, P42, P45, P47, P48, P53, P54, PAIS, PCI, PQC, PSA, RASB, S02, S03, S08, S09, S11, S23, SCOPUS, SSAI, SSAb, SSI, SociolAb, T02, W03, W04, W05.
—BLDSC (6025.934000), CIS, IE, Infotrieve, Ingenta.
Published by: The Nixon Center, 615 L St, Ste 1250, Washington, DC 20036. TEL 856-380-4130, 800-344-7952, backissues@nationalinterest.org, http://www.nixoncenter.org/. Ed. Justine Rosenthal. Pub. Dimitri K Simes. Adv. contact Brooke Leonard. B&W page USD 1,000; trim 7 x 101.

327.94 AUS
DU117.18
NATIONAL OBSERVER. Text in English. 1989. q. bk.rev. back issues avail. **Document type:** *Journal, Trade.* **Description:** Features the latest current affairs with a focus on domestic and international politics, security-related challenges and issues of national cohesion.
Former titles: National Observer North Melbourne (1442-5548); (until 1998): Australia and World Affairs (1033-6192)
Related titles: Online - full text ed.
Indexed: A01, A02, A03, A08, A11, A26, AusPAIS, C12, E08, G08, I05, M01, M02, P27, P34, P48, P54, PCI, PQC, S09, T02, WBA, WMB.
—Ingenta. **CCC.**
Published by: Council for the National Interest, PO Box 751, North Melbourne, VIC 3051, Australia. TEL 61-3-93265757, FAX 61-3-93282877. Ed. Dr. I C F Spry, Q C.

327 GBR ISSN 1353-7113
D1 CODEN: NEPOFN
➤ **NATIONALISM & ETHNIC POLITICS.** Text in English. 1995. q. GBP 337 combined subscription in United Kingdom to institutions (print & online eds.); EUR 447, USD 562 combined subscription to institutions (print & online eds.) (effective 2012). adv. bk.rev. index. back issues avail.; reprint service avail. from PSC. **Document type:** *Journal, Academic/Scholarly.* **Description:** Explores the varied political aspects of nationalism and ethnicity, comparing and contrasting state and community claims and dealing with such factors as citizenship, race, religion, economic development, immigration, language, and the international environment.
Related titles: Online - full text ed.: ISSN 1557-2986. GBP 304 in United Kingdom to institutions; EUR 402, USD 505 to institutions (effective 2012) (from IngentaConnect).
Indexed: A01, A03, A08, A22, AmH&L, CA, E01, ESPM, FamI, GEOBASE, HistAb, I02, I13, I14, IBSS, M10, P30, P34, P42, PSA, PerIslam, R02, RiskAb, S02, S03, SCOPUS, SOPODA, SSA, SSciA, SociolAb, T02.
—IE, Infotrieve, Ingenta. **CCC.**
Published by: Routledge (Subsidiary of: Taylor & Francis Group), 4 Park Sq, Milton Park, Abingdon, Oxon OX14 4RN, United Kingdom. TEL 44-20-70176000, FAX 44-20-70176336, subscriptions@tandf.co.uk, http://www.routledge.com. Ed. William Safran. Adv. contact Linda Hann TEL 44-1344-779945. **Subscr. to:** Taylor & Francis Ltd., Journals Customer Service, Sheepen Pl, Colchester, Essex CO3 3LP, United Kingdom. TEL 44-20-70175544, FAX 44-20-70175198.

327 CZE ISSN 1214-2522
NAVYCHOD. Text in Czech. 2002. 4/yr. CZK 238 (effective 2011). adv. **Document type:** *Magazine, Consumer.*
Related titles: Online - full text ed.: ISSN 1214-2492.
Published by: Na Vychod od Ase, Na Jezerce 26, Prague 4, 140 00, Czech Republic. TEL 420-3-604927439. Ed. Ivana Skalova.

NEAR EAST FOUNDATION. ANNUAL REPORT. *see* BUSINESS AND ECONOMICS—International Development And Assistance

327 USA ISSN 1931-9541
DS41
NEAR EAST QUARTERLY. Text in English. 2006. q. **Document type:** *Newsletter, Consumer.*
Media: Online - full text.
Published by: The Near East Policy Research, Inc, PO Box 11632, Alexandrea, VA 22312. TEL 571-224-5682, FAX 703-997-8996, http://www.neareastpolicy.com/component/option,com_frontpage/Itemid,1.

NEAR EAST REPORT (ONLINE). *see* ETHNIC INTERESTS

327 USA ISSN 0748-4526
HD42 CODEN: NEJOEQ
➤ **NEGOTIATION JOURNAL**; on the process of dispute settlement. Text in English. 1985. q. GBP 605 in United Kingdom to institutions; EUR 767 in Europe to institutions; USD 827 in the Americas to institutions; USD 1,183 elsewhere to institutions; GBP 696 combined subscription in United Kingdom to institutions (print & online eds.); EUR 882 combined subscription in Europe to institutions (print & online eds.); USD 951 combined subscription in the Americas to institutions (print & online eds.); USD 1,362 combined subscription elsewhere to institutions (print & online eds.) (effective 2012). adv. bk.rev. bibl. back issues avail.; reprint service avail. from PSC. **Document type:** *Journal, Academic/Scholarly.* **Description:** Offers insight for professionals in the fields of planning, economics, sociology, social psychology, and public policy.
Related titles: Microfilm ed.: (from PQC); Online - full text ed.: ISSN 1571-9979. GBP 605 in United Kingdom to institutions; EUR 767 in Europe to institutions; USD 827 in the Americas to institutions; USD 1,183 elsewhere to institutions (effective 2012) (from IngentaConnect).
Indexed: A12, A13, A20, A22, A26, ABIn, ABS&EES, ASCA, B01, B06, B07, B09, BibLing, CA, CJPI, CommAb, CurCont, DIP, E-psyche, E01, ESPM, FamI, I13, IBR, IBSS, IBZ, IPARL, LRI, P03, P10, P25, P34, P42, P45, P47, P48, P51, P53, P54, PAIS, PCI, PQC, PRA, PSA, PsycInfo, PsycholAb, RASB, RiskAb, S02, S03, SCOPUS, SOPODA, SSA, SSCI, SociolAb, T02, W07.
—BLDSC (6075.154000), IE, Infotrieve, Ingenta. **CCC.**
Published by: (Harvard Law School, Program on Negotiation), Wiley-Blackwell Publishing, Inc. (Subsidiary of: Wiley-Blackwell Publishing Ltd.), 111 River St, Hoboken, NJ 07030. info@wiley.com, http://www.wiley.com/WileyCDA/. Ed. Michael Wheeler. Adv. contact Kristin McCarthy TEL 201-748-7683.

327 DEU ISSN 0548-2801
NEUE HEIMAT. Text in German. 1973. bi-m. charts; illus.
Indexed: P30.
Published by: (Vereinigung fuer Verbindungen mit Buergern deutscher Herkunft in Ausland), Verlag Zeit im Bild, Julian-Grimau-Allee 10, Dresden, 8010, Germany. Ed. Heinz Vierich. Circ: 12,000.

NEW HAVEN STUDIES IN INTERNATIONAL LAW AND WORLD PUBLIC ORDER. *see* LAW—International Law

327 USA
NEW INTERNATIONAL RELATIONS. Text in English. 200?. irreg. **Document type:** *Monographic series, Academic/Scholarly.* **Description:** Features monographs on international relations, globalization and politics.
Related titles: Online - full text ed.: ISSN 2154-7335.
Published by: C R C Press, LLC (Subsidiary of: Taylor & Francis Group), 6000 Broken Sound Pky, NW, Ste 300, Boca Raton, FL 33487. TEL 561-994-0555, FAX 561-989-9732, journals@crcpress.com, http://www.crcpress.com.

327 GBR ISSN 0305-9529
PN4888.U5
NEW INTERNATIONALIST. Text in English. 1970. m. GBP 36.85 domestic; GBP 37.85 foreign (effective 2009). adv. bk.rev.; film rev. charts; illus.; stat. index. back issues avail.; reprints avail. **Document type:** *Magazine, Consumer.* **Description:** Explores world issues and the relationships between the world's rich and poor.
Formerly (until 1973): Internationalist
Related titles: Microfiche ed.: (from MML); Online - full text ed.: GBP 24.95 (effective 2009).
Indexed: A01, A02, A03, A08, A11, A22, A26, AICP, APW, AltPI, AmHI, B07, BrHumI, C03, C04, C05, CA, CBCARef, CPerI, CWI, DIP, E08, G05, G06, G07, G08, GdIns, H07, I05, I07, IBR, IBZ, ILD, LeftInd, M01, M02, MASUSE, MEA&I, P05, P30, P34, P48, PCI, PQC, PRA, RASB, S09, S23, SPPI, SRRA, T02, W09, WBA, WMB.
—BLDSC (6084.255000), CIS, IE, Infotrieve, Ingenta. **CCC.**
Published by: New Internationalist Publications Ltd., 55 Rectory Rd, Oxford, Berks OX4 1BW, United Kingdom. TEL 44-1858-438896, FAX 44-1858-461739, newint@subscription.co.uk. Eds. Chris Richards, Katherine Ainger, Richard Swift. R&P Veronique Szerauc.

NEW INTERVENTIONS. *see* SOCIOLOGY

327.172 SWE ISSN 1403-3755
NEW ROUTES; a journal of peace research and action. Text in English. 1987. q. SEK 500, EUR 59, USD 52 to individuals; SEK 650, EUR 75, USD 75 to institutions (effective 2003). bk.rev.; Website rev. 30 p./no.; back issues avail. **Document type:** *Journal, Consumer.*
Formerly (until 1996): Life and Peace Review (0284-0200)
Indexed: PerIslam.
Published by: Life and Peace Institute, PO Box 1520, Uppsala, 75145, Sweden. TEL 46-18-169500, FAX 46-18-693059. Ed., R&P Tore Samuelsson. Circ: 800 (paid).

956 USA ISSN 1945-9971
NEW SOCIETY (CAMBRIDGE); harvard college student middle east journal. Text in English. 2007. irreg. **Document type:** *Journal, Academic/Scholarly.*
Published by: Harvard University, Massachusetts Hall, Cambridge, MA 02138. TEL 617-495-1000, president@harvard.edu, http://www.harvard.edu.

327.2 GBR ISSN 0028-6990
NEW WORLD. Text in English. 1958. q. GBP 3 newsstand/cover; free to members (effective 2009). adv. bk.rev. illus. back issues avail. **Document type:** *Newsletter.* **Description:** Aims to support the UN's global campaign to eliminate violence against women.
Related titles: Online - full text ed.: free (effective 2009).
Published by: United Nations Association of Great Britain & Northern Ireland, 3 Whitehall Ct, London, SW1A 2EL, United Kingdom. TEL 44-20-77663444, FAX 44-20-79305893, unysa@una.org.uk. Ed. Veronica Lie. Circ: 7,000.

327.93 NZL ISSN 0110-0262
D839
NEW ZEALAND INTERNATIONAL REVIEW. Text in English. 1976. bi-m. membership; NZD 45 domestic; NZD 60 in Australia & South Pacific; NZD 82 elsewhere (effective 2008 - 2009). adv. bk.rev. Index. back issues avail. **Document type:** *Journal, Academic/Scholarly.* **Description:** Covers international affairs, especially as related to New Zealand.
Related titles: Online - full text ed.
Indexed: A01, A11, A26, AMB, CA, E08, G08, I05, I13, IBSS, INZP, P42, PAIS, PSA, RASB, S09, SPPI, T02.

—Ingenta. **CCC.**
Published by: New Zealand Institute of International Affairs, c/o Victoria University of Wellington, PO Box 600, Wellington, 6140, New Zealand. nziia@vuw.ac.nz. Ed., Adv. contact Ian McGibbon. Circ: 1,500 (controlled).

327.93 NZL
NEW ZEALAND. MINISTRY OF FOREIGN AFFAIRS AND TRADE. ANNUAL REPORT. Text in English. a. free. **Document type:** *Government.*
Former titles (until 2004): New Zealand. Ministry of Foreign Affairs and Trade. Report; New Zealand. Ministry of External Relations and Trade. Report
Related titles: Online - full text ed.
Published by: Ministry of Foreign Affairs and Trade, c/o Publication Officer, Private Bag 18-901, Wellington, New Zealand. TEL 64-4-4398000, FAX 64-4-4398511, enquiries@mfat.govt.nz.

341.21 NZL
NEW ZEALAND. MINISTRY OF FOREIGN AFFAIRS AND TRADE. TREATY SERIES. Text in English. irreg. price varies. **Document type:** *Government.*
Formerly: New Zealand. Ministry of External Relations and Trade. Treaty Series
Published by: Ministry of Foreign Affairs and Trade, c/o Publication Officer, Private Bag 18-901, Wellington, New Zealand. TEL 64-4-4948500, FAX 64-4-4948511.

NEWS TIBET. *see* ETHNIC INTERESTS

327 NGA ISSN 0331-2151
DT515.62
NIGERIA BULLETIN ON FOREIGN AFFAIRS. Text in English. 1971. s-a. NGN 600, USD 50 (effective 2003). adv. bk.rev. bibl. back issues avail. **Document type:** *Bulletin, Academic/Scholarly.* **Description:** Contains a collection of documents, papers, and commentary about Nigerian foreign policy, edited by the Nigerian Institute of International Affairs Library Department.
Indexed: MEA&I.
Published by: (Nigerian Institute of International Affairs, Library Department), N I I A Press, 13-15 Kofo Abayomi Rd., Victory Island, GPO Box 1727, Lagos, Nigeria. TEL 234-1-2615606, FAX 234-1-2611360, http://www.niianet.org. Ed., R&P, Adv. contact U Joy Ogwu.

327.669 NGA ISSN 0078-0685
DT515
NIGERIA YEAR BOOK. Text in English. 1952. a. price varies. adv.
Indexed: RASB.
Published by: Daily Times of Nigeria Ltd., Publications Division, New Isheri Rd., PMB 21340, Ikeja, Agidingbi, Lagos, Nigeria. TEL 234-64-900850-9, FAX 234-64-21333. Ed. Gbenga Odusanya.

327.669 NGA ISSN 0189-0816
DT30.5
NIGERIAN FORUM. Text in English. 1981. q. NGN 250, USD 45 (effective 2003). adv. bk.rev. bibl.; charts; stat. index. back issues avail. **Document type:** *Journal, Academic/Scholarly.* **Description:** Provides factual and authoritative information about current world issues by scholars, statesmen, soldiers, and university students.
Published by: (Nigerian Institute of International Affairs), N I I A Press, 13-15 Kofo Abayomi Rd., Victory Island, GPO Box 1727, Lagos, Nigeria. TEL 234-1-2615606, FAX 234-1-2611360, http://www.niianet.org. Ed., R&P, Adv. contact George A Obiozor. Circ: 3,000. **Dist. in the U.S. by:** First Western Corp., 6323 Beachway Dr, Falls Church, VA 22044.

327.669 NGA ISSN 0331-6262
JX1
NIGERIAN INSTITUTE OF INTERNATIONAL AFFAIRS. LECTURE SERIES. Text in English. 1969. irreg., latest vol.78. price varies. adv. **Document type:** *Monographic series.*
Indexed: ARDT.
Published by: (Nigerian Institute of International Affairs), N I I A Press, 13-15 Kofo Abayomi Rd., Victory Island, GPO Box 1727, Lagos, Nigeria. TEL 234-1-2615606, FAX 234-1-2611360, http://www.niianet.org. Ed., R&P, Adv. contact U Joy Ogwu. **Dist. outside Africa by:** African Books Collective Ltd., The Jam Factory, 27 Park End St, Oxford, Oxon OX1 1HU, United Kingdom. TEL 44-1865-726686, FAX 44-1865-793298.

327.669 NGA ISSN 0331-6254
NIGERIAN INSTITUTE OF INTERNATIONAL AFFAIRS. MONOGRAPH SERIES. Text in English. 1979. irreg., latest vol.15. price varies. adv. charts; stat. back issues avail. **Document type:** *Monographic series.*
Published by: (Nigerian Institute of International Affairs), N I I A Press, 13-15 Kofo Abayomi Rd., Victory Island, GPO Box 1727, Lagos, Nigeria. TEL 234-1-2615606, FAX 234-1-2611360, http://www.niianet.org. Ed., R&P, Adv. contact U Joy Ogwu. **Dist. in the U.S. by:** First Western Corp., 6323 Beachway Dr, Falls Church, VA 22044; **Dist. outside Africa by:** African Books Collective Ltd., The Jam Factory, 27 Park End St, Oxford, Oxon OX1 1HU, United Kingdom. TEL 44-1865-726686, FAX 44-1865-793298.

327.669 NGA ISSN 0331-3646
JZ6.5
NIGERIAN JOURNAL OF INTERNATIONAL AFFAIRS. Abbreviated title: N J I A. Text in English. 1975. s-a. NGN 600, USD 55 (effective 2003). adv. bk.rev. bibl.; charts; stat. index. back issues avail. **Document type:** *Journal, Academic/Scholarly.* **Description:** Publishes scholarly articles on topics in international affairs, with special sections on official documents.
Indexed: ASD, IBSS.
Published by: (Nigerian Institute of International Affairs), N I I A Press, 13-15 Kofo Abayomi Rd., Victory Island, GPO Box 1727, Lagos, Nigeria. TEL 234-1-2615606, FAX 234-1-2611360, http://www.niianet.org. Ed., R&P, Adv. contact U Joy Ogwu. **Dist. in the U.S. by:** First Western Corp., 6323 Beachway Dr, Falls Church, VA 22044.

327.669 NGA ISSN 0331-8524
JQ3081.A1
NIGERIAN JOURNAL OF POLITICAL SCIENCE. Text in English. 1979. s-a. NGN 7.50, USD 12. back issues avail. **Document type:** *Journal, Academic/Scholarly.*
Published by: Ahmadu Bello University, Department of Political Science, Samaru-Zaria, Kaduna, Nigeria. Circ: 3,000.

327 GBR ISSN 1073-6700
JX1974.73
➤ **THE NONPROLIFERATION REVIEW.** Text in English. 1993. 3/yr. GBP 229 combined subscription in United Kingdom to institutions (print & online eds.); EUR 304, USD 382 combined subscription to institutions (print & online eds.) (effective 2012). adv. charts; illus.; maps. 150 p./no. 1 cols./p.; back issues avail.; reprint service avail. from PSC. **Document type:** *Journal, Academic/Scholarly.* **Description:** Features case studies, theoretical analyses, reports, and policy debates on such issues as individual country programs, treaties and export controls, terrorism, and the economic and environmental effects of weapons proliferation.
Formed by the merger of (1991-1993): Missile Monitor (1060-8273); Incorporates (1990-1993): Eye on Supply (1061-1592)
Related titles: Online - full text ed.: ISSN 1746-1766. GBP 206 in United Kingdom to institutions; EUR 274, USD 343 to institutions (effective 2012).
Indexed: A22, CA, E01, I02, I13, LID&ISL, P42, PAIS, PSA, SCOPUS, T02.
—BLDSC (6117.340350), IE, Ingenta. **CCC.**
Published by: (James Martin Center For Nonproliferation Studies USA, Monterey Institute of International Studies, Center for Nonproliferation Studies USA), Routledge (Subsidiary of: Taylor & Francis Group), 4 Park Sq, Milton Park, Abingdon, Oxon OX14 4RN, United Kingdom. TEL 44-20-70176000, FAX 44-20-70176336, subscriptions@tandf.co.uk, http://www.routledge.com. Adv. contact Linda Hann TEL 44-1344-779945. **Subscr. to:** Taylor & Francis Ltd., Journals Customer Service, Sheepen Pl, Colchester, Essex CO3 3LP, United Kingdom. TEL 44-20-70175544, FAX 44-20-70175198, tf.enquiries@tfinforma.com.

327 BEL ISSN 0779-6641
NOORD - ZUID CAHIER; tijdschrift voor ontwikkelingssamenwerking. Text in Flemish. 1974. q. EUR 25 (effective 2005). **Document type:** *Bulletin.* **Description:** Covers all aspects of North-South relations, including population, structural adjustment, food security, democracy.
Formerly: Tijdschrift voor Ontwikkelingssamenwerking
Published by: V.Z.W. WereldMediaHaus, Vlasfabriekstraat 11, Brussel, 1060, Belgium. TEL 32-2-536-1977, FAX 32-2-536-1934, wereldwijd@wereldwijd.ngonet.be. Ed. Bob Hendrickx. Circ: 1,000.

NORD. *see* POLITICAL SCIENCE

327 DEU
NORDEUROPAEISCHE STUDIEN. Text in German. 1986. irreg., latest vol.22, 2010. price varies. **Document type:** *Monographic series, Academic/Scholarly.*
Published by: B W V - Berliner Wissenschafts Verlag GmbH, Markgrafenstr 12-14, Berlin, 10969, Germany. TEL 49-30-8417700, FAX 49-30-84177021, bwv@bwv-verlag.de, http://www.bwv-verlag.de. Ed. Bernd Henningsen.

NORMAN PATERSON SCHOOL OF INTERNATIONAL AFFAIRS. BIBLIOGRAPHY SERIES. *see* POLITICAL SCIENCE—Abstracting, Bibliographies, Statistics

327.11 NOR ISSN 1502-5373
DEN NORSKE ATLANTERHAVSKOMITE. INTERNETT TEKSTER. Text mainly in English. 2000. irreg., latest vol.37, 2007. back issues avail. **Document type:** *Monographic series, Consumer.*
Media: Online - full content.
Published by: Den Norske Atlanterhavskomite/The Norwegian Atlantic Committee, Fridjof Nansens Plass 8, Oslo, 0160, Norway. TEL 47-22-403600, FAX 47-22-403610, post@dnak.org, http://www.dnak.org.

327 MEX ISSN 1870-3550
➤ **NORTEAMERICA**; revista academica del C I S A N - U N A M. Variant title: Centro de Investigaciones sobre America del Norte - Universidad Nacional Autonoma de Mexico. Revista. Text in English, French, Spanish. 2006. s-a. MXN 200 domestic; USD 26 in United States; USD 34 in Canada & Latin America; USD 48 elsewhere (effective 2009). bk.rev. abstr.; bibl.; charts; illus.; maps; stat. back issues avail. **Document type:** *Journal, Academic/Scholarly.* **Description:** Publishes multi- and interdisciplinary academic studies focused on the social sciences and humanities in issues related to North America and its links to the rest of the world. Within analyzed issues it includes elections, foreign policy, border issues, security, minorities, education, human rights, the environment and migration.
Media: Online - full text.
Indexed: A01, C01, F04, T02.
Published by: Universidad Nacional Autonoma de Mexico, Centro de Investigaciones sobre America del Norte (CISAN-UNAM), Pisos 9 y 10 Torre II de Humanidades, Ciudad Universitaria, Coyoacan, D.F., Mexico. TEL 52-5-56230303, FAX 52-5-55500379, http://www.unam.mx/voice/. Ed. Nattie Golubov Figueroa. Circ: 1,000.

➤ **NORTH KOREAN REVIEW.** *see* HISTORY—History Of Asia

327.1 NOR ISSN 1504-2723
NORWAY. NORAD. EVALUERINGSRAPPORT. Text in Multiple languages. 1990. irreg. free. back issues avail. **Document type:** *Monographic series, Government.*
Former titles (until 2004): Norway. Utenriksdepartementet. Evaluation Report (0803-544X); (until 1990): Norway. Royal Norwegian Ministry of Development Cooperation. Evaluation Report (0803-026X); (until 1984): Norway. Norad. Evaluation Report (1503-1268)
Published by: Direktoratet for Utviklingssamarbeid/Norwegian Agency for Development Cooperation, PO Box 8034, Dep, Oslo, 0030, Norway. TEL 47-22-242030, FAX 47-22-242031, postmottag@norad.no, http://www.norad.no.

327 DNK ISSN 1603-7480
NOTAT. Text in Danish. 1973. m. DKK 495 to individuals; DKK 792 to institutions; DKK 372 to students (effective 2009). adv. back issues avail. **Document type:** *Magazine, Consumer.* **Description:** News and debate about EU.
Former titles (until 2004): Det Ny Notat (1395-5896); (until 1995): Notat (0900-7458); (until 1984): Det Ny Notat (0900-744X)
Related titles: Online - full text ed.
Address: Nordkystvejen 2F, Allingaabro, 8961, Denmark. TEL 45-86-481600, FAX 45-86-480233, notat@notat.dk. Eds. Aage Skovrind, Erling Boettcher.

327 ESP ISSN 2013-4428
▼ **NOTES INTERNACIONALS CIDOB.** (Centred'Informacio i Documentacio Internacionals a Barcelona) Text in Catalan. 2009. m. **Document type:** *Bulletin, Academic/Scholarly.*
Media: Online - full text.
Published by: Fundacio C I D O B, C. Elisabets, 12, Barcelona, 08001, Spain. TEL 34-93-3026495, FAX 34-93-3022118, publicaciones@cibod.org, http://www.cibod.org.

327 FRA ISSN 0754-3786
NOUVELLES DU VIETNAM. Text in French. N.S. 1976. q. illus.
Formerly: Bulletin du Vietnam
Indexed: RASB.
Published by: Ambassade de la Republique Socialiste du Vietnam en France, 62 rue Boileau, Paris, 75016, France. Ed. M Aquettaz. Circ: 500.

327.174 USA
NUCLEAR TEXTS AND CONTEXTS. Text in English. 1988. s-a. USD 7.
Address: 3918 Harts Mill Ln, Atlanta, GA 30319. Ed. Daniel L Zins.

NYHETER FRAAN NICARAGUA. *see* HISTORY—History Of North And South America

327 NLD ISSN 1381-4400
O J C D. (Official Journal of the European Communities) Text in English. 1994. 6/yr. EUR 1,450 (effective 2009). **Document type:** *Abstract/Index.* **Description:** Contains the full text of all EU legislation in force passed since 1952, case law from the Court of Justice, and all entries from the Official Journal C Series published since 1990.
Media: CD-ROM.
Indexed: FS&TA.
Published by: Ellis Publications bv, PO Box 1059, Maastricht, 6201 BB, Netherlands. TEL 31-43-3215313, FAX 31-43-3253959, ellis.info@thomson.com, http://www.ellispub.com.

O M D ACTUALITES. (Organisation Mondiale des Douanes) *see* PUBLIC ADMINISTRATION

327 DEU
O S Z E JAHRBUCH. (Organisation fuer Sicherheit und Zusammenarbeit in Europa) Text in German. a. EUR 36 (effective 2004). **Document type:** *Yearbook, Academic/Scholarly.*
Published by: (Universitaet Hamburg, Universitaet Hamburg, Institut fuer Friedensforschung und Sicherheitspolitik), Nomos Verlagsgesellschaft mbH und Co. KG, Waldseestr 3-5, Baden-Baden, 76530, Germany. TEL 49-7221-21040, FAX 49-7221-210427, nomos@nomos.de, http://www.nomos.de.

341.37 BEL
O T A N. MANUEL. (Organisation du Traite de l'Atlantique du Nord) Text in French. irreg.
Related titles: ◆ English ed.: N A T O Handbook. ISSN 0259-4331; ◆ Danish ed.: N A T O Handbogen. ISSN 1015-4892; Multiple languages ed.
Published by: North Atlantic Treaty Organization (N A T O), Office of Information and Press, Blvd Leopold III, Brussels, 1110, Belgium.

355 CZE ISSN 1214-6463
➤ **OBRANA A STRATEGIE/DEFENCE & STRATEGY.** Text in English, Czech, Slovak. 2001. 2/yr. free (effective 2009). abstr.; bibl. back issues avail. **Document type:** *Journal, Academic/Scholarly.* **Description:** Focuses on topics in the areas of security studies, strategic studies, military affairs, international relationships and related subjects.
Related titles: Online - full text ed.: ISSN 1802-7199. 2007. free (effective 2011).
Indexed: CA, I02, P52, T02.
Published by: Univerzita Obrany, Ustav Strategickych a Obrannych Studii/University of Defence, Institute for Strategic and Defence Studies, Kounicova 44, Brno, 612 00, Czech Republic. TEL 420-973-442993, FAX 420-973-443371, libor.frank@unob.cz. Ed., Pub., R&P Libor Frank.

327 COL ISSN 1657-7558
OBSERVATORIO DE ANALISIS DE LOS SISTEMAS INTERNACIONALES. Abbreviated title: O A S I S. Text in Spanish. 1995. a. **Document type:** *Journal, Academic/Scholarly.*
Related titles: Online - full text ed.
Indexed: A01, C01, CA, F03, F04, IBSS, T02.
Published by: Universidad Externado de Colombia, Centro de Investigaciones y Proyectos Especiales, Calle 12 No. 1-17 Este, Bogota, Colombia.

327 ARG ISSN 1852-0103
OBSERVATORIO DE BOLIVIA. Text in Spanish. 2008. q. **Document type:** *Report, Academic/Scholarly.*
Media: Online - full text.
Published by: Centro Argentino de Estudios Internacionales, Lavalle 1646 4o Ofic. 13, Buenos Aires, C1048AAL, Argentina. TEL 34-911-69656393, FAX 34-911-67379606. Ed. Cecilia Pon.

327 ARG
▼ **OBSERVATORIO DE BRASIL.** Text in Spanish. 2010. q. back issues avail. **Document type:** *Report, Academic/Scholarly.*
Media: Online - full text.
Published by: Centro Argentino de Estudios Internacionales, Lavalle 1646 4o Ofic. 13, Buenos Aires, C1048AAL, Argentina. TEL 34-911-69656393, FAX 34-911-67379606. Ed. Pablo Koblum.

327 ARG
▼ **OBSERVATORIO DE CENTROAMERICA.** Text in Spanish. 2009. q. back issues avail. **Document type:** *Report, Academic/Scholarly.*
Media: Online - full text.
Published by: Centro Argentino de Estudios Internacionales, Lavalle 1646 4o Ofic. 13, Buenos Aires, C1048AAL, Argentina. TEL 34-911-69656393, FAX 34-911-67379606. Ed. Santiago Ferrari.

327 ARG
▼ **OBSERVATORIO DE CHILE.** Text in Spanish. 2010. q. back issues avail. **Document type:** *Report, Academic/Scholarly.*
Media: Online - full text.
Published by: Centro Argentino de Estudios Internacionales, Lavalle 1646 4o Ofic. 13, Buenos Aires, C1048AAL, Argentina. TEL 34-911-69656393, FAX 34-911-67379606. Ed. Mariana Reyes.

327 ARG ISSN 1852-0057
OBSERVATORIO DE COLOMBIA. Text in Spanish. 2008. q. back issues avail. **Document type:** *Report, Academic/Scholarly.*
Media: Online - full text.
Published by: Centro Argentino de Estudios Internacionales, Lavalle 1646 4o Ofic. 13, Buenos Aires, C1048AAL, Argentina. TEL 34-911-69656393, FAX 34-911-67379606. Ed. Maria Agustina Ferrari.

P

327 ARG ISSN 1852-0030
OBSERVATORIO DE ECUADOR. Text in Spanish. 2008. q. back issues avail. **Document type:** *Report, Academic/Scholarly.*
Media: Online - full text.
Published by: Centro Argentino de Estudios Internacionales, Lavalle 1646 4o Ofic. 13, Buenos Aires, C1048AAL, Argentina. TEL 34-911-69656393, FAX 34-911-67379606. Ed. Pablo Gambande.

327 ARG
▼ **OBSERVATORIO DE ESTADOS UNIDOS.** Text in Spanish. 2010. q. **Document type:** *Report, Academic/Scholarly.*
Media: Online - full text.
Published by: Centro Argentino de Estudios Internacionales, Lavalle 1646 4o Ofic. 13, Buenos Aires, C1048AAL, Argentina. TEL 34-911-69656393, FAX 34-911-67379606. Ed. Gaston Marando.

327 ARG
▼ **OBSERVATORIO DE GUYANA Y SURINAM.** Text in Spanish. 2010. q. back issues avail. **Document type:** *Report, Academic/Scholarly.*
Media: Online - full text.
Published by: Centro Argentino de Estudios Internacionales, Lavalle 1646 4o Ofic. 13, Buenos Aires, C1048AAL, Argentina. TEL 34-911-69656393, FAX 34-911-67379606. Ed. Matias Magnasco.

327 ARG
▼ **OBSERVATORIO DE INDIA.** Text in Spanish. forthcoming 2011. q. **Document type:** *Report, Academic/Scholarly.*
Media: Online - full text.
Published by: Centro Argentino de Estudios Internacionales, Lavalle 1646 4o Ofic. 13, Buenos Aires, C1048AAL, Argentina. TEL 34-911-69656393, FAX 34-911-67379606.

327 ARG
▼ **OBSERVATORIO DE MEXICO.** Text in Spanish. 2010. q. **Document type:** *Report, Academic/Scholarly.*
Media: Online - full text.
Published by: Centro Argentino de Estudios Internacionales, Lavalle 1646 4o Ofic. 13, Buenos Aires, C1048AAL, Argentina. TEL 34-911-69656393, FAX 34-911-67379606. Ed. Armando Rodriguez Luna.

327 ARG ISSN 1852-0073
OBSERVATORIO DE PARAGUAY. Text in Spanish. 2008. q. back issues avail. **Document type:** *Report, Academic/Scholarly.*
Media: Online - full text.
Published by: Centro Argentino de Estudios Internacionales, Lavalle 1646 4o Ofic. 13, Buenos Aires, C1048AAL, Argentina. TEL 34-911-69656393, FAX 34-911-67379606. Ed. Barbara Quinones Rojas.

327 ARG
▼ **OBSERVATORIO DE PERU.** Text in Spanish. 2009. q. back issues avail. **Document type:** *Report, Academic/Scholarly.*
Media: Online - full text.
Published by: Centro Argentino de Estudios Internacionales, Lavalle 1646 4o Ofic. 13, Buenos Aires, C1048AAL, Argentina. TEL 34-911-69656393, FAX 34-911-67379606. Ed. Melisa Galvano.

327 ARG ISSN 1852-009X
OBSERVATORIO DE URUGUAY. Text in Spanish. 2008. q. **Document type:** *Report, Academic/Scholarly.*
Media: Online - full text.
Published by: Centro Argentino de Estudios Internacionales, Lavalle 1646 4o Ofic. 13, Buenos Aires, C1048AAL, Argentina. TEL 34-911-69656393, FAX 34-911-67379606. Ed. Eugenia Dri.

327 ARG ISSN 1852-0081
OBSERVATORIO DE VENEZUELA. Text in Spanish. 2008. q. **Document type:** *Report, Academic/Scholarly.*
Media: Online - full text.
Published by: Centro Argentino de Estudios Internacionales, Lavalle 1646 4o Ofic. 13, Buenos Aires, C1048AAL, Argentina. TEL 34-911-69656393, FAX 34-911-67379606. Ed. Mercedes Andres.

327 ARG
▼ **OBSERVATORIO DEL CARIBE.** Text in Spanish. 2010. q. **Document type:** *Report, Academic/Scholarly.*
Media: Online - full text.
Published by: Centro Argentino de Estudios Internacionales, Lavalle 1646 4o Ofic. 13, Buenos Aires, C1048AAL, Argentina. TEL 34-911-69656393, FAX 34-911-67379606. Ed. Santiago Ferrari.

327 ARG
▼ **OBSERVATORIO DEL MEDIO AMBIENTE.** Text in Spanish. 2010. q. **Document type:** *Report, Academic/Scholarly.*
Media: Online - full text.
Published by: Centro Argentino de Estudios Internacionales, Lavalle 1646 4o Ofic. 13, Buenos Aires, C1048AAL, Argentina. TEL 34-911-69656393, FAX 34-911-67379606. Ed. Diego Fossati.

327 ARG ISSN 1852-0049
OBSERVATORIO MALVINENSE. Text in Spanish. 2007. q. back issues avail. **Document type:** *Report, Academic/Scholarly.*
Media: Online - full text.
Published by: Centro Argentino de Estudios Internacionales, Lavalle 1646 4o Ofic. 13, Buenos Aires, C1048AAL, Argentina. TEL 34-911-69656393, FAX 34-911-67379606. Ed. Diego Llorente.

327 ARG ISSN 1852-0065
OBSERVATORIO POLAR. Text in Spanish. 2008. q. back issues avail. **Document type:** *Report, Academic/Scholarly.*
Media: Online - full text.
Published by: Centro Argentino de Estudios Internacionales, Lavalle 1646 4o Ofic. 13, Buenos Aires, C1048AAL, Argentina. TEL 34-911-69656393, FAX 34-911-67379606. Ed. Gabriel De Paula.

327 MLT ISSN 1024-6282
➤ **OCCASIONAL PAPERS ON ISLANDS AND SMALL STATES.** Text in English. 1994. irreg., latest vol.13, 1995. USD 40. back issues avail. **Document type:** *Monographic series, Academic/Scholarly.* **Description:** Publishes studies on economic and socio-political issues pertaining to islands and small nations around the world, including sustainable development, the impact of tourism, and environmental concerns.
Published by: Foundation for International Studies, Islands and Small States Institute, St. Paul's St., Valletta, VLT 07, Malta. TEL 356-230551, FAX 356-230551. Ed. Lino Briguglio. Circ: 200.

341 LUX
HC241.2
OFFICE FOR OFFICIAL PUBLICATIONS OF THE EUROPEAN UNION. NEWSLETTER. Text in English. 1992. 2/yr. (2 nos./vol.). free (effective 2005). **Document type:** *Newspaper.* **Description:** Covers economic, technical, and social policy in the EU. Discusses culture, education, women's issues, as well as economy and internal and external trade.
Formerly (until 2002): Eur-Op News (1021-1675)
Related titles: Online - full text ed.; German ed.: ISSN 1021-1667; Spanish ed.: ISSN 1022-8748. 1992; Swedish ed.: ISSN 1028-5245; Dutch ed.: ISSN 1022-8764; Portuguese ed.: ISSN 1022-8772; Finnish ed.: ISSN 1028-5237; French ed.: ISSN 1021-1683; Italian ed.: ISSN 1022-8756.
Published by: European Commission, Office for Official Publications of the European Union, 2 Rue Mercier, Luxembourg, L-2985, Luxembourg. FAX 352-29291, info@publications.europa.eu, http://publications.europa.eu. Circ: 308,500. **Dist. in US by:** Bernan Associates, Bernan, 4611-F Assembly Dr., Lanham, MD 20706-4391. TEL 800-274-4447.

327.17 PER ISSN 1682-4857
OFICINA DE COOPERACION INTERNACIONAL. BOLETIN INFORMATIVO. Key Title: Boletin Informativo - Oficina de Cooperacion Internacional. Text in Spanish. 1999. a. back issues avail.
Media: Online - full text.
Published by: Ministerio de Educacion, Oficina de Cooperacion Internacional, 3er Piso, Pabellon B, Lima, Peru. TEL 51-1-4353900, FAX 51-1-4363524. Ed. Jorge Rodriguez Cuadros.

327.17 DEU ISSN 1866-8798
OLDENBURGER STUDIEN ZUR EUROPAEISIERUNG UND ZUR TRANSNATIONALEN REGULIERUNG. Text in German. 2000. irreg., latest vol.19, 2008. **Document type:** *Monographic series, Academic/Scholarly.*
Formerly (until 2007): Bamberger Beitraege zur Europaforschung und zur Internationalen Politik
Media: Online - full text.
Published by: Centre for Europeanisation and Transnational Regulations Oldenburg, c/o Institut fuer Sozialwissenschaften, Ammerlaender Heerstr 114-118, Raum A6 4-417, Oldenburg, 26129, Germany. TEL 49-441-7982641, FAX 49-441-798192641, christine.meyenberg@uni-oldenburg.de.

327.172 USA ISSN 1522-211X
JX1901
THE ONLINE JOURNAL OF PEACE AND CONFLICT RESOLUTION. Text in English. 1998. bi-m. back issues avail. **Description:** Designed for anyone interested in peace studies and or conflict resolution.
Media: Online - full text.
Indexed: A39, C27, C29, D03, D04, E13, R14, S14, S15, S18.
Published by: Tabula Rasa Institute, Inc. info@trinstitute.org, http://www.trinstitute.org/about.htm. Ed. Dereck Sweetman.

327 NLD ISSN 0030-3232
ONZE WERELD. Text in Dutch. 1957. 10/yr. EUR 49.50 (effective 2010). adv. bk.rev. bibl.; charts; illus.; stat. index.
Published by: (Stichting Onze Wereld), Global Village Media, Spuistraat 239-d, Amsterdam, 1012 VP, Netherlands. TEL 31-20-4621620, FAX 31-20-6936889, http://www.globalvillagemedia.nl. Ed. John Verhoeven. adv.: page EUR 2,995; trim 210 x 297. Circ: 20,606.

327.2 CYP
OPERATIONS IN OIL DIPLOMACY. Variant title: A P S Diplomat Operations in Oil Diplomacy. Text in English. 1972. m. USD 800; includes subscr. to A P S News Service, Strategic Balance in the Middle East, Fate of the Arabian Peninsula, Re-Drawing the Islamic Map. s-a. index. **Document type:** *Bulletin.* **Description:** Provides unique surveys of ruling families involved in oil, trade relations, and factors influencing oil and gas decisions.
Related titles: Online - full text ed.
Published by: Arab Press Service, PO Box 23896, Nicosia, Cyprus. TEL 357-2-351778, FAX 357-2-350265. Ed., Pub. Pierre Shammas.

327 GBR ISSN 0030-4387
D839
➤ **ORBIS (KIDLINGTON)**; a journal of world affairs. Text in English. 1957. 4/yr. EUR 444 in Europe to institutions; JPY 59,000 in Japan to institutions; USD 499 elsewhere to institutions (effective 2012). adv. bk.rev. charts; illus. index. back issues avail.; reprint service avail. from PSC. **Document type:** *Journal, Academic/Scholarly.* **Description:** Contains articles on contemporary international affairs.
Related titles: Microform ed.: (from PQC); Online - full text ed.: ISSN 1873-5282 (from IngentaConnect, ScienceDirect).
Indexed: A01, A02, A03, A08, A20, A22, A25, A26, ABCPolSci, ABS&EES, AMB, Acal, AmH&L, AmHI, B04, BRD, CA, E08, FutSurv, G08, H07, H09, H10, HRIR, HistAb, I05, I13, IBR, IBSS, IBZ, KES, LID&ISL, M01, M02, M05, M10, MEA&I, P02, P06, P10, P27, P30, P34, P42, P47, P48, P53, P54, PAIS, PCI, PQC, PRA, PSA, RASB, S02, S03, S05, S08, S09, S11, SCOPUS, SPAA, SSAI, SSAb, SSI, SociolAb, T02, W03, W05.
—BLDSC (6277.850000), IE, Infotrieve, Ingenta. **CCC.**
Published by: (Foreign Policy Research Institute USA), Pergamon (Subsidiary of: Elsevier Science & Technology), The Blvd, Langford Ln, East Park, Kidlington, Oxford OX5 1GB, United Kingdom. TEL 44-1865-843000, FAX 44-1865-843010, JournalsCustomerServiceEMEA@elsevier.com, http://www.elsevier.nl. Ed. Mackubin Owens. **Subscr. to:** Elsevier BV, Radarweg 29, PO Box 211, Amsterdam 1000 AE, Netherlands. TEL 31-20-4853757, FAX 31-20-4853432.

327.17 DEU ISSN 1868-7989
▼ **ORDNUNGSPOLITISCHE DIALOGE.** Text in German. 2009. irreg. price varies. **Document type:** *Monographic series, Academic/Scholarly.*
Published by: Peter Lang GmbH (Subsidiary of: Peter Lang Publishing Group), Eschborner Landstr 42-50, Frankfurt Am Main, 60489, Germany. TEL 49-69-7807050, FAX 49-69-78070550, zentrale.frankfurt@peterlang.com. Ed. Ralph Wrobel.

327.172 USA
OREGON PEACEWORKER. Text in English. 1988. 10/yr. USD 15 (effective 2000). adv. **Document type:** *Newspaper.*
Published by: Oregon PeaceWorks, 104 Commercial St NE, Salem, OR 97301-3401. TEL 503-371-8002, FAX 503-588-0088. Ed., R&P Peter Bergel. Adv. contact John Exline. Circ: 12,000.

327 BEL ISSN 2030-0832
ORGANISATION INTERNATIONALE ET RELATIONS INTERNATIONALES. Text in French. 1975. a., latest vol.58, 2004. **Document type:** *Monographic series, Academic/Scholarly.*
Published by: (Centre de Recherches sur les Institutions Internationales), Bruylant, Rue de la Regence 67, Bruxelles, 1000, Belgium. TEL 32-2-512-9845, FAX 32-2-511-7202, http://www.bruylant.be.

341 USA
ORGANIZATION OF AMERICAN STATES. GENERAL ASSEMBLY. ACTAS Y DOCUMENTOS. Text in English, Spanish. 1970. a.
Published by: Organization of American States/Organizacion de los Estados Americanos, 1889 F St, NW, Washington, DC 20006. TEL 202-458-3000, rgutierrez@oas.org, http://www.oas.org.

327 ISR ISSN 0792-4615
DS119.7
THE OTHER ISRAEL. Text in English. 1983. bi-m. looseleaf. USD 30 to individuals; USD 50 to institutions; USD 15 to students (effective 2008). adv. 16 p./no.; back issues avail. **Document type:** *Newsletter, Consumer.* **Description:** Covers the Israeli peace movement; comments on events in Israel and the Middle East.
Related titles: E-mail ed.; French ed.: 1990. USD 30 to individuals; USD 50 to institutions; USD 15 to students (effective 2003).
Indexed: AltPI, PerIslam, RASB.
Published by: Israeli Council for Israeli - Palestinian Peace, P O Box 2542, Holon, 58125, Israel. otherisr@actcom.co.il. Eds. Adam Keller, Beate Zilversmidt. R&P, Adv. contact Beate Zilversmidt. Circ: 3,500.

327 USA
OUTPOST. Text in English. 1972. m. membership. bk.rev. illus. back issues avail. **Document type:** *Newsletter.*
Indexed: SPPI.
Published by: Americans for a Safe Israel, 1623 3rd Ave, Ste 205, New York, NY 10128-3638. TEL 212-828-2424, FAX 212-828-1717. Ed. Rael Isaac. Circ: 10,000.

327 FRA ISSN 1636-3671
OUTRE - TERRE; revue francaise de geopolitique. Text in French. 2002. q. EUR 48 in the European Union; EUR 35 in developing nations; EUR 60 elsewhere; EUR 35 in the European Union to students; EUR 50 elsewhere to students (effective 2009). **Document type:** *Journal, Consumer.*
Related titles: Online - full text ed.: ISSN 1951-624X.
Indexed: IBSS.
Published by: Editions Eres, 33 Av. Marcel Dassault, Toulouse, 31500, France. TEL 33-5-61751576, FAX 33-5-61735289, eres@edition-eres.com. Eds. Karine Greth, Stephan Martens. Circ: 1,000.

327 TWN
OUZHOU GUOJI PINGLUN/EUROPEAN JUORNAL OF INTERNATIONAL REVIEW. Text in Chinese. 2005. a. **Document type:** *Journal, Academic/Scholarly.*
Related titles: Online - full text ed.
Published by: Nanhua Daxue, Ouzhou Yanjiuso/Nanhua University, Institute of European Studies, 32, Chung Keng Li, Dalin, Chiayi 62248, Taiwan. TEL 886-5-2721001 ext 2361, http://www.nhu.edu.tw/~europe/.

327.172 DEU
P R I F REPORTS. Text in English. irreg., latest vol.86, 2008. EUR 10 per issue (effective 2009). **Document type:** *Monographic series, Academic/Scholarly.*
Published by: Peace Research Institute Frankfurt, Baseler Str 27-31, Frankfurt Am Main, 60329, Germany. TEL 49-69-959104, FAX 49-69-558481, info@hsfk.de, http://www.hsfk.de.

P S A AND B I S A DIRECTORY. (Political Studies Association / British International Studies Association) *see* POLITICAL SCIENCE

P S R MONITOR (ONLINE). *see* PUBLIC HEALTH AND SAFETY

P S R REPORTS. *see* PUBLIC HEALTH AND SAFETY

325.21 NOR ISSN 1501-9942
PAA FLUKT - WEB. Text in Norwegian. 1991. 3/w. free. illus. **Document type:** *Newsletter, Consumer.* **Description:** Publishes news on political refugee situations worldwide.
Former titles (until 1999): Paa Flukt - Aktuelt (Print Edition) (1500-8401); (until 1998): Paa Flukt - Nyheter (0803-5016)
Media: Online - full text.
Published by: Flyktninghjelpen/Norwegian Refugee Council, Grensen 17, Postboks 6758, St Olavs Plass, Oslo, 0130, Norway. TEL 47-23-109800, FAX 47-23-109801, nrc@nrc.no, http://www.nrc.no. Eds. Lars Torjesen, Petter Nome.

327 CAN ISSN 0030-851X
➤ **PACIFIC AFFAIRS**; an international review of Asia and the Pacific. Text in English. 1928. q. USD 105 to individuals (print or online eds.); USD 215 to institutions (print or online eds.) (effective 2011). adv. bk.rev. illus. index. 200 p./no.; back issues avail.; reprints avail. **Document type:** *Journal, Academic/Scholarly.* **Description:** Peer-reviewed scholarly journal dealing with current affairs in Asia and the Pacific.
Formerly (until 1928): Institute of Pacific Relations. News Bulletin (1530-2199)
Related titles: Microfiche ed.: (from MML); Microform ed.: (from MML, PQC); Online - full text ed.: ISSN 1715-3379 (from IngentaConnect).
Indexed: A01, A02, A03, A08, A20, A22, A25, A26, ABCPolSci, ABS&EES, AMB, APEL, ASCA, AbAn, Acal, AmH&L, AmHI, B04, B14, BAS, BRD, BRI, C03, CA, CBCARef, CBPI, CBRI, CPerI, CurCont, DIP, E08, EI, FamI, G05, G06, G07, G08, G10, GEOBASE, H07, H08, H09, H10, HAb, HistAb, HumInd, I02, I05, I08, I13, IBR, IBSS, IBZ, ILD, KES, LID&ISL, M01, M02, MEA&I, MLA-IB, P02, P06, P10, P13, P14, P27, P30, P34, P42, P45, P47, P48, P53, P54, PAIS, PCI, PQC, PRA, PSA, PerIslam, R02, RASB, S02, S03, S05, S08, S09, S23, SCOPUS, SPPI, SSAI, SSAb, SSCI, SSI, SociolAb, T02, W03, W04, W05, W07.
—BLDSC (6328.700000), IE, Infotrieve, Ingenta. **CCC.**
Published by: University of British Columbia, Pacific Affairs, 1855 West Mall, Ste 376, Vancouver, BC V6T 1Z2, Canada. TEL 604-822-4534, FAX 604-822-9452. Ed. Hyung Gu Lynn. adv.: B&W page USD 250; 5 x 8. Circ: 700 (paid).

327 AUS ISSN 1225-4657
DU1
➤ **PACIFIC FOCUS**; Inha journal of international studies. Text in English. 1986. 3/yr. GBP 204 combined subscription in United Kingdom to institutions (print & online eds.); EUR 259 combined subscription in Europe to institutions (print & online eds.); USD 409 combined subscription in the Americas to institutions (print & online eds.); USD 399 combined subscription elsewhere to institutions (print & online eds.) (effective 2012). reprint service avail. from PSC. **Document type:** *Journal, Academic/Scholarly.* **Description:** Covers all spects of politics, economics, societies and culture of Pacific region and its countries.
Related titles: Online - full text ed.: ISSN 1976-5118. GBP 184 in United Kingdom to institutions; EUR 233 in Europe to institutions; USD 368 in the Americas to institutions; USD 359 elsewhere to institutions (effective 2012) (from IngentaConnect).
Indexed: A22, BAS, CA, E01, P42, SCOPUS, SSCI, T02, W07.
—BLDSC (6329.350000), IE, Ingenta. **CCC.**
Published by: (Inha University, Center for Pacific Studies KOR), Wiley-Blackwell Publishing Asia (Subsidiary of: Wiley-Blackwell Publishing Ltd.), 155 Cremorne St, Richmond, VIC 3121, Australia. TEL 61-3-92743100, FAX 61-3-92743101, melbourne@wiley.com, http://www.wiley.com/WileyCDA/. Ed. Euikon Kim.

327 GBR ISSN 0951-2748
DU29
➤ **THE PACIFIC REVIEW.** Text in English. 1988. 5/yr. GBP 476 combined subscription in United Kingdom to institutions (print & online eds.); EUR 631, USD 791 combined subscription to institutions (print & online eds.) (effective 2012). adv. bk.rev. back issues avail.; reprint service avail. from PSC. **Document type:** *Journal, Academic/Scholarly.* **Description:** Provides an interdisciplinary forum for the exchange of ideas and trends in Pacific politics, history, military strategy, economics and culture.
Related titles: Online - full text ed.: ISSN 1470-1332. GBP 428 in United Kingdom to institutions; EUR 568, USD 712 to institutions (effective 2012) (from IngentaConnect).
Indexed: A01, A03, A08, A20, A22, APEL, AmH&L, AmHI, B21, BAS, BibInd, BrHumI, CA, CurCont, DIP, E01, E17, ESPM, GEOBASE, H07, HistAb, I13, IBR, IBSS, IBZ, L06, LID&ISL, M05, P34, P42, PAIS, PCI, PSA, RASB, S02, S03, SCOPUS, SSCI, SociolAb, T02, W07.
—IE, Infotrieve, Ingenta. **CCC.**
Published by: Routledge (Subsidiary of: Taylor & Francis Group), 4 Park Sq, Milton Park, Abingdon, Oxon OX14 4RN, United Kingdom. TEL 44-20-70176000, FAX 44-20-70176336, subscriptions@tandf.co.uk, http://www.routledge.com. Eds. Christopher W Hughes TEL 44-24-76572631, Richard Higgott TEL 44-24-76524633, Dr. Shaun Breslin TEL 44-24-76572558. **Subscr. in N America to:** Taylor & Francis Inc., Customer Services Dept, 325 Chestnut St, 8th Fl, Philadelphia, PA 19106. TEL 800-354-1420, FAX 215-625-2940; **Subscr. to:** Taylor & Francis Ltd., Journals Customer Service, Sheepen Pl, Colchester, Essex CO3 3LP, United Kingdom. TEL 44-20-70175544, FAX 44-20-70175198, tf.enquiries@tfinforma.com.

327 SGP ISSN 0218-1924
➤ **PACIFIC STRATEGIC PAPERS.** Text in English. 1990. irreg., latest vol.10, 2000. price varies. **Document type:** *Monographic series, Academic/Scholarly.* **Description:** Monograph series on regional issues of current interest in the Asian-Pacific region.
Indexed: CA, PSA.
Published by: (Association of Southeast Asian Nations IND), Institute of Southeast Asian Studies, 30 Heng Mui Keng Terrace, Pasir Panjang, Singapore, 119614, Singapore. TEL 65-6870-2447, FAX 65-6775-6259, pubsunit@iseas.edu.sg, http://www.iseas.edu.sg/. Ed., R&P Mrs. Triena Ong TEL 65-6870-2449.

327 PAK ISSN 0030-980X
DS376 CODEN: PAHOFB
PAKISTAN HORIZON. Text in English. 1948. q. PKR 200, USD 40 (effective 1998). adv. bk.rev. illus. index. reprints avail. **Description:** Facilitates understanding of international affairs and promotes the scientific study of international issues.
Related titles: Microform ed.: (from PQC).
Indexed: A22, ABCPolSci, AMB, AmH&L, BAS, CA, HistAb, IBSS, ILD, M10, MEA&I, P06, P42, PCI, PRA, PerIslam, SCOPUS, T02.
Published by: Pakistan Institute of International Affairs, Aiwan-e-Sadar Rd., P O Box 1447, Karachi, 74200, Pakistan. TEL 92-21-5682891, FAX 92-21-5686069. Ed. Syed Adil Hussain. Pub. Afsar Mehdi. Circ: 1,000.

327 PAK ISSN 1021-2299
DS376
PAKISTAN JOURNAL OF SOCIAL SCIENCE. Text in English. 1974. s-a. **Document type:** *Journal, Academic/Scholarly.* **Description:** International and Pakistan studies.
Indexed: Agr, BAS.
Published by: Quaid-i-Azam University, Faculty Social Sciences, c/o Dr. Naveed-i-Rahat, Deparment of Anthropology, Islamabad, 45320, Pakistan. nrahat@qau.edu.pk, http://www.qau.edu.pk/betaqau/ss.php.

PALESTINE REFUGEES TODAY. *see* SOCIAL SERVICES AND WELFARE

PALESTINE YEARBOOK OF INTERNATIONAL LAW. *see* LAW—International Law

327.06 GBR ISSN 0265-458X
AS2.5
PAN-EUROPEAN ASSOCIATIONS; a directory of multi-national organisations in Europe. Text in English. 1983. irreg., latest vol.3, 1996. GBP 94, USD 188 per issue (effective 2010). **Document type:** *Directory, Trade.* **Description:** Covers information of 2,300 hard-to-find multinational European associations.
—BLDSC (6357.371200). **CCC.**
Published by: C.B.D. Research Ltd., Chancery House, 15 Wickham Rd, Beckenham, Kent BR3 5JS, United Kingdom. TEL 44-20-86507745, FAX 44-20-86500768, cbd@cbdresearch.com.

330.9 DEU ISSN 0932-7592
PANEUROPA DEUTSCHLAND. Text in German. 1977. q. EUR 12 (effective 2006). adv. bk.rev. back issues avail. **Document type:** *Bulletin.*
Formerly: Paneuropa-Jugend in Paneuropa Deutschland
Published by: (Paneuropa Union und Paneuropa-Jugend), Paneuropa Verlag GmbH, Hafnerberg 2, Augsburg, 86152, Germany. TEL 49-821-5024221, FAX 49-821-5024283, pd@paneuropa.org. adv.: color page EUR 2,765, B&W page EUR 2,300; 185 x 270. Circ: 20,000.

329.11 AUT
PANEUROPA OESTERREICH. Text in German. 1976. 7/yr. **Document type:** *Journal, Academic/Scholarly.*
Former titles (until 1992): Oesterreich Paneuropa; (until 1988): Oesterreich Konservativ
Published by: Paneuropa Bewegung Oesterreich, Prinz Eugen-Str 18, Vienna, 1040, Austria. TEL 43-1-50515930, FAX 43-1-505235615, oesterreich@paneuropa.or.at, http://www.paneuropa.at.

341 LUX
HT395.E82
PANORAMA INFOREGIO (ENGLISH EDITION). Text in English. 2000. m.
Formerly (until 2009): Inforegio Panorama (English Edition) (1608-389X)
Related titles: Online - full text ed.; Spanish ed.: Panorama Inforegio (Spanish Edition); Italian ed.: Panorama Inforegio (Italian Edition); German ed.: Panorama Inforegio (German Edition); French ed.: Panorama Inforegio (French Edition).
—BLDSC (4478.881250).
Published by: European Commission, Office for Official Publications of the European Union, 2 Rue Mercier, Luxembourg, L-2985, Luxembourg. TEL 352-29291, FAX 352-29291, http://publications.europa.eu. Ed. Raphael Goulet.

327.362 ESP ISSN 1888-0576
JX1903
PAPELES DE RELACIONES ECOSOCIALES Y CAMBIO GLOBAL. Text in Spanish. 1985. q. **Document type:** *Journal, Academic/Scholarly.*
Former titles (until 2007): Papeles de Cuestiones Internacionales (1885-799X); (until 1996): Papeles para la Paz (0214-8072)
Indexed: I14.
Published by: Fundacion Hogar del Empleado, Centro de Investigacion para la Paz, Duque de Sesto, 40, Madrid, 28009, Spain. TEL 34-91-5763299, FAX 34-91-5774726, http://www.fuhemes/.

327 ESP ISSN 1137-7283
PAPELES DE TRABAJO. ESTUDIOS EUROPEOS. Text in Spanish. 1995. irreg. price varies. back issues avail. **Document type:** *Monographic series, Academic/Scholarly.*
Published by: Fundacion Jose Ortega y Gasset, Fortuny 53, Madrid, 28010, Spain. TEL 34-91-7004100, FAX 34-91-7003530, comunicacion@fog.es, http://www.ortegaygasset.edu/.

327 ESP ISSN 1137-7259
PAPELES DE TRABAJO. RELACIONES INTERNACIONALES. Text in Spanish. 1991. irreg. price varies. back issues avail. **Document type:** *Monographic series, Academic/Scholarly.*
Published by: Fundacion Jose Ortega y Gasset, Fortuny 53, Madrid, 28010, Spain. TEL 34-91-7004100, FAX 34-91-7003530, comunicacion@fog.es, http://www.ortegaygasset.edu/.

328 ESP ISSN 1888-5357
PAPERS I E MED. (Instituto Europeo del Mediterraneo) Text in Multiple languages. 2007. m.
Related titles: Online - full text ed.: ISSN 1988-7981. 2007.
Published by: Instituto Europeo del Mediterraneo/Institut Europeu de la Mediterrania, C Girona 20, 5a. Plana, Barcelona, 08010, Spain. TEL 34-93-2449850, info@iemed.org, http://www.iemed.org/eindex.php. Ed. Jordi Padilla.

325.21 USA
EL PARACAIDISTA; la guia del recien llegado a Miami. Text in English. m. **Description:** Helps those seeking to or recently moved or emigrated to Miami, adapt to their new life. Focuses on health, immigration, work, and housing issues.
Published by: Clave Corporation TEL 305-866-9033, 305-431-8149. Ed. Ira Guevara. Adv. contact Oly Alvarez.

327 PRT ISSN 1646-883X
PARALELO. Text in Portuguese. 2007. irreg. **Document type:** *Magazine, Consumer.*
Published by: Fundacao Luso-Americana para o Desenvolvimento (F L A D), Rua Sacramento a Lapa 21, Lisbon, 1249-090, Portugal. TEL 351-213-935800, FAX 351-213-963358, http://www.flad.pt.

327.2 USA ISSN 0031-2568
PARTNERS (WASHINGTON). Text in English. 1967. q. free. charts; illus. **Description:** Contains news and feature articles about volunteers working promoting broader citizen participation, training community leaders, mobilizing hemispheric collaboration, and strengthening grass roots organizations in the U.S., Latin America, and the Caribbean.
Published by: Partners of the Americas, 1424 K St, N W, Ste 700, Washington, DC 20005. TEL 202-628-3300, FAX 202-628-3306. Ed. Tracy Geoghegan. Circ: 25,000.

327 USA ISSN 1949-9760
PASSPORT (COLUMBUS). Text in English. 1970. 3/yr. free to members (effective 2009). adv. abstr.; bibl. back issues avail. **Document type:** *Newsletter, Trade.* **Description:** Features scholarly articles and contains general material of interest to society members.
Formerly (until 2003): Society for Historians of American Foreign Relations. Newsletter (0740-6169)
Related titles: Online - full text ed.: free (effective 2009).
Indexed: AmH&L, BAS, HistAb.
Published by: Society for Historians of American Foreign Relations (S.H.A.F.R.), c/o Mershon Center, Ohio State University, 1501 Neil Ave, Columbus, OH 43201. TEL 614-292-1951, FAX 614-292-2407, shafr@osu.edu. Eds. Mitch Lerner, Peter L Hahn. adv.: page USD 250; trim 8.5 x 11. Circ: 1,800.

327.17 CAN ISSN 1719-914X
PASSPORT CANADA. ANNUAL REPORT. Text in English. 2001. a. **Document type:** *Government.*
Formerly (until 2005): Canada. Passport Office. Annual Report (1700-9510)
Related titles: Online - full text ed.: Passeport Canada. Rapport Annuel. ISSN 1719-9158. 2000.
Published by: Passport Canada/Passeport Canada, Foreign Affairs Canada, Gatineau, PQ K1A 0G3, Canada. TEL 819-997-8338, 800-567-6868, http://www.ppt.gc.ca.

PATHFINDER (BETHESDA); the geospatial intelligence magazine. *see* MILITARY

327.172 NLD ISSN 1382-3574
PATTERNS IN RECONCILIATION. Text in English. irreg., latest vol.10. EUR 7.50, USD 9.50 newsstand/cover (effective 2009). back issues avail. **Document type:** *Monographic series.* **Description:** Covers topics relating to peace, justice, nonviolence and conflict resolution.
Formerly (until 1994): International Fellowship of Reconciliation. Occasional Paper Series
Published by: International Fellowship of Reconciliation, Spoorstraat 38, Alkmaar, 1815 BK, Netherlands. TEL 31-72-5123014, FAX 31-72-5151102, office@ifor.org. Circ: 750.

327.117 USA
PATTERNS OF GLOBAL TERRORISM. Text in English. a. **Document type:** *Government.*
Related titles: Online - full text ed.
Published by: U.S. Department of State, Office of the Coordinator for Counterterrorism, 2201 C St, N W, Washington, DC 20520. TEL 202-647-6575.

327.172 PER
PAZ. Text in Spanish. N.S. 1993. s-a.
Published by: Centro de Estudios y Accion para la Paz, Gral Santa Cruz, 635, Jesus Maria, Lima, 11, Peru. FAX 51-14-230464. Ed. Augusto Castro.

327.172 CUB ISSN 0864-2052
JZ5511.6
PAZ Y SOBERANIA. Text in Spanish. 1961. q. free. **Description:** Promotes materials on the struggle for peace and freedom and the sovereignty of all cultures.
Indexed: RASB.
Published by: Cuban Movement for Peace and Sovereignty of Peoples, Linea No. 556, Vedado, La Habana, Cuba. TEL 809 32-0506. Ed. Miguel Sosa Herrera.

327.172 USA ISSN 0149-0508
JX1901 CODEN: PCHAEG
➤ **PEACE & CHANGE**; a journal of peace research. Text in English. 1972. q. GBP 367 in United Kingdom to institutions; EUR 466 in Europe to institutions; USD 476 in the Americas to institutions; USD 719 elsewhere to institutions; GBP 423 combined subscription in United Kingdom to institutions (print & online eds.); EUR 537 combined subscription in Europe to institutions (print & online eds.); USD 547 combined subscription in the Americas to institutions (print & online eds.); USD 827 combined subscription elsewhere to institutions (print & online eds.) (effective 2012). adv. bk.rev. illus. Index. back issues avail.; reprints avail. **Document type:** *Journal, Academic/Scholarly.* **Description:** Publishes scholarly and interpretive articles related to the achieving of a peaceful, just, and humane society. Articles relate to peace and war, social change, conflict resolution, and appropriate justice.
Related titles: Online - full text ed.: ISSN 1468-0130. GBP 367 in United Kingdom to institutions; EUR 466 in Europe to institutions; USD 476 in the Americas to institutions; USD 719 elsewhere to institutions (effective 2012) (from IngentaConnect).
Indexed: A01, A02, A03, A08, A22, A26, ABS&EES, AMB, AmH&L, CA, E-psyche, E01, ESPM, HRIR, HistAb, I02, L03, LID&ISL, LeftInd, M05, M07, MEA&I, P10, P27, P34, P42, P47, P48, P53, P54, PAIS, PQC, PRA, PSA, RASB, RILM, RiskAb, S02, S03, S11, SCOPUS, SOPODA, SPAA, SociolAb, T02, V&AA, W04.
—BLDSC (6413.757000), IE, Infotrieve, Ingenta. **CCC.**
Published by: (Consortium on Peace Research, Education and Development), Wiley-Blackwell Publishing, Inc. (Subsidiary of: Wiley-Blackwell Publishing Ltd.), 111 River St, Hoboken, NJ 07030. TEL 201-748-6000, FAX 201-748-6088, info@wiley.com, http://www.wiley.com/WileyCDA/. Ed. Robbie Leiberman. Adv. contact Kristin McCarthy TEL 201-748-7683. **Co-sponsor:** Peace History Society.

327 USA ISSN 1082-7307
JX1901 CODEN: PCSTFR
➤ **PEACE AND CONFLICT STUDIES.** Abbreviated title: P C S. Text in English. 1994. s-a. back issues avail. **Document type:** *Journal, Academic/Scholarly.* **Description:** Contains academic research on conflict analysis and resolution, humanitarian intervention, peacekeeping, global social change and nonviolence.
Formerly (until 1995): Peace and Conflict Studies Notes
Related titles: Online - full text ed.: free (effective 2010).
Indexed: CA, I13, P03, P42, PRA, PSA, PsycInfo, PsycholAb, S02, S03, SCOPUS, SSA, SociolAb, T02.
Published by: (Network of Peace and Conflict Studies), Nova Southeastern University, 3301 College Ave, Fort Lauderdale-Davie, FL 33314. TEL 800-541-6682, help@nova.edu, http://www.nova.edu. Ed. Dr. Honggang Yang.

327 MYS
➤ **PEACE AND DEMOCRACY IN SOUTH ASIA.** Text in English. 2005. s-a. free. **Document type:** *Journal, Academic/Scholarly.* **Description:** Multidisciplinary journal of peace and democracy in the region comprised by Bangladesh, Bhutan, India, Maldives, Nepal, Pakistan and Sri Lanka.
Media: Online - full text.
Published by: Asiawide Network Ed. Ishtiaq Ahmed.

327.172 USA ISSN 0015-9093
JX1965
PEACE AND FREEDOM. Text in English. 1941. q. free to members (effective 2004). adv. bk.rev. charts. 28 p./no.; reprints avail. **Document type:** *Newsletter.* **Description:** Devoted to the women's peace movement in the US and other countries. Covers the empowerment of women, racism, the redirection of US budget priorities, women's history, feminism and peace.
Former titles: Four Lights; Women's International League for Peace and Freedom (Series)
Related titles: Microform ed.: (from PQC); Online - full text ed.
Indexed: A22, A26, APW, AltPI, CWI, E08, FemPer, G08, GW, I05, P19, P42, P45, P48, PQC, PRA, S09.
—CIS, Ingenta.
Published by: Women's International League for Peace and Freedom, 1213 Race St, Philadelphia, PA 19107-1691. TEL 215-563-7110, FAX 215-563-5527, wilpf@wilpf.org, http://www.wilpf.org. Ed., R&P, Adv. contact Theta Pavis TEL 215-563-7110. Circ: 10,000.

327.172 GBR ISSN 0031-3491
PEACE AND FREEDOM NEWS. Text in English. N.S. 1952. irreg. free (effective 2009). bk.rev. back issues avail. **Document type:** *Newsletter.*

P

Indexed: RASB.
Published by: Women's International League for Peace and Freedom, 52-54 Featherstone St, London, EC1Y 8RT, United Kingdom. TEL 44-20-72501968, ukwilpf@hotmail.com, http://www.ukwilpf.org.uk/.

327 JPN
PEACE & POLICY. Text in English. 1996. irreg. **Description:** Provides a forum for the discussion of issues concerning peace, policy, and the rights and responsibilities of global citizenship.
Published by: Toda Institute, 15-3 Samon-cho, Shinjuku-ku, Tokyo, 160-0017, Japan. TEL 81-3-3356-5481, FAX 81-3-3356-5482, todainst@mb.infoweb.or.jp. Ed. Majid Tehranian.

327.172 AUT ISSN 1028-4885
PEACE AND SECURITY; the I I P research quarterly. Text in English. 1964. q. bk.rev. **Document type:** *Journal, Academic/Scholarly.*
Formerly (until 1997): Peace and the Sciences (English Edition) (1017-6888); Which superseded in part (in 1970): Peace and the Sciences (Multilingual Edition) (0031-3513)
Indexed: CPerI, I13, PRA, PerIslam, RASB.
Published by: International Institute for Peace, Moellwaldplatz 5, Vienna, W 1040, Austria. TEL 43-431-5046437, FAX 43-431-5053236, secretariat@iip.at. Eds. Lev Voronkov, Peter Stania. Circ: 500.

327 ETH ISSN 2075-6232
▼ **PEACE AND SECURITY COUNCIL REPORT.** Text in English. 2009. irreg.
Media: Online - full text.
Published by: Institute for Security Studies, PO Box 2329, Addis Ababa, Ethiopia. TEL 251-11-3721154, FAX 251-11-3725954, addisababa@issafrica.org, http://www.issafrica.org/default.php.

327.172 USA
PEACE CHRONICLE. Text in English. 1975. 3/yr. USD 45; includes Peace & Change. adv. **Document type:** *Newsletter.*
Published by: Consortium on Peace Research, Education and Development, c/o Institute for Conflict Analysis & Resolution, George Mason University, 4260 Chainbridge Rd, Ste 315, Fairfax, VA 22030-4444. TEL 703-993-2405. adv.: page USD 150. Circ: 1,000.

327.172 GBR ISSN 1742-0601
JZ5511.2
➤ **PEACE, CONFLICT & DEVELOPMENT**; an interdisciplinary journal. Text in English. 2002. s-a. free (effective 2011). back issues avail. **Document type:** *Journal, Academic/Scholarly.* **Description:** Aims to cover a wide range of topics - human rights, democracy and democratisation, conflict resolution, environment, security, war, culture, identity and community, and other related areas of interest.
Media: Online - full content.
Indexed: A39, C27, C29, CA, D03, D04, E13, P42, PSA, R14, S02, S03, S14, S15, S18, SociolAb, T02.
—CCC.
Published by: University of Bradford, Department of Peace Studies, Pemberton Bldg, Bradford, West Yorkshire BD7 1DP, United Kingdom. TEL 44-1274-235772, FAX 44-1274-235240, course-enquiries@bradford.ac.uk, http://www.brad.ac.uk/acad/peace/index.php.

327.172 USA
PEACE CONVERSION TIMES. Text in English. 1981. q. USD 25 to members. adv. bk.rev. **Document type:** *Newsletter.* **Description:** Devoted to peace, social justice and safe energy. Features action alerts, children's items and a southern California events calendar.
Related titles: Microform ed.
Published by: Alliance for Survival, 1170 Carthay Dr., Norco, CA 92860-1301. Ed. Mel Kernahan. R&P Marion Pack. Circ: 4,000.

327.172 USA ISSN 1930-1251
HC60.5
PEACE CORPS. PERFORMANCE AND ACCOUNTABILITY REPORT. Text in English. 2004. a. **Document type:** *Government.*
Media: Online - full text.
Published by: Peace Corps, Office of Private Sector Initiatives, 1111 20th St, NW, Washington, DC 20526. TEL 800-424-8580.

327.172 USA ISSN 0884-9196
HC60.5
PEACE CORPS TIMES. Text in English. 1978. q. free to qualified personnel (effective 2010). back issues avail. **Document type:** *Newsletter, Government.* **Description:** Provides Peace Corps-related news from the across the globe, and also allows volunteers to share information on their successful projects and endeavors with their fellow volunteers and others in the Peace Corps community.
Related titles: CD-ROM ed.; Online - full text ed.: ISSN 2152-2928. free (effective 2010).
Published by: U.S. Peace Corps, 1111 20th St, NW, Washington, DC 20526. TEL 800-424-8580, psa@peacecorps.gov, https://www.peacecorps.gov. Ed. Mark Huffman.

327.172 USA
PEACE EDUCATION CENTER MONTHLY OF PEACE AND JUSTICE ACTION. Text in English. 1981. 11/yr. USD 5. bk.rev.
Formerly: Peace Education Center Newsletter
Published by: Peace Education Center, 1118 S Harrison, East Lansing, MI 48823. TEL 517-351-4648. Ed. Mary Catharine Knightwright. Circ: 800.

327.172 USA
PEACE GAZETTE. Text in English. 1969. 11/yr. bk.rev. illus. reprints avail. **Description:** Features articles on current peace and justice issues, and highlights urgent political actions and activities.
Published by: Mount Diablo Peace Center, 55 Eckley Ln, Walnut Creek, CA 94596. TEL 925-933-7850, info@mtdpc.org, http://www.mtdpc.org. Ed. Virginia Wheaton.

327.172 CAN ISSN 0826-9521
PEACE MAGAZINE. Text in English. 1985. q. CAD 18.90 domestic; USD 23 in United States; CAD 30 elsewhere (effective 2008). adv. bk.rev. illus. Index. back issues avail.; reprints avail. **Document type:** *Magazine, Consumer.* **Description:** Contains articles on military, peace keeping, and disarmament.
Formerly (until 1985): Peace Calendar (0824-3107)
Related titles: Microfiche ed.: (from MML); Microform ed.: (from MML); Online - full text ed.
Indexed: A01, A26, ABS&EES, AltPI, C03, CBCARef, CBPI, CPerI, G08, I05, MASUSE, P05, P48, PQC, PRA.
—CCC.
Published by: Canadian Disarmament Information Service (CANDIS), PO Box 248, Toronto, ON M5S 2S7, Canada. TEL 416-588-8748. Ed. Metta Spencer. Adv. contact Verda McDonald. Circ: 2,600 (paid); 1,300 (controlled).

327.172 GBR ISSN 1350-3006
JX1901
PEACE MATTERS. Text in English. 1961. q. GBP 7 domestic to non-members; GBP 8 in Europe to non-members; GBP 8.50 elsewhere to non-members; free to members (effective 2009). bk.rev. illus. 20 p./no.; **Document type:** *Newsletter, Consumer.* **Description:** Covers the theory, practice and history of pacifism and nonviolence.
Formerly (until 1993): Pacifist (0048-265X)
Related titles: Microfilm ed.; Online - full content ed.
Published by: Peace Pledge Union, 1 Peace Passage, London, N7 0BT, United Kingdom. TEL 44-20-74249444, FAX 44-20-74826390, maily@ppu.org.uk. Ed. Jan Melichar.

327.172 GBR ISSN 0031-3548
PEACE NEWS FOR NONVIOLENT REVOLUTION. Text in English. 1936. m. (10/yr). GBP 12 domestic to individuals; GBP 17 foreign to individuals; GBP 22 domestic to institutions; GBP 27 foreign to institutions (effective 2009). adv. bk.rev.; dance rev.; music rev.; play rev. back issues avail.; reprints avail. **Document type:** *Newspaper, Trade.* **Description:** Contains reports, analysis and news of nonviolent action and strategies for social change including in depth coverage of pacifism, feminism and environmental concerns.
Formerly (until 1971): Peace News; Incorporates: W R I Newsletter (0085-7882)
Related titles: Microform ed.: (from PQC, RPI); Online - full text ed.
Indexed: AltPI, PRA.
—CCC.
Published by: Peace News Ltd., 5 Caledonian Rd, London, N1 9DY, United Kingdom. TEL 44-20-72783344, FAX 44-20-72780444, news@peacenews.info, http://www.gn.apc.org/peacenews. Eds. Emily Johns, Milan Rai. **Dist. by:** Central Books Ltd., 99 Wallis Rd, London E9 5LN, United Kingdom.

327.172 USA ISSN 0735-4134
B105.P4
PEACE NEWSLETTER; central New York's voice for peace and social justice. Text in English. 1936. m. USD 12 to individuals; USD 15 to institutions. bk.rev. back issues avail. **Document type:** *Newsletter.* **Description:** Provides a forum for articles that discuss issues of concern to the peace movement, and aims to facilitate community interaction.
Related titles: Microform ed.: (from PQC); Online - full text ed.
Indexed: A22, HRIR.
Published by: Syracuse Peace Council, 924 Burnet Ave, Syracuse, NY 13203. TEL 315-472-5478. R&P Bill Mazza. adv.: page USD 700. Circ: 4,500.

327.172 CAN ISSN 0008-4697
JX1904.5
➤ **PEACE RESEARCH**; the Canadian journal of peace and conflict studies. Text in English. 1969. s-a. (in 1 vol., 2 nos./vol.). bk.rev. illus. index. back issues avail.; reprints avail. **Document type:** *Journal, Academic/Scholarly.* **Description:** Contains scientific and scholarly work on world peace, focusing on the problems of violence, war, armaments, peace movements, human rights, developmental issues, environmental security, nonviolence and peace education.
Related titles: Microfiche ed.: (from MML); Microform ed.: (from MML); Online - full text ed.
Indexed: A22, A26, ABS&EES, C03, CBCARef, CBPI, CPerI, DIP, E08, G08, IBR, IBZ, M10, P45, P47, P48, PQC, PRA, S09.
—Ingenta. **CCC.**
Published by: (Menno Simons College USA, Canadian Mennonite University, University of Winnipeg), M.V. Naidu, Ed. & Pub., c/o Menno Simons College, 210-520 Portage Ave, Winnipeg, MB R3C 0G2, Canada. TEL 204-953-3855, FAX 204-783-3699. Eds. John Derksen, Richard McCutcheon.

➤ **PEACE RESEARCH ABSTRACTS.** *see* POLITICAL SCIENCE—Abstracting, Bibliographies, Statistics

327.172 CAN ISSN 0553-4283
JX1901
PEACE RESEARCH REVIEWS. Text in English. 1967. irreg. (approx. 3/yr.). adv. illus. reprints avail. **Document type:** *Monographic series, Academic/Scholarly.* **Description:** Monograph series usually with several hundred references.
Indexed: A22, ABCPolSci, AMB, IBR, IBZ, MEA&I, PRA, RASB.
—IE, Infotrieve, Ingenta.
Published by: Peace Research Institute-Dundas, 25 Dundana Ave, Dundas, ON L9H 4E5, Canada. TEL 905-628-2356, FAX 905-628-1830.

327.172 GBR ISSN 1040-2659
JZ5511.2 CODEN: PEAREC
➤ **PEACE REVIEW**; a journal of social justice. Text in English. 1989. q. GBP 464 combined subscription in United Kingdom to institutions (print & online eds.); EUR 613, USD 769 combined subscription to institutions (print & online eds.) (effective 2012). adv. bk.rev. illus. Index. back issues avail.; reprint service avail. from PSC. **Document type:** *Journal, Academic/Scholarly.* **Description:** Focuses on current issues and controversies that underlie the promotion of a more peaceful world.
Related titles: Online - full text ed.: ISSN 1469-9982. GBP 417 in United Kingdom to institutions; EUR 551, USD 692 to institutions (effective 2012) (from IngentaConnect).
Indexed: A01, A02, A03, A08, A22, AltPI, B21, CA, DIP, E01, E17, ESPM, FamI, H14, I02, I13, IBR, IBZ, LeftInd, M10, MLA-IB, P02, P10, P13, P34, P42, P45, P46, P47, P48, P53, P54, PAIS, PCI, PQC, PRA, PSA, S02, S03, S11, SCOPUS, SOPODA, SSA, SociolAb, T02, W09.
—IE, Infotrieve, Ingenta. **CCC.**
Published by: (University of San Francisco), Routledge (Subsidiary of: Taylor & Francis Group), 4 Park Sq, Milton Park, Abingdon, Oxon OX14 4RN, United Kingdom. TEL 44-20-70176000, FAX 44-20-70176336, info@routledge.co.uk, http://www.routledge.com. Ed. Robert Elias TEL 415-422-6349. Adv. contact Linda Hann TEL 44-1344-779945. Circ: 500.

327.172 USA ISSN 2151-0806
JZ5511.2
➤ **PEACE STUDIES JOURNAL.** Text in English. 2008. q. free (effective 2009). back issues avail. **Document type:** *Journal, Academic/Scholarly.* **Description:** Aims to promote critical scholarly work in the areas of peace, nonviolence, alternatives to violence, and social justice.
Media: Online - full content.
Published by: Central New York Peace Studies Consortium, c/o Peace and Global Studies, Le Moyne College, 1419 Salt Springs Rd, Syracuse, NY 13214. TEL 315-445-4294, info@peaceconsortium.org, http://cnypeacestudies.wordpress.com/. Ed. J Barron Boyd.

327.172 338.4791 NLD ISSN 1878-7754
▼ ➤ **PEACE TOURISM JOURNAL**; the journal of tourism and peace research. Text in English. 2009. s-a. **Document type:** *Journal, Academic/Scholarly.* **Description:** Provides a forum for the study and discussion of tourism and peace issues in tourism and tourism-related areas of leisure, recreation and hospitality studies.
Media: Online - full text.
Published by: International Centre for Peace Through Tourism Research, PO Box 1298, Leeuwarden, 8900 CG, Netherlands. TEL 31-58-2441301, FAX 31-58-2441505. Ed. Omar Moufakkir.

327.172 USA ISSN 1080-9864
JZ5511.2
PEACE WATCH. Text in English. 1988. 3/yr. illus. reprints avail. **Document type:** *Newsletter, Government.* **Description:** Contains short pieces about the Institute's work in promoting peaceful resolution of international conflicts.
Formerly (until 1994): United States Institute of Peace. Journal (1046-7513)
Related titles: Online - full text ed.
Indexed: ABS&EES, PRA, RASB.
—Ingenta.
Published by: U.S. Institute of Peace, 1200 17th St NW, Ste 200, Washington, DC 20036-3011. TEL 202-457-1700, FAX 202-429-6063. Ed. Elizabeth Harper. Circ: 15,000.

327.172 GBR ISSN 1367-9880
PEACEKEEPING. Text in English. 1997. irreg., latest 2009. price varies. back issues avail. **Document type:** *Monographic series, Academic/Scholarly.* **Description:** Covers all aspects of peacekeeping in an up-to-date and accessible way, including the political, operational, developmental, legal and humanitarian issues.
—BLDSC (3062.692070).
Published by: Routledge (Subsidiary of: Taylor & Francis Group), 4 Park Sq, Milton Park, Abingdon, Oxon OX14 4RN, United Kingdom. TEL 44-20-70176000, FAX 44-20-70176336, subscriptions@tandf.co.uk.

327.172 CAN ISSN 1187-3485
JX1
➤ **PEACEKEEPING & INTERNATIONAL RELATIONS.** Text in English. 1972. bi-m. CAD 25; USD 25 foreign (effective 1999). adv. bk.rev. bibl.; illus. Index. reprints avail. **Document type:** *Journal, Academic/Scholarly.*
Incorporates: International Perspectives (0381-4874); Which incorporates: International Canada (0027-0512); Supersedes: External Affairs (0381-4866)
Related titles: Microfiche ed.: (from MML); Microform ed.: (from MML, PQC); Online - full text ed.
Indexed: A01, A02, A03, A08, A12, A22, A26, ABIn, ABS&EES, AMB, AmH&L, BAS, C03, C05, C12, CBCARef, CBPI, CPerI, E08, G08, I02, IBR, IBZ, M01, M02, M05, M10, MEA&I, P02, P06, P10, P27, P42, P45, P47, P48, P51, P53, P54, PAIS, PCI, PQC, PdeR, RASB, S02, S03, S09, S11.
—CCC.
Published by: Canadian PeaceKeeping Press, Pearson Peacekeeping Centre (Subsidiary of: Canadian Institute of Strategic Studies), Cornwallis Park, P O Box 100, Clementsport, NS B0S 1E0, Canada. TEL 902-638-8611, FAX 902-638-8576. Ed. Alex Morrison. R&P, Adv. contact Sue Armstrong. Circ: 1,100 (paid).

➤ **PENN STATE INTERNATIONAL LAW REVIEW.** *see* LAW—International Law

➤ **PEOPLE (KANSAS CITY).** *see* EDUCATION—International Education Programs

327 SWE ISSN 1400-8319
PERGAMENT. Text in Greek, Swedish. 1993. q. (4-5/yr.). SEK 175 (effective 2003). **Description:** Devoted to Greek culture and Swedish-Greek relationship.
Published by: Stiftelsen Grekikskt Kulturcentrum och Arkiv i Sverige, Magnus Ladnaasgatan 49, Stockholm, 11865, Sweden. Pub. Andreas Boukas.

327 USA ISSN 0252-0079
JZ4981
PERMANENT MISSIONS TO THE UNITED NATIONS. Text in English. 1966. s-a. USD 35 per issue (effective 2008). back issues avail. **Document type:** *Directory, Trade.* **Description:** Contains list of the names, addresses and phone numbers of all representatives to the United Nations.
Related titles: French ed.: Missions Permanentes aupres de l'Organisation des Nations Unies. ISSN 0252-0060.
—CCC.
Published by: United Nations Publications, 2 United Nations Plaza, Rm DC2-853, New York, NY 10017. TEL 212-963-8302, 800-253-9646, FAX 212-963-3489, publications@un.org, https://unp.un.org. Circ: 3,000. **Subscr. to:** EBSCO Information Services, PO Box 361, Birmingham, AL 35201. TEL 205-995-1567, 800-633-4931, FAX 205-995-1588.

327 USA ISSN 1071-4154
D34
PERSPECTIVE (BOSTON, 1990). Text in English. 1990. q. free (effective 2010). back issues avail. **Document type:** *Journal, Academic/Scholarly.* **Description:** Contains articles given by eminent contributors from the region.
Related titles: Online - full text ed.
Published by: Boston University, Institute for the Study of Conflict, Ideology & Policy, One Silber Way, Boston, MA 02215. TEL 617-353-2000, http://www.bu.edu/iscip/index.html.

327.071 USA
JX1255
PERSPECTIVE ON ETHICS AND INTERNATIONAL AFFAIRS; education and studies newsletter. Text in English. 1987. s-a. free. reprints avail. **Document type:** *Newsletter.* **Description:** College level curriculum development program for teaching ethics and international affairs.
Formerly: Ethics and International Affairs: Report From the Carnegie Council
Indexed: GSS&RPL, RI-1, RI-2.
Published by: Carnegie Council on Ethics and International Affairs, Merrill House, 170 E 64th St, New York, NY 10021-7478. TEL 212-838-4120, FAX 212-752-2432.

327 CZE ISSN 1210-762X
DAW1051
➤ **PERSPECTIVES**; the Central European review of international affairs. Text in English. 1993. s-a. USD 50; USD 30 per issue (effective 2009). **Document type:** *Journal, Academic/Scholarly.*
Related titles: Microfilm ed.: (from PQC); Online - full text ed.
Indexed: A01, A03, A08, A12, ABIn, CA, I02, IBSS, M07, P02, P10, P42, P45, P47, P48, P51, P53, P54, PQC, R02, RASB, S11, T02.
Published by: Ustav Mezinarodnich Vztahu/Institute of International Relations, Nerudova 3, Prague, 11850, Czech Republic. TEL 420-25-1108111, FAX 420-25-1108222, umvedo@iir.cz. Ed. Petr Kratochvil TEL 420-2-51108101.

327 HKG ISSN 1021-9013
PERSPECTIVES CHINOISES. Text in French. 1979. bi-m. HKD 400 to individuals in Hong Kong & Macau; EUR 60 in Europe to individuals; USD 80 elsewhere to individuals; HKD 600 to institutions in Hong Kong & Macau; EUR 90 in Europe to institutions; USD 120 elsewhere to institutions (effective 2009). **Document type:** *Journal, Academic/Scholarly.*
Former titles (until 1991): Bulletin de Sinologie (1011-2006); (until 1983): Antenne Francaise de Sinologie a Hong Kong. Bulletin Mensuel (0255-5336)
Related titles: Online - full text ed.: ISSN 1996-4609; ◆ English ed.: China Perspectives. ISSN 2070-3449.
Indexed: A01, A34, A36, CABA, E12, G11, GH, I11, IBR, IBSS, IBZ, LT, N02, R12, RRTA, S13, S16, T05, TAR, VS, W11.
—IE, Ingenta.
Published by: Centre d'Etudes Francais sur la Chine Contemporaine/ French Centre for Research on Contemporary China, Rm. 304, Yu Yuet Lai Bldg., 43-55 Wyndham St., Central, Hong Kong. TEL 852-28766910, FAX 852-28153211, cefc@cefc.com.hk, http://www.cefc.com.hk/.

327 FRA ISSN 0243-2331
PERSPECTIVES INTERNATIONALES. Text in French. 1980. irreg. **Document type:** *Monographic series, Academic/Scholarly.*
—**CCC.**
Published by: Presses Universitaires de France, 6 Avenue Reille, Paris, 75685, France. TEL 33-1-58103161, FAX 33-1-45897530, revues@puf.com, http://www.puf.com.

327.4 GBR ISSN 1570-5854
➤ **PERSPECTIVES ON EUROPEAN POLITICS AND SOCIETY**; journal of intra-european dialogue. Text in English. 2000. q. GBP 263 combined subscription in United Kingdom to institutions (print & online eds.); EUR 346, USD 435 combined subscription to institutions (print & online eds.) (effective 2012). adv. bk.rev. back issues avail.; reprint service avail. from PSC. **Document type:** *Journal, Academic/ Scholarly.* **Description:** Aims to promote an intra-European dialogue by giving a voice to scholars in all parts of Europe.
Related titles: Online - full text ed.: ISSN 1568-0258. 2000. GBP 237 in United Kingdom to institutions; EUR 312, USD 391 to institutions (effective 2012) (from IngentaConnect).
Indexed: A01, A03, A08, A22, E01, P34, P42, PSA, S02, S03, SCOPUS, SociolAb, T02.
—BLDSC (6428.142510), IE, Ingenta. **CCC.**
Published by: Routledge (Subsidiary of: Taylor & Francis Group), 4 Park Sq, Milton Park, Abingdon, Oxon OX14 4RN, United Kingdom. TEL 44-20-70176000, FAX 44-20-70176336, subscriptions@tandf.co.uk, http://www.routledge.com. Ed. Dr. Cameron Z Ross TEL 44-1382-385064. Adv. contact Linda Hann TEL 44-1344-779945. **Subscr. to:** Taylor & Francis Ltd., Journals Customer Service, Sheepen Pl, Colchester, Essex CO3 3LP, United Kingdom. TEL 44-20-70175544, FAX 44-20-70175198.

➤ **PERSPEKTIVEN D S**; Zeitschrift fuer Gesellschaftsanalyse und Reformpolitik. (Demokratischen Sozialismus) *see* POLITICAL SCIENCE

327.85 BOL
PERU AHORA. Text in Spanish. 1997. 3/m. free. adv. **Document type:** *Bulletin.* **Description:** Includes up-to-date briefs, opinions and news, official and private, on Peruvian economic, political and cultural issues, Peru-Bolivia relations, Peruvian foreign policy, history and tourism.
Published by: Embajada del Peru en Bolivia, Calle Fernando Guachalla Cdra. 3, Sopocachi, La Paz, Bolivia. TEL 591-2-376773, FAX 591-2-367640. Adv. contact Elmer Schialer. Circ: 250.

327.85 PER
PERU. MINISTERIO DE RELACIONES EXTERIORES. BOLETIN TRIMESTRAL. Text in Spanish. q.
Published by: Ministerio de Relaciones Exteriores, Lima, Peru.

PHILIPPINES CHINESE HISTORICAL ASSOCIATION. ANNALS. *see* HISTORY—History Of Asia

327.599 USA
THE PHILIPPINES: NEWS AND VIEWS. Text in English. 1990. s-m. free. back issues avail. **Description:** Covers Philippine conditions and developments, US-Philippine relations, and Philippine embassy activities.
Published by: Philippine Embassy, 1617 Massachusetts Ave, N W, Washington, DC 20036. TEL 202-483-1414. Ed. MacArthur F Corsino. Circ: 1,000 (controlled).

327.172 100 NLD
PHILOSOPHY OF PEACE. Text in English. irreg. price varies. **Document type:** *Monographic series, Academic/Scholarly.* **Description:** Explores socio-political and ethical perspectives on modern warfare, peacemaking, and conflict resolution.
Related titles: ◆ Series of: Value Inquiry Book Series. ISSN 0929-8436.
Published by: Editions Rodopi B.V., Tijnmuiden 7, Amsterdam, 1046 AK, Netherlands. TEL 31-20-6114821, FAX 31-20-4472979, info@rodopi.nl. Ed. Dr. William C Gay. **Dist. by:** Rodopi - USA, 606 Newark Ave, 2nd fl, Kenilworth, NJ 07033. TEL 908-497-9031, FAX 908-497-9035.

PITT LATIN AMERICAN SERIES. *see* SOCIAL SCIENCES: COMPREHENSIVE WORKS

327 CAN ISSN 1926-6464
PLOUGHSHARES E-NEWSLETTER. Text in English. 2006. a. free (effective 2011). **Document type:** *Newsletter, Trade.*
Media: Online - full text.
Published by: Project Ploughshares, 57 Erb St W, Waterloo, ON N2L 6C2, Canada. TEL 519-888-6541, FAX 519-888-0018, http://www.ploughshares.ca.

327.172 USA
PLOWSHARE NEWS. Text in English. 1979. bi-m. donation. bk.rev. illus. **Document type:** *Newsletter.*
Related titles: Online - full text ed.
Published by: Plowshare Peace and Justice Center, PO Box 4367, Roanoke, VA 24015. TEL 540-989-0393, plowshare@plowshare.org, http://plowshareva.org. Ed. Gary Sandman. Circ: 600.

327.438 DEU ISSN 1863-9712
POLEN-ANALYSEN. Text in German. 2006. bi-w. **Document type:** *Journal, Academic/Scholarly.*
Media: Online - full content.
Published by: Universitaet Bremen, Forschungsstelle Osteuropa/ Bremen University, Research Centre for East European Studies, Klagenfurter Str 3, Bremen, 28359, Germany. TEL 49-421-2187891, FAX 49-421-2183269, publikationsreferat@osteuropa.uni-bremen.de, http://www.forschungsstelle.uni-bremen.de. Ed. Silke Plate.

327 DEU ISSN 0930-4584
POLEN UND WIR; Zeitschrift fuer Deutsch-Polnische Verstaendigung. Text in German. 1984. q. EUR 12; EUR 3 newsstand/cover (effective 2009). adv. bk.rev.; film rev. bibl.; illus. **Document type:** *Magazine, Consumer.*
Published by: Deutsch-Polnische Gesellschaft der Bundesrepublik Deutschland e.V., Im Freihof 3, Huenxe, 46569, Germany. TEL 49-2858-7137, FAX 49-2858-7945, dpgbrd@polen-news.de, http://members.aol.com/dpgbrd/puw.html. Ed. Wulf Schade. Adv. contact Manfred Feustel. Circ: 2,600 (paid and controlled).

POLISH-ANGLOSAXON STUDIES. *see* HISTORY

327.1 POL ISSN 1643-0379
DK4450
THE POLISH FOREIGN AFFAIRS DIGEST/POLSKI PRZEGLAD DYPLOMATYCZNY. Text in English. 2001. q. PLZ 90 domestic; EUR 25 foreign (effective 2005). **Document type:** *Journal, Academic/ Scholarly.*
Related titles: ◆ Translation of: Polski Przeglad Dyplomatyczny. ISSN 1642-4069.
Published by: Polski Instytut Spraw Miedzynarodowych/Polish Institute of International Affairs, ul Warecka 1a, skryt. poczt. nr 1010, Warsaw, 00950, Poland. TEL 48-22-5568000, FAX 48-22-5568099. Ed. Jacek Foks.

327 POL ISSN 1230-4999
D860
➤ **THE POLISH QUARTERLY OF INTERNATIONAL AFFAIRS.** Text in English. 1973. q. PLZ 90 domestic; EUR 25 foreign (effective 2005). adv. bk.rev. bibl. 160 p./no. 1 cols./p.; back issues avail. **Document type:** *Journal, Academic/Scholarly.*
Former titles (until 1993): International Affairs Studies (0867-4493); (until 1991): International Relations (0239-2283); (until 1984): Studies on International Relations (0324-8283)
Related titles: ◆ Polish ed.: Sprawy Miedzynarodowe. ISSN 0038-853X.
Indexed: CA, I13, IBR, IBSS, IBZ, P06, P42, PQC, PSA, RASB, SCOPUS, SociolAb, T02.
—BLDSC (6543.724000), IE, Ingenta.
Published by: Polski Instytut Spraw Miedzynarodowych/Polish Institute of International Affairs, ul Warecka 1a, skryt. poczt. nr 1010, Warsaw, 00950, Poland. TEL 48-22-5568000, FAX 48-22-5568099. Circ: 400. **Dist. by:** Ars Polona, Obroncow 25, Warsaw 03933, Poland. TEL 48-22-5098609, FAX 48-22-5098610, arspolona@arspolona.com.pl, http://www.arspolona.com.pl.

327 CHE ISSN 1661-478X
POLITFOCUS AUSSENPOLITIK. Text in German. 2005. bi-m. CHF 480 (effective 2007). **Document type:** *Journal, Trade.*
Related titles: French ed.: Politfocus Politique Exterieure. ISSN 1661-4798. 2005.
Published by: Ecopolitics GmbH, Schuetzengaesschen 5, Postfach 288, Bern 7, 3000, Switzerland. TEL 41-31-3133434, FAX 41-31-3133435, http://www.ecopolitics.ch.

327 ESP ISSN 0213-6856
DP85.8
POLITICA EXTERIOR. Text in Spanish. 1987. bi-m. EUR 62 (effective 2009). adv. bk.rev. charts; illus. Supplement avail.; back issues avail. **Document type:** *Magazine, Trade.* **Description:** Covers international political affairs.
Related titles: Online - full text ed.
Indexed: A22, I13, I14, P09, PAIS, PCI.
—IE, Infotrieve.
Published by: Estudios de Politica Exterior S.A., Nunez de Balboa 49, 5o Piso, Madrid, 28001, Spain. TEL 34-91-4312628, FAX 34-91-4354027, revista@politicaexterior.com. Ed. Dario Valcarcel. Circ: 10,000. **Dist. by:** Asociacion de Revistas Culturales de Espana, C Covarruvias 9 2o. Derecha, Madrid 28010, Spain. TEL 34-91-3086066, FAX 34-91-3199267, info@arce.es, http://www.arce.es/.

327 BRA ISSN 1518-6660
F2537
POLITICA EXTERNA. Text in Portuguese. 1992. q. USD 30 (effective 2000). bk.rev. back issues avail. **Document type:** *Journal, Academic/ Scholarly.* **Description:** Forum for debate on important international matters and on Brazil's foreign policies.
Indexed: PAIS, PSA.
Address: Rua do Triunfo, 177, Sta. Ifigenia, Sao Paulo, SP 01212-010, Brazil. TEL 55-11-223-6522, FAX 55-11-233-6290, editorial@politicaexterna.com.br, vendas@pazeterra.com.br. Ed. Gilberto Dupas. Pub. Fernando Gesperian.

327 PRT ISSN 0873-6650
D839
➤ **POLITICA INTERNACIONAL.** Text in Portuguese. 1990. s-a. EUR 50 domestic; EUR 80 in the European Union; EUR 90 elsewhere; EUR 40 to students (effective 2002). bk.rev. abstr.; bibl. back issues avail. **Document type:** *Journal, Academic/Scholarly.* **Description:** Dedicated to the study of foreign policy and international relations in a multidisciplinary perspective. Features original articles, essays, and book reviews on a wide range of subjects.
Indexed: I13, PAIS, RASB.
Published by: Centro Interdisciplinar de Estudos Economicos, Palacio Pancas Palha, Travessa do Recolhimento de Lazaro Leitao n.1, Lisbon, Lisboa 1100-044, Portugal. TEL 351-21-811-6000, FAX 351-21-811-6088, pol.int@cidec.pt, http://www.cidec.pt. Ed. Joao Perreira de Sousa. R&P Pedro Aires Oliveira. Circ: 1,500.

327 ITA ISSN 0032-3101
HC59.7
POLITICA INTERNAZIONALE. Text in Italian. 1969. bi-m. adv. bk.rev. index. back issues avail. **Document type:** *Journal, Academic/ Scholarly.* **Description:** Covers relations with developing countries in Africa, Latin America and Middle East.
Related titles: English ed.: ISSN 0393-3024. 1980.
Indexed: AMB, I13, IBR, IBSS, IBZ, PAIS, RASB.
—IE, Infotrieve.
Published by: Institute for Relations with Africa Latin America and the Middle East (IPALMO), Via Del Tritone, 62-B, Rome, RM 00187, Italy. TEL 39-6-6792734, FAX 39-6-6797849.

327 AUS ISSN 1323-5761
HM1 CODEN: CSRDD9
➤ **POLITICAL CROSSROADS.** Text in English. 1978-1991; resumed 1997. s-a. AUD 429 domestic to institutions; AUD 390 in New Zealand to institutions; GBP 220 in Europe to institutions; USD 395 elsewhere to institutions (effective 2008). adv. bk.rev. back issues avail. **Document type:** *Journal, Academic/Scholarly.* **Description:** Focuses on borders, security, terrorism, problems of national identity, issues of migration and citizenship and the economics and politics of resources and trade.
Formerly (until 1991): Crossroads (0334-4649)
Indexed: A22, CA, LID&ISL, P42, PAIS, PSA, SCOPUS, SociolAb, T02.
Published by: James Nicholas Publishers, Pty. Ltd., PO Box 5179, South Melbourne, VIC 3205, Australia. TEL 61-3-96905955, FAX 61-3-96992040, custservice@jnponline.com.

327 GBR ISSN 1365-0580
POLITICAL VIOLENCE. Text in English. 1996. irreg., latest 2009. price varies. **Document type:** *Monographic series, Academic/Scholarly.*
Published by: Routledge (Subsidiary of: Taylor & Francis Group), 4 Park Sq, Milton Park, Abingdon, Oxon OX14 4RN, United Kingdom. TEL 44-20-70176000, FAX 44-20-70176336, subscriptions@tandf.co.uk.

327.1 NLD ISSN 2211-4696
▼ **POLITICAS E GESTAO EM ANALISE.** Text in Portuguese. 2011. a.
Related titles: Online - full text ed.: ISSN 2211-470X; ◆ Translation of: Policy and Management Insights. ISSN 1879-6745.
Published by: European Centre for Development Policy Management/ Centre Europeen de Gestion de Politiques de Developpement, Onze Lieve Vrouweplein 21, Maastricht, 6211 HE, Netherlands. TEL 31-43-3502900, FAX 31-43-3502902, info@ecdpm.org, http://www.ecdpm.org.

327 900 GBR ISSN 2156-7689
JC480
➤ **POLITICS, RELIGION & IDEOLOGY.** Text in English. 2000 (Summer). q. GBP 329 combined subscription in United Kingdom to institutions (print & online eds.); EUR 426, USD 535 combined subscription to institutions (print & online eds.) (effective 2012). adv. bk.rev. annual index. back issues avail.; reprints avail. **Document type:** *Journal, Academic/Scholarly.* **Description:** Provides a forum for the exploration of the politics of illiberal ideologies, both religious and secular.
Formerly (until 2011): Totalitarian Movements and Political Religions (1469-0764)
Related titles: Online - full text ed.: ISSN 2156-7697. GBP 295 in United Kingdom to institutions; EUR 384, USD 482 to institutions (effective 2012) (from IngentaConnect).
Indexed: A01, A02, A03, A08, A22, AmH&L, B21, CA, E01, E17, ESPM, HistAb, I13, IBSS, M05, MLA-IB, P02, P10, P42, P47, P48, P53, P54, PQC, PSA, S02, S03, S11, SCOPUS, SociolAb, T02.
—IE, Ingenta. **CCC.**
Published by: Routledge (Subsidiary of: Taylor & Francis Group), 4 Park Sq, Milton Park, Abingdon, Oxon OX14 4RN, United Kingdom. TEL 44-20-70176000, FAX 44-20-70176336, subscriptions@tandf.co.uk, http://www.routledge.com. Ed. Felix Patrikeeff. Adv. contact Linda Hann TEL 44-1344-779945. **Subscr. to:** Taylor & Francis Ltd., Journals Customer Service, Sheepen Pl, Colchester, Essex CO3 3LP, United Kingdom. TEL 44-20-70175544, FAX 44-20-70175198.

➤ **POLITIKA.** *see* POLITICAL SCIENCE

327 FRA ISSN 0032-342X
JZ11
POLITIQUE ETRANGERE. Text in French. 1936. q. EUR 75 combined subscription domestic to individuals (print & online eds.); EUR 115 combined subscription foreign to individuals (print & online eds.); EUR 110 combined subscription domestic to institutions (print & online eds.); EUR 140 combined subscription foreign to institutions (print & online eds.) (effective 2008). **Document type:** *Journal, Academic/ Scholarly.*
Related titles: Online - full text ed.: ISSN 1958-8992.
Indexed: A22, AmH&L, BAS, CA, CCME, DIP, ELLIS, FR, HistAb, I13, IBR, IBSS, IBZ, LID&ISL, M10, P30, P42, PAIS, PCI, PRA, PSA, PdeR, PerIslam, SociolAb, T02.
—BLDSC (6544.110000), IE, Infotrieve, Ingenta. **CCC.**
Published by: (Institut Francais des Relations Internationales), Armand Colin, 21 Rue du Montparnasse, Paris, 75283 Cedex 06, France. TEL 33-1-44395447, FAX 33-1-44394343, infos@armand-colin.fr. Circ: 4,500.

327 FRA ISSN 1623-6297
POLITIQUE EUROPEENNE. Text in French. 2000. 3/yr. EUR 36.60 domestic; EUR 41.20 foreign (effective 2008). **Document type:** *Journal, Academic/Scholarly.*
Related titles: Online - full text ed.: ISSN 2105-2875. 200?.
Indexed: I13, IBSS.

P

Published by: L' Harmattan, 5 Rue de l'Ecole Polytechnique, Paris, 75005, France. TEL 33-1-43257651, FAX 33-1-43258203.

327 FRA ISSN 0221-2781
D839
POLITIQUE INTERNATIONALE. Text in French; Summaries in English, Spanish. 1978. q. EUR 42 domestic to individuals; EUR 67 DOM-TOM to individuals; EUR 50 in the European Union to individuals; EUR 70 elsewhere to individuals; EUR 55 domestic to institutions; EUR 77 DOM-TOM to institutions; EUR 61 in the European Union to institutions; EUR 83 elsewhere to institutions (effective 2008). adv. bk.rev. reprints avail.
Related titles: Online - full text ed.: ISSN 1961-9073.
Indexed: A22, ABCPolSci, BAS, CA, ELLIS, FR, I13, IBSS, P42, PAIS, PSA, PerIslam, RASB, SCOPUS, SociolAb, T02.
—BLDSC (6544.112000), IE, Infotrieve, Ingenta. **CCC.**
Address: 11 rue du Bois de Boulogne, Paris, 75116, France. TEL 33-1-45001526, FAX 33-1-45003879. Ed., Pub. Patrick Wajsman. Adv. contact Claire Lecardonnel.

327 UKR ISSN 0868-8273
JN6639.A8
POLITYKA I CHAS. Text in Ukrainian. m. USD 130 in United States. **Document type:** *Government.*
Related titles: Online - full text ed.; ◆ English ed.: Politics and the Times.
Indexed: RASB.
—East View.
Published by: Ministerstvo Inostrannykh/Foreign Ministry, Ul Vossoedineniya 15-17, Kiev, Ukraine. TEL 380-44-550-9451, FAX 380-44-550-3144. **Dist. by:** East View Information Services, 10601 Wayzata Blvd, Minneapolis, MN 55305. TEL 952-252-1201, 800-477-1005, FAX 952-252-1202, info@eastview.com, http://www.eastview.com.

327.1 POL ISSN 1642-4069
JZ11.3.P65
➤ **POLSKI PRZEGLAD DYPLOMATYCZNY.** Text in Polish. 2001. bi-m. PLZ 90 domestic; EUR 25 foreign (effective 2005). **Document type:** *Journal, Academic/Scholarly.*
Related titles: ◆ English Translation: The Polish Foreign Affairs Digest. ISSN 1643-0379.
Published by: Polski Instytut Spraw Miedzynarodowych/Polish Institute of International Affairs, ul Warecka 1a, skryt. poczt. nr 1010, Warsaw, 00950, Poland. TEL 48-22-5568000, FAX 48-22-5568099.

327 PRT ISSN 1647-4074
▼ **PORTUGUESE JOURNAL OF INTERNATIONAL AFFAIRS.** Text in English. 2009. s-a. **Document type:** *Magazine, Consumer.*
Related titles: Online - full text ed.: ISSN 1647-5992.
Published by: Instituto Portugues de Relacoes Internacionais e Seguranca/Portuguese Institute of International Relations and Security, Rua Vitorino Nemesio 5, Lisbon, 1750-306, Portugal. http://www.ipris.org.

327 DEU
POTSDAMER TEXTBUECHER. Abbreviated title: P T B. Text in German. 1998. irreg., latest vol.12, 2009. price varies. **Document type:** *Monographic series, Academic/Scholarly.* **Description:** Contains research and studies on comparative international political systems and theories.
Published by: WeltTrends e.V., August-Bebel-Str 89, Potsdam, 14482, Germany. TEL 49-331-9774540, FAX 49-331-9774696, redaktion@welttrends.de, http://www.welttrends.de.

327 FRA ISSN 0760-5439
DS119.76
POUR LA PALESTINE. Text in French. 1979. q. EUR 11 to members; EUR 22 to individuals (effective 2008). **Document type:** *Journal.*
Formerly (until 1983): Bulletin des Amities Franco-Palestiniennes (0241-0540)
Published by: Association France-Palestine Solidarite, 21 ter Rue Voltaire, Paris, 75011, France. TEL 33-1-43721579, afps@france-palestine.org.

▼ **PRAGER SCHRIFTEN ZUR ZEITGESCHICHTE UND ZUM ZEITGESCHEHEN.** *see* HISTORY

327.1 USA ISSN 1949-3223
PRESENTE!. Text in English. 199?. 3/yr. free (effective 2009). adv. back issues avail. **Document type:** *Newspaper, Consumer.* **Description:** Provides information and analysis about events and developments in the Americas in an attempt to get more people involved in the work to change oppressive U.S. foreign policy and to end the racist system of violence and domination.
Formerly (until 2006): S O A Watch Update
Related titles: Online - full text ed.: ISSN 1949-3231.
Published by: S O A Watch, PO Box 4566, Washington, DC 20017. TEL 202-234-3440, FAX 202-636-4505, info@soaw.org. Circ: 110,000.

327 USA
➤ **PRINCETON STUDIES IN COMPLEXITY.** Text in English. 1997. irreg., latest 2009. price varies. charts; illus. back issues avail. **Document type:** *Monographic series, Academic/Scholarly.* **Description:** Examines political, economic, and social challenges to forging and maintaining international relations.
Indexed: CCMJ.
Published by: Princeton University Press, 41 William St, Princeton, NJ 08540. TEL 609-258-4900, 800-777-4726, FAX 609-258-6305, cpriday@pupress.co.uk. Eds. Simon A Levin, Steven H Strogatz. **Subscr. addr. in US:** California - Princeton Fulfillment Services, Inc., 1445 Lower Ferry Rd, Ewing, NJ 08618. TEL 609-883-1759, 800-777-4726, FAX 609-883-7413, 800-999-1958, orders@cpfsinc.com. **Dist. addr. in Canada:** University Press Group.; **Dist. addr. in UK:** John Wiley & Sons Ltd.

327 USA
➤ **PRINCETON STUDIES IN INTERNATIONAL HISTORY AND POLITICS.** Text in English. 1991. irreg., latest 2009. price varies. charts; illus. back issues avail. **Document type:** *Monographic series, Academic/Scholarly.* **Description:** Explores issues and trends in international history and politics.
Published by: Princeton University Press, 41 William St, Princeton, NJ 08540. TEL 609-258-4900, 800-777-4726, FAX 609-258-6305, cpriday@pupress.co.uk. Eds. G John Ikenberry, Marc Trachtenberg. **Subscr. addr. in the US:** California - Princeton Fulfillment Services, Inc., 1445 Lower Ferry Rd, Ewing, NJ 08618. TEL 609-883-1759, 800-777-4726, FAX 609-883-7413, 800-999-1958, orders@cpfsinc.com. **Dist. addr. in Canada:** University Press Group.; **Dist. addr. in UK:** John Wiley & Sons Ltd.

327 RUS ISSN 1560-8913
DK510.763
PRO ET CONTRA. Text in Russian. 1996. q.
—East View.
Published by: Moskovskii Tsentr Carnegie, Tverskaya ul 16/2, Moscow, 125009, Russian Federation. TEL 7-095-9358904, FAX 7-095-9358906, info@carnegie.ru.

327 361.1 FRA ISSN 0015-9743
H3 CODEN: PPOSEQ
PROBLEMES POLITIQUES ET SOCIAUX; articles et documents d'actualite mondiale. Text in French. 1970. m. EUR 89 to individuals; EUR 81 to students (effective 2009). index. **Document type:** *Government.*
Formerly: France. Direction de la Documentation Articles et Documents
Related titles: Microfiche ed.; Online - full text ed.
Indexed: A22, FR, IBSS, ILD, PdeR, RASB.
—BLDSC (6617.871900), IE, Infotrieve, Ingenta, INIST. **CCC.**
Published by: Documentation Francaise, 29-31 Quai Voltaire, Paris, Cedex 7 75344, France. FAX 33-1-40157230. Circ: 4,000.

327.172 NLD ISSN 1871-0352
PROCESNIEUWS. Text in Dutch. 2002. 3/yr. EUR 15 (effective 2010).
Formerly (until 2005): Kernwapens Weg! - ProcesNieuws (1571-683X); Which was formed by the merger of (1984-2002): Procesnieuws (1384-9549); (1977-2002): Kernwapens Weg (1382-1199); Which was formerly (until 1984): N-Bulletin (1382-1679)
Published by: Stichting Tribunaal voor de Vrede, Minahassastraat 1, Postbus 92066, Amsterdam, 1090 AB, Netherlands.

327 GBR ISSN 1740-5823
PROGRAMA CRISIS DE LOS ESTADOS DOCUMENTOS DE TRABAJO. Text in Spanish. 200?. irreg. **Document type:** *Monographic series, Academic/Scholarly.*
Related titles: Online - full text ed.: ISSN 1740-5831; ◆ English ed.: Crisis States Working Papers. Series No.2 (Print). ISSN 1749-1797.
—BLDSC (3487.384150).
Published by: London School of Economics and Political Science, Crisis States Research Centre, Houghton St, Rm U610, London, WC2A 2AE, United Kingdom. csp@lse.ac.uk, http://www.crisisstates.com/.

PROGRESS IN DEVELOPMENT STUDIES. *see* SOCIOLOGY

327.17 DEU ISSN 1867-3945
PROJEKT JUNGES EUROPA. Text in German. 2005. a. EUR 25 (effective 2010). **Document type:** *Journal, Academic/Scholarly.*
Published by: Wehrhahn Verlag, Am Mittelfelde 1, Hannover, 30519, Germany. TEL 49-511-8988906, FAX 49-511-8988245, info@wehrhahn-verlag.de.

327 POL ISSN 0033-2437
DK4010
PRZEGLAD ZACHODNI. Text in Polish, German; Summaries in English. 1945. q. USD 40. bk.rev. bibl.; charts; stat. index.
Indexed: A22, AmH&L, CA, DIP, HistAb, IBR, IBSS, IBZ, MLA-IB, P30, RASB, T02.
—BLDSC (6944.930000), IE, Infotrieve, Ingenta.
Published by: Instytut Zachodni, Stary Rynek 78-79, Poznan, 61772, Poland. Ed. Hanka Dmochowska. Circ: 600.

PSYCHOLOGISTS FOR SOCIAL RESPONSIBILITY. NEWSLETTER. *see* PSYCHOLOGY

327 USA ISSN 1554-0480
PUBLIC JUSTICE REPORT (ONLINE). Text in English. 1977. q. looseleaf. free (effective 2005). bk.rev. 12 p./no. 2 cols./p.; back issues avail. **Document type:** *Newsletter.* **Description:** Analysis and commentary of domestic and international affairs, with the aim of promoting a Christian public philosophy and in pursuit of public justice.
Former titles (until 2005): Public Justice Report (Print) (0742-5325); (until 1980): Public Justice Newsletter
Media: Online - full content.
Published by: Center for Public Justice, 2444 Solomons Island Rd, Ste 201, Annapolis, MD 21401. TEL 410-571-6300, 866-275-8784, FAX 410-571-6365. Ed. Dr. James W Skillen. Circ: 1,500.

327 USA ISSN 1932-6297
PUGWASH OCCASIONAL PAPERS. Text in English. 2000. irreg. **Document type:** *Monographic series, Consumer.*
Published by: Pugwash Conferences on Science and World Affairs, c/o Jeffrey Boutwell, 1111 19th St., NW, Ste 1200, Washington, DC 20036. TEL 202-478-3440, pugwashdc@aol.com, http://www.pugwash.org.

327 BWA ISSN 0256-2316
DT1
➤ **PULA**; Botswana journal of African studies. Text in English. 1978. s-a. USD 20 per issue. bk.rev. back issues avail. **Document type:** *Journal, Academic/Scholarly.* **Description:** Publishes articles devoted primarily to African studies, with emphasis on southern Africa.
Indexed: ASD, IBSS, MLA-IB, P30, PLESA, RASB.
Published by: National Institute of Development Research and Documentation, University of Botswana, Private Bag 0022, Gaborone, Botswana. TEL 267-356364, FAX 267-357573. Ed. T T Fako.

327 IND ISSN 0253-3960
JA26
PUNJAB JOURNAL OF POLITICS. Text in English. 1977. s-a. INR 150 to individuals; INR 300 to institutions (effective 2011). **Document type:** *Journal, Academic/Scholarly.* **Description:** Deals with regional politics, foreign policy and international relations.
Indexed: BAS, CA, HistAb, I13, P30, P42, T02.
Published by: Guru Nanak Dev University Press, c/o Ajaib Singh Brar, Amritsar, 143 005, India. TEL 91-183-2258802, vc@gndu.ac.in, http://www.gndu.ac.in/.

327 ITA ISSN 1125-9663
QUADERNI DI RELAZIONI INTERNAZIONALI. Text in Multiple languages. 1972. s-a. EUR 25 domestic (effective 2011). **Document type:** *Journal, Trade.*
Published by: (Istituto per gli Studi di Politica Internazionale (I S P I)), Universita Bocconi Editore, Egea SpA, Viale Isonzo 25, Milan, MI 20135, Italy. TEL 39-02-58365751, FAX 39-02-58365753, egea.edizioni@uni-bocconi.it, http://www.egeaonline.com.

327.17 ITA ISSN 0394-4204
I QUADERNI DI VENTOTENE. Text in Italian. 1988. irreg. **Document type:** *Journal, Academic/Scholarly.*
Related titles: French ed.: Les Cahiers de Ventotene. ISSN 1825-0521; English ed.: The Ventotene Papers. ISSN 1825-0513.
Published by: Istituto di Studi Federalisti Altiero Spinelli, Via Schina 26, Turin, 10144, Italy. TEL 39-011-4732843, FAX 39-011-4732843, http://www.istitutospinelli.org.

327 ITA ISSN 1973-7696
I QUADERNI EUROPEI. Text in Multiple languages. 2008. irreg. **Document type:** *Monographic series, Academic/Scholarly.*
Media: Online - full text.
Published by: Universita degli Studi di Catania, Centro di Documentazione Europea, Palazzo Hernandez, Via San Lorenzo 4, Catania, Italy. http://www.lex.unict.it/cde/.

327.172 ITA ISSN 1720-402X
QUADERNI SATYAGRAHA; il metodo nonviolento per trascendere i conflitti e costruire la Pace. Text in Italian. 2002. s-a. EUR 15 domestic; EUR 30 foreign (effective 2009). **Document type:** *Journal, Academic/Scholarly.*
Published by: (Universita degli Studi di Pisa, Centro Interdisciplinare di Scienze per la Pace), Edizioni Plus - Universita di Pisa (Pisa University Press), Lungarno Pacinotti 43, Pisa, Italy. TEL 39-050-2212056, FAX 39-050-2212945, http://www.edizioniplus.it. Ed. Rocco Altieri.

327.1 USA ISSN 2153-4306
QUALITY OF LIFE, BALANCE OF POWER, AND NUCLEAR WEAPONS; a statistical yearbook for statesmen and citizens. Text in English. 2008. a. USD 45 per issue (print or online ed.) (effective 2010). back issues avail. **Document type:** *Yearbook, Consumer.* **Description:** Covers all aspects of foundations of power politics in the nuclear age, fundamental forces that drive events in the international news, and seldom-discussed factors that can shift whole economies.
Related titles: Online - full text ed.: ISSN 2153-4322.
Published by: Algora Publishing, 222 Riverside Dr, 16th FL, New York, NY 10025. TEL 212-678-0232, FAX 212-666-3682.

327 AUS ISSN 1837-9338
QUARTERLY ACCESS; your key to international affairs. Abbreviated title: Q A. Text in English. 2007. q. adv. back issues avail. **Document type:** *Journal, Trade.*
Related titles: Online - full text ed.: ISSN 1837-9354. free (effective 2011).
Published by: Australian Institute of International Affairs, Stephen House, 32 Thesiger Ct, Deakin, ACT 2600, Australia. TEL 61-2-62822133, FAX 61-2-62852334, ceo@aiia.asn.au. Ed. Daniel Wilson.

QUESTE ISTITUZIONI; cronache del sistema politico. *see* POLITICAL SCIENCE

327 FRA ISSN 1761-7146
JA11
QUESTIONS INTERNATIONALES. Text in French. 2003. bi-m. **Document type:** *Journal, Academic/Scholarly.*
Indexed: IBSS.
Published by: Documentation Francaise, 29-31 Quai Voltaire, Paris, Cedex 7 75344, France. http://www.ladocumentationfrancaise.fr.

R U S I NEWSBRIEF. (Royal United Services Institute) *see* MILITARY

327 USA ISSN 0882-312X
RANGEL'S REPORTS. Text in English. 1977. q. USD 10. illus.
Formerly (until 1984): Second Republic Newsletter (0146-2547); Supersedes: Bravado
Published by: (Second Republic Research Center (SRRC)), Bravado Feature Service, PO Box 2498, Rockefeller Ctr Sta, New York, NY 10185. Ed. Marc Rangel. Circ: 2,000.

RATEN AMERIKA KENKYU NENPO/ANNALS OF LATIN AMERICAN STUDIES. *see* HISTORY—History Of North And South America

327.172 FIN ISSN 0781-9307
RAUHANTUTKIMUS TANAAN. Text in Multiple languages. 1970. irreg. price varies. back issues avail. **Document type:** *Monographic series, Academic/Scholarly.*
Published by: Suomen Rauhantutkimusyhdistys/Finnish Peace Research Association, c/o Samu Pehkonen, Rauhan- ja Konfliktintutkimuskeskus, TAPRI, Tampereen Yliopisto, Tampere, 33014, Finland.

327 CYP
RE-DRAWING THE ISLAMIC MAP. Variant title: A P S Diplomat Re-Drawing the Islamic Map. Text in English. 1972. m. USD 800; includes subscr. to A P S News Service, Strategic Balance in the Middle East, Fate of the Arabian Peninsula, Operations in Oil Diplomacy. s-a. index. **Document type:** *Bulletin.* **Description:** Surveys Islamic states and political activities.
Related titles: Online - full text ed.
Published by: Arab Press Service, PO Box 23896, Nicosia, Cyprus. TEL 357-2-351778, FAX 357-2-350265. Ed., Pub. Pierre Shammas.

016.32 LUX ISSN 0774-112X
HC241
RECHERCHES UNIVERSITAIRES SUR L'INTEGRATION EUROPEENNE/UNIVERSITY RESEARCH ON EUROPEAN INTEGRATION. Text in English, French. 1963. irreg. price varies. **Document type:** *Abstract/Index.*
Former titles (until 1981): Etudes Universitaires sur l'Integration Europeenne (0071-2213); (until 1967): Recherches et Etudes Universitaires sur l'Integration Europeenne (0776-5568)
Related titles: Online - full text ed.
Published by: European Commission, Office for Official Publications of the European Union, 2 Rue Mercier, Luxembourg, L-2985, Luxembourg. info@publications.europa.eu, http://europa.eu. Circ: 4,000.

327 BRA ISSN 1414-7106
HT390
REDES. Text in Portuguese. 1996. s-a. BRL 30 (effective 2006). back issues avail. **Document type:** *Journal, Academic/Scholarly.*
Published by: (Universidade de Santa Cruz do Sul, Centro de Pesquisa em Desenvolvimento Regional), Editora da Universidade de Santa Cruz do Sul, Av Independencia 2293, Barrio Universitario, Santa Cruz do Sul, RS 96815-900, Brazil. TEL 55-51-37177461, FAX 55-51-37177402, editora@unisc.br. Ed. Heleniza Avila Campos.

REFLECTIONS (WASHINGTON)/REFLEJOS. *see* HISTORY—History Of North And South America

325.21 USA
REFUGEE AND IMMIGRANT RESOURCE DIRECTORY (YEAR). Text in English. 1987. biennial. USD 47.50 (effective 2000). **Document type:** *Directory.* **Description:** Includes information on over 2,250 local, regional and national organizations, associations, agencies, academic programs, research centers, museums and other groups in the United States that offer services providing information and policy analysis about refugees and immigrants.
Published by: Denali Press, PO Box 021535, Juneau, AK 99802-1535. TEL 907-586-6014, FAX 907-463-6780.

325.21 USA
REFUGEE STUDIES CENTER. OCCASIONAL PAPERS. Text in English. 1983. irreg., latest 1996. price varies. back issues avail. **Document type:** *Monographic series.* **Description:** Describes Southeast Asian and other cultures and the problems people face as refugees.
Formerly: Southeast Asian Refugee Studies Project. Occasional Papers
Published by: Refugee Studies Center, University of Minnesota, 330 Humphrey Center, 301 19th Ave S, Minneapolis, MN 55455. TEL 612-625-5535, FAX 612-626-0273. Eds. Daniel Detzner, Karen Yang.

327 CHE ISSN 0252-791X
HV640
REFUGEES. Text in English. 1972. q. free. illus. **Document type:** *Newsletter, Consumer.* **Description:** Describes the problems and plight of refugees around the world.
Incorporates (1982-1983): Refugees Magazine (1014-1235); Former titles (until 1981): U N H C R (0251-6446); (until 1980): H C R Bulletin (0017-615X)
Related titles: Microfiche ed.: 1972 (from CIS); Online - full content ed.; ◆ Spanish ed.: Refugiados. ISSN 1014-0891; ◆ French ed.: Refugies. ISSN 1014-0905; ◆ Italian ed.: Rifugiati. ISSN 1014-0832; ◆ Japanese ed.: Refyujizu. ISSN 1014-1162; ◆ German ed.: Fluchtlinge. ISSN 1014-1154; ◆ Chinese ed.: Nanmin Zazhi. ISSN 1014-5389; ◆ Arabic ed.: Al Lagi'un. ISSN 1014-5370; ◆ Supplement(s): Refugees Magazine. ISSN 1014-1235.
Indexed: A22, C01, HRIR, IIS, RASB, RefugAb.
—IE, Ingenta.
Published by: United Nations High Commissioner for Refugees, Public Information Section, PO Box 2500, Geneva 2, 1211, Switzerland. TEL 41-22-739-81-11, FAX 41-22-739-84-49, http://www.unhcr.ch/. Ed. Ray Wilkinson. Circ: 227,500.

327 CHE ISSN 1014-0891
REFUGIADOS. Text in Spanish. 1983. m.
Related titles: ◆ English ed.: Refugees. ISSN 0252-791X; ◆ French ed.: Refugies. ISSN 1014-0905; ◆ Italian ed.: Rifugiati. ISSN 1014-0832; ◆ Arabic ed.: Al Lagi'un. ISSN 1014-5370; ◆ German ed.: Fluchtlinge. ISSN 1014-1154; ◆ Chinese ed.: Nanmin Zazhi. ISSN 1014-5389; ◆ Japanese ed.: Refyujizu. ISSN 1014-1162.
Published by: United Nations High Commissioner for Refugees, Public Information Section, PO Box 2500, Geneva 2, 1211, Switzerland. TEL 41-22-739-81-11, FAX 41-22-739-84-49, http://www.unhcr.ch/.

327 CHE ISSN 1014-0905
REFUGIES. Text in French. 1972. m.
Former titles (until 1981): H C R. Haut Commissariat des Nations Unies pour les Refugies (0251-6454); (until 1972): H C R Bulletin (Ed. Francaise) (1014-7020)
Related titles: Online - full text ed.: ISSN 1564-8869; ◆ Spanish ed.: Refugiados. ISSN 1014-0891; ◆ Arabic ed.: Al Lagi'un. ISSN 1014-5370; ◆ Japanese ed.: Refyujizu. ISSN 1014-1162; ◆ German ed.: Fluchtlinge. ISSN 1014-1154; ◆ Chinese ed.: Nanmin Zazhi. ISSN 1014-5389; ◆ English ed.: Refugees. ISSN 0252-791X; ◆ Italian ed.: Rifugiati. ISSN 1014-0832.
Indexed: RASB.
Published by: United Nations High Commissioner for Refugees, Public Information Section, PO Box 2500, Geneva 2, 1211, Switzerland. TEL 41-22-739-81-11, FAX 41-22-739-84-49, http://www.unhcr.ch/.

327 CHE ISSN 1014-1162
REFYUJIZU. Text in Japanese. 1986. bi-m.
Related titles: ◆ English ed.: Refugees. ISSN 0252-791X; ◆ French ed.: Refugies. ISSN 1014-0905; ◆ Spanish ed.: Refugiados. ISSN 1014-0891; ◆ Arabic ed.: Al Lagi'un. ISSN 1014-5370; ◆ German ed.: Fluchtlinge. ISSN 1014-1154; ◆ Chinese ed.: Nanmin Zazhi. ISSN 1014-5389; ◆ Italian ed.: Rifugiati. ISSN 1014-0832.
Published by: United Nations High Commissioner for Refugees, Public Information Section, PO Box 2500, Geneva 2, 1211, Switzerland. TEL 41-22-739-81-11, FAX 41-22-739-84-49, http://www.unhcr.ch/.

327.17 BEL ISSN 1780-5414
REGARDS SUR L'INTERNATIONAL/INTERNATIONAL INSIGHTS. Text in French. 2004. irreg., latest vol.9, 2009. price varies. **Document type:** *Monographic series, Academic/Scholarly.*
Published by: P I E - Peter Lang SA, 1 avenue Maurice, 6e etage, Brussels, 1050, Belgium. TEL 32-2-3477236, FAX 32-2-3477237, pie@peterlang.com, http://www.peterlang.net. Ed. Eric Remacle.

327 DEU ISSN 1863-2947
REGENSBURGER STUDIEN ZUR INTERNATIONALEN POLITIK. Text in German. 2006. irreg., latest vol.154, 2010. price varies. **Document type:** *Monographic series, Academic/Scholarly.*
Published by: Verlag Dr. Kovac, Leverkusenstr 13, Hamburg, 22761, Germany. TEL 49-40-3988800, FAX 49-40-39888055, info@verlagdrkovac.de. Ed. Stephan Bierling.

327 323.4 HUN ISSN 0865-557X
REGIO (BUDAPEST, 1990); kisebbseg, politika, tarsadalom. Text in Hungarian. 1990. q. **Document type:** *Journal, Academic/Scholarly.*
Related titles: Online - full text ed.; ◆ English ed.: Regio (Budapest, 1994). ISSN 1219-1701.
Published by: (Teleki Laszlo Alapitvany), Teleki Laszlo Intezet, Szilagyi Erzsebet fasor 22/c, Budapest, 1125, Hungary. TEL 36-1-3915700, FAX 36-1-3915759, tli@tla.hu, http://www.telekiintezet.hu. Ed. Zoltan Kantor.

327 323.4 HUN ISSN 1219-1701
REGIO (BUDAPEST, 1994); minorities, politics, society. Text in English. 1994. a. **Document type:** *Journal, Academic/Scholarly.*
Related titles: Online - full text ed.; ◆ Hungarian ed.: Regio (Budapest, 1990). ISSN 0865-557X.
Indexed: RILM.
Published by: (Teleki Laszlo Alapitvany), Teleki Laszlo Intezet, Szilagyi Erzsebet fasor 22/c, Budapest, 1125, Hungary. TEL 36-1-3915700, FAX 36-1-3915759, tli@tla.hu, http://www.telekiintezet.hu. Ed. Zoltan Kantor.

327 GBR ISSN 1359-7566
JF195.R44 CODEN: RFSTF2
➤ **REGIONAL & FEDERAL STUDIES.** Text in English. 1991. q. GBP 426 combined subscription in United Kingdom to institutions (print & online eds.); EUR 564, USD 709 combined subscription to institutions (print & online eds.) (effective 2012). adv. bk.rev. index. back issues avail.; reprint service avail. from PSC. **Document type:** *Journal, Academic/Scholarly.* **Description:** Covers scholarly research into regional and federal questions which have emerged high on the political agenda in Europe and worldwide.
Formerly (until 1995): Regional Politics and Policy (0959-230X)
Related titles: Online - full text ed.: ISSN 1743-9434. GBP 383 in United Kingdom to institutions; EUR 508, USD 638 to institutions (effective 2012) (from IngentaConnect).
Indexed: A22, ABCPolSci, AmHI, B21, BrHumI, CA, DIP, E01, E17, ESPM, GEOBASE, H07, I02, I13, IBR, IBSS, IBZ, P34, P42, PAIS, PSA, R02, S02, S03, SCOPUS, SOPODA, SSA, SociolAb, T02.
—IE, Ingenta. **CCC.**
Published by: Routledge (Subsidiary of: Taylor & Francis Group), 4 Park Sq, Milton Park, Abingdon, Oxon OX14 4RN, United Kingdom. TEL 44-20-70176000, FAX 44-20-70176336, subscriptions@tandf.co.uk, http://www.routledge.com. Adv. contact Linda Hann TEL 44-1344-779945. **Subscr. to:** Taylor & Francis Ltd., Journals Customer Service, Sheepen Pl, Colchester, Essex CO3 3LP, United Kingdom. TEL 44-20-70175544, FAX 44-20-70175198, tf.enquiries@tfinforma.com.

327.17 BEL ISSN 2030-8787
REGIONAL INTEGRATION AND SOCIAL COHESION. Text in English, French. 2008. irreg., latest vol.4, 2009. price varies. **Document type:** *Monographic series, Academic/Scholarly.*
Published by: P I E - Peter Lang SA, 1 avenue Maurice, 6e etage, Brussels, 1050, Belgium. TEL 32-2-3477236, FAX 32-2-3477237, pie@peterlang.com, http://www.peterlang.net.

327 DEU ISSN 1996-9678
REGIONAL INTEGRATION OBSERVER. Variant title: Z E I Regional Integration Observer. Text in English, German. 2007. q. **Document type:** *Journal, Academic/Scholarly.*
Published by: Zentrum fuer Europaeische Integrationsforschung/Center for European Integration Studies, Walter-Flexstr 3, Bonn, 53113, Germany. TEL 49-228-731886, FAX 49-228-731802, r.meyer@uni-bonn.de.

REGIONAL OUTLOOK: SOUTHEAST ASIA. *see* BUSINESS AND ECONOMICS—Economic Situation And Conditions

341.123 CHE ISSN 1012-7666
REGISTER OF DEVELOPMENT ACTIVITIES OF THE UNITED NATIONS SYSTEM. Text in English. 1987. irreg.
Published by: Coordination Committee of Information Systems, Palais des Nations C552, Geneva, 1211, Switzerland. TEL 41-22-9172804, FAX 41-22-9170248, http://www.acc.unsystem.org/iscc.

327 DEU ISSN 0936-8965
REIHE DER VILLA VIGONI; Deutsch-italienische Studien. Text in German, Italian. 1989. irreg., latest vol.25, 2011. price varies. **Document type:** *Monographic series, Academic/Scholarly.* **Description:** Reports on political, historical and cultural relations between Germany and Italy.
Published by: (Verein der Villa Vigoni e.V.), Max Niemeyer Verlag GmbH (Subsidiary of: Walter de Gruyter GmbH & Co. KG), Pfrondorfer Str 6, Tuebingen, 72074, Germany. TEL 49-7071-98940, FAX 49-7071-989450, info@niemeyer.de, http://www.niemeyer.de.

327 ESP ISSN 1575-8133
RELACIONES ECONOMICAS INTERNACIONALES. Text in Spanish. 1981. s-a. **Document type:** *Government.*
Formerly (until 1999): Direccion General de Relaciones Economicas Internacionales. Boletin Informativo (1575-8125)
Published by: Ministerio de Asuntos Exteriores, Secretaria General Tecnica, Plaza de la Marina Espanola, Madrid, 28013, Spain. http://www.mae.es/.

327 ESP ISSN 1699-3950
JZ9
RELACIONES INTERNACIONALES. Text in Spanish. 2005. q. free (effective 2011). back issues avail. **Document type:** *Journal, Academic/Scholarly.*
Media: Online - full text.
Published by: Asociacion para el Estudio de la Disciplina de Relaciones Internacionales, C Marie Curie, No 1, Ciudad Universitaria de Cantoblanco, Madrid, 28049, Spain. TEL 34-91-4974380, FAX 34-91-4974166, redaccion@relacionesinternacionales.info, http://www.uam.es/.

327 MEX ISSN 0185-0814
JZ9 CODEN: REINFT
RELACIONES INTERNACIONALES. Text in Spanish; Abstracts in English, French, Spanish. 1973. q. MXN 300, USD 110 (effective 2003). bk.rev. bibl. **Description:** Covers political sciences, international relations, global economics and international law.
Related titles: Online - full text ed.
Indexed: C01, CA, DIP, H21, I04, I05, I13, IBR, IBZ, P08, P30, P42, PAIS, PSA, PerIslam, RASB, S02, S03, SOPODA, SociolAb, T02.
Published by: Universidad Nacional Autonoma de Mexico, Facultad de Ciencias Politicas y Sociales, Circuito Cultural Mario de la Cueva, Edif C 2o piso, Ciudad Universitaria, Mexico City, DF 04510, Mexico. TEL 52-5-6229400 ext. 41, FAX 52-5-6228334, cri@socioland.politicas.unam.mx. Ed. Consuelo Davila Perez. Circ: 1,000.

327 BRA ISSN 1413-0149
RELACOES INTERNACIONAIS. Text in Portuguese. 1978. 3/yr. bk.rev. illus. **Document type:** *Journal, Academic/Scholarly.*
Published by: Universidade de Brasilia, Departamento de Ciencia Politica e Relacoes Internacionais, Campus Universitario, Asa Norte, Brasilia, 04359, Brazil. TEL 61-307-2426, FAX 61-274-4117. Circ: 5,000.

328 PRT ISSN 1645-9199
RELACOES INTERNACIONAIS. Text in Portuguese. 2004. q. back issues avail. **Document type:** *Journal, Academic/Scholarly.*
Related titles: Online - full text ed.: free (effective 2011).
Indexed: CA, F04, IBSS, P42, PAIS, PSA, SCOPUS, SociolAb, T02.
Published by: Universidade Nova de Lisboa, Instituto Portugues de Relacoes Internacionais, Rua D. Estefania 195 - 5o. Dto, Lisbon, 1000-155, Portugal. TEL 351-21-3141176, FAX 351-21-3141228, ipri@ipri.pt, http://www.ipri.pt/. Ed. Carmen Fonseca.

327.17 DEU ISSN 1431-3669
RELATIONEN: Internationale Politik in Asien: Probleme - Analysen - Berichte. Text in German. 1995. irreg., latest vol.12, 2006. price varies. **Document type:** *Monographic series, Academic/Scholarly.*
Published by: Trafo Verlag, Finkenstr 8, Berlin, 12621, Germany. TEL 49-30-61299418, FAX 49-30-61299421, info@trafoberlin.de, http://www.trafoberlin.de.

327 FRA ISSN 0335-2013
D410
➤ **RELATIONS INTERNATIONALES.** Text in French; Abstracts in French, English. 1974. q. EUR 83 foreign to institutions (effective 2012). bk.rev. bibl. cum.index: 1974-1994. reprint service avail. from SCH. **Document type:** *Journal, Academic/Scholarly.*
Related titles: Online - full text ed.: ISSN 2105-2654.
Indexed: A22, FR, HistAb, I13, IBSS, P42, PAIS, PCI, PSA, SCOPUS.
—BLDSC (7352.077000), IE, Infotrieve, Ingenta, INIST.
Published by: (Institut Universitaire de Hautes Etudes Internationales, Geneva CHE, Societe d'Etudes Historiques des Relations Internationales Contemporaines), Presses Universitaires de France, 6 Avenue Reille, Paris, 75685, France. TEL 33-1-58103161, FAX 33-1-45897530, revues@puf.com, http://www.puf.com. Ed. Antoine Mares.

➤ **RELIGION AND SECURITY MONOGRAPH SERIES.** *see* RELIGIONS AND THEOLOGY

➤ **THE REPORT. ABU DHABI.** *see* BUSINESS AND ECONOMICS—Production Of Goods And Services

➤ **THE REPORT. AJMAN.** *see* BUSINESS AND ECONOMICS—Production Of Goods And Services

➤ **THE REPORT. BRUNEI DARUSSALAM.** *see* BUSINESS AND ECONOMICS—Production Of Goods And Services

➤ **THE REPORT. KUWAIT.** *see* BUSINESS AND ECONOMICS—Production Of Goods And Services

➤ **THE REPORT. MALAYSIA.** *see* BUSINESS AND ECONOMICS—Production Of Goods And Services

327 USA ISSN 0748-0571
JX1932
REPORT OF A VANTAGE CONFERENCE. Text in English. 1973. irreg. free (effective 2011). **Document type:** *Report, Trade.* **Description:** Discusses the evolving world situation and addresses timely, emerging issues.
Formerly (until 1984): Vantage Conference Report (0145-8833)
Related titles: Online - full text ed.
Published by: The Stanley Foundation, 209 Iowa Ave, Muscatine, IA 52761. TEL 563-264-1500, FAX 563-264-0864, info@stanleyfoundation.org, http://www.stanleyfoundation.org/.

327 330.9 USA ISSN 1043-3856
F1461
REPORT ON GUATEMALA. Text in English. 1978. q. USD 25 domestic to individuals; USD 30 to institutions (effective 2004). adv. bk.rev. 16 p./no.; back issues avail. **Document type:** *Newsletter.* **Description:** Provides scholars, activists, and concerned citizens with in-depth coverage of Guatemalan current events. It's a strong dissident publication on U.S. Central American policy.
Formerly (until 1987): Guatemala!
Related titles: Microfiche ed.
Indexed: HRIR.
Published by: Network in Solidarity with the People of Guatemala, 1830 Connecticut Ave., N W Washington, DC 20009. TEL 202-518-7638, FAX 202-223-8221, sarah_aird@igc.org, http://www.nisgua.org. Ed., R&P Alexandra Durbin. Circ: 800.

THE REPORT. SARAWAK. *see* BUSINESS AND ECONOMICS—Production Of Goods And Services

THE REPORT. SAUDI ARABIA. *see* BUSINESS AND ECONOMICS—Production Of Goods And Services

THE REPORT. SENEGAL. *see* BUSINESS AND ECONOMICS—Production Of Goods And Services

THE REPORT. TAIWAN. *see* BUSINESS AND ECONOMICS—Production Of Goods And Services

THE REPORT. THE PHILIPPINES. *see* BUSINESS AND ECONOMICS—Production Of Goods And Services

RESEARCH PAPERS IN RUSSIAN AND EAST EUROPEAN STUDIES. *see* HISTORY—History Of Europe

RESIST NEWSLETTER. *see* POLITICAL SCIENCE—Civil Rights

327.172 USA
RESOURCE CENTER FOR NONVIOLENCE. CENTER REPORT. Text in English. 1979. 3/yr. donations. bk.rev. **Document type:** *Newsletter.*
Formerly: Resource Center for Nonviolence. Newsletter
Published by: Resource Center for Nonviolence, 515 Broadway, Santa Cruz, CA 95060-4621. TEL 831-423-1626, FAX 831-423-8716. Circ: 3,000.

327 GBR ISSN 0305-6244
HC501 CODEN: RAPEF9
➤ **REVIEW OF AFRICAN POLITICAL ECONOMY.** Abbreviated title: R O A P E. Text in English. 1973. q. GBP 479 combined subscription in United Kingdom to institutions (print & online eds.); EUR 669, USD 840 combined subscription to institutions (print & online eds.) (effective 2012). adv. bk.rev. illus. index. back issues avail.; reprint service avail. from PSC. **Document type:** *Journal, Academic/Scholarly.* **Description:** Provides radical analysis and commentary on trends and issues in Africa.
Related titles: Microfiche ed.; Online - full text ed.: ISSN 1740-1720. GBP 432 in United Kingdom to institutions; EUR 602, USD 756 to institutions (effective 2012) (from IngentaConnect).
Indexed: A12, A17, A22, A35, ABIn, ASD, AgBio, AltPI, B01, B06, B07, B08, B09, B16, C12, C25, CA, CABA, CCA, CurCont, E01, E12, ESPM, EconLit, F08, F12, GEOBASE, H16, I13, I14, IBR, IBSS, IBZ, IIBP, JEL, LeftInd, M10, MLA-IB, N02, P06, P10, P13, P30, P32, P34, P40, P42, P45, P46, P47, P48, P51, P53, P54, PAIS, PCI, PQC, PSA, PerIslam, R12, RASB, RiskAb, S02, S03, S13, S16, SCOPUS, SOPODA, SSA, SSCI, SociolAb, T02, TAR, W07, W11.
—BLDSC (7786.769000), IE, Infotrieve, Ingenta. **CCC.**

P

Published by: Routledge (Subsidiary of: Taylor & Francis Group), 4 Park Sq, Milton Park, Abingdon, Oxon OX14 4RN, United Kingdom. TEL 44-20-70176000, FAX 44-20-70176336, subscriptions@tandf.co.uk, http://www.routledge.com. Adv. contact Linda Hann TEL 44-1344-779945. **Subscr. to:** Taylor & Francis Ltd., Journals Customer Service, Sheepen Pl, Colchester, Essex CO3 3LP, United Kingdom. TEL 44-20-70175544, FAX 44-20-70175198, tf.enquiries@tfinforma.com.

327 CAN ISSN 1718-4835
REVIEW OF EUROPEAN AND RUSSIAN AFFAIRS. Text in English. 2005. s-a. **Document type:** *Journal, Academic/Scholarly.*
Media: Online - full text.
Published by: Carleton University, 1125 Colonel By Dr, Ottawa, ON K1S 5B6, Canada. TEL 613-520-7400, FAX 613-520-7858, info@carleton.ca. Eds. Joan DeBardeleben, Oliver Schmidtke, Piotr Dutkiewicz.

THE REVIEW OF FAITH & INTERNATIONAL AFFAIRS. *see* RELIGIONS AND THEOLOGY

327.17 CHE ISSN 0034-6608
CODEN: ABPGC2
REVIEW OF INTERNATIONAL COOPERATION. Text in English. 1908. q. CHF 100 (effective 2002); includes ICA News. adv. bk.rev. illus.; stat. index. reprints avail. **Document type:** *Journal, Academic/Scholarly.*
Related titles: Microform ed.: (from PQC); Online - full text ed.
Indexed: P06, PCI, RASB.
—IE, Ingenta. **CCC.**
Published by: International Co-Operative Alliance, 15 rte des Morillons, Grand Saconnex, 1218, Switzerland. TEL 41-22-9298888, FAX 41-22-7984122, TELEX 415620-ICA-CH, ica@coop.org. Ed. Iain Williamson. Circ: 4,500.

REVIEW OF INTERNATIONAL POLITICAL ECONOMY. *see* BUSINESS AND ECONOMICS—Economic Situation And Conditions

327 GBR ISSN 0260-2105
K2
➤ **REVIEW OF INTERNATIONAL STUDIES.** Text in English. 1975. q. (plus one supplement). GBP 298, USD 505 to institutions; GBP 330, USD 575 combined subscription to institutions (print & online eds.) (effective 2012). adv. bk.rev. illus. index. back issues avail.; reprint service avail. from PSC. **Document type:** *Journal, Academic/Scholarly.* **Description:** Reviews politics, law, history and other areas of social science in the international arena.
Formerly (until 1981): British Journal of International Studies (0305-8026)
Related titles: Online - full text ed.: ISSN 1469-9044. GBP 290, USD 465 to institutions (effective 2012).
Indexed: A01, A03, A08, A12, A20, A22, ABCPolSci, ABIn, AMB, ASCA, AmH&L, AmHI, BrHumI, CA, CurCont, E01, ESPM, EconLit, H07, HistAb, I13, IBSS, JEL, LID&ISL, LeftInd, P10, P30, P34, P42, P45, P47, P48, P51, P53, P54, PAIS, PCI, PQC, PRA, PSA, PerIslam, RiskAb, S02, S03, S10, SCOPUS, SSCI, SociolAb, T02, W07.
—BLDSC (7790.940000), IE, Infotrieve, Ingenta. **CCC.**
Published by: (British International Studies Association), Cambridge University Press, The Edinburgh Bldg, Shaftesbury Rd, Cambridge, CB2 8RU, United Kingdom. TEL 44-1223-312393, FAX 44-1223-315052, journals@cambridge.org, http://www.cambridge.org/uk. Ed. Nick Rengger. R&P Linda Nicol TEL 44-1223-325702. Adv. contact Rebecca Roberts TEL 44-1223-325083. page GBP 465, page USD 885. Circ: 1,700. **Subscr. to:** Cambridge University Press, 32 Ave of the Americas, New York, NY 10013. TEL 212-337-5000, FAX 212-691-3239, journals_subscriptions@cup.org.

325.21 TZA
REVIEW OF REFUGEE ISSUES. Text in English. 1989. irreg.
Indexed: PLESA.
Published by: University of Dar es Salaam, African Refugee Study Centre, PO Box 35046, Dar Es Salaam, Tanzania.

327 GBR ISSN 2046-6528
LA REVISTA. Text in English. 1951. 3/yr. free to members (effective 2011). adv. bk.rev. illus. index every 5 yrs. back issues avail. **Document type:** *Magazine, Consumer.* **Description:** Publishes articles on matters of Anglo-Spanish interest, Spanish culture, civilization and history.
Former titles (until 2010): Anglo-Spanish Quarterly Review (0003-3383); (until 1959): Anglo-Spanish Review; (until Oct.1958): Anglo-Spanish Society. Quarterly Journal; (until Jun.1958): Anglo-Spanish League of Friendship. Quarterly Journal
Related titles: Online - full text ed.: free (effective 2011).
Published by: Anglo-Spanish Society, 102 Eaton Sq, London, SW1W 9AN, United Kingdom. TEL 44-7903-801576, info@anglospanishsociety.org. Ed. Jimmy Burns. Adv. contact Jose Ivars-Lopez.

REVISTA ARGENTINA DE ESTUDIOS ESTRATEGICOS. *see* MILITARY

327 BRA ISSN 0034-7329
D839
➤ **REVISTA BRASILEIRA DE POLITICA INTERNACIONAL.** Text in Portuguese; Summaries in English, Portuguese. 1958. s-a. adv. bk.rev. cum.index. back issues avail.; reprints avail. **Document type:** *Journal, Academic/Scholarly.*
Related titles: Online - full text ed.: free (effective 2011) (from PQC).
Indexed: A01, A02, A03, A08, A26, AMB, AmH&L, C01, CA, F03, F04, H21, HistAb, I02, I04, I05, IBSS, P08, P34, P42, PCI, PSA, SCOPUS, SSCI, SociolAb, T02, W07.
Published by: Instituto Brasileiro de Relacoes Internacionais, Caixa Postal 4400, Brasilia, DF 70919-970, Brazil. TEL 55-61-21929460, FAX 55-61-33072426, secretaria@ibri-rbpi.org, http://www.ibri-rbpi.org. Ed. Dr. Antonio Carlos Lessa. Circ: 1,000. **Subscr. to:** Susan Bach Serials, Rua Visconde de Caravelas 17, Botafogo, RJ 22271-030, Brazil. TEL 55-21-25372512, sbachserials@sbachbooks.com.br.

327 CHL ISSN 0716-1417
➤ **REVISTA DE CIENCIA POLITICA.** Text in Spanish, English; Abstracts in English. 1979. s-a. CLP 8,000 domestic to individuals; USD 50 foreign to individuals; CLP 20,000 domestic to institutions; USD 130 foreign to institutions; CLP 6,000 domestic to students (effective 2004). back issues avail. **Document type:** *Journal, Academic/Scholarly.*
Related titles: Online - full text ed.: ISSN 0718-090X. 2004. free (effective 2011).
Indexed: A01, CA, F03, F04, IBR, IBSS, IBZ, P34, P42, PAIS, PSA, SCOPUS, SSCI, SociolAb, T02, W07.
Published by: Pontificia Universidad Catolica de Chile, Instituto de Ciencia Politica, Av. Vicuna Mackenna 4860, Santiago, Chile. TEL 56-2-3547818, FAX 56-2-3547813, http://www.puc.cl/icp/. Ed. Dr. David Altman. R&P, Adv. contact David Alvarez.

327 ARG ISSN 1851-9008
REVISTA DE CIENCIA POLITICA. Text in Spanish. 2007. q. **Document type:** *Journal, Academic/Scholarly.*
Media: Online - full text.
Address: Venezuela 472, 1o. Piso "25", Buenos Aires, 1095, Argentina. TEL 541-11-43433379. Ed. Alberto Amadeo Baldioli.

REVISTA DE DERECHO INTERNACIONAL Y CIENCIAS DIPLOMATICAS. *see* LAW—International Law

327 ESP ISSN 1887-4460
REVISTA DE ESTUDIOS INTERNACIONALES MEDITERRANEOS. Text in Spanish, French, Arabic, English. 2007. s-a. free (effective 2011). **Document type:** *Journal, Academic/Scholarly.*
Media: Online - full text.
Published by: (Universidad Autonoma de Madrid, Taller de Estudios Internacionales), Universidad Autonoma de Madrid, Servicio de Publicaciones, Ciudad Universitaria Cantoblanco, Madrid, 28049, Spain. TEL 34-91-4974233, FAX 34-97-4975169, servicio.publicaciones@uam.es, http://www.uam.es/.

327 PRT ISSN 1646-5210
REVISTA DE ESTUDOS EUROPEUS. Text in Portuguese. 2007. s-a. EUR 22 newsstand/cover (effective 2009). **Document type:** *Journal, Academic/Scholarly.*
Published by: Edicoes Almedina, SA, Avenida Fernao de Magalhaes, 584, 5o Andar, Coimbra, 3000-174, Portugal. TEL 351-239-851903, FAX 351-239-436267, editora@almedina.net, http://www.almedina.net.

327 BRA ISSN 2177-3246
▼ **REVISTA DE GEOPOLITICA.** Text in Portuguese, Spanish. 2010. s-a. free (effective 2011). **Document type:** *Journal, Academic/Scholarly.*
Media: Online - full text.
Published by: Universidade Estadual de Ponta Grossa, Editora, Av Carlos Cavalcanti 4748, Campus Universitario de Uvaranas, Ponta Grossa, PR 84030-900, Brazil. TEL 55-42-32203744, http://www.uepg.br/editora/. Ed. Edu Silvestre de Albuquerque.

327 ESP ISSN 1988-7221
REVISTA DE PAZ Y CONFLICTOS. Text in Spanish, English. 2007. a. free (effective 2011). **Document type:** *Journal, Academic/Scholarly.*
Media: Online - full text.
Published by: Universidad de Granada, Instituto de la Paz y los Conflictos, Calle Rector Lopez Argueta s/n, Granada, 18071, Spain. TEL 34-95-8244142, FAX 34-95-8248974, eirene@ugr.es, http://www.ugr.es/~eirene/main.html.

327 COL ISSN 0124-4035
REVISTA DESAFIOS. Text in English. 1999. s-a. COP 53,900 domestic; COP 116,000 foreign (effective 2010). **Document type:** *Journal, Academic/Scholarly.*
Related titles: Online - full text ed.: ISSN 2145-5112.
Indexed: A01, A26, C01, CA, F03, F04, I04, I05, IBSS, T02.
Published by: Universidad del Rosario, Centro de Estudios Politicos e Internacionales, Edificio Santafe Cra 6a No. 14 - 13, 2 piso - oficina 276, Bogota, Colombia. TEL 57-1-3414006 ext 276.

327.72 MEX ISSN 0185-6022
F1236
REVISTA MEXICANA DE POLITICA EXTERIOR. Text in Spanish. 1983. q. back issues avail. **Document type:** *Magazine, Consumer.* **Description:** Covers political and foreign relations issues, along with international human rights, geopolitical, and global economy topics.
Indexed: C01, FR, H21, P08, P42, PAIS, PSA, SociolAb.
Published by: Instituto Matias Romero de Estudios Diplomaticos, Reforma Norte 707, Esq. Av Peralvillo, Col Morelos, Mexico City, 06200, Mexico. TEL 52-55-55269513, FAX 52-55-50623031, http://portal.sre.gob.mx/imr/. Ed. Gabriela Malvido Alvarez.

327 CUB ISSN 0049-4682
D839
REVISTA TRICONTINENTAL. Text in Spanish. 1967. q. USD 22 in the Americas; USD 24 elsewhere. bk.rev. illus. back issues avail. **Document type:** *Newsletter.* **Description:** Presents a wide view concerning political and cultural issues in developing countries.
Related titles: Ed.: Tricontinental Magazine. ISSN 0864-1595; French ed.: Revue Tricontinental. ISSN 0864-1587.
Indexed: C01, HRIR, P06.
Published by: Organization of Solidarity of the Peoples of Africa, Asia, and Latin America, Apdo. Postal 4224 y 6130, Calle C No. 668 e-27 y 29, Vedado, La Habana, Cuba. TEL 537-34048, FAX 537-333985. Ed. Ana Maria Pellon Suarez. Circ: 22,000. **Dist. by:** Ediciones Cubanas, Obispo 527, Havana, Cuba.

327.895 URY
REVISTA URUGUAYA DE ESTUDIOS INTERNACIONALES. Text in Spanish. irreg., latest 1990. USD 5 per issue. adv. bk.rev. **Description:** Covers various issues and history of the Uruguayan territory, also contains essays topics in the field of economy, geopolitics and education.
Published by: Instituto de Estudios Internacionales, Pz. Independencia, 830, Casilla de Correos 903, Montevideo, 11108, Uruguay. Ed. Alphonse Max. Circ: 5,000.

307.341 GBR ISSN 1355-9966
HV639
REVIVAL. Text in English. 1994. s-a. back issues avail. **Document type:** *Newsletter, Academic/Scholarly.* **Description:** Covers proceedings, findings and recommendations from workshops and research projects.
—CCC.
Published by: University of York, Department of Politics, Derwent College, Heslington, York, N W Yorks YO10 5DD, United Kingdom. TEL 44-1904 433542, FAX 44-1904-433563, politics@york.ac.uk. Ed. Gavin Ward.

327 FRA ISSN 0035-0974
DD1
REVUE D'ALLEMAGNE ET DES PAYS DE LANGUE ALLEMANDE. Text in French, German. 1949. q. EUR 52 domestic (effective 2009); EUR 53.40 foreign (effective 2003). adv. bk.rev. bibl.; charts. **Document type:** *Academic/Scholarly.*
Formerly (until 1968): Allemagne (0151-1955)
Indexed: AmH&L, BibInd, CA, DIP, FR, HistAb, I13, IBR, IBSS, IBZ, P30, PAIS, V01.
—INIST.
Published by: Societe d'Etudes Allemandes, 23 Rue du Loess, Strasbourg, Cedex 67037, France. TEL 33-3-88107316, FAX 33-3-88106482. Ed. Christiane Falbisaner-Weeda. Pub. Jean Paul Bled. Circ: 700 (paid).

327 CHE ISSN 0035-1091
K21
REVUE DE DROIT INTERNATIONAL DE SCIENCES DIPLOMATIQUES ET POLITIQUES. Text in English, French, German, Italian. 1923. 3/yr. CHF 180 in Europe; CHF 190 elsewhere (effective 1999). index. reprint service avail. from PSC. **Document type:** *Journal, Academic/Scholarly.*
Related titles: Microfiche ed.: (from IDC).
Indexed: A22, FLP, IBR, IBSS, IBZ, PAIS, PCI, RASB.
—BLDSC (7898.520000), IE, Infotrieve, Ingenta.
Address: Case Postale 151, Lausanne 13, 1000, Switzerland. FAX 41-21-6161358. Ed. C L Heinbach.

327 GBR ISSN 0703-6337
HC241A1R4
➤ **REVUE D'INTEGRATION EUROPEENNE/JOURNAL OF EUROPEAN INTEGRATION.** Text in French. 1977. bi-m. GBP 330 combined subscription in United Kingdom to institutions (print & online eds.); EUR 352, USD 436 combined subscription to institutions (print & online eds.) (effective 2012). adv. bk.rev. reprint service avail. from PSC. **Document type:** *Journal, Academic/Scholarly.* **Description:** Focuses on political, economic, legal and social integration in Western Europe and worldwide.
Formerly (until 1980): Centre d'Etudes et de Documentation Europeennes. Bulletin d'Information Documentaire
Related titles: Online - full text ed.: ISSN 1477-2280. GBP 297 in United Kingdom to institutions; EUR 316, USD 392 to institutions (effective 2012) (from IngentaConnect).
Indexed: A01, A03, A08, A22, CA, E01, ELLIS, I13, IBSS, P34, P42, PSA, PdeR, RASB, S02, S03, SCOPUS, SociolAb, T02.
—BLDSC (4979.606000), IE, Infotrieve, Ingenta. **CCC.**
Published by: Routledge (Subsidiary of: Taylor & Francis Group), 4 Park Sq, Milton Park, Abingdon, Oxon OX14 4RN, United Kingdom. TEL 44-20-7017-6000, FAX 44-20-7017-6336, info@routledge.co.uk, http://www.routledge.com/journals/. Ed. Emil Kirchner. Circ: 400. **Subscr. to:** Taylor & Francis Ltd., Journals Customer Service, Sheepen Pl, Colchester, Essex CO3 3LP, United Kingdom. TEL 44-20-70175544, FAX 44-20-70175198.

327.2 MDG
REVUE DIPLOMATIQUE DE L'OCEAN INDIEN. Text in French. 1982. q. USD 29. adv. bk.rev.
Published by: Communication et Media Ocean Indien, BP 46, Antananarivo, Madagascar. TEL 26120-22536, FAX 26120-34534. Ed. Georges Ranaivosoa. Circ: 3,000.

REVUE DU DROIT DE L'UNION EUROPEENNE. *see* BUSINESS AND ECONOMICS—International Commerce

327 BEL ISSN 1370-0731
JA26
➤ **REVUE INTERNATIONALE DE POLITIQUE COMPAREE.** Text in French. 1994. 4/yr. EUR 105 to individuals; EUR 145 to institutions; EUR 75 to students (effective 2011). bk.rev. abstr. back issues avail. **Document type:** *Journal, Academic/Scholarly.* **Description:** Publishes original articles contributing to the comparative analysis of political phenomena.
Related titles: Online - full text ed.: ISSN 1782-1533.
Indexed: A22, CA, DIP, FR, I13, IBR, IBSS, IBZ, MLA-IB, P42, PAIS, PSA, SCOPUS, SociolAb, T02.
—BLDSC (7925.140000), IE, Ingenta, INIST. **CCC.**
Published by: De Boeck Universite (Subsidiary of: Editis), Fond Jean-Paques 4, Louvain-la-Neuve, 1348, Belgium. TEL 32-10-482511, FAX 32-10-482519, info@superieur.deboeck.com. Ed. Philippe Laurent TEL 32-10-474262.

327 FRA ISSN 1287-1672
JZ11
LA REVUE INTERNATIONALE ET STRATEGIQUE. Text in French. 1991. q. EUR 68 domestic to individuals; EUR 80 foreign to individuals; EUR 46 domestic to students (effective 2010). adv. **Document type:** *Academic/Scholarly.*
Formerly (until 1997): Relations Internationales et Strategiques (1157-5417)
Related titles: Online - full text ed.: ISSN 2104-3876.
Indexed: A22, FR, I13, I14, IBSS, PAIS, SCOPUS.
—BLDSC (7924.820000), IE, Ingenta. **CCC.**
Published by: Institut de Relations Internationales et Strategiques, 2 bis Rue Mercoeur, Paris, 75011, France. TEL 33-1-53276060, FAX 33-1-53276070. Ed. Camille Grand. Pub. Arlea Iris. R&P, Adv. contact Laurent Laborie.

327 ROM ISSN 0048-8178
DR201
REVUE ROUMAINE D'ETUDES INTERNATIONALES. Text in English, French, Russian. 1967. 6/yr. ROL 180, USD 56. bk.rev. bibl.
Related titles: ◆ Romanian ed.: Revista Romana de Studii Internationale. ISSN 1220-2908.
Indexed: AMB, HistAb, IBR, IBZ.
Published by: Academia Romana, Asociatia de Drept International si Relatii Internationale N. Titulescu, Sos. Kiseleff 47, Bucharest, 71268, Romania. TEL 40-1-227462. Circ: 1,500.

327 FRA ISSN 1293-8882
HC59.7
REVUE TIERS MONDE; etudes interdisciplinaires sur les questions de developpement. Text in French. 1960. q. EUR 59 combined subscription domestic to individuals (print & online eds.); EUR 69 combined subscription foreign to individuals (print & online eds.); EUR 99 combined subscription domestic to institutions (print & online eds.); EUR 109 combined subscription foreign to institutions (print & online eds.) (effective 2008). bk.rev. abstr. index. reprint service avail. from SCH. **Document type:** *Journal, Academic/Scholarly.* **Description:** Studies the economic and social problems of Third World countries.
Formerly (until 1996): Tiers Monde (0040-7356)
Related titles: Online - full text ed.
Indexed: A22, BAS, CA, DIP, EI, EconLit, FR, H21, I13, I14, IBR, IBSS, IBZ, ILD, JEL, M10, P08, P30, P34, P42, PAIS, PSA, RASB, S02, S03, SCOPUS, SSA, SociolAb, T02.

—BLDSC (7956.190000), IE, Infotrieve, Ingenta, INIST. **CCC.**
Published by: (Institut d'Etude du Developpement Economique et Social), Armand Colin, 21 Rue du Montparnasse, Paris, 75283 Cedex 06, France. TEL 33-1-44395447, FAX 33-1-44394343, infos@armand-colin.fr.

341.72 CZE ISSN 1214-7737
JC328.6
➤ **REXTER**; odborny casopis pro vyzkum radikalismu, extremismu a terorismu. Text in Czech, Slovak, English. 2002. s-a. free (effective 2011). **Document type:** *Journal, Academic/Scholarly.*
Media: Online - full content.
Indexed: P42.
Published by: Centrum pro Bezpecnostni a Strategicka Studia o.s. Ed. Josef Smolik.

327 CHE ISSN 1014-0832
RIFUGIATI. Text in Italian. 1983. q.
Related titles: ◆ English ed.: Refugees. ISSN 0252-791X; ◆ French ed.: Refugies. ISSN 1014-0905; ◆ Spanish ed.: Refugiados. ISSN 1014-0891; ◆ Arabic ed.: Al Lagi'un. ISSN 1014-5370; ◆ German ed.: Fluchtlinge. ISSN 1014-1154; ◆ Chinese ed.: Nanmin Zazhi. ISSN 1014-5389; ◆ Japanese ed.: Refyujizu. ISSN 1014-1162.
Published by: United Nations High Commissioner for Refugees, Public Information Section, PO Box 2500, Geneva 2, 1211, Switzerland. TEL 41-22-739-81-11, FAX 41-22-739-84-49, http://www.unhcr.ch/.

327 GBR ISSN 1759-6939
➤ **RIVISTA**; the journal of the British-Italian Society. Text in English. 1946. bi-m. free to members (effective 2009). adv. bk.rev.; music rev.; play rev. back issues avail. **Document type:** *Magazine, Consumer.* **Description:** Contains arts reviews and other topics of general interest.
Published by: British-Italian Society, The Offices of Venice in Peril Fund, Hurlingham Studios (Unit 4), Ranelagh Gardens, London, SW6 3PA, United Kingdom. TEL 44-20-81509167, jj@british-italian.org, http://www.british-italian.org/.

327 ITA ISSN 0035-6611
JZ7
RIVISTA DI STUDI POLITICI INTERNAZIONALI. Abbreviated title: R S P I. Text in Italian. 1934. q. EUR 50.65 domestic to individuals; EUR 62 foreign to individuals (effective 2009). adv. bk.rev. bibl. index, cum.index: 1934-1983, 1984-1993. **Document type:** *Journal, Academic/Scholarly.* **Description:** Covers international relations, especially European, at the cultural, social, economic and political level.
Related titles: Online - full text ed.
Indexed: A22, ABCPolSci, BAS, CA, DIP, HistAb, I13, IBR, IBSS, IBZ, P42, PCI, PSA, RASB, SCOPUS, SociolAb, T02.
—IE, Infotrieve.
Address: Via Bruxelles 20, Rome, 00198, Italy. Ed. Maria Grazia Melchionni. Circ: 1,200.

327 POL ISSN 1230-4794
DK4450
➤ **ROCZNIK POLSKIEJ POLITYKI ZAGRANICZNEJ.** Text in Polish. 1991. a. USD 16 per vol. foreign (effective 2004). bibl. 400 p./no. 1 cols./p.; back issues avail. **Document type:** *Journal, Academic/Scholarly.*
Related titles: ◆ English ed.: Yearbook of Polish Foreign Policy. ISSN 1233-9903.
Published by: Akademia Dyplomatyczna/Diplomatic Academy, ul Tyniecka 15/17, Warsaw, 02630, Poland. TEL 48-22-5239086, FAX 48-22-5239027, aleksandra.zieliniecd@msz.gov.pl, http://www.sprawymiedzynarodowe.pl. Ed. Barbara Wizimirska. Adv. contact Aleksandra Zieleniec. Circ: 500.

327 ROM ISSN 1582-8271
JN30
➤ **ROMANIAN JOURNAL OF EUROPEAN AFFAIRS.** Text in English. 2001. q. free (effective 2010). abstr.; bibl.; charts; illus. back issues avail. **Document type:** *Journal, Academic/Scholarly.* **Description:** Focuses on the European integration debate and Romania's role as an Euroepan Union member state.
Related titles: Online - full text ed.: ISSN 1841-4273. 2002. free (effective 2011).
Indexed: IBSS, P42, PSA.
Published by: Institutul European din Romania/European Institute of Romania, 7-9 Bd Regina Elisabeta, Sector 3, Bucharest, 030016, Romania. TEL 40-21-3142696, FAX 40-21-3142666, ier@ier.ro. Ed., Pub., R&P Oana Mocanu.

327 JPN ISSN 0918-7030
DK1
ROSHIA KENKYU/RUSSIAN STUDIES. Text in Japanese. 1957. a. JPY 3,150 newsstand/cover (effective 2005). **Document type:** *Monographic series.*
Former titles (until 1992): Soren Kenkyu/Soviet Studies (0911-8152); (until 1984): Kyosanshugi to Kokusai Seiji (0385-650X); (until 1976): Gekkan Kyosanken Mondai/Communist Bloc Problems (0454-7616); (until 1961): Kiho Kyosanken Mondai/Communist Bloc Problems (0451-937X); (until 1959): Kiho Soren Mondai/Soviet Problems (0489-7617)
Published by: Nihon Kokusai Mondai Kenkyujo/Japan Institute of International Affairs, Kasumigaseki Bldg 11F, 3-2-5 Kasumigaseki, Chiyoda-ku, Tokyo, 100-6011, Japan. TEL 81-3-35037801, FAX 81-3-35037186, jiiajoho@jiia.or.jp, http://www.jiia.or.jp/. **Dist. overseas by:** Japan Publications Trading Co., Ltd., Book Export II Dept, PO Box 5030, Tokyo International, Tokyo 101-3191, Japan. TEL 81-3-32923753, FAX 81-3-32920410, infoserials@jptco.co.jp, http://www.jptco.co.jp.

327.17 RUS
ROSSIYA I SOVREMENNYI MIR. Text in Russian. 1995. q. USD 105 in United States (effective 2004). **Document type:** *Journal, Academic/Scholarly.* **Description:** Coves social and political issues on the problems of the past, present and future of Russia in the spheres of economics, internal and external policy, philosophy, sociology, religion and culture.
Indexed: RASB.
Published by: Rossiiskaya Akademiya Nauk, Institut Nauchnoi Informatsii po Obshchestvennym Naukam, Nakhimovskii pr-t 51/21, Moscow, 117997, Russian Federation. TEL 7-095-1288930, FAX 7-095-4202261, info@inion.ru, http://www.inion.ru. **Dist. by:** East View Information Services, 10601 Wayzata Blvd, Minneapolis, MN 55305. TEL 952-252-1201, 800-477-1005, FAX 952-252-1202, info@eastview.com, http://www.eastview.com.

327 RUS ISSN 1810-6439
DK510.764
ROSSIYA V GLOBAL'NOI POLITIKE; zhurnal o mirovoi politike i mezhdunarodnykh otnosheniyakh. Text in Russian. 2002. q. USD 170 foreign (effective 2005). **Document type:** *Journal, Consumer.* **Description:** Founded by leading Russian experts in international relations, it provides analysis and commentary on Russian and world policy.
Related titles: Online - full content ed.: ISSN 1810-6447.
Address: Nikitskii per. dom 2, Institut Evropy RAN, ofis 113, Moscow, Russian Federation. TEL 7-095-9807353, FAX 7-095-2922318. Ed. Fedor A Luk'yanov. **Dist. by:** East View Information Services, 10601 Wayzata Blvd, Minneapolis, MN 55305. TEL 952-252-1201, 800-477-1005, FAX 952-252-1202, info@eastview.com, http://www.eastview.com.

327 GBR ISSN 0035-8533
AP4
➤ **THE ROUND TABLE**; the commonwealth journal of international affairs. Text in English. 1910. bi-m. GBP 828 combined subscription in United Kingdom to institutions (print & online eds.); EUR 1,231, USD 1,546 combined subscription to institutions (print & online eds.) (effective 2012). adv. bk.rev. index. back issues avail.; reprint service avail. from PSC. **Document type:** *Journal, Academic/Scholarly.* **Description:** Covers of policy issues concerning the contemporary commonwealth and its role in international affairs, with occasional articles on themes of historical interest.
Related titles: Microfiche ed.; Microform ed.: (from PQC); Online - full text ed.: ISSN 1474-029X. GBP 745 in United Kingdom to institutions; EUR 1,109, USD 1,392 to institutions (effective 2012) (from IngentaConnect).
Indexed: A01, A02, A03, A08, A20, A22, A36, ABCPolSci, AmH&L, B21, BAS, C25, CA, CABA, DIP, E01, E12, E17, ESPM, F08, F12, GEOBASE, GH, H09, H10, HistAb, I08, I13, IBR, IBSS, IBZ, LID&ISL, LT, M02, M10, MEA&I, P02, P10, P13, P30, P34, P42, P45, P48, P53, P54, PAIS, PCI, PQC, PRA, PSA, R12, RASB, RRTA, S02, S03, S05, S11, S13, S16, SCOPUS, SPPI, SociolAb, T02, T05, TAR, W11, WBA, WMB.
—IE, Infotrieve, Ingenta. **CCC.**
Published by: Routledge (Subsidiary of: Taylor & Francis Group), 4 Park Sq, Milton Park, Abingdon, Oxon OX14 4RN, United Kingdom. TEL 44-20-70176000, FAX 44-20-70176336, subscriptions@tandf.co.uk, http://www.routledge.com. Ed. Venkat Iyer. Adv. contact Linda Hann TEL 44-1344-779945. **Subscr. to:** Taylor & Francis Ltd., Journals Customer Service, Sheepen Pl, Colchester, Essex CO3 3LP, United Kingdom. TEL 44-20-70175544, FAX 44-20-70175198.

➤ **ROUTLEDGE ADVANCES IN INTERNATIONAL POLITICAL ECONOMY.** *see* BUSINESS AND ECONOMICS—Economic Situation And Conditions

324.2 GBR
ROUTLEDGE E C P R STUDIES IN EUROPEAN POLITICAL SCIENCE. Text in English. 1996. irreg., latest 2009. price varies. bibl. Index. back issues avail. **Document type:** *Monographic series, Academic/Scholarly.* **Description:** Covers topics at the leading edge of current interest in political science and related fields, with contributions from European scholars and others who have presented work at ECPR workshops or research groups.
Published by: (European Consortium for Political Research), Routledge (Subsidiary of: Taylor & Francis Group), 4 Park Sq, Milton Park, Abingdon, Oxon OX14 4RN, United Kingdom. TEL 44-20-70176000, FAX 44-20-70176336, subscriptions@tandf.co.uk.

327 USA
ROUTLEDGE SECURITY IN ASIA SERIES. Text in English. 200?. irreg. **Document type:** *Monographic series, Academic/Scholarly.*
Related titles: Online - full text ed.: ISSN 2155-577X.
Published by: C R C Press, LLC (Subsidiary of: Taylor & Francis Group), 6000 Broken Sound Pky, NW, Ste 300, Boca Raton, FL 33487. TEL 561-994-0555, FAX 561-989-9732, journals@crcpress.com, http://www.crcpress.com.

ROUTLEDGE STUDIES IN DEFENCE AND PEACE ECONOMICS. *see* BUSINESS AND ECONOMICS—International Development And Assistance

327.117 USA
ROUTLEDGE STUDIES IN LIBERTY AND SECURITY. Text in English. 200?. irreg. **Document type:** *Monographic series, Academic/Scholarly.*
Related titles: Online - full text ed.: ISSN 2155-9414.
Published by: C R C Press, LLC (Subsidiary of: Taylor & Francis Group), 6000 Broken Sound Pky, NW, Ste 300, Boca Raton, FL 33487. TEL 561-994-0555, FAX 561-989-9732, journals@crcpress.com, http://www.crcpress.com.

327 GBR ISSN 1754-873X
ROUTLEDGE STUDIES IN MIDDLE EASTERN POLITICS. Text in English. 2004. irreg., latest 2009. price varies. **Document type:** *Monographic series, Academic/Scholarly.* **Description:** Covers issues such as international relations, foreign intervention, security, political Islam, democracy, ideology and public policy.
Published by: Routledge (Subsidiary of: Taylor & Francis Group), 4 Park Sq, Milton Park, Abingdon, Oxon OX14 4RN, United Kingdom. TEL 44-20-70176000, FAX 44-20-70176336, subscriptions@tandf.co.uk.

327 GBR ISSN 1750-7308
ROYAL HOLLOWAY UNIVERSITY OF LONDON. DEPARTMENT OF POLITICS AND INTERNATIONAL RELATIONS. POLITICS AND INTERNATIONAL WORKING PAPERS. Text in English. 2002. q. price varies. back issues avail. **Document type:** *Monographic series, Academic/Scholarly.* **Description:** Provides a forum for the publication of works-in-progress that reflect the research interests of staff and doctoral students in the Department of Politics and International Relations at Royal Holloway.
Related titles: Online - full text ed.: ISSN 1750-7316.
Published by: University of London, Royal Holloway, Department of Politics and International Relations, Royal Holloway, Egham, Surrey TW20 0EX, United Kingdom. TEL 44-1784-443149, FAX 44-1784-434375, Lisa.Dacunha@rhul.ac.uk. Eds. Isabelle Hertner, Lawrence Ampofo, Yasmin Khan.

327 GBR
ROYAL INSTITUTE OF INTERNATIONAL AFFAIRS. BRIEFING PAPERS. Text in English. 1996. irreg. back issues avail. **Document type:** *Proceedings.* **Description:** Presents informed background commentary on issues of topical interest or current research at Chatham House, and responding at very short notice to significant international events.
Related titles: Online - full text ed.: free (effective 2009).
Published by: Royal Institute of International Affairs, Chatham House, 10 St James's Sq, London, SW1Y 4LE, United Kingdom. TEL 44-20-79575700, FAX 44-20-79575710, contact@riia.org, http://www.riia.org.

RUNDBRIEF BILDUNGSAUFTRAG NORD - SUED. *see* EDUCATION

327 RUS ISSN 1810-6374
DK510.764
RUSSIA IN GLOBAL AFFAIRS. Text in English. 2002. q. **Document type:** *Journal, Consumer.*
Related titles: Online - full content ed.
—**CCC.**
Published by: Rossiya v Global'noi Politike, Nikitskii per. dom 2, Institut Evropy RAN, ofis 113, Moscow, Russian Federation. TEL 7-095-9807353, FAX 7-095-2922318, info@globalaffairs.ru, http://www.globalaffairs.ru.

327.47 DEU ISSN 1863-0421
RUSSIAN ANALYTICAL DIGEST. Text in English. 2006. bi-w. free (effective 2011). **Document type:** *Journal, Academic/Scholarly.* **Description:** Covers political, economic, and social developments in Russia and its regions.
Media: Online - full text.
Published by: (Swiss Federal Institute of Technology Zurich, Center for Security Studies CHE), Universitaet Bremen, Forschungsstelle Osteuropa/Bremen University, Research Centre for East European Studies, Klagenfurter Str 3, Bremen, 28359, Germany. TEL 49-421-2187891, FAX 49-421-2183269, publikationsreferat@osteuropa.uni-bremen.de, http://www.forschungsstelle.uni-bremen.de. Ed. Jeronim Perovic.

327 301 USA ISSN 1940-9419
➤ **RUSSIAN JOURNAL OF COMMUNICATION.** Abbreviated title: R J C. Text in English. 2008 (Feb.). irreg. (2-4/yr). USD 149 (effective 2010). bk.rev. reprints avail. **Document type:** *Journal, Academic/Scholarly.* **Description:** Publishes theoretical and empirical papers and essays that advance an understanding of communication in, with and about Russia.
Related titles: Online - full text ed.: ISSN 1940-9427. free (effective 2010).
Published by: (Russian Communication Association RUS), Marquette Books LLC, 3107 E 62nd Ave, Spokane, WA 99223. TEL 509-443-7057, FAX 509-448-2191, journals@marquettejournals.org, http://www.marquettebooks.com. Ed. Igor Klyukanov.

327 AUS
➤ **RUSSIAN POLITICS AND SOCIETY**; international review of Russian studies. Text in English. 1990. s-a. AUD 429 domestic to institutions; AUD 390 in New Zealand to institutions; GBP 148 in Europe to institutions; USD 218 elsewhere to institutions (effective 2006). adv. bk.rev. index. **Document type:** *Journal, Academic/Scholarly.* **Description:** Concerned with all aspects of contemporary Russian society, including the economy, labor and management, Russian foreign policy, political culture and leadership, minorities in Russia, religion, women studies, youth organizations, vocational training, schools and higher education.
Former titles (until 1995): Russian Society; Soviet Society (1034-7437); Soviet Review (1033-6257)
Published by: James Nicholas Publishers, Pty. Ltd., PO Box 5179, South Melbourne, VIC 3205, Australia. TEL 61-3-96905955, FAX 61-3-96992040, custservice@jnponline.com, http://www.jamesnicholaspublishers.com.au. Ed. Joseph Zajda. Pub. Rea Zajda. R&P Mary Berchmans. Adv. contact Irene Schevchenko.

327.47 DEU ISSN 1613-3390
RUSSLANDANALYSEN. Text in German. 2003. w. **Document type:** *Journal, Academic/Scholarly.*
Media: Online - full content.
Published by: Universitaet Bremen, Forschungsstelle Osteuropa/Bremen University, Research Centre for East European Studies, Klagenfurter Str 3, Bremen, 28359, Germany. TEL 49-421-2187891, FAX 49-421-2183269, publikationsreferat@osteuropa.uni-bremen.de, http://www.forschungsstelle.uni-bremen.de. Eds. Hans-Hennig Schroeder, Heiko Pleines.

327 USA ISSN 1945-4716
D839
➤ **THE S A I S REVIEW OF INTERNATIONAL AFFAIRS.** (School of Advanced International Studies) Text in English. 1956-1975; resumed 1981. s-a. USD 98 to institutions (print or online ed.); USD 137.20 combined subscription to institutions (print & online eds.); USD 59 per issue to institutions (effective 2011). adv. bk.rev. illus. index. 224 p./no.; back issues avail.; reprint service avail. from PSC. **Document type:** *Journal, Academic/Scholarly.* **Description:** Analyses contemporary international issues and recent publications on foreign affairs.
Formerly (until 2004): S A I S Review (0036-0775)
Related titles: Online - full text ed.: ISSN 1945-4724.
Indexed: A22, A26, ABCPolSci, ABS&EES, AMB, AmH&L, B04, BAS, BRD, CA, DIP, E01, E08, G06, G07, G08, HistAb, I05, I07, I13, IBR, IBSS, IBZ, LID&ISL, M05, M10, P02, P06, P10, P27, P34, P42, P45, P47, P48, P53, P54, PAIS, PCI, PQC, PSA, S02, S03, S09, S11, SCOPUS, SSAI, SSAb, SSI, SociolAb, T02, W01, W02, W03, W05.
—BLDSC (8070.270000), IE, Infotrieve, Ingenta. **CCC.**
Published by: (The Paul H. Nitze School of Advanced International Studies, Johns Hopkins University, Foreign Policy Institute, School of Advanced International Studies), The Johns Hopkins University Press, 2715 N Charles St, Baltimore, MD 21218. TEL 410-516-6900, FAX 410-516-6968, bjs@press.jhu.edu. Ed. Emily McLeod. Pub. William M Breichner. Circ: 259. **Subscr. to:** PO Box 19966, Baltimore, MD 21211. TEL 410-516-6987, 800-548-1784, FAX 410-516-3866, jrnlcirc@press.jhu.edu.

P

327 ZWE
S A P E S SEMINAR AND OCCASIONAL PAPER SERIES. Text in English. 1989. irreg. (8-10/yr.). price varies. **Document type:** *Monographic series.* **Description:** Short monographs and research papers on issues pertaining to the economy, politics and development of Southern African countries.
Published by: (Southern Africa Political Economy Series), S A P E S Trust, Belgravia, Mt. Pleasant, Deary Ave 4, PO Box MP 111, Harare, Zimbabwe. TEL 263-4-727875, FAX 263-4-732735.

S A V U S A - N I Z A STUDENT PUBLICATION SERIES. (South Africa Vrije Universiteit Strategic Alliances - Nederlands Instituut voor Zuidelijk Afrika) *see* BUSINESS AND ECONOMICS—Economic Situation And Conditions

S A V U S A SERIES. (South Africa Vrije Universiteit Strategic Alliances) *see* BUSINESS AND ECONOMICS—Economic Situation And Conditions

327.1 USA ISSN 1946-827X
S F S NEWS. (School of Foreign Service) Text in English. 2007. q. **Document type:** *Journal, Academic/Scholarly.*
Published by: Georgetown University, School of Foreign Service, 301 InterCultural Ctr, 37th & O St NW, Washington, DC 20057. TEL 202-687-5696, FAX 202-687-1431, http://sfs.georgetown.edu.

327 614.7 JPN ISSN 1341-6510
BQ8400
S G I QUARTERLY. Text in English. 1981-1993; resumed 1995. q. free. adv. **Document type:** *Journal, Academic/Scholarly.* **Description:** Provides information about SGI's activities around the world and to highlight initiatives and perspectives on peace, education and culture.
Formerly (until 1993): S G I. Soka Gakkai International (0288-2930)
Related titles: Online - full content ed.
Indexed: RASB.
Published by: Soka Gakkai International, Josei Toda International Center, 15-3 Samon-cho, Shinjuku-ku, Tokyo, 160-0017, Japan. TEL 81-3-53609831, FAX 81-3-53609885, sgipr@sgi.gr.jp.

327 SWE ISSN 1652-5795
S I D A. WORKING PAPERS. CAPACITY DEVELOPMENT. (Swedish International Development Cooperation Agency) Text in English. 1998. irreg. back issues avail. **Document type:** *Government.*
Related titles: Online - full text ed.
Published by: Styrelsen foer Internationel Utvecklingssamarbete/ Swedish International Development Cooperation Agency (SIDA), Valhallavaegen 199, Stockholm, 10525, Sweden. TEL 46-8-6985000, FAX 46-8-208864, sida@sida.se.

327 SWE ISSN 1654-0700
S I I A PAPERS. (The Swedish Institute of International Affairs) Text in English. 1981. irreg. price varies. back issues avail. **Document type:** *Monographic series, Academic/Scholarly.*
Formerly (until 2007): The Swedish Institute of International Affairs. Conference Papers (0349-7798)
—BLDSC (8276.830000).
Published by: Utrikespolitiska Institutet/The Swedish Institute of International Affairs, Drottning Kristinas Vaeg 37, PO Box 27035, Stockholm, 10251, Sweden. TEL 46-8-51176800, FAX 46-8-51176899, info@ui.se.

327.1745 GBR ISSN 0267-2537
UG447
S I P R I CHEMICAL & BIOLOGICAL WARFARE STUDIES. Text in English. 1985. irreg., latest vol.19, 2001. price varies. back issues avail. **Document type:** *Monographic series, Academic/Scholarly.* **Description:** Series of studies intended primarily for specialists in the field of CBW arms control and for people engaged in other areas of international relations or security affairs whose work could benefit from a deeper understanding of particular CBW matters.
Indexed: LID&ISL.
—BLDSC (8286.040000).
Published by: (Stockholm International Peace Research Institute SWE), Oxford University Press, Great Clarendon St, Oxford, OX2 6DP, United Kingdom. TEL 44-1865-556767, FAX 44-1865-556646, enquiry@oup.co.uk, http://www.oup-usa.org/catalogs/general/series/. **Subscr. in N. America to:** Oxford University Press, 2001 Evans Rd, Cary, NC 27513. TEL 919-677-0977 ext 5777, 800-852-7323, FAX 919-677-1714, jnlorders@oup-usa.org, http://www.us.oup.com.

327.172 SWE ISSN 1652-0432
S I P R I POLICY PAPER. (Stockholm International Peace Research Institute) Text in English. 2002. irreg., latest vol.28, 2011. price varies. back issues avail. **Document type:** *Monographic series.*
Related titles: Online - full text ed.: ISSN 1653-7548.
Published by: Stockholm International Peace Research Institute, Signalistgatan 9, Solna, 16970, Sweden. TEL 46-8-6559700, FAX 46-8-6559733, sipri@sipri.org, http://www.sipri.org.

327 GBR ISSN 1367-1693
S I P R I RESEARCH REPORT. (Stockholm International Peace Research Institute) Text in English. 197?. irreg., latest 2009. price varies. back issues avail. **Document type:** *Monographic series, Academic/ Scholarly.* **Description:** Considers the experiences of those countries which, since the end of the Cold War, have participated in United Nations peacekeeping operations for the first time. They include Germany, Japan, Russia, and the USA. Lessons are drawn from their experience for future peacekeeping operations.
Indexed: LID&ISL.
—BLDSC (8286.100000), IE, Ingenta. **CCC.**
Published by: (Stockholm International Peace Research Institute SWE), Oxford University Press, Great Clarendon St, Oxford, OX2 6DP, United Kingdom. TEL 44-1865-556767, FAX 44-1865-556646, enquiry@oup.co.uk, http://www.oup-usa.org/catalogs/general/series/.

327.172 SWE ISSN 1654-8264
S I P R I UPDATE; global security & arms control. (Stockholm International Peace Research Institute) Text in English. 2008. m. free. back issues avail. **Document type:** *Newsletter, Consumer.*
Media: Online - full content.
Published by: Stockholm International Peace Research Institute, Signalistgatan 9, Solna, 16970, Sweden. TEL 46-8-6559700, FAX 46-8-6559733, sipri@sipri.org.

327 GBR ISSN 0953-0282
S I P R I YEARBOOK; armaments, disarmament and international security. Text in English. 1969. a. price varies. back issues avail.; reprint service avail. from SCH. **Document type:** *Yearbook, Academic/Scholarly.* **Description:** Detailed information on arms and arms control developments in nuclear weapons and world military expenditure.
Former titles (until 1987): World Armaments and Disarmament (0347-2205); (until 1972): S I P R I Yearbook of World Armaments and Disarmament (0579-5508)
Indexed: A22, CA, I13, LID&ISL, P42, PSA, RASB, SCOPUS, T02.
—BLDSC (8286.110000), IE, Ingenta. **CCC.**
Published by: (Stockholm International Peace Research Institute SWE), Oxford University Press, Great Clarendon St, Oxford, OX2 6DP, United Kingdom. TEL 44-1865-556767, FAX 44-1865-556646, enquiry@oup.co.uk, http://www.oup-usa.org/catalogs/general/series/.

327.12 CAN ISSN 1912-1598
S I R C ANNUAL REPORT. (Security Intelligence Review Committee) Text in English. 1985. a. **Document type:** *Government.*
Former titles (until 2005): S I R C Report (1701-0438); (until 2000): Canada. Security Intelligence Review Committee. Annual Report (1497-1933)
Media: Online - full text. **Related titles:** ◆ Print ed.: S I R C Report. ISSN 1701-2287; French ed.: C S A R S. Rapport Annuel. ISSN 1912-1601. 1985.
Published by: Security Intelligence Review Committee/Comite de Surveillance des Activites de Renseignement de Securite, PO Box 2430, Sta. D, Ottawa, ON K1P 5W5, Canada. TEL 613-990-8441, FAX 613-990-5230.

327.12 CAN ISSN 1701-2287
S I R C REPORT. Variant title: Rapport du C S A R S. Text in English. 1985. a. **Document type:** *Government.*
Former titles (until 2000): S I R C Annual Report (1701-2279); (until 1999): Canada. Security Intelligence Review Committee. Annual Report (0833-4129)
Related titles: ◆ Online - full text ed.: S I R C Annual Report. ISSN 1912-1598.
Published by: Security Intelligence Review Committee/Comite de Surveillance des Activites de Renseignement de Securite, PO Box 2430, Sta. D, Ottawa, ON K1P 5W5, Canada. TEL 613-990-8441, FAX 613-990-5230.

SAMSPRAAK. *see* LINGUISTICS

SAN MARINO (REPUBBLICA). DIPARTIMENTO AFFARI ESTERI. NOTIZIA. *see* PUBLIC ADMINISTRATION

327 GBR ISSN 1468-1153
THE SANDHURST CONFERENCE SERIES. Text in English. 2000. irreg., latest 2004. price varies. back issues avail. **Document type:** *Monographic series, Academic/Scholarly.*
—BLDSC (8072.955770).
Published by: Routledge (Subsidiary of: Taylor & Francis Group), 4 Park Sq, Milton Park, Abingdon, Oxon OX14 4RN, United Kingdom. TEL 44-20-70176000, FAX 44-20-70176336, subscriptions@tandf.co.uk. Ed. Matthew Midlane.

SARVODAYA. *see* SOCIAL SERVICES AND WELFARE

327 DEU ISSN 1861-843X
SCHRIFTEN ZU MITTEL- UND OSTEUROPA IN DER EUROPAEISCHEN INTEGRATION. Text in German. 2006. irreg., latest vol.10, 2010. price varies. **Document type:** *Monographic series, Academic/Scholarly.*
Published by: Verlag Dr. Kovac, Leverkusenstr 13, Hamburg, 22761, Germany. TEL 49-40-3988800, FAX 49-40-39888055, info@verlagdrkovac.de. Eds. Gerald Sander, Lubos Tichy.

327.0904 DEU ISSN 1612-9296
SCHRIFTEN ZUR EUROPAPOLITIK. Text in German. 2004. irreg., latest vol.10, 2009. price varies. **Document type:** *Monographic series, Academic/Scholarly.*
Published by: Verlag Dr. Kovac, Leverkusenstr 13, Hamburg, 22761, Germany. TEL 49-40-3988800, FAX 49-40-39888055, info@verlagdrkovac.de.

327 DEU ISSN 1618-0046
SCHRIFTEN ZUR INTERNATIONALEN POLITIK. Text in German. 2001. irreg., latest vol.27, 2010. price varies. **Document type:** *Monographic series, Academic/Scholarly.*
Published by: Verlag Dr. Kovac, Leverkusenstr 13, Hamburg, 22761, Germany. TEL 49-40-3988800, FAX 49-40-39888055, info@verlagdrkovac.de.

327 DEU ISSN 1869-5175
▼ **SCHRIFTENREIHE SICHERHEITSPOLITIK.** Text in German. 2009. irreg., latest vol.4, 2010. price varies. **Document type:** *Monographic series, Academic/Scholarly.*
Published by: Verlag Dr. Koester, Rungestr 22-24, Berlin, 10179, Germany. TEL 49-30-76403224, FAX 49-30-76403227, verlag-koester@t-online.de.

327 AUT
▼ **SCHRIFTENREIHE ZUR INTERNATIONALEN POLITIK.** Text in German. 2009. irreg., latest vol.4, 2011. price varies. **Document type:** *Monographic series, Academic/Scholarly.*
Published by: Boehlau Verlag GmbH & Co.KG., Wiesingerstr 1, Vienna, W 1010, Austria. TEL 43-1-3302427, FAX 43-1-3302432, boehlau@boehlau.at, http://www.boehlau.at.

327 CHE
SCHWEIZERISCHE GESELLSCHAFT FUER AUSSENPOLITIK. SCHRIFTENREIHE. Text in German. 1972. irreg., latest vol.12, 1995. price varies. **Document type:** *Monographic series.*
Published by: (Schweizerische Gesellschaft fuer Aussenpolitik), Verlag Ruegger, Postfach 1470, Zuerich, 8040, Switzerland. TEL 41-1-4912130, FAX 41-1-4931176, info@rueggerverlag.ch.

SEA POWER. *see* MILITARY

SECURITE GLOBALE. *see* SOCIAL SCIENCES: COMPREHENSIVE WORKS

327.1 USA ISSN 0889-4876
SECURITY AFFAIRS. Text in English. 1978. q. per issue contribution. bk.rev. **Document type:** *Newsletter.*
Published by: Jewish Institute for National Security Affairs, 1779 Massachusetts Ave NW, Ste 515, Washington, DC 20036. TEL 202-667-3900, FAX 202-667-0601, info@jinsa.org, http://www.jinsa.org. Ed. James J Colbert.

327.172 GBR ISSN 0967-0106
JX1901 CODEN: SDIAER
➤ **SECURITY DIALOGUE.** Text in English. 1970. bi-m. USD 1,116, GBP 603 combined subscription to institutions (print & online eds.); USD 1,094, GBP 591 to institutions (effective 2011). adv. bk.rev. abstr.; bibl.; illus. Index. back issues avail.; reprint service avail. from PSC. **Document type:** *Journal, Academic/Scholarly.* **Description:** Seeks to provoke reflection through interregional dialogue on issues of global security along a variety of dimensions: the new international system, politics of fusion and fragmentation of states, as well as military, economic, political and environmental aspects.
Formerly (until 1992): Bulletin of Peace Proposals (0007-5035)
Related titles: Microform ed.: (from PQC); Online - full text ed.: ISSN 1460-3640. USD 1,004, GBP 543 to institutions (effective 2011).
Indexed: A01, A03, A08, A20, A22, AMB, ASCA, BAS, CA, CCME, CJA, CurCont, DIP, E01, ESPM, HRIR, HistAb, I13, IBR, IBSS, IBZ, LID&ISL, M10, P30, P34, P42, PAIS, PRA, PSA, Perlslam, RASB, RefugAb, RiskAb, S02, S03, SCOPUS, SOPODA, SPAA, SSCI, SociolAb, T02, V&AA, W07.
—BLDSC (8217.178000), IE, Infotrieve, Ingenta. **CCC.**
Published by: (International Peace Research Institute, Oslo NOR), Sage Publications Ltd. (Subsidiary of: Sage Publications, Inc.), 1 Oliver's Yard, 55 City Rd, London, EC1Y 1SP, United Kingdom. TEL 44-20-73248500, FAX 44-20-73248600, info@sagepub.co.uk, http://www.uk.sagepub.com/home.nav. Ed. J Peter Burgess. adv.: B&W page GBP 400; 140 x 210. **Subscr. in the Americas to:** Sage Publications, Inc., 2455 Teller Rd, Thousand Oaks, CA 91320. TEL 805-499-9774, FAX 805-499-0871, journals@sagepub.com.

327.12 USA ISSN 0963-6412
UA10.5
➤ **SECURITY STUDIES (QUARTERLY).** Text in English. 1991. q. GBP 388 combined subscription in United Kingdom to institutions (print & online eds.); EUR 514, USD 644 combined subscription to institutions (print & online eds.) (effective 2012). adv. bk.rev. index. back issues avail.; reprint service avail. from PSC. **Document type:** *Journal, Academic/Scholarly.* **Description:** Covers international security and the role of force in international politics.
Related titles: Online - full text ed.: ISSN 1556-1852. GBP 349 in United Kingdom to institutions; EUR 463, USD 579 to institutions (effective 2012) (from IngentaConnect).
Indexed: A01, A20, A22, AUNI, CA, CurCont, DIP, E01, ESPM, I02, I13, IBR, IBSS, IBZ, LID&ISL, M05, P02, P10, P34, P42, P47, P48, P53, P54, PAIS, PQC, PSA, RiskAb, S02, S03, S11, SCOPUS, SSCI, T02, W07.
—IE, Ingenta. **CCC.**
Published by: Routledge (Subsidiary of: Taylor & Francis Group), 325 Chestnut St, Ste 800, Philadelphia, PA 19106. TEL 800-354-1420, FAX 215-625-2940, journals@routledge.com, http://www.routledge.com. Ed. William C Wohlforth. Adv. contact Linda Hann TEL 44-1344-779945.

327 GBR ISSN 2047-0304
▼ **SELF KNOWLEDGE GLOBAL RESPONSIBILITY.** Text in English. 2011. 3/yr. GBP 15 domestic to non-members; GBP 19 in Europe to non-members; GBP 22 elsewhere to non-members; GBP 6 per issue domestic to non-members; GBP 7 per issue in Europe to non-members; GBP 8 per issue elsewhere to non-members; free to members (effective 2011). **Document type:** *Journal, Academic/ Scholarly.* **Description:** Aims to present a unique reflection on contemporary life, that of the essential unity of the personal and the global.
Related titles: Online - full text ed.: GBP 3 per issue (effective 2011).
Published by: S K G R, Puckham Barn, Whittington, Cheltenham, GL54 4EX, United Kingdom. Ed. Aaron Cass.

327.663 SEN
SENEGAL. LISTE DU CORPS DIPLOMATIQUE. Text in French. irreg.
Supersedes: Senegal. Service du Protocole. Liste Diplomatique et Consulaire
Published by: Imprimerie Nationale, Rufisque, Senegal.

327 FRA ISSN 1248-2293
SENNACIECA REVUO. Text in Esperanto. 1992. a., latest 2009. bk.rev. **Document type:** *Magazine, Consumer.*
Indexed: MLA-IB.
Published by: Sennacieca Asocio Tutmonda/Worldwide Non-Nationalist Assn., 67 av. Gambetta, Paris, 75020, France. TEL 33-1-47978705, FAX 33-1-47977190, satesperanto@free.fr.

SEQUENCIA; estudos juridicos e politicos. *see* LAW

327 BRA
SERIE CAPISTRANO DE ABREU. Text in Portuguese. 1982. a.
Published by: Colegio Pedro II, Secretaria de Ensino, Campo de Sao Cristovao, 177, Rio De Janeiro, RJ CEP 20291, Brazil.

328 ESP ISSN 2172-1009
SERIE ESTUDIOS INTERNACIONALES Y EUROPEOS DE CADIZ. Text in Spanish. 2004. irreg. **Document type:** *Monographic series, Academic/Scholarly.*
Published by: Dykinson, S.L., C Melendez Valdes, 61, Madrid, 28015, Spain. TEL 34-91-5442869, FAX 34-91-5446040, info@dykinson.com, http://www.dykinson.com/.

327 SGP ISSN 1793-1711
SERIES ON THE IRAQ WAR AND ITS CONSEQUENCES. Text in English. 2003. irreg., latest vol.3, 2010. price varies. back issues avail. **Document type:** *Monographic series, Academic/Scholarly.* **Description:** Provides analyses on the war in Iraq.
Published by: World Scientific Publishing Co. Pte. Ltd., 5 Toh Tuck Link, Singapore, 596224, Singapore. TEL 65-6466-5775, FAX 65-6467-7667, wspc@wspc.com.sg, http://www.worldscientific.com. **Dist. by:** World Scientific Publishing Co., Inc., 27 Warren St, Ste 401-402, Hackensack, NJ 07601. TEL 201-487-9655, 800-227-7562, FAX 201-487-9656, 888-977-2665, wspc@wspc.com; World Scientific Publishing Ltd., 57 Shelton St, London WC2H 9HE, United Kingdom. TEL 44-207-8360888, FAX 44-207-8362020, sales@wspc.co.uk.

341.72 USA ISSN 1940-011X
JZ5511.2
SERVIAM; stability solutions in a dangerous world. Text in English. 2007 (Oct.). bi-m. USD 24.95 (effective 2008). **Document type:** *Magazine, Trade.* **Description:** Covers government policy, law enforcement and industry information for private security contractors in the global stability industry.

Published by: E E I Communications Inc., 66 Canal Center Plaza, Ste 200, Alexandria, VA 22314. TEL 703-683-0683, FAX 703-683-4915. Ed. J Waller.

SHALOM. *see* ETHNIC INTERESTS

327.172 USA ISSN 0197-9116
SHALOM; Jewish peace letter. Text in English. 1962. q. USD 5 (effective 2001). bk.rev. back issues avail. **Document type:** *Newsletter.* **Description:** Addresses the question of peace.
Related titles: Online - full text ed.
Published by: Jewish Peace Fellowship, PO Box 271, Nyack, NY 10960-0271. TEL 914-358-4601, FAX 914-358-4924, jpf@forusa.org, http://www.jewishpeacefellowship.org. Ed., R&P Murray Polner. Circ: 3,000 (controlled).

SHEWAI SHUIWU/INTERNATIONAL TAXATION IN CHINA. *see* BUSINESS AND ECONOMICS—Public Finance, Taxation

327 CHN ISSN 0583-0176
SHIJIE ZHISHI/WORLD AFFAIRS. Text in Chinese. 1934. s-m. USD 98.40 (effective 2009). **Document type:** *Journal, Academic/Scholarly.*
Indexed: RASB.
—East View.
Published by: Shijie Zhishi Chubanshe/World Affairs Press, 51, Ganmian Hutong, Dongcheng-qu, Beijing, 100010, China. TEL 86-10-65265934. Ed. Yao Dongqiao.

327 355 MYS
SHOW DAILY. Text in English. irreg. (distributed daily during exhibitions). free. **Document type:** *Monographic series, Trade.* **Description:** Contains complete coverage of all press conferences, interviews with industry CEOs and top military brass, contract signing ceremonies, official VIP visits, live product demonstrations such as aerial displays and other news worthy items.
Published by: A D P R Consult (M) Sdn. Bhd., 19th Fl, SIME Bank Bldg, No.4 Jalan Sultan Sulaiman, Kuala Lumpur, 50000, Malaysia. TEL 603-22731355, 603-22735315, FAX 603-22735318, info@adprconsult.com, http://www.adprconsult.com/.

328 CHL ISSN 0718-2910
SI SOMOS AMERICANOS. Text in Spanish. 1998. s-a. **Document type:** *Journal, Academic/Scholarly.*
Published by: Universidad Arturo Prat, Instituto de Estudios Internacionales, Ave Manuel Rodriguez Norte 47, Santiago, Chile. TEL 56-2-3832457, FAX 56-2-3832425, http://www.unap.cl/p4_inte/site/edic/base/port/home.html. Ed. Isaac Caro.

327 DEU ISSN 0175-274X
JX1903
SICHERHEIT UND FRIEDEN. Short title: S und F. Text in German. 1983. q. EUR 84 (effective 2011). adv. reprint service avail. from SCH. **Document type:** *Journal, Academic/Scholarly.*
Indexed: CA, DIP, IBR, IBZ, P42, PAIS, PSA, SCOPUS, T02.
—BLDSC (8053.653600). **CCC.**
Published by: Nomos Verlagsgesellschaft mbH und Co. KG, Waldseestr 3-5, Baden-Baden, 76530, Germany. TEL 49-7221-21040, FAX 49-7221-210427, marketing@nomos.de, nomos@nomos.de, http://www.nomos.de. Ed. Patricia Schneider. Adv. contact Bettina Roos. Circ: 800 (paid and controlled).

327 CHN ISSN 1003-3831
AS452.S767
SICHUAN WEIYUE XUEYUAN XUEBAO/SICHUAN INTERNATIONAL STUDIES UNIVERSITY. JOURNAL. Text in Chinese. 1981. bi-m. USD 28.20 (effective 2009). **Document type:** *Journal, Academic/Scholarly.*
Related titles: Online - full text ed.
—BLDSC (5064.436000), East View.
Published by: Sichuan Weiyue Xueyuan/Sichuan International Studies University, Shapingba District, Chongqing, 400031, China. TEL 86-23-65385313. Ed. Renzhe Lan. **Dist. by:** China International Book Trading Corp, 35 Chegongzhuang Xilu, Haidian District, PO Box 399, Beijing 100044, China. TEL 86-10-68412045, FAX 86-10-68412023, cibtc@mail.cibtc.com.cn, http://www.cibtc.com.cn.

327.85 BOL
SIEMPRE PERU. Text in Spanish. 1972. a. free. adv. charts; illus. **Document type:** *Newspaper.* **Description:** Includes articles on Peruvian economic, political and cultural issues, Peru-Bolivia relations, Peruvian foreign policy, history and tourism.
Published by: Embajada del Peru en Bolivia, Calle Fernando Guachalla Cdra. 3, Sopocachi, La Paz, Bolivia. TEL 591-2-376773, FAX 591-2-367640. Adv. contact Elmer Schialer. Circ: 10,000.

327 LBN
AS-SIHAFA WAL-I'LAM/PRESS AND INFORMATION/PRESSE ET INFORMATION. Text in Arabic. 1987. m. USD 3,000 (effective 2001). index. **Document type:** *Consumer.* **Description:** Analyzes Arab world affairs as reported in Arab and international media.
Published by: Dar Naaman lith-Thaqafah, P O Box 567, Jounieh, Lebanon. TEL 961-9-935096, FAX 961-9-935096. Ed. Naji Naaman.

327 UAE
AL-SIJIL AL-SHAHRI LI-AHDATH AL-ALAM/MONTHLY RECORD OF WORLD EVENTS. Text in Arabic. 1981. m. **Description:** Reviews international events and their impact on the U.A.E.
Published by: Ministry of Information and Culture, Information Department, PO Box 17, Abu Dhabi, United Arab Emirates. TEL 453000. Circ: 1,000 (controlled).

327.11 NOR ISSN 0802-6602
D839
DET SIKKERHETSPOLITISKE BIBLIOTEK/SECURITY POLICY LIBRARY/SICHERHEITPOLITISCHE BIBLIOTHEK. Text in Multiple languages. 1986. irreg., latest 2007. back issues avail. **Document type:** *Monographic series, Consumer.*
Related titles: Online - full text ed.: ISSN 1502-2781. 2000.
Published by: Den Norske Atlanterhavskomite/The Norwegian Atlantic Committee, Fridjof Nansens Plass 8, Oslo, 0160, Norway. TEL 47-22-403600, FAX 47-22-403610, post@dnak.org, http://www.dnak.org.

327 TWN ISSN 0377-5321
E183.8.T3
SINO-AMERICAN RELATIONS. Text in Chinese. 1975. q. USD 34. adv. bk.rev. **Document type:** *Academic/Scholarly.*
Indexed: BAS, CLI, MLA-IB.
Published by: Chinese Culture University Press, Chinese Culture University, Hwa Kang, 11114, Taiwan. TEL 886-2-861-5487, FAX 886-2-861-7164. Ed. Yu Tang Daniel Lew. Circ: 1,500.

327 GBR ISSN 0959-2318
U240
➤ **SMALL WARS AND INSURGENCIES.** Text in English. 1990. q. GBP 487 combined subscription in United Kingdom to institutions (print & online eds.); EUR 642, USD 808 combined subscription to institutions (print & online eds.) (effective 2012). adv. bk.rev. index. back issues avail.; reprint service avail. from PSC. **Document type:** *Journal, Academic/Scholarly.* **Description:** Provides a forum to discuss the historical, political, social, economic, and psychological aspects of conflict, short of general war.
Incorporates (1992-2005): Low Intensity Conflict & Law Enforcement (0966-2847)
Related titles: Online - full text ed.: ISSN 1743-9558. GBP 438 in United Kingdom to institutions; EUR 577, USD 727 to institutions (effective 2012) (from IngentaConnect).
Indexed: A22, AmH&L, B21, BAS, CA, E01, E17, ESPM, HistAb, I02, I13, IBR, IBSS, IBZ, LID&ISL, P02, P10, P42, P47, P48, P53, P54, PAIS, PQC, PSA, RiskAb, S02, S03, S11, SCOPUS, SociolAb, T02.
—IE, Infotrieve, Ingenta. **CCC.**
Published by: Routledge (Subsidiary of: Taylor & Francis Group), 4 Park Sq, Milton Park, Abingdon, Oxon OX14 4RN, United Kingdom. TEL 44-20-70176000, FAX 44-20-70176336, subscriptions@tandf.co.uk, http://www.routledge.com. Eds. Paul B Rich, Thomas Mockaitis, Thomas-Durell Young. **Subscr. to:** Taylor & Francis Ltd., Journals Customer Service, Sheepen Pl, Colchester, Essex CO3 3LP, United Kingdom. TEL 44-20-70175544, FAX 44-20-70175198.

➤ **SMALL WARS JOURNAL.** *see* MILITARY

327 NLD ISSN 1385-3376
➤ **SOCIAL, ECONOMIC AND POLITICAL STUDIES OF THE MIDDLE EAST AND ASIA.** Text in Dutch. 1971. irreg., latest vol.105, 2008. price varies. back issues avail. **Document type:** *Monographic series, Academic/Scholarly.* **Description:** Scholarly studies of economic, political, social, religious and historical issues affecting the Middle East, with particular emphasis on development related concerns, the role of women in Islamic societies, recent political history and law in Middle Eastern countries.
Formerly (until 1996): Social, Economic and Political Studies of the Middle East (0085-6193)
Indexed: IZBG.
Published by: Brill, PO Box 9000, Leiden, 2300 PA, Netherlands. TEL 31-71-5353500, FAX 31-71-5317532, cs@brill.nl, http://www.brill.nl. Ed. Dale F Eickelman. R&P Elizabeth Venekamp. **Dist. by:** Turpin Distribution Services Ltd., Pegasus Dr, Stratton Business Park, Biggleswade, Bedfordshire SG18 8QB, United Kingdom. TEL 44-1767-604954, FAX 44-1767-601640, custserv@turpin-distribution.com, http://www.turpin-distribution.com/.

327 USA ISSN 1043-1578
HV6001
➤ **SOCIAL JUSTICE (SAN FRANCISCO)**; a journal of crime, conflict and world order. Text in English. 1974. q. USD 114 domestic to institutions; USD 118 foreign to institutions (effective 2010). adv. bk.rev. charts; stat. back issues avail.; reprint service avail. from PSC. **Document type:** *Journal, Academic/Scholarly.* **Description:** Combines analyses of global issues (peaceful resolution of conflicts, immigration, and human rights) with domestic policy concerns such as reducing crime as well as race and gender discrimination.
Incorporates (197?-1986): Contemporary Marxism (0193-8703); Which was formerly (until 1980): Synthesis (San Francisco) (0193-869X); Formerly (until 1988): Crime and Social Justice (0094-7571); Which incorporated (1965-1975): Issues in Criminology (0021-2385)
Related titles: Microform ed.: (from PQC); Online - full text ed.
Indexed: A01, A02, A03, A08, A20, A21, A22, A25, A26, AC&P, APW, AltPI, AmH&L, B04, BRD, CA, CJA, CJPI, DIP, E02, E03, E07, E08, ERI, EdA, EdI, FR, G05, G06, G07, G08, G10, H09, HRIR, HistAb, I05, I07, IBR, IBSS, IBZ, IPARL, LeftInd, M01, M02, M06, MEA&I, P02, P06, P07, P10, P27, P30, P34, P42, P45, P46, P48, P53, P54, PAIS, PCI, PQC, PRA, PSA, PerIslam, RASB, RI-1, RI-2, S02, S03, S05, S08, S09, S11, S21, S23, SCOPUS, SOPODA, SRRA, SSA, SSAI, SSAb, SSI, SociolAb, T02, W01, W02, W03, W05, W09.
—BLDSC (8318.121300), IE, Infotrieve, Ingenta. **CCC.**
Published by: Global Options, PO Box 40601, San Francisco, CA 94140. TEL 415-550-1703, FAX 510-620-0668. Ed., R&P Gregory Shank. Adv. contact Suzie Dod Thomas TEL 510-620-0660. Circ: 3,500 (paid).

301 USA
SOCIOLOGICAL STUDIES. Text in English. 19??. irreg. back issues avail. **Document type:** *Government.*
Formerly: U S S R Serial Reports: Sociological Studies
Indexed: EIP.
Published by: (Joint Publications Research Service), U.S. Department of Commerce, National Technical Information Service, 5301 Shawnee Rd, Alexandria, VA 22312. TEL 703-605-6000, info@ntis.gov, http://www.ntis.gov.

327 SWE ISSN 1104-5965
SOEDRA AFRIKA. Text in Swedish. 1964. 11/yr. SEK 150 domestic; SEK 200 foreign (effective 2005). adv. bk.rev. illus. cum.index: 1968-1980 (vols.1-55). **Document type:** *Bulletin, Consumer.*
Former titles (until 1994): Afrikabulletinen (0346-9158); (until 1975): Soedra Afrika (0038-0490); (until 1967): Syd- och Sydvaestafrika; Incorporates (1986-1993): Soedra Afrika Nyheter (0283-5738)
Published by: Afrikagrupperna i Sverige/Africa Groups of Sweden, Tegelviksgatan 40, Stockholm, 11641, Sweden. TEL 46-8-4427060, FAX 46-8-6403660, post@afrikagrupperna.se, http://www.afrikagrupperna.se. Ed. Kerstin Bjurman TEL 46-8-4427080. Circ: 3,000.

327.68 ZAF
DT770
SOUTH AFRICAN INSTITUTE OF INTERNATIONAL AFFAIRS. ANNUAL REPORT. Text in English. 1978. a. price varies. **Document type:** *Corporate.*
Former titles: South African Institute of International Affairs. Biennial Report of the National Chairman; (until 1984): South African Institute of International Affairs. Report of the National Chairman; South African Institute of International Affairs. Biennial Council Report; Supersedes (1966-1977): South African Institute of International Affairs. Annual Report (0081-2439)
Published by: South African Institute of International Affairs, PO Box 31596, Braamfontein, Johannesburg 2017, South Africa. TEL 27-11-3392021, FAX 27-11-3392154, info@saiia.org.za, http://www.saiia.org.za.

327.68 GBR ISSN 1022-0461
DT1945
➤ **THE SOUTH AFRICAN JOURNAL OF INTERNATIONAL AFFAIRS.** Variant title: S A J I A. Text in English. 1993. 3/yr. GBP 291 combined subscription in United Kingdom to institutions (print & online eds.); EUR 468, USD 584 combined subscription to institutions (print & online eds.) (effective 2012). adv. bk.rev. back issues avail.; reprint service avail. from PSC. **Document type:** *Journal, Academic/Scholarly.* **Description:** Features original essays and review articles on topics in international affairs.
Formed by the merger of (1977-1992): International Affairs Bulletin (0258-7270); (1975-1992): Southern Africa Record (0377-5445)
Related titles: Online - full text ed.: ISSN 1938-0275. GBP 262 in United Kingdom to institutions; EUR 421, USD 526 to institutions (effective 2012).
Indexed: CA, IBSS, ISAP, LID&ISL, P42, PAIS, PRA, PSA, SCOPUS, T02.
—BLDSC (8338.880000), IE, Ingenta. **CCC.**
Published by: (South African Institute of International Affairs ZAF), Routledge (Subsidiary of: Taylor & Francis Group), 4 Park Sq, Milton Park, Abingdon, Oxon OX14 4RN, United Kingdom. TEL 44-20-70176000, FAX 44-20-70176336, journals@routledge.com, http://www.routledge.com. Ed. Elizabeth Sidiropoulos. Adv. contact Linda Hann TEL 44-1344-779945.

327.68 ZAF ISSN 1026-5651
DT1945
➤ **SOUTH AFRICAN YEARBOOK OF INTERNATIONAL AFFAIRS.** Text in English. 1996. a. ZAR 170 (effective 2003). bk.rev. back issues avail. **Document type:** *Journal, Academic/Scholarly.*
Indexed: CA, P42, PSA, SCOPUS, T02.
Published by: South African Institute of International Affairs, PO Box 31596, Braamfontein, Johannesburg 2017, South Africa. TEL 27-11-3392021, FAX 27-11-3392154, TELEX 4-27291 SA, http://www.wits.ac.za/saiia.html. Ed. Greg Mills. R&P Peter Fabin.

➤ **SOUTH-EAST EUROPE.** *see* BUSINESS AND ECONOMICS—Economic Situation And Conditions

327 GBR ISSN 1360-8746
JN94.A1 CODEN: SESPFS
➤ **SOUTH EUROPEAN SOCIETY & POLITICS.** Text in English. 1996. q. GBP 407 combined subscription in United Kingdom to institutions (print & online eds.); EUR 538, USD 675 combined subscription to institutions (print & online eds.) (effective 2012). adv. bk.rev. back issues avail.; reprint service avail. from PSC. **Document type:** *Journal, Academic/Scholarly.* **Description:** Provides a forum for comparative interdisciplinary (social, economic, political, cultural) studies of southern Europe (principally Portugal, Spain, Italy, and Greece).
Related titles: Online - full text ed.: ISSN 1743-9612. GBP 366 in United Kingdom to institutions; EUR 484, USD 607 to institutions (effective 2012) (from IngentaConnect).
Indexed: A22, B21, CA, E01, E17, ESPM, FR, GEOBASE, HistAb, I13, IBR, IBSS, IBZ, M10, P30, P42, PAIS, PSA, PopulInd, S02, S03, SCOPUS, SOPODA, SSA, SSCI, SociolAb, T02, W07.
—IE, Ingenta, INIST. **CCC.**
Published by: Routledge (Subsidiary of: Taylor & Francis Group), 4 Park Sq, Milton Park, Abingdon, Oxon OX14 4RN, United Kingdom. TEL 44-20-70176000, FAX 44-20-70176336, subscriptions@tandf.co.uk, http://www.routledge.com. Eds. Anna Bosco, Marina Costa Lobo, Susannah Verney. **Subscr. to:** Taylor & Francis Ltd., Journals Customer Service, Sheepen Pl, Colchester, Essex CO3 3LP, United Kingdom. TEL 44-20-70175544, FAX 44-20-70175198.

P

327 NCL ISSN 1017-1983
SOUTH PACIFIC COMMISSION. ANNUAL REPORT. Text in English. 1948. a. free.
Formerly: South Pacific Commission. South Pacific Report (0081-2854)
Related titles: French ed.: Commission de Pacifique Sud. Rapport Annuel. ISSN 0489-9598.
—BLDSC (1450.650000).
Published by: Secretariat of the Pacific Community, PO Box D5, Noumea, Cedex 98848, New Caledonia. TEL 687-262000, FAX 687-263818, spc@spc.int, http://www.spc.int.

327 NCL ISSN 1017-9283
JZ5485
SOUTH PACIFIC CONFERENCE. REPORT. Text in English. 1950. a.
Related titles: French ed.: Conference de Pacifique Sud. Rapport. ISSN 1017-9291.
Published by: Secretariat of the Pacific Community, PO Box D5, Noumea, Cedex 98848, New Caledonia. TEL 687-262000, FAX 687-263818, spc@spc.int, http://www.spc.int.

327 ZWE ISSN 1017-9208
DT1155
SOUTHERN AFRICA. POLITICAL AND ECONOMIC MONTHLY. Short title: S A P E M. Text in English, Portuguese. 1987. m. USD 160 foreign (effective 2003). adv. bk.rev. illus. reprints avail. **Document type:** *Magazine, Academic/Scholarly.* **Description:** Covers politics and current events, social science research, gender issues, and the arts.
Indexed: IIBP, RASB.
Published by: (Southern Africa Political Economy Series), S A P E S Trust, Belgravia, Mt. Pleasant, Deary Ave 4, PO Box MP 111, Harare, Zimbabwe. TEL 263-4-727875, FAX 263-4-732735, sapes@mango.org.

SOVIET (RUSSIAN) MILITARY EXPERIENCE. *see* MILITARY

SPACE NEWS INTERNATIONAL. *see* AERONAUTICS AND SPACE FLIGHT

327 NLD ISSN 2210-2175
▼ ➤ **SPANDA JOURNAL.** Text in English. 2010. q. **Document type:** *Journal, Academic/Scholarly.* **Description:** Aims to increase knowledge and awareness in a variety of disciplines related with individual and social development, culture, education, human rights and the state of the planet.
Media: Online - full text.
Published by: (Spanda Foundation), Spanda Publishing, PO Box 18543, The Hague, 2502 EM, Netherlands. TEL 31-70-3626522, FAX 31-70-3629848. Circ: 1,500.

327.1747 GBR ISSN 1367-7748
JX1974.7
THE SPOKESMAN. Text in English. 1970. q. GBP 20 domestic to individuals; GBP 25 foreign to individuals; GBP 6 per issue (effective 2009). adv. bk.rev. back issues avail. **Document type:** *Journal, Academic/Scholarly.* **Description:** Features independent journalism on peace and nuclear disarmament, human rights and civil liberties, and contemporary politics.
Former titles (until 1995): Peace Register (1367-7756); (until 1993): ENDPapers (0262-7922); (until 1982): Spokesman (0024-5992)
Indexed: AltPI, DIP, HRIR, IBR, IBZ, PAIS.
—BLDSC (8417.630000).
Published by: (Bertrand Russell Peace Foundation), Spokesman Books (Subsidiary of: Bertrand Russell Peace Foundation), Russell House, Bulwell Ln, Nottingham, NG6 0BT, United Kingdom. TEL 44-115-9708318, FAX 44-115-9420433, elfeuro@compuserve.com, http://www.russfound.org. Ed. Ken Coates.

327 POL ISSN 0038-853X
➤ **SPRAWY MIEDZYNARODOWE.** Text in Polish. 1948. q. PLZ 90 domestic; EUR 25 foreign (effective 2005). adv. bk.rev. bibl. back issues avail.; reprints avail. **Document type:** *Journal, Academic/Scholarly.*
Related titles: Microform ed.: (from PQC); ◆ English ed.: The Polish Quarterly of International Affairs. ISSN 1230-4999.
Indexed: BAS, CA, HistAb, P42, PRA, RASB, T02.
Published by: Polski Instytut Spraw Miedzynarodowych/Polish Institute of International Affairs, ul Warecka 1a, skryt. poczt. nr 1010, Warsaw, 00950, Poland. TEL 48-22-5568000, FAX 48-22-5568099. Ed. Henryk Szlajfer. Circ: 900.

➤ **SRI LANKA JOURNAL OF INTERNATIONAL LAW.** *see* LAW—International Law

327.17 GBR ISSN 1746-451X
➤ **ST ANTONY'S INTERNATIONAL REVIEW.** Text in English. 2005. 2/yr. GBP 20 to individuals; GBP 40 to institutions; GBP 10 to students (effective 2011). adv. **Document type:** *Journal, Academic/Scholarly.* **Description:** Features articles on international affairs.
Related titles: Online - full text ed.: ISSN 1746-4528.
Published by: St Antony's College, University of Oxford, Oxford, OX2 6JF, United Kingdom. TEL 44-1865554465, info@stair-journal.org. Ed. Anita Hall.

327 DEU ISSN 1618-629X
ST. POELTNER OSTEUROPA-STUDIEN. Text in German. 2003. irreg., latest vol.3, 2005. price varies. **Document type:** *Monographic series, Academic/Scholarly.*
Published by: Peter Lang GmbH (Subsidiary of: Peter Lang Publishing Group), Eschborner Landstr 42-50, Frankfurt Am Main, 60489, Germany. TEL 49-69-7807050, FAX 49-69-78070550, zentrale.frankfurt@peterlang.com.

327 CAN ISSN 0576-3819
STANDING SENATE COMMMITTEE ON FOREIGN AFFAIRS. PROCEEDINGS. Text in English, French. 1969. 3/w.
Incorporates (1969-1976): Comite Senatorial Permanent des Affaires Etrangeres. Deliberations (0226-8191)
Related titles: Online - full text ed.: ISSN 1498-5691.
Published by: (Senate of Canada, Standing Committee on Foreign Affairs), Supply and Services Canada, Publishing Centre, Ottawa, ON K1A 0S9, Canada.

327.1747 909 USA
STANFORD NUCLEAR AGE SERIES. Text in English. 1989. irreg., latest 2009. price varies. back issues avail. **Document type:** *Monographic series, Academic/Scholarly.* **Description:** Explores ways in which nuclear weapons have affected the course of history, along with issues of nuclear warfare, such as disarmament and maintaining peace.
Published by: Stanford University Press (Subsidiary of: Stanford University), 1450 Page Mill Rd, Palo Alto, CA 94304. TEL 650-723-9434, FAX 650-725-3457, info@www.sup.org. Ed. Martin J Sherwin. **Dist. in Europe by:** Cambridge University Press, The Edinburgh Bldg, Shaftesbury Rd, Cambridge CB2 8RU, United Kingdom. TEL 44-1223-312393, FAX 44-1223-315052, information@cambridge.org, http://www.cambridge.org/uk; **Dist. in the Americas by:** Cambridge University Press Distribution Center, 100 Brookhill Dr, West Nyack, NY 10994. TEL 845-353-7500, FAX 845-353-4141, http://www.cambridge.org.

341.72 USA ISSN 1932-6033
JZ5588
STANFORD UNIVERSITY. CENTER FOR INTERNATIONAL SECURITY AND COOPERATION. CENTER OVERVIEW. Text in English. 200?. a., latest 2008. back issues avail. **Document type:** *Journal, Academic/Scholarly.*
Related titles: Online - full text ed.
Published by: Stanford University, Center for International Security and Cooperation, 616 Serra St E200, Stanford, CA 94305. TEL 650-723-9625, FAX 650-724-5683, tmhill23@stanford.edu.

327.172 USA
STANISLAUS CONNECTIONS. Text in English. 1970. m. USD 25 (effective 2002). adv. bk.rev.; play rev. back issues avail. **Document type:** *Newsletter.* **Description:** Discusses issues of peace, justice and a sustainable environment on local, national and international levels.
Formerly: Modesto Peace - Life Center - Stanislaus Safe Energy Committee. Newsletter
Related titles: Online - full text ed.
Published by: Modesto Peace - Life Center - Stanislaus Safe Energy Committee, PO Box 134, Modesto, CA 95353. TEL 209-529-5750. Eds. Jim Costello, Myrtle Osner TEL 209-522-4967. R&P Jim Costello. Adv. contact Myrtle Osner TEL 209-522-4967. Circ: 3,000.

327.73 USA ISSN 1099-4165
JZ1480.A2
STATE MAGAZINE. Variant title: State. Text in English. 1961. m. (except Aug.-Sep. combined issue). USD 48 domestic; USD 67.20 foreign (effective 2009). illus. reprints avail. **Document type:** *Government.* **Description:** Published to acquaint the State Department's officers and employees, at home and abroad, with developments of interest which may affect operations or personnel.
Former titles (until 1996): State (0278-1859); (until 1980): U.S. Department of State. Newsletter (0041-7629)
Related titles: Microform ed.: (from MIM, PQC); Online - full text ed.: ISSN 1939-3679.
Indexed: A22, A26, ABS&EES, I05, IUSGP, P06, PAIS, PersLit.
—Ingenta.
Published by: U.S. Department of State, 2201 C St NW, Washington, DC 20520. TEL 202-647-4000. Ed. Rob Wiley. **Orders to:** U.S. Government Printing Office, Superintendent of Documents, PO Box 371954, Pittsburgh, PA 15250. TEL 202-512-1800, FAX 202-512-2250, orders@gpo.gov, http://www.access.gpo.gov.

327 ITA ISSN 1825-4985
GLI STATI UNITI D'EUROPA (BARI)/ETATS UNIS D'EUROPE/UNITED STATES OF EUROPE/VEREINIGTEN STAATEN VON EUROPA. Text in Italian. 2003. q. **Document type:** *Magazine, Consumer.*
Published by: Edizioni Dedalo, Viale Luigi Jacobini 5, Bari, BA 70123, Italy. TEL 39-080-5311413, FAX 39-080-5311414, info@edizionidedalo.it, http://www.edizionidedalo.it.

STEIRISCHE KRIEGSOPFER ZEITUNG. *see* MILITARY

327 POL ISSN 0209-0961
D839
STOSUNKI MIEDZYNARODOWE (WARSAW, 1982). Text in Polish; Summaries in English. 1982. irreg., latest vol.20, 1999. price varies. **Document type:** *Academic/Scholarly.*
Indexed: IBSS.
Published by: (Uniwersytet Warszawski, Instytut Stosunkow Miedzynarodowych), Wydawnictwo Naukowe Scholar, Krakowskie Przedmiescie 62, Warsaw, 00322, Poland. TEL 48-22-8289391, FAX 48-22-8289391. Circ: 400. **Dist. by:** Ars Polona, Obroncow 25, Warsaw 03933, Poland. arspolona@arspolona.com.pl.

327 POL ISSN 1509-3077
STOSUNKI MIEDZYNARODOWE (WARSAW, 1999). Text in Polish. 1999. m.
Related titles: Online - full content ed.: Stosunki.pl. ISSN 1689-4480.
Published by: Instytut Badan nad Stosunkami Miedzynarodowymi, ul Ordynacka 11/5, Warsaw, 00364, Poland. TEL 48-22-4981537. Ed. Michal Sikorski.

STRATEGIC AND DEFENCE STUDIES CENTRE. WORKING PAPERS. *see* MILITARY

327 CYP
STRATEGIC BALANCE IN THE MIDDLE EAST. Variant title: A P S Diplomat Strategic Balance in the Middle East. Text in English. 1972. m. USD 800 (effective 2010); includes APS News Service, Fate of the Arabian Peninsula, Operations in Oil Diplomacy, Re-Drawing the Islamic Map. s-a. index. **Document type:** *Journal, Academic/Scholarly.* **Description:** Provides military surveys of the Arab nations, the Palestinian movement, Israel, Iran and the former Soviet Union.
Related titles: Online - full text ed.
Published by: Arab Press Service, PO Box 23896, Nicosia, Cyprus. FAX 357-2-350265. Ed. Pierre Shammas.

327 CAN
STRATEGIC DATALINKS. Text in English. 1987. irreg. (approx. 12/yr.). CAD 3 per issue to non-members; free to members (effective 2005). **Document type:** *Monographic series, Academic/Scholarly.* **Description:** Each issue is a short paper containing a detailed analysis of topical strategic issues.
Published by: Canadian Institute of Strategic Studies, 10 Adelaide St E, Suite 400, Toronto, ON M5C 1J3, Canada. TEL 416-322-8128, FAX 416-322-8129, info@ciss.ca.

STRATEGIC INSIGHTS. *see* MILITARY

355.684 ZAF ISSN 1013-1108
UA10.5
➤ **STRATEGIC REVIEW FOR SOUTHERN AFRICA/STRATEGIESE OORSIG VIR SUIDER AFRIKA.** Text in English, Dutch. 1979. 2/yr. ZAR 150 domestic; USD 60 foreign (effective 2011). bk.rev. bibl.; charts; abstr. back issues avail. **Document type:** *Journal, Academic/Scholarly.* **Description:** Publishes articles on strategic matters relating primarily to South Africa.
Incorporetes (1979-1987): I S S U P Strategiese Oorsig / I S S U P Strategic Review (0250-1961)
Related titles: Online - full text ed.
Indexed: A26, CA, E08, G08, I05, IBSS, ISAP, P42, PSA, S09, SCOPUS, SociolAb, T02.
Published by: University of Pretoria, Institute for Strategic Studies, The Editor, Strategic Review for Southern Africa, University of Pretoria, Pretoria, 0002, South Africa. wilma.martin@up.ac.za. Ed., R&P Mike Hough. Circ: 500.

355 PAK ISSN 1029-0990
U162
➤ **STRATEGIC STUDIES.** Text in English. 1977. q. PKR 180 domestic; USD 50 foreign (effective 2006). adv. bk.rev. **Document type:** *Journal, Academic/Scholarly.* **Description:** Contains research articles on regional and global strategic issues affecting international peace.
Related titles: Online - full text ed.: ISSN 1811-9557. 2000.
Indexed: A26, AMB, I05, IBSS, LID&ISL, M10.
Published by: Institute of Strategic Studies, Sector F-5/2, Islamabad, Pakistan. TEL 92-51-9204423, FAX 92-51-9204658, strategy@isb.paknet.com.pk. Ed. Shireem M Mazari. Circ: 950 (paid and controlled).

327 GBR ISSN 0459-7230
U162
➤ **STRATEGIC SURVEY.** Text in English. 1966. a. GBP 133 combined subscription in United Kingdom to institutions (print & online eds.); EUR 196 combined subscription to institutions (print & online eds.); USD 234 combined subscription in North America to institutions (print & online eds.); USD 245 combined subscription elsewhere to institutions (print & online eds.) (effective 2012). adv. bk.rev. charts. 312 p./no.; back issues avail.; reprint service avail. from PSC. **Document type:** *Journal, Academic/Scholarly.* **Description:** Examines the year's significant events and their importance for international security.
Related titles: Online - full text ed.: ISSN 1476-4997. GBP 120 in United Kingdom to institutions; EUR 177 to institutions; USD 211 in North America to institutions; USD 220 elsewhere to institutions (effective 2012) (from IngentaConnect).
Indexed: A22, CA, E01, I02, P42, PAIS, PSA, R02, SCOPUS, T02.
—IE, Infotrieve, Ingenta, **CCC.**
Published by: (International Institute for Strategic Studies), Routledge (Subsidiary of: Taylor & Francis Group), 4 Park Sq, Milton Park, Abingdon, Oxon OX14 4RN, United Kingdom. TEL 44-20-70176000, FAX 44-20-70176336, subscriptions@tandf.co.uk, http://www.routledge.com. Ed. Alexander Nicoll TEL 44-20-73797676. Adv. contact Linda Hann TEL 44-1344-779945. **Subscr. in N America to:** Taylor & Francis Inc., Customer Services Dept, 325 Chestnut St, 8th Fl, Philadelphia, PA 19106. TEL 215-625-8900, 800-354-1420, FAX 215-625-2940, customerservice@taylorandfrancis.com; **Subscr. outside N America to:** Taylor & Francis Ltd., Journals Customer Service, Sheepen Pl, Colchester, Essex CO3 3LP, United Kingdom. TEL 44-20-70175544, FAX 44-20-70175198, tf.enquiries@tfinforma.com.

320 AUT
▼ **STRATEGIE UND SICHERHEIT.** Text in German. 2010. a. **Document type:** *Journal, Academic/Scholarly.*
Published by: Boehlau Verlag GmbH & Co.KG., Wiesingerstr 1, Vienna, W 1010, Austria. TEL 43-1-3302427, FAX 43-1-3302432, boehlau@boehlau.at, http://www.boehlau.at.

327 DEU ISSN 1612-975X
STRATEGISCHE KULTUR EUROPAS. Text in German. 2004. irreg., latest vol.6, 2009. price varies. **Document type:** *Monographic series, Academic/Scholarly.*
Published by: Peter Lang GmbH (Subsidiary of: Peter Lang Publishing Group), Eschborner Landstr 42-50, Frankfurt Am Main, 60489, Germany. TEL 49-69-7807050, FAX 49-69-78070550, zentrale.frankfurt@peterlang.com. Ed. August Pradetto.

327 AZE
STRATEJI ARASDIRMALAR MERKEZI. ILLERDEKI FEALIYYETINE DAIR JURNAL/JOURNAL ON S A M ACTIVITIES REPORT. Text in Azerbaijani. a. **Document type:** *Report, Government.*
Related titles: Online - full text ed.
Published by: Center for Strategic Studies under the President of the Republic of Azerbaijan/Azerbaycan Respublikasinin Prezidenti yaninda Strateji Arasdirmalar Merkezi (S A M), M. Ibrahimov str. 8, Baku, 1005, Azerbaijan. TEL 994-12-5968239, FAX 994-12-4373458, info@sam.gov.az.

327 ITA ISSN 1970-0903
JN34.5
STUDI SULL'INTEGRAZIONE EUROPEA. Text in Multiple languages. 2006. 3/yr. **Document type:** *Magazine, Consumer.*
Published by: Cacucci Editore, Via D Nicolai 39, Bari, 70122, Italy. TEL 39-080-5214220, FAX 39-080-5234777, info@cacucci.it, http://www.cacucci.it. Eds. Ennio Triggiani, Ugo Villani.

327.2 BEL ISSN 0770-2965
D839
➤ **STUDIA DIPLOMATICA.** Text in French, Dutch, English. 1948. bi-m. EUR 81 domestic; EUR 93 in the European Union; EUR 100 in Europe ouside of European Union; EUR 124 elsewhere (effective 2003). adv. bk.rev. bibl. index, cum.index. back issues avail. **Document type:** *Journal, Academic/Scholarly.* **Description:** Studies issues in international relations.
Formerly: Chronique de Politique Etrangere (0009-6059)
Indexed: A22, ABCPolSci, AMB, BAS, CA, CCME, DIP, ELLIS, IBR, IBSS, IBZ, LID&ISL, P06, P42, PAIS, PSA, RASB, SCOPUS, T02.
—BLDSC (8482.385000), IE, Infotrieve, Ingenta. **CCC.**
Published by: Institut Royal des Relations Internationales/Koninklijk Instituut voor Internationale Relaties, rue de Namur 69, Brussels, B-1000, Belgium. TEL 32-2-2234114, FAX 32-2-2234116. Eds. Mr. Wouter Coussens, Mr. Franklin Dehousse. R&P Mr. Franklin Dehousse. Adv. contact Mrs. Greta Reynaert. Circ: 1,500.

328 ARG ISSN 1669-7405
JL2001
STUDIA POLITICAE. Text in Spanish. 2003. 3/yr. **Document type:** *Journal, Academic/Scholarly.*
Indexed: BRD, CA, P42, S02, S03, SSAI, SSAb, SSI, T02, W03, W05.
Published by: Universidad Catolica de Cordoba, Facultad de Ciencia Politica y Relaciones Internacionales, Obispo Trejo, 323 2o Piso, Cordoba, X5000IYG, Argentina. TEL 54-351-4213213, FAX 54-351-4217800, icda@uccor.edu.ar, http://www.uccor.edu.ar/. Circ: 1,500.

327 DEU ISSN 1618-2847
STUDIEN ZUR EUROPAEISCHEN INTEGRATION. Text in German. 2001. irreg., latest vol.4, 2005. price varies. **Document type:** *Monographic series, Academic/Scholarly.*
Published by: (Europaeisches Zentrum fuer Integrationsforschung e.V.), Shaker Verlag GmbH, Kaiserstr 100, Herzogenrath, 52134, Germany. TEL 49-2407-95960, FAX 49-2407-95969, info@shaker.de.

320 DEU ISSN 1868-6214
▼ **STUDIEN ZUR GESCHICHTE DER EUROPAEISCHEN INTEGRATION/ETUDES SUR L'HISTOIRE DE L'INTEGRATION EUROPEENNE/STUDIES ON THE HISTORY OF EUROPEAN INTEGRATION.** Text in English, French, German. 2009. irreg., latest vol.13, 2011. price varies. **Document type:** *Monographic series, Academic/Scholarly.*
Published by: Franz Steiner Verlag GmbH, Birkenwaldstr 44, Stuttgart, 70191, Germany. TEL 49-711-25820, FAX 49-711-2582290, service@steiner-verlag.de, http://www.steiner-verlag.de.

327 DEU ISSN 1433-8858
STUDIEN ZUR INTERNATIONALEN POLITIK. Text in German. 1997. irreg., latest vol.9, 2009. price varies. **Document type:** *Monographic series, Academic/Scholarly.*
Published by: Peter Lang GmbH (Subsidiary of: Peter Lang Publishing Group), Eschborner Landstr 42-50, Frankfurt Am Main, 60489, Germany. TEL 49-69-7807050, FAX 49-69-78070550, zentrale.frankfurt@peterlang.com, http://www.peterlang.com. Ed. Juergen Schwarz.

327.172 DEU ISSN 1619-5175
STUDIEN ZUR KONFLIKT- UND FRIEDENSFORSCHUNG. Text in German. 2002. irreg., latest vol.6, 2009. price varies. **Document type:** *Monographic series, Academic/Scholarly.*
Published by: Verlag Dr. Kovac, Leverkusenstr 13, Hamburg, 22761, Germany. TEL 49-40-3988800, FAX 49-40-39888055, info@verlagdrkovac.de.

343.85 CHE ISSN 1422-8327
STUDIEN ZUR ZEITGESCHICHTE UND SICHERHEITSPOLITIK/ STUDIES IN CONTEMPORARY HISTORY AND SECURITY POLICY. Text in German, English. 1999. irreg., latest vol.15, 2006. price varies. **Document type:** *Monographic series, Academic/ Scholarly.* **Description:** Contains monographs on issues in Swiss foreign and security policy, international security policy, and conflict research.
Published by: (Forschungsstelle fuer Sicherheitspolitik und Konfliktanalyse), Peter Lang AG (Subsidiary of: Peter Lang Publishing Group), Hochfeldstr 32, Postfach 746, Bern 9, 3000, Switzerland. TEL 41-31-3061717, FAX 41-31-3061727, info@peterlang.com, http://www.peterlang.com.

327 AUT ISSN 1814-568X
STUDIENREIHE KONFLIKTFORSCHUNG. Text in German. 1980. irreg., latest vol.25, 2011. price varies. **Document type:** *Monographic series, Academic/Scholarly.*
Published by: (Institut fuer Konfliktforschung), Wilhelm Braumueller Universitaets-Verlagsbuchhandlung GmbH, Servitengasse 5, Vienna, 1090, Austria. TEL 43-1-3191159, FAX 43-1-3102805, office@braumueller.at. Eds. Anton Pelinka, Ilse Koenig.

STUDIES IN AIR POWER. *see* MILITARY

327.117 363.32 USA ISSN 1057-610X
HM136 CODEN: SCTREO
➤ **STUDIES IN CONFLICT & TERRORISM.** Text in English. 1992. m. GBP 872 combined subscription in United Kingdom to institutions (print & online eds.); EUR 1,151, USD 1,446 combined subscription to institutions (print & online eds.) (effective 2012). adv. bk.rev. index. reprint service avail. from PSC. **Document type:** *Journal, Academic/ Scholarly.* **Description:** Aims to cast new light on the origins and implications of conflict in the 21st Century and to illuminate new approaches and solutions to countering the growth and escalation of contemporary sub-state violence.
Formed by the merger of (1978-1992): Conflict (0149-5941); (1977-1992): Terrorism (0149-0389)
Related titles: Online - full text ed.: ISSN 1521-0731. GBP 784 in United Kingdom to institutions; EUR 1,036, USD 1,301 to institutions (effective 2012) (from IngentaConnect).
Indexed: A01, A20, A22, A25, A26, ABCPolSci, ABS&EES, AMB, AUNI, AmH&L, B04, BAS, BRD, CA, CCME, CJA, CJPI, CurCont, E-psyche, E01, E08, ESPM, G05, G06, G07, G08, HistAb, I02, I05, IBSS, LID&ISL, M05, M06, M07, M10, MEA&I, P02, P03, P10, P27, P30, P34, P42, P47, P48, P53, P54, PAA&I, PAIS, PQC, PRA, PSA, PsycInfo, PsycholAb, RASB, RiskAb, S02, S03, S08, S09, SCOPUS, SOPODA, SSA, SSAI, SSAb, SSCI, SSI, SociolAb, T02, V&AA, W03, W07.
—IE, Infotrieve, Ingenta. **CCC.**
Published by: Taylor & Francis Inc. (Subsidiary of: Taylor & Francis Group), 325 Chestnut St, Ste 800, Philadelphia, PA 19106. TEL 215-625-2940, 800-354-1420, orders@taylorandfrancis.com, http://www.taylorandfrancis.com. Ed. Bruce Hoffman. Adv. contact Linda Hann TEL 44-1344-779945.

327 NLD ISSN 1875-0451
➤ **STUDIES IN E U EXTERNAL RELATIONS.** (European Union) Text in English. 2008. irreg., latest vol.2, 2008. price varies. **Document type:** *Monographic series.* **Description:** Covers the legal, political, trade and historical aspects of the European Union's relations with nonmember states or regions or other international organizations.
Indexed: IZBG.
Published by: Martinus Nijhoff (Subsidiary of: Brill), PO Box 9000, Leiden, 2300 PA, Netherlands. TEL 31-71-5353500, FAX 31-71-5317532, marketing@brill.nl. Ed. Marc Maresceau.

327.17 NLD ISSN 1871-3424
STUDIES IN EUROPEAN DEVELOPMENT CO-OPERATION EVALUATION. Cover title: Triple C Evaluations. Text in English. 2005. irreg., latest vol.8, 2008. EUR 17.90 per vol. (effective 2009). **Document type:** *Monographic series, Academic/Scholarly.*
Published by: Uitgeverij Aksant, Cruquiusweg 31, Amsterdam, Netherlands. TEL 31-20-8500150, FAX 31-20-6656411, info@aksant.nl, http://www.aksant.nl.

327 IRL ISSN 0791-5888
STUDIES IN EUROPEAN UNION (DUBLIN). Text in English. 1991. irreg., latest vol.10, 1997. EUR 19 per issue (effective 2005). **Document type:** *Monographic series, Academic/Scholarly.*
Published by: Institute of European Affairs, Europe House, 8 North Great Georges St., Dublin, 1, Ireland. TEL 353-1-8746756, FAX 353-1-8786880, info@iiea.com, http://www.iiea.com.

327.1 NLD ISSN 1875-0559
▼ ➤ **STUDIES IN FOREIGN POLICY ANALYSIS.** Text in English. 2009. irreg. **Document type:** *Monographic series, Academic/Scholarly.* **Description:** Publishes original, innovative and pathbreaking studies in foreign policy analysis, both monographs and edited volumes, that advance the comparative study of foreign policy.
Indexed: IZBG.
Published by: Martinus Nijhoff (Subsidiary of: Brill), PO Box 9000, Leiden, 2300 PA, Netherlands. TEL 31-71-5353500, FAX 31-71-5317532, marketing@brill.nl. Eds. Bertjan Verbeek, Marijke Breuning.

327.12 GBR ISSN 1368-9916
STUDIES IN INTELLIGENCE. Key Title: Cass Series: Studies in Intelligence. Text in English. 1989. irreg., latest 2009. price varies. back issues avail. **Document type:** *Monographic series, Academic/ Scholarly.* **Description:** Contains scholarly monographs, wartime memoirs, and conference collections, edited by the founding editors of the journal "Intelligence and National Security.".
Published by: Routledge (Subsidiary of: Taylor & Francis Group), 4 Park Sq, Milton Park, Abingdon, Oxon OX14 4RN, United Kingdom. TEL 44-20-70176000, FAX 44-20-70176336, subscriptions@tandf.co.uk. Eds. Christopher Andrew, Richard J Aldrich.

327.12 USA ISSN 1527-0874
JK468.I6
STUDIES IN INTELLIGENCE. Text in English. s-a. back issues avail. **Document type:** *Government.*
Related titles: Microfiche ed.; Online - full text ed.: ISSN 1942-8510.
Indexed: I02.
Published by: U.S. Central Intelligence Agency, Center for the Study of Intelligence, 5852 Port Royal Rd, Springfield, VA 22161. TEL 703-605-6060, http://www.odci.gov/csi/studies/pubs.html/. Ed. Richard Schroeder.

▼ **STUDIES IN INTERNATIONAL INSTITUTIONAL DYNAMICS.** *see* BUSINESS AND ECONOMICS—International Commerce

327.17 USA
STUDIES IN INTERNATIONAL POLICY. Text in English. 1989. irreg., latest 1995. price varies. back issues avail. **Document type:** *Monographic series, Academic/Scholarly.* **Description:** Discusses topics in Asian - US economic policy.
Published by: Stanford University Press (Subsidiary of: Stanford University), 1450 Page Mill Rd, Palo Alto, CA 94304. TEL 650-723-9434, FAX 650-725-3457, info@www.sup.org. **Dist. by:** Cambridge University Press, The Edinburgh Bldg, Shaftesbury Rd, Cambridge CB2 8RU, United Kingdom. TEL 44-1223-312393, FAX 44-1223-315052, information@cambridge.org, http://www.cambridge.org/uk; Cambridge University Press Distribution Center, 100 Brookhill Dr, West Nyack, NY 10994. TEL 845-353-7500, FAX 845-353-4141, http://www.cambridge.org.

327 USA
STUDIES IN INTERNATIONAL POLITICAL ECONOMY. Text in English. 1978. irreg., latest vol.26, 1997. price varies. 380 p./no.; back issues avail. **Document type:** *Monographic series, Academic/Scholarly.* **Description:** Discusses how political policy affects economic conditions.
Incorporates: Science, Technology, and the Changing World Order Series
Published by: University of California Press, Book Series, 2120 Berkeley Way, Berkeley, CA 94704. TEL 510-642-4247, FAX 510-643-7127, foundation@ucpress.edu. **Subscr. to:** California - Princeton Fulfillment Services, Inc., 1445 Lower Ferry Rd, Ewing, NJ 08618. TEL 609-883-1759, 800-777-4726, FAX 800-999-1958, orders@cpfsinc.com.

327 USA ISSN 1529-2568
STUDIES IN INTERNATIONAL RELATIONS. Text in English. 2004. irreg., latest vol.5, 2008. price varies. **Document type:** *Monographic series, Academic/Scholarly.*
Published by: Peter Lang Publishing, Inc. (Subsidiary of: Peter Lang Publishing Group), 29 Broadway, New York, NY 10006. TEL 212-647-7706, 800-770-5264, FAX 212-647-7707, customerservice@plang.com, http://www.peterlang.com.

327 FIN ISSN 1455-1497
DL1141.2
SUOMEN ULKO-JA TURVALLISUUSPOLITIIKKA. Text in Finnish; Text occasionally in English, French, German, Swedish. 1959. s-a. **Document type:** *Government.*
Formerly (until 1995): Finland. Ulkoasiainministerio. Ulkapoliittisia Lausuntoja ja Asiakirjoja (0071-528X)
Published by: Ulkoasiainministerio/Ministry for Foreign Affairs of Finland, Merikasarmi, PO Box 176, Helsinki, 00161, Finland. TEL 90-134151, 358-9-16005, FAX 358-9-16055555, kirjaamo.um@formin.fi. Circ: 2,000.

327 FIN ISSN 0782-8454
E183.8.F5
SUOMI - U S A. Text in Finnish. 1946. q. adv. bk.rev. **Document type:** *Newsletter, Consumer.*
Formerly (until 1985): Suomi - Finland - U S A (0781-447X)
Indexed: RASB.
Published by: Suomi-Amerikka Yhdistysten Liitto/League of Finnish-American Societies, Mechelininkatu 10 A, Helsinki, 00100, Finland. TEL 358-9-41333700, FAX 358-9-408974, sayl@sayl.fi, http:// www.sayl.fi. Ed. Laura Norella-Manninen. adv.: page EUR 2,000. Circ: 13,000 (controlled).

327 GBR ISSN 0039-6338
U162
➤ **SURVIVAL (ABINGDON).** Text in English. 1959. bi-m. GBP 362 combined subscription in United Kingdom to institutions (print & online eds.); EUR 532 combined subscription to institutions (print & online eds.); USD 635 combined subscription in North America to institutions (print & online eds.); USD 667 combined subscription elsewhere to institutions (print & online eds.) (effective 2012). adv. bk.rev. index. 196 p./no.; back issues avail.; reprint service avail. from PSC. **Document type:** *Journal, Academic/Scholarly.* **Description:** Contains original documents, articles and book reviews providing a forum for both policy debate and academic discussion.
Related titles: Microform ed.: (from PQC); Online - full text ed.: ISSN 1468-2699. GBP 325 in United Kingdom to institutions; EUR 479 to institutions; USD 571 in North America to institutions; USD 600 elsewhere to institutions (effective 2012) (from IngentaConnect).
Indexed: A01, A02, A03, A08, A22, A26, AMB, AUNI, AmH&L, B04, BAS, BRD, CA, CCME, CurCont, DIP, E01, E08, G05, G06, G07, G08, HistAb, I02, I05, I13, I14, IBR, IBSS, IBZ, LID&ISL, LeftInd, M05, M06, M07, M10, P02, P10, P27, P30, P34, P42, P47, P48, P53, P54, PAIS, PCI, PQC, PRA, PSA, RASB, S02, S03, S09, S11, SCOPUS, SSAI, SSAb, SSCI, SSI, SociolAb, T02, W03, W07.
—IE, Infotrieve, Ingenta. **CCC.**
Published by: (International Institute for Strategic Studies), Routledge (Subsidiary of: Taylor & Francis Group), 4 Park Sq, Milton Park, Abingdon, Oxon OX14 4RN, United Kingdom. TEL 44-20-70176000, FAX 44-20-70176336, subscriptions@tandf.co.uk, http:// www.routledge.com. Ed. Dana Allin TEL 44-20-73797676. Adv. contact Linda Hann TEL 44-1344-779945. **Subscr. in N America to:** Taylor & Francis Inc., Customer Services Dept, 325 Chestnut St, 8th Fl, Philadelphia, PA 19106. TEL 215-625-8900, 800-354-1420, FAX 215-625-2940, customerservice@taylorandfrancis.com; **Subscr. outside N America to:** Taylor & Francis Ltd., Journals Customer Service, Sheepen Pl, Colchester, Essex CO3 3LP, United Kingdom. TEL 44-20-70175544, FAX 44-20-70175198, tf.enquiries@tfinforma.com.

➤ **SWISS - AMERICAN HISTORICAL SOCIETY. REVIEW.** *see* HISTORY

327.17 USA ISSN 1046-7734
JX1974
SWORDS AND PLOUGHSHARES. Text in English. 1986. s-a. free (effective 2010). **Document type:** *Journal, Academic/Scholarly.* **Description:** Discusses geopolitical issues related to war and peace.
Related titles: Online - full text ed.
Indexed: ABS&EES.
Published by: University of Illinois at Urbana-Champaign, Program in Arms Control, Disarmament, and International Security, 359 Armory Bldg, 505 E Armory Ave, Champaign, IL 61820. TEL 217-333-7086, FAX 217-244-5157, acdis@illinois.edu.

SYDASIEN; tidskrift om Indien, Sri Lanka, Pakistan, Bangladesh, Afghanistan, Nepal, Bhutan och Maldiverna. *see* HISTORY—History Of Asia

327 DNK ISSN 0109-579X
SYDSLESVIG I DAG. Text in Danish. 1946. q. DKK 150, EUR 20 membership (effective 2010). illus. **Document type:** *Magazine, Consumer.*
Formerly (until 1977): Det Braendende Spoergsmaal (0109-5803)
Published by: Sydslesvigsk Udvalg af Maj 1945, Frejasvej 2, Vojens, 6500, Denmark. TEL 45-74-543570, info@sydslesvisk-udvalg.dk, http://www.sydslesvisk-udvalg.dk. Ed. Helge Moosmann TEL 45-74-224745.

327 SYR ISSN 0039-7962
HC497.S8
SYRIE ET MONDE ARABE; etude mensuelle economique, politique et statistique. Text in French, English. 1951. m. USD 380 in Europe; USD 425 elsewhere (effective 2001). charts; stat. Index. back issues avail. **Document type:** *Newsletter, Corporate.*
Indexed: CCME, KES, PAIS, RASB.
Published by: Office Arabe de Presse et de Documentation, 67, Place Chahbandar, PO Box 3550, Damascus, Syria. TEL 963-11-3318237, FAX 963-11-4426021, ofa@net.sy, http://www.ofa-holding.com. Ed. Raghda Bittar. Circ: 1,200 (paid).

327 USA
D860
TAKING SIDES: CLASHING VIEWS IN WORLD POLITICS. Text in English. 1987. biennial. back issues avail. **Document type:** *Catalog, Academic/Scholarly.* **Description:** Presents current controversial issues in a debate-style format designed to stimulate student interest and develop critical thinking skills.
Formerly (until 2008): Taking Sides: Clashing Views on Controversial Issues in World Politics (1094-754X)
Published by: McGraw-Hill, Contemporary Learning Series (Subsidiary of: McGraw-Hill Companies, Inc.), 1221 Ave of the Americas, New York, NY 10020. TEL 212-904-2000, 800-243-6532, FAX 212-512-2000, customer.service@mcgraw-hill.com, http://www.mhhe.com/cls/.

327 ARG ISSN 1851-9792
TEMAS DE POLITICA EXTERIOR, COMERCIO Y RELACIONES INTERNACIONALES. Text in Spanish. 2008. s-a. back issues avail. **Document type:** *Journal, Academic/Scholarly.*
Published by: Asociacion Profesional del Cuerpo Permanente del Servicio Exterior de la Nacion, Esmeralda 1212 1o Piso, Buenos Aires, C1007 ABR, Argentina. TEL 54-11-48198049, apsen@apsen.org.arEsta direccion electronica esta protegida contra spambots. Es necesario activar Javascript para visualizarla apsen@apsen.org.arEsta direccion electronica esta protegida contra spambots. Es necesario activar Javascript para visualizarla, http://www.apcpsen.org.ar/.

327 GBR ISSN 1350-4134
➤ **LE TEMPS MONDIAL/WORLD TIME.** Text in English. 1994. irreg. price varies. **Document type:** *Monographic series, Academic/ Scholarly.* **Description:** Aims to provide an authoritative analysis and interpretation of changes in the world's political and economic scene. The volumes present an interdisciplinary approach encompassing Area Studies, Comparative Politics, History and International Relations.
Published by: Berg Publishers (Subsidiary of: Oxford International Publishers Ltd.), 1st Fl Angel Ct, 81 St Clements St, Oxford, Berks OX4 1AW, United Kingdom. TEL 44-1865-245104, FAX 44-1865-791165, enquiry@bergpublishers.com, http:// www.bergpublishers.com/. **Dist. by:** Turpin Distribution Services Ltd., Pegasus Dr, Stratton Business Park, Biggleswade, Bedfordshire SG18 8QB, United Kingdom. TEL 44-1767-604951, FAX 44-1767-601640, custserv@turpin-distribution.com, http://www.turpin-distribution.com/.

327.17 DEU
TERMINOLOGISCHE SCHRIFTENREIHE/TERMINOLOGICAL SERIES. Text in German. 1982. irreg., latest vol.7, 2009. price varies. **Document type:** *Monographic series, Academic/Scholarly.*
Published by: (Auswaertiges Amt), Walter de Gruyter GmbH & Co. KG, Genthiner Str 13, Berlin, 10785, Germany. TEL 49-30-260050, FAX 49-30-26005251, info@degruyter.com, http://www.degruyter.de.

TERRORISM AND GLOBAL JUSTICE SERIES. *see* CIVIL DEFENSE

327.117 GBR ISSN 0954-6553
HV6431
➤ **TERRORISM AND POLITICAL VIOLENCE.** Text in English. 1989. q. GBP 593 combined subscription in United Kingdom to institutions (print & online eds.); EUR 774, USD 974 combined subscription to institutions (print & online eds.) (effective 2012). adv. bk.rev. index. back issues avail.; reprint service avail. from PSC. **Document type:** *Journal, Academic/Scholarly.* **Description:** Publishes studies of various related forms of violence by rebels and by states, on the links between political violence and organized crime, protest, rebellion, revolution, and human rights.
Related titles: Online - full text ed.: ISSN 1556-1836. GBP 534 in United Kingdom to institutions; EUR 697, USD 877 to institutions (effective 2012) (from IngentaConnect).
Indexed: A20, A22, AmH&L, AmHI, BrHumI, CA, CCME, CJA, CJPI, CurCont, DIP, E01, ESPM, FamI, H07, HistAb, I02, I13, IBR, IBSS, IBZ, LID&ISL, LeftInd, M10, P02, P03, P10, P42, P47, P48, P53, P54, PCI, PQC, PRA, PSA, PerIslam, PsycInfo, RiskAb, S02, S03, S11, SCOPUS, SSCI, SociolAb, T02, W07.
—IE, Infotrieve, Ingenta. **CCC.**
Published by: Routledge (Subsidiary of: Taylor & Francis Group), 4 Park Sq, Milton Park, Abingdon, Oxon OX14 4RN, United Kingdom. TEL 44-20-70176000, FAX 44-20-70176336, subscriptions@tandf.co.uk, http://www.routledge.com. Eds. Alex P Schmid TEL 44-1334-462933, David C Rapoport TEL 310-825-4811. Adv. contact Linda Hann TEL 44-1344-779945. **Subscr. to:** Taylor & Francis Ltd., Journals Customer Service, Sheepen Pl, Colchester, Essex CO3 3LP, United Kingdom. TEL 44-20-70175544, FAX 44-20-70175198.

➤ **TERRORISM: DOCUMENTS OF INTERNATIONAL AND LOCAL CONTROL.** *see* CIVIL DEFENSE

327.593 THA ISSN 0125-6459
DS586
THAILAND. MINISTRY OF FOREIGN AFFAIRS. FOREIGN AFFAIRS NEWSLETTER. Text in Thai. 1977 (no.9). m. free. **Document type:** *Newsletter.*
Formerly: Thailand. Ministry of Foreign Affairs. News Bulletin

P

Published by: Ministry of Foreign Affairs, Department of Information, Bangkok, Thailand. TEL 2226875, FAX 222-1941. Circ: 8,000.

327.1 GRC ISSN 1107-7999
JZ6.5
THESIS; a journal of foreign policy issues. Text in English. 1997. q. USD 20. illus. **Document type:** *Journal, Consumer.* **Description:** Focuses on European politics and culture from a Greek point of view.
Indexed: I13, WTA.
Published by: Ministry of Foreign Affairs, 5 Vas Sofias Ave, Athens, 107 71, Greece. http://www.mfa.gr. Ed. Theodoros I. Theodorou.

THUNDERBIRD INTERNATIONAL BUSINESS REVIEW. *see* BUSINESS AND ECONOMICS

327 CHN ISSN 1008-665X
TIANJIN WAIGUOYU XUEYUAN XUEBAO/TIANJIN FOREIGN STUDIES UNIVERSITY. JOURNAL. Text in Chinese. 1993. bi-m. CNY 7 newsstand/cover (effective 2006). **Document type:** *Journal, Academic/Scholarly.*
Related titles: Online - full text ed.
Published by: Tianjin Waiguoyu Xueyuan/Tianjin Foreign Language Institute, 117 Machang Dao, Hexi Qu, Tianjin, 300204, China. TEL 86-22-23285743.

327 CHN
TIBET STUDIES. Text in English. s-a.
Indexed: BAS.
Published by: Tibetan Academy of Social Sciences, Lhasa, Tibet, China. Ed. Trin Ley Top Gyal. **Dist. by:** China International Book Trading Corp, 35 Chegongzhuang Xilu, Haidian District, PO Box 399, Beijing 100044, China.

327.172 ESP ISSN 0212-8926
TIEMPO DE PAZ. Text in Spanish. 1984. q. **Document type:** *Monographic series, Academic/Scholarly.*
Related titles: Online - full text ed.
Indexed: A01, CA, F03, F04, P34, R15, T02.
Published by: Movimiento por la Paz, el Desarme y la Libertad, Martos 15, Madrid, 28053, Spain. TEL 34-91-4297644, FAX 34-91-5077264, mpdl@mpdl.org.

327 SWE ISSN 1103-8977
TJECKISKA OCH SLOVAKISKA ROESTER. Text in Swedish. 1984. q. SEK 150 (effective 1999). **Document type:** *Bulletin.*
Formerly (until 1993): Roester Fraan Tjeckoslovakien (0282-2520)
Published by: Charta 77 - Stiftelsen, Norrtullsgatan 65, Stockholm, 11345, Sweden. TEL 46-8-7564828, FAX 46-8-7325561. Ed. Frantisek Janouch.

327 JPN ISSN 0916-3085
TOKYO KOKUSAI KENKYU KURABU RONBUNSHU/TOKYO CLUB PAPERS. Text in Japanese. 1988. a. **Document type:** *Academic/Scholarly.*
Published by: Tokyo Club Foundation for Global Studies, 1-9-1 Nihonbashi, Chuo-ku, Tokyo, 103-8011, Japan. tokyoclb@topaz.oca.ne.jp, http://www.tcf.or.jp.

TOPICS IN EUROPEAN STUDIES. *see* BUSINESS AND ECONOMICS—International Commerce

327 CAN ISSN 1920-5457
THE TORONTO GLOBALIST. Text in English. 2005. s-a. back issues avail. **Document type:** *Magazine, Consumer.*
Published by: The Toronto Globalist, 21 Sussex Ave, Rm 526, Toronto, ON M5S 1J6, Canada. TEL 416-500-3242. Ed. Rajiv Sinclair.

327 USA ISSN 1530-1656
JZ6.5
➤ **TOWSON UNIVERSITY JOURNAL OF INTERNATIONAL AFFAIRS.** Text in English. 1967. s-a. USD 3 domestic; USD 5 foreign (effective 2010). bk.rev. bibl. back issues avail. **Document type:** *Journal, Academic/Scholarly.* **Description:** Gives both recognized academics and undergraduate students opportunity to publish their ideas and findings in the field of international affairs and related subjects.
Formerly (until 1997): Towson State Journal of International Affairs (0041-0063)
Indexed: ABS&EES, AmH&L, CA, HistAb, IBR, IBZ, MEA&I, P42, T02.
Published by: Towson State University, Department of Political Science, 8000 York Road, Baltimore, MD 21252. TEL 410-704-3526, FAX 410-704-2960, Polisci@towson.edu.

327 NLD ISSN 0920-2218
KZ745.3
TRACTATENBLAD VAN HET KONINKRIJK DER NEDERLANDEN. Text mainly in Dutch; Text occasionally in English, French. 1951. 200/yr. index. **Document type:** *Government.*
Indexed: KES.
Published by: (Netherlands. Ministerie van Buitenlandse Zaken), Sdu Uitgevers bv, Postbus 20025, The Hague, 2500 EA, Netherlands. TEL 31-70-3789911, FAX 31-70-3854321, sdu@sdu.nl.

947 BEL ISSN 0779-3812
DJK1 CODEN: JANUFR
TRANSITIONS; ex-revue des pays de l'est. Text in French. 1960. 2/yr. EUR 50 (effective 2003). **Document type:** *Academic/Scholarly.*
Former titles (until 1993): Revue des Pays de l'Est (0303-9617); (until 1972): Universite Libre de Bruxelles. Centre d'Etude des Pays de l'Est. Revue du Centre d'Etude des Pays de l'Est et du Centre National pour l'Etude des Etats de l'Est (0008-9699)
Indexed: BAS, CA, DIP, HistAb, IBR, IBSS, IBZ, P42, PAIS, PSA, RASB, S02, S03, SCOPUS, SociolAb, T02.
Published by: Universite Libre de Bruxelles, Institut de Sociologie, Av Jeanne 44, Brussels, 1050, Belgium. TEL 32-2-650-33-60, FAX 32-2-650-35-21, http://www.worldbank.org/html/prddr/trans.html.

327 CZE ISSN 1214-1615
DJK51
TRANSITIONS ONLINE. Text in English; Text occasionally in Russian. 1999. m. (updated daily). USD 48 to individuals; USD 217 public libraries; USD 317 university libraries (effective 2009). **Document type:** *Magazine, Consumer.* **Description:** Provides in-depth analysis of foreign affairs and key political, economic, social and cultural developments in the former Soviet Union, east-central and southeastern Europe.
Media: Online - full text.
Indexed: A01, A03, A08, LeftInd, P34, T02.
Address: Baranova 33, Prague 3, 13000, Czech Republic. TEL 420-2-22780805, FAX 420-2-22780804. Ed. Jeremy Druker.

327 BEL ISSN 0250-4928
AS1 CODEN: WZSUDS
TRANSNATIONAL ASSOCIATIONS/ASSOCIATIONS TRANSNATIONALES. Text in English, French. 1949. q. EUR 45 (effective 2003). adv. bk.rev. bibl.; charts; illus.; stat. index. **Document type:** *Journal, Academic/Scholarly.* **Description:** Covers topics and trends relating to international and transnational organizations, including NGOs, regional associations, legal, social and language issues.
Formerly (until vol.29, 1977): International Associations (0020-6059)
Indexed: P06, PAIS, RASB.
—CASDDS, IE, Ingenta, INIST. **CCC.**
Published by: Union of International Associations/Union des Associations Internationales, Rue Washington 40, Brussels, 1050, Belgium. TEL 32-2-6401808, FAX 32-2-6436199, uia@uia.be, http://www.uia.org. Ed. A Onkelinx.

327 CHE ISSN 0252-9505
TRANSNATIONAL PERSPECTIVES; an independent journal of world politics and social policy. Text in English. 1974. 3/yr. USD 25. bk.rev. illus. **Document type:** *Journal, Academic/Scholarly.*
Formerly: World Federalist (0043-843X)
Related titles: Microfiche ed.
Indexed: HRIR, PAIS, PerIslam, RefugAb.
Address: Case Postale 161, Geneva 16, 1211, Switzerland. TEL 41-33-50047406, FAX 41-33-50047452. Ed., Pub., R&P Rene Wadlow. Circ: 6,000.

327.1 AUS ISSN 1833-3842
TRANSNATIONAL POLICY FORUM REPORT. Text in English. 2004. a. **Document type:** *Report, Academic/Scholarly.*
Published by: Australian National University, Asia-Pacific College of Diplomacy, Coombs Extension (Bldg 8), Canberra, ACT 0200, Australia. TEL 61-2-61257983, FAX 61-2-61257985, ExecutiveOfficer.APCD@anu.edu.au.

341.21 NLD ISSN 1875-9807
THE TRAVAUX PREPARATOIRES OF MULTILATERAL TREATIES. Text in English. 2008. irreg., latest vol.2, 2008. price varies. **Document type:** *Monographic series.*
Indexed: IZBG.
Published by: Martinus Nijhoff (Subsidiary of: Brill), PO Box 9000, Leiden, 2300 PA, Netherlands. TEL 31-71-5353500, FAX 31-71-5317532, marketing@brill.nl.

327.54 SGP ISSN 0082-6316
TRENDS IN SOUTHEAST ASIA. Text in English. 1971. irreg., latest vol.9, 1986. price varies. **Document type:** *Monographic series, Academic/Scholarly.* **Description:** Political trends in Southeast Asia.
Published by: Institute of Southeast Asian Studies, 30 Heng Mui Keng Terrace, Pasir Panjang, Singapore, 119614, Singapore. TEL 65-6870-2447, FAX 65-6775-6259, pubsunit@iseas.edu.sg, http://www.iseas.edu.sg/. Ed., R&P Mrs. Triena Ong TEL 65-6870-2449.

327 USA ISSN 0275-5351
D839
TRIALOGUE (WASHINGTON). Text in English. 1973. irreg., latest no.59, 2009. price varies. back issues avail. **Document type:** *Monographic series, Academic/Scholarly.*
Related titles: Online - full text ed.: free (effective 2010).
Indexed: PAIS, RASB.
Published by: Trilateral Commission, 1156 Fifteenth St, NW, Washington, DC 20005. TEL 202-467-5410, FAX 202-467-5415, https://www.trilateral.org.

327 USA ISSN 1026-5228
TRIANGLE PAPERS. Text in English. 1973. irreg., latest no.62, 2008. price varies. back issues avail. **Document type:** *Monographic series, Academic/Scholarly.*
—BLDSC (9050.202000), IE.
Published by: Trilateral Commission, 1156 Fifteenth St, NW, Washington, DC 20005. TEL 202-467-5410, FAX 202-467-5415, https://www.trilateral.org.

THE TRIBUNE (NEW YORK). *see* WOMEN'S INTERESTS

355 GBR ISSN 0966-9221
JZ5588
TRUST AND VERIFY. Text in English. 1989. q. back issues avail. **Document type:** *Newsletter, Trade.* **Description:** Provides analysis, reviews and news of verification developments.
Related titles: Online - full text ed.: ISSN 2045-2756. free (effective 2011).
Published by: Verification Research, Training and Information Centre, Development House, 56-64 Leonard St, London, EC2A 4LT, United Kingdom. TEL 44-20-70650880, FAX 44-20-70650890, info@vertic.org. Ed. Larry MacFaul.

327 338.91 TUR ISSN 1303-5754
DR603
TURKISH POLICY QUARTERLY. Text in English. 2002. q. USD 180, EUR 140 combined subscription (print & online eds.) (effective 2009). **Document type:** *Journal, Academic/Scholarly.* **Description:** Provides an international forum for practitioners, opinion leaders and researchers on Turkey's foreign policy, international relations and economics. The journal publishes articles on current affairs, opinions, policy pieces, review articles and interviews.
Related titles: Online - full text ed.
Indexed: I14, LeftInd, M10, P42.
Published by: A R I Movement, Cumhuriyet Cad. Pak Apt. No.30 Kat:6 D.13, Elmadag, Istanbul, 80670, Turkey. TEL 90-212-2119071, FAX 90-212-2119083, editor@turkishpolicy.com.

TURKISH REVIEW OF EURASIAN STUDIES. *see* HISTORY—History Of Europe

327 940 950 GBR ISSN 1468-3849
DR401
➤ **TURKISH STUDIES.** Text in English. 2000 (Spring). q. GBP 272 combined subscription in United Kingdom to institutions (print & online eds.); EUR 364, USD 457 combined subscription to institutions (print & online eds.) (effective 2012). bk.rev. annual index. back issues avail.; reprint service avail. from PSC. **Document type:** *Journal, Academic/Scholarly.* **Description:** Covers the history of the Turkish Republic, Turkish politics, government policies and programming, and Turkish international relations and foreign policy.
Related titles: Online - full text ed.: ISSN 1743-9663. GBP 245 in United Kingdom to institutions; EUR 328, USD 411 to institutions (effective 2012) (from IngentaConnect).
Indexed: A01, A03, A08, A22, CA, DIP, E01, ESPM, HistAb, I02, I13, I14, IBR, IBSS, IBZ, LID&ISL, LeftInd, M10, P34, P42, PSA, R02, S02, S03, SCOPUS, SSCI, SSciA, SociolAb, T02, W07.
—IE, Ingenta. **CCC.**
Published by: (The Global Research in International Affairs Center ISR), Routledge (Subsidiary of: Taylor & Francis Group), 4 Park Sq, Milton Park, Abingdon, Oxon OX14 4RN, United Kingdom. TEL 44-20-70176000, FAX 44-20-70176336, subscriptions@tandf.co.uk, http://www.routledge.com. Ed. Barry Rubin TEL 972-9-9602736. Adv. contact Linda Hann TEL 44-1344-779945. **Subscr. to:** Taylor & Francis Ltd., Journals Customer Service, Sheepen Pl, Colchester, Essex CO3 3LP, United Kingdom. TEL 44-20-70175544, FAX 44-20-70175198.

➤ **THE TURKISH TIMES.** *see* ETHNIC INTERESTS

➤ **U C DAVIS JOURNAL OF INTERNATIONAL LAW & POLICY.** *see* LAW

➤ **U C L A JOURNAL OF INTERNATIONAL LAW AND FOREIGN AFFAIRS.** (University of California at Los Angeles) *see* LAW—International Law

327 USA
U N A - U S A POLICY BRIEF. OCCATIONAL PAPERS. (United Nations Association of the United States of America) Variant title: B C U N Briefing. Text in English. 1987. irreg. free (effective 2011). back issues avail. **Document type:** *Report, Government.*
Former titles (until 19??): Business Council for the U N Briefing; (until 1984): F Y I to C E O's
Media: Online - full text.
Published by: United Nations Association of the United States of America & the Business Council for the United Nations, 801 Second Ave, New York, NY 10017. TEL 212-907-1300, FAX 212-682-9185, inquiries@un.org.

327 USA
U N A - U S A WORLD BULLETIN. (United Nations Association of the United States of America) Text in English. 19??. m. free (effective 2011). **Document type:** *Newsletter, Government.*
Formerly: U N A - U S A E-News Update
Media: Online - full text.
Published by: United Nations Association of the United States of America & the Business Council for the United Nations, 801 Second Ave, New York, NY 10017. TEL 212-907-1300, FAX 212-682-9185, inquiries@un.org.

327.2 USA ISSN 0251-7329
JX1977.A1
U N CHRONICLE. (United Nations) Text in English. 1963. q. USD 20 in Africa; USD 30 in Australia, New Zealand, Japan & Europe; USD 40 in North America; USD 55 elsewhere (effective 2011). bk.rev. bibl.; charts; illus. Index. back issues avail. **Document type:** *Journal, Consumer.* **Description:** Contains reports on the wide-ranging activities of the entire UN system as it deals with problems ranging from food and health to nuclear disarmament and the world economy.
Formerly (until 1982): U N Monthly Chronicle (0041-5367); Which superseded (in 1945): United Nations Review (0503-4612); Which was formerly (until 1942): The Inter-allied Review (0735-5610)
Related titles: Online - full text ed.: ISSN 1564-3913. 1997. free (effective 2008); ◆ French ed.: Chronique O N U. ISSN 1025-8523; Spanish ed.: Cronica de las Naciones Unidas. ISSN 0254-8410.
Indexed: A01, A02, A03, A08, A11, A22, A25, A26, ABS&EES, AcaI, B04, BRD, C04, C05, C12, CCME, CLI, CPerI, E07, E08, G05, G06, G07, G08, H09, H14, HRIR, HithInd, I02, I05, I07, I08, JEL, M01, M02, M05, M06, M10, MASUSE, MagInd, P02, P05, P06, P07, P10, P13, P27, P30, P34, P47, P48, P53, P54, PCI, PMR, PQC, PRA, R02, R03, R04, RASB, RGAb, RGPR, S02, S03, S05, S08, S09, S11, S23, SCOPUS, SSAI, SSAb, SSI, T02, TOM, U01, W03, W05, WBA, WMB.
—BLDSC (9083.570000), IE, Infotrieve, Ingenta. **CCC.**
Published by: (United Nations, Department of Public Information), United Nations Publications, 2 United Nations Plaza, Rm DC2-853, New York, NY 10017. TEL 212-963-8302, 800-253-9646, FAX 212-963-3489, publications@un.org, https://unp.un.org. Circ: 7,000. **Subscr. to:** EBSCO Information Services, PO Box 361, Birmingham, AL 35201. TEL 205-995-1567, 800-633-4931, FAX 205-995-1588.

341.734 CHE
U N H C R GLOBAL APPEAL (YEAR). Text in English. a. **Description:** Offers a comprehensive view of the agency's operations and annual requirements.
Published by: United Nations High Commissioner for Refugees, Public Information Section, PO Box 2500, Geneva 2, 1211, Switzerland. TEL 41-22-7398111, http://www.unhcr.ch/.

341.734 CHE
U N H C R GLOBAL REPORT (YEAR). Text in English. a. **Description:** Covers the UNHCR's accomplishments for the year.
Published by: United Nations High Commissioner for Refugees, Public Information Section, PO Box 2500, Geneva 2, 1211, Switzerland. TEL 41-22-7398111, http://www.unhcr.ch/.

341.232 ESP ISSN 1696-2206
JZ5588
➤ **U N I S C I DISCUSSION PAPERS.** (Unidad de Investigacion sobre Cooperacion y Seguridad Internacional) Text in Spanish, English. 2003. q. free (effective 2011). Index. back issues avail. **Document type:** *Journal, Academic/Scholarly.* **Description:** Presents different theoretical perspectives on international relations and security.
Media: Online - full text.
Indexed: CA, H21, I02, I14, IBSS, P08, P42, P45, PAIS, PSA, SociolAb, T02.
—**CCC.**
Published by: (Universidad Complutense de Madrid, Unidad de Investigacion sobre Cooperacion y Seguridad Internacional), Universidad Complutense de Madrid, Servicio de Publicaciones, C/ Obispo Trejo 2, Ciudad Universitaria, Madrid, 28040, Spain. TEL 34-91-3941127, FAX 34-91-3941126, servicio.publicaciones@rect.ucm.es, http://www.ucm.es/publicaciones. Ed. Antonio Marquina.

327 USA
U N NEWS. (United Nations) Text in English; Summaries in Korean. 1997. m. USD 35 (effective 2005). 16 p./no. 3 cols./p.; back issues avail. **Document type:** *Newspaper, Consumer.* **Description:** Provides news related to United Nations responsibilities that affect all people.
Related titles: Online - full text ed.
Published by: International Association of Educators for World Peace, Mastin Lake Station, PO Box 3282, Huntsville, AL 35810-0282. TEL 256-534-5501, FAX 256-536-1018, mercieca@knology.net, info@iaewp.org, http://www.iaewp.org. Ed., Pub. Lee Jon Young. Circ: 30,000.

327.2 USA
U N REFORM CAMPAIGNER; dedicated to building a more effective United Nations system. (United Nations) Text in English. 1976. s-a. USD 10. **Description:** Bipartisan national political organization doing lobbying, electioneering and educational work promoting a more effective United Nations system.
Published by: Campaign for U N Reform, PO Box 15270, Washington, DC 20003-0270. TEL 202-546-3956. Ed. Eric Cox. Circ: 2,000.

327.172 289.9 USA ISSN 1943-2933
U P F TODAY. Text in English. 2007. bi-m. **Document type:** *Magazine, Consumer.*
Related titles: Spanish ed.: ISSN 1943-3123; French ed.: ISSN 1943-2941; Russian ed.: ISSN 1943-3131; Chinese ed.: ISSN 1943-314X.
Published by: Universal Peace Federation, 155 White Plains Rd, Ste 222, Tarrytown, NY 10591. TEL 914-631-1331, FAX 914-631-1308, info@upf.org. Ed. Joy Pople. Pub. Thomas G Walsh.

U S A I D DEVELOPMENTS. *see* BUSINESS AND ECONOMICS—International Development And Assistance

327.174 USA ISSN 8755-7819
JX1974
U.S. ARMS CONTROL AND DISARMAMENT AGENCY. ANNUAL REPORT. Text in English. 1961. a. **Document type:** *Government.*
Former titles: Arms Control (0275-0023); U.S. Arms Control and Disarmament Agency. Annual Report to Congress (0082-8769)
Indexed: LID&ISL.
Published by: U.S. Arms Control and Disarmament Agency, Department of State Bldg, Washington, DC 20451. TEL 202-632-8715.

327 USA ISSN 0164-3886
DS701
U S - CHINA REVIEW. Text in English. 1975. q. USD 32 domestic to individuals; USD 45 foreign to individuals; USD 35 to institutions (effective 2008). adv. bk.rev. **Document type:** *Magazine, Consumer.* **Description:** Features articles on Chinese politics, economics, social trends and culture, as well as on U.S.-China relations.
Incorporates: New China (0161-0643)
Related titles: Online - full text ed.
Indexed: BAS, MEA&I, NPI.
—Ingenta.
Published by: U S - China Peoples Friendship Association, c/o Marge Ketter, membership, 7088 SE Rivers Edge St, Jupiter, FL 33458. TEL 561-747-9487, FAX 561-747-9487, membership@uscpfa.org. Eds. Barbara H Cobb TEL 615-833-9512, Jane Lael TEL 423-314-2777, Marcia Cooper TEL 913-341-5996, Sylvia Krebs TEL 770-949-5112. Circ: 17,000 (controlled).

341 USA ISSN 1093-099X
E183.8.C9
U.S. - CUBA POLICY REPORT. Text in English. 1994. m. USD 75 domestic to individuals; USD 100 foreign to individuals; USD 150 domestic to institutions; USD 175 foreign to institutions (effective 2001). adv. back issues avail. **Document type:** *Bulletin.* **Description:** Washington report on U.S. government policy development toward Cuba including legislation, laws, guidelines, and regulations plus related international perspectives and issues.
—CCC.
Published by: Institute for U.S. Cuba Relations, 1730 M St, N W, Ste 400, Washington, DC 20036. TEL 202-675-6344, FAX 703-790-8266. Ed., Pub., Adv. contact Ralph J Galliano. Circ: 200 (paid); 700 (controlled).

327.2025 USA ISSN 0012-3099
JX1705
U.S. DEPARTMENT OF STATE. DIPLOMATIC LIST. Text in English. q. USD 19 domestic; USD 26.60 foreign (effective 2005). back issues avail. **Document type:** *Directory, Government.* **Description:** Lists foreign diplomats in and around Washington, DC.
Related titles: Microform ed.: (from PMC).
Indexed: A26, I05.
Published by: U.S. Department of State, Office of Information Services, 2201 C Street N W, Washington, DC 20520. TEL 202-655-4000. **Subscr. to:** U.S. Government Printing Office, Superintendent of Documents, PO Box 371954, Pittsburgh, PA 15250. TEL 202-512-1800, FAX 202-512-2250, orders@gpo.gov, http://www.access.gpo.gov.

327 USA ISSN 0023-0790
JX1705
U.S. DEPARTMENT OF STATE. KEY OFFICERS OF FOREIGN SERVICE POSTS; guide for business representatives. Text in English. s-a. USD 5; USD 6.25 foreign (effective 1998). back issues avail. **Document type:** *Directory, Government.* **Description:** Lists key officers at Foreign Service posts, as well as embassies, legations, and consulates general.
Related titles: Online - full text ed.: ISSN 1934-9343. 2000.
Published by: U.S. Department of State, Office of Information Services, 2201 C Street N W, Washington, DC 20520. TEL 202-655-4000. **Subscr. to:** U.S. Government Printing Office, Superintendent of Documents, PO Box 371954, Pittsburgh, PA 15250. TEL 202-512-1800, FAX 202-512-2250.

327.172 USA ISSN 0083-3088
U.S. PEACE CORPS. ANNUAL REPORT. Text in English. 1962. irreg. free.
Published by: U.S. Peace Corps, 1111 20th St, NW, Washington, DC 20526. TEL 202-254-5010. Ed. James C Flanigan.

327.73 USA ISSN 0146-9371
KF30.8
U.S. SENATE. COMMITTEE ON FOREIGN RELATIONS. LEGISLATIVE ACTIVITIES REPORT. Text in English. 19??. biennial. free (effective 2011). **Document type:** *Report, Government.*
Related titles: Online - full text ed.
Published by: U.S. Government Printing Office, 732 N Capitol St, NW, Washington, DC 20401. TEL 202-512-1800, 866-512-1800, FAX 202-512-2104, ContactCenter@gpo.gov.

327 DNK ISSN 1395-3818
➤ **UDENRIGS.** Text in Danish. 1945. q. DKK 250 to individuals; DKK 400 to institutions; DKK 100 per issue (effective 2010). adv. bk.rev. charts; illus.; stat. index. 96 p./no. 2 cols./p.; back issues avail. **Document type:** *Journal, Academic/Scholarly.* **Description:** Analysis and debates of Danish foreign politics.
Former titles (until 1994): Det Udenrigspolitiske Magasin (0903-7845); (until 1988): Fremtiden (0016-1020)
Indexed: PRA.
Published by: Det Udenrigspolitiske Selskab/Danish Foreign Policy Society, Amaliegade 40 A, Copenhagen K, 1256, Denmark. TEL 45-33-148886, FAX 45-33-148520, udenrigs@udenrigs.dk, http://www.udenrigs.dk. Ed. Brita Vibeke Andersen. Circ: 1,800 (paid).

327 DNK ISSN 0109-1654
UDENRIGSPOLITISKE SKRIFTER. Text in Danish. 1954. irreg., latest vol.94, 2006. price varies. back issues avail. **Document type:** *Monographic series, Academic/Scholarly.*
Published by: Det Udenrigspolitiske Selskab/Danish Foreign Policy Society, Amaliegade 40 A, Copenhagen K, 1256, Denmark. TEL 45-33-148886, FAX 45-33-148520, udenrigs@udenrigs.dk, http://www.udenrigs.dk. Eds. Brita Vibeke Andersen, Klaus Carsten Pedersen.

330.904 DNK ISSN 0106-0570
UDVIKLING/DEVELOPMENT. Text in Danish. 1974. 8/yr. free. illus. back issues avail. **Document type:** *Magazine, Government.* **Description:** Highlights official Danish activities in the international development assistance areas.
Incorporates (1986-2003): Danidaavisen (1601-1864)
Related titles: Online - full text ed.: ISSN 1901-5496. 2004.
Published by: Udenrigsministeriet, Dansk International Udviklingsbistand/Ministry of Foreign Affairs of Denmark, Danish International Development Assistance, Asiatisk Plads 2, Copenhagen K, 1448, Denmark. TEL 45-33-920000, FAX 45-33-540533, um@um.dk, http://www.um.dk/da/menu/Udviklingspolitik/OmDanida. Ed. Stefan Katic TEL 45-33-920848.

327.477 DEU ISSN 1862-555X
UKRAINE-ANALYSEN. Text in German. 2006. s-m. **Document type:** *Bulletin, Academic/Scholarly.*
Media: Online - full content.
Published by: Universitaet Bremen, Forschungsstelle Osteuropa/Bremen University, Research Centre for East European Studies, Klagenfurter Str 3, Bremen, 28359, Germany. TEL 49-421-2187891, FAX 49-421-2183269, publikationsreferat@osteuropa.uni-bremen.de, http://www.forschungsstelle.uni-bremen.de. Eds. Heiko Pleines, Matthias Neumann.

327 USA ISSN 0041-6010
DK508.A2
THE UKRAINIAN QUARTERLY; a journal of Ukrainian and international affairs. Text in English. 1944. q. USD 50 to individuals; USD 150 to institutions (effective 2010). bk.rev. cum.index. reprints avail. **Document type:** *Journal, Academic/Scholarly.* **Description:** Provides an outlet for the UCCA to disseminate information and advocate issues.
Incorporates (1948-1970): The Ukrainian Bulletin (0041-5987)
Related titles: Microform ed.: (from PQC).
Indexed: A22, ABS&EES, AmH&L, CA, FR, HistAb, IBR, IBSS, IBZ, L09, MLA, MLA-IB, P06, P30, P42, PAIS, RASB, T02.
—Ingenta.
Published by: Ukrainian Congress Committee of America, Inc., 203 Second Ave, New York, NY 10003. info@ucca.org. Ed. Leonid Rudnytzky.

327 FIN ISSN 1458-994X
ULKOPOLIITTINEN INSTITUUTTI. U P I REPORT. Text in Finnish. 2002. irreg., latest vol.10, 2004. price varies. back issues avail. **Document type:** *Monographic series, Academic/Scholarly.*
Related titles: Online - full text ed.; English ed.
Published by: Ulkopoliittinen Instituutti/Finnish Institute of International Affairs, Mannerheimintie 15 A, Helsinki, 00260, Finland. TEL 358-9-4342070, FAX 358-9-43420769.

327 FIN ISSN 1456-1360
ULKOPOLIITTINEN INSTITUUTTI. U P I WORKING PAPERS. Text in English. 1989. irreg., latest vol.51, 2004. back issues avail. **Document type:** *Monographic series, Academic/Scholarly.*
Formerly (until 1996): Ulkopoliittinen Instituutti. Tutkimusraportteja (1235-6492)
Related titles: Online - full text ed.
Published by: Ulkopoliittinen Instituutti/Finnish Institute of International Affairs, Mannerheimintie 15 A, Helsinki, 00260, Finland. TEL 358-9-4342070, FAX 358-9-43420769, ulkopolitiikka@upi-fiia.fi.

327.4897 FIN ISSN 0501-0659
D839
ULKOPOLITIIKKA/FINNISH JOURNAL OF FOREIGN AFFAIRS/UTRIKESPOLITIK. Text in Finnish. 1961. q. EUR 25 domestic; EUR 18 to students; EUR 28 elsewhere; EUR 7 per issue (effective 2005). adv. bk.rev. **Document type:** *Journal, Academic/Scholarly.* **Description:** Focuses on changes in the international environment, the latest research findings and the background to foreign and security-policy issues.
Indexed: IBSS, RASB.
Published by: Ulkopoliittinen Instituutti/Finnish Institute of International Affairs, Mannerheimintie 15 A, Helsinki, 00260, Finland. TEL 358-9-4342070, FAX 358-9-43420769, http://www.upi-fiia.fi. Ed. Tapani Vaantoranta TEL 358-9-43420720. adv.: B&W page EUR 850, color page EUR 1,150; 210 x 280. Circ: 2,000.

ULUSLARARASI HUKUK VE POLITIKA/REVIEW OF INTERNATIONAL LAW AND POLITICS. *see* LAW—International Law

327 TUR ISSN 1304-7310
➤ **ULUSLARARASI ILISKILER/JOURNAL OF INTERNATIONAL RELATIONS.** Text and summaries in English, Turkish. 2004. q. TRY 60 domestic to individuals; USD 60 foreign to individuals; TRY 200 domestic to institutions; USD 200 foreign to institutions (effective 2010). bk.rev. a. index. back issues avail. **Document type:** *Journal, Academic/Scholarly.* **Description:** Publishes articles on diplomatic history, international relations theories, international law, political economy, regional/current issues to strategic issues.
Related titles: Online - full text ed.: free (effective 2010).
Indexed: A26, CA, G08, HistAb, I05, IBR, IBSS, IBZ, P42, PSA, SCOPUS, SSCI, SociolAb, T02, W07.
—BLDSC (9830.083000).
Published by: Uluslararasi Iliskiler Dergisi, International Relations Council, Sogutozu Cad. No.43, TOBB-ETU, Oda No.364, Sogutozu, Ankara, Turkey. TEL 90-312-2924108, FAX 90-312-2924325, bilgi@uidergisi.com, abone@uidergisi.com. Ed. Mustafa Aydin. R&P Sinem Akgul Acikmese.

341.21 USA ISSN 1540-0107
UNDIPLOMATIC TIMES; the independent newspaper on the United Nations system. Text in English. 1990. m. USD 50 domestic to individuals; USD 60 foreign to individuals; USD 100 to institutions (effective 2002). bk.rev. abstr.; bibl. index, 1991-1998. **Document type:** *Newsletter.* **Description:** Covers the United Nations from an independent, critical perspective. Reviews the activities of General Assembly, Security Council, Economic and Social Council, and Secretary General, along with major documents.
Formerly (until 1999): International Documents Review (1054-4933)
Published by: Impact Communications Consultants, 318 Edgewood Ave, Teaneck, NJ 07666. TEL 201-833-1881, FAX 201-833-1835. Ed., Pub. Bhaskar Menon. Circ: 500 (paid). **Subscr. to:** Ste 1166, 60 E 42nd St, New York, NY 10017.

327 USA
UNESCO ASSOCIATION - U S A NEWSLETTER. Text in English. 1974. bi-m. USD 20. **Document type:** *Newsletter.* **Description:** Conveys the global impact and the importance of understanding America's place in the world by creating an understanding of international issues.
Published by: UNESCO Association - U S A, Inc., 5815 Lawton Ave, Oakland, CA 94618-1510. TEL 510-654-4638, FAX 510-655-1392. Ed. Dorothy Hackbarth.

327 FRA ISSN 1993-8616
THE UNESCO COURIER (ONLINE). Text in Arabic, Chinese, English, Russian, Spanish. 2007. m. **Document type:** *Magazine, Trade.*
Media: Online - full content.
—CCC.
Published by: UNESCO, 7 Place de Fontenoy, Paris, 75352, France. TEL 33-1-45681000, FAX 33-1-45671690, bpi@unesco.org, http://www.unesco.org. Ed. Jasmina Sopova.

327 FRA ISSN 0082-7525
UNESCO REPORT OF THE DIRECTOR - GENERAL ON THE ACTIVITIES OF THE ORGANIZATION. Text in Arabic, English, French, Russian, Spanish. 1959. biennial, latest 2007. price varies.
Related titles: Microfiche ed.: (from CIS).
Indexed: IIS, RASB.
Published by: UNESCO Publishing, 7 place de Fontenoy, Paris, 75352, France. TEL 33-1-45684300, FAX 33-1-45685737, http://publishing.unesco.org/default.aspx. **Dist. in the U.S. by:** Bernan Associates, Bernan, 4611-F Assembly Dr., Lanham, MD 20706-4391. TEL 800-274-4447, FAX 800-865-3450.

339.923 POL ISSN 1506-4832
HC240.25.P7
UNIA & POLSKA; magazyn europejski. Text in Polish. 1998. fortn. **Document type:** *Magazine, Consumer.*
Related titles: Online - full text ed.: ISSN 1689-0175.
Address: ul. Solec 48, III p., Warsaw, 00 382, Poland. TEL 48-22-6254789, FAX 48-22-6252453. Ed. Marek Sarjusz-Wolski. Pub. Krzysztof Bobinski.

327 CAN
UNITED NATIONS ASSOCIATION IN CANADA. LIAISON. Text in English, French. 1975. q. CAD 20 (effective 2000). **Document type:** *Newsletter.* **Description:** Promotes Canadian perspectives, interests and involvement in finding solutions to important global issues.
Formerly (until 1991): United Nations Association in Canada. Quarterly Bulletin
Related titles: Online - full text ed.
Published by: United Nations Association in Canada, 130 Slater St, Ste 900, Ottawa, ON K1P 6E2, Canada. TEL 613-232-5751, FAX 613-563-2455, info@unac.org. Ed. Joan Broughton. Circ: 550.

327 TWN ISSN 0457-8074
DS701
UNITED NATIONS ASSOCIATION OF THE REPUBLIC OF CHINA NEWSLETTER. Text in English. 1950. m. free. **Document type:** *Newsletter.* **Description:** Discusses political reform, trade policy, economics, foreign relations, and news about mainland China and Taiwan.
Published by: United Nations Association of the Republic of China, 101 Ning Po West St, Taipei, Taiwan. TEL 02-301-2654. Ed. Lei Pao Chung. Circ: 1,400.

327.172 USA ISSN 1813-260X
THE UNITED NATIONS BLUE BOOKS SERIES. Text in English. 1995. irreg. USD 29.95 per vol. **Document type:** *Monographic series.* **Description:** Details U.N. efforts at international peace-keeping, human rights monitoring, international development, nonproliferation, and conflict resolutions.
Published by: United Nations Publications, 2 United Nations Plaza, Rm DC2-853, New York, NY 10017. TEL 212-963-8302, 800-253-9646, FAX 212-963-3489, publications@un.org, https://unp.un.org.

327 USA
UNITED NATIONS. CONFERENCE ON TRADE AND DEVELOPMENT. TRADE AND DEVELOPMENT BOARD. OFFICIAL RECORDS. SUPPLEMENTS. Text in English. 1965. irreg. price varies. **Description:** Includes numbered supplements which contain the resolutions and decisions of the Trade and Development Board; reports and resolutions and decisions of its main subsidiary bodies.
Formerly: United Nations. Trade and Development Board. Official Records. Supplements (0082-8483)
Related titles: Microfiche ed.
Published by: (United Nations, Conference on Trade and Development (U N C T A D), Trade and Development Board), United Nations Publications, 2 United Nations Plaza, Rm DC2-853, New York, NY 10017. TEL 212-963-8302, 800-253-9646, FAX 212-963-3489, publications@un.org, https://unp.un.org. Circ: 3,500.

327 USA
UNITED NATIONS. DEPARTMENT OF PUBLIC INFORMATION. PROGRAMME UPDATE. Text in English. fortn.
Published by: Department of Public Information, Centres Programme Section, c/o Leona Forman, Chief, United Nations, Rm S 1060, New York, NY 10017. TEL 212-963-6850.

P

327.174 USA ISSN 0252-5607
JX1974
UNITED NATIONS DISARMAMENT YEARBOOK. Text in English. 1952. a. USD 65 (effective 2008). back issues avail. **Document type:** *Yearbook, Consumer.* **Description:** Contains an annual compilation of text and statistics of disarmament-related resolutions and decisions of the general assembly.
Former titles: United Nations. Disarmament Commission. Yearbook; United Nations. Disarmament Commission. Official Records (0082-8076)
Related titles: Online - full text ed.; Chinese ed.: Guanyu Junhei Guanzhi he Caijun Duobian Xieding de Xiankuang - Lianheguo. ISSN 0252-5577; Russian ed.: Organizatsiya Ob'yedinennyh Natsii. Sostoyanie Mnogostoronnikh Soglashenii o Regulirovanii Vooruzhenii i Razoruzhenii. ISSN 0252-5585; Spanish ed.: Naciones Unidas. Anuario Sobre Desarme. ISSN 0252-5593; French ed.: Nations Unies Annuaire de Desarmement. ISSN 0252-5615.
Indexed: RASB.
—BLDSC (9096.972000). **CCC.**
Published by: (United Nations, Department of Disarmament Affairs), United Nations Publications, 2 United Nations Plaza, Rm DC2-853, New York, NY 10017. TEL 212-963-8302, 800-253-9646, FAX 212-963-3489, publications@un.org, https://unp.un.org.

327.174 USA ISSN 1014-2177
UNITED NATIONS ECONOMIC AND SOCIAL COUNCIL. DISARMAMENT STUDY SERIES. Text in English. 1981. irreg., latest vol.16. price varies.
Related titles: Spanish ed.: Desarme. Serie de Estudios; French ed.: Desarmement. Serie D'etudes. ISSN 0259-2185.
Published by: (United Nations, Economic and Social Council), United Nations Publications, 2 United Nations Plaza, Rm DC2-853, New York, NY 10017. TEL 212-963-8302, 800-253-9646, FAX 212-963-3489, publications@un.org, https://unp.un.org.

341 USA ISSN 0082-8092
HC59
UNITED NATIONS. ECONOMIC AND SOCIAL COUNCIL. OFFICIAL RECORDS. Text in English. 1946. irreg. price varies. back issues avail. **Document type:** *Report, Consumer.* **Description:** Contains complete text of the convention, its final act and related resolutions of the conference and of the United Nations general assembly.
Related titles: CD-ROM ed.; ◆ Supplement to: United Nations Economic and Social Council. Resolutions and Decisions. ISSN 0251-9410.
—CCC.
Published by: (United Nations, Economic and Social Council), United Nations Publications, 2 United Nations Plaza, Rm DC2-853, New York, NY 10017. TEL 212-963-8302, 800-253-9646, FAX 212-963-3489, publications@un.org, https://unp.un.org.

327.320 USA
UNITED NATIONS. GENERAL ASSEMBLY. ANNEXES. Text in Arabic, Chinese, English, French, Russian, Spanish. 194?. a.
Published by: (United Nations General Assembly), United Nations Publications, 2 United Nations Plaza, Rm DC2-853, New York, NY 10017. TEL 212-963-8302, 800-253-9646, FAX 212-963-3489, publications@un.org, https://unp.un.org.

327 USA
UNITED NATIONS. GENERAL ASSEMBLY. OFFICIAL RECORDS. Text in Arabic, Chinese, English, French, Russian, Spanish. a.
Related titles: ◆ Series: United Nations Commission on International Trade Law. Report on the Work of Its Session. ISSN 0251-9127.
Published by: (United Nations General Assembly), United Nations Publications, 2 United Nations Plaza, Rm DC2-853, New York, NY 10017. TEL 212-963-8302, 800-253-9646, FAX 212-963-3489, publications@un.org, https://unp.un.org.

327 USA
UNITED NATIONS. GENERAL ASSEMBLY. PROVISIONAL RECORDS. Text in Arabic, Chinese, English, French, Russian, Spanish. 1946. a.
Published by: (United Nations General Assembly), United Nations Publications, 2 United Nations Plaza, Rm DC2-853, New York, NY 10017. TEL 212-963-8302, 800-253-9646, FAX 212-963-3489, publications@un.org, https://unp.un.org.

327 NZL ISSN 0110-1951
JX1977.2.N5
UNITED NATIONS HANDBOOK (YEAR). Text in English. a. NZD 30 in New Zealand, Australia and South Pacific; USD 20, EUR 16 elsewhere (effective 2009). **Document type:** *Government.* **Description:** Contains a current list of all the organizations in the U.N. with membership roster. Explains their aims, committee structure, and the legal basis for their existence.
Supercedes in part (in 1973): United Nations and Related Agencies Handbook; Which was formerly (until 1968): The United Nations and Specialised Agencies Handbook (0548-9385); (until 1961): United Nations and Specialised Agencies Membership Organisation and Function
Published by: Ministry of Foreign Affairs and Trade, c/o Publication Officer, Private Bag 18-901, Wellington, New Zealand. TEL 64-4-4398000, FAX 64-4-4398511, enquiries@mfat.govt.nz.

341.734 CHE
UNITED NATIONS HIGH COMMISSIONER FOR REFUGEES. MID-YEAR PROGRESS REPORT. Text in English. a. **Description:** Reviews the situation of refugees throughout the world.
Published by: United Nations High Commissioner for Refugees, Public Information Section, PO Box 2500, Geneva 2, 1211, Switzerland. TEL 41-22-739-81-11, FAX 41-22-739-84-49, http://www.unhcr.ch/.

341.734 CHE
UNITED NATIONS HIGH COMMISSIONER FOR REFUGEES. SPECIAL REPORTS. Text in English. irreg.
Published by: United Nations High Commissioner for Refugees, Public Information Section, PO Box 2500, Geneva 2, 1211, Switzerland. TEL 41-22-739-81-11, FAX 41-22-739-84-49, http://www.unhcr.ch/.

327 USA ISSN 0743-9180
UNITED NATIONS ISSUES CONFERENCE. REPORT. Text in English. 1970. a. free (effective 2011). **Document type:** *Report, Trade.* **Description:** Reports discussion of current concern or organizational procedure by groups of officials and academic specialists.
Former titles (until 1984): Conference on United Nations Procedures. Report (0748-2361); (until 1981): Conference on Organization and Procedures of the United Nations. Report
Related titles: Online - full text ed.
Published by: The Stanley Foundation, 209 Iowa Ave, Muscatine, IA 52761. TEL 563-264-1500, FAX 563-264-0864, info@stanleyfoundation.org, http://www.stanleyfoundation.org/.

327 USA ISSN 1948-3104
UNITED NATIONS OF THE NEXT DECADE CONFERENCE. REPORT. Text in English. 1965. a. free (effective 2011). **Document type:** *Report, Trade.* **Description:** Discussion of a major issue and its future implications by groups of officials and international experts.
Former titles (until 1997): United Nations of the Next Decade Conference. Report (0748-433X); (until 1984): Conference on the United Nations of the Next Decade. Report (0069-8733)
Related titles: Online - full text ed.
Published by: The Stanley Foundation, 209 Iowa Ave, Muscatine, IA 52761. TEL 563-264-1500, FAX 563-264-0864, info@stanleyfoundation.org.

UNITED NATIONS RELIEF AND WORKS AGENCY FOR PALESTINE REFUGEES IN THE NEAR EAST. REPORT OF THE COMMISSIONER-GENERAL. *see* SOCIAL SERVICES AND WELFARE

UNITED NATIONS. REPORT OF THE SECRETARY-GENERAL ON THE WORK OF THE ORGANIZATION. *see* LAW—International Law

341 USA ISSN 0082-8416
UNITED NATIONS. SECURITY COUNCIL. OFFICIAL RECORDS. Text in English. 1946. irreg., latest 2007. price varies. Supplement avail.; back issues avail. **Document type:** *Government.* **Description:** Contains information about security council.
Incorporates (in 1946): Journal of the Security Council (1990-2387)
Related titles: French ed.: Nations Unies. Conseil de Securite. Documents Officiels. ISSN 1020-3184. 1946; Spanish ed.: Naciones Unidas. Consejo de Seguridad. Documentos Oficiales. ISSN 1020-3192. 1946; Russian ed.: Organizatsiya Ob'edinennykh Natsii. Sovet Bezopasnosti. Ofitsial'nyi Otchet. ISSN 1020-3206. 1946; Arabic ed.: Al-Umam al-Muttahidat. Maglis al-Amn. Al Wata'iq al-Rasmiyyat. ISSN 1020-3222. 1983; Chinese ed.: Lianheguo. Anquan Lishihui. Zhengshi Jilu. ISSN 1020-3214. 1946.
—CCC.
Published by: (United Nations Security Council), United Nations Publications, 2 United Nations Plaza, Rm DC2-853, New York, NY 10017. TEL 212-963-8302, 800-253-9646, FAX 212-963-3489, publications@un.org, https://unp.un.org.

341.21 USA ISSN 0257-067X
UNITED NATIONS. SECURITY COUNCIL. OFFICIAL RECORDS. SUPPLEMENT. Text in English. 1950. a. USD 22 (effective 2008).
Related titles: French ed.: Nations Unies. Conseil de Securite. Documents Officiels. Supplement. ISSN 0257-0769; Spanish ed.: Naciones Unidas. Consejo de Seguridad. Documentos Oficiales. Suplemento. ISSN 0257-0971; Russian ed.: Organizatsiya Ob'edinennykh Natsii. Sovet Bezopasnosti. Ofitsial'nye Otchety. Dopolnenie. ISSN 0257-1250.
Published by: (United Nations Security Council), United Nations Publications, 2 United Nations Plaza, Rm DC2-853, New York, NY 10017. TEL 212-963-8302, 800-253-9646, FAX 212-963-3489, publications@un.org.

327 USA ISSN 0251-7582
UNITED NATIONS. STATEMENT OF TREATIES AND INTERNATIONAL AGREEMENTS/NATIONS UNIES. RELEVE DES TRAITES ET ACCORDS INTERNATIONAUX. Text in English, French. 1947. m. USD 85 in Africa; USD 180 in Australia, New Zealand & Japan; USD 175 in Europe & N. America; USD 130 elsewhere (effective 2011). **Document type:** *Government.* **Description:** Covers statement of treaties and international agreements registered in accordance with Article 102 of the United Nations Charter.
—CCC.
Published by: United Nations Publications, 2 United Nations Plaza, Rm DC2-853, New York, NY 10017. TEL 212-963-8302, 800-253-9646, FAX 212-963-3489, publications@un.org. **Subscr. to:** EBSCO Information Services, PO Box 361, Birmingham, AL 35201.

341 USA ISSN 0082-8505
UNITED NATIONS. TRUSTEESHIP COUNCIL. OFFICIAL RECORDS/ PROCES-VERBAUX OFFICIELS - NATIONS UNIES, CONSEIL DE TUTELLE. Text in English. 1947. irreg. (39th session), latest 1972. price varies.
Related titles: Microfiche ed.
Published by: (United Nations Trustee Council), United Nations Publications, 2 United Nations Plaza, Rm DC2-853, New York, NY 10017. TEL 212-963-8302, 800-253-9646, FAX 212-963-3489, publications@un.org, https://unp.un.org.

341.06 USA
UNITED NATIONS. TRUSTEESHIP COUNCIL. OFFICIAL RECORDS. ANNEXES - SESSIONAL FASCICLE. Text in English, French. 1946. a.
Published by: (United Nations Trusteeship Council), United Nations Publications, 2 United Nations Plaza, Rm DC2-853, New York, NY 10017. TEL 212-963-8302, 800-253-9646, FAX 212-963-3489, publications@un.org, https://unp.un.org.

341.06 USA
UNITED NATIONS. TRUSTEESHIP COUNCIL. OFFICIAL RECORDS. RESOLUTIONS. Text in English, French. 194?. a.
Published by: (United Nations Trusteeship Council), United Nations Publications, 2 United Nations Plaza, Rm DC2-853, New York, NY 10017. TEL 212-963-8302, 800-253-9646, FAX 212-963-3489, publications@un.org, https://unp.un.org.

341 USA ISSN 0082-8513
UNITED NATIONS. TRUSTEESHIP COUNCIL. OFFICIAL RECORDS. SUPPLEMENTS. Text in English. 1947. irreg. price varies.
Related titles: Microfiche ed.
Published by: (United Nations Trustee Council), United Nations Publications, 2 United Nations Plaza, Rm DC2-853, New York, NY 10017. TEL 212-963-8302, 800-253-9646, FAX 212-963-3489, publications@un.org, https://unp.un.org.

341.06 USA
UNITED NATIONS. TRUSTEESHIP COUNCIL. OFFICIAL RECORDS. VERBATIM RECORDS OF PLENARY MEETINGS. Text in English, French. 194?. a.
Published by: (United Nations Trusteeship Council), United Nations Publications, 2 United Nations Plaza, Rm DC2-853, New York, NY 10017. TEL 212-963-8302, 800-253-9646, FAX 212-963-3489, publications@un.org, https://unp.un.org.

327 USA ISSN 0746-6455
UNITED NATIONS WEEKLY REPORT. Text in English. 1982. w. USD 93. back issues avail.
Published by: Renate B. McCarter, Ed. & Pub., 823 Park Ave, New York, NY 10021. TEL 212-288-8505. Circ: 1,400.

341 USA ISSN 0082-8521
JX1977.A37
UNITED NATIONS. YEARBOOK. Text in English. 1946. a., latest 2002. USD 175 per issue (effective 2008). index. reprints avail. **Description:** Provides information about intergovernmental and expert bodies, major reports, secretariat activities and, in selected cases, the views of the member states.
Related titles: CD-ROM ed.; Online - full text ed.: USD 140 per issue (effective 2008).
Indexed: RASB, RefugAb.
—GNLM. **CCC.**
Published by: (United Nations, Department of Public Information), United Nations Publications, 2 United Nations Plaza, Rm DC2-853, New York, NY 10017. TEL 212-963-8302, 800-253-9646, FAX 212-963-3489, publications@un.org, https://unp.un.org.

327.73 USA
➤ **UNITED STATES IN THE WORLD: FOREIGN PERSPECTIVES.** Text in English. 1975. irreg., latest vol.4, 1988. price varies. adv. bk.rev. reprints avail. **Document type:** *Monographic series, Academic/ Scholarly.*
Published by: University of Chicago, 5801 S Ellis Ave, Chicago, IL 60637. TEL 773-702-7899. Ed. Akira Iriye.

327 USA ISSN 0083-0208
JX1977.2.U5
UNITED STATES PARTICIPATION IN THE UNITED NATIONS; report by the President to Congress. Text in English. 1946. a. **Document type:** *Government.*
Formerly (until 1948): The United States and the United Nations (0272-6769)
Related titles: Series of: International Organization and Conference Series.
Indexed: A26, I05.
Published by: U.S. Department of State, Bureau of International Organization Affairs, 2201 C St, N W, Washington, DC 20520. Ed. Pamela Stroh. **Subscr. to:** U.S. Government Printing Office, Superintendent of Documents, PO Box 371954, Pittsburgh, PA 15250. TEL 202-512-1800, FAX 202-512-2250, orders@gpo.gov, http://www.access.gpo.gov.

327.2 ECU
UNIVERSIDAD DE GUAYAQUIL. ESCUELA DE DIPLOMACIA. REVISTA. Text in Spanish. 1973. irreg.
Indexed: RASB.
Published by: Universidad de Guayaquil, Ave Kennedy interseccion Ave Delta, Guayaquil, Guayas, Ecuador. TEL 593-4-2296589, FAX 593-4-2281559, http://www.ug.edu.ec.

327 DEU ISSN 0341-3233
JZ1242
UNIVERSITAET HAMBURG. INSTITUT FUER INTERNATIONALE ANGELEGENHEITEN. VEROEFFENTLICHUNGEN. Text in German. 1975. irreg., latest vol.25, 2000. price varies. **Document type:** *Proceedings, Academic/Scholarly.*
Published by: (Universitaet Hamburg), Nomos Verlagsgesellschaft mbH und Co. KG, Waldseestr 3-5, Baden-Baden, 76530, Germany. TEL 49-7221-2104-0, FAX 49-7221-210427, nomos@nomos.de, http://www.nomos.de.

UNIVERSITAET HAMBURG. INSTITUT FUER INTERNATIONALE ANGELEGENHEITEN. WERKHEFTE. *see* LAW—International Law

327 BEL
UNIVERSITE DE PAIX; une revue trimestrielle. Text in French. 1976. q. EUR 7 (effective 2005). bk.rev. **Document type:** *Newsletter, Academic/Scholarly.* **Description:** Reports news and information on non-violent conflict resolution methods, including mediation and negotiation, peace education, and peace problems in general.
Formerly (until 1989): U P Informations (0777-8171)
Address: Bd du Nord 4, Namur, 5000, Belgium. TEL 32-81-554140, FAX 32-81-231882, universite.de.paix@skynet.be, http://www.universitedepaix.org. Ed. Francois Bazier. Circ: 4,000.

327 USA ISSN 1552-9665
UNIVERSITY OF CALIFORNIA, BERKELEY. CENTER FOR LATIN AMERICAN STUDIES. POLICY PAPERS. Text in English. 2004. irreg., latest no.28, 2009. free (effective 2010). **Document type:** *Monographic series, Academic/Scholarly.*
Related titles: Online - full text ed.
Published by: University of California, Berkeley, Center for Latin American Studies, 2334 Bowditch St, Berkeley, CA 94720. TEL 510-642-2088, FAX 510-642-3260, clas@berkeley.edu.

UNIVERSITY OF CAMBRIDGE. FACULTY OF ECONOMICS AND POLITICS. RESEARCH PAPER. *see* BUSINESS AND ECONOMICS

327 GBR
UNIVERSITY OF EDINBURGH. DEPARTMENT OF POLITICS. WORKING PAPER SERIES. Text in English. irreg., latest vol.13, 1993. **Document type:** *Monographic series, Academic/Scholarly.*
Published by: University of Edinburgh, Department of Politics, 31 Buccleuch Pl, Edinburgh, Midlothian EH8 9JT, United Kingdom.

327.172 USA
UNIVERSITY OF HAWAII. MATSUNGA INSTITUTE FOR PEACE. ANNUAL REPORT. Text in English. a.
Published by: University of Hawaii, Matsunga Institute for Peace, 2424 Maile Way, Porteus 717, Honolulu, HI 96822. TEL 808-956-7427. Ed. Aimee Harris.

327 GBR ISSN 1754-2839
➤ **UNIVERSITY OF MANCHESTER. THE CENTRE FOR INTERNATIONAL POLITICS. WORKING PAPER SERIES.** Variant title: C I P Working Paper Series. Text in English. 2004. irreg., latest 2006. free (effective 2009). back issues avail. **Document type:** *Monographic series, Academic/Scholarly.* **Description:** Provides a forum for debate and discussion.
Media: Online - full content.
Published by: University of Manchester, Centre for International Politics, Politics, School of Social Science, Oxford Rd, Manchester, M13 9PL, United Kingdom. TEL 44-161-3066000.

327.12 ZAF
➤ **UNIVERSITY OF PRETORIA. INSTITUTE FOR STRATEGIC STUDIES. AD HOC PUBLICATION/UNIVERSITEIT VAN PRETORIA. INSTITUUT VIR STRATEGIESE STUDIES. AD HOC PUBLIKASIE.** Abbreviated title: I S S U P Ad Hoc Publication. Text in Afrikaans, English. 1979. a., latest 2003. ZAR 70 domestic; USD 60 foreign (effective 2003). back issues avail. **Document type:** *Monographic series, Academic/Scholarly.* **Description:** Publishes research in the area of strategic studies, with emphasis on South Africa and the surrounding geographic area.
Published by: University of Pretoria, Institute for Strategic Studies, ISSUP Publications, Pretoria, 0002, South Africa. TEL 27-12-420-2407, FAX 27-12-420-2693, wilma.martin@up.ac.za. Ed., R&P Mike Hough. Circ: 500 (controlled).

327 USA
UNIVERSITY OF WISCONSIN-MILWAUKEE. CENTER FOR LATIN AMERICAN AND CARIBBEAN STUDIES. OCCASIONAL PAPER. Text in English. 19??. irreg., latest no.96, 2009. USD 4 per issue (effective 2010). back issues avail. **Document type:** *Monographic series, Academic/Scholarly.* **Description:** Provides information Center for Latin American and Caribbean Studies.
Related titles: Online - full text ed.: free (effective 2010).
Published by: University of Wisconsin at Milwaukee, Center for Latin American and Caribbean Studies, 2513 E Hartford Ave, Pearse Hall 168, Milwaukee, WI 53201. TEL 414-229-4401, FAX 414-229-2879, clacs@uwm.edu.

327.172 CHE ISSN 1423-6826
UNSERE WELT; Zeitung der Schweizerischen Friedensbewegung. Text in German. 1978. q. CHF 20 domestic; USD 20 foreign (effective 2003). bk.rev. 8 p./no. 5 cols./p.; back issues avail. **Document type:** *Newspaper, Consumer.* **Description:** Provides a newspaper for the Swiss peace movement on disarmament, solidarity and human rights.
Related titles: Online - full text ed.
Published by: Swiss Peace Movement, PO Box 126, Oberburg, 3414, Switzerland. TEL 41344229370, FAX 44134230716, comtex@spectraweb.ch, http://home.sunrise.ch/comtex/uw.htm. Ed. Martin Schwander. Circ: 20,000.

327 SWE ISSN 1650-2035
UPPSALA PEACE RESEARCH PAPERS. Text in English. 2000. irreg., latest vol.8, 2004. SEK 50 per issue (effective 2006). back issues avail. **Document type:** *Monographic series, Academic/Scholarly.*
Related titles: Online - full text ed.
Published by: Uppsala Universitet, Institutionen foer Freds- och Konfliktforskning/University of Uppsala, Department of Peace and Conflict Research, Gamla Torget 3, PO Box 514, Uppsala, 75120, Sweden. TEL 46-18-4710000, FAX 46-18-695102, info@pcr.uu.se.

327.174 GBR ISSN 1740-8083
V E R T I C BRIEF. Text in English. 1999. irreg. back issues avail. **Document type:** *Monographic series.* **Description:** Contains ideas, themes and conclusions that emerged during the Technical Coordination Meeting for legislative and technical assistance facilitators and providers.
Formerly (until 2003): V E R T I C Briefing Paper (1471-7980); Which superseded in part (1992-1999): Confidence Building Matters; (1992-1999): Implementation Matters; (1990-1999): Verification Matters Briefing Papers
Related titles: Online - full text ed.: free (effective 2009).
Published by: Verification Research, Training and Information Centre, Development House, 56-64 Leonard St, London, EC2A 4LT, United Kingdom. TEL 44-20-70650880, FAX 44-20-70650890, info@vertic.org. Ed. Angela Woodward.

355 GBR ISSN 1474-8045
V E R T I C MATTERS. Variant title: V E R T I C Annual Report. Text in English. 1987. irreg., latest 2007. GBP 10 per issue (effective 2009). back issues avail. **Document type:** *Monographic series, Corporate.* **Description:** Covers voluntary transparency measures to increase trust in states' nuclear programme.
Formerly (until 2001): V E R T I C Research Reports; Which superseded in part (1992-1999): Confidence Building Matters; (1992-1999): Implementation Matters; (1990-1999): Verification Matters Briefing Papers
Related titles: Online - full text ed.: free (effective 2009).
Published by: Verification Research, Training and Information Centre, Development House, 56-64 Leonard St, London, EC2A 4LT, United Kingdom. TEL 44-20-70650880, FAX 44-20-70650890, info@vertic.org. Ed. Michael Crowley.

VAART FOERSVAR; foer fred, frihet, framtid. *see* MILITARY

327 SWE ISSN 0042-2134
VAERLDSHORISONT; tidskrift foer FNs ideer. Text in Swedish. 1947. q. SEK 150 (effective 2007). adv. bk.rev. illus. index. **Document type:** *Magazine, Consumer.* **Description:** Directed to inform and be a forum for debate about the UN and UN-related questions.
Incorporates (1970-1974): F N - Studiebladet (0345-3472)
Published by: Svenska FN-Foerbundet/United Nations Association of Sweden, PO Box 15115, Stockholm, 10465, Sweden. TEL 46-8-4622540, FAX 46-8-6418876, info@fn.se. Ed. Lott Jansson. Circ: 8,000.

327 SWE ISSN 0042-2754
D31
VAERLDSPOLITIKENS DAGSFRAAGOR. Text in Swedish. 1940. 12/yr. SEK 370; SEK 50 per issue (effective 2008). charts. back issues avail. **Document type:** *Magazine, Academic/Scholarly.*
Published by: Utrikespolitiska Institutet/The Swedish Institute of International Affairs, Drottning Kristinas Vaeg 37, PO Box 27035, Stockholm, 10251, Sweden. TEL 46-8-51176800, FAX 46-8-51176899, info@ui.se. Ed. Lena Karlsson.

VAESTSAHARA. *see* HISTORY—History Of Africa

327 951.9 KOR ISSN 1228-517X
DS930
VANTAGE POINT; developments in North Korea. Text in English. 1976. m. USD 70; USD 7 newsstand/cover (effective 2004). illus. Index. back issues avail.; reprints avail. **Document type:** *Magazine, Consumer.*
Formerly (until 1978): North Korea Newsletter (1012-4470)
Indexed: BAS, I13, PRA, RASB.
—BLDSC (9145.293100), IE, Ingenta.
Published by: Yonhap News Agency, 85-1 Susong-dong, Jongro-gu, Seoul, Korea, S. FAX 82-2-3983463, http://www.yna.co.kr. Ed. Heung-sik Kim. Pub. Young-sup Chang. Circ: 3,000.

327 DEU ISSN 0042-384X
JZ8
VEREINTE NATIONEN; Zeitschrift fuer die Vereinten Nationen und ihre Sonderorganisationen. Text in German. 1962. bi-m. EUR 63 (effective 2010). adv. bk.rev. charts; stat.; illus. reprint service avail. from SCH. **Document type:** *Journal, Academic/Scholarly.* **Description:** Presents articles, reports and documentation concerning the procedures and actions of the UN.
Indexed: A22, BAS, CA, DIP, IBR, IBZ, P42, PAIS, PRA, PSA, SCOPUS, T02.
—IE, Infotrieve. **CCC.**
Published by: (Deutsche Gesellschaft fuer die Vereinten Nationen), Nomos Verlagsgesellschaft mbH und Co. KG, Waldseestr 3-5, Baden-Baden, 76530, Germany. TEL 49-7221-21040, FAX 49-7221-210427, marketing@nomos.de, nomos@nomos.de, http://www.nomos.de. Ed. Anja Papenfuss. Adv. contact Bettina Roos. page EUR 1,590; trim 190 x 277. Circ: 3,300 (paid and controlled).

327 GBR
VERIFICATION ORGANISATIONS DIRECTORY (YEAR). Text in English. 1999. a. looseleaf. back issues avail. **Document type:** *Directory.* **Description:** Global directory of verification organizations in the fields of arms control and disarmament. Organizations included are involved in either verification or monitoring activity, or verification research.
Published by: Verification Research, Training and Information Centre, Development House, 56-64 Leonard St, London, EC2A 4LT, United Kingdom. TEL 44-20-70650880, FAX 44-20-70650890, info@vertic.org.

327 GBR ISSN 1477-3759
JX1974
VERIFICATION YEARBOOK. Text in English. 1991. irreg., latest 2004. price varies. back issues avail. **Document type:** *Journal, Academic/Scholarly.* **Description:** Covers information about Verification Research, Training and Information Centre.
Former titles (until 2000): Verification (1355-5847); (until 1994): Verification Report (Year) (0963-1607)
—BLDSC (9170.058500).
Published by: Verification Research, Training and Information Centre, Development House, 56-64 Leonard St, London, EC2A 4LT, United Kingdom. TEL 44-20-70650880, FAX 44-20-70650890, info@vertic.org.

327 AUT
VERZEICHNIS DER KONSULARISCHEN VERTRETUNGEN IN OESTERREICH. Text in German. 1973. bi-m. **Document type:** *Directory, Government.*
Published by: Bundesministerium fuer Auswaertige Angelegenheiten, Ballhausplatz 2, Vienna, W 1014, Austria. Circ: (controlled).

327 RUS ISSN 2071-8160
➤ **VESTNIK M G I M O - UNIVERSITETA.** (Moskovskii Gosudarstvennyi Institut Mezhdunarodnyh Otnoshenii) Text in Russian. 2008. bi-m. **Document type:** *Journal, Academic/Scholarly.*
Related titles: Online - full text ed.
Published by: Moskovskii Gosudarstvennyi Institut Mezhdunarodnyh Otnoshenii/Moscow State Institute of International Relations, prospekt Vernadskogo, 76, Moscow, 119454, Russian Federation. TEL 7-495-5046570, http://www.mgimo.ru. Ed. A V Torkunov.

327.172 USA ISSN 1063-9381
JZ5511.2
VETERANS FOR PEACE JOURNAL. Text in English. 1986. q. USD 25 membership (effective 2003); Journal subscr. comes with membership. bk.rev. back issues avail. **Document type:** *Newsletter.* **Description:** Addresses the issues of foreign policy, the cost of war, disarmament, peaceful conflict, and United Nations reform.
Published by: Veterans for Peace, Inc., World Community Center, 438 N Skinker, St Louis, MO 63130. TEL 314-725-6005, FAX 314-725-7103, vfp@igc.org, http://www.veteransforpeace.org/. Ed., R&P Jerry Genesio. Circ: 2,500.

327.172 305.90697 USA
VETERANS FOR PEACE NEWSLETTER. (After vol.3, no.1 (Jun., 2000) publication no longer assigned with vol. & issue nos. First issue with seasonal designation: Winter 2000-2001.) Text in English. 1998. s-a. USD 25 membership (effective 2003); Journal subscr. comes with membership. **Document type:** *Newsletter.*
Related titles: Online - full content ed.
Published by: Veterans for Peace, Inc., World Community Center, 438 N Skinker, St Louis, MO 63130. TEL 314-725-6005, FAX 314-725-7103, vfp@igc.org.

493.21 BEL ISSN 1781-3816
A VIEW FROM BRUSSELS. Text in English. 2004. irreg. **Document type:** *Bulletin, Trade.*
—**CCC.**
Published by: EuroComment, Rue Stevin 186, Brussels, 1000, Belgium. TEL 32-2-7337233, FAX 32-2-7354055, info@eurocomment-diffusion.eu, http://www.eurocomment-diffusion.eu.

327 325 NLD ISSN 1877-8518
VLUCHTELINGENWERK MAGAZINE. Text in Dutch. 1979. q. EUR 20 (effective 2010). **Document type:** *Magazine, Consumer.*
Former titles (until 2009): Contouren (1389-0875); (until 1999): Status (Amsterdam) (0927-7439); (until 1991): Vluchtelingenwerk (0921-3295)
Published by: VluchtelingenWerk Nederland, Postbus 2894, Amsterdam, 1000 CW, Netherlands. TEL 31-20-3467200, FAX 31-20-6178155, info@vluchtelingenwerk.nl, http://www.vluchtelingenwerk.nl.

VOENNYI DIPLOMAT/MILITARY DIPLOMAT. *see* MILITARY

327 304.6 NLD ISSN 1574-6356
VOETSPOREN. Text in Dutch. 2003. q. EUR 20 (effective 2010).
Published by: VluchtelingenWerk Nederland, Postbus 2894, Amsterdam, 1000 CW, Netherlands. TEL 31-20-3467200, FAX 31-20-6178155, info@vluchtelingenwerk.nl, http://www.vluchtelingenwerk.nl.

327 CHN ISSN 1000-9582
VOICE OF FRIENDSHIP/YOUSHENG. Text in English. bi-m. **Document type:** *Journal, Academic/Scholarly.*
Related titles: Online - full text ed.
Published by: Zhongguo Renmin Duiwai Youhao Xiehui/Chinese People's Association for Friendship with Foreign Countries, 1, Taijichang Dajie, Beijing, 100740, China. TEL 86-10-65122782, FAX 86-10-65128354.

327 DEU ISSN 0042-8337
VOLK AUF DEM WEG. Text in German. 1951. m. EUR 30 (effective 2006). bk.rev. illus. **Document type:** *Bulletin, Consumer.*
Published by: Landsmannschaft der Deutschen aus Russland e.V., Raitelsbergstr 49, Stuttgart, 70188, Germany. TEL 49-711-166590, FAX 49-711-2864413, lmdr-ev@t-online.de. Ed. Hans Kampen. Circ: 4,000.

VREDE.NU. *see* LAW—International Law

VREDES MAGAZINE. *see* MILITARY

327.172 NLD ISSN 1879-7288
VREDESEDUCATIE. Running title: Nieuwsbrief Vredeseducatie. Text in Dutch. 200?. a. **Document type:** *Newsletter.*
Published by: (Fort van de Democratie), Stichting Vredeseducatie, Herinneringscentrum Fort De Bilt, Biltsestraatweg 160, Utrecht, 3573 PS, Netherlands. TEL 31-30-2723500, FAX 31-30-2723563, vrede@xs4all.nl, http://www.redeseducatie.nl. Eds. Geu Visser, Jan Durk Tuinier.

VREDESSPIRAAL. *see* RELIGIONS AND THEOLOGY

W C O NEWS. (World Customs Organization) *see* PUBLIC ADMINISTRATION

327 DEU ISSN 1867-3015
W I F I S AKTUELL. (Wissenschaftliches Forum fuer Internationale Sicherheit) Text in German. 1995. irreg., latest vol.44, 2010. price varies. **Document type:** *Monographic series, Academic/Scholarly.*
Published by: (Wissenschaftliches Forum fuer Internationale Sicherheit e.V.), Edition Temmen, Hohenlohestr 21, Bremen, 28209, Germany. TEL 49-421-348430, FAX 49-421-348094, info@edition-temmen.de, http://www.edition-temmen.de. Ed. Horst Temmen.

327 CHN ISSN 1003-3386
WAIJIAO XUEYUAN XUEBAO/FOREIGN AFFAIRS COLLEGE. JOURNAL. Text in Chinese. 1984. q. USD 53.40 (effective 2009). **Document type:** *Journal, Academic/Scholarly.*
Related titles: Online - full content ed.; Online - full text ed.
—East View.
Published by: Waijiao Xueyuan/Foreign Affairs University, Xicheng-qu, 24, Zhanlan Lu, Beijing, 100037, China. http://www.cfau.edu.cn/.

327 CHN
WAISHI TIANDI/FOREIGN AFFAIRS WORLD. Text in Chinese. bi-m. **Description:** Covers China's diplomatic policies. Introduces foreign customs and culture to Chinese people, and Chinese culture to the world.
Published by: Waishi Tiandi Bianjibu, No 72, Renmin Nanlu 2 Duan, Chengdu, Sichuan 610016, China. TEL 86-28-6635186, FAX 86-28-6635194. Ed. Ren Chang An. **Dist. overseas by:** China International Book Trading Corp, 35 Chegongzhuang Xilu, Haidian District, PO Box 399, Beijing 100044, China.

327.2 USA
WASHINGTON - JAPAN JOURNAL. Text in English. 1957. q. USD 15; USD 22 foreign (effective 1999). adv. bk.rev. illus.
Formerly: Japan-America Society of Washington. Bulletin (0021-4299)
Published by: Japan-America Society of Washington Inc., 1020 19th St, N W, LL, Washington, DC 20036-6101. TEL 202-289-8290, FAX 202-789-8265. Ed. Patricia R Kearns. Circ: 3,000.

320 USA ISSN 1064-3028
DS779.15
WASHINGTON JOURNAL OF MODERN CHINA. Text in English. 1992. s-a. USD 30 to individuals; USD 40 to institutions (effective 2011). bk.rev. Index. back issues avail. **Document type:** *Journal, Academic/Scholarly.* **Description:** Focuses on current policy issues relating to China and US-China relations.
Indexed: A01, CA, P42, T02.
Published by: US-China Policy Foundation, 316 Pennsylvania Ave SE, Ste 201-202, Washington, DC 20003. TEL 202-547-8615, FAX 202-547-8853, uscpf@uscpf.org.

327 USA ISSN 0512-610X
DT1
WASHINGTON NOTES ON AFRICA. Text in English. 1972. 3/yr. USD 32 (effective 2003 - 2004). 8 p./no. 3 cols./p.; back issues avail. **Document type:** *Newsletter.* **Description:** Analyzes current policy issues affecting U.S. - Africa relations, especially legislative matters; links economic and social justice themes.
Published by: Washington Office on Africa, 212 E Capitol St NE, Washington, DC 20003-1036. TEL 202-547-7503, FAX 202-547-7505, http://www.woaafrica.org. Ed., R&P Leon Spencer. Circ: 2,600 (paid and controlled).

327 USA ISSN 0278-937X
THE WASHINGTON PAPERS. Text in English. 1972. irreg., latest 2006. price varies. back issues avail. **Document type:** *Monographic series.* **Description:** Offers analyses of international policy issues.
—BLDSC (9263.240000), IE, Ingenta. **CCC.**
Published by: (Center for Strategic and International Studies), Praeger Publishers (Subsidiary of: Greenwood Publishing Group Inc.), 1800 K St, N W, Ste 400, Washington, DC 20006-2294. tech.support@greenwood.com, http://www.greenwood.com.

327.172 USA ISSN 1050-2823
WASHINGTON PEACE LETTER. Text in English. 1963. m. USD 25 (effective 2000). adv. bk.rev. 12 p./no. 4 cols./p.; back issues avail. **Document type:** *Newspaper.* **Description:** Covers news articles, reports and analysis on nonviolent peace and social justice activities at international, national and local levels, especially in the Washington D.C. areas with an antiracist analysis.
Formerly: Washington Peace Center. Newsletter
Published by: Washington Peace Center, 1426 9th St NW, # 306, Washington, DC 20001-3330. TEL 202-234-2000, FAX 202-234-7064, wpc@igc.org. R&P Maria Lya Ramos. adv.: B&W page USD 2,810. Circ: 5,000.

327.2 USA ISSN 0163-660X
D839
➤ **THE WASHINGTON QUARTERLY.** Abbreviated title: T W Q. Text in English. 1978. q. GBP 237 combined subscription in United Kingdom to institutions (print & online eds.); EUR 378 combined subscription to institutions (print & online eds.); USD 385 combined subscription in North America to institutions (print & online eds.); USD 474 combined subscription elsewhere to institutions (print & online eds.) (effective 2012). adv. illus. Index. back issues avail.; reprint service avail. from PSC. **Document type:** *Journal, Academic/Scholarly.* **Description:** Journal of international affairs includes essays on foreign and defense policy, international economics, as well as emerging international issues.
Formerly (until 1978): The Washington Review of Strategic and International Studies (0147-1465)
Related titles: Microform ed.: (from PQC); Online - full text ed.: ISSN 1530-9177. GBP 213 in United Kingdom to institutions; EUR 340 to institutions; USD 346 in North America to institutions; USD 426 elsewhere to institutions (effective 2012).
Indexed: A01, A02, A03, A08, A20, A22, A26, ABCPolSci, ABS&EES, AMB, ASCA, AmH&L, B04, BAS, BRD, C12, CA, CCME, CurCont, E01, E08, FutSurv, G06, G07, G08, HistAb, I05, I13, IBSS, LID&ISL, M01, M02, M05, M06, MASUSE, MEA&I, MLA-IB, P02, P10, P27, P30, P34, P42, P47, P48, P53, P54, PAIS, PCI, PQC, PSA, PerIslam, RASB, S02, S03, S09, S11, SCOPUS, SSAI, SSAb, SSCI, SSI, SociolAb, T02, W03, W05, W07.
—BLDSC (9263.243000), CIS, IE, Infotrieve, Ingenta. **CCC.**
Published by: (Center for Strategic and International Studies), Routledge (Subsidiary of: Taylor & Francis Group), 270 Madison Ave, New York, NY 10016. TEL 212-216-7800, FAX 212-244-1563, orders@taylorandfrancis.com, http://www.routledge.com. Ed. Alexander T J Lennon.

327 USA ISSN 8755-4917
DS63.1
WASHINGTON REPORT ON MIDDLE EAST AFFAIRS; a survey of United States relations with Middle East countries. Text in English. 1982. 8/yr. USD 29 domestic (print or online ed.); USD 35 in Canada; USD 70 elsewhere (effective 2011). adv. bk.rev. illus. back issues avail. **Document type:** *Journal, Academic/Scholarly.* **Description:** Provides nonpartisan coverage of all aspects of Middle Eastern affairs, including political, social, religious, cultural and economic issues, analysis of UN debate and policy, and relevant events in other regions affecting the Middle East and the Islamic world, emphasizing viewpoints not readily available in the mainstream US media.
Related titles: Online - full text ed.
Indexed: A01, A03, A08, A22, A26, DYW, E08, ENW, G06, G07, G08, I02, I05, IJP, J01, LeftInd, M02, M05, M06, M08, M10, P02, P05, P10, P34, P45, P47, P48, P53, P54, PAIS, PQC, PerIslam, S09, SCOPUS, T02.
—BLDSC (9263.245400), IE, Ingenta.
Published by: American Educational Trust (A E T), 1902 18th St, PO Box 53062, Washington, DC 20009. TEL 202-939-6050, 800-368-5788, FAX 202-265-4574, subscriptions@wrmea.com. Pub. Andrew I Killgore.

327 USA ISSN 0275-5599
F1401
WASHINGTON REPORT ON THE HEMISPHERE. Text in English. 1980. fortn. USD 235 to individuals; USD 435 to institutions (effective 2001). bk.rev. index. **Description:** Provides a review of US, Canadian and Latin American relations as well as political, trade, diplomatic, financial, NAFTA, environmental, economic, military, social justice issues and human rights.
Indexed: B16, C03, CBCARef, HRIR, P10, P45, P48, P53, P54, PQC, S11.
Published by: Council on Hemispheric Affairs, 1250 Connecticut Ave NW, # C1, Washington, DC 20036-2603. TEL 202-216-9261, FAX 202-216-9261, coha@coha.org, http://www.coha.org. Ed. Laurence R Birns. Circ: 1,500.

WATER ALTERNATIVES; an interdisciplinary journal on water, politics and development. *see* WATER RESOURCES

327.117 341.734 USA ISSN 1935-8431
U793
WEAPONS OF MASS DESTRUCTION AND TERRORISM. Text in English. 2007 (Mar.). irreg., latest 2008. **Document type:** *Monographic series, Academic/Scholarly.*
Formerly announced as: Terrorism and Weapons of Mass Destruction and Disruption
Published by: McGraw-Hill, Contemporary Learning Series (Subsidiary of: McGraw-Hill Companies, Inc.), 1221 Ave of the Americas, New York, NY 10020. TEL 212-904-2000, FAX 212-512-2000, customer.service@mcgraw-hill.com, http://www.mhhe.com/cls/.

327 USA
WEEKLY INTELLIGENCE NOTES. Abbreviated title: W I Ns. Text in English. 1998. w. free to members (effective 2011). back issues avail. **Document type:** *Newsletter, Consumer.* **Description:** Contains summaries and commentaries covering open-source media reporting on intelligence, counterintelligence, clandestine operations, propaganda and information operations activities.
Media: Online - full text. **Related titles:** E-mail ed.
Published by: Association of Former Intelligence Officers, 6723 Whittier Ave, Ste 200, Mclean, VA 22101. TEL 703-790-0320, FAX 703-991-1278, afio@afio.com.

327 DEU ISSN 1865-7966
WELT-SICHTEN. Text in German. 2007. m. EUR 39 domestic; EUR 51 in Europe; EUR 62.40 elsewhere (effective 2011). adv. bk.rev.; film rev. charts; illus. back issues avail. **Document type:** *Magazine, Consumer.*
Formed by the merger of (1965-2007): Der Ueberblick (0343-0553); (2005-2007): E1ns Entwicklungspolitik (1861-874X)
Related titles: Online - full text ed.
Indexed: DIP, IBR, IBZ.
Published by: Verein zur Foerderung der Entwicklungspolitischen Publizistik e.V., Emil-von-Behring-Str 3, Frankfurt am Main, 60439, Germany. TEL 49-69-58098138, FAX 49-69-58098162, eins@entwicklungspolitik.org, http://www.entwicklungspolitik.org. Ed. Bernd Ludermann. Circ: 13,000.

327 DEU ISSN 0944-8101
D839
➤ **WELTTRENDS**; Zeitschrift fuer internationale Politik. Text in German; Summaries in English. 1993. bi-m. EUR 40; EUR 25 to students; EUR 9.50 newsstand/cover (effective 2011). adv. bk.rev. bibl. index. back issues avail. **Document type:** *Journal, Academic/Scholarly.* **Description:** German-Polish journal for international politics and comparative studies dedicated to supporting a comprehensive intellectual communication among scholars from the East and the West.
Indexed: CA, IBSS, P42, PAIS, PSA, S02, S03, SCOPUS, SociolAb, T02.
Published by: WeltTrends e.V., August-Bebel-Str 89, Potsdam, 14482, Germany. TEL 49-331-9774540, FAX 49-331-9774696. Ed. Raimund Kraemer. Adv. contact Lutz Kleinwaechter. Circ: 900 (paid and controlled). **Co-sponsor:** Instytut Zachodny.

327 DEU ISSN 1861-5139
WELTTRENDS-LEHRTEXTE. Text in German. 2005. irreg., latest vol.15, 2009. price varies. **Document type:** *Monographic series, Academic/Scholarly.*
Published by: (WeltTrends e.V.), Universitaetsverlag Potsdam, Am Neuen Palais 10, Potsdam, 14469, Germany. TEL 49-331-9774458, FAX 49-331-9774625, ubpub@uni-potsdam.de, http://info.ub.uni-potsdam.de/verlag.htm.

327 DEU ISSN 1864-0656
WELTTRENDS-PAPIERE. Text in German. 2007. irreg., latest vol.11, 2009. price varies. **Document type:** *Monographic series, Academic/Scholarly.*
Published by: (WeltTrends e.V.), Universitaetsverlag Potsdam, Am Neuen Palais 10, Potsdam, 14469, Germany. TEL 49-331-9774458, FAX 49-331-9774625, ubpub@uni-potsdam.de, http://info.ub.uni-potsdam.de/verlag.htm.

327 DEU ISSN 1866-0738
WELTTRENDS-THESIS. Text in German. 2008. irreg., latest vol.7, 2009. price varies. **Document type:** *Monographic series, Academic/Scholarly.*
Published by: (WeltTrends e.V.), Universitaetsverlag Potsdam, Am Neuen Palais 10, Potsdam, 14469, Germany. TEL 49-331-9774458, FAX 49-331-9774625, ubpub@uni-potsdam.de, http://info.ub.uni-potsdam.de/verlag.htm.

320 TWN ISSN 0591-2539
➤ **WENTI YU YANJIU/ISSUES AND STUDIES.** Text in Chinese. 1961. bi-m. USD 24 (effective 2003). adv. abstr.; charts; maps; illus.; bibl.; stat. Index. 120 p./no.; back issues avail. **Document type:** *Monographic series, Academic/Scholarly.* **Description:** Focuses on academic analysis of global issues and international affairs.
Related titles: Online - full content ed.
Published by: National Chengchi University, Institute of International Relations, 64 Wanshou Road, Wenshan District, Taipei, 116, Taiwan. TEL 886-2-82377277, FAX 886-2-29378606, iir@nccu.edu.tw. Ed. Szu-Yin Ho. R&P, Adv. contact Yi-Hua Chen. Circ: 376 (paid); 705 (controlled).

327 BEL ISSN 0779-665X
WERELDWIJD; tijdschrift over evangelizatie en ontwikkeling. Text in Dutch. 1970. m. (10/yr.). adv. **Description:** Covers issues pertaining to evangelization and development in the Third World.
Indexed: CERDIC.
Published by: V.Z.W. WereldMediaHaus, Vlasfabriekstraat 11, Brussel, 1060, Belgium. wereldwijd@wereldwijd.ngonet.be. Ed. Gie Goris. Circ: 22,000.

327 DEU
WERKSTATT 3 - PROGRAMM. Text in German. 1979. m. free. **Document type:** *Bulletin.* **Description:** Information about the problems of the relations between industrialized countries and developing countries.
Published by: Verein Werkstatt 3, Nernstweg 32-34, Hamburg, 22765, Germany. TEL 49-40-392191, FAX 49-40-3909866. Circ: 10,000.

327 TWN ISSN 0043-3047
DS895.F7
WEST & EAST/CHUNG-MEI YUEH-K'AN; an independent monthly. Text in Chinese, English. 1956. m. TWD 300, USD 10. adv. charts; stat. **Description:** Sino-American exchange of cultural and economic news.
Indexed: BAS.
Published by: (Sino-American Cultural and Economic Association), Chang Chao Wen-yi, No 23 Hungchow S. Rd, Sec 1, 11th Fl, Taipei, Taiwan. TEL 02-3914200. Ed. Yih Hsien Yu. Circ: 2,400.

327 GBR ISSN 0140-2382
JN94.A1
➤ **WEST EUROPEAN POLITICS.** Abbreviated title: W E P. Text in English. 1978. 5/yr. GBP 654 combined subscription in United Kingdom to institutions (print & online eds.); EUR 852, USD 1,070 combined subscription to institutions (print & online eds.) (effective 2012). adv. bk.rev. illus. index. back issues avail.; reprint service avail. from PSC. **Document type:** *Journal, Academic/Scholarly.* **Description:** Covers all major political and social developments in all Western European countries.
Related titles: CD-ROM ed.; Microfilm ed.: (from PQC); Online - full text ed.: ISSN 1743-9655. GBP 589 in United Kingdom to institutions; EUR 766, USD 963 to institutions (effective 2012) (from IngentaConnect).
Indexed: A01, A02, A03, A08, A20, A22, A25, A26, ABCPolSci, AmHI, B04, BRD, BrHumI, CA, CurCont, DIP, E01, E08, ESPM, FR, G05, G06, G07, G08, GEOBASE, H07, HistAb, I05, I13, IBR, IBSS, IBZ, P02, P10, P27, P30, P34, P42, P47, P48, P53, P54, PAIS, PCI, PQC, PRA, PSA, RASB, RiskAb, S02, S03, S08, S09, S11, S23, SCOPUS, SOPODA, SPAA, SSA, SSAI, SSAb, SSCI, SSI, SSciA, SociolAb, T02, W03, W07.
—IE, Infotrieve, Ingenta. **CCC.**
Published by: Routledge (Subsidiary of: Taylor & Francis Group), 4 Park Sq, Milton Park, Abingdon, Oxon OX14 4RN, United Kingdom. TEL 44-20-70176000, FAX 44-20-70176336, subscriptions@tandf.co.uk, http://www.routledge.com. Eds. Gordon Smith TEL 44-20-74057686, Klaus H Goetz TEL 49-331-9773341, Peter Mair TEL 39-55-4685210. **Subscr. to:** Taylor & Francis Ltd., Journals Customer Service, Sheepen Pl, Colchester, Essex CO3 3LP, United Kingdom. TEL 44-20-70175544, FAX 44-20-70175198.

➤ **WESTERN POLICIES.** *see* POLITICAL SCIENCE

327 USA ISSN 1936-3419
➤ **THE WHITEHEAD JOURNAL OF DIPLOMACY AND INTERNATIONAL RELATIONS.** Text in English. 2000. s-a. bk.rev. Index. back issues avail.; reprints avail. **Document type:** *Journal, Academic/Scholarly.* **Description:** Publishes original scholarship from international leaders, policymakers, and scholars, as well as the views of those who are active in nontraditional applications of diplomacy, including persons from nongovernmental organizations and international business.
Formerly (until 2005): Seton Hall Journal of Diplomacy and International Relations (1538-6589)
Related titles: CD-ROM ed.; Online - full text ed.: ISSN 1936-3427.
Indexed: ABS&EES, CA, P02, P10, P27, P42, P45, P48, P53, P54, PAIS, PQC, PSA, SCOPUS, SociolAb, T02.
—BLDSC (9311.023630), IE.
Published by: Seton Hall University, School of Diplomacy & International Relations, 400 S Orange Ave, S Orange, NJ 07079. TEL 973-275-2258, FAX 973-275-2519, alumni@shu.edu, http://diplomacy.shu.edu. Ed. Kathryn Salucka.

327.092 GBR ISSN 0956-7984
WHO'S WHO IN INTERNATIONAL AFFAIRS. Text in English. 1990. irreg. USD 595 per issue (effective 2009). reprints avail. **Document type:** *Directory, Trade.* **Description:** Profiles 7,000 leading diplomats, politicians, government ministers, heads of state, professors, and journalists.
Published by: (Europa Publications Ltd.), Routledge (Subsidiary of: Taylor & Francis Group), 2 Park Sq, Milton Park, Abingdon, Oxon OX14 4RN, United Kingdom. TEL 44-20-70176000, FAX 44-20-70176699, orders@taylorandfrancis.com.

327 AUT ISSN 1010-1721
WIENER BLAETTER ZUR FRIEDENSFORSCHUNG. Text in German. 1974. 4/yr. adv. bk.rev. **Document type:** *Journal, Academic/Scholarly.*
Indexed: IBR, IBZ.
Published by: Universitaetszentrum fuer Friedenforschung, Universitaetsstr 7-III, Vienna, W 1010, Austria. TEL 43-1-427728201, FAX 43-1-427747493, erwin.bader@univie.ac.at, http://frieden.univie.ac.at. Ed., Adv. contact Sigrid Poellinger. Circ: 500.

WILLAMETTE JOURNAL OF INTERNATIONAL LAW AND DISPUTE RESOLUTION. *see* LAW—International Law

327.172 USA
JX1901
WIN; through revolutionary nonviolence. Text in English. 1945. q. USD 15 to individuals; USD 25 to institutions (effective 2008). adv. bk.rev.; film rev. illus. cum.index. back issues avail.; reprints avail. **Document type:** *Magazine, Consumer.* **Description:** Provides political analysis from a pacifist perspective.
Former titles (until 2007): The Nonviolent Activist (8755-7428); (until 1984): W R L News (0042-9791)
Related titles: Microform ed.: (from PQC).
Indexed: AltPI, HRIR.
Published by: War Resisters League, 339 Lafayette St, New York, NY 10012-2782. TEL 212-228-0450, FAX 212-228-6193. Ed. Francesca Fiorentini.

364.65 GBR ISSN 1472-443X
HV6254
THE WIRE (LONDON, 1963). Text in English. 1963. m. free to members (effective 2009). bk.rev. back issues avail. **Document type:** *Newsletter, Consumer.* **Description:** Summarizes key pieces of research, provides regular World Wide Appeals on individuals at risk, and interviews with human rights defenders.
Former titles (until 2001): Amnesty International News (1363-8246); (until 1995): Amnesty International Newsletter (0308-6887); Amnesty International Monthly (0003-1941); Amnesty International Review
Related titles: Microfiche ed.: (from IDC); Online - full content ed.: free (effective 2009); Arabic ed.: 2001; French ed.: Le Til d'AI. 2001.
Indexed: HRIR, RASB.
—**CCC.**
Published by: Amnesty International U K, 17-25 New Inn Yard, London, EC2A 3EA, United Kingdom. TEL 44-20-70331500, FAX 44-20-70331503, sct@amnesty.org.uk, http://www.amnesty.org.uk. Circ: 30,000.

327 DEU ISSN 1864-6131
WISSENSCHAFTLICHES FORUM FUER INTERNATIONALE SICHERHEIT. SCHRIFTENREIHE. Text in German. 1992. irreg., latest vol.27, 2009. price varies. **Document type:** *Monographic series, Academic/Scholarly.*
Published by: (Wissenschaftliches Forum fuer Internationale Sicherheit e.V.), Edition Temmen, Hohenlohestr 21, Bremen, 28209, Germany. TEL 49-421-348430, FAX 49-421-348094, info@edition-temmen.de, http://www.edition-temmen.de.

327.172 USA
WOMEN STRIKE FOR PEACE. LEGISLATIVE ALERT. Text in English. 1979. 10/yr. looseleaf. USD 25 (effective 2000). bk.rev. back issues avail. **Document type:** *Newsletter.* **Description:** Contains legislative updates and news on peace and human rights issues.
Published by: Women Strike for Peace (Washington), 1111 University Blvd W., Apt. 1005, Silver Spring, MD 20902-3327. TEL 202-543-2660, FAX 202-544-9613. Ed. Edith Villastrigo. Circ: 2,200.

327 BEL
WORKING PARTY REPORTS. Text in English. 1989. irreg., latest vol.21, 1996. back issues avail. **Document type:** *Monographic series, Trade.* **Description:** Publishes the findings of experts from a range of backgrounds on EU policies in the making or in need of reform.
Published by: Centre for European Policy Studies, Pl du Congres 1, Brussels, 1000, Belgium. TEL 32-2-229-3911, FAX 32-2-219-4151, info@ceps.be, http://www.ceps.be/Default.php. Ed. Anne Harrington. R&P Dominic Gilmore.

328 ARG ISSN 1851-6661
WORKSHOP INTERNACIONAL. Text in Spanish. 2008. a. **Document type:** *Monographic series, Academic/Scholarly.*
Published by: Universidad Nacional del Litoral, Bv Pellegrini 2750, Santa Fe, S3000, Argentina. TEL 54-342-4571110, http://www.unl.edu.ar.

327 IND ISSN 0971-8052
AP8
WORLD AFFAIRS. Text in English. 1992. q. USD 40; USD 10 per issue (effective 2011). adv. **Document type:** *Journal, Academic/Scholarly.* **Description:** Covers a broad range of subjects, such as empowerment of the people, health in developing countries, agriculture and bio-technology, information technology, world cultures and human values.
Related titles: Online - full text ed.: ISSN 0974-0937. INR 500 domestic to individuals; INR 700 domestic to institutions; USD 40 foreign (effective 2008).
Indexed: I13, P42, PAIS, PSA, SociolAb.
Published by: Kapur Surya Foundation, Bijwasan Najafgarh Rd, New Delhi, 110 037, India. TEL 91-11-24642969, FAX 91-11-24628994. Ed. Chanda Singh. **Subscr. to:** Indianjournals.com, Divan Enterprises, B-9, Local Shopping Complex, A-Block, Naraina Vihar, Ring Rd, New Delhi 110 028, India. TEL 91-11-25770411, FAX 91-11-25778876, info@indianjournals.com, http://www.indianjournals.com.

327.172 USA ISSN 0043-8200
JX1901
➤ **WORLD AFFAIRS (WASHINGTON)**; a journal of ideas and debate. Text in English. 1834. bi-m. USD 39 (effective 2011). adv. bk.rev. illus. Index. back issues avail.; reprint service avail. from PSC. **Document type:** *Journal, Academic/Scholarly.* **Description:** Provides information about U.S. foreign policy.
Former titles (until 1932): Advocate of Peace Through Justice (2155-7802); (until 1920): The Advocate of Peace (2155-7799); (until 1894): The American Advocate of Peace and Arbitration (2159-5070); (until 1892): American Advocate of Peace (2159-5089); (until 1847): Advocate of Peace (2154-8390); (until 1846): The Advocate of Peace and Universal Brotherhood (2154-8420); The Advocate of Peace (2154-8382); (until 1837): American Advocate of Peace (2159-5062); Which incorporates (1831-1835): The Calumet; Which was formerly (1828-1831): Harbinger of Peace
Related titles: Microform ed.: (from PQC); (from PQC); Online - full text ed.: ISSN 1940-1582.
Indexed: A01, A02, A03, A08, A11, A20, A22, A25, A26, ABCPolSci, ABS&EES, APW, B04, BAS, BRD, C12, CA, DIP, E08, G05, G06, G07, G08, GEOBASE, H09, HistAb, I02, I05, I07, I13, IBR, IBZ, LeftInd, M01, M02, M05, M06, MASUSE, MEA&I, P02, P06, P10, P13, P27, P34, P42, P45, P47, P48, P53, P54, PAIS, PCI, PQC, PRA, PSA, PerIslam, R02, RASB, S02, S03, S05, S08, S09, S11, S23, SCOPUS, SSAI, SSAb, SSI, SociolAb, T02, W03, W05, WBA, WMB.
—BLDSC (9352.430000), IE, Ingenta. **CCC.**
Published by: (American Peace Society), World Affairs Institute (Subsidiary of: American Peace Society), 1319 Eighteenth St, NW, Washington, DC 20036. TEL 202-349-8550. **Subscr. to:** PO Box 465, Hanover, PA 17331. TEL 717-632-3535, FAX 717-633-8920, pubsvc@tsp.sheridan.com.

327 USA ISSN 1523-9810
D839
WORLD AFFAIRS REPORT. Text in English. 1970. d. bk.rev. bibl. reprints avail. **Document type:** *Report, Academic/Scholarly.* **Description:** Contains general information on international relations and world affairs.
Formerly (until 19??): California Institute of International Studies. Report (0068-564X)
Media: Online - full text. **Related titles:** Microfilm ed.: (from PQC).
Indexed: A22, ABCPolSci, AMB, MEA&I, P06.
—Ingenta. **CCC.**
Published by: World Association of International Studies, c/o John Eipper, Department of Modern Languages and Culture, Goldsmith Hall, Adrian College, Michigan, MI 49221. jeipper@stanford.edu, http://wais.stanford.edu/.

WORLD CUSTOMS ORGANIZATION. ANNUAL REPORT; the activities of the WCO. *see* PUBLIC ADMINISTRATION

341.72 GBR
WORLD DEFENCE SYSTEMS; the international review of defence acquisition issues. Text in English. 1999. q. GBP 25, USD 41 (effective 2009). back issues avail. **Document type:** *Magazine, Trade.* **Description:** Combines detailed coverage of the latest developments in defence equipment, systems and products with in-depth analysis of national and international security and defence issues.
Related titles: Online - full content ed.: free (effective 2009).
Indexed: LID&ISL.
Published by: (University of London King's College, Centre for Defence Studies), Sovereign Publications Ltd., 32 Woodstock Grove, London, W12 8LE, United Kingdom. TEL 44-20-76160800, FAX 44-20-77241444, production@sovereign-publications.com. Ed. John Gearson TEL 44-207-8482338. Adv. contact Regi Menezes.

327.205 GBR ISSN 0965-3783
JX1625
WORLD DIRECTORY OF DIPLOMATIC REPRESENTATION. Text in English. 1992. irreg., latest 1992. USD 430 per issue (effective 2009). **Document type:** *Directory.* **Description:** Provides a complete and comprehensive guide to embassies and other government representation in over 150 countries world-wide.
Published by: (Europa Publications Ltd.), Routledge (Subsidiary of: Taylor & Francis Group), 2 Park Sq, Milton Park, Abingdon, Oxon OX14 4RN, United Kingdom. TEL 44-20-70176000, FAX 44-20-70176699, orders@taylorandfrancis.com, http://www.routledge.com.

327 USA ISSN 0277-1527
G122
WORLD FACTBOOK. Text in English. 1981. a. USD 90 in North America; USD 126 elsewhere (effective 2004). back issues avail. **Document type:** *Government.* **Description:** Compiles facts and statistics on the government, people, economy, and geography of more than 250 countries and geographic areas.
Formerly: National Basic Intelligence Factbook (0098-2091)
Related titles: CD-ROM ed.; Microform ed.: (from NTI); Online - full text ed.: ISSN 1553-8133.
Indexed: A01, A02, A03, A08, A11, A33, B07, C04, C05, C12, H05, I02, M01, M02, M04, M05, P01, P05, P42, P45, P47, PQC, R02, U01.
—CIS.
Published by: U.S. Central Intelligence Agency, c/o U S National Technical Information Service, U S Department of Commerce, 5285 Port Royal Rd, Springfield, VA 22161. **Subscr. to:** U.S. Government Printing Office, Superintendent of Documents, PO Box 371954, Pittsburgh, PA 15250. TEL 202-512-1800, FAX 202-512-2250, orders@gpo.gov, http://www.access.gpo.gov. **Dist. by:** Bernan Associates, Bernan, 4611-F Assembly Dr., Lanham, MD 20706-4391. TEL 301-459-0056, 301-459-7666.

327 USA ISSN 0196-2574
WORLD FEDERALIST NEWSLETTER. Text in English. 1976. q. USD 5 (effective 2000). bk.rev. illus. **Document type:** *Newsletter.* **Description:** Discusses options for world peace, economic progress and a livable environment. Also proposes a restructured U.N.
Related titles: Microform ed.: (from PQC).
Published by: World Federalist Association, 418 7th St, S E, Washington, DC 20003. TEL 202-546-3950, FAX 202-546-3749. Ed. Tony Fleming. Circ: 10,000.

327 USA ISSN 0161-2360
CODEN: VAJODH
WORLD GOODWILL COMMENTARY; a bulletin on current trends in world affairs. Text in English. 1968. irreg. donation. bibl. **Document type:** *Journal, Academic/Scholarly.*
Published by: (Lucis Trust), Lucis Publishing Co., 120 Wall St, Fl 24, New York, NY 10005-4001. TEL 212-292-0707. Pub. Sarah McKechnie. Circ: 12,000. **Subscr. to:** Lucis Press Ltd., 3 Whitehall Ct, London SW1A 2DD, United Kingdom.

327 IND ISSN 0043-857X
WORLD INFORMO. Text in English. 1953. m. INR 150 to non-members; free to members (effective 2011). **Document type:** *Newsletter, Trade.*
Published by: United Schools Organisation of India, U S O House, U S O Rd, Jeet Singh Marg, New Delhi, 110 067, India. TEL 91-11-26561103, FAX 91-11-26856283, usousiindia@gmail.com.

327 ZAF ISSN 1819-8600
WORLD JOURNAL OF CONFLICT RESOLUTION. Text in English. 2006. q. USD 120 in Africa to individuals; USD 180 elsewhere to individuals; USD 350 in Africa to institutions; USD 450 elsewhere to institutions; USD 85 in Africa to students; USD 100 elsewhere to students (effective 2007). **Document type:** *Journal, Academic/Scholarly.* **Description:** Explores a variety of national, inter-group and interpersonal conflicts, with a focus on international conflict.
Published by: (World Research Organization), Isis Press, PO Box 1919, Cape Town, 8000, South Africa. TEL 27-21-4471574, FAX 27-86-6219999, orders@unwro.org, http://www.unwro.org/isispress.html.

327 ZAF ISSN 1819-8619
➤ **WORLD JOURNAL OF INTERNATIONAL RELATIONS.** Text in English. 2006. q. USD 120 in Africa to individuals; USD 180 elsewhere to individuals; USD 350 in Africa to institutions; USD 450 elsewhere to institutions; USD 85 in Africa to students; USD 100 elsewhere to students (effective 2007). **Document type:** *Journal, Academic/Scholarly.* **Description:** Aims to foster an awareness of methodological and epistemological questions in the study of international relations, and to reflect research and developments of a conceptual, normative and empirical nature in all the major sub-areas.
Published by: (World Research Organization), Isis Press, PO Box 1919, Cape Town, 8000, South Africa. TEL 27-21-4471574, FAX 27-86-6219999, orders@unwro.org, http://www.unwro.org/isispress.html.

327.172 ZAF ISSN 1991-1300
➤ **WORLD JOURNAL OF PEACE AND SECURITY.** Text in English. 2006. q. USD 120 in Africa to individuals; USD 180 elsewhere to individuals; USD 350 in Africa to institutions; USD 450 elsewhere to institutions; USD 85 in Africa to students; USD 100 elsewhere to students (effective 2007). **Document type:** *Journal, Academic/Scholarly.* **Description:** Publishes theoretical, historical, and policy-oriented articles on the causes and consequences of war, and the sources and conditions of peace, promoting theoretically-based research on policy problems of armed violence, peace building and conflict resolution.
Published by: (World Research Organization), Isis Press, PO Box 1919, Cape Town, 8000, South Africa. TEL 27-21-4471574, FAX 27-86-6219999, orders@unwro.org, http://www.unwro.org/isispress.html.

➤ **WORLD JOURNAL OF PEACE THROUGH TOURISM.** *see* TRAVEL AND TOURISM

341.734 ZAF ISSN 1991-1378
➤ **WORLD JOURNAL OF TERRORISM AND NATIONS.** Text in English. 2006. q. USD 120 in Africa to individuals; USD 180 elsewhere to individuals; USD 350 in Africa to institutions; USD 450 elsewhere to institutions; USD 85 in Africa to students; USD 100 elsewhere to students (effective 2007). **Document type:** *Journal, Academic/Scholarly.* **Description:** Aims to cast new light on the origins and implications of conflict in the twenty-first century and to illuminate new approaches and solutions to countering growth and escalation of contemporary sub-state violence.
Published by: (World Research Organization), Isis Press, PO Box 1919, Cape Town, 8000, South Africa. TEL 27-21-4471574, FAX 27-86-6219999, orders@unwro.org, http://www.unwro.org/isispress.html.

327 USA
WORLD NEIGHBORS IN ACTION; a newsletter for overseas project personnel. Text in English. 1965. s-a. looseleaf. USD 10 (effective 2000). bk.rev. bibl.; charts; illus. cum.index. back issues avail. **Document type:** *Newsletter.*
Related titles: Online - full text ed.; Spanish ed.: Vecinos Mundiales en Accion; French ed.: Voisins Mondiaux en Action.
Published by: World Neighbors, Inc., 4127 N W 122nd St, Oklahoma City, OK 73120-8869. TEL 405-752-9700, FAX 405-752-9393. Ed., R&P Catheryn Koss. Circ: 2,500.

327.1 USA ISSN 0193-3329
D839
WORLD OPINION UPDATE. Text in English. 1977. m. index. **Document type:** *Newsletter, Consumer.*
Published by: (Survey Research Consultants International, Inc.), World Opinion Update, 156 Bulkley St, Williamstown, MA 01267. TEL 413-458-5338, ehh01267@aol.com. Eds. Elizabeth Hann Hastings, Philip K Hastings. Circ: 1,000 (paid).

327 USA ISSN 0895-7452
D839
WORLD OUTLOOK; a journal of international affairs. Text in English. 1985. s-a. USD 10 (effective 2010). bk.rev. back issues avail. **Document type:** *Journal, Academic/Scholarly.* **Description:** Provides a non-partisan forum for original thinking on international affairs.
Indexed: BibInd, IBR, IBZ, PAIS.
—BLDSC (9356.959800), IE, Ingenta. **CCC.**
Published by: Dartmouth College, Trustees, 6048 Dickey Ctr, Dartmouth College, Hanover, NH 03755 . http://www.dartmouth.edu/~trustees/. Ed. Noah Dentzel.

327.172 USA ISSN 0893-0228
WORLD PEACEMAKERS QUARTERLY. Text in English. 1979. q. USD 10. **Document type:** *Newsletter.* **Description:** Presents alternatives for U.S. foreign policy and action based on religious faith.
Published by: World Peacemakers Inc., 11427 Scottsbury Terr, Germantown, MD 20876-6010. TEL 202-265-7582. Ed. William J Price. Circ: 1,000 (controlled).

327.1 USA ISSN 0740-2775
D839
➤ **WORLD POLICY JOURNAL.** Text in English. 1983. q. USD 79 combined subscription to institutions (print & online eds.) (effective 2010). adv. bk.rev. charts; illus.; maps. Index. back issues avail.; reprint service avail. from PSC. **Document type:** *Journal, Academic/Scholarly.* **Description:** Covers progressive international affairs including global security issues, trade and economic policy, environmental concerns and developments in Europe, Latin America, Asia, and Africa. Also contains book reviews, profiles, and reportage.
Related titles: Microform ed.: (from PQC); Online - full text ed.: ISSN 1936-0924. USD 68 to institutions (effective 2010).
Indexed: A01, A02, A03, A08, A20, A22, A25, A26, ABCPolSci, ABS&EES, APW, ASCA, AltPI, AmH&L, B01, B04, B06, B07, B09, BAS, BRD, CA, CCME, ChPerI, CurCont, DIP, E01, E08, ESPM, FutSurv, G05, G06, G07, G08, HRIR, HistAb, I02, I05, I07, I13, IBR, IBZ, LID&ISL, LeftInd, M01, M02, M10, P02, P10, P13, P27, P30, P34, P42, P45, P47, P48, P53, P54, PAIS, PCI, PQC, PRA, PSA, PerIslam, R02, RASB, S02, S03, S08, S09, S11, S23, SCOPUS, SOPODA, SSA, SSAI, SSAb, SSCI, SSI, SSciA, SociolAb, T02, W01, W02, W03, W04, W05, W07.
—BLDSC (9358.073000), IE, Infotrieve. **CCC.**
Published by: (World Policy Institute), Sage Publications, Inc., 2455 Teller Rd, Thousand Oaks, CA 91320. TEL 805-499-9774, FAX 805-499-0871, info@sagepub.com, http://www.sagepub.com/. adv.: B&W page USD 720; 6 x 8.5. Circ: 3,000.

P

327 GBR ISSN 0043-8871
D839
➤ **WORLD POLITICS**; a quarterly journal of international relations. Text in English. 1948. q. GBP 143, USD 260 to institutions; GBP 155, USD 275 combined subscription to institutions (print & online eds.) (effective 2012). adv. illus. Index. 156 p./no.; back issues avail.; reprints avail. **Document type:** *Journal, Academic/Scholarly.* **Description:** Publishes scholarly manuscripts on topics in international relations, comparative politics, political theory, foreign policy and modernization.
Related titles: Microform ed.: (from PQC); Online - full text ed.: ISSN 1086-3338. 1948. GBP 130, USD 230 to institutions (effective 2012).
Indexed: A01, A02, A03, A08, A20, A21, A22, A25, A26, ABCPolSci, ABS&EES, ASCA, AcaI, AmH&L, B04, B14, BRD, BRI, CA, CBRI, CurCont, DIP, E01, E08, EI, ESPM, FutSurv, G08, GEOBASE, H09, H10, HPNRM, HistAb, I05, I13, IBR, IBSS, IBZ, LID&ISL, M01, M02, M06, MEA&I, MagInd, P02, P06, P10, P13, P27, P30, P34, P42, P45, P47, P48, P53, P54, PAA&I, PAIS, PCI, PQC, PRA, PSA, PerIslam, RASB, RI-1, RI-2, RiskAb, S02, S03, S05, S08, S09, S11, SCOPUS, SPAA, SSA, SSAI, SSAb, SSCI, SSI, SSciA, SociolAb, T02, W03, W07.
—BLDSC (9358.080000), IE, Infotrieve, Ingenta. **CCC.**
Published by: (Princeton University, Institute for International and Regional Studies USA), Cambridge University Press, The Edinburgh Bldg, Shaftesbury Rd, Cambridge, CB2 8RU, United Kingdom. TEL 44-1223-312393, FAX 44-1223-315052, journals@cambridge.org, http://www.cambridge.org/uk. Ed. Atul Kohli. R&P Linda Nicol TEL 44-1223-325702. Adv. contact Rebecca Roberts TEL 44-1223-325083. B&W page GBP 250, B&W page USD 370.

325.21 USA ISSN 0197-5439
HV640
WORLD REFUGEE SURVEY; an annual assessment of conditions affecting refugees, asylum seekers and internally displaced persons. Text in English. 1958. a. USD 25 per issue (effective 2005). bk.rev. charts; illus.; stat. 300 p./no. 2 cols./p.; back issues avail. **Description:** Provides a unique source of information on refugee situations around the world. Contains the year's research and on-site documentation by the staff of U.S. Committee for Refugees.
Formerly (until 1980): World Refugee Survey Report (0162-9832)
Related titles: Microfiche ed.: (from CIS).
Indexed: HRIR, RefugAb, SRI.
Published by: U.S. Committee for Refugees, Immigration and Refugee Services of America, 1717 Massachusetts Ave NW, 2nd Flr, Washington, DC 20036-2003. TEL 202-347-3507, FAX 202-347-3418, http://www.refugees.org. Ed. Merrill Smith. Circ: 20,000.

327 GBR ISSN 0043-9134
D410
WORLD TODAY. Text in English. 1925. m. GBP 35 domestic to individuals; USD 65 in US & Canada to individuals; GBP 38 elsewhere to individuals; GBP 110 domestic to institutions; USD 185 in US & Canada to institutions; GBP 125 elsewhere to institutions; GBP 28 domestic to students; USD 50 in US & Canada to students; GBP 30 elsewhere to students (effective 2009). adv. bk.rev. illus. index. 28 p./no. 2 cols./p.; reprints avail. **Document type:** *Magazine, Academic/Scholarly.* **Description:** Features articles that deal with strategic concerns, current issues analysis, and comparative politics.
Formerly (until 1945): Bulletin of International News
Related titles: Microform ed.: (from PQC); Online - full text ed.: free (effective 2009).

Indexed: A01, A02, A03, A08, A11, A20, A22, A25, A26, ABCPolSci, AMB, ASCA, ASD, AmH&L, B04, BAS, BRD, C04, CA, DIP, E08, ELLIS, G08, H09, H10, I05, I13, IBR, IBSS, IBZ, ILD, KES, LID&ISL, LeftInd, M01, M02, M06, MAB, MEA&I, P02, P05, P06, P10, P13, P27, P30, P34, P42, P45, P47, P48, P53, P54, PAA&I, PAIS, PCI, PQC, PRA, PSA, RASB, S05, S08, S09, S11, SCOPUS, SSAI, SSAb, SSI, T02, U01, W01, W02, W03, WBA, WMB.
—BLDSC (9360.150000), IE, Infotrieve, Ingenta. **CCC.**
Published by: Royal Institute of International Affairs, Chatham House, 10 St James's Sq, London, SW1Y 4LE, United Kingdom. TEL 44-20-79575700, FAX 44-20-79575710, contact@riia.org, http://www.riia.org. Ed. Gerrard Cowan. Circ: 10,000.

WORLD TODAY SERIES: MIDDLE EAST AND SOUTH ASIA. *see* HISTORY—History Of Asia

327 USA ISSN 1065-0997
AP2
THE WORLDPAPER; global perspectives from local sources since 1978. Text mainly in English; Text occasionally in Arabic, Chinese, French, Russian, Spanish. 1979. m. bk.rev. index. back issues avail. **Document type:** *Newspaper, Consumer.* **Description:** Contains international news and views on political, social and economic issues of global importance.
Related titles: Online - full text ed.
Indexed: PerIslam.
Published by: World Times, Inc., 225 Franklin St, 26th Fl, Boston, MA 02210. TEL 617-439-5400, FAX 617-439-5415, info@worldtimes.com, http://www.worldtimes.com. Ed. Crocker Snow Jr. Pub. Christine Leblois. R&P Peter Orne TEL 617-439-5442. Adv. contact Kyle Frazier.

327.172 USA ISSN 1047-5338
HC60.5
WORLDVIEW MAGAZINE. Text in English. 1980. q. USD 25 to individuals; USD 35 to institutions (effective 2005). adv. bk.rev. illus. back issues avail. **Document type:** *Magazine, Consumer.* **Description:** Publishes news and opinion about the changing communities of the developing world.
Formerly (until 1988): R P C Voice (0892-1008)
Related titles: Online - full text ed.
Indexed: P10, P48, P53, P54, PQC, PRA.
Published by: National Peace Corps Association, 1900 L St, N W, Ste 205, Washington, DC 20036. TEL 202-293-7728, FAX 202-293-7554, npca@rpev.org, http://www.rpcv.org. Ed., R&P David Arnold. Circ: 17,000 (paid).

XI'AN WAIGUOYU XUEYUAN XUEBAO. *see* LINGUISTICS

327 CHN ISSN 1000-6192
D849
➤ **XIANDAI GUOJI GUANXI.** Text in Chinese; Summaries in English. 1981. m. USD 62.40 (effective 2009). adv. bk.rev. **Document type:** *Academic/Scholarly.* **Description:** Contains comprehensive analyses by prominent Chinese and foreign scholars on various issues on contemporary international relations.
Related titles: CD-ROM ed.; Online - full text ed.; ◆ English ed.: Contemporary International Relations. ISSN 1003-3408.
—East View.
Published by: Xiandai Guoji Guanxi Yanjiusuo/China Institute of Contemporary International Relations, No A-2 Wanshousi, Haidian, Beijing, 100081, China. TEL 86-10-6841-8640, FAX 86-10-6841-8641. Ed. Xu Dan. Adv. contact Zhaoyu Huang. page CNY 1,600; 200 x 140. Circ: 10,000.

341.734 341 RUS
YADERNOE RASPROSTRANENIE. Text in Russian. bi-m.
Published by: Moskovskii Tsentr Carnegie, Tverskaya ul 16/2, Moscow, 125009, Russian Federation. TEL 7-095-9358904, FAX 7-095-9358906, info@carnegie.ru, http://www.carnegie.ru. Ed. Aleksandr Pikaev.

327 USA
YALE GLOBAL ONLINE. Text in English. 2002. irreg. free (effective 2010). **Description:** Aims to analyze and promote debate on all aspects of globalization.
Media: Online - full text.
Published by: Yale University, Center for the Study of Globalization, The Betts House, 393 Prospect St, New Haven, CT 06511. TEL 203-432-1900, FAX 203-432-1200, globalization@yale.edu, http://www.ycsg.yale.edu. Ed. Nayan Chanda.

327 USA
YALE ISRAEL JOURNAL; exploring the history, politics and culture of Israel. Text in English. 2003. s-a. USD 12 (effective 2007). **Document type:** *Magazine, Consumer.*
Address: PO Box 204669, New Haven, CT 06520.

327 USA ISSN 1936-2633
JZ6.5
YALE JOURNAL OF INTERNATIONAL AFFAIRS. Text in English. 2005. s-a. USD 20 domestic to individuals; USD 35 foreign to individuals; USD 40 domestic to institutions; USD 50 foreign to institutions (effective 2011). **Document type:** *Journal, Academic/Scholarly.* **Description:** Presents writing of graduate students, professors, and practitioners within the Yale international affairs and policy community.
Related titles: Online - full text ed.: ISSN 1936-2641.
Indexed: CA, P42, PAIS, PSA, SociolAb, T02.
Published by: Yale University, International Affairs Council, 34 Hillhouse Ave, New Haven, CT 06511. Ed. Mai Truong.

327 384 JPN ISSN 1880-6767
YAMANASHI KOKUSAI KENKYUU/YAMANASHI PREFECTURAL UNIVERSITY. FACULTY OF GLOCAL POLICY MANAGEMENT AND COMMUNICATIONS. BULLETIN. Variant title: Yamanashi Glocal Studies. Text in Japanese. 2006. a. **Document type:** *Journal, Academic/Scholarly.*
Supersedes in part (1967-2005): Yamanashi Kenritsu Joshi Tanki Daigaku Kiyo/Yamanashi Women's Junior College. Bulletin (0385-0331)
Published by: Yamanashi Kenritsu Daigaku/Yamanashi Prefectural University, 5-11-1 Iida, Kofu, Yamanashi 400-0035, Japan. http://www.yamanashi-ken.ac.jp/.

YATAI YANJIU TONGXUN. *see* HISTORY—History Of Asia

327.471 FIN ISSN 1459-0808
DK451.7
YEARBOOK OF FINNISH FOREIGN POLICY. Text in English. 1973-1996; resumed 1998. a., latest 2004. EUR 20 (effective 2003). adv. bk.rev. 148 p./no. 2 cols./p.; **Document type:** *Monographic series, Academic/Scholarly.* **Description:** Presents scholarly articles dealing with Finland's foreign relations, Arctic, Nordic and Baltic cooperation, and relations with and between the EU and Russia.
Former titles (until 2002): Northern Dimensions (1456-1255); (until 1996): Yearbook of Finnish Foreign Policy (0355-0079)
Related titles: Online - full text ed.
Indexed: ABCPolSci, I13, RASB.
Published by: Ulkopoliittinen Instituutti/Finnish Institute of International Affairs, Mannerheimintie 15 A, Helsinki, 00260, Finland. TEL 358-9-4342070, FAX 358-9-4342069. Ed. Tapani Vaantoranta TEL 358-9-43420720. adv.: B&W page EUR 655, color page EUR 990;. Circ: 2,500.

327 DEU ISSN 0084-3814
JX1904 CODEN: YIORD4
YEARBOOK OF INTERNATIONAL ORGANIZATIONS/ANNUAIRE DES ORGANISATIONS INTERNATIONALES. Text in English. 1910. a. (in 6 vols.). USD 1,980 (effective 2009). **Document type:** *Directory, Trade.* **Description:** Provides detailed information for organizations in every field of human endeavor. Lists organizations, administrators, embassies and government agencies concerned with international affairs.
Related titles: ◆ CD-ROM ed.: Yearbook Plus.
Indexed: RASB.
—BLDSC (9414.010000), CASDDS. **CCC.**
Published by: (Union of International Associations/Union des Associations Internationales BEL), De Gruyter Saur (Subsidiary of: Walter de Gruyter GmbH & Co. KG), Mies-van-der-Rohe-Str 1, Munich, 80807, Germany. TEL 49-89-769020, FAX 49-89-76902150, info@degruyter.com.

327.438 POL ISSN 1233-9903
DK4450
➤ **YEARBOOK OF POLISH FOREIGN POLICY.** Text in English. 1993. a. USD 16 per vol. foreign (effective 2004). bibl. 400 p./no. 1 cols./p.; back issues avail. **Document type:** *Journal, Academic/Scholarly.*
Related titles: ◆ Polish ed.: Rocznik Polskiej Polityki Zagranicznej. ISSN 1230-4794.
—BLDSC (9415.556000).
Published by: Akademia Dyplomatyczna/Diplomatic Academy, ul Tyniecka 15/17, Warsaw, 02630, Poland. TEL 48-22-5239086, FAX 48-22-5239027, aleksandra.zieliniecd@msz.gov.pl, http://www.sprawymiedzynarodowe.pl. Ed. Barbara Wizimirska. Adv. contact Aleksandra Zieleniec. Circ: 1,000.

327 DEU
YEARBOOK PLUS. Variant title: Yearbook of International Organizations Plus. Text in German. a. EUR 1,980 (effective 2009). **Document type:** *Directory, Trade.* **Description:** Lists international organizations from around the world, with information on their staff and their publications. Comprises the data in Yearbook of International Organizations and Who's Who in International Organizations.
Media: CD-ROM. **Related titles:** ◆ Print ed.: Yearbook of International Organizations. ISSN 0084-3814.
Published by: (Union of International Associations/Union des Associations Internationales BEL), De Gruyter Saur (Subsidiary of: Walter de Gruyter GmbH & Co. KG), Mies-van-der-Rohe-Str 1, Munich, 80807, Germany. TEL 49-89-769020, FAX 49-89-76902150, info@degruyter.com.

327 CHN
YOU SHENG. Text in Chinese. bi-m.
Related titles: English ed.: Friendly Voices.
Published by: Zhongguo Renmin Duiwai Youhao Xiehui, No 1 Taijichang, Beijing, 100740, China. TEL 5122782. Ed. Gu Zixin.

YOUR UNITED NATIONS; official guidebook. *see* HISTORY

327 382 TWN ISSN 1017-5741
YUANJIAN ZAZHI/GLOBAL VIEWS MONTHLY. Text in Chinese. 1986. m. TWD 1,980 (effective 2007). **Document type:** *Magazine, Consumer.* **Description:** Covers international political and business developments.
Related titles: Online - full text ed.
Published by: Tianxia Yuanjian Chuban Gunfen Youxian Gongsi/Commonwealth Publishing Co., 2F, No. 1, Lane 93 Sung Chiang Rd., Taipei, 104, Taiwan. TEL 886-2-25173688, FAX 886-2-25173685, service@cwgv.com.tw, http://www.bookzone.com.tw.

327 SRB
YUGOSLAVIA. FEDERAL SECRETARIAT FOR FOREIGN AFFAIRS. DIPLOMATIC LIST. Text in French. 1946. a. free. **Document type:** *Directory, Government.*
Formerly (until Mar. 1991): Liste des Membres du Corps Diplomatique a Beograd
Published by: Savezni Sekretarijat za Inostrane Poslove/Federal Secretariat for Foreign Affairs, Belgrade. Circ: 1,000.

327 DEU ISSN 1435-3288
HC240.A1
Z E I DISCUSSION PAPER. Text in English, German. 1998. irreg., latest vol.178, 2007. **Document type:** *Monographic series, Academic/Scholarly.*
Published by: Zentrum fuer Europaeische Integrationsforschung/Center for European Integration Studies, Walter-Flexstr 3, Bonn, 53113, Germany. TEL 49-228-731886, FAX 49-228-731802, r.meyeruni-bonn.de, http://www.zei.de.

327 DEU ISSN 1817-1729
Z E I - E U - TURKEY - MONITOR. (Zentrum fuer Europaeische Integrationsforschung - European Union) Text in English, German. 2005. 3/yr. **Document type:** *Journal, Academic/Scholarly.*
—CCC.
Published by: Zentrum fuer Europaeische Integrationsforschung/Center for European Integration Studies, Walter-Flexstr 3, Bonn, 53113, Germany. TEL 49-228-731886, FAX 49-228-731802, r.meyeruni-bonn.de.

327 DEU
Z E I WORKING PAPERS. Text in English, German. 1997. irreg. **Document type:** *Monographic series, Academic/Scholarly.*
Published by: Zentrum fuer Europaeische Integrationsforschung/Center for European Integration Studies, Walter-Flexstr 3, Bonn, 53113, Germany. TEL 49-228-731886, FAX 49-228-731802, r.meyeruni-bonn.de.

327.1 SVK ISSN 1336-7218
ZAHRANICNA POLITIKA. Variant title: Listy S F P A. Text in Slovak. 1997. bi-m. **Document type:** *Journal, Academic/Scholarly.*
Published by: Slovenska Spolocnost pre Zahranicnu Politiku/Slovak Foreign Policy Association, Panenska 33, Bratislava, 81103, Slovakia. TEL 421-2-54433151, sfpa@sfpa.sk. Ed. Lucia Najslova.

327 CZE ISSN 1210-5600
DB2239
ZAHRANICNI POLITIKA CESKE REPUBLIKY. DOKUMENTY. Text in Czech. 1954. m. **Document type:** *Government.*
Former titles (until 1993): Ceskoslovenska Zahranicni Politika. Dokumenty (0862-8041); (until 1990): Dokumenty k Ceskoslovenske Zahranicni Politice (0012-5202)
Published by: Ministerstvo Zahranicnich Veci Ceske Republiky, Loretanske Namesti 5, Prague 1, 118 00, Czech Republic. TEL 420-2-24181111, info@mzv.cz, http://www.mzv.cz.

327 DNK ISSN 0908-0686
ZAPP JORDEN RUNDT/ZAPP DELE CLIC AL MUNDO/ZAPP MAGAZINE. Text in Danish; Text occasionally in English, Spanish. 1975. q. back issues avail. **Document type:** *Magazine, Consumer.*
Formerly (until 1993): Udkig (0105-0214)
Published by: Mellemfolkeligt Samvirke/Danish Association for International Co-operation, Faelledvej 12, Copenhagen N, 2200, Denmark. TEL 45-77-310000, FAX 45-77-310101, ms@ms.dk. Ed. Bettina Gram.

327 DEU ISSN 1866-2188
ZEITSCHRIFT FUER AUSSEN- UND SICHERHEITSPOLITIK. Text in German. 2008. q. EUR 325.23, USD 400 combined subscription to institutions (print & online eds.) (effective 2012). reprint service avail. from PSC. **Document type:** *Journal, Academic/Scholarly.*
Related titles: Online - full text ed.: ISSN 1866-2196. 2008.
Indexed: A22, E01, SCOPUS.
—IE. **CCC.**
Published by: V S - Verlag fuer Sozialwissenschaften (Subsidiary of: Springer Fachmedien Wiesbaden GmbH), Abraham-Lincoln-Str 46, Wiesbaden, 65189, Germany. TEL 49-611-78780, FAX 49-611-7878400, springerfachmedien-wiesbaden@springer.com, http://www.vs-verlag.de. Circ: 420 (paid).

327 DEU ISSN 0946-7165
JZ8
ZEITSCHRIFT FUER INTERNATIONALE BEZIEHUNGEN. Variant title: Z I B. Text in German. 1994. s-a. EUR 79 (effective 2011). adv. reprint service avail. from SCH. **Document type:** *Journal, Academic/Scholarly.*
Indexed: CA, DIP, I13, IBR, IBSS, IBZ, P42, PSA, RASB, SCOPUS, SociolAb, T02.
—CCC.
Published by: Nomos Verlagsgesellschaft mbH und Co. KG, Waldseestr 3-5, Baden-Baden, 76530, Germany. TEL 49-7221-21040, FAX 49-7221-210427, marketing@nomos.de, nomos@nomos.de, http://www.nomos.de. Adv. contact Bettina Roos. Circ: 800 (paid and controlled).

327 DEU ISSN 0044-2976
ZEITSCHRIFT FUER KULTURAUSTAUSCH; Zeitschrift fuer internationale Perspektiven. Variant title: Kulturaustausch. Text in German. 1952. q. EUR 20 (effective 2008). adv. bk.rev.; rec.rev. bibl.; illus. index. back issues avail. **Document type:** *Magazine, Consumer.* **Description:** Covers all aspects of cultural exchanges between nations.
Formerly (until 1962): Institut fuer Auslandsbeziehungen. Mitteilungen (0936-7349)
Related titles: E-mail ed.; Online - full text ed.
Indexed: ASD, BAS, DIP, FR, I14, IBR, IBZ, MLA-IB, PAIS, PRA, RASB.
—INIST.
Published by: Institut fuer Auslandsbeziehungen e.V., Charlottenplatz 17, Stuttgart, 70173, Germany. TEL 49-711-22250, FAX 49-711-2264346, info@ifa.de. Circ: 6,000.

327.17 DEU ISSN 1610-7780
➤ **ZEITSCHRIFT FUER STAATS- UND EUROPAWISSENSCHAFTEN.** Abbreviated title: Z S E. Text in German. 2003. q. EUR 169 (effective 2011). adv. **Document type:** *Journal, Academic/Scholarly.* **Description:** Covers all aspects of the unification of Europe, including social, political, scientific, legal, economic, and educational issues.
Related titles: Online - full text ed.: ISSN 1612-7013. EUR 188 (effective 2008).
Indexed: A22, A26, E01.
—BLDSC (9486.401500), IE.
Published by: Nomos Verlagsgesellschaft mbH und Co. KG, Waldseestr 3-5, Baden-Baden, 76530, Germany. TEL 49-7221-21040, FAX 49-7221-210427, nomos@nomos.de, http://www.nomos.de. Ed. Jens Hesse. Adv. contact Bettina Roos. Circ: 500 (paid and controlled).

327 DEU
ZENTRUM FUER EUROPAEISCHE INTEGRATIONSFORSCHUNG. SCHRIFTENREIHE. Text in German. 1998. irreg., latest vol.66, 2005. price varies. **Document type:** *Monographic series, Academic/Scholarly.*
Published by: (Zentrum fuer Europaeische Integrationsforschung/Center for European Integration Studies), Nomos Verlagsgesellschaft mbH und Co. KG, Waldseestr 3-5, Baden-Baden, 76530, Germany. TEL 49-7221-21040, FAX 49-7221-210427, nomos@nomos.de, http://www.nomos.de.

327 COL ISSN 0123-8779
ZERO. Text in Spanish. s-a. **Document type:** *Journal, Academic/Scholarly.*
Published by: Universidad Externado de Colombia, Centro de Investigaciones y Proyectos Especiales, Calle 12 No. 1-17 Este, Bogota, Colombia.

ZHONGGUO JIAODIAN/CHINA FOCUS. *see* ETHNIC INTERESTS

327.51 CHN ISSN 1001-2842
DS740.4
ZHONGGUO WAIJIAO/CHINESE FOREIGN AFFAIRS. Text in Chinese. 1978. m. USD 49.90 (effective 2009). 48 p./no.; **Document type:** *Journal, Academic/Scholarly.* **Description:** Covers Chinese diplomatic policies and theories, international relations, and important foreign affairs activities.
Published by: Zhongguo Renmin Daxue Shubao Ziliao Zhongxin/Renmin University of China, Information Center for Social Sciences, Dongcheng-qu, 3, Zhangzizhong Lu, Beijing, 100007, China. TEL 86-10-64039458, FAX 86-10-64015080, center@zlzx.org, http://www.zlzx.org/. **Dist. in US by:** China Publications Service, PO Box 49614, Chicago, IL 60649. TEL 312-288-3291, FAX 312-288-8570; **Dist. by:** China International Book Trading Corp, 35 Chegongzhuang Xilu, Haidian District, PO Box 399, Beijing 100044, China. TEL 86-10-68412045, FAX 86-10-68412023, cibtc@mail.cibtc.com.cn, http://www.cibtc.com.cn.

ZIVIL; Zeitschrift fuer Frieden und Gewaltfreiheit. *see* POLITICAL SCIENCE—Civil Rights

327 DEU ISSN 1614-1954
ZIVILCOURAGE; Das Magazin fuer Pazifismus und Antimilitarismus. Text in German. 1964; N.S. 1975. bi-m. EUR 12 (effective 2009). adv. bk.rev.; film rev. illus. **Document type:** *Magazine, Consumer.*
Formerly: Courage (0011-0388)
Published by: Deutsche Friedensgesellschaft - Vereinigte Kriegsdienstgegnerinnen, Kasseler Str 1a, Frankfurt am Main, 60486, Germany. TEL 49-69-27298231, FAX 49-69-27298232, office@dfg-vk.de, http://www.dfg-vk.de. Ed. Stephan Phillipp. Circ: 6,600 (paid and controlled).

364.65 NOR ISSN 1892-0381
365. Variant title: Trehundreogsekstifem. Text in Norwegian. 1970. q. back issues avail. **Document type:** *Magazine, Consumer.*
Former titles (until 2010): Amnestymagasinet (1504-6923); (until 2007): Amnestynytt (0806-1041); Which incorporated (1996-2000): Herr President (0808-1786); (until 1980): Amnesty Kontakt (0806-1025); (until 1972): Amnesty-Bladet (0806-1017)
Published by: Amnesty International Norge, Grensen 3, Oslo, 0159, Norway. TEL 47-22-402200, FAX 47-22-402250, info@amnesty.no, http://www.amnesty.no.

1066; tidsskrift for historie. *see* HISTORY—History Of Europe

POLLUTION

see ENVIRONMENTAL STUDIES—Pollution

POPULATION STUDIES

see also BIRTH CONTROL

325.1 USA
A C I M NEWSLETTER. Text in English. 1952. 4/yr. free. **Document type:** *Newsletter.*
Formerly: A C I M Dispatch
Published by: American Committee on Italian Migration, 25 Carmine St., New York, NY 10014-4423. TEL 212-247-7373. Ed. Rev. Peter P Polo. Circ: 10,000.

325 DNK ISSN 1729-3561
A E M I JOURNAL. Text in English. 2003. s-a. **Document type:** *Journal, Academic/Scholarly.*
—BLDSC (0719.724050).
Published by: Association of European Migration Institutions, Danish Emigration Archives, Arkivstraede 1, PO Box 1353, Aalborg, Denmark. TEL 45-99314230, FAX 45-98102248, emiarch@emiarch.dk, http://www.aemi.dk. Ed. Hans Storhaug.

A F R A NEWS. *see* POLITICAL SCIENCE—Civil Rights

325 USA
KF4812.A2
A G / B I A DECISIONS LISTING (ONLINE). Text in English. 1940. irreg. price varies. **Document type:** *Government.*
Formerly (1943-2000): U.S. Immigration and Naturalization Service. Administrative Decisions under Immigration and Nationality Laws (Print) (0895-2558)
Media: Online - full content.
Published by: U.S. Department of Justice, Executive Office for Immigration Review, Board of Immigration Appeals, 5107 Leesburg Pike, Ste 2000, Falls Church, VA 22041. http://www.usdoj.gov/eoir/biainfo.htm.

304.6 DEU ISSN 0177-1566
A I D - AUSLAENDER IN DEUTSCHLAND; Informationsdienst zu aktuellen Fragen der Auslaenderarbeit. Text in German. 1984. q. EUR 8 (effective 2002). bk.rev. back issues avail. **Document type:** *Bulletin, Consumer.* **Description:** Provides information for people working toward the integration of foreigners in Germany.
Indexed: DIP.
Published by: Isoplan Institut, Martin-Luther-Str 20, Saarbruecken, 66111, Germany. TEL 49-681-936460, FAX 49-681-9364611, aid-isoplan@t-online.de, http://www.isoplan.de. Ed. Martin Zwick. Circ: 33,000 (controlled). **Co-sponsor:** Bundesministerium fuer Arbeit und Sozialordnung.

A P L I C COMMUNICATOR. *see* LIBRARY AND INFORMATION SCIENCES

304.6 CZE ISSN 0232-0479
➤ **ACTA DEMOGRAPHICA.** Text in Czech. 1977. irreg. **Document type:** *Journal, Academic/Scholarly.*
Indexed: P30.
Published by: Univerzita Karlova v Praze, Prirodovedecka Fakulta, Katedra Demografie a Geodemografie, Albertov 6, Prague 2, 12843, Czech Republic. TEL 420-2-21951418, FAX 420-2-24920657, demodept@natur.cuni.cz, http://boris.natur.cuni.cz/kdgd.

325 944 FRA ISSN 1630-7356
➤ **ACTES DE L'HISTOIRE DE L'IMMIGRATION (PRINT EDITION).** Text in French. 1999. irreg. **Document type:** *Journal, Academic/Scholarly.*
Formerly (until vol.5, 2005): Actes de l'Histoire de l'Immigration (Online Edition)
—**CCC.**
Published by: Ecole Normale Superieure, Equipe Reseaux Savoirs Territoires, 45 Rue d'Ulm, Paris, 75005, France.

304.6 950 NLD ISSN 1879-7180
▼ **ADVANCES IN ASIAN HUMAN-ENVIRONMENTAL RESEARCH.** Text in English. 2010. irreg. **Document type:** *Monographic series, Academic/Scholarly.* **Description:** Explores the complex relationships between physical landscapes, natural resources, and their modification by human land use in various environments of Asia.
Related titles: Online - full text ed.: ISSN 1879-7199.
Published by: Springer Netherlands (Subsidiary of: Springer Science+Business Media), Van Godewijckstraat 30, Dordrecht, 3311 GX, Netherlands. TEL 31-78-6576050, FAX 31-78-6576474. Ed. Marcus Nuesser.

325.1 SWE ISSN 1403-4530
AFRICA FORUM. Text in English. 1997. bi-m. SEK 480 (effective 2003). adv.
Address: PO Box 7018, Malmoe, 20042, Sweden. TEL 46-73-9074348, africaforum@swipnet.se. Ed., Pub. Paul Ahanmisi.

304.6 GHA ISSN 0855-0018
HB850.5.A35
AFRICAN DEMOGRAPHY. Text in English. 1976. biennial. **Document type:** *Journal, Academic/Scholarly.*
Indexed: P30.
Published by: University of Ghana, PO Box LG25, Legon, Accra, Ghana. TEL 233-21-589954, pad@ug.edu.gh, http://www.ug.edu.gh.

304.6 ETH ISSN 0258-980X
AFRICAN POPULATION NEWSLETTER (BILINGUAL EDITION). Text in English, French. 1970. s-a. free. bk.rev. **Document type:** *Newsletter.*
Formed by the 1980 merger of: Informations sur la Population en Afrique (0252-4805); African Population Newsletter (0084-599X)
Indexed: RASB, SSciA.
Published by: (Population Division), United Nations, Economic Commission for Africa/Commission Economique pour l'Afrique, PO Box 3001, Addis Ababa, Ethiopia. TELEX 21029. Circ: 1,500.

AGER; revista de estudios sobre despoblacion y desarrollo rural. *see* BUSINESS AND ECONOMICS—Economic Situation And Conditions

301.32 DEU ISSN 1437-1200
AKADEMIE FUER MIGRATION UND INTEGRATION. BEITRAEGE. Text in German. 1999. irreg., latest vol.12, 2010. price varies. **Document type:** *Monographic series, Academic/Scholarly.*
Published by: (Otto Benecke Stiftung e.V., Akademie fuer Migration und Integration), V & R Unipress GmbH (Subsidiary of: Vandenhoeck und Ruprecht), Robert-Bosch-Breite 6, Goettingen, 37079, Germany. TEL 49-551-5084303, FAX 49-551-5084333, info@vr-unipress.de, http://www.v-r.de/en/publisher/unipress.

325.1 SWE ISSN 1652-7119
AKTUELLT OM MIGRATION; tidskrift foer forskning och debatt. Text in Swedish. 2005. q. **Document type:** *Magazine, Consumer.*
Media: Online - full content.
Published by: Immigrant Institutet, Katrinedalsgatan 43, Boraas, 50451, Sweden. TEL 46-33-136070, FAX 46-33-136075. Ed., Pub. Miguel Benito.

304.6 USA
ALABAMA STATE DATA CENTER NEWSLETTER. Text in English. 1985. q. free. illus. **Document type:** *Newsletter.*
Related titles: Online - full text ed.
Published by: University of Alabama, Center for Business and Economic Research, PO Box 870221, Tuscaloosa, AL 35487-0221. TEL 205-348-6191, FAX 205-348-2951, http://cber.cba.us.edu. Ed. Annette Watters.

304.6 USA ISSN 1063-3790
HA235
ALASKA POPULATION OVERVIEW. Text in English. 1979. a. free (effective 2011). back issues avail. **Document type:** *Report, Government.* **Description:** Population estimates for Alaska and its boroughs and census areas by age and sex. Includes information on historical trends in births, deaths, and migration.
Related titles: Online - full text ed.
Indexed: SRI.
Published by: Department of Labor, Research and Analysis Section, PO Box 115501, Juneau, AK 99811. TEL 907-465-4500, FAX 907-465-4506.

ALLEES ALL AROUND; includes Alley, Ally, Allie, Alyea. *see* GENEALOGY AND HERALDRY

305.851 325 ITA ISSN 1120-0413
JV6005
ALTREITALIE; international journal of studies on the peoples of Italian origin in the world. Text and summaries in Multiple languages. 1989. s-a. free (effective 2009). bk.rev. **Document type:** *Journal, Academic/Scholarly.* **Description:** Devoted to the study of Italian communities in the Americas and Australia on an interdisciplinary basis. Deals with historiography, literature, sociology, demography and ethnology.
Related titles: Online - full text ed.: 1996. free (effective 2011).
Indexed: IBR, IBZ.
Published by: Fondazione Giovanni Agnelli, Via Giuseppe Giacosa 38, Turin, TO 10125, Italy. TEL 39-011-6500500, FAX 39-011-6502777, info@fga.it, http://www.fga.it. Ed., R&P Marcello Pacini. Circ: 1,000.

304.6 AGO
ANGOLA. INSTITUTO NACIONAL DE ESTATISTICA. UNIDADE DE ANALISE DEMOGRAFICA. BOLETIM DEMOGRAFICO. Text in Portuguese. 1987. q.
Published by: Instituto Nacional de Estatistica, Caixa Postal 1215, Luanda, Angola.

316 AGO
ANGOLA. MINISTERIO DA SAUDE. DEPARTAMENTO DE ESTATISTICA. RELATORIO ESTATISTICO. Text in Portuguese. a.
Published by: Ministerio da Saude, Departamento de Estatistica, Rua Diogo Cao, Luanda, Angola.

304.6 FRA ISSN 0066-2062
HB848
ANNALES DE DEMOGRAPHIE HISTORIQUE. Text in English, French. 1964. a. EUR 25 per issue (effective 2009). back issues avail.; reprints avail. **Document type:** *Journal, Academic/Scholarly.*
Formerly (until 1964): Etudes et Chroniques de Demographie Historique (1147-1832)
Related titles: Online - full text ed.: ISSN 1776-2774. 2005; Supplement(s): Annales de Demographie Historique D H. 1970.
Indexed: A22, AmH&L, CA, FR, HistAb, IBR, IBZ, P30, PCI, PopulInd, SCOPUS, T02.
—BLDSC (0971.450000), IE, Infotrieve, Ingenta, INIST. **CCC.**
Published by: (Societe de Demographie Historique), Editions Belin, 8 Rue Ferou, Paris, 75278, France. TEL 33-8-25820111, FAX 33-1-43251829. Ed. Patrice Bourdelais.

ANNUAL REPORT ON THE HEALTH OF THE POPULATION. *see* PUBLIC HEALTH AND SAFETY

304.6 USA
ANNUAL REVIEW OF POPULATION LAW. Text in English. a.
Media: Online - full content.
Published by: Harvard School of Public Health, Department of Population and International Health, 665 Huntington Ave, Boston, MA 02115. http://www.hsph.harvard.edu/Organizations/healthnet/index.html.

304.6 PRT ISSN 1645-8079
ANTECEDENTES, METODOLOGIA E CONCEITOS. CENSOS.. Text in Portuguese. 2003. irreg. **Document type:** *Report, Government.*
Published by: Instituto Nacional de Estatistica, Av Antonio Jose de Almeida 2, Lisbon, 1000-043, Portugal. TEL 351-21-8426100, FAX 351-21-8426380, ine@ine.pt, http://www.ine.pt.

304.6 USA
APPLIED DEMOGRAPHY. Text in English. 2/yr. USD 5 to members; USD 10 to non-members (effective 2001). **Document type:** *Newsletter.* **Description:** Contains articles of interest to demographers working in applied settings, technical articles on demographic analysis, and announcements of related and upcoming news.
Indexed: PopulInd.
Published by: Population Association of America, 8630 Fenton St, Ste 722, Silver Spring, MD 20910. TEL 301-565-6710, FAX 301-565-7850, info@popassoc.org, http://www.popassoc.org/. Ed. Mary Heim. Circ: 560 (paid).

304.6 NLD ISSN 1874-463X
➤ **APPLIED SPATIAL ANALYSIS AND POLICY.** Text in English. 2008. 4/yr. EUR 328 combined subscription to institutions (print & online eds.) (effective 2011). reprint service avail. from PSC. **Document type:** *Journal, Academic/Scholarly.* **Description:** Focuses on the practical application of analytical principles and findings at different spatial scales.
Related titles: Online - full text ed.: ISSN 1874-4621. 2008.
Indexed: A22, A26, E01, E08, GEOBASE, PAIS, S09, SCOPUS.
—IE. **CCC.**
Published by: Springer Netherlands (Subsidiary of: Springer Science+Business Media), Van Godewijckstraat 30, Dordrecht, 3311 GX, Netherlands. TEL 31-78-6576050, FAX 31-78-6576474. Eds. John Stillwell, Mark Birkin.

P

304.6 ARG
ARGENTINA. INSTITUTO NACIONAL DE ESTADISTICA Y CENSOS. CENSO NACIONAL DE POBLACION Y VIVIENDA (YEAR): SERIE A - RESULTADOS PROVISIONALES. Text in Spanish. irreg., latest 1992. ARS 20, USD 32 (effective 1999). **Document type:** *Government.* **Description:** Offers information compiled from the provisional results on the quantity of population and residences.
Published by: Instituto Nacional de Estadistica y Censos, Presidente Julio A Roca 615, Buenos Aires, 1067, Argentina. TEL 54-114-3499662, FAX 54-114-3499621.

304.6 ARG
ARGENTINA. INSTITUTO NACIONAL DE ESTADISTICA Y CENSOS. CENSO NACIONAL DE POBLACION Y VIVIENDA (YEAR): SERIE B - RESULTADOS DEFINITIVOS, CARACTERISTICAS SELECCIONADAS. Text in Spanish. 1992. irreg. (in 37 vols.). **Document type:** *Government.* **Description:** Contains information on the characteristics of residences, homes and demographic aspects of the population.
Related titles: CD-ROM ed.; Diskette ed.
Published by: Instituto Nacional de Estadistica y Censos, Presidente Julio A Roca 615, Buenos Aires, 1067, Argentina. TEL 54-114-3499662, FAX 54-114-3499621.

304.6 ARG
ARGENTINA. INSTITUTO NACIONAL DE ESTADISTICA Y CENSOS. CENSO NACIONAL DE POBLACION Y VIVIENDA (YEAR): SERIE C - PARTE 1. RESULTADOS DEFINITIVOS, CARACTERISTICAS GENERALES. Text in Spanish. 1995. irreg. (in 26 vols.). price varies. **Document type:** *Government.* **Description:** Contains data on availability of electricity, conditions of economic activity, health, marital rates and more.
Related titles: CD-ROM ed.; Diskette ed.
Published by: Instituto Nacional de Estadistica y Censos, Presidente Julio A Roca 615, Buenos Aires, 1067, Argentina. TEL 54-114-3499662, FAX 54-114-3499621.

304.6 ARG
ARGENTINA. INSTITUTO NACIONAL DE ESTADISTICA Y CENSOS. CENSO NACIONAL DE POBLACION Y VIVIENDA (YEAR): SERIE C - PARTE 2. RESULTADOS DEFINITIVOS, CARACTERISTICAS GENERALES. (In 7 regional vols.) Text in Spanish. 1996. irreg. ARS 20, USD 30. **Document type:** *Government.* **Description:** Includes information related to the occupational status of the population.
Related titles: CD-ROM ed.; Diskette ed.
Published by: Instituto Nacional de Estadistica y Censos, Presidente Julio A Roca 615, Buenos Aires, 1067, Argentina. TEL 54-114-3499662, FAX 54-114-3499621.

304.6 ARG
ARGENTINA. INSTITUTO NACIONAL DE ESTADISTICA Y CENSOS. CENSO NACIONAL DE POBLACION Y VIVIENDA (YEAR): SERIE D - RESULTADOS DEFINITIVOS. Text in Spanish. 1996. irreg., latest vol.4, 1998. price varies. **Document type:** *Government.*
Published by: Instituto Nacional de Estadistica y Censos, Presidente Julio A Roca 615, Buenos Aires, 1067, Argentina. TEL 54-114-3499662, FAX 54-114-3499621.

304.6 ARG
ARGENTINA. INSTITUTO NACIONAL DE ESTADISTICA Y CENSOS. CENSO NACIONAL DE POBLACION Y VIVIENDA (YEAR). SERIE E - ENCUESTA POST CENSAL - OMISION. Text in Spanish. 1995. irreg. ARS 15, USD 24 (effective 1999). **Document type:** *Government.* **Description:** Presents estimates on the persons and data omitted from the census.

Published by: Instituto Nacional de Estadistica y Censos, Presidente Julio A Roca 615, Buenos Aires, 1067, Argentina. TEL 54-11-43499200.

304.6 ARG
ARGENTINA. INSTITUTO NACIONAL DE ESTADISTICA Y CENSOS. CENSO NACIONAL DE POBLACION Y VIVIENDA (YEAR). SERIE G - RESULTADOS DEFINITIVOS POR LOCALIDAD. Text in Spanish. 1995. irreg., latest vol.4, 1997. ARS 25, USD 40 (effective 1999). **Document type:** *Government.* **Description:** Offers information on residences and population by sex for all cities and towns.
Related titles: CD-ROM ed.
Published by: Instituto Nacional de Estadistica y Censos, Presidente Julio A Roca 615, Buenos Aires, 1067, Argentina. TEL 54-114-3499662, FAX 54-114-3499650.

304.6 ARG
ARGENTINA. INSTITUTO NACIONAL DE ESTADISTICA Y CENSOS. CENSO NACIONAL DE POBLACION Y VIVIENDA (YEAR). SERIE H. Text in Spanish. 1996. irreg., latest vol.2, 1996. ARS 25, USD 35 (effective 1998). **Document type:** *Government.*
Published by: Instituto Nacional de Estadistica y Censos, Presidente Julio A Roca 615, Buenos Aires, 1067, Argentina. TEL 54-114-3499662, FAX 54-114-3499621.

304.6 ARG
ARGENTINA. INSTITUTO NACIONAL DE ESTADISTICA Y CENSOS. CENSO NACIONAL DE POBLACION Y VIVIENDA (YEAR). SERIE I. Text in Spanish. 1997. irreg. ARS 30, USD 45 (effective 1999). **Document type:** *Government.* **Description:** Presents information on the classification system used by the census.
Published by: Instituto Nacional de Estadistica y Censos, Presidente Julio A Roca 615, Buenos Aires, 1067, Argentina. TEL 54-114-3499662, FAX 54-114-3499621.

304.6 ARG
ARGENTINA. INSTITUTO NACIONAL DE ESTADISTICA Y CENSOS. CENSO NACIONAL DE POBLACION Y VIVIENDA (YEAR). SERIE J. Text in Spanish. 1996. irreg. ARS 20, USD 30 (effective 1999). **Document type:** *Government.*
Published by: Instituto Nacional de Estadistica y Censos, Presidente Julio A Roca 615, Buenos Aires, 1067, Argentina. TEL 54-114-3499662, FAX 54-114-3499621.

304.6 ARG
ARGENTINA. INSTITUTO NACIONAL DE ESTADISTICA Y CENSOS. SERIE ANALISIS DEMOGRAFICO. Text in Spanish. 1995. irreg., latest vol.20, 1999. ARS 15, USD 22 (effective 1999). **Document type:** *Government.* **Description:** Presents analytical information on diverse demographic variables.
Published by: Instituto Nacional de Estadistica y Censos, Presidente Julio A Roca 615, Buenos Aires, 1067, Argentina. TEL 54-114-3499662, FAX 54-114-3499621.

304.6 ARG
ARGENTINA. INSTITUTO NACIONAL DE ESTADISTICA Y CENSOS. SERIE ESTADISTICAS MUNICIPALES. Text in Spanish. 1997. irreg. ARS 30, USD 55 with diskette. **Document type:** *Government.* **Description:** Presents economic, social and demographic information on the municipal level.
Related titles: CD-ROM ed.; Diskette ed.
Published by: Instituto Nacional de Estadistica y Censos, Presidente Julio A Roca 615, Buenos Aires, 1067, Argentina. TEL 54-114-3499662, FAX 54-114-3499621.

ARKLETON RESEARCH PAPERS. *see* SOCIOLOGY

304.6 USA ISSN 0891-6683
ASIA - PACIFIC POPULATION & POLICY. Text in English. 1987. q. back issues avail. **Document type:** *Bulletin, Academic/Scholarly.* **Description:** Summarizes research on population and reproductive health for policymakers and others concerned with the Asia-Pacific region.
Related titles: Online - full text ed.
Indexed: ESPM, GEOBASE, HPNRM, P30, SCOPUS, SSciA.
Published by: (Population and Health Studies), East-West Center, 1601 EW Rd, Honolulu, HI 96848. TEL 808-944-7111, FAX 808-944-7376, ewcbooks@eastwestcenter.org.

304.6 THA ISSN 0259-238X
HA4551
➤ **ASIA - PACIFIC POPULATION JOURNAL.** Text in English. 1986. 3/yr. USD 35 in Africa; USD 55 in Australia, New Zealand & Japan; USD 60 in Europe; USD 50 in North America; USD 40 elsewhere (effective 2011). bk.rev. abstr.; bibl.; charts; illus. back issues avail. **Document type:** *Journal, Academic/Scholarly.* **Description:** Contains 3 full-length original articles plus a note in each issue, or other material such as papers demonstrating the application of a useful methodological approach to the analysis of population research, or news about important developments in the field.
Related titles: Microfiche ed.: (from CIS); Online - full text ed.: ISSN 1564-4278. 1995.
Indexed: APEL, BAS, CA, ESPM, GEOBASE, IIS, P30, P50, P52, P56, PopulInd, RASB, RiskAb, S02, S03, SCOPUS, SSciA, T02.
—BLDSC (1742.261300), IE, Infotrieve, Ingenta.
Published by: United Nations Economic and Social Commission for Asia and the Pacific, Emerging Social Issues Division, Population & Social Integration Section, United Nations Bldg, Rajdamnern Nok Ave, Bangkok, 10200, Thailand. FAX 66-2-2881009, escap-population@un.org, http://www.unescap.org/esid/psis/index.asp. Circ: 2,000. **Subscr. in the Americas to:** EBSCO Information Services, PO Box 361, Birmingham, AL 35201. TEL 205-995-1567, 800-633-4931, FAX 205-995-1588.

➤ **ASIA PACIFIC VIEWPOINT**; specialises in the study of development, change and underdevelopment. *see* BUSINESS AND ECONOMICS—International Development And Assistance

325 PHL ISSN 0117-1968
JV8490 CODEN: APMJES
➤ **ASIAN AND PACIFIC MIGRATION JOURNAL**; a quarterly on human mobility. Text in English. 1992. q. USD 45 (effective 2005). bk.rev. back issues avail. **Document type:** *Journal, Academic/Scholarly.* **Description:** Stimulates research and analysis on migration and refugee movements from and within Asia and the Pacific.
Indexed: A22, AEI, APEL, AbAn, AmH&L, BAS, BibInd, CA, ERA, ESPM, GEOBASE, HPNRM, HistAb, IBR, IBSS, IBZ, IPP, M12, P30, P34, P42, PAIS, PSA, PerIslam, PopulInd, S02, S03, S21, SCOPUS, SOPODA, SSA, SSCI, SSciA, SociolAb, T02, W07.
—BLDSC (1742.354500), IE, Infotrieve, Ingenta, INIST.
Published by: Scalabrini Migration Center, Broadway Centrum, PO Box 10541, Quezon City, 1113, Philippines. TEL 63-2-7243512, FAX 63-2-7214296, smc@smc.org.ph. Ed. Graziano Battistella.

325 PHL ISSN 1013-8064
JV8490 CODEN: ASIME4
ASIAN MIGRANT. Text in English. 1987. irreg., latest 2002, Dec. USD 22. bk.rev. **Document type:** *Monographic series, Academic/Scholarly.* **Description:** Monitors and analyzes the various aspects of Asian migration. Features articles and newsbriefs, research and conference reports, documentation, and NGO news and forum.
Indexed: BAS, IPP, P30, SCOPUS, SOPODA, SociolAb.
—Ingenta.
Published by: Scalabrini Migration Center, Broadway Centrum, PO Box 10541, Quezon City, 1113, Philippines. TEL 63-2-7243512, FAX 63-2-7214296, smc@smc.org.ph. Ed. Graziano Battistella.

325 PHL
ASIAN MIGRATION NEWS. Text in English. bi-w. **Description:** Internet publication aimed at providing scholars, policy makers, advocates and students with a summary of news and events related to migration in Asia.
Media: Online - full text.
Published by: Scalabrini Migration Center, Broadway Centrum, PO Box 10541, Quezon City, 1113, Philippines. TEL 63-2-7243512, FAX 63-2-7214296, smc@smc.org.ph, http://www.smc.org.ph/. Ed. Graziano Battistella.

304.6 GBR ISSN 1744-1730
HB849.65
➤ **ASIAN POPULATION STUDIES.** Text in English. 2005 (Mar.). 3/yr. GBP 202 combined subscription in United Kingdom to institutions (print & online eds.); EUR 287, USD 360 combined subscription to institutions (print & online eds.) (effective 2012). adv. back issues avail.; reprint service avail. from PSC. **Document type:** *Journal, Academic/Scholarly.* **Description:** Publishes original research on matters related to population in this large, complex and rapidly changing region, and welcomes substantive empirical analyses, theoretical works, applied research, and contributions to methodology.
Related titles: Online - full text ed.: ISSN 1744-1749. GBP 182 in United Kingdom to institutions; EUR 258, USD 323 to institutions (effective 2012).
Indexed: A01, A22, A36, CA, CABA, E01, GEOBASE, GH, N02, N03, P10, P27, P46, P48, P50, P52, P53, P54, P56, PQC, R12, S02, S03, SCOPUS, T02, T05, TAR, W11.
—IE, Ingenta. **CCC.**
Published by: (National University of Singapore, Asian Research Institute CHN), Routledge (Subsidiary of: Taylor & Francis Group), 4 Park Sq, Milton Park, Abingdon, Oxon OX14 4RN, United Kingdom. TEL 44-20-70176000, FAX 44-20-70176336, subscriptions@tandf.co.uk, http://www.routledge.com. Ed. Gavin Jones. Adv. contact Linda Hann TEL 44-1344-779945. **Subscr. to:** Taylor & Francis Ltd., Journals Customer Service, Sheepen Pl, Colchester, Essex CO3 3LP, United Kingdom. TEL 44-20-70175544, FAX 44-20-70175198.

304.6 CRI
ASOCIACION DEMOGRAFICA COSTARRICENSE. MEMORIA. Text in Spanish. a.
Published by: Asociacion Demografica Costarricense, Apartado Postal 10203, San Jose, 1000, Costa Rica. TEL 506-31-4425, FAX 506-31-4430.

304.6 AUS ISSN 0819-2588
AUSTRALIAN INSTITUTE OF FAMILY STUDIES. ANNUAL REPORT. Text in English. 1981. a. free (effective 2008). back issues avail. **Document type:** *Report, Consumer.*
Formerly (until 1985): Institute of Family Studies. Annual Report (0726-9870)
Related titles: Online - full text ed.
—CCC.
Published by: Australian Institute of Family Studies, Level 20, 485 La Trobe St, Melbourne, VIC 3000, Australia. TEL 61-3-92147888, FAX 61-3-92147839, afrc@aifs.gov.au, http://www.aifs.gov.au. Circ: 1,000.

304.6 AUS ISSN 1446-9863
HQ706
AUSTRALIAN INSTITUTE OF FAMILY STUDIES. RESEARCH PAPER. Text in English. 2000. irreg. price varies. **Document type:** *Monographic series, Academic/Scholarly.*
Related titles: Online - full text ed.: ISSN 1446-9871.
—CCC.
Published by: Australian Institute of Family Studies, Level 20, 485 La Trobe St, Melbourne, VIC 3000, Australia. TEL 61-3-92147888, FAX 61-3-92147839, fic@aifs.gov.au, http://www.aifs.gov.au.

342.08 USA ISSN 1061-3889
JV6001
BACKGROUNDER (WASHINGTON, DC). Text in English. 1987. irreg. bk.rev. charts; illus.; stat.; tr.lit. cum.index: 1989-1993. **Document type:** *Monographic series, Trade.* **Description:** Covers all immigration issues, from population and environment to economics, social services and immigration law.
Former titles (until 1999): Immigration Review (1073-1997); (until 1994): Scope (1059-6089)
Related titles: Online - full text ed.: free (effective 2010).
Indexed: P30.
Published by: Center for Immigration Studies, 1522 K St, N W, Ste 820, Washington, DC 20005. TEL 202-466-8185, FAX 202-466-8076, center@cis.org, http://www.cis.org/cis.

363.7 USA ISSN 1083-3498
BALANCE ACTIVIST. Text in English. 1973. q. membership. **Document type:** *Newsletter.* **Description:** Covers a variety of U.S. population issues including family planning, immigration reduction, and environmental carrying capacity.
Former titles (until 1995): Balance Report; Balance; (until May 1986): Other Side (Washington)
Indexed: INI.
Published by: Population-Environment Balance, Inc., 2000 P St, N W, Ste 210, Washington, DC 20036-5915. TEL 202-955-5700, FAX 202-955-6161. Ed., R&P Anne E Beale. Circ: 10,000.

BANGLADESH DEVELOPMENT STUDIES. *see* BUSINESS AND ECONOMICS—Economic Situation And Conditions

304.6 IND
BARODA REPORTER. Text in English. 1960. a. bk.rev. abstr.; bibl.; charts; illus.; stat. back issues avail. **Document type:** *Newsletter, Trade.* **Description:** Newsletter of the center, describing research projects and findings.
Related titles: Online - full text ed.: free (effective 2011).
Published by: Population Research Centre, Department of Statistics, Faculty of Science, M S University, Vadodara, Gujarat 390 002, India. TEL 91-265-2794269, FAX 91-265-2795569, prcbaroda@gmail.com, http://www.prcbaroda.org. Ed. Rakesh Srivastava.

304.6 CHN
BEIJING TONGJI NIANJIAN/BEIJING STATISTICAL YEARBOOK. Text in Chinese. a. CNY 280 newsstand/cover (effective 2005). stat. **Document type:** *Yearbook, Government.*
Published by: Beijing Tongji Chubanshe/Beijing Statistics Press, No 75 Yuetan Nanjie, Sanlihe, Beijing, 100826, China. TEL 86-10-63262276, FAX 86-10-63459084, http://www.stats.gov.cn/.

304.6 DEU
BEITRAEGE ZUR BEVOELKERUNGSWISSENSCHAFT. Text in German. 1975. irreg., latest vol.40, 2010. price varies. **Document type:** *Monographic series, Academic/Scholarly.*
Formerly (until 2010): Bundesinstitut fuer Bevoelkerungsforschung. Schriftenreihe (0344-1792)
Published by: (Germany. Bundesinstitut fuer Bevoelkerungsforschung), Ergon Verlag, Keesburgstr 11, Wuerzburg, 97074, Germany. TEL 49-931-280084, FAX 49-931-282872, service@ergon-verlag.de, http://www.ergon-verlag.de.

304.6 BEL
BELGIUM. CENTRUM VOOR BEVOLKINGS- EN GEZINSSTUDIEN. PROGRESS REPORT. Text in Dutch. 1975. a. **Document type:** *Government.*
Formerly: Belgium. Centre d'Etude de la Population et de la Famille. Annual Report
Published by: Centrum voor Bevolkings- en Gezinsstudien/Centre d'Etude de la Population et de la Famille, Markiesstraat 1, Brussels, 1000, Belgium. TEL 32-2-5073569, FAX 32-2-5073419.

BELGIUM. INSTITUT NATIONAL DE STATISTIQUE. SANTE. CAUSES DE DECES. *see* POPULATION STUDIES—Abstracting, Bibliographies, Statistics

BELGIUM. NATIONAAL INSTITUUT VOOR DE STATISTIEK. GEZONDHEID. DOODSOORZAKEN. *see* POPULATION STUDIES—Abstracting, Bibliographies, Statistics

304.6021 BEL ISSN 1379-4043
HA1391
BELGIUM. NATIONAAL INSTITUUT VOOR DE STATISTIEK. MATHEMATISCHE DEMOGRAFIE. STERFTETAFELS. Key Title: Mathematische Demografie. Sterftetafels - Nationaal Instituut voor de Statistiek. Text in Dutch. 1991. bi-m. charts. **Document type:** *Government.*
Former titles (until 2000): Belgium. Nationaal Instituut voor de Statistiek. Bevolkingsstatistieken (1370-1762); (until 1997): Belgium. Nationaal Instituut voor de Statistiek. Sterftetafels (1373-7171)
Related titles: ◆ French ed.: Belgium. Institut National de Statistique. Demographie Mathematique. Tables de Mortalite. ISSN 1379-4051.
Published by: Institut National de Statistique/Nationaal Instituut voor de Statistiek (Subsidiary of: Ministere des Affaires Economiques), Rue de Louvain 44, Brussels, 1000, Belgium. TEL 32-2-548-6211, FAX 32-2-548-6367.

BELIZE. CENTRAL STATISTICAL OFFICE. ABSTRACT OF STATISTICS. *see* POPULATION STUDIES—Abstracting, Bibliographies, Statistics

BELIZE NATIONAL CENSUS REPORT. *see* POPULATION STUDIES—Abstracting, Bibliographies, Statistics

BELIZE NATIONAL POPULATION REPORT. *see* POPULATION STUDIES—Abstracting, Bibliographies, Statistics

325.1 340 USA
BENDER'S IMMIGRATION AND NATIONALITY ACT SERVICE. Text in English. base vol. plus irreg. updates. looseleaf. USD 138 base vol(s). (effective 2008). **Document type:** *Handbook/Manual/Guide, Trade.* **Description:** Contains text of the act set out according to its statutory title and chapter arrangement.
Published by: Matthew Bender & Co., Inc. (Subsidiary of: LexisNexis North America), 1275 Broadway, Albany, NY 12204. TEL 518-487-3000, 800-424-4200, FAX 518-487-3083, international@bender.com, http://bender.lexisnexis.com.

325.1 340 USA
BENDER'S IMMIGRATION REGULATIONS SERVICE. Text in English. 1989. 2 base vols. plus m. updates. looseleaf. USD 325 base vol(s). (effective 2008). **Document type:** *Handbook/Manual/Guide, Trade.* **Description:** Provides up-to-date version of the immigration regulations that can be used as a quick desk reference or conveniently carried to court.
Published by: Matthew Bender & Co., Inc. (Subsidiary of: LexisNexis North America), 1275 Broadway, Albany, NY 12204. TEL 518-487-3000, 800-424-4200, FAX 518-487-3083, international@bender.com, http://bender.lexisnexis.com.

304.6 CHE ISSN 0258-784X
BEVOELKERUNGSBEWEGUNG IN DER SCHWEIZ/MOUVEMENT DE LA POPULATION EN SUISSE. Text in French, German. 1876. a. CHF 12 (effective 2001). **Document type:** *Government.*
Published by: Bundesamt fuer Statistik, Espace de l'Europe 10, Neuchatel, 2010, Switzerland. TEL 41-32-7136011, FAX 41-32-7136012, information@bfs.admin.ch, http://www.admin.ch/bfs.

304.6 DEU
HB848
BEVOELKERUNGSFORSCHUNG AKTUELL. Text in German. 1980. 6/yr. bk.rev. **Document type:** *Journal, Trade.* **Description:** Contains national and international population information and demographic news relevant to policy makers, social scientists, the press and other researchers.
Formerly (until 2010): B I B Mitteilungen (0722-1509)
Indexed: P30, RefZh.

Published by: Bundesinstitut fuer Bevoelkerungsforschung, Friedrich-Ebert-Allee 4, Wiesbaden, 65185, Germany. TEL 49-611-752235, FAX 49-611-753960, bib@destatis.de, http://www.bib-demographie.de. Ed. Bernhard Gueckel. Circ: 1,500 (controlled).

304.6 NLD ISSN 1877-1149
BEVOLKINGSPROGNOSE ROTTERDAM. Cover title: Prognose Bevolking Rotterdam. Text in Dutch. 1989. irreg. EUR 20 per issue (effective 2011). **Document type:** *Report, Government.*
Published by: Centrum voor Onderzoek en Statistiek, Gemeente Rotterdam, Gebouw "De Goudsesingel", 2e etage Goudsesingel 78, Rotterdam, 3011 KD, Netherlands. TEL 31-10-4899500, FAX 31-10-4899501, infocos@sdr.roterdam.nl, http://cos.rotterdam.nl.

304.6 CHN ISSN 1674-5701
BIAOZHUN SHENGHUO/STANDARD LIVING. Text in Chinese. 1964. m. **Document type:** *Journal, Academic/Scholarly.*
Former titles (until 2008): Shijie Biaozhun Xinxi (1002-5774); (until 1986): Guowai Biaozhun Ziliao Baodao
Published by: Zhongguo Biaozhunhua Yanjiuyuan/China National Institute of Standardization, 4, Zhichun Lu, Beijing, 100088, China. TEL 86-10-58811439.

325 413 USA
BILINGUAL DICTIONARY OF IMMIGRATION TERMS (ENGLISH - SPANISH). Text in English, Spanish. 1997. a. USD 19.95 (effective 2000). **Document type:** *Monographic series, Trade.* **Description:** Presents a comprehensive compilation of significant procedural and substantive immigration terms and concepts defined in Spanish and English. Includes flow charts of immigration procedures such as visa application, deportation and exclusion, as well as a Spanish-English index.
Published by: Gould Publications, Inc. (Subsidiary of: LexisNexis North America), 1333 North US Hwy 17-92, Longwood, FL 32750. TEL 800-533-1637, 877-374-2919, FAX 407-695-2906, criminaljustice@lexisnexis.com, http://www.gouldlaw.com.

304.6 618.92 AUS ISSN 1449-8405
BIRTH ANOMALIES SERIES. Variant title: Congenital Anomalies in Australia. Text in English. 1995; N.S. 2004. a., latest vol.3, 2002-2003. AUD 30 per issue (effective 2008). stat. **Document type:** *Monographic series, Government.*
Formerly (until 1999): Birth Defects Series (1321-8352)
Related titles: Online - full text ed.
Indexed: A36, GH.
Published by: Australian Institute of Health and Welfare, National Perinatal Statistics Unit, Level 2, McNevin Dickson Bldg, Gate 6, Avoca St, Randwick Hospitals Campus, Randwick, NSW 2031, Australia. TEL 61-2-93821014, FAX 61-2-93821025, npsu@med.unsw.edu.au.

BOGEON SAHOE YEONGU/HEALTH AND SOCIAL WELFARE REVIEW. *see* SOCIAL SERVICES AND WELFARE

304.6 ESP
BOLETIN MENSUAL DE COYUNTURA (ONLINE). Text in Spanish. 2002. m. back issues avail. **Document type:** *Bulletin, Consumer.*
Media: Online - full text.
Published by: Comunidad de Madrid, Consejeria de Economia y Hacienda, Principe de Vergara, 132 1a. Plata, Madrid, 28002, Spain. TEL 34-91-4207131, FAX 34-91-580-2217, http://www.madrid.org/cs/Satellite?idConsejeria=1109266187242&idListConsj=1109265444710&c=CM_Agrupador_FP&pagename=ComunidadMadrid%2FEstructura&language=es&cid=1109266187242.

304.6 BRA ISSN 1415-0158
BRAZILIAN JOURNAL OF POPULATION STUDIES. Text in English. 1997. s-a. BRL 30 domestic; USD 30 foreign (effective 2006). **Document type:** *Journal, Academic/Scholarly.*
Related titles: Online - full text ed.
Indexed: P30.
Published by: Associacao Brasileira de Estudos Populacionais, Ave Casper Libero, 464 5 andar, Sao Paulo, 01033-000, Brazil. TEL 55-11-21717377, rebep@abep.org.br, http://www.abep.org.br/. Ed. Calos Eugenio Ferreira.

325.2 304.82 SWE ISSN 0345-1798
BRIDGE. Text in English. 1969. q. SEK 120 membership (effective 2003). adv. bk.rev. illus.; bibl. index. **Document type:** *Journal, Consumer.*
Formerly (until 1972): Emigranten
Related titles: ◆ Swedish ed.: Sverige och Amerika. ISSN 2000-4869.
Published by: Samfundet Emigrantforskningens Fraemjande/Society for the Promotion of Emigration Research, PO Box 331, Karlstad, 65108, Sweden. TEL 46-54-617720, 46-54-627726, FAX 46-54-617721, research@emigrantregistret.s.se. Ed., Adv. contact Tommy Hellstrom. Circ: 1,500.

BULGARIA - (YEAR). *see* STATISTICS

BULGARIA: SOTSIALNO-IKONOMICHESKO RAZVITIE. *see* STATISTICS

304.6 CMR ISSN 1013-1396
HB3661.A3
BULLETIN DE LIAISON DE DEMOGRAPHIE AFRICAINE. Text in French. 1971. 3/yr. free. adv. back issues avail. **Document type:** *Government.*
Former titles (until 1978): Demographie Africaine (0151-1394); (until 1977): Demographie en Afrique d'Expression Francaise (0151-1386)
Indexed: P30, Popullnd.
Published by: Institut de Formation et de Recherche Demographiques (I F O R D), BP 1556, Yaounde, Cameroon. TEL 23-29-47, 22-24-71. Circ: 1,000.

BULLETIN ON SOCIAL INTEGRATION POLICIES. *see* GERONTOLOGY AND GERIATRICS

304.6 USA ISSN 0891-2874
C D E WORKING PAPER. Text in English. irreg., latest no.4, 2005. **Document type:** *Monographic series.*
Related titles: Online - full text ed.
Indexed: P30.
Published by: University of Wisconsin at Madison, Center for Demography and Ecology, 4412 Sewell Social Science Bldg, 1180 Observatory Dr, Madison, WI 53706-1393. TEL 608-262-2182, FAX 608-262-8400, cde@ssc.wisc.edu.

C E D P A NETWORK. *see* WOMEN'S INTERESTS

325.1 ESP ISSN 1888-3044
C E I M I G R A. ANUARIO. Text in Spanish. 2007. a. **Document type:** *Monographic series, Academic/Scholarly.*
Published by: Centro de Estudios para la Integracion Social y Formacion de Inmigrantes, Gran Via Fernando el Catolico No. 78, Valencia, 46008, Spain. TEL 34-96-3152220, FAX 34-96-3914353, fundacion@ceimigra.net, http://www.ceimigra.net/.

C H S DEMOGRAPHY/STATISTIQUE DU LOGEMENT AU CANADA: DEMOGRAPHIE. (Canadian Housing Statistics) *see* HOUSING AND URBAN PLANNING—Abstracting, Bibliographies, Statistics

304.6 PRI ISSN 2150-6515
▼ **C I D E DIGITAL.** (Centro de Investigacion Demografica) Text in Spanish, English. 2009 (Nov.). s-a. free (effective 2009). **Document type:** *Journal, Academic/Scholarly.* **Description:** Includes empirical, theoretical, historical and demographic or methodological content relating to any topic on population studies in Puerto Rico.
Media: Online - full text.
Published by: Universidad de Puerto Rico, Centro de Investigacion Demografica, PO Box 365067, San Juan, 00936-5067, Puerto Rico. TEL 787-582-2525, arnaldo.torres1@upr.edu.

CAHIERS DE L'EMIGRATION RUSSE. *see* LITERATURE

362 FRA ISSN 0007-9995
RA18
CAHIERS DE SOCIOLOGIE ET DE DEMOGRAPHIE MEDICALES. Text in French. 1961. q. bk.rev. charts; stat. index. 1 cols./p.; back issues avail. **Document type:** *Magazine, Trade.* **Description:** A bi-lingual and multidisciplinary journal on health sources and systems research.
Indexed: A22, EMBASE, ExcerpMed, FR, IBSS, IndMed, MEDLINE, P30, R10, Reac, SCOPUS.
—BLDSC (2952.240000), GNLM, IE, Infotrieve, Ingenta, INIST. **CCC.**
Published by: Centre de Sociologie et Demographie Medicales, 168A ne de Grenelle, Paris, 75007, France. TEL 33-1-45557377, FAX 33-1-45558794.

342.082 362.82 325.1 FRA ISSN 2102-376X
LES CAHIERS DU SOCIAL. Text in French. 2002. 3/yr. EUR 7 newsstand/cover (effective 2009). **Document type:** *Journal, Trade.* **Description:** Informs the social worker who works with refugees and the integration of immigrants.
Published by: France Terre d'Asile, 24 Rue Marc Seguin, Paris, 75018, France. TEL 33-1-53043999, infos@france-terre-asile.org.

304.6 CAN ISSN 0380-1721
HB3530.Q4
CAHIERS QUEBECOIS DE DEMOGRAPHIE. Text in English. 1975. 2/yr. CAD 25 domestic to individuals; CAD 35 foreign to individuals; CAD 40 domestic to institutions; CAD 45 foreign to institutions (effective 2008). bk.rev. **Document type:** *Journal, Academic/Scholarly.*
Formerly (until 1975): Association des Demographes du Quebec. Bulletin (0380-1713)
Indexed: CA, FR, IBSS, P30, PAIS, PdeR, Popullnd, S02, S03, SCOPUS, SSA, SSciA, SociolAb, T02.
Published by: Association des Demographes du Quebec, c/o Richard Marcoux, Universite Laval, Departement de Sociologie, Pavillon Charles-De Koninck, Local 4491, Quebec, PQ H3T 2A5, Canada. TEL 418-656-5105, FAX 418-656-7390, http://www.demo.umontreal.ca/adq/association.html.

304.6 GBR
CAMBRIDGE GROUP FOR THE HISTORY OF POPULATION AND SOCIAL STRUCTURE. WORKING PAPER SERIES. Text in English. 1995. irreg., latest vol.5, 1997. back issues avail. **Document type:** *Monographic series, Academic/Scholarly.*
Published by: University of Cambridge, Cambridge Group for the History of Population and Social Structure, Sir William Hardy Bldg, Department of Geography, Downing Pl, Cambridge, CB2 3EN, United Kingdom. TEL 44-1223-333181, FAX 44-1223-333183, richard.smith@geog.cam.ac.uk, http://www.hpss.geog.cam.ac.uk.

304.6 CAN ISSN 1911-2408
CANADA, PROVINCES AND TERRITORIES. ANNUAL DEMOGRAPHIC ESTIMATES. Text in English. 2006. a. **Document type:** *Government.*
Media: Online - full text.
Published by: Statistics Canada, Demography Division (Subsidiary of: Statistics Canada/Statistique Canada), Statistical Reference Centre, Rm 1500, Main Building, Holland Avenue, Ottawa, ON K1A 0T6, Canada.

304.6 CAN ISSN 1911-0928
CANADA. STATISTICS CANADA. QUARTERLY DEMOGRAPHIC ESTIMATES. Text in English. 1996. q. **Document type:** *Government.*
Formerly (until 2006): Quarterly Demographic Statistics (1209-1235)
Media: Online - full text. **Related titles:** ◆ Print ed.: Canada. Statistics Canada. Quarterly Demographic Statistics. ISSN 0835-4057; ◆ French ed.: Canada. Statistique Canada. Estimations Demographiques Trimestrielles. ISSN 1911-0936.
Published by: Statistics Canada, Demography Division (Subsidiary of: Statistics Canada/Statistique Canada), Statistical Reference Centre, Rm 1500, Main Building, Holland Avenue, Ottawa, ON K1A 0T6, Canada.

304.6 CAN ISSN 0715-9293
CANADA. STATISTICS CANADA. REPORT ON THE DEMOGRAPHIC SITUATION IN CANADA. Text in English. 1983. a. CAD 31; USD 31 foreign. **Document type:** *Government.* **Description:** Examines population growth at national and provincial levels, marriage and divorce rates, fertility and mortality, international and domestic migration patterns.
Related titles: Microform ed.: (from MML); Online - full text ed.: ISSN 1718-7788. 1994; ◆ French ed.: Canada. Statistiques Canada. Rapport sur l'Etat de la Population du Canada. ISSN 0715-9307.
—**CCC.**
Published by: Statistics Canada, Operations and Integration Division (Subsidiary of: Statistics Canada/Statistique Canada), Circulation Management, 120 Parkdale Ave, Ottawa, ON K1A 0T6, Canada. TEL 613-951-7277, 800-267-6677, FAX 613-951-1584.

CANADA. STATISTIQUES CANADA. RAPPORT SUR L'ETAT DE LA POPULATION DU CANADA. *see* STATISTICS

325.1 CAN
CANADIAN NEWCOMER MAGAZINE. Text in English. 2004. q. free (effective 2004). **Document type:** *Magazine, Consumer.* **Description:** Provides information, advice, entertainment, education and encouragement to new immigrants.
Published by: Canadian Newcomer Magazine Inc., 174 Barrington Ave, Toronto, ON M4C 4Z2, Canada. TEL 416-406-4719. Ed. Dale L Sproule.

304.6 CAN ISSN 0380-1489
HB848 CODEN: CSTPEM
➤ **CANADIAN STUDIES IN POPULATION.** Text in English, French. 1974. s-a. USD 26 in US & Canada to individuals; USD 28 elsewhere to individuals; USD 44 in US & Canada to institutions; USD 46 elsewhere to institutions (effective 2010). bk.rev. illus. index: 1974-1983. back issues avail.; reprints avail. **Document type:** *Journal, Academic/Scholarly.* **Description:** Contains articles on population studies, both methodological and substantive.
Related titles: Online - full text ed.: free (effective 2011).
Indexed: A39, C03, C04, C27, C29, CA, CBCARef, D03, D04, E13, ESPM, HPNRM, P30, P48, P52, P56, PAIS, PQC, Popullnd, R14, S02, S03, S14, S15, S18, SOPODA, SRRA, SSA, SSciA, SociolAb, T02, W09.
—Ingenta. **CCC.**
Published by: (Canadian Popoulation Society), University of Alberta, Department of Sociology, 201 North Power Plant, University of Alberta, Edmonton, AB T6G 2N2, Canada. TEL 780-492-5234, FAX 780-492-7196, http://www.uofaweb.ualberta.ca/. Ed. Frank Trovato.

304.6 LUX ISSN 1683-5042
HC240.A1
CANDIDATE COUNTRIES EUROBAROMETER. Text in English. a.
Formerly: Central and Eastern Eurobarometer
Published by: European Commission, Office for Official Publications of the European Union, 2 Rue Mercier, Luxembourg, L-2985, Luxembourg. FAX 352-29291, info@publications.europa.eu, http://publications.europa.eu.

325 ESP ISSN 0576-8233
DP1
CARTA DE ESPANA; la revista para los espanoles en el extranjero. Text in Spanish. 1960. m. USD 20. adv. bk.rev. **Document type:** *Government.* **Description:** Covers immigration to Spain and emigration to foreign countries.
Formed by the merger (1972-1974): Carta de Espana (World Edition) (1575-0523); (1972-1974): Carta de Espana (Special Edition for the Americas) (1575-0515); Both of which superseded in part in 1972: Carta de Espana (1575-0507)
Published by: Ministerio de Trabajo y Asuntos Sociales, Instituto Espanol de Emigracion, Agustin de Bethencourt 4, Madrid, 28071, Spain. http://www.mtas.es. Ed. Amparo Fernandez Nunez. Circ: 20,000.

CELEBRATE LIFE (STAFFORD). *see* BIRTH CONTROL

304.6 USA
CENSUSCD (YEAR) ESTIMATES, (YEAR) PROJECTIONS, CONSUMER EXPENDITURES, AND PROFILES. Text in English. a. USD 595 per issue for single user (effective 2005). stat. **Document type:** *Government.* **Description:** Covers the changes in American population and compared to the data a previous year and population forecasts 5 years into the future. Also includesconsumer expenditures and Profiles.
Media: CD-ROM.
Published by: GeoLytics, Inc., PO Box 10, East Brunswick, NJ 08816. TEL 732-651-2000, 800-577-6717, FAX 732-651-2721, http://www.geolytics.com/.

304.6 USA
CENSUSCD + MAPS. Text in English. 1998. every 10 yrs. USD 495 for single user (effective 2005). stat.; maps. **Document type:** *Government.* **Description:** Contains normalized Long Form Data and geographical information (Nation, state, county, MCD, place, congress, zip, MSA/CMSA, PMSA, & American Indian).
Media: CD-ROM.
Published by: GeoLytics, Inc., PO Box 10, East Brunswick, NJ 08816. TEL 732-651-2000, 800-577-6717, FAX 732-651-2721, http://www.geolytics.com/.

304.6 USA
CENTER FOR MIGRATION STUDIES. GIOVANNI SCHIAVO COLLECTION. Text in English. 1976. irreg., latest 1993. price varies. back issues avail. **Document type:** *Monographic series, Academic/Scholarly.*
Published by: Center for Migration Studies, 27 Carmine St, New York, NY 10014. TEL 212-675-3993, FAX 212-255-1771, cms@cmsny.org.

304.6 USA
CENTER FOR RURAL POLICY AND DEVELOPMENT. RESEARCH REPORTS. Text in English. irreg., latest 2010. free to members (effective 2010). stat. back issues avail. **Document type:** *Monographic series, Academic/Scholarly.* **Description:** Includes reports on technology, economic development, demography, and education.
Related titles: Online - full content ed.
Published by: Center for Rural Policy and Development, 600 S Fifth St, Ste 211, Saint Peter, MN 56082. TEL 507-934-7700, 877-787-2566, FAX 507-934-7704, crpd@ruralmn.org, http://www.mnsu.edu/ruralmn/index.html.

CENTRE FOR URBAN AND COMMUNITY STUDIES. MAJOR REPORT SERIES. *see* HOUSING AND URBAN PLANNING

CENTRE FOR URBAN AND COMMUNITY STUDIES. RESEARCH PAPERS. *see* HOUSING AND URBAN PLANNING

304.6 PRY ISSN 1017-6047
CENTRO DE DOCUMENTACION Y ESTUDIOS. INFORMATIVO CAMPESINO. Text in Spanish. 1988. m. USD 72.
Published by: Centro de Documentacion y Estudios, Cerro Cara 1426, Casi Pai Peres, Casilla de Correos 2558, Asuncion, Paraguay. TEL 595-21-225000, FAX 595-21-213246, cde@cde.org.py, http://www.cde.org.py/www/index.html. Ed. Quintin Riquelme. Circ: 800. **Dist. by:** D.I.P.P., PO Box 2507, Asuncion, Paraguay.

304.8 ESP ISSN 2172-0487
▼ **CENTRO DE INVESTIGACION Y COOPERACION ESPECIALIZADO EN REMESAS DE EMIGRANTE. WORKING PAPERS.** Key Title: Working Papers (remsas.org). Text in Spanish. 2009. q. back issues avail. **Document type:** *Monographic series, Academic/Scholarly.*
Media: Online - full text.
Published by: Centro de Investigacion y Cooperacion Especializado en Remesas de Emigrantes admin@remesas.org, http://www.remesas.org/.

P

304.6 CHL ISSN 0378-5386
HB3530.5.A3
CENTRO LATINOAMERICANO DE DEMOGRAFIA. BOLETIN DEMOGRAFICO. Text in English, Spanish. 1968. s-a. USD 10. bibl.; charts; stat. back issues avail. **Description:** Reports population projections and estimates, birth and death rates for the Latin American and Caribbean countries.
Related titles: Microfiche ed.: (from CIS).
Indexed: C01, IIS, PAIS, PopulInd.
Published by: United Nations, Centro Latinoamericano de Demografia/ United Nations, Latin American and Demographic Center, Casilla 91, Santiago, Chile. TEL 56-2-210-2000. Circ: 1,000.

304.6 CHL ISSN 0303-1829
HB3530.5.A3
CENTRO LATINOAMERICANO DE DEMOGRAFIA. NOTAS DE POBLACION; revista latinoamericana de demografia. Text in Spanish; Summaries in English. 1973. s-a. USD 20. bk.rev. index. back issues avail. **Description:** Publishes recent studies on population dynamics in Latin America and the Caribbean, information on work in the field of demographics.
Related titles: Microfiche ed.: (from CIS).
Indexed: C01, IIS, P30, PAIS, PopulInd, SCOPUS, SociolAb.
Published by: United Nations, Centro Latinoamericano de Demografia/ United Nations, Latin American and Demographic Center, Casilla 91, Santiago, Chile. TEL 56-2-210-2000. Circ: 1,000.

304.6 CHL ISSN 0503-3934
HA755
CENTRO LATINOAMERICANO DE DEMOGRAFIA. SERIE A/LATIN AMERICAN DEMOGRAPHIC CENTRE. SERIE A. Text in Spanish. 1962. irreg. USD 6 per issue. stat.
Published by: United Nations, Centro Latinoamericano de Demografia/ United Nations, Latin American and Demographic Center, Casilla 91, Santiago, Chile. TEL 56-2-210-2000. Circ: 400.

304.6 CHL ISSN 0503-3942
CENTRO LATINOAMERICANO DE DEMOGRAFIA. SERIE C/LATIN AMERICAN DEMOGRAPHIC CENTRE. SERIE C. Text in Spanish. 1963. irreg. USD 6 per issue. stat.
Published by: United Nations, Centro Latinoamericano de Demografia/ United Nations, Latin American and Demographic Center, Casilla 91, Santiago, Chile. TEL 56-2-210-2000. Circ: 400.

304.6 CHL ISSN 0503-3950
CENTRO LATINOAMERICANO DE DEMOGRAFIA. SERIE D/LATIN AMERICAN DEMOGRAPHIC CENTRE. SERIE D. Text in Spanish. 1962. irreg. USD 6 per issue.
Published by: United Nations, Centro Latinoamericano de Demografia/ United Nations, Latin American and Demographic Center, Casilla 91, Santiago, Chile. TEL 56-2-210-2000. Circ: 400.

304.6 CHL
CENTRO LATINOAMERICANO DE DEMOGRAFIA. SERIE E/LATIN AMERICAN DEMOGRAPHIC CENTRE. SERIE E. Text in Spanish. 1967. irreg. price varies. stat.
Published by: United Nations, Centro Latinoamericano de Demografia/ United Nations, Latin American and Demographic Center, Casilla 91, Santiago, Chile. TEL 56-2-210-2000.

304.6 CHL
CENTRO LATINOAMERICANO DE DEMOGRAFIA. SERIE OI: PUBLICACIONES CONJUNTAS CON INSTITUCIONES NACIONALES DE PAISES DE AMERICA LATINA. Text in Spanish. 1967. irreg. USD 6 per issue. stat.
Published by: United Nations, Centro Latinoamericano de Demografia/ United Nations, Latin American and Demographic Center, Casilla 91, Santiago, Chile. TEL 56-2-210-2000.

304.64 NZL ISSN 1177-7044
CHILD AND YOUTH MORTALITY REVIEW COMMITTEE. REPORT TO THE MINISTER OF HEALTH. Text in English. 2003. a. **Document type:** *Report, Trade.*
Related titles: Online - full text ed.: ISSN 1177-7052.
Published by: Child and Youth Mortality Review Committee, c/o Secretariat, Clinical Services Directorate, Ministry of Health, PO Box 5013, Wellington, New Zealand. TEL 64-4-4708773, cymrc@moh.govt.nz.

304.6 331.11 950 NLD ISSN 1875-936X
HD5830.A6
▼ **THE CHINA POPULATION AND LABOR YEARBOOK.** Variant title: The Chinese Academy of Social Sciences Yearbooks: Population and Labor. Text in English. 2009. a. price varies.
Published by: (Chinese Academy of Social Sciences CHN), Brill, PO Box 9000, Leiden, 2300 PA, Netherlands. TEL 31-71-5353500, FAX 31-71-5317532, cs@brill.nl.

304.6 CHN ISSN 1003-4595
CHINA POPULATION TODAY. Text in English. 1983. bi-m. **Description:** Provides information on China's population and family planning policies, population trends, and family planning and reproductive health in China.
Formerly (until 1991): China Population Newsletter (1000-9043)
Related titles: Online - full text ed.
Indexed: ESPM, HPNRM, P30, SCOPUS, SSciA.
Published by: China Population Information and Research Center, PO Box 2444, Beijing, 100081, China. TEL 86-10-62173519, FAX 86-10-62172101, info@cpirc.org.cn, http://www.cpirc.org.cn.

325 363.96 612.6 BEL ISSN 1027-7412
HQ766.5.E85
CHOICES (LONDON); sexual and reproductive health and rights in Europe. Text in English. 1972. a., latest 2002. free. bk.rev. cum.index: 1972-1976, 1977-1990. back issues avail. **Document type:** *Journal, Academic/Scholarly.* **Description:** Issue-oriented and informative journal, with a focus on sexual and reproductive health and rights.
Formerly (until 1995): Planned Parenthood in Europe (1017-8538); Which superseded in part (1980-1988): Planning Familial en Europe (Ed. Multilingue) (1010-5948); Which was formerly (1972-1979): I P P F Europe Regional Information Bulletin (0306-9303)
Related titles: Online - full content ed.
Indexed: CLFP, CWI, P30.
—BLDSC (3181.538085).
Published by: International Planned Parenthood. European Network, 146 Rue Royale, Brussels, 1000, Belgium. TEL 32-2-2500950, FAX 32-2-2500969, info@ippfen.org, http://www.ippfen.org. Ed. Victoria Rugg. R&P Nicoletta Confalone. Circ: 2,000.

CHRONIC DISEASES NOTES & REPORTS. *see* PUBLIC HEALTH AND SAFETY

304.6 FRA ISSN 1157-4186
HA4030
LA CHRONIQUE DU C E P E D. (Centre Population et Developpement) Text in French. 1991. q. **Document type:** *Magazine, Government.*
Related titles: Online - full text ed.
Indexed: P30, SCOPUS.
Published by: Centre Population et Developpement (C E P E D), 45 Rue des Saints Peres, Paris, 75006, France. TEL 33-1-42864588, FAX 33-1-42863351, contact@ceped.org.

325.1 342.082 CAN ISSN 1495-2114
CITIZENSHIP AND IMMIGRATION MANUALS. Text in English. 1999. q.
Media: CD-ROM.
Published by: Citizenship and Immigration Canada, 6th Fl, 400 University Ave, Toronto, ON M7A 2R9, Canada. TEL 416-327-2422, FAX 416-314-4965, info@mczcr.gov.on.ca.

316.7 CHL ISSN 0718-3348
CIUDAD INVISIBLE. Text in Spanish. 2001. bi-m.
Published by: Ril Editores, Alferez Real 1464, Providencia, Santiago, Chile. TEL 56-2-2238100, FAX 56-2-2254269, ril@rileditores.com, http://www.rileditores.com/.

304.6 PRT ISSN 1647-1709
▼ **CLASSIFICACAO PORTUGUESA DO CONSUMO INDIVIDUAL POR OBJECTIVO.** Text in Portuguese. 2009. irreg. **Document type:** *Report, Government.*
Published by: Instituto Nacional de Estatistica, Av Antonio Jose de Almeida 2, Lisbon, 1000-043, Portugal. TEL 351-21-8426100, FAX 351-21-8426380, ine@ine.pt, http://www.ine.pt.

325 ITA ISSN 2037-9358
COLLANA DI EMIGRAZIONE ITALIANA. Text in Italian. 2008. irreg. **Document type:** *Monographic series, Academic/Scholarly.*
Published by: Editrice Luigi Pellegrini, Via de Rada 67c, Cosenza, CS 87100, Italy. TEL 39-0984-795065, FAX 39-0984-792672, http://www.pellegrinieditore.it.

COLOMBIA. DEPARTAMENTO ADMINISTRATIVO NACIONAL DE ESTADISTICA. ANUARIO DEMOGRAFICO. *see* POPULATION STUDIES—Abstracting, Bibliographies, Statistics

304.6 FRA
COMITE INTERNATIONAL DE COOPERATION DANS LES RECHERCHES NATIONALES EN DEMOGRAPHIE. ACTES DES SEMINAIRES. Text in French, English. 1973. irreg.
Published by: Committee for International Cooperation in National Research in Demography, 133 Boulevard Davout, Paris, 75980 Cedex 20, France. TEL 33-1-56062019, FAX 33-1-56062165, cicred@cicred.org, http://www.cicred.org.

304.6 DEU ISSN 1869-8980
HB848
➤ **COMPARATIVE POPULATION STUDIES.** Text in German; Summaries in English, French, German. 1975. q. free (effective 2011). **Document type:** *Journal, Academic/Scholarly.*
Formerly (until 2010): Zeitschrift fuer Bevoelkerungswissenschaft (0340-2398)
Related titles: Online - full text ed.: ISSN 1869-8999. free (effective 2011).
Indexed: A22, DIP, E01, IBR, IBSS, IBZ, P30, PAIS, PopulInd, RASB, RefZh, SociolAb.
—IE. **CCC.**
Published by: Bundesinstitut fuer Bevoelkerungsforschung, Friedrich-Ebert-Allee 4, Wiesbaden, 65185, Germany. TEL 49-611-752235, FAX 49-611-753960, bib@destatis.de, http://www.bib-demographie.de.

304.6 ESP ISSN 1579-5187
COMUNIDAD DE MADRID. BOLETIN DE POBLACION ACTIVA (DISKETTE). Key Title: Boletin de Poblacion Activa, Comunidad de Madrid. Text in Spanish. 1998. q. **Document type:** *Bulletin, Consumer.*
Formerly (until 2001): Comunidad de Madrid. Boletin de Poblacion Activa (Print) (1139-6261)
Media: Diskette.
Published by: Comunidad de Madrid, Instituto de Estadistica, Principe de Vargara 108, Madrid, 28002, Spain. TEL 34-91-5802540, FAX 34-91-5802664, jestadis@madrid.org, http://www.madrid.org/iestadis/index.htm.

303.4 GBR ISSN 0268-4160
HM104
➤ **CONTINUITY AND CHANGE**; a journal of social structure, law and demography in past societies. Text in English. 1986. 3/yr. GBP 184, USD 312 to institutions; GBP 204, USD 349 combined subscription to institutions (print & online eds.) (effective 2012). adv. bk.rev. illus. 176 p./no. 1 cols./p.; back issues avail.; reprint service avail. from PSC. **Document type:** *Journal, Academic/Scholarly.* **Description:** Covers historical sociology concerned with long-term continuities and discontinuity in the structures of past societies, with emphasis on methodological studies. Combines elements from history, sociology, law, demography, economics, and anthropology.
Related titles: Microform ed.: (from PQC); Online - full text ed.: ISSN 1469-218X. 1997. GBP 177, USD 302 to institutions (effective 2012).
Indexed: A20, A22, ASCA, AmH&L, AmHI, BAS, BrHumI, CA, CurCont, DIP, E01, FamI, GEOBASE, H07, HistAb, IBR, IBSS, IBZ, MLA-IB, P02, P10, P27, P30, P42, P46, P48, P53, P54, PCI, PQC, PSA, PSI, PopulInd, S02, S03, S11, SCOPUS, SOPODA, SSA, SSCI, SociolAb, T02, W07, W09.
—BLDSC (3425.688700), IE, Infotrieve, Ingenta. **CCC.**
Published by: Cambridge University Press, The Edinburgh Bldg, Shaftesbury Rd, Cambridge, CB2 8RU, United Kingdom. TEL 44-1223-312393, FAX 44-1223-315052, journals@cambridge.org, http://www.cambridge.org/uk. Eds. Lloyd Bonfield, Phillipp Schofield, Richard Wall. **Subscr. to:** Cambridge University Press, 32 Ave of the Americas, New York, NY 10013. TEL 212-337-5000, FAX 212-691-3239, journals_subscriptions@cup.org.

➤ **COUNTRY REVIEW. AFGHANISTAN.** *see* BUSINESS AND ECONOMICS—Economic Situation And Conditions

➤ **COUNTRY REVIEW. ALBANIA.** *see* BUSINESS AND ECONOMICS—Economic Situation And Conditions

➤ **COUNTRY REVIEW. ALGERIA.** *see* BUSINESS AND ECONOMICS—Economic Situation And Conditions

➤ **COUNTRY REVIEW. ANDORRA.** *see* BUSINESS AND ECONOMICS—Economic Situation And Conditions

➤ **COUNTRY REVIEW. ANGOLA.** *see* BUSINESS AND ECONOMICS—Economic Situation And Conditions

➤ **COUNTRY REVIEW. ANTIGUA.** *see* BUSINESS AND ECONOMICS—Economic Situation And Conditions

➤ **COUNTRY REVIEW. ARGENTINA.** *see* BUSINESS AND ECONOMICS—Economic Situation And Conditions

➤ **COUNTRY REVIEW. ARMENIA.** *see* BUSINESS AND ECONOMICS—Economic Situation And Conditions

➤ **COUNTRY REVIEW. AUSTRALIA.** *see* BUSINESS AND ECONOMICS—Economic Situation And Conditions

➤ **COUNTRY REVIEW. AUSTRIA.** *see* BUSINESS AND ECONOMICS—Economic Situation And Conditions

➤ **COUNTRY REVIEW. AZERBAIJAN.** *see* BUSINESS AND ECONOMICS—Economic Situation And Conditions

➤ **COUNTRY REVIEW. BAHAMAS.** *see* BUSINESS AND ECONOMICS—Economic Situation And Conditions

➤ **COUNTRY REVIEW. BAHRAIN.** *see* BUSINESS AND ECONOMICS—Economic Situation And Conditions

➤ **COUNTRY REVIEW. BANGLADESH.** *see* BUSINESS AND ECONOMICS—Economic Situation And Conditions

➤ **COUNTRY REVIEW. BARBADOS.** *see* BUSINESS AND ECONOMICS—Economic Situation And Conditions

➤ **COUNTRY REVIEW. BELARUS.** *see* BUSINESS AND ECONOMICS—Economic Situation And Conditions

➤ **COUNTRY REVIEW. BELGIUM.** *see* BUSINESS AND ECONOMICS—Economic Situation And Conditions

➤ **COUNTRY REVIEW. BELIZE.** *see* BUSINESS AND ECONOMICS—Economic Situation And Conditions

➤ **COUNTRY REVIEW. BENIN.** *see* BUSINESS AND ECONOMICS—Economic Situation And Conditions

➤ **COUNTRY REVIEW. BHUTAN.** *see* BUSINESS AND ECONOMICS—Economic Situation And Conditions

➤ **COUNTRY REVIEW. BOLIVIA.** *see* BUSINESS AND ECONOMICS—Economic Situation And Conditions

➤ **COUNTRY REVIEW. BOSNIA HERZEGOVINA.** *see* BUSINESS AND ECONOMICS—Economic Situation And Conditions

➤ **COUNTRY REVIEW. BOTSWANA.** *see* BUSINESS AND ECONOMICS—Economic Situation And Conditions

➤ **COUNTRY REVIEW. BRAZIL.** *see* BUSINESS AND ECONOMICS—Economic Situation And Conditions

➤ **COUNTRY REVIEW. BRUNEI.** *see* BUSINESS AND ECONOMICS—Economic Situation And Conditions

➤ **COUNTRY REVIEW. BULGARIA.** *see* BUSINESS AND ECONOMICS—Economic Situation And Conditions

➤ **COUNTRY REVIEW. BURKINA FASO.** *see* BUSINESS AND ECONOMICS—Economic Situation And Conditions

➤ **COUNTRY REVIEW. BURMA.** *see* BUSINESS AND ECONOMICS—Economic Situation And Conditions

➤ **COUNTRY REVIEW. BURUNDI.** *see* BUSINESS AND ECONOMICS—Economic Situation And Conditions

➤ **COUNTRY REVIEW. CAMBODIA.** *see* BUSINESS AND ECONOMICS—Economic Situation And Conditions

➤ **COUNTRY REVIEW. CAMEROON.** *see* BUSINESS AND ECONOMICS—Economic Situation And Conditions

➤ **COUNTRY REVIEW. CANADA.** *see* BUSINESS AND ECONOMICS—Economic Situation And Conditions

➤ **COUNTRY REVIEW. CAPE VERDE.** *see* BUSINESS AND ECONOMICS—Economic Situation And Conditions

➤ **COUNTRY REVIEW. CENTRAL AFRICAN REPUBLIC.** *see* BUSINESS AND ECONOMICS—Economic Situation And Conditions

➤ **COUNTRY REVIEW. CHAD.** *see* BUSINESS AND ECONOMICS—Economic Situation And Conditions

➤ **COUNTRY REVIEW. CHILE.** *see* BUSINESS AND ECONOMICS—Economic Situation And Conditions

➤ **COUNTRY REVIEW. CHINA.** *see* BUSINESS AND ECONOMICS—Economic Situation And Conditions

➤ **COUNTRY REVIEW. COLOMBIA.** *see* BUSINESS AND ECONOMICS—Economic Situation And Conditions

➤ **COUNTRY REVIEW. COMOROS.** *see* BUSINESS AND ECONOMICS—Economic Situation And Conditions

➤ **COUNTRY REVIEW. CONGO.** *see* BUSINESS AND ECONOMICS—Economic Situation And Conditions

➤ **COUNTRY REVIEW. CONGO DEMOCRATIC REPUBLIC.** *see* BUSINESS AND ECONOMICS—Economic Situation And Conditions

➤ **COUNTRY REVIEW. COSTA RICA.** *see* BUSINESS AND ECONOMICS—Economic Situation And Conditions

➤ **COUNTRY REVIEW. COTE D'IVOIRE.** *see* BUSINESS AND ECONOMICS—Economic Situation And Conditions

➤ **COUNTRY REVIEW. CROATIA.** *see* BUSINESS AND ECONOMICS—Economic Situation And Conditions

➤ **COUNTRY REVIEW. CUBA.** *see* BUSINESS AND ECONOMICS—Economic Situation And Conditions

➤ **COUNTRY REVIEW. CYPRUS.** *see* BUSINESS AND ECONOMICS—Economic Situation And Conditions

➤ **COUNTRY REVIEW. CZECH REPUBLIC.** *see* BUSINESS AND ECONOMICS—Economic Situation And Conditions

➤ **COUNTRY REVIEW. DENMARK.** *see* BUSINESS AND ECONOMICS—Economic Situation And Conditions

➤ **COUNTRY REVIEW. DJIBOUTI.** *see* BUSINESS AND ECONOMICS—Economic Situation And Conditions

➤ **COUNTRY REVIEW. DOMINICA.** *see* BUSINESS AND ECONOMICS—Economic Situation And Conditions

➤ **COUNTRY REVIEW. DOMINICAN REPUBLIC.** *see* BUSINESS AND ECONOMICS—Economic Situation And Conditions

➤ **COUNTRY REVIEW. EAST TIMOR.** *see* BUSINESS AND ECONOMICS—Economic Situation And Conditions

➤ **COUNTRY REVIEW. ECUADOR.** *see* BUSINESS AND ECONOMICS—Economic Situation And Conditions

➤ **COUNTRY REVIEW. EGYPT.** *see* BUSINESS AND ECONOMICS—Economic Situation And Conditions

➤ **COUNTRY REVIEW. EL SALVADOR.** *see* BUSINESS AND ECONOMICS—Economic Situation And Conditions

➤ **COUNTRY REVIEW. EQUATORIAL GUINEA.** *see* BUSINESS AND ECONOMICS—Economic Situation And Conditions

▼ ➤ **COUNTRY REVIEW. ERITREA.** *see* BUSINESS AND ECONOMICS—Economic Situation And Conditions

➤ **COUNTRY REVIEW. ESTONIA.** *see* BUSINESS AND ECONOMICS—Economic Situation And Conditions

➤ **COUNTRY REVIEW. ETHIOPIA.** *see* BUSINESS AND ECONOMICS—Economic Situation And Conditions

➤ **COUNTRY REVIEW. FIJI.** *see* BUSINESS AND ECONOMICS—Economic Situation And Conditions

➤ **COUNTRY REVIEW. FINLAND.** *see* BUSINESS AND ECONOMICS—Economic Situation And Conditions

➤ **COUNTRY REVIEW. FRANCE.** *see* BUSINESS AND ECONOMICS—Economic Situation And Conditions

➤ **COUNTRY REVIEW. GABON.** *see* BUSINESS AND ECONOMICS—Economic Situation And Conditions

➤ **COUNTRY REVIEW. GAMBIA.** *see* BUSINESS AND ECONOMICS—Economic Situation And Conditions

➤ **COUNTRY REVIEW. GEORGIA.** *see* BUSINESS AND ECONOMICS—Economic Situation And Conditions

➤ **COUNTRY REVIEW. GERMANY.** *see* BUSINESS AND ECONOMICS—Economic Situation And Conditions

➤ **COUNTRY REVIEW. GHANA.** *see* BUSINESS AND ECONOMICS—Economic Situation And Conditions

➤ **COUNTRY REVIEW. GREECE.** *see* BUSINESS AND ECONOMICS—Economic Situation And Conditions

➤ **COUNTRY REVIEW. GRENADA.** *see* BUSINESS AND ECONOMICS—Economic Situation And Conditions

➤ **COUNTRY REVIEW. GUATEMALA.** *see* BUSINESS AND ECONOMICS—Economic Situation And Conditions

➤ **COUNTRY REVIEW. GUINEA.** *see* BUSINESS AND ECONOMICS—Economic Situation And Conditions

➤ **COUNTRY REVIEW. GUINEA-BISSAU.** *see* BUSINESS AND ECONOMICS—Economic Situation And Conditions

➤ **COUNTRY REVIEW. GUYANA.** *see* BUSINESS AND ECONOMICS—Economic Situation And Conditions

➤ **COUNTRY REVIEW. HAITI.** *see* BUSINESS AND ECONOMICS—Economic Situation And Conditions

➤ **COUNTRY REVIEW. HOLY SEE.** *see* BUSINESS AND ECONOMICS—Economic Situation And Conditions

➤ **COUNTRY REVIEW. HONDURAS.** *see* BUSINESS AND ECONOMICS—Economic Situation And Conditions

➤ **COUNTRY REVIEW. HUNGARY.** *see* BUSINESS AND ECONOMICS—Economic Situation And Conditions

➤ **COUNTRY REVIEW. ICELAND.** *see* BUSINESS AND ECONOMICS—Economic Situation And Conditions

➤ **COUNTRY REVIEW. INDONESIA.** *see* BUSINESS AND ECONOMICS—Economic Situation And Conditions

➤ **COUNTRY REVIEW. IRAN.** *see* BUSINESS AND ECONOMICS—Economic Situation And Conditions

➤ **COUNTRY REVIEW. IRAQ.** *see* BUSINESS AND ECONOMICS—Economic Situation And Conditions

➤ **COUNTRY REVIEW. IRELAND.** *see* BUSINESS AND ECONOMICS—Economic Situation And Conditions

➤ **COUNTRY REVIEW. ISRAEL.** *see* BUSINESS AND ECONOMICS—Economic Situation And Conditions

➤ **COUNTRY REVIEW. ITALY.** *see* BUSINESS AND ECONOMICS—Economic Situation And Conditions

➤ **COUNTRY REVIEW. JAMAICA.** *see* BUSINESS AND ECONOMICS—Economic Situation And Conditions

➤ **COUNTRY REVIEW. JAPAN.** *see* BUSINESS AND ECONOMICS—Economic Situation And Conditions

➤ **COUNTRY REVIEW. JORDAN.** *see* BUSINESS AND ECONOMICS—Economic Situation And Conditions

➤ **COUNTRY REVIEW. KAZAKHSTAN.** *see* BUSINESS AND ECONOMICS—Economic Situation And Conditions

➤ **COUNTRY REVIEW. KENYA.** *see* BUSINESS AND ECONOMICS—Economic Situation And Conditions

➤ **COUNTRY REVIEW. KIRIBATI.** *see* BUSINESS AND ECONOMICS—Economic Situation And Conditions

➤ **COUNTRY REVIEW. KUWAIT.** *see* BUSINESS AND ECONOMICS—Economic Situation And Conditions

➤ **COUNTRY REVIEW. KYRGYZSTAN.** *see* BUSINESS AND ECONOMICS—Economic Situation And Conditions

➤ **COUNTRY REVIEW. LAOS.** *see* BUSINESS AND ECONOMICS—Economic Situation And Conditions

➤ **COUNTRY REVIEW. LATVIA.** *see* BUSINESS AND ECONOMICS—Economic Situation And Conditions

➤ **COUNTRY REVIEW. LEBANON.** *see* BUSINESS AND ECONOMICS—Economic Situation And Conditions

➤ **COUNTRY REVIEW. LESOTHO.** *see* BUSINESS AND ECONOMICS—Economic Situation And Conditions

➤ **COUNTRY REVIEW. LIBERIA.** *see* BUSINESS AND ECONOMICS—Economic Situation And Conditions

➤ **COUNTRY REVIEW. LIBYA.** *see* BUSINESS AND ECONOMICS—Economic Situation And Conditions

➤ **COUNTRY REVIEW. LIECHTENSTEIN.** *see* BUSINESS AND ECONOMICS—Economic Situation And Conditions

➤ **COUNTRY REVIEW. LITHUANIA.** *see* BUSINESS AND ECONOMICS—Economic Situation And Conditions

➤ **COUNTRY REVIEW. LUXEMBOURG.** *see* BUSINESS AND ECONOMICS—Economic Situation And Conditions

➤ **COUNTRY REVIEW. MACEDONIA.** *see* BUSINESS AND ECONOMICS—Economic Situation And Conditions

➤ **COUNTRY REVIEW. MADAGASCAR.** *see* BUSINESS AND ECONOMICS—Economic Situation And Conditions

➤ **COUNTRY REVIEW. MALAWI.** *see* BUSINESS AND ECONOMICS—Economic Situation And Conditions

➤ **COUNTRY REVIEW. MALAYSIA.** *see* BUSINESS AND ECONOMICS—Economic Situation And Conditions

➤ **COUNTRY REVIEW. MALDIVES.** *see* BUSINESS AND ECONOMICS—Economic Situation And Conditions

➤ **COUNTRY REVIEW. MALI.** *see* BUSINESS AND ECONOMICS—Economic Situation And Conditions

➤ **COUNTRY REVIEW. MALTA.** *see* BUSINESS AND ECONOMICS—Economic Situation And Conditions

➤ **COUNTRY REVIEW. MARSHALL ISLANDS.** *see* BUSINESS AND ECONOMICS—Economic Situation And Conditions

➤ **COUNTRY REVIEW. MAURITANIA.** *see* BUSINESS AND ECONOMICS—Economic Situation And Conditions

➤ **COUNTRY REVIEW. MAURITIUS.** *see* BUSINESS AND ECONOMICS—Economic Situation And Conditions

➤ **COUNTRY REVIEW. MEXICO.** *see* BUSINESS AND ECONOMICS—Economic Situation And Conditions

➤ **COUNTRY REVIEW. MICRONESIA.** *see* BUSINESS AND ECONOMICS—Economic Situation And Conditions

➤ **COUNTRY REVIEW. MOLDOVA.** *see* BUSINESS AND ECONOMICS—Economic Situation And Conditions

➤ **COUNTRY REVIEW. MONACO.** *see* BUSINESS AND ECONOMICS—Economic Situation And Conditions

➤ **COUNTRY REVIEW. MONGOLIA.** *see* BUSINESS AND ECONOMICS—Economic Situation And Conditions

➤ **COUNTRY REVIEW. MOROCCO.** *see* BUSINESS AND ECONOMICS—Economic Situation And Conditions

➤ **COUNTRY REVIEW. MOZAMBIQUE.** *see* BUSINESS AND ECONOMICS—Economic Situation And Conditions

➤ **COUNTRY REVIEW. NAMIBIA.** *see* BUSINESS AND ECONOMICS—Economic Situation And Conditions

➤ **COUNTRY REVIEW. NAURU.** *see* BUSINESS AND ECONOMICS—Economic Situation And Conditions

➤ **COUNTRY REVIEW. NEPAL.** *see* BUSINESS AND ECONOMICS—Economic Situation And Conditions

➤ **COUNTRY REVIEW. NETHERLANDS.** *see* BUSINESS AND ECONOMICS—Economic Situation And Conditions

➤ **COUNTRY REVIEW. NEW ZEALAND.** *see* BUSINESS AND ECONOMICS—Economic Situation And Conditions

➤ **COUNTRY REVIEW. NICARAGUA.** *see* BUSINESS AND ECONOMICS—Economic Situation And Conditions

➤ **COUNTRY REVIEW. NIGER.** *see* BUSINESS AND ECONOMICS—Economic Situation And Conditions

➤ **COUNTRY REVIEW. NIGERIA.** *see* BUSINESS AND ECONOMICS—Economic Situation And Conditions

➤ **COUNTRY REVIEW. NORTH KOREA.** *see* BUSINESS AND ECONOMICS—Economic Situation And Conditions

➤ **COUNTRY REVIEW. NORWAY.** *see* BUSINESS AND ECONOMICS—Economic Situation And Conditions

➤ **COUNTRY REVIEW. OMAN.** *see* BUSINESS AND ECONOMICS—Economic Situation And Conditions

➤ **COUNTRY REVIEW. PAKISTAN.** *see* BUSINESS AND ECONOMICS—Economic Situation And Conditions

➤ **COUNTRY REVIEW. PALAU.** *see* BUSINESS AND ECONOMICS—Economic Situation And Conditions

➤ **COUNTRY REVIEW. PANAMA.** *see* BUSINESS AND ECONOMICS—Economic Situation And Conditions

➤ **COUNTRY REVIEW. PAPUA NEW GUINEA.** *see* BUSINESS AND ECONOMICS—Economic Situation And Conditions

➤ **COUNTRY REVIEW. PARAGUAY.** *see* BUSINESS AND ECONOMICS—Economic Situation And Conditions

➤ **COUNTRY REVIEW. PERU.** *see* BUSINESS AND ECONOMICS—Economic Situation And Conditions

➤ **COUNTRY REVIEW. PHILIPPINES.** *see* BUSINESS AND ECONOMICS—Economic Situation And Conditions

➤ **COUNTRY REVIEW. POLAND.** *see* BUSINESS AND ECONOMICS—Economic Situation And Conditions

➤ **COUNTRY REVIEW. PORTUGAL.** *see* BUSINESS AND ECONOMICS—Economic Situation And Conditions

➤ **COUNTRY REVIEW. QATAR.** *see* BUSINESS AND ECONOMICS—Economic Situation And Conditions

➤ **COUNTRY REVIEW. ROMANIA.** *see* BUSINESS AND ECONOMICS—Economic Situation And Conditions

➤ **COUNTRY REVIEW. RUSSIA.** *see* BUSINESS AND ECONOMICS—Economic Situation And Conditions

➤ **COUNTRY REVIEW. RWANDA.** *see* BUSINESS AND ECONOMICS—Economic Situation And Conditions

➤ **COUNTRY REVIEW. SAIN VICENT AND THE GRENADINES.** *see* BUSINESS AND ECONOMICS—Economic Situation And Conditions

➤ **COUNTRY REVIEW. SAINT KITTS NEVIS.** *see* BUSINESS AND ECONOMICS—Economic Situation And Conditions

➤ **COUNTRY REVIEW. SAINT LUCIA.** *see* BUSINESS AND ECONOMICS—Economic Situation And Conditions

➤ **COUNTRY REVIEW. SAMOA.** *see* BUSINESS AND ECONOMICS—Economic Situation And Conditions

➤ **COUNTRY REVIEW. SAN MARINO.** *see* BUSINESS AND ECONOMICS—Economic Situation And Conditions

➤ **COUNTRY REVIEW. SAO TOME & PRINCIPE.** *see* BUSINESS AND ECONOMICS—Economic Situation And Conditions

➤ **COUNTRY REVIEW. SAUDI ARABIA.** *see* BUSINESS AND ECONOMICS—Economic Situation And Conditions

➤ **COUNTRY REVIEW. SENEGAL.** *see* BUSINESS AND ECONOMICS—Economic Situation And Conditions

➤ **COUNTRY REVIEW. SERBIA.** *see* BUSINESS AND ECONOMICS—Economic Situation And Conditions

➤ **COUNTRY REVIEW. SEYCHELLES.** *see* BUSINESS AND ECONOMICS—Economic Situation And Conditions

➤ **COUNTRY REVIEW. SIERRA LEONE.** *see* BUSINESS AND ECONOMICS—Economic Situation And Conditions

➤ **COUNTRY REVIEW. SINGAPORE.** *see* BUSINESS AND ECONOMICS—Production Of Goods And Services

➤ **COUNTRY REVIEW. SLOVAKIA.** *see* BUSINESS AND ECONOMICS—Economic Situation And Conditions

➤ **COUNTRY REVIEW. SLOVENIA.** *see* BUSINESS AND ECONOMICS—Economic Situation And Conditions

➤ **COUNTRY REVIEW. SOLOMON ISLANDS.** *see* BUSINESS AND ECONOMICS—Economic Situation And Conditions

➤ **COUNTRY REVIEW. SOMALIA.** *see* BUSINESS AND ECONOMICS—Economic Situation And Conditions

➤ **COUNTRY REVIEW. SOUTH AFRICA.** *see* BUSINESS AND ECONOMICS—Economic Situation And Conditions

➤ **COUNTRY REVIEW. SOUTH KOREA.** *see* BUSINESS AND ECONOMICS—Economic Situation And Conditions

➤ **COUNTRY REVIEW. SPAIN.** *see* BUSINESS AND ECONOMICS—Economic Situation And Conditions

➤ **COUNTRY REVIEW. SRI LANKA.** *see* BUSINESS AND ECONOMICS—Economic Situation And Conditions

➤ **COUNTRY REVIEW. SUDAN.** *see* BUSINESS AND ECONOMICS—Economic Situation And Conditions

➤ **COUNTRY REVIEW. SURINAME.** *see* BUSINESS AND ECONOMICS—Economic Situation And Conditions

➤ **COUNTRY REVIEW. SWAZILAND.** *see* BUSINESS AND ECONOMICS—Economic Situation And Conditions

➤ **COUNTRY REVIEW. SWEDEN.** *see* BUSINESS AND ECONOMICS—Economic Situation And Conditions

➤ **COUNTRY REVIEW. SWITZERLAND.** *see* BUSINESS AND ECONOMICS—Economic Situation And Conditions

➤ **COUNTRY REVIEW. SYRIA.** *see* BUSINESS AND ECONOMICS—Economic Situation And Conditions

➤ **COUNTRY REVIEW. TAJIKISTAN.** *see* BUSINESS AND ECONOMICS—Economic Situation And Conditions

➤ **COUNTRY REVIEW. TANZANIA.** *see* BUSINESS AND ECONOMICS—Economic Situation And Conditions

➤ **COUNTRY REVIEW. THAILAND.** *see* BUSINESS AND ECONOMICS—Economic Situation And Conditions

➤ **COUNTRY REVIEW. TOGO.** *see* BUSINESS AND ECONOMICS—Economic Situation And Conditions

➤ **COUNTRY REVIEW. TONGA.** *see* BUSINESS AND ECONOMICS—Economic Situation And Conditions

➤ **COUNTRY REVIEW. TRINIDAD AND TOBAGO.** *see* BUSINESS AND ECONOMICS—Economic Situation And Conditions

➤ **COUNTRY REVIEW. TUNISIA.** *see* BUSINESS AND ECONOMICS—Economic Situation And Conditions

➤ **COUNTRY REVIEW. TURKEY.** *see* BUSINESS AND ECONOMICS—Economic Situation And Conditions

➤ **COUNTRY REVIEW. TURKMENISTAN.** *see* BUSINESS AND ECONOMICS—Economic Situation And Conditions

➤ **COUNTRY REVIEW. TUVALU.** *see* BUSINESS AND ECONOMICS—Economic Situation And Conditions

➤ **COUNTRY REVIEW. UGANDA.** *see* BUSINESS AND ECONOMICS—Economic Situation And Conditions

➤ **COUNTRY REVIEW. UKRAINE.** *see* BUSINESS AND ECONOMICS—Economic Situation And Conditions

➤ **COUNTRY REVIEW. UNITED ARAB EMIRATES.** *see* BUSINESS AND ECONOMICS—Economic Situation And Conditions

➤ **COUNTRY REVIEW. UNITED KINGDOM.** *see* BUSINESS AND ECONOMICS—Economic Situation And Conditions

➤ **COUNTRY REVIEW. UNITED STATES.** *see* BUSINESS AND ECONOMICS—Economic Situation And Conditions

➤ **COUNTRY REVIEW. URUGUAY.** *see* BUSINESS AND ECONOMICS—Economic Situation And Conditions

➤ **COUNTRY REVIEW. UZBEKISTAN.** *see* BUSINESS AND ECONOMICS—Economic Situation And Conditions

➤ **COUNTRY REVIEW. VANUATU.** *see* BUSINESS AND ECONOMICS—Economic Situation And Conditions

➤ **COUNTRY REVIEW. VENEZUELA.** *see* BUSINESS AND ECONOMICS—Economic Situation And Conditions

➤ **COUNTRY REVIEW. VIETNAM.** *see* BUSINESS AND ECONOMICS—Economic Situation And Conditions

➤ **COUNTRY REVIEW. YEMEN.** *see* BUSINESS AND ECONOMICS—Economic Situation And Conditions

➤ **COUNTRY REVIEW. ZAMBIA.** *see* BUSINESS AND ECONOMICS—Economic Situation And Conditions

➤ **COUNTRY REVIEW. ZIMBABWE.** *see* BUSINESS AND ECONOMICS—Economic Situation And Conditions

304.6 MEX ISSN 0187-6171
HA761

CUADERNOS DE POBLACION. Text in Spanish. 1987. a.
Published by: Instituto Nacional de Estadistica, Geografia e Informatica, Secretaria de Programacion y Presupuesto, Prol. Heroe de Nacozari 2301 Sur, Puerta 11, Acceso, Aguascalientes, 20270, Mexico. TEL 49-18-19-48, FAX 491-807-39.

P

CURRENT POPULATION REPORTS. CONSUMER INCOME. INCOME, POVERTY, AND HEALTH INSURANCE COVERAGE IN THE UNITED STATES. *see* SOCIAL SERVICES AND WELFARE

CURRENT POPULATION REPORTS. POPULATION CHARACTERISTICS. EDUCATIONAL ATTAINMENT IN THE UNITED STATES. *see* EDUCATION

304.63 USA ISSN 0272-6505
HA195
CURRENT POPULATION REPORTS. POPULATION CHARACTERISTICS. FERTILITY OF AMERICAN WOMEN. Text in English. a., latest 2006. back issues avail. **Document type:** *Government.*
Formerly (until 1975): Fertility Expectations of American Women
Related titles: Online - full text ed.
Published by: U.S. Census Bureau. Housing and Household Economic Statistics Division, 4600 Silver Hill Rd., Washington, DC 20233. TEL 866-758-1060, http://www.census.gov/hhes/www/hhesdiv.html.

304.6 USA
CURRENT POPULATION REPORTS. POPULATION CHARACTERISTICS. THE FOREIGN-BORN POPULATION IN THE UNITED STATES. Text in English. 1994. a., latest 2003. stat. **Document type:** *Government.*
Formerly (until 1996): Foreign-Born Population
Related titles: Online - full content ed.
Published by: U.S. Census Bureau. Population Division (Subsidiary of: U.S. Department of Commerce), 4600 Silver Hill Rd., Washington, DC 20233. TEL 866-758-1060.

CURRENT POPULATION REPORTS. POPULATION CHARACTERISTICS. VOTING AND REGISTRATION IN THE ELECTION. *see* POLITICAL SCIENCE

CURRENT POPULATION REPORTS: SERIES P-60, CONSUMER INCOME. *see* POPULATION STUDIES—Abstracting, Bibliographies, Statistics

CYPRUS. DEPARTMENT OF STATISTICS AND RESEARCH. DEMOGRAPHIC REPORT. *see* POPULATION STUDIES—Abstracting, Bibliographies, Statistics

CYPRUS. DEPARTMENT OF STATISTICS AND RESEARCH. STATISTICAL ABSTRACT. *see* SOCIAL SCIENCES: COMPREHENSIVE WORKS—Abstracting, Bibliographies, Statistics

325.489 DNK ISSN 0904-2903
DANSKEREN. Text in Danish. 1987. q. DKK 225 (effective 2009). **Document type:** *Magazine, Consumer.*
Related titles: Online - full text ed.: ISSN 1902-357X. 1987.
Published by: Den Danske Forening, Skomagergade 25, Roskilde, 4000, Denmark. TEL 45-86-132401, FAX 45-70-252401, mail@dendanskeforening.dk. Ed. Harry Vinter.

304.6 301.2 HUN ISSN 0011-8249
HB3592.H8
DEMOGRAFIA; review of population sciences. Text in Hungarian; Abstracts and contents page in English, Russian. 1958. q. HUF 264, USD 28. bk.rev. bibl.; charts; stat. index.
Indexed: A20, ESPM, HPNRM, IBSS, P30, PopulInd, RASB, SSciA.
Published by: Kozponti Statisztikai Hivatal, Marketing Oszta'ly, Keleti Karoly utca 5-7, Budapest, 1024, Hungary. TEL 36-1-345-6000, FAX 36-1-345-6699. Ed. Andras Klinger. Circ: 1,000.

304.6 UKR ISSN 0207-0383
HB3608.28
DEMOGRAFICHESKIE ISSLEDOVANIYA; respublikanskii mezhvedomstvennyi sbornik nauchnykh trudov. Text in Russian. 1970. a.
Indexed: P30, RASB.
Published by: (Institut Ekonomiki), Natsional'na Akademiya Nauk Ukrainy, 54 Volodymyrska St, Kyiv, 01601, Ukraine. TEL 380-44-234 5167, FAX 380-44-2343243, prez@nas.gov.ua, http://www.nas.gov.ua.

304.6 DEU ISSN 1613-5822
DEMOGRAFISCHE FORSCHUNG; aus erster Hand. Text in German. 2006. 4/yr. **Document type:** *Journal, Academic/Scholarly.*
Published by: Max-Planck-Institut fuer Demografische Forschung/Max-Planck-Institut for Demographic Research (Subsidiary of: Max-Planck-Institut fuer Gesellschaft zur Foerderung der Wissenschaften), Konrad-Zuse-Str 1, Rostock, 18057, Germany. TEL 49-381-20810, FAX 49-381-2081202, http://www.demogr.mpg.de. Ed. Gabriele M. Doblhammer. Pub. Joshua R Goldstein.

304.6 314 ROM
DEMOGRAPHIC ANALYSIS (YEARS). Text and summaries in English, Romanian. 1999. a. ROL 25,000; USD 15 foreign. charts; stat. **Document type:** *Government.* **Description:** Contains demographic information on Rumania.
Published by: Comisia Nationala pentru Statistica/National Commission for Statistics, Bd. Libertatii 16, Sector 5, Bucharest, 70542, Romania. TEL 40-1-3363370, FAX 40-1-3124873. R&P Ivan Ungureanu Clementina.

304.6 LBN ISSN 0258-1892
HA4556
DEMOGRAPHIC AND RELATED SOCIO-ECONOMIC DATA SHEETS. Text in English. 1976. a.
Published by: United Nations, Economic and Social Commission for Western Asia, PO Box 11-8575, Beirut, Lebanon. TEL 961-1-981301, FAX 961-1-981510, webmaster-eswa@un.org, http://www.escwa.org.lb/.

304.6 USA
DEMOGRAPHIC GUIDE TO ARIZONA (YEAR). Text in English. 1967. a. free. **Document type:** *Government.*
Formerly: Population Estimates of Arizona (0079-3906)
Published by: (Arizona. Population Statistics Unit), Department of Economic Security, Population Statistics Unit, Box 6123, SC-45Z, Phoenix, AZ 85005. TEL 602-542-5984, FAX 602-542-6474. Circ: 2,000.

DEMOGRAPHIC PROFILE OF THE FEDERAL WORKFORCE. *see* BUSINESS AND ECONOMICS—Personnel Management

304.6 DEU ISSN 1435-9871
HB848
➤ **DEMOGRAPHIC RESEARCH.** Text in English. 1999. s-a. free (effective 2011). **Document type:** *Journal, Academic/Scholarly.* **Description:** Publishes demographic research and related material from the full range of disciplines that bear on demography, including the social sciences, the life sciences, mathematics and statistics, policy research, and research on the discipline itself.
Media: Online - full text.
Indexed: A36, CA, CABA, CurCont, D01, E12, ESPM, GH, H05, HPNRM, IBSS, P02, P10, P27, P30, P45, P46, P48, P50, P52, P53, P54, P56, PAIS, PQC, R12, S02, S03, SCOPUS, SSCI, SSciA, SociolAb, T02, T05, TAR, W07, W11.
—**CCC.**
Published by: Max-Planck-Institut fuer Demografische Forschung/Max-Planck-Institut for Demographic Research (Subsidiary of: Max-Planck-Institut fuer Gesellschaft zur Foerderung der Wissenschaften), Konrad-Zuse-Str 1, Rostock, 18057, Germany. TEL 49-381-20810, FAX 49-381-2081202, http://www.demogr.mpg.de. Ed. Nico Keilman. Pub. Joshua R Goldstein.

304.6 DEU ISSN 1613-5520
➤ **DEMOGRAPHIC RESEARCH MONOGRAPHS.** Text in German. 2004. irreg., latest vol.5, 2010. price varies. **Document type:** *Monographic series, Academic/Scholarly.*
—**CCC.**
Published by: (Max-Planck-Institut fuer Demografische Forschung/Max-Planck-Institut for Demographic Research), Springer (Subsidiary of: Springer Science+Business Media), Tiergartenstr 17, Heidelberg, 69121, Germany. TEL 49-6221-4870, FAX 49-6221-345229, subscriptions@springer.com.

304.6 LUX ISSN 0253-6951
DEMOGRAPHIC STATISTICS (YEAR). Text in English. a.
Related titles: Diskette ed.
Indexed: IIS, SSciA.
Published by: European Commission, Statistical Office of the European Communities (E U R O S T A T), Rue Alcide de Gasperi, Luxembourg, 2920, Luxembourg. TEL 352-4301-34526, FAX 352-4301-34415, eurostat-infodesk@cec.eu.int, http://www.europa.eu.int/comm/eurostat.

304.6 USA ISSN 0070-3370
HB881.A1
➤ **DEMOGRAPHY.** Text in English. 1964. q. EUR 99, USD 125 combined subscription to institutions (print & online eds.) (effective 2012). adv. illus. back issues avail.; reprints avail. **Document type:** *Journal, Academic/Scholarly.* **Description:** Publishes articles of general interest to population scientists.
Related titles: Online - full text ed.: ISSN 1533-7790 (from IngentaConnect).
Indexed: A01, A02, A03, A08, A12, A13, A14, A17, A20, A22, A25, A26, A36, ABIn, ABS&EES, APEL, ASCA, ASG, AbAn, AgeL, B01, B02, B04, B06, B07, B08, B09, B15, B17, B18, BAS, BRD, Biostat, C12, C28, CA, CABA, CLFP, ChPerI, Chicano, CurCont, DIP, E01, E08, E12, EMBASE, ESPM, EconLit, EnvAb, EnvInd, ExcerpMed, F09, FR, FamI, G04, G08, GH, H01, H05, H09, HPNRM, I05, IBR, IBSS, IBZ, ILD, INI, IndMed, JEL, M01, M02, MEA&I, MEDLINE, N02, N03, P02, P06, P10, P13, P20, P21, P22, P26, P27, P30, P34, P45, P46, P47, P48, P50, P51, P52, P53, P54, P56, PAIS, PCI, PQC, PRA, PopulInd, R10, R12, RASB, Reac, S02, S03, S05, S08, S09, S11, SCOPUS, SSA, SSAI, SSAb, SSCI, SSI, SSciA, SociolAb, T02, T05, TAR, W01, W02, W03, W05, W07, W09, W11.
—BLDSC (3550.610000), GNLM, IE, Infotrieve, Ingenta. **CCC.**
Published by: (Population Association of America), Springer New York LLC (Subsidiary of: Springer Science+Business Media), 233 Spring St, New York, NY 10013. TEL 212-460-1500, FAX 212-460-1575, journals@springer-ny.com. Ed. Stewart Tolnay.

304.6 314 ROM ISSN 1454-4474
DEMOGRAPHY OF SMALL AND MEDIUM ENTERPRISES. Text and summaries in English, Romanian. 1999. a. ROL 25,000; USD 10 foreign. stat. **Document type:** *Government.* **Description:** Discusses the evolution of small and medium enterprises in Rumania, their birth, development and death.
Published by: Comisia Nationala pentru Statistica/National Commission for Statistics, Bd. Libertatii 16, Sector 5, Bucharest, 70542, Romania. TEL 40-1-3363370, FAX 40-1-3124873. R&P Ivan Ungureanu Clementina.

304.60972 MEX ISSN 0187-7550
HB3531 CODEN: DEMOEX
DEMOS; carta demografica sobre Mexico. Text in Spanish. 1988. a. free. **Description:** Presents demographic analysis, statistical data on topics such as population growth, fertility, mortality, education, health, migration, environmental, employment and population policy.
Related titles: Online - full text ed.
Indexed: C01, CA, P30, P42, S02, S03, SCOPUS, SOPODA, SSciA, SociolAb, T02.
Published by: Universidad Nacional Autonoma de Mexico, Instituto de Investigaciones Sociales, Circuito Mario de la Cueva s-n, 2o Nivel H-06, Ciudad de la Investigacion en Humanidades, Zona Cultural, Mexico City, DF 04510, Mexico. TEL 52-5-6227400, FAX 52-5-6652443, iis@servidor.unam.mx, http://www.unam.mx/iisunam/. Ed. Raul Benitez Zenteno.

304.6 NLD ISSN 0169-1473
HB848
DEMOS (THE HAGUE). Text in Dutch. 1972. 10/yr. free (effective 2009). back issues avail.
Formerly (until 1985): Demografie (0166-574X)
Related titles: Online - full text ed.
Indexed: PopulInd.
Published by: Nederlands Interdisciplinair Demografisch Instituut/Netherlands Interdisciplinary Demographic Institute, Lange Houtstraat 19, The Hague, 2511 CV, Netherlands. TEL 31-70-3565200, FAX 31-70-3647187, info@nidi.nl, http://www.nidi.nl. Ed. Harry Bronsema.

304.6 ITA ISSN 1826-9907
DEMOTRENDS. Text in Multiple languages. 1997. 3/yr. **Document type:** *Journal, Trade.*
Related titles: Online - full text ed.: ISSN 1826-9915.
Published by: Consiglio Nazionale delle Ricerche, Istituto di Ricerche sulla Popolazione e le Politiche Sociali, Via Nizza 128, Rome, 00198, Italy. TEL 39-06-49932805, FAX 39-06-85834506, http://www.irpps.cnr.it.

DENMARK. DANMARKS STATISTIK. BEFOLKNINGENS UDVIKLING/ DENMARK. STATISTICS DENMARK. VITAL STATISTICS. *see* POPULATION STUDIES—Abstracting, Bibliographies, Statistics

304.6 DNK ISSN 1902-8946
DENMARK. DANMARKS STATISTIK. INVANDRERE I DANMARK. Text in Danish. 2007. a. DKK 130 per issue (effective 2008). stat. **Document type:** *Government.* **Description:** Immigration statistics for Denmark.
Related titles: Online - full text ed.: ISSN 1902-8954.
Published by: Danmarks Statistik/Statistics Denmark, Sejroegade 11, Copenhagen OE, 2100, Denmark. TEL 45-39-173917, FAX 45-39-173939, dst@dst.dk. Ed. Annemette Lindhardt Olsen TEL 45-39-173013.

DEREKH; judaica urbinatensia. *see* ETHNIC INTERESTS

948.95 325.9 DNK ISSN 0107-8720
DEUTSCHER VOLKSKALENDER NORDSCHLESWIG. Variant title: Deutscher Volkskalender fuer Nordschleswig. Text in German. 1924. a. DKK 50 per issue (effective 2009). bk.rev. illus. **Document type:** *Yearbook, Consumer.* **Description:** Directed to the German minority in Denmark. Focuses on cultural subjects.
Published by: Deutscher Schul- und Sprachverein fuer Nordschleswig, Vestergade 30, PO Box 242, Aabenraa, 6200, Denmark. TEL 45-73-629171, dssv@dssv.dk, http://www.dssv.dk. Eds. Franz Christiansen, Horst Fries.

304.6 KOR ISSN 1598-8074
➤ **DEVELOPMENT AND SOCIETY.** Text in English. 1972. s-a. abstr.; charts; stat. **Document type:** *Journal, Academic/Scholarly.* **Description:** Provides an international and interdisciplinary forum for new research and ideas on social, cultural, political as well as economic development, including social causes and consequences of development, alternative and sustainable forms of development, and new strategies for improving human conditions.
Former titles (until Dec.1998): Korea Journal of Population and Development (1225-3804); (until 1990): Seoul National University. Population and Development Studies Center. Bulletin
Indexed: BAS, P14, P27, P30, P48, P52, P53, P54, P56, PAIS, PQC, PSA, PopulInd, SCOPUS, SOPODA, SSciA, SociolAb.
—Ingenta.
Published by: Seoul National University. Institute of Social Development and Policy Research, 599 Gwanangno, Gwanak-gu, Seoul, 151-742, Korea, S. TEL 82-2-8806312, FAX 82-2-8736764, isdpr@snu.ac.kr, http://sociology.snu.ac.kr/isdpr/index.php. Ed. Jae-yeol Yee.

➤ **DIASPORA**; a journal of transnational studies. *see* SOCIAL SCIENCES: COMPREHENSIVE WORKS

➤ **DOMESTIC TRAVEL MARKET REPORT.** *see* TRAVEL AND TOURISM

304.6 CAN ISSN 1914-6167
DONNEES SOCIODEMOGRAPHIQUES EN BREF. Text in French. 2004. 3/yr. free. **Document type:** *Bulletin.*
Former titles (until 2004): Bulletin Donnees Sociodemographiques en Bref (1491-6789); (until 1999): Statistiques Donnees Sociodemographiques en Bref (1486-3766)
Published by: Institut de la Statistique du Quebec, 200 chemin Ste Foy, Quebec, PQ G1R 5T4, Canada. TEL 418-691-2401, 800-463-4090, FAX 418-643-4129.

325 SVN ISSN 0353-6777
DR1375
➤ **DVE DOMOVINI.** Text in Slovenian. 1990. s-a. bk.rev. 200 p./no. 1 cols./p.; **Document type:** *Journal, Academic/Scholarly.*
Related titles: English ed.: Two Homelands. ISSN 1581-1220.
Indexed: CA, DIP, FR, IBR, IBSS, IBZ, P42, PSA, S02, S03, SCOPUS, SSA, SSCI, SociolAb, T02, W07.
—INIST.
Published by: (Slovenska Akademija Znanosti in Umetnosti, Znanstvenoraziskovalni Center, Institut za Slovensko Izseljenstvo/ Slovenian Academy of Sciences and Arts, Scientific Research Center, Institute for Slovenian Emigration Studies), Zalozba Z R C/Scientific Research Centre Publishing, Novi trg 2, PO Box 306, Ljubljana, 1001, Slovenia. TEL 386-1-4706474, FAX 386-1-4257794, zalozba@zrc-sazu.si, http://www.zrc-sazu.si/zalozba. Ed. Marjan Drnovsek. Pub. Vojislav Likar TEL 386-1-4706477. Circ: 400.

301.32 USA ISSN 1011-4793
HB3633.3.A3
E S C W A POPULATION BULLETIN. Text in English. 1970. s-a. price varies. bk.rev. back issues avail. **Description:** Presents articles on population and related issues relevant to Arab countries and theoretical and methodological subjects of relevance to population training in the Arab world.
Former titles (until 1985): Population Bulletin of E C W A (0258-1914); (until 198?): United Nations Economic Commission for Western Asia. Population Bulletin (0378-679X); (until 1974): United Nations Economic and Social Office in Beirut. Population Bulletin (0085-7505)
Related titles: Arabic ed.: Al-Lagnat al-iqtisadiyyat wa-al-igtima'iyyat li-garbi Asiya. Al-Nasrat al-Sukkahiyyat. ISSN 1564-7641.
Indexed: P30, PopulInd, SCOPUS.
—**CCC.**
Published by: (United Nations, Economic and Social Commission for Western Asia LBN, Social Development and Population Division), United Nations Publications, 2 United Nations Plaza, Rm DC2-853, New York, NY 10017. TEL 212-963-8302, 800-253-9646, FAX 212-963-3489, publications@un.org, https://unp.un.org. Ed. Walid Halil. Circ: 1,800.

304.6 USA
➤ **EAST - WEST CENTER OCCASIONAL PAPERS: POPULATION AND HEALTH SERIES.** Text in English. 1970. irreg., latest vol.123, 2001. price varies. back issues avail. **Document type:** *Monographic series, Academic/Scholarly.* **Description:** Reports on significant research on population-related issues in the Asia-Pacific region.
Former titles (until 2001): East - West Center Occasional Papers: Population Series; (until 1994): Program on Population. Occasional Papers
Indexed: SRI.
Published by: East-West Center, 1601 EW Rd, Honolulu, HI 96848. TEL 808-944-7111, FAX 808-944-7376, ewcbooks@eastwestcenter.org. Ed. Andrew Mason.

304.6 USA
EAST-WEST CENTER WORKING PAPERS: POPULATION SERIES. Text in English. 19??. irreg., latest 2001. USD 3 per issue (effective 2010). back issues avail. **Document type:** *Monographic series, Academic/Scholarly.* **Description:** Informs interested colleagues about work in progress at the center.
Former titles: Program on Population. Working Papers; (until 1992): East-West Population Institute. Papers (0732-0531); (until 1973): East-West Population Institute. Working Papers
Published by: East-West Center, 1601 EW Rd, Honolulu, HI 96848. TEL 808-944-7111, FAX 808-944-7376, ewcbooks@eastwestcenter.org.

ECONOMIC REVIEW OF TRAVEL IN AMERICA (YEAR). *see* TRAVEL AND TOURISM

304.6 ECU
ECUADOR. INSTITUTO DE ESTADISTICA Y CENSOS. ANUARIO DE ESTADISTICAS VITALES (NACIMIENTOS Y DEFUNCIONES). Text in Spanish. 1954. a. USD 45 (effective 2001). **Document type:** *Yearbook, Government.*
Related titles: Diskette ed.; E-mail ed.
Published by: Instituto Nacional de Estadistica y Censos, Juan Larrea N15-36 y Jose Riofrio, Quito, Ecuador. TEL 593-2-529858, FAX 593-2-509836. Circ: 130.

304.6 ECU ISSN 0070-8909
ECUADOR. INSTITUTO NACIONAL DE ESTADISTICA Y CENSOS. ANUARIO DE ESTADISTICAS VITALES. Text in Spanish. 1954. a. USD 45.
Published by: Instituto Nacional de Estadistica y Censos, Juan Larrea N15-36 y Jose Riofrio, Quito, Ecuador. TEL 593-2-529858, FAX 593-2-509836. Circ: 500.

304.6 ECU
ECUADOR. INSTITUTO NACIONAL DE ESTADISTICA Y CENSOS. ANUARIO DE ESTADISTICAS VITALES (MATRIMONIOS Y DIVORCIOS). Text in Spanish. 1976. irreg. USD 16 (effective 2001). **Document type:** *Yearbook, Government.*
Related titles: Diskette ed.; E-mail ed.
Published by: Instituto Nacional de Estadistica y Censos, Juan Larrea N15-36 y Jose Riofrio, Quito, Ecuador. TEL 593-2-529858, FAX 593-2-509836. Circ: 83.

ECUADOR. INSTITUTO NACIONAL DE ESTADISTICA Y CENSOS. SERIE ESTADISTICA. *see* POPULATION STUDIES—Abstracting, Bibliographies, Statistics

304.6 RUS ISSN 0869-3250
DK509
EKHO KAVKAZA; zhurnal assotsyatsii narodov kavkaza. Text in Russian. 1992. q. USD 136 in the Americas (effective 2000).
Published by: Redaktsiya Ekho Kavkaza, Ul. Novyi Arbat, 19, Moscow, 103025, Russian Federation. TEL 7-095-2037719, FAX 7-095-2035607.

304.6 BRA
ENCONTRO NACIONAL DE ESTUDOS POPULACIONAIS. Text in Portuguese. 1992 (vol.8). biennial. **Document type:** *Proceedings, Academic/Scholarly.* **Description:** Proceedings of the scientific meetings organized by Associacao Brasileira de Estudos Populacionais every two years.
Published by: Associacao Brasileira de Estudos Populacionais (R E B E P), Secretaria Geral, UNICAMP-NEPO, Av Albert Einstein 1300, Campinas, SP 13081-970, Brazil.

304.6 FRA ISSN 0755-7809
HB848
ESPACES - POPULATIONS - SOCIETES. Text and summaries in English, French. 1983. 3/yr. EUR 60 in the European Union to individuals; EUR 72 elsewhere to individuals; EUR 76 in the European Union to institutions; EUR 92 elsewhere to institutions (effective 2010). adv. bk.rev. index. back issues avail. **Document type:** *Academic/Scholarly.* **Description:** Explores the links between space, population and societies.
Related titles: Online - full text ed.: ISSN 2104-3752. 2004.
Indexed: A22, DIP, FR, GEOBASE, HistAb, IBR, IBSS, IBZ, P30, PopulInd, RefZh, SCOPUS.
—BLDSC (3811.327000), IE, Infotrieve, Ingenta, INIST.
Published by: Universite de Lille I (Sciences et Technologies), UFR de Geographie et Amenagement, av. Paul Langevin, Villeneuve D'Ascq, Cedex 59655, France. Ed. Pierre Jean Thumerelle. R&P Jean Pierre Bondue. Adv. contact Nicole Thumerelle Delannoy.

325 ESP ISSN 1139-532X
ESTADISTICAS DEL MOVIMIENTO MIGRATORIO DE LA COMUNIDAD DE MADRID. Text in Spanish. 1997. a. back issues avail. **Document type:** *Bulletin, Consumer.*
Related titles: CD-ROM ed.: ISSN 1579-5195. 2000.
Published by: Comunidad de Madrid, Instituto de Estadistica, Principe de Vargara 108, Madrid, 28002, Spain. TEL 34-91-5802540, jestadis@madrid.org, http://www.madrid.org/iestadis/index.htm.

304.6 COL
ESTUDIOS DE POBLACION. Text in Spanish. 1976. m.
Published by: Asociacion Colombiana para el Estudio de la Poblacion, Departamento de Publicaciones, Carrera 23, 39-82, Bogota, CUND 1, Colombia. Ed. Rafael Salazar Santos. **Co-sponsor:** Consejo de Poblacion.

304.6 BOL
ESTUDIOS DE POBLACION Y DESARROLLO. Text in Spanish. 1974. irreg., latest vol.29, 1985. price varies. **Document type:** *Monographic series, Academic/Scholarly.*
Published by: Centro de Investigaciones Sociales, Casilla 6931 - C.C., La Paz, Bolivia. TEL 591-2-352931. Ed. Antonio Cisneros.

304.6 MEX ISSN 0186-7210
HB3531
➤ **ESTUDIOS DEMOGRAFICOS Y URBANOS.** Text in Spanish; Summaries in English, Spanish. 1967. 3/yr. adv. bk.rev. abstr. **Document type:** *Journal, Academic/Scholarly.*
Superseded in part (in 1984): Demografia y Economia (0185-0148)
Related titles: Online - full text ed.: 2004. free (effective 2011).
Indexed: C01, CA, DIP, FR, H21, IBR, IBSS, IBZ, P08, P09, P30, PAIS, PCI, PopulInd, S02, S03, SCOPUS, SociolAb, T02.
Published by: (Colegio de Mexico), Colegio de Mexico, A.C., Departamento de Publicaciones, Camino al Ajusco 20, Col. Pedregal Santa Teresa, Mexico City, DF 10740, Mexico. TEL 52-5-4493077, FAX 52-5-4493083. Ed., R&P Francisco Gomez Rulz TEL 525-449-3080. Adv. contact Maria Cruz Mora. Circ: 1,000.

304.8 MEX ISSN 0187-6961
ESTUDIOS FRONTIZEROS. Text in Spanish. 1983. s-a. USD 35 in United States; MXN 100 domestic (effective 2006). adv. **Document type:** *Journal, Academic/Scholarly.* **Description:** Covers border studies.
Related titles: Online - full text ed.: free (effective 2011).
Indexed: A01, A26, CA, F03, F04, I04, I05, T02.
Published by: Universidad Autonoma de Baja California, Instituto de Investigaciones Sociales, Mexicali, BAJA CALIFORNIA, Mexico. TEL 52-6-5662985, FAX 52-6-5662985, http://www.uabc.mx/~iis/mainpage.htm. Ed., Adv. contact Guadalupe Sanchez Contreras.

325 ARG ISSN 0326-7458
JV7398
➤ **ESTUDIOS MIGRATORIOS LATINOAMERICANOS.** Text in Spanish. 1985. 3/yr. ARS 15 newsstand/cover domestic; USD 36 in the Americas; USD 36 elsewhere. adv. bk.rev. **Document type:** *Journal, Academic/Scholarly.*
Indexed: AmH&L, C01, CA, DIP, GEOBASE, H21, HistAb, IBR, IBZ, P08, P09, P30, P42, PCI, PSA, PopulInd, S02, S03, SCOPUS, SOPODA, SSA, SociolAb, T02.
—BLDSC (3812.775800).
Published by: Centro de Estudios Migratorios Latinoamericanos (CEMLA), Avda Independencia 20, Buenos Aires, 1099, Argentina. FAX 54-114-3310832. Ed. Fernando Devoto. Pub., Adv. contact Mario Santillo TEL 54-11-4342-6749. Circ: 500.

304.6 ESP ISSN 1889-9609
JV6006
ESTUDOS MIGRATORIOS. Text in Multiple languages. 1995. s-a. EUR 15 (effective 2010). **Document type:** *Journal, Academic/Scholarly.*
Formerly (until 2006): Estudios Migratorios (1136-0291)
Indexed: AmH&L, CA, F04, HistAb, P30, S02, S03, SCOPUS, SociolAb, T02.
Published by: (Universidade de Santiago de Compostela, Servizo de Publicacions e Intercambio Cientifico), Consello da Cultura Galega, Arquivo de Emigracion Galega, Pazo de Raxoi 2a, Praza do Obraidoiro, Santiago de Compostela, 15705, Spain. TEL 34-98-1957202, FAX 34-98-1957205, aemigracion@consellodacultura.org, http://www.consellodacultrua.org/.

304.6 GHA ISSN 0850-5780
HB3661.A3
ETUDE DE LA POPULATION AFRICAINE/AFRICAN POPULATION STUDIES. Text in English, French. s-a. **Document type:** *Journal, Academic/Scholarly.* **Description:** Publishes research on African population, development and related fields.
Related titles: Online - full content ed.: free (effective 2011).
Indexed: A36, CABA, E12, ESPM, GH, HPNRM, IIBP, N02, N03, P30, R12, S02, S03, SCOPUS, SSciA, SociolAb, T02, T05, TAR, W11.
Published by: Union for African Population Studies, 11 Palm St, East Legon, P.M.B CT 224 Cantonments, Accra, Ghana. TEL 233-302-501798, FAX 233-302-501798, uaps@uaps-uepa.org, http:www.uaps.org. Eds. Akoto Eliwo Mandjale, Uche C Isiugo-Abanihe.

EUGENICS SPECIAL INTEREST GROUP BULLETIN. *see* BIOLOGY—Genetics

304.6 USA ISSN 1932-0663
EURASIAN POPULATION AND FAMILY HISTORY. Text in English. 2004. irreg. USD 45 per issue domestic cloth; GBP 29.95 per issue in United Kingdom cloth; USD 23 per issue domestic paper (effective 2009). **Document type:** *Monographic series, Academic/Scholarly.*
Published by: M I T Press, 55 Hayward St, Cambridge, MA 02142. TEL 617-253-5646, FAX 617-258-6779, journals-info@mit.edu.

304.6 LUX ISSN 1012-2249
HN380.5.Z9
EUROBAROMETER (ENGLISH EDITION). Text in English. 197?. s-a.
Related titles: Online - full text ed.; Spanish ed.: Eurobarometro (Spanish Edition). ISSN 1012-2206; Portuguese ed.: Eurobarometro (Portuguese Edition). ISSN 1012-2281; French ed.: Eurobarometre (French Edition). ISSN 1012-2257; Italian ed.: Eurobarometro (Italian Edition). ISSN 1012-2265.
—BLDSC (3829.245800).
Published by: European Commission, Office for Official Publications of the European Union, 2 Rue Mercier, Luxembourg, L-2985, Luxembourg. FAX 352-29291, info@publications.europa.eu, http://publications.europa.eu.

304.6 POL ISSN 1429-7132
HC241
EUROPA XXI. Text in Polish, English. 1998. irreg., latest vol.6, 2001. price varies. **Document type:** *Monographic series, Academic/Scholarly.*
Indexed: FR, IBSS.
Published by: (Centrum Studiow Europejskich), Polska Akademia Nauk, Instytut Geografii i Przestrzennego Zagospodarowania/Polish Academy of Sciences, Institute of Geography and Spatial Organization, Twarda 51/55, Warsaw, 00818, Poland. TEL 48-22-6978844, FAX 48-22-6206221, igipzpan@twarda.pan.pl, http://www.igipz.pan.pl. Ed. Maciej Jakubowski.

304.6 DEU ISSN 1430-0095
EUROPAEISCHE MIGRATIONSFORSCHUNG. Text in German. 1996. irreg., latest vol.6, 2008. price varies. **Document type:** *Monographic series, Academic/Scholarly.*
Published by: Peter Lang GmbH (Subsidiary of: Peter Lang Publishing Group), Eschborner Landstr 42-50, Frankfurt Am Main, 60489, Germany. TEL 49-69-7807050, FAX 49-69-78070550, zentrale.frankfurt@peterlang.com, http://www.peterlang.com. Eds. Manfred Bayer, Wolfgang Mitter.

▼ **EUROPEAN EXPANSION AND INDIGENOUS RESPONSE.** *see* HUMANITIES: COMPREHENSIVE WORKS

EUROPEAN JOURNAL OF MIGRATION AND LAW. *see* LAW—International Law

304.6 NLD ISSN 1381-3579
EUROPEAN STUDIES OF POPULATION. Text in English. 1995. irreg., latest vol.16, 2008. price varies. back issues avail. **Document type:** *Monographic series, Academic/Scholarly.* **Description:** Publishes interdisciplinary demographic research with special emphasis on Europe.
Indexed: HPNRM, SSciA.
—BLDSC (3830.232900).
Published by: (Nederlands Interdisciplinair Demografisch Instituut/Netherlands Interdisciplinary Demographic Institute), Springer Netherlands (Subsidiary of: Springer Science+Business Media), Van Godewijckstraat 30, Dordrecht, 3311 GX, Netherlands. TEL 31-78-6576050, FAX 31-78-6576474, http://www.springer.com. **Co-sponsor:** Centrum voor Bevolkings- en Gezinsstudien, BE.

304.6 CAN ISSN 1706-340X
JV7225.5
FACTS AND FIGURES (YEAR), STATISTICAL OVERVIEW OF THE TEMPORARY RESIDENT AND REFUGEE CLAIMANT POPULATION. Text in English. 1999. a.
Published by: Treasury Board of Canada Secretariat, Corporate Communications/Secretariat du Conseil du Tresor du Canada, West Tower, Rm P-135, 300 Laurier Ave W, Ottawa, ON K1A 0R5, Canada. TEL 613-995-2855, FAX 613-996-0518, services-publications@tbs-sct.gc.ca, http://www.tbs-sct.gc.ca.

325.1 342.082 CAN ISSN 1490-8581
JV7225.5
FACTS AND FIGURES - IMMIGRATION OVERVIEW. Text in English. 1994. irreg.
Published by: Citizenship and Immigration Canada, 6th Fl, 400 University Ave, Toronto, ON M7A 2R9, Canada. TEL 416-327-2422, FAX 416-314-4965, info@mczcr.gov.on.ca.

304.6 FIN ISSN 1455-2191
FAMILY FEDERATION OF FINLAND. POPULATION RESEARCH INSTITUTE. WORKING PAPERS. E. Text in English, Finnish. 1997. irreg. price varies. stat. back issues avail. **Document type:** *Monographic series, Academic/Scholarly.*
Published by: Vaestoliitto, Vaestontutkimuslaitos/Family Federation of Finland. Population Research Institute, PO Box 849, Helsinki, 00101, Finland. TEL 358-9-228050, FAX 358-9-6121211, pop.inst@vaestoliitto.fi, http://www.vaestoliitto.fi.

FEDERAL IMMIGRATION LAWS AND REGULATIONS. *see* LAW

325.1 CAN ISSN 1910-7943
FEE SCHEDULE FOR CITIZENSHIP AND IMMIGRATION SERVICES/ BAREME DES FRAIS POUR LES SERVICES DE CITOYENNETE ET IMMIGRATION. Text in English, French. 199?. a. **Document type:** *Government.*
Published by: Citizenship and Immigration Canada, 6th Fl, 400 University Ave, Toronto, ON M7A 2R9, Canada. TEL 416-327-2422, FAX 416-314-4965, info@mczcr.gov.on.ca.

P

304.6 FIN ISSN 1796-6183
HB848
➤ **FINNISH YEARBOOK OF POPULATION RESEARCH.** Text in English. 1946. a. adv. bk.rev. bibl. back issues avail. **Document type:** *Report, Academic/Scholarly.* **Description:** Includes articles on questions of current interest in demography in Finland. Also population data compiled at the institute, and a bibliography of the Finnish population research.
Former titles (until 2006): Yearbook of Population Research in Finland (0506-3590); (until 1960): Vaestoliiton Vuosikirja
Related titles: Online - full text ed.: ISSN 1796-6191. free (effective 2011).
Indexed: CA, P30, PopulInd, S02, S03, SCOPUS, SSA, SociolAb, T02.
—BLDSC (3929.516000).
Published by: (Suomen Vaestotieteen Yhdistys/Finnish Demografic Society), Vaestoliitto, Vaestontutkimuslaitos/Family Federation of Finland. Population Research Institute, PO Box 849, Helsinki, 00101, Finland. TEL 358-9-228050, FAX 358-9-6121211, pop.inst@vaestoliitto.fi. Ed. Ismo Soederling.

304.6 USA
HB3525.F6
FLORIDA POPULATION STUDIES. Text in English. 1955. 3/yr. USD 70 (effective 2010). **Document type:** *Bulletin, Trade.* **Description:** Contains projections of the Florida population by county through the year 2020, as well as data on the number of Florida households, average household size, and estimates and projections by age, race, and sex.
Formerly (until 1993): University of Florida. Bureau of Economic and Business Research. Population Studies (0071-6030)
Related titles: CD-ROM ed.
Indexed: SRI.
Published by: (Bureau of Economic and Business Research), University of Florida, Office of the President, 226 Tigert Hall, PO Box 113150, Gainesville, FL 32611. TEL 352-392-1311, FAX 352-392-9506, http://www.ufl.edu/. **Co-sponsor:** College of Business Administration.

325 NOR ISSN 1504-0216
FLYKTNINGSREGNSKAPET; alt om mennesker paa flukt over hele verden. Text in Norwegian. 1991-1992; resumed 1994. a. NOK 180 per issue (effective 2006). back issues avail. **Document type:** *Magazine, Consumer.*
Former titles (until 2004): Flyktning (0807-2302); (until 1991): Flukt og Tilflukt (0807-2299)
Related titles: Online - full text ed.: ISSN 1504-5471.
Published by: Flyktninghjelpen/Norwegian Refugee Council, Grensen 17, Postboks 6758, St Olavs Plass, Oslo, 0130, Norway. TEL 47-23-109800, FAX 47-23-109801, nrc@nrc.no.

325.2 ITA ISSN 2038-2243
FONDAZIONE VERGA. ANNALI. Text in Italian. 1984. a. **Document type:** *Journal, Academic/Scholarly.*
Published by: Fondazione Franco Verga, Via Anfiteatro 14, Milan, 20121, Italy. TEL 39-02-8693194, FAX 39-02-86460052, info@fondazioneverga.org, http://www.fondazioneverga.org.

325 SWE ISSN 1404-9007
FORUM FOER MIGRATION OCH KULTUR. Variant title: F O M I K. Text in Swedish. 2000. irreg., latest vol.3, 2003. price varies. back issues avail. **Document type:** *Monographic series, Academic/Scholarly.*
Published by: (Oerebro Universitet, Samhaellsvetenskapliga Institutionen/University of Oerebro. Department of Social and Political Sciences), Oerebro Universitet, Universitetsbiblioteket/University of Oerebro. University Library, Fakultetsgatan 1, Oerebro, 70182, Sweden. TEL 46-19-303240, FAX 46-19-331217, biblioteket@ub.oru.se.

325 DEU
FORUM MIGRATION GESUNDHEIT INTEGRATION. Text in German. 1999. irreg., latest vol.5, 2008. price varies. **Document type:** *Monographic series, Academic/Scholarly.*

Published by: V W B - Verlag fuer Wissenschaft und Bildung, Postfach 110368, Berlin, 10833, Germany. TEL 49-30-2510415, FAX 49-30-2511136, info@vwb-verlag.com, http://www.vwb-verlag.com.

304.6 FRA ISSN 1635-561X
FRANCE. INSTITUT NATIONAL D'ETUDES DEMOGRAPHIQUES. CAHIERS. Text in French. 1946. irreg., latest vol.139, 1997. price varies. **Document type:** *Monographic series, Academic/Scholarly.* **Description:** Presents the results of scientific research on a specific topic within the field of population studies, e.g. languages, or living conditiond of the elderly.
Formerly (until 2002): France. Institut National d'Etudes Demographiques. Cahiers de Travaux et Documents (0071-8823)
Indexed: FR.
—INIST.
Published by: Institut National d'Etudes Demographiques (I N E D), 133 Blvd Davout, Paris, 75980 Cedex 20, France. TEL 33-1-56062000, FAX 33-1-56062199, editions@ined.fr. Ed. H Leridon.

304.6 330.9 327 363.7 MEX ISSN 0187-7372
E183.8.M6
➤ **FRONTERA NORTE.** Text in English, Spanish. 1989. s-a. MXN 500 domestic to individuals; USD 55 domestic to institutions (effective 2009). bk.rev. bibl.; tr.lit.; illus. back issues avail.; reprints avail. **Document type:** *Journal, Academic/Scholarly.* **Description:** Provides information on problems in economy, politics, migration and ecology at the U.S.-Mexico border.
Related titles: Online - full text ed.: free (effective 2011).
Indexed: A01, A26, C01, CA, ChPerl, Chicano, F03, F04, H21, I04, I05, P08, P34, PAIS, SociolAb, T02.
Published by: El Colegio de la Frontra Norte, A.C., Carretera Escenica Tijuana-Ensenada, km. 18.5, San Antonio del Mar, Tijuana, Baja California 22560, Mexico. TEL 52-664-6316300, FAX 52-664-6316327. Ed. Gerardo Ordonez Barba. R&P Rosana Garcia Arteaga A. Circ: 500.

304.6 BRA ISSN 0101-0662
HA973
FUNDACAO INSTITUTO BRASILEIRO DE GEOGRAFIA E ESTATISTICA. BOLETIM DEMOGRAFICO. Text in Portuguese. 1970. q. controlled free circ. charts; stat. cum.index every 5 yrs. back issues avail. **Document type:** *Journal, Academic/Scholarly.*
Formerly (until 1977): Boletim Demografico C B E D (0100-1892)
Indexed: P30, PAIS, PopulInd.
Published by: Fundacao Instituto Brasileiro de Geografia e Estatistica, Av. Beira Mar 436, Rio De Janeiro-, RJ, Brazil. Circ: 400.

GAZETTEER; alphabetical list of localities with statistics on population, number of houses and main source of water supply. *see* BUSINESS AND ECONOMICS—Abstracting, Bibliographies, Statistics

304.6 310 NLD ISSN 1876-9675
GEMEENTE AMSTERDAM. DIENST ONDERZOEK EN STATISTIEK. METROPOOLREGIO AMSTERDAM IN BEELD. Text in Dutch. 2005. a. EUR 15 (effective 2009).
Formerly (until 2008): Regio Amsterdam in Beeld (1876-9667)
Published by: Gemeente Amsterdam, Dienst Onderzoek en Statistiek, Postbus 658, Amsterdam, 1000 AR, Netherlands. TEL 31-20-2510333, FAX 31-20-2510444, algemeen@os.amsterdam.nl, http://www.os.amsterdam.nl.

301.32 ITA ISSN 2035-5556
HB881 CODEN: GNUSA7
GENUS (ONLINE); journal of population studies. Text in English; Summaries in English, French, Italian. 1934. 3/yr. EUR 78 to institutions (effective 2009). adv. bk.rev. bibl. **Document type:** *Journal, Academic/Scholarly.* **Description:** Publishes articles of "pure" demography to further a better knowledge of the interrelationship between demography and biological, social and economic phenomena, connected with the evolution of the population.
Formerly (until 2008): Genus (Print) (0016-6987)
Media: Online - full text.
Indexed: A20, A22, AICP, B25, BAS, BIOSIS Prev, CIS, DIP, FR, HistAb, IBR, IBSS, IBZ, MycolAb, P30, PAIS, PopulInd, RASB, SCOPUS, SSciA.
—BLDSC (4116.700000), IE.
Published by: Universita degli Studi di Roma "La Sapienza", Facolta di Scienze Statistiche Demografiche ed Attuariali, Piazzale Aldo Moro 5, Rome, 00185, Italy. TEL 39-06-4958308, FAX 39-06-491522. Circ: 3,000.

GEOPOLITICAL STUDIES. *see* GEOGRAPHY

GEORGETOWN IMMIGRATION LAW JOURNAL. *see* LAW

GEORGIA VITAL STATISTICS REPORT (ONLINE EDITION). *see* POPULATION STUDIES—Abstracting, Bibliographies, Statistics

GHANA LIVING STANDARDS SURVEY. ROUND REPORT. *see* BUSINESS AND ECONOMICS—Abstracting, Bibliographies, Statistics

GHANA LIVING STANDARDS SURVEY. RURAL COMMUNITIES IN GHANA. *see* BUSINESS AND ECONOMICS—Abstracting, Bibliographies, Statistics

304.6 GHA ISSN 0855-1308
GHANA POPULATION STUDIES. Key Title: University of Ghana Population Studies. Text in English. 1969. irreg., latest vol.10. price varies. **Document type:** *Monographic series, Academic/Scholarly.*
Published by: University of Ghana, Institute of Statistical, Social and Economic Research, PO Box 74, Legon, Ghana.

304.6 USA
GLOBAL POPULATION POLICY DATABASE (YEAR). Text in English. 1987. a. USD 75. **Document type:** *Government.*
Indexed: IIS.
Published by: United Nations, Department of Economic and Social Affairs, Population Division, Rm DC2 1934, New York, NY 10017. TEL 212-963-3230.

301.426 SWE
GOETEBORGS UNIVERSITET. DEMOGRAPHIC RESEARCH INSTITUTE. REPORTS. Text in Swedish. 1974 (no.14). irreg.
Published by: Goeteborgs Universitet, Demographic Research Institute, Viktoriagatan 13, Goeteborg, 41125, Sweden. **Dist. by:** Almqvist & Wiksell International, Gamla Brogatan 26, Stockholm 11285, Sweden.

GREAT BRITAIN. OFFICE FOR NATIONAL STATISTICS. MORTALITY STATISTICS. DEATHS REGISTERED IN (YEAR); review of the registrar general on deaths in England and Wales (Year). *see* POPULATION STUDIES—Abstracting, Bibliographies, Statistics

GREAT BRITAIN. OFFICE FOR NATIONAL STATISTICS. REGIONAL TRENDS. *see* STATISTICS

314 GRL ISSN 0105-0885
HB2576.A3
GREENLAND. GROENLANDS STATISTIK. GROENLANDS BEFOLKNING/KALATDLIT NUNANE INUIT. Text in Danish, Eskimo. 1976. a. free. **Description:** Contains statistics on the population of Greenland.
Related titles: ◆ Series of: Greenland. Groenlands Statistik. Befolkning. ISSN 0904-6860.
Published by: Groenlands Statistik/Kalaallit Nunaanni Naatsorsueqqissaartarfik, PO Box 1025, Nuuk, 3900, Greenland. TEL 299-345564, FAX 299-322954. Circ: 600.

325 USA ISSN 0899-2673
H L I REPORTS. Text in English. 1983. m. looseleaf. donation. adv. charts; illus.; stat.; tr.lit. back issues avail. **Document type:** *Newsletter, Trade.* **Description:** Provides international reservoir of pro-life and pro-family information and perspectives.
Former titles (until 1984): H L I Report; Loveline
Published by: Human Life International, 4 Family Life, Front Royal, VA 22630. TEL 540-635-7884, FAX 540-622-2838. R&P, Adv. contact James Price. Circ: 30,000.

304.6 640 NLD ISSN 1574-003X
HANDBOOK OF POPULATION AND FAMILY ECONOMICS. Text in English. 1997. irreg. **Document type:** *Monographic series, Academic/Scholarly.*
Related titles: Online - full text ed.: ISSN 1875-5682.
Indexed: SCOPUS.
—**CCC.**
Published by: Elsevier BV, North-Holland (Subsidiary of: Elsevier Science & Technology), Sara Burgerhartstraat 25, Amsterdam, 1055 KV, Netherlands. TEL 31-20-4853911, FAX 31-20-4852457, JournalsCustomerServiceEMEA@elsevier.com, http://www.elsevier.com.

HEALTH INFORMATION FOR INTERNATIONAL TRAVEL. *see* PUBLIC HEALTH AND SAFETY

HEALTH REPORTS (ONLINE). *see* PUBLIC HEALTH AND SAFETY

HEALTH REPORTS (PRINT). *see* PUBLIC HEALTH AND SAFETY

304.6 GBR ISSN 1465-1645
➤ **HEALTH STATISTICS QUARTERLY.** Abbreviated title: H S Q. Text in English. 1976. q. USD 258 in North America to institutions; GBP 135 elsewhere to institutions (effective 2011). adv. stat. back issues avail.; reprints avail. **Document type:** *Journal, Government.* **Description:** Contains commentary on the latest findings, topical articles on relevant subjects illustrated with colour charts and diagrams, regularly updated statistical tables and graphs, showing trends and the latest quarterly information: on deaths, childhood mortality, cancer survival, abortions, congenital anomalies, morbidity etc.
Supersedes in part (in 1999): Monitor, Population and Health. DH2 (1366-7637); Which was formerly (until 1996): O P C S Monitor. DH2 (0953-3370)
Related titles: Online - full text ed.: ISSN 2040-1574. free (effective 2011).
Indexed: A12, A17, A26, A36, A39, ABIn, B28, C06, C07, C27, C29, CABA, D03, D04, E08, E12, E13, EMBASE, ExcerpMed, G06, G07, G08, GH, H05, H12, I05, MEDLINE, P20, P21, P22, P27, P30, P41, P48, P50, P51, P52, P53, P54, P56, PQC, R14, S09, S13, S14, S15, S18, SCOPUS, T05, W11.
—BLDSC (4275.201500), IE, Ingenta. **CCC.**
Published by: (Great Britain. Office for National Statistics), Palgrave Macmillan Ltd. (Subsidiary of: Macmillan Publishers Ltd.), Houndmills, Basingstoke, Hants RG21 6XS, United Kingdom. TEL 44-1256-329242, FAX 44-1256-479476, orders@palgrave.com, http://www.palgrave.com. Ed. Myer Glickman TEL 44-20-70142385. Pub. David Bull TEL 44-1256-329242. **Subscr. to:** Subscription Department, Brunel Rd, Houndmills, Basingstoke, Hants RG21 2XS, United Kingdom. TEL 44-1256-357893, FAX 44-1256-328339, subscriptions@palgrave.com.

➤ **HISTORICKA DEMOGRAFIE.** *see* HISTORY—History Of Europe

304.8 FRA ISSN 1142-852X
HOMMES & MIGRATIONS. Text in French. 1950. 6/yr. EUR 49 domestic to individuals; EUR 67 foreign to individuals; EUR 58 domestic to institutions; EUR 77 foreign to institutions (effective 2008). adv. bk.rev. charts; illus.; stat. index, cum.index. **Document type:** *Journal, Academic/Scholarly.*
Former titles (until 1986): Hommes et Migrations. Documents (0223-3290); (until 1964): Documets Nord - Africains (1149-2899); (until 1950): E S N A. Etudes Sociales Nord - Africaines (0423-586X)
Indexed: A22, AMR, FR, I14, IBSS, P30, PAIS, PerIslam, RASB, RILM, RefugAb.
—BLDSC (4326.270000), IE, Ingenta, INIST. **CCC.**
Published by: Amis de Hommes & Migrations, 40 rue de la Duee, Paris, 75020, France. TEL 33-1-47972605, FAX 33-1-47979977. Ed., R&P Philippe Dewitte. Pub. Francois Gremont. Adv. contact Patrice Coulon. Circ: 3,000.

304.6 951 351 HKG ISSN 1011-4521
HONG KONG (YEAR). Variant title: Hong Kong Yearbook. Text in English. a. HKD 106 for 1999 ed. (effective 2001); price varies per edition. **Document type:** *Yearbook, Government.*
Related titles: ◆ Chinese ed.: Xianggang (Year). ISSN 0072-629X.
—BLDSC (4326.347550).
Published by: Information Services Department, 5/F, Murray Bldg, Garden Rd, Hong Kong, Hong Kong. FAX 852-2905-1572, internet@isd.gov.hk, http://www.isd.gov.hk/. **Subscr. to:** Information Services Department, Publications Sales Unit, Rm 402, 4th Fl, Murray Bldg, Garden Rd, Hong Kong, Hong Kong. TEL 852-2537-1910, puborder@isd.gcn.gov.hk, http://www.info.gov.hk/isd/book_e.htm.

304.6 HKG
HONG KONG SPECIAL ADMINISTRATIVE REGION OF CHINA. CENSUS AND STATISTICS DEPARTMENT. DEMOGRAPHIC TRENDS IN HONG KONG. Text in Chinese, English. 1976. irreg., latest 1997. USD 40 newsstand/cover (effective 2001). stat. back issues avail. **Document type:** *Government.* **Description:** Present births, deaths and marriages statistics of the Hong Kong population, together with a comprehensive and in-depth analysis on the fertility, morality and nuptiality trends. The report provides a clear picture on the changing structure of the Hong Kong population. In addition, it also studies the changes in demographic characteristics. Such information is crucial for future planning in such program areas as housing, education, medical and health.
Related titles: Online - full content ed.
Published by: Census and Statistics Department/Zhengfu Tongjichu, Demographic Statistics Section, 7/F Kai Tak Multi-storey Carpark Bldg, 2 Concorde Rd, Kowloon, Hong Kong. TEL 852-2716-8345, FAX 852-2716-0231, demo_1@censtad.gov.hk, http://www.statisticalbookstore.gov.hk. **Subscr. to:** Information Services Department, Publications Sales Unit, Rm 402, 4th Fl, Murray Bldg, Garden Rd, Hong Kong. TEL 852-2842-8844, FAX 852-2598-7482, puborder@isd.gcn.gov.hk, http://www.info.gov.hk/isd/book_e.htm. **Dist. by:** Government Publications Centre, Low Block, Ground Fl, Queensway Government Offices, 66 Queensway, Hong Kong, Hong Kong. TEL 852-2537-1910, FAX 852-2523-7195.

304.6 HKG
HONG KONG SPECIAL ADMINISTRATIVE REGION OF CHINA. CENSUS AND STATISTICS DEPARTMENT. SURVEYS AND YOU. Text in Chinese, English. 2000. irreg. looseleaf. free. stat. **Document type:** *Government.*
Related titles: Online - full content ed.
Published by: Census and Statistics Department/Zhengfu Tongjichu, Economic Surveys Development Section (2), 23/F Chuang's Hung Hom Plaza, 83 Wuhu St, Hung Hom, Kowloon, Hong Kong. TEL 852-2805-6112, FAX 852-2123-1053, esd2_1@censtatd.gov.hk, http://www.info.gov.hk/censtatd, http://www.statisticalbookstore.gov.hk.

HUMAN BIOLOGY (DETROIT); the international journal of population biology and genetics. *see* BIOLOGY—Genetics

HUMAN GEOGRAPHY/JIMBUN-CHIRI. *see* GEOGRAPHY

HUMAN LIFE INTERNATIONAL. SPECIAL REPORT. *see* RELIGIONS AND THEOLOGY—Roman Catholic

304.6 330 DEU ISSN 0721-0086
I F O STUDIEN ZUR BEVOELKERUNGSOEKONOMIE. (Information und Forschung) Text in German. 1981. irreg., latest vol.5, 1988. price varies. **Document type:** *Monographic series, Academic/Scholarly.* **Description:** Publication on population topics.
Published by: I F O Institut fuer Wirtschaftsforschung, Poschingerstr 5, Munich, 81679, Germany. TEL 49-89-92241410, FAX 49-89-92241409, ifo@ifo.de, http://www.ifo.de. Circ: 400.

301.426 IND
I I P S NEWSLETTER. Text in English. 1960. q. bibl.; charts; illus. back issues avail. **Document type:** *Newsletter, Consumer.* **Description:** Contains organization news as well as summaries of new dissertations.
Formerly (until 1978): International Institute for Population Studies. Newsletter (0047-0716)
Related titles: Online - full text ed.
Indexed: SCOPUS.
Published by: International Institute for Population Sciences, Govandi Sta Rd, Deonar, Mumbai, Maharashtra 400 088, India. TEL 91-22-25563255, FAX 91-22-25563257, director@iips.net. Ed. R B Bhagat.

I M C H NEWSLETTER. *see* CHILDREN AND YOUTH—About

325.1 DEU ISSN 0949-4723
JV6004
I M I S - BEITRAEGE. Text in German. irreg. **Document type:** *Monographic series, Academic/Scholarly.*
Indexed: CA, DIP, IBR, IBZ, P42, PAIS, PSA, S02, S03, SociolAb, T02.
Published by: Institut fuer Migrationsforschung und Interkulturelle Studien, IMIS-Fachbereich 2, Neuer Graben 19-21, Osnabrueck, 49069, Germany. TEL 49-541-9694384, FAX 49-541-9694380, imis@uni-osnabrueck.de, http://www.imis.uni-osnabrueck.de.

325 NLD
I M I S C O E DISSERTATIONS. Text in English. irreg. price varies. **Document type:** *Monographic series, Academic/Scholarly.*
Published by: (International Migration, Integration and Social Cohesion in Europe (I M I S C O E)), Amsterdam University Press, Herengracht 221, Amsterdam, 1016 BG, Netherlands. TEL 31-20-4200050, FAX 31-20-4203214, info@aup.nl, http://www.aup.nl.

325 NLD
I M I S C O E REPORTS. (International Migration, Integration and Social Cohesion in Europe) Text in English. irreg. price varies. **Document type:** *Monographic series, Academic/Scholarly.*
Published by: (International Migration, Integration and Social Cohesion in Europe (I M I S C O E)), Amsterdam University Press, Herengracht 221, Amsterdam, 1016 BG, Netherlands. TEL 31-20-4200050, FAX 31-20-4203214, info@aup.nl.

325.1 CAN ISSN 0845-2466
I N S C A N. (International Settlement Canada) Text in English. 1987. q. CAD 25 (effective 2006). **Document type:** *Newsletter.* **Description:** Covers immigration settlement issues. Focuses on immigrant settlement programs and includes information on statistics, opinion polls, conferences, books, videos and other resources for newcomer communities.
Published by: Carleton University, Centre for Peace Action and Migration Research, Research Resource Division for Refugees, A735 Loeb Bldg, 1125 Colonel By Dr, Ottawa, ON K1S 5B6, Canada. TEL 613-520-2717, FAX 613-520-3676.

325 CHE ISSN 1607-338X
JV6006
I O M MIGRATION RESEARCH SERIES. Text in English. 2000. irreg., latest vol.22, 2006. USD 16 per issue (effective 2006). bibl.; charts; illus.; maps; stat. back issues avail.; reprints avail. **Document type:** *Monographic series, Academic/Scholarly.* **Description:** Contains monographs on topics relevant to the issue and management of migration movements.
Indexed: CABA, E12, S13, S16, W11.

—BLDSC (4564.179900).
Published by: International Organization for Migration/Organizacion Internacional para las Migraciones, 17 Rte des Morillons, Geneva 19, 1211, Switzerland. TEL 41-22-7179111, FAX 41-22-7986150, publications@iom.int, http://www.iom.int.

304.8 305.8 SWE ISSN 1404-6857
I & M. (Invandrare & Minoriteter) Text in Swedish. 1974. 6/yr. SEK 170 to individuals; SEK 253 to institutions (effective 2004). adv. bk.rev. back issues avail. **Description:** Describes how different cultures and migration influence Swedish society. Gives background to today's situation and tries to show living conditions for ethnical minorities in the country. Participates in debates on national issues.
Former titles (until 2000): Invandrare och Minoriteter (0346-6566); (until 1976): Nordisk Minoritetsforskning (0345-8318)
Indexed: MLA-IB.
Published by: Stiftelsen Invandrare & Minoriteter, Fittja Gaard, Vaerdshusvaegen 46, Norsborg, 14550, Sweden. TEL 46-8-53176760, FAX 46-8-53173430, info@iochm.com. Ed. Nora Weintraub. Adv. contact Lotta Bolin. B&W page SEK 5,000, color page SEK 7,500; trim 230 x 170. Circ: 1,800.

THE I R C AT WORK. *see* SOCIAL SERVICES AND WELFARE

304.6 FRA ISSN 0771-2022
HB848
I U S S P. NEWSLETTER/U I E S P. BULLETIN. (International Union for the Scientific Study of Population) Text in English, French. 1955. 2/yr. charts; stat. back issues avail. **Document type:** *Newsletter, Trade.*
Formerly (until 1969): Demographe (0011-8273)
Related titles: Online - full text ed.
Indexed: P06, P30.
Published by: International Union for the Scientific Study of Population (I U S S P)/Union Internationale pour l'Etude Scientifique de la Population, 3-5 Rue Nicolas, Paris, 75980, France. TEL 33-1-56062173, FAX 33-1-56062204.

305.8 USA ISSN 0749-5951
IMMIGRANT COMMUNITIES & ETHNIC MINORITIES IN THE UNITED STATES & CANADA. Text in English. 1984. irreg., latest 2008. price varies. back issues avail.; reprints avail. **Document type:** *Monographic series, Trade.* **Description:** Monographs on ethnic enclaves and communities within the United States and Canada.
—BLDSC (4369.637150).
Published by: A M S Press, Inc., Brooklyn Navy Yard, 63 Flushing Ave, Bldg 292, Unit #221, Brooklyn, NY 11205. FAX 718-875-3800, queries@amspressinc.com.

IMMIGRANTS AND MINORITIES. *see* HISTORY

325.1 USA ISSN 1949-9671
E184.A1
THE IMMIGRATION AND ETHNIC HISTORY. NEWSLETTER. Text in English. 1969. s-a. free to members (effective 2009). bk.rev. bibl. back issues avail. **Document type:** *Newsletter.* **Description:** Contains articles of historiographical and pedagogical interest about the field of immigration and ethnic history.
Formerly (until 1998): Immigration History. Newsletter (0579-4374)
Published by: The Immigration and Ethnic History, c/o James M. Bergquist, Editor, Department of History, Villanova University, Villanova, PA 19085. TEL 610-687-0838, FAX 610-519-4450, james.bergquist@villanova.edu.

325 USA
IMMIGRATION AND REFUGEE SERVICES OF AMERICA. ISSUE PAPER SERIES. Text in English. 1985. irreg. (3-5/yr.). USD 4 per issue (effective 2000). adv. **Description:** Reports on critical refugee issues and policy matters.
Formerly: American Council for Nationalities Service. Issue Paper Series
Published by: Immigration and Refugee Services of America, 1717 Massachusetts Ave N W, Ste 200, Washington, DC 20036. TEL 202-347-3507. Ed. Virginia Hamilton. Adv. contact Melissa Wyers.

325.1 USA ISSN 0899-5400
E184.A1
IMMIGRATION DIGEST. Text in English. 1987. irreg. (2-3/yr.), latest no.15. bk.rev.; video rev.; Website rev. bibl.; charts; maps. back issues avail. **Document type:** *Newsletter, Consumer.* **Description:** Provides current information on new resources to link one's immigrant ancestors with their origins: naming patterns and changed name forms, exit documents and where to find them, passenger lists and naturalizations, and administrative boundary maps.
Indexed: GPAI.
Published by: Genealogical Institute, Inc., 56 W Main St, Tremonton, UT 84337. TEL 435-257-3185, 800-377-6058, FAX 435-257-8622, http://www.genealogical-institute.com. Ed., R&P Arlene Eakle. Circ: 500.

IMMIGRATION LAW AND PRACTICE. *see* LAW

IMMIGRATION LAW & PROCEDURE. *see* LAW

IMMIGRATION LAW AND PROCEDURE: DESK EDITION. *see* LAW

325.1 CAN ISSN 0835-3808
KE4454.A45
IMMIGRATION LAW REPORTER (3RD SERIES). Text in English. N.S. 1988. 5/yr. CAD 361 domestic; USD 376 foreign (effective 2011). adv. reprints avail. **Document type:** *Trade.* **Description:** Features timely reporting of decisions of the Immigration Appeal Board and of the Courts in immigration matters. Provides annotations and articles of particular interest to the practitioner, highlighting practice issues and immigration policy.
Published by: Carswell (Subsidiary of: Thomson Reuters Corp.), One Corporate Plz, 2075 Kennedy Rd, Toronto, ON M1T 3V4, Canada. TEL 416-609-8000, 800-387-5164, FAX 416-298-5094, carswell.customerrelations@thomson.com. Ed. Cecil L Rotenberg.

IMMIGRATION PROCEDURES HANDBOOK. *see* LAW

325.1 USA ISSN 1067-3377
KF4802
IMMIGRATION REPORT. Text in English. 1979. m. USD 25 (effective 2006). bk.rev. back issues avail. **Document type:** *Newsletter.* **Description:** Presents news articles and reports dealing with the impact of legal and illegal immigration to the US; tracks immigration-related legislation.
Formerly (until 1990): F A I R Immigration Report (0737-867X)
Published by: Federation for American Immigration Reform, 1666 Connecticut Ave, N W, Ste 400, Washington, DC 20009. TEL 202-328-7004, FAX 202-387-3447, http://www.fairus.org/. Ed. Scipio Garling. R&P Laura Viani. Circ: 45,000.

INDIA. MINISTRY OF HOME AFFAIRS. VITAL STATISTICS DIVISION. SURVEY OF CAUSES OF DEATH (RURAL). *see* POPULATION STUDIES—Abstracting, Bibliographies, Statistics

LES INDICATEURS SOCIAUX (YEAR). *see* BUSINESS AND ECONOMICS—Economic Situation And Conditions

304.6 BRA ISSN 0100-7173
HB3564.S3
INFORME DEMOGRAFICO. Text in Portuguese. 1980. irreg. USD 41.50. **Description:** Devoted to specific topics such as: mortality rates, migration and the fertility rate in the state of Sao Paulo.
Indexed: P30.
Published by: Fundacao Sistema Estadual de Analise de Dados, Av. Casper Libero, 464, Centro, Caixa Postal 8223, Sao Paulo, SP 01033-000, Brazil. Circ: 500.

325.1 ESP ISSN 1888-251X
JV8251
LA INMIGRACION EN ESPANA. Variant title: Anuario de la Inmigracion en Espana. Text in Spanish. 2007. a. EUR 28 (effective 2009). back issues avail. **Document type:** *Yearbook, Consumer.*
Published by: Fundacio C I D O B, C. Elisabets, 12, Barcelona, 08001, Spain. TEL 34-93-3026495, FAX 34-93-3022118, publicaciones@cibod.org, http://www.cibod.org.

304.6 CMR
INSTITUT DE FORMATION ET DE RECHERCHE DEMOGRAPHIQUES. ANNALES. Text in French. 1975. 2/yr. free. back issues avail. **Document type:** *Bulletin.*
Indexed: PopulInd.
Published by: Institut de Formation et de Recherche Demographiques (I F O R D), BP 1556, Yaounde, Cameroon. TEL 23-29-47, 22-24-71. Circ: 500.

304.6 AUT
INSTITUT FUER DEMOGRAPHIE. FORSCHUNGSBERICHTE. Text in German. 1985. irreg., latest vol.32, 2007. price varies. **Document type:** *Monographic series, Academic/Scholarly.*
Published by: Verlag der Oesterreichischen Akademie der Wissenschaften, Postgasse 7/4, Vienna, W 1011, Austria. TEL 43-1-515813402, FAX 43-1-515813400, verlag@oeaw.ac.at.

304.6 AUT
INSTITUT FUER DEMOGRAPHIE. SCHRIFTEN. Text in German. 1977. irreg., latest vol.21, 2007. price varies. **Document type:** *Monographic series, Academic/Scholarly.*
Published by: Verlag der Oesterreichischen Akademie der Wissenschaften, Postgasse 7/4, Vienna, W 1011, Austria. TEL 43-1-515813402, FAX 43-1-515813400, verlag@oeaw.ac.at.

301.32 DEU
INSTITUT FUER MIGRATIONSFORSCHUNG UND INTERKULTURELLE STUDIEN. SCHRIFTEN. Text in German. 1996. irreg., latest vol.15, 2008. price varies. **Document type:** *Monographic series, Academic/Scholarly.*
Published by: (Institut fuer Migrationsforschung und Interkulturelle Studien), V & R Unipress GmbH (Subsidiary of: Vandenhoeck und Ruprecht), Robert-Bosch-Breite 6, Goettingen, 37079, Germany. TEL 49-551-5084303, FAX 49-551-5084333, info@vr-unipress.de, http://www.v-r.de/en/publisher/unipress.

304.6 FRA ISSN 1144-7648
INSTITUT NATIONAL D'ETUDES DEMOGRAPHIQUES. CONGRES ET COLLOQUES. Text in French. 1989. irreg., latest vol.17, 1997. price varies.
Published by: Institut National d'Etudes Demographiques (I N E D), 133 Blvd Davout, Paris, 75980 Cedex 20, France. TEL 33-1-56062000, FAX 33-1-56062199, editions@ined.fr.

325.1 MEX
INSTITUTO PANAMERICANO DE GEOGRAFIA E HISTORIA. SERIE INMIGRACION. Text in Spanish. 1985. irreg., latest vol.6, 1991. price varies.
Published by: Instituto Panamericano de Geografia e Historia, Ex-Arzobispado 29, Col Observatorio, Del Miguel Hidalgo, Mexico City, DF 11860, Mexico. TEL 52-55-52775791, FAX 52-55-52716172, info@ipgh.org.mx, http://www.ipgh.org/.

304.8489 DNK ISSN 1600-8936
INTEGRATIONSSTATUS. Text in Danish. 2000. s-a. stat. **Document type:** *Journal, Trade.*
Related titles: Online - full text ed.
Published by: Catinet- I F K A, Vesterbrogade 24, Copenhagen V, 1620, Denmark. TEL 45-70-202324, FAX 45-70-202423, info@catinet.dk, http://www.catinet.dk.

325 323 CHE ISSN 1726-2224
INTERNATIONAL DIALOGUE ON MIGRATION. Text in English. 2002. irreg. USD 16 per issue (effective 2007). **Document type:** *Proceedings.*
Published by: International Organization for Migration/Organizacion Internacional para las Migraciones, 17 Rte des Morillons, Geneva 19, 1211, Switzerland. TEL 41-22-7179111, FAX 41-22-7986150, publications@iom.int.

304.6 NLD ISSN 1877-9204
▼ **INTERNATIONAL HANDBOOKS OF POPULATION.** Text in English. 2009. irreg., latest vol.2, 2011. price varies. **Document type:** *Monographic series, Academic/Scholarly.* **Description:** Explores topics of vital interest in the area of demography and population.
Published by: Springer Netherlands (Subsidiary of: Springer Science+Business Media), Van Godewijckstraat 30, Dordrecht, 3311 GX, Netherlands. TEL 31-78-6576050, FAX 31-78-6576474. Ed. Dudley L Poston.

304.6 IND
INTERNATIONAL INSTITUTE FOR POPULATION SCIENCES. DIRECTOR'S REPORT. Text in English. 1956. a. **Document type:** *Report, Academic/Scholarly.*
Former titles (until 1974): International Institute for Population Studies. Annual Report; (until 1971): Demographic Training and Research Centre. Annual Report; International Institute for Population Studies. Director's Report
Related titles: Online - full text ed.: free (effective 2011).
Published by: International Institute for Population Sciences, Govandi Sta Rd, Deonar, Mumbai, Maharashtra 400 088, India. TEL 91-22-25563255, FAX 91-22-25563257, director@iips.net.

▼ **INTERNATIONAL JOURNAL OF BORDER SECURITY AND IMMIGRATION POLICY.** *see* LAW—Constitutional Law

INTERNATIONAL JOURNAL OF HEALTH, CULTURE AND MIGRATION. *see* PUBLIC HEALTH AND SAFETY

304.6 363.7 ITA ISSN 2036-7910
▼ **INTERNATIONAL JOURNAL OF HUMAN GEOGRAPHY AND ENVIRONMENTAL STUDIES.** Text in English. 2009. s-a. **Document type:** *Journal, Academic/Scholarly.*
Media: Online - full text.
Published by: Polo Centre of Sustainability, CP 701, Imperia, 18100, Italy. TEL 39-0388-1446069, FAX 39-0331-3128210, polocentre@polosustainability.com, http://www.polosustainability.com.

304.6 USA ISSN 2090-4029
▼ ➤ **INTERNATIONAL JOURNAL OF POPULATION RESEARCH.** Text in English. 2011. USD 195 (effective 2011). **Document type:** *Journal, Academic/Scholarly.* **Description:** Publishes original research articles as well as review articles in all areas of population research.
Related titles: Online - full text ed.: 2011. free (effective 2011).
Published by: Hindawi Publishing Corporation, 410 Park Ave, 15th Fl, PMB 287, New York, NY 10022. FAX 215-893-4392, 866-446-3294, info@hindawi.com.

325 GBR ISSN 0020-7985
JV6001.A1
➤ **INTERNATIONAL MIGRATION.** Text mainly in English; Abstracts in French, Spanish. 1961. 5/yr. GBP 274 in United Kingdom to institutions; EUR 348 in Europe to institutions; USD 457 in the Americas to institutions; USD 536 elsewhere to institutions; GBP 315 combined subscription in United Kingdom to institutions (print & online eds.); EUR 401 combined subscription in Europe to institutions (print & online eds.); USD 526 combined subscription in the Americas to institutions (print & online eds.); USD 616 combined subscription elsewhere to institutions (print & online eds.) (effective 2012). adv. bk.rev. bibl.; charts; stat. index. back issues avail.; reprint service avail. from PSC. **Document type:** *Journal, Academic/Scholarly.* **Description:** Covers the entire field of policy relevance in international migration, giving attention not only to a breadth of topics reflective of policy concerns, but also attention to coverage of all regions of the world and to comparative policy.
Formed by the merger of (1953 -1963): R E M P Bulletin (1605-7805); (1962-1963): Migration (0540-0074); Which was formerly (1961-1962): Migracion (1024-7890)
Related titles: Microfiche ed.: (from CIS); Online - full text ed.: ISSN 1468-2435. GBP 274 in United Kingdom to institutions; EUR 348 in Europe to institutions; USD 457 in the Americas to institutions; USD 536 elsewhere to institutions (effective 2012) (from IngentaConnect).
Indexed: A01, A02, A03, A08, A20, A22, A26, AEI, APEL, ASCA, AmH&L, BibInd, CA, ChPerI, Chicano, CurCont, DRIE, E01, ESPM, EnvAb, FamI, GEOBASE, HPNRM, HistAb, I13, IBSS, IIS, ILD, KES, M10, P06, P30, P34, P42, PAIS, PSA, PerIslam, PopulInd, RefZh, RefugAb, RiskAb, S02, S03, SCOPUS, SOPODA, SRRA, SSA, SSCI, SSciA, SociolAb, T02, W07, W09.
—BLDSC (4544.230000), IE, Infotrieve, Ingenta. **CCC.**
Published by: (International Organization for Migration/Organizacion Internacional para las Migraciones CHE), Wiley-Blackwell Publishing Ltd. (Subsidiary of: John Wiley & Sons, Inc.), 9600 Garsington Rd, Oxford, OX4 2DQ, United Kingdom. TEL 44-1865-776868, FAX 44-1865-714591, customerservices@blackwellpublishing.com. Ed. Elzbieta M Gozdziak. Adv. contact Craig Pickett TEL 44-1865-476267. B&W page GBP 445, B&W page USD 823; 135 x 205. Circ: 2,450.

325 300 USA ISSN 0197-9183
JV6001
➤ **INTERNATIONAL MIGRATION REVIEW;** a quarterly studying sociological, demographic, economic, historical, and legislative aspects of human migration movements and ethnic group relations. Text in English. 1964; N.S. 1966. q. GBP 228 combined subscription in United Kingdom to institutions (print & online eds.); EUR 289 combined subscription in Europe to institutions (print & online eds.); USD 370 combined subscription in the Americas to institutions (print & online eds.); USD 445 combined subscription elsewhere to institutions (print & online eds.) (effective 2012). adv. bk.rev. abstr.; bibl.; charts; stat.; illus. index, cum.index. back issues avail.; reprint service avail. from PSC. **Document type:** *Journal, Academic/Scholarly.* **Description:** Contains articles and research notes on migration and refugee issues.
Formerly (until 1966): International Migration Digest (0538-8716); Which incorporated (in 1973): International Newsletter on Migration (0383-2767); Which was formerly (1971-1972): International Migration Newsletter (0383-2759)
Related titles: Microfilm ed.: (from PQC); Online - full text ed.: ISSN 1747-7379. GBP 194 in United Kingdom to institutions; EUR 247 in Europe to institutions; USD 316 in the Americas to institutions; USD 381 elsewhere to institutions (effective 2012) (from IngentaConnect).
Indexed: A01, A02, A03, A08, A20, A21, A22, A26, A36, ABS&EES, AICP, APEL, ASCA, ASSIA, AbAn, AmH&L, B04, BAS, BRD, C32, CA, CABA, ChPerI, Chicano, CurCont, DIP, E01, E02, E03, E07, E08, EI, ERI, ESPM, EdA, EdI, FR, FamI, G08, G10, GEOBASE, GH, H09, H21, HPNRM, HRA, HRIR, HistAb, I05, IBR, IBSS, IBZ, IIS, M10, MEA&I, N02, N03, P02, P06, P08, P10, P13, P18, P21, P27, P30, P34, P42, P45, P46, P47, P48, P50, P52, P53, P54, P56, PAIS, PCI, PQC, PRA, PSA, PerIslam, PopulInd, R12, RASB, RI-1, RI-2, RefugAb, S02, S03, S05, S09, S11, SCOPUS, SOPODA, SPPI, SRRA, SSA, SSAI, SSAb, SSCI, SSI, SSciA, SUSA, SWR&A, SociolAb, T02, T05, TAR, W01, W02, W03, W07, W09, W11.
—BLDSC (4544.245000), IE, Infotrieve, Ingenta, INIST. **CCC.**
Published by: (Center for Migration Studies), Wiley-Blackwell Publishing, Inc. (Subsidiary of: Wiley-Blackwell Publishing Ltd.), 111 River St, Hoboken, NJ 07030. TEL 201-748-6000, FAX 201-748-6088, info@wiley.com, http://www.wiley.com/WileyCDA/. Ed. Joseph Chamie. Adv. contact Kristin McCarthy TEL 201-748-7683. B&W page USD 412; trim 6 x 9. Circ: 1,037 (paid).

P

325 CHE
INTERNATIONAL ORGANIZATION FOR MIGRATION. ANNUAL REPORT. Text in English. 1969. a. free. reprints avail. **Document type:** *Corporate.* **Description:** Report of the organization covering migration activities, migration for development programs, migration planning, cooperation and research, administration, management, finance, information and publications.
Former titles: International Organization for Migration. Annual Review; Intergovernmental Committee for Migration. Annual Review; Intergovernmental Committee for Migration. Review of Achievements; Intergovernmental Committee for European Migration. Review of Achievements
Related titles: Microfiche ed.: (from CIS); Spanish ed.; French ed.
Indexed: IIS.
Published by: International Organization for Migration/Organizacion Internacional para las Migraciones, 17 Rte des Morillons, Geneva 19, 1211, Switzerland. TEL 41-22-7179111, FAX 41-22-7986150, publications@iom.int. Circ: 5,000.

304.6 CAN ISSN 1492-9759
INTERNATIONAL PRODUCTIVITY MONITOR. Text in English. 2000. s-a. **Document type:** *Journal, Academic/Scholarly.* **Description:** Publishes articles on productivity issues, trends and developments in Canada and other countries and serves as a vehicle for the international discussion of productivity topics.
Related titles: Online - full text ed.: ISSN 1492-9767. 2000. free (effective 2011); French ed.: Observateur International de la Productivite. ISSN 1492-9848.
Indexed: A12, A17, A26, A39, ABIn, C27, C29, CA, D03, D04, E08, E13, EconLit, I05, JEL, P27, P48, P51, P52, P53, P54, P56, PQC, R14, S09, S14, S15, S18, T02.
—BLDSC (4544.982700), IE, Ingenta.
Published by: Centre for the Study of Living Standards, 111 Sparks St, Ste 500, Ottawa, ON K1P 5B5, Canada. TEL 613-233-8891, FAX 613-233-8250, csls@csls.ca.

304.6 NLD ISSN 1871-0395
INTERNATIONAL STUDIES IN POPULATION. Text in English. 2005. irreg., latest vol.7, 2008. price varies. **Document type:** *Monographic series, Academic/Scholarly.*
—BLDSC (4549.795500).
Published by: (International Union for the Scientific Study of Population (I U S S P)/Union Internationale pour l'Etude Scientifique de la Population FRA), Springer Netherlands (Subsidiary of: Springer Science+Business Media), Van Godewijckstraat 30, Dordrecht, 3311 GX, Netherlands. TEL 31-78-6576050, FAX 31-78-6576474.

304.8 305.4 SWE ISSN 0348-6435
INVANDRARKVINNAN. Text in Swedish. 1974. q. SEK 110.
Published by: Riksfoerbundet Internationella Foereningen foer Invandrarkvinnor - R I F F I, Norrtullsgatan 45, Stockholm, 11345, Sweden. TEL 46-8-30-21-89. Ed. Karin Svanebro.

304.6021 IRL ISSN 0790-9969
HA1170.3
IRELAND. CENTRAL STATISTICS OFFICE. POPULATION AND LABOUR FORCE PROJECTIONS. Text in English. 1985. irreg., latest 2004. EUR 15 (effective 2005). **Document type:** *Government.* **Description:** Provides detailed projections in all aspects of the labor force in Ireland.
Related titles: Online - full text ed.
Published by: Ireland. Central Statistics Office/Eire, An Phriomh-Oifig Staidrimh, Skehard Rd, Cork, Ireland. TEL 353-21-4535000, FAX 353-21-4535555, information@cso.ie.

325 CHE ISSN 1661-6065
JV7711
IRISH MIGRATION STUDIES IN LATIN AMERICA. Text in English. 2003. q. free (effective 2011). **Document type:** *Journal, Academic/Scholarly.*
Media: Online - full text.
Indexed: CA, HistAb, T02.
Published by: Society for Irish Latin American Sudies (S I L A S), Maison Rouge, Burtigny, 1268, Switzerland. Ed. Edmundo Murray.

ITALY. ISTITUTO NAZIONALE DI STATISTICA. POPOLAZIONE E MOVIMENTO ANAGRAFICO DEI COMUNI. *see* POPULATION STUDIES—Abstracting, Bibliographies, Statistics

J C W I BULLETIN. *see* LAW

J C W I IMMIGRATION, NATIONALITY AND REFUGEE LAW HANDBOOK. *see* LAW—Constitutional Law

JAARRAPPORT INTEGRATIE. *see* POLITICAL SCIENCE—Civil Rights

JAHRBUCH FUER FRAENKISCHE LANDESFORSCHUNG. *see* HISTORY—History Of Europe

304.6 JPN ISSN 1348-7191
HB848
JAPANESE JOURNAL OF POPULATION. Text in English. 2004. s-a. stat. **Document type:** *Journal, Academic/Scholarly.*
Supersedes in part: Journal of Population and Social Security
Media: Online - full content.
Published by: Kokuritsu Shakai Hosho Jinko Mondai Kenkyusho/ National Institute of Population and Social Security Research, Hibiya Kokusai Bldg 6th Fl, 2-2-3 Uchisaiwaicyo, Chiyoda-ku, Tokyo, Chiyoda-ku 100-0011, Japan. TEL 81-3-35952984, FAX 81-3-35914816, somuka@ipss.go.jp, http://www.ipss.go.jp/.

304.6 CHN ISSN 1671-0061
JIANKANG RENSHENG/HEALTH LIFE. Text in Chinese. 1985. bi-m. USD 12.60 (effective 2009). adv. bk.rev. **Document type:** *Journal, Academic/Scholarly.* **Description:** Covers population studies, information on domestic and foreign populations, pregnancy care, birth control, and contraceptives.
Formerly (until 2000): Renkou yu Yousheng/Population and Better Birth (1005-4820)
Related titles: Online - full text ed.
Published by: Zhejiang Daxue Yixueyuan, 353, Yanan Lu, Hangzhou, 310031, China. Circ: 45,000; 50,000 (paid). **Dist. by:** China International Book Trading Corp, 35 Chegongzhuang Xilu, Haidian District, PO Box 399, Beijing 100044, China. TEL 86-10-68412045, FAX 86-10-68412023, cibtc@mail.cibtc.com.cn, http://www.cibtc.com.cn.

304.6 JPN ISSN 0387-2793
HB848
JINKO MONDAI KENKYU/JOURNAL OF POPULATION PROBLEMS. Text in Japanese; Summaries in English. 1940. q. JPY 2,000 (effective 2006). bk.rev. stat.
Indexed: P30, PopulInd, SCOPUS, SSciA.
Published by: Kokuritsu Shakai Hosho Jinko Mondai Kenkyusho/ National Institute of Population and Social Security Research, Hibiya Kokusai Bldg 6th Fl, 2-2-3 Uchisaiwaicyo, Chiyoda-ku, Tokyo, Chiyoda-ku 100-0011, Japan. TEL 81-3-35952984, FAX 81-3-35914816, somuka@ipss.go.jp, http://www.ipss.go.jp/.

304.6 JPN ISSN 0386-8311
HB3651
JINKOGAKU KENKYU/JOURNAL OF POPULATION STUDIES. Text in Japanese. 1978. s-a. **Document type:** *Journal, Academic/Scholarly.*
Indexed: P30, SCOPUS.
—CCC.
Published by: Nihon Jinko Gakkai/Population Association of Japan, 2-15-14, Tukiji. Chouo-ku, Tokyo, 104-0045, Japan. TEL 81-3-35420360, FAX 81-3-35420362, pajadmin@jarc.net, http://wwwsoc.nii.ac.jp/paj/.

304.6 THA ISSN 0857-2143
HB848
JOURNAL OF DEMOGRAPHY/WARASARN PRACHAKORNSATR. Text in Thai. 1985. s-a. USD 10 (effective 2000). **Document type:** *Academic/Scholarly.*
Indexed: ESPM, HPNRM, SSciA.
Published by: Chulalongkorn University, College of Population Studies, Phyathai Rd, Bangkok, 10330, Thailand. TEL 662-2187342. Circ: 500.

JOURNAL OF ETHNIC AND MIGRATION STUDIES. *see* ETHNIC INTERESTS

JOURNAL OF IDENTITY AND MIGRATION STUDIES. *see* POLITICAL SCIENCE

325.105 NLD ISSN 1488-3473
JV6001
➤ **JOURNAL OF INTERNATIONAL MIGRATION AND INTEGRATION.** Abbreviated title: J I M I. Variant title: Revue de l'Integration et de la Migration Internationale. Text in English, French. 2000. q. EUR 365, USD 523 combined subscription to institutions (print & online eds.) (effective 2012). bk.rev. reprint service avail. from PSC. **Document type:** *Journal, Academic/Scholarly.*
Related titles: Online - full text ed.: ISSN 1874-6365 (from IngentaConnect).
Indexed: A12, A22, A26, ABIn, AmH&L, C03, CA, CBCARef, E01, E08, ESPM, GEOBASE, HistAb, IBSS, P10, P27, P34, P42, P45, P46, P48, P51, P52, P53, P54, P56, PAIS, PQC, PSA, S02, S03, S09, SCOPUS, SSA, SSciA, SociolAb, T02.
—BLDSC (5007.676000), IE. **CCC.**
Published by: (Prairie Centre of Excellence for Research on Immigration and Integration CAN), Springer Netherlands (Subsidiary of: Springer Science+Business Media), Van Godewijckstraat 30, Dordrecht, 3311 GX, Netherlands. TEL 31-78-6576050, FAX 31-78-6576474. Ed. Peter Li.

➤ **THE JOURNAL OF MIGRATION AND REFUGEE ISSUES.** *see* LAW—Constitutional Law

➤ **JOURNAL OF ONE-NAME STUDIES.** *see* GENEALOGY AND HERALDRY

304.6 IDN ISSN 0852-713X
HB3647
➤ **JOURNAL OF POPULATION.** Text in English. 1995. s-a. IDR 40,000 domestic; USD 50 foreign (effective 2000). **Document type:** *Journal, Academic/Scholarly.* **Description:** Covers current issues on demographic topics in Indonesia, ASEAN and other Asian and Pacific countries.
Indexed: HPNRM, PopulInd, S02, S03, SSciA.
—BLDSC (5041.142900), IE, Ingenta.
Published by: (Demographic Institute), University of Indonesia, Faculty of Economics, Gedung A Lt. 2-3, Kampus UI Depok, Depok, 16424, Indonesia. TEL 62-21-787-2911, FAX 62-21-787-2909, demofeui@indo.net.id, rinld@indo.net.id. Ed. Tara H Soeprobo.

304.6 NLD ISSN 1874-7884
➤ **JOURNAL OF POPULATION AGEING.** Text in English. 2008. 4/yr. EUR 343 combined subscription to institutions (print & online eds.) (effective 2011). **Document type:** *Journal, Academic/Scholarly.* **Description:** Focuses on theoretical and empirical research and methodological development. Addresses the broad questions of ageing related to societies worldwide. Targets demographers, development researchers and professionals in sociology, geography, history, economics and health policy.
Related titles: Online - full text ed.: ISSN 1874-7876. 2008 (from IngentaConnect).
Indexed: GEOBASE, P27, P30, P45, P46, P48, P50, P53, P54, PQC, SCOPUS.
—IE. **CCC.**
Published by: Springer Netherlands (Subsidiary of: Springer Science+Business Media), Van Godewijckstraat 30, Dordrecht, 3311 GX, Netherlands. TEL 31-78-6576050, FAX 31-78-6576474, http://www.springer.com. Eds. George Leeson, Sarah Harper.

330 DEU ISSN 0933-1433
HB849.41 CODEN: JPECEW
➤ **JOURNAL OF POPULATION ECONOMICS.** Text in English. 1988. q. EUR 1,084, USD 1,294 combined subscription to institutions (print & online eds.) (effective 2012). adv. illus. back issues avail.; reprint service avail. from PSC. **Document type:** *Journal, Academic/Scholarly.* **Description:** Focuses on the relationship between economics and demographics, and addresses diverse topics in this area.
Related titles: Online - full text ed.: ISSN 1432-1475 (from IngentaConnect).
Indexed: A01, A03, A08, A12, A17, A20, A22, A26, A36, ABIn, APEL, ASCA, B01, B06, B07, B09, CA, CABA, CurCont, E01, E12, ESPM, EconLit, FamI, GH, H01, HPNRM, IBSS, JEL, LT, N02, N03, P10, P21, P27, P30, P34, P47, P48, P50, P51, P52, P53, P54, P56, PCI, PQC, PopulInd, R12, RASB, RRTA, S02, S03, S11, S13, SCOPUS, SSCI, SSciA, T02, T05, W07, W11.
—BLDSC (5041.144000), IE, Infotrieve, Ingenta. **CCC.**
Published by: (European Society for Population Economics), Springer (Subsidiary of: Springer Science+Business Media), Tiergartenstr 17, Heidelberg, 69121, Germany. TEL 49-6221-4870, FAX 49-6221-345229. Ed. Klaus F Zimmermann. **Subscr. in the Americas to:** Springer New York LLC, Journal Fulfillment, PO Box 2485, Secaucus, NJ 07096. TEL 800-777-4643, 201-348-4033, FAX 201-348-4505, journals-ny@springer.com, http://www.springer.com; **Subscr. to:** Springer Distribution Center, Kundenservice Zeitschriften, Haberstr 7, Heidelberg 69126, Germany. TEL 49-6221-3454303, FAX 49-6221-3454229, subscriptions@springer.com.

304.6 NLD ISSN 1443-2447
➤ **JOURNAL OF POPULATION RESEARCH.** Variant title: J P R. Text in English. 1984. q. EUR 313, USD 469 combined subscription to institutions (print & online eds.) (effective 2012). bk.rev. charts; abstr. 100 p./no. 1 cols./p.; back issues avail.; reprint service avail. from PSC. **Document type:** *Journal, Academic/Scholarly.* **Description:** Covers population-related issues and is not restricted to any geography.
Formerly (until 1999): Australian Population Association. Journal (0814-5725)
Related titles: Online - full text ed.: ISSN 1835-9469 (from IngentaConnect).
Indexed: A11, A12, A17, A22, A26, A36, A39, ABIn, AusPAIS, BAS, C27, C29, CA, CABA, D03, D04, E01, E08, E13, ESPM, G08, GEOBASE, GH, H05, HPNRM, I05, IBSS, P10, P21, P27, P30, P33, P39, P42, P46, P48, P51, P52, P53, P54, P56, PQC, PSA, PopulInd, R08, R12, R14, S02, S03, S09, S14, S15, S18, SCOPUS, SSciA, SociolAb, T02, T05, W11.
—BLDSC (5041.145300), IE, Ingenta. **CCC.**
Published by: (Australian Population Association AUS), Springer Netherlands (Subsidiary of: Springer Science+Business Media), Van Godewijckstraat 30, Dordrecht, 3311 GX, Netherlands. TEL 31-78-6576050, FAX 31-78-6576474. Ed. Edith Gray. Circ: 450. **Subscr. to:** Australian Population Association.

➤ **JOURNAL OF REFUGEE STUDIES.** *see* POLITICAL SCIENCE—International Relations

304.6 USA
KANSAS. DEPARTMENT OF HEALTH AND ENVIRONMENT. ANNUAL SUMMARY OF VITAL STATISTICS. Text in English. 1940. a. single copy free. charts; stat. **Document type:** *Government.* **Description:** Summarizes the births, deaths, abortions, marriages and marriage dissolutions that occur in the state. Includes graphs of items of interest and statistical analyses of the vital events.
Related titles: Microfiche ed.: (from CIS).
Indexed: SRI.
Published by: Department of Health and Environment, Center for Health and Environmental Statistics, 900 S W Jackson, Topeka, KS 66612-1290. TEL 913-296-5640, FAX 913-296-7025. Circ: 1,000 (controlled).

304.6 JPN ISSN 0387-3064
HD7227
KIKAN SHAKAI HOSHO KENKYU/QUARTERLY OF SOCIAL SECURITY RESEARCH. Text in Japanese. 1965. q. JPY 2,625 (effective 2006).
Published by: Kokuritsu Shakai Hosho Jinko Mondai Kenkyusho/ National Institute of Population and Social Security Research, Hibiya Kokusai Bldg 6th Fl, 2-2-3 Uchisaiwaicyo, Chiyoda-ku, Tokyo, Chiyoda-ku 100-0011, Japan. TEL 81-3-35952984, FAX 81-3-35914816, somuka@ipss.go.jp, http://www.ipss.go.jp/. **Subscr. to:** 1st Genesis Bldg 5F, 2-31-14 Yushima, Bunkyo-ku, Tokyo 113-0034, Japan. TEL 81-3-58051901, FAX 81-3-58051092.

304.6 JPN ISSN 1343-0742
HD7227
KOKURITSU SHAKAI HOSHO, JINKO MONDAI KENKYUJO NENPO/ NATIONAL INSTITUTE OF POPULATION AND SOCIAL SECURITY RESEARCH. Text in Japanese. 1977. a. free. stat. **Document type:** *Academic/Scholarly.*
Formerly (until 1995): Jinko Mondai Kenkyujo Nenpo/Japan. Institute of Population Problems. Annual Report (0449-0339)
Indexed: P30.
Published by: Kokuritsu Shakai Hosho Jinko Mondai Kenkyusho/ National Institute of Population and Social Security Research, Hibiya Kokusai Bldg 6th Fl, 2-2-3 Uchisaiwaicyo, Chiyoda-ku, Tokyo, Chiyoda-ku 100-0011, Japan. TEL 81-3-35952984, FAX 81-3-35914816, somuka@ipss.go.jp, http://www.ipss.go.jp/.

KONTUR (ONLINE); tidsskrift for kulturstudier. *see* SOCIOLOGY

304.6 CHL ISSN 0717-0165
HN300.O8
➤ **L I D E R.** (Labor Interdisciplinaria de Labor Regional) Variant title: Revista Labor Interdisciplinaria de Labor Regional. Text in Spanish. 1992. s-a. back issues avail. **Document type:** *Journal, Academic/Scholarly.*
Indexed: A01, A26, CA, F03, F04, I04, I05, IBSS, T02.
Published by: Universidad de los Lagos, Centro de Estudios del Desarrollo Local y Regional, Ave Fuschlocher, 1305, Osorno, Chile. TEL 56-64-333583, FAX 56-64-333374. Ed. Juan Sanchez Alvarez. Circ: 350.

➤ **L S M S WORKING PAPER.** (Living Standards Measurement Study) *see* BUSINESS AND ECONOMICS—International Development And Assistance

➤ **LEVEN IN NL.** *see* PUBLIC ADMINISTRATION—Municipal Government

➤ **LIBYA. CENSUS AND STATISTICS DEPARTMENT. GENERAL POPULATION CENSUS.** *see* POPULATION STUDIES—Abstracting, Bibliographies, Statistics

➤ **LIFE IN NEW ZEALAND.** *see* BUSINESS AND ECONOMICS—Labor And Industrial Relations

325.1 370.1 USA ISSN 2159-466X
▼ **LIUXUE YU YIMIN/STUDYING ABROAD AND IMMIGRATION.** Text in Chinese; Abstracts in English. 2010. q. adv. **Document type:** *Journal, Academic/Scholarly.*
Related titles: Online - full text ed.: ISSN 2159-4686. free.
Published by: Hansi Chubanshe/Hans Publishers, 40 E. Main St., Box 275, Newark, DE 19711. TEL 926408-329-4591, http://www.hanspub.org/.

304.6 GBR
LIVERPOOL STUDIES IN EUROPEAN POPULATION. Text in English. 1989. irreg. price varies. back issues avail. **Document type:** *Monographic series, Academic/Scholarly.*
Published by: Liverpool University Press, 4 Cambridge St, Liverpool, L69 7ZU, United Kingdom. TEL 44-151-7942233, FAX 44-151-7942235, lup@liv.ac.uk, http://www.liverpool-unipress.co.uk/.

304.6 GBR ISSN 0143-2974
HB3583
➤ **LOCAL POPULATION STUDIES.** Text in English. 1968. s-a. GBP 4.50 per issue; free to members (effective 2009). adv. bk.rev. bibl.; charts; stat.; maps. back issues avail.; reprints avail. **Document type:** *Journal, Academic/Scholarly.* **Description:** Covers information relating to population within a local or community context.
Formerly (until 1970): Local Population Studies Magazine and Newsletter (0460-2269)
Related titles: Microform ed.: (from PQC); ◆ Supplement(s): Local Population Studies. Supplement. ISSN 0143-2982.
Indexed: CA, EMBASE, ExcerpMed, GEOBASE, HistAb, MEDLINE, P30, PCI, PopulInd, R10, Reac, SCOPUS, T02.
—BLDSC (5290.044700), IE, Infotrieve, Ingenta. **CCC.**
Published by: University of Hertfordshire, College Ln, Hatfield, Herts AL10 9AB, United Kingdom. TEL 44-1707-284800, FAX 44-1707-284115, admissions@herts.ac.uk, http://www.herts.ac.uk. Ed. Nigel Goose. adv.: B&W page GBP 100. Circ: 1,500.

304.6 GBR ISSN 0143-2982
LOCAL POPULATION STUDIES. SUPPLEMENT. Text in English. 1971. irreg.
Related titles: ◆ Supplement to: Local Population Studies. ISSN 0143-2974.
Published by: University of Hertfordshire, L P S General Office, Watford Campus, Aldenham, Watford, Herts WD2 8AT, United Kingdom.

M M W R. (Morbidity and Mortality Weekly Report) *see* PUBLIC HEALTH AND SAFETY

304.6 USA ISSN 2159-4546
M P I DATA HUB. (Migration Policy Institute) Text in English. 2007. **Document type:** *Trade.*
Media: Online - full text.
—CCC.
Published by: Migration Policy Institute, 1400 16th St, NW, Ste 300, Washington, DC 20036. TEL 202-266-1940, FAX 202-266-1900, info@migrationpolicy.org, http://www.migrationpolicy.org.

304.6 PRT ISSN 1646-9488
MADEIRA EM NUMEROS. Text in Portuguese. 1996. a. **Document type:** *Report, Government.*
Published by: Direccao Regional de Estatistica da Madeira, Rua de Joao Gao 4, Funchal, Madeira 9000-071, Portugal. http://estatistica.gov-madeira.pt.

301.32 MYS ISSN 0128-1232
MALAYSIAN JOURNAL OF FAMILY STUDIES. Text in English. 1989. a. USD 10. **Description:** Provides various results of research in the area of family development in Malaysia.
Published by: National Population and Family Development Board, Jalan Raja Laut, PO Box 10416, Kuala Lumpur, 50712, Malaysia. TEL 2937555, FAX 03-2921357. Ed. Ang Eng Suan. Circ: 500.

MALTA. CENTRAL OFFICE OF STATISTICS. DEMOGRAPHIC REVIEW OF THE MALTESE ISLANDS. *see* POPULATION STUDIES—Abstracting, Bibliographies, Statistics

325 AUS ISSN 1449-6461
MANAGING THE BORDER: IMMIGRATION COMPLIANCE. Text in English. 1999. a., latest 2005. **Document type:** *Journal, Government.*
Formerly: Protecting the Border (1445-1344)
Related titles: Online - full text ed.
Published by: Australian Government. Department of Immigration and Multicultural and Indigenous Affairs, PO Box 25, Belconnen, ACT 2616, Australia. TEL 61-2-62641111, FAX 61-2-62644466.

MANITESE. *see* SOCIAL SERVICES AND WELFARE

304.6 CAN ISSN 1924-2441
MANITOBA ABORIGINAL PERSONS. Variant title: Aboriginal People in Manitoba. Text in English. 1989. irreg., latest 2006. USD 50 per issue (effective 2010). back issues avail. **Document type:** *Report, Government.* **Description:** Aims to improve the quality of life and opportunities for Manitoba's Aboriginal and northern people.
Published by: Manitoba Bureau of Statistics, Rm 344, Legislative Bldg, Winnipeg, MB R3C 0V8, Canada. TEL 204-945-3744, 866-626-4862, mgi@gov.mb.ca.

304.6 DEU ISSN 0178-918X
MATERIALIEN ZUR BEVOELKERUNGSWISSENSCHAFT. Text in German. 1977. irreg., latest vol.129, 2010. **Document type:** *Monographic series, Academic/Scholarly.*
Indexed: P30.
Published by: Bundesinstitut fuer Bevoelkerungsforschung, Friedrich-Ebert-Allee 4, Wiesbaden, 65185, Germany. TEL 49-611-752235, FAX 49-611-753960, bib@destatis.de, http://www.bib-demographie.de.

304.6 AUS ISSN 1449-8863
MATERNAL DEATH SERIES. Text in English. 1994. biennial, latest vol.3, 2003-2005. AUD 30 per issue (effective 2008). back issues avail. **Document type:** *Monographic series, Government.* **Description:** Presents an epidemiological overview of maternal deaths in Australia.
Related titles: Online - full text ed.: free (effective 2008).
Indexed: A36, GH.
Published by: Australian Institute of Health and Welfare, National Perinatal Statistics Unit, Level 2, McNevin Dickson Bldg, Gate 6, Avoca St, Randwick Hospitals Campus, Randwick, NSW 2031, Australia. TEL 61-2-93821014, FAX 61-2-93821025, npsu@med.unsw.edu.au. Ed. James King.

304.6 USA ISSN 0889-8480
HB849.51 CODEN: MPSTEG
➤ **MATHEMATICAL POPULATION STUDIES;** an international journal of mathematical demography. Text in English. 1988. q. GBP 924 combined subscription in United Kingdom to institutions (print & online eds.); EUR 942, USD 1,181 combined subscription to institutions (print & online eds.) (effective 2012). adv. reprint service avail. from PSC. **Document type:** *Journal, Academic/Scholarly.* **Description:** Publishes research papers in the mathematical and statistical study of human populations.
Related titles: Microform ed.; Online - full text ed.: ISSN 1547-724X. GBP 831 in United Kingdom to institutions; EUR 848, USD 1,063 to institutions (effective 2012) (from IngentaConnect).
Indexed: A01, A03, A08, A20, A22, CA, CCMJ, CIS, CurCont, E01, ESPM, GEOBASE, MSN, MathR, P30, P48, P50, P52, P54, PQC, PopulInd, S01, SCI, SCOPUS, SSCI, SSciA, ST&MA, T02, W07, Z02.
—IE, Infotrieve, Ingenta. **CCC.**
Published by: Taylor & Francis Inc. (Subsidiary of: Taylor & Francis Group), 325 Chestnut St, Ste 800, Philadelphia, PA 19106. TEL 215-625-2940, 800-354-1420, orders@taylorandfrancis.com, http://www.taylorandfrancis.com. Ed. Noel Bonneuil. Adv. contact Linda Hann TEL 44-1344-779945.

➤ **THE MATURE TRAVELER.** *see* TRAVEL AND TOURISM

➤ **MIGRACIJSKE I ETNICKE TEME/MIGRATION AND ETHNIC THEMES.** *see* SOCIOLOGY

➤ **MIGRACIONES.** *see* SOCIAL SCIENCES: COMPREHENSIVE WORKS

304.8 ESP ISSN 1577-3256
MIGRACIONES Y EXILIOS. Text in Spanish. 2000. a. free membership (effective 2008). back issues avail. **Document type:** *Monographic series, Academic/Scholarly.*
Indexed: MLA-IB.
Published by: Asociacion para el Estudio de los Exilios y Migraciones Ibericos Contemporaneos, C. Senda del Rey, 7, Madrid, 28040, Spain. TEL 34-91-3986736, FAX 34-91-3986718, aemic@iponet.es, http://www.aemic.org/.

MIGRALEX; Zeitschrift fuer Fremden- und Minderheitenrecht. *see* LAW

304.8 ITA ISSN 0391-5492
MIGRANTI-PRESS; settimanale di informazione sulla mobilita umana. Text in Italian. 1979. w. **Document type:** *Newspaper, Consumer.*
Related titles: ◆ Supplement to: Servizio Migranti. ISSN 0037-2803.
Published by: Fondazione Migrantes, Via Aurelia 468, Rome, RM 00165, Italy. TEL 39-06-66398452, FAX 39-06-66398492, http://www.chiesacattolica.it/cci_new/UfficiCEI/.

325 CHE ISSN 1813-2839
JV6008
MIGRATION. Text in English. 1979. q. free (effective 2006). charts; illus.; maps; stat. 20 p./no. 3 cols./p.; back issues avail.; reprints avail. **Document type:** *Newsletter, Academic/Scholarly.* **Description:** Covers current activities of the organization on refugee and migration movements and programs.
Former titles (until 2005): I O M News (1027-7617); (until 1993): I O M Monthly Dispatch; I C M Monthly Dispatch; Intergovernmental Committee for European Migration. Monthly Dispatch
Related titles: Microfiche ed.: (from CIS); Spanish ed.: Migraciones. ISSN 1813-2847; French ed.: Migrations. ISSN 1813-2855.
Indexed: IIS, RefugAb.
Published by: International Organization for Migration/Organizacion Internacional para las Migraciones, 17 Rte des Morillons, Geneva 19, 1211, Switzerland. TEL 41-22-7179111, FAX 41-22-7986150, publications@iom.int, http://www.iom.int. Ed. Jean Philippe Chauzy. Circ: (controlled).

325 NLD ISSN 1873-9113
MIGRATION AND MIGRATION POLICIES IN THE NETHERLANDS. Text in English. 2005. a. price varies.
Published by: Rotterdams Instituut voor Sociaalwetenschappelijk BeleidsOnderzoek/Rotterdam Institute of Social Policy Research, Erasmus Universiteit Rotterdam, Postbus 1738, Rotterdam, 3000 DR, Netherlands. TEL 31-10-4082124, FAX 31-10-4081141, info@risbo.eur.nl, http://www.risbo.nl.

325 USA ISSN 1946-4037
MIGRATION INFORMATION SOURCE; fresh thought. authoritative data. global reach. Text in English. 2002. m. free (effective 2009). adv. back issues avail. **Document type:** *Journal, Academic/Scholarly.* **Description:** Provides a global analysis of international migration and refugee trends.
Media: Online - full content.
—CCC.
Published by: Migration Policy Institute, 1400 16th St, NW, Ste 300, Washington, DC 20036. TEL 202-266-1940, FAX 202-266-1900, info@migrationpolicy.org, http://www.migrationpolicy.org. Ed. Kirin Kalia TEL 202-266-1913. Adv. contact April Siruno TEL 202-266-1908.

325 GBR ISSN 1741-8984
MIGRATION LETTERS; international scholarly letter-type journal of migration studies. Text in English. 2004. s-a. GBP 70 combined subscription domestic to individuals (print & online eds.); GBP 72.50 combined subscription foreign to individuals (print & online eds.); GBP 160 combined subscription domestic to institutions (print & online eds.); GBP 162.50 combined subscription foreign to institutions (print & online eds.) (effective 2009). back issues avail. **Document type:** *Journal, Academic/Scholarly.* **Description:** Topics range from internal migration to transnational mobility and from voluntary to forced migration.
Related titles: Online - full text ed.: ISSN 1741-8992. free (effective 2010).
Indexed: A39, C27, C29, D03, D04, E13, ESPM, IBSS, P48, P54, PQC, R14, S14, S15, S18, SSciA.
—IE.
Address: 172 Strathmore Ave, Luton, LU1 3QW, United Kingdom. TEL 44-787-5211052. Eds. Elli Heikkila, Ibrahim Sirkeci, Jeffrey H Cohen.

325 USA ISSN 1081-9908
CODEN: RMIXEC
MIGRATION NEWS. Text in English. 1994. q. USD 30 domestic; USD 50 foreign (effective 2010). bk.rev. illus. back issues avail.; reprints avail. **Document type:** *Newsletter.* **Description:** Provides a monthly summary of recent immigration developments.
Related titles: Online - full text ed.: Migration Dialogue. ISSN 1081-9916. free (effective 2010).
Published by: University of California, Davis, Department of Agricultural Economics, One Shields Ave, Davis, CA 95616.

325 DNK ISSN 1902-7095
MIGRATION & INTEGRATION. Text in Danish. 2007. irreg. price varies. **Document type:** *Monographic series, Academic/Scholarly.*
Published by: Museum Tusculanum Press, c/o University of Copenhagen, Njalsgade 126, Copenhagen S, 2300, Denmark. TEL 45-35-329109, FAX 45-35-329113, info@mtp.dk, http://www.mtp.dk. Eds. Karen Fog Olwig, Karsten Paerregaard. **Dist. in France by:** Editions Picard, Editions Picard, Paris 75006, France; **Dist. in UK by:** Gazelle Book Services Ltd., White Cross Mills, Hightown, Lancaster LA1 4UU, United Kingdom. TEL 44-1524-68765, FAX 44-1524-63232, sales@gazellebooks.co.uk, http://www.gazellebookservices.co.uk/; **Dist. in US & Canada:** International Specialized Book Services Inc., 920 NE 58th Ave Ste 300, Portland, OR 97213. TEL 503-287-3093, 800-944-6190, FAX 503-280-8832, orders@isbs.com, http://www.isbs.com/.

325 CHE
MIGRATION TRENDS IN CENTRAL AND EASTERN EUROPE. Text in English. 1999. a. USD 35 per vol. (effective 2003). charts; illus.; maps; stat. 200 p./no.; back issues avail.; reprints avail. **Document type:** *Monographic series, Academic/Scholarly.* **Description:** Provides detailed accounts of recent migration trends and policy developments in fifteen countries of Central and Eastern Europe.
Formerly (until 2002): Migration in Central and Eastern Europe (1561-3429)
Published by: (International Centre for Migration Policy Development AUT), International Organization for Migration/Organizacion Internacional para las Migraciones, 17 Rte des Morillons, Geneva 19, 1211, Switzerland. TEL 41-22-7179111, FAX 41-22-7986150, publications@iom.int, http://www.iom.int. **Subscr. to:** United Nations Publications, Sales Office and Bookshop, Bureau E4, Geneva 10 1211, Switzerland. TEL 41-22-917-2614, FAX 41-22-917-0027, unpubli@unog.ch, http://www.unog.ch.

304.6 FRA ISSN 1370-1673
MIGRATIONS EUROPE. Text in French. 1991. m. **Document type:** *Journal, Trade.*
Formerly (until 1993): Informations Europeennes (1370-1665)
Published by: Centre d'Information et d'Etudes sur les Migrations Internationales, 46 rue de Montreuil, Paris, 75011, France. TEL 33-1-43724934, FAX 33-1-43720642, ciemiparis@aol.com, http://members.aol.com/ciemiparis/. Circ: 800.

304.6 FRA ISSN 0995-7367
MIGRATIONS SOCIETE. Text in French. 1989. bi-m. **Description:** Documents international migrations as a factor in the transformation and recomposition of the social, cultural, and religious landscapes.
Formed by the merger of (1981-1989): Presse et Immigres en France (0153-0305); (1981-1989): Dossier Migrations (0249-0145)
Indexed: A22, IBSS.
—BLDSC (5761.541300), IE, Ingenta.
Published by: Centre d'Information et d'Etudes sur les Migrations Internationales, 46 rue de Montreuil, Paris, 75011, France. TEL 33-1-43720140, FAX 33-1-43720642, ciemiparis@aol.com, http://www.ciemi.org/connaitrelesmigrations.htm. Ed. Philippe Farine.

325.1 SWE ISSN 1650-2515
MIGRATIONSVERKETS FOERFATTNINGSSAMLING. Text in Swedish. 1991. irreg. back issues avail. **Document type:** *Monographic series.*
Formerly (until 2000): Statens Invandrarverks Foerfattningssamling (1102-3902)
Related titles: Online - full text ed.
Published by: Migrationsverket/Swedish Immigration Board, Tegelaengsgatan 19 A, Norrkoeping, 60170, Sweden. TEL 46-11-156000, FAX 46-11-108155, migrationsverket@migrationsverket.se.

304.6 RUS
MIGRATSIYA. Text in Russian. q. USD 85 in United States.
Indexed: RASB.
Published by: Izdatel'stvo Gumanitarii, Leninskii pr-t 6, k 301, Moscow, 117933, Russian Federation. TEL 7-095-2369707, FAX 7-095-2368402. Ed. R A Vardanian. **Dist. by:** East View Information Services, 10601 Wayzata Blvd, Minneapolis, MN 55305. TEL 952-252-1201, 800-477-1005, FAX 952-252-1202, info@eastview.com, http://www.eastview.com.

304.8 ARG ISSN 1852-2173
▼ ➤ **MIRADAS EN MOVIMIENTO;** revista virtual sobre migraciones. Text in Spanish; Summaries in English, French, Greek, Italian, Portuguese, Spanish. 2009. s-a. free. bk.rev. abstr.; bibl.; charts; maps; stat. Index. back issues avail. **Document type:** *Journal, Academic/Scholarly.* **Description:** Contains interdisciplinary articles on the cause and effect of migration and public policy.
Media: Online - full text.
Published by: Espacios de Estudios Migratorios, Juan Carlos Gomez 145, Buenos Aires, Argentina. TEL 54-9-43040243, eem@espaciodeestudiosmigratorios.org. Ed. Yahaira Campos Morales.

304.6 USA ISSN 0734-032X
MISSOURI POPULATION ESTIMATES; by county, by age, by sex. Text in English. a. USD 15. **Document type:** *Government.*
Published by: Department of Health, Center for Health Information Management & Epidemiology, PO Box 570, Jefferson City, MO 65102. TEL 314-751-6272. Ed. Garland Land.

325 338.4 GBR ISSN 1745-0101
➤ **MOBILITIES.** Text in English. 2006 (Mar.). 3/yr. GBP 364 combined subscription in United Kingdom to institutions (print & online eds.); EUR 479, USD 603 combined subscription to institutions (print & online eds.) (effective 2012). adv. back issues avail.; reprint service avail. from PSC. **Document type:** *Journal, Academic/Scholarly.* **Description:** Covers both the large-scale movement of peoples, objects, capital and information across the world, as well as the local processes of daily transportation and travel.
Related titles: Online - full text ed.: ISSN 1745-011X. GBP 328 in United Kingdom to institutions; EUR 432, USD 543 to institutions (effective 2012).
Indexed: A01, A22, CA, CurCont, E01, GEOBASE, HRIS, MLA-IB, P50, SCOPUS, SSCI, SociolAb, T02, W07.
—IE, Ingenta. **CCC.**
Published by: Routledge (Subsidiary of: Taylor & Francis Group), 4 Park Sq, Milton Park, Abingdon, Oxon OX14 4RN, United Kingdom. TEL 44-20-70176000, FAX 44-20-70176336, subscriptions@tandf.co.uk, http://www.routledge.com. Eds. John Urry TEL 44-1524-594179, Kevin Hannam TEL 44-191-5153703, Dr. Mimi Sheller TEL 610-957-6143. **Subscr. to:** Taylor & Francis Ltd., Journals Customer Service, Sheepen Pl, Colchester, Essex CO3 3LP, United Kingdom. TEL 44-20-70175544, FAX 44-20-70175198.

P

301.5 GBR ISSN 1364-4947
MONITOR, POPULATION AND HEALTH. ABORTION. Text in English. 1975. m. **Document type:** *Journal, Trade.*
Formerly (until 1998): O P C S Monitor. Abortion (0953-3362)
—CCC.
Published by: Office for National Statistics, Rm 1.101, Government Bldgs, Cardiff Rd, Newport, S Wales NP10 8XG, United Kingdom. TEL 44-845-6013034, FAX 44-1633-652747, info@statistics.gsi.gov.uk, http://www.statistics.gov.uk/default.asp.

MONOGRAFIEEN VREEMDELING EN RECHT. *see* LAW—International Law

MOSELLA. *see* GEOGRAPHY

MOUVEMENT NATUREL DE LA POPULATION DE LA GRECE. *see* POPULATION STUDIES—Abstracting, Bibliographies, Statistics

325 ESP ISSN 2013-8881
MOVIMENTS MIGRATORIS. DADES COMARCALS I MUNICIPALS. Text in Catalan. 1992. a. **Document type:** *Report, Government.*
Related titles: Online - full text ed.: ISSN 2013-4274. 2004.
Published by: Generalitat de Catalunya, Institut d'Estadistica de Catalunya, Via Laietana, 58, Barcelona, 08003, Spain. TEL 34-934-120088, FAX 34-934-123145, questiio@iesc.es, http://www.idescat.es/publications/questiio/questiio.shtm.

MYBODY. *see* BIRTH CONTROL

304.6 AUS
N S W STATE AND REGIONAL INDICATORS. (New South Wales) Text in English. 2005. a. free (effective 2009). stat. back issues avail. **Document type:** *Catalog, Government.* **Description:** Contains statistics on population, education and training, health, housing, crime and justice, labour force, income and expenditure, service provision, community involvement and the environment. Also includes data on the various industries supplying goods and services to the Australian economy, such as agriculture, manufacturing, mining, energy, construction, transport, communication and information technology, retail and wholesale trade, tourism, personal and business services.
Formerly (until Nov.2008): New South Wales in Focus (Print) (1832-2352); Which was formed by the merger of (1981-2004): New South Wales Year Book (0810-9338); Which was formerly (until 1979): Official Year-Book of New South Wales (0085-4441); (1886-1901): Wealth and Progress of New South Wales (0810-9354); (1986-2004): Regional Statistics of New South Wales (0818-2272); Which was formerly (1956-1984): New South Wales. Handbook of Local Statistics (0159-933X)
Media: Online - full text.
Indexed: GeoRef.
Published by: Australian Bureau of Statistics, New South Wales Office, GPO Box 796, Sydney, NSW 2001, Australia. TEL 61-2-92684909, 300-135-070.

325.93 NZL ISSN 1177-2328
N Z A M I NEWS. Text in English. 2005. bi-m. free to members. **Document type:** *Newsletter.*
Published by: New Zealand Association for Migration & Investment, Inc., PO Box 106 560, Auckland City, New Zealand. TEL 64-9-3798050, FAX 64-9-3798055, administrator@nzami.co.nz, http://www.nzami.org.nz/.

304.6 CHN ISSN 1007-032X
NANJING RENKOU GUANLI GANBU XUEYUAN XUEBAO/NANJING COLLEGE FOR POPULATION PROGRAMME MANAGEMENT. JOURNAL. Text in Chinese. 1985. q. CNY 4 newsstand/cover (effective 2006). **Document type:** *Journal, Academic/Scholarly.*
Related titles: Online - full text ed.
Published by: Nanjing Renkou Guanli Ganbu Xueyuan, 10, Suojincun, Nanjing, 210042, China. TEL 86-25-85483043, FAX 86-25-85483142.

304.6 HRV ISSN 1330-7223
NAROD. Text in Croatian. 1995. fortn. **Document type:** *Magazine, Trade.*
Published by: Hrvatski Populacijski Pokret, Ul. Grada Vukovara 226, Zagreb, 10000, Croatia. TEL 385-1-6117144, FAX 385-1-6158687. Ed. Anto Bakovic.

304.6 BGR ISSN 0205-0617
HB3627
NASELENIE/POPULATION. Text in Bulgarian; Summaries in English. 1983. 2/yr. BGL 1.62 per issue; USD 65 foreign (effective 2002). reprint service avail. from IRC. **Document type:** *Journal.*
Indexed: BSLEcon, P30, PopulInd, RASB.
Published by: (Bulgarska Akademiya na Naukite, Institute of Demography), Sofiiski Universitet Sv. Kliment Ohridski, Universitetsko Izdatelstvo/Sofia University St. Kliment Ohridski University Press, Akad G Bonchev 6, Sofia, 1113, Bulgaria. Circ: 800. **Dist. by:** Hemus, 6 Rouski Blvd., Sofia 1000, Bulgaria; **Dist. by:** Sofia Books, ul Silivria 16, Sofia 1404, Bulgaria. TEL 359-2-9586257, info@sofiabooks-bg.com, http://www.sofiabooks-bg.com.

NASELENIE I DEMOGRAFSKI PROTSESI. *see* STATISTICS

NATIONAL HUMAN DEVELOPMENT REPORTS. *see* SOCIAL SCIENCES: COMPREHENSIVE WORKS

NATIONAL INSTITUTE OF CHILD HEALTH AND HUMAN DEVELOPMENT. CENTER FOR POPULATION RESEARCH. PROGRESS REPORT. *see* MEDICAL SCIENCES

304.6 NLD ISSN 0922-7210
NEDERLANDS INTERDISCIPLINAIR DEMOGRAFISCH INSTITUUT. RAPPORT. Key Title: NiDi Rapport. Text in Dutch. 1988. irreg., latest vol.80, 2009. price varies. back issues avail. **Document type:** *Monographic series.*
Supersedes (1973-1988): Nederlands Interuniversitair Demografisch Instituut. Working Papers (0920-9719); (1974-1988): Nederlands Interdisciplinair Demografisch Instituut. Intern Rapport (0925-6954)
Published by: Nederlands Interdisciplinair Demografisch Instituut/ Netherlands Interdisciplinary Demographic Institute, Lange Houtstraat 19, The Hague, 2511 CV, Netherlands. TEL 31-70-3565200, FAX 31-70-3647187, info@nidi.nl, http://www.nidi.nl.

325 CHE
NEW CHALLENGES FOR MIGRATION POLICY IN CENTRAL & EASTERN EUROPE. Text in English. 1997. irreg., latest vol.3, 2002. price varies. charts; illus.; maps; stat. back issues avail.; reprints avail. **Document type:** *Monographic series, Academic/Scholarly.* **Description:** Presents the latest statistics on migration flows into, out of and within the CIS countries.
Formerly (until 2002): Migration in the C I S (1561-5499)
Published by: International Organization for Migration/Organizacion Internacional para las Migraciones, 17 Rte des Morillons, Geneva 19, 1211, Switzerland. TEL 41-22-7179111, FAX 41-22-7986150, publications@iom.int, http://www.iom.int. **Subscr. to:** United Nations Publications, Sales Office and Bookshop, Bureau E4, Geneva 10 1211, Switzerland. TEL 41-22-917-2614, FAX 41-22-917-0027, unpubli@unog.ch, http://www.unog.ch.

NEW ZEALAND HEALTH INFORMATION SERVICE. MORTALITY AND DEMOGRAPHIC DATA. *see* POPULATION STUDIES—Abstracting, Bibliographies, Statistics

304.6 NZL ISSN 0111-199X
HB3692.5.A3
➤ **NEW ZEALAND POPULATION REVIEW.** Text in English. 1974. s-a. free to members (effective 2010). back issues avail. **Document type:** *Journal, Academic/Scholarly.* **Description:** Provides a rich resource of historical perspectives on New Zealand demography.
Former titles (until 1980): New Zealand Population Newsletter (0111-5227); (until 1976): Population
Related titles: Online - full text ed.: ISSN 1179-8149.
Indexed: A11, A26, CA, E08, ESPM, G08, I05, INZP, P30, PopulInd, S02, S03, S09, SCOPUS, SSciA, T02.
—BLDSC (6096.814000).
Published by: Population Association of New Zealand (P A N Z), PO Box 225, Wellington, New Zealand. Alison.reid@arc.govt.nz. Eds. Arvind Zodgekar, Richard Bedford, Ward Friesen.

304.6 NZL ISSN 1179-0873
NEW ZEALAND. STATISTICS NEW ZEALAND. BIRTHS AND DEATHS. Text in English. 1987. q. stat. **Document type:** *Government.* **Description:** Contains statistics on the number of births and deaths registered in New Zealand during the March 2000 year/quarter, along with selected fertility and mortality indices.
Formerly (until Sep.1999): New Zealand. Statistics New Zealand. Vital Statistics
Related titles: Online - full text ed.: ISSN 1178-0436.
Published by: Statistics New Zealand/Te Tari Tatau, Statistics House, The Blvd, Harbour Quays, PO Box 2922, Wellington, 6140, New Zealand. TEL 64-4-9314600, FAX 64-4-9314610, info@stats.govt.nz.

304.6 NZL
NEW ZEALAND. STATISTICS NEW ZEALAND. CENSUS REPORTS. ELECTORAL PROFILE. Text in English. a., latest 2001. NZD 35 (effective 2008). stat. **Document type:** *Government.* **Description:** Provides a report encompassing demographic and economic characteristics of electoral districts.
Published by: Statistics New Zealand/Te Tari Tatau, Statistics House, The Blvd, Harbour Quays, PO Box 2922, Wellington, 6140, New Zealand. TEL 64-4-9314600, FAX 64-4-9314610, info@stats.govt.nz.

304.6 310 NZL ISSN 1179-0954
NEW ZEALAND. STATISTICS NEW ZEALAND. INTERNATIONAL TRAVEL AND MIGRATION. Text in English. m. stat. **Document type:** *Government.*
Formerly (until Jun.2008): New Zealand. Statistics New Zealand. External Migration (1178-0274)
Related titles: Online - full text ed.: ISSN 1179-0407.
Published by: Statistics New Zealand/Te Tari Tatau, Statistics House, The Blvd, Harbour Quays, PO Box 2922, Wellington, 6140, New Zealand. TEL 64-4-9314600, FAX 64-4-9314610, info@stats.govt.nz.

304.6 305.895 NZL
NEW ZEALAND. STATISTICS NEW ZEALAND. NATIONAL ASIAN POPULATION PROJECTIONS. Text in English. 1996. **Document type:** *Government.*
Formerly (until 199?): New Zealand. Statistics New Zealand. Asian Population Projections
Published by: Statistics New Zealand/Te Tari Tatau, Statistics House, The Blvd, Harbour Quays, PO Box 2922, Wellington, 6140, New Zealand. TEL 64-4-9314600, FAX 64-4-9314610, info@stats.govt.nz.

304.6 NZL ISSN 1179-1012
NEW ZEALAND. STATISTICS NEW ZEALAND. NATIONAL POPULATION ESTIMATES. Text in English. 1987. q. stat. **Document type:** *Government.* **Description:** Contains estimates of New Zealand's resident population along with changes in the population age structure and growth rate.
Formerly (until Sep.2001): New Zealand. Statistics New Zealand. Population Estimates
Related titles: Online - full text ed.: ISSN 1178-0576.
Published by: Statistics New Zealand/Te Tari Tatau, Statistics House, The Blvd, Harbour Quays, PO Box 2922, Wellington, 6140, New Zealand. TEL 64-4-9314600, FAX 64-4-9314610, info@stats.govt.nz.

304.6 NZL ISSN 1179-1233
NEW ZEALAND. STATISTICS NEW ZEALAND. SUB-NATIONAL POPULATION ESTIMATES. Text in English. a. stat. **Document type:** *Government.* **Description:** Contains resident population estimates for the 74 territorial authority areas (i.e. cities and districts), regions and urban areas in New Zealand.
Related titles: Online - full text ed.: ISSN 1178-0673.
Published by: Statistics New Zealand/Te Tari Tatau, Statistics House, The Blvd, Harbour Quays, PO Box 2922, Wellington, 6140, New Zealand. TEL 64-4-9314600, FAX 64-4-9314610, info@stats.govt.nz.

304.6 NIC
NICARAGUA. INSTITUTO NACIONAL DE ESTADISTICAS Y CENSOS. BOLETIN DEMOGRAFICO. Text in Spanish. 1978 (no.2). irreg. NIC 15, USD 4 per issue. stat. **Document type:** *Government.*
Formerly: Nicaragua. Oficina Ejecutiva de Encuestas y Censos. Boletin Demografico
Published by: Instituto Nacional de Estadisticas y Censos, Apartado Postal 4031, Managua, Nicaragua.

304.63 USA
NORTH CAROLINA REPORTED PREGNANCIES. Text in English. a. free. **Document type:** *Government.*
Supersedes: North Carolina Reported Abortions (0098-3217)
Published by: U.S. Department of Health and Human Services, State Center for Health Statistics, PO Box 29538, Raleigh, NC 27626-0538. TEL 919-733-4728.

325.1 NOR ISSN 0803-8554
NORWAY. UTLENDINGSDIREKTORATET. AARSMELDING. Variant title: Norway. Utlendingsdirektoratet. Aarsrapport. Text in Norwegian Bokmal. 1988. a. stat. back issues avail. **Document type:** *Report, Government.*
Incorporates in part (2003-2008): Norway. Utlendingsdirektoratet. Tall og Fakta (1504-0127)
Related titles: Online - full text ed.; Norwegian Nynorsk ed.
Published by: Utlendingsdirektoratet/Norwegian Directorate of Immigration, Hausmannsgate 21, Postboks 8108, Oslo, 0032, Norway. TEL 47-23-351500, FAX 47-23-351501, udi@udi.no. Circ: 5,000.

304.6 CAN ISSN 0837-2462
HA747.N9
NOVA SCOTIA. DEPARTMENT OF HEALTH. VITAL STATISTICS. ANNUAL REPORT. Variant title: Vital Statistics. Text in English. 1917. a.
Former titles (until 1982): Province of Nova Scotia. Vital Statistics (0836-9496); (until 1978): Nova Scotia. Annual Report of the Registrar General Containing the Vital Statistics of the Province (0469-0249)
Published by: Nova Scotia. Vital Statistics, PO Box 157, Halifax, NS B3J 2M9, Canada. TEL 902-424-4381, FAX 902-424-0678, vstat@gov.ns.ca.

LA NUEVA LEY DE INMIGRACION. *see* LAW

325.2 ITA
NUOVA PUGLIA EMIGRAZIONE; bimestrale dei pugliesi nel mondo. Text in Italian. 1985. bi-m. **Document type:** *Bulletin, Consumer.*
Formerly (until 1991): Puglia Emigrazione (1120-3412)
Published by: (Associazioni Regionali di Rappresentanza e Tutela degli emigranti e Loro Famiglie), Regione Puglia, Settore Politiche Migratorie, Via Lembo 38/B, Bari, 70124, Italy. TEL 39-080-5402388, FAX 39-080-5402033, pugliaemigrazione@regionepuglia.it. Ed. Angelo Di Summa.

325 DNK ISSN 1902-8385
NY I DANMARK. Text in Danish. 2003. q. free. **Document type:** *Newsletter, Government.*
Formerly (until 2007): I Job Nu (1603-6093)
Related titles: Online - full text ed.: ISSN 1902-9764. 2003.
Published by: Ministeriet for Flygtninge, Indvandrere og Integration/ Ministry of Refugee, Immigration, and Integration, Holbergsgade 6, Copenhagen K, 1057, Denmark. TEL 45-33-923380, FAX 45-33-111239, inm@inm.dk, http://www.inm.dk. Ed. Henrik Thomassen. Circ: 6,000.

304.64 GBR ISSN 0953-4415
O P C S MONITOR. DH3: SUDDEN INFANT DEATH SYNDROME. Text in English. 1980. irreg. **Document type:** *Government.*
—CCC.
Published by: Office of Population Censuses and Surveys, 1 Myddelton St, London, EC1R 1UW, United Kingdom.

L'OBSERVATOIRE DE L'INTEGRATION. *see* SOCIAL SCIENCES: COMPREHENSIVE WORKS

325.1 ESP
OFRIM SUPLEMENTOS. Text in Spanish. irreg. **Document type:** *Bulletin, Consumer.*
Published by: Colegio Oficial de Arquitectos de Galicia, Plaza de Quintana, s-n, Santiago de Compostela, Coruna 15704, Spain. TEL 34-981-580100, FAX 34-981-561655, http://www.coag.es/. Ed. Jose Manuel Rey Pichel.

304.6 ITA ISSN 1972-4527
OLTREOCEANO; rivista sulle migrazioni. Text in Multiple languages. 2007. a. **Document type:** *Journal, Academic/Scholarly.*
Related titles: Online - full text ed.: ISSN 1973-9370.
Published by: (Universita degli Studi di Udine), Forum Editrice Universitaria Udinese, Via Larga 38, Udine, UD 33100, Italy. TEL 39-0432-26001, FAX 39-0432-296756, forum@forumeditrice.it, http://www.forumeditrice.it.

304.6 NLD ISSN 1874-9186
HB848
➤ **THE OPEN DEMOGRAPHY JOURNAL.** Text in English. 2008. irreg. free (effective 2009). **Document type:** *Journal, Academic/Scholarly.* **Description:** Covers all areas of population studies including research on migration and family planning.
Media: Online - full text.
Indexed: ESPM, H05, SSciA, T02.
Published by: Bentham Open (Subsidiary of: Bentham Science Publishers Ltd.), PO Box 294, Bussum, AG 1400, Netherlands. TEL 31-35-6923800, FAX 31-35-6980150, subscriptions@bentham.org.

➤ **LES ORIENTATIONS DE LA POLITIQUE DE L'IMMIGRATION.** *see* PUBLIC ADMINISTRATION

304.6 USA ISSN 0300-6816
HB848
P A A AFFAIRS. Text in English. 1968. q. USD 5 (effective 1999). **Document type:** *Newsletter.* **Description:** General items of interest to members.
Indexed: CLFP.
—CCC.
Published by: Population Association of America, 8630 Fenton St, Ste 722, Silver Spring, MD 20910. TEL 301-565-6710, FAX 301-565-7850, http://www.popassoc.org/. Circ: 3,000.

301.32 MYS ISSN 0127-9068
P O F A M. Text in English. 1969. q. free. abstr.; stat. **Document type:** *Government.* **Description:** Discusses family development, population and family planning.
Formerly (until 1986): Malaysia. National Population and Family Development Board. Bulletin Keluarga (0126-8104)
Published by: National Population and Family Development Board, Jalan Raja Laut, PO Box 10416, Kuala Lumpur, 50712, Malaysia. TEL 2937555, TELEX POPMAL MA 31911. Ed. Raj Abdul Karim.

304.6 USA ISSN 1522-8304
HA201.12
P R B REPORTS ON AMERICA. (Population Reference Bureau) Text in English. 1998. irreg. free (effective 2005).
Published by: Population Reference Bureau, Inc., 1875 Connecticut Ave, NW, Ste 520, Washington, DC 20009-5728. TEL 202-483-1100, 800-877-9881, FAX 202-328-3937, popref@prb.org. R&P Ellen Carnevale.

325 USA ISSN 1072-883X
P R I REVIEW. Text in English. 1991. bi-m. USD 30 donation. adv. back issues avail. **Document type:** *Newsletter.* **Description:** Examines the consequences of world population growth and reports findings.
—BLDSC (6552.484000).

Published by: Population Research Institute, PO Box 1559, Front Royal, VA 22630. TEL 540-622-5240, FAX 540-622-2728, http://www.pop.org. Ed. David Morrison. R&P Tracy Trunk. Adv. contact Vernon Kirby.

304.6 FJI ISSN 1022-4289
HB849.3
PACIFIC P O P I N DIRECTORY; experts, research and institutions. Text in English. 1993. irreg. FJD 10 domestic; FJD 20 foreign (effective 2000). back issues avail. **Document type:** *Directory.*
Published by: Pacific Population Information Network, University of the South Pacific Library, Suva, Fiji. TEL 679-212363, FAX 679-300830, fong_e@usp.ac.fj, http://www.usp.ac.fj/~library. Ed. Elizabeth Reade Fong. R&Ps Elizabeth Reade Fong, Jayshree Mamtora.

PAESI E POPOLI DEL MEDITERRANEO. *see* SOCIOLOGY

304.6 MEX ISSN 1405-7425
HB3532.M39
PAPELES DE POBLACION. Text in Spanish. 1996. q. MXN 400 domestic to institutions; USD 60 to institutions U.S. & Central Am.; USD 70 to institutions Europe and South Am. (effective 2011). **Document type:** *Journal, Academic/Scholarly.*
Related titles: Online - full text ed.: free (effective 2011).
Indexed: C01, CA, H21, P08, P42, PAIS, PSA, S02, S03, SCOPUS, SSCI, SociolAb, T02, W07.
Published by: Universidad Autonoma del Estado de Mexico, Centro de Investigacion y Estudios Avanzados de la Poblacion, Torre Academica. 1er Piso, Cerro de Toatepec, Ciudad Universitaria, Toluca, 50100, Mexico. cieap@uaemex.mx. Ed. Juan Gabino Gonzales Becerril.

PERSPECTIVE GRAND MONTREAL; bulletin d'analyse metropolitaine. *see* PUBLIC ADMINISTRATION—Municipal Government

304.6 FRA ISSN 1993-0232
PERSPECTIVES DES MIGRATIONS INTERNATIONALES. Text in French. 1992. a., latest 2008. EUR 75, GBP 54, USD 116, JPY 10,400 combined subscription print & online eds. (effective 2009). **Document type:** *Directory, Trade.*
Formerly (until 2006): Tendences des Migrations Internationales (1024-7777)
Related titles: Online - full content ed.: EUR 52, GBP 37, USD 81, JPY 7,200 (effective 2009); English ed.: International Migration Outlook. ISSN 1995-3968. 1997.
Published by: Organisation for Economic Cooperation and Development (O E C D)/Organisation de Cooperation et de Developpement Economiques (O C D E), 2 Rue Andre Pascal, Paris, 75775 Cedex 16, France. TEL 33-1-45248200, FAX 33-1-45248500, http://www.oecd.org.

325 NOR ISSN 1891-2230
PERSPEKTIV. Text in Norwegian. 1996. q. NOK 299 (effective 2011). adv. **Document type:** *Magazine, Consumer.*
Former titles (until 2009): Paa Flukt (1504-5463); (until 2005): Paa Flukt Aktuelt (1504-1166); (until 2004): Paa Flukt. Magasin (1501-2255); (until 1998): Paa Flukt (0809-0882)
Related titles: Online - full text ed.: ISSN 1891-1935. 2005; English ed.: Perspective. ISSN 1892-1841. 2010.
Published by: Flyktninghjelpen/Norwegian Refugee Council, Grensen 17, Postboks 6758, St Olavs Plass, Oslo, 0130, Norway. TEL 47-23-109800, FAX 47-23-109801, nrc@nrc.no, http://www.nrc.no. Ed. Roald Hoevring. Circ: 20,000.

304.6 PHL ISSN 1655-8049
HB3649.A3
➤ **PHILIPPINE POPULATION REVIEW.** Text in English. 2002. a. free to qualified personnel. stat.; charts. back issues avail. **Document type:** *Journal, Academic/Scholarly.* **Description:** Forms part of the strategies of the Association, a duly registered professional body, to promote a scientific base for population issues in the country. Discusses technical and substantive topics on theoretical or empirical levels relating to human fertility, mortality, morbidity and migration.
Published by: Philippine Population Association, Behavioral Sciences Department, De La Salle University, 2401 Taft Ave, Manila, Philippines. TEL 63-2-5244611, FAX 63-2-5244611, leer@dlsu.edu.ph. Ed., Pub. Romeo B. Lee.

325.1 CAN ISSN 1497-9284
PLANNING NOW FOR CANADA'S FUTURE. Variant title: Planifier des Maintenant l'Avenir du Canada. Text in English, French. 1979. a.
Former titles (until 2000): Canada. Citizenship and Immigration Canada. Annual Immigration Plan (1209-7330); (until 1997): Canada. Employment and Immigration Canada. Annual Report to Parliament, Immigration Plan (1184-9363); (until 1990): Canada. Employment and Immigration Canada. Annual Report to Parliament on Future Immigration Levels (0825-1991); (until 1983): Canada. Employment and Immigration Canada. Annual Report to Parliament on Immigration Levels (0228-3050)
—CCC.
Published by: Citizenship and Immigration Canada, 6th Fl, 400 University Ave, Toronto, ON M7A 2R9, Canada. TEL 416-327-2422, FAX 416-314-4965, info@mczcr.gov.on.ca.

304.6 ARG ISSN 1668-5458
HB3560.B8
POBLACION DE BUENOS AIRES; revista semestral de datos y estudios demograficos. Text in Spanish. 2004. s-a. stat. **Document type:** *Journal, Government.*
Related titles: Online - full text ed.
Published by: Argentina. Hacienda. Ministrio de Hacienda. Direccion General de Estadistica y Censos, Centro de Documentacion, ubicado en Av. San Juan 1340, Buenos Aires, 1148, Argentina. TEL 54-1-43073547, FAX 54-1-43075661, cdocumentacion_estadistica@buenosaires.gov.ar, http://www.estadistica.buenosaires.gov.ar. Circ: 200.

304.5 CRI ISSN 1659-0201
HB3533
POBLACION Y SALUD EN MESOAMERICA. Text in Spanish. 2003. s-a. free (effective 2011). **Document type:** *Journal, Academic/Scholarly.*
Media: Online - full text.
Indexed: C01.
Published by: Universidad de Costa Rica, Centro Centroamericano de Poblacion, Apdo Postal 2060, San Jose, Costa Rica. revista@ccp.ucr.ac.cr. Ed. Ricardo Chinchilla Arley.

304.6 ARG ISSN 1852-8562
▼ **POBLACION Y SOCIEDAD.** Text in Spanish. 2009. a. back issues avail. **Document type:** *Journal, Academic/Scholarly.*
Media: Online - full text (from SciELO).
Published by: Instituto Superior de Estudios Sociales, San Lorenzo, 429, San Miguel Tucuman, 4000, Argentina. TEL 54-381-4977481, FAX 54-381-4975681, ises@ises.org.ar/, http://www.ises.org.ar/.

304.6 ARG ISSN 0328-3445
POBLACION Y SOCIEDAD. Text in Spanish. 1993. a. **Document type:** *Monographic series, Academic/Scholarly.*
Published by: Fundacion Yocavil, Bernardo Houssay, 102, Yerba Buena, Tucuman, 4107, Argentina. Ed. Alfredo Bolsi.

304.6 FRA ISSN 2108-596X
POLICY & RESEARCH PAPERS. Text in English. 1994. irreg., latest 2009. **Document type:** *Monographic series, Academic/Scholarly.*
Published by: International Union for the Scientific Study of Population (I U S S P)/Union Internationale pour l'Etude Scientifique de la Population, 3-5 Rue Nicolas, Paris, 75980, France. TEL 33-1-56062173, FAX 33-1-56062204, iussp@iussp.org.

304.6 POL ISSN 0867-7905
HB3608.7.A3
POLISH POPULATION REVIEW. Text in English. 1991. s-a. USD 50 per issue foreign (effective 2000). bk.rev. bibl. **Document type:** *Journal, Academic/Scholarly.* **Description:** Presents achievements of Polish scientists and experts in research on demographic phenomena and processes.
Indexed: P30, Populnd, SCOPUS.
Published by: Polskie Towarzystwo Demograficzne/Polish Demographic Society, Al Niepodleglosci 164, Warsaw, 02556, Poland. TEL 48-22-8491251, FAX 48-22-8495312. Ed. Zbigniew Strzelecki. R&P Ewa Fratczak. Circ: 350.

304.6 POL ISSN 1642-0101
POLSKA AKADEMIA NAUK. KOMITET NAUK DEMOGRAFICZNYCH. SEKCJA ANALIZ DEMOGRAFICZNYCH. ZESZYTY NAUKOWE. Text in Polish. 2000. irreg. (2-4/yr.). **Document type:** *Monographic series, Academic/Scholarly.*
Related titles: Online - full text ed.
Published by: (Polska Akademia Nauk, Komitet Nauk Demograficznych, Sekcja Analiz Demograficznych), Polska Akademia Nauk, Komitet Nauk Demograficznych/Polish Academy of Sciences, Committee on Demographic Sciences, Al Niepodleglosci 162, Szkola Glowna Handlowa, Instytut Statystyki i Demografii, Warsaw, 02554, Poland. TEL 48-22-8495397, ewaf@sgh.waw.pl, http://www.knd.pan.pl.

304.6 USA
POPLINE. Text in English. 1979. bi-m. USD 25. **Document type:** *Newsletter.* **Description:** News and feature service provided to more than 2,100 daily newspapers worldwide. Explores, analyzes, and evaluates facts and public policies relating to the problems of world over-population.
Related titles: CD-ROM ed.; Online - full text ed.
Published by: Population Institute, 107 Second St, N E, Washington, DC 20002. TEL 202-544-3300, FAX 202-544-0068. Ed., R&P Harold N Burdett. Circ: 81,000.

304.6 ITA ISSN 1591-4798
POPOLAZIONE E STORIA. Text in Multiple languages. 1979. s-a. EUR 60 to institutions (effective 2009). **Document type:** *Magazine, Consumer.*
Formerly (until 1999): Bollettino di Demografia Storica (1126-9510)
Indexed: P30, SCOPUS.
Published by: (Societa Italiana di Demografia Storica (S I D E S) USA), Forum Editrice Universitaria Udinese, Via Larga 38, Udine, UD 33100, Italy. TEL 39-0432-26001, FAX 39-0432-296756, forum@forumeditrice.it, http://www.forumeditrice.it.

304.6 PRT ISSN 0873-1861
F2659.A1
POPULACAO E SOCIEDADE. Text in Portuguese. 1994. a. EUR 12.80 (effective 2005). **Document type:** *Magazine, Consumer.*
Published by: Edicoes Afrontamento, Lda., Rua de Costa Cabral, 859, Porto, 4200-225, Portugal. TEL 351-22-5074220, FAX 351-22-5074229, editorial@edicoesafrontamento.pt, http://www.edicoesafrontamento.pt. Ed. Fernando Sousa.

304.6 FRA ISSN 1634-2941
HB848
POPULATION (ENGLISH EDITION). Text in English. 1978. q. EUR 90 domestic to individuals; EUR 97 foreign to individuals (effective 2010). illus. **Document type:** *Journal, Academic/Scholarly.*
Former titles (until 2002): Population. English Selection (1169-1018); (until 1989): Selected Papers on Population (0246-4292)
Related titles: Online - full text ed.: (from IngentaConnect); ◆ French ed.: Population (French Edition). ISSN 0032-4663.
Indexed: A01, A22, CA, E01, ESPM, EconLit, GEOBASE, H05, PAIS, S02, S03, SSAI, SSAb, SSI, SSciA, SociolAb, T02, W03, W05.
—IE. **CCC.**
Published by: Institut National d'Etudes Demographiques (I N E D), 133 Blvd Davout, Paris, 75980 Cedex 20, France. TEL 33-1-56062000, FAX 33-1-56062199, editions@ined.fr. Ed. P Festy.

304.6 FRA ISSN 0032-4663
HB881 CODEN: POPUAQ
➤ **POPULATION (FRENCH EDITION).** Text in French. 1946. q. EUR 90 domestic to individuals; EUR 90 DOM-TOM to individuals; EUR 97 foreign to individuals (effective 2010). illus. back issues avail.; reprints avail. **Document type:** *Journal, Academic/Scholarly.*
Incorporates: Demographie et Sciences Humaines (0070-3354)
Related titles: Online - full text ed.: ISSN 1957-7966; ◆ English ed.: Population (English Edition). ISSN 1634-2941.
Indexed: A12, A20, A22, ABIn, B01, B07, BAS, CA, CurCont, ESPM, FR, FamI, HPNRM, HistAb, IBR, IBSS, IBZ, MycolAb, P21, P27, P30, P46, P48, P50, P51, P52, P53, P54, P56, PAIS, PCI, PQC, Populnd, RASB, RILM, RefZh, S02, S03, SCOPUS, SSCI, SSciA, T02, V01, W07.
—BLDSC (6552.000000), IE, Infotrieve, Ingenta, INIST. **CCC.**
Published by: Institut National d'Etudes Demographiques (I N E D), 133 Blvd Davout, Paris, 75980 Cedex 20, France. TEL 33-1-56062000, FAX 33-1-56062199, editions@ined.fr. Ed. P Festy. Circ: 4,500.

304.6 USA ISSN 0197-2235
POPULATION (WASHINGTON); briefing papers on issues of national and international importance in the population field. Text in English. 1976. irreg. price varies. charts; stat.
Indexed: CLFP, HPNRM.
Published by: Population Crisis Committee, 1120 Nineteenth St, N W, Ste 550, Washington, DC 20036. TEL 202-659-1833, FAX 202-293-1795, TELEX 440450. Circ: 55,000.

304.6 ETH
POPULATION AND DEVELOPMENT BULLETIN. Text in English. 1990-1991; resumed 1994. 2/yr. index. **Document type:** *Bulletin, Government.* **Description:** Covers demographic issues relating to development projects and public health initiatives.
Indexed: PLESA.
Published by: Ministry of Planning & Economic Development, Population and Development Planning Unit, PO Box 1037, Addis Ababa, Ethiopia. TEL 251-1-552800, FAX 251-1-553844, TELEX 21531.

304.6 301.32 USA ISSN 0098-7921
HB848
➤ **POPULATION AND DEVELOPMENT REVIEW.** Text in English; Summaries in English, French, Spanish. 1975. q. GBP 154 combined subscription in United Kingdom to institutions (print & online eds.); EUR 196 combined subscription in Europe to institutions (print & online eds.); USD 184 combined subscription in the Americas to institutions (print & online eds.); USD 302 combined subscription elsewhere to institutions (print & online eds.) (effective 2012). bk.rev. abstr.; charts; illus. index, cum.index: vols. 1-20 in 1995. 200 p./no. 1 cols./p.; Supplement avail.; back issues avail.; reprint service avail. from PSC. **Document type:** *Journal, Academic/Scholarly.* **Description:** Focuses on ideas and insights rather than analytical technicalities.
Related titles: Microfilm ed.: (from PQC); Online - full text ed.: ISSN 1728-4457. 1998. GBP 138 in United Kingdom to institutions; EUR 175 in Europe to institutions; USD 165 in the Americas to institutions; USD 270 elsewhere to institutions (effective 2012) (from IngentaConnect).
Indexed: A01, A02, A03, A08, A20, A22, A25, A26, A36, ABCPolSci, ABS&EES, APEL, ASCA, ASG, ASSIA, AmH&L, B02, B04, B15, B17, B18, BA, BAS, BRD, C25, C28, CA, CABA, CLFP, CWI, ChPerI, Chicano, CurCont, D01, DIP, E01, E08, E12, EI, EIP, ERA, ESPM, EconLit, EnvAb, EnvInd, F09, FR, FamI, G04, G05, G06, G07, G08, G10, GEOBASE, GH, HPNRM, HistAb, I05, I07, I14, IBR, IBSS, IBZ, ILD, JEL, MEA&I, N02, P02, P06, P10, P27, P30, P33, P34, P37, P39, P42, P48, P50, P52, P53, P54, P56, PAIS, PCI, PQC, PSA, PerIslam, Populnd, R08, R12, RASB, RefSour, S02, S03, S08, S09, S11, S21, S23, SCOPUS, SFSA, SOPODA, SSA, SSAI, SSAb, SSCI, SSI, SSciA, SUSA, SociolAb, T02, T05, TAR, UAA, VS, W03, W07, W09, W11.
—BLDSC (6552.010000), GNLM, IE, Infotrieve, Ingenta. **CCC.**
Published by: (Population Council), Wiley-Blackwell Publishing, Inc. (Subsidiary of: Wiley-Blackwell Publishing Ltd.), 111 River St, Hoboken, NJ 07030. TEL 201-748-6000, FAX 201-748-6088, info@wiley.com, http://www.wiley.com/WileyCDA/. Eds. Geoffrey McNicoll, Paul Demeny.

➤ **POPULATION AND ENVIRONMENT.** *see* PSYCHOLOGY

➤ **POPULATION & HOUSING CENSUS MAJOR FINDINGS.** *see* POPULATION STUDIES—Abstracting, Bibliographies, Statistics

363.7 USA
POPULATION AND RESOURCE OUTLOOK. Text in English. 1973. q. USD 30 to members (effective 1996). bk.rev. charts; illus.; maps; stat. 4 p./no.; **Document type:** *Newsletter.* **Description:** Includes news and analysis of population issues, with a focus on the United States.
Formerly: Human Survival
Related titles: Online - full content ed.
Published by: Negative Population Growth, 2861 Duke St., # 36, Alexandria, VA 22314-4512. FAX 202-667-8953. Ed. Donald Mann. Circ: 25,000 (paid).

304.6 USA ISSN 1084-6786
POPULATION BRIEFS. Text in English. 1995. 3/yr. free (effective 2010). back issues avail. **Document type:** *Newsletter, Consumer.*
Related titles: Online - full text ed.
Indexed: A26, CWI, E08, G08, H11, H12, I05, P30, S09, SCOPUS.
—CIS.
Published by: Population Council, One Dag Hammarskjold Plz, 9th Fl, New York, NY 10017. TEL 212-339-0500, 877-339-0500, FAX 212-755-6052, publications@popcouncil.org. Ed. Gina Duclayan.

304.6 USA ISSN 0032-468X
HB881.A1 CODEN: POPBA3
POPULATION BULLETIN. Text in English. 1945. q. free to qualified personnel (effective 2010). charts; stat.; illus. back issues avail.; reprints avail. **Document type:** *Journal, Trade.* **Description:** Focuses on national and world issues in the field by recognized authorities.
Related titles: Online - full text ed.
Indexed: A01, A02, A03, A08, A12, A20, A21, A22, A25, A26, A36, ABIn, ABS&EES, ASCA, AcaI, BAS, BRD, C12, CA, CABA, CLFP, CurCont, E08, E12, EI, EIP, ESPM, EconLit, EnvAb, FR, FamI, FutSurv, G08, GEOBASE, GH, H01, H05, H09, HPNRM, I05, JEL, M01, M02, MASUSE, MEA&I, N02, P02, P06, P10, P21, P27, P30, P34, P48, P50, P51, P52, P53, P54, P56, PAIS, PCI, PQC, Populnd, RASB, RI-1, RI-2, RefZh, S02, S03, S05, S08, S09, S11, SCOPUS, SRI, SSAI, SSAb, SSCI, SSI, SSciA, T02, T05, W01, W02, W03, W05, W07, W11.
—BLDSC (6552.200000), IE, Infotrieve, Ingenta.
Published by: Population Reference Bureau, Inc., 1875 Connecticut Ave, NW, Ste 520, Washington, DC 20009. TEL 202-483-1100, 800-877-9881, FAX 202-328-3937, popref@prb.org. Ed. Marlene Lee.

325 USA ISSN 0251-7604
HB848
POPULATION BULLETIN OF THE UNITED NATIONS. Text in English. 1948. irreg., latest 2001. USD 35 per issue (effective 2008). **Document type:** *Journal, Academic/Scholarly.* **Description:** Provides information on population studies, gives a global perspective of demographic issues and an analysis of the direct and indirect implications of population policy.
Related titles: Microfiche ed.: (from CIS); Spanish ed.: Boletin de Poblacion de las Naciones Unidas. ISSN 0251-7590. USD 35 per issue (effective 2008); French ed.: Bulletin Demographique des Nations Unies. ISSN 0251-7612. USD 35 per issue (effective 2008).
Indexed: ARDT, BibInd, IIS, P06, P30, PAIS, Populnd, RASB, SSciA.
—CCC.

P

Published by: (United Nations, Department of Economic and Social Development), United Nations Publications, 2 United Nations Plaza, Rm DC2-853, New York, NY 10017. TEL 212-963-8302, 800-253-9646, FAX 212-963-3489, publications@un.org, https://unp.un.org.

304.6 PNG ISSN 0079-3868
POPULATION CENSUS OF PAPUA NEW GUINEA. POPULATION CHARACTERISTICS BULLETIN SERIES. Text in English. 1966. irreg. PGK 5. **Document type:** *Government.*
Published by: National Statistical Office, Waigani, National Capital District, PO Box 337, Port Moresby, Papua New Guinea. TEL 675-3011226, FAX 675-3251869. Ed. Francis K Kasau. Circ: 842.

304.6 USA ISSN 0361-7858
HB849 CODEN: POPCA6
POPULATION COUNCIL. ANNUAL REPORT. Text in English. 1952. a. free (effective 2010). **Document type:** *Report, Corporate.*
Related titles: Online - full text ed.
Indexed: HPNRM.
Published by: Population Council, One Dag Hammarskjold Plz, 9th Fl, New York, NY 10017. TEL 212-339-0500, FAX 212-755-6052, pubinfo@popcouncil.org. Ed. Gina Duclayan.

595.7 JPN ISSN 1438-3896
QH352 CODEN: PEOCAX
➤ **POPULATION ECOLOGY/KOTAIGUN SEITAIGAKU NO KENKYU.** Text in English. 1962. 3/yr. (in 1 vol., 3 nos./vol.). EUR 452, USD 540 combined subscription to institutions (print & online eds.) (effective 2012). adv. reprint service avail. from PSC. **Document type:** *Journal, Academic/Scholarly.* **Description:** Publishes original research articles and reviews on various aspects of population ecology, such as population dynamics and distribution, evolutionary ecology, ecological genetics, theoretical models, conservation biology, agroecosystem studies, and bioresource management.
Formerly (until 1999): Researches on Population Ecology (0034-5466); Kotaigun Seitai Gakkai Kaiho/Society of Population Ecology. Report (0386-4561)
Related titles: Online - full text ed.: ISSN 1438-390X (from IngentaConnect).
Indexed: A12, A22, A26, A34, A35, A38, ABIn, ASCA, ASFA, AgBio, Agr, AgrForAb, B21, B23, B25, BIOBASE, BIOSIS Prev, C25, C30, CA, CABA, CurCont, E01, E04, E05, E12, E17, ESPM, EntAb, F08, F11, F12, FCA, FS&TA, G11, GEOBASE, GH, H16, HPNRM, IABS, ISR, IndVet, LT, MaizeAb, MycolAb, N02, N04, N05, O01, OR, P02, P10, P27, P30, P32, P33, P38, P40, P48, P50, P51, P52, P53, P54, P56, PGegResA, PHN&I, PQC, R07, R08, R11, R12, R13, RA&MP, S02, S03, S11, S13, S16, S17, SCI, SCOPUS, SSciA, SWRA, SoyAb, T02, TAR, TriticAb, VS, W07, W08, W10, W11, WildRev, Z01.
—IE, Infotrieve, Ingenta, INIST. **CCC.**
Published by: (The Society of Population Ecology/Kotaigun Seitai Gakkai), Springer Japan KK (Subsidiary of: Springer Science+Business Media), No 2 Funato Bldg, 1-11-11 Kudan-kita, Chiyoda-ku, Tokyo, 102-0073, Japan. TEL 81-3-68317000, FAX 81-3-68317001, http://www.springer.jp. Ed. Takashi Saitoh. Circ: 25,000. **Subscr. in the Americas to:** Springer New York LLC, Journal Fulfillment, PO Box 2485, Secaucus, NJ 07096. TEL 800-777-4643, 201-348-4033, FAX 201-348-4505, journals-ny@springer.com, http://www.springer.com; **Subscr. to:** Springer Distribution Center, Kundenservice Zeitschriften, Haberstr 7, Heidelberg 69126, Germany. TEL 49-6221-3454303, FAX 49-6221-3454229, subscriptions@springer.com.

304.6 GBR
POPULATION ESTIMATES SCOTLAND. Text in English. 1958. a. **Document type:** *Government.*
Formerly (until 1987): Annual Estimates of the Population of Scotland (0066-3964)
—BLDSC (6552.239400).
Published by: General Register Office, Scotland, Ladywell House, Ladywell Rd, Edinburgh, EH12 7TF, United Kingdom. TEL 44-131-3144299. Circ: 600.

304.6 300 FRA ISSN 0184-7783
HB848
POPULATION ET SOCIETES. Text in French. 1968. m. EUR 12 domestic to individuals; EUR 12 DOM-TOM to individuals; EUR 18 foreign to individuals (effective 2010). charts; stat. cum.index: 1968-1975, 1976-1981. **Document type:** *Report, Consumer.*
Related titles: ◆ Online - full text ed.: Populations et Societes (Online). ISSN 1950-6236.
Indexed: B01, B07, CA, EMBASE, ESPM, ExcerpMed, FR, HPNRM, IBSS, MEDLINE, P21, P27, P30, P48, P50, P52, P54, P56, PQC, PopulInd, R10, RASB, Reac, RefZh, SCOPUS, SSAI, SSAb, SSI, SSciA, T02, V01, W03, W05.
—IE, INIST. **CCC.**
Published by: Institut National d'Etudes Demographiques (I N E D), 133 Blvd Davout, Paris, 75980 Cedex 20, France. TEL 33-1-56062000, FAX 33-1-56062199, editions@ined.fr. Ed. Michel L Levy. Circ: 40,000.

304.6 CHE ISSN 1660-6043
POPULATION, FAMILY AND SOCIETY/POPULATION, FAMILLE ET SOCIETE. Text in French, English. 2004. irreg., latest vol.12, 2010. price varies. **Document type:** *Monographic series, Academic/Scholarly.*
—BLDSC (6552.277500).
Published by: Peter Lang AG (Subsidiary of: Peter Lang Publishing Group), Hochfeldstr 32, Postfach 746, Bern 9, 3000, Switzerland. TEL 41-31-3061717, FAX 41-31-3061727, info@peterlang.com. Ed. Michel Oris.

301.32 THA ISSN 0252-3639
HB3633.A3
POPULATION HEADLINERS. Text in English. 196?. bi-m. free upon request. charts; illus. **Document type:** *Journal, Academic/Scholarly.*
Former titles: Asian-Pacific Population Programme News (0125-6718); (until 1971): Asian Population Programme News (0084-6821)
Indexed: HPNRM, P30, SCOPUS, SPPI.
Published by: (Population and Rural And Urban Development Division), United Nations Economic and Social Commission for Asia and the Pacific, United Nations Bldg., Rajadamnern Ave., Bangkok, 10200, Thailand. TEL 662-2881174, FAX 662-2883022, unescap@unescap.org, http://www.unescap.org. Circ: 5,500.

304.6 AUS ISSN 1837-6010
POPULATION N S W BULLETIN (ONLINE). Text in English. 2005. s-a. free (effective 2010). back issues avail. **Document type:** *Bulletin, Government.* **Description:** Contains information about new population data, forthcoming data and analysis, and information to help in understanding population data.
Formerly (until 2007): Population N S W Bulletin (Print) (1832-5246)
Media: Online - full text.
Published by: N S W Government, Department of Planning, GPO Box 39, Sydney, NSW 2001, Australia. TEL 61-2-92286111, FAX 61-2-92286455, information@planning.nsw.gov.au.

304.6 THA ISSN 0125-6440
POPULATION NEWSLETTER. Text in Thai. 1969. s-a. free. bk.rev. **Document type:** *Newsletter.*
Published by: Chulalongkorn University, College of Population Studies, Phyathai Rd, Bangkok, 10330, Thailand. TEL 662-2511135, 662-2187342. Circ: 3,500.

304.6 AUS
POPULATION PROJECTIONS FOR LOCAL GOVERNMENT AREAS WITHIN SOUTH AUSTRALIA. Text in English. irreg. **Document type:** *Government.* **Description:** Discusses population projects for local government areas within south Australia.
Former titles (until 19??): Population Projection for South Australia and Statistical Division; South Australia. Department of Environment and Planning. Population Projection for South Australia
Published by: Department for Transport, Urban Planning and the Arts, GPO 1815, Adelaide, SA 5001, Australia.

304.6 AUS ISSN 1449-0161
POPULATION PROJECTIONS TO 2051, QUEENSLAND AND STATISTICAL DIVISIONS. Text in English. 2003. irreg. **Document type:** *Monographic series, Trade.*
Media: Online - full text. **Related titles:** Print ed.: ISSN 1448-675X.
Published by: Queensland Treasury, Office of Economic and Statistical Research, PO Box 15037, City East, QLD 4002, Australia. TEL 61-7-3224-5326, FAX 61-7-3227-7437, oesr@treasury.qld.gov.au, http://www.oesr.qld.gov.au.

325 613.9 USA ISSN 0887-0241
POPULATION REPORTS (ENGLISH EDITION). Text in English. 1973. q. looseleaf. bibl.; charts; illus.; stat. back issues avail.; reprints avail. **Document type:** *Journal, Academic/Scholarly.* **Description:** Provides an overview of important developments in family planning and related health issues.
Formerly: George Washington University. Population Information Program. Population Reports
Related titles: Online - full text ed.; ◆ Spanish ed.: Population Reports (Spanish Edition). ISSN 0887-0268; ◆ Portuguese ed.: Population Reports (Portuguese Edition). ISSN 0887-0276; ◆ French ed.: Population Reports (French Edition). ISSN 0887-025X.
Indexed: A01, A02, A03, A08, A25, A26, A36, CA, CABA, D01, E08, G01, G05, G06, G07, G08, GH, I05, I07, M01, M02, MASUSE, N02, N03, P34, PopulInd, R12, S01, S02, S03, S08, S09, T02, T05, W11.
Published by: Johns Hopkins University, Population Information Program, Bloomberg School of Public Health, 111 Market Pl, Ste 310, Baltimore, MD 21202. TEL 410-659-6300, FAX 410-659-6266, http://www.jhuccp.org.

325 613.9 USA ISSN 0887-025X
POPULATION REPORTS (FRENCH EDITION). Text in French. 1973. 3/yr. looseleaf. USD 2 per issue for developed countries; free in developing nations to qualified personnel (effective 2010). bibl.; charts; illus.; stat. back issues avail. **Document type:** *Monographic series, Academic/Scholarly.*
Formerly: George Washington University. Population Information Program. Population Reports
Related titles: Online - full text ed.; ◆ English ed.: Population Reports (English Edition). ISSN 0887-0241; ◆ Spanish ed.: Population Reports (Spanish Edition). ISSN 0887-0268; ◆ Portuguese ed.: Population Reports (Portuguese Edition). ISSN 0887-0276; Supplement(s): Population Reports. Serie J. Programmes de Planning Familial (French Edition). ISSN 0894-4512. 1975.
Indexed: PopulInd.
Published by: Johns Hopkins University, Population Information Program, Bloomberg School of Public Health, 111 Market Pl, Ste 310, Baltimore, MD 21202. TEL 410-659-6300, FAX 410-659-6266, info@jhuccp.org, http://www.jhuccp.org. Ed. Ward Rinehart.

325 613.9 USA ISSN 0887-0276
POPULATION REPORTS (PORTUGUESE EDITION). Text in Portuguese. 1973. 3/yr. USD 2 per issue for developed nations; free in developing nations to qualified personnel (effective 2010). bibl.; charts; illus.; stat. back issues avail. **Document type:** *Monographic series, Academic/Scholarly.*
Formerly: George Washington University. Population Information Program. Population Reports
Related titles: Online - full text ed.; ◆ English ed.: Population Reports (English Edition). ISSN 0887-0241; ◆ French ed.: Population Reports (French Edition). ISSN 0887-025X; ◆ Spanish ed.: Population Reports (Spanish Edition). ISSN 0887-0268.
Indexed: PopulInd.
Published by: Johns Hopkins University, Population Information Program, Bloomberg School of Public Health, 111 Market Pl, Ste 310, Baltimore, MD 21202. TEL 410-659-6300, FAX 410-659-6266, info@jhuccp.org, http://www.jhuccp.org. Ed. Ward Rinehart. Circ: 14,000.

325 613.9 USA ISSN 0887-0268
POPULATION REPORTS (SPANISH EDITION). Text in Spanish. 1973. 3/yr. looseleaf. USD 2 per issue for developed nations; free in developing nations to qualified personnel (effective 2010). bibl.; charts; illus.; stat. back issues avail. **Document type:** *Monographic series, Academic/Scholarly.*
Formerly: George Washington University. Population Information Program. Population Reports
Related titles: Online - full text ed.; ◆ English ed.: Population Reports (English Edition). ISSN 0887-0241; ◆ French ed.: Population Reports (French Edition). ISSN 0887-025X; ◆ Portuguese ed.: Population Reports (Portuguese Edition). ISSN 0887-0276.
Indexed: PopulInd.
Published by: Johns Hopkins University, Population Information Program, Bloomberg School of Public Health, 111 Market Pl, Ste 310, Baltimore, MD 21202. TEL 410-659-6300, FAX 410-659-6266, info@jhuccp.org, http://www.jhuccp.org. Ed. Ward Rinehart. Circ: 40,000.

304.6 330.9 NLD ISSN 0167-5923
HB848
➤ **POPULATION RESEARCH AND POLICY REVIEW.** Text in English. 1980. bi-m. EUR 877, USD 922 combined subscription to institutions (print & online eds.) (effective 2012). adv. bk.rev. illus. back issues avail.; reprint service avail. from PSC. **Document type:** *Journal, Academic/Scholarly.* **Description:** Promotes the use of empirical research in the analysis and formulation of public policy relevant to demographic issues.
Related titles: Microform ed.: (from PQC); Online - full text ed.: ISSN 1573-7829 (from IngentaConnect).
Indexed: A12, A13, A17, A20, A22, A26, A36, ABIn, APEL, ASCA, Agr, BibInd, BibLing, CA, CABA, CurCont, D01, E01, E03, E07, E12, ERA, ERI, ESPM, EconLit, EnvAb, EnvInd, F08, F12, FamI, GEOBASE, GH, H01, H05, HPNRM, I05, I13, IBSS, IPARL, JEL, LT, M12, N02, N03, P10, P21, P27, P30, P34, P42, P46, P47, P48, P50, P51, P52, P53, P54, P56, PAIS, PCI, PQC, PSA, PopulInd, R12, R17, RRTA, S02, S03, S13, S16, S21, SCOPUS, SOPODA, SSA, SSCI, SSciA, SWR&A, SociolAb, T02, T05, TAR, W07, W09, W11.
—BLDSC (6552.482000), IE, Infotrieve, Ingenta. **CCC.**
Published by: (Southern Demographic Association USA), Springer Netherlands (Subsidiary of: Springer Science+Business Media), Van Godewijckstraat 30, Dordrecht, 3311 GX, Netherlands. TEL 31-78-6576050, FAX 31-78-6576474, http://www.springer.com. Ed. Thomas W Pullum.

304.6 USA
POPULATION RESEARCH CENTER NEWSLETTER. Text in English. 1991 (vol.3, no.1). irreg. **Document type:** *Newsletter.* **Description:** Contains research and administrative news of the center's activities.
Published by: University of Texas at Austin, Population Research Center, Main Bldg 1800, Austin, TX 78712-1088. TEL 512-471-5514, FAX 512-471-4886.

304.6 917.602 USA ISSN 0191-913X
POPULATION RESEARCH CENTER PAPERS. Text in English. 1979. irreg., latest vol.10, no.12. USD 4 per issue. **Document type:** *Monographic series.*
Indexed: HPNRM.
Published by: University of Texas at Austin, Population Research Center, Main Bldg 1800, Austin, TX 78712-1088. TEL 512-471-5514, FAX 512-471-4886.

304.6 CAN
POPULATION RESEARCH LABORATORY. RESEARCH DISCUSSION PAPER SERIES. Text in English. 1973. irreg. free. reprints avail. **Document type:** *Monographic series, Academic/Scholarly.* **Description:** Research papers in the field of population studies, survey research and methodology.
Formerly: Population Research Laboratory. Discussion Paper Series (0317-2473)
Related titles: Microform ed.: (from MML).
Published by: Population Research Laboratory, Department of Sociology, University of Alberta, Edmonton, AB T6G 2H4, Canada. TEL 403-492-4659.

304.6 THA ISSN 1549-0955
➤ **POPULATION REVIEW (ONLINE).** Text in English. 2003. s-a. **Document type:** *Journal, Academic/Scholarly.* **Description:** Covers the fields of sociology, demography, political science, social anthropology, communication and socio-environmental science.
Media: Online - full text.
Indexed: B04, SSAI, SSAb, SSI, W03, W05.
Published by: (Indian Institute for Population Studies IND), Population Review Publications, 3522 2nd fl. rm.2 AL 11B, Lardproa Rd., Klongchang Bangkapi, Bangkok, 10240, Thailand. Ed. Archibald O Haller.

304.6 GBR ISSN 1544-8444
HB1951 CODEN: IJPGFD
➤ **POPULATION, SPACE AND PLACE.** Text in English. 1995. bi-m. GBP 572 in United Kingdom to institutions; EUR 722 in Europe to institutions; USD 1,120 elsewhere to institutions; GBP 629 combined subscription in United Kingdom to institutions (print & online eds.); EUR 795 combined subscription in Europe to institutions (print & online eds.); USD 1,232 combined subscription elsewhere to institutions (print & online eds.) (effective 2010). adv. bk.rev. illus. Index. back issues avail.; reprint service avail. from PSC. **Document type:** *Journal, Academic/Scholarly.* **Description:** Presents key quantitative and qualitative research on population studies of a from a geographical perspective.
Formerly (until 2004): International Journal of Population Geography (1077-3495)
Related titles: Microform ed.: (from PQC); Online - full text ed.: ISSN 1544-8452. GBP 572 in United Kingdom to institutions; EUR 722 in Europe to institutions; USD 1,120 elsewhere to institutions (effective 2010).
Indexed: A20, A28, A34, A36, APA, BrCerAb, C&ISA, CA, CA/WCA, CABA, CIA, CerAb, CivEngAb, CorrAb, CurCont, D01, E&CAJ, E04, E05, E11, E12, EEA, EMA, ESPM, EnvAb, EnvEAb, GEOBASE, GH, H15, H16, HPNRM, I11, I14, IBR, IBSS, IBZ, LT, M&TEA, M09, MBF, METADEX, N02, N03, P30, PAIS, PopulInd, R12, RRTA, S02, S03, S13, S16, S21, SCOPUS, SSCI, SSciA, SociolAb, SolStAb, T02, T04, T05, TAR, W07, W11, WAA.
—IE, Infotrieve, Ingenta, Linda Hall. **CCC.**
Published by: John Wiley & Sons Ltd. (Subsidiary of: John Wiley & Sons, Inc.), 1-7 Oldlands Way, PO Box 808, Bognor Regis, West Sussex PO21 9FF, United Kingdom. TEL 44-1865-778315, FAX 44-1243-843232, cs-journals@wiley.com, http://eu.wiley.com/WileyCDA/. Eds. A M Findlay, P J Boyle. **Subscr. in the Americas to:** John Wiley & Sons, Inc., 111 River St, Hoboken, NJ 07030. subinfo@wiley.com; **Subscr. to:** 1-7 Oldlands Way, PO Box 809, Bognor Regis, West Sussex PO21 9FG, United Kingdom. TEL 44-1865-778054, cs-agency@wiley.com.

304.6 GBR ISSN 0032-4728
HB848 CODEN: POSTA4
➤ **POPULATION STUDIES**; a journal of demography. Text in English. 1947. 3/yr. GBP 184 combined subscription in United Kingdom to institutions (print & online eds.); EUR 243, USD 305 combined subscription to institutions (print & online eds.) (effective 2012). adv. bk.rev. illus. index. back issues avail.; reprint service avail. from PSC. **Document type:** *Journal, Academic/Scholarly.* **Description:** Covers the field of demography, population movements, the effectiveness of birth control programs, fertility and economic and social implications of demographic trends.

Related titles: Online - full text ed.: ISSN 1477-4747. 2002. GBP 166 in United Kingdom to institutions; EUR 218, USD 274 to institutions (effective 2012) (from IngentaConnect).
Indexed: A01, A02, A03, A08, A12, A13, A20, A22, A26, A36, ABIn, AICP, APEL, ARDT, AmH&L, B01, B06, B07, B08, B09, BAS, C28, CA, CABA, CIS, CLFP, CurCont, D01, DIP, E01, E04, E05, E08, E12, EI, EMBASE, ESPM, EconLit, EnvAb, EnvInd, ErgAb, ExcerpMed, FamI, G08, GEOBASE, GH, H05, HPNRM, HistAb, I05, IBR, IBSS, IBZ, JEL, MEA&I, MEDLINE, N02, N03, P02, P06, P10, P26, P30, P33, P34, P42, P48, P51, P52, P53, P54, P56, PAA&I, PAIS, PCI, PQC, PRA, PSA, PopulInd, R08, R12, RASB, S02, S03, S09, S11, SCOPUS, SOPODA, SSA, SSCI, SSciA, SociolAb, T02, T05, TAR, W07, W09, W11.
—IE, Infotrieve, Ingenta, INIST. **CCC.**
Published by: (Population Investigation Committee), Routledge (Subsidiary of: Taylor & Francis Group), 4 Park Sq, Milton Park, Abingdon, Oxon OX14 4RN, United Kingdom. TEL 44-20-70176000, FAX 44-20-70176336, subscriptions@tandf.co.uk, http://www.routledge.com. Adv. contact Linda Hann TEL 44-1344-779945. **Subscr. to:** Taylor & Francis Ltd., Journals Customer Service, Sheepen Pl, Colchester, Essex CO3 3LP, United Kingdom. TEL 44-20-70175544, FAX 44-20-70175198, tf.enquiries@tfinforma.com.

304.6 NLD
POPULATION STUDIES. Text in Dutch. irreg., latest 2007. price varies. **Document type:** *Monographic series, Academic/Scholarly.*
Published by: Rozenberg Publishers, Lindengracht 302 D&E, Amsterdam, 1015 KM, Netherlands. TEL 31-20-6255429, FAX 31-20-6203395, info@rozenbergps.com.

304.6 CAN ISSN 0712-5828
POPULATION STUDIES CENTRE. HIGHLIGHTS. Text in English. 1982. s-a. looseleaf. free. **Document type:** *Newsletter.* **Description:** Presents current projects and publications of the Centre and its associates.
Indexed: HPNRM.
Published by: Population Studies Centre, Rm 3227 SSC, University of Western Ontario, London, ON N6A 5C2, Canada. TEL 519-661-3819, FAX 519-661-3200. Ed. Suzanne Shiel. Circ: 300.

304.6 GBR ISSN 0307-4463
HB3583
➤ **POPULATION TRENDS.** Abbreviated title: P T. Text in English. 1975. q. USD 258 in North America to institutions; GBP 135 elsewhere to institutions (effective 2011). adv. charts; illus.; stat. back issues avail.; reprints avail. **Document type:** *Journal, Government.* **Description:** Contains commentary on the latest findings; topical articles on relevant subjects such as one parent families, cohabitation, fertility differences, international demography, population estimates and projections for different groups.
Incorporates (1997-1998): Monitor, Population and Health. FM2: Marriages in England and Wales During.. (1368-8928); (1977-1998): Monitor, Population and Health. FM2: Divorces in England and Wales During.. (1368-8936); Which superseded in part (in 1997): Marriage and Divorce Statistics. England and Wales (0140-8992); Which superseded in part (in 1977): Registrar General's Statistical Review of England and Wales; Formerly (until 1975): England and Wales. Registrar General. Quarterly Returns
Related titles: Online - full text ed.: ISSN 2040-1590. free (effective 2011).
Indexed: A12, A17, A22, A26, ABIn, B02, B15, B17, B18, EMBASE, ESPM, ExcerpMed, G04, G06, G07, G08, H05, H12, HPNRM, I05, IndMed, MEDLINE, P06, P10, P21, P27, P30, P34, P41, P48, P50, P51, P52, P53, P54, P56, PAIS, PQC, PopulInd, S02, S03, S11, SCOPUS, SSciA.
—BLDSC (6553.250000), IE, Infotrieve, Ingenta. **CCC.**
Published by: (Great Britain. Office for National Statistics), Palgrave Macmillan Ltd. (Subsidiary of: Macmillan Publishers Ltd.), Houndmills, Basingstoke, Hants RG21 6XS, United Kingdom. TEL 44-1256-329242, FAX 44-1256-479476, orders@palgrave.com, http://www.palgrave.com. Ed. Chris W Smith TEL 44-1329-813205. Pub. David Bull TEL 44-1256-329242. **Subscr. to:** Subscription Department, Brunel Rd, Houndmills, Basingstoke, Hants RG21 2XS, United Kingdom. TEL 44-1256-357893, FAX 44-1256-328339, subscriptions@palgrave.com.

304.6 300 FRA ISSN 1950-6236
POPULATIONS ET SOCIETES (ONLINE)/POPULATIONS AND SOCIETIES. Text in French, English. 2000. m. free. **Document type:** *Report, Consumer.*
Media: Online - full text. **Related titles:** ◆ Print ed.: Population et Societes. ISSN 0184-7783.
Published by: Institut National d'Etudes Demographiques (I N E D), 133 Blvd Davout, Paris, 75980 Cedex 20, France. TEL 33-1-56062000, FAX 33-1-56062199, editions@ined.fr.

304.609469 PRT ISSN 0871-8717
PORTUGAL SOCIAL. Text in Portuguese. 1992. a. **Document type:** *Government.* **Description:** Provides statistical data over the period 1985-1989.
Published by: Instituto Nacional de Estatistica, Av Antonio Jose de Almeida 2, Lisbon, 1000-043, Portugal. TEL 351-21-8426100, FAX 351-21-8426380, http://www.ine.pt.

304.6 306.4 PRT ISSN 0873-5921
POVOS E CULTURAS. Text in Portuguese. 1986. a.
Published by: Universidade Catolica Portuguesa, Palma de Cima, Lisbon, 1649-023, Portugal. TEL 351-21-4214000, FAX 351-21-7270256, info@reitoria.ucp.pt, http://www.ucp.pt.

325 342.083 FRA ISSN 1622-4949
PRO ASILE. Text in French. 199?. s-a. EUR 8 per issue (effective 2009). back issues avail. **Document type:** *Journal.*
Published by: France Terre d'Asile, 24 Rue Marc Seguin, Paris, 75018, France. TEL 33-1-53043999, infos@france-terre-asile.org.

304.6 AUS ISSN 1321-9545
PROACTIVE. Text in English. 1994. 3/yr. free (effective 2009). back issues avail. **Document type:** *Newsletter, Government.* **Description:** Provides news and comments for the public researchers of Public Record Office Victoria.
Related titles: Print ed.
Published by: Public Record Office Victoria, PO Box 2100, North Melbourne, VIC 3051, Australia. TEL 61-3-93485600, FAX 61-3-93485656, ask.prov@dvc.vic.gov.au.

304.6 USA ISSN 1941-7586
PROJECT ON GOBAL MIGRATION AND TRANSNATIONAL POLITICS. Variant title: Global Migration and Transnational Politics Series. Text in English. 2008. irreg., latest 2008. free (effective 2009). back issues avail. **Document type:** *Monographic series, Academic/Scholarly.* **Description:** Focuses on how migration trends have changed within the context of global modernity.
Related titles: Online - full text ed.: ISSN 1941-7594.
Published by: George Mason University, Center for Global Studies, 3401 Fairfax Dr, MS 1B9, Arlington, VA 22201. TEL 703-993-9430, FAX 703-993-9431, cgs@gmu.edu.

304.6 301.32 POL ISSN 0079-7189
HB3608.7
➤ **PRZESZLOSC DEMOGRAFICZNA POLSKI**; materialy i studia. Text in Polish; Summaries in English. 1967. irreg., latest vol.28, 2007. price varies. bibl. **Document type:** *Monographic series, Academic/Scholarly.*
Indexed: P30, PopulInd.
Published by: Polska Akademia Nauk, Komitet Nauk Demograficznych/Polish Academy of Sciences, Committee on Demographic Sciences, Al Niepodleglosci 162, Szkola Glowna Handlowa, Instytut Statystyki i Demografii, Warsaw, 02554, Poland. TEL 48-22-8495397, ewaf@sgh.waw.pl. Ed. Marek Gorny. Circ: 300.

304.6 USA ISSN 1097-8194
QUALITY (NEW YORK)/CALIDAD/QUALITE. Text in English. 1989. irreg., latest vol.19, 2006. free (effective 2010). back issues avail. **Document type:** *Monographic series, Academic/Scholarly.* **Description:** Highlights examples of clinical and educational programs which bring a strong commitment, as well as innovative and thoughtful approaches, to the issue of quality care in sexual and reproductive health.
Related titles: Online - full text ed.
Indexed: A26, CWI, H12, I05.
—**CCC.**
Published by: Population Council, One Dag Hammarskjold Plz, 9th Fl, New York, NY 10017. TEL 212-339-0500, 877-339-0500, FAX 212-755-6052, publications@popcouncil.org.

R W I: MATERIALIEN. (Rheinisch-Westfaelisches Institut) *see* SOCIAL SCIENCES: COMPREHENSIVE WORKS

325.1 SWE ISSN 1651-1662
RAPPORT INTEGRATION. Text in Swedish. 2001. a.
Published by: Integrationsverket/Swedish Integration Board, PO Box 633, Norrkoeping, 60114, Sweden. TEL 46-11-361300, FAX 46-11-361301, http://www.integrationsverket.se.

304.6 FRA ISSN 1951-1736
RAPPORT SUR L'EVOLUTION DEMOGRAPHIQUE DE LA FRANCE ET DE L'EUROPE. Text in French. 1970. a. bk.rev. stat. **Document type:** *Academic/Scholarly.*
Formerly (until 2004): Rapport sur la Situation Demographique de la France (1263-476X)
Published by: Institut National d'Etudes Demographiques (I N E D), 133 Blvd Davout, Paris, 75980 Cedex 20, France. TEL 33-1-56062000, FAX 33-1-56062199, editions@ined.fr, http://www.ined.fr. Ed. P Festy. Circ: 2,000.

304.6 FRA
RECENT DEMOGRAPHIC DEVELOPMENTS IN EUROPE AND NORTH AMERICA. Text in French. a. **Description:** Provides an analysis of the structure and evolution of the major components of population: population growth, marriage and divorce, fertility, mortality and migration.
Formerly (until 1992): Recent Demographic Developments in Europe
Related titles: French ed.: Evolution Demographique Recente en Europe et en Amerique du Nord.
Published by: Council of Europe/Conseil de l'Europe, Avenue de l'Europe, Strasbourg, 67075, France. TEL 33-3-88412581, FAX 33-3-88413910, publishing@coe.int, http://www.coe.int.

325 CAN ISSN 0229-5113
HV640.4.C2
REFUGE; Canada's periodical on refugees. Text in English; Abstracts in English, French. 1981. 4/yr. CAD 35 to individuals; CAD 65 to institutions; CAD 20 to students (effective 2004). **Document type:** *Journal, Academic/Scholarly.* **Description:** Dedicated to the encouragement of assistance to refugees by providing a forum for sharing information and opinion on Canadian and international issues pertaining to refugees.
Related titles: Online - full text ed.; French ed.: ISSN 0229-5121.
Indexed: A01, A26, C03, CA, CBCARef, CPerI, E08, ESPM, G08, GEOBASE, HRIR, I05, I13, IBSS, P34, P42, P48, P52, P56, PAIS, PQC, PSA, RefugAb, S02, S03, S09, SCOPUS, SSA, SSciA, SociolAb, T02.
—BLDSC (7336.295000). **CCC.**
Published by: York University, Center for Refugee Studies, Rm 322 York Lanes, 4700 Keele St, North York, ON ON M3J 1P3, Canada. TEL 416-736-5663, FAX 416-736-5837, crs@yorku.ca. Ed. Michael Lanphier. Circ: 1,200.

REFUGEE AND IMMIGRANT RESOURCE DIRECTORY (YEAR). *see* POLITICAL SCIENCE—International Relations

325 USA ISSN 0884-3554
HV640.4.U54
REFUGEE REPORTS. Text in English. 1979. m. USD 50 domestic; USD 55 in Canada; USD 60 elsewhere (effective 2000). bk.rev. **Document type:** *Newsletter.*
Related titles: Microfiche ed.: (from CIS).
Indexed: HRIR, P30, RefugAb, SRI.
Published by: Immigration and Refugee Services of America, 1717 Massachusetts Ave N W, Ste 200, Washington, DC 20036. TEL 202-347-3507. Ed. Virginia Hamilton. Circ: 1,000.

325 342.082 NLD ISSN 1387-6031
REFUGEES AND HUMAN RIGHTS. Text in English. 1997. irreg., latest vol.13, 2007. price varies. **Document type:** *Monographic series, Academic/Scholarly.* **Description:** Explores the nature and causes of forced migration, the modalities and procedures employed when refugees present themselves, and the manner in which their rights are promoted and protected.
Indexed: IZBG.
Published by: Martinus Nijhoff (Subsidiary of: Brill), PO Box 9000, Leiden, 2300 PA, Netherlands. TEL 31-71-5353500, FAX 31-71-5317532, marketing@brill.nl. Ed. Anne F Bayefsky.

304.6 FRA ISSN 1166-5742
RELIEF. Text in French. 1952. q. **Document type:** *Government.*
Former titles (until 1991): Statistiques & Etudes Midi - Pyrenees (0396-0099); (until 1970): Institut National de la Statistique et des Etudes Economiques. Direction Regionale de Toulouse. Bulletin de Statistique (0150-830X); (until 1965): Institut National de la Statistique et des Etudes Economiques. Direction Regionale de Toulouse. Bulletin Regional de Statistique (0532-4718)
Indexed: FR, P30.
Published by: Institut National de la Statistique et des Etudes Economiques, INSEE Midi-Pyrenees, 36 rue des 36 Ponts, Toulouse, Cedex 4 31054, France. TEL 33-61-366136, FAX 33-61-366200.

304.6 CHN
RENKOU XUEKAN/POPULATION JOURNAL. Text in Chinese. 1979. bi-m. CNY 40 domestic; USD 12 in Hong Kong, Macau & Taiwan; USD 21 elsewhere (effective 2007). **Document type:** *Journal, Academic/Scholarly.*
Related titles: Online - full text ed.
Published by: Jilin Daxue/Jilin University, 2699, Qianjin Dajie, Changchun, 130023, China. TEL 86-431-85166391. **Dist. by:** China International Book Trading Corp, 35 Chegongzhuang Xilu, Haidian District, PO Box 399, Beijing 100044, China. TEL 86-10-68412045, FAX 86-10-68412023, cibtc@mail.cibtc.com.cn, http://www.cibtc.com.cn.

304.6 CHN ISSN 1000-6087
HB3654.A3
RENKOU YANJIU/POPULATION RESEARCH. Text in Chinese; Contents page in English. 1977. bi-m. USD 37.20 (effective 2009). **Document type:** *Journal, Academic/Scholarly.* **Description:** Contains papers on population studies and demographics, as well as news of meetings and academic activities.
Related titles: Online - full text ed.
Indexed: P30, RASB.
—East View, Ingenta.
Published by: Zhongguo Renmin Daxue, Renkou Lilun Yanjiusuo/Renmin University of China, Institute of Population Theory, 59, Zhongguancun Dajie, Beijing, 100872, China. **Dist. by:** China International Book Trading Corp, 35 Chegongzhuang Xilu, Haidian District, PO Box 399, Beijing 100044, China. TEL 86-10-68412045, FAX 86-10-68412023, cibtc@mail.cibtc.com.cn, http://www.cibtc.com.cn.

304.6 TWN ISSN 1018-3930
HB848
RENKOU YANJIU TONGXUN/POPULATION NEWSLETTER. Text in Chinese. 1983. s-a. **Document type:** *Newsletter, Academic/Scholarly.*
Published by: Guoli Taiwan Daxue, Renkou yu Xingbei Yanjiu Zhongxin/National Taiwan University, Population And Gender Studies Center, 1, Sec 4, Roosevelt Rd., Taipei, 106, Taiwan. TEL 886-2-23630231 ext 2595, FAX 886-2-23639565, psc@ntu.edu.tw, http://ccms.ntu.edu.tw/~psc/index[1].htm.

304.6 CHN ISSN 1674-1668
HF5410
RENKOU YU FAZHAN (BEIJING). Text in Chinese. 1994. bi-m. **Document type:** *Journal, Academic/Scholarly.*
Formerly (until 2008): Shichang yu Renkou Fenxi/Market and Demographic Analysis (1006-4346)
Related titles: Online - full text ed.
Published by: Beijing Daxue. Renkou Yanjiusuo/Peking University. Institute of Population Research, 5, Yiheyuan Lu, Faxuelou 2/F, Beijing, 100871, China. TEL 86-10-62751974, rkyjs@pku.edu.cn.

304.6 CHN ISSN 1004-8197
HQ766.5.C6
RENKOU YU JIHUA SHENGYU/POPULATION AND FAMILY PLANNING. Text in Chinese. 1993. m. USD 36 (effective 2009). **Document type:** *Journal, Academic/Scholarly.* **Description:** Contains papers on China's population problem, applications of population theory, and the interrelationship between population and development.
Formerly (until 1992): Renkou Dongtai (1003-4579)
Related titles: Online - full text ed.
—East View.
Address: 12, Dahuisi, Beijing, 100081, China. TEL 86-10-62173528, FAX 86-10-62173523.

304.6 339 CHN ISSN 1000-4149
HB3654.A3
RENKOU YU JINGJI/POPULATION & ECONOMICS. Text in Chinese; Contents page in English. 1980. bi-m. USD 37.20 (effective 2009). adv. bk.rev. bibl.; charts; illus.; stat. **Document type:** *Journal, Academic/Scholarly.* **Description:** Features comprehensive studies, demographic analysis, analysis of economic demography population theory, population policies, reproductive health, sustainable development of population, resources and environment, the aged population, the female population, forum on family planning.
Related titles: CD-ROM ed.; Online - full text ed.
Indexed: P30, RASB.
—East View, Ingenta. **CCC.**
Published by: Shoudu Jingji Maoyi Daxue/Capital University of Economics and Business, No. 2 Jintaili, Hongmiao, Chaoyang District, Beijing, 100026, China. TEL 86-10-65976473. Ed. Feng Litian. R&P Tian Xiao Bo. Adv. contact Tian Xiao-BO. Circ: 7,000. **Dist. by:** China Book Publishings Export Corp., PO Box 782, Beijing, China; China International Book Trading Corp, 35 Chegongzhuang Xilu, Haidian District, PO Box 399, Beijing 100044, China. TEL 86-10-68412045, FAX 86-10-68412023, cibtc@mail.cibtc.com.cn, http://www.cibtc.com.cn.

304.6 TWN ISSN 1018-3841
HB3656.A3
➤ **RENKOU ZUEKAN/JOURNAL OF POPULATION STUDIES.** Text in Chinese. 1977. s-a. free. back issues avail. **Document type:** *Journal, Academic/Scholarly.* **Description:** Contains academic research on Taiwan and worldwide population.
Indexed: BAS, CA, ESPM, HPNRM, P42, PSA, PopulInd, S02, S03, SCOPUS, SOPODA, SSA, SSciA, SociolAb, T02.
Published by: Guoli Taiwan Daxue, Renkou yu Xingbei Yanjiu Zhongxin/National Taiwan University, Population And Gender Studies Center, 1, Sec 4, Roosevelt Rd., Taipei, 106, Taiwan. TEL 886-2-23630231 ext 2595, FAX 886-2-23639565, psc@ntu.edu.tw, http://ccms.ntu.edu.tw/~psc/index[1].htm. Circ: 800. **Co-publisher:** Taiwan Renkou Xuehui/Republic of China Population Association.

P

304.6 613.9 CHN ISSN 1674-4462
HB848
RENKOUXUE/DEMOLOGY. Text in Chinese. 1980. bi-m. CNY 60; CNY 10 per issue (effective 2011). 120 p./no.; **Document type:** *Journal, Academic/Scholarly.* **Description:** Covers the history and present situation of Chinese and world population studies. Also covers Chinese birth control policies.
Former titles (until 2009): Renkouxue yu Jihua Shengyu/Population Science and Family Planning (1005-4235); (until 1993): Renkouxue (1001-3458)
Indexed: RASB.
Published by: Zhongguo Renmin Daxue Shubao Ziliao Zhongxin/Renmin University of China, Information Center for Social Sciences, 59, Zhongguancun Dajie, Haidian-qu, Beijing, 100872, China. TEL 86-10-64039458, FAX 86-10-64015080, center@zlzx.org. **Dist. in US by:** China Publications Service, PO Box 49614, Chicago, IL 60649. TEL 312-288-3291, FAX 312-288-8570; **Dist. by:** China International Book Trading Corp, 35 Chegongzhuang Xilu, Haidian District, PO Box 399, Beijing 100044, China. TEL 86-10-68412045, FAX 86-10-68412023, cibtc@mail.cibtc.com.cn, http://www.cibtc.com.cn.

REPORT OF REVIEWABLE DEATHS. *see* SOCIAL SERVICES AND WELFARE

304.6 USA
HQ763
THE REPORTER (WASHINGTON, D.C.). Text in English. 1970. q. adv. bk.rev. charts; stat. back issues avail. **Document type:** *Magazine, Consumer.* **Description:** Contains articles and special features on a range of population-related social, economic and environmental issues.
Former titles (until 2002): The Z P G Reporter (0199-0071); Z P G National Reporter (0049-8718)
Related titles: Online - full text ed.
Indexed: CLFP, EnvAb, EnvInd, P30, SCOPUS.
Published by: Population Connection, 2120 L St, NW, Ste 500, Washington, DC 20037. TEL 202-332-2200, 800-767-1956, FAX 202-332-2302. Ed. Marian Starkey. Circ: 60,000.

REPRODUCTIONS. *see* BIOLOGY

325 NLD ISSN 0080-1623
JV6014
➤ **RESEARCH GROUP FOR EUROPEAN MIGRATION PROBLEMS. PUBLICATIONS.** Text in English. 1951. irreg., latest vol.17, 1972. price varies. **Document type:** *Monographic series, Academic/Scholarly.*
Published by: (Research Group for European Migration Problems), Springer Netherlands (Subsidiary of: Springer Science+Business Media), Van Godewijckstraat 30, Dordrecht, 3311 GX, Netherlands. TEL 31-78-6576050, FAX 31-78-6576474.

304.6 AUS ISSN 1448-6881
RESEARCH MATTERS. Text in English. q. **Document type:** *Newsletter, Government.* **Description:** Explores current issues on populations research as well as highlighting newly released publications, projects and seminars of interest.
Related titles: Online - full text ed.
Published by: Victoria. Department of Planning and Community Development. Strategic Policy Research and Forecasting Division. Spatial Analysis and Research, GPO Box 2392, Melbourne, VIC 3001, Australia. TEL 61-3-92083000, FAX 61-3-92083374, spatialanalysis.research@dpcd.vic.gov.au, http://www.dpcd.vic.gov.au/.

301.426 GBR ISSN 0957-2856
RESEARCH MONOGRAPHS ON HUMAN POPULATION BIOLOGY. Text in English. 1978. irreg., latest 1999. price varies. back issues avail. **Document type:** *Monographic series, Academic/Scholarly.*
Indexed: HPNRM, SSciA.
—BLDSC (7743.356000).
Published by: Oxford University Press, Great Clarendon St, Oxford, OX2 6DP, United Kingdom. TEL 44-1865-556767, FAX 44-1865-556646, enquiry@oup.co.uk, http://www.oup-usa.org/catalogs/general/series/. Ed. Michael A Little. **Orders in N. America to:** Oxford University Press, 2001 Evans Rd, Cary, NC 27513. TEL 919-677-0977 ext 5777, 800-852-7323, FAX 919-677-1714, jnlorders@oup-usa.org, http://www.us.oup.com.

304.6 FRA
HB848
REVIEW OF POPULATION REVIEWS (ONLINE). Text in English. 1976. q. free. bk.rev. back issues avail. **Document type:** *Proceedings, Abstract/Index.*
Formerly (until 200?): Review of Population Reviews (Print) (0379-3311)
Media: Online - full text. **Related titles:** French ed.: Revue des Revues Demographiques. ISSN 0377-8959.
Indexed: PopulInd.
Published by: Committee for International Cooperation in National Research in Demography, 133 Boulevard Davout, Paris, 75980 Cedex 20, France. TEL 33-1-56062019, FAX 33-1-56062165, cicred@cicred.org, http://www.cicred.org. Ed. Philippe Collomb.

304.6 BRA ISSN 0102-3098
HB3563
REVISTA BRASILEIRA DE ESTUDOS DE POPULACAO. Text in Portuguese. 1984. s-a. free to members. **Document type:** *Journal, Academic/Scholarly.*
Related titles: Online - full text ed.: free (effective 2011).
Indexed: C01, IBSS, P30, PopulInd, SCOPUS.
Published by: Associacao Brasileira de Estudos Populacionais (R E B E P), Secretaria Geral, UNICAMP-NEPO, Av Albert Einstein 1300, Campinas, SP 13081-970, Brazil. Ed. Carlos Eugenio Ferreira TEL 55-11-21717377.

REVISTA DE ADMINISTRACAO MUNICIPAL. *see* PUBLIC ADMINISTRATION—Municipal Government

304.6 946 ESP ISSN 1696-702X
HB3619
➤ **REVISTA DE DEMOGRAFIA HISTORICA.** Text in Spanish; Summaries in English. 1983. s-a. EUR 36 domestic to individuals; EUR 48 foreign to individuals; EUR 39 domestic to institutions; EUR 60 foreign to institutions (effective 2008). bk.rev. **Document type:** *Journal, Academic/Scholarly.* **Description:** Covers historical demography, population studies, family history and population history.
Formerly (until 2000): Asociacion de Demografia Historica. Boletin (0213-1145)
Related titles: Online - full text ed.
Indexed: P30, PopulInd, SCOPUS.
Published by: (Asociacion de Demografia Historica), Prensas Universitarias de Zaragoza, C/ Pedro Cerbuna 12, Edificio de Ciencias Geologicas, Zaragoza, 50009, Spain. TEL 34-976-761330, FAX 34-976-761063, puz@posta.unizar.es, http://puz.unizar.es.

➤ **REVISTA DE DERECHO MIGRATORIO Y EXTRANJERIA.** *see* LAW

325.1 CHL ISSN 1022-3045
REVISTA DE LA OIM SOBRE MIGRACIONES EN AMERICA LATINA. (Organizacion Internacional para las Migraciones) Text in Multiple languages. 1983. 3/yr.
Formerly (until 1989): Revista del O I M sobre Migraciones en America Latina (0253-8202)
Indexed: P30.
Published by: (International Organization for Migration/Organizacion Internacional para las Migraciones CHE), Centro de Informacion sobre Migraciones en America Latina, Matilde Salamanca 736, Piso 4, Santiago, Chile. TEL 56-2-2746713, FAX 56-2-2049704, cimal@oimchile.cl.

304.6 BRA ISSN 0101-7217
Z7164.D3
REVISTA DOCPOP; resumos sobre populacao no Brasil. Text in Portuguese. 1982. 2/yr. USD 52.10. bibl. back issues avail. **Description:** Discusses general population, mortality, fertility, migration, spatial distribution, nuptiality and family, characteristics and needs of the population.
Published by: Fundacao Sistema Estadual de Analise de Dados, Av Casper Libero, 464, Centro, Caixa Postal 8223, Sao Paulo, SP 01033-000, Brazil. TEL 011-2292433. Circ: 500.

304.6 MAR ISSN 0851-0024
REVUE DE L'I N S E A. (Institut National de Statistique et d'Economie Appliquee) Text in French. 1977. a.
Published by: Institut National de Statistique et d'Economie Appliquee (INSEA), Charii Allal Al Fassi, Madinat Al Irfane, B.P. 6217, Rabat, Morocco.

325 FRA ISSN 0765-0752
JV6003
➤ **REVUE EUROPEENNE DES MIGRATIONS INTERNATIONALES.** Text in French. 1985. 3/yr. EUR 50 domestic to individuals; EUR 54 elsewhere to individuals; EUR 60 domestic to institutions; EUR 65 elsewhere to institutions (effective 2004). bk.rev. **Document type:** *Academic/Scholarly.*
Indexed: A22, FR, IBSS, P30, PAIS, PopulInd, RASB, SCOPUS.
—BLDSC (7900.169800), IE, Infotrieve, Ingenta, INIST. **CCC.**
Published by: Association pour l'Etude des Migrations Internationales, 99 av. du Recteur Pineau, Poitiers, Cedex 86000, France. TEL 33-5-49454656, FAX 33-5-49454668. Ed. Michelle Guillon. Adv. contact Amir Abdulkarim.

304.6 DEU ISSN 1615-7273
ROSTOCKER BEITRAEGE ZUR DEMOGRAPHIE. Text in German. 2000. irreg., latest vol.2, 2002. price varies. **Document type:** *Monographic series, Academic/Scholarly.*
Published by: Duncker und Humblot GmbH, Carl-Heinrich-Becker-Weg 9, Berlin, 12165, Germany. TEL 49-30-7900060, FAX 49-30-79000631, info@duncker-humblot.de.

304.6 BGD ISSN 1010-3783
HB850.5.B3
RURAL DEMOGRAPHY. Text in English. 1974. s-a. USD 6. charts; stat.
Indexed: CIS, P30, PopulInd.
Published by: (Institute of Statistical Research and Training), University of Dhaka, Ramna, Dhaka, 1000, Bangladesh.

325 USA ISSN 1086-5837
RURAL MIGRATION NEWS. Text in English. 1995. q. USD 30 domestic; USD 50 foreign (effective 2001). back issues avail.
Related titles: Online - full text ed.: ISSN 1086-5845. 1995.
Published by: University of California, Davis, Department of Agricultural Economics, One Shields Ave, Davis, CA 95616. migrant@primal.ucdavis.edu. Ed. Philip Martin.

304.6 RWA
RWANDA. OFFICE NATIONAL DE LA POPULATION. FAMILLE, SANTE, DEVELOPPEMENT/IMBONEZAMULYANGO. Text in French, Kinyarwanda. 1984. q. RWF 550. **Document type:** *Bulletin, Government.*
Indexed: PLESA.
Published by: Office National de la Population, Service de l'Information, BP 914, Kigali, Rwanda.

304.6 USA
S D S U CENSUS DATA CENTER. NEWSLETTER. (South Dakota State University) Text in English. irreg.
Published by: South Dakota State University, Data Center, PO Box 504, Brookings, SD 57006. Ed. James Satterlee.

304.6 DEU ISSN 0942-2455
S O F I D - SOZIALWISSENSCHAFTLICHER FACHINFORMATIONSDIENST. BEVOELKERUNGSFORSCHUNG. Text in German. 1992. s-a. EUR 30 (effective 2008). **Document type:** *Journal, Academic/Scholarly.*
Formed by the merger of (1979-1992): S o F i d - Sozialwissenschaftlicher Fachinformationsdienst. Bevoelkerungsforschung I: Bevoelkerungsforschung Allgemein und Natuerliche Bevoelkerungsbeschreibung (0930-3189); (1979-1992): S o F i d - Sozialwissenschaftlicher Fachinformationsdienst. Bevoelkerungsforschung II: Raeumliche und Sozialoekonomische Bevoelkerungsbeschreibung (0930-3197); Both of which superseded in part (in 1986): Bibliographie Deutschsprachiger Bevoelkerungswissenschaftlicher Literatur (0178-9198)
Published by: Arbeitsgemeinschaft Sozialwissenschaftlicher Institute, Informationszentrum Sozialwissenschaften, Lennestr 30, Bonn, 53113, Germany. TEL 49-228-22810, FAX 49-228-2281121, iz@gesis.org, http://www.gesis.org/IZ/index.htm.

304.6 KOR ISSN 1599-1199
SAENGHWAL SI'GAN JO'SA BO'GO'SEO. JE 2 GWON, SI'GAN DAE'BYEOL HAENGWIJA BIYUL PYEON/KOREA (REPUBLIC). NATIONAL STATISTICAL OFFICE. REPORT ON THE TIME USE SURVEY. VOLUME 2, PARTICIPATION RATES IN ACTIVITIES BY TIME INTERVALS. Text in English, Korean. 2000. quinquennial. USD 36 newsstand/cover (effective 2009). stat. **Document type:** *Government.*
Published by: Tong'gyecheong/Korea National Statistical Office, Government Complex Daejeon, 139 Seonsaro (920 Dunsan 2-dong), Seo-gu, Daejeon, 302-701, Korea, S. TEL 82-42-4814114. **Subscr. to:** The Korean Statistical Association, Rm. 103, Seoul Statistical Branch Office Bldg. 71, Nonhyun-Dong, Kangnam-Ku, Seoul 135701, Korea, S. TEL 82-2-34437954, FAX 82-2-34437957, kosa@nso.go.kr.

304.6 KOR ISSN 1599-0486
HB1482.5.A3
SA'MANG WON'IN TONG'GYE YEONBO/KOREA (REPUBLIC). NATIONAL STATISTICAL OFFICE. ANNUAL REPORT ON THE CAUSE OF DEATH STATISTICS. Text in English. 1982. a. USD 14 newsstand/cover (effective 2009). stat. **Document type:** *Government.*
Published by: Tong'gyecheong/Korea National Statistical Office, Government Complex Daejeon, 139 Seonsaro (920 Dunsan 2-dong), Seo-gu, Daejeon, 302-701, Korea, S. TEL 82-42-4814114. **Subscr. to:** The Korean Statistical Association, Rm. 103, Seoul Statistical Branch Office Bldg. 71, Nonhyun-Dong, Kangnam-Ku, Seoul 135701, Korea, S. TEL 82-2-34437954, FAX 82-2-34437957, kosa@nso.go.kr.

325 PHL
SCALABRINI MIGRATION CENTER. OCCASIONAL PAPERS. Text in English. irreg. **Document type:** *Monographic series, Academic/Scholarly.* **Description:** Contains papers on the study of socio-demographic, economic, political, psychological, historical, legislative and religious aspects of human migration and refugee movements from and within Asia.
Published by: Scalabrini Migration Center, Broadway Centrum, PO Box 10541, Quezon City, 1113, Philippines. TEL 63-2-7243512, FAX 63-2-7214296, smc@smc.org.ph, http://www.smc.org.ph/. Ed. Graziano Battistella.

304.6 USA ISSN 1939-4284
SCIENTISTS, ENGINEERS, AND TECHNICIANS IN THE UNITED STATES. Text in English. 1996. irreg., latest 2001 published in 2005. stat. **Document type:** *Government.*
Media: Online - full content.
Published by: National Science Foundation, Division of Science Resources Statistics, 4201 Wilson Blvd, Ste 965, Arlington, VA 22230. TEL 703-292-8774, FAX 703-292-9092.

SCRITTURE MIGRANTI; rivista di scambi interculturali. *see* LITERATURE

304.6 ARG ISSN 1852-2629
▼ **SERIE DE DOCUMENTOS DE LA DIRECCION NACIONAL DE POBLACION.** Text in Spanish. 2009. irreg. back issues avail. **Document type:** *Bulletin, Consumer.*
Media: Online - full text.
Published by: Ministerio de Interior, Direccion Nacional de Poblacion, 25 de Mayo 145 Piso 2 Ofic. 2002, Buenos Aires, C1003AAP, Argentina. TEL 54-11-43461591, poblacion@mininterior.gov.ar.

SERVICE DE CENTRALISATION DES ETUDES GENEALOGIQUES ET DEMOGRAPHIQUES DE BELGIQUE. NOUVELLES BREVES. *see* GENEALOGY AND HERALDRY

304.6 ITA ISSN 0394-8323
I SERVIZI DEMOGRAFICI; rivista mensile dei servizi di anagrafe, stato civile, elettorale, statistica, e leva dei comuni. Text in Italian. 1982. m. (11/yr.). EUR 148 (effective 2008). **Document type:** *Magazine, Trade.* **Description:** Addresses the problematic issues faced by those in the field of demographic data collection.
Published by: Maggioli Editore, Via del Carpino 8/10, Santarcangelo di Romagna, RN 47822, Italy. TEL 39-0541-628111, FAX 39-0541-622020, editore@maggioli.it, http://www.maggioli.it.

SERVIZIO MIGRANTI. *see* POLITICAL SCIENCE

325 FIN ISSN 0355-3779
SIIRTOLAISUUS/MIGRATION. Text in Finnish, English, Swedish. 1974. q. EUR 10 (effective 2005). adv. bk.rev. illus. 40 p./no. 3 cols./p.; **Document type:** *Journal, Academic/Scholarly.* **Description:** Covers historical, as well as recent trends in population movements, including ethnical issues as a related field.
Indexed: P30.
Published by: Siirtolaisuusinstituutti/Institute of Migration, Linnankatu 61, Turku, 20100, Finland. TEL 358-2-2840440, FAX 358-2-2333460, http://www.migrationsinstitute.fi. Ed. Olavi Koivukangas. Circ: 1,000 (controlled).

325 FIN ISSN 0356-9659
SIIRTOLAISUUSTUTKIMUKSIA, A. Text in Finnish. 1975. irreg. price varies. bk.rev. charts; stat.; illus.; maps. **Document type:** *Monographic series, Academic/Scholarly.* **Description:** Covers historical as well as recent trends in population movements.
Related titles: English ed.: Migration Studies, C. ISSN 0356-780X. 1974; Swedish ed.: Migrationsstudier, B. ISSN 0358-0083. 1975.
Published by: Siirtolaisuusinstituutti/Institute of Migration, Linnankatu 61, Turku, 20100, Finland. TEL 358-2-2840440, FAX 358-2-2333460. Ed. Olavi Koivukangas. Circ: 500.

THE SOCIAL CONTRACT. *see* SOCIOLOGY

304.6 FRA
SOCIO-ECONOMIC DIFFERENTIAL MORTALITY IN INDUSTRIALIZED SOCIETIES. Text in French. 1980. a. free. **Document type:** *Academic/Scholarly.*
Published by: Committee for International Cooperation in National Research in Demography, 133 Boulevard Davout, Paris, 75980 Cedex 20, France. TEL 33-1-56062019, FAX 33-1-56062165, cicred@cicred.org, http://www.cicred.org. Circ: 500.

SOTSIALNI TENDENTSII. *see* STATISTICS

304.6 ZAF
SOUTH AFRICA. STATISTICS SOUTH AFRICA. DOCUMENTED MIGRATION (YEAR). Text in English. irreg., latest 1999. ZAR 50 per issue (effective 2008). stat. **Document type:** *Government.*
Published by: Statistics South Africa/Statistieke Suid-Afrika, Private Bag X44, Pretoria, 0001, South Africa. TEL 27-12-3108911, FAX 27-12-3108500, info@statssa.gov.za, http://www.statssa.gov.za.

304.6 ZAF
SOUTH AFRICA. STATISTICS SOUTH AFRICA. LIVING IN EASTERN CAPE (ONLINE EDITION); selected findings of the (Year) (Month) household survey. Text in English. irreg., latest 1998. free. **Document type:** *Government.*

Formerly: South Africa. Statistics South Africa. Living in Eastern Cape (Print Edition)
Media: Online - full text.
Published by: Statistics South Africa/Statistieke Suid-Afrika, Private Bag X44, Pretoria, 0001, South Africa. TEL 27-12-3108911, FAX 27-12-3108500, info@statssa.gov.za, http://www.statssa.gov.za.

304.6 ZAF
SOUTH AFRICA. STATISTICS SOUTH AFRICA. LIVING IN FREE STATE (ONLINE EDITION); selected findings of the (Year) (Month) household survey. Text in English. irreg., latest 1998. free. **Document type:** *Government.*
Formerly: South Africa. Statistics South Africa. Living in Free State (Print Edition)
Media: Online - full text.
Published by: Statistics South Africa/Statistieke Suid-Afrika, Private Bag X44, Pretoria, 0001, South Africa. TEL 27-12-3108911, FAX 27-12-3108500, info@statssa.gov.za, http://www.statssa.gov.za.

304.6 ZAF
SOUTH AFRICA. STATISTICS SOUTH AFRICA. LIVING IN GAUTENG (ONLINE EDITION); selected findings of the (Year) (Month) household survey. Text in English. irreg. free. **Document type:** *Government.*
Formerly: South Africa. Statistics South Africa. Living in Gauteng (Print Edition)
Media: Online - full text.
Published by: Statistics South Africa/Statistieke Suid-Afrika, Private Bag X44, Pretoria, 0001, South Africa. TEL 27-12-3108911, FAX 27-12-3108500, info@statssa.gov.za, http://www.statssa.gov.za. Ed. Joyce Lestrade-Jefferis.

304.6 ZAF
SOUTH AFRICA. STATISTICS SOUTH AFRICA. LIVING IN KWA-ZULU-NATAL (ONLINE EDITION); selected findings of the (Year) (Month) household survey. Text in English. irreg. free. **Document type:** *Government.*
Formerly: South Africa. Statistics South Africa. Living in Zulu-Natal (Print Edition)
Media: Online - full text.
Published by: Statistics South Africa/Statistieke Suid-Afrika, Private Bag X44, Pretoria, 0001, South Africa. TEL 27-12-3108911, FAX 27-12-3108500, info@statssa.gov.za, http://www.statssa.gov.za.

304.6 ZAF
SOUTH AFRICA. STATISTICS SOUTH AFRICA. LIVING IN LIMPOPO (ONLINE EDITION); selected findings of the (Year) (Month) household survey. Text in English. irreg. free. **Document type:** *Government.*
Media: Online - full text.
Published by: Statistics South Africa/Statistieke Suid-Afrika, Private Bag X44, Pretoria, 0001, South Africa. TEL 27-12-3108911, FAX 27-12-3108500, info@statssa.gov.za, http://www.statssa.gov.za.

304.6 ZAF
SOUTH AFRICA. STATISTICS SOUTH AFRICA. LIVING IN MPUMALANGA (ONLINE EDITION); selected findings of the (Year) (Month) household survey. Text in English. irreg. free. **Document type:** *Government.*
Formerly: South Africa. Statistics South Africa. Living in Mpumalanga (Print Edition)
Media: Online - full text.
Published by: Statistics South Africa/Statistieke Suid-Afrika, Private Bag X44, Pretoria, 0001, South Africa. TEL 27-12-3108911, FAX 27-12-3108500, info@statssa.gov.za, http://www.statssa.gov.za.

304.6
SOUTH AFRICA. STATISTICS SOUTH AFRICA. LIVING IN NORTH WEST (ONLINE EDITION); selected findings of the (Year) (Month) household survey. Text in English. irreg., latest 1998. free. **Document type:** *Government.*
Formerly: South Africa. Statistics South Africa. Living in North West (Print Edition)
Media: Online - full text.
Published by: Statistics South Africa/Statistieke Suid-Afrika, Private Bag X44, Pretoria, 0001, South Africa. TEL 27-12-3108911, FAX 27-12-3108500, info@statssa.gov.za, http://www.statssa.gov.za.

304.6 ZAF
SOUTH AFRICA. STATISTICS SOUTH AFRICA. LIVING IN NORTHERN CAPE (ONLINE EDITION); selected findings of the (Year) (Month) household survey. Text in English. irreg. free. **Document type:** *Government.*
Formerly: South Africa. Statistics South Africa. Living in Northern Cape (Print Edition)
Media: Online - full text.
Published by: Statistics South Africa/Statistieke Suid-Afrika, Private Bag X44, Pretoria, 0001, South Africa. TEL 27-12-3108911, FAX 27-12-3108500, info@statssa.gov.za, http://www.statssa.gov.za.

304.6 ZAF
SOUTH AFRICA. STATISTICS SOUTH AFRICA. LIVING IN SOUTH AFRICA (ONLINE EDITION); selected findings of the (Year) (Month) household survey. Text in English. irreg. free. **Document type:** *Government.*
Formerly: South Africa. Statistics South Africa. Living in South Africa (Print Edition)
Media: Online - full text.
Published by: Statistics South Africa/Statistieke Suid-Afrika, Private Bag X44, Pretoria, 0001, South Africa. TEL 27-12-3108911, FAX 27-12-3108500, info@statssa.gov.za, http://www.statssa.gov.za.

304.6 ZAF
SOUTH AFRICA. STATISTICS SOUTH AFRICA. LIVING IN WESTERN CAPE (ONLINE EDITION); selected findings of the (Year) (Month) household survey. Text in English. irreg. free. **Document type:** *Government.*
Formerly: South Africa. Statistics South Africa. Living in Western Cape (Print Edition)
Media: Online - full text.
Published by: Statistics South Africa/Statistieke Suid-Afrika, Private Bag X44, Pretoria, 0001, South Africa. TEL 27-12-3108911, FAX 27-12-3108500, info@statssa.gov.za, http://www.statssa.gov.za.

304.6 ZAF
SOUTH AFRICA. STATISTICS SOUTH AFRICA. POPULATION CENSUS, (YEAR). EMPLOYMENT EQUITY. Text in English. irreg. ZAR 200 (effective 2007). **Document type:** *Government.*
Media: CD-ROM.
Published by: Statistics South Africa/Statistieke Suid-Afrika, Private Bag X44, Pretoria, 0001, South Africa. TEL 27-12-3108911, FAX 27-12-3108500, info@statssa.gov.za, http://www.statssa.gov.za.

304.6 ZAF
SOUTH AFRICA. STATISTICS SOUTH AFRICA. POPULATION CENSUS, (YEAR). MAGJSTERIAL DISTRICTS BY POPULATION GROUP & GENDER. Text in English. 1996. irreg. free. **Document type:** *Government.*
Published by: Statistics South Africa/Statistieke Suid-Afrika, Private Bag X44, Pretoria, 0001, South Africa. TEL 27-12-3108911, FAX 27-12-3108500, info@statssa.gov.za, http://www.statssa.gov.za.

304.6 ZAF
SOUTH AFRICA. STATISTICS SOUTH AFRICA. POPULATION CENSUS, (YEAR). PRIMARY TABLES EASTERN CAPE (ONLINE EDITION). Text in English. irreg. free. stat. **Document type:** *Government.*
Formerly: South Africa. Statistics South Africa. Primary Tables Eastern Cape (Print Edition)
Media: Online - full text.
Published by: Statistics South Africa/Statistieke Suid-Afrika, Private Bag X44, Pretoria, 0001, South Africa. TEL 27-12-3108911, FAX 27-12-3108500, info@statssa.gov.za, http://www.statssa.gov.za.

304.6 ZAF
SOUTH AFRICA. STATISTICS SOUTH AFRICA. POPULATION CENSUS, (YEAR). PRIMARY TABLES. FREE STATE. Text in English. 1996. irreg., latest 1996. free. stat. **Document type:** *Government.*
Published by: Statistics South Africa/Statistieke Suid-Afrika, Private Bag X44, Pretoria, 0001, South Africa. TEL 27-12-3108911, FAX 27-12-3108500, info@statssa.gov.za, http://www.statssa.gov.za.

304.6 ZAF
SOUTH AFRICA. STATISTICS SOUTH AFRICA. POPULATION CENSUS, (YEAR). PRIMARY TABLES SOUTH AFRICA (ONLINE EDITION). Text in English. 1996. irreg. free. stat. **Document type:** *Government.*
Formerly: South Africa. Statistics South Africa. Population Census, (Year). Primary Tables. South Africa (Print Edition)
Media: Online - full text.
Published by: Statistics South Africa/Statistieke Suid-Afrika, Private Bag X44, Pretoria, 0001, South Africa. TEL 27-12-3108911, FAX 27-12-3108500, info@statssa.gov.za, http://www.statssa.gov.za.

304.6 ZAF
SOUTH AFRICA. STATISTICS SOUTH AFRICA. POPULATION CENSUS, (YEAR). PRIMARY TABLES WESTERN CAPE (ONLINE EDITION). Text in English. irreg. free. stat. **Document type:** *Government.*
Formerly: South Africa. Statistics South Africa. Population Census, (Year). Primary Tables Western Cape (Print Edition)
Media: Online - full text.
Published by: Statistics South Africa/Statistieke Suid-Afrika, Private Bag X44, Pretoria, 0001, South Africa. TEL 27-12-3108911, FAX 27-12-3108500, info@statssa.gov.za, http://www.statssa.gov.za.

304.6 ZAF
SOUTH AFRICA. STATISTICS SOUTH AFRICA. RECORDED DEATHS (YEAR). Text in English. irreg., latest 1999. **Document type:** *Government.* **Description:** Provides a register of manufacturers according to products manufactured in South Africa.
Published by: Statistics South Africa/Statistieke Suid-Afrika, Private Bag X44, Pretoria, 0001, South Africa. TEL 27-12-3108911, FAX 27-12-3108500, info@statssa.gov.za, http://www.statssa.gov.za.

304.6 ZAF
SOUTH AFRICA. STATISTICS SOUTH AFRICA. UNEMPLOYMENT AND EMPLOYMENT (ONLINE EDITION). Text in English. irreg., latest 1994-1997. free. **Document type:** *Government.*
Formerly: South Africa. Statistics South Africa. Employment and Unemployment in South Africa (Print Edition)
Media: Online - full text.
Published by: Statistics South Africa/Statistieke Suid-Afrika, Private Bag X44, Pretoria, 0001, South Africa. TEL 27-12-3108911, FAX 27-12-3108500, info@statssa.gov.za, http://www.statssa.gov.za.

304.6 ZAF
SOUTH AFRICA. STATISTICS SOUTH AFRICA. VILLAGES & TOWNSHIP VITAL STATISTICS NETWORK. Text in English. irreg. free. stat. **Document type:** *Government.*
Published by: Statistics South Africa/Statistieke Suid-Afrika, Private Bag X44, Pretoria, 0001, South Africa. TEL 27-12-3108911, FAX 27-12-3108500, info@statssa.gov.za, http://www.statssa.gov.za.

325.1 NZL ISSN 2230-4673
THE SOUTH AFRICAN; connecting South Africa and New Zealand. Text in English. 2008. bi-m. free (effective 2011). adv. back issues avail. **Document type:** *Magazine, Consumer.*
Media: Online - full text.
Published by: Peter Woodberg, Ed. & Pub. jepwood@xtra.co.nz. Adv. contact Norma Vaz.

304.6 AUS
SOUTH AUSTRALIA. DEPARTMENT OF HOUSING AND URBAN DEVELOPMENT. POPULATION PROJECTIONS BY STATISTICAL DIVISION - DATA SHEETS. Text in English. 1989. irreg. **Document type:** *Government.*
Former titles: South Australia. Department of Housing and Urban Development. State and Regional Projections. Bulletin; South Australia. Department of Environment and Planning. State Regional Projections. Bulletin (1032-8793)
Published by: (South Australia. Information & Data Analysis Branch), Government of South Australia, Department for Families and Communities, GPO Box 292, Adelaide, SA 5001, Australia. TEL 61-8-82268800, FAX 61-8-84139003, enquiries@dfc.sa.gov.a, http://www.dfc.sa.gov.au/.

304.6 USA
SOUTH CAROLINA. STATE DATA CENTER. NEWSLETTER. Text in English. q. **Document type:** *Newsletter.*
Published by: Budget and Control Board, Division of Research & Statistics, Rembert C Dennis Bldg, Rm 425, 1000 Assembly St, Columbia, SC 29201. TEL 803-734-3788, FAX 803-734-3619. Ed. Michael MacFarlane.

314 ZAF ISSN 1682-4482
➤ **SOUTHERN AFRICAN JOURNAL OF DEMOGRAPHY.** Text in English. 1987. irreg., latest vol.9, 2004. price varies. **Document type:** *Journal, Academic/Scholarly.* **Description:** Focuses on the application of mathematical and statistical techniques to the analysis of the population dynamics of the region and on the study of the populations of Southern Africa.
Indexed: ISAP.
Published by: University of Cape Town, Centre for Actuarial Research, Private Bag, Rondebosch, 7701, South Africa. TEL 27-21-6504375, FAX 27-21-6504369. Eds. Rob Dorrington, Tom Moultrie.

304.6 USA
SOUTHERN DEMOGRAPHIC NEWS. Text in English. 1971. q. USD 10 (effective 2000). **Document type:** *Newsletter.* **Description:** Provides news and short articles about population studies and association members and activities.
Former titles: S D A Newsletter; S R D G Newsletter
Published by: Southern Demographic Association, c/o Robert Freymeyer, Department of Sociology, Presbyterian College, Clinton, SC 29325. TEL 864-833-8359. Eds. Barbara Johnson, Robert Freymeyer. Circ: 300.

304.6 USA
SPOTLIGHT ON VIRGINIA. Text in English. 1997. a. **Document type:** *Report, Government.*
Related titles: Online - full text ed.
Published by: University of Virginia, Weldon Cooper Center for Public Service, PO Box 400206, Charlottesville, VA 22904. TEL 434-982-5522, coopercenter@virginia.edu, http://www.coopercenter.org/.

304.6 NLD ISSN 1877-2560
SPRINGER SERIES ON DEMOGRAPHIC METHODS AND POPULATION ANALYSIS. Text in English. 1988. irreg., latest vol.30, 2011. price varies. **Document type:** *Monographic series, Academic/Scholarly.*
Formerly (until 2006): The Plenum Series on Demographic Methods and Popular Analysis (1389-6784)
Published by: Springer Netherlands (Subsidiary of: Springer Science+Business Media), Van Godewijckstraat 30, Dordrecht, 3311 GX, Netherlands. TEL 31-78-6576050, FAX 31-78-6576474. Ed. Kenneth Land.

304.6 NLD ISSN 2211-3215
▼ ➤ **SPRINGERBRIEFS IN POPULATION STUDIES.** Text in English. 2011. irreg., latest vol.2, 2011. EUR 49.95 per vol. (effective 2011). **Document type:** *Monographic series, Academic/Scholarly.* **Description:** Aims to advance research in the field of demography and population studies.
Related titles: Online - full text ed.: ISSN 2211-3223.
Published by: Springer Netherlands (Subsidiary of: Springer Science+Business Media), Van Godewijckstraat 30, Dordrecht, 3311 GX, Netherlands. TEL 31-78-6576050, FAX 31-78-6576474.

➤ **SRBIJA I CRNA GORA ZAVOD ZA STATISTIKU. DEMOGRAFSKA STATISTIKA.** *see* POPULATION STUDIES—Abstracting, Bibliographies, Statistics

304.6 LKA ISSN 1391-3433
HB3636.8.A3
➤ **SRI LANKA JOURNAL OF POPULATION STUDIES.** Text in English. 1998. a. **Document type:** *Journal, Academic/Scholarly.*
Indexed: P30.
Published by: University of Colombo, Department of Demography, PO Box 1490, Colombo, Sri Lanka.

301.3 SRB ISSN 0038-982X
HB848
STANOVNISTVO. Text in Serbian; Abstracts and contents page in English, French, Russian. 1963. s-a. adv. bk.rev. charts; illus.; stat. index. **Document type:** *Journal, Academic/Scholarly.*
Related titles: Online - full text ed.: free (effective 2011).
Indexed: P30, PopulInd, RASB.
Published by: Institut Drustvenih Nauka u Beogradu, Centar za Demografska Istrazivanja, Kraljice Natalije 45, Belgrade, 11000. TEL 381-11-3616001, d.bsukovic@yubc.net, http://www.cei.idn.org.yu. Ed. Mirjana Rasevic.

304.6 USA
STATE OF WORLD POPULATION. Text in English. a.
Indexed: IIS.
Published by: United Nations Population Fund (U N F P A), 220 E 42nd St, New York, NY 10017. TEL 212-297-5000, http://www.unfpa.org. Ed., R&P Alex Marshall TEL 212-297-5020.

STATE PROFILE. *see* BUSINESS AND ECONOMICS—Economic Situation And Conditions

STATE PROFILES; the population and economy of each U S State. *see* STATISTICS

304.6 EGY ISSN 2090-1798
STATISTICS, COMPUTER SCIENCE AND OPERATION RESEARCH. PART V, DEMOGRAPHY. ANNUAL CONFERENCE. Text in English. 1965. a. **Document type:** *Proceedings, Academic/Scholarly.*
Supersedes in part (in 198?): Statistics, Computer Science and Operations Research. Annual Conference (1110-6778)
Published by: Cairo University, Institute of Statistical Studies and Research, 5 Tharwat St, Orman, Giza, Egypt. TEL 20-2-3358496, FAX 20-2-7482533, dean@issr.cu.edu.eg, http://issr.cu.edu.eg.

304.8 ITA ISSN 0039-2936
J1
STUDI EMIGRAZIONE/EMIGRATION STUDIES. Text and summaries in English, French, Italian, Spanish. 1964. 4/yr. EUR 55 domestic; EUR 65 foreign (effective 2009). adv. bk.rev. abstr.; bibl.; charts; stat. index. back issues avail. **Document type:** *Journal, Academic/Scholarly.* **Description:** Explores the phenomenon of massive population displacement.
Indexed: A22, AmH&L, BibInd, CA, ESPM, FR, GEOBASE, HistAb, IBR, IBZ, L&LBA, P30, P34, P42, PAIS, PSA, PopulInd, RefugAb, S02, S03, SCOPUS, SOPODA, SSA, SSciA, SociolAb, T02.
—BLDSC (8481.820000), IE, Infotrieve, Ingenta.
Published by: Centro Studi Emigrazione, Via Dandolo 58, Rome, 00153, Italy. TEL 39-06-5809764, FAX 39-06-5814651. Circ: 1,000.

P

304.6 POL ISSN 0039-3134
HB881.A1
➤ **STUDIA DEMOGRAFICZNE.** Text in English, Polish; Summaries in English. 1963. q. bk.rev. abstr.; charts; stat. **Document type:** *Journal, Academic/Scholarly.* **Description:** Aims to contribute to the high quality demographic research in Poland, with focus on Central and Eastern Europe.
Indexed: IBSS, P30, PopulInd, RASB.
Published by: Polska Akademia Nauk, Komitet Nauk Demograficznych/ Polish Academy of Sciences, Committee on Demographic Sciences, Al Niepodleglosci 162, Szkola Glowna Handlowa, Instytut Statystyki i Demografii, Warsaw, 02554, Poland. TEL 48-22-8495397, ewaf@sgh.waw.pl, http://www.knd.pan.pl. Ed. Irena Kotowska. Circ: 520.

301.3 POL ISSN 0137-5210
STUDIA POLONIJNE. Text in Polish; Summaries in English. 1976. irreg. price varies. index.
Indexed: RASB.
Published by: Katolicki Uniwersytet Lubelski, Towarzystwo Naukowe, ul Gliniana 21, Lublin, 20616, Poland. Circ: 3,125.

304.6 DEU ISSN 1610-9775
STUDIEN ZUR DEMOGRAPHIE UND BEVOELKERUNGSENTWICKLUNG. Text in German. 2003. irreg., latest vol.3, 2010. price varies. **Document type:** *Monographic series, Academic/Scholarly.*
Published by: Verlag Dr. Kovac, Leverkusenstr 13, Hamburg, 22761, Germany. TEL 49-40-3988800, FAX 49-40-39888055, info@verlagdrkovac.de.

301.32 DEU
STUDIEN ZUR HISTORISCHEN MIGRATIONSFORSCHUNG. Text in German. 1995. irreg., latest vol.18, 2006. price varies. **Document type:** *Monographic series, Academic/Scholarly.*
Published by: (Institut fuer Migrationsforschung und Interkulturelle Studien), V & R Unipress GmbH (Subsidiary of: Vandenhoeck und Ruprecht), Robert-Bosch-Breite 6, Goettingen, 37079, Germany. TEL 49-551-5084303, FAX 49-551-5084333, info@vr-unipress.de, http://www.v-r.de/en/publisher/unipress.

304.8 DEU ISSN 1618-6095
STUDIEN ZUR MIGRATIONSFORSCHUNG. Text in German. 2001. irreg., latest vol.12, 2010. price varies. **Document type:** *Monographic series, Academic/Scholarly.*
Published by: Verlag Dr. Kovac, Leverkusenstr 13, Hamburg, 22761, Germany. TEL 49-40-3988800, FAX 49-40-39888055, info@verlagdrkovac.de.

304.6 USA ISSN 1048-163X
➤ **STUDIES IN DEMOGRAPHY.** Text in English. 1987. irreg., latest vol.6, 1993. price varies. back issues avail. **Document type:** *Monographic series, Academic/Scholarly.* **Description:** Discusses family planning, migration, and other phenomena that affect population size.
—CCC.
Published by: University of California Press, Book Series, 2120 Berkeley Way, Berkeley, CA 94704. TEL 510-642-4247, FAX 510-643-7127, foundation@ucpress.edu. **Subscr. to:** California - Princeton Fulfillment Services, Inc., 1445 Lower Ferry Rd, Ewing, NJ 08618. TEL 609-883-1759, 800-777-4726, FAX 800-999-1958, orders@cpfsinc.com.

306.85 USA ISSN 0039-3665
HQ763 CODEN: SFPLA3
➤ **STUDIES IN FAMILY PLANNING.** Text in English. 1963. q. GBP 154 combined subscription in United Kingdom to institutions (print & online eds.); EUR 196 combined subscription in Europe to institutions (print & online eds.); USD 184 combined subscription in the Americas to institutions (print & online eds.); USD 302 combined subscription elsewhere to institutions (print & online eds.) (effective 2012). bk.rev. charts; abstr.; illus. index. 100 p./no.; back issues avail.; reprint service avail. from PSC. **Document type:** *Journal, Academic/Scholarly.* **Description:** Concerned with all aspects of reproductive health, fertility regulation and family planning programs and their relation to health and development in developed and developing countries.
Incorporates: Current Publications in Family Planning (0011-3867)
Related titles: Microform ed.: (from PQC); Online - full text ed.: ISSN 1728-4465. 1998. GBP 138 in United Kingdom to institutions; EUR 175 in Europe to institutions; USD 165 in the Americas to institutions; USD 270 elsewhere to institutions (effective 2012) (from IngentaConnect).
Indexed: A01, A02, A03, A08, A20, A22, A25, A26, A36, ABS&EES, AIDS Ab, AMHA, ASCA, ASSIA, AgrForAb, B21, BAS, CA, CABA, CLFP, CWI, Chicano, CurCont, D01, DIP, E01, E08, E12, EIP, EMBASE, ESPM, EconLit, EnvAb, EnvInd, ExcerpMed, F08, F09, FamI, G05, G06, G07, G08, GEOBASE, GH, H&SSA, H05, H12, H13, HPNRM, I05, I07, I14, IBR, IBSS, IBZ, IndMed, JEL, MEA&I, MEDLINE, N02, N03, P02, P03, P06, P10, P20, P30, P33, P34, P39, P48, P52, P53, P54, P56, PAIS, PCI, PQC, PRA, PopulInd, PsycInfo, PsycholAb, R12, REE&TA, RiskAb, S02, S03, S08, S09, S11, S21, S23, SCOPUS, SFSA, SOPODA, SPPI, SSA, SSCI, SSciA, SociolAb, T02, T05, TAR, W07, W09, W11.
—BLDSC (8490.545000), GNLM, IE, Infotrieve, Ingenta. **CCC.**
Published by: (Population Council), Wiley-Blackwell Publishing, Inc. (Subsidiary of: Wiley-Blackwell Publishing Ltd.), 111 River St, Hoboken, NJ 07030. TEL 201-748-6000, FAX 201-748-6088, info@wiley.com, http://www.wiley.com/WileyCDA/.

325.1 971 CAN ISSN 1914-1459
STUDIES IN IMMIGRATION AND CULTURE. Text in English. 2007. irreg. **Document type:** *Monographic series, Academic/Scholarly.*
Published by: University of Manitoba Press, 301 St. John's College, Winnipeg, MB R3T 2M5, Canada. TEL 204-474-9495, FAX 204-474-7566, uofm_press@umanitoba.ca, http://www.umanitoba.ca/uofmpress/index.html. Ed. Royden Loewen.

304.6 610 GBR ISSN 0072-6400
STUDIES ON MEDICAL AND POPULATION SUBJECTS. Text in English. 1948. irreg., latest no.68, 2005. price varies. reprints avail. **Document type:** *Government.*
Related titles: Online - full text ed.: free.
—IE, Ingenta.
Published by: (Great Britain. Office for National Statistics), Palgrave Macmillan Ltd. (Subsidiary of: Macmillan Publishers Ltd.), Houndmills, Basingstoke, Hants RG21 6XS, United Kingdom. TEL 44-1256-329242, FAX 44-1256-810526, bookenquiries@palgrave.com, http://www.palgrave.com.

325 900 DEU ISSN 0947-5834
STUTTGARTER BEITRAEGE ZUR HISTORISCHEN MIGRATIONSFORSCHUNG. Text in German. 1991. irreg., latest vol.7, 2010. price varies. **Document type:** *Monographic series, Academic/Scholarly.*
Published by: (Stuttgarter Arbeitskreis Historische Migrationsforschung e.V.), Franz Steiner Verlag GmbH, Birkenwaldstr 44, Stuttgart, 70191, Germany. TEL 49-711-25820, FAX 49-711-2582290, service@steiner-verlag.de, http://www.steiner-verlag.de.

325.2 948 304.82 SWE ISSN 2000-4869
SVERIGE OCH AMERIKA. Text in Swedish. 1972. q. SEK 120 domestic membership; SEK 200 elsewhere membership (effective 2010). adv. bk.rev. bibl. Index. **Document type:** *Magazine, Consumer.*
Former titles (until 2009): Bryggan (0345-178X); (until 1972): Emigranten
Related titles: ◆ English ed.: Bridge. ISSN 0345-1798.
Published by: Samfundet Emigrantforskningens Fraemjande/Society for the Promotion of Emigration Research, PO Box 331, Karlstad, 65108, Sweden. TEL 46-54-617720, 46-54-627726, FAX 46-54-617721, research@emigrantregistret.s.se. Ed., Adv. contact Tommy Hellstrom.

325.1 SWE ISSN 1651-1425
SWEDEN. INTEGRATIONSVERKET. SKRIFTSERIE. Text in Swedish. 2002. irreg. back issues avail. **Document type:** *Monographic series, Consumer.*
Related titles: Online - full text ed.
Published by: Integrationsverket/Swedish Integration Board, PO Box 633, Norrkoeping, 60114, Sweden. TEL 46-11-361300, FAX 46-11-361301, http://www.integrationsverket.se.

SWEDEN. MIGRATIONSVERKET. STATISTIK. *see* POPULATION STUDIES—Abstracting, Bibliographies, Statistics

304.6 330.9 TWN ISSN 1016-2224
HA1710.5
TAIWAN STATISTICAL DATA BOOK. Text in English. 1960. a. stat. **Document type:** *Government.* **Description:** Covers key economic and social statistics, including Indicators, area and population, national income, agriculture, industry, science and technology, transportation and communications, money and banking, public finance, prices, external trade, U.S. aid, external resources and outward investment, education, health and medical care, social affairs, and international statistics.
Related titles: Online - full content ed.
Published by: Xingzhengyuan Jingji Jianshe Weiyuanhui/Council for Economic Planning and Development, Executive Yuan, No.3 Baocing Rd., Taipei, 10020, Taiwan. http://www.cepd.gov.tw/. Circ: 4,000.

325 USA ISSN 1078-4179
TEACHER'S PET TERM PAPER. Text in English. 1985. q. free (effective 2000). bk.rev. charts; illus. back issues avail. **Document type:** *Newsletter.*
Published by: Population Connection, 2120 L St, NW, Ste 500, Washington, DC 20037. TEL 202-332-2200, FAX 202-332-2302, info@populationconnections.org, http://www.population connection.org. Ed. Pamela Wasserman. Circ: 15,000.

▼ **TEKSTUITGAVE INTEGRAAL VREEMDELINGENBELEID.** *see* LAW—International Law

304.6 USA
TEXAS POPULATION PERSPECTIVE. Text in English. s-a.?. bk.rev. **Document type:** *Newsletter.* **Description:** Reports on center, students, faculty, and grant funding news.
Published by: University of Texas at Austin, Population Research Center, Main Bldg 1800, Austin, TX 78712-1088. Ed. Jennifer Glick.

THEORETICAL POPULATION BIOLOGY. *see* BIOLOGY

304.6 JPN
TOCHIGI-KEN NO JINKO/POPULATION OF TOCHIGI PREFECTURE. Text in Japanese. 1970. a. free. stat. back issues avail. **Document type:** *Government.*
Published by: Tochigi-ken Kikaku-bu/Tochigi Prefecture, Department of Planning, 1-1-20 Hanawada, Utsunomiya, 320-8501, Japan. Circ: 500.

304.6 USA ISSN 0897-0556
TOWARD THE 21ST CENTURY. Text in English. 1988. q. USD 25. **Document type:** *Monographic series.* **Description:** Discusses population growth and related issues including environment, urban deterioration, food, health and illiteracy.
Published by: Population Institute, 107 Second St, N E, Washington, DC 20002. TEL 202-544-3300, FAX 202-544-0068. R&P Harold N Burdett. Circ: 3,000.

304.6 IRL ISSN 2009-0420
JV7711
TRANSLOCATIONS; the Irish migration, race and social transformation review. Text in English. 2006. s-a.
Related titles: Online - full text ed.: free (effective 2011).
Indexed: A39, C27, C29, D03, D04, E13, R14, S14, S15, S18.
Published by: Dublin City University http://www.dcu.ie. Eds. Bryan Fanning, Ronaldo Munck.

TRENDRAPPORT LANDELIJKE JEUGDMONITOR. *see* SOCIOLOGY

325.1 USA ISSN 1942-3713
THE TRIENNIAL COMPREHENSIVE REPORT ON IMMIGRATION. Text in English. triennial. **Document type:** *Government.*
Formerly (until 1999): President's Comprehensive Triennial Report on Immigration
Related titles: Print ed.: ISSN 1942-3705.
Published by: U.S. Citizenship and Immigration Services (Subsidiary of: U.S. Department of Homeland Security), 425 I St, NW, Washington, DC 20536. http://www.uscis.gov.

304.6 USA ISSN 1944-5199
U S C I S MONTHLY. (United States Citizenship and Immigration Services) Text in English. 2005. m. free (effective 2009). back issues avail. **Document type:** *Newsletter, Trade.* **Description:** Provides important information on USCIS initiatives and programs to the American People and stakeholders.
Formerly (until 2007): U S C I S Today
Media: Online - full content.
Published by: U.S. Citizenship and Immigration Services (Subsidiary of: U.S. Department of Homeland Security), 111 Massachusetts Ave, N W, Washington, DC 20529. TEL 800-375-5283.

U.S. CENTERS FOR DISEASE CONTROL AND PREVENTION. MORBIDITY AND MORTALITY WEEKLY REPORT. RECOMMENDATIONS AND REPORT. *see* PUBLIC HEALTH AND SAFETY

325 USA
JV6414
U.S. CITIZENSHIP AND IMMIGRATION SERVICES. ANNUAL REPORT. Text in English. 1892. a. price varies. **Document type:** *Government.*
Formerly: U.S. Immigration and Naturalization Service. Annual Report (0083-1247)
Related titles: Online - full content ed.
Published by: U.S. Citizenship and Immigration Services (Subsidiary of: U.S. Department of Homeland Security), 425 I St, NW, Washington, DC 20536. http://www.uscis.gov.

U.S. DEPARTMENT OF HEALTH AND HUMAN SERVICES. INDIAN HEALTH SERVICE. TRENDS IN INDIAN HEALTH. *see* NATIVE AMERICAN STUDIES

U.S. DEPARTMENT OF JUSTICE. NATIONAL DRUG INTELLIGENCE CENTER. NATIONAL DRUG THREAT ASSESSMENT. *see* DRUG ABUSE AND ALCOHOLISM

U S MARKET FORECASTS. *see* BUSINESS AND ECONOMICS—Marketing And Purchasing

304.6 NLD ISSN 1878-5271
▼ **UNDERSTANDING POPULATION TRENDS AND PROCESSES.** Text in English. 2009. irreg., latest vol.4, 2011. price varies. **Document type:** *Monographic series, Academic/Scholarly.*
Published by: Springer Netherlands (Subsidiary of: Springer Science+Business Media), Van Godewijckstraat 30, Dordrecht, 3311 GX, Netherlands. TEL 31-78-6576050, FAX 31-78-6576474. Ed. John Stillwell.

304.6 USA ISSN 0082-8041
HA17
UNITED NATIONS. DEMOGRAPHIC YEARBOOK/ANNUAIRE DEMOGRAPHIQUE. Text in English, French. 1949. a. USD 120 (effective 2008). stat. back issues avail.; reprints avail. **Document type:** *Yearbook, Consumer.* **Description:** Provides official national population statistics for over 230 countries and areas of the world.
Related titles: CD-ROM ed.: ISSN 1020-7953; Online - full text ed.: USD 96 (effective 2008); Supplement(s): United Nations. Demographic Yearbook. Supplement. ISSN 1014-9422.
Indexed: IIS, RASB, SSciA.
—CCC.
Published by: (United Nations, Department of Economic and Social Affairs), United Nations Publications, 2 United Nations Plaza, Rm DC2-853, New York, NY 10017. TEL 212-963-8302, 800-253-9646, FAX 212-963-3489, publications@un.org, https://unp.un.org.

301.3 THA ISSN 0066-8451
JX1977
UNITED NATIONS. ECONOMIC AND SOCIAL COMMISSION FOR ASIA AND THE PACIFIC. ASIAN POPULATION STUDIES SERIES. Text in English. 1967. irreg., latest vol.157, 2001. free. **Document type:** *Monographic series, Academic/Scholarly.*
Indexed: IIS, P30, PopulInd.
Published by: (Population and Rural And Urban Development Division), United Nations Economic and Social Commission for Asia and the Pacific, United Nations Bldg., Rajadamnern Ave., Bangkok, 10200, Thailand. http://www.unescap.org. **Subscr. to:** United Nations Publications, Sales Office and Bookshop, Bureau E4, Geneva 10 1211, Switzerland. **Dist. by:** United Nations Publications.; United Nations, Population Division, ESCAP, Bangkok, Thailand.

304.6 USA
UNITED NATIONS POPULATION FUND. ANNUAL REPORT. Cover title: U N F P A (Year) Report. Text in English. a.
Related titles: Microfiche ed.: (from CIS).
Indexed: IIS.
Published by: United Nations Population Fund (U N F P A), 220 E 42nd St, New York, NY 10017. TEL 212-297-5000, http://www.unfpa.org. Ed., R&P Alex Marshall TEL 212-297-5020.

304.6 USA ISSN 0082-805X
JX1977
UNITED NATIONS. POPULATION STUDIES. Text in English. 1948. irreg. price varies. stat. back issues avail. **Document type:** *Monographic series, Government.* **Description:** Provides information on various aspects of population, environment and development, including changes in rural populations and their relationship with development and the environment.
Related titles: Spanish ed.; French ed.
Indexed: HPNRM, JEL, P30, SCOPUS, SSCI, SSciA, W07, WBA.
—BLDSC (6553.105000). **CCC.**
Published by: (United Nations, Department of Economic and Social Affairs), United Nations Publications, 2 United Nations Plaza, Rm DC2-853, New York, NY 10017. TEL 212-963-8302, 800-253-9646, FAX 212-963-3489, publications@un.org, https://unp.un.org.

UNIVERSITY OF DAR ES SALAAM. BUREAU OF RESOURCE ASSESSMENT AND LAND USE PLANNING. ANNUAL REPORT. *see* ENVIRONMENTAL STUDIES

UNIVERSITY OF DAR ES SALAAM. BUREAU OF RESOURCE ASSESSMENT AND LAND USE PLANNING. RESEARCH PAPER. *see* ENVIRONMENTAL STUDIES

UNIVERSITY OF DAR ES SALAAM. BUREAU OF RESOURCE ASSESSMENT AND LAND USE PLANNING. RESEARCH REPORT. *see* ENVIRONMENTAL STUDIES

304.6 NGA
UNIVERSITY OF LAGOS. HUMAN RESOURCES RESEARCH UNIT. MONOGRAPH. Text in English. 1974. irreg. **Document type:** *Monographic series.*
Published by: (University of Lagos), Lagos University Press, Publishing Division, Akoka, PO Box 132, Yaba, Lagos State, Nigeria.

304.6 USA
UNIVERSITY OF MICHIGAN. POPULATION STUDIES CENTER. RESEARCH REPORT SERIES. Text in English. 1981. irreg. (30-35/yr.). price varies. **Document type:** *Monographic series, Academic/Scholarly.* **Description:** Reports the results of current demographic research conducted by PSC associates and affiliates.

Published by: University of Michigan, Population Studies Center, 426 Thompson St, Ann Arbor, MI 48106. TEL 734-763-1543, FAX 734-763-1428, psc-pubs@umich.edu.

UNIVERSITY OF PETROSANI. SOCIAL SCIENCES. ANNALS. *see* SOCIAL SCIENCES: COMPREHENSIVE WORKS

304.6 NZL ISSN 1172-6210
UNIVERSITY OF WAIKATO. POPULATION STUDIES CENTRE. DISCUSSION PAPERS. Variant title: P S C Discussion Papers. Text in English. 1993. irreg., latest vol.65, 2007. **Document type:** *Monographic series, Academic/Scholarly.*
Related titles: Online - full text ed.: ISSN 1178-3141.
Published by: University of Waikato, Population Studies Centre, Private Bag 3015, Hamilton, New Zealand. TEL 64-7-8384040, FAX 64-7-8384621, pscadmin@waikato.ac.nz.

301.3 USA ISSN 0084-0734
UNIVERSITY OF WISCONSIN, MADISON. APPLIED POPULATION LABORATORY. POPULATION NOTES; a look at the demography and geography of Wisconsin. Text in English. 1961. q. free (effective 2010). back issues avail. **Document type:** *Newsletter, Academic/Scholarly.* **Description:** Overview of specific topics concerning Wisconsin's population.
Related titles: Online - full text ed.
Published by: University of Wisconsin at Madison, Applied Population Laboratory, 1450 Linden Dr, Rtm 316, 308 Agricultural Hall, Madison, WI 53706. TEL 608-265-9545, FAX 608-262-6022.

304.8 PER ISSN 0586-5913
URBANIZACION, MIGRACIONES Y CAMBIOS EN LA SOCIEDAD PERUANA. Text in Spanish. 1968. irreg., latest vol.14, 1999. price varies. back issues avail. **Document type:** *Monographic series, Academic/Scholarly.*
Published by: (Instituto de Estudios Peruanos), I E P Ediciones (Subsidiary of: Instituto de Estudios Peruanos), Horacio Urteaga 694, Jesus Maria, Lima, 11, Peru. TEL 51-14-3326194, FAX 51-14-3326173, libreria@iep.org.pe, http://iep.perucultural.org.pe.

UTAH MARRIAGE AND DIVORCE ANNUAL REPORT. *see* POPULATION STUDIES—Abstracting, Bibliographies, Statistics

V I A MAGAZIN; Fachzeitschrift fuer Praktiker. *see* POLITICAL SCIENCE—Civil Rights

304.6 FIN ISSN 0357-4725
VAESTOLIITTO. VAESTONTUTKIMUSLAITOKSEN. JULKAISUSARJA. D/FAMILY FEDERATION OF FINLAND. POPULATION RESEARCH INSTITUTE. PUBLICATIONS. SERIES D. Text in English, Finnish. 1975. irreg. price varies. stat. back issues avail. **Document type:** *Monographic series, Academic/Scholarly.*
Published by: Vaestoliitto, Vaestontutkimuslaitos/Family Federation of Finland. Population Research Institute, PO Box 849, Helsinki, 00101, Finland. TEL 358-9-228050, FAX 358-9-6121211, pop.inst@vaestoliitto.fi, http://www.vaestoliitto.fi.

325.1 305 NLD ISSN 2211-2871
▼ **VERTREKNL.** Text in Dutch. 2011. q. EUR 22.50; EUR 6.50 newsstand/cover (effective 2011). adv. **Document type:** *Magazine, Consumer.*
Published by: Personalia, Valge 3, Leens, 9965 PD, Netherlands. TEL 31-595-572028, FAX 31-595-572231. Ed. Stefan Tibben. Pubs. Mirjam van der Kaaden, Seb van der Kaader.

304.6 AUS ISSN 1834-6650
VICTORIAN POPULATION BULLETIN. Text in English. 1997. a. **Document type:** *Bulletin, Trade.*
Related titles: Online - full text ed.: ISSN 1834-6669.
Published by: Victoria. Department of Planning and Community Development. Strategic Policy Research and Forecasting Division. Spatial Analysis and Research, GPO Box 2392, Melbourne, VIC 3001, Australia. TEL 61-3-96379441, FAX 61-3-96378111, spatialanalysis.research@dpcd.vic.gov.au, http://www.dpcd.vic.gov.au/.

304.6 AUT ISSN 1728-4414
HB3591
VIENNA YEARBOOK OF POPULATION RESEARCH. Text in English, German. 1982. a. EUR 40 (effective 2010). **Document type:** *Journal, Academic/Scholarly.* **Description:** Covers population trends and a broad range of theoretical and methodological issues in population research, particularly those relevant to developments in Austria.
Formerly (until 2003): Demographische Informationen (0259-0883)
Related titles: Online - full text ed.: ISSN 1728-5305. free (effective 2011).
Indexed: P30, SCOPUS, SociolAb.
—IE.
Published by: (Oesterreichische Akademie der Wissenschaften, Vienna Institute of Demography), Verlag der Oesterreichischen Akademie der Wissenschaften, Postgasse 7/4, Vienna, W 1011, Austria. TEL 43-1-515813402, FAX 43-1-515813400, verlag@oeaw.ac.at, http://verlag.oeaw.ac.at.

325 FRA
VILLE - ECOLE - INTEGRATION. Text in French. 1973. 4/yr. bk.rev. bibl. **Description:** Offers information and discussion on education, immigration and educational development of children and adults.
Formerly: Migrants Formation (0335-0894)
Indexed: AMR, FR, RASB, RefugAb.
—INIST.
Published by: Centre National de Documentation Pedagogique, 4 Av du Futuroscope, Teleport 1, B P 80158, Futuroscope, Cedex 86961, France. TEL 33-1-46349000, FAX 33-1-46345544. Ed. Jean Paul Tauvel. **Subscr. to:** CNDP - Abonnement, B.P. 750, Sainte Genevieve Cedex 60732, France. FAX 33-3-44033013.

325 FRA ISSN 1291-7222
Z7164.I3
VILLE - ECOLE - INTEGRATION ACTUALITES. Key Title: V E I Actualites. Text in French. 1974. 10/yr. charts; stat. back issues avail. **Document type:** *Journal, Trade.* **Description:** Provides information briefs on all aspects of immigration.
Formerly: Migrants Nouvelles (0397-944X)
Related titles: CD-ROM ed.
Indexed: RefugAb.
Published by: Centre National de Documentation Pedagogique, 4 Av du Futuroscope, Teleport 1, B P 80158, Futuroscope, Cedex 86961, France. TEL 33-1-46349000, FAX 33-1-46345544. Ed. Jean Paul Tauvel. **Subscr. to:** CNDP - Abonnement, B.P. 750, Sainte Genevieve Cedex 60732, France. FAX 33-3-44033013.

VIVRE ENSEMBLE; bulletin de liaison en pastorale interculturelle. *see* RELIGIONS AND THEOLOGY—Roman Catholic

VLUCHTELINGENWERK MAGAZINE. *see* POLITICAL SCIENCE—International Relations

VOETSPOREN. *see* POLITICAL SCIENCE—International Relations

304.6 IDN ISSN 0125-9679
HB848
WARTA DEMOGRAFI. Text in Indonesian. 1971. q. IDR 30,000 (effective 2000). bk.rev. **Document type:** *Academic/Scholarly.* **Description:** Covers current issues on demographic topics in Indonesia.
Related titles: CD-ROM ed.
Indexed: EI, P30.
Published by: (Demographic Institute), University of Indonesia, Faculty of Economics, Gedung A Lt. 2-3, Kampus UI Depok, Depok, 16424, Indonesia. TEL 62-21-787-2911, FAX 62-21-787-2909, TELEX 69158 UI JKT IA, demofeui@indo.net.id, rinld@indo.net.id. Ed. Tara B Soeprobo. Circ: 600.

304.6 USA
WASHINGTON COUNTS IN THE 21ST CENTURY. Text in English. irreg. free (effective 2006). **Document type:** *Bulletin.*
Former titles (until 1998): Washington Counts (1063-0155); (until 1991): Census Notes
Media: Online - full text.
Indexed: Agr.
Published by: Washington State University, Department of Community & Rural Sociology, Wilson 23, PO Box 644006, Pullman, WA 99164-4006. TEL 509-335-8623, crs@wsu.edu, http://www.crs.wsu.edu. Ed. Dr. Annabel R Kirschner.

WHERE TO LIVE IN AUCKLAND. *see* SOCIOLOGY

304.6 USA ISSN 0738-2340
HA38
WHERE TO WRITE FOR VITAL RECORDS. Text in English. 1982. triennial. price varies. **Document type:** *Directory, Government.*
Formed by the merger of (1965-1982): Where to Write for Divorce Records: United States and Outlying Areas (0565-8454); Which was formerly (until 1965): Where to Write for Divorce Records; (1965-1982): Where to Write for Marriage Records: United States and Outlying Areas (0162-0916); Which was formerly (until 1965): Where to Write for Marriage Records (0565-8462); (19??-1982): Where to Write for Birth and Death Records: United States and Outlying Areas (0098-8022); Which was formerly (until 19??): Where to Write for Birth and Death Records
Published by: U.S. National Center for Health Statistics, Metro IV Bldg, 3311 Toledo Rd, Hyattsville, MD 20782. TEL 301-458-4000, cdcinfo@cdc.gov.

325 SWE ISSN 1650-5743
WILLY BRANDT SERIES OF WORKING PAPERS IN INTERNATIONAL MIGRATION AND ETHNIC RELATIONS. Text in English, Swedish. 2001. irreg. back issues avail. **Document type:** *Monographic series, Academic/Scholarly.*
Related titles: Online - full text ed.
Published by: Malmoe Hoegskola, Internationell Migration och Etniska Relationer/University of Malmoe. School of International Migration and Ethnic Relations, Citadellvaegen 7, Malmoe, 20506, Sweden. TEL 46-40-6657345, FAX 46-40-6657330, info@imer.mah.se, http://www.mah.se/imer.

304.6 USA ISSN 0091-5254
HA711
WISCONSIN POPULATION PROJECTIONS. Text in English. 1969. irreg., latest vol.5, 1993. USD 5. stat. **Document type:** *Government.*
Published by: Department of Administration, Bureau of Program Management, PO Box 7868, Madison, WI 53707. TEL 608-266-1967, FAX 608-267-6931. **Subscr. to:** Document Sales Unit, 202 S Thornton Ave, Madison, WI 53707-7868.

304.6 ZAF
WOMEN & MEN IN SOUTH AFRICA (ONLINE). Text in English. irreg. free. stat. **Document type:** *Government.*
Formerly: Women & Men in South Africa (Print)
Media: Online - full text.
Published by: Statistics South Africa/Statistieke Suid-Afrika, Private Bag X44, Pretoria, 0001, South Africa. TEL 27-12-3108911, FAX 27-12-3108500, info@statssa.gov.za, http://www.statssa.gov.za.

WORLD HEALTH & POPULATION. *see* PUBLIC HEALTH AND SAFETY

325 CHE
WORLD MIGRATION. Text in English. 1999. a. USD 60 per vol. (effective 2003). charts; illus.; stat. back issues avail.; reprints avail. **Document type:** *Monographic series, Academic/Scholarly.* **Description:** Reviews the trends of world migrations over the past year.
Formerly (until 2003): World Migration Report (1561-5502)
Related titles: French ed.: Etat de la Migration dans le Monde. ISSN 1020-8453. 2001.
Published by: International Organization for Migration/Organizacion Internacional para las Migraciones, 17 Rte des Morillons, Geneva 19, 1211, Switzerland. TEL 41-22-7179111, FAX 41-22-7986150, publications@iom.int, http://www.iom.int.

304.6 USA ISSN 0085-8315
HB848
WORLD POPULATION DATA SHEET. Text in English. 1962. a. USD 4.50 (effective 2003). **Document type:** *Bulletin, Consumer.* **Description:** Provides population demographic and social indicators by country.
Related titles: Online - full content ed.
Indexed: EIA, EnerInd, SRI.
—BLDSC (9358.083000).
Published by: Population Reference Bureau, Inc., 1875 Connecticut Ave, NW, Ste 520, Washington, DC 20009-5728. TEL 202-939-5407, FAX 202-328-3937, popref@prb.org, http://www.prb.org. Ed. Carl Haub. R&P Ellen Carnevale.

304.6 951 351 HKG ISSN 0072-629X
DS796.H7
XIANGGANG (YEAR). Variant title: Xianggang Nanbao. Text in Chinese. a., latest 1999. HKD 106 for 1999 Edition (effective 2001); price varies per edition. **Document type:** *Yearbook, Government.*
Former titles (until 1997): Hong Kong: Maijin Xin Jiyuan; (until 1996): Hong Kong: (Year) Nian Huigu; (until 1995): Hong Kong: (Year) Di Huigu; Hong Kong Annual Report (0378-4886)
Related titles: CD-ROM ed.: 1997. HKD 88 (effective 2001); ◆ English ed.: Hong Kong (Year). ISSN 1011-4521.
Published by: Xianggang. Gongwuyuan Shiwuju. Fading Yuwen Shiwubu/Hong Kong. Civil Service Bureau. Official Languages Division, 22/F & 23/F, High Block, Queensway Government Offices, 66 Queensway, Hong Kong, Hong Kong. **Subscr. to:** Information Services Department, Publications Sales Unit, Rm 402, 4th Fl, Murray Bldg, Garden Rd, Hong Kong, Hong Kong. TEL 852-2537-1910, puborder@isd.gcn.gov.hk, http://www.info.gov.hk/isd/book_e.htm.

304.6 CHN ISSN 1007-0672
XIBEI RENKOU/NORTHWEST POPULATION JOURNAL. Text in English. 1980. bi-m. USD 31.20 (effective 2009). **Document type:** *Journal, Academic/Scholarly.*
Related titles: Online - full text ed.
Published by: Lanzhou Daxue, 222, Tianshui Nan Lu, Lanzhou, 730000, China. TEL 86-931-8912629.

304.6 DEU
YEARBOOK MIGRATION. Text in German. 1992. irreg., latest vol.14, 2008. price varies. **Document type:** *Monographic series, Academic/Scholarly.*
Published by: Lit Verlag, Grevener Str/Fresnostr 2, Muenster, 48159, Germany. TEL 49-251-6203222, FAX 49-251-231972, lit@lit-verlag.de, http://www.lit-verlag.de.

323 AUT
YEARBOOK ON ILLEGAL MIGRATION, HUMAN SMUGGLING AND TRAFFICKING IN CENTRAL AND EASTERN EUROPE. Text in English. 1997. a. **Document type:** *Journal, Trade.*
Published by: International Centre for Migration Policy Development, Gonzagagasse 1, 5th Fl, Vienna, 1010, Austria. TEL 43-1-50446770, FAX 43-1-504467775, http://www.icmpd.org.

304.8 914.3 929 USA
YORKER PALATINE NEWSLETTER. Text in English. 1982. q. looseleaf. USD 20 domestic; USD 30 in Canada & Mexico; USD 40 in Europe. back issues avail. **Document type:** *Newsletter.* **Description:** Promotes German immigration to North America. Covers members of the New York Chapter seeking the origin of their German-speaking immigrant ancestors.
Published by: Palatines to America, New York State Chapter, 9666 Elpis Rd, Camden, NY 13316. TEL 315-245-0990. Ed. Eila Schiffer.

325 ZMB ISSN 0084-4802
ZAMBIA. IMMIGRATION DEPARTMENT. REPORT. Text in English. 1964. a. ZMK 100. **Document type:** *Government.* **Description:** Reports on immigration control and the issuance of employment permits in Zambia.
Published by: (Zambia. Immigration Department), Government Printing Department, PO Box 30136, Lusaka, Zambia.

ZDRAVEOPAZVANE. *see* STATISTICS

ZEITLUPE. *see* POLITICAL SCIENCE—Civil Rights

304.6 363.7 CHN ISSN 1002-2104
ZHONGGUO RENKOU ZIYUAN YU HUANJING/CHINA POPULATION RESOURCES AND ENVIRONMENT. Text in Chinese. 1991. bi-m. USD 53.40 (effective 2009). **Document type:** *Journal, Academic/Scholarly.*
Related titles: Online - full text ed.
Indexed: SCOPUS.
—BLDSC (3180.220590), East View, IE.
Address: 88, Wenhua Dong Lu, Jinan, 250014, China. TEL 86-531-2966021, FAX 86-531-2963094.

ZIYUAN KEXUE/RESOURCES SCIENCE. *see* ENVIRONMENTAL STUDIES

POPULATION STUDIES—Abstracting, Bibliographies, Statistics

304.6 CAN ISSN 1485-3809
RA185.A5
ALBERTA VITAL STATISTICS ANNUAL REVIEW. Text in English. 1942. a. stat. **Document type:** *Government.*
Former titles (until 1994): Vital Statistics Annual Report (1188-8571); (until 1990): Vital Statistics Annual Review (0707-7548); (until 1970): Province of Alberta. Department of Health including Vital Statistics Division. Annual Report (0702-9500); (until 1966): Province of Alberta. Department of Public Health including Vital Statistics Division. Annual Report (0824-3840); (until 1954): Province of Alberta. Department of Public Health. Annual Report (0824-3859); (until 1949): Province of Alberta. Department of Public Health, including Vital Statistics Branch. Annual Report (0824-3867)
Related titles: Online - full content ed.
Published by: Alberta Government Services, Communications, 13th Fl Commerce Pl, 10155 102 St, Edmonton, AB T5J 4L4, Canada. TEL 780-415-6051, government.services@gov.ab.ca.

304.6 ASM
AMERICAN SAMOA POPULATION (YEAR). Text in English. a. **Document type:** *Government.*
Published by: (American Samoa. Statistics Division USA), American Samoa Government, Department of Commerce, Pago Pago, 96799, American Samoa. TEL 684-633-5155, FAX 684-633-4195.

304.6 USA
AMERICA'S FAMILIES AND LIVING ARRANGEMENTS. Text in English. a.
Formerly (until 2003): Current Population Reports. Population Characteristics. Children's Living Arrangements and Characteristics (Online)
Media: Online - full text.
Published by: U.S. Census Bureau. Housing and Household Economic Statistics Division. Fertility & Family Statistics Branch (Subsidiary of: U.S. Department of Commerce), 4600 Silver Hill Rd., Washington, DC 20233. TEL 866-758-1060, http://www.census.gov/hhes/www/hhesdiv.html.

304.6 ITA ISSN 1825-6732
ANNUARIO STATISTICO. Text in Italian. 1989. a. **Document type:** *Yearbook, Trade.*
Related titles: Online - full text ed.: ISSN 1825-0440.
Published by: Comune di Verona, Piazza Bra 1, Verona, 37121, Italy. TEL 39-045-8077111, FAX 39-045-8077500, urp@comune.verona.it, http://portale.comune.verona.it.

P

304.6 ESP ISSN 1134-5837
JV8250.A1
ANUARIO DE MIGRACIONES. Text in Spanish. 1984. a. **Document type:** *Directory, Trade.*
Published by: Ministerio de Trabajo y Asuntos Sociales, Centro de Publicaciones, Agustin de Bethencourt 11, Madrid, 28003, Spain. http://www.mtas.es.

304.6 PER
ANUARIO DE NACIMIENTOS. Text in Spanish. a.
Published by: Instituto Nacional de Estadistica, Ave. 28 de Julio 1056, Lima, Peru. Circ: 300.

304.6 ESP ISSN 1135-9846
ANUARIO ESTADISTICO DE ANDALUCIA. Text in Spanish. 1986. a. **Document type:** *Yearbook, Government.*
Related titles: CD-ROM ed.: ISSN 1578-8008. 1999.
Published by: Junta de Andalucia, Consejeria de Economia y Hacienda, Edif. Torretriana, Isla de Cartuja, Sevilla, 41092, Spain. TEL 34-955-065000, http://www.ceh.junta-andalucia.es.

325.1 ESP ISSN 1133-9934
ANUARIO ESTADISTICO DE EXTRANJERIA. Text in Spanish. 1993. a. **Document type:** *Government.*
Related titles: CD-ROM ed.: ISSN 1577-7243. 1999.
Published by: Ministerio del Interior, Secretaria General Tecnica. Area de Estudios, Documentacion y Publicaciones, C Amador de los Rios 7, Madrid, 28071, Spain. TEL 34-91-5371538, FAX 34-91-5371480, estafeta@mir.es, http://www.mir.es/.

304.6 ESP ISSN 1577-5380
ANUARIO SOCIAL DE ESPANA. Text in Spanish. 2000. a. back issues avail. **Document type:** *Directory, Trade.*
Related titles: Online - full text ed.: ISSN 1577-5399. 2000.
Published by: Fundacion la Caixa, Via Laietana 56, Barcelona, 08003, Spain. TEL 34-93-4046076.

318 ARG ISSN 0326-2936
HA954
ARGENTINA. INSTITUTO NACIONAL DE ESTADISTICA Y CENSOS. ANUARIO ESTADISTICO. Text in Spanish. 1948. a. ARS 33, USD 65 (effective 1999). charts; maps. **Document type:** *Government.* **Description:** Contains the principle series of sociodemographic and economic information.
Related titles: CD-ROM ed.: ARS 55, USD 70 (effective 1999); Diskette ed.; Microfiche ed.: (from PQC); English ed.: Statistical Yearbook Republic of Argentina. ISSN 0328-0055.
Published by: Instituto Nacional de Estadistica y Censos, Presidente Julio A Roca 615, Buenos Aires, 1067, Argentina. TEL 54-114-3499662, FAX 54-114-3499621, ces@indec.mecon.ar, http://www.indec.mecon.ar.

304.6 USA
ARIZONA STATE UNIVERSITY. CENTER FOR BUSINESS RESEARCH. POPULATION ESTIMATES AND PROJECTIONS. Text in English. a.
Published by: Arizona State University, Center for Business Research, College of Business, Box 874406, Tempe, AZ 85287-4406. TEL 602-965-3961, FAX 602-965-5458.

304.6 USA ISSN 0364-0728
HA251
ARKANSAS VITAL STATISTICS. Text in English. 1970. a. free. illus.; stat. **Document type:** *Government.*
Formerly: Arkansas. Bureau of Vital Statistics. Annual Report of Births, Deaths, Marriages and Divorces as Reported to the Bureau of Vital Statistics (0094-3576)
Related titles: Microfiche ed.: (from CIS).
Indexed: SRI.
Published by: Minnesota. Department of Health, Center for Health Statistics, Slot 19, 4815 W Markham St, Little Rock, AR 72205-3867. http://www.health.state.mn.us.

325 USA ISSN 1083-0294
HB3633.A3
➤ **ASIA - PACIFIC POPULATION RESEARCH ABSTRACTS.** Text in English. 1995. irreg., latest vol.12, 1998. free (effective 2010). back issues avail. **Document type:** *Monographic series, Academic/Scholarly.* **Description:** Contains abstracts of Asia-Pacific population research reports, which provide a discussion of research on population issues facing the Asia-Pacific region.
Related titles: Online - full text ed.: free (effective 2010).
Indexed: P30.
Published by: East-West Center, 1601 EW Rd, Honolulu, HI 96848. TEL 808-944-7111, FAX 808-944-7376, ewcbooks@eastwestcenter.org. Ed. Sandra E Ward.

304.6021 363.5021 AUS
AUSTRALIA. BUREAU OF STATISTICS. (YEAR) CENSUS OF POPULATION AND HOUSING - A B S VIEWS ON CENSUS CLASSIFICATIONS. Text in English. 1996. irreg. **Document type:** *Government.*
Published by: Australian Bureau of Statistics, Locked Bag 10, Belconnen, ACT 2616, Australia. TEL 61-2-92684909, 61-2-62527037, 300-135-070, FAX 61-2-62528103, client.services@abs.gov.au, http://www.abs.gov.au.

304.6021 AUS
AUSTRALIA. BUREAU OF STATISTICS. 4-SITE CONSULTANCY. Text in English. irreg.
Published by: Australian Bureau of Statistics, Locked Bag 10, Belconnen, ACT 2616, Australia. TEL 61-2-92684909, 61-2-62527037, 300-135-070, FAX 61-2-62528103, client.services@abs.gov.au, http://www.abs.gov.au.

304.6021 363.5021 AUS
AUSTRALIA. BUREAU OF STATISTICS. AN EVALUATION OF THE CENSUS OF POPULATION AND HOUSING. Text in English. 1991. irreg. **Document type:** *Government.*
Related titles: Online - full text ed.
Published by: Australian Bureau of Statistics, Locked Bag 10, Belconnen, ACT 2616, Australia. TEL 61-2-92684909, 61-2-62527037, 300-135-070, FAX 61-2-62528103, client.services@abs.gov.au, http://www.abs.gov.au.

304.6021 AUS
AUSTRALIA. BUREAU OF STATISTICS. AUSTRALIAN DEMOGRAPHIC (ONLINE). Text in English. 1986. irreg., latest 1997. free (effective 2009). **Document type:** *Government.* **Description:** Includes population growth and distribution, age and sex composition, fertility, mortality, international and internal migration.
Formerly: Australia. Bureau of Statistics. Australian Demographic Trends (Print)
Media: Online - full text.
Published by: Australian Bureau of Statistics, Locked Bag 10, Belconnen, ACT 2616, Australia. TEL 61-2-62527037, 61-2-92684909, 300-135-070, FAX 61-2-62528103, client.services@abs.gov.au.

304.6021 AUS
HA3001
AUSTRALIA. BUREAU OF STATISTICS. AUSTRALIAN DEMOGRAPHIC STATISTICS (ONLINE). Text in English. 1979. q. free (effective 2009). stat. **Document type:** *Government.* **Description:** Summarizes the rates of birth, deaths, infant deaths, marriages, divorces, interstate and overseas movements and latest population estimates for Australia.
Former titles (until 199?): Australia. Bureau of Statistics. Australian Demographic Statistics (Print) (1031-055X); (until 1983): Australian Demographic Statistics Quarterly (0159-0294); (until 1979): Australian Bureau of Statistics. Population and Vital Statistics
Media: Online - full text.
Published by: Australian Bureau of Statistics, Locked Bag 10, Belconnen, ACT 2616, Australia. TEL 61-2-92684909, 61-2-62527037, 300-135-070, FAX 61-2-62528103, client.services@abs.gov.au. Circ: 1,072.

304.6021 AUS
AUSTRALIA. BUREAU OF STATISTICS. AUSTRALIAN HISTORICAL POPULATION STATISTICS (ONLINE). Text in English. 2001. irreg., latest 2008. free (effective 2009). back issues avail. **Document type:** *Government.* **Description:** Contains a wide range of demographic data.
Formerly: Australia. Bureau of Statistics. Australian Historical Population Statistics (Print)
Media: Online - full text.
Published by: Australian Bureau of Statistics, Locked Bag 10, Belconnen, ACT 2616, Australia. TEL 61-2-92684909, 61-2-62527037, 300-135-070, FAX 61-2-62528103, client.services@abs.gov.au.

305.82021 AUS
AUSTRALIA. BUREAU OF STATISTICS. AUSTRALIAN STANDARD CLASSIFICATION OF CULTURAL AND ETHNIC GROUPS (ONLINE). Text in English. 2000. quinquennial, latest 2006. free (effective 2009). back issues avail. **Document type:** *Government.* **Description:** Features an explanation of the conceptual basis of the classification, the classification structure, and coding indexes in alphabetical and numerical order.
Formerly: Australia. Bureau of Statistics. Australian Standard Classification of Cultural and Ethnic Groups (Print)
Media: Online - full text.
Published by: Australian Bureau of Statistics, Locked Bag 10, Belconnen, ACT 2616, Australia. TEL 61-2-92684909, 300-135-070, FAX 61-2-92684654, client.services@abs.gov.au.

304.63021 AUS
HB1085
AUSTRALIA. BUREAU OF STATISTICS. BIRTHS, AUSTRALIA (ONLINE). Text in English. 1951. a., latest 2006. free (effective 2009). back issues avail. **Document type:** *Government.* **Description:** Provides detailed statistics on confinements and live births presented in 26 tables.
Former titles (until 2004): Australia. Bureau of Statistics. Births, Australia (Print) (1031-0150); (until 1977): Births; (until 1967): Australian Demographic Review; (until 1955): Monthly Australian Demographic Review
Media: Online - full text.
Published by: Australian Bureau of Statistics, Locked Bag 10, Belconnen, ACT 2616, Australia. TEL 61-2-62525249, FAX 61-2-62526778, subscriptions@abs.gov.au.

304.6021 AUS
AUSTRALIA. BUREAU OF STATISTICS. CANBERRA. A SOCIAL ATLAS. Text in English. 1996. quinquennial, latest 2006. AUD 55 per issue (effective 2009). back issues avail. **Document type:** *Government.* **Description:** Presents colour maps, based on data collected in the 2006 census of population and housing, that highlight key social, demographic and housing characteristics of the population in Canberra and Queanbeyan.
Related titles: Online - full text ed.: free (effective 2009).
Published by: Australian Bureau of Statistics, Locked Bag 10, Belconnen, ACT 2616, Australia. TEL 61-2-92684909, 300-135-070, FAX 61-2-92684654, client.services@abs.gov.au.

304.6021 AUS
RA407.5.A8
AUSTRALIA. BUREAU OF STATISTICS. CAUSES OF DEATH, AUSTRALIA (ONLINE). Text in English. 1962. a., latest 2009. free (effective 2009). back issues avail. **Document type:** *Government.* **Description:** Contains number of deaths by sex and selected age groups classified according to the World Health Organization's International Classification of Diseases.
Former titles (until 2003): Australia. Bureau of Statistics. Causes of Death, Australia (Print) (1031-2005); (until 1978): Australian Bureau of Statistics. Causes of Death (0067-0766)
Media: Online - full text.
Published by: Australian Bureau of Statistics, Locked Bag 10, Belconnen, ACT 2616, Australia. TEL 61-2-62527037, FAX 61-2-92684654, client.services@abs.gov.au. Circ: 476.

304.6021 AUS
AUSTRALIA. BUREAU OF STATISTICS. CENSUS DICTIONARY (ONLINE). Text in English. 1991. quinquennial. free (effective 2009). **Document type:** *Government.* **Description:** Contains the details of the classifications used in the census along with definitions of census concepts and terms.
Formerly: Australia. Bureau of Statistics. Census Dictionary (Print)
Media: Online - full text. **Related titles:** Diskette ed.
Published by: Australian Bureau of Statistics, Locked Bag 10, Belconnen, ACT 2616, Australia. TEL 61-2-62527037, 61-2-92684909, 300-135-070, FAX 61-2-62528103, client.services@abs.gov.au.

304.6021 AUS
AUSTRALIA. BUREAU OF STATISTICS. CENSUS OF POPULATION AND HOUSING: (YEAR) CENSUS SNAPSHOTS. Text in English. 2002. irreg., latest 2002. **Document type:** *Government.*
Related titles: Online - full text ed.
Published by: Australian Bureau of Statistics, Locked Bag 10, Belconnen, ACT 2616, Australia. TEL 61-2-92684909, 61-2-62527037, 300-135-070, FAX 61-2-62528103, client.services@abs.gov.au, http://www.abs.gov.au.

304.6021 363.5021 AUS
AUSTRALIA. BUREAU OF STATISTICS. CENSUS OF POPULATION AND HOUSING: ABORIGINAL AND TORRES STRAIT ISLANDER PEOPLE, AUSTRALIA (ONLINE). Text in English. 1996. quinquennial. free (effective 2009). back issues avail. **Document type:** *Government.* **Description:** Aims to present some important social and economic information about the Indigenous (Aboriginal and Torres Strait Islander) population of Australia.
Formerly: Australia. Bureau of Statistics. Census of Population and Housing: Aboriginal and Torres Strait Islander People, Australia (Print)
Media: Online - full text.
Published by: Australian Bureau of Statistics, Locked Bag 10, Belconnen, ACT 2616, Australia. TEL 61-2-62527037, 61-2-92684909, 300-135-070, FAX 61-2-62528103, client.services@abs.gov.au.

304.6021 363.5021 AUS
AUSTRALIA. BUREAU OF STATISTICS. CENSUS OF POPULATION AND HOUSING: ABORIGINAL AND TORRES STRAIT ISLANDER PEOPLE, AUSTRALIAN CAPITAL TERRITORY (ONLINE). Text in English. 1996. irreg., latest 1996. free (effective 2009). **Document type:** *Government.* **Description:** Presents information on aboriginal and torres strait islander Australians based largely on information from the 1996 and earlier censuses.
Formerly: Australia. Bureau of Statistics. Census of Population and Housing: Aboriginal and Torres Strait Islander People, Australian Capital Territory (Print)
Media: Online - full text.
Published by: Australian Bureau of Statistics, Locked Bag 10, Belconnen, ACT 2616, Australia. TEL 61-2-92684909, 300-135-070, FAX 61-2-92684654, client.services@abs.gov.au.

304.6021 363.5021 AUS
AUSTRALIA. BUREAU OF STATISTICS. CENSUS OF POPULATION AND HOUSING: AUSTRALIA IN PROFILE - A REGIONAL ANALYSIS (ONLINE). Text in English. 1996. quinquennial. free (effective 2009). back issues avail. **Document type:** *Government.* **Description:** Presents commentary and data on a number of key social indicators from the census with the focus on regional distribution and comparisons.
Formerly: Australia. Bureau of Statistics. Census of Population and Housing: Australia in Profile - A Regional Analysis (Print)
Media: Online - full text.
Published by: Australian Bureau of Statistics, Locked Bag 10, Belconnen, ACT 2616, Australia. TEL 61-2-62527037, 61-2-92684909, 300-135-070, FAX 61-2-62528103, client.services@abs.gov.au.

304.6021 AUS
AUSTRALIA. BUREAU OF STATISTICS. CENSUS OF POPULATION AND HOUSING: BASIC COMMUNITY PROFILE. Text in English. 2001. quinquennial, latest 2006. back issues avail. **Document type:** *Government.* **Description:** Consists of 45 tables containing key census characteristics on persons, families and dwellings.
Media: CD-ROM.
Published by: Australian Bureau of Statistics, Locked Bag 10, Belconnen, ACT 2616, Australia. TEL 61-2-92684909, 300-135-070, FAX 61-2-92684654, client.services@abs.gov.au.

304.6021 363.5021 AUS
AUSTRALIA. BUREAU OF STATISTICS. CENSUS OF POPULATION AND HOUSING: CDATA 2001 ADD-ON DATAPACK - EXPANDED COMMUNITY PROFILE (ONLINE). Text in English. 1996. irreg. free. **Document type:** *Government.*
Formerly: Australia. Bureau of Statistics. Census of Population and Housing: CDATA2001 - Full GIS, Australia (CD-ROM)
Media: Online - full text.
Published by: Australian Bureau of Statistics, Locked Bag 10, Belconnen, ACT 2616, Australia. TEL 61-2-92684909, 300-135-070, FAX 61-2-92684654, client.services@abs.gov.au.

304.6021 363.502 AUS
AUSTRALIA. BUREAU OF STATISTICS. CENSUS OF POPULATION AND HOUSING: CDATA2001 ADD-ON DATAPACK - ESTIMATED RESIDENT POPULATION. Text in English. 2001. irreg., latest 2001. price varies. stat. **Document type:** *Government.*
Media: CD-ROM.
Published by: Australian Bureau of Statistics, Locked Bag 10, Belconnen, ACT 2616, Australia. TEL 61-2-62527037, 61-2-92684909, 300-135-070, FAX 61-2-62528103, client.services@abs.gov.au.

304.6021 363.502 AUS
AUSTRALIA. BUREAU OF STATISTICS. CENSUS OF POPULATION AND HOUSING: CDATA2001 ADD-ON DATAPACK - EXPANDED COMMUNITY PROFILE. Text in English. 2001. irreg., latest 2001. price varies. stat. **Document type:** *Government.*
Media: CD-ROM.
Published by: Australian Bureau of Statistics, Locked Bag 10, Belconnen, ACT 2616, Australia. TEL 61-2-62527037, 61-2-92684909, 300-135-070, FAX 61-2-62528103, client.services@abs.gov.au.

304.6021 363.502 AUS
AUSTRALIA. BUREAU OF STATISTICS. CENSUS OF POPULATION AND HOUSING: CDATA2001 ADD-ON DATAPACK - INDIGENOUS PROFILE. Text in English. 2001. irreg., latest 2001. price varies. stat. **Document type:** *Government.*
Media: CD-ROM.
Published by: Australian Bureau of Statistics, Locked Bag 10, Belconnen, ACT 2616, Australia. TEL 61-2-62527037, 61-2-92684909, 300-135-070, FAX 61-2-62528103, client.services@abs.gov.au.

304.6021 363.502 AUS
AUSTRALIA. BUREAU OF STATISTICS. CENSUS OF POPULATION AND HOUSING: CDATA2001 ADD-ON DATAPACK - S E I F A. Text in English. 2001. irreg., latest 2001. price varies. stat. **Document type:** *Government.*
Media: CD-ROM.

Published by: Australian Bureau of Statistics, Locked Bag 10, Belconnen, ACT 2616, Australia. TEL 61-2-62527037, 61-2-92684909, 300-135-070, FAX 61-2-62528103, client.services@abs.gov.au.

304.6021 363.502 AUS
AUSTRALIA. BUREAU OF STATISTICS. CENSUS OF POPULATION AND HOUSING: CDATA2001 ADD-ON DATAPACK - USUAL RESIDENTS PROFILE. Text in English. 2001. irreg., latest 2001. price varies. stat. **Document type:** *Government.*
Media: CD-ROM.
Published by: Australian Bureau of Statistics, Locked Bag 10, Belconnen, ACT 2616, Australia. TEL 61-2-62527037, 61-2-92684909, 300-135-070, FAX 61-2-62528103, client.services@abs.gov.au.

363.502 304.6021 AUS
AUSTRALIA. BUREAU OF STATISTICS. CENSUS OF POPULATION AND HOUSING: CDATA2001 ADD-ON DATAPACK - WORKING POPULATION COMMUNITY PROFILE. Text in English. 2001. irreg., latest 2001. price varies. stat. **Document type:** *Government.*
Media: CD-ROM.
Published by: Australian Bureau of Statistics, Locked Bag 10, Belconnen, ACT 2616, Australia. TEL 61-2-62527037, 61-2-92684909, 300-135-070, FAX 61-2-62528103, client.services@abs.gov.au.

304.6021 363.502 AUS
AUSTRALIA. BUREAU OF STATISTICS. CENSUS OF POPULATION AND HOUSING: CDATA2001 - FULL GIS, AUSTRALIA (CD-ROM). Text in English. 1996. irreg., latest 2001. stat. **Document type:** *Government.* **Description:** Provides a large volume of census small area data (from collection district level) combined with digital geographic and topographic data.
Formerly: Australia. Bureau of Statistics. Census of Population and Housing: CDATA2001 - Full GIS, Australia (Print)
Media: CD-ROM.
Published by: Australian Bureau of Statistics, Locked Bag 10, Belconnen, ACT 2616, Australia. TEL 61-2-92684909, 300-135-070, FAX 61-2-92684654, client.services@abs.gov.au.

304.6021 AUS
AUSTRALIA. BUREAU OF STATISTICS. CENSUS OF POPULATION AND HOUSING: CDATA2001 - QUICKBUILD. Text in English. 2001. quinquennial. **Document type:** *Government.*
Media: CD-ROM.
Published by: Australian Bureau of Statistics, Locked Bag 10, Belconnen, ACT 2616, Australia. TEL 61-2-92684909, 300-135-070, FAX 61-2-92684654, client.services@abs.gov.au, http://www.abs.gov.au.

304.6021 AUS
AUSTRALIA. BUREAU OF STATISTICS. CENSUS OF POPULATION AND HOUSING: CDATA96 ADD-ON DATAPAKS. Text in English. 1996. irreg., latest 1996. price varies. **Description:** Contains containing the indigenous, usual residents, expanded and working population community profiles and estimated resident population.
Media: CD-ROM.
Published by: Australian Bureau of Statistics, Locked Bag 10, Belconnen, ACT 2616, Australia. TEL 61-2-92684909, 300-135-070, FAX 61-2-92684654, client.services@abs.gov.au.

304.6021 363.5021 AUS
AUSTRALIA. BUREAU OF STATISTICS. CENSUS OF POPULATION AND HOUSING: CDATA96 ADD-ON DATAPAKS, AUSTRALIA. Text in English. 1996. irreg., latest 1996. **Document type:** *Government.*
Media: CD-ROM.
Published by: Australian Bureau of Statistics, Locked Bag 10, Belconnen, ACT 2616, Australia. TEL 61-2-92684909, 61-2-62527037, 300-135-070, FAX 61-2-62528103, client.services@abs.gov.au.

304.6021 AUS
AUSTRALIA. BUREAU OF STATISTICS. CENSUS OF POPULATION AND HOUSING: CENSUS BASICS, AUSTRALIA. Text in English. 2001. irreg., latest 2001. **Document type:** *Government.*
Media: CD-ROM.
Published by: Australian Bureau of Statistics, Locked Bag 10, Belconnen, ACT 2616, Australia. TEL 61-2-92684909, 300-135-070, FAX 61-2-92684654, client.services@abs.gov.au.

304.6021 AUS
AUSTRALIA. BUREAU OF STATISTICS. CENSUS OF POPULATION AND HOUSING: CENSUS BASICS, AUSTRALIAN CAPITAL TERRITORY. Text in English. 2001. irreg., latest 2001. **Document type:** *Government.*
Media: CD-ROM.
Published by: Australian Bureau of Statistics, Locked Bag 10, Belconnen, ACT 2616, Australia. TEL 61-2-92684909, 300-135-070, FAX 61-2-92684654, client.services@abs.gov.au.

304.6021 AUS
AUSTRALIA. BUREAU OF STATISTICS. CENSUS OF POPULATION AND HOUSING: CENSUS GEOGRAPHIC AREAS DIGITAL BOUNDARIES, AUSTRALIA (ONLINE). Text in English. 2001. quinquennial. free (effective 2009). back issues avail. **Document type:** *Government.*
Formerly: Australia. Bureau of Statistics. Census of Population and Housing: Census Geographic Areas Digital Boundaries, Australia (Print)
Media: Online - full text.
Published by: Australian Bureau of Statistics, Locked Bag 10, Belconnen, ACT 2616, Australia. TEL 61-2-62527037, 61-2-92684909, 300-135-070, FAX 61-2-62528103, client.services@abs.gov.au.

304.6021 AUS
AUSTRALIA. BUREAU OF STATISTICS. CENSUS OF POPULATION AND HOUSING: CENSUS GUIDE. Text in English. 2001. quinquennial, latest 2006. free (effective 2009). back issues avail. **Document type:** *Government.* **Description:** Includes the census dictionary, information and technical papers, sample community profile structures and an overview of the various hardcopy and electronic products to be released. A simple and intuitive interface presented for users to access the information and web site links also made available.
Media: CD-ROM.
Published by: Australian Bureau of Statistics, Locked Bag 10, Belconnen, ACT 2616, Australia. TEL 61-2-92684909, 300-135-070, FAX 61-2-92684654, client.services@abs.gov.au.

304.6021 363.5021 AUS
AUSTRALIA. BUREAU OF STATISTICS. CENSUS OF POPULATION AND HOUSING: CLASSIFICATION COUNTS, AUSTRALIA. Text in English. 1996. irreg. **Document type:** *Government.*
Related titles: Online - full text ed.
Published by: Australian Bureau of Statistics, Locked Bag 10, Belconnen, ACT 2616, Australia. TEL 61-2-92684909, 61-2-62527037, 300-135-070, FAX 61-2-62528103, client.services@abs.gov.au, http://www.abs.gov.au.

304.6021 AUS
AUSTRALIA. BUREAU OF STATISTICS. CENSUS OF POPULATION AND HOUSING: COLLECTION DISTRICT AND STATISTICAL LOCAL AREA REFERENCE MAPS, AUSTRALIA. Text in English. 1991. quinquennial. price varies. **Document type:** *Government.*
Published by: Australian Bureau of Statistics, Locked Bag 10, Belconnen, ACT 2616, Australia. TEL 61-2-62527037, 61-2-92684909, 300-135-070, FAX 61-2-62528103, client.services@abs.gov.au, http://www.abs.gov.au.

304.6021 363.5021 AUS
AUSTRALIA. BUREAU OF STATISTICS. CENSUS OF POPULATION AND HOUSING: COMMUNITY PROFILES, AUSTRALIA (ONLINE). Text in English. 1996. irreg. free (effective 2009). **Document type:** *Government.*
Formerly: Australia. Bureau of Statistics. Census of Population and Housing: Community Profiles, Australia (Print)
Media: Online - full text.
Published by: Australian Bureau of Statistics, Locked Bag 10, Belconnen, ACT 2616, Australia. TEL 61-2-92684909, 61-2-62527037, 300-135-070, FAX 61-2-62528103, client.services@abs.gov.au.

304.6021 363.502 AUS
AUSTRALIA. BUREAU OF STATISTICS. CENSUS OF POPULATION AND HOUSING: CUSTOMIZED TABLES, AUSTRALIA. Text in English. 1996. irreg. price varies. **Document type:** *Government.*
Published by: Australian Bureau of Statistics, Locked Bag 10, Belconnen, ACT 2616, Australia. TEL 61-2-62527037, 61-2-92684909, 300-135-070, FAX 61-2-62528103, client.services@abs.gov.au, http://www.abs.gov.au.

304.6021 AUS
AUSTRALIA. BUREAU OF STATISTICS. CENSUS OF POPULATION AND HOUSING: DIGITAL BOUNDARIES, AUSTRALIA. Text in English. 1991. quinquennial. price varies. **Document type:** *Government.*
Published by: Australian Bureau of Statistics, Locked Bag 10, Belconnen, ACT 2616, Australia. TEL 61-2-62527037, 61-2-92684909, 300-135-070, FAX 61-2-62528103, client.services@abs.gov.au.

304.6021 363.502 AUS
AUSTRALIA. BUREAU OF STATISTICS. CENSUS OF POPULATION AND HOUSING: EXPANDED COMMUNITY PROFILE. Text in English. 2001. quinquennial. stat. **Document type:** *Government.* **Description:** Contains six separate profiles aimed at providing information on key Census characteristics relating to persons, families and dwellings and covering most topics on the census form.
Related titles: Online - full text ed.
Published by: Australian Bureau of Statistics, Locked Bag 10, Belconnen, ACT 2616, Australia. TEL 61-2-92684909, 61-2-62527037, 300-135-070, FAX 61-2-62528103, client.services@abs.gov.au.

304.6021 363.5021 AUS
AUSTRALIA. BUREAU OF STATISTICS. CENSUS OF POPULATION AND HOUSING: HOUSEHOLD SAMPLE FILE. Text in English. 1996. quinquennial. **Document type:** *Government.* **Description:** Contains census characteristics, for a random sample of person, family, household and dwelling variables.
Media: CD-ROM. **Related titles:** Online - full text ed.: free (effective 2009).
Published by: Australian Bureau of Statistics, Locked Bag 10, Belconnen, ACT 2616, Australia. TEL 61-2-62527037, 61-2-92684909, 300-135-070, FAX 61-2-62528103, client.services@abs.gov.au.

304.6021 AUS
AUSTRALIA. BUREAU OF STATISTICS. CENSUS OF POPULATION AND HOUSING: INDIGENOUS PROFILE. Text in English. 2001. quinquennial, latest 2006. back issues avail. **Document type:** *Government.* **Description:** Contains six separate profiles aimed at providing information on key census characteristics relating to persons, families and dwellings and covering most topics on the census form. The profiles are excellent tools for researching, planning and analysing small and large geographic areas.
Media: CD-ROM.
Published by: Australian Bureau of Statistics, Locked Bag 10, Belconnen, ACT 2616, Australia. TEL 61-2-92684909, 300-135-070, FAX 61-2-92684654, client.services@abs.gov.au.

304.6021 363.5021 AUS
AUSTRALIA. BUREAU OF STATISTICS. CENSUS OF POPULATION AND HOUSING: NATURE AND CONTENT (ONLINE). Text in English. 1996. quinquennial, latest 2006. free (effective 2009). **Document type:** *Government.*
Former titles: Australia. Bureau of Statistics. Census of Population and Housing: Nature and Content; (until 2006): Australia. Bureau of Statistics. Information Paper: Census of Population and Housing: Nature and Content; (until 2001): Australia. Bureau of Statistics. (Year) Census - Nature and Content
Media: Online - full text.
Published by: Australian Bureau of Statistics, Locked Bag 10, Belconnen, ACT 2616, Australia. TEL 61-2-92684909, 61-2-62527037, 300-135-070, FAX 61-2-62528103, client.services@abs.gov.au.

304.6021 363.502 AUS
AUSTRALIA. BUREAU OF STATISTICS. CENSUS OF POPULATION AND HOUSING: PLACE OF ENUMERATION PROFILE. Text in English. 2001. quinquennial. stat. **Document type:** *Government.* **Description:** Contains six separate profiles aimed at providing information on key census characteristics relating to persons, families and dwellings and covering most topics on the census form.

Formerly (until 2006): Australia. Bureau of Statistics. Census of Population and Housing: Usual Residents Profile
Related titles: Online - full text ed.
Published by: Australian Bureau of Statistics, Locked Bag 10, Belconnen, ACT 2616, Australia. TEL 61-2-92684909, 61-2-62527037, 300-135-070, FAX 61-2-62528103, client.services@abs.gov.au.

304.6021 363.5021 AUS
AUSTRALIA. BUREAU OF STATISTICS. CENSUS OF POPULATION AND HOUSING: POPULATION GROWTH AND DISTRIBUTION, AUSTRALIA (ONLINE). Text in English. 1991. quinquennial. free (effective 2009). back issues avail. **Document type:** *Government.*
Former titles: Australia. Bureau of Statistics. Census of Population and Housing: Population Growth and Distribution, Australia (Print); (until 1996): Australia. Bureau of Statistics. Census - Population Growth and Distribution in Australia
Media: Online - full text.
Published by: Australian Bureau of Statistics, Locked Bag 10, Belconnen, ACT 2616, Australia. TEL 61-2-62527037, 61-2-92684909, 300-135-070, FAX 61-2-62528103, client.services@abs.gov.au.

304.6021 363.5021 AUS
AUSTRALIA. BUREAU OF STATISTICS. CENSUS OF POPULATION AND HOUSING: SELECTED CHARACTERISTICS FOR URBAN CENTRES AND LOCALITIES, NEW SOUTH WALES AND AUSTRALIAN CAPITAL TERRITORY (ONLINE). Text in English. 1996. quinquennial, latest 2001. free (effective 2009). back issues avail. **Document type:** *Government.* **Description:** Contains selected 2001 census person, family and dwelling characteristics for all Urban Centres and Localities within New South Wales and the Australian Capital Territory. Also included are ranked tables and reference maps.
Formerly (until 2001): Australia. Bureau of Statistics. Census of Population and Housing: Selected Characteristics for Urban Centres and Localities, New South Wales and Australian Capital Territory (Print)
Media: Online - full text.
Published by: Australian Bureau of Statistics, Locked Bag 10, Belconnen, ACT 2616, Australia. TEL 61-2-92684909, 300-135-070, FAX 61-2-92684654, client.services@abs.gov.au.

304.6021 363.5021 AUS
AUSTRALIA. BUREAU OF STATISTICS. CENSUS OF POPULATION AND HOUSING: SELECTED CHARACTERISTICS FOR URBAN CENTRES, AUSTRALIA (ONLINE). Text in English. 1996. quinquennial. free (effective 2009). back issues avail. **Document type:** *Government.* **Description:** Provides a selection of data for the population and their housing arrangements, for the top 200 urban centres.
Formerly: Australia. Bureau of Statistics. Census of Population and Housing: Selected Characteristics for Urban Centres, Australia (Print)
Media: Online - full text.
Published by: Australian Bureau of Statistics, Locked Bag 10, Belconnen, ACT 2616, Australia. TEL 61-2-92684909, 61-2-62527037, FAX 61-2-62528103, client.services@abs.gov.au.

304.6021 363.5021 AUS
AUSTRALIA. BUREAU OF STATISTICS. CENSUS OF POPULATION AND HOUSING: SELECTED EDUCATION AND LABOUR FORCE CHARACTERISTICS, AUSTRALIA (ONLINE). Text in English. 1996. quinquennial, latest 2001. free (effective 2009). back issues avail. **Document type:** *Government.* **Description:** Presents a range of education and labour force statistics produced from the census of Population and Housing for Australia.
Former titles: Australia. Bureau of Statistics. Census of Population and Housing: Selected Education and Labour Force Characteristics, Australia (Print); Australia. Bureau of Statistics. Census of Population and Housing: Selected Family and Labour Force Characteristics, Australia
Media: Online - full text.
Published by: Australian Bureau of Statistics, Locked Bag 10, Belconnen, ACT 2616, Australia. TEL 61-2-92684909, 61-2-62527037, 300-135-070, FAX 61-2-62528103, client.services@abs.gov.au.

304.6021 363.5021 AUS
AUSTRALIA. BUREAU OF STATISTICS. CENSUS OF POPULATION AND HOUSING: SELECTED EDUCATION AND LABOUR FORCE CHARACTERISTICS FOR STATISTICAL LOCAL AREAS, AUSTRALIAN CAPITAL TERRITORY (ONLINE). Text in English. 1996. irreg., latest 2001. free (effective 2009). back issues avail. **Document type:** *Government.* **Description:** Contains 2001 census population counts and selected education and labour force characteristics for persons in all statistical local areas, statistical sub-divisions and statistical divisions within the Australian Capital Territory.
Former titles (until 2001): Australia. Bureau of Statistics. Census of Population and Housing: Selected Education and Labour Force Characteristics for Statistical Local Areas, Australian Capital Territory (Print); Australia. Bureau of Statistics. Census of Population and Housing: Selected Family and Labour Force Characteristics for Statistical Local Areas, Australian Capital Territory
Media: Online - full text.
Published by: Australian Bureau of Statistics, Locked Bag 10, Belconnen, ACT 2616, Australia. TEL 61-2-92684909, 300-135-070, FAX 61-2-92684654, client.services@abs.gov.au.

304.6021 363.5021 AUS
AUSTRALIA. BUREAU OF STATISTICS. CENSUS OF POPULATION AND HOUSING: SELECTED SOCIAL AND HOUSING CHARACTERISTICS, AUSTRALIA (ONLINE). Text in English. 1996. quinquennial, latest 2001. free (effective 2009). **Document type:** *Government.* **Description:** Presents a range of social and housing statistics produced from the latest Census of Population and Housing for Australia, its states and territories and their regions.
Formerly: Australia. Bureau of Statistics. Census of Population and Housing: Selected Social and Housing Characteristics, Australia (Print)
Media: Online - full text.
Published by: Australian Bureau of Statistics, Locked Bag 10, Belconnen, ACT 2616, Australia. TEL 61-2-92684909, 61-2-62527037, 300-135-070, FAX 61-2-62528103, client.services@abs.gov.au.

P

304.6021 363.5021 AUS
AUSTRALIA. BUREAU OF STATISTICS. CENSUS OF POPULATION AND HOUSING: SELECTED SOCIAL AND HOUSING CHARACTERISTICS FOR STATISTICAL LOCAL AREAS, AUSTRALIAN CAPITAL TERRITORY (ONLINE). Text in English. 1996. quinquennial, latest 2001. free (effective 2009). back issues avail. **Document type:** *Government.* **Description:** Contains 2001 census population counts and selected person, family and dwelling characteristics for all statistical local areas, statistical sub-divisions and statistical divisions within the Australian Capital Territory, as well as ranked tables.
Former titles (untiles 2001): Australia. Bureau of Statistics. Census of Population and Housing: Selected Social and Housing Characteristics for Statistical Local Areas, Australian Capital Territory (Print); Australia. Bureau of Statistics. Census: Selected Social and Housing Characteristics for Statistical Local Areas, Australian Capital Territory
Media: Online - full text.
Published by: Australian Bureau of Statistics, Locked Bag 10, Belconnen, ACT 2616, Australia. TEL 61-2-92684909, 300-135-070, FAX 61-2-92684654, client.services@abs.gov.au.

304.6021 363.5021 AUS
AUSTRALIA. BUREAU OF STATISTICS. CENSUS OF POPULATION AND HOUSING: SOCIO-ECONOMIC INDEXES FOR AREAS, AUSTRALIA. Text in English. 1996. quinquennial. **Document type:** *Government.*
Media: CD-ROM. **Related titles:** Online - full text ed.: free (effective 2009).
Published by: Australian Bureau of Statistics, Locked Bag 10, Belconnen, ACT 2616, Australia. TEL 61-2-62527037, 61-2-92684909, 300-135-070, FAX 61-2-62528103, client.services@abs.gov.au.

304.6021 363.5021 AUS
AUSTRALIA. BUREAU OF STATISTICS. CENSUS OF POPULATION AND HOUSING: THEMATIC PROFILE SERVICE, AUSTRALIA. Text in English. 1996. irreg. price varies. **Document type:** *Government.*
Published by: Australian Bureau of Statistics, Locked Bag 10, Belconnen, ACT 2616, Australia. TEL 61-2-92684909, 61-2-62527037, 300-135-070, FAX 61-2-62528103, client.services@abs.gov.au, http://www.abs.gov.au.

304.6021 363.502 AUS
AUSTRALIA. BUREAU OF STATISTICS. CENSUS OF POPULATION AND HOUSING: TIME SERIES PROFILE. Text in English. 2001. quinquennial. stat. **Document type:** *Government.*
Related titles: Online - full text ed.
Published by: Australian Bureau of Statistics, Locked Bag 10, Belconnen, ACT 2616, Australia. TEL 61-2-92684909, 61-2-62527037, 300-135-070, FAX 61-2-62528103, client.services@abs.gov.au.

304.6021 363.502 AUS
AUSTRALIA. BUREAU OF STATISTICS. CENSUS OF POPULATION AND HOUSING: WORKING POPULATION PROFILE. Text in English. 2003. quinquennial. AUD 10 (effective 2003). stat. back issues avail. **Document type:** *Government.*
Related titles: Online - full text ed.
Published by: Australian Bureau of Statistics, Locked Bag 10, Belconnen, ACT 2616, Australia. TEL 61-2-92684909, 61-2-62527037, 300-135-070, FAX 61-2-62528103, client.services@abs.gov.au.

304.6021 AUS
AUSTRALIA. BUREAU OF STATISTICS. COLLECTION DISTRICT COMPARABILITY LISTING, AUSTRALIA. Text in English. 2001. quinquennial. back issues avail. **Document type:** *Government.*
Media: Online - full text.
Published by: Australian Bureau of Statistics, Locked Bag 10, Belconnen, ACT 2616, Australia. TEL 61-2-92684909, 61-2-62527037, 300-135-070, FAX 61-2-62528103, client.services@abs.gov.au, http://www.abs.gov.au.

304.6021 AUS
AUSTRALIA. BUREAU OF STATISTICS. COMPLETE SET OF SOCIAL ATLASES. Text in English. 1996. quinquennial, latest 2006. AUD 193 (for the full set) (effective 2009). back issues avail. **Description:** Consists of a separate publication for each state and territory that presents colour maps that highlight key characteristics of the population in each capital city and selected regional areas.
Related titles: Online - full text ed.
Published by: Australian Bureau of Statistics, Locked Bag 10, Belconnen, ACT 2616, Australia. TEL 61-2-92684909, 300-135-070, FAX 61-2-92684654, client.services@abs.gov.au.

350.021 AUS
HB1505
AUSTRALIA. BUREAU OF STATISTICS. DEATHS, AUSTRALIA (ONLINE). Text in English. 1967. a., latest 2007. free (effective 2009). illus. **Document type:** *Government.* **Description:** Contains the numbers of deaths classified by age, sex, birthplace, marital status; occupation, month of death, cause of death and usual residence of deceased by state or territory.
Former titles (until 2004): Australia. Bureau of Statistics. Deaths, Australia (Print) (1031-0223); (until 1978): Deaths
Published by: Australian Bureau of Statistics, Locked Bag 10, Belconnen, ACT 2616, Australia. TEL 61-2-92684909, 61-2-62527037, 300-135-070, FAX 61-2-62528103, client.services@abs.gov.au. Circ: 427.

304.6 AUS
AUSTRALIA. BUREAU OF STATISTICS. DEMOGRAPHIC VARIABLES. Text in English. 1993. irreg., latest 1999. free (effective 2009). **Document type:** *Government.*
Formerly (until 1999): Australia. Bureau of Statistics. Standards for Statistics on Age and Sex (Print)
Media: Online - full text.
Published by: Australian Bureau of Statistics, Locked Bag 10, Belconnen, ACT 2616, Australia. TEL 61-2-92684909, 61-2-62527037, 300-135-070, FAX 61-2-62528103, client.services@abs.gov.au.

304.6021 AUS
AUSTRALIA. BUREAU OF STATISTICS. DIRECTORY OF CENSUS STATISTICS (ONLINE). Text in English. 1991. irreg., latest 2003. free (effective 2009). **Document type:** *Directory, Government.* **Description:** Assists users in accessing information from the wealth of statistics collected in the Census of Population and Housing.
Former titles (until 2001): Australia. Bureau of Statistics. Directory of Census Statistics (Print); (until 1991): Census - A Guide to Products and Service
Media: Online - full text.
Published by: Australian Bureau of Statistics, Locked Bag 10, Belconnen, ACT 2616, Australia. TEL 61-2-62527037, FAX 61-2-92684654, client.services@abs.gov.au.

304.6 AUS
AUSTRALIA. BUREAU OF STATISTICS. DIRECTORY OF CHILD AND FAMILY STATISTICS (ONLINE). Text in English. 2000. irreg., latest 2000. free (effective 2009). **Document type:** *Directory, Consumer.* **Description:** Provides descriptive information on various data sources, data items available, frequency of collections, publications produced and any reliability/confidentiality provisions.
Formerly (until 2000): Australia. Bureau of Statistics. Directory of Child and Family Statistics (Print)
Media: Online - full text.
Published by: Australian Bureau of Statistics, Locked Bag 10, Belconnen, ACT 2616, Australia. TEL 61-2-92684909, 300-135-070, FAX 61-2-92684654, client.services@abs.gov.au.

304.6021 AUS
AUSTRALIA. BUREAU OF STATISTICS. EXPERIMENTAL ESTIMATES AND PROJECTIONS OF INDIGENOUS AUSTRALIANS. Text in English. 2003. quinquennial. stat. **Document type:** *Government.*
Published by: Australian Bureau of Statistics, Locked Bag 10, Belconnen, ACT 2616, Australia. TEL 61-2-92684909, 61-2-62527037, 300-135-070, FAX 61-2-62528103, client.services@abs.gov.au, http://www.abs.gov.au.

304.6021 AUS
AUSTRALIA. BUREAU OF STATISTICS. EXPERIMENTAL ESTIMATES OF THE ABORIGINAL AND TORRES STRAIT ISLANDER POPULATION (ONLINE). Text in English. 1991. quinquennial. free (effective 2009). back issues avail. **Document type:** *Government.*
Formerly: Australia. Bureau of Statistics. Experimental Estimates of the Aboriginal and Torres Strait Islander Population (Print)
Media: Online - full text.
Published by: Australian Bureau of Statistics, Locked Bag 10, Belconnen, ACT 2616, Australia. TEL 61-2-92684909, 61-2-62527037, 300-135-070, FAX 61-2-62528103, client.services@abs.gov.au.

304.6021 AUS
AUSTRALIA. BUREAU OF STATISTICS. EXPERIMENTAL PROJECTIONS OF THE ABORIGINAL AND TORRES STRAIT ISLANDER POPULATION (ONLINE). Text in English. 1991. quinquennial. free (effective 2009). **Document type:** *Government.*
Formerly: Australia. Bureau of Statistics. Experimental Projections of the Aboriginal and Torres Strait Islander Population (Print)
Media: Online - full text.
Published by: Australian Bureau of Statistics, Locked Bag 10, Belconnen, ACT 2616, Australia. TEL 61-2-62527037, 61-2-92684909, 300-135-070, FAX 61-2-62528103, client.services@abs.gov.au.

304.6021 AUS
AUSTRALIA. BUREAU OF STATISTICS. HOW AUSTRALIA TAKES A CENSUS (ONLINE). Text in English. 1991. quinquennial. free (effective 2009). back issues avail. **Document type:** *Government.* **Description:** Describes the history of the census, the process by which the census was planned, the way it will be conducted and processed and the type of output that will be available.
Former titles: Australia. Bureau of Statistics. How Australia Takes a Census (Print); (until 2001): Australia. Bureau of Statistics. Census - How Australia Takes a Census
Media: Online - full text.
Published by: Australian Bureau of Statistics, Locked Bag 10, Belconnen, ACT 2616, Australia. TEL 61-2-62527037, 61-2-92684909, 300-135-070, FAX 61-2-62528103, client.services@abs.gov.au.

304.6021 363.5021 AUS
AUSTRALIA. BUREAU OF STATISTICS. INFORMATION PAPER: CENSUS OF POPULATION AND HOUSING - A B S VIEWS ON CENSUS OUTPUT STRATEGY (ONLINE). Text in English. 1996. quinquennial. free (effective 2009). back issues avail. **Document type:** *Government.* **Description:** Sets out the ABS initial views on output strategy options for Census.
Former titles: Australia. Bureau of Statistics. Information Paper: Census of Population and Housing - A B S Views on Census Output Strategy (Print); Australia. Bureau of Statistics. (Year) Census - A B S Views on Census Output
Media: Online - full text.
Published by: Australian Bureau of Statistics, Locked Bag 10, Belconnen, ACT 2616, Australia. TEL 61-2-92684909, 61-2-62527037, 300-135-070, FAX 61-2-62528103, client.services@abs.gov.au.

304.6021 363.5021 AUS
AUSTRALIA. BUREAU OF STATISTICS. INFORMATION PAPER: CENSUS OF POPULATION AND HOUSING, A.B.S. VIEWS ON CONTENT AND PROCEDURES (ONLINE). Text in English. 1996. quinquennial, latest 2011. free (effective 2009). **Document type:** *Government.* **Description:** Designed to initiate public consultation about the content and procedures of the census by seeking comments on views expressed in this publication.
Formerly: Australia. Bureau of Statistics. Information Paper: Census of Population and Housing, A.B.S. Views on Content and Procedures (Print)
Media: Online - full text.
Published by: Australian Bureau of Statistics, Locked Bag 10, Belconnen, ACT 2616, Australia. TEL 61-2-92684909, 61-2-62527037, 300-135-070, FAX 61-2-62528103, client.services@abs.gov.au.

304.6021 AUS
AUSTRALIA. BUREAU OF STATISTICS. INFORMATION PAPER: CENSUS OF POPULATION AND HOUSING - DETAILS OF UNDERCOUNT. Text in English. 1991. quinquennial. free (effective 2009). back issues avail. **Document type:** *Government.* **Description:** Presents estimates of net undercount for the census, as well as information on how the estimates were calculated.
Former titles (until 2006): Australia. Bureau of Statistics. Information Paper: Census of Population and Housing - Undercount; Australia. Bureau of Statistics. Information Paper: Census of Population and Housing, Data Quality - Undercount
Media: Online - full text.
Published by: Australian Bureau of Statistics, Locked Bag 10, Belconnen, ACT 2616, Australia. TEL 61-2-62527037, 61-2-92684909, 300-135-070, FAX 61-2-62528103, client.services@abs.gov.au.

304.6 AUS
AUSTRALIA. BUREAU OF STATISTICS. INFORMATION PAPER - CENSUS OF POPULATION AND HOUSING: LINK BETWEEN AUSTRALIAN STANDARD CLASSIFICATION OF OCCUPATIONS (ASCO) SECOND EDITION AND AUSTRALIAN AND NEW ZEALAND STANDARD CLASSIFICATION OF OCCUPATIONS (ANZSCO). Text in English. 1996. quinquennial, latest 2001. free (effective 2009). back issues avail. **Document type:** *Government.* **Description:** Presents details of a quantitative link between the Australian and New Zealand Standard Classification of Occupations (ANZSCO), first edition and the Australian Standard Classification of Occupations (ASCO), second edition.
Formerly (until 2006): Australia. Bureau of Statistics. Information Paper - Census of Population and Housing: Link Between First and Second Editions of Australian Standard Classification of Occupations (Print)
Media: Online - full text.
Published by: Australian Bureau of Statistics, Locked Bag 10, Belconnen, ACT 2616, Australia. TEL 61-2-92684909, 300-135-070, FAX 61-2-92684654, client.services@abs.gov.au.

304.6021 363.5021 AUS
AUSTRALIA. BUREAU OF STATISTICS. INFORMATION PAPER: CENSUS OF POPULATION AND HOUSING - PROPOSED PRODUCTS AND SERVICES (ONLINE). Text in English. 1996. quinquennial. free (effective 2009). **Document type:** *Government.* **Description:** Provides information on the proposed products and services for Census, and seeks user views on the proposals.
Former titles: Australia. Bureau of Statistics. Information Paper: Census of Population and Housing - Proposed Products and Services (Print); (until 2001): Australia. Bureau of Statistics. (Year) Census of Population and Housing 1996
Media: Online - full text.
Published by: Australian Bureau of Statistics, Locked Bag 10, Belconnen, ACT 2616, Australia. TEL 61-2-92684909, 61-2-62527037, 300-135-070, FAX 61-2-62528103, client.services@abs.gov.au.

304.6021 AUS
AUSTRALIA. BUREAU OF STATISTICS. INFORMATION PAPER: OUTCOMES OF A B S VIEWS ON REMOTENESS CONSULTATION, AUSTRALIA (ONLINE). Text in English. 2001. irreg., latest 2001. free (effective 2009). **Document type:** *Government.* **Description:** Provides seeking the views of users and potential users on five proposals for change to the Australian Standard Geographical Classification (ASGC).
Formerly: Australia. Bureau of Statistics. Information Paper: Outcomes of A B S Views on Remoteness Consultation, Australia (Print)
Media: Online - full text.
Published by: Australian Bureau of Statistics, Locked Bag 10, Belconnen, ACT 2616, Australia. TEL 61-2-92684909, 300-135-070, FAX 61-2-92684654, client.services@abs.gov.au.

304.6021 AUS
JV9125.5
AUSTRALIA. BUREAU OF STATISTICS. MIGRATION, AUSTRALIA (ONLINE). Text in English. 1973. a., latest 1998. free (effective 2009). back issues avail. **Document type:** *Government.* **Description:** Contains information on international and internal migration and the estimated resident population by birthplace.
Former titles (until 200?): Australia. Bureau of Statistics. Migration, Australia (Print) (1322-8765); (until 1995): Australia. Bureau of Statistics. Overseas Arrivals and Departures, Australia (1031-0517); (until 1978): Australia. Bureau of Statistics. Overseas Arrivals and Departures (0310-2378)
Media: Online - full text.
Published by: Australian Bureau of Statistics, Locked Bag 10, Belconnen, ACT 2616, Australia. TEL 61-2-92684909, 61-2-62527037, FAX 61-2-62528103, client.services@abs.gov.au.

304.6021 AUS
AUSTRALIA. BUREAU OF STATISTICS. NATIONAL ABORIGINAL AND TORRES STRAIT ISLANDER SOCIAL SURVEY. Text in English. 200?. irreg., latest 2002. free (effective 2009). stat. **Document type:** *Government.* **Description:** Presents summary results from the 2002 National Aboriginal and Torres Strait Islander Social Survey, on a wide range of topics including family and culture, health, education, employment, income, financial stress, housing, transport and mobility, as well as law and justice.
Formerly (until 2002): Australia. Bureau of Statistics. Indigenous Social Survey (Print)
Media: Online - full text.
Published by: Australian Bureau of Statistics, Locked Bag 10, Belconnen, ACT 2616, Australia. TEL 61-2-92684909, 61-2-62527037, 300-135-070, FAX 61-2-62528103, client.services@abs.gov.au.

340.6021 AUS
AUSTRALIA. BUREAU OF STATISTICS. NATIONAL ABORIGINAL AND TORRES STRAIT ISLANDER SURVEY: UNIT RECORD FILE (ONLINE). Text in English. 1994. irreg., latest 1994. free (effective 2009). **Document type:** *Government.* **Description:** Contains information about the social and economic conditions, cultural status and attitudes of Australia's Indigenous population.
Formerly: Australia. Bureau of Statistics. National Aboriginal and Torres Strait Islander Survey: Unit Record File (Diskette)
Media: Online - full text.

Published by: Australian Bureau of Statistics, Locked Bag 10, Belconnen, ACT 2616, Australia. TEL 61-2-92684909, 61-2-62527037, 300-135-070, FAX 61-2-62528103, client.services@abs.gov.au.

304.6 AUS
AUSTRALIA. BUREAU OF STATISTICS. NATIONAL HEALTH SURVEY: ABORIGINAL AND TORRES STRAIT ISLANDER RESULTS, AUSTRALIA (ONLINE). Text in English. 1995. irreg. free (effective 2009). **Document type:** *Government.* **Description:** Presents selected data about the health of Indigenous and non-Indigenous Australians from the National Health Survey (NHS).
Formerly: Australia. Bureau of Statistics. National Health Survey: Aboriginal and Torres Strait Islander Results, Australia (Online)
Media: Online - full text.
Published by: Australian Bureau of Statistics, Locked Bag 10, Belconnen, ACT 2616, Australia. TEL 61-2-92684909, 61-2-62527037, 300-135-070, FAX 61-2-62528103, client.services@abs.gov.au.

304.6021 AUS
AUSTRALIA. BUREAU OF STATISTICS. NATIONAL HEALTH SURVEY: SF36 POPULATION NORMS, AUSTRALIA (ONLINE). Text in English. 1995. irreg., latest 1995. free (effective 2009). **Document type:** *Government.* **Description:** Contains population norms compiled for the eight dimensions of health covered by the SF36 questionnaire together with the physical and mental health summary scales derived from this instrument.
Formerly: Australia. Bureau of Statistics. National Health Survey: SF36 Population Norms, Australia (Print)
Media: Online - full text.
Published by: Australian Bureau of Statistics, Locked Bag 10, Belconnen, ACT 2616, Australia. TEL 61-2-92684909, 61-2-62527037, 300-135-070, FAX 61-2-62528103, client.services@abs.gov.au.

304.6021 363.5021 AUS
AUSTRALIA. BUREAU OF STATISTICS. NEW SOUTH WALES OFFICE. AUSTRALIAN HOUSING SURVEY: NEW SOUTH WALES - DATA REPORT (ONLINE). Text in English. 1999. irreg. free (effective 2009). **Document type:** *Government.*
Formerly: Australia. Bureau of Statistics. New South Wales Office. Australian Housing Survey: New South Wales - Data Report on Hardcopy
Media: Online - full text.
Published by: Australian Bureau of Statistics, New South Wales Office, GPO Box 796, Sydney, NSW 2001, Australia. TEL 61-2-92684909, 300-135-070, client.services@abs.gov.au.

304.6021 363.5021 AUS
AUSTRALIA. BUREAU OF STATISTICS. NEW SOUTH WALES OFFICE. CENSUS OF POPULATION AND HOUSING: ABORIGINAL AND TORRES STRAIT ISLANDER PEOPLE, NEW SOUTH WALES (ONLINE). Text in English. 1998. quinquennial. free (effective 2009). **Document type:** *Government.* **Description:** Presents information on Aboriginal and Torres Strait Islander Australians based largely on information from the 1996 and earlier censuses.
Formerly: Australia. Bureau of Statistics. New South Wales Office. Census of Population and Housing: Aboriginal and Torres Strait Islander People, New South Wales (Print)
Media: Online - full text.
Published by: Australian Bureau of Statistics, New South Wales Office, GPO Box 796, Sydney, NSW 2001, Australia. TEL 61-2-92684909, 300-135-070, client.services@abs.gov.au.

304.6021 363.5021 AUS
AUSTRALIA. BUREAU OF STATISTICS. NEW SOUTH WALES OFFICE. CENSUS OF POPULATION AND HOUSING: CENSUS BASICS, NEW SOUTH WALES. Text in English. 2001. quinquennial. **Document type:** *Catalog, Government.* **Description:** Contains Census Basic Community Profile data.
Media: CD-ROM.
Published by: Australian Bureau of Statistics, New South Wales Office, GPO Box 796, Sydney, NSW 2001, Australia. TEL 61-2-92684909, 300-135-070.

304.6021 363.5021 AUS
AUSTRALIA. BUREAU OF STATISTICS. NEW SOUTH WALES OFFICE. CENSUS OF POPULATION AND HOUSING: SELECTED CHARACTERISTICS FOR URBAN CENTRES AND LOCALITIES, NEW SOUTH WALES AND AUSTRALIAN CAPITAL TERRITORY (ONLINE). Text in English. 1998. quinquennial. free (effective 2009). back issues avail. **Document type:** *Government.* **Description:** contains data from the Census of Population and Housing for New South Wales and the Australian Capital Territory.
Formerly: Australia. Bureau of Statistics. New South Wales Office. Census of Population and Housing: Selected Characteristics for Urban Centres and Localities, New South Wales and Australian Capital Territory (Print)
Media: Online - full text.
Published by: Australian Bureau of Statistics, New South Wales Office, GPO Box 796, Sydney, NSW 2001, Australia. TEL 61-2-92684909, 300-135-070, client.services@abs.gov.au.

304.6021 363.5021 AUS
AUSTRALIA. BUREAU OF STATISTICS. NEW SOUTH WALES OFFICE. CENSUS OF POPULATION AND HOUSING: SELECTED EDUCATION AND LABOUR FORCE CHARACTERISTICS FOR STATISTICAL LOCAL AREAS, NEW SOUTH WALES AND JERVIS BAY (ONLINE). Text in English. 1998. quinquennial. free (effective 2009). back issues avail. **Document type:** *Government.* **Description:** Presents a range of education and labour force statistics produced from the Census of Population and Housing for New South Wales (NSW).
Formerly: Australia. Bureau of Statistics. New South Wales Office. Census of Population and Housing: Selected Education and Labour Force Characteristics for Statistical Local Areas, New South Wales and Jervis Bay (Print)
Media: Online - full text.
Published by: Australian Bureau of Statistics, New South Wales Office, GPO Box 796, Sydney, NSW 2001, Australia. TEL 61-2-92684909, 300-135-070, client.services@abs.gov.au.

304.6021 AUS
AUSTRALIA. BUREAU OF STATISTICS. NEW SOUTH WALES OFFICE. NEW SOUTH WALES AT A GLANCE (ONLINE). Text in English. 1997. a. free (effective 2009). back issues avail. **Document type:** *Government.* **Description:** Provides summary information about New South Wales, in a series of brief tables.
Former titles (until 2004): Australia. Bureau of Statistics. New South Wales Office. New South Wales at a Glance (Print); (until 1997): Australia. Bureau of Statistics. New South Wales Office. New South Wales in Brief (0725-5039)
Media: Online - full text.
Published by: Australian Bureau of Statistics, New South Wales Office, GPO Box 796, Sydney, NSW 2001, Australia. TEL 61-2-92684909, 300-135-070, client.services@abs.gov.au.

304.6021 AUS
AUSTRALIA. BUREAU OF STATISTICS. NEW SOUTH WALES OFFICE. SYDNEY. A SOCIAL ATLAS. Text in English. 1998. quinquennial. AUD 29 per issue (effective 2009). back issues avail. **Document type:** *Government.* **Description:** Presents colour maps, based on data collected in the Census of Population and Housing, that highlight key social, demographic and housing characteristics of the population in Sydney and two selected regional areas in New South Wales, i.e. Wollongong and the Newcastle-Central Coast region.
Related titles: Online - full text ed.: free (effective 2009).
Published by: Australian Bureau of Statistics, New South Wales Office, GPO Box 796, Sydney, NSW 2001, Australia. TEL 61-2-92684611, 300-135-070, FAX 61-2-92684668, client.services@abs.gov.au.

304.6021 363.5021 AUS
AUSTRALIA. BUREAU OF STATISTICS. NORTHERN TERRITORY OFFICE. CENSUS OF POPULATION AND HOUSING: ABORIGINAL AND TORRES STRAIT ISLANDER PEOPLE, NORTHERN TERRITORY (ONLINE). Text in English. 1996. irreg., latest 1996. free (effective 2009). **Document type:** *Catalog, Government.* **Description:** Covers the demographic and geographic distribution of the population and its growth in recent years.
Formerly: Australia. Bureau of Statistics. Northern Territory Office. Census of Population and Housing: Aboriginal and Torres Strait Islander People, Northern Territory (Print)
Media: Online - full text.
Published by: Australian Bureau of Statistics, Northern Territory Office, GPO BOX 3796, Darwin, N.T. 0801, Australia. TEL 61-2-92684909, 300-135-070.

304.6021 AUS
AUSTRALIA. BUREAU OF STATISTICS. NORTHERN TERRITORY OFFICE. CENSUS OF POPULATION AND HOUSING: CENSUS BASICS, NORTHERN TERRITORY. Text in English. 2001. quinquennial. free (effective 2009). back issues avail. **Document type:** *Catalog, Government.* **Description:** Contains 2001 census basic community profile data.
Media: CD-ROM.
Published by: Australian Bureau of Statistics, Northern Territory Office, GPO BOX 3796, Darwin, N.T. 0801, Australia. TEL 61-2-92684909, 300-135-070.

304.6021 363.5021 AUS
AUSTRALIA. BUREAU OF STATISTICS. NORTHERN TERRITORY OFFICE. CENSUS OF POPULATION AND HOUSING: SELECTED CHARACTERISTICS FOR URBAN CENTRES AND LOCALITIES, NORTHERN TERRITORY (ONLINE). Text in English. 1996. quinquennial, latest 2001. free (effective 2009). back issues avail. **Document type:** *Catalog, Government.* **Description:** Provides a selection of data for the population and their housing arrangements for urban centres/localities and sections of state.
Formerly: Australia. Bureau of Statistics. Northern Territory Office. Census of Population and Housing: Selected Characteristics for Urban Centres and Localities, Northern Territory (Print)
Media: Online - full text.
Published by: Australian Bureau of Statistics, Northern Territory Office, GPO BOX 3796, Darwin, N.T. 0801, Australia.

304.6021 363.5021 AUS
AUSTRALIA. BUREAU OF STATISTICS. NORTHERN TERRITORY OFFICE. CENSUS OF POPULATION AND HOUSING: SELECTED EDUCATION AND LABOUR FORCE CHARACTERISTICS FOR STATISTICAL LOCAL AREAS, NORTHERN TERRITORY (ONLINE). Text in English. 1996. quinquennial, latest 2001. free (effective 2009). back issues avail. **Document type:** *Catalog, Government.* **Description:** Provides a range of education and labour force statistics produced from the 2001 census of population and housing for the Northern Territory.
Former titles: Australia. Bureau of Statistics. Northern Territory Office. Census of Population and Housing: Selected Education and Labour Force Characteristics for Statistical Local Areas, Northern Territory (Print); Australia. Bureau of Statistics. Northern Territory Office. Census of Population and Housing: Selected Family and Labour Force Characteristics for Statistical Local Areas, Northern Territory
Media: Online - full text.
Published by: Australian Bureau of Statistics, Northern Territory Office, GPO BOX 3796, Darwin, N.T. 0801, Australia. TEL 61-2-92684909, 300-135-070.

304.6021 363.5021 AUS
AUSTRALIA. BUREAU OF STATISTICS. NORTHERN TERRITORY OFFICE. CENSUS OF POPULATION AND HOUSING: SELECTED SOCIAL AND HOUSING CHARACTERISTICS FOR STATISTICAL LOCAL AREAS, NORTHERN TERRITORY (ONLINE). Text in English. 1996. quinquennial. free (effective 2009). back issues avail. **Document type:** *Catalog, Government.* **Description:** Focuses on the social and housing characteristics.
Former titles: Australia. Bureau of Statistics. Northern Territory Office. Census of Population and Housing: Selected Social and Housing Characteristics for Statistical Local Areas, Northern Territory (Print); (until 1996): Australia. Bureau of Statistics. Northern Territory Office. Census: Selected Social and Housing Characteristics for Statistical Local Areas, Northern Territory
Media: Online - full text.
Published by: Australian Bureau of Statistics, Northern Territory Office, GPO BOX 3796, Darwin, N.T. 0801, Australia. TEL 61-2-92684909, 300-135-070.

304.6021 363.5021 AUS
AUSTRALIA. BUREAU OF STATISTICS. NORTHERN TERRITORY OFFICE. CENSUS OF POPULATION AND HOUSING: SOCIO-ECONOMIC INDEXES FOR AREAS, NORTHERN TERRITORY. Text in English. 1998. quinquennial. price varies. **Document type:** *Government.*
Media: CD-ROM.
Published by: Australian Bureau of Statistics, Northern Territory Office, GPO BOX 3796, Darwin, N.T. 0801, Australia. TEL 61-2-92684909, 300-135-070, http://www.abs.gov.au.

304.6021 AUS
AUSTRALIA. BUREAU OF STATISTICS. NORTHERN TERRITORY OFFICE. DARWIN AND PALMERSTON. A SOCIAL ATLAS. Text in English. 1996. quinquennial. AUD 29 per issue (effective 2009). back issues avail. **Document type:** *Catalog, Government.* **Description:** Contains a common set of maps for the capital city areas covering topics such as population, cultural diversity, education, labour force, income, families, households and dwellings.
Formerly (until 2000): Australia. Bureau of Statistics. Northern Territory Office. Darwin. A Social Atlas
Related titles: Online - full text ed.: free (effective 2009).
Published by: Australian Bureau of Statistics, Northern Territory Office, GPO BOX 3796, Darwin, N.T. 0801, Australia. TEL 61-2-92684909, 300-135-070.

304.6021 AUS
AUSTRALIA. BUREAU OF STATISTICS. NORTHERN TERRITORY OFFICE. POPULATION PROJECTIONS, NORTHERN TERRITORY (ONLINE). Text in English. 1999. irreg., latest 1999. free (effective 2009). back issues avail. **Document type:** *Catalog, Government.* **Description:** Contains population projections for the Northern Territory by statistical division and major urban areas.
Formerly: Australia. Bureau of Statistics. Northern Territory Office. Population Projections, Northern Territory (Print)
Media: Online - full text.
Published by: Australian Bureau of Statistics, Northern Territory Office, GPO BOX 3796, Darwin, N.T. 0801, Australia. TEL 61-2-92684909, 300-135-070.

304.6021 AUS
HA3007.N675
AUSTRALIA. BUREAU OF STATISTICS. NORTHERN TERRITORY OFFICE. REGIONAL STATISTICS, NORTHERN TERRITORY (ONLINE). Text in English. 1995. a. free (effective 2009). back issues avail. **Document type:** *Catalog, Government.* **Description:** Contains a agriculture and fisheries spreadsheets.
Formerly (until 2004): Australia. Bureau of Statistics. Northern Territory Office. Regional Statistics, Northern Territory (Print) (1324-8723)
Media: Online - full text.
Published by: Australian Bureau of Statistics, Northern Territory Office, GPO BOX 3796, Darwin, N.T. 0801, Australia. TEL 61-2-92684909, 300-135-070.

304.6021 AUS
AUSTRALIA. BUREAU OF STATISTICS. OCCASIONAL PAPER: POPULATION ISSUES, INDIGENOUS AUSTRALIANS (ONLINE). Text in English. 1996. irreg., latest 1996. free (effective 2009). **Document type:** *Government.* **Description:** Examines the issues underlying Indigenous population growth and attempts to quantify elements of population increase.
Formerly: Australia. Bureau of Statistics. Occasional Paper: Population Issues, Indigenous Australians (Print)
Media: Online - full text.
Published by: Australian Bureau of Statistics, Locked Bag 10, Belconnen, ACT 2616, Australia. TEL 61-2-92684909, 61-2-62527037, 300-135-070, FAX 61-2-62528103, client.services@abs.gov.au.

304.6021 AUS
HE104
AUSTRALIA. BUREAU OF STATISTICS. OVERSEAS ARRIVALS AND DEPARTURES, AUSTRALIA (MONTHLY) (ONLINE). Text in English. 1965. m. **Document type:** *Government.* **Description:** Features short summary of visitors arriving and residents departing short-term.
Formerly (until 2004): Australia. Bureau of Statistics. Overseas Arrivals and Departures, Australia (Monthly) (Print) (1031-0495)
Media: Online - full text.
Published by: Australian Bureau of Statistics, Locked Bag 10, Belconnen, ACT 2616, Australia. TEL 61-2-92684909, 61-2-62527037, 300-135-070, FAX 61-2-62528103, client.services@abs.gov.au.

304.6021 AUS
HA3001
AUSTRALIA. BUREAU OF STATISTICS. POPULATION BY AGE AND SEX, AUSTRALIAN STATES AND TERRITORIES (ONLINE). Text in English. 1968. a. free (effective 2009). **Document type:** *Government.* **Description:** Estimates population for each state and territory classified by sex and age.
Former titles: Australia. Bureau of Statistics. Population by Age and Sex, Australian States and Territories (Print) (1329-9115); (until 1997): Australia. Bureau of Statistics. Estimated Resident Population by Sex and Age: States and Territories of Australia (0810-0039)
Media: Online - full text.
Published by: Australian Bureau of Statistics, Locked Bag 10, Belconnen, ACT 2616, Australia. TEL 61-2-92684909, 61-2-62527037, 300-135-070, FAX 61-2-62528103, client.services@abs.gov.au. Circ: 838.

304.6021 AUS
AUSTRALIA. BUREAU OF STATISTICS. POPULATION CHARACTERISTICS, ABORIGINAL AND TORRES STRAIT ISLANDER AUSTRALIANS (ONLINE). Text in English. 2003. quinquennial, latest 2006. free (effective 2009). stat. back issues avail. **Document type:** *Government.* **Description:** Covers indigenous population structure and distribution, mobility, household composition, language and religious affiliation, education, work, income, and housing and transport. It also includes the new topics of need for assistance, unpaid work and dwelling internet connection.
Formerly: Australia. Bureau of Statistics. Population Characteristics, Aboriginal and Torres Strait Islander Australians (Print)
Media: Online - full text.

P

Published by: Australian Bureau of Statistics, Locked Bag 10, Belconnen, ACT 2616, Australia. TEL 61-2-62527037, 61-2-92684909, 300-135-070, FAX 61-2-62528103, client.services@abs.gov.au.

304.6021 AUS
AUSTRALIA. BUREAU OF STATISTICS. POPULATION DISTRIBUTION, ABORIGINAL AND TORRES STRAIT ISLANDER AUSTRALIANS (ONLINE). Text in English. 1996. quinquennial, latest 2006. free (effective 2009). back issues avail. **Document type:** *Government.* **Description:** Presents counts for indigenous Australians from the 2006 census, accompanied by information on data quality to help interpret the data.
Former titles (until 2006): Australia. Bureau of Statistics. Population Distribution, Aboriginal and Torres Strait Islander Australians (Print); (until 2002): Australia. Bureau of Statistics. Population Distribution, Indigenous Australians
Media: Online - full text.
Published by: Australian Bureau of Statistics, Locked Bag 10, Belconnen, ACT 2616, Australia. TEL 61-2-92684909, 61-2-62527037, 300-135-070, FAX 61-2-62528103, client.services@abs.gov.au.

304.6021 AUS
AUSTRALIA. BUREAU OF STATISTICS. POPULATION DISTRIBUTION, AUSTRALIA. Text in English. 1991. irreg. **Document type:** *Government.*
Published by: Australian Bureau of Statistics, Locked Bag 10, Belconnen, ACT 2616, Australia. TEL 61-2-62527037, 61-2-92684909, 300-135-070, FAX 61-2-62528103, client.services@abs.gov.au, http://www.abs.gov.au.

304.6021 AUS
HB3675
AUSTRALIA. BUREAU OF STATISTICS. POPULATION PROJECTIONS, AUSTRALIA (ONLINE). Text in English. 1955. biennial, latest 2006. free (effective 2009). **Document type:** *Government.* **Description:** Contains number and percentage of population at selected ages, sex, sex ratios, mean and median ages.
Former titles (until 199?): Australia. Bureau of Statistics. Population Projections, Australia (Print) (1442-7575); (until 1997): Australia. Bureau of Statistics. Projections of the Populations of Australia, States and Territories (1329-3109); (until 1984): Projections of the Populations of Australia, States and Territories (0816-3391)
Media: Online - full text.
Published by: Australian Bureau of Statistics, Locked Bag 10, Belconnen, ACT 2616, Australia. TEL 61-2-92684909, 61-2-62527037, 300-135-070, FAX 61-2-62528103, client.services@abs.gov.au. Circ: 429.

304.6021 AUS
AUSTRALIA. BUREAU OF STATISTICS. QUEENSLAND OFFICE. BRISBANE. A SOCIAL ATLAS. Text in English. 1996. quinquennial. AUD 29 per issue (effective 2009). back issues avail. **Document type:** *Government.* **Description:** Presents colour maps, based on data collected in the Census of Population and Housing, that highlight key social, demographic and housing characteristics of the population in Brisbane and two selected regional areas in Queensland, i.e. Gold Coast and Sunshine Coast.
Related titles: Online - full text ed.: free (effective 2009).
Published by: Australian Bureau of Statistics, Queensland Office, GPO Box 9817, Brisbane, QLD 4001, Australia. TEL 61-2-92684909, 300-135-070, client.services@abs.gov.au.

304.6021 363.5021 AUS
AUSTRALIA. BUREAU OF STATISTICS. QUEENSLAND OFFICE. CENSUS OF POPULATION AND HOUSING: ABORIGINAL AND TORRES STRAIT ISLANDER PEOPLE, QUEENSLAND (ONLINE). Text in English. 1996. quinquennial. free (effective 2009). **Document type:** *Government.* **Description:** Presents information on Aboriginal and Torres Strait Islander Australians based largely on information from the latest and earlier censuses.
Formerly: Australia. Bureau of Statistics. Queensland Office. Census of Population and Housing: Aboriginal and Torres Strait Islander People, Queensland (Print)
Media: Online - full text.
Published by: Australian Bureau of Statistics, Queensland Office, GPO Box 9817, Brisbane, QLD 4001, Australia. TEL 61-2-92684909, 300-135-070, client.services@abs.gov.au.

304.6021 363.5021 AUS
AUSTRALIA. BUREAU OF STATISTICS. QUEENSLAND OFFICE. CENSUS OF POPULATION AND HOUSING: CDATA2001, QUEENSLAND - FULL GIS. Text in English. 1996. quinquennial. **Document type:** *Government.*
Media: CD-ROM.
Published by: Australian Bureau of Statistics, Queensland Office, GPO Box 9817, Brisbane, QLD 4001, Australia. TEL 61-2-92684909, 300-135-070, client.services@abs.gov.au, http://www.abs.gov.au.

304.6021 AUS
AUSTRALIA. BUREAU OF STATISTICS. QUEENSLAND OFFICE. CENSUS OF POPULATION AND HOUSING: CDATA2001 - QUICKBUILD, QUEENSLAND. Text in English. 2002. quinquennial. **Document type:** *Government.*
Media: CD-ROM.
Published by: Australian Bureau of Statistics, Queensland Office, GPO Box 9817, Brisbane, QLD 4001, Australia. TEL 61-2-92684909, 300-135-070, client.services@abs.gov.au.

304.6021 310 AUS
AUSTRALIA. BUREAU OF STATISTICS. QUEENSLAND OFFICE. CENSUS OF POPULATION AND HOUSING: CENSUS BASICS, QUEENSLAND. Text in English. 2001. quinquennial. **Document type:** *Government.*
Media: CD-ROM.
Published by: Australian Bureau of Statistics, Queensland Office, GPO Box 9817, Brisbane, QLD 4001, Australia. TEL 61-2-92684909, 300-135-070, client.services@abs.gov.au.

304.6021 363.5021 AUS
AUSTRALIA. BUREAU OF STATISTICS. QUEENSLAND OFFICE. CENSUS OF POPULATION AND HOUSING: SELECTED CHARACTERISTICS FOR URBAN CENTRES AND LOCALITIES, QUEENSLAND (ONLINE). Text in English. 1998. quinquennial. free (effective 2009). back issues avail. **Document type:** *Government.* **Description:** Presents a range of social and housing statistics produced from the Census of Population and Housing for Queensland.
Formerly: Australia. Bureau of Statistics. Queensland Office. Census of Population and Housing: Selected Characteristics for Urban Centres and Localities, Queensland (Print)
Media: Online - full text.
Published by: Australian Bureau of Statistics, Queensland Office, GPO Box 9817, Brisbane, QLD 4001, Australia. TEL 61-2-92684909, 300-135-070, client.services@abs.gov.au.

304.6021 363.5021 AUS
AUSTRALIA. BUREAU OF STATISTICS. QUEENSLAND OFFICE. CENSUS OF POPULATION AND HOUSING: SELECTED EDUCATION AND LABOUR FORCE CHARACTERISTICS FOR STATISTICAL LOCAL AREAS, QUEENSLAND (ONLINE). Text in English. 1998. quinquennial. free (effective 2009). back issues avail. **Document type:** *Government.* **Description:** Presents a range of education and labour force statistics produced from the Census of Population and Housing for Queensland.
Former titles: Australia. Bureau of Statistics. Queensland Office. Census of Population and Housing: Selected Education and Labour Force Characteristics for Statistical Local Areas, Queensland (Print); Australia. Bureau of Statistics. Queensland Office. Census of Population and Housing: Selected Family and Labour Force Characteristics for Statistical Local Areas, Queensland
Media: Online - full text.
Published by: Australian Bureau of Statistics, Queensland Office, GPO Box 9817, Brisbane, QLD 4001, Australia. TEL 61-2-92684909, 300-135-070, client.services@abs.gov.au.

304.6021 363.5021 AUS
AUSTRALIA. BUREAU OF STATISTICS. QUEENSLAND OFFICE. CENSUS OF POPULATION AND HOUSING: SELECTED SOCIAL AND HOUSING CHARACTERISTICS FOR STATISTICAL LOCAL AREAS, QUEENSLAND (ONLINE). Text in English. 1996. quinquennial. free (effective 2009). back issues avail. **Document type:** *Government.* **Description:** Presents a range of social and housing statistics produced from the Census of Population and Housing for Queensland.
Former titles: Australia. Bureau of Statistics. Queensland Office. Census of Population and Housing: Selected Social and Housing Characteristics for Statistical Local Areas, Queensland (Print); (until 2001): Australia. Bureau of Statistics. Queensland Office. Census: Selected Social and Housing Characteristics for Statistical Local Areas, Queensland (Print)
Media: Online - full text.
Published by: Australian Bureau of Statistics, Queensland Office, GPO Box 9817, Brisbane, QLD 4001, Australia. TEL 61-2-92684909, 300-135-070, client.services@abs.gov.au.

304.6021 363.5021 AUS
AUSTRALIA. BUREAU OF STATISTICS. QUEENSLAND OFFICE. CENSUS OF POPULATION AND HOUSING: SOCIO-ECONOMIC INDEXES FOR AREAS, QUEENSLAND. Text in English. 1998. quinquennial. price varies. **Document type:** *Government.*
Media: CD-ROM.
Published by: Australian Bureau of Statistics, Queensland Office, GPO Box 9817, Brisbane, QLD 4001, Australia. TEL 61-2-92684909, 300-135-070, client.services@abs.gov.au.

304.6021 AUS
AUSTRALIA. BUREAU OF STATISTICS. QUEENSLAND OFFICE. ESTIMATED RESIDENT POPULATION, QUEENSLAND. Text in English. 1976. irreg. AUD 25. **Description:** Estimated resident population of each local government area, statistical division and statistical district at Census dates with revised intercensal estimates.
Formerly: Estimated Resident Population in Local Authority Areas
Published by: Australian Bureau of Statistics, Queensland Office, GPO Box 9817, Brisbane, QLD 4001, Australia. TEL 61-2-92684909, 300-135-070, http://www.abs.gov.au.

304.6021 AUS
AUSTRALIA. BUREAU OF STATISTICS. QUEENSLAND OFFICE. FERTILITY TRENDS IN QUEENSLAND. Text in English. 1984. irreg. AUD 1.80. **Document type:** *Government.*
Published by: Australian Bureau of Statistics, Queensland Office, GPO Box 9817, Brisbane, QLD 4001, Australia. TEL 61-2-92684909, 300-135-070, http://www.abs.gov.au.

304.6021 310 AUS
AUSTRALIA. BUREAU OF STATISTICS. QUEENSLAND OFFICE. MIGRATION, QUEENSLAND. Text in English. 1996. irreg. **Document type:** *Government.*
Published by: Australian Bureau of Statistics, Queensland Office, GPO Box 9817, Brisbane, QLD 4001, Australia. TEL 61-2-92684909, 300-135-070, client.services@abs.gov.au.

304.6021 310 AUS
AUSTRALIA. BUREAU OF STATISTICS. QUEENSLAND OFFICE. NATIONAL ABORIGINAL AND TORRES STRAIT ISLANDER SURVEY: QUEENSLAND (ONLINE). Variant title: Torres Strait Islanders, Queensland. Text in English. 1994. irreg. free (effective 2009). **Document type:** *Government.*
Formerly: Australia. Bureau of Statistics. Queensland Office. National Aboriginal and Torres Strait Islander Survey: Queensland (Print)
Media: Online - full text.
Published by: Australian Bureau of Statistics, Queensland Office, GPO Box 9817, Brisbane, QLD 4001, Australia. TEL 61-2-92684909, 300-135-070, client.services@abs.gov.au.

304.6021 310 AUS
AUSTRALIA. BUREAU OF STATISTICS. QUEENSLAND OFFICE. POPULATION MOBILITY, QUEENSLAND (ONLINE). Text in English. 2000. irreg. free (effective 2009). **Document type:** *Government.* **Description:** Summarises the results of a survey on mobility of the population, conducted throughout Queensland.
Formerly: Australia. Bureau of Statistics. Queensland Office. Population Mobility, Queensland (Print)
Media: Online - full text.
Published by: Australian Bureau of Statistics, Queensland Office, GPO Box 9817, Brisbane, QLD 4001, Australia. TEL 61-2-92684909, 300-135-070, client.services@abs.gov.au.

304.6021 AUS ISSN 1036-5001
AUSTRALIA. BUREAU OF STATISTICS. QUEENSLAND OFFICE. RECENT POPULATION AND HOUSING TRENDS IN QUEENSLAND. Text in English. 2000. a. **Document type:** *Government.*
Published by: Australian Bureau of Statistics, Queensland Office, GPO Box 9817, Brisbane, QLD 4001, Australia. TEL 61-2-92684909, 300-135-070, client.services@abs.gov.au.

304.6021 AUS ISSN 1833-2498
AUSTRALIA. BUREAU OF STATISTICS. REGIONAL POPULATION GROWTH. AUSTRALIA. Text in English. 1994. a. free (effective 2009). back issues avail. **Document type:** *Government.* **Description:** Population growth in States and Territories, Statistical Divisions, Subdivisions, major population centres, and high growth Statistical Local Areas.
Former titles (until 2006): Australia. Bureau of Statistics. Regional Population Growth, Australia and New Zealand (Print) (1446-3113); (until 2000): Australia. Bureau of Statistics. Regional Population Growth. Australia (1321-179X)
Media: Online - full text.
Published by: Australian Bureau of Statistics, Locked Bag 10, Belconnen, ACT 2616, Australia. TEL 61-2-92684909, 61-2-62527037, FAX 61-2-62528103, client.services@abs.gov.au.

304.6021 310 AUS
AUSTRALIA. BUREAU OF STATISTICS. SOUTH AUSTRALIAN OFFICE. ADELAIDE. A SOCIAL ATLAS. Text in English. 1996. quinquennial. AUD 29 per issue (effective 2009). back issues avail. **Document type:** *Government.* **Description:** Presents colour maps, based on data collected in the Census of Population and Housing, that highlight key social, demographic and housing characteristics of the population in Adelaide.
Related titles: Online - full text ed.: free (effective 2009).
Published by: Australian Bureau of Statistics, South Australian Office, GPO Box 2272, Adelaide, SA 5001, Australia. TEL 61-2-92684909, 300-135-070, client.services@abs.gov.au.

304.6021 363.5021 AUS
AUSTRALIA. BUREAU OF STATISTICS. SOUTH AUSTRALIAN OFFICE. CENSUS OF POPULATION AND HOUSING: ABORIGINAL AND TORRES STRAIT ISLANDER PEOPLE, SOUTH AUSTRALIA (ONLINE). Text in English. 1991. quinquennial, latest 1996. free (effective 2009). back issues avail. **Document type:** *Government.* **Description:** Presents information on Aboriginal and Torres Strait Islander Australians based largely on information from earlier censuses.
Former titles: Australia. Bureau of Statistics. South Australian Office. Census of Population and Housing: Aboriginal and Torres Strait Islander People, South Australia (Print); (until 1996): Australia. Bureau of Statistics. South Australian Office. Census: Aboriginal People in South Australia
Media: Online - full text.
Published by: Australian Bureau of Statistics, South Australian Office, GPO Box 2272, Adelaide, SA 5001, Australia. TEL 61-2-92684909, 300-135-070, client.services@abs.gov.au.

304.6021 363.5021 AUS
AUSTRALIA. BUREAU OF STATISTICS. SOUTH AUSTRALIAN OFFICE. CENSUS OF POPULATION AND HOUSING: CDATA2001, SOUTH AUSTRALIA - FULL GIS. Text in English. 1996. quinquennial, latest 2001. back issues avail. **Document type:** *Government.* **Description:** Provides a large volume of census small area data combined with digital geographic and topographic data.
Formerly (until 2001): Australia. Bureau of Statistics. South Australian Office. Census of Population and Housing: CDATA96, South Australia
Media: CD-ROM.
Published by: Australian Bureau of Statistics, South Australian Office, GPO Box 2272, Adelaide, SA 5001, Australia. TEL 61-2-92684909, 300-135-070, client.services@abs.gov.au.

304.6021 AUS
AUSTRALIA. BUREAU OF STATISTICS. SOUTH AUSTRALIAN OFFICE. CENSUS OF POPULATION AND HOUSING: CENSUS BASICS, SOUTH AUSTRALIA. Text in English. 2001. quinquennial, latest 2001. **Document type:** *Government.*
Media: CD-ROM.
Published by: Australian Bureau of Statistics, South Australian Office, GPO Box 2272, Adelaide, SA 5001, Australia. TEL 61-2-92684909, 300-135-070, client.services@abs.gov.au.

304.6021 363.5021 310 AUS
AUSTRALIA. BUREAU OF STATISTICS. SOUTH AUSTRALIAN OFFICE. CENSUS OF POPULATION AND HOUSING: SELECTED CHARACTERISTICS FOR URBAN CENTRES AND LOCALITIES, SOUTH AUSTRALIA (ONLINE). Text in English. 1998. quinquennial. free (effective 2009). back issues avail. **Document type:** *Government.*
Formerly: Australia. Bureau of Statistics. South Australian Office. Census of Population and Housing: Selected Characteristics for Urban Centres and Localities, South Australia (Print)
Media: Online - full text.
Published by: Australian Bureau of Statistics, South Australian Office, GPO Box 2272, Adelaide, SA 5001, Australia. TEL 61-2-92684909, 300-135-070, client.services@abs.gov.au.

304.6021 363.5021 310 AUS
AUSTRALIA. BUREAU OF STATISTICS. SOUTH AUSTRALIAN OFFICE. CENSUS OF POPULATION AND HOUSING: SELECTED EDUCATION AND LABOUR FORCE CHARACTERISTICS FOR STATISTICAL LOCAL AREAS, SOUTH AUSTRALIA (ONLINE). Text in English. 1998. quinquennial. free (effective 2009). back issues avail. **Document type:** *Government.* **Description:** Presents a range of education and labour force statistics produced from the Census of Population and Housing for South Australia (SA).
Former titles: Australia. Bureau of Statistics. South Australian Office. Census of Population and Housing: Selected Education and Labour Force Characteristics for Statistical Local Areas, South Australia (Print); (until 2000): Australia. Bureau of Statistics. South Australian Office. Census of Population and Housing: Selected Family and Labour Force Characteristics for Statistical Local Areas, South Australia
Media: Online - full text.

Published by: Australian Bureau of Statistics, South Australian Office, GPO Box 2272, Adelaide, SA 5001, Australia. TEL 61-2-92684909, 300-135-070, client.services@abs.gov.au.

304.6021 363.5021 310 AUS
AUSTRALIA. BUREAU OF STATISTICS. SOUTH AUSTRALIAN OFFICE. CENSUS OF POPULATION AND HOUSING: SELECTED SOCIAL AND HOUSING CHARACTERISTICS FOR STATISTICAL LOCAL AREAS, SOUTH AUSTRALIA (ONLINE). Text in English. 1996. quinquennial. free (effective 2009). back issues avail. **Document type:** *Government.* **Description:** Presents a range of social and housing statistics produced from the Census of Population and Housing for South Australia (SA).
Former titles: Australia. Bureau of Statistics. South Australian Office. Census of Population and Housing: Selected Social and Housing Characteristics for Statistical Local Areas, South Australia (Print); Australia. Bureau of Statistics. South Australian Office. Census: Selected Social and Housing Characteristics for Statistical Local Areas, South Australia
Media: Online - full text.
Published by: Australian Bureau of Statistics, South Australian Office, GPO Box 2272, Adelaide, SA 5001, Australia. TEL 61-2-92684909, 300-135-070, client.services@abs.gov.au.

331.021 AUS
AUSTRALIA. BUREAU OF STATISTICS. STANDARD AUSTRALIAN CLASSIFICATION OF COUNTRIES (ONLINE). Abbreviated title: S A C C. Text in English. 1990. irreg., latest 2nd ed. free (effective 2009). **Document type:** *Government.* **Description:** Covers conceptual basis of the classification, the structure of the classification, alphabetical and numerical order coding indexes for population and economic statistics.
Former titles: Australia. Bureau of Statistics. Standard Australian Classification of Countries (Print); (until 1998): Australia. Bureau of Statistics. Australian Standard Classification of Countries for Social Statistics
Media: Online - full text.
Published by: Australian Bureau of Statistics, Locked Bag 10, Belconnen, ACT 2616, Australia. TEL 61-2-62527037, 61-2-92684909, 300-135-070, FAX 61-2-62528103, client.services@abs.gov.au.

304.6021 AUS
AUSTRALIA. BUREAU OF STATISTICS. STATISTICAL GEOGRAPHY: VOLUME 2 - CENSUS GEOGRAPHIC AREAS, AUSTRALIA (ONLINE). Text in English. 1991. quinquennial. free (effective 2009). back issues avail. **Document type:** *Government.* **Description:** Provides an essential reference for understanding and interpreting the geographical context for ABS statistics published on the Census Geographic Areas.
Formerly: Australia. Bureau of Statistics. Statistical Geography: Volume 2 - Census Geographic Areas, Australia (Print)
Media: Online - full text.
Published by: Australian Bureau of Statistics, Locked Bag 10, Belconnen, ACT 2616, Australia. TEL 61-2-62527037, 61-2-92684909, 300-135-070, FAX 61-2-62528103, client.services@abs.gov.au.

304.6021 AUS
AUSTRALIA. BUREAU OF STATISTICS. STATISTICAL GEOGRAPHY: VOLUME 3 - AUSTRALIAN STANDARD GEOGRAPHICAL CLASSIFICATION. URBAN CENTRES AND LOCALITIES (ONLINE). Text in English. 1996. quinquennial. free (effective 2009). back issues avail. **Document type:** *Government.* **Description:** Lists all Urban centres and localities defined within a state or territory in Australia at the time of the census.
Formerly: Australia. Bureau of Statistics. Statistical Geography: Volume 3 - Australian Standard Geographical Classification. Urban Centres and Localities (Print)
Media: Online - full text.
Published by: Australian Bureau of Statistics, Locked Bag 10, Belconnen, ACT 2616, Australia. TEL 61-2-62527037, 61-2-92684909, 300-135-070, FAX 61-2-62528103, client.services@abs.gov.au.

304.6021 363.5021 AUS
AUSTRALIA. BUREAU OF STATISTICS. TASMANIAN OFFICE. CENSUS OF POPULATION AND HOUSING: ABORIGINAL AND TORRES STRAIT ISLANDER PEOPLE, TASMANIA (ONLINE). Text in English. 1996. quinquennial, latest 1996. free (effective 2009). **Document type:** *Government.* **Description:** Presents information on Aboriginal and Torres Strait Islander Australians based largely on information from the 1996 and earlier censuses.
Formerly (until 199?): Australia. Bureau of Statistics. Tasmanian Office. Census of Population and Housing: Aboriginal and Torres Strait Islander People, Tasmania (Print)
Media: Online - full text.
Published by: Australian Bureau of Statistics, Tasmanian Office, GPO Box 66A, Hobart, TAS 7001, Australia. TEL 61-2-92684909, 300-135-070, client.services@abs.gov.au.

304.6021 363.5021 AUS
AUSTRALIA. BUREAU OF STATISTICS. TASMANIAN OFFICE. CENSUS OF POPULATION AND HOUSING: BURNIE AND DEVONPORT SUBURBS (ONLINE). Text in English. 1998. quinquennial, latest 2006. free (effective 2009). **Document type:** *Government.* **Description:** Contains major population census characteristics for Burnie and Devonport suburbs.
Former titles (until 2006): Australia. Bureau of Statistics. Tasmanian Office. Census of Population and Housing: Burnie and Devonport Suburbs; (until 2001): Australia. Bureau of Statistics. Tasmanian Office. Census of Population and Housing: Burnie and Devonport Suburbs (Print)
Media: Online - full text.
Published by: Australian Bureau of Statistics, Tasmanian Office, GPO Box 66A, Hobart, TAS 7001, Australia. TEL 61-2-92684909, 300-135-070, client.services@abs.gov.au.

304.6021 AUS
AUSTRALIA. BUREAU OF STATISTICS. TASMANIAN OFFICE. CENSUS OF POPULATION AND HOUSING: CENSUS BASICS, AUSTRALIA. Text in English. 2001. irreg. **Document type:** *Government.* **Description:** Contains census Basic Community Profile (BCP) data, down to Collection District (CD) level, and digital boundaries.
Media: CD-ROM.
Published by: Australian Bureau of Statistics, Tasmanian Office, GPO Box 66A, Hobart, TAS 7001, Australia. TEL 61-2-92684909, 300-135-070, client.services@abs.gov.au.

304.6021 363.5021 AUS
AUSTRALIA. BUREAU OF STATISTICS. TASMANIAN OFFICE. CENSUS OF POPULATION AND HOUSING: LAUNCESTON SUBURBS (ONLINE). Text in English. 1998. quinquennial, latest 2006. free (effective 2009). **Document type:** *Government.* **Description:** Contains major population census characteristics for Launceston suburbs.
Formerly (until 1996): Census of Population and Housing: Launceston Suburbs (Print)
Media: Online - full text.
Published by: Australian Bureau of Statistics, Tasmanian Office, GPO Box 66A, Hobart, TAS 7001, Australia. TEL 61-2-92684909, 300-135-070, client.services@abs.gov.au.

304.6021 363.5021 AUS
AUSTRALIA. BUREAU OF STATISTICS. TASMANIAN OFFICE. CENSUS OF POPULATION AND HOUSING: SELECTED CHARACTERISTICS FOR URBAN CENTRES AND LOCALITIES, TASMANIA (ONLINE). Text in English. 1998. quinquennial, latest 2003. free (effective 2009). **Document type:** *Government.* **Description:** Presents a range of social and housing statistics produced from the 2001 Census of Population and Housing for Queensland.
Formerly (until 199?): Australia. Bureau of Statistics. Tasmanian Office. Census of Population and Housing: Selected Characteristics for Urban Centres and Localities, Tasmania (Print)
Media: Online - full text.
Published by: Australian Bureau of Statistics, Tasmanian Office, GPO Box 66A, Hobart, TAS 7001, Australia. TEL 61-2-92684909, 300-135-070, client.services@abs.gov.au.

304.6021 363.5021 AUS
AUSTRALIA. BUREAU OF STATISTICS. TASMANIAN OFFICE. CENSUS OF POPULATION AND HOUSING: SELECTED EDUCATION AND LABOUR FORCE CHARACTERISTICS FOR STATISTICAL LOCAL AREAS, TASMANIA (ONLINE). Text in English. 1998. quinquennial, latest 2003. free (effective 2009). **Document type:** *Government.* **Description:** Presents a range of education and labour force statistics produced from the 2001 census of population and housing for Tasmania. For comparative purposes, it includes 1996 census data presented on 2001 census geography.
Formerly (until 199?): Australia. Bureau of Statistics. Tasmanian Office. Census of Population and Housing: Selected Education and Labour Force Characteristics for Statistical Local Areas, Tasmania (Print)
Media: Online - full text.
Published by: Australian Bureau of Statistics, Tasmanian Office, GPO Box 66A, Hobart, TAS 7001, Australia. TEL 61-2-92684909, 300-135-070, client.services@abs.gov.au.

304.6021 363.5021 AUS
AUSTRALIA. BUREAU OF STATISTICS. TASMANIAN OFFICE. CENSUS OF POPULATION AND HOUSING: SELECTED SOCIAL AND HOUSING CHARACTERISTICS FOR STATISTICAL LOCAL AREAS, TASMANIA (ONLINE). Text in English. 1996. quinquennial. free (effective 2009). **Document type:** *Government.* **Description:** Contains 2001 Census population counts and selected person, family and dwelling characteristics for all Statistical Local Areas (SLA), Statistical Sub-divisions (SSD) and Statistical Divisions (SD) within Tasmania, as well as ranked tables.
Formerly (until 2001): Australia. Bureau of Statistics. Tasmanian Office. Census of Population and Housing: Selected Social and Housing Characteristics for Statistical Local Areas, Tasmania (Print)
Media: Online - full text.
Published by: Australian Bureau of Statistics, Tasmanian Office, GPO Box 66A, Hobart, TAS 7001, Australia. TEL 61-2-92684909, 300-135-070, client.services@abs.gov.au.

304.6021 363.5021 AUS
AUSTRALIA. BUREAU OF STATISTICS. TASMANIAN OFFICE. CENSUS OF POPULATION AND HOUSING: SOCIO-ECONOMIC INDEXES FOR AREAS, TASMANIA. Text in English. 1998. quinquennial, latest 2001. price varies. **Document type:** *Government.* **Description:** Provides a method of determining the level of social and economic wellbeing in that region.
Media: CD-ROM.
Published by: Australian Bureau of Statistics, Tasmanian Office, GPO Box 66A, Hobart, TAS 7001, Australia. TEL 61-2-92684909, 300-135-070, client.services@abs.gov.au.

304.6021 AUS
AUSTRALIA. BUREAU OF STATISTICS. TASMANIAN OFFICE. HOBART. A SOCIAL ATLAS. Text in English. 1996. irreg., latest 2006. AUD 29 per issue (effective 2009). **Document type:** *Government.* **Description:** Presents colour maps, based on data collected in the 2006 Census of Population and Housing, that highlight key social, demographic and housing characteristics of the population in Hobart and two selected regional areas in Tasmania.
Related titles: Online - full text ed.: free (effective 2009).
Published by: Australian Bureau of Statistics, Tasmanian Office, GPO Box 66A, Hobart, TAS 7001, Australia. TEL 61-2-92684909, 300-135-070, client.services@abs.gov.au.

304.6021 AUS
AUSTRALIA. BUREAU OF STATISTICS. TASMANIAN OFFICE. POPULATION PROJECTIONS, TASMANIA (ONLINE). Text in English. 1999. irreg., latest 1999. free (effective 2009). **Document type:** *Government.* **Description:** Covers projection results, in terms of population size and growth, and the changing age structure and distribution of the population.
Formerly: Australia. Bureau of Statistics. Tasmanian Office. Population Projections, Tasmania (Print)
Media: Online - full text.
Published by: Australian Bureau of Statistics, Tasmanian Office, GPO Box 66A, Hobart, TAS 7001, Australia. TEL 61-2-92684909, 300-135-070, client.services@abs.gov.au.

304.6021 363.5021 AUS
AUSTRALIA. BUREAU OF STATISTICS. TASMANIAN POPULATION CENSUS DATA: HOBART SUBURBS (ONLINE). Text in English. 1998. quinquennial, latest 2006. free (effective 2009). **Document type:** *Government.* **Description:** Contains major population census characteristics for Hobart suburbs.
Formerly (until 2001): Australia. Bureau of Statistics. Tasmanian Office. Census of Population and Housing: Hobart Suburbs (Print)
Media: Online - full text.
Published by: Australian Bureau of Statistics, Tasmanian Office, GPO Box 66A, Hobart, TAS 7001, Australia. TEL 61-2-92684909, 300-135-070, client.services@abs.gov.au.

304.6021 AUS
AUSTRALIA. BUREAU OF STATISTICS. TOWNS IN TIME: ANALYSIS AND DATA, CENSUS STATISTICS FOR VICTORIA'S TOWNS AND RURAL AREAS. Text in English. 1996. irreg., latest 1981-1996. free (effective 2009). **Document type:** *Government.* **Description:** Provides 1981, 1986, 1991 and 1996 census data for Victoria's 308 towns, 52 'rural balances' of local government areas and the 8 Murray Valley local government areas of New South Wales.
Related titles: Online - full text ed.
Published by: Australian Bureau of Statistics, Victorian Office, GPO Box 2796Y, Melbourne, VIC 3001, Australia. TEL 61-2-62524909, 300-135-070, client.services@abs.gov.au.

304.6021 363.5021 AUS
AUSTRALIA. BUREAU OF STATISTICS. VICTORIAN OFFICE. CENSUS OF POPULATION AND HOUSING: ABORIGINAL AND TORRES STRAIT ISLANDER PEOPLE, VICTORIA (ONLINE). Text in English. 1996. irreg., latest 1996. free (effective 2009). **Document type:** *Government.* **Description:** Presents information on aboriginal and torres strait islander Australians based largely on information from the 1996 and earlier censuses.
Formerly: Australia. Bureau of Statistics. Victorian Office. Census of Population and Housing: Aboriginal and Torres Strait Islander People, Victoria (Print)
Media: Online - full text.
Published by: Australian Bureau of Statistics, Victorian Office, GPO Box 2796Y, Melbourne, VIC 3001, Australia. TEL 61-2-62524909, 300-135-070, client.services@abs.gov.au.

304.6021 AUS
AUSTRALIA. BUREAU OF STATISTICS. VICTORIAN OFFICE. CENSUS OF POPULATION AND HOUSING: CENSUS BASICS, VICTORIA. Text in English. 2001. quinquennial. **Document type:** *Government.* **Description:** Contains 2001 census basic community profile data, down to collection district level, and digital boundaries in mapinfo interchange format (.mid/.mif). A simple Excel viewer tool is also provided to view the data files.
Media: CD-ROM.
Published by: Australian Bureau of Statistics, Victorian Office, GPO Box 2796Y, Melbourne, VIC 3001, Australia. TEL 61-2-62524909, 300-135-070, client.services@abs.gov.au.

304.6021 363.5021 AUS
AUSTRALIA. BUREAU OF STATISTICS. VICTORIAN OFFICE. CENSUS OF POPULATION AND HOUSING: SELECTED CHARACTERISTICS FOR URBAN CENTRES AND LOCALITIES, VICTORIA (ONLINE). Text in English. 1998. irreg., latest 2001. free (effective 2009). **Document type:** *Government.*
Formerly: Australia. Bureau of Statistics. Victorian Office. Census of Population and Housing: Selected Characteristics for Urban Centres and Localities, Victoria (Print)
Media: Online - full text.
Published by: Australian Bureau of Statistics, Victorian Office, GPO Box 2796Y, Melbourne, VIC 3001, Australia. TEL 61-2-62524909, 300-135-070, client.services@abs.gov.au.

304.6021 363.5021 AUS
AUSTRALIA. BUREAU OF STATISTICS. VICTORIAN OFFICE. CENSUS OF POPULATION AND HOUSING: SELECTED EDUCATION AND LABOUR FORCE CHARACTERISTICS FOR STATISTICAL LOCAL AREAS, VICTORIA (ONLINE). Text in English. 1996. irreg., latest 2001. free (effective 2009). back issues avail. **Document type:** *Government.* **Description:** Contains census population counts and selected education and labour force characteristics for persons in all statistical local areas, statistical sub-divisions and statistical divisions within Victoria.
Former titles: Australia. Bureau of Statistics. Victorian Office. Census of Population and Housing: Selected Education and Labour Force Characteristics for Statistical Local Areas, Victoria (Print); Australia. Bureau of Statistics. Victorian Office. Census of Population and Housing: Selected Family and Labour Force Characteristics for Statistical Local Areas, Victoria
Media: Online - full text.
Published by: Australian Bureau of Statistics, Victorian Office, GPO Box 2796Y, Melbourne, VIC 3001, Australia. TEL 61-2-62524909, 300-135-070, client.services@abs.gov.au.

304.6021 363.5021 AUS
AUSTRALIA. BUREAU OF STATISTICS. VICTORIAN OFFICE. CENSUS OF POPULATION AND HOUSING: SELECTED SOCIAL AND HOUSING CHARACTERISTICS FOR STATISTICAL LOCAL AREAS, VICTORIA (ONLINE). Text in English. 1996. irreg., latest 2001. free (effective 2009). back issues avail. **Document type:** *Government.* **Description:** Contains census population counts and selected person, family and dwelling characteristics for all statistical local areas, statistical sub-divisions and statistical divisions thin victoria, as well as ranked tables. Commentary is provided, including comparisons for selected topics and time series comparison.
Former titles: Australia. Bureau of Statistics. Victorian Office. Census of Population and Housing: Selected Social and Housing Characteristics for Statistical Local Areas, Victoria (Print); Australia. Bureau of Statistics. Census: Selected Social and Housing Characteristics for Statistical Local Areas, Victoria
Media: Online - full text.
Published by: Australian Bureau of Statistics, Victorian Office, GPO Box 2796Y, Melbourne, VIC 3001, Australia. TEL 61-2-62524909, 300-135-070, client.services@abs.gov.au.

304.6021 AUS
AUSTRALIA. BUREAU OF STATISTICS. VICTORIAN OFFICE. MELBOURNE. A SOCIAL ATLAS. Text in English. 1998. quinquennial, latest 2006. AUD 29 per issue (effective 2009). back issues avail. **Document type:** *Government.* **Description:** Presents colour maps, based on data collected in the 2006 census of population and housing, that highlight key social, demographic and housing characteristics of the population in Melbourne and a selected regional centre in Victoria.
Related titles: Online - full text ed.: free (effective 2009).

P

Published by: Australian Bureau of Statistics, Victorian Office, GPO Box 2796Y, Melbourne, VIC 3001, Australia. TEL 61-2-62524909, 300-135-070, client.services@abs.gov.au.

304.6021 AUS
AUSTRALIA. BUREAU OF STATISTICS. VICTORIAN OFFICE. MELBOURNE IN FACT - (YEAR) CENSUS STATISTICS FOR MELBOURNE'S NEW LOCAL GOVERNMENT AREAS. Text in English. 1996. irreg., latest 1996. free (effective 2009). **Document type:** *Government.* **Description:** Provides a comprehensive compendium of demographic data which profiles the characteristics and attributes of Melbourne's local government areas. Reflecting local populations in all their diversity of age, education, birthplace, language, industry, occupations, households, dwellings, car usage and ownership, and income.
Related titles: Online - full text ed.
Published by: Australian Bureau of Statistics, Victorian Office, GPO Box 2796Y, Melbourne, VIC 3001, Australia. TEL 61-2-62524909, 300-135-070, client.services@abs.gov.au. **Co-sponsor:** Victoria, Department of Infrastructure.

304.6021 AUS
AUSTRALIA. BUREAU OF STATISTICS. VICTORIAN OFFICE. POPULATION MOBILITY, VICTORIA. Text in English. 1999. irreg. **Document type:** *Government.* **Description:** Provides data on characteristics of people moving to and within Victoria in the last 3 years and the factors influencing their movements. Also provides information on the most recent move, including current and previous place of residence; main reason for moving; main reason for choosing current location; main reason for choosing current dwelling; current dwelling type and current nature of occupancy.
Related titles: Online - full text ed.
Published by: Australian Bureau of Statistics, Victorian Office, GPO Box 2796Y, Melbourne, VIC 3001, Australia. TEL 61-2-62524909, 300-135-070, client.services@abs.gov.au.

304.6021 AUS
AUSTRALIA. BUREAU OF STATISTICS. VICTORIAN OFFICE. REGIONAL VICTORIA IN FACT: CENSUS STATISTICS FOR REGIONAL VICTORIA'S NEW LOCAL GOVERNMENT AREAS. Text in English. 1991. irreg. **Document type:** *Government.*
Published by: Australian Bureau of Statistics, Victorian Office, GPO Box 2796Y, Melbourne, VIC 3001, Australia. TEL 61-2-62524909, 300-135-070, client.services@abs.gov.au. **Co-sponsor:** Victoria, Department of Infrastructure.

304.6021 AUS
AUSTRALIA. BUREAU OF STATISTICS. VICTORIAN OFFICE. VICTORIA IN FUTURE: OVERVIEW. THE VICTORIAN GOVERNMENT'S POPULATION PROJECTIONS (ONLINE). Text in English. 1996. a. free (effective 2009). **Document type:** *Government.* **Description:** Covers total populations, age structure, households, total populations for all Victorian local government areas and dwelling data for metropolitan local government.
Former titles (until 200?): Australia. Bureau of Statistics. Victorian Office. Victoria in Future: Overview. The Victorian Government's Population Projections (Print); Australia. Bureau of Statistics. Victorian Office. Victoria in Future - The Victorian Government's Population Projections for the State's Local Government Areas
Media: Online - full content.
Published by: Victoria. Department of Planning and Community Development. Strategic Policy Research and Forecasting Division. Spatial Analysis and Research, GPO Box 2392, Melbourne, VIC 3001, Australia. TEL 61-3-92083000, FAX 61-3-92083335, spatialanalysis.research@dpcd.vic.gov.au, http://www.dpcd.vic.gov.au/.

304.6021 AUS
AUSTRALIA. BUREAU OF STATISTICS. VICTORIAN OFFICE. VICTORIA IN TIME - (YEAR) CENSUS STATISTICS FOR VICTORIA'S NEW LOCAL GOVERNMENT AREAS. Text in English. 1981. irreg. **Document type:** *Government.* **Description:** Provides a comprehensive compendium of demographic data which profiles the characteristics and attributes of the 78 municipalities that make up Victoria's new local government landscape.
Published by: Australian Bureau of Statistics, Victorian Office, GPO Box 2796Y, Melbourne, VIC 3001, Australia. TEL 61-2-62524909, 300-135-070, client.services@abs.gov.au. **Co-sponsor:** Victoria, Department of Infrastructure.

304.6021 AUS
AUSTRALIA. BUREAU OF STATISTICS. WESTERN AUSTRALIAN OFFICE. CENSUS OF POPULATION AND HOUSING: CENSUS BASICS, WESTERN AUSTRALIA. Text in English. 2002. quinquennial, latest 2002. **Document type:** *Government.*
Media: CD-ROM.
Published by: Australian Bureau of Statistics, Western Australian Office, GPO Box K881, Perth, W.A. 6842, Australia. TEL 61-2-62524909, 300-135-070, client.services@abs.gov.au.

304.6021 363.5021 AUS
AUSTRALIA. BUREAU OF STATISTICS. WESTERN AUSTRALIAN OFFICE. CENSUS OF POPULATION AND HOUSING: SELECTED CHARACTERISTICS FOR URBAN CENTRES AND LOCALITIES, WESTERN AUSTRALIA, COCOS (KEELING) AND CHRISTMAS ISLANDS (ONLINE). Text in English. 1996. quinquennial, latest 2001. free (effective 2009). back issues avail. **Document type:** *Government.* **Description:** Presents a range of social and housing statistics produced from Census of Population and Housing for Queensland.
Formerly: Australia. Bureau of Statistics. Western Australian Office. Census of Population and Housing: Selected Characteristics for Urban Centres and Localities, Western Australia, Cocos (Keeling) and Christmas Islands (Print)
Media: Online - full text.
Published by: Australian Bureau of Statistics, Western Australian Office, GPO Box K881, Perth, W.A. 6842, Australia. TEL 61-2-62524909, 300-135-070, client.services@abs.gov.au.

304.6021 363.5021 AUS
AUSTRALIA. BUREAU OF STATISTICS. WESTERN AUSTRALIAN OFFICE. CENSUS OF POPULATION AND HOUSING: SELECTED EDUCATION AND LABOUR FORCE CHARACTERISTICS FOR STATISTICAL LOCAL AREAS, WESTERN AUSTRALIA, COCOS (KEELING) AND CHRISTMAS ISLANDS (ONLINE). Text in English. 1996. irreg., latest 2001. free (effective 2009). back issues avail. **Document type:** *Government.* **Description:** Presents a range of education and labour force statistics produced from the Census of Population and Housing for Western Australia (WA).
Former titles: Australia. Bureau of Statistics. Western Australian Office. Census of Population and Housing: Selected Education and Labour Force Characteristics for Statistical Local Areas, Western Australia, Cocos (Keeling) and Christmas Islands (Print); (until 2001): Australia. Bureau of Statistics. Western Australian Office. Census of Population and Housing: Selected Family and Labour Force Characteristics for Statistical Local Areas, Western Australia, Cocos (Keeling) and Christmas Islands
Media: Online - full text.
Published by: Australian Bureau of Statistics, Western Australian Office, GPO Box K881, Perth, W.A. 6842, Australia. TEL 61-2-62524909, 300-135-070, client.services@abs.gov.au.

304.6021 363.5021 AUS
AUSTRALIA. BUREAU OF STATISTICS. WESTERN AUSTRALIAN OFFICE. CENSUS OF POPULATION AND HOUSING: SELECTED SOCIAL AND HOUSING CHARACTERISTICS FOR STATISTICAL LOCAL AREAS, WESTERN AUSTRALIA, COCOS (KEELING) AND CHRISTMAS ISLANDS (ONLINE). Text in English. 1996. quinquennial, latest 2001. free (effective 2009). back issues avail. **Document type:** *Government.* **Description:** Presents a range of social and housing statistics produced from Census of Population and Housing for Western Australia and Cocos and Christmas Islands.
Former titles: Australia. Bureau of Statistics. Western Australian Office. Census of Population and Housing: Selected Social and Housing Characteristics for Statistical Local Areas, Western Australia, Cocos (Keeling) and Christmas Islands (Print); (until 2001): Australia. Bureau of Statistics. Western Australian Office. Census: Selected Social and Housing Characteristics for Statistical Local Areas, Western Australia, Cocos (Keeling) and Christmas Islands
Media: Online - full text.
Published by: Australian Bureau of Statistics, Western Australian Office, GPO Box K881, Perth, W.A. 6842, Australia. TEL 61-2-62524909, 300-135-070, client.services@abs.gov.au.

304.6021 363.5021 AUS
AUSTRALIA. BUREAU OF STATISTICS. WESTERN AUSTRALIAN OFFICE. CENSUS OF POPULATION AND HOUSING: SELECTED SOCIAL AND HOUSING CHARACTERISTICS FOR SUBURBS AND POSTAL AREAS, WESTERN AUSTRALIA (ONLINE). Text in English. 1996. irreg., latest 2001. free (effective 2009). back issues avail. **Document type:** *Government.* **Description:** Provides social and housing characteristics for all 'census-derived' suburbs in the Perth/Mandurah region and all 'census-derived' postal areas in Western Australia at the time of the Census. Includes ranking tables.
Former titles: Australia. Bureau of Statistics. Western Australian Office. Census of Population and Housing: Selected Social and Housing Characteristics for Suburbs and Postal Areas, Western Australia (Print); (until 2001): Australia. Bureau of Statistics. Census: Selected Social and Housing Characteristics for Suburbs and Postal Areas, Western Australia
Media: Online - full text.
Published by: Australian Bureau of Statistics, Western Australian Office, GPO Box K881, Perth, W.A. 6842, Australia. TEL 61-2-62524909, 300-135-070, client.services@abs.gov.au.

304.6021 AUS
AUSTRALIA. BUREAU OF STATISTICS. WESTERN AUSTRALIAN OFFICE. PERTH. A SOCIAL ATLAS. Text in English. 1996. quinquennial. AUD 29 per issue (effective 2009). back issues avail. **Document type:** *Government.* **Description:** Presents colour maps, based on data collected in the Census of Population and Housing, that highlight key social, demographic and housing characteristics of the population in the Perth-Mandurah region and two selected regional areas in Western Australia.
Related titles: Online - full text ed.: free (effective 2009).
Published by: Australian Bureau of Statistics, Western Australian Office, GPO Box K881, Perth, W.A. 6842, Australia. TEL 61-2-62524909, 300-135-070, client.services@abs.gov.au.

304.6021 AUS
AUSTRALIA. BUREAU OF STATISTICS. WESTERN AUSTRALIAN OFFICE. STATSEARCH, A REFERENCE GUIDE TO WESTERN AUSTRALIAN STATISTICS (ONLINE). Text in English. 1998. irreg., latest 1998. free (effective 2009). **Document type:** *Government.*
Former titles: Australia. Bureau of Statistics. Western Australian Office. StatSearch, A Reference Guide to Western Australian Statistics (Print); Australia. Bureau of Statistics. Western Australian Office. StatSearch, Western Australia
Media: Online - full text.
Published by: Australian Bureau of Statistics, Western Australian Office, GPO Box K881, Perth, W.A. 6842, Australia. TEL 61-2-62524909, 300-135-070, client.services@abs.gov.au.

304.6021 AUS
AUSTRALIA. BUREAU OF STATISTICS. WESTERN AUSTRALIAN OFFICE. WESTERN AUSTRALIA'S SENIORS. Text in English. 1986. irreg. **Document type:** *Government.* **Description:** Presents a wide range of statistics on the aged in Western Australia.
Formerly: Aged Population in Western Australia
Published by: Australian Bureau of Statistics, Western Australian Office, GPO Box K881, Perth, W.A. 6842, Australia. TEL 61-2-62524909, 300-135-070, client.services@abs.gov.au, http://www.abs.gov.au.

304.6 310 AUS ISSN 1832-7451
AUSTRALIA. DEPARTMENT OF FAMILIES, COMMUNITY SERVICES AND INDIGENOUS AFFAIRS. STATISTICAL PAPER. Variant title: Fa H C S I A Statistical Paper. Text in English. 2006. irreg., latest vol.3, 2006. free (effective 2008). **Document type:** *Government.* **Description:** Designed to meet the needs to policy makers and researchers by providing authoritative and reliable data on customer numbers.
Published by: Australia. Department of Families, Community Services and Indigenous Affairs, GPO Box 7788, Canberra Mail Centre, ACT 2610, Australia. TEL 61-2-62445458, 300-653-227, FAX 61-2-62446589, enquiries@fahcsia.gov.au, http://www.facs.gov.au/internet/facsinternet.nsf.

304.6 GBR ISSN 1464-4533
BASED POPULATION PROJECTIONS FOR WALES. Text in English. 1975. a. free (effective 2009). **Document type:** *Government.*
Former titles (until 199?): Based Population Projections for the Counties and District Health Authorities of Wales (0961-6101); (until 1991): Based Population Projections for the Counties of Wales (0958-9066); (until 1989): Based Household Projections for Counties of Wales (0269-204X); (until 1986): Based Home Population Projections for the Counties of Wales (0262-5180)
Indexed: SSciA.
—BLDSC (1863.855100).
Published by: Welsh Assembly Government, Statistical Directorate, Cathays Park, Cardiff, CF10 3NQ, United Kingdom. TEL 44-29-20825111, 44-1443-845500, stats.info.desk@wales.gsi.gov.uk, http://wales.gov.uk/?lang=en.

304.6 SWE ISSN 1102-4739
BEFOLKNINGSSTATISTIK. DEL 2, INRIKES OCH UTRIKES FLYTTNINGAR. Text in Swedish; Summaries in English. 1911. a. SEK 620. **Document type:** *Government.*
Formerly (until 1992): Sweden. Statistiska Centralbyraan. Befolkningsfoeraendringar (0082-0156)
Published by: Statistiska Centralbyraan/Statistics Sweden, Publishing Unit, Orebro, 70189, Sweden. Circ: 1,600.

304.6 SWE ISSN 1102-4747
BEFOLKNINGSSTATISTIK. DEL 3, FOLKMANGDEN EFTER KON, ALDER OCH MEDBORGARSKAP M M. Text in English; Summaries in English. 1910. a. SEK 330. **Document type:** *Government.*
Former titles (until 1992): Folkmangd 31 dec ..Enligt Indelningen 1 Jan ..Del 3, Fordelning Efter Kon, Alder, Civilstand och Medborgarskap i Kommuner M M (0347-6693); (unitl 1969): Sweden. Statistiska Centralbyraan. Folkmaengd
Published by: Statistiska Centralbyraan/Statistics Sweden, Publishing Unit, Orebro, 70189, Sweden. Circ: 2,700.

304.6021 BEL ISSN 1379-4051
HB1433
BELGIUM. INSTITUT NATIONAL DE STATISTIQUE. DEMOGRAPHIE MATHEMATIQUE. TABLES DE MORTALITE. Key Title: Demographie Mathematique. Tables de Mortalite - Institut National de Statistique. Text in French. 1969. bi-m. charts. back issues avail. **Document type:** *Government.*
Formerly (until 2000): Belgium. Institut National de Statistique. Statistiques Demographiques (0067-5490); Incorporates (1954-1969): Belgium. Institut National de Statistique. Mouvement de la Population des Communes (0067-5458)
Related titles: ◆ Dutch ed.: Belgium. Nationaal Instituut voor de Statistiek. Mathematische Demografie. Sterftetafels. ISSN 1379-4043.
Indexed: P30, PAIS.
Published by: Institut National de Statistique/Nationaal Instituut voor de Statistiek (Subsidiary of: Ministere des Affaires Economiques), Rue de Louvain 44, Brussels, 1000, Belgium. TEL 32-2-548-6211, FAX 32-2-548-6367.

304.6 BEL
BELGIUM. INSTITUT NATIONAL DE STATISTIQUE. PERSPECTIVES DE POPULATION. Key Title: Perspectives de Population - Institut National de Statistique. Text in French. 1976. irreg. charts. back issues avail. **Document type:** *Government.*
Published by: Institut National de Statistique/Nationaal Instituut voor de Statistiek (Subsidiary of: Ministere des Affaires Economiques), Rue de Louvain 44, Brussels, 1000, Belgium. TEL 32-2-548-6211, FAX 32-2-548-6367.

304.64 BEL ISSN 1379-4078
RA407.5.B5
BELGIUM. INSTITUT NATIONAL DE STATISTIQUE. SANTE. CAUSES DE DECES. Text in French. 1976. a. charts. back issues avail. **Document type:** *Government.* **Description:** Analyzes statistical data reflecting the current state and trends in the causes of death in Belgium.
Formerly (until 1994): Belgium. Institut National de Statistique. Statistiques des Causes de Deces (1370-1770)
Related titles: ◆ Dutch ed.: Belgium. Nationaal Instituut voor de Statistiek. Gezondheid. Doodsoorzaken. ISSN 1379-406X.
Published by: Institut National de Statistique/Nationaal Instituut voor de Statistiek (Subsidiary of: Ministere des Affaires Economiques), Rue de Louvain 44, Brussels, 1000, Belgium. TEL 32-2-548-6211, FAX 32-2-5486367.

304.6021 BEL ISSN 1379-406X
BELGIUM. NATIONAAL INSTITUUT VOOR DE STATISTIEK. GEZONDHEID. DOODSOORZAKEN. Text in Dutch. 1976. a. charts. **Document type:** *Government.* **Description:** Analyzes statistical data reflecting the current state and trends in the causes of death in Belgium.
Formerly (until 1994): Belgium. Nationaal Instituut voor de Statistiek. Statistiek van Doodsoorzaken (1370-1789)
Related titles: ◆ French ed.: Belgium. Institut National de Statistique. Sante. Causes de Deces. ISSN 1379-4078.
Published by: Institut National de Statistique/Nationaal Instituut voor de Statistiek (Subsidiary of: Ministere des Affaires Economiques), Rue de Louvain 44, Brussels, 1000, Belgium. TEL 32-2-548-6211, FAX 32-2-548-6367.

BELGIUM. NATIONAAL INSTITUUT VOOR DE STATISTIEK. GEZONDHEID. VERKEERSONGEVALLEN OP DE OPENBARE WEG MET DODEN EN GEWONDEN IN (YEAR). *see* PUBLIC HEALTH AND SAFETY—Abstracting, Bibliographies, Statistics

318.3046 BLZ
BELIZE. CENTRAL STATISTICAL OFFICE. ABSTRACT OF STATISTICS. Text in English. 1980. a. USD 20 (effective 1999). **Document type:** *Government.* **Description:** Contains data relating to the social, demographic, economic, agricultural and climatic situation of Belize.
Related titles: Microfiche ed.: (from PQC).
Published by: Ministry of Finance, Central Statistical Office, Belmopan, Belize. TEL 501-8-22352, FAX 501-8-23206, csogob@btl.net.

304.6 BLZ
BELIZE NATIONAL CENSUS REPORT. Text in English. 1997. irreg. free. **Document type:** *Government.* **Description:** Offers in-depth demographic and socio-economic analysis from the 1991 census data.
Published by: Ministry of Finance, Central Statistical Office, Belmopan, Belize. TEL 501-8-22352, FAX 501-8-23206, csogob@btl.net.

304.6 BLZ
BELIZE NATIONAL POPULATION REPORT. Text in English. 1994. irreg. free. **Document type:** *Government.*
Published by: Ministry of Finance, Central Statistical Office, Belmopan, Belize. TEL 501-8-22352, FAX 501-8-23206.

304.6 BOL
BOLIVIA. INSTITUTO NACIONAL DE ESTADISTICA. ESTADISTICAS REGIONALES DEPARTAMENTALES. Text in Spanish. 1976. a. USD 12.
Published by: Instituto Nacional de Estadistica, Casilla de Correos 6129, La Paz, Bolivia.

304.6021 BWA
BOTSWANA. CENTRAL STATISTICS OFFICE. POPULATION AND HOUSING CENSUS. Text and summaries in English. decennial. charts. back issues avail. **Document type:** *Government.*
Related titles: E-mail ed.; Fax ed.
Published by: Central Statistics Office, c/o Government Statistician, Private Bag 0024, Gaborone, Botswana. TEL 267-31-352200, FAX 267-31-352201, csobots@gov.bw. Ed. G M Charumbira. **Subscr. to:** Government Printer, Private Bag 0081, Gaborone, Botswana. TEL 267-353202, FAX 267-312001, http://www.gov.bw.

304.6 BRA ISSN 0101-2207
HA973
BRAZIL. FUNDACAO INSTITUTO BRASILEIRO DE GEOGRAFIA E ESTADISTICA. ESTATISTICAS DO REGISTRO CIVIL. Text in Portuguese. 1974. a. USD 40. charts; stat. **Document type:** *Government.* **Description:** Furnishes data on births, marriages, deaths, and infant deaths.
Formerly (until 1978): Registro Civil do Brasil (0100-1493); Supersedes (1959-1964): Brazil. Ministerio da Justica. Servico de Estatistica Demografica, Moral e Politica. Registro Civil (0524-3610)
Published by: Fundacao Instituto Brasileiro de Geografia e Estatistica, Centro de Documentacao e Disseminacao de Informacoes, Rua General Canabarro, 706 Andar 2, Maracana, Rio de Janeiro, RJ 20271-201, Brazil. TEL 55-21-2645424, FAX 55-21-2841959.

304.6021 CAN ISSN 0828-2919
HA747.B7
BRITISH COLUMBIA POPULATION FORECAST. Text in English. irreg., latest 1994-2021 ed. CAD 10 per issue (effective 2006). charts; stat. 64 p./no.; **Document type:** *Government.* **Description:** Provides details on British Columbia population growth by age and gender.
Related titles: Online - full text ed.
Published by: Ministry of Finance and Corporate Relations, B C Stats, PO Box 9410, Sta Prov Govt, Victoria, BC V8W 9V1, Canada. TEL 250-387-0359, FAX 250-387-0380, BC.Stats@gov.bc.ca.

BRITISH COLUMBIA REGIONAL INDEX (ONLINE EDITION). *see* BUSINESS AND ECONOMICS—Abstracting, Bibliographies, Statistics

304.6 LBN ISSN 1020-7368
HA4556
BULLETIN ON VITAL STATISTICS IN THE E S C W A REGION/NASRAT AL-IHSA'AT AL HAYAWIYYAT F MINTAQAT AL-LAGNAT AL-IQTISADIYYAT WA-AL-IGTIMA'IYYAT LI-GARBI ASIYA. Text in Arabic, English. 1998. a. USD 30 (effective 2004).
Published by: United Nations, Economic and Social Commission for Western Asia, PO Box 11-8575, Beirut, Lebanon. TEL 961-1-981301, FAX 961-1-981510, webmaster-eswa@un.org, http://www.escwa.org.lb/.

016.3046 016.3637 USA
C S A HUMAN POPULATION & NATURAL RESOURCE MANAGEMENT. Text in English. 2004 (Dec.). base vol. plus m. updates. **Document type:** *Database, Abstract/Index.* **Description:** Explores human population and demography topics, as well as social issues involving natural resource management.
Media: Online - full text.
Published by: ProQuest LLC (Bethesda) (Subsidiary of: Cambridge Information Group), 7200 Wisconsin Ave, Ste 715, Bethesda, MD 20814. TEL 301-961-6700, 800-843-7751, FAX 301-961-6720, journals@csa.com, http://www.csa.com.

304.6021 CAN ISSN 1195-9762
CA1BS91C213
CANADA. STATISTICS CANADA. ANNUAL DEMOGRAPHIC STATISTICS. Text in English. 1993. a.
Published by: Statistics Canada, Demography Division (Subsidiary of: Statistics Canada/Statistique Canada), Statistical Reference Centre, Rm 1500, Main Building, Holland Avenue, Ottawa, ON K1A 0T6, Canada.

310 CAN ISSN 0831-5698
CANADA. STATISTICS CANADA. CANADIAN SOCIAL TRENDS. Text in English. 1986. s-a. CAD 39; CAD 24 per issue (effective 2010). adv. charts; illus.; stat. Index. back issues avail.; reprints avail. **Document type:** *Government.* **Description:** Discusses the social, economic and demographic changes affecting the lives of Canadians and contains the latest figures for major social indicators.
Related titles: Microform ed.: (from MML); Online - full text ed.: ISSN 1481-1634. 1999. free (effective 2010); ◆ French ed.: Tendances Sociales Canadiennes. ISSN 0831-5701.
Indexed: A01, A02, A03, A08, A25, A26, A36, AmH&L, C03, C04, C05, CA, CABA, CBCARef, CBPI, CPerI, E08, E12, G08, GH, I05, LT, M02, N02, P02, P19, P30, P34, P48, P50, P52, PAIS, PCI, PQC, PdeR, PopulInd, RASB, RRTA, S02, S03, S08, S09, S22, SRRA, T02.
—CIS. **CCC.**
Published by: Statistics Canada, Operations and Integration Division (Subsidiary of: Statistics Canada/Statistique Canada), 150 Tunney's Pasture Driveway, Ottawa, ON K1A 0T6, Canada. TEL 613-951-8116, 800-263-1136, FAX 613-951-0581, 877-287-4369, infostats@statcan.gc.ca. **Co-sponsor:** Ministry of Industry and Science.

304.6 CAN ISSN 1708-1440
CANADA. STATISTICS CANADA. CAUSES OF DEATH (OTTAWA, 1997) (ONLINE EDITION). (Catalogue 84-203) Text in English, French. 1960. a. CAD 40.
Former titles (until 2000): Canada. Statistics Canada. Causes of Death. Shelf Tables (Print Edition) (1706-922X); (until 1997): Canada. Statistics Canada. Causes of Death (Ottawa, 1997) (1195-4094); (until 1991): Canada. Statistics Canada. Health Reports. Supplement. Causes of Death (1180-2421); (until 1987): Canada. Statistics Canada. Causes of Death, Provinces by Sex and Canada by Sex and Age (0380-7533); (until 1970): Canada. Bureau of Statistics. Causes of Death, Canada (0575-8122)
Media: Online - full text. **Related titles:** ◆ French ed.: Canada. Statistique Canada. Causes de Deces. ISSN 1708-1459.
Published by: Statistics Canada/Statistique Canada, Communications Division, 3rd Fl, R H Coats Bldg, Ottawa, ON K1A 0A6, Canada. TEL 613-951-7277, FAX 613-951-1584. **Subscr. to:** Publications Sales and Services, Ottawa, ON K1A 0T6, Canada.

304.6 CAN ISSN 1497-7796
CANADA. STATISTICS CANADA. DIVORCES. SHELF TABLES. Text in English. 19??. a.
Former titles (until 1997): Canada. Statistics Canada. Divorces (1195-4159); (until 1991): Canada. Statistics Canada. Health Reports. Supplement. Divorces (1180-3126); Which superseded in part (in 1988): Canada. Statistics Canada. Marriages and Divorces (0825-298X); Which was formerly (until 1982): Canada. Statistics Canada. Vital Statistics. Volume 2: Marriages and Divorces (0700-1460); Which superseded in part (in 1971): Canada. Statistics Canada. Vital Statistics. Preliminary Annual Report (0317-3143); Which was formerly (until 1951): Canada. Statistics Canada. Vital Statistics. Preliminary Annual Report and Fourth Quarter
Published by: Statistics Canada, Health Division (Subsidiary of: Statistics Canada/Statistique Canada), R H Coats Bldg, 18th floor, Ottawa, ON K1A 0T6, Canada. TEL 613-951-8569.

304.6021 CAN ISSN 1712-6452
CANADA. STATISTICS CANADA. MARRIAGES (ONLINE EDITION). Text in English. 1921. a.
Former titles (until 2002): Marriages. Shelf Tables (Print Edition) (1708-9115); (until 1994): Marriages (1195-4140); (until 1991): Health Reports. Supplement. Marriages (1180-3118); Which superseded in part (in 1985): Marriages and Divorces (0825-298X); Which was formerly (until 1981): Vital Statistics. Volume 2, Marriages and Divorces (0700-1460); Which superseded in part (in 1971): Vital Statistics (0527-6438)
Media: Online - full text. **Related titles:** French ed.: Canada. Statistique Canada. Mariages. ISSN 1712-6460. 2002.
Published by: Statistics Canada, Canadian Centre for Health Information (Subsidiary of: Statistics Canada/Statistique Canada), 1500 Rm, Main Bldg, Holland Ave, Ottawa, ON K1A 0T6, Canada. TEL 613-951-8116.

304.64021 CAN
CANADA. STATISTICS CANADA. MORTALITY, SUMMARY LIST OF CAUSES. SHELF TABLES. Text in English, French. 1921. a. CAD 20 (effective 2004).
Former titles (until 1999): Canada. Statistics Canada. Mortality, Summary List of Causes (1195-4108); (until 1991): Health Reports. Supplement. Mortality, Summary List of Causes (1180-2448); (until 1987): Canada. Statistics Canada. Mortality, Summary List of Causes (0825-2998); (until 1982): Canada. Statistics Canada. Vital Statistics. Volume 3: Mortality, Summary List of Causes (0225-7394); (until 1978): Canada. Statistics Canada. Vital Statistics. Volume 3: Deaths (0700-1479); Which superseded in part (in 1971): Canada. Statistics Canada. Vital Statistics (0527-6438)
—CCC.
Published by: (Statistics Canada, Canadian Centre for Health Information), Statistics Canada/Statistique Canada, Publications Sales and Services, Ottawa, ON K1A 0T6, Canada. TEL 613-951-8116, infostats@statcan.gc.ca, http://www.statcan.gc.ca.

304.6 CAN ISSN 0827-9624
HA741
CANADA. STATISTICS CANADA. POSTCENSAL ANNUAL ESTIMATES OF POPULATION BY MARITAL STATUS, AGE, SEX AND COMPONENTS OF GROWTH FOR CANADA, PROVINCES AND TERRITORIES. (Catalog 91-203) Text in English, French. 1983. a. CAD 5, USD 6.
Formerly (until 1984): Canada. Statistics Canada. Postcensal Annual Estimates of Population by Marital Status, Age, Sex and Components of Growth for Canada and the Provinces (0824-9563); Which was formed by the merger of (1924-1983): Canada. Statistics Canada. Estimates of Population for Canada and the Provinces (0708-7012); Which was formerly (until 1977): Canada. Statistics Canada. Estimated Population of Canada by Province (0575-8424); (until 1953): Canada. Dominion Bureau of Statistics. Population of Canada by Provinces (0381-8500); (until 1931): Canada. Dominion Bureau of Statistics. Estimates of Population, Canada (0840-2973); (1944-1983): Canada. Statistics Canada. Estimates of Population by Sex and Age for Canada and the Provinces (0707-3194); Which was formerly (until 1977): Canada. Statistics Canada. Population of Canada and the Provinces by Sex and Age Group (0703-0002); (until 1974): Canada. Dominion Bureau of Statistics. Estimated Population by Sex and Age Group, for Canada and Provinces (0575-8416); (until 1949): Canada. Dominion Bureau of Statistics. Population by Age Group and Sex, Canada (Nine Provinces), 1931 to 1944 (0833-7543); (1976-1983): Canada. Statistics Canada. International and Interprovincial Migration in Canada (0703-6698); (1945-1983): Canada. Statistics Canada. Estimates of Population by Marital Status, Age and Sex, Canada and Provinces (0227-1796); Which was formerly (until 1978): Canada. Statistics Canada. Population Estimates by Marital Status, Age & Sex, Canada and Provinces (0575-934X); (until 1952): Canada. Dominion Bureau of Statistics. Estimated Population by Marital Status and Sex, Canada and Provinces (0318-3939); (until 1947): Canada. Dominion Bureau of Statistics. Estimated Population by Sex and Conjugal Condition for Canada and the Provinces (0833-7535)
Published by: Statistics Canada/Statistique Canada, Communications Division, 3rd Fl, R H Coats Bldg, Ottawa, ON K1A 0A6, Canada. TEL 613-593-7276.

CANADA. STATISTICS CANADA. QUARTERLY DEMOGRAPHIC ESTIMATES. *see* POPULATION STUDIES

304.6021 CAN ISSN 0835-4057
CANADA. STATISTICS CANADA. QUARTERLY DEMOGRAPHIC STATISTICS. Text in English. 1987. q.
Formed by the merger of (1972-1987): Quarterly Estimates of Population for Canada, the Provinces and the Territories (0830-0038); Which was formerly (until 1984): Quarterly Estimates of Population for Canada and Provinces (0706-4705); (1948-1987): Vital Statistics Quarterly (0829-657X); Which was formerly (until 1983): Vital Statistics (0317-3135); (until 1954): Monthly Report of Vital Statistics (0829-6553); (until 1953): Births, Marriages and Deaths in Canada (0837-9092); (until 1949): Monthly Report of Births, Marriages and Deaths in Canada (0837-9017)
Related titles: ◆ Online - full text ed.: Canada. Statistics Canada. Quarterly Demographic Estimates. ISSN 1911-0928.
Published by: Statistics Canada/Statistique Canada, Communications Division, 3rd Fl, R H Coats Bldg, Ottawa, ON K1A 0A6, Canada. TEL 800-263-1136, infostats@statcan.ca, http://www.statcan.gc.ca.

304.6 CAN
CANADA. STATISTICS CANADA. VITAL STATISTICS COMPENDIUM. Text in English. 1993. irreg., latest 1999. CAD 45 (effective 2004).
Formerly (until 1995): Canada. Statistics Canada. Births and Deaths (1201-7353); Which was formed by the merger of (1921-1993): Canada. Statistics Canada. Deaths (1195-4132); Which was formerly (until 1991): Canada. Statistics Canada. Health Reports. Supplement. Deaths (1180-3096); (1921-1993): Canada. Statistics Canada. Births (1195-4124); Which was formerly (until 1991): Canada. Statistics Canada. Supplement. Births (1180-3088); Both of which superseded in part (in 1986): Canada. Statistics Canada. Births and Deaths (0825-2971); Which was formerly (until 1982): Canada. Statistics Canada. Vital Statistics. Volume 1: Births and Deaths (0225-7386); (until 1978): Canada. Statistics Canada. Vital Statistics. Volume 1: Births (0700-1452); Which superseded in part (in 1971): Canada. Dominion Bureau of Statistics. Vital Statistics (0527-6438)
Published by: Statistics Canada/Statistique Canada, Publications Sales and Services, Ottawa, ON K1A 0T6, Canada. TEL 613-951-8116, infostats@statcan.ca, http://www.statcan.gc.ca.

304.6021 CAN ISSN 1708-1459
CANADA. STATISTIQUE CANADA. CAUSES DE DECES. Text in French. 2000. irreg., latest 2003. **Document type:** *Government.*
Media: Online - full text. **Related titles:** ◆ English ed.: Canada. Statistics Canada. Causes of Death (Ottawa, 1997) (Online Edition). ISSN 1708-1440.
Published by: Statistics Canada/Statistique Canada, Communications Division, 3rd Fl, R H Coats Bldg, Ottawa, ON K1A 0A6, Canada. TEL 800-263-1136, infostats@statcan.ca, http://www.statcan.gc.ca.

304.6 ITA ISSN 1121-0958
RA407.5.I8
CAUSE DI MORTE. Text in Italian. 1989. a. **Document type:** *Government.* **Description:** Presents data relevant to the causes of death and infant mortality.
Supersedes in part (in 1989): Statistiche Sanitarie (1121-0990); Which was formerly (until 1985): Annuario di Statistiche Sanitarie (0075-1758)
Published by: Istituto Nazionale di Statistica (I S T A T), Via Cesare Balbo 16, Rome, 00184, Italy. TEL 39-06-46731, http://www.istat.it.

317 CUB
CENSO DE POBLACION Y VIVIENDAS. Text in Spanish. a. free. charts; stat. **Document type:** *Government.*
Published by: (Cuba. Direccion de Informacion y Relaciones Internacionales), Comite Estatal de Estadisticas, Centro de Informacion Cientifico-Tecnica, Almendares No. 156, esq. a Desague, Gaveta Postal 6016, Havana, Cuba.

304.6 BRA ISSN 0104-3145
CENSO DEMOGRAFICO. Text in Portuguese. 1940. decennial (in 7 vols.). USD 200 (effective 1998). charts; stat. **Document type:** *Government.* **Description:** Furnishes information about the number and characteristics of the population, household, fertility, education, health, and more. Issue in 7 parts: Resultados do Universo Relativos as Caracteristicas da Populaco e dos Domicilios; Situacao Demografica, Social e Economica - Primeiras Consideracoes; Resultados da Amostra Relativos as Caracteristicas Gerais da Populaco e Instucao; Familias e Domicilios; Nupcialidade, Fecundidade e Mortalidade; Mao-de-Obra; Migracao.
Published by: Fundacao Instituto Brasileiro de Geografia e Estatistica, Centro de Documentacao e Disseminacao de Informacoes, Rua General Canabarro, 706 Andar 2, Maracana, Rio de Janeiro, RJ 20271-201, Brazil. TEL 55-21-2645424, FAX 55-21-2841959.

304.6 CHL
CHILE. INSTITUTO NACIONAL DE ESTADISTICAS. DEMOGRAFIA. Text in Spanish. 1909. a. CLP 2,700 domestic; USD 18.80 in United States; USD 23.60 elsewhere (effective 1999).
Published by: Instituto Nacional de Estadisticas, Casilla 498, Correo 3, Ave. Bulnes, 418, Santiago, Chile. TEL 56-2-6991441, FAX 56-2-6712169.

325.021 RUS
CHISLENNOST' I MIGRATSIYA NASELENIYA ROSSIISKOI FEDERATSII (YEAR)/POPULATION SIZE AND MIGRATION IN THE RUSSIAN FEDERATION (YEAR). Text in Russian. 1993. a. RUR 330 per issue (effective 2005). **Document type:** *Bulletin, Government.* **Description:** Contains data on administrative and territorial breakdown, area, population density, de facto (present-in-area) and de jure (resident) population and components of their changes for the Russian Federation and its subjects.
Related titles: Online - full content ed.: RUR 354 (effective 2005).
Published by: Gosudarstvennyi Komitet Rossiiskoi Federatsii po Statistike/Federal State Statistics Office, ul Myasnitskaya 39, Moscow, 107450, Russian Federation. TEL 7-095-2074902, FAX 7-095-2074087, stat@gks.ru, http://www.gks.ru.

325.021 RUS
CHISLENNOST' NASELENIYA ROSSIISKOI FEDERATSII PO GORODAM, POSELKAM GORODSKOGO TIPA I RAYONAM (YEAR). Text in Russian. a. RUR 330 per issue (effective 2005). **Document type:** *Bulletin, Government.* **Description:** Contains statistics of population of Russian Federation.
Published by: Gosudarstvennyi Komitet Rossiiskoi Federatsii po Statistike/Federal State Statistics Office, ul Myasnitskaya 39, Moscow, 107450, Russian Federation. TEL 7-095-2074902, FAX 7-095-2074087, stat@gks.ru, http://www.gks.ru.

P

325.021 RUS
CHISLENNOST' NASELENIYA ROSSIISKOI FEDERATSII PO POLU I VOZRASTU (YEAR)/POPULATION SIZE IN THE RUSSIAN FEDERATION BY SEX AND AGE (YEAR). Text in Russian. 1992. a. RUR 385 per issue (effective 2005). **Document type:** *Bulletin, Government.* **Description:** Publishes data related to population size in the Russian Federation. Information is given on de jure (resident) population broken down into urban and rural one. Data are presented by sex, one year age and various ages.
Related titles: Online - full content ed.: RUR 413 (effective 2005).
Published by: Gosudarstvennyi Komitet Rossiiskoi Federatsii po Statistike/Federal State Statistics Office, ul Myasnitskaya 39, Moscow, 107450, Russian Federation. TEL 7-095-2074902, FAX 7-095-2074087, stat@gks.ru, http://www.gks.ru.

304.6 COL
COLOMBIA. DEPARTAMENTO ADMINISTRATIVO NACIONAL DE ESTADISTICA. ANUARIO DEMOGRAFICO. Text in Spanish. a. **Document type:** *Government.*
Published by: Departamento Administrativo Nacional de Estadistica (D A N E), Bancos de Datos, Centro Administrativo Nacional (CAN), Avenida Eldorado, Apartado Aereo 80043, Bogota, CUND, Colombia.

304.6 USA
COMPUTER AND INTERNET USE IN THE UNITED STATES. Text in English. irreg., latest 2007. free (effective 2009). stat. back issues avail. **Document type:** *Government.*
Media: Online - full text.
Published by: U.S. Census Bureau. Population Division. Education & Social Stratification Branch (Subsidiary of: U.S. Department of Commerce) TEL 866-758-1060.

304.6 ITA ISSN 1825-8875
COMUNE DI PISA. ANNUARIO STATISTICO. Text in Italian. 19??. a. **Document type:** *Directory, Trade.*
Former titles (until 1995): Comune di Pisa. Annuario. Bollettino di Statistica (1825-8867); (until 1990): Comune di Pisa. Bollettino Mensile di Statistica (1825-8859)
Published by: Comune di Pisa, Palazzo Gambacorti 2, Pisa, Italy. TEL 39-050-910205.

304.6021 ITA ISSN 2035-2786
COMUNE DI ROMA. ANNUARIO STATISTICO. Text in Italian. 1997. a. **Document type:** *Report, Government.*
Published by: Comune di Roma, Via della Greca 5, Rome, 00186, Italy.

304.6 CRI ISSN 1409-0201
COSTA RICA CALCULO DE POBLACION; por provincia, canton y distrito. Text in Spanish. a. **Description:** Presents vital statistical data on Costa Rica.
Published by: (Costa Rica. Seccion Estadisticas Vitales), Ministerio de Economia Industria y Comercio, Direccion General de Estadistica y Censos, Apdo 10163, San Jose, 1000, Costa Rica.

COUNTY AND CITY EXTRA; annual metro, city and county data book. *see* STATISTICS

304.6 BRA ISSN 0103-4448
HQ792.B7
CRIANCAS E ADOLESCENTES; indicadores sociais. Text in Portuguese. 1987. a. USD 150. **Document type:** *Government.*
Related titles: Diskette ed.: USD 20.
Published by: Fundacao Instituto Brasileiro de Geografia e Estatistica, Centro de Documentacao e Disseminacao de Informacoes, Rua General Canabarro, 706 Andar 2, Maracana, Rio de Janeiro, RJ 20271-201, Brazil. TEL 55-21-2645424, FAX 55-21-2841959.

304.6 USA
CURRENT POPULATION REPORTS. POPULATION CHARACTERISTICS. SCHOOL ENROLLMENT IN THE UNITED STATES. Text in English. a. USD 34. **Document type:** *Government.*
Former titles (until 200?): Current Population Reports. Population Characteristics. School Enrollment in the United States. Social and Economic Characteristics of Students; Current Population Reports: Population Characteristics. School Enrollment: Social and Economic Characteristics of Students; U.S. Bureau of the Census. Current Population Reports: School Enrollment: October (Year) (0082-9528)
Related titles: Online - full text ed.; ◆ Series of: Current Population Reports: Series P-20, Population Characteristics (Print). ISSN 0363-6836.
Published by: U.S. Census Bureau. Housing and Household Economic Statistics Division. Education & Social Stratification Branch (Subsidiary of: U.S. Department of Commerce), 4600 Silver Hill Rd., Washington, DC 20233. TEL 301-763-2464, http://www.census.gov/hhes/www/hhesdiv.html. **Subscr. to:** U.S. Government Printing Office, Superintendent of Documents, PO Box 371954, Pittsburgh, PA 15250. TEL 202-512-1800, FAX 202-512-2250, orders@gpo.gov, http://www.access.gpo.gov.

304.6 USA ISSN 0363-6836
HA195
CURRENT POPULATION REPORTS: SERIES P-20, POPULATION CHARACTERISTICS (PRINT). Text in English. 1947. irreg. back issues avail.; reprints avail. **Document type:** *Government.* **Description:** Compiles current national and, occasionally, local regional data on geographic residence and mobility, fertility, education, school enrollment, marital status and numbers and characteristics of households and families.
Incorporates (in 1987): Current Population Report. Series P-27, Farm Population (1048-6283)
Related titles: ◆ Series: Current Population Reports. Population Characteristics. Household and Family Characteristics; ◆ Current Population Reports. Population Characteristics. School Enrollment in the United States; ◆ Current Population Reports: Population Characteristics. Marital Status and Living Arrangements. ISSN 0146-4213.
Indexed: AmStI, CLFP, P30, PopulInd, SCOPUS.
Published by: U.S. Census Bureau. Population Division (Subsidiary of: U.S. Department of Commerce), 4600 Silver Hill Rd., Washington, DC 20233. TEL 866-758-1060, http://www.census.gov/population/www/. **Subscr. to:** U.S. Government Printing Office, Superintendent of Documents, PO Box 371954, Pittsburgh, PA 15250. TEL 202-512-1800, FAX 202-512-2250, orders@gpo.gov, http://www.access.gpo.gov.

304.6 USA ISSN 0498-8485
HA203
CURRENT POPULATION REPORTS. SERIES P-23, SPECIAL STUDIES. Text in English. 1949. irreg. **Document type:** *Government.*
Formerly: Current Population Reports. Series P-23, Technical Studies
Related titles: Online - full text ed.: ISSN 1555-0699.
Indexed: PopulInd.
Published by: U.S. Census Bureau. Population Division (Subsidiary of: U.S. Department of Commerce), 4600 Silver Hill Rd., Washington, DC 20233. TEL 866-758-1060, http://www.census.gov/population/www/. **Subscr. to:** U.S. Government Printing Office, Superintendent of Documents, PO Box 371954, Pittsburgh, PA 15250. TEL 202-512-1800, FAX 202-512-2250, orders@gpo.gov, http://www.access.gpo.gov.

304.6 USA ISSN 0738-453X
HA195
CURRENT POPULATION REPORTS: SERIES P-25, POPULATION ESTIMATES AND PROJECTIONS. Text in English. 1947. irreg. Supplement avail.; back issues avail.; reprints avail. **Document type:** *Government.* **Description:** Estimates the total population of the U.S. and provides half-year figures broken down by age, color, and sex.
Incorporates (in 1993): Current Population Reports: Series P-26. Population Estimates and Projections
Related titles: Microfiche ed.: (from CIS); Online - full text ed.
Indexed: AmStI, P30, PopulInd.
Published by: U.S. Census Bureau. Population Division (Subsidiary of: U.S. Department of Commerce), 4600 Silver Hill Rd., Washington, DC 20233. TEL 866-758-1060, http://www.census.gov/population/www/.

304.6 USA ISSN 0730-4803
HC110.I5
CURRENT POPULATION REPORTS: SERIES P-60, CONSUMER INCOME. Text in English. 1947. irreg. price varies. **Document type:** *Government.*
Related titles: Online - full text ed.: ISSN 1555-0702; ◆ Series: Current Population Reports: Consumer Income. Money Income of Households, Families and Persons in the United States (Year).
Indexed: P30.
Published by: U.S. Census Bureau (Subsidiary of: U.S. Department of Commerce), 4600 Silver Hill Rd, Washington, DC 20233. **Subscr. to:** U.S. Government Printing Office, Superintendent of Documents, PO Box 371954, Pittsburgh, PA 15250. TEL 202-512-1800, FAX 202-512-2250, orders@gpo.gov, http://www.access.gpo.gov.

301 USA ISSN 0886-5698
HA203
CURRENT POPULATION REPORTS. SERIES P-70, HOUSEHOLD ECONOMIC STUDIES. Text in English. 1983. irreg. USD 16 (effective 2001). reprints avail. **Document type:** *Government.* **Description:** Present statistical trends in American family life. Each issue focuses on a particular social or economic theme.
Related titles: Microfiche ed.: (from CIS); Online - full text ed.: ISSN 1555-0710.
Published by: U.S. Census Bureau (Subsidiary of: U.S. Department of Commerce), 4600 Silver Hill Rd, Washington, DC 20233. **Subscr. to:** U.S. Government Printing Office, Superintendent of Documents, PO Box 371954, Pittsburgh, PA 15250. TEL 202-512-1800, FAX 202-512-2250, orders@gpo.gov, http://www.access.gpo.gov.

304.6 CYP ISSN 0590-4846
HA1950.C9
CYPRUS. DEPARTMENT OF STATISTICS AND RESEARCH. DEMOGRAPHIC REPORT. Text in English, Greek. 1963. a. **Document type:** *Government.* **Description:** Provides population estimates by month: births and fertility statistics, death, and mortality statistics.
Published by: Ministry of Finance, Department of Statistics and Research, 13 Andreas Araouzos St, Nicosia, 1444, Cyprus. TEL 357-2-309318, FAX 357-2-374830.

310 CYP
CYPRUS. DEPARTMENT OF STATISTICS AND RESEARCH. DEMOGRAPHIC SURVEY (YEARS). Text in English. 1980. irreg. **Document type:** *Government.* **Description:** Presents data on the socioeconomic structure of the population, fertility and internal migration.
Formerly (until 1985): Cyprus. Department of Statistics and Research. Multi-Round Demographic Survey. Main Report
Published by: Ministry of Finance, Department of Statistics and Research, 13 Andreas Araouzos St, Nicosia, 1444, Cyprus. TEL 357-2-309301, FAX 357-2-374830.

310 CYP
CYPRUS. DEPARTMENT OF STATISTICS AND RESEARCH. MULTI-ROUND DEMOGRAPHIC SURVEY. MIGRATION IN CYPRUS. Text in English. 1983. irreg. **Document type:** *Government.* **Description:** Analyzes recent and lifetime migration in Cyprus, examining variables such as sex, age, present and previous place of residence, place of birth, type of movement, and reason for moving.
Published by: Ministry of Finance, Department of Statistics and Research, 13 Andreas Araouzos St, Nicosia, 1444, Cyprus. TEL 357-2-309318, FAX 357-2-374830.

CYPRUS. DEPARTMENT OF STATISTICS AND RESEARCH. TOURISM, MIGRATION AND TRAVEL STATISTICS. *see* TRAVEL AND TOURISM—Abstracting, Bibliographies, Statistics

016.3046 012 CHL ISSN 0378-5378
HB3530.5
D O C P A L RESUMENES SOBRE POBLACION EN AMERICA LATINA/D O C P A L LATIN AMERICAN POPULATION ABSTRACTS. Text in English, Spanish. 1977. a. USD 20. back issues avail. **Document type:** *Abstract/Index.* **Description:** Abstracts published and non-published literature on population written in or about Latin America and the Caribbean.
Indexed: PopulInd.
Published by: United Nations, Centro Latinoamericano de Demografia/United Nations, Latin American and Demographic Center, Casilla 91, Santiago, Chile. TEL 56-2-210-2000. Circ: 1,000.

304.60021 RUS
DEMOGRAFICHESKII EZHEGODNIK ROSSII (YEAR)/DEMOGRAPHIC YEARBOOK OF RUSSIA. Text in Russian. a., latest 2005. RUR 440 per issue (effective 2005). **Document type:** *Yearbook, Government.*
Published by: Gosudarstvennyi Komitet Rossiiskoi Federatsii po Statistike/Federal State Statistics Office, ul Myasnitskaya 39, Moscow, 107450, Russian Federation. TEL 7-095-2074902, FAX 7-095-2074087, stat@gks.ru, http://www.gks.ru.

304.6021 CZE ISSN 0011-8265
HB3592.3.A3
DEMOGRAFIE/DEMOGRAPHY; revue pro vyzkum populacniho vyvoje - review of research into population. Text in Czech; Summaries in English. 1959. q. EUR 127, USD 136 foreign (effective 2008). bk.rev. stat. index. **Document type:** *Journal, Government.* **Description:** Overviews and analyzes population trends in the Czech Republic and abroad. Includes information on national population reproduction, migration, training and education, ethnic issues; figures on marriage, divorce, birth, death and abortion rates, as well as other population characteristics.
Supersedes in part: Statistika a Demografie
Indexed: IBSS, P30, PopulInd, RASB, SCOPUS.
Published by: Cesky Statisticky Urad, Na padesatem 81, Prague 10, 10082, Czech Republic. TEL 420-2-74051111, infoservis@czso.cz. Ed. Jirina Ruzkova. Circ: 1,800. **Dist. by:** Myris Trade Ltd., V Stihlach 1311, PO Box 2, Prague 4 14201, Czech Republic.

304.6 GHA
DEMOGRAPHIC AND HEALTH SURVEY (YEAR). Text in English. 1988. irreg., latest 1993. USD 10. **Document type:** *Government.*
Published by: Statistical Service, Information Section, PO Box 1098, Accra, Ghana. TEL 233-21-663758, FAX 233-21-667069.

304.6 AUT ISSN 0258-8676
DEMOGRAPHISCHES JAHRBUCH OESTERREICHS. Text in German. 1951. a. EUR 50 (effective 2004). **Document type:** *Government.* **Description:** Demographic yearbook for Austria.
Formerly: Austria. Statistisches Zentralamt. Die Natuerliche Bevoelkerungsbewegung (0067-2335)
Related titles: ◆ Series of: Beitraege zur Oesterreichischen Statistik. ISSN 0067-2319.
Published by: Statistik Austria, Guglgasse 13, Vienna, W 1110, Austria. TEL 43-1-711280, FAX 43-1-711287728, info@statistik.gv.at, http://www.statistik.at.

DEMOS; carta demografica sobre Mexico. *see* POPULATION STUDIES

314.48 DNK ISSN 1601-0868
HB3611
DENMARK. DANMARKS STATISTIK. BEFOLKNING OG VALG (ONLINE). Text in Danish. 200?. irreg. **Document type:** *Government.*
Formerly (1983-2006): Denmark. Danmarks Statistik. Befolkning og Valg (0108-5530); Which superseded in part (1976-1983): Statistiske Efterretninger A (0105-306X); (1976-1983): Statistiske Efterretninger B (0105-3078); Which both superseded in part (1909-1976): Statistiske Efterretninger (0039-0674)
Media: Online - full content. **Related titles:** ◆ Series of: Denmark. Danmarks Statistik. Statistiske Efterretninger. Indhold (Online).
Indexed: P30.
Published by: Danmarks Statistik/Statistics Denmark, Sejroegade 11, Copenhagen OE, 2100, Denmark. TEL 45-39-173917, FAX 45-39-173939, dst@dst.dk.

304.6 DNK ISSN 1902-049X
HA1473
DENMARK. DANMARKS STATISTIK. BEFOLKNINGENS UDVIKLING/DENMARK. STATISTICS DENMARK. VITAL STATISTICS. Text in Danish; Notes in English. 1931. a. DKK 125 per issue (effective 2008). **Document type:** *Government.*
Formerly (until 2006): Denmark. Danmarks Statistik. Befolkningens Bevaegelser (0070-3478)
Related titles: Online - full text ed.: ISSN 1902-0503. 199?.
Published by: Danmarks Statistik/Statistics Denmark, Sejroegade 11, Copenhagen OE, 2100, Denmark. TEL 45-39-173917, FAX 45-39-173939, dst@dst.dk. Ed. Dorthe Larsen TEL 45-39-173307.

614 363.12509489 DNK ISSN 0070-3516
HE5614.5.D4
DENMARK. DANMARKS STATISTIK. FAERDSELSUHELD/DENMARK. STATISTICS DENMARK. ROAD TRAFFIC ACCIDENTS. Text in Danish, English. 1930. a. DKK 55 per issue (effective 2008). **Document type:** *Government.*
Related titles: Online - full text ed.: ISSN 1601-1120.
Indexed: RASB.
Published by: Danmarks Statistik/Statistics Denmark, Sejroegade 11, Copenhagen OE, 2100, Denmark. TEL 45-39-173917, FAX 45-39-173939, dst@dst.dk.

304.6 DNK ISSN 0904-0234
HA1471
DENMARK. DANMARKS STATISTIK. NOEGLETAL PAA POSTNUMRE/DENMARK. STATISTICS DENMARK. KEY FIGURES BY ZIP CODES; danskerne i tal. Text in Danish. 1985. a. DKK 207 per issue (effective 2008). **Document type:** *Government.* **Description:** Contains Danish population statistics on age, work, income, etc. using zip codes.
Related titles: Online - full text ed.
Published by: Danmarks Statistik/Statistics Denmark, Sejroegade 11, Copenhagen OE, 2100, Denmark. TEL 45-39-173917, FAX 45-39-173939, dst@dst.dk. Ed. Birgitte Andersen TEL 45-39-173681.

304.6 DMA
DOMINICA. MINISTRY OF FINANCE. CENTRAL STATISTICAL OFFICE. ANNUAL DEMOGRAPHIC STATISTICS. Text in English. a. USD 13.50. **Document type:** *Government.*
Published by: Ministry of Finance, Central Statistical Office, Kennedy Ave., Roseau, Dominica. Ed. Michael Murphy.

325 ECU
ECUADOR. INSTITUTO NACIONAL DE ESTADISTICA Y CENSOS. ENCUESTA ANUAL DE MIGRACION INTERNACIONAL. Text in Spanish. a. USD 15 (effective 2001). **Document type:** *Government.*
Related titles: Diskette ed.; E-mail ed.
Published by: Instituto Nacional de Estadistica y Censos, Juan Larrea N15-36 y Jose Riofrio, Quito, Ecuador. TEL 593-2-529858, FAX 593-2-509836. Circ: 85 (paid).

304.6 ECU
ECUADOR. INSTITUTO NACIONAL DE ESTADISTICA Y CENSOS. SERIE ESTADISTICA. Text in Spanish. 1970. quinquennial. USD 27.
Published by: Instituto Nacional de Estadistica y Censos, Juan Larrea N15-36 y Jose Riofrio, Quito, Ecuador. TEL 593-2-529858, FAX 593-2-509836.

304.6 330.9021 ESP ISSN 1136-1611
ESPANA EN CIFRAS. Text in Spanish. 1989. a. price varies. **Document type:** *Government.*

Related titles: French ed.: L' Espagne en Chiffres. ISSN 1137-2338; English ed.: Spain in Figures. ISSN 1137-232X.
Published by: Instituto Nacional de Estadistica (I N E), Paseo de la Castellana 183, Madrid, 28071, Spain. TEL 34-91-5839100.

304.0021 ESP ISSN 0213-3423
ESTADISTICA DEL SUICIDIO EN ESPANA. Text in Spanish. 1913. a., latest 2006. EUR 8. **Document type:** *Bulletin, Government.*
Published by: Instituto Nacional de Estadistica (I N E), Paseo de la Castellana 183, Madrid, 28071, Spain. TEL 34-91-5839100, http://www.ine.es/.

304.6 PAN ISSN 0379-4237
HA851
ESTADISTICA PANAMENA. SITUACION DEMOGRAFICA. SECCION 221. ESTADISTICAS VITALES. Text in Spanish. 1957. a. (in 3 vols.). PAB 3.50 domestic (effective 2000). **Document type:** *Bulletin, Government.* **Description:** Presents data on marriages and divorces, live births and stillbirths, and deaths, arranged by province and by other factors.
Published by: Direccion de Estadistica y Censo, Contraloria General, Apdo. 5213, Panama City, 5, Panama. FAX 507-210-4801. Circ: 900.

325.7287 PAN ISSN 1022-6605
JV7429
ESTADISTICA PANAMENA. SITUACION DEMOGRAFICA. SECCION 231. MOVIMIENTO INTERNACIONAL DE PASAJEROS. Text in Spanish. 1957. a. PAB 1 domestic (effective 2000). **Document type:** *Bulletin, Government.* **Description:** Offers information on the entrance and exiting of passengers at airports, seaports and other land destinations.
Formerly (until 1991): Estadistica Panamena. Situacion Demografica. Seccion 231. Migracion Internacional (0378-4975)
Indexed: P30.
Published by: Direccion de Estadistica y Censo, Contraloria General, Apdo. 5213, Panama City, 5, Panama. FAX 507-210-4801. Circ: 850.

304.6021 ESP ISSN 1138-9001
ESTADISTICAS DE PERMISOS DE TRABAJO A ESTRANJEROS. Text in Spanish. 1985. a. **Document type:** *Government.*
Published by: Ministerio de Trabajo y Asuntos Sociales, Centro de Publicaciones, Agustin de Bethencourt 11, Madrid, 28003, Spain. http://www.mtas.es.

304.6021 ESP ISSN 1696-0459
HB1450.M3
ESTADISTICAS DEL MOVIMIENTO NATURAL DE LA POBLACION DE LA COMUNIDAD DE MADRID. DEFUNCIONES. Text in Spanish. 1990. a. **Document type:** *Government.*
Supersedes in part (in 2003): Estadisticas del Movimiento Natural de Poblacion de la Comunidad de Madrid. Nacimientos, Matrimonios, Defunciones, Mortalidad Segun Causas Multiplas (1579-1785); Which was formerly (until 2001): Estadisticas del Movimiento Natural de Poblacion de la Comunidad de Madrid. Nacimientos, Matrimonios, Defunciones (1137-8433); Which was formed by the merger of (1990-1994): Estadisticas del Movimiento Natural de Poblacion de la Comunidad de Madrid. Nacimientos (1137-8441); (1990-1994): Estadisticas del Movimiento Natural de Poblacion de la Comunidad de Madrid. Matrimonios (1137-8468); (1990-1994): Estadisticas del Movimiento Natural de Poblacion de la Comunidad de Madrid. Defunciones (1137-8476)
Published by: Comunidad de Madrid, Instituto de Estadistica, Principe de Vargara 108, Madrid, 28002, Spain. TEL 34-91-5802540, jestadis@madrid.org, http://www.madrid.org/iestadis/index.htm.

304.6 PRT ISSN 0377-2284
HA1571
ESTATISTICAS DEMOGRAFICAS. Text in Portuguese. 1885. a. EUR 23 (effective 2005). **Document type:** *Government.* **Description:** Provides population estimations and vital statistics.
Published by: Instituto Nacional de Estatistica, Av Antonio Jose de Almeida 2, Lisbon, 1000-043, Portugal. TEL 351-21-8426100, FAX 351-21-8426380, http://www.ine.pt.

304.6021 PRT ISSN 1647-1741
ESTATISTICAS EM SINTESE. BALANCO SOCIAL. Text in Portuguese. 2008. **Document type:** *Report, Government.*
Media: Online - full text.
Published by: Ministerio do Trabalho e da Solidariedade Social, Praca de Londres 2, Lisbon, 1049-056, Portugal. TEL 351-21-8424100, FAX 351-21-8424108, gmtss@mtss.gov.pt, http://www.mtss.gov.pt/.

304.6021 PRT ISSN 1647-175X
ESTATISTICAS EM SINTESE. DEMOGRAFIA DE EMPRESAS, FLUXOS DE EMPREGO. Text in Portuguese. 2008. **Document type:** *Report, Government.*
Media: Online - full text.
Published by: Ministerio do Trabalho e da Solidariedade Social, Praca de Londres 2, Lisbon, 1049-056, Portugal. TEL 351-21-8424100, FAX 351-21-8424108, gmtss@mtss.gov.pt, http://www.mtss.gov.pt/.

304.6021 PRT ISSN 1647-1776
ESTATISTICAS EM SINTESE. GREVES. Text in Portuguese. 2008. **Document type:** *Report, Government.*
Media: Online - full text.
Published by: Ministerio do Trabalho e da Solidariedade Social, Praca de Londres 2, Lisbon, 1049-056, Portugal. TEL 351-21-8424100, FAX 351-21-8424108, gmtss@mtss.gov.pt, http://www.mtss.gov.pt/.

304.6021 PRT ISSN 1647-1784
ESTATISTICAS EM SINTESE. INQUERITO A EXECUCAO DAS ACCOES DE FORMACAO PROFISSIONAL. Text in Portuguese. 2006. **Document type:** *Report, Government.*
Media: Online - full text.
Published by: Ministerio do Trabalho e da Solidariedade Social, Praca de Londres 2, Lisbon, 1049-056, Portugal. TEL 351-21-8424100, FAX 351-21-8424108, gmtss@mtss.gov.pt, http://www.mtss.gov.pt/.

304.6021 PRT ISSN 1647-1806
ESTATISTICAS EM SINTESE. INQUERITO AO EMPREGO NO SECTOR ESTRUTURADO. Text in Portuguese. 2007. **Document type:** *Report, Government.*
Media: Online - full text.
Published by: Ministerio do Trabalho e da Solidariedade Social, Praca de Londres 2, Lisbon, 1049-056, Portugal. TEL 351-21-8424100, FAX 351-21-8424108, gmtss@mtss.gov.pt, http://www.mtss.gov.pt/.

304.6021 PRT ISSN 1647-1822
▼ **ESTATISTICAS EM SINTESE. INQUERITO AOS SALARIOS POR PROFISSOES NA CONTRUCAO.** Text in Portuguese. 2009. **Document type:** *Report, Government.*
Media: Online - full text.
Published by: Ministerio do Trabalho e da Solidariedade Social, Praca de Londres 2, Lisbon, 1049-056, Portugal. TEL 351-21-8424100, FAX 351-21-8424108, gmtss@mtss.gov.pt, http://www.mtss.gov.pt/.

304.6021 PRT ISSN 1647-1814
ESTATISTICAS EM SINTESE. MOBILIDADE DOS TRABALHADORES EM PORTUGAL. Text in Portuguese. 2007. **Document type:** *Report, Government.*
Media: Online - full text.
Published by: Ministerio do Trabalho e da Solidariedade Social, Praca de Londres 2, Lisbon, 1049-056, Portugal. TEL 351-21-8424100, FAX 351-21-8424108, gmtss@mtss.gov.pt, http://www.mtss.gov.pt/.

304.6021 PRT ISSN 1647-1768
ESTATISTICAS EM SINTESE. QUADROS DE PESSOAL. Text in Portuguese. 2008. **Document type:** *Report, Government.*
Media: Online - full text.
Published by: Ministerio do Trabalho e da Solidariedade Social, Praca de Londres 2, Lisbon, 1049-056, Portugal. TEL 351-21-8424100, FAX 351-21-8424108, gmtss@mtss.gov.pt, http://www.mtss.gov.pt/.

304.6021 PRT ISSN 1647-2209
ESTATISTICAS EM SINTESE. SEGURANCA, HIGIENE E SAUDE NO TRABALHO. Text in Portuguese. 2007. **Document type:** *Report, Government.*
Published by: Ministerio do Trabalho e da Solidariedade Social, Praca de Londres 2, Lisbon, 1049-056, Portugal. TEL 351-21-8424100, FAX 351-21-8424108, gmtss@mtss.gov.pt, http://www.mtss.gov.pt/.

325.021 RUS
ESTESTVENNOE DVIZHENIE NASELENIYA ROSSIISKOI FEDERATSII. Text in Russian. q. RUR 220 per issue (effective 2005). **Document type:** *Bulletin, Government.* **Description:** Contains statistical data on the natural migration of the Russian population.
Published by: Gosudarstvennyi Komitet Rossiiskoi Federatsii po Statistike/Federal State Statistics Office, ul Myasnitskaya 39, Moscow, 107450, Russian Federation. TEL 7-095-2074902, FAX 7-095-2074087, stat@gks.ru, http://www.gks.ru.

304.6021 CAN ISSN 1911-2416
ESTIMATIONS DEMOGRAPHIQUES ANNUELLES, CANADA, PROVINCES ET TERRITOIRES. Text in French. 2006. a. **Document type:** *Government.*
Media: Online - full text.
Published by: (Statistics Canada, Demography Division), Statistics Canada/Statistique Canada, Communications Division, 3rd Fl, R H Coats Bldg, Ottawa, ON K1A 0A6, Canada. infostats@statcan.ca, http://www.statcan.gc.ca.

304.6 PRT ISSN 0871-875X
ESTUDOS DEMOGRAFICOS. Text in Portuguese. 1945. s-a. EUR 32 (effective 2005).
Formerly (until 1991): Portugal. Instituto Nacional de Estatistica. Centro de Estudos Demograficos. Revista (0079-4082)
Indexed: IBR, IBZ, P30, PAIS, PopulInd.
Published by: Instituto Nacional de Estatistica, Av Antonio Jose de Almeida 2, Lisbon, 1000-043, Portugal. TEL 351-21-8426100, FAX 351-21-8426380, ine@ine.pt, http://www.ine.pt.

304.6 NLD ISSN 0168-6577
Z7164.D3
➤ **EUROPEAN JOURNAL OF POPULATION/REVUE EUROPEENNE DE DEMOGRAPHIE.** Text and summaries in English, French. 1970-1983; resumed 1985. q. EUR 682, USD 716 combined subscription to institutions (print & online eds.) (effective 2012). adv. bk.rev. illus. index. back issues avail.; reprint service avail. from PSC. **Document type:** *Journal, Academic/Scholarly.* **Description:** Reports and analyzes demographic experiences, including theoretical explanations, research strategies and policy implications.
Formerly (until 1983): European Demographic Information Bulletin (0046-2756)
Related titles: Online - full text ed.: ISSN 1572-9885 (from IngentaConnect).
Indexed: A12, A20, A22, A26, A36, ABIn, ASCA, BibLing, CA, CABA, CurCont, DIP, E01, E12, ERA, ESPM, Faml, GEOBASE, GH, H01, HPNRM, I05, IBR, IBSS, IBZ, N02, P06, P10, P21, P27, P30, P45, P46, P47, P48, P50, P51, P52, P53, P54, P56, PAIS, PCI, PQC, PopulInd, R12, RefZh, S02, S03, S11, S21, SCOPUS, SFSA, SOPODA, SSA, SSCI, SSciA, SociolAb, T02, T05, TAR, W07, W09, W11.
—BLDSC (3829.737500), IE, Infotrieve, Ingenta, INIST. **CCC.**
Published by: (European Association for Population Studies), Springer Netherlands (Subsidiary of: Springer Science+Business Media), Van Godewijckstraat 30, Dordrecht, 3311 GX, Netherlands. TEL 31-78-6576050, FAX 31-78-6576474, http://www.springer.com. Eds. Hill Kulu, Myriam Khlat.

➤ **EUROSTAT STATISTICS IN FOCUS. POPULATION AND SOCIAL CONDITIONS.** *see* BUSINESS AND ECONOMICS—Abstracting, Bibliographies, Statistics

➤ **EUROSTAT STATISTIK KURZ GEFASST. BEVOELKERUNG UND SOZIALE BEDINGUNGEN.** *see* BUSINESS AND ECONOMICS—Abstracting, Bibliographies, Statistics

➤ **EUROSTAT STATISTIQUES EN BREF. POPULATION ET CONDITIONS SOCIALES.** *see* BUSINESS AND ECONOMICS—Abstracting, Bibliographies, Statistics

304.6 BRA ISSN 0103-4731
FAMILIA; indicadores sociais. Text in Portuguese. 1981. a. **Document type:** *Government.*
Published by: Fundacao Instituto Brasileiro de Geografia e Estatistica, Centro de Documentacao e Disseminacao de Informacoes, Rua General Canabarro, 706 Andar 2, Maracana, Rio de Janeiro, RJ 20271-201, Brazil. TEL 55-21-2645424, FAX 55-21-2841959.

304.6 FJI
FIJI. BUREAU OF STATISTICS. FIJI FERTILITY SURVEY. Text in English. 1974. irreg. USD 5 per issue (effective 2000). **Document type:** *Government.*
Published by: Bureau of Statistics, c/o Librarian, Govt. Bldg. 5, PO Box 2221, Suva, Fiji. TEL 679-315-822, FAX 679-303-656.

304.6 FJI
FIJI. BUREAU OF STATISTICS. POPULATION OF FIJI; monograph for the U N World population. Text in English. 1974. irreg. free. **Document type:** *Monographic series, Government.*
Published by: Bureau of Statistics, c/o Librarian, Govt. Bldg. 5, PO Box 2221, Suva, Fiji. TEL 679-315-822, FAX 679-303-656.

FIJI. BUREAU OF STATISTICS. TOURISM AND MIGRATION STATISTICS. *see* TRAVEL AND TOURISM—Abstracting, Bibliographies, Statistics

304.644897 FIN ISSN 0787-0132
FINLAND. TILASTOKESKUS. KUOLEMANSYYT/FINLAND. STATISTICS FINLAND. CAUSES OF DEATH/FINLAND. STATISTIKCENTRALEN. DOEDSORSAKER. Text in English, Finnish, Swedish. 1949. a. EUR 30 (effective 2008). **Document type:** *Government.*
Formerly (until 1988): Sluomen Virallinen Tilasto. 6 B, Kuolemansyyt (0355-2144)
Related titles: Online - full text ed.; ◆ Series of: Finland. Tilastokeskus. Suomen Virallinen Tilasto. ISSN 1795-5165.
Published by: Tilastokeskus/Statistics Finland, Tyopajakatu 13, Statistics Finland, Helsinki, 00022, Finland. TEL 358-9-17341, FAX 358-9-17342279, http://www.stat.fi.

304.6021 FIN ISSN 0785-8205
HB3608.3.A3
FINLAND. TILASTOKESKUS. PERHEET/FINLAND. STATISTICS FINLAND. FAMILIES/FINLAND. STATISTIKCENTRALEN. FAMILJER. Text in English, Finnish, Swedish. 1968. a. EUR 29 (effective 2008). **Document type:** *Government.*
Supersedes in part (in 1989): Finland. Tilastokeskus. Tilastotiedotus - Tilastokeskus. VA, Vaesto (0355-2365)
Related titles: ◆ Series of: Finland. Tilastokeskus. Suomen Virallinen Tilasto. ISSN 1795-5165.
Published by: Tilastokeskus/Statistics Finland, Tyopajakatu 13, Statistics Finland, Helsinki, 00022, Finland. TEL 358-9-17341, FAX 358-9-17342279.

304.6021 FIN ISSN 1239-9663
JV8192.
FINLAND. TILASTOKESKUS. ULKOMAALAISET JA SIIRTOLAISUUS/ FINLAND. STATISTICS FINLAND. ALIENS AND INTERNATIONAL MIGRATION. Text in English, Finnish. 1996. a. **Document type:** *Government.*
Related titles: ◆ Series of: Finland. Tilastokeskus. Suomen Virallinen Tilasto. ISSN 1795-5165.
Published by: Tilastokeskus/Statistics Finland, Tyopajakatu 13, Statistics Finland, Helsinki, 00022, Finland. TEL 358-9-17341, FAX 358-9-17342279, http://www.stat.fi.

403.6021 FIN ISSN 1236-5483
FINLAND. TILASTOKESKUS. VAESTOENNUSTEET/FINLAND. STATISTICS FINLAND. POPULATION PROJECTION/FINLAND. STATISTIKCENTRALEN. BEFOLKNINGSPROGNOSER. Text in English, Finnish, Swedish. 1993. triennial, latest 2007. **Document type:** *Government.*
Related titles: Online - full text ed.; ◆ Series: Finland. Tilastokeskus. Suomen Virallinen Tilasto. ISSN 1795-5165.
Published by: Tilastokeskus/Statistics Finland, Tyopajakatu 13, Statistics Finland, Helsinki, 00022, Finland. TEL 358-9-17341, FAX 358-9-17342279.

304.6021 FIN ISSN 0788-5245
HA1450.5.A1
FINLAND. TILASTOKESKUS. VAESTONMUUTOKSET/FINLAND. STATISTICS FINLAND. VITAL STATISTICS/FINLAND. STATISTIKCENTRALEN. BEFOLKNINGSROERELSEN. Text in English, Finnish, Swedish. 1948. a. EUR 29 (effective 2008). **Document type:** *Government.*
Former titles (until 1990): Finland. Tilastokeskus. Vaestorakenne ja Vaestonmuutokset (0785-4803); (until 1988): Suomen Virallinen Tilasto. 6A, Vaestonmuutokset (0430-5612); (until 1975): Suomen Virallinen Tilasto. 6A, Vaesto (0355-2128)
Published by: Tilastokeskus/Statistics Finland, Tyopajakatu 13, Statistics Finland, Helsinki, 00022, Finland. TEL 358-9-17341, FAX 358-9-17342279, http://www.stat.fi.

304.6021 FIN ISSN 1795-1887
HA1450.5
FINLAND. TILASTOKESKUS. VAESTORAKENNE JA VAESTONMUUTOKSET KUNNITTAIN/FINLAND. STATISTICS FINLAND. POPULATION STRUCTURE AND VITAL STATISTICS BY MUNICIPALITY/FINLAND. STATISTIKCENTRALEN. BEFOLKNINGENS SAMMANSAETTNING OCH BEFOLKNINGSFOERAENDRINGAR KOMMUNVIS. Text in English, Finnish, Swedish. 2004. a. **Document type:** *Government.*
Formed by the merger of (1990-2004): Finland Tilastokeskus. Vaestorakenne (0788-5237); Which superseded in part (in 1990): Finland. Tilastokeskus. Vaestorakenne ja Vaestonmuutokset (0785-4803); (1955-2004): Finland. Tilastokeskus. Vaestonmuutokset Kunnittain (0785-479X); Which superseded in part (in 1988): Finland. Tilastokeskus. Suomen Virallinen Tilasto. 6 A 3. Vaestonmuutokset Kunnittain (0430-5612)
Related titles: Online - full text ed.; ◆ Series of: Finland. Tilastokeskus. Suomen Virallinen Tilasto. ISSN 1795-5165.
Published by: Tilastokeskus/Statistics Finland, Tyopajakatu 13, Statistics Finland, Helsinki, 00022, Finland. TEL 358-9-17341, FAX 358-9-17342279.

304.6 USA
FLORIDA COUNTY RANKINGS. Text in English. 1994. a. USD 60 per issue (effective 2011). maps; stat. back issues avail. **Document type:** *Magazine, Consumer.* **Description:** Summarizes more than 500 ranked county statistical data items, including population, housing, and vital statistics.
Related titles: CD-ROM ed.: USD 50 per issue (effective 2011); E-mail ed.: USD 40 per issue (print or online ed.) (effective 2011); Online - full text ed.
Published by: University of Florida, Bureau of Economic and Business Research, 221 Matherly Hall, PO Box 117145, Gainesville, FL 32611. TEL 352-392-0171, FAX 352-392-4739, info@bebr.ufl.edu.

P

304.6 USA ISSN 1524-234X
HB3525.F6
FLORIDA ESTIMATES OF POPULATION (YEAR). Text in English. 1998. a. maps; stat. back issues avail. **Document type:** *Journal, Government.* **Description:** Contains estimates of resident population as of April 1st for the most recent year for Florida, its cities and counties. Also includes components of population growth and institutional populations.
Formerly (until 1987): Florida Estimates of Population, State, Counties, and Municipalities (0145-4668)
Related titles: Diskette ed.
Published by: (Bureau of Economic and Business Research), University of Florida, Office of the President, 226 Tigert Hall, PO Box 113150, Gainesville, FL 32611. TEL 352-392-1311, FAX 352-392-9506, http://www.ufl.edu/.

304.6 USA
FLORIDA POPULATION PROJECTIONS: AGE, SEX, RACE AND HISPANIC ORIGIN. Text in English. 1989. a. USD 50 per issue (effective 2011). stat. back issues avail. **Document type:** *Government.* **Description:** Provides the demographic breakdown for Florida county resident population through the year 2020. Data are given for five-year age groups by race (black and white only) and sex.
Related titles: CD-ROM ed.: USD 45 per issue (effective 2011); E-mail ed.: USD 40 per issue (print or online ed.) (effective 2011); Online - full text ed.
Published by: University of Florida, Bureau of Economic and Business Research, 221 Matherly Hall, PO Box 117145, Gainesville, FL 32611. TEL 352-392-0171, FAX 352-392-4739, info@bebr.ufl.edu.

310 USA
FLORIDA VITAL STATISTICS. Text in English. 1935. a. first copy free. charts. **Document type:** *Government.* **Description:** Contains data compiled from original records of live births, deaths, fetal deaths, marriages, and dissolutions of marriage. Includes current population figures, extensive analyses of causes of death and historical trends.
Indexed: SRI.
Published by: Florida Department of Health, Bureau of Vital Statistics, Quality Assurance Unit, PO Box 210, Jacksonville, FL 32231-0042. TEL 904-359-6960, FAX 904-359-6697. Circ: 1,500.

▼ **GEMEENTE AMSTERDAM. DIENST ONDERZOEK EN STATISTIEK. METROPOOLREGIO AMSTERDAM IN CIJFERS.** *see* BUSINESS AND ECONOMICS

304.6 USA
GEOGRAPHICAL MOBILITY. Text in English. a. stat. **Document type:** *Government.*
Media: Online - full text.
Published by: U.S. Census Bureau. Housing and Household Economic Statistics Division. Journey-To-Work & Migration Statistics Branch (Subsidiary of: U.S. Department of Commerce) TEL 866-758-1060, http://www.census.gov/population/www/socdemo/journey.html.

304.6 USA
GEORGIA VITAL STATISTICS REPORT (ONLINE EDITION). Text in English. 1947. a. free. back issues avail. **Document type:** *Government.* **Description:** Disseminates selected information by race and age on births, deaths, marriages, divorces, abortions and projected populations for the calendar year.
Former titles: Georgia Vital Statistics Report (Print Edition); (until 1983): Georgia Vital Statistics Data Book; Georgia Vital and Health Statistics (0362-0662); Georgia Vital Morbidity Statistics (0072-1379)
Media: Online - full text.
Indexed: SRI.
Published by: Department of Human Resources, Division of Public Health, 2 Peachtree St, S W, Ste 3 522, Atlanta, GA 30303-3186. TEL 404-657-6300, gdphinfo@ph.dhr.state.ga.us, http://www.ph.dhr.state.ga.us. R&P Wilma Barshaw. Circ: 650 (controlled).

330.9 GHA
GHANA. STATISTICAL SERVICE. POPULATION CENSUS - DEMOGRAPHIC AND ECONOMIC CHARACTERISTICS. Text in English. irreg., latest 1984. USD 90. **Document type:** *Government.*
Published by: Statistical Service, Information Section, PO Box 1098, Accra, Ghana. TEL 233-21-663758, FAX 233-21-667069.

330.9 GHA
GHANA. STATISTICAL SERVICE. POPULATION CENSUS - SPECIAL REPORT ON LOCALITIES. (Comprises 10 regional vols.) Text in English. irreg., latest 1984. USD 75 for 10-vol. set. **Document type:** *Government.*
Published by: Statistical Service, Information Section, PO Box 1098, Accra, Ghana. TEL 233-21-663758, FAX 233-21-667069.

306.0941 GBR ISSN 1754-4777
GREAT BRITAIN. GENERAL HOUSEHOLD SURVEY. Variant title: General Household Survey. Text in English. 1973. a. **Document type:** *Government.*
Former titles (until 2003): Living in Britain (1469-2759); (until 1994): Great Britain. General Household Survey (0952-1003)
Related titles: Online - full text ed.
—BLDSC (4104.345300).
Published by: (Great Britain. Office for National Statistics), Dandy Booksellers Ltd., Units 3 & 4, 31-33 Priory Park Rd, London, NW6 7UP, United Kingdom. TEL 44-20-76242993, FAX 44-20-76245049, enquiries@dandybooksellers.com, http://www.dandybooksellers.com.

304.63021 GBR ISSN 0140-2587
HB993
GREAT BRITAIN. GOVERNMENT STATISTICAL SERVICE. BIRTH STATISTICS. ENGLAND AND WALES. Variant title: Great Britain. Government Statistical Service. Series FM1. Birth Statistics. England and Wales. Text in English. 1974. a., latest vol.38, 2008. stat. back issues avail. **Document type:** *Government.* **Description:** Presents statistics on live births and stillbirths occurring annually in England and Wales.
Supersedes in part (in 1977): Registrar General's Statistical Review of England and Wales
Related titles: Online - full text ed.: free (effective 2010).
—BLDSC (2094.092900).
Published by: (Great Britain. Office of Population Censuses and Surveys), Office for National Statistics, Rm 1.101, Government Bldgs, Cardiff Rd, Newport, S Wales NP10 8XG, United Kingdom. TEL 44-1633-653599, FAX 44-1633-652747, info@statistics.gov.uk, http://www.statistics.gov.uk/default.asp. **Subscr. to:** Palgrave Macmillan Ltd., Subscription Department, Brunel Rd, Houndmills, Basingstoke, Hants RG21 2XS, United Kingdom. TEL 44-1256-357893, FAX 44-1256-328339.

304.640942 GBR ISSN 2040-252X
GREAT BRITAIN. OFFICE FOR NATIONAL STATISTICS. MORTALITY STATISTICS. DEATHS REGISTERED IN (YEAR); review of the registrar general on deaths in England and Wales (Year). Text in English. 2006. a. **Document type:** *Government.* **Description:** Contains data for death rates, cause of death data by sex and age and death registrations by area of residence.
Formed by the merger of (1977-2005): Great Britain. Office for National Statistics. Mortality Statistics. Cause (0265-9670); (1987-2005): Great Britain. Office for National Statistics. Mortality Statistics. General (1469-2805); Which was formerly (1977-1987): Great Britain. HMSO. Mortality Statistics. (0265-9662); (1992-2005): Great Britain. Office for National Statistics. Mortality Statistics. Injury and Poisoning (1469-2791); Which was formerly (1976-1991): Great Britain. HMSO. Mortality Statistics. Accidents and Violence (0267-176X)
Related titles: Online - full text ed.: ISSN 1757-1375.
—BLDSC (5967.453040).
Published by: Office for National Statistics, Rm 1.101, Government Bldgs, Cardiff Rd, Newport, S Wales NP10 8XG, United Kingdom. TEL 44-845-6013034, FAX 44-1633-652747, info@statistics.gsi.gov.uk, http://www.statistics.gov.uk/default.asp.

304.6 GRL ISSN 0904-6860
HA740
GREENLAND. GROENLANDS STATISTIK. BEFOLKNING. Text in Danish. 1989. a. **Description:** Statistics about the population of Greenland.
Related titles: ◆ Series: Greenland. Groenlands Statistik. Befolkningens Bevaegelser. ISSN 1397-6966; ◆ Greenland. Groenlands Statistik. Groenlands Befolkning. ISSN 0105-0885.
Published by: Groenlands Statistik/Kalaallit Nunaanni Naatsorsueqqissaartarfik, PO Box 1025, Nuuk, 3900, Greenland. TEL 299-345564, FAX 299-322954.

304.6 GRL ISSN 1397-6966
GREENLAND. GROENLANDS STATISTIK. BEFOLKNINGENS BEVAEGELSER/INNUTTAASUT NIKERANERAT. Text in Multiple languages. 1996. a. **Document type:** *Government.*
Related titles: ◆ Series of: Greenland. Groenlands Statistik. Befolkning. ISSN 0904-6860.
Published by: Groenlands Statistik/Kalaallit Nunaanni Naatsorsueqqissaartarfik, PO Box 1025, Nuuk, 3900, Greenland. TEL 299-345564, FAX 299-322954.

325 USA ISSN 0271-0684
H I A S STATISTICAL ABSTRACT. (Hebrew Immigrant Aid Society) Text in English. 1973 (vol.14). a. free. charts. **Document type:** *Abstract/Index.*
Indexed: RefugAb.
Published by: H I A S Inc., 333 Seventh Ave, 16th Fl, New York, NY 10001-5004. TEL 212-967-4100, FAX 212-967-4483, info@hias.org, http://www.hias.org. Circ: 1,000.

304.6 KOR ISSN 0075-6873
HA4630.5
HAN'GUG TONG'GYE YEON'GAM/KOREA STATISTICAL YEARBOOK. Text in English, Korean. 1952. a. USD 32 newsstand/cover (effective 2009). **Document type:** *Yearbook, Government.* **Description:** Contains statistical tables including time-series data of 10 or more years compiled by National Statistical Office, other Ministries of the Government and other institutes in Korea.
Formerly (until 1961): Daihan Mingug Tongyei Nyengam (0253-3014)
Related titles: CD-ROM ed.: ISSN 1599-0958. 1999; Online - full text ed.: ISSN 2005-5269. 2008.
Published by: Tong'gyecheong/Korea National Statistical Office, Government Complex Daejeon, 139 Seonsaro (920 Dunsan 2-dong), Seo-gu, Daejeon, 302-701, Korea, S. TEL 82-42-4814114. **Subscr. to:** The Korean Statistical Association, Rm. 103, Seoul Statistical Branch Office Bldg. 71, Nonhyun-Dong, Kangnam-Ku, Seoul 135701, Korea, S. TEL 82-2-34437954, FAX 82-2-34437957, kosa@nso.go.kr.

304.6 KOR ISSN 1599-0907
HN730.5.A85
HAN'GUG UI SAHOE JI'PYO/KOREA (REPUBLIC). NATIONAL STATISTICAL OFFICE. SOCIAL INDICATORS IN KOREA. Text in English, Korean. 1979. a. USD 18 newsstand/cover (effective 2009). **Document type:** *Government.*
Published by: Tong'gyecheong/Korea National Statistical Office, Government Complex Daejeon, 139 Seonsaro (920 Dunsan 2-dong), Seo-gu, Daejeon, 302-701, Korea, S. TEL 82-42-4814114. **Subscr. to:** The Korean Statistical Association, Rm. 103, Seoul Statistical Branch Office Bldg. 71, Nonhyun-Dong, Kangnam-Ku, Seoul 135701, Korea, S. TEL 82-2-34437954, FAX 82-2-34437957, kosa@nso.go.kr.

304.6 USA ISSN 0093-3481
HB3525.H3
HAWAII. DEPARTMENT OF HEALTH. RESEARCH AND STATISTICS OFFICE. R & S REPORT. Key Title: R & S Report (Honolulu). Text in English. 1973. irreg. free. stat. **Document type:** *Government.*
Indexed: P30.
Published by: Department of Health, PO Box 3378, Honolulu, HI 96801. TEL 808-586-4600, FAX 808-586-4606, http://www.hawaii.gov/healthstatistics.

304.6021 PRT ISSN 1646-4060
HOMENS E MULHERES EM PORTUGAL. Text in Portuguese. 2006. irreg. **Document type:** *Report, Government.*
Published by: Instituto Nacional de Estatistica, Av Antonio Jose de Almeida 2, Lisbon, 1000-043, Portugal. TEL 351-21-8426100, FAX 351-21-8426380, ine@ine.pt, http://www.ine.pt.

304.6 331.1 330 HKG ISSN 1011-4033
HONG KONG ANNUAL DIGEST OF STATISTICS. Text in Chinese, English. 1978. a., latest 2000. HKD 68 newsstand/cover (effective 2002). maps; stat. back issues avail. **Document type:** *Government.* **Description:** Provides detailed annual statistical series on various aspects of the social and economic development of Hong Kong. Most of the data is presented for seven years, spanning a period of ten years.
Related titles: Online - full text ed.
Published by: Census and Statistics Department/Zhengfu Tongjichu, General Statistics Section 1(B), 19/F Wanchai Tower, 12 Harbour Rd, Wan Chai, Hong Kong. TEL 852-2582-4068, FAX 852-2827-1708, genenq@censtatd.gov.hk, http://www.statisticalbookstore.gov.hk, http://www.info.gov.hk/censtatd. **Subscr. to:** Information Services Department, Publications Sales Unit, Rm 402, 4th Fl, Murray Bldg, Garden Rd, Hong Kong, Hong Kong. TEL 852-2842-8844, FAX 852-2598-7482, puborder@isd.gcn.gov.hk, http://www.info.gov.hk/isd/book_e.htm. **Dist. by:** Government Publications Centre, Low Block, Ground Fl, Queensway Government Offices, 66 Queensway, Hong Kong, Hong Kong. TEL 852-2537-1910, FAX 852-2523-7195.

304.6 HKG ISSN 0300-418X
HA1950.H6
HONG KONG MONTHLY DIGEST OF STATISTICS. Text in Chinese, English. 1970. m. HKD 576; HKD 48 newsstand/cover (effective 2002). stat. back issues avail. **Document type:** *Government.* **Description:** Contains a collection of up-to-date statistical series on various aspects of the social and economic situation of Hong Kong. Statistics are presented whenever possible in the form of monthly figures for the latest fifteen months for which data are available, together with annual figures for the latest three complete years.
Related titles: Online - full text ed.
Indexed: P30, SCOPUS.
Published by: Census and Statistics Department/Zhengfu Tongjichu, General Statistics Section 1(B), 19/F Wanchai Tower, 12 Harbour Rd, Wan Chai, Hong Kong. TEL 852-2582-4068, FAX 852-2827-1708, genenq@censtatd.gov.hk, http://www.info.gov.hk/censtatd, http://www.statisticalbookstore.gov.hk. Circ: 2,000. **Subscr. to:** Information Services Department, Publications Sales Unit, Rm 402, 4th Fl, Murray Bldg, Garden Rd, Hong Kong, Hong Kong. TEL 852-2842-8844, FAX 852-2598-7482, puborder@isd.gcn.gov.hk, http://www.info.gov.hk/isd/book_e.htm; Government Publications Centre.

304.6021 HKG
HONG KONG SPECIAL ADMINISTRATIVE REGION OF CHINA. CENSUS AND STATISTICS DEPARTMENT. AN OUTLINE OF STATISTICAL DEVELOPMENT. Text in Chinese, English. 1973. a. HKD 84 newsstand/cover (effective 2001). stat. **Document type:** *Government.* **Description:** Provides an updated account of the work and development of the Government Statistical Service (GSS), which comprises the Census and Statistics Department (C&SD) and statistical units in various government departments and policy bureaux. A concise description is given on the organization of the GSS, work of the C&SD, statistical legislation and data dissemination methods. Details are given on recent statistical development in a number of economic and social areas of interest to the public.
Related titles: Online - full content ed.
Published by: Census and Statistics Department/Zhengfu Tongjichu, General Statistics Section 1(A), 19/F Wanchai Tower, 12 Harbour Rd, Wan Chai, Hong Kong. TEL 852-2582-4661, FAX 852-2827-1708, genenq@censtatd.gov.hk, http://www.info.gov.hk/censtatd, http://www.statisticalbookstore.gov.hk. **Subscr. to:** Information Services Department, Publications Sales Unit, Rm 402, 4th Fl, Murray Bldg, Garden Rd, Hong Kong, Hong Kong. TEL 852-2842-8844, FAX 852-2598-7482, puborder@isd.gcn.gov.hk, http://www.info.gov.hk/isd/book_e.htm. **Dist. by:** Government Publications Centre, Low Block, Ground Fl, Queensway Government Offices, 66 Queensway, Hong Kong, Hong Kong. TEL 852-2537-1910, FAX 852-2523-7195.

304.6 HKG
HONG KONG SPECIAL ADMINISTRATIVE REGION OF CHINA. CENSUS AND STATISTICS DEPARTMENT. HONG KONG (YEAR) POPULATION BY-CENSUS; tables for District Board districts and constituency areas: population by age and sex. Text in English. 1981. irreg., latest 1996. HKD 14 newsstand/cover (effective 2001). stat. back issues avail. **Document type:** *Government.* **Description:** Presents the final results of the Population By-census, containing information on resident population by age and sex in each District Board district and Constituency Area.
Related titles: Online - full content ed.; Chinese ed.
Published by: Census and Statistics Department/Zhengfu Tongjichu, Demographic Statistics Section, 7/F Kai Tak Multi-storey Carpark Bldg, 2 Concorde Rd, Kowloon, Hong Kong. TEL 852-2716-8345, FAX 852-2716-0231, demo_1@censtad.gov.hk, http://www.statisticalbookstore.gov.hk, http://www.info.gov.hk/censtatd. **Subscr. to:** Information Services Department, Publications Sales Unit, Rm 402, 4th Fl, Murray Bldg, Garden Rd, Hong Kong, Hong Kong. TEL 852-2842-8844, FAX 852-2598-7482, puborder@isd.gcn.gov.hk, http://www.info.gov.hk/isd/book_e.htm. **Dist. by:** Government Publications Centre, Low Block, Ground Fl, Queensway Government Offices, 66 Queensway, Hong Kong, Hong Kong. TEL 852-2537-1910, FAX 852-2523-7195.

304.6 HKG
HONG KONG SPECIAL ADMINISTRATIVE REGION OF CHINA. CENSUS AND STATISTICS DEPARTMENT. HONG KONG (YEAR) POPULATION BY-CENSUS. BASIC TABLES FOR CONSTITUENCY AREAS: HONG KONG ISLAND. Text in Chinese, English. a. stat. **Document type:** *Government.*
Published by: Census and Statistics Department/Zhengfu Tongjichu, Demographic Statistics Section, 7/F Kai Tak Multi-storey Carpark Bldg, 2 Concorde Rd, Kowloon, Hong Kong. TEL 852-2716-8345, FAX 852-2716-0231, demo_1@censtad.gov.hk, http://www.info.gov.hk/censtatd, http://www.statisticalbookstore.gov.hk. **Subscr. to:** Information Services Department, Publications Sales Unit, Rm 402, 4th Fl, Murray Bldg, Garden Rd, Hong Kong, Hong Kong. TEL 852-2842-8844, FAX 852-2598-7482, puborder@isd.gcn.gov.hk, http://www.info.gov.hk/isd/book_e.htm. **Dist. by:** Government Publications Centre, Low Block, Ground Fl, Queensway Government Offices, 66 Queensway, Hong Kong, Hong Kong. TEL 852-2537-1910, FAX 852-2523-7195.

304.6 HKG
HONG KONG SPECIAL ADMINISTRATIVE REGION OF CHINA. CENSUS AND STATISTICS DEPARTMENT. HONG KONG (YEAR) POPULATION BY-CENSUS. BASIC TABLES FOR CONSTITUENCY AREAS: KOWLOON. Text in Chinese, English. a., latest 2001. stat. **Document type:** *Government.*
Published by: Census and Statistics Department/Zhengfu Tongjichu, Demographic Statistics Section, 7/F Kai Tak Multi-storey Carpark Bldg, 2 Concorde Rd, Kowloon, Hong Kong. TEL 852-2716-8345, FAX 852-2716-0231, demo_1@censtad.gov.hk, http://www.info.gov.hk/censtatd, http://www.statisticalbookstore.gov.hk. **Subscr. to:** Information Services Department, Publications Sales Unit, Rm 402, 4th Fl, Murray Bldg, Garden Rd, Hong Kong, Hong Kong. TEL 852-2842-8844, FAX 852-2598-7482, puborder@isd.gcn.gov.hk, http://www.info.gov.hk/isd/book_e.htm. **Dist. by:** Government Publications Centre, Low Block, Ground Fl, Queensway Government Offices, 66 Queensway, Hong Kong, Hong Kong. TEL 852-2537-1910, FAX 852-2523-7195.

304.6 HKG
HONG KONG SPECIAL ADMINISTRATIVE REGION OF CHINA. CENSUS AND STATISTICS DEPARTMENT. HONG KONG (YEAR) POPULATION BY-CENSUS. BASIC TABLES FOR CONSTITUENCY AREAS: NEW TERRITORIES. Text in Chinese, English. a., latest 2001. stat. **Document type:** *Government.*
Published by: Census and Statistics Department/Zhengfu Tongjichu, Demographic Statistics Section, 7/F Kai Tak Multi-storey Carpark Bldg, 2 Concorde Rd, Kowloon, Hong Kong. TEL 852-2716-8345, FAX 852-2716-0231, demo_1@censtad.gov.hk, http://www.info.gov.hk/censtatd, http://www.statisticalbookstore.gov.hk. **Subscr. to:** Information Services Department, Publications Sales Unit, Rm 402, 4th Fl, Murray Bldg, Garden Rd, Hong Kong, Hong Kong. TEL 852-2842-8844, FAX 852-2598-7482, puborder@isd.gcn.gov.hk, http://www.info.gov.hk/isd/book_e.htm. **Dist. by:** Government Publications Centre, Low Block, Ground Fl, Queensway Government Offices, 66 Queensway, Hong Kong, Hong Kong. TEL 852-2537-1910, FAX 852-2523-7195.

304.6 HKG
HONG KONG SPECIAL ADMINISTRATIVE REGION OF CHINA. CENSUS AND STATISTICS DEPARTMENT. HONG KONG (YEAR) POPULATION BY-CENSUS. BASIC TABLES FOR DISTRICT BOARD DISTRICTS. Text in English. irreg., latest 1996. stat. **Document type:** *Government.*
Published by: Census and Statistics Department/Zhengfu Tongjichu, Demographic Statistics Section, 7/F Kai Tak Multi-storey Carpark Bldg, 2 Concorde Rd, Kowloon, Hong Kong. TEL 852-2716-8345, FAX 852-2716-0231, genenq@censtatd.gov.hk, demo_1@censtad.gov.hk, http://www.statisticalbookstore.gov.hk, http://www.info.gov.hk/censtatd.

304.6 HKG
HONG KONG SPECIAL ADMINISTRATIVE REGION OF CHINA. CENSUS AND STATISTICS DEPARTMENT. HONG KONG (YEAR) POPULATION BY-CENSUS. BASIC TABLES FOR TERTIARY PLANNING UNITS: HONG KONG ISLAND. Text in English. irreg., latest 1996. stat. **Document type:** *Government.*
Published by: Census and Statistics Department/Zhengfu Tongjichu, Demographic Statistics Section, 7/F Kai Tak Multi-storey Carpark Bldg, 2 Concorde Rd, Kowloon, Hong Kong. TEL 852-2716-8345, FAX 852-2716-0231, genenq@censtatd.gov.hk, demo_1@censtad.gov.hk, http://www.statisticalbookstore.gov.hk, http://www.info.gov.hk/censtatd.

304.6 HKG
HONG KONG SPECIAL ADMINISTRATIVE REGION OF CHINA. CENSUS AND STATISTICS DEPARTMENT. HONG KONG (YEAR) POPULATION BY-CENSUS. BASIC TABLES FOR TERTIARY PLANNING UNITS: KOWLOON. Text in English. irreg., latest 1996. stat. **Document type:** *Government.*
Published by: Census and Statistics Department/Zhengfu Tongjichu, Demographic Statistics Section, 7/F Kai Tak Multi-storey Carpark Bldg, 2 Concorde Rd, Kowloon, Hong Kong. TEL 852-2716-8345, FAX 852-2716-0231, genenq@censtatd.gov.hk, demo_1@censtad.gov.hk, http://www.statisticalbookstore.gov.hk, http://www.info.gov.hk/censtatd.

304.6 HKG
HONG KONG SPECIAL ADMINISTRATIVE REGION OF CHINA. CENSUS AND STATISTICS DEPARTMENT. HONG KONG (YEAR) POPULATION BY-CENSUS. BASIC TABLES FOR TERTIARY PLANNING UNITS: NEW TERRITORIES. Text in English. irreg., latest 1996. stat. **Document type:** *Government.*
Published by: Census and Statistics Department/Zhengfu Tongjichu, Demographic Statistics Section, 7/F Kai Tak Multi-storey Carpark Bldg, 2 Concorde Rd, Kowloon, Hong Kong. TEL 852-2716-8345, FAX 852-2716-0231, genenq@censtatd.gov.hk, demo_1@censtad.gov.hk, http://www.statisticalbookstore.gov.hk, http://www.info.gov.hk/censtatd.

304.6 HKG
HONG KONG SPECIAL ADMINISTRATIVE REGION OF CHINA. CENSUS AND STATISTICS DEPARTMENT. HONG KONG (YEAR) POPULATION BY-CENSUS. BOUNDARY MAPS COMPLEMENTARY TO TABLES FOR DISTRICT BOARD DISTRICTS AND CONSTITUENCY AREAS. Text in English. irreg., latest 1996. stat.; maps. **Document type:** *Government.*
Published by: Census and Statistics Department/Zhengfu Tongjichu, Demographic Statistics Section, 7/F Kai Tak Multi-storey Carpark Bldg, 2 Concorde Rd, Kowloon, Hong Kong. TEL 852-2716-8345, FAX 852-2716-0231, genenq@censtatd.gov.hk, demo_1@censtad.gov.hk, http://www.statisticalbookstore.gov.hk, http://www.info.gov.hk/censtatd.

304.6 HKG
HONG KONG SPECIAL ADMINISTRATIVE REGION OF CHINA. CENSUS AND STATISTICS DEPARTMENT. HONG KONG (YEAR) POPULATION BY-CENSUS. BOUNDARY MAPS COMPLEMENTARY TO TABLES FOR TERTIARY PLANNING UNITS AND CONSTITUENCY AREAS. Text in English. irreg., latest 1996. stat.; maps. **Document type:** *Government.*
Published by: Census and Statistics Department/Zhengfu Tongjichu, Demographic Statistics Section, 7/F Kai Tak Multi-storey Carpark Bldg, 2 Concorde Rd, Kowloon, Hong Kong. TEL 852-2716-8345, FAX 852-2716-0231, genenq@censtatd.gov.hk, demo_1@censtad.gov.hk, http://www.statisticalbookstore.gov.hk, http://www.info.gov.hk/censtatd.

304.6 HKG
HONG KONG SPECIAL ADMINISTRATIVE REGION OF CHINA. CENSUS AND STATISTICS DEPARTMENT. HONG KONG (YEAR) POPULATION BY-CENSUS. GRAPHIC GUIDE. Text in English. irreg., latest 1996. stat. **Document type:** *Government.*
Published by: Census and Statistics Department/Zhengfu Tongjichu, Demographic Statistics Section, 7/F Kai Tak Multi-storey Carpark Bldg, 2 Concorde Rd, Kowloon, Hong Kong. TEL 852-2716-8345, FAX 852-2716-0231, demo_1@censtad.gov.hk, genenq@censtatd.gov.hk, http://www.info.gov.hk/censtatd.

304.6 HKG
HONG KONG SPECIAL ADMINISTRATIVE REGION OF CHINA. CENSUS AND STATISTICS DEPARTMENT. HONG KONG (YEAR) POPULATION BY-CENSUS. MAIN REPORT. Text in English. irreg., latest 1996. stat. **Document type:** *Government.*
Published by: Census and Statistics Department/Zhengfu Tongjichu, Demographic Statistics Section, 7/F Kai Tak Multi-storey Carpark Bldg, 2 Concorde Rd, Kowloon, Hong Kong. TEL 852-2716-8345, FAX 852-2716-0231, genenq@censtatd.gov.hk, demo_1@censtad.gov.hk, http://www.statisticalbookstore.gov.hk, http://www.info.gov.hk/censtatd.

304.6 HKG
HONG KONG SPECIAL ADMINISTRATIVE REGION OF CHINA. CENSUS AND STATISTICS DEPARTMENT. HONG KONG (YEAR) POPULATION BY-CENSUS. MAIN TABLES. Text in English. irreg., latest 1996. stat. **Document type:** *Government.*
Published by: Census and Statistics Department/Zhengfu Tongjichu, Demographic Statistics Section, 7/F Kai Tak Multi-storey Carpark Bldg, 2 Concorde Rd, Kowloon, Hong Kong. TEL 852-2716-8345, FAX 852-2716-0231, genenq@censtatd.gov.hk, demo_1@censtad.gov.hk, http://www.statisticalbookstore.gov.hk, http://www.info.gov.hk/censtatd.

304.6 HKG
HONG KONG SPECIAL ADMINISTRATIVE REGION OF CHINA. CENSUS AND STATISTICS DEPARTMENT. HONG KONG (YEAR) POPULATION BY-CENSUS. MAP ON CD-ROM. Text in Chinese, English. irreg., latest 1996. HKD 1,950 per set (effective 2002). stat.; maps. **Document type:** *Government.* **Description:** Contains digital maps of Hong Kong for geographical presentation of statistical data contained in the "Hong Kong 1996 Population By-census: TAB on CD-ROM".
Published by: Census and Statistics Department/Zhengfu Tongjichu, Demographic Statistics Section, 7/F Kai Tak Multi-storey Carpark Bldg, 2 Concorde Rd, Kowloon, Hong Kong. TEL 852-2716-8345, FAX 852-2716-0231, genenq@censtatd.gov.hk, demo_1@censtad.gov.hk, http://www.statisticalbookstore.gov.hk.

304.6 HKG
HONG KONG SPECIAL ADMINISTRATIVE REGION OF CHINA. CENSUS AND STATISTICS DEPARTMENT. HONG KONG (YEAR) POPULATION BY-CENSUS. SUMMARY RESULTS. Text in English. irreg., latest 1996. stat. **Document type:** *Government.*
Published by: Census and Statistics Department/Zhengfu Tongjichu, Demographic Statistics Section, 7/F Kai Tak Multi-storey Carpark Bldg, 2 Concorde Rd, Kowloon, Hong Kong. TEL 852-2716-8345, FAX 852-2716-0231, genenq@censtatd.gov.hk, demo_1@censtad.gov.hk, http://www.info.gov.hk/censtatd, http://www.statisticalbookstore.gov.hk.

304.6 HKG
HONG KONG SPECIAL ADMINISTRATIVE REGION OF CHINA. CENSUS AND STATISTICS DEPARTMENT. HONG KONG (YEAR) POPULATION BY-CENSUS T A B ON CD-ROM. Text in Chinese, English. irreg., latest 1996. HKD 2,430 newsstand/cover (effective 2002). stat. **Document type:** *Government.* **Description:** Contains 324 statistical tables on a broad range of socio-economic characteristics of the population of Hong Kong.
Media: CD-ROM.
Published by: Census and Statistics Department/Zhengfu Tongjichu, Demographic Statistics Section, 7/F Kai Tak Multi-storey Carpark Bldg, 2 Concorde Rd, Kowloon, Hong Kong. TEL 852-2716-8345, FAX 852-2716-0231, genenq@censtatd.gov.hk, demo_1@censtad.gov.hk, http://www.statisticalbookstore.gov.hk.

304.6 HKG
HONG KONG SPECIAL ADMINISTRATIVE REGION OF CHINA. CENSUS AND STATISTICS DEPARTMENT. HONG KONG (YEAR) POPULATION BY-CENSUS. TABLES FOR DISTRICT BOARD DISTRICTS AND CONSTITUENCY AREAS: QUARTERS, HOUSEHOLDS AND POPULATION BY TYPE OF QUARTERS. Text in English. irreg., latest 1996. stat. **Document type:** *Government.*
Published by: Census and Statistics Department/Zhengfu Tongjichu, Demographic Statistics Section, 7/F Kai Tak Multi-storey Carpark Bldg, 2 Concorde Rd, Kowloon, Hong Kong. TEL 852-2716-8345, FAX 852-2716-0231, genenq@censtatd.gov.hk, demo_1@censtad.gov.hk, http://www.statisticalbookstore.gov.hk, http://www.info.gov.hk/censtatd.

304.6 HKG
HONG KONG SPECIAL ADMINISTRATIVE REGION OF CHINA. CENSUS AND STATISTICS DEPARTMENT. HONG KONG (YEAR) POPULATION BY-CENSUS. TABLES FOR TERTIARY PLANNING UNITS: POPULATION BY AGE AND SEX. Text in English. irreg., latest 1996. stat. **Document type:** *Government.*
Published by: Census and Statistics Department/Zhengfu Tongjichu, Demographic Statistics Section, 7/F Kai Tak Multi-storey Carpark Bldg, 2 Concorde Rd, Kowloon, Hong Kong. TEL 852-2716-8345, FAX 852-2716-0231, genenq@censtatd.gov.hk, demo_1@censtad.gov.hk, http://www.statisticalbookstore.gov.hk, http://www.info.gov.hk/censtatd.

304.6 HKG
HONG KONG SPECIAL ADMINISTRATIVE REGION OF CHINA. CENSUS AND STATISTICS DEPARTMENT. HONG KONG (YEAR) POPULATION BY-CENSUS. TABLES FOR TERTIARY PLANNING UNITS: QUARTERS, HOUSEHOLDS AND POPULATION BY TYPE OF QUARTERS. Text in English. irreg., latest 1996. stat. **Document type:** *Government.*
Published by: Census and Statistics Department/Zhengfu Tongjichu, Demographic Statistics Section, 7/F Kai Tak Multi-storey Carpark Bldg, 2 Concorde Rd, Kowloon, Hong Kong. TEL 852-2716-8345, FAX 852-2716-0231, genenq@censtatd.gov.hk, demo_1@censtad.gov.hk, http://www.statisticalbookstore.gov.hk, http://www.info.gov.hk/censtatd.

304.6 HKG
HONG KONG SPECIAL ADMINISTRATIVE REGION OF CHINA. CENSUS AND STATISTICS DEPARTMENT. HONG KONG LIFE TABLES. Text in English. 1961. irreg., latest 2000, projection years 1996-2029. HKD 30 newsstand/cover (effective 2002). stat. **Document type:** *Government.* **Description:** The life table is a statistical device used by statisticians, actuaries, demographers, public health workers and many others to present the mortality experience of a population. It is a valuable tool for studying longevity and for comparing the mortality experience of different countries/territories at a point in time and the mortality level of a population over time. It this report, the life tables for the years 1996 to 1999 are compiled based on actual mortality data. For the future benchmark years 2004, 2009, 2014, 2019, 2024 and 2029, the life tables are compiled based on projected age-sex-specific mortality rates.
Published by: Census and Statistics Department/Zhengfu Tongjichu, Demographic Statistics Section, 7/F Kai Tak Multi-storey Carpark Bldg, 2 Concorde Rd, Kowloon, Hong Kong. TEL 852-2716-8345, FAX 852-2716-0231, genenq@censtatd.gov.hk, demo_1@censtad.gov.hk, http://www.statisticalbookstore.gov.hk, http://www.info.gov.hk/censtatd.

304.6 HKG
HONG KONG SPECIAL ADMINISTRATIVE REGION OF CHINA. CENSUS AND STATISTICS DEPARTMENT. HONG KONG POPULATION PROJECTIONS (YEAR-YEAR). Text in English. 1961. irreg., latest 2000, projection years 2000-2029. HKD 20 newsstand/cover (effective 2002). stat. **Document type:** *Government.* **Description:** This report presents a new set of population projections with the year of population estimates as the population base. The projections have made use of the most up-to-date information on fertility, mortality and migration patterns of the population which has emerged since the last set of population projections was produced. Also, the period of the projections has been extended from 20 years to 30 years. In addition to the projection results, this report also presents a description of the methodology and assumptions used.
Published by: Census and Statistics Department/Zhengfu Tongjichu, Demographic Statistics Section, 7/F Kai Tak Multi-storey Carpark Bldg, 2 Concorde Rd, Kowloon, Hong Kong. FAX 852-2716-0231, demo_1@censtad.gov.hk, genenq@censtatd.gov.hk, http://www.statisticalbookstore.gov.hk, http://www.info.gov.hk/censtatd.

304.6021 HKG
HONG KONG SPECIAL ADMINISTRATIVE REGION OF CHINA. CENSUS AND STATISTICS DEPARTMENT. INDEX NUMBERS OF THE COSTS OF LABOUR AND SELECTED MATERIALS USED IN GOVERNMENT CONTRACTS. Text in Chinese, English. m. free. stat. back issues avail. **Document type:** *Government.*
Related titles: Online - full content ed.
Published by: Census and Statistics Department/Zhengfu Tongjichu, Building, Construction and Real Estate Statistics Section, 15/F Chuang's Hung Hom Plaza, 83 Whuhu St, Hung Hom, Kowloon, Hong Kong. TEL 852-2882-4684, FAX 852-2805-6153, bcre_1@censtatd.gov.hk, http://www.info.gov.hk/censtatd, http://www.statisticalbookstore.gov.hk. **Dist. by:** Government Publications Centre, Low Block, Ground Fl, Queensway Government Offices, 66 Queensway, Hong Kong, Hong Kong. TEL 852-2537-1910, FAX 852-2523-7195.

304.6 HKG
HONG KONG SPECIAL ADMINISTRATIVE REGION OF CHINA. CENSUS AND STATISTICS DEPARTMENT. POPULATION AND HOUSEHOLD STATISTICS ANALYSED BY DISTRICT COUNCIL DISTRICT. Text in Chinese, English. 1997. a., latest 2000. HKD 20 newsstand/cover (effective 2001). stat. back issues avail. **Document type:** *Government.* **Description:** Presents statistics on the demographic and socio-economic characteristics of the population at the District Council district level.
Related titles: Online - full content ed.
Published by: Census and Statistics Department/Zhengfu Tongjichu, General Household Survey Section (1), Fortress Tower Sub-office, 5/F Fortress Tower, 250 King's Rd, North Point, Hong Kong. TEL 852-2887-5512, FAX 852-2508-1501, ghs1_1@censtatd.gov.hk, http://www.statisticalbookstore.gov.hk. **Subscr. to:** Information Services Department, Publications Sales Unit, Rm 402, 4th Fl, Murray Bldg, Garden Rd, Hong Kong, Hong Kong. TEL 852-2842-8844, FAX 852-2598-7482, puborder@isd.gcn.gov.hk, http://www.info.gov.hk/isd/book_e.htm. **Dist. by:** Government Publications Centre, Low Block, Ground Fl, Queensway Government Offices, 66 Queensway, Hong Kong, Hong Kong. TEL 852-2537-1910, FAX 852-2523-7195.

304.6 HKG
HONG KONG SPECIAL ADMINISTRATIVE REGION OF CHINA. CENSUS AND STATISTICS DEPARTMENT. SOCIAL DATA COLLECTED VIA THE GENERAL HOUSEHOLD SURVEY: SPECIAL TOPICS REPORT. Text in Chinese, English. 1983. irreg., latest no.27, 2001. price varies. stat. back issues avail. **Document type:** *Government.* **Description:** Presents the findings of the supplementary enquires conducted via the General Household Survey on a wide range of social topics required by government policy bureaus and departments.
Related titles: Online - full content ed.
Published by: Census and Statistics Department/Zhengfu Tongjichu, Social Analysis and Research Section, 5/F Fortress Tower, 250 King's Rd, North Point, Hong Kong. TEL 852-2887-5503, FAX 852-2508-1501, sar_1@censtatd.gov.hk, http://www.info.gov.hk/censtatd, http://www.statisticalbookstore.gov.hk. **Subscr. to:** Information Services Department, Publications Sales Unit, Rm 402, 4th Fl, Murray Bldg, Garden Rd, Hong Kong, Hong Kong. TEL 852-2842-8844, FAX 852-2598-7482, puborder@isd.gcn.gov.hk, http://www.info.gov.hk/isd/book_e.htm. **Dist. by:** Government Publications Centre, Low Block, Ground Fl, Queensway Government Offices, 66 Queensway, Hong Kong, Hong Kong. TEL 852-2537-1910, FAX 852-2523-7195.

P

304.6 HKG
HONG KONG SPECIAL ADMINISTRATIVE REGION OF CHINA. CENSUS AND STATISTICS DEPARTMENT. WOMEN AND MEN IN HONG KONG - KEY STATISTICS. Text in Chinese, English. 2001. irreg. HKD 46 newsstand/cover (effective 2002). stat. **Document type:** *Government.* **Description:** This bilingual publication contains sex disaggregated statistics and indicators obtained from a variety of sources with a view to painting a picture of the situation of women and men in major economic and social spheres, including: Demographic Characteristics; Marriage, Fertility and Family Conditions; Education Characteristics; Labour Force Characteristics; Employment Earnings; social Welfare; Medical and Health; Law and Order; Participation in Public Affairs.
Published by: Census and Statistics Department/Zhengfu Tongjichu, Technical Secretariat Branch, 21/F Wanchai Tower, 12 Harbour Rd, Wan Chai, Hong Kong. TEL 852-2582 4958, FAX 852-2157 9296, techsec_1@censtatd.gov.hk, http://www.info.gov.hk/censtatd, http://www.info.gov.hk/censtatd, http://www.statisticalbookstore.gov.hk. **Subscr. to:** Information Services Department, Publications Sales Unit, Rm 402, 4th Fl, Murray Bldg, Garden Rd, Hong Kong. TEL 852-2842-8844, FAX 852-2598-7482, puborder@isd.gcn.gov.hk, http://www.info.gov.hk/isd/book_e.htm. **Dist. by:** Government Publications Centre, Low Block, Ground Fl, Queensway Government Offices, 66 Queensway, Hong Kong, Hong Kong. TEL 852-2537-1910, FAX 852-2523-7195.

304.6 BEL
I P D WORKING PAPERS. (Interuniversity Programme in Demography) Text in English. 1975. irreg. (5-10/yr.). price varies. charts; stat.; bibl.; maps. **Document type:** *Monographic series, Academic/Scholarly.* **Description:** Presents research results in pre-publication form. Covers demographic issues relating to Western Europe and Africa, including fertility, family, economic and historical demography, demographic theory, and other topics.
Formerly (until 1983): Demografie
Related titles: Online - full content ed.
Indexed: PopulInd.
Published by: Vrije Universiteit Brussel, Interuniversity Programme in Demography, Pleinlaan 2, Brussels, 1050, Belgium. TEL 32-2-6292040, FAX 32-2-6292420, esvbalck@vub.ac.be. Circ: 200.

325.1021 CAN ISSN 1495-4656
IMMIGRATION HIGHLIGHTS. Text in English. 1990. q. CAD 30 (effective 2006). 9 p./no.; **Document type:** *Government.* **Description:** Features immigrant landings in British Columbia, Vancouver, Victoria and Canada by place of origin and immigration status, with comparative figures for other provinces, as well as analytical articles.
Former titles (until 1999): British Columbia Immigration (1493-1788); (until 1998): Immigration Highlights (1207-4861); (until 1994): British Columbia Immigration Highlights (1184-9215)
Related titles: Online - full text ed.
Published by: Ministry of Finance and Corporate Relations, B C Stats, PO Box 9410, Sta Prov Govt, Victoria, BC V8W 9V1, Canada. TEL 250-387-0359, FAX 250-387-0380, BC.Stats@gov.bc.ca.

304.6 IND
INDIA. MINISTRY OF HOME AFFAIRS. VITAL STATISTICS DIVISION. SURVEY OF CAUSES OF DEATH (RURAL). Text in English. 19??. a. stat. **Document type:** *Government.*
Former titles (until 19??): India. Vital Statistics Division. Causes of Death; (until 1974): India. Ministry of Home Affairs. Vital Statistics Division. Causes of Death: a Survey; (until 1972): India. Vital Statistics Division. Model Registration: Survey of Cause of Death. Report
Published by: Ministry of Home Affairs, Vital Statistics Division, North Block, Central Secretariat, New Delhi, 110 001, India. TEL 91-11-23092161, FAX 91-11-23093750, http://www.mha.nic.in/.

304.6 IND
HA39.I4
INDIA. OFFICE OF THE REGISTRAR GENERAL. SAMPLE REGISTRATION SYSTEM - STATISTICAL REPORT. Text in English. 1964. biennial. charts; stat. **Document type:** *Report, Government.*
Formerly (until 1994): India. Ministry of Home Affairs. Vital Statistics Division. Sample Registration Bulletin (0971-3549); Incorporates: India. Office of the Registrar General. Newsletter (0537-0035)
Indexed: PopulInd.
Published by: Ministry of Home Affairs, Vital Statistics Division, North Block, Central Secretariat, New Delhi, 110 001, India. TEL 91-11-23092161, FAX 91-11-23093750, http://www.mha.nic.in/.

304.6 ESP ISSN 1699-3012
INDICADORES SOCIALES DE ESPANA. Text in Spanish. 1991. a., latest 2005. EUR 11. **Document type:** *Government.*
Formerly (until 1991): Indicadores Sociales (1699-5805)
Published by: Instituto Nacional de Estadistica (I N E), Paseo de la Castellana 183, Madrid, 28071, Spain. TEL 34-91-5839100, http://www.ine.es/.

304.6 ESP ISSN 1697-3259
HA1543
INEBASE. (Instituto Nacional de Estadistica) Text in Spanish. 2004. m. EUR 26 (effective 2010). **Document type:** *Directory, Government.*
Media: Optical Disk.
Published by: Instituto Nacional de Estadistica (I N E), Paseo de la Castellana 183, Madrid, 28071, Spain. TEL 34-91-5839100, http://www.ine.es/.

304.6 KOR ISSN 1599-046X
INGU DONGTAE TONG'GYE YEONBO. CHONG'GWAL CHULSAENG SA'MANG PYEON/KOREA (REPUBLIC). NATIONAL STATISTICAL OFFICE. ANNUAL REPORT ON THE VITAL STATISTICS. VOLUME 1. ON LIVE BIRTHS AND DEATHS. Text in Korean. 1980. a. stat. **Document type:** *Government.*
Published by: Tong'gyecheong/Korea National Statistical Office, Government Complex Daejeon, 139 Seonsaro (920 Dunsan 2-dong), Seo-gu, Daejeon, 302-701, Korea, S. TEL 82-42-4814114. **Subscr. to:** The Korean Statistical Association, Rm. 103, Seoul Statistical Branch Office Bldg. 71, Nonhyun-Dong, Kangnam-Ku, Seoul 135701, Korea, S. TEL 82-2-34437954, FAX 82-2-34437957, kosa@nso.go.kr.

304.6 KOR ISSN 1599-0478
INGU DONGTAE TONG'GYE YEONBO. HON'IN IHON PYEON/KOREA (REPUBLIC). NATIONAL STATISTICAL OFFICE. ANNUAL REPORT ON THE VITAL STATISTICS. VOLUME 2. ON MARRIAGES AND DIVORCES. Text in English, Korean. 2000. a. USD 11 newsstand/cover (effective 2009). stat. **Document type:** *Government.*
Published by: Tong'gyecheong/Korea National Statistical Office, Government Complex Daejeon, 139 Seonsaro (920 Dunsan 2-dong), Seo-gu, Daejeon, 302-701, Korea, S. TEL 82-42-4814114. **Subscr. to:** The Korean Statistical Association, Rm. 103, Seoul Statistical Branch Office Bldg. 71, Nonhyun-Dong, Kangnam-Ku, Seoul 135701, Korea, S. TEL 82-2-34437954, FAX 82-2-34437957, kosa@nso.go.kr.

304.6 KOR ISSN 1228-9019
IN'GU IDONG TONG'GYE YEONBO/KOREA (REPUBLIC). NATIONAL STATISTICAL OFFICE. ANNUAL REPORT ON THE INTERNAL MIGRATION STATISTICS. Text in Korean, English. 1970. a. USD 14 newsstand/cover (effective 2009). **Document type:** *Government.* **Description:** Contains data on internal migrants based on administrative reports to Eups, Myeons and Dongs every month.
Formerly: Korea (Republic). Economic Planning Board. Yearbook of Migration Statistics
Published by: Tong'gyecheong/Korea National Statistical Office, Government Complex Daejeon, 139 Seonsaro (920 Dunsan 2-dong), Seo-gu, Daejeon, 302-701, Korea, S. TEL 82-42-4814114. **Subscr. to:** The Korean Statistical Association, Rm. 103, Seoul Statistical Branch Office Bldg. 71, Nonhyun-Dong, Kangnam-Ku, Seoul 135701, Korea, S. TEL 82-2-34437954, FAX 82-2-34437957.

315 KOR ISSN 1599-1717
HA4630.5
IN'GU JUTAEG CHONG JO'SA JAMJEONG BO'GO'SEO/KOREA (REPUBLIC). NATIONAL STATISTICAL OFFICE. POPULATION AND HOUSING CENSUS REPORT. Text in English, Korean. 1925. quinquennial (published in years ending 2 & 7). USD 1,031 (effective 2006). **Document type:** *Government.*
Published by: Tong'gyecheong/Korea National Statistical Office, Government Complex Daejeon, 139 Seonsaro (920 Dunsan 2-dong), Seo-gu, Daejeon, 302-701, Korea, S. TEL 82-42-4814114, http://www.nso.go.kr. Circ: 1,600. **Subscr. to:** The Korean Statistical Association, Rm. 103, Seoul Statistical Branch Office Bldg. 71, Nonhyun-Dong, Kangnam-Ku, Seoul 135701, Korea, S. TEL 82-2-34437954, FAX 82-2-34437957, kosa@nso.go.kr.

304.6021 PRT ISSN 1647-0443
INQUERITO AS DESPESAS DAS FAMILIAS. Text in Portuguese. 1992-2000; resumed 2008. s-a. **Document type:** *Report, Government.*
Formerly (until 2000): Inquerito aos Orcamentos Familiare (0872-1386)
Published by: Instituto Nacional de Estatistica, Av Antonio Jose de Almeida 2, Lisbon, 1000-043, Portugal. TEL 351-21-8426100, FAX 351-21-8426380, ine@ine.pt, http://www.ine.pt.

304.6 310 ESP ISSN 1698-4595
INSTITUTO NACIONAL DE ESTADISTICA. ENCUESTA DE POBLACION ACTIVA (CD-ROM EDITION). Text in Spanish. 2004. q. EUR 7 (effective 2010). **Document type:** *Government.*
Media: CD-ROM.
Published by: Instituto Nacional de Estadistica (I N E), Paseo de la Castellana 183, Madrid, 28071, Spain. TEL 34-91-5839100, http://www.ine.es/.

304.6 USA
INTERNATIONAL POPULATION REPORTS. Text in English. 1952. irreg., latest 2002. **Document type:** *Monographic series, Government.*
Formerly: Current Population Reports. International Population Reports (0082-9498)
Related titles: Online - full text ed.
Published by: U.S. Census Bureau. Population Division (Subsidiary of: U.S. Department of Commerce), 4600 Silver Hill Rd., Washington, DC 20233. TEL 866-758-1060, http://www.census.gov/population/www/.

304.6021 IRL
IRELAND. CENTRAL STATISTICS OFFICE. CENSUS OF POPULATION. PRINCIPAL DEMOGRAPHIC RESULTS. Text in English. quinquennial. EUR 15 (effective 2005). charts; stat. **Document type:** *Government.* **Description:** Gives the final national census results, classified by age, sex, marital status, household composition, usual residence, and place of birth.
Related titles: Online - full text ed.
Published by: Ireland. Central Statistics Office/Eire, An Phriomh-Oifig Staidrimh, Skehard Rd, Cork, Ireland. TEL 353-21-4535000, FAX 353-21-4535555, information@cso.ie.

304.6021 IRL
IRELAND. CENTRAL STATISTICS OFFICE. CENSUS OF POPULATION. PRINCIPAL SOCIOECONOMIC RESULTS. Text in English. quinquennial. EUR 15 (effective 2005). charts; stat. **Document type:** *Government.* **Description:** Lists national census figures, classified by economic status, employment, unemployment, industries, occupations, education, Irish language, means of travel to work, and school and college.
Related titles: Online - full text ed.
Published by: Ireland. Central Statistics Office/Eire, An Phriomh-Oifig Staidrimh, Skehard Rd, Cork, Ireland. TEL 353-21-4535000, FAX 353-21-4535555, information@cso.ie.

304.6021 IRL
IRELAND. CENTRAL STATISTICS OFFICE. CENSUS OF POPULATION. VOLUME 1: POPULATION CLASSIFIED BY AREA. Text in English. quinquennial. EUR 15 (effective 2005). charts; stat. **Document type:** *Government.* **Description:** Provides census figures, classified by sex, for each province, county, borough, town, district electoral division, urban district, rural district, regional authority area, Gaeltacht area, inhabited island, county electoral area, and constituency in Ireland.
Related titles: Online - full text ed.
Published by: Ireland. Central Statistics Office/Eire, An Phriomh-Oifig Staidrimh, Skehard Rd, Cork, Ireland. TEL 353-21-4535000, FAX 353-21-4535555, information@cso.ie.

304.6021 IRL
IRELAND. CENTRAL STATISTICS OFFICE. CENSUS OF POPULATION. VOLUME 10: EDUCATION AND QUALIFICATIONS. Text in English. quinquennial. EUR 15 (effective 2005). charts; stat. **Document type:** *Government.* **Description:** Compiles census data according to the highest level of education completed and details on the subject of scientific and technological qualifications.
Former titles (until 2006): Ireland. Central Statistics Office. Census of Population. Volume 7: Education and Qualifications; (until 2002): Ireland. Central Statistics Office. Census of Population. Volume 8: Education, Scientific and Technological Qualifications
Related titles: Online - full text ed.
Published by: Ireland. Central Statistics Office/Eire, An Phriomh-Oifig Staidrimh, Skehard Rd, Cork, Ireland. TEL 353-21-4535000, FAX 353-21-4535555, information@cso.ie.

304.6021 IRL
IRELAND. CENTRAL STATISTICS OFFICE. CENSUS OF POPULATION. VOLUME 12: TRAVEL TO WORK, SCHOOL AND COLLEGE. Text in English. quinquennial. EUR 15 (effective 2005). charts; stat. **Document type:** *Government.* **Description:** Compiles census figures according to means of travel to work, school, and college, classified by county and county borough, as well as distance traveled.
Former titles (until 2006): Ireland. Central Statistics Office. Census of Population. Volume 9: Travel to Work, School and College; (until 2002): Ireland. Central Statistics Office. Census of Population. Volume 6: Travel to Work, School and College
Related titles: Online - full text ed.
Published by: Ireland. Central Statistics Office/Eire, An Phriomh-Oifig Staidrimh, Skehard Rd, Cork, Ireland. TEL 353-21-4535000, FAX 353-21-4535555, information@cso.ie.

304.6021 IRL
IRELAND. CENTRAL STATISTICS OFFICE. CENSUS OF POPULATION. VOLUME 2: AGES AND MARITAL STATUS. Text in English. quinquennial. EUR 15 (effective 2005). charts; stat. **Document type:** *Government.* **Description:** Classifies state, county, and local census figures by age and marital status.
Related titles: Online - full text ed.
Published by: Ireland. Central Statistics Office/Eire, An Phriomh-Oifig Staidrimh, Skehard Rd, Cork, Ireland. TEL 353-21-4535000, FAX 353-21-4535555, information@cso.ie.

304.6021 IRL
IRELAND. CENTRAL STATISTICS OFFICE. CENSUS OF POPULATION. VOLUME 3: HOUSEHOLD COMPOSITION, FAMILY UNITS AND FERTILITY. Text in English. quinquennial. EUR 15 (effective 2005). charts; stat. **Document type:** *Government.* **Description:** Analyzes national census figures in the context of: all private households; private households in permanent housing units; private households in temporary housing units; family units and family cycle.
Formerly (until 2006): Ireland. Central Statistics Office. Census of Population. Volume 3: Household Composition and Family Units
Related titles: Online - full text ed.
Published by: Ireland. Central Statistics Office/Eire, An Phriomh-Oifig Staidrimh, Skehard Rd, Cork, Ireland. TEL 353-21-4535000, FAX 353-21-4535555, information@cso.ie.

304.6021 IRL
IRELAND. CENTRAL STATISTICS OFFICE. CENSUS OF POPULATION. VOLUME 4: USUAL RESIDENCE, MIGRATION, BIRTHPLACES AND NATIONALITIES. Text in English. quinquennial. EUR 15 (effective 2005). charts; stat. **Document type:** *Government.* **Description:** Classifies the population by usual residence at census date and one year before census date and by birthplace.
Formerly: Ireland. Central Statistics Office. Census of Population. Volume 4: Usual Residence, Migration and Birthplaces
Related titles: Online - full text ed.
Published by: Ireland. Central Statistics Office/Eire, An Phriomh-Oifig Staidrimh, Skehard Rd, Cork, Ireland. TEL 353-21-4535000, FAX 353-21-4535555, information@cso.ie.

304.6021 IRL
IRELAND. CENTRAL STATISTICS OFFICE. CENSUS OF POPULATION. VOLUME 7: PRINCIPAL ECONOMIC STATUS AND INDUSTRIES. Text in English. quinquennial. EUR 15 (effective 2005). charts; stat. **Document type:** *Government.* **Description:** Classifies persons ages 15 and older according to principal economic status: employed, unemployed, student, as well as by sex, age, and marital status. Results are reported for each province, county and county borough, town, and regional authority area.
Formerly (until 2006): Ireland. Central Statistics Office. Census of Population. Volume 5: Principal Economic Status and Industries
Related titles: Online - full text ed.
Published by: Ireland. Central Statistics Office/Eire, An Phriomh-Oifig Staidrimh, Skehard Rd, Cork, Ireland. TEL 353-21-4535000, FAX 353-21-4535555, information@cso.ie.

304.6021 IRL
IRELAND. CENTRAL STATISTICS OFFICE. CENSUS OF POPULATION. VOLUME 8: OCCUPATIONS. Text in English. quinquennial. EUR 15 (effective 2005). charts; stat. **Document type:** *Government.* **Description:** Supplies details on the number of males and females in each province, county, county borough, urban and rural district, and large town, classified by occupational group and socioeconomic class.
Former titles (until 2006): Ireland. Central Statistics Office. Census of Population. Volume 6: Occupations; Ireland. Central Statistics Office. Census of Population. Volume 7: Occupations
Related titles: Online - full text ed.
Published by: Ireland. Central Statistics Office/Eire, An Phriomh-Oifig Staidrimh, Skehard Rd, Cork, Ireland. TEL 353-21-4535000, FAX 353-21-4535555, information@cso.ie.

304.6021 IRL
IRELAND. CENTRAL STATISTICS OFFICE. CENSUS OF POPULATION. VOLUME 9: IRISH LANGUAGE. Text in English. 1998. quinquennial. EUR 15 (effective 2005). charts; stat. **Document type:** *Government.* **Description:** Gives the number and percentage, for each gender, of Irish speakers ages three and over in each province, county, and county borough, classified by age group, with separate information for the Gaeltacht areas in each county.

Former titles (until 2006): Ireland. Central Statistics Office. Census of Population. Volume 11: Irish Language; Ireland. Central Statistics Office. Census of Population. Volume 9: An Ghaelige - Irish Language
Related titles: Online - full text ed.
Published by: Ireland. Central Statistics Office/Eire, An Phriomh-Oifig Staidrimh, Skehard Rd, Cork, Ireland. TEL 353-21-4535000, FAX 353-21-4535555, information@cso.ie.

304.6021 IRL ISSN 1649-8038
IRELAND. CENTRAL STATISTICS OFFICE. LIVE REGISTER AGE BY DURATION. Text in English. 1987. biennial. charts; stat. **Document type:** *Government.*
Former titles (until 2006): Ireland. Central Statistics Office. Live Register Age by Duration Analysis (1393-5615); (until 1997): Ireland. Central Statistics Office. Half Yearly Age by Duraction Analysis (0791-394X)
Published by: Ireland. Central Statistics Office/Eire, An Phriomh-Oifig Staidrimh, Skehard Rd, Cork, Ireland. TEL 353-21-4535000, FAX 353-21-4535555, information@cso.ie.

304.6021 IRL ISSN 1393-5593
IRELAND. CENTRAL STATISTICS OFFICE. POPULATION AND MIGRATION ESTIMATES. Text in English. 1994. a. charts; illus. **Document type:** *Government.*
Formerly (until 1997): Ireland. Central Statistics Office. Annual Population and Migration Estimates (1393-0788)
Related titles: Online - full text ed.
Published by: Ireland. Central Statistics Office/Eire, An Phriomh-Oifig Staidrimh, Skehard Rd, Cork, Ireland. TEL 353-21-4535000, FAX 353-21-4535555, information@cso.ie.

304.6021 IRL ISSN 0790-7710
HA1170.1
IRELAND. CENTRAL STATISTICS OFFICE. QUARTERLY REPORT ON VITAL STATISTICS/TUARASCAIL CINN RAITHE AR STAIDREAMH BEATHA. Text in English. 186?. q. EUR 28 (effective 2005). **Document type:** *Government.* **Description:** Reports on births, deaths and marriages in each county.
Former titles (until 1986): Ireland. Central Statistics Office. Quarterly Report on Births, Deaths and Marriages and on Certain Infectious Diseases (0790-6811); (until 1956): Ireland. Central Statistics Office. Quarterly Return of the Marriages, Births and Deaths Registered (0790-6803)
Related titles: Online - full text ed.
Published by: Ireland. Central Statistics Office/Eire, An Phriomh-Oifig Staidrimh, Skehard Rd, Cork, Ireland. TEL 353-21-4535000, FAX 353-21-4535555, information@cso.ie.

304.6021 IRL ISSN 0075-062X
HA1141
IRELAND. CENTRAL STATISTICS OFFICE. REPORT ON VITAL STATISTICS - TUARASCAIL AR STAIDREAMH BEATHA. Text in English. 1864. a. EUR 12 (effective 2005). **Document type:** *Government.* **Description:** Provides one of the principal sources of demographic sources of demographic statistics and analyses compiled in Ireland. Reports aggregates and rates per thousands of population for marriages, births, deaths, and infant mortality.
Former titles (until 1955): Ireland. Central Statistics Office. Annual Report of the Registrar-General - Tuarascail an Ard-Chlaraitheora (0790-5963); (until 1938): Ireland. Department of Local Government and Public Health. Annual Report of the Registrar-General (0790-5955); (until 1928): Detailed Annual Report of the Registrar-General for Saorstat Eirann (0790-5947); (until 1923): Detailed Annual Report of the Registrar-General for Ireland (0790-5939)
Related titles: Online - full text ed.
Published by: Ireland. Central Statistics Office/Eire, An Phriomh-Oifig Staidrimh, Skehard Rd, Cork, Ireland. TEL 353-21-4535000, FAX 353-21-4535555, information@cso.ie.

304.6 325 ISR ISSN 0793-3606
HA1931
ISRAEL. CENTRAL BUREAU OF STATISTICS. IMMIGRANT POPULATION FROM FORMER U S S R - DEMOGRAPHIC TRENDS/UKHLUSIYYAT 'OLE B'RIT HA-MO'ATSOT L'SHE'AVAR. M'GAMOT DEMOGRAFIYYOT. Text in English, Hebrew. 1995. irreg., latest 2001. ILS 121. **Document type:** *Government.*
Related titles: Diskette ed.
Published by: Central Bureau of Statistics/Ha-Lishka Ha-Merkazit L'Statistiqa, PO Box 13015, Jerusalem, 91130, Israel. TEL 972-2-6553364, FAX 972-2-6521340.

325.1 ISR ISSN 0302-816X
ISRAEL. CENTRAL BUREAU OF STATISTICS. IMMIGRATION TO ISRAEL/STATISTIQA SHEL 'ALIYYA. Text in English, Hebrew. 1968. irreg., latest 2001. ILS 75. **Document type:** *Government.*
Related titles: Diskette ed.
Published by: Central Bureau of Statistics/Ha-Lishka Ha-Merkazit L'Statistiqa, PO Box 13015, Jerusalem, 91130, Israel. TEL 972-2-6553364, FAX 972-2-6521340.

310 ISR ISSN 0075-1111
HB1254.A3
ISRAEL. CENTRAL BUREAU OF STATISTICS. VITAL STATISTICS. Text in English, Hebrew. 1965. irreg., latest 2001. ILS 30. **Document type:** *Government.*
Related titles: Diskette ed.
Published by: Central Bureau of Statistics/Ha-Lishka Ha-Merkazit L'Statistiqa, PO Box 13015, Jerusalem, 91130, Israel. TEL 972-2-6553364, FAX 972-2-6521340.

304.6 ITA ISSN 1129-7085
HB1429
ITALY. ISTITUTO NAZIONALE DI STATISTICA. ANNUARIO. DECESSI. Text in Italian. 1995. a. **Document type:** *Government.*
Supersedes in part (in 1994): Italy. Istituto Nazionale di Statistica. Annuario. Nascite e Decessi (1126-3075); Which superseded in part (in 1991): Statistiche Demografiche (1121-094X); Which was formerly (until 1984): Annuario di Statistiche Demografiche (0075-1685)
Published by: Istituto Nazionale di Statistica (I S T A T), Via Cesare Balbo 16, Rome, 00184, Italy. TEL 39-06-46731, http://www.istat.it.

301.32 ITA ISSN 1126-3067
ITALY. ISTITUTO NAZIONALE DI STATISTICA. ANNUARIO. MOVIMENTO MIGRATORIO DELLA POPOLAZIONE RESIDENTE; iscrizioni e cancellazioni anagrafiche. Text in Italian. 1988. a. **Document type:** *Government.*
Suprsedes in part (in 1991): Statistiche Demografiche (1121-094X); Which was formerly (until 1984): Annuario di Statistiche Demografiche (0075-1685)
Published by: Istituto Nazionale di Statistica (I S T A T), Via Cesare Balbo 16, Rome, 00184, Italy. TEL 39-06-46731, http://www.istat.it.

304.6 ITA ISSN 1129-7077
HB1009
ITALY. ISTITUTO NAZIONALE DI STATISTICA. ANNUARIO. NASCITE. Text in Italian. 1995. a. **Document type:** *Government.*
Supersedes in part (in 1994): Italy. Istituto Nazionale di Statistica. Annuario. Nascite e Decessi (1126-3075); Which superseded in part (in 1991): Statistiche Demografiche (1121-094X); Which was formerly (until 1984): Annuario di Statistiche Demografiche (0075-1685)
Published by: Istituto Nazionale di Statistica (I S T A T), Via Cesare Balbo 16, Rome, 00184, Italy. TEL 39-06-46731, http://www.istat.it.

304.6 ITA ISSN 0075-1863
HA1363
ITALY. ISTITUTO NAZIONALE DI STATISTICA. POPOLAZIONE E MOVIMENTO ANAGRAFICO DEI COMUNI. Text in Italian. 1950. a. **Document type:** *Government.*
Formerly (until 1964): Italy. Istituto Centrale di Statistica. Popolazione e Circoscrizioni Amministrative dei Comuni (1126-3040)
Related titles: CD-ROM ed.: ISSN 1974-6512; Online - full text ed.: ISSN 1974-6520.
Published by: Istituto Nazionale di Statistica (I S T A T), Via Cesare Balbo 16, Rome, 00184, Italy. TEL 39-06-46731, http://www.istat.it. Circ: 11,000.

304.6 ITA
HA1363
ITALY. ISTITUTO NAZIONALE DI STATISTICA. STATISTICHE DEMOGRAFICHE. Text in Italian. 1951. a. **Document type:** *Government.*
Former titles: Italy. Istituto Centrale di Statistica. Statistiche Demografiche; Italy. Istituto Centrale di Statistica. Annuario di Statistiche Demografiche (0075-1685)
Indexed: RASB.
Published by: Istituto Nazionale di Statistica (I S T A T), Via Cesare Balbo 16, Rome, 00184, Italy. TEL 39-06-46731, http://www.istat.it.

304.6 KOR ISSN 1599-6484
JANGLAE GA'GU CHU'GYE/KOREA (REPUBLIC). NATIONAL STATISTICAL OFFICE. HOUSEHOLD PROJECTIONS. Text in Korean. 2002. quinquennial. USD 6 newsstand/cover (effective 2009). stat. **Document type:** *Government.*
Published by: Tong'gyecheong/Korea National Statistical Office, Government Complex Daejeon, 139 Seonsaro (920 Dunsan 2-dong), Seo-gu, Daejeon, 302-701, Korea, S. TEL 82-42-4814114. **Subscr. to:** The Korean Statistical Association, Rm. 103, Seoul Statistical Branch Office Bldg. 71, Nonhyun-Dong, Kangnam-Ku, Seoul 135701, Korea, S. TEL 82-2-34437954, FAX 82-2-34437957, kosa@nso.go.kr.

304.6 KOR ISSN 1599-4384
JANGLAE IN'GU CHU'GYE/KOREA (REPUBLIC). NATIONAL STATISTICAL OFFICE. POPULATION PROJECTIONS BY PROVINCES. Text in English, Korean. irreg. USD 14 newsstand/cover (effective 2009). **Document type:** *Government.* **Description:** Contains estimates of the population for 30 years by provinces and the estimates of the population by age and sex based on the results of the Population and Housing Census reflecting the reasons for population change.
Published by: Tong'gyecheong/Korea National Statistical Office, Government Complex Daejeon, 139 Seonsaro (920 Dunsan 2-dong), Seo-gu, Daejeon, 302-701, Korea, S. TEL 82-42-4814114. **Subscr. to:** The Korean Statistical Association, Rm. 103, Seoul Statistical Branch Office Bldg. 71, Nonhyun-Dong, Kangnam-Ku, Seoul 135701, Korea, S. TEL 82-2-34437954, FAX 82-2-34437957, kosa@nso.go.kr.

304.6 015 310 JPN ISSN 1349-6794
HA37
JAPAN. MINISTRY OF INTERNAL AFFAIRS AND COMMUNICATIONS. STATISTICS BUREAU. NEWS BULLETIN. Text in English. 1967. every 2 wks. free. bibl. **Document type:** *Bulletin, Government.*
Former titles (until 2004): Japan. Ministry of Public Management, Home Affairs, Posts and Telecommunications. Statistics Bureau. News Bulletin (1348-771X); (until 2003): Japan. Statistics Bureau. Management and Coordination Agency. News Bulletin (0449-5314)
Related titles: Online - full text ed.
Published by: Japan. Ministry of Internal Affairs and Communications. Statistics Bureau/Somucho. Tokeikyoko, 19-1 Wakamatsu-cho, Shinjyuku-ku, Tokyo, 162-8668, Japan. TEL 81-3-5273-2020. **Subscr. to:** Japan Statistical Association, Meito Shinjuku Bldg, 6th Fl, 2-4-6 Shinjuku-ku, Tokyo 169-0073, Japan. TEL 81-3-53323151, http://www.jstat.or.jp/.

304.6 KOR ISSN 1599-2152
JEON'GUG JU'MIN DEUNGLOG IN'GU TONG'GYE/KOREA (REPUBLIC). NATIONAL STATISTICAL OFFICE. RESIDENT OF REGISTRATION POPULATION. Text in English, Korean. 2000. a. USD 14 newsstand/cover (effective 2009). stat. **Document type:** *Government.* **Description:** Contains data on the changes of the size & structure of the population, and the generations by administrative districts after compiling data on residents of registration population as of December 31st of every year.
Published by: Tong'gyecheong/Korea National Statistical Office, Government Complex Daejeon, 139 Seonsaro (920 Dunsan 2-dong), Seo-gu, Daejeon, 302-701, Korea, S. TEL 82-42-4814114. **Subscr. to:** The Korean Statistical Association, Rm. 103, Seoul Statistical Branch Office Bldg. 71, Nonhyun-Dong, Kangnam-Ku, Seoul 135701, Korea, S. TEL 82-2-34437954, FAX 82-2-34437957, kosa@nso.go.kr.

304.6 JPN ISSN 0448-7117
HB3651
JINKO SUIKEI SHIRYO/POPULATION ESTIMATES SERIES. Text in Japanese. 1953. quinquennial. **Document type:** *Monographic series, Government.*
Published by: Japan. Ministry of Internal Affairs and Communications. Statistics Bureau/Somucho. Tokeikyoko, 19-1 Wakamatsu-cho, Shinjyuku-ku, Tokyo, 162-8668, Japan. TEL 81-3-5273-2020, http://www.stat.go.jp.

304.6 JPN
JINKO TOKEI NEMPO/ANNUAL REPORT ON CURRENT POPULATION ESTIMATES. Text in English, Japanese. a. JPY 1,995 (effective 2000). stat. **Document type:** *Report, Government.*
Published by: Japan. Ministry of Internal Affairs and Communications. Statistics Bureau/Somucho. Tokeikyoko, 19-1 Wakamatsu-cho, Shinjyuku-ku, Tokyo, 162-8668, Japan. TEL 81-3-5273-2020.

304.6 JPN ISSN 0286-1410
HB2111
JUMIN KIHON DAICHO JINKO IDO HOKOKU NENPO/ANNUAL REPORT ON THE INTERNAL MIGRATION IN JAPAN DERIVED FROM THE BASIC RESIDENT REGISTERS (YEAR). Text in English, Japanese. 1954. a. JPY 2,940 (effective 2000). stat. **Document type:** *Report, Government.*
Formerly (until 1971): Jumin Kihon Daicho ni Motozuku Jinko Ido Hokoku Nempo/Annual Report on the Internal Migration in Japan Derived from the Basic Resident Registers (0286-1399); (until 1967): Jumin Toroku Jinko Ido Hokoku Nempo (0446-5814)
Related titles: Online - full text ed.: free.
Published by: Japan. Ministry of Internal Affairs and Communications. Statistics Bureau/Somucho. Tokeikyoko, 19-1 Wakamatsu-cho, Shinjyuku-ku, Tokyo, 162-8668, Japan. TEL 81-3-5273-2020. **Subscr. to:** Japan Statistical Association, Meito Shinjuku Bldg, 6th Fl, 2-4-6 Shinjuku-ku, Tokyo 169-0073, Japan. TEL 81-3-53323151, http://www.jstat.or.jp/.

304.6 KEN
KENYA. CENTRAL BUREAU OF STATISTICS. POPULATION CENSUS. Text in English. irreg. KES 1,000. stat. **Document type:** *Government.*
Published by: Ministry of Finance and Planning, Central Bureau of Statistics, PO Box 30266, Nairobi, Kenya. **Subscr. to:** Government Press, Haile Selaissie Ave., PO Box 30128, Nairobi, Kenya. TEL 254-2-334075.

KENYA. CENTRAL BUREAU OF STATISTICS. POPULATIONS AND HOUSING CENSUS (YEAR); population distribution by administrative areas and urban centres. *see* SOCIAL SERVICES AND WELFARE

304.6 GBR ISSN 2041-5508
KEY POPULATION AND VITAL STATISTICS (ONLINE). Text in English. 1986. a. free (effective 2010). stat. back issues avail. **Document type:** *Government.* **Description:** Provides data on resident population, births, maternities, deaths, mortality and migration for local administrative areas and health areas throughout UK, together with explanatory material and illustrative maps.
Former titles (2006): Key Population and Vital Statistics (Print) (1469-2732); (until 1986): Population and Vital Statistics (0951-2497); Which was formed by the merger of (1985-1986): Vital Statistics, Local and Health Areas (0268-9596); Which was formerly (until 1985): Local Authority Vital Statistics; (1974-1986): Great Britain. Office of National Statistics. Population Estimates: England and Wales (0950-7574); Which was formerly (1957-1974): Great Britain. Registrar General. Annual Estimates of the Population of England and Wales and of Local Authority Areas (0301-7141)
Media: Online - full text.
Published by: Office for National Statistics, Rm 1.101, Government Bldgs, Cardiff Rd, Newport, S Wales NP10 8XG, United Kingdom. TEL 44-1633-653599, FAX 44-1633-652747, info@statistics.gsi.gov.uk, http://www.statistics.gov.uk/default.asp.

304.6 KOR ISSN 1739-0923
HA4630.5
KOREA (REPUBLIC). NATIONAL STATISTICAL OFFICE. EXPLORE KOREA THROUGH STATISTICS. Text in English. 1962. a. USD 24 newsstand/cover (effective 2009). stat. **Document type:** *Government.* **Description:** Contains statistical data on population, employment, industry, economy, and society of Korea for English users.
Published by: Tong'gyecheong/Korea National Statistical Office, Government Complex Daejeon, 139 Seonsaro (920 Dunsan 2-dong), Seo-gu, Daejeon, 302-701, Korea, S. TEL 82-42-4814114. **Subscr. to:** The Korean Statistical Association, Rm. 103, Seoul Statistical Branch Office Bldg. 71, Nonhyun-Dong, Kangnam-Ku, Seoul 135701, Korea, S. TEL 82-2-34437954, FAX 82-2-34437957, kosa@nso.go.kr.

304.6 KOR
KOREA (REPUBLIC). NATIONAL STATISTICAL OFFICE. MAJOR STATISTICS BY COUNTY. Text in English, Korean. irreg. stat. **Document type:** *Government.* **Description:** Contains statistics on population, Health & Welfare, Education, etc. of basic governing organizations.
Published by: Tong'gyecheong/Korea National Statistical Office, Government Complex Daejeon, 139 Seonsaro (920 Dunsan 2-dong), Seo-gu, Daejeon, 302-701, Korea, S. TEL 82-42-4814114. **Subscr. to:** The Korean Statistical Association, Rm. 103, Seoul Statistical Branch Office Bldg. 71, Nonhyun-Dong, Kangnam-Ku, Seoul 135701, Korea, S. TEL 82-2-34437954, FAX 82-2-34437957, kosa@nso.go.kr.

330 325 JPN ISSN 0448-3960
KOUSEIROUDOUSHOU. JINKO DOTAI SHAKAI KEIZAIMEN CHOSA HOKOKU/JAPAN. MINISTRY OF HEALTH, LABOUR AND WELFARE. REPORT ON SURVEY OF SOCIO-ECONOMIC ASPECTS ON VITAL EVENTS. Text in Japanese. 1962. a. price varies. stat. **Document type:** *Government.*
Published by: Kouseiroudoushou/Ministry of Health, Labour and Welfare, 1-2-2 Kasumigaseki Chiyoda-ku, Tokyo, 100-8916, Japan. TEL 81-3-52531111, http://www.mhlw.go.jp/. R&P Yoke Kanegae.

304.6 KWT
KUWAIT. CENTRAL STATISTICAL OFFICE. GENERAL POPULATION CENSUS/KUWAIT. AL-IDARAH AL-MARKAZIYYAH LIL-IHSA'. AL-TA'DAD AL-AAM LIL-SUKKAN. Text in Arabic. 1957. irreg. (in 3 vols.), latest vol.7, 1985. KWD 1. **Document type:** *Government.*
Published by: Central Statistical Office/Al-Idarah al-Markaziyyah lil-Ihsa', P O Box 26188, Safat, 13122, Kuwait. TEL 965-2428200, FAX 965-2430464.

P

304.6 KWT
KUWAIT. CENTRAL STATISTICAL OFFICE. VITAL STATISTICS - A SUMMARISED ANALYSIS BULLETIN/KUWAIT. AL-IDARAH AL-MARKAZIYYAH LIL-IHSA'. TAHLIL AL-IHSA'AT AL-HAYAWIYYAH. Variant title: Annual Bulletin for Vital Statistics Analysis. Text in Arabic. 1976. irreg., latest 1986. **Document type:** *Government.* **Description:** Provides statistical information on demographic changes, including birth and death rates, fertility, infant mortality, and marriage and divorce rates.
Published by: Central Statistical Office/Al-Idarah al-Markaziyyah lil-Ihsa', P O Box 26188, Safat, 13122, Kuwait. TEL 965-2428200, FAX 965-2430464.

304.6 KWT
KUWAIT. CENTRAL STATISTICAL OFFICE. VITAL STATISTICS - BIRTHS AND DEATHS/KUWAIT. AL-IDARAH AL-MARKAZIYYAH LIL-IHSA'. AL-IHSA'AT AL-HAYAWIYYAH - AL-MAWALID WAL-WAFAYAT. Text in Arabic, English. 1965. a., latest 1996. **Document type:** *Government.*
Published by: Central Statistical Office/Al-Idarah al-Markaziyyah lil-Ihsa', P O Box 26188, Safat, 13122, Kuwait. TEL 965-2428200, FAX 965-2430464.

KUWAIT. CENTRAL STATISTICAL OFFICE. VITAL STATISTICS - MARRIAGE AND DIVORCE/KUWAIT. AL-IDARAH AL-MARKAZIYYAH LIL-IHSA'. AL-IHSA'AT AL-HAYAWIYYAH - AL-ZAWAJ WAL-TALAQ. *see* MATRIMONY—Abstracting, Bibliographies, Statistics

301.32 310 CYP
LABOUR FORCE AND MIGRATION SURVEY. Text in English. irreg. **Document type:** *Government.* **Description:** Provides a complete set of tables on the demographic characteristics of the population in its various dissections, potential labor force and migration.
Published by: Ministry of Finance, Department of Statistics and Research, 13 Andreas Araouzos St, Nicosia, 1444, Cyprus. TEL 357-2-309318, FAX 357-2-374830.

304.6 LBY ISSN 0075-9236
LIBYA. CENSUS AND STATISTICS DEPARTMENT. GENERAL POPULATION CENSUS. Text in Arabic, English. 1954. decennial. free. **Document type:** *Government.*
Published by: Lybia. Secretariat of Planning, Census and Statistics Department, P O Box 600, Tripoli, Libya.

325 CAN
LOCAL HEALTH AREA POPULATION ESTIMATES AND PROJECTIONS (ONLINE). Text in English. a. price varies. **Document type:** *Government.* **Description:** Provides detailed historical and forecast population statistics by age and gender, including components of change to the year 2021 for 80 sub-provincial areas.
Formerly: Local Health Area Population Estimates and Projections (Print)
Media: Online - full text.
Published by: Ministry of Finance and Corporate Relations, B C Stats, PO Box 9410, Sta Prov Govt, Victoria, BC V8W 9V1, Canada. TEL 250-387-0359, FAX 250-387-0380, BC.Stats@gov.bc.ca.

304.6 LUX ISSN 1019-6471
HC330.A1
LE LUXEMBOURG EN CHIFFRES (YEAR). Text in French. a. free. **Document type:** *Government.* **Description:** Presents figures for territory, climate, population, economic and social situation, and the environment.
Related titles: English ed.: Luxembourg in Figures. ISSN 1019-648X; German ed.: Luxemburg in Zahlen. ISSN 1019-6501; Dutch ed.: Luxemburg in Cijfers. ISSN 1019-6498.
Published by: Service Central de la Statistique et des Etudes Economiques, 13, rue Erasme, Luxembourg, L-1468, Luxembourg. TEL 352-478-4268, FAX 352-464289, http://www.statec.public.lu. Circ: 100,000.

304.6 LUX
LUXEMBOURG. SERVICE CENTRAL DE LA STATISTIQUE ET DES ETUDES ECONOMIQUES. COLLECTION RP: RECENSEMENT DE LA POPULATION ET MOUVEMENT DE LA POPULATION. Text in French. 1962. irreg. price varies. **Document type:** *Government.*
Formerly: Luxembourg. Service Central de la Statistique et des Etudes Economiques. Collection RP: Recensement de la Population (0076-1613)
Published by: Service Central de la Statistique et des Etudes Economiques, 13, rue Erasme, Luxembourg, L-1468, Luxembourg. TEL 352-478-4268, FAX 352-464289, http://www.statec.public.lu.

304.6 LUX ISSN 1012-6643
LUXEMBOURG. SERVICE CENTRAL DE LA STATISTIQUE ET DES ETUDES ECONOMIQUES. INDICATEURS RAPIDES. SERIE E: NAISSANCES, MARIAGES, DIVORCES, DECES. Text in French. q. looseleaf. **Document type:** *Government.*
Published by: Service Central de la Statistique et des Etudes Economiques, 13, rue Erasme, Luxembourg, L-1468, Luxembourg. TEL 352-478-4233, FAX 352-464-289, statec.post@statec.etat.lu, http://www.statec.public.lu.

304.6 LUX
LUXEMBOURG. SERVICE CENTRAL DE LA STATISTIQUE ET DES ETUDES ECONOMIQUES. INDICATEURS RAPIDES. SERIE J: RESULTATS DE L'ENQUETE DE CONJONCTURE. Text in French. m. looseleaf. **Document type:** *Government.*
Published by: Service Central de la Statistique et des Etudes Economiques, 13, rue Erasme, Luxembourg, L-1468, Luxembourg. TEL 352-478-4233, FAX 352-464-289, statec.post@statec.etat.lu, http://www.statec.public.lu.

304.6 MAC
MACAO. DIRECCAO DOS SERVICOS DE ESTATISTICA E CENSOS. CENSOS DA POPULACAO/MACAO. CENSUS AND STATISTICS DEPARTMENT. POPULATION CENSUS. Text in Chinese, Portuguese, English. 1950. every 10 yrs. free. **Document type:** *Government.*
Published by: Direccao dos Servicos de Estatistica e Censos, Alameda Dr Carlos d'Assumcao 411-417, Macao, Macau. TEL 853-3995311, FAX 853-307825, info@dsec.gov.mo, http://www.dsec.gov.mo.

304.6 MAC ISSN 0872-4482
MACAO. DIRECCAO DOS SERVICOS DE ESTATISTICA E CENSOS. ESTATISTICAS DEMOGRAFICAS/MACAO. CENSUS AND STATISTICS DEPARTMENT. DEMOGRAPHIC STATISTICS. Text in Chinese, Portuguese. 1984. q. (plus a. review). free. **Document type:** *Government.* **Description:** Presents the latest figures for movement of population, births, deaths, marriages, divorces and immigration.
Published by: Direccao dos Servicos de Estatistica e Censos, Alameda Dr Carlos d'Assumcao 411-417, Macao, Macau. TEL 853-3995311, FAX 853-307825, info@dsec.gov.mo, http://www.dsec.gov.mo.

304.6 MAC
MACAO. DIRECCAO DOS SERVICOS DE ESTATISTICA E CENSOS. ESTIMATIVAS DA POPULACAO RESIDENTE DE MACAU/ MACAO. CENSUS AND STATISTICS DEPARTMENT. POPULATION ESTIMATES IN MACAO. Text in Chinese, Portuguese. 1991. a. free. **Document type:** *Government.*
Published by: Direccao dos Servicos de Estatistica e Censos, Alameda Dr Carlos d'Assumcao 411-417, Macao, Macau. TEL 853-3995311, FAX 853-307825, info@dsec.gov.mo, http://www.dsec.gov.mo.

304.6 USA
MAINE. DEPARTMENT OF HUMAN SERVICES. POPULATION ESTIMATES FOR MINOR CIVIL DIVISIONS BY COUNTY. Text in English. 1981. a. USD 6. **Document type:** *Government.* **Description:** Population estimates of MCD's.
Published by: (Maine. Office of Data, Research, and Vital Statistics), Department of Human Services, Bureau of Health, State House Sta 11, Augusta, ME 04333. TEL 207-624-5445. Ed. Donald R Lemieux. Circ: 500.

304.6 USA
MAINE. DEPARTMENT OF HUMAN SERVICES. VITAL STATISTICS. Text in English. 1892. a. USD 10.50. **Document type:** *Government.*
Former titles: Maine. Department of Human Services. Bureau of Health Planning and Development. Vital Statistics; Maine. Division of Research and Vital Records. Annual Statistical Report
Related titles: Microfiche ed.: (from CIS).
Indexed: SRI.
Published by: (Maine. Office of Data, Research, and Vital Statistics), Department of Human Services, Bureau of Health, State House Sta 11, Augusta, ME 04333. TEL 207-624-5445. Ed. Donald R Lemieux. Circ: 500.

304.6 MWI ISSN 0076-3306
MALAWI. NATIONAL STATISTICAL OFFICE. POPULATION CENSUS FINAL REPORT. Text in English. 1966. irreg. (approx. every 10 yrs.) (in 6 vols.). MWK 200 per vol. **Document type:** *Government.*
Published by: (Malawi. Commissioner for Census and Statistics), National Statistical Office, PO Box 333, Zomba, Malawi. TEL 265-50-522377, FAX 265-50-523130.

310 MWI
MALAWI. NATIONAL STATISTICAL OFFICE. URBAN HOUSEHOLD EXPENDITURE SURVEY. Text in English. 1968. irreg. MWK 100. **Document type:** *Government.*
Formerly: Malawi. National Statistical Office. Household Income and Expenditure Survey (0076-3276)
Published by: (Malawi. Commissioner for Census and Statistics), National Statistical Office, PO Box 333, Zomba, Malawi. TEL 265-50-522377, FAX 265-50-523130.

304.6 MYS ISSN 0128-0503
HD5822.6
MALAYSIA. DEPARTMENT OF STATISTICS. LABOUR FORCE SURVEY REPORT, MALAYSIA/MALAYSIA. JABATAN PERANGKAAN. LAPORAN PENYIASATAN TENAGA BURUH, MALAYSIA. Text in English, Malay. 1989. a. MYR 24 (effective 1999). **Document type:** *Government.*
Published by: Malaysia. Department of Statistics/Jabatan Perangkaan, Jalan Cenderasari, Kuala Lumpur, 50514, Malaysia. TEL 60-3-294-4264, FAX 60-3-291-4535.

304.6 MYS
MALAYSIA. DEPARTMENT OF STATISTICS. MIGRATION SURVEY REPORT, MALAYSIA/MALAYSIA. JABATAN PERANGKAAN. LAPORAN PENYIASATAN MIGRASI, MALAYSIA. Text in English, Malay. a., latest 1997. MYR 20. **Document type:** *Government.*
Published by: Malaysia. Department of Statistics/Jabatan Perangkaan, Jalan Cenderasari, Kuala Lumpur, 50514, Malaysia. TEL 60-3-294-4264, FAX 30-3-291-4535.

304.6 MYS ISSN 0127-8312
HA4600.6
MALAYSIA. DEPARTMENT OF STATISTICS. QUARTERLY REVIEW OF MALAYSIAN POPULATION STATISTICS/MALAYSIA. JABATAN PERANGKAAN. SARAN PERANGKAAN PENDUDUK SUKU TAHUNAN, MALAYSIA. Text in English. 1986. q. MYR 11 per issue (effective 1999). **Document type:** *Government.*
Published by: Malaysia. Department of Statistics/Jabatan Perangkaan, Jalan Cenderasari, Kuala Lumpur, 50514, Malaysia. TEL 60-3-294-4264, FAX 60-3-291-4535.

304.6 MYS
HA1791
MALAYSIA. DEPARTMENT OF STATISTICS. VITAL STATISTICS, MALAYSIA (YEAR)/MALAYSIA. JABATAN PERANGKAAN. PERANGKAAN PENTING, MALAYSIA. Text in English, Malay. 1963. a. MYR 35. **Document type:** *Government.*
Formerly: Malaysia. Department of Statistics. Vital Statistics, Peninsular Malaysia (0127-466X)
Published by: Malaysia. Department of Statistics/Jabatan Perangkaan, Jalan Cenderasari, Kuala Lumpur, 50514, Malaysia. TEL 60-3-294-4264, FAX 60-3-291-4535. Circ: 800.

304.6 MLT ISSN 0076-3470
MALTA. CENTRAL OFFICE OF STATISTICS. DEMOGRAPHIC REVIEW OF THE MALTESE ISLANDS. Text in English. 1960. a. **Document type:** *Government.*
Published by: Central Office of Statistics, Auberge d'Italie, Merchants' St., Valletta, Malta. FAX 356-248483. **Subscr. to:** Publications Bookshop, Castille Place, Valletta, Malta.

304.6 MUS
MAURITIUS. CENTRAL STATISTICAL OFFICE. DIGEST OF DEMOGRAPHIC STATISTICS. Text in English. 1985. a., latest 1997. MUR 100 per issue (effective 2001). charts. **Document type:** *Government.* **Description:** Provides a statistical overview of the economic situation of Mauritius from a demographic perspective.
Published by: Mauritius. Central Statistical Office, L.I.C. Centre, President John Kennedy St, Port Louis, Mauritius. TEL 230-212-2316, FAX 230-212-4150, cso@intnet.mu, http://statsmauritius.gov.mu. **Subscr. to:** Mauritius. Government Printing Office, Ramtoolah Bldg, Sir S Ramgoolam St, Port Louis, Mauritius. TEL 230-234-5294, 230-242-0234, FAX 230-234-5322.

325.2021 CAN ISSN 1207-4845
MIGRATION HIGHLIGHTS. Text in English. 1990. q. CAD 30 (effective 2006). **Document type:** *Government.* **Description:** Provides detailed current information on the flow of people between B.C. and other provinces and territories. Contains components of population change.
Formerly (until 1994): British Columbia Migration Highlights (1186-7965)
Related titles: Online - full text ed.
Published by: Ministry of Finance and Corporate Relations, B C Stats, PO Box 9410, Sta Prov Govt, Victoria, BC V8W 9V1, Canada. TEL 250-387-0359, FAX 250-387-0380, BC.Stats@gov.bc.ca.

304.6021 GBR ISSN 2040-8544
▼ **MIGRATION STATISTICS QUARTERLY REPORT.** Text in English. 2009. q. free (effective 2010). back issues avail. **Document type:** *Report, Government.* **Description:** Covers summaries of trends from the quarterly publications of migration data by Office for National Statistics (ONS), the home office, department for work and pensions and general register office for Scotland.
Media: Online - full text.
Published by: Office for National Statistics, Rm 1.101, Government Bldgs, Cardiff Rd, Newport, S Wales NP10 8XG, United Kingdom. TEL 44-1633-653599, FAX 44-1633-652747, info@statistics.gov.uk, http://www.statistics.gov.uk/default.asp.

304.6021 USA
MISSOURI MONTHLY VITAL STATISTICS. Text in English. 1967. m. free. charts; stat. **Document type:** *Government.* **Description:** Contains vital statistics data and short analytical article concerning public health issues.
Published by: Department of Health, Center for Health Information Management & Epidemiology, PO Box 570, Jefferson City, MO 65102. TEL 314-751-6272. Ed. Garland Land. Circ: 800.

304.6021 USA ISSN 0098-1974
HA471
MISSOURI VITAL STATISTICS. Text in English. a. free. **Document type:** *Government.* **Description:** Contains tables and graphs.
Related titles: Microfiche ed.: (from CIS).
Indexed: SRI.
Published by: Department of Health, Center for Health Information Management & Epidemiology, PO Box 570, Jefferson City, MO 65102. TEL 314-751-6272. Ed. Garland Land. Circ: 900.

304.6 USA ISSN 0077-1198
HA481
MONTANA VITAL STATISTICS. Text in English. 1954. a. free. **Document type:** *Government.*
Former titles: Montana. State Department of Health. Annual Statistical Supplement (0097-9120); Montana State Board of Health. Annual Statistical Supplement (0097-9112)
Indexed: SRI.
Published by: Montana Department of Public Health and Human Services, Office of Vital Statistics, 111 N Sanders, Helena, MT 59604. TEL 406-444-4228, FAX 406-444-1803, http://www.dphhs.mt.gov. Circ: 850 (controlled).

304.6 MAR
MOROCCO. DIRECTION DE LA STATISTIQUE. POPULATION ACTIVE URBAINE, ACTIVITE, EMPLOI ET CHOMAGE. Text in French. a. MAD 33 (effective 2000). **Document type:** *Government.*
Formerly (until 1995): Morocco. Direction de la Statistique. Population Active Urbaine: Premiers Resultats
Published by: Morocco. Direction de la Statistique, B P 178, Rabat, Morocco. TEL 212-7-77-36-06, FAX 212-7-77-32-17.

304.6 GRC ISSN 0077-6114
MOUVEMENT NATUREL DE LA POPULATION DE LA GRECE. Text in French, Greek. 1956. a., latest 1992. back issues avail. **Document type:** *Government.*
Published by: National Statistical Service of Greece, Statistical Information and Publications Division/Ethniki Statistiki Yperesia tes Ellados, 14-16 Lykourgou St, Athens, 101 66, Greece. TEL 30-1-3289-397, FAX 30-1-3241-102, http://www.statistics.gr, http://www.statistics.gr/Main_eng.asp.

306.4 NLD ISSN 1571-0998
HA1381
NETHERLANDS. CENTRAAL BUREAU VOOR DE STATISTIEK. BEVOKLINGSTRENDS; statistisch kwartaalblad over de demografie van Nederland. Key Title: Bevolkingstrends. Text in Dutch. 1953. q. EUR 50.35; EUR 13.80 newsstand/cover (effective 2008). charts. index. **Document type:** *Government.* **Description:** Provides a statistical survey of population trends and predictions in the Netherlands.
Formerly (until 2003): Netherlands. Centraal Bureau voor de Statistiek. Maandstatistiek van de Bevolking (0168-6240); Supersedes in part (in 1982): Netherlands. Centraal Bureau voor de Statistiek. Maandstatistiek van de Bevolking en Volksgezondheid (0024-8711)
Indexed: A22, ESPM, F09, P30, PopulInd, SCOPUS, SSciA. —IE.
Published by: Centraal Bureau voor de Statistiek, Henri Faasdreef 312, The Hague, 2492 JP, Netherlands. TEL 31-70-3373800, infoserv@cbs.nl.

304.021 NLD ISSN 1569-8033
HB3605
NETHERLANDS. CENTRAAL BUREAU VOOR DE STATISTIEK. DEMOGRAFISCHE KERNCIJFERS PER GEMEENTE. Key Title: Demografische Kerncijfers per Gemeente. Cover title: Population of the Municipalities of the Netherlands. Variant title: Bevolking en Bevolkingsdichtheid der Gemeenten van Nederland. Bevolking en Oppervlakte der Gemeenten van Nederland. Text in Dutch, English. 1920. a. EUR 11.50 (effective 2008). charts; maps. **Document type:** *Government.* **Description:** Surveys statistical changes in the population ranges and densities in Dutch municipalities over the past year.
Formed by the 2001 merger of: Netherlands. Centraal Bureau voor de Statistiek. Bevolking der Gemeenten van Nederland op 1 Januari (Year) (0168-3853); Netherlands. Centraal Bureau voor de Statistiek. Loop van de Bevolking per Gemeente (0920-4318)

Related titles: Diskette ed.: Netherlands. Centraal Bureau voor de Statistiek. Bevolking der Gemeenten van Nederland op 1 Januari (Year) (Diskette). ISSN 0928-4788.
Published by: Centraal Bureau voor de Statistiek, Henri Faasdreef 312, The Hague, 2492 JP, Netherlands. TEL 31-70-3373800, infoserv@cbs.nl, http://www.cbs.nl.

304.6021 NLD ISSN 0924-2686
HA1381
NETHERLANDS. CENTRAAL BUREAU VOOR DE STATISTIEK. STATISTISCH JAARBOEK/NETHERLANDS. CENTRAL BUREAU OF STATISTICS. POCKET YEARBOOK. Text in Dutch, English. 1924. a. **Document type:** *Government.* **Description:** Compiles data on nearly every aspect of community living in the Netherlands, including population, education, unemployment, community, health care, agriculture, and industry.
Formerly (until 1990): Netherlands. Centraal Bureau voor de Statistiek. Statistisch Zakboek (0168-3705)
Related titles: CD-ROM ed.: EUR 22.67 (effective 2000); Online - full text ed.: ISSN 2211-5951.
Published by: Centraal Bureau voor de Statistiek, Henri Faasdreef 312, The Hague, 2492 JP, Netherlands. TEL 31-70-3373800, infoserv@cbs.nl.

304.671021 CAN ISSN 1195-9452
CA2NBSCR17
NEW BRUNSWICK. VITAL STATISTICS. ANNUAL STATISTICAL REPORT/NOUVEAU-BRUNSWICK. STATISTIQUES DE L'ETAT CIVIL. RAPPORT STATISTIQUE ANNUEL. Text in English, French. 1991. a.
Published by: New Brunswick, Department of Health and Wellness, PO Box 5100, Fredericton, NB E3B 5G8, Canada. TEL 506-453-2536, FAX 506-444-4697, http://www.gnb.ca/0051/index-e.asp.

304.6 USA ISSN 0095-5523
HA511
NEW HAMPSHIRE VITAL STATISTICS. Text in English. 1880. a. **Document type:** *Government.*
Indexed: SRI.
Published by: U.S. Department of Health and Human Services, Bureau of Vital Epidemiology and Statistics, 129 Pleasant St, Concord, NH 03301. TEL 603-271-4671. Circ: 350.

352.041021 GBR ISSN 1363-1462
NEW LOCAL GOVERNMENT AREA MONITOR. Text in English. 1996. irreg., latest 1997. **Document type:** *Government.*
Related titles: Online - full text ed.: free (effective 2010).
—CCC.
Published by: Office for National Statistics, Rm 1.101, Government Bldgs, Cardiff Rd, Newport, S Wales NP10 8XG, United Kingdom. TEL 44-845-6013034, FAX 44-1633-652747, info@statistics.gsi.gov.uk, http://www.statistics.gov.uk/default.asp.

319.4 NZL ISSN 1177-438X
HB1323.I42
NEW ZEALAND HEALTH INFORMATION SERVICE. FETAL AND INFANT DEATHS (CD-ROM). Key Title: Fetal and Infant Deaths. Text in English. 1964. a., latest 2004, for the year 2002. stat. **Document type:** *Government.*
Former titles (until 2002): New Zealand Health Information Service. Fetal and Infant Deaths (Print) (0111-8617); (until 1978): New Zealand. Health Statistical Services. Fetal and Infant Deaths; New Zealand. National Health Statistics Centre. Fetal and Infant Deaths
Media: CD-ROM. **Related titles:** Online - full text ed.: ISSN 1177-4770.
Published by: Ministry of Health, Information Directorate, PO Box 5013, Wellington, New Zealand. TEL 64-4-4962000, FAX 64-4-4962340, nzhis-pub@nzhis.govt.nz. Circ: (controlled).

304.64 NZL ISSN 0548-9911
RA407.5.N4
NEW ZEALAND HEALTH INFORMATION SERVICE. MORTALITY AND DEMOGRAPHIC DATA. Text in English. a., latest 1997. stat. **Document type:** *Government.*
Formerly: New Zealand. Health Statistical Services. Mortality and Demographic Data
Published by: Ministry of Health, Information Directorate, PO Box 5013, Wellington, New Zealand. TEL 64-4-8012700, FAX 64-4-8012769, nzhis-pubs@web1.health.govt.nz. Circ: (controlled).

NEW ZEALAND HEALTH INFORMATION SERVICE. SELECTED MORBIDITY DATA FOR PUBLICLY FUNDED HOSPITALS. *see* HEALTH FACILITIES AND ADMINISTRATION—Abstracting, Bibliographies, Statistics

304.6 NZL
NEW ZEALAND. STATISTICS NEW ZEALAND. CENSUS REPORTS. BIRTHPLACES AND ETHNIC ORIGIN. Text in English. quinquennial (issued 2001). NZD 35 (effective 2008). adv. **Document type:** *Government.*
Former titles: New Zealand. Department of Statistics. Population Census: Birthplaces and Ethnic Origin; New Zealand. Department of Statistics. Population Census: Race (0077-9776)
Published by: Statistics New Zealand/Te Tari Tatau, Statistics House, The Blvd, Harbour Quays, PO Box 2922, Wellington, 6140, New Zealand. TEL 64-4-9314600, FAX 64-4-9314610, info@stats.govt.nz.

304.6 NZL
NEW ZEALAND. STATISTICS NEW ZEALAND. CENSUS REPORTS. EDUCATION. Text in English. quinquennial. NZD 35 (effective 2008). **Document type:** *Government.*
Former titles: New Zealand. Department of Statistics. Population Census: Education and Training; New Zealand. Department of Statistics. Population Census: Education (0077-9709)
Related titles: Online - full content ed.
Published by: Statistics New Zealand/Te Tari Tatau, Statistics House, The Blvd, Harbour Quays, PO Box 2922, Wellington, 6140, New Zealand. TEL 64-4-9314600, FAX 64-4-9314610, info@stats.govt.nz.

304.6 305.8 NZL
NEW ZEALAND. STATISTICS NEW ZEALAND. CENSUS REPORTS. ETHNIC GROUPS. Text in English. quinquennial, latest 2001. NZD 29.95 (effective 2000). stat. **Document type:** *Government.* **Description:** Covers demographic, social and economic characteristics of a range of ethnic groups. It also includes education, income and employment information.
Related titles: Online - full content ed.
Published by: Statistics New Zealand/Te Tari Tatau, Statistics House, The Blvd, Harbour Quays, PO Box 2922, Wellington, 6140, New Zealand. TEL 64-4-9314600, FAX 64-4-9314610, info@stats.govt.nz.

304.6 NZL
NEW ZEALAND. STATISTICS NEW ZEALAND. CENSUS REPORTS. FAMILIES AND HOUSEHOLDS. Text in English. quinquennial, latest 2001. NZD 35 (effective 2008). adv. **Document type:** *Government.*
Former titles: New Zealand. Department of Statistics. Population Census: Families and Households; New Zealand. Department of Statistics. Population Census: Households (0077-9725)
Related titles: Online - full content ed.
Published by: Statistics New Zealand/Te Tari Tatau, Statistics House, The Blvd, Harbour Quays, PO Box 2922, Wellington, 6140, New Zealand. TEL 64-4-9314600, FAX 64-4-9314610, info@stats.govt.nz.

304.6 NZL
NEW ZEALAND. STATISTICS NEW ZEALAND. CENSUS REPORTS. GENERAL INFORMATION. Text in English. quinquennial. **Document type:** *Government.*
Formerly: New Zealand. Department of Statistics. Population Census: General Report (0077-9717)
Published by: Statistics New Zealand/Te Tari Tatau, Statistics House, The Blvd, Harbour Quays, PO Box 2922, Wellington, 6140, New Zealand. TEL 64-4-9314600, FAX 64-4-9314610, info@stats.govt.nz, http://www.stats.govt.nz.

304.6 NZL
NEW ZEALAND. STATISTICS NEW ZEALAND. CENSUS REPORTS. INCOMES. Text in English. quinquennial (issued 2001). NZD 35 (effective 2008). adv. **Document type:** *Government.*
Former titles: New Zealand. Statistics New Zealand. Population Census: Incomes and Welfare Payments; New Zealand. Department of Statistics, Population Census: Income and Welfare Payments; New Zealand. Department of Statistics. Population Census: Incomes and Social Security Benefits; New Zealand. Department of Statistics. Population Census: Incomes (0077-9733)
Related titles: Online - full content ed.
Published by: Statistics New Zealand/Te Tari Tatau, Statistics House, The Blvd, Harbour Quays, PO Box 2922, Wellington, 6140, New Zealand. TEL 64-4-9314600, FAX 64-4-9314610, info@stats.govt.nz.

304.6 NZL
NEW ZEALAND. STATISTICS NEW ZEALAND. CENSUS REPORTS. IWI. Text in English. quinquennial, latest 2001. NZD 29.95 (effective 2000). stat. **Document type:** *Government.* **Description:** Covers a wide range of demographic, social and economic characteristics of iwi in New Zealand including topics such as population size, location, age composition, education, employment, income and the characteristics of iwi households and families.
Related titles: Online - full content ed.
Published by: Statistics New Zealand/Te Tari Tatau, Statistics House, The Blvd, Harbour Quays, PO Box 2922, Wellington, 6140, New Zealand. TEL 64-4-9314600, FAX 64-4-9314610, info@stats.govt.nz.

304.6 NZL
NEW ZEALAND. STATISTICS NEW ZEALAND. CENSUS REPORTS. MAORI. Variant title: New Zealand. Statistics New Zealand. Maori Population and Dwellings. Text in English. quinquennial, latest 2001. NZD 35 (effective 2008). stat. **Document type:** *Government.* **Description:** Covers a wide variety of Maori demographic, social and economic characteristics, including education, income, employment and household composition.
Published by: Statistics New Zealand/Te Tari Tatau, Statistics House, The Blvd, Harbour Quays, PO Box 2922, Wellington, 6140, New Zealand. TEL 64-4-9314600, FAX 64-4-9314610, info@stats.govt.nz.

304.6 NZL
NEW ZEALAND. STATISTICS NEW ZEALAND. CENSUS REPORTS. NATIONAL SUMMARY. Text in English. quinquennial, latest 2001. NZD 35 (effective 2008). stat. **Document type:** *Government.* **Description:** Covers a wide variety of demographic, social and economic population characteristics, including ethnic group, income, occupation and household composition.
Related titles: Online - full content ed.
Published by: Statistics New Zealand/Te Tari Tatau, Statistics House, The Blvd, Harbour Quays, PO Box 2922, Wellington, 6140, New Zealand. TEL 64-4-9314600, FAX 64-4-9314610, info@stats.govt.nz.

304.6 NZL
NEW ZEALAND. STATISTICS NEW ZEALAND. CENSUS REPORTS. PACIFIC ISLAND PEOPLE. Text in English. irreg., latest 1996. NZD 29.95 (effective 2008). stat. **Document type:** *Government.* **Description:** Covers demographic, social and economic characteristics of the Cook Islands, Fijian, Niuean, Samoan, Tongan, and Tokelauan ethnic groups.
Related titles: Online - full content ed.
Published by: Statistics New Zealand/Te Tari Tatau, Statistics House, The Blvd, Harbour Quays, PO Box 2922, Wellington, 6140, New Zealand. TEL 64-4-9314600, FAX 64-4-9314610, info@stats.govt.nz, http://www.stats.govt.nz.

304.6 NZL
NEW ZEALAND. STATISTICS NEW ZEALAND. CENSUS REPORTS. PEOPLE BORN OVERSEAS. Variant title: (Year) Census of Population and Dwellings. People Born Overseas. Text in English. irreg., latest 2001. NZD 35 (effective 2008). stat. **Document type:** *Government.* **Description:** Contains statistics outlining the demographics and household composition of New Zealand's immigrant population.
Related titles: Online - full content ed.
Published by: Statistics New Zealand/Te Tari Tatau, Statistics House, The Blvd, Harbour Quays, PO Box 2922, Wellington, 6140, New Zealand. TEL 64-4-9314600, FAX 64-4-9314610, info@stats.govt.nz.

304.6 NZL
NEW ZEALAND. STATISTICS NEW ZEALAND. CENSUS REPORTS. POPULATION AND DWELLING STATISTICS. Text in English. quinquennial (issued 2001). NZD 35 (effective 2008). stat. **Document type:** *Government.*
Formerly: New Zealand. Department of Statistics. Population Census: Dwellings (0077-9695)
Published by: Statistics New Zealand/Te Tari Tatau, Statistics House, The Blvd, Harbour Quays, PO Box 2922, Wellington, 6140, New Zealand. TEL 64-4-9314600, FAX 64-4-9314610, info@stats.govt.nz.

304.6 NZL
NEW ZEALAND. STATISTICS NEW ZEALAND. CENSUS REPORTS. POPULATION STRUCTURE AND INTERNAL MIGRATION. Text in English. 1971. quinquennial (issued 2001). NZD 35 (effective 2008). **Document type:** *Government.*
Formerly: New Zealand. Statistics New Zealand. Population Census: Internal Migration.
Related titles: Print ed.
Published by: Statistics New Zealand/Te Tari Tatau, Statistics House, The Blvd, Harbour Quays, PO Box 2922, Wellington, 6140, New Zealand. TEL 64-4-9314600, FAX 64-4-9314610, info@stats.govt.nz.

304.6 NZL
NEW ZEALAND. STATISTICS NEW ZEALAND. CENSUS REPORTS. REGIONAL SUMMARY. Text in English. quinquennial, latest 2001. NZD 35 (effective 2008). stat. **Document type:** *Government.* **Description:** Covers a range of demographic, social and economic topics together with dwelling and household characteristics. The 30 statistical tables present data at statistical area, regional council area, territorial authority area, urban area and rural area levels.
Related titles: Online - full content ed.
Published by: Statistics New Zealand/Te Tari Tatau, Statistics House, The Blvd, Harbour Quays, PO Box 2922, Wellington, 6140, New Zealand. TEL 64-4-9314600, FAX 64-4-9314610, info@stats.govt.nz.

304.6 NZL ISSN 0077-9784
NEW ZEALAND. STATISTICS NEW ZEALAND. CENSUS REPORTS. RELIGIOUS PROFESSIONS. Text in English. quinquennial. Supplement avail. **Document type:** *Government.*
Published by: Statistics New Zealand/Te Tari Tatau, Statistics House, The Blvd, Harbour Quays, PO Box 2922, Wellington, 6140, New Zealand. TEL 64-4-9314600, FAX 64-4-9314610, info@stats.govt.nz, http://www.stats.govt.nz.

304.6 330 NZL
NEW ZEALAND. STATISTICS NEW ZEALAND. CENSUS REPORTS. UNPAID WORK. Variant title: New Zealand Census of Population and Dwellings. Unpaid Work. Text in English. irreg., latest 1996. NZD 29.95 (effective 2008). stat. **Document type:** *Government.* **Description:** Provides information on unpaid work outside the household by such variables as age, ethnicity, gender and labour force status.
Related titles: Online - full content ed.
Published by: Statistics New Zealand/Te Tari Tatau, Statistics House, The Blvd, Harbour Quays, PO Box 2922, Wellington, 6140, New Zealand. TEL 64-4-9314600, FAX 64-4-9314610, info@stats.govt.nz, http://www.stats.govt.nz.

304.6 NZL
NEW ZEALAND. STATISTICS NEW ZEALAND. CENSUS REPORTS. WORK. Text in English. quinquennial (issued 2001). NZD 35 (effective 2008). adv. **Document type:** *Government.*
Former titles: New Zealand. Statistics New Zealand. Census Reports. Employment and Unemployment; New Zealand, Department of Statistics. Population Census: Industries and Occupations (0077-9741)
Related titles: Online - full content ed.
Published by: Statistics New Zealand/Te Tari Tatau, Statistics House, The Blvd, Harbour Quays, PO Box 2922, Wellington, 6140, New Zealand. TEL 64-4-9314600, FAX 64-4-9314610, info@stats.govt.nz.

304.6 NZL ISSN 0113-3667
HA3171
NEW ZEALAND. STATISTICS NEW ZEALAND. DEMOGRAPHIC TRENDS. Text in English. biennial. NZD 40 (effective 2008). **Document type:** *Government.*
Formerly (until 1987): New Zealand. Department of Statistics. Demographic Trend Bulletin (0112-9155); Which was formed by the 1985 merger of: New Zealand. Department of Statistics. Population and Migration Statistics. Part A. Population (0112-5354); Which was formerly: New Zealand. Department. Population and Migration. Part A: Population (0110-375X); Which superseded in part (in 1973): New Zealand. Department of Statistics. Population and Migration (0077-9903); New Zealand. Department of Statistics. Statistical Report of Population, Migration and Building; (1981-1985): New Zealand. Department of Statistics. Demographic Bulletin (0111-8102); Which was formerly: New Zealand. Department of Statistics. Quarterly Demographic Bulletin (0111-2643); (1977-1979): New Zealand. Department of Statistics. Quarterly Population Bulletin (0110-4055)
Related titles: Online - full text ed.: ISSN 1177-8075.
Indexed: INZP, P30.
—CCC.
Published by: Statistics New Zealand/Te Tari Tatau, Statistics House, The Blvd, Harbour Quays, PO Box 2922, Wellington, 6140, New Zealand. TEL 64-4-9314600, FAX 64-4-9314610, info@stats.govt.nz.

304.6 NIC
NICARAGUA. INSTITUTO NACIONAL DE ESTADISTICAS Y CENSOS. ESTADISTICAS VITALES. Text in Spanish. q. **Document type:** *Government.*
Published by: Instituto Nacional de Estadisticas y Censos, Apartado Postal 4031, Managua, Nicaragua.

304.6 JPN
NIHON NO JINKO/POPULATION CENSUS OF JAPAN. Text in English, Japanese. quinquennial. price varies. **Document type:** *Government.*
Related titles: Online - full text ed.
Published by: Japan. Ministry of Internal Affairs and Communications. Statistics Bureau/Somucho. Tokeikyoko, 19-1 Wakamatsu-cho, Shinjyuku-ku, Tokyo, 162-8668, Japan. TEL 81-3-5273-2020. R&P Akihiko Ito.

NONG'EOB CHONG JO'SA BUNSEOG BO'GO'SEO/KOREA (REPUBLIC). NATIONAL STATISTICAL OFFICE. AGRICULTURAL CENSUS REPORT. *see* AGRICULTURE—Abstracting, Bibliographies, Statistics

NONG'GA GYEONGJE TONG'GYE/KOREA (REPUBLIC). NATIONAL STATISTICAL OFFICE. FARM HOUSEHOLD ECONOMY SURVEY REPORT. *see* BUSINESS AND ECONOMICS—Abstracting, Bibliographies, Statistics

304.6 USA ISSN 0078-1371
NORTH CAROLINA VITAL STATISTICS. Text in English. 1916. a. free. **Document type:** *Government.*
Indexed: SRI.
Published by: U.S. Department of Health and Human Services, State Center for Health Statistics, PO Box 29538, Raleigh, NC 27626-0538. TEL 919-733-4728.

P

304.6021 NOR ISSN 0550-032X
RA407.5.N6
NORWAY. STATISTISK SENTRALBYRAA. DOEDSAARSAKER/ NORWAY. STATISTICS NORWAY. CAUSES OF DEATH. Text in English, Norwegian. 1964. a.
Supersedes in part (in 1964): Norway. Statistisk Sentralbyraa. Helsestatistikk (0332-7906)
Related titles: Online - full text ed.: ISSN 1504-2391; ◆ Series of: Norges Offisielle Statistikk. ISSN 0300-5585.
Published by: Statistisk Sentralbyraa/Statistics Norway, Kongensgate 6, P O Box 8131, Dep, Oslo, 0033, Norway. TEL 47-21-090000, FAX 47-21-094973, ssb@ssb.no.

304.6 NOR ISSN 0332-8015
NORWAY. STATISTISK SENTRALBYRAA. FRAMSKRIVING AV FOLKEMENGDEN/NORWAY. CENTRAL BUREAU OF STATISTICS. POPULATION PROJECTIONS: REGIONAL FIGURES. (Subseries of its Norges Offisielle Statistikk) Text in Norwegian. 1969. triennial. NOK 140 per issue (effective 2004). **Document type:** *Government.*
Related titles: ◆ Series of: Norges Offisielle Statistikk. ISSN 0300-5585.
Published by: Statistisk Sentralbyraa/Statistics Norway, Kongensgate 6, P O Box 8131, Dep, Oslo, 0033, Norway. TEL 47-21-090000, FAX 47-21-094973, ssb@ssb.no, http://www.ssb.no.

O E C D INTERNATIONAL MIGRATION STATISTICS/SOURCE O C D E STATISTIQUES DES MIGRATIONS INTERNATIONALES. (Organisation for Economic Cooperation and Development) *see* BUSINESS AND ECONOMICS—Abstracting, Bibliographies, Statistics

338.021 GBR ISSN 1464-2085
OFFICE FOR NATIONAL STATISTICS. NEWS RELEASE. Text in English. 1989. irreg., latest 2010, Feb. free (effective 2010). back issues avail. **Document type:** *Government.*
Former titles (until 1996): Central Statistical Office. News Release; (until 1994): C S O Bulletin; (until 1991): Central Statistical Office. Business Bulletin
Related titles: Online - full text ed.
—CCC.
Published by: Office for National Statistics, Rm 1.101, Government Bldgs, Cardiff Rd, Newport, S Wales NP10 8XG, United Kingdom. TEL 44-845-6013034, FAX 44-1633-652747, info@statistics.gsi.gov.uk, http://www.statistics.gov.uk/default.asp.

304.6 USA
OKLAHOMA POPULATION ESTIMATES. Text in English. 1967. a. free. charts; stat. **Document type:** *Government.*
Published by: Employment Security Commission, Office of Economic Analysis, 213 Will Rogers Bldg, Oklahoma City, OK 73105. Ed. Roger Jacks. Circ: 850.

304.6 USA
THE OLDER POPULATION IN THE UNITED STATES. Text in English. a. free. **Document type:** *Government.*
Media: Online - full text.
Published by: U.S. Census Bureau. Population Division (Subsidiary of: U.S. Department of Commerce), 4600 Silver Hill Rd., Washington, DC 20233. TEL 866-758-1060.

304.6 325 PNG ISSN 1017-6551
PAPUA NEW GUINEA INTERNATIONAL ARRIVALS AND DEPARTURES. Text in English. 1957. q. PGK 12 domestic; PGK 20 foreign (effective 2005). **Document type:** *Government.* **Description:** Contains statistics compiled from passenger arrival and departure cards; provides a breakdown of persons arriving in Papua New Guinea, by purpose of journey, age, nationality and occupation, overseas address and length of stay in Papua.
Former titles: Papua New Guinea International Migration; Papua New Guinea Overseas Migration (0031-1510); Papua New Guinea Territory. Quarterly Migration Bulletin
Published by: National Statistical Office, Waigani, National Capital District, PO Box 337, Port Moresby, Papua New Guinea. TEL 675-3011200, FAX 675-3251869, http://www.nso.gov.pg/. Ed. Francis Kasau. Circ: 200.

304.6 310 USA
PENNSYLVANIA VITAL STATISTICS. Text in English. 1951. a. free. **Document type:** *Government.*
Formerly: Pennsylvania Natality and Mortality Statistics
Related titles: Microfiche ed.: (from CIS).
Indexed: SRI.
Published by: Department of Health, Bureau of Health Statistics, 555 Walnut St, 6th Fl, Harrisburg, PA 17101-1900. TEL 717-783-2548, FAX 717-772-3258. Circ: 1,000.

304.6021 PRT ISSN 1646-2580
PESSOAS EM NUMEROS. Text in Portuguese. 2005. a. **Document type:** *Report, Government.*
Published by: Instituto Nacional de Estatistica, Av Antonio Jose de Almeida 2, Lisbon, 1000-043, Portugal. TEL 351-21-8426100, FAX 351-21-8426380, ine@ine.pt, http://www.ine.pt.

315 PHL ISSN 0116-1520
HA1821
PHILIPPINE YEARBOOK. Text in English. 1940. biennial. USD 120 (effective 1997). **Document type:** *Government.* **Description:** Presents qualitative and quantitative data on practically all aspects of the country's physiographical, political, social, economic and demographic features in 24 different chapters.
Published by: National Statistics Office, Ramon Magsaysay Blvd, PO Box 779, Manila, Philippines. FAX 63-2-610794. Circ: 1,200.

304.6 PHL
PHILIPPINES. NATIONAL STATISTICS OFFICE. NATIONAL DEMOGRAPHIC SURVEY. Text in English. every 5 yrs. **Document type:** *Government.* **Description:** Analyzes and disseminates demographic data on fertility, family planning, and material and child health.
Published by: National Statistics Office, Ramon Magsaysay Blvd, PO Box 779, Manila, Philippines. FAX 63-2-610794.

315 PHL ISSN 0116-2675
HA1821
PHILIPPINES. NATIONAL STATISTICS OFFICE. VITAL STATISTICS REPORT. Text in English. a., latest 1991. USD 30. 366 p./no.; **Document type:** *Government.* **Description:** A yearly report on vital events like births, deaths, and marriages in the Philippines.
Formerly: Philippines. National Census and Statistics Office. Vital Statistical Report
Published by: National Statistics Office, Ramon Magsaysay Blvd, PO Box 779, Manila, Philippines. FAX 63-2-610794. Circ: 250.

PLACES, TOWNS AND TOWNSHIPS. *see* STATISTICS

304.6021 ESP ISSN 1579-0266
POBLACION DE LOS MUNICIPIOS ESPANOLES. Text in Spanish. 1988. a. EUR 8. **Document type:** *Government.*
Formerly (until 1997): Poblaciones de Derecho de los Municipios Espanoles (1136-2162)
Published by: Instituto Nacional de Estadistica (I N E), Paseo de la Castellana 183, Madrid, 28071, Spain. TEL 34-91-5839100, http://www.ine.es/.

304.6 BLZ
POPULATION & HOUSING CENSUS MAJOR FINDINGS. Text in English. 1991. every 10 yrs. USD 10. **Document type:** *Government.* **Description:** Presents a compendium of statistical tables which represents some of the major results from the census. Some descriptive commentaries and in depth demographic and socio-economic analyses are included.
Formerly: Population Census Major Findings
Published by: Ministry of Finance, Central Statistical Office, Belmopan, Belize. TEL 501-8-22207, FAX 501-8-23206.

304.6 GRC
POPULATION DE LA GRECE AU RECENSEMENT. Text in Greek; Summaries in French. 1920. decennial. back issues avail. **Document type:** *Government.*
Published by: National Statistical Service of Greece, Statistical Information and Publications Division/Ethniki Statistiki Yperesia tes Ellados, 14-16 Lykourgou St, Athens, 101 66, Greece. TEL 30-1-3289-397, FAX 30-1-3241-102, http://www.statistics.gr, http://www.statistics.gr/Main_eng.asp.

301.42 USA
POPULATION INDEX - ON THE WEB. Text in English. irreg. **Document type:** *Bibliography.*
Media: Online - full text.
Published by: Princeton University, Office of Population Research, 21 Prospect Ave, Princeton, NJ 08544-2091. TEL 609-258-4873, FAX 609-258-1655, popindex@princeton.edu.

304.6 PRT ISSN 0379-7007
PORTUGAL. INSTITUTO NACIONAL DE ESTATISTICA. CENTRO DE ESTUDOS DEMOGRAFICOS. CADERNOS. Text in Portuguese. 1976. irreg., latest vol.9, 1988. charts. **Document type:** *Monographic series, Government.* **Description:** Covers demographic studies and comparative methodologies.
Published by: Instituto Nacional de Estatistica, Av Antonio Jose de Almeida 2, Lisbon, 1000-043, Portugal. TEL 351-21-8426100, FAX 351-21-8426380, http://www.ine.pt.

PORTUGAL. INSTITUTO NACIONAL DE ESTATISTICA. RECENSEAMENTO DA POPULACAO E HABITACAO. *see* HOME ECONOMICS

PORTUGAL SOCIAL. *see* POPULATION STUDIES

304.6 PRI
PUERTO RICO. DEPARTMENT OF HEALTH. OFFICE OF HEALTH STATISTICS. DIVISION OF STATISTICS AND REPORTS. ANNUAL VITAL STATISTICS REPORT/INFORME ANUAL DE ESTADISTICAS VITALES. Text in English, Spanish. 1970. a. **Document type:** *Government.* **Description:** Information on population, deaths, births, marriages and divorces by municipality and regions.
Former titles: Puerto Rico. Department of Health. Office of Planning, Evaluation and Reports. Division of Statistics and Reports. Annual Vital Statistics Reports; Puerto Rico. Division of Demographic Registry and Vital Statistics. Annual Vital Statistics Report (0555-6511)
Published by: (Puerto Rico. Division of Statistics USA), Department of Health, Auxiliary Secretariat for Planning, Evaluation, Statistics and Information Systems, P O Box 70184, San Juan, 00936, Puerto Rico. TEL 787-274-7875, FAX 787-274-7877. Circ: 1,100.

325.2 GBR ISSN 1020-4067
HV640
➤ **REFUGEE SURVEY QUARTERLY.** Text in English, French, Spanish. 1982. q. GBP 190 in United Kingdom to institutions; EUR 286 in Europe to institutions; USD 382 in US & Canada to institutions; GBP 190 elsewhere to institutions; GBP 208 combined subscription in United Kingdom to institutions (print & online eds.); EUR 312 combined subscription in Europe to institutions (print & online eds.); USD 416 combined subscription in US & Canada to institutions (print & online eds.); GBP 208 combined subscription elsewhere to institutions (print & online eds.) (effective 2012). adv. bk.rev. 240 p./no.; back issues avail.; reprint service avail. from PSC. **Document type:** *Journal, Academic/Scholarly.* **Description:** Collection of abstracted literature concerning refugees, references to bibliographies, reviews of recent books, basic texts and announcements of new publications, meetings and conferences. Includes a selection of country reports and an expanded section on refugee or human rights related legal documentation.
Formerly (until 1994): Refugee Abstracts (0253-1445)
Related titles: Online - full text ed.: ISSN 1471-695X. GBP 173 in United Kingdom to institutions; EUR 260 in Europe to institutions; USD 347 in US & Canada to institutions; GBP 173 elsewhere to institutions (effective 2012) (from IngentaConnect).
Indexed: A22, E01, ENW, GEOBASE, I02, LeftInd, P10, P42, P45, P48, P50, P52, P53, P54, P56, PAIS, PQC, PSA, S02, S03, SCOPUS, SSA, SSciA, SociolAb, T02.
—BLDSC (7336.345000), IE, Infotrieve, Ingenta. **CCC.**
Published by: (United Nations High Commissioner for Refugees CHE), Oxford University Press, Great Clarendon St, Oxford, OX2 6DP, United Kingdom. TEL 44-1865-556767, FAX 44-1865-556646, enquiry@oup.co.uk, http://www.oxfordjournals.org. Ed. Vincent Chetail. Adv. contact Linda Hann TEL 44-1344-779945. **Subscr. in U.S. to:** Oxford University Press, 2001 Evans Rd, Cary, NC 27513. TEL 919-677-0977 ext 5777, 800-852-7323, FAX 919-677-1714, jnlorders@oup-usa.org, http://www.us.oup.com.

304.6 CAN
REGIONAL POPULATION ESTIMATES AND PROJECTIONS. Text in English. a. CAD 80 per issue (effective 2006). **Document type:** *Government.* **Description:** Provides historical and forecast population by age and sex, including components of change for regional districts.
Published by: Ministry of Finance and Corporate Relations, B C Stats, PO Box 9410, Sta Prov Govt, Victoria, BC V8W 9V1, Canada. TEL 250-387-0359, FAX 250-387-0380, BC.Stats@gov.bc.ca.

304.6 315 TWN
HA1710.5
RENKOU TONGJI JIKAN/DEMOGRAPHY QUARTERLY, REPUBLIC OF CHINA. Text in Chinese, English. 1965. q. TWD 120 (effective 1999). charts; stat. **Document type:** *Government.* **Description:** Contains data of vital statistics produced from centralized tabulation program and monthly data of birth, death and marriage as well as the quarterly data of international migration.
Former titles (until 2006): Taiwan Renkou Tongji Jikan/Taiwan Demography Quarterly Republic of Taiwan (1019-603X); (until Jan. 1975): Taiwan Demography Monthly
Published by: Neizheng Bu, Huzheng Ju/Ministry of the Interior, Department of Population, No.5, Syujhou Rd., Jhongjheng District, Taipei, 100, Taiwan. TEL 886-2-23565000, http://www.moi.gov.tw/. Ed. Ching Chau Su. Pub. Tzu Wen Huang. Circ: 1,400.

REPORT OF THE (YEAR) SURVEY OF FERTILITY IN THAILAND. *see* BUSINESS AND ECONOMICS—Abstracting, Bibliographies, Statistics

304.6 COG
REPUBLIQUE DE CONGO EN QUELQUES CHIFFRES. Text in French. 1980. a. XAF 7,500 per issue. **Document type:** *Government.*
Published by: Centre National de la Statistique et des Etudes Economiques, BP 2031, Brazzaville, Congo, Republic. TEL 242-83-43-24.

304.6 GRC
RESULTATS DU RECENSEMENT DE LA POPULATION ET DES HABITATIONS. Text in French, Greek. 1961. decennial (in 5 vols.). price varies. **Document type:** *Government.*
Published by: National Statistical Service of Greece, Statistical Information and Publications Division/Ethniki Statistiki Yperesia tes Ellados, 14-16 Lykourgou St, Athens, 101 66, Greece. TEL 30-1-3289-397, FAX 30-1-3241-102.

304.6 USA ISSN 0091-3073
HA611
RHODE ISLAND. DEPARTMENT OF HEALTH. VITAL STATISTICS. Text in English. a. free. **Document type:** *Government.*
Formerly: Report of Vital Statistics for Rhode Island (0095-0467)
Indexed: SRI.
Published by: Department of Health, 3 Capitol Hill, Rm 101, Providence, RI 02908-5097. TEL 401-277-2812.

304.6 310 ITA ISSN 0035-6832
HB3599
RIVISTA ITALIANA DI ECONOMIA DEMOGRAFIA E STATISTICA. Text in Italian. 1947. 4/yr. bk.rev. bibl. **Document type:** *Journal, Academic/Scholarly.*
Indexed: CIS, P30, PAIS.
Published by: Societa Italiana di Economia Demografia e Statistica, Piazza Tommaso de Cristoforis 6, Rome, 00159, Italy. sieds@tin.it, http://www.sieds.it. Ed. Giovanni Cariani.

304.6 KOR ISSN 1599-1180
HN730.5.Z9
SAENGHWAL SI'GAN JO'SA BO'GO'SEO. JE 1 GWON, SAENGHWAL SI'GANLYANG PYEON/KOREA (REPUBLIC). NATIONAL STATISTICAL OFFICE. REPORT ON THE TIME USE SURVEY. VOLUME 1, TIME SPENT ON ACTIVITIES. Text in English, Korean. 2000. quadrennial. USD 36 newsstand/cover (effective 2009). stat. **Document type:** *Government.*
Published by: Tong'gyecheong/Korea National Statistical Office, Government Complex Daejeon, 139 Seonsaro (920 Dunsan 2-dong), Seo-gu, Daejeon, 302-701, Korea, S. TEL 82-42-4814114. **Subscr. to:** The Korean Statistical Association, Rm. 103, Seoul Statistical Branch Office Bldg. 71, Nonhyun-Dong, Kangnam-Ku, Seoul 135701, Korea, S. TEL 82-2-34437954, FAX 82-2-34437957, kosa@nso.go.kr.

304.6 KOR ISSN 1599-3361
SAENGMYEONG PYO/KOREA (REPUBLIC). NATIONAL STATISTICAL OFFICE. LIFE TABLES FOR KOREA. Text in Korean. 1993. a. USD 6 newsstand/cover (effective 2009). stat. **Document type:** *Government.* **Description:** Covers statistics on the average life-span of people by age group.
Published by: Tong'gyecheong/Korea National Statistical Office, Government Complex Daejeon, 139 Seonsaro (920 Dunsan 2-dong), Seo-gu, Daejeon, 302-701, Korea, S. TEL 82-42-4814114. **Subscr. to:** The Korean Statistical Association, Rm. 103, Seoul Statistical Branch Office Bldg. 71, Nonhyun-Dong, Kangnam-Ku, Seoul 135701, Korea, S. TEL 82-2-34437954, FAX 82-2-34437957, kosa@nso.go.kr.

304.6 KOR ISSN 1228-9507
HN730.5
SAHOE TONG'GYE JO'SA BO'GO'SEO/KOREA (REPUBLIC). NATIONAL STATISTICAL OFFICE. REPORT ON THE SOCIAL STATISTICS SURVEY. Text in English, Korean. 1997. a. stat. **Document type:** *Government.* **Description:** Provides information on personal views and social concerns of the Korean people for the purpose of evaluating the quality of life.
Published by: Tong'gyecheong/Korea National Statistical Office, Government Complex Daejeon, 139 Seonsaro (920 Dunsan 2-dong), Seo-gu, Daejeon, 302-701, Korea, S. TEL 82-42-4814114. **Subscr. to:** The Korean Statistical Association, Rm. 103, Seoul Statistical Branch Office Bldg. 71, Nonhyun-Dong, Kangnam-Ku, Seoul 135701, Korea, S. TEL 82-2-34437954, FAX 82-2-34437957, kosa@nso.go.kr.

325.2 910.09 LCA
ST. LUCIA. STATISTICAL DEPARTMENT. ANNUAL MIGRATION AND TOURISM STATISTICS. Text in English. 1980. a. XEC 6. **Document type:** *Government.*
Published by: Statistical Department, New Government Bldg, Block C, 2nd Fl, Conway, Castries, St. Lucia. TEL 758-45-22697, FAX 758-45-31648, TELEX 6394 FORAFF. Ed. Bryan Boxill.

325.2 LCA
ST. LUCIA. STATISTICAL DEPARTMENT. QUARTERLY MIGRATION & TOURISM STATISTICS. Text in English. 1980. q. XEC 6 per issue. **Document type:** *Government.*
Published by: Statistical Department, New Government Bldg, Block C, 2nd Fl, Conway, Castries, St. Lucia. TEL 758-45-22697, FAX 758-92-31648, TELEX 6394 FORAFF. Ed. Bryan Boxill.

304.6 LCA
ST. LUCIA. STATISTICAL DEPARTMENT. VITAL STATISTICS REPORT. Text in English. 1984. a. XEC 15. **Document type:** *Government.*
Published by: Statistical Department, New Government Bldg, Block C, 2nd Fl, Conway, Castries, St. Lucia. TEL 758-45-22697, FAX 758-45-31648, TELEX 6394 FORAFF. Ed. Bryan Boxill.

310 CAN ISSN 1188-3642
HA39.C23
SELECTED VITAL STATISTICS AND HEALTH STATUS INDICATORS. ANNUAL REPORT. Text in English. 1927. a. CAD 18 (effective 1997). **Document type:** *Government.* **Description:** Presents comprehensive information and statistical data pertaining to the births, deaths and marriages of British Columbians.
Former titles (until 1990): Vital Statistics of the Province of British Columbia (0702-9446); (until 1944): Report of Vital Statistics of the Province of British Columbia (0229-5164)
Published by: Ministry of Health Services, British Columbia Vital Statistics Agency, 818 Fort St, Victoria, BC V8W 1H8, Canada. TEL 250-952-2558, FAX 250-952-2594. Ed. R J Danderfer. Circ: 1,000.

304.6 SEN
SENEGAL. MINISTERE DE L'ECONOMIE, DES FINANCES ET DU PLAN. POPULATION DU SENEGAL: STRUCTURE PAR AGE ET SEXE ET PROJECTION. Text in French. 1988. irreg. XOF 4,000; XOF 6,000 foreign (effective 1998). **Document type:** *Government.*
Related titles: Series of: Recensement General de la Population et de l'Habitat.
Published by: Ministere de l'Economie des Finances et du Plan, Direction de la Prevision et de la Statistique, BP 116, Dakar, Senegal. TEL 221-21-03-01. Pub. Ibrahima Sarr.

304.6 SEN
SENEGAL. MINISTERE DE L'ECONOMIE, DES FINANCES ET DU PLAN. RAPPORT D'ANALYSE PAR REGION. Text in French. irreg. XOF 4,000; XOF 6,000 foreign (effective 1998). **Document type:** *Government.*
Related titles: Series of: Recensement General de la Population et de l'Habitat.
Published by: Ministere de l'Economie des Finances et du Plan, Direction de la Prevision et de la Statistique, BP 116, Dakar, Senegal. TEL 221-21-03-01. Pub. Ibrahima Sarr.

304.6 SEN
SENEGAL. MINISTERE DE L'ECONOMIE, DES FINANCES ET DU PLAN. RAPPORT NATIONAL. Text in French. irreg. XOF 4,000; XOF 6,000 foreign (effective 1998). **Document type:** *Government.*
Related titles: Series of: Recensement General de la Population et de l'Habitat.
Published by: Ministere de l'Economie des Finances et du Plan, Direction de la Prevision et de la Statistique, BP 116, Dakar, Senegal. TEL 221-21-03-01. Pub. Ibrahima Sarr.

304.6 SEN
SENEGAL. MINISTERE DE L'ECONOMIE, DES FINANCES ET DU PLAN. RECENSEMENT GENERAL DE LA POPULATION ET DE L'HABITAT. Text in French. irreg. **Document type:** *Government.*
Related titles: Series of: Recensement General de la Population et de l'Habitat.
Published by: Ministere de l'Economie des Finances et du Plan, Direction de la Prevision et de la Statistique, BP 116, Dakar, Senegal. TEL 221-21-03-01. Pub. Ibrahima Sarr.

304.6 SEN
SENEGAL. MINISTERE DE L'ECONOMIE, DES FINANCES ET DU PLAN. REPERTOIRE DES VILLAGES PAR REGION. Text in French. irreg. XOF 3,000; XOF 5,000 foreign (effective 1998). **Document type:** *Government.*
Related titles: Series of: Recensement General de la Population et de l'Habitat.
Published by: Ministere de l'Economie des Finances et du Plan, Direction de la Prevision et de la Statistique, BP 116, Dakar, Senegal. TEL 221-21-03-01. Pub. Ibrahima Sarr.

304.6 SEN
SENEGAL. MINISTERE DE L'ECONOMIE, DES FINANCES ET DU PLAN. RESULTATS PROVISOIRES. Text in French. irreg. XOF 2,000; XOF 4,000 foreign (effective 1998). **Document type:** *Government.*
Related titles: Series of: Recensement General de la Population et de l'Habitat.
Published by: Ministere de l'Economie des Finances et du Plan, Direction de la Prevision et de la Statistique, BP 116, Dakar, Senegal. TEL 221-21-03-01. Pub. Ibrahima Sarr.

319 SYC
SEYCHELLES. PRESIDENT'S OFFICE. STATISTICS DIVISION. CENSUS. Text in English. irreg., latest 1977. SCR 80. **Document type:** *Government.*
Published by: (Seychelles. Statistics Division), President's Office, Department of Finance, Box 206, Victoria, Mahe, Seychelles.

304.6 310 SYC
SEYCHELLES. PRESIDENT'S OFFICE. STATISTICS DIVISION. POPULATION AND VITAL STATISTICS. Text in English. 1982. s-a. SCR 5. **Document type:** *Government.*
Published by: (Seychelles. Statistics Division), President's Office, Department of Finance, Box 206, Victoria, Mahe, Seychelles.

SOTSIAL'NO-EKONOMICHESKOE POLOZHENIE DAL'NEVOSTOCHNOGO FEDERAL'NOGO OKRUGA/SOCIO-ECONOMIC SITUATION OF THE FAR EASTERN FEDERAL REGION. *see* BUSINESS AND ECONOMICS—Abstracting, Bibliographies, Statistics

SOTSIAL'NO-EKONOMICHESKOE POLOZHENIE PRIVOLZHSKOGO FEDERAL'NOGO OKRUGA/SOCIO-ECONOMIC SITUATION OF THE VOLGA FEDERAL REGION. *see* BUSINESS AND ECONOMICS—Abstracting, Bibliographies, Statistics

SOTSIAL'NO-EKONOMICHESKOE POLOZHENIE ROSSII/SOCIAL AND ECONOMIC SITUATION IN RUSSIA; ekonomicheskii obzor. *see* BUSINESS AND ECONOMICS—Abstracting, Bibliographies, Statistics

SOTSIAL'NO-EKONOMICHESKOE POLOZHENIE SEVERO-ZAPADNOGO FEDERAL'NOGO OKRUGA/SOCIO-ECONOMIC SITUATION OF THE NORTH-WESTERN FEDERAL REGION. *see* BUSINESS AND ECONOMICS—Abstracting, Bibliographies, Statistics

SOTSIAL'NO-EKONOMICHESKOE POLOZHENIE SIBIRSKOGO FEDERAL'NOGO OKRUGA/SOCIO-ECONOMIC SITUATION OF THE SIBERIAN FEDERAL REGION. *see* BUSINESS AND ECONOMICS—Abstracting, Bibliographies, Statistics

SOTSIAL'NO-EKONOMICHESKOE POLOZHENIE TSENTRAL'NOGO FEDERAL'NOGO OKRUGA/SOCIO-ECONOMIC SITUATION OF THE CENTRAL FEDERAL REGION. *see* BUSINESS AND ECONOMICS—Abstracting, Bibliographies, Statistics

SOTSIAL'NO-EKONOMICHESKOE POLOZHENIE URAL'SKOGO FEDERAL'NOGO OKRUGA/SOCIO-ECONOMIC SITUATION OF THE URAL FEDERAL REGION. *see* BUSINESS AND ECONOMICS—Abstracting, Bibliographies, Statistics

SOTSIAL'NO-EKONOMICHESKOE POLOZHENIE YUZHNOGO FEDERAL'NOGO OKRUGA/SOCIO-ECONOMIC SITUATION OF THE SOUTHERN FEDERAL REGION. *see* BUSINESS AND ECONOMICS—Abstracting, Bibliographies, Statistics

304.6 ZAF
SOUTH AFRICA. STATISTICS SOUTH AFRICA. BIRTHS. Text in English. a., latest 1991. **Document type:** *Government.*
Former titles (until Aug. 1998): South Africa. Central Statistical Service. Births; South Africa. Central Statistical Service. Births - Whites, Coloureds and Asians (0258-7807); South Africa. Central Statistical Service. Report on Births: White, Coloured and Asian; South Africa. Department of Statistics. Report on Births: Whites, Coloureds, Asians; South Africa. Department of Statistics. Report on Births
Published by: Statistics South Africa/Statistieke Suid-Afrika, Private Bag X44, Pretoria, 0001, South Africa. TEL 27-12-3108911, FAX 27-12-3108500, info@statssa.gov.za, http://www.statssa.gov.za.

316.8 ZAF
SOUTH AFRICA. STATISTICS SOUTH AFRICA. DEMOGRAPHIC STATISTICS. Text in English. a., latest 1993. **Document type:** *Government.* **Description:** Presents current demographic information on South Africa.
Formerly (until Aug.1998): South Africa. Central Statistical Service. Demographic Statistics
Published by: Statistics South Africa/Statistieke Suid-Afrika, Private Bag X44, Pretoria, 0001, South Africa. TEL 27-12-3108911, FAX 27-12-3108500, info@statssa.gov.za, http://www.statssa.gov.za.

304.6 ZAF
SOUTH AFRICA. STATISTICS SOUTH AFRICA. OCTOBER HOSUEHOLD SURVEY (YEAR). Text in English. irreg., latest 1997. **Document type:** *Government.*
Published by: Statistics South Africa/Statistieke Suid-Afrika, Private Bag X44, Pretoria, 0001, South Africa. TEL 27-12-3108911, FAX 27-12-3108500, info@statssa.gov.za, http://www.statssa.gov.za.

316.8 ZAF
SOUTH AFRICA. STATISTICS SOUTH AFRICA. POPULATION CENSUS, (YEAR). DWELLINGS. Text in English. 1991. irreg. **Document type:** *Government.*
Formerly (until Aug.1998): South Africa. Central Statistical Service. Population Census. Dwellings
Published by: Statistics South Africa/Statistieke Suid-Afrika, Private Bag X44, Pretoria, 0001, South Africa. TEL 27-12-3108911, FAX 27-12-3108500, info@statssa.gov.za, http://www.statssa.gov.za.

316.8 ZAF
SOUTH AFRICA. STATISTICS SOUTH AFRICA. POPULATION CENSUS, (YEAR). ECONOMIC CHARACTERISTICS OF POPULATION. Text in English. irreg., latest 1991. **Document type:** *Government.*
Former titles (until Aug.1998): South Africa. Central Statistical Service. Population Census. Economic Characteristics of the Population; (until 1991): South Africa. Central Statistical Service. Population Census. Economic Characteristics
Published by: Statistics South Africa/Statistieke Suid-Afrika, Private Bag X44, Pretoria, 0001, South Africa. TEL 27-12-3108911, FAX 27-12-3108500, info@statssa.gov.za, http://www.statssa.gov.za.

316.8 ZAF
SOUTH AFRICA. STATISTICS SOUTH AFRICA. POPULATION CENSUS, (YEAR). HOUSEHOLDS. Text in English. 1991. irreg. **Document type:** *Government.*
Formerly (until Aug.1998): South Africa. Central Statistical Service. Population Census. Households
Published by: Statistics South Africa/Statistieke Suid-Afrika, Private Bag X44, Pretoria, 0001, South Africa. TEL 27-12-3108911, FAX 27-12-3108500, info@statssa.gov.za, http://www.statssa.gov.za.

316.8 ZAF
SOUTH AFRICA. STATISTICS SOUTH AFRICA. POPULATION CENSUS, (YEAR). SELECTED STATISTICAL REGIONS. (Reports avail. for nine statistical regions: Cape Peninsula, No. 03-01-11 (Social Characteristics) & No. 03-01-12 (Economic Characteristics); Port Elizabeth - Uitenhage, No. 03-01-13; Durban - Pinetown - Inanda - Chatsworth, No. 03-01-14; East Rand, No. 03-01-15; Johannesburg - Randburg, No. 03-01-16 (Social Characteristics) & No. 03-01-17 (Economic Characteristics); West Rand, No. 03-01-18; Pretoria - Wonderboom - Soshanguve, No. 03-01-19; Vereeniging - Vanderbijlpark - Sasolburg, No. 03-01-20; Bloemfontein, No. 03-01-21) Text in English. irreg., latest 1991. **Document type:** *Government.* **Description:** Provides statistical data on age, home language, religion and denomination, level of occupation and income by suburb, as well as information on population group and sex, type of dwelling and household size by income group.
Formerly (until Aug.1998): South Africa. Central Statistical Service. Population Census. Selected Statistical Regions
Published by: Statistics South Africa/Statistieke Suid-Afrika, Private Bag X44, Pretoria, 0001, South Africa. TEL 27-12-3108911, FAX 27-12-3108500, info@statssa.gov.za, http://www.statssa.gov.za.

316.8 ZAF
SOUTH AFRICA. STATISTICS SOUTH AFRICA. POPULATION CENSUS, (YEAR). SOCIAL CHARACTERISTICS OF THE POPULATION. Text in English. irreg., latest 1999. **Document type:** *Government.* **Description:** Provides statistical information on the age, home language, marital status, country of birth and citizenship, religion and denomination, level of education, occupation, literacy and income by population group and sex.
Former titles (until Aug.1998): South Africa. Central Statistical Service. Population Census. Social Characteristics; (until 1991): South Africa. Central Statistical Service. Population Census. Social Characteristics
Published by: Statistics South Africa/Statistieke Suid-Afrika, Private Bag X44, Pretoria, 0001, South Africa. TEL 27-12-3108911, FAX 27-12-3108500, info@statssa.gov.za, http://www.statssa.gov.za.

316.8 ZAF
SOUTH AFRICA. STATISTICS SOUTH AFRICA. POPULATION CENSUS, (YEAR). SUMMARISED RESULTS AFTER ADJUSTMENT FOR UNDERCOUNT. Text in English. 1991. irreg. **Document type:** *Government.*
Formerly (until Aug.1998): South Africa. Central Statistical Service. Population Census. Summarised Results After Adjustment for Undercount
Published by: Statistics South Africa/Statistieke Suid-Afrika, Private Bag X44, Pretoria, 0001, South Africa. TEL 27-12-3108911, FAX 27-12-3108500, info@statssa.gov.za, http://www.statssa.gov.za.

306.5 316.8 ZAF
SOUTH AFRICA. STATISTICS SOUTH AFRICA. REPORT ON MARRIAGES AND DIVORCES - WHITES, COLOUREDS AND ASIANS - SOUTH AFRICA. Text in English. 1972. a., latest 1999. **Document type:** *Government.*
Former titles (until 1998): South Africa. Central Statistical Service. Report on Marriages and Divorces - Whites, Coloureds and Asians - South Africa; South Africa. Central Statistical Service. Report on Marriages and Divorces: South Africa; South Africa. Department of Statistics. Report on Marriages and Divorces: South Africa
Published by: Statistics South Africa/Statistieke Suid-Afrika, Private Bag X44, Pretoria, 0001, South Africa. TEL 27-12-3108911, FAX 27-12-3108500, info@statssa.gov.za, http://www.statssa.gov.za.

316.8 ZAF
SOUTH AFRICA. STATISTICS SOUTH AFRICA. STATISTICAL RELEASE. MARRIAGES AND DIVORCES (YEAR). Text in English. a., latest 1996. free. **Document type:** *Government.* **Description:** Provides statistics on marriage and divorce rates in the South African population.
Formerly (until Aug.1998): South Africa. Central Statistical Service. Statistical Release. Marriages and Divorces; Superseded: South Africa. Central Statistical Service. Statistical News Release. Marriages and Divorces - Whites, Coloureds and Asians.
Published by: Statistics South Africa/Statistieke Suid-Afrika, Private Bag X44, Pretoria, 0001, South Africa. TEL 27-12-3108911, FAX 27-12-3108500, info@statssa.gov.za, http://www.statssa.gov.za.

316.8 ZAF
SOUTH AFRICA. STATISTICS SOUTH AFRICA. STATISTICAL RELEASE. MID-YEAR POPULATION ESTIMATES (YEAR). Text in English. a. free. **Document type:** *Government.*
Formerly (until Aug. 1998): South Africa. Central Statistical Service. Statistical Release. Mid-year Estimates (Population)
Published by: Statistics South Africa/Statistieke Suid-Afrika, Private Bag X44, Pretoria, 0001, South Africa. TEL 27-12-3108911, FAX 27-12-3108500, info@statssa.gov.za, http://www.statssa.gov.za.

316.8 ZAF
SOUTH AFRICA. STATISTICS SOUTH AFRICA. STATISTICAL RELEASE. POPULATION CHARACTERISTICS (YEAR); Boipatong, Bophelong, Evaton, Orange Farm, Sebokeng and Sharpeville. Text in English. a., latest 1990. back issues avail. **Document type:** *Government.* **Description:** Sample survey for a specific area to determine population growth since the previous census.
Formerly (until Aug.1998): South Africa. Central Statistical Service. Statistical Release. Population Characteristics (Year)
Published by: Statistics South Africa/Statistieke Suid-Afrika, Private Bag X44, Pretoria, 0001, South Africa. TEL 27-12-3108911, FAX 27-12-3108500, info@statssa.gov.za, http://www.statssa.gov.za.

316.8 ZAF
SOUTH AFRICA. STATISTICS SOUTH AFRICA. STATISTICAL RELEASE. PRELIMINARY RESULTS POPULATION CENSUS (YEAR). Text in English. irreg., latest 1991. **Document type:** *Government.* **Description:** Results listed by enumerator area and population group.
Formerly (until Aug.1998): South Africa. Central Statistical Service. Statistical Release. Preliminary Results Population Census (Year)
Published by: Statistics South Africa/Statistieke Suid-Afrika, Private Bag X44, Pretoria, 0001, South Africa. TEL 27-12-3108911, FAX 27-12-3108500, info@statssa.gov.za, http://www.statssa.gov.za.

316.8 ZAF
SOUTH AFRICA. STATISTICS SOUTH AFRICA. STATISTICAL RELEASE. RECORDED DEATHS. Text in English. a., latest 1995. **Document type:** *Government.*
Former titles (until Aug. 1998): South Africa. Central Statistical Service. Statistical Release. Recorded Deaths; (until 1991): South Africa. Central Statistical Service. Statistical News Release. Deaths - Whites, Coloureds and Asians; South Africa. Central Statistical Service. Statistical News Release. Deaths - Blacks
Published by: Statistics South Africa/Statistieke Suid-Afrika, Private Bag X44, Pretoria, 0001, South Africa. TEL 27-12-3108911, FAX 27-12-3108500, info@statssa.gov.za, http://www.statssa.gov.za.

316.8 ZAF
SOUTH AFRICA. STATISTICS SOUTH AFRICA. STATISTICAL RELEASE. RECORDED LIVE BIRTHS (YEAR). Text in English. a., latest 1995. free. **Document type:** *Government.*
Former titles (until Aug. 1998): South Africa. Central Statistical Service. Statistical Release. Recorded Births; (until 1992): South Africa. Central Statistical Service. Statistical News Release. Birds - Whites, Coloureds and Asians
Published by: Statistics South Africa/Statistieke Suid-Afrika, Private Bag X44, Pretoria, 0001, South Africa. TEL 27-12-3108911, FAX 27-12-3108500, info@statssa.gov.za, http://www.statssa.gov.za.

316.8 ZAF
SOUTH AFRICA. STATISTICS SOUTH AFRICA. STATISTICAL RELEASE. REGIONAL MID-YEAR ESTIMATES - REPUBLIC OF SOUTH AFRICA. Text in English. irreg. **Document type:** *Government.*
Formerly (until Aug. 1998): South Africa. Central Statistical Service. Statistical Release. Regional Mid-year Estimate - Republic of South Africa
Published by: Statistics South Africa/Statistieke Suid-Afrika, Private Bag X44, Pretoria, 0001, South Africa. TEL 27-12-3108911, FAX 27-12-3108500, info@statssa.gov.za, http://www.statssa.gov.za.

316.8 ZAF
SOUTH AFRICA. STATISTICS SOUTH AFRICA. THE PEOPLE OF SOUTH AFRICA POPULATION CENSUS (YEAR). Text in English. irreg., latest 1991. free. **Document type:** *Government.* **Description:** Presents summarized results before adjustment for undercounting.
Formerly (until Aug.1998): South Africa. Central Statistical Service. Population Census (Year)
Published by: Statistics South Africa/Statistieke Suid-Afrika, Private Bag X44, Pretoria, 0001, South Africa. TEL 27-12-3108911, FAX 27-12-3108500, info@statssa.gov.za, http://www.statssa.gov.za.

301.32 916.804 ZAF
SOUTH AFRICA. STATISTICS SOUTH AFRICA. TOURISM AND MIGRATION. Text in English. a., latest 1998. free. **Document type:** *Government.*
Former titles (until Aug. 1998): South Africa. Central Statistical Service. Statistical Release. Tourism and Migration; South Africa. Department of Statistics. Tourism and Migration
Related titles: Diskette ed.: ZAR 15 (effective 1999).
Published by: Statistics South Africa/Statistieke Suid-Afrika, Private Bag X44, Pretoria, 0001, South Africa. TEL 27-12-3108911, FAX 27-12-3108500, info@statssa.gov.za, http://www.statssa.gov.za.

304.6 USA ISSN 0094-6338
HA621
SOUTH CAROLINA VITAL AND MORBIDITY STATISTICS. Text in English. 1972. a. **Document type:** *Government.*
Related titles: Microfiche ed.: (from CIS).
Indexed: SRI.
Published by: (Office of Vital Records and Public Health Statistics), Department of Health and Environmental Control, 2600 Bull St, Columbia, SC 29201. TEL 803-898-3649, FAX 803-898-3661. Circ: 900.

304.6 330.021 ESP ISSN 1887-0872
SPAIN. MINISTERIO DE FOMENTO. ANUARIO ESTADISTICO. Text in Spanish. 1961. a. **Document type:** *Government.*
Former titles (until 1995): Spain. Ministerio de Obras Publicas, Transportes y Medio Ambiente. Anuario Estadistico (1887-0864); (until 1992): Spain. Ministerio de Obras Publicas y Transportes. Anuario Estadistico (1131-9658); (until 1990): Spain. Ministerio de Obras Publicas y Urbanismo. Anuario Estadistico (1131-964X); (until 1987): Las Obras Publicas y el Urbanismo en (Year) (0211-0644); (until 1976): Las Obras Publicas en (Year) (0376-7078)
Published by: Ministerio de Fomento, Centro de Publicaciones, Paseo de la Castellana 67, Madrid, 28029, Spain. http://www.fomento.es.

304.6 SRB
HA1631
SRBIJA I CRNA GORA ZAVOD ZA STATISTIKU. DEMOGRAFSKA STATISTIKA. Text in Serbo-Croatian. 1956. a. **Document type:** *Government.*
Former titles: Yugoslavia. Savezni Zavod za Statistiku. Demografska Statistika (0084-4357); Yugoslavia. Savezni Zavod za Statistiku. Vitalna Statistika
Published by: Srbija i Crna Gora Zavod za Statistiku/Serbia and Montenegro Statistical Office, Kneza Milosa 20, Postanski Fah 203, Belgrade, 11000. TEL 381-11-3617273, FAX 381-11-3617297, http://www.szs.sv.gov.yu. Circ: 600.

304.6 USA ISSN 0276-6566
HA202
STATE AND METROPOLITAN AREA DATA BOOK. Text in English. 1979. irreg., latest 2006, 6th ed. USD 49.50 per issue domestic; USD 69.30 per issue foreign (effective 2009). **Document type:** *Government.* **Description:** Covers more than 1,500 data items for the United States and individual states, counties and metropolitan areas from a variety of sources. Topics include: Age, agriculture, births, business establishments, communications, construction, cost of living, crime, deaths, education, elections, employment, energy, finance, government, health, households, housing, immigration, income, manufactures, marriages and divorces, media, natural resources, population, poverty, race and Hispanic origin, residence, retail sales, science and engineering, social services, tourism, transportation, and veterans.
Related titles: Online - full text ed.: free.
Published by: U.S. Census Bureau (Subsidiary of: U.S. Department of Commerce), 4600 Silver Hill Rd, Washington, DC 20233. **Subscr. to:** U.S. Department of Commerce, National Technical Information Service, 5301 Shawnee Rd, Alexandria, VA 22312. TEL 703-605-6060, FAX 703-605-6880, subscriptions@ntis.gov, http://www.ntis.gov; U.S. Government Printing Office, Superintendent of Documents, PO Box 371954, Pittsburgh, PA 15250. TEL 202-512-1800, FAX 202-512-2250.

STATECO. *see* BUSINESS AND ECONOMICS—Abstracting, Bibliographies, Statistics

304.6 USA ISSN 0081-4741
HA202 CODEN: SASTDA
STATISTICAL ABSTRACT OF THE UNITED STATES (YEAR). Text in English. 1878. a. USD 39 per issue domestic (paperback ed.); USD 54.60 per issue foreign (paperback ed.); USD 43 per issue domestic (hardcover ed.); USD 60.20 per issue foreign (hardcover ed.) (effective 2011). back issues avail.; reprints avail. **Document type:** *Database, Government.* **Description:** Contains an extensive collection of the latest vital statistics and industry trends and an important summary of statistics on the social, political, and economic organization of the U.S.
Related titles: CD-ROM ed.; Microfiche ed.: (from WSH); Microfilm ed.: (from BHP, PQC); Online - full text ed.: free (effective 2011); ◆ Large type ed. 10 pt.: Statistical Abstract of the United States (Large Print Edition). ISSN 1063-1690.
Indexed: RASB.
—CASDDS.
Published by: U.S. Census Bureau (Subsidiary of: U.S. Department of Commerce), 4600 Silver Hill Rd, Washington, DC 20233. TEL 301-763-4636, 800-923-8282, econ@census.gov. **Subscr. to:** U.S. Government Printing Office, Superintendent of Documents.

304.6 JPN ISSN 0081-4792
HA1832
STATISTICAL HANDBOOK OF JAPAN (YEAR). Text in English. 1958. a. JPY 1,575 (effective 1999). stat. back issues avail. **Document type:** *Report, Government.*
Related titles: Online - full text ed.
Published by: (Japan. Ministry of Internal Affairs and Communications. Statistical Research and Training Institute/Somucho. Tokeikenshujo), Japan. Ministry of Internal Affairs and Communications. Statistics Bureau/Somucho. Tokeikyoko, 19-1 Wakamatsu-cho, Shinjyuku-ku, Tokyo, 162-8668, Japan. TEL 81-3-5273-2020, FAX 81-3-5273-1180. R&P Akihiko Ito. **Subscr. to:** Japan Statistical Association, Meito Shinjuku Bldg, 6th Fl, 2-4-6 Shinjuku-ku, Tokyo 169-0073, Japan. TEL 81-3-53323151, http://www.jstat.or.jp/.

317 JAM
STATISTICAL INSTITUTE OF JAMAICA. DEMOGRAPHIC STATISTICS. Text in English. 1971. a. USD 31. stat. back issues avail.
Formerly: Jamaica. Department of Statistics. Demographic Statistics
Published by: Statistical Institute of Jamaica, 9 Swallowfield Rd, Kingston, 5, Jamaica. FAX 809-92-64859. Circ: 126.

304.6 DNK ISSN 1398-9030
STATISTICAL OVERVIEW, MIGRATION AND ASYLUM. Variant title: Migration and Asylum. Text in English. 1998. a. **Document type:** *Government.*
Related titles: Online - full text ed.: ISSN 1903-038X. 2001; ◆ Danish ed.: Tal og Fakta pa Udlaendingeomraadet. ISSN 1902-0945.
Published by: Ministeriet for Flygtninge, Indvandrere og Integration/ Ministry of Refugee, Immigration, and Integration, Holbergsgade 6, Copenhagen K, 1057, Denmark. TEL 45-33-923380, FAX 45-33-111239, inm@inm.dk, http://www.inm.dk. Ed. Henrik Grunnet.

304.6 630 IDN ISSN 0126-2912
HA1811
STATISTICAL YEAR BOOK OF INDONESIA. Text in English, Indonesian. 1976. a. IDR 90,000, USD 39.13. **Document type:** *Government.*
Published by: Central Bureau of Statistics/Biro Pusat Statistik, Jalan Dr. Sutomo No. 8, PO Box 3, Jakarta Pusat, Indonesia. TEL 62-21-372808. Circ: 1,500.

304.6021 PRT ISSN 1647-6778
▼ **STATISTICS PORTUGAL.** Text in English. 2010. irreg. **Document type:** *Report, Government.*
Published by: Instituto Nacional de Estatistica, Av Antonio Jose de Almeida 2, Lisbon, 1000-043, Portugal. TEL 351-21-8426100, FAX 351-21-8426380, ine@ine.pt, http://www.ine.pt.

304.6 DEU ISSN 1430-5054
STATISTISCHE BERICHTE - RHEINLAND-PFALZ. A: BEVOELKERUNG, GESUNDHEITSWESEN, GEBIET, ERWERBSTAETIGKEIT. Text in German. 1951. irreg. **Document type:** *Government.*
Formerly (until 1976): Statistischen Landesamtes Rheinland-Pfalz. Statistische Berichte A (1430-4902); Which superseded in part (in 1956): Statistisches Landesamt Rheinland-Pfalz. Mitteilungen (0482-8887)
Published by: Statistisches Landesamt Rheinland-Pfalz, Mainzerstr 14-16, Bad Ems, 56130, Germany. TEL 49-2603-713240, FAX 49-2603-71193240, pressestelle@statistik.rlp.de.

304.6 DEU
STATISTISCHER JAHRESBERICHT DER STADT MUENSTER. Text in German. 1948. a. EUR 20 (effective 2005). **Document type:** *Yearbook, Government.*
Published by: Stadt Muenster, Amt fuer Stadt- und Regionalentwicklung, Statistik, Stadthaus 3, Albersloher Weg 33, Muenster, 48155, Germany. TEL 49-251-4921201, FAX 49-251-4927905, amt12@stadt-muenster.de, http://www.muenster.de/stadt/stadtentwicklung/index1.html.

SUMMARY HEALTH STATISTICS FOR THE U.S. POPULATION. *see* STATISTICS

325.1 SWE ISSN 1650-1225
SWEDEN. MIGRATIONSVERKET. STATISTIK. Text in Swedish. 2000. a.
Formerly: Statens Invandrarverk. Statistik
Related titles: Online - full text ed.
Published by: Migrationsverket/Swedish Immigration Board, Tegelaengsgatan 19 A, Norrkoeping, 60170, Sweden. TEL 46-11-156000, FAX 46-11-108155, migrationsverket@migrationsverket.se, http://www.migrationsverket.se.

304.6 SWE ISSN 0082-0245
HB2077
SWEDEN. STATISTISKA CENTRALBYRAAN. STATISTISKA MEDDELANDEN. SERIE BE, BEFOLKNING OCH LEVNADSFOERHAALANDEN. Variant title: Sweden. Statistiska Centralbyraan. Serie B, Befolkning och Val. Sweden. Statistiska Centralbyraan. Statistiska Meddelanden. Serie B, Befolkning. Text in Swedish; Summaries in English. 1963. irreg. SEK 500. **Document type:** *Government.*
Formerly (until vol.9, 1965): Sweden. Statistiska Centralbyraan. B
Indexed: P30, PopulInd.
Published by: Statistiska Centralbyraan/Statistics Sweden, Publishing Unit, Orebro, 70189, Sweden. Circ: 1,700.

304.6 CHE
SWITZERLAND. BUNDESAMT FUER STATISTIK. BILANZ DER WOHNBEVOLKERUNG IN DEN GEMEINDEN DER SCHWEIZ - BILAN DEMOGRAPHIQUE DES COMMUNES SUISSES. Text in French. 1981. a. CHF 20 (effective 2001). stat. **Document type:** *Government.*
Formerly: Switzerland. Bundesamt fuer Statistik. Heiraten, Lebendgeborene und Gestorbene in den Gemeinden - Marriages, Naissances et Deces dans les Communes
Related titles: Diskette ed.: CHF 30 (effective 1999).
Published by: Bundesamt fuer Statistik, Espace de l'Europe 10, Neuchatel, 2010, Switzerland. TEL 41-32-7136011, FAX 41-32-7136012, information@bfs.admin.ch, http://www.admin.ch/bfs. Circ: 750.

304.6 DNK ISSN 1902-0945
TAL OG FAKTA PA UDLAENDINGEOMRAADET. Text in Danish. 1997. a. stat. **Document type:** *Government.*
Former titles (until 2005): Noegletal paa Udlaendingeomraadet (1600-5961); (until 2000): Udlaendingestyrelsen. Aarsberetning, Statistiktillaeg (1398-9049)
Related titles: Online - full text ed.: ISSN 1902-0953. 2000; ◆ English ed.: Statistical Overview, Migration and Asylum. ISSN 1398-9030.
Published by: Ministeriet for Flygtninge, Indvandrere og Integration/ Ministry of Refugee, Immigration, and Integration, Holbergsgade 6, Copenhagen K, 1057, Denmark. TEL 45-33-923380, FAX 45-33-111239, inm@inm.dk, http://www.inm.dk. Ed. Henrik Grunnet.

301.32 TZA
TANZANIA. NATIONAL BUREAU OF STATISTICS. MIGRATION STATISTICS. Text in English. 1968-1971; resumed 1979. irreg., latest 1985, for the year 1981. **Document type:** *Government.*
Published by: National Bureau of Statistics, PO Box 796, Dar Es Salaam, Tanzania. TEL 255-22-2122722, FAX 255-22-2130852, itdept@nbs.go.tz, http://www.nbs.go.tz/. **Dist. by:** Government Publications Agency, PO Box 1801, Dar Es Salaam, Tanzania.

310 CAN ISSN 0831-5701
TENDANCES SOCIALES CANADIENNES. Text in French. 1986. q. **Document type:** *Government.*
Related titles: Online - full text ed.: ISSN 1481-1642; ◆ English ed.: Canada. Statistics Canada. Canadian Social Trends. ISSN 0831-5698.
Indexed: C03, CBCARef, P48, P52, P56, PQC.
Published by: Statistics Canada, Operations and Integration Division (Subsidiary of: Statistics Canada/Statistique Canada), Circulation Management, 120 Parkdale Ave, Ottawa, ON K1A 0T6, Canada. TEL 800-267-6677, FAX 613-951-1584, infostats@statcan.ca, http://www.statcan.ca.

304.6021 PRT ISSN 1646-253X
TERRITORIO. REGIAO ALENTEJO. Text in Portuguese. 2005. a. **Document type:** *Report, Government.*
Published by: Instituto Nacional de Estatistica, Av Antonio Jose de Almeida 2, Lisbon, 1000-043, Portugal. TEL 351-21-8426100, FAX 351-21-8426380, ine@ine.pt, http://www.ine.pt.

304.6021 PRT ISSN 1646-2548
TERRITORIO. REGIAO ALGARVE. Text in Portuguese. 2005. a. **Document type:** *Report, Government.*
Published by: Instituto Nacional de Estatistica, Av Antonio Jose de Almeida 2, Lisbon, 1000-043, Portugal. TEL 351-21-8426100, FAX 351-21-8426380, ine@ine.pt, http://www.ine.pt.

304.6021 PRT ISSN 1646-2556
TERRITORIO. REGIAO CENTRO. Text in Portuguese. 2005. a. **Document type:** *Report, Government.*
Published by: Instituto Nacional de Estatistica, Av Antonio Jose de Almeida 2, Lisbon, 1000-043, Portugal. TEL 351-21-8426100, FAX 351-21-8426380, ine@ine.pt, http://www.ine.pt.

304.6021 PRT ISSN 1646-2564
TERRITORIO. REGIAO LISBOA. Text in Portuguese. 2005. a. **Document type:** *Report, Government.*
Published by: Instituto Nacional de Estatistica, Av Antonio Jose de Almeida 2, Lisbon, 1000-043, Portugal. TEL 351-21-8426100, FAX 351-21-8426380, ine@ine.pt, http://www.ine.pt.

304.6021 PRT ISSN 1646-2572
TERRITORIO. REGIAO NORTE. Text in Portuguese. 2005. a. **Document type:** *Report, Government.*
Published by: Instituto Nacional de Estatistica, Av Antonio Jose de Almeida 2, Lisbon, 1000-043, Portugal. TEL 351-21-8426100, FAX 351-21-8426380, ine@ine.pt, http://www.ine.pt.

304.6 USA ISSN 0495-257X
HA651
TEXAS VITAL STATISTICS. Text in English. 1973. a. free. **Document type:** *Government.*
Related titles: Microfiche ed.: (from CIS).
Indexed: SRI.
Published by: Department of Health, Bureau of Vital Statistics, 1100 W 49th St, Austin, TX 78756. TEL 512-458-7111. Circ: 3,000.

310 325 THA
THAILAND. NATIONAL STATISTICAL OFFICE. REPORT OF THE MIGRATION SURVEY. Text in English, Thai. 1992. biennial. price varies. **Document type:** *Government.* **Description:** Contains data on the pattern, rate, flow and direction of migration.
Published by: Thailand. National Statistical Office. Statistical Forecasting Bureau, Larn Luang Rd, Bangkok, 10100, Thailand. TEL 66-2-2810333 ext 1410, 1411, FAX 66-2-2813814, binfopub@nso.go.th, http://www.nso.go.th/. Circ: 500.

304.6 CHL
TRANSICION DE LA FECUNDIDAD EN CHILE. Text in Spanish. 1989. a. CLP 2,000; USD 13.50 in United States; USD 15.90 elsewhere. **Document type:** *Government.*
Published by: Instituto Nacional de Estadisticas, Casilla 498, Correo 3, Ave. Bulnes, 418, Santiago, Chile. TEL 56-2-6991441, FAX 56-2-6712169.

304.6 317.29 TTO ISSN 0564-2612
HA867
TRINIDAD AND TOBAGO. CENTRAL STATISTICAL OFFICE. CONTINUOUS SAMPLE SURVEY OF POPULATION. Text in English. 1964. a. TTD 20 (effective 2000). **Document type:** *Government.*
Related titles: ◆ Series: Trinidad and Tobago. Central Statistical Office. Labour Force by Sex.
Published by: Central Statistical Office, 35-41 Queen St, PO Box 98, Port-of-Spain, Trinidad, Trinidad & Tobago. TEL 868-623-6495, FAX 868-625-3802.

301.32 TTO ISSN 0303-4410
HA867
TRINIDAD AND TOBAGO. CENTRAL STATISTICAL OFFICE. ESTIMATED INTERNAL MIGRATION. BULLETIN. Text in English. 1974. irreg. **Document type:** *Bulletin, Government.*
Published by: Central Statistical Office, 35-41 Queen St, PO Box 98, Port-of-Spain, Trinidad, Trinidad & Tobago. TEL 868-623-6495, FAX 868-625-3802.

304.6 TTO ISSN 0082-6553
HA867
TRINIDAD AND TOBAGO. CENTRAL STATISTICAL OFFICE. POPULATION AND VITAL STATISTICS; REPORT. Text in English. 1953. a. TTD 10, USD 5 (effective 2000). **Document type:** *Government.*

Published by: Central Statistical Office, 35-41 Queen St, PO Box 98, Port-of-Spain, Trinidad, Trinidad & Trobago. TEL 868-623-6495, FAX 868-625-3802.

TURKEY. TURKIYE ISTATISTIK KURUMU. BOSANMA ISTATISTIKLERI/TURKEY. TURKISH STATISTICAL INSTITUTE. DIVORCE STATISTICS. *see* MATRIMONY—Abstracting, Bibliographies, Statistics

TURKEY. TURKIYE ISTATISTIK KURUMU. EVLENME ISTATISTIKLERI (YEAR)/TURKEY. TURKISH STATISTICAL INSTITUTE. MARRIAGE STATISTICS (YEAR). *see* MATRIMONY—Abstracting, Bibliographies, Statistics

315.61 TUR
TURKEY. TURKIYE ISTATISTIK KURUMU. GENEL NUFUS SAYIMI. GECICI SONUCLAR/TURKEY. TURKISH STATISTICAL INSTITUTE. CENSUS OF POPULATION. PRELIMINARY RESULTS. Text in English, Turkish. 1961. irreg., latest 2000. **Document type:** *Government.*
Published by: T.C. Basbakanlik, Turkiye Istatistik Kurumu/Prime Ministry Republic of Turkey, Turkish Statistical Institute, Yucetepe Mah. Necatibey Cad No.114, Cankaya, Ankara, 06100, Turkey. TEL 90-312-4100410, FAX 90-312-4175886, bilgi@tuik.gov.tr, ulka.unsal@tuik.gov.tr, http://www.tuik.gov.tr. Circ: 1,025.

315.61 TUR ISSN 1306-1186
TURKEY. TURKIYE ISTATISTIK KURUMU. GENEL NUFUS SAYIMI; GOC ISTATISTIKLERI (YEAR)/TURKEY. TURKISH STATISTICAL INSTITUTE. CENSUS OF POPULATION; MIGRATION STATISTICS (YEAR). Text in English, Turkish. 1941. irreg. (census year), latest 2000. TRY 14 per issue domestic; USD 20 per issue foreign (effective 2009). **Document type:** *Government.* **Description:** Covers data provided from 2000 General Populations Censes. Migration size by settlement, inter regional and inter provincial migration, social and economic characteristics of migrated population are also indicated.
Formerly: Turkey. Turkish Statistical Institute. Census of Population. Internal Migration by Permanent Residence
Related titles: CD-ROM ed.: TRY 7 per issue domestic; USD 10 per issue foreign (effective 2009).
Published by: T.C. Basbakanlik, Turkiye Istatistik Kurumu/Prime Ministry Republic of Turkey, Turkish Statistical Institute, Yucetepe Mah. Necatibey Cad No.114, Cankaya, Ankara, 06100, Turkey. TEL 90-312-4100410, FAX 90-312-4175886, bilgi@tuik.gov.tr, ulka.unsal@tuik.gov.tr, http://www.tuik.gov.tr. Circ: 1,220.

315.61 TUR
TURKEY. TURKIYE ISTATISTIK KURUMU. GENEL NUFUS SAYIMI. IDARI BOLUNUS/TURKEY. TURKISH STATISTICAL INSTITUTE. CENSUS OF POPULATION. ADMINISTRATIVE DIVISION. Text in English, Turkish. 1928. irreg., latest 2000. **Document type:** *Government.*
Related titles: Diskette ed.
Published by: T.C. Basbakanlik, Turkiye Istatistik Kurumu/Prime Ministry Republic of Turkey, Turkish Statistical Institute, Yucetepe Mah. Necatibey Cad No.114, Cankaya, Ankara, 06100, Turkey. TEL 90-312-4100410, FAX 90-312-4175886, bilgi@tuik.gov.tr, ulka.unsal@tuik.gov.tr, http://www.tuik.gov.tr.

315.61 TUR
TURKEY. TURKIYE ISTATISTIK KURUMU. GENEL NUFUS SAYIMI. NUFUSAN SOSYAL VE EKONOMIK NITELIKLERI/TURKEY. TURKISH STATISTICAL INSTITUTE. CENSUS OF POPULATION. SOCIAL AND ECONOMIC CHARACTERISTICS OF POPULATION. Text in English, Turkish. 1969. irreg., latest 2000. TRY 20 per issue domestic; USD 20 per issue foreign (effective 2009). **Document type:** *Government.* **Description:** Provides social, demographic and economic characteristics of population of Turkey. It includes tables in comparison with the information obtained from previous censuses and also tables by provinces was enriched with graphical presentations and maps.
Related titles: CD-ROM ed.: TRY 10 per issue domestic; USD 10 per issue foreign (effective 2009).
Published by: T.C. Basbakanlik, Turkiye Istatistik Kurumu/Prime Ministry Republic of Turkey, Turkish Statistical Institute, Yucetepe Mah. Necatibey Cad No.114, Cankaya, Ankara, 06100, Turkey. TEL 90-312-4100410, FAX 90-312-4175886, bilgi@tuik.gov.tr, ulka.unsal@tuik.gov.tr, http://www.tuik.gov.tr. Circ: 4,500.

362.28021 TUR ISSN 1300-1159
HA1911
TURKEY. TURKIYE ISTATISTIK KURUMU. INTIHAR ISTATISTIKLERI (YEAR)/TURKEY. TURKISH STATISTICAL INSTITUTE. SUICIDE STATISTICS (YEAR). Key Title: Intihar Istatistikleri. Text in English, Turkish. 1977. a., latest 2007. TRY 10 per issue domestic; USD 20 per issue foreign (effective 2009). **Document type:** *Government.* **Description:** Includes information related to sucides by month of suicide, age, sex, permanent residence, educational level, marital status, occupation group, cause of suicide, method of suicide and dependents.
Related titles: CD-ROM ed.: TRY 5 per issue domestic; USD 10 per issue foreign (effective 2009).
Published by: T.C. Basbakanlik, Turkiye Istatistik Kurumu/Prime Ministry Republic of Turkey, Turkish Statistical Institute, Yucetepe Mah. Necatibey Cad No.114, Cankaya, Ankara, 06100, Turkey. TEL 90-312-4100410, FAX 90-312-4175886, bilgi@tuik.gov.tr, ulka.unsal@tuik.gov.tr, http://www.tuik.gov.tr. Circ: 800.

306.9021 TUR ISSN 1300-1191
HA1911
TURKEY. TURKIYE ISTATISTIK KURUMU. OLUM ISTATISTIKLERI; IL VE ILCE MERKEZLERINDE (YEAR)/TURKEY. TURKISH STATISTICAL INSTITUTE. DEATH STATISTICS; PROVINCIAL AND DISTRICT CENTERS (YEAR). Key Title: Olum Istatistikleri. Text in English, Turkish. 1959. a., latest 2006. TRY 10 per issue domestic; USD 20 per issue foreign (effective 2009). **Document type:** *Government.* **Description:** Includes information related to deaths by month of death, sex, age, permanent residence, cause of death, place where cause of death was determined, marital status, occupation group and infant deaths.
Related titles: CD-ROM ed.: TRY 5 per issue domestic; USD 10 per issue foreign (effective 2009).
Published by: T.C. Basbakanlik, Turkiye Istatistik Kurumu/Prime Ministry Republic of Turkey, Turkish Statistical Institute, Yucetepe Mah. Necatibey Cad No.114, Cankaya, Ankara, 06100, Turkey. TEL 90-312-4100410, FAX 90-312-4175886, bilgi@tuik.gov.tr, ulka.unsal@tuik.gov.tr, http://www.tuik.gov.tr. Circ: 910.

304.6 USA ISSN 1559-7881
U.S.A. STATISTICS IN BRIEF (ONLINE). Text in English. 1972. a. free (effective 2011). stat. back issues avail. **Document type:** *Database, Government.*
Media: Online - full text.
Published by: U.S. Census Bureau (Subsidiary of: U.S. Department of Commerce), 4600 Silver Hill Rd, Washington, DC 20233. TEL 301-763-4636, 800-923-8282, econ@census.gov.

304.6 USA
U.S. BUREAU OF THE CENSUS. CENSUS OF POPULATION AND HOUSING (ONLINE). Text in English. 1790. decennial, latest 2000. free. stat. back issues avail. **Document type:** *Government.*
Former titles (until 2004): U.S. Bureau of the Census. Census of Population and Housing (Print); (until 1985): U.S. Bureau of the Census. Census of Population (0082-9390)
Media: Online - full content.
Published by: U.S. Census Bureau (Subsidiary of: U.S. Department of Commerce), 4600 Silver Hill Rd, Washington, DC 20233. TEL 301-763-4636.

304.6 USA ISSN 1551-8922
HA203
U.S. DEPARTMENT OF HEALTH AND HUMAN SERVICES. NATIONAL CENTER FOR HEALTH STATISTICS. NATIONAL VITAL STATISTICS REPORTS. Text in English. 1952. m. free (effective 2011). Supplement avail.; back issues avail.; reprints avail. **Document type:** *Report, Government.*
Formerly (until 1998): U.S. National Center for Health Statistics. Monthly Vital Statistics Report (0364-0396); Which was formed by the 1952 merger of: Current Mortality Analysis; Monthly Marriage Report; Monthly Vital Statistics Bulletin
Related titles: Microfiche ed.: (from CIS); Online - full text ed.: ISSN 1551-8930; ♦ Supplement(s): U.S. Department of Health and Human Services. National Center for Health Statistics. National Health Statistics Reports.
Indexed: AHCMS, AmStI, CLFP, EMBASE, ExcerpMed, F09, IndMed, MEDLINE, MEDOC, P30, PopulInd, R10, Reac, RehabLit, SCOPUS. —GNLM.
Published by: U.S. Department of Health and Human Services, Centers for Disease Control and Prevention. National Center for Health Statistics, 3311 Toledo Rd, Hyattsville, MD 20782. TEL 800-232-4636, cdcinfo@cdc.gov.

304.6021 325.1021 USA
JV6461
U.S. IMMIGRATION AND NATURALIZATION SERVICE. YEARBOOK OF IMMIGRATION STATISTICS (ONLINE). Text in English. 1978. a. **Document type:** *Yearbook, Government.*
Former titles: U.S. Immigration and Naturalization Service. Yearbook of Immigration Statistics (Print); (until 2002): U.S. Immigration and Naturalization Service. Statistical Yearbook (0743-538X)
Media: Online - full content.
Published by: U.S. Citizenship and Immigration Services (Subsidiary of: U.S. Department of Homeland Security), 425 I St, NW, Washington, DC 20536. http://www.uscis.gov.

U.S. NATIONAL CENTER FOR HEALTH STATISTICS. VITAL AND HEALTH STATISTICS. SERIES 1. PROGRAMS AND COLLECTION PROCEDURES. *see* PUBLIC HEALTH AND SAFETY—Abstracting, Bibliographies, Statistics

U.S. NATIONAL CENTER FOR HEALTH STATISTICS. VITAL AND HEALTH STATISTICS. SERIES 10. DATA FROM THE HEALTH INTERVIEW SURVEY. *see* PUBLIC HEALTH AND SAFETY—Abstracting, Bibliographies, Statistics

U.S. NATIONAL CENTER FOR HEALTH STATISTICS. VITAL AND HEALTH STATISTICS. SERIES 11. DATA FROM THE NATIONAL HEALTH EXAMINATION SURVEY, THE HEALTH AND NUTRITION EXAMINATION SURVEYS, AND THE HISPANIC HEALTH AND NUTRITION EXAMINATION SURVEY. *see* PUBLIC HEALTH AND SAFETY—Abstracting, Bibliographies, Statistics

U.S. NATIONAL CENTER FOR HEALTH STATISTICS. VITAL AND HEALTH STATISTICS. SERIES 14. DATA ON HEALTH RESOURCES. *see* PUBLIC HEALTH AND SAFETY—Abstracting, Bibliographies, Statistics

U.S. NATIONAL CENTER FOR HEALTH STATISTICS. VITAL AND HEALTH STATISTICS. SERIES 2. DATA EVALUATION AND METHODS RESEARCH. *see* PUBLIC HEALTH AND SAFETY—Abstracting, Bibliographies, Statistics

U.S. NATIONAL CENTER FOR HEALTH STATISTICS. VITAL AND HEALTH STATISTICS. SERIES 20. DATA ON MORTALITY. *see* PUBLIC HEALTH AND SAFETY—Abstracting, Bibliographies, Statistics

U.S. NATIONAL CENTER FOR HEALTH STATISTICS. VITAL AND HEALTH STATISTICS. SERIES 21. DATA ON NATALITY, MARRIAGE, AND DIVORCE. *see* PUBLIC HEALTH AND SAFETY—Abstracting, Bibliographies, Statistics

U.S. NATIONAL CENTER FOR HEALTH STATISTICS. VITAL AND HEALTH STATISTICS. SERIES 23. DATA FROM THE NATIONAL SURVEY OF FAMILY GROWTH. *see* PUBLIC HEALTH AND SAFETY—Abstracting, Bibliographies, Statistics

U.S. NATIONAL CENTER FOR HEALTH STATISTICS. VITAL AND HEALTH STATISTICS. SERIES 24. COMPILATIONS OF DATA ON NATALITY, MORTALITY, DIVORCE, AND INDUCED TERMINATIONS OF PREGNANCY. *see* PUBLIC HEALTH AND SAFETY—Abstracting, Bibliographies, Statistics

U.S. NATIONAL CENTER FOR HEALTH STATISTICS. VITAL AND HEALTH STATISTICS. SERIES 3. ANALYTICAL AND EPIDEMIOLOGICAL STUDIES. *see* PUBLIC HEALTH AND SAFETY—Abstracting, Bibliographies, Statistics

U.S. NATIONAL CENTER FOR HEALTH STATISTICS. VITAL AND HEALTH STATISTICS. SERIES 4. DOCUMENTS AND COMMITTEE REPORT. *see* PUBLIC HEALTH AND SAFETY—Abstracting, Bibliographies, Statistics

U.S. NATIONAL CENTER FOR HEALTH STATISTICS. VITAL AND HEALTH STATISTICS. SERIES 5. COMPARATIVE INTERNATIONAL VITAL AND HEALTH STATISTICS REPORTS. *see* PUBLIC HEALTH AND SAFETY—Abstracting, Bibliographies, Statistics

U.S. NATIONAL CENTER FOR HEALTH STATISTICS. VITAL AND HEALTH STATISTICS. SERIES 6. COGNITION AND SURVEY MEASUREMENT. *see* PSYCHOLOGY—Abstracting, Bibliographies, Statistics

314.021 USA ISSN 0251-0030
UNITED NATIONS. POPULATION AND VITAL STATISTICS REPORT. Key Title: United Nations. Statistical Papers. Series A, Population and Vital Statistics Report. Text in English. 1949. s-a. USD 30 in Africa to institutions; USD 80 to institutions in Australia, New Zealand, Japan & Europe; USD 75 in North America to institutions; USD 45 elsewhere to institutions (effective 2011). stat. back issues avail. **Document type:** *Report, Consumer.* **Description:** Provides latest census data, plus worldwide demographic statistics on birth and mortality.
Indexed: IIS.
Published by: (Department of International Economic and Social Affairs (DIESA), United Nations), United Nations Publications, 2 United Nations Plaza, Rm DC2-853, New York, NY 10017. TEL 212-963-8302, 800-253-9646, FAX 212-963-3489, publications@un.org, https://unp.un.org. **Subscr. to:** EBSCO Information Services, PO Box 361, Birmingham, AL 35201. TEL 205-995-1567, 800-633-4931, FAX 205-995-1588.

304.6 USA
UNITED STATES POPULATION PROJECTIONS BY AGE, SEX, RACE, AND HISPANIC ORIGIN. Text in English. irreg. free. stat. **Document type:** *Government.*
Media: Online - full text.
Published by: U.S. Census Bureau. Population Division (Subsidiary of: U.S. Department of Commerce), 4600 Silver Hill Rd., Washington, DC 20233. TEL 866-758-1060, http://www.census.gov/population/www/.

304.6 URY ISSN 0797-3217
URUGUAY. DIRECCION GENERAL DE ESTADISTICA Y CENSOS. ESTADISTICAS VITALES. Text in Spanish. 1961-1974; N.S. 1978. a. **Document type:** *Government.*
Published by: Direccion General de Estadistica y Censos, Montevideo, Uruguay.

304.6 USA ISSN 0148-8694
HB1145.U8
UTAH MARRIAGE AND DIVORCE ANNUAL REPORT. Text in English. a. USD 10. **Document type:** *Government.*
Formerly: Marriage and Divorce in Utah (0093-9641)
Related titles: Microfiche ed.: (from CIS).
Indexed: SRI.
Published by: Department of Health, Bureau of Vital Records, PO Box 142855, Salt Lake City, UT 84114-2855. TEL 801-538-6186.

614 USA ISSN 0500-7720
HA664
UTAH VITAL STATISTICS ANNUAL REPORT. Text in English. a. USD 10. **Document type:** *Government.*
Published by: Department of Health, Bureau of Vital Records, PO Box 142855, Salt Lake City, UT 84114-2855. TEL 801-538-6186. Ed. Cynthia Robinson.

304.6 VUT
VANUATU. STATISTICS OFFICE. CENSUS OF POPULATION (YEAR). BASIC TABLES. Text in English, French. 1972. irreg. USD 25. adv. stat. **Document type:** *Government.*
Former titles: Vanuatu. National Planning and Statistics Office. Census of Population (Year). Base Tables; (until 1983): Vanuatu. Condominium Bureau of Statistics. Census of Population and Housing, Vila and Santo, Preliminary Results
Published by: Statistics Office, PMB 19, Port Vila, Vanuatu. TEL 678-22110, FAX 678-24583. Ed. Jacob Isaiah. Adv. contact Tali Saurei. Circ: 300.

304.6 VUT
VANUATU. STATISTICS OFFICE. OVERSEAS MIGRATION AND TOURISM. Text in English, French. 1972. a. VUV 500, USD 5 (effective 1996). adv. charts; stat. **Document type:** *Government.* **Description:** Presents movements of residents, and arrivals of visitors, people on holidays and people staying in hotels cross-classified by age, sex, nationality, intended length of stay and purpose of visit.
Former titles: Vanuatu. Statistics Office. Overseas Migration; Vanuatu. National Planning and Statistics Office. Overseas Migration; Vanuatu. Bureau of Statistics. Overseas Migration (0259-7543)
Media: Duplicated (not offset).
Published by: Statistics Office, PMB 19, Port Vila, Vanuatu. TEL 678-22110, FAX 678-24583. Ed. Jacob Saurei. Adv. contact Tali Saurei. Circ: 300.

304.6 USA ISSN 0161-8695
HA375
VITAL STATISTICS OF IOWA. Text in English. 1975. a. USD 5 (effective 1999). stat. **Document type:** *Government.*
Formed by the merger of: Iowa Summary of Vital Statistics (0090-5143); Iowa Detailed Report of Vital Statistics (0362-9473)
Related titles: Microfiche ed.
Indexed: SRI.
Published by: Department of Public Health, Center for Health, Des Moines, IA 50319. TEL 515-281-4945, FAX 515-281-4958. Ed. Phyllis Blood. Circ: 400.

VITAL STATISTICS OF THE UNITED STATES. *see* PUBLIC HEALTH AND SAFETY—Abstracting, Bibliographies, Statistics

316 325 ZMB ISSN 0084-4543
JV8975.Z3
ZAMBIA. CENTRAL STATISTICAL OFFICE. MIGRATION STATISTICS. Variant title: Zambia. Central Statistical Office. Migration Statistics: Immigrants and Visitors. Text in English. 1965. a. USD 4. **Document type:** *Government.*
Published by: Central Statistical Office, PO Box 31908, Lusaka, Zambia. TEL 260-1-211231.

316 ZMB ISSN 0084-456X
HA1977.R48
ZAMBIA. CENTRAL STATISTICAL OFFICE. VITAL STATISTICS. Variant title: Zambia. Central Statistical Office. Registered Births, Marriages and Deaths (Vital Statistics). Text in English. 1965. a. USD 1. **Document type:** *Government.*
Published by: Central Statistical Office, PO Box 31908, Lusaka, Zambia. TEL 260-1-211231.

P

321 ZWE
ZIMBABWE. CENTRAL STATISTICAL OFFICE. INEQUALITY AMONG HOUSEHOLDS IN ZIMBABWE. Text in English. a. ZWD 123.20 in Africa; ZWD 160.10 in Europe; ZWD 200.20 elsewhere (effective 2000). **Document type:** *Government.*
Published by: Central Statistical Office, Causeway, PO Box 8063, Harare, Zimbabwe. TEL 263-4-706681, FAX 263-4-728529.

304.6 ZWE
ZIMBABWE. CENTRAL STATISTICAL OFFICE. POVERTY IN ZIMBABWE. Text in English. a. ZWD 394.80 in Africa; ZWD 500.40 in Europe; ZWD 614.80 elsewhere (effective 2000). **Document type:** *Government.*
Published by: Central Statistical Office, Causeway, PO Box 8063, Harare, Zimbabwe. TEL 263-4-706681, FAX 263-4-728529.

ZIMBABWE. CENTRAL STATISTICAL OFFICE. QUARTERLY MIGRATION AND TOURIST STATISTICS. *see* TRAVEL AND TOURISM—Abstracting, Bibliographies, Statistics

321 ZWE
ZIMBABWE. CENTRAL STATISTICAL OFFICE. WOMEN AND MEN IN ZIMBABWE. Text in English. a. ZWD 104.40 in Africa; ZWD 136.10 in Europe; ZWD 170.40 elsewhere (effective 2000). **Document type:** *Government.*
Indexed: CCMJ.
Published by: Central Statistical Office, Causeway, PO Box 8063, Harare, Zimbabwe. TEL 263-4-706681, FAX 263-4-728529.

011 FRA ISSN 1261-0674
50 TITRES SUR.. Text in French. 1995. irreg.
Published by: Centre National de Documentation Pedagogique, 4 Av du Futuroscope, Teleport 1, B P 80158, Futuroscope, Cedex 86961, France. TEL 33-1-46349000, FAX 33-1-46345544, http://www.cndp.fr. Ed. Bernard Piens.

POSTAL AFFAIRS

see COMMUNICATIONS—Postal Affairs

POULTRY AND LIVESTOCK

see AGRICULTURE—Poultry And Livestock

PRINTING

760 DNK ISSN 1603-1083
A G I. (Aktuel Grafisk Information) Variant title: Aktuel Grafisk Information Danmark. Text in Danish. 1970. 13/yr. DKK 850 (effective 2009). adv. **Document type:** *Magazine, Trade.* **Description:** For all who work with graphic production, design and publishing within the graphic arts industry.
Incorporates (1997-2002): Digital Design (1601-2100); Which was formerly (until 1999): On Demand (Koebenhavn) (1397-694X); Former titles (until 1998): A G I Danmark (0909-4717); (until 1994): Aktuel Grafisk Information (0900-3193)
Published by: MediaMind A/S, PO Box 1419, Glostrup, 2600, Denmark. TEL 45-70-253500, FAX 45-70-253595, info@mediamind.dk, http://www.mediamind.dk. Ed. Lis Lykke TEL 45-31-641311. Adv. contact Anders Nygaard Christoffersen TEL 45-31-641213. color page DKK 23,500; trim 210 x 297. Circ: 22,100.

741.6 NOR ISSN 0809-3334
A G I NORSK GRAFISK TIDSSKRIFT. Text in Norwegian. 1970. 5/yr. NOK 900 (effective 2011). adv. **Document type:** *Magazine, Trade.* **Description:** Deals with national and international issues related to graphic arts, typography, prepress (including reproduction, desktop, publishing and computer), printing and bookbinding.
Formerly (until 1997): A G I Norge (1395-4695); Which incorporated (1948-1996): Norsk Grafisk Tidsskrift (0029-1978)
Related titles: Online - full text ed.
Published by: Norske Media AS, PO Box 9231, Groenland, Oslo, 0134, Norway. TEL 47-92-201214. Ed. Marit Helene Gullien. Adv. contact Cato Ingebretsen.

686.2 USA ISSN 2160-0783
THE A P H A NEWSLETTER (ONLINE). Variant title: A P H A Newsletter. Text in English. 1974. q. free (effective 2011). adv. back issues avail. **Document type:** *Newsletter, Trade.*
Former titles (until 2009): A P H A Newsletter (Print) (2160-0767); (until 1986): A P H A Letter (0898-1078)
—Linda Hall.
Published by: American Printing History Association, Grand Central Sta, PO Box 4519, New York, NY 10163. TEL 212-930-9220, publications@printinghistory.org. Ed. Paul Moxon.

686.2 USA
A T F NEWSLETTER. Text in English. 1978. irreg. USD 4; USD 8 foreign (effective 1999). adv. bk.rev. **Document type:** *Newsletter, Trade.* **Description:** Articles on the preservation and promotion of historic hot-metal typecasting equipment and technology.
Published by: American Typecasting Fellowship, PO Box 263, Terra Alta, WV 26764. TEL 304-789-2455. Ed., Pub., R&P, Adv. contact Richard L Hopkins. Circ: 300.

AARETS BEDSTE BOGARBEJDE/SELECTED BOOKS OF THE YEAR; den danske bogdesignpris. *see* PUBLISHING AND BOOK TRADE

ACTAS DE DISENO. *see* ART

686.2 ZAF ISSN 1071-3263
Z244.6.A35
AFRICAN PRINTER. Text in English. 1993. q. ZAR 65 domestic; ZAR 90 in Southern Africa; ZAR 110 elsewhere. adv. **Document type:** *Magazine, Trade.*
Published by: Graphix Publications, PO Box 8147, Johannesburg, 2000, South Africa. TEL 27-11-496-2260, FAX 27-11-496-2266. Ed. Candice Anderson. Pub., Adv. contact Marian Oliver. R&P Neville Pritchars. B&W page USD 2,625, color page USD 2,284; trim 305 x 215. Circ: 8,000 (controlled).

760 SWE ISSN 0347-9846
AKTUELL GRAFISK INFORMATION. Text in Swedish. 1972. 13/yr. SEK 895 domestic; SEK 244 to students; SEK 1,525 in Europe; SEK 1,647 elsewhere (effective 2005). adv. **Document type:** *Magazine, Trade.*
Incorporates (1999-2001): On Demand (Malmoe) (1404-9783); Which supersedes in part (1997-1999): On Demand (Koebenhavn) (1397-694X)
Published by: A G I Aktuel Grafisk Information AB, Lodgatan 1, Malmo, 21124, Sweden. TEL 46-40-127840, FAX 46-40-125820, info@agi.se. Eds. Anna-Mi Wendel, Peter Ollen. Adv. contact Ola Andersson TEL 46-40-124630. color page SEK 24,900; 183 x 268.

686.2 ESP
ALABRENT. Text in Spanish. m. EUR 60 domestic; EUR 80 in Europe; EUR 100 elsewhere (effective 2009). adv. back issues avail. **Document type:** *Magazine, Trade.*
Published by: Alabrent Ediciones S.L., Rbla Josep Tarradellas 1 1s. 4a., Granollers, Barcelona, 08402, Spain. TEL 34-93-8603162, FAX 34-93-8795301, admin@alabrent.com, http://www.alabrent.com/. Ed. Ramon Vilageliv. Pub. Ramon Arnella. Adv. contact Anna Ventura. Circ: 5,000.

686.2 USA ISSN 0744-6616
Z119
AMERICAN PRINTER; the graphic arts managers magazine . Text in English. 1883. m. USD 59 domestic; USD 67 in Canada; USD 84 elsewhere; free domestic to qualified personnel (effective 2011). adv. bk.rev. illus.; tr.lit. back issues avail.; reprints avail. **Document type:** *Magazine, Trade.* **Description:** Covers the printing and lithographic industry including its allied manufacturing and service segments.
Former titles (until 1982): American Printer and Lithographer (0192-9933); (until 1979): Inland Printer - American Lithographer (0020-1502); (until 1961): Inland and American Printer and Lithographer (0096-2562)
Related titles: Microfilm ed.: (from PQC); Online - full text ed.: ISSN 1945-2543.
Indexed: A09, A10, A12, A13, A14, A15, A17, A22, A23, A24, A26, A27, A28, ABIPC, ABIn, APA, B01, B02, B03, B04, B06, B07, B08, B09, B11, B13, B15, B17, B18, BPI, BRD, BrCerAb, BusI, C&ISA, C10, C12, CA/WCA, CIA, CerAb, ChemAb, CivEngAb, CorrAb, E&CAJ, E08, E11, EEA, EMA, ESPM, EngInd, EnvEAb, G04, G06, G07, G08, GALA, H15, I05, L09, M&TEA, M01, M02, M09, MBF, METADEX, MicrocompInd, P10, P13, P16, P52, P53, P54, PQC, PSI, PhotoAb, RASB, S09, S22, SCOPUS, SolStAb, T&II, T02, T03, T04, V02, V03, V04, W01, W02, W03, W05, WAA.
—BLDSC (0853.228100), CIS, IE, Ingenta, Linda Hall. **CCC.**
Published by: Penton Media, Inc., 330 N Wabash Ave, Ste 2300, Chicago, IL 60611. TEL 312-595-1080, FAX 312-595-0295, information@penton.com, http://www.penton.com. Ed. Katherine O'Brien. Pub. Scott Bieda TEL 312-840-8406. adv.: B&W page USD 10,140, color page USD 12,890. Circ: 85,000 (controlled).

760 BRA ISSN 1414-2791
ANUARIO BRASILEIRO DA INDUSTRIA GRAFICA. Text in English, Portuguese. 1996. a. BRL 80, USD 96 (effective 2001). adv. back issues avail. **Document type:** *Directory.* **Description:** Lists the principal 3,300 printing companies and 500 suppliers of that sector.
Published by: (Associacao Brasileira da Industria Grafica/Brazilian Association of Graphic Industry), Clemente e Gramani Editora e Comunicacoes, Rua Marques de Paranagua, 348, 1o. andar, Sao Paulo, SP 01303-905, Brazil. TEL 55-11-3159-3010, 55-11-256-0919, gramani@uol.com.br. Ed. Plinio Gramani Filho. adv.: page USD 4,960; 210 x 280. Circ: 15,000.

760 ARG ISSN 0004-105X
ARGENTINA GRAFICA. Text in Spanish. 1935. 4/yr. USD 7 per issue to non-members. adv. charts; illus.; tr.lit.
Published by: Camara de Industriales Graficos de la Argentina, Cnel. Ramon L. Falcon 1657-59, Buenos Aires, 1405, Argentina. TEL 54-114-6315120. Ed. Lorenzo F Heavey. Circ: 2,500.

686.2 676.3 USA ISSN 1054-2434
Z244.6.L29
ARTES GRAFICAS. Text in Spanish, English, Portuguese. 1967. m. adv. bk.rev. **Document type:** *Magazine, Trade.* **Description:** Provides an international trade publication with technical articles covering the printing, newspaper and graphic arts industries.
Formerly: Industria Grafica y Artes Graficas; Which was formed by the merger of: Industria Grafica (0120-7601); Artes Graficas U S A (0164-1905); Incorporates: Export Graficas U S A (0741-7160); Formerly: Artes Graficas (0004-3494)
Indexed: GALA, PST.
Published by: B 2 B Portales, Inc (Subsidiary of: Carvajal International, Inc.), 901 Ponce De Leon Blvd, Ste 601, Coral Gables, FL 33134. TEL 305-448-6875, FAX 305-448-9942, contactenos@b2bportales.com, http://www.b2bportales.com. Circ: 23,000.

686.2 USA
ASCENDERS. Text in English. q.
Published by: Autologic Incorporated, 2000 Anchor Ct., Newbury Park, CA 91320-1601. TEL 805-498-9611.

ASIA PACIFIC COATINGS JOURNAL. *see* PAINTS AND PROTECTIVE COATINGS

760 BRA ISSN 0103-572X
ASSOCIACAO BRASILEIRA DA INDUSTRIA GRAFICA. REVISTA; arte e industria grafica. Key Title: Revista A B I G R A F. Text in Portuguese. 1949. bi-m. BRL 30 domestic; BRL 50 foreign (effective 2001). adv. back issues avail. **Document type:** *Trade.* **Description:** Covers news, interviews, events, products, and technology in graphic arts, packaging, and converting industries.
Former titles (until 1990): A B I G R A F em Revista (0103-5711); (until 1975): B I G (Boletim da Industria Grafica) (0006-5862)
Published by: (Associacao Brasileira da Industria Grafica/Brazilian Association of Graphic Industry), Clemente e Gramani Editora e Comunicacoes, Rua Marques de Paranagua, 348, 1o. andar, Sao Paulo, SP 01303-905, Brazil. TEL 55-11-3159-3010, 55-11-256-0919, gramani@uol.com.br. Ed. Plinio Gramani Filho. adv.: color page USD 3,890; trim 280 x 210. Circ: 16,000.

AUSTRALIAN PRESS COUNCIL NEWS. *see* JOURNALISM

686.2 AUS ISSN 1328-2573
AUSTRALIAN PRINTER. Abbreviated title: A P. Text in English. 1950. m. (except Jan.). AUD 77 domestic; AUD 165 in New Zealand; AUD 219.45 elsewhere; AUD 9.95 newsstand/cover (effective 2009). adv. bk.rev. illus. Index. back issues avail. **Document type:** *Magazine, Trade.* **Description:** Contains source of all information for the entire printing and graphic communications industry.
Former titles (until 1996): Australian Printer Magazine (1033-1522); (until 1989): Australasian Printer Magazine (1033-1514); (until 1987): The Australasian Printer (0004-8453)
Related titles: Online - full text ed.: free (effective 2009); Supplement(s): Australian Proofing Buyer's Guide.
Indexed: ABIPC, CISA, EngInd, GALA, SCOPUS.
—IE, Ingenta. **CCC.**
Published by: Printer Magazines Pty Ltd., 3/7 Parkes St, PO Box 3665, Parramatta, NSW 2150, Australia. TEL 61-2-96356059, FAX 61-2-96357683, info@i-grafix.com, http://www.printermags.com.au/. Eds. Wayne Robinson, Brian Moore. Pub. Anders Oqvist. Circ: 10,000. **Subscr. to:** ISubscribe Pty Ltd., 25 Lime St, Ste 303, Level 3, Sydney, NSW 2000, Australia. TEL 61-2-92621722, FAX 61-2-92625044, info@isubscribe.com.au, http://www.isubscribe.com.au.

686.2 GBR ISSN 2045-8266
▼ **BANNER REPEATER.** Text in English. 2010. bi-m. **Document type:** *Trade.* **Description:** Brings out on-going series of pamphlets and posters, in tandem with the arts programme, as well as events, performance and lectures commissioned from the project space.
Address: Platform 1, Hackney Downs Network Rail, Dalston Ln, London, E8 1LA, United Kingdom.

686.22 GBR ISSN 0954-9226
Z119
BASELINE (EAST MALLING). Text in English. 1979. 3/yr. GBP 48 domestic; GBP 52 in Europe; GBP 60 elsewhere (effective 2009). adv. **Document type:** *Magazine, Academic/Scholarly.* **Description:** Covers all aspects of typography, including graphic design and art.
Related titles: Online - full text ed.
Indexed: ABM, D05, SCOPUS.
—CCC.
Published by: Bradburne Publishing Ltd., Bradburne House, East Malling, Kent ME19 6DZ, United Kingdom. TEL 44-1732-875200, FAX 44-1732-875300, info@baselinemagazine.com. Ed. Hans Dieter Reichert. Adv. contact Veronika Reichert. B&W page GBP 1,750, color page GBP 2,000.

686.2 384 CHN ISSN 1004-8626
BEIJING YINSHUA XUEYUAN XUEBAO/BEIJING INSTITUTE OF GRAPHIC COMMUNICATION. JOURNAL. Text in Chinese. 1993. bi-m. CNY 8 newsstand/cover (effective 2006). **Document type:** *Journal, Academic/Scholarly.*
Related titles: Online - full text ed.
Published by: Beijing Yinshua Xueyuan/Beijing Institute of Graphic Communication, 25, Huangcun Xinhua Bei Lu, Beijing, 102600, China. TEL 86-10-60261067.

686.2 DEU ISSN 1618-7709
BEITRAEGE ZUR DRUCKGESCHICHTE. Text in German. 2001. irreg., latest vol.5, 2008. price varies. **Document type:** *Monographic series, Academic/Scholarly.*
Published by: Internationaler Arbeitskreis Druck- und Mediengeschichte e.V., c/o Deutsches Zeitungsmuseum, Am Abteihof 1, Wadgassen, 66787, Germany. TEL 49-6834-94230, FAX 49-6834-942320, bosslet@deutsches-zeitungsmuseum.de, http://www.arbeitskreis-druckgeschichte.de.

BIBLIOPHILIA. *see* HISTORY—History Of Europe

BIBLIOTECA DI PARATESTO. *see* PUBLISHING AND BOOK TRADE

BIBLIOTHECA HUNGARICA ANTIQUA. *see* PUBLISHING AND BOOK TRADE

686.2 FRA ISSN 2108-5536
▼ **BIBLIOTHEQUE TYPOGRAPHIQUE.** Text in French, English. 2010. irreg. **Document type:** *Monographic series, Academic/Scholarly.*
Published by: Ypsilon Editeur, 29, Bd de Clichy, Paris, 75009, France. TEL 33-6-29454907, contact@ypsilonediteur.com.

760 USA
BLUE BOOK MARKETING INFORMATION REPORTS. Short title: B B M I R. Text in English. 19??. base vol. plus q. updates. looseleaf. charts; mkt.; stat. **Document type:** *Report, Trade.* **Description:** Presents and analyzes marketing and production data in the graphic arts and suppliers industries.
Related titles: Diskette ed.
Published by: A.F. Lewis Information Services (Subsidiary of: Reed Business Information), 345 Hudson St, 4th Fl, New York, NY 10014. info@gabb.com.

BOGVENNEN/BOOKLOVER. *see* PUBLISHING AND BOOK TRADE

002.09 AUS ISSN 0811-3971
BRANDYWINE DOCUMENTS ON THE HISTORY OF BOOKS & PRINTING. Text in Dutch, English, French, Russian. 1980. irreg. (1-2/yr.). price varies. back issues avail.
Formerly: Brandywine Documents on Printing and Printing History
Published by: Brandywine Press & Archive, 20 Murray Rd., Beecroft, NSW 2119, Australia. TEL (02)86-3627.

686.22 AUS ISSN 0157-5619
BRANDYWINE KEEPSAKE. Text in English, German, Russian. 1979. a. price varies. back issues avail.
Published by: Brandywine Press & Archive, 20 Murray Rd., Beecroft, NSW 2119, Australia. TEL (02)86-3627.

686.22 FRA ISSN 0572-7529
BUREAU INTERNATIONAL DES SOCIETES GERANT LES DROITS D'ENREGISTREMENT ET DE REPRODUCTION MECANIQUE. BULLETIN. Text in French. 1959. irreg.
Published by: Bureau International des Societes Gerant les Droits d'Enregistrement et de Reproduction Mecanique/International Bureau of the Societies Administering the Rights of Mechanical Recording and Reproduction, 56 av. Kleber, Paris, 75116, France. TEL 47-04-57-04, FAX 47-55-11-53.

BUSINESS RATIO REPORT. PAINT & PRINTING INK MANUFACTURERS (YEAR). *see* PAINTS AND PROTECTIVE COATINGS

686.2 658.8 GBR ISSN 1473-527X
BUSINESS RATIO REPORT. PRINTERS - INTERMEDIATE. Text in English. 1978. a., latest no.31, 2008, Mar. GBP 365 per issue (effective 2010). charts; stat. back issues avail. **Document type:** *Report, Trade.* **Description:** Covers companies active as intermediate printers.

Former titles (until 2001): Business Ratio. Printers. Intermediate (1470-3424); (until 2000): Business Ratio Plus: Printers - Intermediate (1354-3385); (until 1994): Business Ratio Report. Printers Intermediate (0261-9423).
Published by: Key Note Ltd. (Subsidiary of: Bonnier Business Information), Harlequin House, 5th Fl, 7 High St, Teddington, Richmond upon Thames, TW11 8EE, United Kingdom. TEL 44-845-5040452, FAX 44-845-5040453, sales@keynote.co.uk.

686.2 658.8 GBR ISSN 1473-5288
BUSINESS RATIO REPORT. PRINTERS - MAJOR. Text in English. 1978. a., latest no.31, 2008, Mar. GBP 365 per issue (effective 2010). charts; stat. back issues avail. **Document type:** *Report, Trade.*
Description: Covers companies active as major printers.
Former titles (until 2001): Business Ratio. Printers. Major (1470-3432); (until 2000): Business Ratio Plus. Printers - Major (1354-5256); (until 1994): Business Ratio Report. Printers - Major (0261-9431)
Published by: Key Note Ltd. (Subsidiary of: Bonnier Business Information), Harlequin House, 5th Fl, 7 High St, Teddington, Richmond upon Thames, TW11 8EE, United Kingdom. TEL 44-845-5040452, FAX 44-845-5040453, sales@keynote.co.uk.

741 MEX ISSN 2007-1663
C C D C. REVISTA. (Centro de Ciencias de Diseno y Construccion) Text in Spanish. 2007. s-a. **Document type:** *Journal, Academic/Scholarly.*
Published by: Universidad Autonoma de Aguascalientes, Centro de Ciencias de Diseno y Construccion, Ave. Universidad # 940, Ciudad Universitaria, Aguascalientes, Aguascalientes 20131, Mexico. TEL 52-449-9107400, http://www.ccdc.uaa.mx/.

C E I M REVISTA. (Confederacion Empresarial de Madrid) *see* ART

686.2 CAN
CANADIAN PRINTER (ONLINE). Text in English. irreg. free (effective 2010). adv.
Media: Online - full text.
Published by: Rogers Publishing Ltd./Les Editions Rogers Limitee, 333 Bloor St. E., 6th Fl., Toronto, ON M4W 1G9, Canada. http://www.rogerspublishing.ca. Ed. Doug Picklyk TEL 416-764-1530.

686.2 USA ISSN 2154-5316
CANVAS; supporting print sales and marketing executives. Text in English. 2007. bi-m. adv. back issues avail. **Document type:** *Magazine, Trade.* **Description:** Provides advice about sales and unparalleled perspective on transforming industry.
Related titles: Online - full text ed.: free (effective 2010).
Published by: Conduit Inc., 2180 Satellite Blvd, Ste 400, Duluth, GA 30097. TEL 678-473-6131. Pub. Mark R Potter.

686.22 NZL ISSN 1175-7507
CAP ONLINE. Text in English. 1994. m. free. **Document type:** *Journal, Trade.* **Description:** Contains in-depth articles for designers and business people, plus the latest news, features and opinions.
Media: Online - full text.
Published by: Jack Yan & Associates, 13 Mamari St, Kilbirnie, PO Box 14-368, Wellington, New Zealand.

686.2 FRA ISSN 0247-039X
Z119
CARACTERE; le magazine des professionnels de l'imprime. Text in French. 1949. a. adv. bk.rev. abstr.; bibl.; charts; illus. index. **Document type:** *Journal, Trade.*
Indexed: A22, ABIPC, EngInd, P&BA, PhotoAb, RefZh, SCOPUS.
—BLDSC (3050.900000), IE, Ingenta, INIST. **CCC.**
Address: 2 Rue Monge, BP 224, Aurillac, Cedex 15002, France. TEL 33-4-71480546, FAX 33-4-71487545, http://www.caractere-sa.fr. Circ: 8,000.

CHINESE MARKETS FOR PRINTING INKS. *see* BUSINESS AND ECONOMICS—Marketing And Purchasing

686.2 CAN ISSN 1918-6606
CHOP. Text in English. 1974. s-a. free to members (effective 2010). **Document type:** *Magazine, Trade.*
Published by: Malespina Printmakers Society, 1555 Duranleau St, Granville Island, Vancouver, BC V6H 3S3, Canada. TEL 604-688-1724, malaspinagallery@telus.net.

CHUBAN YU YINSHUA/PUBLISHING & PRINTING. *see* PUBLISHING AND BOOK TRADE

686.2 BEL ISSN 0772-8220
CICERO; magazine professionnel de la communication graphique. Text in French. 1984. m. adv. illus. **Document type:** *Trade.*
Related titles: Dutch ed.: Cicero (Dutch Edition). ISSN 0772-8239.
Published by: Mema NV, Wielewaasstraat 20, Wilrijk, 2610, Belgium. TEL 32-3-448-0827, FAX 32-3-448-0832, pgermeys@skynet.be. Ed. Piet Germeys. Circ: 8,000 (controlled).

686.2 CHE
TA418.76 CODEN: COTGAV
COATING INTERNATIONAL. Text in German. 1968. m. CHF 192 domestic; CHF 217 foreign; CHF 18 newsstand/cover (effective 2009). adv. **Document type:** *Magazine, Trade.*
Formerly (until 2007): Coating (0590-8450)
Indexed: A22, ABIPC, CIN, CPEI, ChemAb, ChemTitl, EngInd, IPackAb, P&BA, P31, RefZh, SCOPUS, TM, WSCA.
—BLDSC (3292.563000), CASDDS, IE, Infotrieve, Ingenta, INIST.
Published by: Rek & Thomas Medien AG, Schmiedgasse 5, St Gallen, 9001, Switzerland. TEL 41-71-2282011, FAX 41-71-2282014. Ed. Marianne Rek. Pub. Michael Rek. Adv. contact Michael Richardt.

COMMUNICATION ARTS. *see* ADVERTISING AND PUBLIC RELATIONS

686.2 NLD ISSN 0166-7416
COMPRES; lijfblad voor ondernemers in grafimedia. Text in Dutch. 1976. 20/yr. EUR 99; EUR 8 newsstand/cover (effective 2009). adv. **Document type:** *Trade.*
—IE, Infotrieve.
Published by: Uitgeverij Compres b.v., Postbus 55, Leiden, 2300 AB, Netherlands. TEL 31-71-5161515, FAX 31-71-5161535, info@uitgeverijcompres.nl, http://www.uitgeverijcompres.nl. Ed. Hanneke Jelles TEL 31-71-5161524. Pub. Wim Findhammer. Adv. contact Frans van Grondelle TEL 31-71-5161518. B&W page EUR 2,480, color page EUR 4,255; bleed 225 x 285. Circ: 4,129.

CONNOISSEURS GUIDE TO CALIFORNIA WINE. *see* BEVERAGES

CONTEMPORARY PRINT PORTFOLIO; a guide to prices, new editions & sources. *see* ART

621.9 686.2 USA
CONVERTING HOTLINE; connecting buyers and sellers of converting equipment, materials, services and suppliers. Text in English. 1996. m. free to qualified personnel (print or online ed.) (effective 2009). adv. back issues avail. **Document type:** *Magazine, Trade.*
Description: Designed primarily for the entrepreneur whose primary objective is to buy or sell equipment, materials and services.
Related titles: Online - full text ed.
Published by: Industry Marketing Solutions, 809 Central Ave, 2nd Fl, PO Box 893, Fort Dodge, IA 50501. TEL 515-574-2248, 888-247-2007, FAX 515-574-2237, http://www.industrymarketingsolutions.com/. Pub. Steve Scanlan. adv.: B&W page USD 618, color page USD 751; trim 7.625 x 10.75. Circ: 60,000 (controlled).

THE CROUSER REPORT. *see* BUSINESS AND ECONOMICS—Small Business

760 ESP ISSN 2171-6242
▼ **CYAN MAG.** Text in Spanish. 2009. bi-m. back issues avail. **Document type:** *Magazine, Consumer.*
Media: Online - full text.
Published by: Cyan Clous SL Ed. Enrique Alejandro Garde.

760 GBR
D R S NEWS. (Design Research Society) Text in English. m. free to members. **Document type:** *Newsletter, Trade.* **Description:** Includes information on design and design research.
Media: E-mail.
Published by: Design Research Society, Newcastle, NE1 7RU, United Kingdom. TEL 44-191-222-8080, FAX 44-191-222-8580, http://www.designresearchsociety.org/.

686.2 USA ISSN 0889-423X
DEALER COMMUNICATOR; a national link between dealers and their suppliers in the printing and imaging industry. Text in English. 1980. m. USD 30; free to qualified personnel (effective 2007). adv. bk.rev. **Document type:** *Magazine, Trade.* **Description:** Presents news about products for graphic arts dealers and resellers.
Published by: Fichera Publications, 1919 N State Rd 7, Ste 202, Margate, FL 33063. TEL 954-971-4360, 800-327-8999, FAX 954-971-4362. Pub. Orazio M Fichera. R&P, Adv. contact Patricia Leavitt. B&W page USD 5,870, color page USD 6,855. Circ: 9,330 (controlled).

760 MEX ISSN 1405-0439
DEDISENO; diseno, arquitectura, arte. Text in Spanish. 1994. bi-m. adv. back issues avail.
Related titles: Online - full text ed.: ISSN 1605-4822.
Indexed: ABM, SCOPUS.
Published by: Grupo Malabar, Francisco Sosa No. 9, Int. 2, Col. Coyoacan, Mexico, DF, 04000, Mexico. TEL 52-5-6590399, FAX 52-5-6584351, desis@nueve.com.mx, http://www.nueve.com.mx/d. Ed. Luis Moreno. Adv. contact Rocio Perez.

760 NLD ISSN 0923-9790
N6941
DELINEAVIT ET SCULPSIT. Text in Dutch, English, French, German; Summaries in English. 1989. irreg. (2-3/yr.). EUR 60 domestic for 5 issues; EUR 65 in Europe for 5 issues; EUR 85 elsewhere for 5 issues (effective 2008). back issues avail. **Document type:** *Journal, Academic/Scholarly.* **Description:** Deals with the graphic arts of the Netherlands before 1850.
Indexed: B24.
Address: Rijksbureau voor Kunsthistorische Documentatie, Prins Willem-Alexanderhof 26, Postbus 90418, The Hague, 2509 LK, Netherlands. TEL 31-70-3339729, FAX 31-70-3339789, elen@delineavit.nl. Ed. J Bolten. R&P Albert J Elen.

THE DESIGN FIRM DIRECTORY - GRAPHIC DESIGN EDITION; a listing of firms and consultants in graphic design in the U.S. *see* ADVERTISING AND PUBLIC RELATIONS

686.2 GBR ISSN 1752-8445
DESIGN RESEARCH QUARTERLY. Abbreviated title: D R Q. Text in English. 2006. q. free to members (effective 2009). back issues avail. **Document type:** *Journal, Trade.* **Description:** Features the latest research and news in the field of design research.
Media: Online - full content.
Published by: Design Research Society, Newcastle, NE1 7RU, United Kingdom. TEL 44-191-222-8080, FAX 44-191-222-8580, admin@designresearchsociety.org, http://www.designresearchsociety.org/. Ed. Peter Storkerson.

DIE DEUTSCHE SCHRIFT; Zeitschrift zur Foerderung von Gotisch, Schwabacher und Fraktur. *see* ART

686.2 DEU ISSN 0012-1096
TS1080
DEUTSCHER DRUCKER. Text in German. 1965. 38/yr. EUR 145.15 domestic; EUR 191.75 foreign; EUR 6.75 newsstand/cover (effective 2011). adv. bk.rev. abstr.; illus.; pat.; tr.lit.; tr.mk. index. **Document type:** *Magazine, Trade.* **Description:** Trade publication for the printing and paper manufacturing industries, featuring book production and design, graphic arts, media technology, book binding, production development, screen printing, industry news, and reports of events and exhibitions.
Formerly: Papier und Druck (0031-1375)
Related titles: CD-ROM ed.; Online - full text ed.
Indexed: A22, ABIPC, B03, BibCart, CISA, ChemAb, EngInd, P&BA, PROMT, RASB, RefZh, SCOPUS.
—IE, Infotrieve, INIST. **CCC.**
Published by: Deutscher Drucker Verlag GmbH, Postfach 4124, Ostfildern, 73744, Germany. TEL 49-711-448170, FAX 49-711-442099, info@publish.de. Ed. Bernhard Niemela. Adv. contact Michael Bieber. Circ: 9,156 (paid and controlled).

686.2 901 CAN ISSN 0225-7874
DEVIL'S ARTISAN; a journal of the printing arts. Text in English. 1980. s-a. CAD 22 domestic to individuals; USD 22 foreign to individuals; CAD 27 domestic to institutions; USD 27 foreign to institutions; CAD 11 newsstand/cover domestic (effective 2004). **Document type:** *Journal, Academic/Scholarly.* **Description:** Presents information on the craft of printing and bookmaking, on bibliographic and historic matters, and on communicative, sociological, and technical subjects related to printing.
Published by: The Porcupine's Quill, Inc, 68 Main St, Erin, ON N0B 1T0, Canada. TEL 519-833-9158, FAX 519-833-9845, http://www.sentex.net/~pql. Ed. Don McLeod. Pub. Tim Inkster. R&P, Adv. contact Elke Inkster.

686.2 GBR ISSN 1471-5694
DIGITAL DEMAND WORLD; the journal of printing and publishing technology. Text in English. 2000. m. (10/yr). 50 p./no.; **Document type:** *Journal, Trade.*
Formed by the merger of (1997-2000): Journal of Prepress & Printing Technology (1365-7321); (1993-2000): Publishing Technology Review (1351-0177); (1995-2000): Prepress Commentary (1361-2506); Which was formerly (1989-1995): Desktop Publishing Commentary (0957-3178); Which was formed by the merger of (1986-1989): Desktop Publisher (0269-5847); Pira D T P Commentary
Related titles: Online - full text ed.: GBP 750 (effective 2010).
Indexed: Inspec.
—BLDSC (3588.395280). **CCC.**
Published by: IntertechPira, Cleeve Rd, Leatherhead, Surrey KT22 7RU, United Kingdom. TEL 44-1372-802080, FAX 44-1372-802079, info@pira-international.com.

760 AUS ISSN 1834-1764
DIGITAL REPRODUCTION. Text in English. 2006. bi-m. back issues avail. **Document type:** *Magazine, Trade.*
Published by: Dezuma Pty Ltd, PO Box 793, Aspley, QLD 4034, Australia. TEL 61-7-3863-2822, FAX 61-7-3863-2883, http://www.wideformatonline.com/content/view/12/26.

686.2 USA ISSN 1053-3699
DISCOUNT & WHOLESALE PRINTING NEWSLETTER. Text in English. 1990. s-a. looseleaf. USD 6 DOM-TOM (effective 2007). adv. **Document type:** *Newsletter, Trade.* **Description:** Lists sources for discount and wholesale printing.
Published by: Prosperity & Profits Unlimited, PO Box 416, Denver, CO 80201. TEL 303-575-5676, FAX 303-575-1187. Ed. A. Doyle. adv.: page USD 300. Circ: 3,000 (paid and controlled).

686.2 USA
DOCUMENT; mapping the document life cycle. Text in English. 19??. 7/yr. USD 18 domestic; USD 28 in Canada & Mexico; USD 40 elsewhere; free to qualified personnel (print or online ed.) (effective 2009). adv. back issues avail.; reprints avail. **Document type:** *Magazine, Trade.* **Description:** Provides relevant, useful information through all media channels to those responsible for the document process from document creation.
Former titles (until 2003): Document Processing Technology (1081-4078); (until 1993): Document Mailing Technology
Related titles: Online - full text ed.
Indexed: A12, A13, A17, A28, ABIn, APA, BrCerAb, C&ISA, C10, CA/WCA, CIA, CerAb, CivEngAb, CompLI, CorrAb, E&CAJ, E11, EEA, EMA, ESPM, EnvEAb, H15, M&TEA, M09, MBF, METADEX, MicrocompInd, P48, P51, P53, P54, PQC, SolStAb, T02, T04, WAA.
Published by: R B Publishing, Inc., 2901 International Ln, Ste 200, Madison, WI 53704. TEL 608-241-8777, 800-536-1992, FAX 608-241-8666, rbpub@rbpub.com, http://www.rbpub.com. Ed. Allison Lloyd TEL 360-471-3566. Pub. Ken Waddell TEL 608-442-5064. adv.: page USD 5,453; trim 8 x 10.5. **Subscr. to:** PO Box 259098, Madison, WI 53725.

760 006.42 USA
DOCUMENT DESIGN. Text in English. 1997. irreg. **Document type:** *Magazine, Consumer.* **Description:** Explores the constantly evolving boundaries between text and graphics, authors and readers.
Media: Online - full text.
Published by: Whiskey Creek Document Design, RR 1, Box 48A, Hitterdal, MN 56552. TEL 218-962-3202.

686.2 DEU
DRUCK & MEDIEN; Menschen - Technik - Wirtschaft. Text in German. 1999. m. EUR 88 domestic; EUR 114 foreign; EUR 44 to students (effective 2010). adv. bk.rev. bibl.; charts; illus. index. **Document type:** *Magazine, Trade.*
Formerly (until 2004): Druck & Medien Magazin (1439-5703); Which was formed by the merger of (1951-1999): Druckwelt (0012-6519); Which was formerly (1951-1968): Graphische Woche (0432-2657); (1994-1999): O P - Druckmagazin (0948-6461); Which was formerly (1965-1994): Offsetpraxis (0030-0594); (1948-1999): Polygraph (0032-3845); Which was formerly (1945-1948): Klimschs Druckerei-Anzeiger (1438-3632); (1943-1945): Das Deutsche Druckgewerbe (0366-8754); Which was formed by the merger of (1943-1943): Zeitschrift fuer Deutschlands Druckgewerbe (0372-8250); (1927-1943): Klimschs Druckerei-Anzeiger (0368-6094); Which was formerly (1925-1927): Klimschs Allgemeiner Anzeiger fuer Druckereien (1438-3624); (1874-1925): Allgemeiner Anzeiger fuer Druckereien (1438-3616)
Related titles: Online - full text ed.
Indexed: A22, RASB, TM.
—BLDSC (3627.540000), IE, Infotrieve, Ingenta, INIST. **CCC.**
Published by: Haymarket Media GmbH & Co. KG, Weidestr 122a, Hamburg, 22083, Germany. TEL 49-40-69206200, FAX 49-40-69206333, info@haymarket.de, http://www.haymarket.de. Adv. contact Wolfgang Klages. color page EUR 5,150; trim 210 x 297. Circ: 10,733 (controlled).

686.2 CHE
DRUCK BULLETIN. Text in German. q.
Address: Postfach 1116, Zuerich, 8048, Switzerland. TEL 01-9285631, FAX 01-9285630. Ed. Tony Holenstein. Circ: 2,700.

686.2 DEU
DRUCK UND MEDIEN A B C. Text in German. a. **Document type:** *Journal, Trade.*
Formerly: Druck - A B C
Related titles: Online - full text ed.
Published by: Zentral-Fachausschuss Berufsbildung Druck und Medien, Wilhelmshoeher Allee 260, Kassel, 34131, Germany. TEL 49-561-510520, FAX 49-561-5105215, info@zfamedien.de.

686.2 676 DEU ISSN 0946-5235
DRUCK UND PAPIER. Text in German. 1994. 5/yr. **Document type:** *Magazine, Trade.*
Supersedes in part (in 2001): I G Medien Forum (0946-5359); Which was formerly (until 1991): Kontrapunkt (0938-3727); (until 1989): Druck und Papier (0012-6470); Which incorporated (1950-1994): Forum und Technik (0015-7708)
Related titles: Online - full text ed.
Published by: Vereinte Dienstleistungsgewerkschaft, Paula-Thiede-Ufer 10, Berlin, 10179, Germany. TEL 49-30-69560, FAX 49-30-69563141, info@verdi.de, http://www.verdi.de. Ed. Henrik Mueller. Circ: 100,000.

P

686.2 DEU ISSN 0012-6500
Z119
DRUCKSPIEGEL; Das Entscheider-Magazin fuer Premedia, Print und Finishing. Text in German. 1946. 15/yr. EUR 85 domestic; EUR 115 foreign (effective 2009). adv. bk.rev. charts; illus. index. **Document type:** *Magazine, Trade.* **Description:** Provides information on technical developments in the fields of typesetting, data systems technology, computer publishing, typography, printing technology and print converting.
Indexed: GALA, RASB, RefZh, TM.
—CCC.
Published by: Druckspiegel Verlagsgesellschaft mbH und Co., Borsigstr 1-3, Heusenstamm, 63150, Germany. TEL 49-6104-6060, FAX 49-6104-606444, info@kepplermediengruppe.de, http://www.kepplermediengruppe.de. Ed. Johann Sajdowski. Adv. contact Julia Ohlig. B&W page EUR 3,800, color page EUR 5,780; trim 185 x 270. Circ: 13,077 (paid and controlled).

DUTCH DESIGN JAARBOEK. *see* ART

EARLY BOOK SOCIETY. JOURNAL; for the study of manuscripts and printing history. *see* PUBLISHING AND BOOK TRADE

686.2 DEU ISSN 1434-2529
EINKAUFSFUEHRER DRUCK UND PUBLISHING. Text in German. 1997. a. adv. **Document type:** *Directory, Trade.* **Description:** Buyers' guide for the German printing and graphic arts industries.
Published by: Deutscher Drucker Verlag GmbH, Postfach 4124, Ostfildern, 73744, Germany. TEL 49-711-448170, FAX 49-711-442099, info@publish.de, http://www.publish.de. Ed. Johannes Kokot. Circ: 20,000.

760 NLD ISSN 1879-3835
ELEPHANT. Text in English. 2003. q. EUR 64.99; EUR 54.99 to students; EUR 19.95 newsstand/cover (effective 2010). adv. **Document type:** *Magazine, Consumer.*
Formerly (until 2009): Graphic Magazine (1569-4119)
Published by: Frame Publishers, Laan der Hesperiden 68, Amsterdam, 1076 DX, Netherlands. TEL 31-20-4233717, FAX 31-20-4280653. Ed. Marc Valli. Adv. contact Peter Huiberts.

764.8 ESP ISSN 1139-8574
EN SERIGRAFIA. Text in Spanish. 1986. bi-m. EUR 30 domestic; EUR 42 in Europe; EUR 54 elsewhere (effective 2009). **Document type:** *Magazine, Trade.*
Published by: Alabrent Ediciones S.L., Rbla Josep Tarradellas 1 1s. 4a., Granollers, Barcelona, 08402, Spain. TEL 34-93-8603162, FAX 34-93-8795301, alabrenet@alabrenet.es, http://www.alabrent.com/. Circ: 3,000.

760 763 769 FRA ISSN 1772-3345
ENCRES FRAICHES. Text in French. 2003. q. **Document type:** *Newsletter.*
Published by: Actualite de l'Estampe (A D E), 9 Rue de la Republique, Draguignan, 83300, France. contact@actualitedelestampe.fr.

760 FRA ISSN 1774-5160
ETAPES:; graphisme design image creation. Text in French. 1994. 10/yr. EUR 104; EUR 64 to students; EUR 10.70 per issue (effective 2009). adv. **Document type:** *Magazine, Consumer.*
Formerly: Etapes Graphiques (1254-7298)
Published by: Pyramyd N T C V, 15 rue de Turbigo, Paris, 75002, France. TEL 33-1-40260099, FAX 33-1-40260703, http://www.pyramyd.fr. Ed. Patrick Morin. Pub., Adv. contact Michel Chanaud. Circ: 10,000.

760 FRA ISSN 1767-4751
ETAPES: INTERNATIONAL. Text in English. 2005. q. EUR 93, USD 112 to institutions (effective 2008). **Document type:** *Magazine, Trade.*
—CCC.
Published by: Pyramyd N T C V, 15 rue de Turbigo, Paris, 75002, France. TEL 33-1-40260099, FAX 33-1-40260703, form@pyramyd.fr, http://www.pyramyd.fr.

686.2 DEU ISSN 0949-9695
ETIKETTEN-LABELS. Text in German. 1993. bi-m. EUR 88.81 domestic; EUR 103 in Europe; EUR 118 elsewhere (effective 2010). adv. **Document type:** *Magazine, Trade.*
Published by: G & K TechMedia GmbH, Am Stollen 6-1, Gutach-Bleibach, 79261, Germany. TEL 49-7685-918110, FAX 49-7685-909011, info@flexo.de. Ed. Klemens Ehrlitzer. Adv. contact Stefan Nolte. Circ: 3,000 (paid and controlled).

760 CHE
EUREPRO. CONGRESS SUMMARIES. Text in English. a.
Formerly: Union Internationale des Industries Graphiques de Reproduction. Congress Summaries
Published by: Eurepro, Schosshaldenstr 20, Bern 32, 3000, Switzerland. TEL 031-431511.

686.2 GBR
THE EUROPEAN SCREEN PRINTER & DIGITAL IMAGES MAGAZINE. Text in English, German. 1989. 3/yr. GBP 45 (effective 2001). adv. back issues avail. **Document type:** *Magazine, Trade.* **Description:** Offers an in-depth profile on member countries. Covers environmental concerns, E.E.C. legislation, new technology, and developments in Eastern Europe.
Formerly (until 2001): The European Screen Printer Magazine
Published by: Federation of European Screen Printers Association, 7A West St, Reigate, Surrey RH2 9BL, United Kingdom. TEL 44-1737-240788, FAX 44-1737-240770. Ed., Pub. Derek Down. R&P, Adv. contact Nigel Steffens. page GBP 1,200; trim 297 x 210. Circ: 4,500 (controlled).

686.2 DEU
EXPRESSIS VERBIS; a magazine for the graphic arts industry. Text in Danish, English, French, German, Italian, Japanese, Spanish, Dutch, Swedish, Finnish, Russian. 1998. 3/yr. free. 54 p./no.; back issues avail. **Document type:** *Magazine, Trade.* **Description:** Contains articles and features on all aspects of the printing industry.
Published by: Manroland AG, Muehlheimer Strasse 341, Offenbach Am Main, 63075, Germany. TEL 49-69-83050, FAX 49-69-83051440, info@manroland.com, http://www.manroland.com. Ed. Birgit Eisenloeffel. Circ: 130,000 (controlled).

760 BEL
F E B E L G R A TIJDSCHRIFT. Text in Dutch. fortn.
Published by: Federatie van de Belgische Industrie, Dambruggestraat 60, Postbus 1, Antwerp, 2060, Belgium. TEL 2317118.

764.8 GBR
F E S P A WORLD. (Federation of European Screen Printers Associations) Text in English; Summaries in German, French, Spanish. 1991. s-a. free to members (effective 2009). adv. Supplement avail.; back issues avail. **Document type:** *Magazine, Trade.* **Description:** Covers the very latest developments in screen and digital as well as continuing its news on the FESPA and ESMA associations.
Formerly (until 2004): F E S P A Magazine (1681-4703)
Published by: F E S P A Ltd., 7a West St, Reigate, Surrey RH2 9BL, United Kingdom. TEL 44-1737-240788, FAX 44-1737-240770. Ed. Val Hirst TEL 44-1623-882398. Pub. Karen Pooley. Adv. contact Michael Ryan TEL 44-1737-229727. page EUR 2,000.

686.2 DEU ISSN 0015-5322
F O G R A LITERATURDIENST. Text in German. 1955. m. EUR 270 (effective 2005). bk.rev. **Document type:** *Abstract/Index.*
Related titles: Diskette ed.
Indexed: ABIPC, GALA.
Published by: Forschungsgesellschaft Druck e.V., Streitfeldstr 19, Munich, 81673, Germany. TEL 49-89-431820, FAX 49-89-43182100, info@fogra.org, http://www.fogra.org/. Ed. Rainer Pietzsch. Circ: 550.

686.2 DEU
F O G R A LITERATURPROFILE. Text in German. 1975. q. EUR 200 (effective 2005). **Document type:** *Abstract/Index.*
Related titles: Diskette ed.
Published by: Forschungsgesellschaft Druck e.V., Streitfeldstr 19, Munich, 81673, Germany. TEL 49-89-431820, FAX 49-89-43182100, info@fogra.org, http://www.fogra.org/. Ed. Rainer Pietzsch.

686.2 DEU ISSN 0015-5330
F O G R A MITTEILUNGEN. Text in German. 1953. 2/yr. membership. bk.rev. **Document type:** *Bulletin.*
Indexed: ABIPC, GALA.
Published by: Forschungsgesellschaft Druck e.V., Streitfeldstr 19, Munich, 81673, Germany. TEL 49-89-431820, FAX 49-89-43182100, info@fogra.org. Circ: 2,500.

686.2 608.7 DEU
F O G R A PATENTSCHAU. Text in German. 1952. m. EUR 200 (effective 2005). pat.; stat. **Document type:** *Abstract/Index.*
Formerly: Fogra-Patentkurzberichte
Published by: Forschungsgesellschaft Druck e.V., Streitfeldstr 19, Munich, 81673, Germany. TEL 49-89-431820, FAX 49-89-43182100, info@fogra.org, http://www.fogra.org/. Ed. Rainer Pietzsch.

686.2 CHE
FACHHEFTE BULLETIN TECHNIQUE; grafische Industrie und Kommunikationstechnik. Text in German. 1954. 5/yr. CHF 44. adv. bk.rev. bibl.; charts; illus. index.
Formerly: Fachhefte fuer Chemigraphie, Lithographie und Tiefdruck (0014-6374)
Related titles: Ed.: Bulletin Technique. ISSN 0007-5736. 1966. CHF 40.
Indexed: ABIPC, ChemAb, P&BA, TM.
Published by: (Schweizerischer Lithographenbund), Conzett & Huber AG, Baslerstr 30, Zuerich, 8048, Switzerland. TEL 01-522500, FAX 01-4912922. **Co-sponsor:** Verband der Schweizer Druckindustrie.

FINANCIAL SURVEY REPORT. PRINTERS. *see* BUSINESS AND ECONOMICS—Trade And Industrial Directories

686.2 DEU
FINE ART PRINTER. Text in German. 4/yr. EUR 35; EUR 9.50 newsstand/cover (effective 2007). adv. **Document type:** *Magazine, Trade.*
Published by: New Media Magazine Verlag GmbH, Dietlindenstr 18, Munich, 80802, Germany. TEL 49-89-36888180, FAX 49-89-36888181, newmedia@largeformat.de. Ed., Adv. contact Hermann Will. color page EUR 4,039; trim 210 x 297. Circ: 9,200 (paid and controlled).

686.2 USA ISSN 1051-7324
FLEXO; the flexographic technogoly source. Text in English. 1976. m. USD 55 in North America; USD 76 elsewhere (effective 2010). adv. illus. back issues avail.; reprints avail. **Document type:** *Magazine, Trade.* **Description:** Serves the flexographic printing/converting industry, including suppliers, printer-converters, packaging buyers and others involved in the printing and purchasing of materials for labels, packaging, corrugated and related fields.
Formerly (until 1984): Flexographic Technical Journal (0734-6980)
Related titles: Online - full text ed.: free (effective 2010); ◆ Spanish ed.: Flexo Espanol. ISSN 1051-6352.
Indexed: A22, ABIPC, CurPA, EngInd, GALA, SCOPUS.
—BLDSC (3950.678000), IE, Ingenta.
Published by: Foundation of Flexographic Technical Association, 900 Marconi Ave, Ronkonkoma, NY 11779. TEL 631-737-6020, FAX 631-737-6813, memberinfo@flexography.org, http://www.flexography.org. Pub. Bob Moran. Adv. contact Jay Kaible. B&W page USD 2,700, color page USD 3,200; 7 x 10. Circ: 20,000.

686.2 DEU ISSN 1863-6926
FLEXO & GRAVURE ASIA. Text in English. 2002. q. EUR 55.64 domestic; EUR 79 in Europe; EUR 95 elsewhere; EUR 14 per issue (effective 2009). adv. **Document type:** *Magazine, Trade.* **Description:** Serves as an information source on the printing and converting technology.
Published by: G & K TechMedia GmbH, Am Stollen 6-1, Gutach-Bleibach, 79261, Germany. TEL 49-7685-918110, FAX 49-7685-909011, info@flexo.de. adv.: B&W page EUR 1,500, color page EUR 2,500. Circ: 6,000 (paid and controlled).

686.2 USA ISSN 1051-6352
FLEXO ESPANOL. Text in Spanish. 1986. q. USD 55 in North America; USD 76 elsewhere (effective 2005). adv. index. back issues avail. **Description:** Serves the Spanish-speaking flexographic printing-converting industry, including suppliers, printer-converters, packaging buyers and others involved in the printing and purchasing of materials for labels, packaging, corrugated and related fields.
Related titles: ◆ English ed.: Flexo. ISSN 1051-7324.
Published by: Foundation of Flexographic Technical Association, 900 Marconi Ave, Ronkonkoma, NY 11779. TEL 631-737-6020, FAX 631-737-6813, ggilbride@vax.fta-ffta.org. Ed. Graciela Gilbride. Pub. Robert J Moran. Adv. contact Diane Seddio. B&W page USD 1,831, color page USD 2,780. Circ: 7,500.

686.2 DEU ISSN 0949-9709
FLEXO UND GRAVURE INTERNATIONAL. Text in German. 1995. q. EUR 55.64 domestic; EUR 79 in Europe; EUR 100 elsewhere (effective 2010). adv. **Document type:** *Magazine, Trade.*
—BLDSC (3950.678200).
Published by: G & K TechMedia GmbH, Am Stollen 6-1, Gutach-Bleibach, 79261, Germany. TEL 49-7685-918110, FAX 49-7685-909011, info@flexo.de. Ed. Klemens Ehrlitzer. Adv. contact Stefan Nolte. Circ: 10,000 (paid and controlled).

686.2 DEU ISSN 0949-9717
FLEXO- UND TIEF-DRUCK. Text in German. 1990. bi-m. EUR 88.81 domestic; EUR 103 in Europe; EUR 118 elsewhere (effective 2010). **Document type:** *Magazine, Trade.*
Published by: G & K TechMedia GmbH, Am Stollen 6-1, Gutach-Bleibach, 79261, Germany. TEL 49-7685-918110, FAX 49-7685-909011, info@flexo.de. Circ: 4,850 (paid and controlled).

686.2 CHE ISSN 1661-2639
FLEXOPRINT; das Fachmagazin fuer den Verpackungsdruck. Text in German. 1990. m. adv. **Document type:** *Magazine, Trade.*
Published by: Rek & Thomas Medien AG, Schmiedgasse 5, St Gallen, 9001, Switzerland. TEL 41-71-2282011, FAX 41-71-2282014. adv.: B&W page EUR 1,915, color page EUR 2,890; trim 185 x 272. Circ: 6,020 (controlled).

686.2 GBR ISSN 1356-9287
FLEXOTECH. Text in English. 1994. 8/yr. GBP 75 domestic; GBP 120 in Europe; GBP 165 elsewhere (effective 2009). **Document type:** *Journal, Trade.* **Description:** Covers printing and finishing process oh flexography in Europe.
Related titles: Online - full text ed.: free (effective 2009).
Indexed: EngInd, SCOPUS.
—CCC.
Published by: Whitmar Publications Ltd., 30 London Rd, Southborough, Tunbridge Wells, Kent TN4 0RE, United Kingdom. TEL 44-1892-542099, FAX 44-1892-546693, http://www.paperandprint.com. Ed. Robin Meade. Pub. Rob Mulligan. Circ: 5,800.

686.2 USA
FOCUS (SEWICKLEY). Text in English. 1995. q. free to members. bk.rev. charts; illus.; stat. back issues avail. **Document type:** *Newsletter.* **Description:** Focuses on the marketing, business strategies, technology, and application of digital-on-demand printing.
Formerly: Digits
Related titles: Online - full text ed.
Published by: Printing Industries of America, Inc., 200 Deer Run Rd, Sewickley, PA 15143-2600. TEL 412-741-6860, FAX 412-741-2311, membership@printing.org. Circ: 500 (paid).

686.22 USA
THE FONT SITE; a magazine for the type & graphics professional. Text in English. m. **Description:** Presents informative articles on general rules of typography, scanning, 3D objects, and how to create web pages with style.
Media: Online - full text.
Published by: Title Wave Studios, 2787 Sand Dr, Camano Island, WA 98292.

778.1 ESP ISSN 1888-1580
FORMATOS DIGITAL. Text in Spanish. 2004. bi-m. EUR 80 (effective 2009). **Document type:** *Magazine, Consumer.*
Formerly (until 2005): Formatos (1697-736X); Which was formed by the merger of (1995-2003): Reprografia Actual (1139-5176); (2000-2003): Press Graph Serigrafia en la Era Digital (1578-1070)
Published by: (Asociacion Espanola de Reprografia), Ediciones Press Graph S.L., Joanot Martorell 4-10, Sabedell, Barcelona, 08203, Spain. TEL 34-93-7205230, FAX 34-93-7205249, info@pressgraph.es, http://www.pressgraph.es/.

070 USA
FOSSIL; historians of amateur journalism. Text in English. 1904. q. USD 10 (effective 2008). bk.rev.
Published by: Fossils, Inc., 157 S Logan, Denver, CO 80209. http://www.thefossils.org/index.html. Circ: 200.

760 FRA ISSN 0015-9565
LA FRANCE GRAPHIQUE. Short title: F G. Text in French. 1947. m. (11/yr). EUR 67 (effective 2009). bk.rev. charts; illus. index. **Document type:** *Magazine, Trade.* **Description:** Covers graphics and communications equipment.
Incorporates (1997-1999): Guide de la Filiere Graphique (1287-3519)
Indexed: RefZh.
—CCC.
Published by: Editions Techniques pour l'Automobile et l'Industrie (E T A I), 48-50 Rue Benoit Malon, Gentilly, 94250, France. TEL 33-1-56794292, http://www.groupe-etai.com. Circ: 5,000.

686.2 ZAF
G D R. Text in English. m. ZAR 57 in Africa; ZAR 115 elsewhere. adv. **Document type:** *Handbook/Manual/Guide, Trade.*
Indexed: RASB.
Published by: Graphix Publications (Pty) Ltd., PO Box 751119, Garden View, 2047, South Africa. TEL 27-11-622-4800, FAX 27-11-622-2480.

686.2 GBR
G P M U JOURNAL. Text in English. 10/yr.
Published by: Graphic Paper & Media Union, Ossory House, 5 Brereton Rd, Bedford, MK40 1HU, United Kingdom. TEL 01234-219676, FAX 01234-218640. Ed. T Dubbins.

686.2 USA
GANNETT OFFSET QUARTERLY; a newsletter for customers and employees of Gannett Offset companies. Text in English. q.
Published by: Gannett Offset, 6883 Commercial Dr, Springfield, VA 22159. TEL 800-255-1457.

686.20294489 DNK ISSN 1600-2962
GRAFGUIDE. Variant title: A G I Grafguide. Text in Danish. 1996. a. adv. **Document type:** *Catalog, Trade.*
Former titles (until 2000): Grafisk Branchekatalog (1397-9663); (until 1997): Grafisk Telefon- og Fax Katalog (1396-397X)
Related titles: Online - full text ed.: ISSN 1901-8061. 2000.
Published by: MediaMind A/S, PO Box 1419, Glostrup, 2600, Denmark. TEL 45-70-253500, FAX 45-70-253595, info@mediamind.dk, http://www.mediamind.dk.

686.2 HRV ISSN 1330-4127
GRAFICAR. Text in Croatian. 1992. m. **Document type:** *Journal, Trade.*

Published by: Sindikat Graficke i Nakladnicke Djelatnosti Hrvatske, Brescenskoga 4, Zagreb, 10000, Croatia. TEL 385-1-554633, FAX 385-1-4554590. Ed. Veljko Vlahovic.

686.2 ESP ISSN 0017-2901
Z119
GRAFICAS; revista tecnica de las artes del libro. Text in Spanish. 11/yr.
Indexed: ABIPC, Englnd, SCOPUS.
—CCC.
Address: Blasco de Garay, 76 1o, Madrid, 28015, Spain. TEL 1-445-25-64. Ed. F de Pablo Cereceda. Circ: 2,500.

686.2 NLD ISSN 0017-2936
GRAFICUS; onafhankelijk weekblad voor de grafische en communicatie-industrie. Text in Dutch. 1917. 40/yr. EUR 123 (effective 2009). adv. bk.rev. abstr.; charts; illus.; pat.; stat. **Document type:** *Magazine, Trade.* **Description:** Covers the technology, market, and people in the graphic arts and communication industries.
Indexed: KES.
—IE, Infotrieve.
Published by: ManagementMedia B.V., PO Box 1932, Hilversum, 1200 BX, Netherlands. TEL 31-35-6232756, FAX 31-35-6232401, info@managementmedia.nl. Ed. Alex Kunst. Pub. Mike Velleman.

686.2 CAN ISSN 1485-8029
GRAFIKA. Text in English. 1992. m. CAD 49 (effective 2008). **Document type:** *Magazine, Trade.*
Former titles (until 1998): Production Imprimee et Multimedia (1207-5817); (until 1995): Production Imprimee (1192-473X)
Indexed: AIAP.
Published by: Editions Info Presse, 4310, boulevard Saint-Laurent, Montreal, PQ H2W 1Z3, Canada. TEL 514 842-5873, FAX 514 842-2422.

760 SWE ISSN 0346-9727
GRAFIKNYTT. Text in Swedish. 1958. q. SEK 250; SEK 65 per issue (effective 2011). adv. **Document type:** *Magazine, Trade.*
Indexed: B24.
Published by: Grafiska Saellskapet/Swedish Printmakers' Association galleri@grafiskasallakapet.se, http://www.grafiskasallskapet.se. Ed. Bjoern Bredstroem. Adv. contact Eva Engstrand. **Subscr. to:** Hornsgatan 6, Stockholm 11820, Sweden.

760 NLD ISSN 1574-7409
HET GRAFISCH WEEKBLAD. Text in Dutch. 1995. 44/yr. EUR 94 (effective 2009). adv.
Published by: RAI Langfords bv, Postbus 10099, Amsterdam, 1001 EB, Netherlands. TEL 31-20-5042800, FAX 31-20-5042888, http://www.railangfords.nl. Eds. Cees Pfeiffer, Rien Berends. Pub. Ron Brokking. adv.: B&W page EUR 1,995, color page EUR 3,315; 255 x 375. Circ: 7,230.

686.2 DEU ISSN 0936-806X
GRAFISCHE PALETTE. Text in German. 1977. 4/yr. EUR 7.50 newsstand/cover (effective 2011). adv. **Document type:** *Magazine, Trade.*
Published by: Deutscher Drucker Verlag GmbH, Postfach 4124, Ostfildern, 73744, Germany. TEL 49-711-448170, FAX 49-711-442099, info@publish.de, http://www.publish.de. Adv. contact Michael Blind. Circ: 19,518 (controlled).

686.2 DNK ISSN 1904-1454
GRAFISK FREMTID. Text in Danish. 1922. 6/yr. free. adv. **Document type:** *Magazine, Trade.*
Former titles (until 2009): Bogtrykkerne - Distriktsbladene (0106-0619); (until 1977): Vort Medlemsblad (0902-6347)
Related titles: Online - full text ed.: 2006.
Published by: De Grafiske, Roegelvej 1, Brabrand, 8220, Denmark. TEL 45-86-255977, FAX 45-86-255978, kontakt@degrafiske.dk. Eds. Anders Jensen, Anni Kjaer Nielsen. Adv. contacts Joergen Lauge Laugesen, Ole Kristensen.

686.0294489 DNK ISSN 1602-7493
GRAFISK HAANDBOG. Text in Danish. 2001. a. DKK 250 per issue (effective 2008). adv. **Document type:** *Trade.*
Formed by the merger of (1978-2001): Grafisk Leverandoerhaandbog (0905-7986); Which was formerly (until 1990): Leverandoerhaandbogen (0904-5945); (1977-2001): Grafisk Produktionshaandbog (1398-1617); Which was formerly (until 1997): Produktionshaandbogen (0105-7758)
Related titles: Online - full text ed.
Published by: B K Media, Hovedgaden 55 C, Hoersholm, 2970, Denmark. TEL 45-70-209838, FAX 45-36-306261, kh@bkmedia.dk, http://www.bkmedia.dk. Adv. contact Birgit Waltenburg. page DKK 13,100; 144 x 205. Circ: 4,500.

686.2 DNK ISSN 0017-2995
DE GRAFISKE FAG. Text in Danish. 1921. 8/yr. adv. bk.rev. illus. **Document type:** *Magazine, Trade.*
Formerly (until 1991): Bogtrykkerbladet (0006-5730)
Related titles: Online - full text ed.: ISSN 1902-4770. 200?.
Published by: Grafisk Arbejdsgiverforening, Helgavej 26, Odense M, 5230, Denmark. TEL 45-63-127000, FAX 45-63-127080, ga@ga.dk.

686 741.6 SWE ISSN 1650-402X
GRAFISKT FORUM. Text in Swedish. 1962. 10/yr. SEK 924 domestic print ed.; SEK 1,124 domestic print && online eds.; SEK 1,124 foreign print ed.; SEK 1,355 foreign print & online eds.; SEK 693 online ed. (effective 2007). adv. bk.rev. abstr.; charts; illus. index. **Document type:** *Magazine, Trade.*
Former titles (until 2001): Grafiskt Media Forum (1402-8352); (until 1997): Grafiskt Forum (0017-3002); (until 1982): Grafiskt Forum: Med Nordisk Boktryckarekonst; Which was formed by the merger of (1900-1962): Nordisk Boktryckarekonst (0284-3838); (19??-1962): Grafiskt Forum: Svenska Boktryckarfoereningens Meddelanden; Which was formerly (until 1935): Svenska Boktryckarefoereningens Meddelanden
Related titles: Online - full text ed.
Indexed: MLA-IB, P&BA.
Published by: Mentor Online AB, Landskronawaegen 1, PO Box 601, Helsingborg, 25106, Sweden. info@mentoronline.se, http://www.mentoronline.se. Ed. Uffe Berggren. Adv. contact Goeran Holfve TEL 46-42-4901937. color page SEK 22,200; trim 178 x 253. Circ: 3,400 (controlled).

686.2 006.6 ITA ISSN 1591-7096
GRAPH CREATIVE. Text in Italian. 2001. 11/yr. EUR 44 (effective 2009). **Document type:** *Magazine, Trade.*
Formed by the merger of (1989-2000): Creative (1129-227X); (1990-2000): Graph (1594-4832)
Published by: Il Sole 24 Ore Business Media, Via Monte Rosa 91, Milan, 20149, Italy. TEL 39-02-30221, FAX 39-02-312055, info@ilsole24ore.com, http://www.gruppo24ore.com.

686.2 FIN ISSN 1457-9723
GRAPHIC ARTS IN FINLAND (ONLINE). Text in English, Finnish. 1972. 3/yr.
Formerly (until 2001): Graphic Arts in Finland (Print) (0359-2464)
Media: Online - full content.
Published by: (Graphic Industry Research Foundation), Helsinki University, Department of Automation and System Technology, Laboratory of Media Technology, P.O. Box 6400, Helsinki, 02015 HUT, Finland. Ed. Pirkko Oittinen.

686.2 USA ISSN 1047-9325
Z119 CODEN: GAMOE4
GRAPHIC ARTS MONTHLY; applied technology for the printing industry. Text in English. 1929. m. (plus annual Sourcebook). USD 157 domestic; USD 235 in Mexico; USD 264 in Canada; USD 325 elsewhere; USD 10 per issue domestic; USD 20 per issue foreign; free to qualified personnel (print or online ed.) (effective 2009). adv. illus.; tr.lit. index. back issues avail.; reprints avail. **Document type:** *Magazine, Trade.* **Description:** Contains reports on applied technology for printing and allied industries.
Formerly (until 1987): Graphic Arts Monthly and the Printing Industry (0017-3312); Which was formed by the merger of (1928-1937): The Printing Industry; (1929-1937): The Graphic Arts Monthly; Incorporates (in 198?): Business Graphics
Related titles: Microfiche ed.: (from CIS); Online - full text ed.: ISSN 1558-1411; Supplement(s): Graphic Arts Monthly. Buyers' Guide; General Requirements for Applications in Commercial Offset Lithography. ISSN 1544-5933.
Indexed: A01, A02, A03, A08, A09, A10, A12, A13, A14, A15, A17, A22, A23, A26, A27, A30, A31, ABIPC, ABIn, B01, B02, B03, B04, B06, B07, B08, B09, B11, B13, B15, B17, B18, BPI, BRD, BusI, C05, C10, C12, CPerI, CWI, ChemAb, E08, Englnd, G04, G06, G07, G08, GALA, I05, I07, Inspec, L09, M01, M02, MicrocompInd, P02, P10, P13, P16, P34, P48, P51, P53, P54, PQC, PhotoAb, RefZh, ResCtrInd, S09, S23, SCOPUS, SRI, SoftBase, T&II, T02, V02, V03, V04, W01, W02, W03, W05.
—BLDSC (4211.950000), CASDDS, CIS, IE, Infotrieve, Ingenta. **CCC.**
Published by: Reed Business Information (Subsidiary of: Reed Business), 2000 Clearwater Dr, Oak Brook, IL 60523. TEL 630-288-8000, FAX 630-288-8537, corporatecommunications@reedbusiness.com, http://www.reedbusiness.com. Ed. Bill Esler TEL 630-288-8538. Pub. John Bold TEL 630-288-8835. adv.: B&W page USD 15,545, color page USD 14,695; trim 7.875 x 10.5. Circ: 70,100 (paid). **Subscr. to:** Reed Business Information.

070.5 USA ISSN 0884-6901
GRAPHIC COMMUNICATIONS WORLD; the bi-weekly briefing for senior management. Text in English. 1968. s-m. USD 347 to individuals; USD 372 to institutions; USD 177 educational (effective 2006). adv. bk.rev. 4 p./no.; back issues avail. **Document type:** *Newsletter, Trade.* **Description:** Covers new technology and management trends for senior management in the printing and publishing industry.
Related titles: Supplement(s): Financial Report.
Indexed: ABIPC, GALA.
Address: 3313 S Western Ave, Sioux Falls, SD 57105. TEL 605-275-2085, FAX 605-275-2087, jeffreyh@hazlett.com, http://www.hayzlett.com. Pub. Linda Maschino. adv.: page USD 600. Circ: 1,000 (paid).

GRAPHIC COMMUNICATOR. *see* LABOR UNIONS

760 JPN
GRAPHIC DESIGN IN JAPAN. Text in English. a. USD 220.
Published by: Intercontinental Marketing Corp., I.P.O. Box 5056, Tokyo, 100-3191, Japan. TEL 81-3-3661-7458.

▼ **GRAPHIC DESIGN MUSEUM. MUSEUM MAGAZINE.** *see* MUSEUMS AND ART GALLERIES

760 659.1 USA ISSN 0274-7499
NC998.5.A1 CODEN: GDUSE9
GRAPHIC DESIGN: U S A. Text in English. 1965. 10/yr. USD 75 domestic to individuals; USD 100 in Canada to individuals; USD 140 elsewhere to individuals; free to qualified personnel (effective 2010). adv. bk.rev. illus.; tr.lit. **Document type:** *Magazine, Trade.* **Description:** Covers production, advertising, communication, graphic design and art.
Formerly: Graphics: U S A (0017-3428); Incorporates: Graphics: New York
Indexed: GALA.
Published by: Kaye Publishing Corporation, 89 5th Ave, Ste 901, New York, NY 10003. TEL 212-696-4380, FAX 212-969-4564, TELEX gkaye@gdusa.com. Ed., Pub., Adv. contact Gordon Kaye. B&W page USD 4,400, color page USD 5,400; trim 8.5 x 10.875. Circ: 27,250.

686.2 760 CAN ISSN 0227-2806
GRAPHIC MONTHLY. Text in English. 1980. 6/yr. CAD 28. adv. **Document type:** *Handbook/Manual/Guide, Trade.* **Description:** Serves as a reference tool for owners and managers by providing how-to advice and product and service information. Covers news and issues affecting printers today.
Related titles: Microfilm ed.
Published by: North Island Publishing, 1606 Sedlescomb Dr, Unit 8, Mississauga, ON L4X 1M6, Canada. TEL 905-625-7070, FAX 905-625-4856. Ed. Filomena Tamburri. Pub. Alexander Donald. Adv. contact Andrew Luke. B&W page CAD 3,203, color page CAD 4,353; trim 11 x 8.25. Circ: 10,086.

686.2029 CAN ISSN 0828-9638
GRAPHIC MONTHLY ESTIMATORS' & BUYERS GUIDE (ONTARIO EDITION). Text in English. 1984. a. adv. **Document type:** *Directory, Trade.* **Description:** Directory for the graphic arts industry with over 800 listings in 115 categories.
Related titles: Regional ed(s).: Graphic Monthly Estimators' & Buyers Guide (Western Edition). 2001.
Published by: North Island Publishing, 1606 Sedlescomb Dr, Unit 8, Mississauga, ON L4X 1M6, Canada. TEL 905-625-7070, 800-331-7408, FAX 905-625-4856. Circ: 8,000.

070.5 USA
GRAPHIC NEWS. Text in English. 1986. m. membership. bk.rev. **Document type:** *Newsletter.*
Published by: Printing Industry of Minnesota, Inc., 2829 University Ave, S E, Ste 750, Minneapolis, MN 55414-3230. TEL 612-379-6003, FAX 612-379-6030. Ed. Elizabeth A Miller. R&P Elizabeth Miller. Circ: 5,000 (controlled).

686.2 GBR ISSN 0952-4118
GRAPHIC REPRO. Text in English. 1986. m. bk.rev. **Document type:** *Journal, Trade.* **Description:** Reviews technical developments and trade news in the pre-press field, including graphic design, typesetting, color reproduction, proofing, and platemaking.
Address: 99 Maybury Rd, Woking, Surrey GU21 5HX, United Kingdom. TEL 0483-740271, FAX 0483-740397. Ed. N Walker. Circ: 10,000.

766 659 ZAF ISSN 1814-2915
GRAPHIC REPRO ON-LINE. Text in English. 2001. d.
Media: Online - full text.
Published by: Graphic Repro & Print, PO Box 1833, Florida Hills, 1716, South Africa. Ed., Pub. Mike Hilton.

760 USA ISSN 1941-5117
NC1
GRAPHIC TIPS FOR STUDENTS. Text in English. 2008. irreg. free (effective 2009). back issues avail. **Description:** Features articles on basic subjects that all students of graphic design requires.
Media: Online - full content.
Published by: Mara J. Fulmer, Pub., 5523 Jerome Ln, Grand Blanc, MI 48439. mara.fulmer@esmail.mcc.edu. Pub. Mara Jevera Fulmer.

766 659 ZAF ISSN 1814-2923
GRAPHICREPRO.NET E-NEWS. Text in English. 2002. w. free (effective 2006).
Media: Online - full text.
Published by: Graphic Repro & Print, PO Box 1833, Florida Hills, 1716, South Africa. Ed., Pub. Mike Hilton.

686.2 USA
GRAPHICS. Text in English. 1945. bi-m. USD 59. adv.
Published by: Graphic U.S., Inc., 141 Lexington Ave, New York, NY 10016. Ed. Lyle Metzdorf. Circ: 29,000.

686.2 USA
GRAPHICS UPDATE. Text in English. 1985. m. USD 20 to non-members. bk.rev. **Document type:** *Newsletter.*
Published by: Printing Association of Florida, Inc., 6095 NW 167th St., Ste. D7, Hialeah, FL 33015-4313. TEL 305-558-4855, FAX 305-823-8965. Ed. Gene Strul. adv.: B&W page USD 1,264, color page USD 151,680; trim 11 x 8.5. Circ: 10,000 (controlled).

P

686.2 ITA ISSN 0017-3436
GRAPHICUS. Text in Italian. 1911. m. adv. bk.rev. bibl.; charts; illus. index. **Document type:** *Magazine, Trade.*
Formerly (until 1920): Piemonte Grafico (1125-3053)
Indexed: ChemAb, GALA, RASB.
Published by: Alberto Greco Editore, Viale Espinasse 141, Milan, MI 20156, Italy. TEL 39-02-300391, FAX 39-02-30039300, age@gruppodg.com, http://www.ageditore.com. Ed. Marco Picasso. adv.: page EUR 2,250; 210 x 297. Circ: 13,000 (controlled).

GRAPHIS ANNUAL REPORTS. *see* ART

GRAPHIS LOGO. *see* ART

686.2 AUT ISSN 0017-3479
GRAPHISCHE REVUE OESTERREICHS; Fachzeitschrift fuer das gesamte graphische Gewerbe. Text in German. 1899. bi-m. adv. bk.rev. charts; illus. index. **Document type:** *Journal, Trade.*
Published by: Gewerkschaft Druck und Papier, Seidengasse 15-17, Vienna, W 1070, Austria. TEL 43-1-5238231. Ed. Josef Keller. Circ: 4,000.

763 AUT ISSN 0075-2266
Z119
GRAPHISCHE UNTERNEHMUNGEN OESTERREICHS. JAHRBUCH. Text in German. 1930. a. **Document type:** *Directory, Trade.*
Published by: Verband Druck und Medientechnik, Gruenangergasse 4, Vienna, W 1010, Austria. TEL 43-1-5126609, FAX 43-1-513282619. Ed. Hans Inmann. Adv. contact Elisabeth Kraus. Circ: 980.

686.2 ZAF ISSN 1816-0786
GRAPHIX; the monthly journal for the graphic communications industry. Text in English. 1973. m. ZAR 104; ZAR 170 in Africa; ZAR 540 elsewhere. adv. bk.rev. **Document type:** *Journal, Trade.* **Description:** South African journal for the printing and graphic arts industries.
Indexed: ISAP.
Published by: Graphix Publications (Pty) Ltd., PO Box 751119, Garden View, 2047, South Africa. TEL 27-11-622-4800, FAX 27-11-622-2480. Ed. Ruth Longridge. Pub. Brian Strickland. Adv. contact Marion Oliver. Circ: 4,000.

686.2 ZAF
GRAPHIX DIRECT RESPONSE. Text in English. 1990. m. ZAR 65 in southern Africa; ZAR 110 elsewhere. adv. **Document type:** *Newspaper, Trade.*
Published by: Graphix Publications (Pty) Ltd., PO Box 751119, Garden View, 2047, South Africa. TEL 27-11-622-4800, FAX 27-11-622-2480. Ed. Lucia Kaszynska. Pub. Brian Strickland. Adv. contact Christine Raats. Circ: 3,300 (controlled).

686.2 USA ISSN 0894-4946
Z258
GRAVURE; the world's only magazine for the gravure printing industry. Text in English. 1950. bi-m. USD 60 in US & Canada to non-members; USD 116 elsewhere to non-members; free to members (effective 2010). adv. stat.; tr.lit.; illus. 112 p./no. 2 cols./p.; back issues avail.; reprints avail. **Document type:** *Magazine, Trade.* **Description:** Covers topics relating to the gravure printing process including publication, products and packaging.
Former titles (until 1987): Gravure Bulletin (0160-8789); (until 1980): Gravure Technical Association Bulletin (0017-3576)
Related titles: Online - full text ed.: USD 55 to non-members; free to members (effective 2010).
Indexed: ABIPC, Englnd, GALA, P06, SCOPUS.
—BLDSC (4214.150000).
Published by: Gravure Association of America, Inc., 75 W Century Rd, Paramus, NJ 07652. TEL 201-523-6042, FAX 201-523-6048, gaa@gaa.org. Ed. Roger Ynosroza. Adv. contact Emily Dominguez TEL 201-819-2665. B&W page USD 1,813, color page USD 2,777; bleed 8.75 x 11.125.

686.2 USA
GREETING CARD WRITER MAGAZINE. Text in English. 1999. m.
Document type: *Magazine, Trade.*
Media: Online - full content.
Published by: Summerland Ltd., Box 43523, Cincinnati, OH 45243-0523. editor@greetingcardwriter.com, http://www.greetingcardwriter.com. Ed., Pub. Terri See.

760 ESP ISSN 1576-5784
GREM VEINTIUNO. Text in Spanish. 1969. 11/yr. adv. bk.rev.
Former titles (until 1999): Grem (1576-5776); (until 1979): Grem Informa (1576-5768); (until 1976): Grem SAG (1576-575X)
Published by: Asociacion Gremial de Empresarios y Artes Graficas y Manipulados de Papel de Madrid, Edif. Arcade Rufino Gonzalez, 23 Bis 2a. Pl, Puerta 2, Madrid, 28037, Spain. FAX 34-91-2403091.

GUIA DE LA COMUNICACION GRAFICA Y CREATIVA. *see* BUSINESS AND ECONOMICS—Trade And Industrial Directories

GUILD OF BOOK WORKERS JOURNAL. *see* PUBLISHING AND BOOK TRADE

GUOJI XINWENJIE/INTERNATIONAL COMMUNICATION JOURNAL. *see* ADVERTISING AND PUBLIC RELATIONS

LE GUTENBERG; relieur et cartonnier. *see* LABOR UNIONS

686.2 POL ISSN 1505-8328
Z119
GUTENBERG. Text in Polish. 1999. q.
Published by: Polskie Bractwo Kawalerow Gutenberga, Panska 97, Warsaw, 00834, Poland. TEL 48-22-6521747, FAX 48-22-6542608, http://www.bractwogutenberga.pl. Ed. Alina Kuzmina.

686.209 DEU ISSN 0933-6230
GUTENBERG-GESELLSCHAFT. KLEINE DRUCKE. Text in German. 1926. irreg. membership. back issues avail.; reprints avail. **Document type:** *Monographic series, Academic/Scholarly.* **Description:** Contains results of research on the history of printing and activities of the Gutenberg-Gesellschaft.
Published by: Internationale Gutenberg-Gesellschaft e.V., Liebfrauenplatz 5, Mainz, 55116, Germany. TEL 49-6131-226420, FAX 49-6131-233530, info@gutenberg-gesellschaft.de, http://www.gutenberg-gesellschaft.uni-mainz.de. Circ: 2,000.

686.209 DEU ISSN 0072-9094
Z1008
GUTENBERG - JAHRBUCH. Text in German, English, French, Italian, Spanish. 1926. a. EUR 75 per issue (effective 2011). bk.rev. illus. index 1926-1975; 1976-1986; 1987-2000. back issues avail.; reprint service avail. from PSC. **Document type:** *Yearbook, Academic/Scholarly.* **Description:** Research results in the history of printing worldwide.
Indexed: B24, DIP, FR, HistAb, IBR, IBZ, MLA, MLA-IB, P30, PCI, RASB, RILM.
—INIST.
Published by: (Internationale Gutenberg-Gesellschaft), Harrassowitz Verlag, Kreuzberger Ring 7b-d, Wiesbaden, 65205, Germany. TEL 49-611-5300, FAX 49-611-530560, service@harrassowitz.de, http://www.harrassowitz.de. Ed. Stephan Fuessel. Circ: 2,200 (controlled).

HANDBOEKBINDEN. *see* PUBLISHING AND BOOK TRADE

686.2 DEU
HANDBUCH DRUCK MEDIEN BERLIN UND BRANDENBURG. Text in German. 1946. a. EUR 15 (effective 2005). **Document type:** *Directory, Trade.*
Former titles: Handbuch fuer die Druckindustrie Berlin und Brandenburg (0945-0378); (until 1993): Handbuch fuer die Druckindustrie Berlin (0073-0173)
Published by: HandBuch Verlag GmbH, Berliner Str 4a, Hohen Neuendorf, 16540, Germany. TEL 49-3303-509355, FAX 49-3303-509356, info@handbuchverlag.de.

686.2 USA
HOT OFF THE PRESS. Text in English. 1988. 3/yr. **Document type:** *Newsletter.*
Published by: Graham Communications, 40 Oval Rd, Ste 2, Quincy, MA 02170-3813. TEL 617-328-0069, FAX 617-471-1504. Ed., R&P Rob Keane. Pub. John R Graham. Circ: 3,000.

686.3 BEL ISSN 0018-9782
I G F - JOURNAL; journal of the printing, bookbinding and paper workers in all countries. Text in English. 1950. s-a. free.
Incorporates (in 1973): International Graphical Federation. Conference. Proceedings (0074-6169)
Related titles: French ed.; Swedish ed.; Spanish ed.; German ed.
Published by: International Graphical Federation, Bloc 2, Galerie du Centre, Rue des Fripiers 17, Brussels, 1000, Belgium. TEL 32-2-223-18-14, FAX 32-2-223-02-20. Circ: 2,500.

686.2 USA ISSN 1539-137X
I P A BULLETIN. (International Prepress Association) Text in English. 1911. bi-m. USD 20 (effective 2004). adv. bk.rev. charts; illus.; stat. **Document type:** *Journal, Trade.* **Description:** Provides management and technical information on the graphic arts prepress industry.
Former titles (until 2002): Prepress Bulletin (8750-2224); (until 1984): Photoplatemakers Bulletin (0031-8841); (until 1968): Photoengravers Bulletin (0097-5877)
Indexed: ABIPC, Englnd, GALA, PhotoAb, SCOPUS.
Published by: International Prepress Association, 552 W 167 St, South Holland, IL 60473. TEL 708-596-5110, FAX 708-596-5112, bessieipa@earthlink.net, http://www.ipa.org/. Ed., R&P Bessie Halfacre. adv.: B&W page USD 594, color page USD 1,696; 8.25 x 10.25. Circ: 1,650 (paid).

686.2 USA ISSN 1931-1303
I P G E-NEWS. (In-Plant Graphics) Text in English. 2006. s-m. free to qualified personnel (effective 2008). adv. back issues avail. **Document type:** *Newsletter, Trade.*
Media: Online - full text.
Published by: North American Publishing Co., 1500 Spring Garden St., 12th Fl, Philadelphia, PA 19130. TEL 215-238-5300, FAX 215-238-5213, magazinecs@napco.com, http://www.napco.com. Ed. Bob Neubauer TEL 215-238-5321. Pub. Glen Reynolds TEL 215-238-5097.

ICOGRADA MESSAGE BOARD. *see* ART

686.2 AUS
IMAGE MAGAZINE. Text in English. 19??. bi-m. AUD 55 domestic; AUD 70 in New Zealand; AUD 80 elsewhere (effective 2009). adv. back issues avail. **Document type:** *Magazine, Trade.* **Description:** Provides information for screen printers and signmakers in Australia and New Zealand.
Formerly: Australasian Screenprinter Magazine
Published by: Cygnet Publications, PO Box 956, Balcatta, W.A. 6914, Australia. TEL 61-8-94405800, FAX 61-8-94405855, info@imageexpo.com.au. Ed. Ken Pobjoy TEL 61-8-94405700. Adv. contact Stan Kilpin.

686.2 770 USA ISSN 2153-375X
TS155.A1
▼ **THE IMAGING CHANNEL**; the business and people of managed print. Text in English. 2010 (May). bi-m. free to qualified personnel (effective 2011). **Document type:** *Magazine, Trade.* **Description:** For professionals in the managed print and imaging industry.
Related titles: Online - full text ed.: free (effective 2011).
Published by: 1105 Media Inc., 9121 Oakdale Ave, Ste 101, Chatsworth, CA 91311. TEL 818-734-1520, FAX 818-734-1522, info@1105media.com, http://www.1105media.com.

686.2 MEX
IMPRESOR; al servicio de las artes graficas. Text in Spanish. 1977. m. MXN 200, USD 175 (effective 1999). adv. bk.rev. illus.; stat.; tr.lit. **Document type:** *Trade.* **Description:** Covers the graphic arts industry. Includes industry news, new techniques and machinery, politics and cultural notes.
Formerly: Impresor Internacional
Published by: Imprentas Menra, S.A., Sta. Ma. la Rivera 9-103, Mexico City, DF 06400, Mexico. TEL 52-5-5468725, FAX 52-5-5661038. Ed. Joaquin Menendez Rangel. Pub., R&P Joaquin Menendez. Adv. contact Teresa Menendez. Circ: 8,000 (paid).

760 VEN
IMPRIMASE. Text in Spanish. 1958. 6/yr. free. adv. bk.rev.
Published by: Asociacion de Industriales de Artes Graficas de Venezuela, Edificio Camara de Industriales, Piso 2, Esq. Puente Anauco, Apdo. 14.405, Caracas, 1011A, Venezuela. Circ: 2,000.

686.209 DEU
IMPRIMATUR. NEUE FOLGE; ein Jahrbuch fuer Buecherfreunde. Text in German. 1930. biennial. EUR 112 per vol. (effective 2011). adv. **Document type:** *Journal, Academic/Scholarly.*
Formerly: Imprimatur. Jahrbuch fuer Buecherfreunde. Neue Folge (0073-5620)
Indexed: DIP, IBR, IBZ, MLA, MLA-IB, RASB.
Published by: (Gesellschaft der Bibliophilen e.V.), Harrassowitz Verlag, Kreuzberger Ring 7b-d, Wiesbaden, 65205, Germany. TEL 49-611-5300, FAX 49-611-530560, verlag@harrassowitz.de, http://www.harrassowitz.de.

686.22 USA ISSN 1087-2817
Z252.5.O5
IN-PLANT GRAPHICS. Text in English. 1951. m. free to qualified personnel (effective 2008). adv. bk.rev. charts; illus.; stat. back issues avail.; reprints avail. **Document type:** *Magazine, Trade.* **Description:** Written for management and technical personnel connected with basic printing and production processes and techniques in non-commercial printing environments. Examines in-plant and electronic publishing concerns for business, industry and government.
Former titles (until 1996): In-Plant Reproductions (1043-1942); (until 1988): In-Plant Reproductions and Electronic Publishing (0886-3121); (until 1985): In-Plant Productions (0198-9065); (until 1979): Reproductions Review and Methods (0164-4327); Graphic Arts Supplier News (0017-3355); Reproductions Methods; Reproductions Review (0034-4974)
Related titles: Online - full text ed.: free to qualified personnel (effective 2008).
Indexed: A15, A22, A27, ABIPC, ABIn, B03, B11, BPI, BRD, Englnd, GALA, P06, P10, P16, P48, P51, P53, P54, PQC, ResCtrlnd, SCOPUS, W01, W02, W03, W05.
—CIS, IE, Ingenta, Linda Hall. **CCC.**
Published by: North American Publishing Co., 1500 Spring Garden St., 12th Fl, Philadelphia, PA 19130. TEL 215-238-5300, FAX 215-238-5213, magazinecs@napco.com, http://www.napco.com. Ed. Bob Neubauer TEL 215-238-5321. Pub. Glen Reynolds TEL 215-238-5097. Adv. contacts Glen Reynolds TEL 215-238-5097, Maggie Pajak. B&W page USD 6,850, color page USD 8,830; trim 7.75 x 10.5. Circ: 23,600.

686.2 USA ISSN 1071-832X
Z119
IN-PLANT PRINTER; the in-plant management magazine. Text in English. 1961. bi-m. free to qualified personnel. adv. bk.rev. abstr.; charts; illus.; tr.lit. Index. reprints avail. **Document type:** *Magazine, Trade.* **Description:** Covers the non-commercial side of the printing industry-the printing departments in corporations, government agencies, and institutions.
Former titles: In-Plant Printer Including Corporate Imaging; (until 1993): In-Plant Printer and Electronic Publisher (0891-8996); (until 1986): In-Plant Printer (0019-3232); In-Plant Offset Printer
Related titles: Microform ed.: (from PQC); Online - full text ed.
Indexed: A12, A13, A15, A17, A22, ABIPC, ABIn, GALA, P48, P51, P53, P54, PQC, ResCtrlnd, SCOPUS.
—IE, Ingenta, INIST, Linda Hall.
Published by: Innes Publishing Company, PO Box 7280, Libertyville, IL 60048-7280. TEL 847-816-7900, FAX 847-247-8855, meinnes@innespub.com. Ed. Jack Klasnic. Pub., R&P Mary Ellin Innes. Circ: 30,526.

686.2 NOR ISSN 1502-0215
IN-PUBLISH. Text in Norwegian. 1973. m. NOK 560 domestic; NOK 625 in Sweden & Denmark; NOK 670 elsewhere in Sweden & Denmark. adv. **Document type:** *Magazine, Trade.* **Description:** Through specialist articles, interviews and stories, reflects the changing situation and developments in the world of graphics - both nationally and internationally.
Former titles (until 2000): Grafisk Inside (0802-2593); (until 1988): Grafisk (0801-3934)
Related titles: Online - full text ed.: ISSN 1502-0738. 2000.
Published by: Inside Publish AS, Postboks 9076, Groenland, Oslo, 0133, Norway. TEL 47-22-20-80-90, FAX 47-22-20-89-68. Ed. Oeyvind Gloerstad. Adv. contact Bent Skaalerud. B&W page NOK 10,900, color page NOK 13,900; trim 184 x 270. Circ: 3,600.

686.2 NOR
IN-PUBLISH E-NEWS. Text in Norwegian. w. NOK 185 (effective 2000). **Document type:** *Trade.* **Description:** Provides information and content on the graphic arts industry in Norway and elsewhere.
Media: E-mail.
Published by: Inside Publish AS, Postboks 9076, Groenland, Oslo, 0133, Norway. TEL 47-22-20-80-90, FAX 47-22-20-89-68. Ed. Oeyvind Gloerstad. Adv. contact Bent Skaalerud.

INDIAN NEWSPAPER SOCIETY PRESS HANDBOOK (YEAR). *see* JOURNALISM

686.2 USA ISSN 2152-9469
▼ **INDUSTRIAL AND SPECIALTY PRINTING.** Text in English. 2010 (Mar.). bi-m. USD 42 domestic; USD 62 in Canada; USD 65 elsewhere (effective 2011). **Document type:** *Magazine, Trade.* **Description:** Provides news and information for industrial printing professionals.
Published by: S T Media Group International, Inc., 407 Gilbert Ave, Cincinnati, OH 45202. TEL 513-421-2050, FAX 513-421-5144, customer@stmediagroup.com, http://www.stmediagroup.com.

INDUSTRIEGEWERKSCHAFT MEDIEN. SCHRIFTENREIHE FUER BETRIEBSRATE. *see* PUBLISHING AND BOOK TRADE

760 FRA ISSN 1957-1674
INK. Text in French. 2006. irreg. EUR 5 newsstand/cover (effective 2009). **Document type:** *Magazine, Consumer.*
Published by: Ink Magazine, 1 Rue Lemot, Lyon, 69001, France.

686.2 USA ISSN 1093-328X
HD9792.A1 CODEN: INWOFW
INK WORLD; covering the printing inks, coatings and allied industries. Text in English. 1995. m. USD 95 to individuals; free to qualified personnel (effective 2010). adv. back issues avail. **Document type:** *Magazine, Trade.* **Description:** Provides in-depth information on the development, manufacture and sale of all lithographic, flexographic, gravure, radiation-cured, letterpress and specialty inks, coatings and allied products.
Related titles: Online - full text ed.: free to qualified personnel (effective 2008).
Indexed: B01, B02, B03, B11, B15, B17, B18, Englnd, G04, G06, G07, G08, I05, SCOPUS.
—CCC.
Published by: Rodman Publishing, Corp., 70 Hilltop Rd, 3rd Fl, Ramsey, NJ 07446. TEL 201-825-2552, FAX 201-825-0553, info@rodpub.com, http://www.rodmanpublishing .com. Ed. David Savastano. Pubs. Dale Pritchett, Matthew Montgomery TEL 201-825-2552 ext 355. Adv. contact Robert Frederick. B&W page USD 2,600, color page USD 3,900; trim 178 x 253. Circ: 5,185 (controlled).

764.8 USA
INKSIDER. Text in English. 2001. bi-w. adv. back issues avail.
Media: Online - full text.
Published by: Altascopy.com, Box 1292, Dover, DE 19904. FAX 302-678-5825. Ed. Barry Shultz.

686.2 NZL
INKY FINGERS. Text in English. 199?. m. **Document type:** *Magazine, Trade.*
Published by: Printer Magazines Pty. Ltd., Howick, PO Box 39-523, Auckland, New Zealand. TEL 64-9-2716271, FAX 64-9-2716272, info@i-grafix.com, http://www.printermags.com.au/. Ed. Greg Bruce. Circ: 2,000.

686.2 DEU ISSN 1439-5274
INNOVATION UND TECHNIK; Fachzeitung fuer Formenbauer, Formgestalter und Fertigungstechniker, Graveure, Gurtler. Text in German. 1875. m. EUR 81 domestic; EUR 85 foreign; EUR 7.16 newsstand/cover (effective 2008). adv. abstr.; charts; illus. Supplement avail. **Document type:** *Magazine, Trade.*
Formerly (until 1999): Graveur Flexograf (0015-7775)
Published by: Ruehle-Diebener Verlag GmbH und Co. KG, Postfach 700450, Stuttgart, 70574, Germany. TEL 49-711-976670, FAX 49-711-9766749. adv.: B&W page EUR 1,166, color page EUR 2,108; 185 x 255. Circ: 3,440 (paid and controlled).

686.2 JPN ISSN 0020-1758
Z119
INSATSU ZASSHI/JAPAN PRINTER. Text in Japanese. 1918. m. JPY 16,800 (effective 2008). adv. charts; illus. **Document type:** *Magazine, Trade.*
Indexed: ChemAb, JTA.
Published by: (Japanese Society of Printing Science and Technology/ Nippon Insatsu Gakkai), Insatsu Gakkai Shuppanbu Ltd., Tokyo Real Takaracho Bldg 1/F, 4-2-1 Hatchobori, Chuo-ku, Tokyo, 104-0032, Japan. TEL 86-3-35557911, FAX 86-3-35557913. Circ: 5,300.

686.2 JPN ISSN 0020-1766
INSATSUKAI/PRINTING WORLD. Text in Japanese. 1950. m. JPY 24,000 domestic; JPY 39,600 foreign; JPY 1,995 newsstand/cover (effective 2001). adv. illus. back issues avail. **Document type:** *Magazine, Trade.* **Description:** Deals with all aspects within the printing feild including printer's management, administrative and technical staff.
Indexed: ChemAb, SCOPUS.
Published by: Nihon Insatsu Shinbunsha/Japan Printing News Co., Ltd., 16-8 Shintomi 1-chome, Chuo-ku, Tokyo, 104-0041, Japan. TEL 81-3-3553-5681, FAX 81-3-3553-5684. Ed. H Kawauchi. Pub. H Kurihara. R&P H. Kurihara. Adv. contact S Ito. B&W page JPY 130,000, color page JPY 350,000; trim 180 x 260. Circ: 10,000.

INSIDE EDGE. *see* BUSINESS AND ECONOMICS—Management

686.2 USA
INSIDEFINISHING. Text in English. 1992. q. USD 25 domestic; USD 43 in Canada & Mexico; USD 50 elsewhere (effective 2000). adv. **Document type:** *Magazine, Trade.* **Description:** Contains association, industry and government-related news.
Former titles: Finish Line; F S E A Flash Bulletin
Published by: Foil Stamping & Embossing Association, PO Box 12090, Portland, OR 97212. TEL 503-331-6221, FAX 503-331-6928. Ed., R&P, Adv. contact Jeff Peterson TEL 913-266-7076. Circ: 5,000.

686.2 USA ISSN 1044-3746
Z252.5.I49
INSTANT & SMALL COMMERCIAL PRINTER. Text in English. 1982. 12/yr. USD 85 (effective 2000). adv. **Document type:** *Magazine, Trade.*
Formerly: Instant Printer (0744-3854)

Related titles: Microform ed.: (from PQC); Online - full text ed.
Indexed: A15, A22, ABIPC, ABIn, EngInd, GALA, P48, P51, PQC, SCOPUS.
Published by: Innes Publishing Company, PO Box 7280, Libertyville, IL 60048-7280. meinnes@innespub.com. Ed. Anne Marie Mohan. Pub., Adv. contact Dan Innes. R&P Mary Ellin Innes. Circ: 50,953.

THE INTERNATIONAL DIRECTORY OF PRINTING AND GRAPHIC ARTS EQUIPMENT AND SUPPLIES IMPORTERS. *see* BUSINESS AND ECONOMICS—Trade And Industrial Directories

INTERNATIONAL DIRECTORY OF PRIVATE PRESSES. *see* BUSINESS AND ECONOMICS—Trade And Industrial Directories

686.28 GBR ISSN 1756-249X
INTERNATIONAL SIGN MAGAZINE. Abbreviated title: I S M. Text in English. 2007. bi-m. GBP 48 domestic; EUR 88 in Europe; USD 90 in US & Canada; GBP 90 elsewhere (effective 2009). adv. **Document type:** *Magazine, Trade.* **Description:** Features a mix of business news, product updates, technical reports and market analysis.
Related titles: Online - full text ed.: ISSN 1756-2503.
Published by: Open House Publishing Ltd., PO Box 7574, Billericay, Essex CM12 9XF, United Kingdom. TEL 44-1277-650037, FAX 44-8707-621039, sales@intersignmag.com. Pub. Michael Lyons. adv.: page GBP 1,495; trim 210 x 297.

686.2 IRL ISSN 0790-2026
IRISH PRINTER. Text in English. 1959. m. adv. bk.rev. illus. **Document type:** *Magazine, Trade.*
Formerly (until 1975): Modern Irish Printer (0790-2034)
—CCC.
Published by: Jemma Publications Ltd., Marino House, 52 Glasthule Rd., Sandycove, Co. Dublin, Ireland. TEL 353-1-2800000, FAX 353-1-2801818, sales@jemma.ie, edit@jemma.ie. Adv. contact Bryan Beasley. B&W page EUR 1,510, color page EUR 1,870; trim 210 x 297. Circ: 1,682.

ISRAEL BOOK TRADE DIRECTORY; a guide to publishers, booksellers and the book trade in Israel. *see* PUBLISHING AND BOOK TRADE

686.2 ITA ISSN 0021-2784
Z119
ITALIA GRAFICA. Text in Italian. 1946. m. (10/yr.). EUR 60 domestic; EUR 120 in Europe; EUR 140 elsewhere (effective 2011). adv. bk.rev. **Document type:** *Magazine, Trade.*
Related titles: Online - full text ed.
Indexed: GALA.
Published by: (Associazione Nazionale Italiana delle Industrie Grafiche), Tecniche Nuove SpA, Via Eritrea 21, Milan, MI 201, Italy. TEL 39-02-390901, FAX 39-02-7570364, info@tecnichenuove.com. Ed. Alessandro Battaglia. Circ: 12,000.

686.2 JPN ISSN 0072-548X
JAPAN GRAPHIC ARTS. Text and summaries in English. 1959. a. JPY 5,000 newsstand/cover (effective 2001). adv. bk.rev. charts; stat. **Document type:** *Trade.* **Description:** Covers the trends and development in Japanese printing and related industries for printers, traders and managers.
Indexed: ABIPC, GALA, P&BA.
—IE.
Published by: (Japan Federation of Printing Industries), Nihon Insatsu Shinbunsha/Japan Printing News Co., Ltd., 16-8 Shintomi 1-chome, Chuo-ku, Tokyo, 104-0041, Japan. TEL 81-3-3553-5681, FAX 81-3-3553-5684. Ed. H. Kurihara. Pub. H Fujita. R&P H Kurihara. adv.: B&W page JPY 150,000, color page JPY 450,000; trim 180 x 255. Circ: 5,000.

686.221 JPN
JAPAN TYPOGRAPHY ANNUAL/NIHON TAIPOGURAFI NENKAN. Text in Japanese. 1974. a. USD 225 (effective 1999). illus.
Formerly: Nihon Retaringu Nenkan
Published by: (Japan Typography Association), Intercontinental Marketing Corp., I.P.O. Box 5056, Tokyo, 100-3191, Japan. tc9w-ball@asahi-net.or.jp.

JORNADAS DE REFLEXION ACADEMICA EN DISENO Y COMUNICACION. *see* ART

686.2 DEU ISSN 0932-4372
Z119
JOURNAL FUER DRUCKGESCHICHTE/JOURNAL D'HISTOIRE DE L'IMPRIMERIE/JOURNAL OF PRINTING HISTORY. Text in German. 1988. q. **Document type:** *Journal, Academic/Scholarly.*
Published by: Internationaler Arbeitskreis Druck- und Mediengeschichte e.V., c/o Deutsches Zeitungsmuseum, Am Abteihof 1, Wadgassen, 66787, Germany. TEL 49-6834-94230, FAX 49-6834-942320, bosslet@deutsches-zeitungsmuseum.de, http://www.arbeitskreis-druckgeschichte.de. Ed. Sylvia Werfel.

760 USA ISSN 1544-9599
T385
➤ **JOURNAL OF GRAPHIC TECHNOLOGY.** Text in English. 2003. a. **Document type:** *Journal, Academic/Scholarly.*
Related titles: Online - full text ed.: ISSN 1544-9602.
Published by: Technical Association of the Graphic Arts, 200 Deer Run Rd, Sewickley, PA 15143. TEL 800-910-4283, printing@printing.org, http://www.taga.org. Ed. Dr. Juanita Paris.

760 JPN
CODEN: NIGAEV
➤ **JOURNAL OF PRINTING SCIENCE AND TECHNOLOGY.** Text in Japanese; Summaries in English. 1975 (vol.15). bi-m. JPY 16,800 to non-members; JPY 9,000 domestic to members; JPY 150 foreign to members (effective 2001). adv. bk.rev. abstr.; charts; illus. back issues avail. **Document type:** *Journal, Academic/Scholarly.*
Former titles: Japanese Society of Printing Science and Technology. Bulletin (0914-3319); Technical Association of Graphic Arts of Japan. Bulletin (0040-0874)
Indexed: GALA, JTA.
—BLDSC (5042.407000), CASDDS, IE.
Published by: Japanese Society of Printing Science and Technology/ Nippon Insatsu Gakkai, 1-16-8 Shintomi, Chuo-ku, Tokyo, 104-0041, Japan. TEL 81-3-3551-1808, FAX 81-3-3552-7206, http://www.jtpi.or.jp/jspst. Ed. Ken-idi Koseki. R&P Nori Imai. Adv. contact Kan Nakamura.

➤ **KAMI INSATSU PURASUCHIKKU GOMU SEIHIN TOUKEI GEPPOU/MONTHLY REPORT OF PAPER, PRINTING, PLASTICS PRODUCTS AND RUBBER PRODUCTS STATISTICS.** *see* PAPER AND PULP

686.2 GBR
KEY NOTE MARKET REPORT: PRINTING. Variant title: Printing Market Report. Text in English. 1993. irreg., latest 2009, Apr. GBP 460 per issue (effective 2010). **Document type:** *Report, Trade.* **Description:** Provides an overview of a specific UK market segment and includes executive summary, market definition, market size, industry background, competitor analysis, current issues, forecasts, company profiles, and more.
Formerly (until 1995): Key Note Report: Printing (1352-7126)
Related titles: CD-ROM ed.; Online - full text ed.
Published by: Key Note Ltd. (Subsidiary of: Bonnier Business Information), Harlequin House, 5th Fl, 7 High St, Teddington, Richmond upon Thames, TW11 8EE, United Kingdom. TEL 44-845-5040452, FAX 44-845-5040453, info@keynote.co.uk.

LABEL & NARROW WEB. *see* COMPUTERS—Internet

LABEL WORLD. *see* PACKAGING

LABELS AND LABELING; the wider world of narrow web. *see* PACKAGING

686.233 USA
LASERPAGE; news and information for laser printer users. Text in English. 1986. 8/yr. free.
Published by: Landmark Laser Printer Service, 341 W Valley Blvd, Rialto, CA 92376. TEL 909-875-5687. Ed. Warren Whitlock.

LETTERHEAD. *see* ART

760 BEL ISSN 1371-6085
M & C GRAFIEK; vaktijdschrift voor de grafische en aanverwante sectoren. Text in Dutch. 1936. every 3 wks. adv. bk.rev. charts; illus. **Document type:** *Journal, Trade.*
Former titles (until 1996): Compres - Grafiek (0778-6271); (until 1991): Grafiek (0017-2944); (until 1937): Hou Zee (0773-3135)
Related titles: French ed.: M & C Graphique. ISSN 1371-6093. 1991.
Published by: Presstrade bvba, Van de Hautlei 195, Antwerp - Deurne, 2100, Belgium. TEL 32-3-366-0886, FAX 32-3-366-1672. Pub. Koen Goderis. Circ: 5,500.

760 HUN ISSN 0479-480X
Z119
MAGYAR GRAFIKA/HUNGARIAN GRAPHIC ARTS. Text in Hungarian; Summaries in German, Russian. 1957. bi-m. USD 60 (effective 1999). adv. bk.rev. abstr.; bibl.; charts; illus. index. **Document type:** *Trade.*
Indexed: ChemAb, GALA, RASB.
Published by: Papir- es Nyomdaipari Mueszaki Egyesuelet, Fo utca 68, PF 433, Budapest, 1371, Hungary. Ed. Miklos Gara. Adv. contact Sandor Pesti. Circ: 2,200.

686.2 CAN ISSN 0025-0996
LE MAITRE IMPRIMEUR. Text in French. 1937. 10/yr. CAD 30, USD 36. adv. charts; illus. **Document type:** *Magazine, Trade.* **Description:** Covers printing and allied trades, new technological developments, trends in the industry.
Indexed: PdeR.
Published by: Association des Arts Graphiques du Quebec, Inc., 644 boul Cure-Poirier Ouest bur 100, Longueuil, PQ J4J 2H9, Canada. TEL 450-670-9311, FAX 450-670-8762. Ed. Gerard Therien. Adv. contact Jules Cote. B&W page USD 1,800, color page USD 2,400. Circ: 3,959 (controlled).

MALAYSIA PRINTING AND SUPPORTING INDUSTRIES DIRECTORY. *see* BUSINESS AND ECONOMICS—Trade And Industrial Directories

686.2 DEU ISSN 1611-3500
MARKETING EVENT PRAXIS. Text in German. 1996. bi-m. EUR 39; EUR 8 newsstand/cover (effective 2011). adv. **Document type:** *Magazine, Trade.* **Description:** Provides information on merchandising and events products for advertising agencies and marketing departments.
Former titles (until 2003): Multimedia and Event Products (1618-3878); (until 2000): Merchandising and Event Products (1437-5109)
Published by: Verlagshaus Gruber GmbH, Max-Planck-Str 2, Eppertshausen, 64859, Germany. TEL 49-6071-39410, FAX 49-6071-394111, info@verlagshaus-gruber.de, http://www.verlagshaus-gruber.de. Ed. Florian Grimm. adv.: B&W page EUR 1,950, color page EUR 2,650; trim 230 x 297. Circ: 12,000 (paid).

686.2 TUR
MATBAA & TEKNIK. Text in Turkish; Section in English. 1996. m. USD 85 (effective 2009). 150 p./no. 3 cols./p.; **Document type:** *Trade.*
Published by: Iletisim Magazin Gazetecilik San. ve Tic. A.S., Ihlas Holding Merkez Binasi, 29 Ekim Cad. 23, P.K. 34197, Yenibosna - Istanbul, 34197, Turkey. TEL 90-212-4542520, FAX 90-212-4542555, info@img.com.tr, http://www.img.com.tr. Ed. Ahmet Kizil. Pub. Ferruh Isik. R&P Muhsin Yilmaz. Adv. contact Ms. Bahar Sensoz. Circ: 15,085.

MATRIX (HEREFORDSHIRE); a review for printers and bibliophiles. *see* PUBLISHING AND BOOK TRADE

686.2 SWE ISSN 1401-7032
MEDIA GRAFICA. Text in Swedish. 1914. 6/yr. SEK 225 (effective 2000). adv. bk.rev. **Document type:** *Magazine, Trade.*
Formerly (until 1995): Grafisk Faktorstidning (0017-2979)
Published by: Grafiska Faktors- och Tjaenstemannafoerbundet/ Graphical Managers and Overseers Association, Sankt Eriksgatan 26 III, Fack 12069, Stockholm, 10222, Sweden. TEL 46-8-59899097. Ed. Kerstin Orsen. Circ: 3,100 (controlled).

METRO VOICE. *see* COMMUNICATIONS

686.2 NLD ISSN 1876-3464
MOOI MARGINAAL. Text in Dutch. 2004. biennial. EUR 10 per issue (effective 2010). **Document type:** *Catalog.*
Published by: Stichting Laurens Janszoon Coster, Postbus 3316, Haarlem, 2001 DH, Netherlands. TEL 31-23-5247450.

686.2 DEU
NACHDRUCK; aktuelles zur Druckweiterverarbeitung. Text in German. 2003. 3/yr. **Document type:** *Magazine, Trade.*
Published by: (Horizon GmbH), Medienfabrik Guetersloh GmbH, Carl-Bertelsmann-Str 33, Guetersloh, 33311, Germany. TEL 49-5241-2348010, FAX 49-5241-2348022, kontakt@medienfabrik-gt.de, http://www.medienfabrik-gt.de. Ed. Christina Schlehufer.

686.2 DEU ISSN 1617-206X
NARROWEBTECH. Text in English. 1999. q. EUR 55.64 domestic; EUR 79 in Europe; EUR 100 elsewhere; EUR 14 per issue (effective 2009). adv. **Document type:** *Magazine, Trade.* **Description:** Covers all segments of the production of self-adhesive roll labels, tags and similar products, folding carton and narrow-web packaging.
Indexed: RefZh.
Published by: G & K TechMedia GmbH, Am Stollen 6-1, Gutach-Bleibach, 79261, Germany. TEL 49-7685-918110, FAX 49-7685-909011, info@flexo.de. adv.: B&W page EUR 2,600, color page EUR 4,000. Circ: 9,700 (paid and controlled).

NATIONAL AMATEUR. *see* JOURNALISM

763 USA ISSN 0893-4975
NATIONAL ASSOCIATION OF PRINTERS AND LITHOGRAPHERS. SPECIAL REPORTS. Text in English. 197?. irreg. free to members (effective 2011). **Document type:** *Report, Trade.*
Published by: National Association for Printing Leadership, One Meadowlands Plz, Ste 1511, E Rutherford, NJ 07073. TEL 201-634-9600, 800-642-6275, FAX 201-634-0324, http://www.napl.org.

THE NEW BOOKBINDER; journal of designer bookbinders. *see* PUBLISHING AND BOOK TRADE

NEW COLLAGE MAGAZINE. *see* LITERATURE

686.2 USA ISSN 0162-8771
Z119
NEW ENGLAND PRINTER AND PUBLISHER. Text in English. 1938. m. USD 16 (effective 2005). adv. bk.rev. illus.; tr.lit. 3 cols./p.; back issues avail.; reprints avail. **Document type:** *Magazine, Trade.* **Description:** Presents information on regional and national industry and trade association news, a calendar of regional and national events, supplier product-services, and new literature.
Formerly: New England Printer and Lithographer (0028-484X)
Indexed: ABIPC, EngInd, GALA, SCOPUS.
Published by: Printing Industries of New England, 5 Crystal Pond Rd, Southborough, MA 01772-1758. TEL 508-804-4100, FAX 508-804-4119. Ed., Pub. John Scibelli. adv.: B&W page USD 673, color page USD 1,318; trim 11 x 8.5. Circ: 2,012 (paid); 1,445 (controlled); 143 (paid and controlled).

NEW YORK TYPOGRAPHICAL UNION NUMBER SIX. BULLETIN. *see* LABOR UNIONS

686.2 NZL ISSN 1173-9967
NEW ZEALAND PRINTER. Variant title: N Z P. Text in English. 1950. bi-m. adv. **Document type:** *Magazine, Trade.* **Description:** Technical journal circulates to managers of print shops, trade shops, typesetters, art studios, publishers and packaging companies.
Former titles (until 1996): New Zealand Printer Magazine (1171-0829); (until 1987): New Zealand Printer (1033-1514); (until 1984): Australasian Printer (0004-8453)
Related titles: Online - full text ed.
Indexed: ABIX.
Published by: Printer Magazines Pty. Ltd., Howick, PO Box 39-523, Auckland, New Zealand. TEL 64-9-2716271, FAX 64-9-2716272, http://www.printermags.com.au/. Ed. Greg Bruce. Circ: 5,000.

NEWS & VIEWS (PORTLAND). *see* BUSINESS AND ECONOMICS—Marketing And Purchasing

760 GRC
NEWS OF GRAPHIC ARTS. Text in Greek. 1982. m. USD 30. back issues avail.
Published by: Fakinov, 157 Sokratous St, Kallithea, Athens 176 73, Greece. Ed. D Fakinov. Circ: 5,200.

686.2 JPN ISSN 0546-0719
NIHON INSATSU NENKAN/JAPAN PRINTING ART ANNUAL. Text in Japanese. 1957. a. JPY 9,000 newsstand/cover (effective 2001). adv. back issues avail. **Document type:** *Trade.* **Description:** Displays Japanese printing techniques and achievements to the world at large.
Published by: Nihon Insatsu Shinbunsha/Japan Printing News Co., Ltd., 16-8 Shintomi 1-chome, Chuo-ku, Tokyo, 104-0041, Japan. TEL 81-3-3553-5681, FAX 81-3-3553-5684. Ed. K Kitano. Pub. H Kurihara. R&P H. Kurihara. adv.: B&W page JPY 180,000, color page JPY 400,000; trim 180 x 255. Circ: 4,500.

686.2 JPN
NIPPON INSATSU SHINBUN/JAPAN PRINTING NEWS. Text in Japanese. 1943. s-w. JPY 25,200 domestic; JPY 39,600 foreign; JPY 270 newsstand/cover (effective 2001). adv. 4 p./no. 8 cols./p.; back issues avail. **Document type:** *Newspaper, Trade.* **Description:** Provides nation wide coverage of news and events in the prenting business world.
Published by: Nihon Insatsu Shinbunsha/Japan Printing News Co., Ltd., 16-8 Shintomi 1-chome, Chuo-ku, Tokyo, 104-0041, Japan. TEL 81-3-3553-5681, FAX 81-3-3553-5684. Ed. H Arai. Pub. H Kurihara. R&P H. Kurihara. Adv. contact Akiko Ito. B&W page JPY 400,000, color page JPY 600,000; trim 512 x 380. Circ: 15,000.

NOUVELLES DE L'ESTAMPE. *see* ART

686.2 BEL ISSN 0029-4926
NOUVELLES GRAPHIQUES. Text in French. 1950. 22/yr. EUR 50 (effective 2010). adv. bk.rev. charts; illus.; tr.lit. back issues avail. **Document type:** *Magazine, Trade.* **Description:** Covers all aspects of the printing industries in Belgium and Luxembourg.
Related titles: Dutch ed.: Grafisch Nieuws. ISSN 0773-591X.
Indexed: RefZh.
—BLDSC (6176.782800).
Published by: Roularta Media Group, Research Park, Zellik, 1731, Belgium. TEL 32-2-4675611, FAX 32-2-4675757, communication@roularta.be, http://www.roularta.be. adv.: page EUR 2,300. Circ: 8,000 (paid and controlled).

NOVAYA POLIGRAFIYA. *see* ADVERTISING AND PUBLIC RELATIONS

686.2 RUS
NOVOSTI POLIGRAFII. Text in Russian. s-m. USD 145 in United States.
Published by: Izdatel'stvo Tertsiya, Ul Petrovka 26, k 302-304, Moscow, 101429, Russian Federation. TEL 7-095-9237640, FAX 7-095-9237640. Ed. V V Kazartseva. **Dist. by:** East View Information Services, 10601 Wayzata Blvd, Minneapolis, MN 55305. TEL 952-252-1201, 800-477-1005, FAX 952-252-1202, info@eastview.com, http://www.eastview.com.

NOVUM; world of graphic design. *see* ADVERTISING AND PUBLIC RELATIONS

P

NYT FOR BOGVENNER/NEWS FOR BOOKLOVERS. *see* PUBLISHING AND BOOK TRADE

686 AUT ISSN 0029-9170
DAS OESTERREICHISCHE GRAPHISCHE GEWERBE; Journal fuer Druckvorstufe, Druck, Uebersetzungen, Schreibbueros. Text in German. 1949. 10/yr. EUR 46 domestic; EUR 54 foreign; EUR 4.60 newsstand/cover (effective 2005). adv. bk.rev. charts; illus.; tr.lit. index. **Document type:** *Magazine, Trade.*
Published by: Landesinnung Druck, Gruenangergasse 4, Vienna, W 1010, Austria. TEL 43-1-5124985, FAX 43-1-513282619, innung.druck@wkw.at, http://www.druck.or.at. Ed. Hans Inmann. adv.: page EUR 765; trim 185 x 267. Circ: 3,500.

760 MEX
ORIGINA. Text in Spanish. 1998. m. MXN 330 (effective 2002). adv. back issues avail.
Related titles: Online - full text ed.: ISSN 1607-1220. 1998.
Published by: Gilardi Editores, S.A. de C.V., General de Leon No. 48, San Miguel Chapultepect, Mexico, D.F., 11850, Mexico. TEL 52-5-2770694, FAX 52-5-2732475, con-tactp@origina.com.mx. Ed. Rocio Alarcon. Adv. contact Fernando Alvcala. page MXN 44,200. Circ: 10,000.

P C CREATE IT. *see* PHOTOGRAPHY—Computer Applications

P-O-P DESIGN; products and news for high-volume producers of displays, signs and fixtures. (Point-of-Purchase) *see* ADVERTISING AND PUBLIC RELATIONS

686.2 USA ISSN 1536-1039
TS196.7
PACKAGEPRINTING; the package printer's leading resource for business solutions. Text in English. 1974. m. free to qualified personnel (effective 2010). adv. bk.rev. charts; illus.; stat. index. back issues avail.; reprints avail. **Document type:** *Magazine, Trade.* **Description:** Focuses on new machinery and new methods in the specialized field of printing and converting packages, boxes, cartons, bags and cellophane.
Former titles (until 1999): Package Printing & Converting (0895-1608); (until 1987): Package Printing (0163-9234); (until Mar. 1978): Package Printing and Diecutting (0098-7778); Which was formed by the merger of: Diemaking, Diecutting and Converting (0012-2556); Gravure (0017-3568); Flexography Printing and Converting
Related titles: Online - full text ed.: free to qualified personnel (effective 2008).
Indexed: A12, A13, A15, A17, A22, ABIPC, ABIn, B03, B11, BPI, BRD, CurPA, EngInd, GALA, IPackAb, P&BA, P48, P51, P53, P54, PQC, PST, RefZh, SCOPUS, W01, W02, W03, W05.
—BLDSC (6331.978000), IE, Ingenta, Linda Hall. **CCC.**
Published by: North American Publishing Co., 1500 Spring Garden St., 12th Fl, Philadelphia, PA 19130. TEL 215-238-5300, FAX 215-238-5213, magazinecs@napco.com, http://www.napco.com. Ed. Tom Polischuk TEL 215-238-5379. Pub., Adv. contact Brian Ludwick. B&W page USD 5,710, color page USD 7,660; trim 7 x 10. Circ: 24,500.

PACKAGING PRO. *see* PACKAGING

686 FIN ISSN 1235-905X
PAINOMAAILMA. Text in Finnish. 1906. 8/yr. EUR 97 (effective 2002). adv. bk.rev. **Document type:** *Trade.*
Former titles: Kirjapainotaito Graafikko; Graafikko (0017-2731)
Indexed: P&BA.
Published by: Painomaailma Oy, Loennrotinkatu 11 A, Helsinki, 00120, Finland. TEL 358-9-2287-7242, FAX 358-9-603-914, mirja.mantynen@gtl.ttliitot.fi. Ed., R&P, Adv. contact Mirja Mantynen. B&W page EUR 1,370, color page EUR 2,490; trim 210 x 297. Circ: 3,100 (controlled).

PAPER TECHNOLOGY. *see* PAPER AND PULP

PARATESTO. *see* PUBLISHING AND BOOK TRADE

686.2 NLD ISSN 0922-4084
PERS; technisch vakblad voor professionals in druk en print. Text in Dutch. 1988. 20/yr. EUR 99; EUR 8 newsstand/cover (effective 2009). adv. **Document type:** *Magazine, Trade.*
—IE, Infotrieve.
Published by: Uitgeverij Compres b.v., Postbus 55, Leiden, 2300 AB, Netherlands. TEL 31-71-5161515, FAX 31-71-5161535, info@uitgeverijcompres.nl, http://www.uitgeverijcompres.nl. Pub. Wim Findhammer. Adv. contact Frans van Grondelle TEL 31-71-5161518. B&W page EUR 2,800, color page EUR 4,125; bleed 230 x 325. Circ: 4,708.

760 USA ISSN 2159-6212
▼ **THE PIN UP.** Text in English. 2010. q. USD 48 domestic; USD 64 foreign (effective 2011). adv. **Document type:** *Magazine, Trade.*
Related titles: Online - full text ed.: ISSN 2159-6239.
Published by: The Pin Up LLC, 10264 Destino St, Bellflower, CA 90706. press@thepinupmag.com.

686.2 POL ISSN 0373-9864
Z119 CODEN: POLGDZ
POLIGRAFIKA. Text in Polish. 1947. m. EUR 56 foreign (effective 2005). **Document type:** *Magazine, Trade.*
Indexed: ChemAb.
—CASDDS.
Published by: (Stowarzyszenie Inzynierow i Technikow Mechanikow Polskich, Sekcja Poligrafow), Alfa-Print Sp. z o.o., ul Panska 97, Warsaw, 00834, Poland. poligrafika@poligrafika.pl. Ed. Tomasz Mospan. Circ: 2,400. **Dist. by:** Ars Polona, Obroncow 25, Warsaw 03933, Poland. TEL 48-22-5098609, FAX 48-22-5098610, arspolona@arspolona.com.pl, http://www.arspolona.com.pl.

665 RUS ISSN 0204-3513
Z372
➤ **POLIGRAFIST I IZDATEL'.** Text in Russian. 1994. m. RUR 480; USD 95 foreign. adv. bk.rev. **Document type:** *Academic/Scholarly.*
Indexed: RASB.
—East View.
Published by: Printer & Publisher, Sushchevskii Val ul 64, Moscow, 129272, Russian Federation. TEL 7-095-2889317, FAX 7-095-2889444. Ed. Alexei I Ovsiannikov. R&P Tatiana Emelianova. Adv. contact Tatiana V Emelianova. Circ: 7,000. **Dist. by:** East View Information Services, 10601 Wayzata Blvd, Minneapolis, MN 55305. TEL 952-252-1201, 800-477-1005, FAX 952-252-1202, info@eastview.com, http://www.eastview.com.

665 RUS ISSN 0032-2717
CODEN: PLGFAH
POLIGRAFIYA. Text in Russian. 1924. bi-m. USD 99.95. bk.rev. bibl.; charts; illus. index.
Indexed: ABIPC, ChemAb, GALA, RASB, RefZh.
—CASDDS, East View, INIST, Linda Hall. **CCC.**
Address: Sushchevskii Val 64, Moscow, 129272, Russian Federation. TEL 7-095-2024791. Ed. A I Ovsyannikov. Circ: 27,000. **Dist. by:** East View Information Services, 10601 Wayzata Blvd, Minneapolis, MN 55305. TEL 952-252-1201, 800-477-1005, FAX 952-252-1202, info@eastview.com, http://www.eastview.com.

760 ESP ISSN 1695-2448
PRESS - GRAPH; arte, edicion, industria grafica. Text in Spanish. 1994. bi-w. EUR 188 (effective 2009). adv. back issues avail. **Document type:** *Magazine, Trade.* **Description:** Covers color publishing, management, new technology, typography and graphic arts.
Formerly: Press Graph and Imaging (1134-4733); Which was formed by the merger of (1974-1994): Press Graph (1134-4598); (1993-1994): Imaging (1134-4741)
Published by: Ediciones Press Graph S.L., Joanot Martorell 4-10, Sabedell, Barcelona, 08203, Spain. TEL 34-93-7205230, FAX 34-93-7205249, info@pressgraph.es. Ed. Francisco Javier Romero. Adv. contact Joaquina Cervera. Circ: 8,000 (controlled).

686.2 760 CAN
PRESSPECTIVE. Text in English. q. free. **Document type:** *Newsletter.*
Published by: L G M Graphics Inc., 737 Moray St, Winnipeg, MB R3J 9Z9, Canada. TEL 204-889-9050, 800-665-3316, FAX 204-889-9897.

686.2 USA
▼ **PRESSTIME UPDATE.** Text in English. 2009. w. free to members (effective 2011). back issues avail. **Document type:** *Newsletter, Trade.* **Description:** Contains news and information about digital, advertising and content strategy and trends, competitive insights, and timely updates on NAA products and services.
Media: Online - full text. **Related titles:** Microfiche ed.: (from CIS).
Published by: Newspaper Association of America, 4401 Wilson Blvd, Ste 900, Arlington, VA 22203. TEL 571-366-1000, FAX 571-336-1195, membsvc@naa.org.

686.2 GBR ISSN 0032-8529
PRINT. Text in English. 1968. 10/yr. GBP 10. adv. bk.rev. illus. index.
Former titles: Graphical Journal; Incorporates: S L A D E Journal; Which was formerly: Process Journal (0032-9614)
Related titles: Online - full text ed.
Published by: National Graphical Association (N G A), Graphic House 63-67, Bromham Rd, Bedford, Beds MK40 2AG, United Kingdom. FAX 0234-218640. Ed. A D Dubbins.

686.2 AUS ISSN 1446-6554
PRINT 21. Text in English. 1997. bi-m. adv. reprints avail. **Document type:** *Magazine, Trade.* **Description:** Covers news and information for the printing and visual imaging industries in Australia and New Zealand.
Former titles (until 2001): Tecprint (1443-1890); (1997-1999): Print Asia Pacific (1328-0201); Which was formed by the merger of (1986-1997): Ink (South Melbourne) (1030-8318); (1975-1997): Graphix (0314-6685); Which was formerly: Graphic Arts (0310-5792); (1948-1971): Graphic Arts Bulletin (0017-3290)
Related titles: Microform ed.: (from PQC); Online - full text ed.
Indexed: ABIX.
—**CCC.**
Published by: Blueline Media Pty Ltd., PO Box 1636, Potts Point, NSW 2011, Australia. TEL 61-2-93563976, FAX 61-2-93564982. Ed., Pub. Patrick Howard TEL 61-2-93563976. Circ: 7,348.

686.2 GBR
PRINT AND PRODUCTION MANUAL. Text in English. 1986. irreg., latest 2008, 11th ed. GBP 185.25 per vol. (effective 2010). **Document type:** *Handbook/Manual/Guide, Trade.*
—BLDSC (6612.998950).
Published by: IntertechPira, Cleeve Rd, Leatherhead, Surrey KT22 7RU, United Kingdom. TEL 44-1372-802000, FAX 44-1372-802079, info@pira-international.com, http://www.pira-international.com/.

338.47 GBR ISSN 1746-5117
THE PRINT BUSINESS. Text in English. 2005. m. free (effective 2009). adv. back issues avail. **Document type:** *Magazine, Trade.*
Related titles: Online - full text ed.
—**CCC.**
Published by: First City Media Ltd., 28A Jubilee Trade Centre, Jubilee Rd, Letchworth, Herts SG6 1SP, United Kingdom. TEL 44-1462-678300, FAX 44-1462-481622. Ed. Gareth Ward. Pub. Geoff Hall. Adv. contact Tom Vine.

686.2 USA
PRINT BUSINESS REGISTER. Text in English. 1986. s-m. USD 297 in North America; USD 397 elsewhere. **Document type:** *Newsletter, Trade.* **Description:** Follows activities in the commercial printing industry, including mergers and acquisitions, major contracts, installations, bankruptcies, trends, and legal proceedings of note.
Formerly: Print Mergers and Acquisitions
Related titles: Online - full text ed.
Published by: Cygnus Business Media, Inc., 1233 Janesville Ave, PO Box 803, Fort Atkinson, WI 53538. TEL 920-563-6388, FAX 920-563-1702, http://www.cygnusb2b.com. Circ: 650.

686.2 NLD ISSN 0925-3874
PRINT BUYER; inspiratiebron voor marketeers en drukwerkinkopers. Text in Dutch. 1990. 10/yr. EUR 120; EUR 15 newsstand/cover (effective 2009). adv. **Document type:** *Magazine, Trade.*
Published by: Uitgeverij Compres b.v., Postbus 55, Leiden, 2300 AB, Netherlands. TEL 31-71-5161515, FAX 31-71-5161535, info@uitgeverijcompres.nl, http://www.uitgeverijcompres.nl. Ed. Margot Lodewijk. Pub. Wim Findhammer. Adv. contact Frans van Grondelle TEL 31-71-5161518. B&W page EUR 2,105, color page EUR 3,500; bleed 210 x 297. Circ: 4,454.

686.2 NLD
PRINT BUYER GUIDE. Text in Dutch. a. adv. **Document type:** *Directory, Trade.*
Published by: Uitgeverij Compres b.v., Postbus 55, Leiden, 2300 AB, Netherlands. TEL 31-71-5161515, FAX 31-71-5161535, info@uitgeverijcompres.nl, http://www.uitgeverijcompres.nl.

686.2 USA ISSN 0048-5314
Z249
PRINT-EQUIP NEWS. Text in English. 1965. m. adv. illus. **Document type:** *Newspaper, Trade.*
Indexed: GALA.
Published by: P - E N Publications Inc., 215 Allen Ave, Box 5540, Glendale, CA 91201-5540. TEL 818-954-9495, FAX 818-954-0452. Ed. Paul B Kissel. Pub. Richard E Jutras. Adv. contact Jeff Jutras. B&W page USD 1,275, color page USD 1,825. Circ: 25,800.

PRINT MART. *see* MACHINERY

686.2 NLD ISSN 1876-9586
PRINT MATTERS. Text in Dutch. 1987. q. EUR 53 (effective 2009). adv. bk.rev. **Document type:** *Magazine, Trade.* **Description:** Covers development in the graphics industry.
Formerly (until 2008): Graficus Magazine (1382-9068)
Published by: ManagementMedia B.V., PO Box 1932, Hilversum, 1200 BX, Netherlands. TEL 31-35-6232756, FAX 31-35-6232401, info@managementmedia.nl. Ed. Alex Kunst. Pub. Mike Velleman. Circ: 7,000.

686.2 USA ISSN 1938-6206
CODEN: BFLSEP
PRINT PROFESSIONAL. Text in English. 1963. m. free to qualified personnel (effective 2008). adv. bk.rev. tr.lit. back issues avail.; reprints avail. **Document type:** *Magazine, Trade.* **Description:** Provides industry news, new product and technology information as well as market reports for distributors and manufacturers of printed products.
Former titles (until 2007): Business Forms, Labels and Systems (1044-758X); (until 198?): Business Forms and Systems (0745-3914); (until 1982): Business Forms Reporter (0007-6767)
Related titles: Online - full text ed.: ISSN 1940-6010. free to qualified personnel (effective 2008); Regional ed(s).: Business Forms, Labels and Systems (Western News Edition). ISSN 1549-7909.
Indexed: A12, A13, A15, A17, A22, ABIn, B03, B11, CPEI, EngInd, GALA, Inspec, P31, P48, P51, P53, P54, PQC, SCOPUS.
—AskIEEE. **CCC.**
Published by: North American Publishing Co., 1500 Spring Garden St., 12th Fl, Philadelphia, PA 19130. TEL 215-238-5300, FAX 215-238-5213, magazinecs@napco.com, http://www.napco.com. Eds. Nicole Stella, Nichole Stella. Pub. Jim Harvie TEL 215-238-5436. R&P Shirley Baker. adv.: B&W page USD 4,585, color page USD 6,055; 7 x 10. Circ: 12,000.

686.2 USA ISSN 1535-9727
Z244.5
PRINT SOLUTIONS MAGAZINE. Text in English. 1962. m. USD 29 to non-members; free to members (effective 2010); subscr. includes Buyers Guide. adv. bk.rev. illus. index. back issues avail. **Document type:** *Magazine, Trade.* **Description:** Contains management, marketing and sales features to help readers improve their businesses, expand their markets, and learn new ways to sell print and related services.
Formerly (until 2001): Form (0532-1700)
Related titles: Online - full text ed.: ISSN 1535-9735.
Indexed: ABIPC, GALA.
Published by: Print Services & Distribution Association, 433 E Monroe Ave, Alexandria, VA 22301. TEL 703-836-6232, 800-336-4641, FAX 703-836-2241, psda@psda.org, http://www.psda.org. Ed. Peter L Colaianni. Adv. contact Dave Merli. Circ: 13,800.

686.2 DEU ISSN 0944-7482
PRINT UND PRODUKTION; das Magazin fuer Druck und Medien. Text in German. 1988. 10/yr. EUR 50 (effective 2009). adv. **Document type:** *Magazine, Trade.* **Description:** For printers and print buyers.
Formerly (until 1993): Print (0935-5944)
Published by: EuBuCo Verlag GmbH, Geheimrat-Hummel-Platz 4, Hochheim, 65239, Germany. TEL 49-6146-6050, FAX 49-6146-605200, verlag@eubuco.de, http://www.eubuco.de. Ed. Thomas Fasold. Adv. contact Magda Lehmann. color page EUR 5,355, B&W page EUR 3,780; trim 240 x 335. Circ: 12,998 (paid and controlled).

655 DEU
PRINTCOM BRASIL. Text in Portuguese. 2000. 6/yr. adv. **Document type:** *Magazine, Trade.*
Published by: Deutscher Drucker Verlag GmbH, Postfach 4124, Ostfildern, 73744, Germany. TEL 49-711-448170, FAX 49-711-442099, info@publish.de, http://www.publish.de. Pub. Kai Hagenbruch. Circ: 5,000 (controlled).

655 DEU
PRINTCOM LATINA. Text in Spanish. 2007. 4/yr. adv. **Document type:** *Magazine, Trade.*
Published by: Deutscher Drucker Verlag GmbH, Postfach 4124, Ostfildern, 73744, Germany. TEL 49-711-448170, FAX 49-711-442099, info@publish.de, http://www.publish.de. Circ: 8,000 (paid and controlled).

686.2 USA ISSN 0889-4965
THE PRINTER; letterpress news & marketplace. Text in English. 1975. m. USD 30 (effective 2006). **Document type:** *Newsletter, Trade.* **Description:** Contains the advertisements for hobby and craft letterpress for both sides of the Atlantic.
Published by: Michael & Sally Phillips, 337 Wilson St, Findlay, OH 45840. TEL 419-422-4958, FAX 419-420-9353, theprinter4918@hotmail.com. Ed., Pub. M J Phillips.

686.2 USA
PRINTERS EXCHANGE SOUTHWEST. Text in English. 1998. m. free to qualified personnel (effective 2006). adv. back issues avail. **Document type:** *Magazine, Trade.*
Address: PO Box 1016, Alief, TX 77411. TEL 281-498-2433, FAX 281-498-6721, myers-judy@sbcglobal.net. Pub. Judy Myers. adv.: B&W page USD 1,555, color page USD 1,918; trim 8.25 x 10.75. Circ: 10,300 (controlled).

686.2 USA
PRINTER'S INK. Text in English. 1984. q. free (effective 2010). **Document type:** *Newsletter, Academic/Scholarly.* **Description:** Comments on the printing and binding of soft and hard bound books. Provides ideas to help the publisher hold down costs and speed up production time.
Related titles: Online - full text ed.
Published by: Thomson-Shore, Inc., 7300 W Joy Rd, Dexter, Dexter, MI 48130. TEL 734-426-3939, FAX 800-706-4545.

686.2 USA ISSN 1085-3146
PRINTER'S NORTHWEST TRADER. Text in English. 1970. m. USD 10 domestic; USD 48 in Canada (effective 2008). adv. bk.rev.; software rev. tr.lit. 48 p./no. 2 cols./p.; **Document type:** *Magazine, Trade.* **Description:** Serves the print and graphic arts industry in Oregon, Washington, Idaho, Montana, Alaska and Northern California.
Published by: Eagle Newspapers, Inc, 380 SE Spokane St., Ste 101, Portland, OR 97202. TEL 503-283-6175, 800-426-2416, FAX 503-283-1904. Pub. Sandra Hubbard. Adv. contact Rod Stollery. Circ: 5,850 (controlled).

686.209 GBR ISSN 0079-5321
Z119
PRINTING HISTORICAL SOCIETY. JOURNAL. Text in English. 1965; N.S. 2000. a. free to members (effective 2009). **Document type:** *Journal, Academic/Scholarly.*
Incorporates (1980-2000): Printing Historical Society. Bulletin (0144-7505); Which was formerly (until 1980): Printing Historical Society. Newsletter (0556-1515)
Published by: Printing Historical Society, The Secretary, St Bride Institute, Bride Ln, Fleet St, London, EC4Y 8EE, United Kingdom. secretary@printinghistoricalsociety.org.uk. Ed. John Trevitt.

686.209 USA ISSN 0192-9275
Z124.A2
➤ **PRINTING HISTORY.** Text in English. 1979. s-a. free to members (effective 2010). adv. bk.rev. illus. back issues avail.; reprints avail. **Document type:** *Journal, Academic/Scholarly.* **Description:** Features scholarly articles on the history of printing, publishing, books, type, typography, paper and related industries.
Indexed: A26, AmH&L, B04, BrHumI, CA, E08, HistAb, I05, L04, L07, L08, L09, LISTA, LibLit, MLA-IB, PCI, S09, T02.
—BLDSC (6614.050000), Ingenta, Linda Hall.
Published by: American Printing History Association, Grand Central Sta, PO Box 4519, New York, NY 10163. publications@printinghistory.org. Ed. William S Peterson. adv.: page USD 265; 6 x 9.

686.2 USA ISSN 0032-860X
PRINTING IMPRESSIONS. Text in English. 1958. 24/yr. free to qualified personnel (effective 2008). adv. bk.rev. illus. Supplement avail.; reprints avail. **Document type:** *Magazine, Trade.* **Description:** Provides coverage on industry trends, emerging technologies and the news behind the news in the Graphic Arts industry.
Incorporates (1970-197?): Printing Management (0032-8650); Which superseded in part (1958-1970): Printing Production (0191-7749); Which was formerly (1930-1958): Printing Equipment Engineer (0096-9400)
Related titles: Online - full text ed.: free to qualified personnel (effective 2008).
Indexed: A12, A13, A15, A17, A22, ABIPC, ABIn, B03, B11, BPI, BRD, CurPA, EngInd, GALA, P06, P16, P48, P51, P53, P54, PQC, PROMT, SCOPUS, W01, W02, W03, W05.
—BLDSC (6614.100000), IE, Infotrieve, Linda Hall. **CCC.**
Published by: North American Publishing Co., 1500 Spring Garden St., 12th Fl, Philadelphia, PA 19130. TEL 215-238-5300, FAX 215-238-5213, magazinecs@napco.com, http://www.napco.com. Eds. Erik Cagle TEL 215-238-5326, Mark T Michelson TEL 215-238-5329. adv.: B&W page USD 12,970, color page USD 15,130; trim 7 x 10. Circ: 80,491.

760 USA
PRINTING IMPRESSIONS' EXECUTIVE BRIEFING. Text in English. 1997. s-m. USD 249; USD 269 in Canada & Mexico; USD 289 elsewhere.
Related titles: Online - full text ed.
Published by: North American Publishing Co., 1500 Spring Garden St., 12th Fl, Philadelphia, PA 19130. TEL 215-238-5300, FAX 215-238-5457, http://www.napco.com.

686.2 USA ISSN 1556-0163
Z119
PRINTING NEWS. Text in English. 1928. w. free to qualified personnel (effective 2010). bk.rev. illus.; tr.lit. Supplement avail.; back issues avail.; reprints avail. **Document type:** *Magazine, Trade.* **Description:** Contains information on the print and graphic communications industry.
Former titles (until 1997): Printing News - East (1046-8595); (until 1989): Printing News (0032-8626); (until 19??): New York Printing News
Related titles: Online - full text ed.: ISSN 2157-4758. free (effective 2010).
Indexed: A09, A10, A15, ABIPC, ABIn, GALA, I05, P48, P51, PQC, PROMT, SCOPUS, T02, V03, V04.
—**CCC.**
Published by: Cygnus Business Media, Inc., 1233 Janesville Ave, PO Box 803, Fort Atkinson, WI 53538. Kathy.Scott@Cygnusb2b.com, http://www.cygnusb2b.com. Pub. Kelley Holmes TEL 800-616-2252 ext 6104.

686.2 IND ISSN 0401-3956
PRINTING TIMES. Text in English. 1955. m. adv. bk.rev. illus. back issues avail. **Document type:** *Journal, Trade.* **Description:** Features development in printing industry and raw materials like paper, ink, machinery etc., Also cover conferences, seminars, pertaining to printing world wide.
Published by: All India Federation of Master Printers, 605, 6th Fl, Madhuban, 55, Nehru Pl, New Delhi, 110 019, India. TEL 91-11-26451742, FAX 91-11-26451743, aifmp1@gmail.com. Ed. Viren Chhabra. Circ: 2,000 (paid and controlled).

686.2 NLD ISSN 2211-7229
▼ **PRINTIT!.** Text in Dutch. 2010. s-a. adv. **Document type:** *Magazine, Trade.*
Published by: Magenta Publishing, Bijsterhuizen 31-47, Wijchen, 6604 LV, Netherlands. TEL 31-24-3454150, FAX 31-24-3976071, info@kantoornet.nl, http://www.kantoornet.nl. Ed. Joost Heessels. Circ: 15,000.

686.2 GBR
PRINTLINK INTERNATIONAL. Text in Arabic. m. GBP 62. **Document type:** *Handbook/Manual/Guide, Trade.* **Description:** Provides technology guides, in-depth features and analysis for the graphic, printing, converting, finishing and allied industries in the Arab world.
Published by: International Printing Communications Ltd., Crownhill Industry, PO Box 923, Milton Keynes, Bucks MK8 0AY, United Kingdom. TEL 44-1908-561444, FAX 44-1908-569564, TELEX 826373 PRINT G. Ed. M Yousry. Pub. R Ghozzi. adv.: B&W page GBP 1,675, color page GBP 2,075; trim 186 x 272.

PRINTMAKING TODAY. *see* ART

686.2 681.65 GBR
PRINTSHOP. Text in English. 1981 (May, no.6). q. GBP 6.50. adv. illus.
Published by: Franchise Publications, James House, 37 Nottingham Rd, London, SW17 7EA, United Kingdom. Ed. Robert Riding.

069 686.2 USA ISSN 1522-998X
PRINTTHOUGHTS; occasional comments on matters of interest in the print world. Text in English. 1997. irreg., latest vol.2, no.2, April 1997. USD 3.25 (effective 1999). back issues avail. **Document type:** *Monographic series.* **Description:** Contains terminology debasement and questionable professional ethics in the making and selling of fine art prints. Audience is artists, printers, publishers and dealers in the fine art print field.
Published by: Mel Hunter Graphics, Ed.& Pub., 4232 Rte. 7, Ferrisburgh, VT 05456. TEL 802-877-3719, FAX 802-877-2090. R&P Mel Harris. Circ: 250 (paid).

PRINTWEAR. *see* CLOTHING TRADE

686.2 GBR ISSN 0967-2486
PRINTWEAR & PROMOTION. Abbreviated title: P & P. Text in English. 1991. m. GBP 70 domestic; GBP 100 foreign; free to qualified personnel (effective 2009). adv. back issues avail. **Document type:** *Magazine, Trade.*
Formerly (until 1992): Screenprint Wear (0967-2494)
Related titles: Online - full text ed.: free to qualified personnel (effective 2009).
—**CCC.**
Published by: Datateam Publishing Ltd, 15a London Rd, Maidstone, Kent ME16 8LY, United Kingdom. TEL 44-1622-687031, FAX 44-1622-757646, info@datateam.co.uk, http://www.datateam.co.uk. Ed. Deborah Eales TEL 44-1622-699198. Pub. Paul Ryder TEL 44-1622-699105. Adv. contact Tony Gardner TEL 44-1622-699173.

686.2 GBR ISSN 1350-9829
PRINTWEEK. Text in English. 1958. w. GBP 119 (effective 2009). adv. bk.rev. illus. back issues avail.; reprints avail. **Document type:** *Magazine, Trade.* **Description:** Contains print industry news, features, analysis, profiles, research or buying information.
Incorporates (1878-2009): Printing World (0032-8715); Which incorporated (200?-2007): PrintBuyer (1750-4139); (1888-2000): British Printer (0007-1684); Which incorporated: British Bookmaker; British Lithographer; (1964-1981): Printing Today (0264-8075); Which was formerly (1964-1979): Printing Equipment and Materials (0032-8596); PrintWeek was formerly (until 1993): Litho Week (0264-732X); (until 1982): Lithoprinter Week (0264-7168); (until 1979): Lithoprinter (0024-4929)
Related titles: Online - full text ed.
Indexed: A10, A15, ABIn, B01, B07, BrTechI, ChemAb, E11, GALA, P34, P48, P51, P52, PQC, SCOPUS, T04, V03.
—BLDSC (6615.348000), Linda Hall. **CCC.**
Published by: Haymarket Publishing Ltd. (Subsidiary of: Haymarket Media Group), 174 Hammersmith Rd, London, W6 7JP, United Kingdom. TEL 44-20-82674210, info@haymarket.com, http://www.haymarket.com. Ed. Darryl Danielli TEL 44-20-82674473. Circ: 17,080. **Subscr. to:** 12-13 Cranleigh Gardens Industrial Estate, Southall UB1 2DB, United Kingdom. TEL 44-84-51557355, FAX 44-20-86067503, subscriptions@haymarket.com, http://www.haymarketbusinesssubs.com.

686.2 GBR ISSN 0032-9878
PRODUCTION JOURNAL. Text in English. 1958. 10/yr. GBP 32. adv. charts; illus.; stat. index. **Document type:** *Journal, Trade.*
Indexed: A12, A13, A17, ABIPC, ABIn, EngInd, GALA, Inspec, P&BA, P48, P51, P53, P54, PQC, SCOPUS.
—BLDSC (6853.150000).
Published by: (Newspaper Society), Cullum Publishing, 83a Leverstock Green Rd, Hemel Hempstead, Herts HP3 8PR, United Kingdom. TEL 44-1442-233656, FAX 44-171-631-5119. Ed., R&P Gary Cullum. Adv. contact Terry Gunter. Circ: 3,000 (controlled).

686.2 USA ISSN 1530-3497
PROFILES; magazine for professional printing contractors. Text in English. 1999. q. USD 2.95 per issue (effective 2005). adv. 32 p./no.; **Document type:** *Magazine, Trade.*
Published by: Benjamin Moore & Co., Inc., 101 Paragon Dr, Montvale, NJ 07645. TEL 800-344-0400, info@benjaminmoore.com, https://www.benmoorepaints.com/index.asp. Pubs. Jeff Spillane, John Lanzillotti. adv.: color page USD 5,200. Circ: 80,000 (controlled).

760 686.2 ESP ISSN 1575-2240
PROSIGN; tecnologias y materiales para el mercado de la comunicacion visual. Text in Spanish. 1997. 7/yr. EUR 72 domestic; EUR 113 in Europe; EUR 167 elsewhere (effective 2009). **Document type:** *Magazine, Trade.*
Published by: TPI Edita, Ave Manoteras, 26 3a Planta, Madrid, 28050, Spain. TEL 34-91-3396807, FAX 34-91-3396096, info@grupotpi.es, http://www.tpiedita.es.

PUBLISH.DE. *see* PUBLISHING AND BOOK TRADE

PUBLISHING EXECUTIVE. *see* PUBLISHING AND BOOK TRADE

QUAERENDO; a quarterly journal from the Low Countries devoted to manuscripts and printed books. *see* PUBLISHING AND BOOK TRADE

686.2 USA ISSN 0191-4588
Z252.5.I49
QUICK PRINTING; the information source for commercial copyshops and printshops. Text in English. 1977. m. USD 40 domestic; USD 55 in Canada & Mexico; USD 80 elsewhere; free to qualified personnel (effective 2010). adv. charts; illus.; stat. Supplement avail.; back issues avail.; reprints avail. **Document type:** *Magazine, Trade.* **Description:** Focuses on improving efficiency and increasing sales and profits in the print shop.
Related titles: Online - full text ed.: ISSN 1948-5662. free (effective 2009).
Indexed: A09, A10, A15, ABIPC, ABIn, B02, B15, B17, B18, EngInd, G04, G08, GALA, I05, P16, P48, P51, P53, P54, PQC, SCOPUS, T02, V03, V04.
—BLDSC (7216.410000), IE, Ingenta. **CCC.**
Published by: Cygnus Business Media, Inc., 3 Huntington Quadrangle, Ste 301 N, Melville, NY 11747. TEL 800-616-2252, FAX 866-743-5717, http://www.cygnusb2b.com. Pub. Kelley Holmes TEL 800-616-2252 ext 6104. adv.: B&W page USD 4,110, color page USD 5,205; trim 8 x 10.875. Circ: 43,000.

686.2 770 USA
R I T TRAINING UPDATE. (Rochester Institute of Technology) Text in English. q. free. bk.rev. charts; illus. back issues avail. **Document type:** *Newsletter.* **Description:** Provides information on training, seminars, and research for the graphic arts industry.
Former titles: Print R I T Update; T and E News (0895-6529); (until 1986): T and E Center Newsletter (0895-6642); T and E Center (0888-4056); (until 1982): T and E Center Newsletter (0276-9611); (until 1981): G A R C Newsletter (0271-9479)
Related titles: Online - full text ed.
Indexed: ABIPC.
Published by: Rochester Institute of Technology, Center for Integrated Manufacturing Studies, 111 Lomb Memorial Dr, Rochester, NY 14623-5608. TEL 585-475-5101, FAX 585-475-5250, training@cims.rit.edu, http://www.training.rit.edu. Ed., R&P Sandy Richolson. Circ: 30,000.

R S V P: THE DIRECTORY OF ILLUSTRATION AND DESIGN. *see* BUSINESS AND ECONOMICS—Trade And Industrial Directories

686 ITA ISSN 0033-9687
RASSEGNA GRAFICA. Text in Italian. 1950. fortn. (18/yr.). EUR 56 domestic (effective 2008). adv. **Document type:** *Magazine, Trade.*
Related titles: Online - full text ed.
—IE.
Published by: BE-MA Editrice Srl, Via Teocrito 50, Milan, MI 20128, Italy. TEL 39-02-252071, FAX 39-02-27000692, segreteria@bema.it, http://www.bema.it. Circ: 9,400 (controlled).

686.2 USA ISSN 1948-786X
HD9696.2.A1
▼ **REPRINT CONSUMABLES.** Short title: RePrint. Text mainly in English; Text in Chinese. 2009. bi-m. USD 29.90; USD 2.99 per issue (effective 2009). adv. **Document type:** *Magazine, Trade.* **Description:** Publication focused on the printers and consumables industry.
Published by: ReChina Expo, 1621 E St Andrews Pl, Santa Ana, CA 92705. TEL 949-701-6198, FAX 714-259-8600, http://www.rechinaexpo.com/. Circ: 6,000 (controlled).

686.2 CHE
REPRO BULLETIN. Text in German. q. adv. **Document type:** *Trade.*
Published by: Verband Schweizerischer Reprografie-Betriebe/Association Suisses des Ateliers Reprographie, Postfach 319, Zuerich, 8034, Switzerland. TEL 01-2624477. Ed. Viktor Schmid. Adv. contact Rene Collioud.

676.2 686.2 USA ISSN 0736-1238
REPRODUCTION BULLETIN. Text in English. 1954. q. free. bk.rev. pat. cum.index: nos.1-84 (1954-1974). **Document type:** *Bulletin, Trade.* **Description:** Contains items of interest on Diazotpe reproduction processes.
Formerly: Reproduction Paper News Bulletin (0034-4966)
Indexed: ABIPC, ChemAb.
Published by: Andrews Paper & Chemical Co., Inc., 1 Channel Dr, Box 509, Port Washington, NY 11050. TEL 516-767-2800, FAX 516-767-1632. Ed., R&P Peter Muller. Circ: 2,500.

RESEARCH COMMITTEE FOR GRAPHIC SIMULATION AND VISUALIZATION OF MULTIPHASE FLOW. PROCEEDINGS. *see* PHYSICS—Optics

686.2 USA ISSN 1546-4431
TT273
S G I A JOURNAL. Text in English. 1997. q. membership only. **Document type:** *Journal, Trade.*
Published by: Screenprinting & Graphic Imaging Association International, 10015 Main St, Fairfax, VA 22031. TEL 703-385-1335, FAX 703-273-0456. Ed. Johnny Shell. Circ: 13,000.

686.2 USA ISSN 1544-0060
S G I A NEWS. (Screenprinting & Graphic Imaging Association International) Text in English. m. USD 30 to non-members; free to members (effective 2003). **Document type:** *Magazine, Trade.*
Formerly (until 2003): Screenprinting & Graphic Imaging Association International Tabloid (0279-053X)
Published by: Screenprinting & Graphic Imaging Association International, 10015 Main St, Fairfax, VA 22031. TEL 703-385-1335, FAX 703-273-0456, sgia@sgia.org, http://www.sgia.org. Ed. Bruce Joffe. Pub. John M Crawford.

686.2 DEU ISSN 1437-1812
S I P - SIEBDRUCK INFOPOST; Fachzeitschrift fuer Siebdruck, SignMaking und Werbetechnik. Text in German. 1984. 8/yr. EUR 38; EUR 7 newsstand/cover (effective 2008). adv. **Document type:** *Magazine, Trade.* **Description:** Provides decisionmakers and professionals in all sectors of silk-screening and advertising technology with information.
Indexed: TM.
Published by: Verlagshaus Gruber GmbH, Max-Planck-Str 2, Eppertshausen, 64859, Germany. TEL 49-6071-39410, FAX 49-6071-394111, info@verlagshaus-gruber.de, http://www.verlagshaus-gruber.de. Ed. Uwe Heinisch. Adv. contact Ingrid Sonntag. B&W page EUR 1,540, color page EUR 2,240; trim 190 x 265. Circ: 7,500 (paid and controlled).

686.2 GBR
S P A NEWS. Text in English. m. membership. **Document type:** *Newsletter.*
Formerly: Display Producers and Screen Printers Association. Monthly
Published by: Screen Printing Association (UK) Ltd., Association House, 7a West St, Reigate, Surrey RH2 9BL, United Kingdom. TEL 44-1737-240792, FAX 44-1737-240770. Circ: 250.

686.2 DEU
SAECHSISCHES INSTITUT FUER DIE DRUCKINDUSTRIE. HANDBUCH. Text in German. a. **Document type:** *Directory.*
Published by: Saechsisches Institut fuer die Druckindustrie, Arnoldplatz 41, Engelsdorf, 04439, Germany. TEL 0341-2513702, FAX 0341-2513980.

686.2 GBR
SCOTTISH DECORATORS' YEAR BOOK AND REVIEW. Text in English. a. free to members. adv. **Document type:** *Yearbook, Trade.* **Description:** Contains information which is helpful to members but it also records the activities (Minutes etc.) of the Subordinate Committees of the Federation.
Formerly: Scottish Decorators' Review

P

Published by: Scottish Decorators' Federation, Castlecraig Business Park, Players Rd, Stirling, FK7 7SH, United Kingdom. TEL 44-1786-448838, FAX 44-1786-450541, info@scottishdecorators.co.uk, http://www.scottishdecorators.co.uk/. Circ: 500.

686.2 USA ISSN 0036-9594
TT273
SCREEN PRINTING. Text in English. 1953. m. free to qualified personnel (effective 2011). adv. bk.rev. stat.; tr.lit.; illus. Index. back issues avail.; reprints avail. **Document type:** *Magazine, Trade.* **Description:** Aimed at all types of screen printers. Features tips, new products, technology updates, and industry news.
Related titles: Online - full text ed.
Indexed: A&ATA, A22, ABIPC, Englnd, GALA, PhotoAb, SCOPUS.
—BLDSC (8211.759700), IE, Infotrieve, Ingenta, Linda Hall. **CCC.**
Published by: S T Media Group International, Inc., PO Box 1060, Skokie, IL 60076. TEL 847-763-9030, FAX 847-763-4938, customer@stmediagroup.com, http://www.stmediagroup.com. Ed. Gail Flower TEL 513-421-2050. Pub. Steve Duccilli TEL 513-263-9344. Adv. contact Steve Duccill TEL 513-263-9344.

686.2 GBR ISSN 1741-5675
SCREEN PROCESS & DIGITAL IMAGING. Abbreviated title: S P D I. Text in English. 2004. m. GBP 70 domestic; GBP 100 foreign; free to qualified personnel (effective 2009). adv. illus.; tr.lit. back issues avail. **Document type:** *Journal, Trade.*
Incorporates (1999-2004): Digital Display Printing (1474-8916); (1952-2004): Screen Process (0953-3338); Which was formerly (until 1987): Screenprinting (0952-2719); (until 1986): Point of Sale and Screenprinting (0261-1309); (until 1981): Point of Sale News (0036-9586); (until 1970): Screen Printing and Point of Sale News
Related titles: Online - full text ed.: free to qualified personnel (effective 2009).
Indexed: GALA, IPackAb.
—IE. **CCC.**
Published by: Datateam Publishing Ltd, 15a London Rd, Maidstone, Kent ME16 8LY, United Kingdom. TEL 44-1622-687031, FAX 44-1622-757646, info@datateam.co.uk, http://www.datateam.co.uk. Ed. Jon Barrett TEL 44-1622-850044. Pub. Paul Ryder TEL 44-1622-699105. Adv. contact Adam Kinlan TEL 44-1622-699170. page GBP 1,200; trim 229 x 306. Circ: 6,855.

686.2 CAN ISSN 0834-9304
SECOND IMPRESSIONS. Text in English. 1985. bi-m. CAD 24 domestic; CAD 25 in United States; CAD 35 elsewhere (effective 2005). adv. bk.rev. **Document type:** *Magazine, Trade.* **Description:** Explores the different techniques of printing and the influence of new technologies.
Address: 35 Mill Dr, St Albert, AB T8N 1J5, Canada. TEL 780-458-9889, FAX 780-458-9839. Ed., Pub. Loretta Puckrin. adv.: B&W page CAD 1,463, color page CAD 1,950. Circ: 7,500 (paid and controlled).

686.2 006.42 USA ISSN 1080-2207
Z250
SERIF; the magazine of type and typography. Text in English. q. USD 28; USD 32 in Canada & Mexico; USD 36 elsewhere. adv. back issues avail. **Document type:** *Magazine, Trade.* **Description:** Covers the design and use of type.
Related titles: Online - full text ed.: Sans Serif.
Indexed: MLA-IB.
Address: 2038 N Clark St, Ste 377, Chicago, IL 60614. TEL 312-953-3679, FAX 312-803-0698, http://www.quixote.com/.

686.2 DEU ISSN 0178-2835
DER SIEBDRUCK; die Europaeische Fachzeitschrift fuer graphischen und industriellen Siebdruck. Text in German. 1952. m. EUR 48; EUR 6 newsstand/cover (effective 2008). adv. back issues avail. **Document type:** *Magazine, Trade.*
Incorporates (1980-1989): Industrieller Siebdruck und Leiterplattentechnik (0178-3106); (1962-1979): Sieb und Rakel (0342-7013)
Indexed: TM.
—BLDSC (8271.930000), IE, Infotrieve, Ingenta.
Published by: Draeger und Wullenwever Print & Media Luebeck GmbH & Co. KG, Grapengiesserstr 30, Luebeck, 23556, Germany. TEL 49-451-8798887, FAX 49-451-8798893, verlag@draeger.de, http://www.draeger-wullenwever.de. Ed. Michael Ringelsiep. adv.: B&W page EUR 1,430, color page EUR 2,165; trim 172 x 258. Circ: 4,500 (paid and controlled).

764.8 USA ISSN 2158-1533
▼ **SIGN & DIGITAL GRAPHICS.** Text in English. 2009. m. USD 48 for 2 yrs. (effective 2010). adv. **Document type:** *Magazine, Trade.*
Formed by the merger of (1997-2009): Digital Graphics Magazine (1097-5926); (1986-2009): Sign Business (0893-9888)
Published by: National Business Media, Inc., PO Box 1416, Broomfield, CO 80038. TEL 303-469-0424, 800-669-0424, FAX 303-469-5730, rpmpublisher@nbm.com, http://www.nbm.com. Pub. Mary Tohill TEL 303-469-0424 ext 217. Adv. contact Sara Siauw.

764.8 FRA ISSN 1768-3947
SIGN INFO SERI; le magazine de l'expression visuelle. Text in French. 1986. 11/yr. EUR 60 domestic; EUR 95 foreign (effective 2009). **Document type:** *Magazine, Trade.*
Formerly (until 2004): Info Seri (0980-9112)
Published by: Canal Expo, 5 Bd. des Bouvets, Nanterre, 92000, France. TEL 33-1-71113750, FAX 33-1-47290213. Circ: 4,200.

686.2 NLD ISSN 1871-6741
SIGN + SILKSCREEN MAGAZINE. Text in Dutch. 2005. 8/yr. EUR 138 (effective 2008). adv. illus. **Document type:** *Magazine, Trade.*
Formed by the merger of (1952-2005): Silk Screen (0037-5268); (2000-2005): Sign plus (1568-0975); Which was formed by the merger of (1989-2000): Sign & Display (0929-1431); (1997-2000): Digital Sign (1387-4586)
—IE, Infotrieve.
Published by: Eisma Businessmedia bv, Celsiusweg 41, Postbus 340, Leeuwarden, 8901 BC, Netherlands. TEL 31-58-2954854, FAX 31-58-2954875, businessmedia@eisma.nl, http://www.eisma.nl/businessmedia/index.asp. Eds. Hetty Stevens, Marijke Kuypers, Wouter Mooij TEL 31-58-3954853. Pub. Minne Hovenga. adv.: page EUR 1,934; 202 x 268.

686.2 USA ISSN 1091-0832
SIGNS OF THE TIMES & SCREEN PRINTING EN ESPANOL. Text in Spanish. 1997. bi-m. free to qualified personnel (effective 2011). adv. back issues avail. **Document type:** *Magazine, Trade.* **Description:** Offers practical advice on various sign-making and screen-printing techniques and technology (including digital imaging), for Spanish-speaking grapher providers of all skill levels, product specialties, and nationalities.
Formed by the merger of (1993-1997): Screen Printing en Espanol (1070-7239); (1995-1997): Signs of the Times en Espanol (1080-9325)
Related titles: Online - full text ed.; ◆ English ed.: Signs of the Times. ISSN 0037-5063.
—CCC.
Published by: S T Media Group International, Inc., PO Box 1060, Skokie, IL 60076. TEL 847-763-9030, FAX 847-763-4938, customer@stmediagroup.com, http://www.stmediagroup.com. Ed. Nancy Bottoms. Pub. Steve Duccill TEL 513-263-9344.

686.2 SGP ISSN 0129-5152
SINGAPORE PRINTER. Text in English. 1977. irreg. **Document type:** *Monographic series, Trade.*
Published by: Master Printers' Association, 21 Kim Keat Rd #07-01, Singapore, 328805, Singapore. TEL 65-336-4227, 65-336-1401, FAX 65-336-0621, mprinter@pacific.net.sg, http://www.singprint.org.sg/. Ed. Mrs. Tan Soo Buay.

SINGAPORE PRINTING INDUSTRY DIRECTORY. see BUSINESS AND ECONOMICS—Trade And Industrial Directories

764.8 686.2 CHN ISSN 1002-4867
SIWANG YINSHUA/SCREEN PRINTING. Text in Chinese. 1985. m. USD 49.20 (effective 2009). **Description:** Covers the products, technology, market, and developing trends in screen printing and graphic imaging in China.
Related titles: Online - full text ed.
—East View.
Published by: (Beijing Printing Technical Research Institute), China Screenprinting & Graphic Imaging Association, A36 Qianliang Hutong, Eastern District, Beijing, 100010, China. TEL 86-10-64015009, http://www.csgia.org. Circ: 15,000.

SOLAS OCCASIONAL RESEARCH PAPERS IN ART AND DESIGN EDUCATION; an anthology of student research. see ART

SOUTH AFRICAN TYPOGRAPHICAL JOURNAL/SUID-AFRIKAANSE TIPOGRAFIESE JOERNAAL. see LABOR UNIONS

686.2 GBR ISSN 2044-2319
SPECIALIST PRINTING WORLDWIDE. Text in English. 2007. q. GBP 45, EUR 55, USD 80 (effective 2010). adv. **Document type:** *Magazine, Trade.* **Description:** Provides the latest information on techniques of screen and wide format digital printing systems.
Formerly (until 2010): Specialist Printing (1754-6230)
Published by: Chameleon Business Media Ltd., 1 Cantelupe Mews, East Grinstead, West Sussex RH19 3BG, United Kingdom. http://www.cbm-ltd.com. Pub. Debbie Drewery TEL 44-1342-322133. Adv. contact Carol Gibbons TEL 44-1425-617429.

686.2 USA
T A G A NEWSLETTER. Text in English. 19??. q. free to members (effective 2010). back issues avail. **Document type:** *Newsletter, Trade.*
Related titles: Online - full text ed.
Published by: Technical Association of the Graphic Arts, 200 Deer Run Rd, Sewickley, PA 15143. TEL 800-910-4283, printing@printing.org, http://www.taga.org.

686.2 USA ISSN 0082-2299
Z244 CODEN: TAPRAV
T A G A PROCEEDINGS; technical papers presented at annual meeting. Text in English. 1949. a. free to members (effective 2010). index, cum.index: 1949-1996. back issues avail. **Document type:** *Proceedings, Trade.*
Former titles (until 1963): Technical Association of the Graphic Arts. Annual Meeting. Proceedings (0277-5026); (until 1957): Technical Association of the Graphic Arts. Annual Technical Meeting. Proceedings (0370-2375); (until 1951): Technical Association of the Lithographic Industry. Annual Technical Meeting. Proceedings
Indexed: A22, ABIPC, GALA.
—BLDSC (8598.230000), CASDDS, IE, Ingenta, Linda Hall.
Published by: Technical Association of the Graphic Arts, 200 Deer Run Rd, Sewickley, PA 15143. TEL 800-910-4283, printing@printing.org, http://www.taga.org. Circ: 1,000.

T A P P I COATING & GRAPHIC ARTS CONFERENCE PROCEEDINGS. (Technical Association of the Pulp and Paper Industry) see PAPER AND PULP

686.2 DEU
TAG FUER TAG; Sicherheit und Gesundheitsschutz rund um Text, Bild, Druck und Papierverarbeitung. Text in German. 1939. bi-m. free to members (effective 2009). **Document type:** *Magazine, Trade.* **Description:** Informs employers and employees about health and safety protection in the printing industries.
Published by: Berufsgenossenschaft Druck und Papierverarbeitung, Rheinstr 6-8, Wiesbaden, 65185, Germany. TEL 49-611-1310, FAX 49-611-131100, info@bgdp.de. Ed. Michael Boettcher. Circ: 120,000 (controlled).

TECHNICAL COMMUNICATION. see COMMUNICATIONS

686.2 USA
TECHNICAL GUIDEBOOK. Text in English. s-a. membership only. **Document type:** *Handbook/Manual/Guide, Trade.*
Formerly: Technical Guide Book of Screen Printing
Media: CD-ROM.
Published by: Screenprinting & Graphic Imaging Association International, 10015 Main St, Fairfax, VA 22031. TEL 703-385-1335. Pub. John M Crawford.

686.2 CUB
TECNICA GRAFICA. Text in Spanish. q. USD 22 in North America; USD 24 in South America; USD 28 elsewhere.
Published by: (Cuba. Ministerio de Cultura, Cuba. Departamento de Informacion Cientifico-Tecnica, Cuba. CEDE Poligrafico), Ediciones Cubanas, Obispo 527, Havana, Cuba.

686.2 CUB
TECNICA GRAFICA. SUPLEMENTO. Text in Spanish. 3/yr.
Published by: (Cuba. Ministerio de Cultura, Cuba. Departamento de Informacion Cientifico-Tecnica, Cuba. CEDE Poligrafico), Ediciones Cubanas, Obispo 527, Havana, Cuba.

686.2 USA
TEXHAX DIGEST. Text in English. w. back issues avail. **Document type:** *Newsletter.*
Media: Online - full text. **Related titles:** E-mail ed.
Published by: TeX Users Group, 1850 Union St No. 1637, San Francisco, CA 94123. FAX 415-982-8559, http://www.tug.org. Ed. David Osborne.

760 USA
NC997.A1
TRACE (NEW YORK, 1947); A I G A journal of graphic design. Text in English. 1947-1953; resumed 1965. 3/yr. USD 14 to non-members (effective 2002). bk.rev. bibl.; illus. reprints avail. **Document type:** *Journal, Trade.* **Description:** Focuses on criticism, professional practice, review, debate and the history of graphic design.
Former titles (until Jan. 2001): A I G A Journal of Graphic Design (0736-5322); (1965-1982): American Institute of Graphic Arts. Journal (0065-8820); (1947-1953): A I G A Journal (0197-6907)
Indexed: A07, A30, A31, AA, AIAP, ArtInd, B04, SCOPUS.
—Ingenta.
Published by: American Institute of Graphic Arts, 164 Fifth Ave, New York, NY 10010-5900. TEL 212-807-1990, FAX 212-807-1799, http://www.aiga.org. Ed. Andrea Codrington. Pub. Richard Grefe. R&P Marie Finamore. Adv. contact Deborah Aldrich. Circ: 9,000.

686.2 GBR ISSN 1753-4283
TRANSFER. Text in English. 1977. fortn. GBP 63 domestic; EUR 205 in Europe; USD 250 in US & Canada; GBP 137 elsewhere; GBP 9 per issue (effective 2010). adv. **Document type:** *Magazine, Trade.* **Description:** Provides a market place for new and used equipment; products and services targeted at printing and associated trades.
Related titles: Online - full text ed.: free (effective 2010).
Published by: Wilmington Media & Entertainment (Subsidiary of: Wilmington Group Plc), Progressive House, 2 Maidstone Rd, Foots Cray, Sidcup, DA14 5HZ, United Kingdom. TEL 44-20-82697766, FAX 44-20-82697804, investorinfo@wilmington.co.uk, http://www.wilmington.co.uk/. Adv. contact Yvonne Veal TEL 44-20-82697870.

686.2 USA ISSN 0896-3207
Z253.4.T47
TUGBOAT. Text in English. 1980. q. **Document type:** *Journal, Trade.*
—IE.
Published by: TeX Users Group, 1850 Union St No. 1637, San Francisco, CA 94123. TEL 415-982-8449, FAX 415-982-8559, http://www.tug.org.

760 006.42 USA
TYPOFILE. Text in English. 1996. irreg. **Document type:** *Magazine, Consumer.* **Description:** Advances the notion that each new typeface is like a new character and that twentysix shapes can contain the entire knowledge of mankind.
Media: Online - full text. Ed. Daniel Will Harris.

686.2 CZE ISSN 0322-9068
TYPOGRAFIA. Variant title: Polygraf-Typografia. Text in Czech. 1888. m. CZK 600 domestic; CZK 60 per issue domestic (effective 2009). adv. bk.rev. **Document type:** *Magazine, Trade.* **Description:** Covers both the technological and graphical aspects of printing and press work. Includes news on PrePress, Design, Publishing, Photography, Finishing, Paper, as well as employment at publishing and printing companies.
Published by: Kolegium Typografie, Tuchomericka 343, Prague 2, 16400, Czech Republic. typografia@netforce.cz. Ed. Vladislav Najbrt. adv.: B&W page CZK 20,000, color page CZK 25,000.

686.2 CHE ISSN 0041-4840
Z119
TYPOGRAFISCHE MONATSBLAETTER/REVUE SUISSE DE L'IMPRIMERIE/SWISS TYPOGRAPHIC MAGAZINE; Zeitschrift fuer Schrift, Typografie, Gestaltung und Sprache. Text in English, French, German. 1882. bi-m. CHF 133.15 domestic; CHF 154 foreign; CHF 22.55 newsstand/cover (effective 2010). adv. bk.rev. bibl.; charts; illus.; mkt. **Document type:** *Journal, Trade.*
Indexed: A22.
—IE, Infotrieve.
Published by: Comedia die Mediengewerkschaft Schweiz, Monbijoustr 33, Bern, 3011, Switzerland. TEL 41-31-3906611, FAX 41-31-3906691, info@comedia.ch, http://www.comedia.ch. Ed. Lukas Hartmann. Adv. contact Hans Kern. page CHF 1,800; trim 203 x 270. Circ: 3,000 (controlled).

686.2 CHE ISSN 1019-4754
U G R A MITTEILUNGEN. Text in French, German. 1963. 3/yr. CHF 30. bk.rev. bibl.; charts; illus. **Document type:** *Bulletin.* **Description:** Provides professional information for and of the graphics industry.
Indexed: ABIPC, P&BA.
Published by: Verein zur Foerderung Wissenschaftlicher Untersuchungen in der Graphischen Industrie, c/o E M P A, Lerchenfeldstr 5, St. Gallen, 9014, Switzerland. TEL 41-71-7247443, FAX 41-71-2747663. Ed. Walter Steiger. Circ: 3,800.

686.2 USA ISSN 0734-8177
Z232.U6
U.S. GOVERNMENT PRINTING OFFICE. ANNUAL REPORT. Text in English. 19??. a., latest 2008. free (effective 2011). back issues avail. **Document type:** *Report, Government.*
Formerly (until 1980): Annual Report of the Public Printer
Related titles: CD-ROM ed.: Public Printer's Annual Report. ISSN 1930-1065; Online - full text ed.: ISSN 1930-1057.
Published by: U.S. Government Printing Office, 732 N Capitol St, NW, Washington, DC 20401. TEL 202-512-1800, 866-512-1800, FAX 202-512-2104, ContactCenter@gpo.gov.

UNIVERSIDAD DE PALERMO. CENTRO DE ESTUDIOS EN DISENO Y COMUNICACION. CUADERNOS. see ART

686.2 CHE
V S D - MITTEILUNGEN. Text in German. m. CHF 70 (effective 2000). adv. bk.rev. **Document type:** *Bulletin, Trade.*
Published by: Verband der Schweizer Druckindustrie, Schosshaldenstr 20, Bern, 3006, Switzerland. TEL 41-31-3511511, FAX 41-31-3523738.

686.2 CHE
V S F - BULLETIN. Text in German. irreg. **Document type:** *Bulletin.*

Published by: Vereinigung Schweizerischer Formularhersteller, Schosshaldenstr 20, Bern 32, 3000, Switzerland. TEL 031-3511511.

DE VERENIGDE SANDBERGEN. *see* ART

686.2 DEU ISSN 1862-7501
VERSIO!. Text in German. 2002. 2/yr. adv. **Document type:** *Magazine, Trade.*
Formerly (until 2006): Heichlingers
Published by: Deutscher Drucker Verlag GmbH, Postfach 4124, Ostfildern, 73744, Germany. TEL 49-711-448170, FAX 49-711-442099, info@publish.de, http://www.publish.de. Ed. Martina Reinhardt. Adv. contact Michael Blind. Circ: 3,000 (controlled).

686.2 CHE ISSN 1422-9609
VISICOM; print und communication. Text in German, French, Italian. 1998. s-m. CHF 132 domestic; CHF 172 foreign (effective 2008). adv. charts; illus. **Document type:** *Journal, Trade.* **Description:** Articles by Swiss members of the Euro Graphic Press Association.
Formerly (until 1999): Visio (1422-5964); Which was formed by the merger of (1971-1998): Druckindustrie (0046-0737); (1872-1998): Print (1420-391X); Which was formerly (until 1983): Schweizerische Buchdrucker - Zeitung (1421-4660); (until 1899): Verein Schweizerischer Buchdruckereibesitzer. Mitteilungen (1421-489X)
—BLDSC (9240.891400), IE, Ingenta.
Published by: Viscom - Schweizerische Verband fuer Visuelle Kommunikation, Brunngasse 36, Bern, 3011, Switzerland. TEL 41-31-3184500, FAX 41-31-3184501, bern@viscom.ch, http://www.viscom.ch. adv.: B&W page CHF 2,930, color page CHF 4,400; trim 186 x 266. Circ: 20,000.

760 NOR ISSN 0803-8236
VISUELT; tidsskrift for visuell kommunikasjon, illustrasjon og grafisk formgivning. Text in Norwegian. 1975. 6/yr. NOK 480 (effective 2004). **Document type:** *Journal, Trade.*
Former titles (until 1992): Grafisk Design (0802-4006); Which incorporated (1983-1991): Blekkspruten (0800-238X); (until 1989): Norsk Grafisk Design. Bulletin (0801-4027); (until 1983): N G D Medlemsbulletin (0801-5198); (until 1979): N Y T Medlemsbulletin (0801-5201)
Indexed: ABM, SCOPUS.
Published by: G R A F I L L, Kongens Gate 7, Oslo, 0153, Norway. TEL 47-23-103630, FAX 47-23-103631, grafill@grafill.no, http://www.grafill.no. Ed. Judith Naerland TEL 47-22-715437.

686.2 DEU
W A N - I F R A MAGAZINE. Variant title: I F R A Newspaper Techniques. Text in English. 1962. 11/yr. EUR 101 domestic to non-members; EUR 136 in Europe to non-members; EUR 196 elsewhere to non-members (effective 2009). adv. bk.rev. **Document type:** *Magazine, Trade.* **Description:** Contents focus exclusively on problems relating to newspaper organization and production.
Former titles (until 2009): I F R A Magazine; (until 2007): Newspaper Techniques (0019-333X)
Related titles: German ed.: Zeitungstechnik; French ed.: Techniques de Presse.
Indexed: ABIPC, EngInd, P&BA, SCOPUS, TM.
—BLDSC (9261.659715).
Published by: W A N - I F R A, Washingtonplatz 1, Darmstadt, 64287, Germany. TEL 49-6151-7336, FAX 49-6151-733800, info@wan-ifra.org. Adv. contact Bettina Falk. B&W page EUR 2,600; 189 x 268.5. Circ: 8,600.

686.2 USA ISSN 1547-9463
THE WIDE - FORMAT IMAGING; premier source for wide and grand format imaging. Text in English. 1993. m. USD 30 domestic; USD 45 in Canada & Mexico; USD 65 elsewhere; free to qualified personnel (effective 2010). adv. illus.; tr.lit. Supplement avail.; back issues avail.; reprints avail. **Document type:** *Magazine, Trade.* **Description:** Focuses on issues of wide-format and grand-format imaging.
Formerly (until 200?): Modern Reprographics (1068-9257)
Related titles: Online - full text ed.: ISSN 2150-2099. free (effective 2009).
Indexed: A09, A10, A15, ABIn, B02, B15, B17, B18, G04, G08, I05, P48, P51, PQC, T02, V03, V04.
—CCC.
Published by: Cygnus Business Media, Inc., 3 Huntington Quadrangle, Ste 301 N, Melville, NY 11747. TEL 800-308-6397, FAX 631-845-2741, http://www.cygnusb2b.com. Ed. Denise M Gustavson. Pub. Kelley Holmes TEL 800-616-2252 ext 6104. adv.: color page USD 6,525; trim 8 x 10.875. Circ: 17,600.

686.209 DEU ISSN 0724-9586
WOLFENBUETTELER SCHRIFTEN ZUR GESCHICHTE DES BUCHWESENS. Text in German. 1977. irreg., latest vol.43, 2008. price varies. **Document type:** *Monographic series, Academic/Scholarly.*
Published by: (Herzog August Bibliothek), Harrassowitz Verlag, Kreuzberger Ring 7b-d, Wiesbaden, 65205, Germany. TEL 49-611-5300, FAX 49-611-530560, verlag@harrassowitz.de, http://www.harrassowitz.de.

WORLD LEADERS IN PRINT. *see* BUSINESS AND ECONOMICS—Management

WORLD OF PRINT. *see* PUBLISHING AND BOOK TRADE

686.2 658 CHN ISSN 1671-8712
YINSHUA JINGLIREN/PRINTING MANAGER. Text in Chinese. 2001. m. CNY 10, USD 10 per issue (effective 2009). **Document type:** *Magazine, Trade.*
Formerly (until 2002): Dianzi Shangwu Jishu/Electronic Commerce Technology (1009-9581)
Related titles: Online - full text ed.
Published by: Zhongguo Yinshua Kexue Jishu Yanjiusuo, 2, Cuiwei Lu, Beijing, 100036, China. TEL 86-10-88275760, FAX 86-10-88275618.

686.2 CHN ISSN 1003-1960
YINSHUA JISHU/PRINTING TECHNOLOGY. Text in Chinese. 1957. s-m. USD 120, CNY 120 (effective 2009). **Document type:** *Journal, Academic/Scholarly.*
Formerly (until 1979): Yinshua Jishu Ziliao
Related titles: Online - full text ed.
—East View.
Published by: Zhongguo Yinshua Kexue Jishu Yanjiusuo, 2, Cuiwei Lu, Beijing, 100036, China. TEL 86-10-88275760, FAX 86-10-88275618.

686.2 CHN ISSN 1004-6267
Z119
YINSHUA ZAZHI/PRINTING FIELD. Text in Chinese. 1972. bi-m. USD 49.20 (effective 2009). adv. bk.rev. **Document type:** *Trade.* **Description:** For directors, managers, engineers and technicians of research institutes and printing houses.
Related titles: Online - full text ed.
—East View.
Published by: Shanghai Yinshua Jishu Yanjiusuo/Shanghai Printing Technology Institute, No 60 Lane 1209 Xinzha Lu, Shanghai, 200041, China. TEL 86-21-62580014, 86-21-32180191, FAX 86-21-62553562, printmag@printingfield.com, http://www.printingfield.com. Ed. Renchou Gong. Pub. Zhihui Yu. Adv. contact Shihua Ding TEL 86-21-62580018. B&W page USD 1,000, color page USD 2,000; trim 260 x 187. Circ: 15,000. **Dist. by:** China International Book Trading Corp, 35 Chegongzhuang Xilu, Haidian District, PO Box 399, Beijing 100044, China. TEL 86-10-68412045, FAX 86-10-68412023, cibtc@mail.cibtc.com.cn, http://www.cibtc.com.cn/.

686.2 688.8 CHN ISSN 1674-5752
CODEN: ZYYBAO
ZHONGGUO YINSHUA YU BAOZHUANG YANJIU/CHINA PRINTING AND PACKAGING STUDY. Text in Chinese. 1997. bi-m. CNY 156, USD 156; CNY 26, USD 26 per issue (effective 2009). back issues avail. **Document type:** *Journal, Academic/Scholarly.* **Description:** Contains scholarly papers on technological developments in printing and packaging science, covering industry, equipment, new materials, and other related subjects.
Formerly (until 2009): Zhongguo Yinshua Wuzi Shangqing/China Printing Materials Market (1007-516X)
Related titles: Online - full text ed.
Published by: Zhongguo Yinshua Kexue Jishu Yanjiusuo, 2, Cuiwei Lu, Beijing, 100036, China. TEL 86-10-88275760, FAX 86-10-88275618. Ed. Ouyang Yun. Circ: 3,000.

ZUGAKU KENKYU/JOURNAL OF GRAPHIC SCIENCE OF JAPAN. *see* ART

760 POL ISSN 1642-7602
NK1160
2 + 3 D; grafika plus produkt - ogolnopolski kwartalnik projektowy. Text in Polish. 2001. q. EUR 42 foreign (effective 2006). **Document type:** *Magazine, Trade.*
Published by: (Akademia Sztuk Pieknych, Wydzial Form Przemyslowych), Fundacja Rzecz Piekna, ul Smolensk 9, Krakow, 31108, Poland. TEL 48-12-4221546, FAX 48-12-4223444. Ed. Czeslawa Frejlich. Circ: 4,500. **Dist. by:** Ars Polona, Obroncow 25, Warsaw 03933, Poland. TEL 48-22-5098609, FAX 48-22-5098610, arspolona@arspolona.com.pl, http://www.arspolona.com.pl.

760 USA ISSN 2154-9192
NC998.5.A1
365; A I G A year in design. Text in English. 1980. a. USD 65. **Document type:** *Journal, Trade.*
Former titles (until 2001): Graphic Design U S A; (until 1985): A I G A Graphic Design U S A (0275-9470); (until 1980): A I G A Best Books Show; Communication Graphics; Covers; Insides
Published by: (American Institute of Graphic Arts), Watson-Guptill Publications, 770 Broadway, New York, NY 10003-9522. **Subscr. to:** 1685 Oak St, Lakewood, NJ 08701.

PRINTING—Abstracting, Bibliographies, Statistics

686.2 AUS ISSN 0811-3963
BRANDYWINE BIBLIOGRAPHY. Text in English. 1981. irreg. price varies. back issues avail.
Published by: Brandywine Press & Archive, 20 Murray Rd., Beecroft, NSW 2119, Australia. TEL (02)86-3627.

686.2 DEU
F O G R A LITERATUR DATENBANK. Text in German. a. EUR 1,240 to non-members; EUR 620 to members (effective 2005). **Document type:** *Abstract/Index.*
Media: CD-ROM.
Published by: Forschungsgesellschaft Druck e.V., Streitfeldstr 19, Munich, 81673, Germany. TEL 49-89-431820, FAX 49-89-43182100, info@fogra.org, http://www.fogra.org/. Ed. Rainer Pietzsch.

016.665 GBR ISSN 1475-0910
PRESS. Text in English. 2001. bi-m. GBP 950 (effective 2010). bk.rev. abstr.; illus. index. 120 p./no.; **Document type:** *Journal, Abstract/Index.* **Description:** Contains over 1000 of summarised articles across a wide range of topics in printing and publishing business globally.
Formed by the merger of (1946-2001): Printing Abstracts (0031-109X); (1991-2001): World Publishing Monitor (0960-653X); Which was formerly (1983-1991): Electronic Publishing Abstracts (0739-2907)
Related titles: CD-ROM ed.; Microform ed.; Online - full text ed.
—BLDSC (6611.060000), INIST. **CCC.**
Published by: IntertechPira, Cleeve Rd, Leatherhead, Surrey KT22 7RU, United Kingdom. TEL 44-1372-802000, FAX 44-1372-802238, info@pira-international.com.

016.6862 RUS ISSN 0235-2222
Z119
REFERATIVNYI ZHURNAL. IZDATEL'SKOE DELO I POLIGRAFIYA; otdel'nyi vypusk. Text in Russian. 1975. m. USD 684 foreign (effective 2011). **Document type:** *Journal, Abstract/Index.*
Formerly: Referativnyi Zhurnal. Ekonimika, Organizatsiya, Tekhnologiya i Oborudovanie Poligraficheskogo Proizvodstva (0320-5223)
Related titles: CD-ROM ed.; Online - full text ed.
—East View.
Published by: VINITI RAN, ul Usievicha 20, Moscow, 125190, Russian Federation. TEL 7-499-1526113, FAX 7-499-9430060, dir@viniti.ru, http://www.viniti.ru. **Dist. by:** Informnauka Ltd., Ul Usievicha 20, Moscow 125190, Russian Federation. alfimov@viniti.ru.

PRINTING—Computer Applications

see also COMPUTERS—Computer Graphics

COLOR BUSINESS REPORT. *see* COMPUTERS—Computer Graphics

686.2 USA ISSN 1097-4903
COMMUNICATIONS SUPPLIES WEEKLY. Text in English. 1987. w. USD 425; USD 525 foreign (effective 1999). illus.; tr.lit. 12 p./no. 6 cols./p.; back issues avail. **Document type:** *Newsletter.* **Description:** Covers the imaging supplies industries. Coverage includes consumables for electronic printers, copiers, and other imaging equipment for the office, industry and home.
Former titles: Imaging Supplies Monthly (1050-6993); Datek Imaging Supplies Monthly
Published by: CAP Ventures, 97 Libbey Industrial Pkwy., # 300, East Weymouth, MA 02189-3101. TEL 781-871-9000, FAX 781-871-3861. Ed. Cathy Martin. Pub. Scott Phiney.

DIGITAL OUTPUT. *see* PHOTOGRAPHY

686.233 GBR ISSN 1749-9186
DIGITAL PRINTER. Text in English. 2006. 8/yr. GBP 75 domestic; GBP 110 in Europe; GBP 155 elsewhere (effective 2010). **Document type:** *Magazine, Trade.* **Description:** Covers technologies and strategies including successful business models and digital applications.
Related titles: Online - full text ed.: ISSN 2044-0510. free (effective 2010).
—CCC.
Published by: Whitmar Publications Ltd., 30 London Rd, Southborough, Tunbridge Wells, Kent TN4 0RE, United Kingdom. TEL 44-1892-542099, FAX 44-1892-546693, rob.m@whitmar.co.uk. Ed. Simon Eccles TEL 44-1753-865020. Pub. Rob Mulligan.

686.2 USA ISSN 1068-1493
FLASH MAGAZINE; the business of desktop printing. Text in English. 1989. bi-m. USD 29.70; USD 4.95 newsstand/cover. adv. bk.rev. index. back issues avail. **Document type:** *Magazine, Trade.* **Description:** Contains how-to articles on desktop publishing, graphic design, book-on-demand, laser printing, inkjet printers, sublimation, transfer toners, and small business marketing.
Related titles: CD-ROM ed.; Online - full text ed.
Published by: BlackLightning Publishing, Inc., Riddle Pond Rd, West Topsham, VT 05086. TEL 802-439-6462, FAX 802-439-6463. Ed., Pub., R&P Walter Jeffries. Adv. contact Gabe Fekay. page USD 6,000; trim 5.5 x 8.5. Circ: 112,000 (paid).

GOVERNMENT PUBLISHER. *see* PUBLISHING AND BOOK TRADE—Computer Applications

I S & T ANNUAL CONFERENCE. PROCEEDINGS. *see* PHOTOGRAPHY

I S & T NON-IMPACT PRINTING PROCEEDINGS. *see* PHOTOGRAPHY

I S & T - S P I E SYMPOSIUM ON ELECTRONIC IMAGING: SCIENCE AND TECHNOLOGY. ABSTRACTS. *see* PHOTOGRAPHY

621.36705 GBR ISSN 1478-338X
IMAGE REPORTS. Text in English. 1994. m. GBP 2.20 per issue; free to qualified personnel (effective 2010). adv. back issues avail. **Document type:** *Magazine, Trade.*
Former titles (until 2002): Image Reports and Technology for Print (1465-4261); (until 1998): Image Reports and Design Technology (1363-3562)
Related titles: Online - full text ed.: free (effective 2010).
—CCC.
Published by: St. John Patrick Publishers Ltd., 6 Laurence Pountney Hill, London, EC4R 0BL, United Kingdom. TEL 44-20-79338999, FAX 44-20-79338998, info@stjohnpatrick.com, http://www.stjohnpatrick.com. Ed. Lesley Simpson TEL 44-1932-707173. Pub. John Owen TEL 44-20-79338972. Adv. contact Chris Cooke TEL 44-20-79338978.

JOURNAL OF ELECTRONIC IMAGING. *see* PHOTOGRAPHY

THE JOURNAL OF IMAGING SCIENCE AND TECHNOLOGY. *see* PHOTOGRAPHY

686.2 DEU
LARGE FORMAT; digitaler Grossbilddruck & Praesentation. Text in German. 1998. 7/yr. EUR 50 in the European Union; EUR 70 rest of Europe; EUR 85 elsewhere; EUR 7 newsstand/cover (effective 2007). adv. **Document type:** *Magazine, Trade.*
Published by: New Media Magazine Verlag GmbH, Dietlindenstr 18, Munich, 80802, Germany. TEL 49-89-36888180, FAX 49-89-36888181, newmedia@largeformat.de. Ed. Sonja Angerer. Adv. contact Hermann Will. color page EUR 4,039. Circ: 5,200 (paid and controlled).

PREPRESS; world of print. *see* PUBLISHING AND BOOK TRADE—Computer Applications

686.2 USA
PRINT MEDIA GAZETTE; a communication for imaging professionals from Kodak's Printing & Publishing Imaging Print Media Group. Text in English. 1992. bi-m.
Published by: (Professional, Printing and Publishing Imaging), Eastman Kodak Co., 343 State St, Rochester, NY 14650. TEL 716-724-4000, FAX 716-724-9624.

686.21 USA ISSN 0887-7556
PRINTOUT. Text in English. 1977. m. USD 392; USD 592 foreign (effective 1999). adv. illus. index. reprints avail. **Document type:** *Newsletter.* **Description:** Covers company, product and market developments in the computer printer and printer-related industries.
Incorporates (1981-1987): Printout Magazine (0738-6613)
Indexed: ABIPC.
Published by: CAP Ventures, 97 Libbey Industrial Pkwy., # 300, East Weymouth, MA 02189-3101. TEL 781-871-9000, FAX 781-871-3861, nancy_chaponis@capv.com, http://www.capv.com. Eds. Bob Sostillio, Fred Nevin.

686.2 CHN ISSN 1671-9921
SHUMA YINSHUA/DIGITAL PRINTING. Text in Chinese. 1995. m. CNY 5, USD 5 per issue (effective 2009). **Document type:** *Journal, Academic/Scholarly.*
Formerly (until 2002): Zhuomian Chuban yu Sheji (1006-7868)
Related titles: Online - full text ed.
Published by: Zhongguo Yinshua Kexue Jishu Yanjiusuo, 2, Cuiwei Lu, Beijing, 100036, China. TEL 86-10-88275760, FAX 86-10-88275618.

PRODUCTION OF GOODS AND SERVICES

see BUSINESS AND ECONOMICS—Production Of Goods And Services

P

PROTESTANTISM

see RELIGIONS AND THEOLOGY—Protestant

PSYCHIATRY AND NEUROLOGY

see MEDICAL SCIENCES—Psychiatry And Neurology

PSYCHOLOGY

see also MEDICAL SCIENCES—Psychiatry And Neurology

155.282 USA ISSN 1059-0005
A A H A DIALOGUE. (American Association of Handwriting Analysts) Text in English. bi-m. free to members (effective 2005). **Document type:** *Newsletter.*
Published by: American Association of Handwriting Analysts, P O Box 6201, San Jose, CA 95150. AAHAemail@juno.com, http://www.aaha-handwriting.org/. Ed. Ellen Bowers.

155 USA ISSN 1546-9581
A B A NEWSLETTER (KALAMAZOO). (Association for Behavior Analysis) Text in English. 1981. q. free to members (effective 2010). adv. bk.rev. **Document type:** *Newsletter, Trade.* **Description:** Covers association activities, news and conference announcements.
Related titles: Online - full text ed.: ISSN 1729-5297.
Indexed: E-psyche.
Published by: Association for Behavior Analysis International, 550 W Centre Ave, Ste 1, Portage, MI 49024. TEL 269-492-9310, FAX 269-492-9316, mail@abainternational.org, http://www.abainternational.org.

A B S A M E NEWSLETTER. *see* MEDICAL SCIENCES

155.4 GBR
A C A M H OCCASIONAL PAPERS. (Association for Child and Adolescent Mental Health) Text in English. 1989. irreg., latest vol.28, 2009. GBP 7.50 per issue (effective 2009). back issues avail. **Document type:** *Monographic series, Academic/Scholarly.* **Description:** Contains a series of pamphlets based on material presented at selected ACAMH study days.
Formerly (until 2004): Association for Child Psychology and Psychiatry. Occasional Papers (0956-5825)
—BLDSC (6212.040550), IE. **CCC.**
Published by: The Association for Child and Adolescent Mental Health, c/o Ingrid King, Ex. Director, St Saviour's House, 39-41 Union St, London, SE1 1SD, United Kingdom. TEL 44-20-74037458, FAX 44-20-74037081, ingrid.king@acamh.org.uk.

152.4 USA
A D A A HOT SHEET. Text in English. 19??. m. free to members (effective 2010). **Document type:** *Newsletter, Consumer.* **Description:** Contains abstracts of articles about anxiety and related disorders from clinical and scientific journals.
Media: Online - full text.
Published by: Anxiety Disorders Association of America, 8730 Georgia Ave, Ste 600, Silver Spring, MD 20910. TEL 240-485-1001, FAX 240-485-1035, http://www.adaa.org.

A E P APPOINTMENTS BROADSHEET. *see* OCCUPATIONS AND CAREERS

306.85 USA ISSN 1556-1364
RC488.5
A F T A MONOGRAPH SERIES. Text in English. 1980. s-a. USD 16 to non-members (effective 2007). adv. bk.rev. back issues avail. **Document type:** *Newsletter, Trade.* **Description:** Each issue focuses on a theme relating to the mental and physical well-being of families and children. Themes include familes in war zones, immigrant families, and lessons for family therapists in community practice.
Formerly (untl 2005): American Family Therapy Association Newsletter
Related titles: Online - full text ed.: ISSN 1556-1372.
Indexed: E-psyche.
Published by: American Family Therapy Academy, Inc., 1608 20th St NW, 4th Fl, Washington, DC 20009. TEL 202-483-8001, FAX 202-483-8002, afta@afta.org, http://www.afta.org. Ed. Betty Mac Kune-Karrer. adv.: page USD 300. Circ: 1,000.

370.15 USA ISSN 1041-956X
➤ **A H A F JOURNAL.** Text in English. 1967. bi-m. free to members (effective 2010). adv. bk.rev. charts; illus. back issues avail. **Document type:** *Journal, Academic/Scholarly.* **Description:** Covers educational material pertaining to graphology and questioned documents. Includes international graphological "hand-holding" exchange with analysts around the world.
Formerly (until 1985): A H A F News
Indexed: E-psyche.
Published by: American Handwriting Analysis Foundation, PO Box 460385, Escondido, CA 92046. TEL 800-826-7774, ahafpresident@gmail.com, http://www.ahafhandwriting.org.

158 USA
A H P PERSPECTIVE. Text in English. 1962. bi-m. USD 49 membership (effective 2005). adv. bk.rev. back issues avail. **Document type:** *Magazine, Consumer.* **Description:** Aimed at international community of people with diverse talents and interests who are dedicated to building a more humane world.
Formerly: A H P Newsletter
Related titles: Online - full text ed.
Indexed: E-psyche.
Published by: Association for Humanistic Psychology, 1516 Oak St., #320A, Alameda, CA 94501-2947. TEL 415-435-1604, FAX 415-435-2815. Ed., R&P, Adv. contact Kathleen E Erickson. page USD 850. Circ: 5,500 (paid).

A M S STUDIES IN MODERN SOCIETY; political and social issues. (Abrahams Magazine Service) *see* PUBLIC HEALTH AND SAFETY

155.4 610 USA
A N A D: WORKING TOGETHER. Text in English. 1979. q. USD 150 membership (effective 2007). bk.rev. **Document type:** *Newsletter.* **Description:** Discusses issues and challenges facing persons suffering from eating disorders and related afflictions.
Indexed: E-psyche.
Published by: National Association of Anorexia Nervosa and Associated Disorders, PO Box 7, Highland, IL 60035. TEL 847-831-3438, FAX 847-433-4632, anadl@aol.com, http://www.anad.org. Circ: 15,000.

A N R E D. (Anorexia Nervosa & Related Eating Disorders) *see* MEDICAL SCIENCES—Psychiatry And Neurology

A P; tijdschrift over agressie preventie. *see* CRIMINOLOGY AND LAW ENFORCEMENT

150 USA
A P P P A H NEWSLETTER. Text in English. 19??. q. free to members (effective 2010). back issues avail. **Document type:** *Newsletter, Consumer.* **Description:** Contains information, inspiration, and support to persons interested in the growing field of birth psychology.
Related titles: Online - full text ed.: free (effective 2010).
Published by: Association for Pre- & Perinatal Psychology and Health, PO Box 1398, Forestville, CA 95436. TEL 707-887-2838, FAX 707-887-2838, apppah@aol.com. Ed. Marcy Axness.

150 USA ISSN 1946-214X
BF78
A P PSYCHOLOGY. (Advanced Placement) Text in English. 2004. a. **Document type:** *Guide, Trade.*
Published by: Kaplan Inc. (Subsidiary of: Washington Post Co.), 888 7th Ave, New York, NY 10106. TEL 212-997-5886, 800-527-8378, http://www.kaplan.com.

150 USA ISSN 1934-6816
BF78
A P PSYCHOLOGY (HAUPPAGE). (Advanced Placement) Variant title: Barron's A P Psychology. Text in English. 2000. irreg., latest 2007, 3rd ed. USD 16.99 per issue (effective 2008). **Document type:** *Monographic series, Academic/Scholarly.* **Description:** Covers all test topics and presents three full-length practice tests that reflect the actual AP psychology exam in length, subject matter, and difficulty.
Published by: Barron's Educational Series, Inc., 250 Wireless Blvd, Hauppage, NY 11788. TEL 800-645-3476, FAX 631-434-3723, barrons@barronseduc.com.

150 USA ISSN 1050-4672
PJ4503 CODEN: HELIEK
A P S OBSERVER. Text in English. 1988. 10/yr. free to members (effective 2010). adv. illus. back issues avail.; reprints avail. **Document type:** *Magazine, Trade.* **Description:** Designed for the advancement of scientific psychology and its representation at the national and international level.
Related titles: Online - full text ed.: free (effective 2010).
Indexed: E-psyche, P30.
—CCC.
Published by: Association for Psychological Science, 1133 15th St, NW, Ste 1000, Washington, DC 20005. TEL 202-293-9300, FAX 202-293-9350, member@psychologicalscience.org. Ed. Ann Conkle. Pub. Alan G Kraut. adv.: page USD 1,700; 6.75 x 9.25.

378.19405 GBR
A U C C JOURNAL. Text in English. 1999. q. GBP 25 to non-members; GBP 8.50 per issue to non-members; free to members (effective 2009). adv. back issues avail. **Document type:** *Journal, Academic/Scholarly.*
Formerly (until 2002): Association for University and College Counselling. Newsletter and Journal (1469-9850)
Related titles: Online - full text ed.
—CCC.
Published by: Association for University and College Counselling (Subsidiary of: British Association for Counselling & Psychotherapy), BACP House, 15 St John's Business Park, Lutterworth, Leics LE17 4HB, United Kingdom. TEL 44-1455-883300, FAX 44-1455-550243. Ed. Dani Singer. Adv. contact Jeannette Hughes TEL 44-1455-883314.

301.1 150 VEN ISSN 1011-6281
A V E P S O FASCICULO. (Asociacion Venezolana de Psicologia Social) Text in Spanish. 1983. a. back issues avail. **Document type:** *Journal, Academic/Scholarly.*
Indexed: E-psyche, PsycholAb.
Published by: Asociacion Venezolana de Psicologia Social (A V E P S O), Instituto de Psicologia, Centro Comercial los Chaguaramos, Caracas, DF 1040, Venezuela. TEL 6624751; 619811-30, Ext. 2643, 3043. Ed. Beatriz Rodriguez.

ABHIGYAN. *see* SOCIAL SCIENCES: COMPREHENSIVE WORKS

616.89 USA ISSN 1554-2238
ABNORMAL PSYCHOLOGY. Text in English. 2006. irreg., latest 2009. price varies. back issues avail. **Document type:** *Monographic series, Academic/Scholarly.*
Published by: Praeger Publishers (Subsidiary of: Greenwood Publishing Group Inc.), 88 Post Rd W, Westport, CT 06881. TEL 800-368-6868, tech.support@greenwood.com, http://www.greenwood.com. Ed. Thomas Plante.

150 USA ISSN 0192-1088
RC500
➤ **ACADEMY FORUM.** Text in English. 1956. s-a. USD 20 (effective 2010). adv. bk.rev. **Document type:** *Journal, Academic/Scholarly.* **Description:** Provides an opportunity for members to present their views on issues pertaining to practice, social conflict and change, literary criticism, the arts, and the state of the world.
Former titles (until 1978): Academy (0197-5781); (until 1970): American Academy of Psychoanalysis. Newsletter
Related titles: Online - full text ed.: free (effective 2010).
Indexed: E-psyche, MLA-IB.
Published by: American Academy of Psychoanalysis and Dynamic Psychiatry, One Regency Dr, PO Box 30, Bloomfield, CT 06002. TEL 888-691-8281, FAX 860-286-0787, Info@AAPDP.org. Ed. Gerald P Perman.

150.195 ARG ISSN 0329-9147
BF175.4.C84
ACHERONTA; revista de psicoanalisis y cultura. Text in Spanish. 1995. irreg. adv. bk.rev. **Description:** Includes articles on psychology and psychoanalisis, including Freud theory.
Media: Online - full text. **Related titles:** Print ed.: ISSN 0329-8191. 1995.
Address: Coronel Diaz 1785 - 1C, Buenos Aires, 1425, Argentina. http://www.psiconet.com/acheronta/. Ed. Michel Sauval.

150 COL ISSN 0123-9155
BF5
ACTA COLOMBIANA DE PSICOLOGIA. Text in Spanish, Portuguese. 1983. s-a. CLP 15,000 domestic; USD 15 foreign (effective 2010). **Document type:** *Journal, Academic/Scholarly.*
Related titles: Online - full text ed.: ISSN 1909-9711. 2007. free (effective 2011) (from SciELO).
Indexed: C01, P03, PsycInfo, SCOPUS.
Published by: Universidad Catolica de Colombia, Calle 47 No 13-32 1er Piso, Bogota, 29832, Colombia. ediciones@ucatolic.edu.co, http://www.ucatolic.edu.co. Ed. Ernesto Ravelo Contreras.

158 MEX ISSN 0188-8145
BF636.A1 CODEN: ACMPEN
ACTA COMPORTAMENTALIA. Text in Spanish. 1993. s-a.
Indexed: C01, F04, L&LBA, P03, PsycInfo, PsycholAb, SCOPUS, SociolAb, T02.
Published by: (Universidad de Guadalajara, Centro de Estudios e Investigaciones en Comportamiento), Universidad de Guadalajara, Apartado Postal 1-2130, Guadalajara, JALISCO 44600, Mexico. TEL 52-33-36164399, FAX 52-322- 2232982, http://www.cepe.udg.mx/.

ACTA ETHOLOGICA. *see* BIOLOGY—Zoology

ACTA ETHOLOGICA ONLINE. *see* BIOLOGY

ACTA MEDICA ROMANA. *see* MEDICAL SCIENCES

150 NLD ISSN 0001-6918
CODEN: APSOAZ
➤ **ACTA PSYCHOLOGICA.** Text in English. 1941. 9/yr. EUR 1,185 in Europe to institutions; JPY 157,200 in Japan to institutions; USD 1,323 elsewhere to institutions (effective 2012). adv. bk.rev. bibl.; illus. Index. back issues avail.; reprints avail. **Document type:** *Journal, Academic/Scholarly.* **Description:** Publishes original papers reporting on experimental studies, as well as theoretical and review articles, in human experimental psychology.
Related titles: Microform ed.: (from PQC); Online - full text ed.: ISSN 1873-6297 (from IngentaConnect, ScienceDirect).
Indexed: A01, A03, A08, A20, A22, A26, A28, APA, ASCA, B21, BibInd, BrCerAb, C&ISA, CA, CA/WCA, CIA, CIS, CerAb, CivEngAb, CorrAb, CurCont, E&CAJ, E-psyche, E11, EEA, EMA, EMBASE, ESPM, EnvEAb, ErgAb, ExcerpMed, FR, H15, I05, IndMed, L&LBA, M&TEA, M09, MBF, MEA&I, MEDLINE, METADEX, MLA-IB, NSA, P03, P30, PCI, PsycInfo, PsycholAb, R10, RASB, Reac, S02, S03, SCOPUS, SOPODA, SSCI, SociolAb, SolStAb, T02, T04, W07, WAA.
—BLDSC (0661.490000), IE, Infotrieve, Ingenta, INIST. **CCC.**
Published by: Elsevier BV (Subsidiary of: Elsevier Science & Technology), Radarweg 29, PO Box 211, Amsterdam, 1000 AE, Netherlands. TEL 31-20-4853911, FAX 31-20-4852457, JournalsCustomerServiceEMEA@elsevier.com. Eds. B Hommel, J Wagemans, R J Hartsuiker.

152 FIN ISSN 0515-3115
ACTA PSYCHOLOGICA FENNICA. Text in Finnish. 1951. irreg. (1-2/yr.). price varies. **Document type:** *Monographic series, Academic/Scholarly.*
Related titles: ◆ Series: Soveltavan Psykologian Monografioita. ISSN 0783-408X.
Indexed: E-psyche.
—INIST.
Published by: Suomen Psykologinen Seura/Finnish Psychological Society, Liisankatu 16 A, Helsinki, 00170, Finland. TEL 358-9-2782122, FAX 358-9-2781300, psykologia@genealogia.fi. Ed. Marja Vauras. Circ: 700.

150 POL ISSN 1427-969X
BF8.P6
ACTA UNIVERSITATIS LODZIENSIS: FOLIA PSYCHOLOGICA. Text in German, Polish; Summaries in English, German. 1955-1974; N.S. 1980; N.S. 1995. irreg., latest vol.14, 2010. price varies. charts. **Document type:** *Monographic series, Academic/Scholarly.* **Description:** Contains articles from the fields of psychology, as well as proceeding of scientific conferences organized by Department of Pedagogics and Psychology in the University of Lodz.
Supersedes in part (in 1995): Acta Universitatis Lodziensis: Folia Padagogica et Psychologica (0208-6093); Which superseded in part: Uniwersytet Lodzki. Zeszyty Naukowe. Seria 1: Nauki Humanistyczno-Spoleczne (0076-0358)
Indexed: E-psyche.
Published by: (Uniwersytet Lodzki, Wydzial Nauk o Wychowaniu), Wydawnictwo Uniwersytetu Lodzkiego/Lodz University Press, ul Lindleya 8, Lodz, 90-131, Poland. TEL 48-42-6655861, FAX 48-42-6655861, wdwul@uni.lodz.pl, http://www.wydawnictwo.uni.lodz.pl.

ACTA UNIVERSITATIS PALACKIANAE OLOMUCENSIS. GYMNICA. *see* MEDICAL SCIENCES

150 POL ISSN 0137-110X
BF8.P6
ACTA UNIVERSITATIS WRATISLAVIENSIS. PRACE PSYCHOLOGICZNE. Text in Polish. 1972. irreg., latest vol.58, 2006. price varies. **Document type:** *Monographic series, Academic/Scholarly.*
Indexed: E-psyche, RASB.
Published by: (Uniwersytet Wroclawski), Wydawnictwo Uniwersytetu Wroclawskiego Sp. z o.o., pl Uniwersytecki 15, Wroclaw, 50137, Poland. TEL 48-71-3752809, FAX 48-71-3752735, marketing@wuwr.com.pl, http://www.wuwr.com.pl. Ed. Maria Stras Romanowska. Circ: 300.

150 301 FRA ISSN 1765-2723
TA166
ACTIVITES. Text in French, English. 2004. s-a. free (effective 2011). **Document type:** *Journal, Academic/Scholarly.*
Media: Online - full text.
Indexed: P03, PsycInfo.
Published by: Association Recherche et Pratique sur les Activites http://www.activites.org.

▼ **ACTUALIDAD CIENTIFICA - DIAGNOSTICO Y TRATAMIENTO DE LAS ALTERACIONES DEL DESARROLLO.** *see* CHILDREN AND YOUTH—For

150 CRI ISSN 0258-6444
➤ **ACTUALIDADES EN PSICOLOGIA.** Text in Spanish. 1985. a. **Document type:** *Journal, Academic/Scholarly.* **Description:** Contains research on scientific and academic psychology from Costa Rica, Central America and Latin America.

Related titles: Online - full text ed.: free (effective 2011).
Indexed: C01.
—INIST.
Published by: Universidad de Costa Rica, Instituto de Investigaciones Psicologicas, Ciudad Universitaria Rodrigo Facio, San Pedro de Montes de Oca, San Jose, 2060, Costa Rica. TEL 506-207-5567, FAX 506-207-5636, actuapsi@cariari.ucr.ac.cr, http://www.iip.ucr.ac.cr. Ed. N J Tapia Valladares.

150.19 FRA ISSN 1272-1573
ACTUALITE DE LA PSYCHANALYSE. Text in French. 1996. irreg. price varies. back issues avail. **Document type:** *Monographic series, Consumer.*
Published by: Editions Eres, 33 Av. Marcel Dassault, Toulouse, 31500, France. TEL 33-5-61751576, FAX 33-5-61735289, eres@edition-eres.com.

ADLI PSIKIYATRI DERGISI/JOURNAL OF FORENSIC PSYCHIATRY. *see* MEDICAL SCIENCES—Forensic Sciences

ADOLESCENT PSYCHIATRY. *see* MEDICAL SCIENCES—Psychiatry And Neurology

150 ITA ISSN 1828-7654
ADOLESCENZA E PSICOANALISI (PRINT). Abbreviated title: A e P. Text in Italian. 2001-2004; resumed 2006. s-a. **Document type:** *Journal, Academic/Scholarly.*
Formerly (until 2004): Adolescenza e Psicoanalisi (Online) (1592-6001)
Published by: Associazione Romana per la Psicoterapia dell'Adolescenza, Via Ombrone 14, Rome, 00198, Italy. arpad.nov@tiscali.it arpad.nov@tiscali.it, http://www.psychomedia.it/arpad/. Ed. Gianluigi Monniello.

155.4 USA ISSN 1524-6817
BF724.5
ADULTSPAN JOURNAL; development through young, middle, and older adulthood. Text in English. 1999. s-a. GBP 43 in United Kingdom to institutions; EUR 49 in Europe to institutions; USD 60 elsewhere to institutions; GBP 50 combined subscription in United Kingdom to institutions (print & online eds.); EUR 57 combined subscription in Europe to institutions (print & online eds.); USD 69 combined subscription elsewhere to institutions (print & online eds.) (effective 2012). adv. abstr.; bibl. 64 p./no.; back issues avail.; reprint service avail. from PSC. **Document type:** *Journal, Academic/Scholarly.*
Description: Covers development through youth, middle age, and older adulthood.
Related titles: Microfilm ed.; Online - full text ed.: ISSN 2161-0029. GBP 43 in United Kingdom to institutions; EUR 49 in Europe to institutions; USD 60 elsewhere to institutions (effective 2012).
Indexed: A01, A03, A08, A26, ASG, CA, E03, E07, E08, ERI, G08, I05, P25, P27, P43, P48, P50, P54, PQC, S09, SCOPUS, T02.
—CCC.
Published by: (Association for Adult Development and Ageing), American Counseling Association, 5999 Stevenson Ave, Alexandria, VA 22304. TEL 800-347-6647, FAX 703-823-0252, 800-473-2329, http://www.counseling.org. Ed. Catherine B Roland TEL 973-655-7216. Adv. contact Kathy Maguire TEL 703-823-9800 ext 207.

305.9089 153.9 USA ISSN 1042-2021
BF412
ADVANCED DEVELOPMENT. Text in English. 1989. a. price varies. **Document type:** *Journal, Academic/Scholarly.* **Description:** Covers the study of giftedness, advanced development, and undeveloped potential in women.
Indexed: E03, P25, P27, P48, P54, PQC, PsycholAb, T02.
Published by: Institute for the Study of Advanced Development, c/o Gifted Development Center, 1452 Marion St, Denver, CO 80218. TEL 303-837-8378, FAX 303-831-7465.

150 USA ISSN 1086-7015
ADVANCED PSYCHOLOGY TEXTS. Abbreviated title: A P T. Text in English. 199?. irreg., latest vol.4, 2002. price varies. adv. back issues avail.; reprints avail. **Document type:** *Monographic series, Academic/Scholarly.*
Indexed: E-psyche.
—BLDSC (0696.923000). **CCC.**
Published by: Sage Publications, Inc., Books (Subsidiary of: Sage Publications, Inc.), 2455 Teller Rd, Thousand Oaks, CA 91320. TEL 800-818-7243, FAX 800-583-2665, books.claim@sagepub.com.

150 510 SGP ISSN 1793-107X
ADVANCED SERIES ON MATHEMATICAL PSYCHOLOGY. Text in English. 2004. irreg., latest vol.2, 2007. price varies. back issues avail. **Document type:** *Monographic series, Academic/Scholarly.*
Published by: World Scientific Publishing Co. Pte. Ltd., 5 Toh Tuck Link, Singapore, 596224, Singapore. TEL 65-6466-5775, FAX 65-6467-7667, wspc@wspc.com.sg, http://www.worldscientific.com. Eds. E N Dzhafarov, H Colonius. **Dist. by:** World Scientific Publishing Co., Inc., 27 Warren St, Ste 401-402, Hackensack, NJ 07601. TEL 201-487-9655, 800-227-7562, FAX 201-487-9656, 888-977-2665, wspc@wspc.com; World Scientific Publishing Ltd., 57 Shelton St, London WC2H 9HE, United Kingdom. TEL 44-207-8360888, FAX 44-207-8362020, sales@wspc.co.uk.

ADVANCES IN ACCOUNTING BEHAVIORAL RESEARCH. *see* BUSINESS AND ECONOMICS—Accounting

155 USA
BF712
ADVANCES IN APPLIED DEVELOPMENTAL PSYCHOLOGY. Text in English. 1985. irreg. price varies. **Document type:** *Monographic series, Academic/Scholarly.* **Description:** Presents the behavioral and social science communities discussions of current issues facing professionals engaged in the application of behavioral knowledge to the real-life arenas in which they are engaged.
Former titles (until 1993): Annual Advances in Applied Developmental Psychology (1042-2463); (until 1987): Advances in Applied Developmental Psychology (0748-8572)
Indexed: E-psyche, PsycholAb.
—BLDSC (0698.940000). **CCC.**
Published by: Ablex Publishing Corporation (Subsidiary of: Greenwood Publishing Group Inc.), 88 Post Rd W, Westport, CT 06881. TEL 203-226-3571, customer-service@greenwood.com. Ed. Irving Siegel.

155.591 USA ISSN 0099-6246
QP351 CODEN: ADBBBW
➤ **ADVANCES IN BEHAVIORAL BIOLOGY.** Text in English. 1971. irreg., latest vol.58, 2009. price varies. back issues avail. **Document type:** *Monographic series, Academic/Scholarly.*
Indexed: A22, CIN, ChemAb, ChemTitl, E-psyche, P30.
—BLDSC (0699.910000), CASDDS, GNLM, IE, Infotrieve, Ingenta, INIST. **CCC.**
Published by: Springer New York LLC (Subsidiary of: Springer Science+Business Media), 233 Spring St, New York, NY 10013. TEL 212-460-1500, FAX 212-460-1575, service-ny@springer.com.

155 618.92 USA ISSN 0065-2407
BF721 CODEN: ADCDA8
➤ **ADVANCES IN CHILD DEVELOPMENT AND BEHAVIOR.** Text in English. 1963. irreg., latest vol.37, 2009. USD 104 per vol. (effective 2010). adv. index. back issues avail.; reprints avail. **Document type:** *Monographic series, Academic/Scholarly.* **Description:** Aims to ease the task faced by researchers, instructors, and students. Provides scholarly technical articles with reviews, advances in research, and theoretical viewpoints.
Related titles: Online - full text ed.
Indexed: A22, ASCA, B21, BIOSIS Prev, C06, C07, CA, E-psyche, EMBASE, ExcerpMed, IndMed, MEDLINE, MycolAb, NSA, P30, PCI, R10, Reac, SCOPUS, SSCI, T02, W07.
—BLDSC (0703.800000), GNLM, IE, Ingenta, INIST. **CCC.**
Published by: Academic Press (Subsidiary of: Elsevier Science & Technology), 3251 Riverport Ln, Maryland Heights, MO 63043. TEL 314-447-8010, FAX 314-447-8030, JournalCustomerService-usa@elsevier.com, http://www.elsevierdirect.com/imprint.jsp?iid=5. Ed. Patricia Bauer. Adv. contact Tino DeCarlo TEL 212-633-3815.

150 POL ISSN 1895-1171
ADVANCES IN COGNITIVE PSYCHOLOGY. Text in English. 2005. q. free (effective 2011). **Document type:** *Journal, Academic/Scholarly.* **Description:** Devoted to the scientific study of the human mind. Focuses on behavioral, cognitive, and brain studies. Publishes empirical studies, theoretical papers, and critical reviews.
Media: Online - full content.
Indexed: A01, CA, P03, P30, PsycInfo, SCOPUS, T02.
—Linda Hall.
Published by: (Wyzsza Szkola Finansow i Zarzadzania w Warszawie/University of Finance and Management in Warsaw), Vizja Press & IT Ltd., Dzielna 60, Warsaw, 01029, Poland. TEL 48-22-5365453, FAX 48-22-5365468, kozlowski@vizja.pl, http://www.vizja.net.pl. Ed. Piotr Jaskowski.

152 NLD ISSN 1381-589X
BF311
➤ **ADVANCES IN CONSCIOUSNESS RESEARCH.** Text in English. 1995. irreg., latest vol.83, 2011. price varies. back issues avail. **Document type:** *Monographic series, Academic/Scholarly.* **Description:** Provides a forum for scholars from various scientific disciplines and fields of knowledge relating to all aspects of consciousness, including cognitive psychology, linguistics, brain science, and philosophy.
Indexed: E-psyche.
—BLDSC (0704.135000), IE, Ingenta.
Published by: John Benjamins Publishing Co., PO Box 36224, Amsterdam, 1020 ME, Netherlands. TEL 31-20-6304747, FAX 31-20-6739773, customer.services@benjamins.nl. Ed. Maxim I Stamenov. **Dist. in N. America by:** John Benjamins North America Inc., PO Box 960, Herndon, VA 20172-0960. TEL 800-562-5666, FAX 703-661-1501, benjamins@presswarehouse.com.

150 USA ISSN 2155-2622
▼ **ADVANCES IN CULTURE & PSYCHOLOGY.** Text in English. 2010. a. USD 110 per issue (effective 2011). **Document type:** *Journal, Academic/Scholarly.*
Published by: Oxford University Press (Subsidiary of: Oxford University Press), 2001 Evans Rd, Cary, NC 27513. TEL 800-445-9714, FAX 919-677-1303, custserv.us@oup.com. Eds. Chi-yue Chiu, Michele J Gelfand, Ying-yi Hong.

ADVANCES IN EXPERIMENTAL SOCIAL PSYCHOLOGY. *see* SOCIOLOGY

332.1 NLD ISSN 0921-2647
TA166
➤ **ADVANCES IN HUMAN FACTORS - ERGONOMICS.** Text in English. 1984. irreg., latest 1997, vol 21 A&B. price varies. **Document type:** *Monographic series, Academic/Scholarly.* **Description:** Reports on research and development in the specialty field of ergonomics.
Related titles: Online - full text ed.: ISSN 2212-1226.
Indexed: A22, E-psyche, Z02.
—INIST. **CCC.**
Published by: Elsevier BV, North-Holland (Subsidiary of: Elsevier Science & Technology), Sara Burgerhartstraat 25, Amsterdam, 1055 KV, Netherlands. TEL 31-20-4853911, FAX 31-20-4852457, JournalsCustomerServiceEMEA@elsevier.com, http://www.elsevier.com. Ed. Gavriel Salvandy. **Subscr. to:** Elsevier BV, Radarweg 29, PO Box 211, Amsterdam 1000 AE, Netherlands. TEL 31-20-4853757, FAX 31-20-4853432.

150 GBR ISSN 1479-3601
ADVANCES IN HUMAN PERFORMANCE AND COGNITIVE ENGINEERING RESEARCH. Text in English. 2001. irreg., latest vol.7, 2006. price varies. back issues avail. **Document type:** *Monographic series, Academic/Scholarly.* **Description:** Serves as a forum where scientists and practitioners can engage in a dialogue to review, discuss, analyze and debate, the vast number of human performance issues that arise when individuals and groups interact with each other.
Related titles: Online - full text ed.
Indexed: SCOPUS.
—BLDSC (0709.076500), IE, Ingenta. **CCC.**
Published by: Emerald Group Publishing Ltd., Howard House, Wagon Ln, Bingley, W Yorks BD16 1WA, United Kingdom. TEL 44-1274-777700, FAX 44-1274-785201, emerald@emeraldinsight.com. Ed. Eduardo Salas. **Dist. by:** Turpin Distribution Services Ltd., Pegasus Dr, Stratton Business Park, Biggleswade, Bedfordshire SG18 8QB, United Kingdom. TEL 44-1767-604951, FAX 44-1767-601640, custserv@turpin-distribution.com, http://www.turpin-distribution.com/.

ADVANCES IN LEARNING AND BEHAVIORAL DISABILITIES. *see* EDUCATION—Special Education And Rehabilitation

614.58 GBR ISSN 0749-7423
BF501
ADVANCES IN MOTIVATION AND ACHIEVEMENT. Text in English. 1984. irreg., latest vol.16, 2010. price varies. back issues avail. **Document type:** *Monographic series, Academic/Scholarly.* **Description:** Reflects current research and theory concerned with motivation and achievement in work, school, and play.
Related titles: Online - full text ed.
Indexed: E-psyche.
—BLDSC (0709.453000), Ingenta. **CCC.**
Published by: Emerald Group Publishing Ltd., Howard House, Wagon Ln, Bingley, W Yorks BD16 1WA, United Kingdom. TEL 44-1274-777700, FAX 44-1274-785201, emerald@emeraldinsight.com, http://www.emeraldinsight.com. **Dist. by:** Turpin Distribution Services Ltd., Pegasus Dr, Stratton Business Park, Biggleswade, Bedfordshire SG18 8QB, United Kingdom. TEL 44-1767-604951, FAX 44-1767-601640, custserv@turpin-distribution.com, http://www.turpin-distribution.com/.

150 NLD ISSN 0166-4115
CODEN: ADPSEK
➤ **ADVANCES IN PSYCHOLOGY.** Text in English. 1980. irreg., latest vol.139, 2008. price varies. **Document type:** *Monographic series, Academic/Scholarly.* **Description:** Reports on developments and research in clinical and applied psychology.
Related titles: Online - full text ed.
Indexed: A22, E-psyche, FR, SCOPUS.
—BLDSC (0711.065000), IE, Ingenta, INIST. **CCC.**
Published by: Elsevier BV (Subsidiary of: Elsevier Science & Technology), Radarweg 29, PO Box 211, Amsterdam, 1000 AE, Netherlands. TEL 31-20-4853911, FAX 31-20-4852457, JournalsCustomerServiceEMEA@elsevier.com, http://www.elsevier.com. Ed. George Steimach. **Subscr. to:** Radarweg 29, PO Box 211, Amsterdam 1000 AE, Netherlands. TEL 31-20-4853757, FAX 31-20-4853432.

616.89 USA
ADVANCES IN PSYCHOTHERAPY - EVIDENCE-BASED PRACTICE. Text in English. 2005. irreg., latest vol.22, 2010. price varies. **Document type:** *Monographic series, Academic/Scholarly.* **Description:** Contains articles and research on advances in psychotherapy.
Published by: Hogrefe Publishing Corp., 875 Massachusetts Ave, 7th Fl, Cambridge, MA 02139. TEL 866-823-4726, FAX 617-354-6875, customerservices@hogrefe-publishing.com. Ed. Danny Wedding.

ADVANCES IN SCHOOL MENTAL HEALTH PROMOTION. *see* EDUCATION

155.937 362 USA ISSN 0196-1934
BD444
ADVANCES IN THANATOLOGY. Text in English. 1971. q. USD 40 to individuals; USD 80 to institutions (effective 2011). adv. back issues avail. **Document type:** *Journal, Academic/Scholarly.* **Description:** Articles cover life threatening disease, dying, death, bereavement, hospice care, and widowhood.
Formerly (until 1977): Journal of Thanatology (0047-2832)
Related titles: Microform ed.: (from PQC).
Indexed: A22, E-psyche, H09, IBR, IBZ, MLA-IB, P30, S05.
—BLDSC (0711.605000), GNLM, IE.
Published by: Center for Thanatology Research and Education, Inc., 391 Atlantic Ave, Brooklyn, NY 11217. TEL 718-858-3026, FAX 718-852-1846, thanatology@pipeline.com. Ed. Dr. Austin H Kutscher.

150 USA ISSN 0065-3454
QL750 CODEN: ADSBBF
➤ **ADVANCES IN THE STUDY OF BEHAVIOR.** Text in English. 1965. irreg., latest vol.40, 2009. USD 140 per vol. (effective 2010). adv. index. back issues avail.; reprints avail. **Document type:** *Monographic series, Academic/Scholarly.* **Description:** For scientists engaged in the study of animal behavior, including psychologists, neuroscientists, biologists, ethologists, pharmacologists, endocrinologists, ecologists, and geneticists.
Related titles: Online - full text ed.
Indexed: A20, A22, ASCA, Agr, B21, BIOSIS Prev, E-psyche, GeoRef, IBR, IBZ, ISR, MycolAb, NSA, PCI, SCI, SCOPUS, W07, Z01.
—BLDSC (0711.590000), CASDDS, IE, Infotrieve, Ingenta, INIST. **CCC.**
Published by: Academic Press (Subsidiary of: Elsevier Science & Technology), 3251 Riverport Ln, Maryland Heights, MO 63043. TEL 314-447-8010, FAX 314-447-8030, JournalCustomerService-usa@elsevier.com, http://www.elsevierdirect.com/imprint.jsp?iid=5.

616.89 USA ISSN 1552-6208
THE ADVOCATE (ALEXANDRIA). Text in English. 1976. m. free to members (effective 2010). adv. video rev.; bk.rev. abstr. back issues avail. **Document type:** *Newsletter, Trade.* **Description:** Provides practice advances and research highlights, association and chapter news, legislative bulletins and licensure updates.
Related titles: Online - full text ed.
Indexed: A10, A26, E-psyche, E08, I05, S09, V03.
Published by: American Mental Health Counselors Association, 801 N Fairfax St, Ste 304, Alexandria, VA 22314. TEL 703-548-6002, 800-326-2642, FAX 703-548-4775. Ed., Adv. contact Kathleen McCarthy TEL 540-371-7193. Circ: 6,000.

ADVOCATE (BETHESDA). *see* EDUCATION—Special Education And Rehabilitation

616.89 DEU ISSN 1862-4715
➤ **AERZTLICHE PSYCHOTHERAPIE**; und psychosomatische Medizin. Text in German. 2006. 4/yr. EUR 98 to individuals; EUR 136 to institutions; EUR 49 to students; EUR 34 newsstand/cover (effective 2011). adv. **Document type:** *Journal, Academic/Scholarly.*
Published by: Schattauer GmbH, Hoelderlinstr 3, Stuttgart, 70174, Germany. TEL 49-711-229870, FAX 49-711-2298750, info@schattauer.de, http://www.schattauer.com. Ed. Dr. Jan Hueber. Adv. contact Klaus Jansch. B&W page EUR 1,695, color page EUR 2,790; trim 174 x 242. Circ: 2,600 (paid and controlled).

150 COL ISSN 0123-8884
AFFECTIO SOCIETATIS. Text in Spanish. 1998. q. free (effective 2011); free. **Document type:** *Journal, Academic/Scholarly.*
Media: Online - full text.
Published by: Universidad de Antioquia, Departamento de Psicoanalisis, Apartado 1226, Medellin, Colombia. TEL 57-4-210-5770, affectio@antares.udea.edu.co/~affectio. Ed. Diana Patricia Carmona.

P

150 301 NGA
AFRICAN JOURNAL FOR THE PSYCHOLOGICAL STUDY OF SOCIAL ISSUES. Text in English. 1994. s-a. USD 8 domestic; USD 12 foreign (effective 2007). **Document type:** *Journal, Academic/Scholarly.* **Description:** Dedicated to the scientific investigation of psychological and social issues and related phenomenon in Africa.
Related titles: Online - full content ed.
Published by: African Society for the Psychological Study of Social Issues, c/o Prof S.K. Balogun, Editor, Dept of Psychology, University of Ibadan, Ibadan, Nigeria. TEL 234-803-3322424, Shyngle61@yahoo.com. Ed. S K Balogun.

150 796 NGA ISSN 1119-7056
➤ **AFRICAN JOURNAL OF CROSS-CULTURAL PSYCHOLOGY AND SPORT FACILITATION.** Text in English. 1999. a. NGN 5,000 domestic; USD 150 foreign (effective 2007). **Document type:** *Journal, Academic/Scholarly.* **Description:** Publishes empirical studies and theoretical propositions as well as case studies that are community-based and inter/intra-cultural on human behaviour, relationship in the family, workplace, schools and organisations.
Published by: Association of Psychology in Sport and Human Behaviour, c/o Dr Jonathan O Osiki, Editor, University of Ibadan, Ibadan, Nigeria. jonathanosiki@yahoo.co.uk. Ed. Jonathan O Osiki.

➤ **AFTERLOSS**; the monthly newsletter to comfort and care for those who mourn. *see* MEDICAL SCIENCES—Psychiatry And Neurology

150 500 USA ISSN 1741-0754
AGAINST ALL REASON; propaganda, politics, power. Text in English. 2003. irreg., latest vol.3, 2005, Mar. back issues avail. **Document type:** *Journal, Academic/Scholarly.*
Media: Online - full text.
Published by: Human Nature http://human-nature.com/.

616.89 GBR ISSN 1359-1789
RC569.5.A34 CODEN: AVBEFZ
➤ **AGGRESSION AND VIOLENT BEHAVIOR.** Text in English. 1996. 6/yr. EUR 684 in Europe to institutions; JPY 90,900 in Japan to institutions; USD 767 elsewhere to institutions (effective 2012). adv. back issues avail. **Document type:** *Journal, Academic/Scholarly.* **Description:** Provides a multidisciplinary forum for publication of review articles and summary reports of innovative and ongoing clinical research programs relating to the field of aggression and violent behavior.
Related titles: Online - full text ed.: ISSN 1873-6335 (from IngentaConnect, ScienceDirect).
Indexed: A01, A03, A08, A20, A22, A26, ASSIA, AddicA, B21, C06, C07, CA, CJA, CJPI, CurCont, E-psyche, EMBASE, ESPM, ExcerpMed, F09, FR, FamI, H&SSA, H12, I05, IBSS, IPsyAb, NSA, P03, P30, PQC, PsycInfo, PsycholAb, RiskAb, S02, S03, S21, SCOPUS, SSCI, SociolAb, T02, V&AA, W07.
—BLDSC (0736.284200), IE, Infotrieve, Ingenta, INIST. **CCC.**
Published by: Pergamon (Subsidiary of: Elsevier Science & Technology), The Blvd, Langford Ln, East Park, Kidlington, Oxford OX5 1GB, United Kingdom. TEL 44-1865-843000, FAX 44-1865-843010, JournalsCustomerServiceEMEA@elsevier.com. Ed. Cathy Cumberlidge. **Subscr. to:** Elsevier BV, Radarweg 29, PO Box 211, Amsterdam 1000 AE, Netherlands. http://www.elsevier.nl.

350 USA ISSN 0096-140X
BF575.A3 CODEN: AGBEDU
➤ **AGGRESSIVE BEHAVIOR.** Text in English. 1975. bi-m. GBP 1,631 in United Kingdom to institutions; EUR 2,062 in Europe to institutions; USD 3,070 in United States to institutions; USD 3,154 in Canada & Mexico to institutions; USD 3,196 elsewhere to institutions; GBP 1,877 combined subscription in United Kingdom to institutions (print & online eds.); EUR 2,372 combined subscription in Europe to institutions (print & online eds.); USD 3,531 combined subscription in United States to institutions (print & online eds.); USD 3,615 combined subscription in Canada & Mexico to institutions (print & online eds.); USD 3,657 combined subscription elsewhere to institutions (print & online eds.) (effective 2012). adv. bk.rev. bibl.; charts; illus.; abstr. index. back issues avail.; reprint service avail. from PSC. **Document type:** *Journal, Academic/Scholarly.* **Description:** Features articles devoted to the empirical and theoretical analysis of conflict and the scientific understanding of aggression in humans and animals.
Related titles: Microform ed.: (from PQC); Online - full text ed.: ISSN 1098-2337. 1996. GBP 1,567 in United Kingdom to institutions; EUR 1,981 in Europe to institutions; USD 3,070 elsewhere to institutions (effective 2012).
Indexed: A01, A03, A08, A20, A22, A25, A26, A36, AMHA, ASCA, ASSIA, AnBeAb, B21, B25, BIOSIS Prev, BibInd, C06, C07, C28, CA, CABA, CIN, CJA, ChemAb, ChemTitl, CurCont, E-psyche, E08, EMBASE, ESPM, ExcerpMed, FR, FamI, G08, GH, I05, ISR, Inpharma, L&LBA, LT, M06, MEA&I, MEDLINE, MycolAb, N02, N03, NSA, P03, P30, P43, PEI, PRA, PsycInfo, PsycholAb, R12, RRTA, RefZh, RiskAb, S02, S03, S08, S09, SCI, SCOPUS, SSCI, T02, T05, TAR, VITIS, W07, W08, W11, WildRev, Z01.
—BLDSC (0736.285000), CASDDS, GNLM, IE, Infotrieve, Ingenta, INIST. **CCC.**
Published by: (International Society for Research on Agression), John Wiley & Sons, Inc., 111 River St, Hoboken, NJ 07030. TEL 201-748-6000, FAX 201-748-6088, info@wiley.com, http://www.wiley.com/WileyCDA/. Ed. L Rowell Huesmann. Pub., Adv. contact Kim Thompkins TEL 212-850-6921. B&W page USD 772, color page USD 1,009; trim 6.875 x 10. **Subscr. outside the Americas to:** John Wiley & Sons Ltd., The Atrium, Southern Gate, Chichester, West Sussex PO19 8SQ, United Kingdom. TEL 44-1243-779777, 800-243407, FAX 44-1243-775878, cs-journals@wiley.com.

➤ **AGING & MENTAL HEALTH.** *see* GERONTOLOGY AND GERIATRICS

➤ **AGORA**; revista trimestriala de psihopedagogie si asistenta sociala. *see* EDUCATION

158 616.8 BRA ISSN 1516-1498
➤ **AGORA (RIO DE JANEIRO)**; estudos em teoria psicanalitica. Text in Portuguese, Spanish. 1998. bi-m. BRL 30 domestic to individuals; USD 40 foreign to individuals; BRL 40 domestic to institutions; USD 60 foreign to institutions (effective 2005). back issues avail. **Document type:** *Journal, Academic/Scholarly.* **Description:** A discussion forum for research about the themes and most relevant problems of contemporary psychoanalysis.
Related titles: Online - full text ed.: free (effective 2011).
Indexed: P03, PsycInfo, PsycholAb, SCOPUS.
Published by: Universidade Federal do Rio de Janeiro, Programa de Pos-Graduacao em Teoria Psicanalitica, Instituto de Psicologia, Campus Praia Vermelha, Av. Pasteur 250 Fundos, Rio de Janeiro, RJ 22290-240, Brazil. TEL 55-21-38735343, http://www.psicologia.ufrj.br/teoriapsicanalitica/. Ed. Joel Birman. **Subscr. to:** Contra Capa Libraria Limitada, Rua Dias Ferreira, 214, Rio de Janeiro 22431-050, Brazil. TEL 55-21-25114082, FAX 55-21-25114764, ccapa@easynet.com.br, http://www.contracapa.com.br.

➤ **AIDS & BEHAVIOR.** *see* MEDICAL SCIENCES—Allergology And Immunology

➤ **AIDS PREVENTION AND MENTAL HEALTH.** *see* MEDICAL SCIENCES—Communicable Diseases

➤ **AIIKU TSUSHIN/LETTERS OF HUMAN GROWTH.** *see* EDUCATION

150 FRA ISSN 1778-4972
L'AILLEURS DU CORPS. Text in French. 2005. irreg. back issues avail. **Document type:** *Monographic series, Consumer.*
Published by: Editions Eres, 33 Av. Marcel Dassault, Toulouse, 31500, France. TEL 33-5-61751576, FAX 33-5-61735289, eres@edition-eres.com.

AIN SHAMS UNIVERSITY. FACULTY OF EDUCATION. JOURNAL. EDUCATION AND PSYCHOLOGY/MAGALLAT KULLIYYAT AL-TARBIYYAT. TARBIYYA WA'ILM AL-NAFS. *see* EDUCATION

150 BOL ISSN 2077-3161
AJAYU; revista de psicologia. Text in Spanish. 2002. s-a. back issues avail. **Document type:** *Journal, Academic/Scholarly.*
Media: Online - full text (from SciELO).
Published by: Universidad Catolica Boliviana, Departamento de Psicologia, Ave 14 de Septiembre 4876, La Paz, 4805, Bolivia. TEL 59-12-2782222, FAX 59-12-2786707, http://lpz.ucb.edu.bo/Forms/Index.aspx. Ed. Bismarck Pinto.

150 DEU ISSN 0937-4973
AKTUELLE BEITRAEGE ZUR ANGEWANDTEN PSYCHOLOGIE. Text in German. 1991. irreg., latest vol.3, 1996. price varies. **Document type:** *Monographic series, Academic/Scholarly.*
Published by: Centaurus Verlag & Media KG, Kaiser-Joseph-Str 267, Freiburg, 79098, Germany. TEL 49-761-1525861, FAX 49-761-1525868, info@centaurus-verlag.de, http://www.centaurus-verlag.de.

150 DEU ISSN 0943-7282
AKTUELLE PSYCHOLOGISCHE FORSCHUNG. Text in German. 1993. irreg., latest vol.17, 1996. price varies. **Document type:** *Monographic series, Academic/Scholarly.*
Published by: Holos Verlag, Breite Str 47, Bonn, 53111, Germany. TEL 49-228-263020, FAX 49-228-212435, info@holos-verlag.de, http://www.holos-verlag.de.

AKTUELNOSTI IZ NEUROLOGIJE, PSIHIJATRIJE I GRANICNIH PRODUCJA/CURRENT TOPICS IN NEUROLOGY, PSYCHIATRY AND RELATED DISCIPLINES. *see* MEDICAL SCIENCES—Psychiatry And Neurology

ALABAMA COUNSELING ASSOCIATION. JOURNAL. *see* OCCUPATIONS AND CAREERS

150 100 POL ISSN 1230-0802
ALBO ALBO; inspiracje Jungowskie - problemy psychologii i kultury. Text in Polish. 1991. q. 160 p./no.; **Document type:** *Magazine, Consumer.*
Published by: Wydawnictwo Psychologii i Kultury Eneteia, Ul Barborowska 7/15, Warsaw, 01464, Poland. eneteia@scp.pl. Ed. Zenon Dudek. Circ: 1,500.

ALDEAS. *see* CHILDREN AND YOUTH—About

150 BRA ISSN 1413-0394
ALETHEIA. Text in Portuguese. 1995. s-a.
Indexed: A26, B02, B15, B17, B18, G04, I04, I05, IBSS, P03, PsycholAb.
Published by: (Universidade Luterana do Brasil, Departamento de Psicologia), Universidade Luterana do Brasil, Rua Miguel Tostes 101, Bairro Sao Luiz, Canoas RS, 124, Brazil. TEL 55-51-4779118, FAX 55-51-4779115, editora@ulbra.br, http://www.editoradaulbra.com.br.

150 ESP ISSN 1138-3194
ALOMA; revista de psicologia, ciencies de l'educacio i de l'esport Blanquerna. Text in Spanish. 1997. s-a. **Document type:** *Journal, Academic/Scholarly.*
Published by: Universitat Ramon Llull, Facultat de Psicologia i Ciencies de l'Educacio Blanquerna, Cister, 24-34, Barcelona, 08022, Spain. TEL 34-93-2113782, FAX 34-93-2533031, info@url.es, http://www.url.es/.

150 BRA ISSN 0100-1655
ALTER; jornal de estudos psicodinamicos. Text in Portuguese. 1970. s-a. BRL 30 (effective 2006). back issues avail. **Document type:** *Journal, Academic/Scholarly.*
Published by: Sociedade de Psicanalise de Brasilia, SHIS Q1 09 Bloco E1 Sala 105, Centro Clinico do Lago, 71, Brasilia, 625-009, Brazil. TEL 55-61-32482309, FAX 55-61-33641553, http://www.spbsb.org.br/. Ed. Virginia Leone Bicudo.

158 USA ISSN 2152-775X
▼ **ALTERNATIVE & COMPLEMENTARY THERAPY NEWS.** Text in English. 2010 (Mar.). bi-m. USD 36 domestic; USD 65 foreign (effective 2010). adv. back issues avail. **Document type:** *Magazine, Trade.* **Description:** Includes news, events, and articles for practitioners of alternative and complementary therapy.
Related titles: Online - full text ed.: ISSN 2154-7580. free (effective 2010).
Published by: Axley Publishing, PO Box 909, Waldron, AR 72958. TEL 877-767-8537, 888-595-1717. Ed. Debbie Axley. Circ: 10,000.

150.19 USA ISSN 1546-0371
RC500 CODEN: JAAPCC
➤ **AMERICAN ACADEMY OF PSYCHOANALYSIS AND DYNAMIC PSYCHIATRY. JOURNAL.** Text in English. 1973. q. USD 85 combined subscription domestic to individuals (print & online eds.); USD 120 combined subscription foreign to individuals (print & online eds.); USD 490 combined subscription domestic to institutions (print & online eds.); USD 535 combined subscription foreign to institutions (print & online eds.) (effective 2011). adv. bk.rev. index. 180 p./no.; back issues avail.; reprints avail. **Document type:** *Journal, Academic/Scholarly.* **Description:** Contains perspectives on theory and treatment, research, book reviews, and relevant data from neuroscience, the humanities, and the social sciences.
Formerly (until 2003): American Academy of Psychoanalysis. Journal (0090-3604)
Related titles: Microform ed.; Online - full text ed.: ISSN 1943-2852.
Indexed: A01, A03, A08, A20, A22, AMHA, B21, CA, DIP, E-psyche, E01, EMBASE, ExcerpMed, FR, IBR, IBZ, INI, IPsyAb, IndMed, MEDLINE, MLA-IB, NSA, P03, P20, P22, P25, P26, P30, P48, P54, PQC, PSI, PsycInfo, PsycholAb, PsycholRG, R10, Reac, S02, S03, SCOPUS, SWR&A, T02.
—BLDSC (4683.736000), GNLM, IE, Infotrieve, Ingenta, INIST. **CCC.**
Published by: (American Academy of Psychoanalysis and Dynamic Psychiatry), Guilford Publications, Inc., 72 Spring St, 4th Fl, New York, NY 10012. TEL 800-365-7006, FAX 212-966-6708, info@guilford.com. Ed. Dr. Douglas H Ingram. R&P Kathy Kuehl. Adv. contact Marian Robinson. Circ: 900 (paid).

362.28 USA
AMERICAN ASSOCIATION OF SUICIDOLOGY. PROCEEDINGS OF THE ANNUAL MEETING. Text in English. 1975 (8th). a. looseleaf. price varies. back issues avail. **Document type:** *Proceedings.*
Indexed: E-psyche.
Published by: American Association of Suicidology, 5221 Wisconsin Ave, NW, Washington, DC 20015. info@suicidology.org. Ed. Dr. David Lester. Circ: 1,000.

614.58 USA ISSN 0895-8009
CODEN: MAMREB
AMERICAN ASSOCIATION ON MENTAL RETARDATION. MONOGRAPHS. Text in English. 1973. irreg. price varies. **Document type:** *Monographic series, Academic/Scholarly.*
Formerly (until 1987): American Association on Mental Deficiency. Monographs (0098-7123)
Indexed: E-psyche, P30, SCOPUS.
—**CCC.**
Published by: American Association on Intellectual and Developmental Disabilities, 501 3rd St, NW, Ste 200, Washington, DC 20001. TEL 202-387-1968, 800-424-3688, FAX 202-387-2193, anam@aaidd.org, http://www.aamr.org.

AMERICAN BEHAVIORAL SCIENTIST. *see* SOCIAL SCIENCES: COMPREHENSIVE WORKS

158 796 USA
➤ **AMERICAN BOARD OF SPORT PSYCHOLOGY. JOURNAL.** Text in English. 2007. m. **Document type:** *Journal, Academic/Scholarly.* **Description:** Addresses practice, research and methodological issues pertaining to applied sport psychology, athlete assessment and interventions including papers that address ethical issues/concerns.
Media: Online - full text.
Published by: American Board of Sport Psychology, 675 Academy, 2E, New York, NY 10034. TEL 917-680-3994, info@americanboardofsportpsychology.org. Ed. Dr. Roland A Carlstedt.

616.89 USA ISSN 0742-3187
➤ **AMERICAN GROUP PSYCHOTHERAPY MONOGRAPH SERIES.** Text in English. 1983. irreg., latest vol.7. price varies. back issues avail. **Document type:** *Monographic series, Academic/Scholarly.* **Description:** Covers chapters devoted to technique and theory, as well as comprehensive chapters on treatment of borderline adolescents, adolescents with learning disabilities, delinquent adolescents, and group therapy with inpatient populations.
Indexed: E-psyche.
—INIST.
Published by: (American Group Psychotherapy Association), International Universities Press, Inc., 59 Boston Post Rd, Box 1524, PO Box 389, Madison, CT 06443. TEL 203-245-4000, 203-245-4000, FAX 203-245-0775, info@iup.com.

➤ **AMERICAN IMAGO**; psychoanalysis and the human sciences. *see* MEDICAL SCIENCES—Psychiatry And Neurology

➤ **AMERICAN INDIAN AND ALASKA NATIVE MENTAL HEALTH RESEARCH (ONLINE).** *see* NATIVE AMERICAN STUDIES

➤ **AMERICAN JOURNAL OF COMMUNITY PSYCHOLOGY.** *see* SOCIOLOGY

➤ **AMERICAN JOURNAL OF DANCE THERAPY.** *see* DANCE

306.85 USA ISSN 0192-6187
RC488.5 CODEN: IJFPDM
➤ **AMERICAN JOURNAL OF FAMILY THERAPY.** Text in English. 1973. 5/yr. GBP 208 combined subscription in United Kingdom to institutions (print & online eds.); EUR 275, USD 345 combined subscription to institutions (print & online eds.) (effective 2012). adv. bk.rev. illus. index. reprint service avail. from PSC. **Document type:** *Journal, Academic/Scholarly.* **Description:** Provides an interdisciplinary forum for innovation, theory, research and clinical practice in family therapy.
Former titles (until 1979): International Journal of Family Counseling (0147-1775); (until 1977): Journal of Family Counseling (0093-3171)
Related titles: Microform ed.: 1973 (from PQC); Online - full text ed.: ISSN 1521-0383. 1973. GBP 187 in United Kingdom to institutions; EUR 248, USD 311 to institutions (effective 2012) (from IngentaConnect).
Indexed: A01, A02, A03, A08, A20, A22, A25, A26, AMHA, ASCA, B04, BRD, C06, C07, C08, C11, CA, CINAHL, CurCont, E-psyche, E01, E02, E03, E07, E08, ERI, EdA, EdI, F09, FamI, G08, G10, H04, H12, I05, MEA&I, P02, P03, P04, P10, P12, P18, P25, P27, P30, P43, P46, P48, P53, P54, PCI, PQC, PsycInfo, PsycholAb, S02, S03, S08, S09, S11, SCOPUS, SFSA, SOPODA, SSA, SSAI, SSAb, SSCI, SSI, SWR&A, SociolAb, T02, V&AA, W03, W07, W09.
—GNLM, IE, Infotrieve, Ingenta. **CCC.**
Published by: Routledge (Subsidiary of: Taylor & Francis Group), 325 Chestnut St, Ste 800, Philadelphia, PA 19106. TEL 215-625-8900, 800-354-1420, FAX 215-625-2940, orders@taylorandfrancis.com. Ed. S Richard Sauber. **Subsc. to in Europe:** Taylor & Francis Ltd., Journals Customer Service, Sheepen Pl, Colchester, Essex CO3 3LP, United Kingdom. TEL 44-20-70175544, FAX 44-20-70175198, tf.enquiries@tfinforma.com.

301.1 340 USA ISSN 0733-1290
K1 CODEN: AJFPF4
➤ **AMERICAN JOURNAL OF FORENSIC PSYCHOLOGY**; interfacing issues of psychology and law. Text in English. 1983. q. USD 80 domestic to individuals; USD 110 foreign to individuals; USD 105 domestic to institutions; USD 140 foreign to institutions; USD 28 per issue; free to members (effective 2010). bk.rev. 90 p./no. 1 cols./p.; back issues avail.; reprints avail. **Document type:** *Journal, Academic/Scholarly.* **Description:** Features papers that raise new questions and issues in the engaging field of forensic psychology.

Related titles: Microfiche ed.: (from WSH); Microfilm ed.: (from PMC, WSH).
Indexed: A22, CA, CJA, E-psyche, EMBASE, ExcerpMed, P03, P30, PsycInfo, PsycholAb, S02, S03, SCOPUS, T02.
—BLDSC (0824.645000), IE, Infotrieve, Ingenta.
Published by: American College of Forensic Psychiatry, PO Box 130458, Carlsbad, CA 92013. TEL 760-929-9777, FAX 760-929-9803. Circ: 500.

150 USA ISSN 1940-929X
➤ **AMERICAN JOURNAL OF MEDIA PSYCHOLOGY.** Text in English. 2008 (Feb.). a. USD 149 per issue (effective 2010). reprints avail. **Document type:** *Journal, Academic/Scholarly.* **Description:** Publishes theoretical and empirical papers and essays and book reviews that advance an understanding of media effects and processes on individuals in society.
Related titles: Online - full text ed.: ISSN 1940-9303. free (effective 2010).
Published by: Marquette Books LLC, 3107 E 62nd Ave, Spokane, WA 99223. TEL 509-443-7057, FAX 509-448-2191, journals@marquettejournals.org, http://www.marquettebooks.com. Ed. Michael Elasmar.

616.89 USA ISSN 0002-9432
RA790.A1 CODEN: AJORAG
➤ **AMERICAN JOURNAL OF ORTHOPSYCHIATRY**; interdisciplinary approaches to mental health and social justice. Text in English. 1930. q. GBP 251 in United Kingdom to institutions; EUR 293 in Europe to institutions; USD 409 elsewhere to institutions; GBP 289 combined subscription in United Kingdom to institutions (print & online eds.); EUR 338 combined subscription in Europe to institutions (print & online eds.); USD 470 combined subscription elsewhere to institutions (print & online eds.) (effective 2012). bibl.; charts; illus. index, cum.index. back issues avail.; reprint service avail. from PSC. **Document type:** *Journal, Academic/Scholarly.* **Description:** Provides articles that advance the knowledge relevant to mental health and human development from a multidisciplinary and interprofessional perspective.
Related titles: Microform ed.: (from PQC); Online - full text ed.: ISSN 1939-0025. GBP 251 in United Kingdom to institutions; EUR 293 in Europe to institutions; USD 409 elsewhere to institutions (effective 2012).
Indexed: A01, A02, A03, A08, A20, A22, A25, A26, AC&P, AMHA, ASCA, Acal, B04, B05, BDM&CN, BRD, C06, C07, C28, CA, CDA, CLFP, ChemAb, Chicano, CurCont, E-psyche, E01, E06, E08, ECER, EMBASE, ESPM, ExcerpMed, F09, FR, Faml, G08, G10, H09, HospLI, I05, IBSS, INI, ISR, IndMed, Inpharma, MEDLINE, MRefA, P02, P03, P10, P12, P13, P27, P30, P48, P53, P54, PCI, PQC, PRA, PsycInfo, PsycholAb, R10, Reac, RiskAb, S02, S03, S05, S08, S09, S21, SCI, SCOPUS, SFSA, SOPODA, SRRA, SSA, SSAI, SSAb, SSCI, SSI, SWR&A, SociolAb, T02, THA, W03, W07, W09.
—BLDSC (0829.250000), GNLM, IE, Infotrieve, Ingenta, INIST. **CCC.**
Published by: (American Orthopsychiatric Association, Inc.), John Wiley & Sons, Inc., 111 River St, Hoboken, NJ 07030. TEL 201-748-6000, FAX 201-748-6088, info@wiley.com, http://www.wiley.com/WileyCDA/. Eds. Gary B Melton, Oscar A Barbarin. Adv. contact Kristin McCarthy TEL 201-748-7683. **Subscr. to:** American Psychological Association.

➤ **AMERICAN JOURNAL OF PLAY (ONLINE).** *see* LEISURE AND RECREATION

➤ **AMERICAN JOURNAL OF PLAY (PRINT).** *see* LEISURE AND RECREATION

➤ **AMERICAN JOURNAL OF PRIMATOLOGY.** *see* BIOLOGY—Zoology

616.891 USA ISSN 0002-9548
RC321 CODEN: AJPYA8
➤ **THE AMERICAN JOURNAL OF PSYCHOANALYSIS.** Abbreviated title: A J P. Text in English. 1941. q. USD 673 in North America to institutions; GBP 376 elsewhere to institutions (effective 2012). adv. bk.rev. bibl. cum.index: 1941-1965. back issues avail.; reprint service avail. from PSC. **Document type:** *Journal, Academic/Scholarly.* **Description:** Provides a forum for communicating a range of clinical and theoretical concepts of psychoanalysis and for presenting related investigations in allied fields.
Related titles: Microform ed.: (from PQC); Online - full text ed.: ISSN 1573-6741 (from IngentaConnect).
Indexed: A01, A02, A03, A08, A20, A22, A26, B04, BRD, BibLing, CA, CPLI, ChemAb, DIP, E-psyche, E01, E08, EMBASE, ExcerpMed, F09, FR, G08, H13, I05, IBR, IBZ, IndMed, MEA&I, MEDLINE, MLA-IB, P02, P03, P10, P12, P20, P22, P25, P26, P27, P30, P48, P53, P54, PCI, PQC, PsycInfo, PsycholAb, R10, RILM, Reac, S02, S03, S09, SCOPUS, SSAI, SSAb, SSI, SWR&A, T02, W03, W05.
—BLDSC (0835.300000), GNLM, IE, Infotrieve, Ingenta, INIST. **CCC.**
Published by: (Association for the Advancement of Psychoanalysis), Palgrave Macmillan (Subsidiary of: Macmillan Publishers Ltd.), 175 Fifth Ave, New York, NY 10010. TEL 646-307-5151, 888-330-8477, FAX 800-672-2054, bookenquiries@palgrave.com, http://us.macmillan.com/palgrave.aspx. Ed. Giselle Galdi. **Subscr. to:** Palgrave Macmillan Ltd., Subscription Department, Brunel Rd, Houndmills, Basingstoke, Hants RG21 2XS, United Kingdom. TEL 44-1256-357893, FAX 44-1256-812358, subscriptions@palgrave.com.

150 USA ISSN 0002-9556
BF1 CODEN: AJPCAA
➤ **AMERICAN JOURNAL OF PSYCHOLOGY.** Abbreviated title: A J P. Text in English. 1887. q. USD 273 combined subscription to institutions (print & online eds.) (effective 2012). adv. bk.rev. bibl.; charts; stat.; illus.; abstr. cum.index every 25 vols. 168 p./no.; back issues avail.; reprints avail. **Document type:** *Journal, Academic/Scholarly.* **Description:** Features reports of original research in experimental psychology, theoretical presentations, combined theoretical and experimental analyses, historical commentaries, and obituaries of prominent psychologists.
Related titles: Microform ed.: (from MIM, PMC, PQC); Online - full text ed.: ISSN 1939-8298. USD 248 to institutions (effective 2012).
Indexed: A01, A02, A03, A08, A20, A22, A25, A26, AMHA, ASCA, ASSIA, AbAn, Acal, B04, B21, BRD, CA, CBRI, CISA, ChemAb, CommAb, CurCont, DIP, E-psyche, E06, E08, EMBASE, ErgAb, ExcerpMed, FR, G03, G08, GSA, GSI, H09, H10, H11, H12, I05, IBR, IBZ, IPARL, IndMed, M01, M02, M06, MEA&I, MEDLINE, MLA-IB, NSA, P02, P03, P10, P12, P13, P20, P22, P25, P26, P27, P30, P48, P53, P54, PCI, PQC, PersLit, PsycInfo, PsycholAb, R10, RASB, Reac, S02, S03, S05, S08, S09, S23, SCOPUS, SSAI, SSAb, SSCI, SSI, T02, W03, W07.
—BLDSC (0835.500000), IE, Infotrieve, Ingenta, INIST. **CCC.**
Published by: University of Illinois Press, 1325 S Oak St, Champaign, IL 61820. TEL 217-333-0950, 866-244-0626, FAX 217-244-8082, journals@uillinois.edu. Adv. contact Jeff McArdle TEL 217-244-0381.

150 370 USA
▼ **AMERICAN JOURNAL OF PSYCHOLOGY AND EDUCATION.** Text in English. 2010 (Sep.). q. USD 60; USD 15 newsstand/cover (effective 2010). **Document type:** *Journal, Academic/Scholarly.* **Description:** Publishes articles that involve the psychological theory studies and/or its application to the educational process, particularly, the descriptions of empirical research and the presentation of theory designed to either explicate or enhance the educational process. In addition, reviews of educational research are encouraged if the research being reviewed involves the application of psychological science to an important educational issue.
Published by: American Society for Education Science Research, 4301 E Valley Blvd #D2, Los Angeles, CA 90032. TEL 323-9088-554, FAX 323-2278-581, office@asesr.org.

AMERICAN JOURNAL OF SEXUALITY EDUCATION. *see* PHYSICAL FITNESS AND HYGIENE

370.15 USA ISSN 1052-7958
RC500
THE AMERICAN PSYCHOANALYST. Text in English. 1967. q. free to members; USD 80 in US & Canada to non-members; USD 100 elsewhere to non-members (effective 2008). adv. back issues avail. **Document type:** *Newsletter, Trade.* **Description:** Features information of the association, essays on the history of psychoanalysis in America, and interviews with leading analysts.
Formerly: American Psychoanalytic Association. Newsletter
Indexed: E-psyche.
—**CCC.**
Published by: American Psychoanalytic Association, 309 East 49th St, New York, NY 10017. TEL 212-752-0450, FAX 212-593-0571, info@apsa.org. Ed. Janis Chester. adv.: page USD 850; trim 7.25 x 9.75. Circ: 4,000.

616.891 USA ISSN 0003-0651
BF173.A2 CODEN: JAPOAE
➤ **AMERICAN PSYCHOANALYTIC ASSOCIATION. JOURNAL.** Variant title: J A P A. Text in English. 1953. bi-m. USD 528, GBP 311 combined subscription to institutions (print & online eds.); USD 517, GBP 305 to institutions (effective 2011). adv. bk.rev. abstr.; bibl.; charts; illus. index, cum.index: vols.1-22, vols.23-33. Supplement avail.; back issues avail.; reprint service avail. from PSC. **Document type:** *Journal, Academic/Scholarly.* **Description:** Covers articles in clinical and theoretical applied psychoanalytic studies.
Related titles: CD-ROM ed.; Online - full text ed.: ISSN 1941-2460. USD 475, GBP 280 to institutions (effective 2011).
Indexed: A20, A22, AMHA, ASCA, B21, CA, CurCont, DIP, E-psyche, E01, EMBASE, ExcerpMed, F09, FR, Faml, IBR, IBZ, IndMed, MEA&I, MEDLINE, NSA, P03, P30, PsycInfo, PsycholAb, R10, Reac, S02, S03, SCOPUS, SOPODA, SSCI, SociolAb, T02, W07, W09.
—BLDSC (4692.070000), GNLM, IE, Infotrieve, Ingenta, INIST. **CCC.**
Published by: (American Psychoanalytic Association), Sage Publications, Inc., 2455 Teller Rd, Thousand Oaks, CA 91320. TEL 805-499-9774, 800-818-7243, FAX 805-499-0871, 800-583-2665, info@sagepub.com, http://www.sagepub.com. Ed. Steven T Levy. adv.: page USD 630; trim 5 x 8. Circ: 6,500.

150.19 USA
➤ **AMERICAN PSYCHOANALYTIC ASSOCIATION. WORKSHOP SERIES.** Text in English. 1985. irreg., latest vol.9. price varies. back issues avail. **Document type:** *Monographic series, Academic/Scholarly.* **Description:** Covers the problems of therapeutic alliance.
Indexed: E-psyche.
Published by: (American Psychoanalytic Association), International Universities Press, Inc., 59 Boston Post Rd, Box 1524, PO Box 389, Madison, CT 06443. TEL 203-245-4000, FAX 203-245-0775, info@iup.com. Ed. Scott Dowling.

➤ **AMERICAN PSYCHOLOGICAL ASSOCIATION. MEMBERSHIP DIRECTORY.** *see* BIOGRAPHY

150 USA ISSN 0003-066X
BF1 CODEN: AMPSAB
➤ **AMERICAN PSYCHOLOGIST.** Text in English. 1946. 9/yr. USD 310 domestic to individuals; USD 363 foreign to individuals; USD 907 domestic to institutions; USD 1,009 foreign to institutions (effective 2011). adv. illus. index. back issues avail.; reprint service avail. from PSC. **Document type:** *Journal, Academic/Scholarly.* **Description:** Features empirical, theoretical, and practical articles that advance the field of psychology.
Related titles: Microform ed.: (from PMC, PQC); Online - full text ed.: ISSN 1935-990X (from ScienceDirect).
Indexed: A01, A02, A03, A08, A20, A21, A22, A25, A26, ABS&EES, AMHA, ASCA, ASSIA, Acal, AddicA, B01, B02, B04, B06, B07, B09, B15, B17, B18, B21, BRD, C06, C07, C28, CA, CDA, CERDIC, CIS, CJPI, ChemAb, Chicano, CurCont, DIP, E-psyche, E02, E03, E07, E08, EMBASE, ERI, ERIC, EdA, EdI, ExcerpMed, F09, FR, Faml, FutSurv, G04, G08, G10, GeoRef, H09, I05, IBR, IBSS, IBZ, INI, IPARL, IPsyAb, IndMed, M06, MEA&I, MEDLINE, MLA, MLA-IB, NSA, P02, P03, P10, P12, P13, P27, P30, P34, P48, P53, P54, PCI, PQC, PRA, PSI, PersLit, PsycInfo, PsycholAb, R10, RASB, RI-1, RI-2, Reac, S02, S03, S05, S08, S09, S21, SCOPUS, SFSA, SSAI, SSAb, SSCI, SSI, SWR&A, SociolAb, T02, THA, W01, W02, W03, W07, W09.
—BLDSC (0853.400000), GNLM, IE, Infotrieve, Ingenta, INIST. **CCC.**
Published by: American Psychological Association, 750 First St, NE, Washington, DC 20002. TEL 202-336-5500, 800-374-2721, FAX 202-336-5997, journals@apa.org. Ed. Dr. Norman B Anderson. Adv. contact Doug Constant TEL 202-336-5574. Circ: 98,900.

362.29 USA ISSN 0740-0454
➤ **AMERICAN UNIVERSITY STUDIES. SERIES 8. PSYCHOLOGY.** Text in English. 1983. irreg., latest vol.24, 2006. price varies. **Document type:** *Monographic series, Academic/Scholarly.* **Description:** Explores theoretical, practical, and clinical issues in psychology.
Indexed: E-psyche.
Published by: Peter Lang Publishing, Inc. (Subsidiary of: Peter Lang Publishing Group), 29 Broadway, New York, NY 10006. TEL 212-647-7700, 212-647-7706, 800-770-5264, FAX 212-647-7707, customerservice@plang.com.

300 363.25 IND ISSN 0973-175X
AMITY JOURNAL OF BEHAVIOURAL AND FORENSIC SCIENCES. Text in English. 2005. s-a. INR 250 domestic to individuals; USD 85 foreign to individuals; INR 500 domestic to institutions; USD 110 foreign to institutions (effective 2011). **Document type:** *Journal, Academic/Scholarly.*
Related titles: Online - full text ed.: ISSN 0973-9742. INR 100 domestic; USD 75 foreign (effective 2008).
Published by: Amity Institute of Behavioural and Forensic Sciences, Block E2, Amity University Campus, Sector 125, Gautam Budh Nagar, Noida, 201 303, India. TEL 91-120-2445252, aibhas@amity.edu.

370.15 ESP ISSN 0212-9728
➤ **ANALES DE PSICOLOGIA.** Text in English, Spanish. 1955. s-a. back issues avail. **Document type:** *Journal, Academic/Scholarly.* **Description:** Publishes theoretical, empirical and methodological papers covering all aspects related to basic and applied scientific psychology.
Supersedes in part (in 1984): Universidad de Murcia. Anales. Filosofia y Letras (0463-9863)
Related titles: Online - full text ed.: ISSN 1695-2294. free (effective 2011).
Indexed: E-psyche, P03, P09, PCI, PsycInfo, PsycholAb, SCI, SCOPUS, SSCI, W07.
—**CCC.**
Published by: Universidad de Murcia, Servicio de Publicaciones, Edificio Saavedra Fajardo, C/ Actor Isidoro Maiquez 9, Murcia, 30007, Spain. TEL 34-968-363887, FAX 34-968-363414, http://www.um.es/publicaciones/. Circ: 155.

158 PRT ISSN 0870-8231
RC500
ANALISE PSICOLOGICA. Text in Portuguese. 1977. q. USD 77 in Europe; USD 87 elsewhere. adv. bk.rev. **Document type:** *Academic/Scholarly.*
Indexed: A01, CA, E-psyche, P03, PsycInfo, PsycholAb, S02, S03, T02.
Published by: Instituto Superior de Psicologia Aplicada, Rua Jardim do Tabaco 34, Lisbon, 1149-041, Portugal. TEL 351-21-8811700, FAX 351-21-8860954, info@ispa.pt, http://www.ispa.pt. Ed. Frederico Pereira. Adv. contact Jorge Senos.

158 ESP ISSN 0211-7339
ANALISIS Y MODIFICACION DE CONDUCTA. Text in Spanish. 1975. s-a. **Document type:** *Journal, Academic/Scholarly.*
Indexed: P03, PsycholAb, S02, S03.
Published by: Universidad de Huelva, Servicio de Publicaciones, Campus el Carmen, Avenida de las Fuerzas Armadas s/n, Huelva, Andalucia 21071, Spain. TEL 34-95-9018000, publica@uhu.es, http://www.uhu.es/publicaciones/index.html.

150.19 AUS ISSN 1324-5155
ANALYSIS (MELBOURNE). Text in English. 2000. a. AUD 30 domestic Victoria; AUD 35 domestic Other states; AUD 40 foreign (effective 2008). back issues avail. **Document type:** *Journal, Academic/Scholarly.* **Description:** Provides articles that aid psychoanalytic praxis and the development of collaborative work between psychoanalysts and other workers.
Former titles (until 1998): Australian Centre for Psychoanalysis in the Freudian Field. Analysis; (until 1991): Melbourne Centre for Psychoanalytic Research. Analysis (1035-7041)
Published by: Australian Centre for Psychoanalysis, PO Box 509, Carlton South, VIC 3053, Australia. TEL 61-3-93493462, FAX 61-3-93299140, contact@psychoanalysis.org.au. Ed. Megan Williams.

ANALYSIS OF GAMBLING BEHAVIOR. *see* SOCIOLOGY

153.6 USA ISSN 0889-9401
BF455.A1
THE ANALYSIS OF VERBAL BEHAVIOR. Text in English. 1982. a., latest vol.21, 2005. USD 83 to institutions; USD 50 to non-members; free to members (effective 2011). adv. back issues avail.; reprints avail. **Document type:** *Journal, Academic/Scholarly.* **Description:** Covers topics such as elementary verbal operants, multiple control, rule-governed behavior, epistemology, language acquisition, pedagogy, verbal behavior research methodology.
Formerly (until 1985): V B News
Indexed: ERIC, P03, PsycInfo, PsycholAb.
Published by: Association for Behavior Analysis International, 550 W Centre Ave, Ste 1, Portage, MI 49024. TEL 269-492-9310, FAX 269-492-9316, mail@abainternational.org. Ed. Caio Miguel TEL 916-278-6813.

150.19 808.8 USA
ANALYTICAL PSYCHOLOGY CLUB OF NEW YORK. BULLETIN. Text in English. 1938. 8/yr. membership. bk.rev.; film rev. **Description:** Covers club business, programs and brief accounts of talks.
Indexed: E-psyche.
Published by: Analytical Psychology Club of New York, 28 E 39th St, New York, NY 10016. TEL 212-697-7877. Circ: 300.

616.89 DEU ISSN 0945-6740
ANALYTISCHE KINDER- UND JUGENDLICHEN-PSYCHOTHERAPIE; Zeitschrift fuer Theorie und Praxis der Kinder- und Jugendlichen-Psychoanalyse und der tiefenpsychologisch fundierten Psychotherapie. Text in German. 1970. q. EUR 64 (effective 2009). bk.rev. abstr. 136 p./no.; **Document type:** *Journal, Academic/Scholarly.*
Former titles (until 1994): Beitraege zur Analytischen Kinder- und Jugendlichenpsychotherapie (0942-069X); (until 1992): Kind und Umwelt (0721-1791); (until 1980): Beitraege zur Analytischen Kinder- und Jugendlichenpsychotherapie (0343-2777)
Indexed: DIP, E-psyche, IBR, IBZ, P03, PsycInfo, PsycholAb.
—GNLM.

P

Published by: Brandes und Apsel Verlag GmbH, Scheidswaldstr 22, Frankfurt Am Main, 60385, Germany. TEL 49-69-272995170, FAX 49-69-2729951710, brandes-apsel@doodees.de, http://www.brandes-apsel-verlag.de.

150 DEU ISSN 0301-3006
RC500 CODEN: ANAPC4
➤ **ANALYTISCHE PSYCHOLOGIE**; Zeitschrift fuer Psychotherapie und Psychoanalyse. Text in German; Summaries in English, German. 1970. q. EUR 64 domestic; EUR 75 in Europe; EUR 110 elsewhere (effective 2009). bk.rev. bibl. back issues avail. **Document type:** *Journal, Academic/Scholarly.*
Formerly (until 1974): Zeitschrift fuer Analytische Psychologie und ihre Grenzgebiete (0049-8580)
Related titles: Microform ed.: (from PQC); Online - full text ed.: ISSN 1421-9689. CHF 207, EUR 148, USD 159 (effective 2003).
Indexed: A20, A22, ASCA, E-psyche, E01, FR, IBR, IBZ, MLA-IB, P03, P30, PCI, PsycInfo, PsycholAb, S02, S03, SCOPUS.
—GNLM, IE, Infotrieve, Ingenta, INIST. **CCC.**
Published by: Brandes und Apsel Verlag GmbH, Scheidswaldstr 22, Frankfurt Am Main, 60385, Germany. TEL 49-69-272995170, FAX 49-69-2729951710, info@brandes-apsel-verlag.de, http://www.brandes-apsel-verlag.de. Circ: 1,700.

150 410 USA ISSN 0895-366X
ANCHOR POINT MAGAZINE; the practical journal of NLP. Text in English. 1987. m. USD 39 domestic; USD 49 in Canada; USD 59 elsewhere (effective 2005). adv. bk.rev. charts; illus. back issues avail. **Document type:** *Magazine, Trade.*
Indexed: E-psyche.
Published by: Anchor Point Productions, Inc., 259 S 500 E, Salt Lake City, UT 84102-2017. TEL 801-534-1022, 800-544-6480, FAX 801-532-2113, info@nlpanchorpoint.com. Ed. Terry Fieland. Adv. contact Anita Sholiton. Circ: 1,300 (paid).

150 IRN ISSN 2008-0824
➤ **ANDISHAH VA RAFTAR/JOURNAL OF CLINICAL PSYCHOLOY.** Text in English, Persian, Modern. 1996. q. IRR 1,600 domestic; USD 2 foreign (effective 2011). bk.rev. abstr.; bibl.; charts; maps; stat. Index. back issues avail. **Document type:** *Journal, Academic/Scholarly.* **Description:** Explores the science of the mind and behavior, publishing reports of original research in experimental psychology, theoretical presentations, combined theoretical and experimental analyses, and historical commentaries.
Published by: Danishgah-i Azad-i Islami, Vahid-i Rudihin/Islamic Azad University of Iran, Roudehen Branch, 5th Fl., Daneshgah St., Emam Khomeini Ave., Roudehen, Tehran, Iran. TEL 98-221-5726164, FAX 98-221-5726164, andishehvaraftar@yahoo.com, nedasmaeelifar@yahoo.com. Ed. Shahram Vaziri. R&P Farah Lotfi Kashani.

152.47 USA
ANGER MANAGEMENT - CONTROLLING THE VOLCANO WITHIN. Text in English. m. USD 15 (effective 2008). **Document type:** *Newsletter, Consumer.*
Media: Online - full text.
Indexed: E-psyche.
Published by: Anger Management Trauma Association, 98-1247 Kaahumanu St, Ste 223, Aiea, HI 96701. TEL 808-487-5433, FAX 808-487-5444, rhoades@pdchawaii.com, webmaster@anger-management.net.

150 001.3 ITA ISSN 1126-0661
ANIMA. Text in Italian. 1988. a. EUR 31 for 2 yrs. domestic; EUR 50 for 2 yrs. foreign (effective 2009). **Document type:** *Magazine, Consumer.* **Description:** Multidisciplinary forum featuring readings on archetypical psychology, religion, art and humanities.
Indexed: E-psyche, FR.
—INIST.
Published by: Moretti e Vitali Editori, Via Sergentini 6a, Bergamo, BG 24128, Italy. TEL 39-035-251300, FAX 39-035-4329409, http://www.morettievitali.it. Ed. Francesco Donfrancesco.

ANIMAL BEHAVIOUR. *see* BIOLOGY—Zoology

155 DEU ISSN 1435-9448
QL785
➤ **ANIMAL COGNITION.** Text in English. 1998. q. EUR 609, USD 713 combined subscription to institutions (print & online eds.) (effective 2012). adv. back issues avail.; reprint service avail. from PSC. **Document type:** *Journal, Academic/Scholarly.* **Description:** Aims to establish the course of the evolution of intelligence, of the mechanisms, functions and adaptive value of basic and complex cognitive abilities, and of the evolution of intelligent behavior and intelligent systems from invertebrates to humans.
Related titles: Online - full text ed.: ISSN 1435-9456 (from IngentaConnect).
Indexed: A01, A03, A08, A20, A22, A26, B21, B25, BIOSIS Prev, CA, CurCont, E-psyche, E01, E17, EMBASE, ESPM, ExcerpMed, H12, H13, I05, MEDLINE, MycolAb, NSA, P02, P03, P10, P20, P22, P25, P30, P48, P53, P54, PQC, PsycInfo, PsycholAb, SCI, SCOPUS, T02, W07, W08, Z01.
—BLDSC (0903.180000), IE, Infotrieve, Ingenta. **CCC.**
Published by: Springer (Subsidiary of: Springer Science+Business Media), Tiergartenstr 17, Heidelberg, 69121, Germany. TEL 49-6221-4870, FAX 49-6221-345229. Ed. Dr. Tatiana Czeschlik. **Subscr. in the Americas to:** Springer New York LLC, Journal Fulfillment, PO Box 2485, Secaucus, NJ 07096. TEL 800-777-4643, 201-348-4033, FAX 201-348-4505, journals-ny@springer.com, http://www.springer.com; **Subscr. to:** Springer Distribution Center, Kundenservice Zeitschriften, Haberstr 7, Heidelberg 69126, Germany. TEL 49-6221-3454303, FAX 49-6221-3454229, subscriptions@springer.com.

510.71 POL ISSN 1732-1085
ANNALES ACADEMIAE PAEDAGOGICAE CRACOVIENSIS. STUDIA PSYCHOLOGICA. Text in Polish. 1963. irreg., latest 2003. price varies. **Document type:** *Monographic series, Academic/Scholarly.*
Formerly (until 2002): Wyzsza Szkola Pedagogiczna im. Komisji Edukacji Narodowej w Krakowie. Rocznik Naukowo-Dydaktyczny. Prace Psychologiczne (1640-9175)
Indexed: E-psyche.
Published by: (Uniwersytet Pedagogiczny im. Komisji Edukacji Narodowej w Krakowie), Wydawnictwo Naukowe Uniwersytetu Pedagogicznego im. Komisji Edukacji Narodowej w Krakowie, ul Podchorazych 2, Krakow, 30084, Poland. TEL 48-12-6626383, redakcja@wydawnictwoup.pl, http://www.wydawnictwoap.pl. Eds. Jan Kaiser, Leszek Wrona. **Co-sponsor:** Ministerstwo Edukacji Narodowej.

616.8 FRA ISSN 0003-4487
RC321 CODEN: AMPYAT
➤ **ANNALES MEDICO-PSYCHOLOGIQUES**; revue psychiatrique. Text in French. 1843. 10/yr. EUR 484 in Europe to institutions; EUR 407.44 in France to institutions; JPY 57,000 in Japan to institutions; USD 629 elsewhere to institutions (effective 2012). bk.rev. abstr.; illus. index. reprints avail. **Document type:** *Journal, Academic/Scholarly.* **Description:** Deals with topical matters such as the training of psychologists, the relationship between psychiatry and neurology, and the development of psychotherapy.
Incorporates (1986-2002): Annales de Psychiatrie (0768-7559)
Related titles: Online - full text ed.: Annales Medico-Psychologiques, Revue Psychiatrique. ISSN 1769-6631 (from IngentaConnect, ScienceDirect).
Indexed: A01, A03, A08, A20, A22, A26, ASCA, B21, C28, CA, CISA, DBA, E-psyche, EMBASE, ExcerpMed, F09, FR, I05, IndMed, Inpharma, MLA-IB, NSA, P03, P30, PsycInfo, PsycholAb, R10, Reac, S02, S03, SCI, SCOPUS, T02, W07.
—BLDSC (0984.150000), GNLM, IE, Infotrieve, Ingenta, INIST. **CCC.**
Published by: (Societe Medico-Psychologique), Elsevier Masson (Subsidiary of: Elsevier Health Sciences), 62 Rue Camille Desmoulins, Issy les Moulineaux, Cedex 92442, France. TEL 33-1-71165500, FAX 33-1-71165600, infos@elsevier-masson.fr. Ed. Jean-Francois Allilaire. Circ: 2,000.

150 CZE ISSN 1211-3522
LB5
➤ **ANNALES PSYCHOLOGICI.** Variant title: Masarykova Univerzita. Filozoficka Fakulta. Sbornik Praci. P: Rada Psychologicka. Text in Czech, Slovak, English, German. 1996. a. price varies. bk.rev. **Document type:** *Journal, Academic/Scholarly.* **Description:** Covers all aspects of psychology.
Supersedes in part (in 1996): Masarykova Univerzita. Filozoficka Fakulta. Sbornik Praci. I: Rada Pedagogicko - Psychologicka; Which was formerly: Univerzita J.E. Purkyne. Filozoficka Fakulta. Sbornik Praci. I: Rada Pedagogicko - Psychologicka (0068-2705)
Indexed: E-psyche, PsycholAb, SOPODA.
Published by: Masarykova Univerzita, Filozoficka Fakulta/Masaryk University, Faculty of Arts, Arna Novaka 1, Brno, 60200, Czech Republic. TEL 420-549-491111, FAX 420-549-491520, podatelna@phil.muni.cz. Ed. Zuzana Slovackova.

➤ **ANNALES UNIVERSITATIS MARIAE CURIE-SKLODOWSKA. SECTIO J. PAEDAGOGIA - PSYCHOLOGIA.** *see* EDUCATION

➤ **ANNALS OF BEHAVIORAL SCIENCE AND MEDICAL EDUCATION.** *see* EDUCATION

150 FRA ISSN 0003-5033
BF2
➤ **L'ANNEE PSYCHOLOGIQUE.** Text in French; Summaries in English, French. 1894. q. EUR 209 combined subscription domestic to institutions (print & online eds.); EUR 229 combined subscription foreign to institutions (print & online eds.) (effective 2011). bk.rev. charts. index. back issues avail.; reprint service avail. from PSC. **Document type:** *Journal, Academic/Scholarly.* **Description:** Presents original research, critical reviews, bibliographic analyses.
Related titles: Microform ed.; Online - full text ed.: ISSN 1955-2580.
Indexed: A20, A22, BibInd, CurCont, E-psyche, FR, IndMed, MLA-IB, P03, P30, PCI, PsycInfo, PsycholAb, RASB, S02, S03, SCOPUS, SOPODA, SSCI, SociolAb, W07.
—BLDSC (1049.250000), IE, Infotrieve, Ingenta, INIST. **CCC.**
Published by: NecPlus, 1 Pl. du Genie, Paris, 75012, France. TEL 33-6-21152222, jlsoubret@necplus.eu. Circ: 1,500.

155.6 USA ISSN 1094-2610
BF724
ANNUAL EDITIONS: ADOLESCENT PSYCHOLOGY. Variant title: Adolescent Psychology. Text in English. 1997. a. USD 22.25 per issue (effective 2010). illus. back issues avail. **Document type:** *Journal, Academic/Scholarly.*
Related titles: Online - full text ed.
Published by: McGraw-Hill, Contemporary Learning Series (Subsidiary of: McGraw-Hill Companies, Inc.), 1221 Ave of the Americas, New York, NY 10020. TEL 212-904-2000, FAX 212-512-2000, customer.service@mcgraw-hill.com, http://www.mhhe.com/cls/.

ANNUAL EDITIONS: CHILD GROWTH & DEVELOPMENT. *see* MEDICAL SCIENCES—Pediatrics

302 USA ISSN 1069-6407
HQ1073.5.U6
ANNUAL EDITIONS: DYING, DEATH, AND BEREAVEMENT. Text in English. 1993. a. USD 22.25, GBP 18.99 per issue (effective 2010). illus. back issues avail.; reprints avail. **Document type:** *Journal, Academic/Scholarly.*
Related titles: Online - full text ed.
Indexed: E-psyche.
Published by: McGraw-Hill, Contemporary Learning Series (Subsidiary of: McGraw-Hill Companies, Inc.), 1221 Ave of the Americas, New York, NY 10020. TEL 212-904-2000, FAX 212-512-2000, customer.service@mcgraw-hill.com, http://www.mcgraw-hill.com.

ANNUAL EDITIONS: EDUCATIONAL PSYCHOLOGY. *see* EDUCATION

573.6 306.7 USA ISSN 1091-9961
HQ21
➤ **ANNUAL EDITIONS: HUMAN SEXUALITIES.** Key Title: Human Sexuality. Text in English. 1975. a. price varies. illus. back issues avail. **Document type:** *Monographic series, Academic/Scholarly.* **Description:** Contains a compilation of articles selected from magazines, newspapers, and journals, relating to issues dealing with sexuality and society, sexual biology, reproduction, and interpersonal relationships.
Former titles (until 1981): Annual Editions: Readings in Human Sexuality (0163-836X); (until 197?): Focus: Human Sexuality (0147-0655)
Related titles: Online - full text ed.
Indexed: E-psyche.
Published by: McGraw-Hill, Contemporary Learning Series (Subsidiary of: McGraw-Hill Companies, Inc.), 1221 Ave of the Americas, New York, NY 10020. TEL 212-904-2000, FAX 212-512-2000, customer.service@mcgraw-hill.com, http://www.mhhe.com/cls/.

158.105 USA ISSN 0198-912X
BF698.A1
➤ **ANNUAL EDITIONS: PERSONAL GROWTH AND BEHAVIOR.** Text in English. 1975. a. USD 22.25 per issue (effective 2010). illus. index. back issues avail. **Document type:** *Journal, Academic/Scholarly.* **Description:** Covers topics such as the science of psychology; emotion and motivation and development.
Formerly (until 1981): Annual Editions: Readings in Personality and Adjustment (0361-3836)
Related titles: Online - full text ed.
Indexed: E-psyche.
Published by: McGraw-Hill, Contemporary Learning Series (Subsidiary of: McGraw-Hill Companies, Inc.), 1221 Ave of the Americas, New York, NY 10020. TEL 212-904-2000, FAX 212-512-2000, customer.service@mcgraw-hill.com, http://www.mhhe.com/cls/.

150 USA ISSN 0272-3794
BF149
➤ **ANNUAL EDITIONS: PSYCHOLOGY.** Text in English. 1971. a. USD 22.25 per issue (effective 2010). illus. back issues avail. **Document type:** *Journal, Academic/Scholarly.* **Description:** Contains articles that explore the science of psychology; biological bases of behavior; perceptual processes; learning and remembering; cognitive processes; emotion and motivation; development; personality processes; social processes; psychological disorders; and psychological treatments.
Formerly (until 1981): Annual Editions: Readings in Psychology (0197-0542)
Related titles: Online - full text ed.
Indexed: E-psyche.
Published by: McGraw-Hill, Contemporary Learning Series (Subsidiary of: McGraw-Hill Companies, Inc.), 1221 Ave of the Americas, New York, NY 10020. TEL 212-904-2000, FAX 212-512-2000, customer.service@mcgraw-hill.com, http://www.mcgraw-hill.com.

302 USA ISSN 0730-6962
ANNUAL EDITIONS: SOCIAL PSYCHOLOGY. Text in English. 1997. a. USD 22.25 per issue (effective 2010). illus. back issues avail. **Document type:** *Journal, Academic/Scholarly.*
Formerly (until 19??): Annual Editions: Readings in Social Psycholoty
Related titles: Online - full text ed.
Indexed: E-psyche.
Published by: McGraw-Hill, Contemporary Learning Series (Subsidiary of: McGraw-Hill Companies, Inc.), 1221 Ave of the Americas, New York, NY 10020. TEL 212-904-2000, FAX 212-512-2000, customer.service@mcgraw-hill.com, http://www.mcgraw-hill.com.

150 USA ISSN 0092-5055
RC500 CODEN: APSACT
ANNUAL OF PSYCHOANALYSIS. Text in English. 1973. a., latest vol.31. **Document type:** *Journal, Academic/Scholarly.*
Related titles: Online - full text ed.
Indexed: A01, A03, A08, A22, CA, E-psyche, P03, P20, P25, P43, P48, P54, PQC, PsycInfo, PsycholAb.
—BLDSC (1092.900000), GNLM, IE, Ingenta. **CCC.**
Published by: (Chicago Institute for Psychoanalysis), Routledge (Subsidiary of: Taylor & Francis Group), 270 Madison Ave, New York, NY 10016. TEL 212-216-7800, FAX 212-244-1563, orders@taylorandfrancis.com, http://www.routledge-ny.com.

150 USA ISSN 1548-5943
RC467
ANNUAL REVIEW OF CLINICAL PSYCHOLOGY. Text in English. 2005. a. USD 251 combined subscription per issue to institutions (print & online eds.); USD 209 per issue to institutions (print or online ed.) (effective 2012). back issues avail. **Document type:** *Journal, Academic/Scholarly.*
Related titles: Online - full text ed.: ISSN 1548-5951.
Indexed: A26, B21, C06, C07, CurCont, E08, EMBASE, ERA, ExcerpMed, I05, IBR, IBZ, MEDLINE, NSA, P03, P25, P30, P48, PQC, PsycInfo, PsycholAb, R10, Reac, S20, S21, SCI, SCOPUS, SSCI, W07.
—BLDSC (1522.250300), IE. **CCC.**
Published by: Annual Reviews, PO Box 10139, Palo Alto, CA 94303. TEL 650-493-4400, FAX 650-424-0910, 800-523-8635, service@annualreviews.org. Eds. Susan Nolen-Hoeksema TEL 203-432-4500, Samuel Gubins.

150 GBR ISSN 1746-739X
BF39.9
➤ **ANNUAL REVIEW OF CRITICAL PSYCHOLOGY (ONLINE).** Abbreviated title: A R C P. Text in English. 1999. a. free (effective 2011). back issues avail. **Document type:** *Journal, Academic/Scholarly.*
Formerly (until 2006): Annual Review of Critical Psychology (Print) (1464-0538)
Media: Online - full text.
Indexed: A39, C27, C29, D03, D04, E13, R14, S14, S15, S18.
—CCC.
Published by: Manchester Metropolitan University, Discourse Unit, Hathersage Rd, Manchester, M13 0JA, United Kingdom. I.A.Parker@mmu.ac.uk. Ed. Carol Owens.

150 USA ISSN 0066-4308
BF30 CODEN: ARPSAC
➤ **ANNUAL REVIEW OF PSYCHOLOGY.** Text in English. 1950. a. USD 251 combined subscription per issue to institutions (print & online eds.); USD 209 per issue to institutions (print or online ed.) (effective 2012). bibl.; charts; illus.; abstr. index, cum.index. back issues avail.; reprint service avail. from PSC. **Document type:** *Journal, Academic/Scholarly.* **Description:** Synthesizes and filters primary research to identify the principal contributions in the field of psychology.
Related titles: CD-ROM ed.; Microfilm ed.: (from PQC); Online - full text ed.: ISSN 1545-2085.

Indexed: A01, A02, A03, A08, A20, A22, A25, A26, AMHA, ASCA, B01, B02, B06, B07, B09, B15, B17, B18, B21, BAS, BIOSIS Prev, BRD, C06, C07, CA, CDA, CIS, ChemAb, CurCont, DIP, DSHAb, E-psyche, E08, EMBASE, ERA, ExcerpMed, F09, FR, G04, G05, G06, G07, G08, H09, H11, H12, I05, I07, IBR, IBZ, ISR, IndMed, Inpharma, MEDLINE, MLA-IB, MRD, MycolAb, NSA, P02, P03, P10, P12, P13, P19, P20, P22, P24, P25, P26, P27, P30, P43, P48, P53, P54, PCI, PQC, PsycInfo, PsycholAb, R10, RASB, RILM, Reac, S02, S03, S05, S08, S09, S21, S23, SCI, SCOPUS, SOPODA, SSAI, SSAb, SSCI, SSI, SociolAb, T02, W03, W05, W07.
—BLDSC (1528.400000), CASDDS, GNLM, IE, Infotrieve, Ingenta, INIST. **CCC.**
Published by: Annual Reviews, PO Box 10139, Palo Alto, CA 94303. TEL 650-493-4400, FAX 650-424-0910, 800-523-8635, service@annualreviews.org. Eds. Susan T Fiske TEL 609-258-0655, Samuel Gubins.

➤ **ANTHROPOLOGY OF CONSCIOUSNESS.** *see* ANTHROPOLOGY

150 SVN ISSN 0587-5161
B6 CODEN: ATHRAH
ANTHROPOS. Text in Slovenian. 1969. bi-m.
Indexed: RILM, RefZh, SociolAb.
Published by: Drustvo Psihologov Slovenije, Prusnikova 74, Ljubljana, 1210, Slovenia. TEL 386-61-5121727, http://www2.arnes.si/~dpsih/glavna.htm. Ed. Janek Musek.

150 ESP ISSN 0066-5126
➤ **ANUARIO DE PSICOLOGIA.** Text in Spanish, English, French; Summaries in English, French, Spanish. 1969. 3/yr. EUR 38 to individuals; EUR 75 to institutions (effective 2010). bk.rev. 150 p./no.; back issues avail. **Document type:** *Journal, Academic/Scholarly.*
Related titles: Online - full text ed.: ISSN 1988-5253.
Indexed: A01, A22, CA, E-psyche, EMBASE, ExcerpMed, P03, PsycInfo, PsycholAb, R10, Reac, S02, S03, SCOPUS, T02.
—BLDSC (1565.132000), IE, Ingenta, INIST. **CCC.**
Published by: Universitat de Barcelona, Facultat de Psicologia, Passeig de la Vall d'Hebron 171, Barcelona, 08035, Spain. Circ: 1,000.

616.89 ESP ISSN 1699-6410
ANUARIO DE PSICOLOGIA CLINICA Y DE LA SALUD. Text in Spanish. 2004. a. **Document type:** *Yearbook, Academic/Scholarly.*
Media: Online - full text.
Published by: Universidad de Sevilla, Departamento de Personalidad, Evaluacion y Tratamiento Psicologicos, C Camilo Jose Cela, s-n, Sevilla, 41018, Spain. TEL 34-95-4557807, 34-95-4557813, anuarioclin@us.es, http://www.us.es/. Ed. Juan Francisco Rodriguez Testal.

150 340 ESP ISSN 1133-0740
ANUARIO DE PSICOLOGIA JURIDICA. Text in Spanish. 1991. a. EUR 25 domestic to qualified personnel; EUR 32.50 domestic; EUR 60 foreign (effective 2008). **Document type:** *Journal, Academic/Scholarly.*
Related titles: Online - full text ed.: ISSN 2174-0542. 1991.
Indexed: A01, CA, E-psyche, F03, F04, T02.
Published by: Colegio Oficial de Psicologos, Claudio Coello 46, Madrid, 28001, Spain. TEL 34-91-4355212, FAX 34-91-5779172, http://www.cop.es. Ed. Juan Romero.

ANUARIO FILOSOFIA, PSICOLOGIA Y SOCIOLOGIA. *see* PHILOSOPHY

152.46 GBR ISSN 1061-5806
BF575.A6 CODEN: AXSCEP
➤ **ANXIETY, STRESS AND COPING.** Text in English. 1988. 5/yr. GBP 1,035 combined subscription in United Kingdom to institutions (print & online eds.); EUR 1,115, USD 1,394 combined subscription to institutions (print & online eds.) (effective 2012). adv. illus. back issues avail.; reprint service avail. from PSC. **Document type:** *Journal, Academic/Scholarly.* **Description:** Provides a forum for scientific, theoretically important, and clinically significant research reports and conceptual contributions.
Formerly (until 1992): Anxiety Research (0891-7779)
Related titles: Microform ed.; Online - full text ed.: ISSN 1477-2205. GBP 931 in United Kingdom to institutions; EUR 1,004, USD 1,255 to institutions (effective 2012) (from IngentaConnect).
Indexed: A01, A03, A08, A20, A22, ASCA, C06, C07, CA, CJA, CurCont, E-psyche, E01, EMBASE, ErgAb, ExcerpMed, FR, Faml, IPsyAb, MEDLINE, P03, P30, P43, PsycInfo, PsycholAb, R09, R10, Reac, S02, S03, S21, SCOPUS, SD, SOPODA, SSCI, SociolAb, T02, W07.
—BLDSC (1566.612000), GNLM, IE, Infotrieve, Ingenta, INIST. **CCC.**
Published by: (Stress and Anxiety Research Society), Routledge (Subsidiary of: Taylor & Francis Group), 4 Park Sq, Milton Park, Abingdon, Oxon OX14 4RN, United Kingdom. TEL 44-20-70176000, FAX 44-20-70176336, subscriptions@tandf.co.uk, http://www.routledge.com. Eds. Ralf Schwarzer, Aleksandra Luszczynska, Joachim Stoeber. Adv. contact Linda Hann TEL 44-1344-779945. **Subscr. to:** Taylor & Francis Ltd., Journals Customer Service, Sheepen Pl, Colchester, Essex CO3 3LP, United Kingdom. TEL 44-20-70175544, FAX 44-20-70175198.

150.195 ESP ISSN 1699-4825
APERTURAS PSICOANALITICAS. Text in Spanish. 1999. q. free (effective 2011). back issues avail. **Document type:** *Journal, Academic/Scholarly.*
Media: Online - full text.
Address: Diego de Leon, 44 3 Izq, Madrid, 28006, Spain. redaccion@aperturas.org. Ed. Hugo Bleichmar.

150.19 GBR ISSN 0962-1849
RC467
➤ **APPLIED AND PREVENTIVE PSYCHOLOGY;** current scientific perspectives. Abbreviated title: A P P. Text in English. 1992-2001; resumed 2004. 4/yr. EUR 228 in Europe to institutions; JPY 31,900 in Japan to institutions; USD 254 elsewhere to institutions (effective 2012). adv. back issues avail. **Document type:** *Journal, Academic/Scholarly.* **Description:** Focuses on the scientific, epidemiological, or public health approach to psychological problems.
Related titles: Online - full text ed.: ISSN 1873-7293 (from ScienceDirect).
Indexed: A22, A26, ASCA, ASSIA, CA, CurCont, E-psyche, Faml, I05, P30, PsycholAb, SCOPUS, SSCI, T02, THA, W07.
—BLDSC (1571.442000), GNLM, IE, Infotrieve, Ingenta. **CCC.**
Published by: (American Association of Applied and Preventive Psychology), Elsevier Ltd (Subsidiary of: Elsevier Science & Technology), The Blvd, Langford Ln, Kidlington, Oxford, OX5 1GB, United Kingdom. TEL 44-1865-843000, FAX 44-1865-843010, journalscustomerserviceemea@elsevier.com. Ed. David A Smith.

➤ **APPLIED ANIMAL BEHAVIOUR SCIENCE.** *see* BIOLOGY—Zoology

370.15 150 GBR ISSN 0888-4080
BF311 CODEN: ACPSED
➤ **APPLIED COGNITIVE PSYCHOLOGY.** Text in English. 1987. 9/yr. GBP 985 in United Kingdom to institutions; EUR 1,245 in Europe to institutions; USD 1,931 elsewhere to institutions; GBP 1,134 combined subscription in United Kingdom to institutions (print & online eds.); EUR 1,433 combined subscription in Europe to institutions (print & online eds.); USD 2,221 combined subscription elsewhere to institutions (print & online eds.) (effective 2012). adv. bk.rev. charts; illus. index. back issues avail.; reprint service avail. from PSC. **Document type:** *Journal, Academic/Scholarly.* **Description:** Reviews and reports papers dealing with psychological analyses of problems of memory, learning, thinking, language, and consciousness as they are reflected in the real world.
Formerly (until 1987): Human Learning (0277-6707)
Related titles: Microform ed.: (from PQC); Online - full text ed.: ISSN 1099-0720. GBP 985 in United Kingdom to institutions; EUR 1,245 in Europe to institutions; USD 1,931 elsewhere to institutions (effective 2012).
Indexed: A01, A03, A08, A20, A22, AEI, AHCI, ASCA, ASSIA, B21, C28, CA, CPE, CommAb, CurCont, DIP, E-psyche, EMBASE, ERA, ErgAb, ExcerpMed, FR, Faml, IBR, IBZ, L&LBA, MLA-IB, NSA, P02, P03, P10, P12, P30, P43, P48, P53, P54, PCI, PQC, PsycInfo, PsycholAb, R10, RASB, RILM, Reac, RefZh, S02, S03, SCOPUS, SOPODA, SSCI, SociolAb, T02, W07.
—IE, Infotrieve, Ingenta, INIST. **CCC.**
Published by: (Society for Applied Research in Memory and Cognition), John Wiley & Sons Ltd. (Subsidiary of: John Wiley & Sons, Inc.), 1-7 Oldlands Way, PO Box 808, Bognor Regis, West Sussex PO21 9FF, United Kingdom. TEL 44-1865-778315, FAX 44-1243-843232, cs-journals@wiley.com, http://eu.wiley.com/WileyCDA/. Ed. Graham Davies. **Subscr. in the US to:** John Wiley & Sons, Inc., 111 River St, Hoboken, NJ 07030. TEL 201-748-6645, subinfo@wiley.com; **Subscr. to:** 1-7 Oldlands Way, PO Box 809, Bognor Regis, West Sussex PO21 9FG, United Kingdom. TEL 44-1865-778054, cs-agency@wiley.com.

301 USA ISSN 1088-8691
BF712 CODEN: ADSCFM
➤ **APPLIED DEVELOPMENTAL SCIENCE.** Abbreviated title: A D S. Text in English. 1997. q. GBP 347 combined subscription in United Kingdom to institutions (print & online eds.); EUR 462, USD 579 combined subscription to institutions (print & online eds.) (effective 2012). adv. back issues avail.; reprint service avail. from PSC. **Document type:** *Journal, Academic/Scholarly.* **Description:** Synthesis of research and application that reflect the view that individual and family functioning is a combined and interactive product of biology, and the physical and social environments that continuously evolve and change over time.
Related titles: Online - full text ed.: ISSN 1532-480X. GBP 313 in United Kingdom to institutions; EUR 416, USD 521 to institutions (effective 2012).
Indexed: A01, A03, A08, A22, B01, B06, B07, B09, B21, C28, CA, CDA, CPE, CurCont, E-psyche, E01, E03, E17, ERI, ESPM, F09, P03, P10, P12, P26, P30, P34, P43, P48, P53, P54, PAIS, PQC, PsycInfo, PsycholAb, S01, S02, S03, S11, SCOPUS, SSCI, T02, W07.
—BLDSC (1571.946000), IE, Infotrieve, Ingenta. **CCC.**
Published by: Psychology Press (Subsidiary of: Taylor & Francis Inc.), 325 Chestnut St, Ste 800, Philadelphia, PA 19106. TEL 800-354-1420, FAX 215-625-2940, orders@taylorandfrancis.com, http://www.psypress.com. Eds. Celia B Fisher, Richard L Lerner. Adv. contact Linda Hann TEL 44-1344-779945.

➤ **APPLIED ERGONOMICS;** human factors in technology and society. *see* ENGINEERING

616.89 CAN
BF698.A1 CODEN: MCREDA
➤ **APPLIED MULTIVARIATE RESEARCH.** Text in English. 1973. a. USD 29 in North America; USD 35 elsewhere (effective 2009). adv. bk.rev. **Document type:** *Journal, Academic/Scholarly.* **Description:** Publishes methodological and content papers that deal with the application of both classical and more modern multivariate statistical techniques, as well as measurement issues, in applied settings.
Former titles (until 2006): Multivariate Experimental Clinical Research (0147-3964); (until 1976): Journal of Multivariate Experimental Personality and Clinical Psychology (0149-9688)
Indexed: A22, CIS, E-psyche, IBR, IBZ, PsycholAb, SCOPUS.
—BLDSC (1576.205500), GNLM, IE, Ingenta.
Published by: University of Windsor, Department of Psychology, 401 Sunset Avenue, Windsor, ON N9B 3P4, Canada. TEL 519-253-3000 ext 2229, FAX 519-973-7021, djackson@uwindsor.ca. Ed. Dennis L Jackson. Circ: 200.

➤ **APPLIED NEUROPSYCHOLOGY.** *see* MEDICAL SCIENCES—Psychiatry And Neurology

153.1 NLD ISSN 1570-5838
BD312.A4
APPLIED ONTOLOGY. Text in English. 2005. q. USD 686 combined subscription in North America (print & online eds.); EUR 490 combined subscription elsewhere (print & online eds.) (effective 2012). **Document type:** *Journal, Academic/Scholarly.*
Related titles: Online - full text ed.: ISSN 1875-8533.
Indexed: A01, A22, CA, E01, P30, T02.
—IE. **CCC.**
Published by: I O S Press, Nieuwe Hemweg 6B, Amsterdam, 1013 BG, Netherlands. TEL 31-20-6883355, FAX 31-20-6870039, info@iospress.nl, http://www.iospress.nl. Eds. Mark A Musen TEL 650-725-3390, Nicola Guarino TEL 39-461-828486.

APPLIED PSYCHOLINGUISTICS; psychological and linguistic studies across languages and learners. *see* LINGUISTICS

APPLIED PSYCHOLINGUISTICS AND COMMUNICATION DISORDERS. *see* LINGUISTICS

150 USA ISSN 0146-6216
BF39
➤ **APPLIED PSYCHOLOGICAL MEASUREMENT.** Abbreviated title: A P M. Text in English. 1976. 8/yr. USD 961, GBP 564 to institutions; USD 981, GBP 576 combined subscription to institutions (print & online eds.) (effective 2012). adv. bk.rev. illus. Index. back issues avail.; reprint service avail. from PSC. **Document type:** *Journal, Academic/Scholarly.* **Description:** Presents empirical research on the application of techniques of psychological measurement to substantive problems in all areas of psychology and related disciplines.
Related titles: Microfiche ed.: (from PQC); Online - full text ed.: ISSN 1552-3497. USD 883, GBP 518 to institutions (effective 2012).
Indexed: A01, A02, A03, A08, A22, AEI, ASCA, B01, B06, B07, B09, B21, CA, CCMJ, CDA, CIS, CurCont, DIP, E-psyche, E01, E03, ERI, ERIC, Faml, H04, IBR, IBZ, MSN, MathR, NSA, P03, P04, P18, P25, P30, P53, P54, PQC, PsycInfo, PsycholAb, RASB, SCOPUS, SSCI, T02, V02, W07.
—BLDSC (1576.550000), IE, Infotrieve, Ingenta, INIST. **CCC.**
Published by: (Applied Psychological Measurement, Inc.), Sage Publications, Inc., 2455 Teller Rd, Thousand Oaks, CA 91320. TEL 800-818-7243, FAX 800-583-2665, info@sagepub.com, http://www.sagepub.com. Ed. Mark L Davison. **Subscr. overseas to:** Sage Publications Ltd., 1 Oliver's Yard, 55 City Rd, London EC1Y 1SP, United Kingdom. TEL 44-207-3248701, FAX 44-207-3248733, subscription@sagepub.co.uk.

150 USA
APPLIED PSYCHOLOGY. Text in English. 19??. irreg., latest 2008. price varies. adv. back issues avail. **Document type:** *Monographic series, Academic/Scholarly.* **Description:** The series offer publications that emphasize state-of-the-art research and its application to important issues of human behavior in a variety of societal settings.
Related titles: Online - full text ed.
Published by: Psychology Press (Subsidiary of: Taylor & Francis Inc.), 325 Chestnut St, Ste 800, Philadelphia, PA 19106. TEL 800-354-1420, FAX 215-625-2940, orders@taylorandfrancis.com. Eds. Edwin A Fleishman, Jeanette N Cleveland. Adv. contact Linda Hann TEL 44-1344-779945.

158 GBR ISSN 0269-994X
BF636.A1 CODEN: ADPYE4
➤ **APPLIED PSYCHOLOGY;** an international review. Text in English; Abstracts in French. 1951. q. (plus supp.). GBP 756 domestic to institutions; EUR 960 in Europe to institutions; USD 1,269 in the Americas to institutions; USD 1,482 elsewhere to institutions; GBP 832 combined subscription domestic to institutions (print & online eds.); EUR 1,056 combined subscription in Europe to institutions (print & online eds.); USD 1,396 combined subscription in the Americas to institutions (print & online eds.); USD 1,630 combined subscription elsewhere to institutions (print & online eds.) (effective 2009). adv. back issues avail.; reprint service avail. from PSC. **Document type:** *Journal, Academic/Scholarly.* **Description:** Provides a forum for the scholarly exchange of research findings and professional standards and promotes awareness of important professional issues.
Former titles (until 1979): Revue Internationale de Psychologie Appliquee/International Review of Applied Psychology (0035-340X); (until 1968): Association Internationale de Psychologie Appliqee. Bulletin; (until 195?): Association Internationale de Psychotechnique. Bulletin
Related titles: Online - full text ed.: ISSN 1464-0597. GBP 756 domestic to institutions; EUR 960 in Europe to institutions; USD 1,269 in the Americas to institutions; USD 1,482 elsewhere to institutions (effective 2009) (from IngentaConnect); ◆ Supplement to: Applied Psychology: Health and Well-Being. ISSN 1758-0846.
Indexed: A01, A03, A08, A12, A17, A20, A22, A26, ABIn, AMHA, ASCA, ASSIA, B01, B06, B07, B09, BAS, C06, C07, CA, CPM, CurCont, E-psyche, E01, ERA, ESPM, ErgAb, FR, HRA, I05, IPsyAb, M12, P03, P20, P30, P43, P48, P51, P53, P54, PCI, PQC, PsycInfo, PsycholAb, RiskAb, S02, S03, S20, S21, SCOPUS, SFSA, SOPODA, SSCI, SociolAb, T02, V05, W07.
—BLDSC (1576.555000), IE, Infotrieve, Ingenta, INIST. **CCC.**
Published by: (International Association of Applied Psychology, Technion - Israel Institute of Technology, William Davidson Faculty of Industrial Engineering and Management ISR), Wiley-Blackwell Publishing Ltd. (Subsidiary of: John Wiley & Sons, Inc.), 9600 Garsington Rd, Oxford, OX4 2DQ, United Kingdom. TEL 44-1865-776868, FAX 44-1865-714591, customerservices@blackwellpublishing.com. Ed. Sabine Sonnentag. Adv. contact Craig Pickett TEL 44-1865-476267. Circ: 2,000. **Subscr. in N. America to:** Taylor & Francis Inc.

150 GBR ISSN 1758-0846
R726.7
▼ ➤ **APPLIED PSYCHOLOGY: HEALTH AND WELL-BEING.** Text in English. 2009 (Mar.). 3/yr. GBP 298 in United Kingdom to institutions; EUR 381 in Europe to institutions; USD 589 elsewhere to institutions; GBP 344 combined subscription in United Kingdom to institutions (print & online eds.); EUR 438 combined subscription in Europe to institutions (print & online eds.); USD 678 combined subscription elsewhere to institutions (print & online eds.) (effective 2012). **Document type:** *Journal, Academic/Scholarly.* **Description:** Provides readers with articles that present the latest data and best practices in the application of psychology to the promotion of well-being and optimal functioning.
Related titles: Online - full text ed.: ISSN 1758-0854. GBP 298 in United Kingdom to institutions; EUR 381 in Europe to institutions; USD 589 elsewhere to institutions (effective 2012); ◆ Supplement(s): Applied Psychology. ISSN 0269-994X.
Indexed: A01, A22, ASSIA, CA, E01, ESPM, T02.
—IE. **CCC.**
Published by: (International Association of Applied Psychology), Wiley-Blackwell Publishing Ltd. (Subsidiary of: John Wiley & Sons, Inc.), 9600 Garsington Rd, Oxford, OX4 2DQ, United Kingdom. TEL 44-1865-776868, FAX 44-1865-714591, customer@wiley.co.uk, http://www.wiley.com/. Eds. Christopher Peterson, Ralf Schwarzer.

150 345 USA ISSN 1550-3550
HV6789
➤ **APPLIED PSYCHOLOGY IN CRIMINAL JUSTICE.** Abbreviated title: A P C J. Text in English. 2005. s-a. USD 60; USD 20 per issue (effective 2011). **Document type:** *Journal, Academic/Scholarly.* **Description:** Examines the intersection of psychology and criminal justice.
Related titles: Online - full text ed.: ISSN 1550-4409.

P

Indexed: A39, C27, C29, CA, CJA, D03, D04, E13, P03, P30, PsycInfo, R14, S02, S03, S14, S15, S18, SociolAb, T02.
Published by: Sam Houston State University, College of Criminal Justice, 1803 Ave J, Ste 303, Huntsville, TX 77340. TEL 936-294-1111, president@shsu.edu, http://www.shsu.edu. Ed. Randy Garner.

613 USA ISSN 1090-0586
BF319.5.B5 CODEN: APSBFZ
➤ **APPLIED PSYCHOPHYSIOLOGY AND BIOFEEDBACK.** Text in English. 1975. q. EUR 1,047, USD 1,101 combined subscription to institutions (print & online eds.) (effective 2012). adv. bk.rev. illus. Index. back issues avail.; reprint service avail. from PSC. **Document type:** *Journal, Academic/Scholarly.* **Description:** Emphasizes empirical research, basic and applied, in the theory, practice, and evaluation of applied psychophysiology and biofeedback.
Formerly (until 1997): Biofeedback and Self Regulation (0363-3586)
Related titles: Microfilm ed.: (from PQC); Online - full text ed.: ISSN 1573-3270 (from IngentaConnect).
Indexed: A01, A03, A08, A20, A22, A26, AMED, AMHA, ASCA, B21, B25, BIOSIS Prev, BibLing, CA, CurCont, DentInd, E-psyche, E01, E15, E16, EMBASE, ERA, ErgAb, ExcerpMed, FR, H12, H13, I05, IPsyAb, IndMed, Inspec, M12, MEDLINE, MycolAb, NSA, P03, P10, P12, P20, P22, P25, P30, P43, P48, P52, P53, P54, P56, PQC, PsycInfo, PsycholAb, R09, R10, Reac, S19, S20, S21, SCOPUS, SD, SSCI, T02, V05, W07.
—BLDSC (1576.562000), AskIEEE, GNLM, IE, Infotrieve, Ingenta, INIST. **CCC.**
Published by: Springer New York LLC (Subsidiary of: Springer Science+Business Media), 233 Spring St, New York, NY 10013. TEL 212-460-1500, FAX 212-460-1575, service-ny@springer.com, http://www.springer.com/. Ed. Frank Andrasik. adv.: B&W page USD 1,050; trim 7 x 10. Circ: 1,950.

150 DEU
APPLIED RESEARCH IN PSYCHOLOGY AND EVALUATION. Text in English, German. 2008. irreg., latest vol.4, 2009. price varies. **Document type:** *Monographic series, Academic/Scholarly.*
Published by: V & R Unipress GmbH (Subsidiary of: Vandenhoeck und Ruprecht), Robert-Bosch-Breite 6, Goettingen, 37079, Germany. TEL 49-551-5084303, FAX 49-551-5084333, info@vr-unipress.de, http://www.v-r.de/en/publisher/unipress.

APPLIED RESEARCH IN QUALITY OF LIFE. *see* SOCIAL SCIENCES: COMPREHENSIVE WORKS

150.5 FRA ISSN 1774-5314
APPROCHE CENTREE SUR LA PERSONNE. Text in French. 2005. s-a. EUR 33 per issue to individuals; EUR 24 per issue to students (effective 2007). **Document type:** *Journal, Academic/Scholarly.*
Related titles: Online - full text ed.
Published by: Association Francaise de Psychotherapie dans l'Approche Centree sur la Personne (A F P - A C P), 17 Rue Dupin, Paris, 75006, France. secretaire@afpacp.fr.

150 ESP ISSN 0213-3334
➤ **APUNTES DE PSICOLOGIA.** Text in Spanish. 1982. 3/yr. back issues avail. **Document type:** *Journal, Academic/Scholarly.*
Formerly (until 1983): Colegio Oficial de Psicologos, Delegacion de Andalucia Occidental. Boletin Informativo (0213-3342)
Indexed: E-psyche, P03, P30, PsycInfo, PsycholAb, S02, S03.
Published by: (Colegio Oficial de Psicologos, Andalucia Occidental), Colegio Oficial de Psicologos, Claudio Coello 46, Madrid, 28001, Spain. TEL 34-91-4355212, FAX 34-91-5779172, http://www.cop.es. Ed. Francisco Fernandez Serra.

616.89 DEU
ARBEITSHEFTE GRUPPENANALYSE. Text in German. 1991. s-a. EUR 15 per vol. (effective 2010). **Document type:** *Journal, Academic/Scholarly.*
Indexed: E-psyche.
Published by: Foerderverein Gruppentherapie e.V., Spiekerhof 5, Muenster, 48143, Germany. Ed. Regine Scholz.

150.19 DEU ISSN 0721-9628
ARBEITSHEFTE KINDERPSYCHOANALYSE. Text in German. 1982. a. EUR 36 domestic; EUR 40 in Europe; USD 45 elsewhere (effective 2009). bk.rev. back issues avail. **Document type:** *Journal, Academic/Scholarly.* **Description:** Contains articles on psychoanalysis discussing theoretical questions, case studies, and child psychoanalytical work in institutions.
Indexed: E-psyche.
Published by: (Gesamthochschule Kassel, Wissenschaftliches Zentrum II), Brandes und Apsel Verlag GmbH, Scheidswaldstr 22, Frankfurt Am Main, 60385, Germany. TEL 49-69-272995170, FAX 49-69-2729951710, info@brandes-apsel-verlag.de, http://www.brandes-apsel-verlag.de. Circ: 700.

ARCHIV FUER RELIGIONSPSYCHOLOGIE/ARCHIVE FOR THE PSYCHOLOGY OF RELIGION. *see* RELIGIONS AND THEOLOGY

150 CHE ISSN 0003-9640
BF2
ARCHIVES DE PSYCHOLOGIE. Text in English, French. 1901. q. CHF 95 to individuals; CHF 180 to institutions; CHF 75 to students (effective 2005). bk.rev. charts. cum.index irreg. back issues avail. **Document type:** *Journal, Academic/Scholarly.*
Related titles: ◆ Supplement(s): Archives de Psychologie. Monographies. ISSN 0253-0368.
Indexed: A22, DIP, E-psyche, FR, IBR, IBZ, P03, P25, P30, P48, PCI, PQC, PsycholAb, RefZh, SSCI.
—BLDSC (1640.450000), IE, Infotrieve, Ingenta, INIST. **CCC.**
Published by: (Universite de Geneve/University of Geneva), Editions Medecine et Hygiene, Chemin de la Mousse 46, CP 475, Chene-Bourg 4, 1225, Switzerland. TEL 41-22-7029311, FAX 41-22-7029355, abonnements@medhyg.ch, http://www.medhyg.ch. Eds. Helga Kilcher, Jacques Voneche. Circ: 600.

150 CHE ISSN 0253-0368
BF2
ARCHIVES DE PSYCHOLOGIE. MONOGRAPHIES. Text in French. 1973. irreg.
Related titles: ◆ Supplement to: Archives de Psychologie. ISSN 0003-9640.
Indexed: PCI.
Published by: Editions Medecine et Hygiene, Chemin de la Mousse 46, CP 475, Chene-Bourg 4, 1225, Switzerland. TEL 41-22-7029311, FAX 41-22-7029355, http://www.medhyg.ch.

ARCHIVES OF CLINICAL NEUROPSYCHOLOGY. *see* MEDICAL SCIENCES—Psychiatry And Neurology

ARCHIVES OF PSYCHIATRY AND PSYCHOTHERAPY. *see* MEDICAL SCIENCES—Psychiatry And Neurology

362.28 USA ISSN 1381-1118
RC569 CODEN: ASREFQ
➤ **ARCHIVES OF SUICIDE RESEARCH.** Text in English. 1995. q. GBP 232 combined subscription in United Kingdom to institutions (print & online eds.); EUR 308, USD 385 combined subscription to institutions (print & online eds.) (effective 2012). adv. bk.rev. illus. back issues avail.; reprint service avail. from PSC. **Document type:** *Journal, Academic/Scholarly.* **Description:** Features original contributions on the study of suicide and suicide prevention, including pertinent aspects of pharmacotherapy, psychiatry, psychology and sociology.
Related titles: Online - full text ed.: ISSN 1543-6136. GBP 209 in United Kingdom to institutions; EUR 277, USD 346 to institutions (effective 2012) (from IngentaConnect).
Indexed: A01, A22, ASSIA, C06, C07, CA, CurCont, E-psyche, E01, EMBASE, ESPM, ExcerpMed, F09, FamI, IBSS, IPsyAb, MEDLINE, P03, P10, P30, P48, P50, P53, P54, PQC, PsycInfo, PsycholAb, R10, Reac, RiskAb, S02, S03, SCOPUS, SOPODA, SSCI, SociolAb, T02, V&AA, W07.
—GNLM, IE, Infotrieve, Ingenta. **CCC.**
Published by: (International Academy of Suicide Research NLD), Routledge (Subsidiary of: Taylor & Francis Group), 325 Chestnut St, Ste 800, Philadelphia, PA 19106. TEL 800-354-1420, FAX 215-625-2940, journals@routledge.com, http://www.routledge.com. Ed. Barbara Stanley. Adv. contact Linda Hann TEL 44-1344-779945.

➤ **ARCHIVES OF WOMEN'S MENTAL HEALTH.** *see* WOMEN'S HEALTH

306.7 MEX ISSN 1405-1923
➤ **ARCHIVOS HISPANOAMERICANOS DE SEXOLOGIA.** Text in Spanish. 1995. s-a. MXN 80, USD 35 (effective 2000). adv. bk.rev. back issues avail.; reprints avail. **Document type:** *Academic/Scholarly.* **Description:** Designed for educators, psychologists, physicians, social scientists and professionals interested in sex education and sexology. Presents research papers in sexuality, gender issues, rehabilitation and education of the disabled, sex education, therapy and social aspects of sex.
Related titles: Online - full text ed.
Indexed: A01, A26, C01, CA, E-psyche, F03, F04, I04, I05, P03, PsycholAb, T02.
Published by: Instituto Mexicano de Sexologia, TEPIC 86, Col Roma, Mexico City, DF 06760, Mexico. TEL 52-5-5642850, http://www.imesex.edu.mx/. Ed. Dr. Juan Luis Alvarez-Gayou Jurgenson. R&P Juan Luis Alvarez Gayou Jurgenson. Adv. contact Cristina Torices. Circ: 500. **Co-sponsors:** Sociedad Mexicana de Psicologia; Universidad Pedagogica Nacional.

➤ **ARQUIVOS DE SAUDE MENTAL DO ESTADO DE SAO PAULO.** *see* MEDICAL SCIENCES—Psychiatry And Neurology

➤ **ARQUIVOS DE SAUDE MENTAL DO ESTADO DE SAO PAULO. SUPLEMENTO.** *see* MEDICAL SCIENCES—Psychiatry And Neurology

150 FRA ISSN 1269-8105
L'ART DE LA PSYCHOTHERAPIE. Text in French. 1996. irreg. back issues avail. **Document type:** *Monographic series, Consumer.*
Published by: E S F Editeur (Subsidiary of: Reed Business Information France), 2 rue Maurice Hartmann, Issy-les-Moulineaux, 92133 Cedex, France. TEL 33-1-46294629, FAX 33-1-46294633, info@esf-editeur.fr, http://www.esf-editeur.fr.

616.89 GBR ISSN 0197-4556
RC489.A7 CODEN: APCYAJ
➤ **THE ARTS IN PSYCHOTHERAPY.** Text in English. 1973. 5/yr. EUR 843 in Europe to institutions; JPY 111,900 in Japan to institutions; USD 944 elsewhere to institutions (effective 2012). adv. bk.rev. back issues avail.; reprints avail. **Document type:** *Journal, Academic/Scholarly.* **Description:** Discusses innovative research in artistic inquiry and expression and its use in the treatment of mental disorders.
Formerly (until 1980): Art Psychotherapy (0090-9092)
Related titles: Microfilm ed.: (from PQC); Online - full text ed.: ISSN 1873-5878 (from IngentaConnect, ScienceDirect).
Indexed: A01, A03, A07, A08, A20, A22, A26, A30, A31, AA, ABM, AMED, ASCA, ArtInd, CA, CurCont, E-psyche, ECER, EMBASE, ExcerpMed, FR, FamI, I05, IBR, IBZ, MLA-IB, P03, PsycInfo, PsycholAb, RILM, SCOPUS, SSCI, T02, W07.
—BLDSC (1736.825000), GNLM, IE, Infotrieve, Ingenta, INIST. **CCC.**
Published by: Pergamon (Subsidiary of: Elsevier Science & Technology), The Blvd, Langford Ln, East Park, Kidlington, Oxford OX5 1GB, United Kingdom. TEL 44-1865-843000, FAX 44-1865-843010, JournalsCustomerServiceEMEA@elsevier.com. Ed. Robyn Flaum Cruz. **Subscr. to:** Elsevier BV, Radarweg 29, PO Box 211, Amsterdam 1000 AE, Netherlands. http://www.elsevier.nl.

159.9 LTU ISSN 1822-9506
AS IR PSICHOLOGIJA. Text in Lithuanian. 2008. 10/yr. LTL 59 (effective 2011). adv. **Document type:** *Magazine, Trade.*
Published by: UAB Leidykla "Jusu Flintas", V Putvinskio g 34, Kaunas, 44211, Lithuania. TEL 370-37-224489, FAX 370-37-224489, sikstas@flintas.lt, http://www.flintas.lt. Ed. Egidija Seputyte-Vaituleviciene. Adv. contact Saule Peciulyte.

158 AUS ISSN 2150-7686
▼ ➤ **ASIA PACIFIC JOURNAL OF COUNSELLING AND PSYCHOTHERAPY.** Text in English. 2010. s-a. GBP 224 combined subscription in United Kingdom to institutions (print & online eds.); EUR 296, USD 369 combined subscription to institutions (print & online eds.) (effective 2012). **Document type:** *Journal, Academic/Scholarly.* **Description:** Features research and best practice in the field of counseling and psychotherapy from the Asia pacific region.
Related titles: Online - full text ed.: ISSN 2150-7708. GBP 201 in United Kingdom to institutions; EUR 266, USD 332 to institutions (effective 2012).
Indexed: A01, T02.
—CCC.
Published by: (Asian Professional Counselling Association USA), Routledge (Subsidiary of: Taylor & Francis Group), Level 2, 11 Queens Rd, Melbourne, VIC 3004, Australia. TEL 61-03-90098134, FAX 61-03-98668822, http://www.informaworld.com.

150 305.895 USA ISSN 1948-1985
E184.A75
▼ **ASIAN AMERICAN JOURNAL OF PSYCHOLOGY.** Text in English. 2010 (Mar.). q. USD 110 domestic to individuals; USD 137 foreign to individuals; USD 403 domestic to institutions; USD 448 foreign to institutions (effective 2011). adv. back issues avail.; reprints avail. **Document type:** *Journal, Academic/Scholarly.* **Description:** Publishes empirical, theoretical, methodological, and practice oriented articles covering topics relevant to Asian American individuals and communities.
Related titles: Online - full text ed.: ISSN 1948-1993 (from ScienceDirect).
Indexed: P03, P30, PsycInfo, SCOPUS.
—CCC.
Published by: (Asian American Psychological Association), American Psychological Association, 750 First St, NE, Washington, DC 20002. TEL 202-336-5500, 800-374-2721, FAX 202-336-5997, journals@apa.org. Ed. Frederick Leong. Adv. contact Doug Constant TEL 202-336-5574. Circ: 800.

302 HKG ISSN 1560-8255
ASIAN JOURNAL OF COUNSELLING/YAZHOU FUDAO XUEBAO. Text in Chinese, English. 1992. s-a. HKD 100 domestic to individuals; USD 20 foreign to individuals; HKD 150 domestic to institutions; USD 30 foreign to institutions (effective 2004). **Document type:** *Journal, Academic/Scholarly.*
Indexed: P03, PsycInfo, PsycholAb.
—BLDSC (1742.479000).
Published by: (Hong Kong Professional Counselling Association), Hong Kong Institute of Educational Research (Subsidiary of: Chinese University of Hong Kong), The Chinese University of Hong Kong, Ho Tim Building, Room 204, Shatin, New Territories, Hong Kong. TEL 852-2609-6754, FAX 852-2603-6850, hkier@cuhk.edu.hk, http://www.fed.cuhk.edu.hk/~hkier/. Ed. S. Alvin Leung. **Co-publisher:** Hong Kong Professional Counselling Association.

302 AUS ISSN 1367-2223
HM1001
➤ **ASIAN JOURNAL OF SOCIAL PSYCHOLOGY.** Text in English. 1998. q. GBP 369 in United Kingdom to institutions; EUR 470 in Europe to institutions; USD 603 in the Americas to institutions; USD 723 elsewhere to institutions; GBP 426 combined subscription in United Kingdom to institutions (print & online eds.); EUR 541 combined subscription in Europe to institutions (print & online eds.); USD 694 combined subscription in the Americas to institutions (print & online eds.); USD 833 combined subscription elsewhere to institutions (print & online eds.) (effective 2012). bk.rev. Index. back issues avail.; reprint service avail. from PSC. **Document type:** *Journal, Academic/Scholarly.* **Description:** Aims to stimulate research and encourage academic exchanges for the advancement of social psychology in Asia. Publishes both theoretical and empirical papers.
Related titles: Online - full text ed.: ISSN 1467-839X. GBP 369 in United Kingdom to institutions; EUR 470 in Europe to institutions; USD 603 in the Americas to institutions; USD 723 elsewhere to institutions (effective 2012) (from IngentaConnect).
Indexed: A01, A03, A08, A20, A22, A26, C06, C07, C08, CA, CINAHL, CurCont, E-psyche, E01, ESPM, H12, H14, P02, P03, P10, P12, P43, P48, P53, P54, PQC, PsycInfo, PsycholAb, RiskAb, S02, S03, S11, SCOPUS, SSA, SSCI, SociolAb, T02, W07.
—BLDSC (1742.576000), IE, Infotrieve, Ingenta. **CCC.**
Published by: (Asian Association of Social Psychology PHL, The Japanese Group Dynamics Association JPN), Wiley-Blackwell Publishing Asia (Subsidiary of: Wiley-Blackwell Publishing Ltd.), 155 Cremorne St, Richmond, VIC 3121, Australia. TEL 61-3-92743100, FAX 61-3-92743101, melbourne@wiley.com, http://www.wiley.com/WileyCDA/. Ed. James Hou-fu Liu. **Subscr. to:** Wiley-Blackwell Publishing Ltd., Journal Customer Services, 9600 Garsington Rd, PO Box 1354, Oxford OX4 2XG, United Kingdom. TEL 44-1865-778315, FAX 44-1865-471775.

158 USA ISSN 1947-427X
▼ **ASK DEANNA!;** love, life & relationships at its best. Variant title: Ask Deanna! The Magazine. Text in English. 2009. m. USD 25, USD 30; USD 2.99 per issue (effective 2009). **Document type:** *Magazine, Consumer.* **Description:** Advice on relationships by Deanna Michaux, advice columnist.
Published by: JuDe Publishing, 264 LaCienga, No 1283, Beverly Hills, CA 90211. TEL 310-600-9729, judepublishing@yahoo.com.

301.1 150 VEN
ASOCIACION VENEZOLANA DE PSICOLOGIA SOCIAL. REVISTA. Text in Spanish. 1978. q. adv. bk.rev. back issues avail. **Document type:** *Journal, Academic/Scholarly.* **Description:** Features theoretical and methodological papers and information about social psychology in Latin America.
Formerly (until 1994): Asociacion Venezolana de Psicologia Social. Boletin (1011-6273)
Indexed: C01, E-psyche.
Published by: Asociacion Venezolana de Psicologia Social (A V E P S O), Instituto de Psicologia, Centro Comercial los Chaguaramos, Caracas, DF 1040, Venezuela. TEL 619811-30 Ext. 2643. Ed. Leoncio Barrios.

616.8 USA ISSN 1073-1911
BF176
➤ **ASSESSMENT.** Text in English. 1993. q. USD 580, GBP 342 to institutions; USD 592, GBP 349 combined subscription to institutions (print & online eds.) (effective 2012). adv. abstr. back issues avail.; reprint service avail. from PSC. **Document type:** *Journal, Academic/Scholarly.* **Description:** Publishes articles derived from psychometric research, clinical comparisons or theoretical formulations and literature reviews that fall within the broad domain of clinical and applied assessment.
Related titles: Online - full text ed.: ISSN 1552-3489. USD 533, GBP 314 to institutions (effective 2012).
Indexed: A01, A03, A08, A22, ASG, C06, C07, C08, CA, CINAHL, CurCont, E-psyche, E01, E03, EMBASE, ERI, ERIC, ExcerpMed, FamI, IndMed, MEDLINE, P03, P18, P25, P30, P53, P54, PQC, PsycInfo, PsycholAb, R10, Reac, SCOPUS, SSCI, T02, V&AA, W07.
—BLDSC (1746.636200), GNLM, IE, Infotrieve, Ingenta. **CCC.**

Published by: Sage Publications, Inc., 2455 Teller Rd, Thousand Oaks, CA 91320. TEL 800-818-7243, FAX 800-583-2665, info@sagepub.com, http://www.sagepub.com. Ed. R Michael Bagby. **Subscr. to:** Sage Publications Ltd., 1 Oliver's Yard, 55 City Rd, London EC1Y 1SP, United Kingdom. TEL 44-207-3248701, FAX 44-207-3248733, subscription@sagepub.co.uk.

➤ **ASSESSMENT & DEVELOPMENT MATTERS.** *see* BUSINESS AND ECONOMICS—Management

➤ **ASSESSMENT FOR EFFECTIVE INTERVENTION.** *see* EDUCATION—Special Education And Rehabilitation

150 610 USA
BF319.5.B5
ASSOCIATION FOR APPLIED PSYCHOPHYSIOLOGY AND BIOFEEDBACK. PROCEEDINGS OF THE ANNUAL MEETING. Text in English. 1972. a. USD 30 to non-members; USD 15 to members (effective 1999). abstr.; illus. **Document type:** *Proceedings, Abstract/Index.*
Formerly: Biofeedback Society of America. Proceedings of the Annual Meeting (0094-0895)
Media: Online - full content.
Indexed: E-psyche.
Published by: Association for Applied Psychophysiology and Biofeedback, 10200 W 44th Ave, Ste 304, Wheat Ridge, CO 80033. TEL 303-422-8436, FAX 303-422-8894. Ed. Michael Thompson. R&P, Adv. contact Michael P Thompson. Circ: 2,000.

155.937 USA ISSN 1091-4846
ASSOCIATION FOR DEATH EDUCATION & COUNSELING. FORUM NEWSLETTER. Text in English. q. USD 135 individual membership; USD 275 institutional membership (effective 2006). adv. bk.rev. **Document type:** *Newsletter.* **Description:** Provides information on upcoming conventions and events and offers articles relevant to death education and counseling from a multidisciplinary standpoint.
Related titles: Online - full content ed.: free.
Indexed: E-psyche.
Published by: Association for Death Education & Counseling, 60 Revere Dr, Ste 500, Northbrook, IL 60062. TEL 847-509-0403, FAX 847-480-9282, info@adec.org. Ed. Illene C Noppe. Circ: 2,000.

616.891 USA ISSN 0004-542X
RC500
ASSOCIATION FOR PSYCHOANALYTIC MEDICINE. BULLETIN. Text in English. 1961. s-a. bk.rev. cum.index: 1961-1967. back issues avail. **Document type:** *Bulletin, Trade.* **Description:** Features reports of the monthly scientific meetings and theoretical issues found in psychoanalytic journals.
Related titles: Online - full text ed.: free (effective 2010).
Indexed: E-psyche.
Published by: Association for Psychoanalytic Medicine, 335 Central Park W, New York, NY 10024. TEL 718-548-6088, gsagi@mac.com, http://www.theapm.org. Ed. Henry Schwartz.

155.4 USA
ASSOCIATION FOR THE STUDY OF PLAY NEWSLETTER. Text in English. 1974. 3/yr. USD 75 domestic to individual members; USD 80 foreign to individual members; USD 85 to institutional members; USD 65 to students (effective 2007). back issues avail. **Document type:** *Newsletter.* **Description:** Covers social science and humanistic study of play behavior.
Indexed: E-psyche.
Published by: Association for the Study of Play, c/o Laurelle Phillips, Treasurer, Early Childhood Education, East Tennessee State University, Box 70548, Johnson City, TN 37614. TEL 423-439-7903, TASPmembership@museumofplay.org. Ed. Dan Hilliard. Circ: 200.

150.195 FRA ISSN 1775-6871
ASSOCIATION LACANIENNE INTERNATIONALE. CAHIERS. Text in French. 1987. irreg. **Document type:** *Monographic series, Academic/Scholarly.*
Formerly (until 1996): Le Trimestre Psychanalytique (0988-5560)
Published by: Association Lacanienne Internationale, 25 rue de Lille, Paris, 75007, France.

158 ITA
ASSOCIAZIONE ITALIANA STUDI DI MUSICOTERAPIA. BOLLETTINO. Text in Italian. 1982. s-a. **Document type:** *Bulletin, Trade.*
Published by: Associazione Italiana Studi di Musicoterapia, Via Brignole de Ferrari 6-2, Genoa, 16125, Italy. TEL 39-010-206914.

150 FRA ISSN 2104-7588
▼ **LES ATELIERS DE PSYCHOLOGIES MAGAZINE.** Text in French. 2009. irreg. **Document type:** *Monographic series, Consumer.*
Published by: Hachette Livre (Subsidiary of: Lagardere Media), 43, Quai de Grenelle, Paris Cedex 15, 75905, France. TEL 33-1-43923023.

150 ARG ISSN 0329-8221
ATENEO PSICOANALITICO. REVISTA. Text in Spanish. 1997. a. **Document type:** *Monographic series, Academic/Scholarly.*
Published by: Ateneo Psicoanalitico, Ave Pueyrredon 1504 Piso 2-C, Buenos Aires, C1118AAS, Argentina. TEL 54-11-48227410. Ed. Elda Nora Fornari. Circ: 500.

158 USA ISSN 1536-0431
➤ **ATHLETIC INSIGHT.** Text in English. 1999. q. USD 280 to institutions; USD 420 combined subscription to institutions (print & online eds.) (effective 2012). **Document type:** *Journal, Academic/Scholarly.* **Description:** Provides a forum for discussion of topics relevant to the field of sport psychology.
Related titles: Online - full text ed.: ISSN 1947-6299. 2009. USD 280 (effective 2012).
Indexed: A36, A39, C27, C29, CA, CABA, D03, D04, E13, GH, LT, N02, N03, P03, PEI, PsycInfo, PsycholAb, R12, R14, RRTA, S14, S15, S18, SD, T02.
Published by: (Athletic Insight, Inc.), Nova Science Publishers, Inc., 400 Oser Ave, Ste 1600, Hauppauge, NY 11788. TEL 631-231-7269, FAX 631-231-8175, main@novapublishers.com, https://www.novapublishers.com. Eds. Miguel Humara, Robert Schinke.

150 GRC ISSN 1109-6020
➤ **ATHLETIKE PSUHOLOGIA.** Text in Greek. 2002. a. **Document type:** *Journal, Academic/Scholarly.* **Description:** Covers all areas of sports psychology, exercise psychology and motor behavior.
Indexed: SD.
—BLDSC (1765.882255).
Published by: Hellenic Society of Sports Psychology (H S S P), 41 Ethnikis Antistassis Str, Dafne, Athens 172 37, Greece. TEL 30-210-7276053, FAX 30-210-7276054, mpsychou@phed.uoa.gr.

➤ **ATLANTIC JOURNAL OF COMMUNICATION.** *see* SOCIOLOGY

➤ **ATQUE**; materiali tra filosofia e psicoterapia. *see* PHILOSOPHY

616.890405 GBR ISSN 1753-5980
RC475
ATTACHMENT; new directions in psychotherapy and relational psychoanalysis. Text in English. 2007. 3/yr. GBP 45 to individuals; GBP 120 to institutions; GBP 35 to students (effective 2010). back issues avail. **Document type:** *Journal, Trade.* **Description:** Features cultural articles, politics, reviews and poetry relevant to attachment and relational issues.
Related titles: Online - full text ed.: ISSN 2044-3757.
—BLDSC (1772.775250), IE.
Published by: Karnac Books, 118 Finchley Rd, London, NW3 5HT, United Kingdom. TEL 44-20-74311075, FAX 44-20-74359076, shop@karnacbooks.com. Ed. Joseph Schwartz.

155 GBR ISSN 1461-6734
CODEN: AHDTAL
➤ **ATTACHMENT AND HUMAN DEVELOPMENT.** Text in English. 1999. bi-m. GBP 677 combined subscription in United Kingdom to institutions (print & online eds.); EUR 901, USD 1,125 combined subscription to institutions (print & online eds.) (effective 2012). adv. bk.rev. back issues avail.; reprint service avail. from PSC. **Document type:** *Journal, Academic/Scholarly.* **Description:** Provides a new forum for research, case studies and debate for clinicians and academics concerned with the development of social and emotional relationships across the lifespan.
Related titles: Online - full text ed.: ISSN 1469-2988. GBP 609 in United Kingdom to institutions; EUR 810, USD 1,013 to institutions (effective 2012) (from IngentaConnect).
Indexed: A01, A03, A08, A20, A22, B21, C06, C07, C08, CA, CINAHL, CurCont, E-psyche, E01, EMBASE, ExcerpMed, F09, FR, Faml, MEDLINE, NSA, P03, P30, PsycInfo, PsycholAb, SCOPUS, SSCI, T02, W07.
—IE, Infotrieve, Ingenta, INIST. **CCC.**
Published by: (International Attachment Network), Routledge (Subsidiary of: Taylor & Francis Group), 4 Park Sq, Milton Park, Abingdon, Oxon OX14 4RN, United Kingdom. TEL 44-20-70176000, FAX 44-20-70176336, subscriptions@tandf.co.uk, http://www.routledge.com. Ed. Howard Steele TEL 44-20-75045941. Adv. contact Linda Hann TEL 44-1344-779945. **Subscr. to:** Taylor & Francis Ltd., Journals Customer Service, Sheepen Pl, Colchester, Essex CO3 3LP, United Kingdom. TEL 44-20-70175544, FAX 44-20-70175198, tf.enquiries@tfinforma.com.

152 USA ISSN 1047-0387
BF321
➤ **ATTENTION AND PERFORMANCE.** Text in English. 1967. irreg., latest vol.22, 2007. price varies. **Document type:** *Proceedings, Academic/Scholarly.*
Indexed: A20, ASCA, E-psyche, SCOPUS.
—BLDSC (1772.810000). **CCC.**
Published by: (International Association for the Study of Attention and Performance NLD), Oxford University Press (Subsidiary of: Oxford University Press), 2001 Evans Rd, Cary, NC 27513. TEL 919-677-0977, FAX 919-677-1303, orders.us@oup.com, http://www.us.oup.com.

152 USA ISSN 1943-3921
BF233 CODEN: PEPSBJ
➤ **ATTENTION, PERCEPTION & PSYCHOPHYSICS.** Text in English. 1966. 8/yr. EUR 441, USD 502 combined subscription to institutions (print & online eds.) (effective 2012). adv. charts; illus. index. back issues avail.; reprint service avail. from PSC. **Document type:** *Journal, Academic/Scholarly.* **Description:** Contains articles that deal with sensory processes, perception and psychophysics. Some theoretical and evaluative reviews are published.
Formerly (until 2009): Perception & Psychophysics (0031-5117)
Related titles: Microform ed.: (from PQC); Online - full text ed.: ISSN 1943-393X (from IngentaConnect).
Indexed: A01, A03, A08, A20, A22, ASCA, B21, B25, BIOSIS Prev, BibInd, CA, CIS, CMCI, CurCont, DIP, DentInd, E-psyche, EMBASE, ErgAb, ExcerpMed, FR, IBR, IBZ, IndMed, L&LBA, MEDLINE, MLA, MLA-IB, MycolAb, NSA, NSCI, P02, P03, P10, P12, P18, P20, P22, P25, P27, P30, P48, P53, P54, PQC, PsycInfo, PsycholAb, R10, RILM, Reac, SCI, SCOPUS, SOPODA, SSCI, T02, W07.
—BLDSC (1772.812700), GNLM, IE, Infotrieve, Ingenta, INIST, Linda Hall. **CCC.**
Published by: Springer New York LLC (Subsidiary of: Springer Science+Business Media), 233 Spring St, New York, NY 10013. TEL 212-460-1500, FAX 212-460-1575, journals@springer-ny.com, http://www.springer.com. adv.: page USD 145; trim 10.75 x 8. Circ: 1,800.

155.2 ITA ISSN 0394-3747
ATTUALITA GRAFOLOGICA; trimestrale dell'Associazione Grafologica Italiana. Text in Italian. 1981. q. free to members. bk.rev. bibl. 48 p./no. 2 cols./p.; **Document type:** *Bulletin, Trade.* **Description:** Contains news about graphology and psychology initiatives.
Indexed: E-psyche.
Published by: Associazione Grafologica Italiana, Scale San Francesco 8, Ancona, AN 60121, Italy. TEL 39-071-206100. Ed. Pacifico Cristofanelli. Pub. Iride Conficoni. Circ: 1,400 (paid).

150.19 ITA ISSN 1828-1958
ATTUALITA LACANIANA. Text in Italian. 2004. s-a. EUR 39.50 combined subscription domestic to institutions (print & online eds.); EUR 51 combined subscription foreign to institutions (print & online eds.) (effective 2009). **Document type:** *Journal, Academic/Scholarly.*
Related titles: Online - full text ed.: ISSN 1971-8349. 2004.
Published by: Franco Angeli Edizioni, Viale Monza 106, Milan, 20127, Italy. TEL 39-02-2837141, FAX 39-02-26144793, redazioni@francoangeli.it, http://www.francoangeli.it. Ed. Maurizio Mazzotti.

150.195 ARG ISSN 1852-7264
▼ **AUN.** Text in Spanish. 2009. s-m. **Document type:** *Journal, Academic/Scholarly.*
Published by: Foro Analitico del Rio de la Plata, Viamonte, 2790, Buenos Aires, Argentina. TEL 54-11-49645877, farp@fcropfarp@org, http://www.forofarp.org/.

616.89 AUS ISSN 1446-1625
➤ **AUSTRALASIAN JOURNAL OF PSYCHOTHERAPY.** Text in English. 1982. s-a. AUD 60 domestic to individuals; AUD 75 in New Zealand to individuals; AUD 85 elsewhere; AUD 80 domestic to institutions (effective 2009). adv. bk.rev. back issues avail. **Document type:** *Journal, Academic/Scholarly.* **Description:** A journal of clinical and general interest for practitioners and others.
Formerly (until 2001): Australian Journal of Psychotherapy (0728-6155)
Indexed: E-psyche, P03, PsycInfo, PsycholAb.
—GNLM.
Published by: Psychoanalytic Psychotherapy Association of Australia, PO Box 4098, Homebush South, NSW 2140, Australia. theppaa@bigpond.com. Ed. Andrew Leggett TEL 61-7-38390699. Circ: 400 (paid and controlled).

➤ **AUSTRALIAN AND NEW ZEALAND JOURNAL OF FAMILY THERAPY**; innovative and contextual approaches to human problems. *see* SOCIOLOGY

150 AUS ISSN 1835-7601
▼ ➤ **AUSTRALIAN AND NEW ZEALAND JOURNAL OF ORGANISATIONAL PSYCHOLOGY.** Text in English. 2010. irreg. AUD 150 domestic; AUD 134 in New Zealand; AUD 165 elsewhere (effective 2011). **Document type:** *Journal, Academic/Scholarly.* **Description:** Covers the study and practice of organisational psychology encompassing the disciplines of: industrial and organisational (I/O) psychology; work psychology; occupational psychology; personnel psychology; human resource management and development; ergonomics, and vocational psychology; managerial psychology including coaching; and consumer psychology.
Media: Online - full text.
Indexed: A01, CA, T02.
Published by: (The Australian Psychological Society, College of Organisational Psychologists), Australian Academic Press Pty. Ltd., 32 Jeays St, Bowen Hills, QLD 4006, Australia. TEL 61-7-32571176, FAX 61-7-32525908, aap@australianacademicpress.com.au, http://www.australianacademicpress.com.au.

150 AUS ISSN 0816-5122
➤ **AUSTRALIAN EDUCATIONAL AND DEVELOPMENTAL PSYCHOLOGIST.** Abbreviated title: A E D P. Text in English. 1984. s-a. AUD 180 combined subscription domestic (print & online eds.); AUD 165 combined subscription in New Zealand (print & online eds.); AUD 200 combined subscription elsewhere (print & online eds.) (effective 2011). **Document type:** *Journal, Academic/Scholarly.* **Description:** Provides psychological research articles that substantially contribute to the knowledge and practice of education and developmental psychology.
Related titles: Online - full text ed.
Indexed: AEI, CPE, ERO, S21.
—BLDSC (1798.730000), IE, Ingenta.
Published by: (Australian Psychological Society. College of Educational and Developmental Psychologists), Australian Academic Press Pty. Ltd., 32 Jeays St, Bowen Hills, QLD 4006, Australia. TEL 61-7-32571176, FAX 61-7-32525908, info@australianacademicpress.com.au, http://www.australianacademicpress.com.au. Ed. Terry Bowles TEL 61-3-99533117.

150 AUS ISSN 1443-9697
➤ **THE AUSTRALIAN JOURNAL OF COUNSELLING PSYCHOLOGY.** Text in English. 1985-1994; resumed 1999. s-a. free to members. **Document type:** *Journal, Academic/Scholarly.* **Description:** Contains articles that covers original research, reviews or meta-analyses, theoretical, conceptual or ideological issues, psychotherapy that focuses on specific client groups, effects in psychotherapy.
Formerly (until 1999): Australian Counselling Psychologist (0817-7449)
Published by: (Australian Psychological Society. College of Counselling Psychologists), Australian Psychological Society, 257 Collins St, Level 11, Melbourne, VIC 3000, Australia. TEL 61-3-86623300, FAX 61-3-96636177, contactus@psychology.org.au, http://www.psychology.org.au. Ed. Geoff Denham.

➤ **AUSTRALIAN JOURNAL OF EDUCATIONAL AND DEVELOPMENTAL PSYCHOLOGY.** *see* EDUCATION

➤ **AUSTRALIAN JOURNAL OF GUIDANCE AND COUNSELLING.** *see* EDUCATION

150 331 AUS ISSN 1447-574X
➤ **AUSTRALIAN JOURNAL OF ORGANISATIONAL BEHAVIOUR AND MANAGEMENT.** Text in English. 1998. s-a. back issues avail. **Document type:** *Journal, Academic/Scholarly.* **Description:** Aims to act as a learning aid for students of the university and be a forum whereby practitioners and academics can share their knowledge, experiences and ideas.
Formerly (until 2002): Australian Journal of Management and Organisational Behaviour (1440-4567)
Media: Online - full text.
Published by: University of Southern Queensland, The Department of Management & Organisational Behaviour, Toowoomba Campus, Toowoomba, QLD 4350, Australia. TEL 61-7-46312100, FAX 61-7-46312893, HRM@usq.edu.au, http://www.usq.edu.au/faculty/business/dept_hrm/HRMJournal/. Ed. Cec Pedersen TEL 61-7-46312396.

➤ **AUSTRALIAN JOURNAL OF PARAPSYCHOLOGY.** *see* PARAPSYCHOLOGY AND OCCULTISM

150 GBR ISSN 0004-9530
BF1 CODEN: ASJPAE
➤ **AUSTRALIAN JOURNAL OF PSYCHOLOGY.** Abbreviated title: A J P. Text in English. 1949. q. GBP 171 in United Kingdom to institutions; EUR 228 in Europe to institutions; USD 287 elsewhere to institutions; GBP 198 combined subscription in United Kingdom to institutions (print & online eds.); EUR 263 combined subscription in Europe to institutions (print & online eds.); USD 330 combined subscription elsewhere to institutions (print & online eds.) (effective 2012). adv. bk.rev. abstr.; bibl.; charts; illus. index. cum.index approx. every 10 yrs. back issues avail.; reprint service avail. from PSC. **Document type:** *Journal, Academic/Scholarly.* **Description:** Presents articles and book reviews on any topic with a central reference to psychology and an emphasis on academic or archival functions.

P

Related titles: Online - full text ed.: ISSN 1742-9536. GBP 171 in United Kingdom to institutions; EUR 228 in Europe to institutions; USD 287 elsewhere to institutions (effective 2012) (from IngentaConnect); Supplement(s): Australian Journal of Psychology. Monograph Supplement. ISSN 0572-1172.
Indexed: A01, A02, A03, A08, A11, A20, A22, AEI, AMHA, ASCA, ASSIA, AusPAIS, B21, BibInd, C28, CA, CDA, CJPI, CurCont, DIP, DSHAb, E-psyche, E01, ERO, ErgAb, F09, FamI, G10, IBR, IBZ, L&LBA, MEA&I, MLA-IB, NSA, P03, P25, P30, P43, P48, PCI, PQC, PsycInfo, PsycholAb, RASB, S02, S03, S21, SCOPUS, SD, SOPODA, SSCI, SociolAb, T02, W07, W09, WBA, WMB.
—BLDSC (1811.300000), IE, Infotrieve, Ingenta, INIST. **CCC.**
Published by: (Australian Psychological Society AUS), John Wiley & Sons Ltd. (Subsidiary of: John Wiley & Sons, Inc.), 9600 Garsington Rd, Oxford, OX4 2DQ, United Kingdom. TEL 44-1865-776868, FAX 44-1865-714591, cs-journals@wiley.com, http://www.wiley.com.

150 GBR ISSN 0005-0067
BF1 CODEN: AUPCBK
➤ **AUSTRALIAN PSYCHOLOGIST.** Text in English. 1966. q. GBP 180 in United Kingdom to institutions; EUR 239 in Europe to institutions; USD 299 elsewhere to institutions; GBP 207 combined subscription in United Kingdom to institutions (print & online eds.); EUR 275 combined subscription in Europe to institutions (print & online eds.); USD 345 combined subscription elsewhere to institutions (print & online eds.) (effective 2012). adv. bk.rev. abstr.; charts; illus. Index. back issues avail.; reprint service avail. from PSC. **Document type:** *Journal, Academic/Scholarly.* **Description:** Publishes articles of relevance to professional and applied psychology, and generally to Australian psychologists.
Related titles: Online - full text ed.: ISSN 1742-9544. GBP 180 in United Kingdom to institutions; EUR 239 in Europe to institutions; USD 299 elsewhere to institutions (effective 2012) (from IngentaConnect).
Indexed: A01, A02, A03, A08, A11, A20, A22, AEI, ASCA, ASSIA, AusPAIS, B21, C06, C07, CA, CDA, CJPI, CurCont, DIP, E-psyche, E01, E03, ERO, FamI, IBR, IBZ, IPsyAb, NSA, P03, P25, P30, P43, P48, PCI, PQC, PsycInfo, PsycholAb, S02, S03, S21, SCOPUS, SOPODA, SSCI, SociolAb, T02, V&AA, W07.
—BLDSC (1818.350000), IE, Infotrieve, Ingenta. **CCC.**
Published by: (Australian Psychological Society AUS), John Wiley & Sons Ltd. (Subsidiary of: John Wiley & Sons, Inc.), 9600 Garsington Rd, Oxford, OX4 2DQ, United Kingdom. TEL 44-1865-776868, FAX 44-1865-714591, cs-journals@wiley.com, http://www.wiley.com.

➤ **AUTISM**; the international journal of research and practice. *see* MEDICAL SCIENCES—Psychiatry And Neurology

➤ **AUTISM RESEARCH REVIEW INTERNATIONAL.** *see* MEDICAL SCIENCES—Psychiatry And Neurology

150 PER ISSN 1812-9536
AVANCES EN PSICOLOGIA. Text in Spanish. 1997. irreg. **Document type:** *Monographic series, Academic/Scholarly.*
Indexed: CA, F04, T02.
Published by: Universidad Femenina del Sagrado Corazon, Ave Los Frutales 954, Urb Santa Magdalena Sofia, La Molina, Lima, 41, Peru. TEL 51-1-4364641, FAX 51-1-4350853, cinv@unife.edu.pe, http://www.unife.edu.pe.

150 COL ISSN 1794-4724
AVANCES EN PSICOLOGIA LATINOAMERICANA. Text in Spanish. 1982. s-a. COP 53,900 domestic; USD 116 foreign. **Document type:** *Journal, Academic/Scholarly.*
Formerly (until 2004): Avances en Psicologia Clinica Latinoamericana (0120-3797)
Related titles: Online - full text ed.: free (effective 2011).
Indexed: A22, A26, DIP, F04, I04, I05, IBR, IBZ, P03, P30, PsycInfo, PsycholAb, SCOPUS, T02.
—IE, Ingenta. **CCC.**
Published by: (Fundacion para el Avance de la Psicologia), Universidad del Rosario, Editorial, Carretera 7, N 13-41, Oficina 501, Bogota, Colombia. TEL 57-1-2970200, FAX 57-1-3445763, editorial@urosario.edu.co. Ed. Andres M Perez-Acosta. Circ: 300.

B OG B. *see* SOCIOLOGY

150 GBR ISSN 1475-0945
B R A T SERIES IN CLINICAL PSYCHOLOGY. (Behaviour Research and Therapy) Text in English. 2003. irreg., latest vol.3, 2007. price varies. **Document type:** *Monographic series, Academic/Scholarly.* **Description:** Covers abnormal psychology, clinical psychology, and advances in the theory and treatment of psychological disorders.
Published by: Elsevier Ltd (Subsidiary of: Elsevier Science & Technology), The Blvd, Langford Ln, Kidlington, Oxford, OX5 1GB, United Kingdom. TEL 44-1865-843000, FAX 44-1865-843010, http://www.elsevier.com. Ed. S J Rachman.

155.5 FRA ISSN 1621-1227
LE BACHELIER. Text in French. 2000. irreg. back issues avail. **Document type:** *Monographic series, Consumer.*
Published by: Editions Eres, 33 Av. Marcel Dassault, Toulouse, 31500, France. TEL 33-5-61751576, FAX 33-5-61735289, eres@edition-eres.com.

150 JPN ISSN 0386-1856
BAIOFIDOBAKKU KENKYU/JAPANESE JOURNAL OF BIOFEEDBACK RESEARCH. Text in English, Japanese. 1973. a. **Document type:** *Journal, Academic/Scholarly.*
Related titles: Online - full text ed.
Indexed: E-psyche, PsycholAb.
—BLDSC (4651.020000). **CCC.**
Published by: Nihon Baiofidobakku Gakkai/Japanese Society of Biofeedback Research, c/o Toho University, School of Medicine, Department of Medical Informatics, 5-21-6 Omori-Nishi, Ota-ku, Tokyo, 143-8540, Japan. biofeedback@med.toho-u.ac.jp.

158 USA ISSN 1934-3116
THE BALANCING ACT E-NEWSLETTER. Text in English. 1999. m. free (effective 2007). **Document type:** *Newsletter, Consumer.*
Media: Online - full text.
Published by: Summit Consulting Group, Inc., PO Box 1009, E Greenwich, RI 02818-0964. TEL 401-884-2778, FAX 401-884-5068, info@summitconsulting.com, http://www.summitconsulting.com/index.html. Ed. Dr. Alan Weiss.

150 LVA ISSN 1407-768X
➤ **BALTIC JOURNAL OF PSYCHOLOGY/BALTIJAS PSIHOLOGIJAS ZURNALS.** Text in English. 2000. 3/yr. **Document type:** *Journal, Academic/Scholarly.*
Indexed: A01, T02.
—BLDSC (1861.316630), IE.
Published by: Latvijas Universitate, Pedagogijas un Psihologijas Fakultate, Psiholooigijas Katedra/University of Latvia, Faculty of Education and Psychology, Department of Psychology, Jurmalas Gatve 74/76, Riga, 1083, Latvia. http://www.ppf.lu.lv. Eds. Malgozata Rascevska, Solveiga Miezitis.

150 BGD ISSN 1022-7466
BANGLADESH JOURNAL OF PSYCHOLOGY. Text in English. 1968. a. USD 10. reprints avail. **Document type:** *Journal, Academic/Scholarly.* **Description:** Contains research and review articles on all branches of psychology.
Indexed: E-psyche.
Published by: Bangladesh Psychological Association, Dept. of Psychology, University of Dhaka, Dhaka, 1000, Bangladesh. TEL 88-2-864553. Ed. A Khaleque. Circ: 400.

301.1 150 USA ISSN 0197-3533
HM251 CODEN: BASPEG
➤ **BASIC AND APPLIED SOCIAL PSYCHOLOGY.** Abbreviated title: B A S P. Text in English. 1980. q. GBP 519 combined subscription in United Kingdom to institutions (print & online eds.); EUR 693, USD 870 combined subscription to institutions (print & online eds.) (effective 2012). adv. bk.rev. abstr.; bibl.; charts; illus.; stat. back issues avail.; reprint service avail. from PSC. **Document type:** *Journal, Academic/Scholarly.* **Description:** Presents material relevant to basic and applied research in all areas of social psychology in order to bring relevant social psychological studies from other specialties and disciplines to the attention of social psychologists.
Related titles: Online - full text ed.: ISSN 1532-4834. GBP 467 in United Kingdom to institutions; EUR 623, USD 783 to institutions (effective 2012).
Indexed: A01, A03, A08, A20, A22, ASCA, ASSIA, B01, B06, B07, B09, C28, CA, CJPI, CommAb, CurCont, DIP, E-psyche, E01, FR, FamI, IBR, IBZ, P03, P10, P12, P30, P43, P48, P53, P54, PQC, PsycInfo, PsycholAb, RILM, S02, S03, S11, SCOPUS, SSA, SSCI, SociolAb, T02, W07, W09.
—BLDSC (1863.913300), IE, Infotrieve, Ingenta, INIST. **CCC.**
Published by: Psychology Press (Subsidiary of: Taylor & Francis Inc.), 325 Chestnut St, Ste 800, Philadelphia, PA 19106. TEL 800-354-1420, FAX 215-625-2940, orders@taylorandfrancis.com, http://www.psypress.com. Ed. Leonard S Newman. Adv. contact Linda Hann TEL 44-1344-779945.

158 USA
BE YOUR OWN THERAPIST NEWSLETTER. Text in English. m. free (effective 2007). **Document type:** *Newsletter, Consumer.* **Description:** Self-help psychology newsletter featuring tips and suggestions for changing your life.
Media: Online - full text.
Indexed: E-psyche.
Address: TopRankHealing@aol.com. Ed. Thayer White.

150 USA ISSN 1052-0082
BF1
BEHAVIOR ANALYSIS DIGEST. Text in English. 1989. q. USD 8 domestic to individuals; USD 10 foreign to individuals; USD 12 to institutions (effective 2011). **Document type:** *Newsletter, Trade.*
Related titles: Online - full text ed.
Indexed: A01, A03, A08, CA, T02.
Address: Cummings Ctr, Ste 340F, PO Box 7067, Beverly, MA 01915. TEL 978369-2227, FAX 978-369-8584, chase@behavior.org, http://www.behavior.org. Ed. W Joseph Wyatt TEL 304-696-2778.

150 USA ISSN 0738-6729
BF199
➤ **THE BEHAVIOR ANALYST.** Text in English. 1978. s-a. USD 140 to institutions; USD 68 to non-members; free to members (effective 2011). adv. bk.rev. cum.index. back issues avail. **Document type:** *Journal, Academic/Scholarly.* **Description:** Covers articles on theoretical, experimental, and applied topics. Contains literature reviews, re-interpretations of published data, and articles on behaviorism as a philosophy.
Related titles: Audio cassette/tape ed.
Indexed: A20, A22, ASCA, BehAb, CurCont, E-psyche, ERIC, P03, P30, PsycInfo, PsycholAb, SCOPUS, SSCI, W07.
—BLDSC (1876.652500), IE, Infotrieve, Ingenta.
Published by: (Society for the Advancement of Behavior Analysis), Association for Behavior Analysis International, 550 W Centre Ave, Ste 1, Portage, MI 49024. TEL 269-492-9310, FAX 269-492-9316, mail@abainternational.org. Ed. Henry D Schlinger.

150 USA ISSN 1539-4352
RC489.R4
➤ **THE BEHAVIOR ANALYST TODAY**; a context for science with a commitment for change. Text in English. 1999. q. free (effective 2010). adv. back issues avail. **Document type:** *Journal, Academic/Scholarly.* **Description:** Committed to increasing the communication between the sub disciplines within behavior analysis, such as behavioral assessment, work with various populations, basic and applied research.
Media: Online - full text.
Indexed: A01, A03, A08, A26, A39, C27, C29, CA, D03, D04, E03, E13, ERI, ERIC, H12, I05, P03, P30, PsycInfo, R14, S14, S15, S18, T02.
Published by: Behavior Analyst Online, 535 Queen St, Philadelphia, PA 19147. baojournals@aol.com, http://baojournal.com/. Adv. contact Halina Dziewolska TEL 215-462-6737.

150 USA ISSN 1053-8348
BF199 CODEN: BEPHE5
➤ **BEHAVIOR AND PHILOSOPHY.** Text in English. 1973. a. USD 85 per issue domestic; USD 95 per issue foreign (effective 2009). bk.rev. illus. 100 p./no.; reprints avail. **Document type:** *Journal, Academic/Scholarly.* **Description:** Features articles based on the philosophical, metaphysical, and methodological foundations of the study of behavior, brain and mind.
Formerly (until 1990): Behaviorism (0090-4155)
Related titles: Online - full text ed.: ISSN 1943-3328. free (effective 2009).
Indexed: A01, A03, A08, A20, A22, AMHA, ASCA, CA, DIP, E-psyche, FR, IBR, IBZ, MEA&I, P03, P25, P30, P43, P48, PCI, PQC, PhilInd, PsycInfo, PsycholAb, RI-1, RI-2, SCOPUS, T02.
—BLDSC (1876.670000), IE, Infotrieve, Ingenta, INIST.
Published by: Cambridge Center for Behavioral Studies, 550 Newtown Rd, Ste 700, Littleton, MA 01460. TEL 978-369-2227, FAX 978-369-8584, harshbarger@behavior.org. Ed. M Jackson Marr. **Subscr. to:** Boyd Printing Co., 5 Sand Creek Rd, Albany, NY 12205. TEL 518-436-9686 ext 134, 800-877-2693, FAX 518-436-7433, info@boydprinting.com, http://www.boydprinting.com.

302 USA ISSN 1064-9506
BF199
➤ **BEHAVIOR AND SOCIAL ISSUES.** Text in English. 1978. s-a. USD 32 to individuals; USD 75 to institutions; USD 15 to students (effective 2010). bk.rev. illus. 100 p./no. 1 cols./p.; back issues avail. **Document type:** *Journal, Academic/Scholarly.* **Description:** Features scholarly articles that advance the analysis of human social behavior, particularly with application to understanding existing social problems.
Former titles (until 1991): Behavior Analysis and Social Action (1065-1047); (until 1986): Behaviorists for Social Action Journal (0739-5051)
Related titles: Online - full text ed.: 2001. free (effective 2011).
Indexed: A39, B04, C27, C29, CA, D03, D04, E-psyche, E13, P03, P10, P12, P13, P25, P27, P30, P48, P53, P54, PQC, PsycInfo, PsycholAb, R14, S02, S03, S14, S15, S18, SSAI, SSAb, SSI, T02, W03, W05.
—Ingenta.
Published by: Behaviorists for Social Responsibility, JACSW (M/C 309), University of Illinois at Chicago, 1040 W Harrison St, Chicago, IL 60607. TEL 312-996-4629, FAX 312-996-2770, bfsr@bfsr.org, http://www.bfsr.org. Ed. Mark A Mattaini. **Subscr. to:** Boyd Printing Co., 5 Sand Creek Rd, Albany, NY 12205. TEL 800-877-2693, info@boydprinting.com, http://www.boydprinting.com.

150 USA ISSN 0145-4455
BF637.B4
➤ **BEHAVIOR MODIFICATION.** Text in English. 1977. bi-m. USD 1,047, GBP 616 combined subscription to institutions (print & online eds.); USD 1,026, GBP 604 to institutions (effective 2011). adv. bk.rev. illus. index. back issues avail.; reprint service avail. from PSC. **Document type:** *Journal, Academic/Scholarly.* **Description:** Describes assessment and modification techniques for problems in psychiatric, clinical, educational, and rehabilitational settings.
Formerly: Behavior Modification Quarterly
Related titles: Online - full text ed.: ISSN 1552-4167. USD 942, GBP 554 to institutions (effective 2011).
Indexed: A01, A02, A03, A08, A20, A22, AMHA, ASCA, B07, B21, BRD, C06, C07, C08, CA, CINAHL, CurCont, E-psyche, E01, E02, E03, ECER, EMBASE, ERI, ERIC, EdA, EdI, ExcerpMed, FR, FamI, H04, INI, IndMed, L&LBA, MEDLINE, NSA, P02, P03, P04, P10, P12, P18, P25, P26, P30, P48, P53, P54, P55, PQC, PsycInfo, PsycholAb, PsycholRG, R10, Reac, S02, S03, SCOPUS, SFSA, SSA, SSCI, SociolAb, T02, V&AA, V02, W03, W07.
—BLDSC (1876.720000), GNLM, IE, Infotrieve, Ingenta, INIST. **CCC.**
Published by: Sage Publications, Inc., 2455 Teller Rd, Thousand Oaks, CA 91320. TEL 805-499-9774, 800-818-7243, FAX 805-499-0871, 800-583-2665, info@sagepub.com. Eds. Alan S Bellack, Michael Hersen. adv.: color page USD 775, B&W page USD 385; 4.5 x 7.5. Circ: 700 (paid). **Subscr. overseas to:** Sage Publications Ltd., 1 Oliver's Yard, 55 City Rd, London EC1Y 1SP, United Kingdom. TEL 44-207-3248701, FAX 44-207-3248733, info@sagepub.co.uk.

572 USA ISSN 1554-3528
➤ **BEHAVIOR RESEARCH METHODS (ONLINE).** Text in English. 1984. q. EUR 321, USD 376 to institutions (effective 2012). **Document type:** *Journal, Academic/Scholarly.*
Formerly (until 2005): Behavior Research Methods, Instruments, & Computers (Online) (1532-5970)
Media: Online - full text. **Related titles:** Microform ed.: (from PQC).
—BLDSC (1876.825000). **CCC.**
Published by: (Psychonomic Society, Inc.), Springer New York LLC (Subsidiary of: Springer Science+Business Media), 233 Spring St, New York, NY 10013. TEL 212-460-1500, FAX 212-460-1575, service-ny@springer.com.

301.1 USA ISSN 0278-8403
RC489.B4
THE BEHAVIOR THERAPIST. Text in English. 1978. 8/yr. USD 40 to non-members; free to members (effective 2010). adv. bk.rev.; software rev. back issues avail. **Document type:** *Journal, Academic/Scholarly.* **Description:** Aims to be a vehicle of communication among behavioral scientists, educators, practitioners, administrators, students and job seekers.
Formerly (until 19??): Association for Advancement of Behavior Therapy. Newsletter
Related titles: Online - full text ed.: free (effective 2010).
Indexed: A22, E-psyche, P03, PsycInfo, PsycholAb, YAE&RB.
—BLDSC (1876.900000), IE, Infotrieve, Ingenta. **CCC.**
Published by: Association for Behavioral and Cognitive Therapies, 305 7th Ave, 16th Fl, New York, NY 10001. TEL 212-647-1890, FAX 212-647-1865, publications@abct.org. Ed. Drew A Anderson. Adv. contact Stephanie Schwartz TEL 212-647-1890 ext 207.

150 USA ISSN 0005-7894
RC489.B4 CODEN: BHVTAK
➤ **BEHAVIOR THERAPY.** Text in English. 1970. 4/yr. EUR 327 in Europe to institutions; JPY 43,600 in Japan to institutions; USD 395 elsewhere to institutions (effective 2012). illus. Index. back issues avail.; reprints avail. **Document type:** *Journal, Academic/Scholarly.* **Description:** Interdisciplinary journal which presents treatment research covering theory, methodology, clinical and ethical issues.
Related titles: Online - full text ed.: ISSN 1878-1888 (from ScienceDirect).
Indexed: A01, A02, A03, A08, A20, A22, A26, AMHA, ASCA, ASSIA, B21, B25, BIOSIS Prev, BRD, C06, C07, CA, CIS, CurCont, E-psyche, E08, ECER, EMBASE, ERIC, ExcerpMed, F09, FR, FamI, G08, I05, JW-P, MEA&I, MEDLINE, MycolAb, NSA, P02, P03, P10, P12, P27, P30, P48, P53, P54, PCI, PQC, PsycInfo, PsycholAb, R10, Reac, S02, S03, S09, SCOPUS, SSAI, SSAb, SSCI, SSI, T02, THA, W03, W07, W09.
—BLDSC (1876.930000), GNLM, IE, Infotrieve, Ingenta, INIST. **CCC.**
Published by: (Association for Behavioral and Cognitive Therapies), Elsevier Inc. (Subsidiary of: Elsevier Science & Technology), 360 Park Ave S, New York, NY 10010. TEL 212-989-5800, FAX 212-633-3990, usinfo-f@elsevier.com. Ed. Richard G Heimberg. Circ: 3,500.

150 616.8 GBR ISSN 0140-525X
QP360 CODEN: BBSCDH

➤ **BEHAVIORAL AND BRAIN SCIENCES**; an international journal of current research and theory with open peer commentary. Abbreviated title: B B S. Text in English. 1978. bi-m. GBP 643, USD 1,093 to institutions; GBP 703, USD 1,193 combined subscription to institutions (print & online eds.) (effective 2012). adv. bk.rev. charts; illus. index. back issues avail.; reprint service avail. from PSC. **Document type:** *Journal, Academic/Scholarly.* **Description:** Covers psychology, neuroscience, behavioral biology, and cognitive science.

Related titles: Microform ed.: (from PQC); Online - full text ed.: ISSN 1469-1825. GBP 594, USD 1,005 to institutions (effective 2012).

Indexed: A01, A02, A03, A08, A20, A22, A26, ASCA, ArtIAb, B21, B25, BIOBASE, BIOSIS Prev, CA, CMM, CommAb, CurCont, DIP, E-psyche, E01, E07, E08, EMBASE, ESPM, ExcerpMed, FR, G08, H13, I05, IABS, IBR, IBZ, ISR, IndMed, Inpharma, Inspec, L&LBA, MEDLINE, MLA-IB, MycolAb, NSA, NSCI, P02, P03, P10, P12, P20, P22, P25, P30, P48, P52, P53, P54, P56, PCI, PQC, PhilInd, PsycInfo, PsycholAb, R10, RASB, Reac, S02, S03, S09, SCI, SCOPUS, SOPODA, SSCI, SociolAb, T02, THA, Telegen, ToxAb, W07.

—BLDSC (1877.293000), AskIEEE, GNLM, IE, Infotrieve, Ingenta, INIST. **CCC.**

Published by: Cambridge University Press, The Edinburgh Bldg, Shaftesbury Rd, Cambridge, CB2 8RU, United Kingdom. TEL 44-1223-312393, FAX 44-1223-315052, journals@cambridge.org, http://www.cambridge.org/uk. Eds. Barbara L Finlay, Paul Bloom. R&P Linda Nicol TEL 44-1223-325702. adv.: B&W page USD 1,035, color page GBP 1,515, color page USD 2,875, B&W page GBP 545. Circ: 2,100. **Subscr. to:** Cambridge University Press, 32 Ave of the Americas, New York, NY 10013. TEL 212-337-5000, FAX 212-691-3239, journals_subscriptions@cup.org.

➤ **BEHAVIORAL ECOLOGY AND SOCIOBIOLOGY.** *see* ENVIRONMENTAL STUDIES

616.8 USA ISSN 0896-4289
RB152 CODEN: BEMEEF

➤ **BEHAVIORAL MEDICINE**; relating behavior and health. Text in English. 1975. q. GBP 165 combined subscription in United Kingdom to institutions (print & online eds.); EUR 218, USD 272 combined subscription to institutions (print & online eds.) (effective 2012). adv. bk.rev. charts; stat. Index. 40 p./no. 2 cols./p.; back issues avail.; reprint service avail. from PSC. **Document type:** *Journal, Academic/Scholarly.* **Description:** Features for physicians, psychologists, nurses, educators, and all who are concerned with behavioral and social influences on mental and physical health.

Formerly (until 1988): Journal of Human Stress (0097-840X)

Related titles: CD-ROM ed.; Microfilm ed.; Online - full text ed.: ISSN 1940-4026. GBP 149 in United Kingdom to institutions; EUR 197, USD 245 to institutions (effective 2012).

Indexed: A01, A02, A03, A08, A20, A22, A26, A36, AMHA, ASCA, ASSIA, AbAn, B25, BIOSIS Prev, BRD, C06, C07, C08, C11, CA, CABA, CINAHL, CWI, CurCont, DIP, E-psyche, E08, E12, EMBASE, ERIC, ExcerpMed, FR, FamI, G03, G08, GH, GSA, GSI, H04, H11, H12, I05, IBR, IBZ, INI, IndMed, Inpharma, MEA&I, MEDLINE, MycolAb, N02, N03, P03, P10, P12, P19, P20, P22, P24, P25, P26, P30, P35, P43, P48, P53, P54, PQC, PsycInfo, PsycholAb, R10, R12, RASB, Reac, S02, S03, S04, S09, SCI, SCOPUS, SSCI, T02, T05, W03, W05, W07.

—BLDSC (1877.560000), CIS, GNLM, IE, Infotrieve, Ingenta, INIST. **CCC.**

Published by: (Helen Dwight Reid Educational Foundation), Routledge (Subsidiary of: Taylor & Francis Group), 325 Chestnut St, Ste 800, Philadelphia, PA 19106. TEL 215-625-8900, FAX 215-625-2940, journals@routledge.com, http://www.routledge.com.

156 616.8 USA ISSN 0735-7044
BF1 CODEN: BENEDJ

➤ **BEHAVIORAL NEUROSCIENCE.** Text in English. 1921. bi-m. USD 321 domestic to individuals; USD 353 foreign to individuals; USD 1,148 domestic to institutions; USD 1,205 foreign to institutions (effective 2011). adv. charts; illus. index. back issues avail.; reprint service avail. from PSC. **Document type:** *Journal, Academic/Scholarly.* **Description:** Features original papers in the broad field of the biological bases of behavior.

Supersedes in part (in 1983): Journal of Comparative and Physiological Psychology (0021-9940); Which was formerly (until 1947): Journal of Comparative Psychology (0093-4127); Which was formed by the merger of (1917-1921): Psychobiology (0096-9745); (1911-1921): Journal of Animal Behavior (0095-9928)

Related titles: Microform ed.: (from PMC, PQC); Online - full text ed.: ISSN 1939-0084 (from ScienceDirect).

Indexed: A01, A02, A03, A08, A22, A26, A34, A35, A36, A38, ASCA, ASFA, AbAn, AgBio, Agr, AnBeAb, B&AI, B04, B10, B21, B25, BIOSIS Prev, BRD, C25, CA, CABA, ChemAb, ChemoAb, CurCont, D01, DentInd, E-psyche, E08, E12, EMBASE, ExcerpMed, FR, G08, GH, H16, I05, ISR, IndMed, IndVet, Inpharma, MEDLINE, MycolAb, N02, N03, N04, NRN, NSA, NSCI, P02, P03, P10, P12, P27, P30, P37, P48, P53, P54, PQC, PsycInfo, PsycholAb, R07, R10, RA&MP, RASB, Reac, S02, S03, S09, S12, SCI, SCOPUS, SSAI, SSAb, SSI, SoyAb, T02, THA, VS, W03, W07, WildRev.

—BLDSC (1877.610000), CASDDS, GNLM, IE, Infotrieve, Ingenta, INIST. **CCC.**

Published by: American Psychological Association, 750 First St, NE, Washington, DC 20002. TEL 202-336-5500, 800-374-2721, FAX 202-336-5997, journals@apa.org. Ed. Mark S Blumberg. Adv. contact Doug Constant TEL 202-336-5574. Circ: 700.

➤ **BEHAVIORAL RESEARCH IN ACCOUNTING.** *see* BUSINESS AND ECONOMICS—Accounting

155 CHE ISSN 2076-328X

▼ ➤ **BEHAVIORAL SCIENCES.** Text in English. 2011. q. free (effective 2011). **Document type:** *Journal, Academic/Scholarly.* **Description:** Publishes research in the areas of psychology, neuroscience, cognitive science, behavioral biology and behavioral genetics.

Media: Online - full text.

Published by: M D P I AG, Postfach, Basel, 4005, Switzerland. TEL 41-61-6837734, FAX 41-61-3028918, http://www.mdpi.org/. Ed. Dr. John Coverdale.

150 340 GBR ISSN 0735-3936
K2 CODEN: BSLADR

➤ **BEHAVIORAL SCIENCES & THE LAW.** Text in English. 1983. bi-m. GBP 766 in United Kingdom to institutions; EUR 968 in Europe to institutions; USD 1,500 elsewhere to institutions; GBP 881 combined subscription in United Kingdom to institutions (print & online eds.); EUR 1,113 combined subscription in Europe to institutions (print & online eds.); USD 1,726 combined subscription elsewhere to institutions (print & online eds.) (effective 2012). adv. back issues avail.; reprint service avail. from PSC. **Document type:** *Journal, Academic/Scholarly.* **Description:** Provides current and comprehensive information in focused topics at the interface of the law and behavioral sciences.

Related titles: Microform ed.: (from PQC); Online - full text ed.: ISSN 1099-0798. GBP 766 in United Kingdom to institutions; EUR 968 in Europe to institutions; USD 1,500 elsewhere to institutions (effective 2012).

Indexed: A01, A03, A08, A20, A22, A26, ASCA, ASSIA, B04, C06, C07, CA, CJA, CJPI, CLI, CPE, CurCont, E-psyche, EMBASE, ExcerpMed, F09, FamI, G08, H12, I01, I05, ILP, INI, IndMed, L07, L10, LRI, M06, MEDLINE, P02, P03, P10, P12, P30, P34, P42, P43, P48, P53, P54, PAIS, PQC, PSA, PsycInfo, PsycholAb, RI-1, RI-2, S02, S03, SCOPUS, SOPODA, SSCI, SociolAb, T02, W07.

—GNLM, IE, Infotrieve, Ingenta. **CCC.**

Published by: John Wiley & Sons Ltd. (Subsidiary of: John Wiley & Sons, Inc.), 1-7 Oldlands Way, PO Box 808, Bognor Regis, West Sussex PO21 9FF, United Kingdom. customer@wiley.co.uk, http://eu.wiley.com/WileyCDA/. Eds. Alan R Felthous TEL 314-977-4825, Charles Patrick Ewing TEL 716-645-2770. **Subscr. in the Americas to:** John Wiley & Sons, Inc., 111 River St, Hoboken, NJ 07030. TEL 201-748-6645, 800-225-5945, subinfo@wiley.com; **Subscr. to:** 1-7 Oldlands Way, PO Box 809, Bognor Regis, West Sussex PO21 9FG, United Kingdom.

154.6 USA ISSN 1540-2002
RC547

➤ **BEHAVIORAL SLEEP MEDICINE.** Abbreviated title: B S M. Text in English. 2003. q. GBP 279 combined subscription in United Kingdom to institutions (print & online eds.); EUR 371, USD 467 combined subscription to institutions (print & online eds.) (effective 2012). adv. back issues avail.; reprint service avail. from PSC. **Document type:** *Journal, Academic/Scholarly.* **Description:** Addresses behavioral dimensions of normal and abnormal sleep mechanisms and the prevention, assessment, and treatment of sleep disorders and associated behavioral and emotional problems.

Related titles: Online - full text ed.: ISSN 1540-2010. 2003. GBP 251 in United Kingdom to institutions; EUR 334, USD 420 to institutions (effective 2012).

Indexed: A01, A03, A08, A22, ASSIA, CA, CurCont, E01, EMBASE, ExcerpMed, MEDLINE, P03, P10, P30, P43, P48, P53, P54, PQC, PsycInfo, PsycholAb, R10, Reac, SCI, SCOPUS, T02, W07.

—BLDSC (1877.925000), IE, Ingenta. **CCC.**

Published by: Routledge (Subsidiary of: Taylor & Francis Group), 325 Chestnut St, Ste 800, Philadelphia, PA 19106. TEL 800-354-1420, FAX 215-625-8914, journals@routledge.com, http://www.routledge.com. Ed. Kenneth L Lichstein.

370.15 USA ISSN 1532-9518

➤ **BEHAVIORAL TECHNOLOGY TODAY.** Text in English. 2000. irreg., latest vol.5, 2008. free (effective 2009). back issues avail. **Document type:** *Journal, Academic/Scholarly.* **Description:** Provides a medium of communication for the discipline of behavior analysis.

Media: Online - full text.

Indexed: A01, CA, E-psyche, T02.

Published by: Cambridge Center for Behavioral Studies, 550 Newtown Rd, Ste 700, Littleton, MA 01460. TEL 978-369-2227, FAX 978-369-8584, harshbarger@behavior.org. Eds. H S Pennypacker, Murray Sidman. **Subscr. to:** Boyd Printing Co., 5 Sand Creek Rd, Albany, NY 12205. TEL 518-436-9686 ext 134, 800-877-2693, FAX 518-436-7433, info@boydprinting.com, http://www.boydprinting.com.

155.9 304 USA ISSN 1047-8663
BF199

➤ **BEHAVIOROLOGY.** Text in English. 1993. a. back issues avail. **Document type:** *Journal, Academic/Scholarly.* **Description:** Features papers that contribute to the experimental analysis of functional relations between environment and behavior.

Indexed: E-psyche.

Published by: The International Society for Behaviorology, c o Lawrence E Fraley, 5754 Kingwood Pike, Reedsville, WV 26547.

➤ **BEHAVIOUR**; an international journal of behavioural biology. *see* BIOLOGY—Zoology

301.1 150 GBR ISSN 0144-929X
QA75.5 CODEN: BEITD5

➤ **BEHAVIOUR AND INFORMATION TECHNOLOGY**; an international journal on the human aspects of computing. Abbreviated title: B I T. Text in English. 1982. bi-m. GBP 1,180 combined subscription in United Kingdom to institutions (print & online eds.); EUR 1,562, USD 1,960 combined subscription to institutions (print & online eds.) (effective 2012). adv. bk.rev. illus. Index. back issues avail.; reprint service avail. from PSC. **Document type:** *Journal, Academic/Scholarly.* **Description:** Covers all aspects of human-computer interaction.

Related titles: Online - full text ed.: ISSN 1362-3001. GBP 1,062 in United Kingdom to institutions; EUR 1,405, USD 1,764 to institutions (effective 2012) (from IngentaConnect).

Indexed: A01, A03, A08, A10, A20, A22, A28, AHCI, APA, ASCA, B01, B06, B07, B09, B21, BrCerAb, C&ISA, C06, C07, C08, C10, C23, CA, CA/WCA, CIA, CINAHL, CMCI, CMM, CPE, CPEI, CerAb, CivEngAb, CompAb, CompLI, CorrAb, CurCont, E&CAJ, E-psyche, E01, E11, EEA, EMA, ERIC, ESPM, EngInd, EnvEAb, ErgAb, FR, H15, Inspec, L04, L13, LISTA, M&TEA, M09, MBF, METADEX, NSA, P03, P17, P26, P30, P43, P53, P54, PQC, PsycInfo, PsycholAb, RoboAb, S01, SCI, SCOPUS, SSCI, SolStAb, T02, T04, V03, W07, WAA.

—AskIEEE, CASDDS, IE, Infotrieve, Ingenta, INIST, Linda Hall. **CCC.**

Published by: Taylor & Francis Ltd. (Subsidiary of: Taylor & Francis Group), 4 Park Sq, Milton Park, Abingdon, Oxfordshire OX14 4RN, United Kingdom. TEL 44-20-70176000, FAX 44-20-70176336, subscriptions@tandf.co.uk, http://www.taylorandfrancis.com. Ed. Ahmet Cakir. Adv. contact Linda Hann. **Subscr. in N. America to:** Taylor & Francis Inc., Customer Services Dept, 325 Chestnut St, 8th Fl, Philadelphia, PA 19106. TEL 215-625-8900, 800-354-1420, FAX 215-625-2940, customerservice@taylorandfrancis.com; **Subscr. to:** Journals Customer Service, Sheepen Pl, Colchester, Essex CO3 3LP, United Kingdom. TEL 44-20-70175544, FAX 44-20-70175198, tf.enquiries@tfinforma.com.

150 AUS ISSN 0813-4839
RC489.B4 CODEN: BHCAE8

➤ **BEHAVIOUR CHANGE.** Text in English. 1984. q. AUD 258 combined subscription domestic to institutions (print & online eds.); AUD 270 combined subscription in New Zealand to institutions (print & online eds.); AUD 284 combined subscription elsewhere to institutions (print & online eds.) (effective 2011). back issues avail. **Document type:** *Journal, Academic/Scholarly.* **Description:** Provides information about research involving the application of behavioural and cognitive-behavioural principles and techniques to the assessment and treatment of various problems.

Related titles: Online - full text ed.

Indexed: A01, A11, A22, AEI, ASCA, CA, CurCont, E-psyche, EMBASE, ERO, ExcerpMed, FamI, P03, P25, P27, P30, P48, P54, PQC, PsycInfo, PsycholAb, SCOPUS, SOPODA, SSCI, SociolAb, T02, W07.

—BLDSC (1876.679000), GNLM, IE, Infotrieve, Ingenta. **CCC.**

Published by: (Australian Association for Cognitive and Behaviour Therapy), Australian Academic Press Pty. Ltd., 32 Jeays St, Bowen Hills, QLD 4006, Australia. TEL 61-7-32571176, FAX 61-7-32525908, aap@australianacademicpress.com.au, http://www.australianacademicpress.com.au. Ed., Adv. contact Ross G Menzies.

150 GBR ISSN 0005-7967
RC321 CODEN: BRTHAA

➤ **BEHAVIOUR RESEARCH AND THERAPY.** Variant title: Cognitive Behaviour Therapy. Text in English. 1963. 12/yr. EUR 1,994 in Europe to institutions; JPY 264,900 in Japan to institutions; USD 2,231 elsewhere to institutions (effective 2012). adv. bk.rev. charts; illus. index. back issues avail.; reprints avail. **Document type:** *Journal, Academic/Scholarly.* **Description:** Focuses on the application of existing modern learning theory to psychiatric and social problems, relating learning to maladaptive behavior.

Incorporates (1977-1994): Advances in Behaviour Research and Therapy (0146-6402); (1979-1992): Behavioral Assessment (0191-5401)

Related titles: Microfiche ed.: (from MIM); Microfilm ed.: (from PQC); Online - full text ed.: ISSN 1873-622X. 1995 (from IngentaConnect, ScienceDirect).

Indexed: A01, A02, A03, A08, A20, A22, A26, AC&P, AMHA, ASCA, ASFA, ASSIA, Agr, B04, B21, B25, BDM&CN, BIOBASE, BIOSIS Prev, BRD, CA, CDA, CommAb, CurCont, DIP, DentInd, E-psyche, E07, E08, EMBASE, ExcerpMed, F09, FR, FamI, G08, G10, HEA, I05, IABS, IBR, IBZ, ISR, IndMed, JW-P, MEDLINE, MLA, MLA-IB, MycolAb, NSA, P02, P03, P10, P12, P27, P30, P48, P53, P54, PQC, PsycInfo, PsycholAb, R10, Reac, S02, S03, S09, SCOPUS, SOPODA, SSAI, SSAb, SSCI, SSI, SWR&A, SociolAb, T02, THA, W03, W07.

—BLDSC (1876.810000), GNLM, IE, Infotrieve, Ingenta, INIST. **CCC.**

Published by: Elsevier Ltd (Subsidiary of: Elsevier Science & Technology), The Blvd, Langford Ln, Kidlington, Oxford, OX5 1GB, United Kingdom. TEL 44-1865-843000, FAX 44-1865-843010, journalscustomerserviceemea@elsevier.com. Ed. G T Wilson. Circ: 4,300.

150 GBR ISSN 1352-4658
RC489.B4

➤ **BEHAVIOURAL AND COGNITIVE PSYCHOTHERAPY.** Abbreviated title: B C P. Text in English. 1972. 5/yr. GBP 266, USD 499 to institutions; GBP 278, USD 518 combined subscription to institutions (print & online eds.) (effective 2012). adv. bk.rev. back issues avail.; reprint service avail. from PSC. **Document type:** *Journal, Academic/Scholarly.* **Description:** Multidisciplinary original research, of an experimental or clinical nature, that contributes to the theory, practice, and evaluation of behavior therapy.

Former titles (until 1993): Behavioural Psychotherapy (0141-3473); (until 1978): B A B P Bulletin

Related titles: Online - full text ed.: ISSN 1469-1833. 1999. GBP 216, USD 405 to institutions (effective 2012).

Indexed: A01, A03, A08, A20, A22, AMED, AddicA, B21, CA, CurCont, E-psyche, E01, EMBASE, ExcerpMed, FR, MEDLINE, NSA, P03, P25, P30, P48, PQC, PsycInfo, PsycholAb, SCOPUS, SSCI, T02, W07.

—BLDSC (1877.293500), GNLM, IE, Infotrieve, Ingenta, INIST. **CCC.**

Published by: (British Association for Behavioural and Cognitive Psychotherapy), Cambridge University Press, The Edinburgh Bldg, Shaftesbury Rd, Cambridge, CB2 8RU, United Kingdom. TEL 44-1223-312393, FAX 44-1223-315052, journals@cambridge.org, http://www.cambridge.org/uk. Ed. Paul Salkovskis. R&P Linda Nicol TEL 44-1223-325702. Adv. contact Rebecca Roberts TEL 44-1223-325083. page GBP 590, page USD 1,120. Circ: 6,000. **Subscr. to:** Cambridge University Press, 32 Ave of the Americas, New York, NY 10013. TEL 212-337-5000, FAX 212-691-3239, journals_subscriptions@cup.org

➤ **BEHAVIOURAL PHARMACOLOGY.** *see* PHARMACY AND PHARMACOLOGY

150 GBR ISSN 0953-7074

BEHAVIOURAL PSYCHOTHERAPIST. Text in English. 1981. 3/yr. free to members. adv. bk.rev. **Document type:** *Journal, Academic/Scholarly.* **Description:** Gives news of the association's events and allows for the exchange of information among members.

Formerly (until 1987): British Association for Behavioural Psychotherapy. Newsletter (0262-3110)

Indexed: E-psyche.

—BLDSC (1877.740000).

Published by: British Association for Behavioural and Cognitive Psychotherapy, The Globe Centre, PO Box 9, Accrington, BB5 0XB, United Kingdom. TEL 44-1254-875277, FAX 44-1254-239114, babcp@babcp.com, http://www.babcp.org.uk/. Ed., R&P John Rose. Circ: 2,000.

P

150 DEU ISSN 0936-594X
BEITRAEGE ZUR GESCHICHTE DER PSYCHOLOGIE. Text in German. 1991. irreg., latest vol.23, 2007. price varies. **Document type:** *Monographic series, Academic/Scholarly.*
Published by: Peter Lang GmbH (Subsidiary of: Peter Lang Publishing Group), Eschborner Landstr 42-50, Frankfurt Am Main, 60489, Germany. TEL 49-69-7807050, FAX 49-69-78070550, zentrale.frankfurt@peterlang.com. Ed. Helmut Lueck.

150 DEU ISSN 0722-8902
BEITRAEGE ZUR INDIVIDUALPSYCHOLOGIE. Text in German. 1978. irreg., latest vol.34, 2008. price varies. **Document type:** *Monographic series, Academic/Scholarly.*
Indexed: E-psyche.
Published by: Vandenhoeck und Ruprecht, Theaterstr 13, Goettingen, 37073, Germany. TEL 49-551-508440, FAX 49-551-5084422, info@v-r.de.

▼ **BEITRAEGE ZUR PAEDAGOGISCHEN UND REHABILITATIONSPSYCHOLOGIE.** *see* EDUCATION

155.4 DEU ISSN 0340-0123
BEITRAEGE ZUR PSYCHODIAGNOSTIK DES KINDES. Text in German. 1973. irreg., latest 2007. price varies. **Document type:** *Monographic series, Academic/Scholarly.*
Indexed: E-psyche.
Published by: Ernst Reinhardt Verlag, Kemnatenstr 46, Munich, 80639, Germany. TEL 49-89-1780160, FAX 49-89-17801630, webmaster@reinhardt-verlag.de, http://www.reinhardt-verlag.de.

302 DEU ISSN 0173-0967
BEITRAEGE ZUR PSYCHOLOGIE UND SOZIOLOGIE DES KRANKEN MENSCHEN. Text in German. 1974. irreg., latest vol.6, 1986. price varies. **Document type:** *Monographic series, Academic/Scholarly.*
Indexed: E-psyche.
Published by: Ernst Reinhardt Verlag, Kemnatenstr 46, Munich, 80639, Germany. TEL 49-89-1780160, FAX 49-89-17801630, webmaster@reinhardt-verlag.de, http://www.reinhardt-verlag.de. Eds. G Biermann, J von Troschke.

155.2 DEU ISSN 0067-5210
HQ21 CODEN: BSXFAV
BEITRAEGE ZUR SEXUALFORSCHUNG. Text in German. 1952. irreg., latest 2009. price varies. adv. reprint service avail. from IRC. **Document type:** *Monographic series, Academic/Scholarly.*
Indexed: E-psyche, IndMed, P30.
—GNLM.
Published by: (Deutsche Gesellschaft fuer Sexualforschung), Psychosozial Verlag, Walltorstr 10, Giessen, 35390, Germany. TEL 49-641-9699780, FAX 49-641-96997819, info@psychosozial-verlag.de.

302 DEU ISSN 1436-1868
BEITRAEGE ZUR SOZIALPSYCHOLOGIE. Text in German. 1999. irreg., latest vol.11, 2008. price varies. **Document type:** *Monographic series, Academic/Scholarly.*
Published by: Peter Lang GmbH (Subsidiary of: Peter Lang Publishing Group), Eschborner Landstr 42-50, Frankfurt Am Main, 60489, Germany. TEL 49-69-7807050, FAX 49-69-78070550, zentrale.frankfurt@peterlang.com. Eds. Helmut Lueck, Rudolf Miller.

614.58 USA
THE BELL. Text in English. 1980-1993; N.S. 1995. m. USD 40 membership (effective 2007). adv. bk.rev. back issues avail. **Document type:** *Newsletter.* **Description:** Provides information on issues relating to mental health, including research in psychology and psychiatry, the effects of managed mental health care, prevention efforts, legislation and public education.
Supersedes (in 1995): Focus (Alexandria)
Indexed: DYW.
Published by: Mental Health America, 2000 N Beauregard St, 6th Fl, Alexandria, VA 22311. TEL 703-684-7722, 800-969-6642, FAX 703-684-5968, http://www.nmha.org. Ed. Sandy Alexander. Adv. contact Tonya McCreary. Circ: 2,500.

158 DEU ISSN 1439-5916
BERATUNG AKTUELL; Zeitschrift fuer Theorie und Praxis der Beratung. Text in German; Summaries in English. 2000. 4/yr. EUR 26; EUR 21 to students; EUR 8 per issue (effective 2004). adv. **Document type:** *Journal, Academic/Scholarly.* **Description:** Provides information on various types of psychological counseling.
Indexed: E-psyche.
Published by: Junfermann Verlag, Imadstr 40, Paderborn, 33102, Germany. TEL 49-5251-13440, FAX 49-5251-134444, ju@junfermann.de, http://www.junfermann.de. Ed. Dr. Rudolf Sanders. Adv. contact Heike Carstensen.

BEREAVEMENT CARE; an international journal for those who help bereaved people. *see* SOCIAL SERVICES AND WELFARE

HET BESLUIT. *see* PUBLIC HEALTH AND SAFETY

THE BEST TEST PREPARATION FOR THE C L E P. INTRODUCTORY PSYCHOLOGY. (College-Level Examination Program) *see* EDUCATION—Higher Education

150 DEU
▼ **BEWUSSTSEIN, KOGNITION, ERLEBEN.** Text in German. 2009. irreg., latest vol.2, 2010. price varies. **Document type:** *Monographic series, Academic/Scholarly.*
Published by: V W B - Verlag fuer Wissenschaft und Bildung, Postfach 110368, Berlin, 10833, Germany. TEL 49-30-2510415, FAX 49-30-2511136, info@vwb-verlag.com.

150 ESP ISSN 1989-7952
BIBLIOTECA DE PSICOLOGIA. Text in Spanish. 2008. irreg. price varies. **Document type:** *Monographic series, Academic/Scholarly.*
Published by: Sintesis Editorial, Villahermoso, 34, Madrid, 28015, Spain. TEL 34-91-5932098, FAX 34-91-4458696, info@sintesis.com, http://www.sintesis.com/.

150 ITA ISSN 1972-1404
BIBLIOTECA. INCONSCIO E CULTURA. Text in Italian. 1978. irreg., latest vol.21, 1999, numbers not consecutive. price varies. adv. **Document type:** *Monographic series, Academic/Scholarly.*
Formerly (until 1981): Inconscio e Cultura (0391-3198)
Indexed: E-psyche.
Published by: Liguori Editore, Via Posillipo 394, Naples, 80123, Italy. TEL 39-081-7206111, FAX 39-081-7206244, liguori@liguori.it, http://www.liguori.it. Ed. Aldo Carotenuto.

BIBLIOTECA. LO SPECCHIO DI PSICHE. *see* MEDICAL SCIENCES—Psychiatry And Neurology

301.1 150 ITA ISSN 1972-0270
BIBLIOTECA. MENTE E SOCIETA. Text in Italian. 1985. irreg., latest vol.13, 1999. price varies. adv. **Document type:** *Monographic series, Academic/Scholarly.*
Indexed: E-psyche.
Published by: Liguori Editore, Via Posillipo 394, Naples, 80123, Italy. TEL 39-081-7206111, FAX 39-081-7206244, liguori@liguori.it. Ed. Guglielmo Bellelli. Pub. Guido Liguori. Adv. contact Maria Liguori.

150.19 FRA ISSN 1257-9149
BIBLIOTHEQUE JUNGIENNE. Text in French. 1994. irreg. back issues avail. **Document type:** *Monographic series, Academic/Scholarly.*
Published by: Editions Albin Michel, 22 rue Huyghens, Paris, 75014, France. TEL 33-1-42791000, FAX 33-1-43272158, http://www.albin-michel.fr.

158 USA ISSN 1941-4250
BF636.5
BIENNIAL REVIEW OF COUNSELING PSYCHOLOGY. Text in English. 2008 (May). biennial. USD 117 per issue (effective 2010). **Document type:** *Journal, Academic/Scholarly.* **Description:** Covers topics such as adult psychotherapy, multicultural counseling, college counseling and mental-health services, and psychosocial issues and treatment techniques with immigrants.
Related titles: Online - full text ed.
Indexed: P30.
Published by: Routledge (Subsidiary of: Taylor & Francis Group), 325 Chestnut St, Ste 800, Philadelphia, PA 19106. TEL 800-354-1420, FAX 215-625-2940, journals@routledge.com, http://www.routledge.com.

150 CHE ISSN 1424-6279
BIODYNAMIC PSYCHOLOGY AND PSYCHOTHERAPY. Text in English. 2000. irreg., latest vol.2, 2000. price varies. **Document type:** *Monographic series, Academic/Scholarly.*
Published by: Peter Lang AG (Subsidiary of: Peter Lang Publishing Group), Hochfeldstr 32, Postfach 746, Bern 9, 3000, Switzerland. TEL 41-31-3061717, FAX 41-31-3061727, info@peterlang.com. Ed. Mary Molloy.

150 610 USA ISSN 1081-5937
BIOFEEDBACK. Text in English. 1973. q. USD 30 (effective 2011). adv. back issues avail.; reprints avail. **Document type:** *Journal, Academic/Scholarly.* **Description:** Contains original research, conceptual and theoretical articles, evaluative reviews, case studies and clinical notes and observations.
Related titles: Online - full text ed.: ISSN 2158-348X. USD 80 to institutions (effective 2011).
Indexed: A01, CA, E-psyche, P20, P25, P48, P52, P54, P56, PQC, T02.
—IE. **CCC.**
Published by: Association for Applied Psychophysiology and Biofeedback, 10200 W 44th Ave, Ste 304, Wheat Ridge, CO 80033. TEL 303-422-8436, 800-477-8892, aapb@resourcenter.com, http://www.aapb.org. Ed. Donald Moss. Pub. Angie Girdhar.
Co-publisher: Allen Press Inc.

570 NLD ISSN 0301-0511
QP360 CODEN: BLPYAX
➤ **BIOLOGICAL PSYCHOLOGY.** Text in Dutch. 1974. 9/yr. EUR 1,728 in Europe to institutions; JPY 229,500 in Japan to institutions; USD 1,932 elsewhere to institutions (effective 2012). adv. bk.rev. charts. index. back issues avail.; reprints avail. **Document type:** *Journal, Academic/Scholarly.* **Description:** Publishes original scientific papers on the biological aspects of psychological states and processes.
Related titles: Microform ed.: (from PQC); Online - full text ed.: ISSN 1873-6246 (from IngentaConnect, ScienceDirect).
Indexed: A01, A03, A08, A20, A22, A26, ASCA, AddicA, B21, B25, BIOBASE, BIOSIS Prev, BibInd, CA, CIS, ChemAb, CurCont, DIP, DentInd, E-psyche, EMBASE, ExcerpMed, FR, I05, IABS, IBR, IBZ, ISR, IndMed, MEDLINE, MycolAb, NSA, NSCI, P03, P30, PsycInfo, PsycholAb, R10, Reac, S01, SCI, SCOPUS, SSCI, T02, W07.
—BLDSC (2077.560000), CASDDS, GNLM, IE, Infotrieve, Ingenta, INIST. **CCC.**
Published by: Elsevier BV (Subsidiary of: Elsevier Science & Technology), Radarweg 29, PO Box 211, Amsterdam, 1000 AE, Netherlands. TEL 31-20-4853911, FAX 31-20-4852457, JournalsCustomerServiceEMEA@elsevier.com. Ed. O V Lipp.
Subscr. to: Radarweg 29, PO Box 211, Amsterdam 1000 AE, Netherlands. TEL 31-20-4853757, FAX 31-20-4853432.

➤ **BIRD BEHAVIOR**; an international and interdisciplinary multimedia journal. *see* BIOLOGY—Ornithology

➤ **BIRKBECK COLLEGE. SCHOOL OF MANAGEMENT AND ORGANIZATIONAL PSYCHOLOGY. WORKING PAPER SERIES.** *see* BUSINESS AND ECONOMICS—Management

150 618 USA ISSN 0734-3124
RG658
BIRTH PSYCHOLOGY BULLETIN. Text in English. 1979. s-a. free to members (effective 2011). bk.rev. back issues avail. **Document type:** *Bulletin, Academic/Scholarly.* **Description:** Clinical, theoretical, and empirical articles on the psychological impact of pregnancy, birth, and the neonatal period.
Indexed: E-psyche, P30, PsycholAb.
Published by: Association for Birth Psychology, 9115 Ridge Blvd, Brooklyn, NY 11209. TEL 347-517-4607, BirthPsychology@aol.com, http://www.birthpsychology.org.

158 NLD ISSN 1740-1445
BF697.5.B63
➤ **BODY IMAGE.** Text in English. 2004. 4/yr. EUR 398 in Europe to institutions; JPY 52,800 in Japan to institutions; USD 444 elsewhere to institutions (effective 2012). **Document type:** *Journal, Academic/Scholarly.* **Description:** Publishes high-quality, scientific articles on body image and human physical appearance.
Related titles: Online - full text ed.: ISSN 1873-6807 (from IngentaConnect, ScienceDirect).
Indexed: A20, A26, C06, C07, CA, CurCont, EMBASE, ExcerpMed, I05, MEDLINE, P03, P30, PEI, PsycInfo, PsycholAb, SCOPUS, SSCI, T02, W07.
—BLDSC (2117.201700), IE, Ingenta. **CCC.**
Published by: Elsevier BV (Subsidiary of: Elsevier Science & Technology), Radarweg 29, PO Box 211, Radarweg 29, PO Box 211, Amsterdam, 1000 AE, Netherlands. TEL 31-20-4853911, FAX 31-20-4852457, JournalsCustomerServiceEMEA@elsevier.com, http://www.elsevier.nl. Ed. T F Cash.

150 BRA ISSN 1518-5303
➤ **BOLETIM DE INICIACAO CIENTIFICA EM PSICOLOGIA.** Text in Portuguese; Abstracts in English, Portuguese. 2000. a. free (effective 2005). **Document type:** *Journal, Academic/Scholarly.*
Published by: Universidade Presbiteriana Mackenzie (Subsidiary of: Instituto Presbiteriano Mackenzie), Rua da Consolacao 896, Pr.2, Sao Paulo-SP, SP 01302-907, Brazil. TEL 55-11-32368563, FAX 55-11-32368302, http://www.mackenzie.com.br. Ed., R&P Dr. Paulo Afranio Sant'Anna.

150 BRA ISSN 0006-5943
BOLETIM DE PSICOLOGIA. Text in Portuguese, English, Spanish. 1949. bi-m. bibl.; charts. **Document type:** *Journal, Trade.*
Related titles: Online - full text ed.: ISSN 2175-344X.
Indexed: C01, E-psyche.
Published by: Sociedade de Psicologia de Sao Paulo, Av Professor Mello Moraes 1721, Cidade Universitaria, Sao Paulo, SP 05508-030, Brazil. TEL 55-11-30911645, sociedade.psicologia@ig.com.br, http://www.psicologiasp.org.br. Ed. Irai Cristina Boccato Alves.

150 ESP ISSN 0212-8179
BOLETIN DE PSICOLOGIA. Text in Spanish. 1982. q. **Document type:** *Journal, Academic/Scholarly.*
Indexed: P03, PsycholAb, RILM, S02, S03.
Published by: Universitat de Valencia, Facultad de Psicologia, Ave. Blasco Ibanez, 21, 3a. Planta, Valencia, 46010, Spain. TEL 34-96-3864823, FAX 34-96-3864822, http://www.cazorla.uv.es/. Ed. Julio Seoane.

158 ITA ISSN 0006-6761
➤ **BOLLETTINO DI PSICOLOGIA APPLICATA.** Text in Italian. 1954. 3/yr. EUR 75 domestic to institutions; EUR 90 foreign to institutions (effective 2009). adv. bk.rev. bibl.; charts; abstr.; stat. 96 p./no.; back issues avail.; reprints avail. **Document type:** *Journal, Academic/Scholarly.* **Description:** Covers all topics concerning applied psychology in clinical, educational and work fields.
Former titles (until 1959): Bollettino di Psicologia e Sociologia Applicata (1124-660X); (until 1955): Bollettino di Psicologia Applicata (1124-7886)
Related titles: Microform ed.: (from PQC).
Indexed: A01, A22, E-psyche, FR, P03, PsycInfo, PsycholAb, S02, S03, SOPODA, SociolAb.
—BLDSC (2240.700000), IE, Ingenta, INIST.
Published by: Organizzazioni Speciali, Via Fra' Paolo Sarpi 7-A, Florence, 50136, Italy. TEL 39-055-6236501, FAX 39-055-669446, bpa@osnet.it, http://www.osnet.it. Circ: 1,000.

150 ESP ISSN 0210-5934
BORDON; revista de pedagogia. Text in Spanish. 1949. q. free to members. **Document type:** *Journal, Academic/Scholarly.*
Related titles: Online - full text ed.
Indexed: P09, PCI.
Published by: Consejo Superior de Investigaciones Cientificas (C S I C), Sociedad Espanola de Pedagogia, Calle Virtuvio 8, Madrid, 28006, Spain. TEL 34-91-5614839.

150 USA ISSN 0278-2626
QP376
➤ **BRAIN AND COGNITION.** Text in English. 1982. 9/yr. EUR 1,675 in Europe to institutions; JPY 174,700 in Japan to institutions; USD 1,368 elsewhere to institutions (effective 2012). adv. back issues avail.; reprints avail. **Document type:** *Journal, Academic/Scholarly.* **Description:** Presents clinical case histories, original research papers, reviews, notes, and commentaries on neuropsychology.
Related titles: Online - full text ed.: ISSN 1090-2147 (from IngentaConnect, ScienceDirect).
Indexed: A01, A03, A08, A20, A22, A26, ASCA, ASG, AbAn, AgeL, B21, BIOBASE, C06, C07, C08, CA, CDA, CINAHL, CurCont, E-psyche, E01, EMBASE, ERIC, ExcerpMed, FR, Faml, H12, I05, IABS, ISR, IndMed, Inpharma, L&LBA, L11, MEDLINE, MLA-IB, NSA, NSCI, P03, P30, P35, PsycInfo, PsycholAb, R10, RASB, RILM, Reac, SCI, SCOPUS, SOPODA, SSCI, SociolAb, T02, W07.
—BLDSC (2268.032000), GNLM, IE, Infotrieve, Ingenta, INIST. **CCC.**
Published by: Academic Press (Subsidiary of: Elsevier Science & Technology), 3251 Riverport Ln, Maryland Heights, MO 63043. TEL 314-447-8010, FAX 314-447-8030, JournalCustomerService-usa@elsevier.com, http://www.elsevierdirect.com/imprint.jsp?iid=5. Ed. S Segalowitz. Adv. contact Tino DeCarlo TEL 212-633-3815.

150 410 USA ISSN 0093-934X
RC423.A1
➤ **BRAIN AND LANGUAGE.** Text in English. 1974. m. EUR 2,089 in Europe to institutions; JPY 218,200 in Japan to institutions; USD 1,685 elsewhere to institutions (effective 2012). adv. back issues avail.; reprints avail. **Document type:** *Journal, Academic/Scholarly.* **Description:** Presents original theoretical, clinical, and experimental papers on human language and communication, including speech, hearing, reading, writing, and higher language functions as they relate to brain structure and function.
Related titles: Online - full text ed.: ISSN 1090-2155 (from IngentaConnect, ScienceDirect).
Indexed: A01, A03, A08, A20, A22, A26, AMED, ASCA, AbAn, AgeL, B21, BDM&CN, BIOBASE, BibInd, BibLing, C06, C07, C08, CA, CINAHL, CMM, CommAb, CurCont, DentInd, E-psyche, E01, EMBASE, ERIC, ExcerpMed, FR, H12, I05, IABS, IBR, IBZ, IPsyAb, ISR, IndMed, Inpharma, JW-N, L&LBA, L11, MEDLINE, MLA, MLA-IB, NSA, NSCI, P03, P30, PCI, PsycInfo, PsycholAb, R10, RASB, Reac, SCI, SCOPUS, SOPODA, SSCI, T02, W07.
—BLDSC (2268.040000), GNLM, IE, Infotrieve, Ingenta, INIST. **CCC.**
Published by: Academic Press (Subsidiary of: Elsevier Science & Technology), 3251 Riverport Ln, Maryland Heights, MO 63043. TEL 314-447-8010, FAX 314-447-8030, JournalCustomerService-usa@elsevier.com, http://www.elsevierdirect.com/imprint.jsp?iid=5. Ed. S Small. Adv. contact Tino DeCarlo TEL 212-633-3815.

➤ **BRAIN IMPAIRMENT.** *see* MEDICAL SCIENCES—Psychiatry And Neurology

➤ **BREATH SERIES**; a progression of pranayama practices. *see* NEW AGE PUBLICATIONS

158 USA ISSN 1949-2197
▼ **THE BRIEF JOURNAL OF BRIEF THERAPY.** Text in English. forthcoming 2011. a. free (effective 2009). **Document type:** *Journal, Academic/Scholarly.* **Description:** Short articles on psychology and therapy.
Media: Online - full text.
Published by: Mind for Therapy, 111 Fava Dr, West Monroe, LA 71291. TEL 318-801-9296, mthornton@mindfortherapy.com.

616.89 GBR ISSN 0954-0350
➤ **BRITISH ASSOCIATION OF PSYCHOTHERAPISTS. JOURNAL.** Text in English. 1968. q. GBP 123 combined subscription domestic to institutions (print & online eds.); EUR 156 combined subscription in Europe to institutions (print & online eds.); USD 226 combined subscription in the Americas to institutions (print & online eds.); USD 241 combined subscription elsewhere to institutions (print & online eds.) (effective 2009). adv. film rev.; bk.rev. back issues avail.; reprints avail. **Document type:** *Journal, Academic/Scholarly.* **Description:** Covers topics related to Freudian or Jungian psycho-dynamic psychotherapy.
Formerly (until 1988): British Association of Psychotherapists. Bulletin (0268-6643)
Related titles: Online - full text ed.: ISSN 1556-9160. 2006.
Indexed: A01, CA, E-psyche, P03, PsycholAb, T02.
—CCC.
Published by: (British Association of Psychotherapists), Wiley-Blackwell Publishing Ltd. (Subsidiary of: John Wiley & Sons, Inc.), 9600 Garsington Rd, Oxford, OX4 2DQ, United Kingdom. TEL 44-1865-776868, FAX 44-1865-714591, customerservices@blackwellpublishing.com, http://www.wiley.com/. **Subscr. to:** John Wiley & Sons Ltd., 1-7 Oldlands Way, PO Box 809, Bognor Regis, West Sussex PO21 9FG, United Kingdom. TEL 44-1865-778054, cs-agency@wiley.com. **Dist. by:** Turpin Distribution Services Ltd.

301.1 150 GBR ISSN 0144-6657
BF1 CODEN: BJCPDW
➤ **BRITISH JOURNAL OF CLINICAL PSYCHOLOGY.** Abbreviated title: B J C P. Text in English. 1962. q. GBP 250 in United Kingdom to institutions; EUR 369 in Europe to institutions; USD 455 elsewhere to institutions; GBP 306 combined subscription in United Kingdom to institutions (print & online eds.); EUR 451 combined subscription in Europe to institutions (print & online eds.); USD 556 combined subscription elsewhere to institutions (print & online eds.) (effective 2012). adv. bk.rev. charts; illus.; abstr. index. back issues avail.; reprint service avail. from PSC. **Document type:** *Journal, Academic/Scholarly.* **Description:** Aims to reflect the broad role of clinical psychologists and including descriptive studies as well as studies of the aetiology, assessment and amelioration of disorders of all kinds, in all settings, and among all age groups.
Supersedes in part (in 1981): British Journal of Social and Clinical Psychology (0007-1293)
Related titles: Microform ed.: (from PQC, SWZ); Online - full text ed.: ISSN 2044-8260. GBP 265 in United Kingdom to institutions; EUR 392 in Europe to institutions; USD 483 elsewhere to institutions (effective 2012).
Indexed: A01, A02, A03, A08, A20, A22, AC&P, AMED, AMHA, ASCA, ASSIA, AddicA, B21, B28, BDM&CN, BibInd, C06, C07, C08, C11, CA, CINAHL, CIS, CurCont, DIP, DentInd, E-psyche, E01, EMBASE, ExcerpMed, F09, FR, FamI, H04, IBR, IBSS, IBZ, INI, IndMed, L&LBA, MEDLINE, NSA, P03, P20, P22, P24, P25, P26, P30, P43, P48, P54, PQC, PsycInfo, PsycholAb, R10, Reac, RefZh, S02, S03, SCOPUS, SOPODA, SSCI, SociolAb, T02, THA, W07.
—BLDSC (2307.230000), GNLM, IE, Infotrieve, Ingenta, INIST. **CCC.**
Published by: (The British Psychological Society), John Wiley & Sons Ltd. (Subsidiary of: John Wiley & Sons, Inc.), 9600 Garsington Rd, Oxford, OX4 2DQ, United Kingdom. TEL 44-1865-776868, FAX 44-1865-714591, cs-journals@wiley.com, http://www.wiley.com. Eds. Gillian Bradley, Michael Barkham. Adv. contact Julie Neason TEL 44-116-2529580. page GBP 375; trim 174 x 247.

➤ **THE BRITISH JOURNAL OF CRIMINOLOGY**; an international review of crime and society. *see* CRIMINOLOGY AND LAW ENFORCEMENT

155 GBR ISSN 0261-510X
BF712
➤ **BRITISH JOURNAL OF DEVELOPMENTAL PSYCHOLOGY.** Abbreviated title: B J D P. Text in English. 1983. q. GBP 240 in United Kingdom to institutions; EUR 355 in Europe to institutions; USD 439 elsewhere to institutions; GBP 293 combined subscription in United Kingdom to institutions (print & online eds.); EUR 434 combined subscription in Europe to institutions (print & online eds.); USD 536 combined subscription elsewhere to institutions (print & online eds.) (effective 2012). adv. bk.rev. charts; illus.; abstr. index. 160 p./no.; back issues avail.; reprint service avail. from PSC. **Document type:** *Journal, Academic/Scholarly.* **Description:** Features empirical, conceptual, and review articles on all aspects of developmental psychology.
Related titles: Magnetic Tape ed.; Microfiche ed.; Microform ed.: (from PQC, SWZ); Online - full text ed.: ISSN 2044-835X. 1999. GBP 255 in United Kingdom to institutions; EUR 377 in Europe to institutions; USD 466 elsewhere to institutions (effective 2012).
Indexed: A01, A02, A03, A08, A20, A22, AEI, ASCA, ASSIA, B21, B28, B29, BDM&CN, C06, C07, C08, C28, CA, CDA, CINAHL, CurCont, DIP, E-psyche, E01, E03, EMBASE, ERA, ExcerpMed, F09, FR, FamI, IBR, IBSS, IBZ, L&LBA, MEDLINE, NSA, P03, P25, P26, P30, P43, P48, P54, PCI, PQC, PsycInfo, PsycholAb, S02, S03, S20, S21, SCOPUS, SOPODA, SSCI, SociolAb, T02, W07, YAE&RB.
—BLDSC (2307.480000), IE, Infotrieve, Ingenta, INIST. **CCC.**
Published by: (The British Psychological Society), John Wiley & Sons Ltd. (Subsidiary of: John Wiley & Sons, Inc.), 9600 Garsington Rd, Oxford, OX4 2DQ, United Kingdom. TEL 44-1865-776868, FAX 44-1865-714591, cs-journals@wiley.com, http://www.wiley.com. Ed. Margaret Harris. adv.: page GBP 320; trim 174 x 247.

370.15 GBR ISSN 0007-0998
LB1051.A2 CODEN: BJESAE
➤ **BRITISH JOURNAL OF EDUCATIONAL PSYCHOLOGY.** Abbreviated title: B J E P. Text in English. 1911. q. GBP 189 in United Kingdom to institutions; EUR 270 in Europe to institutions; USD 330 elsewhere to institutions; GBP 232 combined subscription in United Kingdom to institutions (print & online eds.); EUR 330 combined subscription in Europe to institutions (print & online eds.); USD 403 combined subscription elsewhere to institutions (print & online eds.) (effective 2012). adv. bk.rev. bibl.; charts; illus.; abstr. index. 144 p./no.; back issues avail.; reprint service avail. from PSC. **Document type:** *Journal, Academic/Scholarly.* **Description:** Focuses on psychological research that makes a significant contribution to the understanding and practice of education. Includes empirical and theoretical studies, action research as well as psychometric and statistical methods.
Former titles (until 1931): Forum of Education; (until 1923): Journal of Experimental Pedagogy and Training College Record
Related titles: Magnetic Tape ed.; Microfiche ed.; Microform ed.: (from SWZ); Online - full text ed.: ISSN 2044-8279. 1999. GBP 201 in United Kingdom to institutions; EUR 287 in Europe to institutions; USD 350 elsewhere to institutions (effective 2012).
Indexed: A01, A02, A03, A08, A20, A22, AEI, AMHA, ASCA, ASSIA, B04, B29, BDM&CN, BRD, C28, CA, CDA, CIS, CPE, ChLitAb, CommAb, CurCont, DIP, E-psyche, E01, E02, E03, E06, E15, EMBASE, ERA, ERI, ERIC, EdA, EdI, ExcerpMed, FR, FamI, HEA, HECAB, IBR, IBZ, IndMed, L&LBA, LT&LA, M12, MEDLINE, MLA-IB, P03, P18, P25, P30, P43, P48, P53, P54, P55, PCI, PQC, PsycInfo, PsycholAb, R10, R17, RASB, RILM, Reac, S02, S03, S19, S20, S21, SCOPUS, SOPODA, SSCI, SociolAb, T02, V05, W03, W07.
—BLDSC (2307.650000), IE, Infotrieve, Ingenta, INIST. **CCC.**
Published by: (The British Psychological Society), John Wiley & Sons Ltd. (Subsidiary of: John Wiley & Sons, Inc.), 9600 Garsington Rd, Oxford, OX4 2DQ, United Kingdom. TEL 44-1865-776868, FAX 44-1865-714591, cs-journals@wiley.com, http://www.wiley.com. Ed. Andrew Tolmie TEL 44-20-76126888. adv.: page GBP 375; trim 174 x 247.

150 GBR ISSN 1476-9808
BRITISH JOURNAL OF EDUCATIONAL PSYCHOLOGY. MONOGRAPH SERIES II. PSYCHOLOGICAL ASPECTS OF EDUCATION - CURRENT TRENDS. Variant title: British Journal of Educational Psychology. Monograph Series 2. Text in English. 2002. irreg., latest no.3. price varies. back issues avail. **Document type:** *Monographic series, Academic/Scholarly.* **Description:** Publishes the inputs to a set of annual conferences on psychological aspects of education, in which invited world-leading researchers provide updates on the latest advances in their fields and consideration of the applied implications.
Related titles: Online - full text ed.
—BLDSC (2307.651001).
Published by: The British Psychological Society, St Andrews House, 48 Princess Rd E, Leicester, LE1 7DR, United Kingdom. TEL 44-116-2549568, FAX 44-116-2271314, enquiries@bps.org.uk, http://www.bps.org.uk.

BRITISH JOURNAL OF GUIDANCE AND COUNSELLING. *see* OCCUPATIONS AND CAREERS

616.8 GBR ISSN 1359-107X
R726.7 CODEN: BJHPFP
➤ **BRITISH JOURNAL OF HEALTH PSYCHOLOGY.** Abbreviated title: B J H P. Text in English. 1996. q. GBP 209 in United Kingdom to institutions; EUR 306 in Europe to institutions; USD 380 elsewhere to institutions; GBP 256 combined subscription in United Kingdom to institutions (print & online eds.); EUR 374 combined subscription in Europe to institutions (print & online eds.); USD 464 combined subscription elsewhere to institutions (print & online eds.) (effective 2012). adv. bk.rev. bibl.; charts; illus.; abstr. index. 104 p./no.; back issues avail.; reprint service avail. from PSC. **Document type:** *Journal, Academic/Scholarly.* **Description:** Covers all areas of psychological factors relating to health and illness across the life span, including experimental and clinical research on aetiology and the management of acute and chronic illness, responses to ill health, screening and medical procedures, research on health behaviour, and psychological aspects of prevention.
Related titles: Magnetic Tape ed.; Microfiche ed.; Online - full text ed.: ISSN 2044-8287. 1999. GBP 222 in United Kingdom to institutions; EUR 325 in Europe to institutions; USD 403 elsewhere to institutions (effective 2012).
Indexed: A01, A02, A03, A08, A20, A22, ASSIA, AddicA, B28, C06, C07, CA, CurCont, DIP, E-psyche, E01, EMBASE, ExcerpMed, FR, FamI, IBR, IBZ, MEDLINE, P03, P20, P22, P25, P26, P30, P43, P48, P50, P54, PQC, PsycInfo, PsycholAb, R09, R10, Reac, RefZh, S02, S03, SCOPUS, SD, SOPODA, SSCI, SociolAb, T02, THA, W07.
—BLDSC (2309.080000), IE, Infotrieve, Ingenta, INIST. **CCC.**
Published by: (The British Psychological Society), John Wiley & Sons Ltd. (Subsidiary of: John Wiley & Sons, Inc.), 9600 Garsington Rd, Oxford, OX4 2DQ, United Kingdom. TEL 44-1865-776868, FAX 44-1865-714591, customer@wiley.co.uk, http://www.wiley.com. Eds. Kavita Vedhara, Paul Bennett. adv.: page GBP 365; trim 174 x 247.

152.8 GBR ISSN 0007-1102
BF1
➤ **BRITISH JOURNAL OF MATHEMATICAL AND STATISTICAL PSYCHOLOGY.** Abbreviated title: B J M S P. Text in English. 1947. 3/yr. GBP 219 in United Kingdom to institutions; EUR 327 in Europe to institutions; USD 405 elsewhere to institutions; GBP 268 combined subscription in United Kingdom to institutions (print & online eds.); EUR 400 combined subscription in Europe to institutions (print & online eds.); USD 494 combined subscription elsewhere to institutions (print & online eds.) (effective 2012). adv. bk.rev. charts; illus. index. back issues avail.; reprint service avail. from PSC. **Document type:** *Journal, Academic/Scholarly.* **Description:** Contains papers on all aspects of quantitative psychology, including mathematical psychology, statistics, psychometrics, psychophysics, and relevant areas of mathematics, computing and computer software.
Former titles (until 1965): British Journal of Statistical Psychology (0950-561X); (until 1953): British Journal of Psychology. Statistical Section
Related titles: Magnetic Tape ed.; Microfiche ed.; Microform ed.: (from PQC, SWZ); Online - full text ed.: ISSN 2044-8317. 1999. GBP 233 in United Kingdom to institutions; EUR 347 in Europe to institutions; USD 430 elsewhere to institutions (effective 2012).
Indexed: A01, A02, A03, A08, A20, A22, AEI, ASCA, B21, BibInd, CA, CCMJ, CIS, CMCI, CompAb, CurCont, DIP, E-psyche, E01, EMBASE, ExcerpMed, FR, IBR, IBZ, IndMed, JCQM, MEDLINE, MResA, MSN, MathR, NSA, P03, P10, P12, P25, P26, P30, P43, P48, P49, P53, P54, PQC, PsycInfo, PsycholAb, RASB, RefZh, S01, SCI, SCOPUS, SSCI, ST&MA, T02, W07, Z02.
—BLDSC (2311.300000), GNLM, IE, Infotrieve, Ingenta, INIST. **CCC.**
Published by: (The British Psychological Society), John Wiley & Sons Ltd. (Subsidiary of: John Wiley & Sons, Inc.), 9600 Garsington Rd, Oxford, OX4 2DQ, United Kingdom. TEL 44-1865-776868, FAX 44-1865-714591, cs-journals@wiley.com, http://www.wiley.com. Eds. Mark Lansdale, Thom Baguley. adv.: page GBP 250; trim 174 x 247.

155.418 792 GBR ISSN 1744-1145
BRITISH JOURNAL OF PLAY THERAPY. Text in English. 2004. s-a. free to members (effective 2009). **Document type:** *Journal, Trade.* **Description:** Contains papers that are of interest to occupational groups using therapeutic play skills.
Published by: The British Association of Play Therapists, 1 Beacon Mews, South Rd, Weybridge, Surrey KT13 9DZ, United Kingdom. TEL 44-1932-828638, FAX 44-1932-820100, info@bapt.uk.com. Ed. Anne Barnes.

150 GBR ISSN 0007-1269
CODEN: BJSGAE
➤ **BRITISH JOURNAL OF PSYCHOLOGY.** Abbreviated title: B J P. Text in English. 1904. q. GBP 321 in United Kingdom to institutions; EUR 480 in Europe to institutions; USD 596 elsewhere to institutions; GBP 393 combined subscription in United Kingdom to institutions (print & online eds.); EUR 586 combined subscription in Europe to institutions (print & online eds.); USD 728 combined subscription elsewhere to institutions (print & online eds.) (effective 2012). adv. bk.rev. bibl.; charts; illus. index. 144 p./no.; back issues avail.; reprint service avail. from PSC. **Document type:** *Journal, Academic/Scholarly.* **Description:** Features reports of empirical studies, critical reviews, and theoretical contributions geared towards academic and research workers in experimental, cognitive and general psychology.
Formerly (until 1953): British Journal of Psychology. General Section (0373-2460); Which superseded in part (in 1920): British Journal of Psychology (0950-5652)
Related titles: Magnetic Tape ed.; Microfiche ed.; Microform ed.: (from PQC); Online - full text ed.: ISSN 2044-8325. GBP 341 in United Kingdom to institutions; EUR 509 in Europe to institutions; USD 632 elsewhere to institutions (effective 2012).
Indexed: A01, A02, A03, A08, A11, A20, A22, A26, AC&P, AEI, AMHA, ASCA, ASSIA, B01, B04, B06, B07, B09, B21, B28, BDM&CN, BRD, C06, C07, C08, CA, CINAHL, CIS, ChemoAb, CurCont, DIP, E-psyche, E01, E08, EMBASE, ERA, ErgAb, ExcerpMed, FR, FamI, G08, H09, H11, H12, I05, IBR, IBSS, IBZ, IndMed, Inspec, L&LBA, M01, M02, MEA&I, MEDLINE, MLA, MLA-IB, NSA, P02, P03, P10, P12, P13, P19, P20, P22, P24, P25, P26, P27, P30, P43, P48, P53, P54, PCI, PQC, PsycInfo, PsycholAb, R10, RASB, Reac, RefZh, S02, S03, S05, S06, S09, S20, S21, S23, SCOPUS, SOPODA, SPPI, SSA, SSAI, SSAb, SSCI, SSI, SociolAb, T02, THA, W03, W05, W07, WBA, WMB.
—BLDSC (2321.000000), IE, Infotrieve, Ingenta, INIST. **CCC.**
Published by: (The British Psychological Society), John Wiley & Sons Ltd. (Subsidiary of: John Wiley & Sons, Inc.), 9600 Garsington Rd, Oxford, OX4 2DQ, United Kingdom. TEL 44-1865-776868, FAX 44-1865-714591, cs-journals@wiley.com, http://www.wiley.com. Ed. Peter Mitchell. adv.: page GBP 375; trim 174 x 247.

301.1 150 GBR ISSN 0144-6665
BF1 CODEN: BJSPDA
➤ **BRITISH JOURNAL OF SOCIAL PSYCHOLOGY.** Abbreviated title: B J S P. Text in English. 1962. q. GBP 240 in United Kingdom to institutions; EUR 355 in Europe to institutions; USD 439 elsewhere to institutions; GBP 293 combined subscription in United Kingdom to institutions (print & online eds.); EUR 434 combined subscription in Europe to institutions (print & online eds.); USD 536 combined subscription elsewhere to institutions (print & online eds.) (effective 2012). adv. bk.rev. charts; illus.; abstr. index. 160 p./no.; back issues avail.; reprint service avail. from PSC. **Document type:** *Journal, Academic/Scholarly.* **Description:** Describes applications of social psychology including research, review and methodological papers in addition to empirical papers of theoretical significance.
Supersedes in part (in 1981): British Journal of Social and Clinical Psychology (0007-1293)
Related titles: Magnetic Tape ed.; Microfiche ed.; Microform ed.: (from PQC); Online - full text ed.: ISSN 2044-8309. 1999. GBP 255 in United Kingdom to institutions; EUR 377 in Europe to institutions; USD 466 elsewhere to institutions (effective 2012).
Indexed: A01, A02, A03, A08, A20, A22, AC&P, AMHA, ASCA, ASSIA, B28, BDM&CN, BibInd, C06, C07, C08, CA, CINAHL, CIS, CommAb, CurCont, DIP, E-psyche, E01, EMBASE, ERA, ExcerpMed, FR, FamI, HECAB, IBR, IBSS, IBZ, IndMed, L&LBA, MEA&I, MEDLINE, MResA, P03, P20, P22, P24, P25, P26, P30, P43, P46, P48, P54, PQC, PsycInfo, PsycholAb, R10, RASB, Reac, S02, S03, S21, SCOPUS, SOPODA, SSA, SSCI, SociolAb, T02, THA, W07.
—BLDSC (2324.784000), GNLM, IE, Infotrieve, Ingenta, INIST. **CCC.**
Published by: (The British Psychological Society), John Wiley & Sons Ltd. (Subsidiary of: John Wiley & Sons, Inc.), 9600 Garsington Rd, Oxford, OX4 2DQ, United Kingdom. TEL 44-1865-776868, FAX 44-1865-714591, cs-journals@wiley.com, http://www.wiley.com. Eds. John Dixon, Jolanda Jetten. adv.: page GBP 340; trim 174 x 247.

➤ **BRITISH JOURNAL OF SPECIAL EDUCATION.** *see* EDUCATION—Special Education And Rehabilitation

150 GBR ISSN 0309-7773
BF11
BRITISH PSYCHOLOGICAL SOCIETY. ANNUAL REPORT. Text in English. 1970. a. free (effective 2009). back issues avail. **Document type:** *Corporate.* **Description:** Describes the society's key achievements in the previous twelve months.
Related titles: Online - full text ed.
Indexed: E-psyche.
—BLDSC (1127.250000).
Published by: The British Psychological Society, St Andrews House, 48 Princess Rd E, Leicester, LE1 7DR, United Kingdom. TEL 44-116-2549568, FAX 44-116-2271314, enquiries@bps.org.uk.

150 GBR ISSN 1754-8837
BF20
BRITISH PSYCHOLOGICAL SOCIETY. CONFERENCE PROCEEDINGS (ONLINE). Text in English. 19??. s-a. free (effective 2009). back issues avail. **Document type:** *Proceedings, Academic/Scholarly.* **Description:** Covers papers and abstracts from all areas of psychology.
Former titles (until 2007): British Psychological Society. Proceedings (Print) (1350-472X); (until 1993): British Psychological Society. Abstracts of Papers (0964-6329)
Media: Online - full text.
Indexed: P25, PQC.
—CCC.
Published by: The British Psychological Society, St Andrews House, 48 Princess Rd E, Leicester, LE1 7DR, United Kingdom. TEL 44-116-2549568, FAX 44-116-2271314, enquiries@bps.org.uk.

BROWN UNIVERSITY CHILD AND ADOLESCENT BEHAVIOR LETTER. *see* CHILDREN AND YOUTH—About

150 BGR ISSN 0861-7813
BULGARSKO SPISANIE PO PSIKHOLOGIA. Text in Bulgarian. 1973. q. **Document type:** *Journal, Academic/Scholarly.*
Formerly (until 1992): Psikhologia (0204-644X)
Indexed: E-psyche, PsycholAb, RASB.
Published by: Druzhestvo na Psikholozite v Bulgaria, 52 Cherkovna St, Sofia, 1505, Bulgaria. office@psychology-bg.org, http://www.psychology-bg.org. Ed. Tatiana Yancheva. Circ: 500.

150 FRA ISSN 0007-4403
BF2
BULLETIN DE PSYCHOLOGIE. Text in French. 1947. bi-m. EUR 85 to individuals; EUR 145 to institutions (effective 2010). adv. bk.rev. abstr.; bibl.; charts. back issues avail.; reprints avail. **Document type:** *Academic/Scholarly.*
Formerly (until 1951): Universite de Paris. Groupe d'Etudes de Psychologie. Bulletin (0242-5432)
Indexed: A22, BibInd, E-psyche, FR, IBR, IBZ, MLA-IB, P03, PsycInfo, PsycholAb, RILM, S02, S03.
—BLDSC (2884.450000), IE, Infotrieve, Ingenta, INIST. **CCC.**
Published by: Universite de Paris I (Pantheon-Sorbonne), 17 rue de la Sorbonne, Paris, 75005, France. TEL 33-1-46989941, petard@claranet.fr. Ed. Marcel Turbiaux. Pub., Adv. contact Jean Pierre Petard. Circ: 700.

375 USA
BUROS DESK REFERENCE. Text in English. 1994. irreg., latest 1996. price varies. back issues avail. **Document type:** *Monographic series, Academic/Scholarly.* **Description:** Contains descriptions and candidly critical reviews of commercially available tests in specific areas. Editions available include School Psychology and Substance Abuse.
Indexed: E-psyche.
Published by: Buros Institute of Mental Measurements, 21 Teachers College Hall, University of Nebraska - Lincoln, Lincoln, NE 68588. TEL 402-472-6203, FAX 402-472-6207, pressmail@unl.edu, http://www.unl.edu/buros/bimm/index.html.

371.3 USA
BUROS - NEBRASKA SERIES ON MEASUREMENT AND TESTING. Text in English. 1982. irreg., latest 2000. price varies. back issues avail. **Document type:** *Monographic series, Academic/Scholarly.* **Description:** Focuses on an individual issue within the assessment field.
Indexed: E-psyche.
Published by: Buros Institute of Mental Measurements, 21 Teachers College Hall, University of Nebraska - Lincoln, Lincoln, NE 68588. TEL 402-472-6203, FAX 402-472-6207, pressmail@unl.edu, http://www.unl.edu/buros/bimm/index.html.

158 NLD ISSN 1872-1710
C. G. JUNG VERENIGING NEDERLAND, INTERDISCIPLINAIRE VERENIGING VOOR ANALYTISCHE PSYCHOLOGIE. JAARBOEK. Text in Dutch. 1984. a. EUR 5 (effective 2008).
Formerly (until 2005): Interdisciplinaire Vereniging voor Analytische Psychologie. Jaarboek (1872-1702)
Published by: C.G. Jung Vereniging Nederland, c/o Wim de Vrij, Platohof 31, Stiens, 9051 KP, Netherlands. w.devrij@wanadoo.nl, http://www.cgjung-vereniging.nl.

150 ITA ISSN 1974-5443
C P D QUADERNI. (Centro Psicologia Dinamica) Text in Italian. 2006. s-a. **Document type:** *Journal, Academic/Scholarly.*
Published by: (Centro di Psicologia Dinamica), Cooperativa Libraria Editrice Universita di Padova (C L E U P), Via G Belzoni 118-3, Padua, PD 35131, Italy. TEL 39-049-650261, FAX 39-049-8753496, info@cleup.it, http://www.cleup.it.

150 GBR ISSN 1747-4973
C T P D C. WORKING PAPER SERIES. Text in English. 2005. m. free (effective 2007). **Document type:** *Monographic series, Academic/Scholarly.*
Media: Online - full text.
Published by: Counselling Training Personal Development Consulting, 49 Rodney St, Liverpool, L1 9EW, United Kingdom. TEL 44-151-7089977, information@ctpdc.co.uk, http://www.ctpdc.co.uk/.

150 PRT ISSN 0871-7516
RC467
CADERNOS DE CONSULTA PSICOLOGICA. Text in Multiple languages. 1985. irreg. **Document type:** *Journal, Academic/Scholarly.*
Published by: Universidade do Porto, Faculdade de Psicologia e Ciencias da Educacao (F P C E U P), Rua do Dr. Manuel Pereira da Silva, Porto, 4200-392, Portugal. TEL 351-22-6079700, FAX 351-22-6079725, http://sigarra.up.pt/fpceup/.

150 BRA ISSN 0103-4251
CADERNOS DE PSICANALISE. Text in Portuguese. 1982. a.
Indexed: P03, PsycInfo, PsycholAb.
Published by: Sociedade de Psicanalise da Cidade do Rio de Janeiro, Rua Saturnino de Brito, 79, Jardim Botanico, Rio de Janeiro, RJ 22470-030, Brazil. TEL 55-21-25122265, comunique@spcrj.org.br.

CADERNOS DE PSICOPEDAGOGIA. *see* EDUCATION

150 FRA ISSN 1779-8450
CAFE PSYCHO. Text in French. 2006. irreg. back issues avail. **Document type:** *Monographic series, Consumer.*
Published by: Editions Eyrolles, 61 Boulevard Saint-Germain, Paris, 75240, France. http://www.editions-eyrolles.com.

616.89156 BEL ISSN 1372-8202
➤ **CAHIERS CRITIQUES DE THERAPIE FAMILIALE ET DE PRATIQUES DE RESEAUX.** Text in French. s-a. EUR 65 (effective 2011). bk.rev. abstr. 200 p./no.; back issues avail. **Document type:** *Journal, Academic/Scholarly.* **Description:** Covers issues relating to family psychotherapy, group therapy, and short-term therapy.
Related titles: Online - full text ed.: ISSN 1782-1398.
Indexed: DIP, E-psyche, IBR, IBZ, P03, PsycInfo, SCOPUS.
Published by: De Boeck Universite (Subsidiary of: Editis), Fond Jean-Paques 4, Louvain-la-Neuve, 1348, Belgium. TEL 32-10-482511, FAX 32-10-482519, info@superieur.deboeck.com. Ed. Mony Elkaim. **Subscr. to:** Acces S.P.R.L., Fond Jean-Paques 4, Louvain-la-Neuve 1348, Belgium. TEL 32-10-482570, FAX 32-10-482519, acces+cde@deboeck.be.

155.4 780 FRA ISSN 1954-4529
LES CAHIERS DE L'EVEIL. Text in French. 2004. a. back issues avail. **Document type:** *Magazine, Consumer.*
Published by: Enfance et Musique, 17 Rue Etienne Marcel, Pantin, 93500, France. TEL 33-1-48103000, FAX 33-1-48103009.

616.89 BEL ISSN 1370-074X
➤ **CAHIERS DE PSYCHOLOGIE CLINIQUE**; une revue interdisciplinaire en psychologie clinique et psychotherapie. Text in French. 1994. s-a. EUR 65 (effective 2011). bk.rev. 230 p./no.; back issues avail. **Document type:** *Journal, Academic/Scholarly.* **Description:** Takes a multidisciplinary approach to the study of clinical psychology and psychotherapy.
Related titles: Online - full text ed.: ISSN 1782-1401.
Indexed: DIP, E-psyche, IBR, IBZ, SCOPUS.
Published by: De Boeck Universite (Subsidiary of: Editis), Fond Jean-Paques 4, Louvain-la-Neuve, 1348, Belgium. TEL 32-10-482511, FAX 32-10-482519, info@superieur.deboeck.com. Eds. Alex Lefebvre, Philippe Van Meerbeeck.

302 FRA ISSN 1772-7642
LES CAHIERS DES F P S. (Facteurs Psychosociaux) Variant title: Les Cahiers des Facteurs Psychosociaux. Text in French. 2005. s-a. **Document type:** *Journal, Trade.*
Published by: Conseil en Analyse du Travail - Etudes et Innovations Sociales (C A T E I S), Le Venitien, 27 Bd Charles Moretti, Marseille, 13014, France. TEL 33-4-91627409, FAX 33-4-91627245.

301.1 150 BEL ISSN 0777-0707
➤ **CAHIERS INTERNATIONAUX DE PSYCHOLOGIE SOCIALE.** Text in French; Summaries in English, French, Spanish. 1989. q. EUR 68 domestic to individuals; EUR 72 foreign to individuals; EUR 95 domestic to institutions; EUR 99 foreign to institutions; EUR 55 domestic to students; EUR 23 per issue domestic; EUR 26 per issue foreign (effective 2005). bk.rev. 128 p./no.; **Document type:** *Monographic series, Academic/Scholarly.* **Description:** Discusses various aspects of social psychology.
Formerly: Les Cahiers de Psychologie Sociale (0774-6288)
Indexed: CA, DIP, E-psyche, FR, IBR, IBZ, P03, PsycInfo, PsycholAb, S02, S03, SCOPUS, SociolAb, T02.
—INIST.
Published by: De Boeck Universite (Subsidiary of: Editis), Fond Jean-Paques 4, Louvain-la-Neuve, 1348, Belgium. TEL 32-10-482511, FAX 32-10-482519, info@superieur.deboeck.com, http://superieur.deboeck.com. Ed. Pierre de Visscher. **Subscr. to:** Acces S.P.R.L., Fond Jean-Paques 4, Louvain-la-Neuve 1348, Belgium. TEL 32-10-482500, FAX 32-10-482519.

150.1954 FRA ISSN 0984-8207
CAHIERS JUNGIENS DE PSYCHANALYSE. Text in French. 1974. 3/yr. EUR 70 domestic; EUR 80 foreign (effective 2008).
Formerly (until 1987): Cahiers de Psychologie Jungienne (0984-8215)
Indexed: PsycholAb.
Published by: Association des Cahiers de Psychologie Jungienne, 6 rue Rampon, Paris, 75011, France. secretariat@cahiers-jungiens.com, http://www.cahiers-jungiens.com/. Ed. Martine Gallard.

150 370 FRA ISSN 2106-5632
CAHIERS PRATIQUES DE PSYCHOLOGIE EN MILIEU EDUCATIF. Text in French. 1994. irreg.
Published by: Association Francaise des Psychologues de l'Education Nationale, 19 Venelle de Kergresk, Quimper, 29000, France. TEL 33-9-75762340, FAX 33-2-98552854, siege.social@afpen.fr.

150 USA ISSN 0890-0302
BF1
THE CALIFORNIA PSYCHOLOGIST. Text in English. m. adv. **Document type:** *Magazine, Trade.* **Description:** Addresses practice concerns and new developments in the field of psychology.
Published by: California Psychological Association, 3835 N Freeway Blvd, Suite 240, Sacramento, CA 95834. TEL 916-286-7979, FAX 916-286-7971. adv.: B&W page USD 800; 7.25 x 9.75. Circ: 5,000.

150 USA ISSN 1087-3414
LB1027.55
➤ **CALIFORNIA SCHOOL PSYCHOLOGIST.** Text in English. 1996. a. USD 20 per issue (effective 2005). **Document type:** *Journal, Academic/Scholarly.* **Description:** Covers research, assessment, consultation, training, service delivery, and other topics important to the profession of school psychology.
Indexed: A26, CA, E03, E08, ERI, H12, I05, P03, P25, P30, P48, PQC, PsycInfo, PsycholAb, S09, T02.
—BLDSC (3015.264000).
Published by: California Association of School Psychologists, 1400 K St., Suite 311, Sacramento, CA 95814. TEL 916-444-1595, FAX 916-444-1597, http://www.casponline.org. Ed. Shane Jimerson.

➤ **CAMBRIDGE SERIES ON HUMAN-COMPUTER INTERACTION.** *see* COMPUTERS

150 CAN ISSN 1192-4179
CANADIAN HEALTH PSYCHOLOGIST. Text in Multiple languages. 1993. irreg.
Related titles: Online - full text ed.
Indexed: C03, CBCARef, CPerI, G08, P48, PQC.
—CIS. **CCC.**
Published by: Canadian Psychological Association, 141 Laurier Ave W, Ste 702, Ottawa, ON K1P 5J3, Canada. TEL 613-237-2144, 888-472-0657, FAX 613-237-1674, cpapub@cpa.ca, http://www.cpa.ca.

150.1953 CAN ISSN 1481-1715
➤ **THE CANADIAN JOURNAL OF ADLERIAN PSYCHOLOGY.** Text in English. 1991. s-a. CAD 35; USD 30 foreign. bk.rev. bibl.; charts; illus.; stat. back issues avail. **Document type:** *Journal, Academic/Scholarly.* **Description:** Provides theoretical and practical information for practicing therapists and counselors who use Adlerian psychology.
Related titles: E-mail ed.; Fax ed.; Online - full text ed.
Indexed: E-psyche.
Published by: Adlerian Psychology Association of British Columbia, No 401-1195 W Broadway, Vancouver, BC V6H 3X5, Canada. TEL 604-874-4614, FAX 604-874-4634. Ed., R&P Steven Slavik. Circ: 500 (paid).

370.15 USA ISSN 0008-400X
CODEN: CJBSAA
➤ **CANADIAN JOURNAL OF BEHAVIOURAL SCIENCE/REVUE CANADIENNE DES SCIENCES DU COMPORTEMENT.** Text in English, French. 1969. q. USD 116 domestic to individuals; USD 143 foreign to individuals; USD 281 domestic to institutions; USD 326 foreign to institutions (effective 2011). adv. bk.rev. charts; tr.lit.; abstr. index. 64 p./no. 2 cols./p.; back issues avail.; reprints avail. **Document type:** *Journal, Academic/Scholarly.* **Description:** Covers abnormal, behavioral, community, counselling, educational, environmental, developmental, health, industrial-organizational, clinical neuropsychological, personality, psychometrics, and social.
Related titles: Microfiche ed.: (from MML); Microform ed.: (from MML, PQC); Online - full text ed.: (from ScienceDirect).
Indexed: A01, A20, A22, A26, AMHA, ASCA, B25, BIOSIS Prev, BRD, C03, C06, C07, C28, CA, CBCARef, CBPI, CPerI, CWPI, CommAb, CurCont, DIP, E-psyche, E08, G08, I05, IBR, IBZ, ISR, MEA&I, MycolAb, P03, P10, P25, P27, P30, P48, P54, PQC, PsycInfo, PsycholAb, S02, S03, S09, S21, SCOPUS, SOPODA, SRRA, SSAI, SSAb, SSCI, SSI, SociolAb, T02, W03, W05, W07, W09.
—BLDSC (3028.700000), CIS, IE, Infotrieve, Ingenta, INIST. **CCC.**
Published by: (Canadian Psychological Association CAN), American Psychological Association, 750 First St, NE, Washington, DC 20002. TEL 202-336-5500, 800-374-2721, journals@apa.org. Ed. Greg Irving. Adv. contact Doug Constant TEL 202-336-5574. Circ: 3,600.

150 301.1 CAN
CANADIAN JOURNAL OF COMMUNITY MENTAL HEALTH (ONLINE)/REVUE CANADIENNE DE SANTE MENTALE COMMUNAUTAIRE. Text in English, French. 1982. s-a. CAD 60 domestic to institutions; USD 65 elsewhere to institutions; CAD 27.50 per issue domestic; USD 30 per issue in United States; USD 32.50 per issue elsewhere (effective 2012). index. **Document type:** *Journal, Academic/Scholarly.* **Description:** Provides a much needed forum for Canadian scholars and practitioners with interest in the promotion of positive mental health and the prevention and treatment of mental health problems in community settings.
Formerly (until 200?): Canadian Journal of Community Mental Health (Print) (0713-3936)
Media: Online - full content.
Indexed: A22, C03, C04, C06, C07, C08, CA, CBCARef, CDA, CINAHL, E-psyche, EMBASE, ExcerpMed, FR, MEDLINE, P03, P30, P48, PAIS, PQC, PsycInfo, PsycholAb, R10, Reac, S02, S03, SCOPUS, SWR&A, T02, V&AA.
—BLDSC (3031.046000), GNLM, IE, Infotrieve, Ingenta. **CCC.**
Published by: (Canadian Periodical for Community Studies Inc.), Wilfrid Laurier University Press, 75 University Ave W, Waterloo, ON N2L 3C5, Canada. TEL 519-884-0710 ext 6124, FAX 519-725-1399, press@wlu.ca, http://www.wlupress.wlu.ca.

158 CAN ISSN 0828-3893
BF637.C6
➤ **CANADIAN JOURNAL OF COUNSELLING/REVUE CANADIENNE DE COUNSELING.** Text in English, French. 1966. q. CAD 55 domestic to individuals; USD 55 foreign to individuals; CAD 95 domestic to institutions; USD 100 foreign to institutions (effective 2011). adv. bk.rev. index. back issues avail.; reprints avail. **Document type:** *Journal, Academic/Scholarly.* **Description:** Publishes current research and reports with relevance to psychological counselling practitioners.
Formerly: Canadian Counsellor (0008-333X)
Related titles: Microfiche ed.: (from MML); Microform ed.: 1967 (from MML, PQC); Online - full text ed.: ISSN 1923-6182.
Indexed: A22, A26, C03, CA, CEI, E-psyche, E03, E07, ERI, ERIC, FamI, HEA, P03, P18, P25, P48, P53, P54, PQC, PsycholAb, T02.
—BLDSC (3031.122000), IE, Infotrieve, Ingenta. **CCC.**
Published by: (Canadian Counselling and Psychotherapy Association/L'Association Canadienne de Counseling et de Psychotherapie), University of Calgary Press, 2500 University Dr NW, Calgary, AB T2N 1N4, Canada. TEL 403-220-7578, FAX 403-282-0085, ucpmail@ucalgary.ca, http://www.uofcpress.com. Ed. Dr. Kevin Alderson. adv.: page CAD 375; 6 x 9. Circ: 3,600 (paid and free).

150 CAN ISSN 1196-1961
BF1 CODEN: CJEPEK
➤ **CANADIAN JOURNAL OF EXPERIMENTAL PSYCHOLOGY/REVUE CANADIENNE DE PSYCHOLOGIE EXPERIMENTALE.** Text in English, French. 1947. q. USD 116 domestic to individuals; USD 143 foreign to individuals; USD 281 domestic to institutions; USD 326 foreign to institutions (effective 2011). adv. bibl.; charts; illus.; abstr. index, cum.index: 1947-1961. 64 p./no. 2 cols./p.; back issues avail.; reprints avail. **Document type:** *Journal, Academic/Scholarly.* **Description:** Publishes original research papers that advance understanding of the broad field of general experimental psychology. This includes, but is not restricted to, cognition, perception, sensorimotor processes, memory, learning, language, decision making, development, and neuroscience.
Former titles (until 1993): Canadian Journal of Psychology (0008-4255); (until 1947): Canadian Psychology Association. Bulletin (0382-8654)
Related titles: Microfiche ed.: (from MML); Microform ed.: (from MML, PQC); Online - full text ed.: ISSN 1878-7290 (from ScienceDirect).
Indexed: A01, A02, A03, A08, A20, A22, A25, A26, AMHA, ASCA, B04, B21, BRD, C03, C06, C07, CA, CBCARef, CBPI, CDA, CPerI, CurCont, DIP, E-psyche, E08, EMBASE, ErgAb, ExcerpMed, FR, FamI, G08, H09, H12, I05, IBR, IBZ, IndMed, M01, M02, MEDLINE, MLA-IB, NSA, P02, P03, P10, P12, P20, P22, P25, P26, P27, P30, P48, P53, P54, PCI, PQC, PdeR, PsycInfo, PsycholAb, R10, RASB, RILM, Reac, S02, S03, S05, S08, S09, S21, SCOPUS, SOPODA, SSAI, SSAb, SSCI, SSI, T02, W01, W02, W03, W05, W07, YAE&RB.
—BLDSC (3031.410000), CIS, GNLM, IE, Infotrieve, Ingenta, INIST, Linda Hall. **CCC.**

Published by: (American Psychological Association USA), Canadian Psychological Association, 141 Laurier Ave W, Ste 702, Ottawa, ON K1P 5J3, Canada. TEL 613-237-2144, 888-472-0657, FAX 613-237-1674, cpa@cpa.ca, http://www.cpa.ca. Ed. Douglas Mewhort. Adv. contact Doug Constant TEL 202-336-5574. Circ: 700.

155.3 616.6 CAN ISSN 1188-4517
HQ57.6.C2 CODEN: CJHSEA

➤ **CANADIAN JOURNAL OF HUMAN SEXUALITY.** Text in English. 1986. q. bk.rev. abstr. back issues avail. **Document type:** *Journal, Academic/Scholarly.* **Description:** Features scholarly articles, research papers, reviews, conference announcements and special theme issue.
Former titles (until 1992): S I E C C A N Journal (0844-3718); (until 1986): Journal - S I E C C A N (0834-0463)
Related titles: Fax ed.; Online - full text ed.
Indexed: A01, A02, A03, A08, A26, ASSIA, C03, C05, C06, C07, C08, C11, CA, CBCARef, CBPI, CDA, CINAHL, CLFP, CPE, CPerl, CWI, E-psyche, E07, E08, EMBASE, ExcerpMed, G01, G08, H04, H11, H12, I05, IBSS, L01, L02, M01, M02, P02, P03, P10, P18, P24, P25, P30, P43, P48, P50, P53, P54, PAIS, PQC, PsycInfo, PsycholAb, R10, Reac, S02, S03, S09, S11, S21, SCOPUS, SFSA, SOPODA, SWR&A, SociolAb, T02, V&AA, W09.
—BLDSC (3031.710000), CIS, GNLM, IE, Infotrieve, Ingenta. **CCC.**
Published by: Sex Information and Education Council of Canada, 850 Coxwell Ave, Toronto, ON M4C 5R1, Canada. TEL 416-466-5304, FAX 416-778-0785, sieccan@web.ca. Circ: 1,000.

154.6 CAN ISSN 1913-4150

➤ **CANADIAN JOURNAL OF HYPNOSIS/REVUE CANADIENNE D'HYPNOSE.** Text in English. 2007. s-a. free. **Document type:** *Journal, Academic/Scholarly.* **Description:** Publishes articles on all aspects of hypnosis in research, education and practice.
Media: Online - full text.
Published by: (Canadian Federation of Clinical Hypnosis), University of Calgary Press, 2500 University Dr NW, Calgary, AB T2N 1N4, Canada. TEL 403-220-7578, FAX 403-282-0085, ucpmail@ucalgary.ca, http://www.uofcpress.com. Ed. L Sabatini.

➤ **CANADIAN JOURNAL OF MUSIC THERAPY/REVUE CANADIENNE DE MUSICOTHERAPIE.** *see* MUSIC

➤ **CANADIAN JOURNAL OF SCHOOL PSYCHOLOGY.** *see* EDUCATION

150 CAN ISSN 0068-9211

CANADIAN MENTAL HEALTH ASSOCIATION. ANNUAL REPORT/ ASSOCIATION CANADIENNE POUR LA SANTE MENTALE. RAPPORT ANNUEL. Text in English. 1926. a. free. **Document type:** *Corporate.*
Indexed: E-psyche.
Published by: Canadian Mental Health Association, 2160 Yonge St, Toronto, ON M4S 2Z3, Canada. TEL 416-484-7750.

150 CAN ISSN 0708-5591
CODEN: CPSGD2

➤ **CANADIAN PSYCHOLOGY/PSYCHOLOGIE CANADIENNE.** Text in English, French. 1950. q. USD 116 domestic to individuals; USD 143 foreign to individuals; USD 281 domestic to institutions; USD 326 foreign to institutions (effective 2011). adv. bk.rev. illus.; abstr. Index. back issues avail.; reprints avail. **Document type:** *Journal, Academic/ Scholarly.* **Description:** Features generalist articles in the areas of theory, research, and practice relevant to a broad cross-section of psychologists.
Former titles (until 1980): Canadian Psychological Review (0318-2096); (until 1975): Canadian Psychologist (0008-4832)
Related titles: Microfiche ed.: (from MML); Microform ed.; Online - full text ed.: ISSN 1878-7304 (from ScienceDirect).
Indexed: A01, A20, A22, A26, ASCA, B04, BRD, C03, C06, CA, CBCARef, CBPI, CPerl, CWPI, CurCont, DIP, E-psyche, E08, Faml, G08, I05, IBR, IBZ, MEA&I, MLA-IB, P03, P10, P25, P27, P30, P48, P54, PAIS, PQC, PsycInfo, PsycholAb, S02, S03, S09, SCOPUS, SOPODA, SSAI, SSAb, SSCI, SSI, SociolAb, T02, W01, W02, W03, W05, W07.
—BLDSC (3044.105000), IE, Infotrieve, Ingenta. **CCC.**
Published by: (American Psychological Association USA), Canadian Psychological Association, 141 Laurier Ave W, Ste 702, Ottawa, ON K1P 5J3, Canada. TEL 613-237-2144, 888-472-0657, FAX 613-237-1674, cpapub@cpa.ca, http://www.cpa.ca. Ed. John Hunsley. Circ: 4,500.

➤ **CANADIAN UNDERGRADUATE JOURNAL OF COGNITIVE SCIENCE.** *see* PHILOSOPHY

➤ **THE CAREER DEVELOPMENT QUARTERLY.** *see* OCCUPATIONS AND CAREERS

➤ **CARIBBEAN JOURNAL OF CRIMINOLOGY & SOCIAL PSYCHOLOGY.** *see* CRIMINOLOGY AND LAW ENFORCEMENT

155.937 618 USA

CARING NOTES; a professional newsletter by S H A R E. Text in English. 1995. q. looseleaf. USD 35 (effective 2000). bk.rev.; video rev.; Website rev. **Document type:** *Newsletter.* **Description:** For SHARE group facilitators and other caregivers, reaching out to the bereaved experiencing a pregnancy loss, stillbirth or neonatal death. Offers professional articles on clinical and psychological aspects of perinatal loss.
Indexed: E-psyche.
Published by: S H A R E Pregnancy & Infant Loss Support National Office, St Joseph Health, 300 First Capitol Dr, Center, MO 63301. TEL 636-947-6164, 800-821-6819, FAX 314-947-7486, share@nationalshareoffice.com, http://www.nationalshareoffice.com. Eds. Catherine A Lammert, Jane Borman. Circ: 150.

150 DEU ISSN 2191-7310

▼ **CARL-STUMPF-GESELLSCHAFT. SCHRIFTENREIHE.** Text in German. forthcoming 2011. irreg. price varies. **Document type:** *Monographic series, Academic/Scholarly.*
Published by: Peter Lang GmbH (Subsidiary of: Peter Lang Publishing Group), Eschborner Landstr 42-50, Frankfurt Am Main, 60489, Germany. TEL 49-69-78070550, FAX 49-69-78070550, zentrale.frankfurt@peterlang.com. Eds. Margret Kaiser-El-Safti, Martin Ebeling.

150.19 155.4 USA

CARNEGIE MELLON SYMPOSIA ON COGNITION SERIES. Variant title: Carnegie Symposium on Cognition. Text in English. 1974. irreg., latest 2008. price varies. adv. back issues avail. **Document type:** *Monographic series, Academic/Scholarly.* **Description:** Research on human perception and action examines sensors and effectors in relative isolation.
Related titles: Online - full text ed.
Indexed: E-psyche, PsycholAb.
Published by: Psychology Press (Subsidiary of: Taylor & Francis Inc.), 325 Chestnut St, Ste 800, Philadelphia, PA 19106. TEL 800-354-1420, FAX 215-625-2940, orders@taylorandfrancis.com. Adv. contact Linda Hann TEL 44-1344-779945.

LE CARNET PSY. *see* MEDICAL SCIENCES—Psychiatry And Neurology

150 CHL ISSN 0717-4985

CASTALIA. Text in Spanish. 1999. s-a. CLP 5,000 domestic; USD 20 foreign (effective 2010). back issues avail. **Document type:** *Journal, Academic/Scholarly.*
Related titles: Online - full text ed.
Published by: Universidad Academia de Humanismo Cristiano, Avenida Condell 343, Providencia, Santiago, Chile. TEL 56-2-7878000, sibacweb@academia.cl, http://www.academia.cl.

150 PRI ISSN 1547-2582

LA CATARSIS DE QUIRON. Text in Spanish. 2002. s-a. back issues avail. **Document type:** *Newsletter.*
Media: Online - full text.
Published by: Catarsis de Quiron, No. 607 Calle Condado, Ste 401, Santurce, 00969, Puerto Rico. correo@catarsisdequiron.com. Ed. Domingo J. Marques.

150.19 ITA ISSN 1128-7918

IL CEFALOPODO. Text in Italian. 1974. a. Supplement avail. **Document type:** *Magazine, Consumer.* **Description:** Essays in psychoanalysis, art and literature.
Formerly (until 1994): Il Piccolo Hans (0390-3206)
Related titles: Supplement(s): Ambulatorio. ISSN 1593-3873. 1999.
Indexed: E-psyche, MLA-IB.
Published by: Moretti e Vitali Editori, Via Sergentini 6a, Bergamo, BG 24128, Italy. TEL 39-035-251300, FAX 39-035-4329409, http://www.morettievitali.it. Ed. Sergio Finzi.

150 FRA ISSN 1292-2048

LA CELIBATAIRE. Text in French. 1998. s-a. EUR 58.77 domestic; EUR 91.94 in the European Union; EUR 112 elsewhere (effective 2012). **Document type:** *Journal, Academic/Scholarly.* **Description:** Deals with society issues; sexual, political, religious, legal, and economic.
Published by: E D P Sciences, 17 Ave du Hoggar, Parc d'Activites de Courtaboeuf, BP 112, Cedex A, Les Ulis, F-91944, France. TEL 33-1-69187575, FAX 33-1-69860678, http://www.edpsciences.org. Ed. Charles Melman.

150 USA

THE CENTER FOR THANATOLOGY. CATALOG. Text in English. s-a. **Document type:** *Catalog, Consumer.*
Published by: Center for Thanatology Research and Education Inc., 391 Atlantic Ave, Brooklyn, NY 11217-1701. TEL 718-858-3026, FAX 718-852-1846, thanatology@pipeline.com, http://www.thanatology.org. Ed. Roberta Halporn.

150 ITA ISSN 1828-4353
BF84

CENTRO STUDI DI PSICOLOGIA E LETTERATURA. GIORNALE STORICO. Text in Italian. 1977. s-a. price varies. adv. **Document type:** *Monographic series, Academic/Scholarly.*
Formerly (until 2005): Giornale Storico di Psicologia Dinamica (0391-2515)
Indexed: A26, E-psyche, I05, P03, PsycInfo, PsycholAb.
Published by: (Centro Studi di Psicologia e Letteratura), Giovanni Fioriti Editore, Via Archimede 179, Rome, 00197, Italy. TEL 39-06-8072063, FAX 39-06-80664609, info@fioriti.it, http://www.fioriti.it.

150 COL ISSN 2011-3080

CES REVISTA PSICOLOGIA. Text in Spanish. 2007. s-a. adv. abstr.; bibl.; charts; illus.; stat. **Document type:** *Journal, Academic/Scholarly.* **Description:** Covers various aspects of psychology, including social sciences, humanities, and health sciences.
Related titles: Online - full text ed.: free (effective 2011).
Indexed: H12, I04, I05.
Published by: Universidad CES, Facultad de Psicologia, Calle 10 A No.22-04, Medellin, Colombia. TEL 57-4-4440555 ext 1402, FAX 57-4-3113578. Ed. Maria Paulina Herrera.

150 CZE ISSN 1211-216X

CESKA AKADEMIE VED. PSYCHOLOGICKY USTAV. BULLETIN. Text in Czech. 1995. irreg. price varies. **Document type:** *Bulletin, Academic/Scholarly.* **Description:** Covers the research of members of the Prague branch of the institute.
Published by: Akademie Ved Ceske Republiky, Psychologicky Ustav, Veveri 97, Brno 1, 60200, Czech Republic. TEL 420-53-2290278, FAX 420-54-9244667, info@psu.cas.cz, http://www.psu.cas.cz.

150 CZE ISSN 0009-062X
BF8.C9 CODEN: CEPSBC

➤ **CESKOSLOVENSKA PSYCHOLOGIE/CZECHOSLOVAK PSYCHOLOGY;** psychological journal for theory and practice. Text mainly in Czech, Slovak; Text occasionally in English, German, Russian; Summaries in English. 1957. bi-m. CZK 222 domestic; USD 44 foreign (effective 2008). adv. bk.rev. charts; illus.; stat. index. **Document type:** *Journal, Academic/Scholarly.* **Description:** Covers all fields of psychology, theoretical and applied. Includes basic research into general and social psychology, survey studies which have been given preference and reports on important conferences and institutes.
Indexed: A01, A20, A22, ASCA, BibLing, CA, CDA, CISA, CurCont, E-psyche, ErgAb, P03, P10, P12, P25, P30, P48, P53, P54, PCI, PQC, PsycInfo, PsycholAb, RASB, S02, S03, SCOPUS, SSCI, T02, W07.
—BLDSC (3122.500000), IE, Infotrieve, Ingenta, INIST.
Published by: Akademie Ved Ceske Republiky, Psychologicky Ustav, Husova 4, Prague, Czech Republic. info@psu.cas.cz, http://www.psu.cas.cz. Eds. D Heller, I Solcova. Circ: 2,800.

➤ **C'EST LA VIE AUSSI.** *see* CHILDREN AND YOUTH—About

150 FRA ISSN 1761-4473

CHAMPS OUVERTS. Text in French. 2003. irreg. back issues avail. **Document type:** *Monographic series, Consumer.*
Published by: Ellebore Editions, B P 60001, Paris, 75560 Cedex 12, France. info@ellebore.fr.

150 POL ISSN 1427-695X

CHARAKTERY; magazyn psychologiczny dla kazdego. Text in Polish. 1997. m. EUR 59 foreign (effective 2006). adv. dance rev.; music rev.; play rev.; tel.rev.; video rev. bibl.; illus. back issues avail. **Description:** Offers practical knowledge indispensable in professional, social and family life.
Address: ul Warszawska 6, Kielce, 25512, Poland. TEL 48-41-3442362, FAX 48-41-3444321, charaktery@charaktery.com.pl. Eds. Andrzej Eliasz, Bogdan Bialek. adv.: color page PLZ 4,800; trim 210 x 297. Circ: 40,000. **Dist. by:** Ars Polona, Obroncow 25, Warsaw 03933, Poland. TEL 48-22-5098609, FAX 48-22-5098610, arspolona@arspolona.com.pl, http://www.arspolona.com.pl.
Co-publisher: Szkola Wyzsza Psychologii Spolecznej w Warszawie/ Warsaw School of Social Psychology.

CHE VUOI?. *see* MEDICAL SCIENCES—Psychiatry And Neurology

616.89 FRA ISSN 1951-5596

LES CHEMINS DE L'INCONSCIENT. Text in French. 2006. irreg. **Document type:** *Monographic series, Academic/Scholarly.*
Published by: Editions Eyrolles, 61 Boulevard Saint-Germain, Paris, 75240, France.

CHILD ABUSE REVIEW. *see* SOCIAL SERVICES AND WELFARE

155.4 GBR ISSN 1475-357X
RJ499.A1

➤ **CHILD AND ADOLESCENT MENTAL HEALTH.** Abbreviated title: C A M H. Text in English. 1996. q. GBP 147 in United Kingdom to institutions; EUR 186 in Europe to institutions; USD 247 in the Americas to institutions; USD 287 elsewhere to institutions; GBP 169 combined subscription in United Kingdom to institutions (print & online eds.); EUR 215 combined subscription in Europe to institutions (print & online eds.); USD 285 combined subscription in the Americas to institutions (print & online eds.); USD 330 combined subscription elsewhere to institutions (print & online eds.) (effective 2012). adv. bk.rev.; software rev. reprint service avail. from PSC. **Document type:** *Journal, Academic/Scholarly.* **Description:** Provides a forum for the exchange of clinical experience, ideas and research.
Formerly (until 2002): Child Psychology and Psychiatry Review (1360-6417); Which superseded in part (in 1996): A C P P Review and Newsletter (1354-5329); Which was formerly (until 1993): Association for Child Psychology and Psychiatry. Newsletter (0265-4520); (until 1983): Association for Child Psychology and Psychiatry. News
Related titles: Online - full text ed.: Child and Adolescent Mental Health (Online). ISSN 1475-3588. 1998. GBP 147 in United Kingdom to institutions; EUR 186 in Europe to institutions; USD 247 in the Americas to institutions; USD 287 elsewhere to institutions (effective 2012) (from IngentaConnect).
Indexed: A01, A03, A08, A22, A26, B28, C06, C07, C08, C28, CA, CINAHL, CurCont, E-psyche, E01, EMBASE, ESPM, ExcerpMed, FR, H12, P03, P30, P43, PsycInfo, PsycholAb, R10, Reac, RiskAb, S02, S03, SCI, SCOPUS, SSCI, T02, W07.
—BLDSC (3172.913520), IE, Ingenta, INIST. **CCC.**
Published by: (The Association for Child and Adolescent Mental Health), Wiley-Blackwell Publishing Ltd. (Subsidiary of: John Wiley & Sons, Inc.), 9600 Garsington Rd, Oxford, OX4 2DQ, United Kingdom. TEL 44-1865-776868, FAX 44-1865-714591, customerservices@blackwellpublishing.com. Eds. Jacqueline Barnes, Paul Stallard, Tamsin Ford. Adv. contact Craig Pickett TEL 44-1865-476267. B&W page USD 925; 175 x 265.

➤ **CHILD AND ADOLESCENT SOCIAL WORK JOURNAL.** *see* SOCIOLOGY

155.4 USA ISSN 0731-7107
RJ504

➤ **CHILD & FAMILY BEHAVIOR THERAPY.** Abbreviated title: C F B T. Text in English. 1978. q. GBP 732 combined subscription in United Kingdom to institutions (print & online eds.); EUR 953, USD 956 combined subscription to institutions (print & online eds.) (effective 2012). adv. bk.rev.; film rev. bibl.; charts; stat.; illus. 120 p./no. 1 cols./p.; back issues avail.; reprint service avail. from PSC. **Document type:** *Journal, Academic/Scholarly.* **Description:** Offers an interdisciplinary journal devoted to research and clinical applications in behavior therapy with children and adolescents, as well as the enhancement of parenting.
Formerly (until 1982): Child Behavior Therapy (0162-1416)
Related titles: Microfiche ed.: (from PQC); Microform ed.; Online - full text ed.: ISSN 1545-228X. GBP 659 in United Kingdom to institutions; EUR 857, USD 860 to institutions (effective 2012).
Indexed: A01, A03, A20, A22, A26, AC&P, AMHA, ASCA, BehAb, C06, C07, C08, C28, CA, CDA, CINAHL, CurCont, E-psyche, E01, E03, E07, ECER, ERI, ERIC, F09, FR, Faml, H12, M02, P02, P03, P10, P12, P30, P48, P53, P54, PQC, PsycInfo, PsycholAb, RehabLit, S02, S03, SCOPUS, SFSA, SOPODA, SSA, SSCI, SWR&A, SociolAb, T02, V&AA, W07.
—BLDSC (3172.915100), GNLM, IE, Infotrieve, Ingenta, INIST. **CCC.**
Published by: Routledge (Subsidiary of: Taylor & Francis Group), 325 Chestnut St, Ste 800, Philadelphia, PA 19106. TEL 215-625-8900, 800-354-1420, FAX 215-625-8914, journals@routledge.com, http://www.routledge.com. Eds. Charles Diament, Cyril M Franks. adv.: B&W page USD 315, color page USD 550; trim 4.375 x 7.125. Circ: 387 (paid).

➤ **CHILD AND YOUTH CARE FORUM;** journal of research and practice in children's services. *see* CHILDREN AND YOUTH—About

➤ **CHILD CARE IN PRACTICE.** *see* CHILDREN AND YOUTH—About

➤ **CHILD DEVELOPMENT.** *see* CHILDREN AND YOUTH—About

➤ **CHILD DEVELOPMENT & ADOLESCENT STUDIES.** *see* MEDICAL SCIENCES—Abstracting, Bibliographies, Statistics

➤ **CHILD DEVELOPMENT PERSPECTIVES.** *see* CHILDREN AND YOUTH—About

155.4 USA ISSN 2090-3987

▼ ➤ **CHILD DEVELOPMENT RESEARCH.** Text in English. 2011. USD 195 (effective 2011). **Document type:** *Journal, Academic/Scholarly.*
Related titles: Online - full text ed.: ISSN 2090-3995. free (effective 2011).
Published by: Hindawi Publishing Corporation, 410 Park Ave, 15th Fl, PMB 287, New York, NY 10022. FAX 215-893-4392, 866-446-3294, hindawi@hindawi.com.

P

➤ **CHILD MALTREATMENT.** *see* CHILDREN AND YOUTH—About

155.4 GBR ISSN 1473-3285

➤ **CHILDREN'S GEOGRAPHIES**; advancing interdisciplinary understanding of younger people's lives. Text in English. 2003 (Mar.). q. GBP 409 combined subscription in United Kingdom to institutions (print & online eds.); EUR 548, USD 686 combined subscription to institutions (print & online eds.) (effective 2012). adv. bk.rev. back issues avail.; reprint service avail. from PSC. **Document type:** *Journal, Academic/Scholarly.* **Description:** Provides an international forum to discuss issues that impact upon the geographical worlds of children and young people under the age of 25 and of their families.
Related titles: Online - full text ed.: ISSN 1473-3277. GBP 368 in United Kingdom to institutions; EUR 493, USD 618 to institutions (effective 2012) (from IngentaConnect).
Indexed: A01, A03, A08, A22, CA, CurCont, E01, SSCI, T02, W07.
—IE, Ingenta. **CCC.**
Published by: Routledge (Subsidiary of: Taylor & Francis Group), 4 Park Sq, Milton Park, Abingdon, Oxon OX14 4RN, United Kingdom. TEL 44-20-70176000, FAX 44-20-70176336, subscriptions@tandf.co.uk, http://www.routledge.com. Ed. Hugh Matthews TEL 44-1604-892810. Adv. contact Linda Hann TEL 44-1344-779945. **Subscr. in N America to:** Taylor & Francis Inc., Customer Services Dept, 325 Chestnut St, 8th Fl, Philadelphia, PA 19106. TEL 215-625-8900, 800-354-1420, FAX 215-625-2940, customerservice@taylorandfrancis.com; **Subscr. to:** Taylor & Francis Ltd., Journals Customer Service, Sheepen Pl, Colchester, Essex CO3 3LP, United Kingdom. TEL 44-20-70175544, FAX 44-20-70175198.

150 130 TWN ISSN 1013-9656
RC321

➤ **CHINESE JOURNAL OF PSYCHOLOGY.** Text in Chinese, English; Abstracts in Chinese, English. 1958. s-a. USD 50 to institutions; TWD 1,000 newsstand/cover (effective 2002). adv. abstr. back issues avail. **Document type:** *Journal, Academic/Scholarly.*
Formerly: Acta Psychologica Taiwanica (0065-1613)
Indexed: A22, ASCA, BAS, E-psyche, P03, PsycInfo, PsycholAb.
—BLDSC (3180.606000), IE, Ingenta, INIST.
Published by: Chinese Psychological Association, c/o Department of Psychology, National Taiwan University, Taipei, 10764, Taiwan. FAX 886-2-2367-2370, cpaatroc@seed.net.tw. Ed., R&P Chengliang Keng. Circ: 500.

➤ **CHOWANNA.** *see* EDUCATION

150 CHL ISSN 0718-4166

CIENCIA PSICOLOGIA. Text in Spanish. 2007. s-a.
Media: Online - full text.
Published by: Universidad Central de Chile, Escuela de Psicologia, Campus La Reina, Carlos Silva, Vildosola 9783, La Reina, Santiago, Chile. TEL 56-2-5826502, http://www.fcsucentral.cl/#. Ed. Carmen Gloria Cabello.

150 ESP ISSN 1135-5956

CIENCIA PSICOLOGICA. Text in Spanish. 1995. s-a. EUR 12; EUR 9 to students. bibl. **Document type:** *Journal, Academic/Scholarly.* **Description:** Publishes scientific articles from the world of psychology and related sciences.
Indexed: E-psyche.
Published by: (Colegio Oficial de Psicologos, Extremadura), Colegio Oficial de Psicologos, Claudio Coello 46, Madrid, 28001, Spain. TEL 34-91-4355212, FAX 34-91-5779172.

150 ESP ISSN 1989-9912

▼ **CLINICA CONTEMPORANEA.** Text in Spanish. 2010. 3/yr. back issues avail. **Document type:** *Magazine, Trade.*
Media: Online - full text.
Published by: Colegio Oficial de Psicologos, Claudio Coello 46, Madrid, 28001, Spain. TEL 34-91-4355212, FAX 34-91-5779172, http://www.cop.es. Ed. Jesus Ramirez Cabanas.

150.19 ESP ISSN 0210-0657
RC475

CLINICA Y ANALISIS GRUPAL; revista de psicoterapia, psicoanalisis y grupo. Text in Spanish; Summaries in English, French. 1976. 3/yr. EUR 42 (effective 2009). adv. bk.rev. index. back issues avail. **Document type:** *Magazine, Academic/Scholarly.*
Indexed: E-psyche, P03, PsycInfo, PsycholAb, RILM.
Published by: Imago Clinica Psicoanalitica, C Pintor Ribera, 20, Baja A, Madrid, 28016, Spain. TEL 34-91-4112020, imago@imagoclinica.com, http://www.imagoclinica.com/imago.asp. Ed. Isabel Sanfeliu. Adv. contact Nicolas Caparros. Circ: 1,500.

158 ESP ISSN 1130-5274
RC467

CLINICA Y SALUD; revista de psicologia clinica y salud. Text in Spanish. 1990. 3/yr. EUR 33.50 domestic to qualified personnel; EUR 43 domestic; EUR 80 foreign (effective 2008). adv. abstr.; bibl. back issues avail. **Document type:** *Journal, Academic/Scholarly.* **Description:** Includes articles and tips on psychology and general health for clinical psychologists to incorporate into their practices.
Related titles: Online - full text ed.: ISSN 2174-0550. 1990.
Indexed: A01, E-psyche, F03, F04, P03, PsycInfo, PsycholAb, T02.
Published by: Colegio Oficial de Psicologos, Claudio Coello 46, Madrid, 28001, Spain. TEL 34-91-4355212, FAX 34-91-5779172. Ed. Hector Gonzalez Ordi.

CLINICAL CASE STUDIES. *see* MEDICAL SCIENCES—Psychiatry And Neurology

155 USA ISSN 1096-4037
RJ503.3 CODEN: CCFPFB

➤ **CLINICAL CHILD AND FAMILY PSYCHOLOGY REVIEW.** Text in English. 1998. q. EUR 346, USD 357 combined subscription to institutions (print & online eds.) (effective 2012). adv. back issues avail.; reprint service avail. from PSC. **Document type:** *Journal, Academic/Scholarly.* **Description:** Covers behavioral issues concerning infants, children, adolescents, and families. Publishes research, review articles, position papers, and conceptual and theoretical articles that explore the psychological treatment of these special populations.
Related titles: Online - full text ed.: ISSN 1573-2827 (from IngentaConnect).
Indexed: A01, A03, A08, A22, A26, Agr, BibLing, C06, C07, C28, CA, CurCont, E-psyche, E01, E03, E07, EMBASE, ERI, ERIC, ExcerpMed, F09, FamI, H12, IndMed, MEDLINE, P03, P20, P22, P25, P30, P43, P48, P50, P54, PQC, PsycInfo, PsycholAb, R10, Reac, S02, S03, SCOPUS, SSCI, T02, W07.
—BLDSC (3286.268350), IE, Infotrieve, Ingenta. **CCC.**
Published by: Springer New York LLC (Subsidiary of: Springer Science+Business Media), 233 Spring St, New York, NY 10013. TEL 212-460-1500, FAX 212-460-1575, service-ny@springer.com. Eds. Ronald J Prinz, Thomas H Ollendick.

➤ **CLINICAL CHILD PSYCHOLOGY & PSYCHIATRY.** *see* CHILDREN AND YOUTH—About

150 616.8 USA ISSN 1745-0179
RC467

➤ **CLINICAL PRACTICE AND EPIDEMIOLOGY IN MENTAL HEALTH.** Text in English. 2005. a. free (effective 2011). adv. back issues avail.; reprints avail. **Document type:** *Journal, Academic/Scholarly.* **Description:** Covers all aspects of clinical and epidemiological research in psychiatry and mental health.
Media: Online - full text.
Indexed: A01, A26, A34, A36, C06, C07, CA, CABA, E12, EMBASE, ExcerpMed, GH, I05, IndVet, N02, N03, P03, P30, PsycInfo, R10, R12, Reac, SCOPUS, T02, T05, VS.
—**CCC.**
Published by: Bentham Science Publishers Ltd., c/o Richard E Morrissy, PO Box 446, Oak Park, IL 60301. Ed. Mauro Giovanni Carta.

150 USA ISSN 0009-9244
BF1

THE CLINICAL PSYCHOLOGIST. Text in English. 19??. q. free to members (effective 2011). back issues avail. **Document type:** *Journal, Academic/Scholarly.* **Description:** Covers clinical psychology, including research, clinical practice, training, and public policy.
Former titles (until 1966): American Psychological Association. Division of Clinical Psychology. Newsletter; (until 1954): American Psychological Association. Division of Clinical and Abnormal Psychology. Newsletter
Related titles: Online - full text ed.
Indexed: P30.
—BLDSC (3286.343000).
Published by: American Psychological Association, Division of Clinical Psychology, PO Box 1082, Niwot, CO 80544. TEL 303-652-3126, FAX 303-652-2723, div12apa@comcast.net.

616.89 GBR ISSN 1328-4207

➤ **CLINICAL PSYCHOLOGIST.** Text in English. 1946. 3/yr. GBP 115 in United Kingdom to institutions; EUR 149 in Europe to institutions; USD 184 elsewhere to institutions; GBP 133 combined subscription in United Kingdom to institutions (print & online eds.); EUR 171 combined subscription in Europe to institutions (print & online eds.); USD 211 combined subscription elsewhere to institutions (print & online eds.) (effective 2012). adv. back issues avail.; reprint service avail. from PSC. **Document type:** *Journal, Academic/Scholarly.* **Description:** Covers a range of topics of broad general relevance to clinical psychologists, including psychopathology, clinical assessment and treatment, as well as commentary on theoretical issues and applied therapies across the lifespan.
Formerly (until 1996): Australian Psychological Society. Clinical College. Newsletter
Related titles: Online - full text ed.: ISSN 1742-9552. GBP 115 in United Kingdom to institutions; EUR 149 in Europe to institutions; USD 184 elsewhere to institutions (effective 2012) (from IngentaConnect).
Indexed: A01, A22, ASSIA, C06, C07, C08, CA, CINAHL, CurCont, E-psyche, E01, ERIC, IBR, IBZ, P03, P48, PQC, PsycInfo, PsycholAb, RehabLit, SCI, SCOPUS, SSCI, T02, W07.
—BLDSC (3286.343100), IE, Ingenta. **CCC.**
Published by: (Australian Psychological Society AUS), Taylor & Francis Ltd. (Subsidiary of: Taylor & Francis Group), 4 Park Sq, Milton Park, Abingdon, Oxfordshire OX14 4RN, United Kingdom. TEL 44-20-70176000, FAX 44-20-70176336, subscriptions@tandf.co.uk, http://www.taylorandfrancis.com. Ed. Justin Kenardy. Adv. contact Linda Hann. **Subscr. in US to:** Taylor & Francis Inc., Customer Services Dept, 325 Chestnut St, 8th Fl, Philadelphia, PA 19106. TEL 215-625-8900, 800-354-1420, FAX 215-625-2940, customerservice@taylorandfrancis.com; **Subscr. to:** Journals Customer Service, Sheepen Pl, Colchester, Essex CO3 3LP, United Kingdom. TEL 44-20-70175544, FAX 44-20-70175198, tf.enquiries@tfinforma.com.

616.89 USA ISSN 0969-5893
RC467 CODEN: CPLSC2

➤ **CLINICAL PSYCHOLOGY**; science and practice. Text in English. 1994. q. GBP 310 combined subscription in United Kingdom to institutions (print & online eds.); EUR 393 combined subscription in Europe to institutions (print & online eds.); USD 483 combined subscription in the Americas to institutions (print & online eds.); USD 607 combined subscription elsewhere to institutions (print & online eds.) (effective 2012). bk.rev. illus. Index. back issues avail.; reprint service avail. from PSC. **Document type:** *Journal, Academic/Scholarly.* **Description:** Publishes topical reviews of research, theory and application, including assessment, intervention, service delivery, and professional issues.
Related titles: Online - full text ed.: ISSN 1468-2850. GBP 281 in United Kingdom to institutions; EUR 359 in Europe to institutions; USD 439 in the Americas to institutions; USD 552 elsewhere to institutions (effective 2012) (from IngentaConnect).
Indexed: A01, A03, A08, A20, A22, A26, ASCA, B21, CA, CurCont, E-psyche, E01, FamI, H13, I05, JW-P, NSA, P03, P10, P12, P20, P25, P30, P48, P53, P54, PQC, PsycInfo, PsycholAb, R10, Reac, SCOPUS, SSCI, T02, W07.
—BLDSC (3286.343400), IE, Infotrieve, Ingenta. **CCC.**
Published by: (American Psychological Association), Wiley-Blackwell Publishing, Inc. (Subsidiary of: Wiley-Blackwell Publishing Ltd.), 111 River St, Hoboken, NJ 07030. TEL 201-748-6000, FAX 201-748-6088, info@wiley.com, http://www.wiley.com/WileyCDA/. Ed. Philip Kendall.

150 GBR ISSN 1746-6008

CLINICAL PSYCHOLOGY & PEOPLE WITH LEARNING DISABILITIES. Text in English. 2003. q. back issues avail. **Document type:** *Newsletter, Academic/Scholarly.* **Description:** Covers papers that make significant and original contributions to the field of clinical psychology and people with learning disabilities.
Related titles: Online - full text ed.: GBP 3.45 per issue to non-members; GBP 2.30 per issue to members (effective 2009).
Published by: The British Psychological Society, St Andrews House, 48 Princess Rd E, Leicester, LE1 7DR, United Kingdom. TEL 44-116-2549568, FAX 44-116-2271314, enquiries@bps.org.uk, http://www.bps.org.uk.

616.89 GBR ISSN 1063-3995
RC467 CODEN: CPPSEO

➤ **CLINICAL PSYCHOLOGY & PSYCHOTHERAPY**; an international journal of theory and practice. Text in English. 1993. bi-m. GBP 551 in United Kingdom to institutions; EUR 689 in Europe to institutions; USD 1,067 elsewhere to institutions; GBP 633 combined subscription in United Kingdom to institutions (print & online eds.); EUR 793 combined subscription in Europe to institutions (print & online eds.); USD 1,227 combined subscription elsewhere to institutions (print & online eds.) (effective 2012). adv. back issues avail.; reprint service avail. from PSC. **Document type:** *Journal, Academic/Scholarly.* **Description:** Presents papers on various presentations within clinical psychology and psychotherapy, with special emphasis on theoretical papers outlining innovations within existing approaches.
Related titles: Microform ed.: (from PQC); Online - full text ed.: ISSN 1099-0879. GBP 551 in United Kingdom to institutions; EUR 689 in Europe to institutions; USD 1,067 elsewhere to institutions (effective 2012).
Indexed: A01, A03, A08, A20, ASCA, B21, C06, C07, CA, CurCont, E-psyche, EMBASE, ExcerpMed, FamI, MEDLINE, NSA, P02, P03, P10, P12, P30, P43, P48, P53, P54, PQC, PsycInfo, PsycholAb, R10, Reac, S02, S03, SCOPUS, SSCI, T02, W07.
—GNLM, IE, Infotrieve, Ingenta. **CCC.**
Published by: John Wiley & Sons Ltd. (Subsidiary of: John Wiley & Sons, Inc.), 1-7 Oldlands Way, PO Box 808, Bognor Regis, West Sussex PO21 9FF, United Kingdom. TEL 44-1865-778315, FAX 44-1243-843232, cs-journals@wiley.com, http://eu.wiley.com/WileyCDA/. Eds. Mick Power, Paul Emmelkamp. **Subscr. to:** John Wiley & Sons, Inc., 111 River St, Hoboken, NJ 07030. TEL 201-748-6645, subinfo@wiley.com; **Subscr. to:** 1-7 Oldlands Way, PO Box 809, Bognor Regis, West Sussex PO21 9FG, United Kingdom. TEL 44-1865-778054, cs-agency@wiley.com.

616.86 GBR ISSN 1747-5732
CODEN: CPLSF5

➤ **CLINICAL PSYCHOLOGY FORUM.** Text in English. 1986. m. adv. reprints avail. **Document type:** *Journal, Academic/Scholarly.* **Description:** Covers regular updates about DCP policy and business in order to inform its membership.
Former titles (until 2005): Clinical Psychology (1473-8279); (until 2001): Clinical Psychology Forum (0269-0144)
Related titles: Online - full text ed.: GBP 4.02 per issue to non-members; GBP 2.88 per issue to members (effective 2009).
Indexed: A22, ASSIA, E-psyche, SCOPUS.
—BLDSC (3286.344050), IE, Ingenta.
Published by: The British Psychological Society, St Andrews House, 48 Princess Rd E, Leicester, LE1 7DR, United Kingdom. TEL 44-116-2549568, FAX 44-116-2271314, enquiries@bps.org.uk. Ed. Craig Wewyes.

616.89 GBR ISSN 0272-7358
RC467 CODEN: CPSRDZ

➤ **CLINICAL PSYCHOLOGY REVIEW.** Text in English. 1981. 8/yr. EUR 1,462 in Europe to institutions; JPY 194,100 in Japan to institutions; USD 1,636 elsewhere to institutions (effective 2012). bk.rev. illus. back issues avail.; reprints avail. **Document type:** *Journal, Academic/Scholarly.* **Description:** Focuses original research and reviews on topics germane to clinical psychology, including psychopathology, psychotherapy, community mental health, behavioral medicine and child development.
Related titles: Microfilm ed.: (from PQC); Online - full text ed.: ISSN 1873-7811 (from IngentaConnect, ScienceDirect).
Indexed: A01, A03, A08, A20, A22, A26, AC&P, CA, CurCont, DokArb, E-psyche, EMBASE, ExcerpMed, F09, FamI, I05, IndMed, MEDLINE, P03, P30, PsycInfo, PsycholAb, R10, Reac, S02, S03, SCOPUS, SSCI, T02, W07.
—BLDSC (3286.345500), GNLM, IE, Infotrieve, Ingenta. **CCC.**
Published by: Pergamon (Subsidiary of: Elsevier Science & Technology), The Blvd, Langford Ln, East Park, Kidlington, Oxford OX5 1GB, United Kingdom. TEL 44-1865-843000, FAX 44-1865-843010, JournalsCustomerServiceEMEA@elsevier.com. **Subscr. to:** Elsevier BV, Radarweg 29, PO Box 211, Amsterdam 1000 AE, Netherlands. TEL 31-20-4853757, FAX 31-20-4853432, http://www.elsevier.nl.

150 GBR ISSN 1479-2524

CLINICAL PSYCHOLOGY TRAINING RESEARCH & DEVELOPMENT. Text in English. q. adv. bk.rev. **Document type:** *Journal, Academic/Scholarly.*
Former titles (until 2002): Psychology Research (0960-2925); (until 1990): Psychology Research on Placement
Indexed: E-psyche.
Published by: Psychology Research, Salomons Centre, Southborough, Broomhill Rd, Tunbridge Wells, Kent TN3 0TG, United Kingdom. TEL 44-1892-515152, FAX 44-1892-539102, 44-1892-539102, CASPD@salomons.org.uk. Adv. contact Jenny Miah.

616.89 USA ISSN 1935-1232
RC514

➤ **CLINICAL SCHIZOPHRENIA & RELATED PSYCHOSES.** Text in English. 2007 (Apr.). q. USD 90 to individuals; USD 180 to institutions; USD 180 combined subscription to individuals (print & online eds.); USD 620 combined subscription to institutions (print & online eds.) (effective 2010). adv. **Document type:** *Journal, Academic/Scholarly.* **Description:** Provides psychiatrists and other healthcare professionals with the latest research and advances in the diagnosis and treatment of schizophrenia and related psychoses.
Related titles: Online - full text ed.: ISSN 1941-2010.
Indexed: A01, CA, EMBASE, ExcerpMed, MEDLINE, P30, R10, Reac, SCOPUS, T02.
—BLDSC (3286.374950), IE. **CCC.**
Published by: Walsh Medical Media, LLC, PO Box 193, Montvale, NJ 07645. TEL 201-931-8411, FAX 201-931-8447. Ed. Peter Buckely. Pub. Paul Walsh. Circ: 20,800 (controlled).

➤ **CLINICAL SOCIOLOGY**; research and practice. *see* SOCIAL SCIENCES: COMPREHENSIVE WORKS

150 USA

CLINICIAN'S TOOLBOX. Text in English. 19??. irreg. price varies. back issues avail. **Document type:** *Monographic series, Academic/Scholarly.* **Description:** Consists of ready-to-use books, manuals and computer programs designed for working practitioners.

Indexed: E-psyche.
Published by: Guilford Publications, Inc., 72 Spring St, 4th Fl, New York, NY 10012. TEL 800-365-7006, FAX 212-966-6708, info@guilford.com. Ed. Edward L Zuckerman.

158 FRA ISSN 1952-210X
CLINIQUE DU TRAVAIL. Text in French. 2006. irreg. back issues avail. **Document type:** *Monographic series, Consumer.*
Published by: Editions Eres, 33 Av. Marcel Dassault, Toulouse, 31500, France. TEL 33-5-61751576, FAX 33-5-61735289, eres@edition-eres.com.

616.89 FRA ISSN 1281-6124
CLINIQUE PSYCHANALITIQUE ET PSYCHO-PATHOLOGIE. Text in French. 1988. a. adv. 200 p./no.; **Document type:** *Academic/Scholarly.* **Description:** Studies practical observations, clinical interventions.
Formerly: Annales des Cliniques Psychologiques (0992-5481)
Indexed: E-psyche.
Published by: (Laboratoire de Cliniques Psychologiques), Presses Universitaires de Rennes, Campus de la Harpe, 2 Rue du Doyen Denis-Leroy, Rennes, Cedex 35044, France. TEL 33-2-99141401, FAX 33-2-99141407. Eds. Francois Sauvagnat, Laurent Ottavi. Adv. contact Jerome Besin.

150 USA ISSN 1080-2622
BF38
CLIO'S PSYCHE. Text in English. 1994. q. free to members (effective 2010). bk.rev.; film rev. back issues avail. **Document type:** *Journal, Academic/Scholarly.* **Description:** Provides interdisciplinary insight for historians, clinicians and lay people on culture, politics, history, war, genocide, etc.
Published by: Psychohistory Forum, 627 Dakota Trail, Franklin Lakes, NJ 07417. TEL 201-891-7486, pelovitz@aol.com. Ed. Paul H Elovitz.

150 GBR ISSN 1752-1882
BF637.P36
➤ **COACHING**; an international journal theory, research and practice. Text in English. 2008. s-a. GBP 114 combined subscription in United Kingdom to institutions (print & online eds.); EUR 179, USD 223 combined subscription to institutions (print & online eds.) (effective 2012). adv. back issues avail.; reprint service avail. from PSC. **Document type:** *Journal, Academic/Scholarly.* **Description:** Aims to develop novel insights and approaches for future research and offers an international forum for debates on policy and practice.
Related titles: Online - full text ed.: ISSN 1752-1890. GBP 103 in United Kingdom to institutions; EUR 161, USD 201 to institutions (effective 2012).
Indexed: A01, A22, B29, CA, E01, PsycInfo, T02.
—IE. **CCC.**
Published by: (Association for Coaching), Routledge (Subsidiary of: Taylor & Francis Group), 4 Park Sq, Milton Park, Abingdon, Oxon OX14 4RN, United Kingdom. TEL 44-20-70176000, FAX 44-20-70176336, subscriptions@tandf.co.uk, http://www.routledge.com/journals/. Eds. Dr. Carol Kauffman, Dr. Tatiana Bachkirova. Adv. contact Linda Hann. **Subscr. to:** Taylor & Francis Ltd., Journals Customer Service, Sheepen Pl, Colchester, Essex CO3 3LP, United Kingdom. TEL 44-20-70175544, FAX 44-20-70175198.

150 GBR ISSN 1748-1104
BF637.P36
THE COACHING PSYCHOLOGIST. Text in English. 2005. 3/yr. free to members (effective 2009). back issues avail. **Document type:** *Journal, Academic/Scholarly.* **Description:** Publishes articles on all aspects of research, theory, practice and case studies in the arena of coaching psychology.
Related titles: Online - full text ed.: GBP 3.45 per issue to non-members (effective 2009).
Indexed: A39, C27, C29, CA, D03, D04, E13, P03, PsycInfo, R14, S14, S15, S18, SD, T02.
Published by: The British Psychological Society, St Andrews House, 48 Princess Rd E, Leicester, LE1 7DR, United Kingdom. TEL 44-116-2549568, FAX 44-116-2271314, sgcpcomm@bps.org.uk, http://www.bps.org.uk. Ed. Siobhain O'Riordan.

150 GBR ISSN 1758-7719
COACHING PSYCHOLOGY INTERNATIONAL. Abbreviated title: C P I. Text in English. 2008. s-a. free (effective 2010). back issues avail. **Document type:** *Journal, Trade.*
Media: Online - full text.
Published by: Society for Coaching Psychology, c/o Sheila Panchal, 28 Darwin Ct, Gloucester Ave, London, NW1 7BG, United Kingdom. sheila@societyforcoachingpsychology.net.

COGNITIO; Kognitions- und neurowissenschaftliche Beitraege zur natuerlichen Sprachverarbeitung. *see* LINGUISTICS

153.4 NLD ISSN 0010-0277
BF311 CODEN: CGTNAU
➤ **COGNITION.** Text in English; Summaries in French. 1972. 12/yr. EUR 1,745 in Europe to institutions; JPY 231,800 in Japan to institutions; USD 1,954 elsewhere to institutions (effective 2012). adv. bibl.; charts; illus. index. back issues avail.; reprints avail. **Document type:** *Journal, Academic/Scholarly.* **Description:** Publishes theoretical and experimental papers covering all aspects of the study of the mind. Includes research papers in the fields of psychology, linguistics, neuroscience, ethology, philosophy and epistemology.
Related titles: Microform ed.: (from PQC); Online - full text ed.: ISSN 1873-7838 (from IngentaConnect, ScienceDirect).
Indexed: A01, A03, A08, A20, A22, A26, AIA, AMED, AMHA, B21, B25, BIOSIS Prev, BibLing, C06, C07, C28, CA, CADCAM, CDA, CPE, CommAb, CurCont, E-psyche, E03, EMBASE, ERI, ERIC, ExcerpMed, FR, FamI, I05, IBR, IBSS, IBZ, IndMed, Inspec, L&LBA, L11, LT&LA, MEDLINE, MLA, MLA-IB, MycolAb, NSA, P03, P30, PCI, PsycInfo, PsycholAb, R10, RASB, RILM, Reac, S02, S03, SCOPUS, SOPODA, SSCI, SociolAb, T02, W07.
—BLDSC (3292.870000), IE, Infotrieve, Ingenta, INIST. **CCC.**
Published by: Elsevier BV (Subsidiary of: Elsevier Science & Technology), Radarweg 29, PO Box 211, Amsterdam, 1000 AE, Netherlands. TEL 31-20-4853911, FAX 31-20-4852457, JournalsCustomerServiceEMEA@elsevier.com, http://www.elsevier.nl. Ed. Gerry T M Altmann.

316 NLD ISSN 1569-5425
COGNITION AND CULTURE BOOK SERIES. Text in English. 2001. irreg. price varies. **Document type:** *Monographic series, Academic/Scholarly.*
Published by: Brill, PO Box 9000, Leiden, 2300 PA, Netherlands. TEL 31-71-5353500, FAX 31-71-5317532, cs@brill.nl.

301.1 150 GBR ISSN 0269-9931
BF309 CODEN: COEMEC
➤ **COGNITION AND EMOTION.** Text in English. 1987. s-m. GBP 1,100 combined subscription in United Kingdom to institutions (print & online eds.); EUR 1,452, USD 1,821 combined subscription to institutions (print & online eds.) (effective 2012). adv. bk.rev. Index. back issues avail.; reprint service avail. from PSC. **Document type:** *Journal, Academic/Scholarly.* **Description:** Explores the interrelationship of cognition and emotion.
Related titles: Online - full text ed.: ISSN 1464-0600. GBP 990 in United Kingdom to institutions; EUR 1,306, USD 1,639 to institutions (effective 2012) (from IngentaConnect).
Indexed: A01, A03, A08, A20, A22, ASCA, ASSIA, B01, B06, B07, B09, B21, BIOBASE, CA, CPE, CommAb, CurCont, E-psyche, E01, EMBASE, ExcerpMed, FR, FamI, IABS, L&LBA, NSA, P03, P30, P43, PCI, PsycInfo, PsycholAb, R10, RASB, Reac, S02, S03, SCOPUS, SOPODA, SSCI, SociolAb, T02, W07.
—GNLM, IE, Infotrieve, Ingenta, INIST. **CCC.**
Published by: Psychology Press (Subsidiary of: Taylor & Francis Ltd.), 27 Church Rd, Hove, E Sussex BN3 2FA, United Kingdom. TEL 44-20-70176000, FAX 44-20-70176717, info@psypress.co.uk, http://www.psypress.com. Eds. Dirk Hermans, Jan De Houwer. Adv. contact Linda Hann TEL 44-1344-779945.

370.152 USA ISSN 0737-0008
LB1060
➤ **COGNITION AND INSTRUCTION.** Text in English. 1984. q. GBP 456 combined subscription in United Kingdom to institutions (print & online eds.); EUR 607, USD 763 combined subscription to institutions (print & online eds.) (effective 2012). adv. back issues avail.; reprint service avail. from PSC. **Document type:** *Journal, Academic/Scholarly.* **Description:** Covers study of foundational issues concerning the mental, socio-cultural, and mediational processes and conditions of learning and intellectual competence.
Related titles: Online - full text ed.: ISSN 1532-690X. GBP 410 in United Kingdom to institutions; EUR 547, USD 687 to institutions (effective 2012).
Indexed: A01, A02, A03, A08, A20, A22, AEI, AHCI, ASCA, B21, BRD, CA, CDA, CPE, ChPerI, CurCont, E-psyche, E01, E02, E03, E09, ERA, ERI, ERIC, EdA, EdI, FamI, L&LBA, NSA, P03, P04, P10, P12, P18, P30, P43, P48, P53, P54, PCI, PQC, PsycInfo, PsycholAb, SCOPUS, SOPODA, SSCI, SociolAb, T02, W03, W07.
—BLDSC (3292.872000), IE, Infotrieve, Ingenta. **CCC.**
Published by: Routledge (Subsidiary of: Taylor & Francis Group), 325 Chestnut St, Ste 800, Philadelphia, PA 19106. TEL 800-354-1420, FAX 215-625-2940, journals@routledge.com, http://www.routledge.com. Ed. Andrea A diSessa. Adv. contact Linda Hann TEL 44-1344-779945.

➤ **COGNITION AND LANGUAGE**; a series in psycholinguistics. *see* LINGUISTICS

153 ROM
BF309
COGNITION, BRAIN, BEHAVIOR. Text in English, French, Romanian. 1997. a. EUR 50 in Eastern Europe to institutions; EUR 60 elsewhere to institutions (effective 2009). **Document type:** *Journal, Academic/Scholarly.*
Formerly (until 2008): Cognitie, Creier, Comportament (1224-8398)
Indexed: A01, CA, IBSS, P03, P25, P48, PQC, PsycInfo, PsycholAb, T02.
—BLDSC (3292.872540), IE.
Published by: (Asociatia de Stiinte Cognitive din Romania/Romanian Association for Cognitive Sciences), Presa Universitara Clujeana/Cluj University Press, 51-st B.P.Hasdeu St, Cluj-Napoca, Romania. TEL 40-264-405352, FAX 40-264-597401, editura@editura.ubbcluj.ro, http://www.editura.ubbcluj.ro. Ed. Mircea Miclea.

153.4 GBR ISSN 1435-5558
➤ **COGNITION, TECHNOLOGY AND WORK.** Text in English. 1999. q. EUR 447, USD 434 combined subscription to institutions (print & online eds.) (effective 2012). back issues avail.; reprint service avail. from PSC. **Document type:** *Journal, Academic/Scholarly.* **Description:** An international journal for the analysis, design and use of joint cognitive systems.
Related titles: Online - full text ed.: ISSN 1435-5566 (from IngentaConnect).
Indexed: A01, A03, A08, A22, A26, B21, CA, CPEI, CompLI, E-psyche, E01, ESPM, ErgAb, H&SSA, I05, Inspec, NSA, P03, P30, PsycInfo, SCOPUS, T02.
—IE, Infotrieve, Ingenta. **CCC.**
Published by: Springer U K (Subsidiary of: Springer Science+Business Media), Ashbourne House, The Guildway, Old Portsmouth Rd, Guildford, Surrey GU3 1LP, United Kingdom. TEL 44-1483-734433, FAX 44-1483-734411, postmaster@svl.co.uk. Eds. Erik Hollnagel, Pietro Cacciabue. Adv. contact Clare Colwell. **Subscr. in the Americas to:** Springer New York LLC, Journal Fulfillment, PO Box 2485, Secaucus, NJ 07096. TEL 201-348-4033, 800-777-4643, FAX 201-348-4505, journals-ny@springer.com, http://www.springer.com; **Subscr. to:** Springer Distribution Center, Kundenservice Zeitschriften, Haberstr 7, Heidelberg 69126, Germany. TEL 49-6221-3454303, FAX 49-6221-3454229, subscriptions@springer.com.

150 ESP ISSN 0214-3550
➤ **COGNITIVA.** Text in English, Spanish. 1988. s-a. EUR 65 per academic year to individuals; EUR 210 per academic year to institutions. adv. **Document type:** *Journal, Academic/Scholarly.* **Description:** Publishes original empirical and theoretical contributions concerning human cognitive processes.
Related titles: Online - full text ed.: ISSN 1579-3702 (from IngentaConnect).
Indexed: A01, A03, A08, A22, CA, E-psyche, E03, ERI, P03, PsycholAb, T02.
—IE, Infotrieve, Ingenta. **CCC.**
Published by: Fundacion Infancia y Aprendizaje, Naranjo de Bulnes 69, Ciudalcampo, San Sebastian de los Reyes, Madrid, 28707, Spain. fundacion@fia.es, http://www.fia.es/. Ed. Dr. Manuel Carreiras. Circ: 1,100.

152.05 USA ISSN 1530-7026
QP360.5 CODEN: CABNC2
➤ **COGNITIVE, AFFECTIVE, & BEHAVIORAL NEUROSCIENCE.** Abbreviated title: C A B N. Text in English. 1964. q. EUR 318, USD 373 combined subscription to institutions (print & online eds.) (effective 2012). adv. illus. back issues avail.; reprint service avail. from PSC. **Document type:** *Journal, Academic/Scholarly.* **Description:** Features original research articles and reviews in the disciplines of cognitive neuroscience and affective neuroscience. Focuses on behavior and brain processes in humans, both normal subjects and patients with brain injury.
Former titles (until 2001): Psychobiology (0889-6313); (until 1987): Physiological Psychology (0090-5046); Which superseded in part (in 1973): Psychonomic Science (0033-3131)
Related titles: Microform ed.: (from PQC); Online - full text ed.: ISSN 1531-135X.
Indexed: A01, A03, A08, A20, A22, ASCA, B21, B25, BIOBASE, BIOSIS Prev, C06, C07, C08, CA, CINAHL, ChemAb, ChemTitl, DIP, E-psyche, EMBASE, ErgAb, ExcerpMed, FR, IABS, IBR, IBZ, ISR, Inpharma, L&LBA, MEDLINE, MycolAb, NSA, NSCI, P03, P20, P22, P25, P30, P48, P54, PQC, PsycInfo, PsycholAb, R10, RASB, Reac, SCI, SCOPUS, T02, W07.
—CASDDS, GNLM, IE, Ingenta, INIST, Linda Hall. **CCC.**
Published by: Springer New York LLC (Subsidiary of: Springer Science+Business Media), 233 Spring St, New York, NY 10013. TEL 212-460-1500, FAX 212-460-1575, journals@springer-ny.com. Ed. Deanna Barch. adv.: B&W page USD 240; trim 8 x 11. Circ: 500.

158 GBR ISSN 1077-7229
RC489.B4 CODEN: CBPRFQ
➤ **COGNITIVE AND BEHAVIORAL PRACTICE.** Text in English. 1994. q. EUR 244 in Europe to institutions; JPY 32,600 in Japan to institutions; USD 295 elsewhere to institutions (effective 2012). adv. **Document type:** *Journal, Academic/Scholarly.* **Description:** Interdisciplinary journal that presents treatment techniques that have been empirically validated. Covers behavior therapy and cognitive therapy.
Related titles: Online - full text ed.: (from ScienceDirect).
Indexed: A20, A22, A26, ASCA, CA, CurCont, E-psyche, EMBASE, ERIC, ExcerpMed, FamI, I05, JW-P, P03, P30, PsycInfo, PsycholAb, R10, Reac, S02, S03, SCOPUS, SSCI, T02, W07.
—BLDSC (3292.872900), IE, Infotrieve, Ingenta. **CCC.**
Published by: (Association for Behavioral and Cognitive Therapies USA), Elsevier Ltd (Subsidiary of: Elsevier Science & Technology), The Blvd, Langford Ln, Kidlington, Oxford, OX5 1GB, United Kingdom. TEL 44-1865-843434, FAX 44-1865-843970, journalscustomerserviceemea@elsevier.com. Ed. Maureen Whittal. adv.: B&W page USD 275.

150 GBR ISSN 1754-470X
➤ **THE COGNITIVE BEHAVIOUR THERAPIST.** Text in English. 2008. q. GBP 108, USD 180 to institutions (effective 2012). back issues avail. **Document type:** *Journal, Academic/Scholarly.* **Description:** Covers clinical and professional issues, which contribute to the theory, practice and evolution of the cognitive and behavioural therapies.
Media: Online - full text.
Indexed: A01, A22, E01, T02.
—**CCC.**
Published by: (British Association for Behavioural and Cognitive Psychotherapies), Cambridge University Press, The Edinburgh Bldg, Shaftesbury Rd, Cambridge, CB2 8RU, United Kingdom. TEL 44-1223-312393, FAX 44-1223-315052, journals@cambridge.org, http://www.cambridge.org/uk. Eds. Mark Freeston, Michael Townend. R&P Linda Nicol TEL 44-1223-325702.

150 GBR ISSN 1650-6073
RC489.C63 CODEN: CBTOAW
➤ **COGNITIVE BEHAVIOUR THERAPY/NORDISK TIDSKRIFT FOER BETEENDETERAPI.** Text in English, Multiple languages. 1971. q. GBP 186 combined subscription in United Kingdom to institutions (print & online eds.); EUR 248, USD 310 combined subscription to institutions (print & online eds.) (effective 2012). adv. bk.rev. charts; illus. 48 p./no.; back issues avail.; reprint service avail. from PSC. **Document type:** *Journal, Academic/Scholarly.* **Description:** Devoted to the application of the behavioural and cognitive sciences to clinical psychology and psychotherapy.
Former titles (until 2002): Scandinavian Journal of Behaviour Therapy (0284-5717); (until 1984): Nordisk Tidskrift foer Beteendeterapi (0345-1402); (until 1975): Beteendeterapi
Related titles: Online - full text ed.: ISSN 1651-2316. GBP 167 in United Kingdom to institutions; EUR 223, USD 279 to institutions (effective 2012) (from IngentaConnect); Supplement(s): Scandinavian Journal of Behavior Therapy. Supplementum. ISSN 0346-8100. 1976.
Indexed: A01, A03, A08, A22, AMED, B25, BIOSIS Prev, CA, E-psyche, E01, EMBASE, ExcerpMed, MEDLINE, MycolAb, P03, P30, P43, P48, P54, PQC, PsycInfo, PsycholAb, R10, Reac, S21, SCOPUS, T02.
—BLDSC (3292.873200), GNLM, IE, Ingenta. **CCC.**
Published by: (Swedish Association for Behaviour Therapy SWE), Routledge (Subsidiary of: Taylor & Francis Group), 4 Park Sq, Milton Park, Abingdon, Oxon OX14 4RN, United Kingdom. TEL 44-20-70176000, FAX 44-20-70176336, subscriptions@tandf.co.uk, http://www.routledge.com. Eds. Gordon J G Asmundson, Per Carlbring TEL 46-1-3282059. Adv. contact Linda Hann TEL 44-1344-779945. Circ: 800. **Subscr. to:** Taylor & Francis Inc., Customer Services Dept, 325 Chestnut St, 8th Fl, Philadelphia, PA 19106. TEL 800-354-1420, FAX 215-625-2940; Taylor & Francis Ltd., Journals Customer Service, Sheepen Pl, Colchester, Essex CO3 3LP, United Kingdom. TEL 44-20-70175544, FAX 44-20-70175198.

152 USA ISSN 2151-2965
BF309
➤ **COGNITIVE CRITIQUE.** Text in English. 19??. s-a. USD 10 per issue (effective 2009). **Document type:** *Journal, Academic/Scholarly.* **Description:** Devoted to perspectives, connections, reviews, controversies, and commentaries in the broad, interdisciplinary field of the cognitive sciences.
Related titles: Online - full text ed.: ISSN 1946-7060. free.
Published by: University of Minnesota, Center for Cognitive Sciences, 221 Elliott Hall, 75 E River Rd, University of Minnesota, Minneapolis, MN 55455. TEL 612-625-9367, FAX 612-626-7253, cogsci@umn.edu, http://www.cogsci.umn.edu/. Ed. Apostolos P Georgopoulos.

370.15 150 GBR ISSN 0885-2014
BF1 CODEN: CODEFI
➤ **COGNITIVE DEVELOPMENT.** Text in English. 1986. 4/yr. EUR 413 in Europe to institutions; JPY 55,000 in Japan to institutions; USD 462 elsewhere to institutions (effective 2012). adv. bk.rev. illus. index. back issues avail.; reprint service avail. from PSC. **Document type:** *Journal, Academic/Scholarly.* **Description:** Examines the development of perception, memory, language, concepts, thinking, problem solving, metacognition, and social cognition.
Related titles: Online - full text ed.: ISSN 1879-226X (from IngentaConnect, ScienceDirect).
Indexed: A01, A03, A08, A20, A22, A26, ASCA, B21, CA, CDA, CPE, CommAb, CurCont, E-psyche, E03, ERA, ERI, ERIC, Faml, I05, IPsyAb, M12, NSA, P03, P30, PsycInfo, PsycholAb, RASB, S20, S21, SCOPUS, SOPODA, SSCI, T02, W07.
—BLDSC (3292.876600), IE, Infotrieve, Ingenta, INIST. **CCC.**
Published by: Elsevier Ltd (Subsidiary of: Elsevier Science & Technology), The Blvd, Langford Ln, Kidlington, Oxford, OX5 1GB, United Kingdom. TEL 44-1865-843000, FAX 44-1865-843010. Ed. Peter Bryant. **Subscr. to:** Elsevier BV, Radarweg 29, PO Box 211, Amsterdam 1000 AE, Netherlands. TEL 31-20-4853757, FAX 31-20-4853432, JournalsCustomerServiceEMEA@elsevier.com, http://www.elsevier.nl.

➤ **COGNITIVE LINGUISTICS**; an interdisciplinary journal of cognitive science. *see* LINGUISTICS

➤ **COGNITIVE LINGUISTICS BIBLIOGRAPHY.** *see* LINGUISTICS

➤ **COGNITIVE LINGUISTICS RESEARCH.** *see* LINGUISTICS

616.89 GBR ISSN 1354-6805
➤ **COGNITIVE NEUROPSYCHIATRY.** Text in English. 1996. bi-m. GBP 541 combined subscription in United Kingdom to institutions (print & online eds.); EUR 716, USD 896 combined subscription to institutions (print & online eds.) (effective 2012). adv. back issues avail.; reprint service avail. from PSC. **Document type:** *Journal, Academic/Scholarly.* **Description:** Promotes the study of cognitive processes underlying psychological and behavioral abnormalities, including psychotic symptoms, with and without organic brain disease.
Related titles: Online - full text ed.: ISSN 1464-0619. GBP 487 in United Kingdom to institutions; EUR 644, USD 807 to institutions (effective 2012) (from IngentaConnect).
Indexed: A01, A03, A08, A22, CA, E-psyche, E01, EMBASE, ExcerpMed, FR, L&LBA, MEDLINE, MLA-IB, P03, P30, P43, P48, PQC, PsycInfo, PsycholAb, R10, Reac, SCOPUS, T02.
—GNLM, IE, Infotrieve, Ingenta, INIST. **CCC.**
Published by: Psychology Press (Subsidiary of: Taylor & Francis Ltd.), 27 Church Rd, Hove, E Sussex BN3 2FA, United Kingdom. TEL 44-20-70176000, FAX 44-20-70176717, info@psypress.co.uk, http://www.psypress.com. Eds. Anthony S David, Peter W Halligan. Adv. contact Linda Hann TEL 44-1344-779945.

150 DEU ISSN 1612-4782
➤ **COGNITIVE PROCESSING**; international quarterly of cognitive science. Text in English. 2000. q. EUR 285, USD 575 combined subscription to institutions (print & online eds.) (effective 2012). reprint service avail. from PSC. **Document type:** *Journal, Academic/Scholarly.* **Description:** Presents the latest results obtained in the manifold disciplines concerned with the different aspects of cognitive processing in natural and artificial systems.
Related titles: Online - full text ed.: ISSN 1612-4790 (from IngentaConnect).
Indexed: A20, A22, A26, B21, BIOBASE, CurCont, E01, EMBASE, ExcerpMed, I05, IABS, L&LBA, MEDLINE, NSA, P03, P30, PsycInfo, PsycholAb, R10, RILM, Reac, SCOPUS, SSCI, W07.
—BLDSC (3292.879850), IE, Ingenta, INIST. **CCC.**
Published by: Springer (Subsidiary of: Springer Science+Business Media), Tiergartenstr 17, Heidelberg, 69121, Germany. TEL 49-6221-4870, FAX 49-6221-345229, subscriptions@springer.com. Ed. Marta O Belardinelli.

153.4 USA ISSN 0010-0285
BF309 CODEN: CGPSBQ
➤ **COGNITIVE PSYCHOLOGY.** Text in English. 1970. 8/yr. EUR 1,129 in Europe to institutions; JPY 117,900 in Japan to institutions; USD 898 elsewhere to institutions (effective 2012). adv. abstr.; bibl.; charts; stat.; illus. back issues avail.; reprints avail. **Document type:** *Journal, Academic/Scholarly.* **Description:** Features articles concerned with advances in the study of memory, language processing, perception, problem solving, and thinking. Presents original empirical, theoretical, and tutorial papers, methodological articles, and critical reviews.
Related titles: Online - full text ed.: ISSN 1095-5623 (from IngentaConnect, ScienceDirect).
Indexed: A01, A02, A03, A08, A20, A22, A26, AMHA, ASCA, ASSIA, B01, B04, B06, B07, B09, B21, BRD, CA, CDA, CommAb, CurCont, DIP, E-psyche, E01, E02, E03, E08, EMBASE, ERA, ERI, ERIC, EdA, Edl, ErgAb, ExcerpMed, FR, G08, H09, I05, IBR, IBZ, IndMed, Inspec, L&LBA, L11, MEA&I, MEDLINE, MLA, MLA-IB, NSA, P02, P03, P10, P12, P18, P27, P30, P48, P53, P54, PQC, PsycInfo, PsycholAb, R10, RASB, RILM, Reac, S02, S03, S05, S09, SCI, SCOPUS, SOPODA, SSAI, SSAb, SSCI, SSI, T02, W03, W07.
—BLDSC (3292.880000), IE, Infotrieve, Ingenta, INIST. **CCC.**
Published by: Academic Press (Subsidiary of: Elsevier Science & Technology), 3251 Riverport Ln, Maryland Heights, MO 63043. TEL 314-447-8010, FAX 314-447-8030, JournalCustomerService-usa@elsevier.com, http://www.elsevierdirect.com/imprint.jsp?iid=5. Ed. Dr. G D Logan.

020 410 USA ISSN 0364-0213
BF311 CODEN: COGSD5
➤ **COGNITIVE SCIENCE**; a multidisciplinary journal. Text in English. 1977. 8/yr. GBP 435 in United Kingdom to institutions; EUR 551 in Europe to institutions; USD 853 elsewhere to institutions; GBP 479 combined subscription in United Kingdom to institutions (print & online eds.); EUR 606 combined subscription in Europe to institutions (print & online eds.); USD 938 combined subscription elsewhere to institutions (print & online eds.) (effective 2010); subscr. includes Topics in Cognitive Science. illus. index. back issues avail.; reprint service avail. from PSC. **Document type:** *Journal, Academic/Scholarly.* **Description:** Publishes articles on such topics as knowledge representation, inference, memory process, learning, problem solving, planning, perception, natural language understanding, connectionism, brain theory, motor control, intentional systems, and other areas of multidisciplinary concern.
Incorporates (in 1984): Cognition and Brain Theory (0193-5488); Which was formerly (until 1980): The S I STM Quarterly Incorporating the Brain Theory Newsletter (0194-0902); Which was formed by the merger of (1975-1978): Brain Theory Newsletter (0363-2741); (1977-1978): S I S T M Quarterly
Related titles: Online - full text ed.: ISSN 1551-6709. GBP 435 in United Kingdom to institutions; EUR 551 in Europe to institutions; USD 853 elsewhere to institutions (effective 2010); subscr. includes Topics in Cognitive Science (from IngentaConnect).
Indexed: A01, A02, A03, A08, A20, A22, A26, AHCI, AIA, ASCA, AbAn, ArtIAb, B01, B06, B07, B09, BibLing, C10, CA, CADCAM, CMCI, CommAb, CurCont, DIP, E-psyche, E01, E03, E07, E08, ERI, ERIC, ErgAb, FR, G08, I05, IBR, IBZ, Inspec, L&LBA, L11, MLA, MLA-IB, P02, P03, P10, P12, P30, P48, P53, P54, PQC, PhilInd, PsycInfo, PsycholAb, RASB, RILM, S09, SCOPUS, SOPODA, SSCI, SociolAb, T02, W07.
—BLDSC (3292.885000), AskIEEE, IE, Infotrieve, Ingenta, INIST. **CCC.**
Published by: (Cognitive Science Society), Wiley-Blackwell Publishing, Inc. (Subsidiary of: Wiley-Blackwell Publishing Ltd.), 111 River St, Hoboken, NJ 07030. TEL 201-748-6000, FAX 201-748-6088, info@wiley.com, http://www.wiley.com/. Adv. contact Kristin McCarthy TEL 201-748-7683.

153 NLD
COGNITIVE SCIENCE. Text in English. irreg. price varies. **Document type:** *Monographic series, Academic/Scholarly.* **Description:** Covers the nature, structure, and justification of knowledge, cognitive architectures and development, brain-mind theories, and consciousness.
Related titles: ◆ Series of: Value Inquiry Book Series. ISSN 0929-8436.
Published by: Editions Rodopi B.V., Tijnmuiden 7, Amsterdam, 1046 AK, Netherlands. TEL 31-20-6114821, FAX 31-20-4472979, info@rodopi.nl. Ed. Francesc Forn i Argimon. **Dist. by:** Rodopi - USA, 606 Newark Ave, 2nd fl, Kenilworth, NJ 07033. TEL 908-497-9031, FAX 908-497-9035.

150 USA ISSN 1556-8237
BF311
COGNITIVE SCIENCE (HAUPPAUGE). Abbreviated title: C S. Text in English. 2004. 2/yr. USD 400; USD 600 combined subscription (print & online eds.) (effective 2012). **Document type:** *Journal, Academic/Scholarly.* **Description:** Brings together interdisciplinary research in memory, cognitive psychology, artificial intelligence, linguistics, philosophy, computer science, neurophysiology, neuroscience, and neuropharmacology.
Related titles: Online - full text ed.: USD 400 to institutions (effective 2012).
Published by: Nova Science Publishers, Inc., 400 Oser Ave, Ste 1600, Hauppauge, NY 11788. TEL 631-231-7269, FAX 631-231-8175, main@novapublishers.com. Ed. Miao-Kun Sun.

150 GBR ISSN 1368-9223
COGNITIVE SCIENCE RESEARCH PAPERS. Text in English. 199?. irreg. **Document type:** *Monographic series.*
—BLDSC (3292.885400), IE, Ingenta.
Published by: University of Birmingham, Edgbaston, Birmingham, B15 2TT, United Kingdom. TEL 44-121-4143344, FAX 44-121-4143971, http://www.bham.ac.uk.

150 USA
➤ **COGNITIVE SCIENCE SERIES: TECHNICAL MONOGRAPHS AND EDITED COLLECTIONS.** Variant title: University of Colorado Institute of Cognitive Science Series. Text in English. 1981. irreg., latest 2007. price varies. adv. bibl.; charts; illus. back issues avail. **Document type:** *Monographic series, Academic/Scholarly.* **Description:** Contains authoritative reference for the theory behind Latent Semantic Analysis (LSA), a burgeoning mathematical method used to analyze how words make meaning, with the desired outcome to program machines to understand human commands via natural language.
Related titles: Online - full text ed.
Indexed: E-psyche, PsycholAb.
Published by: Psychology Press (Subsidiary of: Taylor & Francis Inc.), 325 Chestnut St, Ste 800, Philadelphia, PA 19106. TEL 800-354-1420, FAX 215-625-2940, orders@taylorandfrancis.com. Adv. contact Linda Hann TEL 44-1344-779945.

153 USA
BF311
COGNITIVE SCIENCE SOCIETY. ANNUAL CONFERENCE. PROCEEDINGS (ONLINE). Text in English. 1979. a. free to members (effective 2010). adv. **Document type:** *Proceedings, Academic/Scholarly.*
Former titles (until 2003): Cognitive Science Society. Annual Conference. Proceedings (Print) (1069-7977); (until 1992): Cognitive Science Society. Annual Conference. Program (1047-1316); (until 1985): Cognitive Science Society. Annual Conference. Proceedings; (until 1982): Cognitive Science Society. Annual Conference
Media: Online - full text.
Indexed: E-psyche.
—**CCC.**
Published by: (Cognitive Science Society), Psychology Press (Subsidiary of: Taylor & Francis Inc.), 325 Chestnut St, Ste 800, Philadelphia, PA 19106. TEL 800-354-1420, FAX 215-625-2940, orders@taylorandfrancis.com, http://www.psypress.com. Adv. contact Linda Hann TEL 44-1344-779945.

COGNITIVE SEMIOTICS. *see* LINGUISTICS

150 GBR ISSN 1350-3162
COGNITIVE STUDIES RESEARCH PAPER. Text in English. 1982. irreg. **Document type:** *Monographic series.*
—IE, Ingenta.
Published by: University of Sussex, School of Cognitive and Computing Sciences, Computer Science and Artificial Intelligence, Falmer, Brighton BN1 9QH, United Kingdom. TEL 44-01273-678195, FAX 44-01273-671320.

153 NLD ISSN 0256-663X
COGNITIVE SYSTEMS. Text in Dutch. 1985. irreg. (4 nos./vol.), latest vol.6, no.4, 2004. bk.rev. back issues avail. **Document type:** *Journal, Academic/Scholarly.*
Indexed: E-psyche, PsycholAb.
—BLDSC (3292.892500), IE, Ingenta.
Published by: European Society for the Study of Cognitive Systems, Grote Kruisstraat 2/1, Groningen, 9712 TS, Netherlands. FAX 31-50-3636304, esscs@ppsw.rug.nl, http://www.esscs.org/.

153 USA ISSN 1091-8388
➤ **COGNITIVE TECHNOLOGY.** Text in English. 1996. s-a. USD 60 to individuals; USD 200 to institutions (effective 2005). **Document type:** *Journal, Academic/Scholarly.* **Description:** Provides a forum for scientific analysis of new products that aid in comprehension, perception, memory, problem solving, and reasoning.
Indexed: P03, PsycInfo, PsycholAb.
—BLDSC (4542.172340).
Published by: Practical Memory Institute, 3502 Poplar St, Terre Haute, IN 47803. Ed. Douglas J. Hermann. Pub. Robert Rager.
Co-sponsors: Society for Cognitive Rehabilitation; Society for Applied Research in Memory and Cognition.

150 USA ISSN 0147-5916
BF311 CODEN: CTHRD8
➤ **COGNITIVE THERAPY AND RESEARCH.** Text in English. 1977. bi-m. EUR 1,341, USD 1,387 combined subscription to institutions (print & online eds.) (effective 2012). adv. illus. Index. back issues avail.; reprint service avail. from PSC. **Document type:** *Journal, Academic/Scholarly.* **Description:** Examines the role of cognitive processes in human adaptation and adjustment, drawing from the divergent fields of cognitive psychology, philosophy of science, and behavioral psychotherapy.
Related titles: Microfilm ed.: (from PQC); Online - full text ed.: ISSN 1573-2819 (from IngentaConnect).
Indexed: A01, A03, A08, A20, A22, A26, AMHA, ASCA, B21, B25, BIOSIS Prev, BehAb, BibLing, CA, CurCont, E-psyche, E01, EMBASE, ExcerpMed, FR, Faml, H14, I05, JW-P, MycolAb, NSA, P03, P10, P12, P27, P30, P43, P48, P53, P54, PQC, PsycInfo, PsycholAb, R10, Reac, S02, S03, SCOPUS, SSCI, T02, W07.
—BLDSC (3292.895000), GNLM, IE, Infotrieve, Ingenta, INIST. **CCC.**
Published by: Springer New York LLC (Subsidiary of: Springer Science+Business Media), 233 Spring St, New York, NY 10013. TEL 212-460-1500, FAX 212-460-1575, service-ny@springer.com. Ed. Rick E Ingram.

➤ **COGNITIVISMO CLINICO.** *see* MEDICAL SCIENCES—Psychiatry And Neurology

150 ESP ISSN 1887-9039
COL-LEGI OFICIAL DE PSICOLEGS DE CATALUNYA. REVISTA. Text in Catalan. 1981. m. back issues avail. **Document type:** *Magazine, Trade.*
Former titles (until 2007): Col-legi de Psicolegs, Catalunya. Full Informativ (0214-0462); (until 1983): Col-legi de Psicolegs, Catalunya. Butlleti (0214-0454)
Published by: Col-legi Oficial de Psicolegs de Catalunya, C Rocafort, 120, Barcelona, 08015, Spain. TEL 34-93-2478650, FAX 34-93-2478654, copc.b@copc.es, http://www.copc.org/. Ed. Andres Gonzalez.

150 ESP ISSN 2172-2315
COLECCION PSICOLOGIA. Text in Spanish. 2000. a. **Document type:** *Monographic series, Academic/Scholarly.*
Published by: Ediciones Piramide, Calle Juan Ignacio Luca de Tena 15, Madrid, 28027, Spain. TEL 34-91-3938989, FAX 34-91-7423662, piramide@anaya.es, http://www.edicionespiramide.es.

150.7 ESP ISSN 2172-2919
COLECCION PSICOLOGIA Y PEDAGOGIA. Text in Spanish. 200?. irreg. **Document type:** *Monographic series, Academic/Scholarly.*
Published by: Universidad Publica de Navarra, Servicio de Publicaciones, Campus de Arrosadia, Pamplona, 31006, Spain. TEL 34-948-169000, FAX 34-948-169169, infoweb@unavarra.es.

150 ESP
COLEGIO OFICIAL DE PSICOLOGOS DE MADRID. MONOGRAFIA. Text in Spanish. 1995. irreg. **Document type:** *Monographic series.*
Related titles: Online - full text ed.
Indexed: E-psyche.
Published by: Colegio Oficial de Psicologos, Claudio Coello 46, Madrid, 28001, Spain. TEL 34-91-4355212, FAX 34-91-5779172, http://www.cop.es.

150 ESP ISSN 0213-5973
➤ **COLEXIO OFICIAL DE PSICOLOGOS DE GALICIA. CADERNOS DE PSICOLXIA.** Key Title: Cadernos de Psicolxia. Text in Spanish. 1986. 3/yr. **Document type:** *Journal, Academic/Scholarly.*
Indexed: E-psyche.
Published by: Colexio Oficial de Psicologos, Galicia, Rua Espineira, 10 Bajo, Santiago De Compostela, 15706, Spain. TEL 34-981-534049, FAX 34-981-534983, copgalicia@cop.es, http://www.cop.es/delegaci/cadernos.html. Ed. Elixio Domarco Alvarez.

150 616.8 ITA ISSN 2037-9374
COLLANA DI PSICOLOGIA CLINICA E PSICOTERAPIA PSICOANALITICA. Text in Italian. 2007. irreg. **Document type:** *Monographic series, Academic/Scholarly.*
Published by: Casa Editrice C L U E B, Via Marsala 31, Bologna, BO 40126, Italy. TEL 39-051-220736, FAX 39-051-237758, clueb@clueb.com, http://www.clueb.eu/home.html.

COLLANA DI PSICOLOGIA DELLA RELIGIONE. *see* RELIGIONS AND THEOLOGY

150.19 FRA ISSN 1767-266X
COLLECTION CURSUS. PSYCHANALYSE. Text in French. 2004. irreg. price varies. **Document type:** *Monographic series, Academic/Scholarly.*
Published by: Armand Colin, 21 Rue du Montparnasse, Paris, 75283 Cedex 06, France. TEL 33-1-44395447, FAX 33-1-44394343, infos@armand-colin.fr.

150 FRA ISSN 1258-2476
COLLECTION CURSUS. PSYCHOLOGIE. Variant title: Cursus. Psychologie. Text in French. 1994. irreg. price varies. **Document type:** *Monographic series, Academic/Scholarly.*
Published by: Armand Colin, 21 Rue du Montparnasse, Paris, 75283 Cedex 06, France. TEL 33-1-44395447, FAX 33-1-44394343, infos@armand-colin.fr.

150 FRA ISSN 1778-6479
COLLECTION MEGA ESSENTIALIS. Text in French. 2003. irreg. back issues avail. **Document type:** *Monographic series.*
Related titles: ◆ Series of: Essentialis. ISSN 1264-157X.
Published by: Editions Bernet-Danilo, 42 Allee des Papillons, Meschers, 17132, France. TEL 33-5-46020707, FAX 33-5-46055530, editions@existence.fr.

150 133 CAN ISSN 1912-5771
COLLECTION PSY POPULAIRE. Text in French. 1989. irreg. **Document type:** *Monographic series, Consumer.*
Published by: Editions J C L, 930, Rue Jacques-Cartier Est, Chicoutimi, PQ G7H 7K9, Canada. TEL 418-696-0536, FAX 418-696-3132, http://www.jcl.qc.ca/fr/index.php.

150.198 FRA ISSN 1950-0327
COLLECTION PSYCHOLOGIE TRANSPERSONNELLE. Variant title: Psychologie Transpersonnelle. Text in French. 1987. irreg. EUR 15 newsstand/cover (effective 2009). back issues avail. **Document type:** *Monographic series.*
Formerly (until 2005): Collection Transpersonnel. Serie Psychologie transpersonnelle (1142-6667)
Published by: (Association Francaise du Transpersonnel (A F T)), Editions Trismegiste, 869 route de l'Ocean, Sainte-Eulalie-en-Born, 40200, France.

616.890 FRA ISSN 0989-4330
COLLECTION PSYCHOTHERAPIES CORPORELLES. Text in French. 1988. irreg. **Document type:** *Monographic series, Academic/ Scholarly.*
—**CCC.**
Published by: Elsevier Masson (Subsidiary of: Elsevier Health Sciences), 62 Rue Camille Desmoulins, Issy les Moulineaux, Cedex 92442, France. TEL 33-1-71165500, FAX 33-1-71165600, infos@elsevier-masson.fr, http://www.elsevier-masson.fr.

150 CAN
COLLEGE OF PSYCHOLOGISTS OF ONTARIO. BULLETIN. Text in English. 1973. q. CAD 15 (effective 1999). index. back issues avail. **Document type:** *Bulletin.* **Description:** Covers professional affairs, discipline, licensing, training and public policy.
Formerly: Ontario Board of Examiners in Psychology. Bulletin
Indexed: E-psyche.
Published by: College of Psychologists of Ontario, 1246 Yonge St, Ste 201, Toronto, ON M4T 1W5, Canada. TEL 416-961-8817, 800-489-8388, FAX 416-961-2635. Ed., R&P Dr. Rich Morris. Circ: 2,400 (controlled).

150 USA ISSN 1940-154X
BF1.A4
THE COLLEGE OF ST. ELIZABETH JOURNAL OF THE BEHAVIORAL SCIENCES. Text in English. 2007. a. back issues avail. **Document type:** *Journal, Academic/Scholarly.* **Description:** Publishes student research, both undergraduate and graduate, in fields as diverse as psychology, sociology, and other related social and behavioral sciences.
Media: Online - full text.
Indexed: A01, CA, T02.
Published by: College of St Elizabeth, 2 Convent Rd, Morristown, NJ 07960. TEL 973-290-4000, dbrown@cse.edu. Ed. Patricia Heindel.

150 ITA ISSN 1970-7533
COLLEZIONE DI PSICOLOGIA. Text in Italian. 199?. irreg. price varies. **Document type:** *Monographic series, Academic/Scholarly.*
Published by: Edizioni Angelo Guerini e Associati SpA, Viale Angelo Filippetti 28, Milan, MI 20122, Italy. TEL 39-02-582980, FAX 39-02-58298030, info@guerini.it, http://www.guerini.it.

156 109 USA ISSN 0267-9469
COMMENTS & CRITICISMS. Text in English. 1983. irreg. bk.rev. **Document type:** *Journal, Academic/Scholarly.*
Indexed: E-psyche.
Published by: Prytaneum Press, PO Box 2281, Amarillo, TX 79105. davidsond@juno.com.

616.89 200 USA ISSN 0885-8500
COMMON BOUNDARY; exploring spirituality, psychotherapy, and creativity. Text in English. 1980. bi-m. USD 24.95; USD 35 foreign (effective 1999). adv. bk.rev. back issues avail. **Document type:** *Magazine, Consumer.* **Description:** Publishes articles, news, and research for people interested in the relationship of psychology, spirituality and creativity.
Related titles: Microform ed.: (from PQC).
Indexed: A21, E-psyche, RI-1, RI-2.
—Ingenta.
Published by: Common Boundary, Inc., 4304 East-West Hwy, Bethesda, MD 20814. TEL 301-652-9495, FAX 301-652-0579. Ed. Anne A Simpkinson. Pub. Charles Simpkinson. R&P Anne Simpkinson. Adv. contact Geoff Goldstein. B&W page USD 1,240. Circ: 20,000 (paid).

COMMON GROUND (MILL VALLEY); bay area's magazine for conscious community since 1974. *see* NEW AGE PUBLICATIONS

155.6 USA ISSN 1935-5343
COMMUNICATION & WELLNESS LETTER. Text in English. 2007 (May). bi-m. USD 27.50 (effective 2007). **Document type:** *Newsletter, Consumer.*
Published by: Elder Forest Publishing Group, PO Box 6368, South Bend, IN 46660-6368. TEL 800-428-0552, http://elderforestpublishing.com/ index.html. Pub. Mark Bottita.

370 USA ISSN 0164-775X
COMMUNIQUE (BETHESDA). Text in English. 197?. 8/yr. USD 45 per academic year (effective 2004 - 2005). adv. bk.rev. **Document type:** *Newsletter.* **Description:** Publishes practical professional articles to help school psychologists. Also includes research, job listings, convention information, organizational news, and legislative updates.
Indexed: A26, E-psyche, E03, E07, I05, P18, P48, P53, P54, PQC.
—**CCC.**
Published by: National Association of School Psychologists, 4340 EW Hwy, Ste 402, Bethesda, MD 20814. TEL 301-657-0270, FAX 301-657-0275, publications@naspweb.org, http:// www.nasponline.org. Ed. Paul Mendez. Circ: 19,000 (paid).

COMMUNITY MENTAL HEALTH JOURNAL. *see* SOCIAL SERVICES AND WELFARE

▼ **COMPANION TO COGNITIVE SEMIOTICS.** *see* LINGUISTICS

150 CAN ISSN 1911-4745
QP33
COMPARATIVE COGNITION & BEHAVIOR REVIEWS. Text in English. 2006. irreg. free (effective 2011). **Document type:** *Journal, Academic/Scholarly.*
Media: Online - full text.
Indexed: A01, A39, C27, C29, CA, D03, D04, E13, P03, P30, PsycInfo, R14, S14, S15, S18, T02.
Published by: Comparative Cognition Society http:// www.pigeon.psy.tufts.edu/ccs/default.htm. Eds. Robert Cook, Ronald Weisman.

COMPASS (VICTORIA); a magazine for peer assistance, mentorship and coaching. *see* SOCIAL SERVICES AND WELFARE

155.4 USA
COMPASSION MAGAZINE (COLORADO SPRINGS). Text in English. 1955. q. free (effective 2008). back issues avail. **Description:** News, country reports and photo features covering child development work for ministry's US supporters and friends.
Formerly: Compassion Update (1041-472X)
Published by: Compassion International, 12290 Voyager Pkwy, Colorado Springs, CO 80921. TEL 800-336-7676. Circ: 158,000 (controlled).

150 USA ISSN 1084-2837
➤ **COMPLEXITY IN HUMAN SYSTEMS.** Text in English. 1995. irreg. **Document type:** *Journal, Academic/Scholarly.* **Description:** Focuses on the complexity in human systems with an emphasis on research directed toward the complexity inherent in the parallel processes found in the behaviour of both individuals and groups.
Media: Online - full content.
Published by: Institute for Advanced Interdisciplinary Research, Box 591351, Houston, TX 77259-1351. Ed. Thomas D Nicodemus.

150 PRT ISSN 0872-9662
COMPORTAMENTO ORGANIZACIONAL E GESTAO. Text in Portuguese. 1995. s-a. **Document type:** *Journal, Academic/ Scholarly.*
Indexed: A01, CA, T02.
Published by: Instituto Superior de Psicologia Aplicada, Rua Jardim do Tabaco 34, Lisbon, 1149-041, Portugal. TEL 351-21-8811700, FAX 351-21-8860954, info@ispa.pt, http://www.ispa.pt. Ed. Jorge Gomes. Circ: 1,000.

COMPREHENSIVE PSYCHIATRY. *see* MEDICAL SCIENCES—Psychiatry And Neurology

158 FRA ISSN 1775-6618
COMPRENDRE (PARIS, 2005). Text in French. 2005. irreg. **Document type:** *Monographic series, Academic/Scholarly.*
Published by: Editions Atract, 18 rue Jean-Baptiste-Pigalle, Paris, 75009, France.

150 FRA ISSN 2107-1578
▼ **COMPRENDRE ET AGIR.** Text in French. 2009. irreg. **Document type:** *Monographic series.*
Published by: Editions Eyrolles, 61 Boulevard Saint-Germain, Paris, 75240, France. http://www.editions-eyrolles.com.

COMPUTERS IN HUMAN BEHAVIOR. *see* SOCIOLOGY—Computer Applications

150.195 ARG ISSN 1852-6136
CONCEPTUAL. Text in Spanish. 2000. bi-m. **Document type:** *Journal, Academic/Scholarly.*
Published by: Asociacion de Psicoanalisis de la Plata, Calle 2, No. 1424, Entre 61 y 62, La Plata, 1900, Argentina. TEL 54-221-154181458, http://www.aplp.org.ar/.

150 DEU ISSN 1618-0747
➤ **CONFLICT & COMMUNICATION.** Text in English, German. 2002. s-a. free (effective 2011). back issues avail. **Document type:** *Journal, Academic/Scholarly.* **Description:** Includes theoretical contributions and empirical research results, methodical discussions and practical reflections, reports of experiences and contributions on problematical areas. The problems presented range from social-psychological small-group research to research on internal strife and wars between states, from the analysis of interpersonal communication to research on mass communication and from conflict management to journalism and the new information technologies.
Media: Online - full text.
Indexed: PSA.
Published by: Berlin Regener Publishing House, Ostseestr 109, Berlin, 10409, Germany. TEL 49-30-89379208, FAX 49-30-42856762, verlag@regener-online.de, http://www.regener-online.de. Ed. Wilhelm Kempf.

➤ **CONFLICT & COMMUNICATION ONLINE.** *see* SOCIOLOGY

347.73 302 USA ISSN 1536-5581
KF9084.A15
➤ **CONFLICT RESOLUTION QUARTERLY.** Text in English. 1983. q. GBP 218 in United Kingdom to institutions; EUR 275 in Europe to institutions; USD 350 in United States to institutions; USD 390 in Canada & Mexico to institutions; USD 424 elsewhere to institutions; GBP 252 combined subscription in United Kingdom to institutions (print & online eds.); EUR 318 combined subscription in Europe to institutions (print & online eds.); USD 403 combined subscription in United States to institutions (print & online eds.); USD 443 combined subscription in Canada & Mexico to institutions (print & online eds.); USD 477 combined subscription elsewhere to institutions (print & online eds.) (effective 2012). adv. bk.rev.; software rev.; video rev. back issues avail.; reprint service avail. from PSC. **Document type:** *Journal, Academic/Scholarly.* **Description:** Covers the latest developments in the theory and practice of mediation, dispute resolution and conflict resolution.
Formerly (until 2001): Mediation Quarterly (0739-4098)
Related titles: Microfiche ed.: (from PQC); Online - full text ed.: ISSN 1541-1508. GBP 180 in United Kingdom to institutions; EUR 227 in Europe to institutions; USD 350 elsewhere to institutions (effective 2012).
Indexed: A01, A03, A08, A12, A17, A22, ABIn, ABS&EES, B01, B07, CA, CJA, CMM, E-psyche, E01, FamI, IBSS, IPARL, LRI, P03, P42, P48, P51, P53, P54, PAIS, PCI, PQC, PSA, PsycInfo, PsycholAb, S02, S03, SCOPUS, SOPODA, SSA, SociolAb, T02, V&AA.
—BLDSC (3410.656500), IE, Ingenta. **CCC.**
Published by: (Association for Conflict Resolution), John Wiley & Sons, Inc., 111 River St, Hoboken, NJ 07030. TEL 201-748-6000, FAX 201-748-6088, info@wiley.com, http://www.wiley.com/WileyCDA/. Ed. Susan Summers Raines. Pub., Adv. contact Kim Thompkins TEL 212-850-6921.

150.9 FRA ISSN 0245-8829
CONFLUENTS PSYCHANALYTIQUES. Text in French. 1980. irreg. price varies. **Document type:** *Monographic series, Academic/Scholarly.*
Indexed: E-psyche.
Published by: Editions Les Belles Lettres, 95 Blvd Raspail, Paris, 75006, France. TEL 33-1-44398421, FAX 33-1-45449288, courrier@lesbelleslettres.com, http://www.lesbelleslettres.com. Ed. Alain Mijolla.

150 ARG ISSN 1852-0251
CONGRESO LATINOAMERICANO DE PSICOLOGIA DEL TRABAJO DE LA UNIVERSIDAD DE BUENOS AIRES. Text in Spanish. 2007. a. **Document type:** *Proceedings, Academic/Scholarly.*
Published by: Universidad de Buenos Aires, Facultad de Psicologia, Hipolito Yrigoyen 3241, Buenos Aires, C1207ABQ, Argentina. TEL 55-11-49316900, info@psi.uba.ar, http://www.psi.uba.ar/.

150 SWE ISSN 1650-2302
CONIUNCTIO. Text in Swedish. 2000. a. SEK 100 (effective 2002).
Published by: Svenska C G Jung Stiftelsen, c/o Institutet foer Droempsykologi, Vintervaegen 29, Solna, 16954, Sweden. Ed. Otto von Friesen TEL 46-42-26-16-20.

616.890 GBR ISSN 2044-1320
CONNECT (LONDON, 1999). Text in English. 1999. s-a. free to members (effective 2010). back issues avail. **Document type:** *Newsletter, Trade.* **Description:** Covers any aspect of mental health informatics, information governance, technology, media, communications and user experience.
Media: Online - full text.
Published by: Royal College of Psychiatrists, Mental Health Informatics Special Interest Group, 17 Belgrave Sq, London, SW1X 8PG, United Kingdom. TEL 44-20-72352351, FAX 44-20-72451231, mhisig@rcpsych.ac.uk, http://www.rcpsych.ac.uk/college/ specialinterestgroups/mentalhealthinformatics.aspx. Eds. Fionnbar Lenihan, Matt Evans.

THE CONNECTICUT HOSPICE NEWSLETTER; making today count. *see* PHYSICAL FITNESS AND HYGIENE

302 FRA ISSN 0337-3126
HM251
CONNEXIONS. Text in French. 1972. s-a. EUR 50 domestic to individuals; EUR 60 foreign to individuals; EUR 55 domestic to institutions; EUR 45 domestic to members (effective 2011). back issues avail. **Document type:** *Journal, Academic/Scholarly.*
Former titles (until 199?): Connexions Psychosociologie Sciences Humaines; Connexions - Psychologie - Sciences Humaines
Related titles: Online - full text ed.: ISSN 1776-2804.
Indexed: A22, E-psyche, FR, IBSS, ILD, PsycholAb, RASB, SCOPUS.
—IE, INIST.
Published by: (Association pour la Recherche et Intervention Psychosociologiques), Editions Eres, 33 Av. Marcel Dassault, Toulouse, 31500, France. TEL 33-5-61751576, FAX 33-5-61735289, eres@edition-eres.com. Ed. Jean Claude Rouchy. Circ: 900.

153.4 USA ISSN 1053-8100
BF309 CODEN: COCOF9
➤ **CONSCIOUSNESS AND COGNITION.** Text in English. 1992. q. EUR 874 in Europe to institutions; JPY 91,400 in Japan to institutions; USD 576 elsewhere to institutions (effective 2012). adv. bk.rev. back issues avail.; reprints avail. **Document type:** *Journal, Academic/Scholarly.* **Description:** Provides a forum for a natural-science approach to the issues of consciousness, voluntary control, and self. Features empirical research (in the form of regular articles and short reports) and theoretical articles.
Related titles: Online - full text ed.: ISSN 1090-2376 (from IngentaConnect, ScienceDirect).
Indexed: A01, A03, A08, A20, A22, A26, ASCA, B21, CA, ChemAb, CurCont, E-psyche, E01, EMBASE, ExcerpMed, FR, I05, IndMed, L&LBA, MEDLINE, NSA, P03, P10, P12, P30, P48, P53, P54, PQC, PhilInd, PsycInfo, PsycholAb, R10, Reac, SCOPUS, SOPODA, SSCI, SociolAb, T02, W07.
—BLDSC (3417.864800), GNLM, IE, Infotrieve, Ingenta, INIST. **CCC.**
Published by: Academic Press (Subsidiary of: Elsevier Science & Technology), 3251 Riverport Ln, Maryland Heights, MO 63043. TEL 314-447-8010, FAX 314-447-8030, JournalCustomerService-usa@elsevier.com, http://www.elsevierdirect.com/imprint.jsp?iid=5. Ed. W Banks. Adv. contact Tino DeCarlo TEL 212-633-3815.

152.4 NLD
BF309
➤ **CONSCIOUSNESS & EMOTION BOOK SERIES.** Text in English. 2000. irreg., latest vol.5, 2009. price varies. 320 p./no.; back issues avail. **Document type:** *Monographic series, Academic/Scholarly.* **Description:** Presents thoughtful analysis of the implications of both empirical and experiential (e.g., clinical psychological) approaches to emotion.
Formerly (until 2005): Consciousness & Emotion (1566-5836)
Indexed: A01, A03, A08, CA, DIP, IBR, IBZ, MLA-IB, PsycholAb.
—IE, Ingenta, INIST. **CCC.**
Published by: John Benjamins Publishing Co., PO Box 36224, Amsterdam, 1020 ME, Netherlands. TEL 31-20-6304747, FAX 31-20-6739773, customer.services@benjamins.nl. Eds. Peter Zachar, Ralph D Ellis.

150.19 USA ISSN 1065-9293
BF637.C56
➤ **CONSULTING PSYCHOLOGY JOURNAL**; practice and research. Text in English. 19??. q. USD 98 domestic to individuals; USD 125 foreign to individuals; USD 318 domestic to institutions; USD 363 foreign to institutions (effective 2011). adv. illus. back issues avail.; reprint service avail. from PSC. **Document type:** *Journal, Academic/ Scholarly.* **Description:** Features theoretical and conceptual articles, original research, and in-depth reviews with respect to consultation and its practice.
Former titles (until 1992): American Psychological Association. Division of Consulting Psychology. Journal (1061-4087); American Psychological Association. Division of Consulting Psychology. Bulletin (1049-9067)
Related titles: Online - full text ed.: ISSN 1939-0149 (from ScienceDirect).
Indexed: B01, B06, B07, B09, C06, C07, CA, E-psyche, P03, PsycInfo, PsycholAb, RASB, SCOPUS, T02.
—BLDSC (3424.011000), IE, Ingenta. **CCC.**
Published by: (American Psychological Association, Division 13), American Psychological Association, 750 First St, NE, Washington, DC 20002. TEL 202-336-5500, 800-374-2721, FAX 202-336-5997, journals@apa.org. Ed. Rodney L Lowman. Adv. contact Doug Constant TEL 202-336-5574. Circ: 1,300. **Co-publisher:** Educational Publishing Foundation.

P

➤ **CONTEMPORARY EDUCATIONAL PSYCHOLOGY.** *see* EDUCATION

➤ **CONTEMPORARY ERGONOMICS.** *see* ENGINEERING

306.85 USA ISSN 0892-2764
RC488.5

➤ **CONTEMPORARY FAMILY THERAPY**; an international journal. Text in English. 1979. q. EUR 982, USD 1,029 combined subscription to institutions (print & online eds.) (effective 2012). adv. bk.rev. back issues avail.; reprint service avail. from PSC. **Document type:** *Journal, Academic/Scholarly.* **Description:** Presents the latest theory, research, and practice with an emphasis on examination of the family within the socioeconomic matrix of which it is an integral part.
Formerly (until 1986): International Journal of Family Therapy (0148-8384)
Related titles: Online - full text ed.: ISSN 1573-3335 (from IngentaConnect).
Indexed: A01, A03, A08, A20, A21, A22, A26, ABS&EES, AMHA, ASCA, ASSIA, BibLing, C06, C07, CA, DIP, E-psyche, E01, ERA, F09, FR, FamI, IBR, IBZ, P03, P30, P43, PC&CA, PsycInfo, PsycholAb, RI-1, RI-2, S02, S03, S20, S21, SCOPUS, SFSA, SSA, SWR&A, SociolAb, T02, V&AA.
—BLDSC (3425.181810), GNLM, IE, Infotrieve, Ingenta, INIST. **CCC.**
Published by: Springer New York LLC (Subsidiary of: Springer Science+Business Media), 233 Spring St, New York, NY 10013. TEL 212-460-1500, FAX 212-460-1575, service-ny@springer.com. Ed. Dorothy S Becvar.

➤ **CONTEMPORARY HYPNOSIS.** *see* MEDICAL SCIENCES—Hypnosis

616.89 USA ISSN 0010-7530
RC500 CODEN: CPPSBL

➤ **CONTEMPORARY PSYCHOANALYSIS.** Text in English. 1964. q. USD 70 domestic to individuals; USD 76.50 foreign to individuals; USD 99.50 domestic to institutions; USD 106 foreign to institutions (effective 2010). bk.rev. index. back issues avail. **Document type:** *Journal, Academic/Scholarly.* **Description:** Dedicated to the spirit of mutual respect and inquiry, and therefore also presents a wide variety of other psychoanalytic points of view and empirical research studies.
Indexed: A20, A22, ASCA, CA, CurCont, DIP, E-psyche, ERA, FamI, IBR, IBZ, MEA&I, MLA-IB, P03, P30, PsycInfo, PsycholAb, RefZh, S02, S03, S21, SCOPUS, SOPODA, SSCI, SWR&A, SociolAb, T02, V05, W07.
—BLDSC (3425.230000), GNLM, IE, Infotrieve, Ingenta, INIST. **CCC.**
Published by: William Alanson White Institute of Psychiatry, Psychoanalysis & Psychology, 20 W 74th St, New York, NY 10023. TEL 212-873-0725, FAX 212-362-6967, d.amato@wawhite.org. Ed. Mark J Blechner.

150.19 100 306.4 NLD ISSN 1571-4977

➤ **CONTEMPORARY PSYCHOANALYTIC STUDIES.** Text in English. 2003 (Oct.). irreg., latest vol.8, 2008. price varies. **Document type:** *Monographic series, Academic/Scholarly.* **Description:** Covers all aspects of psychoanalytic inquiry in theoretical, philosophical, applied, and clinical psychoanalysis. Aims to promote open and inclusive dialogue among the humanities and the social-behavioral sciences including such disciplines as philosophy, anthropology, history, literature, religion, cultural studies, sociology, feminism, gender studies, political thought, moral psychology, art, drama, and film, biography, law, economics, biology, and cognitive-neuroscience.
Indexed: A01, T02.
Published by: Editions Rodopi B.V., Tijnmuiden 7, Amsterdam, 1046 AK, Netherlands. TEL 31-20-6114821, FAX 31-20-4472979, info@rodopi.nl. Eds. Roger Frie, Jon Mills. Pub. Mr. Fred van der Zee.

306.7 USA ISSN 1094-5725

CONTEMPORARY SEXUALITY; the international resource for educators, researchers and therapists. Text in English. 1967. m. adv. charts; illus.; stat. **Document type:** *Newsletter, Academic/Scholarly.* **Description:** Publishes research, news and information of interest to sex educators, researchers, and therapists in addition to news and announcements of the association.
Related titles: Online - full text ed.
Indexed: A01, A03, A08, C28, CA, E-psyche, F09, G10, GW, L01, L02, M02, P34, P43, P48, PQC, S02, S03, T02, W09.
—CCC.
Published by: American Association of Sex Educators, Counselors and Therapists, PO Box 5488, Richmond, VA 23220-0488. TEL 319-895-8407, FAX 319-895-6203, aasect@aasect.org, http://www.aasect.org. Ed. Ann Williams. Adv. contact Mary Ann Williams. Circ: 2,100.

150 USA

CONTEMPORARY TOPICS IN VOCATIONAL PSYCHOLOGY. Variant title: Contemporary Topics in Vocational Psychology Series. Text in English. 19??. irreg., latest 2005. price varies. adv. back issues avail. **Document type:** *Monographic series, Academic/Scholarly.* **Description:** Contains career counselors knowledge awareness, and skills to work with diverse girls and women to make their lives as authentic, meaningful, and rewarding.
Related titles: Online - full text ed.
Indexed: E-psyche.
Published by: Psychology Press (Subsidiary of: Taylor & Francis Inc.), 325 Chestnut St, Ste 800, Philadelphia, PA 19106. TEL 800-354-1420, FAX 215-625-2940, orders@taylorandfrancis.com, http://www.psypress.com. Adv. contact Linda Hann TEL 44-1344-779945.

616.89 GBR ISSN 0969-1936

CONTEXT (CANTERBURY); the magazine for family therapy. Text in English. 1989. bi-m. GBP 30 to individuals; GBP 40 domestic to institutions; GBP 45 foreign to institutions; GBP 6.50 per issue; free to members (effective 2009). adv. bk.rev.; film rev.; play rev. index. back issues avail. **Document type:** *Magazine, Consumer.* **Description:** Covers news and views on issues of concern to all professional groups working with children and families in a therapeutic environment.
Indexed: E-psyche.
—CCC.
Published by: A F T Publishing, 7 Executive Ste, St James Ct, Wilderspool Causeway, Warrington, Cheshire WA4 6PS, United Kingdom. TEL 44-1925-444414. Ed. Brian Cade.

150 BRA ISSN 1983-3482
RC467

CONTEXTOS CLINICOS. Text in Portuguese. 2008. s-a. free (effective 2011). **Document type:** *Journal, Academic/Scholarly.*
Media: Online - full text.
Published by: Universidade do Vale do Rio dos Sinos (UNISINOS), Av Unisinos 950, Sao Leopoldo, RS 93022-000, Brazil. TEL 55-51-5908131, FAX 55-51-5908132, http://www.unisinos.br. Ed. Teodoro L M Maycoln.

159 ARG ISSN 1853-0311

▼ **CONTINGENCIA.** Text in Spanish. 2010. a. **Document type:** *Monographic series, Academic/Scholarly.*
Published by: Centro de Investigaciones y Estudios Clinicos, Departamento de Psicoanalisisi y Polititca, Mariano Moreno, 36-38, Cordoba, Argentina. TEL 54-351-4253159, fundaconciec@arnetbiz.com.ar, http://www.cieccordoba.com.ar. Ed. Neolid Ceballos.

150 USA ISSN 0736-2714
BF1

CONTRIBUTIONS IN PSYCHOLOGY. Text in English. 1983. irreg. price varies. bibl. index. back issues avail. **Document type:** *Monographic series, Academic/Scholarly.* **Description:** Contains books that chart the progress of psychology as a discipline going through various changes.
Indexed: E-psyche, P30.
—BLDSC (3461.153000), IE, Infotrieve, Ingenta.
Published by: Greenwood Publishing Group Inc. (Subsidiary of: A B C - C L I O), 88 Post Rd W, PO Box 5007, Westport, CT 06881. TEL 203-226-3571, 800-225-5800, FAX 877-231-6980, sales@greenwood.com. Ed. Paul Pedersen.

155.4 USA

CONTRIBUTIONS TO RESIDENTIAL TREATMENT (CD-ROM EDITION). Text in English. 1957. a. USD 25 (effective 2007). back issues avail. **Document type:** *Proceedings.*
Formerly: Contributions to Residential Treatment (Print Edition)
Media: CD-ROM.
Indexed: E-psyche.
Published by: American Association of Children's Residential Centers, 11700 W. Lake Park Dr, Milwaukee, WI 53224. TEL 877-332-2272, info@aacrc-dc.org. Circ: 200.

150.195 ARG ISSN 1851-5649

➤ **CONTROVERSIAS EN PSICOANALISIS DE NINOS Y ADOLESCENTES.** Text in Spanish, English, French. 2007. s-a. free (effective 2010). **Document type:** *Journal, Academic/Scholarly.* **Description:** Dedicated to child and adolescent psychoanalysis, looking for to generate an interchange between the different perspectives that converge in the field of psychoanalysis.
Media: Online - full text.
Published by: Asociacion Psicoanalitica de Buenos Aires, Maure 1850, Buenos Aires, C1426CUH, Argentina. publicaciones@apdeba.org, http://www.apdeba.org. Ed. Ana Cristina Bison.

150 370 ITA ISSN 1974-1014

COUNSELING. Text in Italian, English. 2008. q. EUR 43.50 domestic to institutions; EUR 55 foreign to institutions (effective 2011). **Document type:** *Journal, Academic/Scholarly.*
Published by: Edizioni Erickson, Via Praga 5, Settore E, Gardolo, TN 38100, Italy. TEL 39-0461-950690, FAX 39-0461-950698, info@erickson.it. Eds. Annamaria Di Fabio, Mario Fulcheri.

COUNSELING AND VALUES. *see* RELIGIONS AND THEOLOGY—Roman Catholic

150 USA ISSN 2150-1378

▼ **COUNSELING OUTCOME RESEARCH AND EVALUATION.** Text in English. 2010 (Mar.). s-a. USD 200 (effective 2010). **Document type:** *Journal, Academic/Scholarly.* **Description:** Provides counselor educators, researchers, educators, and other mental health practitioners with outcome research and program evaluation practices for work with individuals across the lifespan.
Related titles: Online - full text ed.: ISSN 2150-1386. USD 212, GBP 125 to institutions (effective 2011).
Indexed: A22, E01.
—CCC.
Published by: (Association for Assessment in Counseling and Education), Sage Publications, Inc., 2455 Teller Rd, Thousand Oaks, CA 91320. TEL 805-499-9774, FAX 805-499-0871, info@sagepub.com. Ed. Danica G Hays.

158.3 USA ISSN 0011-0000
BF637.C6 CODEN: CPSYB

➤ **THE COUNSELING PSYCHOLOGIST.** Text in English. 1973. 8/yr. USD 982, GBP 578 combined subscription to institutions (print & online eds.); USD 962, GBP 566 to institutions (effective 2011). adv. illus. back issues avail.; reprint service avail. from PSC. **Document type:** *Journal, Academic/Scholarly.* **Description:** Presents timely coverage, especially in new or developing areas of practice and research, of topics of immediate interest to counseling psychologists.
Related titles: Microform ed.: (from PQC); Online - full text ed.: ISSN 1552-3861. USD 884, GBP 520 to institutions (effective 2011).
Indexed: A20, A22, A25, A26, ABS&EES, AMHA, ASCA, ASSIA, B04, BRD, CA, CDA, CurCont, E-psyche, E01, E02, E03, E07, E08, ERI, ERIC, EdA, EdI, FamI, G08, H09, HEA, HRA, I05, MEA&I, P02, P03, P07, P10, P12, P13, P18, P25, P27, P30, P48, P53, P54, PCI, PQC, PsycInfo, PsycholAb, RASB, S02, S03, S05, S08, S09, SCOPUS, SFSA, SSAI, SSAb, SSCI, SSI, SociolAb, T02, V&AA, W01, W02, W03, W07.
—BLDSC (3481.330000), IE, Infotrieve, Ingenta. **CCC.**
Published by: Sage Publications, Inc., 2455 Teller Rd, Thousand Oaks, CA 91320. TEL 805-499-9774, 800-818-7243, FAX 805-499-0871, 800-583-2665, info@sagepub.com. Ed. Nadya A Foad. adv.: color page USD 775, B&W page USD 385; 4.5 x 7.5. Circ: 3,600 (paid and free). **Subscr. outside the Americas to:** Sage Publications Ltd., 1 Oliver's Yard, 55 City Rd, London EC1Y 1SP, United Kingdom. TEL 44-20-73248701, FAX 44-20-73248733, subscription@sagepub.co.uk.

371.42 USA ISSN 1078-8719

COUNSELING TODAY. Text in English. 1958. m. GBP 97 in United Kingdom to institutions; EUR 113 in Europe to institutions; USD 150 elsewhere to institutions (effective 2012). adv. bk.rev.; film rev. 48 p./no.; back issues avail. **Document type:** *Newspaper, Academic/Scholarly.*
Formerly (until 1994): Guidepost (0017-5323)
Related titles: Microfilm ed.; Online - full text ed.: free (effective 2010).
Indexed: A09, A10, A22, CA, E-psyche, E03, ERI, T02, V03, V04.
—CCC.
Published by: American Counseling Association, 5999 Stevenson Ave, Alexandria, VA 22304. TEL 800-347-6647, FAX 703-823-0252, 800-473-2329. Adv. contact Kathy Maguire TEL 703-823-9800 ext 207. **Subscr. to:** PO Box 361, Birmingham, AL 35201. TEL 800-633-4931.

150 GBR ISSN 1473-3145

➤ **COUNSELLING AND PSYCHOTHERAPY RESEARCH**; linking research with practice. Abbreviated title: C P R. Text in English. 2001. q. GBP 320 combined subscription in United Kingdom to institutions (print & online eds.); EUR 461, USD 576 combined subscription to institutions (print & online eds.) (effective 2012). adv. back issues avail.; reprint service avail. from PSC. **Document type:** *Journal, Academic/Scholarly.* **Description:** Publishes research into counselling, psychotherapy, and the use of counselling in allied professions.
Related titles: Online - full text ed.: ISSN 1746-1405. GBP 288 in United Kingdom to institutions; EUR 415, USD 519 to institutions (effective 2012) (from IngentaConnect).
Indexed: A01, A03, A08, A22, B28, C06, C07, C08, CA, CINAHL, E-psyche, E01, P03, P10, P43, P48, P53, P54, PQC, PsycInfo, SCOPUS, T02.
—BLDSC (3481.337570), IE, Ingenta. **CCC.**
Published by: (British Association for Counselling & Psychotherapy), Routledge (Subsidiary of: Taylor & Francis Group), 4 Park Sq, Milton Park, Abingdon, Oxon OX14 4RN, United Kingdom. TEL 44-20-70176000, FAX 44-20-70176336, subscriptions@tandf.co.uk, http://www.routledge.com. Ed. Dr. Andrew Reeves. Adv. contact Jeannette Hughes TEL 44-1455-883314. B&W page GBP 610; 165 x 255. **Subscr. to:** Taylor & Francis Ltd., Journals Customer Service, Sheepen Pl, Colchester, Essex CO3 3LP, United Kingdom. TEL 44-20-70175544, FAX 44-20-70175198.

➤ **COUNSELLING AND PSYCHOTHERAPY RESOURCES DIRECTORY.** *see* BUSINESS AND ECONOMICS—Trade And Industrial Directories

658.385 GBR ISSN 1351-007X

COUNSELLING AT WORK. Text in English. 1993. q. free to members (effective 2009). adv. back issues avail. **Document type:** *Journal, Academic/Scholarly.*
Related titles: Online - full text ed.: free (effective 2009).
—CCC.
Published by: Association for Counselling at Work (Subsidiary of: British Association for Counselling & Psychotherapy), BACP House, 15 St John's Business Park, Lutterworth, Leics LE17 4HB, United Kingdom. TEL 44-870-4435252, FAX 44-870-4435161, bacp@bacp.co.uk, http://www.counsellingatwork.org.uk. adv.: B&W page GBP 420; 170 x 240. Circ: 170.

158 361.3 NLD ISSN 1879-7733

▼ **COUNSELLING MAGAZINE.** Text in Dutch. 2010. q. EUR 25 (effective 2010). adv. **Document type:** *Magazine, Trade.*
Published by: Uitgeverij Kloosterhof Acquisitie Services, Napoleonsweg 128a, Neer, 6086 AJ, Netherlands. TEL 31-475-597151, FAX 31-475-597153, info@kloosterhof.nl, http://www.kloosterhof.nl. adv.: page EUR 850; trim 210 x 297. Circ: 3,000.

150 616.8 GBR ISSN 0951-5070
CODEN: CPQUEZ

➤ **COUNSELLING PSYCHOLOGY QUARTERLY.** Text in English. 1988. q. GBP 784 combined subscription in United Kingdom to institutions (print & online eds.); EUR 1,049, USD 1,317 combined subscription to institutions (print & online eds.) (effective 2012). bk.rev. back issues avail.; reprint service avail. from PSC. **Document type:** *Journal, Academic/Scholarly.* **Description:** Reports on practice, research and theory, it is particularly keen to encourage and publish papers which will be of immediate practical relevance to counselling, clinical, occupational and medical psychologists throughout the world.
Related titles: Microfiche ed.; Online - full text ed.: ISSN 1469-3674. GBP 706 in United Kingdom to institutions; EUR 944, USD 1,185 to institutions (effective 2012) (from IngentaConnect).
Indexed: A01, A02, A03, A08, A22, ASSIA, B21, C06, C07, C08, C11, C12, CA, CINAHL, E-psyche, E01, E03, E17, ERI, ESPM, FR, FamI, H04, H13, P02, P03, P04, P10, P12, P20, P24, P25, P30, P43, P48, P53, P54, PQC, PsycInfo, PsycholAb, R10, Reac, S02, S03, SCOPUS, SOPODA, SociolAb, T02.
—GNLM, IE, Infotrieve, Ingenta, INIST. **CCC.**
Published by: Routledge (Subsidiary of: Taylor & Francis Group), 4 Park Square, Milton Park, Abingdon, Oxon OX14 4RN, United Kingdom. subscriptions@tandf.co.uk, http://www.routledge.com/journals/. Ed. Waseem Alladin. Adv. contact Linda Hann TEL 44-1344-779945. **Subscr. to:** Taylor & Francis Ltd., Journals Customer Service, Sheepen Pl, Colchester, Essex CO3 3LP, United Kingdom. TEL 44-20-70175544, FAX 44-20-70175198, tf.enquiries@tfinforma.com.

158.3 GBR ISSN 1757-2142
BF637.C6

COUNSELLING PSYCHOLOGY REVIEW. Text in English. 1983. q. free to members; GBP 12 to individuals; GBP 20 to institutions (effective 2010). bk.rev. **Document type:** *Journal, Academic/Scholarly.*
Former titles (until 2008): British Psychological Society. Counselling Psychology Section. Review (0269-6975); (until 1986): British Psychological Society. Counselling Psychology Section. Newsletter (0266-6855)
Indexed: A01, CA, P03, PsycInfo, PsycholAb, T02.
—BLDSC (3481.338355), IE, Ingenta. **CCC.**
Published by: The British Psychological Society, Division of Counselling Psychology, St Andrews House, 48 Princess Rd East, Leicester, LE1 7DR, United Kingdom. TEL 44-116-2470787, FAX 44-116-2549568, enquiry@bps.org.uk, http://www.bps.org.uk/dcop/dcop_home.cfm. Ed. Heather Sequeira.

616.89 USA ISSN 1530-5961

COUNSELOR; the magazine for addiction professionals. Text in English. 2000. bi-m. USD 25.95 domestic; USD 31.95 in Canada; USD 40.95 elsewhere (effective 2010). adv. bk.rev. 80 p./no. 3 cols./p.; back issues avail.; reprints avail. **Document type:** *Magazine, Trade.* **Description:** Features articles about mental health counseling, addictions treatment and prevention. Covers the clinical, social and political aspects of addictions.
Formed by the merger of (19??-2000): The Counselor (1047-7314); (1994-2000): Professional Counselor (1086-3397); Which was formerly (1986-1994): Professional Counselor Magazine (1042-7570); N A A D A C Counselor
Related titles: Online - full text ed.
Indexed: E-psyche.

—Ingenta. **CCC.**
Published by: Health Communications, Inc., 3201 SW 15th St, Deerfield, FL 33442. TEL 954-360-0909, 800-851-9100, FAX 954-360-0034, custserv@espcomp.com. Ed. Stephanie Muller. Adv. contact Bob Solomon TEL 212-683-7905. B&W page USD 2,514, color page USD 3,905; trim 8.375 x 10.785. Circ: 19,000 (paid). **Subscr. to:** PO Box 15009, N Hollywood, CA 91615. TEL 818-487-4595, 800-998-0793, FAX 818-487-4550.

COUNSELOR EDUCATION AND SUPERVISION. *see* EDUCATION

616.890 GBR ISSN 2044-4133
▼ **COUPLE AND FAMILY PSYCHOANALYSIS.** Text in English. 2011. s-a. GBP 40 to individuals; GBP 175 to institutions; GBP 200 combined subscription to institutions (print & online eds.) (effective 2011). **Document type:** *Journal, Academic/Scholarly.* **Description:** Provides a forum for disseminating current ideas and research, and for developing clinical practice.
Related titles: Online - full text ed.: ISSN 2044-4141. GBP 150 to institutions (effective 2011).
Published by: Karnac Books, 118 Finchley Rd, London, NW3 5HT, United Kingdom. TEL 44-20-74311075, FAX 44-20-74359076, shop@karnacbooks.com. Ed. Molly Ludlam.

158.24 FRA ISSN 1776-6656
LE COUPLE ET SA FAMILLE. Variant title: Couples Familles et Metamorphoses. Text in French. 2005. irreg. **Document type:** *Monographic series.*
Published by: Editions Eres, 33 Av. Marcel Dassault, Toulouse, 31500, France. TEL 33-5-61751576, FAX 33-5-61735289, eres@edition-eres.com. Pub. Jean Lemaire.

CRACKING THE A P PSYCHOLOGY EXAM. (Advanced Placement) *see* EDUCATION—Higher Education

150 USA ISSN 2150-881X
BF78
CRACKING THE G R E PSYCHOLOGY SUBJECT TEST. (Graduate Record Examination) Text in English. 1995. a., latest 2005, 7th Ed. USD 18.99 per issue (effective 2010).
Formerly (until 2009): Cracking the G R E Psychology Test (1075-2978)
Published by: Princeton Review Publishing, L.L.C. (Subsidiary of: Random House Inc.), 1745 Broadway, New York, NY 10019. TEL 800-733-3000, princetonreview@randomhouse.com, http://www.randomhouse.com/princetonreview.

301.1 150 USA ISSN 1040-0419
➤ **CREATIVITY RESEARCH JOURNAL.** Text in English. 1988. q. GBP 371 combined subscription in United Kingdom to institutions (print & online eds.); EUR 495, USD 623 combined subscription to institutions (print & online eds.) (effective 2012). adv. abstr.; bibl. back issues avail.; reprint service avail. from PSC. **Document type:** *Journal, Academic/Scholarly.* **Description:** Brings out scholarly research capturing the full range of approaches to the study of creativity - behavioral, clinical, cognitive, cross-cultural, developmental, educational, genetic, organizational, psychoanalytic, psychometric, and social.
Related titles: Online - full text ed.: ISSN 1532-6934. GBP 334 in United Kingdom to institutions; EUR 445, USD 561 to institutions (effective 2012).
Indexed: A01, A03, A08, A20, A22, ASCA, CA, CPE, CurCont, E-psyche, E01, E03, ECER, ERI, Faml, P02, P03, P10, P12, P30, P41, P43, P48, P53, P54, PQC, PsycInfo, PsycholAb, SCOPUS, SSCI, T02, W07.
—BLDSC (3487.252000), IE, Infotrieve, Ingenta. **CCC.**
Published by: Routledge (Subsidiary of: Taylor & Francis Group), 325 Chestnut St, Ste 800, Philadelphia, PA 19106. TEL 800-354-1420, FAX 215-625-2940, journals@routledge.com, http://www.routledge.com. Ed. Mark A Runco. Adv. contact Linda Hann TEL 44-1344-779945.

➤ **CRIMINAL JUSTICE & BEHAVIOR.** *see* CRIMINOLOGY AND LAW ENFORCEMENT

362.28 USA ISSN 0227-5910
HV6549
➤ **CRISIS (KIRKLAND)**; the journal of crisis intervention and suicide prevention. Text in English. 1980. bi-m. USD 135, EUR 108 to individuals; USD 244, EUR 190 to institutions; USD 50, EUR 40 per issue; free to members (effective 2011). adv. bk.rev. 48 p./no. 2 cols./p.; back issues avail. **Document type:** *Journal, Academic/Scholarly.* **Description:** Contains articles on the research and clinical aspects of how to prevent suicides, and how to intervene in severe emotional crises.
Related titles: Online - full text ed.: ISSN 2151-2396 (from ScienceDirect).
Indexed: A22, C06, C07, CurCont, DIP, E-psyche, EMBASE, ESPM, ExcerpMed, IBR, IBZ, IPsyAb, IndMed, MEDLINE, P03, P30, PsycInfo, PsycholAb, R10, Reac, RiskAb, SCOPUS, SSCI, W07.
—BLDSC (3487.382350), GNLM, IE, Infotrieve, Ingenta. **CCC.**
Published by: (International Association for Suicide Prevention NZL), Hogrefe Publishing Corp., 875 Massachusetts Ave, 7th Fl, Cambridge, MA 02139. TEL 866-823-4726, FAX 617-354-6875, customservices@hogrefe-publishing.com, http://www.hogrefe.com. Eds. Annette L Beautrais TEL 64-3-3720408, Diego De Leo TEL 61-7-37353382. Adv. contact Gundula von Fintel. Circ: 1,000.

618.92 USA
➤ **CRITICAL ISSUES IN DEVELOPMENTAL & BEHAVIORAL PEDIATRICS.** Text in English. 1987. irreg., latest 1994. price varies. back issues avail. **Document type:** *Monographic series, Academic/Scholarly.*
Formerly: Developmental and Behavioral Pediatrics: Selected Topics
Indexed: E-psyche.
Published by: Springer New York LLC (Subsidiary of: Springer Science+Business Media), 233 Spring St, New York, NY 10013. TEL 212-460-1500, FAX 212-460-1575, service-ny@springer.com.

158 FRA ISSN 1951-512X
CROISSANCE & DEVELOPPEMENT. Text in French. 2006. irreg. back issues avail. **Document type:** *Monographic series, Consumer.*
Published by: Editions Quintessence, rue de la Bastidonne, Aubagne, 13678 Cedex, France. TEL 33-4-42189094, http://www.editions-quintessence.com.

158 NLD ISSN 2210-5417
▼ **CROSS-CULTURAL ADVANCEMENTS IN POSITIVE PSYCHOLOGY.** Text in English. 2010. irreg., latest vol.2, 2011. price varies. **Document type:** *Monographic series, Academic/Scholarly.*
Related titles: Online - full text ed.: ISSN 2210-5425.
Published by: Springer Netherlands (Subsidiary of: Springer Science+Business Media), Van Godewijckstraat 30, Dordrecht, 3311 GX, Netherlands. TEL 31-78-6576050, FAX 31-78-6576474. Ed. Antonella Delle Fave.

156 572 USA ISSN 0710-068X
BF730
CROSS-CULTURAL PSYCHOLOGY BULLETIN. Text in English. 1967. q. free to members (effective 2011). bk.rev. abstr.; bibl. back issues avail. **Document type:** *Newsletter, Consumer.* **Description:** Provides a forum to present and discuss issues relevant to cross-cultural psychology and to the IACCP.
Former titles (until 1981): I A C C P Cross-Cultural Psychology Newsletter (0702-6056); (until 1973): Cross-Cultural Social Psychology Newsletter (0590-1286)
Related titles: Online - full text ed.
Indexed: CDA, E-psyche.
—BLDSC (3488.810000), IE, Ingenta.
Published by: International Association for Cross-Cultural Psychology, c/o Veronica Benet-Martinez, Department of Psychology, Olmsted 1418, University of California, Riverside, CA 92521. TEL 951-827-7776, veronbm@ucr.edu. Ed. Bill Gabrenya.

CROSS-CULTURAL RESEARCH; the journal of comparative social science. *see* SOCIAL SCIENCES: COMPREHENSIVE WORKS

150 USA ISSN 0272-1678
CROSSCURRENTS IN CONTEMPORARY PSYCHOLOGY. Variant title: Crosscurrents in Contemporary Psychology Series. Text in English. 19??. irreg., latest 2003. price varies. adv. back issues avail. **Document type:** *Monographic series, Academic/Scholarly.* **Description:** Derived from original presentations given at a conference in Atlanta, Georgia, under the auspices of the Center for Child Well-Being.
Related titles: Online - full text ed.
Indexed: E-psyche.
Published by: Psychology Press (Subsidiary of: Taylor & Francis Inc.), 325 Chestnut St, Ste 800, Philadelphia, PA 19106. TEL 800-354-1420, FAX 215-625-2940, orders@taylorandfrancis.com, http://www.psypress.com.

150.9 ARG ISSN 0328-364X
CUADERNOS ARGENTINOS DE HISTORIA DE LA PSICOLOGIA. Text in Spanish, English. 1995. a. **Document type:** *Magazine, Academic/Scholarly.*
Indexed: SociolAb.
Published by: Universidad Nacional de San Luis, Facultad de Ciencias Humanas, Avenida Ejercito de los Andes 950, IV Bloque, San Luis, 5700, Argentina. TEL 54-652-30224, histopsi@unsl.edu.ar. Ed. Hugo Klappenbach.

CUADERNOS DE MEDICINA PSICOSOMATICA Y PSIQUIATRIA. *see* MEDICAL SCIENCES—Psychiatry And Neurology

150 CHL ISSN 0718-4123
QP360
CUADERNOS DE NEUROPSICOLOGIA. Text in Spanish. 2007. s-a. free (effective 2011). **Document type:** *Journal, Academic/Scholarly.*
Media: Online - full text.
Indexed: A26, G06, G07, I04, I05.
Published by: Neuropsicologia.cl http://www.neuropsicologia.cl/Web/html/revista.htm. Ed. Roberto E Polanco.

150.195 MEX ISSN 0186-9345
BF173.A2
CUADERNOS DE PSICOANALISIS. Text in Spanish. 1968. q. **Document type:** *Journal, Academic/Scholarly.*
Indexed: C01.
Published by: Sociedad Psicoanalitica de Mexico, A.C., Ave Mexico No 37-403, Col. Hipodromo Condesa, Mexico, D.F., 06100, Mexico. TEL 52-55-52866550, FAX 52-55-52867599, spm@spm.org.mx, http://www.spm.org.mx/spm.html. Ed. Jose Luis Salinas Fernandez.

150 ESP ISSN 0211-3481
CUADERNOS DE PSICOLOGIA/QUADERNS DE PSICOLOGIA. Text in Multiple languages. 1975. s-a. **Document type:** *Journal, Academic/Scholarly.*
Related titles: Online - full text ed.: free (effective 2011).
—CCC.
Published by: Universitat Autonoma de Barcelona, Departament de Psicologia de la Salut, Despatx B5/016b, Bellaterra, 08193, Spain. TEL 34-3-5813831, FAX 34-3-5812125, d.psic.social@uab.cat, http://psicologiasocial.uab.es.

150 COL ISSN 0120-4653
CUADERNOS DE PSICOLOGIA. Text in Spanish. 1976. 2/yr. adv. bk.rev. **Document type:** *Journal, Academic/Scholarly.*
Indexed: E-psyche, PsycholAb.
Published by: Universidad del Valle, Departamento de Psicologia, Apartado Aereo 25360, Cali, VALLE, Colombia. FAX 57-23-392311. Ed. Sonia Meluk.

796.015 ESP ISSN 1578-8423
CUADERNOS DE PSICOLOGIA DEL DEPORTE. Text in Multiple languages. 2001. s-a. **Document type:** *Journal, Academic/Scholarly.*
Related titles: Online - full text ed.
Indexed: CA, F04, P03, PsycInfo, SD, T02.
Published by: Universidad de Murcia, Servicio de Publicaciones, Edificio Saavedra Fajardo, C/ Actor Isidoro Maiquez 9, Murcia, 30007, Spain. TEL 34-968-363887, FAX 34-968-363414, http://www.um.es/publicaciones/.

158 ESP ISSN 0213-7941
CUADERNOS DE TERAPIA FAMILIAR. Text in Spanish. 1987. q. **Document type:** *Magazine, Consumer.*
Published by: Stirpe - Centro de Diagnostico y Terapia Familiar, Paseo de las Delicias 65, Bloque A, Esq. 3, 2o. B, Madrid, 28045, Spain.

150 ARG ISSN 1515-3584
CUADERNOS SOCIALES. Text in Spanish. 1999. a. ARS 30 (effective 2010). **Document type:** *Monographic series, Academic/Scholarly.*
Published by: Universidad Nacional de Rosario, Facultad de Psicologia, Riobaba, 250 Bis, Rosario, Santa Fe, 2000, Argentina. TEL 54-341-4808523. Circ: 500.

150 COL ISSN 2145-9258
▼ ➤ **CULTURA, EDUCACION, SOCIEDAD.** Abbreviated title: C E S. Text in Spanish; Summaries in English, Spanish. 2010. a. **Document type:** *Journal, Academic/Scholarly.* **Description:** Publishes articles that covers: Psychological research; social psychology; educational psychology; clinical psychology; organizational psychology; developmental psychology; environmental psychology; measurement and assessment psychology; cultural and anthropological studies; epistemology and psychological theories.
Published by: Corporacion Universitaria de la Costa, Facultad de Psicologia, Calle 58 No 55-66, Barranquilla, Colombia. http://www.cuc.edu.co. Ed. Omar Fernando Cortes. R&P Maria Gomez De Maury. Circ: 500.

➤ **CULTURAL DIVERSITY & ETHNIC MINORITY PSYCHOLOGY.** *see* SOCIOLOGY

306 GBR ISSN 1354-067X
BF1 CODEN: CUPSFQ
➤ **CULTURE & PSYCHOLOGY.** Text in English. 1995. q. USD 974, GBP 527 combined subscription to institutions (print & online eds.); USD 955, GBP 516 to institutions (effective 2011). adv. back issues avail.; reprint service avail. from PSC. **Document type:** *Journal, Academic/Scholarly.* **Description:** Addresses the centrality of culture to our understanding of human behaviour, identity, intersubjective experiences, emotions, development and language.
Related titles: Online - full text ed.: ISSN 1461-7056. USD 877, GBP 474 to institutions (effective 2011).
Indexed: A01, A02, A03, A08, A20, A22, ASSIA, B01, B06, B07, B09, CA, CommAb, CurCont, DIP, E-psyche, E01, E03, ERI, Faml, H04, IBR, IBSS, IBZ, IPsyAb, L&LBA, P02, P03, P04, P10, P12, P42, P48, P53, P54, PQC, PSA, PsycInfo, PsycholAb, S02, S03, SCOPUS, SOPODA, SSA, SSCI, SociolAb, T02, V02, W07.
—BLDSC (3491.668740), IE, Infotrieve, Ingenta. **CCC.**
Published by: Sage Publications Ltd. (Subsidiary of: Sage Publications, Inc.), 1 Oliver's Yard, 55 City Rd, London, EC1Y 1SP, United Kingdom. TEL 44-20-73248500, FAX 44-20-73248600, info@sagepub.co.uk, http://www.uk.sagepub.com/home.nav. Ed. Jaan Valsiner. **Subscr. in the Americas to:** Sage Publications, Inc., 2455 Teller Rd, Thousand Oaks, CA 91320. TEL 805-499-9774, FAX 805-499-0871, journals@sagepub.com.

➤ **CURRENT CONTENTS: SOCIAL & BEHAVIORAL SCIENCES.** *see* PSYCHOLOGY—Abstracting, Bibliographies, Statistics

150.19 USA ISSN 0963-7214
BF1 CODEN: CDPSE8
➤ **CURRENT DIRECTIONS IN PSYCHOLOGICAL SCIENCE.** Text in English. 1992. bi-m. USD 3,471 to institutions; USD 3,542 combined subscription to institutions (print & online eds.) (effective 2010); Subscr. includes: Psychological Science; Perspectives on Psychological Science; Psychological Science in the Public Interest. illus. back issues avail.; reprint service avail. from PSC. **Document type:** *Journal, Academic/Scholarly.* **Description:** Contains concise reviews of important trends and controversies in psychology.
Related titles: Online - full text ed.: ISSN 1467-8721. USD 3,188 to institutions (effective 2010) (from IngentaConnect).
Indexed: A01, A03, A08, A20, A22, A26, ASCA, ASG, B21, C28, CA, CDA, CurCont, E-psyche, E01, ErgAb, F09, Faml, I05, L&LBA, NSA, P02, P03, P10, P12, P30, P43, P48, P53, P54, PQC, PsycInfo, PsycholAb, RILM, S02, S03, SCOPUS, SSCI, SWR&A, SociolAb, T02, V&AA, W07.
—BLDSC (3496.357000), IE, Infotrieve, Ingenta. **CCC.**
Published by: (Association for Psychological Science), Sage Publications, Inc., 2455 Teller Rd, Thousand Oaks, CA 91320. TEL 805-499-9774, 800-818-7243, FAX 805-499-0871, info@sagepub.com, http://www.sagepub.com. Ed. Randall W Engle. Circ: 15,000.

361 GBR ISSN 0968-4212
CURRENT PERSPECTIVES IN PSYCHOLOGICAL, LEGAL AND ETHICAL ISSUES. Text in English. 1991. irreg. **Document type:** *Monographic series, Academic/Scholarly.*
—BLDSC (3501.280350). **CCC.**
Published by: Jessica Kingsley Publishers, 116 Pentonville Rd, London, N1 9JB, United Kingdom. TEL 44-20-78332307, FAX 44-20-78372917, post@jkp.com, http://www.jkp.com.

150 USA ISSN 1046-1310
BF1
➤ **CURRENT PSYCHOLOGY**; a journal for diverse perspectives on diverse psychological issues. Text in English. 1984. q. EUR 480, USD 626 combined subscription to institutions (print & online eds.) (effective 2012). adv. back issues avail.; reprint service avail. from PSC. **Document type:** *Journal, Academic/Scholarly.* **Description:** Provides an international forum for the rapid dissemination of new psychological information. Includes significant empirical contributions from all areas of psychology.
Formerly (until 1988): Current Psychological Research and Reviews (0737-8262); Which was formed by the merger of (1981-1984): Current Psychological Research (0144-3887); (1981-1984): Current Psychological Reviews (0144-3895)
Related titles: Online - full text ed.: C P Online. ISSN 1936-4733 (from IngentaConnect).
Indexed: A01, A02, A03, A08, A20, A22, A25, A26, ABS&EES, AEI, B01, B06, B07, B09, B25, BIOSIS Prev, CA, CurCont, DIP, E-psyche, E01, E08, FR, Faml, G05, G06, G07, G08, H11, H12, HRIS, I05, I07, IBR, IBZ, M01, M02, MASUSE, MycolAb, P03, P25, P30, P43, P48, PQC, PsycInfo, PsycholAb, S02, S03, S08, S09, SCOPUS, SOPODA, SSCI, SociolAb, T02, W07.
—BLDSC (3501.601000), IE, Infotrieve, Ingenta, INIST. **CCC.**
Published by: Springer New York LLC (Subsidiary of: Springer Science+Business Media), 233 Spring St, New York, NY 10013. TEL 212-460-1500, FAX 212-460-1575, service-ny@springer.com.

150 FRA ISSN 1379-6100
➤ **CURRENT PSYCHOLOGY LETTERS (ONLINE)**; behaviour, brain and cognition. Text in English. 2000. 4/yr. free (effective 2011). bk.rev. abstr. 128 p./no.; back issues avail. **Document type:** *Journal, Academic/Scholarly.* **Description:** Publishes short papers reporting original findings in all areas of cognitive experimental psychology including cognitive psychology, psycholinguistics, cognitive neurosciences, social cognition, cognitive development, cognitive neuropsychology, and comparative cognition.
Formerly (until 2003): Current Psychology Letters (Print) (1376-2095)
Media: Online - full content.
Indexed: A01, CA, L&LBA, P03, P30, PsycInfo, PsycholAb, T02.

P

—BLDSC (3501.670000), IE, Ingenta.
Published by: Revues.org, 3 Place Victor Hugo, Case no 86, Marseille, 13331, France. TEL 33-4-13550355, FAX 33-4-13550341, http://www.revues.org. Ed. Jacques Vauclair.

302 USA ISSN 1088-7423
HM251
➤ **CURRENT RESEARCH IN SOCIAL PSYCHOLOGY.** Abbreviated title: C R I S P. Text in English. 1995. irreg., latest vol.15, no.1, 2009. illus. back issues avail.; reprints avail. **Document type:** *Journal, Academic/Scholarly.* **Description:** Covers a variety of topics in social psychology.
Media: Online - full text.
Indexed: A39, C27, C29, CA, D03, D04, E-psyche, E13, IBSS, P03, PsycInfo, PsycholAb, R14, S02, S03, S14, S15, S18, SCOPUS, SSA, SociolAb, T02.
Published by: University of Iowa, Department of Sociology, 140 Seashore Hall W, Iowa City, IA 52242. TEL 319-335-2502, FAX 319-335-2509, sociology@uiowa.edu, http://www.uiowa.edu/~soc/. Ed. Michael J Lovaglia TEL 319-335-2503.

150.19 USA ISSN 1554-1940
BF173.A2
CURRENT TRENDS IN PSYCHOANALYSIS AND PSYCHOTHERAPY. Text in English. 2005. a. **Document type:** *Journal, Trade.*
Published by: Center for Human Development, 16-21 Split Rock Rd, Fair Lawn, NJ 07410. TEL 212-642-6303, FAX 201-791-1735, CtrHumanDev@aol.com, http://www.thecenterforhumandevelopment.org.

158 BRA ISSN 1981-3252
CURSO DE MEMORIZACAO. Text in Portuguese. 2007. q. BRL 29.90 newsstand/cover (effective 2007). **Document type:** *Magazine, Consumer.*
Published by: Digerati Comunicacao e Tecnologia Ltda., Rua Haddock Lobo 347, 12o andar, Sao Paulo, 01414-001, Brazil. TEL 55-11-32172600, FAX 55-11-32172617, http://www.digerati.com.br.

150 301 CZE ISSN 1802-7962
HM851
CYBERPSYCHOLOGY; journal of psychosocial research in cyberspace. Text in English. 2007. s-a. free (effective 2011). **Document type:** *Journal, Academic/Scholarly.*
Media: Online - full text.
Indexed: A01, CA, T02.
Published by: Masarykova Univerzita, Fakulta Socialnich Studii, Jostova 10, Brno, 602 00, Czech Republic. TEL 420-549-491911, FAX 420-549-491920, info@fss.muni.cz, http://www.fss.muni.cz. Ed. David Smahel.

150 POL ISSN 1425-6460
CZASOPISMO PSYCHOLOGICZNE. Text in Polish. 1995. 3/yr. EUR 33 foreign (effective 2006). **Document type:** *Journal, Academic/Scholarly.*
Published by: (Szkola Wyzsza Psychologii Spolecznej w Warszawie/ Warsaw School of Social Psychology, Stowarzyszenie Psychologia i Architektura), Uniwersytet im. Adama Mickiewicza w Poznaniu, Instytut Psychologii, ul Szamarzewskiego 89, Poznan, 60589, Poland. TEL 48-61-8292307, FAX 48-61-8292107, uampsych@amu.edu.pl, http://www.psychologia.amu.edu.pl. Ed. Augustyn Banka. **Dist. by:** Ars Polona, Obroncow 25, Warsaw 03933, Poland. TEL 48-22-5098609, FAX 48-22-5098610, arspolona@arspolona.com.pl, http://www.arspolona.com.pl.

616.89 DEU ISSN 0935-2066
D G I P - INTERN. (Deutsche Gesellschaft fuer Individualpsychologie) Text in German. 1982. q. EUR 88 membership (effective 2009). adv. bk.rev. 36 p./no.; **Document type:** *Newsletter, Academic/Scholarly.*
Indexed: E-psyche.
Published by: Deutsche Gesellschaft fuer Individualpsychologie e.V., Marktstr 12, Gotha, 99867, Germany. TEL 49-3621-29691, FAX 49-3621-29691, info@dgip.de. Ed., Adv. contact Horst Groener. Circ: 1,800.

D W D NEWSLETTER. *see* GERONTOLOGY AND GERIATRICS

150 CHN ISSN 1004-6100
DAZHONG XINLIXUE/POPULAR PSYCHOLOGY. Text in Chinese. 1982. m. USD 32.40 (effective 2009). **Document type:** *Journal, Academic/Scholarly.*
Indexed: E-psyche.
—East View.
Published by: Huadong Shifan Daxue/East China Normal University, 3663 Zhongshan Beilu, Tianjiabing Jiaoyu Shuyuan, Rm. 1102, Shanghai, 200062, China. TEL 86-21-62232068. **Dist. by:** China International Book Trading Corp, 35 Chegongzhuang Xilu, Haidian District, PO Box 399, Beijing 100044, China. TEL 86-10-68412045, FAX 86-10-68412023, cibtc@mail.cibtc.com.cn, http://www.cibtc.com.cn.

158 CHL ISSN 0717-0173
DE FAMILIAS Y TERAPIAS. Text in Spanish. 1993. s-a. CLP 5,000 newsstand/cover. back issues avail. **Document type:** *Journal, Academic/Scholarly.*
Published by: Instituto Chileno de Terapia Familiar, Ave Larrain 6925, Santiago, Chile. TEL 56-2-2773518, FAX 56-2-2778398, revista@ichtf.cl. Ed. Marta Figueroa.

302 USA ISSN 0748-1187
BF789.D4 CODEN: DESTEA
➤ **DEATH STUDIES**; counseling - research - education - care - ethics. Text in English. 1977. 10/yr. GBP 534 combined subscription in United Kingdom to institutions (print & online eds.); EUR 705, USD 885 combined subscription to institutions (print & online eds.) (effective 2012). bk.rev. abstr.; bibl.; charts; illus. index. back issues avail.; reprint service avail. from PSC. **Document type:** *Journal, Academic/Scholarly.* **Description:** Provides an international and interdisciplinary forum in the field of death studies including refereed papers that cover education, counseling, bioethics, and psychosocial research.
Formerly (until 1985): Death Education (0145-7624)
Related titles: Microform ed.: (from PQC); Online - full text ed.: ISSN 1091-7683. GBP 480 in United Kingdom to institutions; EUR 634, USD 797 to institutions (effective 2012) (from IngentaConnect).
Indexed: A01, A02, A03, A08, A20, A21, A22, A25, A26, AMED, ASCA, ASG, B04, BRD, C06, C07, C08, C11, CA, CERDIC, CINAHL, CPE, CurCont, E-psyche, E01, E02, E03, E07, E08, EMBASE, ERI, ERIC, EdA, EdI, ExcerpMed, F09, FR, FamI, G08, H01, H02, H04, H11, H12, H13, I05, M02, MEDLINE, MLA-IB, P02, P03, P10, P12, P13, P18, P20, P21, P24, P25, P27, P30, P43, P48, P53, P54, PAIS, PC&CA, PCI, PQC, PerIslam, PsycInfo, PsycholAb, R05, R10, RI-1, RI-2, Reac, S02, S03, S08, S09, SCOPUS, SFSA, SOPODA, SSA, SSAI, SSAb, SSCI, SSI, SWR&A, SociolAb, T02, V&AA, W03, W07, WBA, WMB.
—GNLM, IE, Infotrieve, Ingenta, INIST. **CCC.**
Published by: Routledge (Subsidiary of: Taylor & Francis Group), 325 Chestnut St, Ste 800, Philadelphia, PA 19106. TEL 215-625-8900, 800-354-1420, FAX 215-625-2940, orders@taylorandfrancis.com. Ed. Robert A Neimeyer TEL 901-494-1806. **Subscr. in Europe to:** Taylor & Francis Ltd., Journals Customer Service, Sheepen Pl, Colchester, Essex CO3 3LP, United Kingdom. TEL 44-20-70175544, FAX 44-20-70175198, tf.enquiries@tfinforma.com.

150 IND ISSN 0975-8194
▼ ➤ **DELHI PSYCHOLOGIST**; journal of psychological research. Text in English. 2009. s-a. **Document type:** *Journal, Academic/Scholarly.* **Description:** Contains original articles on all aspects of phychological research. It also includes case reports, conference announcements, summary of trials, letters to the editor and conference reports.
Media: Online - full text.
Published by: Action for Human Excellence and Development contact@delhipsychologist.com. Ed. Tej Bahadur Singh.

155.6 NLD ISSN 0926-7182
DENKBEELD; tijdschrift voor psychogeriatrie. Text in Dutch. 1989. bi-m. EUR 71, USD 106 combined subscription to institutions (print & online eds.) (effective 2009). adv. **Document type:** *Journal, Academic/Scholarly.*
Related titles: Online - full text ed.: ISSN 1876-5653.
—IE, Infotrieve.
Published by: Bohn Stafleu van Loghum B.V. (Subsidiary of: Springer Science+Business Media), Postbus 246, Houten, 3990 GA, Netherlands. TEL 31-30-6383830, FAX 31-30-6383999, boekhandels@bsl.nl, http://www.bsl.nl. Ed. L den Hollander. Circ: 3,000.

155.904 616.8 USA ISSN 1091-4269
RC531 CODEN: DEANF5
➤ **DEPRESSION AND ANXIETY (HOBOKEN).** Text in English. 1997. m. GBP 580 in United Kingdom to institutions; EUR 733 in Europe to institutions; USD 967 in United States to institutions; USD 1,079 in Canada & Mexico to institutions; USD 1,135 elsewhere to institutions; GBP 668 combined subscription in United Kingdom to institutions (print & online eds.); EUR 844 combined subscription in Europe to institutions (print & online eds.); USD 1,112 combined subscription in United States to institutions (print & online eds.); USD 1,224 combined subscription in Canada & Mexico to institutions (print & online eds.); USD 1,280 combined subscription elsewhere to institutions (print & online eds.) (effective 2012). adv. back issues avail.; reprint service avail. from PSC. **Document type:** *Journal, Academic/Scholarly.* **Description:** Covers molecular, genetic, biopsychosocial, neurochemical, neuropsychological, physiological, behavioral, sociological, psychodynamic, psychotherapeutic, cognitive and pharmacotherapeutic aspects of mood and anxiety disorders.
Formed by the merger of (1994-1997): Anxiety (1070-9797); (1993-1997): Depression (1062-6417)
Related titles: Online - full text ed.: ISSN 1520-6394. GBP 494 in United Kingdom to institutions; EUR 625 in Europe to institutions; USD 967 elsewhere to institutions (effective 2012).
Indexed: A01, A03, A08, A20, A22, B21, C06, C07, CA, CurCont, E-psyche, EMBASE, ESPM, ExcerpMed, FamI, ISR, IndMed, Inpharma, JW-P, MEDLINE, NSA, P03, P30, P35, P43, PsycInfo, PsycholAb, R10, Reac, RefZh, RiskAb, S02, S03, SCI, SCOPUS, SSCI, T02, W07.
—BLDSC (3554.590040), GNLM, IE, Infotrieve, Ingenta, INIST. **CCC.**
Published by: John Wiley & Sons, Inc., 111 River St, Hoboken, NJ 07030. TEL 201-748-6000, FAX 201-748-6088, info@wiley.com, http://www.wiley.com/WileyCDA/. Ed. Peter P Roy-Byrne. Pub. Kim Thompkins TEL 212-850-6921. Adv. contact Stephen Donohue TEL 781-388-8511. **Subscr. to:** John Wiley & Sons Ltd., The Atrium, Southern Gate, Chichester, West Sussex PO19 8SQ, United Kingdom. TEL 44-1243-779777, 800-243407, FAX 44-1243-775878, cs-journals@wiley.com.

➤ **DEPRESSION AND ANXIETY (NEW YORK).** *see* MEDICAL SCIENCES—Psychiatry And Neurology

➤ **DEPRESSION FRONTIER.** *see* MEDICAL SCIENCES—Psychiatry And Neurology

▼ ➤ **DEPRESSION RESEARCH AND TREATMENT.** *see* MEDICAL SCIENCES—Psychiatry And Neurology

616.89 USA ISSN 0893-8636
RC537 CODEN: DISEER
THE DEPRESSIVE ILLNESS SERIES. Text in English. 1988. irreg., latest vol.4, 1993. price varies. back issues avail. **Document type:** *Monographic series, Academic/Scholarly.*
Indexed: E-psyche.
—CCC.
Published by: Springer New York LLC (Subsidiary of: Springer Science+Business Media), 233 Spring St, New York, NY 10013. TEL 212-460-1500, FAX 212-460-1575, service-ny@springer.com. **Dist. by:** Journal Fulfillment, PO Box 2485, Secaucus, NJ 07096.

150 ESP ISSN 1657-3986
DESDE EL JARDIN DE FREUD. Text in Spanish. 2001. a. USD 12 (effective 2010). **Document type:** *Monographic series, Academic/Scholarly.*
Published by: Universidad Nacional de Colombia, Facultad de Ciencias Humanas, Ciudad Universitaria, Santa Fe de Bogota, 14490, Spain. TEL 57-3-165369, FAX 57-3-165028, http://www.humanas.unal.edu.co/home/. Ed. Luis Bernardo Lopez Caicedo.

152.46 DEU ISSN 1437-2711
DEUTSCHE ANGST-ZEITSCHRIFT; Information und Hilfe bei Angststoerungen. Text in German. 1995. q. EUR 12; EUR 4 newsstand/cover (effective 2009). **Document type:** *Magazine, Trade.*
Formerly (until 1996): Keine Angst!
Published by: Deutsche AngstStoerungenHilfe und -Selbsthilfe, Bayerstr 77a, Munich, 80335, Germany. TEL 49-89-51555315, FAX 49-89-51555316.

150 GBR ISSN 0954-5794
RC454.4 CODEN: DPESBB
➤ **DEVELOPMENT AND PSYCHOPATHOLOGY.** Text in English. 1989. q. GBP 308, USD 557 to institutions; GBP 327, USD 592 combined subscription to institutions (print & online eds.) (effective 2012). adv. back issues avail.; reprint service avail. from PSC. **Document type:** *Journal, Academic/Scholarly.* **Description:** Devoted to the publication of original empirical, theoretical and review papers that address the interrelationship of normal and pathological development in adults and children.
Related titles: Online - full text ed.: ISSN 1469-2198. GBP 267, USD 483 to institutions (effective 2012).
Indexed: A01, A03, A08, A22, AMED, ASCA, B21, BibInd, CA, CJPI, CurCont, E-psyche, E01, EMBASE, ExcerpMed, F09, FamI, INI, IndMed, MEDLINE, NSA, P02, P03, P10, P12, P20, P22, P25, P30, P48, P53, P54, PCI, PQC, PsycInfo, PsycholAb, R10, Reac, S02, S03, SCOPUS, SSCI, T02, W07.
—BLDSC (3578.855000), GNLM, IE, Infotrieve, Ingenta, INIST. **CCC.**
Published by: Cambridge University Press, The Edinburgh Bldg, Shaftesbury Rd, Cambridge, CB2 8RU, United Kingdom. TEL 44-1223-312393, FAX 44-1223-315052, journals@cambridge.org, http://www.cambridge.org/uk. Ed. Dante Cicchetti. R&P Linda Nicol TEL 44-1223-325702. Adv. contact Rebecca Roberts TEL 44-1223-325083. **Subscr. to:** Cambridge University Press, 32 Ave of the Americas, New York, NY 10013. TEL 212-337-5000, FAX 212-691-3239, journals_subscriptions@cup.org.

▼ ➤ **DEVELOPMENTAL COGNITIVE NEUROSCIENCE**; a journal for cognitive, affective and social developmental neuroscience. *see* MEDICAL SCIENCES—Psychiatry And Neurology

155 613.62 USA ISSN 1093-7196
DEVELOPMENTAL DISABILITIES SPECIAL INTEREST SECTION QUARTERLY. Text in English. 197? (vol.12, no.2). q. free to members (effective 2010). adv. **Document type:** *Newsletter, Trade.* **Description:** Focuses on how OT assessment and intervention can facilitate the inclusion of individuals with developmental disabilities in home, school, work, and community life.
Former titles (until 1997): Developmental Disabilities Special Interest Section Newsletter (0279-4098); (until 1981): American Occupational Therapy Association. Developmental Disabilities Specialty Section. Newsletter (0194-6390)
Related titles: Online - full text ed.; ◆ Series: Gerontology Special Interest Section Quarterly. ISSN 1093-717X; ◆ Mental Health Special Interest Section Quarterly. ISSN 1093-7226; ◆ Technology Special Interest Section Quarterly. ISSN 1093-7137; ◆ Work & Industry Special Interest Section Quarterly; ◆ Education Special Interest Section Quarterly. ISSN 1093-7188; ◆ Physical Disabilities Special Interest Section Quarterly. ISSN 1093-7234; ◆ Administration & Management Special Interest Section Quarterly. ISSN 1093-720X; ◆ Sensory Integration Special Interest Section Quarterly. ISSN 1093-7250.
Indexed: C06, C07, C08, CINAHL, P24, P27, P48, P54, PQC.
—CCC.
Published by: American Occupational Therapy Association, Inc., 4720 Montgomery Ln, PO Box 31220, Bethesda, MD 20824. TEL 301-652-2682, 800-377-8555, FAX 301-652-7711, members@aota.org. Ed. Terry K Crowe.

370.15 USA ISSN 8756-5641
CODEN: DENEE8
➤ **DEVELOPMENTAL NEUROPSYCHOLOGY**; an international journal of life-span issues in neuropsychology. Text in English. 1985. bi-m. GBP 955 combined subscription in United Kingdom to institutions (print & online eds.); EUR 1,276, USD 1,600 combined subscription to institutions (print & online eds.) (effective 2012). adv. back issues avail.; reprint service avail. from PSC. **Document type:** *Journal, Academic/Scholarly.* **Description:** Covers issues concerning the structure and function of both the developing and the aging brain.
Related titles: Online - full text ed.: ISSN 1532-6942. GBP 859 in United Kingdom to institutions; EUR 1,148, USD 1,439 to institutions (effective 2012).
Indexed: A01, A03, A08, A20, A22, ASCA, B21, B25, BIOSIS Prev, C06, C07, C08, CA, CDA, CINAHL, CurCont, E-psyche, E01, EMBASE, ESPM, ExcerpMed, FR, FamI, IndMed, L&LBA, MEDLINE, MycolAb, NSA, NSCI, P02, P03, P10, P12, P30, P43, P48, P53, P54, PQC, PsycInfo, PsycholAb, R10, Reac, RiskAb, SCI, SCOPUS, SSCI, T02, ToxAb, W07.
—BLDSC (3579.057300), GNLM, IE, Infotrieve, Ingenta, INIST. **CCC.**
Published by: Psychology Press (Subsidiary of: Taylor & Francis Inc.), 325 Chestnut St, Ste 800, Philadelphia, PA 19106. TEL 800-354-1420, FAX 215-625-2940, orders@taylorandfrancis.com, http://www.psypress.com. Ed. Dennis L Molfese. Adv. contact Linda Hann TEL 44-1344-779945.

➤ **DEVELOPMENTAL PSYCHOBIOLOGY.** *see* BIOLOGY

155 USA ISSN 0012-1649
BF699 CODEN: DEVPA9
➤ **DEVELOPMENTAL PSYCHOLOGY.** Text in English. 1969. bi-m. USD 280 domestic to individuals; USD 312 foreign to individuals; USD 907 domestic to institutions; USD 964 foreign to institutions (effective 2011). adv. bibl.; charts; stat.; illus. back issues avail.; reprint service avail. from PSC. **Document type:** *Journal, Academic/Scholarly.* **Description:** Features articles that advance knowledge and theory about human psychological growth and development from infancy to old age.
Related titles: Microform ed.: (from PQC); Online - full text ed.: ISSN 1939-0599 (from ScienceDirect).
Indexed: A01, A02, A03, A08, A20, A22, A25, A26, A36, AC&P, AMHA, ASCA, ASSIA, B04, B21, BDM&CN, BRD, BibLing, C06, C07, C28, CA, CABA, CDA, CJPI, CPE, ChPerI, Chicano, CommAb, CurCont, DIP, E-psyche, E02, E03, E07, E08, EIA, EMBASE, ERI, ERIC, EdA, EdI, EnerInd, ExcerpMed, F09, FR, FamI, G08, G10, GH, H09, H11, H12, I05, IBR, IBSS, IBZ, IndMed, MEA&I, MEDLINE, MLA, MLA-IB, N02, N03, NSA, P02, P03, P04, P07, P10, P12, P13, P18, P27, P30, P48, P53, P54, P55, PCI, PEI, PQC, PsycInfo, PsycholAb, R10, R12, RASB, Reac, S02, S03, S05, S08, S09, S21, SCOPUS, SFSA, SSAI, SSAb, SSCI, SSI, SWR&A, T02, T05, TAR, W03, W07, W09.
—BLDSC (3579.059000), IE, Infotrieve, Ingenta, INIST. **CCC.**

Published by: American Psychological Association, 750 First St, NE, Washington, DC 20002. TEL 202-336-5500, 800-374-2721, FAX 202-336-5997, journals@apa.org. Ed. Jacquelynne S Eccles. Adv. contact Doug Constant TEL 202-336-5574. Circ: 2,100.

150 USA ISSN 0273-2297
BF721

➤ **DEVELOPMENTAL REVIEW.** Text in English. 1981. q. EUR 629 in Europe to institutions; JPY 65,700 in Japan to institutions; USD 546 elsewhere to institutions (effective 2012). adv. illus. index. back issues avail.; reprints avail. **Document type:** *Journal, Academic/Scholarly.* **Description:** Provides child and developmental, child clinical, and educational psychologists with articles that reflect current thinking and covers scientific developments.
Related titles: Online - full text ed.: ISSN 1090-2406 (from IngentaConnect, ScienceDirect).
Indexed: A01, A03, A08, A20, A22, A26, ASCA, B21, B25, BIOSIS Prev, CA, CDA, CPE, CurCont, DIP, E-psyche, E01, E03, ERA, ERI, ERIC, ESPM, Faml, I05, IBR, IBZ, L&LBA, MycolAb, NSA, P03, P30, PsycInfo, PsycholAb, RASB, RiskAb, S02, S03, S20, S21, SCOPUS, SOPODA, SSCI, SociolAb, T02, W07.
—BLDSC (3579.059780), IE, Infotrieve, Ingenta, INIST. **CCC.**
Published by: Academic Press (Subsidiary of: Elsevier Science & Technology), 3251 Riverport Ln, Maryland Heights, MO 63043. TEL 314-447-8010, FAX 314-447-8030, JournalCustomerService-usa@elsevier.com, http://www.elsevierdirect.com/imprint.jsp?iid=5. Ed. C J Brainerd.

155 GBR ISSN 1363-755X
BF712

DEVELOPMENTAL SCIENCE. Text in English. 1998. bi-m. GBP 716 in United Kingdom to institutions; EUR 909 in Europe to institutions; USD 1,203 in the Americas to institutions; USD 1,402 elsewhere to institutions; GBP 824 combined subscription in United Kingdom to institutions (print & online eds.); EUR 1,046 combined subscription in Europe to institutions (print & online eds.); USD 1,384 combined subscription in the Americas to institutions (print & online eds.); USD 1,613 combined subscription elsewhere to institutions (print & online eds.) (effective 2011). adv. back issues avail.; reprint service avail. from PSC. **Document type:** *Journal, Academic/Scholarly.* **Description:** Contains cutting-edge theory and up-to-the-minute research on scientific developmental psychology from leading thinkers in the field.
Related titles: Online - full text ed.: ISSN 1467-7687. GBP 716 in United Kingdom to institutions; EUR 909 in Europe to institutions; USD 1,203 in the Americas to institutions; USD 1,402 elsewhere to institutions (effective 2011) (from IngentaConnect).
Indexed: A01, A03, A08, A20, A22, A26, B21, CA, CTA, CurCont, E-psyche, E01, EMBASE, ExcerpMed, H12, I05, MEDLINE, NSA, P02, P03, P10, P12, P30, P43, P48, P53, P54, PQC, PsycInfo, PsycholAb, R10, Reac, S01, SCOPUS, SSCI, T02, W07.
—BLDSC (3579.059785), IE, Infotrieve, Ingenta. **CCC.**
Published by: Wiley-Blackwell Publishing Ltd. (Subsidiary of: John Wiley & Sons, Inc.), 9600 Garsington Rd, Oxford, OX4 2DQ, United Kingdom. TEL 44-1865-776868, FAX 44-1865-714591, customerservices@blackwellpublishing.com. Eds. Denis Mareschal, Mark H Johnson. Adv. contact Craig Pickett TEL 44-1865-476267.

150 FRA ISSN 2105-8709
DEVELOPPEMENT PERSONNEL. Text in French. 2006. irreg. **Document type:** *Monographic series, Consumer.*
Published by: Robert Jauze, 41, Rue Barrault, Paris, 75013, France.

150 616.8 FRA ISSN 2103-2874
▼ ➤ **DEVELOPPEMENTS**; revue interdisciplinaire du developpement cognitif normal et pahologique. Text in French. 2009. q. EUR 100 domestic to institutions; EUR 120 in Europe to institutions; EUR 140 elsewhere to institutions (effective 2009). abstr.; illus. **Document type:** *Journal, Academic/Scholarly.*
Related titles: Online - full text ed.
Published by: Editions Solal, 111 Rue Sainte Cecile, Marseille, 13005, France. TEL 33-4-91257785, FAX 33-4-91802958, editions.solal@wanadoo.fr, http://www.editions-solal.fr/. Ed. Andre Cohen.

➤ **DEVIANCE ET SOCIETE.** *see* SOCIOLOGY

➤ **DEVIANT BEHAVIOR**; an interdisciplinary journal. *see* SOCIOLOGY

155.28 DEU ISSN 0012-1924
BF39 CODEN: DGNSAQ

➤ **DIAGNOSTICA**; Zeitschrift fuer Psychologische Diagnostik und Differentielle Psychologie, zugleich Informationsorgan ueber psychologische Tests und Untersuchungsmethoden. Text in German; Summaries in English. 1955. q. EUR 81.95 to individuals; EUR 145.95 to institutions; EUR 36.95 newsstand/cover (effective 2011). adv. bk.rev. bibl.; charts. reprints avail. **Document type:** *Journal, Academic/Scholarly.*
Related titles: Microfiche ed.: (from PQC); Online - full text ed.: ISSN 2190-622X.
Indexed: A20, A22, ASCA, CurCont, DIP, E-psyche, GJP, IBR, IBZ, P03, PsycInfo, PsycholAb, SCOPUS, SSCI, W07.
—BLDSC (3579.670000), GNLM, IE, Infotrieve, Ingenta. **CCC.**
Published by: Hogrefe Verlag GmbH & Co. KG, Rohnsweg 25, Goettingen, 37085, Germany. TEL 49-551-496090, FAX 49-551-4960988, verlag@hogrefe.de. Ed. Olaf Koeller. Circ: 1,200 (paid and controlled).

159 ARG ISSN 1852-5059
DIALOGAR. Text in Spanish. 1994. 3/yr. **Document type:** *Magazine, Trade.*
Published by: Colegio de Psicologos de la Provincia de Cordoba, Ovidio Lagos, 163 - Bo., General Paz, Cordoba, Argentina. TEL 54-351-4222703, FAX 54-351-4259367, http://www.cppc.org.ar/.

▼ **DIALOGOS**; revista cientifica de psicologia, ciencias sociales, humanidades y ciencias de la salud. *see* SOCIAL SCIENCES: COMPREHENSIVE WORKS

306.9 155.937 649 USA ISSN 1533-8886
DIFFERENT KIND OF PARENTING; a 'zine for parents whose children have died. Text in English. 2001 (Jan.). q. USD 8 newsstand/cover (effective 2007). **Document type:** *Magazine, Consumer.* **Description:** Offers an alternative print resource in the form of a 'zine specifically written for parents enduring the death of a child.
Published by: Kota Press, PO Box 514, Vashon Island, WA 98070. TEL 206-251-6706. Ed., R&P Kara L C Jones.

DIPAV QUADERNI; quadrimestrale di psicologia e antropologia culturale. (Dipartimento Psicologia Antropologia Culturale Verona) *see* ANTHROPOLOGY

301.1 USA
THE DIPLOMATE. Text in English. 1981. s-a. looseleaf. membership. bk.rev. **Document type:** *Newsletter.* **Description:** Contains news for members.
Related titles: Online - full text ed.
Indexed: E-psyche.
Published by: American Board of Professional Psychology, 514 E Capitol Ave, Jefferson City, MO 65101-3008. TEL 573-634-5607, 800—255-7792, FAX 573-634-7157, office@abpp.org, http://www.abpp.org. Ed. Robert W Goldberg. Circ: 3,000 (controlled).

616.89 USA ISSN 1062-0788
RC466

➤ **DIRECTIONS IN MENTAL HEALTH COUNSELING.** Text in English. 1991. q. USD 200 per vol. (effective 2010). index. back issues avail.; reprints avail. **Document type:** *Journal, Academic/Scholarly.* **Description:** Presents developments in mental health counseling. Approved by various boards for continuing education credits.
Indexed: E-psyche.
Published by: Hatherleigh Co. Ltd., 62545 State Hwy 10, Hobart, NY 13788. support@hatherleigh.com.

362.28 USA
DIRECTORY OF SUICIDE PREVENTION AND CRISIS INTERVENTION CENTERS. Text in English. a. USD 15 (effective 2000). **Document type:** *Directory.*
Indexed: E-psyche.
Published by: American Association of Suicidology, 5221 Wisconsin Ave, NW, Washington, DC 20015. info@suicidology.org.

150 USA ISSN 1940-901X
DISASTER AND TRAUMA PSYCHOLOGY. Text in English. 2008 (May). irreg., latest 2008. USD 49.95, GBP 34.95 per issue (effective 2010). **Document type:** *Monographic series, Academic/Scholarly.* **Description:** Covers analysis of the psychological and physiological effects of torture.
Published by: Praeger Publishers (Subsidiary of: Greenwood Publishing Group Inc.), 88 Post Rd W, Westport, CT 06881. TEL 800-368-6868, tech.support@greenwood.com. Ed. Gilbert Reyes.

150.19 COL
DISCERNIMIENTO. Text and summaries in Spanish, English. 1998. irreg., latest vol.5, 1999. free. back issues avail. **Description:** Examines various possibilities and potentials in the field of psychology.
Media: Online - full content.
Published by: Universidad del Norte, Division de Humanidades y Ciencias Sociales, Apdo Aereo 1569, Barranquilla, Colombia. http://www.uninorte.edu.co/division/humanidades.

302 GBR ISSN 0957-9265
P302 CODEN: DISOEN

➤ **DISCOURSE & SOCIETY**; an international journal for the study of discourse and communication in their social, political and cultural contexts. Text in English. 1990. bi-m. GBP 775, USD 1,434 combined subscription to institutions (print & online eds.); GBP 760, USD 1,405 to institutions (effective 2010); subscr. includes: Discourse & Communication. adv. back issues avail.; reprint service avail. from PSC. **Document type:** *Journal, Academic/Scholarly.* **Description:** Explores the relevance of discourse analysis to the social sciences, with a particular focus on the political implications of discourse and communication.
Related titles: Online - full text ed.: ISSN 1460-3624. GBP 698, USD 1,291 to institutions (effective 2010).
Indexed: A01, A02, A03, A08, A20, A22, A26, ASCA, B07, BibLing, CA, CMM, CommAb, CurCont, DIP, E-psyche, E01, E08, ESPM, Faml, G08, H04, I05, I13, I14, IBR, IBSS, IBZ, IBibSS, L&LBA, L11, MLA, MLA-IB, P02, P03, P10, P12, P34, P42, P48, P53, P54, PAIS, PCI, PQC, PRA, PSA, PsycInfo, PsycholAb, S02, S03, S09, SCOPUS, SD, SOPODA, SPAA, SSA, SSCI, SSciA, SociolAb, T02, V&AA, V02, W07.
—BLDSC (3595.810000), IE, Infotrieve, Ingenta. **CCC.**
Published by: Sage Publications Ltd. (Subsidiary of: Sage Publications, Inc.), 1 Oliver's Yard, 55 City Rd, London, EC1Y 1SP, United Kingdom. TEL 44-20-73248500, FAX 44-20-73248600, info@sagepub.co.uk, http://www.uk.sagepub.com/home.nav. Ed. Teun A van Dijk. **Subscr. in the Americas to:** Sage Publications, Inc., 2455 Teller Rd, Thousand Oaks, CA 91320. TEL 805-499-9774, FAX 805-499-0871, journals@sagepub.com.

➤ **DISCOURSE STUDIES**; an interdisciplinary journal for the study of text and talk. *see* LINGUISTICS

150.19 SWE ISSN 1101-1408
DIVAN. Text in Swedish. 1990. q. SEK 250 (effective 2007). cum.index: 1990-1995. back issues avail.; reprints avail. **Document type:** *Magazine, Academic/Scholarly.*
Indexed: E-psyche.
Published by: (Psykoanalytiskt Forum Ideell Foerening), Divan, Observationsvaegen 11, Huddinge, 14138, Sweden. TEL 46-8-4620110. Eds. Cecilia Annell, Christian Nilsson, Bengt Warren. Pub. Bengt Warren.

150 COL ISSN 1794-9998
BF5

➤ **DIVERSITAS**; perspectivas en psicologias. Text in English, Spanish, Portuguese. 2005. s-a. **Document type:** *Journal, Academic/Scholarly.*
Related titles: Online - full text ed.
Indexed: C01, F04.
Published by: Universidad Santo Tomas, Facultad de Psicologia, Carrera 9 no 51-11, Bogota, Colombia.

➤ **DOCTOR - PATIENT STUDIES.** *see* MEDICAL SCIENCES

➤ **DOMESTIC VIOLENCE SOURCEBOOK.** *see* CRIMINOLOGY AND LAW ENFORCEMENT

➤ **DOMINI. ERGONOMIA.** *see* ENGINEERING

150 ITA ISSN 1972-0742
DOMINI. PSICOLOGIA CLINICA E LAVORO ISTITUZIONALE. Text in Italian. 2002. irreg. **Document type:** *Monographic series, Academic/Scholarly.*
Published by: Liguori Editore, Via Posillipo 394, Naples, 80123, Italy. TEL 39-081-7206111, FAX 39-081-7206244, liguori@liguori.it, http://www.liguori.it.

153.9 USA ISSN 1930-0425
DON'T REMEMBER THIS; the art of extemporaneous learning. Text in English. 2006. bi-m. USD 12 (effective 2007). **Document type:** *Newsletter, Consumer.*
Published by: Hein Family Enterprises, 522 S. Park St., Casper, WY 82601. TEL 307-472-0208, 888-921-9595, rhein@coffey.com. Ed. Rebecca Lange Hein.

150 JPN ISSN 0389-312X
DOSHISHA SHINRI/DOSHISHA PSYCHOLOGICAL REVIEW. Text in Japanese. 1953. a. **Document type:** *Journal, Academic/Scholarly.*
Indexed: E-psyche.
Published by: Doshisha Daigaku, Shinrigaku Kenkyushitsu, Doshisha University, Department of Psychology, Karasuma-Higashi-iru, Imadegawa-dori Kamigyo-ku, Kyoto, 602-8580, Japan. TEL 81-75-2514095, FAX 81-75-2513077, http://psychology.doshisha.ac.jp/Department/workshop.htm.

150 649 FRA ISSN 1628-464X
LES DOSSIERS DE SPIRALE. Text in French. 2001. irreg. back issues avail. **Document type:** *Monographic series, Consumer.*
Published by: Editions Eres, 33 Av. Marcel Dassault, Toulouse, 31500, France. TEL 33-5-61751576, FAX 33-5-61735289, eres@edition-eres.com.

DOWN SYNDROME RESEARCH AND PRACTICE. *see* MEDICAL SCIENCES—Psychiatry And Neurology

616.8915 USA ISSN 1064-6191
RC489.D72

DRAMASCOPE. Text in English. 1980. 3/yr. free to members. adv. bk.rev. **Document type:** *Newsletter.* **Description:** Publishes news, information, articles and resources of interest to drama and creative arts therapists.
Related titles: Online - full text ed.
Indexed: E-psyche.
Published by: National Association for Drama Therapy (N A D T), 44365 Premier Plaza, Ste 220, Ashburn, VA 20147. Ed. Meredith Dean.

150 GBR ISSN 0263-0672
PN1641

DRAMATHERAPY. Text in English. 1977. 3/yr. GBP 181 combined subscription in United Kingdom to institutions (print & online eds.); EUR 239, USD 298 combined subscription to institutions (print & online eds.) (effective 2012). bk.rev. **Document type:** *Journal, Academic/Scholarly.* **Description:** Presents articles on clinical research, and linking theory and practice, letters and book reviews.
Related titles: Online - full text ed.: GBP 163 in United Kingdom to institutions; EUR 215, USD 269 to institutions (effective 2012).
Indexed: A04, A10, C11, CA, IBT&D, P48, PQC, T02, V03.
—BLDSC (3623.197830). **CCC.**
Published by: The British Association of Dramatherapists, Waverley, Battledown Approach, Cheltenham, Gloucestershire GL52 6RE, United Kingdom. TEL 44-1242-235515, enquiries@badth.org.uk, http://www.badth.org.uk.

DREAM NETWORK JOURNAL; a quarterly publication exploring dreams and myth. *see* NEW AGE PUBLICATIONS

152 USA
➤ **DREAM TIME.** Text in English. 1984. 3/yr. free to members (effective 2010). adv. bk.rev. abstr.; bibl.; charts; illus. back issues avail. **Document type:** *Magazine, Trade.* **Description:** International, multidisciplinary, basic and applied dream research.
Formerly: A S D Newsletter
Indexed: E-psyche.
Published by: Association for the Study of Dreams, 1672 University Ave, Berkeley, CA 94703. TEL 209-724-0889, FAX 209-724-0889, office@asdreams.org, http://www.asdreams.org. Ed. Richard A Russo. Adv. contact Jean Campbell. Circ: 1,000.

158 USA ISSN 1930-0190
THE DREAMERS EDGE. Text in English. 2004. w. **Document type:** *Newsletter, Consumer.* **Description:** Contains motivational material on leadership, strategic planning, change and success.
Media: Online - full text.
Published by: Dream Publications TEL 888-899-5353, FAX 502-899-5354, Conway@DreamHigh.com, http://www.dreamhigh.com. Ed. Conway Stone.

135.3 612.821 USA ISSN 1053-0797
BF1074 CODEN: DRMGEW

➤ **DREAMING.** Text in English. 1991. q. USD 114 domestic to individuals; USD 141 foreign to individuals; USD 632 domestic to institutions; USD 677 foreign to institutions (effective 2011). adv. back issues avail.; reprint service avail. from PSC. **Document type:** *Journal, Academic/Scholarly.* **Description:** Provides a forum for biological and physiological studies involving sleep and dream research, psychological studies, psychoanalytic investigations, and papers on the link between dreams and art, literature, and other human activities.
Indexed: A01, A02, A03, A08, A20, A22, ASCA, BibLing, CA, E-psyche, E01, Faml, MLA-IB, P03, P30, PCI, PsycInfo, PsycholAb, SCOPUS, T02.
—BLDSC (3623.341400), GNLM, IE, Infotrieve, Ingenta. **CCC.**
Published by: (International Association for the Study of Dreams, Educational Publishing Foundation), American Psychological Association, 750 First St, NE, Washington, DC 20002. TEL 202-336-5500, 800-374-2721, journals@apa.org. Ed. Deirdre Barrett. Adv. contact Doug Constant TEL 202-336-5574. Circ: 800.

150 616.8 DNK ISSN 1398-7801
DRIFT; tidsskrift for psychoanalyse. Text in Danish. 1999. 3/yr. DKK 250 domestic to individuals; DKK 300 domestic to institutions; DKK 300 foreign (effective 2009). back issues avail. **Document type:** *Journal, Academic/Scholarly.* **Description:** Aimed towards the academic world and people in the health world with interests in Freudian psychoanalysis and the teachings of Jacques Lacan.
Address: c/o Tommy Thambour, Randboelvej 16, Vanloese, 2720, Denmark. TEL 45-38-793086. Eds. Rene Rasmussen TEL 45-38-799491, Tommy Thambour.

150 USA ISSN 0164-5048
BJ1581

DROMENON; a journal of new ways of being. Text in English. 1994. 4/yr. USD 9.
Related titles: Online - full text ed.
Indexed: E-psyche.

P

Address: c/o Janet Parker, 1458 N W South River Dr, Miami, FL 33125. TEL 305-643-0144. Eds. Jean Houston, Robert Masters.

616.89 NLD ISSN 0167-238X
DTH. Variant title: Directieve Therapie. Text in Dutch. 1981. bi-m. EUR 131, USD 196 combined subscription to institutions (print & online eds.) (effective 2009). adv. bk.rev. **Document type:** *Journal, Academic/Scholarly.*
Related titles: Online - full text ed.: ISSN 1875-6824.
Indexed: A22, E-psyche, E01, SCOPUS.
—GNLM, IE, Infotrieve.
Published by: Bohn Stafleu van Loghum B.V. (Subsidiary of: Springer Science+Business Media), Postbus 246, Houten, 3990 GA, Netherlands. TEL 31-30-6383830, FAX 31-30-6383999, boekhandels@bsl.nl, http://www.bsl.nl. Ed. Alfred Lange. Pub. Daphne Dotsch. R&P Janneke van der Kruijs. adv.: B&W page EUR 704, color page EUR 1,881; trim 95 x 175. Circ: 1,040.

158.7 DEU ISSN 1614-936X
DUISBURGER BEITRAEGE ZUR ARBEITSPSYCHOLOGIE. Text in German. 2005. irreg. price varies. **Document type:** *Monographic series, Academic/Scholarly.*
Published by: Verlag Dr. Kovac, Leverkusenstr 13, Hamburg, 22761, Germany. TEL 49-40-3988800, FAX 49-40-39888055, info@verlagdrkovac.de. Ed. H-P Musahl.

THE DUKE SERIES IN CHILD DEVELOPMENT & PUBLIC POLICY. *see* CHILDREN AND YOUTH—About

150 USA ISSN 1946-7125
➤ **DYNAMICAL PSYCHOLOGY;** an international, interdisciplinary journal of complex mental processes. Text in English. 1994. a. free (effective 2011). back issues avail. **Document type:** *Journal, Academic/Scholarly.*
Formerly (until 1995): PsychoScience (Print)
Media: Online - full text.
Address: c/o Ben Goertzel, Novamente LLC/ Biomind LLC / AGIRI, 14409 Oakvale St, Rockville, MD 20853. ben@goertzel.org, http://goertzel.org/dynapsyc/dynacon.html. Ed. Mark Germine.

➤ **E A P DIGEST.** (Employee Assistance Programs) *see* DRUG ABUSE AND ALCOHOLISM

➤ **E C A RESEARCH IN PRACTICE SERIES.** *see* CHILDREN AND YOUTH—About

152.4 USA ISSN 1947-0568
E F T WITH KIYA. (Emotional Freedom Techniques) Text in English. 200?. m. free (effective 2009). **Document type:** *Newsletter, Consumer.* **Description:** Features Emotional Freedom Techniques essential for life.
Media: Online - full content.
Published by: Kiya L. Immergluck, Pub. http://eft-tap.com/.

150 AUS ISSN 1832-7931
➤ **E - JOURNAL OF APPLIED PSYCHOLOGY.** Abbreviated title: E- J A P. Text in English. 2005. s-a. free (effective 2011). back issues avail. **Document type:** *Journal, Academic/Scholarly.* **Description:** Features original research articles which apply psychological theories to clinical and social issues.
Media: Online - full text.
Indexed: A01, A39, C27, C29, CA, D03, D04, E13, P30, PsycInfo, R14, S14, S15, S18, T02.
Published by: Swinburne University of Technology, Faculty of Life & Social Sciences, H29, PO Box 218, Hawthorn, VIC 3122, Australia. TEL 61-3-86767002, FAX 61-3-98183648, international@swinburne.edu.au, http://www.swinburne.edu.au/lss/.

➤ **E-JOURNAL PHILOSOPHIE DER PSYCHOLOGIE.** *see* PHILOSOPHY

158 NLD ISSN 1871-4315
E K R MAGAZINE. (Elisabeth Kuebler-Ross) Text in Dutch. 1986. q. EUR 24 (effective 2009). adv.
Former titles (until 2004): E K R Nieuws (1571-9375); (until 2002): Stichting Dr. Elisabeth Kuebler-Ross/Shanti Nilaya Nederland. Nieuwsbrief (1386-9744)
Published by: (Stichting Dr. Elisabeth Kuebler-Ross Nederland), EKR-Huis, Halterstraat 3c, Zutphen, 7201 MV, Netherlands. TEL 31-575-545703, FAX 31-575-545704, info@kubler-ross.nl.

150 CZE ISSN 1802-8853
E - PSYCHOLOGIE. Text in Czech, Slovak, English. 2007. q. free (effective 2011). **Document type:** *Journal, Academic/Scholarly.*
Media: Online - full text.
Indexed: A01, CA, T02.
Published by: Ceskomoravska Psychologicka Spolecnost/Czech-Moravian Psychological Society, Kladenska 48, Prague, 160 00, Czech Republic. TEL 420-235-360477, cmps@ecn.cz, http://www.cmps.ecn.cz.

E T D EDUCACAO TEMATICA DIGITAL. *see* EDUCATION

EARLY CHILDHOOD RESEARCH & PRACTICE; an internet journal on the development, care, and education of young children. *see* EDUCATION

EARLY EDUCATION AND DEVELOPMENT. *see* EDUCATION

EATING AND WEIGHT DISORDERS (ONLINE); studies on anorexia, bulimia and obesity. *see* MEDICAL SCIENCES—Psychiatry And Neurology

150 GBR ISSN 1471-0153
RC552.E18 CODEN: EBAEAV
➤ **EATING BEHAVIORS.** Text in English. 2000. 4/yr. EUR 531 in Europe to institutions; JPY 70,500 in Japan to institutions; USD 592 elsewhere to institutions (effective 2012). back issues avail. **Document type:** *Journal, Academic/Scholarly.* **Description:** Cover articles related to human research on the etiology, prevention, and treatment of obesity, binge eating, and eating disorders in adults and children. Studies related to the promotion of healthy eating patterns to treat or prevent medical conditions (e.g., hypertension, diabetes mellitus, cancer) are also acceptable.
Related titles: Online - full text ed.: ISSN 1873-7358 (from IngentaConnect, ScienceDirect).
Indexed: A01, A03, A08, A26, A36, AddicA, C06, C07, CA, CABA, CurCont, D01, E12, EMBASE, ExcerpMed, F10, FR, FS&TA, GH, HEA, I05, LT, MEDLINE, N02, N03, P03, P30, PsycInfo, PsycholAb, R10, R12, RRTA, Reac, S12, SCOPUS, SSCI, SociolAb, SoyAb, T02, T05, W07, W11.
—BLDSC (3646.939080), IE, Ingenta, INIST. **CCC.**
Published by: Pergamon (Subsidiary of: Elsevier Science & Technology), The Blvd, Langford Ln, East Park, Kidlington, Oxford OX5 1GB, United Kingdom. TEL 44-1865-843000, FAX 44-1865-843010, JournalsCustomerServiceEMEA@elsevier.com. Ed. Dr. P Miller TEL 843-792-5547. **Subscr. to:** Elsevier BV, Radarweg 29, PO Box 211, Amsterdam 1000 AE, Netherlands. http://www.elsevier.nl.

616.89 USA ISSN 1064-0266
RC552.E18 CODEN: EDAIAN
➤ **EATING DISORDERS;** the journal of treatment and prevention. Text in English. 1992. 5/yr. GBP 251 combined subscription in United Kingdom to institutions (print & online eds.); EUR 335, USD 419 combined subscription to institutions (print & online eds.) (effective 2012). adv. back issues avail.; reprint service avail. from PSC. **Document type:** *Journal, Academic/Scholarly.* **Description:** Provides a wide range of practical and informative viewpoints for professionals involved in the treatment of and education in eating disorders.
Related titles: Online - full text ed.: ISSN 1532-530X. 1992. GBP 226 in United Kingdom to institutions; EUR 302, USD 378 to institutions (effective 2012) (from IngentaConnect).
Indexed: A01, A03, A08, A22, A34, A36, ASSIA, B21, C06, C07, C08, CA, CABA, CINAHL, E-psyche, E01, E12, EMBASE, ESPM, ExcerpMed, Faml, GH, H&SSA, LT, MEDLINE, N02, N03, P03, P30, P43, PsycInfo, PsycholAb, R09, R10, R12, RRTA, Reac, RiskAb, S02, S03, SCOPUS, SD, SSA, SociolAb, T02, T05, VS.
—IE, Infotrieve, Ingenta. **CCC.**
Published by: Routledge (Subsidiary of: Taylor & Francis Group), 325 Chestnut St, Ste 800, Philadelphia, PA 19106. TEL 800-354-1420, FAX 215-625-2940, journals@routledge.com, http://www.routledge.com. Ed. Leigh Cohn TEL 760-434-7533. Adv. contact Linda Hann TEL 44-1344-779945.

158 ITA ISSN 0394-1310
ECOLOGIA DELLA MENTE. Text in Italian; Summaries in English, Spanish. 1986. s-a. USD 80 domestic to institutions; USD 120 foreign to institutions (effective 2009). adv. **Document type:** *Journal, Academic/Scholarly.*
Indexed: E-psyche, P03, PsycInfo, PsycholAb.
Published by: (Centro Studi di Terapia Familiare e Relazionale), Il Pensiero Scientifico Editore, Via Bradano 3-C, Rome, 00199, Italy. TEL 39-06-862821, FAX 39-06-86282250, pensiero@pensiero.it, http://www.pensiero.it.

370.1 USA ISSN 1040-7413
BF353 CODEN: ECPSEN
➤ **ECOLOGICAL PSYCHOLOGY.** Text in English. 1989. q. GBP 425 combined subscription in United Kingdom to institutions (print & online eds.); EUR 569, USD 711 combined subscription to institutions (print & online eds.) (effective 2012). adv. back issues avail.; reprint service avail. from PSC. **Document type:** *Journal, Academic/Scholarly.* **Description:** Presents empirical, theoretical, and methodological papers in the form of research reports, target articles and commentary.
Related titles: Online - full text ed.: ISSN 1532-6969. GBP 383 in United Kingdom to institutions; EUR 512, USD 641 to institutions (effective 2012).
Indexed: A01, A03, A08, A20, A22, ASCA, B21, B25, BIOSIS Prev, CA, CurCont, E-psyche, E01, E04, E05, ErgAb, MycolAb, NSA, P02, P03, P10, P11, P12, P30, P43, P48, P52, P53, P54, P56, PQC, PsycInfo, PsycholAb, S01, S11, SCOPUS, SSCI, T02, W07.
—BLDSC (3649.050000), IE, Infotrieve, Ingenta. **CCC.**
Published by: (International Society for Ecological Psychology), Routledge (Subsidiary of: Taylor & Francis Group), 325 Chestnut St, Ste 800, Philadelphia, PA 19106. TEL 800-354-1420, FAX 215-625-2940, journals@routledge.com, http://www.routledge.com. Ed. William M Mace. Adv. contact Linda Hann TEL 44-1344-779945.

150 USA ISSN 1942-9347
▼ ➤ **ECOPSYCHOLOGY.** Text in English. 2009 (Spr.). q. USD 402 to institutions (effective 2012). adv. reprints avail. **Document type:** *Journal, Academic/Scholarly.* **Description:** Examines the psychological, spiritual, and therapeutic aspects of human-nature relationships, concern about environmental issues, and responsibility for protecting natural places and other species.
Media: Online - full text.
Indexed: P03, PsycInfo.
—IE. **CCC.**
Published by: Mary Ann Liebert, Inc. Publishers, 140 Huguenot St, 3rd Fl, New Rochelle, NY 10801. TEL 914-740-2100, FAX 914-740-2101, 800-654-3237, info@liebertpub.com. Ed. Thomas Joseph Doherty. Adv. contact Harriet I Matysko TEL 914-740-2182.

150 230 USA ISSN 1930-0379
EDIFICATION; the journal of the Society for Christian Psychology. Text in English. 2005. s-a. **Document type:** *Journal, Consumer.* **Description:** Promotes a distinctly Christian psychology.
Formerly: S C P Newsletter
Indexed: A01, T02.
Published by: (Society of Christian Psychology), American Association of Christian Counselors, PO Box 739, Forest, VA 24551. TEL 434-525-9470, 800-526-8673, FAX 434-525-9480, contactmemberservices@AACC.net, http://www.aacc.net.

158 NGA ISSN 2006-7593
LB1027.5
➤ **EDO JOURNAL OF COUNSELLING.** Text in English. 2008. s-a. NGN 1,000 domestic to individuals; USD 20 foreign to individuals; NGN 1,600 domestic to institutions; USD 24 foreign to institutions (effective 2009). back issues avail.; reprints avail. **Document type:** *Journal, Academic/Scholarly.*
Related titles: Online - full text ed.: free (effective 2011).
Address: Department of Educational Psychology & Curriculum Studies, Faculty o f Education, University of Benin, Benin City, Edo State, Nigeria. TEL 234-80-37190802. Ed. Elizabeth Omotunde Egbochuku. Pub. Oyaziwo Aluede.

➤ **EDUCATION AND PSYCHOLOGY OF THE GIFTED SERIES.** *see* EDUCATION—Special Education And Rehabilitation

➤ **EDUCATION SCIENCES AND PSYCHOLOGY.** *see* EDUCATION

370.15 150 155.4 GBR ISSN 0267-1611
LB1051
➤ **EDUCATIONAL & CHILD PSYCHOLOGY.** Text in English. 1972. q. free to members (effective 2009). back issues avail.; reprint service avail. from PSC. **Document type:** *Journal, Academic/Scholarly.* **Description:** Deals with the research and professional practice of educational and child psychology.
Formerly (until 1984): British Psychology Society. Division of Educational and Child Psychology. Occasional Papers (0144-5219)
Related titles: Online - full text ed.: GBP 4.02 per issue to non-members; GBP 2.88 per issue to members (effective 2009).
Indexed: A22, B29, CA, CPE, E-psyche, E03, P03, PsycInfo, PsycholAb, S21, T02.
—BLDSC (3661.363300), IE, Ingenta. **CCC.**
Published by: The British Psychological Society, St Andrews House, 48 Princess Rd E, Leicester, LE1 7DR, United Kingdom. TEL 44-116-2549568, FAX 44-116-2271314, enquiries@bps.org.uk. Ed. Simon Gibbs.

➤ **EDUCATIONAL AND PSYCHOLOGICAL INTERACTIONS.** *see* EDUCATION

155.28 370.15 USA ISSN 0013-1644
BF1 CODEN: EPMEAJ
➤ **EDUCATIONAL AND PSYCHOLOGICAL MEASUREMENT;** devoted to the development and application of measures of individual differences. Text in English. 1941. bi-m. USD 1,007, GBP 593 combined subscription to institutions (print & online eds.); USD 987, GBP 581 to institutions (effective 2011). adv. bk.rev. bibl.; charts. index. back issues avail.; reprint service avail. from PSC. **Document type:** *Journal, Academic/Scholarly.* **Description:** Discusses problems in the field of measuring individual differences and reports research on the development and use of tests and measurements in education.
Related titles: Microform ed.: (from PQC); Online - full text ed.: ISSN 1552-3888. USD 906, GBP 534 to institutions (effective 2011).
Indexed: A01, A02, A03, A08, A20, A22, A25, A26, AMHA, ASCA, AbAn, Acal, B01, B04, B06, B07, B09, BRD, C06, C07, CA, CCMJ, CIS, CMCI, CPE, ChemAb, Chicano, CurCont, DIP, E-psyche, E01, E02, E03, E06, E07, E08, E09, E16, EAA, ECER, ERA, ERI, ERIC, EdA, Edl, FR, Faml, G08, H04, HEA, HECAB, I05, IBR, IBZ, M12, MEA&I, MLA-IB, MResA, MSN, MathR, P02, P03, P04, P10, P18, P25, P27, P30, P48, P53, P54, P55, PCI, PQC, PersLit, PsycInfo, PsycholAb, RILM, S02, S03, S08, S09, S20, S21, SCI, SCOPUS, SSAI, SSAb, SSCI, SSI, T02, V02, W03, W05, W07.
—BLDSC (3661.366000), IE, Infotrieve, Ingenta, INIST. **CCC.**
Published by: Sage Publications, Inc., 2455 Teller Rd, Thousand Oaks, CA 91320. TEL 805-499-9774, 800-818-7243, FAX 805-499-0871, 800-583-2665, info@sagepub.com. Ed. Xitao Fan. adv.: color page USD 775, B&W page USD 385; 4.5 x 7.5. Circ: 1,250 (paid and free). **Subscr. overseas to:** Sage Publications Ltd., 1 Oliver's Yard, 55 City Rd, London EC1Y 1SP, United Kingdom. TEL 44-207-3248701, FAX 44-207-3248733, subscription@sagepub.co.uk.

370.15 USA ISSN 0046-1520
LB1051 CODEN: EDPSDT
➤ **EDUCATIONAL PSYCHOLOGIST.** Text in English. 1963. q. GBP 409 combined subscription in United Kingdom to institutions (print & online eds.); EUR 547, USD 686 combined subscription to institutions (print & online eds.) (effective 2012). adv. illus. index. back issues avail.; reprint service avail. from PSC. **Document type:** *Journal, Academic/Scholarly.* **Description:** Provides detailed explorations of new educational concepts and accepted educational practices.
Related titles: Microform ed.: (from PQC); Online - full text ed.: ISSN 1532-6985. GBP 368 in United Kingdom to institutions; EUR 492, USD 618 to institutions (effective 2012).
Indexed: A01, A02, A03, A08, A20, A22, AEI, ASCA, B04, BRD, CA, CIS, CPE, CurCont, E-psyche, E01, E02, E03, E06, E09, ERI, ERIC, EdA, Edl, Faml, P03, P04, P10, P18, P25, P30, P43, P48, P53, P54, PCI, PQC, PsycInfo, PsycholAb, SCOPUS, SSCI, T02, W03, W07.
—BLDSC (3661.530000), IE, Infotrieve, Ingenta. **CCC.**
Published by: (American Psychological Association), Routledge (Subsidiary of: Taylor & Francis Group), 325 Chestnut St, Ste 800, Philadelphia, PA 19106. TEL 800-354-1420, FAX 215-625-2940, journals@routledge.com, http://www.routledge.com. Eds. Clark A Chinn, Gale M Sinatra. Adv. contact Linda Hann TEL 44-1344-779945.

➤ **EDUCATIONAL PSYCHOLOGY;** an international journal of experimental educational psychology. *see* EDUCATION

▼ ➤ **EDUCATIONAL PSYCHOLOGY;** critical pedagogical perspectives. *see* EDUCATION

➤ **EDUCATIONAL PSYCHOLOGY (NEW YORK, 1976).** *see* EDUCATION

➤ **EDUCATIONAL PSYCHOLOGY IN PRACTICE.** *see* EDUCATION

➤ **EDUCATIONAL PSYCHOLOGY REVIEW.** *see* EDUCATION

➤ **THE EGYPTIAN JOURNAL OF MENTAL HEALTH.** *see* MEDICAL SCIENCES—Psychiatry And Neurology

➤ **THE EGYPTIAN JOURNAL OF NEUROLOGY, PSYCHIATRY, AND NEUROSURGERY.** *see* MEDICAL SCIENCES—Psychiatry And Neurology

➤ **EINBLICKE (FRANKFURT AM MAIN, 1998);** Beitraege zur Religionspsychologie. *see* RELIGIONS AND THEOLOGY

154.6 USA ISSN 1089-4284
ELECTRIC DREAMS. Text in English. 1994. m. free. back issues avail. **Document type:** *Magazine, Consumer.* **Description:** Publishes dreams, comments on dreams, articles on dream sharing and dreamwork, as well as news on public dream related events both on- and off-line.
Media: Online - full text.
Indexed: E-psyche.
Published by: Dream Gate, 4644 Geary Blvd PMB 171, San Francisco, CA 94118. TEL 415-221-3239, info@dreamgate.com, http://www.dreamgate.com/electric-dreams. Ed., Pub. Richard Catlett Wilkerson.

616.89 CAN ISSN 1492-1103
RC489.C65
➤ **THE ELECTRONIC JOURNAL OF COMMUNICATIVE PSYCHOANALYSIS**; an independent multilingual international publication. Abbreviated title: E J C P. Text in German, Italian, English. 1998. a. free (effective 2007). Website rev. bibl.; abstr. back issues avail. **Document type:** *Journal, Academic/Scholarly.* **Description:** Promotes free scholarly discussion of ideas in psychoanalysis, psychotherapy, psychology, and psychiatry.
Media: Online - full text.
Indexed: E-psyche, EMBASE, ExcerpMed, SCOPUS.
Published by: Electronic Journal of Communicative Psychoanalysis, 2302 W 33rd Ave, Vancouver, BC V6M 1C3, Canada. FAX 604-325-1878. Eds. I Weisberg, J Kahl-Popp, U Berns, V A Bonac.

➤ **THE ELECTRONIC JOURNAL OF HUMAN SEXUALITY.** *see* MEDICAL SCIENCES

➤ **THE ELEMENTARY SCHOOL JOURNAL.** *see* EDUCATION

150 AUT ISSN 1998-2410
ELESTIREL PSIKOLOJI BULTENI. Text in Turkish. 2008. 3/yr. **Document type:** *Journal, Academic/Scholarly.*
Media: Online - full content.
Address: easlitur@ccs.carleton.ca. Eds. Ersin Asliturk, Sertan Batur.

ELSEVIER ERGONOMICS BOOK SERIES. *see* ENGINEERING

152.4 POL
▼ **EMOCJE.** Text in Polish. 2010. bi-m. PLZ 53.42 (effective 2011). **Document type:** *Journal, Academic/Scholarly.* **Description:** Intended for school teachers, psychologists, educators of all levels and parents of school children. Covers psychological, social, health issues and therapy related to the development of young people.
Published by: Dr. Josef Raabe Spolka Wydawnicza z o.o., ul Kurpinskiego 55a, Warsaw, 02-733, Poland. TEL 48-22-8430660, FAX 48-22-8433317, raabe@raabe.com.pl.

150 USA ISSN 1528-3542
BF531 CODEN: EMOTCL
➤ **EMOTION.** Text in English. 2001 (Spring). bi-m. USD 107 domestic to individuals; USD 139 foreign to individuals; USD 512 domestic to institutions; USD 569 foreign to institutions (effective 2011). adv. back issues avail.; reprint service avail. from PSC. **Document type:** *Journal, Academic/Scholarly.* **Description:** Publishes articles that advance knowledge and theory about all aspects of emotional processes, including reports of substantial empirical studies, scholarly reviews, and major theoretical articles.
Related titles: Online - full text ed.: ISSN 1931-1516 (from ScienceDirect).
Indexed: A20, B25, BIOSIS Prev, C06, C07, CurCont, DIP, EMBASE, ExcerpMed, IBR, IBZ, MEDLINE, MycolAb, P03, P30, PsycInfo, PsycholAb, R10, Reac, SCOPUS, SSCI, W07.
—BLDSC (3733.566950), IE, Infotrieve, INIST. **CCC.**
Published by: American Psychological Association, 750 First St, NE, Washington, DC 20002. TEL 202-336-5500, 800-374-2721, journals@apa.org. Ed. Dr. Elizabeth A Phelps. Adv. contact Doug Constant TEL 202-336-5574. Circ: 1,300.

➤ **EMOTION**; Persoenlichkeit - Partnerschaft - Psychologie. *see* WOMEN'S INTERESTS

152.4 GBR ISSN 1754-0739
▼ ➤ **EMOTION REVIEW.** Text in English. 2009 (Jan.). q. USD 766, GBP 414 combined subscription to institutions (print & online eds.); USD 751, GBP 406 to institutions (effective 2011). back issues avail. **Document type:** *Journal, Academic/Scholarly.* **Description:** Features a combination of theoretical, conceptual, and review papers, with commentaries, to enhance debate about critical issues in emotion theory and research.
Related titles: Online - full text ed.: ISSN 1754-0747. 2009. USD 689, GBP 373 to institutions (effective 2011).
Indexed: A22, E01, P30, PsycInfo, SCOPUS.
—IE. **CCC.**
Published by: (International Society for Research on Emotion USA), Sage Publications Ltd. (Subsidiary of: Sage Publications, Inc.), 1 Oliver's Yard, 55 City Rd, London, EC1Y 1SP, United Kingdom. TEL 44-20-73248500, FAX 44-20-73248600, info@sagepub.co.uk, http://www.uk.sagepub.com/home.nav. Eds. James A Russell, Lisa Feldman Barrett.

152.4 NLD ISSN 1878-8084
▼ **EMOTIONS AND STATES OF MIND IN EAST ASIA.** Text in English. 2010. irreg., latest vol.2, 2011. price varies. **Document type:** *Monographic series, Academic/Scholarly.*
Published by: Brill, PO Box 9000, Leiden, 2300 PA, Netherlands. TEL 31-71-5353500, FAX 31-71-5317532, cs@brill.nl. Eds. Cheuk Yin Lee, Paolo Santangelo.

152.4 FRA ISSN 2108-7091
LES EMOTIONS AU MOYEN AGE. Text in French. 2008. irreg. **Document type:** *Journal, Academic/Scholarly.*
Media: Online - full text.
Published by: Le Carnet d'E M M A http://emma.hypotheses.org.

EMPLOYEE ASSISTANCE REPORT; supporting EAP and HR professionals. *see* BUSINESS AND ECONOMICS—Personnel Management

150 FRA ISSN 1761-2861
➤ **L'EN-JE LACANIEN.** Text in French. 2003. s-a. EUR 42 domestic to individuals; EUR 45 domestic to institutions; EUR 30 in South America; EUR 50 elsewhere (effective 2011). back issues avail. **Document type:** *Journal, Academic/Scholarly.*
Related titles: Online - full text ed.: ISSN 1951-6231. 2006.
Published by: Editions Eres, 33 Av. Marcel Dassault, Toulouse, 31500, France. TEL 33-5-61751576, FAX 33-5-61735289, eres@edition-eres.com. Eds. Antonio Quinet, Didier Castanet, Michel Bousseyroux.

158 USA ISSN 2160-4231
▼ **THE ENCHANTED SELF NEWSLETTER.** Text in English. 2011. bi-m. free (effective 2011). back issues avail. **Document type:** *Newsletter, Consumer.*
Media: Online - full text.
Published by: Barbara Becker Holstein, Ed. & Pub., 170 Morris Ave, Long Branch, NJ 07740. TEL 732-571-1200, 877-256-9385, FAX 732-571-1100, barbara@enchantedself.com.

150.19 USA
ENCOUNTERING JUNG. Text in English. 1998. irreg., latest vol.7, 1999. price varies. back issues avail. **Document type:** *Monographic series, Academic/Scholarly.* **Description:** Presents selections from all the published works of C. G. Jung on subjects of continuing interest to contemporary readers, especially in the areas of psychology, spirituality, and personal growth.
Published by: Princeton University Press, 41 William St, Princeton, NJ 08540. TEL 609-258-4900, 800-777-4726, FAX 609-258-6305, cpriday@pupress.co.uk. **Subscr. to:** California - Princeton Fulfillment Services, Inc., 1445 Lower Ferry Rd, Ewing, NJ 08618. TEL 609-883-1759, 800-777-4726, FAX 609-883-7413, 800-999-1958, orders@cpfsinc.com. **Dist. in Canada by:** University Press Group.; **Dist. in Europe & Africa by:** John Wiley & Sons Ltd.

ENCUENTRO ARGENTINO DE HISTORIA DE LA PSIQUIATRIA, LA PSICOLOGIA Y EL PSICOANALISIS. ACTAS. *see* MEDICAL SCIENCES—Psychiatry And Neurology

150 616.8 COL ISSN 2011-1622
ENCUENTRO DE AVANCES EN PSICOLOGIA, GERONTOLOGIA Y NEUROCIENCIAS. Text in Spanish. 2007. s-a. **Document type:** *Journal, Academic/Scholarly.*
Published by: Universidad Pontificia Bolivariana, Seccional Bucaramanga, Autopista Pie de Cuesta Km 7, Bucaramanga, Colombia. TEL 57-7-6796220, http://www.upb.edu.co/.

150 ESP ISSN 0212-453X
ENERGIA. CARACTER Y SOCIEDAD. Text in Spanish. 1983. s-a. **Document type:** *Magazine, Consumer.*
Indexed: RILM.
Published by: Escuela Espanola de Terapia Reichiana, C. Republica de Guinea Ecuatorial, 4-1, Valencia, 46022, Spain. TEL 34-96-3727310, FAX 34-96-3562090, 34-96-3562090, reichiana@cesser.com, http://www.esternet.org/.

150 CHE ISSN 0938-3522
➤ **ENERGIE UND CHARAKTER.** Text in German. 1990. s-a. CHF 60 (effective 2008). adv. bk.rev. index. back issues avail. **Document type:** *Journal, Academic/Scholarly.*
Indexed: E-psyche.
Published by: International Institute for Biosynthesis, Benzenrueti 6, Heiden, 9410, Switzerland. TEL 41-71-8916855, FAX 41-71-8915855, info@biosynthesis.org, http://www.biosynthesis.org. Circ: 1,000 (controlled).

150 USA ISSN 1949-6575
RC489.E53
▼ **ENERGY PSYCHOLOGY**; theory, research, practice, training. Text in English. 2009. 3/yr. USD 99.95; USD 49.95 per issue (effective 2010). **Document type:** *Journal, Academic/Scholarly.* **Description:** For practioners of energy psychology, including emotional freedom techniques.
Published by: Foundation for Epigenetic Medicine, 1490 Mark W Springs Rd, Santa Rosa, CA 95404. TEL 707-486-9961, dawson@soulmedicine.net, http://www.soulmedicineinstitute.org/research.html.

ENFANCE; psychologie, pedagogie, neuro-psychiatrie, sociologie. *see* CHILDREN AND YOUTH—About

ENFANCE & PSY; la revue de tous les professionnels de l'enfance et de l'adolescence. *see* CHILDREN AND YOUTH—About

ENFANCES, FAMILLES, GENERATIONS. *see* SOCIOLOGY

ENGRAMI. *see* MEDICAL SCIENCES—Psychiatry And Neurology

158 MEX ISSN 0185-1594
➤ **ENSENANZA E INVESTIGACION EN PSICOLOGIA.** Text in Spanish. 1975. a. MXN 290, USD 25. adv. bk.rev. abstr.; bibl. index. reprints avail. **Document type:** *Journal, Academic/Scholarly.*
Related titles: Microfilm ed.: (from PQC); Online - full text ed.: free (effective 2011).
Indexed: C01, E-psyche, I04, I05, PsycholAb.
Published by: Consejo Nacional para la Ensenanza e Investigacion en Psicologia, c/o Universidad Iberoamericana, Mexico, PROL PASEO DE LA REFORMA 880, Lomas de Santa Fe, Ciudad De Mexico, DF 01219, Mexico. Ed. Dr. Juan Lafarga. Circ: 1,000.

155.4 ESP ISSN 1575-0841
ENTRE LINEAS (BARCELONA). Text in Spanish, Catalan. 1996. s-a.
Published by: Escola d'Expressio i Psicomotricitat/Asociacion Profesional de Psicomotricistas, C Pere Verges, 1 6o Pl, Barcelona, 08020, Spain. TEL 34-93-2780294, FAX 34-65-5101355, entrelineas.app@wol.es.

150 FRA ISSN 1765-6400
ENTRETIENS. Text in French. 2004. irreg. **Document type:** *Monographic series.*
Published by: Editions Vuibert, 5 Allee de la 2e DB, Paris, 75015, France. TEL 33-1-42794400, FAX 33-1-42794680, http://www.vuibert.com.

150 DEU ISSN 1617-1586
ENTSPANNUNGSVERFAHREN. Text in German. 198?. a. EUR 12.50 (effective 2011). **Document type:** *Journal, Academic/Scholarly.*
Formerly (until 1999): Autogenes Training und Progressive Relaxation (1431-1356)
Published by: Pabst Science Publishers, Am Eichengrund 28, Lengerich, 49525, Germany. TEL 49-5484-97234, FAX 49-5484-550, pabst@pabst-publishers.com, http://www.pabst-publishers.de.

ENVIRONMENT AND BEHAVIOR. *see* SOCIOLOGY

158 FRA ISSN 1773-8156
EPANOUISSEMENT PERSONNEL ET PROFESSIONNEL. Text in French. 2005. irreg. back issues avail. **Document type:** *Monographic series, Consumer.*
Published by: InterEditions (Subsidiary of: Dunod), 5 Rue Laromiguiere, Paris, 75005, France. TEL 33-1-40463500, FAX 33-1-40464995, http://www.intereditions.com/.

152.4 CAN ISSN 1712-3380
EQUILINK. Text in English. 198?. q. CAD 25 membership (effective 2006). **Document type:** *Newsletter.*
Former titles (until 1999): Equilibrium & Link (1717-2160); (until 1998): Equilibrium (Toronto) (1717-2152); (until 1995): Mood Disorders Association of Metropolitan Toronto. Newsletter (1717-2144); (until 1994): Manic-Depressive Association of Metropolitan Toronto. Newsletter (1717-2136)
Indexed: E-psyche.
Published by: Mood Disorders Association of Ontario, 40 Orchard View Blvd, Ste 222, Toronto, ON M4R 1B9, Canada. TEL 416-486-8046, FAX 416-486-8127, info@mooddisorders.on.ca, http://www.mooddisorders.on.ca. Ed. Eric Jonasson.

EQUINE BEHAVIOUR. *see* SPORTS AND GAMES—Horses And Horsemanship

L'ERBAMUSICA; pensare altrimenti la musica e l'educazione. *see* MUSIC

150 ROM ISSN 1454-797X
ERDELYI PSZICHOLOGIAI SZEMLE. Text in Hungarian. q. **Document type:** *Journal, Academic/Scholarly.*
Indexed: P03, PsycInfo, PsycholAb.
Published by: Presa Universitara Clujeana/Cluj University Press, 51-st B.P.Hasdeu St, Cluj-Napoca, Romania. TEL 40-264-405352, http://www.editura.ubbcluj.ro.

155 DEU ISSN 1862-5592
ERGEBNISSE DER RECHTSPSYCHOLOGIE. Text in German. 2006. irreg., latest vol.2, 2007. price varies. **Document type:** *Monographic series, Academic/Scholarly.*
Published by: Shaker Verlag GmbH, Kaiserstr 100, Herzogenrath, 52134, Germany. TEL 49-2407-95960, FAX 49-2407-95969, info@shaker.de.

ERGONOMICS; an international journal of research and practice in human factors and ergonomics. *see* ENGINEERING

ERGONOMICS, HUMAN FACTORS AND SAFETY. *see* ENGINEERING

ERGONOMICS IN DESIGN; the magazine of human factors applications. *see* ENGINEERING

THE ERGONOMIST. *see* ENGINEERING

158.7 DNK ISSN 1602-9968
ERHVERVSPSYKOLOGI; tidsskrift om udvikling, dialog, ledelse, organisation. Text in Danish. 2003. q. DKK 675 (effective 2009); DKK 210 per issue (effective 2008). adv. back issues avail. **Document type:** *Journal, Academic/Scholarly.*
Published by: Dansk Psykologisk Forlag/Danish Psychological Publishers, Kongevejen 155, Virum, 2830, Denmark. TEL 45-35-381655, FAX 45-35-381665, info@dpf.dk. Eds. Birgit Jung, Jacob B Theilgaard. adv.: B&W page DKK 3,000; 170 x 210.

150 USA ISSN 1088-2782
BJ68.E82
ESALEN CATALOG. Text in English. 1961. s-a. USD 15 domestic; USD 25 foreign (effective 2007). **Document type:** *Catalog.*
Related titles: Online - full text ed.: free.
Published by: Esalen Institute, 55000 Highway 1, Big Sur, CA 93920-9616. TEL 831-667-3000 ext 7100, 831-667-3000, info@esalen.org. Ed. Peter Friedberg. Circ: 25,000.

150 ESP ISSN 1989-3809
➤ **ESCRITOS DE PSICOLOGIA (ONLINE)/PSYCHOLOGICAL WRITINGS.** Text in Spanish, English; Summaries in Spanish, English. 1997. 3/yr. free (effective 2011). back issues avail. **Document type:** *Journal, Academic/Scholarly.*
Formerly (until 2009): Escritos de Psicologia (Print) (1138-2635)
Media: Online - full text.
Published by: Universidad de Malaga, Facultad de Psicologia, Campus Universitario de Teatinos, Malaga, 29071, Spain. TEL 34-95-2131332, aljibe@indico.com, http://www.uma.es/. Ed. Rosa Esteve.

150 GBR ISSN 0959-4779
ESSAYS IN COGNITIVE PSYCHOLOGY. Text in English. 1988. irreg., latest 2009. price varies. back issues avail. **Document type:** *Monographic series, Academic/Scholarly.* **Description:** Covers topics such as perception, movement and action, attention, memory, mental representation, language and problem solving.
Indexed: E-psyche.
Published by: Psychology Press (Subsidiary of: Taylor & Francis Ltd.), 27 Church Rd, Hove, E Sussex BN3 2FA, United Kingdom. TEL 44-20-70176000, FAX 44-20-70176717, info@psypress.co.uk. Eds. Alan Baddeley, Johnathan Grainge, Vicki Bruce.

150 GBR ISSN 0959-3977
ESSAYS IN DEVELOPMENTAL PSYCHOLOGY. Text in English. 1990. irreg., latest 2006. price varies. back issues avail. **Document type:** *Monographic series, Academic/Scholarly.* **Description:** Covers topics such as social development, cognitive development, developmental neuropsychology and neuroscience, language development, learning difficulties, developmental psychopathology and applied issues.
Indexed: E-psyche.
Published by: Psychology Press (Subsidiary of: Taylor & Francis Ltd.), 27 Church Rd, Hove, E Sussex BN3 2FA, United Kingdom. TEL 44-20-70176000, FAX 44-20-70176717, info@psypress.co.uk.

360.2 GBR ISSN 1367-5826
ESSAYS IN SOCIAL PSYCHOLOGY. Variant title: Essays in Social Psychology Series. Text in English. 1997 (Sep.). irreg., latest 2005. price varies. back issues avail. **Document type:** *Monographic series, Academic/Scholarly.* **Description:** Designed to meet the need for rapid publication of brief volumes in social psychology.
Published by: Psychology Press (Subsidiary of: Taylor & Francis Ltd.), 27 Church Rd, Hove, E Sussex BN3 2FA, United Kingdom. TEL 44-20-70176000, FAX 44-20-70176717, info@psypress.co.uk. Eds. Miles Hewstone, Monica Biernat.

150 FRA ISSN 1264-157X
ESSENTIALIS. Text in French. 1994. irreg. back issues avail. **Document type:** *Monographic series.*
Related titles: ◆ Series: Collection Mega Essentialis. ISSN 1778-6479.
Published by: Editions Bernet-Danilo, 42 Allee des Papillons, Meschers, 17132, France. TEL 33-5-46020707, FAX 33-5-46055530, editions@existence.fr.

158 FRA ISSN 1966-6187
L'ESSENTIEL DE LA PSYCHO. Text in French. 2008. q. EUR 38 (effective 2010). **Document type:** *Magazine, Consumer.*
Published by: Lafont Presse, 53 Rue du Chemin Vert, Boulogne-Billancourt, 92100, France. TEL 33-1-46102121, FAX 33-1-45792211, http://www.lafontpresse.fr.

150 ESP ISSN 1888-3893
ESTUDIOS DE GESTALT. Text in Spanish. 2007. s-a.
Published by: Mandala Ediciones, C Tarragona, 23, Madrid, 28045, Spain. TEL 34-91-4678528, FAX 34-91-4681501, info@mandalaedicones.com, http://www.mandalaediciones.com/.

ESTUDIOS DE PEDAGOGIA Y PSICOLOGIA. *see* EDUCATION

P

150 ESP ISSN 0210-9395
BF5
➤ **ESTUDIOS DE PSICOLOGIA.** Text in Spanish, English. 1980. 3/yr. EUR 75 to individuals; EUR 250 to institutions. adv. **Document type:** *Journal, Academic/Scholarly.* **Description:** Publishes empirical research, theoretical essays and bibliographic reviews in the field of current general psychology.
Related titles: Online - full text ed.: ISSN 1579-3699 (from IngentaConnect).
Indexed: A01, A03, A08, A22, CA, E-psyche, P03, PsycInfo, PsycholAb, RILM, SCOPUS, SSCI, T02, W07.
—IE, Infotrieve, Ingenta. **CCC.**
Published by: Fundacion Infancia y Aprendizaje, Naranjo de Bulnes 69, Ciudalcampo, San Sebastian de los Reyes, Madrid, 28707, Spain. fundacion@fia.es. Ed. Dr. Alberto Rosa. Circ: 1,100.

150 BRA ISSN 0103-166X
BF5
➤ **ESTUDOS DE PSICOLOGIA (CAMPINAS).** Text in Portuguese; Summaries in Portuguese. 1983. every 4 mos. BRL 40 domestic to individuals; BRL 50 domestic to institutions (effective 2006). bk.rev. 80 p./no.; back issues avail. **Document type:** *Journal, Academic/Scholarly.* **Description:** Provides current research and scientific communications for students and professionals in the fields of psychology and psychiatry.
Related titles: E-mail ed.; Online - full text ed.: free (effective 2011).
Indexed: A22, B21, C01, NSA, P03, PsycInfo, PsycholAb, S02, S03.
—BLDSC (3814.140000), IE, Ingenta.
Published by: Pontificia Universidade Catolica de Campinas, Departamento de Pos-Graduacao em Psicologia, Av John Boyd Dunlop, sin, Jd. Idausurama, Campinas, SP 1305-900, Brazil. TEL 55-19-37298674, FAX 55-19-37298532, revista@puc-campinas.edu.br, http://www.puc-campinas.edu.br/~ipf/revis/index.html. Ed. Marilda E Novaes Lipp.

150 BRA ISSN 1413-294X
BF5
ESTUDOS DE PSICOLOGIA (NATAL). Text in Portuguese. 1996. s-a. **Document type:** *Academic/Scholarly.*
Related titles: Online - full text ed.: ISSN 1678-4669.
Indexed: C01, P03, PsycInfo, PsycholAb, SCOPUS, SociolAb.
Published by: Universidade Federal do Rio Grande do Norte, Departamento de Psicologia, Caixa Postal 1524, Campus Universitario Lagos Nova, Natal, CEP 59072-970, Brazil. http://www.ufrn.br/.

150 BRA ISSN 1676-3041
ESTUDOS E PESQUISAS EM PSICOLOGIA. Text in Portuguese, Spanish. 2001. s-a. **Document type:** *Journal, Academic/Scholarly.*
Related titles: Online - full text ed.: ISSN 1808-4281. free (effective 2011).
Published by: Universidade do Estado do Rio de Janeiro, Instituto de Psicologia, Rua Sao Francisco Xavier 524,, Bloco F, Sala 10005. 3o Andar, Rio de Janeiro, 20550-013, Brazil. TEL 55-21-23340651, http://www.uerj.br.

301.1 150 ITA ISSN 0392-0658
RJ131
ETA EVOLUTIVA; rivista di scienze dello sviluppo. Text in Italian; Summaries in English. 1978. 3/yr. EUR 58 domestic (effective 2009). back issues avail. **Document type:** *Journal, Academic/Scholarly.* **Description:** Contains theoretical work and experimental research on the evolutive age, covering several areas of interest: psychology, sociology, pedagogy, genetics, and psychoanalysis.
Indexed: A22, BibInd, DIP, E-psyche, IBR, IBZ, P03, PsycInfo, PsycholAb, S02, S03.
—BLDSC (3814.194000), IE, Infotrieve, Ingenta.
Published by: Giunti Gruppo Editoriale SpA, Via Bolognese 165, Florence, 50139, Italy. TEL 39-055-5062376, FAX 39-055-5062397, informazioni@giunti.it, http://www.giunti.it. Ed. Bruno Piazzesi. Circ: 1,300.

370.15 150 USA ISSN 1050-8422
BJ1725
➤ **ETHICS & BEHAVIOR.** Text in English. 1991. bi-m. GBP 606 combined subscription in United Kingdom to institutions (print & online eds.); EUR 810, USD 1,012 combined subscription to institutions (print & online eds.) (effective 2012). adv. bk.rev. illus. back issues avail.; reprint service avail. from PSC. **Document type:** *Journal, Academic/Scholarly.* **Description:** Publishes articles on an array of topics pertaining to various moral issues and conduct.
Related titles: Online - full text ed.: ISSN 1532-7019. GBP 546 in United Kingdom to institutions; EUR 729, USD 911 to institutions (effective 2012).
Indexed: A01, A03, A08, A12, A13, A17, A20, A22, ABIn, ASCA, ASSIA, B07, C06, C07, C08, CA, CINAHL, CurCont, E-psyche, E01, ESPM, FamI, H14, L03, P02, P03, P10, P12, P24, P27, P28, P30, P34, P43, P48, P51, P53, P54, PAIS, PQC, PhilInd, PsycInfo, PsycholAb, RiskAb, S02, S03, SCOPUS, SSCI, SociolAb, T02, W07.
—BLDSC (3814.652500), IE, Infotrieve, Ingenta. **CCC.**
Published by: Routledge (Subsidiary of: Taylor & Francis Group), 325 Chestnut St, Ste 800, Philadelphia, PA 19106. TEL 800-354-1420, FAX 215-625-2940, journals@routledge.com, http://www.routledge.com. Ed. Gerald P Koocher. Adv. contact Linda Hann TEL 44-1344-779945.

150 610 DEU ISSN 1435-7909
ETHNOMEDIZIN UND BEWUSSTSEINSFORSCHUNG. Text in German. 1985. irreg., latest 2009. price varies. **Document type:** *Monographic series, Academic/Scholarly.*
Published by: V W B - Verlag fuer Wissenschaft und Bildung, Postfach 110368, Berlin, 10833, Germany. TEL 49-30-2510415, FAX 49-30-2511136, info@vwb-verlag.com.

150 610 DEU ISSN 1435-7917
ETHNOMEDIZIN UND BEWUSSTSEINSFORSCHUNG. HISTORISCHE MATERIALIEN. Text in German. 1986. irreg., latest vol.13, 1996. price varies. **Document type:** *Monographic series, Academic/Scholarly.*
Published by: V W B - Verlag fuer Wissenschaft und Bildung, Postfach 110368, Berlin, 10833, Germany. TEL 49-30-2510415, FAX 49-30-2511136, info@vwb-verlag.com.

155.82 DEU ISSN 0937-4523
ETHNOPSYCHOANALYSE. Text in German. 1990. irreg., latest vol.6, 2000. price varies. bk.rev. **Document type:** *Monographic series, Academic/Scholarly.*
Indexed: DIP, E-psyche, IBR, IBZ.
Published by: Brandes und Apsel Verlag GmbH, Scheidswaldstr 22, Frankfurt Am Main, 60385, Germany. TEL 49-69-272995170, FAX 49-69-2729951710, info@brandes-apsel-verlag.de, http://www.brandes-apsel-verlag.de.

155.8 FRA ISSN 1281-5578
ETHNOPSYCHOLOGIE. Text in French. 1997. irreg. back issues avail. **Document type:** *Monographic series, Consumer.*
Published by: E S F Editeur (Subsidiary of: Reed Business Information France), 2 rue Maurice Hartmann, Issy-les-Moulineaux, 92133 Cedex, France. TEL 33-1-46294629, FAX 33-1-46294633, info@esf-editeur.fr, http://www.esf-editeur.fr.

ETHOLOGY (ONLINE). *see* BIOLOGY—Zoology

ETHOLOGY (PRINT). *see* BIOLOGY—Zoology

155.937 306.9 FRA ISSN 1286-5702
ETUDES SUR LA MORT. Text in French. 1967. s-a. EUR 40 domestic; EUR 60 foreign (effective 2009). back issues avail. **Document type:** *Journal, Academic/Scholarly.*
Former titles (until 1997): Thanatologie (1157-0466); (until 1990): Societe de Thanatologie. Bulletin (0336-1586); (until 1971): Societe de Thanatologie de Langue Francaise. Bulletin (0339-9087)
Related titles: Online - full text ed.: ISSN 1961-8654.
Indexed: FR, SCOPUS.
—INIST. **CCC.**
Published by: (Societe de Thanatologie), Editions L' Esprit du Temps, 115 Rue Anatole France, B P 107, Le Bouscat, 33491 Cedex, France. TEL 33-5-56028419, FAX 33-5-56029131, info@lespritdutemps.com.

150 DEU ISSN 0531-7347
EUROPAEISCHE HOCHSCHULSCHRIFTEN. REIHE 6: PSYCHOLOGIE. Text in German. 1968. irreg., latest vol.761, 2010. price varies. **Document type:** *Monographic series, Academic/Scholarly.*
Indexed: CIS.
—**CCC.**
Published by: Peter Lang GmbH (Subsidiary of: Peter Lang Publishing Group), Eschborner Landstr 42-50, Frankfurt Am Main, 60489, Germany. TEL 49-69-7807050, FAX 49-69-78070550, zentrale.frankfurt@peterlang.com, http://www.peterlang.com.

616.8526 301.1 GBR ISSN 1072-4133
RC552.E18 CODEN: EEDRE8
➤ **EUROPEAN EATING DISORDERS REVIEW.** Text in English. 1986. bi-m. GBP 332 in United Kingdom to institutions; EUR 400 in Europe to institutions; USD 618 elsewhere to institutions; GBP 382 combined subscription in United Kingdom to institutions (print & online eds.); EUR 461 combined subscription in Europe to institutions (print & online eds.); USD 712 combined subscription elsewhere to institutions (print & online eds.) (effective 2012). adv. bk.rev. back issues avail.; reprint service avail. from PSC. **Document type:** *Journal, Academic/Scholarly.* **Description:** Covers all aspects of bulimia and anorexia nervosa for the complete range of professionals who deal with patients suffering from these eating disorders.
Former titles (until 1993): Eating Disorders Review (1067-1633); (until May.1993): British Review of Bulimia and Anorexia Nervosa (0950-3005)
Related titles: Microform ed.: (from PQC); Online - full text ed.: ISSN 1099-0968. GBP 332 in United Kingdom to institutions; EUR 400 in Europe to institutions; USD 618 elsewhere to institutions (effective 2012) (from IngentaConnect).
Indexed: A01, A02, A03, A08, A20, A36, ASCA, C06, C07, C08, CA, CABA, CINAHL, CurCont, E-psyche, EMBASE, ESPM, ExcerpMed, FamI, GH, LT, MEDLINE, N02, N03, P02, P03, P10, P12, P30, P43, P48, P53, P54, PEI, PQC, PsycInfo, PsycholAb, R10, R12, RRTA, Reac, RiskAb, SCOPUS, SSCI, T02, T05, W07, W11.
—GNLM, IE, Infotrieve, Ingenta. **CCC.**
Published by: (Eating Disorders Association), John Wiley & Sons Ltd. (Subsidiary of: John Wiley & Sons, Inc.), 1-7 Oldlands Way, PO Box 808, Bognor Regis, West Sussex PO21 9FF, United Kingdom. TEL 44-1865-778315, FAX 44-1243-843232, cs-journals@wiley.com, http://eu.wiley.com/WileyCDA/. Ed. Robert Palmer. **Subscr. in the Americas to:** John Wiley & Sons, Inc., 111 River St, Hoboken, NJ 07030. TEL 201-748-6645, subinfo@wiley.com; **Subscr. to:** 1-7 Oldlands Way, PO Box 809, Bognor Regis, West Sussex PO21 9FG, United Kingdom. TEL 44-1865-778054, cs-agency@wiley.com.

➤ **EUROPEAN JOURNAL OF AUTOGENIC AND BIONOMIC STUDIES.** *see* MEDICAL SCIENCES—Psychiatry And Neurology

150 NOR ISSN 1502-1149
➤ **EUROPEAN JOURNAL OF BEHAVIOR ANALYSIS.** Variant title: E J O B A. Text in English. 2000. s-a. NOK 100 (effective 2011). back issues avail. **Document type:** *Journal, Academic/Scholarly.*
Indexed: P30.
—BLDSC (3829.722650), IE, Ingenta.
Published by: Norsk Atferdsanalytisk Forening/Norwegian Association for Behaviour Analysis, P O Box 24, Sandefjord, 3209, Norway. TEL 47-33-806570, FAX 47-21-012449, service.nafo@atferd.no, http://www.atferd.no. Eds. Arne Brekstad, Erik Arntzen.

150 616.8 ITA ISSN 2035-2042
EUROPEAN JOURNAL OF CLINICAL PSYCHOLOGY AND PSYCHIATRY. Text in English. 2008. 3/yr. **Document type:** *Journal, Academic/Scholarly.*
Related titles: Online - full text ed.: ISSN 2035-2050.
Published by: Societa Italiana di Psicologia e Psichiatria, Via del Commercio 9, Fano, 61032, Italy. TEL 39-072-11796666, segreteria@sipsi.org, http://www.sipsi.org.

155 GBR ISSN 1740-5629
BF712
➤ **EUROPEAN JOURNAL OF DEVELOPMENTAL PSYCHOLOGY.** Text in English. 2004 (Mar.). bi-m. GBP 417 combined subscription in United Kingdom to institutions (print & online eds.); EUR 554, USD 695 combined subscription to institutions (print & online eds.) (effective 2012). back issues avail.; reprint service avail. from PSC. **Document type:** *Journal, Academic/Scholarly.* **Description:** Contains papers dealing with psychological development during infancy, childhood and adolescence.
Related titles: Online - full text ed.: ISSN 1740-5610. GBP 375 in United Kingdom to institutions; EUR 499, USD 625 to institutions (effective 2012) (from IngentaConnect).
Indexed: A01, A22, CA, CurCont, E01, E03, ERI, P03, P30, P48, PQC, PsycInfo, PsycholAb, SCOPUS, SSCI, T02, W07.
—BLDSC (3829.728282), IE, Ingenta, INIST. **CCC.**
Published by: Psychology Press (Subsidiary of: Taylor & Francis Ltd.), 27 Church Rd, Hove, E Sussex BN3 2FA, United Kingdom. TEL 44-20-70176000, FAX 44-20-70176717, info@psypress.co.uk, http://www.psypress.com. Ed. Willem Koops. Adv. contact Linda Hann TEL 44-1344-779945. **Subscr. to:** Journals Customer Service, Taylor & Francis Group, Rankine Rd, Basingstoke, Hants RG24 8PR, United Kingdom. TEL 44-1256-813002, FAX 44-1256-479438.

155 DEU ISSN 1863-3811
➤ **EUROPEAN JOURNAL OF DEVELOPMENTAL SCIENCE.** Text in English. 2007. q. EUR 59 to individuals; EUR 198 to institutions; EUR 19.90 newsstand/cover (effective 2010). adv. **Document type:** *Journal, Academic/Scholarly.* **Description:** Dedicated to the interdisciplinary study of human development.
Related titles: Online - full text ed.: ISSN 1863-382X. 2007.
Indexed: IBR, IBZ, P30, PsycInfo.
Published by: Vandenhoeck und Ruprecht, Theaterstr 13, Goettingen, 37073, Germany. TEL 49-551-508440, FAX 49-551-5084422, info@v-r.de.

150 GBR ISSN 2040-4204
▼ ➤ **EUROPEAN JOURNAL OF ECOPSYCHOLOGY.** Abbreviated title: E J E. Text in English. 2010. s-a. GBP 8 per issue to individuals; GBP 30 per issue to institutions (print or online ed.); GBP 10 combined subscription per issue to individuals (print & online eds.); GBP 32 combined subscription per issue to institutions (print & online eds.) (effective 2011). **Document type:** *Journal, Academic/Scholarly.* **Description:** Aims to promote discussion about the synthesis of psychological and ecological ideas.
Related titles: Online - full text ed.: GBP 6 per issue (effective 2011).
Address: c/o Paul Stevens, Poole House, Bournemouth University, Fern Barrow, Poole, BH12 5BB, United Kingdom. subscriptions@ecopsychology-journal.eu. Ed. Paul Stevens.

150 370 ESP ISSN 1888-8992
EUROPEAN JOURNAL OF EDUCATION AND PSYCHOLOGY. Text in English, Spanish. 2008. 3/yr. EUR 60 domestic to institutions; EUR 80 foreign to institutions (effective 2009). **Document type:** *Journal, Academic/Scholarly.*
Related titles: Online - full text ed.: ISSN 1989-2209. free (effective 2011).
Indexed: PsycInfo.
Published by: European Journal of Education and Psychology (E J E P), Ctra de Sacramento s/n, Almeria, 04120, Spain. Ed. Maria del Carmen Perez-Fuentes.

156 GBR ISSN 0890-2070
CODEN: FMPLAB
➤ **EUROPEAN JOURNAL OF PERSONALITY.** Text in English; Summaries in English, French, German. 1987. 8/yr. GBP 823 in United Kingdom to institutions; EUR 1,040 in Europe to institutions; USD 1,613 elsewhere to institutions; GBP 947 combined subscription in United Kingdom to institutions (print & online eds.); EUR 1,197 combined subscription in Europe to institutions (print & online eds.); USD 1,855 combined subscription elsewhere to institutions (print & online eds.) (effective 2012). bk.rev. back issues avail.; reprint service avail. from PSC. **Document type:** *Journal, Academic/Scholarly.* **Description:** Reflects all areas of current research in personality psychology with emphasis on human individuality.
Related titles: Microform ed.: (from PQC); Online - full text ed.: ISSN 1099-0984. GBP 823 in United Kingdom to institutions; EUR 1,040 in Europe to institutions; USD 1,613 elsewhere to institutions (effective 2012) (from IngentaConnect).
Indexed: A01, A02, A03, A08, A20, A22, ASCA, ASSIA, B21, BibInd, CA, CurCont, E-psyche, FamI, IBR, IBZ, L&LBA, NSA, P02, P03, P10, P12, P30, P43, P48, P53, P54, PQC, PsycInfo, PsycholAb, RefZh, S02, S03, SCOPUS, SOPODA, SSCI, SociolAb, T02, W07.
—IE, Infotrieve, Ingenta, INIST. **CCC.**
Published by: (European Association of Personality Psychology), John Wiley & Sons Ltd. (Subsidiary of: John Wiley & Sons, Inc.), 1-7 Oldlands Way, PO Box 808, Bognor Regis, West Sussex PO21 9FF, United Kingdom. TEL 44-1865-778315, FAX 44-1243-843232, cs-journals@wiley.com, http://eu.wiley.com/WileyCDA/. Ed. Marco Perugini. **Subscr. in the Americas to:** John Wiley & Sons, Inc., 111 River St, Hoboken, NJ 07030. TEL 201-748-6645, subinfo@wiley.com; **Subscr. to:** 1-7 Oldlands Way, PO Box 809, Bognor Regis, West Sussex PO21 9FG, United Kingdom. TEL 44-1865-778054, cs-agency@wiley.com.

152 USA ISSN 1015-5759
BF176 CODEN: EVRPBI
➤ **EUROPEAN JOURNAL OF PSYCHOLOGICAL ASSESSMENT.** Abbreviated title: E J P A. Text in English. 1985. q. USD 171, EUR 132 to individuals; USD 312, EUR 246 to institutions; USD 104, EUR 82 per issue; free to members (effective 2011). adv. bk.rev. abstr. 100 p./no. 2 cols./p.; back issues avail.; reprints avail. **Document type:** *Journal, Academic/Scholarly.* **Description:** Presents articles on theoretical as well as on practical subjects with regard to psychological assessment and is directed at bot researchers and practitioners.
Formerly (until 1992): Evaluacion Psicologica (0213-3695)
Related titles: Online - full text ed.: ISSN 2151-2426 (from ScienceDirect).
Indexed: A20, A22, AEI, ASCA, CA, CurCont, DIP, E-psyche, IBR, IBZ, P03, P30, PsycInfo, PsycholAb, SCOPUS, SSCI, T02, W07.
—BLDSC (3829.737800), IE, Infotrieve, Ingenta. **CCC.**
Published by: (European Association of Psychological Assessment), Hogrefe Publishing Corp., 875 Massachusetts Ave, 7th Fl, Cambridge, MA 02139. TEL 866-823-4726, FAX 617-354-6875, customerservices@hogrefe-publishing.com, http://www.hogrefe.com. Eds. Dr. Eric E J De Bruyn TEL 31-24-6312123, Dr. Karl Schweizer TEL 49-69-79822081. Adv. contact Gundula von Fintel. Circ: 800.

150 340 ESP ISSN 1889-1861
➤ **THE EUROPEAN JOURNAL OF PSYCHOLOGY APPLIED TO LEGAL CONTEXT.** Text in Multiple languages. 2008. s-a. **Document type:** *Journal, Academic/Scholarly.*
Related titles: Online - full text ed.: ISSN 1989-4007. free (effective 2011).
Indexed: A01, T02.
Published by: Sociedad Espanola de Psicologia Juridica y Forense, Facultad de Psicologia, Campus Universitario s/n, Santiago de Campostela, 15782, Spain. FAX 34-981-528071.

➤ **EUROPEAN JOURNAL OF PSYCHOLOGY OF EDUCATION/JOURNAL EUROPEEN DE PSYCHOLOGIE DE L'EDUCATION.** *see* EDUCATION

150 SWE ISSN 2000-8066
▼ ➤ **EUROPEAN JOURNAL OF PSYCHOTRAUMATOLOGY.** Text in English. 2010. irreg. free (effective 2011). **Document type:** *Journal, Academic/Scholarly.* **Description:** Aims to provide a forum for informative discourse about traumatic stress and its consequences.
Media: Online - full text. **Related titles:** Supplement(s): European Journal of Psychotraumatology. Supplement. ISSN 2000-818X.
Indexed: A01.
Published by: (European Society for Traumatic Stress Studies NLD), Co-Action Publishing, Ripvaegen 7, Jaerfaella, 17564, Sweden. TEL 46-18-4951150, FAX 46-18-4951138, info@co-action.net, http://www.co-action.net. Ed. Miranda Olff.

302 GBR ISSN 0046-2772
HM251 CODEN: EJSPA6
➤ **EUROPEAN JOURNAL OF SOCIAL PSYCHOLOGY.** Text in English. 1971. 7/yr. GBP 671 in United Kingdom to institutions; EUR 850 in Europe to institutions; USD 1,316 elsewhere to institutions; GBP 772 combined subscription in United Kingdom to institutions (print & online eds.); EUR 978 combined subscription in Europe to institutions (print & online eds.); USD 1,514 combined subscription elsewhere to institutions (print & online eds.) (effective 2012). adv. charts. back issues avail.; reprint service avail. from PSC. **Document type:** *Journal, Academic/Scholarly.* **Description:** Promotes communication among social psychology researchers in Europe and provides a bridge between European and other research traditions.
Related titles: Microform ed.: (from PQC); Online - full text ed.: ISSN 1099-0992. GBP 671 in United Kingdom to institutions; EUR 850 in Europe to institutions; USD 1,316 elsewhere to institutions (effective 2012).
Indexed: A01, A02, A03, A08, A20, A21, A22, AMHA, ASCA, ASSIA, BibInd, C06, C07, C08, CA, CINAHL, CommAb, CurCont, DIP, E-psyche, FR, FamI, IBR, IBSS, IBZ, MEA&I, MLA-IB, P02, P03, P10, P12, P30, P34, P43, P48, P53, P54, PCI, PQC, PsycInfo, PsycholAb, RI-1, RefZh, S02, S03, SCOPUS, SOPODA, SSA, SSCI, SociolAb, T02, W07.
—IE, Infotrieve, Ingenta, INIST. **CCC.**
Published by: (European Association of Experimental Social Psychology DEU), John Wiley & Sons Ltd. (Subsidiary of: John Wiley & Sons, Inc.), 1-7 Oldlands Way, PO Box 808, Bognor Regis, West Sussex PO21 9FF, United Kingdom. TEL 44-1865-778315, FAX 44-1243-843232, cs-journals@wiley.com, http://eu.wiley.com/WileyCDA/. Eds. Anne Maass, Russell Spears. **Subscr. to:** John Wiley & Sons, Inc., 111 River St, Hoboken, NJ 07030. subinfo@wiley.com; **Subscr. to:** 1-7 Oldlands Way, PO Box 809, Bognor Regis, West Sussex PO21 9FG, United Kingdom. TEL 44-1865-778054, cs-agency@wiley.com.

158.7 GBR ISSN 1359-432X
HF5548.7 CODEN: EJWPFV
➤ **EUROPEAN JOURNAL OF WORK AND ORGANIZATIONAL PSYCHOLOGY.** Text in English. 1991. bi-m. GBP 644 combined subscription in United Kingdom to institutions (print & online eds.); EUR 855, USD 1,073 combined subscription to institutions (print & online eds.) (effective 2012). bk.rev. abstr. back issues avail.; reprint service avail. from PSC. **Document type:** *Journal, Academic/Scholarly.* **Description:** Aims to act as a bridge between academies who enlarge the knowledge base of work psychology and practitioners who apply this knowledge to clients and organizations.
Formerly (until 1996): European Work and Organizational Psychologist (0960-2003)
Related titles: Online - full text ed.: ISSN 1464-0643. 1996. GBP 580 in United Kingdom to institutions; EUR 769, USD 966 to institutions (effective 2012) (from IngentaConnect).
Indexed: A12, A17, A22, ABIn, B01, B06, B07, B08, B09, B21, CA, CurCont, E-psyche, E01, ESPM, ErgAb, FR, H&SSA, P03, P25, P43, P48, P51, P53, P54, PQC, PsycInfo, PsycholAb, S02, S03, SCOPUS, SOPODA, SSCI, SociolAb, T02, W07.
—IE, Infotrieve, Ingenta, INIST. **CCC.**
Published by: (European Association of Work and Organizational Psychology), Psychology Press (Subsidiary of: Taylor & Francis Ltd.), 27 Church Rd, Hove, E Sussex BN3 2FA, United Kingdom. TEL 44-20-70176000, FAX 44-20-70176717, info@psypress.co.uk, http://www.psypress.com. Ed. Vicente Gonzalez-Roma. Adv. contact Linda Hann TEL 44-1344-779945.

301.15 GBR ISSN 0892-7286
EUROPEAN MONOGRAPHS IN SOCIAL PSYCHOLOGY. Text in English. 1971. irreg., latest 2007. price varies. back issues avail.; reprints avail. **Document type:** *Monographic series, Academic/Scholarly.* **Description:** Promotes the highest quality of writing in European social psychology, and provide an outlet for new research in the field.
Incorporates (1979-1985): European Studies in Social Psychology (0758-7554)
Indexed: E-psyche, PsycholAb.
Published by: (European Association of Experimental Social Psychology DEU), Psychology Press (Subsidiary of: Taylor & Francis Ltd.), 27 Church Rd, Hove, E Sussex BN3 2FA, United Kingdom. TEL 44-20-70176000, FAX 44-20-70176717, info@psypress.co.uk. Ed. Rupert Brown.

150 USA ISSN 1016-9040
BF1 CODEN: EUPSFE
➤ **EUROPEAN PSYCHOLOGIST.** Text in English. 1977. q. USD 178, EUR 138 to institutions; USD 59, EUR 46 per issue (effective 2011). adv. bk.rev. abstr.; tr.lit.; illus. 90 p./no. 2 cols./p.; back issues avail.; reprints avail. **Document type:** *Journal, Academic/Scholarly.* **Description:** Seeks to integrate across all specializations in psychology and to provide a general platform for communication and cooperation among psychologists throughout Europe and worldwide.
Formerly (until 1995): German Journal of Psychology (0705-5870)
Related titles: Online - full text ed.: ISSN 1878-531X (from ScienceDirect).
Indexed: A20, A22, ASSIA, CurCont, DIP, E-psyche, FR, IBR, IBZ, L&LBA, P03, P30, PCI, PsycInfo, PsycholAb, SCOPUS, SSCI, SociolAb, W07.
—BLDSC (3829.842730), IE, Infotrieve, Ingenta, INIST. **CCC.**
Published by: (European Federation of Professional Psychology Associations), Hogrefe Publishing Corp., 875 Massachusetts Ave, 7th Fl, Cambridge, MA 02139. TEL 866-823-4726, FAX 617-354-6875, publishing@hogrefe.com. Ed. Rainer K Silbereisen. adv.: B&W page USD 350; trim 210 x 277. Circ: 2,000.

150 DEU ISSN 1435-9464
EUROPEAN PSYCHOTHERAPY. Text in English. 2000. a. EUR 15 per issue (effective 2009). **Document type:** *Journal, Academic/Scholarly.*
Related titles: Online - full text ed.
Published by: C I P - Medien, Nymphenburger Str. 185, Munchen, D-80634, Germany. TEL 49-89-130793 ext 13, FAX 49-89-132133. Eds. Rainer Krause, Serge Sulz.

150 GBR ISSN 1479-277X
➤ **EUROPEAN REVIEW OF SOCIAL PSYCHOLOGY (ONLINE).** Abbreviated title: E R S P (Online). Text in English. 2003. irreg. GBP 146 in United Kingdom to institutions; EUR 179, USD 224 to institutions (effective 2012). a.index. back issues avail. **Document type:** *Journal, Academic/Scholarly.* **Description:** Contains review articles in the field of social psychology.
Media: Online - full text (from IngentaConnect). **Related titles:** ◆ Print ed.: European Review of Social Psychology (Print). ISSN 1046-3283.
—BLDSC (3829.953300). **CCC.**
Published by: (European Association for Experimental Social Psychology BEL), Psychology Press (Subsidiary of: Taylor & Francis Ltd.), 27 Church Rd, Hove, E Sussex BN3 2FA, United Kingdom. TEL 44-20-70176000, FAX 44-20-70176717, info@psypress.co.uk, http://www.psypress.com. Eds. Miles Hewstone, Wolfgang Stroebe. Adv. contact Linda Hann TEL 44-1344-779945.

301.1 150 GBR ISSN 1046-3283
HM251 CODEN: ERSPEW
➤ **EUROPEAN REVIEW OF SOCIAL PSYCHOLOGY (PRINT).** Abbreviated title: E R S P (Print). Text in English. 1990-199?; N.S. 2003. a. GBP 162 combined subscription in United Kingdom to institutions (print & online eds.); EUR 199, USD 249 combined subscription to institutions (print & online eds.) (effective 2012). back issues avail.; reprint service avail. from PSC. **Document type:** *Journal, Academic/Scholarly.* **Description:** Aims to reflect the dynamism of social psychology in Europe and the attention now paid to European ideas and research.
Related titles: ◆ Online - full text ed.: European Review of Social Psychology (Online). ISSN 1479-277X.
Indexed: A22, CA, CurCont, E01, P03, P46, P48, P54, PCI, PQC, PsycInfo, S02, S03, SCOPUS, SSCI, T02, W07.
—BLDSC (3829.953300), IE, Ingenta. **CCC.**
Published by: (European Association for Experimental Social Psychology BEL), Psychology Press (Subsidiary of: Taylor & Francis Ltd.), 27 Church Rd, Hove, E Sussex BN3 2FA, United Kingdom. TEL 44-20-70176000, FAX 44-20-70176717, info@psypress.co.uk, http://www.psypress.com. Eds. Miles Hewstone, Wolfgang Stroebe. Adv. contact Linda Hann TEL 44-1344-779945. **Subscr. to:** Taylor & Francis Ltd., Journals Customer Service, Sheepen Pl, Colchester, Essex CO3 3LP, United Kingdom. TEL 44-20-70175544, FAX 44-20-70175198, subscriptions@tandf.co.uk, http://www.tandf.co.uk/journals.

150 ROM ISSN 1841-0413
BF1
➤ **EUROPE'S JOURNAL OF PSYCHOLOGY.** Text in English. 2005. q. free (effective 2011). **Document type:** *Journal, Academic/Scholarly.*
Media: Online - full text.
Indexed: A01.
Published by: Universitatea din Bucuresti, Asociatia Studentilor, Bdul M Kogalnicenau 36-46, Sector 5, Bucharest, 050017, Romania. http://www.unibuc.ro. Ed. Vlad Glaveanu.

➤ **EVIDENCE - BASED MENTAL HEALTH;** an international digest of the evidence for mental health clinicians. *see* MEDICAL SCIENCES—Psychiatry And Neurology

155.6 USA ISSN 1935-5386
EVOKE; wellness through life review. Text in English. 2007 (May). bi-m. USD 27.50 (effective 2007). **Document type:** *Newsletter, Consumer.*
Published by: Elder Forest Publishing Group, PO Box 6368, South Bend, IN 46660-6368. TEL 800-428-0552, http://elderforestpublishing.com/index.html. Pub. Mark Bottita.

155 AUT ISSN 0938-2623
➤ **EVOLUTION AND COGNITION.** Text in English. 1991. s-a. EUR 40 (effective 2004). 100 p./no.; back issues avail. **Document type:** *Journal, Academic/Scholarly.* **Description:** Interdisciplinary forum devoted to all aspects of cognition, at both the animal and human level.
Related titles: Microfilm ed.: (from PQC).
Indexed: E-psyche, PhilInd.
—BLDSC (3834.210000), IE, Ingenta. **CCC.**
Published by: Konrad-Lorenz-Institut fuer Evolutions- und Kognitionsforschung, Adolf-Lorenz-Gasse 2, Altenberg, A-3422, Austria. TEL 43-2242-323900, FAX 43-2242-323904, sec@kli.ac.at, http://www.kli.ac.at. Eds. Manfred Wimmer, Rupert Riedl.

150 500 USA ISSN 1474-7049
BF698.95
➤ **EVOLUTIONARY PSYCHOLOGY;** an international journal of evolutionary approaches to psychology and behavior. Text in English. 2003. q. free (effective 2011). back issues avail. **Document type:** *Journal, Academic/Scholarly.* **Description:** Aims to foster communication between experimental and theoretical work, on the one hand, and historical, conceptual and interdisciplinary writings across the whole range of the biological and human sciences, on the other.
Media: Online - full text.
Indexed: A01, A20, A39, CA, CurCont, P03, PsycInfo, SCOPUS, SSCI, T02, W07.
Address: c/o Todd K. Shackelford, Dir., Evolutionary Psychology Laboratory, Oakland University, Department of Psychology, 112 Pryale Hall, Rochester, FL 48309. TEL 248-370-2285, FAX 248-370-4612, shackelf@oakland.edu.

➤ **EVOLVING WOMAN;** A Woman's Guide to Wholeness. *see* WOMEN'S INTERESTS

➤ **EXCEPTIONAL CHILDREN.** *see* EDUCATION—Special Education And Rehabilitation

➤ **EXISTENTIAL ANALYSIS.** *see* PHILOSOPHY

➤ **EXISTENZANALYSE.** *see* MEDICAL SCIENCES—Psychiatry And Neurology

150 ARG ISSN 1852-6519
▼ **EXORDIO;** el psicoanalisis en la cultura. Text in Spanish. 2009. bi-m. **Document type:** *Newsletter, Consumer.*
Published by: Centro de Investigacion y Estudios Clinicos, Mariano Moreno 36-38, Cordoba, Argentina. TEL 54-351-4253159, fundacionciec@arnelbiz.com.ar, http://www.cieccordoba.com.ar/. Ed. Ana Gallegos.

612.67 USA ISSN 0361-073X
QP86 CODEN: EAGRDS
➤ **EXPERIMENTAL AGING RESEARCH.** Text in English. 1975. q. GBP 492 combined subscription in United Kingdom to institutions (print & online eds.); EUR 647, USD 813 combined subscription to institutions (print & online eds.) (effective 2012). adv. bk.rev. illus. index. back issues avail.; reprint service avail. from PSC. **Document type:** *Journal, Academic/Scholarly.* **Description:** Contains scientific papers dealing with age differences and age changes at any point in the adult life span.
Related titles: Microform ed.: (from PQC); Online - full text ed.: ISSN 1096-4657. GBP 443 in United Kingdom to institutions; EUR 582, USD 732 to institutions (effective 2012) (from IngentaConnect).
Indexed: A01, A02, A03, A08, A20, A22, ASCA, ASG, AgeL, B21, B25, BIOBASE, BIOSIS Prev, C06, C07, C08, C11, CA, CINAHL, CIS, ChemAb, CurCont, E-psyche, E01, EMBASE, ErgAb, ExcerpMed, FR, FamI, H04, IABS, ISR, IndMed, Inpharma, L&LBA, MEDLINE, MycolAb, NRN, NSA, P03, P10, P30, P43, P48, P53, P54, PQC, PsycInfo, PsycholAb, R10, Reac, S02, S03, SCI, SCOPUS, T02, W07.
—CASDDS, GNLM, IE, Infotrieve, Ingenta, INIST. **CCC.**
Published by: Taylor & Francis Inc. (Subsidiary of: Taylor & Francis Group), 325 Chestnut St, Ste 800, Philadelphia, PA 19106. TEL 215-625-2940, 800-354-1420, orders@taylorandfrancis.com, http://www.taylorandfrancis.com. Ed. Jeffrey W Elias.

150 615 USA ISSN 1064-1297
RM315 CODEN: ECLPES
➤ **EXPERIMENTAL AND CLINICAL PSYCHOPHARMACOLOGY.** Text in English. 1993. bi-m. USD 167 domestic to individuals; USD 199 foreign to individuals; USD 522 domestic to institutions; USD 579 foreign to institutions (effective 2011). adv. back issues avail.; reprint service avail. from PSC. **Document type:** *Journal, Academic/Scholarly.* **Description:** Advances research and development of theory in psychopharmacology.
Related titles: Online - full text ed.: ISSN 1936-2293 (from ScienceDirect).
Indexed: A22, AddicA, B25, BIOSIS Prev, C06, C07, CIN, ChemAb, ChemTitl, E-psyche, EMBASE, ExcerpMed, FoP, IndMed, MEDLINE, MycolAb, NSCI, P03, P30, PsycInfo, PsycholAb, R10, Reac, SCI, SCOPUS, SSCI, W07.
—BLDSC (3838.654000), GNLM, IE, Infotrieve, Ingenta. **CCC.**
Published by: American Psychological Association, 750 First St, NE, Washington, DC 20002. TEL 202-336-5500, 800-374-2721, journals@apa.org. Ed. Suzette M Evans. Adv. contact Doug Constant TEL 202-336-5574. Circ: 600.

152 USA ISSN 1618-3169
BF3 CODEN: EOTTAO
➤ **EXPERIMENTAL PSYCHOLOGY.** Text in English. 1953. bi-m. USD 366, EUR 284 to institutions; USD 73, EUR 57 per issue (effective 2011). adv. bk.rev. bibl.; charts; illus. 80 p./no. 2 cols./p.; **Document type:** *Journal, Academic/Scholarly.* **Description:** Covers experimental research in psychology. Includes occasional theoretical and review articles.
Former titles (until 2002): Zeitschrift fuer Experimentelle Psychologie (0949-3964); (until 1994): Zeitschrift fuer Experimentelle und Angewandte Psychologie (0044-2712)
Related titles: Online - full text ed.: ISSN 2190-5142 (from ScienceDirect).
Indexed: A20, ASCA, B21, BibInd, CIS, CMCI, CurCont, DIP, E-psyche, EMBASE, ExcerpMed, GJP, IBR, IBZ, IndMed, L&LBA, MEDLINE, NSA, P03, P30, PCI, PsycInfo, PsycholAb, R10, RASB, RILM, Reac, S02, S03, SCOPUS, SSCI, SociolAb, W07.
—BLDSC (3840.092000), GNLM, IE, Infotrieve, INIST. **CCC.**
Published by: Hogrefe Publishing Corp., 875 Massachusetts Ave, 7th Fl, Cambridge, MA 02139. TEL 866-823-4726, FAX 617-354-6875, customservices@hogrefe-publishing.com, http://www.hogrefe.com. Ed. Edgar Erdfelder. Circ: 800 (paid).

150 USA ISSN 1092-0803
BF11
EYE ON PSI CHI. Text in English. 1934. q. USD 15 to non-members; USD 4 per issue to non-members; free to members (effective 2011). **Document type:** *Journal, Academic/Scholarly.*
Formerly (until 1996): Psi Chi Newsletter (0033-2569)
Indexed: E-psyche.
Published by: Psi Chi - The National Honor Society in Psychology, PO Box 709, Chattanooga, TN 37401. TEL 423-756-2044, FAX 877-774-2443, psichi@psichi.org. Circ: 27,000.

153.1 347.91 USA ISSN 1069-0484
RC455.2.F35
F M S FOUNDATION NEWSLETTER. (False Memory Syndrome) Text in English. 1992. 6/yr. USD 30 domestic; USD 35 in Canada; USD 40 elsewhere; USD 15 domestic to students; USD 20 foreign to students (effective 2000). bk.rev. bibl. **Document type:** *Newsletter.* **Description:** Reviews news events, including legal cases involving persons with recovered or repressed memories.
Indexed: E-psyche.
Published by: The False Memory Syndrome Foundation, 1955 Locust Street, Philadelphia, PA 19103-5766. TEL 215-940-1040, FAX 215-940-1042, mail@fmsfonline.org, http://www.memoryandreality.org. Circ: 4,000 (paid).

FACTA UNIVERSITATIS. SERIES PHILOSOPHY, SOCIOLOGY AND PSYCHOLOGY. *see* PHILOSOPHY

FALLING LEAF. *see* MILITARY

306.85 ESP ISSN 2171-8105
▼ **FAMILIA Y PERSONA.** Text in Spanish. 2010. s-a. back issues avail. **Document type:** *Journal, Academic/Scholarly.*
Media: Online - full text.
Published by: Universidad de Malaga, Facultad de Filosofia y Letras, Campus de Teatinos, Malaga, 29071, Spain. candrade@uma.es, http://www.uma.es.

306.85 ESP ISSN 2013-2565
▼ **FAMILIAS SIGLO XXI.** Text in Spanish. 2010. s-a. **Document type:** *Magazine, Consumer.*

Published by: Ediciones Noufront, Santa Joaquina Vedruna, 7 Bajos, Valls, Taragona, 43800, Spain. TEL 34-977-606584, info@edicionesnoufront.com, http://www.edicionesnoufront.com/.

306.85 DEU ISSN 0342-2747
CODEN: FDYNF4

FAMILIENDYNAMIK; Interdisziplinaere Zeitschrift fuer systemorientierte Praxis und Forschung. Text in German. 1976. q. EUR 78; EUR 50 to students; EUR 22 newsstand/cover (effective 2011). adv. abstr.; bibl. 100 p./no.; back issues avail. **Document type:** *Journal, Academic/Scholarly.*
Indexed: DIP, E-psyche, IBR, IBZ, P03, PsycInfo, PsycholAb, SCOPUS.
—GNLM. **CCC.**
Published by: Verlag Klett-Cotta, Rotebuehlstr 77, Stuttgart, 70178, Germany. TEL 49-711-66720, FAX 49-711-66722030, info@klett-cotta.de, http://www.klett-cotta.de. Adv. contact Friederike Kamann. Circ: 3,500 (paid and controlled).

FAMILIENMAGAZIN. *see* CHILDREN AND YOUTH—About

150 306.8 USA ISSN 1066-4807
RC488.5

➤ **THE FAMILY JOURNAL**; counseling and therapy for couples and families. Text in English. 1993. q. USD 765, GBP 450 combined subscription to institutions (print & online eds.); USD 750, GBP 441 to institutions (effective 2011). adv. reprint service avail. from PSC. **Document type:** *Journal, Academic/Scholarly.* **Description:** Emphasizes practical information based on the most up-to-date research and therapies on marriage and family counseling.
Related titles: Online - full text ed.: ISSN 1552-3950. USD 689, GBP 405 to institutions (effective 2011).
Indexed: A01, A02, A03, A08, A22, ASSIA, B07, C06, C07, CA, CJA, CMM, E-psyche, E01, E03, ERI, ERIC, ESPM, F09, FamI, G10, H04, P03, P04, P10, P12, P25, P30, P48, P53, P54, PQC, PsycInfo, PsycholAb, RiskAb, S02, S03, SCOPUS, SFSA, SSA, SWR&A, SociolAb, T02, V02, W09.
—BLDSC (3865.564279), IE, Infotrieve, Ingenta. **CCC.**
Published by: (International Association of Marriage and Family Counselors), Sage Publications, Inc., 2455 Teller Rd, Thousand Oaks, CA 91320. TEL 805-499-9774, 800-818-7243, FAX 805-499-0871, 800-583-2665, info@sagepub.com. Ed. Kaye W Nelson. Circ: 7,000. **Subscr. outside the Americas to:** Sage Publications Ltd., 1 Oliver's Yard, 55 City Rd, London EC1Y 1SP, United Kingdom. TEL 44-20-73248701, FAX 44-20-73248733, subscription@sagepub.co.uk.

306.85 USA ISSN 0014-7370
RC488.5.A1 CODEN: FAPRA

➤ **FAMILY PROCESS.** Text in English. 1962. q. GBP 333 combined subscription in United Kingdom to institutions (print & online eds.); EUR 381 combined subscription in Europe to institutions (print & online eds.); USD 461 combined subscription in the Americas to institutions (print & online eds.); USD 652 combined subscription elsewhere to institutions (print & online eds.) (effective 2012). adv. bk.rev. abstr.; bibl.; charts; illus. index. 128 p./no.; back issues avail.; reprint service avail. from PSC. **Document type:** *Journal, Academic/Scholarly.* **Description:** Covers family mental health and psychotherapy.
Related titles: CD-ROM ed.: USD 99 to individuals; USD 199 to institutions (effective 2000); Online - full text ed.: ISSN 1545-5300. GBP 305 in United Kingdom to institutions; EUR 362 in Europe to institutions; USD 418 in the Americas to institutions; USD 594 elsewhere to institutions (effective 2012) (from IngentaConnect).
Indexed: A01, A02, A03, A08, A20, A22, A26, AMHA, ASCA, C06, C07, C08, C11, CA, CINAHL, CommAb, CurCont, DIP, E-psyche, E01, E07, E08, EMBASE, ESPM, ExcerpMed, F09, FR, FamI, G06, G07, G08, H04, H11, H12, I05, IBR, IBZ, INI, IndMed, MEA&I, MEDLINE, P03, P10, P12, P13, P19, P20, P22, P24, P25, P30, P43, P46, P48, P50, P53, P54, PC&CA, PQC, PsycInfo, PsycholAb, RASB, RiskAb, S02, S03, S09, S21, S23, SCOPUS, SFSA, SOPODA, SSA, SSCI, SWR&A, SociolAb, T02, V&AA, W07.
—BLDSC (3865.576000), GNLM, IE, Infotrieve, Ingenta, INIST. **CCC.**
Published by: (Family Process, Inc.), Wiley-Blackwell Publishing, Inc. (Subsidiary of: Wiley-Blackwell Publishing Ltd.), 111 River St, Hoboken, NJ 07030. TEL 201-748-6000, FAX 201-748-6088, info@wiley.com, http://www.wiley.com/WileyCDA/. Ed. Evan Imber-Black. Adv. contact Kristin McCarthy TEL 201-748-7683. B&W page USD 350; trim 6.75 x 10. Circ: 2,061 (paid).

306.85 USA ISSN 1538-9448
HQ1

FAMILY THERAPY MAGAZINE. Text in English. 1969. bi-m. USD 10 newsstand/cover (effective 2011). adv. reprints avail. **Document type:** *Newsletter, Consumer.*
Former titles (until 2002): Family Therapy News (0277-6464); (until 198?): American Association for Marriage and Family Therapy Newsletter (0273-575X)
Indexed: E-psyche, S02, S03.
—**CCC.**
Published by: American Association for Marriage and Family Therapy, 112 S Alfred St, Alexandria, VA 22314. http://www.aamft.org. Eds. Karen Gautney, Michael Bowers. adv.: B&W page USD 1,400. Circ: 21,000.

▼ **FAR EAST JOURNAL OF PSYCHOLOGY AND BUSINESS.** *see* BUSINESS AND ECONOMICS

158.0 USA ISSN 1949-9175

FEEL FREE TO PROSPER. Text in English. 2006. w. free (effective 2009). **Document type:** *Magazine, Trade.* **Description:** Features articles that provide life-changing wisdom, intriguing articles and valuable information.
Media: Online - full content.
Published by: Marilyn Jenett, Pub. marilyn@feelfreetoprosper.com.

150 TWN

FEICHANG XILIE XINLI CEYAN. Text in English. 2000. m. TWD 88 newsstand/cover (effective 2001). **Document type:** *Magazine, Consumer.* **Description:** Contains monthly psychological and personality tests on love, stress,.
Published by: Jianduan Chuban Qufen Youxian Gongsi/Sharp Point Publishing Ltd., Inc., 231 Xindiansi, Fuyu-Lu 43-Hao 8-Lou, Taipei, Taiwan. TEL 886-2-2218-1582, FAX 886-2-2218-1583, janey@spp.com.tw, http://www.spp.com.tw/.

150 305.4 GBR ISSN 0959-3535
HQ1206 CODEN: FEPSFF

➤ **FEMINISM & PSYCHOLOGY**; an international journal. Abbreviated title: F & P. Text in English. 1991. q. USD 930, GBP 502 combined subscription to institutions (print & online eds.); USD 911, GBP 492 to institutions (effective 2011). adv. bk.rev. illus. back issues avail.; reprint service avail. from PSC. **Document type:** *Journal, Academic/Scholarly.* **Description:** Fosters the development of feminist theory and practice in psychology and represents the concerns of women in a wide range of contexts across the academic-applied 'divide'.
Related titles: Online - full text ed.: ISSN 1461-7161. USD 837, GBP 452 to institutions (effective 2011).
Indexed: A01, A02, A03, A08, A20, A22, ASCA, ASSIA, B07, C06, C07, C08, CA, CINAHL, CurCont, DIP, E-psyche, E01, FamI, FemPer, G10, H04, IBR, IBSS, IBZ, P02, P03, P10, P12, P25, P30, P42, P48, P53, P54, PQC, PSA, PsycInfo, PsycholAb, S02, S03, SCOPUS, SOPODA, SSA, SSCI, SociolAb, T02, V&AA, V02, W07, W09, WSA.
—BLDSC (3905.195980), IE, Infotrieve, Ingenta. **CCC.**
Published by: Sage Publications Ltd. (Subsidiary of: Sage Publications, Inc.), 1 Oliver's Yard, 55 City Rd, London, EC1Y 1SP, United Kingdom. TEL 44-20-73248500, FAX 44-20-73248600, info@sagepub.co.uk, http://www.uk.sagepub.com/home.nav. Eds. Nicola Gavey, Virginia Braun. adv.: B&W page GBP 400; 130 x 205. **Subscr. in the Americas to:** Sage Publications, Inc., 2455 Teller Rd, Thousand Oaks, CA 91320. TEL 805-499-9774, FAX 805-499-0871, journals@sagepub.com.

▼ ➤ **FIGLI FELICI.** *see* CHILDREN AND YOUTH—About

150 BEL

FIGURES OF THE UNCONSCIOUS. Text in Multiple languages. 1998. irreg. price varies. **Document type:** *Academic/Scholarly.*
Published by: Leuven University Press, Blijde Inkomststraat 5, Leuven, 3000, Belgium. TEL 32-16-325345, FAX 32-16-325352, university.press@upers.kuleuven.ac.be, http://www.kuleuven.ac.be/upers.

FILOZOFSKI FAKULTET - ZADAR. RAZDIO FILOZOFIJE, PSIHOLOGIJE, SOCIOLOGIJE I PEDAGOGIJE. RADOVI. *see* EDUCATION

158 USA ISSN 2154-1051

THE FINDING TIME E-ZINE. Text in English. 2006. m. **Document type:** *Magazine, Consumer.* **Description:** Advice and tips on time management for busy people.
Media: Online - full text.
Published by: Finding Time, LLC, PO Box 157, Francestown, NH 03043. TEL 603-547-6696, paula@thetimefinder.com.

FOCUS GROUP KIT. *see* TECHNOLOGY: COMPREHENSIVE WORKS

301.1 150 ITA ISSN 1973-9206

FOGLI DI INFORMAZIONE. Text in Italian; Summaries in English. 1972. 3/yr. USD 30 domestic to individuals; USD 40 domestic to institutions; USD 60 foreign (effective 2008). **Document type:** *Journal, Academic/Scholarly.*
Former titles (until 2006): Fogli di informazione. Documenti e Ricerche per l'Elaborazione di Pratiche Alternative in Campo Psichiatrico e Istituzionale (0393-5418); (until 1980): Fogli di informazione. Documenti di Collegamento e di Verifica per l'Elaborazione di Prassi Alternative nel Campo Istituzionale (1125-078X)
Indexed: E-psyche.
Published by: Associazione Centro Documentazione di Pistoia, Via Pertini, Pistoia, PT 51100, Italy. http://www.centrodocpistoia.it.

FORENSISCHE PSYCHIATRIE, PSYCHOLOGIE, KRIMINOLOGIE. *see* MEDICAL SCIENCES—Psychiatry And Neurology

FORENSISCHE PSYCHIATRIE UND PSYCHOTHERAPIE. *see* MEDICAL SCIENCES—Psychiatry And Neurology

▼ **FORSCHUNGSBERICHTE ARBEITSWISSENSCHAFT, ARBEITSPSYCHOLOGIE.** *see* BUSINESS AND ECONOMICS

150 DEU ISSN 1435-778X

FORSCHUNGSBERICHTE ZUR TRANSKULTURELLEN MEDIZIN UND PSYCHOTHERAPIE. Text in German. 1995. irreg., latest vol.5, 2000. price varies. **Document type:** *Monographic series, Academic/Scholarly.*
Published by: V W B - Verlag fuer Wissenschaft und Bildung, Postfach 110368, Berlin, 10833, Germany. TEL 49-30-2510415, FAX 49-30-2511136, info@vwb-verlag.com.

155.3 DEU ISSN 1435-6783

FORSCHUNGSERGEBNISSE ZUR SEXUALPSYCHOLOGIE. Text in German. 1992. irreg., latest vol.8, 1998. price varies. **Document type:** *Monographic series, Academic/Scholarly.*
Published by: Verlag Dr. Kovac, Leverkusenstr 13, Hamburg, 22761, Germany. TEL 49-40-3988800, FAX 49-40-39888055, info@verlagdrkovac.de.

150 DEU ISSN 1869-6694

▼ **FORSCHUNGSZENTRUMS FUER VERGLEICHENDE GRAPHOLOGIE, FRIAUL- JULISCH VENETIEN. SCHRIFTENREIHE.** Text in German. 2010. irreg., latest vol.3, 2010. price varies. **Document type:** *Monographic series, Academic/Scholarly.*
Published by: Centaurus Verlag & Media KG, Kaiser-Joseph-Str 267, Freiburg, 79098, Germany. TEL 49-761-1525861, FAX 49-761-1525868, info@centaurus-verlag.de, http://www.centaurus-verlag.de.

150.19 DEU ISSN 0178-7667
BF173.A2

➤ **FORUM DER PSYCHOANALYSE**; Zeitschrift fuer klinische Theorie und Praxis. Text in German. 1985. q. EUR 219, USD 244 combined subscription to institutions (print & online eds.) (effective 2012). adv. back issues avail.; reprint service avail. from PSC. **Document type:** *Journal, Academic/Scholarly.* **Description:** Journal for the clinical theory and practice of psychoanalysis.
Related titles: Microform ed.: (from PQC); Online - full text ed.: ISSN 1437-0751 (from IngentaConnect).
Indexed: A20, A22, A26, ASCA, CA, CurCont, DIP, E-psyche, E01, I05, IBR, IBZ, P03, P25, P26, P48, PQC, PsycInfo, PsycholAb, SCOPUS, SSCI, T02, W07.
—BLDSC (4024.098000), GNLM, IE, Infotrieve, Ingenta, INIST. **CCC.**
Published by: Springer (Subsidiary of: Springer Science+Business Media), Tiergartenstr 17, Heidelberg, 69121, Germany. TEL 49-6221-4870, FAX 49-6221-345229. Eds. Dr. C Nedelmann, Dr. J Koerner, Dr. M Ermann. Adv. contact Stephan Kroeck TEL 49-30-827875739. Circ: 2,250 (paid and controlled). **Subscr. in the Americas to:** Springer New York LLC, Journal Fulfillment, PO Box 2485, Secaucus, NJ 07096. TEL 800-777-4643, 201-348-4033, FAX 201-348-4505, journals-ny@springer.com, http://www.springer.com; **Subscr. to:** Springer Distribution Center, Kundenservice Zeitschriften, Haberstr 7, Heidelberg 69126, Germany. TEL 49-6221-3454303, FAX 49-6221-3454229, subscriptions@springer.com.

159.9 DEU

FORUM GEMEINDEPSYCHOLOGIE. Text in German. 1995. 3/yr.
Formerly (until 2007): Gemeindepsychologie-Rundbrief (1430-094X)
Media: Online - full content.
Published by: (Gesellschaft fuer Gemeindepsychologische Forschung und Praxis e.V.), Pabst Science Publishers, Am Eichengrund 28, Lengerich, 49525, Germany. TEL 49-5484-97234, FAX 49-5484-550, pabst@pabst-publishers.com, http://www.pabst-publishers.de.

156 DEU ISSN 0720-0447
BF3

FORUM KRITISCHE PSYCHOLOGIE. Text in German. 1978. s-a. EUR 26; EUR 13 newsstand/cover (effective 2008). adv. back issues avail. **Document type:** *Journal, Academic/Scholarly.*
Indexed: E-psyche.
Published by: Argument-Verlag GmbH, Glashuettenstr 28, Hamburg, 20357, Germany. TEL 49-40-4018000, FAX 49-40-40180020, verlag@argument.de, http://www.argument.de. Ed. Klaus Holzkamp. adv.: B&W page EUR 300. Circ: 425 (paid and controlled).

FOSTERING OUR FUTURE; newsletter for foster carers. *see* SOCIAL SERVICES AND WELFARE

FOUNDATIONS AND TRENDS IN HUMAN-COMPUTER INTERACTION. *see* COMPUTERS

150 BRA ISSN 1984-0292

FRACTAL. REVISTA DE PSICOLOGIA. Text in Portuguese. 2005. irreg. free (effective 2011). **Document type:** *Journal, Academic/Scholarly.*
Formerly (until 2008): U F F. Departamento de Psicologia. Revista (Online) (1980-5489)
Media: Online - full text.
Published by: Universidade Federal Fluminense, Departamento de Psicologia, Campus do Gragoata, Bl O, Sala 334, Niteroi, 24210-350, Brazil. TEL 55-21-26292845. Eds. Marcelo Santana Ferreira, Teresa Cristina Othenio Cordeiro Carreteiro.

158.1 DEU

FREIE ASSOZIATION; Zeitschrift fuer das Unbewusste in Organisation und Kultur. Text in German. q. EUR 17.50 newsstand/cover (effective 2003). **Document type:** *Journal, Academic/Scholarly.*
Published by: Psychosozial Verlag, Walltorstr 10, Giessen, 35390, Germany. TEL 49-641-77819, FAX 49-641-77742, info@psychosozial-verlag.de, http://www.psychosozial-verlag.de.

FREUDIANA. *see* MEDICAL SCIENCES—Psychiatry And Neurology

155 USA ISSN 1089-4365

FROM ANIMALS TO ANIMATS. Text in English. 1991. biennial. price varies. back issues avail. **Document type:** *Proceedings, Academic/Scholarly.* **Description:** Covers the International Conference on Simulation of Adaptive Behavior, including researchers from ethology, psychology, ecology, artificial intelligence, artificial life, robotics, computer science, engineering, and related fields to further understanding of the behaviors and underlying mechanisms that allow adaptation and survival in uncertain environments.
—BLDSC (4040.601800).
Published by: (International Conference on Simulation of Adaptive Behavior GBR), M I T Press, 55 Hayward St, Cambridge, MA 02142. TEL 617-253-5646, FAX 617-258-6779, journals-info@mit.edu, http://mitpress.mit.edu.

155.937 CAN ISSN 1180-3479
HQ1073 CODEN: FRONFI

FRONTIERES; revue quebecoise en etudes sur la mort. Text in English. 1988. 3/yr. adv. bk.rev.; film rev. bibl.; illus.; stat. back issues avail. **Document type:** *Journal, Academic/Scholarly.* **Description:** Discusses death and grieving for professionals and volunteers in the health services.
Related titles: Online - full text ed.: ISSN 1916-0976.
Indexed: CA, E-psyche, FR, PdeR, S02, S03, SSA, SociolAb, T02.
—INIST.
Published by: Universite du Quebec a Montreal, Service des Publications, Succ Centre Ville, C P 8888, Montreal, PQ H3C 3P8, Canada. TEL 514-987-8537, FAX 514-987-0307, frontier@er.uqam.ca. Ed. Diane Laflamme.

150 CHE ISSN 1664-1078

▼ **FRONTIERS IN PSYCHOLOGY.** Text in English. 2010. irreg. free (effective 2011). **Document type:** *Journal, Academic/Scholarly.*
Media: Online - full text.
Indexed: P30.
Published by: Frontiers Research Foundation, Science Park PSE-A, Lausanne, 1015, Switzerland. TEL 41-21-6939202, FAX 41-21-6939201, info@frontiersin.org, http://frontiersin.org. Ed. Axel Cleeremans.

FUKUOKA KYOIKU DAIGAKU KIYO. DAI 4-BUNSATSU, KYOSHOKUKA-HEN/FUKUOKA UNIVERSITY OF EDUCATION. BULLETIN. PART 4, EDUCATION AND PSYCHOLOGY. *see* EDUCATION

150 USA ISSN 1555-2454

FUNDAMENTAL CHANGE. Text in English. 2005. m. free (effective 2007). **Document type:** *Newsletter, Consumer.*
Media: Online - full text.
Published by: Roger Schwarz & Associates, Inc., 600 Market St. Ste 207, Chapel Hill, NC 27516. TEL 919-932-3343, FAX 919-932-3346, info@schwarzassociates.com, http://www.schwarzassociates.com/facilitator/2/Home.

150 ARG ISSN 1515-4467

FUNDAMENTOS EN HUMANIDADES. Text in Spanish. 2000. s-a. ARS 20 (effective 2010). back issues avail. **Document type:** *Journal, Academic/Scholarly.*
Related titles: Online - full text ed.: ISSN 1668-7116. free (effective 2011).
Indexed: A01, A26, CA, F03, F04, I04, I05, T02.
Published by: Universidad Nacional de San Luis, Facultad de Ciencias Humanas, Avenida Ejercito de los Andes 950, IV Bloque, San Luis, 5700, Argentina. TEL 54-652-435512. Circ: 300.

G L C S INK. (Gay and Lesbian Counselling Service) *see* HOMOSEXUALITY

G N I F BRAIN BLOGGER; topics from multidimensional biopsychosocial perspectives. (Global Neuroscience Initiative Foundation) *see* BIOLOGY

G R A P P A F. CAHIERS. (Groupe de Recherche et d'Application des Concepts Psychanalytiques a la Psychiatrie en Afrique Franc) *see* MEDICAL SCIENCES—Psychiatry And Neurology

150 NLD ISSN 1879-5080
▼ **G Z - PSYCHOLOGIE.** Text in Dutch. 2009. 8/yr. adv. **Document type:** *Journal, Trade.*
Related titles: Online - full text ed.: ISSN 1879-5099.
Published by: Benecke, Arena Boulevard 61-75, Amsterdam, 1101 DL, Netherlands. TEL 31-20-7150600, FAX 31-20-6918446, http://www.benecke.nl. Ed. Dr. Jan Derksen.

616.890 AUS ISSN 1832-4975
➤ **GAMBLING RESEARCH.** Text in English. 19??. s-a. free to members (effective 2010). back issues avail. **Document type:** *Journal, Academic/Scholarly.* **Description:** Provides information on gambling and its related issues.
Former titles (until 2003): National Association for Gambling Studies. Journal; (until 1996): National Association for Gambling Studies. Newsletter
Related titles: Online - full text ed.
—BLDSC (4068.573500).
Published by: National Association for Gambling Studies, c/o School of Psychology, University of Adelaide, Adelaide, SA 5005, Australia. TEL 61-8-3034936, FAX 61-8-83033770, nags@nags.org.au. Ed. Paul Delfabbro.

301.1 150 510 USA ISSN 0899-8256
QA269 CODEN: GEBEEF
➤ **GAMES AND ECONOMIC BEHAVIOR.** Text in English. 1989. bi-m. EUR 1,241 in Europe to institutions; JPY 129,700 in Japan to institutions; USD 982 elsewhere to institutions (effective 2012). adv. illus. Index. back issues avail.; reprints avail. **Document type:** *Journal, Academic/Scholarly.* **Description:** Deals with game-theoretic modeling in the social, biological and mathematical sciences. Addresses the beliefs in the importance of interchange of game-theoretic ideas leading to a mathematical science of games and economic behavior.
Related titles: Online - full text ed.: ISSN 1090-2473 (from IngentaConnect, ScienceDirect).
Indexed: A01, A03, A08, A12, A13, A17, A20, A22, A26, ABIn, ASCA, CA, CCMJ, CIS, CurCont, E-psyche, E01, ESPM, EconLit, FamI, I05, IBSS, Inspec, JEL, MSN, MathR, P03, P30, P34, P48, P51, P53, P54, PCI, PQC, PsycInfo, PsycholAb, RASB, RiskAb, S01, SCOPUS, SSCI, T02, W07, Z02.
—BLDSC (4069.168000), AskIEEE, IE, Infotrieve, Ingenta. **CCC.**
Published by: Academic Press (Subsidiary of: Elsevier Science & Technology), 3251 Riverport Ln, Maryland Heights, MO 63043. TEL 314-447-8010, FAX 314-447-8030, JournalCustomerService-usa@elsevier.com, http://www.elsevierdirect.com/imprint.jsp?iid=5. Eds. E Lehrer, Ehud Kalai, M O Jackson.

➤ **GAY AND LESBIAN ISSUES AND PSYCHOLOGY REVIEW.** *see* HOMOSEXUALITY

615.8 NLD ISSN 0167-7454
GEDRAGSTHERAPIE. Text in Dutch. 1982. q. EUR 61 domestic; EUR 74 foreign; EUR 35 domestic to students; EUR 46 foreign to students; EUR 17.65 newsstand/cover (effective 2008). adv. **Document type:** *Academic/Scholarly.*
Indexed: A22, E-psyche, P03, PsycInfo, PsycholAb.
—BLDSC (4095.761600), IE, Infotrieve, Ingenta.
Published by: (Stichting Tijdschrift voor Gedragstherapie), Koninklijke Van Gorcum BV/Royal Van Gorcum BV, PO Box 43, Assen, 9400 AA, Netherlands. TEL 31-592-379555, FAX 31-592-372064, info@vangorcum.nl, http://www.vangorcum.nl. Ed. Theo Bouman. Circ: 2,300.

150 DEU ISSN 1618-8519
GEHIRN UND GEIST; Das Magazin fuer Psychologie und Hirnforschung. Text in German. 2002. 10/yr. EUR 68 domestic; EUR 73 foreign; EUR 55 to students; EUR 7.90 newsstand/cover (effective 2011). adv. **Document type:** *Magazine, Consumer.*
Indexed: IBR, IBZ.
Published by: Spektrum der Wissenschaft Verlagsgesellschaft mbH (Subsidiary of: Verlagsgruppe Georg von Holtzbrinck GmbH), Slevogtstr 3-5, Heidelberg, 69126, Germany. TEL 49-6221-9126600, FAX 49-6221-9126751, redaktion@spektrum.com, http://www.spektrum.de. Ed. Carsten Koenneker. Adv. contact Karin Schmidt. Circ: 25,900 (paid).

158 DEU ISSN 0941-0767
GEISTIG FIT. Text in German. 1991. bi-m. EUR 29.90 domestic; EUR 36.90 foreign (effective 2009). **Document type:** *Journal, Academic/Scholarly.*
Published by: Vless Verlag GmbH, Valentingasse 7-9, Ebersberg, 85560, Germany. TEL 49-8092-864920, FAX 49-8092-864949, info@vless.de.

150 NGA ISSN 1117-7322
GENDER & BEHAVIOUR. Text in English. 2003. a. USD 40 to individuals; USD 80 to institutions (effective 2004). back issues avail. **Document type:** *Journal, Academic/Scholarly.*
Related titles: Online - full text ed.
Indexed: P03, PsycInfo, PsycholAb.
Published by: Ife Center for Psychological Studies-Services, PO Box 1548, Ile-Ife, Osun State, Nigeria. ifepsy@yahoo.com. Ed. Akinsola Olowu.

150.19 616.9 USA ISSN 1091-6318
BF692.2 CODEN: GEPSFQ
➤ **GENDER & PSYCHOANALYSIS**; an interdisciplinary journal. Text in English. 1996. q. adv. bk.rev. charts; illus. back issues avail. **Document type:** *Journal, Academic/Scholarly.* **Description:** Devoted to provide a lively intellectual forum linking and critiquing diverse psychoanalytic views of gender, taking a multidisciplinary approach.
Indexed: AltPI, C06, C07, C08, CINAHL, DIP, E-psyche, EMBASE, ExcerpMed, FemPer, IBR, IBZ, PsycholAb, SCOPUS, SOPODA.
Published by: International Universities Press, Inc., 59 Boston Post Rd, Box 1524, PO Box 389, Madison, CT 06443. TEL 203-245-4000, FAX 203-245-0775, info@iup.com. adv.: page USD 360; 4.25 x 7.

150.9 FRA ISSN 1775-1187
GENEALOGIES DE LA PSYCHOLOGIE. Text in French. 2005. irreg. **Document type:** *Monographic series, Academic/Scholarly.*
Published by: L' Harmattan, 5 Rue de l'Ecole Polytechnique, Paris, 75005, France. TEL 33-1-43257651, FAX 33-1-43258203, http://www.editions-harmattan.fr.

121.3 USA ISSN 0740-9583
BF712
GENETIC EPISTEMOLOGIST. Text in English. 1971. a. free to members. adv. bk.rev. **Document type:** *Newsletter, Trade.* **Description:** Interdisciplinary study of human knowledge and its development.
Formerly (until 2002): Jean Piaget Society. Newsletter
Indexed: E-psyche.
Published by: Jean Piaget Society, Department of Psychology, Franklin and Arshall College, Box 3003, Lancaster, PA 17604. Ed. Ed Reed. Circ: 550 (paid). **Subscr. to:** Wm. M. Gray, Treas, Jean Piaget Society, Dept of Educational Psychology, University of Toledo, Toledo, OH 43606-3390. TEL 419-530-2481.

158 USA ISSN 1541-7557
BF637.C6
GEORGIA JOURNAL OF PROFESSIONAL COUNSELING. Text in English. a.
Published by: Licensed Professional Counselors Association of Georgia, 250 E. Ponce de Leon Ave., Ste. 427, Decatur, GA 30030. TEL 404-370-0200, FAX 404-370-0006, lpca@mindspring.com, http://www.lpcaga.org. Ed. Susan R. Boes.

150 BRA ISSN 1983-8220
GERAIS; revista interinstitucional de psicologia. Text in Portuguese. 2008. s-a. free (effective 2011). **Document type:** *Journal, Academic/Scholarly.*
Media: Online - full text.
Published by: (Universidade Federal de Sao Joao del-Rei (UFSJ), Universidade Federal de Uberlandia, Universidade Federal de Juiz de Fora, Editora), Universidade Federal de Minas Gerais, Av Antonio Carlos 6627, Belo Horizonte, MG 31270, Brazil. TEL 55-31-34994184, FAX 55-31-34994188, http://www.ufmg.br. Ed. Maria Nivalda Carvalho-Freitas.

150 UAE ISSN 1091-1766
GESTALT!. Text in English. 1997. irreg. back issues avail. **Document type:** *Journal, Academic/Scholarly.*
Media: Online - full content.
Indexed: P03, PsycholAb.
Published by: Gestalt Global Corporation http://www.g-g.org/gestalt-global/index.html.

150 DEU ISSN 1615-1518
GESTALT-KRITIK. Text in German. 1992. s-a. **Document type:** *Journal, Academic/Scholarly.*
Related titles: Online - full text ed.: ISSN 1615-1712.
—CCC.
Published by: Gestalt-Institut Koeln, Rurstr 9, Cologne, 50937, Germany. TEL 49-221-416163, FAX 49-221-447652, gik-gestalttherapie@gmx.de.

616.89 USA ISSN 1084-8657
RC489.G4
➤ **GESTALT REVIEW.** Text in English. 1997. 3/yr. USD 55 in US & Canada to individuals; USD 65 elsewhere to individuals; USD 140 in US & Canada to institutions; USD 155 elsewhere to institutions (effective 2010). adv. back issues avail. **Document type:** *Journal, Academic/Scholarly.* **Description:** Concentrates on the Gestalt approach to clinical, family, group and organizational topics.
Related titles: Online - full text ed.: ISSN 1945-4023.
Indexed: A01, CA, E-psyche, P03, P25, P48, PQC, PsycInfo, PsycholAb, T02.
—BLDSC (4163.380000), IE, Ingenta. **CCC.**
Published by: The Gestalt International Study Center, 1035 Cemetery Rd, PO Box 515, S Wellfleet, MA 02663. TEL 508-349-7900, FAX 508-349-7908, office@gisc.org, http://www.gisc.org. Eds. Joseph Melnick, Susan L Fischer. Adv. contact Laurie Fitzpatrick.

150.19 AUT ISSN 0170-057X
BF203
GESTALT THEORY; an international multidisciplinary journal. Text in English, German. 1979. q. EUR 94.10; EUR 52 to students; EUR 25.45 newsstand/cover (effective 2005). adv. bk.rev. **Document type:** *Journal, Academic/Scholarly.*
Indexed: A22, DIP, E-psyche, GJP, IBR, IBZ, P03, P30, PsycInfo, PsycholAb.
—BLDSC (4163.400000), IE, Infotrieve, Ingenta. **CCC.**
Published by: (Society for Gestalt Theory and Its Applications (GTA) DEU), Buchhandlung Krammer, Kaiserstr 13, Vienna, 1070, Austria. TEL 43-1-9852119, FAX 43-1-985211915, buchhandlung_krammer@aon.at, http://www.krammerbuch.at. Eds. H.-J Walter, J Kriz, Gerhard Stemberger. Circ: 550.

GIORNALE DI NEUROPSICHIATRIA DELL'ETA EVOLUTIVA. *see* MEDICAL SCIENCES—Psychiatry And Neurology

150 ITA ISSN 1971-9558
GIORNALE DI PSICOLOGIA/JOURNAL OF PSYCHOLOGY. Text in Multiple languages. 2007. 3/yr. **Document type:** *Journal, Academic/Scholarly.*
Related titles: Online - full text ed.: ISSN 1971-9450. free (effective 2011).
Indexed: PsycInfo.
Published by: Psicotecnica Edizioni, Via Premuda 17, Milan, 20129, Italy. http://www.psicotecnica.it.

GIORNALE ITALIANO DI PSICO-ONCOLOGIA. *see* MEDICAL SCIENCES—Oncology

150.5 ITA ISSN 0390-5349
BF1
GIORNALE ITALIANO DI PSICOLOGIA/ITALIAN JOURNAL OF PSYCHOLOGY. Text in Italian. 1974. q. EUR 140.50 combined subscription domestic to institutions (print & online eds.); EUR 164.50 combined subscription foreign to institutions (print & online eds.) (effective 2009). adv. index. back issues avail. **Document type:** *Journal, Academic/Scholarly.*
Related titles: Online - full text ed.
Indexed: A22, CDA, DIP, E-psyche, IBR, IBZ, L&LBA, P03, PsycInfo, PsycholAb, RILM, RefZh, S02, S03, SCOPUS, SOPODA, SociolAb.
—BLDSC (4178.243000), IE, Ingenta.
Published by: Societa Editrice Il Mulino, Strada Maggiore 37, Bologna, 40125, Italy. TEL 39-051-256011, FAX 39-051-256034, riviste@mulino.it. Ed. Remo Job. Circ: 1,300.

150 ITA ISSN 1720-7681
GIORNALE ITALIANO DI PSICOLOGIA DELL'ORIENTAMENTO. Abbreviated title: G I P O. Text in Multiple languages. 2000. 3/yr. EUR 75 domestic to institutions; EUR 90 foreign to institutions (effective 2009). **Document type:** *Journal, Academic/Scholarly.*
Indexed: P03, PsycInfo.
Published by: Organizzazioni Speciali, Via Fra' Paolo Sarpi 7-A, Florence, 50136, Italy. TEL 39-055-6236501, FAX 39-055-669446, bpa@osnet.it, http://www.osnet.it.

150 616.8 ITA ISSN 2035-2069
GIORNALE ITALIANO DI PSICOLOGIA E PSICHIATRIA. Text in Multiple languages. 2008. q. **Document type:** *Journal, Academic/Scholarly.*
Related titles: Online - full text ed.: ISSN 2035-2077.
Published by: Societa Italiana di Psicologia e Psichiatria, Via del Commercio 9, Fano, 61032, Italy. TEL 39-072-11796666, segreteria@sipsi.org, http://www.sipsi.org.

150 016 SWE ISSN 0301-0996
CODEN: GPSRDB
GOETEBORG PSYCHOLOGICAL REPORTS. Text in English. 1971. irreg. (5-8/yr.). SEK 25, USD 7.50 per issue (effective 2001). **Document type:** *Report, Academic/Scholarly.*
Indexed: CIS, E-psyche, PsycholAb.
Published by: Goeteborgs Universitet, Department of Psychology, P O Box 500, Goeteborg, 40530, Sweden. TEL 46-31-773-1668, FAX 46-31-773-4628. Ed. Anders Biel. Circ: 400.

150 CHE ISSN 0172-3421
GORGO; Zeitschrift fuer archetypische und bildhaftes Denken. Text in German. 1979. 2/yr. CHF 47, EUR 29.50 (effective 2007). adv. bk.rev. illus. **Document type:** *Journal, Academic/Scholarly.*
Indexed: E-psyche.
—CCC.
Published by: Edition I K M AG, Untere Zaeune 1, Zuerich, 8001, Switzerland. TEL 41-1-7502920, FAX 41-1-7502943. Ed. Allan Guggenbuehl. Adv. contact Monika Menne. page CHF 400.

GORILLA. *see* BIOLOGY—Zoology

150 USA ISSN 1540-6881
GRADPSYCH. Text in English. 2003 (May). q. USD 35 domestic to individuals; USD 62 foreign to individuals; USD 70 domestic to institutions; USD 115 foreign to institutions (effective 2011). adv. back issues avail.; reprints avail. **Document type:** *Journal, Academic/Scholarly.* **Description:** Publishes timely articles that give graduate psychology students information to stay current and competitive.
—CCC.
Published by: American Psychological Association, 750 First St, NE, Washington, DC 20002. TEL 202-336-5500, 800-374-2721, journals@apa.org. Ed. Sadie F Dingfelder. Pub. Dr. Rhea K Farberman. Adv. contact Karen Eskew. Circ: 30,000.

150 USA ISSN 1528-5979
BF80.7.U6
GRADUATE PROGRAMS IN PSYCHOLOGY. Text in English. 2001. a. USD 54.95 per issue (effective 2009). **Document type:** *Guide, Trade.*
Supersedes in part (in 19??): Peterson's U-Wire Graduate Studies in Social Sciences & Social Work (1522-6069); Which was formerly (until 19??): Peterson's Compact guides. Graduate Studies in Social Sciences & Social Work
Published by: Thomson Peterson's (Subsidiary of: Thomson Reuters Corp.), Princeton Pike Corporate Center, 2000 Lenox Dr, 3rd Fl, PO Box 67005, Lawrenceville, NJ 08648. TEL 609-896-1800, 800-338-3282 ext 54229, FAX 609-896-4531, custsvc@petersons.com, http://www.petersons.com.

150.71 USA
BF77
GRADUATE STUDY IN PSYCHOLOGY. Text in English. 1969. a. USD 28.95 per issue to non-members; USD 23.95 per issue to members (effective 2010). adv. **Document type:** *Directory, Trade.* **Description:** Offers information about over 500 psychology programs in the United States and Canada, including current facts about programs and degrees offered, admission requirements, application information, financial aid, tuition, and housing.
Former titles (until 1991): Graduate Study in Psychology and Associated Fields (0742-7220); (until 1983): Graduate Study in Psychology (0072-5277)
Indexed: E-psyche, PsycholAb.
Published by: American Psychological Association, 750 First St, NE, Washington, DC 20002. TEL 202-336-5500, 800-374-2721, journals@apa.org.

150 ESP ISSN 1130-6033
PN1
GRAMMA; revista de grafologia y ciencias afines. Text in Spanish. 1980. q. **Document type:** *Journal, Academic/Scholarly.*
Formerly (until 1989): Boletin de Informacion Grafopsicologia (0214-0438)
Published by: Asociacion de Grafopsicologia, Calle Goya 67, 2o derecha, Madrid, 28001, Spain. TEL 34-91-4261422, FAX 34-91-4021315, http://www.asociaciongrafopsicologica.com. Ed. Rafael Martin-Ramos.

150 ITA ISSN 1970-9390
LA GRANDE BIBLIOTECA DELLA PSICOLOGIA. Text in Italian. 2007. w. **Document type:** *Magazine, Consumer.*
Published by: R C S Libri (Subsidiary of: R C S Mediagroup), Via Mecenate 91, Milan, 20138, Italy. TEL 39-02-5095-2248, FAX 39-02-5095-2975, http://rcslibri.corriere.it/libri/index.htm.

155.937 USA ISSN 1559-5064
GRIEF DIGEST. Text in English. 1993. q. USD 30 (effective 2007). **Document type:** *Magazine, Consumer.*
Published by: Centering Corporation, 7230 Maple St, Omaha, NE 68134. TEL 866-218-0101, https://www.centeringcorp.com/catalog/index.php.

155.937 AUS ISSN 1440-6888
GRIEF MATTERS; the Australian journal of grief and bereavement. Text in English. 1998. 3/yr. free to members. adv. back issues avail. **Document type:** *Journal, Academic/Scholarly.* **Description:** Covers all aspects of grief and bereavement.
Related titles: Online - full text ed.
Published by: Australian Centre for Grief and Bereavement, McCulloch House, Monash Medical Centre, 246 Clayton Rd, Clayton, VIC 3168, Australia. TEL 61-3-92652100, FAX 61-3-92652150, info@grief.org.au. Ed. Christopher Hall.

P

616.8 GBR ISSN 0533-3164
RC500
➤ **GROUP ANALYSIS**; the international journal of group-analytic psychotherapy. Text in English. 1967. q. USD 757, GBP 409 combined subscription to institutions (print & online eds.); USD 742, GBP 401 to institutions (effective 2011). adv. bk.rev. back issues avail.; reprint service avail. from PSC. **Document type:** *Journal, Academic/Scholarly.* **Description:** Centered upon the theory, practice and experience of analytic group psychotherapy, using an integrative approach based on the view that we are all primarily group beings.
Related titles: Online - full text ed.: ISSN 1461-717X. USD 681, GBP 368 to institutions (effective 2011).
Indexed: A01, A03, A08, A22, ASSIA, B01, B06, B07, B09, CA, DIP, E-psyche, E01, FamI, H04, HRA, IBR, IBSS, IBZ, P03, P25, PQC, PsycInfo, PsycholAb, S02, S03, S21, SCOPUS, SOPODA, SSA, SociolAb, T02, V02.
—BLDSC (4220.170000), GNLM, IE, Infotrieve, Ingenta, INIST. **CCC.**
Published by: (The Group Analytic Society), Sage Publications Ltd. (Subsidiary of: Sage Publications, Inc.), 1 Oliver's Yard, 55 City Rd, London, EC1Y 1SP, United Kingdom. TEL 44-20-73248500, FAX 44-20-73248600, info@sagepub.co.uk, http://www.uk.sagepub.com/home.nav. Ed. A P (Tom) Ormay. adv.: B&W page GBP 400; 105 x 185. **Subscr. in the Americas to:** Sage Publications, Inc., 2455 Teller Rd, Thousand Oaks, CA 91320. TEL 805-499-9774, FAX 805-499-0871, journals@sagepub.com.

➤ **GROUP & ORGANIZATION MANAGEMENT**; an international journal. *see* EDUCATION

152 USA ISSN 1089-2699
HM131 CODEN: GRDYF7
➤ **GROUP DYNAMICS**; theory, research, and practice. Variant title: Group Dynamics: Theory, Research and Practice. Text in English. 1997. q. USD 98 domestic to individuals; USD 125 foreign to individuals; USD 374 domestic to institutions; USD 419 foreign to institutions (effective 2011). adv. back issues avail.; reprint service avail. from PSC. **Document type:** *Journal, Academic/Scholarly.* **Description:** Covers empirical analyses dealing with topics that extend the knowledge of groups.
Related titles: Online - full text ed.: ISSN 1930-7802 (from ScienceDirect).
Indexed: A22, CA, CurCont, E-psyche, P03, P30, PsycInfo, PsycholAb, S02, S03, S21, SCOPUS, SSCI, SWR&A, T02, W07.
—BLDSC (4220.174600), IE, Infotrieve, Ingenta. **CCC.**
Published by: (Society of Group Psychology and Group Psychotherapy), American Psychological Association, 750 First St, NE, Washington, DC 20002. TEL 202-336-5500, 800-374-2721, journals@apa.org. Ed. Craig D Parks. Adv. contact Doug Constant TEL 202-336-5574. Circ: 600.

158 USA ISSN 1534-5653
HM751
GROUP FACILITATION; a research & application journal. Text in English. 1999 (Win.). a.
Related titles: Online - full text ed.: ISSN 1545-5947.
Indexed: A12, A13, A17, ABIn, B01, B07, CA, H01, P21, P48, P51, P53, P54, PQC, T02.
Published by: International Association of Facilitators, 14985 Glazier Ave. Ste. 550, St. Paul, MN 55124. TEL 952-891-3541, 800-281-9948, FAX 952-891-1800, office@iaf-world.org. Ed. Sandor Schuman.

616.89 USA
GROUP SOLUTION. Text in English. 200?. 3/yr. free to members (effective 2010). **Document type:** *Newsletter, Academic/Scholarly.*
Published by: American Group Psychotherapy Association, 25 E 21st St, 6th Fl, New York, NY 10010. TEL 212-477-2677, 877-668-2472, FAX 212-979-6627, info@agpa.org. Ed. Paul Cox TEL 916-734-7811.

150 FRA ISSN 1275-3424
GROUPES THERAPEUTIQUES. Text in French. 1996. irreg. back issues avail. **Document type:** *Monographic series, Consumer.*
Published by: Editions Eres, 33 Av. Marcel Dassault, Toulouse, 31500, France. TEL 33-5-61751576, FAX 33-5-61735289, eres@edition-eres.com.

GROUPWORK. *see* SOCIAL SERVICES AND WELFARE

616.89 DEU ISSN 0939-4273
GRUPPENANALYSE; Zeitschrift fuer gruppenanalytische Psychotherapie, Beratung und Supervision. Text in German; Summaries in English, German. 1991. 2/yr. EUR 20 (effective 2005). bk.rev. back issues avail. **Document type:** *Journal, Academic/Scholarly.*
Indexed: E-psyche.
Published by: (Institut fuer Gruppenanalyse Heidelberg e.V.), Mattes Verlag GmbH, Postfach 103866, Heidelberg, 69028, Germany. TEL 49-6221-459231, FAX 49-6221-459322, journals@mattes.de, http://www.mattes.de.

302 DEU ISSN 1618-7849
CODEN: GRUPDT
➤ **GRUPPENDYNAMIK UND ORGANISATIONSBERATUNG**; Zeitschrift fuer angewandte Sozialpsychologie. Text in German. 1970. q. EUR 203.74, USD 251 combined subscription to institutions (print & online eds.) (effective 2012). adv. bk.rev. back issues avail.; reprint service avail. from PSC. **Document type:** *Journal, Academic/Scholarly.*
Formerly (until 2000): Gruppendynamik (0046-6514)
Related titles: Online - full text ed.: ISSN 1862-2615.
Indexed: A20, A22, A26, ASCA, CurCont, DIP, E-psyche, E01, GJP, I05, IBR, IBSS, IBZ, P03, PsycInfo, PsycholAb, RefZh, S02, S03, SCOPUS, SSCI, W07.
—BLDSC (4223.459000), IE, Ingenta. **CCC.**
Published by: V S - Verlag fuer Sozialwissenschaften (Subsidiary of: Springer Fachmedien Wiesbaden GmbH), Abraham-Lincoln-Str 46, Wiesbaden, 65189, Germany. TEL 49-611-78780, FAX 49-611-7878400, springerfachmedien-wiesbaden@springer.com, http://www.vs-verlag.de. Circ: 1,000 (paid).

150 ITA ISSN 1826-2589
GRUPPI. Text in Italian. 1999. 3/yr. EUR 73 combined subscription domestic to institutions (print & online eds.); EUR 83.50 combined subscription foreign to institutions (print & online eds.) (effective 2009). **Document type:** *Journal, Academic/Scholarly.*
Related titles: Online - full text ed.: ISSN 1972-4837. 2000.
Indexed: P03, PsycInfo.
Published by: (Confederazione di Organizzazioni Italiane per la Ricerca Analitica sui Gruppi (C O I R A G)), Franco Angeli Edizioni, Viale Monza 106, Milan, 20127, Italy. TEL 39-02-2837141, FAX 39-02-26144793, redazioni@francoangeli.it, http://www.francoangeli.it.

150 ESP ISSN 1885-8392
GUIA DEL PSICOLOGO. Text in Spanish. 1982. m. EUR 36 domestic; EUR 150 foreign (effective 2008). back issues avail. **Document type:** *Magazine, Trade.*
Published by: Colegio Oficial de Psicologos, Claudio Coello 46, Madrid, 28001, Spain. TEL 34-91-4355212, FAX 34-91-5779172, http://www.cop.es. Ed. Jose Ramon Fernandez Hermida.

158 USA ISSN 2153-4748
▼ **A GUIDE TO ACQUIRING WISDOM.** Text in English. 2011 (Mar.). 4/yr. USD 2 per issue (effective 2011). **Document type:** *Guide, Consumer.* **Description:** Advice from the Ancient Curmudgeon, Wendell Prowse.
Published by: Wendell Prowse, Ed. & Pub., 50 Ransom NE, Apt 501, Grand Rapids, MI 49503. TEL 616-589-3263, wendellprowse@yahoo.com. Circ: 30,000.

GUIDE TO PRIVATE SPECIAL EDUCATION. *see* EDUCATION—Special Education And Rehabilitation

616.891 USA ISSN 0884-5808
RC489.M53
HAKOMI FORUM. Text in English. 1984. a. USD 10. adv. bk.rev. cum.index. back issues avail. **Document type:** *Journal, Trade.* **Description:** Journal for therapists with an emphasis on transpersonal, body-centered, cognitive aspects of therapy. Aims to foster the principles of unity, organicity, mind-body holism, mindfulness, and non-violence.
Indexed: E-psyche, PsycholAb.
Published by: Hakomi Institute, PO Box 1873, Boulder, CO 80306. TEL 888-421-6699, HakomiHQ@aol.com, http://www.hakomiinstitute.com. Ed. Gregory J Johanson. R&P, Adv. contact Cedar Barstow. Circ: 1,000.

HAN'GUG SEUPOCEU SIMRI HAGHOEJI/KOREAN JOURNAL OF SPORT PSYCHOLOGY. *see* SPORTS AND GAMES

150 KOR ISSN 1229-0718
BF712
HAN'GUG SIMLIHAG HOEJI. BALDAL/KOREAN JOURNAL OF DEVELOPMENT PSYCHOLOGY. Text in Korean. 1988. s-a. **Document type:** *Journal, Academic/Scholarly.*
Published by: Han'gug Simlihag Hoeji/Korean Psychological Association, Rm. 917, Sung Jie Heights Officetel, 702-13 Yeoksam-Dong Kangnam-Ku, Seoul, 135-080, Korea, S. TEL 82-2-5670102, kpa0102@chol.com, http://www.koreanpsychology.or.kr/.

150 KOR ISSN 1229-0653
HM1001
HAN'GUG SIMLIHAG HOEJI. SAHOE MICH SEONG'GYEOG/KOREAN JOURNAL OF SOCIAL AND PERSONALITY PSYCHOLOGY. Text in Korean. 1982. s-a. **Document type:** *Journal, Academic/Scholarly.*
Published by: Han'gug Simlihag Hoeji/Korean Psychological Association, Rm. 917, Sung Jie Heights Officetel, 702-13 Yeoksam-Dong Kangnam-Ku, Seoul, 135-080, Korea, S. TEL 82-2-5670102, kpa0102@chol.com.

150 KOR ISSN 1226-9875
HAN'GUG SIMRI HAGHOEJI. SAENGMUL MIC SAENGRI/KOREAN JOURNAL OF BIOLOGICAL AND PHYSIOLOGICAL PSYCHOLOGY. Text in Korean. 1989. s-a. **Document type:** *Journal, Academic/Scholarly.*
Published by: Han'gug Simlihag Hoeji/Korean Psychological Association, Rm. 917, Sung Jie Heights Officetel, 702-13 Yeoksam-Dong Kangnam-Ku, Seoul, 135-080, Korea, S. TEL 82-2-5670102, kpa0102@chol.com, http://www.koreanpsychology.or.kr/.

364.3 JPN ISSN 0017-7547
HANZAI SHINRIGAKU KENKYU/JAPANESE JOURNAL OF CRIMINAL PSYCHOLOGY. Text in Japanese; Summaries in English. 1963. 3/yr. **Document type:** *Journal, Academic/Scholarly.*
Indexed: E-psyche, PsycholAb, S02, S03.
Published by: Nihon Hanzai Shinri Gakkai/Japanese Association of Criminal Psychology, c/o International Academic Printing Co., Ltd., 4-4-19, Takadanobaba, Shinjuku-ku, Tokyo, 169-0075, Japan. TEL 81-3-53896239, FAX 81-3-33682822, jacp-post@bunken.co.jp, http://wwwsoc.nii.ac.jp/jacp2/. Circ: 1,200.

158 ITA
▼ **HAPPINESS**; la revista della felicita per cuore anima e corpo. Text in Italian. 2011. bi-m. EUR 39.90 (effective 2011). adv. **Document type:** *Magazine, Consumer.*
Published by: Sprea Editori Srl, Via Torino 51, Cernusco sul Naviglio, MI 20063, Italy. TEL 39-02-92432222, FAX 39-02-92432236, editori@sprea.it, http://www.sprea.it.

158 613.7 FRA ISSN 1965-1015
HARMONIE & BIEN-ETRE. Text in French. 2008. q. EUR 32 for 2 yrs. (effective 2010). **Document type:** *Magazine, Consumer.*
Published by: Lafont Presse, 53 Rue du Chemin Vert, Boulogne-Billancourt, 92100, France. TEL 33-1-46102121, FAX 33-1-45792211, http://www.lafontpresse.fr.

150 NLD
HARTMAN INSTITUTE AXIOLOGY STUDIES. Text in English. irreg. price varies. **Document type:** *Monographic series, Academic/Scholarly.* **Description:** Covers the study, development and application of the formal axiology initiated by Robert Hartman.
Related titles: ◆ Series of: Value Inquiry Book Series. ISSN 0929-8436.
Published by: Editions Rodopi B.V., Tijnmuiden 7, Amsterdam, 1046 AK, Netherlands. TEL 31-20-6114821, FAX 31-20-4472979, info@rodopi.nl. Eds. C Stephen Byrum, Rem B Edwards. **Dist. by:** Rodopi - USA, 606 Newark Ave, 2nd fl, Kenilworth, NJ 07033. TEL 908-497-9031, FAX 908-497-9035.

THE HARVARD MENTAL HEALTH LETTER. *see* MEDICAL SCIENCES—Psychiatry And Neurology

150 GBR ISSN 0266-4771
BF173
➤ **HARVEST**; journal for Jungian studies. Text in English. 1954. a. GBP 20 per issue domestic to institutions; GBP 25 per issue foreign to institutions; GBP 12.50 per issue domestic to non-members; GBP 15 per issue in Europe to non-members; GBP 17.50 per issue elsewhere to non-members; free to members (effective 2010). adv. bk.rev. 200 p./no.; back issues avail. **Document type:** *Journal, Academic/Scholarly.* **Description:** Promotes a specific genre of Jungian writing which makes use of personal experience in a reflexive style in order to develop theoretical and clinical insights.
Related titles: Online - full text ed.
Indexed: E-psyche, MLA-IB, PCI.
Published by: C.G. Jung Analytical Psychology Club, c/o Marilyn Rose, Administrator, PO Box 19017, London, N3 3WY, United Kingdom. TEL 44-20-83433387, FAX 44-20-83433387, admin@jungclub-london.org. Ed. Julian David.

155 JPN ISSN 0915-9029
HATTATSU SHINRIGAKU KENKYU/JAPANESE JOURNAL OF DEVELOPMENTAL PSYCHOLOGY. Text in Japanese; Summaries in English. 1990. 3/yr. **Document type:** *Journal, Academic/Scholarly.*
Indexed: A01, A22, E-psyche, P03, PsycInfo, PsycholAb.
—BLDSC (4651.650000), IE, Ingenta. **CCC.**
Published by: Nihon Hattatsu Shinri Gakkai/Japan Society of Developmental Psychology, 8-5-9-10A, Nishi-Shinjuku, Shinjuku-ku, Tokyo, 160-0023, Japan. TEL 81-3-53485902, http://wwwsoc.nii.ac.jp/jsdp/.

HAWLIYYAT KULLIYYAT AL-ADAB/ANNALS OF THE ARTS AND SOCIAL SCIENCES. *see* HUMANITIES: COMPREHENSIVE WORKS

150 USA ISSN 0278-6133
R726.5
➤ **HEALTH PSYCHOLOGY.** Text in English. 1982. bi-m. USD 179 domestic to individuals; USD 211 foreign to individuals; USD 536 domestic to institutions; USD 593 foreign to institutions (effective 2011). adv. bk.rev. abstr.; bibl.; charts; illus.; stat. back issues avail.; reprint service avail. from PSC. **Document type:** *Journal, Academic/Scholarly.* **Description:** Covers empirical studies that promote the understanding of scientific relationships between behavioral principles and physical health and illness.
Related titles: Online - full text ed.: ISSN 1930-7810 (from ScienceDirect).
Indexed: A20, A22, A26, AIDS Ab, ASSIA, AbAn, AddicA, B21, BRD, C06, C07, C08, C28, CA, CINAHL, CurCont, E-psyche, E08, EMBASE, ERA, ESPM, ExcerpMed, F09, FR, FS&TA, FamI, G08, G10, H&SSA, H11, H12, I05, INI, IndMed, M12, MEDLINE, NRN, P03, P30, PEI, PsycInfo, PsycholAb, R10, RASB, Reac, RiskAb, S02, S03, S09, S20, S21, SCI, SCOPUS, SSAI, SSAb, SSCI, SSI, SWR&A, T02, THA, W03, W07, W09.
—BLDSC (4275.105200), GNLM, IE, Infotrieve, Ingenta, INIST. **CCC.**
Published by: (American Psychological Association, Division 38), American Psychological Association, 750 First St, NE, Washington, DC 20002. TEL 202-336-5500, 800-374-2721, FAX 202-336-5997, journals@apa.org. Ed. Dr. Anne E Kazak. Adv. contact Doug Constant TEL 202-336-5574. Circ: 4,600.

150 GBR ISSN 1743-7199
HEALTH PSYCHOLOGY REVIEW. Abbreviated title: H P R. Text in English. 2007. s-a. GBP 210 combined subscription in United Kingdom to institutions (print & online eds.); EUR 279, USD 347 combined subscription to institutions (print & online eds.) (effective 2012). back issues avail.; reprint service avail. from PSC. **Document type:** *Journal, Academic/Scholarly.* **Description:** Designed for the advancement of the discipline of health psychology and strengthens its relationship to the field of psychology as a whole, as well as to other related academic and professional arenas.
Related titles: Online - full text ed.: ISSN 1743-7202. 2007. GBP 189 in United Kingdom to institutions; EUR 251, USD 313 to institutions (effective 2012).
Indexed: A01, A22, ASSIA, CA, E01, P30, P48, PQC, SCOPUS, T02.
—IE. **CCC.**
Published by: Psychology Press (Subsidiary of: Taylor & Francis Ltd.), 27 Church Rd, Hove, E Sussex BN3 2FA, United Kingdom. TEL 44-20-70176000, FAX 44-20-70176717, info@psypress.co.uk, http://www.psypress.com. Ed. Joop van der Pligt. Adv. contact Linda Hann TEL 44-1344-779945.

150 GRC ISSN 1790-1391
HELLENIC JOURNAL OF PSYCHOLOGY. Text in English. 2004. 3/yr. **Document type:** *Journal, Academic/Scholarly.*
Indexed: P03, PsycInfo, PsycholAb.
—BLDSC (4285.436700), IE.
Published by: (Psychological Society of Northern Greece), Ellenika Grammata - Hellenic Psychological Society, Emm. Benaki 59, Athens, 10681, Greece. TEL 30-210-3891800, FAX 30-210-3836658.

150 331 FIN ISSN 1459-8035
HELSINKI UNIVERSITY OF TECHNOLOGY. LABORATORY OF WORK PSYCHOLOGY AND LEADERSHIP. REPORT/TEKNILLINEN KORKEAKOULU. TYOPSYKOLOGIAN LABORATORIO. REPORT. Text in English, Finnish. 1996. irreg. **Document type:** *Monographic series, Academic/Scholarly.*
Supersedes in part (in 2004): H U T Industrial Management and Work and Organizational Psychology. Report Series (1459-1944); Which was formerly (until 2003): H U T Industrial Management and Work and Organizational Psychology. Working Papers (1239-484X)
Related titles: Online - full text ed.: ISSN 1795-8857.
Published by: Teknillinen Korkeakoulu, Tyopsykologian Laboratorio/Helsinki University of Technology. Laboratory of Work Psychology and Leadership, TUAS House, PO Box 5500, Espoo, 02015, Finland. TEL 358-9-4511.

HENKIMAAILMA. *see* PARAPSYCHOLOGY AND OCCULTISM

150 CAN ISSN 0085-1493
HERE AND NOW; a brief of news from the IPR. Text and summaries in French. 1969. irreg. free. adv. bk.rev. **Document type:** *Bulletin.*
Indexed: E-psyche.
Published by: Institute of Psychological Research, Inc., 34 Fleury St W, Montreal, PQ H3L 1S9, Canada. TEL 514-382-3000, FAX 514-382-3007. Ed. Marie Paule Chevrier. Circ: 2,000 (controlled).

155 JPN
HERUSU SAIKOROJISUTO/HEALTH PSYCHOLOGIST. Text in Japanese. 3/yr.

Indexed: E-psyche.
Published by: Nihon Kenko Shinri Gakkai/Japanese Association of Health Psychology, Waseda University, School of Humanities & Social Sciences, Oda Laboratory, 1-24-1, Toyama, Shinjuku-ku, Tokyo, 162-8644, Japan. http://www.waseda.ac.jp/conference/JAHP/frame.html.

150.195 FRA ISSN 1774-5306
HETERITE. Text in French. 200?. irreg. **Document type:** *Journal, Academic/Scholarly.*
Related titles: Online - full text ed.: free.
Published by: Ecole de Psychanalyse des Forums du Champ Lacanien, 118 rue d'Assas, Paris, 75006, France. TEL 33-1-56242256, FAX 33-1-56242237, http://www.champlacanien.net.

158 USA ISSN 1559-7512
HIDDEN DIMENSIONS INSIGHTS. Text in English. 2004. m. **Document type:** *Newsletter.*
Media: Online - full text.
Published by: Interdevelopmental Institute, 51 Mystic St., Medford, MA 02155. TEL 781-391-2361, http://www.interdevelopmentals.org/index.html. Ed. Dr. Otto Laske.

▼ **HIPNOLOGICA**; revista de hipnosis clinica y experimental. *see* MEDICAL SCIENCES—Hypnosis

150 301.1 USA ISSN 0739-9863
CODEN: HJBSEZ
➤ **HISPANIC JOURNAL OF BEHAVIORAL SCIENCES.** Text in English, Spanish. 1979. q. USD 777, GBP 457 combined subscription to institutions (print & online eds.); USD 761, GBP 448 to institutions (effective 2011). adv. bk.rev.; film rev. illus. index. back issues avail.; reprint service avail. from PSC. **Document type:** *Journal, Academic/Scholarly.* **Description:** Contains empirical articles, case study reports, and scholarly notes of theoretical or methodological interest pertaining to Hispanics. Focuses on the fields of anthropology, linguistics, psychology, public health, and sociology.
Related titles: Microfilm ed.: (from PQC); Online - full text ed.: ISSN 1552-6364. USD 699, GBP 411 to institutions (effective 2011).
Indexed: A01, A02, A03, A08, A20, A22, A26, A36, A37, ASCA, B04, B07, BRD, C06, C07, C08, C28, CA, CABA, CINAHL, CJPI, ChPerl, Chicano, CommAb, CurCont, E-psyche, E01, E02, E03, E07, E08, E12, ERI, ERIC, ESPM, EdA, EdI, F09, FamI, G08, G10, GH, H04, H12, H21, HEA, I05, L&LBA, LT, M08, N02, P02, P03, P04, P08, P09, P10, P18, P24, P25, P27, P30, P48, P53, PCI, PQC, PsycInfo, PsycholAb, R12, RILM, RiskAb, S02, S03, S09, S11, SCOPUS, SFSA, SOPODA, SSA, SSAI, SSAb, SSCI, SSI, SSciA, SWR&A, SociolAb, SoyAb, T02, T05, TAR, V&AA, V02, W03, W07, W09, W11.
—BLDSC (4315.772700), IE, Infotrieve, Ingenta. **CCC.**
Published by: Sage Publications, Inc., 2455 Teller Rd, Thousand Oaks, CA 91320. TEL 805-499-9774, 800-818-7243, FAX 805-499-0871, 800-583-2665, info@sagepub.com. Ed. Dr. Amado M Padilla. adv.: page USD 515; 4.5 x 7.5. Circ: 630 (paid and free). **Subscr. outside the Americas to:** Sage Publications Ltd., 1 Oliver's Yard, 55 City Rd, London EC1Y 1SP, United Kingdom. TEL 44-20-73248701, FAX 44-20-73248733, subscription@sagepub.co.uk.

159.9 DEU ISSN 1615-3901
HISTORISCHE PSYCHOLOGIE. Text in German. 2000. irreg. price varies. **Document type:** *Monographic series, Academic/Scholarly.*
Published by: Centaurus Verlag & Media KG, Kaiser-Joseph-Str 267, Freiburg, 79098, Germany. TEL 49-761-1525861, FAX 49-761-1525868, info@centaurus-verlag.de, http://www.centaurus-verlag.de.

150 NLD ISSN 1572-1914
HISTORY AND PHILOSOPHY OF PSYCHOLOGY. Text in English. 2003. irreg., latest vol.4, 2006. price varies. **Document type:** *Monographic series, Academic/Scholarly.* **Description:** Aims to introduce and analyze the field of history and philosophy of psychology through the investigation of selected topics within the subject area.
Related titles: Online - full text ed.: ISSN 1574-9029.
Published by: Springer Netherlands (Subsidiary of: Springer Science+Business Media), Van Godewijckstraat 30, Dordrecht, 3311 GX, Netherlands. TEL 31-78-6576050, FAX 31-78-6576474. Ed. Man Cheung Chung.

152 USA ISSN 1093-4510
BF81
➤ **HISTORY OF PSYCHOLOGY.** Text in English. 1998. q. USD 110 domestic to individuals; USD 137 foreign to individuals; USD 410 domestic to institutions; USD 455 foreign to institutions (effective 2011). adv. illus. back issues avail.; reprint service avail. from PSC. **Document type:** *Journal, Academic/Scholarly.* **Description:** Addresses all aspects of psychology's past and its interrelationship with the many contexts within which it has emerged and has been practiced.
Related titles: Online - full text ed.: ISSN 1939-0610 (from ScienceDirect).
Indexed: A20, A22, AmH&L, CA, CurCont, E-psyche, EMBASE, ExcerpMed, FR, FamI, HistAb, MEDLINE, P03, P30, PsycInfo, PsycholAb, SCOPUS, SSCI, T02, W07.
—BLDSC (4318.409500), IE, Infotrieve, Ingenta, INIST. **CCC.**
Published by: (American Psychological Association, Division 26), American Psychological Association, 750 First St, NE, Washington, DC 20002. TEL 202-336-5500, 800-374-2721, FAX 202-336-5997, journals@apa.org. Ed. Wade E Pickren. Adv. contact Doug Constant TEL 202-336-5574. Circ: 600.

150 ARG
HOJA INFORMATIVA. Text in Spanish. 1999. m. back issues avail.
Media: Online - full content.
Published by: Universidad de Buenos Aires, Facultad de Psicologia, Hipolito Yrigoyen 3241, Buenos Aires, C1207ABQ, Argentina. TEL 55-11-49316900, info@psi.uba.ar.

150 ESP ISSN 1136-0828
HUARTE DE SAN JUAN. PSICOLOGIA Y PEDAGOGIA. Text in Spanish, Catalan. 1996. irreg. **Document type:** *Journal, Academic/Scholarly.*
Published by: Universidad Publica de Navarra, Facultad de Ciencias Humanas y Sociales, Campus de Arrosadia, Pamplona, 31006, Spain. http://www.unavarra.es.

HUMAN COGNITIVE PROCESSING. *see* LINGUISTICS—Computer Applications

153.6 USA ISSN 0360-3989
P91.3 CODEN: PVBRDX
➤ **HUMAN COMMUNICATION RESEARCH.** Text in English. 1974. q. USD 100 combined subscription in the Americas to individuals (print & online eds.); EUR 107 combined subscription in Europe to individuals (print & online eds.); GBP 71 combined subscription elsewhere to individuals (print & online eds.); GBP 694 combined subscription in United Kingdom to institutions (print & online eds.); USD 1,138 combined subscription in the Americas to institutions (print & online eds.); EUR 881 combined subscription in Europe to institutions (print & online eds.); USD 1,359 combined subscription elsewhere to institutions (print & online eds.) (effective 2010); subscr. includes ommunication Theory and Communication, Culture & Critique and Journal of Communication and Journal of Computer-Mediated Communication. bk.rev. abstr.; illus. back issues avail.; reprint service avail. from PSC. **Document type:** *Journal, Academic/Scholarly.* **Description:** Publishes important research and reports that contribute to the expanding body of knowledge about human communication.
Related titles: Microform ed.: (from PQC); Online - full text ed.: ISSN 1468-2958. GBP 631 in United Kingdom to institutions; USD 1,034 in the Americas to institutions; EUR 801 in Europe to institutions; USD 1,235 elsewhere to institutions (effective 2010) (from IngentaConnect).
Indexed: A01, A02, A03, A08, A20, A22, A26, ASCA, AbAn, B01, B04, B06, B07, B08, B09, BRD, CA, CMM, CommAb, CurCont, E-psyche, E01, E02, E03, E07, E08, ERI, ERIC, EdA, EdI, FR, FamI, G08, G10, H14, I05, IJCS, L&LBA, M06, MEA&I, MLA-IB, P02, P03, P07, P10, P12, P18, P25, P27, P30, P48, P53, P54, PCI, PQC, PsycInfo, PsycholAb, S02, S03, S09, SCOPUS, SFSA, SOPODA, SSA, SSAI, SSAb, SSCI, SSI, SociolAb, T02, W01, W02, W03, W07.
—BLDSC (4336.043000), IE, Infotrieve, Ingenta, INIST. **CCC.**
Published by: (International Communication Association), Wiley-Blackwell Publishing, Inc. (Subsidiary of: Wiley-Blackwell Publishing Ltd.), 111 River St, Hoboken, NJ 07030. TEL 201-748-6000, FAX 201-748-6088, info@wiley.com, http://www.wiley.com/WileyCDA/. Ed. James E Katz.

➤ **HUMAN - COMPUTER INTERACTION (MAHWAH)**; a journal of theoretical, empirical, and methodological issues of user psychology and of system design. *see* COMPUTERS

305.8 USA
HUMAN ETHOLOGY BULLETIN. Text in English. 1974. q. USD 20 membership (effective 2007). adv. bk.rev. back issues avail. **Document type:** *Bulletin, Trade.* **Description:** Publishes essays, brief research reports, listings of current literature, announcements.
Formerly: Human Ethology Newsletter (0739-2036)
Indexed: E-psyche, IBSS.
Published by: International Society for Human Ethology, c/o Dori LeCroy, 175 King St, Charleston, SC 29401. TEL 843-577-9645, karl.grammer@univie.ac.at, http://evolution.anthro.univie.ac.at/ishe.html. Ed., R&P Thomas Alley. Circ: 400 (paid).

HUMAN EVOLUTION, BEHAVIOR, AND INTELLIGENCE. *see* BIOLOGY—Genetics

HUMAN FACTORS; the journal of the human factors and ergonomics society. *see* ENGINEERING

HUMAN FACTORS AND ERGONOMICS IN MANUFACTURING. *see* ENGINEERING—Industrial Engineering

HUMAN FACTORS AND ERGONOMICS SOCIETY ANNUAL MEETING. PROCEEDINGS. *see* ENGINEERING

HUMAN FACTORS AND ERGONOMICS SOCIETY. BULLETIN. *see* ENGINEERING

HUMAN FACTORS AND ERGONOMICS SOCIETY OF AUSTRALIA. ANNUAL CONFERENCE PROCEEDINGS. *see* ENGINEERING

HUMAN FACTORS IN INFORMATION TECHNOLOGY. *see* COMPUTERS—Information Science And Information Theory

616.89 GBR ISSN 1473-4850
➤ **HUMAN GIVENS**; promoting emotional health and clear thinking. Text in English. 1993. q. GBP 30 domestic; GBP 38 foreign; GBP 7 per issue (effective 2009). bk.rev. 52 p./no.; back issues avail. **Document type:** *Journal, Academic/Scholarly.* **Description:** Provides significant articles on human psychology and behaviour including fascinating stories, research findings, new insights, interviews, case histories, research, book reviews and letters.
Former titles (until 2001): The New Therapist (1467-5676); (until 1999): Therapist (1350-4614)
Indexed: AMED.
—BLDSC (4336.110000), IE, Ingenta.
Published by: (European Therapy Studies Institute), Human Givens Publishing Ltd., The Barn, Church Farm, Chalvington, N. Hailsham, E Sussex BN27 3TD, United Kingdom. TEL 44-1323-811662, FAX 44-1323-811486, info@humangivens.com. Eds. Denise Winn TEL 44-20-84505646, Ivan Tyrrell.

➤ **HUMAN MOVEMENT SCIENCE.** *see* MEDICAL SCIENCES

➤ **HUMAN NATURE**; an interdisciplinary biosocial perspective. *see* SOCIAL SCIENCES: COMPREHENSIVE WORKS

150 500 USA ISSN 1476-1084
THE HUMAN NATURE REVIEW. Text in English. 2001. irreg., latest vol.5, 2005, Dec. back issues avail. **Document type:** *Journal, Academic/Scholarly.*
Media: Online - full text.
—CCC.
Published by: Human Nature Eds. Ian Pitchford, Robert M Young.

152 USA ISSN 0895-9285
BF636.A1 CODEN: HPUEAO
➤ **HUMAN PERFORMANCE.** Text in English. 1988. 5/yr. GBP 517 combined subscription in United Kingdom to institutions (print & online eds.); EUR 688, USD 862 combined subscription to institutions (print & online eds.) (effective 2012). adv. back issues avail.; reprint service avail. from PSC. **Document type:** *Journal, Academic/Scholarly.* **Description:** Provides information for behavioral scientists interested in the factors that motivate and influence excellence in human behavior. Publishes research and theory that investigates the nature of goal-directed human activity.
Related titles: Online - full text ed.: ISSN 1532-7043. GBP 465 in United Kingdom to institutions; EUR 620, USD 776 to institutions (effective 2012).
Indexed: A01, A02, A03, A08, A22, ASCA, B01, B06, B07, B09, B21, CA, CurCont, E-psyche, E01, ESPM, ErgAb, FamI, H&SSA, HRA, Inspec, P03, P10, P12, P43, P47, P48, P53, P54, PEI, PQC, PsycInfo, PsycholAb, SCOPUS, SD, SSCI, T02, W07.
—BLDSC (4336.265000), IE, Infotrieve, Ingenta, INIST. **CCC.**
Published by: Routledge (Subsidiary of: Taylor & Francis Group), 325 Chestnut St, Ste 800, Philadelphia, PA 19106. TEL 800-354-1420, FAX 215-625-2940, journals@routledge.com, http://www.routledge.com. Ed. Walter C Borman. Adv. contact Linda Hann TEL 44-1344-779945.

158.2 302 GBR
HUMAN RELATIONS, AUTHORITY AND JUSTICE; experiences and critiques. Text in English. irreg. free. back issues avail. **Document type:** *Journal, Academic/Scholarly.* **Description:** Focuses on bringing psychoanalytic and related psychodynamic approaches to bear on group, institutional, cultural and political processes.
Media: Online - full text.
Indexed: E-psyche.
Published by: Human Nature Trust, 26 Freegrove Rd, London, N7 9RQ, United Kingdom. TEL 44-20-6078306, FAX 44-20-6094837, robert@rmy1.demon.co.uk, http://human-nature.com. Eds. Robert M Young, Toma Tomov.

302.3 USA ISSN 0885-1174
BF575.S75
HUMAN STRESS: CURRENT SELECTED RESEARCH. Text in English. 1986. a. bk.rev. index. back issues avail. **Description:** Articles on biological and behavioral problems related to stress.
Formerly: Human Stress: Current Advances in Research
Indexed: E-psyche.
—BLDSC (4336.466800).
Published by: A M S Press, Inc., Brooklyn Navy Yard, 63 Flushing Ave, Bldg 292, Unit #221, Brooklyn, NY 11205. FAX 718-875-3800, queries@amspressinc.com, http://www.amspressinc.com.

150 GBR ISSN 0960-9830
➤ **HUMAN SYSTEMS**; the journal of systemic consultation and management. Text in English. 1990. q. GBP 30 domestic to individuals; EUR 50 in Europe to individuals; GBP 40 elsewhere to individuals; GBP 40 domestic to institutions; EUR 70 in Europe to institutions; GBP 54 elsewhere to institutions (effective 2009). bk.rev.; software rev.; video rev. back issues avail. **Document type:** *Journal, Academic/Scholarly.* **Description:** Creates a forum for exchanging and developing ideas and practices, investigates and discusses emerging concepts applicable to clinical and organizational practice, and provides a specialist field that includes research and theoretical papers focusing on systematic and constructionist ideas.
Indexed: E-psyche.
—BLDSC (4336.467500). **CCC.**
Published by: (Kensington Consultation Centre), University of Leeds, Leeds Family Therapy and Research Centre, Institute of Psychological Sciences, Leeds, LS2 9JT, United Kingdom. TEL 44-113-3435722, FAX 44-113-3435700, p.boston@leeds.ac.uk, http://www.leeds.ac.uk/lihs/psychiatry/lftrc/index.html. Ed. Peter Stratton. **Subscr. to:** Kensington Consultation Centre, 2 Wyvil Court, Trenchold St, London SW8 2TG, United Kingdom. TEL 44-20-77207301, FAX 44-20-77207302, info@kccfoundation.com, http://www.kcc-international.com/.

➤ **HUMAN SYSTEMS I A C GATEWAY.** (Information Analysis Center) *see* OCCUPATIONAL HEALTH AND SAFETY

150 USA ISSN 0887-3267
➤ **THE HUMANISTIC PSYCHOLOGIST.** Text in English. 1973. q. GBP 127 combined subscription in United Kingdom to institutions (print & online eds.); EUR 170, USD 214 combined subscription to institutions (print & online eds.) (effective 2012). adv. bk.rev. back issues avail.; reprint service avail. from PSC. **Document type:** *Journal, Academic/Scholarly.* **Description:** Publishes contributions that advance the field of humanistic psychology, broadly defined.
Formerly (until 19??): American Psychological Association. Division of Humanistic Psychology. Newsletter
Related titles: Online - full text ed.: ISSN 1547-3333. GBP 114 in United Kingdom to institutions; EUR 153, USD 192 to institutions (effective 2012).
Indexed: A01, A02, A03, A08, A22, CA, E-psyche, E01, FamI, P03, P25, P27, P43, P48, P54, PQC, PsycInfo, PsycholAb, T02.
—BLDSC (4336.530800), IE, Ingenta. **CCC.**
Published by: (American Psychological Association, Division of Humanistic Psychology), Routledge (Subsidiary of: Taylor & Francis Group), 325 Chestnut St, Ste 800, Philadelphia, PA 19106. TEL 800-354-1420, FAX 215-625-2940, journals@routledge.com, http://www.routledge.com. Ed. Scott D Churchill. Adv. contact Linda Hann TEL 44-1344-779945.

➤ **HUMOR**; international journal of humor research. *see* SOCIOLOGY

150 FRA ISSN 1763-9816
HUMUS, SUBJECTIVITE ET LIEN SOCIAL. Text in French. 2003. irreg. back issues avail. **Document type:** *Monographic series, Consumer.*
Published by: Editions Eres, 33 Av. Marcel Dassault, Toulouse, 31500, France. TEL 33-5-61751576, FAX 33-5-61735289, eres@edition-eres.com.

152.4 362.2 USA
HYGEIA; an online journal for pregnancy and neonatal loss. Text in English. 1995. m. (plus d. updates). free. **Document type:** *Magazine, Consumer.* **Description:** Shares information about support groups, resources and references. Provides updates of relevant medical news, reviews, and multidiscipline insights into the nature of pregnancy, perinatal and neonatal loss.
Media: Online - full text.
Indexed: E-psyche, SpeleolAb.
Address: PO Box 3943, Amity Sta, New Haven, CT 06525. Ed., Pub., R&P Dr. Michael R Berman.

HYPNOTHERAPY TODAY. *see* MEDICAL SCIENCES—Hypnosis

150 FRA ISSN 1242-6121
HYPOTHESES. Text in French. 1992. irreg. back issues avail. **Document type:** *Monographic series.*
Published by: Editions Eres, 33 Av. Marcel Dassault, Toulouse, 31500, France. TEL 33-5-61751576, FAX 33-5-61735289, eres@edition-eres.com.

P

150 USA ISSN 1943-0604
BF723.M54
▼ **I E E E TRANSACTIONS ON AUTONOMOUS MENTAL DEVELOPMENT.** (Institute of Electrical and Electronics Engineers) Text in English. 2009 (Mar.). q. USD 610; USD 765 combined subscription (print & online eds.) (effective 2012). adv. back issues avail.; reprints avail. **Document type:** *Journal, Academic/Scholarly.* **Description:** Covers computational modeling of mental development, including mental architecture, theories, algorithms, properties and experiments.
Related titles: Online - full text ed.: ISSN 1943-0612. 2009 (Mar.). USD 555 (effective 2012).
Indexed: CPEI, P30, RefZh, SCOPUS.
—BLDSC (4363.145100), IE. **CCC.**
Published by: I E E E, 445 Hoes Ln, Piscataway, NJ 08854. TEL 732-981-0060, 800-678-4333, FAX 732-562-6380, contactcenter@ieee.org, http://www.ieee.org. Eds. Zhengyou Zhang TEL 425-703-3029, Dawn Melley.

150 NGA ISSN 1117-1421
BF1
➤ **I F E PSYCHOLOGIA**; an international journal. Text in English. 1993. s-a. NGN 1,000 domestic; USD 20 in Africa; USD 40 rest of world (effective 2004). adv. bk.rev. abstr.; bibl.; charts; maps; stat.; tr.lit. 200 p./no.; back issues avail.; reprints avail. **Document type:** *Journal, Academic/Scholarly.* **Description:** Deals with psychology and science.
Related titles: CD-ROM ed.: A P A. 1993; E-mail ed.; Online - full text ed.: Africa Online, INASP London. 1999.
Indexed: A01, E-psyche, P03, P25, P27, P48, P54, PQC, PsycInfo, PsycholAb.
—BLDSC (4363.282195), IE, Ingenta.
Published by: (Psychologia Ltd GHA), I F E Centre for Psychological Studies (I C P S), PO Box 1548, Ile Ife, Osun State, Nigeria. Ed. A A Olowu. Adv. contact Samson Akinyele. page USD 100. Circ: 1,000.

150 BRA ISSN 1807-2526
➤ **I G T NA REDE.** (Instituto de Gestalt - Terapia) Text in Portuguese. 2004. s-a. free (effective 2009). **Document type:** *Journal, Academic/Scholarly.*
Media: Online - full text.
Published by: Instituto de Gestalt - Terapia (I G T), Rua Haddock Lobo 369 Grupo 709, Tijuca, Rio de Janeiro, 20260-141, Brazil. TEL 55-21-25671038, FAX 55-21-25692650. Ed. Marcelo Pinheiro da Silva.

150 DEU ISSN 2190-6734
▼ **I P M B - BEITRAEGE ZUR PSYCHOLOGIE.** (Institut fuer Psychologie - Abteilung fuer Psychologische Methodenlehre und Biopsychologie) Text in German. 2010. irreg. price varies. **Document type:** *Monographic series, Academic/Scholarly.*
Published by: Verlag Dr. Kovac, Leverkusenstr 13, Hamburg, 22761, Germany. TEL 49-40-3988800, FAX 49-40-39888055, info@verlagdrkovac.de, http://www.verlagdrkovac.de.

150 617.7 GBR ISSN 2041-6695
▼ ➤ **I-PERCEPTION.** Text in English. 2010. irreg. free (effective 2011). **Document type:** *Journal, Academic/Scholarly.* **Description:** Journal of human, animal, and machine perception.
Media: Online - full text.
Published by: Pion Ltd., 207 Brondesbury Park, London, NW2 5JN, United Kingdom. TEL 44-20-84590066, FAX 44-20-84516454, http://www.pion.co.uk/.

155 GBR ISSN 2040-5235
BF712
I S S B D BULLETIN. Text in English. 1998. s-a. free to members (effective 2010). back issues avail. **Document type:** *Bulletin, Academic/Scholarly.*
Formerly (until May 2009): International Society for the Study of Behavioral Development. Newsletter
Related titles: Online - full text ed.: ISSN 2040-5243. free (effective 2010).
Published by: (International Society for the Study of Behavioral Development), Sage Publications Ltd. (Subsidiary of: Sage Publications, Inc.), 1 Oliver's Yard, 55 City Rd, London, EC1Y 1SP, United Kingdom. TEL 44-20-73248500, FAX 44-20-73248600, info@sagepub.co.uk, http://www.uk.sagepub.com/home.nav. Ed. Karina Weichold TEL 49-3641-945221.

616.89 USA
I S S D NEWS. Text in English. 1983. bi-m. free to members. back issues avail. **Document type:** *Newsletter.* **Description:** Focuses on recent news from other organizations of interest to members, news for US and international affiliates, and current issues concerning the field of multiple personality and dissociative states.
Formerly: I S S M P and D News (1075-7783)
Indexed: E-psyche.
Published by: International Society for the Study of Dissociation, 8201 Greensboro Dr, Ste 300, McLean, VA 22102. TEL 703-610-9037, FAX 703-610-9005, issd@issd.org, http://www.issd.org/. Circ: 1,500 (paid).

THE I U P JOURNAL OF BEHAVIORAL FINANCE. *see* BUSINESS AND ECONOMICS—Management

150 ESP ISSN 1695-7075
IDEACCION (ONLINE). Text in Spanish. 1994. 3/yr. back issues avail. **Document type:** *Magazine, Academic/Scholarly.*
Formerly (until 2003): Ideaccion (Print) (1134-1548)
Media: Online - full text.
Published by: Centro Psicologico y Educativo Huerta del Rey, Calle del Pio Hortega, 10, Valladolid, Castilla y Leon 47014, Spain. c_h_rey@correo.cop.es, http://www.centrohuertadelrey.com/rv.htm.

370.15 150 USA ISSN 1041-8377
IMAGERY TODAY. Text in English. 1983. s-a. USD 10 (effective 2000).
Indexed: E-psyche.
Published by: (International Imagery Association), Brandon House, Inc., PO Box 240, Bronx, NY 10471. Circ: 14,941.

616.89 FRA ISSN 1628-9676
IMAGINAIRE & INCONSCIENT; etudes psychoterapiques. Text in French. 1970. s-a. EUR 40 domestic; EUR 60 foreign (effective 2009). **Document type:** *Journal, Academic/Scholarly.* **Description:** Covers psychoanalytic techniques involving the waking dream state.
Former titles (until 2001): Etudes Psychanalytiques (1372-8210); (until 1998): Etudes Psychotherapiques (0246-7887)
Related titles: Online - full text ed.
Indexed: DIP, E-psyche, FR, IBR, IBZ, PsycholAb, SCOPUS.
—BLDSC (4368.996070), INIST.
Published by: (Groupe International du Reve-Eveille en Psychanalyse), Editions L' Esprit du Temps, 115 Rue Anatole France, B P 107, Le Bouscat, 33491 Cedex, France. TEL 33-5-56028419, FAX 33-5-56029131, info@lespritdutemps.com.

150 BRA ISSN 1413-666X
H53.B7
IMAGINARIO. Text in Portuguese. 1993. s-a. BRL 60 (effective 2006). back issues avail. **Document type:** *Journal, Academic/Scholarly.*
Related titles: Online - full text ed.: ISSN 1981-1616. 2006.
Published by: Universidade de Sao Paulo, Laboratorio de Estudios do Imaginario, Ave. Prof. Lucio martins Rodriguez, Trav. 4 Bloco 17, Sala 18, Sao Paulo, 05508-900, Brazil. TEL 55-11-30914386, FAX 55-11-30914475, labi@edu.usp.br, http://www.edu.usp.br/. Ed. Maria de Lourdes Beldi de Alcantara.

133 152 USA ISSN 0276-2366
BF311
➤ **IMAGINATION, COGNITION AND PERSONALITY**; consciousness in theory, research, clinical practice. Text in English. 19??. q. USD 402, USD 112 combined subscription to institutions (print & online eds.) (effective 2011). adv. bk.rev. back issues avail.; reprints avail. **Document type:** *Journal, Academic/Scholarly.* **Description:** Examines the diverse uses of imagery, fantasy, consciousness in psychotherapy, behavior modification, and related areas of study.
Former titles (until 1982): Journal of Altered States of Consciousness (0094-5498); (until 1973): International Journal of Altered States of Consciousness
Related titles: Online - full text ed.: ISSN 1541-4477. USD 381 to institutions; USD 106 to individuals (effective 2011).
Indexed: A20, A22, AbAn, C06, C07, CA, DIP, E-psyche, IBR, IBZ, MLA-IB, P03, P10, P12, P25, P30, P48, P53, P54, PQC, PsycInfo, PsycholAb, RASB, RILM, S21, T02.
—BLDSC (4368.996200), IE, Infotrieve, Ingenta. **CCC.**
Published by: Baywood Publishing Co., Inc., 26 Austin Ave, PO Box 337, Amityville, NY 11701. TEL 631-691-1270, 800-638-7819, FAX 631-691-1770, Baywood@baywood.com. Eds. James M Honeycutt, Robert G Kunzendorf.

150 780 649 USA ISSN 2153-7879
IMAGINE (SILVER SPRING). Text in English. 1996. a. free (effective 2010). **Document type:** *Newsletter, Trade.* **Description:** News and information from the American Music Therapy Association Early Childhood section.
Formerly (until Fall 2010): Early Childhood Newsletter (2153-7852)
Media: Online - full text.
Published by: American Music Therapy Association, 8455 Colesville Rd, Ste 1000, Silver Spring, MD 20910. TEL 301-589-3300, FAX 301-589-5175, info@musictherapy.org, http://www.musictherapy.org.

158 USA ISSN 2153-4144
▼ **IMAGINE YOUR POSSIBILITIES.** Text in English. 2010. m. free (effective 2011). **Document type:** *Magazine, Consumer.* **Description:** Advice from Michelle Greene on getting your life unstuck.
Media: Online - full text.
Published by: Michelle Greene, International, 89 Joshua Hill, Windsor, CT 06095. TEL 860-640-4642, mgintl@michellegreene.com, http://www.michellegreene.com/.

IN CHARACTER; a journal of everyday virtues. *see* PHILOSOPHY

IN-FAN-CI-A (CATALAN EDITION). *see* EDUCATION

158 NLD ISSN 1877-5357
▼ ➤ **IN-MIND (DUTCH EDITION).** Text in Dutch. 2010. q. **Document type:** *Journal, Trade.*
Media: Online - full text. **Related titles:** ◆ English ed.: In-Mind (English Edition). ISSN 1877-5306; ◆ Portuguese ed.: In-Mind (Portuguese Edition). ISSN 1877-5322; ◆ German ed.: In-Mind (German Edition). ISSN 1877-5349.
Published by: Hans IJzerman, Ed. & Pub. editor@in-mind.org. Eds. Annemarie Wennekers, Erik Bijleveld, Hans IJzerman, Selin Kesebir.

158 NLD ISSN 1877-5306
➤ **IN-MIND (ENGLISH EDITION).** Text in English. 2006. q. bk.rev. **Document type:** *Journal, Trade.* **Description:** Presents scientific social psychological research.
Media: Online - full text. **Related titles:** ◆ German ed.: In-Mind (German Edition). ISSN 1877-5349; ◆ Portuguese ed.: In-Mind (Portuguese Edition). ISSN 1877-5322; ◆ Dutch ed.: In-Mind (Dutch Edition). ISSN 1877-5357.
Published by: Hans IJzerman, Ed. & Pub. editor@in-mind.org. Eds. Hans IJzerman, Selin Kesebir.

158 NLD ISSN 1877-5349
▼ ➤ **IN-MIND (GERMAN EDITION).** Text in German. 2010. q. **Document type:** *Journal, Trade.*
Media: Online - full text. **Related titles:** ◆ English ed.: In-Mind (English Edition). ISSN 1877-5306; ◆ Portuguese ed.: In-Mind (Portuguese Edition). ISSN 1877-5322; ◆ Dutch ed.: In-Mind (Dutch Edition). ISSN 1877-5357.
Published by: Hans IJzerman, Ed. & Pub. editor@in-mind.org. Eds. Malte Friese, Rene Kopietz, Hans IJzerman, Selin Kesebir.

158 NLD ISSN 1877-5322
▼ ➤ **IN-MIND (PORTUGUESE EDITION).** Text in Portuguese. 2010. q. **Document type:** *Journal, Trade.*
Media: Online - full text. **Related titles:** ◆ English ed.: In-Mind (English Edition). ISSN 1877-5306; ◆ Dutch ed.: In-Mind (Dutch Edition). ISSN 1877-5357; ◆ German ed.: In-Mind (German Edition). ISSN 1877-5349.
Published by: Hans IJzerman, Ed. & Pub. editor@in-mind.org. Eds. Rui Soares Costa, Tomas Palma, Hans IJzerman, Selin Kesebir.

150 AUS ISSN 1441-8754
IN-PSYCH. Text in English. 1979. bi-m. AUD 110 domestic to individuals; AUD 116 foreign to individuals; AUD 125 domestic to institutions; AUD 135 foreign to institutions; free to members (effective 2008). adv. back issues avail. **Document type:** *Bulletin, Trade.* **Description:** Provides latest information on the profession of psychology in Australia.
Formerly (until 1996): Australian Psychological Association. Bulletin (0157-9517); Which incorporated (1984-1988): Professional Psychology Abstracts (0815-3450)
Related titles: Online - full text ed.: free (effective 2008).
Indexed: AEI, IBR, IBZ.
—Ingenta.
Published by: Australian Psychological Society, 257 Collins St, Level 11, Melbourne, VIC 3000, Australia. TEL 61-3-86623300, FAX 61-3-96636177, contactus@psychology.org.au, http://www.psychsociety.com.au/. Ed. Roslyn Crosswell. adv.: color page AUD 2,105; trim 210 x 297.

IN THE FAMILY; the magazine for queer people and their loved ones. *see* HOMOSEXUALITY

150 GBR ISSN 1371-5704
INCLUSION (ENGLISH EDITION). Text in English. a. free. bk.rev. **Document type:** *Bulletin, Consumer.* **Description:** Publishes various pamphlets, position papers, reports of seminars, conferences and more.
Former titles (until 1995): I L S M H News (0772-9367); (until 1984): International League of Societies for Persons with Mental Handicap. News (0772-9626); International League of Societies for the Mentally Handicapped. World Congress Proceedings. (0074-6754)
Related titles: French ed.: Inclusion (French Edition). ISSN 1371-5720; Spanish ed.: Inclusion (Spanish Edition). ISSN 1371-5712; German ed.: Inclusion (German Edition). ISSN 1371-5690.
Indexed: E-psyche.
Published by: Inclusion International, c/o The Rix Centre, University of East London, Docklands Campus, 4-6 University Way, London, E16 2RD, United Kingdom. TEL 44-208-2237709, FAX 44-208-2237411, info@inclusion-international.org, http://www.inclusion-international.org.

158 IND ISSN 0019-4247
BF636.A1
INDIAN ACADEMY OF APPLIED PSYCHOLOGY. JOURNAL. Text in English. 1974 (vol.17). s-a. free to members (effective 2011). charts; stat. index. **Document type:** *Journal, Academic/Scholarly.*
Indexed: E-psyche, ERA, IPsyAb, M12, P03, PsycInfo, PsycholAb, S20, S21.
—BLDSC (4761.900000), IE, Ingenta.
Published by: Indian Academy of Applied Psychology, University of Madras, Department of Educational Management & Applied Psychology, National Institute of Technical Teachers Training & Research, Chennai, Tamil Nadu 600 113, India. iaap_india@yahoo.com, http://www.iaap.org.in. Ed. Panch Ramalingam.

150 IND ISSN 0973-1342
RJ499.A1
➤ **INDIAN ASSOCIATION FOR CHILD AND ADOLESCENT MENTAL HEALTH. JOURNAL.** Abbreviated title: J I A C A M. Text in English. 2005. q. free (effective 2011). adv. back issues avail. **Document type:** *Journal, Academic/Scholarly.* **Description:** Covers all aspects of child and adolescent mental health.
Media: Online - full text.
Indexed: A01, EMBASE, ExcerpMed, R10, Reac, SCOPUS, T02.
Published by: Indian Association for Child and Adolescent Mental Health, c/o Vivek Agarwal, B-1, 10/69, Sector K, Aliganj, Lucknow, 226 024, India. jitendranagpal@rediffmail.com, http://www.childindia.org. Ed., Adv. contact Dr. Pratap Sharan.

158 IND ISSN 0019-5073
BF636.A1 CODEN: IJAPBI
INDIAN JOURNAL OF APPLIED PSYCHOLOGY. Text in English. 1964. a. USD 75 (effective 2011). bk.rev. charts. index. reprints avail. **Document type:** *Journal, Academic/Scholarly.*
Related titles: Microfilm ed.: (from PQC).
Indexed: A22, BAS, E-psyche, IPsyAb, PsycholAb.
—BLDSC (4410.300000), IE, Ingenta.
Published by: (Department of Psychology), University of Madras, c/o Director, Publications Division, University Centenary Bldg, Chepauk, Chennai, Tamil Nadu 600 005, India. TEL 91-44-25399520, FAX 91-44-25366693, vcoffice@unom.ac.in, http://www.unom.ac.in.

152 IND ISSN 0303-2582
RC467
INDIAN JOURNAL OF CLINICAL PSYCHOLOGY. Text in English. 1974. s-a. bk.rev. abstr.; bibl. index. back issues avail. **Document type:** *Journal, Academic/Scholarly.*
Related titles: Online - full text ed.
Indexed: A22, E-psyche, IPsyAb, P30, PsycholAb, PsycholRG.
—BLDSC (4410.750000), IE, Ingenta, INIST.
Published by: Indian Association of Clinical Psychologists, Department of Psychiatry, JSS University, JSS Medical College Hospital, M G Rd, Mysore, 570004, India. iacpsecretary@gmail.com, http://www.iacp.in/.

370.15 150 IND ISSN 0378-1003
L61
INDIAN JOURNAL OF PSYCHOMETRY AND EDUCATION. Text in English. 1970. s-a. bk.rev. bibl.; charts. **Document type:** *Journal, Academic/Scholarly.*
Indexed: E-psyche, IPsyAb, PsycholAb.
—BLDSC (4420.321000), IE, Ingenta.
Published by: Indian Psychometric and Educational Research Association, University of Patna, Dept. of Education, Patna, Bihar 800 004, India. **Subscr. to:** I N S I O Scientific Books & Periodicals, PO Box 7234, Indraprastha HPO, New Delhi 110 002, India. **Dist. by:** Nandini Enterprises, 23-451 Wazirpura, Agra, Uttar Pradesh 282 003, India.

158 USA ISSN 1541-745X
BF697
➤ **INDIVIDUAL DIFFERENCES RESEARCH.** Text in English. 2003 (Apr.). q. USD 75 to individuals; USD 105 to institutions (effective 2010). abstr.; bibl.; mkt.; stat. Index. back issues avail.; reprints avail. **Document type:** *Journal, Academic/Scholarly.* **Description:** Publishes original, scholarly manuscripts investigating the psychology of the individual.
Incorporates: Psychology Research Journal (1553-1678)
Related titles: Online - full text ed.: USD 30 to individuals (effective 2010).
Indexed: A01, A03, A08, ASSIA, B04, CA, P03, P43, PsycInfo, PsycholAb, S02, S03, SCOPUS, SSAI, SSAb, SSI, T02, W03, W05.
—BLDSC (4437.386000).
Address: PO Box 15591, Pittsburgh, TX 15244. TEL 412-736-6551.

150 ZAF ISSN 2079-7222
➤ **INDO - PACIFIC JOURNAL OF PHENOMENOLOGY.** Abbreviated title: I P J P. Text in English. 2001. s-a. ZAR 185.50 to individuals; ZAR 265 to institutions (effective 2011). back issues avail. **Document type:** *Journal, Academic/Scholarly.* **Description:** Intends to be a forum for Southern African, Indian, Australian, Asian, New Zealand and Pacific Island scholars to discuss a broad range of phenomenological issues.
Related titles: Online - full text ed.: ISSN 1445-7377. free (effective 2011).
Indexed: A39, AmHI, C27, C29, CA, D03, D04, E13, H07, R14, S14, S15, S18, T02.
Published by: (Rhodes University, Edith Cowan University AUS), National Inquiry Services Centre, 19 Worcester St., PO Box 377, Grahamstown, 6140, South Africa. TEL 27-46-6229698, FAX 27-46-6229550, publishing@nisc.co.za, http://www.nisc.co.za/. Ed. Christopher R Stones.

150 USA ISSN 1754-9426
HF5548.7
➤ **INDUSTRIAL AND ORGANIZATIONAL PSYCHOLOGY**; perspectives on science and practice. Text in English. 2008 (Mar.). q. GBP 251 combined subscription in United Kingdom to institutions (print & online eds.); EUR 319 combined subscription in Europe to institutions (print & online eds.); USD 505 combined subscription in the Americas to institutions (print & online eds.); USD 491 combined subscription elsewhere to institutions (print & online eds.) (effective 2012). adv. back issues avail.; reprint service avail. from PSC. **Document type:** *Journal, Academic/Scholarly.* **Description:** Aims to cultivate an interactive exchange of ideas of science, practice, and public policy as it relates to the field of industrial and organizational psychology.
Related titles: Online - full text ed.: ISSN 1754-9434. 2008. GBP 219 in United Kingdom to institutions; EUR 277 in Europe to institutions; USD 438 in the Americas to institutions; USD 427 elsewhere to institutions (effective 2012) (from IngentaConnect).
Indexed: A22, B01, B07, CA, CurCont, E01, PsycInfo, SSCI, T02, W07.
—BLDSC (4445.244500), IE. **CCC.**
Published by: (Society for Industrial and Organizational Psychology), Wiley-Blackwell Publishing, Inc. (Subsidiary of: Wiley-Blackwell Publishing Ltd.), 111 River St, Hoboken, NJ 07030. TEL 201-748-6000, FAX 201-748-6088, info@wiley.com, http://www.wiley.com/. Ed. Cynthia McCauley TEL 336-286-4420. Adv. contact Kristin McCarthy TEL 201-748-7683.

158 USA ISSN 0739-1110
HF5548.7
THE INDUSTRIAL-ORGANIZATIONAL PSYCHOLOGIST. Abbreviated title: T I P. Text in English. 1972. q. USD 20 to individuals; USD 30 to institutions (effective 2007). **Document type:** *Magazine, Trade.*
Related titles: Online - full text ed.
Indexed: A01.
—Ingenta. **CCC.**
Published by: Society for Industrial and Organizational Psychology (Subsidiary of: American Psychological Association), 529 Ordway Ave, PO Box 87, Bowling Green, OH 43402. TEL 419-353-0032, FAX 419-352-2645, siop@siop.org. Ed. Wendy Becker.

INFANCIA Y APRENDIZAJE/JOURNAL FOR THE STUDY OF EDUCATION AND DEVELOPMENT; journal for the study of education and development. *see* EDUCATION

155.4 GBR ISSN 1522-7227
HQ771 CODEN: EDPAEA
➤ **INFANT AND CHILD DEVELOPMENT.** Text in English. 1992. 6/yr. GBP 380 in United Kingdom to institutions; EUR 471 in Europe to institutions; USD 730 elsewhere to institutions; GBP 418 combined subscription in United Kingdom to institutions (print & online eds.); EUR 519 combined subscription in Europe to institutions (print & online eds.); USD 803 combined subscription elsewhere to institutions (print & online eds.) (effective 2010). adv. back issues avail.; reprint service avail. from PSC. **Document type:** *Journal, Academic/Scholarly.* **Description:** Publishes theoretical, empirical and methodological papers covering all aspects of psychological development during infancy and early childhood.
Formerly (until 1999): Early Development and Parenting (1057-3593)
Related titles: Microform ed.: (from PQC); Online - full text ed.: ISSN 1522-7219. GBP 380 in United Kingdom to institutions; EUR 471 in Europe to institutions; USD 730 elsewhere to institutions (effective 2010).
Indexed: A01, A03, A08, A22, ASSIA, C06, C07, C08, C22, C28, CA, CINAHL, CMM, CPE, CurCont, E-psyche, F09, FamI, IBR, IBZ, L&LBA, P02, P03, P10, P12, P30, P43, P48, P53, P54, PQC, PsycInfo, PsycholAb, S02, S03, S21, SCOPUS, SSCI, T02, W07.
—GNLM, IE, Infotrieve. **CCC.**
Published by: John Wiley & Sons Ltd. (Subsidiary of: John Wiley & Sons, Inc.), 1-7 Oldlands Way, PO Box 808, Bognor Regis, West Sussex PO21 9FF, United Kingdom. TEL 44-1865-778315, FAX 44-1243-843232, cs-journals@wiley.com, http://eu.wiley.com/WileyCDA/. Eds. Jane Herbert, Mark Bennett. **Subscr. to:** 1-7 Oldlands Way, PO Box 809, Bognor Regis, West Sussex PO21 9FG, United Kingdom. TEL 44-1865-778054, cs-agency@wiley.com; John Wiley & Sons, Inc., 111 River St, Hoboken, NJ 07030. TEL 201-748-6645, subinfo@wiley.com.

618.92 GBR ISSN 0163-6383
BF719 CODEN: IBDEDP
➤ **INFANT BEHAVIOR AND DEVELOPMENT.** Text in English. 1978. 4/yr. EUR 508 in Europe to institutions; JPY 67,500 in Japan to institutions; USD 569 elsewhere to institutions (effective 2012). bk.rev. index. back issues avail.; reprint service avail. from PSC. **Document type:** *Journal, Academic/Scholarly.* **Description:** Presents original, empirical and theoretical studies directed toward the understanding of infancy. Each study is methodologically complete with a documented replicability of results.
Related titles: Online - full text ed.: ISSN 1934-8800 (from IngentaConnect, ScienceDirect).
Indexed: A01, A03, A08, A20, A22, A26, ASCA, B21, B25, BDM&CN, BIOSIS Prev, BibInd, C06, C07, C28, CA, CDA, CPLI, CurCont, DIP, E-psyche, EMBASE, ERA, ExcerpMed, F09, FR, FamI, I05, IBR, IBZ, L&LBA, M12, MEDLINE, MLA, MLA-IB, MycolAb, NSA, P03, P30, PsycInfo, PsycholAb, R10, RILM, Reac, S20, S21, SCOPUS, SOPODA, SSCI, SociolAb, T02, W07.
—BLDSC (4478.270000), GNLM, IE, Infotrieve, Ingenta, INIST. **CCC.**
Published by: (International Society for Infant Studies), Elsevier Ltd (Subsidiary of: Elsevier Science & Technology), The Blvd, Langford Ln, Kidlington, Oxford, OX5 1GB, United Kingdom. TEL 44-1865-843000, FAX 44-1865-843010, journalscustomerserviceemea@elsevier.com. Ed. G Savelsbergh. Circ: 1,500. **Subscr. to:** Elsevier BV, Radarweg 29, PO Box 211, Amsterdam 1000 AE, Netherlands. TEL 31-20-4853757, FAX 31-20-4853432, http://www.elsevier.nl.

➤ **INFANT MENTAL HEALTH JOURNAL.** *see* MEDICAL SCIENCES—Pediatrics

150 ESP ISSN 1138-364X
INFOCOP. Text in Spanish. 1997. 3/yr. adv. back issues avail. **Document type:** *Magazine, Trade.*
Related titles: Online - full text ed.: ISSN 1886-1407.
Published by: Colegio Oficial de Psicologos, Claudio Coello 46, Madrid, 28001, Spain. TEL 34-91-4355212, FAX 34-91-5779172. adv.: page EUR 1,540; 180 x 226. Circ: 51,300.

150 ESP ISSN 0214-347X
INFORMACIO PSICOLOGICA. Text in Spanish, Catalan. 1983. q. back issues avail. **Document type:** *Journal, Academic/Scholarly.*
Formerly (until 1985): Butlleti d'Informacio Psicologica (0214-3461)
Related titles: Online - full text ed.
Published by: Colegio Oficial de Psicologos, Claudio Coello 46, Madrid, 28001, Spain. TEL 34-91-4355212, FAX 34-91-5779172, http://www.cop.es. Circ: 6,000.

302.2 USA ISSN 0740-5502
P87
INFORMATION AND BEHAVIOR. Text in English. 1985. irreg., latest vol.6, 2001. price varies. back issues avail. **Document type:** *Monographic series, Academic/Scholarly.* **Description:** Examines the forms, technologies, organization, and use of information, and how they affect human behavior. Coverage includes the effect of new technology on office and home life, regulation and control of information, and the economics of information.
Indexed: E-psyche, P30.
—**CCC.**
Published by: Transaction Publishers, 35 Berrue Cir, Piscataway, NJ 08854. TEL 732-445-2280, FAX 732-445-3138, trans@transactionpub.com, http://www.transactionpub.com. Ed. Brent D Ruben.

616.890 150 USA ISSN 1086-2099
RC467.7
INSIDER'S GUIDE TO GRADUATE PROGRAMS IN CLINICAL AND COUNSELING PSYCHOLOGY (YEAR). Text in English. 1990. biennial. USD 27.95 per vol. (print or online ed.) (effective 2010). charts; stat. **Document type:** *Directory, Consumer.* **Description:** Outlines strategies for getting into graduate school in psychology and gives an inside look at all to the programs available in the US and Canada.
Formerly (until 1996): Insider's Guide to Graduate Programs in Clinical Psychology (1061-7132)
Related titles: Online - full text ed.
Indexed: E-psyche.
Published by: Guilford Publications, Inc., 72 Spring St, 4th Fl, New York, NY 10012. TEL 800-365-7006, FAX 212-966-6708, info@guilford.com.

INSIGHT-PSICOTERAPIA. *see* MEDICAL SCIENCES—Psychiatry And Neurology

150 FRA ISSN 1778-7807
INSISTANCE. Text in French. 2005. a. EUR 50 for 2 yrs. domestic to individuals; EUR 58 for 2 yrs. foreign; EUR 56 for 2 yrs. domestic to institutions; EUR 40 for 2 yrs. domestic to students (effective 2011). back issues avail. **Document type:** *Journal, Academic/Scholarly.*
Related titles: Online - full text ed.: ISSN 1951-6258.
Published by: (Insistance), Editions Eres, 33 Av. Marcel Dassault, Toulouse, 31500, France. TEL 33-5-61751576, FAX 33-5-61735289, eres@edition-eres.com.

INSPIRATIEKALENDER. *see* BUSINESS AND ECONOMICS—Personnel Management

616.89 CAN ISSN 0832-7475
INSTITUT DE RECHERCHES PSYCHOLOGIQUES. BULLETIN. Key Title: Bulletin I R P. Text in French. 1986. irreg. price varies. **Document type:** *Bulletin.*
Published by: Institut de Recherches Psychologiques, 34 Fleury St W, Montreal, PQ H3L 1S9, Canada. TEL 514-382-3000, FAX 514-382-3007. Eds. Malko von Osten, Marie-Paule Chevrier.

INTEGRATIVE PSYCHOLOGICAL & BEHAVIORAL SCIENCE. *see* MEDICAL SCIENCES—Psychiatry And Neurology

155.4 DEU ISSN 0342-6831
INTEGRATIVE THERAPIE; Zeitschrift fuer vergleichende Psychotherapie und Methodenintegration. Text in German; Summaries in English. 1975. q. EUR 39; EUR 30 to students (effective 2006). adv. bk.rev. index. **Document type:** *Magazine, Academic/Scholarly.*
Indexed: DIP, E-psyche, IBR, IBZ, RILM.
—GNLM.
Published by: (Fritz Perls Institut), Junfermann Verlag, Imadstr 40, Paderborn, 33102, Germany. TEL 49-5251-13440, FAX 49-5251-134444, ju@junfermann.de, http://www.junfermann.de. Ed. Hilarion Petzold. Circ: 2,500.

152.4 BRA ISSN 1809-8002
INTELIGENCIA EMOCIONAL. Text in Portuguese. 2006. m. BRL 19.90 newsstand/cover (effective 2007). adv. **Document type:** *Magazine, Consumer.*
Published by: Digerati Comunicacao e Tecnologia Ltda., Rua Haddock Lobo 347, 12o andar, Sao Paulo, 01414-001, Brazil. TEL 55-11-32172600, FAX 55-11-32172617, http://www.digerati.com.br.

153 FRA ISSN 0769-4113
BF309
INTELLECTICA. Text in French. 1985. s-a.
Indexed: FR, L&LBA, P03, PsycInfo, PsycholAb.
—BLDSC (4531.819070), INIST.
Published by: Association pour la Recherche Cognitive, M S H Paris-Nord, 4 Rue de la Croix Faron, Saint Denis, 93210, France. TEL 33-1-55939306, http://www.arco.asso.fr.

370.15 150 GBR ISSN 0160-2896
BF431 CODEN: NTLLDT
➤ **INTELLIGENCE (KIDLINGTON)**; a multidisciplinary journal. Text in English. 1977. 6/yr. EUR 566 in Europe to institutions; JPY 75,200 in Japan to institutions; USD 634 elsewhere to institutions (effective 2012). bk.rev. Index. back issues avail.; reprint service avail. from PSC. **Document type:** *Journal, Academic/Scholarly.* **Description:** Features original research and theoretical studies and review papers that substantially contribute to the understanding of intelligence. Includes papers in psychometrics, test and measurement, and other empirical and theoretical studies in intelligence and mental retardation.
Related titles: Online - full text ed.: ISSN 1873-7935 (from IngentaConnect, ScienceDirect).
Indexed: A01, A02, A03, A08, A20, A22, A26, AEI, AIA, ASSIA, B21, CA, CDA, CPE, CurCont, DIP, E-psyche, E03, E07, E08, ERI, ERIC, FR, FamI, G08, I05, IBR, IBZ, L&LBA, MLA-IB, NSA, P02, P03, P10, P12, P30, P48, P53, P54, PQC, PsycInfo, PsycholAb, RASB, RILM, S09, SCOPUS, SOPODA, SSCI, SociolAb, T02, W07.
—BLDSC (4531.826500), IE, Infotrieve, Ingenta, INIST. **CCC.**
Published by: Elsevier Ltd (Subsidiary of: Elsevier Science & Technology), The Blvd, Langford Ln, Kidlington, Oxford, OX5 1GB, United Kingdom. TEL 44-1865-843000, FAX 44-1865-843010. Ed. Douglas K Detterman. Circ: 650. **Subscr. to:** Elsevier BV, Radarweg 29, PO Box 211, Amsterdam 1000 AE, Netherlands. TEL 31-20-4853757, FAX 31-20-4853432, JournalsCustomerServiceEMEA@elsevier.com, http://www.elsevier.nl.

153.9 USA ISSN 1930-0441
Z675.A2
INTELLIGENCE INSIGHTS. Text in English. 2005. q. USD 20 to non-members; free to members (effective 2009). adv. back issues avail. **Document type:** *Bulletin, Trade.* **Description:** Designed to support the competitive intelligence practices and the professional development of the Special Library Association's competitive intelligence division members.
Media: Online - full content.
Published by: Special Libraries Association, 331 S Patrick St, Alexandria, VA 22314. sla@sla.org. Ed. Cynthia Cheng Correia TEL 617-479-7862. Adv. contact Tom Seward.

150 BRA ISSN 1981-8076
➤ **INTERACAO EM PSICOLOGIA.** Text in Portuguese. 1997. s-a. free (effective 2011). **Document type:** *Journal, Academic/Scholarly.*
Media: Online - full text.
Published by: Universidade Federal do Parana, Departamento de Psicologia, Praca Santos Andrade 50, Terreo, Curitiba, PR 80020-240, Brazil. TEL 55-41-33102625. Ed. Alexandre Dittrich.

150 BRA ISSN 1413-2907
INTERACOES. Text in Portuguese. 1996. s-a. **Document type:** *Journal, Academic/Scholarly.*
Related titles: Online - full text ed.: ISSN 2175-3504.
Indexed: C01.
Published by: Universidade Sao Marcos, Programa de Pos-graduacao em Psicologia, R. Clovis Bueno de Azevedo, 176, Ipivanga, Sao Paulo, 04266-040, Brazil. TEL 52-11-34910522, editorialinteracoes@smarcos.br, http://www.smarcos.br/. Ed. Ferreira Ricardo Franklin.

150 PRI ISSN 0034-9690
BF1 CODEN: RIPSBZ
➤ **INTERAMERICAN JOURNAL OF PSYCHOLOGY.** Text and summaries in English, Portuguese, Spanish. 1967. s-a. USD 40 domestic; USD 180 foreign (effective 2009). adv. bk.rev. index. back issues avail.; reprints avail. **Document type:** *Journal, Academic/Scholarly.*
Related titles: Online - full text ed.: free (effective 2011).
Indexed: A20, A22, A26, ASCA, B21, C01, CA, Chicano, E-psyche, I04, I05, NSA, P03, P30, PsycInfo, PsycholAb, RILM, S02, S03, SCOPUS, SociolAb, T02.
—BLDSC (4531.889000), IE, Ingenta.
Published by: Interamerican Society of Psychology, Universidad de Puerto Rico, PO Box 23345, San Juan, 00931-3345, Puerto Rico. TEL 787-764-0000, FAX 787-764-2615, http://www.am.org/sipsych/. Ed. Silvia Helena Koller. Circ: 1,500.

150.19 ITA ISSN 1721-0143
INTERAZIONI; clinica e ricerca psicoanalitica su individuo-coppia-famiglia. Text in Italian. 1990. s-a. EUR 39.50 domestic to institutional members; EUR 60.50 foreign to institutions (effective 2009). **Document type:** *Journal, Academic/Scholarly.*
Indexed: DIP, E-psyche, IBR, IBZ, P03, PsycInfo, PsycholAb.
Published by: (Centro di Pscioanalisi Familiare e di Coppia), Franco Angeli Edizioni, Viale Monza 106, Milan, 20127, Italy. TEL 39-02-2837141, FAX 39-02-26144793, redazioni@francoangeli.it, http://www.francoangeli.it.

150 300 ARG ISSN 0325-8203
BF5
INTERDISCIPLINARIA; revista de psicologia y ciencias afines/journal of psychology and related sciences. Text in English, Spanish. 1980. s-a. ARS 35 domestic to individuals; USD 35 foreign to individuals; ARS 50 domestic to institutions; USD 42 foreign to institutions (effective 2010). bk.rev. **Document type:** *Monographic series, Academic/Scholarly.*
Related titles: Online - full text ed.: ISSN 1668-7027. 2003. free (effective 2011) (from SciELO).
Indexed: A01, A26, CA, E-psyche, F03, F04, I04, I05, P03, PsycInfo, PsycholAb, SCOPUS, T02.
Published by: (National Research Council of Argentina), Centro Interamericano de Investigaciones Psicologicas y Ciencias Afines, Tte Gral Juan Peron 2158, Buenos Aires, C1040AAH, Argentina. TEL 54-11-49531477, FAX 54-11-49531477, ciipme@ssdnet.com.ar. Eds. Horacio J A Rimoldi, Maria Cristina Richaud. Circ: 500.

370.15 USA
INTERNATIONAL ASSOCIATION FOR REGRESSION RESEARCH AND THERAPIES. NEWSLETTER. Variant title: A P R T Newsletter. Text in English. 1980. q. free to members (effective 2010). bk.rev. back issues avail. **Document type:** *Newsletter, Trade.* **Description:** Contains the latest IARRT events, news, board activities and updates.
Formerly: Association for Past-Life Research and Therapies. Newsletter (1054-0792)
Related titles: Online - full text ed.
Indexed: E-psyche.

P

Published by: International Association for Regression Research & Therapies, Inc., PO Box 20151, Riverside, CA 92516. TEL 951-784-1570, FAX 951-784-8440, info@iarrt.org. Ed. Dorothy M Neddermeyer.

150 001.3 USA ISSN 2156-0269
BF1
▼ **INTERNATIONAL ASSOCIATION OF TRANSDISCIPLINARY PSYCHOLOGY. JOURNAL.** Variant title: Journal of the International Association of Transdisciplinary Psychology. Text in English. 2009. a. free (effective 2010). **Document type:** *Journal, Academic/Scholarly.* **Description:** Features scholarly work on psychology and architecture, philosophy, cinema, art, literature, theology mythology, and music.
Media: Online - full text.
Published by: International Association of Transdisciplinary Psychology, Mercer County College, LA 129, 1200 Old Trenton Highway, West Windsor, NJ 08550. TEL 609-570-3859, giobbim@mccc.edu.

150 USA ISSN 1094-6039
JA74.5
INTERNATIONAL BULLETIN OF POLITICAL PSYCHOLOGY. Abbreviated title: I B P P. Text in English. 1996 (Nov.). w. free (effective 2010). back issues avail. **Document type:** *Journal, Academic/Scholarly.*
Media: Online - full text. **Related titles:** E-mail ed.
Published by: Embry-Riddle Aeronautical University, Humanities and Social Science Department, 600 S Clyde Morris Blvd, Daytona Beach, FL 32114. TEL 386-226-6790, FAX 386-226-7050, donna.barbie@erau.edu, http://daytonabeach.erau.edu/coas/humanities-social-sciences. Ed. Richard W Bloom.

615.78 USA ISSN 0268-1315
RM315 CODEN: ICLPE4
➤ **INTERNATIONAL CLINICAL PSYCHOPHARMACOLOGY.** Text in English. 1986. bi-m. USD 1,516 domestic to institutions; USD 1,625 foreign to institutions (effective 2011). adv. Index. back issues avail.; reprints avail. **Document type:** *Journal, Academic/Scholarly.* **Description:** Provides an essential link between research and clinical practice throughout psychopharmacology.
Related titles: CD-ROM ed.; Online - full text ed.: ISSN 1473-5857.
Indexed: A22, ASCA, B21, B25, BIOBASE, BIOSIS Prev, CurCont, DBA, E-psyche, E01, EMBASE, ExcerpMed, FoP, IABS, INI, ISR, IndMed, Inpharma, MEDLINE, MycolAb, NSA, NSCI, P03, P30, P35, PsycInfo, PsycholAb, R10, Reac, SCI, SCOPUS, W07.
—BLDSC (4538.674500), GNLM, IE, Infotrieve, Ingenta, INIST. **CCC.**
Published by: Lippincott Williams & Wilkins (Subsidiary of: Wolters Kluwer N.V.), 530 Walnut St, Philadelphia, PA 19106. TEL 215-521-8300, FAX 215-521-8902, customerservice@lww.com, http://www.lww.com. Ed. Dr. Stuart A Montgomery TEL 44-20-85667986. Pub. Phil Daly. Adv. contact Pembe Sevenel. Circ: 138.

150 CHE ISSN 0074-3364
INTERNATIONAL CONGRESS FOR ANALYTICAL PSYCHOLOGY. PROCEEDINGS. Text in English. 1983. triennial. illus.; bibl. Index. back issues avail. **Document type:** *Proceedings, Academic/Scholarly.*
Indexed: E-psyche.
Published by: (International Association for Analytical Psychology), Daimon Verlag AG, Hauptstr 85, Einsiedeln, 8840, Switzerland. TEL 41-55-4122266, FAX 41-55-4122231, daimon@compuserve.com, http://www.daimon.ch. Eds. Mary Ann Mattoon, Robert Hinshaw. R&P Heidy Fassler.

150 GBR ISSN 0085-2112
➤ **INTERNATIONAL CONGRESS OF PSYCHOLOGY. PROCEEDINGS.** (Published by host national organization: Great Britain, 1969; Japan, 1972; France, 1976; German Democratic Republic, 1980; Mexico, 1984; 11/09: Updated by JA) Text in English. quadrennial. USD 125.95 per issue (effective 2009). **Document type:** *Proceedings, Academic/Scholarly.* **Description:** Aims to strengthen the dialog within psychology around the world and to facilitate communication among different areas of psychology and among psychologists from different cultural backgrounds.
Related titles: CD-ROM ed.
Indexed: E-psyche.
Published by: (International Union of Psychological Science DEU), Psychology Press (Subsidiary of: Taylor & Francis Ltd.), 27 Church Rd, Hove, E Sussex BN3 2FA, United Kingdom. TEL 44-20-70176000, FAX 44-20-70176717. Ed. Qicheng Jing et al.

616.89 GBR ISSN 0803-706X
CODEN: IFOPE6
➤ **INTERNATIONAL FORUM OF PSYCHOANALYSIS.** Abbreviated title: I F P. Text in English. 1992. q. GBP 190 combined subscription in United Kingdom to institutions (print & online eds.); EUR 251, USD 315 combined subscription to institutions (print & online eds.) (effective 2012). adv. back issues avail.; reprint service avail. from PSC. **Document type:** *Journal, Academic/Scholarly.* **Description:** Promotes articles demonstrating clinical experience and interest in revising or expanding psychoanalytic theory.
Related titles: Online - full text ed.: ISSN 1651-2324. GBP 172 in United Kingdom to institutions; EUR 226, USD 284 to institutions (effective 2012) (from IngentaConnect).
Indexed: A01, A03, A08, A22, CA, E-psyche, E01, EMBASE, ExcerpMed, MLA-IB, P03, P43, P48, PQC, PsycInfo, PsycholAb, SCOPUS, T02.
—BLDSC (4540.345505), GNLM, IE, Infotrieve, Ingenta. **CCC.**
Published by: (International Federation of Psychoanalytic Societies (IFPS) NOR), Routledge (Subsidiary of: Taylor & Francis Group), 4 Park Sq, Milton Park, Abingdon, Oxon OX14 4RN, United Kingdom. TEL 44-20-70176000, FAX 44-20-70176336, subscriptions@tandf.co.uk, http://www.routledge.com. Ed. Christer Sjodin. Adv. contact Linda Hann TEL 44-1344-779945. Circ: 500. **Subscr. to:** Taylor & Francis Ltd., Journals Customer Service, Sheepen Pl, Colchester, Essex CO3 3LP, United Kingdom. TEL 44-20-70175544, FAX 44-20-70175198, tf.enquiries@tfinforma.com.

306.482 GBR ISSN 1445-9795
➤ **INTERNATIONAL GAMBLING STUDIES.** Abbreviated title: I G S. Text in English. 2001. 3/yr. GBP 276 combined subscription in United Kingdom to institutions (print & online eds.); EUR 364, AUD 530, USD 459 combined subscription to institutions (print & online eds.) (effective 2012). adv. reprint service avail. from PSC. **Document type:** *Journal, Academic/Scholarly.* **Description:** Contains analysis and research in gambling studies, presenting work on the theory, methods, practice and history of gambling.
Related titles: Online - full text ed.: ISSN 1479-4276. 2001. GBP 248 in United Kingdom to institutions; EUR 328, AUD 477, USD 413 to institutions (effective 2012) (from IngentaConnect).
Indexed: A22, ASSIA, CA, E01, H&TI, H06, P03, PsycInfo, SociolAb, T02.
—IE, Ingenta. **CCC.**
Published by: Routledge (Subsidiary of: Taylor & Francis Group), 4 Park Square, Milton Park, Abingdon, Oxon OX14 4RN, United Kingdom. subscriptions@tandf.co.uk, http://www.routledge.com. Ed. Alex Blaszczynski TEL 61-2-90367227. Adv. contact Linda Hann TEL 44-1344-779945. **Subscr. to:** Taylor & Francis Ltd., Journals Customer Service, Sheepen Pl, Colchester, Essex CO3 3LP, United Kingdom. TEL 44-20-70175544, FAX 44-20-70175198, tf.enquiries@tfinforma.com.

150 616.89 USA ISSN 1545-7516
BF203
INTERNATIONAL GESTALT JOURNAL. Text in English. 1978. s-a. USD 50; USD 65 combined subscription (print & CD eds.) (effective 2011). bk.rev. back issues avail. **Document type:** *Journal, Academic/Scholarly.* **Description:** Features articles and reviews relating to the theory and practice of Gestalt therapy.
Formerly (until 2002): The Gestalt Journal (0190-0412)
Related titles: CD-ROM ed.: USD 30 (effective 2011).
Indexed: A22, E-psyche, P03, PsycInfo, PsycholAb.
—BLDSC (4540.610700), IE, Ingenta. **CCC.**
Published by: Center for Gestalt Development, Inc., PO Box 278, Gouldsboro, ME 04607. press@gestalt.org.

155.282 USA ISSN 1552-8138
BF889
INTERNATIONAL HANDWRITING ANALYSIS REVIEW. Text in English. 2002. s-a. free to members (effective 2005).
Published by: American Association of Handwriting Analysts, P O Box 6201, San Jose, CA 95150. AAHAemail@juno.com, http://www.aaha-handwriting.org/.

THE INTERNATIONAL JOURNAL FOR THE PSYCHOLOGY OF RELIGION. *see* RELIGIONS AND THEOLOGY

INTERNATIONAL JOURNAL OF ADOLESCENCE AND YOUTH. *see* CHILDREN AND YOUTH—About

▼ **INTERNATIONAL JOURNAL OF APPLIED BEHAVIORAL ECONOMICS.** *see* BUSINESS AND ECONOMICS

150.19 GBR ISSN 1742-3341
BF173.A2
THE INTERNATIONAL JOURNAL OF APPLIED PSYCHOANALYTIC STUDIES. Text in English. 2004. q. GBP 192 in United Kingdom to institutions; EUR 243 in Europe to institutions; USD 377 elsewhere to institutions; GBP 212 combined subscription in United Kingdom to institutions (print & online eds.); EUR 268 combined subscription in Europe to institutions (print & online eds.); USD 415 combined subscription elsewhere to institutions (print & online eds.) (effective 2010). adv. back issues avail.; reprint service avail. from PSC. **Document type:** *Journal, Academic/Scholarly.* **Description:** Offers a concentrated focus on the subjective and relational aspects of the human unconscious and its expression in human behavior in all its variety.
Related titles: Online - full text ed.: ISSN 1556-9187. 2006. GBP 192 in United Kingdom to institutions; EUR 243 in Europe to institutions; USD 377 elsewhere to institutions (effective 2010).
Indexed: A01, CA, P03, PsycInfo, PsycholAb, SCOPUS, T02.
—IE, Ingenta. **CCC.**
Published by: John Wiley & Sons Ltd. (Subsidiary of: John Wiley & Sons, Inc.), 1-7 Oldlands Way, PO Box 808, Bognor Regis, West Sussex PO21 9FF, United Kingdom. TEL 44-1865-778315, FAX 44-1243-843232, cs-journals@wiley.com, http://eu.wiley.com/WileyCDA/. Eds. Nadia Ramzy, W Twemlow. **Subscr. to:** 1-7 Oldlands Way, PO Box 809, Bognor Regis, West Sussex PO21 9FG, United Kingdom. TEL 44-1865-778054, cs-agency@wiley.com.

THE INTERNATIONAL JOURNAL OF AVIATION PSYCHOLOGY. *see* TRANSPORTATION—Air Transport

150 USA ISSN 1555-7855
RC489.B4
INTERNATIONAL JOURNAL OF BEHAVIORAL AND CONSULTATION THERAPY. Abbreviated title: I J B C T. Variant title: International Journal of Behavioral Consultation and Therapy. Text in English. 2005 (Win.). q. free (effective 2011). adv. back issues avail.; reprints avail. **Document type:** *Journal, Academic/Scholarly.*
Media: Online - full text.
Indexed: A01, A26, A39, C06, C07, C27, C29, CA, D03, D04, E03, E13, ERIC, H12, I05, P03, P30, PsycInfo, R14, S14, S15, S18, T02.
Published by: Behavior Analyst Online, 535 Queen St, Philadelphia, PA 19147. baojournal@aol.com, http://baojournal.com/. Ed. Jack Apsche. Adv. contact Halina Dziewolska TEL 215-462-6737.

155 GBR ISSN 0165-0254
BF712 CODEN: IJBDDY
➤ **INTERNATIONAL JOURNAL OF BEHAVIORAL DEVELOPMENT.** Abbreviated title: I J B D. Text in English. 1978. bi-m. USD 1,596, GBP 863 combined subscription to institutions (print & online eds.); USD 1,564, GBP 846 to institutions (effective 2011). adv. bk.rev. back issues avail.; reprint service avail. from PSC. **Document type:** *Journal, Academic/Scholarly.* **Description:** Promotes the discovery and application of knowledge about developmental processes at all stages of the lifespan, from infancy through old age.
Related titles: Microform ed.: (from PQC); Online - full text ed.: ISSN 1464-0651. USD 1,436, GBP 777 to institutions (effective 2011) (from IngentaConnect); Supplement(s): I S S B D Newsletter.
Indexed: A01, A03, A08, A20, A22, ASCA, ASSIA, B21, B25, BIOSIS Prev, C28, CA, CDA, CPE, ChPerI, CurCont, DIP, E-psyche, E01, E03, EMBASE, ERI, ERIC, ExcerpMed, F09, FR, FamI, IBR, IBZ, IPsyAb, L&LBA, MycolAb, NSA, P03, P30, P43, PCI, PSI, PsycInfo, PsycholAb, R10, RASB, Reac, S02, S03, SCOPUS, SOPODA, SSCI, SociolAb, T02, W07.
—BLDSC (4542.128000), IE, Infotrieve, Ingenta, INIST. **CCC.**
Published by: (International Society for the Study of Behavioral Development), Sage Publications Ltd. (Subsidiary of: Sage Publications, Inc.), 1 Oliver's Yard, 55 City Rd, London, EC1Y 1SP, United Kingdom. TEL 44-20-73248500, FAX 44-20-73248600, info@sagepub.co.uk, http://www.uk.sagepub.com/home.nav. Ed. Marcel AG Van Aken TEL 31-30-2531945. adv.: B&W page GBP 450; 180 x 250. **Subscr. to:** Sage Publications, Inc., 2455 Teller Rd, Thousand Oaks, CA 91320. TEL 805-499-9774, FAX 805-499-0871, journals@sagepub.com.

302 USA ISSN 1070-5503
R726.5 CODEN: IJBMFT
➤ **INTERNATIONAL JOURNAL OF BEHAVIORAL MEDICINE.** Abbreviated title: I J B M. Text in English. 1994. q. EUR 462, USD 692 combined subscription to institutions (print & online eds.) (effective 2012). adv. back issues avail.; reprint service avail. from PSC. **Document type:** *Journal, Academic/Scholarly.* **Description:** Presents research and integrative reviews on interactions among behavioral, psychosocial, environmental, genetic and biomedical factors relevant to health and illness.
Related titles: Online - full text ed.: ISSN 1532-7558 (from IngentaConnect).
Indexed: A01, A02, A03, A08, A20, A22, ASCA, B21, C06, C07, C08, C11, CA, CINAHL, CurCont, E-psyche, E01, EMBASE, ExcerpMed, H04, IPsyAb, MEDLINE, NSA, P02, P03, P10, P12, P20, P22, P24, P25, P30, P43, P48, P53, P54, PQC, PsycInfo, PsycholAb, R09, R10, Reac, S11, SCOPUS, SD, SSCI, T02, W07.
—BLDSC (4542.128700), IE, Infotrieve, Ingenta. **CCC.**
Published by: (International Society of Behavioral Medicine DEU), Springer New York LLC (Subsidiary of: Springer Science+Business Media), 233 Spring St, New York, NY 10013. TEL 212-460-1500, FAX 212-460-1575, service-ny@springer.com. Ed. Joost Dekker. adv.: page USD 400; trim 5 x 8.

150 613.2 GBR ISSN 1479-5868
RM214
➤ **THE INTERNATIONAL JOURNAL OF BEHAVIORAL NUTRITION AND PHYSICAL ACTIVITY.** Text in English. 2004. irreg. free (effective 2010). **Document type:** *Journal, Academic/Scholarly.* **Description:** Covers all aspects of the behavioral features of diet and physical activity.
Related titles: Online - full text ed.: free (effective 2011).
Indexed: A01, A26, A34, A36, A39, C06, C07, C25, C27, C29, CA, CABA, D01, D03, D04, E12, E13, EMBASE, ExcerpMed, F10, FS&TA, FoSS&M, GH, H16, I05, IndVet, LT, N02, N03, N04, P03, P30, P37, P38, PEI, PN&I, PsycInfo, R12, R14, RRTA, S12, S14, S15, S18, SCI, SCOPUS, T02, T05, VS, W07, W11.
—**CCC.**
Published by: (International Society for Behavioral Nutrition and Physcial Activity USA), BioMed Central Ltd. (Subsidiary of: Springer Science+Business Media), 236 Gray's Inn Rd, London, WC1X 8HB, United Kingdom. TEL 44-20-31922000, FAX 44-20-31922010, info@biomedcentral.com, http://www.biomedcentral.com. Eds. Bente Wold, David Crawford, Robert Jeffery.

155.25 GBR ISSN 1364-436X
➤ **INTERNATIONAL JOURNAL OF CHILDREN'S SPIRITUALITY.** Abbreviated title: I J C S. Text in English. 1996. q. GBP 412 combined subscription in United Kingdom to institutions (print & online eds.); EUR 541, USD 679 combined subscription to institutions (print & online eds.) (effective 2012). adv. back issues avail.; reprint service avail. from PSC. **Document type:** *Journal, Academic/Scholarly.* **Description:** Aims to provide an international and multicultural forum for persons involved in research and development of children's and young people's spirituality.
Related titles: Online - full text ed.: ISSN 1469-8455. GBP 370 in United Kingdom to institutions; EUR 487, USD 612 to institutions (effective 2012) (from IngentaConnect).
Indexed: A01, A02, A03, A08, A20, A21, A22, ArtHuCI, B29, C28, CA, CPE, E-psyche, E01, E03, GSS&RPL, P10, P34, P48, P53, P54, PQC, R&TA, SCOPUS, T02, W07.
—IE, Infotrieve, Ingenta. **CCC.**
Published by: (Association for Children's Spirituality), Routledge (Subsidiary of: Taylor & Francis Group), 4 Park Sq, Milton Park, Abingdon, Oxon OX14 4RN, United Kingdom. TEL 44-20-70176000, FAX 44-20-70176336, subscriptions@tandf.co.uk, http://www.routledge.com. Eds. Clive Erricker TEL 44-23-92556926, Jane Erricker TEL 44-1962-827356. Adv. contact Linda Hann TEL 44-1344-779945. **Subscr. in N. America to:** Taylor & Francis Inc., Customer Services Dept, 325 Chestnut St, 8th Fl, Philadelphia, PA 19106. TEL 215-625-8900, 800-354-1420, FAX 215-625-2940, customerservice@taylorandfrancis.com; **Subscr. to:** Taylor & Francis Ltd., Journals Customer Service, Sheepen Pl, Colchester, Essex CO3 3LP, United Kingdom. TEL 44-20-70175544, FAX 44-20-70175198.

616.89 ESP ISSN 1697-2600
INTERNATIONAL JOURNAL OF CLINICAL AND HEALTH PSYCHOLOGY. Text in Spanish, English, Portuguese. 2000. 3/yr. EUR 40 to individuals; EUR 70 to institutions. back issues avail. **Document type:** *Journal, Academic/Scholarly.*
Formerly (until 2003): Revista Internacional de Psicologia Clinica y de la Salud (1576-7329)
Related titles: Online - full text ed.: ISSN 2174-0852. 2001. free (effective 2011).
Indexed: A01, CA, CurCont, P03, P30, PsycInfo, PsycholAb, SCOPUS, SSCI, T02, W07.
—BLDSC (4542.170050), IE, Ingenta. **CCC.**
Published by: (Asociacion Colombiana para el Avance de las Ciencias del Comportamiento COL), Asociacion Espanola de Psicologia Conductual, Ave Madrid s-n, Edif. Eurobequer Bajo, Granada, 18012, Spain. info@aepc.es. Ed. Juan Carlos Sierra.

▼ **INTERNATIONAL JOURNAL OF COGNITIVE LINGUISTICS.** *see* LINGUISTICS

158 USA ISSN 1937-1209
RC489.C63
➤ **INTERNATIONAL JOURNAL OF COGNITIVE THERAPY.** Text in English. 2008 (Feb.). q. USD 95 combined subscription domestic to individuals (print & online eds.); USD 130 combined subscription foreign to individuals (print & online eds.); USD 300 combined subscription domestic to institutions (print & online eds.); USD 345 combined subscription foreign to institutions (print & online eds.) (effective 2011). **Document type:** *Journal, Academic/Scholarly.* **Description:** Addresses all scientific and clinical aspects of cognitive therapy.
Related titles: Online - full text ed.: ISSN 1937-1217.
Indexed: A22, ASSIA, C06, C07, CurCont, E01, P03, P30, PsycInfo, SSCI, W07.
—BLDSC (4542.172370), IE. **CCC.**
Published by: (The International Association for Cognitive Psychotherapy), Guilford Publications, Inc., 72 Spring St, 4th Fl, New York, NY 10012. TEL 800-365-7006, FAX 212-966-6708, info@guilford.com. Ed. John H Riskind. R&P Kathy Kuehl. Adv. contact Marian Robinson. Circ: 900 (paid).

156 USA ISSN 0889-3667
BF671 CODEN: IJCPE8
➤ **INTERNATIONAL JOURNAL OF COMPARATIVE PSYCHOLOGY.** Text in English. 1987. q. back issues avail.; reprints avail. **Document type:** *Journal, Academic/Scholarly.* **Description:** Explores how the study of the development and evolution of behavior elucidates behavior, and investigates relationship of scientific research and theory to fundamental concepts about the evolutionary history and nature of humanity.
Related titles: Online - full text ed.: free (effective 2011).
Indexed: A01, A02, A03, A08, A22, CA, DIP, E-psyche, FR, IBR, IBZ, IPsyAb, P03, P30, P43, PsycInfo, PsycholAb, RASB, RILM, SWR&A, T02.
—BLDSC (4542.172950), IE, Infotrieve, Ingenta, INIST. **CCC.**
Published by: (International Society for Comparative Psychology), eScholarship (Subsidiary of: California Digital Library) Eds. Lauren Highfill, Stan A Kuczaj.

153.42 KOR
THE INTERNATIONAL JOURNAL OF CREATIVITY & PROBLEM SOLVING. Text in English. 1991. s-a. USD 80 to individuals; USD 120 to institutions (effective 2009). bk.rev. **Document type:** *Journal, Academic/Scholarly.* **Description:** Publishes original empirical and theoretical work on human higher-order cognition, with a particular emphasis on creativity.
Former titles (until 2009): Korean Journal of Thinking and Problem Solving (1598-723X); (until 1998): Sa-Go Gaebal Yeon-Gu (1225-3111)
Related titles: Online - full text ed.
Indexed: E-psyche, P03, PsycInfo, PsycholAb.
—BLDSC (4542.178800), IE, Ingenta.
Published by: Korean Association for Thinking Development/Daehan Sago Gaebal Yeonguhoe, Hangaram Core #209, Myung-duk-ro 155, Sueong-1 ga, Daegu, 704-701, Korea, S. TEL 82-53-7665989, FAX 82-53-7665989, kimyung@kmu.ac.kr. Ed. James C Kaufman.

150 GBR ISSN 1754-2863
RC455.4.E8
➤ **INTERNATIONAL JOURNAL OF CULTURE AND MENTAL HEALTH.** Text in English. 2008. s-a. GBP 162 combined subscription in United Kingdom to institutions (print & online eds.); EUR 254, USD 319 combined subscription to institutions (print & online eds.) (effective 2012). adv. reprint service avail. from PSC. **Document type:** *Journal, Academic/Scholarly.* **Description:** Provides an innovative forum, both international and multidisciplinary, for addressing cross-cultural issues and mental health.
Related titles: Online - full text ed.: ISSN 1754-2871. GBP 146 in United Kingdom to institutions; EUR 228, USD 287 to institutions (effective 2012).
Indexed: A22, C06, C07, CA, E01, P10, P30, P46, P48, P53, P54, PQC, PsycInfo, S02, S03, T02.
—IE. **CCC.**
Published by: Routledge (Subsidiary of: Taylor & Francis Group), 4 Park Sq, Milton Park, Abingdon, Oxon OX14 4RN, United Kingdom. TEL 44-20-70176000, FAX 44-20-70176336, subscriptions@tandf.co.uk, http://www.routledge.com. Eds. Dr. David Henderson, K S Bhui. Adv. contact Linda Hann TEL 44-1344-779945. **Subscr. to:** Taylor & Francis Ltd., Journals Customer Service, Sheepen Pl, Colchester, Essex CO3 3LP, United Kingdom. TEL 44-20-70175544, FAX 44-20-70175198.

▼ ➤ **INTERNATIONAL JOURNAL OF CYBER BEHAVIOR, PSYCHOLOGY AND LEARNING.** *see* EDUCATION

➤ **INTERNATIONAL JOURNAL OF DEVELOPMENTAL DISABILITIES.** *see* EDUCATION—Special Education And Rehabilitation

570 155 NLD ISSN 2192-001X
➤ **INTERNATIONAL JOURNAL OF DEVELOPMENTAL SCIENCE.** Text in English. q. USD 306 combined subscription in North America (print & online eds.); EUR 220 combined subscription elsewhere (print & online eds.) (effective 2012). **Document type:** *Journal, Academic/Scholarly.* **Description:** Provides a forum for basic research and application in the field of developmental science.
Related titles: Online - full text ed.: ISSN 2191-7485.
Published by: I O S Press, Nieuwe Hemweg 6B, Amsterdam, 1013 BG, Netherlands. TEL 31-20-6883355, FAX 31-20-6870019, info@iospress.nl, http://www.iospress.nl. Ed. Herbert Scheithauer.

➤ **INTERNATIONAL JOURNAL OF DREAM RESEARCH**; psychological aspects of sleep and dreaming. *see* MEDICAL SCIENCES—Psychiatry And Neurology

➤ **INTERNATIONAL JOURNAL OF EATING DISORDERS.** *see* NUTRITION AND DIETETICS

➤ **THE INTERNATIONAL JOURNAL OF EDUCATIONAL AND PSYCHOLOGICAL ASSESSMENT.** *see* EDUCATION

175 NGA ISSN 1119-7048
➤ **INTERNATIONAL JOURNAL OF EMOTIONAL PSYCHOLOGY AND SPORT ETHICS.** Text in English. a. NGN 5,000 domestic; USD 150 foreign (effective 2007). **Document type:** *Journal, Academic/Scholarly.* **Description:** Presents empirical studies as well as theoretical propositions and case summaries on human emotions and/or feelings, family issues, disabilities, problem of learning-difficulties, intellectual disabilities, behavior disorders, psychosomatic conditions, issues in sports.
Published by: Society for Psychology in Sport and Human Behaviour, c/o Dr J Aizoba, University of Ibadan, PO Box 22968, Ibadan, Nigeria. TEL 234-805-5114889, jaizoba2002@yahoo.co.uk. Ed. Dr. J Aizoba.

➤ **INTERNATIONAL JOURNAL OF EVIDENCE BASED COACHING AND MENTORING.** *see* EDUCATION

➤ **INTERNATIONAL JOURNAL OF FORENSIC PSYCHOLOGY.** *see* MEDICAL SCIENCES—Forensic Sciences

616.8 USA ISSN 0020-7284
RC488 CODEN: IJGPAO
➤ **INTERNATIONAL JOURNAL OF GROUP PSYCHOTHERAPY.** Abbreviated title: I J G P. Text in English. 1951. q. USD 110 combined subscription domestic to individuals (print & online eds.); USD 145 combined subscription foreign to individuals (print & online eds.); USD 560 combined subscription domestic to institutions (print & online eds.); USD 605 combined subscription foreign to institutions (print & online eds.) (effective 2011). adv. bk.rev. abstr.; bibl.; charts; stat.; illus. Index. 144 p./no.; back issues avail.; reprints avail. **Document type:** *Journal, Academic/Scholarly.* **Description:** Features to report and interpret the research and practice of group psychotherapy.
Related titles: Online - full text ed.: ISSN 1943-2836.
Indexed: A20, A22, A25, A26, AMHA, ASCA, ASSIA, B04, BRD, CA, Chicano, CurCont, E-psyche, E01, E08, EMBASE, ExcerpMed, F09, FR, Faml, G08, I05, IBR, IBZ, INI, IndMed, MEDLINE, P02, P03, P10, P12, P13, P20, P22, P25, P27, P30, P48, P53, P54, PQC, PsycInfo, PsycholAb, R10, Reac, S02, S03, S08, S09, SCOPUS, SFSA, SOPODA, SSA, SSAI, SSAb, SSCI, SSI, SWR&A, SociolAb, T02, W03, W07, W09.
—BLDSC (4542.270000), GNLM, IE, Infotrieve, Ingenta, INIST. **CCC.**
Published by: (American Group Psychotherapy Association), Guilford Publications, Inc., 72 Spring St, 4th Fl, New York, NY 10012. TEL 800-365-7006, FAX 212-966-6708, info@guilford.com. Ed. Les R Greene. R&P Kathy Kuehl. Adv. contact Marian Robinson. Circ: 3,500 (paid).

150 305.868 USA ISSN 1939-5841
BF76.5
INTERNATIONAL JOURNAL OF HISPANIC PSYCHOLOGY. Text in English. 2008. q. USD 295 to institutions; USD 442 combined subscription to institutions (print & online eds.) (effective 2012). **Document type:** *Journal, Academic/Scholarly.*
Related titles: Online - full text ed.: USD 295 to institutions (effective 2012).
Published by: Nova Science Publishers, Inc., 400 Oser Ave, Ste 1600, Hauppauge, NY 11788. TEL 631-231-7269, FAX 631-231-8175, main@novapublishers.com. Ed. Cirilo H Garcia.

150.19 GBR ISSN 1940-9052
▼ ➤ **THE INTERNATIONAL JOURNAL OF JUNGIAN STUDIES.** Text in English. 2009 (Mar.). s-a. GBP 163 combined subscription in United Kingdom to institutions (print & online eds.); EUR 259, USD 324 combined subscription to institutions (print & online eds.) (effective 2012). **Document type:** *Journal, Academic/Scholarly.* **Description:** Promotes and develops both Jungian and post-Jungian studies and scholarship on an international basis.
Related titles: Online - full text ed.: ISSN 1940-9060. GBP 147 in United Kingdom to institutions; EUR 233, USD 292 to institutions (effective 2012).
Indexed: A01, CA, P48, PQC, T02.
—CCC.
Published by: (International Association for Jungian Studies), Taylor & Francis Ltd. (Subsidiary of: Taylor & Francis Group), 4 Park Sq, Milton Park, Abingdon, Oxfordshire OX14 4RN, United Kingdom. TEL 44-20-70176000, FAX 44-20-70176336, subscriptions@tandf.co.uk. Ed. Renos K Papadopoulos.

614.58 362.2 USA ISSN 0020-7411
RA790.A1 CODEN: IJMHBV
➤ **INTERNATIONAL JOURNAL OF MENTAL HEALTH.** Abbreviated title: I J M H. Text in English. 1972. q. USD 1,040 combined subscription domestic to institutions (print & online eds.); USD 1,124 combined subscription foreign to institutions (print & online eds.) (effective 2012). adv. bk.rev. back issues avail.; reprint service avail. from PSC. **Document type:** *Journal, Academic/Scholarly.* **Description:** Presents in-depth articles on research, clinical practice, and the organization and delivery of mental health services. Covers both industrial and developing nations.
Related titles: Online - full text ed.: ISSN 1557-9328. 2004 (Apr.). USD 953 to institutions (effective 2012).
Indexed: A01, A03, A08, A20, A22, A26, ABS&EES, AMHA, ASCA, ASSIA, BRD, C06, C07, CA, CDA, E-psyche, E01, E08, Faml, G08, H11, H12, I05, IBR, IBZ, MEA&I, P03, P06, P30, P43, PsycInfo, PsycholAb, S02, S03, S09, SCOPUS, SSAI, SSAb, SSI, SociolAb, T02, W03, W05.
—BLDSC (4542.352000), GNLM, IE, Infotrieve, Ingenta. **CCC.**
Published by: (World Association for Psychosocial Rehabilitation), M.E. Sharpe, Inc., 80 Business Park Dr, Armonk, NY 10504. TEL 914-273-1800, 800-541-6563, FAX 914-273-2106, custserv@mesharpe.com. Ed. Martin Gittelman. Adv. contact Barbara Ladd TEL 914-273-1800.

150 362.2 USA ISSN 1557-1874
RA790.A1
➤ **INTERNATIONAL JOURNAL OF MENTAL HEALTH AND ADDICTION.** Abbreviated title: I J M & A. Text in English. 2006. q. EUR 500, USD 603 combined subscription to institutions (print & online eds.) (effective 2012). back issues avail.; reprint service avail. from PSC. **Document type:** *Journal, Academic/Scholarly.* **Description:** Provides a forum for international debate on mental health and addiction-related issues, and helps make sense of the effects of mental health and addiction on individuals and societies.
Related titles: Online - full text ed.: ISSN 1557-1882. 2003 (from IngentaConnect).
Indexed: A01, A22, A26, A39, Agr, B04, BRD, C27, C29, CA, D03, D04, E01, E13, ERIC, P03, P30, PAIS, PsycInfo, R14, S02, S03, S14, S15, S18, SCOPUS, SSA, SSAI, SSAb, SSI, SociolAb, T02, W01, W02, W03, W05.
—BLDSC (4542.352005), IE, Ingenta. **CCC.**
Published by: Springer New York LLC (Subsidiary of: Springer Science+Business Media), 233 Spring St, New York, NY 10013. TEL 212-460-1500, FAX 212-460-1575, service-ny@springer.com. Ed. Masood Zangeneh.

616.89165 AUS ISSN 1446-5019
➤ **INTERNATIONAL JOURNAL OF NARRATIVE THERAPY AND COMMUNITY WORK.** Text in English. 2002. q. AUD 77 domestic to individuals; AUD 93 foreign to individuals (effective 2009). back issues avail. **Document type:** *Journal, Academic/Scholarly.* **Description:** Provides the practitioners with latest ideas and developments in narrative practice.
Formed by the merger of (1997-2002): Gecko (1328-2123); (1998-2002): Dulwich Centre Journal (1441-1091); Which was formerly (until 1998): Dulwich Centre Newsletter (1030-2883)
Related titles: Online - full text ed.
Indexed: DIP, F09, Faml, IBR, IBZ, PAIS, S02, S03, T02.
—BLDSC (4542.369300). **CCC.**
Published by: Dulwich Centre Publications Pty. Ltd., Hutt St, PO Box 7192, Adelaide, SA 5000, Australia. TEL 61-8-82233966, FAX 61-8-82324441, dulwich@dulwichcentre.com.au. Ed., Pub. Cheryl White.

➤ **INTERNATIONAL JOURNAL OF NEUROPSYCHOPHARMACOLOGY.** *see* PHARMACY AND PHARMACOLOGY

➤ **INTERNATIONAL JOURNAL OF NURSING IN INTELLECTUAL AND DEVELOPMENTAL DISABILITIES.** *see* MEDICAL SCIENCES—Nurses And Nursing

150 AUS ISSN 1440-5377
HD58.7
➤ **INTERNATIONAL JOURNAL OF ORGANISATIONAL BEHAVIOUR.** Text in English. 1998. s-a. **Document type:** *Journal, Academic/Scholarly.*
Media: Online - full text.
Published by: University of Southern Queensland, The Department of Management & Organisational Behaviour, Toowoomba Campus, Toowoomba, QLD 4350, Australia. http://www.usq.edu.au/faculty/business/dept_hrm/HRMJournal/.

150 USA ISSN 1555-6824
➤ **INTERNATIONAL JOURNAL OF PLAY THERAPY.** Text in English. 1992. q. USD 111 domestic to individuals; USD 138 foreign to individuals; USD 415 domestic to institutions; USD 460 foreign to institutions (effective 2011). adv. back issues avail.; reprints avail. **Document type:** *Journal, Academic/Scholarly.* **Description:** Provides information and ideas about clinical interventions used in play therapy.
Related titles: Online - full text ed.: ISSN 1939-0629 (from ScienceDirect).
Indexed: P03, PsycInfo, PsycholAb, SCOPUS.
—BLDSC (4542.470250), IE, Ingenta. **CCC.**
Published by: (Association for Play Therapy, Inc.), American Psychological Association, 750 First St, NE, Washington, DC 20002. TEL 202-336-5500, 800-374-2721, journals@apa.org. Ed. Michael LeBlanc. Adv. contact Doug Constant TEL 202-336-5574. Circ: 5,700.

P

➤ **THE INTERNATIONAL JOURNAL OF PSYCHIATRY IN MEDICINE.** *see* MEDICAL SCIENCES—Psychiatry And Neurology

150.19 GBR ISSN 0020-7578
BF173.A2 CODEN: IJPSAA
➤ **THE INTERNATIONAL JOURNAL OF PSYCHOANALYSIS.** Text in English; Summaries in French, German, Spanish, Italian. 1920. bi-m. GBP 350 combined subscription in United Kingdom to institutions (print & online eds.); EUR 445 combined subscription in Europe to institutions (print & online eds.); USD 644 combined subscription in the Americas to institutions (print & online eds.); USD 685 combined subscription elsewhere to institutions (print & online eds.) (effective 2012). bk.rev.; film rev. abstr.; illus. index. 256 p./no. 1 cols./p.; back issues avail.; reprint service avail. from PSC. **Document type:** *Journal, Academic/Scholarly.* **Description:** Welcomes contributions to psychoanalytic theory and technique, methodology, the history of psychoanalysis, clinical communications, research and life-cycle development, education and professional issues, psychoanalytic psychotherapy, and interdisciplinary studies.
Incorporates (1974-1992): International Review of Psycho-Analysis (0306-2643)
Related titles: Online - full text ed.: ISSN 1745-8315. 1998. GBP 317 in United Kingdom to institutions; EUR 404 in Europe to institutions; USD 586 in the Americas to institutions; USD 623 elsewhere to institutions (effective 2012) (from IngentaConnect).
Indexed: A20, A22, ASCA, BibInd, CA, CurCont, DIP, E-psyche, E01, EMBASE, ExcerpMed, F09, FR, Faml, IBR, IBZ, IndMed, MEA&I, MEDLINE, MLA-IB, P03, P10, P12, P20, P25, P30, P48, P53, P54, PCI, PQC, PsycInfo, PsycholAb, R10, RASB, RILM, Reac, S02, S03, SCOPUS, SOPODA, SSCI, SociolAb, T02, W07.
—BLDSC (4542.498000), GNLM, IE, Infotrieve, Ingenta, INIST. **CCC.**
Published by: (Institute of Psychoanalysis), Wiley-Blackwell Publishing Ltd. (Subsidiary of: John Wiley & Sons, Inc.), 9600 Garsington Rd, Oxford, OX4 2DQ, United Kingdom. TEL 44-1865-776868, FAX 44-1865-714591, customerservices@blackwellpublishing.com. Eds. Dana Birksted-Breen, Robert Michels.

150 USA ISSN 1555-1024
RC489.S43
➤ **INTERNATIONAL JOURNAL OF PSYCHOANALYTIC SELF PSYCHOLOGY.** Abbreviated title: I J P S P. Text in English. 1985 (Win.). q. GBP 186 combined subscription in United Kingdom to institutions (print & online eds.); EUR 245, USD 307 combined subscription to institutions (print & online eds.) (effective 2012). adv. back issues avail.; reprint service avail. from PSC. **Document type:** *Journal, Academic/Scholarly.*
Formerly (until 2006): Progress in Self Psychology (0893-5483)
Related titles: Online - full text ed.: ISSN 1940-9141. GBP 167 in United Kingdom to institutions; EUR 222, USD 277 to institutions (effective 2012) (from IngentaConnect).
Indexed: A01, A22, ASSIA, CA, E01, P03, P48, PQC, PsycInfo, T02.
—BLDSC (4542.502000), IE, Ingenta. **CCC.**
Published by: Routledge (Subsidiary of: Taylor & Francis Group), 325 Chestnut St, Ste 800, Philadelphia, PA 19106. TEL 800-354-1420, FAX 215-625-2940, journals@routledge.com, http://www.routledge.com. Ed. William J Coburn. Adv. contact Linda Hann TEL 44-1344-779945.

150 COL ISSN 2011-7922
INTERNATIONAL JOURNAL OF PSYCHOLOGICAL RESEARCH. Text in English, Spanish. 2008. s-a. **Document type:** *Journal, Academic/Scholarly.*

Related titles: Online - full text ed.: ISSN 2011-2084. free (effective 2011).
Published by: Universidad de San Buenaventura, Medellin, Facultad de Psicologia, Carrera 56 C, 51-90, Barrio de San Benito, Medellin, Colombia. Ed. Mauricio Cuartas.

150 CAN ISSN 1918-7211
▼ **INTERNATIONAL JOURNAL OF PSYCHOLOGICAL STUDIES.** Text in English. 2009. s-a. **Document type:** *Journal, Academic/Scholarly.*
Related titles: Online - full text ed.: ISSN 1918-722X. free (effective 2011).
Indexed: A01, A26, CPerI, I05, P02, P10, P27, P48, P53, P54, PQC, T02.
Published by: Canadian Center of Science and Education, 4915 Bathurst St, Unit 209-309, Toronto, ON M2R 1X9, Canada. TEL 416-208-4027, FAX 416-208-4028, info@ccsenet.org. Ed. Suri Lee.

150 GBR ISSN 0020-7594
BF1 CODEN: IJPSBB
➤ **INTERNATIONAL JOURNAL OF PSYCHOLOGY/JOURNAL INTERNATIONAL DE PSYCHOLOGIE.** Abbreviated title: I J P. Text in English, French. 1965. bi-m. GBP 590 combined subscription in United Kingdom to institutions (print & online eds.); EUR 777, USD 976 combined subscription to institutions (print & online eds.) (effective 2012). adv. abstr.; charts; illus.; stat. back issues avail.; reprint service avail. from PSC. **Document type:** *Journal, Academic/Scholarly.* **Description:** Provides scientific information among sub disciplines of psychology and to foster the development of psychological science around the world.
Related titles: CD-ROM ed.: Psychology: An IUPsyS Global Resource; Microform ed.; Online - full text ed.: ISSN 1464-066X. GBP 530 in United Kingdom to institutions; EUR 699, USD 878 to institutions (effective 2012) (from IngentaConnect).
Indexed: A01, A02, A03, A08, A20, A22, AEI, AMHA, ASCA, ASSIA, B01, B06, B07, B09, BAS, BibInd, C28, CA, Chicano, CurCont, DIP, E-psyche, E01, EMBASE, ERA, ErgAb, ExcerpMed, FamI, IBR, IBZ, IPsyAb, L&LBA, MEA&I, MEDLINE, MLA-IB, P03, P30, P34, P43, PRA, PsycInfo, PsycholAb, R10, RASB, Reac, S02, S03, SCOPUS, SD, SOPODA, SSCI, SociolAb, T02, W07.
—IE, Infotrieve, Ingenta, INIST. **CCC.**
Published by: (International Union of Psychological Science), Psychology Press (Subsidiary of: Taylor & Francis Ltd.), 27 Church Rd, Hove, E Sussex BN3 2FA, United Kingdom. TEL 44-20-70176000, FAX 44-20-70176717, http://www.psypress.com. Ed. Claudia Dalbert. Adv. contact Linda Hann TEL 44-1344-779945. **Subscr. to:** Journals Customer Service, Taylor & Francis Group, Rankine Rd, Basingstoke, Hants RG24 8PR, United Kingdom. TEL 44-1256-813002, FAX 44-1256-479438.

150 LTU ISSN 1941-7233
BF1
➤ **INTERNATIONAL JOURNAL OF PSYCHOLOGY: A BIOPSYCHOSOCIAL APPROACH.** Text in English, Lithuanian. 2008 (Aug.). s-a. free (effective 2008). abstr. **Document type:** *Journal, Academic/Scholarly.* **Description:** Covers the study of the phenomena of human mental processes and behavior through the analysis of psychological issues within the broader context including biological, psychological, and social aspects.
Media: Online - full content.
Indexed: A01, CA, PsycInfo, T02.
Published by: Vytautas Magnus University, Department of General Psychology, K. Donelaicio 52-315, Kaunas, LT-44244, Lithuania. TEL 370-37-327824, FAX 370-37-327824, bpk@smf.vdu.lt. Eds. Aukse Endriulaitiene, Max McFarland. **Co-publisher:** University of Nebraska at Kearney, Department of Counseling and School Psychology.

150 NGA
➤ **INTERNATIONAL JOURNAL OF PSYCHOLOGY AND COUNSELLING.** Text in English. m. free (effective 2010). adv. **Document type:** *Journal, Academic/Scholarly.*
Media: Online - full text.
Published by: Academic Journals, PO Box 73023, Victoria Island, Lagos, Nigeria. service@academicjournals.org. Eds. Narasappa Kumaraswamy, Dr. Shaila Khan, Col. Yazmin Figueroa-Guzmany.

150 USA ISSN 1098-4127
INTERNATIONAL JOURNAL OF PSYCHOLOGY RESEARCH. Text in English. 1995. q. USD 450 to institutions; USD 675 combined subscription to institutions (print & online eds.) (effective 2012). **Document type:** *Journal, Academic/Scholarly.*
Related titles: Online - full text ed.: USD 450 to institutions (effective 2012).
Published by: Nova Science Publishers, Inc., 400 Oser Ave, Ste 1600, Hauppauge, NY 11788. TEL 631-231-7269, FAX 631-231-8175, main@novapublishers.com. Ed. Alexandra M Columbus.

150 616.891 615.1 USA ISSN 1088-6710
➤ **INTERNATIONAL JOURNAL OF PSYCHOPATHOLOGY, PSYCHOPHARMACOLOGY, AND PSYCHOTHERAPY.** Abbreviated title: I J P P P. Text in English. 1996. irreg., latest 1996. free (effective 2011). bk.rev.; software rev.; video rev. illus. reprints avail. **Document type:** *Journal, Academic/Scholarly.* **Description:** Publishes review papers, research reports, case reports, comments and letters to the editor.
Media: Online - full text.
Indexed: E-psyche.
Published by: PsyCom.Net, c/o Ivan Goldberg, 1346 Lexington Ave, New York, NY 10128. Ed. Ivan Goldberg.

150 NLD ISSN 0167-8760
QP360 CODEN: IJPSEE
➤ **INTERNATIONAL JOURNAL OF PSYCHOPHYSIOLOGY.** Text in English. 1983. 12/yr. EUR 2,821 in Europe to institutions; JPY 374,500 in Japan to institutions; USD 3,154 elsewhere to institutions (effective 2012). adv. bk.rev. back issues avail. **Document type:** *Journal, Academic/Scholarly.* **Description:** Covers all aspects of psychophysiology. Aims to integrate the neurosciences and psychological sciences.
Related titles: Microform ed.: (from PQC); Online - full text ed.: ISSN 1872-7697 (from IngentaConnect, ScienceDirect).
Indexed: A01, A03, A08, A20, A22, A26, ASCA, B21, B25, BIOBASE, BIOSIS Prev, CA, CurCont, DIP, E-psyche, EMBASE, ExcerpMed, FR, FamI, GeoRef, I05, IABS, IBR, IBZ, ISR, IndMed, Inpharma, MEDLINE, MycolAb, NSA, NSCI, P03, P30, P35, PsycInfo, PsycholAb, R10, RILM, Reac, SCI, SCOPUS, SSCI, T02, W07.
—BLDSC (4542.506500), GNLM, IE, Infotrieve, Ingenta, INIST. **CCC.**
Published by: (International Organization of Psychophysiology), Elsevier BV (Subsidiary of: Elsevier Science & Technology), Radarweg 29, PO Box 211, Amsterdam, 1000 AE, Netherlands. TEL 31-20-4853911, FAX 31-20-4852457, JournalsCustomerServiceEMEA@elsevier.com, http://www.elsevier.nl. Ed. Connie C Duncan.

150 362.29 GBR ISSN 1475-7192
RA790.A1
➤ **INTERNATIONAL JOURNAL OF PSYCHOSOCIAL REHABILITATION.** Text in English. 1997. a. free (effective 2011). back issues avail. **Document type:** *Journal, Academic/Scholarly.* **Description:** Provides a public forum for practitioners, consumers and researchers to address the multiple service needs of patients and families and help determine what works, for whom under a variety of circumstances.
Media: Online - full content. **Related titles:** Print ed.
Indexed: A01, CA, R09, SCOPUS, T02.
—**CCC.**
Published by: Hampstead Psychological Associates, Ste 12, Islington Business Centre, 14-22 Coleman Fields, London, N1 7AD, United Kingdom.

➤ **THE INTERNATIONAL JOURNAL OF RESEARCH AND REVIEW.** *see* SOCIAL SCIENCES: COMPREHENSIVE WORKS

150 PHL ISSN 2243-7681
▼ ➤ **INTERNATIONAL JOURNAL OF RESEARCH STUDIES IN PSYCHOLOGY.** Text in English. 2012. s-a. PHP 1,200 domestic; USD 30 in Asia & the Pacific; USD 40 elsewhere (effective 2012). Index. back issues avail.; reprints avail. **Document type:** *Journal, Academic/Scholarly.* **Description:** Topics of interests include but not limited to studies that furthers our understanding of the various concepts, issues, and problems of psychology in pre-primary, primary, high school, college, university, and adult individuals. Some other areas of psychology include, clinical, community, developmental, educational, social, organizational, environmental, experimental, family, physiological, positive, psychometric, and other related themes.
Related titles: Online - full text ed.: free.
Published by: Consortia Academia Publishing, Burgos St., Barangay Concepcion, Malabon City, National Capital Region 1470, Philippines. TEL 63-2-5140516. Ed., Pub., R&P, Adv. contact Virginia Pedrasta.

▼ ➤ **INTERNATIONAL JOURNAL OF SCHOOL PSYCHOLOGY.** *see* EDUCATION—Teaching Methods And Curriculum

158 USA ISSN 1091-2851
➤ **INTERNATIONAL JOURNAL OF SELF-HELP AND SELF-CARE.** Abbreviated title: I J S H S C. Text in English. 1999. q. USD 98 combined subscription to individuals (print & online eds.); USD 283 combined subscription to institutions (print & online eds.) (effective 2011). bk.rev. back issues avail.; reprints avail. **Document type:** *Journal, Academic/Scholarly.* **Description:** Designed to link together the wide spectrum of people, issues, and viewpoints involved in the dynamically growing, world-wide self-help movement.
Related titles: Online - full text ed.: ISSN 1541-4450. USD 93 to individuals; USD 270 to institutions (effective 2011).
Indexed: C06, C07, CA, E-psyche, P30, S02, S03, SCOPUS, SSA, SociolAb, T02.
—IE, Ingenta. **CCC.**
Published by: Baywood Publishing Co., Inc., 26 Austin Ave, PO Box 337, Amityville, NY 11701. TEL 631-691-1270, 800-638-7819, FAX 631-691-1770, Baywood@baywood.com. Ed. Fred Massarik.

155.3 USA ISSN 1931-7611
BF692 CODEN: JPSXET
➤ **INTERNATIONAL JOURNAL OF SEXUAL HEALTH.** Abbreviated title: J P H S. Text in English. 1988. q. GBP 600 combined subscription in United Kingdom to institutions (print & online eds.); EUR 779, USD 784 combined subscription to institutions (print & online eds.) (effective 2012). adv. bk.rev. 120 p./no. 1 cols./p.; back issues avail.; reprint service avail. from PSC. **Document type:** *Journal, Academic/Scholarly.* **Description:** Publishes original articles and reviews about human sexuality.
Formerly (until 2007): Journal of Psychology & Human Sexuality (0890-7064)
Related titles: Microform ed.: (from PQC); Online - full text ed.: International Journal of Sexual Health (Online). ISSN 1931-762X. GBP 540 in United Kingdom to institutions; EUR 701, USD 706 to institutions (effective 2012).
Indexed: A01, A03, A22, A36, AbAn, BiolDig, C06, C07, C25, CA, CABA, CurCont, DIP, E-psyche, E01, ESPM, F09, FR, FamI, G10, GH, GW, HEA, IBR, IBZ, IPsyAb, P03, P10, P22, P25, P30, P34, P48, P53, P54, PAIS, PQC, PerIslam, PsycInfo, PsycholAb, R12, RiskAb, S02, S03, S21, SCOPUS, SFSA, SOPODA, SSCI, SWR&A, SociolAb, T02, T05, TAR, V&AA, W07, W11.
—BLDSC (4542.544900), GNLM, IE, Infotrieve, Ingenta, INIST. **CCC.**
Published by: Routledge (Subsidiary of: Taylor & Francis Group), 325 Chestnut St, Ste 800, Philadelphia, PA 19106. TEL 215-625-8900, 800-354-1420, FAX 215-625-8914, http://www.routledge.com. Eds. Eli Coleman, Howard Adler. adv.: B&W page USD 315, color page USD 550; trim 4.375 x 7.125. Circ: 251 (paid).

158 USA ISSN 1612-197X
GV706.4
INTERNATIONAL JOURNAL OF SPORT AND EXERCISE PSYCHOLOGY. Abbreviated title: I J S E P. Text in English. 2003. q. GBP 211 combined subscription in United Kingdom to institutions (print & online eds.); EUR 279, USD 348 combined subscription to institutions (print & online eds.) (effective 2012). adv. back issues avail.; reprint service avail. from PSC. **Document type:** *Journal, Academic/Scholarly.*
Related titles: Online - full text ed.: ISSN 1557-251X. GBP 190 in United Kingdom to institutions; EUR 251, USD 313 to institutions (effective 2012).
Indexed: A26, BRD, C06, C07, CA, E08, G06, G07, G08, I05, P03, P24, P25, P48, PEI, PQC, PsycInfo, PsycholAb, R09, S02, S03, S09, SCOPUS, SD, SSAI, SSAb, SSI, T02, W03, W05.
—BLDSC (4542.680200), IE, Ingenta. **CCC.**
Published by: (International Society of Sport Psychology), Fitness Information Technology Inc., West Virginia University, 275G Coliseum, WVU-PE, PO Box 6116, Morgantown, WV 26506. TEL 304-293-6888, 800-477-4348, FAX 304-293-6658, fitcustomerservice@mail.wvu.edu. Eds. Athanasios G Papaioannou, Jean Cote.

INTERNATIONAL JOURNAL OF SPORT PSYCHOLOGY. *see* MEDICAL SCIENCES—Sports Medicine

152.8 370 USA ISSN 1530-5058
BF176
➤ **INTERNATIONAL JOURNAL OF TESTING.** Abbreviated title: I J T. Text and summaries in English, French. 1974. q. GBP 253 combined subscription in United Kingdom to institutions (print & online eds.); EUR 341, USD 426 combined subscription to institutions (print & online eds.) (effective 2012). adv. back issues avail.; reprint service avail. from PSC. **Document type:** *Journal, Academic/Scholarly.* **Description:** Dedicated to the advancement of theory, research, and practice in testing and assessment in psychology, education, counseling, human resource management, and related disciplines.
Supersedes (in 2001): International Test Commission. Bulletin (1013-9974); Which was formerly (until 1984): International Test Commission. Newsletter (0379-2439)
Related titles: Online - full text ed.: ISSN 1532-7574. GBP 228 in United Kingdom to institutions; EUR 307, USD 384 to institutions (effective 2012).
Indexed: A01, A03, A08, A12, A17, A22, ABIn, AEI, ASSIA, CA, CPE, E-psyche, E01, E03, E09, ERI, ERIC, P03, P10, P18, P43, P48, P51, P53, P54, PQC, PsycInfo, PsycholAb, T02.
—BLDSC (4542.693900), IE, Infotrieve, Ingenta. **CCC.**
Published by: (International Test Commission, Psychological Service Unit GBR), Routledge (Subsidiary of: Taylor & Francis Group), 325 Chestnut St, Ste 800, Philadelphia, PA 19106. TEL 800-354-1420, FAX 215-625-2940, journals@routledge.com, http://www.routledge.com. Eds. Rob R Meijer, Stephen G Sireci. Adv. contact Linda Hann TEL 44-1344-779945.

155.3 USA ISSN 1434-4599
HQ77.9
➤ **THE INTERNATIONAL JOURNAL OF TRANSGENDERISM.** Text in English. 1997. q. USD 403, GBP 306, EUR 397 to institutions (effective 2011). reprint service avail. from PSC. **Document type:** *Journal, Academic/Scholarly.* **Description:** Covers gender dysphoria, improvement in the medical and psychological treatment of transgender individuals, social and legal acceptance of hormonal and surgical sex reassignment, professional and public education on the phenomenon of transgenderism.
Media: Online - full text. **Related titles:** Print ed.: ISSN 1553-2739. USD 448, GBP 340, EUR 441 combined subscription to institutions (print & online eds.) (effective 2011).
Indexed: A01, A03, AmHI, C06, C07, C08, CA, CINAHL, G10, H07, IBSS, L01, L02, M02, P48, P54, PsycholAb, S02, S03, S21, SCOPUS, T02.
—BLDSC (4542.695900). **CCC.**
Published by: (Harry Benjamin International Gender Dysphoria Association), Routledge (Subsidiary of: Taylor & Francis Group), 325 Chestnut St, Ste 800, Philadelphia, PA 19106. TEL 215-625-8900, 800-354-1420, FAX 215-625-8914, journals@routledge.com, http://www.routledge.com. Eds. Dave King, Richard Ekins, Walter O Bockting.

150.5 200 USA ISSN 1321-0122
BF204.7
➤ **INTERNATIONAL JOURNAL OF TRANSPERSONAL STUDIES.** Text in English. 1981. s-a. bk.rev. back issues avail. **Document type:** *Journal, Academic/Scholarly.* **Description:** Concerned with the exploration of higher consciousness, expanded self/identity, spirituality, and human potential.
Formerly (until 1993): Australian Journal of Transpersonal Psychology (0725-0061)
Related titles: Online - full text ed.: ISSN 1942-3241. free (effective 2011).
Indexed: AmHI, E-psyche, H07, SSAI, SSAb, SSI, T02, W03, W05.
—Ingenta.
Published by: Floraglades Foundation, c/o Harris Friedman, 1255 Tom Coker Rd, SW, LaBelle, FL 33935. http://www.floraglades.org. Ed. Glenn Hartelius.

150 NZL ISSN 1179-8602
▼ ➤ **INTERNATIONAL JOURNAL OF WELLBEING.** Text in English. 2011. irreg. free (effective 2011). **Document type:** *Journal, Academic/Scholarly.*
Media: Online - full text.
Address: c/o Aaron Jarden, The Open Polytechnic of New Zealand, 3 Cleary St, Waterloo, New Zealand. Ed. Aaron Jarden.

150 GBR
➤ **INTERNATIONAL LIBRARY OF GROUP ANALYSIS.** Text in English. 1997. irreg., latest 2003. price varies. back issues avail. **Document type:** *Monographic series, Academic/Scholarly.* **Description:** Aims to represent innovative work in group psychotherapy, particularly but not exclusively group analysis.
—BLDSC (4542.922000).
Published by: Jessica Kingsley Publishers, 116 Pentonville Rd, London, N1 9JB, United Kingdom. TEL 44-20-78332307, FAX 44-20-78372917, post@jkp.com. Ed. Malcolm Pines.

150 GBR ISSN 1564-0361
INTERNATIONAL PSYCHOANALYSIS. Text in English. 1992. a. free to members (effective 2009). adv. back issues avail. **Document type:** *Magazine, Trade.* **Description:** Contains information on aspects of professional psychoanalytic life, and administrative news for members of the IPA.
Related titles: Online - full text ed.: ISSN 1564-0051. free (effective 2009).
Indexed: E-psyche.
Published by: International Psychoanalytical Association, Broomhills, Woodside Ln, London, N12 8UD, United Kingdom. TEL 44-20-84468324, FAX 44-20-84454729, ipa@ipa.org.uk. Ed. Silvia Flechner. Adv. contact Robert Stein.

150 USA ISSN 0047-116X
BF1
INTERNATIONAL PSYCHOLOGIST. Text in English. 1959. q. free to members (effective 2011). bk.rev. abstr. back issues avail. **Document type:** *Newsletter, Trade.*
Indexed: E-psyche.
Published by: International Council of Psychologists, Inc., c/o The Chicago School of Professional Psychology, 325 North Wells St, Chicago, IL 60654. http://www.icpweb.org/.

INTERNATIONAL REGISTRY OF ORGANIZATION DEVELOPMENT PROFESSIONALS AND ORGANIZATION DEVELOPMENT HANDBOOK. *see* BUSINESS AND ECONOMICS—Personnel Management

158.7 GBR ISSN 0886-1528
HF5548.7
➤ **INTERNATIONAL REVIEW OF INDUSTRIAL AND ORGANIZATIONAL PSYCHOLOGY.** Text in English. 1986. a. GBP 118 in United Kingdom to institutions; EUR 136 in Europe to institutions; USD 210 elsewhere to institutions (effective 2012). adv. back issues avail.; reprint service avail. from PSC. **Document type:** *Monographic series, Academic/Scholarly.* **Description:** Provides reviews in the field of industrial and organizational psychology.
Related titles: Microform ed.: (from PQC).
Indexed: A22, E-psyche, PCI.
—BLDSC (4547.325000), IE, Infotrieve, Ingenta. **CCC.**
Published by: John Wiley & Sons Ltd. (Subsidiary of: John Wiley & Sons, Inc.), 1-7 Oldlands Way, PO Box 808, Bognor Regis, West Sussex PO21 9FF, United Kingdom. TEL 44-1865-778315, FAX 44-1243-843232, cs-journals@wiley.com. Eds. Gerard P Hodgkinson, Kevin Ford. **Subscr. in the Americas to:** John Wiley & Sons, Inc., 111 River St, Hoboken, NJ 07030. TEL 201-748-6645, subinfo@wiley.com; **Subscr. to:** 1-7 Oldlands Way, PO Box 809, Bognor Regis, West Sussex PO21 9FG, United Kingdom. TEL 44-1865-778054, cs-agency@wiley.com.

150 GBR ISSN 1750-984X
GV706.4
➤ **INTERNATIONAL REVIEW OF SPORT AND EXERCISE PSYCHOLOGY.** Abbreviated title: I R S E P. Text in English. 2008. s-a. GBP 228 combined subscription in United Kingdom to institutions (print & online eds.); EUR 355, USD 446 combined subscription to institutions (print & online eds.) (effective 2012). adv. back issues avail.; reprint service avail. from PSC. **Document type:** *Journal, Academic/Scholarly.* **Description:** Contains critical reviews of the research literature in sport and exercise psychology.
Related titles: Online - full text ed.: ISSN 1750-9858. GBP 205 in United Kingdom to institutions; EUR 319, USD 401 to institutions (effective 2012).
Indexed: A22, C06, C07, CA, E01, P48, P50, PEI, PQC, PsycInfo, SCOPUS, SD, T02.
—IE. **CCC.**
Published by: Routledge (Subsidiary of: Taylor & Francis Group), 4 Park Sq, Milton Park, Abingdon, Oxon OX14 4RN, United Kingdom. TEL 44-20-70176000, FAX 44-20-70176336, subscriptions@tandf.co.uk, http://www.routledge.com. Ed. Aidan Moran. Adv. contact Linda Hann TEL 44-1344-779945. **Subscr. to:** Taylor & Francis Ltd., Journals Customer Service, Sheepen Pl, Colchester, Essex CO3 3LP, United Kingdom. TEL 44-20-70175544, FAX 44-20-70175198.

➤ **INTERNATIONAL SERIES IN THE PSYCHOLOGY OF RELIGION.** *see* RELIGIONS AND THEOLOGY

150 FRA ISSN 2105-1038
INTERNATIONALE DE PSYCHANALYSE DU COUPLE ET DE LA FAMILLE. REVUE/INTERNATIONAL REVIEW OF PSYCHOANALYSIS OF COUPLE AND FAMILY/REVISTA INTERNACIONAL DE PSICOANALISIS DE PAREJA Y FAMILIA. Text in French, English, Spanish. 2007. s-a. **Document type:** *Journal, Academic/Scholarly.*
Media: Online - full text.
Published by: Association Internationale de Psychanalyse de Couple et de Famille, 154 Rue d'Alesia, Paris, 75014, France. info@aipcf.net, http://www.aipcf.net/cgi-bin/index.cgi?page=c1&langue=fra.

302 AUT ISSN 0254-928X
INTERNATIONALE ZEITSCHRIFT FUER SOZIALPSYCHOLOGIE UND GRUPPENDYNAMIK; in Wirtschaft und Gesellschaft. Text in German, English. 1975. q. EUR 32.50 domestic; EUR 39.90 foreign (effective 2005). 48 p./no.; **Document type:** *Journal, Academic/Scholarly.* **Description:** Contains articles and research involving social psychology and group dynamics.
Indexed: DIP, IBR, IBZ.
Published by: Psychologische Gesellschaft fuer Persoenlichkeits und Organisationsentwicklung, Fraungrubergasse 4-5-13, Vienna, 1120, Austria. TEL 43-669-19149514, FAX 43-1-8134182. Ed., R&P Dr. Rudolf Zucha.

150 USA ISSN 1531-2941
RA790.A1
➤ **THE INTERNET JOURNAL OF MENTAL HEALTH.** Text in English. 2001. s-a. free (effective 2011). adv. **Document type:** *Journal, Academic/Scholarly.*
Media: Online - full text.
Indexed: A01, A02, A03, A08, A26, A39, C06, C07, C08, C27, C29, CA, CINAHL, D03, D04, E13, G08, H11, H12, I05, P03, PsycInfo, PsycholAb, R14, S14, S15, S18, SCOPUS, T02.
Published by: Internet Scientific Publications, Llc., 23 Rippling Creek Dr, Sugar Land, TX 77479. TEL 832-443-1193, FAX 281-240-1533, wenker@ispub.com. Ed. Joshua Fogel. R&P Olivier Wenker TEL 832-754-0335.

150 USA ISSN 1933-3315
BF77
INTERNSHIPS IN PSYCHOLOGY; the A P A G S workbook for writing successful applications and finding the right match. Text in English. 199?. irreg., latest 2008. USD 24.95 per issue to non-members; USD 19.95 per issue to members (effective 2010). **Document type:** *Handbook/Manual/Guide, Trade.* **Description:** Provides the resources you will need to successfully navigate the internship application process.
Published by: American Psychological Association, 750 First St, NE, Washington, DC 20002. TEL 202-336-5500, 800-374-2721, journals@apa.org.

158 BRA ISSN 1981-6472
HM1106
➤ **INTERPERSONA**; an international journal on personal relationships. Text in English. 2007. 2/yr. free (effective 2011). bk.rev. Index. back issues avail. **Document type:** *Journal, Academic/Scholarly.*
Media: Online - full text.
Published by: International Center for Interpersonal Relationship Research, Av Fernando Ferrari, 514, Vitoria, 29075-910, Brazil. TEL 55-27-33352501, FAX 55-27-33352501. Ed., Pub., R&P Agnaldo Garcia.

150 302 ESP ISSN 1132-0559
INTERVENCION PSICOSOCIAL. Text in Spanish. 1992. 3/yr. EUR 29 domestic to qualified personnel; EUR 43 domestic; EUR 80 foreign (effective 2008). back issues avail. **Document type:** *Journal, Academic/Scholarly.*
Related titles: Online - full text ed.
Indexed: A01, CA, E-psyche, F03, F04, T02.
Published by: Colegio Oficial de Psicologos, Claudio Coello 46, Madrid, 28001, Spain. TEL 34-91-4355212, FAX 34-91-5779172. Ed. Ferran Casas Aznar.

INTERVENTION IN SCHOOL AND CLINIC. *see* EDUCATION—Special Education And Rehabilitation

150 ARG ISSN 0329-5893
INVESTIGACIONES EN PSICOLOGIA. Text in Spanish. 1996. q. back issues avail. **Document type:** *Journal, Academic/Scholarly.*
Related titles: Online - full text ed.
Published by: Universidad de Buenos Aires, Facultad de Psicologia, Hipolito Yrigoyen 3241, Buenos Aires, C1207ABQ, Argentina. TEL 55-11-49316900, info@psi.uba.ar.

150 ARG ISSN 1515-2138
INVESTIGANDO EN PSICOLOGIA. Text in Spanish. 1998. a. **Document type:** *Monographic series, Academic/Scholarly.*
Published by: Universidad Nacional de Tucuman, Facultad de Psicologia, Ave Benjamin Araoz, 800, San Miguel, Tucuman, 4000, Argentina. TEL 54-381-4310570, FAX 54-381-4310171. Ed. Juan Vicente Garbero.

INZINIERSKA PEDAGOGIKA. *see* EDUCATION—Higher Education

150 ITA ISSN 1971-0461
IPNOSI; rivista italiana di ipnosi clinica e sperimentale. Text in English. 2004. s-a. EUR 29.50 combined subscription domestic to institutions (print & online eds.); EUR 55 combined subscription foreign to institutions (print & online eds.) (effective 2009). **Document type:** *Journal, Academic/Scholarly.*
Related titles: Online - full text ed.: ISSN 1972-4985. 2004.
Published by: Franco Angeli Edizioni, Viale Monza 106, Milan, 20127, Italy. TEL 39-02-2837141, FAX 39-02-26144793, redazioni@francoangeli.it, http://www.francoangeli.it.

150.7 MEX ISSN 2007-1787
IPYE: PSICOLOGIA Y EDUCACION. Text in Spanish. 2007. s-a. **Document type:** *Journal, Academic/Scholarly.*
Published by: Universidad Veracruzana, Instituto de Psicologia y Educacion, Calle Agustin Melgay y Juan escutia s-n, Col. reduccion, Xalapa, Veracruz, Mexico. http://www.uv.mx/ipe/.

IRISH JOURNAL OF PSYCHOLOGICAL MEDICINE. *see* MEDICAL SCIENCES—Psychiatry And Neurology

150 IRL ISSN 0303-3910
BF1 CODEN: IRJPAR
➤ **IRISH JOURNAL OF PSYCHOLOGY.** Text in English. 1971. q. GBP 96 combined subscription in United Kingdom to institutions (print & online eds.); EUR 127, USD 159 combined subscription to institutions (print & online eds.) (effective 2012). bk.rev. bibl.; charts. **Document type:** *Journal, Academic/Scholarly.*
Related titles: Online - full text ed.: GBP 86 in United Kingdom to institutions; EUR 114, USD 143 to institutions (effective 2012).
Indexed: A20, A22, ASCA, E-psyche, FamI, Inpharma, P03, P25, P48, PCI, PQC, PsycInfo, PsycholAb, RILM, SCOPUS, SOPODA, SociolAb.
—BLDSC (4572.200000), IE, Ingenta. **CCC.**
Published by: Psychological Society of Ireland, CX House, 2A Corn Exchange Pl, Poolbeg St, Dublin, 2, Ireland. TEL 353-1-4749160, FAX 353-1-4749161, info@psihq.ie, http://www.psihq.org. Eds. Dr. Barbara Dooley, Dr. Eilis Hennessy. Circ: 1,200.

150 IRL ISSN 0790-4789
THE IRISH PSYCHOLOGIST. Text in English. 197?. m. EUR 45 domestic; EUR 60 in Europe; EUR 70 elsewhere (effective 2006). adv. **Document type:** *Journal, Academic/Scholarly.* **Description:** Contains articles of general interest to psychologists.
Published by: Psychological Society of Ireland, CX House, 2A Corn Exchange Pl, Poolbeg St, Dublin, 2, Ireland. TEL 353-1-4749160, FAX 353-1-4749161, info@psihq.ie, http://www.psihq.org. Ed. Chris Morris. Adv. contact Sinead Lappin. B&W page EUR 1,000. Circ: 1,450 (paid and controlled).

155.4 NLD ISSN 1574-0471
ISSUES IN CLINICAL CHILD PSYCHOLOGY. Text in English. 1993. irreg., latest 2005. price varies. **Document type:** *Monographic series, Academic/Scholarly.* **Description:** Aims to integrate clinical psychology with the development of children, adolescents, and their families and developmental psychopathology.
Published by: Springer Netherlands (Subsidiary of: Springer Science+Business Media), Van Godewijckstraat 30, Dordrecht, 3311 GX, Netherlands. TEL 31-78-6576050, FAX 31-78-6576474. Ed. Michael C Roberts.

364 345 GBR ISSN 1468-4748
➤ **ISSUES IN FORENSIC PSYCHOLOGY.** Text in English. 1981. irreg., latest no.8, 2008. GBP 7 per issue; free to members (effective 2009). back issues avail. **Document type:** *Monographic series, Academic/Scholarly.* **Description:** Conveys recent research and debate in the fields of criminology and legal psychology to an academic readership.
Formerly (until 1999): Issues in Criminological and Legal Psychology (0266-6863)
Related titles: Online - full text ed.: GBP 4.60 per issue to non-members; GBP 3.45 per issue to members (effective 2009).
Indexed: A01, CA, E-psyche, P03, PsycInfo, PsycholAb, T02.
—BLDSC (4584.244500), IE. **CCC.**
Published by: (The British Psychological Society, Division of Forensic Psychology), The British Psychological Society, St Andrews House, 48 Princess Rd E, Leicester, LE1 7DR, United Kingdom. TEL 44-116-2549568, FAX 44-116-2271314, enquiries@bps.org.uk. Eds. Caroline Friendship, Jason Davies.

➤ **ISSUES IN MENTAL HEALTH NURSING.** *see* MEDICAL SCIENCES—Nurses And Nursing

616.89 USA ISSN 1075-0754
RC475
ISSUES IN PSYCHOANALYTIC PSYCHOLOGY. Text in English. 1975. a. USD 28 (effective 2011); price varies. bk.rev. back issues avail. **Document type:** *Journal, Academic/Scholarly.* **Description:** Publishes papers on psychoanalytic theory, technique, and psychotherapy.
Formerly (until 1993): Issues in Ego Psychology (0097-6555)
Indexed: A01, A22, CA, E-psyche, P03, PsycInfo, PsycholAb, T02.
—BLDSC (4584.312950), IE, Ingenta.
Published by: Washington Square Institute, 41-51 E 11th St, New York, NY 10003. TEL 212-477-2600. Ed. Dr. Elliot Kronish.

616.89 USA ISSN 1567-7346
ISSUES IN THE PRACTICE OF PSYCHOLOGY. Text in English. 1996. irreg., latest 2002. price varies. back issues avail. **Document type:** *Monographic series, Academic/Scholarly.* **Description:** Examines professional matters within the mental health services.
Indexed: E-psyche.
Published by: Springer New York LLC (Subsidiary of: Springer Science+Business Media), 233 Spring St, New York, NY 10013. TEL 212-460-1500, FAX 212-460-1575, service-ny@springer.com. Ed. George Stricker.

150 ITA ISSN 1970-0466
ITEMS. LA NEWSLETTER DEL TESTING PSICOLOGICO. Text in Italian. 2006. bi-m. free. **Document type:** *Newsletter, Consumer.*
Media: Online - full text.
Published by: Organizzazioni Speciali, Via Fra' Paolo Sarpi 7-A, Florence, 50136, Italy. TEL 39-055-6236501, FAX 39-055-669446, bpa@osnet.it, http://www.osnet.it.

150.195 ITA ISSN 2038-5196
J E P EUROPEAN JOURNAL OF PSYCHOANALYSIS. Text in English. 1995. s-a. EUR 12.50 to individuals; EUR 25 to institutions (effective 2010). **Document type:** *Journal, Academic/Scholarly.* **Description:** Explores the frontiers of psychoanalytic inquiry.
Formerly (until 2008): Journal of European Psychoanalysis (1125-8217)
Related titles: Online - full text ed.: ISSN 2038-5188.
Indexed: P03, PsycholAb.
Published by: Italian Paths of Culture (I P O C), 159 Viale Martesana, Vimodrome, MI 20090, Italy. ipoc@ipocpress.com.

J O P E. *see* MEDICAL SCIENCES—Dentistry

302 NLD ISSN 2211-9256
JAARBOEK SOCIALE PSYCHOLOGIE. Text in Dutch. 2002. a.
Published by: (Associatie van Sociaal Psychologische Onderzoekers), A S P O Pers, Grote Kruisstraat 2/1, Groningen, 9712 TS, Netherlands. TEL 31-50-3636344, http://www.sociale-psychologie.nl. Ed. Niels van de Ven.

P

150 DEU ISSN 0075-2363
➤ **JAHRBUCH DER PSYCHOANALYSE**; Beitraege zur Theorie, Praxis und Geschichte. Text in German. 1960. 2/yr. EUR 52; EUR 26 to students (effective 2010). adv. back issues avail.; reprint service avail. from SCH. **Document type:** *Journal, Academic/Scholarly.* **Description:** Consists of theoretical, clinical and historical contributions, mainly by psychoanalysts.
Related titles: Supplement(s): Jahrbuch der Psychoanalyse. Beiheft. ISSN 0301-5688. 1973.
Indexed: DIP, IBR, IBZ, P03, PsycInfo, PsycholAb.
—BLDSC (4632.050000), GNLM, INIST. **CCC.**
Published by: Frommann-Holzboog Verlag e.K., Koenig-Karl-Str 27, Stuttgart, 70372, Germany. TEL 49-711-9559690, FAX 49-711-9559691, info@frommann-holzboog.de. Eds. Claudia Frank, Ludger Hermanns. Circ: 700.

➤ **JAHRBUCH DER PSYCHOONKOLOGIE.** *see* MEDICAL SCIENCES—Oncology

301.1 DEU ISSN 0938-183X
RJ504.2
JAHRBUCH FUER PSYCHOANALYTISCHE PAEDAGOGIK. Text in German. 1989. a. **Document type:** *Journal, Academic/Scholarly.*
Indexed: DIP, E-psyche, IBR, IBZ.
Published by: Psychosozial Verlag, Walltorstr 10, Giessen, 35390, Germany. TEL 49-641-77819, FAX 49-641-77742, info@psychosozial-verlag.de, http://www.psychosozial-verlag.de.

150 DEU ISSN 0939-5806
GR880
JAHRBUCH FUER TRANSKULTURELLE MEDIZIN UND PSYCHOTHERAPIE/YEARBOOK OF CROSS-CULTURAL MEDICINE AND PSYCHOTHERAPY. Text in English, German. 1990. a. EUR 34 per vol. (effective 2010). back issues avail. **Document type:** *Yearbook, Academic/Scholarly.* **Description:** Contains research on all aspects of ethnic and alternative healing methods.
Indexed: E-psyche, IBR, IBZ.
—GNLM.
Published by: (Internationales Institut fuer Kulturvergleichende Therapieforschung), V W B - Verlag fuer Wissenschaft und Bildung, Postfach 110368, Berlin, 10833, Germany. TEL 49-30-2510415, FAX 49-30-2511136, info@vwb-verlag.com, http://www.vwb-verlag.com. Ed. Dr. Walter Andritzky.

616.89 DEU ISSN 1861-3217
JAHRBUCH MUSIKTHERAPIE. Text in German. 2005. a. EUR 34 (effective 2010). **Document type:** *Journal, Academic/Scholarly.*
Indexed: RILM.
Published by: Deutsche Musiktherapeutische Gesellschaft e.V., Libauer Str 17, Berlin, 10245, Germany. TEL 49-30-29492493, FAX 49-30-29492494, info@dont-want-spam.musiktherapie.de. Ed. Hanna Schirmer.

150 AUS ISSN 0021-5368
BF76.5 CODEN: JPREAV
➤ **JAPANESE PSYCHOLOGICAL RESEARCH.** Text in English. 1954. q. GBP 205 in United Kingdom to institutions; EUR 261 in Europe to institutions; USD 293 in the Americas to institutions; USD 402 elsewhere to institutions; GBP 236 combined subscription in United Kingdom to institutions (print & online eds.); EUR 300 combined subscription in Europe to institutions (print & online eds.); USD 338 combined subscription in the Americas to institutions (print & online eds.); USD 463 combined subscription elsewhere to institutions (print & online eds.) (effective 2012). adv. abstr.; charts; illus. Index. back issues avail.; reprint service avail. from PSC. **Document type:** *Journal, Academic/Scholarly.* **Description:** Containing original articles, together with news and notes, are intended to raise awareness of psychological research in Japan amongst psychologists worldwide.
Related titles: Online - full text ed.: ISSN 1468-5884. 1954. GBP 205 in United Kingdom to institutions; EUR 261 in Europe to institutions; USD 293 in the Americas to institutions; USD 402 elsewhere to institutions (effective 2012) (from IngentaConnect).

Indexed: A01, A03, A08, A20, A22, A26, ASCA, B21, B25, BAS, BIOSIS Prev, CA, CIS, CurCont, E-psyche, E01, ErgAb, I05, L&LBA, MLA-IB, MycolAb, NSA, P03, P30, P43, PAIS, PsycInfo, PsycholAb, RASB, RILM, RefZh, S02, S03, SCOPUS, SOPODA, SSCI, SociolAb, T02, W07.
—BLDSC (4661.100000), IE, Infotrieve, Ingenta, INIST. **CCC.**
Published by: (Nihon Shinri Gakkai/Japanese Psychological Association JPN), Wiley-Blackwell Publishing Asia (Subsidiary of: Wiley-Blackwell Publishing Ltd.), 155 Cremorne St, Richmond, VIC 3121, Australia. TEL 61-3-92743100, FAX 61-3-92743101, subs@blackwellpublishingasia.com, http://www.wiley.com/WileyCDA/. Ed. Kazuo Shigemasu. Adv. contact Amanda Munce TEL 61-3-83591071. Circ: 6,300. **Dist. by:** Business Center for Academic Societies Japan, 5-16-19 Honkomagome, Bunkyo-ku, Tokyo 113-0021, Japan.

150 CHN
JIANKANG XINLIXUE ZAZHI/HEALTH PSYCHOLOGY JOURNAL. Text in Chinese. 1993. m. CNY 8 newsstand/cover (effective 2007). **Document type:** *Journal, Academic/Scholarly.*
Formerly: Jiankang Xinlixue/Health Psychology Journal (1005-1252)
Related titles: Online - full text ed.
—BLDSC (4275.105192).
Published by: Zhongguo Xinli Weisheng Xiehui/Chinese Association for Mental Health, 5 An Kang Lane, De Sheng Men Wai, Beijing, 100088, China. TEL 86-10-82085385, FAX 86-10-62359838, camh@163bj.com, http://www.camh.org.cn/. **Dist. by:** China International Book Trading Corp, 35 Chegongzhuang Xilu, Haidian District, PO Box 399, Beijing 100044, China. TEL 86-10-68412045, FAX 86-10-68412023, cibtc@mail.cibtc.com.cn, http://www.cibtc.com.cn.

JIAOYU XINLI XUEBAO/BULLETIN OF EDUCATIONAL PSYCHOLOGY. *see* EDUCATION

301.1 JPN ISSN 0387-7973
HM251
JIKKEN SHAKAI SHINRIGAKU KENKYU/JAPANESE JOURNAL OF EXPERIMENTAL SOCIAL PSYCHOLOGY. Text in Japanese. 1960. s-a. **Document type:** *Journal, Academic/Scholarly.*
Formerly (until 1971): Kyoiku, Shakai Shinrigaku Kenkyu/Japanese Journal of Educational & Social Psychology (0387-852X)
Related titles: Online - full text ed.: ISSN 1348-6276.
Indexed: A22, P03, PsycInfo, PsycholAb, S02, S03.
—BLDSC (4651.920000), IE, Ingenta. **CCC.**
Published by: Nippon Gurupu Dainamikkusu Gakkai/Japanese Group Dynamics Association, c/o Kazuya Horike, Dept of Human Sciences, Faculty of Humanity & Social Science, Iwate University, Ueda 3-18-34, Morioka, Iwate 020-8550, Japan. TEL 81-19-6216769, kekehori@iwate-u.ac.jp, http://wwwsoc.nii.ac.jp/jgda/index-j.html.

150 JPN ISSN 0913-4964
JIRITSU KUNREN KENKYU/JAPANESE JOURNAL OF AUTOGENIC THERAPY. Text in Japanese. 1979. a. **Document type:** *Journal, Academic/Scholarly.*
Indexed: P03, PsycInfo, PsycholAb.
—BLDSC (4669.185000), IE. **CCC.**
Published by: Nihon Jiritsu Kunren Gakkai/Japanese Society of Autogenic Therapy, 1-22-1, Sena, Shizuoka, 420-0911, Japan. FAX 81-54-2632750, aki-ito@tokoha-u.ac.jp, http://wwwsoc.nii.ac.jp/jsat/.

150 ARG ISSN 1851-9210
JORNADAS DE PSICOLOGIA INSTITUCIONAL PENSANDO JUNTOS COMO PENSAMOS: UN ANALISIS DE LAS PRACTICAS INSTITUIDAS. Text in Spanish. 2008. biennial. **Document type:** *Proceedings, Academic/Scholarly.*
Media: Optical Disk.
Published by: Universidad de Buenos Aires, Facultad de Psicologia, Hipolito Yrigoyen 3241, Buenos Aires, C1207ABQ, Argentina. TEL 55-11-49316900, info@psi.uba.ar, http://www.psi.uba.ar/.

150 PRT ISSN 1646-365X
JORNAL DE CIENCIAS COGNITIVAS. Text in Portuguese, English. 2005. irreg. free (effective 2011). **Document type:** *Journal, Academic/Scholarly.*
Media: Online - full text.
Published by: Sociedade Portuguesa de Ciencias Cognitivas, Praca da Faculdade de Filosofia 1, Braga, 4710-297, Portugal. jalvespt@iol.pt, http://spcc.no.sapo.pt.

JOSEI SHINSHIN IGAKU/JAPANESE SOCIETY OF PSYCHASOMATIC OBSTETRICS AND GYNECOLOGY. JOURNAL. *see* MEDICAL SCIENCES—Obstetrics And Gynecology

150.195 GBR ISSN 1477-3635
JOURNAL FOR LACANIAN STUDIES. Abbreviated title: J L S. Text in English. 2003. s-a. GBP 19.99 per issue (effective 2010). back issues avail. **Document type:** *Journal, Academic/Scholarly.*
Related titles: Online - full text ed.
—CCC.
Published by: Karnac Books, 118 Finchley Rd, London, NW3 5HT, United Kingdom. TEL 44-20-74311075, FAX 44-20-74359076, shop@karnacbooks.com, http://www.karnacbooks.com. Ed. Dany Nobus. Adv. contact Jo Leedham TEL 44-20-89694454.

158 USA ISSN 0193-3922
BF637.C6
➤ **JOURNAL FOR SPECIALISTS IN GROUP WORK.** Text in English. 1975. q. GBP 229 combined subscription in United Kingdom to institutions (print & online eds.); EUR 302, USD 376 combined subscription to institutions (print & online eds.) (effective 2012). adv. bk.rev. back issues avail.; reprint service avail. from PSC. **Document type:** *Journal, Academic/Scholarly.* **Description:** Includes empirical research, history of group work, work with groups, theoretical discussions and current group literature reviews.
Formerly (until 1978): Together (0161-0333)
Related titles: Microfiche ed.; Online - full text ed.: ISSN 1549-6295. GBP 206 in United Kingdom to institutions; EUR 271, USD 339 to institutions (effective 2012) (from IngentaConnect).
Indexed: A22, ASSIA, C06, C07, C08, CA, CINAHL, CMM, DIP, E-psyche, E01, E03, E09, ERI, ERIC, ESPM, Faml, HEA, IBR, IBZ, P03, P10, P18, P25, P48, P53, P54, PCI, PQC, PsycInfo, PsycholAb, RiskAb, S02, S03, SCOPUS, SOPODA, SSA, SWR&A, SociolAb, T02.
—IE, Infotrieve, Ingenta. **CCC.**
Published by: (American Counseling Association, Association for Specialists in Group Work), Routledge (Subsidiary of: Taylor & Francis Group), 325 Chestnut St, Ste 800, Philadelphia, PA 19106. TEL 800-354-1420, FAX 215-625-2940, journals@routledge.com, http://www.routledge.com. Ed. Sheri Bauman. Adv. contact Linda Hann TEL 44-1344-779945.

158 USA ISSN 1940-624X
▼ ➤ **JOURNAL FOR THE SCHOOL OF PROFESSIONAL COUNSELING.** Text in English. forthcoming 2011 (Jan.). s-a. USD 30 (effective 2008). **Document type:** *Journal, Academic/Scholarly.* **Description:** Focues on research findings that address contemporary, regional, national and international issues that affect the professional therapist and counselor educator.
Related titles: Online - full text ed.: ISSN 1940-6258. forthcoming.
Published by: Lindsey Wilson College, School of Professional Counseling, 210 Lindsey Wilson St, Columbia, KY 42728. TEL 270-384-2126, 800-264-0138, FAX 270-384-8200, http://www.lindsey.edu. Ed. Martin Wesley.

150 USA ISSN 1949-2189
▼ **THE JOURNAL FOR THE STUDY OF HUMAN INTERACTION AND FAMILY THERAPY.** Abbreviated title: S H I F T. Text in English. 2010. a. free (effective 2009). **Document type:** *Journal, Academic/Scholarly.* **Description:** Dedicated to evolving the understanding of human interaction and to advancing the field of family therapy.
Media: Online - full content.
Published by: Mind for Therapy, 111 Fava Dr, West Monroe, LA 71291. TEL 318-801-9296, mthornton@mindfortherapy.com.

155 300 GBR ISSN 0021-8308
HM132
➤ **JOURNAL FOR THE THEORY OF SOCIAL BEHAVIOUR.** Text in English. 1971. q. GBP 423 in United Kingdom to institutions; EUR 537 in Europe to institutions; USD 688 in the Americas to institutions; USD 991 elsewhere to institutions; GBP 487 combined subscription in United Kingdom to institutions (print & online eds.); EUR 617 combined subscription in Europe to institutions (print & online eds.); USD 792 combined subscription in the Americas to institutions (print & online eds.); USD 1,140 combined subscription elsewhere to institutions (print & online eds.) (effective 2012). adv. back issues avail.; reprint service avail. from PSC. **Document type:** *Journal, Academic/Scholarly.* **Description:** Provides original theoretical and methodological articles that examine the links between social structures and human agency embedded in behavioural practices.
Related titles: Online - full text ed.: ISSN 1468-5914. GBP 423 in United Kingdom to institutions; EUR 537 in Europe to institutions; USD 688 in the Americas to institutions; USD 991 elsewhere to institutions (effective 2012) (from IngentaConnect).
Indexed: A01, A03, A08, A20, A22, A26, AMHA, ASCA, B21, CA, CurCont, DIP, E-psyche, E01, FR, Faml, I13, IBR, IBSS, IBZ, MEA&I, MLA-IB, NSA, P03, P30, P42, P43, PCI, PSA, PhilInd, PsycInfo, PsycholAb, S02, S03, S21, SCOPUS, SD, SOPODA, SSA, SSCI, SociolAb, T02, W07.
—BLDSC (5069.076000), IE, Infotrieve, Ingenta, INIST. **CCC.**
Published by: Wiley-Blackwell Publishing Ltd. (Subsidiary of: John Wiley & Sons, Inc.), 9600 Garsington Rd, Oxford, OX4 2DQ, United Kingdom. TEL 44-1865-776868, FAX 44-1865-714591, customerservices@blackwellpublishing.com. Ed. Charles W Smith TEL 718-997-2840. Adv. contact Craig Pickett TEL 44-1865-476267.

150 DEU
➤ **JOURNAL FUER PSYCHOLOGIE (ONLINE).** Text in German. 2007. 3/yr. free (effective 2011). **Document type:** *Journal, Academic/Scholarly.*
Media: Online - full content.
Published by: (Neue Gesellschaft fuer Psychologie), Pabst Science Publishers, Am Eichengrund 28, Lengerich, 49525, Germany. TEL 49-5484-97234, FAX 49-5484-550, pabst@pabst-publishers.com, http://www.pabst-publishers.de.

150 610 301 USA ISSN 1529-5168
QP82
➤ **JOURNAL HUMAN PERFORMANCE IN EXTREME ENVIRONMENTS.** Text in English. 1996. s-a. free to members (effective 2010). back issues avail. **Document type:** *Journal, Academic/Scholarly.* **Description:** Publishes research and findings devoted to the study of human performance and behavior in high-stress environments.
Indexed: A28, APA, BrCerAb, C&ISA, CA, CA/WCA, CIA, CerAb, CivEngAb, CorrAb, E&CAJ, E11, EEA, EMA, ESPM, EnvEAb, ErgAb, GeoRef, H15, M&TEA, M09, MBF, METADEX, P30, PEI, PsycholAb, SCOPUS, SD, SolStAb, T02, T04, WAA.
—BLDSC (5003.419500), Linda Hall.
Published by: The Society for Human Performance in Extreme Environments, 2652 Corbyton Ct, Orlando, FL 32114. TEL 407-381-7762, FAX 386-226-7050, society@hpee.org.

155.4 USA ISSN 0091-0627
RJ499.A1 CODEN: JABCAA
➤ **JOURNAL OF ABNORMAL CHILD PSYCHOLOGY.** Text in English. 1973. 8/yr. EUR 1,599, USD 1,671 combined subscription to institutions (print & online eds.) (effective 2012). adv. bibl.; charts; illus. back issues avail.; reprint service avail. from PSC. **Document type:** *Journal, Academic/Scholarly.* **Description:** Aims to bring together scientists and practicing professionals from a wide range of disciplines to focus on child and adolescent psychopathology.
Related titles: Microfilm ed.: (from PQC); Online - full text ed.: ISSN 1573-2835 (from IngentaConnect).
Indexed: A01, A02, A03, A08, A22, A26, AC&P, AMED, AMHA, ASCA, ASSIA, B21, BDM&CN, BRD, BibLing, C06, C07, C28, CA, CDA, CPE, Chicano, CurCont, DIP, E-psyche, E01, E02, E03, E07, E08, ECER, EMBASE, ERI, ERIC, EdA, EdI, ExcerpMed, F09, FR, Faml, G08, I05, IBR, IBZ, IndMed, L&LBA, M06, MEA&I, MEDLINE, NSA, P02, P03, P04, P07, P10, P12, P13, P18, P19, P20, P22, P25, P26, P27, P30, P48, P53, P54, P55, PCI, PQC, PsycInfo, PsycholAb, R10, Reac, RefZh, S02, S03, S09, SCOPUS, SSAI, SSAb, SSCI, SSI, T02, W03, W05, W07.
—BLDSC (4918.820000), GNLM, IE, Infotrieve, Ingenta, INIST. **CCC.**
Published by: (International Society for Research in Child and Adolescent Psychopathology), Springer New York LLC (Subsidiary of: Springer Science+Business Media), 233 Spring St, New York, NY 10013. TEL 212-460-1500, FAX 212-460-1575, service-ny@springer.com. Ed. John E Lochman.

616.89 USA ISSN 0021-843X
RC321 CODEN: JAPCAC
➤ **JOURNAL OF ABNORMAL PSYCHOLOGY.** Text in English. 1906. q. USD 179 domestic to individuals; USD 206 foreign to individuals; USD 574 domestic to institutions; USD 619 foreign to institutions (effective 2011). adv. charts; illus. index. back issues avail.; reprint service avail. from PSC. **Document type:** *Journal, Academic/Scholarly.* **Description:** Features articles on basic research and theory in the broad field of abnormal behavior, its determinants, and its correlates.
Supersedes in part (in 1965): Journal of Abnormal and Social Psychology (0096-851X); Which was formerly (until 1925): Journal of Abnormal Psychology and Social Psychology (0145-2347); (until 1921): Journal of Abnormal Psychology (0145-2339)
Related titles: Microform ed.: (from PMC, PQC); Online - full text ed.: ISSN 1939-1846 (from ScienceDirect).
Indexed: A01, A02, A03, A08, A20, A22, A25, A26, AC&P, AHCMS, ASCA, ASSIA, Acal, AddicA, B04, B25, BIOSIS Prev, BRD, C06, C07, C28, CA, CIS, CJPI, ChPerI, Chicano, CurCont, DokArb, E-psyche, E08, ECER, EMBASE, ERA, ExcerpMed, F09, FR, Faml, G08, G10, H09, H11, H12, HlthInd, I05, IndMed, JW-P, MEA&I, MEDLINE, MLA, MLA-IB, MycolAb, P02, P03, P10, P12, P13, P27, P30, P48, P50, P53, P54, PCI, PQC, PsycInfo, PsycholAb, R10, RASB, Reac, S02, S03, S05, S08, S09, S20, S21, SCOPUS, SSAI, SSAb, SSCI, SSI, SWR&A, T02, W03, W07, W09.
—BLDSC (4918.840000), IE, Infotrieve, Ingenta, INIST. **CCC.**
Published by: American Psychological Association, 750 First St, NE, Washington, DC 20002. TEL 202-336-5500, 800-374-2721, FAX 202-336-5997, journals@apa.org. Ed. Dr. David Watson. Adv. contact Doug Constant TEL 202-336-5574. Circ: 2,600.

364 USA ISSN 1055-3835
HV9275
➤ **JOURNAL OF ADDICTIONS & OFFENDER COUNSELING.** Text in English. 1980. s-a. GBP 71 in United Kingdom to institutions; EUR 82 in Europe to institutions; USD 100 elsewhere to institutions; GBP 82 combined subscription in United Kingdom to institutions (print & online eds.); EUR 95 combined subscription in Europe to institutions (print & online eds.); USD 115 combined subscription elsewhere to institutions (print & online eds.) (effective 2012). adv. abstr.; bibl.; illus. 48 p./no.; back issues avail.; reprint service avail. from PSC. **Document type:** *Journal, Academic/Scholarly.* **Description:** Covers sexual crime, drug and alcohol abuse, prison overcrowding, and prisoner rehabilitation.
Formerly (until 1990): Journal of Offender Counseling (0275-8598)
Related titles: Microform ed.: (from PQC); Online - full text ed.: ISSN 2161-1874. GBP 71 in United Kingdom to institutions; EUR 82 in Europe to institutions; USD 100 elsewhere to institutions (effective 2012).
Indexed: A01, A02, A03, A08, A22, A26, BRD, C12, CA, CJA, CJPI, E-psyche, E02, E03, E07, E08, ERI, ERIC, EdA, EdI, G08, I05, L03, M01, M02, P03, P04, P07, P18, P25, P43, P48, P53, P54, P55, PQC, PsycInfo, PsycholAb, S02, S03, S09, SCOPUS, SWR&A, T02, W03, W05.
—Ingenta. **CCC.**
Published by: (International Association of Addictions and Offender Counselors), American Counseling Association, 5999 Stevenson Ave, Alexandria, VA 22304. TEL 800-347-6647, FAX 703-823-0252, 800-473-2329. Ed. Stephen Southern TEL 601-925-3841. Adv. contact Kathy Maguire TEL 703-823-9800 ext 207. **Subscr. to:** PO Box 361, Birmingham, AL 35201. TEL 800-633-4931.

➤ **JOURNAL OF ADOLESCENCE.** *see* CHILDREN AND YOUTH—About

155.5 USA ISSN 0743-5584
HQ796
➤ **JOURNAL OF ADOLESCENT RESEARCH.** Abbreviated title: J A R. Text in English. 1986. bi-m. adv. back issues avail.; reprint service avail. from PSC. **Document type:** *Journal, Academic/Scholarly.* **Description:** Takes an interdisciplinary perspective in providing professionals and practitioners with current and relevant information on many aspects of individuals 10-20 years old.
Related titles: Microform ed.; Online - full text ed.: ISSN 1552-6895. USD 793, GBP 466 to institutions (effective 2012).
Indexed: A01, A02, A03, A08, A20, A22, ASCA, Agr, B07, BibAg, C22, C28, CA, CDA, ChPerI, Chicano, CurCont, E-psyche, E01, E03, ERI, ERIC, ESPM, F09, Faml, H04, P02, P03, P04, P10, P18, P25, P30, P48, P53, P54, P55, PQC, PsycInfo, PsycholAb, RILM, RiskAb, S02, S03, SCOPUS, SFSA, SOPODA, SSA, SSCI, SWR&A, SociolAb, T02, THA, V&AA, V02, W07.
—BLDSC (4918.943500), GNLM, IE, Infotrieve, Ingenta. **CCC.**
Published by: Sage Publications, Inc., 2455 Teller Rd, Thousand Oaks, CA 91320. TEL 805-499-9774, 800-818-7243, FAX 805-499-0871, 800-583-2665, info@sagepub.com, http://www.sagepub.com. Ed. Jeffrey Jensen Arnett. **Subscr. outside the Americas to:** Sage Publications Ltd., 1 Oliver's Yard, 55 City Rd, London EC1Y 1SP, United Kingdom. TEL 44-20-73248701, FAX 44-20-73248733, subscription@sagepub.co.uk.

155.6 USA ISSN 1068-0667
HQ799.95 CODEN: JADEEU
➤ **JOURNAL OF ADULT DEVELOPMENT.** Text in English. 1994. q. EUR 602, USD 625 combined subscription to institutions (print & online eds.) (effective 2012). adv. bk.rev. back issues avail.; reprint service avail. from PSC. **Document type:** *Journal, Academic/Scholarly.* **Description:** Brings out theoretical and empirical articles on biological, psychological and sociocultural development in young, middle, and late adulthood.
Related titles: Microfilm ed.: (from PQC); Online - full text ed.: ISSN 1573-3440 (from IngentaConnect).
Indexed: A01, A03, A08, A20, A22, A26, ASCA, ASG, BibLing, C06, C07, CA, CurCont, E-psyche, E01, Faml, G10, I05, P03, P30, P43, PsycInfo, PsycholAb, S02, S03, SCOPUS, SFSA, SSCI, SociolAb, T02, W07.
—BLDSC (4918.943600), IE, Infotrieve, Ingenta. **CCC.**
Published by: (Society for Research in Adult Development), Springer New York LLC (Subsidiary of: Springer Science+Business Media), 233 Spring St, New York, NY 10013. TEL 212-460-1500, FAX 212-460-1575, service-ny@springer.com. Ed. Jack Demick.

152.4 GBR ISSN 1759-6599
▼➤ **JOURNAL OF AGGRESSION, CONFLICT AND PEACE RESEARCH.** Text in English. 2009. q. EUR 689 combined subscription in Europe (print & online eds.); USD 889 combined subscription in the Americas (print & online eds.); GBP 529 combined subscription in the UK & elsewhere (print & online eds.); AUD 999 combined subscription in Australasia (print & online eds.) (effective 2012). adv. back issues avail. **Document type:** *Journal, Academic/Scholarly.* **Description:** Publishes a broad range of practical studies, research articles and review papers on all aspects of aggression, conflict and peace.
Related titles: Online - full text ed.: ISSN 2042-8715.
Indexed: CA, CJPI, I02, P30, PQC, PSA, PsycInfo, T02.
Published by: (University of Central Lancashire), Pier Professional Ltd. (Subsidiary of: Emerald Group Publishing Ltd.), Ste N4, The Old Market, Upper Market St, Hove, BN3 1AS, United Kingdom. TEL 44-1273-783720, FAX 44-1273-783723, info@pierprofessional.com. Eds. Douglas P Fry, Michelle Davies, Nicola Graham-Kevan. adv.: B&W page GBP 350; 160 x 245.

150 USA ISSN 1092-6771
RC569.5.V55 CODEN: JAMTFJ
JOURNAL OF AGGRESSION, MALTREATMENT & TRAUMA. Text in English. 8/yr. GBP 498 combined subscription in United Kingdom to institutions (print & online eds.); EUR 648, USD 662 combined subscription to institutions (print & online eds.) (effective 2012). adv. back issues avail.; reprint service avail. from PSC. **Document type:** *Journal, Academic/Scholarly.*
Incorporates (1998-2008): Journal of Emtional Abuse (1092-6798); Journal of Psychological Trauma (1932-2887); Which was formerly (2002-2007): Journal of Trauma Practice (1536-2922)
Related titles: Online - full text ed.: ISSN 1545-083X. GBP 448 in United Kingdom to institutions; EUR 583, USD 596 to institutions (effective 2012).
Indexed: A01, A03, A22, C06, C07, C08, CA, CINAHL, CJA, CJPI, DIP, E-psyche, E01, E03, EMBASE, ESPM, ExcerpMed, F09, FR, Faml, IBR, IBZ, M02, P03, P30, PQC, PsycInfo, PsycholAb, RefZh, RiskAb, S02, S03, SCOPUS, SSA, SWR&A, SociolAb, T02, V&AA, W09.
—BLDSC (4919.997810), IE, Ingenta, INIST. **CCC.**
Published by: Routledge (Subsidiary of: Taylor & Francis Group), 325 Chestnut St, Ste 800, Philadelphia, PA 19106. TEL 215-625-8900, 800-354-1420, FAX 215-625-8914, journals@routledge.com, http://www.routledge.com. Ed. Dr. Robert A Geffner. adv.: B&W page USD 315, color page USD 550; trim 4.375 x 7.125. Circ: 159 (paid).

616.89 GBR ISSN 0021-8774
BF173.A2 CODEN: JANPA7
➤ **JOURNAL OF ANALYTICAL PSYCHOLOGY.** Abbreviated title: J A P. Text in English. 1955. 5/yr. GBP 349 in United Kingdom to institutions; EUR 444 in Europe to institutions; USD 586 in the Americas to institutions; USD 683 elsewhere to institutions; GBP 402 combined subscription in United Kingdom to institutions (print & online eds.); EUR 510 combined subscription in Europe to institutions (print & online eds.); USD 674 combined subscription in the Americas to institutions (print & online eds.); USD 786 combined subscription elsewhere to institutions (print & online eds.) (effective 2012). adv. bk.rev. bibl. index. back issues avail.; reprint service avail. from PSC. **Document type:** *Journal, Academic/Scholarly.* **Description:** Addresses issues on the leading edge of philosophy, science, religion, and an understanding of the arts.
Related titles: Microfilm ed.; Online - full text ed.: ISSN 1468-5922. GBP 349 in United Kingdom to institutions; EUR 444 in Europe to institutions; USD 586 in the Americas to institutions; USD 683 elsewhere to institutions (effective 2012) (from IngentaConnect).
Indexed: A01, A03, A08, A20, A21, A22, A26, ASCA, BibInd, C06, C07, C28, CA, CurCont, DIP, E-psyche, E01, EMBASE, ExcerpMed, F09, Faml, G10, H12, I05, IBR, IBZ, IndMed, MEA&I, MEDLINE, MLA-IB, P03, P30, P43, PCI, PsycInfo, PsycholAb, R10, RASB, RI-1, RI-2, RILM, Reac, S02, S03, SCOPUS, SSCI, T02, W07, W09, YAE&RB.
—BLDSC (4928.500000), GNLM, IE, Infotrieve, Ingenta, INIST. **CCC.**
Published by: (Society of Analytical Psychology), Wiley-Blackwell Publishing Ltd. (Subsidiary of: John Wiley & Sons, Inc.), 9600 Garsington Rd, Oxford, OX4 2DQ, United Kingdom. TEL 44-1865-776868, FAX 44-1865-714591, customerservices@blackwellpublishing.com. Eds. Michael Horne, Warren Colman. Adv. contact Craig Pickett TEL 44-1865-476267. B&W page GBP 445, B&W page USD 823; 190 x 112. Circ: 1,200.

616.85 152.4 GBR ISSN 0887-6185
RC531 CODEN: JADIE8
➤ **JOURNAL OF ANXIETY DISORDERS.** Text in English. 1987. 8/yr. EUR 904 in Europe to institutions; JPY 120,100 in Japan to institutions; USD 1,010 elsewhere to institutions (effective 2012). illus. index. back issues avail.; reprints avail. **Document type:** *Journal, Academic/Scholarly.* **Description:** Features interdisciplinary research dealing with all aspects of anxiety disorders for all age groups (child, adolescent, adult and geriatric), including assessment, diagnosis, psychosocial and pharmacological treatment, epidemiology and prevention.
Related titles: Microfilm ed.: (from PQC); Online - full text ed.: ISSN 1873-7897 (from IngentaConnect, ScienceDirect).
Indexed: A01, A03, A08, A20, A22, A26, ASCA, ASSIA, B21, B25, BIOSIS Prev, C06, C07, C08, CA, CINAHL, CurCont, E-psyche, EMBASE, ExcerpMed, FR, Faml, H12, I05, IndMed, Inpharma, JW-P, MEDLINE, MycolAb, NSA, P03, P30, PsycInfo, PsycholAb, R10, Reac, S02, S03, SCOPUS, SSCI, T02, W07.
—BLDSC (4939.300000), GNLM, IE, Infotrieve, Ingenta, INIST. **CCC.**
Published by: Pergamon (Subsidiary of: Elsevier Science & Technology), The Blvd, Langford Ln, East Park, Kidlington, Oxford OX5 1GB, United Kingdom. TEL 44-1865-843000, FAX 44-1865-843010, JournalsCustomerServiceEMEA@elsevier.com. Ed. Michel Hersen. **Subscr. to:** Elsevier BV, Radarweg 29, PO Box 211, Amsterdam 1000 AE, Netherlands. http://www.elsevier.nl.

➤ **JOURNAL OF APPLIED ANIMAL WELFARE SCIENCE.** *see* ANIMAL WELFARE

155 USA ISSN 0021-8855
BF636.A1 CODEN: JOABAW
➤ **JOURNAL OF APPLIED BEHAVIOR ANALYSIS.** Text in English. 1968. q. USD 32 to individuals; USD 94 to institutions; USD 16 to students (effective 2010). adv. bk.rev. charts; illus. index. back issues avail.; reprints avail. **Document type:** *Journal, Academic/Scholarly.* **Description:** Covers experimental research about applications of the experimental analysis of behavior to problems of social importance.
Related titles: Microfilm ed.; Online - full text ed.: ISSN 1938-3703.
Indexed: A01, A02, A03, A08, A12, A13, A20, A22, A26, ABIn, AMED, AMHA, ASCA, ASG, B01, B04, B06, B07, B08, B09, BRD, C28, CA, CDA, CIS, CPM, CommAb, CurCont, E-psyche, E02, E03, E06, E07, E08, ECER, EMBASE, ERI, ERIC, EdA, EdI, ExcerpMed, F09, FR, Faml, G08, H09, I05, INI, IndMed, MEA&I, MEDLINE, MLA-IB, P02, P03, P04, P07, P10, P12, P18, P20, P22, P24, P25, P27, P30, P48, P51, P53, P54, P55, PCI, PQC, PsycInfo, PsycholAb, R10, RILM, Reac, S02, S03, S05, S09, SCOPUS, SSAI, SSAb, SSCI, SSI, T02, W01, W02, W03, W05, W07, YAE&RB.
—BLDSC (4940.450000), GNLM, IE, Infotrieve, Ingenta, INIST. **CCC.**
Published by: Society for the Experimental Analysis of Behavior, Inc. (Lawrence), c/o Cathleen C Piazza, Munroe-Meyer Institute, University of Nebraska Medical Ctr, 985450 Nebraska Medical Ctr, Omaha, NE 68198. behavior@mail.ku.edu. Ed. Cathleen C Piazza.

150.1943 USA ISSN 0021-8863
H1 CODEN: JABHAP
➤ **THE JOURNAL OF APPLIED BEHAVIORAL SCIENCE.** Text in English. 1965. q. USD 775, GBP 456 combined subscription to institutions (print & online eds.); USD 760, GBP 447 to institutions (effective 2011). adv. bk.rev. abstr.; charts; illus. index. back issues avail.; reprint service avail. from PSC. **Document type:** *Journal, Academic/Scholarly.* **Description:** Reports the latest interdisciplinary research on behavioral science and its applications to social policy, organization development, and community activity.
Related titles: Online - full text ed.: ISSN 1552-6879. USD 698, GBP 410 to institutions (effective 2011).
Indexed: A12, A14, A17, A20, A22, A25, A26, ABCPolSci, ABIn, ABS&EES, ASSIA, B01, B02, B04, B06, B07, B08, B09, B15, B17, B18, B21, BPIA, BRD, CA, CIS, CJA, CPM, Chicano, CommAb, CurCont, E-psyche, E01, E06, E07, E08, EAA, ErgAb, FR, Faml, G04, G06, G07, G08, H09, HRA, I05, I13, IBR, IBZ, ManagCont, NSA, P02, P03, P30, P42, P48, P51, P53, P54, PCI, PMA, PQC, PRA, PSA, PersLit, PsycInfo, PsycholAb, RASB, S02, S03, S05, S08, S09, S21, SCIMP, SCOPUS, SOPODA, SPAA, SSA, SSAI, SSAb, SSCI, SSI, SWR&A, SociolAb, T02, W03, W07.
—BLDSC (4940.500000), IE, Infotrieve, Ingenta, INIST. **CCC.**
Published by: Sage Publications, Inc., 2455 Teller Rd, Thousand Oaks, CA 91320. TEL 805-499-9774, 800-818-7243, FAX 805-499-0871, 800-583-2665, info@sagepub.com. Ed. Richard W Woodman. Circ: 2,800. **Subscr. overseas to:** Sage Publications Ltd., 1 Oliver's Yard, 55 City Rd, London EC1Y 1SP, United Kingdom. TEL 44-207-3248701, FAX 44-207-3248733, subscription@sagepub.co.uk. **Co-sponsor:** N T L Institute for Applied Behavioral Science.

150 USA ISSN 1071-2089
R726.7
➤ **JOURNAL OF APPLIED BIOBEHAVIORAL RESEARCH.** Text in English. 1993. q. GBP 94 in United Kingdom to institutions; EUR 119 in Europe to institutions; USD 167 in the Americas to institutions; USD 184 elsewhere to institutions; GBP 109 combined subscription in United Kingdom to institutions (print & online eds.); EUR 137 combined subscription in Europe to institutions (print & online eds.); USD 192 combined subscription in the Americas to institutions (print & online eds.); USD 211 combined subscription elsewhere to institutions (print & online eds.) (effective 2012). adv. abstr.; bibl.; charts. index. back issues avail.; reprint service avail. from PSC. **Document type:** *Journal, Academic/Scholarly.* **Description:** Disseminates findings from behavioral science research which have applications to current problems of society. By publishing relevant research and emphasizing excellence of experimental design, as well as potential applicability of experimental results, the journal intends to bridge the theoretical and applied areas of social research.
Related titles: Online - full text ed.: ISSN 1751-9861. GBP 94 in United Kingdom to institutions; EUR 119 in Europe to institutions; USD 167 in the Americas to institutions; USD 184 elsewhere to institutions (effective 2012).
Indexed: A01, A22, B21, CA, E-psyche, E01, ESPM, H&SSA, P03, P30, PEI, PsycInfo, PsycholAb, RiskAb, SCOPUS, T02.
—BLDSC (4940.570000), IE, Infotrieve, Ingenta. **CCC.**
Published by: Wiley-Blackwell Publishing, Inc. (Subsidiary of: Wiley-Blackwell Publishing Ltd.), 111 River St, Hoboken, NJ 07030. TEL 201-748-6000, FAX 201-748-6088, info@wiley.com. Ed. Andrew Baum. Adv. contact Kristin McCarthy TEL 201-748-7683.

155 GBR ISSN 0193-3973
BF636.A1
➤ **JOURNAL OF APPLIED DEVELOPMENTAL PSYCHOLOGY.** Text in English. 1980. 6/yr. EUR 514 in Europe to institutions; JPY 68,000 in Japan to institutions; USD 574 elsewhere to institutions (effective 2012). bk.rev. back issues avail.; reprint service avail. from PSC. **Document type:** *Journal, Academic/Scholarly.* **Description:** Covers study of change in humans over time, bridging the gap between research in developmental psychology and its application.
Related titles: Online - full text ed.: ISSN 1873-7900 (from IngentaConnect, ScienceDirect).
Indexed: A01, A03, A08, A20, A22, A26, ASCA, ASSIA, C28, CA, CDA, CommAb, CurCont, DIP, E-psyche, E03, E16, ERA, ERI, ERIC, F09, FR, Faml, I05, IBR, IBZ, L&LBA, M12, MLA-IB, P03, P30, PAIS, PsycInfo, PsycholAb, S02, S03, S19, S20, S21, SCOPUS, SOPODA, SSCI, SociolAb, T02, W07.
—BLDSC (4942.450000), IE, Infotrieve, Ingenta, INIST. **CCC.**
Published by: Pergamon (Subsidiary of: Elsevier Science & Technology), The Blvd, Langford Ln, East Park, Kidlington, Oxford OX5 1GB, United Kingdom. TEL 44-1865-843000, FAX 44-1865-843010, JournalsCustomerServiceEMEA@elsevier.com. Eds. J Torney-Purta, K Wentzel. **Subscr. to:** Elsevier BV, Radarweg 29, PO Box 211, Amsterdam 1000 AE, Netherlands. TEL 31-20-4853757, FAX 31-20-4853432, http://www.elsevier.nl.

158 USA ISSN 0021-9010
BF1 CODEN: JAPGBP
➤ **JOURNAL OF APPLIED PSYCHOLOGY.** Text in English. 1917. bi-m. USD 280 domestic to individuals; USD 312 foreign to individuals; USD 836 domestic to institutions; USD 893 foreign to institutions (effective 2011). adv. bibl.; charts; illus. index. back issues avail.; reprint service avail. from PSC. **Document type:** *Journal, Academic/Scholarly.*
Related titles: Microform ed.: (from PMC, PQC); Online - full text ed.: ISSN 1939-1854 (from ScienceDirect).
Indexed: A12, A13, A17, A20, A22, A25, A26, ABIn, AC&P, AMHA, ASCA, ASSIA, Acal, B01, B04, B06, B07, B08, B09, B15, B17, B18, BPIA, BRD, C06, C07, C12, C28, CA, CIS, CPM, Chicano, CompAb, CurCont, DIP, DokArb, E-psyche, E06, E08, EAA, EMBASE, ErgAb, ExcerpMed, FR, Faml, G04, G06, G07, G08, G10, H09, H10, H12, HRA, HlthInd, I05, IBR, IBSS, IBZ, ILD, INI, IndMed, M06, MEA&I, MEDLINE, MLA-IB, P02, P03, P10, P12, P13, P21, P27, P30, P34, P48, P51, P53, P54, PCI, PQC, PersLit, PsycInfo, PsycholAb, R10, RASB, RILM, Reac, S02, S03, S05, S08, S09, S21, SCIMP, SCOPUS, SRRA, SSAI, SSAb, SSCI, SSI, T02, W03, W07, W09.
—BLDSC (4947.000000), GNLM, IE, Infotrieve, Ingenta, INIST. **CCC.**
Published by: American Psychological Association, 750 First St, NE, Washington, DC 20002. TEL 202-336-5500, 800-374-2721, FAX 202-336-5997, journals@apa.org. Ed. Steve W J Kozlowski. Adv. contact Doug Constant TEL 202-336-5574. Circ: 2,600.

➤ **JOURNAL OF APPLIED SCHOOL PSYCHOLOGY.** *see* EDUCATION—Special Education And Rehabilitation

158 USA ISSN 0021-9029
HM251 CODEN: JASPBX
➤ **JOURNAL OF APPLIED SOCIAL PSYCHOLOGY.** Text in English. 1971. m. GBP 874 in United Kingdom to institutions; EUR 1,110 in Europe to institutions; USD 1,535 in the Americas to institutions; USD 1,712 elsewhere to institutions; GBP 1,005 combined subscription in United Kingdom to institutions (print & online eds.); EUR 1,278 combined subscription in Europe to institutions (print & online eds.); USD 1,766 combined subscription in the Americas to institutions (print & online eds.); USD 1,970 combined subscription elsewhere to institutions (print & online eds.) (effective 2012). adv. abstr.; charts; illus.; stat. index. back issues avail.; reprint service avail. from PSC. **Document type:** *Journal, Academic/Scholarly.* **Description:** Includes content on laboratory and field research in areas such as health, race relations, discrimination, group processes, population growth, crowding, accelerated cultural change, violence, poverty, environmental stress, helping behavior, effects of the legal system on society and the individual, political participation and extremism.
Related titles: Online - full text ed.: ISSN 1559-1816. GBP 874 in United Kingdom to institutions; EUR 1,110 in Europe to institutions; USD 1,535 in the Americas to institutions; USD 1,712 elsewhere to institutions (effective 2012) (from IngentaConnect).
Indexed: A01, A02, A03, A08, A20, A22, A26, AC&P, ASCA, B01, B04, B06, B07, B09, BRD, C28, CA, CLFP, ChPerI, Chicano, CommAb, CurCont, DIP, E-psyche, E01, E08, F09, FS&TA, Faml, G08, H09, HEA, I05, IBR, IBZ, IPsyAb, MEA&I, MLA-IB, P02, P03, P10, P12, P30, P34, P48, P53, P54, PCI, PQC, PRA, PsycInfo, PsycholAb, RASB, RILM, S02, S03, S05, S09, S21, SCOPUS, SRRA, SSAI, SSAb, SSCI, SSI, SportS, T02, W03, W07, W09.
—BLDSC (4947.080000), IE, Infotrieve, Ingenta. **CCC.**
Published by: Wiley-Blackwell Publishing, Inc. (Subsidiary of: Wiley-Blackwell Publishing Ltd.), 111 River St, Hoboken, NJ 07030. TEL 201-748-6000, FAX 201-748-6088, info@wiley.com. Ed. Andrew Baum. Adv. contact Kristin McCarthy TEL 201-748-7683.

➤ **JOURNAL OF APPLIED SPORT PSYCHOLOGY.** *see* MEDICAL SCIENCES—Sports Medicine

➤ **JOURNAL OF AUTISM AND DEVELOPMENTAL DISORDERS.** *see* EDUCATION—Special Education And Rehabilitation

150 364 USA ISSN 2155-8655
HV6080
➤ **THE JOURNAL OF BEHAVIOR ANALYSIS OF OFFENDER AND VICTIM TREATMENT AND PREVENTION.** Text in English. 2008. q. free (effective 2010). **Document type:** *Journal, Academic/Scholarly.* **Description:** Highlights the role of behavior analysis in adult and juvenile crime prevention, assessment of offenders including risk assessment, and treatment programs.
Media: Online - full text.
Published by: Behavior Analyst Online, 535 Queen St, Philadelphia, PA 19147. TEL 215-462-6737.

155.4 649 USA ISSN 2155-7853
LC4801
JOURNAL OF BEHAVIOR ASSESSMENT AND INTERVENTION IN CHILDREN. Abbreviated title: J E I B I. Text in English. 2004. q. free (effective 2011). **Document type:** *Journal, Academic/Scholarly.*
Formerly (until 2010): Journal of Early and Intensive Behavior Intervention (1554-4893)
Media: Online - full text.
Indexed: A01, A26, A39, C06, C07, C27, C29, CA, D03, D04, E03, E13, ERI, ERIC, H12, I05, P30, R14, S14, S15, S18, T02.
Published by: Behavior Analyst Online, 535 Queen St, Philadelphia, PA 19147. TEL 215-462-6737, http://baojournal.com/.

150 610 300 MEX ISSN 2007-0780
▼➤ **JOURNAL OF BEHAVIOR, HEALTH & SOCIAL ISSUES.** Text in English, Spanish. 2009. s-a. MXN 500 domestic to individuals; USD 40 foreign to individuals; MXN 900, USD 72 domestic to institutions; MXN 150, USD 12 per issue (effective 2011). bk.rev. abstr.; illus.; stat. back issues avail. **Document type:** *Journal, Academic/Scholarly.* **Description:** Publishes original research on: Psychology, psychopharmacology, social psychology, behavioral health, personality, public health, sport psychology, and metanalysis on these subjects.
Related titles: Online - full text ed.
Published by: Asociacion Mexicana de Comportamiento y Salud, Eulalio Pedroza 122, Col. Santa Maria Ahuacatitlan, Cuernavaca, Morelos 62100, Mexico. TEL 52-777-3179988, http://asomexcomsal.blogspot.com/. Ed. Pedro Arriaga Ramirez. Pub. Teresa Rojas. Adv. contact Rosendo Hernandez Castro. Circ: 300.

➤ **JOURNAL OF BEHAVIOR THERAPY AND EXPERIMENTAL PSYCHIATRY;** a journal of experimental psychopathology. *see* MEDICAL SCIENCES—Psychiatry And Neurology

➤ **JOURNAL OF BEHAVIORAL EDUCATION.** *see* EDUCATION

P

150 332 USA ISSN 1542-7560
HG4523
➤ **THE JOURNAL OF BEHAVIORAL FINANCE.** Abbreviated title: J F B. Text in English. 2000. q. GBP 360 combined subscription in United Kingdom to institutions (print & online eds.); EUR 480, USD 602 combined subscription to institutions (print & online eds.) (effective 2012). adv. back issues avail.; reprint service avail. from PSC. **Document type:** *Journal, Academic/Scholarly.* **Description:** Addresses the implications of current research on individual and group emotion, cognition, and action related to individual behavior in the context of financial markets, on the part of both persons in the field and investors.
Formerly (until 2003): Journal of Psychology and Financial Markets (1520-8834)
Related titles: Online - full text ed.: ISSN 1542-7579. GBP 324 in United Kingdom to institutions; EUR 432, USD 542 to institutions (effective 2012) (from IngentaConnect).
Indexed: A12, A13, A17, A22, ABIn, B01, B06, B07, B09, BLI, CA, CurCont, E-psyche, E01, EconLit, JEL, P03, P43, P48, P51, P53, P54, PQC, PsycInfo, PsycholAb, SSCI, T02, W07.
—BLDSC (4951.260500), CIS, IE, Ingenta. **CCC.**
Published by: (Institute of Behavioral Finance), Routledge (Subsidiary of: Taylor & Francis Group), 325 Chestnut St, Ste 800, Philadelphia, PA 19106. TEL 800-354-1420, FAX 215-625-2940, journals@routledge.com, http://www.routledge.com. Ed. Brian Bruce. Adv. contact Linda Hann TEL 44-1344-779945.

➤ **JOURNAL OF BEHAVIORAL HEALTH SERVICES AND RESEARCH.** *see* PUBLIC HEALTH AND SAFETY

➤ **JOURNAL OF BEHAVIORAL MEDICINE.** *see* MEDICAL SCIENCES—Psychiatry And Neurology

150 PAK ISSN 1028-9097
BF636.A1
➤ **JOURNAL OF BEHAVIOURAL SCIENCES.** Text in English. 1990. s-a. **Document type:** *Journal, Academic/Scholarly.* **Description:** Contains original articles, brief reports, review articles and single case studies on different specializations in psychology and allied discipline covering all aspects of human behavior.
Related titles: Online - full text ed.
Indexed: A01, A26, CABA, ERA, GH, H12, I05, LT, P02, P10, P36, P48, P53, P54, PQC, R12, RRTA, S20, T02, W11.
Published by: University of the Punjab, Department of Applied Psychology, PO Box 54590, Lahore, Pakistan. TEL 92-42-9231245, chairperson@appsy.pu.edu.pk, http://www.pu.edu.pk/departments/default.asp?deptid=39. Ed. Rukhsana Kausar.

155.84 USA ISSN 0095-7984
E185.625 CODEN: JBPSE3
➤ **JOURNAL OF BLACK PSYCHOLOGY.** Text in English. 1974. q. USD 659, GBP 388 combined subscription to institutions (print & online eds.); USD 646, GBP 380 to institutions (effective 2011). adv. bk.rev. illus. back issues avail.; reprint service avail. from PSC. **Document type:** *Journal, Academic/Scholarly.* **Description:** Publishes scholarly contributions within the field of psychology on the experience of Black and other minority populations from an Afrocentrist perspective in such issues as cognition, personality, social behavior, child development, education, and clinical application.
Related titles: Microform ed.: (from PQC); Online - full text ed.: ISSN 1552-4558. USD 593, GBP 349 to institutions (effective 2011).
Indexed: A20, A22, A25, A26, AMHA, ASSIA, AbAn, B04, BRD, C06, C07, C08, CA, CINAHL, CurCont, E-psyche, E01, E07, E08, ERIC, ESPM, FamI, G08, H12, HEA, I05, IBSS, IIBP, L&LBA, M08, P02, P03, P10, P12, P13, P18, P24, P25, P27, P30, P48, P53, P54, PCI, PQC, PsycInfo, PsycholAb, RiskAb, S02, S03, S08, S09, SCOPUS, SOPODA, SSA, SSAI, SSAb, SSCI, SSI, SociolAb, T02, V&AA, W03, W07.
—BLDSC (4954.180000), IE, Infotrieve, Ingenta. **CCC.**
Published by: (Association of Black Psychologists), Sage Publications, Inc., 2455 Teller Rd, Thousand Oaks, CA 91320. TEL 805-499-9774, 800-818-7243, FAX 805-499-0871, 800-583-2665, info@sagepub.com. Ed. Kevin Cokley. Circ: 2,600. **Subscr. overseas to:** Sage Publications Ltd., 1 Oliver's Yard, 55 City Rd, London EC1Y 1SP, United Kingdom. TEL 44-207-3248701, FAX 44-207-3248733, subscription@sagepub.co.uk.

158 USA ISSN 1935-1577
RC475
➤ **JOURNAL OF BRIEF, STRATEGIC & SYSTEMIC THERAPIES.** Abbreviated title: J B S S T. Text in English. 2007. s-a. back issues avail. **Document type:** *Journal, Academic/Scholarly.*
Published by: American Association of Brief and Strategic Therapists, 2160 Fletcher Pkwy, Ste M, El Cajon, CA 92020. TEL 619-562-2130, FAX 619-562-2584, members@aabst.org. Ed. Chad Hybarger.

158.7 330 USA ISSN 0889-3268
➤ **JOURNAL OF BUSINESS & PSYCHOLOGY.** Text in English. 1986. q. EUR 948, USD 991 combined subscription to institutions (print & online eds.) (effective 2012). adv. back issues avail.; reprint service avail. from PSC. **Document type:** *Journal, Academic/Scholarly.* **Description:** Highlights empirical research, case studies, and literature reviews dealing with psychological programs implemented in business settings.
Related titles: Online - full text ed.: ISSN 1573-353X (from IngentaConnect).
Indexed: A01, A02, A03, A08, A12, A13, A17, A22, A26, ABIn, ASCA, B01, B02, B06, B07, B08, B09, B17, B18, BPI, BRD, BibLing, C12, CA, CMM, CPE, CommAb, CurCont, DIP, E-psyche, E01, E08, E10, ERA, ESPM, FR, FamI, G04, G08, H01, HRA, I05, IBR, IBZ, P03, P21, P25, P30, P48, P51, P53, P54, PQC, PsycInfo, PsycholAb, RASB, RiskAb, S02, S03, S09, S21, SCOPUS, SSCI, T02, W01, W02, W03, W05, W07.
—BLDSC (4954.661070), IE, Infotrieve, Ingenta. **CCC.**
Published by: (Business Psychology Research Institute), Springer New York LLC (Subsidiary of: Springer Science+Business Media), 233 Spring St, New York, NY 10013. TEL 212-460-1500, FAX 212-460-1575, service-ny@springer.com. Ed. Steven G Rogelberg.

150 658.3 USA ISSN 1069-0727
HF5381.A1 CODEN: JOAAEX
➤ **JOURNAL OF CAREER ASSESSMENT.** Text in English. 1993. q. USD 434, GBP 255 combined subscription to institutions (print & online eds.); USD 425, GBP 250 to institutions (effective 2011). adv. abstr. index. back issues avail.; reprint service avail. from PSC. **Document type:** *Journal, Academic/Scholarly.* **Description:** Focuses on the process and techniques by which counselors and others gain understanding of the individual faced with the necessity of making informed career decisions.
Related titles: Online - full text ed.: ISSN 1552-4590. USD 391, GBP 230 to institutions (effective 2011).
Indexed: A01, A03, A08, A20, A22, AEI, ASCA, CA, CPE, CurCont, E-psyche, E01, E03, ERI, ERIC, FamI, HRA, P03, P18, P25, P48, P53, P54, PQC, PsycInfo, PsycholAb, SCOPUS, SSCI, T02, W07.
—BLDSC (4954.874000), IE, Infotrieve, Ingenta. **CCC.**
Published by: Sage Publications, Inc., 2455 Teller Rd, Thousand Oaks, CA 91320. TEL 805-499-9774, 800-818-7243, FAX 805-499-0871, 800-583-2665, info@sagepub.com. Ed. W Bruce Walsh. adv.: B&W page USD 385, color page USD 775; 5.5 x 8.75. **Subscr. to:** Sage Publications Ltd., 1 Oliver's Yard, 55 City Rd, London EC1Y 1SP, United Kingdom. TEL 44-207-3248701, FAX 44-207-3248733, subscription@sagepub.co.uk.

150 USA ISSN 1936-1521
RJ506.P66
➤ **JOURNAL OF CHILD & ADOLESCENT TRAUMA.** Text in English. 2008 (Apr.). q. GBP 280 combined subscription in United Kingdom to institutions (print & online eds.); EUR 362, USD 370 combined subscription to institutions (print & online eds.) (effective 2012). adv. reprint service avail. from PSC. **Document type:** *Journal, Academic/Scholarly.*
Related titles: Online - full text ed.: ISSN 1936-153X. GBP 252 in United Kingdom to institutions; EUR 326, USD 333 to institutions (effective 2012).
Indexed: A01, A22, C06, C07, CA, E01, P30, PQC, S02, S03, T02.
—BLDSC (4957.425450), IE. **CCC.**
Published by: Routledge (Subsidiary of: Taylor & Francis Group), 325 Chestnut St, Ste 800, Philadelphia, PA 19106. TEL 215-625-8900, 800-354-1420, FAX 215-625-8914, journals@routledge.com, http://www.routledge.com. Ed. Dr. Robert A Geffner. adv.: B&W page USD 315.

150 USA ISSN 1062-1024
RJ499.A1 CODEN: JCFSES
➤ **JOURNAL OF CHILD AND FAMILY STUDIES.** Text in English. 1992. bi-m. EUR 776, USD 819 combined subscription to institutions (print & online eds.) (effective 2012). adv. bk.rev. back issues avail.; reprint service avail. from PSC. **Document type:** *Journal, Academic/Scholarly.* **Description:** Features original papers on basic and applied research, program evaluation, service delivery and policy issues.
Related titles: Online - full text ed.: ISSN 1573-2843 (from IngentaConnect).
Indexed: A01, A02, A03, A08, A22, A25, A26, A36, ASSIA, BRD, BibLing, C06, C07, CA, CABA, CJA, CurCont, E-psyche, E01, E02, E03, E07, E08, ERI, ESPM, EdA, EdI, F09, FamI, G08, GH, I05, IBSS, M01, M02, N02, N03, P02, P03, P04, P07, P10, P12, P18, P25, P27, P30, P34, P43, P48, P53, P54, P55, PQC, PsycInfo, PsycholAb, R12, RiskAb, S02, S03, S08, S09, SCOPUS, SFSA, SOPODA, SSA, SSAI, SSAb, SSCI, SSI, SWR&A, SociolAb, T02, T05, V&AA, W03, W05, W07, W11.
—BLDSC (4957.426000), IE, Infotrieve, Ingenta. **CCC.**
Published by: Springer New York LLC (Subsidiary of: Springer Science+Business Media), 233 Spring St, New York, NY 10013. TEL 212-460-1500, FAX 212-460-1575, service-ny@springer.com. Ed. Nirbhay N Singh.

➤ **JOURNAL OF CHILD LANGUAGE.** *see* CHILDREN AND YOUTH—About

155.4 GBR ISSN 0021-9630
RJ499.A1 CODEN: JPPDAI
➤ **JOURNAL OF CHILD PSYCHOLOGY AND PSYCHIATRY.** Key Title: Journal of Child Psychology and Psychiatry and Allied Disciplines. Abbreviated title: J C P P. Text in English. 1960. m. GBP 549 in United Kingdom to institutions; EUR 696 in Europe to institutions; USD 923 in the Americas to institutions; USD 1,073 elsewhere to institutions; GBP 631 combined subscription in United Kingdom to institutions (print & online eds.); EUR 801 combined subscription in Europe to institutions (print & online eds.); USD 1,062 combined subscription in the Americas to institutions (print & online eds.); USD 1,234 combined subscription elsewhere to institutions (print & online eds.) (effective 2012). adv. bk.rev. charts; illus. index. back issues avail.; reprint service avail. from PSC. **Document type:** *Journal, Academic/Scholarly.* **Description:** Covers both child and adolescent psychology and psychiatry.
Related titles: Microform ed.: (from PQC); Online - full text ed.: ISSN 1469-7610. 1998. GBP 549 in United Kingdom to institutions; EUR 696 in Europe to institutions; USD 923 in the Americas to institutions; USD 1,073 elsewhere to institutions (effective 2012) (from IngentaConnect).
Indexed: A01, A02, A03, A08, A20, A22, A26, AC&P, AEI, AMED, AMHA, ASCA, ASSIA, AddicA, B04, B21, B25, B28, BDM&CN, BIOSIS Prev, BRD, C06, C07, C28, CA, CDA, CommAb, CurCont, E-psyche, E01, E02, E03, E06, E07, E08, ECER, EMBASE, ERI, ERIC, ESPM, EdA, EdI, ExcerpMed, F09, FR, FamI, G08, H&SSA, I05, INI, IPsyAb, IndMed, L&LBA, MEA&I, MEDLINE, MycolAb, P02, P03, P10, P18, P27, P30, P43, P48, P53, P54, PCI, PQC, PsycInfo, PsycholAb, R10, Reac, S02, S03, S09, S21, SCI, SCOPUS, SOPODA, SSAI, SSAb, SSCI, SSI, SociolAb, T02, W03, W07.
—BLDSC (4957.800000), GNLM, IE, Infotrieve, Ingenta, INIST. **CCC.**
Published by: (The Association for Child and Adolescent Mental Health), Wiley-Blackwell Publishing Ltd. (Subsidiary of: John Wiley & Sons, Inc.), 9600 Garsington Rd, Oxford, OX4 2DQ, United Kingdom. TEL 44-1865-776868, FAX 44-1865-714591, customerservices@blackwellpublishing.com. Ed. Tony C Charman. Adv. contact Craig Pickett TEL 44-1865-476267. B&W page USD 823, B&W page GBP 445; 135 x 205. Circ: 4,500.

155.4 616.89 GBR ISSN 0075-417X
➤ **JOURNAL OF CHILD PSYCHOTHERAPY.** Text in English. 1963. 3/yr. GBP 290 combined subscription in United Kingdom to institutions (print & online eds.); EUR 386, USD 486 combined subscription to institutions (print & online eds.) (effective 2012). adv. bk.rev. back issues avail.; reprint service avail. from PSC. **Document type:** *Journal, Academic/Scholarly.* **Description:** Contains articles on theory, technique, and the practice of psychoanalytic psychotherapy with children, young people, and their families.
Related titles: Online - full text ed.: ISSN 1469-9370. GBP 261 in United Kingdom to institutions; EUR 347, USD 437 to institutions (effective 2012) (from IngentaConnect).
Indexed: A01, A03, A08, A22, ASSIA, B21, B29, BiolDig, C28, CA, CDA, E-psyche, E01, E03, E17, EMBASE, ERIC, ESPM, ExcerpMed, FR, FamI, MEA&I, P03, P43, PsycInfo, PsycholAb, R10, Reac, S21, SCOPUS, SWR&A, T02.
—GNLM, IE, Infotrieve, Ingenta, INIST. **CCC.**
Published by: (Association of Child Psychotherapists), Routledge (Subsidiary of: Taylor & Francis Group), 4 Park Sq, Milton Park, Abingdon, Oxon OX14 4RN, United Kingdom. TEL 44-20-70176000, FAX 44-20-70176336, subscriptions@tandf.co.uk, http://www.routledge.com. Eds. Anne Hurley, Viviane Green. Adv. contact Linda Hann TEL 44-1344-779945. **Subscr. to:** Taylor & Francis Ltd., Journals Customer Service, Sheepen Pl, Colchester, Essex CO3 3LP, United Kingdom. TEL 44-20-70175544, FAX 44-20-70175198, tf.enquiries@tfinforma.com.

150.19 USA ISSN 0738-2944
BT732
THE JOURNAL OF CHRISTIAN HEALING. Text in English. 1979. s-a. free (effective 2009). back issues avail. **Document type:** *Journal, Academic/Scholarly.* **Description:** Discuss about the healing of trauma, the cutting edge of science and spirituality and living the Christian healthcare practitioner identity.
Related titles: Online - full text ed.: ISSN 1947-041X.
Published by: Association of Christian Therapists, 6728 Old McLean Village Dr, McLean, VA 22101. TEL 703-556-9222, FAX 703-556-8729, ACTheals@degnon.org. Ed. Douglas W Schoeninger.

155.4 USA ISSN 1537-4416
BF721 CODEN: JCCPD3
➤ **JOURNAL OF CLINICAL CHILD AND ADOLESCENT PSYCHOLOGY.** Abbreviated title: J C C A P. Text in English. 1972. bi-m. GBP 687 combined subscription in United Kingdom to institutions (print & online eds.); EUR 907, USD 1,133 combined subscription to institutions (print & online eds.) (effective 2012). adv. bk.rev. illus. Index. back issues avail.; reprint service avail. from PSC. **Document type:** *Journal, Academic/Scholarly.* **Description:** Features the research and viewpoints of child advocates in all disciplines.
Formerly (until 2001): Journal of Clinical Child Psychology (0047-228X)
Related titles: Microform ed.; Online - full text ed.: ISSN 1537-4424. 2002. GBP 619 in United Kingdom to institutions; EUR 816, USD 1,019 to institutions (effective 2012).
Indexed: A01, A02, A03, A08, A20, A22, A26, AC&P, ASCA, ASSIA, B04, B21, BDM&CN, BRD, CA, CDA, CurCont, E-psyche, E01, E02, E03, E07, E08, ECER, EMBASE, ERI, ERIC, ESPM, EdA, EdI, ExcerpMed, F09, FamI, G08, H&SSA, H11, H12, I05, IndMed, MEA&I, MEDLINE, P02, P03, P10, P12, P27, P30, P43, P48, P53, P54, PEI, PQC, PsycInfo, PsycholAb, R10, Reac, RiskAb, S02, S03, S09, S11, SCOPUS, SFSA, SSAI, SSAb, SSCI, SSI, T02, W03, W07.
—BLDSC (4958.383000), GNLM, IE, Ingenta. **CCC.**
Published by: (American Psychological Association, Society of Clinical Child and Adolescent Psychology. Division 53), Routledge (Subsidiary of: Taylor & Francis Group), 325 Chestnut St, Ste 800, Philadelphia, PA 19106. TEL 800-354-1420, FAX 215-625-2940, journals@routledge.com, http://www.routledge.com. Ed. Paul J Frick. Adv. contact Linda Hann TEL 44-1344-779945.

150 615.5 USA ISSN 2153-4047
▼➤ **JOURNAL OF CLINICAL MINDFULNESS & MEDITATION.** Text in English. 2010 (Nov.). s-a. USD 75 membership (effective 2011). **Document type:** *Journal, Academic/Scholarly.* **Description:** Features clinical research on mindfulness and other forms of meditation.
Media: Online - full text.
Published by: Society for Clinical Mindfulness & Meditation, 440 East McMillan, Cincinnati, OH 45206. TEL 513-602-6126, info@clinical-mindfulness.org. Ed. Richard Sears.

616.891 USA ISSN 1076-044X
CODEN: JCIPEY
➤ **JOURNAL OF CLINICAL PSYCHOANALYSIS.** Text in English. 1992. q. adv. bk.rev. back issues avail. **Document type:** *Journal, Academic/Scholarly.* **Description:** Explains, in jargon-free language, what actually happens in an analysis.
Indexed: E-psyche, EMBASE, ExcerpMed, MLA-IB, PsycholAb, R10, Reac, SCOPUS.
—BLDSC (4958.689000), GNLM, IE, Infotrieve, Ingenta.
Published by: International Universities Press, Inc., 59 Boston Post Rd, Box 1524, PO Box 389, Madison, CT 06443. TEL 203-245-4000, FAX 203-245-0775, info@iup.com.

616.891 USA ISSN 0021-9762
RC321 CODEN: JCPYAO
➤ **JOURNAL OF CLINICAL PSYCHOLOGY.** Text in English. 1945. m. GBP 570 in United Kingdom to institutions; EUR 720 in Europe to institutions; USD 1,032 in United States to institutions; USD 1,116 in Canada & Mexico to institutions; USD 1,116 elsewhere to institutions; GBP 656 combined subscription in United Kingdom to institutions (print & online eds.); EUR 829 combined subscription in Europe to institutions (print & online eds.); USD 1,187 combined subscription in United States to institutions (print & online eds.); USD 1,271 combined subscription in Canada & Mexico to institutions (print & online eds.); USD 1,271 combined subscription elsewhere to institutions (print & online eds.) (effective 2012). adv. bk.rev. charts. index. back issues avail.; reprint service avail. from PSC. **Document type:** *Journal, Academic/Scholarly.* **Description:** Includes research studies, articles on contemporary professional issues, and single case research. Covers psycopathology, psychodiagnostics, and the psychotherapeutic process, as well as psychotherapy effectiveness research, psychological assessment and treatment matching, and clinical outcomes.
Incorporates (1995-1998): In Session: Psychotherapy in Practice (1077-2413)

Related titles: Microform ed.: (from PQC); Online - full text ed.: ISSN 1097-4679. GBP 527 in United Kingdom to institutions; EUR 666 in Europe to institutions; USD 1,032 elsewhere to institutions (effective 2012); Supplement(s): Archives of the Behavioral Sciences. ISSN 0749-8500.
Indexed: A01, A02, A03, A08, A20, A21, A22, A25, A26, ABS&EES, AC&P, AHCMS, AMHA, ASCA, AgeL, B04, BRD, C06, C07, C08, C28, CA, CINAHL, CIS, ChPerI, ChemAb, Chicano, CurCont, DentInd, E-psyche, E02, E03, E06, E07, E08, EMBASE, ERI, EdA, EdI, ExcerpMed, F09, FR, FamI, G08, G10, H09, H11, H12, HospLI, I05, INI, IPsyAb, ISR, IndMed, MEA&I, MEDLINE, P02, P03, P04, P10, P12, P27, P30, P43, P48, P53, P54, PQC, PsycInfo, PsycholAb, R10, RI-1, RI-2, Reac, RefZh, S02, S03, S05, S08, S09, SCOPUS, SFSA, SOPODA, SSAI, SSAb, SSCI, SSI, SWR&A, SociolAb, T02, THA, V&AA, W03, W07, W09.
—BLDSC (4958.690000), GNLM, IE, Infotrieve, Ingenta, INIST. **CCC.**
Published by: John Wiley & Sons, Inc., 111 River St, Hoboken, NJ 07030. TEL 201-748-6000, FAX 201-748-6088, info@wiley.com, http://www.wiley.com/WileyCDA/. Ed. Beverly E Thorn. Pub., Adv. contact Kim Thompkins TEL 212-850-6921. **Subscr. outside the Americas to:** John Wiley & Sons Ltd., The Atrium, Southern Gate, Chichester, West Sussex PO19 8SQ, United Kingdom. TEL 44-1243-779777, FAX 44-1243-775878, cs-journals@wiley.com.

616.89 USA ISSN 1068-9583
RC467 CODEN: JLPSE5
➤ **JOURNAL OF CLINICAL PSYCHOLOGY IN MEDICAL SETTINGS.** Text in English. 1994. q. EUR 539, USD 555 combined subscription to institutions (print & online eds.) (effective 2012). adv. bk.rev. back issues avail.; reprint service avail. from PSC. **Document type:** *Journal, Academic/Scholarly.* **Description:** Explores theoretical and applied research in clinical science, clinical practice and service delivery, education and professional issues.
Related titles: Microfilm ed.: (from PQC); Online - full text ed.: ISSN 1573-3572 (from IngentaConnect).
Indexed: A01, A03, A08, A20, A22, A26, ASCA, BibLing, CA, CurCont, E-psyche, E01, EMBASE, ExcerpMed, FamI, I05, MEDLINE, P03, P30, PsycInfo, PsycholAb, R10, Reac, SCOPUS, SOPODA, SSCI, SociolAb, T02, W07.
—BLDSC (4958.690550), GNLM, IE, Infotrieve, Ingenta. **CCC.**
Published by: (Association of Psychologists in Academic Health Centers, Evanston Hospital, Department of Psychiatry), Springer New York LLC (Subsidiary of: Springer Science+Business Media), 233 Spring St, New York, NY 10013. TEL 212-460-1500, FAX 212-460-1575, service-ny@springer.com. Ed. Barbara A Cubic.

150 796 USA ISSN 1932-9261
GV706.4
➤ **JOURNAL OF CLINICAL SPORT PSYCHOLOGY.** Abbreviated title: J C S P. Text in English. 2007 (Mar.). q. USD 368 domestic to institutions; USD 378 foreign to institutions; USD 426 combined subscription domestic to institutions (print & online eds.); USD 436 combined subscription foreign to institutions (print & online eds.) (effective 2012). back issues avail. **Document type:** *Journal, Academic/Scholarly.* **Description:** Covers topics relating to psychological health and well-being of athletes and coaches, psychological aspects of athletic performance, as well as issues and concerns that connect physical and psychological functioning.
Related titles: Online - full text ed.: ISSN 1932-927X. 2007 (Mar.). USD 368 to institutions (effective 2012).
Indexed: A36, CA, CABA, E12, GH, LT, N02, N03, P03, P30, PsycInfo, RRTA, SD, T02, T05.
—BLDSC (4958.755000), IE. **CCC.**
Published by: Human Kinetics, 1607 N Market St, Champaign, IL 61820. TEL 800-747-4457, FAX 217-351-2674, info@hkusa.com, http://www.humankinetics.com. Ed. Frank L Gardner TEL 215-951-1350. Pub. Rainer Martens. R&P Martha Gullo TEL 217-403-7534. Adv. contact Amy Bleich TEL 217-403-7803.

153.4 NLD ISSN 1567-7095
BF309
➤ **JOURNAL OF COGNITION AND CULTURE.** Text in English. 2001. 2/yr. EUR 222, USD 311 to institutions; EUR 242, USD 339 combined subscription to institutions (print & online eds.) (effective 2012). back issues avail.; reprint service avail. from PSC. **Document type:** *Journal, Academic/Scholarly.* **Description:** Provides an interdisciplinary forum for exploring the mental foundations of culture and the culture foundations of mental life.
Related titles: Online - full text ed.: ISSN 1568-5373. EUR 202, USD 283 to institutions (effective 2012) (from IngentaConnect).
Indexed: A01, A03, A08, A22, AICP, CA, E-psyche, E01, IBSS, IZBG, P03, P30, P43, PsycInfo, PsycholAb, S02, S03, SCOPUS, T02.
—BLDSC (4958.798050), IE, Ingenta. **CCC.**
Published by: Brill, PO Box 9000, Leiden, 2300 PA, Netherlands. TEL 31-71-5353500, FAX 31-71-5317532, cs@brill.nl. Eds. E T Lawson, Pascal Boyer. **Dist. by:** Turpin Distribution Services Ltd., Pegasus Dr, Stratton Business Park, Biggleswade, Bedfordshire SG18 8QB, United Kingdom. TEL 44-1767-604954, FAX 44-1767-601640, custserv@turpin-distribution.com, http://www.turpin-distribution.com/.

155 USA ISSN 1524-8372
➤ **JOURNAL OF COGNITION AND DEVELOPMENT.** Text in English. 2000. q. GBP 352 combined subscription in United Kingdom to institutions (print & online eds.); EUR 469, USD 590 combined subscription to institutions (print & online eds.) (effective 2012). adv. bk.rev. back issues avail.; reprint service avail. from PSC. **Document type:** *Journal, Academic/Scholarly.* **Description:** Provides articles and empirical reports covering the area of cognitive development. Features theoretical essays and reviews of new and significant books.
Related titles: Online - full text ed.: ISSN 1532-7647. 2000. GBP 316 in United Kingdom to institutions; EUR 422, USD 530 to institutions (effective 2012).
Indexed: A01, A03, A08, A20, A22, CA, CPE, CurCont, E01, EMBASE, ERIC, ExcerpMed, FamI, L&LBA, P03, P10, P12, P18, P25, P27, P30, P48, P50, P53, P54, PQC, PsycInfo, PsycholAb, R10, Reac, SCOPUS, SSCI, T02, W07.
—BLDSC (4958.798100), IE, Infotrieve, Ingenta, INIST. **CCC.**
Published by: (Cognitive Development Society), Psychology Press (Subsidiary of: Taylor & Francis Inc.), 325 Chestnut St, Ste 800, Philadelphia, PA 19106. TEL 800-354-1420, FAX 215-625-2940, orders@taylorandfrancis.com, http://www.psypress.com. Ed. Laura L Namy. Adv. contact Linda Hann TEL 44-1344-779945.

616.89142 ROM ISSN 1584-7101
RC489.C63
JOURNAL OF COGNITIVE AND BEHAVIORAL PSYCHOTHERAPIES. Text in English. 2004. s-a. (Mar. & Sept.). USD 25 to individuals; USD 100 to institutions (effective 2009). **Document type:** *Journal, Academic/Scholarly.*
Indexed: A01, A03, A08, A20, CA, IBSS, P03, P25, P27, P30, P48, P54, PQC, PsycInfo, SCOPUS, SSCI, T02, W07.
—BLDSC (4958.798150).
Published by: The International Institute for the Advanced Studies of Psychotherapy and Applied Mental Health, c/o Universitatea Babes-Bolyai, 37 Republicii St, Cluj-Napoca, 400084, Romania. TEL 40-264-744266300, FAX 40-264-595576, danieldavid@psychology.ro. Ed. Daniel David.

JOURNAL OF COGNITIVE EDUCATION AND PSYCHOLOGY. *see* EDUCATION—Teaching Methods And Curriculum

150 004.01 USA ISSN 1555-3434
QA76.9.H85
JOURNAL OF COGNITIVE ENGINEERING AND DECISION MAKING. Text in English. 2007. q. USD 430 to institutions; USD 185 to non-members; USD 100 to members; USD 520 combined subscription to individuals (print & online eds.); USD 225 combined subscription to non-members (print & online eds.); USD 120 combined subscription to members (print & online eds.); USD 46 per issue to non-members; USD 25 per issue to members (effective 2010). adv. **Document type:** *Journal, Academic/Scholarly.* **Description:** Focuses on research that seeks to understand how people engage in cognitive work in real-world settings and on the development of systems that support that work.
Related titles: Online - full text ed.: USD 400 to institutions; USD 170 to non-members; USD 90 to members (effective 2010) (from IngentaConnect).
Indexed: HRIS, PsycInfo.
—CCC.
Published by: Human Factors and Ergonomics Society, PO Box 1369, Santa Monica, CA 90406. TEL 310-394-1811, FAX 310-394-2410, info@hfes.org. Ed. Mica Endsley.

JOURNAL OF COGNITIVE NEUROSCIENCE (ONLINE). *see* MEDICAL SCIENCES—Psychiatry And Neurology

155 GBR ISSN 2044-5911
BF309 CODEN: EJCPEW
➤ **JOURNAL OF COGNITIVE PSYCHOLOGY.** Text in English. 1989. 8/yr. GBP 898 combined subscription in United Kingdom to institutions (print & online eds.); EUR 1,184, USD 1,479 combined subscription to institutions (print & online eds.) (effective 2012). bk.rev. abstr.; stat. back issues avail.; reprints avail. **Document type:** *Journal, Academic/Scholarly.* **Description:** Features reports of empirical work, theoretical contributions and reviews of the literature in all areas of cognitive psychology including applied cognitive psychology.
Former titles (until 2011): European Journal of Cognitive Psychology (0954-1446); (until 1989): European Cognitive Psychology
Related titles: Online - full text ed.: ISSN 2044-592X. 1996. GBP 808 in United Kingdom to institutions; EUR 1,065, USD 1,331 to institutions (effective 2012) (from IngentaConnect).
Indexed: A01, A02, A03, A08, A20, A22, AEI, ASCA, B21, BIOBASE, BibLing, CA, CPE, CurCont, E-psyche, E01, EMBASE, ERA, ErgAb, ExcerpMed, IABS, L&LBA, NSA, P03, P30, P43, PCI, PsycInfo, PsycholAb, R10, Reac, SCOPUS, SOPODA, SSCI, SociolAb, T02, W07.
—GNLM, IE, Infotrieve, Ingenta, INIST. **CCC.**
Published by: (European Society for Cognitive Psychology), Psychology Press (Subsidiary of: Taylor & Francis Ltd.), 27 Church Rd, Hove, E Sussex BN3 2FA, United Kingdom. TEL 44-20-70176000, FAX 44-20-70176717, info@psypress.co.uk, http://www.psypress.com. Ed. Andre Vandierendonck. Adv. contact Linda Hann TEL 44-1344-779945.

616.89 USA ISSN 0889-8391
RC489.C63
➤ **JOURNAL OF COGNITIVE PSYCHOTHERAPY**; an international quarterly. Text in English. 1987. q. USD 90 domestic to individuals; USD 130 foreign to individuals; USD 255 domestic to institutions; USD 295 foreign to institutions; USD 135 combined subscription domestic to individuals (print & online eds.); USD 195 combined subscription foreign to individuals (print & online eds.); USD 385 combined subscription domestic to institutions (print & online eds.); USD 445 combined subscription foreign to institutions (print & online eds.) (effective 2009). adv. bk.rev.; software rev.; video rev.; Website rev. abstr.; bibl. 70 p./no.; back issues avail.; reprints avail. **Document type:** *Journal, Academic/Scholarly.* **Description:** Devoted to the advancement of the clinical practice of cognitive psychotherapy in its broadest sense. Merges theory, research and practice to provide an international forum investigating clinical implications of theoretical developments and research findings.
Related titles: Online - full text ed.: ISSN 1938-887X. USD 80 domestic to individuals; USD 120 foreign to individuals; USD 235 domestic to institutions; USD 275 foreign to institutions (effective 2009) (from IngentaConnect).
Indexed: A01, A03, A22, C06, C07, CA, E-psyche, EMBASE, ExcerpMed, P03, P20, P25, P30, P43, P48, P54, PQC, PsycInfo, PsycholAb, R10, Reac, SCOPUS, SOPODA, SociolAb, T02.
—BLDSC (4958.799200), GNLM, IE, Infotrieve, Ingenta. **CCC.**
Published by: (International Association of Cognitive Psychotherapy), Springer Publishing Company, 11 W 42nd St, 15th Fl, New York, NY 10036. TEL 212-431-4370, FAX 212-941-7842, contactus@springerpub.com. Ed. Steven Taylor. R&P, Adv. contact Jessica Perl. B&W page USD 300; trim 6.75 x 10. Circ: 612 (paid).

616.8914 378.3 USA ISSN 8756-8225
RC451.4.S7
➤ **JOURNAL OF COLLEGE STUDENT PSYCHOTHERAPY.** Abbreviated title: J C S P. Text in English. 1986. q. GBP 625 combined subscription in United Kingdom to institutions (print & online eds.); EUR 812, USD 815 combined subscription to institutions (print & online eds.) (effective 2012). adv. bk.rev. 120 p./no. 1 cols./p.; back issues avail.; reprint service avail. from PSC. **Document type:** *Journal, Academic/Scholarly.* **Description:** Enhances the lives of college and university students by stimulating high-quality practice theory, and research in mental and personal development.

Related titles: Microfiche ed.: (from PQC); Microform ed.; Online - full text ed.: ISSN 1540-4730. GBP 563 in United Kingdom to institutions; EUR 731, USD 734 to institutions (effective 2012).
Indexed: A01, A03, A22, ASSIA, B21, CA, CPE, E-psyche, E01, E03, E17, EAA, ERI, ESPM, FamI, HEA, M02, MLA-IB, P03, P30, PsycInfo, PsycholAb, S02, S03, SCOPUS, SOPODA, SSA, SWR&A, SociolAb, T02, V&AA.
—BLDSC (4958.830000), GNLM, IE, Ingenta. **CCC.**
Published by: Routledge (Subsidiary of: Taylor & Francis Group), 325 Chestnut St, Ste 800, Philadelphia, PA 19106. TEL 215-625-8900, 800-354-1420, FAX 215-625-8914, journals@routledge.com, http://www.routledge.com. Ed. Dr. Leighton C Whitaker. adv.: B&W page USD 315, color page USD 550; trim 4.375 x 7.125. Circ: 253 (paid).

617.8 USA ISSN 0021-9924
RC423.A1 CODEN: JCDIAI
➤ **JOURNAL OF COMMUNICATION DISORDERS.** Text in English. 1967. bi-m. EUR 953 in Europe to institutions; JPY 126,600 in Japan to institutions; USD 1,068 elsewhere to institutions (effective 2012). adv. bk.rev. charts; illus. back issues avail.; reprints avail. **Document type:** *Journal, Academic/Scholarly.* **Description:** Brings out articles on topics related to disorders of speech, language and hearing.
Incorporates (1991-1994): Clinics in Communication Disorders (1054-8505)
Related titles: Microform ed.: (from PQC); Online - full text ed.: ISSN 1873-7994 (from IngentaConnect, ScienceDirect).
Indexed: A01, A03, A08, A20, A22, A26, AMED, ASCA, B25, BDM&CN, BIOSIS Prev, C06, C07, C08, CA, CINAHL, CMM, CurCont, DSHAb, DentInd, E-psyche, E03, ECER, EMBASE, ERI, ERIC, ExcerpMed, FR, FamI, H12, I05, IndMed, L&LBA, L11, MEA&I, MEDLINE, MLA-IB, MycolAb, P03, P30, PsycInfo, PsycholAb, R10, RILM, Reac, RehabLit, SCOPUS, SOPODA, SSCI, T02, W03, W07, YAE&RB.
—BLDSC (4961.600000), GNLM, IE, Infotrieve, Ingenta, INIST. **CCC.**
Published by: Elsevier Inc. (Subsidiary of: Elsevier Science & Technology), 1600 John F Kennedy Blvd, Philadelphia, PA 19103. TEL 215-239-3900, FAX 215-238-7883, JournalCustomerService-usa@elsevier.com. Ed. Luc de Nil. Adv. contact Janine Castle TEL 44-1865-843844.

302 150 GBR ISSN 1052-9284
HM251 CODEN: JLCPEX
➤ **JOURNAL OF COMMUNITY & APPLIED SOCIAL PSYCHOLOGY.** Text in English. 1986. bi-m. GBP 656 in United Kingdom to institutions; EUR 829 in Europe to institutions; USD 1,285 elsewhere to institutions; GBP 754 combined subscription in United Kingdom to institutions (print & online eds.); EUR 954 combined subscription in Europe to institutions (print & online eds.); USD 1,478 combined subscription elsewhere to institutions (print & online eds.) (effective 2012). adv. back issues avail.; reprint service avail. from PSC. **Document type:** *Journal, Academic/Scholarly.* **Description:** Fosters international communication among those concerned with the social psychological analysis and critical understanding of community issues and problems and to develop this understanding in the context of proposals for intervention and social policy.
Formerly (until 1991): Social Behaviour (0885-6249)
Related titles: Microform ed.: (from PQC); Online - full text ed.: ISSN 1099-1298. GBP 656 in United Kingdom to institutions; EUR 829 in Europe to institutions; USD 1,285 elsewhere to institutions (effective 2012).
Indexed: A01, A03, A08, A20, A22, ASCA, ASSIA, C06, C07, CA, CJA, CurCont, DIP, E-psyche, FR, FamI, IBR, IBSS, IBZ, P02, P03, P10, P12, P30, P34, P43, P48, P53, P54, PQC, PsycInfo, PsycholAb, RASB, S02, S03, S21, SCOPUS, SOPODA, SSA, SSCI, SociolAb, T02, W07, W09.
—IE, Infotrieve, Ingenta, INIST. **CCC.**
Published by: John Wiley & Sons Ltd. (Subsidiary of: John Wiley & Sons, Inc.), 1-7 Oldlands Way, PO Box 808, Bognor Regis, West Sussex PO21 9FF, United Kingdom. TEL 44-1865-778315, FAX 44-1243-843232, cs-journals@wiley.com, http://eu.wiley.com/WileyCDA/. Ed. Sandra Schruijer. **Subscr. in the Americas to:** John Wiley & Sons, Inc., 111 River St, Hoboken, NJ 07030. subinfo@wiley.com; **Subscr. to:** 1-7 Oldlands Way, PO Box 809, Bognor Regis, West Sussex PO21 9FG, United Kingdom. TEL 44-1865-778054, cs-agency@wiley.com.

302 USA ISSN 0090-4392
RC467 CODEN: JCPSD9
➤ **JOURNAL OF COMMUNITY PSYCHOLOGY.** Text in English. 1973. 8/yr. GBP 481 in United Kingdom to institutions; EUR 610 in Europe to institutions; USD 897 in United States to institutions; USD 945 in Canada & Mexico to institutions; USD 945 elsewhere to institutions; GBP 554 combined subscription in United Kingdom to institutions (print & online eds.); EUR 702 combined subscription in Europe to institutions (print & online eds.); USD 1,032 combined subscription in United States to institutions (print & online eds.); USD 1,080 combined subscription in Canada & Mexico to institutions (print & online eds.); USD 1,080 combined subscription elsewhere to institutions (print & online eds.) (effective 2012). adv. index. back issues avail.; reprint service avail. from PSC. **Document type:** *Journal, Academic/Scholarly.* **Description:** Devoted to research, evaluation, assessment, and intervention, and review articles that deal with human behavior in community settings. For psychologists, psychiatrists, social workers, counselors and mental health professionals.
Related titles: Microform ed.: (from PQC); Online - full text ed.: ISSN 1520-6629. GBP 457 in United Kingdom to institutions; EUR 579 in Europe to institutions; USD 897 elsewhere to institutions (effective 2012).
Indexed: A01, A02, A03, A08, A20, A22, A36, AMHA, ASCA, C06, C07, C08, C25, C28, CA, CABA, CINAHL, ChPerI, Chicano, CurCont, E-psyche, E12, ERIC, F09, FamI, G10, GH, IBR, IBZ, LT, MEA&I, N02, P02, P03, P10, P12, P30, P34, P43, P48, P53, P54, PQC, PSI, PsycInfo, PsycholAb, R12, RRTA, S02, S03, SCOPUS, SFSA, SRRA, SSCI, T02, T05, TAR, THA, W07, W09, W11.
—BLDSC (4961.750000), IE, Infotrieve, Ingenta. **CCC.**
Published by: John Wiley & Sons, Inc., 111 River St, Hoboken, NJ 07030. TEL 201-748-6000, FAX 201-748-6088, info@wiley.com, http://www.wiley.com/WileyCDA/. Ed. Dr. Raymond P Lorion. Pub., Adv. contact Kim Thompkins TEL 212-850-6921. **Subscr. outside the Americas to:** John Wiley & Sons Ltd., The Atrium, Southern Gate, Chichester, West Sussex PO19 8SQ, United Kingdom. TEL 44-1243-779777, 800-243407, FAX 44-1243-775878, cs-journals@wiley.com.

P

156 USA ISSN 0735-7036
BF1 CODEN: JCOPDT
➤ **JOURNAL OF COMPARATIVE PSYCHOLOGY.** Text in English. 1921. q. USD 107 domestic to individuals; USD 134 foreign to individuals; USD 384 domestic to institutions; USD 429 foreign to institutions (effective 2011). adv. charts; illus. index. back issues avail.; reprint service avail. from PSC. **Document type:** *Journal, Academic/Scholarly.* **Description:** Covers laboratory and field studies of the behavioral patterns of various species as they relate to evolution, development, ecology, control, and functional significance.
Supersedes in part (in 1983): Journal of Comparative and Physiological Psychology (0021-9940); Which was formerly (until 1947): Journal of Comparative Psychology (0093-4127); Which was formed by the merger of (1917-1921): Psychobiology (0096-9745); (1911-1921): Journal of Animal Behavior (0095-9928)
Related titles: Microform ed.: (from PQC); Online - full text ed.: ISSN 1939-2087 (from ScienceDirect).
Indexed: A01, A02, A03, A08, A20, A22, A26, A34, A36, A37, A38, AMHA, ASCA, AbAn, B&AI, B04, B10, B25, BIOSIS Prev, BRD, CA, CABA, ChemAb, CurCont, D01, E-psyche, E08, EMBASE, ExcerpMed, FR, FamI, G01, G08, GH, H09, I05, ISR, IndMed, IndVet, Inpharma, MEDLINE, MycolAb, N02, N03, N04, P02, P03, P10, P12, P27, P30, P33, P37, P48, P53, P54, PCI, PQC, PsycInfo, PsycholAb, R07, R08, R10, RASB, Reac, S01, S02, S03, S05, S09, SCI, SCOPUS, SSAI, SSAb, SSCI, SSI, T02, VS, W03, W07, W08, Z01.
—BLDSC (4963.300000), CASDDS, GNLM, IE, Infotrieve, Ingenta, INIST. **CCC.**
Published by: American Psychological Association, 750 First St, NE, Washington, DC 20002. TEL 202-336-5500, 800-374-2721, FAX 202-336-5997, journals@apa.org. Ed. Dr. Gordon M Burghardt. Adv. contact Doug Constant TEL 202-336-5574. Circ: 700.

153 USA ISSN 1555-9262
BF309
THE JOURNAL OF CONSCIOUS EVOLUTION. Text in English. 2005. 3/yr.
Media: Online - full content.
Published by: Journal of Conscious Evolution, 1610 Westbridge Dr #H-42, Fort Collins, CO 80526. Eds. Allan Combs, Sean M Saiter.

153 500 616.8 GBR ISSN 1355-8250
BF309
➤ **JOURNAL OF CONSCIOUSNESS STUDIES**; controversies in science & the humanities. Text in English. 1994. m. GBP 250, USD 500 combined subscription to institutions (print & online eds.) (effective 2009). bk.rev. back issues avail. **Document type:** *Journal, Academic/Scholarly.* **Description:** Publishes original scholarship and reviews in the new field of consciousness research, integrating developments in the sciences and humanities.
Related titles: Online - full text ed.: (from IngentaConnect).
Indexed: A01, A03, A08, A20, A22, AmHI, ArtHuCI, CA, CurCont, DIP, E-psyche, E01, H07, IBR, IBZ, MLA-IB, P03, PhilInd, PsycInfo, PsycholAb, RILM, SCOPUS, SSCI, T02, W07.
—BLDSC (4965.160000), IE, Ingenta. **CCC.**
Published by: Imprint Academic, PO Box 200, Exeter, Devon EXS 5YX, United Kingdom. TEL 44-1392-851550, FAX 44-1392-851178. Ed. Valerie Gray Hardcastle. Pub. Mr. Keith Sutherland.

155 USA ISSN 1072-0537
BF698.9.P47 CODEN: JCPYES
➤ **JOURNAL OF CONSTRUCTIVIST PSYCHOLOGY.** Text in English. 1988. q. GBP 357 combined subscription in United Kingdom to institutions (print & online eds.); EUR 474, USD 593 combined subscription to institutions (print & online eds.) (effective 2012). adv. reprint service avail. from PSC. **Document type:** *Journal, Academic/Scholarly.* **Description:** Presents empirical research, conceptual analyses, critical reviews, case studies on personal construct theory and related approaches to psychology.
Formerly (until 1994): International Journal of Personal Construct Psychology (0893-603X)
Related titles: Microform ed.: (from PQC); Online - full text ed.: ISSN 1521-0650. GBP 321 in United Kingdom to institutions; EUR 426, USD 534 to institutions (effective 2012) (from IngentaConnect).
Indexed: A01, A03, A08, A20, A22, ASCA, CA, CurCont, E-psyche, E01, FamI, P03, P43, P48, PQC, PsycInfo, PsycholAb, RILM, S02, S03, SCOPUS, SSCI, T02, W07.
—IE, Infotrieve, Ingenta, INIST. **CCC.**
Published by: (Constructivist Psychology Network), Taylor & Francis Inc. (Subsidiary of: Taylor & Francis Group), 325 Chestnut St, Ste 800, Philadelphia, PA 19106. TEL 215-625-2940, 800-354-1420, orders@taylorandfrancis.com, http://www.taylorandfrancis.com. Ed. Robert A Neimeyer. Adv. contact Linda Hann TEL 44-1344-779945.

158.3 USA ISSN 0022-006X
CODEN: JCLPBC
➤ **JOURNAL OF CONSULTING AND CLINICAL PSYCHOLOGY.** Abbreviated title: J C C P. Text in English. 1937. bi-m. USD 280 domestic to individuals; USD 312 foreign to individuals; USD 907 domestic to institutions; USD 964 foreign to institutions (effective 2011). adv. bibl.; charts; illus. index. back issues avail.; reprint service avail. from PSC. **Document type:** *Journal, Academic/Scholarly.* **Description:** Covers research on techniques of diagnosis and treatment in disordered behavior as well as studies of populations of clinical interest.
Formerly (until 1968): Journal of Consulting Psychology (0095-8891)
Related titles: Microform ed.: (from PMC, PQC); Online - full text ed.: ISSN 1939-2117 (from ScienceDirect).
Indexed: A01, A02, A03, A08, A20, A22, A25, A26, A29, AC&P, AMED, AMHA, ASCA, ASSIA, AcaI, AddicA, B20, B21, BRD, C06, C07, C08, C28, CA, CINAHL, CIS, Chicano, CurCont, DIP, DokArb, E-psyche, E02, E03, E06, E07, E08, ECER, EMBASE, ERI, ERIC, ESPM, EdA, EdI, ExcerpMed, F09, FR, FamI, G08, GenetAb, H09, H12, HlthInd, I05, IBR, IBZ, IndMed, JW-P, MEA&I, MEDLINE, MLA-IB, P02, P03, P10, P12, P13, P27, P30, P34, P48, P50, P53, P54, PCI, PQC, PsycInfo, PsycholAb, R10, RASB, Reac, S02, S03, S05, S08, S09, S21, SCOPUS, SFSA, SSAI, SSAb, SSCI, SSI, SWR&A, T02, THA, ViroIAbstr, W03, W07, W09.
—BLDSC (4965.195000), GNLM, IE, Infotrieve, Ingenta, INIST. **CCC.**
Published by: American Psychological Association, 750 First St, NE, Washington, DC 20002. TEL 202-336-5500, 800-374-2721, FAX 202-336-5997, journals@apa.org. Ed. Arthur M Nezu. Adv. contact Doug Constant TEL 202-336-5574. Circ: 2,900.

➤ **JOURNAL OF CONSUMER PSYCHOLOGY.** *see* ADVERTISING AND PUBLIC RELATIONS

➤ **JOURNAL OF CONSUMER SATISFACTION, DISSATISFACTION AND COMPLAINING BEHAVIOR.** *see* BUSINESS AND ECONOMICS—Marketing And Purchasing

616.89 USA ISSN 0022-0116
RC475 CODEN: JCPTBA
➤ **JOURNAL OF CONTEMPORARY PSYCHOTHERAPY**; on the cutting edge of modern developments in psychotherapy. Text in English. 19??. q. EUR 895, USD 921 combined subscription to institutions (print & online eds.) (effective 2012). adv. bk.rev. bibl.; charts. reprint service avail. from PSC. **Document type:** *Journal, Academic/Scholarly.* **Description:** Presents progressive research and clinical papers covering advances in psychotherapeutic concepts and methodology. Offers an eclectic approach to the promotion of emotional health and maturity.
Former titles (until 1968): Long Island Consultation Center. Journal (0458-2365); (until 1960): L I C C Newsletter (0455-0749)
Related titles: Microfilm ed.: (from PQC); Online - full text ed.: ISSN 1573-3564 (from IngentaConnect).
Indexed: A20, A22, A26, BibLing, CA, E-psyche, E01, EMBASE, ExcerpMed, FamI, IBR, IBZ, MEA&I, MLA-IB, P03, P20, P25, P48, P54, PQC, PsycInfo, PsycholAb, R10, RILM, Reac, RefZh, RehabLit, S02, S03, SCOPUS, SWR&A, T02.
—BLDSC (4965.240000), GNLM, IE, Infotrieve, Ingenta, INIST. **CCC.**
Published by: Springer New York LLC (Subsidiary of: Springer Science+Business Media), 233 Spring St, New York, NY 10013. TEL 212-460-1500, FAX 212-460-1575, service-ny@springer.com. Ed. James Overholser.

371.4 USA ISSN 0748-9633
HF5381.A1
➤ **JOURNAL OF COUNSELING & DEVELOPMENT.** Abbreviated title: J C D. Text in English. 1922. q. GBP 212 in United Kingdom to institutions; EUR 244 in Europe to institutions; USD 300 elsewhere to institutions; GBP 244 combined subscription in United Kingdom to institutions (print & online eds.); EUR 281 combined subscription in Europe to institutions (print & online eds.); USD 345 combined subscription elsewhere to institutions (print & online eds.) (effective 2012). abstr.; bibl.; illus. index. 128 p./no.; back issues avail.; reprint service avail. from PSC. **Document type:** *Journal, Academic/Scholarly.* **Description:** Features materials and contains authoritative articles on professional and scientific issues, research of interest to practitioners, and new techniques or practices.
Former titles (until 1984): Personnel and Guidance Journal (0031-5737); (until 1952): Occupations; (until 1933): The Vocational Guidance Magazine; (until 1924): National Vocational Guidance Association Bulletin; (until 1922): National Vocational Guidance Association. Bulletin
Related titles: CD-ROM ed.; Microform ed.: (from PQC); Online - full text ed.: ISSN 1556-6676. GBP 212 in United Kingdom to institutions; EUR 244 in Europe to institutions; USD 300 elsewhere to institutions (effective 2012); Cumulative ed(s).: 1999. USD 295 to non-members; USD 195 to members; USD 495 for multiple user license (effective 2001).
Indexed: A01, A02, A03, A08, A12, A13, A20, A21, A22, A25, A26, A36, ABIn, ASSIA, AcaI, B01, B04, B06, B07, B08, B09, BRD, BRI, C11, C12, C28, CA, CABA, CBRI, ChPerI, Chicano, CurCont, E-psyche, E02, E03, E06, E07, E08, EAA, ECER, ERI, ERIC, EdA, EdI, F09, FamI, G08, G10, GH, H04, HEA, HRA, HlthInd, I05, I06, I07, L09, M01, M02, M06, MagInd, N02, N03, P02, P03, P04, P06, P10, P12, P13, P18, P24, P25, P27, P30, P34, P43, P48, P51, P53, P54, P55, PC&CA, PCI, PQC, PsycInfo, PsycholAb, R04, RASB, RI-1, RI-2, RehabLit, S02, S03, S08, S09, S21, S23, SCOPUS, SFSA, SSAI, SSAb, SSCI, SSI, SWR&A, T02, W03, W05, W07, W09, WorkRelAb.
—BLDSC (4965.445000), IE, Infotrieve, Ingenta. **CCC.**
Published by: American Counseling Association, 5999 Stevenson Ave, Alexandria, VA 22304. TEL 800-347-6647, FAX 703-823-0252, 800-473-2329. Adv. contact Kathy Maguire TEL 703-823-9800 ext 207. Circ: 50,000 (paid).

150 371.4 USA ISSN 0022-0167
➤ **JOURNAL OF COUNSELING PSYCHOLOGY.** Text in English. 1954. q. USD 145 domestic to individuals; USD 172 foreign to individuals; USD 415 domestic to institutions; USD 460 foreign to institutions (effective 2011). adv. bk.rev. bibl.; charts; illus. index. back issues avail.; reprint service avail. from PSC. **Document type:** *Journal, Academic/Scholarly.* **Description:** Covers empirical studies about counseling processes and interventions, theoretical articles about counseling, and studies dealing with evaluation of counseling applications and programs.
Related titles: Microform ed.: (from PQC); Online - full text ed.: ISSN 1939-2168 (from ScienceDirect).
Indexed: A01, A02, A03, A08, A12, A13, A17, A20, A22, A25, A26, ABIn, AC&P, AMHA, ASCA, ASSIA, AddicA, B01, B06, B07, B08, B09, BRD, C06, C07, C28, CA, CBRI, CDA, CMM, ChPerI, Chicano, CurCont, DIP, E-psyche, E02, E03, E06, E07, E08, ERA, ERI, ERIC, EdA, EdI, F09, FR, FamI, G08, G10, H09, HEA, I05, IBR, IBZ, MEA&I, MEDLINE, P02, P03, P07, P10, P12, P18, P27, P30, P48, P51, P53, P54, PCI, PQC, PsycInfo, PsycholAb, R10, RASB, Reac, RehabLit, S02, S03, S05, S08, S09, S20, S21, SCOPUS, SSAI, SSAb, SSCI, SSI, SWR&A, T02, W03, W07, W09.
—BLDSC (4965.450000), IE, Infotrieve, Ingenta, INIST. **CCC.**
Published by: American Psychological Association, 750 First St, NE, Washington, DC 20002. TEL 202-336-5500, 800-374-2721, FAX 202-336-5997, journals@apa.org. Ed. Dr. Brent S Mallinckrodt. Adv. contact Doug Constant TEL 202-336-5574. Circ: 4,800.

616.89 USA ISSN 1533-2691
RC488.5 CODEN: JCTHEV
➤ **JOURNAL OF COUPLE & RELATIONSHIP THERAPY.** Text in English. 2001 (Spr.). q. GBP 427 combined subscription in United Kingdom to institutions (print & online eds.); EUR 554, USD 562 combined subscription to institutions (print & online eds.) (effective 2012). adv. bk.rev. reprint service avail. from PSC. **Document type:** *Journal, Academic/Scholarly.* **Description:** Deals with the study of human bonding and intimacy for couples, therapists, marriage, family and clinical practitioners.
Formerly (until 2002): Journal of Couples Therapy (0897-4446)
Related titles: Microfiche ed.: (from PQC); Microform ed.; Online - full text ed.: ISSN 1533-2683. GBP 385 in United Kingdom to institutions; EUR 499, USD 505 to institutions (effective 2012).
Indexed: A01, A03, A22, C06, C07, C08, CA, CINAHL, CWI, DIP, E-psyche, E01, F09, FamI, IBR, IBZ, M02, P30, P48, P53, P54, PQC, S02, S03, S21, SCOPUS, SFSA, SOPODA, SSA, SWR&A, SociolAb, T02, V&AA.
—BLDSC (4965.454000), GNLM, IE, Ingenta. **CCC.**
Published by: Routledge (Subsidiary of: Taylor & Francis Group), 325 Chestnut St, Ste 800, Philadelphia, PA 19106. TEL 215-625-8900, FAX 215-625-8914, journals@routledge.com, http://www.routledge.com. Ed. Jeffry H Larson. adv.: B&W page USD 315, color page USD 550; trim 4.375 x 7.125. Circ: 161 (paid).

➤ **THE JOURNAL OF CREATIVE BEHAVIOR.** *see* EDUCATION

616.89 USA ISSN 1540-1383
BF636.5
JOURNAL OF CREATIVITY IN MENTAL HEALTH. Text in English. 2005 (Mar.). q. GBP 262 combined subscription in United Kingdom to institutions (print & online eds.); EUR 341, USD 339 combined subscription to institutions (print & online eds.) (effective 2012). reprint service avail. from PSC. **Document type:** *Journal, Academic/Scholarly.* **Description:** Explores how therapeutic approaches can be used to examine and improve on the full range of counseling and therapeutic topics, including loss and grief, blocks to intimacy, the uses and misuses of power and privilege, sexuality, spirituality, addictions, family and gender issues.
Formed by the merger of (1984-2004): The Psychotherapy Patient (0738-6176); (1993-2004): Journal of Psychotherapy in Independent Practice (1522-9580); (2001-2004): Journal of Clinical Activities, Assignments & Handouts in Psychotherapy Practice (1532-3285)
Related titles: Online - full text ed.: ISSN 1540-1391. GBP 236 in United Kingdom to institutions; EUR 307, USD 305 to institutions (effective 2012).
Indexed: A01, A22, C06, C07, CA, E-psyche, E01, E03, ERI, FamI, IBR, IBZ, M02, RefZh, S02, S03, SCOPUS, SSA, SociolAb, T02.
—BLDSC (4965.504000), IE. **CCC.**
Published by: (Association for Creativity in Counseling), Routledge (Subsidiary of: Taylor & Francis Group), 325 Chestnut St, Ste 800, Philadelphia, PA 19106. TEL 215-625-8900, 800-354-1420, FAX 215-625-8914, journals@routledge.com, http://www.routledge.com. Ed. Thelma Duffey.

155 USA ISSN 1088-0755
HV8073
JOURNAL OF CREDIBILITY ASSESSMENT AND WITNESS PSYCHOLOGY. Text in English. 1997. bi-m.?. free (effective 2011). back issues avail. **Document type:** *Journal, Academic/Scholarly.* **Description:** Features original empirical, review, and theoretical work in all areas of the scientific study of credibility assessment and witness psychology.
Media: Online - full text.
Indexed: A39, C27, C29, D03, D04, E-psyche, E13, R14, S14, S15, S18.
Published by: Boise State University, Department of Psychology, 1910 University Drive, Boise, ID 83725. TEL 208-426-1207, FAX 208-426-4386, pjohnso@boisestate.edu, http://sspa.boisestate.edu/psychology. Ed. Charles R Honts.

▼ **JOURNAL OF CRIMINAL PSYCHOLOGY.** *see* CRIMINOLOGY AND LAW ENFORCEMENT

JOURNAL OF CRITICAL PSYCHOLOGY, COUNSELLING, AND PSYCHOTHERAPY. *see* SOCIAL SERVICES AND WELFARE

155.8 USA ISSN 0022-0221
BF728 CODEN: JCPGB5
➤ **JOURNAL OF CROSS-CULTURAL PSYCHOLOGY.** Text in English. 1970. bi-m. USD 1,081, GBP 636 combined subscription to institutions (print & online eds.); USD 1,059, GBP 623 to institutions (effective 2011). adv. bk.rev. charts; illus. cum.index. back issues avail.; reprint service avail. from PSC. **Document type:** *Journal, Academic/Scholarly.* **Description:** Presents behavioral and social research concentrating on psychological phenomena as differentially conditioned by culture, focusing on individual members of cultural groups.
Related titles: Microfilm ed.: (from PQC); Online - full text ed.: ISSN 1552-5422. USD 973, GBP 572 to institutions (effective 2011).
Indexed: A20, A22, A26, ABS&EES, AC&P, AMHA, ASCA, ASSIA, AbAn, B04, BAS, BNNA, BRD, C06, C07, C08, CA, CDA, CINAHL, ChPerI, Chicano, CommAb, CurCont, DIP, E-psyche, E01, E06, E07, E08, F09, FamI, G08, H12, HRA, I05, IBR, IBSS, IBZ, IPsyAb, L&LBA, MEA&I, MLA-IB, P02, P03, P10, P12, P13, P18, P24, P25, P27, P30, P48, P53, P54, PQC, PRA, PsycInfo, PsycholAb, PsycholRG, S02, S03, S09, SCOPUS, SFSA, SOPODA, SSA, SSAI, SSAb, SSCI, SSI, SociolAb, T02, W03, W07.
—BLDSC (4965.670000), IE, Infotrieve, Ingenta, INIST. **CCC.**
Published by: (International Association for Cross-Cultural Psychology), Sage Publications, Inc., 2455 Teller Rd, Thousand Oaks, CA 91320. TEL 805-499-9774, 800-818-7243, FAX 805-499-0871, 800-583-2665, info@sagepub.com. Ed. David R Matsumoto. Circ: 1,500 (paid). **Subscr. overseas to:** Sage Publications Ltd., 1 Oliver's Yard, 55 City Rd, London EC1Y 1SP, United Kingdom. TEL 44-207-3248701, FAX 44-207-3248733, subscription@sagepub.co.uk. **Co-sponsor:** Western Washington University, Center for Cross-Cultural Research.

➤ **JOURNAL OF DEVELOPMENTAL AND BEHAVIORAL PEDIATRICS.** *see* MEDICAL SCIENCES—Pediatrics

616.89 371.92 USA ISSN 1944-4133
BF712
THE JOURNAL OF DEVELOPMENTAL PROCESSES. Abbreviated title: J D P. Text in English. 1997. s-a. back issues avail. **Document type:** *Journal, Academic/Scholarly.* **Description:** Aims to improve the identification, prevention and treatment of disorders that interfere with adaptive developmental and learning processes.
Formerly (until 2006): The Journal of Developmental and Learning Disorders (1529-4137)
Related titles: Online - full text ed.: ISSN 1944-4141.
Indexed: E-psyche.
Published by: (Council of Human Development CAN, Milton and Ethel Harris Research Initiative CAN), Interdisciplinary Council on Developmental & Learning Disorders, 4938 Hampden Ln, Ste 800, Bethesda, MD 20814. TEL 301-656-2667, info@icdl.com.

▼ **JOURNAL OF DISASTER SOCIOLOGY AND PSYCHOLOGY.** *see* SOCIOLOGY

THE JOURNAL OF EARLY ADOLESCENCE. *see* CHILDREN AND YOUTH—About

155.5 USA ISSN 1554-6144
BF721
➤ **JOURNAL OF EARLY CHILDHOOD AND INFANT PSYCHOLOGY.** Text in English. 2005. a. USD 45 membership (effective 2009). **Document type:** *Journal, Academic/Scholarly.*
Indexed: A01, A26, E08, I05, P03, P30, PsycInfo, T02.
—BLDSC (4970.701200), IE.
Published by: (Association of Early Childhood and Infant Psychologists), Pace University Press, 41 Park Row, Rm 1510, New York, NY 10038. TEL 212-346-1405, FAX 212-346-1754, http://www.pace.edu/pace/about-us/pace-publisher. Ed. Dr. Barbara Mowder.

➤ **JOURNAL OF ECONOMIC PSYCHOLOGY.** *see* BUSINESS AND ECONOMICS—Marketing And Purchasing

➤ **JOURNAL OF EDUCATION AND PSYCHOLOGY.** *see* EDUCATION

➤ **JOURNAL OF EDUCATIONAL AND PSYCHOLOGICAL CONSULTATION.** *see* EDUCATION

▼ ➤ **JOURNAL OF EDUCATIONAL, CULTURAL AND PSYCHOLOGICAL STUDIES.** *see* HUMANITIES: COMPREHENSIVE WORKS

➤ **JOURNAL OF EDUCATIONAL PSYCHOLOGY.** *see* EDUCATION

➤ **JOURNAL OF EMPIRICAL RESEARCH ON HUMAN RESEARCH ETHICS.** *see* SOCIOLOGY

371.42 USA ISSN 0022-0787
HF5382.5.U5 CODEN: JECODE
➤ **JOURNAL OF EMPLOYMENT COUNSELING.** Abbreviated title: J E C. Text in English. 1965. q. GBP 106 in United Kingdom to institutions; EUR 122 in Europe to institutions; USD 150 elsewhere to institutions; GBP 122 combined subscription in United Kingdom to institutions (print & online eds.); EUR 141 combined subscription in Europe to institutions (print & online eds.); USD 173 combined subscription elsewhere to institutions (print & online eds.) (effective 2012). adv. bk.rev. abstr.; bibl.; illus. index. 64 p./no.; back issues avail.; reprint service avail. from PSC. **Document type:** *Journal, Academic/Scholarly.* **Description:** Focuses on trends in organizational behavior and state-of-the-art personnel practices.
Related titles: Microform ed.: (from PQC); Online - full text ed.: ISSN 2161-1920. GBP 106 in United Kingdom to institutions; EUR 122 in Europe to institutions; USD 150 elsewhere to institutions (effective 2012).
Indexed: A01, A02, A03, A08, A09, A10, A12, A20, A22, A26, ABIn, ASCA, ASSIA, B01, B06, B07, B08, B09, BPIA, BRD, C12, CA, CurCont, E-psyche, E02, E03, E06, E07, E08, E15, E16, ERA, ERI, ERIC, EdA, EdI, FamI, G08, H01, HEA, HRA, I05, I07, ILD, M01, M02, M12, P03, P04, P07, P10, P12, P18, P25, P43, P48, P51, P53, P54, PQC, PsycInfo, PsycholAb, S02, S03, S09, S19, S20, S21, S23, SCOPUS, SSCI, SWR&A, T02, V03, V04, V05, W03, W05, W07.
—BLDSC (4977.700000), IE, Ingenta. **CCC.**
Published by: (National Employment Counseling Association), American Counseling Association, 5999 Stevenson Ave, Alexandria, VA 22304. TEL 800-347-6647, FAX 703-823-0252, 800-473-2329. Ed. Roberta A Neault TEL 604-856-2386. Circ: 900.

150 GBR ISSN 0272-4944
BF353 CODEN: JEPSEO
➤ **JOURNAL OF ENVIRONMENTAL PSYCHOLOGY.** Text in English. 1981. q. EUR 489 in Europe to institutions; JPY 53,000 in Japan to institutions; USD 434 elsewhere to institutions (effective 2012). adv. bk.rev. illus. back issues avail.; reprint service avail. from PSC. **Document type:** *Journal, Academic/Scholarly.* **Description:** Publishes international research contributions in a broad range of disciplines relating to the study of the transactions and interrelationships between people and their sociophysical surroundings (including man-made and natural environments), as well as relevant applications to the social and biological sciences and the environmental professions.
Related titles: Online - full text ed.: ISSN 1522-9610. USD 374 to institutions (effective 2009) (from IngentaConnect, ScienceDirect).
Indexed: A20, A22, A26, A28, APA, ASCA, ASSIA, BrCerAb, C&ISA, CA, CA/WCA, CIA, CerAb, CivEngAb, CorrAb, CurCont, DIP, E&CAJ, E-psyche, E01, E04, E05, E11, EEA, EMA, ESPM, EnvEAb, ErgAb, FR, FamI, H15, HPNRM, I05, IBR, IBZ, IPsyAb, M&TEA, M09, MBF, METADEX, P03, P30, PollutAb, PsycInfo, PsycholAb, RASB, S02, S03, SCOPUS, SSCI, SSciA, SUSA, SolStAb, T02, T04, W07, W08, WAA.
—BLDSC (4979.389000), IE, Infotrieve, Ingenta, INIST. **CCC.**
Published by: Academic Press (Subsidiary of: Elsevier Science & Technology), 32 Jamestown Rd, Camden, London, NW1 7BY, United Kingdom. TEL 44-20-74244200, FAX 44-20-74832293, corporatesales@elsevier.com.

➤ **JOURNAL OF EVIDENCE-BASED PRACTICES FOR SCHOOLS.** *see* EDUCATION

302 HUN ISSN 1789-2082
JOURNAL OF EVOLUTIONARY PSYCHOLOGY. Text in English. 2002. q. EUR 236, USD 324 combined subscription (print & online eds.) (effective 2012). 95 p./no.; **Document type:** *Journal, Academic/Scholarly.* **Description:** Publishes theoretical and empirical studies from the intersection of two rapidly developing research fields, i.e., cultural psychology and evolutionary psychology. These studies are aimed at investigating generation and transmission of cultural meaning from an evolutionary perspective, or analyzing the role of culture in performing evolutionary tasks.
Formerly (until 2007): Journal of Cultural and Evolutionary Psychology (1589-5254)
Related titles: Online - full text ed.: ISSN 1589-7397. EUR 204, USD 276 (effective 2012).
Indexed: IBR, IBZ, MLA-IB, P03, PsycInfo, PsycholAb, SCOPUS.
—BLDSC (4979.643500), IE, Ingenta. **CCC.**
Published by: Akademiai Kiado Rt. (Subsidiary of: Wolters Kluwer N.V.), Prielle Kornelia u 19/D, Budapest, 1117, Hungary. TEL 36-1-4648222, FAX 36-1-4648221, journals@akkrt.hu. Ed. Tom Dickins.

158 CAN ISSN 1496-9955
JOURNAL OF EXCELLENCE. Text in English. 1998. s-a. CAD 44.95 domestic to individuals; USD 34.95 foreign to individuals; CAD 149.99 domestic to institutions; USD 99.99 foreign to institutions (effective 2001). abstr.; bibl.; charts; stat. back issues avail. **Document type:** *Journal, Consumer.* **Description:** Devoted to nurturing excellence in all human endeavors including sport, performing arts, education, the work place, health and quality living. The goal is education for better people, better performers and a better world.
Related titles: Online - full content ed.
Published by: (International Society for Mental Training and Excellence), Zone of Excellence, PO Box 1807, Chelsea, PQ J9B 1A1, Canada. TEL 819-827-2652, FAX 819-827-2652, excel@zxcel.com. Ed. Louise Zitzelsberger. Pub. Terry Orlick. Circ: 382 (paid); 50 (free).

155.4 152 USA ISSN 0022-0965
BF721 CODEN: JECPAE
➤ **JOURNAL OF EXPERIMENTAL CHILD PSYCHOLOGY.** Text in English. 1964. 12/yr. EUR 1,974 in Europe to institutions; JPY 205,900 in Japan to institutions; USD 1,715 elsewhere to institutions (effective 2012). adv. charts; illus. index. back issues avail.; reprints avail. **Document type:** *Journal, Academic/Scholarly.* **Description:** Covers all aspects child development including psychological research on cognitive, social, and physical development.
Related titles: Online - full text ed.: ISSN 1096-0457 (from IngentaConnect, ScienceDirect).
Indexed: A01, A02, A03, A08, A20, A22, A26, AMHA, ASCA, B25, BDM&CN, BIOSIS Prev, BRD, C28, CA, CDA, CIS, CommAb, CurCont, DIP, E-psyche, E01, E02, E03, E06, E08, EMBASE, ERA, ERI, ERIC, EdA, EdI, ExcerpMed, F09, FR, FamI, G08, H09, H11, H12, I05, IBR, IBZ, IndMed, M12, MEA&I, MEDLINE, MLA-IB, MycolAb, P02, P03, P10, P12, P27, P30, P48, P53, P54, PQC, PsycInfo, PsycholAb, R10, RASB, Reac, S02, S03, S05, S09, S20, S21, SCOPUS, SSAI, SSAb, SSCI, SSI, T02, W01, W02, W03, W07.
—BLDSC (4981.300000), GNLM, IE, Infotrieve, Ingenta, INIST. **CCC.**
Published by: Academic Press (Subsidiary of: Elsevier Science & Technology), 3251 Riverport Ln, Maryland Heights, MO 63043. TEL 314-447-8010, FAX 314-447-8030, JournalCustomerService-usa@elsevier.com, http://www.elsevierdirect.com/imprint.jsp?iid=5. Eds. B P Ackerman, D F Bjorklund.

152 USA ISSN 0097-7403
QL750 CODEN: JPAPDG
➤ **JOURNAL OF EXPERIMENTAL PSYCHOLOGY: ANIMAL BEHAVIOR PROCESSES.** Text in English. 1916. q. USD 107 domestic to individuals; USD 134 foreign to individuals; USD 388 domestic to institutions; USD 433 foreign to institutions (effective 2011). adv. illus. Index. back issues avail.; reprint service avail. from PSC. **Document type:** *Journal, Academic/Scholarly.* **Description:** Covers experimental studies on the basic mechanisms of perception, learning, motivation and performance, especially in nonhuman animals.
Supersedes in part (in 1975): Journal of Experimental Psychology (0022-1015)
Related titles: Microform ed.: (from PQC); Online - full text ed.: ISSN 1939-2184 (from ScienceDirect).
Indexed: A01, A02, A03, A08, A22, A25, A26, A34, A38, ASCA, ASFA, AnBeAb, B21, B25, BIOSIS Prev, BRD, CA, CABA, CDA, ChemoAb, CurCont, DIP, E-psyche, E08, EMBASE, ExcerpMed, FR, G01, G08, GH, H09, I05, IBR, IBZ, ISR, IndMed, IndVet, Inpharma, MEDLINE, MycolAb, N02, N03, N04, NSA, NSCI, P02, P03, P10, P12, P27, P30, P37, P48, P53, P54, PQC, PsycInfo, PsycholAb, RASB, S01, S02, S03, S05, S08, S09, SCI, SCOPUS, SSAI, SSAb, SSCI, SSI, T02, VS, W03, W07, W08, W11, WildRev, Z01.
—BLDSC (4982.501000), IE, Infotrieve, Ingenta, INIST, Linda Hall. **CCC.**
Published by: American Psychological Association, 750 First St, NE, Washington, DC 20002. TEL 202-336-5500, 800-374-2721, FAX 202-336-5997, journals@apa.org. Ed. Anthony Dickinson. Adv. contact Doug Constant TEL 202-336-5574. Circ: 600.

152 USA ISSN 1076-898X
BF180 CODEN: JEPAAY
➤ **JOURNAL OF EXPERIMENTAL PSYCHOLOGY: APPLIED.** Abbreviated title: J E P. Text in English. 1995. q. USD 107 domestic to individuals; USD 134 foreign to individuals; USD 388 domestic to institutions; USD 433 foreign to institutions (effective 2011). adv. back issues avail.; reprint service avail. from PSC. **Document type:** *Journal, Academic/Scholarly.* **Description:** Features empirical investigations in experimental psychology that bridge practically oriented problems and psychological theory.
Related titles: Online - full text ed.: ISSN 1939-2192 (from ScienceDirect).
Indexed: A20, A22, A26, ASCA, ASSIA, B01, B06, B07, B09, BRD, CA, CurCont, DIP, E-psyche, E07, EMBASE, ERIC, ErgAb, ExcerpMed, FamI, IBR, IBZ, IndMed, MEDLINE, P03, P30, PsycInfo, PsycholAb, R10, Reac, S02, S03, SCOPUS, SSAI, SSAb, SSCI, SSI, T02, W03, W07.
—BLDSC (4982.501100), IE, Infotrieve, Ingenta. **CCC.**
Published by: American Psychological Association, 750 First St, NE, Washington, DC 20002. TEL 202-336-5500, 800-374-2721, FAX 202-336-5997, journals@apa.org. Ed. Wendy A Rogers. Adv. contact Doug Constant TEL 202-336-5574. Circ: 900.

152 USA ISSN 0096-3445
BF180 CODEN: JPGEDD
➤ **JOURNAL OF EXPERIMENTAL PSYCHOLOGY: GENERAL.** Text in English. 1916. q. USD 107 domestic to individuals; USD 134 foreign to individuals; USD 388 domestic to institutions; USD 433 foreign to institutions (effective 2011). adv. charts; illus.; stat. index. back issues avail.; reprint service avail. from PSC. **Document type:** *Journal, Academic/Scholarly.* **Description:** Presents reports of interest to all experimental psychologists.
Supersedes in part (in 1975): Journal of Experimental Psychology (0022-1015)
Related titles: Microform ed.: (from PQC); Online - full text ed.: ISSN 1939-2222 (from ScienceDirect).
Indexed: A01, A02, A03, A08, A20, A22, A25, A26, ASCA, B21, B25, BIOSIS Prev, BRD, CA, CDA, CIS, CurCont, DIP, E-psyche, E08, EMBASE, ERIC, ErgAb, ExcerpMed, FR, FamI, G08, H09, H11, H12, I05, IBR, IBZ, IndMed, MEA&I, MEDLINE, MLA-IB, MycolAb, NSA, P02, P03, P10, P12, P27, P30, P48, P53, P54, PCI, PQC, PsycInfo, PsycholAb, R10, RASB, Reac, S02, S03, S05, S08, S09, SCOPUS, SSAI, SSAb, SSCI, SSI, T02, W03, W07, YAE&RB.
—BLDSC (4982.503000), GNLM, IE, Infotrieve, Ingenta, INIST, Linda Hall. **CCC.**
Published by: American Psychological Association, 750 First St, NE, Washington, DC 20002. TEL 202-336-5500, 800-374-2721, FAX 202-336-5997, journals@apa.org. Ed. Dr. Fernanda Ferreira. Adv. contact Doug Constant TEL 202-336-5574. Circ: 1,200.

152.05 USA ISSN 0096-1523
BF311 CODEN: JPHPDH
➤ **JOURNAL OF EXPERIMENTAL PSYCHOLOGY: HUMAN PERCEPTION AND PERFORMANCE.** Text in English. 1916. bi-m. USD 392 domestic to individuals; USD 424 foreign to individuals; USD 1,148 domestic to institutions; USD 1,205 foreign to institutions (effective 2011). adv. back issues avail.; reprint service avail. from PSC. **Document type:** *Journal, Academic/Scholarly.* **Description:** Covers studies on perception, control of action, perceptual aspects of language processing, and related cognitive processes.
Supersedes in part (in 1975): Journal of Experimental Psychology (0022-1015)
Related titles: Microform ed.: (from PQC); Online - full text ed.: ISSN 1939-1277 (from ScienceDirect).
Indexed: A01, A02, A03, A08, A20, A22, A25, A26, AMED, ASCA, ASSIA, B01, B06, B07, B09, B21, B25, BIOSIS Prev, BRD, CA, CDA, CMCI, CommAb, CurCont, DIP, DentInd, E-psyche, E07, E08, EMBASE, ERIC, ErgAb, ExcerpMed, FR, G08, H09, H11, H12, I05, IBR, IBZ, IndMed, L&LBA, MEDLINE, MLA-IB, MycolAb, NSA, NSCI, P02, P03, P10, P12, P27, P30, P48, P53, P54, PQC, PsycInfo, PsycholAb, R10, RASB, RILM, Reac, S02, S03, S05, S08, S09, SCI, SCOPUS, SOPODA, SSAI, SSAb, SSCI, SSI, T02, W03, W07.
—BLDSC (4982.507000), GNLM, IE, Infotrieve, Ingenta, INIST, Linda Hall. **CCC.**
Published by: American Psychological Association, 750 First St, NE, Washington, DC 20002. TEL 202-336-5500, 800-374-2721, FAX 202-336-5997, journals@apa.org. Ed. Dr. Glyn W Humphreys. Adv. contact Doug Constant TEL 202-336-5574. Circ: 900.

152 USA ISSN 0278-7393
LB1051.J647
➤ **JOURNAL OF EXPERIMENTAL PSYCHOLOGY: LEARNING, MEMORY, AND COGNITION.** Text in English. 1916. bi-m. USD 392 domestic to individuals; USD 424 foreign to individuals; USD 1,148 domestic to institutions; USD 1,205 foreign to institutions (effective 2011). adv. back issues avail.; reprint service avail. from PSC. **Document type:** *Journal, Academic/Scholarly.* **Description:** Covers experimental studies on fundamental encoding, transfer, memory, and cognitive processes in human behavior.
Formerly (until Jan.1982): Journal of Experimental Psychology: Human Learning and Memory (0096-1515); Which supersedes in part (in 1975): Journal of Experimental Psychology (0022-1015)
Related titles: Microform ed.: (from PQC); Online - full text ed.: ISSN 1939-1285 (from ScienceDirect).
Indexed: A01, A02, A03, A08, A20, A22, A25, A26, ASCA, B01, B04, B06, B07, B09, B21, B25, BIOSIS Prev, BRD, CA, CDA, CMM, CommAb, CurCont, DIP, E-psyche, E02, E03, E07, E08, EMBASE, ERI, ERIC, EdA, EdI, ErgAb, ExcerpMed, FR, G08, H09, H11, H12, I05, IBR, IBZ, IndMed, L&LBA, MEDLINE, MLA-IB, MycolAb, NSA, NSCI, P02, P03, P10, P12, P27, P30, P48, P53, P54, PQC, PsycInfo, PsycholAb, R10, RILM, Reac, S02, S03, S05, S08, S09, SCI, SCOPUS, SOPODA, SSAI, SSAb, SSCI, SSI, T02, W03, W07.
—BLDSC (4982.509000), GNLM, IE, Infotrieve, Ingenta, INIST, Linda Hall. **CCC.**
Published by: American Psychological Association, 750 First St, NE, Washington, DC 20002. TEL 202-336-5500, 800-374-2721, FAX 202-336-5997, journals@apa.org. Ed. Randi C Martin. Adv. contact Doug Constant TEL 202-336-5574. Circ: 1,100.

302 USA ISSN 0022-1031
HM251 CODEN: JESPAQ
➤ **JOURNAL OF EXPERIMENTAL SOCIAL PSYCHOLOGY.** Text in English. 1965. bi-m. EUR 1,289 in Europe to institutions; JPY 134,400 in Japan to institutions; USD 1,073 elsewhere to institutions (effective 2012). adv. illus. back issues avail.; reprints avail. **Document type:** *Journal, Academic/Scholarly.* **Description:** Covers original research and theory on human social behavior and related phenomena.
Related titles: Online - full text ed.: ISSN 1096-0465 (from IngentaConnect, ScienceDirect).
Indexed: A01, A02, A03, A08, A20, A21, A22, A26, AC&P, ASCA, B02, B04, B17, B18, BRD, CA, CMM, CommAb, CurCont, DIP, E-psyche, E01, E08, FR, FamI, G04, G08, H09, I05, IBR, IBSS, IBZ, MEA&I, P02, P03, P10, P12, P27, P30, P34, P48, P53, P54, PCI, PQC, PRA, PsycInfo, PsycholAb, RASB, RI-1, RI-2, S02, S03, S05, S09, SCOPUS, SSAI, SSAb, SSCI, SSI, T02, W03, W07, W09.
—BLDSC (4982.700000), IE, Infotrieve, Ingenta, INIST. **CCC.**
Published by: Academic Press (Subsidiary of: Elsevier Science & Technology), 3251 Riverport Ln, Maryland Heights, MO 63043. TEL 314-447-8010, FAX 314-447-8030, JournalCustomerService-usa@elsevier.com, http://www.elsevierdirect.com/imprint.jsp?iid=5. Ed. J Cooper.

150 USA ISSN 1058-0476
HQ1 CODEN: JFEIEE
➤ **JOURNAL OF FAMILY AND ECONOMIC ISSUES.** Abbreviated title: J F E I. Text in English. 1978. q. EUR 901, USD 943 combined subscription to institutions (print & online eds.) (effective 2012). adv. bk.rev.; film rev. bibl.; charts; stat.; illus. index. back issues avail.; reprint service avail. from PSC. **Document type:** *Journal, Academic/Scholarly.* **Description:** Features articles that cover family consumer behavior, household division of labor and productivity, the relationship between economic and non economic decisions, and interrelationships between work and family life.
Former titles (until 1991): Lifestyles (0882-3391); (until 1984): Alternative Lifestyles (0161-570X)
Related titles: Online - full text ed.: ISSN 1573-3475 (from IngentaConnect).
Indexed: A12, A13, A22, A26, ABIn, Agr, BibLing, CA, CJPI, CMHR, E-psyche, E01, ECER, ESPM, EconLit, F09, FR, FamI, I05, IBSS, JEL, MEA&I, P03, P10, P12, P25, P27, P30, P48, P51, P53, P54, PAIS, PCI, PQC, PsycInfo, PsycholAb, RASB, RiskAb, S02, S03, SCOPUS, SFSA, SOPODA, SSA, SWR&A, SociolAb, T02, W09.
—BLDSC (4983.645000), IE, Infotrieve, Ingenta, INIST. **CCC.**
Published by: Springer New York LLC (Subsidiary of: Springer Science+Business Media), 233 Spring St, New York, NY 10013. TEL 212-460-1500, FAX 212-460-1575, service-ny@springer.com. Ed. Jing Xiao.

P

▼ *new title* ➤ *refereed* ♦ *full entry avail.*

155 USA ISSN 0893-3200

➤ **JOURNAL OF FAMILY PSYCHOLOGY.** Abbreviated title: J F P. Text in English. 1987. bi-m. USD 167 domestic to individuals; USD 199 foreign to individuals; USD 508 domestic to institutions; USD 565 foreign to institutions (effective 2011). adv. illus. Index. back issues avail.; reprint service avail. from PSC. **Document type:** *Journal, Academic/Scholarly.* **Description:** Delivers a variety of perspectives on the study of family systems, emphasizing empirical research on a wide range of family-related topics.

Related titles: Online - full text ed.: ISSN 1939-1293 (from ScienceDirect).

Indexed: A01, A02, A03, A08, A20, A22, A26, ASCA, ASSIA, AddicA, BRD, C06, C07, C28, CA, CMM, CurCont, E-psyche, E02, E03, E07, E08, EMBASE, ERI, EdA, EdI, ExcerpMed, F09, FR, FamI, G08, G10, I05, IndMed, MEDLINE, P02, P03, P10, P12, P27, P30, P48, P53, P54, PQC, PsycInfo, PsycholAb, R10, RASB, Reac, S02, S03, S09, S21, SCOPUS, SFSA, SOPODA, SSA, SSAI, SSAb, SSCI, SSI, SWR&A, SociolAb, T02, V&AA, W01, W02, W03, W07, W09.

—BLDSC (4983.733000), IE, Infotrieve, Ingenta, INIST. **CCC.**

Published by: American Psychological Association, 750 First St, NE, Washington, DC 20002. TEL 202-336-5500, 800-374-2721, FAX 202-336-5997, journals@apa.org. Ed. Nadine J Kaslow. Adv. contact Doug Constant TEL 202-336-5574. Circ: 2,300.

616.89 USA ISSN 0897-5353
RC488.5 CODEN: JFAPEF

➤ **JOURNAL OF FAMILY PSYCHOTHERAPY**; the official journal of the International Family Therapy Association. Abbreviated title: J F P. Text in English. 1985. q. GBP 550 combined subscription in United Kingdom to institutions (print & online eds.); EUR 717, USD 721 combined subscription to institutions (print & online eds.) (effective 2012). adv. bk.rev. 120 p./no. 1 cols./p.; back issues avail.; reprint service avail. from PSC. **Document type:** *Journal, Academic/Scholarly.* **Description:** Provides an exchange for clinicians across the disciplines to share solutions to difficult family problems. Offers detailed clinical case studies, descriptions of successful treatment programs, innovative strategies in clinical practice.

Formerly (until 1988): Journal of Psychotherapy and the Family (0742-9703)

Related titles: Microfiche ed.: (from PQC); Microform ed.; Online - full text ed.: ISSN 1540-4080. GBP 495 in United Kingdom to institutions; EUR 645, USD 649 to institutions (effective 2012).

Indexed: A01, A03, A22, BiolDig, C06, C07, CA, DNP, E-psyche, E01, E03, EMBASE, ERI, ExcerpMed, F09, FR, FamI, IPARL, IndMed, M02, P03, P30, PC&CA, PsycInfo, PsycholAb, R10, RASB, Reac, RefZh, S02, S03, SCOPUS, SFSA, SOPODA, SSA, SWR&A, SociolAb, T02, V&AA.

—BLDSC (4983.735000), GNLM, IE, Infotrieve, Ingenta, INIST. **CCC.**

Published by: (International Family Therapy Association), Routledge (Subsidiary of: Taylor & Francis Group), 325 Chestnut St, Ste 800, Philadelphia, PA 19106. TEL 215-625-8900, 800-354-1420, FAX 215-625-8914, journals@routledge.com, http://www.routledge.com. Ed. Terry S Trepper. adv.: B&W page USD 315, color page USD 550; trim 4.375 x 7.125. Circ: 272 (paid).

➤ **JOURNAL OF FAMILY STUDIES.** *see* MATRIMONY

➤ **JOURNAL OF FAMILY THERAPY.** *see* MEDICAL SCIENCES—Psychiatry And Neurology

➤ **JOURNAL OF FAMILY VIOLENCE.** *see* CRIMINOLOGY AND LAW ENFORCEMENT

➤ **JOURNAL OF FEMINIST FAMILY THERAPY**; an international forum. *see* WOMEN'S STUDIES

302 USA ISSN 0094-730X
RC423.A1 CODEN: JFDID8

➤ **JOURNAL OF FLUENCY DISORDERS.** Abbreviated title: J F D. Text in English. 1974. q. EUR 748 in Europe to institutions; JPY 99,000 in Japan to institutions; USD 831 elsewhere to institutions (effective 2012). adv. bk.rev. back issues avail.; reprints avail. **Document type:** *Journal, Academic/Scholarly.* **Description:** Provides coverage of clinical, experimental, and theoretical aspects of stuttering, including the remediation techniques.

Related titles: Microform ed.: (from PQC); Online - full text ed.: ISSN 1873-801X (from IngentaConnect, ScienceDirect).

Indexed: A01, A03, A08, A20, A22, A26, AMED, ASCA, B25, BIOSIS Prev, C06, C07, C08, CA, CINAHL, CMM, CommAb, CurCont, DSHAb, E-psyche, EMBASE, ERA, ERIC, ExcerpMed, FR, FamI, I05, L&LBA, L11, M12, MEDLINE, MLA-IB, MycolAb, P03, P30, PsycInfo, PsycholAb, R10, RILM, Reac, RehabLit, S20, SCOPUS, SOPODA, SSCI, T02, W07.

—BLDSC (4984.450000), GNLM, IE, Infotrieve, Ingenta, INIST. **CCC.**

Published by: (International Fluency Association), Elsevier Inc. (Subsidiary of: Elsevier Science & Technology), 1600 John F Kennedy Blvd, Philadelphia, PA 19103. TEL 215-239-3900, FAX 215-238-7883, JournalCustomerService-usa@elsevier.com. Ed. A Craig. Adv. contact Janine Castle TEL 44-1865-843844.

150 345 USA ISSN 1522-8932
RA1148 CODEN: JFPPAI

➤ **JOURNAL OF FORENSIC PSYCHOLOGY PRACTICE.** Abbreviated title: J F P P. Text in English. 2001 (Spr.). q. GBP 379 combined subscription in United Kingdom to institutions (print & online eds.); EUR 492, USD 501 combined subscription to institutions (print & online eds.) (effective 2012). adv. bk.rev. 120 p./no. 1 cols./p.; reprint service avail. from PSC. **Document type:** *Journal, Academic/Scholarly.* **Description:** Presents new programs and techniques, analyzes existing policies and programs in their social context, and evaluates specific institutions and forensic procedures.

Related titles: Online - full text ed.: ISSN 1522-9092. 2002. GBP 341 in United Kingdom to institutions; EUR 443, USD 451 to institutions (effective 2012).

Indexed: A01, A03, A20, A22, CA, CJA, CJPI, CurCont, DIP, E-psyche, E01, EMBASE, ExcerpMed, FR, FamI, IBR, IBZ, M02, P03, P25, P48, PQC, PRA, PsycInfo, PsycholAb, R10, Reac, RefZh, S02, S03, SCOPUS, SSCI, SWR&A, T02, V&AA, W07.

—BLDSC (4984.599100), IE, Ingenta, INIST. **CCC.**

Published by: Routledge (Subsidiary of: Taylor & Francis Group), 325 Chestnut St, Ste 800, Philadelphia, PA 19106. TEL 215-625-8900, 800-354-1420, FAX 215-625-8914, journals@routledge.com, http://www.routledge.com. Ed. Bruce A Arrigo. adv.: color page USD 550, B&W page USD 315; trim 4.375 x 7.125. Circ: 166 (paid).

616.8583406 USA ISSN 1935-9705
RC558 CODEN: JGLPE9

➤ **JOURNAL OF GAY & LESBIAN MENTAL HEALTH.** Abbreviated title: J G L P. Text in English. 1988. q. GBP 259 combined subscription in United Kingdom to institutions (print & online eds.); EUR 337, USD 344 combined subscription to institutions (print & online eds.) (effective 2012). adv. bk.rev. illus. 120 p./no. 1 cols./p.; back issues avail.; reprint service avail. from PSC. **Document type:** *Journal, Academic/Scholarly.* **Description:** Provides a multidisciplinary professional forum for issues relating to the use of psychotherapy for gay, lesbian and bisexual clients. Goal is to facilitate the quality of life for gays and foster effective therapy for those who require support.

Formerly (until 2008): Journal of Gay & Lesbian Psychotherapy (0891-7140)

Related titles: Microfiche ed.: (from PQC); Microfilm ed.; Microform ed.; Online - full text ed.: ISSN 1935-9713. GBP 233 in United Kingdom to institutions; EUR 304, USD 310 to institutions (effective 2012).

Indexed: A01, A02, A03, A08, A22, A26, ASSIA, AbAn, CA, CWI, E-psyche, E01, E08, F09, FamI, G08, GW, I05, L01, L02, M02, M08, P02, P03, P10, P48, P53, P54, PQC, PsycInfo, PsycholAb, S02, S03, S09, S21, SCOPUS, SOPODA, SWR&A, SociolAb, T02.

—BLDSC (4987.635500), GNLM, IE, Ingenta. **CCC.**

Published by: Routledge (Subsidiary of: Taylor & Francis Group), 325 Chestnut St, Ste 800, Philadelphia, PA 19106. TEL 215-625-8900, 800-354-1420, FAX 215-625-8914, journals@routledge.com, http://www.routledge.com. Eds. Dr. Alan Schwartz, Dr. Mary E Barber. adv.: B&W page USD 315, color page USD 550; trim 4.375 x 7.125. Circ: 314 (paid).

150 USA ISSN 0022-1309
BF1 CODEN: JGPSAY

➤ **THE JOURNAL OF GENERAL PSYCHOLOGY**; experimental, physiological, and comparative psychology. Text in English. 1927. q. GBP 202 combined subscription in United Kingdom to institutions (print & online eds.); EUR 268, USD 335 combined subscription to institutions (print & online eds.) (effective 2012). adv. bibl.; charts. index. 110 p./no. 1 cols./p.; back issues avail.; reprint service avail. from PSC. **Document type:** *Journal, Academic/Scholarly.* **Description:** Covers traditional topics such as physiological and comparative psychology, sensation, perception, learning, and motivation, as well as more diverse topics such as cognition, memory, language, aging, and substance abuse, or mathematical, statistical, methodological, and other theoretical investigations.

Related titles: CD-ROM ed.; Microform ed.; Online - full text ed.: ISSN 1940-0888. GBP 182 in United Kingdom to institutions; EUR 241, USD 302 to institutions (effective 2012).

Indexed: A01, A02, A03, A06, A08, A12, A20, A22, A25, A26, ABIn, AC&P, ASCA, B01, B04, B06, B07, B08, B09, B21, BRD, C06, C07, C12, C28, CA, CDA, CIS, CRFR, ChemAb, Chicano, CurCont, DIP, DentInd, E-psyche, E01, E07, E08, ECER, EMBASE, ERA, ErgAb, ExcerpMed, FR, FamI, G05, G06, G07, G08, H09, H10, H11, H12, I05, I07, IBR, IBZ, IPsyAb, IndMed, L&LBA, L09, M01, M02, MEDLINE, MLA-IB, NSA, P02, P03, P10, P12, P20, P22, P25, P26, P27, P30, P43, P48, P51, P53, P54, PCI, PQC, PhilInd, PsycInfo, PsycholAb, R10, RASB, Reac, RefZh, S02, S03, S05, S08, S09, S21, S23, SCOPUS, SOPODA, SSAI, SSAb, SSCI, SSI, SWR&A, SociolAb, T02, W01, W02, W03, W05, W07, W09.

—BLDSC (4989.200000), GNLM, IE, Infotrieve, Ingenta, INIST. **CCC.**

Published by: Routledge (Subsidiary of: Taylor & Francis Group), 325 Chestnut St, Ste 800, Philadelphia, PA 19106. TEL 215-625-8900, FAX 215-625-2940, journals@routledge.com.

150 USA ISSN 1059-7700
RB155.7 CODEN: JGCOET

➤ **JOURNAL OF GENETIC COUNSELING.** Text in English. 1992. bi-m. EUR 676, USD 692 combined subscription to institutions (print & online eds.) (effective 2012). adv. abstr. back issues avail.; reprint service avail. from PSC. **Document type:** *Journal, Academic/Scholarly.* **Description:** Covers psychosocial issues, educational and counseling techniques, legislation and regulations affecting genetic counseling, and other issues related to providing counseling services.

Related titles: Online - full text ed.: ISSN 1573-3599 (from IngentaConnect).

Indexed: A20, A22, A26, ASSIA, B21, BibLing, C06, C07, C08, CA, CINAHL, CurCont, E-psyche, E01, EMBASE, ESPM, ExcerpMed, F09, FamI, GenetAb, H12, MEDLINE, P03, P20, P22, P24, P25, P30, P48, P54, PQC, PsycInfo, PsycholAb, R10, Reac, RiskAb, S02, S03, SCI, SCOPUS, SFSA, SOPODA, SWR&A, SociolAb, T02, W07.

—BLDSC (4989.700000), GNLM, IE, Infotrieve, Ingenta, INIST. **CCC.**

Published by: (National Society of Genetic Counselors, Inc.), Springer New York LLC (Subsidiary of: Springer Science+Business Media), 233 Spring St, New York, NY 10013. TEL 212-460-1500, FAX 212-460-1575, service-ny@springer.com. Ed. Bonnie S LeRoy.

➤ **THE JOURNAL OF GENETIC PSYCHOLOGY.** *see* BIOLOGY—Genetics

130 USA ISSN 0022-1449

JOURNAL OF GRAPHOANALYSIS. Abbreviated title: I G A S Journal. Text in English. 1929. m. free to members (effective 2011). bk.rev. abstr.; bibl.; charts; illus.; tr.lit. **Document type:** *Journal, Academic/Scholarly.*

Indexed: E-psyche.

Published by: International Graphoanalysis Society, 842 Fifth Ave, New Kensington, PA 15068. TEL 724-472-9701, FAX 509-271-1149, greg@igas.com, http://www.igas.com.

JOURNAL OF GROUPS IN ADDICTION & RECOVERY. *see* DRUG ABUSE AND ALCOHOLISM

158 NLD ISSN 1389-4978
BF575.H27 CODEN: JHSOAA

➤ **JOURNAL OF HAPPINESS STUDIES**; an interdisciplinary forum on subjective well-being. Text in English. 2000 (Mar). bi-m. EUR 950, USD 982 combined subscription to institutions (print & online eds.) (effective 2012). adv. bk.rev. reprint service avail. from PSC. **Document type:** *Journal, Academic/Scholarly.* **Description:** Explores the psychological and sociological conditions leading to individual happiness and overall well-being.

Related titles: Online - full text ed.: ISSN 1573-7780 (from IngentaConnect).

Indexed: A01, A02, A03, A08, A12, A20, A22, A26, ABIn, BibLing, CA, CurCont, E01, EconLit, FamI, I05, JEL, P03, P10, P12, P25, P30, P43, P46, P48, P50, P51, P53, P54, PQC, PsycInfo, PsycholAb, S02, S03, SCOPUS, SSA, SSCI, SociolAb, T02, W07.

—BLDSC (4996.623800), IE, Infotrieve, Ingenta. **CCC.**

Published by: (International Society for Quality of Life Studies), Springer Netherlands (Subsidiary of: Springer Science+Business Media), Van Godewijckstraat 30, Dordrecht, 3311 GX, Netherlands. TEL 31-78-6576050, FAX 31-78-6576474, http://www.springer.com. Ed. Robert A Cummins.

616.8 GBR ISSN 1359-1053
R726.7 CODEN: JHPSFC

➤ **JOURNAL OF HEALTH PSYCHOLOGY**; an interdisciplinary, international journal. Text in English. 1996. 8/yr. USD 1,797, GBP 971 combined subscription to institutions (print & online eds.); USD 1,761, GBP 952 to institutions (effective 2011). adv. bk.rev. back issues avail.; reprint service avail. from PSC. **Document type:** *Journal, Academic/Scholarly.* **Description:** Provides an international forum for the best research in health psychology from around the world.

Related titles: Online - full text ed.: ISSN 1461-7277. USD 1,617, GBP 874 to institutions (effective 2011).

Indexed: A01, A02, A03, A08, A20, A22, ASSIA, B07, B21, C06, C07, C08, CA, CINAHL, CurCont, E-psyche, E01, EMBASE, ExcerpMed, FR, FamI, H04, IBSS, MEDLINE, NSA, P03, P30, P34, PsycInfo, PsycholAb, R10, Reac, S02, S03, SCOPUS, SOPODA, SSCI, SociolAb, T02, V02, W07, W09.

—BLDSC (4996.870100), IE, Infotrieve, Ingenta, INIST. **CCC.**

Published by: Sage Publications Ltd. (Subsidiary of: Sage Publications, Inc.), 1 Oliver's Yard, 55 City Rd, London, EC1Y 1SP, United Kingdom. TEL 44-20-73248500, FAX 44-20-73248600, info@sagepub.co.uk, http://www.uk.sagepub.com/home.nav. Ed. David F Marks. adv.: B&W page GBP 400; 140 x 210. **Subscr. in the Americas to:** Sage Publications, Inc., 2455 Teller Rd, Thousand Oaks, CA 91320. TEL 805-499-9774, FAX 805-499-0871, journals@sagepub.com.

▼ ➤ **JOURNAL OF HUMAN SEXUALITY.** *see* HOMOSEXUALITY

371.42 USA ISSN 2159-0311

➤ **JOURNAL OF HUMANISTIC COUNSELING.** Text in English. 1962. s-a. GBP 71 in United Kingdom to institutions; EUR 82 in Europe to institutions; USD 100 elsewhere to institutions; GBP 82 combined subscription in United Kingdom to institutions (print & online eds.); EUR 95 combined subscription in Europe to institutions (print & online eds.); USD 115 combined subscription elsewhere to institutions (print & online eds.) (effective 2012). adv. abstr.; bibl.; illus. 128 p./no.; back issues avail.; reprint service avail. from PSC. **Document type:** *Journal, Academic/Scholarly.* **Description:** Addresses issues and concerns affecting counselors and educators committed to developing humanistic education practices in schools.

Former titles (until 2011): Journal of Humanistic Counseling, Education and Development (1931-0293); (until 1999): Journal of Humanistic Education and Development (0735-6846); (until 1982): Humanist Educator (0362-9783); (until 1975): Student Personnel Association for Teacher Education. Journal (0036-1836); (until 1973): S P A T E (0563-1254)

Related titles: Microform ed.: (from PQC); Online - full text ed.: ISSN 2161-1939. GBP 71 in United Kingdom to institutions; EUR 82 in Europe to institutions; USD 100 elsewhere to institutions (effective 2012).

Indexed: A01, A02, A03, A08, A22, A26, BRD, C28, CA, CPE, E-psyche, E02, E03, E07, E08, ERA, ERI, ERIC, EdA, EdI, FamI, G08, HEA, I05, I06, I07, M01, M02, P04, P18, P30, P43, P48, P53, P54, P55, PQC, PsycholAb, S02, S03, S09, S20, S21, S23, SCOPUS, SWR&A, T02, V05, W03, W05.

—BLDSC (5003.443500), IE, Ingenta. **CCC.**

Published by: (Association for Humanistic Counseling, Education and Development), American Counseling Association, 5999 Stevenson Ave, Alexandria, VA 22304. TEL 800-347-6647, FAX 703-823-0252, 800-473-2329. Ed. Colette T Dollarhide. Adv. contact Kathy Maguire TEL 703-823-9800 ext 207.

150 170 USA ISSN 0022-1678
BF1

➤ **JOURNAL OF HUMANISTIC PSYCHOLOGY.** Text in English. 1961. q. USD 823, GBP 483 combined subscription to institutions (print & online eds.); USD 807, GBP 473 to institutions (effective 2011). adv. bk.rev. stat.; illus. index, cum.index: 1961-1979. back issues avail.; reprint service avail. from PSC. **Document type:** *Journal, Academic/Scholarly.* **Description:** Provides an interdisciplinary forum for contributions and controversies in humanistic psychology as applied to personal growth, interpersonal encounters, social problems, and philosophical issues.

Related titles: Microfilm ed.: (from PQC); Online - full text ed.: ISSN 1552-650X. USD 741, GBP 435 to institutions (effective 2011).

Indexed: A01, A02, A03, A08, A20, A21, A22, A25, A26, ABS&EES, ASCA, ASSIA, B04, B07, BRD, CA, CurCont, E-psyche, E01, E02, E03, E07, E08, ERI, EdA, EdI, FamI, G08, H04, H09, I05, MEA&I, P02, P03, P04, P10, P12, P13, P25, P26, P27, P48, P53, P54, PQC, PRA, PerIslam, PsycInfo, PsycholAb, RASB, RI-1, RI-2, S02, S03, S05, S08, S09, SCOPUS, SOPODA, SSAI, SSAb, SSCI, SSI, T02, V02, W03, W07.

—BLDSC (5003.450000), IE, Infotrieve, Ingenta, INIST. **CCC.**

Published by: (Association for Humanistic Psychology), Sage Publications, Inc., 2455 Teller Rd, Thousand Oaks, CA 91320. TEL 805-499-9774, 800-818-7243, FAX 805-499-0871, 800-583-2665, info@sagepub.com. Ed. Kirk J Schneider. Circ: 1,550 (paid and free). **Subscr. outside the Americas to:** Sage Publications Ltd., 1 Oliver's Yard, 55 City Rd, London EC1Y 1SP, United Kingdom. TEL 44-20-73248701, FAX 44-20-73248733, subscription@sagepub.co.uk.

153.3 615.82 617.1027 USA ISSN 1932-0191

➤ **JOURNAL OF IMAGERY RESEARCH IN SPORT AND PHYSICAL ACTIVITY.** Text in English. 2006 (Feb.). a. USD 325 per issue to institutions; USD 975 per issue to corporations (effective 2011). back issues avail. **Document type:** *Journal, Academic/Scholarly.* **Description:** Features research, reviews, and theoretical or conceptual papers related to understanding the role of imagery in sport, physical activity, exercise, and rehabilitation settings.

Media: Online - full text.

Indexed: A28, APA, BrCerAb, C&ISA, C06, C07, CA/WCA, CABA, CIA, CerAb, CivEngAb, CorrAb, E&CAJ, E11, EEA, EMA, ESPM, EnvEAb, GH, H15, LT, M&TEA, M09, MBF, METADEX, P03, PEI, PsycInfo, RRTA, SCOPUS, SD, SolStAb, T04, WAA.

—**CCC.**

Published by: Berkeley Electronic Press, 2809 Telegraph Ave, Ste 202, Berkeley, CA 94705. TEL 510-665-1200, FAX 510-665-1201, info@bepress.com. Eds. Craig Hall, Sandra Short.

302 USA ISSN 1529-4129
JOURNAL OF IMAGO RELATIONSHIP THERAPY. Text in English. 1996. s-a. adv. bk.rev. **Document type:** *Journal, Academic/Scholarly.* **Description:** Presents research and case studies concerning the use of imago therapy, pioneered by Dr. Harville Hendrix.
Indexed: E-psyche, PsycholAb, SOPODA.
Published by: (Institute for Imago Relationship Therapy), International Universities Press, Inc., Psychosocial Press, 59 Boston Post Rd, Box 1524, PO Box 389, Madison, CT 06443. TEL 203-245-4000, FAX 203-245-0775, info@iup.com. adv.: page USD 375; 4.25 x 7.

301.1 150 IND ISSN 0379-3885
BF1
JOURNAL OF INDIAN PSYCHOLOGY. Text in English. 1977. s-a. **Document type:** *Journal, Academic/Scholarly.*
Formerly: Indian Psychology
Indexed: BAS, E-psyche, IPsyAb, PsycholAb.
—BLDSC (5005.330000), IE, Ingenta.
Published by: (Andhra University, Department of Psychology & Parapsychology), Andhra University Press and Publications, Andhra University, Visakhapatnam, Andhra Pradesh 530 003, India. TEL 91-891-2575464, FAX 91-891-2525611, registrar@andhrauniversity.info. Ed. K MADHU TEL 91-891-2844435. **Subscr. to:** I N S I O Scientific Books & Periodicals.

152 USA ISSN 1614-0001
➤ **JOURNAL OF INDIVIDUAL DIFFERENCES.** Text in English. 1980. q. USD 128, EUR 98 to individuals; USD 208, EUR 164 to institutions; USD 69, EUR 55 per issue (effective 2011). adv. 80 p./no.; back issues avail. **Document type:** *Journal, Academic/Scholarly.* **Description:** Contains articles on individual differences in behavior, emotion, cognition, and their developmental aspects.
Formerly (until 2005): Zeitschrift fuer Differentielle und Diagnostische Psychologie (0170-1789)
Related titles: Online - full text ed.: ISSN 2151-2299 (from ScienceDirect).
Indexed: A20, A22, CurCont, DIP, E-psyche, IBR, IBZ, P03, PsycInfo, PsycholAb, SCOPUS, SSCI, W07.
—BLDSC (5005.348700), GNLM, IE, Ingenta. **CCC.**
Published by: Hogrefe Publishing Corp., 875 Massachusetts Ave, 7th Fl, Cambridge, MA 02139. TEL 866-823-4726, FAX 617-354-6875, customservices@hogrefe-publishing.com, http://www.hogrefe.com. Ed. Dr. Juergen Hennig TEL 49-641-9926150. Adv. contact Gundula von Fintel. Circ: 400 (paid).

150 USA ISSN 1522-2527
BF1
➤ **THE JOURNAL OF INDIVIDUAL PSYCHOLOGY**; the journal of Adlerian theory, research & practice. Text in English. 1982. q. USD 150 domestic to institutions; USD 162 in Canada to institutions; USD 171 elsewhere to institutions (effective 2011). bk.rev. bibl.; charts; stat. Index. 100 p./no.; back issues avail. **Document type:** *Journal, Academic/Scholarly.* **Description:** Provides a forum for the finest dialogue pertaining to Adlerian practices, principles, and theoretical development.
Formerly (until 1998): Individual Psychology (0277-7010); Which was formed by the merger of (1963-1982): The Individual Psychologist (0019-7149); (1957-1982): Journal of Individual Psychology (0022-1805); Which was formerly (until 1957): American Journal of Individual Psychology (0091-7788); (until 1953): Individual Psychology Bulletin; (until 1941): Individual Psychology News (1937-8084); Which superseded (in 1940): International Journal of Individual Psychology
Related titles: Online - full text ed.
Indexed: A01, A02, A03, A08, A20, A22, AMHA, ASCA, AbAn, BibInd, C28, CA, CLFP, DIP, E-psyche, F09, FamI, IBR, IBZ, IndMed, MEA&I, MLA-IB, P03, P26, P30, P43, P48, P54, PCI, PQC, PsycInfo, PsycholAb, S02, S03, SCOPUS, SOPODA, SWR&A, SociolAb, T02.
—BLDSC (5005.350000), GNLM, IE, Infotrieve, Ingenta, INIST. **CCC.**
Published by: (North American Society of Adlerian Psychology), University of Texas Press, Journals Division, PO Box 7819, Austin, TX 78713. TEL 512-471-7233 ext 2, FAX 512-232-7178, journals@uts.cc.utexas.edu, http://www.utexas.edu/utpress/journals/journals.html. Eds. Bill Curlette, Roy Kern. Adv. contact Leah Dixon TEL 512-232-7618.

616.89 USA ISSN 1528-9168
RJ504
➤ **JOURNAL OF INFANT, CHILD AND ADOLESCENT PSYCHOTHERAPY.** Text and summaries in English. 2001. q. GBP 176 combined subscription in United Kingdom to institutions (print & online eds.); EUR 232, USD 290 combined subscription to institutions (print & online eds.) (effective 2012). adv. back issues avail.; reprint service avail. from PSC. **Document type:** *Journal, Academic/Scholarly.* **Description:** Provides a comprehensive overview of child therapy as it is conceptualized and practiced in the 21st century.
Related titles: Online - full text ed.: ISSN 1940-9214. GBP 158 in United Kingdom to institutions; EUR 209, USD 261 to institutions (effective 2012).
Indexed: A01, DIP, F09, IBR, IBZ, P03, P25, P30, P48, PQC, PsycInfo, T02.
—BLDSC (5006.689000), IE, Ingenta. **CCC.**
Published by: Routledge (Subsidiary of: Taylor & Francis Group), 325 Chestnut St, Ste 800, Philadelphia, PA 19106. TEL 800-354-1420, FAX 215-625-2940, journals@routledge.com, http://www.routledge.com. Ed. Kirkland C Vaughans. Adv. contact Linda Hann TEL 44-1344-779945. Circ: 2,500 (paid).

150 100 USA ISSN 1944-5083
➤ **JOURNAL OF INTEGRAL THEORY AND PRACTICE.** Text in English. 2005. q. USD 120 domestic to institutions (print or online ed.); USD 180 foreign to institutions (effective 2010). **Document type:** *Journal, Academic/Scholarly.* **Description:** Contains articles, case studies, integral research, book reviews, critical dialogues, and conference reports related to Integral Theory and its application.
Formerly (until 2008): A Q A L (1554-5814)
Related titles: Online - full text ed.
Indexed: AmHI, CA, H07, T02.
Published by: (Integral Institute), State University of New York Press, 90 State St, Ste 700, Albany, NY 12207. TEL 518-472-5000, FAX 518-472-5038, info@sunypress.edu. Ed. Ken Wilber.

▼ ➤ **THE JOURNAL OF INTERACTIONAL RESEARCH IN COMMUNICATION DISORDERS.** *see* LINGUISTICS

▼ ➤ **THE JOURNAL OF INTERDISCIPLINARY UNDERGRADUATE RESEARCH.** *see* EDUCATION

➤ **JOURNAL OF INTERPERSONAL VIOLENCE**; concerned with the study and treatment of victims and perpetrators of physical and sexual violence. *see* CRIMINOLOGY AND LAW ENFORCEMENT

150 364 GBR ISSN 1544-4759
HV6080
JOURNAL OF INVESTIGATIVE PSYCHOLOGY AND OFFENDER PROFILING. Text in English. 2004. 3/yr. GBP 118 in United Kingdom to institutions; EUR 141 in Europe to institutions; USD 220 elsewhere to institutions; GBP 131 combined subscription in United Kingdom to institutions (print & online eds.); EUR 156 combined subscription in Europe to institutions (print & online eds.); USD 242 combined subscription elsewhere to institutions (print & online eds.) (effective 2010). adv. bk.rev. back issues avail.; reprint service avail. from PSC. **Document type:** *Journal, Academic/Scholarly.* **Description:** Covers the behavioural science contributions to criminal and civil investigations, for researchers and practitioners, also exploring the legal and jurisprudential implications of psychological and related aspects of all forms of investigation.
Related titles: Online - full text ed.: ISSN 1544-4767. GBP 118 in United Kingdom to institutions; EUR 141 in Europe to institutions; USD 220 elsewhere to institutions (effective 2010).
Indexed: A01, A03, A08, CA, CJA, CJPI, P03, P43, PQC, PsycInfo, S02, S03, SCOPUS, T02.
—IE, Ingenta. **CCC.**
Published by: John Wiley & Sons Ltd. (Subsidiary of: John Wiley & Sons, Inc.), 1-7 Oldlands Way, PO Box 808, Bognor Regis, West Sussex PO21 9FF, United Kingdom. TEL 44-1865-778315, FAX 44-1243-843232, cs-journals@wiley.com, http://eu.wiley.com/WileyCDA/. Ed. David Canter TEL 44-1517-943910. **Subscr. to:** 1-7 Oldlands Way, PO Box 809, Bognor Regis, West Sussex PO21 9FG, United Kingdom. TEL 44-1865-778054, cs-agency@wiley.com.

JOURNAL OF INVITATIONAL THEORY AND PRACTICE. *see* EDUCATION

150 USA ISSN 1920-986X
➤ **JOURNAL OF JUNGIAN SCHOLARLY STUDIES.** Text in English. 2005. a. free (effective 2011). **Document type:** *Journal, Academic/Scholarly.* **Description:** Contains topics such as literature, the arts, drama, visual art, myth and fairy tale, pop culture, education,religion, film, music, architecture, psychology, science, masculinity, and Jungian theory itself.
Formerly (until 200?): Jung (1715-7978)
Media: Online - full text.
Indexed: A01, A39, C27, C29, D03, D04, E13, R14, S14, S15, S18, T02.
Published by: The Jungian Society for Scholarly Studies, PO Box 19722, Johnston, RI 02919. fidyk@ualberta.ca. Eds. Christine Herold, Darrell Dobson.

150.1954 USA ISSN 1530-5538
BF173.A2
JOURNAL OF JUNGIAN THEORY AND PRACTICE. Text in English. 1999. s-a. **Document type:** *Journal, Academic/Scholarly.*
Indexed: P03, PsycInfo, PsycholAb.
Published by: C.G. Jung Institute of New York, 28 E 39th St, New York, NY 10016. TEL 212-986-5458, FAX 212-876-0920, cgjunginstitute.ny@verizon.net, http://www.cgjungpage.org/newyork.html, http://www.jungcenter.org.

JOURNAL OF KNOWLEDGE AND BEST PRACTICES IN JUVENILE JUSTICE & PSYCHOLOGY. *see* CRIMINOLOGY AND LAW ENFORCEMENT

155.34 USA ISSN 1553-8605
RC451.4.G39
➤ **JOURNAL OF L G B T ISSUES IN COUNSELING.** (Lesbian Gay Bisexual Transgender) Text in English. 2005 (Fall). q. GBP 205 combined subscription in United Kingdom to institutions (print & online eds.); EUR 267, USD 275 combined subscription to institutions (print & online eds.) (effective 2012). reprint service avail. from PSC. **Document type:** *Journal, Academic/Scholarly.* **Description:** Provides a professional forum for research, best practices, and emerging trends and issues relating to counseling the GLBT community.
Related titles: Online - full text ed.: ISSN 1553-8338. GBP 184 in United Kingdom to institutions; EUR 240, USD 248 to institutions (effective 2012).
Indexed: A01, A03, A22, C06, C07, CA, E01, E03, ERI, ESPM, FamI, IBR, IBZ, L01, L02, M02, P03, P30, P48, P54, PQC, PsycInfo, RiskAb, S02, S03, SCOPUS, T02.
—IE, Ingenta. **CCC.**
Published by: (Association of Lesbian, Gay, Bisexual, Transgender Issues in Counseling), Routledge (Subsidiary of: Taylor & Francis Group), 325 Chestnut St, Ste 800, Philadelphia, PA 19106. TEL 215-625-8900, 800-354-1420, FAX 215-625-8914, journals@routledge.com, http://www.routledge.com. Ed. Dr. Ned Farley.

302 USA ISSN 0261-927X
P40
➤ **JOURNAL OF LANGUAGE AND SOCIAL PSYCHOLOGY.** Text in English. 1982. q. USD 816, GBP 480 combined subscription to institutions (print & online eds.); USD 800, GBP 470 to institutions (effective 2011). bk.rev. index. back issues avail.; reprint service avail. from PSC. **Document type:** *Journal, Academic/Scholarly.* **Description:** Explores the social dimensions of language and the linguistic implications of social life.
Related titles: Online - full text ed.: ISSN 1552-6526. USD 734, GBP 432 to institutions (effective 2011).
Indexed: A01, A02, A03, A08, A20, A22, ASCA, AmHI, B01, B06, B07, B09, BibLing, CA, CJA, CMM, CommAb, CurCont, DIP, E-psyche, E01, E03, ERI, FamI, H07, H14, IBR, IBSS, IBZ, L&LBA, L11, LT&LA, MLA-IB, P02, P03, P10, P25, P26, P30, P42, P48, P53, P54, PCI, PQC, PSA, PsycInfo, PsycholAb, RASB, RefZh, S02, S03, SCOPUS, SOPODA, SSA, SSCI, SociolAb, T02, W07.
—BLDSC (5010.096000), IE, Infotrieve, Ingenta. **CCC.**
Published by: Sage Publications, Inc., 2455 Teller Rd, Thousand Oaks, CA 91320. TEL 805-499-9774, 800-818-7243, FAX 805-499-0871, 800-583-2665, info@sagepub.com. Ed. Howard Giles. Circ: 500. **Subscr. outside the Americas to:** Sage Publications Ltd., 1 Oliver's Yard, 55 City Rd, London EC1Y 1SP, United Kingdom. TEL 44-20-73248701, FAX 44-20-73248733, subscription@sagepub.co.uk.

▼ ➤ **JOURNAL OF LAW AND PSYCHOLOGY.** *see* LAW

➤ **JOURNAL OF LEARNING DISABILITIES.** *see* EDUCATION—Special Education And Rehabilitation

➤ **JOURNAL OF LESBIAN STUDIES.** *see* HOMOSEXUALITY

150 USA ISSN 1532-5024
BF575.D35 CODEN: JPILFC
➤ **JOURNAL OF LOSS & TRAUMA**; international perspectives on stress and coping. Text in English. 1996. 5/yr. GBP 412 combined subscription in United Kingdom to institutions (print & online eds.); EUR 547, USD 687 combined subscription to institutions (print & online eds.) (effective 2012). adv. back issues avail.; reprint service avail. from PSC. **Document type:** *Journal, Academic/Scholarly.* **Description:** Forum on personal losses relating to family, health and aging issues, and interpersonal losses surrounding such areas as marriage and divorce.
Incorporates (1994-2006): Stress, Trauma and Crisis (1543-4613); Which was formerly (until 2004): Crisis Intervention and Time-Limited Treatment (1064-5136); Formerly (until 2001): Journal of Personal & Interpersonal Loss (1081-1443)
Related titles: Online - full text ed.: ISSN 1532-5032. GBP 370 in United Kingdom to institutions; EUR 492, USD 619 to institutions (effective 2012) (from IngentaConnect).
Indexed: A01, A02, A03, A08, A20, A22, ASSIA, C06, C07, CA, CurCont, E-psyche, E01, E03, ERI, ERIC, FamI, P03, P04, P30, P43, P48, P54, PQC, PsycInfo, PsycholAb, S02, S03, SCOPUS, SSCI, SociolAb, T02, V&AA, W07.
—IE, Infotrieve, Ingenta. **CCC.**
Published by: Routledge (Subsidiary of: Taylor & Francis Group), 325 Chestnut St, Ste 800, Philadelphia, PA 19106. TEL 800-354-1420, FAX 215-625-2940, journals@routledge.com, http://www.routledge.com. Ed. John H Harvey TEL 319-335-2473. Adv. contact Linda Hann TEL 44-1344-779945.

➤ **JOURNAL OF MANAGERIAL PSYCHOLOGY.** *see* BUSINESS AND ECONOMICS—Management

306.43 USA ISSN 0194-472X
HQ1
➤ **JOURNAL OF MARITAL AND FAMILY THERAPY.** Text in English. 1975. q. GBP 232 combined subscription in United Kingdom to institutions (print & online eds.); EUR 280 combined subscription in Europe to institutions (print & online eds.); USD 367 combined subscription in the Americas to institutions (print & online eds.); USD 452 combined subscription elsewhere to institutions (print & online eds.) (effective 2012). adv. bk.rev. illus. Index. reprint service avail. from PSC. **Document type:** *Journal, Academic/Scholarly.* **Description:** Provides information about marital and family functioning and the most effective psychotherapeutic treatment of couple and family distress.
Formerly (until 1979): Journal of Marriage and Family Counseling (0094-5102)
Related titles: Microform ed.: (from PQC); Online - full text ed.: ISSN 1752-0606. GBP 211 in United Kingdom to institutions; EUR 268 in Europe to institutions; USD 333 in the Americas to institutions; USD 411 elsewhere to institutions (effective 2012) (from IngentaConnect).
Indexed: A01, A02, A03, A08, A20, A22, A25, A26, AMHA, ASCA, ASSIA, B04, BRD, C06, C07, CA, CERDIC, CurCont, E-psyche, E01, E02, E03, E07, E08, EMBASE, ERI, ERIC, EdA, EdI, ExcerpMed, F09, FamI, G08, H12, I05, INI, IndMed, M01, M02, MEDLINE, P02, P03, P10, P12, P13, P18, P19, P20, P22, P25, P27, P30, P46, P48, P53, P54, PC&CA, PQC, PsycInfo, PsycholAb, RASB, S02, S03, S08, S09, SCOPUS, SFSA, SOPODA, SSA, SSAI, SSAb, SSCI, SSI, SWR&A, SociolAb, T02, W03, W05, W07, W09.
—BLDSC (5012.060000), IE, Infotrieve, Ingenta. **CCC.**
Published by: (American Association for Marriage and Family Therapy), Wiley-Blackwell Publishing, Inc. (Subsidiary of: Wiley-Blackwell Publishing Ltd.), 111 River St, Hoboken, NJ 07030. TEL 201-748-6000, FAX 201-748-6088, info@wiley.com, http://www.wiley.com/WileyCDA/. Ed. Ronald Chenail. Adv. contact Kristin McCarthy TEL 201-748-7683.

150 USA ISSN 0022-2496
BF1 CODEN: JMTPAJ
➤ **JOURNAL OF MATHEMATICAL PSYCHOLOGY.** Text in English. 1964. bi-m. EUR 1,719 in Europe to institutions; JPY 179,400 in Japan to institutions; USD 1,224 elsewhere to institutions (effective 2012). adv. bk.rev. bibl.; charts; illus. Index. back issues avail.; reprints avail. **Document type:** *Journal, Academic/Scholarly.* **Description:** Presents theoretical and empirical research in all areas of mathematical psychology.
Related titles: Online - full text ed.: ISSN 1096-0880 (from IngentaConnect, ScienceDirect).
Indexed: A01, A03, A08, A20, A22, A26, ASCA, B21, BibInd, CA, CCMJ, CDA, CIS, CMCI, CompR, CurCont, DIP, E-psyche, E01, I05, IBR, IBZ, Inspec, JCQM, MSN, MathR, NSA, P03, P30, PsycInfo, PsycholAb, RASB, RILM, S01, SCI, SCOPUS, SSCI, T02, W07, Z02.
—BLDSC (5012.420000), AskIEEE, IE, Infotrieve, Ingenta, INIST. **CCC.**
Published by: (Society for Mathematical Psychology), Academic Press (Subsidiary of: Elsevier Science & Technology), 3251 Riverport Ln, Maryland Heights, MO 63043. TEL 314-447-8010, FAX 314-447-8030, JournalCustomerService-usa@elsevier.com, http://www.elsevierdirect.com/imprint.jsp?iid=5. Ed. J Myung.

302.23 DEU ISSN 1864-1105
P96.P75
➤ **JOURNAL OF MEDIA PSYCHOLOGY**; theories, methods and applications. Text in English. 1989. q. USD 129, EUR 104 to individuals; USD 243, EUR 191 to institutions; USD 79, EUR 64 per issue (effective 2011). adv. bk.rev. index. back issues avail. **Document type:** *Journal, Academic/Scholarly.* **Description:** Publishes original papers, which cover the broad range of media psychological research, including various media, applications, and user groups.
Former titles (until 2008): Zeitschrift fuer Medienpsychologie (1617-6383); (until 2001): Medienpsychologie (0936-7780)
Related titles: Online - full text ed.: ISSN 2151-2388 (from ScienceDirect).
Indexed: DIP, E-psyche, IBR, IBZ, P03, PsycInfo, PsycholAb, RILM, SCOPUS.
—BLDSC (5017.046000), IE. **CCC.**
Published by: Hogrefe Verlag GmbH & Co. KG, Rohnsweg 25, Goettingen, 37085, Germany. TEL 49-551-99950421, FAX 49-551-99950425, verlag@hogrefe.de, http://www.hogrefe.de. Ed. Gary Bente TEL 49-221-4706502. Circ: 600 (paid and controlled).

➤ **JOURNAL OF MEDIA PSYCHOLOGY.** *see* COMMUNICATIONS

P

➤ **JOURNAL OF MEMORY AND LANGUAGE.** *see* LINGUISTICS

362.2 USA ISSN 1040-2861
BF637.C6
➤ **JOURNAL OF MENTAL HEALTH COUNSELING.** Text in English. 1979. q. USD 360 combined subscription domestic to non-members (print & online eds.); USD 385 combined subscription foreign to non-members (print & online eds.); free to members (effective 2010). abstr.; charts. back issues avail.; reprints avail. **Document type:** *Journal, Academic/Scholarly.* **Description:** Features articles with breakthrough research and case studies governed by professional opinion.
Formerly (until 1987): A M H C A Journal (0193-1830)
Related titles: Microfiche ed.; Microfilm ed.; Online - full text ed.: USD 310 (effective 2010).
Indexed: A01, A02, A03, A08, A22, A26, BibInd, C11, C12, CA, CJPI, E-psyche, E03, E07, E08, ERI, ERIC, Faml, G08, H04, HEA, I05, I07, M01, M02, P03, P04, P10, P12, P18, P19, P25, P26, P27, P43, P48, P53, P54, P55, PQC, PsycInfo, PsycholAb, S02, S03, S09, S23, SWR&A, T02, V&AA.
—BLDSC (5017.687000), GNLM, IE, Infotrieve, Ingenta. **CCC.**
Published by: American Mental Health Counselors Association, 801 N Fairfax St, Ste 304, Alexandria, VA 22314. TEL 703-548-6002, 800-326-2642, FAX 703-548-4775. Ed. James R Rogers.

616.89 ITA ISSN 1091-4358
RA790.A1 CODEN: JMHPAR
➤ **JOURNAL OF MENTAL HEALTH POLICY AND ECONOMICS (PRINT EDITION).** Text in English. 1998. q. EUR 500 to institutions (effective 2009). adv. back issues avail. **Document type:** *Journal, Academic/Scholarly.* **Description:** Focuses on the integration of health and economic research in mental health.
Related titles: Online - full text ed.: Journal of Mental Health Policy and Economics (Online Edition). ISSN 1099-176X.
Indexed: AddicA, C06, C07, CurCont, E-psyche, EMBASE, ESPM, EconLit, ExcerpMed, JEL, MEDLINE, P03, P30, PAIS, PsycInfo, PsycholAb, R10, Reac, RiskAb, SCOPUS, SSCI, W07.
—BLDSC (5017.688000), IE, Infotrieve, Ingenta.
Published by: International Center of Mental Health Policy and Economics, Via Daniele Crespi, 7, Milano, 20123, Italy. FAX 39-02-5810-6901. Eds. Agnes Rupp, Massimo Moscarelli. adv.: B&W page GBP 650, color page GBP 1,650.

150 USA ISSN 0364-5541
BF367
JOURNAL OF MENTAL IMAGERY. Text in English. 1977. 4/yr. USD 40 to individuals; USD 90 to institutions (effective 2005). adv. bk.rev. charts. back issues avail.
Indexed: A22, BibInd, DIP, E-psyche, IBR, IBZ, MLA-IB, P03, PCI, PsycInfo, PsycholAb, RASB, SociolAb.
—BLDSC (5017.690000), IE, Infotrieve, Ingenta. **CCC.**
Published by: (International Imagery Association), Brandon House, Inc., PO Box 240, Bronx, NY 10471. Ed. Dr. Akhter Ahsen.

150 121 USA ISSN 0271-0137
BF1
➤ **THE JOURNAL OF MIND AND BEHAVIOR.** Abbreviated title: J M B. Text in English. 1980. q. USD 46 to individuals; USD 158 to institutions; USD 27 to students (effective 2009). adv. bk.rev. abstr.; charts; illus.; stat.; bibl. index in issue #4. 160 p./no. 1 cols./p.; back issues avail.; reprints avail. **Document type:** *Journal, Academic/Scholarly.* **Description:** Presents an interdisciplinary approach within psychology and related fields-building upon the assumption of a unified science.
Indexed: A01, A20, A22, ASCA, BibInd, CA, CommAb, CurCont, DIP, E-psyche, EMBASE, ExcerpMed, Faml, IBR, IBZ, Inspec, L&LBA, MLA-IB, P03, PerIslam, PhilInd, PsycInfo, PsycholAb, R10, Reac, S02, S03, SCOPUS, SOPODA, SSA, SSCI, SWR&A, SociolAb, T02, W07.
—BLDSC (5020.140000), AskIEEE, IE, Infotrieve, Ingenta, INIST. **CCC.**
Published by: Institute of Mind & Behavior, Village Sta, PO Box 522, New York, NY 10014. TEL 212-595-4853. Ed. Dr. Raymond C Russ TEL 207-581-2057.

152.3 USA ISSN 0022-2895
CODEN: JMTBAB
➤ **JOURNAL OF MOTOR BEHAVIOR.** Short title: J M B. Text in English. 1969. bi-m. GBP 228 combined subscription in United Kingdom to institutions (print & online eds.); EUR 301, USD 375 combined subscription to institutions (print & online eds.) (effective 2012). adv. abstr.; bibl.; charts; illus. back issues avail.; reprint service avail. from PSC. **Document type:** *Journal, Academic/Scholarly.* **Description:** Devoted to the understanding of the basic processes underlying motor control and learning.
Related titles: CD-ROM ed.; Microform ed.; Online - full text ed.: ISSN 1940-1027. GBP 205 in United Kingdom to institutions; EUR 270, USD 338 to institutions (effective 2012).
Indexed: A01, A02, A03, A08, A22, A26, AMED, ASCA, B&AI, B10, B25, BIOSIS Prev, BRD, C06, C07, CA, CDA, CurCont, DIP, E-psyche, E01, E07, E08, EMBASE, ERA, ErgAb, ExcerpMed, FR, FoSS&M, G08, I05, IBR, IBZ, ISR, IndMed, MEDLINE, MycolAb, NSCI, P03, P18, P19, P20, P22, P24, P25, P26, P30, P43, P48, P53, P54, PQC, PsycInfo, PsycholAb, R09, R10, RASB, RILM, Reac, RefZh, S04, S09, S20, S21, SCI, SCOPUS, SD, SSCI, SportS, T02, W03, W05, W07.
—BLDSC (5021.050000), IE, Infotrieve, Ingenta, INIST. **CCC.**
Published by: (Helen Dwight Reid Educational Foundation), Routledge (Subsidiary of: Taylor & Francis Group), 325 Chestnut St, Ste 800, Philadelphia, PA 19106. TEL 215-625-8900, FAX 215-625-2940, journals@routledge.com, http://www.routledge.com.

371.9 USA ISSN 0883-8534
LC3701
➤ **JOURNAL OF MULTICULTURAL COUNSELING AND DEVELOPMENT.** Abbreviated title: J M C D. Text in English. 1972. q. GBP 141 in United Kingdom to institutions; EUR 163 in Europe to institutions; USD 200 elsewhere to institutions; GBP 163 combined subscription in United Kingdom to institutions (print & online eds.); EUR 188 combined subscription in Europe to institutions (print & online eds.); USD 230 combined subscription elsewhere to institutions (print & online eds.) (effective 2012). adv. abstr.; bibl.; illus. 64 p./no.; back issues avail.; reprint service avail. from PSC. **Document type:** *Journal, Academic/Scholarly.* **Description:** Covers state-of-the-art multicultural counseling research and reports on applications of the latest theoretical ideas and concepts.
Formerly (until 1985): Journal of Non-White Concerns in Personnel and Guidance (0090-5461)
Related titles: Microform ed.: (from PQC); Online - full text ed.: ISSN 2161-1912. GBP 141 in United Kingdom to institutions; EUR 163 in Europe to institutions; USD 200 elsewhere to institutions (effective 2012).
Indexed: A01, A02, A03, A08, A20, A22, A26, ASCA, B04, BRD, C06, C07, C12, CA, ChPerI, Chicano, CurCont, E-psyche, E02, E03, E07, E08, ENW, ERI, ERIC, EdA, EdI, Faml, G06, G07, G08, HEA, I05, IIBP, M01, M02, M06, P03, P04, P18, P25, P30, P43, P48, P53, P54, P55, PQC, PsycInfo, PsycholAb, S02, S03, S09, SCOPUS, SSCI, SWR&A, T02, W03, W05, W07.
—BLDSC (5021.058000), IE, Ingenta. **CCC.**
Published by: (Association for Multicultural Counseling and Development), American Counseling Association, 5999 Stevenson Ave, Alexandria, VA 22304. TEL 800-347-6647, FAX 703-823-0252, 800-473-2329. Ed. Gargi Roysircar-Sodowsky TEL 603-357-3122. Circ: 2,000.

150 297 USA ISSN 1556-4908
RC451.4.M87
➤ **JOURNAL OF MUSLIM MENTAL HEALTH.** Text in English. 2006 (Sum.). s-a. GBP 177, EUR 234, USD 294 combined subscription to institutions (print & online eds.) (effective 2010). adv. reprint service avail. from PSC. **Document type:** *Journal, Academic/Scholarly.* **Description:** Provides an academic forum for exploring social, cultural, historical, theological, and psychological factors related to the mental health of Muslims in North America as well as that of the global Muslim community.
Related titles: Online - full text ed.: ISSN 1556-5009. USD 279, GBP 168, EUR 222 to institutions (effective 2010).
Indexed: A22, ASSIA, C06, C07, CA, E01, EMBASE, ExcerpMed, I14, IBSS, P03, P30, PsycInfo, R10, Reac, S02, S03, SCOPUS, T02.
—IE, Ingenta. **CCC.**
Published by: Taylor & Francis Inc. (Subsidiary of: Taylor & Francis Group), 325 Chestnut St, Ste 800, Philadelphia, PA 19106. TEL 215-625-2940, 800-354-1420, orders@taylorandfrancis.com, http://www.taylorandfrancis.com. Ed. Mona M Amer. Adv. contact Linda Hann TEL 44-1344-779945.

➤ **JOURNAL OF NEAR-DEATH STUDIES.** *see* PHILOSOPHY

➤ **JOURNAL OF NEUROPSYCHOLOGY.** *see* MEDICAL SCIENCES—Psychiatry And Neurology

302 USA ISSN 1937-321X
QP360.5
JOURNAL OF NEUROSCIENCE, PSYCHOLOGY AND ECONOMICS. Abbreviated title: J N P E. Variant title: NeuroPsychoEconomics. Text in English. 2008. s-a. USD 110 domestic to individuals; USD 137 foreign to individuals; USD 403 domestic to institutions; USD 448 foreign to institutions (effective 2011). adv. back issues avail. **Document type:** *Journal, Academic/Scholarly.*
Related titles: Online - full content ed.: ISSN 1937-3228; Online - full text ed.: (from ScienceDirect); German ed.: ISSN 1861-4523.
Indexed: A01, B01, B07, CA, EMBASE, P03, P30, PsycInfo, SCOPUS, T02.
—**CCC.**
Published by: (Association for NeuroPsychoEconomics), American Psychological Association, 750 First St, NE, Washington, DC 20002. TEL 202-336-5500, 800-374-2721, journals@apa.org. Eds. Martin Reimann, Oliver Schilke. Adv. contact Doug Constant TEL 202-336-5574. Circ: 400.

150 310 USA ISSN 2152-6389
▼ ➤ **JOURNAL OF NON-SIGNIFICANT RESULTS IN THE BEHAVIORAL SCIENCES.** Text in English. 2010 (May). q. free (effective 2011). **Document type:** *Journal, Academic/Scholarly.* **Description:** Features examinations of non-significant results and statistical methods in psychology and the behavioral sciences.
Media: Online - full text.
Published by: College of St Elizabeth, 2 Convent Rd, Morristown, NJ 07960. TEL 973-290-4000, http://www.cse.edu.

301.3 150 USA ISSN 0191-5886
BF353 CODEN: JNVBDV
➤ **JOURNAL OF NONVERBAL BEHAVIOR.** Text in English. 1976. q. EUR 1,022, USD 1,078 combined subscription to institutions (print & online eds.) (effective 2012). adv. illus. back issues avail.; reprint service avail. from PSC. **Document type:** *Journal, Academic/Scholarly.* **Description:** Presents theoretical and empirical research on nonverbal communications, including paralanguage, proxemics, facial expressions, eye contact, face-to-face interaction, and nonverbal emotive expression.
Formerly (until 1979): Environmental Psychology and Nonverbal Behavior (0361-3496)
Related titles: Microform ed.: (from PQC); Online - full text ed.: ISSN 1573-3653 (from IngentaConnect).
Indexed: A01, A02, A03, A08, A20, A22, A26, ASCA, B21, BRD, BibLing, C06, C07, CA, CDA, CJA, CMM, CPE, CommAb, CurCont, E-psyche, E01, E04, E05, E07, E08, Faml, G08, I05, IBR, IBZ, L&LBA, M06, MLA, MLA-IB, NSA, P02, P03, P10, P12, P25, P26, P27, P30, P48, P53, P54, PCI, PQC, PsycInfo, PsycholAb, PsycholRG, S02, S03, S09, SCOPUS, SFSA, SOPODA, SSAI, SSAb, SSCI, SSI, SWR&A, SociolAb, T02, W03, W05, W07.
—BLDSC (5022.843000), IE, Infotrieve, Ingenta, INIST. **CCC.**
Published by: Springer New York LLC (Subsidiary of: Springer Science+Business Media), 233 Spring St, New York, NY 10013. TEL 212-460-1500, FAX 212-460-1575, service-ny@springer.com. Ed. Howard S Friedman.

158 GBR ISSN 0963-1798
HF5548.8 CODEN: JOCCEF
➤ **JOURNAL OF OCCUPATIONAL AND ORGANIZATIONAL PSYCHOLOGY.** Abbreviated title: J O O P. Text in English. 1922. q. GBP 231 in United Kingdom to institutions; EUR 342 in Europe to institutions; USD 426 elsewhere to institutions; GBP 282 combined subscription in United Kingdom to institutions (print & online eds.); EUR 418 combined subscription in Europe to institutions (print & online eds.); USD 520 combined subscription elsewhere to institutions (print & online eds.) (effective 2012). adv. bk.rev. charts; illus.; abstr. index. 128 p./no.; back issues avail.; reprint service avail. from PSC. **Document type:** *Journal, Academic/Scholarly.* **Description:** Examines industrial and organizational psychology as well as describes, and interprets new research about people at work.
Former titles (until 1992): Journal of Occupational Psychology (0305-8107); (until 1975): Occupational Psychology (0029-7976); (until 1938): Human Factors (0301-7397); (until 1932): National Institute of Industrial Psychology. Journal
Related titles: Magnetic Tape ed.; Microfiche ed.; Microform ed.; Online - full text ed.: 1999. GBP 245 in United Kingdom to institutions; EUR 363 in Europe to institutions; USD 452 elsewhere to institutions (effective 2012).
Indexed: A01, A02, A03, A08, A12, A13, A17, A22, A23, A25, A26, ABIn, ADPA, AEI, ASCA, ASSIA, B01, B02, B06, B07, B08, B09, B13, B15, B17, B18, B21, B28, BMT, BPIA, BusI, C06, C07, C12, CA, CIS, CISA, CPM, CurCont, DIP, E-psyche, E01, E08, E10, E15, ERA, ESPM, Emerald, ErgAb, FR, Faml, G04, G06, G07, G08, H&SSA, HRA, HlthInd, I05, IBR, IBSS, IBZ, ILD, IndMed, Inspec, M01, M02, ManagCont, NPPA, P02, P03, P06, P10, P12, P21, P25, P26, P30, P43, P48, P51, P53, P54, PAIS, PCI, PQC, PersLit, PsycInfo, PsycholAb, RASB, S02, S03, S08, S09, S21, SCIMP, SCOPUS, SOPODA, SSCI, SociolAb, T&II, T02, V05, W07.
—BLDSC (5026.082000), AskIEEE, IE, Infotrieve, Ingenta, INIST. **CCC.**
Published by: (The British Psychological Society), John Wiley & Sons Ltd. (Subsidiary of: John Wiley & Sons, Inc.), 9600 Garsington Rd, Oxford, OX4 2DQ, United Kingdom. TEL 44-1865-776868, FAX 44-1865-714591, customer@wiley.co.uk, http://www.wiley.com. Ed. Jan de Jonge. Adv. contact Julie Neason TEL 44-116-2529580. page GBP 360; trim 174 x 247.

150 331.252 155.946 GBR ISSN 1746-0999
JOURNAL OF OCCUPATIONAL PSYCHOLOGY, EMPLOYMENT AND DISABILITY (ONLINE). Text in English. 2002. s-a. GBP 30 to individuals; GBP 65 to corporations (effective 2009). back issues avail. **Document type:** *Journal, Academic/Scholarly.* **Description:** Aims to increase the understanding of, and to provide a forum for sharing good practice in applying occupational psychology to employment and disability.
Media: Online - full text.
Published by: Great Britain. Department for Work and Pensions, Psychology Division, SOL Litigation, Rm 511, New Court, 48 Carey St, London, WC2A 2LS, United Kingdom. enquiries@dwp.gsi.gov.uk. **Subscr. to:** B3 Porterbrook House, 7 Pear St, Sheffield S11 8JF, United Kingdom. TEL 44-114-2597905.

JOURNAL OF OFFENDER REHABILITATION; a multidisciplinary journal of innovation in research, services, and programs in corrections and criminal justice. *see* CRIMINOLOGY AND LAW ENFORCEMENT

302 GBR ISSN 0894-3796
HD6951 CODEN: JORBEJ
➤ **JOURNAL OF ORGANIZATIONAL BEHAVIOR.** Text in English. 1979. 8/yr. GBP 1,307 in United Kingdom to institutions; EUR 1,654 in Europe to institutions; USD 2,561 elsewhere to institutions; GBP 1,504 combined subscription in United Kingdom to institutions (print & online eds.); EUR 1,902 combined subscription in Europe to institutions (print & online eds.); USD 2,946 combined subscription elsewhere to institutions (print & online eds.) (effective 2012). adv. illus. back issues avail.; reprint service avail. from PSC. **Document type:** *Journal, Academic/Scholarly.* **Description:** Aims to report and review the growing research in the industry-organizational behavior fields, and in all topics associated with occupational-organizational behavior.
Formerly (until 1988): Journal of Occupational Behaviour (0142-2774)
Related titles: Microform ed.: (from PQC); Online - full text ed.: ISSN 1099-1379. GBP 1,307 in United Kingdom to institutions; EUR 1,654 in Europe to institutions; USD 2,561 elsewhere to institutions (effective 2012).
Indexed: A12, A13, A14, A17, A18, A20, A22, A26, ABIn, ASCA, ASSIA, B01, B02, B06, B07, B08, B09, B11, B15, B16, B17, B18, BPIA, BusI, CA, CJA, CPM, CommAb, CurCont, DIP, E-psyche, E08, ERA, ESPM, Emerald, ErgAb, Faml, G04, G06, G07, G08, HRA, I05, IBR, IBZ, ILD, Inspec, N06, NPPA, P03, P10, P12, P13, P21, P25, P30, P48, P51, P53, P54, PCI, PMA, PQC, PRA, PsycInfo, PsycholAb, RASB, RiskAb, S02, S03, S09, SCIMP, SCOPUS, SOPODA, SSCI, SociolAb, T&II, T02, W07.
—IE, Infotrieve, Ingenta. **CCC.**
Published by: John Wiley & Sons Ltd. (Subsidiary of: John Wiley & Sons, Inc.), 1-7 Oldlands Way, PO Box 808, Bognor Regis, West Sussex PO21 9FF, United Kingdom. TEL 44-1865-778315, FAX 44-1243-843232, cs-journals@wiley.com, http://eu.wiley.com/WileyCDA/. Ed. Neal M Ashkanasy. **Subscr. in the Americas to:** John Wiley & Sons, Inc., 111 River St, Hoboken, NJ 07030. TEL 201-748-6645, subinfo@wiley.com; **Subscr. to:** 1-7 Oldlands Way, PO Box 809, Bognor Regis, West Sussex PO21 9FG, United Kingdom. TEL 44-1865-778054, cs-agency@wiley.com.

150 USA ISSN 0160-8061
HD58.7 CODEN: JOBMF7
➤ **JOURNAL OF ORGANIZATIONAL BEHAVIOR MANAGEMENT.** Abbreviated title: J O B M. Text in English. 1977. q. GBP 674 combined subscription in United Kingdom to institutions (print & online eds.); EUR 877, USD 880 combined subscription to institutions (print & online eds.) (effective 2012). adv. bk.rev. illus. 120 p./no.; back issues avail.; reprint service avail. from PSC. **Document type:** *Journal, Academic/Scholarly.* **Description:** Deals with behavior management in organizations; provides systematic and effective approaches to behavior management.
Related titles: Microfiche ed.: (from PQC); Microform ed.; Online - full text ed.: ISSN 1540-8604. GBP 606 in United Kingdom to institutions; EUR 789, USD 791 to institutions (effective 2012).
Indexed: A01, A03, A12, A13, A17, A22, A26, ABIn, AHCMS, ASCA, B01, B02, B06, B07, B08, B09, B11, B15, B16, B17, B18, BPIA, BehAb, BusEdI, BusI, C12, CA, CurCont, DIP, E-psyche, E01, E03, E07, E08, EAA, ERI, ERIC, ErgAb, G04, G06, G07, G08, HRA, I05, IBR, IBZ, M&MA, M02, ManagCont, N06, ORMS, P03, P04, P10, P12, P13, P25, P30, P48, P51, P53, P54, PCI, PMA, PQC, PersLit, PsycInfo, PsycholAb, QC&AS, RefZh, S09, SCOPUS, SOPODA, SSCI, T&DA, T&II, T02, W07.
—BLDSC (5027.068000), IE, Infotrieve, Ingenta. **CCC.**
Published by: Routledge (Subsidiary of: Taylor & Francis Group), 325 Chestnut St, Ste 800, Philadelphia, PA 19106. TEL 215-625-8900, 800-354-1420, FAX 215-625-8914, journals@routledge.com, http://www.routledge.com. Ed. Timothy D Ludwig. adv.: B&W page USD 315, color page USD 550; trim 4.375 x 7.125. Circ: 530 (paid).

150 USA ISSN 1949-4890
▼ ➤ **JOURNAL OF ORGANIZATIONAL MORAL PSYCHOLOGY.** Text in English. 2010 (Jan.). q. USD 245 to institutions; USD 367 combined subscription to institutions (print & online eds.) (effective 2012). **Document type:** *Journal, Academic/Scholarly.* **Description:** Features research on topics in organizational moral psychology.
Related titles: Online - full text ed.: USD 245 to institutions (effective 2012).
Published by: Nova Science Publishers, Inc., 400 Oser Ave, Ste 1600, Hauppauge, NY 11788. TEL 631-231-7269, FAX 631-231-8175, journals@novapublishers.com.

150 AUS ISSN 1834-4909
➤ **JOURNAL OF PACIFIC RIM PSYCHOLOGY.** Abbreviated title: J P R P. Text in English. 1984. s-a. USD 150 domestic; USD 165 foreign (effective 2011). adv. bk.rev. back issues avail. **Document type:** *Journal, Academic/Scholarly.* **Description:** Provides scholarly and applied articles on a wide range of issues from climate change to disaster management and poverty reduction with indigenous and minority perspective.
Formerly (until 2005): South Pacific Journal of Psychology (Print) (0257-5434)
Media: Online - full text.
Indexed: A01, CA, E-psyche, SCOPUS, SSCI, T02, W07.
Published by: Australian Academic Press Pty. Ltd., 32 Jeays St, Bowen Hills, QLD 4006, Australia. TEL 61-7-32571176, FAX 61-7-32525908, 61-7-32525908, aap@australianacademicpress.com.au, http://www.australianacademicpress.com.au. Circ: 2,245.

➤ **JOURNAL OF PARAPSYCHOLOGY.** *see* PARAPSYCHOLOGY AND OCCULTISM

➤ **JOURNAL OF PASTORAL CARE & COUNSELING.** *see* RELIGIONS AND THEOLOGY

155.4 GBR ISSN 0146-8693
RJ503.3 CODEN: JPPSDW
➤ **JOURNAL OF PEDIATRIC PSYCHOLOGY.** Text in English. 1976. 10/yr. GBP 659 in United Kingdom to institutions; EUR 990 in Europe to institutions; USD 990 in US & Canada to institutions; GBP 659 elsewhere to institutions; GBP 719 combined subscription in United Kingdom to institutions (print & online eds.); EUR 1,080 combined subscription in Europe to institutions (print & online eds.); USD 1,080 combined subscription in US & Canada to institutions (print & online eds.); GBP 719 combined subscription elsewhere to institutions (print & online eds.) (effective 2012). adv. bk.rev. illus. Index. back issues avail.; reprint service avail. from PSC. **Document type:** *Journal, Academic/Scholarly.* **Description:** Disseminates original research relating broadly to the multidimensional functioning and development of children, adolescents and families or issues related to pediatric health and illness.
Formerly: Pediatric Psychology
Related titles: Microfilm ed.: (from PQC); Online - full text ed.: ISSN 1465-735X. GBP 599 in United Kingdom to institutions; EUR 900 in Europe to institutions; USD 900 in US & Canada to institutions; GBP 599 elsewhere to institutions (effective 2012) (from IngentaConnect).
Indexed: A22, ASCA, BDM&CN, C06, C07, CA, CDA, CurCont, E-psyche, E01, E03, EMBASE, ESPM, ExcerpMed, F09, FR, FamI, INI, IndMed, MEDLINE, P03, P30, PsycInfo, PsycholAb, R10, Reac, RiskAb, S02, S03, SCOPUS, SFSA, SOPODA, SSCI, SWR&A, SociolAb, T02, W07.
—BLDSC (5030.260000), GNLM, IE, Infotrieve, Ingenta, INIST. **CCC.**
Published by: (Society of Pediatric Psychology, Division 54 USA), Oxford University Press, Great Clarendon St, Oxford, OX2 6DP, United Kingdom. TEL 44-1865-556767, FAX 44-1865-556646, enquiry@oup.co.uk, http://www.oxfordjournals.org. Ed. Dennis Drotar TEL 513-636-3936. Pub. Janet Fox.

155.2 USA ISSN 0022-3506
CODEN: JOPEAE
➤ **JOURNAL OF PERSONALITY.** Text in English. 1932. bi-m. GBP 996 in United Kingdom to institutions; EUR 1,264 in Europe to institutions; USD 1,166 in the Americas to institutions; USD 1,951 elsewhere to institutions; GBP 1,145 combined subscription in United Kingdom to institutions (print & online eds.); EUR 1,454 combined subscription in Europe to institutions (print & online eds.); USD 1,341 combined subscription in the Americas to institutions (print & online eds.); USD 2,243 combined subscription elsewhere to institutions (print & online eds.) (effective 2012). bibl.; charts; illus. index. reprint service avail. from PSC. **Document type:** *Journal, Academic/Scholarly.* **Description:** Publishes studies in the fields of personality and behavior dynamics that focus on personality development and individual differences in the cognitive affective and interpersonal domains. Reflects and stimulates growth in new theoretical and methodological approaches.
Formerly (until 1945): Character and Personality (0730-6407)
Related titles: Online - full text ed.: ISSN 1467-6494. GBP 996 in United Kingdom to institutions; EUR 1,264 in Europe to institutions; USD 1,166 in the Americas to institutions; USD 1,951 elsewhere to institutions (effective 2012) (from IngentaConnect).
Indexed: A01, A02, A03, A08, A20, A22, A25, A26, AMHA, ASCA, ASSIA, AcaI, B04, BRD, C06, C07, C28, CA, CommAb, CurCont, DIP, E-psyche, E01, E06, E08, EMBASE, ESPM, ExcerpMed, F09, FR, FamI, G08, G10, H09, I05, IBR, IBSS, IBZ, IndMed, MEA&I, MEDLINE, MLA-IB, P02, P03, P10, P12, P13, P27, P30, P43, P48, P53, P54, PC&CA, PCI, PQC, PRA, PsycInfo, PsycholAb, R10, RASB, Reac, RiskAb, S02, S03, S05, S08, S09, S21, SCOPUS, SFSA, SOPODA, SSAI, SSAb, SSCI, SSI, SociolAb, T02, W03, W07, W09.
—BLDSC (5030.900000), GNLM, IE, Infotrieve, Ingenta, INIST. **CCC.**
Published by: Wiley-Blackwell Publishing, Inc. (Subsidiary of: Wiley-Blackwell Publishing Ltd.), 111 River St, Hoboken, NJ 07030. TEL 201-748-6000, FAX 201-748-6088, info@wiley.com, http://www.wiley.com/WileyCDA/. Ed. Howard Tennen. Adv. contact Kristin McCarthy TEL 201-748-7683.

155.2 USA ISSN 0022-3514
HM251 CODEN: JPSPB2
➤ **JOURNAL OF PERSONALITY AND SOCIAL PSYCHOLOGY.** Text in English. 1965. m. USD 548 domestic to individuals; USD 601 foreign to individuals; USD 1,696 domestic to institutions; USD 1,798 foreign to institutions (effective 2011). adv. charts; stat.; illus. index. back issues avail.; reprint service avail. from PSC. **Document type:** *Journal, Academic/Scholarly.* **Description:** Covers research in three major areas: attitudes and social cognition; interpersonal relations and group processes; and personality processes and individual differences.
Supersedes in part (in 1965): Journal of Abnormal and Social Psychology (0096-851X); Which was formerly (until 1925): The Journal of Abnormal Psychology and Social Psychology (0145-2347); (until 1921): The Journal of Abnormal Psychology (0145-2339)
Related titles: Microform ed.: (from PQC); Online - full text ed.: ISSN 1939-1315 (from ScienceDirect).
Indexed: A01, A02, A03, A08, A12, A20, A21, A22, A25, A26, ABIn, ABS&EES, AMHA, ASCA, ASSIA, AcaI, B01, B02, B06, B07, B09, B15, B17, B18, BAS, BRD, C28, CA, CDA, CIS, CMM, ChPerI, Chicano, CommAb, CurCont, DIP, E-psyche, E08, EAA, EMBASE, ExcerpMed, F09, FR, FamI, G04, G08, G10, H09, HEA, HRA, I05, IBR, IBSS, IBZ, INI, IndMed, M01, M02, MEA&I, MEDLINE, MLA, MLA-IB, MResA, P02, P03, P10, P12, P13, P21, P27, P30, P34, P48, P50, P51, P53, P54, PCI, PQC, PRA, PSI, PsycInfo, PsycholAb, R10, RASB, RI-1, RI-2, RILM, Reac, S02, S03, S05, S08, S09, S21, SCOPUS, SFSA, SOPODA, SRRA, SSA, SSAI, SSAb, SSCI, SSI, SWR&A, SociolAb, SportS, T02, V&AA, W01, W02, W03, W07, W09.
—BLDSC (5030.901000), GNLM, IE, Infotrieve, Ingenta, INIST. **CCC.**
Published by: American Psychological Association, 750 First St, NE, Washington, DC 20002. TEL 202-336-5500, 800-374-2721, FAX 202-336-5997, journals@apa.org. Eds. Dr. Charles M Judd, Jeffry A Simpson, Laura A King. Circ: 2,300.

155.2 USA ISSN 0022-3891
BF698.4
➤ **JOURNAL OF PERSONALITY ASSESSMENT.** Abbreviated title: J P A. Text in English. 1936. bi-m. (in 2 vols.). GBP 456 combined subscription in United Kingdom to institutions (print & online eds.); EUR 607, USD 763 combined subscription to institutions (print & online eds.) (effective 2012). adv. bk.rev. abstr.; bibl.; charts; illus. index. back issues avail.; reprint service avail. from PSC. **Document type:** *Journal, Academic/Scholarly.* **Description:** Presents commentaries, case reports, and research studies dealing with the application of methods of personality assessment.
Former titles (until 1971): Journal of Projective Techniques and Personality Assessment (0091-651X); (until 1963): Journal of Projective Techniques (0885-3126); (until 1950): Rorschach Research Exchange and Journal of Projective Techniques (1068-3402); (until 1947): Rorschach Research Exchange (0893-4037)
Related titles: Microform ed.: (from PQC); Online - full text ed.: ISSN 1532-7752. GBP 410 in United Kingdom to institutions; EUR 547, USD 687 to institutions (effective 2012).
Indexed: A01, A03, A08, A20, A22, AEI, AMHA, ASCA, ASG, ASSIA, B01, B06, B07, B09, B21, CA, CDA, CISA, Chicano, CurCont, E-psyche, E01, ECER, EMBASE, ESPM, ExcerpMed, F09, FR, FamI, G10, H&SSA, INI, IPsyAb, IndMed, MEA&I, MEDLINE, P02, P03, P10, P12, P20, P30, P43, P48, P53, P54, PCI, PQC, PsycInfo, PsycholAb, R09, R10, RASB, Reac, RiskAb, S02, S03, SCOPUS, SD, SSCI, SociolAb, T02, W07, W09.
—BLDSC (5030.950000), GNLM, IE, Infotrieve, Ingenta, INIST. **CCC.**
Published by: (Society for Personality Assessment), Routledge (Subsidiary of: Taylor & Francis Group), 325 Chestnut St, Ste 800, Philadelphia, PA 19106. TEL 800-354-1420, FAX 215-625-2940, journals@routledge.com, http://www.routledge.com. Ed. Gregory J Meyer. Adv. contact Linda Hann TEL 44-1344-779945.

370.15 USA ISSN 0885-579X
RC554
➤ **JOURNAL OF PERSONALITY DISORDERS.** Text in English. 1987. bi-m. USD 115 combined subscription domestic to individuals (print & online eds.); USD 150 combined subscription foreign to individuals (print & online eds.); USD 635 combined subscription domestic to institutions (print & online eds.); USD 680 combined subscription foreign to institutions (print & online eds.) (effective 2011). adv. bk.rev. index. 96 p./no.; back issues avail.; reprints avail. **Document type:** *Journal, Academic/Scholarly.* **Description:** Presents new research, and clinical techniques for assessing, diagnosing and treating personality disorders.
Related titles: Online - full text ed.: ISSN 1943-2763.
Indexed: A01, A03, A08, A22, ASCA, C06, C07, C08, CA, CINAHL, CurCont, DIP, E-psyche, E01, E03, EMBASE, ERI, ExcerpMed, FR, FamI, IBR, IBZ, IndMed, MEDLINE, P03, P18, P20, P22, P24, P25, P26, P27, P30, P48, P53, P54, P55, PQC, PsycInfo, PsycholAb, R10, Reac, S02, S03, SCOPUS, SOPODA, SSCI, SWR&A, SociolAb, T02, W07.
—BLDSC (5030.955000), GNLM, IE, Infotrieve, Ingenta, INIST. **CCC.**
Published by: (International Society for the Study of Personality Disorders), Guilford Publications, Inc., 72 Spring St, 4th Fl, New York, NY 10012. TEL 800-365-7006, FAX 212-966-6708, info@guilford.com. Ed. Paul S Links. R&P Kathy Kuehl. Adv. contact Marian Robinson. Circ: 1,100 (paid).

158.1 DEU ISSN 1866-5888
JOURNAL OF PERSONNEL PSYCHOLOGY. Text in English, German. 2002. q. EUR 199 to institutions; EUR 66 newsstand/cover (effective 2011). adv. **Document type:** *Journal, Academic/Scholarly.* **Description:** Dedicated to international research in psychology as it relates to the working environment and the people who "inhabit" it.
Formerly (until 2009): Zeitschrift fuer Personalpsychologie (1617-6391)
Related titles: Online - full text ed.: ISSN 2190-5150 (from ScienceDirect).
Indexed: CurCont, DIP, E15, E16, ERA, IBR, IBZ, M12, P03, PsycInfo, PsycholAb, S19, S20, S21, SCOPUS, SSCI, V05, W07.
—BLDSC (5030.972000), IE, Ingenta. **CCC.**
Published by: Hogrefe Verlag GmbH & Co. KG, Rohnsweg 25, Goettingen, 37085, Germany. TEL 49-551-496090, FAX 49-551-4960988, verlag@hogrefe.de. Ed. Rolf van Dick. Circ: 600 (paid and controlled).

150 NLD ISSN 0047-2662
BF204.5 CODEN: JPHPAE
➤ **JOURNAL OF PHENOMENOLOGICAL PSYCHOLOGY.** Text in English. 1970. s-a. EUR 152, USD 212 to institutions; EUR 166, USD 232 combined subscription to institutions (print & online eds.) (effective 2012). adv. bk.rev. index. back issues avail.; reprint service avail. from PSC. **Document type:** *Journal, Academic/Scholarly.* **Description:** Publishes articles that advance the discipline of psychology from a phenomenological perspective as understood by scholars who work within the continental sense of phenomenology.
Related titles: Microform ed.: (from PQC); Online - full text ed.: ISSN 1569-1624. EUR 138, USD 193 to institutions (effective 2012) (from IngentaConnect).
Indexed: A01, A02, A03, A08, A20, A22, A26, ASCA, B02, B15, B17, B18, CA, DIP, E-psyche, E01, E08, FR, FamI, G04, G06, G07, G08, I05, IBR, IBZ, IPB, IZBG, P03, P25, P43, P48, PCI, PQC, PhilInd, PsycInfo, PsycholAb, RASB, S09, SCOPUS, T02.
—BLDSC (5034.100000), IE, Infotrieve, Ingenta. **CCC.**
Published by: Brill, PO Box 9000, Leiden, 2300 PA, Netherlands. TEL 31-71-5353500, FAX 31-71-5317532, cs@brill.nl. Ed. Frederick J Wertz. adv.: B&W page USD 150; trim 9 x 6. Circ: 200. **Dist. by:** Turpin Distribution Services Ltd., Pegasus Dr, Stratton Business Park, Biggleswade, Bedfordshire SG18 8QB, United Kingdom. TEL 44-1767-604954, FAX 44-1767-601640, custserv@turpin-distribution.com, http://www.turpin-distribution.com/.

808.81 616.89 GBR ISSN 0889-3675
CODEN: JPTHEK
➤ **JOURNAL OF POETRY THERAPY.** Abbreviated title: J P T. Text in English. 1987. q. GBP 511 combined subscription in United Kingdom to institutions (print & online eds.); EUR 613, USD 769 combined subscription to institutions (print & online eds.) (effective 2012). adv. bk.rev. abstr. back issues avail.; reprint service avail. from PSC. **Document type:** *Journal, Academic/Scholarly.* **Description:** Addresses the use of poetics in health, mental health, education, and other human service settings, focusing on the use of language in therapy.
Related titles: Online - full text ed.: ISSN 1567-2344. GBP 460 in United Kingdom to institutions; EUR 551, USD 692 to institutions (effective 2012) (from IngentaConnect).
Indexed: A22, A26, BibInd, C06, C07, CA, DIP, E-psyche, E01, E03, ERI, FamI, I05, IBR, IBZ, MLA-IB, P48, PQC, S02, S03, SWR&A, SociolAb, T02.
—IE, Infotrieve, Ingenta. **CCC.**
Published by: (National Association for Poetry Therapy USA, Florida State University, School of Social Work USA), Routledge (Subsidiary of: Taylor & Francis Group), 4 Park Sq, Milton Park, Abingdon, Oxon OX14 4RN, United Kingdom. TEL 44-20-70176000, FAX 44-20-70176336, subscriptions@tandf.co.uk, http://www.routledge.com. Ed. Dr. Nicholas Mazza. Adv. contact Linda Hann TEL 44-1344-779945. **Subscr. to:** Taylor & Francis Ltd., Journals Customer Service, Sheepen Pl, Colchester, Essex CO3 3LP, United Kingdom. TEL 44-20-70175544, FAX 44-20-70175198, tf.enquiries@tfinforma.com.

➤ **JOURNAL OF POLICE AND CRIMINAL PSYCHOLOGY.** *see* CRIMINOLOGY AND LAW ENFORCEMENT

150 USA ISSN 1098-3007
RJ505.B4
➤ **JOURNAL OF POSITIVE BEHAVIOR INTERVENTIONS.** Text in English. 1999. q. USD 164, GBP 96 combined subscription to institutions (print & online eds.); USD 161, GBP 94 to institutions (effective 2011). adv. back issues avail.; reprint service avail. from PSC. **Document type:** *Journal, Academic/Scholarly.* **Description:** Provides a forum for researchers, professionals, families, and policymakers concerned with the behavior of individuals with developmental and behavioral disabilities.
Related titles: Microform ed.: (from PQC); Online - full text ed.: ISSN 1538-4772. USD 148, GBP 86 to institutions (effective 2011).
Indexed: A01, A03, A08, A22, A25, A26, B04, BRD, C06, C07, CA, CurCont, E-psyche, E01, E02, E03, E07, E08, E09, E16, ERA, ERI, ERIC, EdA, EdI, G08, I05, P02, P03, P10, P12, P18, P25, P30, P43, P48, P53, P54, P55, PQC, PsycInfo, PsycholAb, S02, S03, S08, S09, S20, S21, SCOPUS, SSCI, T02, V05, W03, W05, W07.
—BLDSC (5041.147700), IE, Ingenta. **CCC.**
Published by: Sage Publications, Inc., 2455 Teller Rd, Thousand Oaks, CA 91320. TEL 805-499-9774, 800-818-7243, FAX 805-499-0871, 800-583-2665, info@sagepub.com, http://www.sagepub.com. Eds. Robert Koegel, V Mark Durand. adv.: page USD 400. Circ: 1,600 (paid and free).

150 GBR ISSN 1743-9760
BF204.6
➤ **THE JOURNAL OF POSITIVE PSYCHOLOGY**; dedicated to furthering research and promoting good practice. Text in English. 2006. bi-m. GBP 371 combined subscription in United Kingdom to institutions (print & online eds.); EUR 538, USD 672 combined subscription to institutions (print & online eds.) (effective 2012). adv. back issues avail.; reprint service avail. from PSC. **Document type:** *Journal, Academic/Scholarly.* **Description:** Provides an interdisciplinary and international forum for the science and application of positive psychology.
Related titles: Online - full text ed.: ISSN 1743-9779. GBP 334 in United Kingdom to institutions; EUR 484, USD 604 to institutions (effective 2012).
Indexed: A01, A22, ASSIA, B07, C06, C07, CA, E01, P03, P30, PsycInfo, SCOPUS, T02.
—IE, Ingenta. **CCC.**
Published by: Routledge (Subsidiary of: Taylor & Francis Group), 4 Park Sq, Milton Park, Abingdon, Oxon OX14 4RN, United Kingdom. TEL 44-20-70176000, FAX 44-20-70176336, subscriptions@tandf.co.uk, http://www.routledge.com. Ed. Robert A Emmons. Adv. contact Linda Hann TEL 44-1344-779945. **Subscr. to:** Taylor & Francis Ltd., Journals Customer Service, Sheepen Pl, Colchester, Essex CO3 3LP, United Kingdom. TEL 44-20-70175544, FAX 44-20-70175198.

➤ **JOURNAL OF PRENATAL & PERINATAL PSYCHOLOGY & HEALTH.** *see* MEDICAL SCIENCES—Obstetrics And Gynecology

P

613 USA ISSN 0278-095X
RA790.A1 CODEN: JPPRDT
➤ **THE JOURNAL OF PRIMARY PREVENTION.** Abbreviated title: J P P. Text in English. 1980. 5/yr. EUR 1,092, USD 1,163 combined subscription to institutions (print & online eds.) (effective 2012). adv. bk.rev. back issues avail.; reprint service avail. from PSC. **Document type:** *Journal, Academic/Scholarly.* **Description:** Presents theoretical, empirical, and methodological research on preventative intervention in human services, and discusses innovative programs and concepts.
Formerly (until 1981): Journal of Prevention (0163-514X)
Related titles: Online - full text ed.: ISSN 1573-6547 (from IngentaConnect).
Indexed: A22, A26, AMHA, B21, BibLing, C06, C07, CA, CJA, CurCont, DIP, E-psyche, E01, E03, E07, EMBASE, ERI, ERIC, ESPM, ExcerpMed, F09, Faml, H&SSA, I05, IBR, IBZ, MEDLINE, P03, P19, P20, P22, P25, P30, P48, P50, P54, PQC, PsycInfo, PsycholAb, R10, Reac, RiskAb, S02, S03, SCOPUS, SOPODA, SSA, SSCI, SWR&A, SociolAb, T02, W07.
—BLDSC (5042.370000), GNLM, IE, Infotrieve, Ingenta. **CCC.**
Published by: (Vermont Conference on Primary Prevention of Psychopathology), Springer New York LLC (Subsidiary of: Springer Science+Business Media), 233 Spring St, New York, NY 10013. TEL 212-460-1500, FAX 212-460-1575, service-ny@springer.com, http://www.springer.com/. Ed. Susan R Tortolero TEL 713-500-9634.

153.4 USA ISSN 1932-6246
QA63
THE JOURNAL OF PROBLEM SOLVING. Text in English. 2006. q. free (effective 2011). **Document type:** *Journal, Academic/Scholarly.* **Description:** Features articles from psychology, neuroscience, computer science and mathematics fields on problem solving abilities in human beings.
Media: Online - full text.
Indexed: A01, E02, EdA, EdI, T02, W03, W05.
Published by: Purdue University Press, Stewart Center 370, 504 W State St, West Lafayette, IN 47907. TEL 765-494-2038, FAX 765-496-2442, pupress@purdue.edu, http://www.thepress.purdue.edu. Ed. Zygmunt Pizlo.

JOURNAL OF PSYCHIATRY, PSYCHOLOGY AND MENTAL HEALTH. *see* MEDICAL SCIENCES—Psychiatry And Neurology

JOURNAL OF PSYCHOACTIVE DRUGS; a multidisciplinary forum. *see* DRUG ABUSE AND ALCOHOLISM

JOURNAL OF PSYCHOEDUCATIONAL ASSESSMENT. *see* EDUCATION

900 150 USA ISSN 0145-3378
HQ768 CODEN: JOPSDP
➤ **JOURNAL OF PSYCHOHISTORY.** Text in English. 1973. q. USD 34 (effective 2011). adv. bk.rev. illus. 110 p./no.; reprints avail. **Document type:** *Journal, Academic/Scholarly.* **Description:** Contains research in the psychological study of history.
Incorporates (1980-1987): Journal of Psychoanalytic Anthropology (0278-2944); Which was formerly (until 1980): Journal of Psychological Anthropology (0161-3308); Formerly (until 1976): History of Childhood Quarterly (0091-4266)
Related titles: Microfilm ed.: (from PQC); Online - full text ed.
Indexed: A01, A20, A21, A22, ASCA, AmH&L, BAS, CA, CDA, CLFP, ChLitAb, CurCont, E-psyche, E06, EMBASE, ExcerpMed, Faml, HistAb, MEA&I, MEDLINE, MLA-IB, P03, P25, P30, P48, PCI, PQC, PsycInfo, PsycholAb, RI-1, RI-2, RefZh, S02, S03, SCOPUS, SOPODA, SSCI, SWR&A, SociolAb, T02, V&AA, W07.
—BLDSC (5043.280000), IE, Infotrieve, Ingenta. **CCC.**
Published by: Association for Psychohistory, Inc., 140 Riverside Dr, Ste 14H, New York, NY 10024. TEL 212-799-2294, FAX 212-799-2294, psychhst@tiac.net. Ed. Lloyd deMause.

➤ **JOURNAL OF PSYCHOLINGUISTIC RESEARCH.** *see* LINGUISTICS

150 IND ISSN 0022-3972
BF1 CODEN: JPSRB8
JOURNAL OF PSYCHOLOGICAL RESEARCHES. Text in English. 1957. 3/yr. bk.rev. charts. index. reprints avail. **Document type:** *Journal, Government.*
Related titles: Microform ed.: (from PQC).
Indexed: A22, BAS, E-psyche, F09, IPsyAb, PsycholAb, S02, S03.
—BLDSC (5043.310000), IE, Ingenta.
Published by: Madras Psychology Society, University of Madras, Department of Psychology, Chennai, Tamil Nadu 600 005, India.

150 USA ISSN 0895-8750
BF698.A1
➤ **JOURNAL OF PSYCHOLOGICAL TYPE.** Abbreviated title: J P T. Text in English. 1977. q. USD 36 to institutions; USD 150 for Academic (effective 2010). adv. back issues avail.; reprints avail. **Document type:** *Journal, Academic/Scholarly.* **Description:** Publishes research, theoretical discussions and applications of psychological type and the Myers-Briggs Type Indicator.
Formerly (until vol.7): Research in Psychological Type
Related titles: Online - full text ed.: ISSN 1938-3290.
Indexed: E-psyche, P03, PsycInfo, PsycholAb.
—IE, Ingenta.
Published by: Center for Applications of Psychological Type, 2815 NW 13th St, Ste 401, Gainesville, FL 32609. TEL 352-375-0160, 800-777-2278, FAX 352-378-0503, customerservice@capt.org.

150 USA ISSN 0022-3980
BF1 CODEN: JOPSAM
➤ **THE JOURNAL OF PSYCHOLOGY**; interdisciplinary and applied. Text in English. 1935. bi-m. GBP 231 combined subscription in United Kingdom to institutions (print & online eds.); EUR 305, USD 382 combined subscription to institutions (print & online eds.) (effective 2012). adv. bibl. index. back issues avail.; reprint service avail. from PSC. **Document type:** *Journal, Academic/Scholarly.* **Description:** Provides forum for genuinely new avenues of thinking and research, particularly with reference to education, industry, management, measurement and assessment.
Related titles: Online - full text ed.: ISSN 1940-1019. GBP 208 in United Kingdom to institutions; EUR 275, USD 343 to institutions (effective 2012).
Indexed: A01, A02, A03, A06, A08, A12, A20, A21, A22, A25, A26, ABIn, AEI, ASSIA, AcaI, B01, B04, B06, B07, B08, B09, BRD, C06, C07, C08, C11, C12, C28, CA, CDA, CERDIC, CINAHL, CIS, ChPerI, ChemAb, Chicano, CommAb, CurCont, DIP, DSHAb, E-psyche, E01, E06, E08, ECER, EMBASE, ERA, ErgAb, ExcerpMed, F09, FR, Faml, G05, G06, G07, G08, G10, H04, H09, H10, H12, HEA, I05, I07, I13, IBR, IBSS, IBZ, IPsyAb, IndMed, M01, M02, M06, M12, MEA&I, MEDLINE, MLA-IB, P02, P03, P10, P12, P20, P22, P24, P25, P26, P27, P30, P42, P43, P48, P51, P53, P54, PCI, PQC, PRA, PsycInfo, PsycholAb, R05, R10, RASB, RI-1, RI-2, RILM, Reac, RefZh, S02, S03, S05, S08, S09, S20, S21, S23, SCOPUS, SD, SOPODA, SSAI, SSAb, SSCI, SSI, SWR&A, SociolAb, T02, W01, W02, W03, W05, W07, W09.
—BLDSC (5043.400000), GNLM, IE, Ingenta, INIST. **CCC.**
Published by: (Helen Dwight Reid Educational Foundation), Routledge (Subsidiary of: Taylor & Francis Group), 325 Chestnut St, Ste 800, Philadelphia, PA 19106. TEL 215-625-8900, FAX 215-625-2940, journals@routledge.com.

150 IND ISSN 0976-4224
▼ **JOURNAL OF PSYCHOLOGY.** Text in English. 2010. s-a. USD 75 domestic (effective 2012). back issues avail. **Document type:** *Journal, Academic/Scholarly.* **Description:** Publishes original papers on current research and practical programmes, short notes, news items, book reviews, reports of meetings and professional announcements on all aspects of social and clinical psychology.
Related titles: Online - full text ed.: free (effective 2012).
Published by: Kamla-Raj Enterprises, 2273 Gali Bari Paharwali, Chawri Bazar, New Delhi, 110 006, India. TEL 91-11-23284126, kre@airtelmail.in.

150 USA ISSN 0733-4273
BR110
➤ **JOURNAL OF PSYCHOLOGY AND CHRISTIANITY.** Abbreviated title: J P C. Text in English. 1982. q. USD 95 to institutions; USD 80 to non-members; free to members (effective 2010). adv. bk.rev. back issues avail.; reprints avail. **Document type:** *Journal, Academic/Scholarly.* **Description:** Investigation of theoretical and applied issues in the relationship of Christianity and the psychological and pastoral professions.
Supersedes (1974-1981): Christian Association for Psychological Studies. Bulletin (0147-7978); Incorporates: Christian Association for Psychological Studies. Proceedings (0092-072X)
Related titles: Microfilm ed.: (from PQC); Online - full text ed.
Indexed: A01, A02, A03, A08, A21, A22, A26, AmHI, B04, BRD, BibInd, CA, ChrPI, DIP, E-psyche, E08, Faml, GSS&RPL, H07, H08, HAb, HumInd, I05, IBR, IBZ, P03, P25, P43, P48, PQC, PSI, PsycInfo, PsycholAb, R&TA, RI-1, RI-2, S02, S03, S09, T02, W03, W05.
—BLDSC (5043.405000), IE, Ingenta. **CCC.**
Published by: Christian Association for Psychological Studies, Inc., PO Box 365, Batavia, IL 60510. TEL 630-639-9478, FAX 630-454-3799, paul.regan@caps.net. Ed., Adv. contact Peter C Hill TEL 562-903-4738.

150 200 USA ISSN 0091-6471
BF1 CODEN: JPSTDG
➤ **JOURNAL OF PSYCHOLOGY AND THEOLOGY**; an evangelical forum for the integration of psychology and theology. Text in English. 1973. q. USD 46 domestic; USD 60 foreign (effective 2011). adv. bk.rev. bibl.; charts; illus. cum index. back issues avail.; reprints avail. **Document type:** *Journal, Academic/Scholarly.* **Description:** Communicates recent scholarly thinking on the interrelationships of psychological and theological concepts and considers the application of these concepts to a variety of professional settings.
Related titles: CD-ROM ed.; Microfilm ed.: (from PQC); Online - full text ed.
Indexed: A01, A02, A03, A08, A20, A21, A22, A26, ASCA, AmHI, ArtHuCI, CA, CCR, CERDIC, ChPerI, ChrPI, CurCont, DIP, E-psyche, E03, E07, E08, ERI, FR, Faml, G08, GSS&RPL, H07, I05, I07, IBR, IBZ, MLA-IB, OTA, P03, P04, P25, P28, P30, P43, P48, P53, P54, PC&CA, PQC, PsycInfo, PsycholAb, PsycholRG, R&TA, R05, RI-1, RI-2, S02, S03, S09, S23, SCOPUS, SSCI, T02, W07.
—BLDSC (5043.420000), IE, Infotrieve, Ingenta.
Published by: Biola University, Rosemead School of Psychology, 13800 Biola Ave, La Mirada, CA 90639-0001. TEL 562-903-4867, FAX 562-906-4864, jpt.subscriptions@biola.edu, http://www.rosemead.edu. Ed. Todd W Hall. Circ: 1,700.

150 ZAF ISSN 1433-0237
BF108.A357
JOURNAL OF PSYCHOLOGY IN AFRICA. Text in English. 1988. 2/yr. bk.rev. **Document type:** *Journal, Academic/Scholarly.* **Description:** Forum for dissemination and utilization of psychological research in Africa and related regions.
Formerly (until 1990): Journal of African Psychology (0795-3097)
Related titles: Online - full text ed.: ISSN 1815-5626 (from IngentaConnect).
Indexed: CA, E-psyche, IBSS, P03, PsycInfo, PsycholAb, S02, S03, SCOPUS, SSCI, SociolAb, T02, W07.
—Ingenta. **CCC.**
Published by: National Inquiry Services Centre, 19 Worcester St., PO Box 377, Grahamstown, 6140, South Africa. TEL 27-46-6229698, FAX 27-46-6229550, publishing@nisc.co.za. Ed. Elias Mpofu.

150 HKG ISSN 1563-3403
BF1
➤ **JOURNAL OF PSYCHOLOGY IN CHINESE SOCIETIES.** Text in English. 1978. s-a. USD 180, USD 24 to individuals; HKD 310, USD 40 to institutions (effective 2001). bk.rev. 155 p./no.; **Document type:** *Journal, Academic/Scholarly.* **Description:** Aims to create a new and integrative forum for discussions and exchanges of research and information across disciplinary and national boundaries by focusing on both differences and similarities in approaches to researching Chinese psychology and empirical data relevant to psychological issues within Chinese societies, including but not limited to social, cognitive, developmental, physiological, and clinical studies.
Formerly (until Feb. 2000): Hong Kong Psychological Society. Bulletin (0379-4490)
Indexed: A01, CA, MLA-IB, P03, P25, P48, PQC, PsycInfo, PsycholAb, T02.
—BLDSC (5043.422000). **CCC.**
Published by: (Hong Kong Psychological Society Ltd.), Zhongwen Daxue Chubanshe/Chinese University Press, The Chinese University of Hong Kong, Shatin, New Territories, Hong Kong. TEL 852-2609-6508, FAX 852-2603-7355, cup@cuhk.edu.hk, http://www.chineseupress.com/. Eds. Leung Y.K. Freedom, Tardif Twila. R&P, Adv. contact Angelina Wong TEL 852-26096500.

150 500 USA ISSN 1939-7062
JOURNAL OF PSYCHOLOGY OF SCIENCE AND TECHNOLOGY (ONLINE). Text in English. 2008. s-a. **Document type:** *Journal, Academic/Scholarly.*
Media: Online - full text.
Published by: (International Society for the Psychology of Science and Technology), Springer Publishing Company, 11 W 42nd St, 15th Fl, New York, NY 10036. TEL 212-431-4370, 877-687-7476, FAX 212-941-7842, journals@springerpub.com, http://www.springerpub.com.

150 USA ISSN 0882-2689
BF698.4 CODEN: JPBAEB
➤ **JOURNAL OF PSYCHOPATHOLOGY AND BEHAVIORAL ASSESSMENT.** Text in English. 1979. q. EUR 1,028, USD 1,066 combined subscription to institutions (print & online eds.) (effective 2012). adv. back issues avail.; reprint service avail. from PSC. **Document type:** *Journal, Academic/Scholarly.* **Description:** Brings out articles on research investigations and clinical case summaries that enhance understanding of psychopathology and mental disorders applicable to all ages.
Formerly (until 1985): Journal of Behavioral Assessment (0164-0305)
Related titles: Microfilm ed.: (from PQC); Online - full text ed.: ISSN 1573-3505 (from IngentaConnect).
Indexed: A01, A03, A08, A20, A22, A26, AMHA, ASCA, ASSIA, B25, BIOSIS Prev, BibLing, C06, C07, CA, CJA, CJPI, CurCont, E-psyche, E01, EMBASE, ExcerpMed, Faml, I05, MycolAb, P03, P25, P30, P48, PQC, PsycInfo, PsycholAb, R10, RASB, Reac, RefZh, S02, S03, SCOPUS, SSCI, SWR&A, T02, W07.
—BLDSC (5043.430000), GNLM, IE, Infotrieve, Ingenta, INIST. **CCC.**
Published by: Springer New York LLC (Subsidiary of: Springer Science+Business Media), 233 Spring St, New York, NY 10013. TEL 212-460-1500, FAX 212-460-1575, service-ny@springer.com, http://www.springer.com/. Ed. Randall Salekin.

➤ **JOURNAL OF PSYCHOPHARMACOLOGY.** *see* PHARMACY AND PHARMACOLOGY

150 301 IND ISSN 0973-5410
HM1001
JOURNAL OF PSYCHOSOCIAL RESEARCH. Text in English. 2006. s-a. **Document type:** *Journal, Academic/Scholarly.*
Indexed: P10, P48, P53, P54, PQC, PsycInfo.
Published by: M D Publications Pvt Ltd, 11 Darya Ganj, New Delhi, 110 002, India. TEL 91-11-41563325, FAX 91-11-23275542, contact@mdppl.com, http://www.mdppl.com.

JOURNAL OF PSYCHOTHERAPY INTEGRATION. *see* MEDICAL SCIENCES—Psychiatry And Neurology

158 USA ISSN 0894-9085
RC489.R3 CODEN: JRCTFK
➤ **JOURNAL OF RATIONAL - EMOTIVE AND COGNITIVE - BEHAVIOR THERAPY.** Text in English. 1966. q. EUR 897, USD 923 combined subscription to institutions (print & online eds.) (effective 2012). adv. bk.rev. illus. back issues avail.; reprint service avail. from PSC. **Document type:** *Journal, Academic/Scholarly.* **Description:** Brings out articles on research, theory, and practice in rational-emotive behavior therapy (REBT) and cognitive behavior therapy (CBT).
Former titles (until 1988): Journal of Rational-Emotive Therapy (0748-1985); (until 1983): Rational Living (0034-0049)
Related titles: Microform ed.: (from PQC); Online - full text ed.: ISSN 1573-6563 (from IngentaConnect).
Indexed: A22, A26, AMHA, ASSIA, B21, BibLing, CA, DIP, E-psyche, E01, FR, Faml, I05, IBR, IBZ, NSA, P03, P20, P25, P27, P30, P48, P54, PQC, PsycInfo, PsycholAb, SCOPUS, T02.
—BLDSC (5046.800000), IE, Infotrieve, Ingenta, INIST. **CCC.**
Published by: Springer New York LLC (Subsidiary of: Springer Science+Business Media), 233 Spring St, New York, NY 10013. TEL 212-460-1500, FAX 212-460-1575, service-ny@springer.com, http://www.springer.com/. Ed. Windy Dryden.

370.1 USA ISSN 1054-0830
RC489.R43
➤ **JOURNAL OF REGRESSION THERAPY.** Text in English. 1986. a. USD 26 per issue (print or online ed.) (effective 2010). bk.rev. back issues avail. **Document type:** *Journal, Academic/Scholarly.* **Description:** Contains articles submitted by professionals in the field of regression therapy.
Related titles: Online - full text ed.: free to members (effective 2010).
Indexed: E-psyche.
Published by: International Association for Regression Research & Therapies, Inc., PO Box 20151, Riverside, CA 92516. TEL 951-784-1570, FAX 951-784-8440, info@iarrt.org. Ed. Lou Siron.

150 AUS ISSN 1838-0956
▼ **JOURNAL OF RELATIONSHIPS RESEARCH.** Text in English. 2010. irreg. AUD 150 domestic; AUD 165 foreign (effective 2011). **Document type:** *Journal, Academic/Scholarly.* **Description:** Covers original articles about all aspects of relationships, social processes and activities that would be of interest to practitioners, researchers, and academics.
Media: Online - full text.
Published by: Australian Academic Press Pty. Ltd., 32 Jeays St, Bowen Hills, QLD 4006, Australia. TEL 61-7-32571176, FAX 61-7-32525908, aap@australianacademicpress.com.au, http://www.australianacademicpress.com.au. Ed. Terry Bowles.

155.3 155.4 GBR ISSN 0264-6838
CODEN: JRIPE3
➤ **JOURNAL OF REPRODUCTIVE AND INFANT PSYCHOLOGY.** Abbreviated title: J R I P. Text in English. 1983. q. GBP 639 combined subscription in United Kingdom to institutions (print & online eds.); EUR 844, USD 1,062 combined subscription to institutions (print & online eds.) (effective 2012). adv. bk.rev. back issues avail.; reprint service avail. from PSC. **Document type:** *Journal, Academic/Scholarly.* **Description:** Reports and reviews research on the psychological, behavioral, medical and social aspects of reproduction, birth and infancy.

Related titles: Online - full text ed.: ISSN 1469-672X. GBP 575 in United Kingdom to institutions; EUR 760, USD 956 to institutions (effective 2012) (from IngentaConnect).
Indexed: A01, A02, A03, A08, A20, A22, B28, C06, C07, C08, CA, CINAHL, CurCont, DIP, E-psyche, E01, EMBASE, ExcerpMed, F09, FR, Faml, H13, IBR, IBZ, P02, P03, P10, P12, P20, P24, P25, P30, P43, P48, P53, P54, PQC, PsycInfo, PsycholAb, R10, Reac, SCOPUS, SOPODA, SSCI, SociolAb, T02, W07, W09.
—BLDSC (5049.620000), GNLM, IE, Infotrieve, Ingenta, INIST. **CCC.**
Published by: (Society for Reproductive and Infant Psychology), Routledge (Subsidiary of: Taylor & Francis Group), 4 Park Sq, Milton Park, Abingdon, Oxon OX14 4RN, United Kingdom. TEL 44-20-70176000, FAX 44-20-70176336, subscriptions@tandf.co.uk, http://www.routledge.com. Ed. Dr. Margaret Redshaw. Adv. contact Linda Hann TEL 44-1344-779945. **Subscr. to:** Taylor & Francis Ltd., Journals Customer Service, Sheepen Pl, Colchester, Essex CO3 3LP, United Kingdom. TEL 44-20-70175544, FAX 44-20-70175198, tf.enquiries@tfinforma.com.

152 USA ISSN 0092-6566
BF1 CODEN: JRPRA6
➤ **JOURNAL OF RESEARCH IN PERSONALITY.** Text in English. 1965. bi-m. EUR 1,076 in Europe to institutions; JPY 112,100 in Japan to institutions; USD 789 elsewhere to institutions (effective 2012). adv. charts. back issues avail.; reprints avail. **Document type:** *Journal, Academic/Scholarly.* **Description:** Examines issues in the field of personality and in related fields basic to the understanding of personality.
Formerly (until 1973): Journal of Experimental Research in Personality (0022-1023)
Related titles: Online - full text ed.: ISSN 1095-7251 (from IngentaConnect, ScienceDirect).
Indexed: A01, A03, A08, A20, A22, A26, AMHA, ASCA, CA, CJA, CommAb, CurCont, DIP, E-psyche, E01, FR, Faml, I05, IBR, IBZ, MEA&I, MLA-IB, P03, P30, PRA, PsycInfo, PsycholAb, RASB, S02, S03, SCOPUS, SSCI, SWR&A, T02, W07, W09.
—BLDSC (5052.025000), GNLM, IE, Infotrieve, Ingenta, INIST. **CCC.**
Published by: Academic Press (Subsidiary of: Elsevier Science & Technology), 3251 Riverport Ln, Maryland Heights, MO 63043. TEL 314-447-8010, FAX 314-447-8030, JournalCustomerService-usa@elsevier.com, http://www.elsevierdirect.com/imprint.jsp?iid=5. Ed. Richard E Lucas. Adv. contact Tino DeCarlo TEL 212-633-3815.

➤ **JOURNAL OF RESEARCH ON ADOLESCENCE.** *see* CHILDREN AND YOUTH—About

➤ **JOURNAL OF RISK AND UNCERTAINTY.** *see* BUSINESS AND ECONOMICS—Economic Systems And Theories, Economic History

➤ **JOURNAL OF RURAL COMMUNITY PSYCHOLOGY (ONLINE).** *see* SOCIOLOGY

150 USA ISSN 1061-0405
BF1
➤ **JOURNAL OF RUSSIAN AND EAST EUROPEAN PSYCHOLOGY.** Abbreviated title: R P O. Text in English. 1962. bi-m. USD 1,348 combined subscription domestic to institutions (print & online eds.); USD 1,456 combined subscription foreign to institutions (print & online eds.) (effective 2012). adv. charts; illus. index. back issues avail.; reprint service avail. from PSC. **Document type:** *Journal, Academic/Scholarly.* **Description:** Contains original submissions and selected translations from the Russian and East European tradition in psychology.
Formerly (until 1992): Soviet Psychology (0038-5751); Which superseded in part (in 1966): Soviet Psychology and Psychiatry (0584-5610)
Related titles: Online - full text ed.: ISSN 1558-0415. 2004 (Feb.). USD 1,257 to institutions (effective 2012).
Indexed: A01, A03, A08, A20, A22, AMHA, B01, B06, B07, B09, CA, E-psyche, E01, IBR, IBZ, P03, P43, PAIS, PsycInfo, PsycholAb, RASB, S02, S03, T02.
—BLDSC (5052.128950), GNLM, IE, Infotrieve, Ingenta. **CCC.**
Published by: M.E. Sharpe, Inc., 80 Business Park Dr, Armonk, NY 10504. TEL 914-273-1800, 800-541-6563, FAX 914-273-2106, custserv@mesharpe.com. Ed. Pentti Hakkarainen. Adv. contact Barbara Ladd TEL 914-273-1800.

615.8 USA ISSN 1089-6457
RC489.S25
➤ **JOURNAL OF SANDPLAY THERAPY.** Abbreviated title: J S T. Text in English. 1991. s-a. USD 52 domestic; USD 63 in Canada; USD 68 in Mexico; USD 77 elsewhere (effective 2010). bk.rev. back issues avail. **Document type:** *Journal, Academic/Scholarly.* **Description:** Contains analytic and psychoanalytic perspectives, clinical cases and theoretical articles on sandplay therapy with children and adults.
Indexed: P03, PsycInfo.
Published by: Sandplay Therapists of America, PO Box 4847, Walnut Creek, CA 94596. TEL 925-478-8103, sta@sanplay.org. Ed. Joyce Camuyrano Cunningham.

370.15 GBR ISSN 0022-4405
LB3013.6 CODEN: JSCPAA
➤ **JOURNAL OF SCHOOL PSYCHOLOGY.** Abbreviated title: J S P. Text in English. 1963. 6/yr. EUR 509 in Europe to institutions; JPY 67,400 in Japan to institutions; USD 572 elsewhere to institutions (effective 2012). adv. bk.rev. abstr.; bibl.; illus. index. back issues avail.; reprints avail. **Document type:** *Journal, Academic/Scholarly.* **Description:** Features original articles on research and practice relevant to the development of school psychology as both a scientific and an applied specialty.
Related titles: Microfilm ed.: (from PQC); Online - full text ed.: ISSN 1873-3506 (from IngentaConnect, ScienceDirect).
Indexed: A01, A03, A08, A20, A22, A26, AEI, AMHA, ASCA, ASSIA, B04, BRD, C28, CA, CIS, CMM, CPE, Chicano, CurCont, E-psyche, E02, E03, E06, ECER, EMBASE, ERA, ERI, ERIC, EdA, Edl, ExcerpMed, Faml, I05, L&LBA, M12, MEDLINE, P03, P30, PCI, PsycInfo, PsycholAb, R10, Reac, S02, S03, S20, S21, SCOPUS, SOPODA, SSCI, SWR&A, SociolAb, T02, W03, W07.
—BLDSC (5052.670000), IE, Infotrieve, Ingenta. **CCC.**
Published by: (Society for the Study of School Psychology USA), Pergamon (Subsidiary of: Elsevier Science & Technology), The Blvd, Langford Ln, East Park, Kidlington, Oxford OX5 1GB, United Kingdom. TEL 44-1865-843000, FAX 44-1865-843010, JournalsCustomerServiceEMEA@elsevier.com. Ed. Edward J Daly III TEL 402-472-5923. **Subscr. to:** Elsevier BV, Radarweg 29, PO Box 211, Amsterdam 1000 AE, Netherlands. http://www.elsevier.nl.

155.3 USA ISSN 0092-623X
RC556 CODEN: JSMTB
➤ **JOURNAL OF SEX & MARITAL THERAPY.** Text in English. 1974. 5/yr. GBP 268 combined subscription in United Kingdom to institutions (print & online eds.); EUR 356, USD 449 combined subscription to institutions (print & online eds.) (effective 2012). adv. bk.rev. illus. index. reprint service avail. from PSC. **Document type:** *Journal, Academic/Scholarly.* **Description:** Provides a contemporary forum on new clinical techniques, conceptualizations and research in sex and marital therapy.
Related titles: Microform ed.: 1974 (from PQC); Online - full text ed.: ISSN 1521-0715. 1974. GBP 241 in United Kingdom to institutions; EUR 320, USD 405 to institutions (effective 2012) (from IngentaConnect).
Indexed: A01, A03, A08, A20, A22, AMHA, ASCA, B28, C06, C07, CA, CurCont, E-psyche, E01, EMBASE, ExcerpMed, F09, FR, Faml, G10, IPsyAb, IndMed, MEA&I, MEDLINE, P03, P30, P43, P48, P50, P53, P54, PQC, PsycInfo, PsycholAb, R10, RASB, Reac, S02, S03, SCOPUS, SFSA, SOPODA, SSCI, SociolAb, T02, W07, W09.
—GNLM, IE, Infotrieve, Ingenta, INIST. **CCC.**
Published by: Routledge (Subsidiary of: Taylor & Francis Group), 325 Chestnut St, Ste 800, Philadelphia, PA 19106. TEL 215-625-8900, FAX 215-625-8914, journals@routledge.com, http://www.routledge.com. Ed. Dr. R Taylor Segraves. Circ: 2,000. **Subscr. addr. in Europe:** Taylor & Francis Ltd., Journals Customer Service, Sheepen Pl, Colchester, Essex CO3 3LP, United Kingdom. TEL 44-20-70175544, FAX 44-20-70175198, tf.enquiries@tfinforma.com.

306.7 USA ISSN 0022-4499
HQ5 CODEN: JSXRAJ
➤ **JOURNAL OF SEX RESEARCH.** Text in English. 1965. bi-m. GBP 302 combined subscription in United Kingdom to institutions (print & online eds.); EUR 399, USD 499 combined subscription to institutions (print & online eds.) (effective 2012). adv. bk.rev. charts; illus.; stat. back issues avail.; reprint service avail. from PSC. **Document type:** *Journal, Academic/Scholarly.* **Description:** Publishes selected research on issues in human sexuality.
Incorporates (in 2007): Annual Review of Sex Research (1053-2528); Formerly (until 196?): Advances in Sex Research (1934-5984)
Related titles: Microfilm ed.: (from PQC); Online - full text ed.: ISSN 1559-8519. GBP 271 in United Kingdom to institutions; EUR 360, USD 449 to institutions (effective 2012).
Indexed: A01, A02, A03, A08, A20, A22, A25, A26, A36, AMHA, ASCA, ASSIA, AbAn, B04, BAS, BRD, C11, CA, CABA, CDA, CLFP, CMM, CWI, ChPerI, Chicano, CurCont, DIP, E-psyche, E01, E08, EMBASE, ExcerpMed, F09, Faml, G08, G10, GH, H04, H11, H12, I05, IBR, IBZ, IPARL, IPsyAb, L01, L02, M01, M02, MEA&I, MEDLINE, MLA-IB, P02, P03, P10, P12, P13, P20, P22, P25, P27, P30, P43, P48, P53, P54, PCI, PQC, PhilInd, PsycInfo, PsycholAb, R10, R12, Reac, S02, S03, S08, S09, SCOPUS, SFSA, SOPODA, SSAI, SSAb, SSCI, SSI, SWR&A, SociolAb, T02, T05, V&AA, W03, W05, W07, W09.
—BLDSC (5064.020000), CIS, GNLM, IE, Infotrieve, Ingenta. **CCC.**
Published by: (Society for the Scientific Study of Sexuality), Routledge (Subsidiary of: Taylor & Francis Group), 325 Chestnut St, Ste 800, Philadelphia, PA 19106. TEL 215-625-8900, 800-354-1420, FAX 215-625-8914, journals@routledge.com, http://www.routledge.com, http://www.tandf.co.uk/journals. Ed. Cynthia Graham. Circ: 1,750.

364.153 GBR ISSN 1355-2600
HQ71 CODEN: JSAGFC
➤ **JOURNAL OF SEXUAL AGGRESSION.** Text in English. 1994. 3/yr. GBP 360 combined subscription in United Kingdom to institutions (print & online eds.); EUR 428, USD 541 combined subscription to institutions (print & online eds.) (effective 2012). adv. bk.rev. back issues avail.; reprint service avail. from PSC. **Document type:** *Journal, Academic/Scholarly.* **Description:** Contains articles on a wide range of topics relating to issues of sexual aggression.
Related titles: Online - full text ed.: ISSN 1742-6545. GBP 323 in United Kingdom to institutions; EUR 386, USD 487 to institutions (effective 2012) (from IngentaConnect).
Indexed: A01, A02, A03, A08, A22, ASSIA, B21, C06, C07, CA, CJA, CJPI, DIP, E-psyche, E01, ERIC, ESPM, FR, Faml, H&SSA, IBR, IBSS, IBZ, P03, P43, PQC, PsycInfo, PsycholAb, S02, S03, SOPODA, SWR&A, SociolAb, T02, V&AA.
—BLDSC (5064.040000), IE, Ingenta, INIST. **CCC.**
Published by: (National Organisation for the Treatment of Abusers, National Association for the Development of Work with Sex Offenders), Routledge (Subsidiary of: Taylor & Francis Group), 4 Park Sq, Milton Park, Abingdon, Oxon OX14 4RN, United Kingdom. TEL 44-20-70176000, FAX 44-20-70176336, subscriptions@tandf.co.uk, http://www.routledge.com. Ed. Dr. Sarah Brown. Adv. contact Linda Hann TEL 44-1344-779945. **Subscr. to:** Taylor & Francis Ltd., Journals Customer Service, Sheepen Pl, Colchester, Essex CO3 3LP, United Kingdom. TEL 44-20-70175544, FAX 44-20-70175198, tf.enquiries@tfinforma.com.

➤ **JOURNAL OF SLEEP RESEARCH (ONLINE).** *see* MEDICAL SCIENCES

➤ **JOURNAL OF SLEEP RESEARCH (PRINT).** *see* MEDICAL SCIENCES

➤ **JOURNAL OF SLEEP RESEARCH. SUPPLEMENT.** *see* MEDICAL SCIENCES

301.1 USA ISSN 0736-7236
RC467 CODEN: JSCPFF
➤ **JOURNAL OF SOCIAL AND CLINICAL PSYCHOLOGY.** Text in English. 1983. 10/yr. USD 170 combined subscription domestic to individuals (print & online eds.); USD 205 combined subscription foreign to individuals (print & online eds.); USD 815 combined subscription domestic to institutions (print & online eds.); USD 860 combined subscription foreign to institutions (print & online eds.) (effective 2011). adv. bk.rev. index. 128 p./no.; back issues avail.; reprints avail. **Document type:** *Journal, Academic/Scholarly.* **Description:** Covers theory, research and practice in the growing interface of social and clinical psychology.
Related titles: Online - full text ed.: ISSN 1943-2771.
Indexed: A01, A03, A08, A20, A22, ASCA, ASSIA, C06, C07, C08, C11, CA, CINAHL, CommAb, CurCont, DIP, E-psyche, E01, E15, E16, ERA, FR, Faml, H04, IBR, IBSS, IBZ, M12, P03, P10, P12, P25, P26, P27, P30, P43, P48, P53, P54, PCI, PQC, PsycInfo, PsycholAb, S02, S03, S19, S20, S21, SCOPUS, SFSA, SOPODA, SSA, SSCI, SWR&A, SociolAb, T02, V&AA, V05, W07.
—BLDSC (5064.718000), GNLM, IE, Infotrieve, Ingenta, INIST. **CCC.**
Published by: Guilford Publications, Inc., 72 Spring St, 4th Fl, New York, NY 10012. TEL 800-365-7006, FAX 212-966-6708, info@guilford.com. Ed. Thomas E Joiner TEL 850-644-1454. R&P Kathy Kuehl. Adv. contact Marian Robinson. Circ: 750 (paid).

➤ **JOURNAL OF SOCIAL AND DEVELOPMENT SCIENCES.** *see* SOCIAL SCIENCES: COMPREHENSIVE WORKS

150 GBR ISSN 0265-4075
HM132 CODEN: JSRLE9
➤ **JOURNAL OF SOCIAL AND PERSONAL RELATIONSHIPS.** Abbreviated title: J S P R. Text in English. 1984. 8/yr. USD 1,680, GBP 908 combined subscription to institutions (print & online eds.); USD 1,646, GBP 890 to institutions (effective 2011). adv. bk.rev. back issues avail.; reprint service avail. from PSC. **Document type:** *Journal, Academic/Scholarly.* **Description:** Multidisciplinary examination of personal relationships, drawing on materials from the fields of social, clinical and developmental psychology, communications, and sociology.
Related titles: Online - full text ed.: ISSN 1460-3608. USD 1,512, GBP 817 to institutions (effective 2011).
Indexed: A01, A02, A03, A08, A20, A22, ASCA, B01, B06, B07, B09, C06, C07, C08, CA, CINAHL, CJA, CMM, CommAb, CurCont, DIP, E-psyche, E01, E03, ERI, F09, Faml, G10, H04, IBR, IBSS, IBZ, P02, P03, P04, P10, P12, P24, P25, P30, P48, P53, P54, PQC, PsycInfo, PsycholAb, RASB, S02, S03, S21, SCOPUS, SFSA, SOPODA, SSA, SSCI, SociolAb, T02, V&AA, V02, W07, W09.
—BLDSC (5064.740000), IE, Infotrieve, Ingenta. **CCC.**
Published by: (International Association for Relationship Research USA), Sage Publications Ltd. (Subsidiary of: Sage Publications, Inc.), 1 Oliver's Yard, 55 City Rd, London, EC1Y 1SP, United Kingdom. TEL 44-20-73248500, FAX 44-20-73248600, info@sagepub.co.uk, http://www.uk.sagepub.com/home.nav. Ed. Paul A Mongeau. adv.: B&W page GBP 400; 130 x 205. **Subscr. in the Americas to:** Sage Publications, Inc., 2455 Teller Rd, Thousand Oaks, CA 91320. TEL 805-499-9774, FAX 805-499-0871, journals@sagepub.com.

➤ **JOURNAL OF SOCIAL AND PSYCHOLOGICAL SCIENCES.** *see* SOCIAL SCIENCES: COMPREHENSIVE WORKS

150 USA ISSN 1933-5377
BF1
JOURNAL OF SOCIAL, EVOLUTIONARY & CULTURAL PSYCHOLOGY. Text in English. 2007. 3/yr. free (effective 2011). **Document type:** *Journal, Academic/Scholarly.*
Media: Online - full text.
Indexed: A39, C27, C29, D03, D04, E13, P03, PsycInfo, R14, S14, S15, S18. Eds. Rosemarie Sokol, Sarah Strout.

302 USA ISSN 0022-4537
HN51 CODEN: JSISAF
➤ **JOURNAL OF SOCIAL ISSUES.** Text in English. 1944. q. GBP 587 in United Kingdom to institutions (print or online ed.); USD 764 in the Americas to institutions (print or online ed.); EUR 746 in Europe to institutions (print or online ed.); USD 1,151 elsewhere to institutions (print or online ed.); GBP 647 combined subscription in United Kingdom to institutions (print & online eds.); USD 840 combined subscription in the Americas to institutions (print & online eds.); EUR 822 combined subscription in Europe to institutions (print & online eds.); USD 1,267 combined subscription elsewhere to institutions (print & online eds.) (effective 2010); subscr. includes Analyses of Social Issues and Public Policy, and Social Issues and Policy Review. adv. abstr.; bibl.; charts; illus. index, cum.index. reprint service avail. from PSC. **Document type:** *Journal, Academic/Scholarly.* **Description:** Focuses on a poverty, housing and health; privacy as a social and psychological concern; youth and violence; and the impact of social class on education.
Related titles: Microfilm ed.: (from PMC, PQC); Online - full text ed.: ISSN 1540-4560. GBP 476 to institutions; USD 619 in the Americas to institutions (effective 2008) (from IngentaConnect).
Indexed: A01, A02, A03, A08, A20, A22, A25, A26, ABCPolSci, AC&P, ASCA, ASG, AbAn, Acal, AmH&L, B04, BAS, BRD, Busl, C28, CA, CJA, CJPI, CLFP, CMM, ChPerI, Chicano, CommAb, CurCont, DIP, E-psyche, E01, E02, E03, E07, E08, EAA, ERI, ESPM, EdA, Edl, F09, Faml, G05, G06, G07, G08, GEOBASE, H09, H10, HRA, I05, I13, IBR, IBSS, IBZ, M06, MEA&I, MLA-IB, MResA, P02, P03, P06, P10, P13, P27, P30, P34, P42, P43, P48, P53, P54, PAIS, PCI, PQC, PRA, PSA, PsycInfo, PsycholAb, R05, RASB, RI-1, RI-2, RiskAb, S02, S03, S05, S08, S09, S11, S21, S23, SCOPUS, SFSA, SOPODA, SRRA, SSA, SSAI, SSAb, SSCI, SSI, SUSA, SWR&A, SociolAb, T02, THA, V&AA, W03, W07, W09.
—BLDSC (5064.755000), IE, Infotrieve, Ingenta, INIST. **CCC.**
Published by: (Society for the Psychological Study of Social Issues), Wiley-Blackwell Publishing, Inc. (Subsidiary of: Wiley-Blackwell Publishing Ltd.), 111 River St, Hoboken, NJ 07030. TEL 201-748-6000, FAX 201-748-6088, info@wiley.com, http://www.wiley.com/WileyCDA/. Ed. Sheri R Levy. Adv. contact Kristin McCarthy TEL 201-748-7683.

301.1 150 USA ISSN 0022-4545
HM251.A1 CODEN: JSPSAG
➤ **THE JOURNAL OF SOCIAL PSYCHOLOGY.** Text in English. 1929. bi-m. GBP 231 combined subscription in United Kingdom to institutions (print & online eds.); EUR 305, USD 382 combined subscription to institutions (print & online eds.) (effective 2012). bibl.; charts; illus. index. back issues avail.; reprint service avail. from PSC. **Document type:** *Journal, Academic/Scholarly.* **Description:** Publishes experimental, empirical and field studies of groups, cultural effects, cross-national problems, and language and ethnicity.
Incorporates (1985-2006): Genetic, Social, and General Psychology Monographs (8756-7547); Which was formerly (1926-1984): Genetic Psychology Monographs (0016-6677)
Related titles: Microfilm ed.: (from PQC); Online - full text ed.: ISSN 1940-1183. GBP 208 in United Kingdom to institutions; EUR 275, USD 343 to institutions (effective 2012).
Indexed: A01, A02, A03, A08, A12, A20, A22, A25, A26, ABIn, ABS&EES, AC&P, AMHA, ASCA, ASG, ASSIA, B01, B04, B06, B07, B08, B09, BAS, BRD, C12, C28, CA, CDA, CMM, CWI, ChPerI, Chicano, CommAb, CurCont, DIP, DSHAb, E-psyche, E01, E02, E03, E06, E07, E08, ECER, EMBASE, ERA, ERI, EdA, Edl, ExcerpMed, F09, FR, Faml, G08, G10, H09, H10, H12, HEA, HRA, I05, I13, IBR, IBSS, IBZ, INI, IPsyAb, IndMed, L&LBA, M01, M02, M06, M12, MEA&I,

P

MEDLINE, MLA-IB, P02, P03, P10, P12, P13, P18, P20, P22, P25, P26, P27, P30, P42, P43, P46, P48, P51, P53, P54, PCI, PQC, PRA, PSA, PSI, PersLit, PsycInfo, PsycholAb, R10, RASB, RILM, Reac, S02, S03, S05, S08, S09, S21, SCOPUS, SD, SFSA, SOPODA, SRRA, SSA, SSAI, SSAb, SSCI, SSI, SWR&A, SociolAb, T02, V&AA, W01, W02, W03, W05, W07, W09.
—BLDSC (5064.800000), CIS, IE, Infotrieve, Ingenta, INIST. **CCC.**
Published by: (Helen Dwight Reid Educational Foundation), Psychology Press (Subsidiary of: Taylor & Francis Inc.), 325 Chestnut St, Ste 800, Philadelphia, PA 19106. TEL 800-354-1420, FAX 215-625-2940, subscriptions@tandf.co.uk.

370.15 150 USA ISSN 1552-4256
HV3000
➤ **JOURNAL OF SOCIAL WORK IN END-OF-LIFE & PALLIATIVE CARE.** Text in English. 1986. q. GBP 354 combined subscription in United Kingdom to institutions (print & online eds.); EUR 459, USD 466 combined subscription to institutions (print & online eds.) (effective 2012). adv. bk.rev. illus. 120 p./no. 1 cols./p.; back issues avail.; reprint service avail. from PSC. **Document type:** *Journal, Academic/Scholarly.* **Description:** Explores the critical issues of psychosocial care for chronically, critically, and terminally ill patients and their family members.
Formerly (until 2005): Loss, Grief & Care (8756-4610)
Related titles: Microfiche ed.: (from PQC); Microform ed.; Online - full text ed.: ISSN 1552-4264. GBP 318 in United Kingdom to institutions; EUR 413, USD 419 to institutions (effective 2012).
Indexed: A01, A03, A22, AMED, ASG, ASSIA, C06, C07, C08, CA, CINAHL, DIP, E-psyche, E01, EMBASE, ExcerpMed, FamI, IBR, IBZ, MEDLINE, P03, P30, PC&CA, PsycInfo, PsycholAb, S02, S03, SCOPUS, SOPODA, SSA, SWR&A, SociolAb, T02.
—BLDSC (5294.735000), GNLM, IE, Infotrieve, Ingenta. **CCC.**
Published by: Routledge (Subsidiary of: Taylor & Francis Group), 325 Chestnut St, Ste 800, Philadelphia, PA 19106. TEL 215-625-8900, 800-354-1420, FAX 215-625-8914, journals@routledge.com, http://www.routledge.com. Ed. Ellen L Csikai. adv.: B&W page USD 315, color page USD 550; trim 4.375 x 7.125. Circ: 232 (paid).

150 616.07 USA ISSN 1932-4731
RC423
➤ **THE JOURNAL OF SPEECH AND LANGUAGE PATHOLOGY AND APPLIED BEHAVIOR ANALYSIS.** Abbreviated title: J S L P - A B A. Text in English. 2006. irreg. free (effective 2011). adv. back issues avail. **Document type:** *Journal, Academic/Scholarly.* **Description:** Brings out research, reviews, and conceptual articles on the use of behavioral techniques and assessment procedures for speech and language disorders including early intervention, speech and language issues related to autism, stroke etc.
Media: Online - full text.
Indexed: A26, A39, C06, C07, C27, C29, CA, CMM, D03, D04, E13, H12, I05, P30, R14, S14, S15, S18, T02.
Published by: Journal of Speech and Language Pathology and Applied Behavior Analysis, c/o Mareile Koenig, 1214 Huntsman Way, Chester Springs, PA 19425. TEL 610-458-5364, FAX 610-458-9949. Ed., Pub. Joe Cautilli.

206.1 USA ISSN 1934-9637
BV4012.2
➤ **JOURNAL OF SPIRITUALITY IN MENTAL HEALTH.** Abbreviated title: A J P C. Text in English. 1952. q. GBP 194 combined subscription in United Kingdom to institutions (print & online eds.); EUR 252, USD 260 combined subscription to institutions (print & online eds.) (effective 2012). adv. bk.rev. 120 p./no. 1 cols./p.; back issues avail.; reprint service avail. from PSC. **Document type:** *Journal, Academic/Scholarly.* **Description:** Aimed at therapists and researchers who are interested in the role and dynamic of religion in the healing process of psychotherapy.
Former titles (until 2006): American Journal of Pastoral Counseling (1094-6098); (until 1997): Journal of Religion in Psychotherapy (1045-5876); (until 1990): Journal of Pastoral Psychotherapy (0886-5477)
Related titles: Microform ed.: (from PQC); Online - full text ed.: ISSN 1934-9645. GBP 175 in United Kingdom to institutions; EUR 227, USD 234 to institutions (effective 2012).
Indexed: A01, A03, A21, A22, ASSIA, C06, C07, CA, CCR, CERDIC, DIP, E-psyche, E01, FR, FamI, GSS&RPL, IBR, IBZ, M02, P48, P53, P54, PC&CA, PQC, PsycholAb, R&TA, RI-1, RefZh, S02, S03, S21, SCOPUS, SWR&A, T02.
—BLDSC (5066.183250), GNLM, IE, Ingenta, INIST. **CCC.**
Published by: Routledge (Subsidiary of: Taylor & Francis Group), 325 Chestnut St, Ste 800, Philadelphia, PA 19106. TEL 215-625-8900, 800-354-1420, FAX 215-625-8914, journals@routledge.com, http://www.routledge.com. Ed. William S Schmidt. adv.: B&W page USD 315, color page USD 550; trim 4.375 x 7.125. Circ: 367 (paid).

150 USA ISSN 0895-2779
GV706.4
➤ **JOURNAL OF SPORT AND EXERCISE PSYCHOLOGY.** Abbreviated title: J S E P. Text in English. 1979. bi-m. USD 468 domestic to institutions; USD 483 foreign to institutions; USD 552 combined subscription domestic to institutions (print & online eds.); USD 567 combined subscription foreign to institutions (print & online eds.) (effective 2012). adv. bk.rev. bibl.; charts; illus.; stat. index. back issues avail.; reprint service avail. from PSC. **Document type:** *Journal, Academic/Scholarly.* **Description:** Multidisciplinary journal designed to stimulate and communicate research and theory. Examines the influence of psychological variables on sport performance and the influence of sport participation on psychological phenomena.
Formerly (until 1988): Journal of Sport Psychology (0163-433X)
Related titles: Online - full text ed.: ISSN 1543-2904. USD 468 to institutions (effective 2012).
Indexed: A01, A02, A03, A08, A20, A22, A26, A36, AMED, ASCA, BRD, C06, C07, CA, CABA, CDA, CurCont, DIP, E-psyche, E02, E03, E07, E08, EMBASE, ERI, EdA, EdI, ErgAb, ExcerpMed, FoSS&M, G08, GH, I05, IBR, IBZ, LT, M01, M02, MEDLINE, N02, N03, P02, P03, P07, P10, P12, P18, P27, P30, P48, P53, P54, PEI, PQC, PsycInfo, PsycholAb, R09, R10, R12, RRTA, Reac, S02, S03, S09, SCI, SCOPUS, SD, SSAI, SSAb, SSCI, SSI, SportS, T02, W01, W02, W03, W07, W11.
—BLDSC (5066.183500), IE, Infotrieve, Ingenta. **CCC.**
Published by: (North American Society for the Psychology of Sport and Physical Activity), Human Kinetics, 1607 N Market St, Champaign, IL 61820. TEL 800-747-4457, FAX 217-351-2674, info@hkusa.com, http://www.humankinetics.com. Ed. Robert C Eklund TEL 850-645-2909. Pub. Rainer Martens. R&P Martha Gullo TEL 217-403-7534. Adv. contact Amy Bleich TEL 217-403-7803.

➤ **JOURNAL OF SPORT BEHAVIOR.** *see* SPORTS AND GAMES

▼ ➤ **JOURNAL OF SPORT PSYCHOLOGY IN ACTION.** *see* MEDICAL SCIENCES—Sports Medicine

158 USA ISSN 2150-279X
▼ **JOURNAL OF STRESS AND SELF-THERAPY.** Text in English. forthcoming 2011. q. **Document type:** *Journal, Academic/Scholarly.* **Description:** Includes studies on the effects of stress on mental health and personal relationships.
Media: Online - full content.
Published by: Kaiser Peer Publishing, PO Box 734, Churchville, NY 14428. TEL 585-393-1464, davidkaiser@spiritualneuroscience.org, http://brainandcosmos.com/info.htm.

616.89 USA ISSN 1195-4396
➤ **JOURNAL OF SYSTEMIC THERAPIES.** Abbreviated title: J S T. Text in English. 1982. q. USD 58 combined subscription domestic to individuals (print & online eds.); USD 73 combined subscription foreign to individuals (print & online eds.); USD 325 combined subscription domestic to institutions (print & online eds.); USD 370 combined subscription foreign to institutions (print & online eds.) (effective 2011). adv. bk.rev. back issues avail. **Document type:** *Journal, Academic/Scholarly.* **Description:** Presents provocative ideas and methods that work with families, individuals and groups. Explores brief therapies, solution-focused models, narrative therapies, constructionism and therapeutic conversations.
Formerly (until 1993): Journal of Strategic and Systematic Therapies (0711-5075)
Related titles: Online - full text ed.: ISSN 1930-6318.
Indexed: A01, A22, CA, E-psyche, E01, FamI, P03, P25, P26, P27, P48, P54, PQC, PsycInfo, PsycholAb, S02, S03, SCOPUS, SSA, SociolAb, T02.
—BLDSC (5068.064000), GNLM, Infotrieve, Ingenta. **CCC.**
Published by: Guilford Publications, Inc., 72 Spring St, 4th Fl, New York, NY 10012. TEL 800-365-7006, FAX 212-966-6708, info@guilford.com. Ed. Jim Duvall TEL 416-972-1935 ext.3342. R&P Kathy Kuehl. Adv. contact Marian Robinson. Circ: 700 (paid).

371.42 USA ISSN 1527-6228
BF637.C6
➤ **JOURNAL OF TECHNOLOGY IN COUNSELING.** Abbreviated title: J T C. Text in English. 1999. a., latest 2008. free (effective 2011). back issues avail. **Document type:** *Journal, Academic/Scholarly.* **Description:** Publishes articles related to the use of technology in training, teaching, and practice of professional counseling.
Media: Online - full text.
Indexed: A39, C27, C29, CA, D03, D04, E03, E13, FamI, R14, S14, S15, S18, SCOPUS, T02.
Published by: Columbus State University, Department of Counseling and Educational Leadership, 4225 University Ave, Jordan Hall, Columbus, GA 31907. TEL 706-568-2222, FAX 706-569-3134.

152 USA ISSN 0022-5002
BF1 CODEN: JEABAU
➤ **JOURNAL OF THE EXPERIMENTAL ANALYSIS OF BEHAVIOR.** Abbreviated title: J E A B. Text in English. 1958. bi-m. USD 32 to individuals; USD 162 to institutions (effective 2010). bk.rev. bibl.; charts. index, cum.index: vols.1-20; 21-40; 41-60. back issues avail. **Document type:** *Journal, Academic/Scholarly.* **Description:** Presents original experiments relevant to the behavior of individual organisms.
Related titles: Microfilm ed.: (from PMC); Online - full text ed.: ISSN 1938-3711.
Indexed: A01, A02, A03, A08, A20, A22, A26, A34, A36, ASCA, AnBeAb, B04, B21, B25, BIOSIS Prev, BRD, CA, CABA, ChemAb, CurCont, D01, DIP, E-psyche, E08, EMBASE, ExcerpMed, FR, G08, GH, H09, I05, IBR, IBZ, ISR, IndMed, IndVet, Inpharma, MEA&I, MEDLINE, MLA-IB, MycolAb, N02, N03, N04, NSA, P02, P03, P10, P12, P15, P20, P22, P25, P27, P30, P33, P37, P48, P52, P53, P54, P56, PQC, PsycInfo, PsycholAb, PsycholRG, R08, R10, RASB, Reac, S02, S03, S05, S09, S12, SCI, SCOPUS, SSAI, SSAb, SSCI, SSI, T02, TriticAb, VS, W03, W07, W11.
—BLDSC (4979.700000), CASDDS, GNLM, IE, Infotrieve, Ingenta, INIST. **CCC.**
Published by: Society for the Experimental Analysis of Behavior, Inc., c/o Monica Bonner, Department of Psychology, Indiana University, Bloomington, IN 47405. TEL 812-336-1257, mbonner@indiana.edu, http://seab.envmed.rochester.edu/society/. Ed. James E Mazur.

➤ **JOURNAL OF THE HISTORY OF SEXUALITY.** *see* SOCIOLOGY

150 USA ISSN 0022-5061
BF1 CODEN: JHBSA5
➤ **JOURNAL OF THE HISTORY OF THE BEHAVIORAL SCIENCES.** Text in English. 1965. q. GBP 288 in United Kingdom to institutions; EUR 365 in Europe to institutions; USD 537 in United States to institutions; USD 565 in Canada & Mexico to institutions; USD 565 elsewhere to institutions; GBP 331 combined subscription in United Kingdom to institutions (print & online eds.); EUR 420 combined subscription in Europe to institutions (print & online eds.); USD 617 combined subscription in United States to institutions (print & online eds.); USD 645 combined subscription in Canada & Mexico to institutions (print & online eds.); USD 645 combined subscription elsewhere to institutions (print & online eds.) (effective 2012). adv. bk.rev. illus. index. back issues avail.; reprint service avail. from PSC. **Document type:** *Journal, Academic/Scholarly.* **Description:** Features articles devoted to the scientific, technical, institutional, and cultural history of the social and behavioral sciences.
Related titles: Microform ed.: (from PQC); Online - full text ed.: ISSN 1520-6696. 1996. GBP 274 in United Kingdom to institutions; EUR 347 in Europe to institutions; USD 537 elsewhere to institutions (effective 2012).
Indexed: A01, A03, A08, A20, A22, ABS&EES, ASCA, AbAn, AmH&L, B21, CA, ChPerI, CommAb, CurCont, E-psyche, EMBASE, ExcerpMed, FR, HistAb, IBR, IBSS, IBZ, IndMed, MEA&I, MEDLINE, MLA-IB, P02, P03, P10, P12, P30, P43, P48, P53, P54, PCI, PQC, PhilInd, PsycInfo, PsycholAb, PsycholRG, RASB, S02, S03, SCOPUS, SOPODA, SSCI, SociolAb, T02, W07.
—BLDSC (5000.600000), GNLM, IE, Infotrieve, Ingenta, INIST. **CCC.**
Published by: John Wiley & Sons, Inc., 111 River St, Hoboken, NJ 07030. TEL 201-748-6000, FAX 201-748-6088, info@wiley.com, http://www.wiley.com/WileyCDA/. Ed. Ian A M Nicholson. Pub. Kim Thompkins TEL 212-850-6921. Adv. contact Kristin McCarthy TEL 201-748-7683. B&W page USD 772, color page USD 1,009; trim 6.875 x 10. **Subscr. outside the Americas to:** John Wiley & Sons Ltd., The Atrium, Southern Gate, Chichester, West Sussex PO19 8SQ, United Kingdom. TEL 44-1243-779777, FAX 44-1243-775878, cs-journals@wiley.com.

➤ **JOURNAL OF THE LEARNING SCIENCES;** a journal of ideas and their applications. *see* EDUCATION

➤ **JOURNAL OF THE PSYCHOLOGY OF RELIGION.** *see* RELIGIONS AND THEOLOGY

150 100 USA ISSN 1068-8471
BF38
JOURNAL OF THEORETICAL & PHILOSOPHICAL PSYCHOLOGY. Text in English. 1982. s-a. USD 98 domestic to individuals; USD 125 foreign to individuals; USD 403 domestic to institutions; USD 448 foreign to institutions (effective 2011). adv. back issues avail.; reprints avail. **Document type:** *Journal, Academic/Scholarly.* **Description:** Encourages and facilities informed exploration and discussion of psychological theories and issues in both their scientific and philosophical dimensions and interrelationships.
Formerly (until 1993): Theoretical and Philosophical Psychology (1068-8455)
Related titles: Online - full text ed.: ISSN 2151-3341 (from ScienceDirect).
Indexed: P03, PhilInd, PsycInfo, PsycholAb, SCOPUS.
—BLDSC (5069.074750), IE, Ingenta. **CCC.**
Published by: American Psychological Association, 750 First St, NE, Washington, DC 20002. TEL 202-336-5500, 800-374-2721, journals@apa.org. Ed. Thomas Teo. Adv. contact Doug Constant TEL 202-336-5574. Circ: 600. **Co-sponsor:** American Psychological Association, Division 24.

▼ **JOURNAL OF TRANCE RESEARCH.** *see* RELIGIONS AND THEOLOGY

150 301 USA ISSN 1947-2668
▼ ➤ **JOURNAL OF TRANSFORMATIVE STUDIES.** Text in English. 2009. s-a. free (effective 2009). **Document type:** *Journal, Academic/Scholarly.* **Description:** A transdisciplinary journal that publishes innovative research combining rigorous scholarship, creativity, and self-inquiry.
Media: Online - full content.
Published by: Integration Press, 2245 C Ashley Crossing Dr, Ste 102, Charleston, SC 29414. FAX 843-556-7753, contact@integrationpress.com contact@integrationpress.com contact@integrationpress.com, http://www.integrationpress.com.

158 USA ISSN 0022-524X
BF1 CODEN: JTPSAN
JOURNAL OF TRANSPERSONAL PSYCHOLOGY. Abbreviated title: J T P. Text in English. 1969. s-a. USD 35 domestic to individuals; USD 45 in Canada & Mexico to individuals; USD 58 elsewhere to individuals (effective 2011). bk.rev. back issues avail.; reprints avail. **Document type:** *Journal, Academic/Scholarly.* **Description:** Focuses on psychological and spiritual states, experiences, practices and concepts.
Related titles: Microform ed.: (from PQC); Online - full text ed.
Indexed: A01, A20, A21, A22, DIP, E-psyche, IBR, IBZ, P03, P25, P48, PCI, PQC, PsycInfo, PsycholAb, PsycholRG, RASB, RI-1, RI-2.
—BLDSC (5069.870000), IE, Infotrieve, Ingenta.
Published by: Association for Transpersonal Psychology, PO Box 50187, Palo Alto, CA 94303. TEL 650-424-8764, FAX 650-618-1851, info@atpweb.org. Ed. Marcie Boucouvalas.

616.852 USA ISSN 1529-9732
RC569.5.M8 CODEN: JTDOAJ
➤ **JOURNAL OF TRAUMA AND DISSOCIATION.** Text in English. 1999. q. GBP 410 combined subscription in United Kingdom to institutions (print & online eds.); EUR 530, USD 541 combined subscription to institutions (print & online eds.) (effective 2012). adv. reprint service avail. from PSC. **Document type:** *Journal, Academic/Scholarly.* **Description:** Provides scientific literature in dissociation, dissociative disorders, psychological trauma, and aspects of memory associated with trauma and dissociation.
Related titles: Online - full text ed.: ISSN 1529-9740. GBP 369 in United Kingdom to institutions; EUR 477, USD 487 to institutions (effective 2012).
Indexed: A01, A03, A22, BiolDig, C06, C07, CA, CJPI, CurCont, DIP, E-psyche, E01, EMBASE, ExcerpMed, F09, FR, IBR, IBZ, MEDLINE, P03, P25, P30, P48, PQC, PsycInfo, PsycholAb, R10, Reac, RefZh, S02, S03, SCOPUS, SSCI, SWR&A, T02, W07.
—BLDSC (5070.511000), IE, Ingenta, INIST. **CCC.**
Published by: (International Society for the Study of Dissociation), Routledge (Subsidiary of: Taylor & Francis Group), 325 Chestnut St, Ste 800, Philadelphia, PA 19106. TEL 215-625-8900, 800-354-1420, FAX 215-625-8914, http://www.routledge.com. Ed. Jennifer J Freyd. adv.: B&W page USD 315, color page USD 550; trim 4.375 x 7.125. Circ: 1,601 (paid).

370.15 150 USA ISSN 0894-9867
RC552.P67 CODEN: JTSTEB
➤ **JOURNAL OF TRAUMATIC STRESS.** Text in English. 1988. bi-m. GBP 551 in United Kingdom to institutions; EUR 697 in Europe to institutions; USD 967 in United States to institutions; USD 1,027 in Canada & Mexico to institutions; USD 1,078 elsewhere to institutions; GBP 635 combined subscription in United Kingdom to institutions (print & online eds.); EUR 803 combined subscription in Europe to institutions (print & online eds.); USD 1,112 combined subscription in United States to institutions (print & online eds.); USD 1,172 combined subscription in Canada & Mexico to institutions (print & online eds.); USD 1,223 combined subscription elsewhere to institutions (print & online eds.) (effective 2012). adv. bk.rev. back issues avail.; reprint service avail. from PSC. **Document type:** *Journal, Academic/Scholarly.* **Description:** Examines the biopsychosocial aspects of trauma through theoretical formulations, research, treatment, prevention, education and training, and legal and policy concerns.

Related titles: Microfilm ed.: (from PQC); Online - full text ed.: ISSN 1573-6598. GBP 494 in United Kingdom to institutions; EUR 625 in Europe to institutions; USD 967 elsewhere to institutions (effective 2012) (from IngentaConnect).
Indexed: A01, A03, A08, A20, A22, A26, ASCA, B21, BibLing, C06, C07, C28, CA, CurCont, E-psyche, E01, EMBASE, ESPM, ExcerpMed, F09, FR, Faml, G10, H&SSA, INI, IndMed, MEDLINE, P03, P10, P12, P20, P22, P25, P30, P34, P43, P48, P53, P54, PQC, PsycInfo, PsycholAb, R10, Reac, RiskAb, S02, S03, SCOPUS, SOPODA, SSCI, SWR&A, SociolAb, T02, W07.
—BLDSC (5070.520000), GNLM, IE, Infotrieve, Ingenta, INIST. **CCC.**
Published by: (International Society for Traumatic Stress Studies), John Wiley & Sons, Inc., 111 River St, Hoboken, NJ 07030. TEL 201-748-6000, FAX 201-748-6088, info@wiley.com, http://www.wiley.com/WileyCDA/. Ed. Paula P Schnurr. Pub., Adv. contact Kim Thompkins TEL 212-850-6921.

150 AUS ISSN 1838-9902
▼ ➤ **JOURNAL OF TROPICAL PSYCHOLOGY.** Text in English. 2011. s-a. AUD 150 domestic; AUD 165 foreign (effective 2011). **Document type:** *Journal, Academic/Scholarly.* **Description:** Publishes psychological research in tropical zone countries and regions.
Media: Online - full text.
Published by: Australian Academic Press Pty. Ltd., 32 Jeays St, Bowen Hills, QLD 4006, Australia. TEL 61-7-32571176, FAX 61-7-32525908, aap@australianacademicpress.com.au, http://www.australianacademicpress.com.au. Ed. Robert Morgan.

150 301 GBR ISSN 2151-5581
▼ ➤ **JOURNAL OF TRUST RESEARCH.** Text in English. forthcoming 2011 (Mar.). s-a. GBP 212 combined subscription in United Kingdom to institutions (print & online eds.); EUR 281, USD 351 combined subscription to institutions (print & online eds.) (effective 2012). **Document type:** *Journal, Academic/Scholarly.* **Description:** Addresses the nature, form, base and role of trust as well as the mechanism and stage of trust-building and trust repair at and across personal, group, organizational, community and national levels.
Related titles: Online - full text ed.: ISSN 2151-559X. forthcoming 2011 (Mar.). GBP 191 in United Kingdom to institutions; EUR 253, USD 316 to institutions (effective 2012).
—**CCC.**
Published by: Taylor & Francis Ltd. (Subsidiary of: Taylor & Francis Group), 4 Park Sq, Milton Park, Abingdon, Oxfordshire OX14 4RN, United Kingdom. TEL 44-20-70176000, FAX 44-20-70176336, info@tandf.co.uk.

150 USA ISSN 2154-8730
▼ **JOURNAL OF UNIFIED PSYCHOTHERAPY AND CLINICAL SCIENCE.** Text in English. forthcoming 2011 (Jan.). q. **Document type:** *Journal, Academic/Scholarly.* **Description:** Devoted to the exploration and explication of the component domains of human personality functioning and dysfunctioning.
Media: Online - full text.
Published by: Unified Psychotherapy Project, 2901 Boston St, No 410, Baltimore, MD 21224-4889. TEL 410-583-1221, steve@cantoncove.com.

158 USA ISSN 0001-8791
HF5381.A1 CODEN: JVBHA2
➤ **JOURNAL OF VOCATIONAL BEHAVIOR.** Text in English. 1971. bi-m. EUR 1,557 in Europe to institutions; JPY 162,800 in Japan to institutions; USD 1,220 elsewhere to institutions (effective 2012). adv. illus. index. back issues avail.; reprints avail. **Document type:** *Journal, Academic/Scholarly.* **Description:** Features empirical and theoretical articles that expand knowledge of vocational behavior and career development across the life span.
Related titles: Online - full text ed.: ISSN 1095-9084 (from IngentaConnect, ScienceDirect).
Indexed: A12, A13, A14, A17, A20, A22, A26, ABIn, AEI, ASCA, CA, ChPerl, Chicano, CurCont, DIP, E-psyche, E01, E03, E06, ERI, ERIC, Faml, G10, HEA, I05, IBR, IBZ, MEA&I, P03, P30, P42, P48, P51, P53, P54, PQC, PSA, PersLit, PsycInfo, PsycholAb, RASB, S02, S03, SCOPUS, SOPODA, SSA, SSCI, SociolAb, T02, W07, W09.
—BLDSC (5072.510000), IE, Infotrieve, Ingenta. **CCC.**
Published by: Academic Press (Subsidiary of: Elsevier Science & Technology), 3251 Riverport Ln, Maryland Heights, MO 63043. TEL 314-447-8010, FAX 314-447-8030, JournalCustomerService-usa@elsevier.com, http://www.elsevierdirect.com/imprint.jsp?iid=5. Ed. Mark L Savickas.

615.851 NLD ISSN 1052-2263
HD7255.A2 CODEN: JVREFA
➤ **JOURNAL OF VOCATIONAL REHABILITATION.** Text in English. 1991. bi-m. (in 2 vols., 3 nos./vol.). USD 784 combined subscription in North America (print & online eds.); EUR 560 combined subscription elsewhere (print & online eds.) (effective 2012). bk.rev. abstr.; illus. back issues avail. **Document type:** *Journal, Academic/Scholarly.* **Description:** Topics range from supported employment to psychiatric impairment, vocational training, and physical disability.
Related titles: Microform ed.: (from PQC); Online - full text ed.: ISSN 1878-6316 (from IngentaConnect).
Indexed: A01, A03, A08, A22, AMED, C06, C07, C08, CA, CINAHL, E-psyche, E01, E03, ECER, EMBASE, ERI, ExcerpMed, P03, P34, PsycInfo, PsycholAb, R09, S02, S03, SCOPUS, T02.
—BLDSC (5072.512400), GNLM, IE, Infotrieve, Ingenta. **CCC.**
Published by: I O S Press, Nieuwe Hemweg 6B, Amsterdam, 1013 BG, Netherlands. TEL 31-20-6883355, FAX 31-20-6870019, info@iospress.nl. Ed. Paul H Wehman TEL 804-828-1851. **Subscr. to:** I O S Press, Inc, 4502 Rachael Manor Dr, Fairfax, VA 22032-3631. sales@iospress.com; Globe Publication Pvt. Ltd., C-62 Inderpuri, New Delhi 100 012, India. TEL 91-11-579-3211, 91-11-579-3212, FAX 91-11-579-8876, custserve@globepub.com, http://www.globepub.com; Kinokuniya Co Ltd., Shinjuku 3-chome, Shinjuku-ku, Tokyo 160-0022, Japan. FAX 81-3-3439-1094, journal@kinokuniya.co.jp, http://www.kinokuniya.co.jp.

➤ **JOURNAL OF YOUTH AND ADOLESCENCE**; a multidisciplinary research publication. *see* CHILDREN AND YOUTH—About

➤ **JOURNAL OF YOUTH STUDIES.** *see* CHILDREN AND YOUTH—About

➤ **JOURNALS OF GERONTOLOGY. SERIES B: PSYCHOLOGICAL SCIENCES & SOCIAL SCIENCES.** *see* GERONTOLOGY AND GERIATRICS

➤ **JUDGMENT AND DECISION MAKING.** *see* BUSINESS AND ECONOMICS

158 USA ISSN 1934-2039
BF175.4.C84
➤ **JUNG JOURNAL**; culture & psyche. Text in English. 1979. q. USD 191 combined subscription to institutions (print & online eds.) (effective 2012). adv. back issues avail.; reprint service avail. from PSC. **Document type:** *Journal, Academic/Scholarly.* **Description:** Provides a dialogue between culture, as reflected in art, literature, science, and world events, and contemporary Jungian views of the dynamic relationship between the cultural and personal aspects of the human psyche.
Formerly (until 2007): The San Francisco Jung Institute Library Journal (0270-6210)
Related titles: Online - full text ed.: ISSN 1934-2047. USD 172 to institutions (effective 2012).
Indexed: A01, A03, A08, A20, A22, ArtHuCI, CA, CurCont, E01, MLA-IB, P03, P10, P25, P27, P45, P46, P48, P53, P54, PQC, PsycInfo, SCOPUS, W07.
—IE. **CCC.**
Published by: (C G Jung Institute of San Francisco, C.G. Jung Institute, Virginia Allan Detloff Library), University of California Press, Journals Division, 2000 Ctr St, Ste 303, Berkeley, CA 94704. TEL 510-643-7154, 877-262-4226, FAX 510-642-9917, customerservice@ucpressjournals.com. Ed. Dyane Sherwood. Adv. contact Jennifer Rogers TEL 510-642-6188. Circ: 756. **Subscr. to:** 149 5th Ave, 8th Fl, New York, NY 10010. participation@jstor.org.

155 301.1 MYS ISSN 0127-8029
BF8.M35
JURNAL PSIKOLOGI MALAYSIA. Text in English, Malay. 1972. a. USD 15. **Document type:** *Journal, Academic/Scholarly.* **Description:** Discusses various fields of psychology such as social, developmental, physiological, industrial, counseling, and others particularly relevant to Malaysia.
Indexed: E-psyche.
—Ingenta.
Published by: Universiti Kebangsaan Malaysia/National University of Malaysia, 43600 UKM, Bangi, Selangor 43600, Malaysia. http://www.ukm.my.

JYVASKYLA STUDIES IN EDUCATION, PSYCHOLOGY AND SOCIAL RESEARCH. *see* EDUCATION

▼ **K B M JOURNAL OF COGNITIVE SCIENCE.** *see* MEDICAL SCIENCES—Psychiatry And Neurology

152.4 JPN
KANJO SHINRIGAKU KENKYU. Text in Japanese. 1993. irreg. **Document type:** *Journal, Academic/Scholarly.*
Published by: Japan Society for Research on Emotions, Department of Psychology, Doshisha University, Kamigyo-ku, Kyoto, 602-8580, Japan. jsre@psychology.doshisha.ac.jp, http://psychology.doshisha.ac.jp/JSREHome/JSREtop.html.

KARDIAGRAM. *see* RELIGIONS AND THEOLOGY

371.4 JPN ISSN 0914-8337
KAUNSERINGU KENKYU/JAPANESE JOURNAL OF COUNSELING SCIENCE. Text in Japanese. 1968. s-a. **Document type:** *Journal, Academic/Scholarly.*
Formerly (until 1987): Sodangaku Kenkyu (0385-860X)
Indexed: A22, P03, PsycInfo, PsycholAb.
—BLDSC (4651.464000), IE, Ingenta.
Published by: Nihon Kaunseringu Gakkai/Japanese Association of Counseling Science, 3-29-1 Otsuka, Bunkyo-ku, Tokyo, 112-0012, Japan. http://wwwsoc.nii.ac.jp/jacs2/. **Subscr. to:** c/o Academic Business Center, 5-16-9 Hon Komagome, Bunkyo-ku, Tokyo 113-8622, Japan. TEL 81-3-58145811.

150 JPN ISSN 0915-0625
KAZOKU SHINRIGAKU KENKYU/JAPANESE JOURNAL OF FAMILY PSYCHOLOGY. Text in Japanese. 1987. s-a. **Document type:** *Journal, Academic/Scholarly.*
Indexed: PsycholAb, S02, S03.
—BLDSC (4651.925000). **CCC.**
Published by: Nihon Kazoku Shinri Gakkai/Japanese Association of Family Psychology, 2-40-7, Hongo, Bunkyo-ku, YG Bldg. 5th Fl., Tokyo, 113-0033, Japan. jafp2nd@abox2.so-net.ne.jp.

150 JPN ISSN 0917-3323
KENKO SHINRIGAKU KENKYU/JAPANESE JOURNAL OF HEALTH PSYCHOLOGY. Text in Japanese. 1988. s-a. **Document type:** *Journal, Academic/Scholarly.*
Indexed: P03, PsycInfo, PsycholAb.
—BLDSC (4655.150000). **CCC.**
Published by: Nihon Kenko Shinri Gakkai/Japanese Association of Health Psychology, Waseda University, School of Humanities & Social Sciences, Oda Laboratory, 1-24-1, Toyama, Shinjuku-ku, Tokyo, 162-8644, Japan. http://www.waseda.ac.jp/conference/JAHP/frame.html.

KEY DATA ON ADOLESCENCE (YEAR); the latest information and statistics about young people today. *see* CHILDREN AND YOUTH—About

302 GBR ISSN 1531-2569
KEY READINGS IN SOCIAL PSYCHOLOGY. Text in English. 1999. irreg., latest 2009. price varies. back issues avail. **Document type:** *Monographic series, Academic/Scholarly.* **Description:** Provides undergraduate and graduate students with key articles in each area of social psychology.
—**CCC.**
Published by: Psychology Press (Subsidiary of: Taylor & Francis Ltd.), 27 Church Rd, Hove, E Sussex BN3 2FA, United Kingdom. TEL 44-20-70176000, FAX 44-20-70176717, info@psypress.co.uk. Ed. Arie W Kruglanski.

150 PAK ISSN 2075-6933
▼ **KHYBER BEHAVIOURAL STUDIES.** Text in English. 2009 (Dec.). a. **Document type:** *Journal, Academic/Scholarly.* **Description:** Publishes papers in the disciplines of Psychology, Psychiatry, Sociology, Social Work, Anthropology, Political Science, Economics, Journalism, Education, IR, Management and other behavioural sciences focusing on human behaviour and interaction.
Published by: University of Peshawar, Department of Psychology, Peshawar, N-WFP 25120, Pakistan. http://psychology.upesh.edu.pk/index.html.

DAS KIND. *see* CHILDREN AND YOUTH—About

616.89 DEU ISSN 0942-6051
CODEN: KINDF9
KINDERANALYSE. Text in German. 1992. q. EUR 68; EUR 56 to students; EUR 21 newsstand/cover (effective 2011). adv. abstr.; bibl. 100 p./no.; back issues avail. **Document type:** *Journal, Academic/Scholarly.*
Indexed: DIP, E-psyche, IBR, IBZ, P03, PsycInfo, PsycholAb, SCOPUS.
—BLDSC (5095.570000), GNLM.
Published by: Verlag Klett-Cotta, Rotebuehlstr 77, Stuttgart, 70178, Germany. TEL 49-711-66720, FAX 49-711-66722030, info@klett-cotta.de, http://www.klett-cotta.de. Eds. Kai von Klitzing, Michael Guenter. Adv. contact Friederike Kamann. Circ: 1,500 (paid and controlled).

150 JPN ISSN 0287-7651
KISO SHINRIGAKU KENKYU/JAPANESE JOURNAL OF PSYCHONOMIC SCIENCE. Text in Japanese. 1982. s-a. JPY 25,000 (effective 2003). **Document type:** *Journal, Academic/Scholarly.*
Indexed: P03, P30, PsycInfo, PsycholAb.
—BLDSC (4658.310000).
Published by: Nihon Kiso Shinri Gakkai/Japanese Psychonomic Society, 3-8-8, Takadanobaba, Shinjuku-ku, Tokyo, 169-0075, Japan. TEL 86-3-53896239, FAX 86-3-33682822, kisoshin-post@bunken.co.jp, http://wwwsoc.nii.ac.jp/psychono/index.html.

159.9 DEU ISSN 1860-0379
KLEINE LEBENSHELFER. Text in German. 2004. irreg., latest vol.50, 2005. price varies. **Document type:** *Monographic series, Academic/Scholarly.*
Published by: Centaurus Verlag & Media KG, Kaiser-Joseph-Str 267, Freiburg, 79098, Germany. TEL 49-761-1525861, FAX 49-761-1525868, info@centaurus-verlag.de, http://www.centaurus-verlag.de.

150.198 CAN ISSN 1499-0970
➤ **KLEINIAN STUDIES.** Text in English. 2000. a. **Document type:** *Journal, Academic/Scholarly.* **Description:** Publishes writings related to Kleinian theory and practice.
Media: Online - full content.
Indexed: PsycholAb.
Address: dcarveth@yorku.ca, http://human-nature.com/ksej/. Ed. Donald L. Carveth.

155 DEU ISSN 1864-6050
➤ **KLINISCHE DIAGNOSTIK UND EVALUATION.** Text in German. 2008. q. EUR 79 to individuals; EUR 158 to institutions; EUR 24.90 newsstand/cover (effective 2011). adv. **Document type:** *Journal, Academic/Scholarly.*
Indexed: IBR, IBZ.
Published by: Vandenhoeck und Ruprecht, Theaterstr 13, Goettingen, 37073, Germany. TEL 49-551-508440, FAX 49-551-5084422, info@v-r.de. Ed. Elmar Braehler. Circ: 400 (paid).

156 JPN ISSN 0913-8013
KODO BUNSEKIGAKU KENKYU/JAPANESE JOURNAL OF BEHAVIOR ANALYSIS. Text in Japanese; Text occasionally in English. 1986. s-a. JPY 7,000 to individuals for membership; JPY 8,000 to institutions for membership; JPY 4,000 to students for membership (effective 2005). bk.rev. **Document type:** *Journal, Academic/Scholarly.* **Description:** Publishes applied, experimental, practical, and theoretical research articles in behavior analysis.
Indexed: P03, PsycInfo, PsycholAb.
—BLDSC (5100.721750). **CCC.**
Published by: Nihon Kodo Bunseki Gakkai/Japanese Association for Behavior Analysis, Department of Psychology, Sophia University, 7-1 Kioi-cho, Chiyoda-ku, Tokyo, 102-8554, Japan. FAX 81-3-32383658, yoshia-n@sophia.ac.jp. Ed. Yoshihiro Fujiwara.

616.89 JPN ISSN 0910-6529
➤ **KODO RYOHO KENKYU/JAPANESE JOURNAL OF BEHAVIOR THERAPY.** Text in English, Japanese; Summaries in English. 1974. s-a. membership. adv. bk.rev. Index. back issues avail. **Document type:** *Journal, Academic/Scholarly.* **Description:** Covers experimental and clinical research in behavior therapy.
Indexed: A22, E-psyche, PsycholAb.
—BLDSC (4651.010000), IE, Ingenta.
Published by: Nihon Kodo Ryoho Gakkai/Japanese Association of Behavior Therapy, c/o Waseda University, Faculty of Human Sciences, Shimada Laboratory, 2-579-15 Mikajima, Tokorozawa, Saitama 359-1192, Japan. FAX 81-4-29476758, jabt07-09@list.waseda.jp, http://wwwsoc.nii.ac.jp/jabt/. Circ: 1,200.

159.9 DEU ISSN 0935-4107
KOELNER ARBEITEN ZUR WIRTSCHAFTSPSYCHOLOGIE. Text in German. 1989. irreg., latest vol.17, 2005. price varies. **Document type:** *Monographic series, Academic/Scholarly.*
Published by: Peter Lang GmbH (Subsidiary of: Peter Lang Publishing Group), Eschborner Landstr 42-50, Frankfurt Am Main, 60489, Germany. TEL 49-69-7807050, FAX 49-69-78070550, zentrale.frankfurt@peterlang.com. Ed. Gerd Wiendieck.

150 DEU ISSN 0949-1821
GN502
KOELNER BEITRAEGE ZUR ETHNOPSYCHOLOGIE UND TRANSKULTURELLEN PSYCHOLOGIE. Text in German. 1995. irreg., latest vol.7, 2008. price varies. **Document type:** *Monographic series, Academic/Scholarly.*
Indexed: AnthLit, E-psyche.
Published by: V & R Unipress GmbH (Subsidiary of: Vandenhoeck und Ruprecht), Robert-Bosch-Breite 6, Goettingen, 37079, Germany. TEL 49-551-5084303, FAX 49-551-5084333, info@vr-unipress.de, http://www.v-r.de/en/publisher/unipress. Ed. Hannes Stubbe.

KOELNER ZEITSCHRIFT FUER SOZIOLOGIE UND SOZIALPSYCHOLOGIE. *see* SOCIOLOGY

370.15 150 DNK ISSN 0906-6225
KOGNITION & PAEDAGOGIK. Text in Danish. 1991. q. DKK 400 to individuals (effective 2009); DKK 116 per issue (effective 2008). adv. bk.rev. 80 p./no.; back issues avail. **Document type:** *Journal, Academic/Scholarly.*
Published by: (Aarhus Universitet, Center for Kognitiv Forskning og Paedagogik), Dansk Psykologisk Forlag/Danish Psychological Publishers, Kongevejen 155, Virum, 2830, Denmark. TEL 45-35-381655, FAX 45-35-381665, info@dpf.dk. Eds. Frans Oersted Andersen, Hans Henrik Knoop. adv.: B&W page DKK 3,000; 170 x 240.

P

616.89 ITA ISSN 1593-0041
KOINOS. GRUPPO E FUNZIONE ANALITICA. Text in Italian. s-a. EUR 40 domestic to individuals; EUR 65 foreign to individuals; EUR 46 domestic to institutions; EUR 76 foreign to institutions (effective 2009). **Document type:** *Journal, Academic/Scholarly.*
Formerly (until 1990): Gruppo e Funzione Analitica (1593-0068)
Indexed: E-psyche.
Published by: (Istituto Italiano di Psicanalisi di Gruppo), Edizioni Borla Srl, Via delle Fornaci 50, Rome, RM 00165, Italy. TEL 39-06-39376728, FAX 39-06-39376620, borla@edizioni-borla.it, http://www.edizioni-borla.it.

150 JPN ISSN 1349-6905
KOKORO NO SHOMONDAI RONSOU/MIND/SOUL INTERFACES. Text in Japanese. 2004. irreg. **Document type:** *Journal, Academic/Scholarly.*
Media: Online - full content.
Published by: Kokoro no Shomondai Koukyuukai/Mind - Soul Explorers http://www.h4.dion.ne.jp/~kokoro_s/.

616.8 JPN ISSN 0023-2807
KOKORO TO SHAKAI/MIND AND SOCIETY. Text in Japanese. 1931. q. back issues avail. **Document type:** *Journal, Academic/Scholarly.*
Supersedes in part (in 1969): Seishin Eisei/Mental Hygiene
Indexed: E-psyche.
Published by: Nihon Seishin Eiseikai/Japan Mental Health Society, 91 Bentencho, Shinjyuku-ku, Tokyo, 162-0851, Japan. z-seisin@dc4.so-net.ne.jp.

150 DEU ISSN 0720-1079
➤ **KONTEXT**; Zeitschrift fuer Systematische Therapie und Familientherapie. Text in German. 1979. 4/yr. EUR 57 to individuals; EUR 114 to institutions; EUR 46 to students; EUR 17.90 newsstand/cover (effective 2011). adv. **Document type:** *Journal, Academic/Scholarly.*
Indexed: DIP, E-psyche, IBR, IBZ.
—GNLM.
Published by: (Deutschen Gesellschaft Systemische Therapie und Familientherapie e.V.), Vandenhoeck und Ruprecht, Theaterstr 13, Goettingen, 37073, Germany. TEL 49-551-508440, FAX 49-551-5084422, info@v-r.de. Ed. Sandra Englisch. Circ: 3,700 (paid and controlled).

➤ **KOTAPRESS JOURNAL.** *see* LITERATURE—Poetry

➤ **KOTSU SHINRIGAKU KENKYU/JAPANESE JOURNAL OF TRAFFIC PSYCHOLOGY.** *see* TRANSPORTATION—Roads And Traffic

158 DEU ISSN 1865-4517
KUNST, GESTALTUNG UND THERAPIE. Text in German. 2008. irreg., latest vol.2, 2009. price varies. **Document type:** *Monographic series, Academic/Scholarly.*
Published by: Frank und Timme GmbH, Wittelsbacherstr 27a, Berlin, 10707, Germany. TEL 49-30-88667911, FAX 49-30-86398731, info@frank-timme.de.

616.89 DEU ISSN 0177-4352
KUNST UND THERAPIE. Text in German. 1982. irreg. **Document type:** *Monographic series, Academic/Scholarly.*
Indexed: P30.
Published by: Koelner Schule fuer Kunsttherapie e.V., Rennbahnstr 117, Cologne, 50737, Germany. TEL 49-221-131108, FAX 49-221-375538, info@koelnerschule.de, http://www.koelnerschule.de.

KYIVS'KYI NATSIONAL'NYI UNIVERSYTET IMENI TARASA SHEVCHENKA. VISNYK. SOTSIOLOHIYA, PSYKHOLOHIYA, PEDAHOHIKA. *see* SOCIOLOGY

370.15 150 JPN ISSN 0021-5015
LB1051 CODEN: JJEPAP
➤ **KYOIKU SHINRIGAKU KENKYU/JAPANESE JOURNAL OF EDUCATIONAL PSYCHOLOGY.** Text in Japanese; Contents page in English. 1953. q. subscr. incld. with membership. adv. bk.rev. charts. **Document type:** *Journal, Academic/Scholarly.*
Indexed: A20, A22, ASCA, BAS, CDA, CurCont, E-psyche, MLA-IB, P03, PsycInfo, PsycholAb, S02, S03, SCOPUS, SSCI, W07.
—BLDSC (4651.750000), IE, Ingenta. **CCC.**
Published by: Nihon Kyoiku Shinri Gakkai/Japanese Association of Educational Psychology, 5F 1st Yaguchi Bldg., 2-11-7,Hongo,Bunkyoku, Tokyo, 113-0033, Japan. TEL 81-3-38181534, FAX 81-3-38181575, kyoshin@wb3.so-net.ne.jp, http://wwwsoc.nii.ac.jp/jaep/. Circ: (controlled).

➤ **KYOIKU SHINRIGAKU NENPO/ANNUAL REPORT OF EDUCATIONAL PSYCHOLOGY IN JAPAN.** *see* EDUCATION

616.89 JPN ISSN 0285-4562
KYUSHU DAIGAKU SHINRI RINSHO KENKYU/KYUSHU UNIVERSITY. PSYCHOLOGICAL CLINIC. ARCHIVES. Text in Japanese. 1982. a. for sale only to clinician. **Document type:** *Academic/Scholarly.*
Indexed: E-psyche.
Published by: (Shinri Kyoiku Sodanshitsu), Kyushu Daigaku, Kyoikugakubu, 19-1 Hakozaki 6-chome, Higashi-ku, Fukuoka-shi, 812-8581, Japan. TEL 81-92-642-3144, FAX 81-92-646-4330. Ed. Seiichi Tajima.

THE L D READER. (Learning Disabilities) *see* EDUCATION—Special Education And Rehabilitation

150 SWE
L I U-P E K-R. (Linkoepings Universitet. Institutionen foer Beteendevetenskap och Laerande. Reports) Text in English, Swedish. 1984. irreg. back issues avail. **Document type:** *Monographic series, Academic/Scholarly.*
Former titles (until 2007): Linkoepings Universitet. Institutionen foer Beteendevetenskap (1650-3643); (until 2000): Linkoepings Universitet. Institutionen foer Pedagogik och Psykologi (1404-8183); (until 1994): Universitetet i Linkoeping. Institutionen foer Pedagogik och Psykologi. Rapport (0282-4957); Which incorporated (1985-1993): Universitetet i Linkoeping. Institutionen foer Pedagogik och Psykologi. Arbetsrapport (0283-0787); Which was formerly (until 1985): Universitetet i Linkoeping. Pedagogiska Institutionen. Arbetsrapport (0281-7438); (1975-1984): Universitetet i Linkoeping. Pedagogiska Institutionen. Rapport (0348-4785)
Related titles: Online - full text ed.
Published by: Linkoepings Universitet, Institutionen foer Beteendevetenskap och Laerande/University of Linkoeping, Department of Behavioural Sciences and Learning, Campus Valla, Linkoeping, 58183, Sweden. TEL 46-13-281000, FAX 46-13-282145, http://www.ibl.liu.se.

150.195 USA ISSN 1049-7749
RC500
LACANIAN INK. Text in English. 1990. s-a. USD 20 domestic to individuals; USD 36 foreign to individuals; USD 40 domestic to institutions; USD 56 foreign to institutions (effective 2004). back issues avail. **Document type:** *Journal, Academic/Scholarly.*
Indexed: A01, E-psyche, T02.
—BLDSC (5142.758000).
Published by: (Lacan Circle of New York), Wooster Press, 133 Wooster St, 7R, New York, NY 10012. perfume@lacan.com, http://www.lacan.com/woosterp.htm. Ed. Josefina Ayerza.

150.195 USA
➤ **LACANIAN STUDIES**; a journal of lacanian studies. Text in English. 1987. s-a. bk.rev. **Document type:** *Journal, Academic/Scholarly.* **Description:** Dedicated to the study of Jacques Lacan's oral teaching as presented in the seminars (1953-81) and the Ecrits (1966).
Former titles (until 1997): Askew; Newsletter of the Freudian Field (0894-1750)
Related titles: Online - full content ed.: free membership (effective 2003).
Indexed: E-psyche.
Published by: (Foundation Freudian Field), Ellie Ragland, Ed. & Pub., 502 W Rockcreek Dr, Columbia, MO 65203-1664. TEL 573-445-1655, FAX 573-882-5785. Eds. Ellie Ragland, Eve Moore. R&P Ellie Ragland. Circ: 300 (paid).

150 ARG ISSN 1852-1770
LAGOM-PSI. Text in Spanish. 2008. s-a. back issues avail. **Document type:** *Bulletin, Academic/Scholarly.*
Media: Online - full text.
Published by: Colegio de Psicologos de la Provincia de Buenos Aires, Rivadavia 154 3o. Piso, San Isidro, Buenos Aires, Argentina. TEL 54-11-47322050, FAX 54-11-47473251, cpsi@sion.com, http://www.cpsi.org.ar/.

▼ **LANDSCAPES OF VIOLENCE**; an interdisciplinary journal devoted to the study of violence, conflict, and trauma. *see* POLITICAL SCIENCE—Civil Rights

LANGUAGE AND COGNITIVE PROCESSES. *see* LINGUISTICS

LANGUAGE, CULTURE AND COGNITION. *see* LINGUISTICS

LATERALITY; asymmetries of body, brain and cognition. *see* MEDICAL SCIENCES—Psychiatry And Neurology

152.4 646 AUS ISSN 1832-2999
LAUGH WHILE YOU WAIT. Text in English. 2005. m. **Document type:** *Magazine, Consumer.*
Published by: VIG-LAX International, PO Box 35, Sandown Village, VIC 3171, Australia. TEL 61-3-95470380, FAX 61-3-95475524, contactus@laughwhileuwait.com.

808.87 USA ISSN 0731-1788
LAUGHING MATTERS. Text in English. 1981. q. USD 15. bk.rev. illus. cum.index. back issues avail.
Indexed: E-psyche.
Published by: Saratoga Institute, Humor Project, 480 Broadway, 210, Saratoga Springs, NY 12866-2230. TEL 518-587-8770. Ed. Dr. Joel Goodman. Circ: 10,000.

LAW AND HUMAN BEHAVIOR. *see* LAW

LAW AND PSYCHOLOGY REVIEW. *see* LAW

158 USA ISSN 1941-4005
LB2342.92
LEADERSHIP EXCHANGE. Text in English. 2003. q. USD 41 combined subscription to members (print & online eds.) (effective 2010). adv. back issues avail. **Document type:** *Magazine, Trade.* **Description:** Delivers expert news and analysis on the most timely and sensitive issues in student affairs.
Related titles: Online - full text ed.: ISSN 1937-8947.
—**CCC.**
Published by: National Association of Student Personnel Administrators, 111 K St, NE, 10th Fl, Washington, DC 20002. TEL 202-265-7500, FAX 202-898-5737, office@naspa.org, naspa@tasco1.com. Adv. contact Fred Comparato TEL 614-204-5994.

THE LEADERSHIP QUARTERLY. *see* BUSINESS AND ECONOMICS—Management

591.5 USA ISSN 1543-4494
QL785 CODEN: ALBVAB
➤ **LEARNING & BEHAVIOR.** Abbreviated title: L & B. Text in English. 1964. q. EUR 255, USD 297 combined subscription to institutions (print & online eds.) (effective 2012). adv. illus. back issues avail.; reprint service avail. from PSC. **Document type:** *Journal, Academic/Scholarly.* **Description:** Features experimental and theoretical contributions and critical reviews concerning fundamental processes of learning and behavior in nonhuman and human animals.
Formerly (until 2003): Animal Learning & Behavior (0090-4996); Which superseded in part (in 1973): Psychonomic Science (0033-3131)
Related titles: Microform ed.: (from PQC); Online - full text ed.: ISSN 1543-4508 (from IngentaConnect).
Indexed: A01, A02, A03, A08, A20, A22, A26, ASCA, ASFA, Agr, AnBeAb, B04, B21, B25, BIOBASE, BIOSIS Prev, BRD, CA, ChemoAb, CurCont, E-psyche, E07, E08, EMBASE, ESPM, EntAb, ExcerpMed, FR, G03, G08, GSA, GSI, I05, IABS, IBR, IBZ, ISR, Inpharma, MEDLINE, MycolAb, NSA, P02, P03, P10, P12, P15, P20, P22, P25, P26, P27, P30, P48, P52, P53, P54, P56, PQC, PsycInfo, PsycholAb, R10, Reac, S09, S10, SCI, SCOPUS, SSCI, T02, ToxAb, W03, W07, WildRev, Z01.
—BLDSC (5179.325855), IE, Ingenta, INIST, Linda Hall. **CCC.**
Published by: Springer New York LLC (Subsidiary of: Springer Science+Business Media), 233 Spring St, New York, NY 10013. TEL 212-460-1500, FAX 212-460-1575, journals@springer-ny.com. Ed. Geoffrey Hall. adv.: B&W page USD 240; trim 8 x 11. Circ: 800.

➤ **LEARNING AND INDIVIDUAL DIFFERENCES**; journal of psychology and education. *see* EDUCATION

➤ **LEARNING AND INSTRUCTION.** *see* EDUCATION

➤ **LEARNING AND MOTIVATION.** *see* EDUCATION

153.1 HUN ISSN 1789-3186
➤ **LEARNING & PERCEPTION.** Text in English. 2008. s-a. (in 1 vol., 2 nos./vol.). EUR 238, USD 334 combined subscription (print & online eds.) (effective 2012). **Document type:** *Journal, Academic/Scholarly.* **Description:** Concerned with various aspects of human learning, memory and perception. Coverage includes, but is not limited to experimental, neuropsychological and neuropsychiatric studies on human cognition.
Related titles: Online - full content ed.: ISSN 2060-9175. EUR 206, USD 288 (effective 2012).
Indexed: P30.
Published by: Akademiai Kiado Rt. (Subsidiary of: Wolters Kluwer N.V.), Prielle Kornelia u 19/D, Budapest, 1117, Hungary. TEL 36-1-4648222, FAX 36-1-4648221, journals@akkrt.hu, http://www.akademiai.com. Ed. Mihaly Racsmany.

➤ **LEARNING DISABILITY PRACTICE.** *see* EDUCATION—Special Education And Rehabilitation

153.1 GBR
LEARNING IN DOING; social, cognitive and computational perspectives. Text in English. 1987. irreg., latest 2009. price varies. back issues avail.; reprints avail. **Document type:** *Monographic series, Academic/Scholarly.* **Description:** Examines cognitive theories of knowledge representation and educational practice in schools and in the workplace, along with the current and future nature of learning.
Published by: Cambridge University Press, The Edinburgh Bldg, Shaftesbury Rd, Cambridge, CB2 8RU, United Kingdom. TEL 44-1223-312393, FAX 44-1223-315052, journals@cambridge.org, http://www.cambridge.org/uk. Eds. Christian Heath, John Seely Brown, Roy Pea.

LEBENDIGE SEELSORGE; Zeitschrift fuer alle Fragen der Seelsorge. *see* RELIGIONS AND THEOLOGY—Protestant

158 364 614.19 GBR ISSN 1355-3259
K12 CODEN: LCPSFX
➤ **LEGAL AND CRIMINOLOGICAL PSYCHOLOGY.** Abbreviated title: L C P. Text in English. 1996. s-a. GBP 158 in United Kingdom to institutions; EUR 213 in Europe to institutions; USD 264 elsewhere to institutions; GBP 193 combined subscription in United Kingdom to institutions (print & online eds.); EUR 260 combined subscription in Europe to institutions (print & online eds.); USD 323 combined subscription elsewhere to institutions (print & online eds.) (effective 2012). adv. bk.rev. abstr. 128 p./no.; back issues avail.; reprint service avail. from PSC. **Document type:** *Journal, Academic/Scholarly.* **Description:** Covers theoretical, empirical and review studies in the field as broadly defined. Topics include new legislation, victimology, theories of delinquency, public attitudes, mental health and the law, policing and crime detection.
Related titles: Magnetic Tape ed.; Microfiche ed.; Online - full text ed.: ISSN 2044-8333. 1999. GBP 168 in United Kingdom to institutions; EUR 226 in Europe to institutions; USD 280 elsewhere to institutions (effective 2012).
Indexed: A01, A03, A08, A22, ASSIA, CA, CJA, CJPI, CurCont, DIP, E-psyche, E01, EMBASE, ExcerpMed, FamI, IBR, IBZ, L03, P03, P20, P25, P43, P48, P54, PQC, PsycInfo, PsycholAb, S02, S03, SCOPUS, SSA, SSCI, SociolAb, T02, W07.
—BLDSC (5181.312110), IE, Infotrieve, Ingenta, INIST. **CCC.**
Published by: (The British Psychological Society), John Wiley & Sons Ltd. (Subsidiary of: John Wiley & Sons, Inc.), 9600 Garsington Rd, Oxford, OX4 2DQ, United Kingdom. TEL 44-1865-776868, FAX 44-1865-714591, customer@wiley.co.uk, http://www.wiley.com. Ed. Aldert Vrij. adv.: page GBP 220; trim 174 x 247.

153.1 DEU
LEIPZIG SERIES IN COGNITIVE SCIENCES. Text in German. 2000. irreg., latest vol.4, 2002. price varies. **Document type:** *Monographic series, Academic/Scholarly.*
Published by: Leipziger Universitaetsverlag GmbH, Oststr 41, Leipzig, 04317, Germany. TEL 49-341-9900440, FAX 49-341-9900440, info@univerlag-leipzig.de.

LEISURE SCIENCES; an interdisciplinary journal. *see* LEISURE AND RECREATION

649 155.4 FRA ISSN 1146-061X
LA LETTRE DE L'ENFANCE ET DE L'ADOLESCENCE; revue du GRAPE. Key Title: Groupe de Recherche et d'Action pour l'Enfance. La Lettre. Text in French. 1990. 4/yr. EUR 38 domestic; EUR 50 foreign (effective 2011). back issues avail. **Document type:** *Journal, Academic/Scholarly.*
Related titles: Online - full text ed.: ISSN 1951-6304.
Published by: (Groupe de Recherche et d'Action pour l'Enfance (GRAPE)), Editions Eres, 33 Av. Marcel Dassault, Toulouse, 31500, France. TEL 33-5-61751576, FAX 33-5-61735289, eres@edition-eres.com, http://www.edition-eres.com. Ed. Francoise Petitot. Circ: 1,100.

150 PER ISSN 1729-4827
LIBERABIT. Variant title: Revista de Psicologia Liberabit. Text in Spanish. a. **Document type:** *Journal, Academic/Scholarly.*
Related titles: Online - full text ed.: ISSN 2223-7666. 2009. free (effective 2011) (from SciELO).
Published by: Universidad de San Martin de Porres, Facultad de Ciencias de la Comunicacion, Turismo y Psicologia, Ave Tomas marsano 242, Anexos 2037 Surquillo, Lima, 36, Peru. TEL 511-513-6300, FAX 511-242-5899, liberabit@psicologia.usmp.edu.pe. Ed. Jesus Romero Croce.

301.1 150 GBR ISSN 0267-7172
LIBERTARIAN ALLIANCE. PSYCHOLOGICAL NOTES. Text in English. 1988. irreg., latest 2000. back issues avail. **Document type:** *Monographic series, Trade.*
Related titles: Online - full text ed.: ISSN 2042-2784. free (effective 2009).
Indexed: E-psyche.
Published by: Libertarian Alliance, 2 Lansdowne Row, Ste 35, London, W1J 6HL, United Kingdom. TEL 44-7956-472199. Ed. Nigel Meek.

158 USA ISSN 2150-1971
LIFEEXCELLENCE NEWSLETTER. Text in English. 2001. bi-w. free (effective 2009). back issues avail. **Document type:** *Newsletter, Trade.* **Description:** Aims to inspire and support people who are committed to improving performance and achieving greater success in their lives.
Media: Online - full content.

Published by: LifeExcellence, Llc, PO Box 700424, Plymouth, MI 48170. TEL 734-254-9970, FAX 734-254-9973, info@lifeexcellence.com, http://www.lifeexcellence.com.

LIMITE. *see* PHILOSOPHY

150 USA ISSN 1534-7508
LIVING & LEARNING; effective strategies for behavior change. Text in English. 2001. s-a. **Document type:** *Journal, Academic/Scholarly.*
Description: Aims to empower caring people to become more effective in solving society's problems.
Indexed: E-psyche.
Published by: Cambridge Center for Behavioral Studies, 550 Newtown Rd, Ste 700, Littleton, MA 01460. TEL 978-369-2227, FAX 978-369-8584, harshbarger@behavior.org. Ed. Katharine B. Daugherty.

616.85882 USA
LIVING IN THE SPECTRUM: AUTISM & ASPERGER'S. Text in English. 2004. a. USD 16.95 (effective 2005). **Document type:** *Journal, Magazine, Consumer.*
Published by: Mindscape Productions, Llc, 4022 Custer Ave, Royal Oak, MI 48073. TEL 248-288-2242, FAX 248-288-3021, info@mindscapeproductions.com, http://www.mindscapeproducations.com. Ed., R&P Lecia Macryn.

155 USA ISSN 1935-701X
LIVING WITH LOSS MAGAZINE. Text in English. 1987. q. USD 32 domestic; USD 49 foreign (effective 2007). **Document type:** *Magazine, Consumer.* **Description:** Contains articles, stories and poems written and submitted by the bereaved for the bereaved.
Formerly (until 2006): Bereavement (0897-9588)
Published by: Bereavement Publishing, Inc., P O Box 61, Montrose, CO 81402. TEL 888-604-4673, FAX 970-252-1776.

LONGITUDINAL RESEARCH IN THE SOCIAL AND BEHAVIORAL SCIENCES; an interdisciplinary series. *see* SOCIAL SCIENCES: COMPREHENSIVE WORKS

LUND STUDIES IN PSYCHOLOGY OF RELIGION. *see* RELIGIONS AND THEOLOGY

150 DEU ISSN 0933-3347
BF173.A2
LUZIFER-AMOR; Zeitschrift zur Geschichte der Psychoanalyse. Text in German. 1988. s-a. EUR 30; EUR 18 newsstand/cover (effective 2009). adv. bk.rev. back issues avail. **Document type:** *Journal, Academic/Scholarly.*
Indexed: DIP, E-psyche, EMBASE, ExcerpMed, IBR, IBZ, MEDLINE, P03, P30, PsycInfo, PsycholAb, R10, Reac, SCOPUS.
—GNLM. **CCC.**
Published by: Edition Diskord (Subsidiary of: Brandes und Apsel Verlag GmbH), Scheidswaldstr 22, Frankfurt am Main, 60385, Germany. TEL 49-69-272995170, FAX 49-69-2729951710, info@brandes-apsel-verlag.de, http://www.edition-diskord.de. Ed. Ludger Hermanns. R&P Gerd Kimmerle. Circ: 800.

158 618.92 NOR ISSN 0801-1346
MAGASINET VOKSNE FOR BARN. Text in Norwegian. 1921. 5/yr. NOK 275; NOK 60 per issue (effective 2007). adv. bk.rev. bibl. back issues avail. **Document type:** *Magazine, Consumer.*
Incorporates (1996-2006): Voksne for Boern. Bulletin (0809-1293); Former titles (until 2005): Temamagasinet for Foraeldre om.. (1502-475X); (until 2000): Sinnets Helse (0049-0563); (until 1960): Mentalhygiene og Folkehelse (0332-7876); (until 1954): Folkehelseforeningens Tidsskrift (0332-7884)
Related titles: Online - full text ed.: ISSN 1890-2499. 2005.
Indexed: E-psyche.
—CCC.
Published by: Voksne for Barn, Stortorvet 10, Oslo, 0155, Norway. TEL 47-23-100610, FAX 47-23-100611, vfb@vfb.no. Eds. Ingeborg Vea, Randi Talseth. Circ: 4,500.

150 HUN ISSN 0025-0279
BF8.H8
MAGYAR PSZICHOLOGIAI SZEMLE/HUNGARIAN PSYCHOLOGICAL REVIEW. Text in Hungarian; Summaries in English. 1928. q. EUR 109, USD 147 combined subscription (print & online eds.) (effective 2011). adv. bk.rev. abstr.; illus. index. 160 p./no.; back issues avail. **Document type:** *Journal, Academic/Scholarly.* **Description:** Latest Hungarian and occasional foreign results in fields of general and evolutionary, medical, pedagogical, social psychology, psychology of art, and criminal psychology research.
Related titles: Online - full text ed.: ISSN 1588-2799. EUR 92, USD 126 (effective 2011).
Indexed: CISA, E-psyche, MLA-IB, P03, PsycInfo, PsycholAb, RASB, S02, S03, SCOPUS, SOPODA, SociolAb.
—Ingenta.
Published by: (Budapesti Muszaki es Gazdasagtudomanyi Egyetem, Kognitiv Tudomanyi Tanszek, Magyar Tudomanyos Akademia/ Hungarian Academy of Sciences), Akademiai Kiado Rt. (Subsidiary of: Wolters Kluwer N.V.), Prielle Kornelia u 19/D, Budapest, 1117, Hungary. TEL 36-1-4648222, FAX 36-1-4648221, journals@akkrt.hu. Ed. Csaba Pleh.

MAJALAT ADDERASAT ATTARBAWIAH WANNAFSIAH/JOURNAL OF EDUCATIONAL AND PSYCHOLOGICAL STUDIES. *see* EDUCATION

MAJALLAH-I RAVANPIZISHKI VA RAVANSHINASI-I BALINI-I IRAN/IRANIAN JOURNAL OF PSYCHIATRY AND CLINICAL PSYCHOLOGY. *see* MEDICAL SCIENCES—Psychiatry And Neurology

150 IRQ ISSN 1816-1790
MAJALLAT AL-'ULUM AL-NAFSIYYAT/JOURNAL OF PSYCHOLOGICAL SCIENCES. Text in Arabic, English. 1994. q. **Document type:** *Journal, Academic/Scholarly.*
Published by: Jami'at Baghdad, Psychological Research Center (Subsidiary of: Jami'at Baghdad/University of Baghdad), University of Baghdad Complex, Baghdad, Iraq. TEL 964-1-7786678, FAX 964-1-7785162, psychocenter@hotmail.com, http://www.psychocenteriraq.com.

150 BHR ISSN 1726-3670
LB1051
MAJALLAT AL-'ULUM AL-TARBAWIYYAT WA-AL-NAFSIYYAT/ JOURNAL OF EDUCATIONAL & PSYCHOLOGICAL SCIENCES. Text in English. 2002. q. **Document type:** *Journal, Academic/ Scholarly.*
Related titles: Online - full text ed.: ISSN 1726-5231. free (effective 2011).
Published by: University of Bahrain, College of Education, Kingdom of Bahrain, Bahrain. jeps@edu.uob.bh.

150 USA ISSN 1940-3267
MAKING SENSE OF PSYCHOLOGY. Text in English. 2008 (Mar.). irreg., latest 2008. USD 49.95, GBP 34.95 per issue (effective 2010). **Document type:** *Monographic series, Academic/Scholarly.* **Description:** Provides resources for handling harmful situations facing adolescents, offering practical and straightforward methods to aid one in negotiating positive paths for those in distress.
Published by: Praeger Publishers (Subsidiary of: Greenwood Publishing Group Inc.), 88 Post Rd W, Westport, CT 06881. TEL 800-368-6868, tech.support@greenwood.com. Ed. Carol Korn-Bursztyn.

616.89 GBR ISSN 0955-386X
MALCOLM MILLAR LECTURE IN PSYCHOTHERAPY. Text in English. 1980. irreg. **Document type:** *Monographic series, Academic/ Scholarly.*
Formerly (until 1988): Malcolm Millar Lecture (0144-1663)
—CCC.
Published by: University of Aberdeen, Department of Mental Health, Royal Cornhill Hospital, Aberdeen, AB25 2ZD, United Kingdom. TEL 44-1224-557951, FAX 44-1224-557400, mental.health.FH@abdn.ac.uk, http://www.abdn.ac.uk/mentalhealth/ DepartmentofMentalHealth.shtml.

MALTRATTAMENTO E ABUSO ALL'INFANZIA. *see* CHILDREN AND YOUTH—About

MANAGEMENT KINDEROPVANG. *see* CHILDREN AND YOUTH—About

MANKIND QUARTERLY. *see* ANTHROPOLOGY

158 USA ISSN 2150-5004
▼ **MARIE JUNE INSPIREME.** Text in English. 2009. q. USD 3.50 per issue (effective 2009). adv. back issues avail. **Document type:** *Magazine, Consumer.* **Description:** Features life inspiring articles essential for life.
Media: Online - full content.
Published by: Marie June and Associates, Inc, PO Box 19577, Detroit, MI 48219. june@mariejuneandassociates.com, http://www.mariejuneandassociates.com. Ed. June Williams.

150 658 USA
MASSACHUSETTS PSYCHOLOGIST. Text in English. 1993. m. Free to qualified subscribers. adv. back issues avail. **Document type:** *Magazine, Trade.* **Description:** Targets business and marketplace issues that affect clinical practices.
Related titles: Online - full content ed.
Address: P O Box 812068, Wellesley, MA 02482-0013. TEL 781-237-9909, feedback@masspsy.com, http://www.masspsy.com. Pub. Denise M. Yocum.

MATERIALIEN AUS DER BILDUNGSFORSCHUNG. *see* EDUCATION

MATHEMATICAL THINKING AND LEARNING; an international journal. *see* MATHEMATICS

616.89 DNK ISSN 0109-646X
➤ **MATRIX**; nordisk tidsskrift for psykoterapi. Text in Danish, Norwegian, Swedish; Abstracts in English. 1984. q. DKK 395 to individuals (effective 2009); DKK 130 per issue (effective 2008). bk.rev. 80 p./no.; back issues avail. **Document type:** *Journal, Academic/Scholarly.*
Indexed: E-psyche, P03, PsycInfo.
Published by: (Dansk Psykolog Forening/Danish Psychological Association), Dansk Psykologisk Forlag/Danish Psychological Publishers, Kongevejen 155, Virum, 2830, Denmark. TEL 45-35-381655, FAX 45-35-381665, info@dpf.dk. Eds. Anne Lindhardt, Svein Tjelta.

155 USA ISSN 1556-665X
MCGRAW-HILL SERIES IN DEVELOPMENTAL PSYCHOLOGY. Text in English. 199?. irreg. price varies. back issues avail. **Document type:** *Monographic series, Academic/Scholarly.*
Published by: McGraw-Hill Companies, Inc., 1221 Ave of the Americas, 43rd fl, New York, NY 10020. TEL 212-512-2000, customer.service@mcgraw-hill.com, http://www.mcgraw-hill.com. Ed. Ross Thompson.

MEASUREMENT AND EVALUATION IN COUNSELING AND DEVELOPMENT. *see* EDUCATION

302.23 USA ISSN 1521-3269
P96.P75
➤ **MEDIA PSYCHOLOGY.** Text in English. 1999. q. GBP 491 combined subscription in United Kingdom to institutions (print & online eds.); EUR 655, USD 823 combined subscription to institutions (print & online eds.) (effective 2012). adv. back issues avail.; reprint service avail. from PSC. **Document type:** *Journal, Academic/Scholarly.* **Description:** Publishes theoretical and empirical research in the area where the fields of psychology and media communication intersect.
Related titles: Online - full text ed.: ISSN 1532-785X. GBP 442 in United Kingdom to institutions; EUR 590, USD 740 to institutions (effective 2012) (from IngentaConnect).
Indexed: A01, A03, A08, A20, A22, ArtHuCI, BRD, CA, CMM, CommAb, CurCont, E-psyche, E01, F01, F02, FamI, P03, P10, P12, P25, P27, P30, P48, P53, P54, PQC, PsycInfo, PsycholAb, S02, S03, S11, SCOPUS, SSAI, SSAb, SSCI, SSI, T02, W03, W07.
—BLDSC (5525.258750), IE, Infotrieve, Ingenta. **CCC.**
Published by: Routledge (Subsidiary of: Taylor & Francis Group), 325 Chestnut St, Ste 800, Philadelphia, PA 19106. TEL 800-354-1420, FAX 215-625-2940, journals@routledge.com, http://www.routledge.com. Adv. contact Linda Hann TEL 44-1344-779945.

150 ARG ISSN 1668-3897
MEDIODICHO. Text in Spanish. 1996. s-a. **Document type:** *Journal, Academic/Scholarly.*
Published by: Escuela de la Orientacion Lacaniana, Caseros 950, Cordoba, 5000, Argentina. eolcordoba@eolcba.com.ar, http://www.eolcba.com.ar/.

150 UKR
➤ **MEDITSINSKAYA PSIKHOLOGIYA/MEDICAL PSYCHOLOGY**; nauchno-prakticheskii zhurnal. Text in Russian, Ukrainian. 2006. q. USD 77 foreign (effective 2006). **Document type:** *Journal, Academic/ Scholarly.*
Published by: (Khar'kovskoe Meditsinskoe Obshchestvo), Khar'kovskaya Meditsinskaya Akademiya Poslediplomnogo Obrazovaniya, ul Mironositskaya 81/85, Khar'kov, Ukraine. TEL 380-57-7005002, FAX 380-57-7007685. Ed. V V Krishtal'. Circ: 500.
Dist. by: East View Information Services, 10601 Wayzata Blvd, Minneapolis, MN 55305. TEL 952-252-1201, 800-477-1005, FAX 952-252-1202, info@eastview.com, http://www.eastview.com.

616.890 133 NLD ISSN 1878-920X
MEMORIE. Text in Dutch. 198?. bi-m. EUR 55 (effective 2011). **Document type:** *Magazine, Trade.*
Formerly (until 2009): Nederlandse Vereniging van Reincarnatie Therapeuten. Het Bulletin (1570-9752)
Published by: Nederlandse Vereniging van Reincarnatie Therapeuten, c/o Gerda van Middendorp, Sec., Kleine Beer 47, Zeewolde, 3893 DG, Netherlands. TEL 31-6-25288716, http://www.reincarnatietherapie.nl. Ed. Henk Muda TEL 31-24-3775259.

152 GBR ISSN 0965-8211
BF371 CODEN: MEMOFV
➤ **MEMORY.** Text in English. 1993. 8/yr. GBP 812 combined subscription in United Kingdom to institutions (print & online eds.); EUR 1,072, USD 1,348 combined subscription to institutions (print & online eds.) (effective 2012). back issues avail.; reprint service avail. from PSC. **Document type:** *Journal, Academic/Scholarly.* **Description:** Covers high-quality research in all areas of memory, including experimental studies and developmental, educational, neuropsychological, clinical, and social research on memory.
Related titles: Online - full text ed.: ISSN 1464-0686. GBP 731 in United Kingdom to institutions; EUR 965, USD 1,213 to institutions (effective 2012) (from IngentaConnect).
Indexed: A01, A03, A08, A20, A22, AMED, ASCA, B21, BIOBASE, CA, CurCont, E-psyche, E01, EMBASE, ErgAb, ExcerpMed, FamI, IABS, IndMed, L&LBA, MEDLINE, NSA, P03, P30, P43, PsycInfo, PsycholAb, R10, Reac, SCOPUS, SOPODA, SSCI, SociolAb, T02, W07.
—IE, Infotrieve, Ingenta, INIST. **CCC.**
Published by: Psychology Press (Subsidiary of: Taylor & Francis Ltd.), 27 Church Rd, Hove, E Sussex BN3 2FA, United Kingdom. TEL 44-20-70176000, 44-1273-207411, FAX 44-20-70176717, info@psypress.co.uk, http://www.psypress.co.uk. Eds. Martin A Conway, Susan E Gathercole. Adv. contact Linda Hann TEL 44-1344-779945. **Subscr. in N. America to:** Taylor & Francis Inc., Customer Services Dept, 325 Chestnut St, 8th Fl, Philadelphia, PA 19106. TEL 215-625-8900, 800-354-1420, FAX 215-625-2940; **Subscr. outside of N. America to:** Taylor & Francis Ltd., Journals Customer Service, Sheepen Pl, Colchester, Essex CO3 3LP, United Kingdom. TEL 44-20-70175544, FAX 44-20-70175198, subscriptions@tandf.co.uk, http://www.tandf.co.uk/journals.

P

152 USA ISSN 0090-502X
BF371 CODEN: MYCGAO
➤ **MEMORY AND COGNITION.** Abbreviated title: M & C. Text in English. 1964. 8/yr. EUR 420, USD 472 combined subscription to institutions (print & online eds.) (effective 2012). adv. bibl.; illus. back issues avail.; reprint service avail. from PSC. **Document type:** *Journal, Academic/Scholarly.* **Description:** Covers human memory, learning, conceptual processes, psycholinguistics, and problem solving, along with reports of work in computer simulation and experimental social psychology.
Supersedes in part (in 1973): Psychonomic Science (0033-3131)
Related titles: Microform ed.: (from PQC); Online - full text ed.: ISSN 1532-5946 (from IngentaConnect).
Indexed: A01, A02, A03, A08, A12, A20, A22, A26, ABIn, ASCA, B01, B06, B07, B09, B21, BRD, C06, C07, C08, CA, CDA, CINAHL, CommAb, CurCont, DIP, E-psyche, E07, E08, EMBASE, ErgAb, ExcerpMed, FR, G08, H12, I05, IBR, IBZ, IndMed, L&LBA, MEA&I, MEDLINE, MLA, MLA-IB, NSA, P02, P03, P07, P10, P12, P20, P22, P24, P25, P27, P30, P48, P51, P53, P54, PQC, PsycInfo, PsycholAb, R10, RASB, RILM, Reac, S02, S03, S09, SCOPUS, SOPODA, SSAI, SSAb, SSCI, SSI, T02, W03, W07.
—BLDSC (5678.300000), GNLM, IE, Infotrieve, Ingenta, INIST, Linda Hall. **CCC.**
Published by: Springer New York LLC (Subsidiary of: Springer Science+Business Media), 233 Spring St, New York, NY 10013. TEL 212-460-1500, FAX 212-460-1575, journals-ny@springer.com. Ed. James Nairne. Circ: 1,700.

153.1 GBR ISSN 1750-6980
BF371
➤ **MEMORY STUDIES.** Text in English. 2008 (Jan.). 4/yr. USD 585, GBP 316 combined subscription to institutions (print & online eds.); USD 573, GBP 310 to institutions (effective 2011). adv. back issues avail.; reprint service avail. from PSC. **Document type:** *Journal, Academic/ Scholarly.* **Description:** Examines the social, cultural, cognitive, political and technological shifts affecting how, what and why individuals, groups and societies remember, and forget.
Related titles: Online - full text ed.: ISSN 1750-6999. USD 527, GBP 284 to institutions (effective 2011).
Indexed: A22, B21, E01, NSA, SCOPUS.
—BLDSC (5678.372000), IE. **CCC.**
Published by: Sage Publications Ltd. (Subsidiary of: Sage Publications, Inc.), 1 Oliver's Yard, 55 City Rd, London, EC1Y 1SP, United Kingdom. TEL 44-20-73248500, FAX 44-20-73248600, info@sagepub.co.uk, http://www.uk.sagepub.com/home.nav. Ed. Andrew Hoskins. adv.: B&W page GBP 350; 130 x 205. **Subscr. in the americas to:** Sage Publications, Inc., 2455 Teller Rd, Thousand Oaks, CA 91320. TEL 805-499-9774, FAX 805-499-0871, journals@sagepub.com.

➤ **MENNINGER CLINIC. BULLETIN**; a journal for the mental health professions. *see* MEDICAL SCIENCES—Psychiatry And Neurology

➤ **MENNINGER PERSPECTIVE.** *see* MEDICAL SCIENCES—Psychiatry And Neurology

➤ **MENS SANA MONOGRAPHS.** *see* MEDICAL SCIENCES—Psychiatry And Neurology

153.9 FRA ISSN 1771-8813
MENSANS; le journal de Mensa. Text in French. 2005. bi-m. **Document type:** *Magazine, Consumer.*
Published by: Mensa France, 20 Rue Leonard de Vinci, Paris, 75116, France. TEL 033-6-61226878, informations@mensa.fr.

614.58 790.1 USA
THE MENTAL EDGE. Text in English. q. USD 29.95 domestic (effective 2007). **Document type:** *Newsletter, Trade.* **Description:** Covers specific procedures to enhance sports performance and discusses how top athletes use mental training to boost their athletic skills.
Published by: Mental Edge, 18607 Ventura Blvd, Ste 310, Tarzana, CA 91356. Ed. J P Erickson.

613.7 158 NLD ISSN 1755-2966
RA790.A1
➤ **MENTAL HEALTH AND PHYSICAL ACTIVITY.** Text in English. 2008. s-a. EUR 150 in Europe to institutions; JPY 24,800 in Japan to institutions; USD 200 elsewhere to institutions (effective 2012). **Document type:** *Journal, Academic/Scholarly.* **Description:** Aims to foster the inter-disciplinary development and understanding of the mental health and physical activity field.
Related titles: Online - full text ed.: 2008 (from ScienceDirect).
Indexed: CA, EMBASE, ExcerpMed, P30, PsycInfo, SCOPUS, T02.
—IE. **CCC.**
Published by: Elsevier BV (Subsidiary of: Elsevier Science & Technology), Radarweg 29, PO Box 211, Amsterdam, 1000 AE, Netherlands. TEL 31-20-4853911, FAX 31-20-4852457, JournalsCustomerServiceEMEA@elsevier.com. Eds. Adrian Taylor, Guy Faulkner.

➤ **MENTAL HEALTH AND SOCIAL INCLUSION.** *see* SOCIAL SERVICES AND WELFARE

616.89 USA
MENTAL HEALTH DISORDERS SOURCEBOOK. Text in English. 1995. irreg., latest 2005, 3rd ed. USD 84 3rd ed. (effective 2008). charts. Index. **Document type:** *Handbook/Manual/Guide, Consumer.* **Description:** Basic information about schizophrenia, depression, bipolar disorder, panic disorder, obsessive-compulsive disorder, phobias and other anxiety disorders, paranoia and other personality disorders, eating disorders, and sleep disorders, along with information about treatment and therapies.
Published by: Omnigraphics, Inc., PO Box 31-1640, Detroit, MI 48231. TEL 313-961-1340, 800-234-1340, FAX 313-961-1383, 800-875-1340, info@omnigraphics.com. Ed. Karen Bellenir.

MENTAL HEALTH IN FAMILY MEDICINE. *see* MEDICAL SCIENCES—Psychiatry And Neurology

MENTAL HEALTH LAW BULLETIN. *see* LAW—Civil Law

150 USA
MENTAL HEALTH LIBRARY SERIES. Text in English. 1992. irreg., latest vol.4, 2003. price varies. back issues avail. **Document type:** *Monographic series, Academic/Scholarly.*
Indexed: E-psyche.
Published by: International Universities Press, Inc., 59 Boston Post Rd, Box 1524, PO Box 389, Madison, CT 06443. TEL 203-245-4000, FAX 203-245-0775, info@iup.com.

MENTAL HEALTH MATTERS. *see* MEDICAL SCIENCES—Psychiatry And Neurology

616.89 CAN ISSN 1196-5304
MENTAL HEALTH MATTERS. Text in English, French. q. **Document type:** *Newsletter.* **Description:** Audience consists of members of the association, people who have had mental illness, mental health professionals, and family members.
Formerly (until 1994): Canadian Mental Health Association. National Office. Newsletter (1196-0337)
Published by: Canadian Mental Health Association, 2160 Yonge St, Toronto, ON M4S 2Z3, Canada. TEL 416-484-7750, FAX 416-484-4617. Ed. Nancy MacMillan. Circ: 1,500 (controlled).

150 GBR ISSN 1363-4682
MENTAL HEALTH OCCUPATIONAL THERAPY. Text in English. 1996. 3/yr. **Document type:** *Journal, Academic/Scholarly.*
Indexed: C06, C07, C08, CA, CINAHL, T02.
—BLDSC (5678.583740), IE, Ingenta.
Published by: Association of Occupational Therapists in Mental Health (Subsidiary of: College of Occupational Therapists Ltd.), 120 Wilton Rd, London, SW1V 1JZ, United Kingdom. TEL 44-20-72338322, admin@aotmh.org, http://www.cot.org.uk/specialist/aotmh/intro.php. Ed. Jane Clewes.

155.82 GBR ISSN 1367-4676
RC455.4.R4 CODEN: MHRCA2
➤ **MENTAL HEALTH, RELIGION & CULTURE.** Text in English. 1998. bi-m. GBP 874 combined subscription in United Kingdom to institutions (print & online eds.); EUR 1,155, USD 1,452 combined subscription to institutions (print & online eds.) (effective 2012). adv. back issues avail.; reprint service avail. from PSC. **Document type:** *Journal, Academic/Scholarly.* **Description:** Publishes empirically-based work exploring the relationships between mental health and aspects of religion and culture, and discussing conceptual and philosophical aspects.
Related titles: Online - full text ed.: ISSN 1469-9737. GBP 786 in United Kingdom to institutions; EUR 1,040, USD 1,306 to institutions (effective 2012) (from IngentaConnect).
Indexed: A01, A03, A08, A22, C06, C07, C08, CA, CINAHL, E-psyche, E01, P03, P30, P43, P48, P50, P53, P54, PQC, PsycInfo, PsycholAb, S02, S03, SCOPUS, SSA, SociolAb, T02.
—IE, Infotrieve, Ingenta. **CCC.**
Published by: Routledge (Subsidiary of: Taylor & Francis Group), 4 Park Sq, Milton Park, Abingdon, Oxon OX14 4RN, United Kingdom. TEL 44-20-70176000, FAX 44-20-70176336, subscriptions@tandf.co.uk, http://www.routledge.com. Adv. contact Linda Hann TEL 44-1344-779945. **Subscr. to:** Taylor & Francis Ltd., Journals Customer Service, Sheepen Pl, Colchester, Essex CO3 3LP, United Kingdom. TEL 44-20-70175544, FAX 44-20-70175198, tf.enquiries@tfinforma.com.

614.58 GBR
MENTAL HEALTH RESEARCH REVIEW (ONLINE). Text in English. 1994. irreg., latest vol.9, 2003. free (effective 2010). **Document type:** *Monographic series, Academic/Scholarly.* **Description:** Presents mental health care research carried out by the PSSRU and the Centre for the Economics of Mental Health (CEMH).
Formerly (until 2003): Mental Health Research Review (Print) (1353-2650)
Media: Online - full text.
Indexed: E-psyche.
—CCC.
Published by: Personal Social Services Research Unit, University of Kent at Canterbury, Cornwallis Bldg, George Allen Wing, Canterbury, Kent CT2 7NF, United Kingdom. TEL 44-1227-827672, FAX 44-1227-827038, pssru@kent.ac.uk.

THE MENTAL HEALTH REVIEW JOURNAL. *see* MEDICAL SCIENCES—Psychiatry And Neurology

MENTAL HEALTH REVIEW TRIBUNALS FOR ENGLAND AND WALES. ANNUAL REPORT. *see* PUBLIC HEALTH AND SAFETY

370.15 613.62 USA ISSN 1093-7226
MENTAL HEALTH SPECIAL INTEREST SECTION QUARTERLY. Text in English. 197? (vol.12, no.4). q. free to members (effective 2010). adv. **Document type:** *Newsletter, Trade.* **Description:** Provides a networking and information forum for occupational therapy practitioners providing services to address mental health disorders and psychosocial dysfunction in a wide range of settings.
Former titles (until 1997): Mental Health Special Interest Section Newsletter (0279-4136); (until 1981): American Occupational Therapy Association. Mental Health Specialty Section. Newsletter (0194-6382)
Related titles: Online - full text ed.; ◆ Series: Developmental Disabilities Special Interest Section Quarterly. ISSN 1093-7196; ◆ Gerontology Special Interest Section Quarterly. ISSN 1093-717X; ◆ Technology Special Interest Section Quarterly. ISSN 1093-7137; ◆ Work & Industry Special Interest Section Quarterly; ◆ Education Special Interest Section Quarterly. ISSN 1093-7188; ◆ Physical Disabilities Special Interest Section Quarterly. ISSN 1093-7234; ◆ Administration & Management Special Interest Section Quarterly. ISSN 1093-720X; ◆ Sensory Integration Special Interest Section Quarterly. ISSN 1093-7250.
Indexed: C06, C07, C08, CINAHL, E-psyche, P24, P27, P48, P54, PQC.
—BLDSC (5678.585742). **CCC.**
Published by: American Occupational Therapy Association, Inc., 4720 Montgomery Ln, PO Box 31220, Bethesda, MD 20824, TEL 301-652-2682, 800-377-8555, FAX 301-652-7711, members@aota.org. Ed. Linda Olson.

MENTAL HEALTH TODAY. *see* MEDICAL SCIENCES—Psychiatry And Neurology

362.2 301.1 USA ISSN 1058-1103
RC321
MENTAL HEALTH WEEKLY; news for policy and program decision-makers. Text in English. 1991. w. GBP 2,714 in United Kingdom to institutions; EUR 3,432 in Europe to institutions; USD 5,125 in United States to institutions; USD 5,269 in Canada & Mexico to institutions; USD 5,317 elsewhere to institutions; GBP 3,122 combined subscription in United Kingdom to institutions (print & online eds.); EUR 3,949 combined subscription in Europe to institutions (print & online eds.); USD 5,897 combined subscription in United States to institutions (print & online eds.); USD 6,041 combined subscription in Canada & Mexico to institutions (print & online eds.); USD 6,089 combined subscription elsewhere to institutions (print & online eds.) (effective 2012). adv. 8 p./no.; back issues avail.; reprints avail. **Document type:** *Newsletter, Trade.* **Description:** Covers the latest news and analysis of public policy, business trends and treatment issues affecting mental health administrators in the public, private and nonprofit sectors.
Incorporates (198?-1991): Addiction Program Management (0897-4934); (1970-1991): Behavior Today (0005-7924); Which incorporated (197?-198?): Sexuality Today (0148-883X); (197?-198?): Marriage and Divorce Today (0148-8821)
Related titles: E-mail ed.; Online - full text ed.: ISSN 1556-7583. GBP 2,616 in United Kingdom to institutions; EUR 3,308 in Europe to institutions; USD 5,125 elsewhere to institutions (effective 2012).
Indexed: A01, A02, A03, A08, A26, C06, C07, C08, C12, C28, CA, CINAHL, E-psyche, E08, ECER, G06, G07, G08, H01, H03, H04, H11, H12, I05, M01, M02, M06, P34, PersLit, S02, S03, S09, S23, SWR&A, T02.
—BLDSC (5678.590200), IE. **CCC.**
Published by: John Wiley & Sons, Inc., 111 River St, Hoboken, NJ 07030. TEL 201-748-6000, FAX 201-748-6088, info@wiley.com, http://www.wiley.com/WileyCDA/. Pub. Sue Lewis.

153.93 370 USA ISSN 0076-6461
Z5814.P8
MENTAL MEASUREMENTS YEARBOOK. Text in English. 1938. biennial. price varies. back issues avail. **Document type:** *Yearbook, Trade.* **Description:** Contains descriptions and candidly critical reviews of commercially available test instruments. Reviews done by professionals in the assessment, measurement or subject area.
Former titles (until 1940): Rutgers University. School of Education. Mental Measurements Yearbook; (until 1938): Educational, Psychological, and Personality Tests
Related titles: Fax ed.; Online - full text ed.
Indexed: E-psyche.
—BLDSC (5678.605000).
Published by: Buros Institute of Mental Measurements, 21 Teachers College Hall, University of Nebraska - Lincoln, Lincoln, NE 68588. TEL 402-472-6203, FAX 402-472-6207, pressmail@unl.edu, http://www.unl.edu/buros/bimm/index.html.

MENTALHIGIENE ES PSZICHOSZOMATIKA/JOURNAL OF MENTAL HEALTH AND PSYCHOSOMATICS. *see* MEDICAL SCIENCES—Psychiatry And Neurology

MENTALITIES/MENTALITES; an interdisciplinary journal. *see* HISTORY

150 ESP ISSN 1699-0579
MENTE SANA. Text in Spanish. 2005. m. **Document type:** *Magazine, Consumer.*
Published by: R B A Edipresse, Perez Galdos 36, Barcelona, 08012, Spain. TEL 34-93-4157374, FAX 34-93-2177378, http://www.rbaedipresse.es. Ed. Jorge Bucay.

302 BRA ISSN 1414-1868
MENTE SOCIAL. Text in Portuguese. 1996. s-a. **Document type:** *Journal, Academic/Scholarly.* **Description:** Publishes the research on social psychology done by UGF professors and graduate students.
Published by: Universidade Gama Filho, Rua Manoel Vitorino 625, Piedade, Rio de Janeiro, RJ 20748-900, Brazil. TEL 55-21-32137735, FAX 55-21-32137731, http://www.ugf.br.

150 ESP ISSN 1695-0887
MENTE Y CEREBRO. Text in Spanish. 2002. q. EUR 30 domestic (effective 2010). adv. bk.rev. 96 p./no.; **Document type:** *Journal, Academic/Scholarly.*
Published by: Prensa Cientifica S.A., Muntaner, 339, pral. 1a, Barcelona, 08021, Spain. TEL 34-93-4143344, FAX 34-93-4145413, http://www.investigacionyciencia.es/.

MERIDIAN; Fachzeitschrift fuer Astrologie. *see* NEW AGE PUBLICATIONS

150 301 USA ISSN 0272-930X
HQ1 CODEN: MPQUA5
➤ **MERRILL - PALMER QUARTERLY;** journal of developmental psychology. Text in English. 1954. q. USD 85 to individuals; USD 190 to institutions; USD 27 to students (effective 2009). adv. charts; illus. index. reprints avail. **Document type:** *Journal, Academic/Scholarly.* **Description:** Publishes theoretical and empirical papers in the areas of human development and family-child relationships.
Former titles (until 1960): Merrill - Palmer Quarterly of Behavior and Development (0026-0150); (until 1958): Merrill - Palmer Quarterly (0272-9679)
Related titles: Microform ed.: (from PQC); Online - full text ed.: ISSN 1535-0266.
Indexed: A01, A02, A03, A08, A20, A22, A26, AEI, AMHA, ASCA, B04, BDM&CN, BRD, C28, CA, CDA, CPE, CommAb, CurCont, DIP, DSHAb, E-psyche, E01, E02, E03, E06, E07, E08, ECER, ERA, ERI, ERIC, EdA, EdI, F09, FamI, G08, I05, IBR, IBZ, L&LBA, MEA&I, MLA-IB, P03, P18, P25, P30, P48, P53, P54, P55, PQC, PSI, PsycInfo, PsycholAb, S02, S03, S09, S19, S20, S21, SCOPUS, SFSA, SOPODA, SSCI, SWR&A, SociolAb, T02, V&AA, W03, W05, W07, W09.
—BLDSC (5682.280000), IE, Infotrieve, Ingenta, INIST. **CCC.**
Published by: (Merrill - Palmer Institute), Wayne State University Press, The Leonard N Simons Bldg, 4809 Woodward Ave, Detroit, MI 48201. TEL 313-577-6120, 800-978-7323, FAX 313-577-6131, http://wsupress.wayne.edu/. Ed. Gary Ladd. R&P Mary Garcia TEL 313-577-6257. Adv. contact Alison Reeves. Circ: 400 (paid).

150 FRA ISSN 1951-7572
MES CONSULTATIONS PSY. Text in French. 2006. irreg. back issues avail. **Document type:** *Monographic series, Consumer.*
Published by: Editions Solar, 12 av. d'Italie, Paris, 75627 Cedex 13, France. edito@solar.tm.fr, contact@solar.tm.fr, http://www.solar.tm.fr.

MES TISSAGES. *see* SOCIOLOGY

METAPHOR AND SYMBOL. *see* LINGUISTICS

150 USA ISSN 1931-5716
METAPSYCHOLOGY ONLINE REVIEWS. Text in English. 1998. w. **Document type:** *Journal, Consumer.*
Media: Online - full text.
Published by: Mental Help Net, 570 Metro Place N, Dublin, OH 43017. TEL 614-764-0143, FAX 614-764-0362, webmaster@cmhc.com.

METHODOLOGIA; pensiero linguaggio modelli - thought language models. *see* LINGUISTICS

150 300 USA ISSN 1614-1881
➤ **METHODOLOGY;** European journal of research methods for the behavioral and social sciences. Text in English. 2005. a. ((includes 4 quarterly online issues)). USD 212, EUR 169 to institutions (effective 2011). adv. **Document type:** *Journal, Academic/Scholarly.* **Description:** Provides a platform for interdisciplinary exchange of methodological research and applications in the different fields, including new methodological approaches, review articles, software information, and instructional papers that can be used in teaching.
Related titles: Online - full text ed.: ISSN 1614-2241 (from ScienceDirect).
Indexed: CurCont, P03, P30, PsycInfo, PsycholAb, SCOPUS, SSCI, W07.
—CCC.
Published by: (European Association of Methodology DEU), Hogrefe Publishing Corp., 875 Massachusetts Ave, 7th Fl, Cambridge, MA 02139. TEL 866-823-4726, FAX 617-354-6875, customerservices@hogrefe-publishing.com, http://www.hogrefe.com. Eds. Dr. Joop Hox, Dr. Manuel Ato. Circ: 700 (paid).

355 USA ISSN 0899-5605
U22.3
➤ **MILITARY PSYCHOLOGY.** Text in English. 1989. q. GBP 862 combined subscription in United Kingdom to institutions (print & online eds.); EUR 1,146, USD 1,432 combined subscription to institutions (print & online eds.) (effective 2012). adv. back issues avail.; reprint service avail. from PSC. **Document type:** *Journal, Academic/Scholarly.* **Description:** Seeks to facilitate the scientific development of military psychology by encouraging communication between researchers and practitioners.
Related titles: Online - full text ed.: ISSN 1532-7876. GBP 776 in United Kingdom to institutions; EUR 1,032, USD 1,289 to institutions (effective 2012).
Indexed: A01, A02, A03, A08, A20, A22, ASCA, B21, C06, C07, C08, C11, CA, CINAHL, CMCI, CurCont, E-psyche, E01, ESPM, ErgAb, FamI, H&SSA, H04, I02, M05, M07, P02, P03, P10, P12, P24, P30, P43, P47, P48, P53, P54, PQC, PRA, PsycInfo, PsycholAb, SCOPUS, SSCI, T02, W07.
—BLDSC (5768.167000), IE, Infotrieve, Ingenta. **CCC.**
Published by: (American Psychological Association, Division 19), Routledge (Subsidiary of: Taylor & Francis Group), 325 Chestnut St, Ste 800, Philadelphia, PA 19106. TEL 800-354-1420, FAX 215-625-2940, journals@routledge.com, http://www.routledge.com. Ed. Armando X Estrada. Adv. contact Linda Hann TEL 44-1344-779945.

➤ **MIMESIS (BAURU);** revista da area de ciencias humanas. *see* SOCIAL SCIENCES: COMPREHENSIVE WORKS

150.19 300 USA ISSN 1071-6866
➤ **MIND AND HUMAN INTERACTION;** windows between history, culture, politics, and psychoanalysis. Text in English. 1989. q. USD 30 domestic to individuals; USD 50 foreign to individuals; USD 60 domestic to institutions; USD 80 foreign to institutions (effective 2011). back issues avail. **Document type:** *Journal, Academic/Scholarly.* **Description:** Seeks to open windows between psychoanalysis and politics, history, sociology, anthropology and other social sciences disciplines.
—IE, Ingenta.
Published by: University of Virginia, Health System, Center for the Study of Mind and Human Interaction, PO Box 800657, Charlottesville, VA 22908. TEL 434-982-1045, FAX 434-982-2524, mind@virginia.edu. Ed. Dr. Lisa Aronson.

153.1 USA ISSN 1555-7308
RC321
MIND, MOOD & MEMORY. Variant title: Maintaining Mental Fitness from Middle Age and Beyond. Text in English. 2005. m. USD 39 domestic; USD 49 in Canada; USD 59 elsewhere (effective 2010). **Document type:** *Magazine, Consumer.* **Description:** Devoted to the mental health concerns of men and women approaching their 60th birthday and beyond.
Related titles: Online - full text ed.
Indexed: A26, E08, G06, G07, G08, H11, H12, I05, S09.
Published by: (Massachusetts General Hospital), Belvoir Media Group, LLC, PO Box 5656, Norwalk, CT 06856. TEL 203-857-3100, 800-424-7887, FAX 203-857-3103, customer_service@belvoir.com, http://www.belvoir.com. **Subscr. to:** Palm Coast Data, LLC, 11 Commerce Blvd, Palm Coast, FL 32164. TEL 386-445-4662, 866-848-2412, http://www.palmcoastdata.com.

158 USA ISSN 1868-8527
RC489.M43
▼ ➤ **MINDFULNESS.** Text in English. 2010. 4/yr. EUR 332, USD 448 combined subscription to institutions (print & online eds.) (effective 2012). **Document type:** *Journal, Academic/Scholarly.*
Related titles: Online - full text ed.: ISSN 1868-8535. 2010 (from IngentaConnect).
Indexed: A26, H12, P30, SCOPUS.
—IE. **CCC.**
Published by: Springer New York LLC (Subsidiary of: Springer Science+Business Media), 233 Spring St, New York, NY 10013. TEL 212-460-1500, FAX 212-460-1575, journals-ny@springer.com. Ed. Nirbhay Singh.

158 USA ISSN 1948-5050
▼ **MINDFULNESS MONTHLY.** Text in English. 2009. m. free (effective 2009). **Document type:** *Newsletter, Consumer.* **Description:** Designed to help you live a more purposeful, peaceful and powerful life.
Media: Online - full content.
Published by: Success Visionary Media, Inc., 4626 Centerplace Dr, No 112, Ste 502, Greeley, CO 80634. TEL 970-372-2229, joshua@joshuaaragon.com, http://www.successvisionary.com/.

155.4 USA ISSN 0076-9266
BF721 CODEN: MSCRBG
➤ **MINNESOTA SYMPOSIA ON CHILD PSYCHOLOGY SERIES.** Text in English. 1966. irreg., latest vol.35, 2009. price varies. back issues avail. **Document type:** *Proceedings.*
Indexed: A20, ASCA, PCI, PsycholAb, SSCI, W07.
—BLDSC (5810.490000). **CCC.**
Published by: (Institute of Child Development), John Wiley & Sons, Inc., 111 River St, Hoboken, NJ 07030. TEL 201-748-6000, FAX 201-748-5915.

➤ **MIRACLES MAGAZINE**; miracles, mysticism, metaphysics & mirth. *see* NEW AGE PUBLICATIONS

616.89 DEU ISSN 0342-3174
BF3
MITEINANDER LEBEN LERNEN; Zeitschrift fuer Tiefenpsychologie, Persoenlichkeitsbildung und Kulturforschung. Text in German. 1976. bi-m. **Document type:** *Journal, Academic/Scholarly.*
Formerly (until 1976): Leben Lernen (0341-8286)
Indexed: E-psyche.
Published by: Institut fuer Tiefenpsychologie, Eichenallee 6, Berlin, 14050, Germany. TEL 49-30-102588, FAX 49-30-3023034, verlag@itgg-berlin.de, http://www.itgg-berlin.de. Ed. Josef Rattner.

158.7 DNK ISSN 1901-7642
MOBBEMAGASINET. Text in Danish. 2006. s-a. free. **Document type:** *Magazine, Trade.*
Related titles: Online - full text ed.
Published by: Socialt Udviklingscenter/Social Development Centre, Nr. Farimagsgade 13, Copenhagen K, 1364, Denmark. TEL 45-33-934450, FAX 45-33-935450, sus@sus.dk. Eds. Dorthe Perlt, Hanne Juel Nielsen. Circ: 10,000.

150 USA ISSN 0361-5227
RC500
➤ **MODERN PSYCHOANALYSIS.** Text in English. 1976. s-a. adv. bk.rev. Index. back issues avail.; reprints avail. **Document type:** *Journal, Academic/Scholarly.* **Description:** Dedicated to extending the theory and practice of psychoanalysis to the full range of emotional disorders.
Related titles: Online - full text ed.
Indexed: A01, A02, A03, A08, A22, CA, CPLI, DIP, E-psyche, IBR, IBZ, MEA&I, P03, P25, P43, P48, PQC, PsycInfo, PsycholAb, T02.
—BLDSC (5894.420000), IE, Ingenta.
Published by: (Center for Modern Psychoanalytic Studies), International Universities Press, Inc., 59 Boston Post Rd, Box 1524, PO Box 389, Madison, CT 06443. TEL 203-245-4000, FAX 203-245-0775, info@iup.com. adv.: page USD 580; 4.25 x 7. Circ: 1,000 (paid).

150 SWE ISSN 2000-4087
▼ **MODERN PSYKOLOGI.** Text in Swedish. 2009. 6/yr. SEK 365; SEK 68 per issue (effective 2010). adv. **Document type:** *Magazine, Consumer.*
Published by: Modern Psykologi i Sverige AB, Folkunggatan 122, Stockholm, 11630, Sweden. TEL 46-770-457151, http://www.modernpsykologi.wordpress.com. Ed. Jonas Mattson.

150 CZE ISSN 1802-2073
MOJE PSYCHOLOGIE. Text in Czech. 2006. m. CZK 552 (effective 2011). adv. **Document type:** *Magazine, Consumer.*
Published by: Mlada Fronta, Mezi Vodami 1952/9, Prague 4, 14300, Czech Republic. TEL 420-2-25276201, FAX 420-2-25276222, online@mf.cz. Ed. Martina Svecova. Adv. contact Martina Kratka.

150 FRA ISSN 1778-7890
LE MONDE DE L'INTELLIGENCE. Text in French. 2005. bi-m. EUR 60 combined subscription to individuals (print & online eds.) (effective 2010). **Document type:** *Magazine, Consumer.* **Description:** Brings together themes dealing with the brain's function, psychology, and personal development. A practical and culturally-centered publication for the general consumer.
Related titles: Online - full text ed.
Published by: Mondeo Publishing, 3 av. de l'Opera, Paris, 75001, France. TEL 33-1-55350689, redaction@mondeo.fr.

150 USA ISSN 1529-4978
BF1
MONITOR ON PSYCHOLOGY. Text in English. 19??. m. USD 50 domestic to individuals; USD 103 foreign to individuals; USD 93 domestic to institutions; USD 195 foreign to institutions (effective 2011). adv. charts; illus.; tr.lit. back issues avail.; reprints avail. **Document type:** *Magazine, Consumer.* **Description:** Reports on the science, practice, and social responsibility activities of psychology, including latest legislative developments affecting mental health, education, and research support.
Former titles (until 2000): A P A Monitor (0001-2114); (until 1970): Washington Report
Related titles: Online - full text ed.: free with subscr. to print ed.
Indexed: A22, F09.
—BLDSC (5908.960250), IE. **CCC.**
Published by: American Psychological Association, 750 First St, NE, Washington, DC 20002. TEL 202-336-5500, 800-374-2721, journals@apa.org. Ed. Sara Martin. Adv. contact Karen Eskew.

150 RUS ISSN 2072-8514
➤ **MOSKOVSKII GOSUDARSTVENNYI OBLASTNOI UNIVERSITET. VESTNIK. SERIYA PSIKHOLOGICHESKIE NAUKI.** Variant title: Vestnik M G O U. Seriya Psikhologicheskie Nauki. Text in Russian; Summaries in Russian, English. 2006. q. RUR 1,000 (effective 2011). bibl.; charts; illus.; maps. back issues avail. **Document type:** *Journal, Academic/Scholarly.* **Description:** Intended for scientists, researchers, teachers of high schools, undergraduate and post graduate students. Publishes results of scientific research in the field of Psychology, including dissertation research, conferences and seminars.
Related titles: Online - full text ed.
Indexed: RefZh.
Published by: Moskovskii Gosudarstvennyi Oblastnoi Universitet/ Moscow State Regional University, ul Radio, dom 10A, komn. 98, Moscow, Russian Federation. TEL 7-499-7235631, FAX 7-499-2614341, http://www.mgou.ru. Ed. Aleksandr Bulgakov.

155.6 RUS ISSN 0137-0936
➤ **MOSKOVSKII GOSUDARSTVENNYI UNIVERSITET. VESTNIK. SERIYA 14: PSIKHOLOGIYA.** Text in Russian. 1977. q. USD 113 in North America; USD 164 combined subscription in North America (print & online eds.) (effective 2011). **Document type:** *Journal, Academic/Scholarly.*
Related titles: Online - full text ed.
Indexed: E-psyche, RASB, RILM.
—BLDSC (0032.697100), East View, INIST.
Published by: (Moskovskii Gosudarstvennyi Universitet im. M.V. Lomonosova, Fakul'tet Psikhologii/M.V. Lomonosov Moscow State University, Department of Psychology), Izdatel'stvo Moskovskogo Gosudarstvennogo Universiteta im. M. V. Lomonosova/Publishing House of Moscow State University, B Nikitskaya 5/7, Moscow, 103009, Russian Federation. TEL 7-095-2295091, FAX 7-095-2036671, kd_mgu@rambler.ru, http://www.msu.ru/depts/MSUPubl. **Dist. by:** East View Information Services, 10601 Wayzata Blvd, Minneapolis, MN 55305. TEL 952-252-1201, 800-477-1005, FAX 952-252-1202, info@eastview.com, http://www.eastview.com.

150 USA ISSN 0146-7239
BF683 CODEN: MOEMDJ
➤ **MOTIVATION AND EMOTION.** Text in English. 1977. q. EUR 930, USD 956 combined subscription to institutions (print & online eds.) (effective 2012). adv. back issues avail.; reprint service avail. from PSC. **Document type:** *Journal, Academic/Scholarly.* **Description:** Publishes theoretical papers and original research reports of either a basic or applied nature from any area of psychology or other behavioral science.
Related titles: Microfilm ed.: (from PQC); Online - full text ed.: ISSN 1573-6644 (from IngentaConnect).
Indexed: A01, A03, A08, A12, A20, A22, A26, ABIn, ASCA, ASSIA, BibInd, BibLing, CA, CDA, CommAb, CurCont, DIP, E-psyche, E01, FamI, GenetAb, I05, IBR, IBZ, P03, P10, P12, P25, P27, P30, P43, P48, P51, P53, P54, PQC, PsycInfo, PsycholAb, RI-1, RI-2, RefZh, SCOPUS, SSCI, T02, W07.
—BLDSC (5969.060000), IE, Infotrieve, Ingenta, INIST. **CCC.**
Published by: Springer New York LLC (Subsidiary of: Springer Science+Business Media), 233 Spring St, New York, NY 10013. TEL 212-460-1500, FAX 212-460-1575, service-ny@springer.com, http://www.springer.com/. Ed. Richard M Ryan.

155.4 DEU
MULTIMIND - N L P AKTUELL. Text in German. 1992. bi-m. EUR 39 (effective 2004). adv. bk.rev. index. back issues avail. **Document type:** *Magazine, Academic/Scholarly.*
Indexed: E-psyche.
Published by: Junfermann Verlag, Imadstr 40, Paderborn, 33102, Germany. TEL 49-5251-13440, FAX 49-5251-134444, ju@junfermann.de, http://www.junfermann.de. Adv. contact Stefanie Empfing. B&W page EUR 1,000; trim 184 x 265. Circ: 5,500 (paid and controlled).

152 USA ISSN 0027-3171
BF39 CODEN: MVBRAV
➤ **MULTIVARIATE BEHAVIORAL RESEARCH.** Text in English. 1966. bi-m. GBP 547 combined subscription in United Kingdom to institutions (print & online eds.); EUR 727, USD 908 combined subscription to institutions (print & online eds.) (effective 2012). adv. illus. index. back issues avail.; reprint service avail. from PSC. **Document type:** *Journal, Academic/Scholarly.* **Description:** Reports results of behavioral research employing multivariate methods.
Related titles: Microform ed.: (from PQC); Online - full text ed.: ISSN 1532-7906. GBP 492 in United Kingdom to institutions; EUR 654, USD 817 to institutions (effective 2012).
Indexed: A01, A03, A08, A20, A22, AEI, ASCA, B01, B06, B07, B09, BibInd, Biostat, CA, CIS, CMCI, CommAb, CurCont, DIP, E-psyche, E01, E03, ERI, ERIC, FamI, IBR, IBZ, JCQM, MEA&I, P03, P10, P12, P30, P43, P48, P52, P53, P54, PQC, PsycInfo, PsycholAb, S02, S03, SCI, SCOPUS, SOPODA, SSCI, SociolAb, T02, W07.
—BLDSC (5983.300000), IE, Infotrieve, Ingenta, INIST. **CCC.**
Published by: (Society of Multivariate Experimental Psychology), Psychology Press (Subsidiary of: Taylor & Francis Inc.), 325 Chestnut St, Ste 800, Philadelphia, PA 19106. TEL 800-354-1420, FAX 215-625-2940, orders@taylorandfrancis.com, http://www.psypress.com. Ed. Joseph Lee Rodgers TEL 405-325-4597. Adv. contact Linda Hann TEL 44-1344-779945.

▼ ➤ **MUSIC AND MEDICINE.** *see* MEDICAL SCIENCES

➤ **MUSIC THERAPY NOW.** *see* MUSIC

➤ **MUSIC THERAPY PERSPECTIVES.** *see* MUSIC

➤ **MUSIKPSYCHOLOGIE.** *see* MUSIC

616.89 DEU ISSN 0172-5505
ML3920
➤ **MUSIKTHERAPEUTISCHE UMSCHAU**; Forschung und Praxis der Musiktherapie. Text in German; Summaries in English. 4/yr. EUR 67 to individuals; EUR 134 to institutions; EUR 50 to students; EUR 24.90 newsstand/cover (effective 2011). adv. **Document type:** *Journal, Academic/Scholarly.* **Description:** Publication containing studies in music oriented therapy, and its application in medicine, psychotherapy, and psychology.
Indexed: A22, DIP, DokArb, E-psyche, IBR, IBZ, IIMP, M11, MusicInd, P03, PsycInfo, PsycholAb, RILM.
—GNLM, IE. **CCC.**
Published by: (Deutsche Gesellschaft fuer Musiktherapie), Vandenhoeck und Ruprecht, Theaterstr 13, Goettingen, 37073, Germany. TEL 49-551-508440, FAX 49-551-5084422, info@v-r.de. Ed. Volker Bernius. Circ: 2,000 (paid and controlled).

➤ **N H S A DIALOG**; a research-to-practice journal for the early intervention field. (National Head Start Association) *see* EDUCATION—Special Education And Rehabilitation

150 USA ISSN 1048-6925
N Y S P A NOTEBOOK. (New York State Psychological Association) Text in English. 1989. bi-m. free to qualified personnel (effective 2010). back issues avail. **Document type:** *Magazine, Trade.* **Description:** Aims to explain the diverse world of psychology and its specialties to audiences and to advance knowledge about psychology.
Related titles: Online - full text ed.
Indexed: P03.
—BLDSC (6169.845000).
Published by: Foundation of the New York State Psychological Association, 6 Automation Ln, Ste 103, Albany, NY 12205. TEL 518-437-1040, 800-732-3933, FAX 518-437-0177, nyspa@nyspa.org.

150 USA ISSN 0028-7687
➤ **N Y S PSYCHOLOGIST.** (New York State) Text in English. 1948. a. free to members (effective 2010). bk.rev. charts; illus.; stat.; tr.lit. back issues avail. **Document type:** *Journal, Academic/Scholarly.* **Description:** Covers all aspects of trends and research in psychology and the future of psychology.
Formerly (until 1954): New York State Psychological Association. Bulletin
Related titles: Online - full text ed.
Indexed: E-psyche, PsycholAb.
Published by: Foundation of the New York State Psychological Association, 6 Automation Ln, Ste 103, Albany, NY 12205. TEL 518-437-1040, 800-732-3933, FAX 518-437-0177, nyspa@nyspa.org. Ed. John Hogan.

P

150 IRQ ISSN 1815-6762
AL NAFS WA-AL-HAYAT/JOURNAL OF PSYCHE AND LIFE. Text in Arabic, English. 1992. bi-m. **Document type:** *Journal, Academic/Scholarly.*
Published by: Jami'at Baghdad, Psychological Research Center (Subsidiary of: Jami'at Baghdad/University of Baghdad), University of Baghdad Complex, Baghdad, Iraq. TEL 964-1-7786678, FAX 964-1-7785162, psychocenter@hotmail.com, http://www.psychocenteriraq.com.

370.15 150 USA ISSN 1067-1161
NATIONAL CHARACTER LABORATORY NEWSLETTER. Text in English. 1971. q. USD 5 (effective 2000). bk.rev. abstr.; bibl.; stat. **Document type:** *Newsletter.* **Description:** Reports research results on character, and encourages and coordinates further research.
Indexed: E-psyche.
Published by: National Character Laboratory, 4635 Leeds Ave, El Paso, TX 79903. TEL 915-562-5046. Ed. A J Stuart Jr. Circ: 150.

150.19 USA ISSN 0077-5339
BF173.A2
NATIONAL PSYCHOLOGICAL ASSOCIATION FOR PSYCHOANALYSIS. BULLETIN. Text in English. 1950. biennial. free to members. **Document type:** *Bulletin.*
Indexed: E-psyche.
Published by: National Psychological Association for Psychoanalysis, Inc., 150 W 13th St, New York, NY 10011. TEL 212-924-7440, FAX 212-989-7543, http://www.npap.org. Circ: 7,000.

150.19 USA
NATIONAL PSYCHOLOGICAL ASSOCIATION FOR PSYCHOANALYSIS. NEWS AND REVIEWS. Text in English. 1970. 3/yr. free to members. **Document type:** *Newsletter.*
Indexed: E-psyche.
Published by: National Psychological Association for Psychoanalysis, Inc., 150 W 13th St, New York, NY 10011. TEL 212-924-7440, FAX 212-989-7543, http://www.npap.org. Ed. Harvey A Kaplan. Circ: 1,000.

150 USA ISSN 0099-2151
NATIONAL REGISTER OF HEALTH SERVICE PROVIDERS IN PSYCHOLOGY. Text in English. 1975. biennial.
Published by: Council for the National Register of Health Services Providers in Psychology, 1120 G St NW Ste 330, Washington, DC 20005. TEL 202-783-7663, FAX 202-347-0550, support@nationalregister.org, http://www.nationalregister.org.

154.6 GBR ISSN 1179-1608
▼ ➤ **NATURE AND SCIENCE OF SLEEP.** Text in English. 2009. a. free (effective 2011). back issues avail. **Document type:** *Journal, Academic/Scholarly.* **Description:** Covers all aspects of sleep science and sleep medicine, including the neurophysiology and functions of sleep, the genetics of sleep, sleep and society, biological rhythms and dreaming.
Media: Online - full text.
Indexed: P30.
—**CCC.**
Published by: Dove Medical Press Ltd., Beechfield House, Winterton Way, Macclesfield, SK11 0JL, United Kingdom. Ed. Steven A Shea.

153.1534 USA ISSN 0146-7875
BF683 CODEN: NSMPB3
NEBRASKA SYMPOSIUM ON MOTIVATION. Text in English. 1953. a., latest vol.52, 2007. index, cum.index. back issues avail. **Document type:** *Monographic series, Academic/Scholarly.* **Description:** Includes timely paper topics for the Nebraska Symposium which deal with all aspects of motivation.
Formerly (until 1954): Current Theory and Research in Motivation (0070-2099)
Indexed: A22, ASCA, CA, E-psyche, EMBASE, ExcerpMed, IndMed, MEDLINE, P30, PCI, PsycholAb, R10, Reac, SCOPUS, SSCI, W07.
—BLDSC (6068.380000), IE, Infotrieve, Ingenta. **CCC.**
Published by: University of Nebraska Press, 1111 Lincoln Mall, Lincoln, NE 68588. TEL 402-472-3581, FAX 402-472-6214, pressmail@unl.edu.

158 NLD ISSN 1574-602X
NEDERLANDSE WERKGEMEENSCHAP VOOR INDIVIDUALPSYCHOLOGIE. NIEUWSBRIEF. Text in Dutch. 3/yr. EUR 25 membership (effective 2010).
Former titles (until 2004): Individual Psychologische Verkenningen (1382-5089); (until 1991): Nederlandse Werkgemeenschap voor Individual Psychologie. Mededelingenblad (1382-5070)
Published by: Nederlandse Werkgemeenschap voor Individualpsychologie, Potgieterlaan 21, Hazerswoude Rijndijk, 2394 VA, Netherlands. TEL 31-71-3416110, orgadvkulker@planet.nl, http://www.individualpsychologie.nl.

NEODIDAGMATA. *see* EDUCATION—Teaching Methods And Curriculum

NEURO-PSYCHOANALYSIS; an interdisciplinary journal for psychoanalysis and the neurosciences. *see* MEDICAL SCIENCES—Psychiatry And Neurology

NEUROBIOLOGY OF LEARNING AND MEMORY. *see* MEDICAL SCIENCES—Psychiatry And Neurology

NEUROPSYCHOLOGICAL REHABILITATION. *see* MEDICAL SCIENCES—Psychiatry And Neurology

150 FRA
NEUROPSYCHOLOGIE. Text in French. 2008. q. EUR 295 combined subscription domestic to institutions print & online eds.; EUR 311 combined subscription in the European Union to institutions print & online eds.; EUR 319 combined subscription elsewhere to institutions print & online eds. (effective 2011). **Document type:** *Journal, Academic/Scholarly.*
Related titles: Online - full text ed.
Published by: John Libbey Eurotext, 127 Av. de la Republique, Montrouge, 92120, France. TEL 33-1-46730660, FAX 33-1-40840999, contact@jle.com, http://www.john-libbey-eurotext.fr. Ed. Francis Eustache.

NEUROPSYCHOLOGY. *see* MEDICAL SCIENCES—Psychiatry And Neurology

NEUROPSYCHOLOGY AND COGNITION. *see* MEDICAL SCIENCES—Psychiatry And Neurology

616.8 GBR ISSN 1380-3395
CODEN: JCENE8
➤ **NEUROPSYCHOLOGY, DEVELOPMENT AND COGNITION. SECTION A: JOURNAL OF CLINICAL AND EXPERIMENTAL NEUROPSYCHOLOGY.** Abbreviated title: J C E N. Cover title: Journal of Clinical and Experimental Neuropsychology. Text in English. 1994. 10/yr. GBP 1,775 combined subscription in United Kingdom to institutions (print & online eds.); EUR 2,344, USD 2,945 combined subscription to institutions (print & online eds.) (effective 2012). bk.rev. abstr.; illus. Index. back issues avail.; reprint service avail. from PSC. **Document type:** *Journal, Academic/Scholarly.* **Description:** Features original empirical research comprising methodological and theoretical papers, critical reviews, and case studies.
Supersedes in part (in 1994): Journal of Clinical and Experimental Neuropsychology (0168-8634); Which was formerly (until 1985): Journal of Clinical Neuropsychology (0165-0475)
Related titles: Online - full text ed.: ISSN 1744-411X. GBP 1,597 in United Kingdom to institutions; EUR 2,110, USD 2,651 to institutions (effective 2012) (from IngentaConnect).
Indexed: A01, A03, A08, A20, A22, ASCA, AgeL, CA, CDA, CurCont, E-psyche, E01, ECER, EMBASE, ExcerpMed, FR, Faml, ISR, IndMed, Inpharma, L&LBA, MEDLINE, NSCI, P03, P30, P43, PsycInfo, PsycholAb, R10, Reac, RefZh, SCI, SOPODA, SSCI, T02, THA, W07.
—GNLM, IE, Ingenta, INIST. **CCC.**
Published by: Psychology Press (Subsidiary of: Taylor & Francis Ltd.), 27 Church Rd, Hove, E Sussex BN3 2FA, United Kingdom. TEL 44-20-70176000, FAX 44-20-70176717, info@psypress.co.uk, http://www.psypress.com. Eds. Daniel Tranel, Wilfred G van Gorp. Adv. contact Linda Hann TEL 44-1344-779945.

618.97 GBR ISSN 1382-5585
QP360.5 CODEN: AGCOEW
➤ **NEUROPSYCHOLOGY, DEVELOPMENT AND COGNITION. SECTION B: AGING, NEUROPSYCHOLOGY AND COGNITION**; a journal on normal and dysfunctional development. Cover title: Aging, Neuropsychology and Cognition. Text in English. 1994. bi-m. GBP 724 combined subscription in United Kingdom to institutions (print & online eds.); EUR 965, USD 1,214 combined subscription to institutions (print & online eds.) (effective 2012). abstr. back issues avail.; reprint service avail. from PSC. **Document type:** *Journal, Academic/Scholarly.* **Description:** Features research in normal and dysfunctional aspects of cognitive development in adulthood and aging, integrating theory, method and research findings in the fields of cognitive gerontology and neuropsychology.
Formerly (until 1996): Neuropsychology, Development, and Cognition. Section B, Aging and Cognition (0928-9917); Which superseded in part (in 1994): Journal of Clinical and Experimental Neuropsychology (0168-8634); Which was formerly (until 1985): Journal of Clinical Neuropsychology (0165-0475)
Related titles: Online - full text ed.: ISSN 1744-4128. GBP 651 in United Kingdom to institutions; EUR 868, USD 1,092 to institutions (effective 2012) (from IngentaConnect).
Indexed: A01, A03, A08, A20, A22, ASCA, ASG, AgeL, C06, C07, CA, CurCont, E-psyche, E01, EMBASE, ExcerpMed, L&LBA, MEDLINE, P03, P30, P43, PsycInfo, PsycholAb, R10, Reac, RefZh, SCOPUS, SOPODA, SSCI, T02, W07.
—BLDSC (0736.364400), IE, Infotrieve, Ingenta, INIST. **CCC.**
Published by: Psychology Press (Subsidiary of: Taylor & Francis Ltd.), 27 Church Rd, Hove, E Sussex BN3 2FA, United Kingdom. TEL 44-20-70176000, FAX 44-20-70176717, info@psypress.co.uk, http://www.psypress.com. Eds. Linas A Bieliauskas, Martin Sliwinski. Adv. contact Linda Hann TEL 44-1344-779945. **Subscr. in Europe to:** Taylor & Francis Ltd., Journals Customer Service, Sheepen Pl, Colchester, Essex CO3 3LP, United Kingdom. TEL 44-20-70175544, FAX 44-20-70175198, subscriptions@tandf.co.uk, http://www.tandf.co.uk/journals; **Subscr. in N. America to:** Taylor & Francis Inc., Customer Services Dept, 325 Chestnut St, 8th Fl, Philadelphia, PA 19106. TEL 215-625-8900, 800-354-1420, FAX 215-625-2940.

616.8 155.4 GBR ISSN 0929-7049
CODEN: CHNEFJ
➤ **NEUROPSYCHOLOGY, DEVELOPMENT, AND COGNITION. SECTION C: CHILD NEUROPSYCHOLOGY**; a journal on normal and abnormal development in childhood and adolescence. Text and summaries in English. 1995. bi-m. GBP 604 combined subscription in United Kingdom to institutions (print & online eds.); EUR 801, USD 1,000 combined subscription to institutions (print & online eds.) (effective 2012). bk.rev. abstr. index. back issues avail.; reprint service avail. from PSC. **Document type:** *Journal, Academic/Scholarly.* **Description:** Features research on the neuropsychological dimension of development in childhood and adolescence, and promotes the integration of theories, methods and research findings in child and developmental neuropsychology.
Supersedes in part (in 1994): Journal of Clinical and Experimental Neuropsychology (0168-8634); Which was formerly: Journal of Clinical Neuropsychology (0165-0475)
Related titles: Microfilm ed.: (from SWZ); Online - full text ed.: ISSN 1744-4136. GBP 544 in United Kingdom to institutions; EUR 721, USD 901 to institutions (effective 2012) (from IngentaConnect).
Indexed: A01, A03, A08, A20, A22, B21, CA, E-psyche, E01, EMBASE, ExcerpMed, IndMed, L&LBA, MEDLINE, NSA, NSCI, P03, P30, P43, PsycInfo, PsycholAb, R10, Reac, RefZh, SCI, SCOPUS, SOPODA, T02, W07.
—BLDSC (3172.944795), IE, Infotrieve, Ingenta, INIST. **CCC.**
Published by: Psychology Press (Subsidiary of: Taylor & Francis Ltd.), 27 Church Rd, Hove, E Sussex BN3 2FA, United Kingdom. TEL 44-20-70176000, FAX 44-20-70176717, info@psypress.co.uk, http://www.psypress.com. Ed. Michael Westerveld. Adv. contact Linda Hann TEL 44-1344-779945. **Subscr. in N America to:** Taylor & Francis Inc., Customer Services Dept, 325 Chestnut St, 8th Fl, Philadelphia, PA 19106. TEL 215-625-8900, 800-354-1420, FAX 215-625-2940, customerservice@taylorandfrancis.com; **Subscr. to:** Journals Customer Service, Taylor & Francis Group, Rankine Rd, Basingstoke, Hants RG24 8PR, United Kingdom. TEL 44-1256-813002, FAX 44-1256-479438, enquiries@tandf.co.uk.

616.8 GBR ISSN 1385-4046
CODEN: CLNEEC
➤ **NEUROPSYCHOLOGY, DEVELOPMENT AND COGNITION. SECTION D: THE CLINICAL NEUROPSYCHOLOGIST.** Cover title: The Clinical Neuropsychologist. Text in English. 1987. 8/yr. GBP 926 combined subscription in United Kingdom to institutions (print & online eds.); EUR 1,219, USD 1,525 combined subscription to institutions (print & online eds.) (effective 2012). Supplement avail.; back issues avail.; reprint service avail. from PSC. **Document type:** *Journal, Academic/Scholarly.* **Description:** Covers all matters relevant to the practicing clinical neuropsychologist.
Formerly (until 1995): Clinical Neuropsychologist (0920-1637)
Related titles: Online - full text ed.: ISSN 1744-4144. GBP 833 in United Kingdom to institutions; EUR 1,097, USD 1,372 to institutions (effective 2012) (from IngentaConnect).
Indexed: A01, A03, A08, A20, A22, ASCA, BibInd, CA, CDA, CurCont, E-psyche, E01, ECER, EMBASE, ExcerpMed, IndMed, L&LBA, MEDLINE, NSCI, P03, P30, P43, PsycInfo, PsycholAb, R10, Reac, RefZh, SCI, SCOPUS, SOPODA, SSCI, T02, W07.
—BLDSC (3286.310680), GNLM, IE, Infotrieve, Ingenta, INIST. **CCC.**
Published by: (American Academy of Clinical Neurophysiology USA), Psychology Press (Subsidiary of: Taylor & Francis Ltd.), 27 Church Rd, Hove, E Sussex BN3 2FA, United Kingdom. TEL 44-20-70176000, FAX 44-20-70176717, info@psypress.co.uk, http://www.psypress.com. Eds. Jerry J Sweet, Russell M Bauer. Adv. contact Linda Hann TEL 44-1344-779945. **Subscr. in Europe to:** Taylor & Francis Ltd., Journals Customer Service, Sheepen Pl, Colchester, Essex CO3 3LP, United Kingdom. TEL 44-20-70175544, FAX 44-20-70175198, subscriptions@tandf.co.uk, http://www.tandf.co.uk/journals; **Subscr. in N. America to:** Taylor & Francis Inc., Customer Services Dept, 325 Chestnut St, 8th Fl, Philadelphia, PA 19106. TEL 215-625-8900, 800-354-1420, FAX 215-625-2940.

➤ **NEUROPSYCHOLOGY REVIEW.** *see* MEDICAL SCIENCES—Psychiatry And Neurology

150 GBR ISSN 2042-9096
▼ **NEW ASSOCIATIONS.** Text in English. 2009. 3/yr. GBP 10 domestic; GBP 16 foreign (effective 2010). adv. back issues avail. **Document type:** *Magazine, Consumer.* **Description:** Provides news, analysis and opinion relevant to the full spectrum of psychoanalytically-informed practice.
Published by: British Psychoanalytic Council, Unit 7, 19-23 Wedmore St, London, N19 4RU, United Kingdom. TEL 44-20-75619240, mail@psychoanalytic-council.org. Adv. contact Leanne Cannon.

NEW BABYLON: STUDIES IN THE SOCIAL SCIENCES. *see* SOCIAL SCIENCES: COMPREHENSIVE WORKS

210 USA
NEW CRUCIBLE; a magazine about man and his environment. Variant title: Crucible. Text in English. 1964. irreg. USD 24 (effective 2005). adv. bk.rev. **Document type:** *Magazine, Consumer.* **Description:** Deals with the total human environment including all ecological factors impacting upon man such as political, psychological, religious, and physical.
Incorporates: Naturalist (8756-3592); Former titles: Crucible and Scientific Atheist (8756-1247); Scientific Atheist
Indexed: E-psyche.
Published by: De Young Press, RR 1 Box 76, Stark, KS 66775-9802. Eds. Garry De Young, Garry De Young. R&P Mary De Young. Adv. contact Gary De Young. Circ: 2,500.

155.4 USA ISSN 1520-3247
BF721 CODEN: NDCDDI
NEW DIRECTIONS FOR CHILD AND ADOLESCENT DEVELOPMENT. Text in English. 1978. q. GBP 217 in United Kingdom to institutions; EUR 273 in Europe to institutions; USD 343 in United States to institutions; USD 383 in Canada & Mexico to institutions; USD 417 elsewhere to institutions; GBP 251 combined subscription in United Kingdom to institutions (print & online eds.); EUR 315 combined subscription in Europe to institutions (print & online eds.); USD 398 combined subscription in United States to institutions (print & online eds.); USD 438 combined subscription in Canada & Mexico to institutions (print & online eds.); USD 472 combined subscription elsewhere to institutions (print & online eds.) (effective 2012). bibl. Index. back issues avail.; reprint service avail. from PSC. **Document type:** *Journal, Academic/Scholarly.* **Description:** Covers the latest findings in developmental psychology; addresses children's cognitive, social, moral, and emotional growth.
Formerly (until 1998): New Directions for Child Development (0195-2269)
Related titles: Microfiche ed.: (from PQC); Online - full text ed.: ISSN 1534-8687. GBP 179 in United Kingdom to institutions; EUR 225 in Europe to institutions; USD 343 elsewhere to institutions (effective 2012).
Indexed: A01, A03, A08, A22, ASSIA, Agr, C28, CA, CDA, CPE, E-psyche, E01, E03, EMBASE, ERI, ERIC, ExcerpMed, F09, IndMed, L&LBA, MEDLINE, MLA-IB, P04, P30, PsycholAb, S02, S03, SCOPUS, SOPODA, SSA, SociolAb, T02.
—BLDSC (6083.323000), GNLM, IE, Infotrieve, Ingenta. **CCC.**
Published by: Jossey-Bass Inc., Publishers (Subsidiary of: John Wiley & Sons, Inc.), 111 River St, Hoboken, NJ 07030. TEL 201-748-6000, FAX 201-748-6088, info@wiley.com. Eds. Lene Arnett Jensen, Reed W Larson.

153.4 GBR
NEW DIRECTIONS IN COGNITIVE SCIENCE. Text in English. 1990. irreg., latest vol.12, 2007. price varies. **Document type:** *Proceedings, Academic/Scholarly.*
Formerly (until 2002): Vancouver Studies in Cognitive Science (0847-0502)
Indexed: E-psyche, PCI.
Published by: Oxford University Press, Great Clarendon St, Oxford, OX2 6DP, United Kingdom. TEL 44-1865-556767, FAX 44-1865-556646, enquiry@oup.co.uk, http://www.oup-usa.org/catalogs/general/series/.

150 USA ISSN 1932-5649
RC437.2
NEW DIRECTIONS IN PSYCHOANALYTIC WRITING. Text in English. 2002. s-a. **Document type:** *Journal, Academic/Scholarly.*
Formerly (until 2006): New Directions Journal
Related titles: Online - full text ed.: ISSN 1932-5657.
Published by: Washington Center for Psychoanalysis, 4545 42nd St NW, #209, Washington, DC 20016. TEL 202-237-1854, FAX 202-237-1856, center@wcpweb.org, http://www.wcpweb.org.

158 USA
NEW HARVEST NEWSLETTER. Text in English. bi-m. free. **Document type:** *Newsletter.* **Description:** Provides assistance with abuse recovery, stress management, chemical dependency, crisis intervention, communication skills, and trauma recovery.
Media: Online - full text.
Indexed: E-psyche.
Published by: Personal Development Center Associates, 6345 Balboa Blvd, Ste 212, Encino, CA 91316. TEL 818-996-6820, FAX 818-776-0312, KLKenneyPhD@aol.com. Ed. Karen Kenney.

150 GBR ISSN 0732-118X
BF1
➤ **NEW IDEAS IN PSYCHOLOGY.** Text in English. 1983. 3/yr. EUR 763 in Europe to institutions; JPY 101,400 in Japan to institutions; USD 853 elsewhere to institutions (effective 2012). back issues avail. **Document type:** *Journal, Academic/Scholarly.* **Description:** Provides a forum for theorizers striving to integrate the fragmented ideas and theories currently found in theoretical psychology.
Related titles: Microfilm ed.: (from PQC); Online - full text ed.: ISSN 1873-3522 (from IngentaConnect, ScienceDirect).
Indexed: A01, A03, A08, A20, A22, A26, AEI, ASCA, ASSIA, B21, BibInd, CA, CurCont, E-psyche, I05, NSA, P03, P30, PCI, PsycInfo, PsycholAb, RASB, SCOPUS, SSCI, T02, W07.
—BLDSC (6084.249500), IE, Infotrieve, Ingenta, INIST. **CCC.**
Published by: Pergamon (Subsidiary of: Elsevier Science & Technology), The Blvd, Langford Ln, East Park, Kidlington, Oxford OX5 1GB, United Kingdom. TEL 44-1865-843000, FAX 44-1865-843010, JournalsCustomerServiceEMEA@elsevier.com. Eds. M Bickhard, R L Campbell. **Subscr. to:** Elsevier BV, Radarweg 29, PO Box 211, Amsterdam 1000 AE, Netherlands. TEL 31-20-4853757, FAX 31-20-4853432, http://www.elsevier.nl.

150 USA ISSN 1931-793X
➤ **THE NEW SCHOOL PSYCHOLOGY BULLETIN.** Text in English. 2005. s-a. **Document type:** *Journal, Academic/Scholarly.*
Related titles: Online - full text ed.: ISSN 1931-7948. 2003. free (effective 2011).
Published by: The New School for Social Research, 65 Fifth Ave, New York, NY 10003. TEL 212-229-5700, http://www.socialresearch.newschool.edu. Eds. Alexander Kriss, Jennifer Doran.

301.1 150 ZAF ISSN 1812-6731
BF1
➤ **NEW VOICES IN PSYCHOLOGY.** Text in English. 1974. a. ZAR 40 per issue domestic to individuals; USD 15 per issue foreign to individuals; ZAR 60 per issue domestic to institutions; USD 40 per issue foreign to institutions (effective 2006). adv. bk.rev. back issues avail. **Document type:** *Journal, Academic/Scholarly.* **Description:** Includes scientific articles and synopses of psychology's sub-disciplines from students and lecturers.
Formerly (until 2004): U N I S A Psychologia (0256-8896)
Indexed: E-psyche, ISAP.
Published by: (University of South Africa), UniSA Press, PO Box 392, Pretoria, 0003, South Africa. TEL 27-12-4292953, FAX 27-12-4293449, unisa-press@unisa.ac.za, http://www.unisa.ac.za/press. Ed., Adv. contact Henning Viljoen. B&W page ZAR 400. Circ: 16,000.

370.15 USA ISSN 1555-8924
LB1027.5
➤ **NEW YORK STATE SCHOOL COUNSELING JOURNAL.** Text in English. 2005. s-a. **Document type:** *Journal, Trade.*

Published by: New York State School Counselor Association, PO Box 217, Leicester, NY 14481. info@nyssca.org.

➤ **THE NEW ZEALAND JOURNAL OF MUSIC THERAPY.** *see* MUSIC

150 NZL ISSN 1179-7924
NEW ZEALAND JOURNAL OF PSYCHOLOGY (ONLINE). Abbreviated title: N Z J P. Text in English. 1972. 3/yr. free to members (effective 2010). adv. back issues avail. **Document type:** *Journal, Academic/ Scholarly.*
Media: Online - full text.
Indexed: PsycInfo.
Published by: New Zealand Psychological Society, Level 4, AMP Chambers, 187 Featherston St, PO Box 4092, Wellington, 6140, New Zealand. TEL 64-4-4734884, FAX 64-4-4734889, office@psychology.org.nz. Ed. John Fitzgerald. adv.: page NZD 420; 185 x 250.

150 ITA ISSN 1828-1842
NEWSLETTER DI PSICOLOGIA POSITIVA. Text in Italian. 2005. irreg. **Document type:** *Newsletter, Trade.*
Published by: Societa Italiana di Psicologia Positiva, c/o Scuola Asipse, Via Settembrini 2, Milan, 20124, Italy. TEL 39-02-2043880, http://www.psicologiapositiva.it.

362.28 USA
NEWSLINK (WASHINGTON). Text in English. q. membership. **Description:** Provides suicide prevention information.
Indexed: E-psyche.
Published by: American Association of Suicidology, 5221 Wisconsin Ave, NW, Washington, DC 20015. info@suicidology.org. Circ: 1,500.

158.3 NGA ISSN 1118-4035
RC466.83.N6
NIGERIAN JOURNAL OF CLINICAL AND COUNSELLING PSYCHOLOGY. Text in English. 1995. s-a. USD 18 (effective 2004). back issues avail. **Document type:** *Journal, Academic/Scholarly.* **Description:** Publishes articles concerned with the psychological, social, behavioral, medical, pediatric and ethical aspects of the applied field of clinical and counseling psychology.
Related titles: Online - full text ed.
Published by: University of Ibadan, Department of Guidance and Counselling, Ibadan, Nigeria. http://www.ui.edu.ng/. Ed. Helen Nwagwu.

616.89 JPN
NIHON KODO RYOHO GAKKAI NYUZU RETA/JAPANESE ASSOCIATION OF BEHAVIOR THERAPY. NEWSLETTER. Text in Japanese. s-a. **Document type:** *Newsletter, Academic/Scholarly.*
Indexed: E-psyche.
Published by: Nihon Kodo Ryoho Gakkai/Japanese Association of Behavior Therapy, c/o Waseda University, Faculty of Human Sciences, Shimada Laboratory, 2-579-15 Mikajima, Tokorozawa, Saitama 359-1192, Japan. FAX 81-4-29476758, jabt07-09@list.waseda.jp, http://wwwsoc.nii.ac.jp/jabt/.

NIHON SEIKAGAKU GAKKAI NYUSU/JAPANESE SOCIETY OF SEXUAL SCIENCE NEWS. *see* MEDICAL SCIENCES

NIJMEGEN C N S; proceedings of the Cognitive Neuroscience Master of the Radboud University. *see* MEDICAL SCIENCES—Psychiatry And Neurology

153 JPN ISSN 1348-7264
➤ **NINCHI SHINRIGAKU KENKYUU/JAPANESE JOURNAL OF COGNITIVE PSYCHOLOGY.** Text in Japanese. 2004. s-a. membership. abstr. **Document type:** *Journal, Academic/Scholarly.*
Indexed: P03, PsycInfo.
—BLDSC (6113.213800).
Published by: Nihon Ninchi Shinri Gakkai/Japanese Society for Cognitive Psychology, Yoshida-Honmachi, Sakyo 2-309, Kyoto University, Graduate School of Informatics, Kyoto, 606-8501, Japan. g-office@cogpsy.jp.

➤ **NINGEN KOGAKU/JAPANESE JOURNAL OF ERGONOMICS.** *see* BUSINESS AND ECONOMICS—Labor And Industrial Relations

150 ESP ISSN 1135-6901
EL NINO. Text in Spanish. 1994. a. **Document type:** *Newsletter, Consumer.*
Published by: Instituto del Campo Freudiano, Via Laietana 64 2n 2a., Barcelona, Cataluna 08003t, Spain. TEL 34-934-121489, secretaria@scb.icf.net, http://www.scb-icf.net/.

NIPPON GEIJUTSU RYOHO GAKKAISHI/JAPANESE BULLETIN OF ARTS THERAPY. *see* ART

616.89 617 JPN ISSN 0917-950X
NO SHINKEI GEKA JANARU/JAPANESE JOURNAL OF NEUROSURGERY. Text in Japanese; Summaries in English, Japanese. 1992. q. JPY 24,469; JPY 2,039 newsstand/cover (effective 2007). adv. **Document type:** *Journal, Academic/Scholarly.*
Indexed: A22, E-psyche, EMBASE, ExcerpMed, INIS AtomInd, R10, Reac, SCOPUS.
—BLDSC (4656.643000), GNLM, IE, Ingenta.
Published by: (Nihon No Shinkei Geka Konguresu/Japanese Congress of Neurological Surgeons), Miwa-Shoten Ltd., 6-17-9 Hongo, Bunkyo-ku, Hongou Tsuna Bldg. 4F, Tokyo, 113-0033, Japan. TEL 81-3-38167796, FAX 81-3-38167756, info@miwapubl.com, http://www.miwapubl.com/.

THE NOETIC JOURNAL. *see* PHYSICS

003.75 300 USA ISSN 1090-0578
BF1 CODEN: NDPSFS
➤ **NONLINEAR DYNAMICS, PSYCHOLOGY, AND LIFE SCIENCES.** Text in English. 1997. q. USD 225 to institutions (print or online ed.); USD 250 combined subscription to institutions (print & online eds.); USD 25 per issue; free to members (effective 2009). adv. bk.rev. back issues avail. **Document type:** *Journal, Academic/Scholarly.* **Description:** Contains applications of nonlinear dynamics research to problems in the psychological, life and social sciences.
Related titles: Online - full text ed.: ISSN 1573-6652 (from IngentaConnect).
Indexed: A22, BibLing, CA, CurCont, E-psyche, E01, EMBASE, EconLit, ExcerpMed, JEL, MEDLINE, MSN, P03, P30, PsycInfo, PsycholAb, R10, Reac, S01, SCOPUS, SSCI, T02, W07.
—BLDSC (6117.316720), IE, Infotrieve, Ingenta. **CCC.**
Published by: Society for Chaos Theory in Psychology & Life Sciences, c/o Matthijs Koopmans, 525 West 238 St, Apt 4A, Bronx, NY 10463. mkoopmans@aol.com. Ed. Stephen J Guastello TEL 414-288-6900.

150 DNK ISSN 1904-0016
BF8.D3 CODEN: NOPSAW
➤ **NORDIC PSYCHOLOGY (ONLINE);** theory, research, practice. Text in English. 1949. q. DKK 500 (effective 2009). adv. bk.rev. bibl.; charts; illus.; stat. index. 80 p./no.; back issues avail. **Document type:** *Journal, Academic/Scholarly.* **Description:** Aims to reflect the particular "Northern Light", which in Scandinavia is characterized by special working approaches used by psychologists in Northern welfare societies.
Former titles (until Jan.2009): Nordic Psychology (Print) (1901-2276); (until 2006): Nordisk Psykologi (0029-1463)
Media: Online - full text.
Indexed: A20, A22, ASCA, ASSIA, CA, ChemAb, E-psyche, MLA-IB, P03, P30, PCI, PsycInfo, PsycholAb, RASB, S02, S03, SCOPUS, SOPODA, SSCI, SociolAb, T02, W07.
—BLDSC (6117.927740), IE, Infotrieve. **CCC.**
Published by: (Dansk Psykolog Forening/Danish Psychological Association, Sveriges Psykologfoerbund/Swedish Psychological Association SWE, Norsk Psykologforening/Norwegian Psychological Association NOR, Salfraedingafelag Islands/Icelandic Psychological Association ISL, Suomen Psykologiliitto/Finnish Psychological Association FIN), Dansk Psykologisk Forlag/Danish Psychological Publishers, Kongevejen 155, Virum, 2830, Denmark. TEL 45-35-381655, FAX 45-35-381665, info@dpf.dk. Eds. Peter Elsass, Klaus Nielsen.

150 NOR ISSN 0332-6470
NORSK PSYKOLOGFORENING. TIDSSKRIFT/NORWEGIAN PSYCHOLOGICAL ASSOCIATION. JOURNAL. Text in Norwegian. 1964. m. NOK 1,350 to individuals; NOK 1,600 to institutions; NOK 150 per issue (effective 2011). adv. bk.rev. index. back issues avail. **Document type:** *Magazine, Trade.*
Formerly (until 1973): Psykologen (0800-6598)
Indexed: A22, E-psyche, P03, PsycInfo, PsycholAb, S02, S03.
—BLDSC (8822.340000), IE, Ingenta.
Published by: Norsk Psykologforening/Norwegian Psychological Association, PO Box 419, Sentrum, Oslo, 0103, Norway. TEL 47-23-103130, FAX 47-22-424292, npfpost@psykologforeningen.no, http://www.psykologiforeningen.no. Ed. Bjoernar Olsen. Circ: 7,500.

150 NOR ISSN 0809-781X
➤ **NORSK TIDSSKRIFT FOR ATFERDSANALYSE.** Variant title: N T A. Text in Norwegian. 1986. q. NOK 160 (effective 2011). bk.rev. **Document type:** *Journal, Academic/Scholarly.* **Description:** Membership journal with timely and professional articles related to psychology.
Formerly (until 2006): Diskriminanten (0801-0536)
Related titles: Online - full text ed.
Published by: Norsk Atferdsanalytisk Forening/Norwegian Association for Behaviour Analysis, P O Box 24, Sandefjord, 3209, Norway. TEL 47-33-806570, FAX 47-21-012449, service.nafo@atferd.no, http://www.atferd.no. Ed. Boerge Stroemgren.

158 370.15 306.43 USA ISSN 1527-7143
➤ **NORTH AMERICAN JOURNAL OF PSYCHOLOGY.** Text in English. 1999. 3/yr. USD 30 to individuals; USD 65 to institutions (effective 2011). bk.rev. abstr. back issues avail. **Document type:** *Journal, Academic/Scholarly.* **Description:** Publishes original studies in a wide variety of areas of psychology, as well as education and sociology. Includes interviews with renowned psychologists and reviews, with an editorial bias favoring topics of broad concern to social scientists.
Related titles: Online - full text ed.
Indexed: A01, A03, A08, A12, A26, ABIn, B01, B06, B07, B09, CA, H12, I05, L&LBA, P03, P25, P43, P48, P51, P53, P54, PAIS, PQC, PsycInfo, PsycholAb, S02, S03, SCOPUS, T02.
—BLDSC (6148.172000).
Address: 240 Harbor Dr, Winter Garden, FL 34787. TEL 407-877-8364.

150.1953 USA ISSN 0889-9428
NORTH AMERICAN SOCIETY OF ADLERIAN PSYCHOLOGY. NEWSLETTER. Text in English. 1967. bi-m. USD 20 to non-members (effective 2000). bk.rev. **Document type:** *Newsletter.* **Description:** Contains information on news and activities of the Society. Covers recent conventions in the field.
Indexed: E-psyche.
Published by: North American Society of Adlerian Psychology, 614 Old W Chocolate Ave, Hershey, PA 17033. TEL 312-629-8801, FAX 312-629-8859. Ed., R&P Jerianne Garber. Circ: 1,000.

150 POL ISSN 0867-7980
➤ **NOWINY PSYCHOLOGICZNE.** Text in Polish. 1981. q. PLZ 77 domestic (effective 2007). **Document type:** *Journal, Academic/ Scholarly.*
Published by: Polskie Towarzystwo Psychologiczne, ul Stawki 5-7, Warsaw, 00183, Poland. ptp@engram.psych.uw.edu.pl, http://www.ptp.org.pl. Ed. Anna Strzalkowska.

150 ARG ISSN 1852-4613
NUESTRA CIENCIA. Text in Spanish. 1995. 3/yr. **Document type:** *Magazine, Trade.*
Published by: Colegio de Psicologos de la Provincia de Cordoba, Ovidio Lagos, 163 - Bo., General Paz, Cordoba, Argentina. TEL 54-351-4222703, FAX 54-351-4259367, http://www.cppc.org.ar/.

NUTRITION HEALTH REVIEW; the consumer's medical journal. *see* NUTRITION AND DIETETICS

150 618.92 JPN ISSN 0918-7065
NYUUYOUJI IGAKU, SHINRIGAKU KENKYUU/JAPANESE JOURNAL OF MEDICAL AND PSYCHOLOGICAL STUDY OF INFANTS. Text in Japanese. 1992. a. **Document type:** *Journal, Academic/Scholarly.*
—CCC.
Published by: Nyuyoji Igaku Shinrigaku Kenkyukai/Japanese Association for Medical and Psychological Study of Infants, c/o Nagoya University School of Education, Graduate School of Education & Human Development, 65 Tsurumai-cho, Showa-ku, Nagoya, 466-8550, Japan. TEL 81-52-7815111 ext 2643.

150 USA
O P A NEWSGRAM. Text in English. 1959. 10/yr. USD 35 to non-members (effective 2000). adv. bk.rev. **Document type:** *Newsletter.*
Former titles: Oregon Psychology; Oregon Psychological Association. Newsletter (0471-9336)
Indexed: E-psyche.
Published by: Oregon Psychological Association, 147 S E 102nd Ave, Portland, OR 97216-2703. Ed. Rodger Bufford. Adv. contact Rod Harriman. Circ: 700 (controlled).

▼ **OBSHCHESTVO: SOTSIOLOGIYA, PSIKHOLOGIYA, PEDAGOGIKA/SOCIETY: SOCIOLOGY, PSYCHOLOGY, PEDAGOGICS.** *see* SOCIOLOGY

150 SWE ISSN 1651-1328
OEREBRO STUDIES IN PSYCHOLOGY. Text in English; Text occasionally in Swedish. 2002. irreg., latest vol.7, 2006. SEK 180 per issue (effective 2006). back issues avail. **Document type:** *Monographic series, Academic/Scholarly.*
Published by: Oerebro Universitet, Universitetsbiblioteket/University of Oerebro. University Library, Fakultetsgatan 1, Oerebro, 70182, Sweden. TEL 46-19-303240, FAX 46-19-331217, biblioteket@ub.oru.se. Ed. Joanna Jansdotter.

150 USA ISSN 0472-7290
THE OHIO PSYCHOLOGIST. Text in English. 19??. bi-m. **Document type:** *Journal, Academic/Scholarly.* **Description:** Covers state-wide and national issues that affect psychologists and consumers.
Published by: Ohio Psychological Association, 395 E Broad, Suite 310, Columbus, OH 43215. TEL 614-224-0034, 800-783-1983, FAX 614-224-2059.

OKEE-KRANT; de duidelijkste krant voor jou. *see* MEDICAL SCIENCES—Psychiatry And Neurology

614.58 USA
OKLAHOMA. DEPARTMENT OF MENTAL HEALTH AND SUBSTANCE ABUSE SERVICES. ANNUAL REPORT. Text in English. a. free. **Document type:** *Government.*
Former titles: Oklahoma. Department of Mental Health. Annual Report; Mental Health Care in Oklahoma. Annual Report
Indexed: E-psyche.
Published by: Department of Mental Health, Biometrics Division, P O Box 53277, Oklahoma City, OK 73105. TEL 405-522-3908, FAX 405-522-3650. Ed. Rosemary Brown. Circ: 1,000.

150.19 ITA ISSN 1126-0653
BF173.A2
L'OMBRA; tracce e percorsi a partire da Jung. Text in Italian. 1996. s-a. EUR 13 domestic; EUR 50 foreign (effective 2009). **Document type:** *Magazine, Consumer.* **Description:** Covers studies in psychoanalysis since Jung.
Indexed: E-psyche.
Published by: Moretti e Vitali Editori, Via Sergentini 6a, Bergamo, BG 24128, Italy. TEL 39-035-251300, FAX 39-035-4329409, http://www.morettievitali.it. Ed. Fulvio Salza.

155.937 USA ISSN 0030-2228
BF789.D4 CODEN: OMGABX
➤ **OMEGA: JOURNAL OF DEATH AND DYING.** Text in English. 1970. 8/yr. USD 158 combined subscription to individuals (print & online eds.); USD 560 combined subscription to institutions (print & online eds.) (effective 2011). bk.rev. abstr.; bibl.; charts; illus. Index. back issues avail.; reprints avail. **Document type:** *Journal, Academic/ Scholarly.* **Description:** Provides guide for clinicians, social workers, and health professionals dealing with problems in crisis management, such as terminal illness, fatal accidents, catastrophes, suicide and bereavement.
Related titles: Online - full text ed.: ISSN 1541-3764. USD 151 to individuals; USD 532 to institutions (effective 2011).
Indexed: A01, A02, A03, A08, A20, A21, A22, A25, A26, AMED, ASCA, ASG, ASSIA, AbAn, AgeL, B04, BRD, C06, C07, C08, CA, CINAHL, CMCI, CurCont, DIP, E-psyche, E02, E03, E07, E08, EMBASE, ERI, EdA, EdI, ExcerpMed, F09, G08, H04, H09, H11, H12, I05, IBR, IBZ, MEDLINE, MLA-IB, P02, P03, P04, P10, P12, P13, P27, P30, P48, P53, P54, PCI, PQC, PsycInfo, PsycholAb, RI-1, RI-2, RILM, S02, S03, S05, S08, S09, SCOPUS, SOPODA, SSA, SSAI, SSAb, SSCI, SSI, SociolAb, T02, V&AA, W03, W07, W09.
—BLDSC (6256.425000), GNLM, IE, Infotrieve, Ingenta, INIST. **CCC.**
Published by: Baywood Publishing Co., Inc., 26 Austin Ave, PO Box 337, Amityville, NY 11701. TEL 631-691-1270, 800-638-7819, FAX 631-691-1770, Baywood@baywood.com. Ed. Kenneth J Doka.

364 345 USA ISSN 1948-5115
▼ **OPEN ACCESS JOURNAL OF FORENSIC PATHOLOGY.** Text in English. 2009. a. free (effective 2011). **Document type:** *Journal, Academic/Scholarly.*
Media: Online - full text.
Address: gregdeclue@me.com, http://gregdeclue.myakkatech.com. Pub. Gregory DeClue.

150 NLD ISSN 1874-2300
BF1
➤ **THE OPEN BEHAVIORAL SCIENCE JOURNAL.** Text in English. 2007. irreg. free (effective 2011). **Document type:** *Journal, Academic/Scholarly.*
Media: Online - full text.
Indexed: A01, A39, AnBeAb, C27, C29, D03, D04, E13, NSA, R14, S14, S15, S18.
Published by: Bentham Open (Subsidiary of: Bentham Science Publishers Ltd.), PO Box 294, Bussum, AG 1400, Netherlands. TEL 31-35-6923800, FAX 31-35-6980150, subscriptions@bentham.org. Ed. Kiyofumi Yamada.

150 NLD ISSN 1874-3501
BF1
➤ **THE OPEN PSYCHOLOGY JOURNAL.** Text in English. 2008. irreg. free (effective 2011). **Document type:** *Journal, Academic/Scholarly.*
Media: Online - full text.
Indexed: A01, A39, C27, C29, D03, D04, E13, NSA, R14, S14, S15, S18.
Published by: Bentham Open (Subsidiary of: Bentham Science Publishers Ltd.), PO Box 294, Bussum, AG 1400, Netherlands. TEL 31-35-6923800, FAX 31-35-6980150, subscriptions@bentham.org.

150.19 302.3 GBR ISSN 1474-2780
ORGANISATIONAL AND SOCIAL DYNAMICS; an international journal for the integration of psychoanalytic, systemic and group behavior perspectives. Text in English. 2001. s-a. GBP 120 to institutions; GBP 40 to non-members; free to members (effective 2010). adv. back issues avail. **Document type:** *Journal, Academic/Scholarly.* **Description:** Aims to contribute to the development of a deeper understanding of organizational and social processes, and of their effect on the individual.
Related titles: Online - full text ed.: ISSN 2044-3765.
Indexed: E-psyche.
—BLDSC (6289.355000), IE, Ingenta. **CCC.**

P

Published by: (O P U S), Karnac Books, 118 Finchley Rd, London, NW3 5HT, United Kingdom. TEL 44-20-74311075, FAX 44-20-74359076, shop@karnacbooks.com. Eds. Anne-Marie Cummins, Michael Moskowitz. Adv. contact Fernando Marques. B&W page GBP 100; 110 x 195.

ORGANISATIONSBERATUNG, SUPERVISION, COACHING. *see* BUSINESS AND ECONOMICS—Personnel Management

ORGANIZATIONAL BEHAVIOR AND HUMAN DECISION PROCESSES. *see* BUSINESS AND ECONOMICS—Management

150 610 DEU ISSN 1612-0531
ORGANIZATIONAL PSYCHOLOGY AND HEALTH CARE. Text in German. 1999. irreg., latest vol.5, 2007. price varies. **Document type:** *Monographic series, Academic/Scholarly.*
Published by: Rainer Hampp Verlag, Marktplatz 5, Mering, 86415, Germany. TEL 49-8233-4783, FAX 49-8233-30755, info@rhverlag.de, http://www.rhverlag.de.

150 GBR ISSN 2041-3866
▼ ➤ **ORGANIZATIONAL PSYCHOLOGY REVIEW.** Text in English. forthcoming 2011 (Feb.). q. USD 792, GBP 428 combined subscription to institutions (print & online eds.); USD 776, GBP 419 to institutions (effective 2011). **Document type:** *Journal, Academic/Scholarly.* **Description:** Publishes original articles on organizational psychology, including applied, industrial, occupational, personnel, and work psychology as well as organizational behavior.
Related titles: Online - full text ed.: ISSN 2041-3874. forthcoming. USD 713, GBP 385 to institutions (effective 2011).
—IE. **CCC.**
Published by: (European Association of Work and Organizational Psychology), Sage Publications Ltd. (Subsidiary of: Sage Publications, Inc.), 1 Oliver's Yard, 55 City Rd, London, EC1Y 1SP, United Kingdom. TEL 44-20-73248500, FAX 44-20-73248600, info@sagepub.co.uk, http://www.uk.sagepub.com/home.nav. Ed. Daan van Knippenberg.

150 ARG ISSN 1515-6877
ORIENTACION Y SOCIEDAD; revista internacional y interdisciplinaria de orientacion vocacional ocupacional. Text in Spanish. 1999. s-a. **Document type:** *Journal, Academic/Scholarly.*
Related titles: Online - full text ed.: ISSN 1851-8893. 2003. free (effective 2011) (from SciELO).
Published by: Universidad Nacional de la Plata, Facultad de Humanidades y Ciencias de la Educacion, Calle 48 entre 6 y 7, 1er Subsuelo, La Plata, Buenos Aires 1900, Argentina. TEL 54-221-4230125, ceciroz@.fahce.unlp.edu.ar, http://www.publicaciones.fahce.unlp.edu.ar. Circ: 500.

158.3 FRA ISSN 0249-6739
➤ **ORIENTATION SCOLAIRE ET PROFESSIONNELLE.** Text in French. 1972. q. EUR 66 domestic to individuals; EUR 78 foreign to individuals; EUR 33 domestic to students; EUR 39 foreign to students (effective 2010). adv. bk.rev. abstr.; bibl.; charts; stat. index. back issues avail. **Document type:** *Journal, Academic/Scholarly.*
Formerly (until 1972): B I N O P Bulletin (0005-3147)
Related titles: Online - full text ed.
Indexed: A22, E-psyche, FR, P03, PsycInfo, PsycholAb, RASB, RefZh, S02, S03.
—BLDSC (6291.213000), IE, Infotrieve, INIST.
Published by: Institut National d'Etude du Travail et d'Orientation Professionnelle, 41 rue Gay Lussac, Paris, 75005, France. TEL 33-1-44107877, FAX 33-1-44107911, inetop-osp@cnam.fr. Ed. Serge Blanchard. Pub. Jean Guichard. Adv. contact Renee Delblond. Circ: 2,000. **Co-sponsor:** Institut National des Arts et Metiers.

➤ **OUR GIFTED CHILDREN.** *see* CHILDREN AND YOUTH—About

158 USA ISSN 2155-3882
OUR WAY. Text in English. 2008. q. USD 6.99 per issue (effective 2010). **Document type:** *Magazine, Consumer.* **Description:** Provides behavioral health information for people of color and professionals who work with people of color.
Published by: Overbrook Therapy Associates, PO Box 1415, Philadelphia, PA 19105. TEL 215-510-1063, publisher@ourwaymagazine.com.

150 JPN ISSN 0387-4605
OYO SHINRIGAKU KENKYU/JAPANESE JOURNAL OF APPLIED PSYCHOLOGY. Text in English. 1965. a. subscr. incld. with membership. **Document type:** *Journal, Academic/Scholarly.*
Formerly (until 1975): Nihon Oyo Shinri Gakkai Kaiho (0388-1172)
—**CCC.**
Published by: Nihon Oyo Shinri Gakkai/Japan Association of Applied Psychology, 4-4-19 Takadanobaba, Shinjuku-ku, Tokyo, 169-0075, Japan. TEL 81-3-53896491, FAX 81-3-33682822, jaap-post@bunken.co.jp, http://wwwsoc.nii.ac.jp/jaap/.

P S!; populaer psykologi och medicin. *see* MEDICAL SCIENCES

150 USA
P S C P NEWSLETTER. Text in English. 1971. q. free to members. **Document type:** *Newsletter.* **Description:** Keeps its readers informed of important issues in the field of psychology.
Formerly: P S C P Times
Indexed: E-psyche.
Published by: Philadelphia Society of Clinical Psychologists, 302 Cottman St, 2nd Fl, Jenkintown, PA 19046. TEL 215-885-2562, FAX 215-885-1797, info@philadelphiapsychology.org, http://www.philadelphiapsychology.org. Circ: 200.

PAEDAGOGISCHE PSYCHOLOGIE UND ENTWICKLUNGSPSYCHOLOGIE. *see* EDUCATION

370.15 150 DNK ISSN 1903-0002
➤ **PAEDAGOGISK PSYKOLOGISK TIDSSKRIFT/JOURNAL OF SCHOOL PSYCHOLOGY.** Text in Danish. 1964. bi-m. DKK 430 to non-members; DKK 285 to students; DKK 120 per issue (effective 2009). adv. bk.rev. abstr.; bibl. index. 80 p./no.; Supplement avail.; back issues avail. **Document type:** *Journal, Academic/Scholarly.*
Former titles (until 2008): Psykologisk Paedagogisk Raadgivning (0906-219X); (until 1991): Skolepsykologi (0037-6493)
Related titles: Online - full text ed.: ISSN 1903-6906. 199?.
Indexed: E-psyche, FamI, P03, PsycInfo, PsycholAb, S02, S03, SWR&A.
Published by: (Paedagogiske Psykologers Forening), Forlaget Skolepsykologi, Havrevaenget 9, Herfoelge, 4681, Denmark. TEL 46-25-577655. Ed. Palle Kristian Johansen.

150 370 BRA ISSN 0103-863X
➤ **PAIDEIA**; cadernos de psicologia e educacao. Text in Portuguese. 1991. 3/yr. BRL 40 to individuals; BRL 90 to institutions; BRL 25 to students (effective 2010). **Document type:** *Journal, Academic/Scholarly.* **Description:** Publishes original contributions on varied subjects in psychology, education and related areas.
Related titles: Online - full text ed.: ISSN 1982-4327. 2006. free (effective 2011).
Indexed: C01, P03, PsycInfo.
Published by: Universidade de Sao Paulo, Faculdade de Filosofia Ciencias e Letras de Ribeirao Preto, Av Bandeirantes 3900, Monte Alegre, Ribeirao Preto, SP 14040-901, Brazil. Ed., R&P, Adv. contact Manoel Antonio dos Santos.

150 PAK ISSN 1019-438X
➤ **PAKISTAN JOURNAL OF CLINICAL PSYCHOLOGY.** Text in English. 1992. s-a. back issues avail. **Document type:** *Journal, Academic/Scholarly.* **Description:** Publishes experimental, clinical and theoretical articles, social surveys, comments and special reviews of clinical issues in psychology.
Related titles: CD-ROM ed.
Indexed: A26, E-psyche, ExtraMED, I05.
Published by: University of Karachi, Institute of Clinical Psychology, 118, Block 20 Abul Asar Hafeez Jalindhri Rd, Gulistan-e-Jauhar, Karachi, 75290, Pakistan. TEL 92-21-34613584, FAX 92-21-34615369, http://www.uok.edu.pk/research_institutes/icp/faculty.php. Ed. Riaz Ahmad. Circ: 500.

150 PAK ISSN 1016-0604
PAKISTAN JOURNAL OF PSYCHOLOGICAL RESEARCH. Text in English. s-a. **Document type:** *Journal, Academic/Scholarly.*
Related titles: Online - full text ed.
Indexed: H12, I05, P02, P25, P54, PsycInfo.
Published by: National Institute of Psychology, c/o Quaid-i-Azam University (New Campus), Shahdra Rd. (off Main Murree Rd.), Islamabad, Pakistan. TEL 92-51-90644031, FAX 92-51-2896012, nip@nip.edu.pk, http://www.nip.edu.pk/. Ed. Anila Kamal.

150 PAK ISSN 0030-9869
BF1
➤ **PAKISTAN JOURNAL OF PSYCHOLOGY.** Text in English. 1965-1976 (Dec.); resumed 1979. 2/yr. adv. bk.rev. charts. back issues avail. **Document type:** *Journal, Academic/Scholarly.* **Description:** Publishes theoretical and research articles covering a wide range of issues in psychology.
Related titles: CD-ROM ed.
Indexed: A26, BAS, E-psyche, ExtraMED, I05, P30, P36, PsycholAb.
Published by: University of Karachi, Institute of Clinical Psychology, 118, Block 20 Abul Asar Hafeez Jalindhri Rd, Gulistan-e-Jauhar, Karachi, 75290, Pakistan. TEL 92-21-34613584, FAX 92-21-34615369, http://www.uok.edu.pk/research_institutes/icp/faculty.php. Ed. Riaz Ahmad. Circ: 500.

150 PAK ISSN 1727-4931
HM1027.P18
➤ **PAKISTAN JOURNAL OF SOCIAL AND CLINICAL PSYCHOLOGY.** Text in English. 1964. a. (q. until 2003). PKR 250 domestic to individuals; USD 25 foreign to individuals; PKR 300 domestic to institutions; USD 30 foreign to institutions (effective 2010). bk.rev. charts; stat. back issues avail. **Document type:** *Journal, Academic/Scholarly.*
Former titles (until 2003): Psychology Quarterly (0033-3093); Journal of Psychology
Related titles: Online - full text ed.
Indexed: A26, E-psyche, I05, P36, PsycInfo, PsycholAb.
Published by: Government College University, Department of Psychology, Lahore, Pakistan. TEL 92-111-000010 ext 307, 309, FAX 92-42-9213341. Ed. Kausar Suhail. Circ: 300.

➤ **PAKISTAN PSYCHOLOGICAL ABSTRACTS.** *see* ABSTRACTING AND INDEXING SERVICES

➤ **PALO ALTO REVIEW**; journal of ideas. *see* EDUCATION

150.72 ESP ISSN 1699-437X
LC189.8
PAPELES DE TRABAJO SOBRE CULTURA, EDUCACION Y DESARROLLO HUMANO/WORKING PAPERS ON CULTURE, EDUCATION AND HUMAN DEVELOPMENT. Text in Spanish. 2005. m. free (effective 2011). back issues avail. **Document type:** *Monographic series, Academic/Scholarly.*
Media: Online - full text.
—**CCC.**
Published by: Universidad Autonoma de Madrid, Departamento de Psicologia Evolutiva y de la Educacion, Ciudad Universitaria de Canto Blanco, Madrid, 28049, Spain. TEL 34-91-4975000, http://www.uam.es/centros/psicologia/paginas/departamentos/evolutiva/default.html. Ed. David Poveda.

150 ESP ISSN 0214-7823
➤ **PAPELES DEL PSICOLOGO.** Text in Spanish. 1981. bi-m. EUR 10 (effective 2010). **Document type:** *Journal, Academic/Scholarly.*
Formerly (until 1989): Colegio Oficial de Psicologos. Delegacion de Madrid. Papeles del Colegio (0211-7851)
Related titles: Online - full text ed.: free (effective 2011).
Indexed: E-psyche, PsycInfo, SCOPUS.
—**CCC.**
Published by: Colegio Oficial de Psicologos, Claudio Coello 46, Madrid, 28001, Spain. TEL 34-91-4355212, FAX 34-91-5779172.

150 AUT ISSN 1021-5573
➤ **PAPERS ON SOCIAL REPRESENTATIONS. THREAD OF DISCUSSION/TEXTES SUR LES REPRESENTATIONS SOCIALES. ESPACE DE DISCUSSION.** Text in Multiple languages. 1992. 3/yr. **Document type:** *Journal, Academic/Scholarly.* **Description:** Publishes empirical, theoretical, methodological and discussion papers in the fields of social representation theory, cultural psychology, discourse and communication theory, social construction, societal psychology and related areas.
Related titles: Online - full text ed.: free (effective 2011).
Indexed: CA, S02, S03, T02.
Published by: Johannes Kepler Universitaet Linz, Institut fuer Paedagogik und Psychologie, Altenbergerstrasse 69, Linz, A-4040, Austria.

150 360 USA ISSN 1946-6560
HV6626.2
▼ ➤ **PARTNER ABUSE.** Text in English. 2010 (Jan.). q. USD 130 domestic to individuals; USD 195 foreign to individuals; USD 310 domestic to institutions; USD 370 foreign to institutions (effective 2010). **Document type:** *Journal, Academic/Scholarly.* **Description:** Provides new research on physical and emotional partner abuse, including mutual abuse, female perpetrators, male victims, alternative intervention programs, and abuse in the LGBT community.
Related titles: Online - full text ed.: ISSN 1946-6579. 2010 (Jan.) (from IngentaConnect).
Indexed: ASSIA, P30, SSA.
Published by: Springer Publishing Company, 11 W 42nd St, 15th Fl, New York, NY 10036. TEL 212-431-4370, FAX 212-941-7842, contactus@springerpub.com, http://www.springerjournals.com. Ed. John Hamel.

150 JPN ISSN 1348-8406
PASONARITI KENKYUU/JAPANESE JOURNAL OF PERSONALITY. Text in Japanese. 1993. s-a. JPY 4,000 membership (effective 2005). **Document type:** *Journal, Academic/Scholarly.*
Formerly (until 2003): Seikaku Shinrigaku Kenkyu
Related titles: Online - full text ed.: ISSN 1349-6174. free (effective 2011).
Indexed: A01, A39, C27, C29, D04, E13, S14, S15, S18.
Published by: Nihon Pasonariti Shinri Gakkai/Japan Society of Personality Psychology, c/o International AcademicPrinting Co., Ltd., 3-8-8, Takadanobaba,Shinjuku-ku, Tokyo, Japan. TEL 81-3-53896243, FAX 81-3-33682822, office-jimukyoku@jspp.gr.jp, http://wwwsoc.nii.ac.jp/jspp/.

150 200 USA ISSN 0031-2789
BV4012
➤ **PASTORAL PSYCHOLOGY.** Text in English. 1950. bi-m. EUR 1,096, USD 1,143 combined subscription to institutions (print & online eds.) (effective 2012). adv. bk.rev.; film rev. back issues avail.; reprint service avail. from PSC. **Document type:** *Journal, Academic/Scholarly.* **Description:** Brings out psychological, behavioral, social, and human sciences research into critical engagement with pastoral concerns (local, institutional, societal, political, international, and other).
Related titles: Microfilm ed.: (from PQC); Online - full text ed.: ISSN 1573-6679 (from IngentaConnect).
Indexed: A01, A02, A03, A08, A20, A21, A22, A26, ASSIA, BibLing, CA, CCR, ChrPI, DIP, E-psyche, E01, FamI, GSS&RPL, IBR, IBZ, P03, P25, P28, P30, P43, P48, P53, P54, PQC, PhilInd, PsycInfo, PsycholAb, R&TA, RI-1, RI-2, S02, S03, SCOPUS, T02.
—BLDSC (6409.300000), IE, Infotrieve, Ingenta. **CCC.**
Published by: Springer New York LLC (Subsidiary of: Springer Science+Business Media), 233 Spring St, New York, NY 10013. TEL 212-460-1500, FAX 212-460-1575, service-ny@springer.com, http://www.springer.com/. Ed. Lewis R Rambo.

➤ **PASTORALPSYCHOLOGIE UND SPIRITUALITAET.** *see* RELIGIONS AND THEOLOGY

150 USA ISSN 1574-048X
PATH IN PSYCHOLOGY SERIES. Variant title: Publications for the Advancement of Theory and History in Psychology Series. Text in English. 1982. irreg., latest 2009. price varies. **Document type:** *Monographic series, Academic/Scholarly.*
Indexed: E-psyche.
Published by: Springer Netherlands (Subsidiary of: Springer Science+Business Media), Van Godewijckstraat 30, Dordrecht, 3311 GX, Netherlands. TEL 31-78-6576050, FAX 31-78-6576474. Ed. Robert W Rieber.

301.1 USA
PATHWAYS (BETHESDA); DC resources. Text in English. 1978. 4/yr. USD 10. adv. bk.rev.
Published by: Pathways, 30405, Bethesda, MD 20824-0405. TEL 301-656-3127, FAX 301-656-3023, pathwaysmag@earthlink.net. Ed. Lou de Sabla. Circ: 40,000.

PATIENT REPORTED OUTCOMES NEWSLETTER. *see* MEDICAL SCIENCES

150 USA ISSN 1078-1919
JX1901
➤ **PEACE AND CONFLICT**; journal of peace psychology. Text in English. 1995. q. GBP 352 combined subscription in United Kingdom to institutions (print & online eds.); EUR 469, USD 590 combined subscription to institutions (print & online eds.) (effective 2012). adv. bk.rev. illus. Index. back issues avail.; reprint service avail. from PSC. **Document type:** *Journal, Academic/Scholarly.* **Description:** Reflects the essential reality of human consciousness and social and societal relations.
Related titles: Online - full text ed.: ISSN 1532-7949. GBP 316 in United Kingdom to institutions; EUR 422, USD 530 to institutions (effective 2012).
Indexed: A22, B04, BRD, CA, CMM, E-psyche, E01, ESPM, GEOBASE, I02, I13, IBSS, P02, P03, P10, P12, P27, P34, P42, P47, P48, P53, P54, PAIS, PQC, PRA, PSA, PsycInfo, PsycholAb, RiskAb, S02, S03, SCOPUS, SSA, SSAI, SSAb, SSI, SociolAb, T02, W01, W02, W03.
—BLDSC (6413.759000), IE, Infotrieve, Ingenta. **CCC.**
Published by: (American Psychological Association, Division 48), Routledge (Subsidiary of: Taylor & Francis Group), 325 Chestnut St, Ste 800, Philadelphia, PA 19106. TEL 800-354-1420, FAX 215-625-2940, journals@routledge.com, http://www.routledge.com. Ed. Richard V Wagner.

150 USA ISSN 1935-4894
JZ5511.2
PEACE PSYCHOLOGY. Text in English. s-a. **Document type:** *Newsletter, Consumer.*
Formerly (until 200?): Peace Psychology Bulletin
Published by: American Psychological Association, Division 48, 750 First St, NE, Washington, DC 20002-4242. TEL 202-336-6013, FAX 202-218-3599, division@apa.org, http://www.apa.org/about/division/div48.html. Ed. Dr. J W Heuchert.

PEDAGOGIES MAGAZINE; le premier magazine des parents d'ados. *see* CHILDREN AND YOUTH—About

370.5 155.4 SWE ISSN 0346-5004
PEDAGOGISK-PSYKOLOGISKA PROBLEM. Text in Swedish. 1964. irreg. back issues avail. **Document type:** *Monographic series, Academic/Scholarly.*
Indexed: E-psyche, PsycholAb.

Published by: Malmoe Hoegskola, Laerarutbildningen/Malmoe University. School of Teacher Education, Nordenskioeldgatan 10, Malmo, 20045, Sweden. TEL 46-40-6657000.

150 370 USA ISSN 1941-7934
▼ ➤ **PEDAGOGY AND THE HUMAN SCIENCES.** Abbreviated title: P H S. Text in English. 2009. s-a. free (effective 2011). **Document type:** *Journal, Academic/Scholarly.* **Description:** Devoted to the study of teaching and learning in psychology and other social sciences.
Media: Online - full text.
Published by: Merrimack College, Department of Psychology, 315 Turnpike St, North Andover, MA 01845. TEL 978-837-5000, http://www.merrimack.edu/academics/liberal_arts/Psychology/Pages/default.aspx. Ed. Debra A Harkins.

➤ **THE PEER BULLETIN.** *see* SOCIAL SERVICES AND WELFARE

150 613.7 USA ISSN 1070-6674
PELIZZA'S POSITIVE PRINCIPLES FOR BETTER LIVING. Text in English. 1993. q. looseleaf. USD 29.95 for 3 yrs. (effective 2006). adv. bk.rev. **Document type:** *Newsletter, Consumer.* **Description:** Provides information and tips to maximize personal and professional productivity.
Indexed: E-psyche.
Published by: Pelizza & Associates, PO Box 225, North Chatham, NY 12132. Eds. Bonnie Pelizza, Phillip Niles. Pub. John Pelizza. R&P Bonnie Pelizza. Adv. contacts Bonnie Pelizza, Bonnie Pelizza. Circ: 3,000 (paid).

150 COL ISSN 1657-8961
BF5
➤ **PENSAMIENTO PSICOLOGICO.** Text in Spanish. 2005. s-a. **Document type:** *Journal, Academic/Scholarly.*
Related titles: Online - full text ed.: free (effective 2011).
Indexed: H21, P08.
Published by: Pontificia Universidad Javeriana, Cali, Facultad de Psicologia, Calle 18, No 118-250, Edificio el Saman, 3er Piso, Cali, Colombia. TEL 57-3-218200.

150 ITA ISSN 1129-2644
PER ME. Text in Italian. 1999. m. EUR 23 (effective 2004). **Document type:** *Magazine, Consumer.*
Published by: Arnoldo Mondadori Editore SpA, Via Mondadori 1, Segrate, 20090, Italy. TEL 39-02-66814363, FAX 39-030-3198412, http://www.mondadori.com.

150 617.7 GBR ISSN 0301-0066
BF311 CODEN: PCTNBA
➤ **PERCEPTION.** Text in English. 1972. m. USD 1,370 combined subscription in the Americas (print & online eds.); GBP 770 combined subscription elsewhere (print & online eds.) (effective 2012). bk.rev. index. back issues avail.; reprints avail. **Document type:** *Journal, Academic/Scholarly.* **Description:** Reports experimental results and theoretical ideas in the fields of animal, human and machine perception, and artificial intelligence.
Related titles: CD-ROM ed.; Online - full text ed.: ISSN 1468-4233. 2000. USD 1,340 in the Americas; GBP 740 elsewhere (effective 2012).
Indexed: A20, A22, AHCI, BibInd, CPerI, CommAb, CurCont, DIP, DentInd, E-psyche, EMBASE, ErgAb, ExcerpMed, FR, IBR, IBZ, IndMed, MEA&I, MEDLINE, NSCI, P03, P30, PCI, PhotoAb, PsycInfo, PsycholAb, R10, Reac, SCI, SCOPUS, SSCI, W07.
—BLDSC (6423.150000), GNLM, IE, Infotrieve, Ingenta, INIST. **CCC.**
Published by: Pion Ltd., 207 Brondesbury Park, London, NW2 5JN, United Kingdom. TEL 44-20-84590066, FAX 44-20-84516454, sales@pion.co.uk, http://www.pion.co.uk/. Eds. Peter Thompson, Tim Meese, Tom Troscianko.

152 USA ISSN 0031-5125
BF311 CODEN: PMOSAZ
➤ **PERCEPTUAL AND MOTOR SKILLS.** Text in English. 1949. bi-m. USD 580 domestic; USD 595 foreign; USD 630 combined subscription domestic (print & online eds.); USD 645 combined subscription foreign (print & online eds.) (effective 2011). charts; illus.; abstr.; stat. Index. 352 p./no.; back issues avail.; reprints avail. **Document type:** *Journal, Academic/Scholarly.* **Description:** Encourages scientific originality and creativity. Includes experimental or theoretical articles dealing with perception or motor skills, especially as affected by experience.
Former titles (until 1952): Perceptual and Motor Skills Research Exchange (0885-6524); Motor Skills Research Exchange
Related titles: Microform ed.; Online - full text ed.: ISSN 1558-688X. USD 530 (effective 2011).
Indexed: A01, A02, A03, A08, A20, A22, A26, AMED, ASCA, AbAn, AgeL, B04, B21, BDM&CN, BRD, C06, C07, C08, CA, CDA, CINAHL, CIS, ChPerI, ChemoAb, Chicano, CommAb, CurCont, DIP, DSHAb, DentInd, E-psyche, E02, E03, E07, E08, E16, ECER, EMBASE, ERA, ERI, EdA, EdI, ErgAb, ExcerpMed, F09, FR, FamI, G08, H09, H12, HEA, HRIS, I05, IBR, IBZ, INI, IPsyAb, IndMed, M12, MEDLINE, MLA, MLA-IB, P02, P03, P10, P12, P24, P27, P30, P48, P53, P54, PCI, PEI, PQC, PsycInfo, PsycholAb, R10, RASB, RILM, Reac, S02, S03, S05, S09, S20, S21, SCOPUS, SD, SOPODA, SSAI, SSAb, SSCI, SSI, SportS, T02, W03, W07, W09.
—BLDSC (6423.300000), GNLM, IE, Infotrieve, Ingenta, INIST, Linda Hall. **CCC.**
Published by: Ammons Scientific Ltd., PO Box 9229, Missoula, MT 59807. TEL 406-728-1710, FAX 406-541-2704, ejournalservices@ammonsscientific.com, http://www.ammonsscientific.com. Eds. Carol H Ammons TEL 406-728-1702, Douglas Ammons, S A Isbell TEL 406-728-1702. R&P S A Isbell TEL 406-728-1702. Circ: 1,800.

150.19 ITA ISSN 1970-6049
PERCORSI DI PSICANALISI. Key Title: Percorsi. Text in Italian. 1996. a. EUR 18 (effective 2011). **Document type:** *Journal, Academic/Scholarly.*
Published by: (Universita degli Studi di Pisa, Dipartimento di Anglistica), Edizioni E T S, Piazza Carrara 16-19, Pisa, Italy. TEL 39-050-29544, FAX 39-050-20158, info@edizioniets.it, http://www.edizioniets.it. Ed. Giuliana Bertelloni.

150.195 BRA ISSN 0103-6815
PERCURSO; revista de psicanalise. Text in Portuguese. 1988. s-a. BRL 60 (effective 2004).
Indexed: P03, PsycInfo, PsycholAb.
Published by: Instituto Sedes Sapientiae, Departamento de Psicanalise, R. Ministro de Godoy, 1484, Sao Paulo, SP 05015-900, Brazil. TEL 55-11-38662730.

150 GBR ISSN 1477-9757
PERSON-CENTERED AND EXPERIENTIAL PSYCHOTHERAPIES/ REVISTA DE LA ASOCIACION MUNDIAL PARA PSICOTERAPIA Y ORIENTACION CENTRADAS EN LA PERSONA Y EXPERIENCIAL/ ZEITSCHRIFT DES WELTVERBANDES FUR PERSONZENTRIERTE UND EXPERIENZIELLE PSYCHOTHERAPIE. Abbreviated title: P C E P. Text in English. 2002. q. GBP 234 combined subscription in United Kingdom to institutions (print & online eds.); EUR 309, USD 386 combined subscription to institutions (print & online eds.) (effective 2012). back issues avail. **Document type:** *Journal, Academic/Scholarly.* **Description:** Aims to encourage, and disseminate worldwide, new work on person-centered and experiential therapies, including philosophy, theory, practice, training and research.
Related titles: Online - full text ed.: ISSN 1752-9182. GBP 211 in United Kingdom to institutions; EUR 279, USD 348 to institutions (effective 2012).
Indexed: A01, CA, P03, PsycInfo, T02.
—BLDSC (6427.772000), IE, Ingenta. **CCC.**
Published by: (World Association for Person-Centered and Experiential Psychotherapy and Counseling), P C C S Books Ltd., 2 Cropper Row, Alton Rd, Ross-on-Wye, HR9 5LA, United Kingdom. TEL 44-1989-763900, FAX 44-1989-763901, contact@pccs-books.co.uk.

150 USA ISSN 1932-4820
➤ **THE PERSON-CENTERED JOURNAL.** Text in English. 1992. a., latest 2006. free to members (effective 2010). back issues avail. **Document type:** *Journal, Academic/Scholarly.* **Description:** Contains articles and research that supports the development and application of the person-centered approach.
Related titles: Online - full text ed.: ISSN 1932-4839.
Published by: The Association for the Development of the Person-Centered Approach, 2865 Shimmering Bay St, Laughlin, NV 89029. TEL 702-298-9215, adpca@cmaaccess.com.

150 FIN ISSN 1795-2476
PERSONA GRATA. Text in Finnish. 2005. a., latest 2007. **Document type:** *Monographic series, Academic/Scholarly.*
Published by: (Suomen Psykologiliitto/Finnish Psychological Association), Edita Publishing Oy/Edita Publishing Ltd., PO Box 700, Edita, 00043, Finland. TEL 358-20-45000, FAX 358-20-4502380, tiedotus@edita.fi, http://www.edita.fi.

158 USA ISSN 1940-0012
BF637.S8
PERSONAL DEVELOPMENT. Text in English. 2007 (Nov.). m. USD 29.97 (effective 2007). **Document type:** *Magazine, Consumer.*
Published by: Red Mat Publishing, LLC, PO Box 1276, Belmar, NJ 08099-5276. TEL 856-931-1249, 800-273-6725, http://www.redmatpublishing.com. Ed. Ann McGuire.

150 GBR ISSN 0191-8869
BF698.A1 CODEN: PEIDD9
➤ **PERSONALITY AND INDIVIDUAL DIFFERENCES.** Text in English. 1980. 16/yr. EUR 2,656 in Europe to institutions; JPY 352,400 in Japan to institutions; USD 2,971 elsewhere to institutions (effective 2012). adv. back issues avail.; reprints avail. **Document type:** *Journal, Academic/Scholarly.* **Description:** Covers experimental, theoretical and review articles that aim to integrate the major factors of personality with empirical paradigms from experimental, physiological, animal, clinical, educational, criminological or industrial psychology.
Related titles: Microform ed.: (from PMC, PQC); Online - full text ed.: ISSN 1873-3549. 199? (from IngentaConnect, ScienceDirect).
Indexed: A01, A03, A08, A20, A22, A26, ABS&EES, ASCA, ASSIA, AddicA, B21, BibInd, C28, CA, CommAb, CurCont, E-psyche, E03, ERI, F09, FR, FamI, HRA, I05, IPsyAb, NSA, P03, P30, PSI, PsycInfo, PsycholAb, RASB, RILM, S02, S03, SCOPUS, SSCI, T02, V&AA, W07.
—BLDSC (6428.010500), GNLM, IE, Infotrieve, Ingenta, INIST. **CCC.**
Published by: (International Society for the Study of Individual Differences USA), Pergamon (Subsidiary of: Elsevier Science & Technology), The Blvd, Langford Ln, East Park, Kidlington, Oxford OX5 1GB, United Kingdom. TEL 44-1865-843000, FAX 44-1865-843010, JournalsCustomerServiceEMEA@elsevier.com. Eds. P A Vernon, S B G Eysenck. **Subscr. to:** Elsevier BV, Radarweg 29, PO Box 211, Amsterdam 1000 AE, Netherlands. TEL 31-20-4853757, FAX 31-20-4853432, http://www.elsevier.nl.

150 USA ISSN 0146-1672
BF698.A1
➤ **PERSONALITY AND SOCIAL PSYCHOLOGY BULLETIN.** Text in English. 1975. m. USD 1,561, GBP 918 combined subscription to institutions (print & online eds.); USD 1,530, GBP 900 to institutions (effective 2011). illus. back issues avail.; reprint service avail. from PSC. **Document type:** *Journal, Academic/Scholarly.* **Description:** Publishes theoretical articles and empirical reports of research in all areas of personality and social psychology.
Formerly: American Psychological Association. Division of Personality and Social Psychology. Proceedings
Related titles: Microform ed.: (from PQC); Online - full text ed.: ISSN 1552-7433. USD 1,405, GBP 826 to institutions (effective 2011).
Indexed: A20, A22, A26, AMHA, ASCA, ASSIA, B04, BRD, C06, C07, CA, CIS, Chicano, CommAb, CurCont, DIP, E-psyche, E01, E02, E03, E07, E08, EMBASE, ERI, ESPM, EdA, EdI, ExcerpMed, F09, FamI, G08, H09, HRA, I05, IBR, IBZ, M06, MEDLINE, P02, P03, P10, P12, P13, P25, P27, P30, P42, P48, P53, P54, PCI, PQC, PSA, PSI, PsycInfo, PsycholAb, R10, RASB, RILM, Reac, RiskAb, S02, S03, S05, S09, S21, SCOPUS, SFSA, SSA, SSAI, SSAb, SSCI, SSI, SociolAb, T02, V&AA, W01, W02, W03, W07, W09.
—BLDSC (6428.011500), IE, Infotrieve, Ingenta. **CCC.**
Published by: (Society for Personality and Social Psychology), Sage Publications, Inc., 2455 Teller Rd, Thousand Oaks, CA 91320. TEL 805-499-9774, 800-818-7243, FAX 805-499-0871, 800-583-2665, info@sagepub.com. Ed. Shinobu Kitayama. Circ: 4,250 (paid).

155.28 302 USA ISSN 1088-8683
BF698.A1 CODEN: PSPRFG
PERSONALITY AND SOCIAL PSYCHOLOGY REVIEW. Text in English. 1997. q. USD 569, GBP 335 combined subscription to institutions (print & online eds.); USD 558, GBP 328 to institutions (effective 2011). adv. back issues avail.; reprint service avail. from PSC. **Document type:** *Journal, Academic/Scholarly.* **Description:** Publishes theory-based reviews and offers integrative theoretical formulations in personality and social psychology.
Related titles: Online - full text ed.: ISSN 1532-7957. USD 512, GBP 302 to institutions (effective 2011).
Indexed: A01, A02, A03, A08, A20, A22, B01, B06, B07, B09, CA, CMM, CurCont, E-psyche, E01, EMBASE, ESPM, ExcerpMed, FamI, MEDLINE, P02, P03, P10, P12, P27, P30, P43, P48, P53, P54, PQC, PsycInfo, PsycholAb, R10, Reac, RiskAb, S02, S03, S11, SCOPUS, SOPODA, SSA, SSCI, SociolAb, T02, W07.
—BLDSC (6428.011530), IE, Infotrieve, Ingenta, INIST. **CCC.**
Published by: (Society for Personality and Social Psychology), Sage Publications, Inc., 2455 Teller Rd, Thousand Oaks, CA 91320. TEL 805-499-9774, 800-818-7243, FAX 805-499-0871, 800-583-2665, info@sagepub.com, http://www.sagepub.com. Ed. Galen Bodenhausen. adv.: page USD 475; trim 7 x 10. **Subscr. outside the Americas to:** Sage Publications Ltd., 1 Oliver's Yard, 55 City Rd, London EC1Y 1SP, United Kingdom. TEL 44-20-73248701, FAX 44-20-73248733, subscription@sagepub.co.uk.

150 616.890 USA ISSN 1949-2715
RC554
▼ ➤ **PERSONALITY DISORDERS;** theory, research, and treatment. Abbreviated title: P D T R T. Text in English. 2010 (Jan.). q. USD 110 domestic to individuals; USD 137 foreign to individuals; USD 403 domestic to institutions; USD 448 foreign to institutions (effective 2010). adv. back issues avail.; reprints avail. **Document type:** *Journal, Academic/Scholarly.* **Description:** Publishes a wide range of research on personality disorders and related psychopathology from a categorical and/or dimensional perspective including laboratory and treatment outcome studies.
Related titles: Online - full text ed.: ISSN 1949-2723. 2010 (Jan.) (from ScienceDirect).
Indexed: P03, P30, PsycInfo, SCOPUS.
—**CCC.**
Published by: American Psychological Association, 750 First St, NE, Washington, DC 20002. TEL 202-336-5500, 800-374-2721, journals@apa.org. Ed. Carl W Lejuez. Adv. contact Doug Constant TEL 202-336-5574.

156 IND ISSN 0970-8111
PERSONALITY STUDY AND GROUP BEHAVIOUR. Text in English. 1981. a. INR 150 per issue to individuals; INR 300 per issue to institutions (effective 2011). **Document type:** *Journal, Academic/Scholarly.* **Description:** Examines research reports and other related scholarly endeavors which have a theoretical, empirical orientation.
Indexed: E-psyche, PsycholAb.
Published by: Guru Nanak Dev University Press, Press & Publications Department, Amritsar, Punjab 143 005, India. TEL 91-183-258802, FAX 91-183-258819, dcse.gndu@yahoo.com.

155 USA ISSN 2159-8096
▼ **PERSONALITY TYPE IN DEPTH.** Abbreviated title: P T D. Text in English. 2010. bi-m. free (effective 2011). back issues avail. **Document type:** *Magazine, Trade.* **Description:** Aims to encourage discourse, exploration, and experimentation relating to the use of personality type in fostering human development.
Media: Online - full text.
Published by: Type Resource, 36 Pauline Rd, Louisville, KY 40206. TEL 502-893-3677, 800-456-6284, FAX 502-893-3673, info@type-resources.com, http://www.type-resources.com. Eds. Carol Shumate, Mark Hunziker.

158 USA ISSN 0031-5826
HF5549.A2 CODEN: PPSYAQ
➤ **PERSONNEL PSYCHOLOGY;** a journal of applied research. Text in English. 1948. q. GBP 293 in United Kingdom to institutions; EUR 371 in Europe to institutions; USD 457 in the Americas to institutions; USD 573 elsewhere to institutions; GBP 338 combined subscription in United Kingdom to institutions (print & online eds.); EUR 428 combined subscription in Europe to institutions (print & online eds.); USD 526 combined subscription in the Americas to institutions (print & online eds.); USD 659 combined subscription elsewhere to institutions (print & online eds.) (effective 2012). adv. bk.rev. charts; illus. index. 280 p./no.; back issues avail.; reprint service avail. from PSC. **Document type:** *Journal, Academic/Scholarly.* **Description:** Research articles on industrial psychology, employees and the workplace.
Related titles: Microform ed.: (from PQC); Online - full text ed.: ISSN 1744-6570. GBP 293 in United Kingdom to institutions; EUR 371 in Europe to institutions; USD 457 in the Americas to institutions; USD 573 elsewhere to institutions (effective 2012) (from IngentaConnect).
Indexed: A12, A13, A14, A17, A20, A22, A23, A26, ABIn, ASCA, B01, B02, B04, B06, B07, B08, B09, B13, B14, B15, B17, B18, BPI, BPIA, BRD, BRI, BusI, C12, CA, CBRI, CPM, CurCont, E-psyche, E01, E03, E07, E08, E10, EAA, ERI, Emerald, FamI, G04, G06, G07, G08, H01, H02, HRA, I05, L09, M06, ManagCont, P03, P21, P25, P43, P48, P51, P53, P54, PCI, PMA, PQC, PersLit, PsycInfo, PsycholAb, RASB, S02, S03, S09, SCIMP, SCOPUS, SSCI, T&DA, T02, W01, W02, W03, W07, WorkRelAb.
—BLDSC (6428.095000), IE, Infotrieve, Ingenta, INIST. **CCC.**
Published by: Wiley-Blackwell Publishing, Inc. (Subsidiary of: Wiley-Blackwell Publishing Ltd.), 111 River St, Hoboken, NJ 07030. TEL 201-748-6000, FAX 201-748-6088, info@wiley.com, http://www.wiley.com/WileyCDA/. Ed. Michael J Burke. Adv. contact Kristin McCarthy TEL 201-748-7683.

150 ARG ISSN 1668-7175
PERSPECTIVAS EN PSICOLOGIA; revista de psicologia y ciencias afines. Text in Spanish. 2004. a. USD 20 (effective 2010). back issues avail. **Document type:** *Journal, Academic/Scholarly.*
Indexed: A01, CA, F03, F04.
Published by: Universidad Nacional de Mar del Plata, Facultad de Psicologia, Complejo Universitario - Funes 3250, Cuerpo V - Nivel II, Mar de Plata, Argentina. psisecoo@mdp.edu.ar, http://www2.mdp.edu.ar/psicologia/. Ed. Maria Cristina Belloc. Circ: 300.

301.1 150 COL ISSN 0120-3878
BF5
PERSPECTIVAS EN PSICOLOGIA. Text in Spanish. 1982. a. COP 4,000 (effective 2007). bk.rev. **Document type:** *Journal, Academic/Scholarly.*
Related titles: English ed.
Indexed: E-psyche, PsycholAb.
Published by: Universidad de Manizales, Facultad de Psicologia, Apartado Aereo 868, Manizales, CAL, Colombia. http://umanizales.edu.co. Ed. Luis Fernando Ospina Carvajal.

PERSPECTIVES IN LAW AND PSYCHOLOGY. *see* LAW

P

153 USA ISSN 1556-4495
PERSPECTIVES ON COGNITIVE SCIENCE. Text in English. 1995. irreg., latest 2002. price varies. back issues avail. **Document type:** *Monographic series.*
Published by: Praeger Publishers (Subsidiary of: Greenwood Publishing Group Inc.), 88 Post Rd W, Westport, CT 06881. TEL 800-368-6868, info@greenwood.com, http://www.greenwood.com. Ed. Peter Slezak.

150 USA ISSN 1745-6916
BF1
PERSPECTIVES ON PSYCHOLOGICAL SCIENCE. Text in English. 2006. q. USD 3,471 to institutions; USD 3,542 combined subscription to institutions (print & online eds.) (effective 2010); Subscr. includes: Psychological Science; Current Directions in Psychological Science; Psychological Science in the Public Interest. reprint service avail. from PSC. **Document type:** *Journal, Academic/Scholarly.* **Description:** Publishes an eclectic mix of provocative reports and articles, including broad integrative reviews, overviews of research programs, meta-analyses, theoretical statements, book reviews, and articles on topics such as the philosophy of science, opinion pieces about major issues in the field, autobiographical reflections of senior members of the field, and even occasional humorous essays and sketches.
Related titles: Online - full text ed.: ISSN 1745-6924. USD 3,188 to institutions (effective 2010) (from IngentaConnect).
Indexed: A01, A20, A22, A26, B21, C06, C07, CA, CurCont, E01, I05, NSA, P03, P30, PsycInfo, SCOPUS, SSCI, T02, V&AA, W07.
—BLDSC (6428.161240), IE, Ingenta. **CCC.**
Published by: (Association for Psychological Science), Sage Publications, Inc., 2455 Teller Rd, Thousand Oaks, CA 91320. TEL 805-499-9774, FAX 805-499-0871, info@sagepub.com, http://www.sagepub.com. Ed. Ed Dien.

150 PRT ISSN 0874-0070
A PESSOA COMO CENTRO. Variant title: Revista de Estudos Rogerianos. Text in Portuguese. 1998. s-a. EUR 15 to individuals; EUR 20 to institutions (effective 2006). back issues avail. **Document type:** *Journal, Academic/Scholarly.*
Indexed: CA, T02.
Published by: Associacao Portuguesa de Psicoterapia Centrada na Pessoa e Counselling, Ave Estados Unidos da America, 137 7 Dto, Lisbon, 1700-173, Portugal. TEL 351-21-7939381, FAX 351-21-7819234, revista@appcpc.com. Ed. Odete Nunes. Circ: 1,000.

616.890 FRA ISSN 1295-1005
PETITE BIBLIOTHEQUE DE PSYCHANALYSE. Text in French. 1999. irreg. back issues avail. **Document type:** *Monographic series, Academic/Scholarly.*
Published by: Presses Universitaires de France, 6 Avenue Reille, Paris, 75685, France. TEL 33-1-58103161, FAX 33-1-45897530.

PHARMACOLOGY, BIOCHEMISTRY AND BEHAVIOR. *see* PHARMACY AND PHARMACOLOGY

616.89 PHL ISSN 1655-1702
➤ **PHILIPPINE JOURNAL OF COUNSELING PSYCHOLOGY.** Text in English. 1987. a. adv. bk.rev. **Document type:** *Journal, Academic/Scholarly.* **Description:** Publishes original contributions on counseling in different populations. Emphasizes empirical studies on counseling techniques and intervention strategies; the development and validation of assessment instruments; group treatment programs; and counselor education and supervision. Also accepts reviews, concept papers, and research notes.
Indexed: E-psyche.
Published by: Philippine Association for Counselor Education, Research & Supervision (PACERS), c/o Counseling and Educational Psychology Department, A1609 Gonzalez Hall, De La Salle University, 2401 Taft Ave., Malate, Manila, Philippines. pjcp@ymail.com. Ed. John Addy S. Garcia. Circ: 300.

150 PHL ISSN 0115-3153
CODEN: PJPSDM
➤ **PHILIPPINE JOURNAL OF PSYCHOLOGY.** Text in English. 1968. s-a. USD 20 (effective 2007). adv. charts; illus. **Document type:** *Journal, Academic/Scholarly.*
Related titles: Online - full text ed.
Indexed: BAS, E-psyche, IPP, PsycholAb.
Published by: Psychological Association of the Philippines, Philippine Social Science Council (PSSC) Bldg, Commonwealth Ave, Diliman, Quezon City, Philippines. TEL 63-2-4538257, pap@mozcom.com, http://www.philippinepsychology.net/pap/. Ed. Emma Concepcion D. Liwag. Circ: 175.

156 GBR ISSN 0951-5089
BF38
➤ **PHILOSOPHICAL PSYCHOLOGY.** Text in English. 1988. bi-m. GBP 1,064 combined subscription in United Kingdom to institutions (print & online eds.); EUR 1,403, USD 1,763 combined subscription to institutions (print & online eds.) (effective 2012). adv. bk.rev. abstr. back issues avail.; reprint service avail. from PSC. **Document type:** *Journal, Academic/Scholarly.* **Description:** Deals with the application of philosophical psychology to the cognitive and brain sciences, and to areas of applied psychology.
Related titles: Online - full text ed.: ISSN 1465-394X. GBP 957 in United Kingdom to institutions; EUR 1,263, USD 1,587 to institutions (effective 2012) (from IngentaConnect).
Indexed: A01, A02, A03, A08, A20, A22, ASCA, AddicA, C12, CA, CurCont, DIP, E-psyche, E01, H14, IBR, IBZ, IPB, L&LBA, P02, P03, P10, P12, P25, P28, P30, P43, P48, P53, P54, PCI, PQC, PhilInd, PsycInfo, PsycholAb, RASB, S02, S03, S11, SCOPUS, SOPODA, SSCI, SociolAb, T02, W07.
—IE, Infotrieve, Ingenta, INIST. **CCC.**
Published by: Routledge (Subsidiary of: Taylor & Francis Group), 4 Park Sq, Milton Park, Abingdon, Oxon OX14 4RN, United Kingdom. TEL 44-20-70176000, FAX 44-20-70176336, subscriptions@tandf.co.uk, http://www.routledge.com. Eds. Cees van Leeuwen, William Bechtel. Adv. contact Linda Hann TEL 44-1344-779945. **Subscr. in N America to:** Taylor & Francis Inc., Customer Services Dept, 325 Chestnut St, 8th Fl, Philadelphia, PA 19106. TEL 215-625-8900, 800-354-1420, FAX 215-625-2940, customerservice@taylorandfrancis.com; **Subscr. to:** Taylor & Francis Ltd., Journals Customer Service, Sheepen Pl, Colchester, Essex CO3 3LP, United Kingdom. TEL 44-20-70175544, FAX 44-20-70175198, tf.enquiries@tfinforma.com.

➤ **PHILOSOPHY AND PSYCHOLOGY.** *see* PHILOSOPHY

➤ **PHILOSOPHY OF SEX AND LOVE.** *see* PHILOSOPHY

➤ **PHILOSOPHY, PSYCHIATRY & PSYCHOLOGY.** *see* PHILOSOPHY

➤ **PLAY THERAPY.** *see* MEDICAL SCIENCES—Psychiatry And Neurology

➤ **PLENUM SERIES IN REHABILITATION AND HEALTH.** *see* MEDICAL SCIENCES—Physical Medicine And Rehabilitation

153.9 USA ISSN 1572-5642
PLENUM SERIES ON HUMAN EXCEPTIONALITY. Text in English. 1999. irreg., latest 2010. price varies. back issues avail. **Document type:** *Monographic series, Academic/Scholarly.* **Description:** Explores the psychological, social, cultural, educational, and legal aspects of human exceptionality.
Published by: Springer New York LLC (Subsidiary of: Springer Science+Business Media), 233 Spring St, New York, NY 10013. TEL 212-460-1500, FAX 212-460-1575, service-ny@springer.com. Eds. Donald H Saklofske, Moshe Zeidner.

150 POL ISSN 0079-2993
BF1 CODEN: PPBUDY
POLISH PSYCHOLOGICAL BULLETIN. Text in English. 1970. q. bibl. **Document type:** *Journal, Academic/Scholarly.*
Related titles: Online - full text ed.: ISSN 1641-7844. free (effective 2011).
Indexed: A20, A22, BibLing, E-psyche, P03, PsycInfo, PsycholAb, RASB. —BLDSC (6543.723000), IE, Ingenta, INIST.
Published by: Polska Akademia Nauk, Komitet Nauk Psychologicznych, Ul Stawki 5-7, pok. 316, Warsaw, 00183, Poland. **Dist. by:** Ars Polona, Obroncow 25, Warsaw 03933, Poland. TEL 48-22-5098609, FAX 48-22-5098610, arspolona@arspolona.com.pl, http://www.arspolona.com.pl.

POLITICAL PSYCHOLOGY. *see* POLITICAL SCIENCE

▼ **POPULAR ENTERTAINMENT STUDIES.** *see* MUSIC

158 NLD ISSN 0199-0039
HB848 CODEN: PENVDK
➤ **POPULATION AND ENVIRONMENT.** Text in English. 1978. q. EUR 889, USD 907 combined subscription to institutions (print & online eds.) (effective 2012). adv. bk.rev. charts; illus. index. reprint service avail. from PSC. **Document type:** *Journal, Academic/Scholarly.* **Description:** Explores relationships between population and societal, cultural, and physical environments. Covers demographic variables linked to lifestyle, law, health, business, economics, and international relations.
Former titles (until vol.4, 1981): Journal of Population (0146-1052); Population (New York)
Related titles: Microfilm ed.: (from PQC); Online - full text ed.: ISSN 1573-7810 (from IngentaConnect).
Indexed: A01, A02, A03, A08, A12, A13, A17, A20, A22, A25, A26, A34, A36, A37, ABIn, ASCA, AgrForAb, B01, B06, B07, B08, B09, BA, BRD, BibLing, C25, CA, CABA, CLFP, CurCont, DIP, E-psyche, E01, E04, E05, E08, E12, ESPM, EnvAb, EnvInd, F08, F11, F12, FamI, G02, G03, G08, G11, GEOBASE, GH, GSA, GSI, GSS&RPL, H01, H16, HEA, HPNRM, I05, I11, IBR, IBSS, IBZ, LT, M01, M02, MaizeAb, N02, N03, P02, P03, P05, P10, P21, P25, P26, P30, P32, P34, P42, P46, P48, P51, P52, P53, P54, P56, PAIS, PCI, PGegResA, PQC, PSA, PollutAb, PopulInd, PsycInfo, PsycholAb, R11, R12, RRTA, S02, S03, S04, S08, S09, S11, S13, S16, SCOPUS, SOPODA, SSA, SSCI, SSciA, SUSA, SWR&A, SociolAb, T02, T05, TAR, W03, W05, W07, W09, W10, W11.
—BLDSC (6552.022000), IE, Infotrieve, Ingenta, INIST. **CCC.**
Published by: (California State University, Long Beach, Department of Psychology USA, American Psychological Association, Division of Population and Environmental Psychology USA), Springer Netherlands (Subsidiary of: Springer Science+Business Media), Van Godewijckstraat 30, Dordrecht, 3311 GX, Netherlands. TEL 31-78-6576050, FAX 31-78-6576474, http://www.springer.com. Ed. Lori M Hunter.

➤ **POSITIVE THINKING**; attitude is everything. *see* PHYSICAL FITNESS AND HYGIENE

158 USA ISSN 1938-7725
PRACTICAL AND APPLIED PSYCHOLOGY. Text in English. 2008 (May). irreg., latest 2008. USD 44.95, GBP 31.95 per issue (effective 2010). back issues avail. **Document type:** *Monographic series, Academic/Scholarly.*
Published by: Praeger Publishers (Subsidiary of: Greenwood Publishing Group Inc.), 88 Post Rd W, Westport, CT 06881. TEL 800-368-6868, tech.support@greenwood.com, http://www.greenwood.com. Ed. Judy Kuriansky.

150 USA ISSN 1873-0450
PRACTICAL RESOURCES FOR THE MENTAL HEALTH PROFESSIONAL. Text in English. 1998. irreg., latest 2010. price varies. **Document type:** *Monographic series, Academic/Scholarly.*
Related titles: Online - full text ed.: ISSN 1877-0592.
Published by: Academic Press (Subsidiary of: Elsevier Science & Technology), 3251 Riverport Ln, Maryland Heights, MO 63043. TEL 314-447-8010, FAX 314-447-8030, http://www.elsevierdirect.com/imprint.jsp?iid=5.

150.19 GBR
PRACTICE OF PSYCHOTHERAPY SERIES. Text in English. 2002. irreg. price varies. back issues avail. **Document type:** *Monographic series, Academic/Scholarly.* **Description:** Explains psychoanalytic concepts, their relevance to everyday life, and their ability to illuminate the nature of human society and culture.
Published by: Karnac Books, 118 Finchley Rd, London, NW3 5HT, United Kingdom. TEL 44-20-74311075, FAX 44-20-74359076, shop@karnacbooks.com.

150 USA ISSN 1553-0124
RC465
➤ **PRAGMATIC CASE STUDIES IN PSYCHOTHERAPY.** Abbreviated title: P C S P. Text in English. 2005. q. free (effective 2011). **Document type:** *Journal, Academic/Scholarly.* **Description:** Provides knowledge about psychotherapy process and outcome, for both researchers and practitioners.
Media: Online - full text.
Indexed: A01, A39, C27, C29, CA, D03, D04, E13, P03, PsycInfo, R14, S14, S15, S18, T02.
Published by: Rutgers University Libraries, Graduate School of Applied and Professional Psychology, Rutgers University, 152 Frelinghuysen Rd, Piscataway, NJ 08854. TEL 732-445-2000, FAX 732-445-4888, http://www.libraries.rutgers.edu. Ed. Daniel B Fishman.

150 ITA ISSN 1120-9380
LA PRATICA ANALITICA; saggi di psicologia junghiana. Text in Italian. 1977. irreg. price varies. **Document type:** *Monographic series, Academic/Scholarly.*
Indexed: E-psyche.
Published by: Centro Italiano di Psicologia Analitica, Via Donizetti 1A, Milan, 20122, Italy.

150 FRA ISSN 1286-1286
➤ **PRATIQUES EN SANTE MENTALE.** Text in French. 1953. q. EUR 41 domestic; EUR 54 foreign (effective 2009). **Document type:** *Journal, Academic/Scholarly.*
Formerly (until 1998): Revue Pratique de Psychologie de la Vie Sociale et d'Hygiene Mentale (0556-803X)
Indexed: E-psyche, FR.
—INIST.
Published by: Federation d'Aide a la Sante Mentale Croix-Marine, 31 Rue d'Amsterdam, Paris, 75008, France. TEL 33-1-45960636, FAX 33-1-45960605, http://www.croixmarine.com.

150 FRA ISSN 1269-1763
BF2
PRATIQUES PSYCHOLOGIQUES. Text in French. 1995. 4/yr. EUR 153 in Europe to institutions; EUR 143.98 in France to institutions; JPY 19,600 in Japan to institutions; USD 196 elsewhere to institutions (effective 2012). **Document type:** *Journal, Academic/Scholarly.* **Description:** Publishes thematic issues covering all fields of psychology and concentrates on the applications in the psychological practice.
Related titles: Online - full text ed.: (from ScienceDirect).
Indexed: A26, CA, FR, I05, P03, PsycInfo, PsycholAb, SCI, SCOPUS, SSCI, T02, W07.
—IE, Ingenta, INIST. **CCC.**
Published by: (Societe Francaise de Psychologie), Elsevier Masson (Subsidiary of: Elsevier Health Sciences), 62 Rue Camille Desmoulins, Issy les Moulineaux, Cedex 92442, France. TEL 33-1-71165500, FAX 33-1-71165600, infos@elsevier-masson.fr. Ed. Dana Castro.

150 CHL ISSN 0717-473X
PRAXIS. Text in Spanish. 1999. s-a. **Document type:** *Journal, Academic/Scholarly.*
Published by: Universidad Diego Portales, Manuel Rodriguez Sur, 415, Santiago, Chile. TEL 56-2-6762000, revista.praxis@udp.cl, http://www.udp.cl/. Ed. Ricardo Lopez Perez. Circ: 500.

PRAXIS DER KINDERPSYCHOLOGIE UND KINDERPSYCHIATRIE; Ergebnisse aus Psychoanalyse, Psychologie und Familientherapie. *see* MEDICAL SCIENCES—Psychiatry And Neurology

343.95 DEU ISSN 0939-9062
PRAXIS DER RECHTSPSYCHOLOGIE. Text in German. 1991. s-a. EUR 33; EUR 20 newsstand/cover (effective 2011). **Document type:** *Journal, Academic/Scholarly.*
Published by: Deutscher Psychologen Verlag GmbH, Am Koellnischen Park 2, Berlin, 10179, Germany. TEL 49-30-209166410, FAX 49-30-209166413, verlag@psychologenverlag.de.

PRAXIS SPIEL UND GRUPPE. *see* EDUCATION

PREVENTING SUICIDE; the national journal. *see* PUBLIC HEALTH AND SAFETY

PREVENTION IN PRACTICE LIBRARY. *see* MEDICAL SCIENCES

THE PREVENTION RESEARCHER. *see* SOCIAL SERVICES AND WELFARE

150 RUS
PRIKLADNAYA PSIKHOLOGIYA. Text in Russian. 1997. bi-m.
Published by: (Rossiiskaya Akademiya Nauk, Obshchestvo Psikhologov), Izdatelstvo Magistr, Donskaya 26, korp.8, Moscow, 117419, Russian Federation. TEL 7-095-2988564, FAX 7-095-9545182. Ed. Yu. Zabrodin. **Co-sponsor:** Ministerstvo Truda i Sotsial'nogo Razvitiya Rossiiskoi Federatsii.

150 USA ISSN 0164-5056
RC489.P67
PRIMAL INSTITUTE NEWSLETTER. Text in English. 1973. q. bk.rev. index. back issues avail. **Document type:** *Newsletter, Trade.* **Description:** Contains personal narratives and experiences of patients and therapists involved with primal therapy. Also discusses scientific, medical and psychological discoveries relating to primal therapy.
Formerly (until 1978): Journal of Primal Therapy (0091-9772)
Indexed: E-psyche.
—GNLM.
Published by: Primal Institute, 10379 W Pico Blvd, Los Angeles, CA 90064-2608. TEL 310-785-9456, FAX 310-785-9481, info@primalinstitute.com. Ed., R&P Vivian Janov. Circ: 1,600.

PRIMATES; journal of primatology. *see* BIOLOGY—Zoology

306.85 DEU ISSN 0175-2960
PRO FAMILIA MAGAZIN; die Zeitschrift fuer Sexualpaedagogik, Sexualberatung und Familienplanung. Text in German. 1981. q. EUR 19.50 domestic; EUR 21.50 foreign; EUR 5.10 newsstand/cover (effective 2008). adv. bk.rev. back issues avail. **Document type:** *Magazine, Consumer.*
Formerly (until 1983): Sexualpaedagogik und Familienplanung (0721-1228); Which was formed by the merger of (1969-1981): Sexualpaedagogik (0344-5380); Which was formerly (until 1977): Medien und Sexual Paedagogik (0343-0189); (until 1973): Sexual Paedagogik (0343-0421); (1971-1981): Pro Familia Informationen (0721-1198)
Related titles: Online - full text ed.
Indexed: DIP, E-psyche, IBR, IBZ, P30.
—GNLM.
Published by: Pro Familia - Deutsche Gesellschaft fuer Familienplanung, Sexualpaedagogik und Sexualberatung, Stresemannallee 3, Frankfurt am Main, 60596, Germany. TEL 49-69-639002, FAX 49-69-639852, info@profamilia.de. adv.: B&W page EUR 1,015, color page EUR 1,565. Circ: 7,000 (controlled).

158.1 HRV ISSN 1331-2774
PRO MENTE CROATICA. Text in Croatian. 1997. q. **Document type:** *Journal, Academic/Scholarly.*
Published by: Pro Mente d.o.o., Slavka Batusica 5, Zagreb, 10000, Croatia. TEL 385-1-3894430. Ed. Miro Jakovljevic.

PROBLEME DE PEDAGOGIE CONTEMPORANA. *see* EDUCATION

158.7 USA
PROFESSIONAL PRACTICE SERIES. Text in English. irreg. (approx. biennial). **Document type:** *Monographic series.* **Description:** Generates better understanding of contemporary issues in human resources management. Case studies, longitudinal and empirical research and theoretical frameworks illustrate how organizations can respond to diversity, manage change, and use communication to function effectively.
Published by: Society for Industrial and Organizational Psychology (Subsidiary of: American Psychological Association), 529 Ordway Ave, PO Box 87, Bowling Green, OH 43402. Ed. Douglas W Bray.

150 USA ISSN 0735-7028
RC467
➤ **PROFESSIONAL PSYCHOLOGY: RESEARCH AND PRACTICE.** Text in English. 1969. bi-m. USD 145 domestic to individuals; USD 177 foreign to individuals; USD 480 domestic to institutions; USD 537 foreign to institutions (effective 2011). adv. illus. index. back issues avail.; reprint service avail. from PSC. **Document type:** *Journal, Academic/Scholarly.* **Description:** Contains articles on techniques and practices used in the application of psychology, including applications of research, standards of practice, interprofessional relations, delivery of services, and training.
Formerly (until 1983): Professional Psychology (0033-0175)
Related titles: Microform ed.: (from PQC); Online - full text ed.: ISSN 1939-1323 (from ScienceDirect).
Indexed: A01, A02, A03, A08, A20, A22, A26, AHCMS, AMHA, ASCA, ASSIA, B04, BRD, CA, ChPerl, Chicano, CommAb, CurCont, E-psyche, E08, FR, Faml, G08, I05, MEA&I, P02, P03, P10, P12, P27, P30, P34, P48, P53, P54, PQC, PsycInfo, PsycholAb, RASB, RI-1, RI-2, RILM, S02, S03, S09, SCOPUS, SSAI, SSAb, SSCI, SSI, T02, W03, W07.
—BLDSC (6864.211000), IE, Infotrieve, Ingenta, INIST. **CCC.**
Published by: American Psychological Association, 750 First St, NE, Washington, DC 20002. TEL 202-336-5500, 800-374-2721, FAX 202-336-5997, journals@apa.org. Ed. Dr. Michael C Roberts. Adv. contact Doug Constant TEL 202-336-5574. Circ: 5,000.

➤ **PROFESSIONAL SCHOOL COUNSELING.** *see* EDUCATION

155.4 USA
PROGRESS NOTES. Text in English. 1976. 3/yr. membership. adv. **Document type:** *Newsletter, Trade.*
Formerly: Society of Pediatric Psychology. Newsletter
Indexed: E-psyche.
Published by: Society of Pediatric Psychology, Division 54 (Subsidiary of: American Psychological Association), c/o Martha Hagen, Admin. Officer, PO Box 170231, Atlanta, GA 30317. http://www.apa.org/divisions/div54/. Ed. Dr. Daniel L Clay. Circ: 1,000.

▼ **THE PROVIDENT.** *see* RELIGIONS AND THEOLOGY—Protestant

150 POL ISSN 0048-5675
BF26 CODEN: PRZPBF
➤ **PRZEGLAD PSYCHOLOGICZNY/PSYCHOLOGICAL REVIEW.** Text in Polish; Summaries in English, Russian. 1952. q. PLZ 100 domestic; EUR 80 foreign (effective 2007). bk.rev. index. reprints avail. **Document type:** *Journal, Academic/Scholarly.*
Related titles: Microform ed.: (from PQC).
Indexed: Acal, CMCI, E-psyche, IBR, IBZ, P03, PsycInfo, PsycholAb, RASB, S02, S03.
—INIST.
Published by: Polskie Towarzystwo Psychologiczne, ul Stawki 5-7, Warsaw, 00183, Poland. ptp@engram.psych.uw.edu.pl, http://www.ptp.org.pl. Ed. Andrzej Sekowski. Circ: 2,200. **Dist. by:** Ars Polona, Obroncow 25, Warsaw 03933, Poland. TEL 48-22-5098609, FAX 48-22-5098610, arspolona@arspolona.com.pl, http://www.arspolona.com.pl.

150 USA ISSN 1089-4136
BF1
➤ **PSI CHI JOURNAL OF UNDERGRADUATE RESEARCH.** Text in English. 1996. q. USD 20 to individuals; USD 40 to institutions (effective 2010). **Document type:** *Journal, Academic/Scholarly.*
Indexed: A01, CA, T02.
Published by: Psi Chi - The National Honor Society in Psychology, PO Box 709, Chattanooga, TN 37401. TEL 423-756-2044, FAX 877-774-2443, psichi@psichi.org.

150 BRA ISSN 1676-7314
➤ **PSIC.** Text in Portuguese, Spanish. 1999. s-a. **Document type:** *Journal, Academic/Scholarly.*
Related titles: Online - full text ed.: free (effective 2011).
Published by: Vetor Editora Psico - Pedagogica, Rua Cubatao 48, Vila Mariana, Sao Paulo, 04013-000, Brazil. info@vetoreditora.com.br. Ed. Fermino Fernandes Sisto.

150 BRA ISSN 1413-0556
➤ **PSICANALISE E UNIVERSIDADE/PSYCHOANALYSIS AND UNIVERSITY.** Text in Portuguese. 1993. s-a. 180 p./no.; back issues avail. **Document type:** *Academic/Scholarly.*
Published by: (Pontificia Universidade Catolica de Sao Paulo), Nucleo de Estudos e Pesquisas em Psicanalise, Rua Monte Alegre, 984, Perdizes, Sao Paulo, SP 05014-001, Brazil. TEL 55-11-38628213, FAX 55-11-36708501, psiclini@pucsp.br. Ed. Maria Lucia Vieira Violante. Circ: 500. **Co-publisher:** Via Lettera Editora e Libraria Ltda.

302 ITA ISSN 1724-0751
➤ **PSICHIATRIA DI COMUNITA.** Text in Italian. 2002. q. **Document type:** *Journal, Academic/Scholarly.*
Related titles: Online - full text ed.
—BLDSC (6945.832000), IE, Ingenta.
Published by: Centro Scientifico Editore, Via Borgone 57, Turin, 10139, Italy. TEL 39-011-3853656, FAX 39-011-3853244, cse@cse.it, http://www.cse.it. Ed. F Asioli.

➤ **PSICHIATRIA E PSICOTERAPIA (ROME)/ANALYTIC PSYCHOTHERAPY AND PSYCHOPATHOLOGY.** *see* MEDICAL SCIENCES—Psychiatry And Neurology

150 LTU ISSN 1392-0359
PSICHOLOGIJA. Text in Lithuanian, English. 1980. a. **Document type:** *Journal, Academic/Scholarly.*
Formerly (until 1992): Lietuvos T S R Aukstuju Mokyklu Mokslo Darbai. Psichologija (0202-3318); Which superseded in part: Lietuvos T S R Aukstuju Mokyklu Mokslo Darbai. Pedagogika ir Psichologija (0204-2126)
Related titles: Online - full text ed.: free (effective 2011).
Indexed: A01, CA, P03, PsycInfo, T02.
—INIST.
Published by: (Vilniaus Universitetas/Vilnius University), Vilniaus Universiteto Leidykla, Universiteto g 1, Vilnius, 2734, Lithuania. TEL 370-5-2687260, FAX 370-5-2123939, leidykla@leidykla.vu.lt, http://www.leidykla.vu.lt.

150 BRA ISSN 0103-5371
BF5
PSICO. Text in Portuguese. 1971. 3/yr. BRL 38 (effective 2007). **Document type:** *Journal, Academic/Scholarly.*
Related titles: Online - full text ed.: ISSN 1980-8623. free (effective 2011).
Indexed: P03, PsycInfo, PsycholAb, S02, S03.
Published by: (Pontificia Universidade Catolica do Rio Grande do Sul, Instituto de Psicologia), Editora da P U C R S, Avenida Ipiranga 6681, Predio 33, Porto Alegre, RS 90619-900, Brazil. http://www.pucrs.br/edipucrs/.

150 ARG ISSN 0328-5324
PSICO LOGOS; revista de psicologia. Text in Spanish. 1991. a. back issues avail. **Document type:** *Monographic series, Academic/Scholarly.*
Published by: Universidad Nacional de Tucuman, Facultad de Psicologia, Ave Benjamin Araoz, 800, San Miguel, Tucuman, 4000, Argentina. TEL 54-381-4310570, FAX 54-381-4310171. Ed. Emma Sarubi de Rearte.

150 BRA ISSN 1413-8271
PSICO-USF. (Psicologia Universidade Sao Francisco) Text in Portuguese. 1996. s-a. back issues avail. **Document type:** *Journal, Academic/Scholarly.*
Related titles: Online - full text ed.: ISSN 2175-3563. free (effective 2011).
Indexed: C01.
Published by: (Universidade Sao Francisco, Programa de Pos-Graduacao em Psicologia), Universidade Sao Francisco, Editora, Ave Sao Francisco de Assis, 218, Jardim Sao Jose, Braganca Paulista, SP 12916-900, Brazil. TEL 55-11-40348448, FAX 55-11-40341825, edusf@saofrancisco.edu.br, http://www.saofrancisco.edu.br/. Ed. Anna Elisa de Villemor-Amaral.

150 ITA ISSN 1971-0364
PSICOANALISI (MILAN). Text in Italian. 2006. s-a. EUR 54 domestic to institutions; EUR 110 foreign to institutions (effective 2009). **Document type:** *Journal, Academic/Scholarly.*
Related titles: Online - full text ed.: ISSN 1972-490X.
Published by: (Associazione Italiana di Psicoanalisi), Franco Angeli Edizioni, Viale Monza 106, Milan, 20127, Italy. TEL 39-02-2837141, FAX 39-02-26144793, redazioni@francoangeli.it, http://www.francoangeli.it.

158 ITA ISSN 2038-422X
PSICOANALISI E METODO; materiali per il piacere della psicoanalisi. Text in Italian. 1983. a. EUR 20 domestic; EUR 30 foreign (effective 2011). bk.rev. back issues avail. **Document type:** *Journal, Academic/Scholarly.*
Formerly (until 1992): Materiali per il Piacere della Psicoanalisi (0394-8102)
Related titles: Online - full text ed.
Indexed: E-psyche.
Published by: (Associazione Materiali per il Piacere della Psicoanalisi), Edizioni E T S, Piazza Carrara 16-19, Pisa, Italy. TEL 39-050-29544, FAX 39-050-20158, info@edizioniets.it, http://www.edizioniets.it.

150.19 200 ITA ISSN 1972-151X
PSICOANALISI RELIGIOSA. Text in Italian. 2007. a. **Document type:** *Journal, Academic/Scholarly.*
Related titles: Online - full text ed.: ISSN 1972-5906.
Published by: Fabrizio Serra Editore (Subsidiary of: Accademia Editoriale), c/o Accademia Editoriale, Via Santa Bibbiana 28, Pisa, 56127, Italy. TEL 39-050-542332, FAX 39-050-574888, accademiaeditoriale@accademiaeditoriale.it, http://www.libraweb.net.

150.195 ARG ISSN 0325-819X
BF173.A2
PSICOANALISIS. Text in Spanish. 1979. s-a. ARS 60 domestic; USD 50 in the Americas; USD 60 elsewhere (effective 2004).
Related titles: Online - full text ed.
Indexed: A01, A26, CA, I04, I05, P03, PsycInfo, PsycholAb, T02.
Published by: Asociacion Psicoanalitica de Buenos Aires, Maure 1850, Buenos Aires, C1426CUH, Argentina. TEL 54-11-47757867, FAX 54-11-47757985, publicaciones@apdeba.org, http://www.apdeba.org.

159.9 ARG ISSN 1851-7854
PSICOANALISISI DE LAS CONFIGURACIONES VINCULARES. Text in Spanish. 2008. s-a. **Document type:** *Journal, Academic/Scholarly.*
Media: Online - full text.
Published by: Asociacion Argentina de Psicologia y Psicoterapia de Grupo, Arevalo, 1840, Buenos Aires, C1414CQL, Argentina. TEL 54-11-47710247, FAX 54-11-47746465, secretaria@aappg.org.ar.

▼ **PSICOART**; rivista online di arte e psicologia. *see* ART

150 ITA ISSN 0392-2952
PSICOBIETTIVO. Text in Italian. 1981. 3/yr. EUR 65 combined subscription domestic to institutions (print & online eds.); EUR 84.50 combined subscription foreign to institutions (print & online eds.) (effective 2009). **Document type:** *Journal, Academic/Scholarly.*
Related titles: Online - full text ed.: ISSN 1972-487X.
Published by: Franco Angeli Edizioni, Viale Monza 106, Milan, 20127, Italy. TEL 39-02-2837141, FAX 39-02-26144793, redazioni@francoangeli.it, http://www.francoangeli.it.

150 ARG ISSN 0327-2273
PSICODIAGNOSTICO DE RORSCHACH; y otras tecnicas proyectivas. Text in Spanish. 1969. a. **Document type:** *Monographic series, Academic/Scholarly.*
Formerly (until 1981): Rorschach en la Argentina (0327-537X)
Published by: Asociacion Argentina de Psicodiagnostico de Rorschach, Uriarte, 2221, Buenos Aires, 1425, Argentina. TEL 54-11-47774927, FAX 54-11-47770351, aapro@ciudad.com.ar, http://www.asoc-arg-rorschach.com.ar/. Ed. Norma Menestrina.

150 VEN ISSN 0124-0137
➤ **PSICOGENTE.** Variant title: Revista Psicogente. Text in Spanish. 1998. s-a. **Document type:** *Journal, Academic/Scholarly.*
Related titles: Online - full text ed.: ISSN 2027-212X. free (effective 2011).
Published by: Universidad Simon Bolivar, Instituto de Investigaciones, Calle 59, No 50-132, Caracas, Venezuela.

150 370 BRA ISSN 1413-8557
PSICOLGIA ESCOLAR E EDUCACIONAL. Text in Multiple languages. 1996. s-a. **Document type:** *Journal, Academic/Scholarly.*
Related titles: Online - full text ed.: ISSN 2175-3539.
Published by: Associacao Brasileira de Psicolgia Escolar e Educacional (A B R A P E E), Mogi-Guacu 569, Chacara da Barra, Campinas, SP 13090-605, Brazil. TEL 55-19-32957112, http://www.abrapee.psc.br. Ed. Maria Cristina Rodrigues Azevedo Joly.

150 ESP ISSN 1130-1481
PSICOLOGEMAS. Text in Spanish. 1987. s-a. **Document type:** *Journal, Academic/Scholarly.*
Indexed: PsycholAb.
Published by: Universitat de Valencia, Facultad de Psicologia, Ave. Blasco Ibanez, 21, 3a. Planta, Valencia, 46010, Spain. TEL 34-96-3864823, FAX 34-96-3864822.

150 BRA ISSN 1518-5923
HD58.7
PSICOLOGIA. Text in Portuguese. 2001. bi-m. **Document type:** *Journal, Academic/Scholarly.*
Published by: Universidade Federal de Santa Catarina, Programa de Pos-Graduacao em Psicologia, Campus Universitario, Trindade, Florianopolis, 88040-500, Brazil. TEL 55-44-37219984, rev-pot@cfh.ufsc.br, http://cfh.ufsc.br/.

150 PRT ISSN 0873-4976
BF5
PSICOLOGIA (BRAGA). Text in Portuguese. 1996. 3/yr. **Document type:** *Journal, Academic/Scholarly.*
Indexed: P03, PsycInfo, PsycholAb.
Published by: Universidade do Minho, Largo do Paco, Braga, 4704-553, Portugal. TEL 351-253-601109, FAX 351-253-601105, http://www.uminho.pt.

150 PRT ISSN 0874-2049
BF5
➤ **PSICOLOGIA (LISBON).** Text in Portuguese. 1980. irreg. **Document type:** *Journal, Academic/Scholarly.*
Indexed: E-psyche, P03, PsycInfo, PsycholAb, S02, S03.
Published by: Associacao Portuguesa de Psicologia, Avenida das Forcas Armadas, Lisbon, 1649-026, Portugal. TEL 351-21-7941474, app@appsicologia.org, http://www.appsicologia.org.

➤ **PSICOLOGIA E SOCIEDADE.** *see* SOCIAL SCIENCES: COMPREHENSIVE WORKS

150 BRA ISSN 0103-7013
PSICOLOGIA ARGUMENTO. Text in Portuguese. 1982. s-a. **Document type:** *Journal, Academic/Scholarly.*
Indexed: C01.
Published by: Pontificia Universidade Catolica do Parana, Rua Imaculada Conceicao 1155, Prado Velho, Curitiba, PR 80215-901, Brazil. TEL 55-41-32711515, http://www.pucpr.br.

616.89 BRA ISSN 0103-5665
RC467
PSICOLOGIA CLINICA. Text in Portuguese. 1986. s-a. **Document type:** *Journal, Academic/Scholarly.*
Related titles: Online - full text ed.: free (effective 2011).
Indexed: P03, PsycInfo, PsycholAb, SCOPUS.
Published by: Pontificia Universidade Catolica do Rio de Janeiro, Departamento de Psicologia, Rua Marques de Sao Vicente 225, Edificio Cardeal Lerne, sala 201, Gavea, RJ 22453-900, Brazil. TEL 55-21-31141183, FAX 55-21-31141187, psidir@psi.puc-rio.br, http://sphere.rdc.puc-rio.br/sobrepuc/depto/psicologia/index.html. Ed. Ana Maria Rudge.

158 ITA ISSN 1824-078X
PSICOLOGIA CLINICA DELLO SVILUPPO. Text in Italian. 1997. 3/yr. EUR 96 combined subscription domestic to institutions (print & online eds.); EUR 146.50 combined subscription foreign to institutions (print & online eds.) (effective 2009). **Document type:** *Journal, Academic/Scholarly.*
Related titles: Online - full text ed.
Indexed: E-psyche, P03, PsycInfo, PsycholAb.
Published by: Societa Editrice Il Mulino, Strada Maggiore 37, Bologna, 40125, Italy. TEL 39-051-256011, FAX 39-051-256034, riviste@mulino.it. Ed. Cesare Cornoldi.

150 ESP ISSN 1132-9483
CODEN: PCONFN
➤ **PSICOLOGIA CONDUCTUAL/BEHAVIORAL PSYCHOLOGY**; revista internacional de psicologia clinica y de la salud. Text in Spanish; Summaries in Spanish, English. 1993. 3/yr. EUR 18 domestic; EUR 20 foreign (effective 2009). adv. bk.rev. abstr. back issues avail. **Document type:** *Journal, Academic/Scholarly.* **Description:** Directed to psychologists, psychiatrists, social workers and others interested in clinical and/or health psychology from an empirical standpoint, mainly cognitive, behavioral or cognitive-behavioral.
Related titles: Online - full text ed.
Indexed: A22, A26, E08, I04, I05, P03, P30, PsycInfo, PsycholAb, SCOPUS, SSCI, W07.
—BLDSC (6945.850000), IE, Ingenta.
Published by: Fundacion VECA, Asociacion Psicologia Iberoamericana de Clinica y Salud, Apartado de Correos 1245, Granada, 18080, Spain. TEL 34-902-117486, FAX 34-902-117486, apicsa@attglobal.net, http://www.apicsa.com. Ed. Dr. Vicente E Caballo. Circ: 1,000.

150 ITA ISSN 0390-346X
PSICOLOGIA CONTEMPORANEA. Text in Italian. 1974. bi-m. EUR 21.60 domestic (effective 2009). adv. **Document type:** *Magazine, Consumer.*
Indexed: DIP, E-psyche, IBR, IBZ.
Published by: Giunti Gruppo Editoriale SpA, Via Bolognese 165, Florence, 50139, Italy. TEL 39-055-5062376, FAX 39-055-5062397, informazioni@giunti.it, http://www.giunti.it. Ed. Anna Oliverio Ferraris.

155.4 PRT ISSN 1647-4120
▼ **PSICOLOGIA DA CRIANCA E DO ADOLESCENTE.** Text in Portuguese. 2010. s-a. **Document type:** *Journal, Academic/Scholarly.*
Published by: Universidade Lusiada de Lisboa, Rua da Junqueira 188-198, Lisbon, 1349-001, Portugal. TEL 351-213-611527, FAX 351-213-638307, editora@lis.ulusiada.pt, http://editora.lis.ulusiada.pt.

P

150 613.7 ITA ISSN 1721-0321
PSICOLOGIA DELLA SALUTE; quadrimestrale di psicologia e scienze della salute. Text in Italian. 1998. 3/yr. EUR 56 combined subscription domestic to institutions (print & online eds.); EUR 84.50 combined subscription foreign to institutions (print & online eds.) (effective 2009). **Document type:** *Journal, Academic/Scholarly.*
Related titles: Online - full text ed.: ISSN 1972-5167.
Indexed: DIP, IBR, IBZ.
Published by: Franco Angeli Edizioni, Viale Monza 106, Milan, 20127, Italy. TEL 39-02-2837141, FAX 39-02-26144793, redazioni@francoangeli.it, http://www.francoangeli.it.

PSICOLOGIA DELL'EDUCAZIONE. *see* EDUCATION

150.19 COL ISSN 0123-417X
BF108.C7
➤ **PSICOLOGIA DESDE EL CARIBE.** Text in Spanish. 1997. s-a. **Document type:** *Journal, Academic/Scholarly.* **Description:** Showcases academic scholarship and research in psychology of interest to professors and students in the field conducted in northern Colombia.
Related titles: Online - full text ed.: ISSN 2145-9428. 2006. free (effective 2011) (from SciELO).
Indexed: A01, A26, CA, F03, F04, I04, I05, T02.
Published by: (Universidad del Norte, Division de Humanidades y Ciencias Sociales), Universidad del Norte, Ediciones Uninorte, Km 5 Via a Puerto Colombia, Barranquilla, Colombia. TEL 57-5-3509218, FAX 57-5-3509489, ediciones@uninorte.edu.co, http://www.uninorte.edu.co. Ed. Carlos De los Reyes.

150 ITA ISSN 2035-1089
PSICOLOGIA & BENESSERE. Text in Italian. 2008. q. **Document type:** *Journal, Academic/Scholarly.*
Related titles: Online - full text ed.: ISSN 2035-1097.
Published by: Societa Italiana di Psicologia e Psichiatria (S I P S I), Via del Commercio 9, Fano, 61032, Italy. TEL 39-072-11796666, segreteria@sipsi.org, http://www.sipsi.org.

158.7 ITA ISSN 0048-5691
HF5548.8
PSICOLOGIA E LAVORO. Text in Italian. 1968. 3/yr. EUR 48 domestic; EUR 54 foreign (effective 2009). back issues avail. **Document type:** *Journal, Academic/Scholarly.* **Description:** Focuses on psycology in workplace settings through research and opinion articles.
Indexed: E-psyche, PsycholAb.
Published by: Patron Editore, Via Badini 12, Quarto Inferiore, BO 40050, Italy. TEL 39-051-767003, FAX 39-051-768252, info@patroneditore.com, http://www.patroneditore.com. Ed. Enzo Spaltro.

PSICOLOGIA E SCUOLA; giornale italiano di psicologia dell'educazione e pedagogia sperimentale. *see* EDUCATION

150 ITA ISSN 0394-2856
PSICOLOGIA E SOCIETA. Text in Italian. 1920. q. **Document type:** *Journal, Academic/Scholarly.*
Former titles (until 1975): Rivista di Psicologia Sociale e Archivio Italiano di Psicologia Generale e del Lavoro (0390-6728); (until 1954): Archivio Italiano di Psicologia Generale e del Lavoro (1122-0295); (until 1942): Archivio Italiano di Psicologia (1126-828X)
Indexed: S02, S03.
Published by: Universita degli Studi di Torino, Istituto Superiore di Psicologia Sociale, Via Verdi 10, Turin, 10124, Italy. TEL 39-011-6706111, http://www.unito.it.

150 PRT ISSN 0874-2391
PSICOLOGIA, EDUCACAO E CULTURA. Text in Portuguese. 1998. s-a. **Document type:** *Journal, Academic/Scholarly.*
Indexed: P03, PsycInfo, PsycholAb, S02, S03.
Published by: Colegio Internato dos Carvalhos, Rua do Padrao 83, Carvalhos, 4415, Portugal. TEL 351-22-7860460, FAX 351-22-7860461, http://www.cic.pt.

155.4 370.15 ESP ISSN 1135-755X
PSICOLOGIA EDUCATIVA; revista de los psicologos de la educacion. Text in Spanish. 1995. s-a. EUR 23 domestic to qualified personnel; EUR 30.50 domestic; EUR 63 foreign (effective 2008). back issues avail. **Document type:** *Journal, Academic/Scholarly.*
Related titles: Online - full text ed.: ISSN 2174-0526. 1995.
Indexed: A01, CA, E-psyche, F03, F04, T02.
Published by: Colegio Oficial de Psicologos, Claudio Coello 46, Madrid, 28001, Spain. TEL 34-91-4355212, FAX 34-91-5779172. Ed. Jesus Ramirez Cabanas.

150 BRA ISSN 1413-7372
PSICOLOGIA EM ESTUDO. Text in Portuguese. 1996. s-a.
Related titles: Online - full text ed.: free (effective 2011).
Indexed: C01, P03, P30, PsycInfo, PsycholAb, S02, S03, SCOPUS, SociolAb.
Published by: Universidade Estadual de Maringa, Departamento do Psicologia, Av. Colombo, 5790, Maringa, PR 87020-900, Brazil. proj-psysite@uem.br, http://www.dpi.uem.br/DPI/indexdpi.htm.

150 BRA ISSN 1677-1168
BF5
➤ **PSICOLOGIA EM REVISTA.** Text in Portuguese, Spanish; Summaries in English, Portuguese. 1993. s-a. bk.rev. back issues avail. **Document type:** *Journal, Academic/Scholarly.* **Description:** Publishes scientific articles that contribute to the development of psychology while focusing on diversity and a critical view of reality.
Formerly (until 2001): Cadernos de Psicologia (0104-4370)
Related titles: Online - full text ed.: ISSN 1678-9563. 2002. free (effective 2011).
Published by: (Pontificia Universidade Catolica de Minas Gerais), Editora P U C Minas, Rua Padre Pedro Evangelista 377, Belo Horizonte, 30535-490, Brazil. TEL 55-31-33758189, FAX 55-31-33766498, editora@pucminas.br, http://www.pucminas.br/editora/. Ed. Ilka Franco Ferrari.

150 MEX ISSN 1405-0943
PSICOLOGIA IBEROAMERICANA. Text in Spanish. 1988; N.S. 1993. q. MXN 70 (effective 2010). bibl.; illus. 70 p./no.; **Document type:** *Journal, Academic/Scholarly.* **Description:** Presents contributions in the research, teaching, and profession of psychology.
Formerly (until 1993): Universidad Iberoamericana. Departamento de Psicologia. Revista
Indexed: C01, E-psyche.
Published by: (Universidad Iberoamericana, Departamento de Psicologia), Plaza y Valdes Editores, Cedro 299, Col. Santa Maria la Ribera, Mexico City, DF 06400, Mexico. ventas@plazayvaldes.com. Ed. Alberto S Segrera. Circ: 1,000.

150 ITA ISSN 0393-1064
PSICOLOGIA ITALIANA. Text in Italian. 1910. 3/yr. **Document type:** *Journal, Academic/Scholarly.* **Description:** Explores all branches of psychological science and the many forms it can assume in society. Includes news, opinion, and discussion.
Formerly (until 1979): Rivista di Psicologia (0393-0610)
Indexed: E-psyche, S02, S03.
Published by: Societa Italiana di Psicologia, Via Tagliamento 76, Rome, 00198, Italy. TEL 39-06-8845136, http://www.sips.it.

340.19 ESP ISSN 2172-3087
PSICOLOGIA JURIDICA. Text in Spanish. 1994. irreg. **Document type:** *Monographic series, Academic/Scholarly.*
Published by: Ediciones Piramide, Calle Juan Ignacio Luca de Tena 15, Madrid, 28027, Spain. TEL 34-91-3938989, FAX 34-91-7423662, piramide@anaya.es, http://www.edicionespiramide.es.

150 ESP ISSN 1138-0853
PSICOLOGIA POLITICA. Text in Spanish. 1990. s-a. **Document type:** *Journal, Academic/Scholarly.*
Related titles: Online - full text ed.: free (effective 2011).
Indexed: CA, P03, P42, PSA, PsycInfo, PsycholAb, S02, S03, SCOPUS, SSA, SociolAb, T02.
Published by: Promolibro, Psyli.com, C/San Juan de la Cruz 9, Valencia, 46009, Spain. TEL 34-96-3662017, FAX 34-96-3665132, info@psyli.com, http://www.psyli.com. Ed. Adela Garzon.

158 ESP ISSN 1576-5148
PSICOLOGIA PRACTICA. Text in Spanish. 1999. m. EUR 26.40 domestic; EUR 69 in Europe; EUR 84 elsewhere (effective 2009). adv. **Document type:** *Magazine, Consumer.* **Description:** Assists readers in dealing with self-help issues such as stress, anxiety, and self-esteem through possible solutions as provided by psychologists and other specialists.
Formerly (until 2000): Psicologia Salud Natural (1575-1678)
Published by: Globus Comunicacion (Subsidiary of: Bonnier AB), Covarrubias 1, Madrid, 28010, Spain. TEL 34-91-4471202, FAX 34-91-4471043, txhdez@globuscom.es, http://www.globuscom.es. Ed. Pepa Castro. adv.: color page EUR 2,827; trim 19.8 x 27. Circ: 158,000.

150 BRA ISSN 0102-7972
BF5
➤ **PSICOLOGIA: REFLEXAO E CRITICA.** Text in Portuguese. 1986. s-a. BRL 75 domestic; USD 50 foreign; BRL 40 newsstand/cover domestic; USD 25 newsstand/cover foreign (effective 2000). bk.rev. back issues avail. **Document type:** *Journal, Academic/Scholarly.* **Description:** Provides research reports, theoritical studies, article reviews, and other information pertaining to the field of psychology.
Related titles: Online - full text ed.: free (effective 2011).
Indexed: A26, B21, C01, E-psyche, ESPM, I04, I05, NSA, P03, PsycInfo, PsycholAb, S02, S03, SCOPUS, SSCI, ToxAb, W07.
Published by: Universidade Federal do Rio Grande do Sul, Curso de Pos-Graduacao em Psicologia, Rua Ramiro Barcelos, 2600 Sala 110, Porto Alegre, RGS 90035-003, Brazil. TEL 55-51-316-5246, FAX 55-51-330-4797. Eds. Cleonice Bosa, Silivia Helena Koller. R&P Silivia Helena Koller.

150 BRA ISSN 1413-4063
➤ **PSICOLOGIA REVISTA.** Text in Portuguese, Spanish; Summaries in English, Portuguese. 1995. s-a. looseleaf. BRL 20, USD 10 (effective 2002). adv. bk.rev. abstr.; bibl.; illus.; stat. back issues avail. **Document type:** *Journal, Academic/Scholarly.* **Description:** Deals with broad subjects in the area of psychology and discusses new challenges.
Published by: (Pontificia Universidade Catolica de Sao Paulo, Faculdade de Fonoaudiologia), Pontificia Universidade Catolica de Sao Paulo, Rua Monte Alegre 984, Sao Paolo, 05010-001, Brazil. TEL 55-11-38733359, boltim@uol.com.br.

150 PRT ISSN 1645-0086
PSICOLOGIA, SAUDE E DOCENCAS. Text in Portuguese, English. 2000. s-a. EUR 15 (effective 2006). back issues avail. **Document type:** *Journal, Academic/Scholarly.*
Media: Online - full text.
Published by: Sociedade Portuguesa de Psicologia da Saude, Ave Fonste Pereira de Melo No. 35 11 B, Lisbon, 1050-1118, Portugal. Ed. Jose Luis Ribeiro.

150 ARG ISSN 1851-3441
PSICOLOGIA SIN FRONTERAS. Text in Spanish. 2006. s-a.
Media: Online - full text.
Published by: Universidad Nacional de San Luis, Facultad de Ciencias Humanas, Avenida Ejercito de los Andes 950, IV Bloque, San Luis, 5700, Argentina. TEL 54-652-435512, 54-652-30224, histopsi@unsl.edu.ar, http://humanas.unsl.edu.ar/.

370.15 150 BRA
BF5
➤ **PSICOLOGIA: TEORIA E PESQUISA/PSYCHOLOGY: THEORY AND RESEARCH.** Text in Portuguese; Summaries in English, Portuguese. 1985. q. USD 66 to individuals (effective 2009). adv. bk.rev. back issues avail. **Document type:** *Journal, Academic/Scholarly.* **Description:** Publishes research reports, theoretical studies, reports of professional experience, critical reviews, and technical notes related to psychology.
Related titles: CD-ROM ed.; Online - full text ed.: free (effective 2011).
Indexed: C01, E-psyche, P03, PsycholAb, S02, S03, SCOPUS. —INIST.
Published by: Universidade de Brasilia, Instituto de Psicologia, Campus Universitario, Brasilia, DF 70910900, Brazil. TEL 55-61-2746455, FAX 55-61-2736378. Ed. Josele Abreu-Rodrigues.

150 BRA ISSN 1516-3687
➤ **PSICOLOGIA: TEORIA E PRATICA.** Text in Portuguese. 1999. s-a. free (effective 2011). bk.rev. 100 p./no.; **Document type:** *Journal, Academic/Scholarly.*
Related titles: CD-ROM ed.; Online - full text ed.: Revista de Psicologia: Teoria e Pratica. ISSN 1980-6906.
Indexed: A01, C01, CA, F03, F04, L&LBA, P03, PsycInfo, PsycholAb, S02, S03, SSA, SociolAb, T02.
Published by: Universidade Presbiteriana Mackenzie (Subsidiary of: Instituto Presbiteriano Mackenzie), Rua da Consolacao 896, Pr.2, Sao Paulo-SP, SP 01302-907, Brazil. FAX 55-11-32368302, 55-11-32142582, biblio.per@mackenzie.br, http://www.mackenzie.com.br. Eds. Maria Cristina Triguero Veloz Teixeira, Maria Leonor Espinosa Eneas.

150 ESP ISSN 1130-8877
PSICOLOGIA. TEXT I CONTEXT. Text in Spanish, Catalan. 1990. 3/yr. **Document type:** *Magazine, Trade.*
Published by: Col-legi Oficial de Psicolegs de Catalunya, C Rocaford, 120, Barcelona, 08015, Spain. TEL 34-93-2478650, FAX 34-93-2478654, copc.b@copc.es, http://www.copc.org/.

150 BRA ISSN 0103-6564
BF5
PSICOLOGIA U S P. (Universidade de Sao Paulo) Text in Portuguese. 1990. s-a. back issues avail. **Document type:** *Journal, Academic/Scholarly.* **Description:** Publishes works which aim to contribute to the knowledge and development of psychology and related fields, such as theoretical articles and essays emphasizing some classical issues such as memory, family, conscience and the unconscious.
Related titles: Online - full text ed.: ISSN 1678-5177. free (effective 2011).
Indexed: SCOPUS.
Published by: Universidade de Sao Paulo, Instituto de Psicologia, Ave. Prof. Lucio Martins Rodrigues, Trav.4, 399 Bl. 23, Cidade Universitaria, Sao Paulo, SP 05508-900, Brazil. TEL 55-11-8184452, FAX 55-11-8184462, revpsico@edu.usp.br. Ed. Ana Maria Loffredo.

150 MEX ISSN 1405-5082
PSICOLOGIA Y CIENCIA SOCIAL. Text in Spanish. 1997. s-a. **Document type:** *Journal, Academic/Scholarly.*
Media: Online - full text.
Indexed: C01.
Published by: Universidad Nacional Autonoma de Mexico, Facultad de Estudios Profesionales Iztacala, Ave de los Barrios No. 1, Tlanepantla, Edo. de Mexico, 54090, Mexico. TEL 52-55-56231199, FAX 52-55-56231205. Ed. Rosario Rspinosa Salcido.

PSICOLOGIA Y PSICOPEDAGOGIA. *see* EDUCATION

150 MEX ISSN 1405-1109
PSICOLOGIA Y SALUD. Text in Spanish. 1987. s-a. **Document type:** *Journal, Academic/Scholarly.*
Related titles: Online - full text ed.: free (effective 2011).
Indexed: A26, C01, I04, I05.
Published by: Universidad Veracruzana, Instituto de Investigaciones Psicologicas, Calle Dr. Luis Castelazo Ayala s-n, Xalapa, Veracruz, 91190, Mexico. TEL 52-228-8418900, FAX 52-228-8418914, http://www.uv.mx/iip/. Ed. Rafael Bulle-Goyrir.

150 PRI ISSN 1948-559X
▼ ➤ **PSICOLOGIAS/PSYCHOLOGIES.** Variant title: Psicologia(s). Psicologias Revista. Text in Spanish. 2009. a. free (effective 2009). **Document type:** *Journal, Academic/Scholarly.* **Description:** Research on psychology from Puerto Rico.
Media: Online - full content.
Published by: University of Puerto Rico, Rio Piedras Campus, PO Box 23345, San Juan, 00931-23345, Puerto Rico. TEL 787-594-1778, hfiguero@coqui.net, http://www.uprrp.edu/.

152 ESP ISSN 0211-2159
BF38.5
➤ **PSICOLOGICA**; journal of methodology and experimental psychology. Text mainly in Spanish; Text occasionally in English. 1980. s-a. EUR 36 (effective 2009). adv. bk.rev. abstr.; bibl. back issues avail. **Document type:** *Journal, Academic/Scholarly.* **Description:** Includes articles on experimental psychology as well as the methodological and statistical aspects of psychology.
Related titles: Online - full text ed.: ISSN 1576-8597. free (effective 2011).
Indexed: A26, E-psyche, E07, ERIC, I04, I05, L&LBA, P03, P09, PCI, PsycInfo, PsycholAb, SCOPUS, SSCI, W07.
—CCC.
Published by: Universitat de Valencia, Departamento de Metodologia. Facultad de Psicologia, Avda Blasco Ibanez, 21, Valencia, 46010, Spain. TEL 34-96-3864420, FAX 34-96-3864697, psicologica@uve.es, http://www.uv.es./psicologica.

150 616.8 ITA ISSN 1723-3844
PSICOMOTRICITA; terapia, prevenzione, formazione. Text in Italian. 1997. 3/yr. EUR 24 to individuals; EUR 28 domestic to institutions; EUR 40 foreign to institutions (effective 2008). **Document type:** *Journal, Academic/Scholarly.*
Published by: Edizioni Erickson, Via Praga 5, Settore E, Gardolo, TN 38100, Italy. TEL 39-0461-950690, FAX 39-0461-950698, info@erickson.it. Ed. Marina Massenz.

PSICOONCOLOGIA. *see* MEDICAL SCIENCES—Oncology

PSICOPEDAGOGIA. *see* EDUCATION

150 300 001.3 CHL ISSN 0718-6924
PSICOPERSPECTIVAS (ONLINE); individuo y sociedad. Text in Spanish, English. 2002. s-a. free (effective 2011). **Document type:** *Journal, Academic/Scholarly.*
Formerly (until 2007): Psicoperspectivas (Print) (0717-7798)
Media: Online - full text.
Indexed: F04, H21, P08.
Published by: Pontificia Universidad Catolica de Valparaiso, Avenida Brasil 2950, Valparaiso, 4059, Chile. TEL 56-32-273000, FAX 56-32-212746, http://www.ucv.cl. Ed. Veronica Lopez.

150 384 616.891 ITA ISSN 1828-5171
PSICOTECH. Text in Italian. 2000. s-a. EUR 47.50 combined subscription domestic to institutions (print & online eds.); EUR 77 combined subscription foreign to institutions (print & online eds.) (effective 2009). **Document type:** *Journal, Academic/Scholarly.*
Related titles: Online - full text ed.: ISSN 1971-8438. 2003.
Published by: (Societa Italiana di Psicotecnologie & Clinica dei Nuovi Media), Franco Angeli Edizioni, Viale Monza 106, Milan, 20127, Italy. TEL 39-02-2837141, FAX 39-02-26144793, redazioni@francoangeli.it, http://www.francoangeli.it.

616.85 ITA ISSN 1126-1072
PSICOTERAPIA COGNITIVA E COMPORTAMENTALE. Text in Italian. 1995. 3/yr. EUR 35 to individuals; EUR 50 domestic to institutions; EUR 62 foreign to institutions (effective 2008). **Document type:** *Journal, Academic/Scholarly.* **Description:** Publishes articles contributing to the theoretical knowledge and progress of clinical practice in cognitive and behavioral psychotherapy.
Indexed: P03, PsycInfo, PsycholAb, R10, Reac, SCOPUS.
—BLDSC (6945.864500), IE, Ingenta.
Published by: (Fondazione Salvatore Maugeri, Istituto di Terapia Cognitiva e Comportamentale), Edizioni Erickson, Via Praga 5, Settore E, Gardolo, TN 38100, Italy. TEL 39-0461-950690, FAX 39-0461-950698, info@erickson.it. Ed. Ezio Sanavio.

PSICOTERAPIA, PSICOTERAPIE; la lettera della psicoterapia italiana. *see* MEDICAL SCIENCES—Psychiatry And Neurology

150 ESP ISSN 0214-9915
BF5
➤ **PSICOTHEMA: REVISTA DE PSICOLOGIA.** Text in English, Spanish. 1989. q. EUR 45 domestic to individuals; EUR 60 foreign to individuals; EUR 150 domestic to institutions; EUR 160 foreign to institutions (effective 2010). adv. bk.rev.; software rev. stat. back issues avail.; reprints avail. **Document type:** *Journal, Academic/Scholarly.*
Related titles: Online - full text ed.: ISSN 1886-144X. free (effective 2011).
Indexed: A01, A20, A22, A26, ASCA, B02, B15, B17, B18, CA, CurCont, E-psyche, EMBASE, ExcerpMed, F03, F04, G04, H12, I04, I05, MEDLINE, P03, P09, P30, PCI, PsycInfo, PsycholAb, R10, RILM, Reac, S02, S03, SCOPUS, SSCI, T02, W07.
—BLDSC (6945.865500), IE, Ingenta. **CCC.**
Published by: (Colegio Oficial de Psicologos, Asturias), Colegio Oficial de Psicologos, Claudio Coello 46, Madrid, 28001, Spain. TEL 34-91-4355212, FAX 34-91-5779172, http://www.cop.es. Circ: 2,000.

158.1 HRV ISSN 1330-8777
PSIHA. Text in Croatian. 1995. m. **Document type:** *Journal, Academic/Scholarly.*
Address: J. Sibeliusa 8, Zagreb, 10000, Croatia. TEL 385-1-382269, FAX 385-1-221436. Ed. Jovan Bamburac.

150 SRB ISSN 0048-5705
BF8.S4 CODEN: PSIHAE
PSIHOLOGIJA. Text in Multiple languages. 1968. q. **Document type:** *Journal, Academic/Scholarly.*
Related titles: Online - full text ed.: free (effective 2011).
Indexed: SCOPUS, SSCI, W07.
Published by: Drustvo Psihologa Srbije/Serbian Society of Psychology

150 HRV ISSN 1332-0742
PSIHOLOGIJSKE TEME/PSYCHOLOGICAL TOPICS; evolucijska psihologija. Text in Croatian, English. 2003. s-a. free (effective 2011). **Document type:** *Journal, Academic/Scholarly.*
Media: Online - full text.
Indexed: A01, CA, P02, P03, P10, P48, P53, P54, PQC, PsycInfo, SCOPUS, T02.
Published by: Sveuciliste u Rijeci, Filozofski Fakultet/University of Rijeka, Faculty of Philosophy, Trg Ivana Klobucarica 1, Rijeka, 51000, Croatia. ured@uniri.hr, http://www.ffri.hr.

150 SVN ISSN 1318-1874
PSIHOLOSKA OBZORJA/HORIZONS OF PSYCHOLOGY. Text in Slovenian. 1992. s-a.
Indexed: E-psyche, P03, PsycInfo, PsycholAb.
Published by: Drustvo Psihologov Slovenije, Prusnikova 74, Ljubljana, 1210, Slovenia. TEL 386-61-5121727, http://www2.arnes.si/~dpsih/glavna.htm. Ed. Valentin Bucik.

616.890 HRV ISSN 0350-3186
PSIHOTERAPIJA. Text in Croatian. 1971. s-a. **Document type:** *Journal, Academic/Scholarly.*
Indexed: A26, EMBASE, ExcerpMed, P30, R10, Reac, SCOPUS.
Published by: Sveuciliste u Zagrebu, Medicinski Fakultet, Klinicki Bolnicki Centar, Klinika za za Psiholosku Medicinu, Kispaticeva 12, Zagreb, 10000, Croatia. TEL 385-1-2332825, FAX 385-1-2335818, http://www.mef.hr/katedre/psihijat/zavod/klinike.htm.

150 ARG ISSN 1850-339X
RC321
PSIKEBA; revista de psicoanalisis y estudios culturales. Text in Spanish. 2006. irreg. free (effective 2011). **Document type:** *Journal, Academic/Scholarly.*
Media: Online - full text.

150 CHL ISSN 0717-0297
PSIKHE. Text in Spanish, English. 1992. s-a. back issues avail. **Document type:** *Journal, Academic/Scholarly.* **Description:** Aims at divulging empirical and theoretical work in different areas of scientific and professional psychology.
Related titles: Online - full text ed.: ISSN 0718-2228. 2005. free (effective 2011) (from SciELO).
Indexed: A01, CA, F03, F04, P03, PsycInfo, PsycholAb, S02, S03, SCOPUS, T02.
Published by: Pontificia Universidad Catolica de Chile, Escuela de Psicologia, Ave. Vicuna Mackenna 4860, Santiago, Chile. FAX 56-2-6864843, psykhe@puc.cl. Eds. Maria Rosa Lissi, Neva Milicic Muller.

150 RUS ISSN 2075-7999
➤ **PSIKHOLOGICHESKIE ISSLEDOVANIYA/PSYCHOLOGICAL STUDIES.** Text in Russian, English. 2008. bi-m. free. abstr.; bibl.; illus. back issues avail. **Document type:** *Journal, Academic/Scholarly.* **Description:** Publishes original articles on various branches of psychology.
Media: Online - full text.
Published by: (Rossiiskaya Akademiya Obrazovaniya, Psikhologicheskii Institut/Russian Academy of Education, Institute of Psychology), Izdatel'stvo Soliton, Sudostroitel'naya ul 49-3-507, Moscow, 115407, Russian Federation. TEL 7-985-9284314, solitonpress@gmail.com. Ed. Tat'yana Martsinkovskaya. Pub. Svetlana P'yankova.

100 RUS ISSN 0205-9592
BF8.R8
➤ **PSIKHOLOGICHESKII ZHURNAL.** Text in Russian. 1980. bi-m. **Document type:** *Journal, Academic/Scholarly.*
Related titles: Online - full text ed.
Indexed: A20, CurCont, E-psyche, P30, RASB, RefZh, S02, S03, SCOPUS, SSCI, W07.
—BLDSC (0134.678000), East View, INIST. **CCC.**
Published by: (Rossiiskaya Akademiya Nauk/Russian Academy of Sciences), Izdatel'stvo Nauka, Profsoyuznaya ul 90, Moscow, 117864, Russian Federation. secret@naukaran.ru.

➤ **PSIKHOLOGIYA ZRELOSTI I STARENIYA**; nauchno-prakticheskii zhurnal. *see* GERONTOLOGY AND GERIATRICS

150 GRC ISSN 1106-5737
PSUHOLOGIA/PSYCHOLOGY; the journal of the Hellenic Psychological Society. Text in Greek. 1992. q. free to members; EUR 25.70 domestic to individuals; EUR 85 foreign to individuals; EUR 44 domestic to institutions; EUR 125 foreign to institutions (effective 2004). **Document type:** *Journal, Academic/Scholarly.*
Indexed: P03, PsycInfo, PsycholAb.
—BLDSC (6945.980900).
Published by: Ellenika Grammata - Hellenic Psychological Society, Emm. Benaki 59, Athens, 10681, Greece. TEL 30-210-3891800, FAX 30-210-3836658.

158 NLD ISSN 1385-7630
PSY; tijdschrift over geestelijke gezondheid en verslaving. Text in Dutch. 1996. 11/yr. EUR 42.50; EUR 25.50 to students (effective 2008). adv. **Document type:** *Journal, Academic/Scholarly.*
Formed by the merger of (1995-1996): Mentaal (1382-3000); (1993-1996): Gazet (1382-3620); Which was formerly (1973-1993): G G Z Nieuwsbrief (0929-3663); (1992-1996): Buitengewoon (1381-2599); Which was formerly (1987-1992): Nederlandse Vereniging van Beschermede Woonvormen (N V B W). Nieuwsbrief; (1993-1996): Addictum (0929-7375); Which was formed by the merger of (1989-1993): Cadans (1380-7900); (1985-1993): JoJo Info Bulletin (1380-7943); (1990-1993): Kommissie Gezamenlijk Overlag Drugshulpverlenigsinstellingen (K G O D). Nieuwsbrief (1381-0049)
Indexed: E-psyche.
—Infotrieve.
Published by: G G Z Nederland, Postbus 1556, Amersfoort, 3800 BN, Netherlands. TEL 31-33-4608953, FAX 31-33-4608956, info@ggznederland.nl, http://www.ggznederland.nl. Ed. Michaja Langelaan. adv.: B&W page EUR 2,240, color page EUR 2,840; 220 x 265. Circ: 30,000.

150 USA ISSN 1088-5870
NX165
➤ **PSYART**; an online journal for the psychological study of the arts. Text in English. 1997. a. free (effective 2011). **Document type:** *Journal, Academic/Scholarly.* **Description:** Focused on psychological studies of the arts: literature, film, visual arts, or music.
Media: Online - full text.
Indexed: A01, CA, D03, D04, E13, MLA-IB, P03, P25, P48, PQC, PsycInfo, PsycholAb, R14, S18, T02.
Published by: University of Florida, Office of the President, 226 Tigert Hall, PO Box 113150, Gainesville, FL 32611. TEL 352-392-1311, FAX 352-392-9506, http://www.ufl.edu/. Eds. Murray M Schwartz, Norman Holland.

155 USA ISSN 1554-0138
BF1
PSYCCRITIQUES (ONLINE). Text in English. 1956. w. free to members (effective 2010). adv. bk.rev.; film rev. illus. index. reprint service avail. from PSC. **Document type:** *Academic/Scholarly.* **Description:** Delivera approximately 20 reviews of psychological books, most from the current copyright year.
Formerly (until 2005): Contemporary Psychology: A P A Review of Books (Print) (0010-7549)
Media: Online - full text. **Related titles:** Microform ed.
Indexed: A20, A22, A26, AMHA, ASCA, CBRI, CIS, ChPerl, Chicano, DIP, G08, H11, H12, IBR, IBZ, P03, PCI, RASB, SCOPUS, W09.
—IE, Ingenta, INIST. **CCC.**
Published by: American Psychological Association, 750 First St, NE, Washington, DC 20002. TEL 202-336-5500, 800-374-2721, FAX 202-336-5997, journals@apa.org.

370.15 USA ISSN 1091-4781
PSYCH DISCOURSE. Text in English. 1970. m. USD 95 to individuals; USD 110 to institutions (effective 2000); free to members of ABPsi. adv. back issues avail. **Document type:** *Newsletter, Trade.* **Description:** Covers news of member and chapter activities. Includes original articles, letters and essays.
Formerly: Association of Black Psychologists Newsletter
Indexed: E-psyche.
Published by: Association of Black Psychologists, PO Box 55999, Washington, DC 20040-5999. TEL 202-722-0808, 202-722-0808. Ed., R&P Dr. Halford H Fairchild. Adv. contact Rosa Wright. page USD 650; trim 9 x 7. Circ: 1,500.

150 FRA ISSN 1770-0078
➤ **PSYCHANALYSE.** Text in French. 2004. 3/yr. EUR 52 domestic; EUR 65 foreign (effective 2011). back issues avail. **Document type:** *Journal, Academic/Scholarly.*
Related titles: Online - full text ed.: ISSN 1951-6320.
Published by: Editions Eres, 33 Av. Marcel Dassault, Toulouse, 31500, France. TEL 33-5-61751576, FAX 33-5-61735289, eres@edition-eres.com.

150.19 FRA ISSN 1951-7599
LA PSYCHANALYSE A L'OUVRAGE. Text in French. 2006. irreg. back issues avail. **Document type:** *Monographic series.*
Published by: Editions Eres, 33 Av. Marcel Dassault, Toulouse, 31500, France. TEL 33-5-61751576, FAX 33-5-61735289, eres@edition-eres.com.

PSYCHANALYSE ET ECRITURE. *see* LITERATURE

150 FRA ISSN 1778-5413
PSYCHANALYSE ET FAITS SOCIAUX. Text in French. 2005. **Document type:** *Monographic series.*
Published by: L' Harmattan, 5 Rue de l'Ecole Polytechnique, Paris, 75005, France. TEL 33-1-43257651, FAX 33-1-43258203.

150 BRA ISSN 1415-1138
PSYCHE; revista de psicanalise. Text in Portuguese. 1997. a. **Document type:** *Monographic series, Academic/Scholarly.*
Related titles: Online - full text ed.: ISSN 2175-3571.
Indexed: C01.
Published by: Universidade Sao Marcos, Centro de Estudos e Pesquisa em Psicanalise, Rua Clovis Buenos de Azevedo, 176, Sao Paulo, Brazil. TEL 55-11-34910523, psiqu@smarcos.br. Ed. Daniel Delouya.

150.19 DEU ISSN 0033-2623
BF173.A2 CODEN: PSYEDK
➤ **PSYCHE**; Zeitschrift fuer Psychoanalyse und ihre Anwendungen. Text in German. 1947. 11/yr. EUR 128; EUR 102 to students; EUR 13.90 newsstand/cover (effective 2010). adv. bk.rev.; Website rev. abstr.; bibl.; charts. index. back issues avail.; reprints avail. **Document type:** *Journal, Academic/Scholarly.*
Indexed: A20, A22, ASCA, CurCont, DIP, GJP, IBR, IBZ, IndMed, MLA-IB, P03, P30, PsycInfo, PsycholAb, R10, RASB, Reac, S02, S03, SCOPUS, SSCI, W07.
—BLDSC (6946.115000), GNLM, IE, Ingenta, INIST. **CCC.**
Published by: Verlag Klett-Cotta, Rotebuehlstr 77, Stuttgart, 70178, Germany. TEL 49-711-66720, FAX 49-711-66722030, info@klett-cotta.de, http://www.klett-cotta.de. Ed. Bernd Schwibs. Adv. contact Friederike Kamann. Circ: 4,500 (paid and controlled).

513 USA ISSN 1039-723X
BF201
➤ **PSYCHE (ONLINE)**; an interdisciplinary journal of research on consciousness. Text in English. 1993. irreg. free (effective 2010). **Document type:** *Journal, Academic/Scholarly.* **Description:** Dedicated to supporting the interdisciplinary exploration of the nature of consciousness and its relation to the brain.
Media: Online - full text.
Indexed: A39, C27, C29, D03, D04, E13, P03, PhilInd, PsycInfo, PsycholAb, R14, S14, S15, S18, SCOPUS.
Published by: Association for the Scientific Study of Consciousness ocarter@unimelb.edu.au. Ed. Stephanie Ortigue.

150 BEL
PSYCHE & BREIN. Text in Dutch. bi-m. EUR 6.95 newsstand/cover (effective 2009). **Document type:** *Magazine, Consumer.*
Published by: Uitgeverij Cascade, Katwilgweg 2 bus 5, Antwerpen, 2050, Belgium. TEL 32-36-802561, FAX 32-36-802564. Ed. Leen Lampo. Circ: 20,000.

PSYCHIATRIC AND PSYCHOLOGICAL EVIDENCE. *see* LAW

PSYCHIATRIC REHABILITATION JOURNAL. *see* MEDICAL SCIENCES—Psychiatry And Neurology

PSYCHIATRY PSYCHOLOGY AND LAW. *see* MEDICAL SCIENCES—Psychiatry And Neurology

150 600 ITA ISSN 1720-7525
BF1
➤ **PSYCHNOLOGY.** Text in English. 2002. 3/yr. free (effective 2011). **Document type:** *Journal, Academic/Scholarly.* **Description:** Publishes contributions on the relationship between humans and technology.
Media: Online - full text.
Indexed: A01, CA, P03, PsycInfo, PsycholAb, T02.
Published by: Psychnology http://www.psychnology.org/index.php. Eds. Anna Spagnolli, Giuseppe Riva, Luciano Gamberini.

616.89 ZAF ISSN 1023-0548
➤ **PSYCHO-ANALYTIC PSYCHOTHERAPY IN SOUTH AFRICA.** Text in English. 1992. 2/yr. ZAR 80 domestic to individuals; USD 15 foreign to individuals; ZAR 100 domestic to institutions; USD 20 foreign to institutions (effective 2001). adv. bk.rev. back issues avail. **Document type:** *Journal, Academic/Scholarly.* **Description:** Publishes articles of interest to psychotherapists working psycho-analytically in South Africa.
Indexed: A01, E-psyche, ISAP, P03, P25, P48, PQC, PsycInfo, PsycholAb, T02.
—BLDSC (6946.269760), IE, Ingenta.
Address: PO Box 16115, Vlaeberg, Cape Town 8018, South Africa. TEL 27-21-4232550, FAX 27-21-4232550, http://www.psa.za.org. Ed. Trevor Lubbe.

150 FRA ISSN 2108-8942
▼ **PSYCHO ET DEVELOPPEMENT PERSONNEL.** Text in French. 2010. bi-m. EUR 6.95 per issue (effective 2010). **Document type:** *Magazine, Consumer.*
Published by: Euro Services Internet, 60 rue Vitruve, Paris, 75020, France. FAX 33-1-55253101.

PSYCHO-LINGUA. *see* LINGUISTICS

PSYCHO-ONCOLOGIE. *see* MEDICAL SCIENCES—Oncology

PSYCHO-ONCOLOGY; journal of the psychological, social and behavioral dimensions of cancer. *see* MEDICAL SCIENCES—Oncology

150 FRA ISSN 1255-1546
PSYCHO-PEDAGOGIE. Text in French. 1993. irreg. back issues avail. **Document type:** *Monographic series, Consumer.*
Published by: Editions Fleurus, 15-27 Rue Moussorgski, Paris, 75018, France. TEL 33-1-53263335, FAX 33-1-53263336, editionsfleurus@fleurus-mame.fr.

150 AUS ISSN 1833-5659
PSYCHO-SOCIAL UPDATE. Text in English. 2006. q. **Document type:** *Newsletter.*
Published by: International Program for Psycho-Social Health Research (I P P - S H R), PO Box 1307, Kenmore, QLD 4069, Australia. http://www.ipp-shr.cqu.edu.au/index.php.

150.19 DEU ISSN 1615-8393
PSYCHOANALYSE; Texte zur Sozialforschung. Text in German. 1997. 2/yr. EUR 20; EUR 12 newsstand/cover (effective 2011). adv. **Document type:** *Journal, Academic/Scholarly.*
Formerly (until 2000): Texte aus dem Colloquium Psychoanalyse
Published by: Pabst Science Publishers, Am Eichengrund 28, Lengerich, 49525, Germany. TEL 49-5484-97234, FAX 49-5484-550, pabst@pabst-publishers.com, http://www.pabst-publishers.de. Ed. Oliver Decker.

616.89 NLD ISSN 0924-6290
➤ **PSYCHOANALYSE EN CULTUUR/PSYCHOANALYSIS AND CULTURE.** Text in Dutch, English. 1990. irreg., latest 2008. price varies. illus. back issues avail. **Document type:** *Monographic series, Academic/Scholarly.* **Description:** Examines the interaction of psychoanalysis and culture.
Indexed: E-psyche.
Published by: Rozenberg Publishers, Lindengracht 302 D&E, Amsterdam, 1015 KM, Netherlands. TEL 31-20-6255429, FAX 31-20-6203395, info@rozenbergps.com, http://www.rozenbergps.com.

P

150.19 CHE ISSN 0944-2154
PSYCHOANALYSE IM DIALOG. Text in German. 1993. irreg., latest vol.13, 2009. price varies. **Document type:** *Monographic series, Academic/Scholarly.*
Published by: Peter Lang AG (Subsidiary of: Peter Lang Publishing Group), Hochfeldstr 32, Postfach 746, Bern 9, 3000, Switzerland. TEL 41-31-3061717, FAX 41-31-3061727, info@peterlang.com, http://www.peterlang.com.

150 DEU
PSYCHOANALYSE UND KOERPER. Text in German. 2/yr. EUR 25; EUR 14.90 newsstand/cover (effective 2003). **Document type:** *Journal, Academic/Scholarly.*
Published by: Psychosozial Verlag, Walltorstr 10, Giessen, 35390, Germany. TEL 49-641-77819, FAX 49-641-77742, info@psychosozial-verlag.de, http://www.psychosozial-verlag.de. Ed. Dr. Peter Geissler.

PSYCHOANALYSIS AND HISTORY. *see* HISTORY

302 GBR ISSN 1088-0763
BF175.4.C84
➤ **PSYCHOANALYSIS, CULTURE & SOCIETY.** Added title page title: P C S. Variant title: Journal for the Psychoanalysis of Culture & Society. Text in English. 1996. q. USD 530 in North America to institutions; GBP 285 elsewhere to institutions (effective 2011). adv. bk.rev. illus. back issues avail.; reprint service avail. from PSC. **Document type:** *Journal, Academic/Scholarly.* **Description:** Publishes works that employ psychoanalytic theories, concepts to address the psychological roots or consequences of social and cultural phenomena in such a way as to promote beneficial social change.
Related titles: Online - full text ed.: ISSN 1543-3390 (from IngentaConnect).
Indexed: A01, A03, A08, A22, A26, CA, E-psyche, E01, E08, G08, I05, MLA-IB, P03, P10, P25, P42, P48, P53, P54, PQC, PSA, PsycInfo, PsycholAb, S09, S21, SociolAb, T02.
—BLDSC (5043.264000), IE, Ingenta. **CCC.**
Published by: (Kent State University, Department of English USA, Association for the Psychoanalysis of Culture and Society USA), Palgrave Macmillan Ltd. (Subsidiary of: Macmillan Publishers Ltd.), Houndmills, Basingstoke, Hants RG21 6XS, United Kingdom. TEL 44-1256-329242, FAX 44-1256-479476, orders@palgrave.com, http://www.palgrave.com. Eds. Lynne Layton, Peter Redman. Pub. Guy Edwards. Circ: 400. **Subscr. to:** Subscription Department, Brunel Rd, Houndmills, Basingstoke, Hants RG21 2XS, United Kingdom. TEL 44-1256-357893, FAX 44-1256-328339, subscriptions@palgrave.com.

150.19 616.891 USA
PSYCHOANALYTIC CROSSCURRENTS. Text in English. 1985. irreg., latest 1994. price varies. **Document type:** *Monographic series, Academic/Scholarly.* **Description:** Explores the close and necessary relationship between the two theories and illustrate how they have developed the language of therapy and affected the practice of both psychoanalysis and developmental psychology.
Indexed: E-psyche.
Published by: New York University Press, 838 Broadway, 3rd Fl, New York, NY 10003. TEL 212-998-2575, 800-996-6987, FAX 212-995-3833, information@nyupress.org.

616.89 USA ISSN 1048-1885
RC500
➤ **PSYCHOANALYTIC DIALOGUES**; the international journal of relational perspectives. Text in English. 1991. bi-m. GBP 285 combined subscription in United Kingdom to institutions (print & online eds.); EUR 375, USD 474 combined subscription to institutions (print & online eds.) (effective 2012). adv. back issues avail.; reprint service avail. from PSC. **Document type:** *Journal, Academic/Scholarly.* **Description:** Features facilitating debate among theoreticians and clinicians working within this array of relational perspectives.
Related titles: Online - full text ed.: ISSN 1940-9222. GBP 257 in United Kingdom to institutions; EUR 338, USD 426 to institutions (effective 2012) (from IngentaConnect).
Indexed: A01, A03, A08, A20, A22, CA, CurCont, DIP, E-psyche, E01, H13, IBR, IBZ, P02, P03, P10, P20, P25, P43, P48, P53, P54, PQC, PsycInfo, PsycholAb, S02, S03, SCOPUS, SSCI, T02, W07.
—BLDSC (6946.267000), IE, Infotrieve, Ingenta. **CCC.**
Published by: Routledge (Subsidiary of: Taylor & Francis Group), 325 Chestnut St, Ste 800, Philadelphia, PA 19106. TEL 800-354-1420, FAX 215-625-2940, journals@routledge.com, http://www.routledge.com. Eds. Dr. Anthony Bass, Stephen Seligman, Dr. Steven H Cooper.

150 USA ISSN 0735-1690
RC500
➤ **PSYCHOANALYTIC INQUIRY**; a topical journal for mental health professionals. Abbreviated title: P I. Text in English. 1980. bi-m. GBP 334 combined subscription in United Kingdom to institutions (print & online eds.); EUR 438, USD 548 combined subscription to institutions (print & online eds.) (effective 2012). adv. back issues avail.; reprint service avail. from PSC. **Document type:** *Journal, Academic/Scholarly.* **Description:** Focuses a specific topic in psychoanalysis, psychotherapy, infant research or child development.
Related titles: Online - full text ed.: ISSN 1940-9133. GBP 301 in United Kingdom to institutions; EUR 394, USD 493 to institutions (effective 2012) (from IngentaConnect).
Indexed: A01, A03, A08, A20, A22, ASCA, ASSIA, CA, CurCont, DIP, E-psyche, E01, FamI, H13, IBR, IBZ, MLA-IB, P02, P03, P10, P12, P20, P25, P43, P48, P53, P54, PQC, PsycInfo, PsycholAb, SCOPUS, SSCI, T02, W07.
—BLDSC (6946.269000), GNLM, IE, Infotrieve, Ingenta, INIST. **CCC.**
Published by: Routledge (Subsidiary of: Taylor & Francis Group), 325 Chestnut St, Ste 800, Philadelphia, PA 19106. TEL 800-354-1420, FAX 215-625-2940, journals@routledge.com, http://www.routledge.com. Eds. Dr. Melvin Bornstein, Dr. Joseph D Lichtenberg. Adv. contact Linda Hann TEL 44-1344-779945.

150.19 616.890 USA ISSN 1551-806X
BF173
PSYCHOANALYTIC PERSPECTIVES; a journal of integration and innovation. Text in English. 2003. s-a.
Published by: National Institute for the Psychotherapies, 330 W 58th St, Ste 300, New York, NY 10019. TEL 212-582-1566, FAX 212-586-1272, info@nipinst.org, http://www.nipinst.org/.

150 616.8 USA ISSN 0736-9735
BF173.A2 CODEN: RCUFAC
➤ **PSYCHOANALYTIC PSYCHOLOGY.** Text in English. 1984. q. USD 110 domestic to individuals; USD 137 foreign to individuals; USD 555 domestic to institutions; USD 600 foreign to institutions (effective 2011). adv. bk.rev. abstr.; bibl. 600 p./no.; back issues avail.; reprint service avail. from PSC. **Document type:** *Journal, Academic/Scholarly.* **Description:** Serves as a resource for original contributions that reflect and broaden the interaction between psychoanalysis and psychology.
Related titles: Online - full text ed.: ISSN 1939-1331 (from ScienceDirect).
Indexed: A20, A22, ASCA, ASSIA, BibInd, CurCont, E-psyche, EMBASE, ExcerpMed, FR, FamI, MLA-IB, P03, P30, PsycInfo, PsycholAb, R10, Reac, SCOPUS, SSCI, W07.
—BLDSC (6946.269600), GNLM, IE, Infotrieve, Ingenta, INIST. **CCC.**
Published by: American Psychological Association, 750 First St, NE, Washington, DC 20002. TEL 202-336-5500, 800-374-2721, FAX 202-336-5997, journals@apa.org. Ed. Elliot L Jurist. Adv. contact Doug Constant TEL 202-336-5574. Circ: 3,300.

616.890 GBR ISSN 0266-8734
RC475 CODEN: PPSSFD
➤ **PSYCHOANALYTIC PSYCHOTHERAPY.** Text in English. 1984. q. GBP 185 combined subscription in United Kingdom to institutions (print & online eds.); EUR 243, USD 308 combined subscription to institutions (print & online eds.) (effective 2012). adv. bk.rev. 104 p./no.; back issues avail.; reprint service avail. from PSC. **Document type:** *Journal, Academic/Scholarly.* **Description:** Promotes standards of excellence and to act as a vehicle for the exchange of views and the dissemination of research throughout the public sphere.
Related titles: Online - full text ed.: ISSN 1474-9734. GBP 166 in United Kingdom to institutions; EUR 219, USD 277 to institutions (effective 2012) (from IngentaConnect).
Indexed: A01, A22, BibInd, C06, C07, CA, E01, EMBASE, ExcerpMed, P03, P30, P48, PAIS, PQC, PsycInfo, PsycholAb, R10, Reac, S21, SCOPUS, T02.
—IE, Infotrieve, Ingenta. **CCC.**
Published by: (Association for Psychoanalytic Psychotherapy in the National Health Service), Routledge (Subsidiary of: Taylor & Francis Group), 4 Park Sq, Milton Park, Abingdon, Oxon OX14 4RN, United Kingdom. TEL 44-20-70176000, FAX 44-20-70176336, subscriptions@tandf.co.uk, http://www.routledge.com. Ed. Dr. Maureen Marks. Adv. contact Linda Hann TEL 44-1344-779945. **Subscr. to:** Taylor & Francis Ltd., Journals Customer Service, Sheepen Pl, Colchester, Essex CO3 3LP, United Kingdom. TEL 44-20-70175544, FAX 44-20-70175198, tf.enquiries@tfinforma.com.

616.89 USA ISSN 0033-2828
BF173.A2 CODEN: PSQAAX
➤ **PSYCHOANALYTIC QUARTERLY.** Text in English. 1932. q. USD 112 in North America to individuals; USD 130 elsewhere to individuals; USD 245 in North America to institutions; USD 275 elsewhere to institutions (effective 2010). bk.rev. abstr.; bibl. index, cum.index: vols.1-35, 36-45, 46-55. back issues avail.; reprints avail. **Document type:** *Journal, Academic/Scholarly.* **Description:** Original contributions in the field of theoretical, clinical, and applied psychoanalysis. Departments include book reviews, abstracts, notes.
Indexed: A20, A21, A22, ABS&EES, ASCA, ASD, BibInd, CA, CPLI, CurCont, E-psyche, EMBASE, ExcerpMed, F09, FR, FamI, IPsyAb, IndMed, MEA&I, MEDLINE, MLA-IB, P03, P30, PsycInfo, PsycholAb, R10, RASB, RI-1, RI-2, Reac, RefZh, S02, S03, SCOPUS, SOPODA, SSCI, SWR&A, SociolAb, T02, W07.
—BLDSC (6946.270000), GNLM, IE, Infotrieve, Ingenta, INIST. **CCC.**
Published by: Psychoanalytic Quarterly, Inc., c/o Matthew Baile, The Sheridan Press, PO Box 465, Hanover, PA 17331. TEL 717-633-8974, 800-617-1932, FAX 717-633-8920, matt.baile@sheridan.com. Ed. Henry F Smith.

150 616.89 USA ISSN 0033-2836
BF1 CODEN: PSREAG
➤ **THE PSYCHOANALYTIC REVIEW.** Text in English. 1914. bi-m. USD 99 combined subscription domestic to individuals (print & online eds.); USD 134 combined subscription foreign to individuals (print & online eds.); USD 620 combined subscription domestic to institutions (print & online eds.); USD 665 combined subscription foreign to institutions (print & online eds.) (effective 2011). adv. bk.rev.; film rev.; play rev. bibl. index. 160 p./no.; back issues avail.; reprints avail. **Document type:** *Journal, Academic/Scholarly.* **Description:** Covers contemporary psychoanalytical theory and practice, and psychoanalytical themes in art, film and literature.
Formerly (until 1963): Psychoanalysis and the Psychoanalytic Review (0885-7830); Which was forme by the merger of (1913-1958): The Psychoanalytic Review (0886-795X); (1952-1958): Psychoanalysis (0555-5523)
Related titles: Microform ed.: (from PQC); Online - full text ed.: ISSN 1943-3301.
Indexed: A01, A03, A08, A20, A21, A22, ABS&EES, AC&P, AES, AbAn, CA, DIP, E-psyche, E01, EMBASE, ExcerpMed, F09, FR, FamI, G10, IBR, IBZ, IndMed, MEA&I, MEDLINE, MLA-IB, P03, P20, P22, P25, P26, P30, P48, P54, PCI, PQC, PsycInfo, PsycholAb, R10, RASB, RI-1, RI-2, RILM, Reac, RefZh, S02, S03, SCOPUS, SOPODA, SSCI, SWR&A, SociolAb, T02, W09, YAE&RB.
—BLDSC (6946.273000), GNLM, IE, Infotrieve, Ingenta, INIST. **CCC.**
Published by: (National Psychological Association for Psychoanalysis, Inc.), Guilford Publications, Inc., 72 Spring St, 4th Fl, New York, NY 10012. TEL 800-365-7006, FAX 212-966-6708, info@guilford.com. Ed. Alan Barnett. R&P Kathy Kuehl. Adv. contact Marian Robinson. Circ: 900 (paid).

➤ **PSYCHOANALYTIC SOCIAL WORK.** *see* SOCIAL SERVICES AND WELFARE

155.4 USA ISSN 0079-7308
BF721 CODEN: PYACAZ
THE PSYCHOANALYTIC STUDY OF THE CHILD. Text in English. 1945. a. USD 75 per issue (effective 2010). reprints avail. **Document type:** *Journal, Academic/Scholarly.* **Description:** Contains original papers in psychoanalytic theory and practice, brings together findings from all areas of analytic research and offers a rich mixture of clinical and theoretical material.
Indexed: A01, A02, A03, A08, A20, A22, ASCA, B04, BRD, C28, CA, E-psyche, E02, E03, E06, EMBASE, ERI, EdA, EdI, ExcerpMed, F09, FR, FamI, IndMed, M01, M02, MEDLINE, MLA-IB, P03, P20, P22, P25, P30, P48, P54, PCI, PQC, PsycInfo, PsycholAb, R10, RILM, Reac, SCOPUS, SSCI, T02, W03, W07, YAE&RB.
—BLDSC (6946.275000), GNLM, IE, Infotrieve, Ingenta, INIST.
Published by: Yale University Press, PO Box 209040, New Haven, CT 06520. TEL 203-432-0960, 800-405-1619, FAX 203-432-0948, customer.care@triliteral.org, http://yalepress.yale.edu/home.asp.

PSYCHOANALYTISCHE BLAETTER. *see* MEDICAL SCIENCES—Psychiatry And Neurology

158.1 DEU ISSN 1616-8836
PSYCHOANALYTISCHE FAMILIENTHERAPIE; Zeitschrift fuer Paar-, Familien- und Sozialtherapie. Text in German. 2000. s-a. EUR 14.90 newsstand/cover (effective 2003). **Document type:** *Journal, Academic/Scholarly.*
Published by: Psychosozial Verlag, Walltorstr 10, Giessen, 35390, Germany. TEL 49-641-77819, FAX 49-641-77742, info@psychosozial-verlag.de, http://www.psychosozial-verlag.de.

616.89 USA
PSYCHODRAMA NETWORK NEWS. Text in English. q. USD 15 (effective 2006). adv. bk.rev. **Document type:** *Newsletter.*
Indexed: E-psyche.
Published by: American Society of Group Psychotherapy and Psychodrama, 301 N Harisson St, Ste 508, Princeton, NJ 08540. TEL 609-452-1339, FAX 732-605-7033, asgpp@asgpp.org, http://www.asgpp.org. Ed. Eduardo Garcia. Circ: 800.

616.89 DEU ISSN 1618-7830
➤ **PSYCHODYNAMISCHE PSYCHOTHERAPIE.** Text in German. 2002. 4/yr. EUR 92 to individuals; EUR 138 to institutions; EUR 51 to students; EUR 32 newsstand/cover (effective 2011). adv. **Document type:** *Journal, Academic/Scholarly.*
Indexed: P03, PsycInfo, PsycholAb.
Published by: (Fachgesellschaft fuer Tiefenpsychologisch Fundierte Psychotherapie e.V.), Schattauer GmbH, Hoelderlinstr 3, Stuttgart, 70174, Germany. TEL 49-711-229870, FAX 49-711-2298750, info@schattauer.de, http://www.schattauer.com. Ed. Dr. Jan Hueber. Adv. contact Nicole Doerr. Circ: 1,550 (paid and controlled).

150 ITA ISSN 1722-8093
PSYCHOFENIA; ricerca ed analisi psicologica. Text in Italian. 1998. s-a. EUR 24 to individuals; EUR 30 to institutions (effective 2011). **Document type:** *Journal, Academic/Scholarly.*
Related titles: Online - full text ed.: ISSN 1720-1632. free (effective 2011).
Published by: (Universita degli Studi del Salento, Coordinamento S I B A), Pensa MultiMedia, Via A M Caprioli 8, Lecce, 73100, Italy. TEL 39-0832-230435, FAX 39-0832-230896, http://www.pensamultimedia.it. Ed. Antonio Godino.

150 155.67 AUS ISSN 1346-3500
RC451.4.A5
➤ **PSYCHOGERIATRICS.** Text in English. 2001. q. GBP 276 in United Kingdom to institutions; EUR 351 in Europe to institutions; USD 448 in the Americas to institutions; USD 541 elsewhere to institutions; GBP 318 combined subscription in United Kingdom to institutions (print & online eds.); EUR 404 combined subscription in Europe to institutions (print & online eds.); USD 516 combined subscription in the Americas to institutions (print & online eds.); USD 623 combined subscription elsewhere to institutions (print & online eds.) (effective 2012). adv. back issues avail.; reprint service avail. from PSC. **Document type:** *Journal, Academic/Scholarly.* **Description:** Covers all aspects of psychogeriatrics and related fields.
Related titles: Online - full text ed.: ISSN 1479-8301. GBP 276 in United Kingdom to institutions; EUR 351 in Europe to institutions; USD 448 in the Americas to institutions; USD 541 elsewhere to institutions (effective 2012) (from IngentaConnect).
Indexed: A01, A03, A08, A22, A26, ASG, B21, C06, C07, CA, E01, EMBASE, ESPM, ExcerpMed, H13, I05, MEDLINE, NSA, P02, P03, P10, P12, P20, P30, P48, P53, P54, PQC, PsycInfo, PsycholAb, R10, Reac, RiskAb, SCI, SCOPUS, T02, W07.
—BLDSC (6946.277347), IE, Ingenta. **CCC.**
Published by: (Japanese Psychogeriatric Society JPN), Wiley-Blackwell Publishing Asia (Subsidiary of: Wiley-Blackwell Publishing Ltd.), 155 Cremorne St, Richmond, VIC 3121, Australia. TEL 61-3-92743100, FAX 61-3-92743101, melbourne@wiley.com, http://www.wiley.com/WileyCDA/. Ed. Masatoshi Takeda.

150 JPN ISSN 0033-2852
BF1 CODEN: PYLGAY
➤ **PSYCHOLOGIA/PUSHIKOROGIA**; an international journal of psychology in the Orient. Text in English. 1957. q. JPY 8,000 domestic to individuals; JPY 7,000 foreign to individuals; JPY 11,000 domestic to institutions; JPY 10,000 foreign to institutions (effective 2001). adv. bk.rev. index. 75 p./no.; back issues avail.; reprints avail. **Document type:** *Journal, Academic/Scholarly.* **Description:** Publishes symposia, general surveys, reviews, brief reports, notes and discussions, as well as representative original works in very broad field of psychology.
Related titles: Online - full text ed.: ISSN 1347-5916.
Indexed: A20, A22, ASCA, ASD, BAS, BibInd, CurCont, E-psyche, FamI, IBR, IBZ, IPsyAb, L&LBA, MEA&I, MLA-IB, P03, P30, PCI, PsycInfo, PsycholAb, RASB, S02, S03, SCOPUS, SOPODA, SSCI, SociolAb, W07.
—BLDSC (6946.278000), IE, Ingenta, INIST.
Published by: Psychologia Society/Pushikorogia-kai, Dept of Cognitive Psychology in Education, Graduate School of Education, Kyoto University, Yoshida-Honmachi, Sakyo-ku, Kyoto, 606-8501, Japan. Ed. Masuo Koyasu. Circ: 900.

370.15 SVK ISSN 0555-5574
RJ499.A1 CODEN: PPDIB6
➤ **PSYCHOLOGIA A PATOPSYCHOLOGIA DIETATA.** Text in Slovak, Czech; Summaries in English, German. 1966. q. EUR 74.40 in Europe; EUR 83 elsewhere (effective 2011). bk.rev. **Document type:** *Journal, Academic/Scholarly.*
Indexed: BibLing, E-psyche, P03, PsycInfo, PsycholAb, S02, S03.
—BLDSC (6946.279000), IE, Ingenta.

Published by: (Vyskumny Ustav Detskej Psychologie a Patopsychologie/ Research Institute for Child Psychology and Pathopsychology), Slovak Academic Press Ltd., Nam Slobody 6, PO Box 57, Bratislava, 81005, Slovakia. TEL 421-2-55421729, FAX 421-2-55565862, sap@sappress.sk, http://www.sappress.sk. Ed. Vladimir Dockal. Circ: 800. **Dist. by:** Slovart G.T.G. s.r.o., Krupinska 4, PO Box 152, Bratislava 85299, Slovakia. TEL 421-2-63839472, FAX 421-2-63839485, info@slovart-gtg.sk, http://www.slovart-gtg.sk.

150 576.5 POL

PSYCHOLOGIA, ETOLOGIA, GENETYKA. Text in Polish. s-a. PLZ 20 per issue (effective 2003). **Document type:** *Journal, Academic/ Scholarly.*

Published by: (Uniwersytet Warszawski, Interdyscyplinarne Centrum Genetyki Zachowania), Wydawnictwo Naukowe Scholar, Krakowskie Przedmiescie 62, Warsaw, 00322, Poland. TEL 48-22-6357404 ext 218, FAX 48-22-8289391, info@scholar.com.pl, http:// www.scholar.com.pl.

150 ESP ISSN 2171-6609

▼ **PSYCHOLOGIA LATINA.** Text in Spanish. 2010. s-a. back issues avail. **Document type:** *Journal, Academic/Scholarly.*

Media: Online - full text. **Related titles:** ◆ Supplement to: The Spanish Journal of Psychology. ISSN 1138-7416.

Published by: (Universidad Complutense de Madrid, Facultad de Psicologia), Universidad Complutense de Madrid, Servicio de Publicaciones, C/ Obispo Trejo 2, Ciudad Universitaria, Madrid, 28040, Spain. TEL 34-91-3941127, FAX 34-91-3941126, servicio.publicaciones@rect.ucm.es, http://www.ucm.es/ publicaciones. Ed. Javier Bandres Ponce.

150 POL ISSN 1895-6297

➤ **PSYCHOLOGIA ROZWOJOWA.** Text in Polish. 1993. q. **Document type:** *Journal, Academic/Scholarly.*

Formerly (until 2000): Kwartalnik Polskiej Psychologii Rozwojowej (1231-2835)

Published by: (Polskie Towarzystwo Psychologiczne, Sekcja Psychologii Rozwojowej), Wydawnictwo Uniwersytetu Jagiellonskiego/ Jagiellonian University Press, ul Grodzka 26, Krakow, 31044, Poland. TEL 48-12-4312364, FAX 48-12-4301995, wydaw@if.uj.edu.pl. Ed. Maria Kielar-Turska.

150 PRT ISSN 0871-4657

PSYCHOLOGICA. Text in Portuguese. 1988. q. EUR 28 domestic to individuals; EUR 40 in Europe to individuals; EUR 49 rest of world to individuals; EUR 36 domestic to institutions; EUR 48 in Europe to institutions; EUR 57 rest of world to institutions (effective 2007). back issues avail. **Document type:** *Journal, Academic/Scholarly.*

Indexed: P03, PsycInfo.

Published by: Universidade de Coimbra, Faculdade de psicologia e de Ciencias da Educacao, Rua do colegio Novo, Coimbra, 3001-802, Portugal. psychologica@fpce.uc.pt. Ed. Eduardo Joao Ribeiro.

150 BEL ISSN 0033-2879
BF30 CODEN: PBELAN

➤ **PSYCHOLOGICA BELGICA.** Text and summaries in English. 1954. q. free (effective 2005). adv. abstr. cum.index. Supplement avail.; back issues avail. **Document type:** *Journal, Academic/Scholarly.*

Related titles: Online - full text ed.: (from IngentaConnect).

Indexed: A20, A22, ASCA, CISA, CMCI, CurCont, E-psyche, P03, P30, PsycInfo, PsycholAb, RILM, SCOPUS, SSCI, W07.

—BLDSC (6946.287000), IE, Infotrieve, Ingenta, INIST. **CCC.**

Published by: Societe Belge de Psychologie/Belgische Vereniging voor Psychologie, Tiensestraat 102, Leuven, 3000, Belgium. TEL 32-16-326013, FAX 32-16-326118, betty.vandenbaviere@psy.kuleuven.ac.be. Ed., R&P, Adv. contact Axel Cleeremans. Circ: 450.

152 USA ISSN 1040-3590
RC467 CODEN: PYASEJ

➤ **PSYCHOLOGICAL ASSESSMENT.** Text in English. 1989. q. USD 167 domestic to individuals; USD 194 foreign to individuals; USD 459 domestic to institutions; USD 504 foreign to institutions (effective 2011). adv. illus. back issues avail.; reprint service avail. from PSC. **Document type:** *Journal, Academic/Scholarly.* **Description:** Original empirical articles concerning clinical assessment and evaluations.

Supersedes in part (in 1989): Journal of Consulting and Clinical Psychology (0022-006X); Which was formerly (1937-1968): Journal of Consulting Psychology (0095-8891)

Related titles: Online - full text ed.: ISSN 1939-134X (from ScienceDirect).

Indexed: A01, A02, A03, A08, A20, A22, A26, ASCA, BRD, C06, C07, C28, CA, CurCont, E-psyche, E02, E03, E07, E08, EMBASE, ERI, ERIC, EdA, EdI, ErgAb, ExcerpMed, F09, FR, FamI, G08, I05, IndMed, MEDLINE, P02, P03, P10, P12, P27, P30, P48, P53, P54, PQC, PsycInfo, PsycholAb, R10, RASB, Reac, S02, S03, S09, SCOPUS, SSAI, SSAb, SSCI, SSI, SWR&A, T02, W01, W02, W03, W07.

—BLDSC (6946.293500), GNLM, IE, Infotrieve, Ingenta, INIST. **CCC.**

Published by: American Psychological Association, 750 First St, NE, Washington, DC 20002. TEL 202-336-5500, 800-374-2721, FAX 202-336-5997, journals@apa.org. Ed. Cecil R Reynolds. Adv. contact Doug Constant TEL 202-336-5574. Circ: 3,000.

150 USA ISSN 0033-2909
BF1 CODEN: PSBUAI

➤ **PSYCHOLOGICAL BULLETIN.** Text in English. 1904. bi-m. USD 280 domestic to individuals; USD 312 foreign to individuals; USD 765 domestic to institutions; USD 822 foreign to institutions (effective 2011). adv. charts; illus. index. back issues avail.; reprint service avail. from PSC. **Document type:** *Journal, Academic/Scholarly.* **Description:** Comprehensive and integrative reviews and interpretations of critical substantive and methodological issues and practical problems from all the areas of psychology.

Related titles: Microform ed.: (from PMC, PQC); Online - full text ed.: ISSN 1939-1455 (from ScienceDirect).

Indexed: A01, A02, A03, A08, A12, A13, A20, A22, A25, A26, ABIn, AC&P, AEI, AMHA, ASCA, ASSIA, AcaI, AddicA, B01, B02, B06, B07, B08, B09, B15, B17, B18, B21, BRD, C28, CA, CDA, CIS, CMCI, CurCont, DIP, E-psyche, E02, E03, E07, E08, EAA, EMBASE, ERI, ERIC, ESPM, EdA, EdI, ErgAb, ExcerpMed, FR, FamI, G04, G08, G10, H&SSA, H09, H10, I05, IBR, IBSS, IBZ, ISR, IndMed, Inpharma, M06, MEA&I, MEDLINE, MLA, MLA-IB, MResA, NSA, P02, P03, P10, P12, P13, P21, P27, P30, P48, P50, P51, P53, P54, PCI, PQC, PRA, PsycInfo, PsycholAb, R10, RASB, Reac, S02, S03, S05, S08, S09, S21, SCI, SCOPUS, SSAI, SSAb, SSCI, SSI, SWR&A, T02, W03, W07, W09.

—BLDSC (6946.300000), GNLM, IE, Infotrieve, Ingenta, INIST. **CCC.**

Published by: American Psychological Association, 750 First St, NE, Washington, DC 20002. TEL 202-336-5500, 800-374-2721, FAX 202-336-5997, journals@apa.org. Ed. Stephen P Hinshaw. Adv. contact Doug Constant TEL 202-336-5574. Circ: 2,200.

150 340 USA ISSN 1938-971X
K16

PSYCHOLOGICAL INJURY AND LAW. Text in English. 2008 (Mar.). 4/yr. USD 517 combined subscription to institutions (print & online eds.) (effective 2011). back issues avail.; reprint service avail. from PSC. **Document type:** *Journal, Academic/Scholarly.* **Description:** Covers articles and scholarly exchanges about issues pertaining to the interface of psychology and law in the area of trauma, injury, and their psychological impact.

Related titles: Online - full text ed.: ISSN 1938-9728. 2008 (Mar.) (from IngentaConnect).

Indexed: A22, E01, P30, SCOPUS.

—IE. **CCC.**

Published by: Springer New York LLC (Subsidiary of: Springer Science+Business Media), 233 Spring St, New York, NY 10013. TEL 212—460-1500, FAX 212-460-1575, service-ny@springer.com, http://www.springer.com. Ed. Gerald Young.

370.15 150 USA ISSN 1047-840X
BF1 CODEN: PINQEY

➤ **PSYCHOLOGICAL INQUIRY**; an international journal of peer commentary and review. Text in English. 1990. q. GBP 508 combined subscription in United Kingdom to institutions (print & online eds.); EUR 675, USD 847 combined subscription to institutions (print & online eds.) (effective 2012). adv. bk.rev. illus. back issues avail.; reprint service avail. from PSC. **Document type:** *Journal, Academic/ Scholarly.* **Description:** Publishes theoretical and issue-oriented articles in the areas of personality, social, developmental, health, and clinical psychology.

Related titles: Online - full text ed.: ISSN 1532-7965. GBP 457 in United Kingdom to institutions; EUR 607, USD 762 to institutions (effective 2012).

Indexed: A01, A03, A08, A20, A22, ASCA, B01, B06, B07, B09, CA, CurCont, E-psyche, E01, FamI, P02, P03, P10, P12, P20, P30, P43, P48, P53, P54, PCI, PQC, PsycInfo, PsycholAb, S02, S03, SCOPUS, SOPODA, SSCI, SociolAb, T02, W07.

—BLDSC (6946.380000), IE, Infotrieve, Ingenta. **CCC.**

Published by: Psychology Press (Subsidiary of: Taylor & Francis Inc.), 325 Chestnut St, Ste 800, Philadelphia, PA 19106. TEL 800-354-1420, FAX 215-625-2940, orders@taylorandfrancis.com, http:// www.psypress.com. Ed. Ronnie Janoff-Bulman. Adv. contact Linda Hann TEL 44-1344-779945.

150 USA ISSN 1082-989X
BF38.5

➤ **PSYCHOLOGICAL METHODS.** Text in English. 1996. q. USD 107 domestic to individuals; USD 134 foreign to individuals; USD 415 domestic to institutions; USD 460 foreign to institutions (effective 2011). adv. illus. Index. back issues avail.; reprint service avail. from PSC. **Document type:** *Journal, Academic/Scholarly.* **Description:** Devoted to the development and dissemination of methods for collecting, analyzing, understanding and interpreting psychological data.

Related titles: Online - full text ed.: ISSN 1939-1463 (from ScienceDirect).

Indexed: A20, A22, A26, ASSIA, CA, CIS, CurCont, E-psyche, E03, E07, EMBASE, ERI, ERIC, ErgAb, ExcerpMed, FR, FamI, IndMed, MEDLINE, P03, P30, PsycInfo, PsycholAb, R10, Reac, S02, S03, SCOPUS, SSCI, SWR&A, T02, W07.

—BLDSC (6946.485000), IE, Infotrieve, Ingenta, INIST. **CCC.**

Published by: American Psychological Association, 750 First St, NE, Washington, DC 20002. TEL 202-336-5500, 800-374-2721, FAX 202-336-5997, journals@apa.org. Ed. Dr. Scott E Maxwell. Adv. contact Doug Constant TEL 202-336-5574. Circ: 1,800.

150 USA ISSN 0033-2925
BF173.A2

PSYCHOLOGICAL PERSPECTIVES; a semiannual journal of Jungian thought. Text in English. 1970. q. GBP 167 combined subscription in United Kingdom to institutions (print & online eds.); EUR 218, USD 274 combined subscription to institutions (print & online eds.) (effective 2012). adv. bk.rev.; film rev.; video rev. index. back issues avail.; reprint service avail. from PSC. **Document type:** *Journal, Academic/Scholarly.* **Description:** Offers original articles, interviews, fiction writing, book, video and film reviews, art, illustrations and poetry which are attracting a growing interest and audiences worldwide.

Related titles: Microform ed.: (from PQC); Online - full text ed.: ISSN 1556-3030. GBP 151 in United Kingdom to institutions; EUR 197, USD 246 to institutions (effective 2012) (from IngentaConnect).

Indexed: A01, A22, CA, E-psyche, E01, FamI, MLA-IB, P03, P48, PQC, PsycInfo, PsycholAb, T02.

—BLDSC (6946.510000), IE, Ingenta. **CCC.**

Published by: (C.G. Jung Institute of Los Angeles), Taylor & Francis Inc. (Subsidiary of: Taylor & Francis Group), 325 Chestnut St, Ste 800, Philadelphia, PA 19106. TEL 215-625-2940, 800-354-1420, orders@taylorandfrancis.com, http://www.taylorandfrancis.com. Eds. Gilda Frantz, Margaret Johnson.

150 152 USA ISSN 0033-2933
BF1 CODEN: PYRCAI

➤ **THE PSYCHOLOGICAL RECORD.** Text in English. 1937. q. USD 50 domestic to individuals; USD 60 foreign to individuals; USD 160 domestic to institutions; USD 170 foreign to institutions; USD 40 domestic to students; USD 50 foreign to students (effective 2009). bk.rev. Index. back issues avail.; reprints avail. **Document type:** *Journal, Academic/Scholarly.* **Description:** Covers psychological theory and research concerned with a broad range of scientific topics in the discipline.

Related titles: Microform ed.: (from PQC); Online - full text ed.

Indexed: A01, A02, A03, A08, A20, A22, A25, A26, ABS&EES, AC&P, AMHA, ASCA, ASG, ASSIA, B01, B04, B06, B07, B09, B25, BAS, BIOSIS Prev, BRD, C28, CA, CDA, CurCont, DIP, E-psyche, E02, E03, E07, E08, ERI, ERIC, EdA, EdI, G08, H09, HEA, I05, IBR, IBZ, IndMed, L&LBA, M01, M02, MEA&I, MLA-IB, MycolAb, P02, P03, P07, P10, P12, P13, P25, P26, P27, P30, P43, P48, P53, P54, PCI, PQC, PsycInfo, PsycholAb, RefZh, S02, S03, S05, S08, S09, SCOPUS, SOPODA, SSAI, SSAb, SSCI, SSI, SociolAb, T02, W03, W05, W07.

—BLDSC (6946.520000), IE, Infotrieve, Ingenta, INIST. **CCC.**

Published by: The Psychological Record, Southern Illinois University, PO Box 4609, Carbondale, IL 62901. FAX 618-453-8271. Ed. Ruth Anne Rehfeldt.

150 USA ISSN 0033-2941
BF21 CODEN: PYRTAZ

➤ **PSYCHOLOGICAL REPORTS.** Text in English. 1955. bi-m. USD 580 domestic; USD 530 foreign; USD 630 combined subscription domestic (print & online eds.); USD 645 combined subscription foreign (print & online eds.) (effective 2011). charts; illus.; stat.; abstr. 352 p./no.; back issues avail.; reprints avail. **Document type:** *Journal, Academic/Scholarly.* **Description:** Publishes experimental, theoretical, and speculative articles in the field of general psychology.

Related titles: Online - full text ed.: ISSN 1558-691X. USD 530 (effective 2011).

Indexed: A01, A02, A03, A08, A20, A21, A22, A26, ABS&EES, AC&P, AMHA, ASCA, ASD, AgeL, B01, B04, B06, B07, B09, BRD, C06, C07, C08, C28, C4, CA, CERDIC, CINAHL, CIS, CLFP, ChPerI, Chicano, CurCont, DIP, DentInd, E-psyche, E02, E03, E07, E08, E16, EMBASE, ERA, ERI, EdA, EdI, ErgAb, ExcerpMed, F09, FR, FamI, G08, G10, H09, H12, HEA, I05, IBR, IBZ, INI, IPsyAb, IndMed, M12, MEA&I, MEDLINE, MLA-IB, P02, P03, P10, P12, P30, P34, P48, P53, P54, PCI, PQC, PRA, PSI, PsycInfo, PsycholAb, R10, RASB, RI-1, RI-2, RILM, Reac, S02, S03, S05, S09, S20, S21, SCOPUS, SSAI, SSAb, SSCI, SSI, T02, THA, V05, W03, W07, W09.

—BLDSC (6946.525000), GNLM, IE, Infotrieve, Ingenta, INIST. **CCC.**

Published by: Ammons Scientific Ltd., PO Box 9229, Missoula, MT 59807. TEL 406-728-1710, FAX 406-541-2704, ejournalservices@ammonsscientific.com, http:// www.ammonsscientific.com. Eds. Carol H Ammons TEL 406-728-1702, Douglas Ammons, S A Isbell TEL 406-728-1702. R&P S A Isbell TEL 406-728-1702. Circ: 1,800. **Co-publisher:** Ammons Scientific, Ltd.

150 DEU ISSN 0340-0727
BF3 CODEN: PSREDJ

➤ **PSYCHOLOGICAL RESEARCH**; an international journal of perception, attention, memory and action. Text in English. 1921. bi-m. EUR 1,570, USD 1,544 combined subscription to institutions (print & online eds.) (effective 2012). cum.index: vols.1-36. back issues avail.; reprint service avail. from PSC. **Document type:** *Journal, Academic/ Scholarly.* **Description:** Publishes articles that contribute to a basic understanding of human perception, attention, memory and action. Emphasizes the theoretical implications of the research reported.

Supersedes (in 1974): Psychologische Forschung (0033-3026)

Related titles: Microform ed.: (from PQC); Online - full text ed.: ISSN 1430-2772 (from IngentaConnect).

Indexed: A01, A03, A08, A12, A20, A22, A26, ABIn, ASCA, B01, B06, B07, B09, B21, B25, BIOSIS Prev, CA, CMCI, CurCont, DIP, E-psyche, E01, EMBASE, ExcerpMed, H12, I05, IBR, IBZ, IndMed, MEA&I, MEDLINE, MycolAb, NSA, P03, P10, P12, P20, P22, P25, P30, P43, P48, P51, P53, P54, PCI, PQC, PsycInfo, PsycholAb, R10, RASB, RILM, Reac, S02, S03, SCOPUS, SSCI, T02, W07.

—BLDSC (6946.527000), IE, Infotrieve, Ingenta, INIST. **CCC.**

Published by: Springer (Subsidiary of: Springer Science+Business Media), Tiergartenstr 17, Heidelberg, 69121, Germany. TEL 49-6221-4870, FAX 49-6221-345229. Ed. Bernhard Hommel. **Subscr. in the Americas to:** Springer New York LLC, Journal Fulfillment, PO Box 2485, Secaucus, NJ 07096. TEL 800-777-4643, 201-348-4033, FAX 201-348-4505, journals-ny@springer.com, http://www.springer.com; **Subscr. to:** Springer Distribution Center, Kundenservice Zeitschriften, Haberstr 7, Heidelberg 69126, Germany. TEL 49-6221-3454303, FAX 49-6221-3454229, subscriptions@springer.com.

150 USA ISSN 0033-295X
BF1 CODEN: PSRVAX

➤ **PSYCHOLOGICAL REVIEW.** Text in English. 1894. q. USD 179 domestic to individuals; USD 206 foreign to individuals; USD 629 domestic to institutions; USD 674 foreign to institutions (effective 2011). adv. bibl.; charts; illus. index. back issues avail.; reprint service avail. from PSC. **Document type:** *Journal, Academic/Scholarly.* **Description:** Includes articles that make theoretical contributions to all areas of scientific psychology.

Related titles: Microform ed.: (from PMC, PQC); Online - full text ed.: ISSN 1939-1471 (from ScienceDirect).

Indexed: A01, A02, A03, A08, A20, A22, A23, A24, A25, A26, AEI, AcaI, AddicA, B02, B04, B13, B15, B17, B18, BRD, C28, CA, CDA, CIS, CLFP, CMCI, CPM, CurCont, DIP, E-psyche, E02, E03, E07, E08, EMBASE, ERI, ERIC, EdA, EdI, ErgAb, ExcerpMed, FR, FamI, G04, G08, H09, H10, H11, H12, I05, IBR, IBSS, IBZ, ISR, IndMed, Inpharma, L&LBA, M01, M02, MEA&I, MEDLINE, MLA, MLA-IB, P02, P03, P10, P12, P13, P27, P30, P48, P53, P54, PCI, PQC, PhilInd, PsycInfo, PsycholAb, R10, RASB, RILM, Reac, S02, S03, S05, S08, S09, S21, SCI, SCOPUS, SSAI, SSAb, SSCI, SSI, SWR&A, SociolAb, T02, W03, W07, WorkRelAb, YAE&RB.

—BLDSC (6946.530000), GNLM, IE, Infotrieve, Ingenta, INIST. **CCC.**

Published by: American Psychological Association, 750 First St, NE, Washington, DC 20002. TEL 202-336-5500, 800-374-2721, FAX 202-336-5997, journals@apa.org. Ed. John R Anderson. Adv. contact Doug Constant TEL 202-336-5574. Circ: 2,100.

150.19 USA ISSN 0956-7976
BF1 CODEN: PSYSET

➤ **PSYCHOLOGICAL SCIENCE.** Text in English. 1990. m. USD 3,471 to institutions; USD 3,542 combined subscription to institutions (print & online eds.) (effective 2010); subscr. includes Psychological Science in the Public Interest, Current Directions in Psychological Science, & Perspectives on Psychological Science. adv. bk.rev. illus. back issues avail.; reprint service avail. from PSC. **Document type:** *Journal, Academic/Scholarly.* **Description:** Provides a forum for research, theory and application in psychology and the closely related behavioral, cognitive, neural and social sciences.

Related titles: Online - full text ed.: ISSN 1467-9280. USD 3,188 to institutions (effective 2010) (from IngentaConnect); ◆ Supplement(s): Psychological Science in the Public Interest. ISSN 1529-1006.

Indexed: A01, A02, A03, A08, A20, A22, A25, A26, ASCA, B01, B04, B06, B07, B09, B21, BRD, C28, CA, CMM, CurCont, E-psyche, E01, E08, EMBASE, ErgAb, ExcerpMed, F09, FamI, G08, HEA, I05, IBSS, IndMed, L&LBA, MEDLINE, NSA, P02, P03, P10, P12, P27, P30, P43, P48, P53, P54, PQC, PerIslam, PsycInfo, PsycholAb, R10, RASB, RILM, Reac, S02, S03, S08, S09, SCOPUS, SD, SOPODA, SSAI, SSAb, SSCI, SSI, SWR&A, SociolAb, T02, V&AA, W01, W02, W03, W07.

P

—BLDSC (6946.530300), IE, Infotrieve, Ingenta. **CCC.**
Published by: (Association for Psychological Science), Sage Publications, Inc., 2455 Teller Rd, Thousand Oaks, CA 91320. TEL 805-499-9774, FAX 805-499-0871, 800-583-2665, info@sagepub.com, http://www.sagepub.com. Ed. Robert V Kail.

150 USA ISSN 1057-0721
PSYCHOLOGICAL SCIENCE AGENDA. Text in English. 1988. bi-m. free (effective 2010). back issues avail. **Document type:** *Newsletter.* **Description:** Discusses current news in the field of psychological science research and events at the American Psychological Association's Science Directorate.
Formerly (until 1991): Science Agenda (1040-404X)
Related titles: Online - full text ed.
Indexed: E-psyche.
—**CCC.**
Published by: American Psychological Association, 750 First St, NE, Washington, DC 20002. TEL 202-336-5500, 800-374-2721, journals@apa.org. Ed. David A Rosenbaum.

302 USA ISSN 1529-1006
BF636.A1
PSYCHOLOGICAL SCIENCE IN THE PUBLIC INTEREST. Abbreviated title: P S P I. Text in English. 2000. 3/yr. USD 4,260 to institutions; USD 4,347 combined subscription to institutions (print & online eds.); USD 174 per issue to institutions; free to members (effective 2011); Subscr. includes: Psychological Science; Current Directions in Psychological Science; Perspectives on Psychological Science. adv. back issues avail.; reprint service avail. from PSC. **Document type:** *Journal, Academic/Scholarly.* **Description:** Provides definitive assessments of topics where psychological science may have the potential to inform and improve the lives of individuals and the well-being of society.
Related titles: Online - full text ed.: ISSN 2160-0031. USD 3,912 to institutions (effective 2011) (from IngentaConnect); ◆ Supplement to: Psychological Science. ISSN 0956-7976.
Indexed: A01, A02, A03, A08, A22, A26, B01, B06, B07, B09, CA, E-psyche, E01, ESPM, I05, L&LBA, P03, P10, P30, P34, P43, P48, P53, P54, PQC, PsycInfo, PsycholAb, RiskAb, S02, S03, SCOPUS, T02.
—BLDSC (6946.530350), IE, Infotrieve, Ingenta. **CCC.**
Published by: (Association for Psychological Science), Sage Publications, Inc., 2455 Teller Rd, Thousand Oaks, CA 91320. TEL 805-499-9774, 800-818-7243, FAX 805-499-0871, info@sagepub.com, http://www.sagepub.com. Ed. Elaine F Walker.

150 USA ISSN 1541-1559
RA790.A1
PSYCHOLOGICAL SERVICES. Text in English. 2004. q. USD 98 domestic to individuals; USD 125 foreign to individuals; USD 403 domestic to institutions; USD 448 foreign to institutions (effective 2011). adv. back issues avail.; reprint service avail. from PSC. **Document type:** *Journal, Academic/Scholarly.* **Description:** Data-based articles on psychological services in any service delivery setting, thereby broadening the usual parameter limited to a government agency.
Related titles: Online - full text ed.: ISSN 1939-148X (from ScienceDirect).
Indexed: ASSIA, C06, C07, P03, P30, PsycInfo, PsycholAb, SCOPUS.
—BLDSC (6946.530375), IE, Ingenta. **CCC.**
Published by: (American Psychological Association, Division 18, Educational Publishing Foundation), American Psychological Association, 750 First St, NE, Washington, DC 20002. TEL 202-336-5500, 800-374-2721, journals@apa.org. Ed. Dr. Patrick H DeLeon. Adv. contact Doug Constant TEL 202-336-5574. Circ: 900.

150 IND ISSN 0033-2968
BF1
➤ **PSYCHOLOGICAL STUDIES.** Text in English. 1956. 3/yr. EUR 160, USD 242 combined subscription to institutions (print & online eds.) (effective 2012). adv. bk.rev. charts; illus.; stat. index. reprint service avail. from PSC. **Document type:** *Journal, Academic/Scholarly.* **Description:** Aims to provide a forum for research encompassing all areas of psychology. It focuses on the centrality of co-construction of cultural and psychological processes and facilitates understanding psychology from diverse theoretical perspectives.
Related titles: Online - full text ed.: ISSN 0974-9861 (from IngentaConnect).
Indexed: A22, ASD, BAS, E-psyche, E01, IPsyAb, P03, P30, PsycInfo, PsycholAb, SCOPUS.
—BLDSC (6946.531100), IE, Infotrieve, Ingenta, Linda Hall. **CCC.**
Published by: (National Academy of Psychology), Springer (India) Private Ltd. (Subsidiary of: Springer Science+Business Media), 212, Deen Dayal Upadhyaya Marg, 3rd Fl, Gandharva Mahavidyalaya, New Delhi, 110 002, India. TEL 91-11-45755888, FAX 91-11-45755889. Ed. Girishwar Misra. Circ: 500.

150 DEU ISSN 2190-0493
BF3
➤ **PSYCHOLOGICAL TEST AND ASSESSMENT MODELING.** Text in English. 1953. q. EUR 60; EUR 15 newsstand/cover (effective 2011). adv. bk.rev. abstr.; bibl.; charts. index, cum.index every 10 yrs. Supplement avail.; reprints avail. **Document type:** *Journal, Academic/Scholarly.* **Description:** Publishes original articles on all aspects and disciplines of psychology.
Former titles (until 2010): Psychology Science Quarterly (1866-6140); (until 2008): Psychology Science (1614-9947); (until 2003): Psychologische Beitraege (0033-3018); Which incorporated: Cognitive Processing
Related titles: Online - full text ed.: ISSN 2190-0507. free (effective 2011).
Indexed: A20, CIS, DIP, E-psyche, ErgAb, GJP, IBR, IBZ, P03, P25, P26, P30, P48, P54, PCI, PQC, PsycInfo, PsycholAb, RILM, RefZh, S02, S03, SCOPUS, SOPODA, SociolAb.
—BLDSC (6946.531150), IE, Infotrieve, Ingenta, INIST. **CCC.**
Published by: (Deutsche Gesellschaft fuer Psychologie), Pabst Science Publishers, Am Eichengrund 28, Lengerich, 49525, Germany. TEL 49-5484-97234, FAX 49-5484-550, pabst@pabst-publishers.com, http://www.pabst-publishers.de. Ed. Klaus D Kubinger. Circ: 1,410 (paid).

150 USA ISSN 1942-9681
RC530
▼ **PSYCHOLOGICAL TRAUMA;** theory, research, and practice. Text in English. 2009 (Mar.). q. USD 110 domestic to individuals; USD 137 foreign to individuals; USD 403 domestic to institutions; USD 448 foreign to institutions (effective 2011). adv. back issues avail.; reprints avail. **Document type:** *Journal, Academic/Scholarly.* **Description:** Publishes empirical research results on the psychological effects of trauma. Intended for the professionals involved in the use of experimental and correlational methods and qualitative analysis.
Related titles: Online - full text ed.: ISSN 1942-969X. 2009 (Mar.) (from ScienceDirect).
Indexed: CurCont, P03, P30, PsycInfo, SCOPUS, SSCI, W07.
—**CCC.**
Published by: (Trauma Psychology - Division 56), American Psychological Association, 750 First St, NE, Washington, DC 20002. TEL 202-336-5500, 800-374-2721, journals@apa.org. Ed. Steven N Gold. Adv. contact Doug Constant TEL 202-336-5574. Circ: 1,800.

150 FRA ISSN 1145-1882
PSYCHOLOGIE CLINIQUE. Text in French. 1989. s-a. EUR 42.65 combined subscription domestic (print & online eds.); EUR 70.14 combined subscription in the European Union (print & online eds.); EUR 92 combined subscription elsewhere (print & online eds.) (effective 2012). **Document type:** *Journal, Academic/Scholarly.*
Related titles: Online - full text ed.
—INIST.
Published by: E D P Sciences, 17 Ave du Hoggar, Parc d'Activites de Courtaboeuf, BP 112, Cedex A, Les Ulis, F-91944, France. TEL 33-1-69187575, FAX 33-1-69860678, http://www.edpsciences.org.

150 FRA ISSN 1265-5449
PSYCHOLOGIE CLINIQUE ET PROJECTIVE. Text in French. 1952. s-a. **Document type:** *Journal, Academic/Scholarly.*
Former titles (until 1993): Societe Francaise du Rorschach et des Methodes Projectives. Bulletin (0373-6261); (until 1962): Groupement Francais du Rorschach. Bulletin (1148-828X)
Indexed: DIP, E-psyche, FR, IBR, IBZ, P03, PsycInfo, PsycholAb.
—BLDSC (6946.531870), INIST.
Published by: Dunod, 5 rue Laromiguiere, Paris, 75005, France. TEL 33-1-40463500, FAX 33-1-40464995, infos@dunod.com, http://www.dunod.com. **Subscr. to:** Societe de Periodiques Specialises. TEL 33-2-54504612, FAX 33-2-54504611.

PSYCHOLOGIE DE L'INTERACTION. *see* MEDICAL SCIENCES—Psychiatry And Neurology

150 DEU
PSYCHOLOGIE DER MENSCH-TIER-BEZIEHUNG. Text in German. 2006. irreg., latest vol.5, 2009. price varies. **Document type:** *Monographic series, Academic/Scholarly.*
Published by: S. Roderer Verlag, In der Obern Au 12, Regensburg, 93055, Germany. TEL 49-941-7992270, FAX 49-941-795198, info@roderer-verlag.de, http://roderer-verlag.de.

150 AUT ISSN 1998-9970
PSYCHOLOGIE DES ALLTAGSHANDELNS/PSYCHOLOGY OF EVERYDAY ACTIVITY. Text in English, German. 2008. q. EUR 50; EUR 15 newsstand/cover (effective 2009). **Document type:** *Journal, Academic/Scholarly.*
Published by: Innsbruck University Press, Technikerstr 21a, EG, Innsbruck, 6020, Austria. TEL 43-512-5079096, FAX 43-512-5079812, iup@uibk.ac.at, http://www.uibk.ac.at/iup/index.html. Ed. Pierre Sachse.

150 CZE ISSN 1212-9607
PSYCHOLOGIE DNES. Text in Czech. 1995. m. CZK 484 (effective 2009). **Document type:** *Magazine, Consumer.*
Formerly (until 1999): Propsy (1211-5886)
Related titles: Online - full text ed.
Published by: Portal, Klapkova 2, Prague 8, 18200, Czech Republic. TEL 420-2-83028111, FAX 420-2-83028112, naklad@portal.cz.

150 FRA ISSN 1420-2530
PSYCHOLOGIE DU TRAVAIL ET DES ORGANISATIONS. Text in French. 1994. 4/yr. EUR 75 combined subscription domestic to individuals print & online eds.; EUR 80 combined subscription in the European Union to individuals print & online eds.; EUR 85 combined subscription elsewhere to individuals print & online eds.; EUR 115 combined subscription domestic to institutions print & online eds.; EUR 120 combined subscription in the European Union to institutions print & online eds.; EUR 125 combined subscription elsewhere to institutions print & online eds.; EUR 55 combined subscription domestic to students print & online eds.; EUR 60 combined subscription in the European Union to students print & online eds.; EUR 65 combined subscription elsewhere to students print & online eds. (effective 2009). **Document type:** *Journal, Academic/Scholarly.* **Description:** Deals with the individual, social, psychological and structural aspects of work in social organisation.
Related titles: Online - full text ed.: ISSN 1778-3631.
Indexed: A26, CA, I05, P03, PsycholAb, SCOPUS, SSCI, T02, W07.
—BLDSC (6946.532360), IE, Ingenta, INIST. **CCC.**
Published by: Association Internationale de Psychologie du Travail de Langue Francaise (A I P T L F), Universite Lille 3, UFR Psychologie, BP 60149, Villeneuve d'Ascq, cedex 59653, France. TEL 33-3-20416968, g.masclet@revue-pto.com.

150 NLD ISSN 1873-1791
BF8.D8 CODEN: GEGEE6
PSYCHOLOGIE & GEZONDHEID. Text in Dutch, English. 1973. 5/yr. EUR 130, USD 195 combined subscription to institutions (print & online eds.) (effective 2009). adv. bk.rev. bibl.; charts; illus. index. **Document type:** *Magazine, Trade.* **Description:** Offers advice to professionals in all areas of caring for persons with both physical and mental disorders.
Former titles (until 2007): Gedrag en Gezondheid (0921-5360); (until 1986): Gedrag (0377-7308); Which was formed by the merger of (1956-1973): Hypothese (0018-8352); (1970-1973): Nijmeegs Tijdschrift voor Psychologie (0029-0475); Which was formerly (1952-1969): Gawein (0016-5271)
Related titles: Online - full text ed.: ISSN 1876-8741.
Indexed: A20, A22, E-psyche, IBR, IBZ, P03, P30, PsycInfo, PsycholAb, SCI, W07.
—IE, Infotrieve, Ingenta. **CCC.**
Published by: Bohn Stafleu van Loghum B.V. (Subsidiary of: Springer Science+Business Media), Postbus 246, Houten, 3990 GA, Netherlands. TEL 31-30-6383872, FAX 31-30-6383991, boekhandels@bsl.nl. adv.: page EUR 519; trim 130 x 210. Circ: 500 (controlled).

PSYCHOLOGIE & EDUCATION. *see* EDUCATION

PSYCHOLOGIE ET NEUROPSYCHIATRIE DU VIEILLISSEMENT. *see* MEDICAL SCIENCES—Psychiatry And Neurology

150 FRA ISSN 0033-2984
BF2 CODEN: PSFRAT
PSYCHOLOGIE FRANCAISE. Text in French. 1956. 4/yr. EUR 171 in Europe to institutions; EUR 160.63 in France to institutions; JPY 22,600 in Japan to institutions; USD 220 elsewhere to institutions (effective 2012). bibl.; charts; illus. index. reprints avail. **Document type:** *Journal, Academic/Scholarly.* **Description:** Publishes reviews of original investigations and articles covering theoretical reflection regarding the practice of psychology.
Related titles: Online - full text ed.: ISSN 1873-7277 (from ScienceDirect).
Indexed: A22, A26, BibInd, CA, DIP, E-psyche, FR, I05, IBR, IBZ, P03, PsycInfo, PsycholAb, RASB, S02, S03, SCOPUS, SSCI, T02, W07.
—BLDSC (6946.532200), IE, Infotrieve, Ingenta, INIST. **CCC.**
Published by: (Societe Francaise de Psychologie), Elsevier Masson (Subsidiary of: Elsevier Health Sciences), 62 Rue Camille Desmoulins, Issy les Moulineaux, Cedex 92442, France. TEL 33-1-71165500, FAX 33-1-71165600, infos@elsevier-masson.fr. Ed. Denis Brouillet. Circ: 2,800.

150 DEU ISSN 0340-1677
➤ **PSYCHOLOGIE HEUTE.** Text in German. 1974. m. EUR 59; EUR 5.90 newsstand/cover (effective 2010). adv. bk.rev. bibl.; charts; illus.; stat. index. **Document type:** *Journal, Academic/Scholarly.* **Description:** Covers the behavioral sciences.
Indexed: DIP, E-psyche, IBR, IBZ, RASB.
—BLDSC (6946.532240), IE, Infotrieve. **CCC.**
Published by: Julius Beltz GmbH & Co. KG, Werderstr 10, Weinheim, 69469, Germany. TEL 49-6201-6007200, FAX 49-6201-6007201, info@beltz.de, http://www.beltz.de. Ed., R&P Heiko Ernst. Adv. contact Claudia Klinger. B&W page EUR 3,580, color page EUR 6,140; trim 210 x 280. Circ: 92,621 (paid and controlled).

150 NLD ISSN 1389-8051
PSYCHOLOGIE MAGAZINE. Text in Dutch. 1982. m. (11/yr.). EUR 53.50 (effective 2008). adv. back issues avail. **Document type:** *Consumer.* **Description:** Covers current psychological knowledge for an educated lay readership.
Formerly (until 1999): Psychologie (0167-6598)
Indexed: E-psyche.
—IE, Infotrieve.
Published by: Weekbladpers B.V., Postbus 2994, Amsterdam, 1000 CZ, Netherlands. TEL 31-20-5518542, FAX 31-20-4212476. Eds. Ruud Hollander, Sterre van Leer. Adv. contact Gerda de Graaff.

301.1 150 CAN ISSN 0714-3494
BF2P69
PSYCHOLOGIE PREVENTIVE. Text in English. 1982. s-a. CAD 16 domestic to individuals; CAD 20 foreign to individuals; CAD 12 domestic to institutions; CAD 25 foreign to institutions (effective 2000). adv. bk.rev. index. back issues avail. **Document type:** *Journal, Consumer.* **Description:** Covers problems of family, youth, education and health.
Indexed: E-psyche, PdeR.
Published by: Societe de Recherche en Orientation Humaine Inc., 2120 E Rue Sherbrooke, Bur 212, Montreal, PQ H2K 1C3, Canada. TEL 514-523-5677, FAX 514-523-9999, frederike.d@sympatico.ca. Ed. Yves Brissette. Pub., R&P Moncef Guitouni. Circ: 1,000.

158 CZE ISSN 1803-8670
HF5548.8 CODEN: PSVPB2
PSYCHOLOGIE PRO PRAXI/APPLIED INDUSTRIAL PSYCHOLOGY; casopis pro pomoc hospodarske praxi. Text in Czech; Summaries in English, German. 1966. s-a. CZK 160 (effective 2010). bk.rev. abstr.; bibl.; charts; illus.; stat. index. **Document type:** *Journal, Academic/Scholarly.* **Description:** Aims to widen the scientific focus on various topics of applied psychology, or psychological theory for the practice.
Formerly (until Jan. 2009): Psychologie v Ekonomicke Praxi (0033-300X)
Related titles: Microform ed.
Indexed: CISA, E-psyche, ErgAb, PsycholAb, RASB, S02, S03.
—INIST.
Published by: (Univerzita Karlova v Praze, Filozoficka Fakulta/Charles University in Prague, Faculty of Philosophy), Nakladatelstvi Karolinum, Ovocny trh 3/5, Prague 1, 11636, Czech Republic. TEL 420-224491275, FAX 420-224212041, cupress@cuni.cz, http://cupress.cuni.cz. Eds. Hedvika Boukalova, Ilona Gillernova. Circ: 500.

302 DEU ISSN 1612-488X
PSYCHOLOGIE UND GESELLSCHAFT. Text in German. 2003. irreg., latest vol.9, 2010. price varies. **Document type:** *Monographic series, Academic/Scholarly.*
Published by: Peter Lang GmbH (Subsidiary of: Peter Lang Publishing Group), Eschborner Landstr 42-50, Frankfurt Am Main, 60489, Germany. TEL 49-69-7807050, FAX 49-69-78070550, zentrale.frankfurt@peterlang.com, http://www.peterlang.com. Ed. Martin Schweer.

150 DEU ISSN 0170-0537
BF3
PSYCHOLOGIE UND GESELLSCHAFTSKRITIK. Text in German. 1977. 3/yr. EUR 40; EUR 13 newsstand/cover (effective 2011). adv. bk.rev. index. back issues avail. **Document type:** *Journal, Academic/Scholarly.* **Description:** Critique of mainstream psychology in theory and practice; social foundation of psychology.
Formerly (until 1978): Psychologie und Gesellschaft (0342-0981)
Indexed: DIP, E-psyche, IBR, IBZ.
Published by: (Initiative Kritischer Psychologinnen und Psychologen e.V.), Pabst Science Publishers, Am Eichengrund 28, Lengerich, 49525, Germany. TEL 49-5484-97234, FAX 49-5484-550, pabst@pabst-publishers.com, http://www.pabst-publishers.de. Ed. Ulrich Kobbe. Circ: 2,750.

PSYCHOLOGIES; pour mieux vivre notre vie. *see* WOMEN'S INTERESTS

150 ESP

PSYCHOLOGIES; vive mejor tu vida. Text in Spanish. 2005. m. EUR 2.95 newsstand/cover (effective 2009). back issues avail. **Document type:** *Magazine, Consumer.*

Related titles: Online - full text ed.

Published by: Prisma Publicaciones, Ave Diagonal, 477 3a. pl, Barcelona, 08360, Spain. TEL 34-93-2704550, FAX 34-93-2704581, redaccioncyu@historiayvida.com, http://www.[rismapublicaciones.com/. Circ: 91,267.

PSYCHOLOGIES. *see* WOMEN'S INTERESTS

158 305.4 ZAF ISSN 1993-2839

PSYCHOLOGIES. Text in English. 2007. bi-m. ZAR 132.85 domestic; ZAR 222.42 in Namibia; ZAR 358.02 in Zimbabwe; ZAR 330.42 elsewhere; ZAR 29.95 newsstand/cover (effective 2007). adv. **Document type:** *Magazine, Consumer.* **Description:** For women who are interested in the way they think, behave, change and connect. Focuses on self-accomplishment, better living and relationships.

Published by: Media24 Ltd., Naspers Centre, 40 Heerengracht St, PO Box 1802, Cape Town, 8000, South Africa. TEL 27-21-4461415, http://www.media24.com. Ed. Tracy Melass TEL 27-21-4461411. Pub. Mari Lategan. Adv. contact Anneli Moolman TEL 27-21-4465064.

PSYCHOLOGIES MAGAZINE. *see* WOMEN'S INTERESTS

150 DEU ISSN 1435-666X

PSYCHOLOGISCHE FORSCHUNGSERGEBNISSE. Text in German. 1991. irreg., latest vol.148, 2010. price varies. **Document type:** *Monographic series, Academic/Scholarly.*

Published by: Verlag Dr. Kovac, Leverkusenstr 13, Hamburg, 22761, Germany. TEL 49-40-3988800, FAX 49-40-39888055, info@verlagdrkovac.de.

150 DEU ISSN 0033-3042
BF3

➤ **PSYCHOLOGISCHE RUNDSCHAU**; Offizielles Orgen des Deutschen Gesellschaft fuer Psychologie zugleich Informationsorgan des Berufsverbandes Deutscher Psychologinnen und Psychologen. Text in German; Summaries in English. 1949. q. EUR 61.95 to individuals; EUR 133.95 to institutions; EUR 33.95 newsstand/cover (effective 2011). adv. abstr.; charts. index. reprints avail. **Document type:** *Journal, Academic/Scholarly.*

Related titles: Online - full text ed.: ISSN 2190-6238.

Indexed: A20, A22, ASCA, BibInd, CDA, CurCont, DIP, E-psyche, ERA, IBR, IBZ, MLA-IB, P03, P30, PCI, PsycInfo, PsycholAb, RASB, S02, S03, S20, S21, SCOPUS, SSCI, W07.

—IE, Infotrieve, INIST.

Published by: (Deutsche Gesellschaft fuer Psychologie), Hogrefe Verlag GmbH & Co. KG, Rohnsweg 25, Goettingen, 37085, Germany. TEL 49-551-496090, FAX 49-551-4960988, verlag@hogrefe.de. Circ: 6,200 (paid). **Co-sponsor:** Berufsverband Deutscher Psychologinnen und Psychologen e.V.

150 DEU ISSN 1434-7423

PSYCHOLOGISCHE STUDIEN. Text in German. 1998. irreg., latest vol.2, 2008. price varies. **Document type:** *Monographic series, Academic/Scholarly.*

Published by: Centaurus Verlag & Media KG, Kaiser-Joseph-Str 267, Freiburg, 79098, Germany. TEL 49-761-1525861, FAX 49-761-1525868, info@centaurus-verlag.de, http://www.centaurus-verlag.de.

150 GBR ISSN 0952-8229
BF1

➤ **THE PSYCHOLOGIST.** Text in English. 1988. m. GBP 60 domestic to non-members; GBP 70 foreign to non-members; free to members (effective 2009). adv. bk.rev.; software rev. abstr. back issues avail.; reprint service avail. from PSC. **Document type:** *Journal, Academic/Scholarly.* **Description:** Contains articles on issues and events of general psychological interest, society news, regular columns on the media, computer and software news.

Former titles (until 1988): British Psychological Society. Bulletin (0007-1692); (until 1953): British Psychological Society. Quarterly Bulletin

Related titles: Microform ed.: (from PQC); Online - full text ed.: GBP 3.45 per issue to non-members; free to members (effective 2009).

Indexed: A01, A20, A22, AMED, ASCA, CA, CurCont, E-psyche, ErgAb, FamI, P03, P10, P19, P25, P26, P30, P34, P48, P53, P54, PQC, PsycInfo, PsycholAb, SCOPUS, SSCI, T02, W07.

—BLDSC (6946.534680), IE, Infotrieve, Ingenta. **CCC.**

Published by: The British Psychological Society, St Andrews House, 48 Princess Rd E, Leicester, LE1 7DR, United Kingdom. TEL 44-116-2549568, FAX 44-116-2271314, enquiry@bps.org.uk, http://www.bps.org.uk. Ed. Jon Sutton TEL 44-116-2529573. Adv. contact Sarah Stainton TEL 44-116-2529552. page GBP 1,100; 190 x 248.

371.42 GBR

PSYCHOLOGIST APPOINTMENT. Text in English. 19??. m. free to members (effective 2009). adv. **Document type:** *Journal, Trade.* **Description:** Features jobs in psychology across the whole spectrum of the discipline, both applied and academic.

Which was formerly (until 2007): Appointments Memorandum

Related titles: Online - full content ed.

Published by: B P S Communications Ltd. (Subsidiary of: The British Psychological Society), St Andrews House, 48 Princess Rd E, Leicester, LE1 7DR, United Kingdom. TEL 44-116-2549568, FAX 44-116-2470787, enquiry@psychapp.co.uk. adv.: page GBP 2,495.

150 GBR ISSN 1468-4756
BF121

THE PSYCHOLOGIST IN WALES. Text in English. 1984. a. free to members (effective 2009). back issues avail. **Document type:** *Journal, Academic/Scholarly.* **Description:** Designed for all the members of The British Psychological Society who are resident in Wales.

Formerly (until 1989): British Psychological Society. Welsh Branch. Bulletin

Published by: The British Psychological Society. Welsh Branch, c/o M Everson, 47 Courtlands, Park Rd, Barry, CF62 6NT, United Kingdom. TEL 44-7738-329664, wales@bps.org.uk, http://www.bps.org.uk/welsh/welsh_home.cfm. Ed. Dr. Enlli Thomas.

150 USA ISSN 1088-7156
HF5549.A2

➤ **THE PSYCHOLOGIST-MANAGER JOURNAL.** Abbreviated title: T P M J. Text in English. 1997. q. GBP 302 combined subscription in United Kingdom to institutions (print & online eds.); EUR 399, USD 499 combined subscription to institutions (print & online eds.) (effective 2012). adv. bk.rev. back issues avail.; reprint service avail. from PSC. **Document type:** *Journal, Academic/Scholarly.* **Description:** Designed for members of the Society of Psychologists in Management (SPIM) and others with similar interests. Presents as a hybrid between a journal and a professional guide to managerial practice.

Related titles: Online - full text ed.: ISSN 1550-3461. GBP 271 in United Kingdom to institutions; EUR 360, USD 449 to institutions (effective 2012).

Indexed: A01, A02, A03, A08, A12, A17, A22, ABIn, CA, E01, P03, P25, P43, P48, P51, P53, P54, PQC, PsycInfo, PsycholAb, T02.

—BLDSC (6946.534710), IE, Ingenta. **CCC.**

Published by: (Society of Psychologists in Management), Psychology Press (Subsidiary of: Taylor & Francis Inc.), 325 Chestnut St, Ste 800, Philadelphia, PA 19106. TEL 800-354-1420, FAX 215-625-2940, orders@taylorandfrancis.com, http://www.psypress.com. Ed. William D Siegfried Jr. Adv. contact Linda Hann TEL 44-1344-779945.

150 USA

PSYCHOLOGISTS FOR SOCIAL RESPONSIBILITY. NEWSLETTER. Text in English. 1982. q. USD 45 membership (effective 2007). **Document type:** *Newsletter.* **Description:** Networking newsletter for professional psychologists, students of psychology, and others interested in conflict resolution and prevention of war.

Related titles: Online - full content ed.

Indexed: E-psyche.

Published by: Psychologists for Social Responsibility, 208 "I" Street, NE, Ste B, Washington, DC 20002. TEL 202-543-5347, FAX 202-543-5348, psysr@psysr.org. Ed. Anne Anderson.

159.9 FRA ISSN 0555-5736

LE PSYCHOLOGUE. Text in French. 1958. irreg. **Document type:** *Monographic series, Academic/Scholarly.*

—CCC.

Published by: Presses Universitaires de France, 6 Avenue Reille, Paris, 75685, France. TEL 33-1-58103161, FAX 33-1-45897530, revues@puf.com, http://www.puf.com.

150 USA ISSN 2152-7180

▼ **PSYCHOLOGY (IRVINE).** Text in English. 2009. q.

Related titles: Online - full text ed.: ISSN 2152-7199. free (effective 2011).

Indexed: E08, I05, P10, PQC.

Published by: Scientific Research Publishing, Inc., 5005 Paseo Segovia, Irvine, CA 92603. TEL 408-329-4591, service@scirp.org, http://www.scirp.org. Eds. Annett Christine Korner, Martin Drapeau.

PSYCHOLOGY AND AGING. *see* GERONTOLOGY AND GERIATRICS

150 IND ISSN 0971-3336
BF1 CODEN: PDSOEI

➤ **PSYCHOLOGY AND DEVELOPING SOCIETIES.** Text in English. 1989. s-a. USD 326, GBP 176 combined subscription to institutions (print & online eds.); USD 319, GBP 172 to institutions (effective 2011). adv. bk.rev. abstr. back issues avail.; reprint service avail. from PSC. **Document type:** *Journal, Academic/Scholarly.* **Description:** Provides an international forum for psychologists concerned with problems of developing societies. Publishes theoretical, empirical, and review papers that further our understanding of the problems of these societies.

Related titles: Online - full text ed.: ISSN 0973-0761. USD 293, GBP 158 to institutions (effective 2011).

Indexed: A22, ASD, E-psyche, E01, ESPM, IBSS, IPsyAb, L&LBA, P03, P30, PAIS, PerIslam, PsycInfo, PsycholAb, RiskAb, SCOPUS, SOPODA, SociolAb.

—BLDSC (6946.535321), IE, Infotrieve, Ingenta. **CCC.**

Published by: (University of Allahabad, Center for Advanced Study in Psychology), Sage Publications India Pvt. Ltd. (Subsidiary of: Sage Publications, Inc.), M-32 Market, Greater Kailash-I, PO Box 4215, New Delhi, 110 048, India. TEL 91-11-6444958, FAX 91-11-6472426, editors@indiasage.com, http://www.indiasage.com/. Ed. Ajit K Dalal. adv.: page USD 75. Circ: 500. **Subscr. in Europe to:** Sage Publications Ltd., 1 Oliver's Yard, 55 City Rd, London EC1Y 1SP, United Kingdom. TEL 44-207-3248701, FAX 44-207-3248733, subscription@sagepub.co.uk; **Subscr. in the Americas to:** Sage Publications, Inc., 2455 Teller Rd, Thousand Oaks, CA 91320. TEL 805-499-9774, FAX 805-499-0871, journals@sagepub.com.

155 GBR ISSN 0887-0446
R726.7 CODEN: PSHEE4

➤ **PSYCHOLOGY & HEALTH.** Text in English. 1987. 10/yr. GBP 1,506 combined subscription in United Kingdom to institutions (print & online eds.); EUR 1,586, USD 1,992 combined subscription to institutions (print & online eds.) (effective 2012). adv. illus. back issues avail.; reprint service avail. from PSC. **Document type:** *Journal, Academic/Scholarly.* **Description:** Promotes the study and application of psychological approaches to health and illness.

Related titles: Microform ed.; Online - full text ed.: ISSN 1476-8321. GBP 1,355 in United Kingdom to institutions; EUR 1,428, USD 1,792 to institutions (effective 2012) (from IngentaConnect).

Indexed: A01, A02, A03, A08, A20, A22, A36, ASCA, C06, C07, C08, C11, CA, CABA, CINAHL, CurCont, D01, E-psyche, E01, E12, EMBASE, ExcerpMed, FamI, GH, H04, LT, MEDLINE, N02, N03, P03, P30, P43, PQC, PsycInfo, PsycholAb, R10, R12, RRTA, Reac, S02, S03, SCOPUS, SD, SSCI, T02, T05, W07, W11.

—BLDSC (6946.535325), GNLM, IE, Infotrieve, Ingenta, INIST. **CCC.**

Published by: (European Health Psychology Society PRT), Routledge (Subsidiary of: Taylor & Francis Group), 4 Park Sq, Milton Park, Abingdon, Oxon OX14 4RN, United Kingdom. TEL 44-20-70176000, FAX 44-20-70176336, subscriptions@tandf.co.uk, http://www.routledge.com. Eds. Lucy Yardley, Rona Moss-Morris. Adv. contact Linda Hann TEL 44-1344-779945. **Subscr. to:** Taylor & Francis Ltd., Journals Customer Service, Sheepen Pl, Colchester, Essex CO3 3LP, United Kingdom. TEL 44-20-70175544, FAX 44-20-70175198, tf.enquiries@tfinforma.com.

301.1 150 USA ISSN 0742-6046
HF5415.34 CODEN: PSMAFI

➤ **PSYCHOLOGY & MARKETING.** Text in English. 1984. m. GBP 1,155 in United Kingdom to institutions; EUR 1,461 in Europe to institutions; USD 1,819 in United States to institutions; USD 1,939 in Canada & Mexico to institutions; USD 2,041 elsewhere to institutions; GBP 1,313 combined subscription in United Kingdom to institutions (print & online eds.); EUR 1,660 combined subscription in Europe to institutions (print & online eds.); USD 2,093 combined subscription in United States to institutions (print & online eds.); USD 2,213 combined subscription in Canada & Mexico to institutions (print & online eds.); USD 2,315 combined subscription elsewhere to institutions (print & online eds.) (effective 2012). adv. illus. Index. back issues avail.; reprint service avail. from PSC. **Document type:** *Journal, Academic/Scholarly.* **Description:** Promotes an understanding of the nature and operation of psychological principles, as applied to strategies in the marketing industry.

Related titles: Microform ed.: (from PQC); Online - full text ed.: ISSN 1520-6793. 1996. GBP 1,042 in United Kingdom to institutions; EUR 1,318 in Europe to institutions; USD 1,819 elsewhere to institutions (effective 2012).

Indexed: A12, A13, A14, A15, A17, A18, A20, A22, ABIn, ASCA, B01, B04, B06, B07, B08, B09, B11, BPI, BRD, C12, CA, CMM, CommAb, CurCont, E-psyche, FamI, IBR, IBZ, P03, P21, P25, P48, P51, P53, P54, PCI, PQC, PsycInfo, PsycholAb, S02, S03, SCOPUS, SSCI, T02, W01, W02, W03, W07.

—BLDSC (6946.535340), IE, Infotrieve, Ingenta. **CCC.**

Published by: John Wiley & Sons, Inc., 111 River St, Hoboken, NJ 07030. TEL 201-748-6000, FAX 201-748-6088, info@wiley.com, http://www.wiley.com/WileyCDA/. Ed. Dr. Ronald Jay Cohen TEL 954-567-8530. Adv. contact Kim Thompkins TEL 212-850-6921. B&W page USD 772, color page USD 1,009; trim 6.875 x 10. **Subscr. outside the Americas to:** John Wiley & Sons Ltd., The Atrium, Southern Gate, Chichester, West Sussex PO19 8SQ, United Kingdom. TEL 44-1243-779777, 800-243407, FAX 44-1243-775878, cs-journals@wiley.com.

616.8 BRA ISSN 1984-3054

PSYCHOLOGY & NEUROSCIENCE. Text in English. 2008. s-a. **Document type:** *Journal, Academic/Scholarly.*

Related titles: Online - full text ed.: ISSN 1983-3288. free (effective 2011).

Indexed: PsycInfo, SCOPUS.

Published by: Casa do Psicologo Livraria e Editora, Rua Mourato Coelho 1059, Pinheiro, SP, Brazil. TEL 55-11-38131425, http://www.casadopsicologo.com.br. Eds. A. Pedro M. Cruz, Dora Fix Ventura.

150 616.8 USA ISSN 1944-2718

PSYCHOLOGY & PSYCHIATRY JOURNAL. Text in English. 2008. w. **Document type:** *Newsletter, Trade.*

Related titles: Online - full text ed.: ISSN 1944-2726.

Indexed: H11, I05, P20, P25, P48, P54, PQC.

Published by: NewsRx, 2727 Paces Ferry Rd SE, Ste 2-440, Atlanta, GA 30339. TEL 770-435-8286, 800-726-4550, FAX 770-435-6800, pressrelease@newsrx.com, http://www.newsrx.com.

616.89 150 GBR ISSN 1476-0835
RC321 CODEN: PPTRCC

➤ **PSYCHOLOGY & PSYCHOTHERAPY**; theory, research & practice. Text in English. 1904. q. GBP 246 in United Kingdom to institutions; EUR 365 in Europe to institutions; USD 451 elsewhere to institutions; GBP 300 combined subscription in United Kingdom to institutions (print & online eds.); EUR 446 combined subscription in Europe to institutions (print & online eds.); USD 551 combined subscription elsewhere to institutions (print & online eds.) (effective 2012). adv. bk.rev. charts; illus.; abstr. index. 144 p./no.; back issues avail.; reprint service avail. from PSC. **Document type:** *Journal, Academic/Scholarly.* **Description:** Covers original theory and research from psychodynamic and interpersonal psychology.

Former titles (until 2002): British Journal of Medical Psychology (0007-1129); (until 1923): British Journal of Medical Psychology. Medical Section; (until 1920): British Journal of Psychology (0950-5652)

Related titles: Magnetic Tape ed.; Microfiche ed.; Microform ed.: (from PQC, SWZ); Online - full text ed.: ISSN 2044-8341. 1999. GBP 261 in United Kingdom to institutions; EUR 387 in Europe to institutions; USD 479 elsewhere to institutions (effective 2012).

Indexed: A01, A03, A08, A20, A22, AMHA, ASCA, ASSIA, B21, B28, BDM&CN, BibInd, C06, C07, C08, CA, CINAHL, ChemAb, CurCont, DIP, DentInd, E-psyche, E01, EMBASE, ExcerpMed, F09, FR, FamI, IBR, IBZ, INI, ISR, IndMed, Inpharma, MEA&I, MEDLINE, MLA-IB, NSA, P03, P20, P22, P25, P26, P30, P43, P48, P54, PQC, PhilInd, PsycInfo, PsycholAb, R10, RILM, Reac, RefZh, S02, S03, SCI, SCOPUS, SOPODA, SSCI, SociolAb, T02, THA, W07.

—BLDSC (6946.535380), GNLM, IE, Infotrieve, Ingenta, INIST. **CCC.**

Published by: (The British Psychological Society), John Wiley & Sons Ltd. (Subsidiary of: John Wiley & Sons, Inc.), 9600 Garsington Rd, Oxford, OX4 2DQ, United Kingdom. TEL 44-1865-776868, FAX 44-1865-714591, customer@wiley.com.uk, http://www.wiley.com. Ed. Steven Jones. adv.: page GBP 340; trim 174 x 247.

155.3 GBR ISSN 1941-9899

▼ **PSYCHOLOGY & SEXUALITY.** Text in English. 2010 (Jan.). 3/yr. GBP 201 combined subscription in United Kingdom to institutions (print & online eds.); EUR 291, USD 364 combined subscription to institutions (print & online eds.) (effective 2012). **Document type:** *Journal, Academic/Scholarly.* **Description:** Aims to fulfil the requirement for an international journal, publishing high-quality quantitative and qualitative psychological research on sexualities.

Related titles: Online - full text ed.: ISSN 1941-9902. GBP 181 in United Kingdom to institutions; EUR 262, USD 328 to institutions (effective 2012).

Indexed: A01, PQC, T02.

—CCC.

Published by: Taylor & Francis Ltd. (Subsidiary of: Taylor & Francis Group), 4 Park Sq, Milton Park, Abingdon, Oxfordshire OX14 4RN, United Kingdom. TEL 44-20-70176000, FAX 44-20-70176336, subscriptions@tandf.co.uk. Eds. Darren Langdridge, Meg Barker.

150 GBR ISSN 2041-5893

PSYCHOLOGY & SOCIETY. Text in English. 2008. irreg. free (effective 2011). **Document type:** *Journal, Academic/Scholarly.*

Media: Online - full text.

P

Published by: University of Cambridge, Department of Social and Developmental Psychology, Free School Lane, Cambridge, CB2 3RQ, United Kingdom. http://www.sdp.cam.ac.uk. Eds. Brady Wagoner, Julian Oldmeadow.

302 USA ISSN 0885-7423
GV706

PSYCHOLOGY AND SOCIOLOGY OF SPORT: CURRENT SELECTED RESEARCH. Text in English. 1986. a. index. back issues avail.; reprints avail. **Document type:** *Journal, Academic/Scholarly.* **Description:** Research on contemporary problems of interest to behavioral scientists in the area of sport.
Indexed: E-psyche.
—BLDSC (6946.535430).
Published by: A M S Press, Inc., Brooklyn Navy Yard, 63 Flushing Ave, Bldg 292, Unit #221, Brooklyn, NY 11205. FAX 718-875-3800, queries@amspressinc.com, http://www.amspressinc.com.

616.89 ZAF

➤ **PSYCHOLOGY BULLETIN.** Text in English. 1990. s-a. **Document type:** *Journal, Academic/Scholarly.*
Formerly (until vol.3, no.1, 1993): Psychology Quarterly
Indexed: E-psyche.
Published by: (University of the Western Cape, History Department, Department of Psychology), Psychology Resource Centre, Private Bag X17, Bellville, 7353, South Africa. TEL 27-21-9592453, ykleinhans@uwc.ac.za, http://ww3.uwc.ac.za/index.asp. Eds. Ashley van Niekerk, Norman Duncan. Circ: 1,000 (controlled).

345 GBR ISSN 1068-316X
HV6080 CODEN: PCLAE2

➤ **PSYCHOLOGY, CRIME AND LAW.** Text in English. 1994. 8/yr. GBP 630 combined subscription in United Kingdom to institutions (print & online eds.); EUR 674, USD 844 combined subscription to institutions (print & online eds.) (effective 2012). adv. back issues avail.; reprint service avail. from PSC. **Document type:** *Journal, Academic/Scholarly.* **Description:** Aims to promote the study and application of psychological approaches to crime, criminal and civil law, and the influence of law on behavior.
Related titles: Online - full text ed.: ISSN 1477-2744. GBP 567 in United Kingdom to institutions; EUR 607, USD 760 to institutions (effective 2012) (from IngentaConnect).
Indexed: A01, A03, A08, A20, A22, ASCA, AddicA, CA, CJA, CJPI, CurCont, E-psyche, E01, I02, IBSS, L03, P03, P25, P43, P48, PQC, PsycInfo, PsycholAb, R02, S02, S03, SCOPUS, SSCI, T02, V&AA, W07.
—BLDSC (6946.535550), IE, Infotrieve, Ingenta, INIST. **CCC.**
Published by: (European Association of Psychology and Law DEU), Routledge (Subsidiary of: Taylor & Francis Group), 4 Park Sq, Milton Park, Abingdon, Oxon OX14 4RN, United Kingdom. TEL 44-20-70176000, FAX 44-20-70176336, subscriptions@tandf.co.uk, http://www.routledge.com. Adv. contact Linda Hann TEL 44-1344-779945. **Subscr. to:** Taylor & Francis Ltd., Journals Customer Service, Sheepen Pl, Colchester, Essex CO3 3LP, United Kingdom. TEL 44-20-70175544, FAX 44-20-70175198, tf.enquiries@tfinforma.com.

616.89 GBR ISSN 1354-8506
R726.5 CODEN: PHMEFL

➤ **PSYCHOLOGY, HEALTH & MEDICINE.** Text in English. 1996. bi-m. GBP 770 combined subscription in United Kingdom to institutions (print & online eds.); EUR 1,007, USD 1,257 combined subscription to institutions (print & online eds.) (effective 2012). adv. bk.rev. back issues avail.; reprint service avail. from PSC. **Document type:** *Journal, Academic/Scholarly.* **Description:** Provides a forum to report on issues of psychology and health in practice.
Related titles: Online - full text ed.: ISSN 1465-3966. GBP 693 in United Kingdom to institutions; EUR 906, USD 1,132 to institutions (effective 2012) (from IngentaConnect).
Indexed: A01, A02, A03, A08, A20, A22, ASSIA, B21, C06, C07, C08, C11, CA, CINAHL, CurCont, E-psyche, E01, EMBASE, ESPM, ExcerpMed, FR, H&SSA, H04, MEDLINE, P03, P24, P25, P30, P43, P48, PQC, PsycInfo, PsycholAb, R09, R10, Reac, RiskAb, S02, S03, SCI, SCOPUS, SD, SOPODA, SSCI, SociolAb, T02, W07.
—IE, Infotrieve, Ingenta, INIST. **CCC.**
Published by: Routledge (Subsidiary of: Taylor & Francis Group), 4 Park Sq, Milton Park, Abingdon, Oxon OX14 4RN, United Kingdom. TEL 44-20-70176000, FAX 44-20-70176336, subscriptions@tandf.co.uk, http://www.routledge.com. Ed. Lorraine Sherr. Adv. contact Linda Hann TEL 44-1344-779945. **Subscr. to:** Taylor & Francis Ltd., Journals Customer Service, Sheepen Pl, Colchester, Essex CO3 3LP, United Kingdom. TEL 44-20-70175544, FAX 44-20-70175198, tf.enquiries@tfinforma.com.

150 ZAF ISSN 1015-6046

PSYCHOLOGY IN SOCIETY. Text in English. 1983. 3/yr. **Document type:** *Journal, Academic/Scholarly.*
Related titles: Online - full text ed.: free (effective 2011).
Address: Box 17285, Congella, 4013, South Africa. TEL 27-31-2602531. Ed. Grahame Hayes.

150 ESP ISSN 1137-9685

PSYCHOLOGY IN SPAIN. Text in English. 1997. a. free (effective 2005). back issues avail. **Document type:** *Journal, Academic/Scholarly.* **Description:** Disseminates selected articles published in Colegio Oficial de Psicologos (COP - Spanish Psychological Association) journals.
Related titles: Online - full text ed.: free (effective 2011).
Indexed: E-psyche, P03, PsycInfo, PsycholAb.
—**CCC.**
Published by: Colegio Oficial de Psicologos, Conde de Penalver, 45 Planta 5, Madrid, 28008, Spain. http://www.cop.es. Ed. Jose Ramon Fernandez Hermida.

370.15 USA ISSN 0033-3085
LB1101

➤ **PSYCHOLOGY IN THE SCHOOLS.** Text in English. 1964. 8/yr. GBP 423 in United Kingdom to institutions; EUR 535 in Europe to institutions; USD 786 in United States to institutions; USD 828 in Canada & Mexico to institutions; USD 828 elsewhere to institutions; GBP 487 combined subscription in United Kingdom to institutions (print & online eds.); EUR 616 combined subscription in Europe to institutions (print & online eds.); USD 905 combined subscription in United States to institutions (print & online eds.); USD 947 combined subscription in Canada & Mexico to institutions (print & online eds.); USD 947 combined subscription elsewhere to institutions (print & online eds.) (effective 2012). adv. bk.rev. bibl.; illus.; abstr. Index. back issues avail.; reprint service avail. from PSC. **Document type:** *Journal, Academic/Scholarly.* **Description:** Focuses on the issues confronting school psychologists, teachers, counselors, administrators, and other personnel workers in schools and colleges, public and private organizations.
Related titles: Microform ed.: (from PQC); Online - full text ed.: ISSN 1520-6807. GBP 402 in United Kingdom to institutions; EUR 508 in Europe to institutions; USD 786 elsewhere to institutions (effective 2012).
Indexed: A01, A02, A03, A08, A20, A22, ABS&EES, AEI, AMHA, ASCA, ASSIA, BRD, C28, CA, CPE, Chicano, CurCont, DIP, E-psyche, E02, E03, E06, EAA, ECER, ERI, ERIC, EdA, EdI, F09, FR, FamI, IBR, IBZ, L&LBA, P03, P04, P30, P43, PAIS, PsycInfo, PsycholAb, S02, S03, SCOPUS, SOPODA, SSCI, SociolAb, T02, W03, W07.
—BLDSC (6946.536400), IE, Infotrieve, Ingenta, INIST. **CCC.**
Published by: John Wiley & Sons, Inc., 111 River St, Hoboken, NJ 07030. TEL 201-748-6000, FAX 201-748-6088, info@wiley.com, http://www.wiley.com/WileyCDA/. Ed. David E McIntosh. Pub., Adv. contact Kim Thompkins TEL 212-850-6921. B&W page USD 1,241, color page USD 1,576; trim 6.875 x 10. **Subscr. outside the Americas to:** John Wiley & Sons Ltd., The Atrium, Southern Gate, Chichester, West Sussex PO19 8SQ, United Kingdom. TEL 44-1243-779777, 800-243407, FAX 44-1243-775878, cs-journals@wiley.com.

150 USA ISSN 1931-5694
BF1

➤ **PSYCHOLOGY JOURNAL.** Text in English. 2007 (Mar.). q. back issues avail. **Document type:** *Journal, Academic/Scholarly.*
Formed by the merger of (2005-2007): Journal of Worry and Affective Experience (1546-0924); (2004-2007): Counseling and Clinical Psychology Journal (1931-2091)
Indexed: A01, A02, A03, A08, CA, S02, S03, SSA, SociolAb, T02.
Published by: Psychological Publishing, PO Box 176, Natchitoches, LA 71458.

150 GBR ISSN 1475-7257

PSYCHOLOGY LEARNING & TEACHING. Text in English. 2001. 3/yr. adv. back issues avail.; reprints avail. **Document type:** *Journal, Academic/Scholarly.*
Related titles: ◆ Online - full text ed.: Psychology Learning & Teaching (Online).
Indexed: B29, PsycInfo.
Published by: Symposium Journals (Subsidiary of: wwwords Ltd), PO Box 204, Didcot, Oxford, OX11 9ZQ, United Kingdom. TEL 44-1235-818062, FAX 44-1235-817275, info@symposium-journals.co.uk, http://www.symposium-journals.co.uk/.

150 GBR

PSYCHOLOGY LEARNING & TEACHING (ONLINE). Text in English. 2001. 3/yr. USD 50 to individuals; USD 490 to libraries (effective 2011). **Document type:** *Journal, Academic/Scholarly.*
Media: Online - full text. **Related titles:** ◆ Print ed.: Psychology Learning & Teaching. ISSN 1475-7257.
Published by: Symposium Journals (Subsidiary of: wwwords Ltd), PO Box 204, Didcot, Oxford, OX11 9ZQ, United Kingdom. TEL 44-1235-818062, FAX 44-1235-817275, info@symposium-journals.co.uk, http://www.symposium-journals.co.uk/.

PSYCHOLOGY OF ADDICTIVE BEHAVIORS. *see* DRUG ABUSE AND ALCOHOLISM

150 700 USA ISSN 1931-3896
BH1

PSYCHOLOGY OF AESTHETICS, CREATIVITY, AND THE ARTS. Text in English. 2007. q. USD 97 domestic to individuals; USD 124 foreign to individuals; USD 410 domestic to institutions; USD 455 foreign to institutions (effective 2011). adv. illus. back issues avail. **Document type:** *Journal, Academic/Scholarly.* **Description:** Devoted to promoting scholarship on how individuals participate in the creation and appreciation of artistic endeavor.
Related titles: Online - full text ed.: ISSN 1931-390X (from ScienceDirect).
Indexed: A07, A20, A30, A31, AA, ArtHuCI, ArtInd, CA, CurCont, P03, PsycInfo, SCOPUS, SSCI, T02, W07.
—BLDSC (9830.071000), IE. **CCC.**
Published by: (American Psychological Association, Division 10), American Psychological Association, 750 First St, NE, Washington, DC 20002. TEL 202-336-5500, 800-374-2721, journals@apa.org. Eds. James C Kaufman, Jeffrey Smith, Lisa F Smith. Circ: 600.

THE PSYCHOLOGY OF EDUCATION REVIEW. *see* EDUCATION

150 POL ISSN 1234-2238
BF455.A1

➤ **PSYCHOLOGY OF LANGUAGE AND COMMUNICATION.** Text in English. 1997. s-a. EUR 31 foreign (effective 2011). **Document type:** *Journal, Academic/Scholarly.*
Related titles: Online - full text ed.: free (effective 2011).
Indexed: L&LBA, MLA-IB, SCOPUS.
—Linda Hall.
Published by: Uniwersytet Warszawski, Wydzial Psychologii/University of Warsaw, Faculty of Psychology, ul Stawki 5/7, Warsaw, 00183, Poland. TEL 48-22-5549722, http://www.psychology.pl. Ed. Barbara Bokus.

152.5 USA ISSN 0079-7421
BF683 CODEN: PYLMAI

PSYCHOLOGY OF LEARNING AND MOTIVATION: ADVANCES IN RESEARCH AND THEORY. Text in English. 1967. irreg., latest vol.52, 2010. USD 130 per vol. (effective 2010). back issues avail.; reprints avail. **Document type:** *Monographic series, Academic/Scholarly.*
Related titles: Online - full text ed.: ISSN 1557-802X.
Indexed: A20, A22, ASCA, B21, BIOSIS Prev, BRD, CA, DIP, E-psyche, E02, E03, E06, ERI, EdA, EdI, IBR, IBZ, MycolAb, NSA, PCI, SCOPUS, SSCI, T02, W03, W07.
—BLDSC (6946.535700), IE, Ingenta, INIST. **CCC.**
Published by: Academic Press (Subsidiary of: Elsevier Science & Technology), 3251 Riverport Ln, Maryland Heights, MO 63043. TEL 314-447-8010, FAX 314-447-8030, JournalCustomerService-usa@elsevier.com, http://www.elsevierdirect.com/imprint.jsp?iid=5.

155 USA ISSN 1524-9220
BF692.5

PSYCHOLOGY OF MEN & MASCULINITY. Text in English. 2000. q. USD 110 domestic to individuals; USD 137 foreign to individuals; USD 410 domestic to institutions; USD 455 foreign to institutions (effective 2011). adv. back issues avail.; reprint service avail. from PSC. **Document type:** *Journal, Academic/Scholarly.* **Description:** Devoted to the dissemination of research, theory and clinical scholarship that advances the discipline of the psychology of men and masculinity.
Related titles: Online - full text ed.: ISSN 1939-151X (from ScienceDirect).
Indexed: ASSIA, C06, C07, CA, CurCont, P03, P30, PsycInfo, PsycholAb, SCOPUS, SSCI, T02, W07.
—BLDSC (6946.535760), IE, Infotrieve, Ingenta. **CCC.**
Published by: (American Psychological Association, Division 51), American Psychological Association, 750 First St, NE, Washington, DC 20002. TEL 202-336-5500, 800-374-2721, FAX 202-336-5997, journals@apa.org. Ed. Ronald F Levant. Adv. contact Doug Constant TEL 202-336-5574. B&W page USD 250, color page USD 1,225; trim 7 x 10. Circ: 700.

PSYCHOLOGY OF MUSIC. *see* MUSIC

150 200 USA ISSN 1941-1022
BL53.A1

▼ ➤ **PSYCHOLOGY OF RELIGION AND SPIRITUALITY.** Text in English. 2009. q. USD 110 domestic to individuals; USD 137 foreign to individuals; USD 403 domestic to institutions; USD 448 foreign to institutions (effective 2011). adv. back issues avail.; reprints avail. **Document type:** *Journal, Academic/Scholarly.* **Description:** Contains articles related to the psychological aspects of religion and spirituality.
Related titles: Online - full text ed.: ISSN 1943-1562 (from ScienceDirect).
Indexed: ArtHuCI, CurCont, P03, PsycInfo, SCOPUS, SSCI, W07.
—**CCC.**
Published by: (American Psychological Association, Division 36), American Psychological Association, 750 First St, NE, Washington, DC 20002. TEL 202-336-5500, 800-374-2721, journals@apa.org. Ed. Ralph L Piedmont. Adv. contact Doug Constant TEL 202-336-5574. Circ: 1,400.

150 613.71 NLD ISSN 1469-0292
GV206.4

➤ **PSYCHOLOGY OF SPORT AND EXERCISE.** Text in English. 1997. 6/yr. EUR 504 in Europe to institutions; JPY 66,800 in Japan to institutions; USD 561 elsewhere to institutions (effective 2012). back issues avail. **Document type:** *Journal, Academic/Scholarly.* **Description:** Provides an international forum for scholarly reports in the psychology of sport and exercise.
Formerly (until 2000): European Yearbook of Sport Psychology (1433-1462)
Related titles: Online - full text ed.: (from IngentaConnect, ScienceDirect).
Indexed: A01, A03, A08, A20, A26, A36, CA, CABA, CurCont, E12, ESPM, ErgAb, FoSS&M, GH, I05, LT, N02, N03, P03, P30, PEI, PsycInfo, PsycholAb, R12, RRTA, RiskAb, S02, S03, SCI, SCOPUS, SD, SSCI, T02, T05, W07.
—BLDSC (6946.536590), IE, Ingenta. **CCC.**
Published by: (European Federation of Sport Psychology DEU), Elsevier BV (Subsidiary of: Elsevier Science & Technology), Radarweg 29, PO Box 211, Amsterdam, 1000 AE, Netherlands. TEL 31-20-4853911, FAX 31-20-4852457, JournalsCustomerServiceEMEA@elsevier.com, http://www.elsevier.nl. Eds. Dorothee Alfermann, Martin Hagger. **Subscr. to:** Radarweg 29, PO Box 211, Amsterdam 1000 AE, Netherlands. TEL 31-20-4853757, FAX 31-20-4853432.

150 USA ISSN 2152-0828

▼ ➤ **PSYCHOLOGY OF VIOLENCE.** Text in English. forthcoming 2011 (Mar.). q. USD 110 domestic to individuals; USD 137 foreign to individuals; USD 403 domestic to institutions; USD 448 foreign to institutions (effective 2011). adv. **Document type:** *Journal, Academic/Scholarly.* **Description:** Devoted to research on violence and extreme aggression, including identifying the causes of violence from a psychological framework, finding ways to prevent or reduce violence, and developing practical interventions and treatments.
Related titles: Online - full text ed.: ISSN 2152-081X. forthcoming 2011 (Mar.) (from ScienceDirect).
Indexed: P30, PsycInfo.
—**CCC.**
Published by: American Psychological Association, 750 First St, NE, Washington, DC 20002. TEL 202-336-5500, 800-374-2721, FAX 202-336-5997, journals@apa.org. Ed. Sherry Hamby. Adv. contact Doug Constant TEL 202-336-5574.

158 DEU ISSN 2211-1522

▼ ➤ **PSYCHOLOGY OF WELL-BEING**; theory, research and practice. Text in English. 2011. irreg. free (effective 2011). **Document type:** *Journal, Academic/Scholarly.* **Description:** Devoted to understanding the biopsychosocial and behavioural factors leading to enhanced well-being.
Published by: SpringerOpen (Subsidiary of: Springer Science+Business Media), Tiergartenstr 17, Heidelberg, 69121, Germany. info@springeropen.com, http://www.springeropen.com. Eds. Dianne Vella-Brodrick, Nikki Rickard.

155 305.4 USA ISSN 0361-6843
HQ1206 CODEN: PWOQDY

➤ **PSYCHOLOGY OF WOMEN QUARTERLY.** Text in English. 1976. q. USD 369, GBP 217 combined subscription to institutions (print & online eds.); USD 362, GBP 213 to institutions (effective 2011). adv. bk.rev. illus. Index. back issues avail.; reprint service avail. from PSC. **Document type:** *Journal, Academic/Scholarly.* **Description:** Publishes current and important findings in the field of psychology of women and gender.
Related titles: Microform ed.: (from PQC); Online - full text ed.: ISSN 1471-6402. USD 332, GBP 195 to institutions (effective 2011) (from IngentaConnect).

Indexed: A01, A02, A03, A08, A20, A22, A25, A26, A36, ABS&EES, AMHA, ASCA, ASSIA, AbAn, B04, B21, BRD, C06, C07, C25, CA, CABA, CDA, CLFP, Chicano, CommAb, CurCont, DIP, E-psyche, E01, E02, E03, E07, E08, E12, ERI, ERIC, ESPM, EdA, EdI, F09, FR, FamI, FemPer, G08, G10, GH, H&SSA, H09, HEA, HRA, I05, IBR, IBSS, IBZ, L01, L02, LT, N02, N03, P02, P03, P04, P07, P10, P12, P13, P24, P27, P30, P43, P48, P53, P54, PCI, PQC, PsycInfo, PsycholAb, R12, RILM, RRTA, RiskAb, S02, S03, S05, S08, S09, S21, SCOPUS, SFSA, SOPODA, SSA, SSAI, SSAb, SSCI, SSI, SWR&A, SociolAb, T02, T05, V&AA, W01, W02, W03, W06, W07, W09, W11, WSA, WSI.
—BLDSC (6946.538000), IE, Infotrieve, Ingenta, INIST. **CCC.**
Published by: (American Psychological Association, Society for the Psychology of Women. Division 35), Wiley-Blackwell Publishing, Inc. (Subsidiary of: Wiley-Blackwell Publishing Ltd.), 111 River St, Hoboken, NJ 07030. TEL 201-748-6000, FAX 201-748-6088, info@wiley.com, http://www.wiley.com/WileyCDA/. Ed. Janice D Yoder. Adv. contact Kristin McCarthy TEL 201-748-7683.

150 GBR ISSN 1466-3724
PSYCHOLOGY OF WOMEN SECTION REVIEW. Abbreviated title: P O W S Review. Text in English. 1988. s-a. free to members (effective 2009). back issues avail. **Document type:** *Journal, Academic/Scholarly.* **Description:** Provides a forum for discussion of issues and debates around all aspects of the psychology of women in research, teaching and professional practice.
Formerly (until 1999): British Psychological Society. Psychology of Women Section. Newsletter (1362-6345)
Related titles: Online - full text ed.: GBP 3.45 per issue to non-members; GBP 2.30 per issue to members (effective 2009).
—BLDSC (6946.538500).
Published by: The British Psychological Society, St Andrews House, 48 Princess Rd E, Leicester, LE1 7DR, United Kingdom. TEL 44-116-2549568, FAX 44-116-2271314, enquiries@bps.org.uk.

150 USA ISSN 1076-8971
K16
➤ **PSYCHOLOGY, PUBLIC POLICY, AND LAW.** Text in English. 1995. q. USD 107 domestic to individuals; USD 134 foreign to individuals; USD 527 domestic to institutions; USD 572 foreign to institutions (effective 2011). adv. illus. back issues avail.; reprint service avail. from PSC. **Document type:** *Journal, Academic/Scholarly.* **Description:** Links psychological science with policy and law. Evaluates the contributions of psychology to policy and law issues, assesses policy alternatives, and articulates research needs in psychology that address policy and legal issues.
Related titles: Online - full text ed.: ISSN 1939-1528 (from ScienceDirect).
Indexed: A22, ASCA, CA, CurCont, E-psyche, FamI, P03, P30, P34, PsycInfo, PsycholAb, S02, S03, SCOPUS, SSCI, T02, V&AA, W07.
—BLDSC (6946.536170), CIS, IE, Infotrieve, Ingenta. **CCC.**
Published by: American Psychological Association, 750 First St, NE, Washington, DC 20002. TEL 202-336-5500, 800-374-2721, FAX 202-336-5997, journals@apa.org. Eds. Ronald Roesch, Mary-Grace Mendoza. Circ: 2,100.

150 AUS ISSN 1838-658X
▼ **PSYCHOLOGY RESEARCH.** Text in English. 2010. q. **Document type:** *Journal, Trade.*
Published by: St. Plum-Blossom Press Pty Ltd., 45 Centre Rd, Brighton E, VIC 3187, Australia. TEL 61-4-23370166, FAX 61-4-23370166.

150 USA ISSN 2159-5542
▼ **PSYCHOLOGY RESEARCH.** Text in English. 2011. m. **Document type:** *Journal, Academic/Scholarly.*
Related titles: Online - full text ed.: ISSN 2159-5550.
Published by: David Publishing Co., Inc., 1840 Industrial Dr, Ste 160, Libertyville, IL 60048. TEL 847-281-9822, FAX 847-281-9855, order@davidpublishing.com, http://www.davidpublishing.com.

150 GBR ISSN 1750-3469
PSYCHOLOGY REVIEW. Text in English. 1994. q. GBP 26.95 domestic; GBP 33 in Europe; GBP 38 elsewhere (effective 2010). adv. **Document type:** *Journal, Academic/Scholarly.* **Description:** Focuses on the core content of the AQA (A) specification, although the intention is to address topics that will still be relevant to centers following other specifications.
Former titles (until 2006): A Q A (A) Psychology Review (1746-6504); (until 2005): Psychology Review (1354-1129)
Related titles: Online - full text ed.: free to qualified personnel (effective 2010).
Indexed: E-psyche, G05, G06, G07, G08, I05, I07, S06, S23.
—BLDSC (6946.536375), IE, Ingenta. **CCC.**
Published by: Philip Allan Updates, Market Pl, Deddington, Banbury, Oxon OX15 0SE, United Kingdom. TEL 44-1869-338652, FAX 44-1869-337590, sales@philipallan.co.uk. **Subscr. to:** Turpin Distribution, Pegasus Dr, Stratton Business Park, Biggleswade, Bedfordshire SG18 8TQ, United Kingdom. TEL 44-1767-604974, FAX 44-845-0095840, custserv@turpin-distribution.com.

370.15 150 GBR ISSN 0965-948X
➤ **PSYCHOLOGY TEACHING REVIEW.** Abbreviated title: P T R. Text in English. 1992. a. free to members (effective 2009). back issues avail. **Document type:** *Journal, Academic/Scholarly.* **Description:** Focuses on research and theoretical issues surrounding the teaching of psychology whether in schools, colleges of further education, universities or elsewhere.
Related titles: Online - full text ed.: GBP 4.02 per issue to non-members; GBP 2.88 per issue to members (effective 2009).
Indexed: B29, ERA, P03, PsycInfo, R17, S21.
—IE, Ingenta.
Published by: The British Psychological Society, St Andrews House, 48 Princess Rd E, Leicester, LE1 7DR, United Kingdom. TEL 44-116-2549568, FAX 44-116-2271314, enquiries@bps.org.uk. Ed. Paul Sander.

150 USA ISSN 0033-3107
BF1 CODEN: PSTOAM
PSYCHOLOGY TODAY; for a healthier life. Text in English. 1967-1989 (Dec.); resumed 1991. bi-m. USD 15.97 domestic; USD 23.97 in Canada; USD 27.97 elsewhere (effective 2009). adv. bk.rev. bibl.; charts; illus.; stat. Index. reprints avail. **Document type:** *Magazine, Consumer.* **Description:** Provides a forum for popular psychology, primarily for laypersons. Explores the emotional, physical and spiritual aspects of daily life.
Incorporates (in 1969): Careers Today
Related titles: CD-ROM ed.; Microfiche ed.: (from NBI); Online - full text ed.
Indexed: A01, A02, A03, A08, A11, A12, A13, A17, A20, A21, A22, A25, A26, ABIn, ARG, AcaI, B01, B04, B05, B06, B07, B08, B09, BRD, BiolDig, C03, C05, C06, C07, C08, C12, CBCARef, CBPI, CBRI, CCR, CINAHL, CLFP, CPerI, Chicano, E-psyche, E08, ECER, F09, FutSurv, G05, G06, G07, G08, G10, GSS&RPL, H03, H04, H09, H11, H12, HECAB, HlthInd, I05, I06, I07, IPARL, M01, M02, M05, M06, MASUSE, MEA&I, MLA-IB, MagInd, MusicInd, P02, P10, P12, P13, P19, P24, P25, P26, P27, P30, P43, P47, P48, P51, P53, P54, PCI, PMR, PQC, PRA, PersLit, R03, R04, R05, R06, RASB, RGAb, RGPR, RI-1, RI-2, S02, S03, S05, S06, S08, S09, S23, SCOPUS, SSAI, SSAb, SSI, SportS, T02, TOM, U01, W01, W02, W03, W05, W09, WBA, WMB.
—BLDSC (6946.537000), IE, Infotrieve, Ingenta.
Published by: Sussex Publishers Inc., 115 E 23rd St, 9th Fl, New York, NY 10010. TEL 212-260-7210, FAX 212-260-7445. Ed. Kaja Perina. Adv. contact John Thomas. color page USD 20,055, B&W page USD 13,755; trim 8 x 10.5. Circ: 79,313. **Dist. in UK by:** Comag, Tavistock Rd, W Drayton, Middlesex UB7 7QE, United Kingdom.

150 NLD ISSN 0033-3115
DE PSYCHOLOOG. Text in Dutch. 1966. m. (11/yr.). EUR 61 domestic to individuals; EUR 91 foreign to individuals; EUR 115 domestic to institutions; EUR 132.95 foreign to institutions (effective 2008). adv. bk.rev. abstr.; bibl. index, cum.index. **Document type:** *Magazine, Academic/Scholarly.*
Indexed: A22, E-psyche, P03, PsycholAb, S02, S03.
—BLDSC (6946.539300), IE, Infotrieve, Ingenta.
Published by: (Nederlands Instituut van Psychologen/Netherlands Psychological Association), Koninklijke Van Gorcum BV/Royal Van Gorcum BV, PO Box 43, Assen, 9400 AA, Netherlands. TEL 31-592-379555, FAX 31-592-372064, info@vangorcum.nl, http://www.vangorcum.nl. adv.: B&W page EUR 1,290, color page EUR 2,990; trim 205 x 275. Circ: 14,500.

150 USA ISSN 0033-3123
BF1
➤ **PSYCHOMETRIKA.** Text in English. 1936. q. EUR 248, USD 308 combined subscription to institutions (print & online eds.) (effective 2012). adv. bk.rev. abstr.; bibl.; charts; illus. index. back issues avail.; reprint service avail. from PSC. **Document type:** *Journal, Academic/Scholarly.* **Description:** Features articles devoted to the advancement of theory and methodology for behavioral data in psychology, education and the social and behavioral sciences generally.
Related titles: Microform ed.: (from PQC); Online - full text ed.: ISSN 1860-0980 (from IngentaConnect).
Indexed: A12, A22, A26, ABIn, ASCA, B21, BibInd, CA, CCMJ, CDA, CIS, CMCI, CurCont, DIP, E-psyche, E01, E03, ERIC, ErgAb, FR, I05, IBR, IBZ, JCQM, MEA&I, MSN, MathR, NSA, P03, P20, P25, P30, P48, P51, P53, P54, PCI, PQC, PsycInfo, PsycholAb, RASB, S02, S03, SCI, SCOPUS, SSCI, ST&MA, T02, W07, Z02.
—BLDSC (6946.540000), GNLM, IE, Infotrieve, Ingenta, INIST. **CCC.**
Published by: (Psychometric Society), Springer New York LLC (Subsidiary of: Springer Science+Business Media), 233 Spring St, New York, NY 10013. TEL 212-460-1500, FAX 212-460-1575, service-ny@springer.com.

➤ **PSYCHOMUSICOLOGY**; a journal of music cognition. *see* MUSIC

150 USA ISSN 1069-9384
BF1 CODEN: PBUREN
➤ **PSYCHONOMIC BULLETIN & REVIEW.** Abbreviated title: P B & R. Text in English. 1964. bi-m. EUR 325, USD 367 combined subscription to institutions (print & online eds.) (effective 2012). adv. illus. Index. back issues avail.; reprint service avail. from PSC. **Document type:** *Journal, Academic/Scholarly.* **Description:** Features theoretical and review articles on topics in all areas of experimental psychology.
Formerly (until 1994): Psychonomic Society. Bulletin (0090-5054); Which superseded in part (in 1973): Psychonomic Science (0033-3131)
Related titles: Microform ed.: N.S. (from PQC); Online - full text ed.: ISSN 1531-5320 (from IngentaConnect).
Indexed: A01, A03, A08, A20, A22, ASCA, B21, B25, BIOSIS Prev, CA, CIS, CurCont, DIP, E-psyche, E01, EMBASE, ErgAb, ExcerpMed, FR, HEA, IBR, IBZ, IndMed, L&LBA, MEA&I, MEDLINE, MLA, MLA-IB, MycolAb, NSA, P02, P03, P10, P12, P20, P22, P25, P30, P48, P53, P54, PQC, PsycInfo, PsycholAb, R10, RILM, Reac, SCOPUS, SOPODA, SSCI, SociolAb, T02, W07.
—BLDSC (6946.540550), CASDDS, GNLM, IE, Infotrieve, Ingenta, INIST, Linda Hall. **CCC.**
Published by: Springer New York LLC (Subsidiary of: Springer Science+Business Media), 233 Spring St, New York, NY 10013. TEL 212-460-1500, FAX 212-460-1575, journals-ny@springer.com. Ed. Robert M Nosofsky. Circ: 2,400.

612.8 DEU ISSN 1430-8169
PSYCHOPHYSIOLOGIE IN LABOR UND FELD. Text in German. 1996. irreg., latest vol.15, 2006. price varies. **Document type:** *Monographic series, Academic/Scholarly.*
Published by: Peter Lang GmbH (Subsidiary of: Peter Lang Publishing Group), Eschborner Landstr 42-50, Frankfurt Am Main, 60489, Germany. TEL 49-69-7807050, FAX 49-69-78070550, zentrale.frankfurt@peterlang.com, http://www.peterlang.com. Eds. Jochen Fahrenberg, Michael Myrtek.

158 AUT ISSN 1434-1883
RC321
➤ **PSYCHOPRAXIS**; Zeitschrift fuer praktische Psychiatrie und Grenzgebiete. Text in German. 1998. bi-m. EUR 71, USD 93 combined subscription to institutions (print & online eds.) (effective 2012). adv. back issues avail.; reprint service avail. from PSC. **Document type:** *Journal, Academic/Scholarly.*
Related titles: Online - full text ed.: ISSN 1613-7590.
Indexed: A22, A26, E-psyche, E01.
—IE. **CCC.**
Published by: Springer Wien (Subsidiary of: Springer Science+Business Media), Sachsenplatz 4-6, Vienna, W 1201, Austria. TEL 43-1-33024150, FAX 43-1-3302426, journals@springer.at, http://www.springer.at. Ed. Hans Zapotoczky. Adv. contact Gabriele Popernitsch. color page EUR 3,130; trim 210 x 297. Circ: 6,783 (paid). **Subscr. in the Americas to:** Springer New York LLC, Journal Fulfillment, PO Box 2485, Secaucus, NJ 07096. TEL 800-777-4643, 201-348-4033, FAX 201-348-4505, journals-ny@springer.com, http://www.springer.com; **Subscr. to:** Springer Distribution Center, Kundenservice Zeitschriften, Haberstr 7, Heidelberg 69126, Germany. TEL 49-6221-3454303, FAX 49-6221-3454229, subscriptions@springer.com.

301.1 150 CHE ISSN 1420-620X
PSYCHOSCOPE. Text in French, German. 1980. 10/yr. CHF 85; CHF 48 to students (effective 2007). adv. bk.rev. **Document type:** *Journal, Trade.*
Formerly (until 1991): Schweizer Psychologen. Bulletin (1013-5987)
Indexed: E-psyche.
Published by: Foederation der Schweizer Psychologen, Choisystr 11, Bern 14, 3000, Switzerland. TEL 41-31-3888800, FAX 41-31-3888801, fsp@psychologie.ch. Eds. Annett Jucker, Vadim Frosio. adv.: page CHF 1,800; trim 190 x 276. Circ: 6,300 (paid and controlled).

616.890 152.4 CHE ISSN 1680-1970
HM1001
PSYCHOSOCIAL NOTEBOOK. Text in English. 2000. irreg., latest 2004. USD 25 per issue (effective 2004). **Document type:** *Monographic series, Academic/Scholarly.*
Published by: International Organization for Migration/Organizacion Internacional para las Migraciones, 17 Rte des Morillons, Geneva 19, 1211, Switzerland. TEL 41-22-7179111, FAX 41-22-7986150, publications@iom.int, http://www.iom.int.

301.1 150 DEU ISSN 0171-3434
RC475
PSYCHOSOZIAL; Zeitschrift fuer Analyse, Praevention und Therapie psychosozialer Konflikte und Krankheiten. Text in German. 1978. q. EUR 16 newsstand/cover (effective 2003). adv. bk.rev. **Document type:** *Journal, Academic/Scholarly.*
Indexed: A22, DIP, E-psyche, IBR, IBZ.
—GNLM, IE, Infotrieve.
Published by: Psychosozial Verlag, Walltorstr 10, Giessen, 35390, Germany. TEL 49-641-77819, FAX 49-641-77742, info@psychosozial-verlag.de, http://www.psychosozial-verlag.de. Ed. Hans-Juergen Wirth. Pub. Hans Juergen Wirth. R&P Stephan Vogel. Circ: 4,500.

PSYCHOTERAPIA. *see* MEDICAL SCIENCES—Psychiatry And Neurology

PSYCHOTHERAPEUT; Fachzeitschrift fuer Aerzte und Psychologen in der Praxis und Klinik. *see* MEDICAL SCIENCES—Psychiatry And Neurology

150.19 DEU ISSN 1611-0773
PSYCHOTHERAPEUTENJOURNAL. Text in German. 2002. 4/yr. EUR 72 domestic; EUR 75 foreign; EUR 43 to students; EUR 20 newsstand/cover (effective 2011). adv. **Document type:** *Journal, Academic/Scholarly.*
Published by: (Bundespsychotherapeutenkammer), Verlagsgruppe Huethig Jehle Rehm GmbH (Subsidiary of: Sueddeutscher Verlag GmbH), Emmy-Noether-Str 2, Munich, 80992, Germany. TEL 49-89-5485206, FAX 49-89-548528230, info@hjr-verlag.de, http://www.huethig-jehle-rehm.de. Ed. Karin Welsch. Adv. contact Claudia Kampmann-Schroeder. Circ: 37,290 (paid and controlled).

616.89 AUT ISSN 0943-1950
RC475 CODEN: PSFOEO
➤ **PSYCHOTHERAPIE FORUM.** Text in German. 1993. q. EUR 82, USD 90 combined subscription to institutions (print & online eds.) (effective 2010). adv. back issues avail.; reprint service avail. from PSC. **Document type:** *Journal, Academic/Scholarly.*
Related titles: Online - full text ed.: ISSN 1613-7604 (from IngentaConnect).
Indexed: A22, A26, DIP, E-psyche, E01, IBR, IBZ, P03, PsycInfo.
—GNLM, IE. **CCC.**
Published by: Springer Wien (Subsidiary of: Springer Science+Business Media), Sachsenplatz 4-6, Vienna, W 1201, Austria. TEL 43-1-33024150, FAX 43-1-3302426, journals@springer.at, http://www.springer.at. Ed. O Frischenschlager. Adv. contact Elise Haidenthaller. color page EUR 3,130; trim 210 x 297. Circ: 6,000 (paid). **Subscr. in the Americas to:** Springer New York LLC, Journal Fulfillment, PO Box 2485, Secaucus, NJ 07096. TEL 800-777-4643, 201-348-4033, FAX 201-348-4505, journals-ny@springer.com, http://www.springer.com; **Subscr. to:** Springer Distribution Center, Kundenservice Zeitschriften, Haberstr 7, Heidelberg 69126, Germany. TEL 49-6221-3454303, FAX 49-6221-3454229, subscriptions@springer.com.

616.89 DEU ISSN 1860-0271
PSYCHOTHERAPIE UND SEELSORGE; Magazin fuer Psychotherapie und Seelsorge. Text in German. 2005. 4/yr. EUR 32; EUR 9.90 newsstand/cover (effective 2011). adv. **Document type:** *Journal, Academic/Scholarly.*
Indexed: IBR, IBZ.
Published by: Bundes Verlag GmbH, Bodenborn 43, Witten, 58452, Germany. TEL 49-2302-930930, FAX 49-2302-93093689, info@bundes-verlag.de, http://www.bundes-verlag.de. Ed. Hanna Schott. Adv. contact Thilo Cunz. Circ: 5,000 (paid).

616.8914 302 DEU ISSN 1436-4638
PSYCHOTHERAPIE UND SOZIALWISSENSCHAFT; Zeitschrift fuer Qualitative Forschung. Text in English, German. 1999. s-a. EUR 22.90 per vol. (effective 2009). adv. **Document type:** *Journal, Academic/Scholarly.*
Indexed: DIP, IBR, IBSS, IBZ, P03, PsycInfo, PsycholAb.
Published by: Psychosozial Verlag, Walltorstr 10, Giessen, 35390, Germany. TEL 49-641-9699780, FAX 49-641-96997819, info@psychosozial-verlag.de, http://www.psychosozial-verlag.de. Ed. Ulrich Streeck. adv.: B&W page EUR 400. Circ: 900 (paid and controlled).

616.89 CHE ISSN 0251-737X
CODEN: PSYTEW
PSYCHOTHERAPIES. Text in French. 1981. q. CHF 120 to individuals; CHF 185 to institutions; CHF 85 to students (effective 2007). adv. bk.rev. back issues avail.; reprints avail. **Document type:** *Journal, Academic/Scholarly.*
Related titles: Online - full text ed.
Indexed: A22, E-psyche, EMBASE, ExcerpMed, FR, INI, P03, P25, P48, PQC, PsycInfo, PsycholAb, R10, Reac, SCOPUS.
—BLDSC (6946.558400), GNLM, IE, Infotrieve, Ingenta, INIST. **CCC.**

P

Published by: Editions Medecine et Hygiene, Chemin de la Mousse 46, CP 475, Chene-Bourg 4, 1225, Switzerland. TEL 41-22-7029311, FAX 41-22-7029355, abonnements@medhyg.ch, http://www.medhyg.ch. Circ: 900.

616.890 DEU

▼ **PSYCHOTHERAPIEWISSENSCHAFT IN FORSCHUNG, PROFESSION UND KULTUR.** Text in German. 2011. irreg. price varies. **Document type:** *Monographic series, Academic/Scholarly.*
Published by: Waxmann Verlag GmbH, Steinfurter Str 555, Muenster, 48159, Germany. TEL 49-251-265040, FAX 49-251-2650426, info@waxmann.com. Ed. Bernd Rieken.

616.89 USA ISSN 0033-3204
RC475 CODEN: PSYOAD

➤ **PSYCHOTHERAPY**; theory, research, practice, training. Text in English. 1963. q. USD 128 domestic to individuals; USD 155 foreign to individuals; USD 363 domestic to institutions; USD 408 foreign to institutions (effective 2011). adv. bk.rev. charts. index. back issues avail.; reprint service avail. from PSC. **Document type:** *Journal, Academic/Scholarly.* **Description:** Offers a wide variety of articles relevant to the field of psychotherapy, both theoretical contributions and research studies.
Related titles: Online - full text ed.: ISSN 1939-1536 (from ScienceDirect).
Indexed: A20, A22, AMHA, ASCA, ASSIA, C06, C07, CIN, ChemAb, CurCont, E-psyche, EMBASE, ExcerpMed, F09, FamI, MEDLINE, MLA-IB, P03, P30, PsycInfo, PsycholAb, R10, Reac, S02, S03, SCOPUS, SSCI, W07.
—BLDSC (6946.558530), GNLM, IE, Infotrieve, Ingenta. **CCC.**
Published by: American Psychological Association, 750 First St, NE, Washington, DC 20002. TEL 202-336-5500, 800-374-2721, journals@apa.org. Ed. Mark J Hilsenroth. Adv. contact Doug Constant TEL 202-336-5574. Circ: 3,200 (controlled).

150 USA ISSN 0163-1543
RC475 CODEN: TOLED5

PSYCHOTHERAPY FINANCES. Text in English. 1974. m. USD 79 (effective 2008). bk.rev.
Formerly (until 1977): Psychotherapy Economics (0092-184X)
Indexed: C33, CA, E-psyche, S02, S03, SWR&A, T02.
Published by: Ridgewood Financial Institute, Inc., 14255 US Hwy 1, Suite 286, Juno Beach, FL 33408. TEL 800-869-8450, FAX 561-743-3504. Ed. John Klein. Pub. Herbert E Klein. Circ: 7,000.

616.89156 USA ISSN 1535-573X
RC488.5

PSYCHOTHERAPY NETWORKER; the magazine for today's helping professional. Text in English. 197?. bi-m. USD 18 domestic; USD 24 foreign (effective 2010). adv. bk.rev. illus. back issues avail.; reprints avail. **Document type:** *Magazine, Trade.* **Description:** Designed for social workers, psychologists, therapists and educators.
Formerly (until Mar.2001): Family Therapy Networker (0739-0882); (until 1982): Family Therapy Network Newsletter; (until 197?): Family Therapy Practice Network Newsletter; Family Shtick
Related titles: Online - full text ed.
Indexed: A22, APW, E-psyche, MLA-IB, P10, P12, P27, P48, P53, P54, PQC, S02, S03, SFSA, SWR&A, T02.
—BLDSC (6946.559180), IE, Ingenta.
Published by: Family Therapy Network, Inc., 5135 MacArthur Blvd NW, Washington, DC 20016. TEL 202-537-8950, 888-408-2452, FAX 202-537-6869, http://www.psychotherapynetworker.org/. Ed. Richard Simon. Adv. contact Mike McKenna. B&W page USD 2,555, color page USD 3,375; trim 8.375 x 10.675. Circ: 55,000.

616.89 GBR ISSN 1050-3307
RC475 CODEN: PRSECG

➤ **PSYCHOTHERAPY RESEARCH.** Text in English. 1991. bi-m. GBP 311 combined subscription in United Kingdom to institutions (print & online eds.); EUR 410, USD 517 combined subscription to institutions (print & online eds.) (effective 2012). adv. back issues avail.; reprint service avail. from PSC. **Document type:** *Journal, Academic/Scholarly.* **Description:** Seeks to enhance the development, scientific quality, and social relevance of psychotherapy research and to foster the use of research findings in practice, education, and policy formulation.
Related titles: Online - full text ed.: ISSN 1468-4381. GBP 280 in United Kingdom to institutions; EUR 369, USD 465 to institutions (effective 2012) (from IngentaConnect).
Indexed: A01, A03, A08, A20, A22, ASCA, CA, CurCont, E-psyche, E01, EMBASE, ExcerpMed, FamI, MEDLINE, P03, P25, P26, P30, P48, P54, PQC, PsycInfo, PsycholAb, R10, Reac, SCOPUS, SSCI, T02, W07.
—GNLM, IE, Infotrieve, Ingenta. **CCC.**
Published by: (Society for Psychotherapy Research USA), Routledge (Subsidiary of: Taylor & Francis Group), 4 Park Sq, Milton Park, Abingdon, Oxon OX14 4RN, United Kingdom. TEL 44-20-70176000, FAX 44-20-70176336, subscriptions@tandf.co.uk, http://www.routledge.com. Eds. Clara E Hill, Paulo P P. Machado. Adv. contact Linda Hann TEL 44-1344-779945. **Subscr. in N America to:** Taylor & Francis Inc., Customer Services Dept, 325 Chestnut St, 8th Fl, Philadelphia, PA 19106. TEL 215-625-8900, 800-354-1420, FAX 215-625-2940, customerservice@taylorandfrancis.com; **Subscr. outside N America to:** Taylor & Francis Ltd., Journals Customer Service, Sheepen Pl, Colchester, Essex CO3 3LP, United Kingdom. TEL 44-20-70175544, FAX 44-20-70175198, tf.enquiries@tfinforma.com.

150 GBR ISSN 1747-1761

PSYCHOTHERAPY SECTION REVIEW. Text in English. 2005. s-a. GBP 2.82 per issue (effective 2009). **Document type:** *Journal, Academic/Scholarly.* **Description:** Provides a forum within the Society for psychologists and others who share an interest in psychotherapeutic psychology.
Formerly (until 2005): British Psychological Society. Psychotherapy Section. Newsletter (0965-5662)
—BLDSC (6946.559480).
Published by: The British Psychotherapy Society, Psychotherapy Section, St Andrews House, 48 Princess Rd East, Leics, LE1 7DR, United Kingdom. TEL 44-116-2549568, FAX 44-116-2271314, enquiry@bps.org.uk. Ed. Adrian Hemmings.

150 BEL ISSN 1245-2092

➤ **PSYCHOTROPES**; revue internationale des toxicomanies et des addictions. Text in French. q. EUR 85 (effective 2011). bk.rev. abstr.; bibl. 128 p./no.; back issues avail. **Document type:** *Journal, Academic/Scholarly.*
Related titles: Online - full text ed.: ISSN 1782-1487.
Indexed: DIP, E-psyche, EMBASE, ExcerpMed, IBR, IBZ, SSA, SociolAb.
—BLDSC (6946.559532).
Published by: De Boeck Universite (Subsidiary of: Editis), Fond Jean-Paques 4, Louvain-la-Neuve, 1348, Belgium. TEL 32-10-482511, FAX 32-10-482519, info@superieur.deboeck.com.

150 363.7 ESP ISSN 2171-1976

PSYECOLOGY; revista bilingue de psicologia ambiental - bilingual journal of environmental psychology. Text in English, Spanish. 2000. 3/yr. **Document type:** *Journal, Academic/Scholarly.*
Formerly (until 2009): Medio Ambiente y Comportamiento Humano (1576-6462)
Related titles: Online - full text ed.: ISSN 1989-9386. free (effective 2011).
Published by: Fundacion Infancia y Aprendizaje, Naranjo de Bulnes 69, Ciudalcampo, San Sebastian de los Reyes, Madrid, 28707, Spain. fundacion@fia.es, http://www.fia.es/.

150 DNK ISSN 0107-1211

PSYKE & LOGOS. Text in Danish; Abstracts in English. 1980. 2/yr. DKK 325 (effective 2008). bk.rev. cum index:1989-2003. 400 p./no.; back issues avail. **Document type:** *Monographic series, Academic/Scholarly.*
Indexed: E-psyche, P03, PsycInfo, PsycholAb, RILM.
—BLDSC (6946.559790), IE, Ingenta.
Published by: Dansk Psykologisk Forlag/Danish Psychological Publishers, Kongevejen 155, Virum, 2830, Denmark. TEL 45-35-381655, FAX 45-35-381665, info@dpf.dk. Eds. Bo Moehl, Jan Toennesvang, Peter Berliner.

616.89 362.2 SWE ISSN 0033-3212

PSYKISK HAELSA/MENTAL HEALTH. Text in Swedish. 1960. q. SEK 300, SEK 200 to members (effective 2004). bk.rev. **Document type:** *Academic/Scholarly.*
Indexed: E-psyche, PsycholAb, S02, S03.
Published by: Svenska Foereningen foer Psykisk Haelsa/Swedish Association for Mental Health, Saltmaetargatan 5 2, PO Box 3445, Stockholm, 10369, Sweden. TEL 46-8-347065, FAX 46-8-328875, info@sfph.se. Ed. Eggert Nielsen. Circ: 6,000.

150 SWE ISSN 1650-7398

➤ **PSYKOANALYTISK TID/SKRIFT.** Text in Swedish. 2002. q. SEK 300 (effective 2005). back issues avail. **Document type:** *Journal, Academic/Scholarly.*
Published by: Freudianska Foereningen, Stora Nygatan 13, Goeteborg, 41108, Sweden. TEL 46-31-155470, info@freudianska.org. Ed., Pub. Per Magnus Johansson.

150 DNK ISSN 0901-7089

PSYKOLOG NYT. Text in Danish. 1947. 23/yr. DKK 1,150 (effective 2009). adv. bk.rev. tr.lit. cum.index: 1997-2002. **Document type:** *Bulletin, Trade.*
Formerly (until 1986): Dansk Psykolog Nyt (0011-6432)
Related titles: Online - full text ed.
Indexed: E-psyche, PsycholAb.
Published by: Dansk Psykolog Forening/Danish Psychological Association, Stockholmgade 27, Copenhagen OE, 2100, Denmark. TEL 45-35-269955, FAX 45-35-259737, dp@dp.dk. Eds. Joergen Carl, Arne Groenborg Johansen. adv.: color page DKK 11,570; 237 x 176. Circ: 8,169 (controlled).

150 305.4 DNK ISSN 1603-9203

PSYKOLOGI; indsigt, mentalt velvaere, personlig udvikling. Text in Danish. 2004. 8/yr. DKK 395 (effective 2008). **Document type:** *Magazine, Consumer.*
Related titles: Online - full text ed.
Published by: Aller Media A/S, Havneholmen 33, Copenhagen V, 1561, Denmark. TEL 45-72-342000, FAX 45-72-342003, info@aller.dk, http://www.aller.dk. Ed. Camilla Lindeman. Adv. contact Alice Ferdman. Circ: 20,561.

150 FIN ISSN 1456-7768

PSYKOLOGI. Text in Finnish. 1973. 8/yr. EUR 35 domestic; EUR 45 elsewhere (effective 2007). adv. **Document type:** *Magazine, Trade.*
Former titles (until 1999): Psykologiuutiset (0357-1467); (until 1976): Suomen Psykologiliitto ry. Jasentiedote
Published by: Suomen Psykologiliitto/Finnish Psychological Association, Bulevardi 30 B 3, Helsinki, 00120, Finland. TEL 358-9-61229122, FAX 358-9-61229161, http://www.psyli.fi. Ed. Riitta Elf. Adv. contact Riitta Malmstroem.

150 FIN ISSN 0355-1067

PSYKOLOGIA. Text in Finnish; Summaries in English. 1966. bi-m. EUR 45 domestic; EUR 50 foreign; EUR 20 to students (effective 2005). adv. back issues avail. **Document type:** *Magazine, Academic/Scholarly.*
Indexed: A22, P03, PsycInfo, PsycholAb, S02, S03.
—BLDSC (6946.559900), IE, Ingenta.
Published by: Suomen Psykologinen Seura/Finnish Psychological Society, Liisankatu 16 A, Helsinki, 00170, Finland. TEL 358-9-2782122, FAX 358-9-2781300. Ed. Jukka Tontti. adv.: page EUR 420. Circ: 3,000.

150 DNK ISSN 0906-2483

PSYKOLOGISK SET. Text in Danish. 1982. q. DKK 310 to individuals; DKK 440 to institutions; DKK 238 to students; DKK 95 per issue (effective 2008). bk.rev. illus. back issues avail. **Document type:** *Journal, Academic/Scholarly.*
Formerly (until 1991): Psykologi (0107-8755)
Indexed: E-psyche, PsycholAb.
Published by: Frydenlund, Hyskenstraede 10, Copenhagen K, 1207, Denmark. TEL 45-33-932422, FAX 45-33-932412, post@frydenlund.dk, http://www.frydenlund.dk. Eds. Pernille Stroebaek, Allan Westerling.

150 NOR ISSN 1501-7508

PSYKOLOGISK TIDSSKRIFT. Text in Norwegian. 1997. 3/yr. NOK 130; NOK 45 per issue (effective 2011). bk.rev. back issues avail. **Document type:** *Magazine, Academic/Scholarly.*
Published by: Norges Teknisk-Naturvitenskapelige Universitet, Psykologisk Institutt/Norwegian University of Science and Technology, Department of Psychology, Dragvoll, Trondheim, 7491, Norway. TEL 47-48-106548, psykologi@svt.ntnu.no, http://www.ntnu.no/psykologi. Ed. Cecilie Liseth.

150 SWE ISSN 0280-9702

PSYKOLOGTIDNINGEN. Text in Swedish. 1954. 10/yr. SEK 600 domestic; SEK 700 foreign; SEK 60 per issue (effective 2011). adv. bk.rev. charts; illus. **Document type:** *Magazine, Trade.*
Former titles (until 1983): Psykolognytt/Psychologist News (0033-3220); (until 1959): Meddelanden fraan Sveriges Psykologfoerbund
Related titles: Online - full text ed.: 2003.
Published by: Sveriges Psykologfoerbund/Swedish Psychological Association, PO Box 3287, Stockholm, 10365, Sweden. TEL 46-8-56706400, FAX 46-8-56706490, post@psykologforbundet.se. Ed., Pub. Eva Brita Jaernefors TEL 46-8-56706457. Adv. contact Niklas Nilsson TEL 46-8-58786531. Circ: 10,400.

150 CAN ISSN 1187-1180

PSYNOPSIS. Text in French, English. q. USD 21.40 domestic; USD 30 foreign (effective 2006). adv. **Document type:** *Newspaper, Trade.*
Formerly (until 1990): Canadian Psychological Association. Highlights (0834-2261)
Indexed: A01, C03, C04, CBCARef, P48, PQC.
—CCC.
Published by: Canadian Psychological Association, 141 Laurier Ave W, Ste 702, Ottawa, ON K1P 5J3, Canada. TEL 613-237-2144, FAX 613-237-1674, cpa@cpa.ca. adv.: B&W page USD 1,150, color page USD 2,195; 10 x 16. Circ: 5,800 (paid).

150 HUN ISSN 0230-0508
BF8.H8

➤ **PSZICHOLOGIA/PSYCHOLOGY.** Text in Hungarian. 1981. q. EUR 122, USD 168 combined subscription (print & online eds.) (effective 2011). **Document type:** *Journal, Academic/Scholarly.* **Description:** Offers a scientific forum for basic research in psychology and its related applications.
Related titles: Online - full content ed.: EUR 104, USD 143 (effective 2011).
Indexed: P03, PsycInfo, PsycholAb.
Published by: (Magyar Tudomanyos Akademia, Pszichologiai Kutatointezete/Hungarian Academy of Sciences, Institute of Psychology), Akademiai Kiado Rt. (Subsidiary of: Wolters Kluwer N.V.), Prielle Kornelia u 19/D, Budapest, 1117, Hungary. TEL 36-1-4648222, FAX 36-1-4648221, journals@akkrt.hu. Ed. Bea Ehmann.

150 HUN ISSN 0079-7464

PSZICHOLOGIAI TANULMANYOK/PSYCHOLOGICAL STUDIES. Text in Hungarian; Summaries in English, German. 1958. irreg., latest vol.20, 2005. price varies. back issues avail. **Document type:** *Monographic series, Academic/Scholarly.*
Indexed: E-psyche, PsycholAb, RASB, S02, S03.
Published by: Akademiai Kiado Rt. (Subsidiary of: Wolters Kluwer N.V.), Prielle Kornelia u 19/D, Budapest, 1117, Hungary. TEL 36-1-4648222, FAX 36-1-4648221, journals@akkrt.hu, http://www.akademiai.com.

PULSE OF THE PLANET. *see* ENVIRONMENTAL STUDIES

150 BRA ISSN 1517-5316

PULSIONAL REVISTA DE PSICANALISE. Text in Portuguese. 1998. q. BRL 130 (effective 2007). **Document type:** *Journal, Academic/Scholarly.*
Indexed: C01.
Published by: Editora Escuta, Rua Dr. Homen de Melo 446, Sao Paulo, SP, Brazil. TEL 55-11-38658950, FAX 55-11-36751190, pulsional@uol.com.br. Ed. Manoel Tosta Berlink.

PURE POWER; when training + science = peak performance. *see* PHYSICAL FITNESS AND HYGIENE

150 GBR ISSN 2044-0820

Q M I P BULLETIN. (Qualitative Methods in Psychology) Text in English. 2006. s-a. GBP 2.30 per issue to non-members; free to members (effective 2011). back issues avail. **Document type:** *Bulletin, Trade.* **Description:** Includes events, reviews of qualitative psychologist conferences, stories of new initiatives for raising the profile of qualitative methods, research reports and book reviews.
Formerly (until 2010): Q M i P Newsletter (1751-2662)
Published by: The British Psychological Society, St Andrews House, 48 Princess Rd E, Leicester, LE1 7DR, United Kingdom. TEL 44-116-2549568, FAX 44-116-2271314, enquiries@bps.org.uk.

150 ITA ISSN 1121-0737

QUADERNI DI GESTALT. Text in Multiple languages. 1985. s-a. **Document type:** *Journal, Academic/Scholarly.*
Related titles: Online - full text ed.: ISSN 2035-6994.
Published by: Franco Angeli Edizioni, Viale Monza 106, Milan, 20127, Italy. TEL 39-02-2837141, FAX 39-02-26144793, redazioni@francoangeli.it, http://www.francoangeli.it.

150 ITA ISSN 1592-8535

QUADERNI DI PSICOLOGIA, ANALISI TRANSAZIONALE E SCIENZE UMANE. Text in Multiple languages. 1990. 3/yr. **Document type:** *Monographic series, Academic/Scholarly.*
Formerly (until 1996): Centro di Psicologia e Analisi Transazionale. Quaderni (1592-8969)
Published by: Mimesis Edizioni, Via Risorgimento 33, Sesto San Giovanni, MI 20099, Italy. http://www.mimesisedizioni.it.

150 USA ISSN 0033-5010
BF173.A2

QUADRANT. Text in English. 1967. s-a. USD 32 (effective 2011). adv. bk.rev. charts; illus. back issues avail.; reprints avail. **Document type:** *Journal, Academic/Scholarly.* **Description:** Contains articles and reviews on analytical psychology and related subjects.
Formerly: Journal of Contemporary Jungian Thought
Related titles: Online - full text ed.
Indexed: E-psyche, MLA, PsycholAb.
—Ingenta.
Published by: C.G. Jung Foundation for Analytical Psychology, Inc., 28 E 39th St, New York, NY 10016. TEL 212-697-6430, FAX 212-953-3989, info@cgjungny.org. Ed. Kathryn Madden.

150 ITA ISSN 1972-2338

QUALE PSICOLOGIA. Text in Multiple languages. 1992. s-a. **Document type:** *Journal, Academic/Scholarly.*
Published by: Istituto per lo Studio delle Psicoterapie (I S P), Via Tuscia 25, Rome, 00191, Italy. TEL 39-06-3294350, FAX 39-06-36303637, i.psicoterapie@tiscalinet.it, http://www.istitutopsicoterapie.it.

150 GBR ISSN 1478-0887
BF1.A4
QUALITATIVE RESEARCH IN PSYCHOLOGY. Text in English. 2004. q. GBP 234 combined subscription in United Kingdom to institutions (print & online eds.); EUR 310, USD 388 combined subscription to institutions (print & online eds.) (effective 2012). adv. back issues avail.; reprint service avail. from PSC. **Document type:** *Journal, Academic/Scholarly.* **Description:** Dedicated to exploring and expanding the territory of qualitative psychological research, strengthening its identity within the international research community and defining its place within the undergraduate and graduate curriculum.
Related titles: Online - full text ed.: ISSN 1478-0895. GBP 211 in United Kingdom to institutions; EUR 279, USD 349 to institutions (effective 2012) (from IngentaConnect).
Indexed: A01, A22, CA, E01, P03, P10, P12, P25, P48, P53, P54, PQC, PsycInfo, SCOPUS, T02.
—BLDSC (7168.124410), IE, Ingenta. **CCC.**
Published by: Routledge (Subsidiary of: Taylor & Francis Group), 4 Park Sq, Milton Park, Abingdon, Oxon OX14 4RN, United Kingdom. TEL 44-20-70176000, FAX 44-20-70176336, subscriptions@tandf.co.uk, http://www.routledge.com. Eds. Brendan Gough, David E A Giles, Martin Packer. **Subscr. to:** Taylor & Francis Ltd., Journals Customer Service, Sheepen Pl, Colchester, Essex CO3 3LP, United Kingdom. TEL 44-20-70175544, FAX 44-20-70175198, tf.enquiries@tfinforma.com.

150 GBR ISSN 1747-0218
BF180
➤ **THE QUARTERLY JOURNAL OF EXPERIMENTAL PSYCHOLOGY.** Abbreviated title: Q J E P. Text in English. 2006. m. GBP 850 combined subscription in United Kingdom to institutions (print & online eds.); EUR 1,358, USD 1,698 combined subscription to institutions (print & online eds.) (effective 2012). adv. reprint service avail. from PSC. **Document type:** *Journal, Academic/Scholarly.* **Description:** Features original articles on any topic within the field of experimental psychology and covers the areas of learning, memory, motivation and cognitive processes in both non-human and human animals.
Formed by the merger of (1981-2005): Quarterly Journal of Experimental Psychology. Section A: Human Experimental Psychology (0272-4987); (1981-2005): Quarterly Journal of Experimental Psychology. Section B: Comparative and Physiological Psychology (0272-4995); Both of which superseded in part (in 1981): Quarterly Journal of Experimental Psychology (0033-555X)
Related titles: Online - full text ed.: ISSN 1747-0226. GBP 765 in United Kingdom to institutions; EUR 1,223, USD 1,528 to institutions (effective 2012).
Indexed: A01, A02, A03, A08, A20, A22, A26, B01, B04, B06, B07, B09, B21, B25, BIOSIS Prev, BRD, CA, CurCont, E01, E08, EMBASE, ExcerpMed, G08, H12, I05, IBR, IBZ, L&LBA, L11, MEDLINE, MycolAb, NSA, NSCI, P03, P30, P43, PsycInfo, PsycholAb, R10, Reac, S02, S03, S09, SCI, SCOPUS, SSAI, SSAb, SSCI, SSI, T02, W03, W07.
—IE, Ingenta, INIST. **CCC.**
Published by: (The Experimental Psychology Society), Psychology Press (Subsidiary of: Taylor & Francis Ltd.), 27 Church Rd, Hove, E Sussex BN3 2FA, United Kingdom. TEL 44-20-70176000, FAX 44-20-70176717, info@psypress.co.uk, http://www.psypress.com. Eds. A Mike Burton, Simon Killcross. Adv. contact Linda Hann TEL 44-1344-779945.

158 NLD ISSN 2210-2094
▼ **QUEST PSYCHOLOGIE.** Text in Dutch. 2010. q. EUR 25 (effective 2011). **Document type:** *Magazine, Consumer.*
Published by: G + J/R B A Publishing BV (Subsidiary of: Gruner + Jahr AG & Co), Gebouw Stede, Dalsteindreef 82 t/m 92, Diemen, 1112 XC, Netherlands. TEL 31-20-7943500, FAX 31-20-7943501, info@genj.nl, http://www.genj.nl.

158 FRA ISSN 1777-6988
QUESTION PSYCHO. Text in French. 2005. q. EUR 32 for 2 yrs. (effective 2010). **Document type:** *Magazine, Consumer.*
Published by: Lafont Presse, 53 Rue du Chemin Vert, Boulogne-Billancourt, 92100, France. TEL 33-1-46102121, FAX 33-1-45792211.

QUESTIONS D'ADOS. *see* CHILDREN AND YOUTH—About

152.4 BRA ISSN 1676-8965
R B S E. REVISTA BRASILEIRA DE SOCIOLOGIA DA EMOCAO. Text in Portuguese. 2002. 3/yr. back issues avail. **Document type:** *Journal, Academic/Scholarly.*
Media: Online - full text.
Indexed: SCOPUS, SociolAb.
Published by: Universidade Federal da Paraiba, Grupo de Pesquisa em Antropologia e Sociologia das Emocoes, Caixa Postal 5144, Joao Pessoa, Paraiba 58051-900, Brazil. grem@cchla.ufpb.br, http://www.cchla.ufpb.br/grem/Index.html. Ed. Mauro Guilheme Pinheiro.

R O S - INFO. (Raadgivning om Spiseforstyrrelser) *see* MEDICAL SCIENCES—Psychiatry And Neurology

301.1 150 ITA ISSN 1125-5196
RASSEGNA DI PSICOLOGIA. Text in Italian. 1984. 3/yr. EUR 41.50 domestic; EUR 63.50 foreign (effective 2008). **Document type:** *Journal, Academic/Scholarly.*
Related titles: Online - full text ed.: ISSN 1974-4854.
Indexed: E-psyche, IBR, IBZ, P03, PsycInfo, PsycholAb, S02, S03.
Published by: (Universita degli Studi di Roma "La Sapienza", Dipartimenti di Psicologia e Psicologia dei Processi di Sviluppo e Socializzazione), Carocci Editore, Via Sardegna 50, Rome, 00187, Italy. TEL 39-06-42818417, FAX 39-06-42747931, clienti@carocci.it, http://www.carocci.it. Ed. Clotilde Pontecorvo Piperno.

150.19 USA ISSN 1559-5145
BF173.A2
➤ **(RE)-TURN**; a journal of Lacanian studies. Text in English. 2003 (Win.). a. free to members (effective 2010). back issues avail. **Document type:** *Journal, Academic/Scholarly.* **Description:** Explores the theories of French psychoanalyst, Jacques Lacan, within the context of a variety of fields, including clinical psychoanalysis, philosophy, critical studies, theatre, politics, music, visual arts, mass media, communications, religion, and literature.
Related titles: Online - full text ed.
Indexed: A01.
Published by: University of Missouri Press, 2910 LeMone Blvd, Columbia, MO 65201. TEL 573-882-7641, FAX 573-884-4498, upress@umsystem.edu, http://press.umsystem.edu/. Ed. Ellie Ragland.

➤ **READING AND WRITING**; an interdisciplinary journal. *see* LINGUISTICS

➤ **READING PSYCHOLOGY**; an international quarterly. *see* EDUCATION

150.19 FRA ISSN 1767-5448
RECHERCHES EN PSYCHANALYSE. Text in French. 2004. s-a. back issues avail. **Document type:** *Journal, Academic/Scholarly.*
Related titles: Online - full text ed.: ISSN 1965-0213.
Indexed: P03.
Published by: (Universite de Paris VII, Ecole Doctorale), Editions L' Esprit du Temps, 115 Rue Anatole France, B P 107, Le Bouscat, 33491 Cedex, France. TEL 33-5-56028419, FAX 33-5-56029131, info@lespritdutemps.com.

614.58 616.8 340 DEU ISSN 0724-2247
CODEN: RPESBT
RECHT & PSYCHIATRIE. Text in German. 1983. q. EUR 49 domestic; EUR 57 foreign; EUR 33 to students; EUR 19.90 newsstand/cover (effective 2008). adv. back issues avail. **Document type:** *Journal, Academic/Scholarly.* **Description:** Examines law and psychiatry.
Indexed: DIP, E-psyche, IBR, IBZ, P03, PsycInfo, PsycholAb, S02, S03, SCI, SCOPUS, SSCI, W07.
—GNLM. **CCC.**
Published by: Psychiatrie Verlag GmbH, Thomas-Mann-Str 49a, Bonn, 53111, Germany. TEL 49-228-725340, FAX 49-228-7253420, verlag@psychiatrie.de, http://www.psychiatrie.de. Ed. Helmut Pollaehne. Adv. contact Cornelia Brodmann. page EUR 500; trim 210 x 297. Circ: 1,150 (paid).

155.4 USA ISSN 1089-5701
HV741 CODEN: RCYOFU
➤ **RECLAIMING CHILDREN AND YOUTH.** Text in English. 1992. q. USD 50 to individuals; USD 100 combined subscription to libraries (print & online eds.) (effective 2010). back issues avail. **Document type:** *Journal, Academic/Scholarly.* **Description:** Interdisciplinary journal networking practitioners and policy leaders from diverse backgrounds who serve children and youth in conflict with self, family, school and community. Articles blend research with practical wisdom and a holistic perspective.
Formerly (until 1995): Journal of Emotional and Behavioral Problems (1064-7023)
Related titles: Microform ed.: (from PQC); Online - full text ed.: USD 25 (effective 2010).
Indexed: A01, A02, A03, A08, A22, A25, A26, B04, BRD, C28, CA, CJPI, E-psyche, E02, E03, E07, E08, ECER, ERI, ERIC, EdA, EdI, G05, G06, G07, G08, H13, I05, I06, I07, P02, P04, P07, P10, P18, P20, P25, P48, P53, P54, P55, PQC, S02, S03, S08, S09, S23, SCOPUS, SOPODA, SociolAb, T02, V&AA, W03.
—BLDSC (7309.659000), IE, Ingenta. **CCC.**
Published by: Reclaiming Youth, 104 N Main St, PO Box 57, Lennox, SD 57039. TEL 605-647-2532, 888-647-2532, FAX 605-647-5212, bookstore@reclaiming.com, http://www.reclaiming.com. Ed. Larry K Brendtro. **Subscr. to:** Compassion Publications, Ltd.

158 USA ISSN 1947-2773
▼ **RECOVERING THE SELF**; a journal of hope and healing. Text in English. 2009. q. USD 29.95 domestic; USD 38.95 in Canada and U.K.; USD 9.95 per issue (effective 2009). **Document type:** *Journal, Consumer.* **Description:** Short stories, essays, poems, memoir, history, and art related to self-help topics.
Published by: Loving Healing Press, 5145 Pontiac Trail, Ann Arbor, MI 48105-9279. TEL 734-662-6864, FAX 734-663-6861, info@lovinghealing.com, http://www.lovinghealing.com.

RECOVERY TODAY; the newsmagazine for today's recovering community. *see* DRUG ABUSE AND ALCOHOLISM

RECREARTE; revista internacional de creatividad aplicada total. *see* EDUCATION

150 ESP ISSN 1135-8793
REDES (BARCELONA). Text in Spanish. 1996. s-a. EUR 60 domestic to individuals; EUR 100 elsewhere to individuals; EUR 180 elsewhere to institutions (effective 2009). **Document type:** *Journal, Trade.*
Published by: (Escuela Vasco - Navarra de Terapia Familiar), Red Espanola y Latinoamericana de Escuelas Sistemicas, Mallorca 489 Entresuelo 2, Barcelona, 08013, Spain. correo@redrelates.org, http://www.redrelates.org/.

REFLECTIONS (LONG BEACH); narratives of professional helping. *see* EDUCATION—Special Education And Rehabilitation

REFLEXIVE SOZIALPSYCHOLOGIE. *see* SOCIOLOGY

155.916 USA ISSN 0090-5550
RM930.A1
➤ **REHABILITATION PSYCHOLOGY.** Text in English. 1954. q. USD 107 domestic to individuals; USD 134 foreign to individuals; USD 465 domestic to institutions; USD 510 foreign to institutions (effective 2011). adv. bk.rev.; film rev. charts; illus. back issues avail.; reprint service avail. from PSC. **Document type:** *Journal, Academic/Scholarly.* **Description:** Takes an interdisciplinary approach in addressing psychosocial and behavioral aspects of rehabilitation; covers topics that relate to the experience of chronic illness and disability throughout the lifespan.
Former titles (until 1972): Psychological Aspects of Disability (0091-178X); (until 1969): American Psychological Association. Division 22. Psychological Aspects of Disability. Bulletin (0091-1763); (until 196?): American Psychological Association. National Council on the Psychological Aspects of Disability. Bulletin
Related titles: Online - full text ed.: ISSN 1939-1544 (from ScienceDirect).
Indexed: A20, A22, AMED, ASCA, ASSIA, B04, BRD, C06, C07, C08, CA, CINAHL, CurCont, E-psyche, EMBASE, ExcerpMed, FamI, MEDLINE, P03, P30, PsycInfo, PsycholAb, R10, Reac, RehabLit, S02, S03, SCOPUS, SSAI, SSAb, SSCI, SSI, SWR&A, SociolAb, T02, W03, W07, YAE&RB.
—BLDSC (7350.290000), GNLM, IE, Infotrieve, Ingenta. **CCC.**
Published by: (American Psychological Association, Division 22), American Psychological Association, 750 First St, NE, Washington, DC 20002. TEL 202-336-5500, 800-374-2721, FAX 202-336-5997, journals@apa.org. Ed. Dr. Timothy R Elliott. Adv. contact Doug Constant TEL 202-336-5574. Circ: 1,700.

159.9 DEU ISSN 1434-7458
REIHE PSYCHODIAGNOSTIK. Text in German. 1998. irreg. price varies. **Document type:** *Monographic series, Academic/Scholarly.*
Published by: Centaurus Verlag & Media KG, Kaiser-Joseph-Str 267, Freiburg, 79098, Germany. TEL 49-761-1525861, FAX 49-761-1525868, info@centaurus-verlag.de, http://www.centaurus-verlag.de.

302 URY ISSN 0797-9754
BF5
➤ **RELACIONES**; revista al tema del hombre. Text in Spanish. 1984. m. USD 60 foreign (effective 2003). adv. bk.rev.; dance rev.; music rev.; play rev. 32 p./no.; back issues avail. **Document type:** *Academic/Scholarly.* **Description:** Devoted to human sciences.
Published by: Editorial Periodica S.R.L., Avda. Luis A. de Herrera, 1042, Ap. 708, Montevideo, 11300, Uruguay. TEL 598-2-6221108, FAX 598-2-6221108. Ed. Saul Paciuk. Adv. contact Rosa Verdier. B&W page USD 700; 25 x 36. Circ: 3,000.

▼ ➤ **RELIGION, BRAIN & BEHAVIOR.** *see* RELIGIONS AND THEOLOGY

155.4 370.15 616.891 USA ISSN 1531-5479
RJ506.B44
REPORT ON EMOTIONAL & BEHAVIORAL DISORDERS IN YOUTH. Variant title: Emotional & Behavioral Disorders in Youth. Text in English. 2000. q. USD 179.95 (effective 2010). back issues avail. **Document type:** *Newsletter, Trade.* **Description:** Designed for school counselors, social workers, psychologists, psychiatrists, educators, and other professionals who work with troubled children and adolescents.
Related titles: Online - full text ed.: ISSN 2156-9304.
—**CCC.**
Published by: Civic Research Insitute, PO Box 585, Kingston, NJ 08528. TEL 609-683-4450, FAX 609-683-7291, order@civicresearchinstitute.com. Eds. Eric J Bruns, Eric W Trupin.

616.89 DEU ISSN 0344-9602
➤ **REPORT PSYCHOLOGIE.** Text in German. 1974. 10/yr. EUR 54 domestic; EUR 72 foreign; EUR 37.80 to students; EUR 7.45 newsstand/cover (effective 2011). adv. bk.rev. 72 p./no. **Document type:** *Journal, Academic/Scholarly.*
Indexed: DIP, E-psyche, IBR, IBZ.
—GNLM.
Published by: Deutscher Psychologen Verlag GmbH, Am Koellnischen Park 2, Berlin, 10179, Germany. TEL 49-30-209166410, FAX 49-30-209166413, verlag@psychologenverlag.de, http://www.psychologenverlag.de.

P

155.3 USA
REPRESENTATIONS BOOKS SERIES. Text in English. 1987. irreg., latest vol.8, 1999. price varies. back issues avail. **Document type:** *Monographic series, Academic/Scholarly.* **Description:** Examines sexuality throughout Western history.
Indexed: E-psyche.
Published by: University of California Press, Book Series, 2120 Berkeley Way, Berkeley, CA 94704. TEL 510-642-4247, FAX 510-643-7127, foundation@ucpress.edu. **Orders to:** California - Princeton Fulfillment Services, Inc., 1445 Lower Ferry Rd, Ewing, NJ 08618. TEL 609-883-1759, 800-777-4726, FAX 800-999-1958, orders@cpfsinc.com.

RESEARCH IN COMMUNITY AND MENTAL HEALTH. *see* PUBLIC HEALTH AND SAFETY

RESEARCH IN ETHICAL ISSUES IN ORGANIZATIONS. *see* BUSINESS AND ECONOMICS—Management

155 USA ISSN 1542-7609
BF713
RESEARCH IN HUMAN DEVELOPMENT. Abbreviated title: R H D. Text in English. 2004. q. GBP 251 combined subscription in United Kingdom to institutions (print & online eds.); EUR 333, USD 420 combined subscription to institutions (print & online eds.) (effective 2012). adv. back issues avail.; reprint service avail. from PSC. **Document type:** *Journal, Academic/Scholarly.* **Description:** Seeks to promote a shift away from research focused on development at particular stages (early childhood, adolescence, middle age, older adulthood) and from separate fields of inquiry to a more inclusive, integrative, and interdisciplinary approach to the study of human development across the entire life span.
Related titles: Online - full text ed.: ISSN 1542-7617. 2004. GBP 226 in United Kingdom to institutions; EUR 300, USD 378 to institutions (effective 2012).
Indexed: A22, CA, CurCont, E01, FamI, P03, P10, P30, P48, P53, P54, PQC, PsycInfo, S02, S03, SSCI, T02, W07.
—BLDSC (7741.314500), IE, Ingenta. **CCC.**
Published by: (Society for the Study of Human Development), Psychology Press (Subsidiary of: Taylor & Francis Inc.), 325 Chestnut St, Ste 800, Philadelphia, PA 19106. TEL 800-354-1420, FAX 215-625-2940, orders@taylorandfrancis.com, http://www.psypress.com. Ed. Carolyn Aldwin. Adv. contact Linda Hann TEL 44-1344-779945.

302 USA ISSN 0191-3085
HD28
➤ **RESEARCH IN ORGANIZATIONAL BEHAVIOR.** Text in English. 1979. a. EUR 206 in Europe to institutions; JPY 31,800 in Japan to institutions; USD 289 elsewhere to institutions (effective 2012). back issues avail. **Document type:** *Journal, Academic/Scholarly.* **Description:** Covers issues from individual emotion and cognition to social movements and networks.
Related titles: Online - full text ed.: (from ScienceDirect).
Indexed: A12, A13, A14, A17, A20, A22, ABIn, ASCA, B01, B06, B07, B09, CA, E-psyche, ILD, P48, P51, P53, P54, PQC, PsycholAb, S02, S03, SCOPUS, SSCI, T02, W07.
—BLDSC (7750.600000), IE, Ingenta. **CCC.**
Published by: J A I Press Inc. (Subsidiary of: Elsevier Science & Technology), 360 Park Ave S, New York, NY 10010. TEL 212-989-5800, FAX 212-633-3990, usinfo-f@elsevier.com. Eds. Arthur Brief, Barry Staw.

150 GBR ISSN 1750-1571
RESEARCH INSITUTE FOR HEALTH & SOCIAL CHANGE. REPORTS AND OCCASIONAL PAPERS. Variant title: R I H S C Research Reports and Occasional Papers. Text in English. 1995. irreg., latest 2008. price varies. back issues avail. **Document type:** *Monographic series, Academic/Scholarly.*

Former titles (until 2004): Community and Organisational Psychology Research Group. Occasional Papers (1746-2479); (until 2002): Interpersonal Organisational Development Research Group. Occasional Papers (1359-9089)
Published by: Manchester Metropolitan University, Research Institute for Health and Social Change, c o David Brown, Rm E53d, Elizabeth Gaskell Campus, Manchester Metropolitan University, Hathersage Rd, Manchester, M13 0JA, United Kingdom. TEL 44-161-2472774, FAX 44-161-2476842, rihsc@mmu.ac.uk, http://www.rihsc.mmu.ac.uk/.

152.4 NLD ISSN 1746-9791
RESEARCH ON EMOTION IN ORGANIZATIONS. Text in English. 2005. a. price varies. **Document type:** *Monographic series, Academic/Scholarly.*
Related titles: Online - full text ed.
Indexed: SCOPUS.
—BLDSC (7738.975000), IE. **CCC.**
Published by: Elsevier BV (Subsidiary of: Elsevier Science & Technology), Radarweg 29, PO Box 211, Amsterdam, 1000 AE, Netherlands. TEL 31-20-4853911, FAX 31-20-4852457, JournalsCustomerServiceEMEA@elsevier.com. Eds. Charmine Hartel, Neal Ashkanasy, Wilfred Zerbe.

RESEARCH ON SOCIAL WORK PRACTICE. *see* SOCIOLOGY

150.19 100 USA ISSN 1059-3551
THE RESHAPING OF PSYCHOANALYSIS; from Sigmund Freud to Ernest Becker. Text in English. 1992. irreg., latest vol.11, 2003. price varies. **Document type:** *Monographic series, Academic/Scholarly.* **Description:** Studies of Freud and neo-Freudians such as Ernest Becker, concerned with the reshaping and revitalization of psychoanalysis.
Indexed: E-psyche.
Published by: Peter Lang Publishing, Inc. (Subsidiary of: Peter Lang Publishing Group), 29 Broadway, New York, NY 10006. TEL 212-647-7706, 212-647-7700, 800-770-5264, FAX 212-647-7707, customerservice@plang.com, http://www.peterlang.com. Ed. Barry R Arnold.

158 NLD ISSN 2210-2833
▼ **RETHINKING RESEARCH AND PROFESSIONAL PRACTICES IN TERMS OF RELATIONALITY, SUBJECTIVITY AND POWER.** Text in English. 2010. irreg. **Document type:** *Monographic series, Academic/Scholarly.*
Media: Online - full text.
Published by: Bentham Science Publishers Ltd., PO Box 294, Bussum, 1400 AG, Netherlands. TEL 31-35-6923800, FAX 31-35-6980150, sales@bentham.org, http://www.bentham.org. Ed. Bronwyn Davies.

REVIEW OF COGNITIVE LINGUISTICS. *see* LINGUISTICS

150 616.8 100 800 USA ISSN 0361-1531
RC321 CODEN: REXPB4
➤ **REVIEW OF EXISTENTIAL PSYCHOLOGY AND PSYCHIATRY.** Text in English. 1961. 3/yr. USD 36 domestic to individuals; USD 56 foreign to individuals; USD 198 domestic to institutions; USD 228 foreign to institutions (effective 2009). adv. bk.rev. cum. index. back issues avail.; reprints avail. **Document type:** *Journal, Academic/Scholarly.* **Description:** Applies existential and phenomenological approaches to the study of problems in human existence.
Former titles (until 1971): Human Inquiries (0363-2326); (until 1969): Review of Existential Psychology and Psychiatry (0034-656X)
Indexed: A22, DIP, E-psyche, IBR, IBZ, IPB, MLA-IB, PhilInd, PsycholAb.
—BLDSC (7790.550000), IE, Ingenta. **CCC.**
Address: PO Box 15680, Seattle, WA 98115. TEL 206-367-5764, FAX 206-365-3036. Ed., Pub., R&P, Adv. contact Keith Hoeller. B&W page USD 295; trim 6 x 9. Circ: 300 (paid).

152 USA ISSN 1089-2680
BF1
➤ **REVIEW OF GENERAL PSYCHOLOGY.** Text in English. 1997. q. USD 110 domestic to individuals; USD 137 foreign to individuals; USD 415 domestic to institutions; USD 460 foreign to institutions (effective 2011). adv. 100 p./no. 1 cols./p.; back issues avail.; reprint service avail. from PSC. **Document type:** *Journal, Academic/Scholarly.* **Description:** Includes innovative theoretical, conceptual, and methodological articles that cross-cut the traditional subdisciplines of psychology.
Related titles: Online - full text ed.: ISSN 1939-1552 (from ScienceDirect).
Indexed: A20, A22, ASSIA, CurCont, E-psyche, FR, P03, P30, PsycInfo, PsycholAb, SCOPUS, SSCI, W07.
—BLDSC (7790.741000), IE, Infotrieve, Ingenta, INIST. **CCC.**
Published by: (American Psychological Association, Division 1), American Psychological Association, 750 First St, NE, Washington, DC 20002. TEL 202-336-5500, 800-374-2721, journals@apa.org. Ed. Dr. Douglas K Candland. Adv. contact Doug Constant TEL 202-336-5574. Circ: 1,400.

▼ ➤ **REVIEW OF PHILOSOPHY AND PSYCHOLOGY.** *see* PHILOSOPHY

150 HRV ISSN 1330-6812
BF8.S4 CODEN: RPSHDY
REVIEW OF PSYCHOLOGY. Text in English. 1971. s-a. HRK 70 domestic to individuals; EUR 25 foreign to individuals; HRK 140 domestic to institutions; EUR 35 foreign to institutions (effective 2002). adv. bk.rev. **Document type:** *Journal, Academic/Scholarly.* **Description:** Publishes original scientific papers, theoretical contributions and critical surveys of research in all fields of psychology and related disciplines, as well as relevant professional papers and news.
Formerly (until 1991): Revija za Psihologiju (0352-1605)
Indexed: E-psyche, P03, PsycInfo, PsycholAb.
Published by: (Drustvo Psihologa S R Hrvatske/Croatian Psychologica), Naklada Slap, Dr F Tudmana 33, Jastrebarsko, 10450, Croatia. nslap@nakladaslap.com, http://www.nakladaslap.com. Ed. Vladimir Kolesaric. Circ: 1,000.

150 ARG ISSN 1852-4206
BF1.A4
▼ **REVISTA ARGENTINA DE CIENCIAS DEL COMPORTAMIENTO.** Text in English, Portuguese, Spanish. 2009. q. free (effective 2011). back issues avail. **Document type:** *Journal, Academic/Scholarly.*
Media: Online - full text.
Published by: Universidad Nacional de Cordoba, Facultad de Psicologia, Enfermera Gordillo s/n, Ciudad Universitaria, Cordoba, 5000, Argentina. Ed. Marcos Cupani.

150 ARG ISSN 0327-6716
REVISTA ARGENTINA DE CLINICA PSICOLOGICA. Text in Spanish. 1992. 3/yr. USD 190 in Latin America to individuals; USD 210 elsewhere to individuals; USD 240 in Latin America to institutions; USD 250 elsewhere to institutions (effective 2007). **Document type:** *Journal, Academic/Scholarly.*
Indexed: C01, CA, F04, P03, PsycInfo, PsycholAb, SCI, SCOPUS, SSCI, T02, W07.
—BLDSC (7841.160000).
Published by: Fundacion Aigle, Virrey Olaguer y Feliu 2679, Buenos Aires, Argentina. TEL 54-11-47813897, fundacion@aigle.org.ar, http://www.aigle.org.ar. Ed. Lilian Corrado. Circ: 1,000.

150 ARG ISSN 0557-6466
BF5
REVISTA ARGENTINA DE PSICOLOGIA. Text in Spanish. 1969. a. **Document type:** *Journal, Academic/Scholarly.*
Published by: Asociacion de Psicologos de Buenos Aires, Azcuenaga 7676, 5o Piso, Buenos Aires, Argentina. TEL 54-11-49539840, http://www.psicologos.org.ar.

REVISTA ARGENTINA DE PSICOPEDAGOGIA. *see* EDUCATION

REVISTA ARGENTINA DE PSIQUIATRIA Y PSICOLOGIA DE LA INFANCIA Y DE LA ADOLESCENCIA. *see* MEDICAL SCIENCES—Psychiatry And Neurology

150 BRA ISSN 1807-8338
REVISTA BRASILEIRA DE ANALISE DO COMPORTAMENTO. Text in Multiple languages. 2005. s-a. **Document type:** *Journal, Academic/Scholarly.* **Description:** Aims to disseminate behavior analysis in Brazil and abroad.
Published by: Instituto Brasiliense de Analise do Comportamento, 910 Sul Mix Park Sul, Bloco F, Salas 119-129, Brasilia, Brazil. TEL 55-61-32425250, http://www.ibac.com.br. Pub. Joao Claudio Todorov.

150 616.8 BRA ISSN 1517-8668
REVISTA BRASILEIRA DE ANALISE TRANSACIONAL. Text in Portuguese. 1988. a. **Document type:** *Journal, Academic/Scholarly.*
Published by: Uniao Nacional de Analistas Transacionais (U N A T), Rua Saldanha Marinho 33 Conj 402, Bairro Menino Deus, Porto Alegre, RS 90160-240, Brazil. TEL 55-51-32234190, http://www.unat.com.br.

150.195 616.8917 BRA ISSN 0486-641X
RC500
REVISTA BRASILEIRA DE PSICANALISE. Text in Portuguese. 1928. q. **Document type:** *Journal, Academic/Scholarly.*
Related titles: Online - full text ed.: ISSN 2175-3601.
Indexed: P03, PsycInfo, PsycholAb, S02, S03.
Published by: Associacao Brasileira de Psicanalise, Rua Sergipe, 475, 8 andar, Sala 807, Sao Paulo, SP 01243-001, Brazil. TEL 55-11-36618709, FAX 55-11-36619473, abp@abp.org.br, http://www.abp.org.br/. Ed. Leopold Nosek.

158.1 ESP ISSN 0212-9205
REVISTA CATALANA DE PSICOANALISI. Text in Catalan. 1984. s-a. EUR 44 (effective 2009).
Indexed: P03, PsycInfo, PsycholAb.
Published by: Institut de Psicoanalisi de Barcelona, Alacanta, 27 Entr. B, Barcelona, Catalunya 08022, Spain. Ed. Julia Coromines.

REVISTA CHILENA DE NEUROPSICOLOGIA. *see* MEDICAL SCIENCES—Psychiatry And Neurology

150.195 CHL ISSN 0716-3649
➤ **REVISTA CHILENA DE PSICOANALISIS.** Text in Spanish. 1979. s-a. **Document type:** *Journal, Academic/Scholarly.*
Indexed: P03, PsycInfo, PsycholAb.
Published by: Asociacion Psicoanalitica Chilena, Avenida Hammarskjold 3269, 20 Piso, Vitacura, Santiago, Chile. TEL 56-2-2639631, FAX 56-2-2078926.

150 CHL ISSN 0716-3630
REVISTA CHILENA DE PSICOLOGIA. Text in Spanish. 1978. a. **Document type:** *Journal, Academic/Scholarly.*
Published by: Colegio de Psicologos de Chile, Ricardo Matte Perez 492, Providencia, Santiago, Chile. TEL 56-2-2746997, FAX 56-2-2747034, info@colegiopsicologos.cl, http://www.colegiopsicologos.cl.

150 CHL ISSN 0718-3666
REVISTA CHILENA DE PSICOLOGIA CLINICA/CHILEAN JOURNAL OF CLINICAL PSYCHOLOGY. Text in Spanish. 2006. s-a. **Document type:** *Journal, Academic/Scholarly.*
Related titles: Online - full text ed.: ISSN 0718-3674.

150 COL ISSN 0121-5469
BF5
REVISTA COLOMBIANA DE PSICOLOGIA. Text in Spanish; Summaries in English, French, Spanish. 1956. a. COP 47,000 domestic; USD 60 in Latin America; USD 130 elsewhere (effective 2011). adv. bk.rev. abstr.; bibl.; illus. **Document type:** *Journal, Academic/Scholarly.* **Description:** Includes original papers and clinical case work on psychology.
Formerly: Revista de Psicologia (0120-2901)
Related titles: Online - full text ed.: free (effective 2011) (from SciELO).
Indexed: E-psyche.
Published by: Universidad Nacional de Colombia, Departamento de Psicologia, Apdo Aereo 14490, Bogota DC, Colombia. TEL 57-1-3681565, FAX 57-1-2225285. Ed. Telmo Eduardo Pena-Corral. Circ: 1,000.

301.1 150 CUB ISSN 0257-4322
REVISTA CUBANA DE PSICOLOGIA. Text in Spanish; Summaries in English, Spanish. 1983. 3/yr. **Document type:** *Journal, Academic/Scholarly.*
Related titles: Online - full text ed.
Indexed: A01, A26, C01, C32, CA, E-psyche, F03, F04, I04, I05, RASB, T02.
—INIST.
Published by: Universidad de La Habana, Calle San Lazaro esq L Vedado, Havana, 4, Cuba. TEL 53-7-3231, http://www.uh.cu. **Dist. by:** Ediciones Cubanas, Obispo 527, Havana, Cuba.

150 ESP ISSN 0212-9876
REVISTA DE ANALISIS TRANSACCIONAL Y PSICOLOGIA HUMANISTA. Text in Spanish. 1981. 3/yr. EUR 30 (effective 2008). **Document type:** *Magazine, Consumer.*
Published by: Asociacion Espanola de Analisis Transaccional de Madrid, Isaac Peral, 16 Bajo Izq., Madrid, 28015, Spain.

150 ESP ISSN 0211-0040
BF85
REVISTA DE HISTORIA DE LA PSICOLOGIA. Text in Spanish. 1980. q. EUR 35 (effective 2011). **Document type:** *Journal, Academic/Scholarly.*
Indexed: A22, AmH&L, HistAb, P03, P09, P30, PCI, PhilInd, PsycInfo, PsycholAb.
—IE, Infotrieve, Ingenta. **CCC.**
Published by: Universitat de Valencia, Facultad de Psicologia, Ave. Blasco Ibanez, 21, 3a. Planta, Valencia, 46010, Spain. TEL 34-96-3864823, FAX 34-96-3864822, http://www.cazorla.uv.es/.

150 PER ISSN 1560-909X
REVISTA DE INVESTIGACION EN PSICOLOGIA. Text in Spanish. 1998. s-a. back issues avail. **Document type:** *Journal, Academic/Scholarly.*
Related titles: Online - full text ed.: ISSN 1609-7475. 1998 (from SciELO).
Indexed: A26, I04, I05.
Published by: Universidad Nacional Mayor de San Marcos, Instituto de Investigaciones Psicologicas, Ave German Amezaga s-n, Lima, 1, Peru. TEL 51-1-6197000 ext. 3217, FAX 51-1-6197000 ext. 3202. Ed. Diego Oswaldo Orellana Manrique.

616.89 BRA ISSN 0102-4205
REVISTA DE PSICANALISE INTEGRAL. Text in Portuguese. 1978. s-a. adv. illus. 100 p./no.; **Document type:** *Journal, Academic/Scholarly.*
Formerly: Analytical Trilogy
Indexed: E-psyche.
Published by: Sociedad Internacional de Trilogia Analitica, Av Reboucas 3819, Jardim Paulistano, Sao Paulo, 05401- 450, Brazil. TEL 55-11-30323616, http://www.trilogiaanalitica.com.br.

616.89 ARG ISSN 0034-8740
RC321
REVISTA DE PSICOANALISIS. Text in Spanish; Summaries in English, French. 1943. 6/yr. ARS 88 (effective 2010). bk.rev. abstr. index. **Document type:** *Journal, Academic/Scholarly.*
Indexed: C01, E-psyche, IBR, IBZ, P03, P30, PsycInfo, PsycholAb, S02, S03.
—IE, Ingenta, INIST.
Published by: Asociacion Psicoanalitica Argentina, Rodriguez Pena 1674, Buenos Aires, 1021, Argentina. TEL 54-11-48123518, FAX 54-11-48140079, http://www.apa.org.ar.

150 616.89 ESP ISSN 1135-3171
REVISTA DE PSICOANALISIS (MADRID). Text in Spanish. 1985. s-a. EUR 60 domestic; EUR 70 in Europe; EUR 50 in the Americas; EUR 75 rest of world (effective 2008). **Document type:** *Journal, Academic/Scholarly.*
Formerly (until 1995): Revista de Psicoanalisis de Madrid (0214-0063)
Indexed: P03, PsycInfo, PsycholAb.
Published by: Asociacion Psicoanalitica de Madrid, Velazquez, 94, Madrid, 28006, Spain. TEL 34-91-4310533, apma@ono.com, http://www.apmadrid.com/. Ed. Francisco Granados.

REVISTA DE PSICODIDACTICA. *see* EDUCATION

150 CHL ISSN 0716-8039
REVISTA DE PSICOLOGIA. Text in Spanish. 1990. s-a. back issues avail. **Document type:** *Journal, Academic/Scholarly.*
Related titles: Online - full text ed.
Published by: Universidad de Chile, Departamento de Psicologia, Ignacio Carrera Pinto, 1045, Santiago, Chile. TEL 56-2-6850331, revpsico@uchile.cl, http://www.csociales.uchile.cl/psicologia/. Ed. German Rozas.

150 ARG ISSN 1669-2438
➤ **REVISTA DE PSICOLOGIA.** Text in English, Spanish. 2005. 2/yr. ARS 30 to individuals; ARS 60 to institutions. bk.rev. back issues avail. **Document type:** *Journal, Academic/Scholarly.*
Indexed: CA, F04, T02.
Published by: Pontificia Universidad Catolica Argentina, Facultad de Psicologia y Educacion, Avda Alicia Moreau de Justo 1500, Buenos Aires, Argentina. TEL 54-11-43490200. Ed. Gustavo Daniel Belaustegui. Adv. contact Pablo Alavarez Imaz.

150 PER ISSN 0254-9247
➤ **REVISTA DE PSICOLOGIA.** Text in Spanish. 1983. s-a. USD 30 (effective 2003). adv. **Document type:** *Academic/Scholarly.*
Related titles: Online - full text ed.: ISSN 1609-7564. 1997.
Indexed: A01, A26, CA, E-psyche, F03, F04, I04, I05, P03, PsycInfo, PsycholAb, T02.
Published by: (Departamento de Humanidades), Pontificia Universidad Catolica del Peru, Avenuda Universitaria, Cdra 18 s/n, san Miguel, Lima, 32, Peru. TEL 51-14-626390, FAX 51-14-611785, http://www.pucp.edu.pe. Ed. Cecilia Thorne. Circ: 1,000.

616.89 VEN ISSN 1316-0923
BF5
➤ **REVISTA DE PSICOLOGIA.** Text in Spanish. 1974-199?; resumed 1995. q. **Document type:** *Journal, Academic/Scholarly.* **Description:** Covers general, scholarly, clinical, educational, industrial, and social psychology.
Formerly (until 19??): Psicologia (0798-4308)
Related titles: Online - full text ed.: free (effective 2011).
Indexed: C01, E-psyche.
Published by: Universidad Central de Venezuela, Escuela de Psicologia, Apdo 47589, Caracas, 1041-A, Venezuela.

150 ESP ISSN 0214-4859
REVISTA DE PSICOLOGIA DE LA SALUD/JOURNAL OF HEALTH PSYCHOLOGY. Text in Spanish. 1989. s-a. **Document type:** *Journal, Academic/Scholarly.*
Published by: Universidad Miguel Hernandez, Departamento de Psicologia de Salud, Crta Nacional N-332 s-n, San Juan de Alicante, 03550, Spain. TEL 34-96-5919466, FAX 34-96-5919475, psicologia.salud@umh.es, http://medicina.umh.es/.

150 796 ESP ISSN 1132-239X
➤ **REVISTA DE PSICOLOGIA DEL DEPORTE.** Text in Spanish. 1992. s-a. back issues avail. **Document type:** *Journal, Academic/Scholarly.*
Related titles: Online - full text ed.
Indexed: A01, CA, F03, F04, P03, PsycInfo, PsycholAb, SCOPUS, SD, SSCI, T02, W07.
Published by: (Universitat de les Illes Balears, Departament de Psicologia, Federacion Espanola de Psicologia del Deporte), Universitat de les Illes Balears, Servei de Publicacions i Intercanvi Cientific, Carr. de Valdemosa, Km. 7.5, Palma de Mallorca, 07071, Spain. TEL 34-971-173000, FAX 34-971-173190, informacio@uib.es.

150 331.3 ESP ISSN 1576-5962
REVISTA DE PSICOLOGIA DEL TRABAJO Y DE LAS ORGANIZACIONES. Text in Spanish. 1985. 3/yr. EUR 33.50 domestic to qualified personnel; EUR 43 domestic; EUR 80 foreign (effective 2008). back issues avail. **Document type:** *Journal, Academic/Scholarly.*
Former titles (until 1999): Psicologia del Trabajo y Organizaciones (1135-0806); (until 1993): Revista de Psicologia del Trabajo y de las Organizaciones (0213-3628)
Related titles: Online - full text ed.: ISSN 2174-0534. 1985.
Indexed: A01, CA, E-psyche, F03, F04, P03, PsycInfo, PsycholAb, S02, S03, T02.
Published by: Colegio Oficial de Psicologos, Claudio Coello 46, Madrid, 28001, Spain. TEL 34-91-4355212, FAX 34-91-5779172. Ed. Adolfo Hernandez Gordillo.

150 ESP ISSN 0373-2002
BF5 CODEN: RPGAAI
➤ **REVISTA DE PSICOLOGIA GENERAL Y APLICADA.** Text in Spanish; Summaries in English, Spanish. 1946. q. EUR 42 domestic; EUR 51 in Europe; EUR 69 in the Americas (effective 2009). bk.rev. bibl.; charts. **Document type:** *Journal, Academic/Scholarly.* **Description:** Reviews clinical and applied psychology.
Related titles: Online - full text ed.: IberPsicologia. 1996.
Indexed: A22, CIS, E-psyche, IBR, IBZ, MLA-IB, P03, P09, P30, PCI, PsycInfo, PsycholAb, S02, S03, SOPODA, SociolAb.
—IE, Infotrieve, INIST. **CCC.**
Published by: Federacion Espanola de Asociaciones de Psicologia, Seminario de Psicologia Basica, Facultad de Filosofia, Edif. A, Desp. 41, Universidad Complutense, Madrid, 28040, Spain. TEL 34-91-3946016, fedap@fedap.es, http://www.fedap.es/. Ed. Helio Carpintero. Pub. Jose Pascual.

150 ESP ISSN 0213-4748
HM1001
➤ **REVISTA DE PSICOLOGIA SOCIAL.** Text in Multiple languages. 1986. 3/yr. EUR 75 to individuals; EUR 250 per issue to institutions. adv. **Document type:** *Journal, Academic/Scholarly.* **Description:** Publishes articles on empirical and theoretical research concerning the study of behavior from a theoretical perspective.
Related titles: Online - full text ed.: ISSN 1579-3680 (from IngentaConnect).
Indexed: A01, A03, A08, A22, CA, E-psyche, P03, PsycInfo, PsycholAb, S02, S03, SCOPUS, SSCI, T02, W07.
—IE, Infotrieve, Ingenta. **CCC.**
Published by: Fundacion Infancia y Aprendizaje, Naranjo de Bulnes 69, Ciudalcampo, San Sebastian de los Reyes, Madrid, 28707, Spain. fundacion@fia.es. Ed. Dr. Morales Francisco. Circ: 1,100.

➤ **REVISTA DE PSICOLOGIA SOCIAL APLICADA.** *see* SOCIOLOGY

301.1 MEX ISSN 0188-6533
REVISTA DE PSICOLOGIA SOCIAL Y PERSONALIDAD. Text in Spanish. 1985. 2/yr. USD 10.
Indexed: E-psyche, PsycholAb.
Published by: Asociacion Mexicana de Psicologia Social, Ciudad Universitaria, Mexico, D.F., 04510, Mexico. TEL 52-55-56222326, amepso@servidor.unam.mx, http://www.geocities.com/amepsomx/index.html. Ed. Gabina Villagran.

150 MEX ISSN 2007-1833
▼ **REVISTA DE PSICOLOGIA Y CIENCIAS DEL COMPORTAMIENTO.** Text in Spanish. 2009. s-a. **Document type:** *Journal, Academic/Scholarly.*
Published by: Universidad Autonoma de Tamaulipas, Unidad Academica de Ciencias Juridicas y Sociales, Matamoros 8 y 9, Col. Centro, Ciudad Victoria, Tamaulipas 87000, Mexico. TEL 52-834-3181800, http://www.uacjs.uat.edu.mx/.

REVISTA DE PSICOLOGIA Y EDUCACION. *see* EDUCATION

150 ESP ISSN 1136-5420
BF5
REVISTA DE PSICOPATOLOGIA Y PSICOLOGIA CLINICA. Text in Spanish. 1996. q. **Document type:** *Journal, Academic/Scholarly.*
Related titles: Online - full text ed.
Indexed: A01, CA, P03, PsycInfo, PsycholAb, T02.
—BLDSC (7870.180050).
Published by: Asociacion Espanola de Psicologia Clinica y Psicopatologia, Beato Galves, 3, 4o., Valencia, 46007, Spain. Eds. Amparo Belloch, Cristina Botella.

REVISTA DE PSICOTERAPIA PSICOANALITICA. *see* MEDICAL SCIENCES—Psychiatry And Neurology

158 ESP ISSN 0211-0822
REVISTA DE PSICOTERAPIA Y PSICOSOMATICA. Text in Spanish. 1978. s-a. EUR 25 (effective 2009). back issues avail. **Document type:** *Journal, Academic/Scholarly.*
Formerly (until 1980): Instituto de Estudios Psicosomaticos y Psicoterapia Medica. Boletin (0211-0814)
Published by: Instituto de Estudios Psicosomaticos y Psicoterapia Medica, Apdo de Correos 3076, Madrid, 28080, Spain. TEL 34-91-5445081, ieppm@inicia.es, http://www.ieppm.org. Ed. Rafael Cruz Roche.

150 ROM ISSN 0034-8759
BF8.R7
REVISTA DE PSIHOLOGIE. Text in Romanian, French, English. 1955. q. bk.rev. index. **Document type:** *Journal, Academic/Scholarly.*
Related titles: Online - full text ed.: free (effective 2011).
Indexed: CDA, CISA, E-psyche, ErgAb, IBR, IBZ, P03, PsycInfo, PsycholAb, RASB, RefZh, S02, S03.
—BLDSC (7870.200000), INIST.
Published by: (Academia Romana/Romanian Academy, Institutul de Psihologie), Editura Academiei Romane/Publishing House of the Romanian Academy, Calea 13 Septembrie 13, Sector 5, Bucharest, 050711, Romania. TEL 40-21-3188146, FAX 40-21-3182444, edacad@ear.ro. Ed. Constantin Voicu. Circ: 1,400. **Dist. by:** Rodipet S.A. TEL 40-21-2224126, 40-21-2226407, rodipet@rodipet.ro.

REVISTA ELECTRONICA DE INVESTIGACION EDUCATIVA Y PSICOPEDAGOGICA/ELECTRONIC JOURNAL OF RESEARCH IN EDUCATIONAL PSYCHOLOGY. *see* EDUCATION

150 ESP ISSN 1137-8492
BF1
REVISTA ELECTRONICA DE PSICOLOGIA. Key Title: Psicologia.com. Text in Spanish. 1997. q. free to qualified personnel (effective 2010). back issues avail. **Document type:** *Journal, Academic/Scholarly.* **Description:** Publishes papers on pscyhology research.
Media: Online - full text.
Published by: InterSalud, Apdo de Correos 227, Palmova, Mallorca, 07181, Spain. info@intersalud.es, http://www.intersalud.es/.

150 ESP ISSN 1576-4214
REVISTA ESPANOLA DE MOTIVACION Y EMOCION/SPANISH JOURNAL OF MOTIVATION AND EMOTION. Text in Multiple languages. 2000. a. **Document type:** *Journal, Academic/Scholarly.*
Related titles: Online - full text ed.: Revista Electronica de Motivacion y Emocion. ISSN 1138-493X.
Published by: Universidad Nacional de Educacion a Distancia, Bravo Murillo 38, Madrid, Spain. TEL 34-91-3986000, FAX 34-91-3986600, http://www.uned.es/.

150 616.8 ESP ISSN 1139-9872
REVISTA ESPANOLA DE NEUROPSICOLOGIA. Text in Multiple languages. 1999. q. **Document type:** *Journal, Academic/Scholarly.*
Indexed: FR.
Published by: (Universidad de Sevilla, Facultad de Psicologia), Universidad de Sevilla, Secretariado de Publicaciones, Calle Porvenir 27, Sevilla, 41013, Spain.

REVISTA ESPANOLA DE ORIENTACION Y PSICOPEDAGOGIA. *see* EDUCATION

REVISTA GALEGO-PORTUGUESA DE PSICOLOXIA E EDUCACION/ GALICIAN-PORTUGUESE JOURNAL FOR THE STUDY OF PSYCHOLOGY AND EDUCATION. *see* EDUCATION

150 ESP ISSN 1135-3848
REVISTA IBEROAMERICANA DE DIAGNOSTICO Y EVALUACION PSICOLOGICA. Text in Spanish. 1995. s-a. free membership (effective 2008). back issues avail. **Document type:** *Journal, Academic/Scholarly.*
Related titles: Online - full text ed.
Indexed: P03, PsycInfo, PsycholAb, SSCI, W07.
Published by: A I D E P, Ave. de la Merced, 109-131, Salamanca, 37005, Spain. FAX 34-23-294607, ridep@aided.org, http://www.aidep.org/. Ed. Maria M Casullo.

150 ESP ISSN 1886-8576
REVISTA IBEROAMERICANA DE PSICOLOGIA DEL EJERCICIO Y EL DEPORTE. Text in Spanish. 2006. s-a. **Document type:** *Journal, Trade.*
Published by: Wanceulen Editorial Deportiva, Cristo del Desamparo y Abandono 56, Seville, 41006, Spain. TEL 34-95-4921511, FAX 34-95-4921059, infoeditorial@wanceleuen.com, http://www.wanceulen.com.

150 ESP ISSN 2171-2069
▼ **REVISTA IBEROAMERICANA DE PSICOLOGIA Y SALUD.** Text in English, Spanish. 2010. s-a. **Document type:** *Journal, Academic/Scholarly.*
Related titles: Online - full text ed.: ISSN 1989-9246. free (effective 2011).
Published by: Sociedad Universitaria de Investigacion en Psicologia y Salud, Universidad de A Coruna, Escuela Universitaria de Fisioterapia, Campus de Oza, A Coruna, 15006, Spain.

150 MEX ISSN 0187-7690
REVISTA INTERCONTINENTAL DE PSICOLOGIA Y EDUCACION. Text in Spanish. 1988. s-a. **Document type:** *Journal, Academic/Scholarly.*
Related titles: Online - full text ed.: free (effective 2011).
Indexed: C01, P03, PsycholAb.
Published by: Universidad Intercontinental, Insurgentes Sur 4303, Col Santa Ursula Xitla, Del Tlalpan, Mexico, D.F., 14420, Mexico. TEL 52-55-54871300, http://www.uic.edu.mx. Ed. Rosa Maria Torres Hernandez.

150 ESP ISSN 1577-7057
BF1
REVISTA INTERNACIONAL DE PSICOLOGIA Y TERAPIA PSICOLOGICA/INTERNATIONAL JOURNAL OF PSYCHOLOGY AND PSYCHOLOGICAL THERAPY. Text in English, Spanish. 2001. s-a. EUR 30 domestic to individuals; USD 40 in Latin America to individuals; EUR 70 domestic to institutions; USD 80 in Latin America to institutions (effective 2010). bk.rev. back issues avail. **Document type:** *Journal, Academic/Scholarly.* **Description:** Publishes empirical and theoretical contributions on any topic related to psychology.
Related titles: Online - full text ed.: free (effective 2011).
Indexed: A01, CA, E-psyche, H21, P03, P08, P30, PsycInfo, PsycholAb, SCOPUS, T02.
—BLDSC (4542.506050), IE. **CCC.**
Address: Universidad de Almeria, Facultad de Humanidades, Edificio A, Almeria, 04120, Spain. FAX 34-950-015471. Ed. Jesus Gil Roales-Nieto.

150 COL ISSN 0120-0534
BF5 CODEN: RLPSBM
➤ **REVISTA LATINOAMERICANA DE PSICOLOGIA.** Text in Spanish; Abstracts in English. 1969. 3/yr. adv. bk.rev.; Website rev. abstr.; bibl.; illus.; stat. index. **Document type:** *Journal, Academic/Scholarly.* **Description:** International journal of all areas of psychology.
Related titles: Online - full text ed.: free (effective 2011).
Indexed: A01, A02, A03, A08, A20, A22, A26, ASCA, C01, CA, CurCont, DIP, E-psyche, F04, I04, I05, IBR, IBZ, P03, P30, PsycInfo, PsycholAb, S02, S03, SCOPUS, SSCI, T02, W07.
—BLDSC (7863.513000), IE, Infotrieve, Ingenta. **CCC.**
Published by: Fundacion Universitaria Konrad Lorenz, Carrera 9 bis No. 62-43, Bogota, Colombia. TEL 57-1-3472311, FAX 57-1-3472311 ext. 131, http://www.fukl.edu/. Circ: 2,500.

150 BRA ISSN 1518-6148
REVISTA MAL-ESTAR E SUBJETIVIDADE. Text in Portuguese. 2000. s-a. back issues avail. **Document type:** *Journal, Academic/Scholarly.*
Related titles: Online - full text ed.: free (effective 2011).
Indexed: C01, SociolAb.
Published by: Universidade de Fortaleza, Laboratorio de Clinica do Social e do Sujeito, Ave Washigton Soares, 1321, Bloco N Sala 12, Bairro Edson Queiroz, Fortaleza, 60811-905, Brazil. TEL 55-85-34773219, cmps@unfor.br, http://www.unifor.br/. Ed. Henrique Figuereido Carneiro.

150 MEX ISSN 0185-4534
BF199
➤ **REVISTA MEXICANA DE ANALISIS DE LA CONDUCTA/MEXICAN JOURNAL OF BEHAVIOR ANALYSIS.** Text in English, Spanish. 1975. q. MXN 450 domestic to individuals; USD 36 foreign to individuals; MXN 500 domestic to institutions; USD 72 foreign to institutions; MXN 180, USD 15 per issue (effective 2011). adv. bk.rev. bibl.; charts; illus.; stat.; abstr. index. back issues avail. **Document type:** *Journal, Academic/Scholarly.* **Description:** Presents original research in behavior analysis and technical notes on diverse subjects of interest to behavioral scientists.
Related titles: Online - full text ed.
Indexed: AMHA, C01, CIS, E-psyche, F04, P03, PsycInfo, PsycholAb, T02.
Published by: Sociedad Mexicana de Analisis de la Conducta/Mexican Society of Behavior Analysis, Calle Zaragoza 91-2, Deleg. Tlalpan, Mexico City, DF 14268, Mexico. TEL 52-777-3179988, http://www.smac.org.mx/. Ed. Rocio Hernandez-Pozo. Adv. contact Rosendo Hernandez Castro. Circ: 650.

150 MEX ISSN 2007-0926
▼ **REVISTA MEXICANA DE INVESTIGACION EN PSICOLOGIA.** Text in Spanish. 2010. s-a. **Document type:** *Journal, Academic/Scholarly.*
Related titles: Online - full text ed.: free (effective 2011).
Published by: Universidad de Guadalajara, Centro Universitario de la Cienaga, Av Universidad 1115, Col Lindavista, Ocotlan, Jalisco 47820, Mexico. http://cuci.udg.mx. Ed. Pedro Solis-Camara.

150 MEX ISSN 0185-6073
➤ **REVISTA MEXICANA DE PSICOLOGIA/MEXICAN JOURNAL OF PSYCHOLOGY.** Text in English, Spanish; Summaries in English, Spanish. 1984. s-a. USD 20 domestic; USD 40 foreign (effective 2000); USD 10 newsstand/cover. adv. back issues avail.; reprints avail. **Document type:** *Journal, Academic/Scholarly.* **Description:** Publishes original articles representing different theoretical and methodological approaches as well as contributions from different applied fields of psychology.
Indexed: A20, A22, ASCA, C01, Chicano, CurCont, E-psyche, P03, PsycInfo, PsycholAb, S02, S03, SCOPUS, SSCI, W07.
—BLDSC (7866.402000), IE, Ingenta.
Published by: Sociedad Mexicana de Psicologia, Indiana No. 260, Despacho 608, Mexico City, DF 03710, Mexico. TEL 52-5-5989566, FAX 52-5-6234046, http://www.psicologia.org.mx/. Ed. Dr. Roberto A Prado Alcala. adv.: page USD 150. Circ: 500 (paid).

P

150 PER ISSN 1726-9415
REVISTA PERUANA DE PSICOLOGIA. Text in Spanish. 2002. a. **Document type:** *Journal, Academic/Scholarly.*
Published by: Colegio de Psicologos del Peru, Jr Mateo Pumacahua 936, Jesus Maria, Lima, Peru. TEL 51-1-3305231, colegiopsicologosperu@terra.com.pe, http://www.colegiopsicologosperu.org.

150.19 PRT ISSN 0873-9129
REVISTA PORTUGUESA DE PSICANALISE; orgao da Sociedade Portuguesa de Psicanalise. Text in Portuguese. 1985. irreg., latest 2004. price varies.
Indexed: E-psyche, P03, PsycInfo, PsycholAb.
Published by: (Sociedade Portuguesa de Psicanalise), Edicoes Afrontamento, Lda., Rua de Costa Cabral, 859, Porto, 4200-225, Portugal. TEL 351-22-5074220, FAX 351-22-5074229, editorial@edicoesafrontamento.pt, http://www.edicoesafrontamento.pt. Ed. Jaime Milheiro.

150 PRT ISSN 0874-4696
REVISTA PORTUGUESA DE PSICOSSOMATICA. Text in Portuguese. 1999. s-a. **Document type:** *Journal, Academic/Scholarly.*
Published by: Sociedade Portuguesa de Psicossomatica, Rua Prof. Arsenio Cordeiro No. 7, 4o. Esq, Lisbon, 1600-595, Portugal. rmnscoelho@mail.telepac.pt, http://psychosomatic.med.up.pt/spps/.

150 ARG ISSN 1851-9083
REVISTA PSIENCIA. Text in Spanish. 2008. s-a. **Document type:** *Journal, Academic/Scholarly.*
Related titles: Online - full text ed.: ISSN 1851-9644. free (effective 2011).
Published by: Coband - Asociacion para el Avance de la Ciencia Psicologica, Av Nazca 1425, 1o B, Buenos Aires, C1416ASD, Argentina. contacto@coband.org, http://coband.org/. Ed. Ezequiel Benito.

150 PRI ISSN 1946-2026
BF5
REVISTA PUERTORRIQUENA DE PSICOLOGIA. Text in Spanish. 1983. a. **Document type:** *Journal, Academic/Scholarly.*
Related titles: Online - full text ed.: free (effective 2011).
Indexed: P30.
Published by: Asociacion de Psicologia de Puerto Rico, Ave Munoz Rivera 500, Condominio El Centro II Oficina 230, Hato Rey, 00918, Puerto Rico.

150 ROM ISSN 1582-6694
REVISTA ROMANA DE PSIHOTERAPII COGNITIVE SI COMPORTAMENTALE. Text in Romanian. 2001. a. **Document type:** *Journal, Academic/Scholarly.*
Indexed: PsycholAb.
Published by: Presa Universitara Clujeana/Cluj University Press, 51-st B.P.Hasdeu St, Cluj-Napoca, Romania. TEL 40-264-405352, http://www.editura.ubbcluj.ro.

150 ARG ISSN 1515-3894
REVISTA UNIVERSITARIA DE PSICOANALISIS. Text in Spanish. 1999. a. back issues avail. **Document type:** *Monographic series, Academic/Scholarly.*
Published by: Universidad de Buenos Aires, Facultad de Psicologia, Hipolito Yrigoyen 3241, Buenos Aires, C1207ABQ, Argentina. TEL 55-11-49316900, info@psi.uba.ar, http://www.psi.uba.ar/. Circ: 1,500.

150.195 616.8917 URY ISSN 0484-8268
BF173.A2
REVISTA URUGUAYA DE PSICOANALISIS. Text in Spanish. 1956. q. **Document type:** *Journal, Academic/Scholarly.*
Indexed: P03, P30, PsycInfo, PsycholAb.
Published by: Asociacion Psicoanalitica del Uruguay, Canelones 1571, Casilla de Correos 813, Montevideo, Uruguay. TEL 598-2-4007418, FAX 598-2-4080439, publicaciones@apuruguay.com.

150 URY ISSN 0797-4876
REVISTA URUGUAYA DE PSICOLOGIA. Text in Spanish. 1978. s-a. bk.rev. **Document type:** *Journal, Academic/Scholarly.*
Indexed: E-psyche, PsychoIAb.
Published by: (Asociacion de Psicologos Universitarios del Uruguay), Editorial Imago s.r.l., Treinta Y Tres, 1324, Montevideo, 11007, Uruguay. Ed. Ricardo Landeira.

159 ESP ISSN 2171-6676
▼ **REVISTA VINCULOS.** Text in Spanish. 2009. s-a. back issues avail. **Document type:** *Magazine, Academic/Scholarly.*
Published by: Instituto de Tecnicas de Grupo y Psicodrama, C San Martin de Porres, No. 12, OB, Madrid, 28035, Spain. TEL 34-91-3164216, FAX 34-91-3164727, itqp@itqp.org, http://www.itgpsicodrama.org/index.html. Ed. Pablo Poblacion.

REVUE DE NEUROPSYCHOLOGIE NEUROSCIENCES COGNITIVES ET CLINIQUES. *see* MEDICAL SCIENCES—Psychiatry And Neurology

REVUE DE PSYCHOEDUCATION. *see* EDUCATION

150 FRA ISSN 0297-1194
RC488.A1
➤ **REVUE DE PSYCHOTHERAPIE PSYCHANALYTIQUE DE GROUPE.** Text in French. 1985. s-a. EUR 50 domestic to individuals; EUR 60 foreign to individuals; EUR 55 domestic to institutions; EUR 45 foreign to members (effective 2011). back issues avail. **Document type:** *Journal, Academic/Scholarly.* **Description:** Contains reviews concerning groups dealing with psychoanalytic psychotherapy.
Related titles: Online - full text ed.: ISSN 1776-2863.
Indexed: PsycInfo, SCOPUS.
—INIST.
Published by: (Revue de Psychotherapie Psychanalytique de Groupe), Editions Eres, 33 Av. Marcel Dassault, Toulouse, 31500, France. TEL 33-5-61751576, FAX 33-5-61735289, eres@edition-eres.com. Eds. Jacqueline Falguiere, Jean Claude Rouchy. Circ: 700.

302 FRA ISSN 1920-3128
▼ **LA REVUE DE SYNERGOLOGIE.** Text in French. 2009. bi-m. **Document type:** *Journal, Academic/Scholarly.*
Published by: Institut Europeen de Synergologie, 21 Rue Brey, Paris, 75017, France. TEL 33-1-55371605, paris@synergologie.org, http://www.synergologie.org.

155.4 780 FRA ISSN 1779-515X
LA REVUE DES INITIATIVES. Text in French. 2003. a. back issues avail. **Document type:** *Magazine, Consumer.*
Published by: Enfance et Musique, 17 Rue Etienne Marcel, Pantin, 93500, France. TEL 33-1-48103000, FAX 33-1-48103009.

159.19 FRA
REVUE DU CHAMP LACANIEN. Text in French. irreg. EUR 20 newsstand/cover (effective 2010). **Document type:** *Journal, Academic/Scholarly.*
Published by: Ecole de Psychanalyse des Forums du Champ Lacanien, 118 rue d'Assas, Paris, 75006, France. TEL 33-1-56242256, FAX 33-1-56242237, http://www.champlacanien.net.

158 FRA ISSN 1162-9088
BF636.A1
➤ **REVUE EUROPEENE DE PSYCHOLOGIE APPLIQUEE/EUROPEAN REVIEW OF APPLIED PSYCHOLOGY.** Text in Multiple languages. 1950. 4/yr. EUR 298 in Europe to institutions; EUR 286.97 in France to institutions; JPY 38,800 in Japan to institutions; USD 354 elsewhere to institutions (effective 2012). adv. bk.rev. bibl.; charts; illus. index. **Document type:** *Journal, Academic/Scholarly.* **Description:** Devoted to European developments in applied psychology.
Formerly (until 1990): Revue de Psychologie Appliquee (0035-1709)
Related titles: Online - full text ed.: (from ScienceDirect).
Indexed: A20, A22, A26, ASCA, B21, CA, CDA, E-psyche, ErgAb, FR, Faml, I05, Inspec, NSA, P03, P30, PsycInfo, PsycholAb, S02, S03, SCOPUS, SSCI, T02, W07.
—BLDSC (3829.942000), IE, Infotrieve, Ingenta, INIST. **CCC.**
Published by: Elsevier Masson (Subsidiary of: Elsevier Health Sciences), 62 Rue Camille Desmoulins, Issy les Moulineaux, Cedex 92442, France. TEL 33-1-71165500, FAX 33-1-71165600, infos@elsevier-masson.fr. Ed. Jacques Py.

616.89 FRA ISSN 0035-2942
➤ **REVUE FRANCAISE DE PSYCHANALYSE.** Text in French; Abstracts in French, English, Italian, German, Spanish. 1926. 5/yr. EUR 127 domestic; EUR 148 foreign (effective 2012). adv. abstr.; bibl.; charts. index. back issues avail.; reprints avail. **Document type:** *Journal, Academic/Scholarly.* **Description:** Covers all aspects of psychoanalysis.
Related titles: Online - full text ed.: ISSN 2105-2964. 200?; Supplement(s): Congres de Psychanalyse des Langues Romanes. Rapports.
Indexed: A20, A22, ASCA, E-psyche, FR, IBR, IBSS, IBZ, IndMed, P03, P30, PCI, PsycInfo, PsycholAb, RASB, RILM, S02, S03, SCOPUS.
—BLDSC (7904.280000), GNLM, IE, Infotrieve, Ingenta, INIST. **CCC.**
Published by: (Societe Psychanalytique de Paris), Presses Universitaires de France, 6 Avenue Reille, Paris, 75685, France. TEL 33-1-58103161, FAX 33-1-45897530, revues@puf.com, http://www.puf.com. Ed. Denys Ribas.

150 FRA ISSN 1375-6249
REVUE FRANCOPHONE DE CLINIQUE COMPORTEMENTALE ET COGNITIVE. Text in French. 1996. q. **Document type:** *Journal, Academic/Scholarly.*
Indexed: P03, PsycInfo.
—BLDSC (7904.498800).
Published by: Association Francophone de Formation et de Recherche en Therapie Comportementale et Cognitive, 10 Avenue Gantin, Rumilly, 74150, France. TEL 33-4-50645175, http://www.afforthecc.org/. Ed. Sylvie Blairy.

301.1 150 FRA ISSN 0992-986X
CODEN: RIPSE4
REVUE INTERNATIONALE DE PSYCHOLOGIE SOCIALE/ INTERNATIONAL REVIEW OF SOCIAL PSYCHOLOGY. Text in English, French. 1976. q. EUR 63 domestic to individuals; EUR 71 foreign to individuals; EUR 95 to institutions (effective 2009). **Document type:** *Journal, Academic/Scholarly.* **Description:** Publishes critical overviews, theoretical notes, and empirical research from all areas of social psychologie.
Formerly (until 1988): Psychologie et Education (0151-2137)
Indexed: E-psyche, FR, P03, PsycInfo, PsycholAb, S02, S03, SCOPUS, SSCI, W07.
—BLDSC (7925.260000), IE, Ingenta, INIST. **CCC.**
Published by: Presses Universitaires de Grenoble, 1041 Rue des Residences, Grenoble, 38040, France. TEL 33-4-76825651, FAX 33-4-76827835, pug@oug.fr.

REVUE INTERNATIONALE DE PSYCHOSOCIOLOGIE. *see* SOCIOLOGY

158 CAN ISSN 0225-9885
BF636 A1R42
REVUE QUEBECOISE DE PSYCHOLOGIE. Text in English, French. 1980. 3/yr. CAD 46.01 domestic to individuals; CAD 65 foreign to individuals; CAD 63.26 domestic to institutions; CAD 28.76 to students (effective 2003).
Indexed: FR, P03, PsycholAb, S02, S03.
—INIST.
Published by: Universite du Quebec a Montreal, Departement de Psychologie, CP 6128, Montreal, PQ H3C 3J7, Canada. TEL 514-343-6663, FAX 514-343-2285, revuepsy@uqtr.ca. **Subscr. to:** c/o Sonia Boucher, 1100, av. Beaumont, Bureau 510, Mont-Royal, PQ H3P 3H5, Canada. TEL 514-738-1881, 800-363-2644, ext 238, revue.qc.psy@sympatico.ca.

150 ROM ISSN 1844-2382
➤ **REVUE ROUMAINE DE PSYCHANALYSE/ROMANIAN JOURNAL OF PSYCHOANALYSIS.** Text in English, French. 2008. s-a. USD 20 to institutions; ROL 45 per issue (effective 2011). bk.rev. abstr.; bibl. back issues avail.; reprints avail. **Document type:** *Journal, Academic/ Scholarly.* **Description:** Publishes original articles on current clinical and theoretical topics, reviews of classical psychoanalysis subjects, casuistry presentations, and interdisciplinary studies.
Related titles: Online - full text ed.
Published by: (Societatii Romane de Psihanaliza/Romanian Society of Psychoanalysis), Editura Renaissance, Str. Trestiana 1, Bl.32, Ap.41, Sect.4, Bucuresti, 040371, Romania. TEL 40-74-4652118, editurarenaissance@yahoo.com, http://www.editurarenaissance.ro/. Ed. Gianina Micu. Pub. Sorin Alexandru Sontea. R&P Brindusa Orasanu. Circ: 250.

➤ **RICERCA DI SENSO**; analisi esistenziale e logoterapia frankliana. *see* MEDICAL SCIENCES—Psychiatry And Neurology

616.89 ITA ISSN 0391-6081
RICERCHE DI PSICOLOGIA. Text in Italian; Summaries in English, Italian. 1967. q. EUR 81.50 combined subscription domestic to institutions; EUR 121 combined subscription foreign to institutions (effective 2009). adv. bk.rev. **Document type:** *Journal, Academic/ Scholarly.*
Former titles (until 1972): Annali di Psicologia (0390-7163); (until 1967): Universita degli Studi di Milano. Istituto di Psicologia. Annali (0391-996X)
Related titles: Online - full text ed.: ISSN 1972-5620.
Indexed: A22, DIP, E-psyche, IBR, IBZ, P03, PsycInfo, PsycholAb, S02, S03.
—BLDSC (7966.430000), IE, Ingenta.
Published by: (Universita degli Studi di Milano), Franco Angeli Edizioni, Viale Monza 106, Milan, 20127, Italy. TEL 39-02-2837141, FAX 39-02-26144793, redazioni@francoangeli.it, http://www.francoangeli.it.

155.4 ITA ISSN 1121-9602
RICHARD E PIGGLE; studi psicoanalitici del bambino e dell'adolescente. Text in Italian. 1993. 3/yr. USD 170 domestic to institutions; USD 220 foreign to institutions (effective 2009). adv. 128 p./no.; **Document type:** *Journal, Academic/Scholarly.*
Related titles: Online - full text ed.
Indexed: E-psyche, P03, PsycInfo, PsycholAb.
Published by: (Associazione Italiana di Psicoterapia Psicoanalitica Infantile), Il Pensiero Scientifico Editore, Via Bradano 3-C, Rome, 00199, Italy. TEL 39-06-862821, FAX 39-06-86282250, pensiero@pensiero.it, http://www.pensiero.it.

618.89 JPN ISSN 0389-3723
RINSHO SEISHIN BYORI/JAPANESE JOURNAL OF PSYCHOPATHOLOGY. Text in Japanese. 1980. 3/yr. JPY 4,600 (effective 2007). **Document type:** *Journal, Academic/Scholarly.*
Indexed: E-psyche.
—CCC.
Published by: (Nihon Seishin Byouri Gakkai/Japanese Society of Psychopathology), Seiwa Shoten Co. Ltd., 2-5 Kamitakaido, 1-chome, Suginami-ku, Tokyo, 168-0074, Japan.

150 JPN ISSN 0035-5496
RINSHOU SHINRIGAKU KENKYUU/JAPANESE JOURNAL OF CLINICAL PSYCHOLOGY. Text in Japanese. 1967. 3/yr. **Document type:** *Journal, Academic/Scholarly.*
—CCC.
Published by: Nihon Shinri Rinshou Gakkai/Association of Japanese Clinical Psychology, 2-40-14 Hongo, Bunkyo-ku, Yamazaki Bldg 501, Tokyo, 113-0033, Japan. TEL 81-3-38175851, FAX 81-3-38177800, http://www.u-netsurf.ne.jp/pajcp/.

158 ITA ISSN 1128-0689
RISORSA UOMO; rivista di psicologia del lavoro e dell'organizzazione. Text in Italian. 1993. q. EUR 63 combined subscription domestic to institutions (print & online eds.); EUR 97 combined subscription foreign to institutions (print & online eds.) (effective 2009). **Document type:** *Journal, Academic/Scholarly.*
Related titles: Online - full text ed.: ISSN 1972-5205.
Indexed: E-psyche, IBR, IBZ, P03, PsycInfo.
Published by: Franco Angeli Edizioni, Viale Monza 106, Milan, 20127, Italy. TEL 39-02-2837141, FAX 39-02-26144793, redazioni@francoangeli.it, http://www.francoangeli.it.

616.89 AUT ISSN 1019-1976
RISS; Zeitschrift fuer Psychoanalyse. Text in German. 1986. 3/yr. EUR 35 (effective 2007). **Document type:** *Journal, Academic/Scholarly.*
Indexed: E-psyche, MLA-IB.
Published by: Verlag Turia und Kant, Schottengasse 3A/5/DG1, Vienna, 1010, Austria. TEL 43-1-5320766, FAX 43-1-5320768, info@turia.at, http://www.turia.at. Circ: 300.

616.89 ITA ISSN 0035-6492
RIVISTA DI PSICOANALISI/ITALIAN PSYCHOANALYTICAL SOCIETY. JOURNAL. Text in Italian. 1955. q. EUR 70 domestic to individuals; EUR 80 foreign to individuals; EUR 115 domestic to institutions; EUR 125 foreign to institutions (effective 2009). bk.rev. bibl.; charts. index. reprints avail. **Document type:** *Journal, Academic/Scholarly.* **Description:** Covers research and study in the field of psychoanalysis.
Related titles: Online - full text ed.: ISSN 1974-4722; English ed.
Indexed: DIP, E-psyche, IBR, IBZ, P03, P30, PsycInfo, PsycholAb, SSCI, W07.
—GNLM.
Published by: (Societa Psicoanalitica Italiana), Edizioni Borla Srl, Via delle Fornaci 50, Rome, RM 00165, Italy. TEL 39-06-39376728, FAX 39-06-39376620, borla@edizioni-borla.it, http://www.edizioni-borla.it. Circ: 1,500.

150.19 ITA ISSN 0392-9787
RIVISTA DI PSICOLOGIA ANALITICA. Text in Italian. 1970. s-a. EUR 40 domestic to institutions; EUR 80 foreign to institutions (effective 2009). bk.rev. **Document type:** *Journal, Academic/Scholarly.* **Description:** Covers research and study in the field of analytical psychology.
Related titles: Online - full text ed.: ISSN 1972-6449.
Indexed: E-psyche.
Published by: Gruppo di Psicologia Analitica, Vicolo dei Serpenti 14, Rome, 00184, Italy. Circ: 1,500.

RIVISTA DI PSICOTERAPIA RELAZIONALE. *see* MEDICAL SCIENCES—Psychiatry And Neurology

616.89 ITA ISSN 1129-275X
➤ **RIVISTA ITALIANA DI ANALISI TRANSAZIONALE E METODOLOGIE PSICOTERAPEUTICHE.** Text in Italian; Summaries in English. 1981. s-a. bk.rev. bibl. index. back issues avail. **Document type:** *Journal, Academic/Scholarly.* **Description:** Presents theoretical research on transactional analysis as a philosophy and scientific theory. Reports on its application in psychiatry, medicine, in schools and in the training of adults.
Indexed: E-psyche.
Published by: Societa Italiana di Metodologie Psicoterapeutiche e Analisi Transazionale, Via Filippo Nicolai 70, Rome, 00136, Italy. TEL 39-06-35344043, FAX 39-06-35402495, simpat.scuola@flashnet.it. Ed. Maria Teresa Romanini. Circ: 1,000 (paid).

➤ **RIVISTA ITALIANA DI ERGONOMIA.** *see* ENGINEERING

150 ITA ISSN 1721-6664
RIVISTA ITALIANA DI GRUPPOANALISI; accordi analitici tra individuo, gruppo e istituzioni. Text in Italian. 1986. 3/yr. EUR 61.50 combined subscription domestic to institutions (print & online eds.); EUR 97 combined subscription foreign to institutions (print & online eds.) (effective 2009). **Document type:** *Journal, Academic/Scholarly.*
Related titles: Online - full text ed.: ISSN 1972-5264.
Published by: Franco Angeli Edizioni, Viale Monza 106, Milan, 20127, Italy. TEL 39-02-2837141, FAX 39-02-26144793, redazioni@francoangeli.it, http://www.francoangeli.it.

150 ITA ISSN 1120-2750
RIVISTA MEDICA ITALIANA DI PSICOTERAPIA ED IPNOSI. Text in Italian. 1989. s-a. EUR 26 (effective 2005). **Document type:** *Journal, Academic/Scholarly.*
Published by: Societa Medica Italiana di Psicoterapia ed Ipnosi (S M I P I), Via Porrettana 466, Casalecchio di Reno, BO 40033, Italy. TEL 39-051-573046, FAX 39-051-932309.

150 USA ISSN 1192-5604
BF698.8.R5
RORSCHACHIANA; yearbook of the International Rorschach Society. Text in English. 1945. a., latest vol.32, 2010. USD 172, EUR 132 combined subscription to institutions (print & online eds.) (effective 2011). **Document type:** *Journal, Academic/Scholarly.* **Description:** Provides updates on current uses of the Rorschach instrument in various countries and highlights recent results of research and theory.
Related titles: Online - full text ed.: ISSN 2151-206X (from ScienceDirect).
Indexed: P03, PsycInfo, SCOPUS.
—CCC.
Published by: (International Rorschach Society FRA), Hogrefe Publishing Corp., 875 Massachusetts Ave, 7th Fl, Cambridge, MA 02139. TEL 866-823-4726, FAX 617-354-6875, customservices@hogrefe-publishing.com. Ed. Sadegh Nashat. Circ: 3,500 (paid).

150 GBR ISSN 1361-2204
ROUTLEDGE PROGRESS IN PSYCHOLOGY. Text in English. 1996. irreg., latest 2000. price varies. back issues avail. **Document type:** *Monographic series, Academic/Scholarly.*
Indexed: E-psyche.
Published by: Routledge (Subsidiary of: Taylor & Francis Group), 4 Park Sq, Milton Park, Abingdon, Oxon OX14 4RN, United Kingdom. TEL 44-20-70176000, FAX 44-20-70176336, subscriptions@tandf.co.uk.

150 ITA ISSN 1828-1974
IL RUOLO TERAPEUTICO; rivista quadrimestrale di clinica e formazione psicoanalitica. Text in Italian. 1972. 3/yr. EUR 73 combined subscription domestic to institutions (print & online eds.); EUR 80 combined subscription foreign to institutions (print & online eds.) (effective 2009). **Document type:** *Journal, Academic/Scholarly.*
Related titles: Online - full text ed.: ISSN 1972-5159.
Indexed: E-psyche, IBR, IBZ.
Published by: Franco Angeli Edizioni, Viale Monza 106, Milan, 20127, Italy. TEL 39-02-2837141, FAX 39-02-26144793, redazioni@francoangeli.it, http://www.francoangeli.it.

302 USA ISSN 1556-4851
RUSSELL SAGE FOUNDATION SERIES ON TRUST. Text in English. irreg. prices vary.
Published by: Russell Sage Foundation, 112 E 64th St, New York, NY 10021. TEL 212-750-6000, FAX 212-371-4761, http://www.russellsage.org.

158 USA
➤ **RUTGERS SERIES ON SELF AND SOCIAL IDENTITY.** Text in English. 1997. irreg., latest 2001. price varies. back issues avail. **Document type:** *Monographic series, Academic/Scholarly.* **Description:** Examines issues in psychology relating to social identity and self-perception.

Published by: Oxford University Press (Subsidiary of: Oxford University Press), 198 Madison Ave, New York, NY 10016. orders.us@oup.com, http://www.us.oup.com.

150 NLD ISSN 1874-9062
➤ **S**; journal of the Jan van Eyck Circle for Lacanian ideology critique. Text in English. 2008. a. free (effective 2011). **Document type:** *Journal, Academic/Scholarly.*
Media: Online - full text.
Published by: Jan van Eyck Academie, Academieplein 1, Maastricht, 6211 KM, Netherlands. TEL 31-43-3503737, FAX 31-43-3503799, info@janvaneyck.nl, http://www.janvaneyck.nl. Ed. Sigi Joettkandt.

158 ZAF ISSN 0258-5200
HF5548.8
S A JOURNAL OF INDUSTRIAL PSYCHOLOGY. (South Africa) Text in English. 1975. 3/yr. **Document type:** *Journal, Academic/Scholarly.* **Description:** Aims to publish research in all the areas of specialization in the field of Industrial Psychology in South Africa.
Formerly (until 1986): Perspectives in Industrial Psychology
Related titles: Online - full text ed.: free (effective 2011).
Indexed: A01, ISAP, T02.
Published by: (Rand Afrikaans University, Department of Human Resource Management), OpenJournals Publishing, Postnet Ste 55, Private Bag X22, Tygervalley, 7536, South Africa. TEL 27-021-9754684, FAX 27-021-9753448. Ed. Gert Roodt.

616.89 USA ISSN 1543-1088
RD594.3
➤ **S C I PSYCHOSOCIAL PROCESS.** (Spinal Cord Injury) Text in English. 1988. q. bk.rev. charts; illus. **Document type:** *Journal, Academic/Scholarly.* **Description:** For psychologists and social workers who cares for spinal cord injured persons.
Indexed: C06, C07, C08, CINAHL, E-psyche, SWR&A.
—IE, Ingenta. **CCC.**
Published by: (American Association of Spinal Cord Injury Psychologists and Social Workers), United Spinal Association, 75-20 Astoria Blvd, Ste 120, Jackson Heights, NY 11370. TEL 800-404-2898, 718-803-3782, FAX 718-803-0414, info@unitedspinal.org, http://www.unitedspinal.org.

158.1 IND ISSN 0971-6610
S I S JOURNAL OF PROJECTIVE PSYCHOLOGY & MENTAL HEALTH. Text in English. 1994. s-a. INR 500 domestic to institutions; USD 60 foreign to institutions; INR 150, INR 25 per issue; free to members (effective 2011). bk.rev. **Document type:** *Journal, Academic/Scholarly.* **Description:** Focuses on the development of inkblot tests and personality assessment in clinical, counseling, cross-cultural, organizational, and health psychology settings.
Indexed: A01, P03, P25, P48, PQC, PsycInfo, PsycholAb, T02.
Published by: Somatic Inkblot Society, Sector-15 Post Office, PO Box 1107, Chandigarh, 160 015, India. TEL 91-172-710985, FAX 91-172-710986, sisdubey@rediffmail.com.

S R C D DEVELOPMENTS NEWSLETTER. *see* CHILDREN AND YOUTH—About

154.7 JPN ISSN 0581-3131
SAIMINGAKU KENKYU/JAPANESE JOURNAL OF HYPNOSIS. Text in Japanese. 1956. s-a. JPY 7,000 membership (effective 2005). **Document type:** *Journal, Academic/Scholarly.*
Indexed: P03, PsycholAb.
Published by: Nihon Saimin Igaku Shinri Gakkai/Japanese Society of Hypnosis, University of Tsukuba, Kasai Laboratory, 3-29-1 Otsuka, Bunkyo-ku, Tokyo, 112-0012, Japan. jsh@human.tsukuba.ac.jp, http://wwwsoc.nii.ac.jp/jsh/.

150 661.86 ITA ISSN 1592-0216
SALUTE E PREVENZIONE; rassegna italiana delle tossicodipendenze. Short title: S & P. Text in Italian. 1983. 3/yr. EUR 47 domestic to institutions; EUR 65 foreign to institutions (effective 2009). **Document type:** *Journal, Academic/Scholarly.*
Published by: Franco Angeli Edizioni, Viale Monza 106, Milan, 20127, Italy. TEL 39-02-2837141, FAX 39-02-26144793, redazioni@francoangeli.it, http://www.francoangeli.it.

150 IND ISSN 0971-3492
SAMIKSHA. Text in English. 1947. irreg., latest vol.53. bk.rev. back issues avail. **Document type:** *Journal, Academic/Scholarly.* **Description:** Presents scientific discussion of various aspects of psychoanalysis and related subjects.
Indexed: ASD, E-psyche, IPsyAb, PsycholAb.
Published by: Indian Psychoanalytical Society, 14 Parsibagan Ln, Kolkata, West Bengal 700 009, India. TEL 91-33-23508788.

150 370 301 RUS ISSN 1995-0047
➤ **SANKT-PETERBURGSKII UNIVERSITET. VESTNIK. SERIYA 12. PSIKHOLOGIYA, SOTSIOLOGIYA, PEDAGOGIKA.** Text in Russian. 1946. q. **Document type:** *Journal, Academic/Scholarly.*
Supersedes in part (in 2008): Sankt-Peterburgskii Universitet. Vestnik. Seriya 6. Filosofiya, Politologiya, Sotsiologiya, Psikhologiya, Pravo (1560-1390); Which was formerly (until June 1991): Leningradskii Universitet. Vestnik. Seriya 6. Filosofiya, Politologiya, Teoriya i Istoriya Sotsializma, Sotsiologiya, Psikhologiya, Pravo (1560-1811); (until 1990): Leningradskii Universitet. Vestnik. Seriya: Istoriya K P S S, Nauchnyi Kommunizm, Filosofiya, Pravo (0233-7541); Which superseded in part (in 1985): Leningradskii Universitet. Vestnik. Seriya: Ekonomika, Filosofiya i Pravo (0024-0818)
Published by: (Sankt-Peterburgskii Gosudarstvennyi Universitet, Fakul'tet Psikhologii/Saint-Petersburg State University, Department of Psyhology), Izdatel'skii Dom Sankt-Peterburgskogo Gosudarstvennogo Universiteta, V.O., 6-ya liniya, dom 11/21, komn 319, St Petersburg, 199004, Russian Federation. TEL 7-812-3252604, press@unipress.ru, http://www.unipress.ru. Ed. N A Gulyaeva.

150 CAN ISSN 0383-6320
CODEN: SMQUEK
➤ **SANTE MENTALE AU QUEBEC.** Text in French; Summaries in English, French. 1976. s-a. CAD 48.42, EUR 32 to institutions (effective 2011). **Document type:** *Journal, Academic/Scholarly.* **Description:** Publishes articles on experimental research and social innovation. Aims to fulfill the needs in development of scientific, academic and clinical knowledge.
Related titles: Online - full text ed.: ISSN 1708-3923.
Indexed: A22, A26, C06, C07, C08, CA, CINAHL, CPerI, E-psyche, EMBASE, ExcerpMed, FR, H12, I05, INI, MEDLINE, P30, PdeR, R10, Reac, S02, S03, SCOPUS, SOPODA, SWR&A, SociolAb, T02.
—BLDSC (8075.341000), GNLM, IE, Infotrieve, Ingenta, INIST. **CCC.**
Published by: Revue Sante Mentale au Quebec, Succ. Place d'Armes, C.P. 548, Montreal, PQ H2Y 3H3, Canada. TEL 514-843-2015, FAX 514-843-2160. Ed. Jean-Francois Saucier. Circ: 1,200.

616.89 CAN ISSN 1718-2050
THE SATIR JOURNAL. Text in English. 2006. 3/yr. USD 65 to individuals; CAD 55, USD 50 to individual members; USD 180 to institutions (effective 2007). **Document type:** *Journal, Academic/Scholarly.*
Related titles: Online - full text ed.: ISSN 1718-2069.
Indexed: A01, CA, T02.
Published by: Satir Institute of the Pacific, 13686 94A Avenue, Surrey, BC V3V 1N1, Canada. TEL 604-634-0572, sjeditor@shaw.ca, http://www.satirpacific.org.

150 GBR ISSN 0036-5564
BF1 CODEN: SJPYA2
➤ **SCANDINAVIAN JOURNAL OF PSYCHOLOGY.** Text in English. 1960. bi-m. GBP 649 in United Kingdom to institutions; EUR 824 in Europe to institutions; USD 1,182 in the Americas to institutions; USD 1,378 elsewhere to institutions; GBP 747 combined subscription in United Kingdom to institutions (print & online eds.); EUR 948 combined subscription in Europe to institutions (print & online eds.); USD 1,360 combined subscription in the Americas to institutions (print & online eds.); USD 1,585 combined subscription elsewhere to institutions (print & online eds.) (effective 2012). adv. bibl.; charts; illus. index, cum.index every 5 yrs. back issues avail.; reprint service avail. from PSC. **Document type:** *Journal, Academic/Scholarly.* **Description:** Devoted to original scientific contributions from all fields of psychology.
Related titles: Online - full text ed.: ISSN 1467-9450. GBP 649 in United Kingdom to institutions; EUR 824 in Europe to institutions; USD 1,182 in the Americas to institutions; USD 1,378 elsewhere to institutions (effective 2012) (from IngentaConnect); Supplement(s): Scandinavian Journal of Psychology. Supplementum. ISSN 0281-0573.
Indexed: A01, A03, A08, A20, A22, A26, AMHA, ASCA, AddicA, B04, B21, BehAb, BibInd, C06, C07, CA, CDA, CIS, CurCont, DentInd, E-psyche, E01, EMBASE, ERA, ESPM, ErgAb, ExcerpMed, FR, FamI, H12, I05, IndMed, MEA&I, MEDLINE, MLA-IB, NSA, P03, P30, P43, PCI, PsycInfo, PsycholAb, R10, RASB, Reac, RiskAb, S02, S03, SCOPUS, SOPODA, SSCI, SociolAb, T02, THA, W07.
—BLDSC (8087.520000), GNLM, IE, Infotrieve, Ingenta, INIST. **CCC.**
Published by: (Psychological Associations of Denmark, Finland, Norway and Sweden), Wiley-Blackwell Publishing Ltd. (Subsidiary of: John Wiley & Sons, Inc.), 9600 Garsington Rd, Oxford, OX4 2DQ, United Kingdom. TEL 44-1865-776868, FAX 44-1865-714591, customerservices@blackwellpublishing.com. Ed. Jerker Ronnberg TEL 46-13-282107. Adv. contact Craig Pickett TEL 44-1865-476267.

370.15 USA ISSN 1866-2625
LB3430
▼ ➤ **SCHOOL MENTAL HEALTH.** Text in English. 2009. q. EUR 193, USD 290 combined subscription to institutions (print & online eds.) (effective 2012). adv. back issues avail.; reprint service avail. from PSC. **Document type:** *Journal, Academic/Scholarly.* **Description:** Brings out research related to prevention, education, and treatment practices that target the emotional and behavioral health of children in the education system.
Related titles: Online - full text ed.: ISSN 1866-2633. 2009 (from IngentaConnect).
Indexed: A22, E01, P30, PsycInfo, SCOPUS.
—IE. **CCC.**
Published by: Springer New York LLC (Subsidiary of: Springer Science+Business Media), 233 Spring St, New York, NY 10013. TEL 212-460-1500, FAX 212-460-1575, service-ny@springer.com, http://www.springer.com. Ed. Steven W Evans.

155.4 USA ISSN 0160-5585
CODEN: SPSYDS
SCHOOL PSYCHOLOGIST. Text in English. 19??. q. adv. **Document type:** *Newsletter, Trade.* **Description:** Provides information members and the field of school psychology as well as support and promote research in practice in school psychology and education.
Related titles: Online - full content ed.
Published by: American Psychological Association, Division of School Psychology, Division 16, School Psychology, c/o Division Service, 750 First Street N.E., Washington, DC 20002-4242. Ed. Linda A Reddy TEL 201-692-2649. adv.: page USD 600.

SCHOOL PSYCHOLOGY INTERNATIONAL. *see* EDUCATION—Teaching Methods And Curriculum

370.15 USA ISSN 1045-3830
LB1027.55 CODEN: SPSQE5
➤ **SCHOOL PSYCHOLOGY QUARTERLY.** Abbreviated title: S P Q. Text in English. 1986. q. USD 116 domestic to individuals; USD 143 foreign to individuals; USD 415 domestic to institutions; USD 460 foreign to institutions (effective 2011). adv. bk.rev. illus. index. 128 p./no.; back issues avail.; reprints avail. **Document type:** *Journal, Academic/Scholarly.* **Description:** Focuses on the scientific understanding of school psychology; covers new concepts in enhancing life experiences of children, families and schools.
Formerly (until 1990): Professional School Psychology (0886-3016)
Related titles: Online - full text ed.: ISSN 1939-1560 (from ScienceDirect).
Indexed: A01, A03, A08, A22, ASCA, CA, CPE, CurCont, E-psyche, E01, E03, ERI, ERIC, FamI, P02, P03, P18, P25, P30, P48, P53, P54, P55, PQC, PsycInfo, PsycholAb, S21, SCOPUS, SOPODA, SSAI, SSAb, SSCI, SSI, SociolAb, T02, W03, W07.
—BLDSC (8092.926500), IE, Infotrieve, Ingenta. **CCC.**
Published by: (American Psychological Association, Division of School Psychology), American Psychological Association, 750 First St, NE, Washington, DC 20002. TEL 202-336-5500, 800-374-2721, journals@apa.org. Ed. Randy W Kamphaus. Adv. contact Doug Constant TEL 202-336-5574. Circ: 2,500 (paid).

370.15 USA ISSN 0279-6015
LB1051
➤ **SCHOOL PSYCHOLOGY REVIEW.** Abbreviated title: S P R. Text in English. 1972. q. free to members (effective 2010). adv. bk.rev. abstr.; bibl.; charts; stat.; illus. back issues avail.; reprints avail. **Document type:** *Journal, Academic/Scholarly.* **Description:** Covers research, training, and practice in school psychology.
Formerly (until 1980): School Psychology Digest (0160-5569)
Related titles: Microform ed.: (from PQC); Online - full text ed.
Indexed: A01, A02, A03, A08, A22, A26, ASCA, B04, BRD, CA, CMM, CPE, CurCont, E02, E03, E06, E07, E08, ERI, ERIC, EdA, EdI, FamI, G08, I05, M01, M02, P03, P04, P07, P18, P25, P30, P43, P48, P53, P54, P55, PQC, PsycInfo, PsycholAb, S02, S03, S09, SCOPUS, SSCI, T02, W03, W05, W07.
—BLDSC (8092.926600), IE, Infotrieve, Ingenta. **CCC.**
Published by: National Association of School Psychologists, 4340 EW Hwy, Ste 402, Bethesda, MD 20814. TEL 301-657-0270, FAX 301-657-0275, publications@naspweb.org. Ed. Thomas J Power TEL 215-590-7447.

158.7 DEU ISSN 1611-2806
SCHRIFTEN ZUR ARBEITS-, BETRIEBS- UND ORGANISATIONSPSYCHOLOGIE. Text in German. 2003. irreg., latest vol.51, 2010. price varies. **Document type:** *Monographic series, Academic/Scholarly.*
Published by: Verlag Dr. Kovac, Leverkusenstr 13, Hamburg, 22761, Germany. TEL 49-40-3988800, FAX 49-40-39888055, info@verlagdrkovac.de.

150 CHE
SCHRIFTEN ZUR ARBEITSPSYCHOLOGIE. Text in German. 1953. irreg., latest vol.65, 2008. price varies. **Document type:** *Monographic series, Academic/Scholarly.*
Published by: (Universitaet Innsbruck, Institut fuer Psychologie AUT), Verlag Hans Huber AG (Subsidiary of: Hogrefe Verlag GmbH & Co. KG), Laenggassstr 76, Bern 9, 3000, Switzerland. TEL 41-31-3004500, FAX 41-31-3004590, verlag@hanshuber.com, http://verlag.hanshuber.com.

150 DEU ISSN 2190-412X
▼ **SCHRIFTEN ZUR DIFFERENZIELLEN PSYCHOLOGIE.** Text in German. 2010. irreg. price varies. **Document type:** *Monographic series, Academic/Scholarly.*
Published by: Verlag Dr. Kovac, Leverkusenstr 13, Hamburg, 22761, Germany. TEL 49-40-3988800, FAX 49-40-39888055, info@verlagdrkovac.de.

155 DEU ISSN 1617-2078
SCHRIFTEN ZUR ENTWICKLUNGSPSYCHOLOGIE. Text in German. 2001. irreg., latest vol.22, 2009. price varies. **Document type:** *Monographic series, Academic/Scholarly.*
Published by: Verlag Dr. Kovac, Leverkusenstr 13, Hamburg, 22761, Germany. TEL 49-40-3988800, FAX 49-40-39888055, info@verlagdrkovac.de.

158 DEU ISSN 1618-8012
SCHRIFTEN ZUR MEDIZINISCHEN PSYCHOLOGIE. Text in German. 2002. irreg., latest vol.24, 2010. price varies. **Document type:** *Monographic series, Academic/Scholarly.*
Published by: Verlag Dr. Kovac, Leverkusenstr 13, Hamburg, 22761, Germany. TEL 49-40-3988800, FAX 49-40-39888055, info@verlagdrkovac.de.

SCHRIFTEN ZUR MUSIKPSYCHOLOGIE UND MUSIKAESTHETIK. *see* MUSIC

SCHRIFTEN ZUR PAEDAGOGISCHEN PSYCHOLOGIE. *see* EDUCATION

150 DEU ISSN 1618-2715
SCHRIFTEN ZUR SOZIALPSYCHOLOGIE. Text in German. 2001. irreg., latest vol.21, 2010. price varies. **Document type:** *Monographic series, Academic/Scholarly.*
Published by: Verlag Dr. Kovac, Leverkusenstr 13, Hamburg, 22761, Germany. TEL 49-40-3988800, FAX 49-40-39888055, info@verlagdrkovac.de.

302 794 DEU ISSN 1611-2814
SCHRIFTEN ZUR SPORTPSYCHOLOGIE. Text in German. 2003. irreg., latest vol.3, 2008. price varies. **Document type:** *Monographic series, Academic/Scholarly.*
Published by: Verlag Dr. Kovac, Leverkusenstr 13, Hamburg, 22761, Germany. TEL 49-40-3988800, FAX 49-40-39888055, info@verlagdrkovac.de.

302 795 DEU ISSN 1861-759X
SCHRIFTENREIHE ZUR GLUECKSSPIELFORSCHUNG. Text in German. 2006. irreg., latest vol.5, 2010. price varies. **Document type:** *Monographic series, Academic/Scholarly.*
Published by: Peter Lang GmbH (Subsidiary of: Peter Lang Publishing Group), Eschborner Landstr 42-50, Frankfurt Am Main, 60489, Germany. TEL 49-69-7807050, FAX 49-69-78070550, zentrale.frankfurt@peterlang.com. Ed. Tilman Becker.

155.3 610 BRA ISSN 1415-3211
SCIENTIA SEXUALIS. Text in Portuguese. 1997. s-a. **Document type:** *Journal, Academic/Scholarly.* **Description:** Publishes the results of research on human sexual behavior by UGF professors and graduate students.
Published by: Universidade Gama Filho, Rua Manoel Vitorino 625, Piedade, Rio de Janeiro, RJ 20748-900, Brazil. TEL 55-21-32137735, FAX 55-21-32137731, http://www.ugf.br.

150 USA ISSN 1538-4985
RC467
THE SCIENTIFIC REVIEW OF MENTAL HEALTH PRACTICE. Abbreviated title: S R M H P. Text in English. 2002 (Mar.). s-a. USD 60 in US & Canada; USD 70 elsewhere (effective 2010). back issues avail. **Document type:** *Journal, Academic/Scholarly.* **Description:** Focuses in distinguishing scientifically supported claims from scientifically unsupported claims in clinical psychology, psychiatry, social work, and allied disciplines.
Related titles: Online - full text ed.
Indexed: A01, CA, P03, PsycInfo, T02.
—BLDSC (8203.917000).
Published by: Prometheus Books Inc., 59 John Glenn Dr, Amherst, NY 14228. TEL 716-691-0133, 800-421-0351, FAX 716-691-0137, marketing@prometheusbooks.com, http://www.prometheusbooks.com. Ed. Scott O Lillienfeld TEL 404-727-1125. **Subscr. to:** Commission for Scientific Medicine and Mental Health, c/o Barry Karr, PO Box 741, Amherst, NY 14226. TEL 716-636-4869 ext 217, FAX 716-636-1733, bkarr@centerforinquiry.net, http://www.srmhp.org.

616.8 USA ISSN 0164-7393
THE SCRIPT. Text in English. 19??. 9/yr. free to members (effective 2010). **Document type:** *Newsletter, Trade.* **Description:** Offers articles and interviews; editorial columns; news about organizational activities, such as workshops, conferences, and elections; information on training; and announcements of awards and special events.

P

Related titles: Online - full text ed.: free (effective 2010).
Indexed: E-psyche.
Published by: International Transactional Analysis Association, 2186 Rheem Dr, B-1, Pleasanton, CA 94588. TEL 925-600-8110, FAX 925-600-8112, itaa@itaa-net.org. Ed. Laurie Hawkes.

155.2 ITA ISSN 0391-4224
SCRITTURA (URBINO); rivista di problemi grafologici. Text in Italian. 1971. q. EUR 28 (effective 2009). bk.rev. index. 100 p./no.; **Document type:** *Magazine, Trade.*
Indexed: E-psyche.
Published by: Istituto Grafologico G. Moretti, Piazza San Francesco, 7, Urbino, PS 61029, Italy. info@grafologia.it, http://www.grafologia.it.

150 PRT ISSN 1647-7367
▼ **SE.. NAO.** Text in Portuguese. 2010. s-a. **Document type:** *Magazine, Trade.*
Published by: (Associacao Portuguesa de Psicanalise e Psicoterapia Psicanalitica), Coisas de Ler Editora, Rua Professor Egas Moniz Lote 4, Cave Traseira, Vialonga, 2625-659, Portugal. TEL 351-211-919350, FAX 351-211-919349, info@coisasdeler.pt, http://www.coisasdeler.pt.

SEEING AND PERCEIVING; an international journal on computation, perception, attention and action. *see* MATHEMATICS—Computer Applications

150 571 JPN ISSN 0289-2405
SEIRI SHINRIGAKU TO SEISHIN SEIRIGAKU/JAPANESE JOURNAL OF PHYSIOLOGICAL PSYCHOLOGY AND PSYCHOPHYSIOLOGY. Text in Japanese. 1983. s-a. JPY 7,500 membership (effective 2005). **Document type:** *Journal, Academic/Scholarly.*
Indexed: P03, PsycInfo, PsycholAb.
Published by: Nihon Seiri Shinri Gakkai/Japanese Society of Physiological Psychology and Psychophysiology, c/o Waseda University, School of Sports Sciences, 2-579-15 Mikajima, Tokorozawa, Saitama 359-1192, Japan. jspp@list.waseda.jp, http://www.pplab.org/jspp/.

158 DEU ISSN 1863-530X
SELBSTMANAGEMENT-LETTER. Text in German. 2003. w. free (effective 2011). **Document type:** *Newsletter, Trade.*
Media: E-mail.
Published by: Orgenda Verlag fuer Persoenliche Weiterentwicklung (Subsidiary of: V N R Verlag fuer die Deutsche Wirtschaft AG), Theodor Heuss Str 2-4, Bonn, 53177, Germany. TEL 49-228-9550140, FAX 49-228-3696001, info@orgenda.de, http://www.orgenda.de.

616.89 DEU ISSN 1615-343X
SELBSTPSYCHOLOGIE/SELF PSYCHOLOGY; europaeische Zeitschrift fuer psychoanalytische Therapie und Forschung. Text in German, English. 2000. q. EUR 64 domestic; EUR 75 in Europe; EUR 110 elsewhere (effective 2009). **Document type:** *Journal, Academic/Scholarly.* **Description:** Contains articles on various aspects of psychoanalytical therapy and research.
Indexed: DIP, IBR, IBZ, P03, PsycInfo, PsycholAb.
—BLDSC (8230.479500).
Published by: Brandes und Apsel Verlag GmbH, Scheidswaldstr 22, Frankfurt Am Main, 60385, Germany. TEL 49-69-272995170, FAX 49-69-2729951710, info@brandes-apsel-verlag.de, http://www.brandes-apsel-verlag.de.

152 GBR ISSN 1529-8868
BF697
➤ **SELF AND IDENTITY.** Text in English. 2002. q. GBP 345 combined subscription in United Kingdom to institutions (print & online eds.); EUR 458, USD 574 combined subscription to institutions (print & online eds.) (effective 2012). back issues avail.; reprint service avail. from PSC. **Document type:** *Journal, Academic/Scholarly.* **Description:** Features articles dedicated to the study of social and psychological processes, such as, cognition, motivation, emotion, and interpersonal behavior that involve the human capacity for self-awareness, self-representation, and self-regulation.
Related titles: Online - full text ed.: ISSN 1529-8876. 2002. GBP 311 in United Kingdom to institutions; EUR 412, USD 517 to institutions (effective 2012) (from IngentaConnect).
Indexed: A01, A03, A08, A22, CA, CurCont, E-psyche, E01, P03, P10, P30, P43, P48, P53, P54, PQC, PsycInfo, PsycholAb, SCOPUS, SSCI, T02, W07.
—IE, Infotrieve, Ingenta. **CCC.**
Published by: (International Society for Self and Identity USA), Psychology Press (Subsidiary of: Taylor & Francis Ltd.), 27 Church Rd, Hove, E Sussex BN3 2FA, United Kingdom. TEL 44-20-70176000, FAX 44-20-70176717, info@psypress.co.uk, http://www.psypress.com. Ed. Mark Alicke. Adv. contact Linda Hann TEL 44-1344-779945. **Subscr. in N. America to:** Taylor & Francis Inc., Customer Services Dept, 325 Chestnut St, 8th Fl, Philadelphia, PA 19106. TEL 215-625-8900, 800-354-1420, FAX 215-625-2940, customerservice@taylorandfrancis.com; **Subscr. to:** Taylor & Francis Ltd., Journals Customer Service, Sheepen Pl, Colchester, Essex CO3 3LP, United Kingdom. TEL 44-20-70175544, FAX 44-20-70175198, subscriptions@tandf.co.uk.

301.1 150 GBR ISSN 0306-0497
SELF & SOCIETY; a forum for contemporary psychology. Text in English. 1973. q. GBP 4.50 newsstand/cover to non-members; free to members (effective 2009). adv. bk.rev. back issues avail. **Document type:** *Journal, Academic/Scholarly.* **Description:** Discusses human potential and research work in psychology and sociology: promotes a holistic view of life and the importance of the individual.
Indexed: E-psyche, RASB.
—BLDSC (8235.350000), IE, Ingenta. **CCC.**
Published by: Association for Humanistic Psychology in Britain, BM Box 3582, London, WC1N 3XX, United Kingdom. TEL 44-7758-617149, admin@ahpb.org.uk. Ed. Julian Nangle.

150 360 USA
SELF-HELP 2000. Text in English. 1977. q. bk.rev. **Document type:** *Newsletter, Consumer.* **Description:** Covers trends in the burgeoning self-help movement, describes mutual support group activities, and discusses the theoretical underpinnings of self-help mutual support.
Formerly (until 2000): Self Help Reporter Newsletter
Indexed: E-psyche.
Published by: National Self Help Clearinghouse, Graduate School and University Center, City University of New York, 365 Fifth Ave, Suite 3300, New York, NY 10016. TEL 212-817-1822, info@selfhelpweb.org. Ed. Audrey Gartner. Circ: 1,000 (paid).

SELF-HELP MAGAZINE. *see* SOCIAL SERVICES AND WELFARE

THE SELF-HELP SOURCEBOOK; your guide to community and online support group. *see* SOCIAL SERVICES AND WELFARE

SEMIOTIC AND COGNITIVE STUDIES. *see* PHILOSOPHY

154.6 POL ISSN 1641-6007
➤ **SEN/SLEEP.** Text in Polish, English. 2001. q. EUR 18 to individuals; EUR 25 to institutions (effective 2011). **Document type:** *Journal, Academic/Scholarly.* **Description:** Intended for specialists involved in sleep disorder management, including family doctors. Contains original papers (clinical as well as experimental), reviews, case reports and letters to editor.
Related titles: Online - full content ed.: ISSN 1644-3306. PLZ 14 to individuals; PLZ 52 to institutions (effective 2007).
Indexed: C06, C07, EMBASE, ExcerpMed, R10, Reac, SCOPUS.
—BLDSC (8239.560000).
Published by: (Polskie Towarzystwo Badan nad Snem/Polish Sleep Research Society), Wydawnictwo Via Medica, ul Swietokrzyska 73, Gdansk, 80180, Poland. TEL 48-58-3209494, FAX 48-58-3209460, redakcja@viamedica.pl, http://www.viamedica.pl. Ed. Zbigniew Nowicki.

150.18 GBR ISSN 1741-4725
➤ **SENSORY FORMATIONS.** Text in English. 2003 (Dec.)-200?; N.S. 2004. irreg., latest 2009. price varies. **Document type:** *Monographic series, Academic/Scholarly.* **Description:** Aims to enhance our understanding of the role of the senses in history, culture and aesthetics.
Published by: Berg Publishers (Subsidiary of: Oxford International Publishers Ltd.), 1st Fl Angel Ct, 81 St Clements St, Oxford, Berks OX4 1AW, United Kingdom. TEL 44-1865-245104, FAX 44-1865-791165, enquiry@bergpublishers.com. Ed. David Howes.

150 PRT ISSN 1645-6378
SER. Text in Portuguese. 199?. irreg. **Document type:** *Journal, Academic/Scholarly.*
Published by: Instituto Superior de Psicologia Aplicada, Rua Jardim do Tabaco 34, Lisbon, 1149-041, Portugal. TEL 351-21-8811700, FAX 351-21-8860954, info@ispa.pt, http://www.ispa.pt.

SERENITY MATTERS. *see* NEW AGE PUBLICATIONS

THE SERIES ON SOCIAL EMOTIONAL LEARNING. *see* EDUCATION

150.19 ITA ISSN 1124-3899
RC500
SETTING. Text in Italian. 1990. s-a. EUR 47.50 combined subscription domestic to institutions (print & online eds.); EUR 59 combined subscription foreign to institutions (print & online eds.) (effective 2009). **Document type:** *Journal, Academic/Scholarly.* **Description:** Publishes studies of the association covering the field of psychoanalysis.
Formerly (until 1995): Associazione di Studi Psicoanalitici. Quaderni (1124-3902)
Related titles: Online - full text ed.: ISSN 1972-5175.
Indexed: E-psyche.
Published by: (Associazione di Studi Psicoanalitici), Franco Angeli Edizioni, Viale Monza 106, Milan, 20127, Italy. TEL 39-02-2837141, FAX 39-02-26144793, redazioni@francoangeli.it, http://www.francoangeli.it.

155.3 USA ISSN 1554-222X
SEX, LOVE AND PSYCHOLOGY. Text in English. 2007. irreg., latest 2010. price varies. back issues avail. **Document type:** *Monographic series, Academic/Scholarly.* **Description:** Each volume focuses on a different aspect of sex psychology. Topics include how memories affect relationships, the impact of health and public policy on our image of sex, teens and HIV, and transsexuality.
Published by: Praeger Publishers (Subsidiary of: Greenwood Publishing Group Inc.), 88 Post Rd W, Westport, CT 06881. TEL 800-368-6868, tech.support@greenwood.com, http://www.greenwood.com. Ed. Judy Kuriansky.

306.7 USA ISSN 0360-0025
HQ768 CODEN: SROLDH
➤ **SEX ROLES**; a journal of research. Text in English. 1975. m. EUR 1,763, USD 1,840 combined subscription to institutions (print & online eds.) (effective 2012). adv. bk.rev. bibl.; charts; illus. Index. back issues avail.; reprint service avail. from PSC. **Document type:** *Journal, Academic/Scholarly.* **Description:** Covers original research, theory, and reviews concerned with the underlying processes and consequences of gender role socialization, perceptions, and attitudes.
Related titles: Microfilm ed.: (from PQC); Online - full text ed.: ISSN 1573-2762 (from IngentaConnect).
Indexed: A01, A02, A03, A08, A20, A22, A26, ABS&EES, AMHA, ASCA, AbAn, B04, BRD, BibLing, C28, CA, CDA, CMCI, Chicano, CurCont, DIP, E-psyche, E01, E02, E03, E07, E08, E16, ERA, ERI, ESPM, EdA, EdI, F09, FR, FamI, FemPer, G08, G10, H09, HEA, I05, IBR, IBZ, L01, L02, M01, M02, M06, M12, MEA&I, MLA-IB, P02, P03, P10, P12, P18, P25, P27, P30, P34, P42, P46, P48, P53, P54, PCI, PQC, PSA, PsycInfo, PsycholAb, RASB, RILM, RefZh, RiskAb, S02, S03, S05, S09, S19, S20, S21, SCOPUS, SFSA, SOPODA, SSA, SSAI, SSAb, SSCI, SSI, SWR&A, SociolAb, T02, V05, W01, W02, W03, W05, W07, W09, WSA.
—BLDSC (8254.457000), GNLM, IE, Infotrieve, Ingenta, INIST. **CCC.**
Published by: Springer New York LLC (Subsidiary of: Springer Science+Business Media), 233 Spring St, New York, NY 10013. TEL 212-460-1500, FAX 212-460-1575, service-ny@springer.com. Ed. Irene Hanson Frieze.

306.7 USA ISSN 1079-0632
RC560.S47 CODEN: SAJTEY
➤ **SEXUAL ABUSE**; a journal of research and treatment. Text in English. 1988. q. USD 843, GBP 496 combined subscription to institutions (print & online eds.); USD 826, GBP 486 to institutions (effective 2011). adv. illus. back issues avail.; reprint service avail. from PSC. **Document type:** *Journal, Academic/Scholarly.* **Description:** Publishes clinical and theoretical material relating to the field of sexual abuse. Addresses causes, treatment and consequences for both perpetrators and victims.
Formerly (until 1995): Annals of Sex Research (0843-4611)
Related titles: Online - full text ed.: ISSN 1573-286X. USD 759, GBP 446 to institutions (effective 2011) (from IngentaConnect).
Indexed: A20, A22, A26, BibLing, C06, C07, CA, CJPI, CurCont, E-psyche, E01, EMBASE, ESPM, ExcerpMed, F09, FamI, H12, IndMed, MEDLINE, P03, P30, PQC, PsycInfo, PsycholAb, R10, Reac, RiskAb, S02, S03, SCOPUS, SSA, SSCI, SociolAb, T02, W07.
—BLDSC (8254.482000), GNLM, IE, Infotrieve, Ingenta. **CCC.**
Published by: (Association for the Treatment of Sexual Abusers), Sage Publications, Inc., 2455 Teller Rd, Thousand Oaks, CA 91320. TEL 805-499-9774, 800-818-7243, FAX 805-499-0871, 800-583-2665, info@sagepub.com. Ed. Howard Barbaree. **Subscr. outside the Americas to:** Sage Publications Ltd., 1 Oliver's Yard, 55 City Rd, London EC1Y 1SP, United Kingdom. TEL 44-20-73248701, FAX 44-20-73248733, subscription@sagepub.co.uk.

150 614.1 364.3 AUS ISSN 1833-8488
➤ **SEXUAL ABUSE IN AUSTRALIA AND NEW ZEALAND.** Text in English. 2008 (Jul.). s-a. AUD 80; AUD 40 per issue (effective 2011). bk.rev. Index. back issues avail. **Document type:** *Journal, Academic/Scholarly.* **Description:** Contains articles on the psychological and social factors that impact on sexual offending and sexual abuse, and the victims of sexual offending. Covers risk assessment and profiling of offenders and offenses, treatment and custody issues, pure and applied research into features associated with sexual offending and sexual abuse, and impact of offending and abuse on victim/survivors and treatment for such persons.
Indexed: ASSIA.
Published by: Australia News Zealand Association for the Treatment of Sexual Abuse (A N Z A T S A), PO Box K1330, Haymarket, NSW 1240, Australia. TEL 61-416-418636, info@anzatsa.org. Ed., R&P Douglas Boer.

616.89 USA ISSN 1072-0162
RC560.S43 CODEN: SACECK
➤ **SEXUAL ADDICTION & COMPULSIVITY**; the journal of treatment and prevention. Text in English. 1994. q. GBP 208 combined subscription in United Kingdom to institutions (print & online eds.); EUR 274, USD 344 combined subscription to institutions (print & online eds.) (effective 2012). bk.rev. index. reprint service avail. from PSC. **Document type:** *Journal, Academic/Scholarly.* **Description:** Features articles that deal with topics pertaining to the growing disorder of sexual addiction and compulsivity.
Related titles: Online - full text ed.: ISSN 1532-5318. 1994. GBP 187 in United Kingdom to institutions; EUR 246, USD 310 to institutions (effective 2012) (from IngentaConnect).
Indexed: A01, A03, A08, A22, ASSIA, C06, C07, C08, CA, CINAHL, CJA, CJPI, E-psyche, E01, ESPM, FamI, G10, L03, P03, P43, PQC, PsycInfo, PsycholAb, RiskAb, S02, S03, SCOPUS, SociolAb, T02, V&AA.
—IE, Infotrieve, Ingenta. **CCC.**
Published by: (The Society for the Advancement of Sexual Health), Routledge (Subsidiary of: Taylor & Francis Group), 325 Chestnut St, Ste 800, Philadelphia, PA 19106. TEL 215-625-8900, 800-354-1420, FAX 215-625-2940, orders@taylorandfrancis.com. Ed. Charles Samenow. **Subsc. in Europe:** Taylor & Francis Ltd. tf.enquiries@tfinforma.com.

155.3 610 GBR ISSN 1468-1994
➤ **SEXUAL AND RELATIONSHIP THERAPY.** Text in English. 1986. q. GBP 496 combined subscription in United Kingdom to institutions (print & online eds.); EUR 735, USD 926 combined subscription to institutions (print & online eds.) (effective 2012). adv. bk.rev. illus.; stat. index, cum.index. back issues avail.; reprint service avail. from PSC. **Document type:** *Journal, Academic/Scholarly.* **Description:** Provides an active, multidisciplinary forum for review and debate across the spectrum of sexual and relationship dysfunctions and therapies.
Formerly (until 2000): Sexual and Marital Therapy (0267-4653)
Related titles: Microfiche ed.; Online - full text ed.: ISSN 1468-1749. GBP 446 in United Kingdom to institutions; EUR 661, USD 833 to institutions (effective 2012) (from IngentaConnect).
Indexed: A01, A02, A03, A08, A22, ASSIA, B21, BAS, C06, C07, C08, C11, CA, CINAHL, CurCont, E-psyche, E01, E17, ESPM, F09, FR, FamI, H04, H13, L01, L02, P03, P10, P20, P24, P25, P30, P43, P48, P53, P54, PQC, PsycInfo, PsycholAb, S02, S03, S21, SCOPUS, SFSA, SOPODA, SSCI, SociolAb, T02, V&AA, W07, W09.
—GNLM, IE, Infotrieve, Ingenta, INIST. **CCC.**
Published by: (British Association for Sexual and Relationship Therapy), Routledge (Subsidiary of: Taylor & Francis Group), 4 Park Sq, Milton Park, Abingdon, Oxon OX14 4RN, United Kingdom. TEL 44-20-70176000, FAX 44-20-70176336, subscriptions@tandf.co.uk, http://www.routledge.com. Ed. Dr. Alessandra Iantaffi. Adv. contact Linda Hann TEL 44-1344-779945. **Subscr. to:** Taylor & Francis Ltd., Journals Customer Service, Sheepen Pl, Colchester, Essex CO3 3LP, United Kingdom. TEL 44-20-70175544, FAX 44-20-70175198, tf.enquiries@tfinforma.com.

306.7 DEU ISSN 1862-2941
➤ **SEXUAL OFFENDER TREATMENT.** Text in English. 2006. irreg. (2-3/yr.). free (effective 2011). **Document type:** *Journal, Academic/Scholarly.* **Description:** Promotes the research of and treatment for sexual offenders.
Media: Online - full text.
Published by: (International Association for the Treatment of Sexual Offenders AUT), Pabst Science Publishers, Am Eichengrund 28, Lengerich, 49525, Germany. TEL 49-5484-97234, FAX 49-5484-550, pabst@pabst-publishers.com, http://www.pabst-publishers.de. Eds. Michael Miner, Reinhard Eher.

306.7 GBR ISSN 1363-4607
HQ21
➤ **SEXUALITIES**; studies in culture and society. Text in English. 1998. bi-m. USD 1,116, GBP 603 combined subscription to institutions (print & online eds.); USD 1,094, GBP 591 to institutions (effective 2011). adv. bk.rev. illus. Index. back issues avail.; reprint service avail. from PSC. **Document type:** *Journal, Academic/Scholarly.* **Description:** Publishes work of an analytical and ethnographic nature which describes, analyzes, theorizes and provides a critique on the changing nature of the social organization of human sexual experience in the late modern world.
Related titles: Online - full text ed.: ISSN 1461-7382. USD 1,004, GBP 543 to institutions (effective 2011).

Indexed: A01, A03, A08, A20, A22, B07, CA, CMM, CurCont, DIP, E-psyche, E01, ESPM, FR, FamI, H04, I13, I14, IBR, IBSS, IBZ, L01, L02, MLA-IB, P03, P30, P34, PsycInfo, PsycholAb, RiskAb, S02, S03, SCOPUS, SSA, SSCI, SociolAb, T02, V02, W07, W09.
—BLDSC (8254.485170), IE, Infotrieve, Ingenta, INIST. **CCC.**
Published by: Sage Publications Ltd. (Subsidiary of: Sage Publications, Inc.), 1 Oliver's Yard, 55 City Rd, London, EC1Y 1SP, United Kingdom. TEL 44-20-73248500, FAX 44-20-73248600, info@sagepub.co.uk, http://www.uk.sagepub.com/home.nav. Ed. Ken Plummer. adv.: B&W page GBP 400; 130 x 205. **Subscr. in the Americas to:** Sage Publications, Inc., 2455 Teller Rd, Thousand Oaks, CA 91320. TEL 805-499-9774, FAX 805-499-0871, journals@sagepub.com.

302 JPN ISSN 0916-1503
SHAKAI SHINRIGAKU KENKYU/JAPANESE JOURNAL OF SOCIAL PSYCHOLOGY. Text in Japanese. 1960. s-a. JPY 8,000 membership (effective 2006). **Document type:** *Journal, Academic/Scholarly.*
Formerly (until 1984): Nenpo Shakai Shinrigaku/Japanese Annals of Social Psychology (0548-1589)
Indexed: P03, PsycInfo, PsycholAb, S02, S03, SCOPUS.
—BLDSC (8254.567500). **CCC.**
Published by: Nihon Shakai Shinri Gakkai/Japanese Society of Social Psychology, c/o International Academic Printing Co., 4-4-19 Takadanobaba, Shinjuku-ku, Tokyo, 169 0075, Japan. TEL 81-3-53896217, FAX 81-3-33682822, jssp-post@bunken.co.jp, http://wwwsoc.nii.ac.jp/jssp/.

150 CHN ISSN 1674-5418
SHAONIAN XIN SHIJIE/PSYCHOLOGY WORLD FOR JUVENILE. Text in Chinese. 2005. m. **Document type:** *Journal, Academic/Scholarly.*
Formerly (until 2008): Shaoer Keji Bolan/Science Review for Children (1672-836X)
Published by: (Tianjin Shifan Daxue/Tianjin Normal University), Qingshaonian Keji Bolan Zazhishe, 241, Weijin Lu, Tianjin Shifan Daxue, Tianjin, 300074, China. TEL 86-22-23541101, http://202.113.96.10/kjbl/homepage/index.htm.

155.937 618 USA
SHARING (ST. CHARLES); the official newsletter of S H A R E. Text in English. 1978. bi-m. looseleaf. USD 20 donation (effective 2001). bk.rev.; film rev.; video rev.; Website rev. bibl. reprints avail. **Document type:** *Newsletter.* **Description:** Provides guidance in bereavement following the death of a baby through miscarriage, stillbirth or newborn death. Includes writing from parents and information on support groups.
Formerly: S H A R E Newsletter
Indexed: E-psyche.
Published by: S H A R E Pregnancy & Infant Loss Support National Office, St Joseph Health, 300 First Capitol Dr, Center, MO 63301. TEL 636-947-6164, 800-821-6819, share@nationalshareoffice.com, http://www.nationalshareoffice.com. Ed. Sue Friedeck. R&P Catherine Lammert. Circ: 4,500.

SHEHUI XINLI KEXUE/SCIENCE OF SOCIAL PSYCHOLOGY. *see* LAW

SHINKEI SHINRIGAKU/JAPANESE JOURNAL OF NEUROPSYCHOLOGY. *see* MEDICAL SCIENCES—Psychiatry And Neurology

150 JPN ISSN 0386-1058
BF8.J3 CODEN: SHHYDJ
➤ **SHINRIGAKU HYORON/JAPANESE PSYCHOLOGICAL REVIEW.** Text in Japanese; Abstracts occasionally in English. 1957. q. illus. **Document type:** *Journal, Academic/Scholarly.* **Description:** Contains review articles on experimental psychology.
Indexed: E-psyche, P03, PsycInfo, PsycholAb.
—BLDSC (4661.150000).
Published by: (Department of Psychology), Shinrigaku Hyoron Kankokai, c/o Kyoto University, Department of Psychology, Yoshida-Honmachi, Sakyo-ku, Kyoto, 606-8501, Japan. FAX 81-75-753-2835. Ed. Naoyuki Osaka. Circ: 2,500 (controlled).

150 JPN ISSN 0021-5236
BF8.J3 CODEN: SHKEA5
➤ **SHINRIGAKU KENKYU/JAPANESE JOURNAL OF PSYCHOLOGY.** Text in Japanese; Summaries in English. 1926. bi-m. membership. adv. abstr.; charts; illus. Index. **Document type:** *Journal, Academic/Scholarly.*
Indexed: A20, A22, ASCA, C28, CA, E-psyche, EMBASE, ExcerpMed, INI, IndMed, L&LBA, MEDLINE, P03, P30, PsycInfo, PsycholAb, R10, RASB, Reac, S02, S03, SCOPUS, SOPODA, SSCI, SociolAb, T02.
—BLDSC (4658.300000), GNLM, IE, Infotrieve, Ingenta, INIST.
Published by: Nihon Shinri Gakkai/Japanese Psychological Association, 5-23-13-7F Hongo, Bunkyo-Ku, Tokyo, 113, Japan. TEL 81-3-38143953, FAX 81-3-38143954, psychj@ceres.ocn.ne.jp. Circ: 8,000.

616.89 ESP ISSN 0210-1696
SIGLO CERO. Text in Spanish. 1967. bi-m. EUR 36 domestic; EUR 46 in Europe; EUR 70 elsewhere (effective 2008). back issues avail. **Document type:** *Journal, Academic/Scholarly.*
Formerly (until 1972): Federacion Espanola de Asociaciones Protectoras de Subnormales. Boletin (1139-9597)
Published by: Confederacion Espanola de Organizacion en Favor de las Personas con Discapacidad Intelectual, General Peron 32-1, Madrid, 28020, Spain. TEL 34-91-5567413, FAX 34-91-5974105, feaps@feaps.org, http://www.feaps.org/. Ed. Miguel Angel Verduro.

150 ESP ISSN 1888-279X
SILENOS. Text in Spanish. 2002. a. **Document type:** *Journal, Academic/Scholarly.*
Formerly (until 2007): Clinica y Pensamiento (1579-0622)
Published by: (Asociacion Espanola de Psicoanalisis del Campo Lacaniano), Exlibris Ediciones, S.L., C. Infanta Mercedes, 92-bajo, Madrid, 28020, Spain. TEL 34-91-5717051, FAX 34-91-5716913, exlibris@exlibrisediciones.com, http://www.exlibrisediciones.com/inicio.htm.

158 DEU ISSN 1868-6141
SIMPLIFY SELBSTMANAGEMENT. Text in German. 2003. m. EUR 14.95 per issue (effective 2011). **Document type:** *Newsletter, Consumer.*
Formerly (until 2008): Simplify Yourself (1619-3032)
Published by: Orgenda Verlag fuer Persoenliche Weiterentwicklung (Subsidiary of: V N R Verlag fuer die Deutsche Wirtschaft AG), Theodor Heuss Str 2-4, Bonn, 53177, Germany. TEL 49-228-9550140, FAX 49-228-3696001, info@orgenda.de.

154.6 USA ISSN 1531-3034
RA786
SLEEP REVIEW; the journal for sleep specialists. Text in English. 2000. 8/yr. free domestic to qualified personnel (effective 2011). adv. back issues avail. **Document type:** *Journal, Trade.* **Description:** Publishes information on the clinical as well as the business management side of sleep medicine.
Related titles: Online - full text ed.
Indexed: A26, B02, B15, B17, B18, G04, H01, H11, H12, I05.
—CCC.
Published by: Allied Healthcare Group (Subsidiary of: Ascend Media), 6100 Ctr Dr, Ste 1020, Los Angeles, CA 90045. TEL 310-642-4400, FAX 310-641-4444, http://www.alliedhealthjournals.com. Ed. Franklin Holman TEL 310-642-4400, ext 232. Pub. Darren Sextro TEL 913-894-6923. Adv. contact Dave Jeans TEL 303-856-3067. Circ: 20,500.

302 USA ISSN 1046-4964
HM133 CODEN: SGREE3
➤ **SMALL GROUP RESEARCH**; an international journal of theory, investigation and application. Text in English. 1970. bi-m. USD 899, GBP 529 combined subscription to institutions (print & online eds.); USD 881, GBP 518 to institutions (effective 2011). adv. bk.rev. charts; abstr. index. back issues avail.; reprint service avail. from PSC. **Document type:** *Journal, Academic/Scholarly.* **Description:** Addresses three vital areas of study: the psychology of small groups, communication within small groups, and the organizational behavior of small groups. Brings together research that probes all aspects of small group functioning, including processes, dynamics, outcomes, and relationship to environment.
Formerly: Small Group Behavior (0090-5526); Incorporates: International Journal of Small Group Research (8756-0275); Comparative Group Studies (0010-4108)
Related titles: Microform ed.: (from PQC); Online - full text ed.: ISSN 1552-8278. USD 809, GBP 476 to institutions (effective 2011).
Indexed: A01, A02, A03, A08, A20, A22, AMHA, ASCA, ASSIA, B01, B06, B07, B09, CA, CMM, CommAb, CurCont, E-psyche, E01, E03, ERA, ERI, FR, FamI, H04, HRA, MEA&I, P02, P03, P04, P10, P12, P25, P48, P53, P54, PMA, PQC, PsycInfo, PsycholAb, R17, RASB, S02, S03, S21, SCOPUS, SOPODA, SSA, SSCI, SWR&A, SociolAb, T02, V02, W07.
—BLDSC (8309.995000), IE, Infotrieve, Ingenta, INIST. **CCC.**
Published by: Sage Publications, Inc., 2455 Teller Rd, Thousand Oaks, CA 91320. TEL 805-499-9774, 800-818-7243, FAX 805-499-0871, 800-583-2665, info@sagepub.com. Eds. Aaron M Brower, Joann Keyton. adv.: color page USD 775, B&W page USD 385; 4.5 x 7.5. Circ: 800 (paid). **Subscr. overseas to:** Sage Publications Ltd., 1 Oliver's Yard, 55 City Rd, London EC1Y 1SP, United Kingdom. TEL 44-207-3248701, FAX 44-207-3248733, subscription@sagepub.co.uk.

➤ **SMITH COLLEGE STUDIES IN SOCIAL WORK.** *see* SOCIAL SERVICES AND WELFARE

150 USA ISSN 2159-8142
➤ **SOCIAL ACTION/ACCION SOCIAL.** Abbreviated title: J S A C P. Variant title: The Journal for Social Action in Counseling and Psychology. Text in English, Spanish. 2007. s-a. free (effective 2011). bk.rev. back issues avail. **Document type:** *Journal, Academic/Scholarly.* **Description:** Aims to highlight 'engaged scholarship' and the very important social change work done by professionals and activists.
Media: Online - full text.
Indexed: CA, P43.
Published by: Lewis & Clark College, Graduate School of Education and Counseling, Department of Counseling Psychology, Rogers Hall, 0615 S W Palatine Hill Rd, MSC 86, Portland, OR 97219. TEL 503-768-6060, FAX 503-768-6065, cpsy@lclark.edu, http://www.lclark.edu/graduate/departments/counseling_psychology/. Eds. Rebecca L Toporek, Tod Sloan.

302 GBR ISSN 1751-9004
HM1033
➤ **SOCIAL AND PERSONALITY PSYCHOLOGY COMPASS.** Text in English. 2008. bi-m. GBP 594 in United Kingdom to institutions; EUR 754 in Europe to institutions; USD 1,044 in the Americas to institutions; USD 1,163 elsewhere to institutions (effective 2012). back issues avail. **Document type:** *Journal, Academic/Scholarly.* **Description:** Publishes surveys of current research and theory from across the entire discipline.
Media: Online - full text.
Indexed: A01, P03, P30, PsycInfo.
—BLDSC (8318.053605), IE.
Published by: Wiley-Blackwell Publishing Ltd. (Subsidiary of: John Wiley & Sons, Inc.), 9600 Garsington Rd, Oxford, OX4 2DQ, United Kingdom. TEL 44-1865-776868, FAX 44-1865-714591, customerservices@blackwellpublishing.com. Ed. Jerry Suls.

150 USA ISSN 1941-7985
SOCIAL AND PSYCHOLOGICAL ISSUES; challenges and solutions. Text in English. 2008 (Sep.). irreg., latest 2010. price varies. back issues avail. **Document type:** *Monographic series, Academic/Scholarly.*
Published by: Praeger Publishers (Subsidiary of: Greenwood Publishing Group Inc.), 88 Post Rd W, Westport, CT 06881. TEL 800-368-6868, tech.support@greenwood.com, http://www.greenwood.com. Ed. Albert Roberts.

302 NZL ISSN 0301-2212
HM1 CODEN: SBHPAF
➤ **SOCIAL BEHAVIOR AND PERSONALITY**; an international journal. Text in English. 1973. 8/yr. USD 1,280 combined subscription (print & online eds.) (effective 2011). adv. bibl.; illus.; mkt.; stat. 104 p./no.; back issues avail.; reprints avail. **Document type:** *Journal, Academic/Scholarly.* **Description:** Brings out papers on all aspects of social psychology, developmental psychology, and personality.
Incorporates (1984-1991): Psychology and Human Development (1011-5021); (1978-1990): Third Force Psychology
Related titles: CD-ROM ed.; Microform ed.: (from PQC); Online - full text ed.: ISSN 1179-6391. USD 1,152 (effective 2011) (from IngentaConnect).
Indexed: A01, A02, A03, A08, A20, A22, A26, AC&P, ASCA, ASSIA, AddicA, BAS, BibInd, CA, CDA, CMM, CurCont, DIP, E-psyche, E15, E16, ERA, FamI, G06, G07, HEA, I05, IBR, IBZ, IndMed, M12, P03, P25, P26, P30, P34, P43, P46, P48, P54, PQC, PsycInfo, PsycholAb, R17, S02, S03, S19, S20, S21, SCOPUS, SD, SOPODA, SSA, SSCI, SociolAb, SportS, T02, V05, W07.
—BLDSC (8318.054500), IE, Infotrieve, Ingenta. **CCC.**
Published by: Society for Personality Research (Inc.), 30 Summerhill Dr, PO Box 1539, Palmerston North, 4440, New Zealand. TEL 64-6-3555736, FAX 64-6-3555424. Ed. Robert A C Stewart. Circ: 1,600.

155 USA ISSN 0278-016X
BF311
➤ **SOCIAL COGNITION.** Text in English. 1983. bi-m. USD 125 combined subscription domestic to individuals (print & online eds.); USD 160 combined subscription foreign to individuals (print & online eds.); USD 640 combined subscription domestic to institutions (print & online eds.); USD 685 combined subscription foreign to institutions (print & online eds.) (effective 2011). adv. bk.rev. abstr. index. 96 p./no.; back issues avail.; reprints avail. **Document type:** *Journal, Academic/Scholarly.* **Description:** Features reports on empirical research, self-perception, self-concept, social neuroscience, person-memory integration, social schemata, the development of social cognition, and the role of affect in memory and perception.
Related titles: Online - full text ed.: ISSN 1943-2798.
Indexed: A01, A02, A03, A08, A20, A22, A26, ASCA, ASSIA, CA, CMM, CommAb, CurCont, DIP, E-psyche, E01, E08, E15, E16, ERA, FR, FamI, G08, I05, IBR, IBZ, L&LBA, M12, MLA-IB, P02, P03, P10, P12, P25, P27, P30, P43, P48, P53, P54, PQC, PsycInfo, PsycholAb, RASB, S02, S03, S09, S19, S20, S21, SCOPUS, SOPODA, SSA, SSCI, SociolAb, T02, V05, W07.
—BLDSC (8318.073000), IE, Infotrieve, Ingenta, INIST. **CCC.**
Published by: (International Social Cognition Network), Guilford Publications, Inc., 72 Spring St, 4th Fl, New York, NY 10012. TEL 800-365-7006, FAX 212-966-6708, info@guilford.com. Ed. Jeffrey W Sherman. R&P Kathy Kuehl. Adv. contact Marian Robinson. Circ: 800 (paid).

➤ **SOCIAL COGNITIVE AND AFFECTIVE NEUROSCIENCE (ONLINE).** *see* MEDICAL SCIENCES—Psychiatry And Neurology

150 GBR ISSN 1553-4510
HM1176
➤ **SOCIAL INFLUENCE.** Text in English. 2006 (Jan.). q. GBP 177 combined subscription in United Kingdom to institutions (print & online eds.); EUR 248, USD 312 combined subscription to institutions (print & online eds.) (effective 2012). back issues avail.; reprint service avail. from PSC. **Document type:** *Journal, Academic/Scholarly.* **Description:** Covers conformity, norms, interpersonal influence, persuasion, power, propaganda, social movements, resistance to influence and influence across cultures, among others.
Related titles: Online - full text ed.: ISSN 1553-4529. GBP 159 in United Kingdom to institutions; EUR 223, USD 281 to institutions (effective 2012).
Indexed: A22, ASSIA, CA, CurCont, E01, P03, PsycInfo, S02, S03, SCOPUS, SSCI, T02, W07.
—IE, Ingenta. **CCC.**
Published by: Psychology Press (Subsidiary of: Taylor & Francis Ltd.), 27 Church Rd, Hove, E Sussex BN3 2FA, United Kingdom. TEL 44-20-70176000, FAX 44-20-70176717, info@psypress.co.uk, http://www.psypress.com. Ed. Kipling D Williams. Adv. contact Linda Hann TEL 44-1344-779945.

155 USA ISSN 1075-7031
HQ792.U5
SOCIAL POLICY REPORT. Text in English. 19??. q. free to members (effective 2010). **Document type:** *Journal, Academic/Scholarly.*
Formerly (until 1987): Society for Research in Child Development. Washington Report
Related titles: Online - full text ed.: free (effective 2011).
Indexed: A39, C27, C29, D03, D04, E03, E13, P30, R14, S14, S15, S18, T02.
—Infotrieve. **CCC.**
Published by: Society for Research in Child Development, University of Michigan, 3131 S State St, Ste 302, Ann Arbor, MI 48108-1623. TEL 734-998-6578, FAX 734-998-6569, srcd@umich.edu.

302 USA ISSN 1948-5506
BF698.A1
▼ **SOCIAL PSYCHOLOGICAL AND PERSONALITY SCIENCE.** Abbreviated title: S P P S. Text in English. 2010 (Jan.). q. USD 800, GBP 471 combined subscription to institutions (print & online eds.); USD 784, GBP 462 to institutions (effective 2011). **Document type:** *Journal, Academic/Scholarly.* **Description:** Contains unique short reports in social and personality psychology. Aims to publish short reports of single studies, or very succinct reports of multiple studies.
Related titles: Online - full text ed.: ISSN 1948-5514. 2010. USD 720, GBP 424 to institutions (effective 2011).
Indexed: A22, ASSIA, E01, P30.
—CCC.
Published by: (Association for Research in Personality, Society of Experimental and Social Psychology, European Association of Experimental Social Psychology DEU, Society for Personality and Social Psychology), Sage Publications, Inc., 2455 Teller Rd, Thousand Oaks, CA 91320. TEL 805-499-9774, FAX 805-499-0871, info@sagepub.com. Ed. Vincent Y A Yzerbyt.

302 USA ISSN 1571-3091
HM251
➤ **SOCIAL PSYCHOLOGICAL APPLICATIONS TO SOCIAL ISSUES.** Text in English. 1990. irreg., latest 2002. price varies. back issues avail. **Document type:** *Monographic series, Academic/Scholarly.*
Formerly (until 1988): Applied Social Psychology Annual (0196-4151)
Indexed: E-psyche, PsycholAb.
—BLDSC (8318.145900). **CCC.**
Published by: Springer New York LLC (Subsidiary of: Springer Science+Business Media), 233 Spring St, New York, NY 10013. TEL 212-460-1500, FAX 212-460-1575, service-ny@springer.com.

P

302 DEU ISSN 1864-9335
HM251
➤ **SOCIAL PSYCHOLOGY.** Text in German; Summaries in English. 1970. q. USD 145, EUR 114 to individuals; USD 296, EUR 228 to institutions; USD 99, EUR 76 per issue (effective 2011). adv. bk.rev.; Website rev. abstr.; bibl. back issues avail.; reprint service avail. from SCH. **Document type:** *Journal, Academic/Scholarly.* **Description:** Dedicated to international research in social psychology. Serves as a forum for scientific discussion and debate.
Formerly (until 2008): Zeitschrift fuer Sozialpsychologie (0044-3514)
Related titles: Online - full text ed.: ISSN 2151-2590 (from ScienceDirect).
Indexed: A20, A22, ASCA, CA, CRCL, CurCont, E-psyche, GJP, IBR, IBZ, P03, P42, PSA, Phillnd, PsycInfo, PsycholAb, RASB, S02, S03, SCOPUS, SOPODA, SSA, SSCI, SociolAb, T02, W07.
—BLDSC (8318.145960), IE, Infotrieve, Ingenta. **CCC.**
Published by: Hogrefe Verlag GmbH & Co. KG, Rohnsweg 25, Goettingen, 37085, Germany. TEL 49-551-99950421, FAX 49-551-99950425, verlag@hogrefe.de, http://www.hogrefe.de. Ed. Dr. Gerd Bohner TEL 49-521-1064437. Circ: 500 (paid).

302 GBR ISSN 1368-4574
SOCIAL PSYCHOLOGY. Text in English. 199?. irreg., latest 2006. price varies. back issues avail.; reprints avail. **Document type:** *Monographic series, Academic/Scholarly.* **Description:** Focuses on a specific key area of social psychology. Provides a review of the empirical, theoretical and practical issues in that field.
Published by: Psychology Press (Subsidiary of: Taylor & Francis Ltd.), 27 Church Rd, Hove, E Sussex BN3 2FA, United Kingdom. TEL 44-20-70176000, FAX 44-20-70176717, info@psypress.co.uk, http://www.psypress.com.

SOCIAL PSYCHOLOGY OF EDUCATION; an international journal. *see* EDUCATION

SOCIAL PSYCHOLOGY QUARTERLY. *see* SOCIOLOGY

SOCIAL SERVICE JOBS. *see* OCCUPATIONS AND CAREERS

302 USA
SOCIAL WORK PRACTICE WITH CHILDREN AND FAMILIES. Text in English. 19??. irreg. price varies. **Document type:** *Monographic series, Academic/Scholarly.* **Description:** Features detailed discussions of assessment, intervention, and professional and value issues.
Related titles: Online - full text ed.
Indexed: E-psyche.
Published by: Guilford Publications, Inc., 72 Spring St, 4th Fl, New York, NY 10012. TEL 800-365-7006, FAX 212-966-6708, info@guilford.com. Ed. Nancy Boyd Webb.

150 ESP ISSN 1130-4561
SOCIEDAD ESPANOLA DEL RORSCHACH Y METODOS PROYECTIVOS. REVISTA. Text in Spanish. 1988. a. **Document type:** *Journal, Trade.*
Published by: Sociedad Espanola del Rorschach y Metodos Proyectivos, Fernando Agullo, 24, Barcelona, Cataluna 08021, Spain.

616.891 BRA ISSN 1413-4438
SOCIEDADE PSICANALITICA DE PORTO ALEGRE. REVISTA DE PSICANALISE. Text in Portuguese. 1993. q. BRL 75 domestic; USD 45 foreign (effective 2006). back issues avail. **Document type:** *Journal, Academic/Scholarly.*
Indexed: C01, P03, PsycInfo, PsycholAb.
Published by: Sociedade Psicanalititca de Porto Alegre, Rua Gen Andrade Neves, 14-802, Porto Alegre, RS 90010-210, Brazil. TEL 55-51-32243340, sppa@sppa.org.br, http://www.sppa.org.br/. Ed. Cesar Luis De Souza Brito.

150 ESP ISSN 1135-1268
SOCIETAT VALENCIANA DE PSICOLOGIA. ANUARI DE PSICOLOGIA. Key Title: Anuari de Psicologia de la Societat Valenciana de Psicologia. Text in Spanish, Catalan. 1995. a. **Document type:** *Journal, Academic/Scholarly.*
Published by: Societat Valenciana de Psicologia, Blasco Ibanez, 21, Valencia, 46010, Spain.

150.19 FRA ISSN 1953-6623
SOCIETE FRANCAISE DE PSYCHANALYSE ADLERIENNE. BULLETIN. Text in French. 1971. 3/yr. EUR 11 per issue (effective 2007). back issues avail. **Document type:** *Bulletin.*
Formerly (until 2004): Societe Francaise de Psychologie Adlerienne. Le Bulletin (0154-7208)
Published by: Societe Francaise de Psychanalyse Adlerienne, 5 Passage Gambetta, Paris, 75020, France. TEL 33-1-43616302, FAX 33-1-43616302.

SOCIETY AND ANIMALS; journal of human - animal studies. *see* ANIMAL WELFARE

SOCIETY FOR COMPANION ANIMAL STUDIES. JOURNAL. *see* ANIMAL WELFARE

150 USA ISSN 0037-976X
LB1103 CODEN: MSCDA7
➤ **SOCIETY FOR RESEARCH IN CHILD DEVELOPMENT. MONOGRAPHS.** Text in English. 1936. 3/yr. USD 609 in the Americas (print or online ed.); GBP 435 in United Kingdom (print or online ed.); EUR 553 in Europe (print or online ed.); USD 852 elsewhere (print or online ed.); USD 670 combined subscription in the Americas (print & online eds.); GBP 479 combined subscription in United Kingdom (print & online eds.); EUR 608 combined subscription in Europe (print & online eds.); USD 938 combined subscription elsewhere (print & online eds.) (effective 2010); subscr. includes Child Development & Child Development Perspectives. back issues avail.; reprints avail. **Document type:** *Monographic series, Academic/Scholarly.* **Description:** Presents in-depth research studies and findings in child development and related disciplines.
Related titles: Microform ed.: (from PQC); Online - full text ed.: ISSN 1540-5834 (from IngentaConnect).
Indexed: A01, A02, A03, A08, A20, A22, A26, AMHA, ASCA, BDM&CN, BRD, C06, C07, C08, C28, CA, CDA, CINAHL, DIP, E-psyche, E01, E02, E03, E06, E07, EMBASE, ERI, ERIC, EdA, EdI, ExcerpMed, FR, Faml, H12, IBR, IBZ, IndMed, L&LBA, MEA&I, MEDLINE, P03, P04, P10, P12, P18, P30, P43, P48, P53, P54, PCI, PQC, PsycInfo, PsycholAb, R10, Reac, S02, S03, SCOPUS, SOPODA, SSCI, SociolAb, T02, W03, W07.
—BLDSC (5914.820000), GNLM, IE, Infotrieve, Ingenta, INIST. **CCC.**
Published by: (Society for Research in Child Development), Wiley-Blackwell Publishing, Inc. (Subsidiary of: Wiley-Blackwell Publishing Ltd.), 111 River St, Hoboken, NJ 07030. TEL 201-748-6000, FAX 201-748-6088, info@wiley.com. Ed. W Andrew Collins.

➤ **SOCIOLOGUS**; Zeitschrift fuer empirische Ethnosoziologie und Ethnopsychologie. *see* SOCIOLOGY

➤ **SOMATICS**; magazine - journal of the mind - body arts and sciences. *see* PHYSICAL FITNESS AND HYGIENE

➤ **SOMNO - JOURNAL.** *see* MEDICAL SCIENCES

➤ **SOMNOLOGIE/SOMNOLOGY**; Schlafforschung und Schlafmedizin. *see* MEDICAL SCIENCES

➤ **SOTSIONIKA, MENTOLOGIYA I PSIKHOLOGIYA LICHNOSTI.** *see* SOCIOLOGY

150 ZAF ISSN 0081-2463
BF1 CODEN: SAJPDL
➤ **SOUTH AFRICAN JOURNAL OF PSYCHOLOGY/SUID-AFRIKAANSE TYDSKRIF VIR SIELKUNDE.** Text and summaries in English. 1970. q. adv. bk.rev. bibl.; charts; illus.; stat. **Document type:** *Journal, Academic/Scholarly.* **Description:** Publishes empirical research, theoretical and methodological papers, review articles and short communications in the field of psychology.
Incorporates (in July 1983): Psychologia Africana (0079-7332); (in Jan. 1979): South African Psychologist; Which was formerly: Journal of Behavioural Science (0075-4145)
Related titles: Online - full text ed.
Indexed: A01, A02, A03, A08, A20, A22, ASCA, CA, CurCont, DIP, E-psyche, ErgAb, Faml, IBR, IBZ, IPsyAb, ISAP, P03, P30, P43, PCI, PsycInfo, PsycholAb, RASB, S02, S03, S21, SCOPUS, SRRA, SSCI, T02, W07.
—BLDSC (8339.750000), IE, Infotrieve, Ingenta, INIST.
Published by: (Psychological Society of South Africa), UniSA Press, PO Box 392, Pretoria, 0003, South Africa. TEL 27-12-4292953, FAX 27-12-4293449, unisa-press@unisa.ac.za, http://www.unisa.ac.za/press. Circ: 1,500.

150 BGD ISSN 1025-773X
SOUTH ASIAN JOURNAL OF PSYCHOLOGY. Text in English. 1996. s-a. USD 50 (effective 2000). **Document type:** *Journal, Academic/Scholarly.* **Description:** Publishes articles in all branches of psychology.
Indexed: E-psyche.
Published by: South Asian Association of Psychologists, 601 Eastern Valley, 28/6 New Eskaton Rd, Dhaka, 1000, Bangladesh. TEL 880-2-864553, FAX 880-2-865583. Ed. Arun K Sen. R&P, Adv. contact Muhammad R Ali TEL 880-2-883240.

153 FIN ISSN 0783-408X
SOVELTAVAN PSYKOLOGIAN MONOGRAFIOITA. Text in Finnish. 1987. irreg. price varies. back issues avail. **Document type:** *Monographic series, Academic/Scholarly.*
Related titles: ◆ Series of: Acta Psychologica Fennica. ISSN 0515-3115.
Published by: Suomen Psykologinen Seura/Finnish Psychological Society, Liisankatu 16 A, Helsinki, 00170, Finland. TEL 358-9-2782122, FAX 358-9-2781300, psykologia@genealogia.fi, http://www.psykologienkustannus.fi/sps.

301.1 616.8 360 DEU ISSN 0171-4538
SOZIALPSYCHIATRISCHE INFORMATIONEN. Text in German. 1971. q. EUR 30; EUR 22 to students; EUR 9.90 newsstand/cover (effective 2008). adv. back issues avail. **Document type:** *Journal, Academic/Scholarly.* **Description:** A journal for people working in psychiatry: psychiatrists, doctors, social workers and nurses.
Indexed: E-psyche, IBR, IBZ.
—GNLM.
Published by: Psychiatrie Verlag GmbH, Thomas-Mann-Str 49a, Bonn, 53111, Germany. TEL 49-228-725340, FAX 49-228-7253420, verlag@psychiatrie.de, http://www.psychiatrie.de. Ed. Dr. Helmut Haselbeck. Adv. contact Cornelia Brodmann. B&W page EUR 650, color page EUR 1,137. Circ: 2,250 (paid and controlled).

150 ESP ISSN 1138-7416
BF1.S68
➤ **THE SPANISH JOURNAL OF PSYCHOLOGY.** Text in English. 1998. s-a. EUR 42 domestic to institutions; EUR 50 in Europe to institutions; EUR 69 elsewhere to institutions (effective 2011). back issues avail. **Document type:** *Journal, Academic/Scholarly.* **Description:** Aims to disseminate empirical research and methodological proposals in different areas of specialization within psychology.
Related titles: CD-ROM ed.; Online - full text ed.: ISSN 1988-2904. free; ◆ Supplement(s): Psychologia Latina. ISSN 2171-6609.
Indexed: A20, A26, E-psyche, EMBASE, ExcerpMed, FR, H21, I04, I05, IBSS, L&LBA, MEDLINE, P03, P08, P20, P22, P25, P27, P30, P48, P54, PQC, PsycInfo, PsycholAb, R10, Reac, SCOPUS, SSCI, W07.
—BLDSC (8361.737590), IE, Ingenta, INIST. **CCC.**
Published by: (Universidad Complutense de Madrid, Facultad de Psicologia), Universidad Complutense de Madrid, Servicio de Publicaciones, C/ Obispo Trejo 2, Ciudad Universitaria, Madrid, 28040, Spain. TEL 34-91-3941127, FAX 34-91-3941126, servicio.publicaciones@rect.ucm.es, http://www.ucm.es/publicaciones. Ed. Javier Bandres Ponce.

150 USA ISSN 1387-5868
BF469 CODEN: SCCOFX
SPATIAL COGNITION AND COMPUTATION. Text in English. 1999. q. GBP 298 combined subscription in United Kingdom to institutions (print & online eds.); EUR 396, USD 498 combined subscription to institutions (print & online eds.) (effective 2012). adv. back issues avail.; reprint service avail. from PSC. **Document type:** *Journal, Academic/Scholarly.* **Description:** Aims to concentrate the presentation of research into spatial cognition and computation, and to explicitly encourage an interdisciplinary dialogue.
Related titles: Online - full text ed.: ISSN 1573-9252. GBP 268 in United Kingdom to institutions; EUR 357, USD 448 to institutions (effective 2012) (from IngentaConnect).
Indexed: A01, A20, A22, B21, CA, CurCont, E-psyche, E01, Inspec, L&LBA, NSA, P03, P30, PsycInfo, PsycholAb, SCOPUS, SSCI, T02, W07.
—BLDSC (8361.785150), IE, Infotrieve, Ingenta, Linda Hall. **CCC.**
Published by: Taylor & Francis Inc. (Subsidiary of: Taylor & Francis Group), 325 Chestnut St, Ste 800, Philadelphia, PA 19106. TEL 215-625-2940, 800-354-1420, customerservice@taylorandfrancis.com, http://www.taylorandfrancis.com. Eds. Anthony G Cohn, Dan Montello. Adv. contact Linda Hann TEL 44-1344-779945.

SPINDET; sprogpsykologisk information og debat. *see* LINGUISTICS

158 135 NLD ISSN 1871-5494
SPIRITUELE SCHEURKALENDER. Cover title: Happinez Spirituele Scheurkalender. Text in Dutch. 2005. a. EUR 15.95 (effective 2009).
Published by: (Happinez), Uitgeverij Ten Have, Postbus 5018, Kampen, 8260 GA, Netherlands. TEL 31-38-3392500, http://www.uitgeverijtenhave.nl.

796.01 GBR ISSN 1745-4980
SPORT AND EXERCISE PSYCHOLOGY REVIEW. Text in English. 2005. s-a. free to members (effective 2009). bk.rev. back issues avail. **Document type:** *Journal, Academic/Scholarly.* **Description:** Presents news bulletins, research and professional practice articles, conference reports and other topical items of interest to sport and exercise psychologists.
Indexed: CA, PEI, SD, T02.
—BLDSC (8419.364150), IE.
Published by: The British Psychological Society, Division of Sport and Exercise Psychology, St Andrews House, 48 Princess Rd E, Leicester, LE1 7DR, United Kingdom. TEL 44-116-2549568, FAX 44-116-2271314, enquiry@bps.org.uk.

150.19 790.1 USA ISSN 0888-4781
CODEN: SPPSEU
➤ **THE SPORT PSYCHOLOGIST.** Short title: T S P. Text in English. 1987. q. USD 368 domestic to institutions; USD 378 foreign to institutions; USD 426 combined subscription domestic to institutions (print & online eds.); USD 436 combined subscription foreign to institutions (print & online eds.) (effective 2012). adv. bk.rev. bibl.; charts; illus. back issues avail.; reprint service avail. from PSC. **Document type:** *Journal, Academic/Scholarly.* **Description:** Designed for educational and clinical sport psychologists. Focuses on applied research and practical application of results in providing psychological services to coaches and athletes.
Related titles: Online - full text ed.: ISSN 1543-2793. USD 368 to institutions (effective 2012).
Indexed: A01, A03, A08, A20, A22, A36, ASCA, CA, CABA, CurCont, DIP, E-psyche, E12, FoSS&M, GH, IBR, IBZ, LT, N03, P02, P03, P10, P12, P48, P53, P54, PEI, PQC, PsycInfo, PsycholAb, R09, R12, RRTA, SCI, SCOPUS, SD, SOPODA, SSCI, SociolAb, SportS, T02, W07.
—BLDSC (8419.638000), IE, Infotrieve, Ingenta. **CCC.**
Published by: (International Society of Sport Psychology), Human Kinetics, 1607 N Market St, Champaign, IL 61820. TEL 800-747-4457, FAX 217-351-2674, info@hkusa.com, http://www.humankinetics.com. Ed. Ian Maynard TEL 44-114-2254339. Pub. Rainer Martens. R&P Martha Gullo TEL 217-403-7534. Adv. contact Amy Bleich TEL 217-403-7803.

150 796 DEU ISSN 0721-4111
SPORTPSYCHOLOGIE. Text in German. 1990. irreg., latest vol.7, 2004. price varies. **Document type:** *Monographic series, Academic/Scholarly.*
Published by: Peter Lang GmbH (Subsidiary of: Peter Lang Publishing Group), Eschborner Landstr 42-50, Frankfurt Am Main, 60489, Germany. TEL 49-69-7807050, FAX 49-69-78070550, zentrale.frankfurt@peterlang.com. Eds. Frank Haensel, Henning Haase.

SPORTS RAGE ADVISORY. *see* SPORTS AND GAMES

150 USA ISSN 0362-0522
BF173.A2 CODEN: SAATDM
➤ **SPRING JOURNAL**; a journal of archetype and culture. Text in English. 1941. s-a. USD 35 domestic; USD 54 foreign (effective 2011). bk.rev.; play rev.; film rev. back issues avail.; reprint service avail. from PSC. **Document type:** *Journal, Academic/Scholarly.* **Description:** Contains seminal articles on archetypal psychology that examine culture from an archetypal point of view. As the oldest journal on Jungian psychology, examines critically Jung's ideas in the light of post-Jungian developments.
Indexed: A22, E-psyche, MLA-IB, PMR, PsycholAb.
—Ingenta. **CCC.**
Published by: Spring Journal, Inc., 627 Ursulines St #7, New Orleans, LA 70116. TEL 504-524-5117, FAX 504-558-0088, customerservice@springjournalandbooks.com.

➤ **SPRINGER SERIES: FOCUS ON MEN.** *see* MEN'S HEALTH

150 370 DEU ISSN 1860-4498
STANDARDWERKE AUS PSYCHOLOGIE UND PAEDAGOGIK. REPRINTS. Text in German. 2005. irreg., latest vol.4, 2007. price varies. **Document type:** *Monographic series, Academic/Scholarly.*
Published by: Waxmann Verlag GmbH, Steinfurter Str 555, Muenster, 48159, Germany. TEL 49-251-265040, FAX 49-251-2650426, info@waxmann.com. Ed. Detlef H. Rost.

STATE PLAN FOR DEVELOPMENTAL DISABILITIES. *see* SOCIAL SERVICES AND WELFARE

150 SWE ISSN 0562-1089
STOCKHOLM STUDIES IN EDUCATIONAL PSYCHOLOGY. Text in Multiple languages. 1957. irreg., latest vol.27, 1997. price varies. back issues avail. **Document type:** *Monographic series, Academic/Scholarly.*
Related titles: ◆ Series of: Acta Universitatis Stockholmiensis. ISSN 0346-6418.
Published by: Stockholms Universitet, Acta Universitatis Stockholmiensis, c/o Stockholms Universitetsbibliotek, Universitetsvaegen 10, Stockholm, 10691, Sweden. TEL 46-8-162800, FAX 46-8-157776, http://www.sub.su.se. Ed. Margaretha Fathli. **Dist. by:** Eddy.se AB, Norra Kyrkogatan 3, Visby 62155, Sweden. TEL 46-498-253900, FAX 46-498-249789, info@eddy.se, order@eddy.se, http://www.eddy.se, http://acta.bokorder.se.

150 SWE ISSN 0585-3591
STOCKHOLM STUDIES IN PSYCHOLOGY. Text in English. 1958. irreg., latest 2010. price varies. **Document type:** *Monographic series, Academic/Scholarly.*
Related titles: ◆ Series of: Acta Universitatis Stockholmiensis. ISSN 0346-6418.

Published by: (Stockholms Universitet, Psykologiska Institutionen/ Stockholm University, Department of Psychology), Stockholms Universitet, Acta Universitatis Stockholmiensis, c/o Stockholms Universitetsbiblioteket, Universitetsvaegen 10, Stockholm, 10691, Sweden. TEL 46-8-162800, FAX 46-8-157776, http://www.sub.su.se. Ed. Margaretha Fathli. **Dist. by:** Eddy.se AB, Norra Kyrkogatan 3, Visby 62155, Sweden. TEL 46-498-253900, FAX 46-498-249789, info@eddy.se, order@eddy.se, http://acta.bokorder.se.

155 SWE ISSN 1652-5639
STOCKHOLMS UNIVERSITET. PEDAGOGISKA INSTITUTIONEN. UTVECKLINGSPSYKOLOGISKA SEMINARIET. SKRIFTSERIEN. Text in Swedish. 1975. irreg., latest vol.75, 2008. back issues avail. **Document type:** *Monographic series, Academic/Scholarly.*
Formerly (until 1999): Stockholm Universitet. Pedagogiska Institutionen. Utvecklingspsykologiska Seminariet. Rapport (0281-661X)
Published by: Stockholms Universitet, Pedagogiska Institutionen/ Stockholm University, Department of Education, Stockholm, 10691, Sweden. TEL 46-8-162000, FAX 46-8-158354, info@ped.su.se, http://www.ped.su.se.

150 USA ISSN 1933-9186
STRESS CLUB. Text in English. 2006. w. free (effective 2008). **Document type:** *Magazine, Consumer.*
Media: Online - full text.
Published by: Stress Club Magazine http://www.stressclub.com/show/home.html.

STRESS MANAGEMENT FOR LAW ENFORCEMENT; behind the shield: combating trauma. *see* CRIMINOLOGY AND LAW ENFORCEMENT

150 616.8 SWE ISSN 0280-2783
➤ **STRESSFORSKNINGSRAPPORTER/STRESS RESEARCH REPORTS.** Text in English, Swedish. 1967. irreg., latest vol.319, 2006. price varies. index. back issues avail. **Document type:** *Monographic series, Academic/Scholarly.*
Formerly (until 1981): Rapporter fraan Laboratoriet foer Klinisk Stressforskning (0303-7185)
Related titles: Online - full text ed.
Indexed: E-psyche.
—BLDSC (8474.141000).
Published by: (Karolinska Institutet, Avdelingen foer Stressforskning), Institutet foer Psykosocial Medicin, Granits Vaeg 8, PO Box 230, Stockholm, 17177, Sweden. TEL 46-8-52482000, FAX 46-8-344143, registrator@ipm.ki.se, http://www.imp.ki.se. Ed. Toeres Theorell.

302 USA ISSN 1070-5511
QA278 CODEN: SEMTC7
➤ **STRUCTURAL EQUATION MODELING**; a multidisciplinary journal. Abbreviated title: S E M. Text in English. 1994. q. GBP 564 combined subscription in United Kingdom to institutions (print & online eds.); EUR 752, USD 943 combined subscription to institutions (print & online eds.) (effective 2012). adv. bk.rev. back issues avail.; reprint service avail. from PSC. **Document type:** *Journal, Academic/ Scholarly.* **Description:** Covers all academic disciplines with an interest in structural equation modeling, including psychology, sociology, educational research, political science, economics, management and business/marketing.
Related titles: Online - full text ed.: ISSN 1532-8007. GBP 508 in United Kingdom to institutions; EUR 677, USD 849 to institutions (effective 2012).
Indexed: A01, A03, A08, A22, A36, CA, CCMJ, CIS, CMCI, CurCont, E-psyche, E01, ERIC, GH, Inspec, MSN, MathR, P03, P10, P27, P30, P43, P48, P53, P54, PQC, PsycInfo, PsycholAb, S02, S03, SCI, SCOPUS, SSCI, SociolAb, T02, W07.
—BLDSC (8477.210000), IE, Infotrieve, Ingenta. **CCC.**
Published by: Psychology Press (Subsidiary of: Taylor & Francis Inc.), 325 Chestnut St, Ste 800, Philadelphia, PA 19106. TEL 800-354-1420, FAX 215-625-2940, orders@taylorandfrancis.com, http://www.psypress.com. Ed. George A Marcoulides. Adv. contact Linda Hann TEL 44-1344-779945.

➤ **STUDI DI PSICOLOGIA DELL'EDUCAZIONE.** *see* EDUCATION

150.19 ITA ISSN 1828-5147
STUDI JUNGHIANI. Text in Multiple languages. 1988. s-a. EUR 44 domestic to institutions; EUR 64 foreign to institutions (effective 2009). adv. **Document type:** *Journal, Academic/Scholarly.*
Related titles: Online - full text ed.: ISSN 1971-8411.
Indexed: E-psyche.
Published by: (Associazione Italiana di Psicologia Analitica), Franco Angeli Edizioni, Viale Monza 106, Milan, 20127, Italy. TEL 39-02-2837141, FAX 39-02-26144793, redazioni@francoangeli.it, http://www.francoangeli.it. Circ: 500.

150 100 POL ISSN 1642-2473
BF8.P6
STUDIA PSYCHOLOGICA. Text in Polish. 1983. a. **Document type:** *Journal, Academic/Scholarly.*
Formerly (until 2000): Studia z Psychologii (0239-8516)
Published by: (Uniwersytet Kardynala Stefana Wyszynskiego, Wydzial Filozofii Chrzescijanskiej), Wydawnictwo Uniwersytetu Kardynala Stefana Wyszynskiego, Ul Dewajtis 5, Warsaw, 01815, Poland. wydawnictwo@uksw.edu.pl, http://www.uksw.edu.pl/wydawn/wydawnictwo.htm.

150 BEL
STUDIA PSYCHOLOGICA. Text in Multiple languages. 1954. irreg. price varies. **Document type:** *Academic/Scholarly.*
Published by: Leuven University Press, Blijde Inkomststraat 5, Leuven, 3000, Belgium. TEL 32-16-325345, FAX 32-16-325352, university.press@upers.kuleuven.ac.be, http://www.kuleuven.ac.be/upers.

150 SVK ISSN 0039-3320
BF8.S55 CODEN: STPSAK
➤ **STUDIA PSYCHOLOGICA**; journal for basic research in psychological sciences. Text in English; Summaries in Czech, Slovak, English. 1958. 5/yr. EUR 187.40 in Europe; EUR 196 elsewhere (effective 2011). adv. bk.rev. charts; illus. index. **Document type:** *Journal, Academic/Scholarly.* **Description:** Publishes original experimental and theoretical studies about results of investigations carried out in Slovakia and abroad in the field of basic psychological research.
Indexed: A01, A20, ASCA, CA, CDA, CurCont, E-psyche, FamI, L&LBA, P03, P25, P27, P30, P46, P48, P54, PQC, PsycInfo, PsycholAb, RASB, S02, S03, SCOPUS, SD, SOPODA, SSCI, SociolAb, T02, W07.
—BLDSC (8483.202000), IE, Infotrieve, Ingenta, INIST.
Published by: (Slovenska Akademia Vied, Ustav Experimentalnej Psychologie/Slovak Academy of Sciences, Institute of Experimental Psychology), Slovak Academic Press Ltd., Nam Slobody 6, PO Box 57, Bratislava, 81005, Slovakia. TEL 421-2-55421729, FAX 421-2-55565862, sap@sappress.sk, http://www.sappress.sk. Ed. Viera Bacova. Circ: 1,300. **Dist. by:** Slovart G.T.G. s.r.o., Krupinska 4, PO Box 152, Bratislava 85299, Slovakia. TEL 421-2-63839472, FAX 421-2-63839485, info@slovart-gtg.sk, http://www.slovart-gtg.sk.

➤ **STUDIA PSYCHOLOGICA ET PAEDAGOGICA. SERIES ALTERA.** *see* EDUCATION

150 SWE ISSN 0586-8858
BF8.S9
STUDIA PSYCHOLOGICA UPSALIENSIA. Text in Multiple languages. 1969. irreg., latest vol.20, 2001. price varies. back issues avail. **Document type:** *Monographic series, Academic/Scholarly.*
Related titles: ◆ Series of: Acta Universitatis Upsaliensis. ISSN 0346-5462.
Published by: Uppsala Universitet, Acta Universitatis Upsaliensis/ University Publications from Uppsala, PO Box 256, Uppsala, 75105, Sweden. TEL 46-18-4716804, FAX 46-18-4716804, acta@ub.uu.se, http://www.ub.uu.se/upu/auu/index.html. Ed. Bengt Landgren. **Dist. by:** Almqvist & Wiksell International.

150 POL ISSN 0081-685X
BF26 CODEN: SPSLBL
➤ **STUDIA PSYCHOLOGICZNE.** Text in Polish; Summaries in English, Polish. 1956. s-a. PLZ 10 domestic; USD 18 foreign (effective 2000 & 2001). **Document type:** *Academic/Scholarly.* **Description:** Works concerning historical and experimental psychology, theoretical and methodological problems, social perception, personal communication.
Indexed: DIP, E-psyche, IBR, IBZ, P03, PsycInfo, PsycholAb, RASB, S02, S03.
—INIST.
Published by: Polska Akademia Nauk, Instytut Psychologii, Ul Podlesna 61, Warsaw, 01673, Poland. TEL 48-22-8340907, FAX 48-22-8340907, jacekj@atos.psychpan.waw.pl. Ed. Magdalena Marszal-Wisniewska. Pub. Jacek Jarymowicz.

➤ **STUDIA UNIVERSITATIS BABES-BOLYAI. PSYCHOLOGIA - PAEDAGOGIA.** *see* EDUCATION

➤ **STUDIEN UND BERICHTE.** *see* EDUCATION

159.9 DEU ISSN 0721-4170
STUDIEN ZUR PAEDAGOGISCHEN UND PSYCHOLOGISCHEN INTERVENTION. Text in German. 1980. irreg., latest vol.10, 2008. price varies. **Document type:** *Monographic series, Academic/ Scholarly.*
Published by: Peter Lang GmbH (Subsidiary of: Peter Lang Publishing Group), Eschborner Landstr 42-50, Frankfurt Am Main, 60489, Germany. TEL 49-69-7807050, FAX 49-69-78070550, zentrale.frankfurt@peterlang.com.

159.9 DEU ISSN 1435-1595
STUDIEN ZUR PSYCHOLOGIE UND KRIMINALITAET. Text in German. 2005. irreg. price varies. **Document type:** *Monographic series, Academic/Scholarly.*
Published by: Peter Lang GmbH (Subsidiary of: Peter Lang Publishing Group), Eschborner Landstr 42-50, Frankfurt Am Main, 60489, Germany. TEL 49-69-7807050, FAX 49-69-78070550, zentrale.frankfurt@peterlang.com. Ed. Thilo Eisenhardt.

158 DEU ISSN 1435-6805
STUDIEN ZUR STRESSFORSCHUNG. Text in German. 1993. irreg., latest vol.29, 2010. price varies. **Document type:** *Monographic series, Academic/Scholarly.*
Published by: Verlag Dr. Kovac, Leverkusenstr 13, Hamburg, 22761, Germany. TEL 49-40-3988800, FAX 49-40-39888055, info@verlagdrkovac.de.

155.9 DEU ISSN 1861-1494
STUDIEN ZUR UMWELTPSYCHOLOGIE. Text in German. 2005. irreg., latest vol.2, 2005. price varies. **Document type:** *Monographic series, Academic/Scholarly.*
Published by: Verlag Dr. Kovac, Leverkusenstr 13, Hamburg, 22761, Germany. TEL 49-40-3988800, FAX 49-40-39888055, info@verlagdrkovac.de.

STUDIES DI GESTALT THERAPY. *see* MEDICAL SCIENCES—Psychiatry And Neurology

155.5 GBR ISSN 1466-4801
STUDIES IN ADOLESCENT DEVELOPMENT. Text in English. 1999. irreg., latest 2006. price varies. back issues avail. **Document type:** *Monographic series, Academic/Scholarly.* **Description:** Aims to respond to the recent shifts in the social and ecological environment of adolescents and in the new theoretical perspectives within the social science by providing a range of books, each of which deals in-depth with an aspect of current interest within the field of adolescent development.
Published by: (European Association for Research on Adolescence), Psychology Press (Subsidiary of: Taylor & Francis Ltd.), 27 Church Rd, Hove, E Sussex BN3 2FA, United Kingdom. TEL 44-20-70176000, FAX 44-20-70176717, info@psypress.co.uk. Eds. Inge Seiffge-Krenke, Leon B Hendry TEL 44-1443-482356, Marion Kloep TEL 44-1443-482419.

153.4 121 NLD ISSN 0924-0780
STUDIES IN COGNITIVE SYSTEMS. Text in English. 1988. irreg., latest vol.30, 2003. price varies. **Document type:** *Monographic series, Academic/Scholarly.* **Description:** Presents studies devoted to the investigation and exploration of knowledge, information and dataprocessing systems of all kinds.
Indexed: E-psyche, Z02.
Published by: Springer Netherlands (Subsidiary of: Springer Science+Business Media), Van Godewijckstraat 30, Dordrecht, 3311 GX, Netherlands. TEL 31-78-6576050, FAX 31-78-6576474. Ed. James H Fetzer.

STUDIES IN EATING DISORDERS: AN INTERNATIONAL SERIES. *see* MEDICAL SCIENCES—Psychiatry And Neurology

STUDIES IN EDUCATIONAL SCIENCES. *see* EDUCATION

STUDIES IN THE PSYCHOLOGY OF RELIGION. *see* RELIGIONS AND THEOLOGY

STUDIES IN THEORETICAL PSYCHOLINGUISTICS. *see* LINGUISTICS

STUDIES OF ARGUMENTATION IN PRAGMATICS AND DISCOURSE ANALYSIS. *see* LINGUISTICS

STUDIES ON NEUROPSYCHOLOGY, DEVELOPMENT AND COGNITION. *see* MEDICAL SCIENCES—Psychiatry And Neurology

150.19 GBR ISSN 1755-6341
BF39.9
➤ **SUBJECTIVITY**; international journal of critical psychology. Text in English. 2001 (Oct.). q. USD 562 in North America to institutions; GBP 331 elsewhere to institutions (effective 2011). adv. bk.rev. 192 p./no.; back issues avail.; reprint service avail. from PSC. **Document type:** *Journal, Academic/Scholarly.* **Description:** Provides a forum for new research in the rapidly expanding field of critical psychology, including such topics as feminist psychology, the anti-psychiatry movement, and black socio-political thought.
Formerly (until 2008): Critical Psychology (1471-4167)
Related titles: Online - full text ed.: ISSN 1755-635X (from IngentaConnect).
Indexed: A01, A22, A26, CA, E-psyche, E01, I05, IBSS, MLA-IB, P25, P48, PQC, SociolAb, T02.
—BLDSC (8503.225000), IE.
Published by: Palgrave Macmillan Ltd. (Subsidiary of: Macmillan Publishers Ltd.), Houndmills, Basingstoke, Hants RG21 6XS, United Kingdom. TEL 44-1256-329242, FAX 44-1256-479476, orders@palgrave.com, http://www.palgrave.com. Pub. Ros Pyne TEL 44-1256-303524. Circ: 400. **Subscr. to:** Subscription Department, Brunel Rd, Houndmills, Basingstoke, Hants RG21 2XS, United Kingdom. TEL 44-1256-357893, FAX 44-1256-328339, subscriptions@palgrave.com.

158 ARG ISSN 1666-244X
SUBJETIVIDAD Y PROCESOS COGNITIVOS. Text in Spanish. 2001. s-a. back issues avail. **Document type:** *Journal, Academic/Scholarly.*
Related titles: Online - full text ed.: ISSN 1852-7310. 2001 (from SciELO).
Published by: Universidad de Ciencias Empresariales y Sociales, Departamento de Investigacion, Paraguay, 1401 9o. Piso, Buenos Aires, 1061, Argentina. TEL 54-114-8130228, informes@uces.edu.ar. Circ: 1,000.

SUCCESS (NEW YORK); what achievers read. *see* OCCUPATIONS AND CAREERS

297.13 USA ISSN 1534-2379
BP189
➤ **SUFISM**; the science of the soul. Text in English. 1998. 2/yr. USD 15.95 to non-members; free to members (effective 2010). back issues avail. **Document type:** *Journal, Academic/Scholarly.* **Description:** Contains theoretical and research articles pertaining to the beneficial effects of Sufi psychology and application of methods in everyday life, with emphasis on the helping professions.
Published by: (Sufi Psychology Association), M T O Shahmaghsoudi Publications, PO Box 19922, Sacramento, CA 95827. TEL 916-368-5530, FAX 916-923-1201, info@mto-publications.com, http://mto-publications.org. Ed. Cheryl Crumpler.

150.19 USA
SUGGESTION. Text in English. 1962. a. free to members (effective 2011). bk.rev. **Document type:** *Bulletin, Trade.* **Description:** Contains articles covering topics presented at our conference, along with other issues.
Indexed: E-psyche.
Published by: Association to Advance Ethical Hypnosis, AAEH National Headquarters, 9 The Crossway, Yonkers, NY 10701. TEL 914-476-8131, joann4@optonline.net.

362.28 USA ISSN 0363-0234
RC569 CODEN: SLBEDP
➤ **SUICIDE AND LIFE-THREATENING BEHAVIOR.** Text in English. 1970. bi-m. GBP 487 in United Kingdom to institutions; EUR 562 in Europe to institutions; USD 690 elsewhere to institutions; GBP 535 combined subscription in United Kingdom to institutions (print & online eds.); EUR 618 combined subscription in Europe to institutions (print & online eds.); USD 759 combined subscription elsewhere to institutions (print & online eds.) (effective 2012). adv. abstr.; bibl.; illus. Index. back issues avail.; reprint service avail. from PSC. **Document type:** *Journal, Academic/Scholarly.* **Description:** Biological, statistical, psychological and sociological approaches to the full range of suicide issues.
Former titles (until 1976): Suicide (0360-1390); (until 1975): Life Threatening Behavior (0047-4592)
Related titles: Microform ed.: (from PQC); Online - full text ed.: ISSN 1943-278X. GBP 487 in United Kingdom to institutions; EUR 562 in Europe to institutions; USD 690 elsewhere to institutions (effective 2012).
Indexed: A01, A02, A03, A08, A20, A22, A26, AC&P, AMHA, ASCA, ASG, AbAn, B04, B25, BIOSIS Prev, BRD, C06, C07, CA, CERDIC, CJA, CMHR, CMM, Chicano, CurCont, E-psyche, E01, E02, E03, E07, E08, EMBASE, ERI, ERIC, EdA, EdI, ExcerpMed, F09, FR, FamI, G08, H12, H13, I05, INI, IndMed, M01, M02, M06, MEDLINE, MycolAb, P02, P03, P10, P12, P13, P18, P20, P22, P25, P27, P30, P46, P48, P50, P53, P54, PCI, PQC, PsycInfo, PsycholAb, R10, RILM, Reac, S02, S03, S09, SCOPUS, SFSA, SOPODA, SSA, SSAI, SSAb, SSCI, SSI, SociolAb, T02, V&AA, W03, W07, W09.
—BLDSC (8514.141000), GNLM, IE, Infotrieve, Ingenta, INIST. **CCC.**
Published by: (American Association of Suicidology), John Wiley & Sons, Inc., 111 River St, Hoboken, NJ 07030. TEL 201-748-6000, 800-825-7550, FAX 201-748-5915, info@wiley.com, http://www.wiley.com/WileyCDA/. Ed. Thomas E Joiner TEL 850-644-1454.

150 POL ISSN 1895-3786
➤ **SUICYDOLOGIA/SUICIDOLOGY.** Text in Polish, English. 2005. a. **Document type:** *Journal, Academic/Scholarly.*
Related titles: Online - full text ed.: ISSN 1895-6505.
Published by: (Polskie Towarzystwo Suicydologiczne/Polish Suicidogical Society), Wydawnictwo Via Medica, ul Swietokrzyska 73, Gdansk, 80180, Poland. TEL 48-58-3209494, FAX 48-58-3209460, redakcja@viamedica.pl, http://www.viamedica.pl. Ed. Brunon Holyst.

150 CHL ISSN 0718-0446
SUMA PSICOLOGIA UST. (Universidad de Santo Tomas) Text in Spanish. 2003. s-a. **Document type:** *Journal, Academic/Scholarly.*
Indexed: C01.
Published by: Universidad de Santo Tomas, Escuela de Psicologia, Ave Ejercito 146, Barrio, Santiago, Chile. TEL 56-2-3625000, FAX 56-2-3601376, admision@santotoma.cl, http://www.ust.cl/ust/.

P

150 COL ISSN 0121-4381
SUMA PSICOLOGICA. Text in Spanish. 1994. s-a. COP 26,400 domestic; USD 30 foreign (effective 2008). back issues avail. **Document type:** *Journal, Academic/Scholarly.*
Related titles: Online - full text ed.: free (effective 2011).
Indexed: A01, CA, F03, F04, T02.
Published by: Fundacion Universitaria Konrad Lorenz, Carrera 9 bis No. 62-43, Bogota, Colombia. Ed. Gladys S Martinez.

SURDITES. *see* HANDICAPPED—Hearing Impaired

150 HRV ISSN 1331-9264
➤ **SUVREMENA PSIHOLOGIJA.** Text in Croatian. 1998. s-a. HRK 70 domestic to individuals; EUR 25 foreign to individuals; HRK 140 domestic to institutions; HRK 35 foreign to institutions (effective 2008). **Document type:** *Journal, Academic/Scholarly.*
Indexed: L&LBA, P03, PsycInfo, SCOPUS, SSCI, SociolAb, W07.
—BLDSC (8553.619000).
Published by: Naklada Slap, Dr F Tudmana 33, Jastrebarsko, 10450, Croatia. nslap@nakladaslap.com, http://www.nakladaslap.com. Ed. Predrag Zarevski.

616.89 SWE ISSN 0346-8968
SVENSKA FOERENINGEN FOER PSYKISK HAELSA. MONOGRAFSERIE. Text in Swedish. 1971. irreg. price varies. back issues avail. **Document type:** *Monographic series.*
Published by: Svenska Foereningen foer Psykisk Haelsa/Swedish Association for Mental Health, Saltmaetargatan 5 2, PO Box 3445, Stockholm, 10369, Sweden. TEL 46-8-347065, FAX 46-8-328875, info@sfph.se, http://www.sfph.se.

150 CHE ISSN 1421-0185
➤ **SWISS JOURNAL OF PSYCHOLOGY.** Text in French, German; Abstracts in English, German. 1942. 4/yr. CHF 219 domestic to institutions; EUR 146 in Europe to institutions (effective 2011). bk.rev. abstr.; bibl.; charts. 48 p./no.; **Document type:** *Journal, Academic/Scholarly.* **Description:** Serves as a forum for the scientific discussion of all areas of psychology and their applications.
Former titles (until 1993): Schweizerische Zeitschrift fuer Psychologie (1421-0177); (until 1986): Psychologie (1421-0169); (until 1967): Schweizerische Zeitschrift fuer Psychologie und ihre Anwendungen (0036-7869)
Related titles: Online - full text ed.: ISSN 1662-0879 (from ScienceDirect).
Indexed: A20, ASCA, BibInd, CurCont, DIP, E-psyche, FamI, GJP, IBR, IBZ, P03, P30, PsycInfo, PsycholAb, RASB, RILM, S02, S03, SCOPUS, SSCI, W07.
—BLDSC (8576.760500), IE, Infotrieve, Ingenta, INIST. **CCC.**
Published by: (Societe Suisse de Psychologie), Verlag Hans Huber AG (Subsidiary of: Hogrefe Verlag GmbH & Co. KG), Laenggassstr 76, Bern 9, 3000, Switzerland. TEL 41-31-3004500, FAX 41-31-3004590, verlag@hanshuber.com, http://www.hanshuber.com. Ed. Adrian Bangerter. Circ: 750 (paid and controlled).

150 USA
SWISS MONOGRAPHS IN PSYCHOLOGY. Text in English. irreg., latest vol.4, 2005. price varies. **Document type:** *Monographic series, Academic/Scholarly.*
Indexed: E-psyche.
Published by: (Swiss Psychological Society), Hogrefe Publishing Corp., 875 Massachusetts Ave, 7th Fl, Cambridge, MA 02139. TEL 866-823-4726, FAX 617-354-6875, customservices@hogrefe-publishing.com, http://www.hogrefe.com.

616.890 NLD ISSN 1874-9666
SYMFOCUS. Text in Dutch. 2007. q. free (effective 2010).
Published by: Symfora Groep, Postbus 3051, Amersfoort, 3800 DB, Netherlands. TEL 31-33-4609609, FAX 31-33-4650463, pr@symfora.nl, http://www.symfora.nl. Circ: 4,500.

616.890 AUS ISSN 1442-7818
SYNERGY. Text in English. 1996. 3/yr. free (effective 2008). back issues avail. **Document type:** *Magazine, Consumer.* **Description:** Features a variety of articles that highlight different approaches to treating mental illness.
Formerly (until 1998): Synapse (1440-3099)
Related titles: Online - full text ed.: free (effective 2008).
Indexed: C06, C07, C08, CINAHL.
Published by: Australian Transcultural Mental Health Network, Locked Bag 7118, Parramatta, NSW 2150, Australia. TEL 61-2-98403333, FAX 61-2-98403388, info@mmha.org.au.

616.89 DEU ISSN 0724-7923
BF173.A2
SYSTEM UBW; Zeitschrift fuer klassische Psychoanalyse. Text in German; Summaries in English, French. 1983. irreg. EUR 6.80 per issue (effective 2008). bk.rev. 100 p./no.; back issues avail. **Document type:** *Magazine, Academic/Scholarly.* **Description:** Scientific periodical for psychoanalysis in the tradition of Sigmund Freud.
Indexed: DIP, E-psyche, IBR, IBZ, MLA-IB, RASB.
—GNLM.
Published by: Ahriman Verlag GmbH, Postfach 6569, Freiburg Im Breisgau, 79041, Germany. TEL 49-761-502303, FAX 49-761-502247, ahriman@t-online.de. **Dist. by:** Thanilo Verlag und Vertriebs GmbH, Postfach 710, Freiburg Im Breisgau 79007, Germany. TEL 49-761-502247, thanilo@t-online.de.

150 USA ISSN 1940-2422
HQ18.U5
TAKING SIDES: CLASHING VIEWS IN HUMAN SEXUALITY. Text in English. 1986. biennial. illus. **Document type:** *Catalog, Academic/Scholarly.* **Description:** Presents current controversial issues in a debate-style format designed to stimulate student interest and develop critical thinking skills.
Formerly (until 2008): Taking Sides: Clashing Views on Controversial Issues in Human Sexuality (1098-5387)
Indexed: E-psyche.
Published by: McGraw-Hill, Contemporary Learning Series (Subsidiary of: McGraw-Hill Companies, Inc.), 1221 Ave of the Americas, New York, NY 10020. TEL 212-904-2000, 800-243-6532, FAX 212-512-2000, customer.service@mcgraw-hill.com, http://www.mhhe.com/cls/.

155 USA ISSN 1559-2642
BF713
TAKING SIDES: CLASHING VIEWS IN LIFESPAN DEVELOPMENT. Text in English. 2006. biennial. back issues avail. **Document type:** *Catalog, Academic/Scholarly.* **Description:** Presents current controversial issues in a debate-style format designed to stimulate student interest and develop critical thinking skills.
Related titles: Online - full text ed.
Published by: McGraw-Hill, Contemporary Learning Series (Subsidiary of: McGraw-Hill Companies, Inc.), 1221 Ave of the Americas, New York, NY 10020. TEL 212-904-2000, 800-243-6532, FAX 212-512-2000, customer.service@mcgraw-hill.com, http://www.mhhe.com/cls/.

158 USA ISSN 2152-9701
BF698.A1
▼ **TAKING SIDES: CLASHING VIEWS IN PERSONALITY PSYCHOLOGY.** Text in English. 2010 (May). biennial. USD 23.99 per issue (effective 2010). **Document type:** *Academic/Scholarly.* **Description:** Presents debates and issues in personality psychology for college students.
Related titles: Online - full text ed.: ISSN 2152-971X.
Published by: McGraw-Hill Higher Education (Subsidiary of: McGraw-Hill Companies, Inc.), 2 Penn Plaza, New York, NY 10121. TEL 212-512-2000, http://catalogs.mhhe.com/mhhe/home.do.

302 USA
HM251
TAKING SIDES: CLASHING VIEWS IN SOCIAL PSYCHOLOGY. Text in English. 2005. irreg., latest 2010, 3rd ed. back issues avail. **Document type:** *Catalog, Academic/Scholarly.* **Description:** Presents current controversial issues in a debate-style format designed to stimulate student interest and develop critical thinking skills.
Formerly (until 2006): Taking Sides: Clashing Views on Controversial Issues in Social Psychology (1550-6169)
Published by: McGraw-Hill, Contemporary Learning Series (Subsidiary of: McGraw-Hill Companies, Inc.), 1221 Ave of the Americas, New York, NY 10020. TEL 212-904-2000, 800-243-6532, FAX 212-512-2000, customer.service@mcgraw-hill.com, http://www.mhhe.com/cls/.

150 USA
BJ1012
TAKING SIDES: CLASHING VIEWS ON MORAL ISSUES. Text in English. 1988. irreg., latest 2010, 12th ed. illus. back issues avail. **Document type:** *Catalog, Academic/Scholarly.* **Description:** Designed to introduce students to current controversies in moral philosophy.
Formerly (until 2006): Taking Sides: Clashing Views on Controversial Moral Issues (1094-7604)
Published by: McGraw-Hill, Contemporary Learning Series (Subsidiary of: McGraw-Hill Companies, Inc.), 1221 Ave of the Americas, New York, NY 10020. TEL 212-904-2000, 800-243-6532, FAX 212-512-2000, customer.service@mcgraw-hill.com, http://www.mhhe.com/cls/.

150 USA
BF149
TAKING SIDES: CLASHING VIEWS ON PSYCHOLOGICAL ISSUES. Text in English. 1980. irreg., latest 2010, 16th ed. illus. back issues avail. **Document type:** *Catalog, Academic/Scholarly.* **Description:** Designed to introduce students to controversies in psychology.
Formerly (until 2006): Taking Sides: Clashing Views on Controversial Psychological Issues (1098-5409)
Indexed: E-psyche.
Published by: McGraw-Hill, Contemporary Learning Series (Subsidiary of: McGraw-Hill Companies, Inc.), 1221 Ave of the Americas, New York, NY 10020. TEL 212-904-2000, 800-243-6532, FAX 212-512-2000, customer.service@mcgraw-hill.com, http://www.mhhe.com/cls/.

TE AWATEA REVIEW. *see* CRIMINOLOGY AND LAW ENFORCEMENT

150.71 USA ISSN 0098-6283
BF77
➤ **TEACHING OF PSYCHOLOGY.** Text in English. 1974. q. USD 568, GBP 334 combined subscription to institutions (print & online eds.); USD 557, GBP 327 to institutions (effective 2011). adv. bk.rev.; film rev. bibl.; charts; illus. index. back issues avail.; reprint service avail. from PSC. **Document type:** *Journal, Academic/Scholarly.* **Description:** Provides information to improving the learning-teaching process at all educational levels: from secondary through college and graduate school, to continuing education.
Related titles: Microform ed.: (from PQC); Online - full text ed.: ISSN 1532-8023. USD 511, GBP 301 to institutions (effective 2011).
Indexed: A01, A02, A03, A08, A20, A22, ABS&EES, ASCA, B04, BRD, CA, CPE, CurCont, E-psyche, E01, E02, E03, E09, ERI, ERIC, EdA, EdI, FamI, P03, P04, P10, P18, P20, P25, P30, P43, P48, P53, P54, PQC, PsycInfo, PsycholAb, PsycholRG, S02, S03, SCOPUS, SSCI, T02, W03, W07.
—BLDSC (8614.330000), IE, Infotrieve, Ingenta. **CCC.**
Published by: (Society for the Teaching of Psychology Share, American Psychological Association), Sage Publications, Inc., 2455 Teller Rd, Thousand Oaks, CA 91320. TEL 805-499-9774, 800-818-7243, FAX 805-499-0871, 800-583-2665, info@sagepub.com, http://www.sagepub.com.

158 FRA ISSN 1295-1552
TECHNIQUES DE DEVELOPPEMENT PERSONNEL. Text in French. 1999. irreg. back issues avail. **Document type:** *Monographic series, Consumer.*
Published by: InterEditions (Subsidiary of: Dunod), 5 Rue Laromiguiere, Paris, 75005, France. TEL 33-1-40463500, FAX 33-1-40464995, http://www.intereditions.com/.

370.15 USA ISSN 1540-0182
L11
➤ **TECHNOLOGY, INSTRUCTION, COGNITION AND LEARNING.** Abbreviated title: T I C L. Text in French. 1968. q. EUR 76 in Europe to individuals; JPY 11,100 in Japan to individuals; USD 65 elsewhere to individuals; EUR 549 combined subscription in Europe to institutions (print & online eds.); JPY 65,206 combined subscription in Japan to institutions (print & online eds.); USD 658 combined subscription elsewhere to institutions (print & online eds.) (effective 2011). adv. bk.rev.; software rev. index. back issues avail.; reprints avail. **Document type:** *Journal, Academic/Scholarly.* **Description:** Promotes and disseminates advances in theory and research at the intersection of four focus disciplines such as technology, instruction, cognition and learning.
Former titles (until 2002): Journal of Structural Learning and Intelligent Systems (1027-1015); (until 1997): Journal of Structural Learning (0022-4774)
Related titles: CD-ROM ed.; Microform ed.; Online - full text ed.: ISSN 1540-0174.
Indexed: A01, A03, A08, A20, B07, C23, CA, CPE, CommAb, DIP, E-psyche, E03, ERI, IBR, IBZ, P43, PsycholAb, SociolAb, T02, Z02.
—BLDSC (8758.877000), IE, Ingenta, INIST. **CCC.**
Published by: (International Study Group for Mathematics Learning CHE, Association for Educational Communications and Technology), Old City Publishing, Inc., 628 N 2nd St, Philadelphia, PA 19123. TEL 215-925-4390, FAX 215-925-4371, info@oldcitypublishing.com. **Co-sponsor:** Structural Learning Society.

▼ ➤ **TECHNOLOGY, PSYCHOLOGY, AND HEALTH.** *see* MEDICAL SCIENCES

➤ **TEILHABE;** Die Fachzeitschrift der Lebenshilfe. *see* EDUCATION—Special Education And Rehabilitation

150 158.7 CAN
TELL-A-TYPE. Text in English. q. free to members (effective 2004). **Document type:** *Newsletter.*
Indexed: E-psyche.
Published by: Ontario Association for the Application of Personality Type, 116 Viceroy Rd, Unit B1, Concord, ON L4K 2M2, Canada. TEL 905-760-1339, info@oaapt.ca.

150 ESP ISSN 1137-7682
TEMAS DE PSICOANALISIS. Text in Spanish. 1996. a. **Document type:** *Magazine, Consumer.*
Published by: Sociedad Espanola de Psicoanalisis, Alacant, 27 Entlo. B, Barcelona, 08022, Spain.

150.195 616.8917 BRA ISSN 0101-4838
TEMPO PSICANALITICO. Text in Portuguese. 1978. s-a.
Indexed: P03, PsycInfo, PsycholAb, SSCI, W07.
Published by: Sociedade de Psicanalise Iracy Doyle, Rua Visconde de Piraja 156 s/307, Rio de Janeiro, RJ 22410-000, Brazil. spid@spid.com.br.

TEORIE & MODELLI; rivista di storia e metodologia della psicologia. *see* MATHEMATICS

TERAPIA FAMILIARE; rivista interdisciplinare di ricerca ed intervento relazionale. *see* LAW—Family And Matrimonial Law

150 CHL ISSN 0716-6184
TERAPIA PSICOLOGICA. Text in Spanish. 1982. s-a. CLP 10,000 domestic to individuals; USD 20 foreign to individuals; CLP 20,000 domestic to institutions; USD 35 foreign to institutions (effective 2011). **Document type:** *Journal, Academic/Scholarly.*
Related titles: Online - full text ed.: ISSN 0718-4808. 2007. free (effective 2011) (from SciELO).
Indexed: EMBASE, ExcerpMed, P03, PsycInfo, PsycholAb, SCOPUS.
Published by: Sociedad Chilena de Psicolgia Clinica, Ricardo Matte Perez 492, Providencia, Santiago, Chile. TEL 56-2-2090286, FAX 56-2-2698328, sochpscl@entelchile.net, http://sociedadchilenadepsicologiaclinica.cl. Ed. Pablo Vera-Villarroel.

TESTIMONI; quindicinale di informazione e aggiornamento per istituti di vita consacrata. *see* RELIGIONS AND THEOLOGY

371.3 USA ISSN 0361-025X
Z5814.E9
TESTS IN PRINT. Abbreviated title: T I P. Text in English. 1961. irreg., latest vol.7, 2006. USD 325 per issue (effective 2010). bibl. cum.index. back issues avail. **Document type:** *Directory, Trade.* **Description:** Lists over 4,000 test instruments that are commercially available in English. Includes description of tests, intended population, scores available, current pricing, and publisher name and address.
Indexed: E-psyche.
Published by: Buros Institute of Mental Measurements, 21 Teachers College Hall, University of Nebraska - Lincoln, Lincoln, NE 68588. TEL 402-472-6203, FAX 402-472-6207, pressmail@unl.edu, http://www.unl.edu/buros/bimm/index.html.

302 DEU
TEXTE ZUR SOZIALPSYCHOLOGIE. Text in German. 199?. irreg., latest vol.9, 2004. price varies. **Document type:** *Monographic series, Academic/Scholarly.*
Published by: Waxmann Verlag GmbH, Steinfurter Str 555, Muenster, 48159, Germany. TEL 49-251-265040, FAX 49-251-2650426, info@waxmann.com. Ed. Ulrich Wagner.

156 DEU ISSN 0934-5272
HM291
THEMENZENTRIERTE INTERAKTION. Text and summaries in English, German. 1987. s-a. EUR 18.50 per issue (effective 2009). adv. bk.rev. back issues avail. **Document type:** *Journal, Academic/Scholarly.*
Indexed: E-psyche.
Published by: Psychosozial Verlag, Walltorstr 10, Giessen, 35390, Germany. TEL 49-641-9699780, FAX 49-641-96997819, info@psychosozial-verlag.de, http://www.psychosozial-verlag.de. adv.: B&W page EUR 550; trim 120 x 180. Circ: 2,700 (paid).

THEORIA; a Swedish journal of philosophy. *see* PHILOSOPHY

150 DEU ISSN 1866-0398
THEORIEN UND METHODEN DER PSYCHOLOGIE. Text in German. 2008. irreg., latest vol.3, 2009. price varies. **Document type:** *Monographic series, Academic/Scholarly.*
Published by: Verlag Dr. Kovac, Leverkusenstr 13, Hamburg, 22761, Germany. TEL 49-40-3988800, FAX 49-40-39888055, info@verlagdrkovac.de.

370.15 150 GBR ISSN 0959-3543
BF1 CODEN: THPSEJ
➤ **THEORY & PSYCHOLOGY.** Text in English. 1990. bi-m. USD 1,131, GBP 612 combined subscription to institutions (print & online eds.); USD 1,108, GBP 600 to institutions (effective 2011). adv. bk.rev. back issues avail.; reprint service avail. from PSC. **Document type:** *Journal, Academic/Scholarly.* **Description:** Fosters theoretical dialogue and innovation within psychology, focusing on the emergent themes at the center of contemporary psychological debate.
Related titles: Online - full text ed.: ISSN 1461-7447. USD 1,018, GBP 551 to institutions (effective 2011).
Indexed: A01, A03, A08, A20, A22, AEI, ASCA, B07, CA, CurCont, DIP, E-psyche, E01, FamI, H04, IBR, IBSS, IBZ, L&LBA, P02, P03, P10, P12, P25, P30, P48, P53, P54, PQC, PsycInfo, PsycholAb, RASB, S02, S03, SCOPUS, SOPODA, SSCI, SociolAb, T02, V02, W07.

—BLDSC (8814.628600), IE, Infotrieve, Ingenta. **CCC.**
Published by: Sage Publications Ltd. (Subsidiary of: Sage Publications, Inc.), 1 Oliver's Yard, 55 City Rd, London, EC1Y 1SP, United Kingdom. TEL 44-20-73248500, FAX 44-20-73248600, info@sagepub.co.uk, http://www.uk.sagepub.com/home.nav. Ed. Henderikus J Stam. adv.: B&W page GBP 400; 130 x 205. **Subscr. in the Americas to:** Sage Publications, Inc., 2455 Teller Rd, Thousand Oaks, CA 91320. TEL 805-499-9774, FAX 805-499-0871, journals@sagepub.com.

➤ **THERAPEUTIC RECREATION JOURNAL.** *see* PHYSICAL FITNESS AND HYGIENE

158.1 DEU ISSN 1434-8977
THERAPIE KREATIV; Zeitschrift fuer kreative Sozio- und Psychotherapie. Text in German. 1991. 3/yr. EUR 20 domestic; EUR 21.50 foreign; EUR 10.50 newsstand/cover (effective 2008). **Document type:** *Journal, Trade.*
Formerly (until 1998): Sozialtherapie (0940-3213)
Published by: Affenkoenig Verlag und Vertrieb, Balderbruchweg 35, Neukirchen-Vluyn, 47506, Germany. TEL 49-2845-4635, FAX 49-2845-4635, info@affenkoenig.de, http://www.affenkoenig.de. Eds. Gabriele Frick-Baer, Martin Lenz.

614.58 USA ISSN 1540-2770
RC488.5
THE THERAPIST. Text in English. 1989. bi-m. USD 36 to non-members (effective 2005). bk.rev. charts; illus.; stat.; tr.lit. **Document type:** *Magazine, Trade.* **Description:** For and about CA licensed marriage, family and child therapists.
Formerly (until 2005): California Therapist (1062-8193)
Indexed: E-psyche.
Published by: California Association of Marriage and Family Therapists, 7901 Raytheon Rd, San Diego, CA 92111-1606. TEL 858-292-2638, FAX 858-292-2666, infocenter@camft.org, http://www.camft.org. Ed. Mary Riemersma. R&P, Adv. contact Eileen Schuster. Circ: 27,500 (paid and free).

150 USA ISSN 1061-4362
THERAPISTS REPORT. Text in English. 1985. q. USD 49 (effective 2000). adv. back issues avail. **Document type:** *Newsletter.* **Description:** Disseminates information to behavioral therapists on what is new in the behavioral sciences.
Indexed: E-psyche.
Published by: American Association of Behavioral Therapists, PO Box 1737, Ormond Beach, FL 32175-1735. Ed., Pub., R&P, Adv. contact Dan J Allen. Circ: 1,000.

616.89 GBR ISSN 1748-7846
➤ **THERAPY TODAY**; for counselling and psychotherapy professionals. Text in English. 19??. 10/yr. GBP 69 domestic to non-members; GBP 84 foreign to non-members; GBP 8.50 per issue to non-members; free to members (effective 2010). adv. bk.rev. index. 67 p./no. 3 cols./p.; back issues avail. **Document type:** *Journal, Academic/Scholarly.* **Description:** Provides a forum counselling and psychotherapy professionals and those interested in therapy.
Former titles (until 2005): C P J - Counselling and Psychotherapy Journal (1474-5372); (until 2001): Counselling (0264-9977); (until 1981): Counselling News (0963-0767)
Related titles: Diskette ed.; Online - full text ed.
Indexed: A01, A03, A08, A22, B28, C06, C07, C08, CA, CINAHL, E-psyche, P43, T02.
—BLDSC (8814.767900), IE, Ingenta. **CCC.**
Published by: British Association for Counselling & Psychotherapy, BACP House, 15 St John's Business Park, Lutterworth, Leicestershire LE17 4HB, United Kingdom. TEL 44-1455-883300, FAX 44-1455-550243, bacp@bacp.co.uk, http://www.bacp.co.uk. Ed. Sarah Browne TEL 44-1455-883317. Adv. contact Jeannette Hughes TEL 44-1455-883314. B&W page GBP 870, color page GBP 1,450; 240 x 156. Circ: 31,634.

150 AUS ISSN 1837-9796
▼ **THINK AND GROW RICH INC.** Text in English. 2010. s-a. free in Australia & New Zealand to qualified personnel (effective 2011). adv. **Document type:** *Magazine, Consumer.* **Description:** Helps to assist in creating and manifesting wealth and abundance as per the principles originally taught by Napoleon Hill.
Related titles: Online - full text ed.: ISSN 1837-980X.
Published by: Napoleon Hill Australia, PO Box 352, Tewantin, QLD 4565, Australia. TEL 61-7-35039021, 800-701-519, enquiries@21stca.com.au. Adv. contact Kirsten Pride TEL 61-3-86160270.

150 100 GBR ISSN 1354-6783
BF441 CODEN: THREFM
➤ **THINKING & REASONING.** Text in English. 1995. q. GBP 387 combined subscription in United Kingdom to institutions (print & online eds.); EUR 513, USD 643 combined subscription to institutions (print & online eds.) (effective 2012). bk.rev. 96 p./no.; back issues avail.; reprint service avail. from PSC. **Document type:** *Journal, Academic/Scholarly.* **Description:** Features articles dedicated to the understanding of human thought processes, particularly reasoning.
Related titles: Online - full text ed.: ISSN 1464-0708. GBP 348 in United Kingdom to institutions; EUR 462, USD 578 to institutions (effective 2012) (from IngentaConnect).
Indexed: A01, A03, A08, A20, A22, B01, B06, B07, B09, CA, CurCont, E-psyche, E01, ErgAb, FR, Inspec, L&LBA, P03, P43, PsycInfo, PsycholAb, SCOPUS, SOPODA, SSCI, SociolAb, T02, W07.
—AskIEEE, IE, Infotrieve, Ingenta, INIST. **CCC.**
Published by: Psychology Press (Subsidiary of: Taylor & Francis Ltd.), 27 Church Rd, Hove, E Sussex BN3 2FA, United Kingdom. TEL 44-20-70176000, FAX 44-20-70176717, info@psypress.co.uk, http://www.psypress.com. Ed. Jonathan St B T Evans. Adv. contact Linda Hann TEL 44-1344-779945. **Subscr. to:** Taylor & Francis Ltd., Journals Customer Service, Sheepen Pl, Colchester, Essex CO3 3LP, United Kingdom. TEL 44-20-70175544, FAX 44-20-70175198, subscriptions@tandf.co.uk, http://www.tandf.co.uk/journals; **Subsct. in N. America to:** Taylor & Francis Inc., Customer Services Dept, 325 Chestnut St, 8th Fl, Philadelphia, PA 19106. TEL 215-625-8900, 800-354-1420, FAX 215-625-2940, customerservice@taylorandfrancis.com.

158 133 GBR ISSN 2045-516X
THRESHOLDS; counselling with spirit. Text in English. 200?. q. free to members (effective 2010). back issues avail. **Document type:** *Journal, Trade.* **Description:** Contains the information of medicine, culture, spirituality and transformation towards therapeutic learning groups.
Formerly (until 2007): Reflections
Published by: British Association for Counselling & Psychotherapy, BACP House, 15 St John's Business Park, Lutterworth, Leicestershire LE17 4HB, United Kingdom. TEL 44-1455-883300, FAX 44-1455-550243, bacp@bacp.co.uk, http://www.bacp.co.uk.

150 BEL ISSN 1378-8647
TIJDSCHRIFT KLINISCHE PSYCHOLOGIE. Text in Dutch. 1971. q. EUR 35 (effective 2005). **Document type:** *Journal, Academic/Scholarly.*
Published by: Uitgeverij Acco, Brusselsestraat 153, Leuven, 3000, Belgium. TEL 32-16-628000, FAX 32-16-628001, uitgeverij@acco.be, http://www.acco.be. Ed. Johan Vereycken.

158 616.89 NLD ISSN 1380-7161
TIJDSCHRIFT VOOR CLIENTGERICHTE PSYCHOTHERAPIE. Text in Dutch. 1984. q. EUR 44 to individuals; EUR 69 to institutions; EUR 15 newsstand/cover to institutions (effective 2009). **Document type:** *Journal, Academic/Scholarly.* **Description:** Examines client-directed psychotherapy.
Former titles (until 1994): V R T - Periodiek (0165-9014); (until 1989): Vereniging voor Rogeriaanse Therapie. Mededelingenblad (0923-9189)
Published by: (Vereniging voor Clientgerichte Psychotherapie te Utrecht), De Tijdstroom Uitgeverij, Janskerkhof 26, Utrecht, 3500 AT, Netherlands. TEL 31-30-2364450, FAX 31-30-2369354, info@tijdstroom.nl, http://www.tijdstroom.nl. **Co-sponsor:** Vlaamse Vereniging voor Clientgerichte Psychotherapie te Leuven, BE.

616.890 NLD ISSN 1871-1391
TIJDSCHRIFT VOOR NEUROPSYCHOLOGIE; diagnostiek, behandeling en onderzoek. Text in Dutch. 2006. 3/yr. EUR 50.75 to individuals; EUR 72 to institutions; EUR 36.50 to students (effective 2009). adv. **Document type:** *Journal, Trade.*
Published by: Boom Uitgevers Amsterdam, Prinsengracht 747-751, Amsterdam, 1017 JX, Netherlands. TEL 31-20-6226107, FAX 31-20-6253327, info@uitgeverijboom.nl, http://www.uitgeverijboom.nl. Adv. contact Michiel Klaasen TEL 31-20-5200122. B&W page EUR 575; trim 140 x 210. Circ: 2,500.

TIROLER SCHULE. *see* EDUCATION

150 USA
TODAY (BUFFALO); good mental health for a healty community. Text in English. m. free (effective 2004). **Document type:** *Newspaper, Consumer.* **Description:** Contains valuable information on mental health events and happenings in Erie County as well as resources and information on topics that are important to you.
Indexed: E-psyche.
Published by: Mental Health Association of Erie County, 999 Delaware Ave, Buffalo, NY 14209-1892. TEL 716-886-1242, FAX 716-881-6428. Ed. TeNeathia L Wesolowski. Circ: 3,000.

150.19 370.15 371.3 USA ISSN 1098-9277
TODAY'S SCHOOL PSYCHOLOGIST. Text in English. 1997. m. USD 185 (print or email ed.) (effective 2008). **Document type:** *Newsletter, Trade.* **Description:** Contains information to tackle day-to-day challenges - from identifying students with learning disorders to interpreting assessment data.
Related titles: E-mail ed.; Online - full text ed.
Indexed: E-psyche.
—CIS. **CCC.**
Published by: L R P Publications, Inc., 747 Dresher Rd, Ste 500, PO Box 980, Horsham, PA 19044. TEL 215-784-0860, 800-341-7874, FAX 215-784-9639, techsup@lrp.com, http://www.lrp.com. Ed. Cara Kraft.

615.85 NLD ISSN 1566-0273
TOEGANG TOT DE PSYCHOTHERAPIE INTERNATIONAAL. Text in Dutch. 1994. q. EUR 154.30 to individuals; EUR 240.10 to institutions; EUR 77.15 to students (effective 2007). **Document type:** *Journal, Academic/Scholarly.*
Formerly (until 1999): Psychotherapie (1381-5180)
Published by: Bohn Stafleu van Loghum B.V. (Subsidiary of: Springer Science+Business Media), Postbus 246, Houten, 3990 GA, Netherlands. TEL 31-30-6383872, FAX 31-30-6383991, boekhandels@bsl.nl, http://www.bsl.nl. Ed. P Spinhoven.

150 JPN ISSN 0040-8743
BF1 CODEN: TPSFAD
➤ **TOHOKU PSYCHOLOGICA FOLIA.** Text in English. 1933. a. per issue exchange basis. charts; illus. Index. **Document type:** *Journal, Academic/Scholarly.* **Description:** Contains full paper and short research notes, technical or instrument notes, and letters on the study of psychology.
Indexed: B25, BIOSIS Prev, CDA, E-psyche, FR, L&LBA, MycolAb, P03, PsycInfo, PsycholAb, RefZh, S02, S03, SCOPUS, SOPODA, SociolAb.
—BLDSC (8862.350000), INIST.
Published by: Tohoku University, Graduate School of Arts & Letters, Department of Psychology/Tohoku Daigaku, Bungakubu Shinrigaku Kyoshitsu, Kawauchi 27-1, Aoba-ku, Sendai, 980-8576, Japan. TEL 81-22-7956048, FAX 81-22-7953703, http://www.sal.tohoku.ac.jp/psychology/index-j.html. Ed. Yoshiaki Nihei. Circ: 525.

302 ARG
TOPIA REVISTA; psicoanalisis, sociedad y cultura. Text in Spanish. 1991. 3/yr. ARS 15 domestic; USD 30 foreign (effective 2007). adv. bk.rev. **Document type:** *Magazine, Consumer.*
Indexed: E-psyche.
Address: Juan Maria Gutierrez, 3809 3o A, Buenos Aires, 1425, Argentina.

020 USA ISSN 1756-8757
BF311
▼ ➤ **TOPICS IN COGNITIVE SCIENCE.** Text in English. 2009 (Jan.). q. **Document type:** *Journal, Academic/Scholarly.* **Description:** Covers all areas of cognitive science including cognitive modeling, cognitive neuroscience, cognitive anthropology, and cognitive science and philosophy.
Related titles: Online - full text ed.: ISSN 1756-8765. 2009.
—CCC.
Published by: (Cognitive Science Society), Wiley-Blackwell Publishing, Inc. (Subsidiary of: Wiley-Blackwell Publishing Ltd.), Commerce Pl, 350 Main St, Malden, MA 02148. TEL 781-388-8206, FAX 781-388-8232, info@wiley.com, http://www.wiley.com/WileyCDA/. Ed. Wayne D Gray.

➤ **TOPIQUE**; revue Freudienne. *see* MEDICAL SCIENCES—Psychiatry And Neurology

➤ **TOPOI**; an international review of philosophy. *see* PHILOSOPHY

150 616.8 JPN ISSN 1345-4501
TORANSUPASONARU SHINRIGAKU/SEISHIN IGAKU/JAPANESE JOURNAL OF TRANSPERSONAL PSYCHOLOGY/PSYCHIATRY. Text in Japanese. 2000. a. **Document type:** *Journal, Academic/Scholarly.*
—BLDSC (6113.130000).
Published by: Nihon Toransupasonaru Shinrigaku/Seishin Igakkai/Japanese Association for Transpersonal Psychology/Psychiatry, Ritsumeikan University, Graduate School of Letters, 56-1 Toji-in Kitamachi Kita-ku, Kyoto-shi, Kyoto 603-8577, Japan. FAX 86-75-466-3231, jatp@mail.goo.ne.jp.

TOTAL HEALTH; for longevity. *see* NUTRITION AND DIETETICS

370.15 USA ISSN 1931-3918
BF77
➤ **TRAINING AND EDUCATION IN PROFESSIONAL PSYCHOLOGY.** Text in English. 2006. q. USD 116 domestic to individuals; USD 143 foreign to individuals; USD 415 domestic to institutions; USD 460 foreign to institutions (effective 2011). adv. back issues avail. **Document type:** *Journal, Academic/Scholarly.* **Description:** Dedicated to enhancing supervision and training provided by psychologists. It publishes manuscripts that contribute to and advance professional psychology education.
Related titles: Online - full text ed.: ISSN 1931-3926 (from ScienceDirect).
Indexed: C06, CA, CurCont, P03, PsycInfo, SCOPUS, SSCI, T02, W03, W07.
—CCC.
Published by: (Association of Psychology Postdoctoral and Internship Centers), American Psychological Association, 750 First St, NE, Washington, DC 20002. TEL 202-336-5500, 800-374-2721, journals@apa.org. Ed. Emil R Rodolfa. Adv. contact Doug Constant TEL 202-336-5574. Circ: 1,600.

616.89 361.06 GBR
TRAINING IN COUNSELLING & PSYCHOTHERAPY. Text in English. 1984. a., latest 2008. GBP 19 per issue to non-members; GBP 17 per issue to members (effective 2010). **Document type:** *Directory, Trade.*
Published by: British Association for Counselling & Psychotherapy, BACP House, 15 St John's Business Park, Lutterworth, Leicestershire LE17 4HB, United Kingdom. TEL 44-1455-883300, FAX 44-1455-550243, bacp@bacp.co.uk, http://www.bacp.co.uk.

616.8 370 USA ISSN 0362-1537
RC489.T7
TRANSACTIONAL ANALYSIS JOURNAL. Abbreviated title: T A J. Text in English. 1970. q. USD 60 to non-members; free to members (effective 2010). bk.rev. abstr.; charts. Index. back issues avail.; reprints avail. **Document type:** *Journal, Academic/Scholarly.* **Description:** Covers the theory, principles, and practice of transactional analysis, including scholarly articles on related topics on the research into the nature of human change; insightful book reviews; and a yearly author and subject index. Theme issues covers subjects such as case studies, violence, core concepts in transactional analysis, "For Our Clients," and the schizoid process.
Formerly (until 1971): Transactional Analysis Bulletin (0041-1051)
Related titles: Microform ed.: (from PQC).
Indexed: A01, A20, A22, ASCA, E-psyche, IPsyAb, P03, P25, P48, PQC, PsycInfo, PsycholAb.
—BLDSC (9020.564000), GNLM, IE, Infotrieve, Ingenta.
Published by: International Transactional Analysis Association, 2186 Rheem Dr, B-1, Pleasanton, CA 94588. TEL 925-600-8110, FAX 925-600-8112, itaa@itaa-net.org.

155.34 USA ISSN 1083-0006
TRANSGENDER TAPESTRY. Text in English. 1978. q. donation. adv. bk.rev. illus. back issues avail.; reprints avail. **Document type:** *Magazine, Consumer.* **Description:** Covers a wide range of gender topics, from medical and psychological care to family and partner issues.
Former titles (until 1995): TV-TS Tapestry; (until 198?): Tapestry (0884-9749)
Related titles: Online - full text ed.
Indexed: AltPI, CA, E-psyche, G10, GW, L01, L02, P48, PQC, T02.
Published by: International Foundation for Gender Education, Inc., PO Box 540229, Waltham, MA 02454. TEL 781-899-2212, info@ifge.org, http://www.ifge.org. Ed. Denise Leclair.

616.890 FRA ISSN 1286-7802
TRANSITION. Text in French. 1998. irreg. back issues avail. **Document type:** *Monographic series, Consumer.*
Published by: Editions Eres, 33 Av. Marcel Dassault, Toulouse, 31500, France. TEL 33-5-61751576, FAX 33-5-61735289, eres@edition-eres.com.

301 DEU ISSN 1435-7844
TRANSKULTURELLE PSYCHOFORUM. Text in German. 1997. irreg., latest vol.16, 2009. price varies. **Document type:** *Monographic series, Academic/Scholarly.*
Indexed: E-psyche.
Published by: V W B - Verlag fuer Wissenschaft und Bildung, Postfach 110368, Berlin, 10833, Germany. TEL 49-30-2510415, FAX 49-30-2511136, info@vwb-verlag.com, http://www.vwb-verlag.com.

152 USA ISSN 1869-6716
▼ ➤ **TRANSLATIONAL BEHAVIORAL MEDICINE**; practice, policy, research. Text in English. 2011. q. EUR 399, USD 490 combined subscription to institutions (print & online eds.) (effective 2012). **Document type:** *Journal, Academic/Scholarly.*
Related titles: Online - full text ed.: ISSN 1613-9860. 2011.
—CCC.
Published by: Springer New York LLC (Subsidiary of: Springer Science+Business Media), 233 Spring St, New York, NY 10013. TEL 212-460-1500, FAX 212-460-1575, journals-ny@springer.com. Ed. Bonnie Spring.

P

155.4 USA ISSN 1534-0333
RJ506.P55
TRAUMA AND LOSS: RESEARCH AND INTERVENTIONS; journal of the National Institute for Trauma and Loss in Children. Text in English. 2001 (Spring). s-a. USD 40 domestic to non-members; USD 65 in Canada to non-members; USD 75 elsewhere to non-members; free to members (effective 2001). adv.
Related titles: Online - full text ed.: ISSN 1930-2851.
Indexed: S02, S03, T02.
Published by: The National Institute for Trauma and Loss in Children, 900 Cook Road, Grosse Pointe Woods, MI 48236. TEL 313-885-0390, 877-306-5256, http://www.tlcinst.org. Ed. Cathy A. Malchiodi.

155 DEU ISSN 1863-7167
TRAUMA UND GEWALT; Forschung und Praxisfelder. Text in German. 2007. 4/yr. EUR 88; EUR 62 to students; EUR 23 newsstand/cover (effective 2010). adv. **Document type:** *Journal, Academic/Scholarly.*
Indexed: PsycInfo.
Published by: Verlag Klett-Cotta, Rotebuehlstr 77, Stuttgart, 70178, Germany. TEL 49-711-66720, FAX 49-711-66722030, info@klett-cotta.de, http://www.klett-cotta.de. Ed. Frank Wagner. Adv. contact Friederike Kamann.

320.82 FRA ISSN 0041-1868
T58.A2 CODEN: TRHUAH
➤ **LE TRAVAIL HUMAIN.** Text in French; Abstracts in English, French. 1933. q. EUR 90 foreign to institutions (effective 2012). bk.rev. charts; illus. index. reprint service avail. from SCH. **Document type:** *Journal, Academic/Scholarly.* **Description:** Covers ergonomics, organization of work, personnel recruitment, and occupational health and safety.
Related titles: Online - full text ed.: ISSN 2104-3663.
Indexed: A20, A22, ASCA, B25, BIOSIS Prev, CDA, CIS, CISA, CMCI, ChemAb, CurCont, DIP, E-psyche, ErgAb, FR, IBR, IBZ, ILD, MycolAb, P03, P30, PAIS, PsycInfo, PsycholAb, RASB, RefZh, S02, S03, SCI, SCOPUS, SSCI, W07.
—BLDSC (9027.300000), IE, Infotrieve, Ingenta, INIST. **CCC.**
Published by: Presses Universitaires de France, 6 Avenue Reille, Paris, 75685, France. TEL 33-1-58103161, FAX 33-1-45897530, revues@puf.com, http://www.puf.com. Ed. Francoise Darses. Circ: 1,500.

➤ **TRAVAILLER**; revue internationale de psychopathologie et de psychodynamique du travail. *see* MEDICAL SCIENCES—Psychiatry And Neurology

153 GBR ISSN 1364-6613
QP360.5 CODEN: TCSCFK
➤ **TRENDS IN COGNITIVE SCIENCES.** Text in English. 1997. m. EUR 1,827 in Europe to institutions; JPY 253,400 in Japan to institutions; USD 2,043 elsewhere to institutions (effective 2012). adv. bk.rev.; software rev. illus. back issues avail.; reprints avail. **Document type:** *Journal, Academic/Scholarly.* **Description:** Explores all the cognitive sciences, bringing together such diverse disciplines as psychology, psychiatry, the neurosciences, artificial intelligence, philosophy, and anthropology.
Related titles: Online - full text ed.: ISSN 1879-307X (from IngentaConnect, ScienceDirect).
Indexed: A01, A03, A08, A20, A22, A26, B21, BIOBASE, CA, CPEI, CurCont, E-psyche, EMBASE, EngInd, ErgAb, ExcerpMed, FR, I05, IABS, ISR, MEDLINE, NSA, NSCI, P03, P30, PsycInfo, PsycholAb, R10, Reac, S01, SCI, SCOPUS, SSCI, T02, W07.
—BLDSC (9049.559000), IE, Infotrieve, Ingenta, INIST. **CCC.**
Published by: Elsevier Ltd., Trends Journals (Subsidiary of: Elsevier Science & Technology), 84 Theobald's Rd, London, WC1X 8RR, United Kingdom. TEL 44-20-76114000, FAX 44-20-76114485, JournalsCustomerServiceEMEA@elsevier.com, http://www.elsevier.com. Ed. Stavroula Kousta. Adv. contact James Kenney TEL 44-20-74244216.

616.89 DEU ISSN 1619-3970
➤ **TRIERER PSYCHOLOGISCHE BERICHTE.** Text and summaries in English, German. 1974. irreg. free. cum.index: 1974-1998. **Document type:** *Journal, Academic/Scholarly.*
Related titles: Online - full text ed.
Indexed: E-psyche.
Published by: Universitaet Trier, Fachgebiet Psychologie, Universitaetsring 15, Trier, 54296, Germany. TEL 49-651-2010, FAX 49-651-2014299, kanzler@uni-trier.de, http://www.psychologie.uni-trier.de. Eds. Horst Graeser, Reinhold Scheller. Circ: 100.

152.4 USA
TRIUMPH NEWSLETTER. Text in English. 1990. m. free (effective 2010). bk.rev. **Document type:** *Newsletter, Consumer.* **Description:** Designed for people interested in learning about anxiety and anxiety-related disorders.
Formerly: A D A A Reporter (Print)
Media: Online - full text.
Indexed: E-psyche.
Published by: Anxiety Disorders Association of America, 8730 Georgia Ave, Ste 600, Silver Spring, MD 20910. TEL 240-485-1001, FAX 240-485-1035.

150.195 VEN ISSN 1316-7219
TROPICOS; revista de psicoanalisis. Text in Spanish. 1998. s-a.
Indexed: PsycholAb.
Published by: Sociedad Psicoanalitica de Caracas, Centro Empresarial Los Ruices, Piso 5, Avenida Principal de Los Ruices, Oficina 505, Caracas, Miranda 1071, Venezuela. TEL 58-212-2395901, FAX 58-212-2395618, spdecaracas@telcel.net.ve, http://www.spcaracas.com/.

THE TRUTH (CHATTANOOGA). *see* CRIMINOLOGY AND LAW ENFORCEMENT

TURNING POINT (LONG BEACH). *see* BUSINESS AND ECONOMICS—Management

150 FIN ISSN 0356-8741
TURUN YLIOPISTO. PSYKOLOGIAN TUTKIMUKSIA. Short title: Psykologian Tutkimuksia. Text in Finnish. 1976. irreg. price varies. **Document type:** *Monographic series, Academic/Scholarly.*
Indexed: E-psyche.
Published by: Turun Yliopisto, Psykologian Laitos/University of Turku, Department of Psychology, Assistentinkatu 7, Turku, 20500, Finland. TEL 358-2-33351, FAX 358-2-3335060, http://www.psy.utu.fi. Ed. P Niemi. Circ: 500.

150 CAN ISSN 1913-4126
➤ **TUTORIALS IN QUANTITATIVE METHODS FOR PSYCHOLOGY.** Text in English, French. 2005. s-a. free (effective 2011). **Document type:** *Journal, Academic/Scholarly.*
Media: Online - full text.
Published by: Universite de Montreal, Faculte des Arts et des Sciences, Succ Centre Ville, C P 6128, Montreal, PQ H3C 3J7, Canada. TEL 514-343-5970, FAX 514-343-7716. Ed. Denis Cousineau.

150.19 USA ISSN 8756-4963
CODEN: TYREE4
THE TYPE REPORTER; a monthly publication on psychological type. Text in English. 1984. 5/yr. USD 24.95 (effective 2004). bk.rev. charts; illus. back issues avail. **Document type:** *Newsletter, Consumer.* **Description:** Covers personality type, and how it influences you in all the stages of life, from growing up to growing old, and all the settings of life from the workplace to your favorite vacation spot.
Indexed: E-psyche.
Published by: Type Reporter, Inc., 11314 Chapel Rd, Fairfax Station, VA 22039. TEL 703-764-5370, FAX 703-425-1240. Ed. Susan Scanlon. Circ: 3,000.

616.8914 USA ISSN 1538-960X
➤ **THE U S A BODY PSYCHOTHERAPY JOURNAL.** Text in English. 2002 (May). s-a. USD 35 to non-members; USD 15 per issue; free to members (effective 2010). **Document type:** *Journal, Academic/Scholarly.* **Description:** Fosters research and scholarship in body psychotherapy and in the related disciplines of clinical practice and inquiry.
Indexed: E-psyche.
Published by: U. S. Association for Body Psychotherapy, 8639 B 16th St, Ste 119, Silver Spring, MD 20910. TEL 202-466-1619, usabp@usabp.org.

150 100 370 RUS
➤ **UDMURTSKII UNIVERSITET. VESTNIK. SERIYA 3: FILOSOHIYA, PSIKHOLOGIYA, PEDAGOGIKA.** Text in Russian. 2008. s-a. RUR 200 per issue domestic (effective 2010). **Document type:** *Journal, Academic/Scholarly.*
Related titles: Online - full text ed.
Published by: Udmurtskii Gosudarstvennyi Universitet/Udmurt State University, Universitetskaya Str., 1, Izhevsk, 426034, Russian Federation. TEL 7-341-682061, ob@uni.udm.ru, http://v4.udsu.ru.

370.15 LTU ISSN 1392-639X
UGDYMO PSICHOLOGIJA/EDUCATIONAL PSYCHOLOGY. Text in Lithuanian. 1998. a. **Document type:** *Journal, Academic/Scholarly.*
Indexed: CA, E03, ERI, MLA-IB, T02.
Published by: (Vilniaus Pedagoginis Universitetas, Psichologijos Didaktikos Katedra), Vilniaus Pedagoginio Universiteto Leidykla, T Sevcenkos g 31, Vilnius, 2009, Lithuania. TEL 370-5-2333593, leidykla@vpu.lt.

150 GBR ISSN 2046-9527
THE UK MISSING PERSON BEHAVIOUR STUDY. Text in English. 19??. irreg. free (effective 2011). back issues avail. **Document type:** *Report, Trade.*
Formerly (until 2004): Missing Person Behaviour. A UK Study
Media: Online - full text.
Published by: The Centre for Search Research, Office 03, Wansbeck Enterprise Workspace, Green Ln, Ashington, Northumberland NE63 0EE, United Kingdom. TEL 44-1670-528141, daveprkns@googlemail.com.

150.19 USA ISSN 1087-0830
BF173.A2
UMBR(A); a journal of the unconscious. Text in English. 1996. a. USD 10 domestic to individuals; USD 14 in Canada to individuals; USD 16 in South America to individuals; USD 16 in Europe to individuals; USD 18 in Australia to individuals; USD 18 domestic to institutions; USD 22 in Canada to institutions; USD 24 in South America to institutions; USD 24 in Europe to institutions; USD 26 in Australia to institutions (effective 2003).
Indexed: MLA-IB.
Published by: State University of New York at Buffalo, Center for the Study of Psychoanalysis and Culture, 409 Clemens Hall, Buffalo, NY 14260-4610.

159.9 DEU ISSN 1434-3304
UMWELTPSYCHOLOGIE. Text in German. 1997. s-a. EUR 22; EUR 12 newsstand/cover (effective 2011). **Document type:** *Journal, Academic/Scholarly.*
Published by: Pabst Science Publishers, Am Eichengrund 28, Lengerich, 49525, Germany. TEL 49-5484-97234, FAX 49-5484-550, pabst@pabst-publishers.com, http://www.pabst-publishers.de.

150 FRA ISSN 1956-0206
L'UNIVERS PSYCHOLOGIQUE. Text in French. 2007. irreg. **Document type:** *Monographic series, Consumer.*
Published by: Editions Larousse, 21 rue du Montparnasse, Paris, 75283 Cedex 06, France. TEL 33-1-44394400, FAX 33-1-44394343, http://www.editions-larousse.fr.

158 ARG ISSN 0329-5885
BF5
UNIVERSIDAD DE BUENOS AIRES. FACULTAD DE PSICOLOGIA. ANUARIO DE INVESTIGACIONES. Key Title: Anuario de Investigaciones - Facultad de Psicologia. Universidad de Buenos Aires. Text in Spanish. 1989. a. back issues avail. **Document type:** *Journal, Academic/Scholarly.*
Related titles: Online - full text ed.: ISSN 1851-1686. 1989. free (effective 2011) (from SciELO).
Published by: Universidad de Buenos Aires, Facultad de Psicologia, Hipolito Yrigoyen 3241, Buenos Aires, C1207ABQ, Argentina. TEL 55-11-49316900, info@psi.uba.ar, http://www.psi.uba.ar/. Ed. Nelida Cervone.

159 PER ISSN 2078-7189
UNIVERSIDAD DE SAN MARTIN DE PORRES. ESCUELA PROFESIONAL DE PSICOLOGIA. CUADERNOS DE INVESTIGACION. Text in Spanish. 2000. irreg. **Document type:** *Monographic series, Academic/Scholarly.*
Published by: Universidad de San Martin de Porres, Escuela Profesional de Psicologia, Ave Tomas Marsano, 242, Lima, 34, Peru. http://www.psicologia.usmp.edu.pe/.

UNIVERSIDAD DE SEVILLA. SERIE: FILOSOFIA Y PSICOLOGIA. *see* PHILOSOPHY

150 ARG ISSN 1853-0354
▼ **UNIVERSIDAD NACIONAL DE CORDOBA. FACULTAD DE PSICOLOGIA. ANUARIO DE INVESTIGACIONES.** Text in Spanish. 2010. a. **Document type:** *Proceedings, Academic/Scholarly.*
Published by: Universidad Nacional de Cordoba, Facultad de Psicologia, Enfermera Gordillo s/n, Ciudad Universitaria, Cordoba, 5000, Argentina. TEL 54-11-49575887.

UNIVERSIDAD NACIONAL DE ROSARIO. CENTRO DE INVESTIGACIONES DE FILOSOFIA JURIDICA Y FILOSOFIA SOCIAL. REVISTA. *see* LAW

150 PER ISSN 2218-4732
▼ **UNIVERSIDAD NACIONAL MAYOR DE SAN MARCOS. INSTITUTO DE INVESTIGACIONES PSICOLOGICAS. REVISTA.** Text in Spanish. 2010. a. **Document type:** *Journal, Academic/Scholarly.*
Media: Online - full text.
Published by: Universidad Nacional Mayor de San Marcos, Instituto de Investigaciones Psicologicas, Ave German Amezaga s-n, Lima, 1, Peru. TEL 51-1-6197000 ext. 3217, FAX 51-1-6197000 ext. 3202, http://www.unmsm.edu.pe/psicologia/publicaciones2.htm.

150 PRT ISSN 1647-2284
UNIVERSIDADE AUTONOMA DE LISBOA. ANAIS. SERIE PSICOLOGIA. Key Title: Anais. Serie Psicologia. Text in Portuguese. 2005. irreg. **Document type:** *Monographic series, Academic/Scholarly.*
Published by: Universidade Autonoma de Lisboa, Rua de Santa Marta 56, Lisbon, 1169-023, Portugal. TEL 351-21-3177646, FAX 351-21-177603, http://www.universidade-autonoma.pt.

UNIVERSIDADE DE SAO PAULO. REVISTA DE TERAPIA OCUPACIONAL. *see* MEDICAL SCIENCES—Physical Medicine And Rehabilitation

150 ITA ISSN 1721-3134
UNIVERSITA DI LECCE. DIPARTIMENTO DI SCIENZE PEDAGOGICHE PSICOLOGICHE E DIDATTICHE. STUDI E RICERCHE. Text in Italian. 1975. irreg. **Document type:** *Monographic series, Academic/Scholarly.*
Formerly (until 1998): Universita degli Studi di Lecce. Facolta di Magistero. Istituto di Psicologia-Sociologia-Igiene. Studi e Ricerche (1125-0208)
Published by: (Universita degli Studi del Salento, Dipartimento di Scienze Pedagogiche Psicologiche e Didattiche), Piero Manni Editori, Via Umberto I 47-51, Cesario di Lecce, LE 73016, Italy. TEL 39-0832-205577, FAX 39-0832-200373, http://www.mannieditori.it.

150 COL ISSN 1657-9267
BF5
UNIVERSITAS PSYCHOLOGICA. Text in Spanish, English. 2002. 3/yr. COP 18,000 domestic; USD 16 foreign (effective 2006). **Document type:** *Journal, Academic/Scholarly.*
Related titles: Online - full text ed.: free (effective 2011).
Indexed: A01, C01, CA, F03, F04, I04, I05, P03, PsycInfo, SCOPUS, SSCI, T02, W07.
—BLDSC (9101.396000).
Published by: Pontificia Universidad Javeriana, Faculta de Psicologia, Carrera 5a No 39-00, Edif. Manuel Briceno, Bogota, Colombia. TEL 57-1-3208320, http://www.javeriana.edu.co/. Ed. Wilson Lopez.

150 ESP ISSN 1130-3522
UNIVERSITAS TARRACONENSIS. REVISTA DE PSICOLOGIA. Key Title: Revista de Psicologia Universitas Tarraconensis. Text in Spanish, English. 1976. s-a. back issues avail. **Document type:** *Journal, Academic/Scholarly.*
Former titles (until 1986): Universitas Tarragonensis. Revista de Psicologia, Pedagogia y Filosofia (1130-3514); (until 1982): Universitas Tarragonensis. Serie Filosofia, Pedagogia y Psicologia (1130-3506); (until 1981): Universitas Tarragonensis. Facultat de Filosofia i Lletres. Diviso de Filosofia i Ciencies de l'Educacio (1130-3492); Which superseded in part (in 1977): Universitas Tarragonensis (0211-3368)
Related titles: Online - full text ed.
Indexed: PsycholAb, RILM.
Published by: Universitat Rovira i Virgili, Departament de Psicologia, Carr. de Valls, s-n, Tarragona, 43007, Spain. TEL 34-977-558075, FAX 34-977-558088, tarraconensis@fcep.urv.es.

150 370 ROM ISSN 1582-313X
B8.R8
UNIVERSITATEA DIN CRAIOVA. ANALELE. SERIA: PSIHOLOGIE, PEDAGOGIE. Text in Romanian. 1997. s-a. **Document type:** *Academic/Scholarly.*
Supersedes in part (in 2000): Universitatea din Craiova. Analele. Seria: Filozofie, Sociologie, Psihologie, Pedagogie (1582-1633); Which was formed by the merger of (1995-1997): Universitatea din Craiova. Analele. Seria: Filozofie, Sociologie (1224-3590); (1996-1997): Universitatea din Craiova. Analele. Seria: Psihologie, Pedagogie (1224-5690)
Published by: Universitatea din Craiova/University of Craiova, Str A.I. Cuza 13, Craiova, 200585, Romania. TEL 40-251-414398, FAX 40-251-411688, relint@central.ucv.ro, http://www.ucv.ro.

UNIVERSITATII "SPIRU HARET". ANALELE. SERIA SOCIOLOGIE-PSIHOLOGIE/SPIRU HARET UNIVERSITY. ANNALS. SOCIOLOGY-PSYCHOLOGY STUDIES. *see* SOCIAL SCIENCES: COMPREHENSIVE WORKS

150 USA ISSN 2159-2829
▼ **UNIVERSITY OF FLORIDA. JOURNAL OF PSYCHOLOGICAL SCIENCE.** Text in English. 2010. s-a. free (effective 2011). **Document type:** *Journal, Academic/Scholarly.* **Description:** Provides constructive, peer reviewed environment where undergraduate and graduate psychology students at the University of Florida can display their research throughout the academic year.
Media: Online - full text.
Published by: University of Florida, Psi Chi and Psychology Club osoutullo@ufl.edu, http://www.psych.ufl.edu/~psichi/. Ed. Sarah Righi.

150 SWE
BF21 CODEN: RPUSB7
UNIVERSITY OF STOCKHOLM. DEPARTMENT OF PSYCHOLOGY. REPORTS (ONLINE). Text in English. 1964. irreg., latest vol.866, 2003. USD 25. index. back issues avail. **Document type:** *Monographic series, Academic/Scholarly.*

Former titles (until 2004): University of Stockholm. Department of Psychology. Report (Print) (0345-0139); (until 1975): University of Stockholm. Psychological Laboratories. Reports (0081-5756)
Media: Online - full content.
Indexed: E-psyche, PsycholAb.
Published by: Stockholms Universitet, Psykologiska Institutionen/ Stockholm University, Department of Psychology, Stockholms Universitet, Stockholm, 10691, Sweden. TEL 46-8-162000, FAX 46-8-161002. Circ: 500.

150 FIN ISSN 0359-0216
UNIVERSITY OF TURKU. PSYCHOLOGICAL RESEARCH REPORTS. Key Title: Psychological Research Reports. Text in English. 1963. irreg. price varies. **Document type:** *Monographic series, Academic/ Scholarly.*
Supersedes (in 1981): Turun Yliopisto. Psykologian Laitos. Reports (0356-8733)
Indexed: E-psyche.
Published by: Turun Yliopisto, Psykologian Laitos/University of Turku, Department of Psychology, Assistentinkatu 7, Turku, 20500, Finland. TEL 358-2-333351, FAX 358-2-3335060, http://www.psy.utu.fi. Circ: 500.

150 SVK ISSN 0083-419X
BF26 CODEN: PSYAD8
UNIVERZITA KOMENSKEHO. FILOZOFICKA FAKULTA. ZBORNIK: PSYCHOLOGICA. Text in Slovak; Summaries in English, German. 1961. irreg. free domestic (effective 2005). **Document type:** *Academic/Scholarly.* **Description:** Covers all aspects of psychology.
Indexed: E-psyche, PsycholAb, RASB.
Published by: Univerzita Komenskeho, Filozoficka Fakulta, Ustredna Kniznica, Gondova 2, Bratislava, 81801, Slovakia. Circ: 400.

UNIWERSYTET IM. ADAMA MICKIEWICZA. PSYCHOLOGIA-PEDAGOGIKA. *see* EDUCATION

158.7 POL ISSN 1428-8664
BF8.P6
➤ **UNIWERSYTET SLASKI W KATOWICACH. PRACE NAUKOWE. PSYCHOLOGIA. BADANIA I APLIKACJE.** Text in Polish; Summaries in English, Russian. 1980. irreg., latest vol.6, 2004. price varies. **Document type:** *Monographic series, Academic/Scholarly.* **Description:** Provides social psychological studies of human behaviour at work, especially on interpersonal relations, trust, injustice, leadership, and resistance to change. Also covers attitudes to work and stress.
Formerly (until 1997): Uniwersytet Slaski w Katowicach. Prace Naukowe. Psychologiczne Problemy Funkcjonowania Czlowieka w Sytuacji Pracy (0208-5569)
Indexed: E-psyche, RASB.
Published by: (Uniwersytet Slaski w Katowicach), Wydawnictwo Uniwersytetu Slaskiego w Katowicach, ul Bankowa 12B, Katowice, 40007, Poland. TEL 48-32-2596915, FAX 48-32-2582735, TELEX 0315584 uskpl, wydawus@us.edu.pl, https://wydawnictwo.us.edu.pl. Ed. Zofia Radajczak.

150 ARG ISSN 1669-3795
UNO MISMO. Text in Spanish. 2005. m. ARS 6.50 newsstand/cover (effective 2008).
Published by: Producciones Publiexpress, Magallanes 1346, Buenos Aires, C1288ABB, Argentina. TEL 54-11-43031484, FAX 54-11-43031280, rrhh@publiexpress.com.ar, http://www.publiexpress.com.ar/. Ed. Claudia Gonzalez. Circ: 19,000.

150 ESP ISSN 1133-8121
BF173.A2
UNO POR UNO; revista de psiconalisis. Text in Spanish. 1989. s-a.
Published by: Editorial/Eolia, Muntaner, 499, Barcelona, 35004, Spain. Ed. Miguel Bassols.

155.5 SWE ISSN 1654-8507
VAARA TONAARINGAR. Text in Swedish. 2006. s-a. adv. **Document type:** *Magazine, Consumer.* **Description:** Aimed at parents with teenagers.
Related titles: Online - full text ed.: ISSN 1653-7009.
Published by: Protelma AB, Kungsgatan 84, Stockholm, 11227, Sweden. TEL 46-8-50635650, FAX 46-8-50635651, info@varatonaringar.se. Ed., Adv. contact Pia Bohlin TEL 46-8-50635653. page SEK 19,900; 240 x 325.

150 DEU ISSN 0931-3249
VERHALTENSEFFEKTIVITAET UND STRESS. Text in German. 1987. irreg., latest vol.20, 1992. price varies. **Document type:** *Monographic series, Academic/Scholarly.*
—CCC.
Published by: Peter Lang GmbH (Subsidiary of: Peter Lang Publishing Group), Eschborner Landstr 42-50, Frankfurt Am Main, 60489, Germany. TEL 49-69-7807050, FAX 49-69-78070550, zentrale.frankfurt@peterlang.com, http://www.peterlang.com.

616.89 DEU ISSN 0721-7234
VERHALTENSTHERAPIE UND PSYCHOSOZIALE PRAXIS. Text in German; Summaries in English. 19??. q. EUR 15 newsstand/cover (effective 2009). bk.rev. abstr.; bibl. back issues avail. **Document type:** *Journal, Academic/Scholarly.* **Description:** Focuses on behavior therapy (associated with the German Association of Behavior Therapy) and aims at an audience of psychologists, social workers and public health employees.
Former titles (until 1981): Deutsche Gesellschaft fuer Verhaltenstherapie. Mitteilungen (0173-7791); (until 1976): Gesellschaft zur Foerderung der Verhaltenstherapie. Mitteilungen (0173-7813)
Indexed: E-psyche, P03, PsycInfo, PsycholAb.
—GNLM.
Published by: (Deutsche Gesellschaft fuer Verhaltenstherapie), D G V T - Verlag, Hechinger Str 203, Tuebingen, 72072, Germany. TEL 49-7071-792850, FAX 49-7071-792851, dgvt-verlag@dgvt.de, http://www.dgvt.de/verlag/. Circ: 6,000.

150 FRA ISSN 1771-6055
VIE INTERIEURE. Text in French. 2003. irreg. back issues avail. **Document type:** *Monographic series, Consumer.*
Published by: Editions du Fayet, 5 Chemin de la Basse Valiere, Ampuis, 69420, France.

VIERTELJAHRESSCHRIFT FUER HEILPAEDAGOGIK UND IHRE NACHBARGEBIETE. *see* EDUCATION—Special Education And Rehabilitation

VIOLENCE AND VICTIMS. *see* SOCIOLOGY

150 USA
VISIONS (SAN FRANCISCO). Text in English. 1987. s-a. free. adv. tr.lit. **Document type:** *Newsletter.* **Description:** Covers the following areas of psychology: clinical, organizational, forensic, health, cross-cultural, and multicultural. Intended for CSPP alumni as well as outside audiences.
Indexed: E-psyche.
Published by: California School of Professional Psychology, 2728 Hyde St No. 100, San Francisco, CA 94109. TEL 415-346-4500, FAX 415-931-8322. Ed., R&P, Adv. contact Meryl Ginsberg. Circ: 8,000 (controlled).

152 USA ISSN 1064-5578
AM7.V56
➤ **VISITOR STUDIES**; theory, research, and practice. Text in English. 1988. s-a. GBP 154 combined subscription in United Kingdom to institutions (print & online eds.); EUR 205, USD 256 combined subscription to institutions (print & online eds.) (effective 2012). adv. back issues avail.; reprint service avail. from PSC. **Document type:** *Journal, Academic/Scholarly.* **Description:** Features articles, focusing on visitor research, visitor studies, evaluation studies, and research methodologies.
Related titles: Online - full text ed.: ISSN 1934-7715. GBP 138 in United Kingdom to institutions; EUR 184, USD 230 to institutions (effective 2012).
Indexed: A22, A37, ASSIA, CA, CABA, E-psyche, E01, E12, F08, F12, H&TI, H06, LT, P10, P48, P53, P54, PQC, RRTA, S13, S16, SCOPUS, T02, W11.
—IE. **CCC.**
Published by: (Visitor Studies Association), Routledge (Subsidiary of: Taylor & Francis Group), 325 Chestnut St, Ste 800, Philadelphia, PA 19106. TEL 800-354-1420, FAX 215-625-2940, journals@routledge.com, http://www.routledge.com. Eds. Dr. Jan Packer, Roy Ballantyne. Adv. contact Linda Hann TEL 44-1344-779945.

150 GBR ISSN 1350-6285
BF241 CODEN: VICOF6
➤ **VISUAL COGNITION.** Text in English. 1994. 10/yr. GBP 788 combined subscription in United Kingdom to institutions (print & online eds.); EUR 1,042, USD 1,307 combined subscription to institutions (print & online eds.) (effective 2012). back issues avail.; reprint service avail. from PSC. **Document type:** *Journal, Academic/Scholarly.* **Description:** Features research papers on all aspects of visual cognition, including studies of visual object and face recognition, texture and surface perception, perceptual organization, visual attention, visual memory, and much more.
Related titles: Online - full text ed.: ISSN 1464-0716. GBP 709 in United Kingdom to institutions; EUR 938, USD 1,176 to institutions (effective 2012) (from IngentaConnect).
Indexed: A01, A03, A08, A20, A22, B07, B21, BIOBASE, CA, CMM, CommAb, CurCont, E-psyche, E01, EMBASE, ErgAb, ExcerpMed, FR, IABS, Inspec, L&LBA, NSA, P03, P30, P43, PsycInfo, PsycholAb, R10, Reac, SCOPUS, SOPODA, SSCI, T02, W07.
—AskIEEE, IE, Infotrieve, Ingenta, INIST. **CCC.**
Published by: Psychology Press (Subsidiary of: Taylor & Francis Ltd.), 27 Church Rd, Hove, E Sussex BN3 2FA, United Kingdom. TEL 44-20-70176000, FAX 44-20-70176717, info@psypress.co.uk, http://www.psypress.com. Ed. John M Henderson. Adv. contact Linda Hann TEL 44-1344-779945. **Subscr. in N. America to:** Taylor & Francis Inc., Customer Services Dept, 325 Chestnut St, 8th Fl, Philadelphia, PA 19106. TEL 215-625-8900, 800-354-1420, FAX 215-625-2940, customerservice@taylorandfrancis.com; **Subscr. to:** Taylor & Francis Ltd., Journals Customer Service, Sheepen Pl, Colchester, Essex CO3 3LP, United Kingdom. TEL 44-20-70175544, FAX 44-20-70175198, subscriptions@tandf.co.uk, http://www.tandf.co.uk/journals.

➤ **VITA DELL'INFANZIA.** *see* EDUCATION

158 FRA ISSN 1773-8164
VIVRE EN FAMILLE. Text in French. 2005. irreg. back issues avail. **Document type:** *Monographic series, Consumer.*
Published by: InterEditions (Subsidiary of: Dunod), 5 Rue Laromiguiere, Paris, 75005, France. TEL 33-1-40463500, FAX 33-1-40464995, http://www.intereditions.com/.

158 FRA ISSN 1952-0778
VIVRE & COMMUNIQUER. Text in French. 2006. irreg. back issues avail. **Document type:** *Monographic series, Consumer.*
Published by: InterEditions (Subsidiary of: Dunod), 5 Rue Laromiguiere, Paris, 75005, France. TEL 33-1-40463500, FAX 33-1-40464995, http://www.intereditions.com/.

616.89 USA ISSN 0042-8272
RC475
➤ **VOICES (NEW BERN)**; the art and science of psychotherapy. Text in English. 1965. q. USD 55 domestic to individuals; USD 65 in Canada to individuals; USD 75 elsewhere to individuals (effective 2010). adv. bk.rev. illus. cum.index. reprints avail. **Document type:** *Journal, Academic/Scholarly.*
Related titles: Audio cassette/tape ed.: 1965; Microform ed.: 1965 (from PQC).
Indexed: A22, E-psyche, PsycholRG.
—BLDSC (9251.465000), GNLM, IE, Ingenta. **CCC.**
Published by: American Academy of Psychotherapists, 605 Poole Dr, Garner, NC 27529. TEL 919-779-5051, FAX 919-779-5642, aap@mgmt4u.com. Eds. Doris Jackson, Penelope Norton. Circ: 1,500.

➤ **VOPROSY PSIKHOLINGVISTIKI.** *see* LINGUISTICS

150 RUS ISSN 0042-8841
BF8.R8 CODEN: VOPSAI
➤ **VOPROSY PSIKHOLOGII.** Text in Russian; Summaries in English. 1955. bi-m. USD 105 foreign (effective 2005). 10 p./no.; **Document type:** *Journal, Academic/Scholarly.*
Indexed: A20, A22, ASCA, CDA, CurCont, E-psyche, L&LBA, MLA-IB, P03, P30, PsycInfo, PsycholAb, RASB, RILM, RefZh, S02, S03, SCOPUS, SOPODA, SSCI, SociolAb, W07.
—East View, IE, Ingenta, INIST. **CCC.**
Published by: Redaktsiya Zhurnala Voprosy Psikhologii, ul Mokhovaya 9-V, Moscow, 125009, Russian Federation. Ed., R&P E.V. Shchedrina. Pub. E V Shchedrina. **Dist. by:** M K - Periodica, ul Gilyarovskogo 39, Moscow 129110, Russian Federation. TEL 7-095-2845008, FAX 7-095-2813798, info@periodicals.ru, http://www.mkniga.ru.

➤ **WASHINGTON COUNSELETTER.** *see* OCCUPATIONS AND CAREERS

155.937 USA
WE NEED NOT WALK ALONE. Text in English. 1998. q. USD 20 (effective 2007). **Document type:** *Magazine, Consumer.* **Description:** Focuses on grief-related issues and features poetry and original articles by bereaved parents, siblings, grandparents, and professionals.
Formed by the merger of (1993-1998): S T A G E S Sibling Newsletter; We Need Not Walk Alone Newsletter; Which was formerly: Compassionate Friends National Newsletter; Compassionate Friends Newsletter
Indexed: E-psyche.
Published by: Compassionate Friends, Inc., PO Box 3696, Oak Brook, IL 60522. TEL 630-990-0010, 877-969-0010, FAX 630-990-0246, http://www.compassionatefriends.org/index.html. Ed. Wayne Loder. R&P Terry Eubanks.

WELFARE WORLD. *see* SOCIAL SERVICES AND WELFARE

152 DEU ISSN 1435-7860
WELTEN DES BEWUSSTSEINS/WORLDS OF CONSCIOUSNESS. Text in German. 1993. irreg., latest vol.10, 2000. price varies. **Document type:** *Monographic series, Academic/Scholarly.*
Published by: V W B - Verlag fuer Wissenschaft und Bildung, Postfach 110368, Berlin, 10833, Germany. TEL 49-30-2510415, FAX 49-30-2511136, info@vwb-verlag.com.

301 AUT ISSN 0257-3601
BF173.A2
WERKBLATT; Zeitschrift fuer Psychoanalyse und Gesellschaftskritik. Text in German. 1984. 2/yr. EUR 21; EUR 12.50 newsstand/cover (effective 2005). 128 p./no.; **Document type:** *Journal, Academic/ Scholarly.*
Indexed: E-psyche.
Address: Ludwig Schmederer Platz 1, Salzburg, Sa 5020, Austria. vertrieb@werkblatt.at.

158 AUT
WIENER BEITRAEGE ZUR MUSIKTHERAPIE. Text in German. 1997. irreg., latest vol.8, 2008. price varies. **Document type:** *Monographic series, Academic/Scholarly.*
Published by: Praesens VerlagsgesmbH, Wehlistr 154/12, Vienna, W 1020, Austria. TEL 43-1-720703506, FAX 43-1-25330334660, m.ritter@praesens.at, http://www.praesens.at.

158 NLD ISSN 2210-9404
▼ **WIJSHEDEN VOOR ELKE DAG.** Text in Dutch. 2010. a. EUR 8.99 (effective 2010).
Published by: Uitgeverij Verba, Birkstraat 143A, Soest, 3768 HE, Netherlands. TEL 31-33-4943909, FAX 31-33-4655174, info@uitgeverijdelantaarn.nl, http://www.ruitenbergboek.nl.

150 GBR ISSN 1939-5078
▼ ➤ **WILEY INTERDISCIPLINARY REVIEWS. COGNITIVE SCIENCE.** Text in English. 2010. bi-m. **Document type:** *Journal, Academic/ Scholarly.*
Related titles: Online - full text ed.: ISSN 1939-5086.
Indexed: P30.
—IE. **CCC.**
Published by: John Wiley & Sons Ltd. (Subsidiary of: John Wiley & Sons, Inc.), 9600 Garsington Rd, Oxford, OX4 2DQ, United Kingdom. TEL 44-1865-776868, FAX 44-1865-714591, customer@wiley.co.uk, http://www.wiley.com.

616.58 USA
WILLIAM ALANSON WHITE INSTITUTE OF PSYCHIATRY, PSYCHOANALYSIS & PSYCHOLOGY. RECORD. Text in English. 1966. s-a. free to members (effective 2010). bk.rev. illus. **Document type:** *Newsletter.* **Description:** Reports on the professional activities of the White Institute and its members, and provides summaries of papers presented at meetings of the professional societies associated with the Institute.
Formerly (until 1994): W A W Newsletter (0042-9511)
Indexed: E-psyche.
Published by: William Alanson White Institute of Psychiatry, Psychoanalysis & Psychology, 20 W 74th St, New York, NY 10023. TEL 212-873-0725, FAX 212-362-6967, d.amato@wawhite.org.

150 USA ISSN 1933-8295
B945.J24
➤ **WILLIAM JAMES STUDIES.** Text in English. 2006. a. free (effective 2011). back issues avail.; reprints avail. **Document type:** *Journal, Academic/Scholarly.*
Media: Online - full text.
Indexed: A39, AmHI, B04, C27, C29, D03, D04, E13, H07, H08, HAb, HumInd, PhilInd, R14, S14, S15, S18, T02, W03, W05.
Published by: (William James Society), University of Illinois Press, 1325 S Oak St, Champaign, IL 61820. TEL 217-333-0950, 866-244-0626, FAX 217-244-8082, uipress@uillinois.edu, http://www.press.uillinois.edu. Ed. Linda Simon.

➤ **WINGSPAN (NORTH LAKE)**; journal of the male spirit. *see* MEN'S STUDIES

150 330 DEU ISSN 1866-9042
▼ **WIRTSCHAFTSPSYCHOLOGIE (BERLIN).** Text in German. 2009. irreg., latest vol.3, 2010. price varies. **Document type:** *Monographic series, Academic/Scholarly.*
Published by: Logos Verlag Berlin, Comeniushof, Gubener Str 47, Berlin, 10243, Germany. TEL 49-30-42851090, FAX 49-30-42851092, redaktion@logos-verlag.de.

302 DEU ISSN 0945-182X
WIRTSCHAFTSPSYCHOLOGIE (FRANKFURT AM MAIN). Text in German. 1995. irreg., latest vol.14, 2008. price varies. **Document type:** *Monographic series, Academic/Scholarly.*
Published by: Peter Lang GmbH (Subsidiary of: Peter Lang Publishing Group), Eschborner Landstr 42-50, Frankfurt Am Main, 60489, Germany. TEL 49-69-7807050, FAX 49-69-78070550, zentrale.frankfurt@peterlang.com, http://www.peterlang.com. Ed. Detlev Liepmann.

158.7 DEU ISSN 1615-7729
➤ **WIRTSCHAFTSPSYCHOLOGIE (LENGERICH).** Text in German. 1993. q. EUR 45; EUR 12.50 newsstand/cover (effective 2011). adv. **Document type:** *Journal, Academic/Scholarly.*
Formerly (until 1999): Arbeit Betrieb Organisation Aktuell (0945-6201)
Indexed: DIP, IBR, IBZ.

P

Published by: Pabst Science Publishers, Am Eichengrund 28, Lengerich, 49525, Germany. TEL 49-5484-97234, FAX 49-5484-550, pabst@pabst-publishers.com, http://www.pabst-publishers.de. Ed. Theo Wehner. Circ: 3,800 (paid and controlled).

159.9 DEU ISSN 1611-9207
WIRTSCHAFTSPSYCHOLOGIE AKTUELL. Text in German. 2001. 4/yr. EUR 72 domestic; EUR 75 foreign; EUR 36 to students; EUR 21.45 newsstand/cover (effective 2011). adv. **Document type:** *Journal, Academic/Scholarly.*
Formerly (until 2003): Wirtschaftspsychologie (1618-9507)
Published by: Deutscher Psychologen Verlag GmbH, Am Koellnischen Park 2, Berlin, 10179, Germany. TEL 49-30-209166410, FAX 49-30-209166413, verlag@psychologenverlag.de, http://www.psychologenverlag.de.

158.7 DEU ISSN 0721-0213
WIRTSCHAFTSPSYCHOLOGISCHE SCHRIFTEN. Text in German. 1972. irreg., latest vol.14, 2005. price varies. **Document type:** *Monographic series, Academic/Scholarly.*
Published by: Duncker und Humblot GmbH, Carl-Heinrich-Becker-Weg 9, Berlin, 12165, Germany. TEL 49-30-7900060, FAX 49-30-79000631, info@duncker-humblot.de.

150 DEU ISSN 1861-7735
WISSENSCHAFTLICHE BEITRAEGE AUS DEM TECTUM-VERLAG. REIHE PSYCHOLOGIE. Text in German. 1999. irreg., latest vol.19, 2010. price varies. **Document type:** *Monographic series, Academic/Scholarly.*
Published by: Tectum Wissenschaftsverlag Marburg, Biegenstr 4, Marburg, 35037, Germany. TEL 49-6421-481523, FAX 49-6421-43470, email@tectum-verlag.de.

150 DEU ISSN 1431-0325
WISSENSCHAFTLICHE SCHRIFTENREIHE PSYCHOLOGIE. Text in German. 1994. irreg., latest vol.18, 2007. price varies. **Document type:** *Monographic series, Academic/Scholarly.*
Published by: Verlag Dr. Koester, Rungestr 22-24, Berlin, 10179, Germany. TEL 49-30-76403224, FAX 49-30-76403227, verlag-koester@t-online.de.

150 GBR ISSN 1754-9787
WOMAN AND PSYCHOLOGY. Text in English. 1997. irreg., latest 2008. price varies. back issues avail. **Document type:** *Monographic series, Academic/Scholarly.* **Description:** Covers topics such as postnatal depression and eating disorders and addressing a wide range of theories and methodologies.
Published by: Routledge (Subsidiary of: Taylor & Francis Group), 4 Park Sq, Milton Park, Abingdon, Oxon OX14 4RN, United Kingdom. TEL 44-20-70176000, FAX 44-20-70176336, subscriptions@tandf.co.uk, http://www.routledge.com. Ed. Jane Ussher.

158 305.4 USA ISSN 0270-3149
RC451.4.W6 CODEN: WOTHDJ
➤ **WOMEN & THERAPY**; a feminist quarterly. Abbreviated title: W T. Text in English. 1982. q. GBP 711 combined subscription in United Kingdom to institutions (print & online eds.); EUR 927, USD 931 combined subscription to institutions (print & online eds.) (effective 2012). adv. bk.rev. illus. 120 p./no. 1 cols./p.; back issues avail.; reprint service avail. from PSC. **Document type:** *Journal, Academic/Scholarly.* **Description:** Explores the multidimensional relationship between women and therapy, with a feminist orientation. Publishes descriptive, theoretical, clinical, and empirical perspectives on the topic and the therapeutic process.
Formerly: Women - Counseling Therapy and Mental Health Services
Related titles: Microfiche ed.: (from PQC); Microform ed.; Online - full text ed.: ISSN 1541-0315. GBP 641 in United Kingdom to institutions; EUR 834, USD 837 to institutions (effective 2012).
Indexed: A01, A02, A03, A08, A20, A22, A25, A26, ABS&EES, ASCA, AltPI, C06, C07, C08, CA, CINAHL, CWI, CurCont, DIP, E-psyche, E01, E08, F09, FR, FamI, FemPer, G08, G10, GW, H11, H12, HEA, I05, IBR, IBZ, L01, L02, M01, M02, P02, P03, P10, P24, P25, P30, P46, P48, P53, P54, PCI, PQC, PsycInfo, PsycholAb, RefZh, S02, S03, S08, S09, SCOPUS, SFSA, SSA, SSCI, SWR&A, SociolAb, T02, V&AA, W06, W07, W09, WSA, WSI.
—BLDSC (9343.276000), GNLM, IE, Infotrieve, Ingenta, INIST. **CCC.**
Published by: Routledge (Subsidiary of: Taylor & Francis Group), 325 Chestnut St, Ste 800, Philadelphia, PA 19106. TEL 215-625-8900, 800-354-1420, FAX 215-625-8914, journals@routledge.com, http://www.routledge.com. Ed. Ellyn Kaschak. adv.: B&W page USD 315, color page USD 550; trim 4.375 x 7.125. Circ: 433 (paid).

➤ **WOMEN'S MENTAL HEALTH & DEVELOPMENT.** *see* WOMEN'S HEALTH

150 305.4 USA ISSN 1931-0021
WOMEN'S PSYCHOLOGY. Text in English. 2006 (Fall). irreg., latest 2010. price varies. back issues avail. **Document type:** *Monographic series, Academic/Scholarly.*
Published by: Praeger Publishers (Subsidiary of: Greenwood Publishing Group Inc.), 88 Post Rd W, Westport, CT 06881. TEL 800-368-6868, tech.support@greenwood.com, http://www.greenwood.com. Ed. Michele Paludi.

158.7 GBR ISSN 0267-8373
HF5548.85
➤ **WORK AND STRESS.** Text in English. 1987. q. GBP 387 combined subscription in United Kingdom to institutions (print & online eds.); EUR 509, USD 640 combined subscription to institutions (print & online eds.) (effective 2012). adv. back issues avail.; reprint service avail. from PSC. **Document type:** *Journal, Academic/Scholarly.* **Description:** Features academic papers relating to stress, health and safety, and associated areas and scholarly articles of concern to the policy-makers, managers and trades unionists who have to deal with such issues.
Related titles: Online - full text ed.: ISSN 1464-5335. GBP 348 in United Kingdom to institutions; EUR 458, USD 576 to institutions (effective 2012) (from IngentaConnect).
Indexed: A01, A02, A03, A08, A20, A22, A36, ASCA, B01, B06, B07, B09, B21, C06, C07, C08, C11, CA, CABA, CINAHL, CPM, CurCont, E-psyche, E01, E04, E05, ESPM, ErgAb, FR, FamI, GH, H&SSA, H04, HRA, IBSS, OR, P03, P30, P43, P50, PsycInfo, PsycholAb, R09, R12, S02, S03, SCOPUS, SD, SOPODA, SSA, SSCI, SociolAb, T02, T05, W07, W11.
—GNLM, IE, Infotrieve, Ingenta, INIST. **CCC.**
Published by: (European Academy of Occupational Health Psychology), Routledge (Subsidiary of: Taylor & Francis Group), 4 Park Sq, Milton Park, Abingdon, Oxon OX14 4RN, United Kingdom. TEL 44-20-70176000, FAX 44-20-70176336, subscriptions@tandf.co.uk, http://www.routledge.com. Adv. contact Linda Hann TEL 44-1344-779945. **Subscr. in N. America to:** Taylor & Francis Inc., Customer Services Dept, 325 Chestnut St, 8th Fl, Philadelphia, PA 19106. TEL 215-625-8900, 800-354-1420, FAX 215-625-2940, customerservice@taylorandfrancis.com; **Subscr. to:** Taylor & Francis Ltd., Journals Customer Service, Sheepen Pl, Colchester, Essex CO3 3LP, United Kingdom. TEL 44-20-70175544, FAX 44-20-70175198, tf.enquiries@tfinforma.com.

150 306 USA ISSN 1932-6270
RC455.4.E8
WORLD CULTURAL PSYCHIATRY RESEARCH REVIEW. Text in English. 2006. q. free (effective 2011). **Document type:** *Journal, Academic/Scholarly.* **Description:** Features articles from psychiatric research and clinical practice based on various cultural and psychological perspectives.
Media: Online - full text.
Published by: World Association of Cultural Psychiatry, 1356 Lusitana St, 4th Fl, Honolulu, HI 96813. treasurer@waculturalpsy.org, http://www.waculturalpsy.org. Ed. Goffredo Bartocci.

616.89 614.582 USA
WORLD FEDERATION FOR MENTAL HEALTH. ANNUAL REPORT. Text in English. 1984. a. USD 15 membership developing countries; USD 35 membership; USD 35 to libraries (effective 2006). **Description:** Reviews the organization's international activities of the past year.
Related titles: Online - full content ed.
Indexed: E-psyche.
Published by: World Federation for Mental Health, PO Box 16810, Alexandria, VA 22302. TEL 703-838-7525, FAX 703-519-7648, info@wfmh.com. Ed. Dr. Eugene B Brody. Circ: 3,000 (controlled).

616.89 614.582 USA
WORLD FEDERATION FOR MENTAL HEALTH. NEWSLETTER. Text in English. 1948. q. USD 15 membership developing countries; USD 35 membership; USD 35 to libraries (effective 2006). bibl. **Document type:** *Newsletter.* **Description:** Provides members with information on the federation's activities at the United Nations, the World Health Organization, and around the world. Comments on mental health issues and contains a calendar of events.
Related titles: Online - full content ed.
Indexed: E-psyche.
Published by: World Federation for Mental Health, PO Box 16810, Alexandria, VA 22302. TEL 703-838-7525, FAX 703-519-7648, info@wfmh.com. Ed. Dr. Eugene B Brody. Circ: 4,000.

150 USA
WRITE-UP. Text in English. 1972. bi-m. free to members (effective 2011). bk.rev. back issues avail. **Document type:** *Newsletter, Trade.* **Description:** Discusses topics of interest pertaining to the study of handwriting.
Formerly: National Society for Graphology Newsletter
Indexed: E-psyche.
Published by: National Society for Graphology, 250 W 57th St, Ste 1228A, New York, NY 10107. TEL 212-265-1148, http://www.handwriting.org/nsg/nsgmain.html.

WRITING SYSTEMS RESEARCH. *see* LINGUISTICS

150 DEU ISSN 0170-9453
WUERZBURGER PSYCHOLOGISCHE UNTERSUCHUNGEN. Text in German. 1972. irreg., latest vol.5, 1981. price varies. **Document type:** *Monographic series, Academic/Scholarly.*
Published by: Peter Lang GmbH (Subsidiary of: Peter Lang Publishing Group), Eschborner Landstr 42-50, Frankfurt Am Main, 60489, Germany. TEL 49-69-7807050, FAX 49-69-78070550, zentrale.frankfurt@peterlang.com, http://www.peterlang.com. Ed. Ernst Wehner.

150 370 CHN ISSN 1001-4918
XINLI FAZHAN YU JIAOYU. Abbreviated title: Psychological Development and Education. Text in Chinese. 1985. q. CNY 60 (effective 2009). **Document type:** *Journal, Academic/Scholarly.*
Related titles: Online - full text ed.
Published by: Beijing Shifan Daxue/Beijing Normal University, 19, Xinjiekouwai Dajie, Beijing, 100875, China. TEL 86-10-58807700.

150 CHN ISSN 1671-6981
BF8.C5
XINLI KEXUE/PSYCHOLOGICAL SCIENCE. Text in Chinese. 1965. bi-m. USD 66.60 (effective 2009). **Document type:** *Journal, Academic/Scholarly.*
Formerly: Xinli Kexue Tongxun/Information on Psychological Sciences (1000-6648)
Related titles: Online - full text ed.
Indexed: E-psyche, P03, PsycInfo, PsycholAb.
—BLDSC (6946.530330), East View, IE, Ingenta.
Address: 3663, Zhongshan Beilu, Shanghai, 200062, China. TEL 86-21-62232236. **Dist. by:** China International Book Trading Corp, 35 Chegongzhuang Xilu, Haidian District, PO Box 399, Beijing 100044, China. TEL 86-10-68412045, FAX 86-10-68412023, cibtc@mail.cibtc.com.cn, http://www.cibtc.com.cn.

155 CHN ISSN 0439-755X
BF8.C5
➤ **XINLI XUEBAO/ACTA PSYCHOLOGICA SINICA.** Text in Chinese; Summaries in English. 1956. bi-m. USD 159.60 (effective 2009). adv. **Document type:** *Journal, Academic/Scholarly.* **Description:** Covers the basic theories of psychology, general, medical, physiological, child, and educational psychology. Also covers the history of psychology, and contains evaluations of academic studies and information on current academic activities.
Related titles: Online - full text ed.
Indexed: E-psyche, P03, P30, PsycInfo, PsycholAb, RASB, RILM.
—BLDSC (0661.498000), IE.
Published by: Zhongguo Kexueyuan Xinlin Yanjiuso, Dewai Beishatan, Beijing, 100101, China. TEL 86-10-64850861. Circ: 32,000. **Dist. by:** China International Book Trading Corp, 35 Chegongzhuang Xilu, Haidian District, PO Box 399, Beijing 100044, China. TEL 86-10-68412045, FAX 86-10-68412023, cibtc@mail.cibtc.com.cn, http://www.cibtc.com.cn.

➤ **XINLI YANJIU/PSYCHOLOGICAL RESEARCH.** *see* MEDICAL SCIENCES—Psychiatry And Neurology

150 CHN ISSN 1672-0628
XINLI YU XINGWEI YANJIU/STUDIES OF PSYCHOLOGY AND BEHAVIOR. Text in Chinese. 2003. quadrennial. USD 16.40 (effective 2009). **Document type:** *Journal, Academic/Scholarly.*
Published by: Tianjin Shifan Daxue, Xinli yu Xingwei Yanjiuyuan/Tianjin Normal University, Academy of Psychology and Behavior, 241, Weijin Lu, Balitai Jiao-qu, 106 Xinxiang, Tianjin, 300074, China. TEL 86-22-23541213, http://202.113.102.136/.

150 613.7 CHN ISSN 1673-6796
XINLI YUEKAN/PSYCHOLOGIES. Text in Chinese. 1980. m. CNY 210 (effective 2009). **Document type:** *Magazine, Consumer.*
Formerly (until 2006): Jiankang Guwen/A Guide to Good Health (1003-000X)
Related titles: Online - full content ed.
Published by: Beijing Bierde Guanggao Youxian Gongsi/Beijing Hachette Advertising Co., Ltd. (Subsidiary of: Hachette Filipacchi Medias S.A.), 19, Deguomen wai Dajie, Guoji Dasha 2202, Beijing, 100004, China.

XINLING SHIJIE/MIND WORLD. *see* MEDICAL SCIENCES—Psychiatry And Neurology

150 CHN ISSN 1001-2532
XINLIXUE/PSYCHOLOGY. Text in Chinese. 1978. m. USD 72.10 (effective 2009). 88 p./no.; **Document type:** *Journal, Academic/Scholarly.* **Description:** Contains reprints of articles on psychology and related fields.
Indexed: E-psyche.
Published by: Zhongguo Renmin Daxue Shubao Ziliao Zhongxin/Renmin University of China, Information Center for Social Sciences, Dongcheng-qu, 3, Zhangzizhong Lu, Beijing, 100007, China. TEL 86-10-64039458, FAX 86-10-64015080, center@zlzx.org, http://www.zlzx.org/. **Dist. by:** China International Book Trading Corp, 35 Chegongzhuang Xilu, Haidian District, PO Box 399, Beijing 100044, China. TEL 86-10-68412045, FAX 86-10-68412023, cibtc@mail.cibtc.com.cn, http://www.cibtc.com.cn.

150 USA ISSN 2160-7273
▼ **XINLIXUE JINZHAN/ADVANCES IN PSYCHOLOGY.** Text in Chinese; Abstracts in English. 2011. q. **Document type:** *Journal, Academic/Scholarly.*
Related titles: Online - full text ed.: ISSN 2160-7281. free (effective 2011).
Published by: Hansi Chubanshe/Hans Publishers, 40 E. Main St., Box 275, Newark, DE 19711. TEL 926408-329-4591. Eds. Kai-ping Peng, Lin Chen.

150 CHN ISSN 1003-5184
XINLIXUE TANXIN/PSYCHOLOGICAL EXPLORATION. Text in Chinese. 1998. q. CNY 32 domestic; USD 8 in Hong Kong, Macau & Taiwan; USD 14 elsewhere (effective 2007). **Document type:** *Journal, Academic/Scholarly.*
Related titles: Online - full text ed.
Published by: Jiangxi Shifan Daxue/Jiangxi Normal University, 437 Beijing Xilu, Nanchang, Jiangxi 330027, China. TEL 86-791-8120281. **Dist. by:** China International Book Trading Corp, 35 Chegongzhuang Xilu, Haidian District, PO Box 399, Beijing 100044, China. TEL 86-10-68412045, FAX 86-10-68412023, cibtc@mail.cibtc.com.cn, http://www.cibtc.com.cn.

YOGA INTERNATIONAL. *see* NEW AGE PUBLICATIONS

155.4 CHN ISSN 1006-3595
YOU'ER ZHILI SHIJIE/INFANTS' INTELLIGENCE WORLD. Text in Chinese. 1986. s-m. (m. before 2002). USD 72 (effective 2009). adv. Index. back issues avail. **Document type:** *Consumer.*
Media: Large Type (14 pt.).
Indexed: E-psyche.
—East View.
Published by: Zhejiang Shaonian Ertong Chubanshe/Zhejiang Juvenile and Children's Publishing House, Zhejiang Distribution Bureau, Rm 909 & 910, No.347 Tiyuchang Rd, Hangzhou, Zhejiang Province, China. TEL 86-571-85102968, FAX 86-571-85176984, zjsrs@mail.hz.zj.cn, http://www.ses.zjcb.com. Eds. Mingjun Chen, Wen Chen. Pub. Chunyue Chen. R&P Ying Wu TEL 86-571-5102968. Adv. contact Mingjun Chen. color page CNY 20,000; trim 187 x 216. Circ: 450,000. **Dist. by:** China International Book Trading Corp, 35 Chegongzhuang Xilu, Haidian District, PO Box 399, Beijing 100044, China. TEL 86-10-68412045, FAX 86-10-68412023, cibtc@mail.cibtc.com.cn, http://www.cibtc.com.cn/.

150 158 DEU ISSN 0932-4089
➤ **ZEITSCHRIFT FUER ARBEITS- UND ORGANISATIONSPSYCHOLOGIE.** Short title: A & O. Text in German; Summaries in English. 1956. q. EUR 106.95 to individuals; EUR 190.95 to institutions; EUR 47.95 newsstand/cover (effective 2011). adv. bk.rev. bibl.; charts. **Document type:** *Journal, Academic/Scholarly.*
Formerly (until 1987): Psychologie und Praxis (0033-2992)
Related titles: Online - full text ed.: ISSN 2190-6270.
Indexed: ASCA, ASD, BAS, CISA, CurCont, DIP, DokArb, E-psyche, FR, GJP, IBR, IBZ, IPsyAb, P03, PsycInfo, PsycholAb, S02, S03, SCOPUS, SSCI, W07.
—IE, Infotrieve, INIST. **CCC.**
Published by: Hogrefe Verlag GmbH & Co. KG, Rohnsweg 25, Goettingen, 37085, Germany. TEL 49-551-496090, FAX 49-551-4960988, verlag@hogrefe.de. Ed. Conny Antoni. Circ: 2,200 (paid and controlled).

370.15 150 DEU ISSN 0049-8637
L31 CODEN: ZEPPBI
➤ **ZEITSCHRIFT FUER ENTWICKLUNGSPSYCHOLOGIE UND PAEDAGOGISCHE PSYCHOLOGIE.** Text in German; Summaries in English. 1969. q. EUR 81.95 to individuals; EUR 145.95 to institutions; EUR 36.95 newsstand/cover (effective 2011). adv. bk.rev. abstr.; bibl. **Document type:** *Journal, Academic/Scholarly.*
Related titles: Online - full text ed.: ISSN 2190-6262.
Indexed: A20, A22, ASCA, CDA, CPE, CurCont, DIP, E-psyche, E15, E16, ERA, GJP, IBR, IBZ, M12, P03, P30, PsycInfo, PsycholAb, RILM, S02, S03, S19, S20, S21, SCOPUS, SSCI, V05, W07.
—BLDSC (9458.600000), IE, Infotrieve, Ingenta.
Published by: Hogrefe Verlag GmbH & Co. KG, Rohnsweg 25, Goettingen, 37085, Germany. TEL 49-551-496090, FAX 49-551-4960988, verlag@hogrefe.de. Ed. Bettina Hannover. Circ: 2,000 (paid and controlled).

616.89 DEU ISSN 1619-5515
➤ **ZEITSCHRIFT FUER EVALUATION.** Text in German. 2002. s-a. EUR 32; EUR 19 newsstand/cover (effective 2011). **Document type:** *Journal, Academic/Scholarly.*
Indexed: DIP, IBR, IBZ, SCOPUS, SSCI, W07.
—CCC.
Published by: Waxmann Verlag GmbH, Steinfurter Str 555, Muenster, 48159, Germany. TEL 49-251-265040, FAX 49-251-2650426, info@waxmann.com, http://www.waxmann.com. Ed. Stefanie Kihm.

150 DEU ISSN 0943-8149
ZEITSCHRIFT FUER GESUNDHEITSPSYCHOLOGIE. Text in German. 1993. q. EUR 81.95 to individuals; EUR 190.95 to institutions; EUR 43.95 newsstand/cover (effective 2011). adv. bk.rev. abstr.; bibl.; illus. **Document type:** *Journal, Academic/Scholarly.*
Related titles: Online - full text ed.: ISSN 2190-6289.
Indexed: DIP, E-psyche, IBR, IBZ, P03, PsycInfo, PsycholAb, SCOPUS, SSCI, W07.
—GNLM. **CCC.**
Published by: Hogrefe Verlag GmbH & Co. KG, Rohnsweg 25, Goettingen, 37085, Germany. TEL 49-551-496090, FAX 49-551-4960988, verlag@hogrefe.de. Ed. Carl-Walter Kohlmann TEL 49-7171-983418. Circ: 1,600 (paid and controlled).

150 DEU ISSN 0342-393X
BF3
➤ **ZEITSCHRIFT FUER INDIVIDUALPSYCHOLOGIE.** Text in German. 1976. q. EUR 64 to individuals; EUR 128 to institutions; EUR 51 to students; EUR 17.90 newsstand/cover (effective 2011). adv. bk.rev. reprints avail. **Document type:** *Journal, Academic/Scholarly.*
Indexed: DIP, E-psyche, IBR, IBZ, P03, PsycInfo, PsycholAb.
—GNLM. **CCC.**
Published by: Vandenhoeck und Ruprecht, Theaterstr 13, Goettingen, 37073, Germany. TEL 49-551-508440, FAX 49-551-5084422, info@v-r.de. Ed. Ulla Breuer. Circ: 2,400 (paid and controlled).

616.89 DEU ISSN 1616-3443
ZEITSCHRIFT FUER KLINISCHE PSYCHOLOGIE UND PSYCHOTHERAPIE - FORSCHUNG UND PRAXIS. Text in German; Summaries in English. 1972. q. EUR 106.95 to individuals; EUR 190.95 to institutions; EUR 47.95 newsstand/cover (effective 2011). adv. bk.rev. **Document type:** *Journal, Academic/Scholarly.*
Formerly (until 2000): Zeitschrift fuer Klinische Psychologie - Forschung und Praxis (0084-5345)
Related titles: Online - full text ed.: ISSN 2190-6297.
Indexed: A20, A22, ASCA, CurCont, DIP, E-psyche, GJP, IBR, IBZ, P03, PsycInfo, PsycholAb, RILM, S02, S03, SCOPUS, SSCI, W07.
—BLDSC (9467.782000), GNLM, IE, Ingenta, INIST. **CCC.**
Published by: Hogrefe Verlag GmbH & Co. KG, Rohnsweg 25, Goettingen, 37085, Germany. TEL 49-551-496090, 49-551-496090, FAX 49-551-4960988, verlag@hogrefe.de. Ed. Norbert Kathmann. Circ: 3,600 (paid and controlled).

150 DEU ISSN 0940-5569
➤ **ZEITSCHRIFT FUER MEDIZINISCHE PSYCHOLOGIE.** Text in German. 1992. q. EUR 162 (effective 2009). adv. bk.rev. 48 p./no. 3 cols./p.; back issues avail. **Document type:** *Journal, Academic/Scholarly.*
Related titles: Online - full text ed.: ISSN 1875-9246.
Indexed: A22, DIP, E-psyche, IBR, IBZ, P03, P30, PsycInfo, PsycholAb, SCOPUS.
—BLDSC (9469.895000), GNLM, IE.
Published by: Akademische Verlagsgesellschaft Aka GmbH, Neue Promenade 6, Berlin, 10178, Germany. TEL 49-30-24729840, FAX 49-30-24729840, http://www.aka-verlag.de. Ed. H Faller. Pub. H Schulz.

150 CHE ISSN 1016-264X
➤ **ZEITSCHRIFT FUER NEUROPSYCHOLOGIE.** Text in German; Summaries in English. 1990. 4/yr. CHF 288 domestic to institutions; EUR 192 in Europe to institutions (effective 2011). adv. bk.rev.; Website rev. 96 p./no.; **Document type:** *Journal, Academic/Scholarly.*
Related titles: Online - full text ed.: ISSN 1664-2902.
Indexed: E-psyche, NSCI, P03, PsycInfo, PsycholAb, SCI, W07.
—GNLM, IE. **CCC.**
Published by: Verlag Hans Huber AG (Subsidiary of: Hogrefe Verlag GmbH & Co. KG), Laenggassstr 76, Bern 9, 3000, Switzerland. TEL 41-31-3004500, FAX 41-31-3004590, verlag@hanshuber.com, http://www.hanshuber.com. Ed. Dr. Lutz Jaencke. Circ: 2,100 (paid).

370.15 CHE ISSN 1010-0652
LB1051 CODEN: ZPPSE5
➤ **ZEITSCHRIFT FUER PAEDAGOGISCHE PSYCHOLOGIE.** Text in English, German. 1987. q. CHF 288 domestic to institutions; EUR 192 in Europe to institutions (effective 2011). adv. bk.rev. back issues avail. **Document type:** *Journal, Academic/Scholarly.*
Related titles: Online - full text ed.: ISSN 1664-2910.
Indexed: A22, ASCA, CPE, CurCont, DIP, E-psyche, E16, ERA, IBR, IBZ, L&LBA, P03, PsycInfo, PsycholAb, S20, S21, SCOPUS, SOPODA, SSCI, SociolAb, W07.
—BLDSC (9475.803000), IE, Ingenta.
Published by: Verlag Hans Huber AG (Subsidiary of: Hogrefe Verlag GmbH & Co. KG), Laenggassstr 76, Bern 9, 3000, Switzerland. TEL 41-31-3004500, FAX 41-31-3004590, verlag@hanshuber.com, http://www.hanshuber.com. Eds. Andreas Knapp, Detlef H. Rost. Circ: 450 (paid).

➤ **ZEITSCHRIFT FUER PSYCHIATRIE, PSYCHOLOGIE UND PSYCHOTHERAPIE.** see MEDICAL SCIENCES—Psychiatry And Neurology

➤ **ZEITSCHRIFT FUER PSYCHOANALYTISCHE THEORIE UND PRAXIS.** see MEDICAL SCIENCES—Psychiatry And Neurology

616.89 DEU ISSN 1619-5507
➤ **ZEITSCHRIFT FUER PSYCHODRAMA UND SOZIOMETRIE.** Text in German. 2002. s-a. EUR 157.01, USD 194 combined subscription to institutions (print & online eds.) (effective 2012). adv. reprint service avail. from PSC. **Document type:** *Journal, Academic/Scholarly.*
Related titles: Online - full text ed.: ISSN 1862-2526.
Indexed: A22, A26, DIP, E01, I05, IBR, IBSS, IBZ, P03, PsycInfo, SCOPUS.
—IE, Ingenta. **CCC.**
Published by: V S - Verlag fuer Sozialwissenschaften (Subsidiary of: Springer Fachmedien Wiesbaden GmbH), Abraham-Lincoln-Str 46, Wiesbaden, 65189, Germany. TEL 49-611-78780, FAX 49-611-7878400, springerfachmedien-wiesbaden@springer.com, http://www.vs-verlag.de. Circ: 790 (paid).

150 DEU ISSN 2190-8370
QP351
➤ **ZEITSCHRIFT FUER PSYCHOLOGIE - JOURNAL OF PSYCHOLOGY.** Text in German. 1944. q. EUR 212 to institutions; EUR 64.95 newsstand/cover (effective 2011). adv. bk.rev. bibl.; charts; illus. index. back issues avail.; reprints avail. **Document type:** *Journal, Academic/Scholarly.* **Description:** Publishes papers on experimental and theoretical psychology.
Formerly (until 2007): Zeitschrift fuer Psychologie mit Zeitschrift fuer Angewandte Psychologie (0044-3409); Which was formed by the merger of (1903-1944): Zeitschrift fuer Angewandte Psychologie und Charakterkunde (0323-8296); Which was formerly (until 1935): Zeitschrift fuer Angewandte Psychologie (0948-5503); (until 1916): Zeitschrift fuer Angewandte Psychologie und Psychologische Sammelforschung (0948-549X); (until 1907): Beitraege zur Psychologie der Aussage (0948-5481); (1890-1944): Zeitschrift fuer Psychologie (0323-8342); Which was formerly (until 1940): Zeitschrift fuer Psychologie und Physiologie des Sinnesorgane. 1. Abteilung. Zeitschrift fuer Psychologie (0233-2353); Which superseded in part (in 1906): Zeitschrift fuer Psychologie und Physiologie der Sinnesorgane (0233-2302)
Related titles: Online - full text ed.: ISSN 2151-2604 (from ScienceDirect).
Indexed: A20, A22, ASCA, BibInd, CurCont, DIP, E-psyche, E06, GJP, H09, H10, IBR, IBZ, IndMed, L&LBA, MLA-IB, P03, P30, PCI, PsycInfo, PsycholAb, RASB, S02, S03, S05, SCOPUS, SOPODA, SSCI, SociolAb, W07.
—BLDSC (5043.380000), IE, Infotrieve, Ingenta, INIST. **CCC.**
Published by: Hogrefe Verlag GmbH & Co. KG, Rohnsweg 25, Goettingen, 37085, Germany. TEL 49-551-99950421, FAX 49-551-99950425, verlag@hogrefe.de. Ed. Bernd Leplow. Circ: 800 (paid and controlled).

616.89 DEU ISSN 1611-9568
ZEITSCHRIFT FUER PSYCHOTRAUMATOLOGIE UND PSYCHOLOGISCHE MEDIZIN. Abbreviated title: Z P P M. Text in German. q. EUR 59; EUR 39 to students; EUR 19 newsstand/cover (effective 2006). adv. **Document type:** *Journal, Academic/Scholarly.*
Published by: Roland Asanger Verlag GmbH, Boedldorf 3, Kroening, 84178, Germany. TEL 49-8744-7262, FAX 49-8744-967755, verlag@asanger.de, http://www.asanger.de. Ed. Christiane Eichenberg. Adv. contact Sabine Zercher. page EUR 500; trim 135 x 224. Circ: 1,000 (paid and controlled).

ZEITSCHRIFT FUER SEXUALFORSCHUNG. see MEDICAL SCIENCES

150 790.1 DEU ISSN 1612-5010
ZEITSCHRIFT FUER SPORTPSYCHOLOGIE. Text in German. 1987. q. EUR 64.95 to individuals; EUR 117.95 to institutions; EUR 29.95 newsstand/cover (effective 2011). **Document type:** *Journal, Academic/Scholarly.*
Former titles (until 2004): Psychologie und Sport (0945-6031); (until 1994): Sportpsychologie (0932-1608)
Related titles: Online - full text ed.: ISSN 2190-6300.
Indexed: CA, DIP, E-psyche, IBR, IBZ, P03, PEI, PsycInfo, PsycholAb, SCOPUS, SD, SSCI, T02, W07.
—BLDSC (9486.400550), IE, Ingenta.
Published by: (Arbeitsgemeinschaft fuer Sportpsychologie), Hogrefe Verlag GmbH & Co. KG, Rohnsweg 25, Goettingen, 37085, Germany. TEL 49-551-496090, FAX 49-551-4960988, verlag@hogrefe.de. Ed. Markus Raab. Circ: 700 (paid and controlled).

616.89 DEU
ZEITSCHRIFT FUER SYSTEMISCHE THERAPIE UND BERATUNG. Text in German. 1982. q. EUR 33; EUR 9 newsstand/cover (effective 2011). adv. **Document type:** *Journal, Academic/Scholarly.*
Formerly (until 200?): Zeitschrift fuer Systemische Therapie (0723-9505)
Indexed: DIP, E-psyche, IBR, IBZ.
—GNLM, IE.
Published by: Verlag Modernes Lernen Borgmann KG, Schleefstr 14, Dortmund, 44287, Germany. TEL 49-231-128008, FAX 49-231-125640, info@verlag-modernes-lernen.de. Ed. Cornelia Tsirigotis. Pub. Dieter Borgmann.

616.89 DEU
ZEITSCHRIFT FUER TRANSAKTIONSANALYSE. Text in German; Summaries in English. 1984. q. EUR 39 to individuals; EUR 34 to students (effective 2004). index. back issues avail. **Document type:** *Magazine, Academic/Scholarly.*
Formerly: Zeitschrift fuer Transaktionsanalyse in Theorie und Praxis (0176-9855)
Indexed: E-psyche.
Published by: (Deutsche Gesellschaft fuer Transaktions-Analyse e.V.), Junfermann Verlag, Imadstr 40, Paderborn, 33102, Germany. TEL 49-5251-13440, FAX 49-5251-134444, ju@junfermann.de, http://www.junfermann.de.

ZHONGGUO XING KEXUE/CHINESE JOURNAL OF HUMAN SEXUALITY. see BIOLOGY—Physiology

150 CHN ISSN 1000-6729
➤ **ZHONGGUO XINLI WEISHENG ZAZHI/CHINESE MENTAL HEALTH JOURNAL.** Text in Chinese; Abstracts in English. 1987. m. (bi-m. until 2002). USD 49.20 (effective 2009). adv. **Document type:** *Journal, Academic/Scholarly.* **Description:** Publishes postgraduate dissertations, research articles, and clinical practices in the fields of medicine, psychology, pedagogy and sociology, focusing on mental health issues.
Related titles: Online - full text ed.
Indexed: A22, E-psyche, P03, PsycInfo, PsycholAb, S02, S03.
—BLDSC (3181.015100), East View, IE, Ingenta.
Published by: Zhongguo Xinli Weisheng Xiehui/Chinese Association for Mental Health, 5 An Kang Lane, De Sheng Men Wai, Beijing, 100088, China. TEL 86-10-82085385, FAX 86-10-62359838, camh@163bj.com. Ed. Ruicong Peng. adv.: page USD 800. Circ: 15,000 (paid). **Dist. by:** China International Book Trading Corp, 35 Chegongzhuang Xilu, Haidian District, PO Box 399, Beijing 100044, China. TEL 86-10-68412045, FAX 86-10-68412023, cibtc@mail.cibtc.com.cn, http://www.cibtc.com.cn.

150 DEU ISSN 0724-3766
ZWISCHENSCHRITTE; Beitraege zu einer morphologischen Psychologie. Text in German. 1982. a. EUR 16 (effective 2007). adv. bk.rev.; film rev.; play rev. bibl.; illus. back issues avail. **Document type:** *Journal, Academic/Scholarly.*
Indexed: DIP, E-psyche, IBR, IBZ.
Published by: (Arbeitskreis Morphologische Psychologie e.V.), Psychosozial Verlag, Walltorstr 10, Giessen, 35390, Germany. TEL 49-641-9699780, FAX 49-641-96997819, info@psychosozial-verlag.de, http://www.psychosozial-verlag.de. Circ: 1,500.

PSYCHOLOGY—Abstracting, Bibliographies, Statistics

150 USA
BEHAVIORAL PARENTING ABSTRACTS. Text in English. 2002. q. back issues avail. **Document type:** *Newsletter, Academic/Scholarly.* **Description:** Contains a reviews of parent training literature and special topics.
Published by: Cambridge Center for Behavioral Studies, 550 Newtown Rd, Ste 700, Littleton, MA 01460. TEL 978-369-2227, FAX 978-369-8584, harshbarger@behavior.org. Ed. Timothy R Vollmer.

310 150 JPN ISSN 0385-7417
BF76.5
➤ **BEHAVIORMETRIKA.** Text mainly in English. 1974. s-a. USD 40 (effective 2001). back issues avail. **Document type:** *Journal, Academic/Scholarly.*
Related titles: Online - full text ed.: ISSN 1349-6964. free (effective 2011).
Indexed: A39, B21, C27, C29, CA, CCMJ, CIS, D03, D04, E-psyche, E13, JCQM, MSN, MathR, NSA, P03, P30, P42, PSA, PsycInfo, PsycholAb, R14, S02, S03, S14, S15, S18, SOPODA, ST&MA, SociolAb, T02, Z02.
—BLDSC (1878.070000), IE, Infotrieve, Ingenta.
Published by: Nihon Kodo Keiryo Gakkai/Behaviormetric Society of Japan, 6-7 Minami-Azabu 4-chome, Minato-ku, Tokyo, 106-0047, Japan. FAX 81-3-5421-8707, yoshino@ism.ac.jp. Ed. Yutaka Kanou.

016.3011 DEU ISSN 1436-2104
Z7203
BIBLIOGRAPHIE PSYCHOLOGISCHER LITERATUR AUS DEN DEUTSCHSPRACHIGEN LAENDERN. Text in German. 1972. a. EUR 238 per vol. (effective 2011). back issues avail. **Document type:** *Bibliography.* **Description:** Lists sources in the German-language psychological literature.
Formerly (until 1996): Bibliographie der Deutschsprachigen Psychologischen Literatur (0303-5999)
—GNLM.
Published by: (Universitaet Trier, Leibniz-Zentrum fuer Psychologische Information und Dokumentation), Vittorio Klostermann, Frauenlobstr 22, Frankfurt Am Main, 60487, Germany. TEL 49-69-9708160, FAX 49-69-708038, verlag@klostermann.de, http://www.klostermann.de.

016.15 USA ISSN 0742-681X
BIBLIOGRAPHIES AND INDEXES IN PSYCHOLOGY. Text in English. 1984. irreg. price varies. back issues avail. **Document type:** *Monographic series, Bibliography.*
Indexed: E-psyche.
Published by: Greenwood Publishing Group Inc. (Subsidiary of: A B C - C L I O), 88 Post Rd W, PO Box 5007, Westport, CT 06881. TEL 203-226-3571, 800-225-5800, FAX 877-231-6980, sales@greenwood.com, http://www.greenwood.com.

150 USA ISSN 2155-1677
CABELL'S DIRECTORY OF PUBLISHING OPPORTUNITIES IN PSYCHOLOGY AND PSYCHIATRY. Text in English. 2005. irreg. (in 2 vols.), latest 2005-2006. USD 249.95 per issue (effective 2011). **Document type:** *Directory, Bibliography.*
Formerly (until 2007): Cabell's Directory of Publishing Opportunities in Psychology
Related titles: Online - full text ed.
Published by: Cabell Publishing, Inc., PO Box 5428, Beaumont, TX 77726. TEL 409-898-0575, FAX 409-866-9554, publish@cabells.com, https://cabells.com.

152 USA ISSN 8756-3207
RC467
CLINICIAN'S RESEARCH DIGEST; briefings in behavioral science. Abbreviated title: C R D. Text in English. 1983. m. USD 107 domestic to individuals; USD 160 foreign to individuals; USD 277 domestic to institutions; USD 379 foreign to institutions (effective 2011). adv. back issues avail.; reprints avail. **Document type:** *Newsletter, Trade.* **Description:** Reviews over 100 journals each month and highlights the most relevant articles.
Related titles: Online - full text ed.
Indexed: E-psyche.
Published by: American Psychological Association, 750 First St, NE, Washington, DC 20002. TEL 202-336-5500, 800-374-2721, journals@apa.org. Ed. Dr. Thmoas E Joiner.

016.5 ESP
COLEGIO OFICIAL DE PSICOLOGOS DE MADRID. SELECCIONES DE PRENSA. Text in Spanish. m. (11/yr.). EUR 59 domestic to qualified personnel; EUR 69 domestic; EUR 190 foreign (effective 2004). **Document type:** *Abstract/Index.* **Description:** Summarizes the most noteworthy articles on psychology from more than 90 daily and 35 weekly newspapers and at least 195 magazines and journals.
Media: CD-ROM.
Indexed: E-psyche.
Published by: Colegio Oficial de Psicologos, Claudio Coello 46, Madrid, 28001, Spain. TEL 34-91-4355212, FAX 34-91-5779172, http://www.cop.es. Ed. Javier Martinez.

016.15 USA ISSN 0092-6361
CURRENT CONTENTS: SOCIAL & BEHAVIORAL SCIENCES. Short title: C C: S & B S. Text in English. 1969 (Jan.). w. Index. **Document type:** *Journal, Academic/Scholarly.* **Description:** Tables of contents of the world's leading publications covering social and behavioral sciences.
Former titles (until 1974): Current Contents: Behavioral, Social and Educational Sciences (0011-3387); (until 1971): Current Contents: Behavioral, Social & Management Sciences (0590-384X); (until 1969): Current Contents: Education (0590-3866)
Related titles: Diskette ed.: ISSN 1062-3140; Magnetic Tape ed.: ISSN 1079-1248; Online - full text ed.: ISSN 1086-640X.
Indexed: A20, PopulInd, RASB.
—BLDSC (3496.209500).
Published by: Thomson Reuters (Subsidiary of: Thomson Reuters Corp.), 1500 Spring Garden, 4th Fl, Philadelphia, PA 19130. TEL 215-386-0100, 800-336-4474, FAX 215-386-2911, general.info@thomson.com.

P

ERGONOMICS ABSTRACTS ONLINE. *see* ENGINEERING—Abstracting, Bibliographies, Statistics

016.150 USA ISSN 1040-2144
Z7204.P8
INTERNATIONAL ABSTRACTS IN ANALYTICAL PSYCHOLOGY. Text in English. 1986. a. USD 24.95 per issue (effective 2010). **Document type:** *Monographic series, Academic/Scholarly.*
Published by: Chiron Publications, c/o Lantern Books, 128 Second Pl, Garden Ste, Brooklyn, NY 11231. chiron@rcn.com, http://www.chironpublications.com.

150 016.614 USA ISSN 1085-2352
RA421 CODEN: JPICFJ
➤ **JOURNAL OF PREVENTION AND INTERVENTION IN THE COMMUNITY.** Abbreviated title: J P I C. Text in English. 1976. s-a. GBP 939 combined subscription in United Kingdom to institutions (print & online eds.); EUR 1,221, USD 1,234 combined subscription to institutions (print & online eds.) (effective 2012). adv. bk.rev. abstr.; bibl.; illus. cum.index. 120 p./no. 1 cols./p.; back issues avail.; reprint service avail. from PSC. **Document type:** *Journal, Academic/Scholarly.* **Description:** Deals with the application of the philosophy of prevention in mental health and other human services.
Former titles (until 1996): Prevention in Human Services (0270-3114); (until 1981): Community Mental Health Review (0363-1605)
Related titles: Microfiche ed.: (from PQC); Microform ed.; Online - full text ed.: ISSN 1540-7330. GBP 846 in United Kingdom to institutions; EUR 1,099, USD 1,111 to institutions (effective 2012).
Indexed: A01, A03, A22, B21, C06, C07, C08, CA, CDA, CINAHL, CJA, DIP, E-psyche, E01, E03, E17, EMBASE, ERI, ESPM, ExcerpMed, FamI, H&SSA, IBR, IBZ, MEDLINE, P03, P30, P34, PsycInfo, PsycholAb, RefZh, RiskAb, S02, S03, SCOPUS, SSA, SWR&A, SociolAb, T02.
—BLDSC (5042.227300), GNLM, IE, Infotrieve, Ingenta, INIST. **CCC.**
Published by: Routledge (Subsidiary of: Taylor & Francis Group), 325 Chestnut St, Ste 800, Philadelphia, PA 19106. TEL 215-625-8900, 800-354-1420, FAX 215-625-8914, journals@routledge.com, http://www.routledge.com. Ed. Joseph R Ferrari. Circ: 207 (paid).

152 USA ISSN 0272-0582
P C R; films and video in the behavioral sciences. (Psychological Cinema Register) Text in English. 1944. a. **Document type:** *Catalog.*
Indexed: E-psyche.
Published by: Pennsylvania State University, Audio-Visual Services, University Park, PA 16802. TEL 800-826-0132. Circ: 9,000.

016.15 PAK
PAKISTAN PSYCHOLOGICAL ABSTRACTS (ONLINE). Text in English. base vol. plus irreg. updates. **Document type:** *Database, Abstract/Index.* **Description:** Contains non-evaluative summaries of articles, research monographs, books, and theses related to psychology published in or conducted in Pakistan.
Media: Online - full text. **Related titles:** ◆ Print ed.: Pakistan Psychological Abstracts. ISSN 2075-6011.
Published by: National Institute of Psychology, c/o Quaid-i-Azam University (New Campus), Shahdra Rd. (off Main Murree Rd.), Islamabad, Pakistan. TEL 92-51-90644031, FAX 92-51-2896012, nip@nip.edu.pk.

150 USA ISSN 1350-4126
HM132 CODEN: PRRLEY
➤ **PERSONAL RELATIONSHIPS.** Text in English. 1994. q. GBP 412 in United Kingdom to institutions; EUR 523 in Europe to institutions; USD 516 in the Americas to institutions; USD 807 elsewhere to institutions; GBP 474 combined subscription in United Kingdom to institutions (print & online eds.); EUR 602 combined subscription in Europe to institutions (print & online eds.); USD 593 combined subscription in the Americas to institutions (print & online eds.); USD 929 combined subscription elsewhere to institutions (print & online eds.) (effective 2012). adv. back issues avail.; reprint service avail. from PSC. **Document type:** *Journal, Academic/Scholarly.* **Description:** Promotes scholarship in personal relationships through a broad range of disciplines, including psychology, psychiatry, communication studies, sociology, anthropology, and family studies.
Related titles: Online - full text ed.: ISSN 1475-6811. GBP 412 in United Kingdom to institutions; EUR 523 in Europe to institutions; USD 516 in the Americas to institutions; USD 807 elsewhere to institutions (effective 2012) (from IngentaConnect).
Indexed: A01, A03, A08, A20, A22, A26, ASCA, CA, CurCont, E-psyche, E01, F09, FamI, I05, P03, P30, P43, PsycInfo, PsycholAb, S02, S03, SCOPUS, SOPODA, SSCI, SWR&A, SociolAb, T02, W07.
—BLDSC (6427.885200), IE, Infotrieve, Ingenta. **CCC.**
Published by: (International Association for Relationship Research), Wiley-Blackwell Publishing, Inc. (Subsidiary of: Wiley-Blackwell Publishing Ltd.), Commerce Pl, 350 Main St, Malden, MA 02148. TEL 781-388-8206, FAX 781-388-8232, info@wiley.com, http://www.wiley.com/WileyCDA/. Ed. Lorne Campbell. adv.: B&W page USD 450; trim 6.75 x 10. Circ: 850 (paid).

016.15 USA
PROQUEST PSYCHOLOGY JOURNALS. Text in English. base vol. plus d. updates. **Document type:** *Database, Abstract/Index.*
Media: Online - full text.
Published by: ProQuest (Subsidiary of: Cambridge Information Group), 789 E Eisenhower Pky, PO Box 1346, Ann Arbor, MI 48106. TEL 734-761-4700, 800-521-0600, FAX 734-997-4040, 888-241-5612, info@proquest.com, http://www.proquest.com.

016.15 ESP ISSN 1988-0073
PSICODOC; lo mejor de la psicologia al instante. Text in Spanish. 1997. irreg. back issues avail. **Document type:** *Abstract/Index.* **Description:** Compiles some 27,000 bibliographic references from more than 200 Spanish-language scholarly and trade publications and the proceedings of 100 congresses.
Media: CD-ROM. **Related titles:** Online - full text ed.: ISSN 1988-0065. 2002.
Indexed: E-psyche.
Published by: Colegio Oficial de Psicologos, Claudio Coello 46, Madrid, 28001, Spain. TEL 34-91-4355212, FAX 34-91-5779172, http://www.cop.es.

016.15 USA
PSYCFIRST. Text in English. 19??. base vol. plus m. updates. **Document type:** *Database, Abstract/Index.* **Description:** Provides the three most recent years of citations from the PsycInfo database.
Media: Online - full text.
Published by: American Psychological Association, 750 First St, NE, Washington, DC 20002. TEL 202-336-5500, 800-374-2721, journals@apa.org.

016.15 016.6168 USA
PSYCHOLOGY & BEHAVIORAL SCIENCES COLLECTION. Text in English. base vol. plus w. updates. **Document type:** *Database, Abstract/Index.* **Description:** Concentrate on topics in emotional and behavioral characteristics, psychiatry & psychology, mental processes, anthropology, and observational & experimental methods.
Media: Online - full text.
Published by: EBSCO Publishing (Subsidiary of: EBSCO Industries, Inc.), 10 Estes St, PO Box 682, Ipswich, MA 01938. TEL 800-653-2726, FAX 978-356-6565, information@ebscohost.com.

016.15 USA
PSYCHOLOGY MODULE. Text in English. base vol. plus d. updates. **Document type:** *Database, Abstract/Index.*
Media: Online - full text.
Published by: ProQuest (Subsidiary of: Cambridge Information Group), 789 E Eisenhower Pky, PO Box 1346, Ann Arbor, MI 48106. TEL 734-761-4700, 800-521-0600, FAX 734-997-4040, 888-241-5612, info@proquest.com, http://www.proquest.com.

016.15 USA
PSYCINFO. Text in English. 19??. base vol. plus w. updates. free to members (effective 2010). **Document type:** *Database, Abstract/Index.* **Description:** Provides systematic coverage of the psychological literature from the 1800s to the present.
Media: Online - full text.
Published by: American Psychological Association, 750 First St, NE, Washington, DC 20002. TEL 202-336-5500, 800-374-2721, journals@apa.org.

370.15 USA
PSYCINFO NEWS. Text in English. 1981. q. free (effective 2010). **Document type:** *Newsletter.* **Description:** Contains search tips and news about forthcoming and existing PsycINFO products.
Related titles: Online - full text ed.
Published by: American Psychological Association, 750 First St, NE, Washington, DC 20002. TEL 202-336-5500, 800-374-2721, journals@apa.org.

016.158 USA
BF636.A1
PSYCSCAN: APPLIED PSYCHOLOGY (ONLINE). (Subset of PsycINFO) Text in English. 1981. base vol. plus m. updates. USD 59 to non-members (effective 2008). adv. **Document type:** *Database, Abstract/Index.* **Description:** Abstracts from a cluster of subscriber-selected journals in general area of applied psychology.
Formerly (until 200?): PsycSCAN: Applied Psychology (Print) (0271-7506)
Media: Online - full content.
Published by: American Psychological Association, 750 First St, NE, Washington, DC 20002. TEL 800-374-2721, journals@apa.org.

016.158 USA
PSYCSCAN: BEHAVIOR ANALYSIS AND THERAPY (ONLINE). (Subset of PsycINFO) Text in English. 1995. base vol. plus m. updates. USD 59 to non-members (effective 2008). **Document type:** *Database, Abstract/Index.* **Description:** Lists abstracts from subscriber selected journals in basic and applied research in behavioral psychology and related topics.
Formerly (until 200?): PsycSCAN: Behavior Analysis and Therapy (Print) (1078-3946)
Media: Online - full text.
Published by: American Psychological Association, 750 First St, NE, Washington, DC 20002. TEL 800-374-2721, journals@apa.org.

016.61689 USA
RC467
PSYCSCAN: CLINICAL PSYCHOLOGY (ONLINE). Text in English. 1980. base vol. plus m. updates. USD 59 to non-members (effective 2008). adv. back issues avail. **Document type:** *Database, Abstract/Index.* **Description:** Abstracts from subscriber-selected journals of interest to clinical psychologists.
Formerly (until 2008): PsycSCAN: Clinical Psychology (Print) (0197-1484)
Media: Online - full text.
Published by: American Psychological Association, 750 First St, NE, Washington, DC 20002. TEL 800-374-2721, journals@apa.org.

016.155 USA
PSYCSCAN: DEVELOPMENTAL PSYCHOLOGY (ONLINE). Text in English. 1980. base vol. plus m. updates. USD 59 to non-members (effective 2008). adv. **Document type:** *Database, Abstract/Index.* **Description:** Abstracts from subscriber-selected journals of interest to developmental psychologists.
Formerly (until 200?): PsycSCAN: Developmental Psychology (Print) (0197-1492)
Media: Online - full text.
Published by: American Psychological Association, 750 First St, NE, Washington, DC 20002. TEL 800-374-2721, journals@apa.org.

016.6167 USA
PSYCSCAN: LEARNING DISORDERS AND MENTAL RETARDATION (ONLINE). (Subset of PsycINFO) Text in English. 1982. base vol. plus d. updates. USD 59 to non-members (effective 2008). adv. **Document type:** *Database, Abstract/Index.* **Description:** Abstracts articles on learning disorders, communication disorders, and mental retardation, drawn from the subscriber-selected journals.
Formerly (until 200?): PsycSCAN: Learning Disabilities - Mental Retardation (Print) (0730-1928)
Media: Online - full text.
Published by: American Psychological Association, 750 First St, NE, Washington, DC 20002. TEL 800-374-2721, journals@apa.org.

016.150195 USA
PSYCSCAN: PSYCHOANALYSIS (ONLINE). (Subset of PsycINFO) Text in English. 1986. base vol. plus m. updates. USD 59 to non-members (effective 2008). adv. **Document type:** *Database, Abstract/Index.* **Description:** Covers international literature in the field of psychoanalysis, including advances in psychoanalytic theory, therapy and interpretation, as well as the history of psychoanalysis.
Former titles (until 2008): Psychoanalytic Abstracts (Print) (1066-9884); (until 1993): PsycSCAN: Psychoanalysis (0889-5236)
Media: Online - full text.
—**CCC.**
Published by: American Psychological Association, 750 First St, NE, Washington, DC 20002. TEL 800-374-2721, journals@apa.org.

016.15 RUS ISSN 0869-4133
REFERATIVNYI ZHURNAL. PSIKHOLOGIYA; razdel-tom. Text in Russian. 1990. m. USD 507.60 foreign (effective 2011). **Document type:** *Journal, Abstract/Index.*
Related titles: CD-ROM ed.; Online - full text ed.
—East View.
Published by: VINITI RAN, ul Usievicha 20, Moscow, 125190, Russian Federation. TEL 7-499-1526113, FAX 7-499-9430060, dir@viniti.ru, http://www.viniti.ru. **Dist. by:** Informnauka Ltd., Ul Usievicha 20, Moscow 125190, Russian Federation. alfimov@viniti.ru.

150 DEU
TESTZENTRALE TESTKATALOG. Text in German. a. **Document type:** *Catalog, Academic/Scholarly.* **Description:** Contains information on a wide variety of diagnostic tests available to psychologists.
Related titles: CD-ROM ed.
Indexed: E-psyche.
Published by: (Testzentrale), Hogrefe Verlag GmbH & Co. KG, Rohnsweg 25, Goettingen, 37085, Germany. TEL 49-551-496090, FAX 49-551-4960988, verlag@hogrefe.de, http://www.hogrefe.de. Circ: 110,000 (paid).

153.021 USA
U.S. NATIONAL CENTER FOR HEALTH STATISTICS. VITAL AND HEALTH STATISTICS. SERIES 6. COGNITION AND SURVEY MEASUREMENT. Text in English. 1989. irreg., latest vol.8. free (effective 2011). back issues avail. **Document type:** *Monographic series, Government.* **Description:** Comprises research from the National Laboratory for Collaborative Research in Cognition and Survey Measurement, using methods of cognitive science to design, evaluate, and test survey instruments.
Related titles: Online - full text ed.
Published by: U.S. National Center for Health Statistics, Data Dissemination Branch, Centers for Disease Control and Prevention, 3311 Toledo Rd, Rm 5407, Hyattsville, MD 20782. TEL 301-436-8500, 800-232-4636, FAX 301-436-4258, nchsed@cdc.gov.

PUBLIC ADMINISTRATION

see also HOUSING AND URBAN PLANNING ; POLITICAL SCIENCE ; PUBLIC ADMINISTRATION—Computer Applications ; PUBLIC ADMINISTRATION—Municipal Government ; SOCIAL SERVICES AND WELFARE

351 USA ISSN 0896-3134
E740
A D A TODAY; a newsletter for liberal activists. Text in English. 1947. q. USD 20 to non-members (effective 2000). **Document type:** *Newsletter, Government.* **Description:** Political and governmental news and commentary from liberal viewpoint, including congressional voting records and ratings.
Formerly: A D A World (0001-0871)
Related titles: Microform ed.: (from MIM, PQC).
Published by: Americans for Democratic Action, 1625 K St N W, Ste 210, Washington, DC 20006. TEL 202-785-5980, FAX 202-785-5969. Ed., R&P Mike Alpern. Circ: 40,000.

351 DEU ISSN 0941-9225
A K P - ALTERNATIVE KOMMUNALPOLITIK; Fachzeitschrift fuer alternative Kommunalpolitik. Text in German. 1982. bi-m. EUR 52; EUR 9 newsstand/cover (effective 2008). adv. bk.rev. back issues avail. **Document type:** *Journal, Trade.*
Formerly (until 1992): Alternative Kommunalpolitik (0722-5474)
Published by: Alternative Kommunalpolitik, Luisenstr 40, Bielefeld, 33602, Germany. TEL 49-521-177517, FAX 49-521-177568, akp@akp-redaktion.de, http://www.gruene.de/akp-redaktion/index.htm. adv.: B&W page EUR 1,250, color page EUR 1,595; trim 180 x 250. Circ: 4,000 (paid and controlled).

A P A I S: AUSTRALIAN PUBLIC AFFAIRS INFORMATION SERVICE (ONLINE). *see* PUBLIC ADMINISTRATION—Abstracting, Bibliographies, Statistics

351.1 AUT
A P A - JOURNAL. OEFFENTLICHE HAND. Text in German. w. EUR 380 combined subscription for print & online eds. (effective 2003). **Document type:** *Journal, Trade.*
Related titles: Online - full text ed.
Published by: Austria Presse Agentur, Gunoldstr 14, Vienna, W 1190, Austria. TEL 43-1-360600, FAX 43-1-360603099, kundenservice@apa.at, http://www.apa.at.

351.94 AUS ISSN 1835-2480
A P S JOBS. (Australian Public Service) Text in English. w. free (effective 2008). **Document type:** *Government.* **Description:** Offers a gateway to a challenging and rewarding careers in the Australian Public Service.
Former titles: A P S Employment Gazette; Commonwealth of Australia Gazette. Public Service (Online) (1445-3894)
Media: Online - full text.
Published by: Australian Government. Attorney-General's Department, Central Office, 3-5 National Circuit, Barton, ACT 2600, Australia. TEL 61-2-62506666, FAX 61-2-62505900, http://www.ag.gov.au.

A P W A REPORTER. *see* ENGINEERING—Civil Engineering

353.53497 CAN ISSN 1701-5367
E96.5
ABORIGINAL HEAD START ON RESERVE PROGRAM. NATIONAL ANNUAL REPORT. Text in English. 2000. a.
Published by: (Health Canada, Aboriginal Head Start on Reserve Program), Health Canada, First Nations and Inuit Health Branch, 60 Queen St, Suite 1400, Postal Locator 3914A, Ottawa, ON K1A 0K9, Canada. TEL 613-946-8081, 866-509-1769, FAX 613-954-9953, 800-949-2718, http://hc-sc.gc.ca/fnihb-dgspni/fnihb/.

351 AUS ISSN 1443-3117
ABOUT THE HOUSE. Text in English. 1999. 5/yr. free. **Document type:** *Magazine, Government.*
Related titles: Online - full text ed.
Published by: Parliament of Australia, House of Representatives, Parliament House, Canberra, ACT 2600, Australia. TEL 800-139-299, FAX 61-2-62778521, liaison.reps@aph.gov.au.

ABSTRACTS OF PUBLIC ADMINISTRATION, DEVELOPMENT AND ENVIRONMENT. *see* PUBLIC ADMINISTRATION—Abstracting, Bibliographies, Statistics

ABU DHABI. DA'IRAT AT-TAKHTIT. AL-KITAB AL-IHSA'I AS-SANAWI/ ABU DHABI. DEPARTMENT OF PLANNING. STATISTICAL YEARBOOK. *see* PUBLIC ADMINISTRATION—Abstracting, Bibliographies, Statistics

ACADEMY OF BUSINESS AND ECONOMICS. JOURNAL. *see* BUSINESS AND ECONOMICS—International Commerce

351 FRA ISSN 1278-5083
ACCENTS. Text in French. 198?. m. **Document type:** *Consumer.*
Former titles (until 1994): La Lettre du Conseil General Bouches-du-Rhone (1163-2275); (until 1988): Les Nouvelles des Bouches-du-Rhone (0983-8155)
Related titles: Supplement(s): Les Cahiers d'Accents. ISSN 2116-6250. 2011.
Published by: Conseil General des Bouches-du-Rhone, Hotel du Departement, 52, Av de Saint-Just, Marseille Cedex 20, 13256, France. TEL 33-4-13311313, 33-4-13311537.

352.71 CAN ISSN 1486-3103
ACCESS AND PRIVACY DIRECTORY. Text in English. 1988. irreg.
Former titles (until 1998): Access Guide to Government Records and Information (1187-4317); (until 1991): Access Guide (1187-4333)
Published by: Minister of Culture, Heritage and Citizenship, Access & Privacy Services, Government Records Office, Archives of Manitoba, 3-200 Vaughan St, Winnipeg, MB R3C 1T5, Canada. TEL 204-945-3738, 800-617-3588, FAX 204-948-2008, govrecs@gov.mb.ca.

352.53 USA
ACCOUNTING FOR GOVERNMENT CONTRACTS: COST ACCOUNTING STANDARDS. Text in English. 1981. base vol. plus s-a. updates. looseleaf. USD 315 base vol(s). (effective 2008). Supplement avail. **Document type:** *Handbook/Manual/Guide, Trade.* **Description:** Provides detailed analysis for implementing and complying with cost accounting standards for federal government procurement contracts.
Related titles: Online - full text ed.
Published by: Matthew Bender & Co., Inc. (Subsidiary of: LexisNexis North America), 1275 Broadway, Albany, NY 12204. TEL 518-487-3000, 800-424-4200, FAX 518-487-3083, international@bender.com, http://bender.lexisnexis.com. Ed. Lane K Anderson.

352.53 USA
ACCOUNTING FOR GOVERNMENT CONTRACTS: FEDERAL ACQUISITION REGULATION. Text in English. 1985. base vol. plus a. updates. looseleaf. USD 350 base vol(s). (effective 2008). Supplement avail. **Document type:** *Handbook/Manual/Guide, Trade.* **Description:** Covers all aspects of government contract accounting, with particular emphasis on the Federal Acquisition Regulation.
Related titles: CD-ROM ed.; Supplement(s): U.S. Department of Energy Acquisition Regulation.
Published by: (U.S. General Services Administration), Matthew Bender & Co., Inc. (Subsidiary of: LexisNexis North America), 1275 Broadway, Albany, NY 12204. TEL 518-487-3000, 800-424-4200, FAX 518-487-3083, international@bender.com, http://bender.lexisnexis.com. Ed. Lane K Anderson. **Subscr. to:** U.S. Government Printing Office, Superintendent of Documents, PO Box 371954, Pittsburgh, PA 15250. TEL 202-512-1800, FAX 202-512-2250.

ACCOUNTING FOR PUBLIC UTILITIES. *see* BUSINESS AND ECONOMICS—Accounting

352.5 CAN ISSN 1489-3568
CA1P35-111
ACHIEVEMENTS. Variant title: Realisations. Text in English, French. 1997. a. **Description:** Highlights the major achievements of the year and illustrates the support of key government priorities.
Published by: Public Works and Government Services Canada/Travaux Publics et Services Gouvernementaux Canada, Place du Portage, Phase III, 11 Laurier St, Gatineau, PQ K1A 0S5, Canada. Questions@pwgsc.gc.ca, http://www.pwgsc.gc.ca/text/home-e.html. **Subscr. to:** Canadian Government Publishing Centre, Publishing and Depository Services, Public Works and Government Services Canada, Ottawa, ON K1A 0S5, Canada. TEL 613-941-5995, 800-635-7943, FAX 613-954-5779, 800-565-7757, publications@pwgsc.gc.ca, http://publications.gc.ca.

352 COL ISSN 2027-2677
ACOMPANAMIENTO Y FORTALECIMIENTO DE LAS JUSTAS DE ACCION COMUNAL JAC Y DE LAS JUNTAS ADMINISTRADORAS LOCALES JAL. Text in Spanish. 2008. m. **Document type:** *Magazine, Consumer.*
Published by: Escuela Superior de Administracion Publica, Centro de Investigaciones en Administracion Publica, Diagonal 40, 46-A-37, Bogota, CUND, Colombia. TEL 57-1-2202790.

328 284 USA
ACT AND INFORM. Text in English. bi-m. **Document type:** *Newsletter.* **Description:** Publishes legislative updates on national policy proposals.
Published by: Church Women United, 475 Riverside Dr, Rm 500, New York, NY 10115. TEL 212-870-2347, 800-298-5551, FAX 212-870-2338, cwu@churchwomen.org, http://www.churchwomen.org.

351 340 POL ISSN 0137-1134
K16
ACTA UNIVERSITATIS WRATISLAVIENSIS. PRZEGLAD PRAWA I ADMINISTRACJI. Text in English, German, Polish; Summaries in English, French, German, Polish. 1972. irreg., latest vol.82, 2010. price varies. **Document type:** *Monographic series, Academic/Scholarly.*
Indexed: RASB.
Published by: (Uniwersytet Wroclawski), Wydawnictwo Uniwersytetu Wroclawskiego Sp. z o.o., pl Uniwersytecki 15, Wroclaw, 50137, Poland. TEL 48-71-3752809, FAX 48-71-3752735, marketing@wuwr.com.pl, http://www.wuwr.com.pl. Ed. Mariusz Jablonski. Circ: 250.

351 FIN ISSN 1235-7863
ACTA WASAENSIA. ADMINISTRATIVE SCIENCE/ACTA WASAENSIA. HALLINTOTIEDE. Text in English, Finnish. 1984. irreg., latest vol.9, 2004. price varies. back issues avail. **Document type:** *Monographic series, Academic/Scholarly.*
Related titles: ◆ Series of: Acta Wasaensia. ISSN 0355-2667.
Published by: Vaasan Yliopisto/University of Vaasa, PO Box 700, Vaasa, 65101, Finland. TEL 358-6-3248111, FAX 358-6-3248187, http://lipas.uwasa.fi/.

ACTION ON POVERTY TODAY. *see* SOCIAL SERVICES AND WELFARE

351 BEL ISSN 1783-6077
ACTION PUBLIQUE/PUBLIC ACTION. Text in French, English. 2007. irreg., latest vol.5, 2009. price varies. **Document type:** *Monographic series, Academic/Scholarly.*
Published by: P I E - Peter Lang SA, 1 avenue Maurice, 6e etage, Brussels, 1050, Belgium. TEL 32-2-3477236, FAX 32-2-3477237, pie@peterlang.com, http://www.peterlang.net. Eds. Jean-Louis Genard, Steve Jacob.

351 AUS ISSN 0727-6311
KU13
ACTS OF THE PARLIAMENT OF THE COMMONWEALTH OF AUSTRALIA. Text in English. 1901. irreg. **Document type:** *Government.*
Indexed: P30.
Published by: Australia. Department of Finance and Administration, John Gorton Bldg, King Edward Terrace, Parkes, ACT 2600, Australia. TEL 61-2-62153657, 61-2-62152222, http://www.finance.gov.au.

351 FRA ISSN 2107-0075
▼ **L'ACTU' DE LA BRIE DES TEMPLIERS.** Text in French. 2009. s-a. **Document type:** *Newsletter, Government.*
Published by: Communaute de Communes de la Brie des Templiers, 2, Place de l'Ile de France, Coulommiers, 77120, France. TEL 33-1-64753090, FAX 33-1-64200067, http: www.cc-briedestempliers.fr.

351 ARG ISSN 0325-724X
ACTUALIDAD ADMINISTRATIVA. Text in Spanish. 1977. q. **Document type:** *Journal, Academic/Scholarly.*
Published by: Universidad Nacional de Salta, Escuela de Administracion Publica, Av Buenos Aires 177, Salta, 4400, Argentina. http://www.unsa.edu.ar.

351 ESP ISSN 1887-0287
ADMINISTRACION & CIUDADANIA (GALLEGAN EDITION). Text in Gallegan. 1992. 3/yr. EUR 72 to individuals; EUR 108 to institutions (effective 2009). back issues avail. **Document type:** *Journal, Academic/Scholarly.*
Supersedes in part (in 2005): Regap (1132-8371); Which was formed by the 1992 merger of: Regap (Spanish Edition) (1131-7191); Regap (Gallegan Edition) (1131-7183)
Related titles: Online - full text ed.: ISSN 1887-5289. 2006.
Published by: Escola Galega de Administracion Publica, Poligono de Fontinas, Rua de Madrid, 2-4, Santiago de Compostela, Coruna 15707, Spain. TEL 34-81-546040, FAX 34-81-546347, egap@xunta.es.

351 ESP ISSN 1887-0279
JA26
ADMINISTRACION & CIUDADANIA (SPANISH EDITION). Text in Spanish, Gallegan. 1992. 3/yr.
Supersedes in part (in 2005): Regap (1132-8371); Which was formed by the 1992 merger of: Regap (Spanish Edition) (1131-7191); Regap (Gallegan Edition) (1131-7183)
Related titles: Online - full text ed.: ISSN 1887-5270. 2006.
Published by: Escola Galega de Administracion Publica, Poligono de Fontinas, Rua de Madrid, 2-4, Santiago de Compostela, Coruna 15707, Spain. TEL 34-81-546040, FAX 34-81-546347, egap@xunta.es.

351 ARG
ADMINISTRACION PUBLICA Y SOCIEDAD. Text in Spanish. q. **Document type:** *Academic/Scholarly.*
Published by: Universidad Nacional de Cordoba, Instituto de Investigacion y Formacion en Administracion Publica, Casilla de Correo 1088, Cordoba, 5000, Argentina. TEL 54-51-433-4084, FAX 54-51-433-4089, iifap@eco.uncor.edu. Ed. Diana Cernotto.

351 338 COL ISSN 0120-3754
JA5
ADMINISTRACION Y DESARROLLO. Text in Spanish. 1962. s-a. COP 4,000. adv. bk.rev. bibl.; charts; stat. **Document type:** *Academic/Scholarly.*
Indexed: C01, FR.
Published by: Escuela Superior de Administracion Publica, Centro de Investigaciones en Administracion Publica, Diagonal 40, 46-A-37, Bogota, CUND, Colombia. TEL 57-1-2224700, FAX 57-1-2224356. Ed. Julio Roballo Lozano. Circ: 2,000.

ADMINISTRATIE SI MANAGEMENT PUBLIC/ADMINISTRATION AND PUBLIC MANAGEMENT REVIEW. *see* BUSINESS AND ECONOMICS—Management

351 FRA ISSN 0223-5439
ADMINISTRATION; revue d'etude et d'information. Text in French. 1946. q. **Document type:** *Journal, Government.*
Former titles (until 1961): Ministere de l'Interieur. Association du Corps Prefectoral et des Administrateurs Civils. Bulletin d'information (0765-829X); (until 1950): Ministere de l'Interieur. Association du Corps Prefectoral et des Administrateurs Civils (0765-8281); (until 1947): Ministere de l'Interieur. Association des Fonctionnaires (0765-8273)
Indexed: A22, FR, I13, IBSS, SPAA.
—BLDSC (0681.952000), IE, Ingenta.
Published by: Association du Corps Prefectoral et des Hauts Fonctionnaires du Ministere de l'Interieur, 1 bis place des Saussaies, Paris, 75008, France. TEL 33-1-49273019, FAX 33-1-40076820, acphfmi@interieur.gouv.fr, http://www.acphfmi.interieur.gouv.fr.

351 IRL ISSN 0001-8325
ADMINISTRATION. Text in English. 1953. q. EUR 68 (effective 2003). adv. bk.rev. charts. index. **Document type:** *Journal, Trade.* **Description:** Covers all aspects of public affairs.
Indexed: ABCPolSci, CA, DIP, Emerald, FR, I13, IBR, IBSS, IBZ, P06, P42, PADDI, PAIS, PCI, PSA, S02, S03, SPAA, SSA, SocioIAb, T02.
—BLDSC (0681.950000), IE, Ingenta.
Published by: Institute of Public Administration, 57-61 Lansdowne Rd., Ballsbridge, Dublin, 4, Ireland. TEL 353-1-6686233, FAX 353-1-6689135, http://www.ipa.ie. Ed. Tony McNamara. Adv. contact Eileen Kelly. Circ: 2,500 (paid).

351 USA ISSN 0095-3997
JA3
➤ **ADMINISTRATION & SOCIETY.** Abbreviated title: A A S. Text in English. 1969. 8/yr. USD 1,208, GBP 711 to institutions; USD 1,233, GBP 726 combined subscription to institutions (print & online eds.) (effective 2012). adv. abstr.; bibl.; charts; tr.lit. index. back issues avail.; reprint service avail. from PSC. **Document type:** *Journal, Academic/Scholarly.* **Description:** Brings you the latest research on public and human services organizations, their administrative processes, and their effects on society, as well as reports and theoretical analysis of administrative issues at the federal, state, and local levels as well.
Formerly (until 1974): Journal of Comparative Administration (0021-9932)
Related titles: Microfilm ed.: (from PQC); Online - full text ed.: ISSN 1552-3039. USD 1,110, GBP 653 to institutions (effective 2012).
Indexed: A01, A03, A08, A12, A17, A20, A22, A25, A26, ABCPolSci, ABIn, ASCA, AmH&L, B01, B02, B04, B06, B07, B08, B09, B15, B17, B18, BAS, BPIA, BRD, BusI, CA, CMM, CWI, CurCont, E01, E02, E03, E07, E08, EI, EIA, ERI, EdA, EdI, EnerInd, FamI, G04, G06, G07, G08, H04, I05, I13, IBSS, MEA&I, ManagCont, P02, P03, P04, P06, P30, P34, P42, P48, P51, P53, P54, PAA&I, PAIS, PCI, PQC, PRA, PSA, PersLit, PsycInfo, PsycholAb, RASB, RefZh, S02, S03, S08, S09, S21, SCOPUS, SOPODA, SPAA, SSA, SSAI, SSAb, SSCI, SSI, SUSA, SocioIAb, T&II, T02, V02, W03, W07.
—BLDSC (0681.957000), IE, Infotrieve, Ingenta. **CCC.**
Published by: Sage Publications, Inc., 2455 Teller Rd, Thousand Oaks, CA 91320. TEL 800-818-7243, FAX 800-583-2665, info@sagepub.com, http://www.sagepub.com. Ed. Gary L Wamsley. **Subscr. overseas to:** Sage Publications Ltd., 1 Oliver's Yard, 55 City Rd, London EC1Y 1SP, United Kingdom. TEL 44-207-3248701, FAX 44-207-3248733, subscription@sagepub.co.uk.

➤ **ADMINISTRATION DES DIRECTIONS REGIONALES DE L'INDUSTRIE, DE LA RECHERCHE ET DE L'ENVIRONNEMENT. ANNUAIRE.** *see* ENERGY

351 649 USA ISSN 1942-4957
ADMINISTRATION ON CHILDREN, YOUTH AND FAMILIES. FAMILY AND YOUTH SERVICES BUREAU. REPORT TO CONGRESS ON THE YOUTH PROGRAMS OF THE FAMILY AND YOUTH SERVICES BUREAU FOR FISCAL YEARS (YEAR). Text in English. biennial. **Document type:** *Government.*
Related titles: Online - full content ed.
Published by: Administration on Children, Youth and Families, Family and Youth Services Bureau (Subsidiary of: U.S. Department of Health and Human Services, Administration for Children and Families), National Clearinghouse on Families & Youth, PO Box 13505, Silver Spring, MD 20911-3050. TEL 301-608-8098, info@ncfy.com, http://ncfy.acf.hhs.gov/.

351 BEL ISSN 0771-4084
KJK2711.3
ADMINISTRATION PUBLIQUE. Text in French. 1976. q. EUR 150 (effective 2004). bk.rev. **Document type:** *Journal, Trade.* **Description:** Reviews laws and cases in public administration.
Formerly: Recueil de Jurisprudence du Droit Administratif et du Conseil d'Etat
Indexed: A22, ELLIS, FR, IBSS.
—IE.
Published by: Bruylant, Rue de la Regence 67, Bruxelles, 1000, Belgium. TEL 32-2-512-9845, FAX 32-2-511-7202.

351.71447 CAN ISSN 1481-4420
ADMINISTRATION PUBLIQUE AU QUEBEC. Text in English. biennial. CAD 39.95 (effective 2001). **Document type:** *Directory.* **Description:** Contains listings of provincial and national government offices in Quebec.
Formerly: Pouvoirs Publics au Quebec (1183-482X)
Published by: Quebec dans le Monde, C P 8503, Sainte Foy, PQ G1V 4N5, Canada. TEL 418-659-5540, FAX 418-659-4143.

351.5492 BGD
ADMINISTRATIVE AFFAIRS IN BANGLADESH. Text in Bengali. 1979. a. USD 5.
Published by: (Center for Administrative Studies), University of Dhaka, Ramna, Dhaka, 1000, Bangladesh.

352.63 USA
ADMINISTRATIVE ASSISTANTS ASSOCIATION OF THE U.S. HOUSE OF REPRESENTATIVES. NEWSLETTER. Text in English. q. **Document type:** *Newsletter.*
Published by: Administrative Assistants Association of the U.S. House of Representatives, 225 Cannon, Washington, DC 20515. TEL 202-225-3831.

351 IND ISSN 0302-2986
JA26
ADMINISTRATIVE CHANGE. Text in English. 1973. 2/yr. **Document type:** *Journal, Academic/Scholarly.*
Indexed: I13, SPAA.
Published by: University of Rajasthan, JLN Marg, Jaipur, Rajasthan 302 055, India. TEL 91-141-2711070, info@uniraj.ernet.in, http://www.uniraj.ac.in/.

351 371.2 362 USA
▼ ➤ **ADMINISTRATIVE ISSUES JOURNAL: EDUCATION, PRACTICE, AND RESEARCH.** Text in English. forthcoming 2011 (Feb.). s-a. free. abstr.; stat.; bibl.; charts; illus. Index. back issues avail. **Document type:** *Journal, Academic/Scholarly.* **Description:** Covers multidisciplinary issues in administration, containing articles in: business administration, health care administration, education administration, nursing administration and public administration.
Published by: Southwestern Oklahoma State University, 100 Campus Dr., Weatherford, OK 73096. TEL 580-774-7175. Ed. Tami Moser. Pub. Marci Grant. R&P Trisha Wald.

P

351 USA ISSN 0001-8392
HD28 CODEN: ASCQAG
➤ **ADMINISTRATIVE SCIENCE QUARTERLY.** Abbreviated title: A S Q. Text in English. 1956. q. USD 80 domestic to individuals; USD 96 foreign to individuals; USD 230 domestic to institutions; USD 246 foreign to institutions; USD 38 domestic to students; USD 54 foreign to students; free to members (effective 2009). adv. bk.rev. charts; illus. cum.index: 1956-1985. back issues avail.; reprints avail. **Document type:** *Journal, Academic/Scholarly.* **Description:** Publishes the best theoretical and empirical papers based on dissertations and on the evolving and new work of more established scholars, as well as interdisciplinary work in organizational theory, and informative book reviews.
Related titles: Microform ed.: (from PQC); Online - full text ed.: ISSN 1930-3815. USD 75 to individuals; USD 220 to institutions (effective 2009).
Indexed: A12, A13, A14, A17, A20, A22, A23, A25, A26, ABCPolSci, ABIn, ASCA, AmH&L, B01, B02, B04, B06, B07, B08, B09, B13, B15, B16, B17, B18, BAS, BPI, BPIA, BRD, BusI, C12, CA, CPM, CurCont, DIP, E-psyche, E02, E03, E07, E08, E10, EAA, EI, ERI, EdA, EdI, Emerald, FR, FamI, G04, G06, G07, G08, H01, H09, HRA, I05, I13, IBR, IBSS, IBZ, KES, M&MA, MCR, MEA&I, ManagCont, N06, ORMS, P02, P03, P06, P10, P13, P21, P25, P27, P30, P34, P42, P45, P48, P51, P53, P54, PAA&I, PAIS, PCI, PMA, PQC, PRA, PSA, PersLit, PsycInfo, PsycholAb, QC&AS, RASB, S02, S03, S05, S08, S09, S11, SCIMP, SCOPUS, SOPODA, SPAA, SSA, SSAI, SSAb, SSCI, SSI, SWR&A, SociolAb, T02, W01, W02, W03, W05, W07.
—BLDSC (0696.517000), IE, Infotrieve, Ingenta. **CCC.**
Published by: Cornell University, Johnson Graduate School of Management, 130 E Seneca St, Ste 400, Ithaca, NY 14850. TEL 607 254-7143, FAX 607 254-7100, helpdesk@johnson.cornell.edu. Ed. Hayagreeva Rao. Adv. contact Sally A Iacovelli. page USD 500; 5.5 x 8.75. **Subscr.to:** Allen Press Inc., PO Box 1897, Lawrence, KS 66044. TEL 785-843-1235, FAX 785-843-1274.

350 USA ISSN 1084-1806
JA1
➤ **ADMINISTRATIVE THEORY & PRAXIS**; a quarterly journal of dialogue in public administration theory. Abbreviated title: A T P. Text in English. 1978. q. USD 378 combined subscription domestic to institutions (print & online eds.); USD 414 combined subscription foreign to institutions (print & online eds.) (effective 2012). back issues avail.; reprint service avail. from PSC. **Document type:** *Journal, Academic/Scholarly.* **Description:** Features articles that critically examine the emerging and enduring topics in public administration theory.
Formerly (until 1993): Dialogue (2154-2945)
Related titles: Online - full text ed.: ISSN 1949-0461. USD 328 to institutions (effective 2012).
Indexed: A01, A03, A08, A12, A13, A17, ABIn, B01, B06, B07, B09, CA, P10, P34, P42, P45, P48, P51, P53, P54, PQC, PRA, PSA, S02, S03, SPAA, SociolAb, T02.
—BLDSC (0696.528000), IE, Ingenta.
Published by: M.E. Sharpe, Inc., 80 Business Park Dr, Armonk, NY 10504. TEL 914-273-1800, 800-541-6563, FAX 914-273-2106, custserv@mesharpe.com. Ed. Thomas J Catlaw.

➤ **ADVIES OVER HET MACROBUDGET HUISHOUDELIJKE WMO-HULP (YEAR).** *see* BUSINESS AND ECONOMICS—Accounting

➤ **ADVOCATE (VIRGINIA).** *see* GERONTOLOGY AND GERIATRICS

351.7 658 NLD ISSN 1871-6830
AEDES CORPORATIE INFORMATIE. ONDERNEMEN. Variant title: Corporatieinformatie. Text in Dutch. 2003. irreg. (up to 40/yr.). EUR 355.40 to non-members; EUR 335.40 to members (effective 2008).
Published by: Aedes Vereniging van Woningcorporaties, Postbus 611, Hilversum, 1200 AP, Netherlands. TEL 31-35-6268200, FAX 31-35-6268211, publicaties@aedes.nl, http://www.aedesnet.nl.

351.7 331 NLD ISSN 1871-6849
AEDES CORPORATIE INFORMATIE. WERKEN. Text in Dutch. 1998. irreg. (up to 40/yr.). EUR 355.40 to non-members; EUR 335.40 to members (effective 2008).
Published by: Aedes Vereniging van Woningcorporaties, Postbus 611, Hilversum, 1200 AP, Netherlands. TEL 31-35-6268200, FAX 31-35-6268211, publicaties@aedes.nl, http://www.aedesnet.nl.

351.7 330 NLD ISSN 1871-6814
AEDES CORPORATIE INFORMATIE. WONEN. Text in Dutch. 1998. irreg. (up to 40/yr.). EUR 355.40 to non-members; EUR 335.40 to members (effective 2008).
Published by: Aedes Vereniging van Woningcorporaties, Postbus 611, Hilversum, 1200 AP, Netherlands. TEL 31-35-6268200, FAX 31-35-6268211, publicaties@aedes.nl, http://www.aedesnet.nl.

351.6 MAR ISSN 0007-9588
JQ1871.A1
AFRICAN ADMINISTRATIVE STUDIES. Text in English. 1966. s-a. USD 40 (effective 2000). **Document type:** *Bulletin, Academic/Scholarly.*
Related titles: ◆ French ed.: Cahiers Africains d'Administration Publique; English ed.; Arabic ed.; French ed.
Indexed: ASD, CCA, FR, I13, IBSS, MEA&I, P06, P30, PAIS.
Published by: Centre Africain de Formation et de Recherche Administratives pour le Developpement/African Training and Research Centre in Administration for Development, B P 310, Tangier, 90001, Morocco. TEL 212-9-307269, FAX 212-9-325785, 212-9-322707. Ed. Lizette Michael.

AFRICAN SECURITY REVIEW; a working paper series. *see* MILITARY

351 BOL ISSN 1609-6940
AGENCIA BOLIVIANA DE INFORMACION. Text in Spanish. 1995. d. back issues avail.
Media: Online - full text.
Published by: Ministerio de la Presidencia, Unidad de Comunicacion, Ave. Camacho No. 1485, La Paz, Bolivia. TEL 591-2-2200402, FAX 591-2-2200383, mig@comunica.gov.bo.

351 ARG ISSN 1666-7166
AGENDA IMPOSITIVA, LABORAL, PREVISIONAL Y SOCIETARIA. Text in Spanish. 2002. m. ARS 120 (effective 2006). **Document type:** *Magazine, Trade.*
Published by: La Ley, S.A., Tucuman 1471, Buenos Aires, 1050, Argentina. TEL 54-11-43784838, FAX 54-11-43720953, atencionalcliente@laley.com.ar, http://www.laley.com.ar/. Ed. Alejandro Lopez.

351 CHL ISSN 0718-123X
AGENDA PUBLICA; reflexion y analisis sobre gobierno y asuntos publicos. Text in Spanish. 2002. irreg. back issues avail. **Document type:** *Journal, Academic/Scholarly.*
Media: Online - full text.
Published by: Universidad de Chile, Instituto de Asuntos Publicos, Santa Lucia 240, Santiago, Chile. TEL 56-2-9771502, FAX 56-2-6648536, inap@uchile.cl, http://www.inap.uchile.cl/. Ed. Daniel Grimaldi Toro.

351.761 USA ISSN 0892-9084
HA221
ALABAMA COUNTY DATA BOOK. Text in English. 1976. a. free. charts; stat. **Document type:** *Government.*
Related titles: Microfiche ed.: (from CIS).
Indexed: SRI.
Published by: Department of Economic and Community Affairs, PO Box 5690, Montgomery, AL 36103-5690. TEL 205-242-5493, FAX 205-242-0776. Ed., R&P Parker Collins. Circ: 3,500.

351.761 USA ISSN 1072-7620
HA221
ALABAMA MUNICIPAL DATA BOOK. Text in English. every 5 yrs. free. **Document type:** *Government.*
Published by: Department of Economic and Community Affairs, PO Box 5690, Montgomery, AL 36103-5690. TEL 205-242-5493, FAX 205-242-0776. R&P Parker Collins.

ALASKA LEGISLATIVE DIGEST. *see* POLITICAL SCIENCE

ALASKA. LEGISLATURE. BUDGET AND AUDIT COMMITTEE. ANNUAL REPORT. *see* POLITICAL SCIENCE

ALBERTA. ALBERTA INFRASTRUCTURE AND TRANSPORTATION. ANNUAL REPORT. *see* TRANSPORTATION

352.74 CAN ISSN 1497-0732
ALBERTA. ALBERTA INNOVATION AND SCIENCE. ANNUAL REPORT. Text in English. 1998. a.
Formerly (until 2000): Alberta. Ministry of Science, Research and Information Technology. Annual Report (1481-3793)
Published by: Alberta Innovation and Science, 10365 97 St, 9th Fl, Edmonton, AB T5J 3W7, Canada. TEL 780-427-0285, FAX 780-415-9824, is.inq@gov.ab.ca.

ALBERTA ENVIRONMENT. ANNUAL REPORT. *see* ENVIRONMENTAL STUDIES

ALBERTA FINANCE MINISTRY. QUARTER FISCAL UPDATE. *see* BUSINESS AND ECONOMICS—Banking And Finance

353.37 CAN ISSN 1492-9635
HV6722.C23
ALBERTA GAMING. ANNUAL REPORT. Text in English. 2000. a.
Published by: Alberta Gaming, 50 Corriveau Ave, Saint Albert, AB T8N 3T5, Canada. TEL 780-447-8600.

354.3 CAN ISSN 1703-8634
HD9502.C33
ALBERTA. MINISTRY OF SUSTAINABLE RESOURCE DEVELOPMENT. ANNUAL REPORT. Text in English. 1996. a. **Document type:** *Government.*
Supersedes in part (in 2002): Alberta. Alberta Resource Development. Annual Report (1492-871X); Which was formerly (until 2000): Alberta. Ministry of Energy. Annual Report (1482-5899); Which was formed by the 1996 merger of: Public Utilities Board Alberta. Annual Report (0383-3690); (1986-1996): Alberta. Alberta Energy. Annual Report (0832-6878); Which superseded in part (in 1986): Alberta Energy and Natural Resources. Annual Report (0700-2645); Which was formed by the merger of part of (1973-1975): Alberta Lands and Forests. Annual Report (0383-4204); Which was formerly (until 1972): Department of Lands and Forests of the Province of Alberta. Annual Report (0401-2577); (1972-1975): Alberta Mines and Minerals. Annual Report (0383-4190); Which was formerly (until 1971): Department of Mines and Minerals of the Province of Alberta. Annual Report (0401-2585); Both Department of Lands and Forests of the Province of Alberta. Annual Report & Department of Mines and Minerals of the Province of Alberta. Annual Report superseded (1939-1949): Department of Lands and Mines of the Province of Alberta. Annual Report (0383-4182)
Indexed: GeoRef.
—Linda Hall.
Published by: Alberta. Ministry of Sustainable Resource Development, Information Centre, 9920 108 St, Main Flr, Edmonton, AB T5K 2M4, Canada. TEL 780-944-0313, FAX 780-427-4407, http://www3.gov.ab.ca/srd/.

ALBERTA SENIOR ANNUAL REPORT. *see* GERONTOLOGY AND GERIATRICS

ALCOHOLIC BEVERAGE CONTROL - STATE CAPITALS. *see* LAW

ALGEMENE WET BESTUURSRECHT EN AANVERWANTE REGELGEVING. *see* LAW

ALLIANCE (ENGLISH EDITION). *see* LABOR UNIONS

351 NLD ISSN 1877-7198
ALLROUND BLAUW. Text in Dutch. 2008. bi-m. EUR 19.95; EUR 4.95 newsstand/cover (effective 2011). adv. **Document type:** *Magazine, Trade.*
Published by: Ter Hoeve Uitgevers, Postbus 154, Velp, 6880 AD, Netherlands. TEL 31-26-3615959, FAX 31-26-3882312, info@terhoeveuitgevers.nl, http://www.terhoeveuitgevers.nl. Eds. Gerda Preusting, Foeke Wagenaar.

351 BLZ
AMANDALA. Text in English. 1970. w. BZD 85 domestic weeken's edition; USD 85 foreign weeken's edition; BZD 60 domestic mid-week's edition; USD 60 foreign mid-week's edition (effective 2005). adv. back issues avail. **Document type:** *Newspaper, Consumer.* **Description:** Community service publication.
Related titles: Online - full text ed.: ISSN 1563-8049.
Published by: Amandala Press, 3304 Partridge St, PO Box 15, Belize City, Belize. TEL 501-202-4476, FAX 501-222-4702, editor@amandala.com.bz. Ed. Russell Vellos. Pub., R&P Evan X Hyde TEL 501-2-24472. Adv. contact Jacinta Hyde Garnett. B&W page USD 540. Circ: 10,000.

▼ **AMERICAN ECONOMIC JOURNAL: ECONOMIC POLICY.** *see* BUSINESS AND ECONOMICS

351.73 USA ISSN 0275-0740
JK1
➤ **AMERICAN REVIEW OF PUBLIC ADMINISTRATION.** Abbreviated title: A R P A. Text in English. 1967. bi-m. USD 899, GBP 529 to institutions; USD 917, GBP 540 combined subscription to institutions (print & online eds.) (effective 2012). adv. bk.rev. bibl. back issues avail.; reprint service avail. from PSC. **Document type:** *Journal, Academic/Scholarly.* **Description:** Includes theory-based empirical research, commentaries on pressing issues, reviews or syntheses of research and conceptual-theoretical discussions on or over the boundaries of traditional public administration.
Formerly (until 1981): Midwest Review of Public Administration (0026-346X)
Related titles: Microform ed.: (from PQC); Online - full text ed.: ISSN 1552-3357. USD 825, GBP 486 to institutions (effective 2012).
Indexed: A12, A13, A17, A20, A22, A26, A28, ABCPolSci, ABIn, APA, ASCA, B01, B02, B06, B07, B08, B09, B11, B15, B17, B18, BPIA, BrCerAb, BusI, C&ISA, CA, CA/WCA, CIA, CLI, CerAb, CivEngAb, CorrAb, CurCont, DIP, E&CAJ, E01, E08, E11, EEA, EMA, ESPM, EnvEAb, FamI, G04, G06, G07, G08, H04, H15, I05, I13, IBR, IBZ, LRI, M&TEA, M09, MBF, METADEX, ManagCont, P03, P34, P42, P48, P51, P53, P54, PAA&I, PAIS, PCI, PQC, PSA, PSI, PersLit, PsycInfo, RiskAb, S02, S03, S09, SCOPUS, SPAA, SSCI, SociolAb, SolStAb, T&II, T02, T04, V02, W07, WAA.
—BLDSC (0853.800000), IE, Infotrieve, Ingenta, Linda Hall. **CCC.**
Published by: (Georgia State University, School of Public Administration and Urban Studies), Sage Publications, Inc., 2455 Teller Rd, Thousand Oaks, CA 91320. TEL 800-818-7243, FAX 800-583-2665, info@sagepub.com, http://www.sagepub.com. Eds. Andrew Glassberg, Guy Adams, John Clayton Thomas. **Subscr. outside the Americas to:** Sage Publications Ltd., 1 Oliver's Yard, 55 City Rd, London EC1Y 1SP, United Kingdom. TEL 44-20-73248701, FAX 44-20-73248733, subscription@sagepub.co.uk. **Co-sponsors:** University of Missouri at Columbia; University of Missouri, St. Louis.

351 USA
AMERICAN SOCIETY FOR PUBLIC ADMINISTRATION. SECTION ON INTERNATIONAL AND COMPARATIVE ADMINISTRATION. OCCASIONAL PAPERS. Text in English. 1974. irreg., latest 1992. USD 3 per issue. back issues avail.; reprints avail.
Published by: (Section on International and Comparative Administration), American Society for Public Administration, 1301 Pennsylvania Ave NW, Ste 840, Washington, DC 20004. TEL 202-393-7878. Ed. Richard Ryan. Circ: 550.

328.12 USA ISSN 1084-5437
JK2495
AMERICAN SOCIETY OF LEGISLATIVE CLERKS AND SECRETARIES. JOURNAL. Text in English. 1995. s-a. **Document type:** *Journal, Trade.*
—CCC.
Published by: American Society of Legislative Clerks and Secretaries, 7700 E First Place, Denver, CO 80230. TEL 303-856-1485, FAX 303-364-7800, natalie.odonnell@ncsl.org, http://www.ncsl.org/programs/legismgt/aslcs/cshome.htm.

AMERICAN VETERAN. *see* MILITARY

351.561 TUR ISSN 1300-1795
AMME IDARESI DERGISI/JOURNAL OF PUBLIC ADMINISTRATION. Text in Turkish. 1968. q. **Document type:** *Journal, Academic/Scholarly.*
Indexed: SSCI, W07.
Published by: Turkiye ve Orta Dogu Amme Idaresi Enstitusu, TODAIE 85, Cad No: 8, Yucetepe, Ankara, 06100, Turkey. TEL 90-312-2317360, FAX 90-312-2313881, todaie@todaie.gov.tr.

351 ITA ISSN 0044-8141
AMMINISTRARE. Text in Italian. 1986. 3/yr. EUR 132.50 combined subscription domestic to institutions (print & online eds.); EUR 178.50 combined subscription foreign to institutions (print & online eds.) (effective 2009). adv. index. back issues avail. **Document type:** *Journal, Academic/Scholarly.*
Related titles: Online - full text ed.
Indexed: DoGi, FR, I13, IBR, IBZ.
Published by: (Istituto per la Scienza dell' Amministrazione Pubblica (I S A P)), Societa Editrice Il Mulino, Strada Maggiore 37, Bologna, 40125, Italy. TEL 39-051-256011, FAX 39-051-256034, riviste@mulino.it. Ed. Ettore Rotelli. Circ: 1,200.

351 ITA ISSN 1122-0635
JS7.I8
AMMINISTRAZIONE CIVILE. Text in Italian. 1993. bi-m. EUR 76 (effective 2008). **Document type:** *Magazine, Trade.* **Description:** The four divisions Dottrina, Casistica, Documenti and Informazioni contain writings on the events concerning public administration at both the local and national level, including conference and publication announcements.
Indexed: DoGi.
Published by: (Ministero dell'Interno), Maggioli Editore, Via del Carpino 8/10, Santarcangelo di Romagna, RN 47822, Italy. TEL 39-0541-628111, FAX 39-0541-622020, editore@maggioli.it, http://www.maggioli.it.

351.45 ITA ISSN 0303-9722
L'AMMINISTRAZIONE ITALIANA. Text in Italian. 1945. m. EUR 180 domestic; EUR 250 foreign (effective 2009). adv. bk.rev. index. **Document type:** *Journal, Trade.* **Description:** Covers local and national Italian administration.
Indexed: DoGi.
Published by: Societa Tipografica Barbieri Noccioli & C., Casella Postale, 759, Empoli, FI 50053, Italy. Circ: 3,000.

351 NLD ISSN 1871-2606
AMPERSAND. Text in Dutch. 1999. irreg.
Formerly (until 2004): Beleidsberichten (1389-6857)
Published by: B&A Groep, Postbus 829, The Hague, 2501 CV, Netherlands. TEL 31-70-3029500, FAX 31-70-3029501, info@bagroep.nl.

351 CHE ISSN 0003-2115
AMTLICHER ANZEIGER. Text in German. 1968. w. adv. bk.rev.
Published by: H. Akerets Erben AG, Postfach, Duebendorf, 8600, Switzerland. Circ: 12,100.

351 DEU
AMTSBLATT DER REGIERUNG VON UNTERFRANKEN. Text in German. 1956. m. EUR 23; EUR 2 newsstand/cover (effective 2006). bk.rev. **Document type:** *Government.*

Published by: Regierung von Unterfranken, Peterplatz 9, Wuerzburg, 97070, Germany. TEL 49-931-38000, FAX 49-931-3802222, buecherei@reg-ufr.bayern.de, http://www.regierung.unterfranken.bayern.de. Circ: 600.

351 DEU ISSN 0934-8964
AMTSBLATT DER STADT MOENCHENGLADBACH. Text in German. 1975. 2/m. EUR 20.45 (effective 2006). back issues avail. **Document type:** *Bulletin, Government.*
Published by: Presse- und Informationsamt, Weiherstr 21, Moenchengladbach, 41050, Germany. TEL 49-2161-252565, http://www.moenchengladbach.de. Circ: 1,000 (paid).

351.43 DEU ISSN 0949-2585
AMTSBLATT DES HESSISCHEN KULTUSMINISTERIUMS. Text in German. 1963. m. EUR 32 (effective 2008). adv. **Document type:** *Newsletter, Trade.*
Former titles (until 1995): Amtsblatt des Hessischen Kultusministers und des Hessischen Ministers fuer Wissenschaft und Kunst (0177-669X); (until 1984): Amtsblatt des Hessischen Kultusministers (0930-5726)
Published by: (Hessisches Kultusministerium), A. Bernecker Verlag, Unter dem Schoeneberg 1, Melsungen, 34212, Germany. TEL 49-5661-7310, FAX 49-5661-731111, info@bernecker.de, http://www.bernecke.de. adv.: B&W page EUR 670.

351 DEU
AMTSBLATT DES LANDKREISES DILLINGEN AN DER DONAU. Text in German. bi-m.
Published by: Landkreis Dillingen an der Donau, Grosse Allee 24, Dillingen, 89407, Germany. TEL 09071-51-138.

351 DEU
AMTSBLATT DES LANDKREISES HOF. Text in German. 1972. s-m. **Document type:** *Government.*
Published by: Landratsamt Hof, Schaumbergstr 14, Hof, 95032, Germany. TEL 49-9281-570, FAX 49-9281-58340, poststelle@landkreis-hof.de. Circ: 500.

354.3 ARG ISSN 0302-5705
QH113
ANALES DE PARQUES NACIONALES. Text in Spanish. 1945. irreg., latest vol.17, 1995. ARS 20, USD 20; or exchange basis. illus.; maps. **Document type:** *Monographic series, Government.* **Description:** Contains information on the national parks of the country.
Supersedes (in 1955): Natura (0470-3685)
Published by: Administracion de Parques Nacionales, Avda. Santa Fe 690, Buenos Aires, 1059, Argentina. TEL 54-114-3110303, 54-11-45151361, FAX 54-114-3158412, biblioteca@parquesnacionales.gov.ar. Circ: 4,000.

352 ESP ISSN 1575-5266
ANALISIS LOCAL. Text in Spanish. 1995. bi-m.
Published by: Analistas Financieros Internacionales, Espanoleto, 19, Madrid, 28010, Spain. TEL 34-91-5200100, FAX 34-91-5200121, info@afi.es, http://www.grupoanalistas.com/.

ANALYSES OF SOCIAL ISSUES AND PUBLIC POLICY. *see* SOCIOLOGY

351.73 USA ISSN 0747-5187
HJ9
AN ANALYSIS OF THE PRESIDENT'S BUDGETARY PROPOSALS FOR FISCAL YEAR. Text in English. 1979. a. USD 9 per issue (effective 2004). **Document type:** *Government.*
Published by: U S Congress, Congressional Budget Office, Ford House Bldg, 4th Fl, Second and D Sts, SW, Washington, DC 20515. TEL 202-226-2602, FAX 202-226-2714, webmaster@cbo.gov, http://www.cbo.gov.

ANBUDSJOURNALEN; Sveriges marknadsdatabas foer offentlig upphandling. *see* BUSINESS AND ECONOMICS—Marketing And Purchasing

ANDERSON'S OHIO E P A ON CD-ROM. (Environmental Protection Agency) *see* ENVIRONMENTAL STUDIES—Toxicology And Environmental Safety

351 CHN ISSN 1009-0746
ANHUI ZHENGBAO/JOURNAL OF THE ANHUI. Text in Chinese. 1952. s-a. **Document type:** *Magazine, Government.*
Related titles: Online - full text ed.
Published by: Anhui Sheng Renmin Zhengfu Bangongting/The People's Government of Anhui Province, 221, Changjiang Zhong Lu, Hefei, 230001, China. TEL 86-551-2601224, english@ah.gov.cn.

ANNOTATED BRITISH COLUMBIA RESIDENTIAL TENANCY ACT. *see* HOUSING AND URBAN PLANNING

351.493 BEL ISSN 0066-2461
ANNUAIRE ADMINISTRATIF ET JUDICIAIRE DE BELGIQUE/ ADMINISTRATIEF EN GERECHTELIJK JAARBOEK VOOR BELGIE. Text in Dutch, French. 1869. a., latest 2004. EUR 195 per vol. (effective 2004). **Document type:** *Directory, Trade.*
Published by: Bruylant, Rue de la Regence 67, Bruxelles, 1000, Belgium. TEL 32-2-512-9845, FAX 32-2-511-7202, http://www.bruylant.be. Circ: 7,500.

351 FRA ISSN 0291-4700
ANNUAIRE DES COLLECTIVITES LOCALES. Text in French. 1981. a. price varies. **Document type:** *Directory, Government.*
Indexed: FR, I13, IBSS.
—INIST.
Published by: Centre National de la Recherche Scientifique, 15 Rue Malebranche, Paris, 75005, France. TEL 33-1-53102700, FAX 33-1-53102727.

351.025 FRA ISSN 1770-1813
ANNUAIRE DES SERVICES PUBLICS DES LANDES. Text in French. a. **Document type:** *Directory.*
Former titles (until 2000): Annuaire Administratif des Services Publics des Landes (1255-6092); (until 199?): Annuaire des Services de l'Etat du Departement des Landes (1240-0491)
Published by: Editions O P A S, 41 rue Saint Sebastien, Paris, 75011, France.

351 FRA ISSN 0221-5918
ANNUAIRE EUROPEEN D'ADMINISTRATION PUBLIQUE. Text in French. a. price varies. adv. bk.rev. index. **Document type:** *Directory, Academic/Scholarly.*
Indexed: FR, IBR, IBSS, IBZ.
—INIST.
Published by: (Universite d'Aix-Marseille Iii (Universite de Droit, d'Economie et des Sciences), Centre de Recherches Administratives), Centre National de la Recherche Scientifique, Campus Gerard-Megie, 3 Rue Michel-Ange, Paris, 75794, France. TEL 33-1-44964000, FAX 33-1-44965390, http://www.cnrseditions.fr. Circ: 1,500 (controlled). **Co-sponsor:** Universite d'Aix-Marseille III (Universite de Droit, d'Economie et des Sciences).

351.6721 GAB
ANNUAIRE NATIONAL OFFICIEL DE LA REPUBLIQUE GABONAISE. Text in French. 1973. a. XOF 5,000. adv. illus.; stat. **Document type:** *Government.*
Published by: Agence Havas Gabon, BP 213, Libreville, Gabon. Circ: 5,000.

351 USA
JK1
➤ **ANNUAL EDITIONS: PUBLIC POLICY AND ADMINISTRATION.** Text in English. 1990. a. USD 22.25, GBP 18.99 per issue (effective 2010). illus. **Document type:** *Journal, Academic/Scholarly.* **Description:** Covers such topics as: dealing with government and organizational behavior, public management practices and information systems technology, along with public finance, budgeting and productivity improvement.
Formerly (until 2007): Annual Editions: Public Administration (1052-7532)
Related titles: Online - full text ed.
Published by: McGraw-Hill, Contemporary Learning Series (Subsidiary of: McGraw-Hill Companies, Inc.), 1221 Ave of the Americas, New York, NY 10020. TEL 212-904-2000, FAX 212-512-2000, customer.service@mcgraw-hill.com, http://www.mcgraw-hill.com.

➤ **ANNUAL EDITIONS: STATE & LOCAL GOVERNMENT.** *see* POLITICAL SCIENCE

342.06 USA ISSN 0275-200X
KF5365
ANNUAL REPORT OF THE FEDERAL LABOR RELATIONS AUTHORITY AND THE FEDERAL SERVICE IMPASSES PANEL FOR THE FISCAL PERIOD. Text in English. 1979. a.
Published by: U.S. Federal Labor Relations Authority, 607 Fourteenth St, N W, Washington, DC 20424-0001. http://www.flra.gov/.

ANNUAL REPORT ON THE ADMINISTRATION OF PRISONS IN KENYA. *see* CRIMINOLOGY AND LAW ENFORCEMENT

998 351.93 NZL ISSN 1174-3948
ANTARCTICA NEW ZEALAND. ANNUAL REPORT. Text in English. 1997. a. free (effective 2008). **Document type:** *Report, Trade.* **Description:** Details the work of Antarctica New Zealand, including scientific highlights and environmental initiatives. It also reports on education, media, the artists' program and our international involvement in Antarctic Treaty forums.
Related titles: Online - full text ed.: ISSN 1177-9462.
Published by: Antarctica New Zealand, Private Bag 4745, Christchurch, 8140, New Zealand. TEL 64-3-3580200, FAX 64-3-3580211, info@antarcticanz.govt.nz.

342.06 URY ISSN 0797-0463
KHU3230.A15
ANUARIO DE DERECHO ADMINISTRATIVO. Text in Spanish. 1987. a. price varies.
Published by: Fundacion de Cultura Universitaria, 25 de Mayo 568, Montevideo, 11003, Uruguay. TEL 598-2-9161152, FAX 598-2-9152549.

351 ARG ISSN 0328-5855
JL2001
➤ **APORTES**; para el estado y la administracion gubernamental. Text in Spanish. 1994. q. USD 50; USD 60 in North America; USD 70 in Europe; USD 80 elsewhere. adv. bk.rev. **Document type:** *Academic/Scholarly.* **Description:** Creates a discussion forum for reseachers, professionals and officers interested in government reform processes. Includes a variety of perspectives from different disciplines and ideological points of view, prioritizing quality and originality.
Published by: Asociacion de Administradores Gubernamentales, Sarmiento 517, 6 E, Buenos Aires, 1041, Argentina. TEL 54-114-3945588. Ed. Jorge Iragui. Adv. contact Ana Perez Luzuriaga.

352 COL ISSN 2011-2483
APUNTES DE GOBIERNO. Text in Spanish. 2007. 3/yr.
Published by: Universidad de Antioquia, Escuela de Gobierno y Politicas Publicas de Antioquia, Carrera 44 No. 48-72, Edif. San Ignacio Ofic. 308-309, Antioquia, Colombia. TEL 57-4-2394656, FAX 57-4-2396603, http://www.escuelagobierno.org/.

351.93 027 NZL ISSN 1175-8686
CD2573
ARCHIVES NEW ZEALAND. STATEMENT OF INTENT. Text in English. 1996. a.
Formerly (until 2003): Archives New Zealand. Departmental Forecast Report (1175-5520); Which superseded in part (in 2002): New Zealand. Department of Internal Affairs. Departmental Forecast Report (1173-5015)
Related titles: Online - full text ed.: ISSN 1177-9497. free (effective 2009).
Published by: Archives New Zealand, 10 Mulgrave St, Thorndon, PO Box 12-050, Wellington, New Zealand. TEL 64-4-4995595, FAX 64-4-4956210, enquiries@archives.govt.nz.

328.791 USA ISSN 0744-7477
ARIZONA CAPITOL TIMES. Text in English. 1946. w. (Fri.). USD 51 in state; USD 61 out of state (effective 2005). adv. **Document type:** *Newspaper, Consumer.* **Description:** Covers Arizona political, legislative and state agency news.
Formerly: Arizona Legislative Review
Indexed: A16, ABIn, G08, I05, L03, P48, P51, PQC, R01.
—CIS.
Published by: Arizona News Service, Inc. (Subsidiary of: Dolan Media Co.), 1835 W Adams, Phoenix, AZ 85007. TEL 602-258-7026, FAX 602-253-7636, http://www.aznewsservice.com. Adv. contact Brenda Abraham. Circ: 20,000 (paid).

351 USA ISSN 1557-4601
HC107.A6
ARIZONA'S ECONOMY. Abbreviated title: A R. Text in English. 1952. q. free (effective 2008); free in U.S. charts; illus. **Description:** Provides current analysis of business conditions and forecasts of future economic activity in Arizona.
Former titles (until 1990): Arizona Review (0004-1629); (until 1965): Arizona Review of Business and Public Administration; (until 1959): Arizona Business and Economic Review
Related titles: Online - full text ed.
Indexed: IPARL, P06, PAIS.
Published by: University of Arizona, College of Business and Public Administration, Economic and Business Research Center, Eller College of Management, McClelland Hall, PO Box 210108, Tucson, AZ 85721. TEL 520-621-2165, FAX 520-621-8105, EBRPublications@eller.arizona.edu, http://www.eller.arizona.edu. Circ: 3,200.

351 347 USA ISSN 2154-610X
ARKANSAS GOVERNMENT REGISTER. Text in English. 2000. m. **Document type:** *Government.* **Description:** A compilation of information about official Arkansas state government actions.
Formerly (until 2005): Weil's Arkansas Government Register (1531-2208)
Published by: LexisNexis (Subsidiary of: Reed Elsevier Group plc), 1016 W Ninth Ave, 1st Fl, King of Prussia, PA 19406. TEL 215 564-1788, 800 448-1515, customer.support@lexisnexis.com.

351.767 USA
ARKANSAS STATE DIRECTORY. Text in English. 1973. biennial. USD 10. adv. **Document type:** *Directory.* **Description:** Directory of State of Arkansas government offices plus a section on federal government offices within Arkansas.
Published by: Prestige Press, 4271 E 43rd St, North Little Rock, AR 72117-2536. TEL 501-945-0866, FAX 501-945-5000. Circ: 4,000.

354.75 USA
THE ART OF COMMUNICATION. Text in English. q. free to members (effective 2005). adv. **Document type:** *Newsletter.* **Description:** Aimed at county government officials involved with disseminating public information.
Related titles: Online - full content ed.
Published by: National Association of County Information Officers, c/o Mecklenburg Country Public Service and Information, 600 E Fourth St, Charlotte, NC 28202. TEL 704-336-2597, diehldc@co.mecklenburg.nc.us, http://www.NACIO.org. adv.: page USD 350; 7.5 x 9.75.

351 CAN ISSN 1499-8009
ARTICLE DOCUMENTAIRE. Text in French. irreg. **Document type:** *Monographic series, Academic/Scholarly.*
Related titles: Online - full content ed.; ◆ English ed.: Backgrounder. ISSN 1499-7983.
Published by: C.D. Howe Institute/Institut C.D. Howe, 125 Adelaide St East, Toronto, ON M5C 1L7, Canada. TEL 416-865-1904, FAX 416-865-1866, publicat@cdhowe.org, http://www.cdhowe.org.

351 HKG
ASIAN PACIFIC JOURNAL OF PUBLIC ADMINISTRATION/YA TAI GONG GONG XING ZHENG XUE. Text in English. 1979. a. (s-a. until 2006). HKD 165 domestic; USD 42 in Asia; USD 47 elsewhere (effective 2008). bk.rev. back issues avail. **Document type:** *Journal, Academic/Scholarly.*
Former titles (until 2004): Asian Journal of Public Administration (0259-8272); (until 1983): Hong Kong Journal of Public Administration (0252-9165)
Indexed: BAS, CA, FR, HongKongiana, I13, IBSS, PAA&I, PAIS, PSA, SPAA.
—BLDSC (1742.575000). **CCC.**
Published by: Hong Kong University, Department of Politics and Public Administration, Pokfulam Rd, Hong Kong, Hong Kong. TEL 852-28592393, FAX 852-28583550, http://www.hku.hk/ppaweb/index.htm. Eds. Ian Thynne, John P Burns. Circ: 500. **Co-publisher:** Charles Darwin University, Governance Programme.

351.7 USA ISSN 1095-6468
ASSESSING NEW FEDERALISM; issues and options for states. Text in English. 1997. irreg. back issues avail. **Document type:** *Monographic series, Academic/Scholarly.* **Description:** Consists of articles exploring changing social policies.
Related titles: Online - full text ed.
Published by: Urban Institute, 2100 M St, NW, Washington, DC 20037. TEL 202-833-7200, FAX 202-467-5775, paffairs@ui.urban.org, http://www.urban.org.

354.71 CAN ISSN 0844-7195
CA1FA2
AUDITOR GENERAL OF CANADA. REPORT OF THE AUDITOR GENERAL OF CANADA TO THE HOUSE OF COMMONS. MAIN POINTS. Variant title: Bureau du Verificateur General du Canada. Rapport du Verificateur General du Canada a la Chambre des Communes. Points Saillants. Text in English, French. 1988. a.
Published by: Office of the Auditor General of Canada/Bureau du Verificateur General du Canada, 240 Sparks St, Ottawa, ON K1A 0G6, Canada. TEL 613-952-0213, 888-761-5953, FAX 613-954-0696, communications@oag-bvg.gc.ca, distribution@oag-bvg.gc.ca, http://www.oag-bvg.gc.ca.

354.71 CAN ISSN 0821-8110
HJ9921
AUDITOR GENERAL OF CANADA. REPORT TO THE HOUSE OF COMMONS. Text in English. 1973. a.
Former titles (until 1979): Auditor General of Canada. Annual Report to the House of Commons (0707-3097); (until 1978): Auditor General of Canada. Report to the House of Commons (0317-4875)
Related titles: CD-ROM ed.: ISSN 1200-6866; Online - full text ed.: ISSN 1701-5413.
Published by: Office of the Auditor General of Canada/Bureau du Verificateur General du Canada, 240 Sparks St, Ottawa, ON K1A 0G6, Canada. TEL 613-952-0213, 888-761-5953, FAX 613-954-0696, communications@oag-bvg.gc.ca, distribution@oag-bvg.gc.ca, http://www.oag-bvg.gc.ca.

351 CAN ISSN 1719-6264
AUDITOR GENERAL, REPORT TO THE HOUSE OF ASSEMBLY. (SUMMARY). Text in English. 1997. a., latest 2005. **Document type:** *Government.*
Published by: Newfoundland and Labrador, Office of the Auditor General, PO Box 8700, St. John's, NF A1B 4J6, Canada. TEL 709-729-2700, FAX 709-729-5970, http://www.ag.gov.nl.ca/ag.

351 CAN ISSN 1719-6256
AUDITOR GENERAL. REPORT TO THE HOUSE OF ASSEMBLY ON THE OPERATIONS OF THE OFFICE OF THE AUDITOR GENERAL. Text in English. 2002. a., latest 2005. **Document type:** *Government.*

P

Published by: Newfoundland and Labrador, Office of the Auditor General, PO Box 8700, St. John's, NF A1B 4J6, Canada. TEL 709-729-2700, FAX 709-729-5970, http://www.ag.gov.nl.ca/ag.

351 657 ESP ISSN 1136-517X
HJ60
AUDITORIA PUBLICA. Text in Spanish. 1995. 3/yr. **Document type:** *Journal, Trade.*
Published by: Parlamento de Navarra, Camara de Comptos de Navarra, C/ Ansoleaga 10, Pamplona, 31001, Spain. TEL 34-848-421400, FAX 34-848-421433, http://www.cfnavarra.es/camara.comptos/.

351 DEU ISSN 1867-7002
AUSBILDUNG PRUEFUNG FACHPRAXIS (LANDESTEIL BADEN-WUERTTEMBERG EDITION); Zeitschrift fuer die staatliche und kommunale Verwaltung. Abbreviated title: A P F. Text in German. 1975. m. EUR 129.60; EUR 17 newsstand/cover (effective 2010). adv. **Document type:** *Magazine, Trade.*
Formerly (until 2009): Ausbildung Pruefung Fortbildung (Baden-Wuerttemberg Edition) (1612-3980)
Published by: Richard Boorberg Verlag GmbH und Co. KG, Scharrstr 2, Stuttgart, 70563, Germany. TEL 49-711-73850, FAX 49-711-7385100, mail@boorberg.de. Ed. Susanne Sonntag. Adv. contact Roland Schulz. Circ: 1,560 (paid and controlled).

351 DEU ISSN 1867-7010
AUSBILDUNG PRUEFUNG FACHPRAXIS (LANDESTEIL BAYERN EDITION); Zeitschrift fuer die staatliche und kommunale Verwaltung. Text in German. 1975. m. EUR 129.60; EUR 17 newsstand/cover (effective 2010). adv. **Document type:** *Magazine, Trade.*
Formerly (until 2009): Ausbildung Pruefung Fortbildung (Bayern Edition) (0344-3825)
Indexed: IBR, IBZ.
Published by: Richard Boorberg Verlag GmbH und Co. KG, Scharrstr 2, Stuttgart, 70563, Germany. TEL 49-711-73850, FAX 49-711-7385100, mail@boorberg.de. Ed. Susanne Sonntag. Adv. contact Roland Schulz.

351 DEU ISSN 0946-8870
AUSBILDUNG PRUEFUNG FORTBILDUNG (BERLIN EDITION); Zeitschrift fuer die staatliche und kommunale Verwaltung. Text in German. 199?. m. adv. **Document type:** *Magazine, Trade.*
Indexed: DIP, IBR, IBZ.
Published by: Richard Boorberg Verlag GmbH und Co. KG, Scharrstr 2, Stuttgart, 70563, Germany. TEL 49-711-73850, FAX 49-711-7385100, mail@boorberg.de, http://www.boorberg.de. Ed. Susanne Sonntag. Adv. contact Roland Schulz.

351 DEU ISSN 0944-8438
AUSBILDUNG PRUEFUNG FORTBILDUNG (BRANDENBURG EDITION); Zeitschrift fuer die staatliche und kommunale Verwaltung. Abbreviated title: A P F (Ausgabe Brandenburg). Text in German. 1993. m. adv. **Document type:** *Magazine, Trade.*
Indexed: IBR, IBZ.
Published by: Richard Boorberg Verlag GmbH und Co. KG, Scharrstr 2, Stuttgart, 70563, Germany. TEL 49-711-73850, FAX 49-711-7385100, mail@boorberg.de, http://www.boorberg.de. Ed. Susanne Sonntag. Adv. contact Roland Schulz.

351 DEU ISSN 0947-2401
AUSBILDUNG PRUEFUNG FORTBILDUNG (SACHSEN-ANHALT EDITION); Zeitschrift fuer die staatliche und kommunale Verwaltung. Abbreviated title: A P F (Ausgabe Sachsen-Anhalt). Text in German. 1995. m. adv. **Document type:** *Magazine, Trade.*
Indexed: IBR, IBZ.
Published by: Richard Boorberg Verlag GmbH und Co. KG, Scharrstr 2, Stuttgart, 70563, Germany. TEL 49-711-73850, FAX 49-711-7385100, mail@boorberg.de, http://www.boorberg.de. Ed. Susanne Sonntag. Adv. contact Roland Schulz.

351 DEU ISSN 0943-2418
AUSBILDUNG PRUEFUNG FORTBILDUNG (SACHSEN EDITION); Zeitschrift fuer die staatliche und kommunale Verwaltung. Abbreviated title: A P F (Ausgabe Sachsen). Text in German. 1992. m. adv. **Document type:** *Magazine, Trade.*
Indexed: IBR, IBZ.
Published by: Richard Boorberg Verlag GmbH und Co. KG, Scharrstr 2, Stuttgart, 70563, Germany. TEL 49-711-73850, FAX 49-711-7385100, mail@boorberg.de, http://www.boorberg.de. Ed. Susanne Sonntag. Adv. contact Roland Schulz.

351 DEU ISSN 0943-2426
AUSBILDUNG PRUEFUNG FORTBILDUNG (THUERINGEN EDITION); Zeitschrift fuer die staatliche und kommunale Verwaltung. Abbreviated title: A P F (Ausgabe Thueringen). Text in German. 1993. m. adv. bk.rev. back issues avail. **Document type:** *Magazine, Trade.*
Indexed: IBR, IBZ.
Published by: Richard Boorberg Verlag GmbH und Co. KG, Scharrstr 2, Stuttgart, 70563, Germany. TEL 49-711-73850, FAX 49-711-7385100, mail@boorberg.de, http://www.boorberg.de. Ed. Peter Neumann. Circ: 1,560 (paid and controlled).

AUSTIN REPORT. *see* POLITICAL SCIENCE

351 AUS ISSN 1447-9125
AUSTRALASIAN PARLIAMENTARY REVIEW. Text in English. 1980. irreg. **Document type:** *Journal, Academic/Scholarly.*
Former titles (until 2000): Legislative Studies (0816-9152); (until 198?): Legislative Studies Newsletter (0159-527X)
Related titles: Online - full text ed.
Published by: Australasian Study of Parliament Group, c/o Dr. Anthony Marinac, Senate, Parliament House, Canberra, ACT 2600, Australia. Anthony.Marinac@aph.gov.au.

351.94035 AUS ISSN 1447-8722
RA371
AUSTRALIA. DEPARTMENT OF HEALTH AND AGEING. ANNUAL REPORT. Text in English. 1988. a. free (effective 2008). back issues avail. **Document type:** *Government.*
Formerly (until 2002): Australia. Commonwealth Department of Health and Aged Care. Annual Report (1443-0509); Which superseded in part (in 1998): Australia. Department of Human Services and Health. Annual Report (1323-0093); Which superseded in part (in 1993): Australia. Department of Health, Housing, Local Government and Community Services. Annual Report (1321-4950); Which was formerly (until 1992): Department of Health, Housing and Community Services. Annual Report (1037-4825); (until 1991): Department of Community Services and Health. Annual Report (1032-1659); Which was formed by the merger of (1985-1988): Commonwealth Department of Health. Annual Report (0816-7621); (1985-1988): Department of Community Services. Annual Report (1032-7916); Which was formerly (until 1986): Department of Community Services. Report for the Period (0815-8894)
Related titles: Online - full text ed.: free (effective 2008).
Published by: Australia. Department of Health and Ageing, GPO Box 9848, Canberra, ACT 2601, Australia. TEL 61-2-62897181, FAX 61-2-62897177, enquiries@health.gov.au.

351 AUS ISSN 1832-0848
AUSTRALIA. DEPARTMENT OF PARLIAMENTARY SERVICES. ANNUAL REPORT. Text in English. 2004. a. free (effective 2008). **Document type:** *Government.* **Description:** Contains information about the Australian department of parliamentary services.
Formed by the merger of (1983-2004): Joint House Department. Annual Report (0812-213X); (1983-2004): Department of the Parliamentary Reporting Staff. Annual Report (0812-2571); (1991-2004): Department of the Parliamentary Library. Annual Report (1038-3824)
Related titles: Online - full text ed.: free (effective 2008).
Published by: Australia. Department of Parliamentary Services, Parliament House, Canberra, ACT 2600, Australia. TEL 61-2-62777111, Visitor.Services@aph.gov.au.

AUSTRALIA. DEPARTMENT OF THE TREASURY. FOREIGN INVESTMENT REVIEW BOARD. REPORT. *see* BUSINESS AND ECONOMICS—Investments

351 AUS ISSN 1834-9854
AUSTRALIA. DEPTARTMENT OF PARLIAMENTARY SERVICES. PARLIAMENTARY LIBRARY. RESEARCH PAPER. Text in English. 2007. a. **Document type:** *Government.* **Description:** Publishes research conducted on the matters concerning the issues before Parliament.
Formed by the merger of (2004-2007): Australia. Deptartment of Parliamentary Services. Parliamentary Library. Research Note (1449-8456); Which was formerly (until 2004): Australia. Department of the Parliamentary Library. Information and Research Services. Research Note (1328-8016); (1995-1996): Australia. Parliamentary Research Service. Research Note (1323-5664); (2004-2007): Australia. Deptartment of Parliamentary Services. Parliamentary Library. Research Brief (1832-2883); Which was formerly (until 2004): Australia. Department of Parliamentary Sevices. Information and Research Services. Current Issues Brief (1449-8472); (until 2004): Australia. Department of the Parliamentary Library. Information and Research Services. Current Issues Brief (1440-2009); (until 1997): Australia. Parliamentary Research Service. Current Issues Brief (1321-1560); (1991-1993): Australia. Parliamentary Research Service. Issues Brief (1323-8434)
Related titles: Online - full text ed.
Published by: Parliament of Australia, Parliamentary Library, Parliament House, Canberra, ACT 2600, Australia. TEL 61-2-62777111.

353.9 AUS
AUSTRALIA. OFFICE OF HOUSING. SUMMARY OF HOUSING ASSISTANCE PROGRAMS. Text in English. 1939. a. **Document type:** *Government.* **Description:** Provides detailed descriptions and statistics on housing assistance activities during the annual year.
Formerly: Australia. Department of Planning and Development. Annual Report
Related titles: Online - full content ed.
Published by: Department of Human Services, Office of Housing, 50 Lonsdale St, Melbourne, VIC 3000, Australia. TEL 61-3-90960000, 300-650-172, housing@dhs.vic.gov.au, http://www.housing.vic.gov.au.

342.06 340 AUS ISSN 0816-3030
AUSTRALIAN ADMINISTRATIVE LAW. Abbreviated title: A L. Text in English. 1979. base vol. plus updates 4/yr. looseleaf. AUD 1,185.80 base vol(s). (effective 2008). adv. back issues avail. **Document type:** *Handbook/Manual/Guide, Trade.* **Description:** Contains all-important legislation relating to Commonwealth administrative law, and extracts from other relevant federal legislation.
Related titles: CD-ROM ed.; Online - full text ed.: AUD 1,239.70 (effective 2008).
Published by: LexisNexis Butterworths (Subsidiary of: LexisNexis Asia Pacific), Level 9, Tower 2, 475-495 Victoria Ave, Locked Bag 2222, Chatswood Delivery Ctr, Chatswood, NSW 2067, Australia. TEL 61-2-94222174, FAX 61-2-94222405, customer.relations@lexisnexis.com.au. Ed. D C Pearce.

351 AUS ISSN 1832-9802
AUSTRALIAN CAPITAL TERRITORY. EMERGENCY SERVICES AUTHORITY. ANNUAL REPORT. Text in English. 2005. a. **Document type:** *Corporate.* **Description:** Contains information on emergency management and related support arrangements in the Australian capital territory.
Formerly: Australian Capital Territory. Department of Justice and Community Services. Annual Report
Related titles: Online - full text ed.
Published by: Australian Capital Territory, Emergency Services Authority, 123 - 125 Carruthers St, PO Box 104, Curtin, ACT 2605, Australia. TEL 61-2-62078444, FAX 61-2-62078447, esahaveyoursay@act.gov.au, http://www.esa.act.gov.au.

351.94 AUS ISSN 0313-6647
JA26
➤ **AUSTRALIAN JOURNAL OF PUBLIC ADMINISTRATION.** Abbreviated title: A J P A. Text in English. 1937. q. GBP 178 in United Kingdom to institutions; EUR 225 in Europe to institutions; USD 257 in the Americas to institutions; USD 348 elsewhere to institutions; GBP 205 combined subscription in United Kingdom to institutions (print & online eds.); EUR 259 combined subscription in Europe to institutions (print & online eds.); USD 296 combined subscription in the Americas to institutions (print & online eds.); USD 401 combined subscription elsewhere to institutions (print & online eds.) (effective 2012). adv. bk.rev. charts; stat. cum.index: 1938-1976. back issues avail.; reprint service avail. from PSC. **Document type:** *Journal, Academic/Scholarly.* **Description:** Covers the research, reflection and commentary in federal, state, local and inter-governmental sectors.
Formerly (until 1976): Public Administration (0033-328X)
Related titles: Online - full text ed.: ISSN 1467-8500. GBP 178 in United Kingdom to institutions; EUR 225 in Europe to institutions; USD 257 in the Americas to institutions; USD 348 elsewhere to institutions (effective 2012) (from IngentaConnect).
Indexed: A11, A12, A17, A20, A22, A26, ABIn, AEI, ASCA, AusPAIS, B01, B06, B07, B08, B09, C12, CA, CurCont, E01, E08, ESPM, FR, Faml, G08, I05, I13, IBSS, P06, P34, P42, P48, P51, P53, P54, PAA&I, PAIS, PCI, PQC, PSA, RiskAb, S09, SCOPUS, SPAA, SSCI, SociolAb, T02, W07, WBA, WMB.
—BLDSC (1811.500000), IE, Infotrieve, Ingenta. **CCC.**
Published by: (Institute of Public Administration Australia), Wiley-Blackwell Publishing Asia (Subsidiary of: Wiley-Blackwell Publishing Ltd.), 155 Cremorne St, Richmond, VIC 3121, Australia. TEL 61-3-92743100, FAX 61-3-92743101, subs@blackwellpublishingasia.com, http://www.wiley.com/WileyCDA/. Eds. John Wanna, Patrick Bishop. Adv. contact Daniel Nash TEL 61-3-83591071. Circ: 5,700.

351 330 AUS ISSN 1832-424X
AUSTRALIAN PUBLIC POLICY PROGRAM WORKING PAPER. Text in English. 2003. irreg., latest vol.2, 2008. free (effective 2009). back issues avail. **Document type:** *Monographic series, Academic/Scholarly.*
Media: Online - full text.
Published by: University of Queensland, Risk and Sustainable Management Group, Colin Clark Bldg, No 39, St. Lucia, QLD 4072, Australia. FAX 61-7-33657299, rsmg@uq.edu.au.

351 DEU ISSN 1434-8152
B F H - N V. (Bundesfinanzhof - Nicht Veroeffentlichten) Text in German. 1985. m. EUR 285.60 (effective 2010). **Document type:** *Journal, Government.*
Formerly (until 1998): B F H - N V. Sammlung der Entscheidungen des Bundesfinanzhofs (0179-0498)
Published by: Rudolf Haufe Verlag GmbH & Co. KG, Hindenburgstr 64, Freiburg, 79102, Germany. TEL 49-761-36830, FAX 49-761-3683105, online@haufe.de, http://www.haufe.de.

B F S AKTUELL/ACTUALITES O F S. *see* PUBLIC ADMINISTRATION—Abstracting, Bibliographies, Statistics

B S L BULLETIN. *see* BUSINESS AND ECONOMICS—Economic Situation And Conditions

351.43 DEU ISSN 1860-3017
KKB1050
B W - WOCHE; landespolitische Wochenzeitung. (Baden-Wuerttemberg) Text in German. 1952. w. EUR 47.60; EUR 1.70 newsstand/cover (effective 2006). adv. **Document type:** *Newspaper, Consumer.* **Description:** Covers all political and parliamentary information for the state of Baden-Wuerttemberg.
Formerly (until 2004): Staatsanzeiger fuer Baden-Wuerttemberg (0404-603X)
Published by: Staatsanzeiger fuer Baden-Wuerttemberg GmbH, Breitscheidstr 69, Stuttgart, 70176, Germany. TEL 49-711-666010, FAX 49-711-6660119, verlag@staatsanzeiger.de, http://www.staatsanzeiger-verlag.de. Circ: 16,926 (paid).

351 CAN ISSN 1499-7983
BACKGROUNDER. Text in English. 1988. irreg. free. **Document type:** *Monographic series, Academic/Scholarly.* **Description:** Comments on Canadian policy issues.
Related titles: Online - full text ed.: ISSN 1499-7991. 1996; ◆ French ed.: Article Documentaire. ISSN 1499-8009.
Indexed: C03, CBCABus, P48, PQC.
Published by: C.D. Howe Institute/Institut C.D. Howe, 125 Adelaide St East, Toronto, ON M5C 1L7, Canada. TEL 416-865-1904, FAX 416-865-1866, publicat@cdhowe.org, http://www.cdhowe.org.

351.5365 BHR
BAHRAIN. MINISTRY OF INFORMATION. OFFICIAL GAZETTE/ BAHRAIN. WIZARAT AL-ISTI'LAMAT. AL-JARIDAH AL-RASMIYAH. Text in Arabic. 1957. w. **Document type:** *Government.*
Published by: Ministry of Information, P O Box 253, Isa Town, Bahrain. TEL 981555, FAX 682777, TELEX 8399.

351 BGD
BANGLADESH GAZETTE. Text in Bengali. 1947. w. BDT 30 per issue (effective 2008). **Document type:** *Government.* **Description:** Contains orders, notifications, announcements, advertisements & statistics resolutions of government issued & incorporated of the week.
Formerly (until 1971): Dacca Gazette
Related titles: Online - full text ed.; Supplement(s): Bangladesh Gazette. Extraordinary.
Published by: Bangladesh Forms And Publications Office (Subsidiary of: Bangladesh Government Press), Tejgaon, Dhaka, 1208, Bangladesh. info@bgpress.gov.bd.

351.5492 BGD
BANGLADESH JOURNAL OF PUBLIC ADMINISTRATION. Text in Bengali. 1987. s-a. BDT 40, USD 10. bk.rev. abstr.; bibl.; charts. **Description:** Contains articles, research, and comments.
Incorporates: Administrative Science Review (0001-8406)
Related titles: Online - full text ed.
Indexed: BAS, P06.
Published by: Bangladesh Public Administration Training Centre, c/o Mr. Shaikh Altaf Ali, BPATC, Savar, Dhaka, 1343, Bangladesh. TEL 880-2-7711609, 880-2-7710010, FAX 880-2-7710029, zakir@bpatc.org, http://www.bpatc.org/. Ed. Mustafa Abdur Rahman. Circ: 750.

BARBADOS. LEGISLATURE. HOUSE OF ASSEMBLY. MINUTES OF PROCEEDINGS. *see* POLITICAL SCIENCE

BARBADOS. LEGISLATURE. SENATE. MINUTES OF PROCEEDINGS. *see* POLITICAL SCIENCE

BARBADOS. REGISTRATION OFFICE. REPORT ON VITAL STATISTICS & REGISTRATIONS. *see* PUBLIC ADMINISTRATION—Abstracting, Bibliographies, Statistics

351 342.492 NLD ISSN 1871-627X
BASISADMINISTRATIE PERSOONSGEGEVENS EN REISDOCUMENTEN KWALITEITSBROCHURE. Key Title: BPRkwaliteitsbrochure. Variant title: B P R Kwaliteitsbrochure. Text in Dutch. 1993. irreg., latest vol.42, 2008.
Formerly (until 1999): G B A Kwaliteitsbrochure (1873-8648)
Published by: Agentschap Basisadministratie Persoonsgegevens en Reisdocumenten, Postbus 10451, The Hague, 2501 HL, Netherlands. TEL 31-70-3613100, FAX 31-70-3560066, agentschap@bprbzk.nl, http://www.bprbzk.nl.

351 DEU ISSN 0723-7022
DER BAYERISCHE BUERGERMEISTER. Text in German. 1917. m. EUR 159.95 domestic; EUR 169.95 foreign (effective 2011). adv. back issues avail. **Document type:** *Magazine, Trade.*
Former titles (until 1977): Der Bayerische Buergermeister. Ausgabe A (0341-390X); (until 1949): Der Bayerische Buergermeister (0723-7030)
Published by: Verlagsgruppe Huethig Jehle Rehm GmbH (Subsidiary of: Sueddeutscher Verlag GmbH), Emmy-Noether-Str 2, Munich, 80992, Germany. TEL 49-89-5485206, FAX 49-89-548528230, info@hjr-verlag.de, http://www.huethig-jehle-rehm.de. Adv. contact Stefan Jaitner. B&W page EUR 655; trim 210 x 297. Circ: 2,500.

BAYERISCHE VERWALTUNGSBLAETTER; Zeitschrift fuer oeffentliches Recht und oeffentliche Verwaltung. *see* LAW

351 DEU
BAYERISCHER GEMEINDETAG. Text in German. 1948. m. EUR 33 (effective 2009). adv. **Document type:** *Magazine, Trade.*
Former titles (until 2004): Bay G T Zeitung; (until 1995): Bayerischer Gemeindetag
Address: Dreschstr 8, Munich, 80805, Germany. TEL 49-89-3600090, FAX 49-89-365603, baygt@bay-gemeindetag.de. adv.: B&W page EUR 1,030, color page EUR 2,410. Circ: 6,300 (controlled).

351 DEU ISSN 0934-6465
J357.R1
BAYERISCHES STAATSMINISTERIUM DES INNERN. ALLGEMEINES MINISTERIALBLATT. Text in German. 1949. bi-w. bk.rev. **Document type:** *Government.*
Formerly (until 1988): Bayerisches Staatsministerium des Innern. Ministerialamtsblatt der Bayerischen Inneren Verwaltung (0005-7185)
Published by: Staatsministerium des Innern, Odeonsplatz 3, Munich, 80539, Germany. TEL 49-89-2192-01, FAX 49-89-21921-2885. Ed. Peter Abholzer. Circ: 8,500.

351.43 DEU ISSN 0934-3652
BEAMTENRECHT. Text in German. 1973. 9 base vols. plus irreg. updates. price varies. **Document type:** *Monographic series, Trade.*
Published by: Erich Schmidt Verlag GmbH & Co. (Berlin), Genthiner Str 30 G, Berlin, 10785, Germany. TEL 49-30-2500850, FAX 49-30-250085305, esv@esvmedien.de, http://www.esv.info.

351 NLD ISSN 0921-8459
BEDRIJFSHULPVERLENING. Text in Dutch. 4/yr. adv. **Document type:** *Trade.*
Formerly (until 1983): Nederlandse Vereniging Zelfbescherming Bedrijven en Inrichtingen. Mededelingenblad (1385-8548)
—IE, Infotrieve.
Published by: Nederlandse Vereniging Bedrijfshulpverlening, Prins Bernhardweg 21, Postbus 34, Lochem, 7240 AA, Netherlands. TEL 71-573-256570, FAX 71-573-255980, bhv@vnb-bhv.nl. adv.: page EUR 300; 185 x 270. Circ: 750.

BEHEMOTH; a journal on civilisation. *see* POLITICAL SCIENCE

351 CHN ISSN 1009-2862
BEIJING SHI RENMIN ZHENGFU GONGBAO/PEOPLE'S GOVERNMENT OF BEIJING MUNICIPALITY. GAZETTE. Text in Chinese. 2000. s-m. **Document type:** *Newspaper, Government.*
Related titles: E-mail ed.; Online - full text ed.
Published by: Beijing Shi Renmin Zhengfu Bangongting, 2, Zhengyi Lu, Beijing, 100744, China. TEL 86-10-65192756, FAX 86-10-65192760.

351 CHN ISSN 1008-7621
BEIJING XINGZHENG XUEYUAN XUEBAO/BEIJING ADMINISTRATIVE COLLEGE. JOURNAL. Text in Chinese. 1999. bi-m. **Document type:** *Journal, Academic/Scholarly.*
Related titles: Online - full text ed.
Published by: Beijing Xingzheng Xueyuan/Beijing Administrative College, 6, Chegongzhuang Dajie, Beijing, 100044, China. TEL 86-10-68007412, FAX 86-10-68006709, http://www.bac.gov.cn/webnew/swdx/about/Detail.aspx?NodeID=28&ID=205.

351 DEU ISSN 0940-676X
BEITRAEGE ZUM BEAMTENRECHT. Text in German. 1991. irreg., latest vol.10, 2008. price varies. **Document type:** *Monographic series, Academic/Scholarly.*
Published by: Duncker und Humblot GmbH, Carl-Heinrich-Becker-Weg 9, Berlin, 12165, Germany. TEL 49-30-7900060, FAX 49-30-79000631, info@duncker-humblot.de.

328 DEU ISSN 0720-6674
BEITRAEGE ZUM PARLAMENTSRECHT. Text in German. 1979. irreg., latest vol.65, 2008. price varies. **Document type:** *Monographic series, Academic/Scholarly.*
Published by: Duncker und Humblot GmbH, Carl-Heinrich-Becker-Weg 9, Berlin, 12165, Germany. TEL 49-30-7900060, FAX 49-30-79000631, info@duncker-humblot.de.

368.4 362.6 BEL ISSN 1375-4424
BEKNOPT OVERZICHT VAN DE SOCIALE ZEKERHEID IN BELGIE/SURVEY OF SOCIAL SECURITY IN BELGIUM. Text in Dutch. 1999. a., latest 2003. EUR 10 per issue (effective 2003). charts; stat. back issues avail. **Document type:** *Monographic series, Government.* **Description:** Summarizes, as completely as possible, the social security regulations in Belgium as they apply to employed persons, self-employed persons, civil servants, miners, and sailors. Outlines the structure, organization, and financing of these schemes and explains each of the social security branches, along with other social assistance programs.
Related titles: Online - full content ed.; French ed.: Apercu de la Securite Sociale en Belgique. ISSN 1375-4416.
Published by: Ministere Federal des Affaires Sociales de la Sante Publique et de l'Environnement, Service des Publications/Federaal Ministerie van Sociale Zaken, Volksgezondheid en Leefmilieu, Publicaties Dienst, Rue de la Vierge Noire 3C, Zwarte Lievevrouwstraat 3C, Brussels, 1000, Belgium. TEL 32-2-509-8552, FAX 32-2-509-8016, roland.vanlaere@minisoc.fed.be, http://www.socialsecurity.fgov.be/bib/homehome.htm.

362.6 368.4 BEL ISSN 0775-0234
DE BELGISCH TIJDSCHRIFT VOOR SOCIALE ZEKERHEID/BELGIAN SOCIAL SECURITY JOURNAL. Text in Dutch; Abstracts in Dutch, English. 1959. q. EUR 19 domestic; EUR 22.50 foreign (effective 2003). bk.rev. abstr.; bibl.; charts. back issues avail. **Document type:** *Government.* **Description:** Contains articles about social security, social rights and benefits regarding old age, disability, unemployment, judicial protection, medical care and child benefits.
Related titles: ◆ French ed.: Revue Belge de Securite Sociale. ISSN 0035-0834.
—IE, Infotrieve.
Published by: Ministere Federal des Affaires Sociales de la Sante Publique et de l'Environnement, Service des Publications/Federaal Ministerie van Sociale Zaken, Volksgezondheid en Leefmilieu, Publicaties Dienst, Rue de la Vierge Noire 3C, Zwarte Lievevrouwstraat 3C, Brussels, 1000, Belgium. TEL 32-2-509-8552, FAX 32-2-509-8016, roland.vanlaere@minisoc.fed.be, http://www.socialsecurity.fgov.be/bib/homehome.htm.

368.4 362.6 BEL ISSN 1374-8254
BELGIUM. FEDERAAL MINISTERIE VAN SOCIALE ZAKEN, VOLKSGEZONDHEID EN LEEFMILIEU. ALGEMEEN VERSLAG OVER DE SOCIALE ZEKERHEID. Text in Dutch. a. EUR 9 per issue domestic (effective 2003). charts; stat. back issues avail. **Document type:** *Government.* **Description:** Offers an annual assessment of the accounts of social security funds in Belgium. Describes the income redistribution produced by social security and offers policy makers and scientific researchers a comprehensive reference source. Contains a methodological note and a survey of the major political measures taken during the year.
Related titles: ◆ French ed.: Belgium. Ministere Federal des Affaires Sociales, de la Sante Publique et de l'Environnement. Rapport General sur la Securite Sociale. ISSN 1374-8262.
Published by: Ministere Federal des Affaires Sociales de la Sante Publique et de l'Environnement, Service des Publications/Federaal Ministerie van Sociale Zaken, Volksgezondheid en Leefmilieu, Publicaties Dienst, Rue de la Vierge Noire 3C, Zwarte Lievevrouwstraat 3C, Brussels, 1000, Belgium. TEL 32-2-509-8552, FAX 32-2-509-8016, roland.vanlaere@minisoc.fed.be, http://www.socialsecurity.fgov.be/bib/homehome.htm. Ed. Hendrik Larmuseau. R&P Roland Van Laere.

BELGIUM. FEDERAAL MINISTERIE VAN SOCIALE ZAKEN, VOLKSGEZONDHEID EN LEEFMILIEU. TEGEMOETKOMINGEN AAN GEHANDICAPTEN/BENEFITS FOR THE DISABLED. *see* HANDICAPPED

352.63 BEL
BELGIUM. HOGE RAAD VOOR DE MIDDENSTAND. JAARVERSLAG. Text in Dutch. 1951. a. free. **Document type:** *Government.*
Formerly: Belgium. Hoge Raad voor de Middenstand. Jaarverslag van de Secretaris Generaal
Related titles: ◆ French ed.: Belgium. Conseil Superieur des Classes Moyennes. Rapport Annuel. ISSN 0067-5393.
Published by: Hoge Raad voor de Middenstand, WTC Tower III, 2nd Fl, Bd Emile Jacqmain 158, Brussels, 1000, Belgium. TEL 32-2-2083404, FAX 32-2-2083405. Ed., R&P Marc Hoogmartens.

BELGIUM. MINISTERE FEDERAL DES AFFAIRES SOCIALES, DE LA SANTE PUBLIQUE ET DE L'ENVIRONNEMENT. RAPPORT GENERAL SUR LA SECURITE SOCIALE. *see* INSURANCE

351 HUN ISSN 1218-8956
BELUGYI SZEMLE. Text in Hungarian. 1963. m.
Former titles (until 1995): Rendeszeti Szemle (1215-167X); (until 1991): Belugyi Szemle (0133-6738)
Indexed: S02, S03.
Published by: Belugyminiszterium, Horanszky Utca 6, Budapest, 1085, Hungary. TEL 36-1-4411000, FAX 36-1-3339199.

337.1492 BEL
BENELUX NEWSLETTER. Text in Dutch, French. 1989. irreg. (4-5/yr.). **Description:** Reports on the activities of the Benelux Secretariat.
Indexed: RASB.
Published by: Benelux Economic Union, Rue de la Regence 39, Brussels, 1000, Belgium. TEL 32-2-5193811, FAX 32-2-5134206.

351 BEL ISSN 0005-8777
BENELUX PUBLIKATIEBLAD/BULLETIN BENELUX. Text in Dutch, French. 1958. irreg. (approx. 3/yr.). looseleaf. Supplement avail.
—BLDSC (2834.520000).
Published by: Benelux Economic Union, Rue de la Regence 39, Brussels, 1000, Belgium. TEL 32-2-5193811, FAX 32-2-5134206.

351 330 NLD ISSN 1878-7851
HET BENOEMINGSRECHT VOOR DE SOCIAAL-ECONOMISCHE RAAD. Cover title: Benoemingsrecht Sociaal-Economische Raad. Variant title: Advies het Benoemingsrecht voor de Sociaal-Economische Raad. Text in Dutch. 2008. triennial. EUR 7.50 per issue (effective 2011). **Document type:** *Report, Government.*
Published by: Sociaal-Economische Raad, Postbus 90405, The Hague, 2509 LK, Netherlands. TEL 31-70-3499499, FAX 31-70-3832535, ser.info@ser.nl, http://www.ser.nl.

351 NLD ISSN 1574-1672
BESTUUR RENDEMENT. Text in Dutch. 1998. m. (11/yr.). EUR 179; EUR 24 newsstand/cover (effective 2010). adv.
Former titles (until 2005): Goed Bestuur Stichting en Vereniging (1569-0954); (until 1999): Praktijkbrief Goed Bestuur Stichting en Vereniging (1387-3687)
Related titles: ◆ Supplement(s): Dossier Bestuur Rendement. ISSN 1872-3306.
Published by: Rendement Uitgeverij BV (Subsidiary of: Springer Netherlands), Postbus 27020, Rotterdam, 3003 LA, Netherlands. TEL 31-10-2433933, FAX 31-10-2439028. Pub. Marnix Hoogerwerf. Adv. contact Ralph Pennenburg. B&W page EUR 1,495; trim 210 x 297. Circ: 3,000.

351 NLD ISSN 0167-0689
BESTUURSFORUM; maandblad voor christen-democratische gemeente- en provinciepolitiek. Text in Dutch. 1977. 10/yr. EUR 30 (effective 2008). adv. bk.rev.; Website rev. illus. 32 p./no.; back issues avail. **Document type:** *Journal, Government.* **Description:** Covers topics relating to public administration and local government from a Christian-Democratic point of view.
Formed by the merger of (1928-1977): Magistratuur (0922-6125); (1934-1977): Gemeentebeleid (0922-6141); (1973-1977): Gemeente en Gewest (0922-6133)
Related titles: Online - full text ed.
Indexed: ELLIS.
—IE, Infotrieve.
Published by: C D A - bestuurdersvereniging, Buitenom 18, PO Box 30453, The Hague, 2500 GL, Netherlands. TEL 31-70-3424890, FAX 31-70-3643417, info@cda-bestuurdersvereniging.nl. Ed., R&P, Adv. contact Carmen T Boersma. Circ: 3,350 (paid).

351 NLD ISSN 0927-3387
➤ **BESTUURSKUNDE.** Text in Dutch. 1992. 4/yr. EUR 73.50 (effective 2008). adv. 152 p./no.; **Document type:** *Journal, Academic/Scholarly.* **Description:** Covers issues relating to public administration at the local and central levels.
—IE, Infotrieve.
Published by: (Vereniging voor Bestuurskunde), Reed Business bv (Subsidiary of: Reed Business), Van Bylandthuis, Benoordenhoutseweg 46, Den Haag, 2596 BC, Netherlands. TEL 31-70-441-5166, FAX 31-70-441-5916, info@reedbusiness.nl, http://www.reedbusiness.nl. Circ: 1,400.

351 NLD ISSN 0165-7194
BESTUURSWETENSCHAPPEN. Text in Dutch. 1947. 6/yr. EUR 77.50 to individuals; EUR 90 to institutions (effective 2008). adv. index. **Document type:** *Trade.*
Indexed: ELLIS, KES, T02.
—IE, Infotrieve.
Published by: Sdu Uitgevers bv, Postbus 20025, The Hague, 2500 EA, Netherlands. TEL 31-70-3789911, FAX 31-70-3854321, sdu@sdu.nl. Ed. Dr. P J M de Goede.

351.758 USA ISSN 0894-9697
BILL SHIPP'S GEORGIA. Text in English. 1987. w. USD 195; USD 205 both print and online eds. (effective 2000). adv. **Document type:** *Newsletter.* **Description:** Covers Georgia government, politics and business.
Related titles: Online - full text ed.: USD 149.
Published by: Word Merchants, Inc., PO Box 440755, Kennesaw, GA 30144-9513. TEL 770-422-2543, FAX 770-422-0227. Ed., Pub. Bill Shipp. R&P, Adv. contact Michelle Cobb.

328.777 USA ISSN 1077-4807
BILL STATUS SHEET. Text in English. 1985. w. (while legislature is in session). looseleaf. USD 198 (effective 1999). **Description:** Describes current status of all bills pending before the Iowa State Legislature.
Published by: Iowa Legislative News Service, PO Box 8370, Des Moines, IA 50301-8370. TEL 515-288-4676, FAX 515-266-6626. Ed., Pub., R&P Jack Hunt.

351 NLD ISSN 0167-1146
BINNENLANDS BESTUUR; onafhankelijk weekblad voor ambtenaren en bestuurders bij de overheid. Text in Dutch. 1980. w. (48/yr.). EUR 187 to non-members; EUR 112 to members (effective 2009). adv. **Document type:** *Trade.*
Incorporates: Binnenlands Bestuur Management (0922-3193)
Related titles: ◆ Supplement(s): Jong en Ambtenaar. ISSN 1877-217X.
Indexed: T02.
—IE, Infotrieve.
Published by: Kluwer B.V. (Subsidiary of: Wolters Kluwer N.V.), Postbus 23, Deventer, 7400 GA, Netherlands. TEL 31-570-673555, FAX 31-570-691555, info@kluwer.nl, http://www.kluwer.nl. adv.: B&W page EUR 4,841, color page EUR 5,835; bleed 210 x 297. Circ: 48,024.

P

328 FRA ISSN 1957-6587
LES BIOGRAPHIES.COM. DOCUMENTATION ELECTORALE. Text in French. 200?. irreg. EUR 355 base vol(s).; EUR 530 (effective 2009).
Formerly (until 200?): Encyclopedie Periodique Economique Politique et Administrative. Documentation Electorale (0767-9815)
Published by: Societe Generale de Presse, 13 Avenue de l'Opera, Paris Cedex 01, 75001, France. TEL 33-1-40151789, FAX 33-1-40151715, http://www.sgpresse.fr.

LES BIOGRAPHIES.COM. LE CONSEIL D'ETAT. *see* BIOGRAPHY

LES BIOGRAPHIES.COM. LE CONSEIL ECONOMIQUE SOCIAL ET ENVIRONNEMENTAL. *see* BIOGRAPHY

351.72 POL ISSN 1233-717X
BIULETYN ZAMOWIEN PUBLICZNYCH. Text in Polish. 1995. w. price on request. **Document type:** *Bulletin.*
Related titles: Online - full content ed.: ISSN 1689-3808.
Published by: Urzed Zamowien Publicznych/Public Procurement Office, Al Szucha 2/4, Warsaw, 00582, Poland. TEL 48-22-4587777, FAX 48-22-4587700, die@uzp.gov.pl, http://www.uzp.gov.pl. **Dist. by:** Ars Polona, Obroncow 25, Warsaw 03933, Poland. TEL 48-22-5098609, FAX 48-22-5098610, arspolona@arspolona.com.pl, http://www.arspolona.com.pl.

BLACKS IN GOVERNMENT - NEWS. *see* ETHNIC INTERESTS

BLAUW. *see* LAW

351 DEU
BLICKPUNKT D S T G NORDRHEIN-WESTFALEN. (Deutsche Steuer-Gewerkschaft) Text in German. 1985. 9/yr. adv. **Document type:** *Magazine, Trade.*
Former titles (until 2000): Blickpunkt D S T G; (until 1990): Die Steuer-Gewerkschaft in Nordrhein-Westfalen
Published by: Deutsche Steuer-Gewerkschaft, Landesverband Nordrhein-Westfalen, Elisabethstr 40, Duesseldorf, 40217, Germany. TEL 49-211-906950, FAX 49-211-9069522, dstg.nrw@t-online.de. adv.: B&W page EUR 970; trim 185 x 270. Circ: 24,000 (controlled).

▼ **BLOOMBERG LAW REPORTS. CONGRESSIONAL MONITOR.** *see* LAW

BOARD OF IMMIGRATION APPEALS. INTERIM DECISIONS (ONLINE). *see* LAW—Constitutional Law

351 MAC
BOLETIM OFICIAL. Text in Portuguese. 1838. w.
Address: Rua da Imprensa Nacional, CP 33, Macau. TEL 853-573822, FAX 853-596802. Ed. Antonio de Vasconcelos Mendes Liz.

351 301 VEN
BOLETIN REFORME. Text in Spanish. 1997. w. **Description:** Publishes summaries of the activities of the public administrations of many Latin American countries.
Related titles: Online - full text ed.
Published by: Centro Latinoamericano de Administracion para el Desarrollo, C. Herrera Toro, Qta. CLAD, Sector Los Naranjos, Las Mercedes, Apdo. Postal 4181, Caracas, 1010-A, Venezuela. TEL 58-212-9924064, FAX 58-212-9918427, cedai@clad.org.ve.

THE BOOK OF THE STATES. *see* POLITICAL SCIENCE

351 FRA ISSN 1147-1999
JN2303
BOTTIN ADMINISTRATIF. Text in French. 1943. a., latest 2009. **Document type:** *Directory, Trade.*

Published by: (Societe Bottin Administratif), LexisNexis JurisClasseur, Relation Clients, 141 rue de Javel, Paris, Cedex 15 75747, France. TEL 33-1-45589200, FAX 33-1-45589400, relation.clients@lexisnexis.fr, http://www.lexisnexis.fr/lexisnexisjurisclasseur/juris_liste_revue.htm. Ed. Patrice Soulie.

351.77 614.77 SWE
BQ. Text in Swedish. 1966. q. free (effective 2007). back issues avail. **Document type:** *Magazine, Government.*
Formerly (until 2007): Straalskyddsnytt (0280-0357)
Related titles: Online - full text ed.
Published by: Statens Straalskyddsinstitut/Swedish Radiation Protection Authority, Solna Strandvaeg, Stockholm, 17116, Sweden. TEL 46-8-7297100, FAX 46-8-7297108, ssi@ssi.se. Ed. Mattias Skjoeld TEL 46-8-7299167.

354.3 BRA ISSN 0101-5680
HD1741.B8
BRAZIL. DEPARTAMENTO NACIONAL DE OBRAS CONTRA AS SECAS. RELATORIO. Cover title: Relatorio D N O C S. Text in Portuguese. 1945. a. free. bk.rev. charts; illus.; stat.
Media: Duplicated (not offset).
Published by: Departamento Nacional de Obras Contra as Secas, Av Duque de Caxias, 1700, sala 413, Caixa Postal 1441 AG CENTRO, Fortaleza, CE 60035-111, Brazil.

354.3 CAN ISSN 1705-9348
BRITISH COLUMBIA. AGRICULTURAL LAND COMMISSION. ANNUAL SERVICE PLAN REPORT. Text in English. 1974. a.
Former titles (until 2003): British Columbia. Land Reserve Commission. Annual Report (1496-8584); (until 2001): British Columbia. Provincial Agricultural Land Commission. Annual Report (1998) (1489-4092); Which incorporated (1996-1999): British Columbia. Forest Land Commission. Annual Report (1480-9958); (until 1998): British Columbia. Provincial Agricultural Land Commission. A L C Annual Report (1480-9966); (until 1996): British Columbia. Provincial Agricultural Land Commission. Annual Report (0708-4048); (until 1978): Provincial Land Commission. Annual Report (0703-2374)
Published by: British Columbia Provincial Agricultural Land Commission, 133-4940 Canada Way, Burnaby, BC V5G 4K6, Canada. TEL 604-660-7000, FAX 604-660-7033, http://www.alc.bc.ca.

351.71 CAN ISSN 1495-8864
BRITISH COLUMBIA ASSESSMENT AUTHORITY. ANNUAL PERFORMANCE REPORT AND A REPORT OF THE CREATION OF THE ASSESSMENT ROLL. Text in English. 1974. a.
Former titles (until 1999): British Columbia Assessment Authority. Report on the Creation of the Assessment Roll and Financial Statements (1485-9785); (until 1997): British Columbia Assessment Authority. Annual Report (0383-5049)
Published by: British Columbia Assessment Authority, 1537 Hillside Ave, Victoria, BC V8T 4Y2, Canada. TEL 250-595-6211, info@bcassessment.ca.

354.71 CAN ISSN 0710-7412
HV9309.B7
BRITISH COLUMBIA BOARD OF PAROLE. ANNUAL REPORT. Text in English. 1981. a.
Published by: (Province of British Columbia, Board of Parole), British Columbia. Ministry of Attorney General, Communications Branch, PO Box 9206, Stn Prov Govt, Victoria, BC V8W 9J1, Canada. TEL 250-387-1866, FAX 250-387-6411, EnquiryBC@gov.bc.ca, http://www.gov.bc.ca/ag/.

328.711 CAN ISSN 0825-6187
BRITISH COLUMBIA. LEGISLATIVE ASSEMBLY. DEBATES (HANSARD DAILY). Text in English. 1968. d. (during sessions). CAD 298. **Document type:** *Government.*
Formerly (until 1981): Unrevised Synoptic Report of the Proceedings of the Legislative Assembly (0825-6098)
Published by: (New Brunswick. Legislative Assembly/Assemblee Legislative), Crown Publications Inc., 521 Fort St, Victoria, BC BC V8W 1E7, Canada. TEL 250-386-4636, FAX 250-386-0221, crown@pinc.com, http://www.crownpub.bc.ca.

328.711 CAN
BRITISH COLUMBIA. LEGISLATIVE ASSEMBLY. DEBATES (HANSARD PAPERBOUND). Text in English. irreg. CAD 200. **Document type:** *Government.*
Published by: (New Brunswick. Legislative Assembly/Assemblee Legislative), Crown Publications Inc., 521 Fort St, Victoria, BC BC V8W 1E7, Canada. TEL 250-386-4636, FAX 250-386-0221, crown@pinc.com, http://www.crownpub.bc.ca.

351 340 CAN ISSN 0825-6179
BRITISH COLUMBIA. LEGISLATIVE ASSEMBLY. DEBATES (HANSARD SESSIONAL EDITION)/JOURNAL DES DEBATS. Text in English, French. 1895. a.
Formerly (until 1979): Synoptic Report of the Proceedings of the Legislative Assembly of the Province of New Brunswick (0703-9832)
Published by: (New Brunswick. Legislative Assembly/Assemblee Legislative), Crown Publications Inc., 521 Fort St, Victoria, BC BC V8W 1E7, Canada. TEL 250-386-4636, FAX 250-386-0221, crown@pinc.com, http://www.crownpub.bc.ca.

328.71 CAN ISSN 1924-2905
BRITISH COLUMBIA. LEGISLATIVE ASSEMBLY. HANSARD SERVICES. INDEX TO DEBATES. Variant title: Index, Official Report of Debates of the Legislative Assembly, Hansard. Text in English. 1973. d. USD 396; USD 2.85 per issue (effective 2010). back issues avail. **Document type:** *Report, Government.*
Published by: Legislative Assembly of British Columbia, Hansard Services, 612 Government St, Victoria, BC V8V 1X4, Canada. TEL 250-387-3681, FAX 250-356-5095, hansard.services@leg.bc.ca.

328.711 CAN ISSN 0706-0629
BRITISH COLUMBIA. LEGISLATIVE ASSEMBLY. JOURNALS. Text in English. 1815. a. price varies. back issues avail. **Document type:** *Government.*
Formerly (until 1892): House of Assembly of the Province of New Brunswick. Journal (1185-4766)
Related titles: French ed.: L' Assemblee Legislative du Nouveau-Brunswick. Journeaux. ISSN 0319-9223.
Published by: (New Brunswick. Legislative Assembly/Assemblee Legislative), Crown Publications Inc., 521 Fort St, Victoria, BC BC V8W 1E7, Canada. TEL 250-386-4636, FAX 250-386-0221, crown@pinc.com, http://www.crownpub.bc.ca.

BRITISH COLUMBIA. LEGISLATIVE ASSEMBLY. SELECT STANDING COMMITTEE ON ABORIGINAL AFFAIRS. REPORT OF PROCEEDINGS (HANSARD). *see* ETHNIC INTERESTS

BRITISH COLUMBIA. LEGISLATIVE ASSEMBLY. SELECT STANDING COMMITTEE ON EDUCATION. REPORT OF PROCEEDINGS (HANSARD). *see* EDUCATION

BRITISH COLUMBIA. LEGISLATIVE ASSEMBLY. SELECT STANDING COMMITTEE ON FINANCE AND GOVERNMENT SERVICES. REPORT OF PROCEEDINGS (HANSARD). *see* BUSINESS AND ECONOMICS—Public Finance, Taxation

BRITISH COLUMBIA. LEGISLATIVE ASSEMBLY. SELECT STANDING COMMITTEE ON HEALTH. REPORT OF PROCEEDINGS (HANSARD). *see* PUBLIC HEALTH AND SAFETY

328.711 CAN ISSN 1185-3026
BRITISH COLUMBIA. LEGISLATIVE ASSEMBLY. THIRD READING BILLS. Text in English. w. CAD 80. **Document type:** *Government.*
Published by: (New Brunswick. Legislative Assembly/Assemblee Legislative), Crown Publications Inc., 521 Fort St, Victoria, BC BC V8W 1E7, Canada. TEL 250-386-4636, FAX 250-386-0221, crown@pinc.com, http://www.crownpub.bc.ca.

351.71 CAN ISSN 0709-4531
HV5309.B7
BRITISH COLUMBIA LIQUOR DISTRIBUTION BRANCH. FINANCIAL STATEMENTS. Text in English. 196?. a.
Former titles (until 1978): British Columbia Liquor Administration Branch. Financial Statements (0319-8154); (until 1974): British Columbia Liquor Control Board. Financial Statements (0319-8162)
Published by: British Columbia Liquor Distribution Branch, 2625 Rupert St, Vancouver, BC V5M 3T5, Canada. TEL 604-252-3000, FAX 604-252-3044.

351.71 CAN ISSN 0837-6859
HG6142.B7
BRITISH COLUMBIA LOTTERY CORPORATION. ANNUAL REPORT. Text in English. 1986. a.
Published by: British Columbia Lottery Corporation, 74 W Seymour St, Kamloops, BC V2C 1E2, Canada. TEL 250-828-5500, FAX 250-828-5631.

353.40971 CAN ISSN 1499-0210
KEB475.A13
BRITISH COLUMBIA. MINISTRY OF ATTORNEY GENERAL. ANNUAL PERFORMANCE REPORT. Text in English. 1974. a.
Former titles (until 2001): British Columbia. Ministry of the Attorney-General. Annual Report (0704-6022); (until 1976): British Columbia. Department of the Attorney-General. Annual Report (0704-6030)
Published by: British Columbia, Ministry of Attorney General, PO Box 9282, Stn Prov Govt, Victoria, BC V8W 9J7, Canada. TEL 604-660-2421, FAX 250-387-1753, http://www.gov.bc.ca/bvprd/bc/channel.do?action=ministry&channelID=-8378&navId=NAV_ID_province.

354.4 CAN ISSN 1705-9275
BRITISH COLUMBIA. MINISTRY OF ENERGY AND MINES. ANNUAL SERVICE PLAN REPORT. Text in English. 1994. a.
Formerly (until 2003): British Columbia. Ministry of Energy and Mines. Annual Report (1481-7152); Which superseded in part in 1997: British Columbia. Ministry of Employment and Investment. Annual Report (1203-9195); Which was formerly (until 1994): British Columbia. Ministry of Economic Development, Small Business and Trade. Annual Report (1192-7232); (until 1992): British Columbia. Ministry of Regional and Economic Development. Annual Report (1181-6546); (until 1990): British Columbia. Ministry of Regional Development and Minister of State for Mainland/Southwest. Annual Report (1181-6538); (until 1989): British Columbia. Ministry of Economic Development. Annual Report (0838-3855); (until 1987): British Columbia. Ministry of Industry and Small Business Development. Annual Report (0711-5490); (until 1979): British Columbia. Ministry of Economic Development. Annual Report (0704-674X); (until 1976): Government of British Columbia. Department of Economic Development. Annual Report (0318-8302); (until 1974): British Columbia. Department of Industrial Development, Trade and Commerce. Annual Report (0318-8310); (until 1969): Province of British Columbia. Department of Industrial Development, Trade and Commerce. Annual Report and Summary of Economic Activity
Published by: British Columbia, Ministry of Energy and Mines, c/o Communications Coordinator, Stn Prov Govt, PO Box 9324, Victoria, BC V8W 9N3, Canada. http://www.gov.bc.ca/bvprd/bc/channel.do?action=ministry&channelID=-8383&navId=NAV_ID_province.

351.71 CAN ISSN 1708-0266
BRITISH COLUMBIA. MINISTRY OF FINANCE. ANNUAL SERVICE PLAN REPORT. Text in English. 2002. a.
Formerly (until 2003): British Columbia. Ministry of Finance. Annual Report (1703-5031); Which superseded in part: British Columbia. Ministry of Finance and Corporate Relations. Annual Performance Report (1499-0962); Which was formerly (until 2001): British Columbia. Ministry of Finance and Corporate Relations. Annual Report (0835-7315); (until 1987): British Columbia. Ministry of Consumer and Corporate Affairs. Annual Report (0381-1506); (until 1976): British Columbia Department of Consumer Services. Annual Report (0319-3063)
Published by: Ministry of Finance, PO Box 9417, Stn Prov Govt, Victoria, BC V8W 9V1, Canada. TEL 250-387-7848, FAX 250-356-0206, http://www.gov.bc.ca/fin/.

352.4971 CAN ISSN 1705-6071
CA2BC FN .B776 .ENG
BRITISH COLUMBIA. MINISTRY OF FINANCE. BUDGET AND FISCAL PLAN. Text in English. a.
Formerly (until 2005): British Columbia. Ministry of Finance and Corporate Relations. Budget Reports (1207-5841); Which superseded in part (in 1995): B.C. Budget (0823-2008); Which was formerly (until 1994): Province of British Columbia Budget (0229-5253); (until 1981): British Columbia Budget (0382-1986); (until 1976): Province of British Columbia. Budget Speech (0382-1978)
Published by: Ministry of Finance, PO Box 9417, Stn Prov Govt, Victoria, BC V8W 9V1, Canada. TEL 250-387-7848, FAX 250-356-0206, http://www.gov.bc.ca/fin/.

352.4971 CAN ISSN 1705-6063
BRITISH COLUMBIA. MINISTRY OF FINANCE. BUDGET SPEECH. Text in English. a.
Formerly (until 2002): British Columbia. Ministry of Finance and Corporate Relations. Budget Speech (0825-0650); Which superseded in part (in 1995): B.C. Budget (0823-2008); Which was formerly (until 1994): Province of British Columbia Budget (0229-5253); (until 1981): British Columbia Budget (0382-1986); (until 1976): Province of British Columbia. Budget Speech (0382-1978)
Published by: Ministry of Finance, PO Box 9417, Stn Prov Govt, Victoria, BC V8W 9V1, Canada. TEL 250-387-7848, FAX 250-356-0206, http://www.gov.bc.ca/fin/.

354.71 CAN ISSN 1192-2176
HJ13
BRITISH COLUMBIA. MINISTRY OF FINANCE. QUARTERLY REPORT ON THE ECONOMY, FISCAL SITUATION AND CROWN CORPORATIONS. Text in English. q.
Former titles (until 1992): Province of British Columbia. Ministry of Finance and Corporate Relations. Quarterly Financial Report (0833-1375); (until 1986): Ministry of Finance, Victoria. Quarterly Financial Report (0228-5983); (until 1980): British Columbia Quarterly Financial Report (0383-5596)
Published by: Ministry of Finance, PO Box 9417, Stn Prov Govt, Victoria, BC V8W 9V1, Canada. TEL 250-387-7848, FAX 250-356-0206, http://www.gov.bc.ca/fin/.

354.71 388 CAN ISSN 1705-8929
BRITISH COLUMBIA. MINISTRY OF TRANSPORTATION. ANNUAL SERVICE PLAN. Text in English. 1980. a.
Former titles (until 2003): British Columbia. Ministry of Transportation. Annual Report (1703-3985); (until 2002): British Columbia. Ministry of Transportation and Highways. Annual Performance Report (1499-0164); (until 2001): British Columbia. Ministry of Transportation and Highways. Annual Report (1180-5315); (until 1986): British Columbia. Minister of Transportation and Highways. Report (0706-1897); Which superseded in part (in 1980): British Columbia. Minister of Transportation, Communications and Highways. Report (0708-7691)
Published by: British Columbia Ministry of Transportation, PO Box 9055, Stn Prov Govt, Victoria, BC V8W 9E2, Canada. TEL 250-387-1978, FAX 250-356-2290.

351.71 CAN ISSN 1208-7920
BRITISH COLUMBIA. OFFICE OF THE AUDITOR GENERAL. ANNUAL REPORT. Text in English. 1978. a.
Former titles (until 1994): British Columbia. Office of the Auditor General. Annual Report to the Legislative Assembly of British Columbia (1190-9366); (until 1989): British Columbia. Office of the Auditor General. Annual Report of the Auditor General of British Columbia to the Legislative Assembly (1190-9358); (until 1987): Province of British Columbia. Office of the Auditor General. Report of the Auditor General (0708-5222)
Published by: British Columbia Office of the Auditor General, 8 Bastion Square, Victoria, BC V8V 1X4, Canada. TEL 250-387-6803, FAX 250-387-1230, bcauditor@bcauditor.com.

352.88 CAN ISSN 0712-0508
BRITISH COLUMBIA. OFFICE OF THE OMBUDSMAN. PUBLIC REPORT SERIES. Key Title: Public Report - Ombudsman of British Columbia. Text in English. 1979. irreg., latest vol.36. price varies. back issues avail. **Document type:** *Government.*
Published by: Office of the Ombudsman, PO Box 9039, Stn Prov Govt, Victoria, BC V8W 9A5, Canada. TEL 250-356-5725, FAX 250-660-1691.

351.711 CAN
BRITISH COLUMBIA PUBLIC SECTOR; of official personnel in federal, provincial and municipal governments in the Province of British Columbia. Text in English. 1978. a. CAD 395. adv. **Document type:** *Directory, Government.*
Formerly: British Columbia List
Published by: B and C List (1982) Ltd., 8278 Manitoba St, Vancouver, BC V5X 3A2, Canada. TEL 604-482-3100, FAX 604-482-3130. Ed. Laurette I Garn. R&P S Hyman. Adv. contact H Barry Hyman. Circ: 1,500.

353 USA ISSN 1934-1954
JL421
BRITISH COLUMBIA STAFF DIRECTORY. Text in English. 1978. a. USD 250 (effective 2008). reprints avail. **Document type:** *Directory, Government.* **Description:** A directory of official personnel in federal state and local government within British Columbia.
Former titles (until 2006): British Columbia Public Sector (1189-5292); (until 1990): British Columbia List of Federal, Provincial and Municipal Personnel in the British Columbia Public Sector (0849-3073); (until 1989): British Columbia List of Official Personnel in Federal, Provincial and Municipal Governments in the Province of British Columbia (0711-7442)
Published by: C Q Press, Inc. (Subsidiary of: Sage Publications, Inc.), 2300 N St, NW, Ste 800, Washington, DC 20037. TEL 202-729-1900, 866-427-7737, FAX 800-380-3810, customerservice@cqpress.com, http://www.cqpress.com. Ed. Barbara Rogers.

BRITISH COLUMBIA UTILITIES COMMISSION. ANNUAL REPORT. *see* ENERGY

351 FRA ISSN 2104-2926
BRIVE LE PHARE. Text in French. 2008. 11/yr. EUR 11 (effective 2011). **Document type:** *Consumer.*
Published by: Brive Envie, BP 4001, Brive Cedex, 19101, France. http://www.brive-envie.fr.

351 USA ISSN 1934-1156
THE BROOKINGS INSTITUTION. POLICY BRIEF. Text in English. 1996. m. back issues avail. **Document type:** *Newsletter, Academic/Scholarly.*
Related titles: Online - full text ed.; Print ed.: ISSN 1934-1164. —CCC.
Published by: Brookings Institution Press, 1775 Massachusetts Ave, NW, Washington, DC 20036. TEL 202-797-6000, 800-275-1447, FAX 202-536-3623, communications@brookings.edu.

BROOKINGS PAPERS ON EDUCATION POLICY (YEAR) (ONLINE). *see* EDUCATION—School Organization And Administration

351 CAN ISSN 1910-8486
CA1BT31-2
BUDGET DES DEPENSES. PARTIE I ET II. PLAN DE DEPENSES DU GOUVERNEMENT ET BUDGET PRINCIPAL DES DEPENSES/ESTIMATES. PART I AND II. THE GOVERNMENT EXPENDITURE PLAN AND THE MAIN ESTIMATES. Text in French, English. 1999. a. **Document type:** *Government.*

Published by: Treasury Board of Canada Secretariat, Corporate Communications/Secretariat du Conseil du Tresor du Canada, West Tower, Rm P-135, 300 Laurier Ave W, Ottawa, ON K1A 0R5, Canada. TEL 613-995-2855, FAX 613-996-0518, services-publications@tbs-sct.gc.ca, http://www.tbs-sct.gc.ca.

351 USA ISSN 0499-0803
S21
BUDGET ESTIMATES FOR THE UNITED STATES DEPARTMENT OF AGRICULTURE. Text in English. 19??. a. **Document type:** *Government.*
Published by: U.S. Government Printing Office, 732 N Capitol St, NW, Washington, DC 20401. TEL 202-512-1800, 866-512-1800, FAX 202-512-2104, ContactCenter@gpo.gov, http://www.gpo.gov.

336.73 USA
BUDGET OF THE UNITED STATES GOVERNMENT. HISTORICAL TABLES. Text in English. a. **Document type:** *Government.* **Description:** Contains the Budget Message of the President, information on the President's budget and management priorities, and budget overviews organized by agency, including assessments of their performance.
Related titles: Online - full content ed.
Published by: Executive Office of the President of the United States, Office of Management and Budget, 725 17th St., NW, Washington, DC 20503. TEL 202-395-3080, FAX 202-395-3888, http://www.whitehouse.gov/omb/index.html. **Subscr. to:** U.S. Government Printing Office, Superintendent of Documents, PO Box 371954, Pittsburgh, PA 15250. TEL 202-512-1800, FAX 202-512-2250, orders@gpo.gov, http://www.access.gpo.gov.

351 USA
BUDGET SENSE. Text in English. m. free. charts. **Document type:** *Newsletter, Government.* **Description:** Covers key issues from the Governor's Budget Office.
Related titles: Online - full content ed.
Published by: Commonwealth of Pennsylvania, Governor's Budget Office, Verizon Tower, 303 Walnut St, 7th Fl, Harrisburg, PA 17101. TEL 717-265-8067, FAX 717-783-3368, shooper@state.pa.us.

343.034 CAN ISSN 1202-6379
BUDGET SPEECH. Text in English. 1906. a. **Document type:** *Government.*
Former titles (until 1992): Budget Address (0822-1979); (until 1980): Budget address of the Honourable ..., Provincial Treasurer, Presented at the .. Session of the .. Legislature of the Province of Alberta in the Legislative Assembly of Alberta (0822-1960); (until 1973): Budget Address (0382-1366); (until 1971): Budget Speech (0382-1374)
Related titles: Online - full content ed.
Published by: Alberta Finance Ministry, Rm 426, Terrace Bldg, 9515 - 107 St., Edmonton, AB T5K 2C3, Canada. TEL 780-427-3035, FAX 780-427-1147, http://www.finance.gov.ab.ca/.

BUFFALO PUBLIC INTEREST LAW JOURNAL. *see* LAW

351.43 DEU ISSN 0942-5985
BULA; Entscheidungs-Informationen fuer Bund - Land - Kreis - Kommune. Text in German. 1982. 8/yr. EUR 30 (effective 2007). adv. **Document type:** *Journal, Trade.* **Description:** Furnishes purchasing agencies of the German Government with information about market developments and innovative products.
Related titles: Online - full text ed.: EUR 50 (effective 2005).
Published by: Rolf Soll Verlag GmbH, Postfach 650680, Hamburg, 22366, Germany. TEL 49-40-6068820, FAX 49-40-60688288, info@soll.de. Ed., Pub. Rolf Soll. R&P Claudia Regine Soll. Adv. contact Claudia-Regine Soll. B&W page EUR 2,520, color page EUR 3,550; trim 190 x 280. Circ: 10,298 (paid and controlled).

353.7 CAN ISSN 1203-0996
BULLETIN INFOACTION. Text in English. 1994. irreg.
Published by: Office of the Commissioner of Official Languages, Rm 1421 110 O Connor St, Ottawa, ON K1A 0T8, Canada. TEL 613-996-6368, FAX 613-943-2255, http://ocol-clo.gc.ca.

BUNDESAKADEMIE FUER OEFFENTLICHE VERWALTUNG. AKADEMIEBRIEF (ONLINE). *see* LAW

BUNDESAMT FUER STATISTIK. INFO. *see* PUBLIC ADMINISTRATION—Abstracting, Bibliographies, Statistics

351 DEU
BUNDESMINISTERIUM FUER BILDUNG UND FORSCHUNG. BUNDESBERICHT FORSCHUNG UND INNOVATION. Text in English. 1979. biennial. free (effective 2009). **Document type:** *Report, Trade.*
Former titles (until 2008): Germany. Bundesministerium fuer Bildung, Wissenschaft, Forschung und Technologie. Bundesbericht Forschung (0300-2047); Germany. Bundesministerium fuer Forschung und Technologie. Bundesbericht Forschung; Germany (Federal Republic, 1949-). Bundesministerium fuer Bildung und Wissenschaft. Forschungsbericht der Bundesregierung
Related titles: German ed.
Published by: Bundesministerium fuer Bildung und Forschung, Hannoversche Str 28-30, Berlin, 10115, Germany. TEL 49-30-18570, FAX 49-30-18575503, information@bmbf.bund.de, http://www.bmbf.de.

BURGERZAKEN EN RECHT. *see* LAW—Civil Law

BUSINESS AND POLITICS (ONLINE). *see* BUSINESS AND ECONOMICS

BUTTERWORTHS LOCAL GOVERNMENT REPORTS. *see* LAW

351.1 MAR
C A F R A D WEB NEWS LETTER. (Centre Africain de Formation et de Recherche Administratives pour le Developpement) Text in English. 2002. m. **Document type:** *Newsletter, Government.* **Description:** Covers activities of the centre, announcements and discussion on major developments and trends in Public Administration and Governance in Africa and world-wide.
Media: Online - full text.
Published by: Centre Africain de Formation et de Recherche Administratives pour le Developpement (C A F R A D)/African Training and Research Centre in Administration for Development, P O Box 310, Tangier, 90001, Morocco. TEL 212-39-322707, FAX 212-39-325785, cafrad@cafrad.org, http://www.cafrad.org/.

351 FRA ISSN 2107-5476
C A R A 'MAG'. (Communaute d'Agglomeration Royan Atlantique) Text in French. 1996. q. **Document type:** *Magazine, Consumer.*
Former titles (until 2008): Pays Royannais (1638-7686); (2001-2002): Intercom (1629-6591); (until 1998): La Lettre Intercommunale du Pays Royannais (1285-1493)
Related titles: Online - full text ed.: ISSN 2107-6960. 2010.
Published by: Communaute d'Agglomeration Royan Atlantique, 107, Av de Rochefort, Royan, 17200, France. TEL 33-5-46221920, FAX 33-5-46056034, contact@agglo-royan.fr, http://www.agglo-royan.fr.

353.53 USA
C B A NEWSNOTES. Text in English. irreg.
Published by: Congressional Black Associates, 1504 Longworth, Washington, DC 20515. TEL 202-225-5865.

351 FRA ISSN 1964-8405
C C B B POINT COM. (Communaute de Communes du Pays Bellegardien) Text in French. 2003. s-a. **Document type:** *Newsletter, Consumer.*
Related titles: Supplement(s): Edition "Special S C O T". ISSN 2108-2499. 2008.
Published by: Communaute de Communes du Pays Bellegardien, 5 Rue des Papetiers, Bellegarde-sur-Valserine, 01200, France. TEL 33-4-50481978, FAX 33-4-50480922, info@ccpb01.fr, http://www.cc-bassinbellegardien.fr/accueil.

328 NLD ISSN 1572-3844
C D VERZAMELING NEDERLANDSE WETGEVING. Key Title: Cd V N W. Text in Dutch. 200?. q. EUR 229 (effective 2009).
Media: CD-ROM.
Published by: Sdu Uitgevers bv, Postbus 20025, The Hague, 2500 EA, Netherlands. TEL 31-70-3789911, FAX 31-70-3854321, sdu@sdu.nl, http://www.sdu.nl/.

C I S INDEX TO PUBLICATIONS OF THE UNITED STATES CONGRESS. *see* PUBLIC ADMINISTRATION—Abstracting, Bibliographies, Statistics

354.4 CAN ISSN 1704-5592
C N S C ANNUAL REPORT. Variant title: Canadian Nuclear Safety Commission. Report on Public Proceedings and Decisions. Text in English. 1947. a.
Former titles (until 2002): Canadian Nuclear Safety Commission. Annual Report (1700-8042); (until 2001): Canada. Atomic Energy Control Board. A E C B Annual Report (1493-5872); (until 1998): Canada. Atomic Energy Control Board. Annual Report (0704-1578)
Related titles: Online - full text ed.: ISSN 1912-0753.
Published by: Canadian Nuclear Safety Commission/Commission Canadienne de Surete Nucleaire, 280 Slater St, PO Box 1046, Sta B, Ottawa, ON K1P 5S9, Canada. TEL 613-995-5894, 800-668-5284, FAX 613-995-5086, info@cnsc-ccsn.gc.ca, http://www.nuclearsafety.gc.ca.

C O S S A WASHINGTON UPDATE. *see* PUBLIC ADMINISTRATION—Abstracting, Bibliographies, Statistics

C P E R. (California Public Employee Relations) *see* BUSINESS AND ECONOMICS—Labor And Industrial Relations

351 FRA ISSN 2109-0793
C P L INFOS. (Carrefour des Pays Lorrains) Text in French. 1999. m. **Document type:** *Newsletter, Consumer.*
Formerly (until 2010): Reseau Infos (2107-2906)
Published by: Carrefour des Pays Lorrains, 7, Rue Alexandre III, BP 22, Colombey-les-Belles, 54170, France. TEL 33-3-83528062, FAX 33-3-83528434, http://cpl.asso.fr.

C Q HOUSE ACTION REPORTS. *see* POLITICAL SCIENCE

C Q TODAY. (Congressional Quarterly) *see* POLITICAL SCIENCE

C Q WEEKLY. (Congressional Quarterly) *see* POLITICAL SCIENCE

351 FRA ISSN 2106-9581
C R E A LE MAG. (Communaute d'Agglomeration Rouen-Elbeuf-Austreberthe) Key Title: Crea le Mag. Text in French. 198?. m. **Document type:** *Magazine, Consumer.*
Former titles (until 2010): Agglo (1621-5389); (until 1999): District 2000 (1269-3855); (until 1995): S I V O M 2000 (1168-8637); (until 199?): La Lettre de l'Agglomeration Rouennaise (0999-629X)
Published by: La C R E A, 14 Bis Ave Pasteur, Rouen Cedex 1, 76006, France. http://www.la-crea.fr.

354.7 GBR
C R I OCCASIONAL PAPERS. (Centre for the Study of Regulated Industries) Text in English. 1997. irreg., latest vol.24, 2005. GBP 10 per issue (effective 2010). back issues avail. **Document type:** *Monographic series, Trade.* **Description:** Contains reviews various aspects of the regulation of utilities, transportation industries, and mail services.
Supersedes (in 1997): C R I Discussion Papers
Related titles: Online - full text ed.: free (effective 2010).
Published by: University of Bath, Centre for the Study of Regulated Industries, c/o Jan Marchant, School of Management University of Bath, Bath, BA2 7AY, United Kingdom. TEL 44-1225-383221, FAX 44-1225-386271, mnsjsm@management.bath.ac.uk, http://www.bath.ac.uk/cri/index.html.

354.8 GBR ISSN 1362-9948
C R I PROCEEDINGS SERIES. Variant title: C R I Conference and Seminar Proceedings. Text in English. 1992. irreg., latest vol.34, 2007. GBP 15 per issue (effective 2010). back issues avail. **Document type:** *Proceedings, Trade.* **Description:** Provides a forum for persons interested in debating regulatory matters.
Related titles: Online - full text ed.: free (effective 2010).
—IE, Ingenta.
Published by: University of Bath, Centre for the Study of Regulated Industries, c/o Jan Marchant, School of Management University of Bath, Bath, BA2 7AY, United Kingdom. TEL 44-1225-386742, FAX 44-1225-386743, mnsjsm@management.bath.ac.uk, http://www.bath.ac.uk/cri/index.html. Ed. Peter Vass TEL 44-1225-386271.

351 USA
C R P C INFO. Text in English. 1967. m. free.
Published by: Capital Region Planning Commission, 333 N 19th St, Box 3355, Baton Rouge, LA 70821. TEL 504-383-5203. Ed. Sidney L Gray. Circ: 719.

352.68 USA ISSN 1521-7272
JK2403
C S G STATE DIRECTORY. DIRECTORY I. ELECTIVE OFFICIALS. Variant title: C S G State Directory I(Council of State Governments). Text in English. 1963. a. USD 65 per issue (effective 2009). **Document type:** *Directory, Government.* **Description:** Provides a lists names, parties, addresses, and districts of state legislators, as well as elected officials with state-wide jurisdiction.
Former titles (until 1998): State Leadership Directory. State Elective Officials Directory I (1090-1159); (until 1996): State Elective Officials and the Legislatures (0191-9466); (until 1977): Selected State Officials and the Legislatures (0191-944X); (until 1975): State Elective Officials and the Legislatures (0191-9431)
Related titles: Diskette ed.; Online - full text ed.
—CCC.
Published by: Council of State Governments, 2760 Research Park Dr, PO Box 11910, Lexington, KY 40578. TEL 859-244-8000, 800-800-1910, FAX 859-244-8001, info@csg.org, http://www.csg.org/.

C S G STATE DIRECTORY. DIRECTORY II, LEGISLATIVE LEADERSHIP, COMMITTEES & STAFF. *see* POLITICAL SCIENCE

352.63 USA ISSN 1521-7264
JK2403
C S G STATE DIRECTORY. DIRECTORY III, ADMINISTRATIVE OFFICIALS. Variant title: C S G State Directory III(Council of State Governments). Text in English. 1961. a. USD 65 per issue (effective 2009). **Document type:** *Directory, Government.* **Description:** Provides a lists names, titles, addresses, and telephone numbers of thousands of administrators in more than 150 areas of state government.
Former titles (until 1998): State Leadership Directory. State Administrative Officials Classified by Function Directory III (1095-5097); (until 1996): State Administrative Officials Classified by Function (0191-9423); (until 1967): Administrative Officials Classified by Functions (0191-9458)
Related titles: CD-ROM ed.; Diskette ed.
Published by: Council of State Governments, 2760 Research Park Dr, PO Box 11910, Lexington, KY 40578. TEL 859-244-8000, 800-800-1910, FAX 859-244-8001, info@csg.org, http://www.csg.org/.

328 USA
C S S P CONGRESSIONAL SOURCEBOOK. Text in English. 1994. a. membership. **Document type:** *Directory.* **Description:** Includes information on each member of Congress: e-mail, address, district phone number, D.C. office staff, address and fax, committee and subcommittee assignments and addresses, district maps, committee staff names, and related information.
Published by: Council of Scientific Society Presidents, 1155 16th St, N W, Washington, DC 20036. TEL 202-872-4452, FAX 202-872-4079, http://www.science-presidents.org. Circ: 500 (controlled).

C T A P PUBLICATION. *see* TRANSPORTATION

351 MAR
CAHIERS AFRICAINS D'ADMINISTRATION PUBLIQUE. Text in French. 1966. s-a. USD 40 (effective 2000). bk.rev. bibl. **Document type:** *Academic/Scholarly.*
Related titles: ◆ English ed.: African Administrative Studies. ISSN 0007-9588; English ed.; Arabic ed.
Indexed: ASD, PerIslam.
Published by: Centre Africain de Formation et de Recherche Administratives pour le Developpement/African Training and Research Centre in Administration for Development, B P 310, Tangier, 90001, Morocco. TEL 212-9-307269, FAX 212-9-322707, 212-9-325785. Ed. Dr. Tijjani Muhammad Bande. Circ: 2,000.

CALIFORNIA AND NEW YORK TAX ANALYSIS (ONLINE EDITION). *see* BUSINESS AND ECONOMICS—Public Finance, Taxation

CALIFORNIA CORRIDORS. *see* TRANSPORTATION

▼ **CALIFORNIA JOURNAL OF POLITICS AND POLICY.** *see* POLITICAL SCIENCE

354.35 USA ISSN 0891-382X
HT169.C2
CALIFORNIA PLANNING AND DEVELOPMENT REPORT. Text in English. 1986. m. USD 249; USD 349 combined subscription print & online eds. (effective 2004). **Document type:** *Newsletter, Trade.* **Description:** Covers local government, real estate and urban planning issues, and environmental issues.
Related titles: Online - full text ed.
Indexed: B02, B15, B17, B18, G04, G06, G07, G08, I05, M06.
Published by: Solimar Research Group, Inc., 973 E Main St, Ventura, CA 93001. TEL 805-643-7700, FAX 805-643-7782. Ed. Paul Shigley. Pub., R&P William Fulton. Circ: 700 (paid).

353 USA ISSN 1934-5011
JK8730
CALIFORNIA STAFF DIRECTORY. Text in English. 1992. a. USD 250 (effective 2008). back issues avail.; reprints avail. **Document type:** *Directory, Government.* **Description:** A directory of official personnel in federal state and local government within California.
Formerly (until 2006): California Public Sector (1073-0915)
Published by: C Q Press, Inc. (Subsidiary of: Sage Publications, Inc.), 2300 N St, NW, Ste 800, Washington, DC 20037. TEL 202-729-1900, 866-427-7737, FAX 800-380-3810, customerservice@cqpress.com, http://www.cqpress.com. Ed. Barbara Rogers.

351 340 USA ISSN 0091-5548
JK8730
CALIFORNIA'S LEGISLATURE. Text in English. 1942. irreg.
Formerly (until 1969): The Legislature of California
Published by: The California State Assembly, State Capitol, P O Box 942849, Sacramento, CA 94249-0000. http://www.assembly.ca.gov/defaulttext.asp.

351 GBR
CAMBRIDGESHIRE COUNTY COUNCIL. LOCAL PERFORMANCE PLAN. Text in English. 1999. a., latest 2003. charts; stat. **Document type:** *Government.* **Description:** Aims to establishes funding targets for the following year.
Related titles: Online - full content ed.
Published by: Cambridgeshire County Council, Strategic Planning Section, Shire Hall, Castle Hill, Cambridge, CB3 0AP, United Kingdom. TEL 44-345-0455200, FAX 44-1223-717201, http://www.cambridgeshire.gov.uk.

351 GBR
CAMBRIDGESHIRE COUNTY COUNCIL. MEDIUM TERM SERVICE PRIORITIES. Text in English. 19??. a., latest 2006. charts.
Document type: *Government.* **Description:** Aims to establishes budget priorities over the ensuing three years.
Related titles: Online - full content ed.
Published by: Cambridgeshire County Council, Strategic Planning Section, Shire Hall, Castle Hill, Cambridge, CB3 0AP, United Kingdom. TEL 44-345-0455200, FAX 44-1223-717201, http://www.cambridgeshire.gov.uk.

CAMBRIDGESHIRE COUNTY COUNCIL. ROAD NETWORK MANAGEMENT PLAN. *see* TRANSPORTATION—Roads And Traffic

CAMBRIDGESHIRE COUNTY COUNCIL. ROAD SAFETY PLAN (YEAR). *see* TRANSPORTATION—Roads And Traffic

CAMBRIDGESHIRE COUNTY COUNCIL. SOCIAL SERVICES DEPARTMENT. CAMBRIDGESHIRE COMMUNITY CARE PLAN. *see* SOCIAL SERVICES AND WELFARE

CAMBRIDGESHIRE COUNTY COUNCIL. SOCIAL SERVICES DEPARTMENT. CHILDREN'S SERVICES PLAN. *see* SOCIAL SERVICES AND WELFARE

CAMBRIDGESHIRE COUNTY COUNCIL. SOCIAL SERVICES DEPARTMENT. SOCIAL SERVICES SERVICE PLAN. *see* SOCIAL SERVICES AND WELFARE

CAMBRIDGESHIRE COUNTY COUNCIL. STATE OF THE ENVIRONMENT REPORTS. *see* ENVIRONMENTAL STUDIES

CAMBRIDGESHIRE COUNTY COUNCIL. TRAFFIC MONITORING REPORT (YEAR). *see* TRANSPORTATION—Roads And Traffic

CAMEROON. DIRECTION DE LA STATISTIQUE ET DE LA COMPTABILITE NATIONALE. BULLETIN TRIMESTRIEL DE CONJONCTURE. *see* PUBLIC ADMINISTRATION—Abstracting, Bibliographies, Statistics

351.71 CAN ISSN 1483-6742
S133
CANADA. AGRICULTURE AND AGRI-FOOD CANADA. PERFORMANCE REPORT. Text in English, French. 1996. a.
Related titles: Online - full text ed.: ISSN 1490-1714.
Published by: (Canada. Agriculture and Agri-Food Canada), Treasury Board of Canada Secretariat, Corporate Communications/Secretariat du Conseil du Tresor du Canada, West Tower, Rm P-135, 300 Laurier Ave W, Ottawa, ON K1A 0R5, Canada. TEL 613-995-2855, FAX 613-996-0518, services-publications@tbs-sct.gc.ca, http://www.tbs-sct.gc.ca.

354.2799 CAN ISSN 1497-6609
CANADA BUSINESS SERVICE CENTRES. ANNUAL REPORT/ CENTRES DE SERVICES AUX ENTREPRISES DU CANADA. RAPPORT ANNUEL. Text in English, French. 2000. a. **Document type:** *Government.*
Related titles: Online - full text ed.: ISSN 1497-6234; ISSN 1497-6242.
Published by: Canada Business Service Centres, Industry Canada, 235 Queen St, Ottawa, ON K1A 0H5, Canada. FAX 613-954-5463, webmaster@cbsc.org.

354.08 CAN ISSN 1200-2569
CANADA. CANADIAN HERITAGE. ANNUAL REPORT ON THE OPERATION OF THE CANADIAN MULTICULTURALISM ACT. Text in English, French. 1989. a.
Formerly (until 1993): Multiculturalism and Citizenship Canada. Annual Report (0848-418X)
Related titles: Online - full text ed.: ISSN 1497-7400.
Published by: Canadian Heritage/Patrimoine Canadien, 15 Eddy St, Gatineau, PQ K1A 0M5, Canada. TEL 819-997-0055, 866-811-0055.

354.071 CAN ISSN 1196-7323
P119.32
CANADA. CANADIAN HERITAGE. OFFICIAL LANGUAGES ANNUAL REPORT/CANADA. PATRIMOINE CANADIEN. RAPPORT ANNUEL LANGUES OFFICIELLES. Text in English, French. 1989. a.
Formerly (until 1994): Canada. Department of the Secretary of State. Official Languages Annual Report (0846-7331)
Published by: (Canadian Heritage, Official Languages Support Programs Branch), Canadian Heritage/Patrimoine Canadien, 15 Eddy St, Gatineau, PQ K1A 0M5, Canada. TEL 819-997-0055, 866-811-0055.

351.71 CAN ISSN 1483-9377
CA1BT31-4 24
CANADA. CANADIAN HERITAGE. PERFORMANCE REPORT. Text in English, French. 1997. a.
Related titles: Online - full text ed.: ISSN 1490-1730.
Published by: (Canadian Heritage/Patrimoine Canadien), Treasury Board of Canada Secretariat, Corporate Communications/Secretariat du Conseil du Tresor du Canada, West Tower, Rm P-135, 300 Laurier Ave W, Ottawa, ON K1A 0R5, Canada. TEL 613-995-2855, FAX 613-996-0518, services-publications@tbs-sct.gc.ca, http://www.tbs-sct.gc.ca.

CANADA. CHAMBRE DES COMMUNES. COMITE PERMANENT DES RESSOURCES NATURELLES. PROCES-VERBAL (FRENCH ONLINE EDITION). *see* EARTH SCIENCES

CANADA. CHAMBRE DES COMMUNES. COMITE PERMANENT DES RESSOURCES NATURELLES. PROCES-VERBAL (FRENCH PRINT EDITION). *see* EARTH SCIENCES

353.484 CAN ISSN 1483-6858
CA1BT31-4 32
CANADA. CITIZENSHIP AND IMMIGRATION CANADA. PERFORMANCE REPORT. Text in English, French. 1997. a.
Related titles: Online - full text ed.: ISSN 1490-4071.
Published by: (Citizenship and Immigration Canada), Treasury Board of Canada Secretariat, Corporate Communications/Secretariat du Conseil du Tresor du Canada, West Tower, Rm P-135, 300 Laurier Ave W, Ottawa, ON K1A 0R5, Canada. TEL 613-995-2855, FAX 613-996-0518, services-publications@tbs-sct.gc.ca, http://www.tbs-sct.gc.ca.

353.4 CAN ISSN 1700-5353
HV8158.7.R69
CANADA. COMMISSION FOR PUBLIC COMPLAINTS AGAINST THE R C M P. ANNUAL REPORT. (Royal Canadian Mounted Police) Variant title: Canada. Commission des Plaintes du Public contre la G R C. Rapport Annuel. Text in English, French. 1989. a.
Formerly (until 2001): Royal Canadian Mounted Police. Public Complaints Commission. Annual Report (1182-3305)
Related titles: Online - full text ed.: ISSN 1700-5361.
Published by: Canada. Commission for Public Complaints Against the R C M P, PO Box 3423, Sta D, Ottawa, ON K1P 6L4, Canada. TEL 613-952-1471, 800-267-6637, FAX 613-952-8045, org@cpc-cpp.gc.ca, http://www.cpc-cpp.gc.ca.

353.7 CAN ISSN 0382-1161
JL25
CANADA. COMMISSIONER OF OFFICIAL LANGUAGES. ANNUAL REPORT. Text in English, French. 1971. a. free. **Document type:** *Government.*
Published by: Office of the Commissioner of Official Languages, 344 Slater St, Ottawa, ON K1A 0T8, Canada. TEL 613-996-6368, FAX 613-993-5082. Ed., R&P, Adv. contact Diane Rioux.

351.71 CAN ISSN 1483-6866
CA1BT31-4 37
CANADA. DEPARTMENT OF FINANCE. PERFORMANCE REPORT. Text in English, French. 1997. a.
Related titles: Online - full text ed.: ISSN 1490-2397.
Published by: (Canada. Canada, Department of Finance/Ministere des Finances Canada), Treasury Board of Canada Secretariat, Corporate Communications/Secretariat du Conseil du Tresor du Canada, West Tower, Rm P-135, 300 Laurier Ave W, Ottawa, ON K1A 0R5, Canada. TEL 613-995-2855, FAX 613-996-0518, services-publications@tbs-sct.gc.ca.

351.71 639.2 CAN ISSN 1483-6696
CA1BT31-4 4
CANADA. DEPARTMENT OF FISHERIES AND OCEANS. PERFORMANCE REPORT. Text in English. 1996. a.
Related titles: Online - full text ed.: ISSN 1490-1595.
Published by: (Canada. Fisheries and Oceans Canada), Treasury Board of Canada Secretariat, Corporate Communications/Secretariat du Conseil du Tresor du Canada, West Tower, Rm P-135, 300 Laurier Ave W, Ottawa, ON K1A 0R5, Canada. TEL 613-995-2855, FAX 613-996-0518, services-publications@tbs-sct.gc.ca, http://www.tbs-sct.gc.ca.

353.13 CAN ISSN 1483-8540
CA1BT31-4 38
CANADA. DEPARTMENT OF FOREIGN AFFAIRS AND INTERNATIONAL TRADE. PERFORMANCE REPORT. Text in English, French. 1997. a.
Related titles: Online - full text ed.: ISSN 1490-2443.
Indexed: LID&ISL.
Published by: (Canada, Department of Foreign Affairs and International Trade), Treasury Board of Canada Secretariat, Corporate Communications/Secretariat du Conseil du Tresor du Canada, West Tower, Rm P-135, 300 Laurier Ave W, Ottawa, ON K1A 0R5, Canada. TEL 613-995-2855, FAX 613-996-0518, services-publications@tbs-sct.gc.ca, http://www.tbs-sct.gc.ca.

351.71 347.013 CAN ISSN 1483-7781
CA1BT31-4 39
CANADA. DEPARTMENT OF JUSTICE. PERFORMANCE REPORT. Text in English, French. 1997. a.
Related titles: Online - full text ed.: ISSN 1490-2370.
Published by: (Canada, Department of Justice/Ministere de la Justice du Canada), Treasury Board of Canada Secretariat, Corporate Communications/Secretariat du Conseil du Tresor du Canada, West Tower, Rm P-135, 300 Laurier Ave W, Ottawa, ON K1A 0R5, Canada. TEL 613-995-2855, FAX 613-996-0518, services-publications@tbs-sct.gc.ca.

355.60971 CAN ISSN 1483-7102
CA1BT31-4 50
CANADA. DEPARTMENT OF NATIONAL DEFENCE. PERFORMANCE REPORT. Text in English, French. 1997. a.
Related titles: Online - full text ed.: ISSN 1490-2346.
Published by: (Canada. Department of National Defence), Treasury Board of Canada Secretariat, Corporate Communications/Secretariat du Conseil du Tresor du Canada, West Tower, Rm P-135, 300 Laurier Ave W, Ottawa, ON K1A 0R5, Canada. TEL 613-995-2855, FAX 613-996-0518, services-publications@tbs-sct.gc.ca, http://www.tbs-sct.gc.ca.

354.3 CAN ISSN 1483-6793
CA1BT31-4 3
CANADA. ENVIRONMENT CANADA. PERFORMANCE REPORT. Text in English, French. 1996. a.
Related titles: Online - full text ed.: ISSN 1490-1307.
Published by: (Canada. Environment Canada/Environnement Canada), Treasury Board of Canada Secretariat, Corporate Communications/Secretariat du Conseil du Tresor du Canada, West Tower, Rm P-135, 300 Laurier Ave W, Ottawa, ON K1A 0R5, Canada. TEL 613-995-2855, FAX 613-996-0518, services-publications@tbs-sct.gc.ca, http://www.tbs-sct.gc.ca.

351.73 CAN ISSN 0705-9485
CANADA GAZETTE: PART 3. Text in English, French. 1974. m. CAD 28.50; CAD 37.05 foreign (effective 1997).
Related titles: Microform ed.: (from MML); Online - full text ed.: ISSN 1491-9710.
—CCC.
Published by: Government of Canada Publications, Publishing and Depository Services, Public Works and Government Services Canada, Ottawa, ON K1A 0S9, Canada.

344.71 351.71 CAN ISSN 1483-8346
CA1BT31-4 41
CANADA. HAZARDOUS MATERIALS INFORMATION REVIEW COMMISSION. PERFORMANCE REPORT. Text in English, French. 1997. a.
Related titles: Online - full text ed.: ISSN 1490-4934.
Published by: (Canada. Hazardous Materials Information Review Commission), Treasury Board of Canada Secretariat, Corporate Communications/Secretariat du Conseil du Tresor du Canada, West Tower, Rm P-135, 300 Laurier Ave W, Ottawa, ON K1A 0R5, Canada. TEL 613-995-2855, FAX 613-996-0518, services-publications@tbs-sct.gc.ca.

353.60971 CAN ISSN 1483-779X
CA1BT31-4 42
CANADA. HEALTH CANADA. PERFORMANCE REPORT. Text in English, French. 1997. a.
Related titles: Online - full text ed.: ISSN 1490-1560.
Published by: (Canada. Health Canada/Sante Canada), Treasury Board of Canada Secretariat, Corporate Communications/Secretariat du Conseil du Tresor du Canada, West Tower, Rm P-135, 300 Laurier Ave W, Ottawa, ON K1A 0R5, Canada. TEL 613-995-2855, FAX 613-996-0518, services-publications@tbs-sct.gc.ca.

CANADA. HOUSE OF COMMONS. STANDING COMMITTEE ON JUSTICE AND HUMAN RIGHTS. MINUTES OF PROCEEDINGS. *see* LAW

CANADA. HOUSE OF COMMONS. STANDING COMMITTEE ON NATIONAL DEFENCE. MINUTES OF PROCEEDINGS. *see* MILITARY

CANADA. HOUSE OF COMMONS. STANDING COMMITTEE ON NATURAL RESOURCES. MINUTES OF PROCEEDINGS (ENGLISH ONLINE EDITION). *see* EARTH SCIENCES

CANADA. HOUSE OF COMMONS. STANDING COMMITTEE ON NATURAL RESOURCES. MINUTES OF PROCEEDINGS (ENGLISH PRINT EDITION). *see* EARTH SCIENCES

CANADA. HOUSE OF COMMONS. STANDING COMMITTEE ON VETERANS AFFAIRS. MINUTES OF PROCEEDINGS. *see* SOCIAL SERVICES AND WELFARE

CANADA. HOUSE OF COMMONS. SUBCOMMITTEE ON PARLIAMENT HILL SECURITY. MINUTES OF PROCEEDINGS. *see* CRIMINOLOGY AND LAW ENFORCEMENT—Security

351.71 CAN
CANADA. HUMAN RESOURCES AND SOCIAL DEVELOPMENT. PERFORMANCE REPORT. Text in English, French. 1997. a.
Formed by the merger of: Canada. Social Development Canada. Performance Report (1714-437X); Canada. Human Resources and Skills Development Canada. Performance Report (1714-4361); Which both superseded in part (in 2004): Canada. Human Resources Development Canada. Performance Report (1483-7161)
Published by: (Human Resources and Social Development Canada), Treasury Board of Canada Secretariat, Corporate Communications/ Secretariat du Conseil du Tresor du Canada, West Tower, Rm P-135, 300 Laurier Ave W, Ottawa, ON K1A 0R5, Canada. TEL 613-995-2855, FAX 613-996-0518, services-publications@tbs-sct.gc.ca.

353.53497 CAN ISSN 1706-3124
CANADA. INDIAN AND NORTHERN AFFAIRS CANADA. ALBERTA REGION YEAR IN REVIEW. Text in English, French. 1999. a.
Formerly (until 2002): Canada. Department of Indian Affairs and Northern Development. Alberta Region. Year in Review (1497-3596)
Published by: (Indian and Northern Affairs Canada, Alberta Region), Indian and Northern Affairs Canada/Affaires Indiennes et du Nord Canada, Terrasses de la Chaudiere, 10 Wellington St, N Tower, Rm 1210, Gatineau, PQ K1A 0H4, Canada. TEL 800-567-9604, infopubs@ainc-inac.gc.ca.

CANADA INDUSTRIAL RELATIONS BOARD. PERFORMANCE REPORT/CONSEIL CANADIEN DES RELATIONS INDUSTRIELLES. RAPPORT SUR LE RENDEMENT. *see* BUSINESS AND ECONOMICS—Labor And Industrial Relations

353.7 CAN ISSN 1495-5970
CA1C12-X1
CANADA. INDUSTRY CANADA. ACHIEVEMENT REPORT: PART VII, SECTION 41, OFFICIAL LANGUAGES ACT. Variant title: Canada. Industrie Canada. Etat de Realisations: Partie VII, Article 41, Loi sur les Langues Officielles. Text in English, French. 1999. a.
Related titles: Online - full text ed.: ISSN 1912-2721. 2002; French ed.: Canada. Industrie Canada. Etat de Realisations. Mise en Oeuvre de l'Article 41 de la Loi sur les Langues Officielles. ISSN 1912-2748. 2002.
Published by: Industry Canada/Industrie Canada, Distribution Services, Communications & Marketing Branch, Rm 268D, West Tower, C.D. Howe Bldg., 235 Queen St, Ottawa, ON K1A 0H5, Canada. TEL 613-947-7466, FAX 613-954-6436, publications@ic.gc.ca.

354 CAN ISSN 1483-9814
CA1BT31-4 45
CANADA. INDUSTRY CANADA. PERFORMANCE REPORT. Text in English, French. 1997. a.
Related titles: Online - full text ed.: ISSN 1490-1471.
Published by: (Canada. Industry Canada/Industrie Canada), Treasury Board of Canada Secretariat, Corporate Communications/Secretariat du Conseil du Tresor du Canada, West Tower, Rm P-135, 300 Laurier Ave W, Ottawa, ON K1A 0R5, Canada. TEL 613-995-2855, FAX 613-996-0518, services-publications@tbs-sct.gc.ca, http://www.tbs-sct.gc.ca.

350 CAN
CANADA. MINISTER OF PUBLIC WORKS AND GOVERNMENT SERVICES CANADA. ESTIMATES (YEAR). Text in English. a. CAD 70. **Document type:** *Proceedings.* **Description:** Covers the spending plan of the Government of Canada.
Published by: (Canada. Public Works and Government Services Canada/Travaux Publics et Services Gouvernementaux Canada), Government of Canada Publications, Publishing and Depository Services, Public Works and Government Services Canada, Ottawa, ON K1A 0S9, Canada. TEL 819-956-4800, FAX 819-994-1498, http://publications.gc.ca.

353.77 CAN ISSN 1483-8869
CA1BT31-4 49
CANADA. NATIONAL BATTLEFIELDS COMMISSION. PERFORMANCE REPORT. Text in English, French. 1997. a.
Related titles: Online - full text ed.: ISSN 1490-6147.
Published by: (Canada. National Battlefields Commission), Treasury Board of Canada Secretariat, Corporate Communications/Secretariat du Conseil du Tresor du Canada, West Tower, Rm P-135, 300 Laurier Ave W, Ottawa, ON K1A 0R5, Canada. TEL 613-995-2855, FAX 613-996-0518, services-publications@tbs-sct.gc.ca.

354.4 CAN ISSN 0825-0170
NE12-3
CANADA. NATIONAL ENERGY BOARD. INFORMATION BULLETINS. Text in English. 1984. irreg. **Document type:** *Monographic series, Government.*
Formerly (until 1983): Canada. National Energy Board. Staff Papers
Published by: National Energy Board/Office National de l'Energie, 444 Seventh Ave, S W, Calgary, AB T2P 0X8, Canada. TEL 403-299-3562, FAX 403-292-5576.

CANADA. NATIONAL ENERGY BOARD. PERFORMANCE REPORT. *see* ENERGY

354.4 CAN ISSN 0821-8641
CANADA. NATIONAL ENERGY BOARD. REGULATORY AGENDA. Text in English, French. 1982. m. free. **Document type:** *Government.*
Description: Provides information on recent hearing reports, forthcoming regulatory actions, and the status of ongoing proceedings.
Published by: National Energy Board/Office National de l'Energie, 444 Seventh Ave, S W, Calgary, AB T2P 0X8, Canada. TEL 403-292-4800, FAX 403-292-5503. Circ: 1,500.

353.39 CAN ISSN 1483-6807
CA1BT31-4 8
CANADA. NATIONAL PAROLE BOARD. PERFORMANCE REPORT. Text in English, French. 1996. a.
Related titles: Online - full text ed.: ISSN 1490-6279.
Published by: (Canada. National Parole Board), Treasury Board of Canada Secretariat, Corporate Communications/Secretariat du Conseil du Tresor du Canada, West Tower, Rm P-135, 300 Laurier Ave W, Ottawa, ON K1A 0R5, Canada. TEL 613-995-2855, FAX 613-996-0518, services-publications@tbs-sct.gc.ca, http://www.tbs-sct.gc.ca.

354.3 CAN ISSN 1483-6718
CA1BT31-4 9
CANADA. NATURAL RESOURCES CANADA. PERFORMANCE REPORT. Text in English, French. 1996. a.
Related titles: Online - full text ed.: ISSN 1490-2524.
Published by: (Canada. Natural Resources Canada/Ressources Naturelles Canada), Treasury Board of Canada Secretariat, Corporate Communications/Secretariat du Conseil du Tresor du Canada, West Tower, Rm P-135, 300 Laurier Ave W, Ottawa, ON K1A 0R5, Canada. TEL 613-995-2855, FAX 613-996-0518, services-publications@tbs-sct.gc.ca, http://www.tbs-sct.gc.ca.

352.439 CAN ISSN 1483-9636
HJ13
CANADA. OFFICE OF THE AUDITOR GENERAL. PERFORMANCE REPORT. Text in English, French. 1997. a.
Related titles: Online - full text ed.: ISSN 1490-3342.
Published by: (Office of the Auditor General of Canada/Bureau du Verificateur General du Canada), Treasury Board of Canada Secretariat, Corporate Communications/Secretariat du Conseil du Tresor du Canada, West Tower, Rm P-135, 300 Laurier Ave W, Ottawa, ON K1A 0R5, Canada. TEL 613-995-2855, FAX 613-996-0518, services-publications@tbs-sct.gc.ca, http://www.tbs-sct.gc.ca.

351.71 CAN ISSN 1483-9237
CA1BT31-4 60
CANADA. OFFICE OF THE COMMISSIONER OF OFFICIAL LANGUAGES. PERFORMANCE REPORT. Text in English, French. 1997. a.
Related titles: Online - full text ed.: ISSN 1490-6082.
Published by: (Canada. Office of the Commissioner of Official Languages), Treasury Board of Canada Secretariat, Corporate Communications/Secretariat du Conseil du Tresor du Canada, West Tower, Rm P-135, 300 Laurier Ave W, Ottawa, ON K1A 0R5, Canada. TEL 613-995-2855, FAX 613-996-0518, services-publications@tbs-sct.gc.ca.

353.71 364 CAN ISSN 1483-8826
CA1BT31-4 61
CANADA. OFFICE OF THE CORRECTIONAL INVESTIGATOR. PERFORMANCE REPORT. Text in English, French. 1997. a.
Related titles: Online - full text ed.: ISSN 1490-6295.
Published by: (Office of the Correctional Investigator), Treasury Board of Canada Secretariat, Corporate Communications/Secretariat du Conseil du Tresor du Canada, West Tower, Rm P-135, 300 Laurier Ave W, Ottawa, ON K1A 0R5, Canada. TEL 613-995-2855, FAX 613-996-0518, services-publications@tbs-sct.gc.ca, http://www.tbs-sct.gc.ca.

351 CAN ISSN 1910-684X
CANADA. OFFICE OF THE SENATE ETHICS OFFICER. ANNUAL REPORT/CANADA. BUREAU DU CONSEILLER SENATORIAL EN ETHIQUE. RAPPORT ANNUEL. Text in English, French. 2006. a. **Document type:** *Government.*
Published by: Canada, Office of the Senate Ethics Officer, Thomas D'Arcy McGee Bldg, 90 Sparks St, Rm 526, Ottawa, ON K1P 5B4, Canada. TEL 613-947-3566, 800-267-7362, FAX 613-947-3577, cse-seo@sen.parl.gc.ca, http://www.sen.parl.gc.ca/seo-cse/eng/Home-e.html.

328.71 CAN ISSN 0704-5638
CANADA. PARLIAMENT. CHAMBRE DES COMMUNES. DEBATS. Text in French. d.
Related titles: ◆ English ed.: Canada. Parliament. House of Commons Debates. ISSN 0704-5603.
Published by: (Canada. Canada, House of Commons), Supply and Services Canada, Publishing Centre, Ottawa, ON K1A 0S9, Canada.

328.71 CAN ISSN 0704-5603
J103
CANADA. PARLIAMENT. HOUSE OF COMMONS DEBATES. Text in English. 1951. d.
Related titles: CD-ROM ed.: ISSN 1201-169X; ◆ French ed.: Canada. Parliament. Chambre des Communes. Debats. ISSN 0704-5638.
Published by: (Canada. Canada, House of Commons), Supply and Services Canada, Publishing Centre, Ottawa, ON K1A 0S9, Canada.

328 CAN ISSN 0707-9311
J103.
CANADA. PARLIAMENT. HOUSE OF COMMONS. JOURNALS/ CANADA. PARLEMENT. CHAMBRE DES COMMUNES. JOURNAUX. Text in English, French. 1977. irreg.
Formed by the merger of (1868-1977): House of Commons of Canada. Journals (0707-929X); Which was formerly (until 1949): House of Commons of the Dominion of Canada. Journals (1494-6408); (1868-1977): Chambre des Communes du Canada (0707-9338); Which was formerly (until 1874): Chambre des Communes de la Puissance du Canada. Journaux (0707-932X)
Related titles: CD-ROM ed.: Canada. Parliament. House of Commons. Electronic Journals. ISSN 1494-4499. 1999. CAD 49.95 (effective 2005); Online - full text ed.: ISSN 1486-911X.
Published by: Canada, House of Commons (Subsidiary of: Parliament), Information Service, Ottawa, ON K1A 0A9, Canada. TEL 613-992-4793, info@parl.gc.ca, http://www.parl.gc.ca.

328.71 CAN ISSN 0848-2659
J103
CANADA. PARLIAMENT. HOUSE OF COMMONS. ORDER PAPER AND NOTICE PAPER. Text in English, French. irreg.
Formerly (until 1988): Canada. Parliament. House of Commons. Order Paper and Notices (0317-8420)
Related titles: Online - full text ed.: ISSN 1493-3446.
Published by: Canada, House of Commons (Subsidiary of: Parliament), Information Service, Ottawa, ON K1A 0A9, Canada. TEL 613-992-4793, info@parl.gc.ca.

354 CAN ISSN 1707-8369
J103
CANADA. PARLIAMENT. HOUSE OF COMMONS. STANDING COMMITTEE ON GOVERNMENT OPERATIONS AND ESTIMATES. Text in English. 2001. irreg. **Document type:** *Government.*
Supersedes in part (in 2002): Canada. Parliament. House of Commons. Standing Committee on Transport and Government Operations. Minutes of Proceedings (1706-3302); Which was formed by the merger of (1965-2001): Canada. Parliament. House of Commons. Standing Committee on Transport. Minutes of Proceedings (1204-5187); Which was formerly (until 1995): Canada. Parliament. House of Commons. Standing Committee on Transport. Minutes of Proceedings and Evidence (0826-3531); (until 1979): Canada. Parliament. House of Commons. Standing Committee on Transport and Communications. Minutes of Proceedings and Evidence (0576-3665); (1988-2001): Canada. Parliament. House of Commons. Standing Committee on Government Operations. Minutes of Proceedings (1196-9474); Which was formerly (until 1995): Canada. Parliament. House of Commons. Standing Committee on Government Operations. Minutes of Proceedings and Evidence (1200-0086); (until 1994): Canada. Parliament. House of Commons. Standing Committee on Consumer and Corporate Affairs and Government Operations (0844-8590); Which was formed by the merger of (1986-1988): Canada. Parliament. House of Commons. Standing Committee on Consumer and Corporate Affairs and Government Operations. Minutes of Proceedings and Evidence (0834-9878); (1986-1988): Canada. Parliament. House of Commons. Standing Committee on Government Operations. Minutes of Proceedings and Evidence (0840-2299)
Related titles: Online - full text ed.: ISSN 1706-3930.
Published by: (House of Commons, Standing Committee on Government Operations and Estimates), Canada, House of Commons (Subsidiary of: Parliament), Information Service, Ottawa, ON K1A 0A9, Canada. TEL 613-992-4793, info@parl.gc.ca, http://www.parl.gc.ca.

CANADA. PARLIAMENT. HOUSE OF COMMONS. STANDING COMMITTEE ON PUBLIC SAFETY AND NATIONAL SECURITY. MINUTES OF PROCEEDINGS. *see* CRIMINOLOGY AND LAW ENFORCEMENT—Security

CANADA. PARLIAMENT. HOUSE OF COMMONS. STANDING COMMITTEE ON TRANSPORT, INFRASTRUCTURE AND COMMUNITIES. MINUTES OF PROCEEDINGS. *see* TRANSPORTATION

328.71 CAN ISSN 1204-9484
CA1Y4F25
CANADA. PARLIAMENT. SENATE. ORDER PAPER AND NOTICE PAPER/FUEILLETON ET FEUILLETON DES AVIS. Text in English, French. 19??. irreg.
Supersedes in part (in 1996): Canada. Parliament. Senate. Minutes of the Proceedings of the Senate (0384-2266); Which incorporated (19??-1976): Proces-Verbaux du Senat (0384-2274)
Published by: Senate of Canada, Information Service, Ottawa, ON K1A 0A9, Canada. TEL 613-992-4793, info@parl.gc.ca, http://www.parl.gc.ca.

354.71 615 CAN ISSN 0847-4397
CA1RG79-1
CANADA. PATENTED MEDICINE PRICES REVIEW BOARD. ANNUAL REPORT. Text in English, French. 1989. a.
Related titles: Online - full content ed.: ISSN 1495-0561.
Published by: Canada. Patented Medicine Prices Review Board/Conseil d'Examen du Prix des Medicaments Brevetes, Standard Life Centre, 333 Laurier Ave W, Ste 1400, PO Box L40, Ottawa, ON K1P 1C1, Canada. TEL 613-952-7360, 877-861-2350, FAX 613-952-7626, pmprb@pmprb-cepmb.gc.ca, http://www.pmprb-cepmb.gc.ca.

354.759 CAN ISSN 0825-396X
CANADA POST CORPORATION. ANNUAL REPORT. Variant title: Societe Canadienne des Postes. Rapport Annuel. Text in English, French. 1967. a.
Former titles (until 1983): Canada Post. Annual Report (0848-6581); (until 1971): Canada. Post Office Department. Annual Report (0848-7030)
Published by: Canada Post Corporation, 4567 Dixie Rd, Mississauga, ON L4W 1S2, Canada. http://www.canadapost.ca/.

352.24 CAN ISSN 1484-0774
CA1BT31-4 65
CANADA. PRIVY COUNCIL OFFICE. PERFORMANCE REPORT. Text in English, French. 1997. a.
Related titles: Online - full text ed.: ISSN 1490-4101.
Published by: (Government of Canada, Privy Council Office/ Gouvernement du Canada. Bureau du Conseil Prive), Treasury Board of Canada Secretariat, Corporate Communications/Secretariat du Conseil du Tresor du Canada, West Tower, Rm P-135, 300 Laurier Ave W, Ottawa, ON K1A 0R5, Canada. TEL 613-995-2855, FAX 613-996-0518, services-publications@tbs-sct.gc.ca, http://www.tbs-sct.gc.ca.

351 CAN ISSN 1719-6469
CANADA. PUBLIC SERVICE INTEGRITY OFFICE. ANNUAL REPORT TO PARLIAMENT. Text in English. 2003. a.
Media: Online - full text. **Related titles:** ◆ Print ed.: Public Service Integrity Office. Annual Report to Parliament. ISSN 1709-7274; Ed.: Canada. Bureau de l'Integrite de la Fonction Publique. Rapport Annuel au Parlement. ISSN 1719-6477.
Published by: Canada, Public Service Integrity Office, 60 Queen St., Ste 605, Ottawa, ON, Canada. TEL 613-941-6400, 866-941-6400, FAX 613-941-6535, http://www.psio-bifp.gc.ca/index_e.php.

351 CAN ISSN 0590-9449
CANADA. PUBLIC SERVICE STAFF RELATIONS BOARD. ANNUAL REPORT. Text in English, French. 1968. a.
Related titles: Online - full text ed.: ISSN 1493-8200.
Published by: Canada. Public Service Staff Relations Board, PO Box 1525, Sta. B, Ottawa, ON K1P 5V2, Canada. TEL 613-990-1800, FAX 613-990-1849, mail.courrier@pssrb-crtfp.gc.ca.

352.68 CAN ISSN 1483-9385
CA1BT31-4 67
CANADA. PUBLIC SERVICE STAFF RELATIONS BOARD. PERFORMANCE REPORT. Text in English, French. 1997. a.
Related titles: Online - full text ed.: ISSN 1490-5248.
Published by: (Canada. Public Service Staff Relations Board), Treasury Board of Canada Secretariat, Corporate Communications/Secretariat du Conseil du Tresor du Canada, West Tower, Rm P-135, 300 Laurier Ave W, Ottawa, ON K1A 0R5, Canada. TEL 613-995-2855, FAX 613-996-0518, services-publications@tbs-sct.gc.ca, http://www.tbs-sct.gc.ca.

CANADA. PUBLIC SERVICE STAFFING TRIBUNAL. ESTIMATES. PART III. REPORT ON PLANS AND PRIORITIES/CANADA. SECRETARIAT DU CONSEIL DU TRESOR DU CANADA. BUDGET DES DEPENSES. PARTIE III. RAPPORT SUR LES PLANS ET LES PRIORITES. *see* BUSINESS AND ECONOMICS—Public Finance, Taxation

352.5 CAN ISSN 1483-6734
CA1BT31-4 68 2006
CANADA. PUBLIC WORKS AND GOVERNMENT SERVICES CANADA. PERFORMANCE REPORT. Text in English, French. 1997. a.
Related titles: Online - full text ed.: ISSN 1490-2419.
Published by: (Canada. Public Works and Government Services Canada/Travaux Publics et Services Gouvernementaux Canada), Treasury Board of Canada Secretariat, Corporate Communications/ Secretariat du Conseil du Tresor du Canada, West Tower, Rm P-135, 300 Laurier Ave W, Ottawa, ON K1A 0R5, Canada. TEL 613-995-2855, FAX 613-996-0518, services-publications@tbs-sct.gc.ca, http://www.tbs-sct.gc.ca.

352.7 CAN ISSN 1494-5150
CANADA. RURAL SECRETARIAT. ANNUAL REPORT TO PARLIAMENT. Variant title: Working Together in Rural Canada. Text in English, French. 2000. a.
Published by: Agriculture and Agri-Food Canada, Rural Secretariat, 1525 Carling Ave, 3rd Flr, Ottawa, ON K1A 0C5, Canada. TEL 888-781-2222, FAX 800-884-9899, rs@agr.gc.ca.

351.71 CAN ISSN 1719-1785
CA1BT31-4 21
CANADA SCHOOL OF PUBLIC SERVICE. PERFORMANCE REPORT. Text in English, French. 1997. a.
Formerly (until 2005): Canadian Centre for Management Development. Performance Report (1484-0626)
Published by: (Canada School of Public Service), Treasury Board of Canada Secretariat, Corporate Communications/Secretariat du Conseil du Tresor du Canada, West Tower, Rm P-135, 300 Laurier Ave W, Ottawa, ON K1A 0R5, Canada. TEL 613-995-2855, FAX 613-996-0518, services-publications@tbs-sct.gc.ca.

P

353.9 CAN ISSN 1483-6874
CA1BT31-4 74
CANADA. SOLICITOR GENERAL CANADA. PERFORMANCE REPORT. Text in English, French. 1997. a.
Published by: (Public Safety Canada), Treasury Board of Canada Secretariat, Corporate Communications/Secretariat du Conseil du Tresor du Canada, West Tower, Rm P-135, 300 Laurier Ave W, Ottawa, ON K1A 0R5, Canada. TEL 613-995-2855, FAX 613-996-0518, services-publications@tbs-sct.gc.ca, http://www.tbs-sct.gc.ca.

CANADA. STATISTICS CANADA. CANADIAN CULTURE IN PERSPECTIVE: A STATISTICAL OVERVIEW/CANADA. STATISTIQUE CANADA. LE CANADA, SA CULTURE, SON PATRIMOINE ET SON IDENTITE: PERSPECTIVE STATISTIQUE. *see* PUBLIC ADMINISTRATION—Abstracting, Bibliographies, Statistics

353.71 346.134 CAN ISSN 1483-667X
CA1BT31-4 13
CANADA. STATUS OF WOMEN CANADA. PERFORMANCE REPORT. Text in English, French. 1996. a.
Related titles: Online - full text ed.: ISSN 1490-5221.
Published by: (Status of Women Canada/Condition Feminine Canada), Treasury Board of Canada Secretariat, Corporate Communications/ Secretariat du Conseil du Tresor du Canada, West Tower, Rm P-135, 300 Laurier Ave W, Ottawa, ON K1A 0R5, Canada. TEL 613-995-2855, FAX 613-996-0518, services-publications@tbs-sct.gc.ca.

351.71 CAN ISSN 1483-7552
CA1BT31-4 76
CANADA. TAX COURT. PERFORMANCE REPORT. Text in English, French. 1997. a.
Related titles: Online - full text ed.: ISSN 1490-3849.
Published by: (Tax Court of Canada), Treasury Board of Canada Secretariat, Corporate Communications/Secretariat du Conseil du Tresor du Canada, West Tower, Rm P-135, 300 Laurier Ave W, Ottawa, ON K1A 0R5, Canada. TEL 613-995-2855, FAX 613-996-0518, services-publications@tbs-sct.gc.ca.

351.71 CAN ISSN 1483-6351
CA1BT31-4 14
CANADA. TRANSPORT CANADA. PERFORMANCE REPORT. Text in English, French. 1996. a.
Related titles: Online - full text ed.: ISSN 1490-1617.
Published by: (Transport Canada/Transports Canada), Treasury Board of Canada Secretariat, Corporate Communications/Secretariat du Conseil du Tresor du Canada, West Tower, Rm P-135, 300 Laurier Ave W, Ottawa, ON K1A 0R5, Canada. TEL 613-995-2855, FAX 613-996-0518, services-publications@tbs-sct.gc.ca.

354.71 CAN ISSN 1189-7546
HD4007.5
CANADA. TREASURY BOARD. CROWN CORPORATIONS AND OTHER CORPORATE INTERESTS OF CANADA. Text in English. 1954. a.
Supersedes in part (in 1992): Public Accounts of Canada (0319-3306)
Related titles: Online - full text ed.: ISSN 1487-010X.
Published by: (Canada. Treasury Board), Treasury Board of Canada Secretariat, Corporate Communications/Secretariat du Conseil du Tresor du Canada, West Tower, Rm P-135, 300 Laurier Ave W, Ottawa, ON K1A 0R5, Canada. TEL 613-995-2855, FAX 613-996-0518, services-publications@tbs-sct.gc.ca, http://www.tbs-sct.gc.ca.

352.40971 CAN ISSN 1483-670X
CA1BT31-4 15
CANADA. TREASURY BOARD. PERFORMANCE REPORT. Text in English, French. 1996. a.
Related titles: Online - full text ed.: ISSN 1490-1498.
Published by: (Canada. Treasury Board), Treasury Board of Canada Secretariat, Corporate Communications/Secretariat du Conseil du Tresor du Canada, West Tower, Rm P-135, 300 Laurier Ave W, Ottawa, ON K1A 0R5, Canada. TEL 613-995-2855, FAX 613-996-0518, services-publications@tbs-sct.gc.ca.

352.46071 CAN ISSN 1209-336X
CANADA. TREASURY BOARD. PROGRAM EXPENDITURE DETAIL: A PROFILE OF DEPARTMENTAL SPENDING. Variant title: Canada. Conseil du Tresor. Detail des Depenses de Programmes: Profil des Depenses des Ministeres. Text in English, French. 1996. a.
Published by: (Canada. Treasury Board), Treasury Board of Canada Secretariat, Corporate Communications/Secretariat du Conseil du Tresor du Canada, West Tower, Rm P-135, 300 Laurier Ave W, Ottawa, ON K1A 0R5, Canada. TEL 613-995-2855, FAX 613-996-0518, services-publications@tbs-sct.gc.ca.

352.46 CAN
CANADA. TREASURY BOARD SECRETARIAT. ESTIMATES. PART I: GOVERNMENT EXPENDITURE PLAN AND HIGHLIGHTS BY MINISTRY/CANADA CONSEIL DU TRESOR. BUDGET DES DEPENSES. PARTIE I: PLAN DE DEPENSES DU GOUVERNEMENT ET POINTS SAILLANTS PAR PORTEFEUILLE. Text in English, French. 1977. a. free. charts; stat. **Document type:** *Government.*
Former titles: Canada. Treasury Board Secretariat. Estimates. Part I: Government Expenditures Plan; Canada. Treasury Board Secretariat. Federal Expenditure Plan (0706-6007)
Published by: Treasury Board, 140 O Connor St, Ottawa, ON K1A 0R5, Canada. TEL 613-995-2855. R&P Robert Mellon.

354.8 CAN
CANADA. TREASURY BOARD SECRETARIAT. ESTIMATES. PART II: ESTIMATES/CANADA. CONSEIL DU TRESOR. PARTIE II: BUDGET DES DEPENSES PRINCIPAL. Text in English. a. CAD 60. stat. **Document type:** *Government.*
Published by: (Canada. Treasury Board), Government of Canada Publications, Publishing and Depository Services, Public Works and Government Services Canada, Ottawa, ON K1A 0S9, Canada. TEL 819-956-5365, FAX 819-956-5134.

352.4 CAN ISSN 1706-6166
HJ13
CANADA. TREASURY BOARD SECRETARIAT. ESTIMATES. PART III: REPORT ON PLANS AND PRIORITIES/SECRETARIAT DU CONSEIL DU TRESOR. BUDGET DES DEPENSES. PARTIE III: RAPPORT SUR LES PLANS ET LES PRIORITES. Variant title: T B S Plans and Priorities. Text in English, French. 1983. a.
Incorporates (1983-1998): Treasury Board Secretariat. Federal Regulatory Plan (0833-7322); Which was formerly (until 1987): Canada. Treasury Board. Regulatory Agendas (0823-1923)
Published by: (Canada. Treasury Board), Treasury Board of Canada Secretariat, Corporate Communications/Secretariat du Conseil du Tresor du Canada, West Tower, Rm P-135, 300 Laurier Ave W, Ottawa, ON K1A 0R5, Canada. TEL 613-995-2855, FAX 613-996-0518, services-publications@tbs-sct.gc.ca.

353.538 CAN ISSN 1483-6815
CA1BT31-4 16
CANADA. VETERANS AFFAIRS CANADA. PERFORMANCE REPORT. Text in English, French. 1996. a.
Related titles: Online - full text ed.: ISSN 1490-5523.
Published by: (Veterans Affairs Canada/Anciens Combattants Canada), Treasury Board of Canada Secretariat, Corporate Communications/Secretariat du Conseil du Tresor du Canada, West Tower, Rm P-135, 300 Laurier Ave W, Ottawa, ON K1A 0R5, Canada. TEL 613-995-2855, FAX 613-996-0518, services-publications@tbs-sct.gc.ca.

353.96 CAN ISSN 1483-9849
CA1BT31-4 22
CANADIAN CENTRE FOR OCCUPATIONAL HEALTH AND SAFETY. PERFORMANCE REPORT. Text in English, French. 1997. a.
Related titles: Online - full text ed.: ISSN 1490-5981.
Published by: (Canadian Centre for Occupational Health and Safety (C C O H S)/Centre Canadien d'Hygiene et de Securite au Travail), Treasury Board of Canada Secretariat, Corporate Communications/Secretariat du Conseil du Tresor du Canada, West Tower, Rm P-135, 300 Laurier Ave W, Ottawa, ON K1A 0R5, Canada. TEL 613-995-2855, FAX 613-996-0518, services-publications@tbs-sct.gc.ca, http://www.tbs-sct.gc.ca.

354.73 CAN ISSN 0382-2281
CANADIAN COMMERCIAL CORPORATION. ANNUAL REPORT. Text in English. 1961. a.
Related titles: Online - full text ed.: ISSN 1701-9036.
Published by: Corporation Commerciale Canadienne/Canadian Commercial Corporation, 1100-50 O'Connor St, Ottawa, ON K1A 0S6, Canada. TEL 613-996-0034, 800-748-8191, FAX 613-995-2121.

354.3 CAN ISSN 1483-9652
CA1BT31-4 23
CANADIAN ENVIRONMENTAL ASSESSMENT AGENCY. PERFORMANCE REPORT. Text in English, French. 1997. a.
Related titles: Online - full text ed.: ISSN 1490-5469.
Published by: (Canadian Environmental Assessment Agency), Treasury Board of Canada Secretariat, Corporate Communications/Secretariat du Conseil du Tresor du Canada, West Tower, Rm P-135, 300 Laurier Ave W, Ottawa, ON K1A 0R5, Canada. TEL 613-995-2855, FAX 613-996-0518, services-publications@tbs-sct.gc.ca, http://www.tbs-sct.gc.ca.

351.71 CAN ISSN 0045-4893
CANADIAN GOVERNMENT PROGRAMS AND SERVICES. Text in English. 1970. bi-m. looseleaf. CAD 740 (effective 2008). index. **Document type:** *Handbook/Manual/Guide, Trade.* **Description:** Authoritative guide to federal government organizations, programs and services, government relations. Information on all departments: structure, key personnel with addresses and phone numbers, jurisdictions, responsibilities, budgets, etc.
Formerly (until 1972): Canadian Government Organization Manual (0384-580X)
Indexed: C03, CBCABus, PQC.
—CIS.
Published by: C C H Canadian Ltd. (Subsidiary of: Wolters Kluwer N.V.), 90 Sheppard Ave E, Ste 300, North York, ON M2N 6X1, Canada. TEL 416-224-2248, 800-268-4522, FAX 416-224-2243, 800-461-4131, cservice@cch.ca.

353.7 CAN ISSN 1497-5637
CANADIAN HERITAGE. PUBLICATIONS ASSISTANCE PROGRAM. ACTIVITY REPORT. Text in English. 1999. a.
Related titles: Online - full text ed.: ISSN 1497-4762.
Published by: Canadian Heritage, Publications Assistance Program (Subsidiary of: Canadian Heritage/Patrimoine Canadien), 15 Eddy St, 15-4-F, Gatineau, PQ K1A 0M5, Canada. TEL 819-997-4974, 800-641-9221, FAX 819-997-4995, pap@pch.gc.ca.

353.480971 CAN ISSN 1483-7412
CA1BT31-4 25
CANADIAN HUMAN RIGHTS COMMISSION. PERFORMANCE REPORT. Text in English, French. 1997. a.
Related titles: Online - full text ed.: ISSN 1490-5485.
Published by: (Canadian Human Rights Commission/Commission Canadienne des Droits de la Personne), Treasury Board of Canada Secretariat, Corporate Communications/Secretariat du Conseil du Tresor du Canada, West Tower, Rm P-135, 300 Laurier Ave W, Ottawa, ON K1A 0R5, Canada. TEL 613-995-2855, FAX 613-996-0518, services-publications@tbs-sct.gc.ca.

353.48 323 CAN ISSN 1494-0132
CA1HR61-1
CANADIAN HUMAN RIGHTS TRIBUNAL. ANNUAL REPORT. Text in English, French. 1998. a.
Related titles: Online - full text ed.: ISSN 1494-524X.
Published by: Canadian Human Rights Tribunal/Tribunal Canadien des Droits de la Personne, 160 Elgin St, 11th Fl, Ottawa, ON K1A 1J4, Canada. TEL 613-995-1707, FAX 613-995-3484, registrar@chrt-tcdp.gc.ca, http://www.chrt-tcdp.gc.ca.

353.6274 CAN ISSN 1701-073X
RA184
CANADIAN INSTITUTES OF HEALTH RESEARCH. PERFORMANCE REPORT. Variant title: Instituts de Recherche en Sante du Canada. Rapport sur le Rendement. Text in English, French. 1997. a.
Formerly (until 2001): Medical Research Council. Performance Report (1483-7129)
Related titles: Online - full text ed.: ISSN 1701-0748.
Published by: (Canadian Institutes of Health Research (C I H R)/Instituts de Recherche en Sante au Canada (I R S C)), Treasury Board of Canada Secretariat, Corporate Communications/Secretariat du Conseil du Tresor du Canada, West Tower, Rm P-135, 300 Laurier Ave W, Ottawa, ON K1A 0R5, Canada. TEL 613-995-2855, FAX 613-996-0518, services-publications@tbs-sct.gc.ca, http://www.tbs-sct.gc.ca.

353.33 CAN ISSN 1483-9482
CA1BT31-4 26
CANADIAN INTERGOVERNMENTAL CONFERENCE SECRETARIAT. PERFORMANCE REPORT. Text in English, French. 1997. a.
Related titles: Online - full text ed.: ISSN 1490-6244.
Published by: (Canadian Intergovernmental Conference Secretariat/ Secretariat des Conferences Intergouvernementales Canadiennes), Treasury Board of Canada Secretariat, Corporate Communications/ Secretariat du Conseil du Tresor du Canada, West Tower, Rm P-135, 300 Laurier Ave W, Ottawa, ON K1A 0R5, Canada. TEL 613-995-2855, FAX 613-996-0518, services-publications@tbs-sct.gc.ca, http://www.tbs-sct.gc.ca.

351 CAN ISSN 0846-7986
CANADIAN INTERGOVERNMENTAL CONFERENCE SECRETARIAT. REPORT TO GOVERNMENTS/RAPPORT AUX GOUVERNEMENTS. Text in English, French. a.
Related titles: Online - full text ed.: ISSN 1719-6205; French ed.: Secretariat des Conferences Intergouvernementales Canadiennes. Rapport aux Gouvernements. ISSN 1719-6213. 1997.
Published by: Canadian Intergovernmental Conference Secretariat/ Secretariat des Conferences Intergouvernementales Canadiennes, P.O. Box 488, Station A, Ottawa, ON K1N 8V5, Canada. TEL 613-995-2341, FAX 613-996-6091, info@scics.gc.ca.

351.71 382 CAN ISSN 1483-7315
CA1BT31-4 28
CANADIAN INTERNATIONAL TRADE TRIBUNAL. PERFORMANCE REPORT. Text in English, French. 1997. a.
Related titles: Online - full text ed.: ISSN 1490-554X.
Published by: (Canada. Canadian International Trade Tribunal), Treasury Board of Canada Secretariat, Corporate Communications/Secretariat du Conseil du Tresor du Canada, West Tower, Rm P-135, 300 Laurier Ave W, Ottawa, ON K1A 0R5, Canada. TEL 613-995-2855, FAX 613-996-0518, services-publications@tbs-sct.gc.ca, http://www.tbs-sct.gc.ca.

351.71 CAN ISSN 0834-1516
H62.5.C2 CODEN: CJPEE8
➤ **CANADIAN JOURNAL OF PROGRAM EVALUATION/REVUE CANADIENNE D'EVALUATION DE PROGRAMME.** Text and summaries in English, French. 1986. s-a. CAD 165 domestic to individuals; USD 165 foreign to individuals; CAD 210 domestic to institutions; USD 210 foreign to institutions (effective 2011). adv. bk.rev. charts; stat. 150 p./no.; back issues avail.; reprints avail. **Document type:** *Journal, Academic/Scholarly.* **Description:** Publishes articles on all aspects of the theory and practice of evaluation, including methodology, evaluation standards, implementation of evaluations, reporting and use of studies, and the audit or meta-evaluation of evaluation.
Related titles: Online - full text ed.
Indexed: C03, CA, CBCARef, CWPI, E-psyche, E03, ERI, P03, P42, P48, PAA&I, PQC, PsycInfo, PsycholAb, S02, S03, SCOPUS, SOPODA, SPAA, SWR&A, SociolAb, T02.
—BLDSC (3034.650000), IE, Ingenta. **CCC.**
Published by: (Canadian Evaluation Society), University of Calgary Press, 2500 University Dr NW, Calgary, AB T2N 1N4, Canada. TEL 403-220-7578, FAX 403-282-0085, http://www.uofcpress.com. Ed. J Bradley Cousins TEL 613-562-5800 ext 4036. adv.: page CAD 300. Circ: 1,700 (paid and free).

351.71 333.792 CAN ISSN 1701-0764
HD9698.C2
CANADIAN NUCLEAR SAFETY COMMISSION. PERFORMANCE REPORT/COMMISSION CANADIENNE DE SURETE NUCLEAIRE. RAPORT SUR LE RENDEMENT. Text in English, French. 1997. a.
Formerly (until 2000): Canada. Atomic Energy Control Board. Performance Report (1483-7366)
Related titles: Online - full text ed.: ISSN 1701-0772.
Published by: (Canadian Nuclear Safety Commission/Commission Canadienne de Surete Nucleaire), Treasury Board of Canada Secretariat, Corporate Communications/Secretariat du Conseil du Tresor du Canada, West Tower, Rm P-135, 300 Laurier Ave W, Ottawa, ON K1A 0R5, Canada. TEL 613-995-2855, FAX 613-996-0518, services-publications@tbs-sct.gc.ca, http://www.tbs-sct.gc.ca.

328.71 CAN ISSN 0714-8143
CA1BT40 R26
CANADIAN PARLIAMENTARY HANDBOOK. Text in French, English. 1982. a., latest vol.21, 2002. CAD 93.05 domestic; USD 91.96 in United States; USD 94.12 elsewhere (effective 2005). back issues avail.
Published by: Borealis Press Limited, 110 Bloomingdale St, Ottawa, ON K2C 4A4, Canada. TEL 613-789-9299, FAX 613-789-9747, borealis@istar.ca, http://www.borealispress.com. Circ: 1,000 (paid).

CANADIAN PARLIAMENTARY REVIEW. *see* POLITICAL SCIENCE

351.71 USA ISSN 0008-4840
➤ **CANADIAN PUBLIC ADMINISTRATION/ADMINISTRATION PUBLIQUE DU CANADA.** Abbreviated title: C P A. Text in English, French. 1958. q. GBP 193 in United Kingdom to institutions; EUR 245 in Europe to institutions; USD 351 in the Americas to institutions; USD 378 elsewhere to institutions; GBP 223 combined subscription in United Kingdom to institutions (print & online eds.); EUR 282 combined subscription in Europe to institutions (print & online eds.); USD 404 combined subscription in the Americas to institutions (print & online eds.); USD 435 combined subscription elsewhere to institutions (print & online eds.) (effective 2012). adv. bk.rev. bibl. index. back issues avail.; reprint service avail. from PSC. **Document type:** *Journal, Academic/Scholarly.*
Related titles: Microfiche ed.: (from MML); Microfilm ed.: (from MML); Microform ed.: (from MML); Online - full text ed.: ISSN 1754-7121. GBP 193 in United Kingdom to institutions; EUR 245 in Europe to institutions; USD 351 in the Americas to institutions; USD 378 elsewhere to institutions (effective 2012) (from IngentaConnect).
Indexed: A01, A02, A03, A08, A20, A22, A26, ABCPolSci, ASCA, AmH&L, BPIA, BusI, C03, CA, CBCARef, CBPI, CPerI, CurCont, E01, E08, EAA, FR, G06, G07, G08, HistAb, I05, I13, IBR, IBSS, IBZ, ICLPL, M01, M02, ManagCont, P06, P30, P34, P42, P48, PAA&I, PAIS, PCI, PQC, PSA, RASB, S09, SCOPUS, SPAA, SSCI, SociolAb, T02, W07.
—BLDSC (3044.150000), IE, Infotrieve, Ingenta. **CCC.**
Published by: (Institute of Public Administration of Canada/Institut d'Administration Publique du Canada CAN), Wiley-Blackwell Publishing, Inc. (Subsidiary of: Wiley-Blackwell Publishing Ltd.), 111 River St, Hoboken, NJ 07030. TEL 201-748-6000, FAX 201-748-6088, info@wiley.com. Ed. Barbara Wake Carroll TEL 905-688-5550 ext 5415. Adv. contact Kristin McCarthy TEL 201-748-7683.

➤ **CANADIAN RADIO-TELEVISION AND TELECOMMUNICATIONS COMMISSION. PERFORMANCE REPORT.** *see* COMMUNICATIONS

354.79 CAN ISSN 1483-9822
CA1BT31-4 30
CANADIAN SPACE AGENCY. PERFORMANCE REPORT. Text in English, French. 1997. a.
Related titles: Online - full text ed.: ISSN 1490-4527.
Published by: (Canadian Space Agency), Treasury Board of Canada Secretariat, Corporate Communications/Secretariat du Conseil du Tresor du Canada, West Tower, Rm P-135, 300 Laurier Ave W, Ottawa, ON K1A 0R5, Canada. TEL 613-995-2855, FAX 613-996-0518, services-publications@tbs-sct.gc.ca, http://www.tbs-sct.gc.ca.

CANADIAN TRANSPORTATION AGENCY. PERFORMANCE REPORT. *see* TRANSPORTATION

CANADIAN WOMEN'S HEALTH NETWORK. BULLETIN. *see* WOMEN'S HEALTH

351 FRA ISSN 2108-8551
▼ **CANAL 31.** Text in French. 2010. irreg. **Document type:** *Magazine, Consumer.*
Published by: Conseil General de Haute-Garonne, 1, Bd de la Marquette, Toulouse Cedex 9, 31090, France. TEL 33-5-34333231, contact@cg31.fr, http://www.haute-garonne.fr.

307.336 FRA ISSN 1774-9883
CAP QUARTIERS; journal des conseils de quartier du XIe. Text in French. 2005. irreg. **Document type:** *Journal, Trade.*
Published by: Mairie du XIe Arrondissement de Paris, Place Leon-Blum, Paris, 75011, France.

351 NZL ISSN 0110-5655
THE CAPITAL LETTER. Text in English. 1978. w. NZD 393.50 (effective 2001). **Document type:** *Newsletter.*
Published by: Liberty Holdings, PO Box 1881, Auckland 1, New Zealand. TEL 64-9-3071287, 800-658-765, FAX 64-9-3732634, customerservices@nbr.co.nz, http://www.nbr.co.nz.

351 USA
THE CAPITOL. Text in English. 2007 (Nov.). 15/yr. USD 48 (effective 2009). **Document type:** *Magazine, Trade.* **Description:** Covers New York state politics. Targets the politicians, lobbyists, unions and staffers.
Published by: Manhattan Media, LLC, 63 W 38th St, Ste 206, New York, NY 10018. TEL 212-268-8600, FAX 212-268-9049, information@manhattanmedia.com.

321.023 USA ISSN 2152-8489
JK2403
CAPITOL IDEAS. Text in English. 1958. bi-m. USD 42; USD 7 per issue (effective 2010). adv. illus. index. reprints avail. **Document type:** *Magazine, Trade.* **Description:** Covers events and developments in the administrative, legislative and judicial branches of state government.
Former titles (until 2010): State News (1549-3628); (until 2004): State Government News (0039-0119); Which incorporated (in 1978): Legislative Session Sheet (0193-3833); States and Nation; Which was formerly (until 1962): Washington Bulletin; (until 1961): Washington Legislative Bulletin; (199?-2001): State Trends; Which was formerly (until 199?): State Trends Bulletin
Related titles: Microfiche ed.: (from WSH); Online - full text ed.: free (effective 2010).

Indexed: A01, A22, A26, APD, C12, EIA, EnerInd, G05, G06, G07, G08, I02, I05, I06, I07, IPARL, M01, M02, M06, ManagCont, P06, P34, P42, PAIS, R02, S23, T02.
—Ingenta. **CCC.**
Published by: Council of State Governments, 2760 Research Park Dr, PO Box 11910, Lexington, KY 40578. TEL 859-244-8000, 800-800-1910, FAX 859-244-8001, info@csg.org. Pub. David Adkins.

351.764 USA ISSN 0889-4841
CAPITOL UPDATE. Text in English. 1981. bi-w. **Document type:** *Newsletter, Government.* **Description:** Reports on Texas government, politics and business.
Related titles: E-mail ed.: USD 79 (effective 2011).
Published by: Texas State Directory Press, Inc., 1800 Nueces St, Austin, TX 78701. TEL 512-477-5698, FAX 512-473-2447.

351 ITA ISSN 0008-610X
U4
IL CARABINIERE. Text in Italian. 1948. m. (11/yr.). adv. bk.rev. charts; illus.; stat. **Document type:** *Magazine, Trade.*
Indexed: MLA-IB.
Published by: L' Arma dei Carabinieri, Viale Romania 45, Rome, 00197, Italy. TEL 39-06-80985297, FAX 39-06-80985296, http://www.carabinieri.it. Circ: 220,000.

351.75231 USA
CAROLINA REPORT. Text in English. 1986. m. USD 48 (effective 2000). **Document type:** *Newsletter.* **Description:** Covers South Carolina electoral politics, legislative affairs and public policy issues.
Published by: Broach, Mijeski and Associates, PO Box 12074, Rock Hill, SC 29731. TEL 803-323-2200. Ed., Pub., R&P Glen Broach.

351.029 USA ISSN 1080-4919
JK6
CARROLL'S FEDERAL DIRECTORY; executive, legislative, and judicial. Text in English. 1976. bi-m. USD 450 (effective 2011). **Document type:** *Directory, Government.* **Description:** Directory of nearly 40,000 key officials in executive, legislative, and judicial branches of US federal government.
Former titles (until 1995): Federal Executive Directory (0270-563X); (until 1980): Federal Executive Telephone Directory (0363-5384)
Related titles: CD-ROM ed.: USD 730; Online - full text ed.: ISSN 1944-3617.
Published by: Carroll Publishing, 4701 Sangamore Rd, Ste S 155, Bethesda, MD 20816. TEL 800-336-4240, FAX 301-263-9801, info@carrollpub.com.

351 USA ISSN 1096-1771
JK404
CARROLL'S FEDERAL ORGANIZATION CHARTS. Text in English. 19??. base vol. plus updates every 6 wks. looseleaf. USD 1,550 (effective 2011). charts. **Document type:** *Directory, Government.* **Description:** Organization charts identifying nearly 12,000 key individuals of departments and offices of the civil branch of the federal government.
Former titles (until 199?): Federal Organization Service (0741-5109); (until 1976): Federal Organization Service - Civil
Related titles: CD-ROM ed.; Online - full text ed.: ISSN 1521-169X.
Published by: Carroll Publishing, 4701 Sangamore Rd, Ste S 155, Bethesda, MD 20816. TEL 800-336-4240, 800-336-4240, FAX 301-263-9801, info@carrollpub.com.

351.029 USA ISSN 1082-3182
JK723.E9
CARROLL'S FEDERAL REGIONAL DIRECTORY. Text in English. 1984. s-a. USD 425 (effective 2011). maps. **Document type:** *Directory, Government.* **Description:** Directory of over 23,000 key officials in regional field offices of US Cabinet departments, Congress, the courts, federal administrative agencies, and mailing bases.
Formerly (until 1995): Federal Regional Executive Directory (0742-1729)
Related titles: CD-ROM ed.: USD 730; Online - full text ed.: ISSN 1944-3625.
Published by: Carroll Publishing, 4701 Sangamore Rd, Ste S 155, Bethesda, MD 20816. TEL 800-336-4240, FAX 301-263-9801, info@carrollpub.com.

351.025 USA ISSN 1539-6339
JK723.E9
CARROLL'S FEDERAL REGIONAL DIRECTORY (YEAR) ANNUAL. Text in English. 1983. a. USD 295 per issue (effective 2004). **Document type:** *Directory, Government.* **Description:** Covers approximately 63,000 individuals in the executive, legislative and judicial branches of federal government plus their regional field offices.
Supersedes in part (in 2002): Carroll's Federal Regional Directory (Annual) (1543-9062); Which was formerly (until 1996): Carroll's Federal Directory (Year) Annual (1093-2089); (until 1995): Federal Executive Directory Annual (1056-7275); Which superseded in part (in 1991): Federal/State Executive Directory (0887-4727); Which was fomerly (until 1984): Annual Federal/State Executive Directory (0734-4651)
Related titles: CD-ROM ed.; Online - full content ed.
Published by: Carroll Publishing, 4701 Sangamore Rd, Ste S 155, Bethesda, MD 20816. TEL 800-336-4240, 800-336-4240, FAX 301-263-9801, info@carrollpub.com, http://www.carrollpub.com.

351.46 ESP
CARTA LOCAL; boletin informativo. Text in Spanish. 1968. m. adv. bk.rev. illus. back issues avail. **Document type:** *Bulletin, Government.* **Description:** Contains administrative, economic, and judicial information. Includes interviews.
Former titles (until 1990): Informacion Iberoamericana; Instituto de Estudios de Administracion Local. Oficina Tecnica de la O I C I. Boletin de Informacion; Instituto de Estudios de Administracion Local. Secretariado Iberoamericano de Municipios. Boletin de Informacion (0210-0975)
Published by: Federacion Espanola de Municipios y Provincias, Nuncio, 8, Madrid, 28005, Spain. TEL 34-91-3643700, FAX 34-91-3655482, femp@femp.es, http://www.femp.es/. R&P Jesus Diaz Lobo. Circ: 14,500. **Co-sponsor:** Ministerio para las Administraciones Publicas.

351.72921 CYM
CAYMAN ISLANDS ANNUAL REPORT AND OFFICIAL HANDBOOK. Text in English. 1972. a. KYD 32, USD 40 (effective 2001). **Document type:** *Yearbook, Government.* **Description:** Official report on operations of Cayman Islands Government, giving a comprehensive picture of life in the islands.
Formerly: Cayman Islands. Government Information Services. Annual Report
Published by: Government Information Services, Cricket Square, Elguin Ave, George Town, Grand Cayman, Cayman Isl. TEL 345-949-8092, FAX 345-949-5936, susan.watler@gov.ky. Ed. E Patricia Ebanks. Circ: 1,000.

CAYMAN ISLANDS. LEGISLATIVE ASSEMBLY. MINUTES. *see* POLITICAL SCIENCE

CENTER FOR LAW IN THE PUBLIC INTEREST. NEWSLETTER. *see* POLITICAL SCIENCE

351 GBR
CENTRE FOR PUBLIC SERVICE MANAGEMENT. RESEARCH REPORT. Text in English. 1998. irreg. GBP 10 per issue.
Published by: Centre for Public Service Management, Liverpool John Moores University, Liverpool Business School, Liverpool, Merseyside L3 5UZ, United Kingdom. TEL 44-151-231-3440, FAX 44-151-709-3156.

351 658 CAN ISSN 1487-3052
➤ **CENTRE ON GOVERNANCE.** Text in English, French. 1998. s-a. price varies. adv. bibl. back issues avail. **Document type:** *Monographic series, Academic/Scholarly.*
Published by: (Centre on Governance), University of Ottawa Press/ Presses de l'Universite d'Ottawa, 542 King Edward, Ottawa, ON K1N 6N5, Canada. TEL 613-562-5246, FAX 613-562-5247, press@uottawa.ca, paquet@admin.uottawa.ca. Ed. Vicki Bennett. R&P Martine Beauchesne. Adv. contact Elizabeth Thebaud. Circ: 800.

351 USA ISSN 0730-9805
JK2075.C22
CERTIFIED LIST OF CANDIDATES FOR THE DIRECT PRIMARY ELECTION. Text in English. biennial.
Published by: California. Secretary of State, 1500 11th St, Sacramento, CA 95814. TEL 916-653-6814.

CHAIRE GLAVERBEL D'ETUDES EUROPEENNES. ACTES. *see* POLITICAL SCIENCE—International Relations

351 CHN ISSN 1009-1955
CHANG'AN/PEACE & ORDER. Text in Chinese. 1980. m. CNY 57.60; CNY 4.80 per issue (effective 2009). **Document type:** *Magazine, Government.*
Published by: (Zhongyang Shehui Zhian Zonghe Zhili Weiyuanhui, Zhonggong Zhongyang Zhengfa Weiyuanhui), Chang'an Zazhishe, Dongcheng-qu, 14, Beichizi Dajie, Beijing, 100006, China. TEL 86-10-65270650. **Subscr. to:** 1, Huajiadi Jia, Beijing 100102, China. TEL 86-10-64728501.

351 CHN ISSN 1671-363X
CHANGZHOU NIANJIAN/CHANGZHOU ALMANAC. Text in Chinese. 1991. a. **Document type:** *Yearbook, Government.*
Related titles: Online - full text ed.
Published by: Changzhou Shi Renmin Zhengfu BanGongsi, 180, Juqian Jie, Changzhou, 213003, China. czic@czmail.gov.cn, http://www.changzhou.gov.cn/.

CHARITABLE GAMING IN ALBERTA (YEAR/YEAR) IN REVIEW. *see* SPORTS AND GAMES

CHARTERED INSTITUTE OF PUBLIC FINANCE AND ACCOUNTANCY. LOCAL GOVERNMENT COMPARATIVE STATISTICS. ESTIMATES. *see* PUBLIC ADMINISTRATION—Abstracting, Bibliographies, Statistics

CHECKLIST OF OFFICIAL PUBLICATIONS OF THE STATE OF NEW YORK (ONLINE). *see* PUBLIC ADMINISTRATION—Abstracting, Bibliographies, Statistics

354.7 CHN ISSN 1001-599X
HD2763.A2
CHENGSHI GONGYONG SHIYE/PUBLIC UTILITIES. Text in Chinese. 1987. bi-m. USD 21.60 (effective 2009). adv. **Document type:** *Journal, Academic/Scholarly.* **Description:** Covers the developments and events in the field of public transit, taxi, ferry, and metro services, town gas and urban water supplies in China.
Related titles: Online - full text ed.
—East View.
Published by: Shanghai Gongyong Shiye Yanjiusuo/Shanghai Municipal Research Institute of Public Utilities, 706 Hengshan Rd, Shanghai, 200030, China. adv.: page USD 600. **Dist. by:** China International Book Trading Corp, 35 Chegongzhuang Xilu, Haidian District, PO Box 399, Beijing 100044, China. TEL 86-10-68412045, FAX 86-10-68412023, cibtc@mail.cibtc.com.cn, http://www.cibtc.com.cn.

352.63 USA ISSN 0746-7761
THE CHIEF CIVIL SERVICE LEADER. Text in English. 1897. w. (Tue.). USD 22 domestic; USD 32 foreign. adv. 12 p./no. 8 cols./p.; back issues avail. **Document type:** *Newspaper, Trade.* **Description:** Concentrates on the civil services field, reaching police officers, firefighters, school teachers, sanitation and postal employees.
Formerly: Chief (0009-3807)
Published by: New York Civil Service Employees Publishing Co., Inc., 277 Broadway, Ste 1506, New York, NY 10007. TEL 212-962-2690, FAX 212-962-2556. Ed. Richar Steier. Pub. James Prial. R&P Richard Steier. Adv. contact Edward B Prial. Circ: 43,916 (paid).

351 CAN ISSN 0227-8073
JL338
CHIEF ELECTORAL OFFICER. ANNUAL REPORT. Key Title: Annual Report of the Chief Electoral Officer Administering the Election Finances and Contributions Disclosure Act. Text in English. a. **Document type:** *Government.*
Formerly (until 1978): Chief Electoral Officer Administering the Election Finances and Contributions Disclosure Act. Rapport (0708-6504)
Related titles: Online - full content ed.
Published by: Office of the Chief Electoral Officer, Ste 100, 11510 Kingsway Ave, Edmonton, AB T5G 2Y5, Canada. FAX 780-427-7191, info@electionsalberta.ab.ca, http://www.electionsalberta.ab.ca/.

351.71 CAN ISSN 1716-6144
CHILD AND YOUTH OFFICER FOR BRITISH COLUMBIA. ANNUAL REPORT. Text in English. 2003. a.
Formerly (until 2004): British Columbia. Office for Children and Youth. Annual Report (1708-4458); Which was formed by the merger of (1997-2001): British Columbia. Children's Commission. Annual Report (1480-4980); (1996-2001): British Columbia. Office of the Child, Youth and Family Advocate. Annual Report (1205-7010)
Published by: Child and Youth Officer for British Columbia, PO Box 9207, Stn Prov Govt, Victoria, BC V8W 9J1, Canada. TEL 250-356-0831, 800-476-3933, FAX 250-356-0837, cyo@gov.bc.ca, http://gov.bc.ca/cyo/.

CHILDREN'S ADVOCATE. *see* CHILDREN AND YOUTH—About

351.51092 JPN
CHINA DIRECTORY (YEAR)/CHUGOKU SOSHIKIBETSU JINMEIBO/ ZHONGGUO ZUZHIBIE RENMINGBU. Text in Chinese, English. 1971. a. JPY 16,000, USD 110. bk.rev. index. back issues avail. **Document type:** *Directory.* **Description:** Organization-based directory of 10,000 Chinese leaders and 2,000 organizations. Covers state council structural reforms, new cabinet members and other changes of the past year; names listed in Chinese and Pinyin romanization.
Published by: R P Printings, 1-10-22 Shimo-Noge, Takatsu-ku, Kawasaki-shi, Kanagawa-ken 213-0006, Japan. TEL 81-44-833-4421, FAX 81-4-833-4422. Circ: 2,500.

350 650 TWN ISSN 0009-4579
➤ **CHINESE JOURNAL OF ADMINISTRATION.** Text in Chinese, English. 1963. s-a. TWD 400 domestic to individuals; USD 20 foreign to individuals; TWD 800 domestic to libraries; USD 40 foreign to libraries (effective 2003). bk.rev. charts; illus. **Document type:** *Journal, Academic/Scholarly.* **Description:** Provides a forum for exchanging ideas and information among administrators, scholars, and others interested in public and business administration and related fields.
Formerly: Zhongguo Xingzheng (1017-575X)
Indexed: BAS.
Published by: National Chengchi University, Center for Public and Business Administration Education, 187 Chin Hua St, Taipei, Taiwan. TEL 886-2-23940690, FAX 886-2-23975219, http://www.cpbae.nccu.edu.tw/. Ed. Jay N Shih. Pub. Bau-Tschung Dung. Circ: 1,500.

351.51 USA ISSN 1539-6754
➤ **CHINESE PUBLIC ADMINISTRATION REVIEW.** Abbreviated title: CPAR. Text in English. 2002 (Jan./Mar.). q. back issues avail. **Document type:** *Journal, Academic/Scholarly.* **Description:** Addresses the issues of Chinese public administration: administrative reform, public policy, administrative law, public productivity improvement, performance measurement, civil service, etc.
Indexed: CA, P42, T02.
Published by: (American Society for Public Administration, Section on Chinese Public Administration), Rutgers University, Newark, National Center for Public Productivity, School of Public Affairs and Administration Rutgers University, Campus at Newark, Center for Urban and Public Service, 111 Washington St, Newark, NJ 07102. TEL 973-353-5093, FAX 973-353-5907, ncpp@andromeda.rutgers.edu, http://www.ncpp.us/.

P

351 CHN ISSN 1004-8383
CHONGQING NIANJIAN/CHONGQING YEARBOOK. Text in Chinese. 1987. a. **Document type:** *Yearbook, Government.*
Published by: Chongqing Shi Renmin Zhengfu/Chongqing Municipal People's Government, 3-1, Jiangxin Dong Lu, 9/F, Baiyexing Dasha, Chongqing, 400020, China. TEL 86-23-67761342, http://www.cq.gov.cn/.

351 CHN ISSN 1674-5272
CHUTIAN ZHUREN/MASTER OF SOUTH CHINA. Text in Chinese. 1993. m. **Document type:** *Magazine, Government.*
Published by: Hubei Sheng Renmin Daibiao Dahui Changwu Weiyuanhui/Standing Committee of the People's Congress of Hubei Province, Wuchang-qu, Shuiguohu, Shengwei Dayuan, Wuhan, 430071, China. TEL 86-27-87893759, FAX 86-27-87893759.

351 VEN ISSN 1316-371X
F2331.Z9
➤ **CIENCIAS DE GOBIERNO.** Text in Spanish. 1997. s-a. USD 12 domestic; USD 25 in Latin America; USD 35 in US & Canada; USD 40 elsewhere (effective 2003). Website rev. 150 p./no.; **Document type:** *Journal, Academic/Scholarly.* **Description:** Promotes the progress of study in the area of governmental science to improve the quality of local, regional and national governments.
Indexed: C01, CA, H21, I13, P08, P42, PSA, SociolAb, T02.
Published by: Instituto Zuliano de Estudios Politicos, Economicos y Sociales, Av. 18, entre C. 77 y 78, Edif. Lieja, Piso 1, Maracaibo, Venezuela. TEL 58-261-7186258, FAX 58-261-7186261. Ed. Guillermo Garcia.

351 USA ISSN 1936-007X
HT123
CITYSCAPE (WASHINGTON, D.C.); a journal of policy development and research. Text in English. 1994. 3/yr. free (effective 2010). back issues avail. **Document type:** *Journal, Trade.* **Description:** Focuses on ideas, policies, and programs for revitalizing cities and regions, renewing their infrastructure, and creating economic opportunities.
Related titles: Online - full text ed.: ISSN 1939-1935.
Indexed: EconLit, JEL, P48, P51, P53, P54, PQC.
Published by: U.S. Department of Housing and Urban Development, Office of Policy Development and Research, PO Box 23268, Washington, DC 20026. TEL 800-245-2691, FAX 202-708-9981, helpdesk@huduser.org, http://www.huduser.org/portal/index.html.

352 ESP ISSN 1133-4762
HT395.S7
CIUDAD Y TERRITORIO: ESTUDIOS TERRITORIALES. Text in Spanish; Summaries in English. 1993. q. bk.rev. bibl.; illus. **Document type:** *Journal, Academic/Scholarly.* **Description:** Forum for the spatial disciplines that touch upon either the town and country planning, human geography, administering of territory or urbanism.
Formed by the merger of (1970-1993): Ciudad y Territorio (0210-0487); (1981-1993): Estudios Territoriales (0211-6871)
Indexed: A22, FR, GeoRef, IECT, P09, PCI, SpeleolAb.
—IE. **CCC.**
Published by: Ministerio de Fomento, Centro de Publicaciones, Paseo de la Castellana 67, Madrid, 28029, Spain. http://www.fomento.es.

351 CAN ISSN 0829-772X
JS1701
CIVIC PUBLIC WORKS. Text in English. 1949. bi-m. CAD 36. adv. bk.rev. bibl.; charts; illus.; mkt.; tr.lit. index.

Formerly: Civic Administration (0009-7764); Incorporates: Civic Public Works Reference Manual and Buyer's Guide; Which was formerly: Civic Municipal Reference Manual and Purchasing Guide (0069-4258); Civic Administration's Municipal Reference Manual and Purchasing Guide
Related titles: Microfiche ed.: (from MML); Microform ed.: (from MML).
Indexed: C03, CBCABus, CBPI, P06, PQC.
—CCC.
Published by: Healthcare and Financial Publishing (Subsidiary of: Rogers Publishing Ltd./Les Editions Rogers Limitee), 777 Bay Street, 5th Fl, Toronto, ON M5W 1A7, Canada. TEL 416-596-5953, FAX 416-593-3193. Ed. Alex Jenkins. Pub. David J Fidler. Circ: 13,500.

351.93 387.7 NZL ISSN 1177-6072
CIVIL AVIATION AUTHORITY OF NEW ZEALAND. ANNUAL REPORT. Text in English. 1993. a. **Document type:** *Corporate.*
Related titles: Online - full text ed.: ISSN 1177-9403.
Published by: Civil Aviation Authority of New Zealand, PO Box 31-441, Lower Hutt, 5040, New Zealand. TEL 64-4-5699400, FAX 64-4-5692024, info@caa.govt.nz.

CIVIL AVIATION AUTHORITY OF NEW ZEALAND. STATEMENT OF INTENT. *see* TRANSPORTATION—Air Transport

352.63 USA
CIVIL SERVICE NEWS. Text in English. irreg. free.
Formerly: Civil Service News Releases (0009-8019)
Media: Duplicated (not offset).
Published by: U.S. Office of Personnel Management, Office of Public Policy, 1900 E St, Rm 5F10, Washington, DC 20415. TEL 202-632-1212.

352.63 MUS
CIVIL SERVICE NEWS. Text in English, French. m.
Indexed: CRIA, CRICC.
Published by: Federation of Civil Service Unions, 10 La Chausee, Port Louis, Mauritius.

351 PHL ISSN 0300-3620
JQ1412
CIVIL SERVICE REPORTER. Text in English. 1956. q. free. bk.rev. charts; illus.; stat. 24 p./no.; back issues avail. **Document type:** *Government.* **Description:** Serves as the official publication of the Civil Service Commission. Carries news, memorandum, announcements and more.
Related titles: Fax ed.
Indexed: IPP.
Published by: Civil Service Commission, Constitution Hills, Diliman, Quezon City Mm, 1128, Philippines. FAX 63-2-931-4180, pid@csc.gov.ph, http://www.csc.gov.ph. Ed. Theresa C Fernandez. Circ: 3,000.

CIVIL SERVICE REWARDS. *see* BUSINESS AND ECONOMICS—Labor And Industrial Relations

351 FRA ISSN 1275-7705
CIVIQUE. Text in French. 1990. m. **Document type:** *Magazine, Government.* **Description:** Internal publication of France's Ministere de l'Interieur.
Formerly (until 1997): Civic (1146-0210)
Indexed: FR.
Published by: France. Ministere de l'Interieur, 6 rue Canbaceres, Paris, 75008, France. TEL 33-01-49273134, FAX 33-01-47420936.

351 CAN ISSN 1910-8729
CLAUSES ET CONDITIONS UNIFORMISEES D'ACHAT. Text in French. 2002. irreg. **Document type:** *Monographic series, Trade.*
Media: Online - full text.
Published by: Public Works and Government Services Canada/Travaux Publics et Services Gouvernementaux Canada, Place du Portage, Phase III, 11 Laurier St, Gatineau, PQ K1A 0S5, Canada. TEL 800-622-6232, Questions@pwgsc.gc.ca, http://www.pwgsc.gc.ca/text/home-e.html.

CODE OF MARYLAND REGULATIONS. *see* LAW

361.6 BEL ISSN 1782-1207
CODEX OPENBARE HULPVERLENING. HULPDIENSTEN. Text in Dutch. 1992. irreg. **Document type:** *Trade.*
Published by: Die Keure NV, Kleine Pathoekeweg 3, Bruges, 8000, Belgium. TEL 32-50-471272, FAX 32-50-335154, juridische.uitgaven@diekeure.be, http://www.diekeure.be.

361.6 BEL ISSN 1782-1215
CODEX OPENBARE HULPVERLENING. INTERVENTIE. Text in Dutch. 1992. irreg. **Document type:** *Trade.*
Published by: Die Keure NV, Kleine Pathoekeweg 3, Bruges, 8000, Belgium. TEL 32-50-471272, FAX 32-50-335154, juridische.uitgaven@diekeure.be, http://www.diekeure.be.

614.4 BEL ISSN 1782-1193
CODEX OPENBARE HULPVERLENING. PREVENTIE. Text in Dutch. 1992. irreg. **Document type:** *Trade.*
Published by: Die Keure NV, Kleine Pathoekeweg 3, Bruges, 8000, Belgium. TEL 32-50-471272, FAX 32-50-335154, juridische.uitgaven@diekeure.be, http://www.diekeure.be.

342.57 BEL ISSN 0778-0680
CODEX PUBLIEK RECHT. Text in Dutch. 1990. a. **Document type:** *Trade.*
Published by: Die Keure NV, Kleine Pathoekeweg 3, Bruges, 8000, Belgium. TEL 32-50-471272, FAX 32-50-335154, juridische.uitgaven@diekeure.be, http://www.diekeure.be.

343.025 USA
COGGINS, WILKINSON AND LESHY'S FEDERAL PUBLIC LAND AND RESOURCES LAW. Text in English. 19??. a. USD 32 per issue (effective 2010). **Document type:** *Journal, Trade.* **Description:** Covers federal public land and resources laws.
Related titles: ◆ Series of: University Casebook Series.
Published by: Thomson West (Subsidiary of: Thomson Reuters Corp.), 610 Opperman Dr, Eagan, MN 55123. TEL 651-687-7000, 800-344-5008, west.customer.service@thomson.com.

COLLANA DI SUDI AZIENDALI E DI MARKETING. SEZIONE IMPRESE DI SERVIZI E AZIENDE PUBBLICHE. *see* BUSINESS AND ECONOMICS

COLOMBIA. DEPARTAMENTO ADMINISTRATIVO NACIONAL DE ESTADISTICA. DIVISION POLITICO-ADMINISTRATIVA. *see* PUBLIC ADMINISTRATION—Abstracting, Bibliographies, Statistics

354.8 USA
COLORADO. GENERAL SUPPORT SERVICES. DIVISION OF ACCOUNTS & CONTROL. COMPREHENSIVE ANNUAL FINANCIAL REPORT. Text in English. 1876. a. free. **Document type:** *Government.*
Formerly: Colorado. Department of Administration. Division of Accounts and Control. Comprehensive Annual Financial Report
Indexed: SRI.
Published by: General Support Services, Division of Accounts & Control, 1525 Sherman St, Ste 250, Denver, CO 80203-1717. TEL 303-866-3894, FAX 303-866-4233. Circ: 500.

351 347 USA
COLORADO REGISTER. Text in English. m. **Document type:** *Government.* **Description:** A compilation of information about official Colorado state government actions.
Published by: LexisNexis (Subsidiary of: Reed Elsevier Group plc), 1016 W Ninth Ave, 1st Fl, King of Prussia, PA 19406. TEL 215 564-1788, 800 448-1515, customer.support@lexisnexis.com, http://www.lexisnexis.com.

351 FRA ISSN 2107-4607
COMCOM INFOS. Text in French. 1996. 3/yr. **Document type:** *Bulletin, Consumer.*
Formerly (until 2008): Communaute de Communes de la Region Pouance-Combree (1287-7964)
Published by: Communaute de Communes de la Region Pouance-Combree, 13, Place de la Madeleine, Pouance, 49420, France. TEL 33-2-41923519, FAX 33-2-41927697, http://www.cc-pouance-combree.fr/Pouance.

351 REU
COMMENTAIRES DES PRINCIPALES DECISIONS DU TRIBUNAL ADMINISTRATIF DE LA REUNION. Text in French. 1974. a.
Related titles: Series of: Dossiers du Centre d'Etudes.
Published by: Centre Universitaire de la Reunion, Centre d'Etudes Administratives, 24, 26 av. de la Victoire, Saint-denis, Reunion. Circ: 150.

351 FRA ISSN 1952-9759
COMMISSION D'ACCES AUX DOCUMENTS ADMINISTRATIFS. RAPPORT D'ACTIVITE. Text in French. 1981. a.
Formerly (until 2005): L'Acces aux Documents Administratifs (0766-5601)
Published by: (Commission d'Acces aux Documents Administratifs), Documentation Francaise, 29-31 Quai Voltaire, Paris, Cedex 7 75344, France. TEL 33-1-40157000, FAX 33-1-40157230, http://www.ladocumentationfrancaise.fr.

COMMISSION DE LA FONCTION PUBLIQUE DU CANADA. RAPPORT ANNUEL. POINTS SAILLANTS. *see* OCCUPATIONS AND CAREERS

351 CAN ISSN 1719-5268
COMMISSION SPECIALE SUR LA LOI ELECTORALE. JOURNAL DES DEBATS. Text in French. 2005. irreg. **Document type:** *Proceedings, Government.*
Published by: Assemblee Nationale de Quebec, Parliament Bldg, 1045, rue des Parlementaires, Quebec, PQ G1A 1A4, Canada. TEL 418-643-7239, 866-337-8837, FAX 418-646-4271, http://www.assnat.qc.ca/eng/index.html.

351 361 USA
COMMONWEALTH; politics, ideas and civic life in Massachusetts. Text in English. 1996. q. USD 50 (effective 2011). **Document type:** *Magazine, Consumer.* **Description:** Aims to develop a public agenda for Massachusetts that promotes the growth and vitality of the middle class. It has four primary initiatives: economic prosperity, lifelong learning, safe neighborhoods and civic renewal. Includes articles, interviews, news and books reviews.
Related titles: Online - full text ed.
Published by: The Massachusetts Institute for a New Common Wealth, 18 Tremont St, Ste 1120, Boston, MA 02108. info@massinc.org. Ed. Bruce Mohl.

351 USA ISSN 0010-3349
JK8702
THE COMMONWEALTH. Text in English. 1925. bi-w. free to members. **Document type:** *Magazine, Consumer.*
Indexed: A22, P06, PAIS.
—Linda Hall.
Published by: Commonwealth Club of California, 595 Market St, San Francisco, CA 94105. TEL 415-5976700, FAX 415-5976729, club@commonwealthclub.org. Circ: 17,000 (controlled).

351 USA
COMMONWEALTH CLUB OF CALIFORNIA. TRANSACTIONS. Text in English. irreg.
Published by: Commonwealth Club of California, 595 Market St, San Francisco, CA 94105.

351 GBR ISSN 0958-8558
JN248
COMMONWEALTH MINISTERS REFERENCE BOOK (YEAR). Text in English. 1989. a. GBP 35 per issue (effective 2009). back issues avail. **Document type:** *Government.* **Description:** Provides the information on key aspects of policy issues for all commonwealth ministers, from trade to transport.
Published by: Commonwealth Secretariat, Marlborough House, Pall Mall, London, SW1Y 5HX, United Kingdom. TEL 44-20-77476500, FAX 44-20-79300827, info@commonwealth.int. Ed. Tom Baird TEL 44-20-77476136.

351.94 AUS
COMMONWEALTH OF AUSTRALIA GAZETTE. PERIODIC. Text in English. 1977. irreg. free (effective 2008). **Document type:** *Newspaper, Government.* **Description:** Contains detailed government notices of non-urgent nature. Also covers business issues.
Formerly (until 1977): Australia. Australian Government Gazette. Periodic
Related titles: Online - full text ed.: free to members (effective 2008).
Published by: Australian Government. Attorney-General's Department, Central Office, 3-5 National Circuit, Barton, ACT 2600, Australia. TEL 61-2-62506666, FAX 61-2-62505900.

350 AUS ISSN 0727-4181
J905
COMMONWEALTH OF AUSTRALIA. PARLIAMENT. PARLIAMENTARY PAPER. Text in English. 1901. irreg., latest 1998. price varies. back issues avail. **Document type:** *Monographic series, Government.* **Description:** Discusses issues related to the Australian Commonwealth Government.
Related titles: ◆ Series: Parliamentary Handbook of the Commonwealth of Australia. ISSN 0813-541X.
Indexed: GeoRef, SpeleolAb.
Published by: Parliament of Australia, Parliment House, Canberra, ACT 2600, Australia. TEL 61-2-62777111.

354.9 AUS ISSN 0814-7124
J905
COMMONWEALTH OMBUDSMAN AND DEFENCE FORCE OMBUDSMAN. ANNUAL REPORTS. Text in English. 1978. a. free (effective 2009). back issues avail. **Document type:** *Yearbook, Government.* **Description:** Reports on the various activities and performance of the Ombudsman's office.
Formerly (until 1984): Commonwealth Ombudsman. Annual Report (0156-739X)
Related titles: Online - full text ed.: free (effective 2009).
—CCC.
Published by: Commonwealth Ombudsman, GPO Box 442, Canberra, ACT 2601, Australia. TEL 300-362-072, FAX 61-2-62497829, ombudsman@ombudsman.gov.au.

351.6897 MWI
COMMONWEALTH PARLIAMENTARY ASSOCIATION. MALAWI BRANCH. CONFERENCE. REPORT OF PROCEEDINGS. Text in English. irreg. **Document type:** *Proceedings.*
Published by: Commonwealth Parliamentary Association, Malawi Branch, c/o Parliament of Malawi, PO Box 80, Zomba, Malawi.

351.6897 MWI
COMMONWEALTH PARLIAMENTARY ASSOCIATION. MALAWI BRANCH. EXECUTIVE COMMITTEE. ANNUAL REPORT. Text in English. a. **Document type:** *Corporate.*
Published by: Commonwealth Parliamentary Association, Malawi Branch, c/o Parliament of Malawi, PO Box 80, Zomba, Malawi.

351 USA ISSN 1077-4467
COMMONWEALTH REGISTER. Text in English. 1982. 85/yr. USD 275 (effective 2000). adv. back issues avail. **Document type:** *Government.* **Description:** Reports on the Pennsylvania General Assembly.
Formerly: Legislative Reporter
Related titles: E-mail ed.; Fax ed.
Published by: 51st Associates, 216 Briggs St, Harrisburg, PA 17102. TEL 717-238-1222, FAX 717-238-9512. Ed., R&P Deborah Shoemaker. Circ: 400 (paid).

354.9 AUS ISSN 1031-8585
JQ4049.S2
COMMONWEALTH SUPERANNUATION ADMINISTRATION. ANNUAL REPORT. Text in English. 1994. a. free (effective 2009). back issues avail. **Document type:** *Yearbook, Government.* **Description:** Contains detailed statistical and performance related data as well as financial statements.
Supersedes in part (in 1987): Superannuation Fund Investment Trust and the Commissioner for Superannuation. Annual Reports (0155-9605)
Related titles: Online - full text ed.: free (effective 2009).
—CCC.
Published by: Commonwealth Superannuation Administration, PO Box 22, Belconnen, ACT 2616, Australia. TEL 61-2-62729081, FAX 61-2-62729612, publications@comsuper.gov.au.

351 FRA ISSN 2108-159X
COMMUNAUTE DE COMMUNES DU FLORENTINOIS. BULLETIN D'INFORMATION. Text in French. 2005. s-a. **Document type:** *Bulletin, Consumer.*
Published by: Communaute de Communes du Florentinois, BP 162, Saint-Florentin, 89600, France. TEL 33-3-86350857, cc-florentinois@wanadoo.fr.

351 FRA ISSN 2106-5349
COMMUNAUTE DE COMMUNES DU LUSSACOIS. LE JOURNAL D'INFORMATION. Text in French. 1998. a. **Document type:** *Consumer.*
Formerly (until 2009): Communaute de Communes du Lussacois. Le Bulletin (1957-2611)
Published by: Communaute de Communes du Lussacois, 3, Av de l'Europe, Lussac-les-Chateaux, 86320, France. TEL 33-5-49487415, FAX 33-5-49849797, cclussacois@cq86.fr, http://www.cclussacois.fr.

351 FRA ISSN 2108-3223
COMMUNAUTE DE COMMUNES DU PAYS BIGOUDEN SUD. MAGAZINE. Text in French. 1998. 3/yr. **Document type:** *Magazine, Consumer.*
Formerly (until 2010): Le Pays Bigouden Sud (1297-7918)
Published by: Communaute de Communes du Pays Bigouden Sud, BP 82035, Pont l'Abbe Cedex, 29122, France. TEL 33-2-98871442, FAX 33-2-98823793, info@cc-pays-bigouden-sud.fr, http://www.cc-pays-bigouden-sud.fr.

910.202 FRA ISSN 2107-4305
COMMUNAUTE DE COMMUNES VARENNES FORTERRE. LA LETTRE D'INFORMATIONS. Text in French. 2004. a., latest 2009. **Document type:** *Newsletter, Consumer.*
Published by: Communaute de Communes Varennes Forterre, 18 Rue de Vouroux, Varennes-sur-Allier, 03150, France. TEL 33-4-70450099, FAX 33-4-70456436, varennes-forterre@wanadoo.fr.

COMMUNICATION CANADA. PERFORMANCE REPORT. *see* COMMUNICATIONS

352.63 CAN ISSN 0707-9133
COMMUNICATOR (ST. JOHN'S). Text in English. 1976. m. membership. bk.rev. illus. **Document type:** *Newsletter.*
Former titles: N A P E Journal (0381-6826); N A P E News (0318-1723)
Published by: Newfoundland Association of Public Employees, P O Box 8100, St. John's, NF A1B 3M9, Canada. TEL 709-754-0700, FAX 709-754-0726. Ed. Trudi Brake. Circ: 19,000.

COMMUNITY DEVELOPMENT JOURNAL; an international forum. *see* SOCIAL SERVICES AND WELFARE

353.6 USA ISSN 1934-4864
COMMUNITY HEALTH FUNDING REPORT. Abbreviated title: C H F. Text in English. 2004. bi-w. USD 479 combined subscription (print & online eds.) (effective 2008). 18 p./no. 2 cols./p.; back issues avail.; reprints avail. **Document type:** *Newsletter, Trade.* **Description:** Highlights funding sources for a wide range of healthcare concerns, including substance abuse, teen pregnancy, minority healthcare, maternal/child health, chronic illness, mental health and HIV/AIDS programs.
Formerly (until 2006): Community Health Funding Week (1553-2941); Which was formed by the merger of (197?-2004): Health Grants & Contracts Weekly (0194-2352); (1990-2004): Community Health Funding Report (1052-6552); Which incorporated (1988-1993): Public Assistance Funding Report (1056-7100); Which was formerly (until 1991): Public Assistance Success (1050-3447); Which incorporated (1988-1991): Helping the Homeless (1050-3439)
Related titles: Online - full text ed.: ISSN 1934-4872. USD 439 (effective 2008).
Indexed: H02, N06.
—CCC.
Published by: (Community Development Services, Inc.), C D Publications, Inc., 8204 Fenton St, Silver Spring, MD 20910. TEL 301-588-6380, 800-666-6380, FAX 301-588-6385, info@cdpublications.com. Eds. Chet Dembeck, David Adler. Pub. Mike Gerecht.

COMMUNITY RELATIONS REPORT. *see* COMMUNICATIONS

351 USA ISSN 1936-0002
COMPASS (CAMBRIDGE). Text in English. 19??. s-a. **Document type:** *Journal, Academic/Scholarly.*
Formerly (until 2003): Leadership
Published by: Harvard University, John F. Kennedy School of Government, 79 John F Kennedy St, PO Box 142, Cambridge, MA 02138. TEL 617-495-1100, cpl@ksg.harvard.edu, http://www.ksg.harvard.edu/leadership.

351 347 ARG ISSN 1852-8961
▼ **COMPENDIO TRIBUTARIO ARGENTINO.** Text in Spanish. 2010. a. **Document type:** *Handbook/Manual/Guide, Trade.*
Published by: La Ley, S.A., Tucuman 1471, Buenos Aires, 1050, Argentina. TEL 54-11-43784838, FAX 54-11-43720953, atencionalcliente@laley.com.ar, http://www.laley.com.ar/.

351.71 343.71 CAN ISSN 1483-7544
CA1BT31-4 34
COMPETITION TRIBUNAL OF CANADA. PERFORMANCE REPORT. Text in English, French. 1997. a.
Related titles: Online - full text ed.: ISSN 1490-5566.
Published by: (Competition Tribunal of Canada), Treasury Board of Canada Secretariat, Corporate Communications/Secretariat du Conseil du Tresor du Canada, West Tower, Rm P-135, 300 Laurier Ave W, Ottawa, ON K1A 0R5, Canada. TEL 613-995-2855, FAX 613-996-0518, services-publications@tbs-sct.gc.ca.

351 PRT ISSN 1646-9569
OS COMPROMISSOS I N E. (Instituto Nacional de Estatistica) Text in Portuguese. 2008. a. **Document type:** *Report, Government.*
Published by: Instituto Nacional de Estatistica, Av Antonio Jose de Almeida 2, Lisbon, 1000-043, Portugal. TEL 351-21-8426100, FAX 351-21-8426380, ine@ine.pt, http://www.ine.pt.

CONCLUSIONSONLINE. *see* BUSINESS AND ECONOMICS—Banking And Finance

CONFLICT OF INTEREST AND POST-EMPLOYMENT CODE FOR PUBLIC OFFICE HOLDERS. *see* PHILOSOPHY

354.710099505 CAN ISSN 0840-0180
CA1 YM 32-1/ 79-3
CONFLICT OF INTEREST RULES FOR FEDERAL LEGISLATORS. Text in English. 1979. irreg. **Document type:** *Government.*
Related titles: Online - full content ed.
Published by: Library of Parliament, Parliamentary Research Branch, Information Service, Ottawa, ON K1A 0A9, Canada.

351.597 VNM
CONG BAO/OFFICIAL GAZETTE. Text in Vietnamese. 1994. s-m. VND 2,784,000 domestic; USD 336 foreign (effective 2000). adv. **Document type:** *Government.* **Description:** Contains legal documents, including laws, ordinances, decrees, decisions, circulars, and more.
Related titles: English Translation: Socialist Republic of Vietnam. Office Gazette.
Published by: (Socialist Republic of Vietnam. Office of the Government), Vietnam News Agency, 5 Ly Thuong Kiet St, Hanoi, Viet Nam. TEL 84-4-8248670, FAX 84-4-8248672, vnnews@vnagency.com.vn, http://www.vnagency.com.vn/. Ed., Pub., Adv. contact Nguyen Vu Quang.

351 PER ISSN 1609-9788
CONGRESO DE LA REPUBLICA DEL PERU. Text in Spanish. irreg.
Media: Online - full text.
Address: Plaza Bolivar, Ave Abancay s-n, Lima, Peru. cchuma@congreso.gob.pe.

351 USA
CONGRESS. Text in English. 1978. s-a. free. bk.rev. illus. **Document type:** *Newsletter.* **Description:** Covers activities of the center relating to the study of Congress and its leaders.
Formerly (until 1997): Dirksen Congressional Center. Report
Published by: Dirksen Congressional Center, 301 S Fourth St, Ste A, Pekin, IL 61554-4219. TEL 309-347-7113, FAX 309-347-6432. Ed. Linda Sams. Circ: 10,000.

CONGRESS AND THE NATION. *see* POLITICAL SCIENCE

CONGRESS & THE PRESIDENCY; a journal of capital studies. *see* POLITICAL SCIENCE

351 FRA
CONGRESS OF LOCAL AND REGIONAL AUTHORITIES OF EUROPE. ADOPTEDTEXTS. Text in French, English, German, Italian, Russian. 1957. a. USD 24 newsstand/cover (effective 2009). bk.rev. **Document type:** *Proceedings.*
Former titles (until 1994): Standing Conference of Local and Regional Authorities of Europe. Texts Adopted; European Conference of Local and Regional Authorities. Texts Adopted; European Conference of Local Authorities. Texts Adopted (0071-2639)
Published by: Congress of Local and Regional Authorities of Europe, Publishing Division, Palais de l'Europe, Strasbourg, Cedex 67075, France. TEL 33-3-88412581, FAX 33-3-88413910, publishing@coe.int. **Dist. in US by:** Manhattan Publishing Co., PO Box 650, Croton On Hudson, NY 10520.

351 FRA
CONGRESS OF LOCAL AND REGIONAL AUTHORITIES OF EUROPE. OFFICIAL REPORTS OF DEBATES. Text in French, English. 1962. a. USD 29 newsstand/cover (effective 2009). bk.rev. **Document type:** *Proceedings.*
Former titles (until 1994): Standing Conference of Local and Regional Authorities of Europe. Official Reports of Debates; European Conference of Local and Regional Authorities. Official Reports of Debates; European Conference of Local Authorities. Official Reports of Debates (0071-2620)
Published by: Congress of Local and Regional Authorities of Europe, Publishing Division, Palais de l'Europe, Strasbourg, Cedex 67075, France. TEL 33-3-88412581, FAX 33-3-88413910, publishing@coe.int. **Dist. in US by:** Manhattan Publishing Co., PO Box 650, Croton On Hudson, NY 10520.

351 USA ISSN 0733-0200
CONGRESSIONAL ACTIVITIES. Text in English. 1935. w. USD 1,250 (effective 2000). **Document type:** *Newspaper.*
Related titles: Online - full text ed.
Published by: Oliphant Washington Service, PO Box 9808, Friendship Sta, Washington, DC 20016. TEL 202-298-7226, FAX 202-333-5006. Ed., Pub. John Oliphant. Circ: 100.

328.73 USA
G1201.F7
CONGRESSIONAL DISTRICT ATLAS (PRINT). Text in English. 1960. irreg. USD 68 per issue (effective 2009). **Document type:** *Government.* **Description:** Contains maps and tables that depict the boundaries and geographic relationships of congressional districts.
Former titles: Congressional District Atlas (DVD); (until 199?): Congressional District Atlas (Print) (0090-8061); (until 1964): Congressional District Atlas of the United States (0748-4828)
Published by: (U.S. Census Bureau), Bernan Press, 4611-F Assembly Dr, Lanham, MD 20706-4391. TEL 301-459-2255, 800-865-3457, FAX 301-459-0056, bpress@bernan.com.

352 USA ISSN 0589-3151
JK1011
CONGRESSIONAL PICTORIAL DIRECTORY. Text in English. 1951. biennial. USD 33.50 per issue domestic; USD 46.90 per issue foreign (effective 2011). **Document type:** *Directory, Government.*
Formerly (until 1965): Pocket Congressional Directory (0190-9959)
Published by: U.S. Government Printing Office, 732 N Capitol St, NW, Washington, DC 20401. TEL 202-512-1800, 866-512-1800, FAX 202-512-2104, ContactCenter@gpo.gov, http://www.gpo.gov.

351.73 USA ISSN 0364-7544
KF35
CONGRESSIONAL RECORD INDEX. Abbreviated title: U.S. Congress. C R I. Text in English. 19??. bi-w. (when Congress in session). **Document type:** *Government.*
Formerly (until 1873): Index to the Congressional Globe
Published by: U.S. Government Printing Office, 732 N Capitol St, NW, Washington, DC 20401. TEL 202-512-1800, 866-512-1800, FAX 202-512-2104, ContactCenter@gpo.gov, http://www.gpo.gov.

354.3 USA ISSN 0887-1914
CONGRESSIONAL REPORT: SCIENCE, ENERGY & ENVIRONMENT. Text in English. 1985. s-m. USD 360. **Document type:** *Newsletter.* **Description:** Briefings of Congressional events concerning science, energy and the environment.
Published by: J. Anthony Malone, Ed. & Pub., 11300 Weddington St, North Hollywood, CA 91601. TEL 818-509-0384.

CONGRESSIONAL RESEARCH SERVICE. SELECTED REPORTS. *see* POLITICAL SCIENCE

CONGRESSIONAL STAFF DIRECTORY. *see* POLITICAL SCIENCE

351.092 USA ISSN 0191-1422
JK1083 CODEN: CYBOD4
CONGRESSIONAL YELLOW BOOK; who's who in Congress, including committees and key staff. Text in English. 1975. q. USD 475 (effective 2008). illus.; maps. Index. **Document type:** *Directory, Trade.* **Description:** Provides information for any office working with the U.S Congress and lists over 10,000 individuals who work and serve on Capitol Hill.
Formerly (until 1976): Directory of Key Congressional Aides (0099-1376)
Related titles: CD-ROM ed.; Online - full text ed.: USD 925 (effective 2008).
—CASDDS. **CCC.**
Published by: Leadership Directories, Inc, 104 Fifth Ave, 2nd Fl, New York, NY 10011. TEL 212-627-4140, FAX 212-645-0931, info@leadershipdirectories.com. Ed. Ericka J Claflin.

351 347 USA
CONNECTICUT GOVERNMENT REGISTER. Text in English. 2001. m. **Document type:** *Government.* **Description:** A compilation of information about official Connecticut state government actions.
Formerly (until 2005): Weil's Connecticut Government Register (1537-5021)
Published by: LexisNexis (Subsidiary of: Reed Elsevier Group plc), 1016 W Ninth Ave, 1st Fl, King of Prussia, PA 19406. TEL 215 564-1788, 800 448-1515, customer.support@lexisnexis.com.

351.93 333.72 NZL ISSN 1173-5627
S918.N45
CONSERVATION ACTION. Text in English. 1994. a. back issues avail. **Document type:** *Handbook/Manual/Guide, Consumer.* **Description:** Provides an easy-to-read snapshot of conservation work undertaken during the year.
Incorporates (1990-1993): New Zealand. Department of Conservation. Corporate Plan (1170-3970)
Related titles: Online - full text ed.: ISSN 1178-3567.
Published by: New Zealand, Department of Conservation, PO Box 10420, Wellington, 6143, New Zealand. TEL 64-4-4710726, FAX 64-4-3813057, enquiries@doc.govt.nz.

CONSERVATION DU PATRIMOINE. *see* ANTHROPOLOGY

352.53 ITA ISSN 1122-3235
I CONTRATTI DELLO STATO E DEGLI ENTI PUBBLICI; rivista trimestrale di contrattualistica pubblica. Text in Italian. 1992; N.S. 1995. q. EUR 146 (effective 2009). **Document type:** *Magazine, Trade.* **Description:** Provides information from judicial institutes regarding contract law.
Published by: Maggioli Editore, Via del Carpino 8/10, Santarcangelo di Romagna, RN 47822, Italy. TEL 39-0541-628111, FAX 39-0541-622020, editore@maggioli.it, http://www.maggioli.it.

352.53 GBR
CONTRAX WEEKLY U K. Text in English. 1994. w. **Document type:** *Magazine, Trade.* **Description:** Provides information on public sector tenders and contracts in the UK.
Formerly: Contrax Weekly (1356-0239)
Related titles: Diskette ed.: GBP 496; Online - full text ed.: GBP 496.
—CCC.
Published by: B I P Solutions Ltd, Medius, 60 Pacific Quay, Glasgow, G51 1DZ, United Kingdom. TEL 44-141-3328247, FAX 44-141-3312652, bip@bipsolutions.com, http://www.bipsolutions.com.

CONTROVERSIAL ISSUES IN PUBLIC POLICY SERIES. *see* POLITICAL SCIENCE

351 320 MEX ISSN 1405-1435
H8.S7
CONVERGENCIA; revista de ciencias sociales. Text in Spanish. 1993. q. MXN 360 domestic; MXN 450 foreign (effective 2011). **Document type:** *Journal, Academic/Scholarly.*
Related titles: Online - full text ed.: 1999. free (effective 2011) (from SciELO).
Indexed: A01, C01, CA, F03, F04, H21, IBSS, P08, P34, P42, PSA, S02, S03, SCOPUS, SSA, SSCI, SociolAb, T02, W07.
—IE.
Published by: Universidad Autonoma del Estado de Mexico, Centro de Investigacion y Estudios Avanzados en Ciencias Politicas y Administracion Publica, Cerro de Coatepec s/n, Ciudad Universitaria, Toluca, 50000, Mexico. TEL 52-722-2159280. Ed. Eduardo Sandoval Forero.

THE COPENHAGEN DIPLOMATIC LIST. *see* POLITICAL SCIENCE—International Relations

352.749 CAN ISSN 1483-9830
CA1BT31-4 35
COPYRIGHT BOARD CANADA. PERFORMANCE REPORT. Text in English, French. 1997. a.
Related titles: Online - full text ed.: ISSN 1490-473X.
Published by: (Copyright Board of Canada/Commission du Droit d'Auteur Canada), Treasury Board of Canada Secretariat, Corporate Communications/Secretariat du Conseil du Tresor du Canada, West Tower, Rm P-135, 300 Laurier Ave W, Ottawa, ON K1A 0R5, Canada. TEL 613-995-2855, FAX 613-996-0518, services-publications@tbs-sct.gc.ca, http://www.tbs-sct.gc.ca.

353.39 CAN ISSN 1483-7439
CA1BT31-4 36
CORRECTIONAL SERVICE CANADA. PERFORMANCE REPORT. Text in English, French. 1997. a.
Related titles: Online - full text ed.: ISSN 1490-4667.
Published by: (Correctional Service of Canada/Service Correctionnel Canada), Treasury Board of Canada Secretariat, Corporate Communications/Secretariat du Conseil du Tresor du Canada, West Tower, Rm P-135, 300 Laurier Ave W, Ottawa, ON K1A 0R5, Canada. TEL 613-995-2855, FAX 613-996-0518, services-publications@tbs-sct.gc.ca, http://www.tbs-sct.gc.ca.

351 FRA ISSN 2105-5882
COTE S C O T. (Schema de Coherence Territoriale) Text in French. 2003. irreg. **Document type:** *Newsletter, Consumer.*
Formerly (until 2009): Acteurs et Pratiques (1773-3545)
Published by: Etablissement Public du S C O T de la Region Urbaine de Grenoble, 21, Rue Lesdiguieres, Grenoble, 38000, France. TEL 33-4-76288639, FAX 33-4-76472001, http://www.region-grenoble.org.

COUNCIL OF JEWISH ORGANIZATIONS IN CIVIL SERVICE. COUNCIL NEWS. *see* ETHNIC INTERESTS

351.41 GBR
COUNCILS, COMMITTEES AND BOARDS: INCLUDING GOVERNMENT AGENCIES & AUTHORITIES. Text in English. 1970. irreg., latest 2004, 13 ed. GBP 163 per issue (effective 2010). index. **Document type:** *Directory, Trade.* **Description:** Contains lists of 1,300 official and semi-official bodies in the UK.
Formerly (until 1998): Councils, Committees and Boards (0070-1211)
—BLDSC (3481.250000). **CCC.**
Published by: C.B.D. Research Ltd., Chancery House, 15 Wickham Rd, Beckenham, Kent BR3 5JS, United Kingdom. TEL 44-20-86507745, FAX 44-20-86500768, cbd@cbdresearch.com.

351 USA ISSN 1094-4907
E154.5
COUNTIES U S A; a directory of United States counties. Text in English. 1997. irreg., latest 2006, 3rd ed. USD 135 3rd ed. (effective 2008). charts; maps; stat. **Document type:** *Directory, Consumer.* **Description:** Lists persons and agencies for each of the more than 3,100 counties in the United States, arranged by state. Includes contact information for the governor, lieutenant governor, secretary of state, and attorney general, along with data on the state supreme court, the state library, and the US senators and representatives.
Published by: Omnigraphics, Inc., PO Box 31-1640, Detroit, MI 48231. TEL 313-961-1340, 800-234-1340, FAX 313-961-1383, 800-875-1340, info@omnigraphics.com. Pub. Frederick G Ruffner Jr.

352.13 USA
THE COUNTY ADMINISTRATOR. Text in English. 1953. m. membership. adv. bk.rev. **Document type:** *Newsletter.* **Description:** Covers issues affecting county governments.
Published by: National Association of County Administrators, Mort McBain, 500 Forest St, Wausau, WI 54403-5554. TEL 715-261-1402, FAX 715-261-1515. Ed. Alan Siegel. Circ: 500.

COUNTY COMPASS. *see* ETHNIC INTERESTS

P

352 USA ISSN 0011-0353
JS451.T4
COUNTY PROGRESS; the business magazine for county officials. Text in English. 1923. m. USD 20 domestic; USD 30 foreign (effective 2006). adv. illus. 56 p./no. 3 cols./p.; reprints avail. **Document type:** *Magazine, Trade.* **Description:** Covers criminal justice, juvenile justice, healthcare, technology, road construction and maintenance, and grants.
Related titles: Supplement(s): Texas County Directory.
Indexed: P06.
Published by: (County Judges and Commissioners Association of Texas), Zachry Associates, 500 Chestnut St., Ste 2000, PO Box 1739, Abilene, TX 79604-1739. TEL 325-673-4822, FAX 325-677-2631. Ed. Julie Anderson. Pub. H C Zachry. R&P Kimberly Snyder. Adv. contact Amy Brittain. B&W page USD 600, color page USD 1,300. Circ: 3,600 (paid and controlled).

CRACKING THE A P U.S. GOVERNMENT AND POLITICS EXAM. (Advanced Placement, United States) *see* EDUCATION—Higher Education

CRIMINOLOGY AND PUBLIC POLICY. *see* CRIMINOLOGY AND LAW ENFORCEMENT

351 900 321.87 NZL ISSN 1179-6588
CROWN & KORU; supporting the monarchy of New Zealand. Text in English. 1996. q. free to members (effective 2010). **Document type:** *Journal, Academic/Scholarly.* **Description:** Contains information on the constitutional Monarchy of New Zealand.
Former titles (until 2010): Monarchy New Zealand (1174-8435); (until 1998): Monarchist League of New Zealand. Newsletter; (until 1997): Monarchist League of New Zealand. Members Newsletter
Related titles: Online - full text ed.: free (effective 2010).
Published by: Monarchy New Zealand, PO Box 128-519, Remuera, Auckland, 1541, New Zealand. TEL 64-9-5234408, FAX 64-9-5234405, enquiries@monarchy.org.nz, http://www.monarchy.org.nz. Ed. Dr. Noel Cox TEL 64-9-9219999 ext 5209.

351 ESP
CUADERNOS DE ADMINISTRACION LOCAL. Text in Spanish. 2001. m.
Published by: Federacion Espanola de Municipios y Provincias, Nuncio, 8, Madrid, 28005, Spain. TEL 34-91-3643700, FAX 34-91-3655482, femp@femp.es, http://www.femp.es/. Ed. Gonzalo Brun.

351 ARG ISSN 0326-0003
CUADERNOS DE ADMINISTRACION PUBLICA. Text in Spanish. 1975. bi-m. back issues avail. **Document type:** *Journal, Academic/Scholarly.*
Published by: Universidad Catolica de Cordoba, Instituto de Ciencias de la Administracion, Obispo Trejo 323 Piso 1, Cordoba, 5000, Argentina. TEL 54-351-4213213, http://www.uccor.edu.ar/modelo.php?param=1.9&new_window=1.

351 ESP ISSN 1576-0529
JN8101
CUADERNOS DE GOBIERNO Y ADMINISTRACION. Text in Spanish. 2000. s-a. **Document type:** *Journal, Academic/Scholarly.*
Published by: Universidad Rey Juan Carlos, Facultad de Ciencias Juridicas y Sociales, Campus de Vicalvaro, P. Artilleros, s-n, Madrid, 28032, Spain. TEL 34-91-3019800, FAX 34-91-7750342, fcjsinfo@fcjs.urjc.es, http://www.urjc.es/.

320 ESP ISSN 1131-7744
CUADERNOS REPUBLICANOS. Text in Spanish. 1989. q. back issues avail. **Document type:** *Journal, Academic/Scholarly.*
Related titles: Online - full text ed.
Published by: Centro de Investigaciones de Estudios Republicanos, C Zabaleta 7-1o C, Madrid, 28002, Spain. TEL 34-91-5153589.

351 AUS ISSN 1838-3424
CULTURAL FUNDING IN AUSTRALIA. Text in English. 1991. a., latest 2009. free (effective 2011). back issues avail. **Document type:** *Report, Government.* **Description:** Presents information about cultural funding by each of the three levels of government in Australia such as Federal Government, State and Territory Government, and Local Government.
Related titles: Online - full text ed.: ISSN 1838-3432.
Published by: (Cultural Ministers Council, Statistics Working Group), Australia Council for the Arts, PO Box 788, Strawberry Hills, NSW 2012, Australia. TEL 61-2-92159000, 800-226-912, FAX 61-2-92159111, mail@australiacouncil.gov.au, http://www.australiacouncil.gov.au.

351 COL ISSN 2011-4605
CUNDINAMARCA. CORAZON DE COLOMBIA. Text in Spanish. 1996. w. **Document type:** *Magazine, Consumer.*
Published by: Gobernacion de Cundinamarca, Calle 26 No. 51-53, Bogota, Colombia. TEL 57-1-4260000.

351.85 FIN ISSN 1796-9263
CUPOREN VERKKOJULKAISUJA. Text in Finnish. 2007. irreg., latest vol.2, 2007. back issues avail. **Document type:** *Monographic series, Consumer.*
Media: Online - full content.
Published by: Kulttuuripoliittisen Tutkimuksen Edistamissaatio/The Finnish Foundation for Cultural Policy Research, Talberginkatu 1 C 137, Helsinki, 00180, Finland. TEL 358-9-77460441, FAX 358-9-77460437, info@cupore.fi.

351 NLD ISSN 1727-0707
CURRENT EUROPEAN ISSUES. Text in English; Text occasionally in French. 1997. irreg., latest 2003. price varies. back issues avail. **Document type:** *Monographic series, Academic/Scholarly.* **Description:** Examines in-depth issues relating to all areas of public administration.
Published by: European Institute of Public Administration/Institut Europeen d'Administration Publique, PO Box 1229, Maastricht, 6201 BE, Netherlands. TEL 31-43-3296222, FAX 31-43-3296296, eipa@eipa-nl.com.

CURRENT POPULATION REPORTS. POPULATION CHARACTERISTICS. VOTING AND REGISTRATION IN THE ELECTION. *see* POLITICAL SCIENCE

352.448 USA
CUSTOMS REGULATIONS OF THE UNITED STATES. Text in English. base vol. plus irreg. updates. looseleaf. USD 123 (effective 2001). **Document type:** *Government.* **Description:** Contains regulations made and published for the purpose of carrying out customs laws administered by the U.S. Customs Service.
Published by: U.S. Customs Service, National Support Staff, Rm B338, 1301 Constitution Ave, N W, Washington, DC 20229. **Subscr. to:** U.S. Government Printing Office, Superintendent of Documents, PO Box 371954, Pittsburgh, PA 15250. TEL 202-512-1800, FAX 202-512-2250, orders@gpo.gov, http://www.access.gpo.gov.

CYPRUS. DEPARTMENT OF STATISTICS AND RESEARCH. FUNCTIONS AND SERVICES. *see* PUBLIC ADMINISTRATION—Abstracting, Bibliographies, Statistics

352.4 CYP
CYPRUS. MINISTRY OF FINANCE. ANNUAL REPORT. Text in Greek. 1990. a. stat. **Document type:** *Government.* **Description:** Includes reports from all departments of the Ministry of Finance.
Incorporates (in 1991): Cyprus. Department of Customs and Excise. Annual Report
Published by: Ministry of Finance, Department of Statistics and Research, Nicosia, Cyprus. Ed., Pub. Panayiotis Tilliros.

351 DEU ISSN 1867-8254
D B B - REPORT. (Deutscher Beamtenbund) Text in German. 1952. q. membership. adv. bk.rev. stat. back issues avail. **Document type:** *Newsletter, Government.*
Former titles (until 2003): D B B Mitteilungen fuer den Oeffentlichen Dienst (0721-8206); (until 1981): Beamte im Lande Bremen (0005-7401)
Published by: Deutscher Beamtenbund, Landesbund Bremen e.V., Kontorhaus, Rembertistr 28, Bremen, 28203, Germany. TEL 49-421-700043, FAX 49-421-702826, dbb.bremen@ewetel.net. Circ: 10,000 (controlled).

351 USA
D E S ACTIVITIES REPORT. (Arizona Department of Economic Security) Text in English. 1973. a. illus. **Document type:** *Government.*
Formerly: Arizona. Department of Economic Security. Annual Report (0094-0712)
Published by: Arizona Department of Economic Security, Research Administration, Site Code 733A, Box 6123, Phoenix, AZ 85005. TEL 602-542-4791.

351 USA
D H S DAILY OPEN SOURCE INFRASTRUCTURE REPORT. Text in English. d. free. **Document type:** *Newsletter, Government.*
Media: Online - full content.
Published by: U.S. Department of Homeland Security, Washington, DC 20528. TEL 202-312-3421.

D L A P S. (Defense Logistics Agency Publishing System) *see* PUBLIC ADMINISTRATION—Abstracting, Bibliographies, Statistics

336.2 DEU
D S T G MAGAZIN. Text in German. 1952. 10/yr. free to members (effective 2009). adv. **Document type:** *Magazine, Trade.*
Former titles (until 2001): Die Steuer-Gewerkschaft (0178-207X); (until 1973): Der Steuerbeamte (0178-2088)
Published by: Deutsche Steuer-Gewerkschaft, Friedrichstr 169-170, Berlin, 10117, Germany. TEL 49-30-206256650, FAX 49-30-206256601, stgv@dstg-verlag.de. adv.: B&W page EUR 2,549.45, color page EUR 4,239. Circ: 75,300 (paid and controlled).

DAGENS SAMHAELLE; kommunernas och landstingets tidning. *see* PUBLIC ADMINISTRATION—Municipal Government

328.748025 USA
DAILY BULLETIN. Text in English. 1935. irreg. back issues avail. **Document type:** *Bulletin, Trade.* **Description:** Provides clear and concise summaries of bills, committee substitutes, and amendments and a complete record of all floor action taken every day.
Related titles: E-mail ed.: USD 50 per week to individuals; USD 25 per week to institutions (effective 2010).
Published by: University of North Carolina at Chapel Hill, School of Government, Knapp-Sanders Bldg, Campus Box 3330, Chapel Hill, NC 27599. TEL 919-966-5381, FAX 919-962-0654, sales@sog.unc.edu, http://sog.unc.edu.

DAILY COMPILATION OF PRESIDENTIAL DOCUMENTS. *see* POLITICAL SCIENCE

328.76318 USA
KFI1212.D3
DAILY LEGISLATIVE REPORT (BATON ROUGE). Text in English. 1974. d. (when in session). USD 300. **Document type:** *Newsletter.*
Published by: Legiscon, PO Box 1643, Baton Rouge, LA 70821. TEL 504-343-9828, FAX 504-338-5243. Ed. Jim Lee. Circ: 300.

328.76212 USA
DAILY LEGISLATIVE REPORT (JACKSON). Text in English. d. (when in session). USD 395 to non-members; USD 150 to members. **Document type:** *Newsletter.*
Published by: Mississippi Economic Council, PO Box 23276, Jackson, MS 39225. TEL 601-969-0022, FAX 601-353-0247. Ed. Blake Wilson.

328 USA ISSN 0277-4917
DAILY LEGISLATIVE REPORT (SPRINGFIELD). Text in English. 1939. d. (when in session). looseleaf. USD 825 (effective 2008).
Published by: State Capital Information Service, Inc., PO Box 2455, Springfield, IL 62705-2455. TEL 217-523-6422, scis@scisinc.com, http://www.scisinc.com.

328.77356 USA
DAILY LEGISLATIVE REPORTER. Text in English. 1936. d. price varies. index. back issues avail.
Published by: Journal Record Newspaper, 222 N Robinson Ave, Oklahoma City, OK 73102-9020. TEL 405-521-1405, FAX 405-521-0457. Ed. David Mauser.

DAILY TERRITORIAL. *see* BUSINESS AND ECONOMICS

351 CHN ISSN 1671-3001
DALIAN NIANJIAN/DALIAN YEARBOOK. Text in Chinese. 1990. a. **Document type:** *Yearbook, Government.*
Published by: Zhonggong Dalian Shi Weiyuanhui/Dalian Committee of the Chinese Poeple's Political Consultative Conference, 138, Changjiang Lu, Dalian, 116001, China. http://www.dlzx.gov.cn/index.do. **Co-sponsor:** Dalian Shi Shizhi Bangongshi.

328 660 NLD ISSN 1567-5017
DANGEROUS SUBSTANCES CD. Text in English. 1999. s-a. EUR 995 (effective 2009). **Description:** Covers legislation and proposed legislation on the classification, packaging and labelling of dangerous preparations.
Media: CD-ROM.
Published by: Ellis Publications bv, PO Box 1059, Maastricht, 6201 BB, Netherlands. TEL 31-43-3215313, FAX 31-43-3253959, ellis.info@thomson.com.

DANMARKS NATIONALBANK. DANISH GOVERNMENT BORROWING AND DEBT. *see* BUSINESS AND ECONOMICS—Banking And Finance

351 DNK ISSN 0902-6681
HJ56
DANMARKS NATIONALBANK. STATENS LAANTAGNING OG GAELD. Text in Danish. 1924. a. free. back issues avail. **Document type:** *Consumer.* **Description:** Reports on the Danish government's borrowing and debt.
Formerly (until 1987): Finansministeriet. Danske Statslaan (0105-4554)
Related titles: Online - full content ed.: ISSN 1398-3873; ◆ English ed.: Danmarks Nationalbank. Danish Government Borrowing and Debt. ISSN 1399-2023.
Published by: Danmarks Nationalbank, Havnegade 5, Copenhagen K, 1093, Denmark. TEL 45-33-636363, FAX 45-33-637103, kommunikation@nationalbanken.dk.

351 ROM ISSN 2068-5459
▼ ➤ **DANUBIUS UNIVERSITAS. ACTA. ADMINISTRATIO.** Key Title: Acta Universitatis Danubius: Administratio. Text in English, French. 2010. irreg. free (effective 2011). **Document type:** *Journal, Academic/Scholarly.*
Media: Online - full text.
Published by: Universitatea "Danubius" Galati/Danubius University of Galati, B-dul Galati nr. 3, Galati, 800654, Romania. TEL 40-749-084355. Ed. Mirela Costache.

351 NLD ISSN 1877-9026
DE DATALOODS EN ZIJN MACHINEKARMER. Text in Dutch. 2004. biennial. EUR 52.50 per issue (effective 2011).
Published by: Kluwer B.V. (Subsidiary of: Wolters Kluwer N.V.), Postbus 23, Deventer, 7400 GA, Netherlands. TEL 31-570-673449, FAX 31-570-691555, info@kluwer.nl, http://www.kluwer.nl.

DATATILSYNET. AARSBERETNING. *see* COMPUTERS—Computer Security

DAVID HUME PAPER. *see* POLITICAL SCIENCE

352.63 CAN ISSN 1488-8173
A DAY IN THE LIFE OF THE PUBLIC SERVICE OF CANADA. Variant title: Journee dans la Vie de la Fonction Publique du Canada. Text in English, French. 1999. irreg.
Related titles: Online - full text ed.: ISSN 1488-8181.
Published by: Leadership Network, 122 Bank St, 3rd Fl, Ottawa, ON K1A 0R5, Canada. TEL 613-996-1353, FAX 613-996-2228, http://leadership.gc.ca.

DCWATCH. (District of Columbia) *see* POLITICAL SCIENCE

351 AUS ISSN 1833-6825
DEBATES OF THE LEGISLATIVE ASSEMBLY FOR THE AUSTRALIAN CAPITAL TERRITORY, WEEKLY HANSARD. Text in English. 1989. w. **Document type:** *Proceedings, Government.* **Description:** Provides information on proceedings of the legislative assembly and the evidence taken during hearings of the legislative assembly committees.
Formerly: A C T House of Assembly (Australia). Hansard
Related titles: Online - full text ed.: ISSN 1833-6833.
Published by: Australian Capital Territory, Legislative Assembly, GPO Box 1020, Canberra, ACT 2601, Australia. TEL 61-2-62050439, FAX 61-2-62053109, secretariat@parliament.act.gov.au, http://www.parliament.act.gov.au/index.asp.

351 CAN ISSN 1910-944X
DEBATES OF THE SENATE OF CANADA. HANSARD. Text in English. 1996. irreg. **Document type:** *Government.*
Media: Online - full text. **Related titles:** Print ed.: ISSN 0704-5565. 187?; French ed.: Debats du Senat. Hansard. ISSN 1910-9458; Supplement(s): Index des Debats du Senat. ISSN 1912-4775; Senate Debate Indexes. ISSN 1912-4767. 1993.
Published by: Senate of Canada, Information Service, Ottawa, ON K1A 0A9, Canada. TEL 613-992-4793, info@parl.gc.ca, http://www.parl.gc.ca.

351 CAN ISSN 0847-4273
J107
DEBATS DE L'ASSEMBLEE LEGISLATIVE. EDITION REVISEE. Text in French. 1868. irreg. **Document type:** *Proceedings, Government.*
—CCC.
Published by: Assemblee Nationale de Quebec, Parliament Bldg, 1045, rue des Parlementaires, Quebec, PQ G1A 1A4, Canada. TEL 418-643-7239, 866-337-8837, FAX 418-646-4271, http://www.assnat.qc.ca/eng/index.html.

DECIDEUR PUBLIC; systemes d'information. *see* LIBRARY AND INFORMATION SCIENCES

351 347 USA ISSN 1092-2245
KFD36
DELAWARE GOVERNMENT REGISTER. Text in English. 1996. m. back issues avail. **Document type:** *Government.* **Description:** Covers executive orders of the Governor, Attorney General opinions, public laws enacted, public utility and environmental orders enacted, banking and insurance agency information, emergency rules, and gubernatorial appointments of state officials and board-commission members.
Published by: LexisNexis (Subsidiary of: Reed Elsevier Group plc), 1016 W Ninth Ave, 1st Fl, King of Prussia, PA 19406. TEL 215 564-1788, 800 448-1515, customer.support@lexisnexis.com.

351.624 SDN
DEMOCRATIC REPUBLIC OF THE SUDAN GAZETTE/AL-JARIDAH AR-RASMIYAH LI-JUMHURIYAT AS-SUDAN AD-DIMUQRATIYAH. Text in Arabic, English. m. **Document type:** *Government.*
Indexed: RASB.
Published by: Attorney General, Attorney General's Chambers, P O Box 302, Khartoum, Sudan.

DEMOCRATIC REPUBLIC OF THE SUDAN GAZETTE. LEGISLATIVE SUPPLEMENT. *see* POLITICAL SCIENCE

351 DEU ISSN 1863-7590
DENKMALPFLEGE-INFORMATIONEN. Text in German. 2006. irreg. bk.rev. **Document type:** *Bulletin, Government.*
Formed by the merger of (1975-2006): Denkmalpflege-Informationen. Ausgabe A (1617-3147); (1975-2006): Denkmalpflege-Informationen. Ausgabe B (1617-3155)

Published by: Bayerisches Landesamt fuer Denkmalpflege, Hofgraben 4, Munich, 80539, Germany. TEL 49-89-21140, FAX 49-89-2114300, poststelle@blfd.bayern.de, http://www.blfd.bayern.de. Circ: 3,000 (controlled).

DENMARK. FINANSMINISTERIET. AFTALER OM DEN KOMMUNALE OG REGIONALE OEKONOMI. *see* BUSINESS AND ECONOMICS—Public Finance, Taxation

328.9489 DNK ISSN 0903-6946
JN7269
DENMARK. FOLKETINGET. PRAESIDIET. FOLKETINGSTIDENDE. AARBOG OG REGISTRE. Text in Danish. 1988. a. price varies. **Document type:** *Yearbook, Government.*
Formed by the merger of (1954-1988): Folketingstidende (0904-0307); (1899-1988): Denmark. Folketinget. Folketingsaarbog (0084-9707); Which was formerly (until 1954): Rigsdagsaarbog (0901-4748); (until 1943): Aarbog for Rigssamlingen
Related titles: Online - full text ed.
Published by: Folketinget/Danish Parliament, Christiansborg, Copenhagen K, 1240, Denmark. TEL 45-33-375500, folketinget@ft.dk, http://www.ft.dk. **Dist. by:** Schultz Information A-S, Herstedvang 12, Albertslund 2620, Denmark. TEL 45-43-632300, FAX 45-43-631963, schultz@schultz-information.dk, http://www.schultz-information.dk.

354.9406 AUS ISSN 0157-8340
JQ4042
DEPARTMENT OF THE PRIME MINISTER AND CABINET. ANNUAL REPORT. Text in English. 1979. a. **Document type:** *Bulletin, Government.*
—CCC.
Published by: Department of the Prime Minister and Cabinet, One National Circuit, Barton, ACT 2600, Australia. TEL 61-2-62715111, FAX 61-2-62715414, anne.hazell@pmc.gov.au.

328.45 ITA
I DEPUTATI E SENATORI DEL PARLAMENTO REPUBBLICANO. ANNUARIO. Text in Italian. 1992. a. EUR 90 (effective 2009). **Document type:** *Directory.* **Description:** Contains information on the Italian Parliament and government.
Related titles: CD-ROM ed.
Published by: Editoriale Italiana, Via Vigliena 10, Rome, 00192, Italy. TEL 39-06-3230177, FAX 39-06-3211359, info@editoriale.it, http://www.editoriale.it. Ed. Giordano Treveri Gennari.

▼ **DERECHO DE LA SEGURIDAD NACIONAL.** *see* LAW

351 DEU ISSN 0340-8604
K30
DEUTSCHE NOTAR-ZEITSCHRIFT; Verkuendungsblatt der Bundesnotarkammer. Text in German. 1948. m. EUR 96; EUR 9.20 newsstand/cover (effective 2011). adv. back issues avail.; reprints avail. **Document type:** *Journal, Trade.*
Indexed: IBR, IBZ.
Published by: (Bundesnotarkammer), Verlag C.H. Beck oHG, Wilhelmstr 9, Munich, 80801, Germany. TEL 49-89-381890, FAX 49-89-38189398, abo.service@beck.de, http://www.beck.de. Circ: 7,220 (paid).

352 DEU ISSN 0344-2489
DEUTSCHER STAEDTETAG. REIHE E: BEITRAEGE ZUR STADTENTWICKLUNG. Variant title: D S T Beitraege zur Stadtentwicklung. Text in German. 1972. irreg., latest vol.32, 2000. price varies. **Document type:** *Monographic series, Academic/Scholarly.*
Published by: Deutscher Staedtetag, Im Klapperhof 23, Cologne, 50670, Germany. TEL 49-221-37710, FAX 49-221-3771128, staedtetag@staedtetag.de.

351 DEU ISSN 0070-4423
DEUTSCHES BEAMTEN-JAHRBUCH. BUNDESAUSGABE. Text in German. 1968. 2 base vols. plus updates 3/yr. looseleaf. EUR 99 base vol(s).; EUR 45 updates (effective 2010). bk.rev. **Document type:** *Trade.*
Related titles: CD-ROM ed.; Online - full text ed.
Published by: (Deutscher Beamtenbund), Walhalla Fachverlag, Haus an der Eisernen Bruecke, Regensburg, 93042, Germany. TEL 49-941-56840, FAX 49-941-5684111, walhalla@walhalla.de. Ed. Thomas Mischlewitz. Circ: 4,600 (paid).

DEUTSCHES VERWALTUNGSBLATT. *see* LAW

351 GTM
DIARIO DE CENTRO AMERICA. Text in Spanish. 1880. irreg. USD 54. adv. bk.rev.
Formerly: Guatemalteco
Related titles: Online - full text ed.: ISSN 1563-8391.
Address: 18 Calle No. 6-72, Zona 1, Guatemala City, Guatemala. Ed. Luis Mendizabal R. Circ: 10,000.

351 USA
DICKINSON'S F D A UPDATES. (Federal Drug Administration) Text in English. w. USD 580 domestic; USD 690 elsewhere (effective 2005). **Document type:** *Newsletter, Trade.*
Media: Fax.
Published by: Ferdic Inc., PO Box 28, Camp Hill, PA 17011. TEL 717-731-1426, FAX 717-731-1427, info@fdaweb.com, http://www.fdaweb.com. Ed., Pub. James G Dickinson TEL 520-684-3112.

351.03 FRA
DICTIONNAIRE DES COMMUNES (LAVAUZELLE ET CIE). Text in French. quadrennial.
Published by: Editions Charles Lavauzelle, Le Prouet, BP 8, Panazol, 87350, France. TEL 33-5-55584545, FAX 33-5-55584525.

351.43 DEU
DAS DIENST- UND TARIFRECHT DER SOZIALVERSICHERUNGSTRAEGER. Text in German. 4 base vols. plus updates 6/yr. EUR 329 base vol(s).; EUR 50 updates (effective 2010). adv. **Document type:** *Trade.*
Related titles: CD-ROM ed.
Published by: Walhalla Fachverlag, Haus an der Eisernen Bruecke, Regensburg, 93042, Germany. TEL 49-941-56840, FAX 49-941-5684111, walhalla@walhalla.de. Ed. Klaus M Dauderstaedt. adv.: B&W page EUR 245. Circ: 500 (controlled).

351 DEU
DIENSTSTELLEN DES FREISTAATES BAYERN. Text in German. 1980. a. EUR 24.30 (effective 2011). **Document type:** *Government.*
Former titles (until 2001): Verzeichnis der Dienststellen des Freistaates Bayern; (until 1998): Die Dienststellen des Freistaates Bayern in den Kreisfreien Staedten und Landkreisen
Published by: Bayerisches Landesamt fuer Statistik und Datenverarbeitung, Neuhauser Str 8, Munich, 80331, Germany. TEL 49-89-2119205, FAX 49-89-2119410, poststelle@statistik.bayern.de, http://www.statistik.bayern.de.

351 USA ISSN 0733-0227
DIGEST OF ACTIVITIES OF CONGRESS. Text in English. 1935. w. USD 300 (effective 2000). **Document type:** *Newspaper.*
Related titles: Online - full text ed.
Published by: Oliphant Washington Service, PO Box 9808, Friendship Sta, Washington, DC 20016. TEL 202-298-7226, FAX 202-333-5006. Ed., Pub. John Oliphant. Circ: 200.

352.68 CYP
DIMOSIOS YPALLILOS/CIVIL SERVANT. Text in Greek. 1965. fortn. adv. bk.rev. **Document type:** *Bulletin, Government.*
Published by: Cyprus Civil Servants Association, 3 Demetrios Severis Ave, Nicosia, Cyprus. TEL 357-2-442393, FAX 357-2-665199. Ed., R&P Priamos Loizides TEL 357-2-667260. Circ: 14,000.

DIPLOMATIC BULLETIN. *see* POLITICAL SCIENCE—International Relations

320 DEU ISSN 0949-040X
DIPLOMATISCHES MAGAZIN. Text in German. 1995. m. EUR 78.68; EUR 4.90 newsstand/cover (effective 2009). adv. **Document type:** *Magazine, Trade.*
Published by: Diplomatisches Magazin Verlagsgesellschaft mbH, Zimmerstr 56, Berlin, 10117, Germany. TEL 49-30-26393085, FAX 49-30-2186934. Ed. Corinna Schlag. Pub. Irene Ernst. adv.: B&W page EUR 2,800, color page EUR 3,800; trim 210 x 297. Circ: 12,000 (controlled).

DIRECTORIO DE EJECUTIVAS. *see* BUSINESS AND ECONOMICS—Trade And Industrial Directories

351.025 MEX
DIRECTORIO DEL GOBIERNO. Text in Spanish. 1983. irreg., latest vol.27, 2001. USD 330 (effective 2001). Supplement avail. **Document type:** *Directory.* **Description:** Lists names, with job titles, urls, phone and fax numbers of federal, state and municipal government personnel and executive, legislative and judicial branch personnel. Indexed by surname and keyword of agencies.
Related titles: E-mail ed.: USD 140 for 6 mos. (effective 2001).
Published by: Ibcon S.A., Gutemberg 224, Col Anzures, Mexico City, DF 11590, Mexico. TEL 52-5-2554577, FAX 52-5-2554577, ibcon@infosel.net.mx, http://www.ibcon.com.mx. Ed. Gabriel Zaid.

351.51025 HKG ISSN 1021-691X
DIRECTORY OF CHINESE GOVERNMENT ORGANS. Text in English. 1989. biennial. USD 110. **Document type:** *Directory, Government.* **Description:** Features comprehensive and authoritative coverage of the various institutions of the Chinese government.
Published by: Xinhua News Agency, c/o Current Publications Ltd, 1503 Enterprise Bldg, 228 Queen's Rd Central, GPO Box 9848, Hong Kong, Hong Kong.

352.140 GBR
▼ **THE DIRECTORY OF ENGLISH REGIONAL & LONDON GOVERNMENT.** Text in English. 2009. a. GBP 315 combined subscription per issue (print & CD-ROM eds.); GBP 265 per issue (effective 2009). adv. back issues avail. **Document type:** *Directory, Trade.* **Description:** Designed to be a guide to the system of regional government in England outside London.
Formed by the merger of (2002-2009): The Directory of English Regional Government (1471-3586); (2000-2009): The Directory of London Government (1468-4179)
Related titles: CD-ROM ed.: GBP 280 per issue (effective 2009).
—CCC.
Published by: Carlton Publishing & Printing Ltd., Maple House, Maple View, Steeds Ln, Kingsnorth, TN26 1NQ, United Kingdom. TEL 44-1923-800801, FAX 44-1923-800802, info@carlton-group.co.uk.

351.796 USA
DIRECTORY OF IDAHO GOVERNMENT OFFICIALS. Text in English. a. USD 20 (effective 2000). adv. **Document type:** *Directory.*
Published by: Association of Idaho Cities, 3100 S Vista Ave, Ste 310, Boise, ID 83705. TEL 208-344-8594, FAX 208-344-8677. Ed. Ken Harward. R&P Tondee P Clark. adv.: page USD 750; trim 11 x 8.5.

351.789 USA
DIRECTORY OF NEW MEXICO MUNICIPAL OFFICIALS. Text in English. a. USD 35. adv. **Document type:** *Directory.* **Description:** Contains names, addresses of all incorporated municipalities and elected and appointed officials in New Mexico.
Formerly: Directory of Municipal Officials of New Mexico (0070-5888)
Published by: New Mexico Municipal League, 1229 Paseo de Peralta, Box 846, Santa Fe, NM 87504-0846. TEL 505-982-5573, FAX 505-984-1392. Ed. William F Fulginiti. Circ: 1,400.

328.41 GBR ISSN 1465-4768
JN1572.A12
THE DIRECTORY OF NORTHERN IRELAND GOVERNMENT. Text in English. 1999. a. GBP 325 combined subscription per issue (print & CD-ROM eds.); GBP 255 per issue (effective 2010). adv. **Document type:** *Directory, Trade.* **Description:** Provides information on the Northern Ireland Government and assembly.
Related titles: CD-ROM ed.: GBP 280 per issue (effective 2010).
—CCC.
Published by: Carlton Publishing & Printing Ltd., Maple House, Maple View, Steeds Ln, Kingsnorth, TN26 1NQ, United Kingdom. TEL 44-1923-800801, FAX 44-1923-800802, info@carlton-group.co.uk.

351 USA ISSN 1098-6901
DIRECTORY OF OFFICIAL NEW JERSEY. Text in English. 1998. a. USD 72.95 per issue; USD 199 combined subscription per issue (print & CD-ROM eds.) (effective 2011). **Document type:** *Directory, Trade.* **Description:** Provides a guide to municipal, county, and state officials, parks, museums, post offices, authorities and planning boards.
Related titles: CD-ROM ed.; Online - full text ed.
Published by: Research Communications, Inc., 6818 Oasis Pass, Ste 101, Austin, TX 78731. TEL 512-266-0067, 800-331-5076, FAX 512-266-2696, researchcomm@austin.rr.com, http://www.researchcomm.com/.

328.411 GBR ISSN 1465-4776
JN1187
THE DIRECTORY OF SCOTTISH GOVERNMENT. Text in English. 1999. a. GBP 315 combined subscription per issue (print & CD-ROM eds.); GBP 245 per issue (effective 2009). adv. **Document type:** *Directory, Trade.* **Description:** Provides information on the Scottish Government.
Related titles: CD-ROM ed.: GBP 280 per issue (effective 2009).
—CCC.
Published by: Carlton Publishing & Printing Ltd., Maple House, Maple View, Steeds Ln, Kingsnorth, TN26 1NQ, United Kingdom. TEL 44-1923-800801, FAX 44-1923-800802, info@carlton-group.co.uk.

351 USA ISSN 0440-4947
JK9330
DIRECTORY OF STATE, COUNTY, AND FEDERAL OFFICIALS. Text in English. 1964. a. price varies. **Document type:** *Directory, Government.*
Published by: Legislative Reference Bureau, State Capitol, Rm 005, Honolulu, HI 96813. TEL 808-587-0690, FAX 808-587-0699, lrb@capitol.hawaii.gov.

328.025 GBR ISSN 1477-3023
THE DIRECTORY OF U K PARLIAMENTS AND ASSEMBLIES. Variant title: The Guide to U K Parliaments and Assemblies. Text in English. 2003. a. GBP 315 combined subscription per issue (print & CD-ROM eds.); GBP 255 per issue (effective 2009). adv. **Document type:** *Directory, Trade.* **Description:** Provides information on the UK Parliaments and Assemblies.
Related titles: CD-ROM ed.: GBP 280 per issue (effective 2009).
—CCC.
Published by: Carlton Publishing & Printing Ltd., Maple House, Maple View, Steeds Ln, Kingsnorth, TN26 1NQ, United Kingdom. TEL 44-1923-800801, FAX 44-1923-800802, info@carlton-group.co.uk.

328.429 GBR ISSN 1465-4784
THE DIRECTORY OF WELSH GOVERNMENT. Text in English. 2000. a. GBP 315 combined subscription per issue (print & CD-ROM eds.); GBP 245 per issue (effective 2009). adv. **Document type:** *Directory, Trade.* **Description:** Provides information on the Welsh Assembly Government.
Related titles: CD-ROM ed.: GBP 280 per issue (effective 2009).
—CCC.
Published by: Carlton Publishing & Printing Ltd., Maple House, Maple View, Steeds Ln, Kingsnorth, TN26 1NQ, United Kingdom. TEL 44-1923-800801, FAX 44-1923-800802, info@carlton-group.co.uk.

328.775 USA
DIRECTORY OF WISCONSIN LEGISLATIVE AND CONGRESSIONAL DISTRICTS. Text in English. 19??. biennial. USD 1.95 per issue (effective 2011). maps. **Document type:** *Directory, Government.* **Description:** Contains maps of congressional, senate, and assembly districts, along with the names and addresses of persons representing each district.
Published by: Wisconsin Taxpayers Alliance, 401 N Lawn Ave, Madison, WI 53704. TEL 608-241-9789, FAX 608-241-5807, wistax@wistax.org.

351.44 FRA ISSN 1779-9708
DIRIGER UN SERVICE DES AFFAIRES CULTURELLES. Text in French. 2005. 2 base vols. plus updates 4/yr. looseleaf. EUR 169 (effective 2011). **Document type:** *Trade.*
Related titles: CD-ROM ed.: ISSN 2103-6276. 2009.
Published by: Reseau Territorial, BP 215, Voiron, Cedex 38506, France. TEL 33-4-76657136, FAX 33-4-76050163, info@territorial.fr.

351 FRA ISSN 2104-9114
▼ **DIRIGER UNE INTERCO.** Text in French. 2009. s-a. EUR 169 (effective 2011). **Document type:** *Trade.*
Published by: Reseau Territorial, BP 215, Voiron, Cedex 38506, France. TEL 33-4-76657136, FAX 33-4-76050163, info@territorial.fr, http://www.territorial.fr.

351 USA ISSN 1930-9821
KF5698.Z9
DISCRETIONARY LAND USE CONTROLS; avoiding invitations to abuse of discretion. Text in English. 1997. a., latest 2006. USD 190 per issue (effective 2008). **Description:** Provides guidance about discretionary land use control and local government land use decision-making.
Published by: Thomson West (Subsidiary of: Thomson Reuters Corp.), 610 Opperman Dr, Eagan, MN 55123. TEL 651-687-7000, 800-328-4880, FAX 651-687-6674, west.support@thomson.com.

DISTRICT COURT MONTHLY DIGEST. *see* LAW

351.43 DEU ISSN 0934-506X
DISZIPLINARRECHT DES BUNDES UND DER LAENDER. Text in German. 1974. 6 base vols. plus irreg. updates. EUR 198 base vol(s). (effective 2009). **Document type:** *Monographic series, Trade.*
Published by: Erich Schmidt Verlag GmbH & Co. (Berlin), Genthiner Str 30 G, Berlin, 10785, Germany. TEL 49-30-2500850, FAX 49-30-250085305, esv@esvmedien.de, http://www.esv.info.

351.83 NLD ISSN 2212-1773
DIVOSA MONITOR. Text in Dutch. 2005. a. **Document type:** *Report, Trade.*
Formerly (until 2007): W W B Monitor (1874-4885)
Published by: (Centrum voor Arbeid en Beleid), Verenigingsbureau Divosa, Postbus 407, Utrecht, 3500 AK, Netherlands. TEL 31-30-2332337, FAX 31-30-2333726, cb@divosa.nl, http://www.divosa.nl. Ed. Liny Bruijnzeel.

352 ARG ISSN 1851-9296
DOCUMENTOS DE TRABAJO DE CONTABILIDAD SOCIAL. Text in Spanish. 2008. bi-m. back issues avail. **Document type:** *Monographic series, Academic/Scholarly.*
Published by: Universidad de Buenos Aires, Facultad de Ciencias Economicas, Ave. Cordoba No. 2122, Buenos Aires, 1120, Argentina. TEL 54-11-43706130, FAX 54-11-43706131, web@econ.uba.ar, http://www.econ.uba.ar/. Ed. Luisa Fronti de Garcia.

352 ARG ISSN 1851-3727
DOCUMENTOS Y APORTES EN ADMINISTRACION PUBLICA Y GESTION ESTATAL. Text in Spanish. 2001. a. back issues avail. **Document type:** *Monographic series, Academic/Scholarly.*
Media: Online - full text (from SciELO).
Published by: Universidad Nacional del Litoral, Facultad de Ciencias Economicas Comerciales y Politicas, Moreno 2557, Santa Fe, 53000FTE, Argentina. TEL 54-342-4571156, magadpub@fce.unl.edu.ar, http://www.unl.edu.ar/.

P

DOCUMENTS TO THE PEOPLE OF NEW YORK STATE. *see* LIBRARY AND INFORMATION SCIENCES

354.7 DOM
DOMINICAN REPUBLIC. SECRETARIA DE ESTADO DE OBRAS PUBLICAS Y COMUNICACIONES. OPC. Text in Spanish. 1972. irreg. free. adv. index.
Formerly: Dominican Republic. Secretaria de Obras Publicas y Comunicaciones. Estadistica (0070-7066)
Published by: Secretaria de Estado de Obras Publicas y Comunicaciones, c/o Director General de Programacion y Proyectos, Santo Domingo, Dominican Republic. Circ: 1,000.

351 NLD ISSN 1872-3306
DOSSIER BESTUUR RENDEMENT. Text in Dutch. 2006. 4/yr. EUR 105 (effective 2010).
Related titles: ◆ Supplement to: Bestuur Rendement. ISSN 1574-1672.
Published by: Rendement Uitgeverij BV (Subsidiary of: Springer Netherlands), Postbus 27020, Rotterdam, 3003 LA, Netherlands. TEL 31-10-2433933, FAX 31-10-2439028.

351 NLD ISSN 2210-951X
DOSSIER LEERPLICHT, KWALIFICATIEPLICHT EN R M C. (Regionale Meld- en Coordinatiefunctie) Text in Dutch. 2007. a. EUR 29.95 (effective 2010).
Published by: Kluwer B.V. (Subsidiary of: Wolters Kluwer N.V.), Postbus 4, Alphen aan den Rijn, 2400 MA, Netherlands. TEL 31-172-466633, info@kluwer.nl, http://www.kluwer.nl.

352.190 FRA ISSN 1957-6234
DRACENIE POINT MAG. Key Title: Dracenie.M@g. Text in French. 2005. irreg. **Document type:** *Magazine, Government.*
Formerly (until 2007): Dracenie Point Communication (1774-5098)
Published by: Communaute d'Agglomeration Dracenoise, B.P. 129, Draguignan, 83004 Cedex, France. TEL 33-4-94501620, FAX 33-4-94603471, contact@dracenie.com.

342.44 FRA ISSN 0419-7461
K21
DROIT ADMINISTRATIF. Text in French. 1952. m. EUR 165 domestic; EUR 178.20 foreign (effective 2008).
Formerly (until 1962): Revue Pratique de Droit Administratif (0482-833X)
Related titles: Online - full text ed.: ISSN 1963-0220.
Published by: LexisNexis JurisClasseur, Relation Clients, 141 rue de Javel, Paris, Cedex 15 75747, France. TEL 33-1-45589200, FAX 33-1-45589400, relation.clients@lexisnexis.fr, http://www.lexisnexis.fr/lexisnexisjurisclasseur/juris_liste_revue.htm.

351.5357 UAE
DUBAI. HUKUMAT DUBAI. AL-JARIDAH AL-RASMIYYAH/DUBAI. GOVERNMENT OF DUBAI. OFFICIAL GAZETTE. Text in Arabic, English. 1965. 6/yr. **Description:** Publishes all local laws and local government decisions.
Published by: Hukumat Dubai/Government of Dubai, PO Box 446, Dubai, United Arab Emirates. TEL 531073. Ed. Ablah Al Rusan. Circ: 500.

351 340 USA ISSN 1937-9439
K4
DUKE JOURNAL OF CONSTITUTIONAL LAW & PUBLIC POLICY. Text in English. 2006. a. back issues avail. **Document type:** *Journal, Academic/Scholarly.* **Description:** Aims to enhance the community's understanding of constitutional law and public policy and to arm practitioners with arguments and proposals for reform.
Related titles: Online - full text ed.: ISSN 1937-9498. free (effective 2009).
Indexed: A01, A26, I05, L03, T02.
Published by: Duke University, School of Law, Science Dr & Toverview Rd, PO Box 90372, Durham, NC 27708. TEL 919-613-7224, 919-613-7101, 919-613-7006, FAX 919-681-8460, publications@law.duke.edu. Ed. Robb Giddings.

351 DEU ISSN 0946-7483
DURCHBLICK; Zeitschrift fuer den oeffentlichen Dienst in Rheinland-Pfalz. Text in German. 1949. 10/yr. free to members (effective 2009). adv. 8 p./no.; **Document type:** *Magazine, Trade.*
Formerly (until 1993): Der Beamte in Rheinland-Pfalz (0005-741X)
Published by: Deutscher Beamtenbund, Landesbund Rheinland-Pfalz, Adam-Karrillon-Str 62, Mainz, 55118, Germany. TEL 49-6131-611356, FAX 49-6131-679995, post@dbb-rlp.de, http://www.dbb-rlp.de. Ed. Malte Hestermann. adv.: B&W page EUR 1,040, color page EUR 2,000; trim 185 x 270. Circ: 30,000 (controlled).

351.438 POL
DZIENNIK URZEDOWY MINISTRA FINANSOW. Text in Polish. 1950. irreg., latest vol.2, 2003. price varies.
Formerly (until 2001): Poland. Ministerstwo Finansow. Dziennik Urzedowy (0137-7922)
Published by: Grupa Wydawnicza INFOR Sp. z o.o., Ul Okopowa 58/72, Warsaw, 01042, Poland. TEL 48-22-7613030, FAX 48-22-7613031, bok@infor.pl, http://www.infor.pl.

351.438 POL
DZIENNIK URZEDOWY MINISTRA SPRAWIEDLIWOSCI. Text in Polish. 1946. irreg., latest vol.5, 2002. price varies. **Description:** Publishes official regulations issued by the Ministry of Justice.
Formerly (until 2001): Poland. Ministerstwo Sprawiedliwosci. Dziennik Urzedowy (0137-8627)
Published by: (Poland. Ministerstwo Sprawiedliwosci), Grupa Wydawnicza INFOR Sp. z o.o., Ul Okopowa 58/72, Warsaw, 01042, Poland. TEL 48-22-7613030, FAX 48-22-7613031, bok@infor.pl, http://www.infor.pl.

351.438 344.046 POL
DZIENNIK URZEDOWY MINISTRA SRODOWISKA I GLOWNEGO INSPEKTORA OCHRONY SRODOWISKA. Text in Polish. irreg., latest vol.3, 2002.
Formerly (until 2001): Poland. Ministerstwo Administracji, Gospodarki Terenowej i Ochrony Srodowiska. Dziennik Urzedowy (0137-7523)
Published by: Grupa Wydawnicza INFOR Sp. z o.o., Ul Okopowa 58/72, Warsaw, 01042, Poland. TEL 48-22-7613030, FAX 48-22-7613031, bok@infor.pl, http://www.infor.pl.

351.438 POL ISSN 1643-5672
DZIENNIK URZEDOWY MINISTRA ZDROWIA. Text in Polish. 1948. irreg., latest vol.10, 2002. EUR 61 foreign (effective 2006). **Document type:** *Newspaper, Government.*
Former titles (until 2001): Poland. Ministerstwo Zdrowia. Dziennik Urzedowy (1643-5664); (until 1999): Poland. Ministerstwo Zdrowia i Opieki Spolecznej. Dziennik Urzedowy (0551-2727); (until 1960): Poland. Ministerstwo Zdrowia. Dziennik Urzedowy (1643-5656)
Published by: Grupa Wydawnicza INFOR Sp. z o.o., Ul Okopowa 58/72, Warsaw, 01042, Poland. TEL 48-22-7613030, FAX 48-22-7613031, bok@infor.pl, http://www.infor.pl. **Dist. by:** Ars Polona, Obroncow 25, Warsaw 03933, Poland. TEL 48-22-5098609, FAX 48-22-5098610, arspolona@arspolona.com.pl, http://www.arspolona.com.pl.

351 NLD ISSN 0923-9278
E C D P M OCCASIONAL PAPER. Text in English, French. 1989. irreg.
Published by: European Centre for Development Policy Management/ Centre Europeen de Gestion de Politiques de Developpement, Onze Lieve Vrouweplein 21, Maastricht, 6211 HE, Netherlands. TEL 31-43-3502900, FAX 31-43-3502902, info@ecdpm.org, http://www.ecdpm.org.

351 USA ISSN 1553-7005
E H S LEGISLATIVE ALERT. (Environmental Health Safety) Text in English. 2004. d. price varies based on number of users. **Document type:** *Newsletter, Trade.*
Media: E-mail. **Related titles:** Online - full text ed.
—CCC.
Published by: The Bureau of National Affairs, Inc., 1801 S Bell St, Arlington, VA 22202. TEL 703-341-3000, 800-372-1033, FAX 703-341-4634, bnaplus@bna.com.

351 NLD
E I P A ANNUAL REPORT. Text in English, French. 1997. a. **Document type:** *Report, Academic/Scholarly.*
Related titles: Online - full text ed.
Published by: European Institute of Public Administration/Institut Europeen d'Administration Publique, PO Box 1229, Maastricht, 6201 BE, Netherlands. TEL 31-43-3296222, FAX 31-43-3296296, eipa@eipa-nl.com, http://www.eipa.eu.

351 NLD ISSN 1025-6253
E I P A SCOPE. Text in English, French. 1992. 3/yr. free (effective 2009). **Document type:** *Journal, Academic/Scholarly.* **Description:** Discusses topics in public administration, both applied and theoretical. Lists forthcoming seminars and conferences.
Related titles: Online - full text ed.
Indexed: PAIS.
Published by: European Institute of Public Administration/Institut Europeen d'Administration Publique, PO Box 1229, Maastricht, 6201 BE, Netherlands. TEL 31-43-3296222, FAX 31-43-3296296, eipa@eipa-nl.com. Eds. Cosimo Monda, Dr. Edward Best, Dr. Phedan Nicolaides.

351 NLD
E I P A WORKING PAPERS. Text in English. irreg., latest 2008. price varies. back issues avail. **Document type:** *Monographic series, Academic/Scholarly.* **Description:** Examines a specific issues in national public administration.
Related titles: Online - full text ed.: free.
Published by: European Institute of Public Administration/Institut Europeen d'Administration Publique, PO Box 1229, Maastricht, 6201 BE, Netherlands. TEL 31-43-3296222, FAX 31-43-3296296, eipa@eipa-nl.com.

332 CZE ISSN 1213-6344
E-MAIL NOVINY PRO MESTA A OBCE. Text in Czech. 2000. fortn. free. **Document type:** *Newsletter, Trade.*
Media: E-mail.
Published by: Verlag Dashoefer s.r.o., Na Prikope 18, PO Box 756, Prague 1, 11121, Czech Republic. TEL 420-224-197333, FAX 420-224-197555, info@dashofer.cz, http://www.dashofer.cz.

352 CAN ISSN 1710-4416
LES EAUX VIVES. Text in French, English. 2004. q. **Document type:** *Newsletter, Consumer.*
Published by: Montreal, Arrondissement de l'Ile-Bizard - Sainte-Genevieve, 350, Montee de l'Eglise, L'Ile-Bizard, PQ H9C 1G9, Canada. TEL 514-620-6331, FAX 514-620-8198, http://ville.montreal.qc.ca/portal/page?_pageid=65,38111&_dad=portal&_schema=PORTAL.

331.12 351.7 USA
ECONOMIC RESTRUCTURING AND THE JOB MARKET; a series on labor trends and their policy implications. Text in English. 1997. irreg., latest 1997. back issues avail. **Document type:** *Monographic series, Academic/Scholarly.*
Related titles: Online - full text ed.: free (effective 2010).
Published by: Urban Institute, 2100 M St, NW, Washington, DC 20037. TEL 202-833-7200, FAX 202-467-5775, paffairs@ui.urban.org.

ECONOMY TRANSDISCIPLINARY COGNITION. *see* BUSINESS AND ECONOMICS—Economic Systems And Theories, Economic History

ECOPOLIS; la revue de la gouvernance environnementale. *see* ENERGY

321.023 USA ISSN 1071-8478
ECOS; the environmental communique of the states. Text in English. 1993. bi-m. back issues avail. **Document type:** *Journal, Government.* **Description:** Contains information on significant policy, budget and legislative initiatives on the environment in all the fifty states of US.
—CCC.
Published by: Council of State Governments, 2760 Research Park Dr, PO Box 11910, Lexington, KY 40578. TEL 859-244-8000, 800-800-1910, FAX 859-244-8001, info@csg.org. Ed. Krista Rinehart.

351 DEU
EDITION SOZIALPLANUNG. Text in German. 2008. irreg. price varies. **Document type:** *Monographic series, Academic/Scholarly.*
Published by: Paulo Freire Verlag, Unterm Berg 65a, Oldenburg, 26123, Germany. TEL 49-441-381674, FAX 49-441-9330056, pfv@freire.de, http://www.paulo-freire-verlag.de.

351.7284 SLV
EL SALVADOR. MINISTERIO DEL INTERIOR. MEMORIA DE LABORES. Text in Spanish. a. **Document type:** *Government.*
Published by: Ministerio del Interior, Centro del Gobierno, San Salvador, El Salvador.

352.68 USA
ELDER LAW BULLETIN. Text in English. 1995. irreg., latest vol.8, 2009. **Document type:** *Bulletin, Academic/Scholarly.* **Description:** Discusses the often-confusing interplay between North Carolina's laws regarding spousal support and responsibility and the provisions of the federal Medicaid statute that apply to income and assets of a married couple when one spouse is a nursing home patient and applies for Medicaid payment for nursing home care while the other spouse continues to live in the community.
Related titles: Online - full text ed.: free (effective 2010).
Published by: University of North Carolina at Chapel Hill, School of Government, Knapp-Sanders Bldg, Campus Box 3330, Chapel Hill, NC 27599. TEL 919-966-5381, FAX 919-962-0654, sales@sog.unc.edu, http://www.sogpubs.unc.edu.

351 AUS ISSN 1320-8616
ELECTION FUNDING AUTHORITY OF NEW SOUTH WALES. ANNUAL REPORT. Text in English. 1982. a. **Document type:** *Government.*
Related titles: Online - full text ed.: ISSN 1834-1748. 2000.
Published by: Australia. New South Wales. Election Funding Authority, GPO Box 832, Sydney, NSW 2001, Australia. TEL 61-2-9290-5999, 1300-135-736, FAX 61-2-9290-5991, enquiries@efa.nsw.gov.au, http://www.efa.nsw.gov.au/home.

363.34525 USA ISSN 2156-2490
EMERGENCY MANAGEMENT (FOLSOM); strategy & leadership in critical times. Text in English. 2006. bi-m. free to qualified personnel (effective 2010). adv. back issues avail. **Document type:** *Magazine, Trade.* **Description:** Addresses the intergovernmental community of stakeholders with timely editorial insight and expertise to support their mission-critical roles in joint operations and planning.
Formerly (until 2010): Government Technology's Emergency Management
Related titles: Online - full text ed.: free (effective 2010).
Indexed: I02, R02.
Published by: e.Republic, Inc., 100 Blue Ravine Rd, Folsom, CA 95630. TEL 916-932-1300, FAX 916-932-1470, info@erepublic.com, http://www.erepublic.com. Ed. Jim McKay. Pub. Scott M Fackert TEL 916-932-1416.

EMERGENCY PREPAREDNESS NEWS; contingency planning - crisis management - disaster relief. *see* CIVIL DEFENSE

EMPIRE STATE REPORT; the magazine of politics and policy for New York State. *see* POLITICAL SCIENCE

EMPLOYMENT AND PAYROLLS IN WASHINGTON STATE BY COUNTY AND INDUSTRY; industries covered by the Employment Security Act and federal employment covered by Title 5, U.S.C. 85. *see* BUSINESS AND ECONOMICS—Abstracting, Bibliographies, Statistics

351.71 CAN ISSN 1493-4884
EMPLOYMENT EQUITY IN THE FEDERAL PUBLIC SERVICE/EQUITE EN EMPLOI DANS LA FONCTION PUBLIQUE FEDERALE. Text in English, French. 1993. a. **Document type:** *Government.*
Formerly (until 1997): Employment Equity in the Public Service. Annual Report (1202-2454)
Related titles: Online - full text ed.: ISSN 1486-973X.
Published by: Canada Public Service Agency/Agence de la Fonction Publique du Canada, L'Esplanade Laurier, Rm P-135, West Tower, 300 Laurier Ave West, Ottawa, ON K1A 0R5, Canada. TEL 613-995-2855, FAX 613-996-0518, services-publications@tbs-sct.gc.ca, http://www.psagency-agencefp.gc.ca/index_e.asp.

351 ESP ISSN 1138-6819
LA EMPRESA. Text in Spanish. 1984. s-a. back issues avail.
Formerly (until 1996): I C A D E (Instituto Catolico de Administracion y Direccion de Empresas) (0212-7377)
Published by: Universidad Pontificia Comillas de Madrid, Comision de Publicaciones, C Alberto Aguilera, 23, Madrid, 28015, Spain. TEL 34-91-5422800, http://www.upcomillas.es/.

351.03 USA ISSN 0092-8380
JK468.C7
ENCYCLOPEDIA OF GOVERNMENTAL ADVISORY ORGANIZATIONS. Text in English. 1973. a. USD 910 (effective 2009). back issues avail. **Document type:** *Monographic series, Academic/Scholarly.* **Description:** Directory of contractors, consultants and other advisory businesses and organizations for the U.S. government.
Related titles: Online - full text ed.
—BLDSC (3738.592300).
Published by: Gale (Subsidiary of: Cengage Learning), 27500 Drake Rd, Farmington Hills, MI 48331. TEL 248-699-4253, 800-877-4253, FAX 877-363-4253, gale.customerservice@cengage.com, http://gale.cengage.com. Ed. Donna Batten.

352.14 FRA ISSN 1775-9471
ENCYCLOPEDIE DES COLLECTIVITES LOCALES. Text in French. 2004. 3/yr. EUR 222,800 base vol(s). print & CD-Rom eds.; incl. six month subscription; EUR 896 print & CD-Rom eds. (effective 2009). **Document type:** *Directory.*
Formerly (until 2004): Collectivites Locales (1760-9771)
Published by: Editions Dalloz, 31-35 rue Froidevaux, Paris, Cedex 14 75685, France. TEL 33-1-40645454, FAX 33-1-40645497, http://www.dalloz.fr.

352.4 DNK ISSN 0107-0061
ENDELIG BETAENKNING OVER STATSREGNSKABET FOR FINANSAARET. Text in Danish. 1868. a. **Document type:** *Government.* **Description:** Annual audit report of the state finances.
Supersedes in part (in 1977): Betaenkning over Statsregnskabet for Finansaaret (0901-9111)
Published by: Folketinget, Statsrevisoratet, Prins Joergens Gaard 2, Copenhagen K, 1240, Denmark. TEL 45-33-375500, FAX 45-33-375995. **Dist. by:** Schultz Information A-S. schultz@schultz-information.dk, http://www.schultz-information.dk.

354 CAN ISSN 0848-5267
CA1CC396
ENTERPRISE CAPE BRETON CORPORATION. ANNUAL REPORT. Text in English, French. 1989. a.
Supersedes in part: Cape Breton Development Corporation. Annual Report (0228-4723); Which incorporated (1967-1970): Societe de Developpement du Cap-Breton. Rapport Annuel (0228-4731)
Related titles: Online - full text ed.: ISSN 1497-5084.

Published by: Enterprise Cape Breton Corporation/Societe d'Expansion du Cap-Breton, Commerce Tower, 3rd Fl, 15 Dorchester St, Sydney, NS B1P 6T7, Canada. TEL 902-564-3600, 800-705-3926, FAX 902-564-3825, ecbcinfo@ecbc.cag.

354.3 GBR ISSN 0263-774X
H97
➤ **ENVIRONMENT AND PLANNING C: GOVERNMENT AND POLICY.** Text in English. 1983. bi-m. USD 662 combined subscription in the Americas (print & online eds.); GBP 374 combined subscription elsewhere (print & online eds.) (effective 2012). bk.rev. index. 156 p./no.; back issues avail.; reprints avail. **Document type:** *Journal, Academic/Scholarly.* **Description:** Multidisciplinary, international approach to the study of theoretical economic, political, legal, fiscal and social issues related to government activities.
Related titles: CD-ROM ed.; Online - full text ed.: ISSN 1472-3425. USD 649 in the Americas; GBP 359 elsewhere (effective 2012).
Indexed: A01, A02, A03, A08, A20, A22, ASCA, ASFA, CA, CurCont, E04, E05, ESPM, EconLit, EnerRev, FR, G02, GEOBASE, IBSS, JEL, P30, P34, P42, PAIS, PCI, PRA, PollutAb, SCOPUS, SPAA, SSCI, SSciA, SUSA, T02, W07.
—BLDSC (3791.105600), IE, Infotrieve, Ingenta. **CCC.**
Published by: Pion Ltd., 207 Brondesbury Park, London, NW2 5JN, United Kingdom. TEL 44-20-84590066, FAX 44-20-84516454, sales@pion.co.uk, http://www.pion.co.uk/.

354.3 CAN ISSN 1205-6928
GE190.C2
ENVIRONMENTAL COMMISSIONER OF ONTARIO. ANNUAL REPORT. Text in English. 1995. a. free (effective 2004).
Published by: Environmental Commissioner of Ontario, 1075 Bay St., Suite 605, Toronto, ON M5S 2B1, Canada. TEL 416-325-3377, 800-701-6454, FAX 416-325-3370, inquiry@eco.on.ca.

354.3 HKG
ENVIRONMENTAL HONG KONG (YEAR). Text in English. a. HKD 17.
Published by: Government Publications Centre, G.P.O. Bldg, Ground Fl, Connaught Pl, Hong Kong, Hong Kong. TEL 5-8428801. **Subscr. to:** Director of Information Services, Information Services Dept., 1 Battery Path G-F, Central, Hong Kong, Hong Kong.

EQUALITY STATE ALMANAC. *see* BUSINESS AND ECONOMICS—Economic Situation And Conditions

EQUIPEMENT, TRANSPORT ET SERVICES INFOS. *see* TRANSPORTATION

351 DEU
ERFURTER BEITRAEGE ZU DEN STAATSWISSENSCHAFTEN. Text in German. 2003. irreg., latest vol.8, 2008. price varies. **Document type:** *Monographic series, Academic/Scholarly.*
Published by: Walter de Gruyter GmbH & Co. KG, Genthiner Str 13, Berlin, 10785, Germany. TEL 49-30-26005220, FAX 49-30-26005251, info@degruyter.com, http://www.degruyter.de.

351 ESP ISSN 1888-4407
ESCOLA INNOVACIO. Text in Multiple languages. 2007. m.
Published by: Generalitat de Catalunya, Escola d'Administracio Publica de Catalunya, C de Girona, 20, Barcelona, 08010, Spain. TEL 34-93-5672323, FAX 34-93-5672350, eapc@gencat.cat, http://www.eapc.es/.

353 PRT ISSN 1647-1369
ESFERA. Text in Portuguese. 2008. a.
Published by: Universidade de Evora, Largo dos Colegiais 2, Evora, 7004-516, Portugal. TEL 351-266-740800.

351 ITA ISSN 1971-999X
ESPROPRIONLINE. Text in Italian. 2007. w. **Document type:** *Newsletter, Consumer.*
Related titles: Online - full text ed.: ISSN 1971-9817.
Published by: Exeo Srl, Via Garibaldi 129, Piove di Sacco, PD 35028, Italy. TEL 39-049-9711446.

352 GBR ISSN 1369-0078
ESSEX RECORD OFFICE PUBLICATION. Text in English. 1946. irreg. **Document type:** *Monographic series, Consumer.*
—BLDSC (3812.050000), IE.
Published by: Essex Record Office Publications, Wharf Rd, Chelmsford, Essex CM2 6YT, United Kingdom. TEL 44-1245-244644, FAX 44-1245-244655, ero.enquiry@essex.gov.uk, http://www.essexcc.gov.uk/vip8/ecc/ECCWebsite/dis/gui.jsp?channelOid=13813&guideOid=14806.

351 CHL ISSN 0717-6759
JA5
➤ **ESTADO, GOBIERNO, GESTION PUBLICA.** Text in Spanish, English. 2002. 2/yr. **Document type:** *Journal, Academic/Scholarly.*
Related titles: Online - full text ed.: ISSN 0717-8980. free (effective 2011).
Indexed: C01, P42, PSA.
Published by: Universidad de Chile, Instituto de Asuntos Publicos, Santa Lucia 240, Santiago, Chile. TEL 56-2-9771502, FAX 56-2-6648536. Ed., R&P Eduardo Araya Moreno. Circ: 500 (paid and controlled).

351 FRA ISSN 1772-7626
L'ETAT EN BOURGOGNE. Text in French. 1996-199?; resumed 2005. q. **Document type:** *Newsletter, Consumer.*
Formerly (until 199?): Lettre de la Prefecture de Region et des Services de l'Etat en Bourgogne (1277-6262)
Related titles: CD-ROM ed.: L' Etat en Bourgogne en.. (Year). ISSN 2103-6519. 200?.
Published by: Bourgogne. Prefecture de la Region de Bourgogne - Prefecture de la Cote d'Or, Service Communication, 55 Rue de la Prefecture, Dijon Cedex, 21041, France. TEL 33-3-80446400, http://www.bourgogne.gouv.fr/fr.

351 174 USA ISSN 0279-2869
KF4568.A6
ETHICS IN GOVERNMENT REPORTER. Text in English. 1980. 4 base vols. plus m. updates. looseleaf. USD 1,181 (effective 2006). bk.rev. back issues avail. **Document type:** *Journal, Trade.* **Description:** Presents federal ethics laws and government publications of interest including cases.
—**CCC.**
Published by: C C H Inc. (Subsidiary of: Wolters Kluwer N.V.), 2700 Lake Cook Rd, Riverwoods, IL 60015. TEL 847-267-7000, cust_serv@cch.com, http://www.cch.com.

351.4 BEL ISSN 1370-7868
EURO-GUIDE: YEARBOOK OF THE INSTITUTIONS OF THE EUROPEAN UNION AND OF THE OTHER EUROPEAN ORGANIZATIONS/ANNUAIRE DES INSTITUTIONS DE L'UNION EUROPEENNE ET DES AUTRES ORGANISATIONS EUROPEENNES. Text in English, French. 1977. a., latest 2004, 21 ed. USD 275 per vol. (effective 2005). adv. index. **Document type:** *Directory.* **Description:** Provides information on the structure and operation of the European Union and on 20 other European organizations, which contribute to European integration: political, economic, scientific, technical, and military. Also includes names and addresses of key people.
Formerly (until 1996): Yearbook of the European Communities and Other European Organizations (0771-7962)
—BLDSC (3829.231530).
Published by: Editions Delta, Rue Scailquin 55, Brussels, 1210, Belgium. TEL 32-2-217-5555, FAX 32-2-217-9393, editions.delta@skynet.be. Ed. Georges Francis Seingry. Circ: 8,000. **Dist. by:** Bernan Associates, Bernan, 4611-F Assembly Dr., Lanham, MD 20706-4391. TEL 301-459-2255, 800-274-4447, FAX 301-459-0056, query@bernan.com, http://www.bernan.com.

352.73 FRA ISSN 1778-8358
EUROFUNDING. COOPERATION INTERNATIONALE. Cover title: Cooperation internationale. Text in French. 200?. a., latest 2010. EUR 165.65 per issue (effective 2010). **Description:** Features an analysis of hundreds of European Union funds that are available.
Related titles: ◆ English ed.: Eurofunding. International Cooperation. ISSN 1778-8331.
Published by: Welcomeurope, 38 rue Leon, Paris, 75018, France. TEL 33-1-42546064, FAX 33-1-42547004, http://www.welcomeurope.com.

352.73 FRA ISSN 1778-834X
EUROFUNDING. EDUCATION FORMATION RECHERCHE. Text in French. 200?. a., latest 2010. EUR 146.65 per issue (effective 2010).
Published by: Welcomeurope, 38 rue Leon, Paris, 75018, France. TEL 33-1-42546064, FAX 33-1-42547004, http://www.welcomeurope.com.

352.73 FRA ISSN 1778-8331
EUROFUNDING. INTERNATIONAL COOPERATION. Text in English. 200?. a. EUR 146.65 per issue (effective 2010). **Description:** Features an analysis of hundreds of European Union funds that are available.
Related titles: ◆ French ed.: Eurofunding. Cooperation Internationale. ISSN 1778-8358.
Published by: Welcomeurope, 38 rue Leon, Paris, 75018, France. TEL 33-1-42546064, FAX 33-1-42547004, http://www.welcomeurope.com.

352.73 FRA ISSN 1778-8366
EUROFUNDING. PUBLIC SECTOR. Text in English. 200?. a. EUR 146.65 per issue (effective 2010).
Published by: Welcomeurope, 38 rue Leon, Paris, 75018, France. TEL 33-1-42546064, FAX 33-1-42547004, http://www.welcomeurope.com.

351 725 NLD ISSN 1875-290X
EUROPA NOSTRA. ANNUAL REPORT. Text in English, French. 19??. a.
Published by: Europa Nostra, Lange Voorhout 35, The Hague, 2514 EC, Netherlands. TEL 31-70-3024050, FAX 31-70-3617865, info@europanostra.org.

EUROPEAN PARLIAMENT. GROUP OF THE EUROPEAN PEOPLE'S PARTY. CHRISTIAN DEMOCRAT GROUP. REPORT ON THE ACTIVITIES. *see* POLITICAL SCIENCE

EUROPEAN PARLIAMENT'S OFFICIAL HANDBOOK. *see* POLITICAL SCIENCE

351 BEL ISSN 1376-0890
EUROPEAN POLICY/CITE EUROPEENNE. Text in English, French. 1993. irreg., latest vol.46, 2009. price varies. **Document type:** *Monographic series, Academic/Scholarly.*
Published by: P I E - Peter Lang SA, 1 avenue Maurice, 6e etage, Brussels, 1050, Belgium. TEL 32-2-3477236, FAX 32-2-3477237, pie@peterlang.com, http://www.peterlang.net. Ed. Pascaline Winand.

EUROPEAN POLICY RESEARCH PAPERS. *see* POLITICAL SCIENCE

EUROPEAN UNION POLITICS. *see* POLITICAL SCIENCE—International Relations

EUROSOCIAL REPORTS. *see* SOCIAL SERVICES AND WELFARE

352.63 CAN ISSN 1922-9364
EXCHANGE. Text in English. 1982. q. free to members (effective 2010). adv. bk.rev. back issues avail. **Document type:** *Magazine, Trade.* **Description:** Designed to share information, exchanging ideas on practices, enhancing professional development and building networks.
Formerly (until 2010): Chapter 290 (1482-7344)
Related titles: Online - full text ed.: free (effective 2010).
Published by: Local Government Management Association of British Columbia, 7th Fl, 620 View St, Victoria, BC V8W 1J6, Canada. TEL 250-383-7032, FAX 250-383-4879, office@lgma.ca. Ed. Therese Mickelson. Adv. contact Randee Platz.

343.0552 CAN ISSN 1926-0164
EXCISE AND G S T/H S T NEWS. (Goods and Services Tax - Harmonized Sales Tax) Text in English. 1991. q. free (effective 2011). back issues avail. **Document type:** *Trade.*
Former titles (until 2005): G S T/H S T News (Online) (1498-198X); (until 1997): Excise/G S T News (1498-1971)
Media: Online - full text.
Published by: Canada Revenue Agency/Agence du Revenu du Canada, International Tax Services Office, 2204 Walkley Rd, Ottawa, ON K1A 1A8, Canada. TEL 613-952-3741, 800-959-2221, FAX 613-941-2505.

352.53 USA
EXCLUDED PARTIES LIST SYSTEM. Abbreviated title: E P L S. Text in English. 1988. d. free (effective 2011). **Document type:** *Government.* **Description:** Identifies parties who are not permitted to receive Federal contracts, certain subcontracts, and certain types of Federal financial and nonfinancial assistance and benefits. Reasons for exclusion are given.
Former titles (until 200?): List of Parties Excluded from Federal Procurement and Nonprocurement Programs (Print) (1057-5774); (until 1988): Consolidated List of Debarred, Suspended, and Ineligible Contractors as of; (until 1982): Consolidated List of Current Administrative Debarments by Executive Agencies
Media: Online - full text.

Published by: U.S. General Services Administration, One Constitution Sq, 1275 First St, NE, Washington, DC 20417. TEL 866-606-8220, fbo.support@gsa.gov, http://www.gsa.gov.

351 AUS ISSN 1838-3076
▼ **EXECUTIVE COMPLIANCE NEWS. INDEPENDENT NEWS FOR PUBLIC SECTOR.** Text in English. 2010. w. AUD 1,200 combined subscription (online & email eds.) (effective 2011). **Document type:** *Newsletter, Trade.* **Description:** Provides news and analysis impacting on the public sector.
Media: Online - full text. **Related titles:** E-mail ed.
Published by: Thomson Reuters (Professional) Australia Limited (Subsidiary of: Thomson Reuters Corp.), PO Box 3502, Rozelle, NSW 2039, Australia. TEL 61-2-85877980, FAX 61-2-85877981, LTA.Service@thomsonreuters.com.

EXPORT DEVELOPMENT CANADA. ANNUAL REPORT (PRINT EDITION). *see* BUSINESS AND ECONOMICS—International Commerce

F C C RECORD. *see* COMMUNICATIONS

F C N L WASHINGTON NEWSLETTER. *see* POLITICAL SCIENCE

352.68 USA ISSN 0895-3619
F E W'S NEWS AND VIEWS. Text in English. 1987. bi-m. USD 12. adv. bk.rev. bibl.; illus.
Former titles: News and Views from Federally Employed Women (0162-2471); F E W's News and Views (0046-3477)
Related titles: Online - full text ed.
Indexed: GW, P48, PQC.
Published by: Federally Employed Women Inc., 1666 K St NW, Ste. 440, Washington, DC 20006-1242. TEL 202-898-0994, FAX 202-898-0998, execdir@few.org. Ed. Michael J Varhola. Circ: 10,000.

F L R A REPORTS OF CASE DECISIONS. F S I P RELEASES AND ADMINISTRATIVE LAW JUDGE DECISIONS. *see* LAW—Constitutional Law

F T C NEWSNOTES. (Federal Trade Commission) *see* BUSINESS AND ECONOMICS—Production Of Goods And Services

F T C WATCH. (Federal Trade Commission) *see* BUSINESS AND ECONOMICS—International Commerce

351 330 AUS ISSN 1832-1593
FAIR TRADING ADMINISTRATION CORPORATION, BUILDING INSURERS' GUARANTEE CORPORATION. ANNUAL REPORTS. Text in English. 2004. a. free (effective 2009). back issues avail. **Document type:** *Government.*
Related titles: Online - full text ed.
Published by: N S W Office of Fair Trading, PO Box 972, Parramatta, NSW 2124, Australia. TEL 61-2-98950111, FAX 61-2-98950222.

351 FRA ISSN 2107-4690
▼ **FAIRE MIEUX ENSEMBLE.** Text in French. 2009. s-a. **Document type:** *Newsletter, Consumer.*
Published by: Communaute d'Agglomeration Europ'Essonne, 30 Av Carnot, Massy, 91300, France. TEL 33-1-80380230, FAX 33-1-80380231.

328 SWE ISSN 0283-4251
JN7934
FAKTA OM FOLKVALDA. Text in Swedish. 1984. quinquennial. SEK 75 per issue (effective 2007). **Document type:** *Trade.* **Description:** News about the newly elected members of the Swedish Parliament.
Formerly (until 1986): Riksdagen (0282-0714)
Published by: Riksdagsfoervaltningen, Jakobsgatan 6, Stockholm, 10012, Sweden. TEL 46-8-7864000, FAX 46-8-7866195, riksdaginformation@riksdagen.se, http://www.riksdagen.se.

FAMILY RELATIONS - STATE CAPITALS. *see* LAW—Family And Matrimonial Law

FARM BUREAU NEWS. *see* AGRICULTURE

FARM POLICY JOURNAL. *see* AGRICULTURE

351 MEX ISSN 1563-7468
FEDERACION. DIARIO OFICIAL (ONLINE EDITION). Text in Spanish. 1899. d. **Document type:** *Newspaper, Government.*
Former titles (until 199?): Federacion. Diario Oficial (Print Edition); (until 1987): Gobierno Constitucional de los Estados Unidos Mexicanos. Diario Oficial (0187-1404); (until 1926): Secretaria de Gobernacion. Diario Oficial (0187-1390); (until 1917): Gobierno Constitucional de los Estados Unidos Mexicanos. Diario Oficial (0187-1382); (until 1917): Gobierno Provisional de la Republica Mexicana. Diario Oficial (0187-1374); (until 1915): Estados Unidos Mexicanos. Diario Oficial (0187-134X); (until 1903): Supremo Gobierno de los Estados Unidos Mexicanos. Diario Oficial (0187-1331)
Media: Online - full text.
Published by: Estados Unidos Mexicanos, Secretaria de la Funcion Publica, Insurgentes Sur 1735, Col Guadalupe Inn, Delegacion Alvaro Obregon, Mexico City, DF 01020, Mexico. TEL 52-55-30033000, 800-475-2393, quejas@funcionpublica.gob.mx, http://www.funcionpublica.gob.mx.

354.75 USA ISSN 1068-7386
KF844.7
FEDERAL ACQUISITION REGULATION (WASHINGTON). Key Title: Federal Information Resources Management Regulation and Bulletins through Transmittal Circular. Short title: F A R. Text in English. 1991. base vol. plus irreg. updates. looseleaf. **Document type:** *Government.* **Description:** Compiles procurement and contracting regulations for A.D.P. and telecommunications equipment and services to be used in conjunction with general procurement and contracting regulations in the F.A.R. Includes information on construction and leases. Complete text in first chapter of Title 48 of the Code of Federal Regulations available in Central libraries and GSA Business Service Centers.
Related titles: CD-ROM ed.: USD 78 (effective 2001); Online - full text ed.: ISSN 1555-015X. free (effective 2011); ◆ Supplement(s): Defense F A R Supplement.
Published by: U.S. General Services Administration, One Constitution Sq, 1275 First St, NE, Washington, DC 20417. TEL 866-606-8220, fbo.support@gsa.gov, http://www.gsa.gov.

FEDERAL ACTION AFFECTING THE STATES - STATE CAPITALS. *see* LAW

FEDERAL ADMINISTRATIVE LAW. *see* LAW—Constitutional Law

P

351 USA
HC110.P63
FEDERAL AID TO STATES FOR FISCAL YEAR. Text in English. a. **Document type:** *Government.*
Former titles (until 1998): Federal Expenditures by State for Fiscal Year (0737-7444); (until 1981): Geographic Distribution of Federal Funds in Summary (0162-1734)
Published by: U.S. Census Bureau. Governments Division. Federal Programs Branch (Subsidiary of: U.S. Department of Commerce), 4600 Silver Hill Rd., Washington, DC 20233. TEL 301-763-1565.

FEDERAL & FOUNDATION ASSISTANCE MONITOR; semi-monthly report on federal and private grant opportunities. *see* LAW

FEDERAL AVIATION REGULATIONS. PART 11, GENERAL RULE-MAKING PROCEDURES. *see* AERONAUTICS AND SPACE FLIGHT

352.4 USA ISSN 0898-0071
FEDERAL BUDGET REPORT. Text in English. 1981. fortn. USD 375 domestic; USD 390 foreign (effective 2000). **Document type:** *Newsletter, Trade.* **Description:** Provides analyses of congressional and presidential budget activities.
—CCC.
Published by: Fleishman-Hillard, Inc., PO Box 66115, Washington, DC 20035. TEL 202-828-9712, FAX 202-233-8199. Ed. Stanley Collender.

351.753 354.35 USA ISSN 0275-6404
HJ9013.W2
FEDERAL CAPITAL IMPROVEMENTS PROGRAM FOR THE NATIONAL CAPITAL REGION. Text in English. a. **Document type:** *Government.*
Related titles: Online - full content ed.
Published by: U.S. National Capital Planning Commission, 401 9th St NW, N Lobby Ste 500, Washington, DC 20576. TEL 202-482-7200, FAX 202-482-7272, info@ncpc.gov, http://www.ncpc.gov. Ed. Marybeth Murphy.

351 USA ISSN 1534-441X
FEDERAL CONTRACTS DAILY. Text in English. 2001. d. USD 2,348 domestic (effective 2005 - 2006). back issues avail. **Document type:** *Newsletter, Trade.* **Description:** Covers policies and regulations affecting the federal acquisition of goods and services.
Media: Online - full text.
—CCC.
Published by: The Bureau of National Affairs, Inc., 1801 S Bell St, Arlington, VA 22202. TEL 703-341-3000, 800-372-1033, FAX 703-341-4634, 800-253-0332, bnaplus@bna.com. Ed. Gregory C McCaffery.

352.53 USA ISSN 0014-9063
KF849.A1
FEDERAL CONTRACTS REPORT. Text in English. 1964 (Feb.). w. looseleaf. USD 2,431 (effective 2010 - 2011). bk.rev. index. 45 p./no.; back issues avail. **Document type:** *Report, Trade.* **Description:** Provides practical guidance on day-to-day labor relations questions. Includes current reports on employee relations and union developments.
Related titles: Online - full text ed.: ISSN 1523-5696. 1996 (Feb.). USD 2,795 (effective 2010 - 2011).
—CCC.
Published by: The Bureau of National Affairs, Inc., 1801 S Bell St, Arlington, VA 22202. TEL 703-341-3000, 800-372-1033, FAX 703-341-4634, bnaplus@bna.com.

351.025 USA ISSN 0360-3512
JK6
THE FEDERAL DIRECTORY. Text in English. 1973. irreg. USD 95. **Document type:** *Directory, Trade.*
Formerly (until 1975): Federal Telephone Directory (0093-674X)
Published by: Consolidated Directories, Inc, 3221 Ryan St, Ste C, Lake Charles, LA 70605. TEL 318-477-7283.

352.68 USA ISSN 0014-9071
FEDERAL EMPLOYEE. Text in English. 1917. m. USD 15. adv. illus. **Document type:** *Newsletter.* **Description:** Focuses on civil service work.
Indexed: PersLit.
Published by: National Federation of Federal Employees, 1016 16th St, N W, Washington, DC 20036. TEL 202-862-4400. Ed., R&P Dawn Vance Adams. Circ: 80,000.

352.68 USA ISSN 0071-4127
JK671
FEDERAL EMPLOYEES ALMANAC. Text in English. 1954. a. USD 16.95 per issue (effective 2008). **Description:** Guide to the rules and policies that govern federal employees' rights, benefits and pay.
Related titles: CD-ROM ed.
Published by: Federal Employees News Digest, Inc. (Subsidiary of: 1105 Media Inc.), 610 Herndon Pkwy, Ste 400, Herndon, VA 20170-5400. TEL 703-707-8434, 800-989-3363, FAX 703-707-8474, customerservice@federaldaily.com. Ed. Sheila McCormick. Pub. Stephen Young. Circ: 140,000.

352.68 USA ISSN 1065-0970
HD8008.A1
FEDERAL EMPLOYEES NEWS DIGEST. Text in English. 1951. w. USD 97 (effective 2008). adv. s-a. index. back issues avail. **Document type:** *Newsletter.* **Description:** Provides an overview of events that affect the careers of federal employees.
Formerly (until 1991): Weekly Federal Employees News Digest (0430-1692); Incorporates (1983-1991): Federal Employee Weekly Up-date (1043-1993); Which was formerly (until 1988): Federal Personnel Guide Weekly News Up-date (0745-841X)
Related titles: Online - full text ed.
Indexed: PersLit.
Published by: Federal Employees News Digest, Inc. (Subsidiary of: 1105 Media Inc.), 610 Herndon Pkwy, Ste 400, Herndon, VA 20170-5400. TEL 703-707-8434, 800-989-3363, FAX 703-707-8474, customerservice@federaldaily.com. Ed. Sheila McCormick. Pub. Stephen Young. Adv. contact Scott Thompson. Circ: 35,000.

352.68021 USA ISSN 8756-7156
JK639
FEDERAL EMPLOYMENT STATISTICS. BIENNIAL REPORT OF EMPLOYMENT BY GEOGRAPHIC AREA. Text in English. 1966. biennial. stat.
Former titles (until 1982): Federal Civilian Workforce Statistics. Annual Report of Employment by Geographic Area (0148-8597); (until 1975): Employment by Geographic Area. Annual Report (0148-8600); Annual Report of Federal Civilian Employment by Geographic Area (0090-6263)
Indexed: CISI.
Published by: U.S. Office of Personnel Management, Compliance and Investigations Group, Work Force Analysis and Statistics Division, 1900 E St, NW, Washington, DC 20415. TEL 202-606-1800.

351 174 USA ISSN 1080-210X
KF4568.A6
FEDERAL ETHICS REPORT. Text in English. 1994. m. USD 398 (effective 2006). bk.rev. back issues avail. **Document type:** *Newsletter, Government.* **Description:** Covers current events, cases and stories regarding federal government ethics.
Indexed: A01, A12, A13, A17, ABIn, P34, P48, P51, P53, P54, PQC.
—CCC.
Published by: C C H Inc. (Subsidiary of: Wolters Kluwer N.V.), 2700 Lake Cook Rd, Riverwoods, IL 60015. TEL 847-267-7000, cust_serv@cch.com, http://www.cch.com. Circ: 400.

352.4 USA
FEDERAL FUNDS INFORMATION FOR STATES NEWSLETTER. Text in English. 8/yr. USD 250. **Document type:** *Newsletter.*
Published by: National Governors' Association, 444 N Capitol St, Washington, DC 20001. TEL 202-624-5849. **Co-sponsor:** National Conference of State Legislatures.

351.71 CAN ISSN 1205-6294
JL111.E93
FEDERAL GUIDEBOOK. Text in English. 1985. a. CAD 59.95. **Description:** Authoritative handbook providing comprehensive information on the Canadian Federal Government.
Former titles (until 1996): Canadian Federal Government Handbook (1189-4709); (until 1992): Ottawa's Senior Executives Guide (0826-8355)
Related titles: Online - full text ed.
Published by: Globe Information Services, 444 Front St W, Toronto, ON M5V 2S9, Canada. TEL 416-585-5250, FAX 416-585-5249. Ed. Mary Ferguson.

FEDERAL MOTOR VEHICLE FLEET REPORT. *see* TRANSPORTATION—Automobiles

320 USA ISSN 2154-7858
▼ **FEDERAL P M FOCUS**; advancing government project and program management. Text in English. 2010. m. **Document type:** *Journal, Trade.* **Description:** Contains new resources devoted to meeting the unique demands of managing government projects.
Related titles: Online - full text ed.: ISSN 2154-7866. 2010. USD 129 (effective 2010).
Published by: Management Concepts, 8230 Leesburg Pike, Vienna, VA 22182. TEL 703-790-9595, FAX 703-790-1371.

351.973 USA
THE FEDERAL PAPER. Text in English. w. adv. **Document type:** *Newsletter, Consumer.* **Description:** Covers the White House and federal agencies as well as their interaction with Congress, lobbyists, defense, technology, and the private sector. Features news, analysis and profiles and more. Written for people with the federal government and Congress.
Related titles: Online - full content ed.
Published by: Public Sector Media, 1150 18th St NW, Ste 475, Washington, DC 20036. TEL 202-449-3300, FAX 202-530-0070. adv.: B&W page USD 8,000, color page USD 9,000; trim 10.5 x 15.

FEDERAL PERSONNEL GUIDE; employment, pay, benefits, postal service, civil service. *see* BUSINESS AND ECONOMICS—Personnel Management

351.092 USA ISSN 1061-3153
JK6
FEDERAL REGIONAL YELLOW BOOK; who's who in the federal government's departments, agencies, diplomatic missions, military installations and service academies outside of Washington, DC. Text in English. 1993. s-a. USD 355 (effective 2008). illus. **Document type:** *Directory, Trade.* **Description:** Provides contact information for over 45,000 regional directors and administrative staff members at federal departments and agencies and includes field offices, regional headquarters, military installations, U.S. embassies and foreign service posts.
Related titles: CD-ROM ed.; Online - full text ed.; ◆ Supplement to: Federal Yellow Book. ISSN 0145-6202.
—CCC.
Published by: Leadership Directories, Inc, 104 Fifth Ave, 2nd Fl, New York, NY 10011. TEL 212-627-4140, FAX 212-645-0931, info@leadershipdirectories.com. Ed. Thomas J Zurla.

FEDERAL REGISTER. *see* LAW

FEDERAL REGULATORY DIRECTORY. *see* POLITICAL SCIENCE

FEDERAL RESEARCH IN PROGRESS DATABASE. *see* ENGINEERING

FEDERAL RULES SERVICE. *see* LAW

352.63025 USA ISSN 0735-3324
JK723.E9 CODEN: FSDIEM
FEDERAL STAFF DIRECTORY. Text in English. 1982. 3/yr. USD 288 per issue (effective 2008). index. back issues avail.; reprints avail. **Document type:** *Directory.* **Description:** Lists 34,000 federal, executive, and military personnel from the White House, Departments, and independent and quasi-agencies, including 2,600 biographies of key decision makers. Also includes descriptions of each agency's responsibility with symbols to indicate which positions are presidential appointments.
Related titles: CD-ROM ed.; Online - full text ed.: free (effective 2008).
—CASDDS.
Published by: C Q Press, Inc. (Subsidiary of: Sage Publications, Inc.), 2300 N St, NW, Ste 800, Washington, DC 20037. TEL 202-729-1900, 866-427-7737, FAX 800-380-3810, customerservice@cqpress.com, http://www.cqpress.com. Ed. Penny Perry.

FEDERAL STATUTES ANNOTATIONS. *see* PUBLIC ADMINISTRATION—Abstracting, Bibliographies, Statistics

354.7 USA ISSN 0014-9233
FEDERAL TIMES. Text in English. 1965. w. adv. bk.rev. illus. reprints avail. **Document type:** *Newspaper, Government.* **Description:** Serving all federal government workers and US Postal employees.
Related titles: Microform ed.: (from PQC); Online - full text ed.: ISSN 1943-5789.
Indexed: A22, C12, M01, M02, M05, P34, PersLit, T02.
—CCC.
Published by: Army Times Publishing Co. (Subsidiary of: Gannett Company, Inc.), 6883 Commercial Dr, Springfield, VA 22159. TEL 703-642-7330, 800-368-5718. Eds. Steve Watkins, Tobias Naegele. adv.: B&W page USD 6,980, color page USD 8,980; trim 10.75 x 12.5. Circ: 38,000 (paid).

351 USA
FEDERAL TRAVEL REGULATION. Text in English. base vol. plus irreg. updates. looseleaf. USD 347 (effective 2001). **Document type:** *Government.* **Description:** Covers Federal civilian employee entitlements and allowances for per diem, travel, transportation, and relocation allowances under Chapter 57 of Title 5, U.S. Code. These entitlements and allowances are set forth in the FTR, FPMR 101-7.
Published by: U.S. General Services Administration, Office of Governmentwide Policy, 1800 F St, NW, Washington, DC 20405. TEL 202-501-1538, ftrtravel.chat@gsa.gov. **Subscr. to:** U.S. Government Printing Office, Superintendent of Documents, PO Box 371954, Pittsburgh, PA 15250. TEL 202-512-1800, FAX 202-512-2250, orders@gpo.gov, http://www.access.gpo.gov.

352.63025 USA ISSN 0145-6202
JK6 CODEN: FYBOD3
FEDERAL YELLOW BOOK; who's who in the federal departments and agencies. Text in English. 1976. q. USD 475 (effective 2008). adv. illus. Index. **Document type:** *Directory, Government.* **Description:** Provides contact information for over 45,000 U.S. federal positions located within the Washington, D.C. metropolitan area.
Related titles: CD-ROM ed.; Online - full text ed.; ◆ Supplement(s): Federal Regional Yellow Book. ISSN 1061-3153.
—CASDDS. **CCC.**
Published by: Leadership Directories, Inc, 104 Fifth Ave, 2nd Fl, New York, NY 10011. TEL 212-627-4140, FAX 212-645-0931, info@leadershipdirectories.com. Ed. Thomas J Zurla. Circ: 12,000.

352.68 USA ISSN 0736-8151
E172
THE FEDERALIST. Text in English. 1980. q. free to members (effective 2010). bk.rev. **Document type:** *Newsletter, Academic/Scholarly.* **Description:** Carries news and features pertaining to historians and professionals in related fields (archivists, librarians, records managers, teachers) who are employed in the federal government.
Published by: Society for History in the Federal Government, PO Box 14139, Washington, DC 20044. benjamin.guterman@nara.gov.

FEDNEWS. *see* LABOR UNIONS

351.9611 FJI
FIJI ROYAL GAZETTE. Text in English. w. USD 105. **Document type:** *Government.*
Related titles: Microfilm ed.: (from PQC).
Published by: Government Printing Department, PO Box 98, Suva, Fiji.

351.9611 FJI
FIJI TODAY. Text in English. a. free. **Document type:** *Government.*
Formerly: Fiji Information
Published by: Ministry of Information Broadcasting Television and Telecommunications, Govt. Bldgs, PO Box 2225, Suva, Fiji. TEL 679-211368, FAX 679-303146. Ed. Eliki Bomani.

351 FRA ISSN 2106-8151
▼ **LE FIL SUD ESTUAIRE.** Text in French. 2009. q. **Document type:** *Newsletter, Consumer.*
Published by: Sud Estuaire-Communaute de Communes, 6 Bl Dumesnildot, BP 3014, Paimboeuf, 44560, France. TEL 33-2-40277012, FAX 33-2-40277933, info@cc-sudestuaire.fr, http://www.cc-sudestuaire.fr.

352.63 USA
JK2474
FINANCES OF SELECTED STATE AND LOCAL GOVERNMENT EMPLOYEE RETIREMENT SYSTEMS (ONLINE). Text in English. a. free. **Document type:** *Government.*
Formerly (until 1992): Finances of Employee Retirement Systems of State and Local Governments (Print) (0096-3224)
Media: Online - full text. **Related titles:** Microfiche ed.
Indexed: AmStI.
Published by: U.S. Census Bureau. Governments Division (Subsidiary of: U.S. Department of Commerce), 4600 Silver Hill Rd., Washington, DC 20233. TEL 888-529-1963.

354.8 CAN ISSN 1704-8176
CA1FC1
FINANCIAL CONSUMER AGENCY OF CANADA. ANNUAL REPORT/ AGENCE DE LA CONSOMMATION EN MATIERE FINANCIERE DU CANADA. RAPPORT ANNUEL. Text in English, French. 2002. a.
Related titles: Online - full text ed.: ISSN 1706-0532.
Published by: Financial Consumer Agency of Canada/Agence de la Consommation en Matiere Financiere du Canada, 427 Laurier Ave W, 6th Flr, Ottawa, ON K1R 1B9, Canada. TEL 613-996-5454, FAX 613-941-1436.

351 368 336 SWE ISSN 1102-7460
FINANSINSPEKTIONENS FOERFATTNINGSSAMLING. Variant title: F F F S. Text in Swedish. 1977. irreg. back issues avail. **Document type:** *Trade.*
Formerly (until 1991): Bankinsspektionen och Foesaekringsinspektionens Foerfattningssamling (0349-358X)
Related titles: Online - full text ed.
Published by: Finansinspektionen/Swedish Financial Supervisory Authority, PO Box 670, Stockholm, 11385, Sweden. TEL 46-8-7878000, FAX 46-8-241335, finansinspektionen@fi.se. Ed. Maria Feldt TEL 46-8-7878046.

328 FIN ISSN 1239-1638
JN7397
FINLAND. EDUSKUNNAN KANSLIA. JULKAISU/FINLAND. RIKSDAGENS KANSLI. PUBLIKATIONER/FINLAND. THE PARLIAMENTARY OFFICE. PUBLICATIONS. Text in English, Finnish, Swedish. 1996. irreg. **Document type:** *Monographic series, Government.*
Related titles: Online - full text ed.: ISSN 1795-7230. 2000.
Published by: Suomen Eduskunta/Finnish Parliament, Mannerheimintie 30, Helsinki, 00102, Finland. TEL 358-9-4321, FAX 358-9-4322274, eduskunta@eduskunta.fi.

353 354 FIN ISSN 0789-0893
FINLAND. OIKEUSMINISTERIO. TIETOHALLINTOTOIMISTO. A. Text in Finnish. 1979. irreg. **Document type:** *Monographic series, Government.*
Formerly (until 1990): Finland. Oikeusministerio. Tietojarjestelmayksikko. A (0358-6022)
Published by: Oikeusministerio/Ministry of Justice, PO Box 25, Government, Helsinki, 00023, Finland. TEL 358-9-16003, FAX 358-9-16067730, om-tiedot@om.fi, http://www.om.fi.

353 354 FIN ISSN 0359-6729
FINLAND. OIKEUSMINISTERIO. TIETOJARJESTELMAYKSIKKO. B. Text in Finnish. 1979. irreg. **Document type:** *Monographic series, Government.*
Published by: Oikeusministerio/Ministry of Justice, PO Box 25, Government, Helsinki, 00023, Finland. TEL 358-9-16003, FAX 358-9-16067730, om-tiedot@om.fi, http://www.om.fi.

351 FIN ISSN 0782-6036
FINLAND. STATSRAADETS KANSLI. PUBLIKATIONSSERIE. Text in Swedish. 1985. irreg. free. back issues avail. **Document type:** *Monographic series, Government.*
Related titles: Online - full text ed.; ◆ English ed.: Finland. The Prime Minister's Office. Publication. ISSN 0783-1609; ◆ Finnish ed.: Finland. Valtioneuvoston Kanslia. Julkaisusarja. ISSN 0782-6028.
Published by: Valtioneuvoston Kanslia/Prime Minister's Office, Snellmaninkatu 1 A, PO Box 23, Helsinki, 00023, Finland. TEL 358-9-16001, FAX 358-9-16022165, info@vnk.fi. **Dist. by:** Yliopistopaino, Kirjamyynti ja Asiakaspalvelu, Vuorikatu 3 A, II krs., Helsinki, Finland. TEL 358-9-70102363, FAX 358-9-70102374, books@yliopistopaino.fi, http://www.yliopistopaino.fi.

351 FIN ISSN 0782-6028
FINLAND. VALTIONEUVOSTON KANSLIA. JULKAISUSARJA. Text in Finnish. 1959. irreg. free. back issues avail. **Document type:** *Monographic series, Government.*
Former titles (until 1985): Finland. Valtioneuvoston Kanslia. Julkaisuja (0355-8878); Which incorporated (1975-1985): Finland. Valtioneuvoston Kanslia. Monisteita (0357-4113); (until 1972): Finland. Valtakunnansuunnittelutoimisto. Julkaisusarja. Sarja A (0071-5360)
Related titles: Online - full text ed.; ◆ English ed.: Finland. The Prime Minister's Office. Publication. ISSN 0783-1609; ◆ Swedish ed.: Finland. Statsraadets Kansli. Publikationsserie. ISSN 0782-6036.
Published by: Valtioneuvoston Kanslia/Prime Minister's Office, Snellmaninkatu 1 A, PO Box 23, Helsinki, 00023, Finland. TEL 358-9-16001, FAX 358-9-16022165, info@vnk.fi. **Dist. by:** Yliopistopaino, Kirjamyynti ja Asiakaspalvelu, Vuorikatu 3 A, II krs., Helsinki, Finland. TEL 358-9-70102363, FAX 358-9-70102374, books@yliopistopaino.fi, http://www.yliopistopaino.fi.

351 363.7 FIN ISSN 1796-1645
FINLAND. YMPARISTOMINISTERIO. YMPARISTOHALLINNON OHJEITA. Text in Finnish. 2006. irreg. back issues avail. **Document type:** *Government.*
Related titles: Online - full text ed.: ISSN 1796-1653.
Published by: Ymparistoministerio/Ministry of the Environment, Kasarmikatu 25, PO Box 35, Valtioneuvosto, 00023, Finland. TEL 358-20-690160, FAX 358-9-16039320.

351 FIN ISSN 1235-9343
FINLANDS KOMMUNTIDNING. Text in Finnish, Swedish. 1993. 9/yr. EUR 46 (effective 2005). adv. **Document type:** *Magazine, Consumer.*
Formed by the merger of (1970-1993): Finlands Kommunaltidskrift (0355-6093); (1918-1993): Kommuntidningen (0780-7627); Which was formerly (until 1984): Kommunaltidningen (0355-9882); (until 1931): Kommunaltidning foer Finands Svenska Landskommuner
Related titles: Online - full text ed.
Published by: Suomen Kuntaliitto/Finlands Kommunalfoerbund, Kommunernas Hus, Andra Linjen 14, Helsinki, 00530, Finland. TEL 358-9-7717711, FAX 358-9-7712291, http://www.kommunerna.net. Ed. Berndt Laangvik. Adv. contact Jonny Aastrand. B&W page EUR 980, color page EUR 1,915; 210 x 297. Circ: 3,000.

351.771 USA
KFO431.A6
FINLEY'S OHIO MUNICIPAL SERVICE. Text in English. 19??. bi-m. USD 574.56 (effective 2011). **Document type:** *Newsletter, Trade.* **Description:** Commentary on municipal tort liability, municipal financing, environmental and property law affecting municipalities, and public employee collective bargaining; judicial and legislative developments tracked.
Former titles (until 2002): Marburger & Hunt's Ohio Municipal Service; (until 2001): Babbit's Ohio Municipal Service (1088-2006); (until 1996): Gotherman's Ohio Municipal Service (0739-6937)
—CCC.
Published by: West Publishing Corporation (Subsidiary of: Thomson Reuters), 610 Opperman Dr, Eagan, MN 55123. TEL 651-687-7000, 800-344-5008.

FLEMING'S CANADIAN LEGISLATURES. *see* LAW

351.759 USA
FLORIDA ADMINISTRATIVE PRACTICE. Text in English. 1979. irreg., latest 2009, 8th ed. looseleaf. USD 175 combined subscription per issue (print & CD-ROM eds.) (effective 2010). **Document type:** *Handbook/Manual/Guide, Trade.* **Description:** Provides a discussion of the procedural aspects of administrative litigation.
Related titles: CD-ROM ed.
Published by: The Florida Bar, 651 E Jefferson St, Tallahassee, FL 32399. TEL 850-561-5600, 800-342-8060, FAX 850-561-9416, flabarwm@flabar.org, http://www.floridabar.org.

351.3 USA
FLORIDA. DEPARTMENT OF HEALTH. VITAL NEWS. Cover title: Vital News. Text in English. q. free. charts. **Document type:** *Newsletter, Government.*
Former titles: Florida. Department of Health. Vital News and Quarterly Vital Statistics Report; Florida. Department of Health and Rehabilitative Service. Vital News and Quarterly Vital Statistics Report
Published by: Florida Department of Health, Bureau of Vital Statistics, Quality Assurance Unit, PO Box 210, Jacksonville, FL 32231-0042. TEL 904-359-6940, FAX 904-359-6648.

351.759025 USA
FLORIDA DIRECTORY. Text in English. 1991. a. USD 65 to libraries; USD 75 elsewhere. **Document type:** *Directory.* **Description:** Lists the state's elected and appointed officials at all levels. Includes demographic and media information for each county including one or more major city.
Published by: Florida Communications Network, Inc., 7998 W Highway 318, Reddick, FL 32686. Ed. John Hotaling. Pub. Jon Mills. Circ: 350.

351.759 USA ISSN 0430-7801
FLORIDA PUBLIC DOCUMENTS. Text in English. 1968. m. (plus a. cumulation). free to qualified libraries. bibl. **Document type:** *Government.*
Formerly: Florida State Documents (0071-6014)
Published by: State Library, Documents Section, 500 S Bronough St, Tallahassee, FL 32399. TEL 850-487-2651, FAX 850-487-6242. Ed. Cay Hohmeister. Circ: (controlled).

351.775 USA
FOCUS (MADISON, 1972). Text in English. 1972. 27/yr. USD 54.97; free to qualified personnel (effective 2011). **Document type:** *Newsletter, Government.* **Description:** Covers Wisconsin legislative issues, as well as state and local government.
Former titles (until 19??): Your Wisconsin Government in Focus; Your Wisconsin Government
Published by: Wisconsin Taxpayers Alliance, 401 N Lawn Ave, Madison, WI 53704. TEL 608-241-9789, FAX 608-241-5807, wistax@wistax.org.

FOCUS HAAGLANDEN. *see* BUSINESS AND ECONOMICS—Macroeconomics

351 SWE ISSN 0015-8585
K6
➤ **FOERVALTNINGSRAETTSLIG TIDSKRIFT.** Text in Swedish. 1938. 4/yr. SEK 590; SEK 140 per issue (effective 2010). abstr.; bibl. **Document type:** *Journal, Academic/Scholarly.*
Related titles: Online - full text ed.
Indexed: FLP.
Published by: (Foervaltningsraettslig Tidskrift Foerening), Eddy.se AB, Norra Kyrkogatan 3, Visby, 62155, Sweden. TEL 46-498-253900, FAX 46-498-249789, info@eddy.se, http://www.eddy.se. Ed. Lars Bejstram.

351 DNK ISSN 0906-4893
JN7261
FOLKETINGET EFTER VALGET. Text in Danish. 1956. irreg., latest 2007. illus. **Document type:** *Government.* **Description:** Covers changes in the Danish Parliament after each major election.
Former titles (until 1991): Folketingets Haandbog (0109-6354); (until 1984): Folketinget (0107-9670)
Related titles: Online - full text ed.
Published by: Folketinget/Danish Parliament, Christiansborg, Copenhagen K, 1240, Denmark. TEL 45-33-375500, folketinget@ft.dk. **Dist. by:** Schultz Boghandel.

FOLKHAELSORAPPORT. *see* PUBLIC HEALTH AND SAFETY

FONCTION PUBLIQUE. *see* LABOR UNIONS

342.5 SWE ISSN 0346-6086
FRAAN RIKSDAG & DEPARTEMENT; rakt og relevant om politiken i Sverige och E U. Variant title: R och D. Text in Swedish. 1973. 38/yr. SEK 595 domestic; SEK 750 in the European Union; SEK 708 elsewhere (effective 2007). adv. Index. **Document type:** *Magazine, Consumer.*
Formerly (until 1976): Departementnytt (0345-2298)
Related titles: Online - full text ed.
Published by: Riksdagsfoervaltningen, Jakobsgatan 6, Stockholm, 10012, Sweden. TEL 46-8-7864000, FAX 46-8-7866195, riksdaginformation@riksdagen.se, http://www.riksdagen.se. Eds. Christian Carlstroem TEL 46-8-7865344, Nils Funcke TEL 46-8-7865784. Adv. contact Karin Aakerblom TEL 46-8-109585. B&W page SEK 21,100, color page SEK 27,800; 220 x 287. Circ: 14,300 (controlled).

351.775 USA
THE FRAMEWORK OF YOUR WISCONSIN GOVERNMENT. Text in English. 1955. irreg. USD 3 per issue (effective 2011). **Document type:** *Monographic series, Government.* **Description:** Describes Wisconsin state and local government. Contains charts, illustrations and diagrams. Includes questions and projects.
Published by: Wisconsin Taxpayers Alliance, 401 N Lawn Ave, Madison, WI 53704. TEL 608-241-9789, FAX 608-241-5807, wistax@wistax.org.

FRANCE. ASSEMBLEE NATIONALE. BULLETIN. BILAN DE SESSION. *see* POLITICAL SCIENCE

351 FRA ISSN 0182-788X
FRANCE. CONSEIL D'ETAT. ETUDES ET DOCUMENTS. Text in French. 1947. a. reprint service avail. from SCH. **Document type:** *Government.*
Indexed: IBSS.
Published by: (France. Le Conseil d'Etat), Documentation Francaise, 29-31 Quai Voltaire, Paris, Cedex 7 75344, France. TEL 33-1-40157000, http://www.ladocumentationfrancaise.fr.

351.44 FRA ISSN 0339-9338
FRANCE. CONSEIL NATIONAL DE LA COMPTABILITE. BULLETIN TRIMESTRIEL. Text in French. 1970. q.
Published by: Conseil National de la Comptabilite, c/o Imprimerie Nationale, Etablissement de Douai. Route d'Auby, Flers En Escrebieux, 59128, France.

FRANCE FORUM. *see* POLITICAL SCIENCE

351.44 FRA ISSN 0182-7502
FRANCE. LE MEDIATEUR DE LA REPUBLIQUE. RAPPORT ANNUEL. Text in French. 1973. a.
Related titles: Online - full text ed.
Published by: France. Mediateur de la Republique, 7 Rue Saint-Florentin, Paris, 75008, France. TEL 33-1-55352424, FAX 33-1-55352425.

351.44 FRA ISSN 0240-4729
FRANCE. MINISTERE DE L'INTERIEUR. REPERTOIRE MENSUEL. Text in French. 1979. m. (11/yr.). EUR 105 (effective 2009). **Document type:** *Journal, Government.*
Formerly (until 1979): France. Ministere de l'Interieur. Bulletin Officiel (0151-0789)
Indexed: FR.
Published by: (France. France. Ministere de l'Interieur), Imprimerie Paul Dupont, 4ter Rue du Bouloi, Paris, 75001, France. TEL 33-1-42360687, FAX 33-1-42360155, abo@paul-dupont.fr, http://www.paul-dupont.fr/.

352.63 FRA ISSN 2101-2490
FRANCE. MINISTERE DU TRAVAIL, DES RELATIONS SOCIALES, DE LA FAMILLE ET DE LA SOLIDARITE ET DE LA VILLE. MINISTERE DE L'AGRICULTURE ET DE LA PECHE. CONVENTIONS COLLECTIVES. BULLETIN OFFICIEL. Text in French. 1983. w. charts. **Document type:** *Directory, Government.*
Former titles (until 2009): France. Ministere du Travail, des Relations Sociales, de la Famille et de la Solidarite. Ministere de l'Agriculture et de la Peche. Conventions Collectives. Bulletin Officiel (2101-2482); (until 2008): France. Ministere du Travail, des Relations Sociales et de la Solidarite. Ministere de l'Agriculture et de la Peche. Conventions Collectives. Bulletin Officiel (2101-2474); (until 2007): France. Ministere de l'Emploi, de la Cohesion Sociale et du Logement. Ministere de l'Agriculture et de la Peche. Conventions Collectives. Bulletin Officiel (1953-6534); (until 2005): France. Ministere de l'Emploi, du Travail et de la Cohesion Sociale. Ministere de l'Agriculture, de l'Alimentation, de la Peche et des Affaires Rurales. Conventions Collectives. Bulletin Officiel (1776-7008); (until 2004): France. Ministere des Affaires Sociales, du Travail et de la Solidarite. Conventions Collectives. Bulletin Officiel (1764-8505); (until 2002): France. Ministere de l'Emploi et de la Solidarite. Conventions Collectives. Bulletin Officiel (1283-5013); (until 1997): France. Ministere du Travail et des Affaires Sociales. Ministere de l'Agriculture, de la Peche et de l'Alimentation. Conventions Collectives. Bulletin Officiel (1282-7851); (until 1995): France. Ministere du Travail, du Dialogue Social et de la Partecipation. Ministere de l'Agriculture, de la Peche et de l'Alimentation. Conventions Collectives. Bulletin Officiel (1267-4303); (until 1995): France. Ministere du Travail, de l'Emploi et de la Formation Professionnelle. Ministere de l'Agriculture et de la Foret. Conventions Collectives. Bulletin Officiel (0992-812X); (until 1988): France. Ministere des Affaires Sociales et de l'Emploi. Conventions Collectives. Bulletin Officiel (0298-234X); (until 1986): France. Ministere du Travail, de l'Emploi et de la Formation Professionnelle. Conventions Collectives. Bulletin Officiel (0753-1761); (until 1984): France. Ministere Charge de l'Emploi. Conventions Collectives. Bulletin Officiel (0759-0083); (until 1983): France. Ministere Charge de l'Emploi et du Travail. Conventions Collectives (0755-7450)
Published by: (France. France. Ministere des Affaires Sociales de la Sante et de la Ville), France. Direction des Journaux Officiels, 26 rue Desaix, Paris, 75727 Cedex 15, France. TEL 33-1-40587500, info@journal-officiel.gouv.fr, http://www.journal-officiel.gouv.fr.

320 351 USA ISSN 1939-7992
JK1
FRANK. Text in English. 2007. s-a. **Document type:** *Magazine, Consumer.*
Published by: University of Arkansas, Clinton School of Public Service, 1200 President Clinton Ave, Little Rock, AR 72201. TEL 501-683-5200, http://clintonschool.uasys.edu. Ed. Patrick Kennedy.

351 380.1029 CAN ISSN 0845-096X
JL269.5.R4
FREEDOM OF INFORMATION AND PRIVACY BRANCH. DIRECTORY OF INSTITUTIONS, ONTARIO. Text in English. a.
Former titles (until 1990): Management Board of Cabinet. Directory of Institutions (1187-2144); (until 1988): Directory of Government Ministries, Agencies and Affiliated Agencies (0845-0951)
Published by: (Ontario, Access and Privacy Office), Queen's Printer for Ontario, Publications Ontario, 50 Grosvenor St, Toronto, ON M7A 1N8, Canada. TEL 416-326-5300, FAX 613-566-2234, http://pubont.stores.gov.on.ca/.

FREEDOM OF INFORMATION AND PROTECTION OF PRIVACY ACT. ANNUAL REPORT. *see* LAW

328.37 DEU ISSN 0409-1426
FREIE UNIVERSITAET BERLIN. INSTITUT FUER STAATSLEHRE, STAATS- UND VERWALTUNGSRECHT. STUDIEN UND GUTACHTEN. Text in German. 1963. irreg., latest vol.18, 2006. price varies. **Document type:** *Monographic series, Academic/Scholarly.*
Published by: (Freie Universitaet Berlin, Institut fuer Staatslehre, Staats- und Verwaltungsrecht), Duncker und Humblot GmbH, Carl-Heinrich-Becker-Weg 9, Berlin, 12165, Germany. TEL 49-30-7900060, FAX 49-30-79000631, info@duncker-humblot.de.

351 USA
FRONTLINE. Text in English. 1972. q. back issues avail. **Document type:** *Newsletter, Trade.*
Formerly (until 2000): M A S S Media
Media: Online - full content.
Published by: National Council of Social Security Management Associations, 418 C St, N E, Washington, DC 20002. TEL 202-547-8530, FAX 202-547-8532, president@ncssma.org. Circ: 4,600.

351.7 USA
THE FUTURE OF THE PUBLIC SECTOR; a series on the long-term forces affecting U.S. social policy. Text in English. 1996. irreg., latest 1999. back issues avail. **Document type:** *Monographic series, Academic/Scholarly.* **Description:** Includes maintaining quality in health care as costs are contained; the implications of shifting responsibilities from the federal level to the states; and how can governments determine the public will in complex policy issues.
Related titles: Online - full text ed.: free (effective 2010).
Published by: Urban Institute, 2100 M St, NW, Washington, DC 20037. TEL 202-833-7200, FAX 202-467-5775, paffairs@ui.urban.org.

352.379 MEX ISSN 1405-7697
G C D: LA REVISTA DE LA SEGURIDAD. Text in Spanish. 1998. m. MXN 25 newsstand/cover (effective 2000).
Published by: Sistema Opalo, Patricio Sanz 1130, Col Del Valle, Mexico, D.F. 03100, Mexico. TEL 52-5-575-2036, FAX 52-5-559-8102, gcd@diamante.com.mx. Ed. Enriqueta Carlon Dominguez.

351 USA ISSN 0016-3619
JS302
G R A REPORTER. Text in English. 1949. q. USD 75 (effective 2000 - 2001). illus. **Document type:** *Newsletter, Trade.*
Published by: Governmental Research Association, Inc., 402 Samford Hall, Samford University, Birmingham, AL 35229-7017. TEL 205-726-2482. Circ: 300.

P

352.53 USA ISSN 0095-5620
TS199.U5
G S A SUPPLY CATALOG. (General Services Administration) Text in English. a. (plus irreg. updates). USD 33; USD 41.25 foreign. **Document type:** *Catalog, Government.* **Description:** Lists office products, tools, furniture used by the federal government that are available from G.S.A. supply and distribution facilities. Contains full ordering information, including prices.
—Linda Hall.
Published by: U.S. General Services Administration, Federal Supply Service, Office of Public Affairs, 18th and F Sts NW, Washington, DC 20405. **Subscr. to:** U.S. Government Printing Office, Superintendent of Documents, PO Box 371954, Pittsburgh, PA 15250. TEL 202-512-1800, FAX 202-512-2250, orders@gpo.gov.

351 MEX ISSN 0185-8599
JL1224
GACETA MEXICANA DE ADMINISTRACION PUBLICA ESTATAL Y MUNICIPAL. Text in Spanish. 1981. s-a. MXN 28 per issue (effective 2006). **Document type:** *Bulletin, Government.*
Related titles: Online - full text ed.
Indexed: FR.
Published by: Instituto Nacional de Administracion Publica, Km. 14.5 Carretera Libre Mexico-Toluca, Col. Palo Alto, Del. Cuajimalpa, Mexico, D.F., 05110, Mexico. TEL 52-55-50812690, FAX 52-55-55700532.

351 POL ISSN 1428-8257
GAZETA SAMORZADU I ADMINISTRACJI. Text in Polish. 1999. bi-w. PLZ 84 (effective 2001). **Document type:** *Newspaper.*
Published by: Grupa Wydawnicza INFOR Sp. z o.o., Ul Okopowa 58/72, Warsaw, 01042, Poland. TEL 48-22-5304208, 48-22-5304450, bok@infor.pl. Ed. Jolanta Adamczyk. Adv. contact Waldemar Krakowiak.

351.691 MDG ISSN 0255-9536
GAZETIM-PANJAKAN'NY REPOBLIKA DEMOKRATIKA MALAGASY/ JOURNAL OFFICIEL DE LA REPUBLIQUE DEMOCRATIQUE DE MADAGASCAR. Text in French, Malagasy. 1888. w. (in 3 vols.). MGF 546,880. **Document type:** *Government.*
Formerly: Gazetim-panjakan'ny Repoblika Malagasy (1017-2203)
Published by: Imprimerie Nationale, BP 38, Antananarivo, 101, Madagascar. TEL 236-75. Ed. Raymond Rajaonarivo. Pub. Honoree Elianne Ralalaharison. R&P Gilbert Rakotonandrasana.

351 ITA ISSN 2037-4054
GAZZETTA AMMINISTRATIVA DEI COMUNI DELLE PROVINCE E DELLE REGIONI D'ITALIA. Text in Italian. 2008. q. **Document type:** *Journal, Trade.*
Related titles: Online - full text ed.: ISSN 2037-4062.
Published by: Gazzetta Amministrativa, Via G Nicotera, Rome, 00195, Italy. TEL 39-06-3242351, FAX 39-06-3242356, info@gazzettaamministrativa.it.

GELSENKIRCHEN IM SPIEGEL DER STATISTIK. *see* PUBLIC ADMINISTRATION—Abstracting, Bibliographies, Statistics

351 NLD ISSN 0165-7895
DE GEMEENTESTEM; tweewekelijks tijdschrift aan de belangen der gemeenten in Nederland gewijd. Key Title: Gemeente-stem. Text in Dutch. 1851. 22/yr. EUR 322; EUR 497.70 combined subscription (print & online eds.) (effective 2009). adv. **Document type:** *Journal, Trade.*
Related titles: Online - full text ed.: EUR 384 (effective 2009).
—IE, Infotrieve.
Published by: Kluwer B.V. (Subsidiary of: Wolters Kluwer N.V.), Postbus 4, Alphen aan den Rijn, 2400 MA, Netherlands. TEL 31-172-466633, info@kluwer.nl, http://www.kluwer.nl.

351 DEU
DIE GEMEINDE (STUTTGART); Zeitschrift fuer die Staedte und Gemeinden, fuer Stadtraete, Gemeinderaete und Ortschaftsraete. Text in German. 1877. s-m. EUR 135; EUR 80 to students; EUR 8 newsstand/cover (effective 2007). adv. bk.rev. stat. **Document type:** *Magazine, Trade.*
Published by: Gemeindetag Baden-Wuerttemberg, Panoramastr 33, Stuttgart, 70174, Germany. TEL 49-711-225720, FAX 49-711-2257247. adv.: B&W page EUR 1,100, color page EUR 1,940. Circ: 4,500 (paid and controlled).

351.43 DEU ISSN 0943-7878
GEMEINDEORDNUNG FUER DAS LAND SACHSEN-ANHALT. Text in German. 1993. 2 base vols. plus updates 2/yr. EUR 98 base vol(s).; EUR 36.80 updates per issue (effective 2009). **Document type:** *Monographic series, Trade.*
Published by: Erich Schmidt Verlag GmbH & Co. (Berlin), Genthiner Str 30 G, Berlin, 10785, Germany. TEL 49-30-2500850, FAX 49-30-250085305, esv@esvmedien.de, http://www.erich-schmidt-verlag.de.

351.43 DEU ISSN 0944-1131
GEMEINDEORDNUNG FUER DEN FREISTAAT SACHSEN. Text in German. 1993. 3 base vols. plus updates 3/yr. EUR 98 base vol(s).; EUR 36.90 updates per issue (effective 2009). **Document type:** *Monographic series, Trade.*
Published by: Erich Schmidt Verlag GmbH & Co. (Berlin), Genthiner Str 30 G, Berlin, 10785, Germany. TEL 49-30-2500850, FAX 49-30-250085305, esv@esvmedien.de, http://www.erich-schmidt-verlag.de.

351.43 DEU ISSN 0939-4729
GEMEINSAMES MINISTERIALBLATT DES AUSWAERTIGEN AMTES, DES BUNDESMINISTERS DES INNERN, DES BUNDESMINISTERS FUER ERNAEHRUNG, LANDWIRTSCHAFT UND FORSTEN, DES BUNDESMINISTERS FUER INNERDEUTSCHE BEZIEHUNGEN, DES BUNDESMINISTERS FUER JUGEND, FAMILIE, FRAUEN UND GESUNDHEIT, DES BUNDESMINISTERS FUER UMWELT, NATURSCHUTZ UND REAKTORSICHERHEIT, DES BUNDESMINISTERS FUER RAUMORDNUNG, BAUWESEN UND STAEDTEBAU. Text in German. 1957. 40/yr. EUR 73; EUR 2 per issue (effective 2011). **Document type:** *Bulletin, Trade.*
Former titles (until 1986): Gemeinsames Ministerialblatt des Auswaertigen Amtes, des Bundesministers des Innern, des Bundesministers fuer Ernaehrung, Landwirtschaft und Forsten, des Bundesministers fuer Jugend, Familie und Gesundheit, des Bundesministers fuer Raumordnung, Bauwesen und Staedtebau, des Bundesministers fuer Innerdeutsche Beziehungen, des Bundesministers fuer Forschung und Technologie (0341-1435); (until 1972): Gemeinsames Ministerialblatt des Auswaertigen Amtes, des Bundesministers des Innern, des Bundesministers fuer Jugend, Familie und Gesundheit, des Bundesministers fuer Staedtebau und Wohnungswesen, des Bundesministers fuer Innerdeutsche Beziehungen, des Bundesministers fuer Bildung und Wissenschaft, des Bundesministers fuer Wirtschaftliche Zusammenarbeit (0341-1427); (until 1969): Gemeinsames Ministerialblatt des Auswaertigen Amtes, des Bundesministers des Innern, des Bundesministers fuer Wohnungswesen und Staedtebau, des Bundesministers fuer Vertriebene, Fluechtlinge und Kriegsgeschaedigte, des Bundesministers fuer Gesamtdeutsche Fragen, des Bundesministers fuer Angelegenheiten des Bundesrates und der Laender, des Bundesministers fuer Familie und Jugend (0177-557X); (until 1965): Gemeinsames Ministerialblatt des Auswaertigen Amtes, des Bundesministers des Innern, des Bundesministers fuer Wohnungswesen, Staedtebau und Raumordnung, des Bundesministers fuer Vertriebene, Fluechtlinge und Kriegsgeschaedigte, des Bundesministers fuer Gesamtdeutsche Fragen, des Bundesministers fuer Angelegenheiten des Bundesrates und der Laender, des Bundesministers fuer Familie und Jugend (0177-431X); (until 1962): Gemeinsames Ministerialblatt des Auswaertigen Amtes, des Bundesministers des Innern, des Bundesministers fuer Vertriebene, Fluechtlinge und Kriegsgeschaedigte, des Bundesministers fuer Wohnungswesen, Staedtebau und Raumordnung, des Bundesministers fuer Gesamtdeutsche Fragen, des Bundesministers fuer Angelegenheiten des Bundesrates und der Laender, des Bundesministers fuer Familien- und Jugendfrage (0177-4069); (until 1961): Gemeinsames Ministerialblatt des Auswaertigen Amtes, des Bundesministers des Innern, des Bundesministers fuer Vertriebene, Fluechtlinge und Kriegsgeschaedigte, des Bundesministers fuer Wohnungsbau, des Bundesministers fuer Gesamtdeutsche Fragen, des Bundesministers fuer Angelegenheiten des Bundesrates und der Laender, des Bundesministers fuer Familien- und Jugendfragen (0177-3704)
Indexed: A22.
—IE.
Published by: Carl Heymanns Verlag KG (Subsidiary of: Wolters Kluwer Deutschland GmbH), Luxemburger Str 449, Cologne, 50939, Germany. TEL 49-221-943730, FAX 49-221-94373901, marketing@heymanns.com, http://www.heymanns.com.

GEOGRAPHIC DISTRIBUTION OF V A EXPENDITURES. (Veterans Administration) *see* MILITARY

GEOGRAPHICAL CODE OF GREECE; by eparchy, municipality, commune and locality. *see* PUBLIC ADMINISTRATION—Abstracting, Bibliographies, Statistics

351.758 USA ISSN 1066-0119
GEORGIA COUNTY GOVERNMENT. Text in English. 1947. m. USD 45 to non-members; free to members (effective 2006). adv. cum.index: 1986-1993. **Document type:** *Magazine, Government.* **Description:** For local elected officials of Georgia counties and state agency managerial staff. Covers legislative developments at state and local levels, local government administration, service delivery programs, strategies for efficient operations, environmental compliance and public works projects.
Related titles: Online - full content ed.
Published by: Association County Commissioners of Georgia, 50 Hurt Pl, Ste 1000, Atlanta, GA 30303. TEL 404-522-5022, 800-858-2224, FAX 404-525-2477. Ed., R&P Kay R Morgareidge TEL 770-963-1796. Adv. contact Jane Cronic. B&W page USD 500. Circ: 4,850.

351 347 USA ISSN 1946-830X
GEORGIA GOVERNMENT REGISTER. Text in English. 2001. m. USD 914 (effective 2011). **Document type:** *Government.* **Description:** A compilation of information about official Georgia state government actions.
Formerly (until 2005): Weil's Georgia Government Register (1535-220X)
Published by: LexisNexis (Subsidiary of: Reed Elsevier Group plc), 1016 W Ninth Ave, 1st Fl, King of Prussia, PA 19406. TEL 215 564-1788, 800 448-1515, customer.support@lexisnexis.com.

351 USA ISSN 2152-4130
▼ ➤ **GEORGIA JOURNAL OF PUBLIC POLICY.** Text in English. 2010 (June). s-a. USD 100 (effective 2010). **Document type:** *Journal, Academic/Scholarly.*
Media: Online - full text.
Published by: (Kennesaw State University), Berkeley Electronic Press, 2809 Telegraph Ave, Ste 202, Berkeley, CA 94705. TEL 510-665-1200, FAX 510-665-1201, info@bepress.com, http://www.bepress.com/.

➤ **GEORGIA SCHOOL LAW DECISIONS.** *see* EDUCATION—School Organization And Administration

351 CAN ISSN 1910-6459
GEORGIA STRAIT ALLIANCE. ANNUAL REPORT. Text in English. 1996. a. **Document type:** *Government.*
Published by: Georgia Strait Alliance, 201-195 Commercial St, Nanaimo, BC V9R 5G5, Canada. TEL 250-753-3459, FAX 250-753-2567, gsa@georgiastrait.org, http://www.georgiastrait.org.

351 USA ISSN 1523-9764
➤ **GERMAN POLICY STUDIES/POLITIKFELDANALYSE.** Abbreviated title: G P S. Text in English, German. 2000. q. adv. bk.rev. back issues avail. **Document type:** *Journal, Academic/Scholarly.* **Description:** Acts as a bridge between Anglo-Saxon and Continental-European-German tradition in policy research.
Media: Online - full text.
Indexed: A01, A03, A08, A12, A17, A26, ABIn, B01, B06, B07, B09, CA, E08, G08, I05, P10, P34, P42, P48, P51, P53, P54, PQC, S09, T02.
—CCC.
Published by: Southern Public Administration Education Foundation, Inc., 122 W High St, Elizabethtown, PA 17022. TEL 717-689-6126, spaef@spaef.com.

351 CAN ISSN 1703-9193
GESTION DU MINISTERE DE LA CULTURE ET DES COMMUNICATIONS DU QUEBEC. RAPPORT ANNUEL (YEAR). Text in French. 1994. a.
Formerly (until 2002): Quebec. Ministere de la Culture et des Communications. Rapport Annuel (1201-3595); Which was formed by the merger of (197?-1994): Quebec. Ministere des Communications. Rapport Annuel (0707-915X); Which was formerly (until 1977): Quebec. Ministere des Communications. Rapport des Activites (0380-4461); (until 1974): Quebec. Ministere des Communications. Rapport Annuel (0380-447X); (1962-1994): Quebec. Ministere de la Culture. Rapport Annuel (1209-0700); Which was formerly (until 1993): Quebec. Ministere des Affaires Culturelles. Rapport Annuel (1209-0697); (until 1983): Quebec. Ministere des Affaires Culturelles. Rapport Culturelle (0714-4083); (until 1982): Quebec. Ministere des Affaires Culturelles. Rapport Annuel (0225-6428); (until 1978): Quebec. Ministere des Affaires Culturelles. Rapport des Activite (0701-7138); (until 1976): Quebec. Ministere des Affaires Culturelles. Rapport Annuel (0701-7146); (until 1969): Quebec. Rapport du Ministere des Affaires Culturelles (0481-2921); (until 1963): Quebec. Ministere des Affaires Culturelles de la Province. Rapport Annuel (0709-9150)
Published by: Ministere de la Culture et des Communications du Quebec, 225, Grande Allee Est, Bloc B, 2e etage, Quebec, PQ G1R 5G5, Canada. TEL 418-380-2363, FAX 418-380-2364, http://www.mcc.gouv.qc.ca/minister/administration_citoyen.htm.

351 FRA ISSN 1628-6073
GESTION PUBLIQUE. Text in French. 2001. irreg. **Document type:** *Monographic series, Consumer.*
Published by: E S F Editeur (Subsidiary of: Reed Business Information France), 2 rue Maurice Hartmann, Issy-les-Moulineaux, 92133 Cedex, France. TEL 33-1-46294629, FAX 33-1-46294633, info@esf-editeur.fr, http://www.esf-editeur.fr.

351 ESP ISSN 1134-6035
➤ **GESTION Y ANALISIS DE POLITICAS PUBLICAS.** Text in Spanish; Summaries in English, Spanish. 1994. s-a. EUR 27.03 to individuals; EUR 15 newsstand/cover to individuals (effective 2010). bk.rev. abstr. back issues avail.; reprints avail. **Document type:** *Journal, Government.* **Description:** Publishes interdisciplinary contributions in the area and analysis of issues and cases of special interest to professionals in public policy and administration.
Indexed: FR.
Published by: Instituto Nacional de Administracion Publica, Atocha 106, Madrid, 28012, Spain. TEL 34-91-2739100, FAX 34-91-2739270, publicaciones@inap.map.es. Pub. Alfonso Fernandez Burgos. Circ: 500.

351 MEX ISSN 0188-8234
HD28
GESTION Y ESTRATEGIA. Text in Spanish. 1992. s-a.
Related titles: Online - full text ed.: Gestion y Estrategia. Edicion para Internet. ISSN 1606-8459.
Indexed: A01, CA, F03, F04, T02.
Published by: Universidad Autonoma Metropolitana - Azcapotzalco, Departamento de Humanidades, Ave. San Pablo 180, Col Reynosa Tamaulipas, Mexico, D.F., DF 02200, Mexico. TEL 52-5-53189125, FAX 52-5-53947506, cshenlinea@correo.azc.uam.mx, http://www-azc.uam.mx/enlinea2/enlihome.htm. Ed. Anahi Gallardo Velazquez.

GESTION Y POLITICA PUBLICA. *see* POLITICAL SCIENCE

THE GHANA DIGEST. *see* POLITICAL SCIENCE

307.336 FRA ISSN 1774-0452
GIB'ECHOS. Text in French. 2005. 3/yr. **Document type:** *Journal, Trade.*
Published by: Maison de la Gibauderie, 111 rue de la Gibauderie, Poitiers, 86000, France.

GILDEA REVIEW. *see* ENVIRONMENTAL STUDIES—Waste Management

GLOBAL ECONOMY JOURNAL. *see* BUSINESS AND ECONOMICS—Macroeconomics

351 USA ISSN 1523-9756
➤ **GLOBAL VIRTUE ETHICS REVIEW.** Text in English. 1999. q. bk.rev. back issues avail. **Document type:** *Journal, Academic/Scholarly.* **Description:** Explores how ethics can be enhanced to upgrade the quality of professional organizations.
Media: Online - full text.
Indexed: A12, A17, A26, ABIn, E08, G08, I05, P21, P48, P51, P53, P54, PQC, R05, S09.
—CCC.
Published by: Southern Public Administration Education Foundation, Inc., 122 W High St, Elizabethtown, PA 17022. TEL 717-689-6126, spaef@spaef.com. Ed. Cynthia E Lynch.

351 NLD ISSN 1574-1982
GOED BESTUUR. Text in Dutch. 2005. q. EUR 187.50 (effective 2009). adv.
Supersedes in part (in 2005): Goed Bestuur Stichting en Vereniging (1569-0954); Which was formerly (until 1999): Praktijkbrief Goed Bestuur Stichting en Vereniging (1387-3687)
Published by: Mediawerf Uitgevers, Nicolaas Witsenstraat 5, Amsterdam, 1017 ZE, Netherlands. TEL 31-20-4687126, FAX 31-20-4687128, http://www.mediawerf.nl. Ed. Jan Schoenmakers. Pub. Klazinus Lagerwerf.

351.485 SWE ISSN 1651-5242
GOETEBORG UNIVERSITY. SCHOOL OF PUBLIC ADMINISTRATION. S P A WORKING PAPERS. Text in English. 2002. irreg., latest vol.15, 2006. back issues avail. **Document type:** *Monographic series, Academic/Scholarly.*
Related titles: Online - full text ed.
Published by: Goeteborgs Universitet, Foervaltningshoegskolan/ Goeteborg University, School of Public Administration, PO Box 712, Goeteborg, 40530, Sweden. TEL 46-31-7860000, FAX 46-31-7864719.

351 SWE ISSN 1653-1264
GOETEBORGS UNIVERSITET. CENTRUM FOER FORSKNING OM OFFENTLIG SEKTOR. RAPPORT. Text in Swedish. 1993. irreg. back issues avail. **Document type:** *Monographic series, Academic/ Scholarly.*
Formerly (until 2005): Goeteborgs Universitet. Centrum foer Forskning om Offentlig Sektor. Rapport (Print Edition) (1104-327X)
Media: Online - full content.
Published by: Goeteborgs Universitet, Centrum foer Forskning om Offentlig Sektor/University of Goeteborg. Center for Public Sector Research, Pilgatan 19 A, PO Box 720, Goeteborg, 40530, Sweden. TEL 46-31-7734142, FAX 46-31-7734480, office@cefos.gu.se.

351 SWE ISSN 1401-7199
GOETEBORGS UNIVERSITET. FOERVALTNINGSHOEGSKOLAN. RAPPORTER. Text in Swedish. 1996. irreg., latest vol.86, 2006. price varies. **Document type:** *Monographic series, Academic/Scholarly.*
Published by: Goeteborgs Universitet, Foervaltningshoegskolan/ Goeteborg University, School of Public Administration, PO Box 712, Goeteborg, 40530, Sweden. TEL 46-31-7860000, FAX 46-31-7864719.

GOETTINGER STATISTIK. see PUBLIC ADMINISTRATION—Abstracting, Bibliographies, Statistics

351 CHN ISSN 1672-6162
GONGGONG GUANLI XUEBAO/JOURNAL OF PUBLIC MANAGEMENT. Text in Chinese. 2004. q. CNY 10 newsstand/cover (effective 2006). **Document type:** *Journal, Academic/Scholarly.*
Related titles: Online - full text ed.
Published by: Ha'erbin Gongye Daxue Guanli Xueyuan, 13, Fayuan Jie, Ha'erbin, 150001, China.

351 CHN ISSN 1008-3251
GONGGONG XINGZHENG/PUBLIC ADMINISTRATION. Text in English. 1999. bi-m. USD 63.80 (effective 2009). **Document type:** *Journal, Academic/Scholarly.*
—East View.
Published by: Zhongguo Renmin Daxue Shubao Ziliao Zhongxin/Renmin University of China, Information Center for Social Sciences, Dongcheng-qu, 3, Zhangzizhong Lu, Beijing, 100007, China. TEL 86-10-64039458, FAX 86-10-64015080, http://www.zlzx.org/. **Dist. in the US by:** China Publications Service, PO Box 49614, Chicago, IL 60649. TEL 312-288-3291, FAX 312-288-8570; **Dist. outside of China by:** China International Book Trading Corp, 35 Chegongzhuang Xilu, Haidian District, PO Box 399, Beijing 100044, China. TEL 86-10-68412045, FAX 86-10-68412023, cibtc@mail.cibtc.com.cn, http://www.cibtc.com.cn/.

351 CHN ISSN 1674-2486
JQ1501.A1
GONGGONG XINGZHENG PINGLUN/JOURNAL OF PUBLIC ADMINISTRATION. Text in Chinese. 2008. bi-m. CNY 60; CNY 10 per issue (effective 2009). **Document type:** *Journal, Academic/Scholarly.*
Related titles: Online - full text ed.
Published by: Zhongshan Daxue Xingzheng Guangli Yanjiu Zhongxin/Center for Public Administration Research of Sun Yatsen University, 135, Xingangxi Rd., Guangzhou, 510275, China. TEL 86-20-84038746, FAX 86-20-84038746, http://cpac.zsu.edu.cn/.

GONGSHANG XINGZHENG GUANLI/ADMINISTRATION FOR INDUSTY AND COMMERCE. see BUSINESS AND ECONOMICS

354.71 CAN ISSN 0706-2869
GOUVERNEMENT DU QUEBEC. MINISTERE DES FINANCES. COMPTES PUBLICS. Text in French. 1942. a. **Document type:** *Journal, Trade.*
Supersedes in part (in 1977): Comptes Publics de la Province de Quebec (0382-3091)
—CCC.
Published by: Gouvernement du Quebec. Ministere des Finances, 12, rue Saint-Louis, Quebec, PQ G1R 5L3, Canada. TEL 418-528-9323, FAX 418-646-1631, info@finances.gouv.qc.ca, http://www.finances.gouv.qc.ca.

GOVERNANCE; an international journal of policy, administration, and institutions. see POLITICAL SCIENCE

351 CAN ISSN 1916-5714
GOVERNANCE AND RECORDKEEPING AROUND THE WORLD. Text in English. 2007. m. free (effective 2011). **Document type:** *Newsletter, Government.* **Description:** Explores and highlights issues pertaining to government and recordkeeping practices in the public and private sector.
Media: Online - full text.
Published by: Library and Archives Canada, 395 Wellington St, Ottawa, ON K1A 0N4, Canada. TEL 613-996-5115, 866-578-7777, FAX 613-995-6274, http://www.collectionscanada.gc.ca/index-e.html.

▼ **THE GOVERNANCE MENTOR.** see BUSINESS AND ECONOMICS

GOVERNMENT ACCOUNTING AND AUDITING DISCLOSURE MANUAL. see BUILDING AND CONSTRUCTION—Carpentry And Woodwork

351 USA ISSN 1048-1389
GOVERNMENT ACCOUNTING & AUDITING UPDATE. Text in English. 1990. m. USD 355 (effective 2008). **Document type:** *Newsletter, Trade.* **Description:** Contains current analysis of the latest government accounting and auditing requirements, clear explanations of how they affect your work, and practical guidance on how to adapt to these changes and prepare for those that will come later.
Related titles: Online - full text ed.: USD 300 (effective 2008).
—CCC.
Published by: R I A (Subsidiary of: Thomson Reuters Corp.), PO Box 6159, Carol Stream, IL 60197. TEL 800-323-8724, ria.customerservices@thomson.com, http://ria.thomsonreuters.com. Ed. Raj Rangavajan.

GOVERNMENT ACCOUNTING AND FINANCIAL REPORTING MANUAL. see BUSINESS AND ECONOMICS—Accounting

351.092 USA ISSN 1078-9812
JK1118
GOVERNMENT AFFAIRS YELLOW BOOK; who's who in government affairs. Text in English. 1995. s-a. USD 355 (effective 2008). illus. **Document type:** *Directory, Trade.* **Description:** Provides names, titles, addresses, emails, direct-dial phone numbers, fax numbers, career histories and additional information for over 26,000 government affairs professionals.
Related titles: CD-ROM ed.; Online - full text ed.
—CCC.
Published by: Leadership Directories, Inc, 104 Fifth Ave, 2nd Fl, New York, NY 10011. TEL 212-627-4140, FAX 212-645-0931, info@leadershipdirectories.com. Ed. Catherine Shih.

GOVERNMENT AND OPPOSITION; an international journal of comparative politics. see POLITICAL SCIENCE

351 GBR ISSN 1470-0735
GOVERNMENT BUSINESS. Abbreviated title: G B. Text in English. 1995. m. adv. back issues avail. **Document type:** *Magazine, Trade.* **Description:** Contains need-to-know features, news and case studies that explain the commercial issues affecting local and central government operation and procurement.
Formerly (until 2000): Finance & Administration (1356-2541)
Related titles: Online - full text ed.: free (effective 2009).
Published by: Public Sector Publishing Ltd., 226 High Rd, Loughton, Essex IG10 1ET, United Kingdom. TEL 44-20-85320055, FAX 44-20-85320066, info@psp-media.co.uk, http://www.psp-media.co.uk. Ed. Sofie Lidefjard TEL 44-20-85325707. Pub. John O'Leary TEL 44-20-85325731. Adv. contact David Morgan TEL 44-20-85012397. page GBP 2,495.

352.53 USA
GOVERNMENT CONTRACTS; law, administration and procedure. Text in English. 1962. 17 base vols. plus q. updates. looseleaf. USD 1,918 base vol(s). (effective 2008). **Document type:** *Handbook/Manual/Guide, Trade.* **Description:** Features extensive coverage of the law and regulation of the business of government contracting or federal acquisition. Government Contracts: Law, Administration and Procedure addresses nearly every aspect of government contract law and practice, with references to the history and policies underlying current principles as well as current references to applicable statutes, regulations and case decisions. More than a mere "case finder" or primary source compilation, this treatise provides a thorough discussion from experienced practitioners that places case law and regulations in the context most useful to attorneys, contract administrators and other professionals.
Related titles: CD-ROM ed.: USD 1,166 (effective 2002).
Published by: Matthew Bender & Co., Inc. (Subsidiary of: LexisNexis North America), 1275 Broadway, Albany, NY 12204. TEL 518-487-3000, 800-424-4200, FAX 518-487-3083, international@bender.com, http://bender.lexisnexis.com. Ed. Thomas Toubey.

351 USA ISSN 0072-5153
GOVERNMENT CONTRACTS MONOGRAPHS. Text in English. 1961. irreg., latest vol.13, 1980. price varies. **Document type:** *Monographic series.*
Published by: George Washington University, Government Contracts Program, 2100 Pennsylvania Ave, N W, Ste 250, Washington, DC 20052. TEL 202-223-2772, FAX 202-223-1387.

GOVERNMENT CONTRACTS REPORTER (ONLINE). see LAW

GOVERNMENT EMPLOYEE RELATIONS REPORT. see BUSINESS AND ECONOMICS—Labor And Industrial Relations

351 USA ISSN 0017-2626
JK1 CODEN: GVEXAW
GOVERNMENT EXECUTIVE. Text in English. 1969. m. USD 58 to individuals; free to qualified personnel (effective 2010). adv. bk.rev. charts; illus. index. back issues avail.; reprints avail. **Document type:** *Magazine, Trade.* **Description:** Covers the business of the federal government, including news and trends at the executive level, technology, management, and innovations.
Incorporates (1994-2001): Federal Technology Source; (2000-2002): Procurement Preview; Which was formerly (until 2000): The Top 200 Federal Contractors
Related titles: Microform ed.: (from PQC); Online - full text ed.: ISSN 2152-6702.
Indexed: A09, A10, A12, A13, A17, A22, A26, ABIn, ABS&EES, AUNI, AgeL, B01, B02, B06, B07, B08, B09, B15, B17, B18, BPIA, BusI, G04, G05, G06, G07, G08, I05, M02, M05, M07, P02, P10, P34, P47, P48, P51, P53, P54, PAIS, PQC, PersLit, RASB, T&II, T02, V03, V04.
—BLDSC (4204.100000), Infotrieve, Ingenta. **CCC.**
Published by: National Journal Group, Inc., The Watergate 600 New Hampshire Ave, NW, Washington, DC 20037. TEL 202-266-7000, FAX 202-739-8511, subscriptions@nationaljournal.com, http://www.nationaljournal.com. Ed. Amelia Gruber.

351 TZA
GOVERNMENT GAZETTE. Text in English. 1964. w. **Document type:** *Government.* **Description:** Contains official announcements.
Address: PO Box 261, Zanzibar, Tanzania.

351.6982 MUS
GOVERNMENT GAZETTE OF MAURITIUS. Text in English. irreg., latest vol.34, 1981. index.
Published by: Government Printing Office, Elizabeth II Ave, Port Louis, Mauritius.

351.6982 MUS
GOVERNMENT GAZETTE OF MAURITIUS. LEGAL SUPPLEMENT. ACT. Text in English. irreg., latest vol.2, 1981.
Published by: Government Printing Office, Elizabeth II Ave, Port Louis, Mauritius.

351.6982 MUS
GOVERNMENT GAZETTE OF MAURITIUS. LEGAL SUPPLEMENT. GOVERNMENT NOTICE. Text in English. irreg.
Published by: Government Printing Office, Elizabeth II Ave, Port Louis, Mauritius.

351.6982 MUS
GOVERNMENT GAZETTE OF MAURITIUS. LEGAL SUPPLEMENT. PROCLAMATION. Text in English. irreg., latest vol.3, 1981.
Published by: Government Printing Office, Elizabeth II Ave, Port Louis, Mauritius.

351.6982 MUS
GOVERNMENT GAZETTE OF MAURITIUS. SPECIAL LEGAL SUPPLEMENT. A BILL. Text in English. irreg., latest vol.7, 1981.
Published by: Government Printing Office, Elizabeth II Ave, Port Louis, Mauritius.

351.410285 GBR ISSN 1464-3235
GOVERNMENT I T. (Information Technology) Text in English. 1997. q. free to qualified personnel (effective 2009). adv. **Document type:** *Magazine, Trade.* **Description:** Examines information and communication technology at local and central government level.
Related titles: Online - full text ed.
—CCC.
Published by: GovNet Communications, St. James Bldg, Oxford St, Manchester, M1 6PP, United Kingdom. TEL 44-161-2113000, FAX 44-161-2113008, website@govnet.co.uk. Ed. Felicity King-Evans TEL 44-161-2113452. Adv. contact Sharon Randhawa.

354.8 USA ISSN 0072-517X
HJ389.5
GOVERNMENT IN HAWAII; a handbook of financial statistics. Text in English. 1954. a. USD 15 (effective 2000).
Published by: Tax Foundation of Hawaii, 126 Queen St, Ste 304, Honolulu, HI 96813-4415. Ed. Lowell L Kalapa. Circ: 3,500.

351 USA
GOVERNMENT INFORMATION INSIDER. Text in English. m.
Published by: O M B Watch, 1742 Connecticut Ave, N W, Washington, DC 20009.

351 GBR ISSN 0740-624X
Z688.G6 CODEN: GIQUEO
➤ **GOVERNMENT INFORMATION QUARTERLY**; an international journal of information technology management, policies, and practices. Text in English. 1982. 4/yr. EUR 574 in Europe to institutions; JPY 75,900 in Japan to institutions; USD 639 elsewhere to institutions (effective 2012). adv. bk.rev. illus. back issues avail.; reprint service avail. from PSC. **Document type:** *Journal, Academic/Scholarly.* **Description:** Covers information and telecommunications policy, information management, information technology planning and management, and e-government practices, policies and issues relevant to all levels of government within the United States and abroad.
Incorporates (1994-2004): Journal of Government Information (1352-0237); Which was formerly (until vol.21, 1994): Government Publications Review (0277-9390); Which was formed by the merger of (1980-1981): Government Publications Review. Part A: Research Articles (0196-335X); (1980-1981): Government Publications Review. Part B: Acquisitions Guide to Significant Government Publications at All Levels (0196-3368); Both of which superseded in part (in 1980): Government Publications Review (0093-061X)
Related titles: Microform ed.: (from PQC); Online - full text ed.: ISSN 1872-9517 (from IngentaConnect, ScienceDirect).
Indexed: A20, A22, A26, ASCA, B01, B04, B06, B07, B08, B09, BRD, C10, C12, CA, CommAb, CurCont, E03, ERIC, H01, I02, I05, I13, ISTA, Inspec, L03, L04, L07, L08, L13, LIMI, LISTA, LibLit, M01, M02, M05, P30, P34, P42, PAIS, PSA, R02, S02, S03, SCOPUS, SSCI, SociolAb, T02, W03, W05, W07.
—BLDSC (4204.235000), AskIEEE, IE, Infotrieve, Ingenta, INIST. **CCC.**
Published by: Elsevier Ltd (Subsidiary of: Elsevier Science & Technology), The Blvd, Langford Ln, Kidlington, Oxford, OX5 1GB, United Kingdom. TEL 44-1865-843000, FAX 44-1865-843010, journalscustomerserviceemea@elsevier.com. Ed. John Carlo Bertot TEL 301-314-9145.

351 CAN ISSN 1491-8781
HJ795.A6
GOVERNMENT OF ALBERTA ANNUAL REPORT. Text in English. 1998. a. **Document type:** *Government.*
Formed by the merger of (1996-1998): Government of Alberta. Annual Report (1208-7815); (1996-1998): Measuring Up. Annual Report on the Performance of the Government of Alberta (1482-9673); Which was formerly (until 1995): Measuring up. Annual Report (1204-1920)
Related titles: Print ed.
Published by: Alberta Finance Ministry, Rm 426, Terrace Bldg, 9515 - 107 St., Edmonton, AB T5K 2C3, Canada. TEL 780-427-3035, FAX 780-427-1147.

351 CAN ISSN 1912-8185
P40.5.L362
GOVERNMENT OF SASKATCHEWAN FRENCH-LANGUAGE SERVICES POLICY. ANNUAL REPORT/POLITIQUE DE SERVICES EN LANGUE FRANCAISE DU GOUVERNEMENT DE LA SASKATCHEWAN. Text in English. 2006. a. **Document type:** *Report, Trade.*
Published by: Saskatchewan Government Relations, 1855 Victoria Ave, Regina, SK S4P 3T2, Canada. TEL 306-787-2635, info@gr.gov.sk.ca, http://www.gr.gov.sk.ca/default.htm.

351 CAN ISSN 1719-5187
GOVERNMENT ON-LINE. Text in English. 2003. a., latest 2006. **Document type:** *Government.*
Media: Online - full text. **Related titles:** Print ed.: ISSN 1707-7982; French ed.: ISSN 1719-5195.
Published by: Government of Canada, Service Canada, Ottawa, ON K1A 0J9, Canada. TEL 800-635-7943, canadasite@canada.gc.ca, http://www.canada.gc.ca, http://publications.gc.ca.

352.53 GBR
GOVERNMENT OPPORTUNITIES. Abbreviated title: G O. Text in English. 1993. m. GBP 50.40 to qualified personnel; GBP 4.20 per issue (effective 2009). adv. back issues avail. **Document type:** *Magazine, Trade.* **Description:** Provides information on government service contracts for a large range of activities.
Formerly (until 1995): Market Testing Bulletin (1357-1001)
Related titles: Diskette ed.; Online - full text ed.: free (effective 2009).
—BLDSC (4204.343000). **CCC.**
Published by: B I P Solutions Ltd, Medius, 60 Pacific Quay, Glasgow, G51 1DZ, United Kingdom. TEL 44-141-3328247, FAX 44-141-3312652, bip@bipsolutions.com, http://www.bipsolutions.com. Adv. contact Jenny Coombes. page GBP 1,500; trim 210 x 297. Circ: 8,287 (controlled).

351.025 USA ISSN 1091-9643
JK6
GOVERNMENT PHONE BOOK U S A. Text in English. 1992. a., latest 16th ed. USD 285 (effective 2008). **Document type:** *Directory, Trade.* **Description:** Directory listings of more than 257,000 government offices. Entries include direct telephone numbers and complete mailing addresses. Fax numbers and e-mail and web site addresses are provided as available.
Formerly (until 1997): The Government Directory of Addresses and Telephone Numbers (1062-1466)
Published by: (Carroll Publishing), Omnigraphics, Inc., PO Box 31-1640, Detroit, MI 48231. TEL 313-961-1340, 800-234-1340, FAX 313-961-1383, 800-875-1340, info@omnigraphics.com, http://www.omnigraphics.com. Pub. Frederick G Ruffner Jr.

352.53 USA ISSN 1078-0769
JK1673
GOVERNMENT PROCUREMENT. Text in English. 1993. bi-m. USD 33 domestic; USD 42 in Canada; USD 50 elsewhere; free domestic to qualified personnel (effective 2011). **Document type:** *Magazine, Trade.* **Description:** Provides of ideas, information and experience pertinent to US and Canadian government purchasing professionals involved with the standards and ethics of the government purchasing department.
Related titles: Online - full text ed.: ISSN 1931-6712.
Indexed: A12, A26, ABIn, B01, B06, B07, B08, B09, C12, E08, G06, G07, G08, H01, I02, I05, M01, M02, M05, M06, P34, P53, P54, PQC, R02, S09, T02.
—CCC.

P

Published by: Penton Media, Inc., 1300 E 9th St, Cleveland, OH 44114. TEL 216-696-7000, FAX 216-696-3432, information@penton.com, http://www.penton.com. Circ: 20,000 (paid and controlled).

351 USA ISSN 0017-2642
GOVERNMENT PRODUCT NEWS. Text in English. 1962. 13/yr. USD 59 domestic; USD 67 in Canada; USD 84 foreign; free domestic to qualified personnel (effective 2011). adv. tr.lit. reprints avail. **Document type:** *Magazine, Trade.* **Description:** Contains news, ideas, applications and literature of products and services utilized in government functions.
Former titles: Government Product News and Purchasing Digest; Government Purchasing Digest (0017-2650)
Related titles: Microform ed.: (from PQC); Online - full text ed.
Indexed: A09, A10, A15, A22, ABIn, B01, B02, B06, B07, B08, B09, B15, B17, B18, G04, G06, G07, G08, I05, M01, M02, M05, PQC, S22, T&II, T02, V03, V04.
—CCC.
Published by: Penton Media, Inc., 1300 E 9th St, Cleveland, OH 44114. TEL 216-696-7000, FAX 216-696-3432, information@penton.com, http://www.penton.com. adv.: B&W page USD 13,500, color page USD 15,200; trim 15 x 10.5. Circ: 85,000 (controlled).

GOVERNMENT PURCHASING GUIDE. *see* BUSINESS AND ECONOMICS—Marketing And Purchasing

GOVERNMENT RELATIONS (ONLINE). *see* BUSINESS AND ECONOMICS—Management

GOVERNMENT STANDARD. *see* LABOR UNIONS

351 004 GBR ISSN 1747-5805
GOVERNMENT TECHNOLOGY; the business magazine for government technology. Abbreviated title: G T. Text in English. 200?. m. free to qualified personnel (effective 2009). adv. back issues avail. **Document type:** *Magazine, Trade.* **Description:** Contains features, news and case studies that explain the administrative and commercial issues affecting IT in Central and Local Government.
Related titles: Online - full text ed.: free (effective 2009).
Published by: Public Sector Publishing Ltd., 226 High Rd, Loughton, Essex IG10 1ET, United Kingdom. TEL 44-20-85320055, FAX 44-20-85320066, info@psp-media.co.uk, http://www.psp-media.co.uk. Ed. Sofie Lidefjard TEL 44-20-85325707. Pub. Jesse Sandh TEL 44-20-85325735. Adv. contact Sally Brockman TEL 44-20-85325732. page GBP 2,495.

351.778 USA ISSN 0148-4664
JK5401
GOVERNMENTAL AFFAIRS NEWSLETTER. Text in English. 1966. 11/yr. USD 15. **Document type:** *Newsletter.* **Description:** Covers Missouri government and politics.
Published by: University of Missouri, Governmental Affairs Program, Professional Bldg, Rm 206, Columbia, MO 65211. TEL 314-882-6401. Ed. Richard Dohm.

GOVERNMENTAL RISK MANAGEMENT MANUAL. *see* BUSINESS AND ECONOMICS—Management

351 USA ISSN 0883-3753
GOVERNMENTS OF ALABAMA. Text in English. 1983. a. USD 150 per issue (effective 2010). stat. **Document type:** *Report, Trade.* **Description:** Covers significant cities, counties, schools and utility districts in state. Analysis Includes up to 651 ratios in tax-based services & employment, fee-based services & education & employment, utility services & employment, high performance evaluation, debt management, early warning indicators, national & state rankings, county area analysis, total funds flow, and general overview.
Published by: Municipal Analysis Services, Inc., PO Box 13453, Austin, TX 78711. TEL 512-327-3328, FAX 413-740-1294, munilysis@hotmail.com, http://sites.google.com/site/gregmichels.

351 USA ISSN 0883-3761
GOVERNMENTS OF ARKANSAS. Text in English. 1983. a. USD 150 per issue (effective 2010). stat. **Document type:** *Report, Trade.* **Description:** Covers significant cities, counties, schools and utility districts in state. Analysis Includes up to 651 ratios in tax-based services & employment, fee-based services & education & employment, utility services & employment, high performance evaluation, debt management, early warning indicators, national & state rankings, county area analysis, total funds flow, and general overview.
Published by: Municipal Analysis Services, Inc., PO Box 13453, Austin, TX 78711. TEL 512-327-3328, FAX 413-740-1294, munilysis@hotmail.com, http://sites.google.com/site/gregmichels.

351 USA ISSN 0883-377X
GOVERNMENTS OF CALIFORNIA. Text in English. 1983. a. USD 150 per issue (effective 2010). stat. **Document type:** *Report, Trade.* **Description:** Covers significant cities, counties, schools and utility districts in state. Analysis Includes up to 651 ratios in tax-based services & employment, fee-based services & education & employment, utility services & employment, high performance evaluation, debt management, early warning indicators, national & state rankings, county area analysis, total funds flow, and general overview.
Published by: Municipal Analysis Services, Inc., PO Box 13453, Austin, TX 78711. TEL 512-327-3328, FAX 413-740-1294, munilysis@hotmail.com, http://sites.google.com/site/gregmichels.

351 USA ISSN 0883-3788
GOVERNMENTS OF COLORADO. Text in English. 1983. a. USD 150 per issue (effective 2010). stat. **Document type:** *Report, Trade.* **Description:** Covers significant cities, counties, schools and utility districts in state. Analysis Includes up to 651 ratios in tax-based services & employment, fee-based services & education & employment, utility services & employment, high performance evaluation, debt management, early warning indicators, national & state rankings, county area analysis, total funds flow, and general overview.
Published by: Municipal Analysis Services, Inc., PO Box 13453, Austin, TX 78711. TEL 512-327-3328, FAX 413-740-1294, munilysis@hotmail.com, http://sites.google.com/site/gregmichels.

351 USA ISSN 0883-3796
GOVERNMENTS OF CONNECTICUT. Text in English. 1983. a. USD 150 per issue (effective 2010). stat. **Document type:** *Report, Trade.* **Description:** Covers significant cities, counties, schools and utility districts in state. Analysis Includes up to 651 ratios in tax-based services & employment, fee-based services & education & employment, utility services & employment, high performance evaluation, debt management, early warning indicators, national & state rankings, county area analysis, total funds flow, and general overview.
Published by: Municipal Analysis Services, Inc., PO Box 13453, Austin, TX 78711. TEL 512-327-3328, FAX 413-740-1294, munilysis@hotmail.com, http://sites.google.com/site/gregmichels.

351 USA ISSN 0883-380X
GOVERNMENTS OF FLORIDA. Text in English. 1983. a. USD 150 per issue (effective 2010). stat. **Document type:** *Report, Trade.* **Description:** Covers significant cities, counties, schools and utility districts in state. Analysis Includes up to 651 ratios in tax-based services & employment, fee-based services & education & employment, utility services & employment, high performance evaluation, debt management, early warning indicators, national & state rankings, county area analysis, total funds flow, and general overview.
Published by: Municipal Analysis Services, Inc., PO Box 13453, Austin, TX 78711. TEL 512-327-3328, FAX 413-740-1294, munilysis@hotmail.com, http://sites.google.com/site/gregmichels.

351 USA ISSN 0883-3818
GOVERNMENTS OF GEORGIA. Text in English. 1983. a. USD 150 per issue (effective 2010). stat. **Document type:** *Report, Trade.* **Description:** Covers significant cities, counties, schools and utility districts in state. Analysis Includes up to 651 ratios in tax-based services & employment, fee-based services & education & employment, utility services & employment, high performance evaluation, debt management, early warning indicators, national & state rankings, county area analysis, total funds flow, and general overview.
Published by: Municipal Analysis Services, Inc., PO Box 13453, Austin, TX 78711. TEL 512-327-3328, FAX 413-740-1294, munilysis@hotmail.com, http://sites.google.com/site/gregmichels.

351 USA ISSN 0883-3826
GOVERNMENTS OF ILLINOIS. Text in English. 1983. a. USD 150 per issue (effective 2010). stat. **Document type:** *Report, Trade.* **Description:** Covers significant cities, counties, schools and utility districts in state. Analysis Includes up to 651 ratios in tax-based services & employment, fee-based services & education & employment, utility services & employment, high performance evaluation, debt management, early warning indicators, national & state rankings, county area analysis, total funds flow, and general overview.
Published by: Municipal Analysis Services, Inc., PO Box 13453, Austin, TX 78711. TEL 512-327-3328, FAX 413-740-1294, munilysis@hotmail.com, http://sites.google.com/site/gregmichels.

351 USA ISSN 0883-3834
GOVERNMENTS OF INDIANA. Text in English. 1983. a. USD 150 per issue (effective 2010). stat. **Document type:** *Report, Trade.* **Description:** Covers significant cities, counties, schools and utility districts in state. Analysis Includes up to 651 ratios in tax-based services & employment, fee-based services & education & employment, utility services & employment, high performance evaluation, debt management, early warning indicators, national & state rankings, county area analysis, total funds flow, and general overview.
Published by: Municipal Analysis Services, Inc., PO Box 13453, Austin, TX 78711. TEL 512-327-3328, FAX 413-740-1294, munilysis@hotmail.com, http://sites.google.com/site/gregmichels.

351 USA ISSN 0883-3842
GOVERNMENTS OF IOWA. Text in English. 1983. a. USD 150 per issue (effective 2010). stat. **Document type:** *Report, Trade.* **Description:** Covers significant cities, counties, schools and utility districts in state. Analysis Includes up to 651 ratios in tax-based services & employment, fee-based services & education & employment, utility services & employment, high performance evaluation, debt management, early warning indicators, national & state rankings, county area analysis, total funds flow, and general overview.
Published by: Municipal Analysis Services, Inc., PO Box 13453, Austin, TX 78711. TEL 512-327-3328, FAX 413-740-1294, munilysis@hotmail.com, http://sites.google.com/site/gregmichels.

351 USA ISSN 0883-3850
GOVERNMENTS OF KANSAS. Text in English. 1983. a. USD 150 per issue (effective 2010). stat. **Document type:** *Report, Trade.* **Description:** Covers significant cities, counties, schools and utility districts in state. Analysis Includes up to 651 ratios in tax-based services & employment, fee-based services & education & employment, utility services & employment, high performance evaluation, debt management, early warning indicators, national & state rankings, county area analysis, total funds flow, and general overview.
Published by: Municipal Analysis Services, Inc., PO Box 13453, Austin, TX 78711. TEL 512-327-3328, FAX 413-740-1294, munilysis@hotmail.com, http://sites.google.com/site/gregmichels.

351 USA ISSN 0883-3869
GOVERNMENTS OF KENTUCKY. Text in English. 1983. a. USD 150 per issue (effective 2010). stat. **Document type:** *Report, Trade.* **Description:** Covers significant cities, counties, schools and utility districts in state. Analysis Includes up to 651 ratios in tax-based services & employment, fee-based services & education & employment, utility services & employment, high performance evaluation, debt management, early warning indicators, national & state rankings, county area analysis, total funds flow, and general overview.
Published by: Municipal Analysis Services, Inc., PO Box 13453, Austin, TX 78711. TEL 512-327-3328, FAX 413-740-1294, munilysis@hotmail.com, http://sites.google.com/site/gregmichels.

351 USA ISSN 0883-3877
JS451.L8
GOVERNMENTS OF LOUISIANA. Text in English. 1983. a. USD 150 per issue (effective 2010). stat. **Document type:** *Report, Trade.* **Description:** Covers significant cities, counties, schools and utility districts in state. Analysis Includes up to 651 ratios in tax-based services & employment, fee-based services & education & employment, utility services & employment, high performance evaluation, debt management, early warning indicators, national & state rankings, county area analysis, total funds flow, and general overview.
Published by: Municipal Analysis Services, Inc., PO Box 13453, Austin, TX 78711. TEL 512-327-3328, FAX 413-740-1294, munilysis@hotmail.com, http://sites.google.com/site/gregmichels.

351 USA ISSN 0883-3885
GOVERNMENTS OF MAINE. Text in English. 1983. a. USD 150 per issue (effective 2010). stat. **Document type:** *Report, Trade.* **Description:** Covers significant cities, counties, schools and utility districts in state. Analysis Includes up to 651 ratios in tax-based services & employment, fee-based services & education & employment, utility services & employment, high performance evaluation, debt management, early warning indicators, national & state rankings, county area analysis, total funds flow, and general overview.
Published by: Municipal Analysis Services, Inc., PO Box 13453, Austin, TX 78711. TEL 512-327-3328, FAX 413-740-1294, munilysis@hotmail.com, http://sites.google.com/site/gregmichels.

351 USA ISSN 0883-3893
GOVERNMENTS OF MASSACHUSETTS. Text in English. 1983. a. USD 150 per issue (effective 2010). stat. **Document type:** *Report, Trade.* **Description:** Covers significant cities, counties, schools and utility districts in state. Analysis Includes up to 651 ratios in tax-based services & employment, fee-based services & education & employment, utility services & employment, high performance evaluation, debt management, early warning indicators, national & state rankings, county area analysis, total funds flow, and general overview.
Published by: Municipal Analysis Services, Inc., PO Box 13453, Austin, TX 78711. TEL 512-327-3328, FAX 413-740-1294, munilysis@hotmail.com, http://sites.google.com/site/gregmichels.

351 USA ISSN 0883-3907
GOVERNMENTS OF MICHIGAN. Text in English. 1983. a. USD 150 per issue (effective 2010). stat. **Document type:** *Report, Trade.* **Description:** Covers significant cities, counties, schools and utility districts in state. Analysis Includes up to 651 ratios in tax-based services & employment, fee-based services & education & employment, utility services & employment, high performance evaluation, debt management, early warning indicators, national & state rankings, county area analysis, total funds flow, and general overview.
Published by: Municipal Analysis Services, Inc., PO Box 13453, Austin, TX 78711. TEL 512-327-3328, FAX 413-740-1294, munilysis@hotmail.com, http://sites.google.com/site/gregmichels.

351 USA ISSN 0883-3915
GOVERNMENTS OF MINNESOTA. Text in English. 1983. a. USD 150 per issue (effective 2010). stat. **Document type:** *Report, Trade.* **Description:** Covers significant cities, counties, schools and utility districts in state. Analysis Includes up to 651 ratios in tax-based services & employment, fee-based services & education & employment, utility services & employment, high performance evaluation, debt management, early warning indicators, national & state rankings, county area analysis, total funds flow, and general overview.
Published by: Municipal Analysis Services, Inc., PO Box 13453, Austin, TX 78711. TEL 512-327-3328, FAX 413-740-1294, munilysis@hotmail.com, http://sites.google.com/site/gregmichels.

351 USA ISSN 0883-3923
GOVERNMENTS OF MISSISSIPPI. Text in English. 1983. a. USD 150 per issue (effective 2010). stat. **Document type:** *Report, Trade.* **Description:** Covers significant cities, counties, schools and utility districts in state. Analysis Includes up to 651 ratios in tax-based services & employment, fee-based services & education & employment, utility services & employment, high performance evaluation, debt management, early warning indicators, national & state rankings, county area analysis, total funds flow, and general overview.
Published by: Municipal Analysis Services, Inc., PO Box 13453, Austin, TX 78711. TEL 512-327-3328, FAX 413-740-1294, munilysis@hotmail.com, http://sites.google.com/site/gregmichels.

351 USA ISSN 0883-3931
GOVERNMENTS OF MISSOURI. Text in English. 1983. a. USD 150 per issue (effective 2010). stat. **Document type:** *Report, Trade.* **Description:** Covers significant cities, counties, schools and utility districts in state. Analysis Includes up to 651 ratios in tax-based services & employment, fee-based services & education & employment, utility services & employment, high performance evaluation, debt management, early warning indicators, national & state rankings, county area analysis, total funds flow, and general overview.
Published by: Municipal Analysis Services, Inc., PO Box 13453, Austin, TX 78711. TEL 512-327-3328, FAX 413-740-1294, munilysis@hotmail.com, http://sites.google.com/site/gregmichels.

351 USA ISSN 0883-394X
GOVERNMENTS OF NEBRASKA. Text in English. 1983. a. USD 150 per issue (effective 2010). stat. **Document type:** *Report, Trade.* **Description:** Covers significant cities, counties, schools and utility districts in state. Analysis Includes up to 651 ratios in tax-based services & employment, fee-based services & education & employment, utility services & employment, high performance evaluation, debt management, early warning indicators, national & state rankings, county area analysis, total funds flow, and general overview.
Published by: Municipal Analysis Services, Inc., PO Box 13453, Austin, TX 78711. TEL 512-327-3328, FAX 413-740-1294, munilysis@hotmail.com, http://sites.google.com/site/gregmichels.

350 USA ISSN 0883-3958
GOVERNMENTS OF NEW JERSEY. Text in English. 1983. a. USD 150 per issue (effective 2010). stat. **Document type:** *Report, Trade.* **Description:** Covers significant cities, counties, schools and utility districts in state. Analysis Includes up to 651 ratios in tax-based services & employment, fee-based services & education & employment, utility services & employment, high performance evaluation, debt management, early warning indicators, national & state rankings, county area analysis, total funds flow, and general overview.
Published by: Municipal Analysis Services, Inc., PO Box 13453, Austin, TX 78711. TEL 512-327-3328, FAX 413-740-1294, munilysis@hotmail.com, http://sites.google.com/site/gregmichels.

351 USA ISSN 0883-3966
GOVERNMENTS OF NEW YORK. Text in English. 1983. a. USD 150 per issue (effective 2010). stat. **Document type:** *Report, Trade.* **Description:** Covers significant cities, counties, schools and utility districts in state. Analysis Includes up to 651 ratios in tax-based services & employment, fee-based services & education & employment, utility services & employment, high performance evaluation, debt management, early warning indicators, national & state rankings, county area analysis, total funds flow, and general overview.
Published by: Municipal Analysis Services, Inc., PO Box 13453, Austin, TX 78711. TEL 512-327-3328, FAX 413-740-1294, munilysis@hotmail.com, http://sites.google.com/site/gregmichels.

351 USA ISSN 0883-3974
GOVERNMENTS OF NORTH DAKOTA. Text in English. 1983. a. USD 150 per issue (effective 2010). stat. **Document type:** *Report, Trade.* **Description:** Covers significant cities, counties, schools and utility districts in state. Analysis Includes up to 651 ratios in tax-based services & employment, fee-based services & education & employment, utility services & employment, high performance evaluation, debt management, early warning indicators, national & state rankings, county area analysis, total funds flow, and general overview.
Published by: Municipal Analysis Services, Inc., PO Box 13453, Austin, TX 78711. TEL 512-327-3328, FAX 413-740-1294, munilysis@hotmail.com, http://sites.google.com/site/gregmichels.

351 USA ISSN 0883-3982
GOVERNMENTS OF OHIO. Text in English. 1983. a. USD 150 per issue (effective 2010). stat. **Document type:** *Report, Trade.* **Description:** Covers significant cities, counties, schools and utility districts in state. Analysis Includes up to 651 ratios in tax-based services & employment, fee-based services & education & employment, utility services & employment, high performance evaluation, debt management, early warning indicators, national & state rankings, county area analysis, total funds flow, and general overview.
Published by: Municipal Analysis Services, Inc., PO Box 13453, Austin, TX 78711. TEL 512-327-3328, FAX 413-740-1294, munilysis@hotmail.com, http://sites.google.com/site/gregmichels.

351 USA ISSN 0883-3990
GOVERNMENTS OF OKLAHOMA. Text in English. 1983. a. USD 150 per issue (effective 2010). stat. **Document type:** *Report, Trade.* **Description:** Covers significant cities, counties, schools and utility districts in state. Analysis Includes up to 651 ratios in tax-based services & employment, fee-based services & education & employment, utility services & employment, high performance evaluation, debt management, early warning indicators, national & state rankings, county area analysis, total funds flow, and general overview.
Published by: Municipal Analysis Services, Inc., PO Box 13453, Austin, TX 78711. TEL 512-327-3328, FAX 413-740-1294, munilysis@hotmail.com, http://sites.google.com/site/gregmichels.

351 USA ISSN 0883-4008
GOVERNMENTS OF PENNSYLVANIA. Text in English. 1983. a. USD 150 per issue (effective 2010). stat. **Document type:** *Report, Trade.* **Description:** Covers significant cities, counties, schools and utility districts in state. Analysis Includes up to 651 ratios in tax-based services & employment, fee-based services & education & employment, utility services & employment, high performance evaluation, debt management, early warning indicators, national & state rankings, county area analysis, total funds flow, and general overview.
Published by: Municipal Analysis Services, Inc., PO Box 13453, Austin, TX 78711. TEL 512-327-3328, FAX 413-740-1294, munilysis@hotmail.com, http://sites.google.com/site/gregmichels.

351 USA ISSN 0883-4016
JS451.S8
GOVERNMENTS OF SOUTH DAKOTA. Text in English. 1983. a. USD 150 per issue (effective 2010). stat. **Document type:** *Report, Trade.* **Description:** Covers significant cities, counties, schools and utility districts in state. Analysis Includes up to 651 ratios in tax-based services & employment, fee-based services & education & employment, utility services & employment, high performance evaluation, debt management, early warning indicators, national & state rankings, county area analysis, total funds flow, and general overview.
Published by: Municipal Analysis Services, Inc., PO Box 13453, Austin, TX 78711. TEL 512-327-3328, FAX 413-740-1294, munilysis@hotmail.com, http://sites.google.com/site/gregmichels.

351 USA ISSN 0883-4024
HJ9317
GOVERNMENTS OF TENNESSEE. Text in English. 1983. a. USD 150 per issue (effective 2010). stat. **Document type:** *Report, Trade.* **Description:** Covers significant cities, counties, schools and utility districts in state. Analysis Includes up to 651 ratios in tax-based services & employment, fee-based services & education & employment, utility services & employment, high performance evaluation, debt management, early warning indicators, national & state rankings, county area analysis, total funds flow, and general overview.
Published by: Municipal Analysis Services, Inc., PO Box 13453, Austin, TX 78711. TEL 512-327-3328, FAX 413-740-1294, munilysis@hotmail.com, http://sites.google.com/site/gregmichels.

351 USA ISSN 0883-4032
HJ9011.T4
GOVERNMENTS OF TEXAS. Text in English. 1983. a. USD 150 per issue (effective 2010). stat. **Document type:** *Report, Trade.* **Description:** Covers significant cities, counties, schools and utility districts in state. Analysis Includes up to 651 ratios in tax-based services & employment, fee-based services & education & employment, utility services & employment, high performance evaluation, debt management, early warning indicators, national & state rankings, county area analysis, total funds flow, and general overview.
Published by: Municipal Analysis Services, Inc., PO Box 13453, Austin, TX 78711. TEL 512-327-3328, FAX 413-740-1294, munilysis@hotmail.com, http://sites.google.com/site/gregmichels.

351 USA ISSN 0883-4091
GOVERNMENTS OF THE CAROLINAS. Text in English. 1983. a. USD 150 per issue (effective 2010). stat. **Document type:** *Report, Trade.* **Description:** Covers significant cities, counties, schools and utility districts in state. Analysis Includes up to 651 ratios in tax-based services & employment, fee-based services & education & employment, utility services & employment, high performance evaluation, debt management, early warning indicators, national & state rankings, county area analysis, total funds flow, and general overview.
Published by: Municipal Analysis Services, Inc., PO Box 13453, Austin, TX 78711. TEL 512-327-3328, FAX 413-740-1294, munilysis@hotmail.com, http://sites.google.com/site/gregmichels.

351 USA ISSN 0883-4121
GOVERNMENTS OF THE NORTHEAST. Text in English. 1983. a. USD 150 per issue (effective 2010). stat. **Document type:** *Report, Trade.* **Description:** Covers significant cities, counties, schools and utility districts in state. Analysis Includes up to 651 ratios in tax-based services & employment, fee-based services & education & employment, utility services & employment, high performance evaluation, debt management, early warning indicators, national & state rankings, county area analysis, total funds flow, and general overview.
Published by: Municipal Analysis Services, Inc., PO Box 13453, Austin, TX 78711. TEL 512-327-3328, FAX 413-740-1294, munilysis@hotmail.com, http://sites.google.com/site/gregmichels.

351 USA ISSN 0883-4105
GOVERNMENTS OF THE NORTHWEST. Text in English. 1983. a. USD 150 per issue (effective 2010). stat. **Document type:** *Report, Trade.* **Description:** Covers significant cities, counties, schools and utility districts in state. Analysis Includes up to 651 ratios in tax-based services & employment, fee-based services & education & employment, utility services & employment, high performance evaluation, debt management, early warning indicators, national & state rankings, county area analysis, total funds flow, and general overview.
Published by: Municipal Analysis Services, Inc., PO Box 13453, Austin, TX 78711. TEL 512-327-3328, FAX 413-740-1294, munilysis@hotmail.com, http://sites.google.com/site/gregmichels.

351 USA ISSN 0883-4113
GOVERNMENTS OF THE WEST. Text in English. 1983. a. USD 150 per issue (effective 2010). stat. **Document type:** *Report, Trade.* **Description:** Covers significant cities, counties, schools and utility districts in state. Analysis Includes up to 651 ratios in tax-based services & employment, fee-based services & education & employment, utility services & employment, high performance evaluation, debt management, early warning indicators, national & state rankings, county area analysis, total funds flow, and general overview.
Published by: Municipal Analysis Services, Inc., PO Box 13453, Austin, TX 78711. TEL 512-327-3328, FAX 413-740-1294, munilysis@hotmail.com, http://sites.google.com/site/gregmichels.

351 USA ISSN 0883-4040
GOVERNMENTS OF VERMONT. Text in English. 1983. a. USD 150 per issue (effective 2010). stat. **Document type:** *Report, Trade.* **Description:** Covers significant cities, counties, schools and utility districts in state. Analysis Includes up to 651 ratios in tax-based services & employment, fee-based services & education & employment, utility services & employment, high performance evaluation, debt management, early warning indicators, national & state rankings, county area analysis, total funds flow, and general overview.
Published by: Municipal Analysis Services, Inc., PO Box 13453, Austin, TX 78711. TEL 512-327-3328, FAX 413-740-1294, munilysis@hotmail.com, http://sites.google.com/site/gregmichels.

351 USA ISSN 0883-4059
GOVERNMENTS OF VIRGINIA. Text in English. 1983. a. USD 150 per issue (effective 2010). stat. **Document type:** *Report, Trade.* **Description:** Covers significant cities, counties, schools and utility districts in state. Analysis Includes up to 651 ratios in tax-based services & employment, fee-based services & education & employment, utility services & employment, high performance evaluation, debt management, early warning indicators, national & state rankings, county area analysis, total funds flow, and general overview.
Published by: Municipal Analysis Services, Inc., PO Box 13453, Austin, TX 78711. TEL 512-327-3328, FAX 413-740-1294, munilysis@hotmail.com, http://sites.google.com/site/gregmichels.

351 USA ISSN 0883-4067
GOVERNMENTS OF WASHINGTON. Text in English. 1983. a. USD 150 per issue (effective 2010). stat. **Document type:** *Report, Trade.* **Description:** Covers significant cities, counties, schools and utility districts in state. Analysis Includes up to 651 ratios in tax-based services & employment, fee-based services & education & employment, utility services & employment, high performance evaluation, debt management, early warning indicators, national & state rankings, county area analysis, total funds flow, and general overview.
Published by: Municipal Analysis Services, Inc., PO Box 13453, Austin, TX 78711. TEL 512-327-3328, FAX 413-740-1294, munilysis@hotmail.com, http://sites.google.com/site/gregmichels.

351 USA ISSN 0883-4075
GOVERNMENTS OF WEST VIRGINIA. Text in English. 1983. a. USD 150 per issue (effective 2010). stat. **Document type:** *Report, Trade.* **Description:** Covers significant cities, counties, schools and utility districts in state. Analysis Includes up to 651 ratios in tax-based services & employment, fee-based services & education & employment, utility services & employment, high performance evaluation, debt management, early warning indicators, national & state rankings, county area analysis, total funds flow, and general overview.
Published by: Municipal Analysis Services, Inc., PO Box 13453, Austin, TX 78711. TEL 512-327-3328, FAX 413-740-1294, munilysis@hotmail.com, http://sites.google.com/site/gregmichels.

351 USA ISSN 0883-4083
HJ9011.W6
GOVERNMENTS OF WISCONSIN. Text in English. 1983. a. USD 150 per issue (effective 2010). stat. **Document type:** *Journal, Academic/Scholarly.* **Description:** Covers significant cities, counties, schools and utility districts in state. Analysis Includes up to 651 ratios in tax-based services & employment, fee-based services & education & employment, utility services & employment, high performance evaluation, debt management, early warning indicators, national & state rankings, county area analysis, total funds flow, and general overview.
Published by: Municipal Analysis Services, Inc., PO Box 13453, Austin, TX 78711. TEL 512-327-3328, FAX 413-740-1294, munilysis@hotmail.com, http://sites.google.com/site/gregmichels.

307.336 FRA ISSN 1774-5357
LE GRAND SAINT-BARTHELEMY. Text in French. 2005. s-a. **Document type:** *Journal, Trade.*
Published by: Association Act Emploi, 26 rue Raphael, Marseille, 13008, France.

352.73 USA
GRANTS POLICY DIRECTIVES. Text in English. 1992. base vol. plus irreg. updates. looseleaf. USD 219 includes Grants Administration Manual (effective 2001). **Document type:** *Government.* **Description:** Comprised of individual directives outlining key policies pertinent to administering discretionary and mandatory grant programs funded by the HHS. Issued as an instrument of internal department management to provide guidance on grants management issues. As directives are issued, chapters in the Grants Administration Manual will be superseded.
Supersedes in part (in 1992): U.S. Department of Health and Human Services. Grants Administration Manual
Related titles: Online - full text ed.: 1992; ◆ Supplement(s): U.S. Department of Health and Human Services. Grants Administration Manual.
Published by: U.S. Department of Health and Human Services, Office of Grants Management, 200 Independence Avenue, S.W., Washington, DC 20201. TEL 202-690-6377, FAX 202-690-6902, gnet@os.dhhs.gov. **Subscr. to:** U.S. Government Printing Office, Superintendent of Documents, PO Box 371954, Pittsburgh, PA 15250. TEL 202-512-1800, FAX 202-512-2250, orders@gpo.gov, http://www.access.gpo.gov.

351.1 GBR
GREAT BRITAIN. DEPARTMENT FOR ENVIRONMENT, FOOD & RURAL AFFAIRS. DEPARTMENTAL REPORTS. Text in English. irreg. GBP 34.55 per issue (effective 2010). back issues avail. **Document type:** *Government.* **Description:** Contains reports to parliament, including a foreword from Department Secretary and an executive summary from Permanent Secretary, highlighting key successes over the past year, new strategies, and report on the progress against strategic objectives.
Published by: (Great Britain. Department for Environment, Food & Rural Affairs), The Stationery Office, St Crispins, Duke St, Norwich, NR3 1PD, United Kingdom. TEL 44-1603-622211, FAX 44-870-6005533, customer.services@tso.co.uk, http://www.tso.co.uk. **Subscr. to:** PO Box 29, Norwich NR3 1GN, United Kingdom. TEL 44-870-6005522.

354.3 GBR
GREAT BRITAIN. DEPARTMENT OF THE ENVIRONMENT. PLANNING INSPECTORATE. EXECUTIVE AGENCY. BUSINESS AND CORPORATE PLAN. Text in English. a. **Document type:** *Government.*
Formed by the 1995 merger of: Great Britain. Department of the Environment. Planning Inspectorate. Executive Agency. Corporate Plan; Great Britain. Department of the Environment. Planning Inspectorate. Executive Agency. Business Plan
Published by: Department of the Environment, Planning Inspectorate, Tollgate House, Houlton St, Bristol, Avon BS2 9DJ, United Kingdom. TEL 44-117-9878927. **Co-sponsor:** Welsh Office. Planning Inspectorate.

GREAT BRITAIN. DEPARTMENT OF TRANSPORT. ANNUAL REPORT. *see* ENVIRONMENTAL STUDIES

GREAT BRITAIN. DEPARTMENT OF TRANSPORT, LOCAL GOVERNMENT, AND THE REGIONS. PLANNING POLICY GUIDANCE NOTES. *see* TRANSPORTATION

GREAT BRITAIN. H M CUSTOMS & EXCISE. MANAGEMENT PLAN. *see* BUSINESS AND ECONOMICS—Public Finance, Taxation

GREAT BRITAIN. H M TREASURY. CIVIL SERVICE STATISTICS (ONLINE). *see* PUBLIC ADMINISTRATION—Abstracting, Bibliographies, Statistics

353.4 GBR ISSN 1477-3120
GREAT BRITAIN. HOME OFFICE. DEVELOPMENT AND PRACTICE REPORTS (ONLINE). Text in English. 2002. irreg., latest 2007. free (effective 2009). back issues avail. **Document type:** *Monographic series, Government.*
Formerly (until 19??): Great Britain. Home Office. Development and Practice Reports (Print)
Media: Online - full text.
—CCC.
Published by: Great Britain. Home Office, Research Development and Statistics, Direct Communications Unit, 2 Marsham St, London, SW1P 4DF, United Kingdom. TEL 44-20-70354848, publications.rds@homeoffice.gsi.gov.uk, http://www.homeoffice.gov.uk/rds/index.htm.

P

353.4 GBR
GREAT BRITAIN. HOME OFFICE. RESEARCH, DEVELOPMENT AND STATISTICS DIRECTORATE. FINDINGS (ONLINE). Text in English. 1992. irreg. free (effective 2010). **Document type:** *Monographic series, Government.* **Description:** Summarizes research conducted by the Research and Planning Unit on the criminal justice system and community relations.
Former titles (until 200?): Great Britain. Home Office. Research, Development and Statistics Directorate. Findings (Print) (1473-8406); (until 2001): Great Britain. Home Office. Research, Development and Statistics Directorate. Research Findings; (until 1998): Great Britain. Home Office. Research and Statistics Directorate. Research Findings (1364-6540); (until 1996): Great Britain. Home Office. Research and Planning Unit. Research Findings (1355-5995)
Media: Online - full text.
—BLDSC (3927.734150). **CCC.**
Published by: Great Britain. Home Office, Research Development and Statistics, Direct Communications Unit, 2 Marsham St, London, SW1P 4DF, United Kingdom. TEL 44-20-72732084, FAX 44-20-72730211, http://www.homeoffice.gov.uk/rds/index.htm.

328.42 GBR ISSN 0309-8826
J301
GREAT BRITAIN. HOUSE OF COMMONS. PARLIAMENTARY DEBATES. WEEKLY HANSARD. Key Title: Parliamentary Debates, Hansard. House of Commons Official Report. Text in English. 1892. w. GBP 440 (effective 2010). Index. **Document type:** *Government.* **Description:** Transcripts of the oral arguments presented in the House of Commons.
Formerly (until 1943): Parliamentary Debates, Official Report. House of Commons (0309-9016); Which superseded in part (in 1909): Parliamentary Debates. Authorised Edition (0309-9032)
Related titles: Alternate Frequency ed(s).: Great Britain. House of Commons. Parliamentary Debates (Weekly Edition). ISSN 0261-8303. w.
Published by: (Great Britain. Parliament. House of Commons), The Stationery Office, St Crispins, Duke St, Norwich, NR3 1PD, United Kingdom. TEL 44-1603-622211, customer.services@tso.co.uk, http://www.tso.co.uk. **Subscr. to:** PO Box 29, Norwich NR3 1GN, United Kingdom. TEL 44-870-6005522, FAX 44-870-6005533, subscriptions@tso.co.uk.

GREAT BRITAIN. HOUSE OF LORDS. PARLIAMENTARY DEBATES. *see* POLITICAL SCIENCE

GREAT BRITAIN. OFFICE OF FAIR TRADING. ANNUAL REPORT AND RESOURCE ACCOUNTS. *see* BUSINESS AND ECONOMICS—International Commerce

351.41 GBR ISSN 0072-7032
GREAT BRITAIN. PUBLIC WORKS LOAN BOARD. ANNUAL REPORT. Text in English. 1875. a. free (effective 2009). back issues avail. **Document type:** *Government.*
Related titles: Online - full text ed.
—BLDSC (1402.065000). **CCC.**
Published by: Public Works Loan Board, UK Debt Management Office, Eastcheap Ct, 11 Philpot Ln, London, EC3M 8UD, United Kingdom. TEL 44-845-3576610, FAX 44-845-3576509, pwlb@dmo.gsi.gov.uk, http://www.dmo.gov.uk/index.aspx?page=PWLB/Introduction.

GRIEPHAN BERLIN KONTAKT; Informationen zum Geschaeft mit dem Staat. *see* BUSINESS AND ECONOMICS—Trade And Industrial Directories

352 FRA ISSN 2108-3967
GROUPE MAJORITE MUNICIPALE, SOCIALISTES ET APPARENTES. LA LETTRE. Text in French. 200?. m. **Document type:** *Newsletter, Government.*
Formerly (until 2008): La Lettre des Elus Socialistes (1952-7950)
Published by: Groupe Majorite Municipale Socialistes et Apparentes, 13 Place de l'Hotel de Ville (1er etage), Saint-Etienne, 42000, France. TEL 33-4-77479270, majorite.municipale-socialiste.apparentes@orange.fr, http://www.majorite-municipale-st-etienne.fr/index.htm.

THE GUARDIAN (LOS ANGELES). *see* POLITICAL SCIENCE

351 BRA ISSN 1414-3461
GUIA DE FORNECEDORES MUNICIPAIS. Text in Portuguese. 1989. m. adv. back issues avail. **Document type:** *Magazine, Trade.* **Description:** Features articles on public administration and government issues.
Related titles: Online - full text ed.
Published by: Editora Guia de Fornecedores Ltda., Av Doutor Adolfo Pinto, 109 Andar 4, B Funda, Sao Paulo, SP 01156-050, Brazil. TEL 55-11-3824-9655, FAX 55-11-826-9789. Ed. Eduardo David Airton. Adv. contact Camila Nunez. page USD 4,208; trim 14.25 x 10.5. Circ: 11,000.

351 ITA
GUIDA AGLI ACQUISTI PER GLI ENTI PUBBLICI. Text in Italian. 1991. a. free to qualified personnel. charts; stat. **Document type:** *Directory, Trade.*
Related titles: Online - full text ed.
Published by: Kompass Italia SpA, Strada del Lionetto 6, Turin, TO 10146, Italy. TEL 39-011-4353536, FAX 39-011-4353535, kompass.to@seat.it, http://www.kompassitalia.com.

351 ITA
GUIDAZZURRA REPERTORI. Text in Italian. m. price varies. **Document type:** *Monographic series, Government.*
Related titles: Special ed(s).: Guidazzurra Amministrazione Centrale dello Stato.
Published by: D'Anselmi Editore Srl, Via Vigliena 10, Rome, RM 00192, Italy. TEL 39-06-3220020, FAX 39-06-3220025, danselmi@interbusiness.it.

351 CAN ISSN 1910-8982
GUIDE DES APPROVISIONNEMENTS. Text in French. 2002. s-a. **Document type:** *Handbook/Manual/Guide, Trade.*
Media: Online - full text. **Related titles:** Ed.: Supply Manual. ISSN 1910-8974.
Published by: Public Works and Government Services Canada/Travaux Publics et Services Gouvernementaux Canada, Place du Portage, Phase III, 11 Laurier St, Gatineau, PQ K1A 0S5, Canada. TEL 800-622-6232, Questions@pwgsc.gc.ca, http://www.pwgsc.gc.ca/text/home-e.html.

352 CAN ISSN 1910-3093
GUIDE DU CITOYEN. Text in French. 2005. a. **Document type:** *Directory, Consumer.*
Published by: Ville de Mont-Tremblant, 1145, rue de Saint-Jovite, Mont-Tremblant, PQ J8E 1V1, Canada. TEL 819-425-8614, info@villedemont-tremblant.qc.ca, http://www.villedemont-tremblant.qc.ca/jahia/Jahia/pid/2.

328 CAN ISSN 1491-6983
CA2PQXF400G76
GUIDE DU POUVOIR AU QUEBEC. Text in French. 1995. a. CAD 34.95 (effective 2005).
Formerly: Bottin du Pouvoir a Quebec (1201-7094)
Published by: Publications Mass-Media, 30 Grande-Allee Ouest, Quebec, PQ G1R 2G6, Canada. TEL 418-522-8182, FAX 418-529-7548. Ed. Denis Massicotte.

352.14 FRA ISSN 1775-9536
LE GUIDE JURIDIQUE DE L'ELU LOCAL. Text in French. 2002. irreg. looseleaf. **Document type:** *Directory, Trade.*
Published by: Editions Weka, 249 Rue de Crimee, Paris, 75935 Cedex 19, France.

GUIDE TO EUROPEAN COMMUNITY GRANTS AND LOANS. *see* BUSINESS AND ECONOMICS—International Development And Assistance

354.4 GBR
JN106
▼ **THE GUIDE TO EXECUTIVE AGENCIES & PUBLIC BODIES "QUANGOS"**; your guide to public bodies. Text in English. 2009. a. GBP 315 combined subscription per issue (print & CD-ROM eds.); GBP 265 per issue (effective 2009). adv. **Document type:** *Directory, Trade.* **Description:** Provides essential information and an invaluable insight into this aspect of government.
Formed by the merger of (1997-2009): The Guide to Public Bodies "Quangos" (1367-0808); (1995-2009): The Guide to the Executive Agencies (1360-6689)
Related titles: CD-ROM ed.: GBP 280 per issue (effective 2009).
—CCC.
Published by: Carlton Publishing & Printing Ltd., Maple House, Maple View, Steeds Ln, Kingsnorth, TN26 1NQ, United Kingdom. TEL 44-1923-800801, FAX 44-1923-800802, info@carlton-group.co.uk.

351 791.43 CAN ISSN 1494-9113
GUIDE TO FEDERAL PROGRAMS FOR THE FILM AND VIDEO SECTOR. Text in English. 1998. a., latest 2003. **Document type:** *Government.*
Related titles: Online - full content ed.
Published by: Canadian Heritage/Patrimoine Canadien, 15 Eddy St, Gatineau, PQ K1A 0M5, Canada. TEL 819-997-0055, 866-811-0055, http://www.pch.gc.ca.

352.53 USA
GUIDE TO GOVERNMENT CONTRACTING. Text in English. 1991. base vol. plus m. updates. USD 625 base vol(s). (effective 2004). **Description:** Provides a layman's explanation of the contracting process without the full text of laws and regulations, so don't need to spend time wading through more cumbersome references.
Published by: C C H Inc. (Subsidiary of: Wolters Kluwer N.V.), 2700 Lake Cook Rd, Riverwoods, IL 60015. TEL 847-267-7000, 800-449-6439, cust_serv@cch.com, http://www.cch.com. Pub. Stacey Caywood.

351.969 USA ISSN 0072-8454
JQ6121
GUIDE TO GOVERNMENT IN HAWAII. Text in English. 1961. irreg., latest 2007. price varies. **Document type:** *Handbook/Manual/Guide, Government.*
Published by: Legislative Reference Bureau, State Capitol, Rm 005, Honolulu, HI 96813. TEL 808-587-0690, FAX 808-587-0699, lrb@capitol.hawaii.gov.

351.969 USA ISSN 1085-0325
Z1223.Z7
GUIDE TO GOVERNMENT INFORMATION AVAILABLE ON THE INTERNET. Text in English. irreg.
Published by: Ryan Information Management Press, 1049 Ackerman Ave, Syracuse, NY 13210-3035. TEL 315-475-3630, jryan@mailbox.syr.edu.

351.782 USA ISSN 0091-0716
JK6630
GUIDE TO NEBRASKA STATE AGENCIES. Text in English. 1973. irreg. free. **Document type:** *Directory, Government.*
Media: Online - full content. **Related titles:** Print ed.
Published by: Nebraska Publications Clearinghouse, c/o Nebraska Library Commission, 1200 N St, 120, Lincoln, NE 68508-2023. TEL 402-471-4017, FAX 402-471-2083. Ed., R&P Beth Goble. Circ: 300.

351 USA ISSN 1931-8529
JZ5514
GUIDE TO SPECIALISTS. Text in English. 1993. a. **Document type:** *Guide, Trade.*
Published by: U.S. Institute of Peace, 1200 17th St NW, Ste 200, Washington, DC 20036-3011. TEL 202-457-1700, FAX 202-429-6063, usiprquests@usip.org, http://www.usip.org.

351.94 AUS ISSN 1836-148X
A GUIDE TO THE AUSTRALIAN GOVERNMENT; structure, organisations and key people. Text in English. 1921. a. **Document type:** *Directory, Government.*
Former titles (until 2003): Commonwealth Government Directory (1030-3170); (until 1987): Commonwealth Government Directory. Volume I, Offices and Personnel (0810-3615); (until 1977): Commonwealth Government Directory (0725-5403); (until 1976): Guide to Commonwealth Government Departments and Authorities (1035-7777); (until 1975): Australian Government Directory (0311-2918); (until 1973): Directory to the Office of the Governor-General, the Parliament, the Executive Government, the Judiciary, Departments and Authorities (1035-7742); (until 1961): Federal Guide (1035-7734)
Related titles: Online - full text ed.: Government Online Directory.
Published by: Australian Government. Information Office. Department of Finance and Deregulation, John Gorton Building, King Edward Terr., Parkes, ACT 2600, Australia. TEL 61-2-62152222, http://www.finance.gov.au/. Circ: 4,000.

352.114 GBR ISSN 1364-2855
THE GUIDE TO THE GOVERNANCE OF BRITAIN IN EUROPE. Text in English. 1997. a. GBP 315 combined subscription per issue (print & CD-ROM eds.); GBP 255 per issue (effective 2009). adv. **Document type:** *Directory, Trade.* **Description:** Contains address, emails, telephone and fax numbers, professional and political careers, staff contacts for European parliament.
Related titles: CD-ROM ed.: GBP 280 per issue (effective 2009).
—CCC.
Published by: Carlton Publishing & Printing Ltd., Maple House, Maple View, Steeds Ln, Kingsnorth, TN26 1NQ, United Kingdom. TEL 44-1923-800801, FAX 44-1923-800802, info@carlton-group.co.uk.

328.410 GBR ISSN 1362-5241
JN617
THE GUIDE TO THE HOUSE OF LORDS. Text in English. 1996. a. GBP 315 combined subscription per issue (print & CD-ROM eds.); GBP 255 per issue (effective 2009). adv. **Document type:** *Directory, Trade.* **Description:** Contains information on the structure, procedures and work of the house of lords - CVs on members of the house of lords.
Related titles: CD-ROM ed.: ISSN 1475-5122. GBP 280 (effective 2009).
—CCC.
Published by: Carlton Publishing & Printing Ltd., Maple House, Maple View, Steeds Ln, Kingsnorth, TN26 1NQ, United Kingdom. TEL 44-1923-800801, FAX 44-1923-800802, info@carlton-group.co.uk.

GUIDE TO U S GOVERNMENT PUBLICATIONS. *see* PUBLIC ADMINISTRATION—Abstracting, Bibliographies, Statistics

GULF WAR REVIEW; information for veterans who served in Desert Shield - Desert Storm. *see* ENVIRONMENTAL STUDIES—Toxicology And Environmental Safety

H K KOMMUNALBLADET. (Handels- og Kontorfunktionaerernes Forbund) *see* LABOR UNIONS

H S R & D RESEARCH BRIEFS. (Health Services Research and Development) *see* MILITARY

353.3 364.4 USA ISSN 1553-3670
UA10.5
H S TODAY; insight & analysis for homeland security policy makers. Text in English. 2004 (May). m. USD 49.95 domestic; USD 69.95 in Canada; USD 99.95 elsewhere; free to qualified personnel (effective 2005). adv. **Document type:** *Magazine, Trade.*
Indexed: I02.
Published by: K M D Media LLC, 6800 Fleetwood Rd, Ste 114, McLean, VA 22101. TEL 800-503-6506, FAX 866-503-5758. Ed. David Silverberg TEL 703-757-0520. Pub. Kimberley S Hanson-Brown. adv.: B&W page USD 6,100, color page USD 7,650; trim 8.125 x 10.875. Circ: 28,431 (controlled).

351 FIN ISSN 0355-7448
HALLINTO. Text in Finnish. 1959. 6/yr. EUR 44 domestic; EUR 49 in Scandinavia and Baltic countries; EUR 53 in Europe; EUR 55 elsewhere (effective 2005). adv. **Document type:** *Magazine, Trade.*
Former titles (until 1974): R-Muistio (1235-0753); (until 1973): Valtionhallion R-Muistio (0506-3868); Incorporates (1986-1995): Aluekehitys (1237-069X); Which was formerly (until 1994): Aluekehitys ja Hallinto (0787-4588); (until 1990): Ajankohtaista Aluepolitiikasta (0782-9140)
Published by: Stellatum Oy, Tyopajankatu 6 A, Helsinki, 00580, Finland. TEL 358-9-8689700, FAX 358-9-86897070, info@stellatum.fi, http://www.stellatum.fi. adv.: B&W page EUR 1,100, color page EUR 1,600; 180 x 255. Circ: 2,500.

HAMLINE JOURNAL OF PUBLIC LAW AND POLICY. *see* LAW

351 NLD ISSN 1871-5729
HANDBOEK UITKERINGSBEREKENING WET WERK EN BIJSTAND. Key Title: Handboek Uitkeringsberekening WWB. Text in Dutch. 199?. a. EUR 31 (effective 2009).
Published by: Langhenkel Groep, Postbus 40127, Zwolle, 8004 DC, Netherlands. TEL 31-38-4677200, FAX 31-38-4677222, info@langhenkel.nl, http://www.langhenkel.nl/.

351 NLD ISSN 2210-2043
HANDBOEK WET WERK EN BIJSTAND EN WET INVESTEREN IN JONGEREN. Text in Dutch. 200?. s-a. EUR 59 per issue (effective 2010).
Formerly (until 2010): De Wet Werk en Bijstand (1871-5737)
Published by: (Langhenkel Opleiding en Training), Langhenkel Groep, Postbus 40127, Zwolle, 8004 DC, Netherlands. TEL 31-38-4677200, FAX 31-38-4677222, info@langhenkel.nl, http://www.langhenkel.nl/.

351 355 330 NLD ISSN 1574-0013
HANDBOOK OF DEFENSE ECONOMICS. Text in English. 1995. irreg., latest vol.2, 2007. price varies. **Document type:** *Monographic series, Academic/Scholarly.*
Related titles: Online - full text ed.: ISSN 1875-5623.
Indexed: SCOPUS.
—CCC.
Published by: Elsevier BV, North-Holland (Subsidiary of: Elsevier Science & Technology), Sara Burgerhartstraat 25, Amsterdam, 1055 KV, Netherlands. TEL 31-20-4853911, FAX 31-20-4852457, JournalsCustomerServiceEMEA@elsevier.com, http://www.elsevier.com.

351.43 DEU ISSN 0948-5945
HANDBUCH DER LEITUNGS- UND WEGERECHTE. Text in German. 1995. 2 base vols. plus a. updates. EUR 98 base vol(s).; EUR 34.80 updates per issue (effective 2009). **Document type:** *Monographic series, Trade.*
Published by: Erich Schmidt Verlag GmbH & Co. (Berlin), Genthiner Str 30 G, Berlin, 10785, Germany. TEL 49-30-2500850, FAX 49-30-250085305, esv@esvmedien.de, http://www.erich-schmidt-verlag.de.

328.492 657 NLD ISSN 1879-7571
HANDLEIDING REGELGEVING ACCOUNTANCY. Variant title: H R A. Text in Dutch. 1996. biennial. EUR 180 (effective 2010).
Formerly (until 2007): Richtlijnen voor de Accountantscontrole (1572-591X)
Published by: (Nederlandse Orde van Accountants-Administratieconsulenten), Koninklijk Nederlands Instituut van Registeraccountants, Postbus 7984, Amsterdam, 1008 AD, Netherlands. TEL 31-20-3010301, FAX 31-20-3010302, nivra@nivra.nl, http://www.nivra.nl.

351 CHN ISSN 1674-2540
HANGZHOU ZHENGBAO. Text in Chinese. 1999. m. **Document type:** *Government.*
Related titles: Online - full text ed.
Published by: Hangzhou Shi Renmin Zhengfu Bangongting, 318, Huancheng Bei Lu, Hangzhou, 310026, China. TEL 86-571-85252566, FAX 86-571-85252536.

328.71 CAN ISSN 1922-592X
HANSARD. Text in English. 2007. irreg. free (effective 2010). back issues avail. **Document type:** *Proceedings, Government.* **Description:** Addresses the daily transcript of the proceedings of the House of Assembly.
Related titles: Online - full text ed.
Published by: House of Assembly of Newfoundland and Labrador, PO Box 8700, St. John's, NF A1B 4J6, Canada. TEL 709-729-2129, legcounsel@gov.nl.ca.

351 USA ISSN 1081-0463
E185.86
➤ **HARVARD JOURNAL OF AFRICAN AMERICAN PUBLIC POLICY.** Text in English. 1989. a. USD 20 per issue to individuals; USD 40 per issue to institutions (effective 2010). adv. **Document type:** *Journal, Academic/Scholarly.* **Description:** Provides a comprehensive and interdisciplinary examination of the interaction between public policy and the African American experience.
Related titles: Online - full text ed.
Indexed: A01, A03, A08, A26, CA, E08, G08, H05, I05, IIBP, P34, P42, P45, PAIS, S09, T02.
Published by: Harvard University, John F. Kennedy School of Government, 79 John F Kennedy St, PO Box 142, Cambridge, MA 02138. TEL 617-496-8655, FAX 617-384-9555. Ed. Timothy Cunningham. adv.: B&W page USD 300; trim 5 x 8.

320 USA ISSN 1535-0215
H96
➤ **HARVARD KENNEDY SCHOOL REVIEW.** Text in English. 2000. a. USD 10 per issue to individuals; USD 20 per issue to institutions (effective 2010). adv. **Document type:** *Journal, Academic/Scholarly.* **Description:** Brings creative ideas and challenging perspectives into the public realm by publishing the work of Kennedy School students.
Related titles: Online - full text ed.
Indexed: A01, A03, A08, A26, CA, E07, E08, G08, I05, P34, P42, PAIS, S09, T02.
Published by: Harvard University, John F. Kennedy School of Government, 79 John F Kennedy St, PO Box 142, Cambridge, MA 02138. TEL 617-496-8655, FAX 617-384-9555, cpl@ksg.harvard.edu. Ed. Melinda Kuritzky. Pub. Martha Foley TEL 617-496-0320.

351 347 USA ISSN 1939-9715
KFH34.5
HAWAII GOVERNMENT REGISTER. Text in English. 1998. m. USD 914 (effective 2011). back issues avail. **Document type:** *Government.* **Description:** Covers executive orders of the governor, Attorney General opinions, public laws enacted, public utility and environmental orders enacted, banking and insurance agency information, emergency rules, and gubernatorial appointments of state officials and board-commission members.
Formerly (until 2005): Weil's Hawaii Government Register (1097-8550)
Published by: LexisNexis (Subsidiary of: Reed Elsevier Group plc), 1016 W Ninth Ave, 1st Fl, King of Prussia, PA 19406. TEL 215 564-1788, 800 448-1515, customer.support@lexisnexis.com.

HAWAII. LEGISLATIVE AUDITOR. SPECIAL REPORTS. *see* POLITICAL SCIENCE

HAWAII. LEGISLATIVE REFERENCE BUREAU. REPORT. *see* POLITICAL SCIENCE

351.764 USA ISSN 1071-5401
HAWVER'S CAPITOL REPORT. Variant title: Capitol Report. Text in English. 1993. 40/yr. USD 200 domestic (effective 2001). 8 p./no.; **Document type:** *Newsletter, Government.* **Description:** Covers political and state government news of Kansas.
Published by: Hawver News Company, LLC, 3823 SW Wood Valley Dr, Topeka, KS 66610-1124. TEL 785-267-5500, 785-233-9888, FAX 785-267-1099, hawvernews@hawvernews.com. Ed. Martin Hawver.

HEALTH MATTERS. *see* PUBLIC HEALTH AND SAFETY

614 CAN ISSN 1496-466X
RA395.C2
HEALTH POLICY RESEARCH. Text in Multiple languages. 2001. 3/yr.
Related titles: Online - full text ed.: ISSN 1499-3503. 2001.
Published by: Health Canada/Sante Canada, Address Locator 0900C2, Ottawa, ON K1A OK9, Canada. TEL 613-957-2991, FAX 613-941-5366, http://www.hc-sc.gc.ca.

HEALTHCARE PARLIAMENTARY MONITOR (ONLINE). *see* MEDICAL SCIENCES

310 352 FIN ISSN 0788-1576
Z674.5.F5
HELSINGIN KAUPUNGIN TIETOKESKUKSEN NELJANNESVUOSIJULKAISU. KVARTTI/CITY OF HELSINKI URBAN FACTS. QUARTERLY/HELSINGFORS STADS FAKTACENTRAL. KVARTALSPUBLIKATION. Key Title: Kvartti. Variant title: Helsinki Quarterly. Text in Finnish, Swedish; Text occasionally in English. 1979. q. bk.rev. abstr.; stat. 102 p./no.; back issues avail. **Document type:** *Bulletin, Consumer.* **Description:** Information on the population and urban culture of Helsinki.
Former titles (until 1990): Helsingin Kaupungin Tilastokeskuksen. Neljannesvuosijulkaisu (0781-0490); (until 1984): Helsingin Kaupungin Titokeskuksen. Neljannesvuosikatsaus (0357-3362)
Related titles: Online - full text ed.: ISSN 1796-7279.
Published by: Helsingin Kaupungin Tietokeskus/City of Helsinki Urban Facts, PO Box 5500, Helsinki, 00099, Finland. TEL 358-9-3101612, FAX 358-9-31036601, tietokeskus.kirjaamo@hel.fi, http://www.hel2.fi/tietokeskus/kaupunkitilastot/index.html. Eds. Asta Manninen, Vesa Keskinen. R&P Asta Manninen. Circ: 800 (controlled).

352 FIN ISSN 1455-7258
HELSINGIN KAUPUNGIN TIETOKESKUS. KESKUSTELUALOITTEITA/CORE INDICATORS FOR SUSTAINABLE DEVELOPMENT IN HELSINKI. Text in English, Finnish. 1990. irreg. **Document type:** *Monographic series, Consumer.*
Formerly (until 1998): Helsingin Kaupungin Tietokeskuksen Keskustelualoitteita (0788-1541)
Related titles: Online - full text ed.: ISSN 1458-5707.
Indexed: SSciA.
Published by: Helsingin Kaupungin Tietokeskus/City of Helsinki Urban Facts, PO Box 5500, Helsinki, 00099, Finland. TEL 358-9-3101612, FAX 358-9-31036601, tietokeskus.kirjaamo@hel.fi, http://www.hel2.fi/tietokeskus/kaupunkitilastot/index.html.

351 USA ISSN 0272-1155
JC573
HERITAGE LECTURES. Text in English. 1980. irreg., latest no.1171, 2010. index. back issues avail. **Document type:** *Monographic series, Trade.* **Description:** Covers lectures given political figures, academics, and issue experts from around the world to promote conservative public policies.
Related titles: Online - full text ed.: free (effective 2010).
Published by: The Heritage Foundation, 214 Massachusetts Ave NE, Washington, DC 20002-4999. TEL 202-546-4400, FAX 202-546-8328, info@heritage.org.

HIGH COURT OF AUSTRALIA. ANNUAL REPORT. *see* LAW—Judicial Systems

HIGHWAY FINANCING & CONSTRUCTION - STATE CAPITALS. *see* LAW

HIGHWAY TAXES AND FEES (YEAR). *see* TRANSPORTATION

351.73 USA ISSN 1521-1568
THE HILL. Text in English. 1993. 3/w. (Tue., Wed. & Thu. when Congress is in session. Wed. when Congress is not in session.). USD 185 domestic; USD 235 in Canada; USD 600 elsewhere (effective 2006). adv. 32 p./no. 3 cols./p.; **Document type:** *Newspaper, Government.* **Description:** Discusses what legislation is up for consideration, as well as the policy makers, aides, lobbyists, and other deal makers behind the issues, all in a nonpartisan and non-ideological manner.
Related titles: Online - full text ed.
Indexed: A26, E08, G06, G07, G08, I05, I06, I07, M02, P05, S09, S23. —CIS. **CCC.**
Published by: Capitol Hill Publishing Corp. (Subsidiary of: News Communications, Inc.), 1625 K St., Ste. 900, Washington, DC 20006. TEL 202-628-8500, 800-284-3437, FAX 202-628-8503. Ed. Hugo Gurdon. Pub. James Finkelstein.

354.94 AUS ISSN 1832-8482
HISTORY TRUST OF SOUTH AUSTRALIA. ANNUAL REPORT. Text in English. 1978. a. free (effective 2009). back issues avail. **Document type:** *Government.* **Description:** Covers annual information about the History Trust of South Australia.
Formerly (until 1982): Constitutional Museum Trust. Report (0156-6997)
Related titles: Online - full text ed.
Published by: History Trust of South Australia, GPO Box 1836, Adelaide, SA 5001, Australia. TEL 61-8-82039888, FAX 61-8-82039883, staff@history.sa.gov.au.

351 DEU ISSN 0561-6271
HOCHSCHULE SPEYER. SCHRIFTENREIHE. Text in German. 1949. irreg., latest vol.198, 2009. price varies. **Document type:** *Monographic series, Academic/Scholarly.*
Formerly (until 1950): Schriftenreihe der Akademie Speyer (0174-8807)
Published by: Duncker und Humblot GmbH, Carl-Heinrich-Becker-Weg 9, Berlin, 12165, Germany. TEL 49-30-7900060, FAX 49-30-79000631, info@duncker-humblot.de.

351 941.1 GBR
HOLYROOD NEWS. Text in English. 1991. w. mkt. back issues avail. **Document type:** *Newsletter, Consumer.* **Description:** Scotland's news and parliamentry journal and RP planner, aimed at the public affairs and corporate relations market.
Related titles: E-mail ed.; Fax ed.; Online - full content ed.
Published by: Holyrood Group Ltd., 26 Forth St., Edinburgh, EH1 3LH, United Kingdom. TEL 44-131-5551999, FAX 44-131-5503863. Pub. Julia Clarke. Adv. contact James Campbell.

351 GBR ISSN 1366-2627
HOME OFFICE CIRCULAR. Text in English. 1955. irreg., latest 2009. back issues avail. **Document type:** *Government.*
—CCC.
Published by: Great Britain. Home Office, Direct Communications Unit, 2 Marsham St, London, SW1P 4DF, United Kingdom. TEL 44-20-70354848, FAX 44-20-70354745, public.enquiries@homeoffice.gsi.gov.uk.

HOME OFFICE. RESEARCH AND STATISTICS DIRECTORATE. STATISTICAL BULLETIN (ONLINE). *see* PUBLIC ADMINISTRATION—Abstracting, Bibliographies, Statistics

HOMELAND SECURITY AFFAIRS. *see* PUBLIC HEALTH AND SAFETY

352.379 USA ISSN 1554-737X
HV6432.4
HOMELAND SECURITY FUNDING WEEK. Text in English. 2003. s-m. USD 469 (effective 2005).
Former titles (until 2005): Homeland Security Funding Report (1554-7280); (until 2004): State & Local Homeland Security Funding Report (1543-5067)
—CCC.
Published by: C D Publications, Inc., 8204 Fenton St, Silver Spring, MD 20910. TEL 301-588-6380, 800-666-6380, FAX 301-588-6385, subscriptions@cdpublications.com, http://www.cdpublications.com. Ed. Alice Lipowicz. Pub. Mike Gerecht.

353.3 364.4 USA ISSN 1554-3234
➤ **THE HOMELAND SECURITY REVIEW.** Text in English. 2006 (Winter). q. USD 179 (effective 2011). bk.rev. back issues avail. **Document type:** *Journal, Academic/Scholarly.* **Description:** Devoted to the discussion and analysis of issues related to the subject of Homeland Security. The Review publishes feature articles, commentaries and articles focusing on the field of Homeland Security.
Related titles: Online - full text ed.: ISSN 1554-3242.
Indexed: CA, CJA, I02, P05, T02.
Published by: California University of Pennsylvania, Institute for Law & Public Policy, 250 University Ave, California, PA 15419. TEL 724-938-4000, FAX 724-938-5239. Ed. Charles P Nemeth.

351.7283 HND
HONDURAS. CONGRESO NACIONAL. BOLETIN. Text in Spanish. irreg., latest vol.18, 1982.
Published by: Congreso Nacional, Oficina de Boletines y Publicaciones, Tegucigalpa DC, Honduras.

HONG KONG (YEAR). *see* POPULATION STUDIES

351.5125 HKG
HONG KONG. GOVERNMENT PUBLICATION CENTRE. INQUIRY REPORTS. Text in English. irreg., latest 1984. price varies.
Related titles: Chinese ed.
Published by: Government Publications Centre, G.P.O. Bldg, Ground Fl, Connaught Pl, Hong Kong, Hong Kong. TEL 842-8801. **Subscr. to:** Director of Information Services, Information Services Dept., 1 Battery Path G-F, Central, Hong Kong, Hong Kong.

HONG KONG. LAW REFORM COMMISSION. REPORT. *see* LAW

354.8 HKG
HONG KONG. LEGISLATIVE COUNCIL. FINANCE COMMITTEE. REPORT. Text in English. a. HKD 160.
Published by: (Hong Kong. Legislative Council, Hong Kong. Finance Committee), Government Publications Centre, G.P.O. Bldg, Ground Fl, Connaught Pl, Hong Kong, Hong Kong. TEL 842-8801. **Subscr. to:** Director of Information Services, Information Services Dept., 1 Battery Path G-F, Central, Hong Kong, Hong Kong.

328.5125 HKG
HONG KONG. LEGISLATIVE COUNCIL. PROCEEDINGS. Text in English. w. price varies. **Document type:** *Proceedings.*
Related titles: Chinese ed.
Published by: (Hong Kong. Legislative Council), Government Publications Centre, G.P.O. Bldg, Ground Fl, Connaught Pl, Hong Kong, Hong Kong. TEL 842-8801. **Subscr. to:** Director of Information Services, Information Services Dept., 1 Battery Path G-F, Central, Hong Kong, Hong Kong.

328.5125 HKG
HONG KONG. LEGISLATIVE COUNCIL. PUBLIC WORKS SUB-COMMITTEE. REPORT. Text in English. a. HKD 200.
Published by: (Hong Kong. Legislative Council, Hong Kong. Public Works Sub-Committee), Government Publications Centre, G.P.O. Bldg, Ground Fl, Connaught Pl, Hong Kong, Hong Kong. TEL 842-8801. **Subscr. to:** Director of Information Services, Information Services Dept., 1 Battery Path G-F, Central, Hong Kong, Hong Kong.

351.5125 HKG
HONG KONG. PUBLIC SERVICE COMMISSION. CHAIRMAN'S REPORT. Text in English. a. HKD 35.
Published by: (Zambia. Public Service Commission MUS), Government Publications Centre, G.P.O. Bldg, Ground Fl, Connaught Pl, Hong Kong, Hong Kong. TEL 842-8801, FAX 845-9078. **Subscr. to:** Director of Information Services, Information Services Dept., 1 Battery Path G-F, Central, Hong Kong, Hong Kong.

352.63 HKG
HONG KONG. STANDING COMMISSION ON CIVIL SERVICE SALARIES AND CONDITIONS OF SERVICE. CIVIL SERVICE PAY. Text in English. irreg., latest vol.20, 1988. price varies.
Related titles: Chinese ed.
Published by: (Hong Kong. Standing Commission on Civil Service Salaries and Conditions of Service), Government Publications Centre, G.P.O. Bldg, Ground Fl, Connaught Pl, Hong Kong, Hong Kong. TEL 842-8801. **Subscr. to:** Director of Information Services, Information Services Dept., 1 Battery Path G-F, Central, Hong Kong, Hong Kong.

354.2 HKG
HONG KONG. URBAN COUNCIL. PROCEEDINGS. Text in English. m. price varies. **Document type:** *Proceedings.*
Related titles: Chinese ed.
Published by: (Hong Kong. Urban Council), Government Publications Centre, G.P.O. Bldg, Ground Fl, Connaught Pl, Hong Kong, Hong Kong. TEL 842-8801, FAX 845-9078. **Subscr. to:** Director of Information Services, Information Services Dept., 1 Battery Path G-F, Central, Hong Kong, Hong Kong.

307.336 FRA ISSN 1774-4970
HORIZON OUEST; journal d'information des quartiers Koenigshoffen, Montagne Verte, Elsau. Text in French. 2005. q. free (effective 2006). **Document type:** *Bulletin, Trade.*
Published by: Animation, Valorisation et Communication, 84 route des Romains, Strasbourg, 67200, France.

352.34 USA
HORIZONS (COLUMBUS); the newsletter of the Mid-Ohio Regional Planning Commission. Text in English. 1969. q. free. illus.; tr.lit.
Former titles (until 1990): Mid-Ohio Review; Regional Review
Indexed: ChemAb.
Published by: Mid-Ohio Regional Planning Commission, 285 E Main St, Columbus, OH 43215-5272. TEL 614-228-2663, FAX 614-621-2401. Ed. Jan Hiltner. Circ: 5,300.

351 330.9 FRA ISSN 1958-3370
HORIZONS STRATEGIQUES. Text mainly in French; Text occasionally in English. 2006. q. EUR 36 (effective 2009). back issues avail. **Document type:** *Journal, Government.*
Related titles: Online - full text ed.: free.
Indexed: IBSS.
Published by: (France. Centre d'Analyse Strategique), Documentation Francaise, 29-31 Quai Voltaire, Paris, Cedex 7 75344, France. TEL 33-1-40157000, http://www.ladocumentationfrancaise.fr.

HOTLINE (WASHINGTON). *see* POLITICAL SCIENCE

351 USA ISSN 0740-8269
KF31.8
HOUSE COMMITTEE ON RULES. SURVEY OF ACTIVITIES. Key Title: Survey of Activities of the House Committee on Rules. Text in English. 19??. biennial. **Document type:** *Government.*
Published by: U.S. Government Printing Office, 732 N Capitol St, NW, Washington, DC 20401. TEL 202-512-1800, 866-512-1800, FAX 202-512-2104, ContactCenter@gpo.gov, http://www.gpo.gov.

353.55 GBR ISSN 0309-0426
JN101
HOUSE MAGAZINE. Text in English. 1976. w. GBP 195 domestic; GBP 227 in Europe; GBP 237 elsewhere (effective 2009). adv. bk.rev. back issues avail. **Document type:** *Magazine, Trade.* **Description:** Provides a forum for news, views and comment by members of the Commons and Lords, commentators and leading figures from the political world.
—CCC.

P

Published by: Dod's Parliamentary Communications Ltd., Westminster Tower, 3rd Fl, 3 Albert Embankment, London, SE1 7SP, United Kingdom. TEL 44-20-70917500, FAX 44-20-70917505, uk@dods.co.uk, http://www.dods.co.uk. Adv. contact Lenny Rolles TEL 44-20-70917579. B&W page GBP 3,310.85, color page GBP 4,417.15; 210 x 270.

351.4 GBR ISSN 1368-8456
HOUSE OF COMMONS. LIBRARY. RESEARCH PAPER. Text in English. 1993. irreg. back issues avail. **Document type:** *Monographic series, Academic/Scholarly.*
—BLDSC (7752.135000). **CCC.**
Published by: House of Commons, Library, London, SW1A 0AA, United Kingdom. hcinfo@parliament.uk, http://www.publications.parliament.uk/pa/cm/cmpubns.htm.

HOUSING AND URBAN POLICY STUDIES. *see* HOUSING AND URBAN PLANNING

HOUSING NEW ZEALAND CORPORATION. ANNUAL REPORT. *see* HOUSING AND URBAN PLANNING

HOUSING NEW ZEALAND CORPORATION. STATEMENT OF INTENT. *see* HOUSING AND URBAN PLANNING

HUME OCCASIONAL PAPERS. *see* POLITICAL SCIENCE

351 CHN ISSN 1674-2478
HUNAN ZHENGBAO. Text in Chinese. 1949. s-m. **Document type:** *Magazine, Government.*
Published by: Hu'nan Sheng Renmin Zhengfu Bangongting, 69, Wu-Yi Zhong Lu, Changsha, 410011, China. TEL 86-731-2211243, FAX 86-731-2212222.

353.46 HKG
I C A C COMMISSIONER'S ANNUAL REPORT. Text in English. 1985. a. HKD 18.
Related titles: Chinese ed.
Published by: (Hong Kong. Independent Commission Against Corruption), Government Publications Centre, G.P.O. Bldg, Ground Fl, Connaught Pl, Hong Kong, Hong Kong. TEL 842-8801. **Subscr. to:** Director of Information Services, Information Services Dept., 1 Battery Path G-F, Central, Hong Kong, Hong Kong.

351.4 UKR
I C P S NEWSLETTER. Text in English. w. **Document type:** *Newsletter, Academic/Scholarly.* **Description:** Contains information for clients and partners on current research, projects, and events at ICPS.
Published by: International Centre for Policy Studies, vul Pymonenka 13A, Kiev, 04050, Ukraine. TEL 380-44-4844410, FAX 380-44-4844402, astarynsky@icps.kiev.ua. Ed. Olha Lvova.

351 IND ISSN 0536-1761
I I P A NEWSLETTER. Text in English. 1957. m. INR 10 domestic; USD 4 foreign (effective 2011). **Document type:** *Newsletter, Consumer.* **Description:** Features national and international news of public administration and allied matters.
Published by: Indian Institute of Public Administration, Indraprastha Estate, Ring Rd, New Delhi, 110 002, India. TEL 91-11-23702400, FAX 91-11-23702440, diriipa@bol.net.in. Ed. Rakesh Hooja.

I L O JOINT COMMITTEE ON THE PUBLIC SERVICE. REPORT. (International Labour Organization) *see* BUSINESS AND ECONOMICS—Labor And Industrial Relations

352.63 IRL
I M P A C T NEWS. Text in English. 1951. 10/yr. membership. adv. bk.rev. **Document type:** *Newsletter, Trade.* **Description:** Covers labor unions, labor & industrial relations and public administration.
Formerly: I P C S News
Published by: Irish Municipal Public and Civil Trade Union, Nerney's Ct., Dublin, 1, Ireland. TEL 353-1-8171500, FAX 353-1-8171501. Ed., R&P Bernard Harbor. Adv. contact Frank Bambrick TEL 353-1-4534011. Circ: 33,000.

I P M N NEWSLETTER. *see* BUSINESS AND ECONOMICS—Management

351 GBR
I P P R NEWSLETTER. Text in English. w. membership. **Document type:** *Newsletter.*
Media: E-mail.
Published by: Institute for Public Policy Research, 30 - 32 Southampton St, Covent Garden, London, WC2E 7RA, United Kingdom. TEL 44-20-74706100, FAX 44-20-74706111, http://www.ippr.org.

351 CAN ISSN 1920-9428
▼ **I R P P STUDY.** Text in English, French. 2010. irreg.
Related titles: Online - full text ed.
Published by: Institute for Research on Public Policy/Institut de Recherches Politiques, 1470 Peel St, Ste 200, Montreal, PQ H3A 1T1, Canada. TEL 514-985-2461, FAX 514-985-2559, irrp@irrp.org, http://www.irpp.org.

351.796 USA
IDAHO PUBLIC AFFAIRS DIGEST. Text in English. 1996. w. looseleaf. USD 62 (effective 2011). index. back issues avail. **Document type:** *Newsletter, Trade.*
Former titles (until 2003): Idaho Monthly Public Affairs Digest; (until 2000): Idaho Public Affairs Aigest; Which was formed by the merger of (1995-1996): Idaho Digest (1083-0766); (1993-1996): Idaho Government Digest; Which was formerly (until 1993): Idaho Regulatory Letter (1050-9666)
Related titles: E-mail ed.
Published by: Ridenbaugh Press, PO Box 834, Carlton, OR 97111. TEL 503-852-0010, stapilus@ridenbaugh.com.

351 SAU
AL-IDARAH AL-AAMAH. Text in Arabic; Summaries in English. a. SAR 20, USD 8. abstr. **Description:** Publishes research on a variety of issues in public administration.
Published by: Ma'had al-Idarah al-Aamah/Institute of Public Administration, Recruiting Office, P O Box 205, Riyadh, 11141, Saudi Arabia. TEL 966-1-476-7305, FAX 966-1-479-2136, esl@ipa.edu.sa.

351 UAE
AL-IDARAH WAL-TANMIYAH/ADMINISTRATION AND DEVELOPMENT. Text in Arabic. 1986. 2/yr. **Description:** Presents research and analysis on administration and development in the U.A.E.
Published by: Institute of Administration and Development, PO Box 779, Abu Dhabi, United Arab Emirates. TEL 654665, TELEX 23718. Ed. Said Khalifa Al Ghaith. Circ: 2,000.

351 OMN
AL-IDARI; dawriyyah mutakhassisah fi majal al-aloom al-idariyah. Text in Arabic. q. OMR 8; OMR 20 to institutions. bibl. **Description:** Specialized research concerning issues in public administration.
Published by: Institute of Public Administration, Ruwi, P O Box 1994, Muscat, 112, Oman. TEL 968-602252, FAX 968-698763, TELEX 5105 ON.

IKAGAKU OYO KENKYU ZAIDAN KENKYU HOKOKU/SUZUKEN MEMORIAL FOUNDATION. RESEARCH PAPERS. *see* PUBLIC HEALTH AND SAFETY

351.773 USA ISSN 0191-104X
ILLINOIS BLUE BOOK. Text in English. biennial. **Document type:** *Government.*
Former titles (until 1952): Blue Book of the State of Illinois; (until 1903): List of State Officers of the State of Illinois, with an Appendix
Published by: Illinois Office of the Secretary of State, 213 State Capitol, Springfield, IL 62706. http://www.sos.state.il.us.

353 USA ISSN 1938-4890
JK5730
ILLINOIS STAFF DIRECTORY. Text and summaries in English. 2001. a. USD 250 (effective 2008). back issues avail.; reprints avail. **Document type:** *Directory, Government.* **Description:** A directory of official personnel in federal, state and local government within Illinois.
Formerly (until 2006): Illinois Public Sector (1701-1299)
Published by: C Q Press, Inc. (Subsidiary of: Sage Publications, Inc.), 2300 N St, NW, Ste 800, Washington, DC 20037. TEL 202-729-1900, 866-427-7737, FAX 800-380-3810, customerservice@cqpress.com, http://www.cqpress.com. Ed. Barbara Rogers.

351.8153 BRA
IMPRENSA OFICIAL DO ESTADO DO RIO DE JANEIRO. Text in Portuguese. 1975. d. BRL 4,800. adv.
Related titles: Microfilm ed.
Published by: (Rio de Janeiro, Brazil (State). Secretaria Extraordinaria de Comunicacao Social), Imprensa Oficial, Rua Margues de Olinda, 15, Niteroi, RJ, Brazil. TEL 021-719-1122. Circ: 17,900.

351 RWA
IMVAHO. Text in Kinyarwanda. 1960. w.
Published by: Office Rwandais d'Information, BP 83, Kigali, Rwanda. TEL 75724. Circ: 51,000.

INCIDENT PREVENTION; providing safety information to utilities, municipalities and telcom. *see* OCCUPATIONAL HEALTH AND SAFETY

351 DNK ISSN 1902-598X
INCITAMENT; om effektivitet, oganisation og ledelse i den offentlige sektor. Text in Danish. 1989. q. free (effective 2007). back issues avail. **Document type:** *Magazine, Government.*
Former titles (until 2007): Styrelsen (1603-5550); (until 2003): Nyt fra Oekonomistyrelsen (1396-5328); (until 1996): RSavisen (0905-345X)
Related titles: Online - full text ed.: ISSN 1902-5998.
Published by: Oekonomistyrelsen/Danish Agency for Governmental Management, Landgreven 4, Copenhagen K, 1017, Denmark. TEL 45-33-928000, oes@oes.dk. Ed. Theresa Kjaerside. Circ: 5,500.

328.748025 USA ISSN 0160-0656
KFN7410
INDEX OF LEGISLATION. Text in English. 19??. a. includes subscr. with Daily Bulletin. 139 p./no.; **Document type:** *Bulletin, Government.* **Description:** Includes a cumulative report of the status of all bills with local bills organized by county and public bills by subject categories that include each chapter of the General Statutes, appropriations, constitutional amendments, studies, and joint resolutions.
Published by: University of North Carolina at Chapel Hill, School of Government, Knapp-Sanders Bldg, Campus Box 3330, Chapel Hill, NC 27599. TEL 919-966-5381, FAX 919-962-0654, sales@sog.unc.edu, http://sog.unc.edu.

351.54 IND ISSN 0073-6171
JQ245
INDIA. CENTRAL VIGILANCE COMMISSION. REPORT. Text in English, Hindi. 1965. a. free (effective 2011). back issues avail. **Document type:** *Report, Trade.*
Related titles: Online - full text ed.: free (effective 2011).
Published by: Central Vigilance Commission, Satarkata Bhavan, A-Block, GPO Complex, INA, New Delhi, Delhi 110 023, India. TEL 91-11-24651001, FAX 91-11-24651010, vigilance@nic.in, http://www.cvc.nic.in.

351.54 IND ISSN 0073-6236
JQ245
INDIA. UNION PUBLIC SERVICE COMMISSION. ANNUAL REPORT. Text in English, Hindi. 1951. a. free (effective 2011). back issues avail. **Document type:** *Report, Academic/Scholarly.*
Related titles: Online - full text ed.
Published by: Union Public Service Commission, Minto Rd, New Delhi, India.

351.54 IND ISSN 0019-5561
➤ **INDIAN JOURNAL OF PUBLIC ADMINISTRATION.** Abbreviated title: I J P A. Text in English. 1955. q. INR 425 domestic to individuals; USD 120 foreign to individuals; INR 700 domestic to institutions; USD 240 foreign to institutions; INR 120 per issue domestic to individuals; USD 30 per issue foreign to individuals; INR 175 per issue domestic to institutions; USD 80 per issue foreign to institutions (effective 2011). bk.rev. abstr.; bibl. index. **Document type:** *Journal, Academic/Scholarly.*
Indexed: A22, ABCPolSci, BAS, BibInd, EI, FR, IBSS, ILD, P06, P30, PAA&I, PCI, RASB.
—BLDSC (4420.350000), IE, Infotrieve, Ingenta.
Published by: Indian Institute of Public Administration, Indraprastha Estate, Ring Rd, New Delhi, 110 002, India. TEL 91-11-23702400, FAX 91-11-23702440, diriipa@bol.net.in. Ed. S L Goel.

328.772 USA ISSN 1076-8661
INDIANA LEGISLATIVE INSIGHT. Text in English. 1989. 44/yr. USD 375 by email; USD 475 by fax (effective 2005). bk.rev. **Document type:** *Newsletter.* **Description:** Reports on activities in the legislative and executive branches of Indiana state government and on state politics.
Related titles: Online - full text ed.
Published by: INGroup, PO Box 383, Noblesville, IN 46061-0383. TEL 317-817-9997, FAX 317-817-9998. Circ: 400.

351.598 IDN
INDONESIA. DEPARTEMEN PENERANGAN. SIARAN UMUM. Text in Indonesian. irreg.
Published by: Department of Information, Jl. Merdeka Barat 7, Jakarta, Indonesia.

354 CAN ISSN 1709-7258
INDUSTRY CANADA. MAKING A DIFFERENCE - CONTRIBUTING TO THE QUALITY OF LIFE OF CANADIANS/INDUSTRIE CANADA. PARTENAIRE INDISPENSABLE - NOTRE CONTRIBUTION A LA QUALITE DE VIE DES CANADIENS. Text in English, French. 1999. a.
Formerly (until 2003): Industry Canada. Making a Difference - Our Priorities (1494-8583)
Published by: Industry Canada/Industrie Canada, Distribution Services, Communications & Marketing Branch, Rm 268D, West Tower, C.D. Howe Bldg., 235 Queen St, Ottawa, ON K1A 0H5, Canada. TEL 613-947-7466, FAX 613-954-6436, publications@ic.gc.ca.

352 CAN ISSN 1911-7787
INFO LA PECHE. Text in French, English. 2002. m. **Document type:** *Newsletter, Consumer.*
Published by: Municipality of La Peche/Municipalite de la Peche, 1, rue Principale Ouest, La Peche, PQ J0X 2W0, Canada. TEL 819-456-2161, FAX 819-456-4534, http://www.villelapeche.qc.ca.

354.7 CAN ISSN 1205-5166
CA1BT51-3/15
INFO SOURCE. DIRECTORY OF FEDERAL GOVERNMENT ENQUIRY POINTS. Text in English. 1995. a.
Published by: Treasury Board of Canada Secretariat, Corporate Communications/Secretariat du Conseil du Tresor du Canada, West Tower, Rm P-135, 300 Laurier Ave W, Ottawa, ON K1A 0R5, Canada. TEL 613-995-2855, FAX 613-996-0518, services-publications@tbs-sct.gc.ca, http://www.tbs-sct.gc.ca.

354.7 CAN ISSN 1188-7907
CA1BT51-3-11
INFO SOURCE. GUIDE TO SOURCES OF FEDERAL GOVERNMENT INFORMATION/INFO SOURCE. GUIDE DES SOURCES DE RENSEIGNEMENTS FEDERAUX. Text in English, French. 1991. a.
Published by: Treasury Board of Canada Secretariat, Corporate Communications/Secretariat du Conseil du Tresor du Canada, West Tower, Rm P-135, 300 Laurier Ave W, Ottawa, ON K1A 0R5, Canada. TEL 613-995-2855, FAX 613-996-0518, services-publications@tbs-sct.gc.ca, http://www.tbs-sct.gc.ca.

354.71 CAN ISSN 1184-8111
KE5325
INFO SOURCE. SOURCE DE RENSEIGNEMENTS FEDERAUX. Text in French. 1991. a.
Related titles: ◆ English ed.: Info Source. Sources of Federal Government Information. ISSN 1184-8103; ◆ Supplement(s): Info Source Bulletin. ISSN 0825-2238.
Published by: Treasury Board of Canada Secretariat, Corporate Communications/Secretariat du Conseil du Tresor du Canada, West Tower, Rm P-135, 300 Laurier Ave W, Ottawa, ON K1A 0R5, Canada. TEL 613-995-2855, FAX 613-996-0518, services-publications@tbs-sct.gc.ca, http://www.tbs-sct.gc.ca.

354.7 CAN ISSN 1188-7893
INFO SOURCE. SOURCES OF FEDERAL EMPLOYEE INFORMATION. Text in Multiple languages. 1991. a.
Published by: Treasury Board of Canada Secretariat, Corporate Communications/Secretariat du Conseil du Tresor du Canada, West Tower, Rm P-135, 300 Laurier Ave W, Ottawa, ON K1A 0R5, Canada. TEL 613-995-2855, FAX 613-996-0518, services-publications@tbs-sct.gc.ca, http://www.tbs-sct.gc.ca.

354.71 CAN ISSN 1184-8103
INFO SOURCE. SOURCES OF FEDERAL GOVERNMENT INFORMATION. Text in English. 1991. a.
Incorporates (1995-1999): Info Source. Directory of Federal Government Databases (1205-5158)
Related titles: ◆ French ed.: Info Source. Source de Renseignements Federaux. ISSN 1184-8111; ◆ Supplement(s): Info Source Bulletin. ISSN 0825-2238.
Published by: Treasury Board of Canada Secretariat, Corporate Communications/Secretariat du Conseil du Tresor du Canada, West Tower, Rm P-135, 300 Laurier Ave W, Ottawa, ON K1A 0R5, Canada. TEL 613-995-2855, FAX 613-996-0518, services-publications@tbs-sct.gc.ca, http://www.tbs-sct.gc.ca.

351.83 362 NLD ISSN 1874-5598
INFO WET MAATSCHAPPELIJKE ONDERSTEUNING. Text in Dutch. 2005. a. EUR 40.92 (effective 2009).
Published by: Elsevier Overheid (Subsidiary of: Reed Business bv), Postbus 152, Amsterdam, 1000 AD, Netherlands. TEL 31-20-5159222, FAX 31-20-5159145, Gemeente.nu@reedbusiness.nl, http://www.elsevieroverheid.nl.

349.2 DEU ISSN 1610-0468
➤ **INFORMATIONSDIENST OEFFENTLICHES DIENSTRECHT.** Text in German. 1992. 24/yr. EUR 199 (effective 2011). **Document type:** *Journal, Academic/Scholarly.*
Formerly (until 2002): Oeffentliches Dienstrecht (0941-7907)
Published by: Hermann Luchterhand Verlag GmbH (Subsidiary of: Wolters Kluwer Deutschland GmbH), Heddesdorfer Str 31, Neuwied, 56564, Germany. TEL 49-2631-8012222, FAX 49-2631-8012223, info@luchterhand.de, http://www.luchterhand.de.

351 ARG ISSN 1852-8457
INFORME ESTADISTICO DE LA SEGURIDAD SOCIAL. ADMINISTRACION PUBLICA. Text in Spanish. 2008. m. back issues avail. **Document type:** *Bulletin, Consumer.*
Media: Online - full text.
Published by: Caja de Jubilaciones, Pensiones y Retiros de Cordoba, Gral. Alvear 15, Centro, Cordoba, X5000ILA, Argentina.

▼ **INFORME ESTADISTICO DE LA SEGURIDAD SOCIAL. AUTORIDADES DEL PODER EJECUTIVO Y LEGISLATIVO Y LEGISLADORES.** *see* SOCIAL SERVICES AND WELFARE

351 CAN ISSN 1715-3816
➤ **THE INNOVATION JOURNAL.** Text in English. 1995. 3/yr. free. bk.rev. **Document type:** *Journal, Academic/Scholarly.* **Description:** Devoted to sharing ideas and information about public sector innovation. Aims to encourage innovation which will improve the quality, efficiency or effectiveness of government administration and policy.
Media: Online - full text.
Indexed: B01, B07, CA, PSA, S02, S03, SCOPUS, SSAI, SSAb, SSI, T02, W03, W05.
Published by: The Innovation Journal Ed. Eleanor Glor.

351 DEU ISSN 1618-9876
INNOVATIVE VERWALTUNG; das Fachmedium fuer erfolgreiches Verwaltungsmanagement. Text in German. 1978. 10/yr. EUR 155; EUR 88 to students (effective 2011). adv. bk.rev. reprint service avail. from PSC. **Document type:** *Magazine, Trade.*
Former titles (until 2002): V O P (1431-9985); (until 1996): V O P - Verwaltungsfuehrung (0946-9036); (until 1994): V O P - Verwaltungsfuehrung, Organisation, Personal (0946-9028); (until 1982): V O P - Verwaltungsfuehrung, Organisation, Personalwesen (0170-7140)
Indexed: A12, A13, A17, ABIn, P48, P51, P53, P54, PQC.
—CCC.
Published by: Betriebswirtschaftlicher Verlag Dr. Th. Gabler GmbH (Subsidiary of: Springer Fachmedien Wiesbaden GmbH), Abraham-Lincoln-Str 46, Wiesbaden, 65189, Germany. TEL 49-611-78780, FAX 49-611-7878400, springerfachmedien-wiesbaden@springer.com, http://www.gabler.de. Ed. Michael Kloeker. Adv. contact Eva Hanenberg. Circ: 7,047 (paid and controlled).

351 ITA ISSN 2035-4509
INNOVAZIONE. Text in Italian. 2003. fortn. **Document type:** *Magazine, Trade.*
Published by: Centro Nazionale per l'Informatica nella Pubblica Amministrazione (C N I P A), Viale Carlo Marx 31/49, Rome, 00137, Italy. TEL 39-800-254-009, http://www.cnipa.gov.it.

351 ITA ISSN 1828-2024
INNOV@ZIONE. P A. (Public Administration) Text in Italian. 2004. m. (11/yr.). EUR 30 domestic (effective 2009). **Document type:** *Magazine, Trade.*
Published by: Soiel International, Via Martiri Oscuri 3, Milan, MI 20125, Italy. TEL 39-02-26148855, FAX 39-02-26149333, info@soiel.it, http://www.soiel.it.

INQUERITO MENSAL DE CONJUNTURA A CONSTRUCAO E OBRAS PUBLICAS. *see* PUBLIC ADMINISTRATION—Abstracting, Bibliographies, Statistics

351.761 USA ISSN 0884-030X
INSIDE ALABAMA POLITICS. Text in English. 1985. w. USD 95 (effective 2011). **Document type:** *Newsletter, Trade.* **Description:** Takes readers behind the scenes of Alabama politics to give the facts, background, people, and politics behind the headlines.
Related titles: Online - full text ed.
Published by: (Inside Alabama Politics, Inc.), P M T Publishing Inc., 3729 Cottage Hill Rd, Ste H, Mobile, AL 36609. TEL 251-473-6269, FAX 251-479-8822, http://pmtpublishing.com.

351.774 USA ISSN 1052-8857
INSIDE MICHIGAN POLITICS. Text in English. 1987. bi-w. USD 180 (effective 2005). back issues avail.; reprints avail. **Document type:** *Newsletter, Trade.* **Description:** Covers Michigan government, politics and business.
Address: 2029 S Waverly Rd, Lansing, MI 48917-4263. TEL 517-487-6665, 800-715-7873, FAX 517-487-3830, impbb@tir.com. Ed., Pub., R&P William S Ballenger. Circ: 1,170 (paid and controlled).

351 NLD ISSN 1874-9992
INSPECTIEBERICHT. Text in Dutch. 2005. irreg., latest vol.4, 2008.
Published by: Ministerie van Veiligheid en Justitie, Inspectie Openbare Orde en Veiligheid, Postbus 20301, The Hague, 2500 EH, Netherlands. TEL 31-70-4266261, FAX 31-70-4266990.

351 ESP ISSN 1560-5264
INSTITUCIONES Y DESARROLLO. Text in Spanish, English, Catalan. 1998. s-a. EUR 40 domestic; EUR 54 in Europe; EUR 70 elsewhere (effective 2002). back issues avail. **Document type:** *Magazine, Consumer.*
Related titles: Online - full text ed.
Published by: Instituto Internacional de Gobernabilidad, Corsega, 255, 5o. 1a., Barcelona, Cataluna 08036, Spain. TEL 34-93-2370388, FAX 34-93-2376026, iig@iigov.org, http://www.iigov.org/. Ed. Cesar Yanez.

351 DEU
INSTITUT FUER VERWALTUNG UND VERWALTUNGSRECHT IN DEN NEUEN BUNDESLAENDERN. SCHRIFTEN. Text in German. 1993. irreg., latest vol.3, 1997. price varies. **Document type:** *Monographic series, Academic/Scholarly.*
Published by: (Institut fuer Verwaltung und Verwaltungsrecht in den Neuen Bundeslaendern e.V.), B W V - Berliner Wissenschafts Verlag GmbH, Markgrafenstr 12-14, Berlin, 10969, Germany. TEL 49-30-8417700, FAX 49-30-84177021, bwv@bwv-verlag.de, http://www.bwv-verlag.de.

351 CAN ISSN 1719-9093
INSTITUTE FOR RESEARCH ON PUBLIC POLICY. ANNUAL REPORT. Text in English. 1999. a. free. **Document type:** *Report.*
Media: Online - full text. **Related titles:** Print ed.: ISSN 0827-1321. 1973.
Published by: Institute for Research on Public Policy/Institut de Recherches Politiques, 1470 Peel St, Ste 200, Montreal, PQ H3A 1T1, Canada. TEL 514-985-2461, FAX 514-985-2559, irrp@irrp.org.

INSTITUTE FOR STRATEGIC STUDIES. BULLETIN/INSTITUUT VIR STRATEGIESE STUDIES. BULLETIN. *see* POLITICAL SCIENCE—International Relations

351 IRL ISSN 0073-9596
JN1400
INSTITUTE OF PUBLIC ADMINISTRATION, DUBLIN. ADMINISTRATION YEARBOOK AND DIARY. Text mainly in English; Some issues in Irish. 1967. a. EUR 65 (effective 2003). adv. **Document type:** *Directory, Trade.*
—BLDSC (0696.300000).
Published by: Institute of Public Administration, 57-61 Lansdowne Rd., Ballsbridge, Dublin, 4, Ireland. TEL 353-1-6686233, FAX 353-1-6689135, http://www.ipa.ie. Ed. Tony McNamara. Adv. contact Eileen Kelly. Circ: 10,700 (paid).

351 IRL ISSN 0073-9588
INSTITUTE OF PUBLIC ADMINISTRATION, DUBLIN. ANNUAL REPORT. Text mainly in English; Some issues in Irish. 1958. a. free. **Document type:** *Corporate.*
Published by: Institute of Public Administration, 57-61 Lansdowne Rd., Ballsbridge, Dublin, 4, Ireland. TEL 353-1-6686233, FAX 353-1-6689135, mcnamara@ipa.ie, http://www.ipa.ie. Ed. Tony McNamara. Circ: 2,000.

351 IRL ISSN 1393-6190
INSTITUTE OF PUBLIC ADMINISTRATION, DUBLIN. DISCUSSION PAPER. Variant title: C P M R. Discussion Paper. Text in English. 1977. irreg. **Document type:** *Monographic series.*
Published by: (Institute of Public Administration, Committee for Public Management Research), Institute of Public Administration, 57-61 Lansdowne Rd., Ballsbridge, Dublin, 4, Ireland. TEL 353-1-6686233, FAX 353-1-6689135, http://www.ipa.ie.

351 IRL ISSN 1393-9424
INSTITUTE OF PUBLIC ADMINISTRATION, DUBLIN. RESEARCH REPORT. Variant title: C P M R. Research Report. Text in English. 1998. irreg. **Document type:** *Monographic series.*
Published by: (Institute of Public Administration, Committee for Public Management Research), Institute of Public Administration, 57-61 Lansdowne Rd., Ballsbridge, Dublin, 4, Ireland. TEL 353-1-6686233, FAX 353-1-6689135, http://www.ipa.ie.

351 SDN ISSN 0073-9618
INSTITUTE OF PUBLIC ADMINISTRATION, KHARTOUM. OCCASIONAL PAPERS. Text in English. 1964. irreg.
Published by: Institute of Public Administration, P O Box 1492, Khartoum, Sudan.

351 SDN ISSN 0073-9626
INSTITUTE OF PUBLIC ADMINISTRATION, KHARTOUM. PROCEEDINGS OF THE ANNUAL ROUND TABLE CONFERENCE. Text in Arabic, English. 1959. irreg. **Document type:** *Proceedings.*
Published by: Institute of Public Administration, P O Box 1492, Khartoum, Sudan.

INSTITUTO NACIONAL DE ESTADISTICA. BOLETIM MENSAL DE ESTADISTICA. *see* PUBLIC ADMINISTRATION—Abstracting, Bibliographies, Statistics

351 PRT ISSN 1646-7558
INSTITUTO NACIONAL DE ESTATISTICA. Text in Portuguese. 200?. a. **Document type:** *Report, Government.*
Related titles: Special ed(s).: O Instituto Nacional de Estatistica (Abridged Edition). ISSN 1647-0303. 2008.
Address: Av Antonio Jose de Almeida 2, Lisbon, 1000-043, Portugal. TEL 351-21-8426100, FAX 351-21-8426380, ine@ine.pt, http://www.ine.pt.

351 USA ISSN 0074-106X
INTER-UNIVERSITY CASE PROGRAM. CASE STUDY. Text in English. 1951. irreg. price varies.
Published by: Inter-University Case Program, Inc., PO Box 229, Syracuse, NY 13210. Ed. E A Bock.

351 USA ISSN 2154-6649
INTERGOVERNMENTAL SOLUTIONS NEWSLETTER. Text in English. 200?. s-a. free (effective 2010). back issues avail. **Document type:** *Newsletter, Government.* **Description:** Focuses in depth on a topic of particular interest and current relevance to the intergovernmental IT community with articles and analysis from government officials and academic, non-profit, and industry organizations.
Former titles (until 2004): O I S Newsletter (1559-6818); (until 200?): Intergovernmental Solutions Newsletter
Media: Online - full text. **Related titles:** ◆ Print ed.: United States. General Services Administration. Office of Intergovernmental Solutions. Newsletter. ISSN 1559-6699.
Published by: U.S. General Services Administration, Office of Citizen Services and Communications, 1800 F St, NW, Washington, DC 20405. TEL 800-488-3111, FAX 800-465-1416, rodsm.ncsc@gsa.gov.

INTERINSTITUTIONAL DIRECTORY. WHO'S WHO IN THE EUROPEAN UNION?. *see* BIOGRAPHY

352.48 USA ISSN 0743-2844
JK864
THE INTERIOR BUDGET IN BRIEF. Text in English. 19??. a. free (effective 2011). back issues avail. **Document type:** *Report, Government.*
Formerly: Budget Highlights
Related titles: Online - full text ed.
Published by: U.S. Department of the Interior, 1849 C St., NW, Washington, DC 20240. TEL 202-208-3100.

352.68 USA
INTERNATIONAL ASSOCIATION OF CLERKS, RECORDERS, ELECTION OFFICIALS, AND TREASURERS. NEWS. Text in English. q. membership. **Document type:** *Newsletter, Trade.*
Published by: International Association of Clerks, Recorders, Election Officials, and Treasurers, 2400 Augusta Dr, Ste 250, Houston, TX 77057. TEL 800-890-7368, FAX 713-789-1897, tjsthree@msn.com, http://www.iacreot.com. Circ: 1,400.

351 341 USA ISSN 1077-8497
E179.5
INTERNATIONAL BOUNDARY COMMISSION. JOINT ANNUAL REPORT. Text in English. 1978. a.
Formerly (until 1986): Canada and the United States Annual Joint Report (0732-7404)
Published by: International Boundary Commission, 1250 23rd St, Ste 100, Washington, DC 20037. TEL 202-736-9102, FAX 202-736-9015.

351 NLD ISSN 1382-4414
➤ **INTERNATIONAL INSTITUTE OF ADMINISTRATIVE SCIENCES MONOGRAPHS.** Text in English. 1995. irreg., latest vol.30, 2009. price varies. back issues avail. **Document type:** *Monographic series, Academic/Scholarly.*
Related titles: Online - full text ed.: ISSN 1879-8446.
—BLDSC (4541.305500). **CCC.**
Published by: (International Institute of Administrative Sciences), I O S Press, Nieuwe Hemweg 6B, Amsterdam, 1013 BG, Netherlands. TEL 31-20-6883355, FAX 31-20-6870039, info@iospress.nl. **Subscr. to:** I O S Press, Inc, 4502 Rachael Manor Dr, Fairfax, VA 22032-3631. sales@iospress.com. **Dist. by:** Ohmsha Ltd. TEL 81-3-32330641, http://www.ohmsha.co.jp.

351 BEL ISSN 0074-6479
INTERNATIONAL INSTITUTE OF ADMINISTRATIVE SCIENCES. REPORTS OF THE INTERNATIONAL CONGRESS. Text in English. 1910. triennial. **Document type:** *Proceedings.*
Published by: International Institute of Administrative Sciences, Rue Defacqz 1, Bte 11, Brussels, 1000, Belgium. TEL 32-2-536-0880, FAX 32-2-537-9702, http://www.iiasiisa.be.

351 USA ISSN 1547-4844
HF1
➤ **INTERNATIONAL JOURNAL OF BUSINESS AND PUBLIC ADMINISTRATION.** Text in English. 2004. s-a. (2-3/yr.). USD 30 per issue (effective 2009). **Document type:** *Journal, Academic/Scholarly.*
Indexed: B01, T02.
Published by: International Academy of Business and Public Administration Disciplines (I A B P A D), PO Box 295, Ruston, LA 71273. TEL 318-255-1491, FAX 318-255-9415, iabpad_conference@suddenlink.net, http://www.iabpad.com. Eds. Raja Nassar, Abdalla Hagen.

▼ ➤ **INTERNATIONAL JOURNAL OF BUSINESS AND PUBLIC MANAGEMENT.** *see* BUSINESS AND ECONOMICS—Management

➤ **INTERNATIONAL JOURNAL OF ELECTRONIC DEMOCRACY.** *see* POLITICAL SCIENCE

351 629.8 GBR ISSN 1742-7509
➤ **INTERNATIONAL JOURNAL OF ELECTRONIC GOVERNANCE.** Text in English. 2007. 4/yr. EUR 494 to institutions (print or online ed.); EUR 672 combined subscription to institutions (print & online eds.) (effective 2012). bk.rev. charts; illus.; abstr.; bibl. **Document type:** *Journal, Academic/Scholarly.* **Description:** Publishes articles that present current research and practice in all areas of electronic governance.
Related titles: Online - full text ed.: ISSN 1742-7517 (from IngentaConnect).
Indexed: A26, A28, APA, BrCerAb, C&ISA, CA, CA/WCA, CIA, CerAb, CivEngAb, CorrAb, E&CAJ, E11, EEA, EMA, ESPM, EnvEAb, H15, I05, M&TEA, M09, MBF, METADEX, P42, RiskAb, SolStAb, T02, T04, WAA.
—BLDSC (4542.231250), IE. **CCC.**
Published by: Inderscience Publishers, PO Box 735, Olney, Bucks MK46 5WB, United Kingdom. TEL 44-1234-240519, FAX 44-1234-240515, editorial@inderscience.com. Ed. Panagiotis Georgiadis. **Subscr. to:** World Trade Centre Bldg, 29 Rte de Pre-Bois, Case Postale 856, Geneva 15 1215, Switzerland. FAX 41-22-7910885, subs@inderscience.com.

351 004 USA ISSN 1548-3886
T49.5
➤ **INTERNATIONAL JOURNAL OF ELECTRONIC GOVERNMENT RESEARCH.** Text in English. 2005. q. USD 210 to individuals; USD 595 to institutions; USD 275 combined subscription to individuals (print & online eds.); USD 860 combined subscription to institutions (print & online eds.) (effective 2012). **Document type:** *Journal, Academic/Scholarly.* **Description:** Publishes high-quality, original research about electronic government.
Related titles: Online - full text ed.: ISSN 1548-3894. 2005. USD 140 to individuals; USD 595 to institutions (effective 2012).
Indexed: A12, A17, A26, A28, ABIn, APA, BrCerAb, C&ISA, CA, CA/WCA, CIA, CerAb, CivEngAb, CorrAb, E&CAJ, E11, EEA, EMA, ESPM, EnvEAb, H15, I05, IBSS, Inspec, L13, M&TEA, M09, MBF, METADEX, P17, P21, P27, P42, P48, P51, P52, P53, P54, PQC, PSA, SCOPUS, SolStAb, T02, T04, WAA.
—BLDSC (4542.231300), IE, Ingenta, Linda Hall. **CCC.**
Published by: (Information Resources Management Association), I G I Global, 701 E Chocolate Ave, Ste 200, Hershey, PA 17033. TEL 717-533-8845 ext 100, 866-342-6657, FAX 717-533-8661, cust@igi-global.com. Ed. Vishanth Weerakkody.

▼ ➤ **INTERNATIONAL JOURNAL OF ENERGY ECONOMICS AND POLICY.** *see* ENERGY

351 GBR ISSN 1740-2816
➤ **INTERNATIONAL JOURNAL OF FORESIGHT AND INNOVATION POLICY.** Abbreviated title: I J F I P. Text in English. 2004. 4/yr. EUR 494 to institutions (print or online ed.); EUR 672 combined subscription to institutions (print & online eds.) (effective 2012). abstr.; bibl.; charts; stat.; illus. back issues avail. **Document type:** *Journal, Academic/Scholarly.* **Description:** Aims to further develop insight into the role of strategic intelligence in innovation policy and practice by acting as a scientific forum and contributing to the interaction between researchers, policy makers and actors involved in innovation processes.
Related titles: Online - full text ed.: ISSN 1740-2824 (from IngentaConnect).
Indexed: A26, A28, APA, B02, B15, B17, B18, BrCerAb, C&ISA, CA, CA/WCA, CIA, CerAb, CivEngAb, CorrAb, E&CAJ, E08, E11, EEA, EMA, ESPM, EnvEAb, G04, G08, H15, I05, Inspec, M&TEA, M09, MBF, METADEX, S09, SCOPUS, SolStAb, T02, T04, WAA.
—BLDSC (4542.257350), IE, Ingenta, Linda Hall. **CCC.**
Published by: Inderscience Publishers, PO Box 735, Olney, Bucks MK46 5WB, United Kingdom. TEL 44-1234-240519, FAX 44-1234-240515, editorial@inderscience.com. Ed. Dr. M A Dorgham. **Subscr. to:** World Trade Centre Bldg, 29 Rte de Pre-Bois, Case Postale 856, Geneva 15 1215, Switzerland. FAX 41-22-7910885, subs@inderscience.com.

350.7232 USA
INTERNATIONAL JOURNAL OF GOVERNMENT AUDITING (ONLINE). Text in English, French, German, Spanish. 1999. q. free (effective 2008). **Document type:** *Journal, Trade.* **Description:** Dedicated to the advancement of government auditing procedures and techniques.
Media: Online - full text.
Published by: International Organization of Supreme Audit Institutions, c/o U S General Accounting Office, 441 G St, N W, Rm 7814, Washington, DC 20548. TEL 202-512-4707, FAX 202-512-4021, spel@gao.gov, http://www.intosai.org. Ed. Donald R Drach.

351.4105 GBR ISSN 1754-8187
THE INTERNATIONAL JOURNAL OF LEADERSHIP IN PUBLIC SERVICE. Text in English. 2005. q. EUR 689 combined subscription in Europe (print & online eds.); USD 889 combined subscription in the Americas (print & online eds.); GBP 529 combined subscription in the UK & elsewhere (print & online eds.); AUD 999 combined subscription in Australasia (print & online eds.) (effective 2012). adv. back issues avail. **Document type:** *Journal, Academic/Scholarly.* **Description:** Brings together leaders, academics and policy makers to disseminate and debate approaches to leadership and improving public services.
Formerly (until 2007): The British Journal of Leadership in Public Services (1747-9886)
Related titles: Online - full text ed.: ISSN 2042-8642 (from IngentaConnect).
Indexed: A01, CA, N06, P34, P42, S02, S03, T02.
—BLDSC (4542.314525), IE, Ingenta. **CCC.**

P

Published by: (International Initiative for Mental Health Leadership NZL), Pier Professional Ltd. (Subsidiary of: Emerald Group Publishing Ltd.), Ste N4, The Old Market, Upper Market St, Hove, BN3 1AS, United Kingdom. TEL 44-1273-783720, FAX 44-1273-783723, info@pierprofessional.com. Eds. Mark Davidson, Steve Onyett. Adv. contact Paul Somerville TEL 44-1273-783724. B&W page GBP 350; 160 x 245.

351 USA ISSN 1093-4537
HD28 CODEN: IJOTFD
➤ **INTERNATIONAL JOURNAL OF ORGANIZATION THEORY AND BEHAVIOR.** Text in English. 1998. q. USD 295 domestic to individuals print or online ed.; USD 395 domestic to libraries print or online ed.; USD 305 foreign to individuals print or online ed.; USD 405 foreign to libraries print or online ed. (effective 2009). bk.rev. abstr.; bibl.; charts; illus. 140 p./no. 1 cols./p.; back issues avail. **Document type:** *Journal, Academic/Scholarly.* **Description:** Includes organization theory, group theory and behavior organization, work motivation, individual decision-making, organization development, and performance review and measurement.
Related titles: Online - full text ed.: ISSN 1532-4273.
Indexed: A09, A10, A12, A13, A17, A22, ABIn, B01, B06, B07, B08, B09, B16, CA, DIP, E01, HRA, I13, IBR, IBZ, N06, P02, P10, P16, P27, P42, P48, P51, P53, P54, PQC, S02, S03, SCOPUS, SPAA, SociolAb, T02, V03, V04.
—BLDSC (4542.435100), IE, Ingenta. **CCC.**
Published by: PrAcademics Press, 21760 Mountain Sugar Ln, Boca Raton, FL 33433. TEL 561-362-9183, FAX 561-391-9572, AdMin@PrAcademicsPress.com, http://www.pracademics.com. Eds. Jack Rabin, Khi V Thai TEL 561-297-4007. Pub. Xuan H Thai. Circ: 200 (paid).

351 USA ISSN 0190-0692
JA1.A1 CODEN: IJPADR
➤ **INTERNATIONAL JOURNAL OF PUBLIC ADMINISTRATION.** Text in English. 1979. 14/yr. GBP 2,519 combined subscription in United Kingdom to institutions (print & online eds.); EUR 3,325, USD 4,178 combined subscription to institutions (print & online eds.) (effective 2012). adv. reprint service avail. from PSC. **Document type:** *Journal, Academic/Scholarly.* **Description:** Presents a forum for academicians and practitioners in management and administration to share theoretical issues as well as applications of concepts and theories.
Related titles: Microform ed.: (from RPI); Online - full text ed.: ISSN 1532-4265. GBP 2,267 in United Kingdom to institutions; EUR 2,992, USD 3,760 to institutions (effective 2012) (from IngentaConnect).
Indexed: A12, A13, A17, A20, A22, A26, ABIn, ABS&EES, ASG, B01, B02, B06, B07, B08, B09, B15, B17, B18, BPIA, CA, DIP, E-psyche, E01, E08, G04, G06, G07, G08, I05, I08, I13, IBR, IBZ, M06, ManagCont, P10, P34, P42, P48, P51, P53, P54, PAA&I, PAIS, PQC, PRA, PSA, PSI, PersLit, S02, S03, S09, SCOPUS, SPAA, SUSA, SociolAb, T02.
—IE, Infotrieve, Ingenta. **CCC.**
Published by: Taylor & Francis Inc. (Subsidiary of: Taylor & Francis Group), 325 Chestnut St, Ste 800, Philadelphia, PA 19106. TEL 215-625-2940, 800-354-1420, orders@taylorandfrancis.com, http://www.taylorandfrancis.com. Ed. Colin Talbot. Adv. contact Linda Hann TEL 44-1344-779945.

351 GBR ISSN 1740-0600
➤ **INTERNATIONAL JOURNAL OF PUBLIC POLICY.** Abbreviated title: I J P P. Text in English. 2005. 6/yr. (in 2 vols., 4 nos./vol.). EUR 593 to institutions (print or online ed.); EUR 830 combined subscription to institutions (print & online eds.) (effective 2012). abstr.; bibl.; charts; illus.; stat. back issues avail. **Document type:** *Journal, Academic/ Scholarly.* **Description:** Proposes and fosters discussion on public policy issues facing nation states and national and supranational organizations, including governments, and how these diverse groups approach and solve common public policy problems.
Related titles: Online - full text ed.: ISSN 1740-0619 (from IngentaConnect).
Indexed: A26, A28, APA, B02, B15, B17, B18, B21, BrCerAb, C&ISA, CA/WCA, CIA, CerAb, CivEngAb, CorrAb, E&CAJ, E08, E11, EEA, EMA, ESPM, EconLit, EnvEAb, G04, G08, H&SSA, H15, I05, Inspec, JEL, M&TEA, M09, MBF, METADEX, P30, S09, SCOPUS, SolStAb, T04, WAA.
—BLDSC (4542.509105), IE, Ingenta, Linda Hall. **CCC.**
Published by: Inderscience Publishers, PO Box 735, Olney, Bucks MK46 5WB, United Kingdom. TEL 44-1234-240519, FAX 44-1234-240515, editorial@inderscience.com. Ed. Dr. M A Dorgham. **Subscr. to:** World Trade Centre Bldg, 29 Rte de Pre-Bois, Case Postale 856, Geneva 15 1215, Switzerland. FAX 41-22-7910885, subs@inderscience.com.

351 USA ISSN 1949-2332
▼ ➤ **INTERNATIONAL JOURNAL OF PUBLIC PROCUREMENT.** Text in English. 2011 (Apr.). q. USD 375; USD 700 combined subscription (print & online eds.) (effective 2011). **Document type:** *Journal, Academic/Scholarly.* **Description:** Features research on procurement policy, procurement strategic planning and scheduling, contract formation, contract administration, evaluation, and procurement methods and techniques around the world.
Related titles: Online - full text ed.: ISSN 1949-2340. 2010 (Mar.).
Published by: PrAcademics Press, 21760 Mountain Sugar Ln, Boca Raton, FL 33433. TEL 561-362-9183, FAX 561-391-9572, info@pracademics.com, http://www.pracademics.com. Ed. Khi V Thai TEL 561-297-4007.

351 GBR ISSN 1741-1041
➤ **INTERNATIONAL JOURNAL OF PUBLIC SECTOR PERFORMANCE MANAGEMENT.** Abbreviated title: I J P S P M. Text in English. 2007 (May). 4/yr. EUR 494 to institutions (print or online ed.); EUR 672 combined subscription to institutions (print & online eds.) (effective 2012). abstr.; bibl.; charts; illus. back issues avail. **Document type:** *Journal, Academic/Scholarly.* **Description:** Proposes and fosters discussion on performance management in the public sector, with an emphasis on the implementation of performance management technologies.
Related titles: Online - full text ed.: ISSN 1741-105X (from IngentaConnect).
Indexed: A26, A28, APA, B02, B15, B17, B18, BrCerAb, C&ISA, CA/WCA, CIA, CerAb, CivEngAb, CorrAb, E&CAJ, E11, EEA, EMA, ESPM, EnvEAb, G04, H15, I05, M&TEA, M09, MBF, METADEX, SCOPUS, SolStAb, T04, WAA.
—BLDSC (4542.509252), IE. **CCC.**

Published by: Inderscience Publishers, PO Box 735, Olney, Bucks MK46 5WB, United Kingdom. TEL 44-1234-240519, FAX 44-1234-240515, editorial@inderscience.com. Ed. Robert Fouchet. **Subscr. to:** World Trade Centre Bldg, 29 Rte de Pre-Bois, Case Postale 856, Geneva 15 1215, Switzerland. FAX 41-22-7910885, subs@inderscience.com.

351 658 USA ISSN 1096-7494
JA1
➤ **INTERNATIONAL PUBLIC MANAGEMENT JOURNAL.** Abbreviated title: I P M J. Text in English. 1998. q. GBP 275 combined subscription in United Kingdom to institutions (print & online eds.); EUR 364, USD 457 combined subscription to institutions (print & online eds.) (effective 2012). adv. back issues avail.; reprint service avail. from PSC. **Document type:** *Journal, Academic/Scholarly.* **Description:** Features work from scholars around the world who conduct research in the areas of public management and government reform, comparative public administration, organizational theory, and organizational behavior.
Related titles: Online - full text ed.: ISSN 1559-3169. GBP 248 in United Kingdom to institutions; EUR 328, USD 411 to institutions (effective 2012) (from IngentaConnect).
Indexed: A12, A17, A20, A22, ABIn, B01, B06, B07, B09, CA, CurCont, E01, IBR, IBZ, P34, P42, P48, P51, P53, P54, PAIS, PQC, PSA, SCOPUS, SPAA, SSCI, SociolAb, T02, W07.
—BLDSC (4545.380000), IE, Infotrieve, Ingenta. **CCC.**
Published by: (International Public Management Network), Routledge (Subsidiary of: Taylor & Francis Group), 325 Chestnut St, Ste 800, Philadelphia, PA 19106. TEL 800-354-1420, FAX 215-625-2940, journals@routledge.com, http://www.routledge.com. Ed. Steven Kelman. Adv. contact Linda Hann TEL 44-1344-779945.

351 GBR ISSN 0020-8523
JA1.A1
➤ **INTERNATIONAL REVIEW OF ADMINISTRATIVE SCIENCES;** an international journal of comparative public administration. Abbreviated title: I R A S. Text in English. 1953. q. GBP 636, USD 1,177 to institutions; GBP 649, USD 1,201 combined subscription to institutions (print & online eds.) (effective 2012). adv. bk.rev. bibl. index. cum.index every 5 yrs. back issues avail.; reprint service avail. from PSC. **Document type:** *Journal, Academic/Scholarly.* **Description:** Presents comparative studies and national monographs on international administration, national civil services, controls on central government, administrative reform, public finance, regionalization and the history of administration.
Formerly (until 1957): Progress in Public Administration (0552-3060)
Related titles: Online - full text ed.: ISSN 1461-7226. GBP 584, USD 1,081 to institutions (effective 2012); ◆ French ed.: Revue Internationale des Sciences Administratives. ISSN 0303-965X; Spanish ed.: Revista Internacional de Ciencias Administrativas. ISSN 0255-3635.
Indexed: A12, A17, A20, A22, ABCPolSci, ABIn, ASCA, BAS, BPIA, BibInd, CA, CPM, CurCont, DIP, E01, EI, FLP, GEOBASE, I13, I14, IBR, IBSS, IBZ, ILD, KES, MEA&I, ManagCont, P06, P42, P48, P51, P53, P54, PAA&I, PAIS, PCI, PQC, PRA, PSA, SCOPUS, SPAA, SSCI, SociolAb, T02, W07.
—BLDSC (4545.900000), IE, Ingenta. **CCC.**
Published by: (International Institute of Administrative Sciences BEL), Sage Publications Ltd. (Subsidiary of: Sage Publications, Inc.), 1 Oliver's Yard, 55 City Rd, London, EC1Y 1SP, United Kingdom. TEL 44-20-73248500, FAX 44-20-73248600, info@sagepub.co.uk, http://www.uk.sagepub.com/home.nav. Ed. Christopher Pollitt. **Subscr. in the Americas to:** Sage Publications, Inc., 2455 Teller Rd, Thousand Oaks, CA 91320. TEL 805-499-9774, FAX 805-499-0871, journals@sagepub.com.

➤ **INTERNATIONAL REVIEW OF COMPARATIVE PUBLIC POLICY.** *see* POLITICAL SCIENCE

351 KOR ISSN 1229-4659
JA26
INTERNATIONAL REVIEW OF PUBLIC ADMINISTRATION. Text in English. 1996. s-a. membership. bk.rev. **Document type:** *Journal, Trade.*
Formerly (until 1999): Korean Review of Public Administration (1226-4431)
Indexed: I13, P42, SCOPUS.
—BLDSC (4547.522000), IE, Ingenta.
Published by: Han'gug Haeng'jeong Haghoe/Korean Association for Public Administration, Ste. 1609, Gwanghwamun Ssangyong Platinum Bldg. 156, Jeokeon-dong, Jongno-gu, Seoul, 110-052, Korea, S. TEL 82-2-7364977, FAX 82-2-7382190, kapa21@kapa21.or.kr. Eds. Jae Kim, Suk-Won Won Lee.

INTERNATIONAL RISK GOVERNANCE COUNCIL BOOKSERIES. *see* BUSINESS AND ECONOMICS—Management

INTERNATIONAL UPDATE. *see* SOCIAL SERVICES AND WELFARE

328.777 USA ISSN 0738-9450
IOWA LEGISLATIVE NEWS SERVICE BULLETIN. Text in English. 1979. d. (during session; bi-m., during interim). looseleaf. USD 495 (effective 2007). reprints avail. **Document type:** *Bulletin.* **Description:** Provides abstracts of each bill and study bill introduced. Tracks committee and floor action on bills. Reports on interim committees, and provides other related information.
Related titles: Online - full text ed.; Alternate Frequency ed(s).: Iowa Legislative News Service Bulletin (Interim Report Edition). ISSN 0740-3151.
Published by: Iowa Legislative News Service, PO Box 8370, Des Moines, IA 50301-8370. TEL 515-288-4676, FAX 515-266-6626, ialns.news@gmail.com. Ed., Pub. Jack Hunt.

IOWA OFFICIAL REGISTER. *see* PUBLIC ADMINISTRATION—Abstracting, Bibliographies, Statistics

351.415 IRL ISSN 0790-1070
IRELAND, A DIRECTORY. Text in English. 1975. a. price varies. adv. index.
Formerly (until 1981): Ireland, a Directory and Yearbook (0332-2300)
Published by: Institute of Public Administration, 57-61 Lansdowne Rd., Ballsbridge, Dublin, 4, Ireland. TEL 353-1-6686233, FAX 353-1-6689135, http://www.ipa.ie. Ed. Daniel Sullivan. Circ: 8,500.

IRELAND. ENVIRONMENTAL PROTECTION AGENCY. REPORT. *see* ENVIRONMENTAL STUDIES

351.415 IRL
IRELAND. PUBLIC SERVICE ADVISORY COUNCIL. REPORT. Text in English. 1975. a. **Document type:** *Government.*

Published by: (Ireland. Public Service Advisory Council), Government Publications Sales Office, Sun Alliance House, Molesworth St., Dublin, 2, Ireland.

351 IRL
IRIS OIFIGIUIL. Text in English, Irish. fortn. EUR 5.71 newsstand/cover (effective 2005). adv. 10 p./no. 2 cols./p.; Supplement avail.; back issues avail. **Document type:** *Newspaper, Government.*
Formerly (until 1922): Dublin Gazette
Published by: (Publications Section), Government Supplies Agency, Postal Trade Section, 51 St. Stephen's Green, Dublin, 2, Ireland. TEL 353-1-6476838, FAX 353-1-6476842. Circ: 600.

IRISH LAW REPORTS MONTHLY. *see* LAW—Civil Law

351 USA ISSN 1932-3921
IRVING B. HARRIS GRADUATE SCHOOL OF PUBLIC POLICY STUDIES. WORKING PAPER SERIES. Text in English. 19??. irreg. **Document type:** *Monographic series, Academic/Scholarly.*
Related titles: Online - full text ed.
Published by: University of Chicago, Irving B Harris Graduate School of Public Policy Studies, 1155 E 60th St, Chicago, IL 60637. TEL 773-702-8400, harrisschool@uchicago.edu.

351 ITA ISSN 1970-6332
ITALY. SENATO DELLA REBUBBLICA. ARCHIVIO STORICO. CARTEGGI. Text in Italian. 2003. irreg. **Document type:** *Monographic series, Government.*
Published by: (Senato della Repubblica), Rubbettino Editore, Viale Rosario Rubbettino 10, Soveria Mannelli, CZ 88049, Italy. TEL 39-0968-662034, FAX 39-0968-662055, segreteria@rubbettino.it, http://www.rubbettino.it.

351.43 DEU
J V B - PRESSE. (Justizvollzugsbediensteten) Text in German. bi-m. adv.
Published by: Landesverband der Bayerischen Justizvollzugsbediensteten e.V., Koenigreichweg 24, Straubing, 94315, Germany. TEL 49-9421-923401, FAX 49-9421-923402, http://www.jvb-bbb.de. adv.: B&W page EUR 164. Circ: 3,100 (controlled).

351.492 NLD ISSN 2210-8890
▼ **JAARBOEK ACTIEVE CULTUURPARTICIPATIE.** Text in Dutch. 2010. a.
Published by: Fonds voor Cultuurparticipatie, Postbus 465, Utrrecht, 3500 AL, Netherlands. TEL 31-30-2336030, info@cultuurparticipatie.nl.

351 NLD ISSN 1871-0034
JAARBOEK KENNISSAMENLEVING. Text in Dutch. 2005. a. EUR 29.90 (effective 2009).
Published by: Uitgeverij Aksant, Cruquiusweg 31, Amsterdam, Netherlands. TEL 31-20-8500150, FAX 31-20-6656411, info@aksant.nl, http://www.aksant.nl.

328 AUT
JAHRBUCH DES OESTERREICHISCHEN PARLAMENTS; Daten - Fakten - Analysen. Text in German. 1994. irreg. **Document type:** *Government.*
Published by: (Oesterreichische Parlamentarische Gesellschaft), Manz'sche Verlags- und Universitaetsbuchhandlung GmbH, Johannesgasse 23, Vienna, W 1010, Austria. TEL 43-1-53161-0, FAX 43-1-53161-181. Ed. Guenther Schefbeck.

JAPAN'S AND I C H GUIDELINES FOR NEW DRUG REGISTRATION (YEAR). *see* PHARMACY AND PHARMACOLOGY

351.5357 UAE
AL-JARIDAH AR-RASMIYYAH LI-DAWLAT AL-IMARAT AL-ARABIYYAH AL-MUTTAHIDAH/UNITED ARAB EMIRATES. OFFICIAL GAZETTE. Text in Arabic. 1971. m. cum.index: 1971-1985. **Description:** Publishes laws and governmental decisions from all U.A.E. Ministries.
Published by: Wizarat al-Dawlah li-Shu'un Majlis al-Wuzara'/State Ministry of Cabinet Affairs, PO Box 899, Abu Dhabi, United Arab Emirates. TEL 651113, FAX 661172. Ed. Ahmad Muhammad Hamza. Circ: 13,000.

JAVNA UPRAVA. *see* LAW

351 320 300 CHN
JIANGHUAI - WENZHAI. Text in Chinese. 2004. m. **Document type:** *Magazine, Government.*
Formed by the 2004 merger of: Anhui Gongzuo; (1957-2003): Dangyuan Shenghuo (1006-236X)
Published by: Zhonggong Anhui Sheng Wei, Jianghuai Zazhishe, 1, Hongxin Lu, 8/F, Shengweiban Gongting Fuwu Luo, Hefei, 230001, China. TEL 86-551-2608426, FAX 86-551-2608426.

352.8 USA ISSN 1546-4660
RA997.A1
JOINT COMMISSION INTERNATIONAL ACCREDITATION STANDARDS FOR THE CARE CONTINUUM. Text in English. 2003. biennial. USD 95 per issue (effective 2011). **Document type:** *Handbook/Manual/Guide, Trade.*
Related titles: Online - full text ed.: USD 75 per issue (effective 2011).
Published by: Joint Commission Resources, Inc. (Subsidiary of: Joint Commission on Accreditation of Healthcare Organizations), 1515 W 22nd St, Ste 1300W, Oak Brook, IL 60523. TEL 630-268-7400, jcrcustomerservice@pbd.com.

330.9 USA ISSN 0162-5888
HC106.5
THE JOINT ECONOMIC REPORT. Text in English. 196?. a. **Document type:** *Report, Government.*
Supersedes in part: Annual Report on the Economic Report of the President
Published by: (U.S. Congress), U.S. Government Printing Office, 732 N Capitol St, NW, Washington, DC 20401. TEL 202-512-1800, 866-512-1800, FAX 202-512-2104, ContactCenter@gpo.gov, http://www.gpo.gov.

351 331.1 NLD ISSN 1877-217X
JONG EN AMBTENAAR. Text in Dutch. 2008. a.
Related titles: ◆ Supplement to: Binnenlands Bestuur. ISSN 0167-1146.
Published by: Kluwer B.V. (Subsidiary of: Wolters Kluwer N.V.), Postbus 23, Deventer, 7400 GA, Netherlands. TEL 31-570-673449, FAX 31-570-691555, info@kluwer.nl, http://www.kluwer.nl.

351.44949 MCO ISSN 1010-8742
JOURNAL DE MONACO. Text in French. 1858. w. **Document type:** *Bulletin, Government.* **Description:** Official government bulletin of the Principality of Monaco.

Published by: Monaco. Ministere d'Etat, Place de la Visitation, Monaco, MC 98015, Monaco. TEL 377-93-158090. Ed. Rainier Imperti.

352 FRA ISSN 2109-5582

▼ **LE JOURNAL DES ACTEURS DE LA VILLE.** Text in French. 2010. bi-m. **Document type:** *Consumer.*
Published by: Trajectoires Ressources, Maison des Metiers de la Ville, 13 Av Leon Blum, Montbeliard, 25200, France. TEL 33-3-81967475.

351 CAN ISSN 0709-3632
J107

JOURNAL DES DEBATS. Text in French. 1868. irreg. **Document type:** *Proceedings, Government.*
Former titles (until 1970): Assemblee Nationale du Quebec. Debats (0709-3624); (until 1969): Assemblee Legislative du Quebec. Debats (0709-3616); (until 1895): Assemblee Legislative de la Province de Quebec. Debats (0844-2169); (until 1889): Legislature de la Province de Quebec. Debats (0844-2142); (until 1881): Legislature Provinciale de la Province de Quebec. Debats (0844-2134); (until 1879): Assemblee Legislative Quebec. Debats (0844-2126)
Published by: Assemblee Nationale de Quebec, Parliament Bldg, 1045, rue des Parlementaires, Quebec, PQ G1A 1A4, Canada. TEL 418-643-7239, 866-337-8837, FAX 418-646-4271, http://www.assnat.qc.ca/eng/index.html.

JOURNAL OF ACCOUNTING, ETHICS & PUBLIC POLICY. *see* BUSINESS AND ECONOMICS—Accounting

351 AUS ISSN 1834-3511

➤ **JOURNAL OF ADMINISTRATION AND GOVERNANCE.** Text in English. 2006. s-a. **Document type:** *Journal, Academic/Scholarly.*
Related titles: Online - full text ed.: ISSN 1834-352X. free (effective 2011).
Indexed: A39, C27, C29, D03, D04, E13, R14, S14, S15, S18.
Published by: (Network of Asia-Pacific Schools and Institutes of Public Administration and Governance MYS), Monash University, Department of Management, PO Box 197, Caulfield East, VIC 3145, Australia. Ed. Dr. Sharif As-Saber.

351 GBR ISSN 1387-6988
H97 CODEN: JCPAFP

JOURNAL OF COMPARATIVE POLICY ANALYSIS; research and practice. Abbreviated title: J C P A. Text in English. 1999. q. GBP 607 combined subscription in United Kingdom to institutions (print & online eds.); EUR 807, USD 1,012 combined subscription to institutions (print & online eds.) (effective 2012). adv. back issues avail.; reprint service avail. from PSC. **Document type:** *Journal, Academic/Scholarly.* **Description:** Addresses issues of public policy and public administration that are explicitly comparative; covers studies that (1) contribute to theory development, (2) present theory-based empirical research, (3) offer comparative evaluations of research methods, (4) derive the practice implications of theory-based research, and (5) use conceptual heuristics to interpret practice.
Related titles: Online - full text ed.: ISSN 1572-5448. GBP 547 in United Kingdom to institutions; EUR 726, USD 911 to institutions (effective 2012) (from IngentaConnect).
Indexed: A12, A13, A22, A26, ABIn, BibLing, CA, E01, ESPM, I13, IBSS, P34, P42, P47, P48, P51, P53, P54, PQC, RiskAb, S02, S03, SWR&A, T02.
—BLDSC (4963.280000), IE, Infotrieve, Ingenta. **CCC.**
Published by: Routledge (Subsidiary of: Taylor & Francis Group), 4 Park Sq, Milton Park, Abingdon, Oxon OX14 4RN, United Kingdom. TEL 44-20-70176000, FAX 44-20-70176336, subscriptions@tandf.co.uk, http://www.routledge.com. Ed. Iris Geva-May TEL 604-291-4948. Adv. contact Linda Hann TEL 44-1344-779945. **Subscr. to:** Taylor & Francis Ltd., Journals Customer Service, Sheepen Pl, Colchester, Essex CO3 3LP, United Kingdom. TEL 44-20-70175544, FAX 44-20-70175198.

351 LKA ISSN 0047-2360

JOURNAL OF DEVELOPMENT ADMINISTRATION. Text in English. 1970. s-a. LKR 60, USD 15. bk.rev. bibl.; charts.
Indexed: BAS, SLSI.
Published by: Sri Lanka Institute of Development Administration (SLIDA), c/o Additional Director (R.C. and P.), 28-10 Longdon Place, Colombo, 7, Sri Lanka. Ed. K P Vimaladharma. Circ: 1,000.

JOURNAL OF DRUG POLICY ANALYSIS; a journal of substance abuse control policy. *see* DRUG ABUSE AND ALCOHOLISM

JOURNAL OF EUROPEAN PUBLIC POLICY. *see* POLITICAL SCIENCE

JOURNAL OF HEALTH MANAGEMENT. *see* MEDICAL SCIENCES

351 USA ISSN 1933-1681
JF1525.A8

➤ **JOURNAL OF INFORMATION TECHNOLOGY & POLITICS.** Text in English. 2004 (Spring). q. GBP 373 combined subscription in United Kingdom to institutions (print & online eds.); EUR 485, USD 491 combined subscription to institutions (print & online eds.) (effective 2012). reprint service avail. from PSC. **Document type:** *Journal, Academic/Scholarly.* **Description:** Focuses on the application and practice of using information technology to enhance the delivery of public services and information.
Formerly (until 2007): Journal of E-Government (1542-4049)
Related titles: Online - full text ed.: ISSN 1933-169X. GBP 336 in United Kingdom to institutions; EUR 436, USD 442 to institutions (effective 2012).
Indexed: A01, A03, A22, A28, APA, BrCerAb, C&ISA, C10, CA, CA/WCA, CIA, CerAb, CivEngAb, CorrAb, E&CAJ, E01, E11, EEA, EMA, ESPM, EnvEAb, FamI, H15, IBR, IBSS, IBZ, L04, L13, LISTA, M&TEA, M02, M09, MBF, METADEX, P34, P42, PAIS, PSA, RiskAb, SCOPUS, SolStAb, T02, T04, WAA.
—BLDSC (5006.791000), IE, Linda Hall. **CCC.**
Published by: Routledge (Subsidiary of: Taylor & Francis Group), 325 Chestnut St, Ste 800, Philadelphia, PA 19106. TEL 215-625-8900, 800-354-1420, FAX 215-625-8914, journals@routledge.com, http://www.routledge.com. Ed. Stuart W Shulman.

➤ **JOURNAL OF INTEGRATED CARE;** practical evidence for service development. *see* SOCIAL SERVICES AND WELFARE

352.34 USA ISSN 0276-8739
H97

➤ **JOURNAL OF POLICY ANALYSIS AND MANAGEMENT.** Text in English. 1981. q. GBP 729 in United Kingdom to institutions; EUR 925 in Europe to institutions; USD 1,278 in United States to institutions; USD 1,318 in Canada & Mexico to institutions; USD 1,352 elsewhere to institutions; GBP 832 combined subscription in United Kingdom to institutions (print & online eds.); EUR 1,058 combined subscription in Europe to institutions (print & online eds.); USD 1,470 combined subscription in United States to institutions (print & online eds.); USD 1,510 combined subscription in Canada & Mexico to institutions (print & online eds.); USD 1,544 combined subscription elsewhere to institutions (print & online eds.) (effective 2012). adv. bk.rev. illus. index. back issues avail.; reprint service avail. from PSC. **Document type:** *Journal, Academic/Scholarly.* **Description:** Encompasses issues and practices in policy analysis and public management for practitioners, researchers, economists, operations researchers, and consultants.
Formed by the merger of (1975-1981): Policy Analysis (0098-2067); (1940-1981): Public Policy (0033-3646)
Related titles: Online - full text ed.: ISSN 1520-6688. GBP 650 in United Kingdom to institutions; EUR 826 in Europe to institutions; USD 1,278 elsewhere to institutions (effective 2012).
Indexed: A12, A13, A14, A18, A20, A22, A26, ABCPolSci, ABIn, ABS&EES, AHCMS, ASCA, AmH&L, B01, B02, B04, B06, B07, B09, B11, B15, B17, B18, BAS, BPIA, BRD, BusI, CA, CurCont, DIP, E02, E03, E07, E08, EIA, EMBASE, ERI, ERIC, EconLit, EdA, EdI, EnerInd, ExcerpMed, FR, FamI, FutSurv, G04, G06, G07, G08, H05, H09, I05, I13, IBR, IBSS, IBZ, JEL, M06, MCR, MEA&I, MEDLINE, P02, P03, P06, P10, P27, P30, P34, P42, P45, P47, P48, P51, P53, P54, PAA&I, PAIS, PCI, PQC, PRA, PSA, PsycInfo, RASB, S02, S03, S05, S09, S11, SCOPUS, SOPODA, SPAA, SSA, SSAI, SSAb, SSCI, SSI, SSciA, SUSA, SWR&A, SociolAb, T&II, T02, W01, W02, W03, W07.
—BLDSC (5040.841400), IE, Infotrieve, Ingenta. **CCC.**
Published by: (Association for Public Policy Analysis and Management), John Wiley & Sons, Inc., 111 River St, Hoboken, NJ 07030. FAX 201-748-6088, info@wiley.com, http://www.wiley.com/WileyCDA/. Ed. Maureen Pirog. Adv. contact Kim Thompkins TEL 212-850-6921. **Subscr. outside the Americas to:** John Wiley & Sons Ltd.

➤ **JOURNAL OF POLICY HISTORY.** *see* POLITICAL SCIENCE

351 USA ISSN 2161-7104

▼ ➤ **JOURNAL OF PUBLIC ADMINISTRATION AND GOVERNANCE.** Text in English. 2011. q. free. bk.rev. abstr.; bibl. Index. back issues avail. **Document type:** *Journal, Academic/Scholarly.* **Description:** Aims to provide analysis of developments in the organizational, administrative, and policy sciences as they apply to government and governance.
Media: Online - full text.
Published by: Macrothink Institute, Inc., 5348 Vegas Dr, Ste 825, Las Vegas, NV 89108. TEL 702-953-1852, FAX 702-387-2666, info@macrothink.org. Ed. Saleh Ahmed. Pub. Wenwu Zhao.

351 320.6 NGA

➤ **JOURNAL OF PUBLIC ADMINISTRATION AND POLICY RESEARCH.** Text in English. m. free (effective 2010). adv. **Document type:** *Journal, Academic/Scholarly.*
Media: Online - full text.
Published by: Academic Journals, PO Box 73023, Victoria Island, Lagos, Nigeria. service@academicjournals.org. Eds. Dr. Assembe Mvondo, Dr. Dacian C Dragos, Dr. Maitreyee B Roy.

351 GBR ISSN 1053-1858
JA1 CODEN: JPRTEC

➤ **JOURNAL OF PUBLIC ADMINISTRATION RESEARCH AND THEORY.** Variant title: J - P A R T. Text in English. 1991. q. GBP 307 in United Kingdom to institutions; EUR 462 in Europe to institutions; USD 492 in US & Canada to institutions; GBP 307 elsewhere to institutions; GBP 335 combined subscription in United Kingdom to institutions (print & online eds.); EUR 504 combined subscription in Europe to institutions (print & online eds.); USD 537 combined subscription in US & Canada to institutions (print & online eds.); GBP 335 combined subscription elsewhere to institutions (print & online eds.) (effective 2012). adv. bk.rev. index. back issues avail.; reprint service avail. from PSC. **Document type:** *Journal, Academic/Scholarly.* **Description:** Aims to embrace the organizational, administrative, and policy sciences as they apply to government and governance.
Related titles: Microfilm ed.: (from PQC); Online - full text ed.: ISSN 1477-9803. GBP 279 in United Kingdom to institutions; EUR 420 in Europe to institutions; USD 448 in US & Canada to institutions; GBP 279 elsewhere to institutions (effective 2012) (from IngentaConnect).
Indexed: A12, A13, A17, A22, A26, ABIn, B01, B04, B06, B07, B08, B09, BRD, C12, CA, CurCont, E01, E08, G08, H01, I05, I13, IBSS, P02, P10, P27, P34, P42, P45, P48, P51, P53, P54, PAIS, PQC, PSA, S02, S03, S09, S11, SCOPUS, SOPODA, SPAA, SSA, SSAI, SSAb, SSCI, SSI, SociolAb, T02, W03, W07.
—BLDSC (5043.490500), IE, Infotrieve, Ingenta. **CCC.**
Published by: (Public Management Research Association USA), Oxford University Press, Great Clarendon St, Oxford, OX2 6DP, United Kingdom. TEL 44-1865-556767, FAX 44-1865-556646, enquiry@oup.co.uk, http://www.oxfordjournals.org. Eds. Craig Thomas, H George Frederickson. Adv. contact Linda Hann TEL 44-1344-779945. **Subscr. to:** Transaction Distribution Center, The State University of New Jersey, 35 Berrue Cir, Piscataway, NJ 08854. TEL 732-445-2280, FAX 732-445-3138, trans@transactionpub.com, http://www.transactionpub.com.

351 USA ISSN 1540-823X
LC221.2.M8

THE JOURNAL OF PUBLIC AFFAIRS. Text in English. 1997. a. **Document type:** *Journal, Trade.* **Description:** Addresses public affairs issues in the broadest sense in academe, the professional world, and personal experience.
Formerly (until 2001): S M S U Journal of Public Affairs (1096-5602)
Related titles: Online - full text ed.
Indexed: A01, A03, A08, CA, CMM, P34, PAIS.
Published by: Southwest Missouri State University, Department of English, 901 S National Ave, Springfield, MO 65897. TEL 417-836-5000, http://www.missouristate.edu/.

351 GBR ISSN 1472-3891
HD59

➤ **JOURNAL OF PUBLIC AFFAIRS.** Text in English. 2001. q. GBP 269 in United Kingdom to institutions; EUR 312 in Europe to institutions; USD 484 elsewhere to institutions; GBP 309 combined subscription in United Kingdom to institutions (print & online eds.); EUR 360 combined subscription in Europe to institutions (print & online eds.); USD 557 combined subscription elsewhere to institutions (print & online eds.) (effective 2012). adv. reprint service avail. from PSC. **Document type:** *Journal, Academic/Scholarly.* **Description:** Provides an international, peer-reviewed forum for submissions examining best practice, new thinking and developments, and applied research in the field.
Related titles: Online - full text ed.: ISSN 1479-1854. GBP 269 in United Kingdom to institutions; EUR 312 in Europe to institutions; USD 484 elsewhere to institutions (effective 2012) (from IngentaConnect).
Indexed: A01, A03, A08, A12, A17, A22, ABIn, B01, B06, B07, B09, CA, CMM, CommAb, E01, IBR, IBSS, IBZ, P34, P42, P47, P48, P51, P53, P54, PAIS, PQC, SCOPUS, T02.
—IE, Ingenta. **CCC.**
Published by: John Wiley & Sons Ltd. (Subsidiary of: John Wiley & Sons, Inc.), 1-7 Oldlands Way, PO Box 808, Bognor Regis, West Sussex PO21 9FF, United Kingdom. TEL 44-1865-778315, FAX 44-1243-843232, cs-journals@wiley.com, http://eu.wiley.com/WileyCDA/. Eds. Danny Moss, Phil Harris. **Subscr. to:** 1-7 Oldlands Way, PO Box 809, Bognor Regis, West Sussex PO21 9FG, United Kingdom. TEL 44-1865-778054, cs-agency@wiley.com.

351.071 379 USA ISSN 1523-6803
JF1338.A2

➤ **JOURNAL OF PUBLIC AFFAIRS EDUCATION.** Abbreviated title: J P A E. Text in English. 1995. q. USD 50 to individuals; USD 125 to institutions; USD 40 to students (effective 2011). bk.rev. back issues avail. **Document type:** *Journal, Academic/Scholarly.* **Description:** Promotes the change in teaching, learning, and quality in public affairs education.
Formerly (until 1998): Journal of Public Administration Education (1087-7789)
Related titles: Online - full text ed.: free (effective 2011).
Indexed: B04, BRD, CA, CPE, DIP, E02, E03, ERI, EdA, EdI, IBR, IBZ, P34, P42, PAIS, PSA, SCOPUS, SOPODA, SPAA, T02, W03, WorkRelAb.
—BLDSC (5043.490600), IE, Ingenta.
Published by: National Association of Schools of Public Affairs and Administration, 1029 Vermont Ave, NW, Ste 1100, Washington, DC 20005. TEL 202-628-8965, FAX 202-626-4978, naspaa@naspaa.org. Ed. David Schultz.

P

332 658 351 USA ISSN 1096-3367
HJ101 CODEN: PBFMEZ

➤ **JOURNAL OF PUBLIC BUDGETING, ACCOUNTING & FINANCIAL MANAGEMENT.** Text in English. 1989. q. USD 295 domestic to individuals print or online ed.; USD 305 foreign to individuals print or online ed.; USD 395 domestic to institutions print or online ed.; USD 405 foreign to institutions print or online ed. (effective 2009). bk.rev. abstr.; bibl.; charts; illus. back issues avail. **Document type:** *Journal, Academic/Scholarly.* **Description:** Covers theories and practices in the fields of public budgeting, governmental accounting, and financial management.
Formerly (until 1997): Public Budgeting and Financial Management (1042-4741)
Related titles: Online - full text ed.: ISSN 1945-1814.
Indexed: A10, A12, A17, A22, ABIn, ATI, B01, B06, B07, B08, B09, BLI, C12, CA, H01, P21, P34, P48, P51, P53, P54, PAIS, PQC, R02, SPAA, T02, V03.
—BLDSC (5043.491000), IE, Ingenta. **CCC.**
Published by: PrAcademics Press, 21760 Mountain Sugar Ln, Boca Raton, FL 33433. TEL 561-362-9183, FAX 561-391-9572, AdMin@PrAcademicsPress.com, http://www.pracademics.com. Eds. Jack Rabin, Khi V Thai TEL 561-297-4007. Pub. Xuan H Thai. R&P Helene Kreamer. Circ: 500 (paid).

351 USA ISSN 1535-0118
JF1525.P85

➤ **JOURNAL OF PUBLIC PROCUREMENT.** Text in English. 2001. q. USD 295 domestic to individuals (print or online ed.); USD 305 foreign to individuals (print or online ed.); USD 395 domestic to libraries (print or online ed.); USD 405 foreign to libraries (print or online ed.) (effective 2009). bk.rev. abstr.; bibl.; charts; illus. 135 p./no. 1 cols./p.; back issues avail. **Document type:** *Journal, Academic/Scholarly.* **Description:** Focuses on the development of theories and concepts to enhance equity, efficiency and transparency in government procurement.
Related titles: Online - full text ed.: ISSN 2150-6930.
Indexed: A01, A12, A13, A17, ABIn, CA, I02, P10, P34, P42, P48, P51, P53, P54, PAIS, PQC, SociolAb, T02.
—BLDSC (5043.645500), IE, Ingenta.
Published by: (Florida Atlantic University, School of Public Administration), PrAcademics Press, 21760 Mountain Sugar Ln, Boca Raton, FL 33433. TEL 561-362-9183, FAX 561-391-9572, info@pracademics.com. Ed. Khi V Thai TEL 561-297-4007.

➤ **JOURNAL OF PUBLIC WORKS & INFRASTRUCTURE.** *see* BUSINESS AND ECONOMICS—Management

340 USA ISSN 1939-5922
HD61

➤ **JOURNAL OF RISK AND GOVERNANCE.** Text in English. 2008. q. USD 295 to institutions; USD 442 combined subscription to institutions (print & online eds.) (effective 2012). **Document type:** *Journal, Academic/Scholarly.* **Description:** Focuses on the intersection of risk and governance research in its broadest sense.
Related titles: Online - full text ed.: USD 295 to institutions (effective 2012).
Published by: Nova Science Publishers, Inc., 400 Oser Ave, Ste 1600, Hauppauge, NY 11788. TEL 631-231-7269, FAX 631-231-8175, main@novapublishers.com. Ed. Matthias Beck.

351 PAK ISSN 0047-2751
HC440.5.A1

➤ **JOURNAL OF RURAL DEVELOPMENT AND ADMINISTRATION;** rural development, public administration development. (JORDA) (Rural Development, Public Administration Development) Text in English. 1977 (vol.12). q. USD 40 (effective 2001). adv. bk.rev. bibl.; charts; stat. 100 p./no.; **Document type:** *Journal, Academic/Scholarly.*

Formerly: Academy Quarterly
Indexed: ARDT, BAS, CABA, E12, FS&TA, I11, R12, REE&TA, S13, S16, W11.
—Ingenta.
Published by: Pakistan Academy for Rural Development, Academy Town, Peshawar, Pakistan. TEL 91-9216200, FAX 91-9216278, nipard@paknet.ptc.pk. Ed. Shahid Tanveer. R&P Abdul Ihsan. adv.: page USD 100; 6 x 5. Circ: 1,000.

351 GIN ISSN 0533-5701
JOURNAL OFFICIEL DE GUINEE. Text in French. 1958. fortn. USD 16. adv. illus.; stat.
Indexed: RASB.
Published by: Patrice Lumumba Printing Office, BP 156, Conakry, Guinea. Circ: 700.

351.668 CIV
JOURNAL OFFICIEL DE LA COTE D'IVOIRE. Text in French. w.
Related titles: Microfilm ed.: (from PQC).
Published by: Service Autonome des Journaux Officiels, BP V70, Abidjan, Ivory Coast. TEL 22-67-76. Circ: 1,000.

351.6771 DJI
JOURNAL OFFICIEL DE LA REPUBLIQUE DE DJIBOUTI. Text in French. 1977. irreg. DJF 5,720. adv.
Published by: Secretaire General du Gouvernement, Djibouti, Djibouti. **Subscr. to:** Impr. Administrative, BP 268, Djibouti, Djibouti.

351.6711 CMR
JOURNAL OFFICIEL DE LA REPUBLIQUE DU CAMEROUN/OFFICIAL GAZETTE OF THE REPUBLIC OF CAMEROON. Text in English, French. 1946. fortn. XAF 30,000 domestic; XAF 130,000 in Europe; XAF 150,000 in North America. **Document type:** *Government.*
Description: Carries presidential decrees, orders, decisions, the laws of the nation, parliamentary debates and decisions, Ministerial trial texts, diplomatic and financial agreements with foreign partners.
Related titles: Microfilm ed.: (from BHP).
Indexed: RASB.
Address: Offical Gazette Department, Presidence de la Republique, Yaounde, Cameroon. FAX 237-215218. Ed. Njika Lucas Ivo. Pub. Joseph Marcel Ndi. Circ: 4,000.

351.6626 NER
JOURNAL OFFICIEL DE LA REPUBLIQUE DU NIGER. Text in French. 1960. fortn.
Address: BP 116, Niamey, Niger. TEL 227-72-39-30. Ed. Bonkoula Aminatou Mayaki. Circ: 800.

351.663 SEN
JOURNAL OFFICIEL DE LA REPUBLIQUE DU SENEGAL. Text in French. 1856. w.
Indexed: RASB.
Address: Rufisque, Senegal.

328.4 FRA ISSN 0242-6765
J341
JOURNAL OFFICIEL DE LA REPUBLIQUE FRANCAISE. DEBATS PARLAMENTAIRES. ASSEMBLEE NATIONALE. COMPTE RENDU INTEGRAL. Variant title: Les Debats et Documents de l'Assemble Nationale. Text in French. 1980. 3/w. **Document type:** *Journal, Government.*
Published by: France. Direction des Journaux Officiels, 26 rue Desaix, Paris, 75727 Cedex 15, France. TEL 33-1-40587500, info@journal-officiel.gouv.fr, http://www.journal-officiel.gouv.fr.

351.6721 GAB
JOURNAL OFFICIEL DE LA REPUBLIQUE GABONAISE. Text in French. 1959. fortn.
Address: BP 563, Libreville, Gabon. Ed. Emmanuel Obame.

351.6683 BEN
JOURNAL OFFICIEL DE LA REPUBLIQUE POPULAIRE DU BENIN. Text in French. fortn.
Indexed: RASB.
Address: Porto Novo, Benin.

351.675711 RWA
JOURNAL OFFICIEL DE LA REPUBLIQUE RWANDAISE. Text in French. 1979 (vol.18). s-m.
Indexed: RASB.
Published by: Service des Affaires Juriques de la Presidence de la Republique, Kigali, Rwanda. **Subscr. to:** Imprimerie Nationale du Rwanda, BP 351, Kigali, Rwanda.

328.7101 CAN ISSN 0703-2579
J103
JOURNALS OF THE SENATE OF CANADA. Text in English. 1868. irreg.
Published by: Queen's Printer, Confederation Bldg, PO Box 8700, St. John's, NF A1B 4J6, Canada. TEL 709-729-3649, FAX 709-729-1900, gp@wst.gov.nf.ca.

JUDICIAL BUSINESS OF THE UNITED STATES COURTS: (YEAR) REPORT OF THE DIRECTOR. *see* LAW—Constitutional Law

JUDICIAL STAFF DIRECTORY. *see* LAW—Judicial Systems

352.33 CHN
JUECE/DECISION MAKING. Text in Chinese. 1993. m. CNY 120; CNY 10 per issue (effective 2009). **Document type:** *Journal, Academic/Scholarly.*
Formerly: Anhui Juece Zixun (1005-5940)
Published by: Anhui Juece Zixun Zazhishe, 15, Huizhou Dadao, C-21, Tianhui Dasha, Hefei, 230001, China. TEL 86-551-2663266, FAX 86-551-2663260.

351 ESP ISSN 0212-5803
KKT5321.A15
JUNTA DE ANDALUCIA. BOLETIN OFICIAL. Abbreviated title: B O J A. Text in Spanish. 1979. 2/w. back issues avail. **Document type:** *Bulletin, Government.*
Published by: Junta de Andalucia, Consejeria de la Presidencia, Torretriana, Isla de la Cartuja, Sevilla, 41092, Spain. TEL 34-955-064562, FAX 34-955-065000, informacion@juntadeandalucia.es, http://junta-andalucia.es/.

351 LUX ISSN 1810-4657
JURISNEWS - REGARD SUR LE DROIT ADMINISTRATIF. Text in French. 2004. 8/yr. EUR 59 to individuals (effective 2008). 8 p./no.; **Document type:** *Newsletter, Trade.*
Published by: Editions Promoculture, PO Box 1142, Luxembourg, L-1011, Luxembourg. TEL 352-480691, FAX 352-400950, info@promoculture.lu, http://www.promoculture.lu. Ed. Georges Gudenburg.

JURISPRUDENCIJA/JURISPRUDENCE. *see* LAW

▼ **JURISPRUDENTIE SOCIALE ZEKERHEID.** *see* INSURANCE

JURISPRUDENTIE VOOR GEMEENTEN. *see* LAW

JUTA - STATE LIBRARY INDEX TO THE GOVERNMENT GAZETTE. *see* PUBLIC ADMINISTRATION—Abstracting, Bibliographies, Statistics

351 DEU
K O M B A JAHRBUCH NORDRHEIN-WESTFALEN. (Kommunalbeamten) Text in German. 1976. 2 base vols. plus updates 3/yr. looseleaf. EUR 79 base vol(s).; EUR 30 updates (effective 2010). adv. **Document type:** *Trade.*
Related titles: CD-ROM ed.; Online - full text ed.
Published by: Walhalla Fachverlag, Haus an der Eisernen Bruecke, Regensburg, 93042, Germany. TEL 49-941-56840, FAX 49-941-5684111, walhalla@walhalla.de. Ed. Reinhard Neffke. adv.: page EUR 390. Circ: 1,000 (paid).

351 DEU ISSN 1616-8127
K W I - ARBEITSHEFTE. (Kommunalwissenschaftliches Institut) Text in German. 2000. irreg., latest vol.14, 2007. price varies. **Document type:** *Monographic series, Academic/Scholarly.*
Published by: (Universitaet Potsdam, Kommunalwissenschaftliches Institut), Universitaetsverlag Potsdam, Am Neuen Palais 10, Potsdam, 14469, Germany. TEL 49-331-9774458, FAX 49-331-9774625, ubpub@uni-potsdam.de, http://info.ub.uni-potsdam.de/verlag.htm.

351 DEU ISSN 1439-8907
K W I - GUTACHTEN. (Kommunalwissenschaftliches Institut) Text in German. 2006. irreg., latest vol.3, 2008. price varies. **Document type:** *Monographic series, Academic/Scholarly.*
Related titles: Online - full text ed.: ISSN 1866-5462.
Published by: (Universitaet Potsdam, Kommunalwissenschaftliches Institut), Universitaetsverlag Potsdam, Am Neuen Palais 10, Potsdam, 14469, Germany. TEL 49-331-9774458, FAX 49-331-9774625, ubpub@uni-potsdam.de, http://info.ub.uni-potsdam.de/verlag.htm.

351 DEU ISSN 1438-566X
K W I - INFO. (Kommunalwissenschaftliches Institut) Text in German. 1999. irreg., latest vol.7, 2006. price varies. **Document type:** *Monographic series, Academic/Scholarly.*
Published by: (Universitaet Potsdam, Kommunalwissenschaftliches Institut), Universitaetsverlag Potsdam, Am Neuen Palais 10, Potsdam, 14469, Germany. TEL 49-331-9774458, FAX 49-331-9774625, ubpub@uni-potsdam.de, http://info.ub.uni-potsdam.de/verlag.htm.

351 DEU ISSN 1611-3969
K W I - PROJEKTBERICHTE. (Kommunalwissenschaftliches Institut) Text in German. 2003. irreg., latest vol.11, 2006. price varies. **Document type:** *Monographic series, Academic/Scholarly.*
Published by: (Universitaet Potsdam, Kommunalwissenschaftliches Institut), Universitaetsverlag Potsdam, Am Neuen Palais 10, Potsdam, 14469, Germany. TEL 49-331-9774458, FAX 49-331-9774625, ubpub@uni-potsdam.de, http://info.ub.uni-potsdam.de/verlag.htm.

352.669 NGA
KANO STATE OF NIGERIA GAZETTE. Text in English. 1967. irreg. looseleaf. **Document type:** *Government.*
Formerly: Northern Nigeria Gazette
Related titles: Diskette ed.; E-mail ed.; Fax ed.; Supplement(s): ISSN 0331-1805. 1969.
Published by: Federal Government Press, Mobil Rd., Apapa, Lagos, Nigeria. TEL 234-1-7744335. Circ: 2,500.

KANSAS JOURNAL OF LAW & PUBLIC POLICY. *see* LAW

351 USA ISSN 2156-4590
KANSAS LEGISLATURE. LEGISLATIVE DIVISION OF POST AUDIT. PERFORMANCE AUDIT REPORT. Text in English. 19??. irreg. **Document type:** *Government.* **Description:** Provides answers to the questions raised by individual legislators or legislative committees about potential problem areas in state agencies or programs.
Formerly (until 1980): Program Audit Report
Related titles: Online - full text ed.: free (effective 2010).
Published by: Legislative Division of Post Audit, 800 SW Jackson St, Ste 1200, Topeka, KS 66612. TEL 785-296-3792, FAX 785-296-4482, LPA@lpa.ks.gov.

351.49457 CHE
KANTON ZUERICH. STAATSKALENDER. Text in German. a. **Document type:** *Government.* **Description:** Information and reference bulletin for the inhabitants of the Swiss state of Zurich.
Published by: (Zuerich. Kanton Zuerich), Kretz AG, General Wille-Str 147, Postfach, Feldmeilen, 8706, Switzerland. TEL 41-1-9237656, FAX 41-1-9237657, info@kretzag.ch. Circ: 8,500 (controlled).

KANTONE UND STAEDTE DER SCHWEIZ. STATISTISCHE UEBERSICHTEN/CANTONS ET VILLES SUISSES. DONNEES STATISTIQUES. *see* PUBLIC ADMINISTRATION—Abstracting, Bibliographies, Statistics

352 GRL ISSN 1602-0286
KANUKOKA. NUTAARSIASSAT. (Kalaallit Nunaanni Kommuneqarfiit Kattuffiat) Text in Danish, Inuktitut. 2000. q. back issues avail. **Document type:** *Newsletter, Government.* **Description:** Newsletter about local government activities in Greenland.
Related titles: Online - full text ed.: ISSN 1602-1282. 2002.
Published by: Kalaallit Nunaanni Kommunequarfiit Kattuffiat/Association of Greenlandic Communities, P. H. Lundsteensvej 2, PO Box 10, Nuuk, 3900, Greenland. TEL 299-32-2100, FAX 299-32-4036.

351 DEU ISSN 1432-4903
KANZLEIFUEHRUNG PROFESSIONELL. Text in German. 1997. m. EUR 73.50 for 6 mos. (effective 2010). **Document type:** *Journal, Trade.*
Related titles: Online - full text ed.
Published by: (I W W - Institut fuer Wirtschaftspublizistik), Vogel Business Media GmbH & Co.KG, Max-Planck-Str 7-9, Wuerzburg, 97064, Germany. TEL 49-931-4180, FAX 49-931-4182750, info@vogel.de, http://www.vogel-media.de. Ed. Christiane Noecker. **Subscr. to:** DataM-Services GmbH, Fichtestr 9, Wuerzburg 97074, Germany. TEL 49-931-417001, FAX 49-931-4170499, http://www.datam-services.de.

KASSELER STATISTIK. *see* PUBLIC ADMINISTRATION—Abstracting, Bibliographies, Statistics

354.8 KEN
KENYA. CENTRAL BUREAU OF STATISTICS. DISTRICT DEVELOPMENT PLAN. (Consists of 1 vol. for each of 47 districts.) Text in English. irreg. KES 300. **Document type:** *Government.*
Published by: Ministry of Finance and Planning, Central Bureau of Statistics, PO Box 30266, Nairobi, Kenya. **Subscr. to:** Government Press, Haile Selaissie Ave., PO Box 30128, Nairobi, Kenya. TEL 254-2-334075.

351.6762 KEN
KENYA GAZETTE. Text in English. 1898. w. KES 558. index. Supplement avail.; back issues avail.; reprints avail. **Document type:** *Newspaper, Government.*
Related titles: Microfilm ed.: (from PQC).
Indexed: RASB.
Published by: (Kenya. Office of the President), Government Press, Haile Selaissie Ave., PO Box 30128, Nairobi, Kenya. Circ: 8,000.

351.6762 KEN
KENYA GAZETTE SUPPLEMENT. Text in English. irreg. (in 3 vols.). index. Supplement avail. **Document type:** *Government.*
Published by: Government Printing and Stationery Department, PO Box 30128, Nairobi, Kenya. TEL 254-2-334075.

353.5 KEN ISSN 0378-8938
KENYA. MINISTRY OF COOPERATIVES AND SOCIAL SERVICES. SESSIONAL PAPERS. Text in English. irreg., latest 1994. price varies. back issues avail. **Document type:** *Monographic series, Government.*
Published by: Ministry of Cooperatives and Social Services, Nairobi, Kenya. **Subscr. to:** Government Press, Haile Selaissie Ave., PO Box 30128, Nairobi, Kenya. TEL 254-2-334075.

354.8 KEN
KENYA. MINISTRY OF FINANCE AND PLANNING. BUDGET SPEECH BY MINISTER FOR FINANCE AND PLANNING. Text in English. a. **Document type:** *Government.*
Former titles: Kenya. Ministry of Finance and Economic Planning. Budget Speech; Kenya. Ministry of Finance. Speech Delivered to the National Assembly, Presenting the Budget
Published by: Ministry of Finance and Planning, PO Box 30266, Nairobi, Kenya. **Orders to:** Government Press, Haile Selaissie Ave., PO Box 30128, Nairobi, Kenya. TEL 254-2-334075.

354.8 KEN
KENYA. MINISTRY OF FINANCE AND PLANNING. NATIONAL DEVELOPMENT PLAN. Text in English. irreg. KES 550. **Document type:** *Government.*
Published by: Ministry of Finance and Planning, P O Box 30266, Nairobi, Kenya. **Subscr. to:** Government Press, Haile Selaissie Ave., PO Box 30128, Nairobi, Kenya. TEL 254-2-334075.

352.4 KEN
KENYA. MINISTRY OF FINANCE AND PLANNING. PLAN IMPLEMENTATION REPORT. Text in English. 1973. irreg. **Document type:** *Government.*
Published by: Ministry of Finance and Planning, P O Box 30266, Nairobi, Kenya. TEL 254-2-334075. **Subscr. to:** Government Press, Haile Selaissie Ave., PO Box 30128, Nairobi, Kenya.

KENYA. MINISTRY OF HOUSING. ANNUAL REPORT. *see* HOUSING AND URBAN PLANNING

352.193 KEN
KENYA. OFFICE OF THE DISTRICT COMMISSIONER. ANNUAL REPORT. Text in English. a.
Published by: Office of the District Commissioner, S. Nyanza District, PO Box 1, Homa Bay, Kenya.

KENYA. PUBLIC SERVICE COMMISSION. ANNUAL REPORT. *see* SOCIAL SERVICES AND WELFARE

351 USA
KEYSTONE CONNECTION. Text in English. 1979. 2/yr. free. charts; illus. **Document type:** *Newsletter, Government.* **Description:** Reports on government issues and other relevant information for state and local government officials and agencies, as well as nonprofit organizations. Also reports on economic development efforts, strategies and achievements.
Former titles (until 1995): Community Affairs; (until 1987): D C A Reports
Published by: Department of Community & Economic Development, c/o Lynn Lawson, Press Secretary, Rm 453, Forum Bldg, Harrisburg, PA 17120. TEL 717-788-1182, FAX 717-772-4559. Circ: 24,000.

351 368.4 NLD ISSN 1879-9159
▼ **DE KLEINE GIDS HANDHAVING SOCIALE ZEKERHEID.** Text in Dutch. 2009. a. EUR 13.95 (effective 2009).
Published by: Kluwer B.V. (Subsidiary of: Wolters Kluwer N.V.), Postbus 23, Deventer, 7400 GA, Netherlands. TEL 31-570-673449, FAX 31-570-691555, info@kluwer.nl, http://www.kluwer.nl.

351 NLD ISSN 1879-9396
▼ **DE KLEINE GIDS RISICO- EN CRISISCOMMUNICATIE.** Text in Dutch. 2009. a. EUR 12.40 (effective 2010).
Published by: Kluwer B.V. (Subsidiary of: Wolters Kluwer N.V.), Postbus 23, Deventer, 7400 GA, Netherlands. TEL 31-570-673449, FAX 31-570-691555, info@kluwer.nl, http://www.kluwer.nl.

351.492 NLD ISSN 2211-3924
▼ **DE KLEINE GIDS VOOR DE BUITENGEWOON OPSPORINGSAMBTENAAR (BOA).** Text in Dutch. 2011. a. EUR 13.90 (effective 2011).
Published by: Kluwer B.V. (Subsidiary of: Wolters Kluwer N.V.), Postbus 4, Alphen aan den Rijn, 2400 MA, Netherlands. TEL 31-172-466633, info@kluwer.nl, http://www.kluwer.nl.

KNIGHT'S GUIDE TO BEST VALUE AND PUBLIC PROCUREMENT. *see* LAW

KOELNER STATISTISCHE NACHRICHTEN. SONDERHEFTE. *see* PUBLIC ADMINISTRATION—Abstracting, Bibliographies, Statistics

352 AUS ISSN 1832-2859
KOGARAHLIFE. Text in English. 2000. bi-m. free to qualified personnel (effective 2009). **Document type:** *Newsletter, Consumer.*
Description: Covers news for celebrating and supporting a variety of community, health, charity and environmental projects and initiatives.
Related titles: Audio CD ed.; Online - full text ed.: free (effective 2009); Large type ed.
Published by: Kogarah Council, 2 Belgrave St, Locked Bag 8, Kogarah, NSW 2217, Australia. TEL 612-93309400, FAX 612-93309560, kmcmail@kogarah.nsw.gov.au.

354.6 IND
THE KOLKATA GAZETTE. Text in English. 1784. w. Supplement avail.; back issues avail. **Document type:** *Newspaper, Government.*
Formerly (until 2001): Calcutta Gazette (0045-3838)
Related titles: Microfiche ed.: (from IDC).
Published by: (West Bengal. Commerce & Industries Department), Government Press, Publication Branch, 38 Gopal Nagar Rd., Alipore, Kolkata, West Bengal 700 027, India.

351.43 DEU ISSN 1867-0822
▼ **KOMMUNALE VERWALTUNGSSTEUERUNG.** Text in German. 2009. irreg., latest vol.7, 2011. price varies. **Document type:** *Monographic series, Academic/Scholarly.*
Published by: Erich Schmidt Verlag GmbH & Co. (Berlin), Genthiner Str 30 G, Berlin, 10785, Germany. TEL 49-30-2500850, FAX 49-30-250085305, vertrieb@esvmedien.de.

351 DEU
KOMMUNALLEASING MAGAZIN. Text in German. 2003. bi-m. EUR 49.50 to institutions (effective 2011). adv. **Document type:** *Magazine, Trade.*
Published by: Verlag Peter Baranec, Grabenstr 34, Neunkirchen, 66538, Germany. TEL 49-6821-140234, FAX 49-180-506033835990. Ed., Pub. Peter Baranec. adv.: color page EUR 3,900; trim 210 x 297. Circ: 5,350 (paid).

351 DEU ISSN 1615-4924
KOMMUNALTECHNIK; Zeitschrift fuer das Technische Rathaus. Text in German. 1998. bi-m. EUR 45 (effective 2009). adv. **Document type:** *Magazine, Trade.*
Published by: Beckmann Verlag GmbH & Co. KG, Heidecker Weg 112, Lehrte, 31275, Germany. TEL 49-5132-85910, FAX 49-5132-859125, info@beckmann-verlag.de, http://www.beckmann-verlag.de. Ed. Hans-Guenter Doerpmund. Pub. Jan-Klaus Beckmann. Adv. contact Edward Kurdzielewicz. B&W page EUR 2,960, color page EUR 3,848; trim 190 x 270. Circ: 14,361 (paid and controlled).

351.485 SWE ISSN 1654-7373
KOMMUNER OCH LANDSTING. Text in Swedish. 2008. a. SZL 195 per issue (effective 2008). **Document type:** *Consumer.*
Published by: Dagens Samhaelle AB, Peter Myndes Backe 12, Stockholm, 11882, Sweden. TEL 46-8-4527300, FAX 46-8-6423013, http://www.dagenssamhalle.se. Ed. Lena Hoerngren TEL 46-8-4527301.

351.485 SWE ISSN 1654-8361
KOMMUNINFO OBIZ. Text in Swedish. 2007. q. SEK 98 (effective 2008). adv. **Document type:** *Magazine, Consumer.*
Related titles: Online - full text ed.
Published by: Komuninfo AB, Oestra Kyrkogatan 16, Umeaa, 90330, Sweden. TEL 46-90-717660, FAX 46-90-717669, info@kommuninfo.se. adv.: page SEK 26,900; 185 x 240. Circ: 25,000 (controlled).

KOMPENDIUM DER FINANZSTATISTIK. *see* PUBLIC ADMINISTRATION—Abstracting, Bibliographies, Statistics

351 HRV ISSN 1331-6303
KOMUNALNI VJESNIK. Text in Croatian. 1985. m. **Document type:** *Newspaper, Trade.*
Published by: Otvoreno Sveuciliste, Ul. Grada Vukovara 68, Zagreb, 10000, Croatia. Ed. Kresimir Kosic.

352.68 DNK ISSN 0085-2589
JN7104
KONGELIG DANSK HOF- OG STATSKALENDER; statshaandbog for kongeriget Danmark. Spine title: Hof- og Statskalender. Text in Danish. 1734. a. price varies. adv. **Document type:** *Government.* **Description:** Information about the Danish royal family, Danish authorities, boards, councils, state committees and local authorities as well as information about Danish embassies, the EU, other international organizations, and the Danish constitution.
Formerly (until 1809): Dansk Hof- og Statskalender
—CCC.
Published by: Ministeriet for Videnskab, Teknologi og Udvikling, IT- og Telestyrelsen, Holsteinsgade 63, Copenhagen OE, 2100, Denmark. TEL 45-35-450000, FAX 45-35-450001, itst@itst.dk, http://www.itst.dk. **Dist. by:** Danmark.dk's Netboghandel. sp@itst.dk.

351 NLD ISSN 0920-2064
KONINGRIJK DER NEDERLANDEN. STAATSBLAD. Text in Dutch. 1816. irreg. **Document type:** *Bulletin, Government.*
Published by: Sdu Uitgevers bv, Postbus 20025, The Hague, 2500 EA, Netherlands. TEL 31-70-3789911, FAX 31-70-3854321, sdu@sdu.nl.

320.6 KOR ISSN 1225-5017
H96
➤ **KOREAN JOURNAL OF POLICY STUDIES.** Text in English. 1986. s-a. USD 40 to individuals; USD 80 to institutions (effective 2009). **Document type:** *Journal, Academic/Scholarly.*
Formerly (until 1987): Chongch'aek Nonch'ong
Related titles: Online - full text ed.
Published by: Seoul National University, Graduate School of Public Administration, Bldg. 57, San 56-1, Sillim-dong, Gwanak-gu, Seoul, 151-742, Korea, S. TEL 82-2-8805633, FAX 82-2-8823998, http://gspa.snu.ac.kr/. **Co-publisher:** Advanced Center for Administrative Development.

351 DEU ISSN 0939-2041
CODEN: ACCOE4
KREIS WESEL. JAHRBUCH. Text in German. 1979. a. EUR 8.80 (effective 2009). **Document type:** *Journal, Trade.*
Formerly (until 1990): Heimatkalender des Kreises Wesel (0173-797X)
Published by: (Oberkreisdirektor des Kreises Wesel), Mercator-Verlag (Subsidiary of: Gert Wohlfarth GmbH), Stresemannstr 20-22, Duisburg, 47051, Germany. TEL 49-203-305270, FAX 49-203-30527820, info@wohlfarth.de, http://www.mercator-verlag.de.

351.85 FIN ISSN 1795-1739
KULTTUURIPOLIITTISEN TUTKIMUKSEN EDISTAMISSAATIO. CUPORE JULKAISUJA. Variant title: Cupore. Julkaisuja. Text mainly in Finnish; Text occasionally in English. 2004. irreg., latest vol.13, 2007. back issues avail. **Document type:** *Monographic series, Consumer.*
Related titles: Online - full text ed.
Published by: Kulttuuripoliittisen Tutkimuksen Edistamissaatio/The Finnish Foundation for Cultural Policy Research, Talberginkatu 1 C 137, Helsinki, 00180, Finland. TEL 358-9-77460441, FAX 358-9-77460437, info@cupore.fi.

KUTLWANO/MUTUAL UNDERSTANDING. *see* POLITICAL SCIENCE

351.5367 KWT ISSN 0023-575X
KUWAIT AL-YOUM/KUWAIT TODAY. Text in Arabic. 1954. w. **Document type:** *Government.* **Description:** Review of Kuwaiti official decrees, laws, decisions, and tenders.
Indexed: RASB.
Published by: Ministry of Information/Wizarat al-'Islam, 193, Safat, 13002, Kuwait. TEL 965-4842167, FAX 965-4831044. Circ: 5,000.

351 ZAF
KWAZULU NATAL. OFFISIELE KOERANT/KWAZULU NATAL. OFFICIAL GAZETTE. Text in Afrikaans, English. 1994 (no.4971). w. **Document type:** *Government.*
Supersedes: Natal. Offisiele Koerant - Official Gazette
Published by: (Northern Cape (Province). Provincial Administration), Natal Witness Printing and Publishing Co., Longmarketstraat 244, Pietermaritzburg, KwaZulu-Natal 3201, South Africa.

351.43 DEU ISSN 1864-0192
L K R Z; Zeitschrift fuer Landes- und Kommunalrecht Hessen - Rheinland-Pfalz - Saarland. Text in German. 2007. m. EUR 128 (effective 2011). adv. **Document type:** *Journal, Trade.*
Published by: Nomos Verlagsgesellschaft mbH und Co. KG, Waldseestr 3-5, Baden-Baden, 76530, Germany. TEL 49-7221-21040, FAX 49-7221-210427, nomos@nomos.de, http://www.nomos.de. Ed. Siegfried Jutzi. Adv. contact Bettina Roos. Circ: 900 (paid and controlled).

351 ITA ISSN 1827-3270
L'AGORA ON LINE. Text in Italian. 2005. s-m. **Document type:** *Journal, Academic/Scholarly.*
Media: Online - full text.
Published by: Associazione Centro Studi Agora, Via Armando Diaz 43D, Palermo, 90100, Italy. TEL 39-091-475028, postmaster@centroagora.org.

354.34 ZAF ISSN 1023-702X
LAND INFO. Text in English. 1994. bi-m. free. bk.rev. illus. back issues avail. **Document type:** *Government.* **Description:** Contents deals with government's land reform programs. Looks to inform parliamentarians and stakeholders.
Related titles: E-mail ed.
Published by: Department of Land Affairs, Directorate: Communication Services, Private Bag X833, Pretoria, 0001, South Africa. FAX 27-12-3233693, http://wn.apc.org/dla/. Ed., R&P Marissa Greeff TEL 27-12-3128561. Circ: 6,000.

LAND INFORMATION NEW ZEALAND. STATEMENT OF INTENT. *see* HOUSING AND URBAN PLANNING

351 AUS ISSN 1834-1403
LAND MANAGEMENT CORPORATION. ANNUAL REPORT. Text in English. 1999. a. **Document type:** *Report, Trade.*
Related titles: Online - full text ed.: ISSN 1834-1543. 2006.
Published by: South Australia, Land Management Corporation, GPO Box 698, Adelaide, SA 5001, Australia. TEL 61-8-8207-0801, FAX 61-8-8207-0830, info@lmc.sa.gov.au, http://www.lmc.sa.gov.au.

351 DEU ISSN 0939-0014
LANDES- UND KOMMUNALVERWALTUNG; Verwaltungsrecht-Zeitschrift fuer die Laender Berlin, Brandenburg, Mecklenburg-Vorpommern, Sachsen, Sachsen-Anhalt und Thueringen. Abbreviated title: L K V. Text in German. 1991. m. EUR 198; EUR 18.50 newsstand/cover (effective 2011). back issues avail.; reprint service avail. from SCH. **Document type:** *Journal, Trade.*
Incorporates (1991-2005): Zeitschrift fuer Vermoegens- und Immobilienrecht (1432-8933); Which was formerly: Zeitschrift fuer Vermoegens- und Investitionsrecht (0940-6867); Which incorporated (1990-200?): Deutsch - Deutsche Rechtszeitschrift (0937-9371)
Related titles: CD-ROM ed.
Indexed: DIP, IBR, IBZ.
Published by: Verlag C.H. Beck oHG, Wilhelmstr 9, Munich, 80801, Germany. TEL 49-89-381890, FAX 49-89-38189398, abo.service@beck.de, http://www.beck.de. Circ: 1,100 (paid). **Co-publisher:** Nomos Verlagsgesellschaft mbH und Co. KG.

351 AUT ISSN 0023-7876
LANDESAMTSBLATT FUER DAS BURGENLAND. Text in German. 1921. w. looseleaf. adv. index. **Document type:** *Government.*
Published by: Amt der Burgenlaendischen Landesregierung, Landesarchiv und Landesbibliothek, Europaplatz 1, Eisenstadt, B 7000, Austria. TEL 43-2682-6002351, FAX 43-2682-6002058, post.kultur@bgld.gv.at, http://www.burgenland.at.

LANDESGESETZE BRANDENBURG. *see* LAW—Civil Law

LANDESGESETZE FREISTAAT SACHSEN. *see* LAW—Civil Law

LANDESGESETZE FREISTAAT THUERINGEN. *see* LAW—Civil Law

LANDESGESETZE MECKLENBURG-VORPOMMERN. *see* LAW—Civil Law

LANDESGESETZE SACHSEN-ANHALT. *see* LAW—Civil Law

351 DEU
LANDESHAUPTSTADT STUTTGART. AMTSBLATT. Text in German. 1901. w. EUR 24.60 (effective 2006). bk.rev. charts. back issues avail. **Document type:** *Journal, Government.*
Formerly: Stuttgart. Amtsblatt
Published by: Landeshauptstadt Stuttgart, Presse- und Informationsamt, Rathauspassage 2, Stuttgart, 70173, Germany. TEL 49-711-2162316, FAX 49-711-2167705, info@stuttgart.de. Circ: 43,000.

353.55 DEU ISSN 0342-2259
DER LANDKREIS; Zeitschrift fuer kommunale Selbstverwaltung. Text in German. 1930. m. EUR 91.70; EUR 11.95 newsstand/cover (effective 2010). adv. bk.rev. bibl.; illus.; tr.lit. **Document type:** *Journal, Trade.*
Related titles: Regional ed(s).: Der Landkreis (Bavarian State Edition). ISSN 0340-9880; Der Landkreis (Rheinland-Pfalz Edition). ISSN 0172-9640; Der Landkreis (Hessian State Edition). ISSN 3403-3246.
Indexed: GeoRef, PAIS, SpeleolAb.
—CCC.
Published by: (Deutscher Landkreistag), W. Kohlhammer GmbH, Hessbruehlstr 69, Stuttgart, 70565, Germany. TEL 49-711-78630, FAX 49-711-78638204, kohlhammerkontakt@kohlhammer.de, http://www.kohlhammer.de. Eds. Daniela Willrodt, Hans-Guenter Henneke. Adv. contact Sabine Zinke. Circ: 1,847 (paid and controlled).

353.7 CAN ISSN 1485-6212
LANGUAGE RIGHTS. Text in English, French. 1995. biennial.
Related titles: Online - full content ed.: ISSN 1498-9379.
Published by: Office of the Commissioner of Official Languages, 344 Slater St, Ottawa, ON K1A 0T8, Canada. TEL 613-996-6368, 877-996-6368, FAX 613-993-5082, message@ocol-clo.gc.ca, http://ocol-clo.gc.ca.

328 USA ISSN 1068-2716
KF85
LEGISBRIEFS. Text in English. 1993. 48/yr. USD 79 to non-members; free to members (effective 2011). **Document type:** *Newsletter, Trade.* **Description:** Provides detailed coverage of specific issues facing state legislatures.
Indexed: EMBASE, ExcerpMed, MEDLINE, P30, SCOPUS.
—CCC.
Published by: National Conference of State Legislatures, 7700 E First Pl, Denver, CO 80230. TEL 303-364-7700, FAX 303-364-7800, ncslnet-admin@ncsl.org, http://www.ncsl.org/.

328.763 USA
LEGISCON STATEHOUSE REPORT. Text in English. 1975. w. USD 300. **Document type:** *Newsletter.* **Description:** Covers Louisiana executive branch activity, interim legislative action and judicial decisions affecting state government.
Published by: Legiscon, PO Box 1643, Baton Rouge, LA 70821. TEL 504-343-9828, FAX 504-338-5243. Ed. James A Lee.

351.73 USA ISSN 0736-5985
KF4650.A29
LEGISLATION ON FOREIGN RELATIONS. Text in English. 1957. irreg., latest 2008. price varies. **Document type:** *Government.*
Formerly (until 1976): Legislation on Foreign Relations, with Explanatory Notes
Published by: U.S. Government Printing Office, 732 N Capitol St, NW, Washington, DC 20401. TEL 202-512-1800, 866-512-1800, FAX 202-512-2104, ContactCenter@gpo.gov, http://www.gpo.gov.

LEGISLATION REVIEW DIGEST. *see* LAW

351 CAN ISSN 0542-5492
J109
LEGISLATIVE ASSEMBLY OF MANITOBA. DEBATES AND PROCEEDINGS. Text in English. 1958. irreg.
Published by: (Legislative Assembly of Manitoba), Queen's Printer, Manitoba, 200 Vaughan St, Winnipeg, MB R3C 1T5, Canada. TEL 204-945-3101, FAX 204-945-7172, statpub@gov.mb.ca, http://www.gov.mb.ca/chc/statpub/.

328 342 CAN ISSN 1922-9755
LEGISLATIVE ASSEMBLY OF MANITOBA. SPECIAL COMMITTEE ON SENATE REFORM. Text in English, French. 2008. irreg. free (effective 2010). **Document type:** *Report, Government.*
Related titles: Online - full text ed.
Published by: Legislative Assembly of Manitoba, Rm 237 Legislative Bldg, 450 Broadway, Winnipeg, MB R3C 0V8, Canada. TEL 204-945-3636, FAX 204-948-2507, clerkla@leg.gov.mb.ca, http://www.gov.mb.ca/legislature/.

328 342 CAN ISSN 1922-9615
▼ **LEGISLATIVE ASSEMBLY OF MANITOBA. SUBCOMMITTEE ON SENATE ELECTIONS.** Text in English. 2009. irreg. free (effective 2010). **Document type:** *Government.*
Related titles: Online - full text ed.
Published by: Legislative Assembly of Manitoba, Rm 237 Legislative Bldg, 450 Broadway, Winnipeg, MB R3C 0V8, Canada. TEL 204-945-3636, FAX 204-948-2507, clerkla@leg.gov.mb.ca, http://www.gov.mb.ca/legislature/.

351 CAN ISSN 1192-0025
LEGISLATIVE ASSEMBLY OF ONTARIO COMMITTEES, INDEX. Text in English. 1989. irreg.
Formerly (until 199?): Legislature of Ontario. Committees, Index (1192-0017)
Published by: Ontario, Legislative Assembly, Queen's Park, Toronto, ON M7A 1A2, Canada. TEL 416-325-7500, FAX 416-325-7489, http://www.ontla.on.ca/index.htm.

LEGISLATIVE ASSEMBLY OF THE NORTHWEST TERRITORIES. HANSARD. *see* LAW—Civil Law

LEGISLATIVE ASSEMBLY OF THE PROVINCE OF ALBERTA. VOTES AND PROCEEDINGS. *see* LAW

351 340.56 CAN ISSN 0714-4652
LEGISLATIVE ASSEMBLY OF THE PROVINCE OF SASKATCHEWAN. JOURNALS. Text in English. 1906. 3/w.
Published by: (The Legislative Assembly of Saskatchewan), Queen's Printer, Province of Saskatchewan, 8th Floor, Chateau Tower, 1920 Broad St, Regina, SK S4P 3V7, Canada. TEL 306-787-6894, 800-226-7302, FAX 306-798-0835, qprinter@justice.gov.sk.ca, http://www.qp.gov.sk.ca.

THE LEGISLATIVE GAZETTE. *see* POLITICAL SCIENCE

351 340 669 USA
LEGISVIEWS. Text in English. q. **Document type:** *Newsletter, Trade.*
Published by: Steel Recycling Institute, 680 Andersen Drive, Pittsburgh, PA 15220-2700. TEL 800-876-7274, sri@recycle-steel.org, http://www.recycle-steel.org.

351.425 GBR
LEICESTERSHIRE COUNTY COUNCIL. REVENUE BUDGET, CAPITAL PROGRAMME AND PROVISIONAL PROGRAMMES. Text in English. irreg. **Description:** Provides information for members, officers and members of the public on the County Council's planned revenue and capital expenditure and it's financing.
Published by: Leicester County Council, County Hall, Glenfield, Leicester, LE3 8RA, United Kingdom. TEL 44-116-232-3232, information@leics.gov.uk, http://www.leics.gov.uk/.

351 AUT
DIE LEISTUNGEN DER STADT WIEN. Text in German. 1863. a. EUR 14.53 (effective 2003). illus.; stat. index. 300 p./no.; back issues avail. **Document type:** *Yearbook, Government.*
Formerly (until 2003): Die Verwaltung der Stadt Wien (1028-0685)
Published by: Statistisches Amt der Stadt Wien, Volksgartenstrasse 3, Vienna, 1010, Austria. TEL 43-1-4000-88629, FAX 43-1-4000-7166, post@m66.magwien.gv.at, http://www.statistik.wien.at. Ed., R&P Gerlinde Haydn. Circ: 700.

351 CAN ISSN 1910-6890
LESLIE HARRIS CENTRE OF REGIONAL POLICY AND DEVELOPMENT. ANNUAL REPORT. Text in English. 2001. a., latest 2005. **Document type:** *Report, Academic/Scholarly.*

P

Formerly (until 2004): Memorial University of Newfoundland. Public Policy Research Centre. Annual Report (1701-8382)
Published by: Memorial University of Newfoundland, Leslie Harris Centre of Regional Policy and Development, 4th Flr, Spencer Hall, St. John's, NF A1C 5S7, Canada. FAX 709-737-3734, harriscentre@mun.ca, http://www.mun.ca/harriscentre/index.php.

LESOTHO LAW JOURNAL; a journal of law and development. *see* LAW

351 340 CAN ISSN 1702-8957
LESSONS LEARNED/LECONS APPRISES. Text in English, French. 2001. irreg.
Published by: Canada Department of Justice, Research and Statistics Division, 284 Wellington St, Ottawa, ON K1A 0H8, Canada. TEL 613-946-0460, FAX 613-941-1845, rsd.drs@justice.gc.ca.

352.150 FRA ISSN 1969-6027
LA LETTRE DE L'ETAT EN VENDEE. Text in French. 1995. bi-m. **Document type:** *Bulletin, Trade.*
Former titles (until 2008): L' Etat en Vendee (1774-9921); (until 2005): Prefecture de Vendee (1264-6695)
Media: Online - full content.
Published by: Prefecture de Vendee, 29 rue Delille, Cedex 9, La Roche-sur-Yon, 85922, France. TEL 33-2-51367085.

351 FRA ISSN 2108-2553
LA LETTRE DU SECTEUR PUBLIC. Text in French. 2007. 40/yr. EUR 280 (effective 2010). **Document type:** *Newsletter, Government.*
Published by: Les Editions du Secteur Public, 27 Rue des Sablons, Paris, 75116, France. TEL 33-1-47271185, FAX 33-1-43540009, contact@lalettredusecteurpublic.fr, http://www.lalettredusecteurpublic.fr.

LIBRARY DEVELOPMENTS. *see* LIBRARY AND INFORMATION SCIENCES

LICENSEE CONTRACTOR AND VENDOR INSPECTION STATUS REPORT. *see* ENERGY—Nuclear Energy

351.71 663.1 CAN ISSN 1713-0514
LIQUOR CONTROL BOARD OF ONTARIO. ANNUAL REPORT. Text in English. 1927. a.
Former titles (until 2001): L C B O Annual Report (1209-3718); (until 1993): Liquor Control Board of Ontario. Annual Report (0838-3391); (until 1987): Liquor Control Board of Ontario. Report (0383-3259)
Published by: Liquor Control Board of Ontario, 55 Lake Shore Blvd E, Toronto, ON M5E 1A4, Canada. TEL 416-365-5900, 800-668-5226, infoline@lcbo.com, http://www.lcbo.com.

354.71 CAN ISSN 0710-8648
HV5087.C2
LIQUOR DISTRIBUTION BRANCH. ANNUAL REPORT. Text in English. 1978. a.
Supersedes in part: Liquor Distribution Branch and Liquor Control and Licensing Branch. Annual Report (0706-3997); Which was formerly (until 1977): Province of British Columbia. Liquor Administration Branch. Department of the Attorney-General. Annual Report (0319-8138)
Published by: British Columbia Liquor Distribution Branch, 2625 Rupert St, Vancouver, BC V5M 3T5, Canada. TEL 604-252-3000, FAX 604-252-3044, http://www.bcliquorstores.com.

351 AUS
LIST OF AUSTRALIAN GOVERNMENT BODIES AND GOVERNANCE RELATIONSHIPS AS AT 31 DECEMBER (YEAR). Text in English. 2004. a., latest 2004. free. **Document type:** *Government.* **Description:** Lists the details of the statutory and non-statutory bodies, companies, incorporated associations and trusts that the Australian Government controls or has an interest in, at a formal level, including through holding shares or an ability to appoint directors.
Formerly: List of Australian Government Bodies (1449-7956)
Published by: Australia. Department of Finance and Administration, John Gorton Bldg, King Edward Terrace, Parkes, ACT 2600, Australia. TEL 61-2-62153657.

LIST OF BOOKS AND ARTICLES CATALOGUED. *see* PUBLIC ADMINISTRATION—Abstracting, Bibliographies, Statistics

LIST OF MATERIALS ACCEPTABLE FOR USE ON SYSTEMS OF R U S ELECTRIFICATION BORROWERS. *see* ENERGY—Electrical Energy

LIST OF MATERIALS ACCEPTABLE FOR USE ON TELECOMMUNICATIONS SYSTEMS OF R U S BORROWERS. *see* COMMUNICATIONS

351 USA ISSN 1080-0948
KF4920.Z95
LOBBYING, POLITICAL ACTION COMMITTEES & CAMPAIGN FINANCE; 50 state handbook. Text in English. 1995. a. USD 189 (effective 2008). **Document type:** *Handbook/Manual/Guide, Trade.* **Description:** Covers the regulations and laws covering campaign contributions and proper contact with elected officials in each of the fifty states and the federal government.
Published by: Thomson West (Subsidiary of: Thomson Reuters Corp.), 610 Opperman Dr, Eagan, MN 55123. TEL 651-687-7000, 800-344-5008, FAX 651-687-6674, west.support@thomson.com, http://west.thomson.com.

351 AUS ISSN 1832-4169
LOCAL GOVERNMENT IN VICTORIA (YEAR). Text in English. 2001. a., latest 2005. **Document type:** *Government.* **Description:** Brings together information from councils' annual reports to provide a snapshot of the current position of the sector.
Published by: Department for Victorian Communities (Subsidiary of: Sport and Recreation Victoria), GPO Box 2392, Melbourne, VIC 3001, Australia. TEL 61-3-96517026, FAX 61-3-96517269, http://www.dvc.vic.gov/local_gov.htm.

351.94 AUS ISSN 1832-9187
LOCAL GOVERNMENT POSTAL ELECTIONS REPORT. Spine title: Postal Elections. Text in English. 1997. biennial. **Description:** Provides information of postal election report under by the local government.
Published by: Western Australian Electoral Commission, GPO Box F316, Perth, W.A. 6841, Australia. TEL 61-8-92140400, FAX 61-8-92260577, waec@waec.wa.gov.au, http://www.waec.wa.gov.au.

LOTTERY, PARIMUTUEL & CASINO REGULATION - STATE CAPITALS. *see* LAW

342.06 USA
LOUISIANA ADMINISTRATIVE CODE. Text in English. irreg. USD 1,080 (effective 2000); includes supplement. adv. **Document type:** *Government.*
Published by: Division of Administration, Office of the State Register, PO Box 94095, Baton Rouge, LA 70804-9095. TEL 225-342-5015. Ed. Vickie Moreau. R&P, Adv. contact Catherine Friloux TEL 225-342-5016. Circ: 2,000.

342.06 USA ISSN 0098-8545
KFL34.A2
LOUISIANA REGISTER. Text in English. 1975. m. USD 65 (effective 2000). index. back issues avail. **Document type:** *Government.*
Published by: Division of Administration, Office of the State Register, PO Box 94095, Baton Rouge, LA 70804-9095. TEL 225-342-5015. Ed., R&P, Adv. contact Catherine Friloux TEL 225-342-5016. Circ: 957.

351 340 USA ISSN 1536-5778
K12
LOYOLA JOURNAL OF PUBLIC INTEREST LAW. Text in English. 1995. s-a. USD 10 domestic; USD 20 foreign (effective 2010). back issues avail.; reprint service avail. from WSH. **Document type:** *Journal, Academic/Scholarly.* **Description:** Covers the issues faced by the poor, children, the elderly, and all others who are unable to afford legal representation.
Formerly (until 2000): Loyola Poverty Law Journal
Related titles: Online - full text ed.
Indexed: A01, A26, E08, G08, I01, I05, ILP, L03, LRI, T02, W03, W05.
Published by: Loyola University New Orleans, College of Law, 7214 St Charles Ave, PO Box 901, New Orleans, LA 70118. TEL 504-861-5550. Eds. Ryan Higgins, Matthew Menendez.

351.4935 LUX ISSN 1021-058X
LUXEMBOURG. MINISTERE D'ETAT. BULLETIN D'INFORMATION ET DE DOCUMENTATION. Text in French. 1945. q. free.
Formerly (until 1991): Luxembourg. Ministere d'Etat. Bulletin de Documentation (0251-4001)
Published by: Ministere d'Etat, 3 rue du Saint Esprit, Luxembourg, L-1475, Luxembourg. TEL 352-4782181, FAX 352-470285.

353.9 USA
M A P A ANNUAL REPORT. Text in English. 1969. a. free (effective 2011). **Document type:** *Report, Government.*
Related titles: Online - full text ed.
Published by: Omaha - Council Bluffs Metropolitan Area Planning Agency, 2222 Cuming St, Omaha, NE 68102. TEL 402-444-6866, FAX 402-342-0949, mapa@mapacog.org.

351 USA
M A P A COMMUNITY ASSISTANCE REPORT. Text in English. 19??. a. free (effective 2011). **Document type:** *Report, Government.*
Related titles: Online - full text ed.
Published by: Omaha - Council Bluffs Metropolitan Area Planning Agency, 2222 Cuming St, Omaha, NE 68102. TEL 402-444-6866, FAX 402-342-0949, mapa@mapacog.org.

351 624 NLD
M I R T PROJECTENBOEK. (Meerjarenprogramma Infrastructuur, Ruimte en Transport) Text in Dutch. 1989. a.
Former titles (until 2008): M I T/S N I P-Projectenboek (1874-8627); (until 2004): M I T Projectenboek (1571-2087); (until 2000): Meerjarenprogramma Infrastructuur en Transport (0926-4833)
Published by: (Ministerie van Verkeer en Waterstaat), Sdu Uitgevers bv, Postbus 20025, The Hague, 2500 EA, Netherlands. TEL 31-70-3789911, FAX 31-70-3854321, sdu@sdu.nl, http://www.sdu.nl/.

351 330 EGY ISSN 1110-225X
MAGALLAT AL-BUHUTH AL-IDARIYYAT/ADMINISTRATIVE RESEARCH REVIEW. Text in Arabic. 1983. irreg. price varies (effective 2004). **Document type:** *Journal, Academic/Scholarly.*
Published by: Sadat Academy for Management Sciences, Maadi Entrance, Cornish El-Nile, P O Box 2222, Maadi Cairo, Egypt. TEL 20-2-3501261, FAX 20-2-3501033. Ed. Dr. Hamdi Abdel-Azhim.

351 347 USA ISSN 1071-3387
KFM36
MAINE GOVERNMENT REGISTER. Text in English. 1991. m. USD 914 (effective 2011). back issues avail. **Document type:** *Government.* **Description:** Covers executive orders of the Governor, Attorney General opinions, public laws enacted, public utility and environmental orders enacted, banking and insurance agency information, emergency rules, and gubernatorial appointments of state officials and board-commission members.
Published by: LexisNexis (Subsidiary of: Reed Elsevier Group plc), 1016 W Ninth Ave, 1st Fl, King of Prussia, PA 19406. TEL 215 564-1788, 800 448-1515, customer.support@lexisnexis.com.

351.598 IDN ISSN 0125-9652
JA26
MAJALAH ADMINISTRASI NEGARA; Indonesian journal of public administration. Text in Indonesian. 1959. q. IDR 6,000. adv. bibl.; illus.
Published by: Lembaga Administrasi Negara, Jl. Veteran 10, Jakarta, Indonesia. Circ: 1,000.

352.4 MWI
MALAWI. ECONOMIC PLANNING DIVISION. MID-YEAR ECONOMIC REVIEW. Text in English. 1971. a. **Document type:** *Government.*
Published by: (Malawi. Economic Planning Division), Government Printer, PO Box 37, Zomba, Malawi.

351.6897 MWI
MALAWI GAZETTE SUPPLEMENT CONTAINING ACTS. Text in English. irreg. **Document type:** *Government.*
Published by: Government Printer, PO Box 37, Zomba, Malawi.

351.6897 MWI
MALAWI GAZETTE SUPPLEMENT CONTAINING BILLS. Text in English. irreg. **Document type:** *Government.*
Published by: Government Printer, PO Box 37, Zomba, Malawi.

351.6897 MWI
MALAWI GAZETTE SUPPLEMENT CONTAINING REGULATIONS, RULES, ETC. Text in English. irreg. **Document type:** *Government.*
Published by: Government Printer, PO Box 37, Zomba, Malawi.

351.6897 MWI
MALAWI GOVERNMENT DIRECTORY. Text in English. a. **Document type:** *Directory, Government.*
Published by: Government Printer, PO Box 37, Zomba, Malawi.

351.6897 MWI
MALAWI GOVERNMENT GAZETTE. Text in English. 1894. w. MWK 12.60. index. **Document type:** *Government.*
Published by: Ministry of Finance, PO Box 30049, Lilongwe, Malawi. TEL 265-782199. **Orders to:** Government Printer, PO Box 37, Zomba, Malawi. TEL 265-50-523155.

MALAWI. GOVERNMENT PRINTER. CATALOGUE OF PUBLICATIONS. *see* PUBLIC ADMINISTRATION—Abstracting, Bibliographies, Statistics

MALTA. DEPARTMENT OF INFORMATION. REPORTS ON THE WORKING OF GOVERNMENT DEPARTMENTS. *see* PUBLIC ADMINISTRATION—Abstracting, Bibliographies, Statistics

351 IND ISSN 0047-570X
JA26
MANAGEMENT IN GOVERNMENT. Abbreviated title: M I G. Text in English. 1960. q. bk.rev. abstr.; bibl.; charts; illus. back issues avail.; reprints avail. **Document type:** *Journal, Government.* **Description:** Covers public policy, personnel management, human resource development, administrative management, and other topics related to government management.
Indexed: BAS, CLOSS, G08, KES, PAA&I.
Published by: Department of Administrative Reforms and Public Grievances, Sardar Patel Bhawan, Parliament St., New Delhi, 110 001, India. TEL 91-11-23401441, ak.marwaha@nic.in.

MANAGER. *see* BUSINESS AND ECONOMICS—Management

351 USA ISSN 1551-2819
MANAGING IN TODAY'S GOVERNMENT. Text in English. 2003 (Jul.). m. **Document type:** *Newsletter, Trade.*
Published by: Dartnell Corp. (Subsidiary of: L R P Publications, Inc.), 2272 Airport Rd S, Naples, FL 34112. TEL 800-477-4030, custserve@lrp.com, http://www.dartnellcorp.com/.

351.0711 GBR ISSN 0260-4388
MANCHESTER TRAINING HANDBOOKS. Text in English. 1981. irreg. GBP 4.50 domestic; GBP 7.50 foreign (effective 2000). **Document type:** *Bulletin.* **Description:** Training handbooks designed to assist those involved in development administration and public sector management in the Third World.
Published by: University of Manchester, Institute for Development Policy and Management, Crawford House, Precinct Centre, Oxford Rd, Manchester, Lancs M13 9GH, United Kingdom. TEL 44-161-275-2800, FAX 44-161-273-8829, http://www.sed.manchester.ac.uk/idpm/. Ed. Ron Clarke.

352.439 CAN ISSN 1706-2675
HJ13
MANITOBA. OFFICE OF THE AUDITOR GENERAL. OPERATIONS OF THE OFFICE. Text in English. 1996. a.
Formerly (until 2002): Manitoba. Provincial Auditor. Operations of the Office (1485-5089); Which superseded in part in 1997: Manitoba. Office of the Provincial Auditor. Annual Report on Public Accounts and the Operations (1482-7417)
Published by: Manitoba. Office of the Auditor General, 500-330 Portage Ave, Winnipeg, MB R3C 0C4, Canada. TEL 204-945-3790, FAX 204-945-2169, contact@oag.mb.ca.

354.27 352.88 CAN ISSN 1493-7220
MANITOBA. OMBUDSMAN MANITOBA. ANNUAL REPORT. Text in English, French. 1970. a.
Former titles (until 1998): Manitoba. Ombudsman Manitoba. Annual Report of the Ombudsman Presented to the Legislature Pursuant to Section 42 of the Ombudsman Act (1196-8516); (until 1985): Manitoba. Office of the Ombudsman. Annual Report of the Ombudsman (0714-7236); (until 1979): Manitoba. Office of the Ombudsman. Report of the Ombudsman (0701-7073)
Published by: Ombudsman Manitoba, 750-500 Portage Ave, Winnipeg, MB R3C 3X1, Canada. TEL 204-982-9130, 800-665-0531, FAX 204-942-7803.

351 CAN ISSN 0464-8625
MANITOBA. PUBLIC UTILITIES BOARD. ANNUAL REPORT. Text in English. 1928. a.
Supersedes in part (in 1960): Municipal and Public Utility Board. Annual Report (0383-4883)
Published by: Manitoba Public Utilities Board, 330 Portage Ave, Rm 400, Winnipeg, MB R3C 0C4, Canada. TEL 204-945-2638, 866-854-3698, FAX 204-945-2643, publicutilities@gov.mb.ca, http://www.gov.mb.ca/finance/cca/publutil.

351 DEU ISSN 1430-905X
MANNHEIMER SCHRIFTEN ZUR VERWALTUNGS- UND VERSORGUNGSWIRTSCHAFT. Text in German. 1996. irreg., latest vol.22, 2010. price varies. **Document type:** *Monographic series, Academic/Scholarly.*
Published by: Centaurus Verlag & Media KG, Kaiser-Joseph-Str 267, Freiburg, 79098, Germany. TEL 49-761-1525861, FAX 49-761-1525868, info@centaurus-verlag.de, http://www.centaurus-verlag.de.

MANUAL ON UNIFORM TRAFFIC CONTROL DEVICES. *see* TRANSPORTATION

353.9 NZL ISSN 1177-7575
MARITIME NEW ZEALAND. ANNUAL REPORT. Text in English. 1994. a. **Document type:** *Corporate.*
Former titles (until 2005): Maritime Safety Authority of New Zealand. Annual Report (1176-8347); (until 2004): Maritime Safety Authority of New Zealand. Report (1176-4554)
Related titles: Online - full text ed.: ISSN 1177-7583.
Published by: Maritime New Zealand, Level 8, gen-i Tower, 109 Featherston St, PO Box 27006, Wellington, New Zealand. TEL 64-4-4730111, FAX 64-4-4941263, enquiries@maritimenz.govt.nz, http://www.maritimenz.govt.nz.

MARYLAND. GENERAL ASSEMBLY. STATE DEPARTMENT OF LEGISLATIVE REFERENCE. LIBRARY AND INFORMATION SERVICES DIVISION. MARYLAND DOCUMENTS. *see* PUBLIC ADMINISTRATION—Abstracting, Bibliographies, Statistics

MARYLAND. HOUSE OF DELEGATES. JOURNAL OF PROCEEDINGS. REGULAR SESSION. *see* POLITICAL SCIENCE

351 USA ISSN 2151-4232
▼ **THE MARYLAND JOURNAL**; a journal of public policy and public finance analysis. Text in English. 2011. a. USD 25 per issue domestic to individuals; USD 35 per issue foreign to individuals; USD 35 per issue domestic to institutions; USD 45 per issue foreign to institutions (effective 2011). adv. **Document type:** *Journal, Academic/Scholarly.* **Description:** Features research and case studies on public policy and finance in Maryland.
Related titles: Online - full text ed.: ISSN 2151-4240.
Published by: Maryland Public Policy Institute, 1 Research Ct, Ste 450, Rockville, MD 20850. TEL 240-686-3510, csummers@mdpolicy.org, http://mdpolicy.org/.

351.752 USA ISSN 0094-4491
MARYLAND MANUAL; a guide to Maryland state government. Variant title: Manual-State of Maryland. Text in English. 1896. biennial. USD 20. charts; illus.; stat. index. back issues avail.
Published by: State Archives, 350 Rowe Blvd, Annapolis, MD 21401. TEL 301-974-3916, FAX 301-974-3895. Ed. Diane P Frese. Circ: 8,000.

328.752 USA ISSN 0360-2834
KFM1236
MARYLAND REGISTER. Text in English. 1974. bi-w. USD 190 (effective 2006). index. **Document type:** *Government.* **Description:** Official text of all proposed, adopted and emergency regulations, court rules, governor's executive orders, agency hearing and meeting notices.
Published by: Division of State Documents, Secretary of State, 1700 Margaret Ave, Annapolis, MD 21401. TEL 410-974-2486, 800-633-9657, FAX 410-974-2546, statedocs@sos.state.md.us, http://www.sos.state.md.us. Ed. Dennis Schnepfe. Circ: 1,600.

351.752 USA ISSN 1042-1564
THE MARYLAND REPORT. Text in English. 1989. q. USD 225 (effective 2001). **Document type:** *Newsletter.* **Description:** News, analysis of Maryland government, politics and business.
Former titles: Bruce Bortz's Maryland Report; Maryland Report
Related titles: Microfiche ed.: (from BHP).
—CCC.
Published by: Bancroft Information Group, Inc., PO Box 65360, Baltimore, MD 21209. TEL 410-358-0658, FAX 410-764-1967, bruceb@bancroftpress.com. Ed. Bruce L Bortz. Circ: 200 (paid).

328.752 USA
MARYLAND REPORT'S GUIDEBOOK TO MARYLAND LEGISLATORS. Text in English. quadrennial. USD 298 book; USD 99 update service (effective 2000).
Formerly: Yearbook of Maryland Legislators
Published by: Bancroft Information Group, Inc., PO Box 65360, Baltimore, MD 21209. TEL 410-358-0658, FAX 410-764-1967, bruceb@bancroftpress.com. Ed. Bruce Bortz.

MARYLAND. SENATE. JOURNAL OF PROCEEDINGS. REGULAR SESSION. *see* POLITICAL SCIENCE

MASSACHUSETTS CIVIL SERVICE REPORTER. *see* LAW

MASSACHUSETTS PRACTICE SERIES. *see* LAW

MASSACHUSETTS PRACTICE SERIES. ADMINISTRATIVE LAW AND PRACTICE. *see* LAW

MASSACHUSETTS PRACTICE SERIES. TAXATION. *see* BUSINESS AND ECONOMICS—Public Finance, Taxation

MASSACHUSETTS TAXPAYERS FOUNDATION. STATE BUDGET TRENDS. *see* PUBLIC ADMINISTRATION—Abstracting, Bibliographies, Statistics

352.88 MUS
MAURITIUS. OMBUDSMAN. ANNUAL REPORT. Text in English. irreg., latest 1996.
Formerly: Mauritius. Ombudsman. Report
Published by: (Mauritius. Ombudsman), Government Printing Office, La Tour Koenig, Pointe aux Sables, Port Louis, Mauritius. TEL 234-53-20, FAX 234-53-22.

351.6982 MUS
MAURITIUS. PUBLIC SERVICE COMMISSION. ANNUAL REPORT. Text in English. triennial. MUR 50 (effective 1998).
Published by: (Zambia. Public Service Commission), Government Printing Office, La Tour Koenig, Pointe aux Sables, Port Louis, Mauritius. TEL 234-53-20, FAX 234-53-22.

351 361 FRA ISSN 1769-9657
MEDIATEUR ACTUALITES. Text in French. 2004. 10/yr. **Document type:** *Newsletter, Consumer.*
Published by: France. Mediateur de la Republique, 7 Rue Saint-Florentin, Paris, 75008, France. TEL 33-1-55352424, FAX 33-1-55352425.

351.51249 USA ISSN 1548-6591
JQ1501.A1
➤ **MEI-ZHONG GONGGONG GUANLI/JOURNAL OF U S-CHINA PUBLIC ADMINISTRATION.** Key Title: Mei Zhong Gong Gong Guan Li. Text in Chinese. 2004. m. **Document type:** *Journal, Trade.*
Related titles: Online - full text ed.: ISSN 1935-9691.
Indexed: A01, CA, P34, PAIS, PSA, T02.
Published by: David Publishing Co., Inc., 1840 Industrial Dr, Ste 160, Libertyville, IL 60048. TEL 847-281-9822, FAX 847-281-9855, order@davidpublishing.com, http://www.davidpublishing.com.

351 FRA ISSN 1957-6471
MEMENTO DE L'ACTION CULTURELLE. Text in French. 2003. 2 base vols. plus updates 4/yr. looseleaf. EUR 119 base vol(s).; EUR 33 updates per month (effective 2009). **Document type:** *Trade.*
Published by: Editions Weka, 249 Rue de Crimee, Paris, 75935 Cedex 19, France. TEL 33-1-53351717, FAX 33-1-53351701.

351.77 NLD ISSN 1871-1200
MEMO MESTREGELS. Text in Dutch. 2005. a. EUR 28.82 (effective 2009).
Published by: Kluwer B.V. (Subsidiary of: Wolters Kluwer N.V.), Postbus 23, Deventer, 7400 GA, Netherlands. TEL 31-570-673555, FAX 31-570-691555, info@kluwer.nl, http://www.kluwer.nl.

354.8 FRA ISSN 0999-2588
MEMORIAL DES PERCEPTEURS ET RECEVEURS DES COMMUNES. Text in French. 1826. m. EUR 100 (effective 2009). index. **Document type:** *Journal, Government.* **Description:** Comments on the official literature and decisions of the Ministry regarding local finances.
Published by: Imprimerie Paul Dupont, 4ter Rue du Bouloi, Paris, 75001, France. TEL 33-1-42360687, FAX 33-1-42360155, abo@paul-dupont.fr, http://www.paul-dupont.fr/.

354 NZL ISSN 1172-7969
MENAAKI WHENUA LANDCARE RESEARCH NEW ZEALAND. STATEMENT OF CORPORATE INTENT. Text in English. 1993. a. **Document type:** *Corporate.*
Related titles: Online - full text ed.
Published by: Landcare Research New Zealand/Manaaki Whenua, Gerald St, PO Box 40, Lincoln, 7640, New Zealand. TEL 64-3-3219999, FAX 64-3-3219998.

363.6 388 USA ISSN 1930-1588
HG4961
MERGENT PUBLIC UTILITY & TRANSPORTATION MANUAL. Variant title: Public Utility and Transportation Manual. Text in English. 2003. a. USD 1,395 (effective 2008).
Formed by the merger of (2001-2002): Mergent Public Utility Manual (1540-1316); Which was formerly (until 2000): Moody's Public Utility Manual (0545-0241); Which superseded in part: Moody's Manual of Investments, American and Foreign. Public Utility Securities; (2001-2002): Mergent Transportation Manual (1546-6000); Which was formerly: Moody's Transportation Manual (0545-025X)
Related titles: Online - full text ed.
Published by: Mergent, Inc., 60 Madison Ave, New York, NY 10010. TEL 800-937-1398, customerservice@mergent.com, http://www.mergent.com.

351 RUS
MERIYA MOSKVY. VESTNIK. Text in Russian. 24/yr. USD 235 in United States (effective 2000).
Published by: Vestnik Merii Moskvy, Tverskaya ul 13 komn 804, Moscow, 103032, Russian Federation. TEL 7-095-2927870. **Dist. by:** East View Information Services, 10601 Wayzata Blvd, Minneapolis, MN 55305. TEL 952-252-1201, 800-477-1005, FAX 952-252-1202, info@eastview.com, http://www.eastview.com.

351 CAN ISSN 1718-5726
MESSAGER REGIONAL DE COMTE. Text in English. 2003. 3/yr. **Document type:** *Newsletter, Consumer.*
Published by: M R C de Maskinonge, 651, boule Saint-Laurent Est, Louiseville, PQ J5V 1J1, Canada. TEL 819-228-9461, FAX 819-228-2193, mrcinfo@mrc-maskinonge.qc.ca, http://www.mrc-maskinonge.qc.ca/portail.

354.3 CAN ISSN 1704-1244
QC875.C2
METEOROLOGICAL SERVICE OF CANADA. ANNUAL REPORT. Text in English. 2001. a.
Related titles: Online - full text ed.: ISSN 1702-9279.
Published by: Environment Canada, Meteorological Service of Canada (Subsidiary of: Environment Canada/Environnement Canada), National Office, Ottawa, ON K1A 0H3, Canada. TEL 819-997-2800, FAX 819-953-2225, enviroinfo@ec.gc.ca, http://www.ec.gc.ca. **Subscr. to:** Inquiry Centre, 70 Cremazie St, Gatineau, PQ K1A 0H3, Canada. TEL 819-997-2800, 800-668-6767, FAX 819-994-1412.

351 ESP ISSN 2013-0309
METODOLOGIES I RECERQUES. Text in Catalan, Spanish. 2008. irreg. back issues avail. **Document type:** *Monographic series, Academic/Scholarly.*
Related titles: Online - full text ed.: ISSN 2013-7435. 2008.
Published by: Universitat Autonoma de Barcelona, Institut d'Estudis Regionals i Metropolitans de Barcelona, Campus de Bellaterra, Placa Nord, Edif. MRA, Planta 2, Bellaterra, 08193, Spain. TEL 34-93-586-8880, FAX 34-93-5814433, iermb@uab.cat, http://www.iermb.uab.es/index.asp.

MICHIGAN. DEPARTMENT OF SOCIAL SERVICES. ASSISTANCE PAYMENTS STATISTICS. *see* SOCIAL SERVICES AND WELFARE

352 USA ISSN 0091-1933
MICHIGAN MANUAL. Text in English. 1960. biennial.
Published by: Michigan Department of State, Lansing, MI 48918. secretary@michigan.gov, http://www.michigan.gov/sos.

MICHIGAN STATE EMPLOYEES' RETIREMENT SYSTEM. *see* BUSINESS AND ECONOMICS—Labor And Industrial Relations

351 USA ISSN 2157-7854
MILESTONES (WASHINGTON). Text in English. 2008. q. free (effective 2010). back issues avail. **Document type:** *Newsletter, Government.* **Description:** Contains major achievements, project round-up from countries around the world, and staff perspectives.
Media: Online - full text.
Published by: Millennium Challenge Corporation, 875 Fifteenth St NW, Washington, DC 20005. TEL 202-521-3600.

MILLER-MCCUNE; turning research into solutions. *see* POLITICAL SCIENCE

328 USA
MILLS CAPITOL OBSERVER. Text in English. 1972. w. **Document type:** *Newsletter, Government.* **Description:** Reports on New Mexico legislative activity and politics.
Formerly: Ernie Mills' Legislative Report
Address: PO Box 5141, Santa Fe, NM 87502. Pub. Lorene Mills.

MINING AND PETROLEUM LEGISLATION SERVICE (COMMONWEALTH). *see* MINES AND MINING INDUSTRY

328 AUS
MINING AND PETROLEUM LEGISLATION SERVICE (NEW SOUTH WALES / AUSTRALIAN CAPITAL TERRITORY). Text in English. 3 base vols. plus irreg. updates. looseleaf. AUD 1,320 (effective 2008). **Document type:** *Handbook/Manual/Guide, Trade.* **Description:** Covers resource that brings together legislation and regulations relating to all forms of mining, mineral exploration, onshore and offshore petroleum and pipelines in Australia.
Related titles: ◆ Series of: Mining and Petroleum Legislation Service.
Published by: (Australian Mining and Petroleum Law Association Ltd.), Lawbook Co. (Subsidiary of: Thomson Reuters (Professional) Australia Limited), PO Box 3502, Rozelle, NSW 2039, Australia. TEL 61-2-85877980, 300-304-195, FAX 61-2-85877981, 300-304-196, LTA.Service@thomsonreuters.com, http://www.thomson.com.au.

328 AUS
MINING AND PETROLEUM LEGISLATION SERVICE (QUEENSLAND). Text in English. 2 base vols. plus irreg. updates. looseleaf. AUD 1,100 (effective 2008). **Document type:** *Handbook/Manual/Guide, Trade.* **Description:** Covers resource that brings together legislation and regulations relating to all forms of mining, mineral exploration, onshore and offshore petroleum and pipelines in Australia.
Related titles: ◆ Series of: Mining and Petroleum Legislation Service.
Published by: (Australian Mining and Petroleum Law Association Ltd.), Lawbook Co. (Subsidiary of: Thomson Reuters (Professional) Australia Limited), PO Box 3502, Rozelle, NSW 2039, Australia. TEL 61-2-85877980, 300-304-195, FAX 61-2-85877981, 300-304-196, LTA.Service@thomsonreuters.com, http://www.thomson.com.au.

328 AUS
MINING AND PETROLEUM LEGISLATION SERVICE (SOUTH AUSTRALIA / NORTHERN TERRITORY). Text in English. 3 base vols. plus irreg. updates. looseleaf. AUD 715 (effective 2008). **Document type:** *Handbook/Manual/Guide, Trade.* **Description:** Covers resource that brings together legislation and regulations relating to all forms of mining, mineral exploration, onshore and offshore petroleum and pipelines in Australia.
Related titles: ◆ Series of: Mining and Petroleum Legislation Service.
Published by: (Australian Mining and Petroleum Law Association Ltd.), Lawbook Co. (Subsidiary of: Thomson Reuters (Professional) Australia Limited), PO Box 3502, Rozelle, NSW 2039, Australia. TEL 61-2-85877980, 300-304-195, FAX 61-2-85877981, 300-304-196, LTA.Service@thomsonreuters.com, http://www.thomson.com.au.

328 AUS
MINING AND PETROLEUM LEGISLATION SERVICE (VICTORIA / TASMANIA). Text in English. 3 base vols. plus irreg. updates. looseleaf. AUD 1,177 (effective 2004). **Document type:** *Handbook/Manual/Guide, Trade.* **Description:** Covers resource that brings together legislation and regulations relating to all forms of mining, mineral exploration, onshore and offshore petroleum and pipelines in Australia.
Related titles: ◆ Series of: Mining and Petroleum Legislation Service.
Published by: (Australian Mining and Petroleum Law Association Ltd.), Lawbook Co. (Subsidiary of: Thomson Reuters (Professional) Australia Limited), PO Box 3502, Rozelle, NSW 2039, Australia. TEL 61-2-85877980, 300-304-195, FAX 61-2-85877981, 300-304-196, LTA.Service@thomsonreuters.com, http://www.thomson.com.au.

P

328 AUS
MINING AND PETROLEUM LEGISLATION SERVICE (WESTERN AUSTRALIA MINING ONLY). Text in English. 2 base vols. plus irreg. updates. looseleaf. AUD 1,100 (effective 2008). **Document type:** *Handbook/Manual/Guide, Trade.* **Description:** Covers resource that brings together legislation and regulations relating to all forms of mining, mineral exploration, onshore and offshore petroleum and pipelines in Australia.
Related titles: ◆ Series of: Mining and Petroleum Legislation Service (Western Australia).
Published by: (Australian Mining and Petroleum Law Association Ltd.), Lawbook Co. (Subsidiary of: Thomson Reuters (Professional) Australia Limited), PO Box 3502, Rozelle, NSW 2039, Australia. TEL 61-2-85877980, 300-304-195, FAX 61-2-85877981, 300-304-196, LTA.Service@thomsonreuters.com, http://www.thomson.com.au.

328 AUS
MINING AND PETROLEUM LEGISLATION SERVICE (WESTERN AUSTRALIA PETROLEUM ONLY). Text in English. base vol. plus irreg. updates. looseleaf. AUD 770 (effective 2008). **Document type:** *Handbook/Manual/Guide, Trade.* **Description:** Covers resource that brings together legislation and regulations relating to all forms of mining, mineral exploration, onshore and offshore petroleum and pipelines in Australia.
Related titles: ◆ Series of: Mining and Petroleum Legislation Service (Western Australia).
Published by: (Australian Mining and Petroleum Law Association Ltd.), Lawbook Co. (Subsidiary of: Thomson Reuters (Professional) Australia Limited), PO Box 3502, Rozelle, NSW 2039, Australia. TEL 61-2-85877980, 300-304-195, FAX 61-2-85877981, 300-304-196, LTA.Service@thomsonreuters.com, http://www.thomson.com.au.

328 AUS
MINING AND PETROLEUM LEGISLATION SERVICE (WESTERN AUSTRALIA). Text in English. 1990. 2 base vols. plus irreg. updates. looseleaf. AUD 1,870 (effective 2008). **Document type:** *Handbook/Manual/Guide, Trade.* **Description:** Covers resource that brings together legislation and regulations relating to all forms of mining, mineral exploration, onshore and offshore petroleum and pipelines in Australia.
Related titles: ◆ Series of: Mining and Petroleum Legislation Service; ◆ Series: Mining and Petroleum Legislation Service (Western Australia Petroleum Only); ◆ Mining and Petroleum Legislation Service (Western Australia Mining Only).
Published by: (Australian Mining and Petroleum Law Association Ltd.), Lawbook Co. (Subsidiary of: Thomson Reuters (Professional) Australia Limited), PO Box 3502, Rozelle, NSW 2039, Australia. TEL 61-2-85877980, 300-304-195, FAX 61-2-85877981, 300-304-196, LTA.Service@thomsonreuters.com, http://www.thomson.com.au.

351.776 USA
MINNESOTA GOVERNMENT REPORT. Text in English. 1978. s-w. USD 270. **Description:** Covers Minnesota state government.
Address: PO Box 441, Willernie, MN 55090. TEL 651-426-6339. Ed. Jean L Dawson.

351.776 USA ISSN 1061-0987
JK6130
MINNESOTA GUIDEBOOK TO STATE AGENCY SERVICES. Text in English. 1977. quadrennial. USD 14.98 (effective 2000). index.
Published by: Department of Administration, Print Communications Division, 117 University Ave., St. Paul, MN 55155. TEL 651-297-3000, 800-657-3757, FAX 651-297-7260. Ed. Robin Panlener. Circ: 10,000.

MINNESOTA RULES. SUPPLEMENT. *see* POLITICAL SCIENCE

MINNESOTA STATE REGISTER. *see* LAW

MINORITY AGING. *see* GERONTOLOGY AND GERIATRICS

351 347 USA ISSN 1094-0685
KFM6636
MISSISSIPPI GOVERNMENT REGISTER. Text in English. 1997. m. back issues avail. **Document type:** *Government.* **Description:** Covers executive orders of the Governor, Attorney General opinions, public laws enacted, public utility and environment orders enacted, banking and insurance agency information, emergency rules, and gubernatorial appointments of state officials and board-commissioned members.
Published by: LexisNexis (Subsidiary of: Reed Elsevier Group plc), 1016 W Ninth Ave, 1st Fl, King of Prussia, PA 19406. TEL 215 564-1788, 800 448-1515, customer.support@lexisnexis.com.

MISSOURI STATE GOVERNMENT PUBLICATIONS. *see* PUBLIC ADMINISTRATION—Abstracting, Bibliographies, Statistics

384 351 USA ISSN 1543-3854
JF1525.A8
MOBILE GOVERNMENT. Text in English. 2001. q. includes with subscr. Government Technology. **Document type:** *Magazine, Trade.* **Description:** Gives state and local government the information edge and helps them to move from traditional-based to mobile-based business organizations.
Related titles: ◆ Supplement to: Government Technology. ISSN 1043-9668.
Published by: e.Republic, Inc., 100 Blue Ravine Rd, Folsom, CA 95630. TEL 916-932-1300, FAX 916-932-1470, getinfo@govtech.net, http://www.govtech.net/.

351 DEU ISSN 1865-7192
DER MODERNE STAAT; Zeitschrift fuer Public Policy, Recht und Management. Text in German. 2008. 2/yr. EUR 110 to institutions; EUR 165 combined subscription to institutions (print & online eds.) (effective 2010). **Document type:** *Journal, Academic/Scholarly.*
Related titles: Online - full text ed.
Indexed: IBR, IBZ.
Published by: Verlag Barbara Budrich, Stauffenbergstr 7, Leverkusen, 51379, Germany. TEL 49-2171-344594, FAX 49-2171-344693, info@budrich-verlag.de, http://www.budrich-verlag.de. Ed. Bernhard Blanke.

351.42 GBR ISSN 2045-5526
MODUS. Text in English. 1991. 10/yr. free to members. adv. back issues avail. **Document type:** *Magazine, Consumer.* **Description:** Contains all the latest news relevant to the profession and the members of the Institution of Chartered Surveyor.
Former titles (until Sep.2010): R I C S Business (1740-486X); (until 2002): Chartered Surveyor Monthly (0964-3311)
Related titles: Online - full text ed.
Indexed: RICS.
—BLDSC (5900.372500), IE, Ingenta. **CCC.**
Published by: (Royal Institution of Chartered Surveyors (R I C S)), Sunday Publishing, Studio 2, 1st Fl, Enterprise House, 1-2 Hatfields, London, SE1 9PG, United Kingdom. TEL 44-20-77932460, hello@sundaypublishing.com, http://www.sundaypublishing.com/. Ed. Victoria Brookes. Adv. contact Lucie Inns TEL 44-20-77932477. Circ: 95,256.

351 USA ISSN 1523-570X
MONEY & POLITICS REPORT. Text in English. 1997. d. USD 1,344 (effective 2010 - 2011). back issues avail. **Document type:** *Newsletter, Trade.* **Description:** Covers campaign finance, lobbying, and government ethics issues at federal, state, and local levels.
Formerly (until 1999): B N A's Money & Politics Report (Print) (1096-6889)
Media: Online - full text.
—CCC.
Published by: The Bureau of National Affairs, Inc., 1801 S Bell St, Arlington, VA 22202. TEL 703-341-3000, 800-372-1033, FAX 703-341-4634, bnaplus@bna.com.

351.438 POL ISSN 0137-771X
HD3517.7
MONITOR SPOLDZIELCZY. Text in Polish. 1948. bi-m. EUR 54 foreign (effective 2005). **Document type:** *Government.*
Published by: Krajowa Rada Spoldzielcza, ul Jasna 1, Warsaw, 00013, Poland. TEL 48-22-8267221, http://www.spoldzielczosc.pl. **Dist. by:** Ars Polona, Obroncow 25, Warsaw 03933, Poland. TEL 48-22-5098609, FAX 48-22-5098610, arspolona@arspolona.com.pl, http://www.arspolona.com.pl.

354.7 USA
MONTANA. DEPARTMENT OF COMMERCE. PROFESSIONAL AND OCCUPATIONAL LICENSING BUREAU. PUBLIC SAFETY DIVISION. BIENNIAL REPORT. Text in English. biennial. **Document type:** *Government.*
Formerly: Montana. Department of Business Regulation. Annual Report (0093-8246)
Published by: (Montana. Public Safety Division), Montana Department of Commerce, Professional and Occupational Licensing Bureau, 111 N Jackson, Helena, MT 59620-0407. TEL 406-444-3737, FAX 406-444-1667.

354.8 USA ISSN 0090-9912
HJ3835.M9
MONTANA. OFFICE OF THE LEGISLATIVE AUDITOR. STATE OF MONTANA BOARD OF INVESTMENTS. REPORT ON EXAMINATION OF FINANCIAL STATEMENTS. Key Title: State of Montana Investment Program. Report on Audit. Text in English. a. free. stat. **Document type:** *Government.*
Published by: Office of the Legislative Auditor, PO Box 201705, Helena, MT 59620-1705. TEL 406-444-3122.

351 BGD
MONTHLY PRATIRODHA. Text in Bengali. 1976. s-m. BDT 36. adv. bk.rev.
Formerly: Pakshika Pratirodha
Published by: Ministry of Home Affairs, Jatiya Gram Pratirakaha Committee, Khilgoan, Dhaka, 1219, Bangladesh. Ed. Jahangir Habibullah.

351 RUS ISSN 2073-2643
➤ **MOSKOVSKII GOSUDARSTVENNYI UNIVERSITET. VESTNIK. SERIYA 21: UPRAVLENIE (GOSUDARSTVO I OBSHCHESTVO).** Text in Russian. 2003. q. USD 142 in North America; USD 206 combined subscription in North America (print & online eds.) (effective 2011). **Document type:** *Journal, Academic/Scholarly.*
Related titles: Online - full text ed.
Published by: (Moskovskii Gosudarstvennyi Universitet im. M.V. Lomonosova, Fakul'tet Gosudarstvennogo Upravleniya), Izdatel'stvo Moskovskogo Gosudarstvennogo Universiteta im. M. V. Lomonosova/Publishing House of Moscow State University, B Nikitskaya 5/7, Moscow, 103009, Russian Federation. TEL 7-095-2295091, FAX 7-095-2036671, kd_mgu@rambler.ru, http://www.msu.ru/depts/MSUPubl. Ed. A V Surin. **Dist. by:** East View Information Services, 10601 Wayzata Blvd, Minneapolis, MN 55305. TEL 952-252-1201, 800-477-1005, FAX 952-252-1202, info@eastview.com, http://www.eastview.com.

351.4731 381 RUS ISSN 1606-1489
MOSKVA: MER I BIZNES. Text in Russian. 1999. w. free (effective 2004). **Document type:** *Consumer.*
Media: Online - full text.
Published by: Al'yans Midiya, Bolotnaya ul 12, str 3, Moscow, 115035, Russian Federation. TEL 7-095-2345380, FAX 7-095-2345363, allmedia@allmedia.ru, http://www.businesspress.ru, http://allmedia.ru.

MOTOR VEHICLE REGULATION - STATE CAPITALS. *see* TRANSPORTATION—Automobiles

351 CAN ISSN 0464-8617
JS4.M3
THE MUNICIPAL BOARD. ANNUAL REPORT. Text in English. 1928. a.
Supersedes in part (in 1960): Municipal and Public Utility Board. Annual Report (0383-4883)
Published by: Manitoba Municipal Board, 1144-363 Broadway Ave, Winnipeg, MB R3C 3N9, Canada. TEL 204-945-2941, FAX 204-948-2235, http://www.gov.mb.ca/municipalboard.

351 CAN
MUNICIPAL OPEN LINE. Text in English. 1964. m. bk.rev. **Document type:** *Newsletter.*
Related titles: Online - full text ed.
Published by: Union of Nova Scotia Municipalities, 1809 Barrington Street, Suite 1106, Halifax, NS B3J 3K8, Canada. TEL 902-423-8331, FAX 902-425-5592, mainunsm@eastlink.ca. Ed. Ken Simpson. Circ: 880.

351 310 CAN ISSN 0319-4183
MUNICIPAL STATISTICS. ANNUAL REPORT; for New Brunswick. Text in English, French. 193?. a.
Formerly (until 1950): Municipal Corporations of the Province of New Brunswick. Annual Report (0319-4191)
Published by: New Brunswick, Office of the Department of Environment and Local Government, P O Box 6000, Fredericton, NB E3B 5H1, Canada. TEL 506-453-2690, FAX 506-457-4991.

352.07 CAN ISSN 0713-4800
MUNICIPALITE. Text in French. 1969. m. **Document type:** *Journal, Trade.*
Former titles (until 1982): Nouvelle Revue Municipalite Quebec (0227-3888); (until 1980): Municipalite Quebec (0227-3896); (until 1979): Municipalite (0226-7713)
—CCC.
Published by: Ministere des Affaires Municipales et des Regions Quebec, 10, rue Pierre-Olivier-Chauveau, Quebec, PQ G1R 4J3, Canada. TEL 418-691-2019, FAX 418-643-7385, communications@mamr.gouv.qc.ca.

328 USA
N A C R C BULLETIN. Text in English. q. membership. **Document type:** *Newsletter.* **Description:** Contains legislative updates and conference notes.
Formerly: N A C R C News
Published by: National Association of County Recorders, Election Officials, and Clerks, PO Box 75099, Colorado Springs, CO 80970-5099. TEL 719-550-0751. Circ: 1,000 (controlled).

351.71 382 CAN ISSN 1483-8079
CA1BT31-4 47
N A F T A. CANADIAN SECTION. PERFORMANCE REPORT. (North Atlantic Free Trade Agreement) Text in English, French. 1997. a.
Related titles: Online - full text ed.: ISSN 1490-5051.
Published by: (N A F T A Secretariat, Canadian Section), Treasury Board of Canada Secretariat, Corporate Communications/Secretariat du Conseil du Tresor du Canada, West Tower, Rm P-135, 300 Laurier Ave W, Ottawa, ON K1A 0R5, Canada. TEL 613-995-2855, FAX 613-996-0518, services-publications@tbs-sct.gc.ca.

N A S A O NEWSLETTER. *see* AERONAUTICS AND SPACE FLIGHT

351 USA
N C L G FOCUS. Text in English. 1982. q. free. **Document type:** *Newsletter.* **Description:** Covers issues of interest to senior state officials.
Formerly (until 1993): N C L G Newsletter
Published by: (National Conference of Lieutenant Governors), Gail B. Manning, Ed. & Pub., 2760 Research Park Dr, Box 11910, Lexington, KY 40578-1910. Circ: 550. **Co-sponsor:** Council of State Governments.

N C S L A MINUTES OF ANNUAL MEETING. *see* BEVERAGES

N C S L A OFFICIAL DIRECTORY. *see* BEVERAGES

651 USA ISSN 1932-5827
JK2679
N C S L'S GUIDE TO LEADERS AND LEGISLATURES. (National Conference of State Legislatures) Text in English. 1986. a. USD 20 per issue to non-members; free to members (effective 2011). **Document type:** *Handbook/Manual/Guide, Trade.*
Former titles (until 200?): N C S L Leaders and Media Guide; (until 2002): Directory of Legislative Leaders (1051-4988)
Related titles: Online - full text ed.: USD 20 per issue (effective 2008).
Published by: National Conference of State Legislatures, 7700 E First Pl, Denver, CO 80230. TEL 303-364-7700, FAX 303-364-7800, ncslnet-admin@ncsl.org.

N E M A NEWS. *see* CIVIL DEFENSE

N L R B ADVICE MEMORANDUM REPORTER. *see* LAW

N T L-MAGASINET. (Norsk Tjenestemannslag) *see* BUSINESS AND ECONOMICS—Labor And Industrial Relations

351 UKR ISSN 1812-514X
NARODNYI DEPUTAT. Text in Ukrainian. 2004. m. **Document type:** *Journal.*
Published by: Deputats'kyi Klub Parlament, a/s 30, Kyiv, 01025, Ukraine. TEL 380-44-2559263, FAX 380-44-2559264, dkp@nardep.com. Circ: 10,000.

351 CHE
LE NATIONAL. Text in French. 1947. 15/yr. CHF 47. **Document type:** *Bulletin.*
Published by: Parti Radical - Democratique Neuchatelois, 1 rue de Flandres, Neuchatel, 2000, Switzerland. TEL 41-32-7246691, FAX 41-32-7246784. Ed., Pub. Damien Cottier. adv.: page CHF 2,500. Circ: 4,500.

351.6894 ZMB
NATIONAL ARCHIVES OF ZAMBIA. CALENDARS OF THE DISTRICT NOTEBOOKS. Text in English. irreg. (in 4 vols.). ZMK 500. **Document type:** *Government.*
Published by: National Archives, Ridgeway, PO Box RW 50010, Lusaka, Zambia. Ed. P M Mukula.

352 GBR
NATIONAL ASSEMBLY FOR WALES. PLANNING DIVISION. PLANNING POLICY WALES. TECHNICAL ADVICE NOTE. Text in English. 19??. irreg. back issues avail. **Description:** Provides advice on good design.
Formerly: National Assembly for Wales. Planning Division. Planning Guidance (Wales). Technical Advice Note (Wales)
Related titles: Online - full text ed.
Published by: The National Assembly for Wales, Planning Division, Cathays Park, Cardiff, CF10 3NQ, United Kingdom. TEL 44-1443-845500, http://wales.gov.uk/topics/planning/policy/?lang=en.

NATIONAL ASSOCIATION OF BLACKS WITHIN GOVERNMENT. NEWSLETTER. *see* ETHNIC INTERESTS

351 USA
NATIONAL ASSOCIATION OF REGIONAL COUNCILS. SPECIAL REPORT. Variant title: National Association of Regional Councils. Transportation Research Board. Special Report. Text in English. 1967. irreg., latest vol.294, 2008. back issues avail. **Document type:** *Monographic series, Trade.* **Description:** Addresses state association activities and involvement in state-development strategies.
Formerly (until 19??): National Service to Regional Councils. Special Report (0550-5976)
Related titles: Online - full text ed.
Published by: National Association of Regional Councils, 777 N Capitol St NE, Ste 305, Washington, DC 20002. TEL 202-986-1032, FAX 202-986-1038, fred@narc.org, http://www.narc.org.

NATIONAL ASSOCIATION OF STATE BOARDS OF ACCOUNTANCY. STATE BOARD REPORT. *see* BUSINESS AND ECONOMICS—Accounting

NATIONAL CONFERENCE ON PUBLIC RETIREMENT SYSTEMS. PROCEEDINGS RECORD. *see* BUSINESS AND ECONOMICS—Labor And Industrial Relations

NATIONAL GUIDE TO GOVERNMENT. *see* POLITICAL SCIENCE

353.690973 USA ISSN 0270-6768
NATIONAL INTELLIGENCE REPORT; the biweekly on Medicare policy for laboratories, blood banks & physician services. Abbreviated title: N I R. Variant title: Clinical Labs/Blood Banks. Text in English. 1979. bi-w. looseleaf. USD 514 combined subscription in US & Canada (print & online eds.); USD 614 combined subscription elsewhere (print & online eds.) (effective 2009). adv. charts. back issues avail. **Document type:** *Newsletter, Trade.* **Description:** Covers third-party payment and billing news, C.L.I.A. developments, system fraud and abuse. Aimed at laboratory and hospital administrators, attorneys, physicians, and blood bank directors.
Related titles: Online - full text ed.: USD 30 per issue (effective 2008).
Indexed: B01, B06, B07, B09, I02, M05, P34, T02.
—CCC.
Published by: Institute of Management & Administration, Inc., One Washington Park, Ste 1300, Newark, NJ 07102. TEL 973-718-4700, FAX 973-622-0595, subserve@ioma.com. Ed. Bowman Cox. Circ: 2,000.

NATIONAL REPORTER SYSTEM. FEDERAL RULES DECISIONS. *see* LAW

351.71 CAN ISSN 1483-7463
CA1BT31-4 53
NATIONAL RESEARCH COUNCIL CANADA. PERFORMANCE REPORT. Text in English, French. 1997. a.
Related titles: Online - full text ed.: ISSN 1490-3407.
Published by: (National Research Council Canada (N R C)/Conseil National de Recherches Canada (C N R C)), Treasury Board of Canada Secretariat, Corporate Communications/Secretariat du Conseil du Tresor du Canada, West Tower, Rm P-135, 300 Laurier Ave W, Ottawa, ON K1A 0R5, Canada. TEL 613-995-2855, FAX 613-996-0518, services-publications@tbs-sct.gc.ca.

354.274 CAN ISSN 1483-8834
HC120.E5
NATIONAL ROUND TABLE ON THE ENVIRONMENT AND THE ECONOMY. PERFORMANCE REPORT. Text in English, French. 1997. a.
Related titles: Online - full text ed.: ISSN 1490-6058.
Published by: (National Round Table on the Environment and the Economy/Table Ronde Nationale sur l'Environnement et l'Economie), Treasury Board of Canada Secretariat, Corporate Communications/ Secretariat du Conseil du Tresor du Canada, West Tower, Rm P-135, 300 Laurier Ave W, Ottawa, ON K1A 0R5, Canada. TEL 613-995-2855, FAX 613-996-0518, services-publications@tbs-sct.gc.ca, http://www.tbs-sct.gc.ca.

NATIONAL SCIENCE FOUNDATION. ACTIVE FUNDING OPPORTUNITIES. *see* SCIENCES: COMPREHENSIVE WORKS

351 NLD ISSN 1875-7561
NATIONALE VEILIGHEID EN CRISISBEHEERSING. Text in Dutch. 200?. bi-m. free (effective 2011).
Formerly (until 2008): Nieuwsbrief Crisisbeheersing (1871-2843)
Related titles: Online - full text ed.: Magazine Nationale Veiligheid en Crisisbeheersing. ISSN 1875-7553.

Published by: (Ministerie van Veiligheid en Justitie, Ministerie van Binnenlandse Zaken en Koninkrijksrelaties, Directie Crisisbeheersing), Ministerie van Binnenlandse Zaken en Koninkrijksrelaties, Schedeldoekshaven 200, Postbus 20011, The Hague, 2500 EA, Netherlands. TEL 31-70-4266426, FAX 31-70-3639153, info@minbzk.nl, http://www.minbzk.nl. Ed. Geert Wismans.

NATIONALRATSWAHLEN (YEAR)/ELECTIONS AU CONSEIL NATIONAL (YEAR); Uebersicht und Analyse. *see* PUBLIC ADMINISTRATION—Abstracting, Bibliographies, Statistics

NATURAL HAZARDS CENTER. SPECIAL PUBLICATIONS (ONLINE). *see* SOCIAL SCIENCES: COMPREHENSIVE WORKS

351.71 CAN ISSN 1483-9350
CA1BT31-4 55
NATURAL SCIENCES AND ENGINEERING RESEARCH COUNCIL OF CANADA. PERFORMANCE REPORT. Text in English, French. 1997. a.
Related titles: Online - full text ed.: ISSN 1490-6007.
Published by: (Natural Sciences and Engineering Research Council of Canada/Conseil de Recherches en Sciences Naturelles et en Genie du Canada), Treasury Board of Canada Secretariat, Corporate Communications/Secretariat du Conseil du Tresor du Canada, West Tower, Rm P-135, 300 Laurier Ave W, Ottawa, ON K1A 0R5, Canada. TEL 613-995-2855, FAX 613-996-0518, services-publications@tbs-sct.gc.ca.

351.4652 ESP ISSN 1130-5894
NAVARRA. BOLETIN OFICIAL/NAFARROAKO ALDIZKARI. Text in Spanish. 1838. 3/w. EUR 90 (effective 2009). **Document type:** *Bulletin, Government.*
Former titles (until 1975): Boletin Oficial de la Provincia de Navarra (1130-5878); (until 1846): Boletin Oficial de Pamplona (1130-5886)
Related titles: Online - full text ed.; Basque ed.: Nafarroako Aldizkari Ofiziala. ISSN 1130-586X.
Published by: (Gobierno de Navarra, Departamento de Presidencia Justicia e Interior), Gobierno de Navarra, Fondo de Publicaciones, Calle de la Navas de Tolosa 21, Pamplona, Navarra 31002, Spain. TEL 34-9848-427121, FAX 34-9848-427123, fondo.publicaciones@cfnavarra.es.

351 MNG ISSN 1674-2680
NEIMENGGU RENDA. Text in Chinese. 2001. m. **Document type:** *Government.*
Published by: (Neimenggu Zizhiqu Renda Changweihui Bangongting CHN), Neimenggu Renda Zazhishe, 3, Zhongshan Dong Lu, Hohhot, 010020, Mongolia. TEL 976-471-6600642, FAX 976-471-6600641.

351.336 USA
NELSON A. ROCKEFELLER INSTITUTE OF GOVERNMENT. STATE FISCAL BRIEF. Text in English. 1991. irreg., latest vol.72, 2005. **Document type:** *Monographic series, Government.*
Related titles: Online - full text ed.: free (effective 2010).
Published by: (Center for the Study of States), Nelson A. Rockefeller Institute of Government, 411 State St, Albany, NY 12203. TEL 518-443-5522, FAX 518-443-5788, info@rockinst.org, http://www.rockinst.org.

351 NLD ISSN 1872-2458
NETHERLANDS. MINISTERIE VAN ALGEMENE ZAKEN. BELEIDSPROGRAMMA. Text in Dutch. 2002. a.
Published by: (Tweede Kamer de Staten-Generaal, Ministerie van Algemene Zaken), Sdu Uitgevers bv, Postbus 20025, The Hague, 2500 EA, Netherlands. TEL 31-70-3789911, FAX 31-70-3854321, sdu@sdu.nl, http://www.sdu.nl/.

351 NLD ISSN 1877-7090
NETHERLANDS. MINISTERIE VAN BINNENLANDSE ZAKEN EN KONINKRIJKSRELATIES. CIRCULAIRE PROVINCIEFONDS. Variant title: Circulaire Provinciefonds. Text in Dutch. 200?. 3/yr.
Published by: Ministerie van Binnenlandse Zaken en Koninkrijksrelaties, Schedeldoekshaven 200, Postbus 20011, The Hague, 2500 EA, Netherlands. TEL 31-70-4266426, FAX 31-70-3639153, info@minbzk.nl, http://www.minbzk.nl.

351 NLD ISSN 1874-8104
NETHERLANDS. MINISTERIE VAN ONDERWIJS, CULTUUR EN WETENSCHAP. ACTIEPLAN CULTUURBEREIK. Text in Dutch. 2005. irreg.
Published by: Ministerie van Onderwijs, Cultuur en Wetenschap, Postbus 16375, The Hague, 2500 BJ, Netherlands. TEL 31-70-4123456, FAX 31-70-4123450, ocwinfo@postbus51.nl, http://www.minocw.nl/.

352.745 CAN ISSN 1489-2707
NETWORKS OF CENTRES OF EXCELLENCE. ANNUAL REPORT. Text in English, French. 1994. a.
Related titles: Online - full text ed.: ISSN 1498-220X.
Published by: Networks of Centres of Excellence/Reseaux de Centres d'Excellence, 350 Albert St, Ottawa, ON K1A 1H5, Canada. TEL 613-995-6010, FAX 613-992-7356, info@nce.gc.ca.

351 DEU ISSN 1860-2339
NEUE STAATSWISSENSCHAFTEN. Text in German. 2005. irreg., latest vol.13, 2010. price varies. **Document type:** *Monographic series, Academic/Scholarly.*
Published by: Mohr Siebeck GmbH & Co. KG, Wilhelmstr 18, Tuebingen, 72074, Germany. TEL 49-7071-9230, FAX 49-7071-51104, info@mohr.de.

NEVADA. OFFICE OF LEGISLATIVE AUDITOR. BIENNIAL REPORT. *see* POLITICAL SCIENCE

354.71 CAN ISSN 1192-3563
NEW BRUNSWICK. DEPARTMENT OF FINANCE. ANNUAL REPORT. Variant title: Nouveau-Brunswick. Ministere des Finances. Rapport Annuel. Text in English, French. 1992. a.
Published by: New Brunswick, Department of Finance, Centennial Bldg, PO Box 6000, Fredericton, NB E3B 5H1, Canada. TEL 506-453-2451, FAX 506-457-4989, http://www.gnb.ca/0024/index-e.asp.

352.48 CAN ISSN 1200-2321
NEW BRUNSWICK. DEPARTMENT OF FINANCE. BUDGET. Text in English, French. a.
Former titles (until 1992): The New Brunswick Budget (0833-5680); (until 1983): New Brunswick. Department of Finance. Provincial Budget Speech (0702-3324); (until 1977): New Brunswick. Department of Finance. Budget Speech (0470-861X)
Published by: New Brunswick, Department of Finance, Centennial Bldg, PO Box 6000, Fredericton, NB E3B 5H1, Canada. TEL 506-453-2451, FAX 506-457-4989, http://www.gnb.ca/0024/index-e.asp.

354 330 CAN ISSN 0700-2467
NEW BRUNSWICK. DEPARTMENT OF FINANCE. MAIN ESTIMATES. Text in English, French. 1959. a.
Former titles (until 1973): New Brunswick. Department of Finance. Estimates (0700-2475); (until 1967): New Brunswick. Department of Finance. Ordinary and Capital Account Budget (0700-2483); (until 1966): New Brunswick. Department of Finance. Revenue and Capital Account Budget (0470-8628); Incorporates (1988-1993): Nouveau Brunswick. Ministere des Finances. Budget Principal (1196-3026)
Published by: New Brunswick, Department of Finance, Centennial Bldg, PO Box 6000, Fredericton, NB E3B 5H1, Canada. TEL 506-453-2451, FAX 506-457-4989, http://www.gnb.ca/0024/index-e.asp.

354.71 CAN ISSN 0382-1420
NEW BRUNSWICK. OFFICE OF THE AUDITOR GENERAL. REPORT OF THE AUDITOR GENERAL TO THE LEGISLATIVE ASSEMBLY. Variant title: Rapport du Verificateur General a l'Assemblee Legislative. Text in English, French. 1968. a.
Published by: (New Brunswick, Office of the Auditor General), Queen's Printer for New Brunswick, 670 King St, Room 117, Fredericton, NB E3B 5H1, Canada. TEL 506-453-2520, FAX 506-457-7899, queens.printer@gnb.ca.

351 CAN ISSN 1196-3271
NEW BRUNSWICK. OFFICE OF THE OMBUDSMAN. ANNUAL REPORT/NOUVEAU-BRUNSWICK. BUREAU DE L'OMBUDSMAN. RAPPORT ANNUEL. Text in English, French. 1968. a.
Formerly (until 1988): Report of the Ombudsman (0550-628X)
Published by: New Brunswick, Office of the Ombudsman, Sterling House, P O Box 6000, Fredericton, NB E3B 5H1, Canada. TEL 506-453-2789, 888-465-1100, FAX 506-453-5599, nbombud@gnb.ca, http://www.gnb.ca/0073/index-e.asp.

351 USA
NEW DIRECTIONS IN PUBLIC ADMINISTRATION RESEARCH. Text in English. 1987. s-a. USD 33. back issues avail. **Description:** Covers new methods and research fields in public administration.
Published by: Florida Atlantic University, College of Urban and Public Affairs, 111 E. Las Olas Blvd., # 101A, Ft Lauderdale, FL 33301-2206. TEL 305-355-5219. Ed. Jay Mendell. Circ: 300.

353 USA ISSN 1527-5051
JK2930
NEW HAMPSHIRE GOVERNMENT DIRECTORY. Text in English. 2000. a.
Published by: Putney Press, PO Box 430, Newfane, VT 05345-0430. TEL 802-365-7991, 800-639-6074, FAX 802-365-7996, ppress@sover.net. Ed. Linda Antonowicz. Pubs. Ellen Roffman, Gary Roffman.

351 352 347 USA ISSN 1089-2613
KFN1236
NEW HAMPSHIRE GOVERNMENT REGISTER. Text in English. 1996. m. back issues avail. **Document type:** *Government.* **Description:** Provides information about official New Hampshire state government actions.
Published by: LexisNexis (Subsidiary of: Reed Elsevier Group plc), 1016 W Ninth Ave, 1st Fl, King of Prussia, PA 19406. TEL 215 564-1788, 800 448-1515, customer.support@lexisnexis.com.

NEW JERSEY ADMINISTRATIVE CODE. *see* LAW

NEW JERSEY ADMINISTRATIVE CODE. ADMINISTRATIVE LAW. *see* LAW

NEW JERSEY ADMINISTRATIVE CODE. AGRICULTURE. *see* LAW

NEW JERSEY ADMINISTRATIVE CODE. ALCOHOL BEVERAGE CONTROL. *see* LAW

NEW JERSEY ADMINISTRATIVE CODE. BANKING. *see* LAW

NEW JERSEY ADMINISTRATIVE CODE. CASINO CONTROL COMMISSION. *see* LAW

NEW JERSEY ADMINISTRATIVE CODE. COMMERCE, ENERGY & ECONOMIC DEVELOPMENT. *see* LAW

NEW JERSEY ADMINISTRATIVE CODE. COMMUNITY AFFAIRS. *see* LAW

NEW JERSEY ADMINISTRATIVE CODE. CORRECTIONS. *see* LAW

NEW JERSEY ADMINISTRATIVE CODE. EDUCATION. *see* LAW

NEW JERSEY ADMINISTRATIVE CODE. ENVIRONMENTAL PROTECTION. *see* LAW

NEW JERSEY ADMINISTRATIVE CODE. FULL CODE INDEX. *see* LAW

NEW JERSEY ADMINISTRATIVE CODE. GUBERNATORIAL EXEC ORDERS. *see* LAW

NEW JERSEY ADMINISTRATIVE CODE. HEALTH. *see* LAW

NEW JERSEY ADMINISTRATIVE CODE. HIGHER EDUCATION. *see* LAW

NEW JERSEY ADMINISTRATIVE CODE. HUMAN SERVICES. *see* LAW

NEW JERSEY ADMINISTRATIVE CODE. INSURANCE. *see* LAW

NEW JERSEY ADMINISTRATIVE CODE. LABOR. *see* LAW

NEW JERSEY ADMINISTRATIVE CODE. LAW & PUBLIC SAFETY. *see* LAW

NEW JERSEY ADMINISTRATIVE CODE. MILITARY & VETERANS AFFAIRS. *see* LAW

NEW JERSEY ADMINISTRATIVE CODE. N J P D E S PROGRAM RULES ONLY. (New Jersey Pollutant Discharge Elimination System) *see* LAW

NEW JERSEY ADMINISTRATIVE CODE. OTHER AGENCIES. *see* LAW

NEW JERSEY ADMINISTRATIVE CODE. PERSONNEL. *see* LAW

NEW JERSEY ADMINISTRATIVE CODE. PUBLIC UTILITIES. *see* LAW

NEW JERSEY ADMINISTRATIVE CODE. STATE. *see* LAW

NEW JERSEY ADMINISTRATIVE CODE. TRANSPORTATION. *see* LAW

NEW JERSEY ADMINISTRATIVE CODE. TREASURY - GENERAL. *see* LAW

NEW JERSEY ADMINISTRATIVE CODE. TREASURY - TAXATION. *see* LAW

351 USA
NEW JERSEY COMPREHENSIVE ANNUAL FINANCIAL REPORT. Text in English. a. **Document type:** *Government.*
Formerly: State of New Jersey Annual Financial Report
Indexed: SRI.
Published by: Department of the Treasury, Division of Budget and Accounting, Office of Management and Budget, CN 221, Trenton, NJ 08625.

NEW JERSEY. LEGALIZED GAMES OF CHANCE CONTROL COMMISSION. REPORT. *see* LEISURE AND RECREATION

353 USA ISSN 1934-502X
JK3530
NEW JERSEY STAFF DIRECTORY. Text in English. 19??. a. USD 250 (effective 2008). reprints avail. **Document type:** *Directory, Government.*
Formerly (until 2006): New Jersey State Legistature, Office of Legislative Services Staff Directory
Published by: C Q Press, Inc. (Subsidiary of: Sage Publications, Inc.), 2300 N St, NW, Ste 800, Washington, DC 20037. TEL 202-729-1900, 866-427-7737, FAX 800-380-3810, customerservice@cqpress.com, http://www.cqpress.com. Ed. Barbara Rogers.

NEW RESOURCES. *see* PUBLIC ADMINISTRATION—Abstracting, Bibliographies, Statistics

352 AUS
NEW SOUTH WALES ADMINISTRATIVE LAW. Variant title: N S W Administrative Law. Text in English. 1996. base vol. plus q. updates. looseleaf. AUD 1,830 (effective 2008). **Document type:** *Handbook/Manual/Guide, Trade.* **Description:** Provides commentary on administrative law remedies in New South Wales.
Published by: Lawbook Co. (Subsidiary of: Thomson Reuters (Professional) Australia Limited), PO Box 3502, Rozelle, NSW 2039, Australia. TEL 61-2-85877980, 300-304-195, FAX 61-2-85877981, 300-304-196, LTA.Service@thomsonreuters.com, http://www.thomson.com.au.

351 363.7 333.72 AUS ISSN 1835-3606
NEW SOUTH WALES. DEPARTMENT OF ENVIRONMENT AND CLIMATE CHANGE. ANNUAL REPORT. Text in English. 2003. a. free (effective 2009). 180 p./no.; back issues avail. **Document type:** *Government.* **Description:** Provides information to the Parliament and the public about activities, performance and finances of the department.
Formerly (until 2007): New South Wales, Australia. Department of Environment and Conservation. Annual Report (1832-0988); Which was formed by the merger of (1992-2003): New South Wales. Environment Protection Authority. Annual Report (1321-652X); (1990-1992): New South Wales. Ministry for the Environment. Annual Report (1037-4469); Which was formerly (until 1990): New South Wales. Office of the Minister for the Environment. Annual Report; (1967-2003): New South Wales. National Parks and Wildlife Service. Annual Report (0158-0965)
Published by: Department of Environment and Climate Change, 59-61 Goulburn St, PO Box A290, Sydney, NSW 1232, Australia. TEL 61-2-99955000, FAX 61-2-99955999, info@environment.nsw.gov.au.

354.0994 AUS ISSN 1833-8801
NEW SOUTH WALES. DEPARTMENT OF LANDS. ANNUAL REPORT. Text in English. 2003. a. free (effective 2009). back issues avail. **Document type:** *Government.* **Description:** Contains reports on performance highlights against land's corporate strategic objectives as well as detailed performance outcomes against specific objectives.
Media: Online - full text. **Related titles:** Print ed.
Published by: Department of Lands, GPO Box 15, Sydney, NSW 2001, Australia. TEL 61-2-92286666, FAX 61-2-92334357.

328 AUS ISSN 1838-6598
NEW SOUTH WALES. DEPARTMENT OF PARLIAMENTARY SERVICES. ANNUAL REPORT. Text in English. 2002. a. free (effective 2011). **Document type:** *Report, Government.* **Description:** Provides logistical support and advice to members of Parliament, the Departments of the Legislative Council and Legislative Assembly and the public to ensure an effective working Parliament.
Related titles: Online - full text ed.: ISSN 1838-6601. free (effective 2011).
Published by: Australia. Department of Parliamentary Services, Parliament House, Canberra, ACT 2600, Australia. TEL 61-2-62777111, Visitor.Services@aph.gov.au.

NEW SOUTH WALES. DEPARTMENT OF PRIMARY INDUSTRIES. ANNUAL REPORT. *see* AGRICULTURE

351.94 AUS ISSN 1833-8348
NEW SOUTH WALES. PREMIER'S DEPARTMENT. STRATEGIC MANAGEMENT CALENDAR. Text in English. 2003. a. **Document type:** *Government.* **Description:** Summarizes the main planning, budgeting and reporting processes and requirements over the financial year.
Media: Online - full text.
Published by: New South Wales, The Department of Premier and Cabinet, GPO Box 5341, Sydney, NSW 2001, Australia. TEL 61-2-92285239, FAX 61-2-92283935, contact_us@premiers.nsw.gov.au, http://www.premiers.nsw.gov.au.

NEW SOUTH WALES. PUBLIC EMPLOYMENT OFFICE. OCCASIONAL PAPER. *see* BUSINESS AND ECONOMICS—Labor And Industrial Relations

NEW YORK CODES, RULES AND REGULATIONS. *see* LAW

NEW YORK RED BOOK. *see* POLITICAL SCIENCE

352.73 USA
NEW YORK SEA GRANT INSTITUTE. ANNUAL REPORT. Text in English. 1972-1986; resumed 1992. a. adv. bk.rev. illus. back issues avail. **Document type:** *Report, Trade.*
Formerly (until 1974): New York State Sea Grant Program. Annual Report (0360-3326)
Related titles: Online - full text ed.
Published by: New York Sea Grant Institute, 121 Discovery Hall, State University of New York at Stony Brook, Stony Brook, NY 11794. TEL 631-632-6905, FAX 631-632-6917, nyseagrant@stonybrook.edu.

P

353 USA ISSN 1933-6578
JK3430
NEW YORK STAFF DIRECTORY. Text in English. 1994. a. USD 250 (effective 2008). reprints avail. **Document type:** *Directory, Government.* **Description:** A directory of official personnel in federal state and local government within New York.
Formerly (until 2001): New York Public Sector (1073-5682)
Published by: C Q Press, Inc. (Subsidiary of: Sage Publications, Inc.), 2300 N St, NW, Ste 800, Washington, DC 20037. TEL 202-729-1900, 866-427-7737, FAX 800-380-3810, customerservice@cqpress.com, http://www.cqpress.com. Ed. Barbara Rogers.

351 328 USA
NEW YORK STATE REPORT. Text in English. 1950. s-m. looseleaf. USD 450 (effective 2003). adv. back issues avail. **Document type:** *Newsletter.* **Description:** Covers current New York State legislation, new laws, vetoes, and executive orders.
Published by: New York Legislative Service, Inc., 15 Maiden Ln., Ste. 1000, New York, NY 10038-5117. TEL 212-962-2826, FAX 212-962-1420, http://www.nyls.org. Ed., R&P Laird M Ehlert. Pub., Adv. contact Laird Ehlert. Circ: 100 (paid).

328 USA ISSN 1094-513X
K14
NEW YORK UNIVERSITY JOURNAL OF LEGISLATION AND PUBLIC POLICY. Variant title: Journal of Legislation and Public Policy. Text in English. 1998. s-a. USD 30 domestic; USD 34 foreign; USD 14 per issue domestic; USD 16 per issue foreign (effective 2009). back issues avail.; reprint service avail. from WSH. **Document type:** *Journal, Academic/Scholarly.* **Description:** Covers the analysis of legislation and the influence of public policy on the lawmaking process.
Related titles: Microform ed.: (from WSH); Online - full text ed.
Indexed: A26, CLI, FamI, G08, I01, ILP, LRI, P30.
—CIS, Ingenta.
Published by: New York University School of Law, Tax Law Office, 110 W Third St, New York, NY 10012. TEL 212-998-6480, FAX 212-995-4032, law.taxprograms@nyu.edu. Ed. Laura Miller.

354.93 NZL ISSN 1177-0368
NEW ZEALAND. COMMERCE COMMISSION. STATEMENT OF INTENT. Text in English. 1998. a.
Formerly (until 2006): New Zealand. Commerce Commission. Annual Plan
Published by: Commerce Commission, 44-52 The Terrace, PO Box 2351, Wellington, New Zealand. TEL 64-4-9243600, FAX 64-4-9243700.

NEW ZEALAND COMPUTER CRIME AND SECURITY SURVEY. *see* COMPUTERS—Computer Security

351.93 340 NZL ISSN 1176-2128
NEW ZEALAND. CROWN LAW OFFICE. STATEMENT OF INTENT. Text in English. 1996. a.
Formerly (until 2004): New Zealand. Crown Law Office. Departmental Forecast Report (1173-518X)
Related titles: Online - full text ed.: ISSN 1178-377X.
Published by: Crown Law Office, Unisys House, 56 The Terrace, PO Box 2858, Wellington, New Zealand. TEL 64-4-4721719, FAX 64-4-4733482.

351.93 NZL ISSN 1174-3654
HJ7169.5
NEW ZEALAND CUSTOMS SERVICE. ANNUAL REPORT. Text in English. 1989. a. **Document type:** *Government.*
Formerly (until 1997): New Zealand Customs. Annual Report (0114-6769)
Related titles: Online - full text ed.: ISSN 1177-6455.
Published by: New Zealand Customs Service, Private Bag 1928, Dunedin, New Zealand. TEL 64-3-4779251, FAX 64-3-4776773, nzcs.publications@customs.govt.nz.

353.55 NZL ISSN 1177-0503
NEW ZEALAND. DEPARTMENT OF BUILDING AND HOUSING. ANNUAL REPORT. Text in English. 2006. a. free (effective 2007).
Supersedes (in 2003): New Zealand. Ministry of Housing. Report (Year) (1172-7063)
Related titles: Online - full text ed.: ISSN 1177-8148.
Published by: New Zealand Department of Building and Housing, PO Box 10-729, Wellington, 6143, New Zealand. TEL 64-4-4940260, FAX 64-4-4940290, info@dbh.govt.nz.

351.93 NZL ISSN 1177-2069
NEW ZEALAND. DEPARTMENT OF THE PRIME MINISTER AND CABINET. ANNUAL REPORT. Text in English. a. **Document type:** *Corporate.*
Formerly (until 2005): New Zealand. Department of the Prime Minister and Cabinet. Report (1173-4590); Which was formed by the 1990 merger of: New Zealand. Report of the Cabinet Office (Year); New Zealand. Report of the Prime Minister's Office (Year)
Published by: New Zealand. Department of the Prime Minister and Cabinet, Executive Wing, Parliament Bldgs, Wellington, New Zealand. TEL 64-4-4719700, FAX 64-4-4992109.

351.93 NZL ISSN 1175-8295
NEW ZEALAND. EDUCATION REVIEW OFFICE. STATEMENT OF INTENT. Text in English. 1996. a. **Document type:** *Journal, Trade.*
Formerly (until 2003): New Zealand. Education Review Office. Departmental Forecast Report (1173-4639)
Related titles: Online - full text ed.: ISSN 1177-8806.
Published by: Education Review Office, Level 1, Sybase House, 101 Lambton Quay, Box 2799, Wellington, 6140, New Zealand. TEL 64-4-4992489, FAX 64-4-4992482, info@ero.govt.nz.

351.93 363.7 NZL ISSN 1177-4630
NEW ZEALAND. ENVIRONMENTAL RISK MANAGEMENT AUTHORITY. PERSPECTIVE. Text in English. 1998. 3/yr. **Document type:** *Newsletter.*
Related titles: Online - full text ed.: ISSN 1177-4649.
Published by: E R M A New Zealand, PO Box 131, Wellington, 6140, New Zealand. TEL 64-4-9162426, FAX 64-4-9140433, info@ermanz.govt.nz. Ed. Mark Walles.

353.5331 NZL ISSN 1177-102X
NEW ZEALAND. FAMILIES COMMISSION. ANNUAL REPORT. Text in English. 2005. a. **Document type:** *Corporate.*
Related titles: Online - full text ed.: ISSN 1177-6528.
Published by: Families Commission, Level 6, Public Trust Bldg, 117-125 Lambton Quay, PO Box 2839, Wellington, New Zealand. TEL 64-4-9177040, FAX 64-4-9177059, enquiries@nzfamilies.org.nz, http://www.nzfamilies.org.nz.

353.5331 NZL ISSN 1176-8126
NEW ZEALAND. FAMILIES COMMISSION. STATEMENT OF INTENT. Text in English. 2005. a. **Document type:** *Corporate.*
Related titles: Online - full text ed.: ISSN 1177-9853.
Published by: Families Commission, Level 6, Public Trust Bldg, 117-125 Lambton Quay, PO Box 2839, Wellington, New Zealand. TEL 64-4-9177040, FAX 64-4-9177059, enquiries@nzfamilies.org.nz, http://www.nzfamilies.org.nz.

351 328 NZL ISSN 0111-5650
KUQ7
NEW ZEALAND GAZETTE. Text in English. 1853. w. (Thu.). NZD 198 (main Thursday edition) (effective 2008); NZD 261 (main Thursday edition plus supplements & special eds.); NZD 165 (Customs edition) (effective 2001). **Document type:** *Newspaper, Government.* **Description:** Divided into commercial and government notices, covering business proceedings, bankruptcies, land transfer notices, departmental and parliamentary notices.
Formerly (until 1856): New Zealand Government Gazette
Related titles: Online - full content ed.: ISSN 1177-8415; Special ed(s).: New Zealand Gazette. Special Edition. Queen's Birthday Honours; New Zealand Gazette. Special Edition. New Year Honours; New Zealand Gazette Customs Edition. NZD 165 (effective 2005); ◆ Supplement(s): New Zealand Gazette. Supplement. Racing Board Notices; ◆ New Zealand Gazette. Supplement. Anglers Notices; ◆ New Zealand Gazette. Supplement. Regulations; ◆ New Zealand Gazette. Supplement. Power Company Disclosure Information; ◆ New Zealand Gazette. Supplement. Casino Control Notices; ◆ New Zealand Gazette. Supplement. Tax Evaders.
Indexed: Inpharma.
Published by: Department of Internal Affairs, New Zealand Gazette Office, Level 13, Prime Property Tower, 86-90 Lambton Quay, PO Box 805, Wellington, 6011, New Zealand. TEL 64-4-4702930, FAX 64-4-4702932.

NEW ZEALAND GAZETTE. SUPPLEMENT. ANGLERS NOTICES. *see* SPORTS AND GAMES—Outdoor Life

NEW ZEALAND GAZETTE. SUPPLEMENT. CASINO CONTROL NOTICES. *see* SPORTS AND GAMES

NEW ZEALAND GAZETTE. SUPPLEMENT. POWER COMPANY DISCLOSURE INFORMATION. *see* BUSINESS AND ECONOMICS—Trade And Industrial Directories

NEW ZEALAND GAZETTE. SUPPLEMENT. RACING BOARD NOTICES. *see* SPORTS AND GAMES

351 NZL
NEW ZEALAND GAZETTE. SUPPLEMENT. REGULATIONS. Text in English. irreg. NZD 261 combined subscription inclds. Gazette, supplements & special eds. (effective 2005). **Document type:** *Government.*
Related titles: ◆ Supplement to: New Zealand Gazette. ISSN 0111-5650.
Published by: Department of Internal Affairs, New Zealand Gazette Office, Level 13, Prime Property Tower, 86-90 Lambton Quay, PO Box 805, Wellington, 6011, New Zealand. TEL 64-4-4702930, FAX 64-4-4702932, gazette@parliament.govt.nz, http://www.gazette.govt.nz/diawebsite.nsf.

NEW ZEALAND GAZETTE TRADE LISTS. PUBLIC VALUERS. *see* BUSINESS AND ECONOMICS—Trade And Industrial Directories

351 NZL
NEW ZEALAND GOVERNMENT, LOCAL BODY & COMMERCIAL TENDER; a private weekly newsletter monitoring the tenders market nationwide. Text in English. w. **Document type:** *Newsletter, Government.*
Formerly (until Jun.2003): New Zealand Government & Local Body Tender
Published by: Liberty Holdings, PO Box 1881, Auckland 1, New Zealand. TEL 64-9-3071287, 800-658-765, FAX 64-9-3732634, customerservices@nbr.co.nz, http://www.nbr.co.nz.

328.37 NZL
NEW ZEALAND. HOUSE OF REPRESENTATIVES. ACTS. Text in English. irreg. looseleaf. price varies. **Document type:** *Government.* **Description:** Published 10-12 days following Royal Assent.
Published by: New Zealand. House of Representatives, Parliament Buildings, Molesworth St, Wellington, 6160, New Zealand. TEL 64-4-4719999, FAX 64-4-4712551. **Dist. by:** Legislation Direct, PO Box 12357, Wellington 6144, New Zealand. TEL 64-4-5680005, FAX 64-4-5680003, ldorders@legislationdirect.co.nz, http://www.legislationdirect.co.nz/.

328.37 NZL
NEW ZEALAND. HOUSE OF REPRESENTATIVES. ORDER PAPER. Text in English. d. **Document type:** *Government.* **Description:** Covers the daily agenda of the House, including the day's 12 oral questions to be answered by Ministers.
Published by: New Zealand. House of Representatives, Parliament Buildings, Molesworth St, Wellington, 6160, New Zealand. TEL 64-4-4719999, FAX 64-4-4712551.

328.37 NZL
NEW ZEALAND. HOUSE OF REPRESENTATIVES. PARLIAMENTARY BILLS. Text in English. irreg. price varies. **Document type:** *Government.* **Description:** Includes all Supplementary Order Papers.
Published by: (New Zealand. New Zealand. House of Representatives), Legislation Direct, PO Box 12357, Wellington, 6144, New Zealand. TEL 64-4-5680005, FAX 64-4-5680003, ldorders@legislationdirect.co.nz.

328.37 NZL ISSN 0113-1176
J941
NEW ZEALAND. HOUSE OF REPRESENTATIVES. PARLIAMENTARY BULLETIN. Text in English. 1979. w. **Document type:** *Bulletin, Government.* **Description:** Covers activities in the House of Representatives and select committees.
Incorporates (1991-2003): New Zealand. House of Representatives. Journals (1171-0241); Formerly (until 1986): New Zealand. House of Representatives. Weekly Bulletin (0110-9103)
Published by: New Zealand. House of Representatives, Parliament Buildings, Molesworth St, Wellington, 6160, New Zealand. TEL 64-4-4719999, FAX 64-4-4712551, http://www.parliament.nz/.

328 NZL
NEW ZEALAND. HOUSE OF REPRESENTATIVES. PARLIAMENTARY PAPERS. Text in English. irreg. **Document type:** *Government.* **Description:** Publishes select committee reports.
Published by: New Zealand. House of Representatives, Parliament Buildings, Molesworth St, Wellington, 6160, New Zealand. TEL 64-4-4719999, FAX 64-4-4712551.

328 NZL
NEW ZEALAND. HOUSE OF REPRESENTATIVES. REGULATIONS. Text in English. irreg. looseleaf. price varies. **Document type:** *Government.* **Description:** Keeps subscribers current with regulations, legislation created by delegated powers from Parliament.
Published by: New Zealand. House of Representatives, Parliament Buildings, Molesworth St, Wellington, 6160, New Zealand. TEL 64-4-4719999, FAX 64-4-4712551, http://www.parliament.nz/. **Dist. by:** Legislation Direct, PO Box 12357, Wellington 6144, New Zealand. TEL 64-4-5680005, FAX 64-4-5680003, ldorders@legislationdirect.co.nz, http://www.legislationdirect.co.nz/.

328.37 NZL
NEW ZEALAND. HOUSE OF REPRESENTATIVES. SPEAKER'S RULINGS. Text in English. irreg. **Document type:** *Government.* **Description:** Rulings from the Speaker show how the Standing Orders have been applied and interpreted.
Published by: New Zealand. House of Representatives, Parliament Buildings, Molesworth St, Wellington, 6160, New Zealand. TEL 64-4-4719999, FAX 64-4-4712551.

328 347 NZL
NEW ZEALAND. HOUSE OF REPRESENTATIVES. SUPPLEMENTARY ORDER PAPER. Text in English. irreg. NZD 2.30 per issue (effective 2008). **Document type:** *Government.* **Description:** Provides up-to-date information on SOPs, the vehicle for altering a bill in New Zealand's Parliament.
Published by: New Zealand. House of Representatives, Parliament Buildings, Molesworth St, Wellington, 6160, New Zealand. TEL 64-4-4719999, FAX 64-4-4712551. **Dist. by:** Legislation Direct, PO Box 12357, Wellington 6144, New Zealand. TEL 64-4-5680005, FAX 64-4-5680003, ldorders@legislationdirect.co.nz, http://www.legislationdirect.co.nz/.

354.93 NZL ISSN 1171-302X
NEW ZEALAND INSTITUTE OF PUBLIC ADMINISTRATION. RESEARCH PAPERS. Text in English. 1979. irreg. price varies. adv. bk.rev. back issues avail. **Document type:** *Monographic series, Academic/Scholarly.*
Formerly (until 1991): Public Sector Research Papers (0111-1523)
Published by: Institute of Public Administration New Zealand, PO Box 5032, Wellington, New Zealand. TEL 64-4-4636940, FAX 64-4-4636939, admin@ipanz.org.nz, http://www.ipanz.org.nz/.

NEW ZEALAND. LAND TRANSPORT SAFETY AUTHORITY. RULES. *see* TRANSPORTATION

354.50993 NZL ISSN 1177-701X
NEW ZEALAND. MINISTRY OF AGRICULTURE AND FORESTRY. POLICY NEWS. Abbreviated title: M A F Policy News. Text in English. 1994. bi-m. free (effective 2009). **Document type:** *Newsletter.*
Former titles (until 2006): M A F R M Update (Online); (until 2006): New Zealand. Ministry of Agriculture and Forestry Resource Management Update (Print) (1174-8869); (until 1999): Forestry R M Update (1173-2725)
Media: Online - full text.
Published by: Ministry of Agriculture and Forestry, MAF Policy, PO Box 2526, Wellington, New Zealand. TEL 64-4-8940657, FAX 64-4-8940742.

351.93 338 NZL ISSN 1176-4007
NEW ZEALAND. MINISTRY OF ECONOMIC DEVELOPMENT. REPORT. Text in English. 1988. a. **Description:** Annual Report presented to the House of Representatives Pursuant to Section 39 of the Public Finance Act 1989.
Formerly (until 2000): New Zealand. Ministry of Commerce. Report (0114-7471)
Related titles: Online - full text ed.: ISSN 1178-3052.
Published by: Ministry of Economic Development, PO Box 1473, Wellington, 6011, New Zealand. TEL 64-4-4720030, FAX 64-4-4734638, info@med.govt.nz.

351.93 347 NZL ISSN 1178-2730
NEW ZEALAND. MINISTRY OF JUSTICE. ANNUAL REPORT. Text in English. 1996. a. **Document type:** *Government.*
Related titles: Online - full text ed.: ISSN 1178-2749.
Published by: Ministry of Justice, PO Box 180, Wellington, New Zealand. TEL 64-4-9188800, FAX 64-4-9188820, publications@justice.govt.nz.

351.93 NZL ISSN 1178-3451
NEW ZEALAND. MINISTRY OF MAORI DEVELOPMENT. STATEMENT OF INTENT (ONLINE). Text in English. 2003. a.
Media: Online - full text. **Related titles:** ◆ Print ed.: New Zealand. Ministry of Maori Development. Statement of Intent (Print). ISSN 1176-2381; ◆ Maori ed.: Panui Whainga. ISSN 1178-3516.
Published by: New Zealand. Te Puni Kokiri/New Zealand. Ministry of Maori Development, PO Box 3943, Wellington, New Zealand. TEL 64-4-8196000, FAX 64-4-8196299, info@tpk.govt.nz.

351.93 NZL ISSN 1176-2381
NEW ZEALAND. MINISTRY OF MAORI DEVELOPMENT. STATEMENT OF INTENT (PRINT). Text in English. 1995. a.
Formerly (until 2003): New Zealand. Ministry of Maori Development. Departmental Forecast Report (1173-4809)
Related titles: ◆ Online - full text ed.: New Zealand. Ministry of Maori Development. Statement of Intent (Online). ISSN 1178-3451.
Published by: New Zealand. Te Puni Kokiri/New Zealand. Ministry of Maori Development, PO Box 3943, Wellington, New Zealand. TEL 64-4-8196000, FAX 64-4-8196299, info@tpk.govt.nz.

351.93 NZL ISSN 1175-9895
HN930.5
NEW ZEALAND. MINISTRY OF SOCIAL DEVELOPMENT. ANNUAL REPORT. Text in English. 2002. a. **Document type:** *Government.*
Related titles: Online - full text ed.: ISSN 1178-3389.
Published by: Ministry of Social Development, PO Box 1556, Wellington, New Zealand. TEL 64-4-9163300, FAX 64-4-9180099, information@msd.govt.nz.

354.76 NZL ISSN 1177-1550
NEW ZEALAND. MINISTRY OF TRANSPORT. ANNUAL REPORT. Text in English. 1969. a. **Description:** Provides information about the Ministry of Transport, reports on the Ministry's achievements over the course of the year against its targets, and provides financial statements and management information.
Formerly (until 2005): New Zealand. Report of the Ministry of Transport (0085-4123); Which was formed by the 1969 merger of: New Zealand. Report of the Department of Transport; (1965-1968): New Zealand. Report of the Department of Civil Aviation (0548-9350); Which was formerly (until 1965): New Zealand. Report of the Air Department. Civil Aviation, Meteorological Service and Accidents Investigation Branch
Published by: Ministry of Transport, PO Box 3175, Wellington, New Zealand. TEL 64-4-4721253, FAX 64-4-4733697, info@transport.govt.nz.

328.93 NZL ISSN 1176-3914
NEW ZEALAND. PARLIAMENTARY COUNSEL OFFICE. REPORT. Text in English. 1990. a.
Related titles: Online - full text ed.: ISSN 1177-6625.
Published by: Parliamentary Counsel Office, Level 12, Reserve Bank Bldg, 2 The Terrace, PO Box 18 070, Wellington, New Zealand. TEL 64-4-4729639, FAX 64-4-4991724, contact.pco@parliament.govt.nz.

328.93 NZL ISSN 1176-3884
NEW ZEALAND. PARLIAMENTARY COUNSEL OFFICE. STATEMENT OF INTENT. Text in English. 1997. a.
Former titles (until 2004): New Zealand. Parliamentary Counsel Office. Departmental Forecast Report (1174-3484); (until 1998): New Zealand. Parliamentary Counsel Office. Forecast Financial Statements (1173-5155)
Related titles: Online - full text ed.: ISSN 1177-7001.
Published by: Parliamentary Counsel Office, Level 12, Reserve Bank Bldg, 2 The Terrace, PO Box 18 070, Wellington, New Zealand. TEL 64-4-4729639, FAX 64-4-4991724, contact.pco@parliament.govt.nz.

NEW ZEALAND. PATENT OFFICE. JOURNAL (CD-ROM). *see* PATENTS, TRADEMARKS AND COPYRIGHTS

351.93 364 NZL ISSN 1177-1526
NEW ZEALAND POLICE. ANNUAL REPORT. Text in English. a.
Formerly (until 2004): New Zealand Police. Report
Related titles: Online - full text ed.
Published by: New Zealand Police, PO Box 3017, Wellington, 6140, New Zealand. TEL 64-4-4749499, FAX 64-4-4987400.

351.93 362.6 NZL ISSN 1177-3960
NEW ZEALAND POSITIVE AGEING STRATEGY. ANNUAL REPORT AND ACTION PLAN. Text in English. 2005. a. **Document type:** *Government.*
Formed by the merger of (2002-2005): New Zealand Positive Ageing Strategy. Annual Report (1176-0125); (2002-2005): New Zealand Positive Ageing Strategy. Action Plan (1176-0192)
Related titles: Online - full text ed.: ISSN 1177-5793.
Published by: Ministry of Social Development, Office for Senior Citizens, PO Box 1556, Wellington, New Zealand. TEL 64-4-9163758, FAX 64-4-9163778, osc@msd.govt.nz.

351.93 362.6 NZL ISSN 1177-5505
NEW ZEALAND POSITIVE AGEING STRATEGY. HIGHLIGHTS. Variant title: Achieving Positive Ageing and the Year Ahead. Text in English. 2006. a. **Document type:** *Government.*
Related titles: Online - full text ed.: ISSN 1177-5866.
Published by: Ministry of Social Development, Office for Senior Citizens, PO Box 1556, Wellington, New Zealand. TEL 64-4-9163758, FAX 64-4-9163778, osc@msd.govt.nz.

353.80993 NZL ISSN 1172-823X
NEW ZEALAND QUALIFICATIONS AUTHORITY. ANNUAL REPORT. Text in English. 1990. a.
Related titles: Online - full text ed.: ISSN 1177-7966.
Published by: New Zealand Qualifications Authority, PO Box 160, Wellington, 6140, New Zealand. TEL 64-4-4633000, FAX 64-4-4633112, helpdesk@nzqa.govt.nz.

328 NZL ISSN 1173-0714
NEW ZEALAND STATUTORY REGULATIONS: QUARTERLY SUMMARY. Text in English. ceased 2003; resumed 1994. q. index. **Document type:** *Government.* **Description:** Summarizes Statutory Regulations. Includes department of administration, date of notification, and acts passed.
Published by: Legislation Direct, PO Box 12357, Wellington, 6144, New Zealand. TEL 64-4-496-5655, FAX 64-4-496-5698, ldorders@legislationdirect.co.nz, http://www.legislationdirect.co.nz/.

353.53 USA
NEWS FROM CONGRESSIONAL BLACK ASSOCIATES. Text in English. q. **Description:** Informs members of the black community of federal government activities.
Published by: Congressional Black Associates, 1504 Longworth, Washington, DC 20515. TEL 202-225-5865.

NGUOI DAI BIEU NHAN DAN/PEOPLE'S DEPUTY. *see* POLITICAL SCIENCE

353.1 DEU ISSN 0341-3497
NIEDERSAECHSISCHES GESETZ- UND VERORDNUNGSBLATT. Text in German. 1947. irreg. EUR 56.30 (effective 2010). **Document type:** *Journal, Trade.*
Published by: Schluetersche Verlagsgesellschaft mbH und Co. KG, Hans-Boeckler-Allee 7, Hannover, 30173, Germany. TEL 49-511-85500, FAX 49-511-85501100, info@schluetersche.de, http://www.schluetersche.de.

353.9 DEU ISSN 0341-3500
NIEDERSAECHSISCHES MINISTERIALBLATT. Text in German. 1951. w. EUR 130.40 (effective 2010). **Document type:** *Journal, Trade.*
Published by: Schluetersche Verlagsgesellschaft mbH und Co. KG, Hans-Boeckler-Allee 7, Hannover, 30173, Germany. TEL 49-511-85500, FAX 49-511-85501100, info@schluetersche.de, http://www.schluetersche.de.

351 BEL
NIEUW KLIMAAT. Text in Dutch. 1958. bi-m. adv. bk.rev.
Published by: Verbond Vlaams Overheidspersoneel, Rykeklazenstraat 45, Brussels, 1000, Belgium. Ed. P Stoppie. Circ: 6,500.

351 NLD ISSN 1877-2293
NIEUWSBRIEF I O O V. (Inspectie Openbare Orde en Veiligheid) Text in Dutch. 2002. irreg.
Published by: Ministerie van Veiligheid en Justitie, Inspectie Openbare Orde en Veiligheid, Postbus 20301, The Hague, 2500 EH, Netherlands. TEL 31-70-4267343, FAX 31-70-4266990.

351 JPN ISSN 0548-1570
NIPPON GYOSEI KENKYU NENPO/JAPANESE SOCIETY FOR PUBLIC ADMINISTRATION. ANNALS. Text in Japanese. 1692. a. JPY 7,000 membership (effective 2006). bibl. **Document type:** *Journal, Academic/Scholarly.*
Published by: Nippon Gyosei Gakkai/Japanese Society for Public Administration, c/o Kyoto University, Faculty of Law, Yoshidahonmachi, Sakyo-ku, Kyoto, 606-8501, Japan. TEL 81-75-7533213, FAX 81-20-46690556, jspa@mbn.nifty.com, http://wwwsoc.nii.ac.jp/jaspa/.

351.1106 KEN
NON-GOVERNMENTAL ORGANIZATIONS REGULATIONS (YEAR). Text in English. irreg., latest 1992. KES 55. **Document type:** *Government.*
Published by: Government Press, Haile Selaissie Ave., PO Box 30128, Nairobi, Kenya.

351.687355 ZAF
NOORD-KAAP. PROVINSIALE KOERANT/NORTHERN CAPE. PROVINCIAL GAZETTE. Text in Afrikaans, English. 1994. w. **Document type:** *Government.*
Supersedes in part: Kaap die Goeie Hoop. Provinsiale Koerant - Cape of Good Hope. Provincial Gazette
Published by: Provincial Administration, c/o Government Printer, Private Bag X85, Pretoria, 0001, South Africa.

351.682 ZAF
NOORD-TRANSVAAL. PROVINSIALE KOERANT/NORTHERN TRANSVAAL. PROVINCIAL GAZETTE. Text in Afrikaans, English, Sotho, Northern, Tsonga. 1994. w. **Document type:** *Government.*
Supersedes in part: Transvaal. Provinsiale Koerant
Published by: Provincial Administration, c/o Government Printer, Private Bag X85, Pretoria, 0001, South Africa.

NORD. *see* POLITICAL SCIENCE

NORDRHEIN-WESTFAELISCHE VERWALTUNGSBLAETTER; Zeitschrift fuer oeffentliches Recht und oeffentliche Verwaltung. *see* LAW

354.8 DEU
NORDRHEIN-WESTFALEN. FINANZMINISTERIUM. FINANZ REPORT. Text in German. 1991. 2/yr. **Document type:** *Government.*
Published by: Finanzministerium des Landes Nordrhein-Westfalen, Jaegerhofstr 6, Duesseldorf, 40479, Germany. TEL 49-211-49722325, FAX 49-211-49722300. Ed. Marie Luise Hoffmann. Circ: 40,000.

351.9482 NFK
NORFOLK ISLAND GOVERNMENT GAZETTE. Text in English. 1942. w. back issues avail. **Document type:** *Newspaper.*
Published by: Administration Offices, Kingston, 2899, Norfolk Isl. TEL 61-7232-22001, FAX 61-7232-23177.

351.1422 GBR ISSN 1749-4702
NORK QUARTERLY. Text in English. 1926. q. free to members (effective 2009). adv. **Document type:** *Magazine, Consumer.*
Published by: Nork Ratepayers' and Residents' Association, c/o Mr. George W. Hinton, Ed., 9 Nork Gardens, Nork, Banstead, Surrey SM7 1NZ, United Kingdom. TEL 44-1737-354309, george.hinton@nork-residents.org.uk. Ed., Adv. contact George W Hinton. page GBP 51.25.

351 USA
NORTH CAROLINA MANUAL. Text in English. 1901. biennial. USD 24.49 (effective 2000). **Document type:** *Government.*
Published by: Secretary of State, Publications Division, PO Box 29622, Raleigh, NC 27626-0622. TEL 919-807-2149. Circ: 5,000 (controlled).

351.756 USA
NORTH CAROLINA. SECRETARY OF STATE. DIRECTORY OF STATE AND COUNTY OFFICIALS. Text in English. 1936. a. USD 10.50 (effective 2000). **Document type:** *Directory, Government.*
Published by: Secretary of State, Publications Division, PO Box 29622, Raleigh, NC 27626-0622. TEL 919-807-2149. Circ: 10,000 (controlled).

351 JPN
NORTH KOREA DIRECTORY (YEAR); comprehensive guide to North Korean organizations and leadership. Text in English, Chinese. 1988. a. JPY 6,000, USD 60. **Document type:** *Directory.* **Description:** Lists personnel and structural changes in North Korea's government, state organs, political parties, and mass organizations. Lists names in Chinese characters, Roman letters, and Japanese hiragana. Includes approximately 5000 North Korean leaders.
Published by: R P Printings, 1-10-22 Shimo-Noge, Takatsu-ku, Kawasaki-shi, Kanagawa-ken 213-0006, Japan. TEL 81-44-833-4421, FAX 81-44-833-4422.

351.416 GBR
NORTHERN IRELAND JUDICIAL APPOINTMENTS OMBUDSMAN ANNUAL REPORT. Text in English. 1970. a. price varies. **Document type:** *Government.*
Formerly: Northern Ireland. Commissioner for Complaints. Annual Report
Published by: (Northern Ireland Judicial Appointments Ombudsman IRL), The Stationery Office, St Crispins, Duke St, Norwich, NR3 1PD, United Kingdom. TEL 44-1603-622211, FAX 44-870-6005533, customer.services@tso.co.uk, http://www.tso.co.uk. Circ: 170. **Subscr. to:** PO Box 29, Norwich NR3 1GN, United Kingdom. TEL 44-870-6005522.

351 AUS
NORTHERN TERRITORY. DEPARTMENT OF LANDS AND PLANNING. ANNUAL REPORT. Text in English. 2002. a. free (print or online ed.) (effective 2010). back issues avail. **Document type:** *Report, Government.* **Description:** Provides a record of the activities and achievements of the Department of Planning and Infrastructure and its Government Business Divisions Construction Division and Darwin Bus Service for the each financial year.
Formerly (until 200?): Northern Territory. Department of Planning and Infrastructure. Annual Report; Which superseded in part (in 2006): Northern Territory. Department of Infrastructure, Planning and Environment. Annual Report (1832-214X); Which was formed by the merger of (1996-2002): Northern Territory. Department of Parks and Wildlife Commission. Annual Report; (1979-2002): Northern Territory. Department of Transport and Works. Annual Report (0810-3933); (1995-2002): Northern Territory. Department of Lands, Planning & Environment. Annual Report (1327-5674); Which was formerly (until 1995): Northern Territory. Department of Lands, Housing and Local Government. Annual Report (1321-604X); Which was formed by the merger of (1991-1993): Northern Territory. Office of Local Government. Annual Report (1037-8898); (1989-1993): Northern Territory. Department of Lands and Housing. Annual Report (1035-638X); Which was formerly (until 1989): Northern Territory. Department of Lands and Housing. Annual Report (1031-5578); (1981-1987): Northern Territory. Department of Lands. Annual Report (0727-5676)
Related titles: Online - full text ed.: ISSN 1837-5804.
Published by: Northern Territory, Department of Lands and Planning, GPO Box 2520, Darwin, N.T. 0801, Australia. TEL 61-8-89995511, FAX 61-8-89247044, feedback.dpi@nt.gov.au.

351 AUS ISSN 1834-0571
NORTHERN TERRITORY. DEPARTMENT OF NATURAL RESOURCES, ENVIRONMENT AND THE ARTS. ANNUAL REPORT. Text in English. 2006. a. free (print or online ed.) (effective 2009). back issues avail. **Document type:** *Report, Trade.* **Description:** Provides a record of the Department of Natural Resources, Environment and The Arts and the Territory Wildlife Parks Government Business Division's achievements for the each financial year.
Supersedes in part (in 2005): Northern Territory. Department of Infrastructure, Planning and Environment. Annual Report (1832-214X); Which was formed by the merger of (1996-2001): Northern Territory. Department of Parks and Wildlife Commission. Annual Report; (1996-2001): Northern Territory. Department of Lands, Planning & Environment. Annual Report (1327-5674); (1979-2001): Northern Territory. Department of Transport and Works. Annual Report (0810-3933)
Related titles: Online - full text ed.
Published by: Northern Territories, Department of Natural Resources, Environment and the Arts, PO Box 496, Palmerston, N.T. 0831, Australia. TEL 61-8-89995511, http://www.nt.gov.au/nreta/index.html.

351.44 AUS ISSN 1833-1467
NORTHERN TERRITORY GRANTS COMMISSION. ANNUAL REPORT. Text in English. 1993. a., latest 2005. free (effective 2009). back issues avail. **Document type:** *Government.*
Formerly (until 1995): Northern Territory Local Government Grants Commission. Annual Report (1321-389X); Which was formed by the merger (1987-1992): Northern Territory Local Government Grants Commission. Financial Statements for the Year Ended (1032-8637); (1991-1992): Annual Report - Office of Local Government (1037-8898)
Related titles: CD-ROM ed.; Online - full text ed.: ISSN 1835-4440.
Published by: Northern Territory Grants Commission, GPO Box 4621, Darwin, N.T. 0801, Australia. http://www.grantscommission.nt.gov.au.

351 FRA ISSN 1263-2325
NOTES DU CENTRE DE PROSPECTIVE ET DE VEILLE SCIENTIFIQUE. EQUIPEMENT. Text in French. 1994. irreg., latest vol.18, 2003. **Document type:** *Monographic series.*
—INIST.
Published by: Centre de Prospective et de Veille Scientifique, Tour Pascal B, La Defense, 92055 Cedex 04, France. TEL 33-1-40816323, FAX 33-1-40811444, CPVS.DRAST@equipement.gouv.fr. Ed. Jacques Theys.

351 USA ISSN 0883-3648
K14
NOTRE DAME JOURNAL OF LAW, ETHICS & PUBLIC POLICY. Abbreviated title: N D J L E P P. Text in English. 1984. s-a. USD 35 domestic; USD 40 in Canada; USD 42 elsewhere (effective 2009). back issues avail.; reprint service avail. from WSH. **Document type:** *Journal, Academic/Scholarly.* **Description:** Explores the legal, ethical, and policy considerations within the framework of the Judeo-Christian intellectual and moral tradition.
Related titles: Microfiche ed.: (from WSH); Microform ed.: (from WSH); Online - full text ed.
Indexed: A22, A26, B04, BRD, CA, CJA, CLI, FamI, G08, I01, I05, ILP, LRI, P30, P34, P42, PAIS, PSA, PhilInd, RI-1, RI-2, S02, S03, SCOPUS, SOPODA, SSA, SociolAb, T02, W03, W05.
—BLDSC (6175.405000), CIS, IE, Infotrieve, Ingenta.
Published by: University of Notre Dame, Thomas J. White Center on Law and Government, Notre Dame Law School, Notre Dame, IN 46556. TEL 574-631-4888, FAX 574-631-6371. Ed. Noah J Stanzione.

352.8 GBR
NOTTINGHAM TRENT UNIVERSITY. CENTRE FOR RESEARCH INTO REGULATION, ORGANIZATION AND LAW. OCCASIONAL PAPERS IN ECONOMICS. Text in English. irreg., latest no.96-11. **Document type:** *Monographic series, Academic/Scholarly.*
Published by: Nottingham Trent University, Centre for Research into Regulation, Organization and Law, Burton St., Nottingham, NG1 4BU, United Kingdom. TEL 44-115-941-8418, FAX 44-115-948-6808.

351 CAN ISSN 1718-4894
NOUVELLES SUR LES PROCHAINES ETAPES. Text in French. 2005. q. **Document type:** *Newsletter, Government.*
Media: Online - full text. **Related titles:** English ed.: The Way Forward.
Published by: Public Works and Government Services Canada/Travaux Publics et Services Gouvernementaux Canada, Place du Portage, Phase III, 11 Laurier St, Gatineau, PQ K1A 0S5, Canada. TEL 800-622-6232, Questions@pwgsc.gc.ca, http://www.pwgsc.gc.ca/text/home-e.html.

354 CAN
NOVA SCOTIA. DEPARTMENT OF ECONOMIC DEVELOPMENT AND TOURISM. ANNUAL REPORT. Text in English. 1971. a. free. **Document type:** *Government.*
Former titles: Nova Scotia. Department of Economic Development. Annual Report; Nova Scotia. Department of Industry, Trade and Technology. Annual Report; Nova Scotia. Department of Development. Annual Report
Published by: Department of Economic Development, P O Box 519, Halifax, NS B3J 2R7, Canada. TEL 902-424-8922, FAX 902-424-5739, TELEX 019-22548. Ed., R&P Mary Jane Fumerton. Circ: 300 (controlled).

351 CAN ISSN 1910-4243
NOVA SCOTIA. DEPARTMENT OF TRANSPORTATION AND PUBLIC WORKS. ACCOUNTABILITY REPORT. Text in English. a. **Document type:** *Government.*

P

Former titles (until 2001): Nova Scotia. Department of Transportation and Communications. Annual Report (1184-9932); (until 1988): Nova Scotia Department of Transportation. Annual Report (0823-9169); (until 1980): Nova Scotia Department of Highways. Annual Report (0701-7693); (until 1971): Nova Scotia. Annual Report of the Department of Highways (0701-7707); Which superseded in part (1946-1956): Annual Report of the Department of Highways and Public Works. Nova Scotia (0701-7723); Which was formerly: Department of Highways and Public Works. Report
Published by: Nova Scotia, Department of Transportation and Public Works, PO Box 186, Halifax, NS B3J 2N2, Canada. TEL 902-424-2297, FAX 902-424-0532, tpwpaff@gov.ns.ca, http://www.gov.ns.ca/tran/default.asp.

352.88 CAN ISSN 0380-5670
NOVA SCOTIA. OFFICE OF THE OMBUDSMAN. ANNUAL REPORT. Text in English. 1971. a. free. **Document type:** *Government.*
Published by: Office of the Ombudsman, Lord Nelson Bldg, Ste 300, 5675 Spring Garden Rd, P O Box 2152, Halifax, NS B3J 3B7, Canada. TEL 902-424-6780, FAX 902-424-6675. Ed. Douglas G Ruck. Circ: 500.

321.023 AUS ISSN 1442-3030
NOW AND THEN. Text in English. 1988. bi-m. back issues avail. **Document type:** *Newsletter.* **Description:** Provides up-to-date information about new research tools and resources, services and seminars, exhibitions and other activities taking place at state records.
Formerly (until 1999): Archivista (1032-1330)
Related titles: Online - full text ed.: free (effective 2009).
Published by: State Records Authority of New South Wales, PO Box R625, Royal Exchange, NSW 1225, Australia. info@records.nsw.gov.au.

NUERNBERGER STATISTIK AKTUELL. *see* PUBLIC ADMINISTRATION—Abstracting, Bibliographies, Statistics

351 USA
O M B WATCHER. (Office of Management and Budget) Text in English. 1983. bi-m. USD 35 to individuals. **Document type:** *Newsletter.* **Description:** News of OMB activities.
Published by: O M B Watch, 1742 Connecticut Ave, N W, Washington, DC 20009. TEL 202-234-8494, FAX 202-234-8584. Ed. Patrick Lester. R&P Barbara Western.

351 BEL ISSN 1782-1843
O M D ACTUALITES. (Organisation Mondiale des Douanes) Text in French. 1983. bi-m. free. **Document type:** *Magazine, Trade.*
Related titles: Online - full text ed.; ◆ Supplement to: W C O News. ISSN 1782-1851.
Published by: World Customs Organization (W C O)/Organisation Mondiale des Douanes (O M D), Rue du Marche 30, Brussels, 1210, Belgium. TEL 32-2-209-9211, FAX 32-2-209-9292, information@wcoomd.org, http://www.wcoomd.org.

O R E S WORKING PAPER SERIES. (Office of Research, Evaluation and Statistics) *see* SOCIAL SERVICES AND WELFARE

354.8 332.1 CAN ISSN 1701-0802
HG185.C2
O S F I ANNUAL REPORT. (Office of the Superintendent of Financial Institutions) Variant title: Rapport Annuel du B S I F. Text in English, French. 1988. a.
Formerly (until 2000): Office of the Superintendent of Financial Institutions. Annual Report (0842-4659)
Related titles: Online - full text ed.: ISSN 1701-0810.
Published by: Canada. Office of the Superintendent of Financial Institutions, 255 Albert St, 13th Flr, Ottawa, ON K1A 0H2, Canada. TEL 613-990-7655, FAX 613-952-8219, pub@osfi-bsif.gc.ca.

351 NLD ISSN 1385-1187
O T B WERKDOCUMENT. (Onderzoeksinstituut Technische Bestuurskunde) Text in Dutch. 1988; N.S. 1996. irreg., latest vol.2, 2001. price varies. back issues avail. **Document type:** *Monographic series, Academic/Scholarly.* **Description:** Discusses public-administration issues as they pertain to the construction industry.
Former titles (until 1996): Onderzoeksinstituut O T B. Werkdocument (1383-8016); (until 1992): Onderzoeksinstituut voor Technische Bestuurskunde. Werkdocument (0923-9871)
Published by: (Onderzoeksinstituut OTB), Delft University Press (Subsidiary of: I O S Press), Nieuwe Hemweg 6B, Amsterdam, 1013 BG, Netherlands. TEL 31-20-6883355, FAX 31-20-6870039, info.dupress@iospress.nl.

351 320 COL ISSN 1657-8651
JL2801
➤ **OBSERVATORIO DE POLITICAS, EJECUCION Y RESULTADOS DE LA ADMINISTRACION PUBLICA.** Text in Spanish. 2001. a. COP 40,000 domestic; USD 40 foreign (effective 2011). Index. back issues avail. **Document type:** *Journal, Academic/Scholarly.*
Related titles: Online - full text ed.: free (effective 2011).
Indexed: A01, C01, CA, F03, F04, IBSS, P42, T02.
Published by: (Universidad Externado de Colombia, Facultad de Finanzas, Gobierno y Relaciones Internacionales), Universidad Externado de Colombia, Departamento de Publicaciones, Calle 12, No 1-17 Este, Bogota, Colombia. TEL 57-1-3420288, 57-1-2826066, publicaciones@uexternado.edu.co. Ed. Javier Torres. R&P Carolina Esguerra. **Dist. by:** Siglo del Hombre Editores, Cra. 32 No.25-46/50, Bogota, D.C., Colombia. TEL 57-1-3377700, FAX 57-1-3377665, info@siglodelhombre.com, http://www.siglodelhombre.com.

351 DEU ISSN 1869-9421
▼ **OEFFENTLICHE UNTERNEHMEN UND OEFFENTLICHES WIRTSCHAFTSRECHT.** Text in German. 2010. irreg. price varies. **Document type:** *Monographic series, Academic/Scholarly.*
Published by: Verlag Dr. Kovac, Leverkusenstr 13, Hamburg, 22761, Germany. TEL 49-40-3988800, FAX 49-40-39888055, info@verlagdrkovac.de.

DIE OEFFENTLICHE VERWALTUNG; Zeitschrift fuer oeffentliches Recht und Verwaltungswissenschaft. *see* LAW

351 SWE ISSN 2000-8058
OFFENTLIG FOERVALTNING; scandinavian journal of public administartion. Text in Multiple languages. 1997. q. **Document type:** *Journal, Academic/Scholarly.*
Formerly (until 2010): Kommunal Ekonomi och Politik (1402-8700)
Related titles: Online - full text ed.
Published by: Goeteborgs Universitet, Foervaltningshoegskolan/Goeteborg University, School of Public Administration, PO Box 712, Goeteborg, 40530, Sweden. TEL 46-31-7860000, FAX 46-31-7864719, http://www.spa.gu.se.

351 SWE ISSN 1653-3674
OFFENTLIGA AFFAERER; affaerstidningen foer offentlig sektor. Text in Swedish. 1993. q. SEK 299 (effective 2007). adv. **Document type:** *Magazine, Trade.*
Former titles (until 2005): Stat och Kommuninformation (1650-7789); (until 2001): Svensk Kommuninformation (1403-3798)
Related titles: Online - full text ed.
Published by: Hexanova Media Group, Fiskhamnsgatan 2, Goeteborg, 414588, Sweden. TEL 46-31-7190500, FAX 46-31-7751589, info@hexanova.se, http://www.hexanova.se. Ed. Anita Sanderholm. Pub. Urban Nilsson. Adv. contact Thelma Infante TEL 46-31-7751592. page SEK 29,950; 185 x 270.

OFFICE FOR NATIONAL STATISTICS. U.K. SERVICE SECTOR. *see* PUBLIC ADMINISTRATION—Abstracting, Bibliographies, Statistics

OFFICE OF THE REGISTRAR OF LOBBYISTS. ESTIMATES. PART III: REPORT ON PLANS AND PRIORITIES/BUREAU DU DIRECTEUR DES LOBBYISTES. BUDGET DES DEPENSES. PARTIE III: RAPPORT SUR LES PLANS ET LES PRIORITES. *see* BUSINESS AND ECONOMICS—Public Finance, Taxation

351.71 332 CAN ISSN 1483-8559
CA1BT31-4 62
OFFICE OF THE SUPERINTENDENT OF FINANCIAL INSTITUTIONS CANADA. PERFORMANCE REPORT. Text in English, French. 1997. a.
Related titles: Online - full text ed.: ISSN 1490-5841.
Published by: (Canada. Canada. Office of the Superintendent of Financial Institutions), Treasury Board of Canada Secretariat, Corporate Communications/Secretariat du Conseil du Tresor du Canada, West Tower, Rm P-135, 300 Laurier Ave W, Ottawa, ON K1A 0R5, Canada. TEL 613-995-2855, FAX 613-996-0518, services-publications@tbs-sct.gc.ca.

351.881 GUY ISSN 0030-0314
OFFICIAL GAZETTE OF GUYANA. Text in English. 1966. w. looseleaf. USD 533. adv. stat.
Published by: (Guyana. Public Communications Agency), Ministry of Information and Culture, Brickdam 18, PO Box 1023, Georgetown, Guyana. Circ: 1,156.

351.771 USA ISSN 0163-0008
OHIO MONTHLY RECORD. Abbreviated title: O M R. Text in English. 1977. m. looseleaf. USD 128.25 (effective 2011). **Document type:** *Trade.* **Description:** Contains the full text of new administrative agency rules, with research aids—including notes to recent Ohio and federal court decisions and agency opinions.
Related titles: Supplement(s): Ohio Administrative Code.
Published by: West Publishing Corporation (Subsidiary of: Thomson Reuters), 610 Opperman Dr, Eagan, MN 55123. TEL 651-687-7000, 800-344-5008.

349 USA ISSN 1063-990X
OHIO REPORT. Text in English. 19??. d. USD 2,750; USD 240 per month (effective 2009). **Document type:** *Government.* **Description:** Provides detailed coverage of every bill in the General Assembly and closely tracks the intricate workings of the executive and judicial branches.
Related titles: Online - full text ed.: ISSN 1946-1585.
Published by: Gongwer News Service, Inc., 17 S High St, Ste 630, Columbus, OH 43215. TEL 614-221-1992, FAX 614-221-7844, gongwer@gongwer-oh.com, http://www.gongwer-oh.com.

351.771 USA
OHIO UNITED WAY. ADMINISTRATIVE REPORT. Text in English. 1976. 24/yr. looseleaf. USD 45 (effective 2000). s-a. index. back issues avail. **Document type:** *Newsletter.*
Published by: Ohio United Way, 88 E Broad St, Ste 620, Columbus, OH 43215-3506. TEL 614-224-8146, FAX 614-224-6597. Ed. Willie Verhoff. R&P Wilfred Verhoff. Circ: 500.

351 FIN ISSN 0357-1084
OHOI. Text in Finnish. 1978. q. EUR 24 (effective 2006). adv. back issues avail. **Document type:** *Magazine, Government.* **Description:** Quarterly information on the current work and activities at the Ministry of Justice in Finland.
Related titles: Online - full text ed.
Published by: Oikeusministerio/Ministry of Justice, PO Box 25, Government, Helsinki, 00023, Finland. TEL 358-9-16003, FAX 358-9-16067730, om-tiedot@om.fi. Eds. Eeva Vallisaari TEL 358-9-16087606, Pirkko Kauppinen TEL 358-9-16067605. adv.: page EUR 500. Circ: 8,000.

OKLAHOMA AGENCIES, BOARDS AND COMMISSIONS. *see* POLITICAL SCIENCE

351.766 USA ISSN 0890-1007
THE OKLAHOMA CONSTITUTION. Text in English. 1979. q. USD 10 (effective 2002). **Description:** Reports on Oklahoma government and political news.
Published by: The Oklahoma Constitution, P.O. Box 53482, Oklahoma City, OK 73152. TEL 405-366-1125, okconsti@aol.com. Ed. Steve Byas.

351 CAN ISSN 1912-7723
OMBUDSMAN MANITOBA. ANNUAL REPORTS AND OTHER PUBLICATIONS. Text in English. 2005. a. **Document type:** *Report, Trade.*
Media: CD-ROM.
Published by: Ombudsman Manitoba, 750-500 Portage Ave, Winnipeg, MB R3C 3X1, Canada. TEL 204-982-9130, 800-665-0531, FAX 204-942-7803, http://www.ombudsman.mb.ca.

ON THE IMPLEMENTATION OF THE EUROPEAN COMMISSION'S EXTERNAL ASSISTANCE (YEAR). ANNUAL REPORT. *see* BUSINESS AND ECONOMICS—International Development And Assistance

360 351 CAN ISSN 0704-2663
ONTARIO ADVISORY COUNCIL ON SENIOR CITIZENS. ANNUAL REPORT. Text in English. 1975. a.
Published by: (Ontario Advisory Council on Senior Citizens), Ontario, Legislative Assembly, Queen's Park, Toronto, ON M7A 1A2, Canada. TEL 416-325-7500, FAX 416-325-7489, http://www.ontla.on.ca/index.htm.

354.7 CAN ISSN 1483-2623
HJ13.O6
ONTARIO BUDGET. BUDGET PAPERS. Text in English. 1953. a. **Document type:** *Government.*
Former titles (until 1995): Ontario Budget (0381-2332); (until 1971): Budget Ontario (0381-2324); (until 1968): Budget Statement Ontario (0381-2316)
Published by: Ontario Ministry of Finance, Frost Bldg S, 7th Flr, 7 Queen's Park Cres, Toronto, ON M7A 1Y7, Canada. TEL 800-263-7965, FAX 905-433-6777, http://www.gov.on.ca/fin.

354.7 CAN ISSN 0828-3877
ONTARIO ECONOMIC ACCOUNTS. Text in English. 1977. q.
Former titles (until 1987): Ontario. Ministry of Treasury and Economics. Economic Accounts (0715-9390); (until 1982): Economic Accounts Bulletin (0228-4634); (until 1980): Bulletin. Ontario Economic Accounts (0702-0023)
Published by: Ontario Ministry of Finance, Frost Bldg S, 7th Flr, 7 Queen's Park Cres, Toronto, ON M7A 1Y7, Canada. TEL 800-263-7965, FAX 905-433-6777, http://www.gov.on.ca/fin.

354.71 388.1 CAN ISSN 0701-9971
HE5635.O5
ONTARIO HIGHWAY TRANSPORT BOARD. ANNUAL REPORT. Text in English. 1958. a.
Incorporates (1988-1989): Commission des Transports Routiers de l'Ontario. Rapport Annuel (0847-4060); Former titles (until 1971): Ontario Department of Transport. Annual Report (0703-6159); (until 1967): Ontario. Department of Transport. Annual Report of the Minister of Transport (0703-6167); (until 1964): Ontario Department of Transport. Annual Report (0474-1773)
Published by: Ontario Highway Transport Board, 151 Bloor St. W., 10th Flr., Toronto, ON M5S 2T5, Canada. TEL 416-326-6732, FAX 416-326-6738, ohtb@mto.gov.on.ca, http://www.ohtb.gov.on.ca.

351 CAN ISSN 1715-4316
ONTARIO LEGISLATIVE ASSEMBLY. SELECT COMMITTEE ON ELECTORAL REFORM. OFFICIAL REPORT OF DEBATES, HANSARD/JOURNAL DES DEBATS (HANSARD). Text in English. 2005. irreg. **Document type:** *Government.*
Published by: Ontario, Legislative Assembly, Queen's Park, Toronto, ON M7A 1A2, Canada. TEL 416-325-7500, FAX 416-325-7489, http://www.ontla.on.ca/index.htm.

353.37 CAN ISSN 1499-4887
ONTARIO LOTTERY AND GAMING CORPORATION. ANNUAL REPORT. Text in English. 1995. a.
Formerly (until 2001): Ontario Casino Corporation. Annual Report (1204-041X); Which incorporated (1976-1998): Ontario Lottery Corporation. Annual Report (0706-0076)
Published by: Ontario Lottery and Gaming Corporation, 4120 Yonge St, Suite 420, Toronto, ON M2P 2B8, Canada. TEL 416-224-1772, http://www.olgc.ca.

351.713 CAN ISSN 1198-824X
JS1789
ONTARIO MUNICIPAL DIRECTORY. Text in English, French. 1948. a. CAD 7.50. charts; stat. index. **Document type:** *Directory.*
Formerly: Ontario. Provincial-Municipal Affairs Secretariat. Municipal Directory. (0318-0743)
Related titles: French ed.: Annuaire Municipal de l'Ontario. ISSN 1209-0891.
Published by: (Provincial-Municipal Affairs Secretariat), Ministry of Municipal Affairs, 777 Bay St, Toronto, ON M5G 2E5, Canada. TEL 416-585-4286.

353 USA ISSN 1934-1946
ONTARIO STAFF DIRECTORY. Text in English. 1988. a. USD 250 (effective 2008). reprints avail. **Document type:** *Directory, Government.* **Description:** A directory of official personnel in federal state and local government within Ontario.
Formerly (until 2006): Ontario Public Sector (0841-0798)
Published by: C Q Press, Inc. (Subsidiary of: Sage Publications, Inc.), 2300 N St, NW, Ste 800, Washington, DC 20037. TEL 202-729-1900, 866-427-7737, FAX 800-380-3810, customerservice@cqpress.com, http://www.cqpress.com. Ed. Barbara Rogers.

351.687355 ZAF
OOS-KAAP. PROVINSIALE KOERANT/EASTERN CAPE. PROVINCIAL GAZETTE. Text in Afrikaans, English. 1994. w. **Document type:** *Government.*
Supersedes in part: Kaap die Goeie Hoop. Provinsiale Koerant - Cape of Good Hope. Provincial Gazette
Published by: Provincial Administration, c/o Government Printer, Private Bag X85, Pretoria, 0001, South Africa.

351.682 ZAF
OOS-TRANSVAAL. PROVINSIALE KOERANT/EASTERN TRANSVAAL. PROVINCIAL GAZETTE. Text in Afrikaans, English. 1994. w. **Document type:** *Government.*
Supersedes in part: Transvaal. Provinsiale Koerant
Published by: Provincial Administration, c/o Government Printer, Private Bag X85, Pretoria, 0001, South Africa.

352.68 NLD ISSN 0925-7322
➤ **OPENBAAR BESTUUR.** Text in Dutch. 1991. m. (11/yr.). EUR 162; EUR 81 to students (effective 2008). adv. bk.rev. index. back issues avail. **Document type:** *Academic/Scholarly.* **Description:** Articles of interest to civil servants at the central, provincial and municipal levels, as well as to scholars of public administration.
Formed by the merger of: Tijdschrift voor Openbaar Bestuur (0165-1226); Bestuur (0167-6733); Which was formerly: Centraal Instituut Vorming en Opleiding Bestuursdiensten-blad (0922-3045)
Indexed: ELLIS.
—IE.
Published by: Kluwer B.V. (Subsidiary of: Wolters Kluwer N.V.), Postbus 4, Alphen aan den Rijn, 2400 MA, Netherlands. TEL 31-172-466405, FAX 31-172-466577, http://www.kluwer.nl.

351 ESP ISSN 1989-8703
▼ **OPINAR.** Text in Spanish. 2010. s-a. **Document type:** *Newsletter, Consumer.*
Media: Online - full text.
Published by: Capitulo Espanol del Club de Roma, Grupo Valenciano http://www.clubderoma.net/grval/.

351 658 CAN ISSN 1910-7706
OPTIMUM ONLINE; the journal of public sector management. Text in English, French. q. free (effective 2011). **Document type:** *Journal, Academic/Scholarly.*
Media: Online - full text. **Related titles:** French ed.: ISSN 1910-7692. 1998.
Indexed: A01, ATI, B02, B15, B17, B18, C03, C05, CA, CBCABus, CPerl, G04, G08, I05, P34, P48, P53, P54, PQC, T02.
Published by: (University of Ottawa, Centre on Governance), The Summit Group, 100-263 Holmwood Ave, Ottawa, ON K1S 2P8, Canada. TEL 613-688-0763, 800-575-1146, FAX 613-688-0767.

351.685 ZAF
ORANJE-VRYSTAAT. PROVINSIALE KOERANT/ORANGE FREE STATE. PROVINCIAL GAZETTE. Text in Afrikaans, English. 1994. w. **Document type:** *Government.*
Published by: Provincial Administration, PO Box 517, Bloemfontein, 9300, South Africa.

351 CAN ISSN 1926-1683
ORDER OF CANADA INVESTITURE/ORDE DU CANADA, REMISE DES DECORATIONS. Text in English. 19??. s-a. free (effective 2011). **Document type:** *Government.* **Description:** Designed to recognize a lifetime of outstanding achievement, dedication to the community and service to the nation.
Published by: Governor General of Canada, Rideau Hall, 1 Sussex Dr, Ottawa, ON K1A 0A1, Canada. TEL 613-993-8200, 800-465-6890, FAX 613-998-8760, info@gg.ca.

328 DEU ISSN 0474-3385
ORDO POLITICUS. Text in German. 1965. irreg., latest vol.36, 2001. price varies. **Document type:** *Monographic series, Academic/Scholarly.*
Published by: Duncker und Humblot GmbH, Carl-Heinrich-Becker-Weg 9, Berlin, 12165, Germany. TEL 49-30-7900060, FAX 49-30-79000631, info@duncker-humblot.de.

351.795 USA ISSN 0196-4577
JK9031
OREGON BLUE BOOK. Text in English. 1904. biennial. USD 19 (effective 2005). **Document type:** *Directory, Government.* **Description:** Provides a record of Oregon's government, businesses, and people. Chronicles its society, providing a sense of how Oregonians live their lives.
Published by: Minnesota Secretary of State, 225 Capitol St N E, Ste 180, Salem, OR 97310. TEL 503-986-2234, FAX 503-378-4991. Ed., R&P Tim Torgerson TEL 503-373-0701. Circ: 30,000.

351.795 USA
OREGON BULLETIN. Text in English. m. USD 75 (effective 2000). **Document type:** *Government.* **Description:** Contains notices of proposed rulemaking, text of new, amended and temporary rules, resumes of the administrative rule orders, special notices and an index.
Related titles: Online - full text ed.
Published by: Secretary of State, Archives, Archives Bldg, 800 N E Summer St, Salem, OR 97310. TEL 503-373-0701, FAX 503-378-4118. Ed. Tim Torgerson. R&P Roy Turnbaugh. Circ: 370 (paid); 30 (controlled).

OREGON. PUBLIC UTILITY COMMISSIONER. OREGON UTILITY STATISTICS. *see* PUBLIC ADMINISTRATION—Abstracting, Bibliographies, Statistics

351.795 USA
OREGON. SECRETARY OF STATE. ADMINISTRATIVE RULES COMPILATION. Text in English. 16 base vols. plus m. updates. USD 350; USD 300 for base vols. (effective 2000). **Document type:** *Government.* **Description:** Contains the complete text of both permanent and temporary Administrative Rules of all 177 state agencies, boards and commissions.
Related titles: Online - full text ed.
Published by: Secretary of State, Archives, Archives Bldg, 800 N E Summer St, Salem, OR 97310. TEL 503-373-0701, FAX 503-378-4118. Ed. Phil Keisling. R&P Roy Turnbaugh.

351.44 325 FRA ISSN 1957-5750
LES ORIENTATIONS DE LA POLITIQUE DE L'IMMIGRATION. Text in French. 2005. a. **Document type:** *Government.*
Published by: (Comite Interministeriel de Controle de l'Immigration), Documentation Francaise, 29-31 Quai Voltaire, Paris, Cedex 7 75344, France. TEL 33-1-40157000, FAX 33-1-40157230.

351 DEU
DAS ORTS- UND GERICHTSVERZEICHNIS; mit den zustaendigen Finanzaemtern. Text in German. 1996. a. EUR 24.80 (effective 2010). **Document type:** *Directory, Trade.*
Related titles: CD-ROM ed.
Published by: Verlag Dr. Otto Schmidt KG, Gustav-Heinemann-Ufer 58, Cologne, 50968, Germany. TEL 49-221-93738460, FAX 49-221-93738943, info@otto-schmidt.de.

351.71 CAN ISSN 0702-8210
F1034.2
OTTAWA LETTER. Text in English. bi-w. looseleaf. CAD 800 (effective 2008). index. **Document type:** *Newsletter, Trade.* **Description:** Reports on what is going on in Parliament and government departments, tracks progress of Bills through Parliament, highlights the economy and weekly foreign exchange rates.
Formerly: View from Ottawa (0049-6383)
Related titles: Online - full text ed.
Indexed: C03, CBCARef, PQC.
Published by: C C H Canadian Ltd. (Subsidiary of: Wolters Kluwer N.V.), 90 Sheppard Ave E, Ste 300, North York, ON M2N 6X1, Canada. TEL 416-224-2248, 800-268-4522, FAX 416-224-2243, 800-461-4131, cservice@cch.ca. Ed. Ken Pole.

328.71384 CAN
OTTAWA UPDATE. Text in English. 1986. w. looseleaf. CAD 700. back issues avail. **Document type:** *Newsletter.* **Description:** Reports the status of federal legislation and government operations. Includes coverage of Parliamentary Committee activity and overall reaction from opposition parties and non-governmental organizations.
Formerly: Ottawa Weekly Update (0840-9196)
Related titles: Online - full text ed.
Published by: (Informetrica Limited), Publinet, P O BOX 828, Sta B, Ottawa, ON K1P 5P9, Canada. TEL 613-238-4831, FAX 613-238-7698. Ed. Rennie MacKenzie. Pub. Michael McCracken.

OUTPUT. *see* HOUSING AND URBAN PLANNING

351.66925 NGA
OYO STATE. ESTIMATES INCLUDING BUDGET SPEECH AND MEMORANDUM. Short title: Oyo State of Nigeria Estimates. Text in English. a. NGN 40. **Document type:** *Government.*
Formerly: Western State. Estimates Including Budget Speech and Memorandum
Published by: Government Printer, Ibadan, Oyo, Nigeria.

351.66925 NGA
OYO STATE OF NIGERIA GAZETTE. Text in English. irreg. NGN 30. Supplement avail. **Document type:** *Government.*
Formerly: Western State. Gazette
Published by: Government Printer, Ibadan, Oyo, Nigeria. TEL 234-22-411216.

351 USA ISSN 1041-6323
JK1
P A TIMES. (Public Administration) Text in English. 1978. m. free to members. adv. reprints avail. **Description:** Reports on current developments, innovative programs, and relevant issues in the field of public service.
Former titles (until 1987): Public Administration Times (0149-8797); (1951-1978): Public Administration News and Views (0033-3328); A S P A News and Views (0360-4233); Incorporates: Public Administration Recruiter (0033-3336)
Related titles: Online - full text ed.
Indexed: A09, A10, B01, B06, B07, B08, B09, C12, M01, M02, P34, PersLit, T02, V03, V04.
—CCC.
Published by: American Society for Public Administration, 1301 Pennsylvania Ave NW, Ste 840, Washington, DC 20004. TEL 202-393-7878, FAX 202-638-4952. Ed. Sheila McCormick. adv.: B&W page USD 4,595. Circ: 13,000.

351 NLD ISSN 0920-4865
P B O BLAD. (Publiek Rechtelijke Bedrijfsorganisatie) Key Title: PBO-blad. Text in Dutch. 1950. w. free (effective 2010). **Document type:** *Newspaper, Trade.*
Formerly (until 1987): Mededelingen- en Verordeningblad Bedrijfsorganisatie (0920-4857); Which was formed by the 1984 merger of: Verordeningenblad Bedrijfsorganisatie (0489-2534); Mededelingenblad Bedrijfsorganisatie (0025-6862)
Indexed: KES.
Published by: Sociaal-Economische Raad, Postbus 90405, The Hague, 2509 LK, Netherlands. TEL 31-70-3499499, FAX 31-70-3832535, ser.info@ser.nl, http://www.ser.nl.

352.63 USA ISSN 0732-1988
HD8011.N4
P E R B NEWS. Text in English. 1968. m. USD 25. **Document type:** *Newsletter.*
Published by: Public Employment Relations Board, 80 Wolf Rd, Albany, NY 12205. FAX 518-457-2664. Ed. R Rosen. Circ: 400.

362.1 USA ISSN 1930-6490
HN79.C23
P P I C STATEWIDE SURVEY. (Public Policy Institute of California) Text in English. 1998. irreg. free (effective 2010). **Document type:** *Newsletter, Consumer.*
Related titles: Online - full text ed.: free (effective 2010).
Published by: Public Policy Institute of California, 500 Washington St, Ste 600, San Franscisco, CA 94111. TEL 415-291-4400, FAX 415-291-4401, http://www.ppic.org/main/home.asp.

351 GBR
HD4645
P S L G BUILDING. (Public Service & Local Government) Text in English. 19??. m. free domestic (effective 2009). adv. illus. back issues avail. **Document type:** *Magazine, Government.* **Description:** Provides key local authority decision makers with essential news, views and technical information.
Former titles (until 2006): Public Sector and Local Government Magazine; (until 2001): P S L G (0144-4212); (until 1977): Public Service and Local Government Appointments
Indexed: A22.
—BLDSC (6969.230000), IE, Ingenta.
Published by: Unity Media PLC, Becket House, Vestry Rd, Sevenoaks, Kent TN14 5EJ, United Kingdom. TEL 44-1732-748000, FAX 44-1732-748001, http://www.unity-media.com/. Ed. Jo White TEL 44-1732-748039. Pub. Colin Wilkinson. Adv. contact Paul Ingleby TEL 44-1732-748067. color page GBP 1,950; trim 210 x 297. Circ: 15,000.

P T R C PERSPECTIVES. (Planning and Transport Research and Computation) *see* TRANSPORTATION—Roads And Traffic

351.6822 ZAF
P W V. PROVINSIALE KOERANT/P W V. PROVINCIAL GAZETTE. (Pretoria Witwatersrand Vaal) Cover title: Provinsiale Koerant - die Provinsie Transvaal. Text in Afrikaans, English. 1994 (vol.237, no.5009). w. **Document type:** *Government.*
Incorporates (in 1995): Gauteng. Provinsiale Koerant; Supersedes in part: Transvaal. Provinsiale Koerant
Published by: Provincial Administration, c/o Government Printer, Private Bag X85, Pretoria, 0001, South Africa.

351.5491 PAK ISSN 0078-8333
PAKISTAN. NATIONAL ASSEMBLY. DEBATES. OFFICIAL REPORT. Text in English, Urdu. 1962. irreg., latest 1999. PKR 0.50 (effective 2001). **Document type:** *Proceedings.*
Published by: National Assembly, Islamabad, Pakistan. TEL 92-51-9205626, FAX 92-51-9204673, assembly@isb.paknet.com.pk. **Dist. by:** Manager of Publications.

PANAMA. TRIBUNAL ELECTORAL. MEMORIA. *see* POLITICAL SCIENCE

351.93 NZL ISSN 1178-3516
PANUI WHAINGA. Text in Maori. 2003. a.
Media: Online - full text. **Related titles:** ◆ English ed.: New Zealand. Ministry of Maori Development. Statement of Intent (Online). ISSN 1178-3451.
Published by: New Zealand. Te Puni Kokiri/New Zealand. Ministry of Maori Development, PO Box 3943, Wellington, New Zealand. TEL 64-4-8196000, FAX 64-4-8196299, info@tpk.govt.nz.

351 ESP ISSN 1137-7224
PAPELES DE TRABAJO. ADMINISTRACION PUBLICA. Text in Spanish. 1991. irreg. price varies. back issues avail. **Document type:** *Monographic series, Academic/Scholarly.*
Published by: Fundacion Jose Ortega y Gasset, Fortuny 53, Madrid, 28010, Spain. TEL 34-91-7004100, FAX 34-91-7003530, comunicacion@fog.es.

352.44361 FRA ISSN 0296-1830
PARIS. BULLETIN MUNICIPAL OFFICIEL - BULLETIN DEPARTEMENTAL OFFICIEL. Key Title: Bulletin Municipal Officiel de la Ville de Paris, Bulletin Departemental Officiel du Departement de Paris. Text in French. 1985. 104/yr. **Document type:** *Bulletin.*
Formed by the 1985 merger of: Paris (Departement). Bulletin Departement Officiel - Arrets (0762-4689); Paris (City). Bulletin Municipal Officiel (0152-0377); Which was formerly: Paris (City). Bulletin Municipal Officiel. Deliberations du Conseil de Paris (0151-8267)
Published by: (Paris. Service des Publications Administratives), Ville de Paris, Cabinet du Maire, Hotel de Ville, Annexe Napoleon, Bureau 267, Paris, 75004, France. TEL 33-1-42765261, FAX 33-1-42766489. Ed. P Ribeyrolles. Circ: 5,600.

351 NLD ISSN 1871-1928
PARKEER. Text in Dutch. 2005. bi-m. EUR 65 (effective 2010). adv. **Document type:** *Magazine, Trade.*
Published by: Parkeermagazine BV (Subsidiary of: Arko Uitgeverij BV), Postbus 616, Nieuwegein, 3430 AP, Netherlands. TEL 31-30-7073030, FAX 31-30-6052618, http://www.parkeermagazine.nl/. Eds. Peter Bekkering, Jan van den Broek. Pub. Arend Jan Kornet. Adv. contact Wim Elbertse. color page EUR 2,295; 200 x 267. Circ: 8,000.

328.43 DEU
PARLAMENTARIUM. Text in German. 1987. a. EUR 49 (effective 2010). adv. **Document type:** *Trade.*
Published by: Walhalla Fachverlag, Haus an der Eisernen Bruecke, Regensburg, 93042, Germany. TEL 49-941-56840, FAX 49-941-5684111, walhalla@walhalla.de. adv.: B&W page EUR 3,330, color page EUR 5,050. Circ: 3,450 (paid and controlled).

328.4652 ESP
PARLAMENTO DE NAVARRA. BOLETIN. Text in Spanish. 1980. irreg. includes Diario de Sesiones. **Document type:** *Bulletin, Government.*
Published by: Parlamento de Navarra, Calle Navas de Tolosa 1, Pamplona, 31002, Spain. TEL 34-948-209209, FAX 34-948-228444, registro@parlamento-navarra.es.

328.4652 ESP
PARLAMENTO DE NAVARRA. DIARIO DE SESIONES. Text in Spanish. 1980. irreg. **Document type:** *Journal, Government.*
Published by: Parlamento de Navarra, Calle Navas de Tolosa 1, Pamplona, 31002, Spain. TEL 34-948-209209, FAX 34-948-228444, registro@parlamento-navarra.es, http://www.parlamento-navarra.es.

351 RUS
PARLAMENTSKAYA GAZETA. Text in Russian. 1998. 224/yr. USD 598 in United States (effective 2007). **Document type:** *Newspaper, Government.* **Description:** A daily newspaper of the Federal Assembly of the Russian Federation. Alongside with material of general interest it publishes detailed information on activities of the Russian parliament, laws and resolutions passed by the State Duma and the Federation Council.
Related titles: Microfilm ed.: (from EVP); Online - full text ed.
Published by: (Federal'noe Sobranie Rossiiskoi Federatsii/Federal Assembly of the Russian Federation), Parlamentskaya Gazeta, Yamskogo Polya 1-ya ulitsa, dom 28, Moscow, 125124, Russian Federation. TEL 7-495-2575090, FAX 7-495-2575082. Ed. L P Kravchenko. **Dist. by:** East View Information Services, 10601 Wayzata Blvd, Minneapolis, MN 55305. TEL 952-252-1201, 800-477-1005, FAX 952-252-1202, info@eastview.com, http://www.eastview.com.

328.43 DEU ISSN 0553-3163
PARLAMENTSSPIEGEL. Text in German. 1957. a. **Document type:** *Directory, Trade.*
—CCC.
Published by: Landtag Nordrhein-Westfalen, Platz des Landtags 1, Duesseldorf, 40221, Germany. TEL 49-211-8840, FAX 49-211-8843021.

THE PARLIAMENT MAGAZINE; politics, policy and people. *see* POLITICAL SCIENCE

THE PARLIAMENT MAGAZINE'S REGIONAL REVIEW. *see* POLITICAL SCIENCE

THE PARLIAMENT MAGAZINE'S RESEARCH REVIEW. *see* POLITICAL SCIENCE

PARLIAMENTARY BULLETIN FOR LOCAL GOVERNMENT EXECUTIVES. *see* POLITICAL SCIENCE

328.4294 AUS ISSN 0155-6290
J911
PARLIAMENTARY DEBATES. Text in English. 1879; N.S. 1901; N.S. 1952. w. back issues avail. **Document type:** *Government.* **Description:** Presents parliamentary debates on amendments to the law.
Related titles: Diskette ed.
Indexed: AEI, IMMAb.
Published by: Hansard Parliamentary Debates New South Wales, c/o Editor of Debates, Sydney, Macquarie St, Parliament House, NSW 2000, Australia.

328 340 NZL ISSN 0111-5642
PARLIAMENTARY DEBATES (WELLINGTON). Variant title: Hansard (Parliamentary Debates). New Zealand Parliamentary Debates (Hansard). Text in English. irreg. **Document type:** *Government.* **Description:** Provides transcripts of debates in the House of Representatives.
Published by: New Zealand. House of Representatives, Parliament Buildings, Molesworth St, Wellington, 6160, New Zealand. TEL 64-4-4719999, FAX 64-4-4712551.

PARLIAMENTARY NAMES & NUMBERS; your guide to governments in Canada. *see* POLITICAL SCIENCE

PARLIAMENTARY YEARBOOK. *see* POLITICAL SCIENCE

351.1 USA ISSN 0899-9252
PATHWAYS (CHESTNUT HILL). Text in English. 1977. q. **Document type:** *Newsletter.*
Formerly (until 1986): Pathpapers (0738-6265)
Indexed: P30.
Published by: Pathfinder International, 9 Galen St, Suite 217, Watertown, MA 02472. TEL 617-924-7200, FAX 617-924-3833, information@pathfind.org. Ed. Michelle Badash.

P

351.5955 BRN
PELITA BRUNEI. Text in Malay. 1956. w. free (effective 2005). **Document type:** *Newspaper, Government.* **Description:** Reports on government, social and business events.
Related titles: Online - full text ed.: ISSN 1563-812X.
Published by: Information Department, Prime Minister's Office, BB 3510, Berakas Old Airport, 2041, Brunei Darussalam. TEL 673-2-380527, FAX 673-2-381004, http://www.brunet.bn/news/pelita. Ed. Haju Dimbang Bakar. Circ: 40,000.

328.748025 USA
PENNSYLVANIA CHAMBER OF BUSINESS AND INDUSTRY. LEGISLATIVE DIRECTORY. Text in English. 1987. a. USD 16.50 per issue to non-members (effective 2007). **Document type:** *Directory.* **Description:** Provides information and addresses of Pennsylvania elected officials at state and federal levels.
Published by: Pennsylvania Chamber of Business and Industry, 417 Walnut St, Harrisburg, PA 17101. TEL 717-255-3252, 800-225-7224, FAX 717-255-3298, info@pachamber.org.

351 USA ISSN 0275-8814
THE PENNSYLVANIA MANUAL. Text in English. 1928. biennial.
Published by: Pennsylvania, Department of General Services, PA Historic and Museum Commission, Keystone Building, 400 North St, Harrisburg, PA 17120-0053. TEL 717-787-5109.

351.835 IRL ISSN 1649-8690
PENSIONS BOARD. ANNUAL REPORT AND ACCOUNTS/ TUARASCAIL BHLIANTUIL AGUS CUNTAIS. Text in English. 1991. a.
Published by: Pensions Board, Verschoyle House, 28/30 Lower Mount St, Dublin, 2, Ireland. TEL 353-1-6131900, pb@pensionsboard.ie.

PENTRU PATRIE. *see* CRIMINOLOGY AND LAW ENFORCEMENT

351 HUN ISSN 0031-496X
PENZUGYI SZEMLE. Text in Hungarian; Summaries in German, Russian. 1963. m. HUF 5,000 domestic (effective 2008). bk.rev. charts. **Document type:** *Journal, Government.*
Indexed: IBSS, NumL, RASB.
Published by: Allami Szamvevoszek/State Audit Office of Hungary, Becsi u 5, Budapest, 1052, Hungary. TEL 36-1-4849104, FAX 36-1-4849200, hinglјn@asz.hu. Circ: 6,500.

351 USA ISSN 2158-2572
PEPPERDINE POLICY REVIEW. Text in English. 2008. a. back issues avail. **Document type:** *Journal, Trade.* **Description:** Aims to publish the scholarly research, innovative policy solutions, and insightful commentary that School of Public Policy students offers.
Related titles: Online - full text ed.: ISSN 1946-7192. free (effective 2010).
Indexed: P10, P21, P48, P50, P53, P54, PQC.
Published by: Pepperdine University, School of Public Policy, 24255 Pacific Coast Hwy, Malibu, CA 90263. TEL 310-506-7490, FAX 310-506-7494, christina.ramirez@pepperdine.edu.

351 BRA
PERFIL DA ADMINISTRACAO FEDERAL. Text in Portuguese. 1974. s-a. USD 12 per issue. adv.
Published by: Editora Visao Ltda., Rua Alvaro de Carvalho, 354, Centro, Sao Paulo, SP 01050-070, Brazil. TEL 256-5011, FAX 258-1919. Circ: 31,000.

353.93 BRA ISSN 0006-9469
PERNAMBUCO. SECRETARIA DO SANEAMENTO, HABITACAO E OBRAS. BOLETIM TECNICO. Text in Portuguese. bi-m. free. adv. bk.rev. charts; illus.; stat.
Published by: Secretaria do Saneamento Habitacao e Obras, Av Cruz Cabuga, 1111, S Amaro, Recife, PE 50040-000, Brazil.

351.593 THA ISSN 0125-3689
PHATTHANABORIHANSAT/THAI JOURNAL OF DEVELOPMENT ADMINISTRATION. Text in English, Thai. 1960. q. adv. bk.rev. abstr.; charts; illus.; stat. Index. **Document type:** *Journal, Academic/ Scholarly.*
Formerly: Thai Journal of Public Administration
Indexed: BAS.
Published by: National Institute of Development Administration, 118 Moo3, Sereethai Rd., Khwaeng Klong-Chan, Khet Bangkapi, Bangkok, 10240, Thailand. TEL 66-2-7273000, FAX 66-2-3758798, nisnida@nida.nida.ac.th. Ed. Juree Vichit Vadakan. Circ: 1,500.

PHILIPPINE JOURNAL OF DEVELOPMENT. *see* BUSINESS AND ECONOMICS

351.599 PHL ISSN 0031-7675
JA26
➤ **PHILIPPINE JOURNAL OF PUBLIC ADMINISTRATION**; University of the Philippines, journal of the national college of public administration and governance. Text in English. 1957. q. PHP 500; USD 50 foreign (effective 2001). bk.rev. bibl.; charts. index. reprints avail. **Document type:** *Journal, Academic/Scholarly.*
Formerly: University of the Philippines. College of Public Administration. (Publication) (0079-9254)
Related titles: Microform ed.: (from PQC).
Indexed: A22, ABCPolSci, APEL, BAS, CA, DIP, HistAb, IBR, IBZ, IPP, P06, P30, P34, P42, PAA&I, PAIS, PCI, PSA, S02, S03, SOPODA, SSA, SociolAb, T02.
—Ingenta.
Published by: University of the Philippines, National College of Public Administration and Governance, Dilliman, Quezon City, 1101, Philippines. TEL 63-2-927-9085, FAX 63-2-928-3861, TELEX CPAUP. Ed. Victoria A Bautista. Circ: 1,000.

➤ **PHILOSOPHY AND PUBLIC POLICY QUARTERLY.** *see* PHILOSOPHY

354.3 GBR
THE PLANNING INSPECTORATE ANNUAL REPORT AND ACCOUNTS; House of Commons papers. Text in English. a. GBP 19.15 per issue (effective 2010). **Document type:** *Government.*
Former titles: Planning Inspectorate Executive Agency. Annual Report; Great Britain. Planning Inspectorate Executive Agency. Annual Report and Accounts for the Year Ended .. (1352-2035); (until 1992): Chief Planning Inspector's Report (0956-0807)
Published by: (Great Britain. Planning Inspectorate, Publications Centre), The Stationery Office, St Crispins, Duke St, Norwich, NR3 1PD, United Kingdom. TEL 44-1603-622211, FAX 44-870-6005533, customer.services@tso.co.uk, http://www.tso.co.uk.

351 AUS ISSN 1832-3219
PLANNING PERMIT ACTIVITY IN VICTORIA. Text in English. 2004. a. free (effective 2008). **Document type:** *Bulletin, Government.*
Published by: Victoria. Department of Sustainability and Environment, 8 Nicholson St, East Melbourne, VIC 3002, Australia. TEL 61-3-53325000, customer.service@dse.vic.gov.au, http://www.dse.vic.gov.au/dse/index.htm.

351.1 PRT ISSN 1647-6824
PLANO DE ACTIVIDADES PARA (YEAR). Text in Portuguese. 2004. a. **Document type:** *Report, Government.*
Published by: Entidade Reguladora dos Servicos de Agua e Resiiduos (E R S A R), Centro Empresarial Torres de Lisboa, Rua Tomas da Fonseca, Torre G - 8o, Lisbon, 1600-209, Portugal. TEL 351-210-052200, FAX 351-210-052259, geral@ersar.pt, http://www.ersar.pt.

POLICY AND POLITICS; an international journal. *see* POLITICAL SCIENCE

352 360 AUS ISSN 1833-0959
POLICY BITES. Text in English. 2005. irreg. **Description:** Provides a short overview of the latest findings of recent research and Melbourne Citymission's policy positions on social issues.
Published by: Melbourne Citymission, Research and Social Policy Unit (Subsidiary of: Melbourne Citymission), 19 King St, Melbourne, VIC 3000, Australia. TEL 61-3-8625-4444, FAX 61-3-8625-4410, information@mcm.org.au, http://www.melbournecitymission.org.au/index.htm.

POLICY OPTIONS. *see* POLITICAL SCIENCE

351 USA ISSN 1085-7087
JK404
➤ **POLICY PERSPECTIVES (WASHINGTON, D.C., 1994)**; the George Washington university journal of public administration. Text in English. 1994 (Spr.). a. back issues avail. **Document type:** *Journal, Academic/Scholarly.* **Description:** Publishes articles on a wide range of topics important to public policy, and aims to be accessible to interested readers within and outside the Trachtenberg community.
Related titles: Online - full text ed.: free (effective 2011).
—Ingenta.
Published by: George Washington University, The Trachtenberg School of Public Policy and Public Administration, 805 21st St NW, Suite 602A, Washington, DC 20052. tspppa@gwu.edu, http://www.tspppa.gwu.edu. Ed. Andrea Leung.

352.34 USA ISSN 0163-108X
H1
POLICY STUDIES REVIEW ANNUAL. Text in English. 1977. irreg., latest vol.14, 2005. price varies. bibl. back issues avail. **Document type:** *Monographic series, Academic/Scholarly.* **Description:** Presents research and analysis in a wide variety of policy areas, including defense and national security, health care cost containment, work and labor information, the environment, immigration, and poverty.
Indexed: A22, PCI.
—CCC.
Published by: Transaction Publishers, 35 Berrue Cir, Piscataway, NJ 08854. TEL 732-445-2280, FAX 732-445-3138, trans@transactionpub.com, http://www.transactionpub.com. Ed. Robert F Rich.

351 SWE ISSN 1403-476X
POLISHOEGSKOLAN. FORSKNINGSRAPPORT. Text in Swedish. 1994. irreg. **Document type:** *Monographic series, Academic/Scholarly.*
Supersedes in part (in 1998): P H S Forskningsrapport (1402-6112); Which was formerly (until 1996): P H S-Rapport (1400-0261)
Published by: Polishoegskolan/Swedish National Police Academy, Soerentorp, Stockholm, 17082, Sweden. TEL 46-8-4019000, FAX 46-8-4016655, diarie@phs.police.se, http://www.polishogskolan.polisen.se.

351 MEX ISSN 1405-1060
JL1201
POLITICA Y GOBIERNO. Text in Spanish. 1994. s-a. MXN 306, USD 65 for 2 yrs. to individuals; MXN 380, USD 150 for 2 yrs. to institutions (effective 2009). **Document type:** *Academic/Scholarly.* **Description:** Presents theories, studies, and experience stories in the sphere of public policy studies and the management of government organizations.
Related titles: Online - full text ed.
Indexed: A01, C01, CA, F03, F04, H21, I13, P08, P34, P42, PAIS, S02, S03, SCOPUS, T02.
Published by: Centro de Investigacion y Docencia Economicas, Carretera Mexico-Toluca Km. 16.5, Apdo. Postal 116-114, Mexico City, DF 01130, Mexico. TEL 52-5-7279800, FAX 52-5-7279885, arellano@dis1.cide.mx, http://www.cide.mx.

POLITICAL PULSE. *see* POLITICAL SCIENCE

POLITICAL REPORT. *see* POLITICAL SCIENCE

320.6 ARG ISSN 1851-4936
POLITICAS PUBLICAS. Text in Spanish. 2007. q.
Media: Online - full text.
Published by: Instituto de Politicas Publicas, Solis 1388, Buenos Aires, Argentina. TEL 54-11-41376603, revista@ipoliticaspublicas.org.

POLITICS AND THE LIFE SCIENCES. *see* POLITICAL SCIENCE

POLITIQUE ECONOMIQUE ET SOCIALE. *see* POLITICAL SCIENCE

351.74 NLD ISSN 1874-5776
PRAKTIJKWIJZER TOEZICHT EN OPSPORING. Text in Dutch. 2002. a. EUR 9.95 (effective 2009).
Published by: Nederlands Instituut voor Opleiding van Opsporingsambtenaren, Postbus 13, Maartensdijk, 3738 ZL, Netherlands. TEL 31-346-217421, FAX 31-346-210741, info@nivoo.nl, http://www.nivoo.nl. Circ: 8,000.

351 IND ISSN 0971-6246
PRASHASNIKA. Text in English, Hindi. 1972. q. bk.rev. bibl. **Document type:** *Journal, Government.* **Description:** Covers a wide range of subjects of interest to both administrators and academics.
Indexed: PAA&I.
Published by: Harishchandra Mathur State Institute of Public Administration, Jawahar Lal Nehru Marg, Jaipur, Rajasthan 302 017, India. TEL 91-141-2704950, FAX 91-141-2705420, hcmripa@sancharnet.in.

351 AUS ISSN 1449-9142
THE PRESS GALLERY GUIDE. Text in English. 2004. q. **Document type:** *Handbook/Manual/Guide, Trade.*
Published by: Morrison, Croxford, Chambers & Associates, PO BOX 4778, Kingston, ACT 2604, Australia. http://mccanda.com.au.

351 FIN ISSN 0783-1609
FINLAND. THE PRIME MINISTER'S OFFICE. PUBLICATION. Text in English. 1986. irreg. free. back issues avail. **Document type:** *Monographic series, Government.*
Related titles: Online - full text ed.; ◆ Swedish ed.: Finland. Statsraadets Kansli. Publikationsserie. ISSN 0782-6036; ◆ Finnish ed.: Finland. Valtioneuvoston Kanslia. Julkaisusarja. ISSN 0782-6028.
Published by: Valtioneuvoston Kanslia/Prime Minister's Office, Snellmaninkatu 1 A, PO Box 23, Helsinki, 00023, Finland. TEL 358-9-16001, FAX 358-9-16022165, info@vnk.fi. **Dist. by:** Yliopistopaino, Kirjamyynti ja Asiakaspalvelu, Vuorikatu 3 (4 krs., Helsinki, Finland. TEL 358-9-70102363, FAX 358-9-70102374, books@yliopistopaino.fi, http://www.yliopistopaino.fi.

352.3 CAN
PRINCE EDWARD ISLAND. DEPARTMENT OF COMMUNITY AND CULTURAL AFFAIRS. ANNUAL REPORT. Text in English. 1970. a. free. **Document type:** *Government.*
Former titles: Prince Edward Island. Department of Community Affairs. Annual Report (0701-6956); (until 1980): Prince Edward Island. Department of the Environment Annual Report (0085-5138); Prince Edward Island. Water Authority. Annual Report
Published by: Department of Environmental Resources, P O Box 2000, Charlottetown, PE C1A 7N8, Canada. Circ: 150.

351.717 CAN
PRINCE EDWARD ISLAND. DEPARTMENT OF DEVELOPMENT AND TECHNOLOGY. ANNUAL REPORT. Text in English. 1971. a., latest 2006. free (effective 2008).
Published by: Department of Development and Technology, PO Box 2000, Charlottetown, PE C1A 7N8, Canada. TEL 902-892-4137.

351 CAN
PRINCE EDWARD ISLAND. ISLAND REGULATORY & APPEALS COMMISSION. ANNUAL REPORT. Text in English. 1961. a. free.
Formerly: Prince Edward Island. Public Utilities Commission. Annual Report (0079-5151)
Published by: Island Regulatory & Appeals Commission, P O Box 577, Charlottetown, PE C1A 7L1, Canada. TEL 902-892-3501, FAX 902-566-4076. Ed. Wayne D Cheverie. Circ: 325.

PRIORITERINGSCENTRUM. RAPPORT. *see* PUBLIC HEALTH AND SAFETY

351 AUS ISSN 1321-6163
PROCEEDINGS OF THE LEGISLATIVE ASSEMBLY FOR THE AUSTRALIAN CAPITAL TERRITORY. DIGEST. Text in English. 1990. a. **Document type:** *Proceedings, Government.* **Description:** Provides digest of proceedings of the legislative assembly for the Australian capital territory.
Formerly: Malot's Guide to the Session of the Legislative Assembly for the Australian Capital Territory
Related titles: Online - full text ed.: ISSN 1833-6841. 2004.
Published by: Australian Capital Territory, Legislative Assembly, GPO Box 1020, Canberra, ACT 2601, Australia. TEL 61-2-62050439, FAX 61-2-62053109, secretariat@parliament.act.gov.au, http://www.parliament.act.gov.au/index.asp.

352.63 CAN ISSN 0318-0646
PROFESSIONAL INSTITUTE OF THE PUBLIC SERVICE OF CANADA. COMMUNICATIONS. Text in English, French. 1975. q. free. **Document type:** *Newsletter.*
Related titles: English ed.: Institut Professionel de la Fonction Publique du Canada. ISSN 0820-7658.
Published by: Professional Institute of the Public Service of Canada, 53 Auriga Dr, Nepean, ON K2E 8C3, Canada. TEL 613-228-6310, FAX 613-228-9048. Ed., Pub., R&P Chantal Lecours. Circ: 29,000 (controlled).

351 CAN ISSN 1912-3515
PROFIL DE LOCALISATION DE L'EFFECTIF, DES DIRIGEANTS, DES BUREAUX CENTRAUX DES MINISTERES ET DES SIEGES SOCIAUX DES ORGANISMES GOUVERNEMENTAUX. Text in French. 1997. irreg. **Document type:** *Monographic series, Trade.*
Published by: Commission de la Capitale Nationale du Quebec, 525, Boul. Rene-Levesque Est R C, Quebec, PQ G1R 5S9, Canada. TEL 418-528-0773, 800-442-0773, FAX 418-528-0833, commission@capitale.gouv.qc.ca, http://www.capitale.gouv.qc.ca/default.html.

351.68 ZAF
PROFILE. Text in English. 1994. irreg. **Document type:** *Government.* **Description:** Contains biographies of role-players in the South African government.
Published by: South African Communication Service, Private Bag X745, Pretoria, 0002, South Africa. TEL 27-12-3142105, FAX 27-12-3233831. Ed. H de Jager. R&P G van Schalkwyk TEL 27-12-3142137.

PROFILE OF ELECTORAL DISTRICTS (ONLINE EDITION). *see* PUBLIC ADMINISTRATION—Abstracting, Bibliographies, Statistics

PROFILES OF WORLDWIDE GOVERNMENT LEADERS. *see* POLITICAL SCIENCE

PROGRAM ON ENVIRONMENT AND BEHAVIOR MONOGRAPH SERIES. *see* SOCIOLOGY

PROGRAMMADIRECTIE RUIMTE VOOR DE RIVIER. VOORTGANGSRAPPORTAGE. *see* WATER RESOURCES

351 CAN ISSN 0701-5984
PROTECTEUR DU CITOYEN. RAPPORT ANNUEL. Text in French. 1969. a.
Related titles: English ed.: ISSN 1189-9522.
Published by: Quebec. Assemblee Nationale. Protecteur du Citoyen, 525, boul. Rene-Levesque Est, Bureau 1.25, Quebec, PQ G1R 5Y4, Canada. TEL 418-643-2688, 800-463-5070, FAX 418-643-8759, http://www.ombuds.gouv.qc.ca/fr/index.asp.

354.71 CAN ISSN 0828-2277
PROVINCE OF ALBERTA. OFFICE OF THE OMBUDSMAN. ANNUAL REPORT TO THE LEGISLATIVE ASSEMBLY. Text in English. 1967. a.
Former titles (until 1984): Alberta. Annual Report of the Ombudsman (0828-2781); (until 1976): Alberta. Report of the Ombudsman (0319-8197); (until 1974): Province of Alberta. Ombudsman. Annual Report (0319-8189); (until 1972): Alberta. Report of the Ombudsman (0319-8170)

Published by: Alberta. Office of the Ombudsman, 10303 Jasper Ave NW, Suite 2800, Edmonton, AB T5J 5C3, Canada. TEL 780-427-2756, FAX 780-427-2759.

354 CAN ISSN 0383-4948
PROVINCE OF NEW BRUNSWICK. DEPARTMENT OF SUPPLY AND SERVICES. ANNUAL REPORT/PROVINCE DU NOUVEAU-BRUNSWICK. MINISTERE DE L'APPROVISIONNEMENT ET DES SERVICES. RAPPORT ANNUEL. Text in English, French. a.
Former titles (until 1973): Province of New Brunswick. Department of Public Works. Annual Report (0383-493X); (until 1968): Province of New Brunswick. Department of Public Works. Buildings (0383-4921); (until 1966): Province of New Brunswick. Department of Public Works. Report (0383-4913); New Brunswick. Minister of Public Works. Annual Report
Published by: New Brunswick, Department of Supply and Services, Marysville Pl, 4th Flr, PO Box 6000, Fredericton, NB E3B 5H1, Canada. TEL 506-453-3742, FAX 506-444-4400, http://www.gnb.ca/0099/index-e.asp.

354.71 CAN ISSN 0702-8148
HJ13
PROVINCE OF NOVA SCOTIA. PUBLIC ACCOUNTS. Text in English. a.
Published by: Nova Scotia, Department of Finance, PO Box 187, Halifax, NS B3J 2N3, Canada. TEL 902-424-5554, FAX 902-434-0635.

352.4 CAN ISSN 1707-6633
PROVINCE OF ONTARIO ANNUAL REPORT AND FINANCIAL STATEMENTS. Text in English. 1996. a.
Formerly (until 2002): Province of Ontario. Annual Report (1206-0429)
Published by: Ontario Ministry of Finance, Frost Bldg S, 7th Flr, 7 Queen's Park Cres, Toronto, ON M7A 1Y7, Canada. TEL 800-263-7965, FAX 905-433-6777, http://www.gov.on.ca/fin.

354.35 ITA ISSN 1722-5523
PROVINCIA NUOVA. Text in Italian. 1971. bi-m. free. adv. illus.
Document type: *Magazine, Consumer.*
Published by: Provincia di Cremona, Corso Vittorio Emanuele II, 17, Cremona, 26100, Italy. http://www.provincia.cremona.it. Circ: 140,000 (controlled).

PROVINCIAL AUDITOR SASKATCHEWAN. REPORT OF THE PROVINCIAL AUDITOR TO THE LEGISLATIVE ASSEMBLY OF SASKATCHEWAN. *see* BUSINESS AND ECONOMICS—Public Finance, Taxation

354.71 CAN ISSN 0827-1089
JL435
PROVINCIAL CAPITAL COMMISSION. ANNUAL REPORT. Text in English. 1985. a.
Published by: British Columbia Provincial Capital Commission, 613 Pandora Ave, Victoria, BC V8W 1N8, Canada. TEL 250-953-8800, FAX 250-386-1303g, info.pcc@bcpcc.com.

328 ZAF ISSN 1994-4551
PROVINCIAL GAZETTE. KWAZULU-NATAL PROVINCE. Text in Multiple languages. 2007. w. ZAR 148.50 (effective 2007).
Published by: South Africa. Government Printing Works, 149 Bosman St, Private Bag X85, Pretoria, 0001, South Africa. TEL 27-12-3344507, FAX 27-12-3238805.

PROVINCIAL LEGISLATIVE RECORD. *see* POLITICAL SCIENCE

351 GBR ISSN 0033-3298
JA8 CODEN: PUADDD
➤ **PUBLIC ADMINISTRATION**; an international quarterly covering public administration throughout the world. Text in English. 1922. q. GBP 663 in United Kingdom to institutions; EUR 841 in Europe to institutions; USD 1,320 in the Americas to institutions; USD 1,543 elsewhere to institutions; GBP 763 combined subscription in United Kingdom to institutions (print & online eds.); EUR 967 combined subscription in Europe to institutions (print & online eds.); USD 1,518 combined subscription in the Americas to institutions (print & online eds.); USD 1,775 combined subscription elsewhere to institutions (print & online eds.) (effective 2012). adv. bk.rev. illus. index, cum.index 1953-1962. back issues avail.; reprint service avail. from PSC. **Document type:** *Journal, Academic/Scholarly.* **Description:** Presents articles on public administration, public policy and public management.
Formerly (until 1926): Journal of Public Administration
Related titles: Microform ed.: (from PQC); Online - full text ed.: ISSN 1467-9299. GBP 663 in United Kingdom to institutions; EUR 841 in Europe to institutions; USD 1,320 in the Americas to institutions; USD 1,543 elsewhere to institutions (effective 2012) (from IngentaConnect).
Indexed: A12, A13, A17, A20, A22, A26, ABCPolSci, ABIn, ADPA, B01, B02, B04, B06, B07, B08, B09, B15, B17, B18, BAS, BPIA, BRD, BrHumI, CA, CMM, CPM, CurCont, E01, E08, ESPM, Emerald, FR, G04, G06, G07, G08, GEOBASE, H01, H09, I05, I13, IBSS, Inspec, KES, MEA&I, ManagCont, P02, P06, P10, P27, P30, P34, P42, P48, P51, P53, P54, PAIS, PCI, PQC, PRA, PSA, PSI, PersLit, RASB, RiskAb, S02, S03, S05, S09, S11, SCOPUS, SPAA, SSAI, SSAb, SSCI, SSI, SUSA, SociolAb, T&II, T02, W03, W07, WBA, WMB.
—BLDSC (6962.400000), IE, Infotrieve, Ingenta. **CCC.**
Published by: Wiley-Blackwell Publishing Ltd. (Subsidiary of: John Wiley & Sons, Inc.), 9600 Garsington Rd, Oxford, OX4 2DQ, United Kingdom. TEL 44-1865-776868, FAX 44-1865-714591, customerservices@blackwellpublishing.com. Adv. contact Craig Pickett TEL 44-1865-476267. B&W page GBP 445, B&W page USD 823; 112 x 190. Circ: 1,500.

351 USA ISSN 1087-0091
JA1
➤ **PUBLIC ADMINISTRATION AND MANAGEMENT.** Text in English. 1996. s-a. free (effective 2011). bk.rev. illus. back issues avail.; reprints avail. **Document type:** *Journal, Academic/Scholarly.* **Description:** Brings out articles which will be of interest to both scholars and practitioners in the fields of public administration and management.
Media: Online - full text.
Indexed: A12, A13, A17, A39, ABIn, B01, B07, C27, C29, CA, D03, D04, E13, H01, P21, P48, P51, P53, P54, PQC, R14, S14, S15, S18, SCOPUS, T02.
—**CCC.**
Published by: Southern Public Administration Education Foundation, Inc., 122 W High St, Elizabethtown, PA 17022. TEL 717-689-6126, spaef@spaef.com. Ed. Gregory McNeal.

351 HKG
PUBLIC ADMINISTRATION AND POLICY; a Hong Kong and Asia-Pacific journal. Text in English. 1992. s-a. HKD 110 domestic; USD 25 foreign; HKD 70 newsstand/cover domestic; USD 15 newsstand/cover foreign (effective 2003). **Document type:** *Journal, Academic/Scholarly.* **Description:** Devoted to the integration of the theories and practice of public administration and management, with special emphasis on Hong Kong, China, and the Asia-Pacific region.
Formerly (until 1998): Hong Kong Public Administration (1022-0275)
Indexed: Emerald, I13, IBSS.
Published by: City University of Hong Kong, Department of Public and Social Administration, Tat Chee Ave, Kowloon, Hong Kong. TEL 852-2788-8929, FAX 852-2788-8926, sa@plink.cityu.edu.hk. Ed. Ahmed-Safiql Huque.

351 USA
PUBLIC ADMINISTRATION AND PUBLIC POLICY. Text in English. 1978. irreg., latest 2010. price varies. back issues avail. **Document type:** *Monographic series, Academic/Scholarly.*
Indexed: RASB.
Published by: C R C Press, LLC (Subsidiary of: Taylor & Francis Group), 6000 Broken Sound Pky, NW, Ste 300, Boca Raton, FL 33487. TEL 800-272-7737, FAX 800-374-3401, orders@crcpress.com.

351 USA
PUBLIC ADMINISTRATION BRIEFING. Text in English. 1990. m.
Published by: Kentucky State University, School of Public Affairs, Center for Public Policy Research, Frankfort, KY 40601. TEL 502-227-6117. Ed. Manindra Mohapatra.

351 BGR
PUBLIC ADMINISTRATION JOURNAL. Text in English. irreg.
Published by: Institute of Public Administration and European Integration, 18 Vitosha Blvd, Sofia, 1000, Bulgaria.

351 USA ISSN 0734-9149
JA1
➤ **PUBLIC ADMINISTRATION QUARTERLY.** Abbreviated title: P A Q. Text in English. 1977. q. USD 155 to individuals; USD 230 to institutions (effective 2010). bk.rev. back issues avail.; reprint service avail. from PSC. **Document type:** *Journal, Academic/Scholarly.*
Formerly (until 1983): Southern Review of Public Administration (0147-8168)
Related titles: Microform ed.: (from PQC); Online - full text ed.
Indexed: A12, A13, A17, A18, A22, A26, ABIn, B01, B06, B07, B08, B09, BPIA, C12, CA, I05, Inspec, ManagCont, P10, P34, P42, P48, P51, P53, P54, PAIS, PCI, PQC, PRA, PSA, PersLit, S02, S03, SPAA, SociolAb, T02.
—BLDSC (6962.595000), AskIEEE, IE, Infotrieve, Ingenta. **CCC.**
Published by: Southern Public Administration Education Foundation, Inc., 122 W High St, Elizabethtown, PA 17022. TEL 717-689-6126, spaef@spaef.com. Ed. T Aaron Wachhaus.

351 USA ISSN 0033-3352
JK1
➤ **PUBLIC ADMINISTRATION REVIEW.** Abbreviated title: P A R. Text in English. 1940. bi-m. GBP 412 in United Kingdom to institutions; EUR 522 in Europe to institutions; USD 415 in the Americas to institutions; USD 807 elsewhere to institutions; GBP 474 combined subscription in United Kingdom to institutions (print & online eds.); EUR 600 combined subscription in Europe to institutions (print & online eds.); USD 477 combined subscription in the Americas to institutions (print & online eds.); USD 929 combined subscription elsewhere to institutions (print & online eds.) (effective 2012). adv. bk.rev. illus. index, irreg. cum.index. back issues avail.; reprint service avail. from PSC. **Document type:** *Journal, Academic/Scholarly.* **Description:** Presents authoritative research and articles on current issues.
Related titles: Microform ed.: (from MIM, PQC); Online - full text ed.: ISSN 1540-6210. GBP 412 in United Kingdom to institutions; EUR 522 in Europe to institutions; USD 415 in the Americas to institutions; USD 807 elsewhere to institutions (effective 2012) (from IngentaConnect).
Indexed: A12, A13, A14, A17, A20, A22, A25, A26, ABCPolSci, ABIn, ABS&EES, Acal, AmH&L, B01, B02, B04, B06, B07, B08, B09, B14, B15, B17, B18, BPI, BPIA, BRD, C12, CA, CBRI, CLI, CurCont, DIP, E01, E02, E03, E07, E08, E10, EAA, ERI, ESPM, EconLit, EdA, EdI, FR, FamI, G04, G06, G07, G08, H01, H09, H10, HRA, I03, I05, I13, IBR, IBSS, IBZ, IPARL, JEL, LRI, M06, MEA&I, ManagCont, P02, P03, P06, P07, P10, P13, P18, P25, P27, P30, P34, P42, P45, P48, P51, P53, P54, PAA&I, PAIS, PCI, PQC, PSA, PsycInfo, PsycholAb, RASB, RiskAb, S02, S03, S05, S08, S09, S11, S21, SCOPUS, SPAA, SSAI, SSAb, SSCI, SSI, SUSA, SWR&A, SociolAb, T02, W01, W02, W03, W05, W07, W09.
—BLDSC (6962.600000), IE, Infotrieve, Ingenta. **CCC.**
Published by: (American Society for Public Administration), Wiley-Blackwell Publishing, Inc. (Subsidiary of: Wiley-Blackwell Publishing Ltd.), 111 River St, Hoboken, NJ 07030. TEL 201-748-6000, FAX 201-748-6088, info@wiley.com. Ed. Richard J Stillman.

351 PAK ISSN 0033-3344
JQ629.A58
PUBLIC ADMINISTRATION REVIEW; journal of the national institute of public administration. Text in English. 1963. 2/yr. PKR 350 domestic; USD 50 foreign; INR 150 newsstand/cover (effective 2001). bk.rev. 160 p./no.; back issues avail.; reprints avail. **Document type:** *Journal, Government.*
Related titles: Microform ed.: (from PQC); Online - full text ed.
Indexed: ABCPolSci, BAS, FutSurv, PAA&I, PSI, PersLit, T&II.
Published by: National Institute of Public Administration, Regional Office, 78 Shahrah-e-Quaid-i-Azam, Lahore, 54000, Pakistan. TEL 92-42-9200921, FAX 92-42-9200926, nipalhr@wol.net.pk, http://www.nipalahore.gov.pk. Ed. Tamgha Malik.

354.940006094 AUS ISSN 1832-0066
PUBLIC ADMINISTRATION TODAY. Abbreviated title: P A T. Text in English. 1973. q. AUD 93.50 to non-members; free to members (effective 2008). back issues avail. **Document type:** *Journal, Academic/Scholarly.* **Description:** Discusses public sector management in Australia.
Former titles (until 2004): Canberra Bulletin of Public Administration (0811-6318); (until 1982): Australian Institute of Public Administration. Newsletter (0727-3703); (until 1980): Royal Institute of Public Administration. A.C.T. Group. Newsletter (0310-6373)
Indexed: AusPAIS.
—Ingenta.
Published by: Institute of Public Administration Australia, First Fl, SEQWater Bldg, 240 Margaret St, City East, PO Box 15624, Brisbane, QLD 4002, Australia. TEL 61-7-32282800, FAX 61-7-32282888, info@ipaa.org.au, http://www.ipaa.org.au. Ed. Russell Ayres TEL 61-2-62491137.

659.205 GBR ISSN 1748-541X
PUBLIC AFFAIRS NEWS. Text in English. 1994. m. GBP 155 domestic; GBP 175 in Europe; GBP 184 elsewhere (effective 2009). adv. back issues avail. **Document type:** *Magazine, Trade.* **Description:** Provides news coverage from across the profession in the UK, Brussels, the enlarged European Union and around the world.
Formerly (until 2004): Public Affairs Newsletter (1470-0115)
Published by: Dod's Parliamentary Communications Ltd., Westminster Tower, 3rd Fl, 3 Albert Embankment, London, SE1 7SP, United Kingdom. TEL 44-20-70917500, FAX 44-20-70917505, uk@dods.co.uk, http://www.dods.co.uk. Ed. Ian Hall TEL 44-20-70917522. Pub. Gerry Murray TEL 44-20-70917500. Adv. contact Rob Ellis TEL 44-20-70917609.

PUBLIC ASSISTANCE & WELFARE TRENDS - STATE CAPITALS. *see* LAW

354.8 USA ISSN 0275-1100
HJ2052.A2
➤ **PUBLIC BUDGETING AND FINANCE.** Text in English. 1981. q. GBP 325 in United Kingdom to institutions; EUR 411 in Europe to institutions; USD 411 in the Americas to institutions; USD 633 elsewhere to institutions; GBP 374 combined subscription in United Kingdom to institutions (print & online eds.); EUR 473 combined subscription in Europe to institutions (print & online eds.); USD 473 combined subscription in the Americas to institutions (print & online eds.); USD 729 combined subscription elsewhere to institutions (print & online eds.) (effective 2012). adv. bk.rev. abstr. back issues avail.; reprint service avail. from PSC. **Document type:** *Journal, Academic/Scholarly.* **Description:** Fundamental journal of theory and practice in financial management and budgeting at all levels of U.S. government.
Related titles: Online - full text ed.: ISSN 1540-5850. GBP 325 in United Kingdom to institutions; EUR 411 in Europe to institutions; USD 411 in the Americas to institutions; USD 633 elsewhere to institutions (effective 2012) (from IngentaConnect).
Indexed: A12, A13, A17, A22, A26, ABIn, ATI, B01, B02, B04, B06, B07, B08, B09, B15, B17, B18, BPI, BPIA, BRD, C12, CA, CPM, CREJ, E01, E07, ESPM, EconLit, G04, G06, G07, G08, H01, I05, JEL, P34, P42, P48, P51, P53, P54, PAIS, PQC, PSA, RiskAb, SCOPUS, SPAA, SUSA, T02, W01, W02, W03.
—BLDSC (6962.825000), IE, Infotrieve, Ingenta. **CCC.**
Published by: (American Association for Budget and Program Analysis, Association for Budgeting and Financial Management), Wiley-Blackwell Publishing, Inc. (Subsidiary of: Wiley-Blackwell Publishing Ltd.), 111 River St, Hoboken, NJ 07030. TEL 201-748-6000, FAX 201-748-6088, info@wiley.com. Ed. John L Mikesell TEL 812-855-0732. Adv. contact Kristin McCarthy TEL 201-748-7683.
Co-sponsor: American Society for Public Administration, Section on Budgeting and Financial Management.

P

351 USA ISSN 1944-3455
HD30.2
➤ **PUBLIC C I O**; technology leadership in the public sector. (Chief Information Officer) Text in English. 2003. q. free (effective 2008). adv. back issues avail. **Document type:** *Journal, Academic/Scholarly.* **Description:** Focuses solely on the management issues, technology strategies, and political hurdles unique to the government C-level executive.
Related titles: Online - full text ed.
Indexed: B01, CA, T02.
Published by: e.Republic, Inc., 100 Blue Ravine Rd, Folsom, CA 95630. TEL 916-932-1300, FAX 916-932-1470, getinfo@govtech.net, http://www.govtech.net/. Eds. Steve Towns TEL 916-932-1333, Tod Newcombe TEL 413-567-2408. Pub. Jon Fyffe TEL 916-932-1300. adv.: color page USD 14,990, B&W page USD 13,220; trim 9 x 10.75. Circ: 24,684.

352.68 USA ISSN 0033-345X
HD8011.N4
PUBLIC EMPLOYEE PRESS. Abbreviated title: P E P. Text in English. 1947. m. (Jul./Aug. combined). bk.rev. illus. back issues avail. **Document type:** *Newspaper, Trade.*
Formerly (until 19??): Spotlight
Related titles: Online - full text ed.: free (effective 2009).
Published by: A F L - C I O, American Federation of State, County & Municipal Employees, 125 Barclay St, New York, NY 10007. TEL 212-815-1000, pubaffairs@afscme.org, http://www.afscme.org.

352.68 USA
PUBLIC EMPLOYMENT LAW BULLETIN. Text in English. 1994. irreg., latest vol.37, 2009. price varies. back issues avail. **Document type:** *Bulletin, Academic/Scholarly.* **Description:** Explains the law governing the ability of North Carolina local government employers to offer domestic partner benefits.
Formerly (until 2005): Public Personnel Law Bulletin
Related titles: Online - full text ed.: free (effective 2010).
Published by: University of North Carolina at Chapel Hill, School of Government, Knapp-Sanders Bldg, Campus Box 3330, Chapel Hill, NC 27599. TEL 919-966-5381, FAX 919-962-0654, sales@sog.unc.edu, http://sog.unc.edu.

351 GBR ISSN 0963-5076
PUBLIC GENERAL ACTS & GENERAL SYNOD MEASURES. Text in English. a., latest 2007. GBP 330 per issue (effective 2010). **Document type:** *Government.* **Description:** Contains 5 parts: 1: PGA chapters 1-3; 2: PGA chapters 4-14; 3: PGA chapters 15-27; 4: PGA chapters 28-31, General Synod Measures 1; 5: Table V of Origins and Destinations (if applicable): Table VI - Effect of Legislation; General Index.
Formerly (until 1972): Public General Acts
Published by: The Stationery Office, St Crispins, Duke St, Norwich, NR3 1PD, United Kingdom. TEL 44-1603-622211, FAX 44-870-6005533, customer.services@tso.co.uk, http://www.tso.co.uk. **Subscr. to:** PO Box 29, Norwich NR3 1GN, United Kingdom. TEL 44-870-6005522.

172.2 USA ISSN 1099-9922
JK468.E7
PUBLIC INTEGRITY. Text in English. 1996. q. USD 399 combined subscription domestic to institutions (print & online eds.); USD 431 combined subscription foreign to institutions (print & online eds.) (effective 2012). adv. bk.rev. 136 p./no.; back issues avail.; reprint service avail. from PSC. **Document type:** *Journal, Academic/Scholarly.* **Description:** Provides information on the fundamental questions of integrity in American democracy. Covers issues ranging from ethical conduct of public officials to legislative updates and includes original studies, cases, commentaries, and more.
Formerly (until 1999): Public Integrity Annual (1098-0695)
Related titles: Online - full text ed.: ISSN 1558-0989. 2004 (Jan.). USD 350 to institutions (effective 2012).
Indexed: A01, A03, A08, A22, CA, E01, I13, P34, P42, PAIS, PSA, SCOPUS, SPAA, SociolAb, T02.
—BLDSC (6967.097200), IE, Ingenta. **CCC.**
Published by: (American Society for Public Administration), M.E. Sharpe, Inc., 80 Business Park Dr, Armonk, NY 10504. TEL 914-273-1800, 800-541-6563, FAX 914-273-2106, custserv@mesharpe.com. Ed. James S Bowman. Adv. contact Barbara Ladd TEL 914-273-1800. **Dist. in Europe by:** Perseus Books Group; **Dist. in the US by:** HarperCollins Publishers, Order Department. **Co-sponsors:** Council of State Governments; International City/County Management Association.

353 USA
PUBLIC LAWS. Text in English. 19??. irreg. USD 307 domestic; USD 429.80 foreign (effective 2009). back issues avail. **Document type:** *Government.*
Related titles: Online - full text ed.
Published by: National Archives and Records Administration, U.S. Office of the Federal Register, 8601 Adelphi Rd, College Park, MD 20740. TEL 202-741-6000, FAX 202-741-6012, fedreg.info@nara.gov, http://www.federalregister.gov. **Subscr. to:** U.S. Government Printing Office, Superintendent of Documents, PO Box 371954, Pittsburgh, PA 15250. TEL 202-512-1800, FAX 202-512-2250, orders@gpo.gov, http://www.access.gpo.gov.

PUBLIC MANAGEMENT AND POLICY ASSOCIATION. REVIEW. *see* POLITICAL SCIENCE

351 658 USA
PUBLIC MANAGEMENT BULLETIN. Text in English. 1998. irreg., latest no.4, 2009. back issues avail. **Document type:** *Bulletin, Academic/Scholarly.* **Description:** Describes the distinctive approach taken in this benchmarking project and reports many of the project's key findings.
Related titles: Online - full text ed.: free (effective 2010).
Published by: University of North Carolina at Chapel Hill, School of Government, Knapp-Sanders Bldg, Campus Box 3330, Chapel Hill, NC 27599. TEL 919-966-5381, FAX 919-962-0654, sales@sog.unc.edu, http://sog.unc.edu.

PUBLIC MANAGEMENT REVIEW (ONLINE). *see* BUSINESS AND ECONOMICS—Management

PUBLIC MANAGEMENT REVIEW (PRINT); an international journal of research and theory. *see* BUSINESS AND ECONOMICS—Management

351.092 USA ISSN 1061-7639
JK1
THE PUBLIC MANAGER; the journal for practitioners. Text in English. 1972. q. USD 35 domestic to individuals; USD 52 in Canada & Mexico to individuals; USD 85 elsewhere to individuals; USD 65 domestic to institutions; USD 81 in Canada & Mexico to institutions; USD 82 elsewhere to institutions (effective 2005). adv. bk.rev. charts; illus. index. 64 p./no.; back issues avail.; reprints avail. **Document type:** *Journal, Trade.*
Formerly (until Spring 1992): Bureaucrat (0045-3544)
Related titles: Online - full text ed.
Indexed: A01, A02, A03, A08, A12, A13, A14, A17, A22, A26, ABCPolSci, ABIn, B01, B02, B04, B06, B07, B08, B09, B15, B17, B18, BPI, BPIA, BRD, BusI, CA, DIP, E08, G04, G06, G07, G08, H01, I05, I13, IBR, IBZ, M06, P06, P10, P21, P34, P42, P45, P48, P51, P53, P54, PAA&I, PAIS, PQC, PSA, RASB, S09, S11, SCOPUS, SPAA, SociolAb, T&DA, T&II, T02, UAA, W01, W02, W03.
—BLDSC (6967.760000), IE, Infotrieve, Ingenta. **CCC.**
Published by: Bureaucrat, Inc., 12007 Titian Way, Potomac, MD 20854. TEL 301-279-9445, FAX 301-251-5872, tnovo@aol.com. Ed. Warren Master. Pub., Adv. contact T W Novotny. Circ: 4,000 (paid).

352.4 GBR ISSN 0954-0962
HC251
➤ **PUBLIC MONEY AND MANAGEMENT**; integrating theory and practice in public management. Abbreviated title: P M M. Text in English. 1981. bi-m. GBP 768 combined subscription in United Kingdom to institutions (print & online eds.); EUR 984, USD 1,282 combined subscription to institutions (print & online eds.) (effective 2012). adv. bk.rev. illus. back issues avail.; reprint service avail. from PSC. **Document type:** *Journal, Academic/Scholarly.* **Description:** Publishes articles which contribute new knowledge as a basis for policy or management improvements or which reflect on evidence from public service management and finance.
Formerly (until 1988): Chartered Institute of Public Finance and Accountancy. Public Money (0261-1252)
Related titles: Online - full text ed.: ISSN 1467-9302. GBP 691 in United Kingdom to institutions; EUR 885, USD 1,154 to institutions (effective 2012) (from IngentaConnect).
Indexed: A12, A13, A17, A22, A26, ABIn, ASCA, ATI, B01, B04, B06, B07, B08, B09, B21, BPI, BRD, C12, CA, CPM, CurCont, DIP, E01, ESPM, Emerald, FR, H&SSA, IBR, IBSS, IBZ, P34, P42, P48, P51, P53, P54, PAIS, PCI, PQC, RiskAb, SCOPUS, SPAA, SSCI, SociolAb, T02, W01, W02, W03, W07.
—BLDSC (6967.781000), IE, Infotrieve, Ingenta. **CCC.**
Published by: (Chartered Institute of Public Finance and Accountancy, Public Management and Policy Association, Public Finance Foundation), Routledge (Subsidiary of: Taylor & Francis Group), 4 Park Sq, Milton Park, Abingdon, Oxon OX14 4RN, United Kingdom. TEL 44-20-70176000, FAX 44-20-70176336, subscriptions@tandf.co.uk, http://www.routledge.com. Adv. contact Linda Hann TEL 44-1344-779945. **Subscr. to:** Taylor & Francis Ltd., Journals Customer Service, Sheepen Pl, Colchester, Essex CO3 3LP, United Kingdom. TEL 44-20-70175544, FAX 44-20-70175198, tf.enquiries@tfinforma.com.

351 CAN ISSN 1715-9067
JL86
PUBLIC OPINION RESEARCH IN THE GOVERNMENT OF CANADA. ANNUAL REPORT. Text in English. 2002. a. **Document type:** *Report, Trade.*
Media: Online - full text. **Related titles:** Print ed.: ISSN 1709-9463.
Published by: (Communication Canada, Public Works and Government Services Canada, Government Information Services Branch), Public Works and Government Services Canada/Travaux Publics et Services Gouvernementaux Canada, Place du Portage, Phase III, 11 Laurier St, Gatineau, PQ K1A 0S5, Canada. TEL 800-622-6232, Questions@pwgsc.gc.ca, http://www.pwgsc.gc.ca/text/home-e.html.

PUBLIC ORGANIZATION REVIEW. *see* BUSINESS AND ECONOMICS—Management

352.23 USA ISSN 0079-7626
J80
PUBLIC PAPERS OF THE PRESIDENTS OF THE UNITED STATES. Text in English. 1957. irreg., latest 2004. price varies. index. back issues avail. **Document type:** *Government.* **Description:** contains the papers and speeches of the president of the United States that were issued by the office of the press secretary during the specified time period.
Related titles: Online - full text ed.
Published by: National Archives and Records Administration, U.S. Office of the Federal Register, 8601 Adelphi Rd, College Park, MD 20740. TEL 202-741-6000, FAX 202-741-6012, fedreg.info@nara.gov, http://www.federalregister.gov. **Orders to:** U.S. Government Printing Office, Superintendent of Documents.

351 658 USA ISSN 1530-9576
JF1411
➤ **PUBLIC PERFORMANCE AND MANAGEMENT REVIEW.** Abbreviated title: P P M R. Text in English. 1975. q. USD 580 combined subscription domestic to institutions (print & online eds.); USD 612 combined subscription foreign to institutions (print & online eds.) (effective 2012). adv. bk.rev. abstr.; illus. Index. back issues avail.; reprint service avail. from PSC. **Document type:** *Journal, Academic/Scholarly.* **Description:** Provides a scholarly forum that addresses a broad range of factors influencing the performance of public and nonprofit organizations and agencies.
Former titles (until 2000): Public Productivity and Management Review (1044-8039); (until 1989): Public Productivity Review (0361-6681)
Related titles: Microform ed.: (from PQC); Online - full text ed.: ISSN 1557-9271. 2004 (Feb.). USD 515 to institutions (effective 2012).
Indexed: A12, A13, A14, A17, A22, A26, ABIn, ADPA, B01, B02, B06, B07, B09, B11, B15, B16, B17, B18, BPI, BPIA, BRD, CA, CurCont, E01, E08, Emerald, G04, G06, G07, G08, I05, P10, P34, P42, P48, P51, P53, P54, PAIS, PCI, PMA, PQC, PSA, PersLit, S09, SPAA, SSCI, SociolAb, T02, UAA, W01, W02, W03, W05, W07.
—BLDSC (6967.887000), IE, Infotrieve, Ingenta. **CCC.**
Published by: (American Society for Public Administration, Section on Management Science and Policy Analysis, Section on Management Science), M.E. Sharpe, Inc., 80 Business Park Dr, Armonk, NY 10504. TEL 914-273-1800, 800-541-6563, FAX 914-273-2106, custserv@mesharpe.com. Ed. Marc Holzer. Adv. contact Barbara Ladd TEL 914-273-1800. **Co-sponsor:** Rutgers University, Newark, National Center for Public Productivity.

351 GBR ISSN 0952-0767
JA8
PUBLIC POLICY AND ADMINISTRATION. Abbreviated title: P P A. Text in English. 1972. q. USD 685, GBP 370 combined subscription to institutions (print & online eds.); USD 671, GBP 363 to institutions (effective 2011). adv. back issues avail.; reprint service avail. from PSC. **Document type:** *Journal, Academic/Scholarly.* **Description:** Aims to publish original material within the broad field of public policy and administration.
Former titles (until 1986): Public Administration Bulletin (0144-2171); (until 1972): P A C Bulletin
Related titles: Online - full text ed.: ISSN 1749-4192. USD 617, GBP 333 to institutions (effective 2011).
Indexed: A22, CA, E01, ESPM, IBSS, P42, PAIS, PSA, RiskAb, SCOPUS, SPAA, SSciA, SociolAb, T02.
—BLDSC (6968.309000), IE, Ingenta. **CCC.**
Published by: (U K Joint University Council Public Administration Committee), Sage Publications Ltd. (Subsidiary of: Sage Publications, Inc.), 1 Oliver's Yard, 55 City Rd, London, EC1Y 1SP, United Kingdom. TEL 44-20-73248500, FAX 44-20-73248600, info@sagepub.co.uk, http://www.uk.sagepub.com/home.nav. Eds. Duncan McTavish, Karen Johnston Miller. adv.: B&W page GBP 350; 150 x 205.

351 GBR ISSN 1754-9590
PUBLIC POLICY AND POLITICS. Text in English. 2001. irreg., latest 2009. price varies. back issues avail. **Document type:** *Monographic series.*
Published by: Palgrave Macmillan Ltd. (Subsidiary of: Macmillan Publishers Ltd.), Houndmills, Basingstoke, Hants RG21 6XS, United Kingdom. TEL 44-1256-329242, FAX 44-1256-810526, bookenquiries@palgrave.com, http://www.palgrave.com. **Dist. by:** Palgrave Macmillan, 175 Fifth Ave, New York, NY 10010.

PUBLIC POLICY AND SOCIAL WELFARE. *see* POLITICAL SCIENCE

351 362.1 USA
PUBLIC POLICY FORUM. RESEARCH REPORTS. Text in English. irreg. (8-18/yr.). charts; stat. **Description:** Covers education, tax and economic development policy, transportation, public safety, health, public infrastructure and other quality of life concerns.
Related titles: Online - full text ed.
Published by: Public Policy Forum, 633 W Wisconsin Ave, Ste 406, Milwaukee, WI 53203-1918. TEL 414-276-8240, FAX 414-276-9962, jslaske@publicpolicyforum.org. Circ: 1,500.

342 GBR ISSN 0963-8245
K16
PUBLIC PROCUREMENT LAW REVIEW. Text in English. 1992. bi-m. GBP 785, EUR 1,035, USD 1,350 (effective 2012). **Document type:** *Journal, Academic/Scholarly.* **Description:** Provides up-to-date information and analysis on the procurement systems in the European Union and EFTA, via a pan-European team of legal contributors. Information relating to international agreement on public procurement, such as the GPA, and procurement in other major trading countries, such as the US, is also included.
Indexed: ELJI, LJI, T02.
—BLDSC (6968.391000), IE, Ingenta. **CCC.**
Published by: Sweet & Maxwell Ltd. (Subsidiary of: Thomson Reuters Corp.), 100 Avenue Rd, London, NW3 3PF, United Kingdom. TEL 44-20-73937000, FAX 44-20-74491144, sweetandmaxwell.customer.services@thomson.com. Eds. Adrian Brown, Steen Treumer, Sue Arrowsmith. **Subscr. outside the UK to:** PO Box 1000, Andover SP10 9AF, United Kingdom. TEL 44-20-73938051, sweetandmaxwell.international.queries@thomson.com.

PUBLIC RISK. *see* BUSINESS AND ECONOMICS—Management

351 NZL ISSN 0110-5191
JA8 CODEN: CNEUET
PUBLIC SECTOR. Text in English. 1978. q. NZD 115 to individual members (effective 2008). adv. bk.rev. charts. cum.index. **Document type:** *Journal, Academic/Scholarly.* **Description:** Includes general articles, reports on emerging issues or debates, news briefs, information about IPANZ's events, opinion pieces and letters to the editor.
Formerly (until vol.40, 1978): New Zealand Journal of Public Administration (0028-8357)
Related titles: Microform ed.; Online - full text ed.
Indexed: CA, I13, INZP, P06, P42, PCI, SCOPUS, T02.
—CCC.
Published by: Institute of Public Administration New Zealand, PO Box 5032, Wellington, New Zealand. TEL 64-4-4636940, FAX 64-4-4636939, admin@ipanz.org.nz. Eds. Rose Northcott, Shelly Farr Biswell. Circ: 1,135.

351 USA
PUBLIC SECTOR. Text in English. 1976. q. free. bibl.; charts; illus.; stat. back issues avail. **Description:** Covers current issues of interest to government officials: growth management, tax reform, economic development and solid waste management.
Indexed: ABCPolSci.
Published by: Auburn University, Center for Governmental Services, 2232 Haley Center, Auburn University, Auburn, AL 36849. TEL 205-844-1913, FAX 205-844-1919. Ed. Charles Spindler. Circ: 3,000 (controlled).

351.41 GBR ISSN 1477-9331
PUBLIC SECTOR EXECUTIVE; the independent journal for government & health care professionals. Abbreviated title: P S E. Text in English. 2002. bi-m. free to qualified personnel (effective 2009). adv. **Document type:** *Magazine, Trade.* **Description:** Explains and assess the public sector's efficiency drive, and feature regular interviews with the leading authorities on public spending.
—CCC.
Published by: Cognitive Publishing Ltd., Ste 102, International House, 82-86 Deansgate, Manchester, Lancashire M3 2ER, United Kingdom. TEL 44-161-8336320, FAX 44-161-8320571, info@cognitivepublishing.com, http://www.cognitivepublishing.com. Ed. Stephen Lewis. Adv. contact Chris Greenhalgh. Circ: 7,001.

351 CAN ISSN 1183-1081
PUBLIC SECTOR MANAGEMENT/MANAGEMENT ET SECTEUR PUBLIC. Text in English, French. 1979. q. CAD 30 to non-members (effective 2006); free to members. adv. **Document type:** *Magazine, Consumer.* **Description:** Informs of the latest developments in the area of public management at all spheres of government and abreast of the activities of the Institute across the country and internationally.
Formerly (until 1990): Institute of Public Administration of Canada. Bulletin (0380-3988)
Published by: Institute of Public Administration of Canada/Institut d'Administration Publique du Canada, 1075 Bay St, Ste 401, Toronto, ON M5S 2B1, Canada. TEL 416-924-8787, FAX 416-924-4992, ntl@ipaciapc.ca, http://www.ipaciapc.ca. Ed. Geoffrey McIlroy. R&P, Adv. contact Joseph Galimberti. Circ: 3,000.

352.63 AUS
PUBLIC SECTOR REVIEW. Text in English. 1888. bi-m. free to members (effective 2009). adv. bk.rev. illus. back issues avail. **Document type:** *Newspaper.* **Description:** Provides information about public sectors.
Former titles (until 1994): Public Service Review (0033-3786); (until 1969): Public Service; (until 1962): South Australian Public Service Review; (until 1945): Public Service Review; (until 1892): The Public Service Journal and Railway Review, South Australia; (until 1889): The Public Service Journal, South Australia
Related titles: Online - full text ed.: free (effective 2009).
Published by: Public Service Association of South Australia Inc., GPO Box 2170, Adelaide, SA 5001, Australia. TEL 61-8-82053200, 800-811-457, FAX 61-8-82236509, enquiry@cpsu.asn.au. Circ: 25,200.

351.4105 GBR ISSN 1749-5784
PUBLIC SECTOR REVIEW (MACCLESFIELD). Abbreviated title: P S R. Text in English. 2004. s-m. GBP 30 per issue (effective 2009). **Document type:** *Magazine, Trade.* **Description:** Promotes best value/best practice and highlights policy changes and the latest advice on financing options for central and local government spending such as direct investment, PPP/PFI and other strategic procurement partnerships with the private sector.
Related titles: ◆ Supplement(s): Public Sector Procurement. ISSN 1754-7849.
Published by: Ten Alps Publishing (Subsidiary of: Ten Alps Group), Trelawney House, Chestergate, Macclesfield, Cheshire SK11 6DW, United Kingdom. TEL 44-1625-613000, FAX 44-1625-511446, info@tenalpspublishing.com, http://www.tenalpspublishing.com. Ed. Anitha Narayan TEL 44-1625-667602. Adv. contact Glyn Jackson TEL 44-1625-613000.

351.415 IRL ISSN 0790-1232
PUBLIC SECTOR TIMES. Text in English. 1983. m. **Document type:** *Newspaper.*
Published by: (Irish Public & Civil Service), Bradan Publishing Ltd., 1 Eglinton Rd., Bray, Co. Wicklow, Ireland. TEL 353-1-2869111, FAX 353-1-2869074. Ed. James D Fitzmaurice. Adv. contact Lesley Kavanagh. Circ: 17,000.

351.41 GBR ISSN 1744-1781
PUBLIC SERVANT; the publication for today's public service leaders. Text in English. 2004. m. GBP 60 to members; GBP 41.40 to non-members (effective 2010). adv. back issues avail. **Document type:** *Magazine, Trade.* **Description:** Provides news, analysis and opinion on the topics that matter to public sector managers.
Related titles: Online - full text ed.
—CCC.

Published by: P S C A International Ltd., Ebenezer House, Rycroft, Newcastle-under-Lyme, Staffs ST5 2UB, United Kingdom. TEL 44-1782-630200, FAX 44-1782-625533, mailbox@publicservice.co.uk. Ed. David Allaby TEL 44-1782-711000. Adv. contact Gerrod Mellor TEL 44-1782-630200. Circ: 13,688.

352.68 GUY
PUBLIC SERVANT. Text in English. 1977 (vol.4). m.
Published by: Guyana Public Service Union, Regent Rd & New Garden St 160, Georgetown, Guyana. TEL 2-61770.

351 CAN ISSN 1912-0842
PUBLIC SERVICE COMMISSION OF CANADA. ANNUAL REPORT (ONLINE). Text in English. 1996. a.
Media: Online - full text. **Related titles:** Braille ed.: ISSN 1487-1459; ◆ Print ed.: Public Service Commission of Canada. Annual Report (Print). ISSN 0701-7820; French ed.: Commission de la Fonction Publique du Canada. Rapport Annuel (En ligne). ISSN 1912-0850.
Published by: Public Service Commission of Canada/Commission de la Fonction Publique du Canada, 300 Laurier Ave W, Ottawa, ON K1A OM7, Canada. TEL 613-992-9562, FAX 613-992-9352, info-com@psc-cfp.gc.ca, http://www.psc-cfp.gc.ca.

351.1 CAN ISSN 0701-7820
CA1SCF1
PUBLIC SERVICE COMMISSION OF CANADA. ANNUAL REPORT (PRINT). Text in English. 1909. a. **Document type:** *Government.*
Former titles (until 1967): Public Service Commission of Canada. Annual Report of the Commissioners (0576-3983); (until 1966): Civil Service Commission of Canada. Annual Report (0701-7839)
Related titles: Braille ed.: ISSN 1487-1459; ◆ Online - full text ed.: Public Service Commission of Canada. Annual Report (Online). ISSN 1912-0842.
Published by: Public Service Commission of Canada/Commission de la Fonction Publique du Canada, 300 Laurier Ave W, Ottawa, ON K1A OM7, Canada. TEL 613-992-9562, FAX 613-992-9352, info-com@psc-cfp.gc.ca.

351 CAN ISSN 1912-0613
PUBLIC SERVICE COMMISSION OF CANADA. ANNUAL REPORT. HIGHLIGHTS. Text in English. 200?. a. **Document type:** *Report, Trade.*
Related titles: Online - full text ed.: ISSN 1912-0710.
Published by: Public Service Commission of Canada/Commission de la Fonction Publique du Canada, 300 Laurier Ave W, Ottawa, ON K1A OM7, Canada. TEL 613-992-9562, FAX 613-992-9352, info-com@psc-cfp.gc.ca, http://www.psc-cfp.gc.ca.

351.71 CAN ISSN 1483-8850
CA1BT31-4 66
PUBLIC SERVICE COMMISSION OF CANADA. PERFORMANCE REPORT. Text in English, French. 1997. a.
Related titles: Online - full text ed.: ISSN 1490-4144.
Published by: (Public Service Commission of Canada/Commission de la Fonction Publique du Canada), Treasury Board of Canada Secretariat, Corporate Communications/Secretariat du Conseil du Tresor du Canada, West Tower, Rm P-135, 300 Laurier Ave W, Ottawa, ON K1A 0R5, Canada. TEL 613-995-2855, FAX 613-996-0518, services-publications@tbs-sct.gc.ca.

351 CAN ISSN 1709-7274
CA1PG1
PUBLIC SERVICE INTEGRITY OFFICE. ANNUAL REPORT TO PARLIAMENT/BUREAU DE L'INTEGRITE DE LA FONCTION PUBLIQUE. RAPPORT ANNUEL AU PARLEMENT. Text in English, French. 2003. a., latest 2005. **Document type:** *Government.*
Related titles: ◆ Online - full text ed.: Canada. Public Service Integrity Office. Annual Report to Parliament. ISSN 1719-6469.
Published by: Canada, Public Service Integrity Office, 60 Queen St., Ste 605, Ottawa, ON, Canada. TEL 613-941-6400, 866-941-6400, FAX 613-941-6535, http://www.psio-bifp.gc.ca/index_e.php.

351.41 GBR ISSN 1470-5257
JN425
PUBLIC SERVICE REVIEW. CENTRAL GOVERNMENT. Text in English. 2000. s-a. GBP 50 (effective 2011). adv. back issues avail. **Document type:** *Magazine, Trade.* **Description:** Provides anyone with a professional interest in the worlds of Westminster and Whitehall with editorial from the Members of Parliament and senior civil servants tasked with the decision-making and management at the heart of the country's day-to-day running.
Related titles: Online - full text ed.: ISSN 2045-8819. free (effective 2011).
—CCC.
Published by: P S C A International Ltd., Ebenezer House, Rycroft, Newcastle-under-Lyme, Staffs ST5 2UB, United Kingdom. TEL 44-1782-630200, FAX 44-1782-625533, mailbox@publicservice.co.uk. Ed. Amy Caddick. Adv. contact Gerrod Mellor TEL 44-1782-630200. Circ: 7,485.

352.56 GBR ISSN 1743-016X
PUBLIC SERVICE REVIEW. CONSTRUCTION. Text in English. 2004. s-a. adv. back issues avail. **Document type:** *Magazine, Trade.* **Description:** Highlights the importance of the construction industry to the UK economy, offering articles and insights that analyse procurement issues, spread and promote Best Practice and Best Value, and disseminate policy changes.
—CCC.
Published by: P S C A International Ltd., Ebenezer House, Rycroft, Newcastle-under-Lyme, Staffs ST5 2UB, United Kingdom. TEL 44-1782-630200, FAX 44-1782-625533, mailbox@publicservice.co.uk. Ed. Lisa Carnwell. Adv. contact Gerrod Mellor TEL 44-1782-630200.

321.02 GBR ISSN 1473-9275
PUBLIC SERVICE REVIEW. DEVOLVED GOVERNMENT. Text in English. 2001. 3/yr. GBP 100 (effective 2010). adv. back issues avail. **Document type:** *Magazine, Trade.* **Description:** Provides a biannual glimpse at the tremendous progress and regeneration being experienced in sectors from science and technology to environmental policy.
Related titles: Online - full text ed.: free (effective 2009).
—CCC.
Published by: P S C A International Ltd., Ebenezer House, Rycroft, Newcastle-under-Lyme, Staffs ST5 2UB, United Kingdom. TEL 44-1782-630200, FAX 44-1782-625533, mailbox@publicservice.co.uk. Ed. Jonathan Miles. Adv. contact Gerrod Mellor TEL 44-1782-630200. Circ: 3,567.

351.4 GBR ISSN 1472-3395
PUBLIC SERVICE REVIEW. EUROPEAN UNION. Text in English. 2001. s-a. GBP 50 (effective 2011). adv. back issues avail. **Document type:** *Magazine, Trade.* **Description:** Provides a balanced view of the alternative methods of procurement across the European Union as well as on the variety of issues affecting the public sector throughout Europe.
Related titles: Online - full text ed.: ISSN 2046-6110. free (effective 2011).
—CCC.
Published by: P S C A International Ltd., Ebenezer House, Rycroft, Newcastle-under-Lyme, Staffs ST5 2UB, United Kingdom. TEL 44-1782-630200, FAX 44-1782-625533, mailbox@publicservice.co.uk. Ed. Jonathan Miles. Adv. contact Gerrod Mellor TEL 44-1782-630200.

352.40 GBR ISSN 1478-6699
PUBLIC SERVICE REVIEW. FINANCE. Text in English. 2003. s-a. back issues avail. **Document type:** *Magazine, Trade.* **Description:** Features articles that analyse public sector financial issues, thereby spreading and promoting best practice and best value. It disseminates policy changes and forecasts future developments, offering guidance on policy information, whilst profiling the leading private sector solution providers.
—CCC.
Published by: P S C A International Ltd., Ebenezer House, Rycroft, Newcastle-under-Lyme, Staffs ST5 2UB, United Kingdom. TEL 44-1782-630200, FAX 44-1782-625533, mailbox@publicservice.co.uk. Eds. Lisa Carnwell, Matthew D'Arcy TEL 44-1782-740088.

381 GBR ISSN 1747-5872
PUBLIC SERVICE REVIEW: TRADE AND INDUSTRY. Text in English. 2002. s-a. adv. back issues avail. **Document type:** *Magazine, Trade.* **Description:** Features articles that seek to bring opinion from major figures within government and the civil service, academics and industry with a hand in driving the economy forward.
Formerly (until 2005): Public Service Review. Department of Trade and Industry (1474-8029)
—CCC.
Published by: P S C A International Ltd., Ebenezer House, Rycroft, Newcastle-under-Lyme, Staffs ST5 2UB, United Kingdom. TEL 44-1782-630200, FAX 44-1782-625533, mailbox@publicservice.co.uk. Ed. Lisa Carnwell. Adv. contact Gerrod Mellor TEL 44-1782-630200.

351.953 CAN ISSN 1499-6499
PUBLIC SERVICE STAFF RELATIONS BOARD. SUMMARIES OF DECISIONS. Text in English, French. 1982. s-a.
Formerly (until 2000): Public Service Staff Relations Board Decisions (0822-1790)
Published by: Canada. Public Service Staff Relations Board, PO Box 1525, Sta. B, Ottawa, ON K1P 5V2, Canada. TEL 613-990-1800, FAX 613-990-1849, mail.courrier@pssrb-crtfp.gc.ca, http://www.pssrb-crtfp.gc.ca/.

PUBLIC UTILITIES FORTNIGHTLY; energy, money, power. *see* ENVIRONMENTAL STUDIES—Waste Management

351 USA ISSN 1087-724X
HD3881
➤ **PUBLIC WORKS MANAGEMENT & POLICY.** Text in English. 1996. q. USD 724, GBP 426 combined subscription to institutions (print & online eds.); USD 710, GBP 417 to institutions (effective 2011). reprint service avail. from PSC. **Document type:** *Journal, Academic/Scholarly.* **Description:** Dedicated to publishing analysis, research and opinions to help shape the diverse public works profession. Contains innovative, thought-provoking scholarship written in accessible language and with direct relevance to practice and policy.
Related titles: Online - full text ed.: ISSN 1552-7549. USD 652, GBP 383 to institutions (effective 2011).
Indexed: A22, A28, A32, APA, B01, B06, B07, B08, B09, BrCerAb, C&ISA, CA, CA/WCA, CIA, CerAb, CivEngAb, CorrAb, E&CAJ, E01, E11, EEA, EMA, ESPM, EnvEAb, H04, H15, HRIS, IBR, IBZ, M&TEA, M09, MBF, METADEX, P34, P42, PAIS, PSA, PollutAb, SCOPUS, SPAA, SSciA, SUSA, SolStAb, T02, T04, V02, WAA.
—BLDSC (6970.123000), IE, Infotrieve, Ingenta, Linda Hall. **CCC.**
Published by: Sage Publications, Inc., 2455 Teller Rd, Thousand Oaks, CA 91320. TEL 805-499-9774, 800-818-7243, FAX 805-499-0871, 800-583-2665, info@sagepub.com. Ed. Richard G Little. **Subscr. in Asia to:** Sage Publications Ltd., 1 Oliver's Yard, 55 City Rd, London EC1Y 1SP, United Kingdom. TEL 44-207-3248701, FAX 44-207-3248733, subscription@sagepub.co.uk; **Subscr. in Europe to:** Sage Publications India Pvt. Ltd., M-32 Market, Greater Kailash-I, PO Box 4215, New Delhi 110 048, India. **Co-sponsor:** American Public Works Association.

351.494 CHE ISSN 0080-7249
DQ1
PUBLICUS; Schweizer Jahrbuch des oeffentlichen Lebens. Text in French, German. 1958. a. CHF 85; CHF 150 combined subscription (print & online eds.) (effective 2009). adv. index. **Document type:** *Directory, Consumer.* **Description:** Summaries include science and culture, sports, economic and political organizations in Switzerland.
Related titles: CD-ROM ed.: CHF 198 (effective 2003); Online - full text ed.: CHF 85 (effective 2009).
—CCC.
Published by: Schwabe und Co. AG, Steinentorstr 13, Basel, 4010, Switzerland. TEL 41-61-2789565, FAX 41-61-2789566, verlag@schwabe.ch, http://www.schwabe.ch. Ed. Bernard Hess. Circ: 6,500.

PUBLIUS; the journal of federalism. *see* POLITICAL SCIENCE

351 NLD ISSN 2210-7606
PUNT. Text in Dutch. 2003. 3/yr.
Related titles: Online - full text ed.: ISSN 2210-7614.
Published by: C M O Groningen, Postbus 2266, Groningen, 9704 CG, Netherlands. TEL 31-50-5770101, info@cmogroningen.nl.

351.93 363.7 NZL ISSN 1177-4665
TE PUTARA. Text in English. 2003. 3/yr. **Document type:** *Newsletter.*
Related titles: Online - full text ed.: ISSN 1177-4673.
Published by: E R M A New Zealand, PO Box 131, Wellington, 6140, New Zealand. TEL 64-4-9162426, FAX 64-4-9140433, info@ermanz.govt.nz. Eds. David Venables, Linda Faulkner.

351 CAN ISSN 1924-3464
Q S T AND G S T / H S T REBATES. (Quebec Sales Tax and Goods and Services Tax / Harmonized Sales Tax Rebates) Text in English. 2003. irreg. free (effective 2010). **Document type:** *Government.*
Published by: Revenu Quebec, 3800, rue de Marly, Gatineau, PQ G1X 4A5, Canada. TEL 418-659-4692, 800-488-2323.

351.5363 QAT
QATAR YEARBOOK. Text in Arabic, English, French. 1976. biennial. free. charts; illus.; maps; stat.; tr.lit. **Document type:** *Government.* **Description:** Covers the various activities of all ministries and public institutions in Qatar, as well as many private sector industrial and commercial enterprises. Also includes historic and geographic information, as well as local contact numbers.
Published by: Ministry of Foreign Affairs, Information & Research Department, P O Box 5147, Doha, Qatar. TEL 974-440345, FAX 974-445070, TELEX 4552. Ed. Hussien Ahmed. R&P Hussien Ahmad TEL 972-420456. Circ: 15,000.

352 CAN ISSN 1719-8631
QUEBEC (PROVINCE). MINISTERE DES AFFAIRES MUNICIPALES ET DES REGIONS. RAPPORT ANNUEL DE GESTION. Text in French. 1999. a., latest 2005. **Document type:** *Government.*
Former titles (until 2005): Quebec (Province). Ministere des Affaires Municipales, du Sport et du Loisir. Rapport Annuel de Gestion (1719-3532); (until 2004): Quebec (Province). Ministere des Affaires Municipales et de la Metropole. Rapport Annuel de Gestion (1705-0650); (until 2002): Quebec (Province). Ministere des Affaires Municipales et de la Metropole. Rapport Annuel (1492-5567); Which was formed by the merger of (19??-1999): Quebec (Province). Ministere des Affaires Municipales. Rapport Annuel (0481-472X); Which incorporated (1966-1967): Quebec Department of Municipal Affairs. Annual Report (0481-4355); (1997-1999): Quebec (Province). Ministere de la Metropole. Rapport Annuel (1480-3712)
Related titles: Online - full text ed.: ISSN 1912-0036. 2002.
Published by: Quebec, Ministere des Affaires Municipales et des Regions, 10, rue Pierre-Olivier-Chauveau, Quebec, PQ G1R 4J3, Canada. TEL 418-691-2019, FAX 418-643-7385, communications@mamr.gouv.qc.ca, http://www.mamr.gouv.qc.ca/accueil.asp.

351 401 CAN ISSN 1708-2781
PC3601
QUEBEC. CONSEIL SUPERIEUR DE LA LANGUE FRANCAISE. RAPPORT ANNUEL DE GESTION. Text in French. 1978. a. **Document type:** *Report, Trade.*
Former titles (until 2002): Quebec. Conseil de la Langue Francaise. Rapport Annuel de Gestion (1707-3839); (until 2001): Quebec. Conseil de la Langue Francaise. Rapport Annuel (0229-9259)
Published by: Quebec. Conseil Superieur de la Langue Francaise, 800, place D'Youville, 13 etage, Quebec, PQ G1R 3P4, Canada. TEL 418-643-2740, FAX 418-644-7654, cslfq@cslf.gouv.qc.ca, http://www.cslf.gouv.qc.ca.

P

351 CAN ISSN 1719-8607
TD171.5.C22
QUEBEC. MINISTERE DU DEVELOPPEMENT DURABLE, ENVIRONNEMENT ET PARCS. RAPPORT ANNUEL DE GESTION. Text in French. 1994. a., latest 2005. **Document type:** *Government.*
Former titles (until 2005): Quebec. Ministere de l'Environnement. Rapport Annuel de Gestion (1711-1889); (until 2002): Quebec. Ministere de l'Environnement. Rapport Annuel (1496-6948); (until 2000): Quebec. Ministere de l'Environnement et de la Faune. Rapport Annuel (1201-7388); Which was formed by the merger of (1973-1994): Quebec. Ministere de l'Environnement. Rapport Annuel (0228-4952); Which was formerly (until 1980): Services de Protection de l'Environnement.Rapport Annuel (0226-3629); (19??-1994): Quebec. Ministere du Loisir, de la Chasse et de la Peche. Rapport Annuel (0228-6793); Which was formerly (until 1979): Quebec. Ministere du Tourisme, de la Chasse et de la Peche. Rapport Annuel (0481-2786); (until 1963): Quebec. Ministre de la Chasse et des Pecheries Concernant les Activites de la Chasse. Rapport General
Published by: Quebec, Ministere du Developpement Durable, Environnement et Parcs, Edifice Marie-Guyart, 29e etage, 675, boule. Rene-Levesque Est, Quebec, PQ G1R 5V7, Canada. TEL 418-521-3830, 800-561-1616, FAX 418-646-5974, info@mddep.gouv.qc.ca, http://www.mddep.gouv.qc.ca/index.asp.

351 CAN ISSN 1911-0642
QUEBEC. MINISTERE DU REVENU. PLAN D'ACTION. Text in French. 2005. a. **Document type:** *Government.*
Published by: Quebec, Ministere du Revenu, 3800, rue de Marly, Quebec, PQ G1X 4A5, Canada. http://www.revenu.gouv.qc.ca/fr/ministere/index.asp.

QUEBEC. MINISTERE DU TRAVAIL. RAPPORT ANNUEL DE GESTION (YEAR). *see* BUSINESS AND ECONOMICS—Labor And Industrial Relations

351 CAN ISSN 1719-3869
JC599.C22
QUEBEC PROVINCE. MINISTERE DE L'IMMIGRATION ET DES COMMUNAUTES CULTURELLES. RAPPORT ANNUEL DE GESTION. Text in French. 1994. a.
Former titles (until 2005): Quebec Province. Ministere des Relations avec les Citoyens et de l'Immigration. Rapport Annuel de Gestion (1711-1005); (until 2001): Quebec Province. Ministere des Relations avec les Citoyens et de l'Immigration. Rapport Annuel (1485-5291); Which superseded in part (in 1997): Quebec Province. Ministere des Affaires Internationales, de l'Immigration et des Communautes Culturelles. Rapport Annuel (1201-3005); Which was formed by the merger of (1982-1994): Quebec Province. Ministere des Communautes Culturelles et de l'Immigration. Rapport Annuel (0820-0637); Which was formerly (until 1982): Quebec Province. Ministere de l'Immigration. Rapport Annuel (0383-4433); (until 1969): Quebec. Secretariat de la Province. Rapport Annuel (0481-2956); (1989-1994): Quebec Province. Ministere des Affaires Internationales. Rapport Annuel (0848-4848); Which was formerly (until 1989): Quebec Province. Ministere des Relations Internationales. Rapport Annuel (0833-7403); (until 1985): Quebec Province. Ministere des Affaires Intergouvernementales. Rapport Annuel (0711-947X); (until 1969): Quebec Province. Ministere des Affaires Intergouvernementales. Rapport (0711-9461); (until 1968): Quebec Province. Ministere des Affaires Federales-Provinciales. Rapport

Published by: Quebec, Ministere de l'Immigration et des Communautes Culturelles, 360, rue McGill, Montreal, PQ H2Y 2E9, Canada. direction.communications@micc.gouv.qc.ca, http://www.micc.gouv.qc.ca.

351 CAN ISSN 1714-5457
QUEBEC PROVINCE. MINISTERE DES RELATIONS INTERNATIONALES. RAPPORT ANNUEL DE GESTION. Text in French. 1994. a.
Formerly (until 2001): Quebec Province. Ministere des Relations Internationales. Rapport Annuel (1491-0063); Which superseded in part (in 1997): Quebec Province. Ministere des Affaires Internationales, de l'Immigration et des Communautes Culturelles. Rapport Annuel (1201-3005); Which was formed by the merger of (1982-1994): Quebec Province. Ministere des Communautes Culturelles et de l'Immigration. Rapport Annuel (0820-0637); Which was formerly (until 1982): Quebec Province. Ministere de l'Immigration. Rapport Annuel (0383-4433); (until 1969): Quebec. Secretariat de la Province. Rapport Annuel (0481-2956); (1989-1994): Quebec Province. Ministere des Affaires Internationales. Rapport Annuel (0848-4848); Which was formerly (until 1989): Quebec Province. Ministere des Relations Internationales. Rapport Annuel (0833-7403); (until 1985): Quebec Province. Ministere des Affaires Intergouvernementales. Rapport Annuel (0711-947X); (until 1969): Quebec Province.Ministere des Affaires Intergouvernementales. Rapport (0711-9461); (until 1968): Quebec Province. Ministere des Affaires Federales-Provinciales. Rapport
Published by: Quebec, Ministere des Relations Internationales, Edifice Hector-Fabre, 525, bl Rene-Levesque Est, Quebec, PQ G1R 5R9, Canada. TEL 418-649-2300, FAX 418-649-2656, http://www.mri.gouv.qc.ca/en/index.asp.

352 351 AUS
QUEENSLAND ADMINISTRATIVE LAW. Variant title: Q L D Administrative Law. Text in English. 1995. base vol. plus irreg. updates. looseleaf. AUD 778 (effective 2008). **Document type:** *Handbook/Manual/Guide, Trade.* **Description:** Provides commentary on administrative law remedies in Queensland.
Incorporates: Queensland Administrative Reports
Published by: Lawbook Co. (Subsidiary of: Thomson Reuters (Professional) Australia Limited), PO Box 3502, Rozelle, NSW 2039, Australia. TEL 61-2-85877980, 300-304-195, FAX 61-2-85877981, 300-304-196, LTA.Service@thomsonreuters.com, http://www.thomson.com.au.

353.80994 AUS ISSN 1835-0402
QUEENSLAND. DEPARTMENT OF EDUCATION, TRAINING AND THE ARTS. ANNUAL REPORT. Text in English. 2004. a. free (effective 2009). **Description:** Details of fulfilling the department's commitment to accountability and transparency.
Formerly (until 2007): Queensland. Department of Education and the Arts. Annual Report (1833-8445); Which was formed by the merger of (1987-2003): Queensland. Department of Education. Annual Report (1033-9744); Which was formerly (until 1987): Minister for Education. Annual Report (0159-379X); (until 1978): Minister for Education and Cultural Activities. Annual Report (0157-0412); Which was formed by the 2003 merger of: Arts Queensland. Annual Report
Related titles: CD-ROM ed.; Online - full text ed.: ISSN 1835-0410.
Published by: Queensland, Department of Education, Training and the Arts, PO Box 15033, City East, QLD 4002, Australia. TEL 61-7-32370111.

351.764 USA
QUORUM REPORT (ONLINE). Variant title: Harvey Kronberg's Quorum Report. Text in English. 1982. s-m. USD 275 (effective 2006). bk.rev. **Document type:** *Newsletter, Trade.* **Description:** Reports on Texas government and politics.
Formerly: Quorum Report (Print) (0882-3456)
Published by: Quorum Report, PO Box 8, Austin, TX 78767. TEL 512-292-8191, FAX 512-292-0099. Ed., Pub. Harvey Kronberg.

352.63 CAN ISSN 0033-6734
R A NEWS. (Recreation Association) Text in English. 1942. 4/yr. CAD 15. adv. bk.rev. illus. **Description:** Wellbeing magazine, aims to inform members and recruit potential members.
Published by: Recreation Association of the Public Service of Canada, 2451 Riverside Dr, Ottawa, ON K1H 7X7, Canada. TEL 613-733-5100, FAX 613-733-3310. Ed., R&P, Adv. contact Jane Proudfoot. Circ: 100 (paid); 40,000 (controlled).

351 ZAF
R D P VISION. (Reconstruction and Development Programme) Text in English. 1995. m.?. **Document type:** *Government.*
Indexed: ISAP.
Published by: (Gauteng Province. Communications Directorate), Gauteng Provincial Government, Office of the Premier, Private Bag X61, Marshalltown, Johannesburg 2107, South Africa.

351 331 ITA ISSN 1825-8557
R I P IMPIEGO E DIRIGENZA PUBBLICA. Text in Italian. 2005. q. EUR 100 combined subscription (print & online eds.) (effective 2011). **Document type:** *Journal, Trade.*
Related titles: Online - full text ed.
Published by: Gedit Edizioni, Via Irnerio 12/5, Bologna, 40126, Italy. TEL 39-051-421874, FAX 39-051-4210565, http://www.gedit.it.

352.63 TUN ISSN 0330-9932
R T A P. (Revue Tunisienne d'Administration Publique) Text in Arabic, French. 1967-1976; resumed 1985. s-a. TND 7; USD 15 foreign. abstr.; stat. back issues avail. **Document type:** *Academic/Scholarly.* **Description:** Covers administration activities, such as modernization and reformation and innovations in public services.
Formerly: Servir (0035-4120)
Indexed: FR.
Published by: Ecole Nationale d'Administration, Centre de Recherches et d'Etudes Administratives, Mutuelleville, 24 Ave., Dr. Calmette, Tunis, 1002, Tunisia. TEL 216-1-846-167, FAX 787-205. R&P Ayadh Chaouachi. Circ: 2,000.

R Y; rakennettu ymparisto. *see* BUILDING AND CONSTRUCTION

354.79 CAN ISSN 1494-6785
TL796.5C2R34
RADARSAT ANNUAL REVIEW. Text in English, French. 1997. a.
Related titles: Online - full text ed.: ISSN 1701-5979.
Published by: Canadian Space Agency, John H Chapman Space Centre, 6767 Route de l'Aeroport, Saint-Hubert, PQ J3Y 8Y9, Canada. TEL 450-926-4800, FAX 450-926-4352, http://www.space.gc.ca.

351 CAN ISSN 1709-6227
RAPPORT ANNUEL DE GESTION (YEAR). Text in French. 1979. a.
Formerly (until 2001): Rapport Annuel (0711-0022)
Published by: Ministere des Ressources Naturelles, de la Faune et des Parcs, 5700, 4e Avenue Ouest, B302, Charlesbourg, ON G1H 6R1, Canada. TEL 418-627-8600, 866-248-6936, FAX 418-643-0720, service.citoyens@mrnfp.gouv.qc.ca, http://www.mrnfp.gouv.qc.ca.

351 NLD ISSN 2210-6324
RAPPORT BIJ DE NEDERLANDSE E U-LIDSTAATVERKLARING. Text in Dutch. 2006. a.
Published by: (Algemene Rekenkamer, Tweede Kamer de Staten-Generaal), Sdu Uitgevers bv, Postbus 20025, The Hague, 2500 EA, Netherlands. TEL 31-70-3789911, FAX 31-70-3854321, sdu@sdu.nl, http://www.sdu.nl/.

351 DEU ISSN 0942-2110
RAUMORDNUNGS- UND LANDESPLANUNGSRECHT DES BUNDES UND DER LAENDER. Text in German. 1979. 2 base vols. plus updates 2/yr. looseleaf. EUR 98 base vol(s).; EUR 33.80 updates per issue (effective 2009). **Document type:** *Monographic series, Trade.*
Published by: Erich Schmidt Verlag GmbH & Co. (Berlin), Genthiner Str 30 G, Berlin, 10785, Germany. TEL 49-30-2500850, FAX 49-30-250085305, vertrieb@esvmedien.de, http://www.erich-schmidt-verlag.de.

351 DEU
RECHT DES OEFFENTLICHEN DIENSTES BRANDENBURG. Text in German. 3 base vols. plus updates 6/yr. looseleaf. EUR 269 base vol(s).; EUR 69 updates (effective 2010). adv. **Document type:** *Trade.*
Related titles: CD-ROM ed.; Online - full text ed.
Published by: Walhalla Fachverlag, Haus an der Eisernen Bruecke, Regensburg, 93042, Germany. TEL 49-941-56840, FAX 49-941-5684111, walhalla@walhalla.de. Ed. Klaus M Dauderstaedt. adv.: page EUR 500. Circ: 2,600.

351 DEU
RECHT DES OEFFENTLICHEN DIENSTES MECKLENBURG-VORPOMMERN. Text in German. 3 base vols. plus updates 6/yr. looseleaf. EUR 269 base vol(s).; EUR 69 updates (effective 2010). adv. **Document type:** *Trade.*
Related titles: CD-ROM ed.; Online - full text ed.
Published by: Walhalla Fachverlag, Haus an der Eisernen Bruecke, Regensburg, 93042, Germany. TEL 49-941-56840, FAX 49-941-5684111, walhalla@walhalla.de. Ed. Klaus M Dauderstaedt. adv.: page EUR 500. Circ: 2,600.

351 DEU
RECHT DES OEFFENTLICHEN DIENSTES SACHSEN. Text in German. 3 base vols. plus updates 6/yr. looseleaf. EUR 269 base vol(s).; EUR 69 updates (effective 2010). adv. **Document type:** *Trade.*
Related titles: CD-ROM ed.; Online - full text ed.
Published by: Walhalla Fachverlag, Haus an der Eisernen Bruecke, Regensburg, 93042, Germany. TEL 49-941-56840, FAX 49-941-5684111, walhalla@walhalla.de. Ed. Klaus M Dauderstaedt. adv.: page EUR 500. Circ: 2,600.

351 DEU
RECHT DES OEFFENTLICHEN DIENSTES SACHSEN-ANHALT. Text in German. 3 base vols. plus updates 6/yr. looseleaf. EUR 269 base vol(s).; EUR 69 updates (effective 2010). adv. **Document type:** *Trade.*
Related titles: CD-ROM ed.; Online - full text ed.
Published by: Walhalla Fachverlag, Haus an der Eisernen Bruecke, Regensburg, 93042, Germany. TEL 49-941-56840, FAX 49-941-5684111, walhalla@walhalla.de. Ed. Klaus M Dauderstaedt. adv.: page EUR 500. Circ: 2,600.

351 DEU
RECHT DES OEFFENTLICHEN DIENSTES THUERINGEN. Text in German. 3 base vols. plus updates 6/yr. looseleaf. EUR 269 base vol(s).; EUR 69 updates (effective 2010). adv. **Document type:** *Trade.*
Related titles: CD-ROM ed.; Online - full text ed.
Published by: Walhalla Fachverlag, Haus an der Eisernen Bruecke, Regensburg, 93042, Germany. TEL 49-941-56840, FAX 49-941-5684111, walhalla@walhalla.de. Ed. Klaus M Dauderstaedt. adv.: page EUR 500. Circ: 2,600.

351 DEU ISSN 0034-1339
KK5571.2
➤ **RECHT IM AMT**; Zeitschrift fuer den oeffentlichen Dienst. Text in German. 1954. bi-m. EUR 120; EUR 27 newsstand/cover (effective 2011). adv. bk.rev. index. reprint service avail. from SCH. **Document type:** *Journal, Academic/Scholarly.*
Indexed: DIP, IBR, IBZ.
—CCC.
Published by: Hermann Luchterhand Verlag GmbH (Subsidiary of: Wolters Kluwer Deutschland GmbH), Heddesdorfer Str 31, Neuwied, 56564, Germany. TEL 49-2631-8012222, FAX 49-2631-8012223, info@luchterhand.de, http://www.luchterhand.de. Adv. contacts Marcus Kipp, Margret Sock-Freiberg. Circ: 1,350 (paid and controlled).

351 DEU ISSN 0481-9357
RECHT UND ORGANISATION DER PARLAMENTE. Text in German. 1958. 6 base vols. plus updates 3/yr. looseleaf. EUR 198 base vol(s).; EUR 49.80 updates per issue (effective 2009). **Document type:** *Monographic series, Trade.*
Published by: Erich Schmidt Verlag GmbH & Co. (Berlin), Genthiner Str 30 G, Berlin, 10785, Germany. TEL 49-30-2500850, FAX 49-30-250085305, vertrieb@esvmedien.de, http://www.erich-schmidt-verlag.de.

352.1 DEU ISSN 0344-7871
RECHT UND POLITIK; Vierteljahreshefte fuer Rechts- und Verwaltungspolitik. Text in German. 1965. q. EUR 40; EUR 32 to students; EUR 14 newsstand/cover (effective 2010). adv. bk.rev. reprint service avail. from SCH. **Document type:** *Journal, Academic/Scholarly.* **Description:** Deals with legal and political problems and the background of legislation, administration and jurisdiction in social, educational and civic matters.
Indexed: CA, DIP, IBR, IBZ, P42, PRA, PSA, SCOPUS, SociolAb, T02.
—BLDSC (7309.376500), IE, Infotrieve.
Published by: B W V - Berliner Wissenschafts Verlag GmbH, Markgrafenstr 12-14, Berlin, 10969, Germany. TEL 49-30-8417700, FAX 49-30-84177021, bwv@bwv-verlag.de, http://www.bwv-verlag.de. Ed. Hendrick Wassermann. Circ: 1,000 (paid and controlled).

328 NLD ISSN 1871-4293
RECHTSPRAAK NOTARIAAT. Text in Dutch. 1829. m. (11/yr.). EUR 302; EUR 360 combined subscription (print & online eds.); EUR 151 to students; EUR 28.75 newsstand/cover (effective 2009). back issues avail. **Document type:** *Trade.* **Description:** Covers recent jurisprudence and ministerial decisions relating to inheritance and gift law and taxation, civil law, income and asset taxation.
Former titles (until 2006): Periodiek Woordenboek (1387-6155); (until 1997): Periodiek Woordenboek van Administraitieve en Gerechtlijke Beslissingen (0165-0785)
Related titles: Online - full text ed.: EUR 300 (effective 2009).
Published by: Kluwer B.V. (Subsidiary of: Wolters Kluwer N.V.), Postbus 23, Deventer, 7400 GA, Netherlands. TEL 31-570-673555, FAX 31-570-691555, info@kluwer.nl, http://www.kluwer.nl. Ed. J Hopmans.

RECOGNITION OF EXCELLENCE IN AGING RESEARCH, COMMITTEE REPORT, REPORT OF THE SPECIAL COMMITTEE ON AGING, UNITED STATES SENATE. *see* SOCIAL SERVICES AND WELFARE

351 537 PRT ISSN 1646-7612
REDES ENERGETICAS NACIONAIS. RELATORIO E CONTAS. Text in Portuguese. 2007. a. **Document type:** *Report, Government.*
Published by: Redes Energeticas Nacionais, Avenida dos Estados Unidos da America 55, Lisbon, 1749-061, Portugal. TEL 351-210-013500, FAX 351-210-013310, http://www.ren.pt.

351 VEN ISSN 1315-2378
JA5
➤ **REFORMA Y DEMOCRACIA.** Text in Spanish; Summaries in English. 1994. 3/yr. VEB 90 domestic; USD 60 in Latin America and the Caribbean; USD 70 elsewhere (effective 2009). back issues avail. **Document type:** *Journal, Academic/Scholarly.* **Description:** Discusses governance, democracy and states issues about Latin America countries.
Related titles: Online - full text ed.
Indexed: C01, FR, SSCI, W07.
Published by: Centro Latinoamericano de Administracion para el Desarrollo, C. Herrera Toro, Qta. CLAD, Sector Los Naranjos, Las Mercedes, Apdo. Postal 4181, Caracas, 1010-A, Venezuela. TEL 58-212-9924064, FAX 58-212-9918427, cedai@clad.org.ve. Ed. Nuria Cunill Grau. Circ: 800.

351.44 FRA ISSN 0337-7091
JN2301
REGARDS SUR L'ACTUALITE; mensuel de la vie publique en France. Text in French. 1969. 10/yr. EUR 52 to individuals; EUR 43 to students (effective 2009). bibl. **Document type:** *Government.*
Formerly (until 1975): Politique Interieure de la France (0556-4034)
Related titles: Microfiche ed.
Indexed: A22, ELLIS, FR, IBSS, P30, RASB.
—BLDSC (7336.440000), IE, Infotrieve, Ingenta.
Published by: Documentation Francaise, 29-31 Quai Voltaire, Paris, Cedex 7 75344, France. FAX 33-1-40157230.

REGENSBURGER BEITRAEGE ZUM STAATS- UND VERWALTUNGSRECHT. *see* LAW

351 SWE ISSN 0345-9896
KKV18.A35
REGERINGSRAETTENS AARSBOK. Variant title: R Aa. Text in Swedish. 1909. a. **Document type:** *Government.*
Incorporates (in 1978): Raettsfall och Notiser fraan Regeringsraetten (0348-4246)
Published by: (Sweden. Domstolsverket), Fritzes Offentliga Publikationer (Subsidiary of: Norstedts Juridik AB), c/o Norstedts Juridik AB, Stockholm, 10647, Sweden. TEL 46-8-690-9090, FAX 46-8-690-9191.

351 330.9 FRA ISSN 1267-5059
REGION ET DEVELOPPEMENT. Text in Multiple languages. 1995. s-a. EUR 37 domestic; EUR 40 foreign (effective 2008). **Document type:** *Journal, Trade.*
Indexed: IBSS, JEL.
Published by: L' Harmattan, 5 Rue de l'Ecole Polytechnique, Paris, 75005, France. TEL 33-1-43257651, FAX 33-1-43258203.

351 GBR
REGIONAL REVIEW (LONDON); Europe's regions and cities. Text in English. 2006. q. GBP 38 (effective 2009). adv. back issues avail. **Document type:** *Magazine, Trade.* **Description:** Provides news and analysis of regional policy legislation and developments at EU, national and regional levels.
Related titles: Online - full text ed.: free.
Published by: Dod's Parliamentary Communications Ltd., Westminster Tower, 3rd Fl, 3 Albert Embankment, London, SE1 7SP, United Kingdom. TEL 44-20-70917500, FAX 44-20-70917505, uk@dods.co.uk, http://www.dods.co.uk. Ed. Martha Moss TEL 32-2-2850829. Adv. contact Stephen Hayter TEL 44-20-70917668. B&W page GBP 5,975, color page GBP 6,700; 210 x 270.

351 ITA ISSN 1971-7989
REGIONE DEL VENETO. BOLLETTINO UFFICIALE. Text in Italian. 1970. bi-w. **Document type:** *Bulletin, Consumer.*
Related titles: Online - full text ed.: ISSN 1971-7997. 2004.
Published by: Regione del Veneto, Palazzo Balbi, Dorsoduro 3901, Venice, 30123, Italy. TEL 39-041-2792910, FAX 39-041-2792917, http://www.regione.veneto.it.

351.4565 ITA
REGIONE UMBRIA. BOLLETTINO UFFICIALE. Text in Italian. w. Supplement avail. **Document type:** *Bulletin, Consumer.*
Related titles: Online - full text ed.
Published by: Regione Umbria, Corso Vannucci 96, Perugia, PG 06121, Italy. TEL 39-0755-043507, FAX 39-0755-043500, http://www.regione.umbria.it.

351 RUS
L452.A2
REGIONOLOGIYA. Text in Russian; Abstracts in English; Summaries in English. 1992. q. RUR 600 for 6 mos. domestic; USD 217 foreign (effective 2011). adv. **Document type:** *Journal, Academic/Scholarly.* **Description:** Focuses on the processes of change in the Russian regions, problems with the current federal structure, the interrelation of federal and local authorities and bodies, as well as regional policy in the spheres of science, education, and culture.
Indexed: RASB.
Published by: Institut Regionologii, ul Bogdana Khmel'nitskogo 39a, Saransk, Mordovia 430005, Russian Federation. TEL 7-342-328614, FAX 7-342-473995. Ed. Aleksandr Sukharev. Circ: 1,500. **Dist. by:** East View Information Services, 10601 Wayzata Blvd, Minneapolis, MN 55305. TEL 952-252-1201, 800-477-1005, FAX 952-252-1202, info@eastview.com, http://www.eastview.com.

351 SWE ISSN 0280-1647
REGISTER OVER GAELLANDE S F S-FOERFATTNINGAR. Text in Swedish. 1974. a., latest 2005.
Published by: Thomson Fakta (Subsidiary of: Thomson Reuters Corp.), Haelsingegatan 43, PO Box 6430, Stockholm, 11382, Sweden. TEL 46-8-58767000, FAX 46-8-58767171, thomsonfakta.info@thomson.com, http://www.thomsonfakta.se.

REGULATION & GOVERNANCE. *see* LAW

REGULATORY FOCUS. *see* MEDICAL SCIENCES

351.93 NZL ISSN 1177-0953
THE REGULATORY REVIEW. Text in English. 2004. 3/yr. free (effective 2009). **Document type:** *Newsletter.* **Description:** Provides information about the Regulatory Policy Team, its work programme, and how they can help you.
Media: Online - full text.
Published by: Ministry of Economic Development, PO Box 1473, Wellington, 6011, New Zealand. TEL 64-4-4720030, FAX 64-4-4734638, info@med.govt.nz.

354.9 AUS ISSN 0728-7216
J905
REMUNERATION TRIBUNAL. ANNUAL REPORT. Text in English. 1981. a., latest 2007. free (effective 2009). back issues avail. **Document type:** *Yearbook, Government.* **Description:** Highlights the activities of the remuneration tribunal for the financial year.
Related titles: Online - full text ed.: free (effective 2009).
—CCC.
Published by: Remuneration Tribunal, PO Box 281, Civic Square, ACT 2608, Australia. TEL 61-2-61217965, FAX 61-2-62184056, enquiry@remtribunal.gov.au.

351.51 CHN
RENMIN ZHENGXIE BAO/JOURNAL OF THE C P P C C. Text in Chinese. 1996. d. CNY 198, USD 92 (effective 2005). **Document type:** *Newspaper, Government.*
Published by: (China, People's Republic. Zhongguo Renmin Zhengzhi Xieshang Huiyi), Renmin Zhengxie Bao, no.1, Alley 6, Jianguo Lu Jianguo, 703, Shaanxi Sheng Zhengxiebangong Dalou, Xi'an, 710001, China. TEL 86-29-87419139, FAX 86-29-87419187. **Dist. by:** China International Book Trading Corp, 35 Chegongzhuang Xilu, Haidian District, PO Box 399, Beijing 100044, China. TEL 86-10-68412045, FAX 86-10-68412023, cibtc@mail.cibtc.com.cn, http://www.cibtc.com.cn.

351.44 FRA ISSN 0765-0078
REPERTOIRE DE L'ADMINISTRATION FRANCAISE. Text in French. 1945. a., latest 1999. EUR 38 newsstand/cover (effective 2009). **Document type:** *Government.*
Former titles: Repertoire Permanent de l'Administration Francaise; France. Delegation Generale a la Recherche Scientifique et Technique. Repertoire Permanent de l'Administration Publique (0080-1186)
Related titles: Microfiche ed.
—INIST.
Published by: Documentation Francaise, 29-31 Quai Voltaire, Paris, Cedex 7 75344, France. FAX 33-1-40157230, http://www.ladocumentationfrancaise.fr. Circ: 10,000.

REPERTOIRE DES TEXTES LEGISLATIFS ET REGLEMENTAIRES ET DES REPONSES AUX QUESTIONS ECRITES CONCERNANT LA REUNION. *see* POLITICAL SCIENCE

REPORT OF REVIEWABLE DEATHS. *see* SOCIAL SERVICES AND WELFARE

351 NZL ISSN 0111-6053
REPORT OF THE ADMINISTRATOR OF TOKELAU. Text in English. a. free. **Document type:** *Government.*
Former titles (until 1981): Tokelau (0110-2761); (until 1977): Report on the Tokelau Islands
Published by: Ministry of Foreign Affairs and Trade, c/o Publication Officer, Private Bag 18-901, Wellington, New Zealand. TEL 64-4-4398000, FAX 64-4-4398511, enquiries@mfat.govt.nz.

351 170 CAN ISSN 1706-1806
JL111.E84
REPORT OF THE ETHICS COUNSELLOR ON THE ACTIVITIES OF THE OFFICE OF THE ETHICS COUNSELLOR/RAPPORT DU CONSEILLER EN ETHIQUE SUR LES ACTIVITES DU BUREAU DU CONSEILLER EN ETHIQUE. Variant title: Ethics Counsellor Annual Report. Text in English, French. 2002. a.
Published by: Canada Office of the Ethics Counsellor, 22nd Floor, 66 Slater St, Ottawa, ON K1A 0C9, Canada. TEL 613-995-0721, FAX 613-995-7308, ethics@ic.gc.ca, http://strategis.ic.gc.ca/epic/internet/inoec-bce.nsf/en/Home.

351 USA ISSN 0145-1928
J87
REPORT OF THE SECRETARY OF THE COMMONWEALTH TO THE GOVERNOR AND GENERAL ASSEMBLY OF VIRGINIA. Text in English. 1925. a. USD 30 (effective 2005).
Related titles: Online - full text ed.: USD 25 (effective 2005).
Published by: Virginia. Secretary of the Commonwealth, PO Box 2454, Richmond, VA 23218-2454. TEL 804-786-2441, socmail@governor.virginia.gov.

351.5957 SGP
REPUBLIC OF SINGAPORE GOVERNMENT GAZETTE. Text in English. 1959. w. SGD 2,548.54 (effective 2007). **Document type:** *Newspaper, Government.*
Related titles: Online - full text ed.
Published by: S N P Corporation Ltd., 1 Kim Seng Promenade, #18-01 Great World City East Tower, Singapore, 237994, Singapore. TEL 65-68269600, FAX 65-68203341, http://www.snpcorp.com.

351 PHL
REPUBLIC OF THE PHILIPPINES. OFFICE OF THE PRESS SECRETARY. BUREAU OF COMMUNICATIONS SERVICES. POLICY STATEMENTS. Text in English. irreg., latest 2003, May.
Formerly: Republic of the Philippines. Department of Public Information. Bureau of National and Foreign Information. Policy Statements
Related titles: Online - full content ed.
Published by: Republic of the Philippines. Office of the Press Secretary. Bureau of Communications Services, PCS Bldg. 310 San Rafael St., Malacanang Palace Complex, San Miguel, Manila 1005, Philippines. TEL 63-2-7342120, FAX 63-2-7342118, mail@bcs.gov.ph.

351 USA
REPUBLICAN LIBERTY; free enterprise, individual freedom & limited government. Text in English. bi-m. **Document type:** *Newsletter.*
Related titles: Online - full content ed.
Published by: Republican Liberty Caucus, 611 Pennsylvania Ave SE #370, Washington, DC 20003. TEL 954-458-7655, rlc@rlc.org, http://www.rlc.org/.

RESEARCH IN PUBLIC POLICY ANALYSIS AND MANAGEMENT. *see* POLITICAL SCIENCE

REVIEW OF BUSINESS RESEARCH. *see* BUSINESS AND ECONOMICS—International Commerce

352.68 USA ISSN 0734-371X
JK765
REVIEW OF PUBLIC PERSONNEL ADMINISTRATION; the journal of public human resource management. Text in English. 1980. q. USD 802, GBP 472 combined subscription to institutions (print & online eds.); USD 786, GBP 463 to institutions (effective 2011). back issues avail.; reprint service avail. from PSC. **Document type:** *Journal, Academic/Scholarly.* **Description:** Focuses on the study and practice of personnel management in public organizations.
Related titles: Online - full text ed.: ISSN 1552-759X. USD 722, GBP 425 to institutions (effective 2011).
Indexed: A12, A13, A17, A22, A26, ABCPolSci, ABIn, B01, B02, B06, B07, B08, B09, B11, B15, B17, B18, CA, CurCont, E01, E07, G04, G06, G07, G08, I05, P07, P34, P42, P48, P51, P53, P54, PAIS, PMA, PQC, PSA, PersLit, SCOPUS, SPAA, SSCI, SociolAb, T02, UAA, V02, W07.
—BLDSC (7794.164000), IE, Ingenta. **CCC.**
Published by: Sage Publications, Inc., 2455 Teller Rd, Thousand Oaks, CA 91320. TEL 805-499-9774, 800-818-7243, FAX 805-499-0871, 800-583-2665, info@sagepub.com. Ed. Stephen E Condrey. Circ: 200 (paid). **Subscr. outside the Americas to:** Sage Publications Ltd., 1 Oliver's Yard, 55 City Rd, London EC1Y 1SP, United Kingdom. TEL 44-20-73248701, FAX 44-20-73248733, subscription@sagepub.co.uk.

REVIEW OF THE ENVIRONMENTAL PERFORMANCE OF THE ELECTRICITY COMMISSION. *see* ENERGY

REVIEW OF URBAN & REGIONAL DEVELOPMENT STUDIES. *see* BUSINESS AND ECONOMICS—International Development And Assistance

353 FIN ISSN 1796-9212
REVIISORI. Text in Finnish. 2007. q. **Document type:** *Magazine, Government.*
Related titles: Online - full text ed.: ISSN 1796-9670.
Published by: Valtiontalouden Tarkastusvirasto/National Audit Office of Finland, Antinkatu 1, PO Box 1119, Helsinki, 00101, Finland. TEL 358-9-4321, FAX 358-9-4325820, kirjaamo@vtv.fi. Ed. Esa Tammelin.

351 ESP ISSN 1133-4797
K19
REVISTA ARAGONESA DE ADMINISTRACION PUBLICA. Text in Spanish. 1992. s-a. EUR 21.04 (effective 2009). back issues avail.
Related titles: Online - full text ed.
Published by: Diputacion General de Aragon, Instituto Aragones de Administracion Publica, Paseo Maria Agustin, 36, Zaragoza, 50004, Spain. TEL 34-976-761396, webadmin@aragob.es, http://www.aragob.es/. Ed. Jose Manuel Aspas.

351 BRA ISSN 1517-2007
REVISTA BRASILEIRA DE ADMINISTRACAO. Text in Portuguese. 1989. 3/yr. **Document type:** *Journal, Government.*
Published by: Conselho Federal de Administracao, SAUS Quadra 1 Lote L, Brasilia, 70070-932, Brazil. TEL 55-61-32181800, FAX 55-61-32181833, cfa@cfa.org.br, http://www.cfa.org.br.

351 BRA ISSN 1516-7429
REVISTA BRASILEIRA DE ADMINISTRACAO PUBLICA E DE EMPRESAS. Text in Portuguese. 1995. s-a. **Document type:** *Journal, Academic/Scholarly.*
Formerly (until 1998): Cadernos de Administracao (1516-1420)
Published by: Universidade de Brasilia, Departamento de Administracao, Instituto Central de Ciencias, Campus Universitario Darcy Ribeiro, Asa Norte, Brasilia, 70910-900, Brazil. TEL 55-61-3072342, FAX 55-61-2748647, adm@unb.br, http://www.unb.br/fa/adm/.

REVISTA BRASILEIRA DE CONTABILIDADE. *see* BUSINESS AND ECONOMICS—Accounting

351 BRA ISSN 2179-8338
▼ ➤ **REVISTA BRASILEIRA DE POLITICAS PUBLICAS/BRAZILIAN JOURNAL OF PUBLIC POLICY.** Text in Portuguese; Text occasionally in English, Spanish. 2011. s-a. bk.rev. abstr.; bibl. back issues avail. **Document type:** *Journal, Academic/Scholarly.* **Description:** Covers the scientific and doctrinal aspects related to the interaction between public policy and law, covering issues related to governance, integration, citizen participation, development and other issues involving the state, society and law.
Related titles: Online - full text ed.: ISSN 2236-1677. free.
Published by: Centro Universitario de Brasilia, SEPN 707/907 Bloco III, Terreo, Campus do UniCEUB, Brasilia, DF 70970-075, Brazil. TEL 55-61-39661350, FAX 55-61-39661200, http://www.uniceub.br/. Ed. Alice Rocha da Silva. Pub., R&P Rodrigo Peres. Circ: 500.

➤ **REVISTA CATALANA DE DRET PUBLIC.** *see* LAW

351 CRI
REVISTA CENTROAMERICANA DE ADMINISTRACION PUBLICA; revista del I C A P. Text in Spanish. 1981. s-a. USD 7 (effective 2000). adv. bk.rev. bibl. **Document type:** *Journal, Government.*
Published by: Instituto Centroamericano de Administracion Publica, Apdo 10025, San Jose, 1000, Costa Rica. TEL 506-234-1011, FAX 506-225-2049. Ed. Rethelny Figueroa de Jain. Adv. contact Lidiette Salas Solano. Circ: 1,500.

351 CHL ISSN 0717-313X
REVISTA CHILENA COOPERACION. Text in Spanish. 1991. q. **Document type:** *Magazine, Government.*
Formerly (until 1995): Cooperacion (0716-9248)
Published by: Gobierno de Chile, Agencia de Cooperacion Internacional (A G C I), Teatinos 950, Piso 11, Santiago, Chile. TEL 56-2-3990900, FAX 56-2-39909922, http://www.agci.cl.

351 CHL ISSN 0717-070X
JL2631
REVISTA CHILENA DE ADMINISTRACION PUBLICA. Text in Spanish. 1994. q. **Document type:** *Magazine, Government.*
Published by: Colegio de Administradores Publicos de Chile, Augustinas 1533, Off 311, Santiago, Chile. TEL 56-2-6986404, FAX 56-2-6716976, cadeministradorespublicos@entelchile.net, http://www.colegioap.cl/Contacto/SolicitudIngreso.asp.

351 BRA ISSN 0034-7612
JA5
REVISTA DE ADMINISTRACAO PUBLICA. Abbreviated title: R A P. Text in Portuguese; Summaries in English. 1967. bi-m. adv. bk.rev. bibl. **Document type:** *Journal, Academic/Scholarly.* **Description:** Previews administrative matters and issues. Analyzes theories and practices.
Related titles: Online - full text ed.: free (effective 2011).
Indexed: C01, SCOPUS.
Published by: Fundacao Getulio Vargas, Editora, Praia de Botafogo 190, 14o Andar, Botafogo, Rio de Janeiro, RJ 22250-900, Brazil. TEL 55-21-25595542, FAX 55-21-25595532, editora@fgv.br, http://www.editora.fgv.br. Ed. Deobrah Monaes Zouain. Adv. contact Else Flejlau. Circ: 2,000.

351 PRI ISSN 0034-7620
JA5
REVISTA DE ADMINISTRACION PUBLICA. Text in Spanish. 1964. s-a. USD 8 to individuals; USD 10 to institutions; USD 6 to students (effective 2000). bk.rev. **Document type:** *Academic/Scholarly.* **Description:** Promotes the study, research and dissemination of information in the field of public affairs and public administration.
Indexed: ABCPolSci, ELLIS.
Published by: Universidad de Puerto Rico, Escuela Graduada de Administracion Publica, Apartado 21839, Estacion U.P.R., Rio Piedras, 00931, Puerto Rico. TEL 787-764-0000, FAX 787-763-7510, admipubl@upracd.upr.clu.edu. Ed. Emerito Rivera Torres. Circ: 1,000.

P

351 MEX ISSN 0482-5209
REVISTA DE ADMINISTRACION PUBLICA/JOURNAL OF PUBLIC ADMINISTRATION. Text in Spanish. 1956. 4/yr. cum.index. **Document type:** *Journal, Trade.*
Indexed: C01.
Published by: Universidad Nacional Autonoma de Mexico, Instituto de Investigaciones Juridicas, Circuito Mario de la Cueva S/N, Ciudad Universitaria, Mexico City, 04510, Mexico. TEL 52-5-56227474 ext 1704, FAX 52-5-6652193, http://www.unam.mx.

351 ESP ISSN 0034-7639
K19
REVISTA DE ADMINISTRACION PUBLICA. Text in Spanish. 1950. 3/yr. EUR 53 (effective 2007). bk.rev. abstr.; bibl. index, cum.index. back issues avail. **Document type:** *Journal, Academic/Scholarly.*
Related titles: CD-ROM ed.: ISSN 1697-2449. 2004; Online - full text ed.: ISSN 1989-0656. 1950; Optical Disk - DVD ed.: ISSN 1697-2457. 2004.
Indexed: A22, ABCPolSci, FLP, FR, IBR, IBSS, IBZ, P09, PAIS, PCI, RASB.
—IE, Infotrieve, INIST. **CCC.**
Published by: Centro de Estudios Politicos y Constitucionales, Plaza de la Marina Espanola 9, Madrid, 28071, Spain. TEL 34-91-5401950, FAX 34-91-5419574, public@cepc.es. Ed. Eduardo Garcia de Enterria. R&P Julian Sanchez Garcia. Circ: 2,000.

351 ROM ISSN 2067-1695
▼ **REVISTA DE ADMINISTRATIE PUBLICA SI POLITICI SOCIALE/PUBLIC ADMINISTRATION AND SOCIAL POLICIES REVIEW.** Text in Romanian, English. 2009. q. **Document type:** *Journal, Academic/Scholarly.*
Related titles: Online - full text ed.: free (effective 2011).
Published by: Universitatea de Vest "Vasile Goldis"/"Vasile Goldis" University Press, B dul Revolutiei 94-96, Arad, 310025, Romania. http://uvvg.ro/editura/.

351.71 URY ISSN 0797-0056
REVISTA DE ADMINISTRATION PUBLICA URUGUAYA. Text in Spanish. 1986. 3/yr. **Document type:** *Magazine, Trade.*
Indexed: FR, PAIS.
Published by: Presidencia de la Republica, Oficina Nacional del Servicio Civil, Luis Alberto de Herrera 3350, piso 1, Montevideo, 11600, Uruguay. TEL 598-2-4872110, http://www.onsc.gub.uy/.

351 PRT ISSN 1646-9119
▼ **REVISTA DE DIREITO PUBLICO.** Text in Portuguese. 2009. s-a. **Document type:** *Journal, Trade.*
Published by: (Instituto de Direito Publico), Edicoes Almedina, SA, Avenida Fernao de Magalhaes, 584, 5o Andar, Coimbra, 3000-174, Portugal. TEL 351-239-851903, FAX 351-239-436267, editora@almedina.net, http://www.almedina.net.

346.1 BRA ISSN 1678-7102
K19
➤ **REVISTA DE DIREITO PUBLICO DA ECONOMIA.** Text in Portuguese. 2003. q. BRL 582 (effective 2008). **Document type:** *Journal, Academic/Scholarly.*
Published by: Editora Forum Ltda, Av Afonso Pena 2770, 16o Andar, Funcionarios, Belo Horizonte, MG, Brazil. TEL 55-31-21214900, FAX 55-31-21214931, editoraforum@editoraforum.com.br, http://www.editoraforum.com.br. Ed. Egon Bockmann Moreira. Pub. Luis Claudio Rodrigues Ferreira. Circ: 300 (paid).

351 ESP ISSN 1137-9022
REVISTA DE GESTION PUBLICA Y PRIVADA. Text in Spanish. 1997. a. EUR 13.52 (effective 2009). **Document type:** *Journal, Academic/Scholarly.*

Published by: (Universidad de Zaragoza, Escuela Universitaria de Estudios Empresariales), Prensas Universitarias de Zaragoza, C/ Pedro Cerbuna 12, Edificio de Ciencias Geologicas, Zaragoza, 50009, Spain. TEL 34-976-761330, FAX 34-976-761063, puz@posta.unizar.es, http://puz.unizar.es, http://puz.unizar.es.

351 ESP ISSN 0212-5056
PC3801
REVISTA DE LLENGUA I DRET. Text in Spanish, Catalan. 1983. bi-m. back issues avail. **Document type:** *Journal, Academic/Scholarly.*
Related titles: Online - full text ed.: ISSN 2013-1453. 1983. free (effective 2011).
Indexed: L&LBA, SCOPUS.
Published by: Escola d'Administracio Publica de Catalunya, C. de Girona, 20, Barcelona, 08010, Spain. TEL 34-93-5672323, FAX 34-93-5672350, publicacions.eapc@gencat.cat, http://www.eapc.es/auto.html.

REVISTA D'ESTUDIS AUTONOMICS I FEDERALS. *see* LAW—Constitutional Law

351 CHL ISSN 0718-0241
JA5
REVISTA ENFOQUES; ciencia politica y administracion publica. Key Title: Enfoques. Text in Spanish. 2003. s-a. **Document type:** *Journal, Academic/Scholarly.*
Related titles: Online - full text ed.: free (effective 2011).
Indexed: PSA.
Published by: Universidad Central de Chile, Toesca 1783, Santiago, Chile. TEL 56-2-5826000, http://www.ucentral.cl. Circ: 300.

▼ **REVISTA EUROPEA DE HISTORIA DE LAS IDEAS POLITICAS Y DE LAS INSTITUCIONES PUBLICAS.** *see* POLITICAL SCIENCE

REVISTA GESTION. *see* BUSINESS AND ECONOMICS—Management

351 MEX
➤ **REVISTA LEGISLATIVA DE ESTUDIOS SOCIALES Y DE OPINION PUBLICA.** Text in Spanish. 2008. s-a. free (effective 2011). **Document type:** *Journal, Academic/Scholarly.* **Description:** Analyzes various topics involving public opinion as it relates to legislative activities.
Published by: Camara de Diputados, Centro de Estudios Sociales y de Opinion Publica, Av Congreso de la Union 66, Edificio I, 1er piso, Colonia El Parque, Mexico D.F., 15969, Mexico. TEL 55-50-360000 ext 55237, FAX 55-50-360000 ext 55251, gustavo.meixueiro@congreso.gob.mx.

613 PRT ISSN 0870-9025
RA511
REVISTA PORTUGUESA DE SAUDE PUBLICA. Text in Portuguese. 1983. a. **Document type:** *Monographic series, Academic/Scholarly.*
Indexed: CA, H05, S02, S03, T02.
Published by: Universidade Nova de Lisboa, Escola Nacional de Saude Publica, Ave Padre Cruz, Lisbon, 1600-560, Portugal. TEL 351-217-512100, FAX 351-217-582754, http://www.ensp.unl.pt/ensp.

351 ROM ISSN 1454-1378
REVISTA TRANSILVANA DE STIINTE ADMINISTRATIVE. Text in Romanian. 1998. s-a. **Document type:** *Journal, Academic/Scholarly.*
Related titles: Online - full text ed.: free (effective 2011); ◆ English ed.: Transylvanian Review of Administrative Sciences. ISSN 1842-2845.
Indexed: A01, CA.
Published by: Universitatea "Babes-Bolyai", Facultatea de Stiinte Politice, Administrative si ale Comunicari, 71 Gen Traian Mosoiu Str, Cluj - Napoca, 400132, Romania.

351 ESP ISSN 0211-9560
K8
REVISTA VASCA DE ADMINISTRACION PUBLICA. Key Title: Herri-Arduralaritzazko Euskal Aldizkaria. Text in Multiple languages. 1981. 3/yr. **Document type:** *Magazine, Academic/Scholarly.*
Indexed: FR, P09, PCI.
—CCC.
Published by: Instituto Vasco de Administracion Publica. Onate, Ave Universidad, s-n, Onati, 20560, Spain. TEL 34-943-782000, arqifalpenak-ivap@ivap.es, http://www.ivap.com/.

351 FRA ISSN 0035-0672
JA11
LA REVUE ADMINISTRATIVE. Text in French. 1948. bi-m. EUR 128 domestic to individuals; EUR 141.92 foreign to individuals; EUR 150 domestic to institutions; EUR 160.30 foreign to institutions (effective 2009). adv. bk.rev.; rec.rev. bibl.; tr.lit. index. reprint service avail. from SCH. **Document type:** *Journal, Academic/Scholarly.*
Related titles: Microform ed.: (from SWZ).
Indexed: A22, BAS, FLP, FR, I13, IBSS, PAIS, PCI, RASB.
—IE, Infotrieve, INIST.
Published by: Presses Universitaires de France, 6 Avenue Reille, Paris, 75685, France. TEL 33-1-58103161, FAX 33-1-45897530, revues@puf.com. Ed. Francois Monnier.

362.6 368.4 BEL ISSN 0035-0834
HD7186
REVUE BELGE DE SECURITE SOCIALE/BELGIAN SOCIAL SECURITY JOURNAL. Text in French; Abstracts in French, Dutch. 1959. q. EUR 19 domestic; EUR 22.50 foreign (effective 2003). bk.rev. abstr.; bibl.; charts. back issues avail. **Document type:** *Magazine, Consumer.* **Description:** Contains articles about social security, social rights and benefits regarding old age, disability, unemployment, judicial protection, medical care and child benefits.
Related titles: ◆ Dutch ed.: De Belgisch Tijdschrift voor Sociale Zekerheid. ISSN 0775-0234.
Indexed: FR, IBR, IBSS, IBZ, ILD, PAIS, RASB, WBSS.
Published by: Ministere Federal des Affaires Sociales de la Sante Publique et de l'Environnement, Service des Publications/Federaal Ministerie van Sociale Zaken, Volksgezondheid en Leefmilieu, Publicaties Dienst, Rue de la Vierge Noire 3C, Zwarte Lievevrouwstraat 3C, Brussels, 1000, Belgium. TEL 32-2-509-8552, FAX 32-2-5098016, roland.vanlaere@minisoc.fed.be, http://www.socialsecurity.fgov.be/bib/homehome.htm. Ed. Jean-Paul Hamoir TEL 32-2-5098019.

353.93 FRA ISSN 0245-9469
REVUE DE DROIT SANITAIRE ET SOCIAL. Text in French. 1958. q. EUR 175 (effective 2009). bk.rev. index. reprint service avail. from SCH. **Document type:** *Journal, Academic/Scholarly.*
Former titles (until 1980): Revue Trimestrielle de Droit Sanitaire et Social (0035-4325); (until 1965): Revue de l'Aide Sociale (0998-5077)
Indexed: A22, FR, IBSS.
—IE. CCC.
Published by: Editions Dalloz, 31-35 rue Froidevaux, Paris, Cedex 14 75685, France. TEL 33-1-40645454, FAX 33-1-40645497, http://www.dalloz.fr. Ed. F Moneger.

351.44 FRA ISSN 0152-7401
JS41
➤ **REVUE FRANCAISE D'ADMINISTRATION PUBLIQUE.** Text in French. 1967. q. EUR 67.50 (effective 2009). adv. bk.rev. abstr.; bibl. back issues avail. **Document type:** *Journal, Academic/Scholarly.* **Description:** Details on all aspects of comparative public administration: city management and international cooperation, immigration and health, civil servants, telecommunications, the environment, foreign relations, modernisation.
Formerly (until 1977): Institut International d'Administration Publique. Bulletin (0020-2355)
Related titles: Microfiche ed.; Online - full text ed.
Indexed: A22, ABCPolSci, CA, DIP, ELLIS, FR, I13, IBR, IBSS, IBZ, P42, PSA, RASB, SCIMP, SCOPUS, T02.
—BLDSC (7902.240000), IE, Infotrieve, Ingenta. CCC.
Published by: Ecole Nationale d'Administration, 1 Rue Sainte-Marguerite, Strasbourg, 67080, France. TEL 33-3-69204860, FAX 33-3-88214439, http://www.ena.fr/accueil.php. Circ: 2,000. **Subscr. to:** Documentation Francaise. **Dist. by:** Documentation Francaise.

351 BEL ISSN 0303-965X
REVUE INTERNATIONALE DES SCIENCES ADMINISTRATIVES. Text in French. 1928. q. EUR 140 (effective 2004). **Document type:** *Journal, Academic/Scholarly.* **Description:** Presents comparative studies and national monographs on international administration, national civil services, controls on central government, administrative reform, public finance, regionalization and the history of administration.
Related titles: ◆ English ed.: International Review of Administrative Sciences. ISSN 0020-8523; Spanish ed.: Revista Internacional de Ciencias Administrativas. ISSN 0255-3635.
Indexed: A22, IBR, IBZ, RASB.
—Infotrieve.
Published by: (Institut International des Sciences Administratives), Bruylant, Rue de la Regence 67, Bruxelles, 1000, Belgium. TEL 32-2-512-9845, FAX 32-2-511-7202. Circ: 5,000.

RHEINLAND-PFALZ HEUTE. *see* PUBLIC ADMINISTRATION—Abstracting, Bibliographies, Statistics

351 USA ISSN 1932-4669
JK3230
THE RHODE ISLAND GOVERNMENT OWNER'S MANUAL. Text in English. 1868. biennial, latest 2008. **Document type:** *Government.*
Formerly (until 1996): State of Rhode Island and Providence Plantations. Manual (0197-4238); (until 1974): Manual, with Rules and Orders, for the Use of the General Assembly of the State of Rhode Island (0190-5309)
Published by: Rhode Island, Secretary of State. Office of Public Information, 82 Smith St, State House Room 38, Providence, RI 02903. TEL 401-222-3983, FAX 401-222-1356, publicinfo@sec.state.ri.us.

351 347 USA ISSN 1071-3395
KFR36
RHODE ISLAND GOVERNMENT REGISTER. Text in English. 1992. m. back issues avail. **Document type:** *Government.* **Description:** Covers executive orders of the Governor, Attorney General opinions, public laws enacted, public utility and environmental orders enacted, banking and insurance agency information, emergency rules, and gubernatorial appointments of state officials and board-commission members.
Published by: LexisNexis (Subsidiary of: Reed Elsevier Group plc), 1016 W Ninth Ave, 1st Fl, King of Prussia, PA 19406. TEL 215 564-1788, 800 448-1515, customer.support@lexisnexis.com.

RIFORMA AMMINISTRATIVA. *see* BUSINESS AND ECONOMICS—Management

RIGHTS REVIEW. *see* SOCIAL SERVICES AND WELFARE

351 NLD ISSN 1872-0005
RIJK VERANTWOORD. Text in Dutch. a.
Published by: (Algemene Rekenkamer, Tweede Kamer de Staten-Generaal), Sdu Uitgevers bv, Postbus 20025, The Hague, 2500 EA, Netherlands. TEL 31-70-3789911, FAX 31-70-3854321, sdu@sdu.nl, http://www.sdu.nl/.

351 USA ISSN 1944-4079
▼ **RISKS, HAZARDS & CRISIS IN PUBLIC POLICY.** Text in English. 2010. q. USD 300 to institutions; USD 900 to corporations (effective 2011). **Document type:** *Journal, Academic/Scholarly.* **Description:** Analyzes the ways that societies deal with both unpredictable and predictable events as public policy questions, which include topics such as governance, loss and liability, administrative practices, agenda setting, and the social and cultural contexts in which hazards, risks and crises are perceived and defined.
Announced as: Crisis & Risk in Public Policy
Media: Online - full text.
—CCC.
Published by: (Policy Studies Organization), Berkeley Electronic Press, 2809 Telegraph Ave, Ste 202, Berkeley, CA 94705. TEL 510-665-1200, FAX 510-665-1201, info@bepress.com, http://www.bepress.com/. Ed. Heather M Bell.

RISKWATCH. *see* BUSINESS AND ECONOMICS—Management

351 ITA ISSN 0035-5763
RIVISTA AMMINISTRATIVA DELLA REPUBBLICA ITALIANA. Text in Italian. 1850. m. EUR 148 (effective 2009). **Document type:** *Magazine, Trade.*
Related titles: Supplement(s): Rivista Amministrativa della Regione Campania. ISSN 1828-5570. 1995. EUR 42 (effective 2007); Rivista Amministrativa della Regione Toscana. ISSN 1828-5589. 2000. EUR 42 (effective 2007); Rivista Amministrativa della Regione Veneto. ISSN 1828-5554. 1995. EUR 42 (effective 2007); Rivista Amministrativa della Regione Lombardia. ISSN 1828-5562. 1995. EUR 42 (effective 2007).
Indexed: DoGi, PAIS.
Published by: Istituto Editoriale Regioni Italiane, Via Barnaba Tortolini 34, Rome, 00197, Italy. TEL 39-06-8070155, FAX 39-06-8077267.

RIVISTA ITALIANA DI COMUNICAZIONE PUBBLICA. *see* COMMUNICATIONS

351 ITA ISSN 0391-190X
JA18
RIVISTA TRIMESTRALE DI SCIENZA DELL'AMMINISTRAZIONE; analisi delle istituzioni e delle politiche pubbliche. Text in English, French, Italian. 1954; N.S. 1972. q. EUR 81 combined subscription domestic to institutions (print & online eds.); EUR 115 combined subscription foreign to institutions (print & online eds.) (effective 2009). adv. bk.rev. bibl.; charts; illus. index. **Document type:** *Journal, Academic/Scholarly.*
Formerly (until 1972): Scienza e la Tecnica della Organizzazione nella Pubblica Amministrazione (0036-8873)
Related titles: Online - full text ed.: ISSN 1972-4942. 2000.
Indexed: A22, DoGi, I13, IBR, IBZ.
—IE.
Published by: Franco Angeli Edizioni, Viale Monza 106, Milan, 20127, Italy. TEL 39-02-2837141, FAX 39-02-26144793, redazioni@francoangeli.it, http://www.francoangeli.it. Circ: 1,500.

351 USA
ROCKEFELLER REPORTS. Text in English. 1991. irreg., latest 2006. price varies. back issues avail. **Document type:** *Monographic series, Government.* **Description:** Covers reports on various topics in government and public administration.
Related titles: Online - full text ed.
Published by: Nelson A. Rockefeller Institute of Government, 411 State St, Albany, NY 12203. TEL 518-443-5522, FAX 518-443-5788, info@rockinst.org. **Dist. by:** State University of New York Press, c/o CUP Services, PO Box 6525, Ithaca, NY 14851. TEL 607-277-2211, 800-666-2211, FAX 607-277-6292, 800-688-2877, orderbook@cupserv.org, http://www.sunypress.edu/.

ROMANIAN JOURNAL OF FISCAL POLICY. *see* BUSINESS AND ECONOMICS—Banking And Finance

351 ROM ISSN 2066-4885
JN26
▼ ➤ **ROMANIAN REVIEW OF EUROPEAN GOVERNANCE STUDIES.** Text in English. 2009. s-a. free (effective 2011). back issues avail. **Document type:** *Journal, Academic/Scholarly.* **Description:** Covers the field of International Relations and European Studies, including governance and multi-level governance, theories of European integration, European policies, civil society and case studies on Central and Eastern Europe.
Media: Online - full text.
Published by: Universitatea "Babes-Bolyai", Centrul "Altiero Spinelli" de Studiere a Organizarii Europene (CASSOE), tr. Mihail Kogalniceanu, nr. 1, Cladirea Centrala, et. III, cam. 305/307, Cluj-Napoca, 400084, Romania. TEL 40-264-405300 ext 5264, contact@cassoe.ro.

➤ **ROUTLEDGE STUDIES IN GOVERNANCE AND PUBLIC POLICY.** *see* POLITICAL SCIENCE

351 CAN ISSN 0714-1211
ROYAL CANADIAN MINT. ANNUAL REPORT. Text in English, French. a.
Formerly (until 1975): Master of Royal Canadian Mint. Report (0381-422X)
Published by: Royal Canadian Mint, 320 Sussex Dr, Ottawa, ON K1A 0GB, Canada. info@mint.ca, http://www.rcmint.ca.

354.71 CAN ISSN 0837-4589
CA1JS74-1
ROYAL CANADIAN MOUNTED POLICE. EXTERNAL REVIEW COMMITTEE. ANNUAL REPORT. Text in Multiple languages. 1987. a.
Published by: (Royal Canadian Mounted Police, External Review Committee), Royal Canadian Mounted Police/Gendarmerie Royale du Canada, 1200 Vanier Parkway, Ottawa, ON K1A 0R2, Canada. TEL 613-998-6307, FAX 613-993-3098, http://www.rcmp.ca.

353.36 CAN ISSN 1483-9679
HV7641
ROYAL CANADIAN MOUNTED POLICE. EXTERNAL REVIEW COMMITTEE. PERFORMANCE REPORT. Text in English, French. 1997. a.
Related titles: Online - full text ed.: ISSN 1490-540X.
Published by: (Royal Canadian Mounted Police, External Review Committee), Treasury Board of Canada Secretariat, Corporate Communications/Secretariat du Conseil du Tresor du Canada, West Tower, Rm P-135, 300 Laurier Ave W, Ottawa, ON K1A 0R5, Canada. TEL 613-995-2855, FAX 613-996-0518, services-publications@tbs-sct.gc.ca, http://www.tbs-sct.gc.ca.

353.36 CAN ISSN 1483-6661
CA1BT31-4 11
ROYAL CANADIAN MOUNTED POLICE. PERFORMANCE REPORT. Text in English, French. 1996. a.
Related titles: Online - full text ed.: ISSN 1490-4128.
Published by: (Royal Canadian Mounted Police/Gendarmerie Royale du Canada), Treasury Board of Canada Secretariat, Corporate Communications/Secretariat du Conseil du Tresor du Canada, West Tower, Rm P-135, 300 Laurier Ave W, Ottawa, ON K1A 0R5, Canada. TEL 613-995-2855, FAX 613-996-0518, services-publications@tbs-sct.gc.ca, http://www.tbs-sct.gc.ca.

354.71 CAN ISSN 0703-8623
CODEN: RGNBEV
THE ROYAL GAZETTE (NEW BRUNSWICK). Text in English, French. w.
Related titles: Online - full content ed.
Published by: Queen's Printer for New Brunswick, 670 King St, Room 117, Fredericton, NB E3B 5H1, Canada. TEL 506-453-2520, FAX 506-457-7899, queens.printer@gnb.ca.

351 USA ISSN 0730-9902
KF4996
RULES ADOPTED BY THE COMMITTEES OF THE HOUSE OF REPRESENTATIVES. Text in English. biennial.
Published by: (U.S. Congress), U.S. Government Printing Office, 732 N Capitol St, NW, Washington, DC 20401. TEL 202-512-1800, FAX 202-512-2104.

RURAL SOCIETY; the journal of research into rural and regional social issues in Australia. *see* SOCIOLOGY

RWANDA. DIRECTION GENERALE DE LA STATISTIQUE. RAPPORT ANNUEL. *see* PUBLIC ADMINISTRATION—Abstracting, Bibliographies, Statistics

354.94 AUS ISSN 1832-8296
S A WATER. ANNUAL REPORT. (South Australian) Text in English. 1929. a. back issues avail. **Document type:** *Report, Trade.* **Description:** Highlights the performance of the department against the Australian Drinking Water Guidelines and provides a comparison to previous years.
Formerly (until 1995): South Australia. Engineering and Water Supply Department. Annual Report (0728-7879)
Related titles: Online - full text ed.: ISSN 1833-9980. free (effective 2009).
Indexed: GeoRef.
Published by: South Australian Water Corporation, EDS Ctr, 108 N Terrace, Adelaide, SA 5000, Australia. TEL 300-650-950, FAX 61-8-70033329, customerservice@sawater.com.au.

351 NLD ISSN 1876-6455
S C (THE HAGUE). (Staatscourant) Text in Dutch. 1814. w. EUR 134; EUR 395 combined subscription (print & online eds.) (effective 2011). **Document type:** *Newspaper, Government.*
Former titles (until 2008): Staatscourant (1569-2531); (until 2001): Nederlandse Staatscourant (1566-7235); (until 2000): Staatscourant (0169-5037); (until 1985): Nederlandsche Staatscourant (0920-1424)
Related titles: Online - full text ed.: EUR 339 (effective 2011).
Published by: Sdu Uitgevers bv, Postbus 20025, The Hague, 2500 EA, Netherlands. TEL 31-70-3789911, FAX 31-70-3854321, sdu@sdu.nl, http://www.sdu.nl/. Ed. Martijn van der Kooij.

351 NLD ISSN 1877-9689
S C REGISTER. (StaatsCourant) Variant title: Register Officiele Publicaties en S C. Text in Dutch. 2002. s-a. EUR 255 (effective 2011).
Formerly (until 2009): Register Parlementaire Publicaties en Staatscourant (1571-0076); Which was formed by the merger of (1988-2002): Register op de Staatscourant en het Staatsblad (0922-341X); (1990-2002): Register Parlementaire Publikaties (0925-5184)
Published by: Sdu Uitgevers bv, Postbus 20025, The Hague, 2500 EA, Netherlands. TEL 31-70-3789911, FAX 31-70-3854321, sdu@sdu.nl, http://www.sdu.nl/. Ed. Dr. D Mentink.

SAIGAI NO JITTAI TO SHOBO NO GENKYO/ANNUAL REPORT OF FIRE AND DISASTER PREVENTION. *see* FIRE PREVENTION

351.4549 SMR ISSN 0036-4223
SAN MARINO (REPUBBLICA) BOLLETTINO UFFICIALE. Text in Italian. 1924. m. bk.rev. index. **Document type:** *Government.* **Description:** Reviews the legislative activity of the Republic of San Marino.
Published by: Dipartimento Affari Istituzionali, San Marino, 47890, San Marino. TEL 39-549-882234. Circ: 1,100 (controlled).

351.4549 SMR
SAN MARINO (REPUBBLICA). DIPARTIMENTO AFFARI ESTERI. NOTIZIA. Text in Italian. 1978. m. free. **Document type:** *Government.*
Formerly: San Marino (Repubblica). Segreteria di Stato per gli Affari Esteri. Notizia; Supersedes (1959-1978): San Marino (Repubblica). Segreteria di Stato per gli Affari Esteri. Notiziario (0558-4477)
Published by: Dipartimento Affari Esteri, Ufficio Stampa, Palazzo Begni - Belluzzi, San Marino, 47890, San Marino. Ed. Pier Roberto De Biagi.

353.63 CAN ISSN 1491-6967
RC261.A1
SASKATCHEWAN CANCER AGENCY. ANNUAL REPORT. Text in English. a.
Former titles (until 1998): Saskatchewan Cancer Foundation. Annual Report (0715-013X); (until 1980): Saskatchewan Cancer Commission. Annual Report (0703-0029); (until 1973): Saskatchewan Cancer Commission. Report (0703-0010)
Published by: Saskatchewan Cancer Agency, 2631 28th Ave, Suite 400, Regina, SK S4S 6X3, Canada. TEL 306-585-1831, FAX 306-584-2733, http://www.scf.sk.ca.

351 CAN ISSN 1701-4018
SASKATCHEWAN CULTURE, YOUTH AND RECREATION. ANNUAL REPORT. Text in English. 1994. a.
Former titles (until 2001): Saskatchewan. Saskatchewan Municipal Affairs, Culture and Housing. Annual Report (1494-9008); (until 1999): Saskatchewan. Saskatchewan Municipal Government. Annual Report (1208-2740); Which was formed by the merger of (1981-1994): Saskatchewan Rural Development. Annual Report (0831-9073); Which was formerly (until 1983): Saskatchewan Rural Affairs. Annual Report (0715-2167); (1991-1994): Saskatchewan. Saskatchewan Community Services. Annual Report (1191-1476); Which was formed by the merger of (1985-1991): Northern Affairs Secretariat. Annual Report (0836-9437); (1910-1991): Saskatchewan. Saskatchewan Community Services. Annual Report (0715-2159); Which superseded in part (in 1981): Saskatchewan Municipal Affairs. Annual Report (0708-5370); Which was formerly (until 1978): Department of Municipal Affairs of the Province of Saskatchewan. Annual Report (0702-0767); (until 1977): Department of Municipal Affairs and of the Community Capital Fund of the Province of Saskatchewan. Annual Report (0701-6387); Which superseded in part (in 1975): Department of Municipal Affairs and of the Municipal Road Assistance Authority of the Province of Saskatchewan. Annual Report (0701-6379); Which was formerly (until 1957): Department of Municipal Affairs of the Province of Saskatchewan. Annual Report (0701-6360)
Published by: Saskatchewan Culture, Youth and Recreation, 1919 Saskatchewan Dr, 4th floor, Regina, SK S4P 3V7, Canada. TEL 306-787-5729, FAX 306-798-0033, info@cyr.gov.sk.ca.

351 CAN ISSN 1910-8648
JL301.A1
SASKATCHEWAN GOVERNMENT RELATIONS. ANNUAL REPORT. Text in English. 2005. a., latest 2006. **Document type:** *Government.*
Supersedes in part (2003-2005): Saskatchewan Government Relations and Aboriginal Affairs. Annual Report (1713-2061)
Published by: Saskatchewan Government Relations, 1855 Victoria Ave, Regina, SK S4P 3T2, Canada. TEL 306-787-2635, info@gr.gov.sk.ca, http://www.gr.gov.sk.ca/default.htm.

351 CAN ISSN 0317-7319
SASKATCHEWAN. OFFICE OF THE OMBUDSMAN. ANNUAL REPORT. Text in English. 1973. a.
Published by: Office of the Ombudsman, 2401 Saskatchewan Dr, Ste 150, Regina, SK S4P 3V7, Canada. TEL 306-787-6211, 800-667-7180, http://www.legassembly.sk.ca/officers/ombuds.htm.

SASKATCHEWAN PROVINCIAL BUDGET. *see* BUSINESS AND ECONOMICS—Public Finance, Taxation

SCHRIFTEN ZUM BAU- UND VERGABERECHT. *see* LAW

351 DEU ISSN 0343-8228
SCHRIFTEN ZUR OEFFENTLICHEN VERWALTUNG UND OEFFENTLICHEN WIRTSCHAFT. Text in German; Summaries in English, French, Russian. 1974. irreg., latest vol.181, 2003. price varies. **Document type:** *Monographic series, Academic/Scholarly.*
Published by: Nomos Verlagsgesellschaft mbH und Co. KG, Waldseestr 3-5, Baden-Baden, 76530, Germany. TEL 49-7221-2104-0, FAX 49-7221-210427, nomos@nomos.de, http://www.nomos.de. Eds. P Friedrich, Peter Eichhorn.

351 DEU ISSN 0720-7506
SCHRIFTEN ZUR VERWALTUNGSWISSENSCHAFT. Text in German. 1975. irreg., latest vol.14, 1999. price varies. **Document type:** *Monographic series, Academic/Scholarly.*
Published by: Duncker und Humblot GmbH, Carl-Heinrich-Becker-Weg 9, Berlin, 12165, Germany. TEL 49-30-7900060, FAX 49-30-79000631, info@duncker-humblot.de.

351 AUT
SCHRIFTENREIHE VERWALTUNGSRECHT. Text in German. 1989. irreg., latest vol.8, 2005. price varies. **Document type:** *Monographic series, Academic/Scholarly.*
Published by: (Institut fuer Foederalismus), Wilhelm Braumueller Universitaets-Verlagsbuchhandlung GmbH, Servitengasse 5, Vienna, 1090, Austria. TEL 43-1-3191159, FAX 43-1-3102805, office@braumueller.at. Ed. Peter Bussjaeger.

SCHRIFTENREIHE ZUM OEFFENTLICHEN RECHT UND ZU DEN POLITISCHEN WISSENSCHAFTEN. *see* POLITICAL SCIENCE

350 DEU
SCHRIFTENREIHE ZUR MODERNISIERUNG DER LANDESVERWALTUNG IN BRANDENBURG. Text in German. 2003. irreg., latest vol.2, 2003. price varies. **Document type:** *Monographic series, Academic/Scholarly.*
Published by: Universitaetsverlag Potsdam, Am Neuen Palais 10, Potsdam, 14469, Germany. TEL 49-331-9774458, FAX 49-331-9774625, ubpub@uni-potsdam.de, http://info.ub.uni-potsdam.de/verlag.htm.

351 DEU ISSN 0342-7722
SCHWARTZSCHE VAKANZEN-ZEITUNG. Text in German. 1871. 3/m. adv. **Document type:** *Bulletin, Trade.*
Published by: Fachbuchhandlung Otto Schwartz GmbH, Annastr 7, Goettingen, 37075, Germany. TEL 49-551-31051, FAX 49-551-372812. adv.: B&W page EUR 1,600, color page EUR 2,440.

342.92 CHE ISSN 1424-1692
DIE SCHWEIZERISCHE KOMMUNAL REVUE. Abbreviated title: S K R. Text in German. 1995. q. CHF 33 domestic; CHF 45 foreign; CHF 11 newsstand/cover (effective 2002). adv. **Document type:** *Magazine, Trade.*
Published by: Trend Verlags AG, Steinenvorstadt 67, Basel, 4001, Switzerland. TEL 41-61-2262626, FAX 41-61-2262600, redaktion@trendverlag.ch, http://www.trendverlag.ch. Ed., Pub. Bruno Ruessli. Adv. contact Barbara Hopf. B&W page CHF 5,100, color page CHF 6,375; trim 210 x 297. Circ: 10,000 (paid and controlled).

351 CHE
SCHWEIZERISCHES ZENTRALBLATT FUER STAATS- UND VERWALTUNGSRECHT. Text in German. m. CHF 138 domestic; CHF 163 foreign (effective 2001). **Document type:** *Bulletin, Trade.*
Formerly: Schweizerisches Zentralblatt fuer Staats- und Gemeindeverwaltung (0036-7990)
—CCC.
Published by: Schulthess Juristische Medien AG, Zwinglipatz 2, Zuerich, 8022, Switzerland. TEL 41-1-2519336, FAX 41-1-2616394, zs.verlag@schulthess.com, http://www.schulthess.com. Circ: 1,800.

354.274 CAN ISSN 1702-3025
SCIENCE AND TECHNOLOGY FOR SUSTAINABLE DEVELOPMENT. 5NR BIENNIAL REPORT/SCIENCES ET LA TECHNOLOGIE AU SERVICE DU DEVELOPPEMENT DURABLE, RAPPORT BISANNUEL DES 5RN. Text in English, French. 1996. biennial.
Former titles (until 2001): Science and Technology for Sustainable Development. Annual Report (1702-3017); (until 1999): Memorandum of Understanding on Science and Technology for Sustainable Development. Annual Report (1493-6569); (until 1998): Annual Report on the Memorandum of Understanding among the Four Natural Resources Departments on Science and Technology for Sustainable Development (1209-4056)
Published by: (Canada. Health Canada/Sante Canada, Canada. Agriculture and Agri-Food Canada, Canada. Natural Resources Canada/Ressources Naturelles Canada, Canada. Fisheries and Oceans Canada), Environment Canada/Environnement Canada, 351 St Joseph Blvd, 18th Fl, Place Vincent Massey, Hull, PQ K1A 0H3, Canada. TEL 819-997-2800, 800-668-6767, FAX 819-953-2225, enviroinfo@ec.gc.ca, http://www.ec.gc.ca.

351 500 600 USA
SCIENCE AND TECHNOLOGY IN CONGRESS (ONLINE). Text in English. 2000. irreg. (3-9/issue). free. back issues avail. **Document type:** *Newsletter, Government.* **Description:** Provides information to Congress on current science and technology issues.
Media: Online - full content.
Published by: American Association for the Advancement of Science, Center for Science, Technology, and Congress, 1200 New York Ave, NW, Washington, DC 20005. TEL 202-289-4950, FAX 202-326-6661.

SCIENCE PROGRESS. *see* SCIENCES: COMPREHENSIVE WORKS

351.411 GBR ISSN 1462-1657
SCOTLAND'S YEAR BOOK. Text in English. 1931. a. GBP 19.50. **Document type:** *Yearbook, Consumer.*
Former titles (until 1997): Scotland's Regions (0305-6562); (until 1974): County and Municipal Year Book for Scotland (0070-1300)
Published by: William Culross & Son Ltd., Queen St, Coupar Angus, Perthshire PH13 9DF, United Kingdom. TEL 44-1828-627266, admin@culross.co.uk, http://www.culross.co.uk/.

351.41 GBR ISSN 1741-1203
SCOTTISH PLANNING POLICY. Text in English. 1993. irreg., latest 2010. **Document type:** *Monographic series, Trade.*
Formerly (until 2002): National Planning Policy Guideline (1350-6153)
—BLDSC (8211.064000). **CCC.**
Published by: The Scottish Government, St. Andrew's House, Regent Rd, Edinburgh, EH1 3DG, United Kingdom. TEL 44-8457-741741, FAX 44-1397-795001, ceu@scotland.gsi.gov.uk.

351 CAN ISSN 1480-5189
JL71
SCOTT'S GOVERNMENT INDEX. Text in English. 1972. 3/yr. CAD 499 domestic; USD 499 foreign (effective 2008). **Document type:** *Directory, Trade.*
Former titles (until 1998): Corpus Government Index (1209-7659); (until 1997): Corpus Administrative Index (0703-7384)
Related titles: CD-ROM ed.: CAD 499 domestic; USD 499 foreign (effective 2008).
Published by: Business Information Group, 12 Concorde Pl, Ste 800, Toronto, ON M3C 4J2, Canada. TEL 416-442-2122, 800-668-2374, FAX 416-442-2191, orders@businessinformationgroup.ca.

352.38 USA ISSN 1939-1986
SECRECY NEWS. Text in English. 2000. irreg. (2-3/wk.). **Document type:** *Bulletin, Trade.* **Description:** Challenges excessive secrecy in government and research, and promotes public oversight and free exchange of information in science and technology research in government, defense and intelligence.
Formed by the merger of (1991-2000): Secrecy & Government Bulletin (Print) (1061-0340); (1991-2000): Secrecy & Government Bulletin (Online) (1939-1994)
Media: Online - full content.
Published by: Federation of American Scientists, 1725 DeSales St, NW, 6th Fl, Washington, DC 20036. TEL 202-546-3300, FAX 202-675-1010, fas@fas.org. Ed. Steven Aftergood.

351 USA ISSN 1930-4439
HV6432.4
SEMIANNUAL REPORT TO THE CONGRESS. Text in English. 2003. s-a. **Document type:** *Government.*
Related titles: Online - full text ed.: ISSN 1930-4447.
Published by: U.S. Department of Homeland Security, Office of Inspector General, Washington, DC 20528.

SENATE ELECTION LAW GUIDEBOOK. *see* LAW

354.71 CAN ISSN 0826-7839
HN101
SENATE OF CANADA. STANDING SENATE COMMITTEE ON SOCIAL AFFAIRS, SCIENCE AND TECHNOLOGY. PROCEEDINGS. Text in English, French. 1984. irreg., latest vol.66, 2002.
Related titles: Online - full text ed.: ISSN 1498-5578.
Published by: (Senate of Canada, Standing Committee on Social Affairs, Science and Technology), Supply and Services Canada, Printing and Publishing, 270 Albert St, Ottawa, ON K1A 0S9, Canada.

351 DEU ISSN 0722-5725
SENIOREN ZEITSCHRIFT. Text in German. 1974. q. back issues avail. **Document type:** *Government.*
Published by: Stadt Frankfurt, Dezernat Soziales, Jugend und Wohnungswesen, Eschersheimer Landstr 42-44, Frankfurt Am Main, 60322, Germany. TEL 069-21233405. Ed. Maria Schuster.

353.537 354.08 CAN ISSN 1191-6737
SENIORS' GUIDE TO FEDERAL PROGRAMS AND SERVICES. Text in English. 1988. a. **Description:** Includes information on disease prevention, nutrition, safety, consumer products and legal matters, housing and transportation, employment and pensions, travel and recreation opportunities, and volunteer and cultural activities.
Related titles: Online - full content ed.: ISSN 1493-7476.
Published by: Health Canada, Division of Aging and Seniors, Locator 1908A1, Ottawa, ON K1A 1B4, Canada. TEL 613-952-7606, FAX 613-957-9938, seniors@hc-sc-gc.ca, http://www.hc-sc.gc.ca/seniors-aines/.

351 AUS ISSN 1832-2166
SERVICE TASMANIA BOARD. ANNUAL REPORT. Text in English. 2004. a. free (effective 2009). back issues avail. **Document type:** *Government.* **Description:** Provides achievements of Tasmania, Department of Premier and Cabinet, Service Board for each financial year.
Media: Online - full text.
Published by: Tasmania, Department of Premier and Cabinet, Service Board, GPO Box 123, Hobart, TAS 7001, Australia. TEL 61-3-62327148, FAX 61-3-62336534, STU@dpac.tas.gov.au, http://www.service.tas.gov.au.

SERVICES AND BENEFITS. *see* MILITARY

SERVICES ET AVANTAGES. *see* MILITARY

351.4 GBR ISSN 0266-8343
J301 CODEN: SINDES
SESSIONAL INFORMATION DIGEST. Text in English. 1984. a. GBP 5.50 per issue (effective 2009). back issues avail. **Document type:** *Bulletin, Government.*
—BLDSC (8253.159100). **CCC.**
Published by: (House of Commons, Public Information Office), The Stationery Office, St Crispins, Duke St, Norwich, NR3 1PD, United Kingdom. TEL 44-1603-622211, FAX 44-870-6005533, customer.services@tso.co.uk, http://www.tso.co.uk. Ed. Mary Durkin.

352.53 USA ISSN 1068-5715
SET-ASIDE ALERT. Text in English. 1993. bi-w. USD 497 (effective 2011). back issues avail. **Document type:** *Newsletter, Trade.* **Description:** Covers US federal and state policies and programs for contracting with small and small, disadvantaged businesses and the 8(a) set-aside program.
Related titles: Online - full text ed.
Indexed: A26, G06, G07, G08, I05.
—CCC.
Published by: Business Research Services, Inc., 7720 Wisconsin Ave, Ste 213, Bethesda, MD 20814. TEL 301-229-5561, 800-845-8420, FAX 301-229-6133, brspubs@sba8a.com, http://www.sba8a.com/.

SETTING COURSE; a congressional management guide. *see* POLITICAL SCIENCE

SEX OFFENDER LAW REPORT. *see* LAW—Criminal Law

352.4 SYC
SEYCHELLES. MINISTRY OF FINANCE. BUDGET ADDRESS. Text in Creoles and Pidgins, English, French. a. USD 50.
Formerly: Seychelles. Office of the President. Budget Address
Published by: Ministry of Finance, PO Box 313, Victoria, Mahe, Seychelles. TEL 248-382000, FAX 248-225265, TELEX 2363 FINTUR SZ.

P

351.5357 UAE
AS-SIJIL ASH-SHAHRI LI-AHDATH DAWLAT AL-IMARAT AL-ARABIYYAH AL-MUTTAHIDAH/MONTHLY RECORD FOR THE EVENTS OF THE UNITED ARAB EMIRATES. Text in Arabic. 1979. m. **Description:** Reports activities of the rulers of the U.A.E., legislative, civil service, cabinet, and economic developments, and international concerns.
Published by: Ministry of Information and Culture, Information Department, PO Box 17, Abu Dhabi, United Arab Emirates. TEL 453000. Circ: 1,000 (controlled).

351.5957 SGP ISSN 0129-3109
JQ745.S5
SINGAPORE GOVERNMENT DIRECTORY. Text in English. 1960. biennial. USD 50 per issue (effective 2008). **Document type:** *Directory, Government.*
Formerly (until 1981): Republic of Singapore Government Directory; (until 1961): Colony of Singapore. Directory
Published by: (Singapore. Ministry of Culture), Marshall Cavendish Business Information Pty. Ltd. (Subsidiary of: Times Publishing Group), Times Centre, 1 New Industrial Rd, Singapore, 536196, Singapore. TEL 65-6213-9288, FAX 65-6285-0161, bizinfo@sg.marshallcavendish.com, http://www.marshallcavendish.com/.

351 ESP ISSN 1139-9929
SISTEMA ADMINISTRATIVO. AVANCE MENSUAL. Text in Spanish. 1996. m. **Document type:** *Directory, Trade.*
Published by: La Ley (Subsidiary of: Wolters Kluwer N.V.), Calle Collado Mediano 9, Las Rozas, Madrid 28230, Spain. FAX 34-902-420012, clientes@laley.net, http://www.laley.net.

351 MKD ISSN 0354-1622
KKZ5401.5
SLUZBEN VESNIK NA REPUBLIKA MAKEDONIJA. Text in Macedonian. 1945. irreg.
Formerly (until 1991): Sluzben Vesnik na Socijalisticka Republika Makedonija (0037-7147)
Indexed: RASB.
Address: 29 Noemvri 10-a, Skopje, Macedonia.

351 USA ISSN 0273-4982
Q11
SMITHSONIAN YEAR. Text in English. 1965. a. free (effective 2004). **Document type:** *Magazine, Trade.*
Formerly (until 1979): Smithsonian Institution. Programs and Activities (0190-714X); Which superseded in part (in 1977): Smithsonian Year (0096-8404); Which was formed by the merger of (1846-1965): Smithsonian Institution. Board of Regents. Annual Report (0096-4093); (1907-1965): United States National Museum. Annual Report (0273-0243); Which was formerly (until 1951): Report on the Progress and Condition of the United States National Museum (0198-6104)
Indexed: P30, R04.
—Linda Hall. **CCC.**
Published by: Smithsonian Institution, Office of Public Affairs, 900 Jefferson Dr, Rm 2410, Washington, DC 20560. TEL 202-357-2627.

SOCIAAL - ECONOMISCH BELEID. *see* POLITICAL SCIENCE

352.745 CAN ISSN 1483-7471
CA1BT31-4 73
SOCIAL SCIENCES AND HUMANITIES RESEARCH COUNCIL OF CANADA. PERFORMANCE REPORT. Text in English, French. 1997. a.
Related titles: Online - full text ed.: ISSN 1490-5108.
Published by: (Social Sciences and Humanities Research Council of Canada), Treasury Board of Canada Secretariat, Corporate Communications/Secretariat du Conseil du Tresor du Canada, West Tower, Rm P-135, 300 Laurier Ave W, Ottawa, ON K1A 0R5, Canada. TEL 613-995-2855, FAX 613-996-0518, services-publications@tbs-sct.gc.ca, http://www.tbs-sct.gc.ca.

SOCIETY OF GOVERNMENT ECONOMISTS. BULLETIN. *see* BUSINESS AND ECONOMICS

351 GBR ISSN 0038-0121
HD82
➤ **SOCIO-ECONOMIC PLANNING SCIENCES.** Text in English. 1967. 4/yr. EUR 893 in Europe to institutions; JPY 118,400 in Japan to institutions; USD 995 elsewhere to institutions (effective 2012). bk.rev. charts; illus.; stat.; abstr. index. back issues avail.; reprints avail. **Document type:** *Journal, Academic/Scholarly.* **Description:** Designed to the application of quantitative analysis to interdisciplinary decision problems arising in the area of socioeconomic planning and development.
Related titles: Microfiche ed.: (from MIM); Microfilm ed.: (from PQC); Online - full text ed.: ISSN 1873-6041 (from IngentaConnect, ScienceDirect).
Indexed: A01, A03, A08, A22, A26, ABCPolSci, AHCMS, AIAP, ASCA, B01, B02, B06, B07, B09, B17, B18, BPIA, BusI, CA, CMCI, CPM, CREJ, EAA, ESPM, FR, G04, G06, G07, G08, GEOBASE, I05, IBSS, JCQM, MCR, MEA&I, ManagCont, ORMS, P06, P30, P34, P42, PAIS, PSA, QC&AS, RASB, RiskAb, S02, S03, SCOPUS, SOPODA, SSA, SUSA, SociolAb, T&II, T02.
—BLDSC (8319.576000), IE, Infotrieve, Ingenta, INIST. **CCC.**
Published by: Pergamon (Subsidiary of: Elsevier Science & Technology), The Blvd, Langford Ln, East Park, Kidlington, Oxford OX5 1GB, United Kingdom. TEL 44-1865-843000, FAX 44-1865-843010, JournalsCustomerServiceEMEA@elsevier.com. Ed. Barnett R Parker. **Subscr. to:** Elsevier BV, Radarweg 29, PO Box 211, Amsterdam 1000 AE, Netherlands. TEL 31-20-4853757, FAX 31-20-4853432, http://www.elsevier.nl.

➤ **SORKINS DIRECTORY OF BUSINESS & GOVERNMENT (CHICAGO EDITION).** *see* BUSINESS AND ECONOMICS—Production Of Goods And Services

➤ **SOURCE BOOK OF AMERICAN STATE LEGISLATION.** *see* POLITICAL SCIENCE

351 USA ISSN 1932-1309
JK468.P76
THE SOURCEBOOK TO PUBLIC RECORD INFORMATION. Text in English. 1999. a., latest 10th ed. USD 49 per issue (effective 2011). 1972 p./no.; **Document type:** *Handbook/Manual/Guide, Consumer.*
Formed by the merger of (1992-1999): Sourcebook of County Court Records; (199?-1999): Sourcebook of State Public Records; Sourcebook of Federal Courts, U.S. District and Bankruptcy; Sourcebook of County Asset/Lien Records
Published by: B R B Publications, Inc., PO Box 27869, Tempe, AZ 85285. TEL 800-929-3811, FAX 800-929-4981, brb@brbpub.com, http://www.brbpub.com.

353.5 ZAF
SOUTH AFRICA. DIRECTORATE: INTERNAL PEACE INSTITUTIONS. ANNUAL REPORT. Text in English. 1993. a. **Document type:** *Government.*
Published by: (South Africa. Directorate: Internal Peace Institutions), South Africa. Government Printing Works, 149 Bosman St, Private Bag X85, Pretoria, 0001, South Africa.

SOUTH AFRICA. OFFICE OF THE AUDITOR-GENERAL. REPORT OF THE AUDITOR-GENERAL. *see* BUSINESS AND ECONOMICS—Public Finance, Taxation

352.88 ZAF
SOUTH AFRICA. OFFICE OF THE OMBUDSMAN. ANNUAL REPORT. Text in English. a. **Document type:** *Government.*
Published by: (South Africa. Office of the Ombudsman), South Africa. Government Printing Works, 149 Bosman St, Private Bag X85, Pretoria, 0001, South Africa.

SOUTH AFRICA. STATISTICS SOUTH AFRICA. FINAL SOCIAL ACCOUNTING MATRIX FOR SOUTH AFRICA. *see* PUBLIC ADMINISTRATION—Abstracting, Bibliographies, Statistics

SOUTH AFRICA. STATISTICS SOUTH AFRICA. STATISTICAL RELEASE. CENTRAL GOVERNMENT: REVENUE OF THE STATE REVENUE AND OTHER REVENUE ACCOUNTS. *see* PUBLIC ADMINISTRATION—Abstracting, Bibliographies, Statistics

SOUTH AFRICA. STATISTICS SOUTH AFRICA. STATISTICAL RELEASE. FINANCIAL STATISTICS OF LOCAL AUTHORITIES AND REGIONAL SERVICES COUNCILS AND JOINT SERVICES BOARDS. *see* PUBLIC ADMINISTRATION—Abstracting, Bibliographies, Statistics

SOUTH AFRICA. STATISTICS SOUTH AFRICA. STATISTICAL RELEASE. NATIONAL GOVERNMENT EXPENDITURE. *see* PUBLIC ADMINISTRATION—Abstracting, Bibliographies, Statistics

351.68 ZAF
SOUTH AFRICAN GOVERNMENT DIRECTORY. Text in English. s-a. **Document type:** *Directory.* **Description:** Contains information on ministries, deputy ministries, national government departments, provincial governments, and other government organizations.
Published by: South African Communication Service, Private Bag X745, Pretoria, 0002, South Africa. TEL 27-12-3142105, FAX 27-12-3233831. R&P E C Muller.

351 AUS ISSN 1832-9055
SOUTH AUSTRALIA. DEPARTMENT OF TRANSPORT ENERGY AND INFRASTRUCTURE. ANNUAL REPORT. Text in English. 2000. a., latest 2007. **Document type:** *Government.*
Former titles (until 2004): South Australia. Department of Transport and Urban Planning. Annual Report (1448-7357); (until 2003): South Australia. Department for Transport, Urban Planning and the Arts. Annual Report (1445-6672); Which incorporated (in 19??): South Australia. Passenger Transport Board. Annual Report
Related titles: CD-ROM ed.: ISSN 1832-9063. 2003; Online - full text ed.: ISSN 1445-6680.
Published by: South Australia, Department for Transport, Energy & Infrastructure, PO Box 1, Walkerville, SA 5081, Australia. TEL 61-8-82048200, FAX 61-8-82048216, dtei.enquiries@saugov.sa.gov.au, http://www.transport.sa.gov.au.

351.94 AUS ISSN 0038-2906
THE SOUTH AUSTRALIAN GOVERNMENT GAZETTE. Text in English. 1839. w. AUD 274; AUD 5.40 per issue (effective 2008). adv. charts; stat. s-a. index. back issues avail. **Document type:** *Newspaper, Trade.*
Formerly (until 1839): South Australian Gazette and Colonial Register
Related titles: Online - full text ed.
Indexed: AESIS.
Published by: Government Publishing SA, Department of the Premier and Cabinet, Plaza Level, Riverside Bldg, North Terrace, PO Box 9, Adelaide, SA 5000, Australia. TEL 61-8-82071045, FAX 61-8-82071040.

352.14 USA
JS39
SOUTH DAKOTA COUNTY COMMENT. Text in English. 1953. m. USD 10. adv. bk.rev. **Document type:** *Newsletter.*
Former titles: South Dakota Counties County Government; (until 1992): S D A C C County Comment (1049-7838); (until vol.36, no.5, 1990): South Dakota Journal of County Government
Published by: South Dakota Association of Counties, 207 E Capitol, Ste 203, Pierre, SD 57501. TEL 605-224-4554. Ed. Dennis Henson. R&P, Adv. contact Bernie Ripperger. Circ: 1,000.

SOZIAL- UND WIRTSCHAFTSPOLITIK. *see* POLITICAL SCIENCE

351 BRA ISSN 1807-3131
JL2429.A8
SP.GOV. Text in Portuguese. 2004. q. **Document type:** *Government.*
Related titles: Online - full text ed.: ISSN 1807-314X.
Published by: Fundacao do Desenvolvimento Administrativo, Rua Cristiano Viana, 428 CEP 05411-902, Sao Paulo, Brazil. FAX 55-11-30819082, caf@fundap.sp.gov.br. Ed. Cristina Penz.

351 ESP ISSN 0212-033X
SPAIN. BOLETIN OFICIAL DEL ESTADO. Text in Spanish. 1936. d. (except Sun.). index. **Document type:** *Government.*
Formed by the 1936 merger of: Spain. Junta de Defensa Nacional. Boletin Oficial (0212-128X); Gaceta de la Republica (0212-1271); Which was formerly: Gaceta de Madrid (0212-1220)
Related titles: CD-ROM ed.: ISSN 1138-7432; Microfiche ed.: ISSN 1138-4018; Microfilm ed.: ISSN 1138-400X (from BHP, PQC); Online - full text ed.; Optical Disk ed.: ISSN 1695-9299. 2003; Optical Disk - DVD ed.: ISSN 1577-8681. 2001.
Indexed: RASB.
Published by: Agencia Estatal Boletin Oficial del Estado, Imprenta Nacional, Avenida de Manoteras 54, Madrid, 28050, Spain. TEL 34-91-3841747, FAX 34-91-3841769, info@boe.es, http://www.boe.es.

351 ESP ISSN 0212-5897
HJ60
SPAIN. MINISTERIO DE ECONOMIA Y HACIENDA. BOLETIN OFICIAL. Text in Spanish. 1850. w. **Document type:** *Bulletin, Government.*
Formerly (until 1983): Spain. Ministerio de Hacienda. Boletin Oficial (0211-7592)
Related titles: CD-ROM ed.: ISSN 2171-4584. 2008.
Published by: Ministerio de Economia y Hacienda, Alcala 9, Madrid, 28071, Spain. TEL 34-91-5958348, FAX 34-91-5958869, http://www.minhac.es.

351 USA ISSN 1082-3417
SPECIAL DATA ISSUE. Text in English. 1987. irreg., latest 2005. price varies. **Document type:** *Monographic series, Trade.* **Description:** Provides current information on the management and functions of local government web site.
Related titles: Online - full content ed.
Published by: International City/County Management Association, 777 N Capitol St NE, Ste 500, Washington, DC 20002. TEL 202-289-4262, 800-745-8780, FAX 202-962-3500, info@icma.org, http://icma.org/en/icma/home.

351 CAN ISSN 1910-8737
SPECIAL SENATE COMMITTEE ON SENATE REFORM. PROCEEDINGS (ONLINE EDITION). Text in English. 2006. irreg. **Document type:** *Government.*
Media: Online - full text. **Related titles:** ◆ Print ed.: Special Senate Committee on Senate Reform. Proceedings (Print Edition). ISSN 1910-8052; French ed.: Deliberations du Comite Senatorial Special sur la Reforme du Senat. ISSN 1910-8745.
Published by: Senate of Canada, Special Senate Committee on Senate Reform (Subsidiary of: Senate of Canada), Senate Reform, The Senate, Ottawa, ON K1A 0A4, Canada. TEL 613-990-0088, FAX 613-947-2104, senreform@sen.parl.gc.ca, http://www.parl.gc.ca/common/Committee_SenHome.asp?Language=E&Parl=39&Ses=1&comm_id=599.

351 CAN ISSN 1910-8052
JL155
SPECIAL SENATE COMMITTEE ON SENATE REFORM. PROCEEDINGS (PRINT EDITION). Text in English. 2006. irreg. **Document type:** *Government.*
Related titles: ◆ Online - full text ed.: Special Senate Committee on Senate Reform. Proceedings (Online Edition). ISSN 1910-8737.
Published by: Senate of Canada, Special Senate Committee on Senate Reform (Subsidiary of: Senate of Canada), Senate Reform, The Senate, Ottawa, ON K1A 0A4, Canada. TEL 613-990-0088, FAX 613-947-2104, senreform@sen.parl.gc.ca, http://www.parl.gc.ca/common/Committee_SenHome.asp?Language=E&Parl=39&Ses=1&comm_id=599.

351.43 DEU ISSN 1862-250X
SPEYERER SCHRIFTEN ZUR VERWALTUNGSWISSENSCHAFT. Text in German. 2006. irreg., latest vol.8, 2009. price varies. **Document type:** *Monographic series, Academic/Scholarly.*
Published by: Peter Lang GmbH (Subsidiary of: Peter Lang Publishing Group), Eschborner Landstr 42-50, Frankfurt Am Main, 60489, Germany. TEL 49-69-7807050, FAX 49-69-78070550, zentrale.frankfurt@peterlang.com. Ed. Rainer Pitschas.

SPORT LOKAAL. *see* SPORTS AND GAMES

351.5493 LKA
SRI LANKA GOVERNMENT GAZETTE. Text in English. 1802. w. **Description:** Official government bulletin.
Published by: Government Press, P O Box 507, Colombo, Sri Lanka. TEL 1-93611. Circ: 54,000.

351 DEU ISSN 1618-0909
STAATLICHE FOERDERUNG DER ALTERSVORSORGE UND VERMOEGENSBILDUNG. Text in German. 1981. irreg. looseleaf. price varies. **Document type:** *Monographic series, Trade.*
Formerly (until 2001): Kommentar zur Staatlichen Sparfoerderung und Vermoegensbildung (0934-7992)
Published by: Erich Schmidt Verlag GmbH & Co. (Berlin), Genthiner Str 30 G, Berlin, 10785, Germany. TEL 49-30-2500850, FAX 49-30-250085305, esv@esvmedien.de, http://www.esv.info.

351 NLD ISSN 1570-8470
STAATSALMANAK. Text in Dutch. 1860. a. EUR 147.84 (effective 2009). adv.
Former titles (until 2002): Staatsalmanak voor het Koninkrijk der Nederlanden (0921-7428); (until 1958): Officiele Staatsalmanak voor het Koninkrijk der Nederlanden (1873-8214); (until 1954): Staatsalmanak voor het Koningrijk der Nederlanden (1872-8472)
Published by: Sdu Uitgevers bv, Postbus 20025, The Hague, 2500 EA, Netherlands. TEL 31-70-3789911, FAX 31-70-3854321, sdu@sdu.nl, http://www.sdu.nl/. adv.: B&W page EUR 1,795, color page EUR 2,695; trim 170 x 244. Circ: 3,900.

351 DEU ISSN 1862-3204
STAATSRECHT.INFO. Text in German. 2004. m. **Document type:** *Journal, Academic/Scholarly.*
Formerly (until 2006): Der Staat, das Recht und Mehr (1860-6997)
Media: Online - full content.
Address: c/o Johannes Rux, Universitaetsstr 150, NA 6/36, Bochum, 44780, Germany. TEL 49-234-3226818, FAX 49-234-3214359. Ed. Johannes Rux.

STAB; jurisprudentie tijdschrift op het gebied van ruimtelijke ordening, milieubeheer en water. *see* HOUSING AND URBAN PLANNING

351 DEU ISSN 0942-3672
STADT DUISBURG. GESCHAEFTSBERICHT (YEAR). Text in German. 1963. a. free. charts; illus.; maps; stat. back issues avail. **Document type:** *Bulletin, Government.* **Description:** Publishes articles of interest to urban researchers, practitioners, planners and policy makers.
Formerly (until 1989): Stadt Duisburg. Verwaltungsbericht (0932-8955)
Published by: Stadt Duisburg Amt fuer Statistik Stadtforschung und Europaangelegenheiten, Die Oberbuergermeisterin, Bismarckstr 150-158, Duisburg, 47049, Germany. TEL 49-203-283-4502, FAX 49-203-283-4404, a.rauser@stadt-duisburg.de, http://www.uni-duisburg.de/duisburg/statistik. Circ: 2,000.

STADT DUISBURG. MATERIALEN ZUR STADTFORSCHUNG. *see* PUBLIC ADMINISTRATION—Abstracting, Bibliographies, Statistics

STADT DUISBURG. PROGRAMM-INFORMATIONS-DIENST. FOERDERPROGRAMME; Foerderprogramme des Bundes, des Landes Nordrhein-Westfalen und der Europaeischen Union in Duisburg. *see* PUBLIC ADMINISTRATION—Abstracting, Bibliographies, Statistics

STADT FREIBURG IM BREISGAU. AMT FUER STATISTIK UND EINWOHNERWESEN. JAHRESHEFT. *see* PUBLIC ADMINISTRATION—Abstracting, Bibliographies, Statistics

351 DEU ISSN 0940-0990
STADT UND GEMEINDE. Text in German. 1946. 10/yr. EUR 78; EUR 7.50 newsstand/cover (effective 2010). adv. bk.rev. index. **Document type:** *Magazine, Trade.*
Former titles (until 1990): Staedte- und Gemeindebund (0342-7706); (until 1973): Staedtebund (0038-903X)
Published by: (Deutscher Staedte- und Gemeindebund), Winkler & Stenzel GmbH, Schulze-Delitzsch-Str. 35, Burgwedel, 30938, Germany. TEL 49-5139-89990, FAX 49-5139-899950, info@winkler-stenzel.de, http://www.winkler-stenzel.de. adv.: B&W page EUR 1,510, color page EUR 2,410; trim 170 x 262. Circ: 5,950 (paid and controlled).

STADTFORSCHUNG UND STATISTIK; Zeitschrift des Verbandes Deutscher Staedtestatistiker. *see* PUBLIC ADMINISTRATION—Abstracting, Bibliographies, Statistics

351 DEU ISSN 0342-6106
STAEDTE- UND GEMEINDERAT; die Fachzeitschrift fuer Kommunal- und Landespolitik in Nordrhein-Westfalen. Text in German. 1947. 10/yr. EUR 49; EUR 5 newsstand/cover (effective 2006). adv. **Document type:** *Magazine, Trade.*
Former titles (until 1971): Der Gemeinderat (0342-6092); (until 1955): Gemeindetag Westfalen (0342-6084); (until 1949): Gemeindetag Nordrhein-Westfalen (0342-6076)
Published by: Krammer Verlag Duesseldorf AG, Goethestr 75, Duesseldorf, 40237, Germany. TEL 49-211-91493, FAX 49-211-9149450, krammer@krammerag.de, http://www.krammerag.de. adv.: color page EUR 1,890, B&W page EUR 1,080; trim 210 x 297. Circ: 2,108 (paid and controlled).

STAFO-NYTT. *see* BUSINESS AND ECONOMICS—Labor And Industrial Relations

THE STAKEHOLDER; public values in public service. *see* POLITICAL SCIENCE

STANDING ORDERS OF THE HOUSE OF COMMONS INCLUDING THE CONFLICT OF INTEREST CODE FOR MEMBERS/REGLEMENT PROVISOIRE DE LA CHAMBRE DES COMMUNES. *see* LAW—Constitutional Law

STANDING SENATE COMMITTEE ON NATIONAL FINANCE. PROCEEDINGS/DELIBERATIONS DU COMITE SENATORIAL PERMANENT DES FINANCES NATIONALES. *see* BUSINESS AND ECONOMICS—Public Finance, Taxation

351 CAN ISSN 1702-0921
UA 600.
STANDING SENATE COMMITTEE ON NATIONAL SECURITY AND DEFENCE. PROCEEDINGS/DELIBERATIONS DU COMITE SENATORIAL PERMANENT DE LA SECURITE NATIONALE ET DE LA DEFENSE. Text in English, French. 2001. irreg.
Formerly (until 2001): Standing Senate Committee on Defence and Security. Proceedings (1700-4012)
Related titles: Online - full content ed.: ISSN 1702-093X.
Published by: Senate of Canada, Standing Committee on National Security and Defence, The Senate, Ottawa, ON K1A 0A4, Canada. TEL 613-990-0088, 800-267-7362, FAX 613-947-2104, defence@sen.parl.gc.ca, http://sen.parl.gc.ca.

351 DNK ISSN 1901-5518
STAT & KOMMUNE INDKOEB. Text in Danish. 1982. 10/yr. DKK 235 (effective 2009). adv. **Document type:** *Trade.*
Former titles (until 2006): Stat, Amt og Kommune Information (1395-1297); (until 1994): Amt og Kommune Information (0903-2800)
Published by: Danja Media, Rundforbivej 2, Vedbaek, 2950, Denmark. TEL 45-43-433121, FAX 45-45-650599, saki@saki.dk, http://www.saki.dk. Ed., Adv. contact Dan Morrison. page DKK 15,900; 266 x 360. Circ: 7,534 (controlled).

351 NOR ISSN 0803-0103
JN7461
STAT & STYRING; tidsskrift for politikk og forvaltning. Text in Norwegian. 1956. q. NOK 350 to individuals; NOK 730 to institutions; NOK 270 to students (effective 2010). back issues avail. **Document type:** *Journal, Academic/Scholarly.* **Description:** Focuses on government and leadership issues.
Formerly (until 1991): Administrasjonsnytt (0400-518X)
Related titles: Online - full text ed.: ISSN 0809-750X. NOK 830 (effective 2010).
Published by: Universitetsforlaget AS/Scandinavian University Press (Subsidiary of: Aschehoug & Co.), Sehesteds Gate 3, P O Box 508, Sentrum, Oslo, 0105, Norway. TEL 47-24-147500, FAX 47-24-147501, post@universitetsforlaget.no, http://www.universitetsforlaget.no. Ed. Jan Erik Grindheim. Circ: 1,200.

351 USA
JK2403
STATE & LOCAL GOVERNMENT (WASHINGTON); guide to current issues and activities. Text in English. 1985. a. USD 32.95 per issue (effective 2008). reprints avail. **Description:** Contains thirty nine articles, which cover significant issues facing state and local government.
Formerly (until 2000): State Government (Washington) (0888-8590)
Related titles: Online - full text ed.
Published by: C Q Press, Inc. (Subsidiary of: Sage Publications, Inc.), 2300 N St, NW, Ste 800, Washington, DC 20037. TEL 202-729-1900, FAX 800-380-3810, customerservice@cqpress.com. Ed. Kevin B Smith.

353.3 364.4 USA
STATE & LOCAL GOVERNMENT INFORMATION SECURITY. Text in English. 2004. irreg. USD 400 combined subscription (print & CD-ROM eds.) (effective 2008). **Document type:** *Newsletter, Trade.* **Description:** Designed to help managers and officers to quickly and easily implement a comprehensive, written information security program.
Formerly (until 2005): State and Local Government Homeland Security Update (1553-6602)
Related titles: CD-ROM ed.
Published by: Sheshunoff Information Services Inc. (Subsidiary of: Thompson Publishing Group), 807 Las Cimas Pky, Ste 300, Austin, TX 78746. TEL 512-472-2244, 800-456-2340, FAX 512-305-6575, info.sis@sheshunoff.com. Ed. Iris Arnold.

328 USA
STATE CAPITOLS REPORT; the weekly briefing on news from the 50 states. Text in English. w. USD 1,200. **Document type:** *Newsletter.* **Description:** Reports on the legislation, leadership, politics, personalities of all 50 state capitols.
Related titles: Fax ed.; Online - full text ed.
Published by: (Information for Public Affairs, Inc.), State Net, 2101 K St, Sacramento, CA 95816. TEL 916-444-0840, FAX 916-446-5369. Ed. John Borland. Pub. Jud Clark.

351.769 USA ISSN 0585-1173
JK5330
STATE DIRECTORY OF KENTUCKY. Text in English. 1966. a. USD 18 to individuals; USD 15 to libraries. **Document type:** *Directory, Government.*
Published by: Directories, Inc., PO Box 988, Crestwood, KY 40014-0988. TEL 502-241-8256. Ed. Mary Mary McKay Wright. Pub. Mary Mckay Wright. Circ: 5,000 (controlled).

351 USA
STATE FISCAL BRIEF (NEW YORK). Text in English. 1993. m. back issues avail. **Document type:** *Bulletin, Government.*
Published by: Nelson A. Rockefeller Institute of Government, 411 State St, Albany, NY 12203. TEL 518-443-5522, FAX 518-443-5788, info@rockinst.org, http://www.rockinst.org.

328.744 USA ISSN 1070-7719
JK3101
STATE HOUSE WATCH. Text in English. 1982. 20/yr. USD 75 to individuals; USD 125 to institutions. adv. **Document type:** *Newsletter.* **Description:** Covers Massachusetts human service legislation and budgets, including housing, health care, children and families, senior citizens, disabilities and mental health.
Published by: Massachusetts Human Service Coalition, Inc., 37 Temple Pl, 3rd Fl, Boston, MA 02111. TEL 617-482-6119, FAX 617-695-1295. Ed. Susan Cahill. R&P Jen Douglas. Adv. contact Susan Grue. Circ: 700.

STATE LEGISLATIVE REPORT (DENVER). *see* POLITICAL SCIENCE

STATE LEGISLATIVE REPORT (WASHINGTON, DC). *see* WOMEN'S INTERESTS

328 USA ISSN 0898-7297
JK2495
STATE LEGISLATIVE SOURCEBOOK; a resource guide to legislative information in the fifty states. Text in English. 1985. a. (Jan.). USD 177 (effective 2006). **Document type:** *Directory, Government.* **Description:** Contains sources of information on legislatures in the 50 states, D.C. and Puerto Rico. Includes where to get copies of bills, bill subscription services, tracking and monitoring services, legislative websites.
Published by: Government Research Service, PO Box 2067, Topeka, KS 66601-2067. TEL 785-232-7720, FAX 785-232-1615. Ed. Lynn Hellebust.

320 USA ISSN 1521-8457
STATE NET CAPITOL JOURNAL; news & views from the 50 states. Text in English. 1998. w. free to qualified personnel (effective 2010). back issues avail. **Document type:** *Magazine, Consumer.* **Description:** Provides a comprehensive look at the issues and politics driving state governments all over the country.
Media: E-mail. **Related titles:** Fax ed.; Online - full text ed.: free (effective 2010).
Published by: State Net, 2101 K St, Sacramento, CA 95816. TEL 916-444-0840, 800-726-4566, FAX 916-446-5369, info@statenet.com. Ed. Rich Ehisen.

352.38 USA ISSN 0099-2410
Z1223.5.L7
STATE OF LOUISIANA PUBLIC DOCUMENTS. Key Title: Public Documents (Baton Rouge). Text in English. 1948. s-a. free. **Document type:** *Bibliography.*
Published by: State Library, Recorder of Documents, State Library of Louisiana, Box 131, Baton Rouge, LA 70821. TEL 504-342-4929, FAX 504-342-3547. Ed. Stacey S Hathaway Bell. Circ: 300.

351.93 NZL ISSN 1177-3812
THE STATE OF OUR FISHERIES. Variant title: New Zealand. Ministry of Fisheries. Annual Summary. Text in English. 2006. a. **Document type:** *Report, Trade.* **Description:** Reports on the management of New Zealand's fisheries now and into the future.
Published by: New Zealand Ministry of Fisheries, ASB Bank House, 101-103 The Terrace, PO Box 1020, Wellington, New Zealand. TEL 64-4-4702600, FAX 64-4-4702601, comms@fish.govt.nz.

351.73025 USA ISSN 0899-2207
JK2403
STATE YELLOW BOOK; who's who in the executive, and legislative branches of the 50 state governments. Text in English. 1975. q. USD 475 (effective 2008). illus. Index. **Document type:** *Directory, Trade.* **Description:** Provides contact information for 53,000 state officials, legislators and administrators in governor's offices, key departments and bureaus, boards and commissions and state assemblies.
Former titles (until 1989): State Information Book (0896-8128); State Information and Federal Region Book
Related titles: CD-ROM ed.; Online - full text ed.
—CCC.
Published by: Leadership Directories, Inc., 104 Fifth Ave, 2nd Fl, New York, NY 10011. TEL 212-627-4140, FAX 212-645-0931, info@leadershipdirectories.com. Ed. Leslie M Godfrey. Circ: 3,800.

351 USA ISSN 0091-1402
JK6655
STATEHOUSE OBSERVER. Text in English. 1972. q. free. stat.; illus. **Document type:** *Newsletter, Government.*
Related titles: Microfiche ed.
Published by: State Personnel Department, PO Box 94905, Lincoln, NE 68509. TEL 402-471-4112. Ed., R&P Kitty Policky. Circ: 18,000.

351 SWE ISSN 0375-250X
J406 CODEN: SOUTBE
STATENS OFFENTLIGA UTREDNINGAR. Variant title: Government Official Reports. S O U. Text in Swedish. 1922. irreg. price varies. **Document type:** *Monographic series, Government.*
Related titles: Online - full text ed.; ◆ Series: Kunskapslaeget paa Kaernavfallsomraadet. ISSN 0284-6373.
Indexed: INIS AtomInd.
Published by: Regeringskansliet Kommitteservice, Karlavaegen 30, Stockholm, 10333, Sweden. TEL 46-8-4051000. **Subscr. to:** Fritzes Offentliga Publikationer. http://www.fritzes.se.

351.77 616.07 SWE ISSN 0282-4434
STATENS STRAALSKYDDSINSTITUT. S S I-RAPPORT. Text mainly in Swedish; Text occasionally in English. 1985. irreg., latest 2007. price varies. back issues avail. **Document type:** *Monographic series, Government.*
Formed by the merger of (1978-1984): Statens Straalskyddsinstitut. Kvartalsrapport (0281-1421); (1979-1984): Statens Straalskyddsinstitut. Arbetsdokument (0281-1359)
Related titles: Online - full text ed.: 2000.
Published by: Statens Straalskyddsinstitut/Swedish Radiation Protection Authority, Solna Strandvaeg, Stockholm, 17116, Sweden. TEL 46-8-7297100, FAX 46-8-7297108, ssi@ssi.se.

STATISTICAL REVIEW OF GOVERNMENT IN UTAH. *see* PUBLIC ADMINISTRATION—Abstracting, Bibliographies, Statistics

351.71 CAN ISSN 1483-6289
CA1BT31-4 12
STATISTICS CANADA. PERFORMANCE REPORT. Text in English, French. 1996. a.
Related titles: Online - full text ed.: ISSN 1490-3474.
Published by: (Canada. Statistics Canada/Statistique Canada), Treasury Board of Canada Secretariat, Corporate Communications/Secretariat du Conseil du Tresor du Canada, West Tower, Rm P-135, 300 Laurier Ave W, Ottawa, ON K1A 0R5, Canada. TEL 613-995-2855, FAX 613-996-0518, services-publications@tbs-sct.gc.ca.

351 310 USA ISSN 2151-7509
▼ ➤ **STATISTICS, POLITICS, AND POLICY.** Text in English. 2010. a. USD 375 per issue to institutions; USD 1,125 per issue to corporations (effective 2010). **Document type:** *Journal, Academic/Scholarly.* **Description:** Presents research articles that explore statistical thinking and methods applied to public policy issues as well as commentary pieces and innovative policy ideas on public issues.
Media: Online - full text.
Published by: Berkeley Electronic Press, 2809 Telegraph Ave, Ste 202, Berkeley, CA 94705. TEL 510-665-1200, FAX 510-665-1201, info@bepress.com.

➤ **STATISTISCHE INFORMATION/INFORMATIONS STATISTIQUES**; Katalog der verfuegbaren Publikationen zur Bundesstatistik. *see* PUBLIC ADMINISTRATION—Abstracting, Bibliographies, Statistics

➤ **STATISTISCHE NACHRICHTEN DER STADT NUERNBERG.** *see* PUBLIC ADMINISTRATION—Abstracting, Bibliographies, Statistics

➤ **STATISTISCHES JAHRBUCH DER STADT NUERNBERG.** *see* PUBLIC ADMINISTRATION—Abstracting, Bibliographies, Statistics

➤ **STATISTISCHES JAHRBUCH FUER DIE BUNDESREPUBLIK DEUTSCHLAND.** *see* PUBLIC ADMINISTRATION—Abstracting, Bibliographies, Statistics

➤ **STATISTISCHES JAHRBUCH RHEINLAND-PFALZ.** *see* PUBLIC ADMINISTRATION—Abstracting, Bibliographies, Statistics

➤ **STATISTISCHES JAHRBUCH SCHLESWIG-HOLSTEIN.** *see* PUBLIC ADMINISTRATION—Abstracting, Bibliographies, Statistics

351 NOR ISSN 1503-9358
STATSNOEKKELEN (YEAR); din veiviser i stat og kommune. Text in Norwegian. 2004. a. **Document type:** *Directory, Consumer.*
Published by: Argus A/S, Parkveien 51 A, Oslo, 0256, Norway. TEL 47-21-513100, FAX 47-21-513102, info@argusgruppen.no, http://www.argusmedia.com.

351 BEL ISSN 1377-4204
STATUUTENZAKBOEKJE OVERHEIDSPERSONEEL. Text in Dutch. 1991. a. EUR 71.99 (effective 2003). **Document type:** *Trade.*
Formerly (until 2000): Ambtenarenzakboekje (1377-4190)
Published by: Kluwer Uitgevers (Subsidiary of: Wolters Kluwer Belgique), Ragheno Business Park, Motstraat 30, Mechelen, B-2800, Belgium. TEL 32-15-800-94571, info@kluwer.be, http://www.kluwer.be. Eds. Frank Franceus, Martine Van Sande, Paul Berckx.

STEDELIJKE EN REGIONALE VERKENNINGEN. *see* HOUSING AND URBAN PLANNING

STEFAN CEL MARE UNIVERSITY OF SUCEAVA. FACULTY OF ECONOMICS AND PUBLIC ADMINISTRATION. THE ANNALS. *see* BUSINESS AND ECONOMICS

351 AUT ISSN 0039-1050
STEIRISCHE GEMEINDE-NACHRICHTEN. Text in German. 1948. m. adv. bk.rev. charts; stat. index.
Published by: Steiermaerkischer Gemeindebund, Burgring 18, Graz, St 8010, Austria. Ed. Dr. Hermine Jarz.

STEPPING UP. *see* LABOR UNIONS

336.2 DEU ISSN 0178-2096
DIE STEUER-WARTE. Text in German. 1921. 10/yr. EUR 39.90; EUR 4.90 newsstand/cover (effective 2009). **Document type:** *Journal, Trade.*
Published by: Deutsche Steuer-Gewerkschaft, Friedrichstr 169-170, Berlin, 10117, Germany. TEL 49-30-206256650, FAX 49-30-206256601, stgv@dstg-verlag.de.

351 ITA ISSN 1126-5825
STORIA AMMINISTRAZIONE COSTITUZIONE. Text in Italian. 1993. a. **Document type:** *Journal, Academic/Scholarly.*
Published by: Istituto per la Scienza dell' Amministrazione Pubblica (I S A P), Piazza Castello 3, Milan, 20121, Italy. TEL 39-02-86464455, FAX 39-02-86464464, isapmi@tin.it, http://www.isapistituto.it.

STRATEGIC AUDIT OF VICTORIAN GOVERNMENT AGENCIES' ENVIRONMENTAL MANAGEMENT SYSTEMS. *see* ENVIRONMENTAL STUDIES

▼ **STRATEGIC BEHAVIOR AND THE ENVIRONMENT.** *see* ENVIRONMENTAL STUDIES

351.71 GBR ISSN 0264-1496
STRATHCLYDE PAPERS ON GOVERNMENT AND POLITICS. Text in English. 1983. irreg., latest vol.120, 2003. GBP 4 per issue (effective 2009). back issues avail. **Document type:** *Monographic series.*

P

Published by: University of Strathclyde, Department of Government, McCance Bldg, 16 Richmond St, Glasgow, G1 1XQ, United Kingdom. TEL 44-141-5482733, FAX 44-141-5525677, contact-government@strath.ac.uk. Ed. Robert Johns.

352.4 GBR ISSN 0266-0172
STRATHCLYDE REGIONAL COUNCIL. ANNUAL REPORT & FINANCIAL STATEMENT. Text in English. 1980. a. free.
Formerly: Strathclyde's Budget (0260-8065)
Published by: Strathclyde Regional Council, Public Relations Department, Strathclyde House, 20 India St, Glasgow, G2 4PF, United Kingdom. Ed. Neil McIntosh. Circ: 10,000.

351.624 SDN
SUDAN JOURNAL OF ADMINISTRATION AND DEVELOPMENT. Text in Arabic, English. 1965. a.
Published by: Institute of Public Administration, P O Box 1492, Khartoum, Sudan.

352.49624 SDN
SUDAN. MINISTRY OF FINANCE AND NATIONAL ECONOMY. ANNUAL BUDGET SPEECH, PROPOSALS FOR THE GENERAL BUDGET AND THE DEVELOPMENT BUDGET. Text in English. a. **Document type:** *Government.*
Published by: Ministry of Finance and National Economy, P O Box 298, Khartoum, Sudan.

352.49624 SDN
SUDAN. MINISTRY OF FINANCE AND NATIONAL ECONOMY. GENERAL BUDGET: REVIEW, PRESENTATION AND ANALYSIS. Text in English. irreg. **Document type:** *Government.*
Published by: Ministry of Finance and National Economy, P O Box 298, Khartoum, Sudan.

352.5 CAN ISSN 1481-4935
HF5437.A2
SUMMIT; Canada's magazine on public sector planning. Text in English. 1998 (Nov.). q. CAD 21.95 domestic; USD 21.95 in United States (effective 2006). **Document type:** *Magazine, Trade.* **Description:** Contains up-to-date news on the latest trends in public sector purchasing.
Related titles: Online - full text ed.
Indexed: A12, A13, A17, ABIn, B01, B02, B15, B17, B18, C03, CBCABus, CPerI, G04, G08, I05, P21, P48, P51, P53, P54, PQC.
—CCC.
Published by: The Summit Group, 100-263 Holmwood Ave, Ottawa, ON K1S 2P8, Canada. TEL 613-688-0763, 800-575-1146, FAX 613-688-0767.

SURVEY OF STATE RETIREMENT SYSTEMS. *see* BUSINESS AND ECONOMICS—Labor And Industrial Relations

328 SWE ISSN 0346-5470
J406
SVERIGES RIKSDAG. AARSBOK. Variant title: Riksdagens Aarsbok. Text in Swedish. 1906. a. free. illus.; stat. **Document type:** *Yearbook, Government.* **Description:** Summaries of the Parliamentary desicions in Sweden.
Former titles (until 1974): Riksdag (0346-5527); (until 1949): Lagtima Riksdagen
Related titles: Audio cassette/tape ed.
Published by: Sveriges Riksdag/The Swedish Parliament, Stockholm, 10012, Sweden. TEL 46-8-7864000, FAX 46-8-7865871, rigsdagsinformation@riksdagen.se. **Dist. by:** Sveriges Riksdag, Tryckeriexpeditionen.

351 SWE ISSN 1653-0942
SVERIGES RIKSDAG. RAPPORTER. Text in Swedish. 1994. irreg., latest 2007. back issues avail. **Document type:** *Monographic series, Government.*
Formerly (until 2005): Sveriges Riksdag. Utredningar (1104-6414)
Related titles: Online - full text ed.
Published by: Sveriges Riksdag/The Swedish Parliament, Stockholm, 10012, Sweden. TEL 46-8-7864000, FAX 46-8-7865871, rigsdagsinformation@riksdagen.se.

328 USA
T I P R O TARGET NEWSLETTER. Text in English. irreg. (approx. every 6 wks.). USD 5 per issue to non-members. adv. **Document type:** *Newsletter.* **Description:** Reports on industry-related topics, with emphasis on government legislation and rulings.
Published by: Texas Independent Producers & Royalty Owners Association, 515 Congress Ave, Ste 1910, Austin, TX 78701. TEL 512-477-4452, FAX 512-476-8070. Ed. Chris Thibodeau. adv.: B&W page USD 895, color page USD 1,000; trim 11 x 8.5. Circ: 2,500 (paid).

351 FRA ISSN 1254-5678
T P DE FRANCE. ANNALES. (Travaux Publics) Text in French. 1881. m. adv. bk.rev. bibl.; illus.
Formerly (until 1989): T P Annales (0039-8462)
Published by: (Federation Nationale des Travaux Publics et des Syndicats Affilies), Centre de l'Industrie Francaise des Travaux Publics, 3 rue de Berri, Paris, 75008, France. Circ: 1,600.

T R'S LAST-MILE TELECOM REPORT. *see* COMMUNICATIONS

354.71 CAN ISSN 1709-2841
HE215.A15
T S B ANNUAL REPORT TO PARLIAMENT/B S T RAPPORT ANNUEL AU PARLEMENT. (Transportation Safety Board) Text in English, French. 1984. a.
Former titles (until 1994): Bureau de la Securite des Transports du Canada. Rapport Annuel (1186-2270); (until 1990): Canadian Aviation Safety Board. Annual Report (0837-2616)
Published by: Transportation Safety Board of Canada, 200 Promenade de Portage, Place du Centre 4th Fl, Gatineau, PQ KIA 1K8, Canada. TEL 819-994-3741, FAX 819-997-2239.

351 352 USA ISSN 2152-3851
JK2403
▼ **TAKING SIDES: CLASHING VIEWS ON STATE AND LOCAL GOVERNMENT ISSUES.** Text in English. forthcoming 2011. biennial. USD 26 per issue (effective 2010). **Document type:** *Academic/Scholarly.* **Description:** Presents differing views and controversies on state and local government and public administration issues for students.
Published by: McGraw-Hill Higher Education (Subsidiary of: McGraw-Hill Companies, Inc.), 2 Penn Plaza, New York, NY 10121. TEL 212-512-2000, http://catalogs.mhhe.com/mhhe/home.do.

351 AUS ISSN 1446-2508
KU2562
TALKING NATIVE TITLE. Text in English. 2001. q. free (effective 2009). back issues avail. **Document type:** *Newsletter, Government.* **Description:** Covers the native Australian issues and native title claims.
Formed by the merger of (1999-200?): South Australia Native Title News; (1997-2001): Queensland Native Title News; (1999-2001): Victoria/Tasmania Native Title News; (1998-2001): N S W Native Title News
Related titles: Online - full text ed.
Published by: National Native Title Tribunal, Media Unit, GPO Box 9973, Perth, W.A. 6848, Australia. TEL 61-8-92687272, 800-640-501, FAX 61-8-92687299, enquiries@nntt.gov.au.

352 FIN ISSN 1458-557X
TAMPERE. Text in Finnish. 1993. q. **Document type:** *Magazine, Consumer.*
Related titles: Online - full text ed.: ISSN 1458-6991.
Published by: Tampereen Kaupunki/City of Tampere, PO Box 487, Helsinki, 33101, Finland. TEL 358-20-7166030, FAX 358-20-7166710. Ed. Aila Rajamaki.

351.678 TZA ISSN 0856-0323
TANZANIA OFFICIAL GAZETTE. Text in English, Swahili. 1940. w. TZS 33,300. **Document type:** *Newspaper, Government.*
Published by: Ministry of Information and Broadcasting, The Government Bookshop, PO Box 1801, Dar Es Salaam, Tanzania. TEL 255-51-32038, TELEX GOVTSHOP. Ed. H Hadji. Circ: 6,000.

TARIEFADVIES VOOR DE LEVERING VAN WARMTE AAN KLEINVERBRUIKERS. *see* ENERGY

328 MEX
TARJETA; analisis y debate parlamentario. Text in Spanish. 1994. bi-m.
Published by: Enkidu Editores S.A. de C.V., YACATAS 236-1, Col Narvarte, Mexico City, DF 03020, Mexico. TEL 525-6398381. Ed. Mario Valencia Hernandez.

TASCHENBUCH DES OEFFENTLICHEN LEBENS; Deutschland. *see* PUBLIC ADMINISTRATION—Abstracting, Bibliographies, Statistics

TASCHENBUCH DES OEFFENTLICHEN LEBENS. EUROPA UND INTERNATIONALE ZUSAMMENSCHLUESE. *see* PUBLIC ADMINISTRATION—Abstracting, Bibliographies, Statistics

351 DEU
TASCHENBUCH FUER DEN OEFFENTLICHEN DIENST (TOED). Text in German. 1965. 3 base vols. plus updates 9/yr. looseleaf. EUR 192 base vol(s).; EUR 58 updates (effective 2010). adv. **Document type:** *Trade.*
Former titles: B A T: Taschenbuch fuer den Oeffentlichen Dienst (0082-1888); Taschenbuch fuer den Oeffentilichen Dienst
Related titles: CD-ROM ed.; Online - full text ed.
Published by: Walhalla Fachverlag, Haus an der Eisernen Bruecke, Regensburg, 93042, Germany. TEL 49-941-56840, FAX 49-941-5684111, walhalla@walhalla.de. Ed. Joerg Effertz. adv.: B&W page EUR 460. Circ: 3,500 (controlled).

351.43 DEU
TASCHENLEXIKON STAATS- UND VERWALTUNGSRECHTLICHER ENTSCHEIDUNGEN. Text in German. irreg. price varies. **Document type:** *Monographic series, Trade.*
Published by: Erich Schmidt Verlag GmbH & Co. (Berlin), Genthiner Str 30 G, Berlin, 10785, Germany. TEL 49-30-2500850, FAX 49-30-250085305, esv@esvmedien.de, http://www.esv.info.

351 AUS ISSN 1448-9023
TASMANIA. DEPARTMENT OF PREMIER AND CABINET. ANNUAL REPORT. Text in English. 1989. a. free (effective 2009). **Document type:** *Government.* **Description:** Provides achievements of Tasmania, Department of Premier and Cabinet for each financial year.
Related titles: Online - full text ed.: ISSN 1448-9031.
Published by: Tasmania, Department of Premier and Cabinet, GPO Box 123, Hobart, TAS 7001, Australia. TEL 61-3-62333738, FAX 61-3-62332769, Secretary@dpac.tas.gov.au.

TASMANIA. DEPARTMENT OF PRIMARY INDUSTRIES AND WATER. ANNUAL REPORT. *see* ENVIRONMENTAL STUDIES

630 AUS ISSN 1327-7081
TASMANIA. DEPARTMENT OF PRIMARY INDUSTRIES, WATER AND ENVIRONMENT. ANNUAL REPORT. Text in English. 1928. a. back issues avail. **Document type:** *Government.* **Description:** Covers the operations of the department and financial statements.
Former titles: Tasmania. Department of Primary Industry and Fisheries. Annual Report; Tasmania. Department of Primary Industry. Annual Report; (until 1990): Tasmania. Department of Agriculture. Annual Report (0082-1993)
Related titles: Online - full text ed.
Published by: Department of Primary Industry & Fisheries, Corporate Planning Unit, 1 Franklin Wharf, GPO Box 44, Hobart, TAS 7001, Australia. TEL 61-3-62338451, FAX 61-3-62335482, pi.enquiries@dpiwe.tas.gov.au, http://www.dpiwe.tas.gov.au/.

351 AUS ISSN 1448-9066
TASMANIA. OFFICE OF THE STATE SERVICE COMMISSIONER. ANNUAL REPORT. Text in English. 2001. a. free (effective 2009). back issues avail. **Document type:** *Government.* **Description:** Provides achievements of Tasmania, Office of the State Service Commissioner for each financial year.
Related titles: Online - full text ed.: ISSN 1448-9074. 2003.
Published by: Tasmania, Office of the State Service Commissioner, PO Box 621, Hobart, TAS 7001, Australia. TEL 61-3-62333637, FAX 61-3-62332693, ossc@dpac.tas.gov.au.

351.946 AUS ISSN 0039-9795
TASMANIAN GOVERNMENT GAZETTE. Text in English. 1836. w. adv. back issues avail. **Document type:** *Newspaper, Government.*
Former titles (1907): Tasmania. Hobart Gazette; (until 1881): Hobart Town Gazette
Related titles: Online - full text ed.
Published by: Printing Authority of Tasmania, GPO Box 307, Hobart, TAS 7000, Australia. TEL 61-3-62333289, 800-030-940, FAX 61-3-62164294, sales@thepat.com.au, http://www.pat.tas.gov.au/. Circ: 1,400.

351 AUS ISSN 1834-3023
TASMANIAN STATE SERVICE EVALUATION REPORT. Text in English. 2006. a. **Document type:** *Government.*
Related titles: Online - full text ed.: ISSN 1834-3031.
Published by: Tasmania, Office of the State Service Commissioner, Level 2/144 Macquarie St, Hobart, TAS 7001, Australia. TEL 61-3-62333637, FAX 61-3-62332693, ossc@dpac.tas.gov.au, http://www.ossc.tas.gov.au.

352.13 USA
TAUBMAN CENTER FOR STATE AND LOCAL GOVERNMENT. REPORT. Text in English. 1985. a. free (effective 2006).
Former titles (until 1998): Taubman Center for State and Local Government. Annual Report; (until 1991): State and Local News; (until 1990): Taubman Center for State and Local Government. Newsletter (1046-2198); (until 1989): State, Local, and Intergovernmental Report (0895-8041)
Related titles: Online - full content ed.
Published by: Harvard University, Taubman Center for State and Local Government, 79 John F Kennedy St, Cambridge, MA 02138. TEL 617-495-2199, FAX 617-496-1722, http://www.ksg.havard.edu/taubmancenter. Eds. Arnold M Howitt, Phineas Baxandall. Circ: 6,000.

TAXATION AND REVENUE POLICIES - STATE CAPITALS. *see* BUSINESS AND ECONOMICS—Public Finance, Taxation

TE MANGAI PAHO. ANNUAL REPORT. *see* COMMUNICATIONS

351.0711 GBR ISSN 0144-7394
JF1338.A2
➤ **TEACHING PUBLIC ADMINISTRATION.** Text in English. 1979. 2/yr. bk.rev. **Document type:** *Journal, Academic/Scholarly.* **Description:** Covers conceptions, approaches, and practices in public administration education, teaching and training.
Formerly: Public Administration Teacher
Indexed: P34.
—BLDSC (8614.332000), IE, Ingenta.
Published by: (Joint University Council, Public Administration Committee, Sheffield Hallam University, Policy Research Centre), Sage Publications Ltd. (Subsidiary of: Sage Publications, Inc.), 1 Oliver's Yard, 55 City Rd, London, EC1Y 1SP, United Kingdom. TEL 44-20-73248500, FAX 44-20-73248600, info@sagepub.co.uk, http://www.uk.sagepub.com/home.nav. Ed. Michael Hunt. R&P Jenny Chambers. Circ: 250.

➤ **TECHNISCH-BESTUURSKUNDIGE VERKENNINGEN.** *see* ENVIRONMENTAL STUDIES

351 342.066 NLD ISSN 1877-4512
▼ **TEKSTUITGAVE UITVOERING SOCIALE ZEKERHEID EN BESTUURSRECHT.** Variant title: Uitvoering Sociale Zekerheid en Bestuursrecht. Text in Dutch. 2009. s-a. EUR 50 per vol. (effective 2011).
Published by: Kluwer B.V. (Subsidiary of: Wolters Kluwer N.V.), Postbus 23, Deventer, 7400 GA, Netherlands. TEL 31-570-673449, FAX 31-570-691555, info@kluwer.nl, http://www.kluwer.nl.

▼ **TEKSTUITGAVE VEILIGHEID EN CRISISBEHEERSING.** *see* CRIMINOLOGY AND LAW ENFORCEMENT—Security

▼ **TEKSTUITGAVE WETGEVING SOCIALE VERZEKERINGEN.** *see* INSURANCE

328.71 CAN ISSN 1200-3654
TELEVISION AND THE HOUSE OF COMMONS. Text in English. 1990. a. CAD 16.50 (effective 2006).
Published by: Library of Parliament, Parliamentary Research Branch, Information Service, Ottawa, ON K1A 0A9, Canada. TEL 613-992-4793, 866-599-4999, info@parl.gc.ca, http://www.parl.gc.ca.

351.768 USA
TENNESSEE COUNTY NEWS. Text in English. 1980. bi-m. USD 10. adv. **Document type:** *Newspaper.*
Published by: Tennessee County Services Association, 226 Capitol Blvd, Ste 700, Nashville, TN 37219. Ed., Adv. contact Kelly Thompson. Pub. Bob Worksley. Circ: 4,000.

351.768 USA ISSN 0194-1240
THE TENNESSEE JOURNAL; the weekly insiders newsletter on Tennessee government, politics & business. Text in English. 1974. w. USD 247 (effective 2008); subscr. includes Tennessee Tax Guide. back issues avail. **Document type:** *Newsletter, Trade.* **Description:** Gives an insider's view of Tennessee government and politics.
Published by: M. Lee Smith Publishers LLC, 5201 Virginia Way, PO Box 5094, Brentwood, TN 37024. TEL 615-661-0246, 800-274-6774, FAX 615-373-5183, custserv@mleesmith.com. Ed. Ed Cromer. Circ: 1,400.

352.68 USA ISSN 0040-4640
TEXAS PUBLIC EMPLOYEE. Text in English. 1946. q. free to members. adv. illus. **Document type:** *Magazine, Consumer.*
Published by: Texas Public Employees Association, 512 East 11th St, Ste 100, Austin, TX 78701. TEL 512-476-2691, 888-367-8732, FAX 512-476-1338, mail@tpea.org. Ed., Pub., Adv. contact Bill Warren. Circ: 20,000.

TEXAS REGISTER. *see* LAW

351 USA ISSN 1942-5589
JK4830
TEXAS STAFF DIRECTORY. Text in English. 2004. biennial. USD 450 per issue (effective 2008). **Document type:** *Directory, Government.* **Description:** A Directory of official personnel in federal state and local government within Texas.
Formerly (until 2006): Texas Public Sector (1713-6458)
Published by: C Q Press, Inc. (Subsidiary of: Sage Publications, Inc.), 2300 N St, NW, Ste 800, Washington, DC 20037. TEL 202-729-1900, 866-427-7737, FAX 800-380-3810, customerservice@cqpress.com, http://www.cqpress.com.

351.764 USA ISSN 0363-7530
JK4830
TEXAS STATE DIRECTORY. Text in English. 1940. a. USD 34.95 per issue (effective 2011). **Document type:** *Directory, Government.* **Description:** Lists personnel at all levels of government in Texas.
Related titles: Online - full text ed.: 2006.
Published by: Texas State Directory Press, Inc., 1800 Nueces St, Austin, TX 78701. TEL 512-477-5698, FAX 512-473-2447.

352.14 USA ISSN 1084-5356
JS39
TEXAS TOWN & CITY. Text in English. 1914. 11/yr. USD 30 to non-members; USD 15 to members (effective 2010). adv. bk.rev. illus. index. back issues avail. **Document type:** *Magazine, Trade.* **Description:** Provides timely information for the Texas City Official.

Former titles (until 1994): T M L Texas Town & City (1040-6565); (until 1984): Texas Town & City (0040-473X); (until 1959): Texas Municipalities
Indexed: IPARL.
Published by: Texas Municipal League, 1821 Rutherford Ln, Ste 400, Austin, TX 78754. TEL 512-231-7400, FAX 512-719-7490. Ed. Karla Vining. Pub. Frank Sturz. Adv. contact Laurie Dodson. B&W page USD 675; 7 x 10. Circ: 11,015.

351.764 USA ISSN 0890-5924
CODEN: ACLSER
TEXAS WEEKLY. Text in English. 1984. 48/yr. USD 250 print or online ed. (effective 2006). back issues avail.; reprints avail. **Document type:** *Newsletter, Consumer.* **Description:** Nonpartisan reports on Texas government and politics.
Related titles: Online - full text ed.: USD 250 (effective 2001).
Published by: P P S, Inc., PO Box 1484, Austin, TX 78767-1484. TEL 512-288-6598, FAX 512-288-9557. Ed. Ross Ramsey.

351.593 THA
THAI GOVERNMENT ORGANIZATIONAL DIRECTORY. Text in English, Thai. irreg. free. **Document type:** *Directory, Government.*
Formerly: Organizational Directory of the Government of Thailand (0475-2015)
Published by: Office of the Prime Minister, Public Relations Department, 236 Vibhavadi Rungsit Rd, Huai Kwang, Bangkok, 10400, Thailand.

THINK TANK DIRECTORY; guide to nonprofit public policy research organizations. *see* POLITICAL SCIENCE

THIS WEEK IN WASHINGTON (ONLINE). *see* POLITICAL SCIENCE

351 CHN ISSN 1674-6570
TIANJIN REN-DA. Text in Chinese. 2002. m. **Document type:** *Magazine, Government.*
Related titles: Online - full text ed.
Published by: Tianjin Shi Ren-Da Chang-Wei-Hui, 201, Jiefang Bei Lu, Tianjin, 300042, China. TEL 86-22-23326455, FAX 86-22-23326784.

351.492 NLD ISSN 1879-8705
▼ **TIJDSCHRIFT VOOR TOEZICHT.** Text in Dutch. 2010. q. EUR 99 (effective 2010). adv. **Document type:** *Journal, Trade.*
Related titles: Online - full text ed.: ISSN 1879-8713.
Published by: Boom Juridische Uitgevers, Postbus 85576, The Hague, 2508 CG, Netherlands. TEL 31-70-3307033, FAX 31-70-3307030, info@bju.nl, http://www.boomuitgeversdenhaag.nl. Ed. A T Ottow.

328.5173 MNG
TORIYN MEDEELEL/STATE INFORMATION. Text in Mongol. 1991. bi-m. **Document type:** *Government.* **Description:** Covers presidential and governmental decrees, state laws, and parliamentary news.
Published by: State Great Hural - Parliament of Mongolia, c/o Parliamentary Secretariat, State House, Ulan Bator, Mongolia. TEL 976-1-327016, FAX 976-1-310011, TELEX 79309 GOVER MH. Ed. N Rinchindorj.

328.4371 ARG ISSN 1850-9762
TRAMITE PARLAMENTARIO. Text in Spanish. 1989. d. **Document type:** *Bulletin, Consumer.*
Published by: Camara de Diputados de la Nacion, Ave Rivadavia 1864, Buenos Aires, C1033AAU, Argentina. TEL 54-11-63107100, http://www.diputados.gov.ar/.

351 ESP
TRAMITE PARLAMENTARIO Y MUNICIPAL. Text in Spanish. m. **Document type:** *Magazine, Trade.*
Published by: Grupo Intereconomia, S.A., Paseo de la Castellana, no 36-38, Planta 1, Madrid, 28046, Spain. TEL 34-90-2996611, redaccion@intereconomia.com, http://www.grupointereconomia.com. Ed. Berta Molina.

351 ZAF
TRANSACT; a monthly analysis of law-making in South Africa's transitional parliament. Text in English. 1994. m. ZAR 270; USD 250 foreign. bk.rev. **Document type:** *Journal, Academic/Scholarly.*
Published by: Centre for Policy Studies, PO Box 12266, Queenswood, Pretoria 0121, South Africa. TEL 27-12-3336252, FAX 27-12-3339248. Circ: 60,000.

351 003.54 658 GBR ISSN 1750-6166
➤ **TRANSFORMING GOVERNMENT**; people, process and policy. Text in English. 2007. q. EUR 339 combined subscription in Europe (print & online eds.); USD 479 combined subscription in the Americas (print & online eds.); GBP 239 combined subscription in the UK & elsewhere (print & online eds.); AUD 639 combined subscription in Australasia (print & online eds.) (effective 2012). back issues avail.; reprint service avail. from PSC. **Document type:** *Journal, Academic/Scholarly.* **Description:** Publishes leading scholarly research on the subject of technology integration and management of Government, and how this impacts on organizations and people.
Related titles: Online - full text ed.: ISSN 1750-6174 (from IngentaConnect).
Indexed: A12, A17, A22, ABIn, E01, P48, P51, P53, P54, PAIS, PQC, SCOPUS.
—BLDSC (9020.679500), IE. **CCC.**
Published by: Emerald Group Publishing Ltd., Howard House, Wagon Ln, Bingley, W Yorks BD16 1WA, United Kingdom. TEL 44-1274-777700, FAX 44-1274-785201, information@emeraldinsight.com. Ed. Zahir Irani. Pub. Nicola Codner.

351.71 363.12 CAN ISSN 1483-7773
CA1BT31-4 77
TRANSPORTATION SAFETY BOARD OF CANADA. PERFORMANCE REPORT. Text in English, French. 1997. a.
Related titles: Online - full text ed.: ISSN 1490-6201.
Published by: (Transportation Safety Board of Canada), Treasury Board of Canada Secretariat, Corporate Communications/Secretariat du Conseil du Tresor du Canada, West Tower, Rm P-135, 300 Laurier Ave W, Ottawa, ON K1A 0R5, Canada. TEL 613-995-2855, FAX 613-996-0518, services-publications@tbs-sct.gc.ca.

351 ROM ISSN 1842-2845
TRANSYLVANIAN REVIEW OF ADMINISTRATIVE SCIENCES. Text in English. 2005. 3/yr.
Related titles: Online - full text ed.: free (effective 2011); ◆ Romanian ed.: Revista Transilvana de Stiinte Administrative. ISSN 1454-1378.
Indexed: A01, CA, SCOPUS, SSCI, W07.
Published by: Universitatea "Babes-Bolyai", Facultatea de Stiinte Politice, Administrative si ale Comunicari, 71 Gen Traian Mosoiu Str, Cluj - Napoca, 400132, Romania.

TRENDINFO. *see* PUBLIC ADMINISTRATION—Abstracting, Bibliographies, Statistics

TRENTINO; rivista della provincia autonoma di Trento. *see* ENVIRONMENTAL STUDIES

351.72983 TTO
TRINIDAD AND TOBAGO GAZETTE. Text in English. 1962. w. TTD 18.
Related titles: Microfilm ed.: (from PQC).
Published by: Government Printery, Sales Section, 48 St Vincent St, Port-of-Spain, Trinidad, Trinidad & Tobago.

351.561 TUR ISSN 0041-3925
TURK IDARE DERGISI/JOURNAL OF TURKISH ADMINISTRATION. Text in Turkish. 1928. bi-m. adv. bk.rev. bibl. index. **Document type:** *Government.* **Description:** Includes articles, translations, research, news, and regulations related to the ministry of interior and governors in Turkey.
Formerly: Idare Dergisi
Related titles: Online - full text ed.: free (effective 2009).
Published by: Iqisleri Bakanligi, A P K Baskanligi Yayin ve Dokumantasyon Dairesi/Ministry of Interior, Board of Publication, Paris Caddesi Alidede Sokak 8-3, Asagi Ayranci, Ankara, Turkey. TEL 90-312-4308893, FAX 90-312-4308896, tid@icisleri.gov.tr. Ed. Mualla Erkul. Circ: 3,000 (paid).

TURKEY. TURKIYE ISTATISTIK KURUMU. BUTCELER - BELEDIYELER, IL OZEL IDARLER VE KOYLER (YEAR)/TURKEY. TURKISH STATISTICAL INSTITUTE. BUDGETS - MUNICIPAL AND SPECIAL PROVINCIAL ADMINISTRATIONS AND VILLAGES (YEAR). *see* PUBLIC ADMINISTRATION—Abstracting, Bibliographies, Statistics

TURKEY. TURKIYE ISTATISTIK KURUMU. KESIN HESAPLAR - BELEDIYELER VE IL OZEL IDARELERI (YEAR)/TURKEY. TURKISH STATISTICAL INSTITUTE. FINAL ACCOUNTS - MUNICIPALITIES AND SPECIAL PROVINCIAL ADMINISTRATIONS (YEAR). *see* PUBLIC ADMINISTRATION—Abstracting, Bibliographies, Statistics

TURKEY. TURKIYE ISTATISTIK KURUMU. MAHALLI IDARELER SECIMI/TURKEY. TURKISH STATISTICAL INSTITUTE. ELECTIONS OF LOCAL ADMINISTRATIONS. *see* PUBLIC ADMINISTRATION—Abstracting, Bibliographies, Statistics

351 TUR ISSN 0251-2955
JQ1801.A1
TURKISH PUBLIC ADMINISTRATION ANNUAL. Text in English. 1974. a.
Indexed: FR, PAIS.
Published by: Institute of Public Administration for Turkey and the Middle East, 1 Numarali Cadde, No 8, Yucetepe, Ankara, 06100, Turkey.

351 NLD ISSN 2211-517X
▼ **TWAALF.** Text in Dutch. 2009. s-a.
Published by: Raad van Twaalf, c/o Kunst Centraal, Postbus 160, Bunnnik, 3980 CD, Netherlands. TEL 31-30-6595520. Ed. Martje Lamme. Circ: 1,500 (controlled).

U K ENVIRONMENT NEWS. *see* ENVIRONMENTAL STUDIES—Pollution

U.S. CODE CONGRESSIONAL AND ADMINISTRATIVE NEWS. *see* LAW

351 USA
U.S. CONGRESS. REPORTS ON PUBLIC BILLS. Text in English. irreg. USD 3,538 per session of congress (effective 2001). **Document type:** *Government.*
Published by: U.S. Congress, Washington, DC 20515. **Subscr. to:** U.S. Government Printing Office, Superintendent of Documents, PO Box 371954, Pittsburgh, PA 15250. TEL 202-512-1800, FAX 202-512-2250, orders@gpo.gov, http://www.access.gpo.gov.

351 USA ISSN 1931-2822
KF12
U.S. CONGRESSIONAL SERIAL SET. Text in English. 1817. irreg. **Document type:** *Government.* **Description:** Contains the House and Senate documents and the House and Senate reports bound by session of congress.
Published by: U.S. Government Printing Office, 732 N Capitol St, NW, Washington, DC 20401. TEL 202-512-1800, 866-512-1800, FAX 202-512-2104, ContactCenter@gpo.gov, http://www.gpo.gov.

U.S. DEPARTMENT OF AGRICULTURE. BOARD OF CONTRACT APPEALS. ANNUAL REPORT. *see* AGRICULTURE

U.S. DEPARTMENT OF AGRICULTURE. BUDGET SUMMARY AND ANNUAL PERFORMANCE PLAN. *see* AGRICULTURE

U.S. DEPARTMENT OF AGRICULTURE. PERFORMANCE AND ACCOUNTABILITY REPORT. *see* AGRICULTURE

U.S. DEPARTMENT OF ENERGY. WESTERN AREA POWER ADMINISTRATION. ANNUAL PERFORMANCE REPORT. *see* ENERGY

U.S. DEPARTMENT OF ENERGY. WESTERN AREA POWER ADMINISTRATION. ANNUAL REPORT. *see* ENERGY

351 615 332 USA
U.S. DEPARTMENT OF HEALTH AND HUMAN SERVICES. FOOD AND DRUG ADMINISTRATION. PRESCRIPTION DRUG USER FEE ACT. FINANCIAL REPORT TO CONGRESS. Text in English. 1995. a. free (effective 2011). **Document type:** *Report, Government.* **Description:** Reports annually on the financial aspects of its implementation of the Prescription Drug User Fee Act of 1992.
Related titles: Online - full text ed.
Published by: U.S. Department of Health and Human Services, Food and Drug Administration, 10903 New Hampshire Ave, Silver Spring, MD 20993. TEL 301-796-8240, 888-463-6332, druginfo@fda.hhs.gov.

351 615 USA
U.S. DEPARTMENT OF HEALTH AND HUMAN SERVICES. FOOD AND DRUG ADMINISTRATION. PRESCRIPTION DRUG USER FEE ACT. PERFORMANCE REPORT TO CONGRESS. Text in English. 1995. a. free (effective 2011). back issues avail. **Document type:** *Report, Government.* **Description:** Updates the Agency's review performance on the application submissions and evaluates its performance in reviewing application submissions and meeting other PDUFA performance goals.
Related titles: Online - full text ed.
Published by: U.S. Department of Health and Human Services, Food and Drug Administration, 10903 New Hampshire Ave, Silver Spring, MD 20993. TEL 301-796-8240, 888-463-6332, druginfo@fda.hhs.gov.

352.73 USA
U.S. DEPARTMENT OF HEALTH AND HUMAN SERVICES. GRANTS ADMINISTRATION MANUAL. Text in English. 1988. base vol. plus irreg. updates. looseleaf. **Document type:** *Government.* **Description:** Provides guidelines on the fiscal and administrative aspects of grant management to H.H.S. granting agencies. In the process of being phased out by Grants Policy Directives. As individual directives are issued, respective chapters are superseded.
Related titles: Online - full text ed.; ◆ Supplement to: Grants Policy Directives.
Published by: U.S. Department of Health and Human Services, 200 Independence Ave, SW, Washington, DC 20201. TEL 202-619-0257, 877-696-6775, http://www.hhs.gov/.

U.S. DEPARTMENT OF HOMELAND SECURITY. PRIVACY OFFICE. (YEAR) ANNUAL FREEDOM OF INFORMATION ACT REPORT TO THE ATTORNEY GENERAL OF THE UNITED STATES. *see* LAW

323.448 USA
U.S. DEPARTMENT OF HOMELAND SECURITY. PRIVACY OFFICE. REPORT TO CONGRESS. Text in English. a. **Document type:** *Government.*
Related titles: Online - full content ed.
Published by: U.S. Department of Homeland Security, Privacy Office, Washington, DC 20528. TEL 703-235-0780, FAX 703-235-0442, privacy@dhs.gov, http://www.dhs.gov/xabout/structure/editorial_0338.shtm.

U.S. DEPARTMENT OF HOUSING AND URBAN DEVELOPMENT. SECRETARY'S ESSAYS. *see* HOUSING AND URBAN PLANNING

U.S. DEPARTMENT OF JUSTICE. ATTORNEY GENERAL OF THE UNITED STATES. ANNUAL REPORT. *see* LAW

U.S. DEPARTMENT OF JUSTICE. OFFICE OF THE ATTORNEY GENERAL. STRATEGIC PLAN. *see* CRIMINOLOGY AND LAW ENFORCEMENT

352.53 USA
U.S. DEPARTMENT OF THE INTERIOR. INTERIOR BOARD OF CONTRACT APPEALS. Text in English. 1970. base vol. plus irreg. updates. **Document type:** *Government.*
Published by: U.S. Department of the Interior, Board of Contract, 1849 C St, NW, Washington, DC 20240. TEL 202-208-3100, feedback@ios.doi.gov, http://www.doi.gov.

353.53 USA
U.S. DEPARTMENT OF THE INTERIOR. INTERIOR BOARD OF INDIAN APPEALS. Abbreviated title: I B I A. Text in English. 1970. irreg. **Document type:** *Database, Government.*
Published by: U.S. Department of the Interior, Board of Contract, 1849 C St, NW, Washington, DC 20240. TEL 202-208-3100, feedback@ios.doi.gov, http://www.doi.gov.

351 USA
U.S. DEPARTMENT OF THE INTERIOR. INTERIOR BOARD OF LAND APPEALS. Text in English. 1970. irreg. **Document type:** *Database, Government.*
Published by: U.S. Department of the Interior, Board of Contract, 1849 C St, NW, Washington, DC 20240. TEL 202-208-3100, feedback@ios.doi.gov, http://www.doi.gov.

351 332 USA
U.S. DEPARTMENT OF THE TREASURY. FINANCIAL MANAGEMENT SERVICE. FINANCIAL REPORT OF THE UNITED STATES GOVERNMENT. Text in English. 19??. a. free (effective 2011). **Document type:** *Government.*
Former titles: Consolidated Financial Statements of the United States Government; United States Government Consolidated Financial Statements
Related titles: Online - full text ed.
Published by: U.S. Department of the Treasury, Financial Management Service, 401 14th St, SW, Washington, DC 20227. TEL 202-874-6950.

U.S. DEPARTMENT OF VETERANS AFFAIRS. FISCAL YEAR (YEAR) PERFORMANCE AND ACCOUNTABILITY REPORT. *see* MILITARY

351 363.7 USA
U.S. ENVIRONMENTAL PROTECTION AGENCY. OFFICE OF RESEARCH AND DEVELOPMENT. SUPERFUND INNOVATIVE TECHNOLOGY EVALUATION PROGRAM. ANNUAL REPORT TO CONGRESS. Text in English. 1997. a. **Document type:** *Government.*
Related titles: Online - full content ed.
Published by: U.S. Environmental Protection Agency, Office of Research and Development, National Risk Management Research Laboratory, Superfund Innovative Technology Evaluation, 26 W. Martin Luther King Dr., Mail Stop: G75, Cincinnati, OH 45268. parker.randy@epa.gov, http://www.epa.gov/ord/. **Dist. by:** National Service Center for Environmental Publications, PO Box 42419, Cincinnati, OH 45242-0419. TEL 513-489-8190, 800-490-9198, FAX 513-489-8695, ncepimal@one.net, http://www.epa.gov/ncepihom/ordering.htm.

354.7 USA ISSN 0094-8411
KF1987.A329 CODEN: EARGDG
U.S. EXPORT ADMINISTRATION REGULATIONS. Variant title: Export Administration Bulletin. Text in English. 1941-1987; resumed 199?. base vol. plus irreg. updates. looseleaf. USD 193 (effective 2005). **Document type:** *Government.* **Description:** Compiles official regulations and policies governing the export licensing of commodities and technical data.
Formerly: Export Control Regulations (0082-8947)
Related titles: CD-ROM ed.: USD 93.50 (effective 2005).
—CASDDS.
Published by: U.S. Department of Commerce, Bureau of Industry and Security, 14th St and Constitution Ave, NW, Washington, DC 20230. **Alt. subscr. addr.:** U.S. Department of Commerce, National Technical Information Service, 5301 Shawnee Rd, Alexandria, VA 22312. TEL 800-363-2068, subscriptions@ntis.gov; **Subscr. to:** U.S. Government Printing Office, Superintendent of Documents, PO Box 371954, Pittsburgh, PA 15250. TEL 202-512-1800, FAX 202-512-2250, orders@gpo.gov, http://www.access.gpo.gov.

U.S. FARM CREDIT ADMINISTRATION. PERFORMANCE AND ACCOUNTABILITY REPORT. *see* AGRICULTURE—Agricultural Economics

U.S. FEDERAL TRADE COMMISSION. BUREAU OF COMPETITION. SUMMARY OF AGREEMENTS FILED IN F Y (YEAR). *see* PHARMACY AND PHARMACOLOGY

351 USA
U.S. FEDERAL TRADE COMMISSION. PERFORMANCE AND ACCOUNTABILITY REPORT. Text in English. 19??. a. free (effective 2011). back issues avail. **Document type:** *Report, Government.*
Media: Online - full content.
Published by: U.S. Federal Trade Commission, 600 Pennsylvania Ave, NW, Washington, DC 20580. TEL 202-326-2222, HSRhelp@hsr.gov.

351 USA
U.S. FEDERAL TRADE COMMISSION. PERFORMANCE PLAN, FISCAL YEAR (YEAR) THROUGH FISCAL YEAR (YEAR), AND PRESIDENT'S MANAGEMENT AGENDA. Text in English. 19??. a., latest 2008. free (effective 2011). back issues avail. **Document type:** *Report, Government.*
Formerly: Annual Performance Plan Objectives by Program
Media: Online - full text.
Published by: U.S. Federal Trade Commission, 600 Pennsylvania Ave, NW, Washington, DC 20580. TEL 202-326-2222, HSRhelp@hsr.gov.

351 USA
U.S. FEDERAL TRADE COMMISSION. STRATEGIC PLAN. Text in English. 19??. every 5 yrs., latest Fiscal Year 2009-2014. free (effective 2011). back issues avail. **Document type:** *Report, Government.*
Media: Online - full text.
Published by: U.S. Federal Trade Commission, 600 Pennsylvania Ave, NW, Washington, DC 20580. TEL 202-326-2222, HSRhelp@hsr.gov.

U.S. GENERAL ACCOUNTING OFFICE. OFFICE OF PUBLIC AFFAIRS. MONTH IN REVIEW (ONLINE). *see* PUBLIC ADMINISTRATION—Abstracting, Bibliographies, Statistics

351 USA ISSN 0097-7799
HC110.P63
U.S. GENERAL SERVICES ADMINISTRATION. CATALOG OF FEDERAL DOMESTIC ASSISTANCE. Key Title: Catalog of Federal Domestic Assistance. Text in English. 1965. base vol. plus a. updates. looseleaf. **Document type:** *Catalog, Government.* **Description:** Listing of 1,300 government grants and assistance programs of more than 50 Federal agencies. Indexed by agency, function, subject and applicant eligibility to help state and local government groups and nonprofit organizations locate potential federal assistance.
Former titles (until 1969): Catalog of Federal Assistance Programs; (until 1967): Catalog of Federal Programs for Individual and Community Improvement
Related titles: CD-ROM ed.: USD 75; USD 45 newsstand/cover (effective 2001); Diskette ed.: USD 50 newsstand/cover; USD 85 (effective 2001); Magnetic Tape ed.; Online - full text ed.: ISSN 1555-0192. free (effective 2011).
Published by: U.S. General Services Administration, One Constitution Sq, 1275 First St, NE, Washington, DC 20417. TEL 866-606-8220, fbo.support@gsa.gov, http://www.gsa.gov.

328.73 USA
U.S. HOUSE OF REPRESENTATIVES. COMMITTEE ON GOVERNMENT REFORM. LEGISLATIVE CALENDAR. Text in English. 1995. a. **Document type:** *Government.*
Formed by the merger of (1979-1995): U.S. House of Representatives. Committee on Post Office and Civil Service. Legislative Calendar (0364-4235); (1954-1995): U.S. House of Representatives. Committee on Government Operations. Legislative Calendar (0364-4278); (19??-1995): U.S. House of Representatives. Committee on the District of Columbia. Legislative Calendar (0364-4227)
Published by: (U.S. House of Representatives, Committee on Government Reform), U.S. Government Printing Office, 732 N Capitol St, NW, Washington, DC 20401. TEL 202-512-1800, 866-512-1800, FAX 202-512-2104, ContactCenter@gpo.gov, http://www.gpo.gov.

351 USA ISSN 0148-0006
KF31.8
U.S. HOUSE OF REPRESENTATIVES. COMMITTEE ON STANDARDS OF OFFICIAL CONDUCT. SUMMARY OF ACTIVITIES. REPORT. Key Title: Summary of Activities. A Report of the Committee on Standards of Official Conduct, United States House of Representatives. Text in English. 1977. biennial. back issues avail. **Document type:** *Report, Government.*
Published by: U.S. Government Printing Office, 732 N Capitol St, NW, Washington, DC 20401. TEL 202-512-1800, 866-512-1800, FAX 202-512-2104, ContactCenter@gpo.gov, http://www.gpo.gov.

344 USA
U.S. HOUSE OF REPRESENTATIVES. COMMITTEE ON TRANSPORTATION AND INFRASTRUCTURE. LEGISLATIVE CALENDAR. Text in English. 1975. a. **Document type:** *Government.*
Formerly (until 1995): U.S. House of Representatives. Committee on Public Works and Transportation. Legislative Calendar (0364-9660)
Published by: (U.S. House of Representatives, Committee on Transportation and Infrastructure), U.S. Government Printing Office, 732 N Capitol St, NW, Washington, DC 20401. TEL 202-512-1800, 866-512-1800, FAX 202-512-2104, ContactCenter@gpo.gov, http://www.gpo.gov.

351 USA ISSN 0272-6211
U.S. HOUSE OF REPRESENTATIVES. FINANCIAL DISCLOSURE REPORTS OF MEMBERS. Text in English. 19??. irreg. USD 78 per issue domestic; USD 109.20 per issue elsewhere (effective 2011). **Document type:** *Report, Government.*
Published by: (U.S. House of Representatives), U.S. Government Printing Office, 732 N Capitol St, NW, Washington, DC 20401. TEL 202-512-1800, 866-512-1800, FAX 202-512-2104, ContactCenter@gpo.gov, http://www.gpo.gov.

351 USA
U.S. HOUSE OF REPRESENTATIVES. RULES OF THE COMMITTEE ON EDUCATION AND LABOR, U.S. HOUSE OF REPRESENTATIVES. Text in English. a. **Document type:** *Government.*
Former titles (until 2005): U.S. House of Representatives. Rules of the Committee on Education and the Workforce; (until 199?): U.S. House of Representatives. Committee on Education and Labor. Rules of the Committee on Education and Labor
Related titles: Online - full content ed.
Published by: U.S. House of Representatives, Committee on Education and Labor, 2181 Rayburn House Office Bldg, Washington, DC 20515. TEL 202-225-3725, http://edlabor.house.gov/. **Subscr. to:** U.S. Government Printing Office, Superintendent of Documents, PO Box 371954, Pittsburgh, PA 15250. TEL 202-512-1800, FAX 202-512-2250, orders@gpo.gov, http://www.access.gpo.gov/.

U.S. HOUSING MARKET CONDITIONS. *see* HOUSING AND URBAN PLANNING

351 USA
U.S. LARGEST CITIES, COUNTIES & STATES. Text in English. 19??. a. USD 235 per issue (effective 2010). stat. **Document type:** *Report, Trade.*
Published by: Municipal Analysis Services, Inc., PO Box 13453, Austin, TX 78711. TEL 512-327-3328, FAX 413-740-1294, munilysis@hotmail.com, http://sites.google.com/site/gregmichels.

352 USA ISSN 0271-9797
JK631
U.S. MERIT SYSTEMS PROTECTION BOARD. ANNUAL REPORT. Text in English. 1979. a.
Published by: U.S. Merit Systems Protection Board, 1120 Vermont Ave NW, Ste 816, Washington, DC 20419. TEL 202-653-6772, FAX 202-653-6203.

U.S. NUCLEAR REGULATORY COMMISSION. ANNUAL REPORT TO CONGRESS. *see* ENERGY—Nuclear Energy

U.S. NUCLEAR REGULATORY COMMISSION. RULES AND REGULATIONS. *see* ENERGY—Nuclear Energy

U.S. OFFICE OF PERSONNEL MANAGEMENT. NEGOTIABILITY DETERMINATIONS BY THE FEDERAL LABOR RELATIONS AUTHORITY. *see* BUSINESS AND ECONOMICS—Labor And Industrial Relations

351 USA ISSN 2155-0662
U.S. PUBLIC BUILDINGS SERVICE. CHILD CARE DIVISION. CENTER NEWS. Text in English. 19??. q. free (effective 2010). back issues avail. **Document type:** *Newsletter, Academic/Scholarly.*
Published by: U.S. General Services Administration, Public Buildings Service, Child Care Division, 1800 F St, NW, Washington, DC 20405. TEL 866-606-8220, fbo.support@gsa.gov, http://www.gsa.gov/Portal/gsa/ep/contentView.do?contentId=28420&programPage=/ep/program/gsaBasic.jsp&channelId=-24687&ooid=8355&pageTypeId=17114&P=PLCC&programId=15688&contentType=GSA_BASIC.

351.73 USA ISSN 0364-5886
J37
U.S. SENATE. CALENDAR OF BUSINESS. Text in English. 19??. d. (when Senate in session). free (effective 2011). back issues avail. **Document type:** *Government.*
Related titles: Online - full text ed.: ISSN 1944-303X.
Published by: U.S. Government Printing Office, 732 N Capitol St, NW, Washington, DC 20401. TEL 202-512-1800, 866-512-1800, FAX 202-512-2104, ContactCenter@gpo.gov.

351 USA
U.S. SENATE. COMMITTEE ON FOREIGN RELATIONS. MEMBERSHIP AND JURISDICTION OF SUBCOMMITTEES. Text in English. 19??. biennial. **Document type:** *Government.*
Former titles (until 1977): U.S. Senate. Committee on Foreign Relations. Subcommittees; (until 1971): U.S. Senate. Committee on Foreign Relations. Consultative Subcommittees; (until 1963): U.S. Senate. Committee on Foreign Relations. Subcommittees; (until 1961): U.S. Senate. Committee on Foreign Relations. Subcommittees for Consultative Purposes
Related titles: Online - full content ed.
Published by: U.S. Senate, Committee on Foreign Relations, Dirksen Senate Office Bldg, Washington, DC 20510-6225. **Subscr. to:** U.S. Government Printing Office, Superintendent of Documents, PO Box 371954, Pittsburgh, PA 15250. TEL 202-512-1800, FAX 202-512-2250, orders@gpo.gov, http://www.access.gpo.gov/.

351 365.34 USA
U.S. SENATE. COMMITTEE ON GOVERNMENTAL AFFAIRS. RULES OF PROCEDURE OF THE COMMITTEE ON HOMELAND SECURITY AND GOVERNMENTAL AFFAIRS, UNITED STATES SENATE/RULES OF PROCEDURE OF THE COMMITTEE ON HOMELAND SECURITY AND GOVERNMENTAL AFFAIRS, UNITED STATES SENATE. Text in English. biennial. **Document type:** *Government.*
Formerly (until 2005): U.S. Congress. Senate. Committee on Governmental Affairs. Rules of Procedure of the Committee on Governmental Affairs, United States Senate
Related titles: Online - full content ed.
Published by: U.S. Senate, Committee on Governmental Affairs, SD 340, Washington, DC 20510-6250. TEL 202-224-4751, FAX 202-224-9682. **Subscr. to:** U.S. Government Printing Office, Superintendent of Documents, PO Box 371954, Pittsburgh, PA 15250. TEL 202-512-1800, FAX 202-512-2250, orders@gpo.gov, http://www.access.gpo.gov/.

346.73 USA
U.S. SENATE. COMMITTEE ON SMALL BUSINESS AND ENTREPRENEURSHIP. LEGISLATIVE CALENDAR. Text in English. 19??. a. **Document type:** *Government.*
Formerly (until 2001): U.S. Senate. Committee on Small Business. Legislative Calendar (0739-6104)
Published by: (U.S. Senate, Committee on Small Business and Entrepreneurship), U.S. Government Printing Office, 732 N Capitol St, NW, Washington, DC 20401. TEL 202-512-1800, 866-512-1800, FAX 202-512-2104, ContactCenter@gpo.gov, http://www.gpo.gov.

351 347 USA
U.S. VIRGIN ISLANDS GOVERNMENT REGISTER. Text in English. m. USD 308 (effective 2011). **Document type:** *Government.* **Description:** A compilation of information about official U.S. Virgin Islands government actions.
Published by: LexisNexis (Subsidiary of: Reed Elsevier Group plc), 1016 W Ninth Ave, 1st Fl, King of Prussia, PA 19406. TEL 215 564-1788, 800 448-1515, customer.support@lexisnexis.com.

351 USA ISSN 1559-4661
UNIFIED AGENDA OF FEDERAL REGULATORY AND DEREGULATORY ACTIONS. Text in English. 19??. s-a. **Document type:** *Government.*
Media: Online - full text.
Published by: U.S. General Services Administration, Office of Governmentwide Policy. Regulatory Information Service Center, 7th & D Sts, SW, Washington, DC 20407. RISC@gsa.gov.

351.711 CAN ISSN 0082-7746
UNION OF BRITISH COLUMBIA MUNICIPALITIES. MINUTES OF ANNUAL CONVENTION. Text in English. 1904. a. free.
Published by: Union of British Columbia Municipalities, 10551 Shellbridge Way, Suite 60, Richmond, BC V6X 2W9, Canada. TEL 604-270-8226, FAX 604-270-9116, ubcm@civicnet.bc.ca.

354.3 USA
UNITED STATES. BUREAU OF LAND MANAGEMENT. ANNUAL REPORT ON PERFORMANCE AND ACCOUNTABILITY. Text in English. 1980. a. free (effective 2011). **Document type:** *Government.* **Description:** Describes management of U.S. public lands. Includes Bureau's accomplishments, issues, goals for the preceding fiscal year.
Former titles (until 2004): United States. Bureau of Land Management. Annual Report; Managing the Nation's Public Lands
Related titles: Online - full text ed.
Published by: (Bureau of Land Management), U.S. Department of the Interior, 1849 C St., NW, Washington, DC 20240. TEL 202-208-3100, feedback@ios.doi.gov, http://www.doi.gov.

UNITED STATES DEPARTMENT OF TRANSPORTATION. OFFICE OF INSPECTOR GENERAL. SEMIANNUAL REPORT TO THE CONGRESS. *see* TRANSPORTATION

UNITED STATES. DEPARTMENT OF VETERANS AFFAIRS. HEALTH SERVICES RESEARCH AND DEVELOPMENT SERVICE. FORUM. *see* MILITARY

351 USA ISSN 1944-138X
UNITED STATES. FEDERAL HOUSING FINANCE BOARD. OFFICE OF INSPECTOR GENERAL. SEMIANNUAL REPORT. Text in English. 19??. s-a. free (effective 2009). back issues avail. **Document type:** *Government.*
Media: Online - full content.
Published by: U.S. Federal Housing Finance Board, Office of Inspector General, 1625 Eye St, N W, Washington, DC 20006. TEL 202-408-2544, 800-793-7724, FAX 202-408-2972.

351 USA ISSN 1559-6699
JK468.A8
UNITED STATES. GENERAL SERVICES ADMINISTRATION. OFFICE OF INTERGOVERNMENTAL SOLUTIONS. NEWSLETTER. Text in English. 200?. irreg. **Document type:** *Newsletter, Government.*
Related titles: ◆ Online - full text ed.: Intergovernmental Solutions Newsletter. ISSN 2154-6649.
Published by: U.S. General Services Administration, Office of Citizen Services and Communications, 1800 F St, NW, Washington, DC 20405. http://www.usaservices.gov/.

351 USA
UNITED STATES GOVERNMENT ACCOUNTABILITY OFFICE. ABSTRACTS OF REPORTS AND TESTIMONY: FISCAL YEAR (YEAR). Text in English. a. free (effective 2011). back issues avail. **Document type:** *Report, Government.*
Formerly (until 2004): U.S. General Accounting Office. Abstracts of Reports and Testimony: Fiscal Year (Year)
Related titles: Online - full text ed.
Published by: United States Government Accountability Office, 441 G St, NW, Washington, DC 20548. TEL 202-512-3000, contact@gao.gov.

351 USA
UNITED STATES GOVERNMENT ACCOUNTABILITY OFFICE. MONTH IN REVIEW. Text in English. 2003. m. free (effective 2011). **Document type:** *Report, Government.* **Description:** Contains comprehensive list of all reports, testimony, correspondence, and other publications issued by GAO during the previous month, grouped according to subject categories.
Related titles: Online - full text ed.
Published by: United States Government Accountability Office, 441 G St, NW, Washington, DC 20548. TEL 202-512-3000, contact@gao.gov.

351.021 USA
UNITED STATES GOVERNMENT ACCOUNTABILITY OFFICE. REPORTS AND TESTIMONY. Text in English. 19??. m. free (effective 2011). **Document type:** *Report, Government.* **Description:** Summarizes reports available through the G.A.O.
Formerly (until 2004): U.S. General Accounting Office. Reports and Testimony
Related titles: Online - full text ed.
Published by: United States Government Accountability Office, 441 G St, NW, Washington, DC 20548. TEL 202-512-3000, contact@gao.gov.

352.4 USA
UNITED STATES GOVERNMENT ACCOUNTABILITY OFFICE. TODAY'S REPORTS. Text in English. 1995. d. back issues avail. **Document type:** *Report, Government.* **Description:** Listing of released GAO reports and testimony.
Formerly (until 19??): G A O Daybook
Media: Online - full text.
Published by: United States Government Accountability Office, 441 G St, NW, Washington, DC 20548. TEL 202-512-3000, contact@gao.gov.

320 USA
THE UNITED STATES GOVERNMENT INTERNET DIRECTORY. Text in English. 1997. a. USD 65 per issue (effective 2011). back issues avail. **Document type:** *Directory, Trade.*
Former titles (until 2010): E-Government and Web Directory (2152-9434); (until 2009): United States Government Internet Manual (1547-2892); (until 2004): Government Information on the Internet (1529-594X)
Published by: Bernan Press, 15200 NBN Way, PO Box 191, Blue Ridge Summit, PA 17214. TEL 301-459-7666, 800-865-3457, FAX 301-459-6988, 800-865-3450, customercare@bernan.com.

UNITED STATES GOVERNMENT MANUAL. *see* POLITICAL SCIENCE

351 USA ISSN 1559-467X
UNITED STATES GOVERNMENT POLICY AND SUPPORTING POSITIONS. Text in English. 1960. every 4 yrs. free (effective 2011). **Document type:** *Government.*
Media: Online - full text.

Published by: U.S. Government Printing Office, 732 N Capitol St, NW, Washington, DC 20401. TEL 202-512-1800, 866-512-1800, FAX 202-512-2104, ContactCenter@gpo.gov, http://www.gpo.gov.

351.73 USA ISSN 0147-3883
KF31.8
UNITED STATES HOUSE OF REPRESENTATIVES. COMMITTEE ON APPROPRIATIONS. REPORT OF COMMITTEE ACTIVITIES. Text in English. 19??. biennial. **Document type:** *Government.*
Published by: (U.S. House of Representatives, Committee on Appropriations), U.S. Government Printing Office, 732 N Capitol St, NW, Washington, DC 20401. TEL 202-512-1800, 866-512-1800, FAX 202-512-2104, ContactCenter@gpo.gov, http://www.gpo.gov.

351.73 USA
KF22
UNITED STATES HOUSE OF REPRESENTATIVES. COMMITTEE ON FINANCE. LEGISLATIVE CALENDAR. Text in English. 19??. a. **Document type:** *Government.*
Former titles (until 2001): United States House of Representatives. Committee on Banking and Financial Services. Legislative Calendar; (until 1995): United States House of Representatives. Committee on Banking, Finance, and Urban Affairs. Legislative Calendar (0190-5473); (until 1977): United States House of Representatives. Committee on Banking, Currency, and Housing. Legislative Calendar (0364-9652); (until 1975): United States House of Representatives. Committee on Banking and Currency. Legislative Calendar
Published by: (U.S. House of Representatives, Committee on Finance), U.S. Government Printing Office, 732 N Capitol St, NW, Washington, DC 20401. TEL 202-512-1800, 866-512-1800, FAX 202-512-2104, ContactCenter@gpo.gov, http://www.gpo.gov.

351 USA ISSN 1931-2830
JZ4997.5.U6
UNITED STATES PARTICIPATION IN THE UNITED NATIONS; report by the secretary of state to the congress. Text in English. 2002. a. free (effective 2011). back issues avail. **Document type:** *Report, Government.*
Related titles: Online - full text ed.
Published by: U.S. Department of State, 2201 C St NW, Washington, DC 20520. TEL 202-647-4000, 800-877-8339.

328.73 338.1 USA ISSN 0147-4103
KF21
UNITED STATES SENATE. COMMITTEE ON AGRICULTURE, NUTRITION AND FORESTRY. LEGISLATIVE CALENDAR. Text in English. 19??. biennial. free (effective 2011). **Document type:** *Government.*
Formerly (until 1977): United States Senate. Committee on Agriculture and Forestry. Legislative Calendar (0364-4170)
Related titles: Online - full text ed.
Published by: (U.S. Senate, Committee on Agriculture, Nutrition and Forestry), U.S. Government Printing Office, 732 N Capitol St, NW, Washington, DC 20401. TEL 202-512-1800, 866-512-1800, FAX 202-512-2104, ContactCenter@gpo.gov, http://www.gpo.gov.

351.73 USA ISSN 0364-4197
KF21.B35
UNITED STATES SENATE. COMMITTEE ON BANKING, HOUSING, AND URBAN AFFAIRS. LEGISLATIVE CALENDAR. Text in English. 19??. biennial. free (effective 2011). **Document type:** *Government.*
Formerly (until 1971): Legislative Calendar
Related titles: Online - full text ed.
Published by: U.S. Government Printing Office, 732 N Capitol St, NW, Washington, DC 20401. TEL 202-512-1800, 866-512-1800, FAX 202-512-2104, ContactCenter@gpo.gov, http://www.gpo.gov.

328.73 USA
UNITED STATES SENATE. COMMITTEE ON HOMELAND SECURITY AND GOVERNMENTAL AFFAIRS. LEGISLATIVE CALENDAR. Text in English. 19??. irreg. free (effective 2011). **Document type:** *Government.*
Former titles (until 2006): United States Senate. Committee on Governmental Affairs. Legislative Calendar (0147-6572); (until 1977): United States Senate. Committee on Government Operations. Legislative Calendar (0364-4251); (until 195?): Legislative Calendar
Related titles: Online - full text ed.
Published by: (U.S. Senate, Committee on Governmental Affairs), U.S. Government Printing Office, 732 N Capitol St, NW, Washington, DC 20401. TEL 202-512-1800, 866-512-1800, FAX 202-512-2104, ContactCenter@gpo.gov, http://www.gpo.gov.

351 COL ISSN 0465-4773
UNIVERSIDAD DE MEDELLIN. FACULTAD DE CIENCIAS ADMINISTRATIVAS. REVISTA. Text in Spanish. 1973. q. charts; illus.
Published by: Universidad de Medellin, Facultad de Ciencias Administrativas, Calle 31 No. 83b-150, Medellin, ANT, Colombia. Ed. Orlando Vasquez Castro.

351 PAN
UNIVERSIDAD DE PANAMA. FACULTAD DE ADMINISTRACION PUBLICA Y COMERCIO. REVISTA. Text in Spanish. q. illus.
Published by: Universidad de Panama, Facultad de Administracion Publica y Comercio, Estafeta Universitaria, Panama City, Panama.

351 ARG
UNIVERSIDAD NACIONAL DEL LITORAL. FACULTAD DE CIENCIAS DE LA ADMINISTRACION. REVISTA. Text in Spanish. 1969. a.
Published by: Universidad Nacional del Litoral, Facultad de Ciencias de la Administracion, 25 de Mayo, 1783, Santa Fe, Argentina. http://www.unl.edu.ar/.

351 NOR ISSN 0803-0200
UNIVERSITETET I BERGEN. INSTITUTT FOR ADMINISTRASJON OG ORGANISASJONSVITENSKAP. NOTAT. Text in English, Norwegian. 1981. irreg. price varies. back issues avail. **Document type:** *Monographic series, Academic/Scholarly.*
Formerly (until 1987): Universitetet i Bergen. Institutt for Administrasjon og Organisasjonskunnkap. Notater (1504-484X)
Published by: Universitetet i Bergen, Institutt for Administrasjon og Organisasjonsvitenskap/University of Bergen. Department of Administration and Organization Theory, Christies Gt. 17, Bergen, 5007, Norway. TEL 47-55-582175, FAX 47-55-589890, post@aorg.uib.no.

UNIVERSITY OF BIRMINGHAM. SCHOOL OF PUBLIC POLICY. OCCASIONAL PAPERS. *see* POLITICAL SCIENCE

351 340 USA
UNIVERSITY OF CALIFORNIA HASTINGS COLLEGE OF LAW. PUBLIC LAW RESEARCH INSTITUTE. REPORTS. Text in English. 1994. irreg., latest 2004. price varies. back issues avail.; reprints avail. **Document type:** *Monographic series, Academic/Scholarly.* **Description:** Publishes student research into public-law issues affecting state and local governments.
Formerly: University of California at San Francisco. Hastings College of Law. Public Law Research Institute. Reports
Related titles: Online - full text ed.
Published by: (Public Law Research Institute), University of California, San Francisco, Hastings College of the Law, 100 McAllister St, Ste 405, San Francisco, CA 94102. TEL 415-565-4639, lawbooks@uchastings.edu.

UNIVERSITY OF CALIFORNIA. INSTITUTE OF GOVERNMENTAL STUDIES LIBRARY. ACCESSIONS LIST. *see* PUBLIC ADMINISTRATION—Abstracting, Bibliographies, Statistics

352 SWE ISSN 1653-3895
UNIVERSITY OF GOETEBORG. CENTER FOR PUBLIC SECTOR RESEARCH. WORKING PAPERS. Text in English. 2005. irreg., latest vol.5, 2006. back issues avail. **Document type:** *Monographic series, Academic/Scholarly.*
Media: Online - full content.
Published by: Goeteborgs Universitet, Centrum foer Forskning om Offentlig Sektor/University of Goeteborg. Center for Public Sector Research, Pilgatan 19 A, PO Box 720, Goeteborg, 40530, Sweden. TEL 46-31-7734142, FAX 46-31-7734480, office@cefos.gu.se.

351.789 USA ISSN 0194-2670
JK8001
UNIVERSITY OF NEW MEXICO. DIVISION OF GOVERNMENT RESEARCH. MONOGRAPH SERIES. Text in English. 1946. irreg., latest vol.86, 1981. free. bk.rev. abstr. **Document type:** *Monographic series, Government.*
Indexed: P06.
Published by: University of New Mexico, Division of Government Research, 1920 Lomas Blvd N E, Albuquerque, NM 87131-6025. TEL 505-277-3305, FAX 505-277-6540. Ed. Robert U Anderson. Circ: 600.

354.35 GBR ISSN 0951-385X
UNIVERSITY OF NEWCASTLE-UPON-TYNE. DEPARTMENT OF TOWN AND COUNTRY PLANNING. WORKING PAPER SERIES. Text in English. 1987. irreg. **Document type:** *Monographic series.*
Published by: University of Newcastle upon Tyne, Department of Town and Country Planning, Newcastle upon Tyne, Tyne and Wear NE1 7RU, United Kingdom. TEL 44-191-232-8511, FAX 44-191-261-1182. Ed. Tim Shaw.

UNIVERSITY OF PRETORIA. INSTITUTE FOR STRATEGIC STUDIES. AD HOC PUBLICATION/UNIVERSITEIT VAN PRETORIA. INSTITUUT VIR STRATEGIESE STUDIES. AD HOC PUBLIKASIE. *see* POLITICAL SCIENCE—International Relations

UNIVERSITY OF ST. THOMAS JOURNAL OF LAW & PUBLIC POLICY. *see* LAW

UNIVERSITY OF TEXAS, AUSTIN. LYNDON B. JOHNSON SCHOOL OF PUBLIC AFFAIRS. POLICY RESEARCH PROJECT REPORT SERIES. *see* POLITICAL SCIENCE

351.599 PHL
UNIVERSITY OF THE PHILIPPINES. COLLEGE OF PUBLIC ADMINISTRATION. PUBLIC ADMINISTRATION OCCASIONAL PAPERS AND SPECIAL STUDIES SERIES. Text in English. irreg. price varies. **Document type:** *Monographic series.*
Formerly: University of the Philippines. College of Public Administration. Public Administration Special Studies Series
Published by: University of the Philippines, College of Public Administration, Diliman, P.O. Box 198, Quezon City, Philippines. TEL 95-13-53.

351 DEU ISSN 0042-0611
UA710
UNTERRICHTSBLAETTER FUER DIE BUNDESWEHRVERWALTUNG; Zeitschrift fuer Ausbildung, Fortbildung und Verwaltungspraxis. Text in German. 1961. m. EUR 151 domestic; EUR 156 foreign; EUR 11 newsstand/cover (effective 2011). adv. bk.rev. bibl.; charts; illus.; stat. index. **Document type:** *Magazine, Trade.*
Published by: (Germany. Bundesministerium der Verteidigung), R. v. Decker's Verlag Huethig GmbH (Subsidiary of: Sueddeutscher Verlag GmbH), Im Weiher 10, Heidelberg, 69121, Germany. TEL 49-6221-4890, FAX 49-6221-489279, info@hjr-verlag.de, http://www.huethig-jehle-rehm.de. Ed. Michael Streffer. Adv. contact Isabell Henze. Circ: 2,000 (paid and controlled).

351 ITA ISSN 1825-5833
UOMINI COMUNICAZIONE P A. (Pubblica Amministrazione) Text in Italian. 2003. a. **Document type:** *Directory, Trade.*
Published by: Editoriale Genesis, Via Vincenzo Monti 15, Milan, 20123, Italy. TEL 39-02-48194401, FAX 39-02-4818658.

351.485 SWE ISSN 1654-725X
UPPHANDLING24. Text in Swedish. 2007. 8/yr. SEK 1,795 (effective 2011). adv. **Document type:** *Magazine, Trade.*
Published by: I D G AB (Subsidiary of: I D G Communications Inc.), Karlbergsvaegen 77-81, Stockholm, 10678, Sweden. TEL 46-8-4536000, FAX 46-8-4536005, kundservice@idg.se, http://www.idg.se. Ed. Bo Nordlin. Adv. contact Asa Johansson.

351 GBR ISSN 1753-5069
HT101
URBAN RESEARCH & PRACTICE. Text in English. 2008. 3/yr. GBP 188 combined subscription in United Kingdom to institutions (print & online eds.); EUR 293, USD 371 combined subscription to institutions (print & online eds.) (effective 2012). adv. bk.rev. back issues avail.; reprint service avail. from PSC. **Document type:** *Journal, Academic/Scholarly.* **Description:** Focuses on urban policy.
Related titles: Online - full text ed.: ISSN 1753-5077. GBP 170 in United Kingdom to institutions; EUR 264, USD 334 to institutions (effective 2012).
Indexed: A01, A22, CA, E01, P42, T02.
—IE. **CCC.**
Published by: (European Urban Research Association DEU), Routledge (Subsidiary of: Taylor & Francis Group), 4 Park Sq, Milton Park, Abingdon, Oxon OX14 4RN, United Kingdom. FAX 44-20-70176336, subscriptions@tandf.co.uk, http://www.routledge.com. Ed. Rob Atkinson TEL 44-117-3283359. Adv. contact Linda Hann TEL 44-1344-779945. **Subscr. to:** Taylor & Francis Ltd., Journals Customer Service, Sheepen Pl, Colchester, Essex CO3 3LP, United Kingdom. TEL 44-20-70175544, FAX 44-20-70175198.

352.1 USA ISSN 0882-4738
KFU440.A73
UTAH. DIVISION OF ADMINISTRATIVE RULES. UTAH STATE BULLETIN. Text in English. 1973. s-m. USD 174 (effective 2001). **Document type:** *Bulletin, Government.* **Description:** Contains the administrative rules and executive branch notices of the state government.
Former titles (until 1985): State of Utah Bulletin (0886-9650); (until 1978): Utah Administrative Rule Making Bulletin (0093-8955)
Related titles: Online - full text ed.
Published by: Division of Administrative Rules, PO Box 141007, Salt Lake City, UT 84114-1007. TEL 801-538-3218, FAX 801-538-1773, rulesonline@state.ut.us, http://www.rules.state.ut.us/publicat/bulletin.htm. Ed. Nancy Lancaster. Circ: 175. **Subscr. to:** Legislative Printing, P O Box 140107, Salt Lake City, UT 84114-0107. TEL 801-538-1103, FAX 801-538-1728.

352.56 USA
UTILITIES LAW REPORTER. Text in English. 3 base vols. plus bi-m. updates. USD 2,970 base vol(s). (effective 2004). **Description:** Covers the federal laws and regulations governing gas and electric public utilities, as well as federal and state court cases.
Formerly: Utilities Law Reports (0162-1718)
—**CCC.**
Published by: C C H Inc. (Subsidiary of: Wolters Kluwer N.V.), 2700 Lake Cook Rd, Riverwoods, IL 60015. TEL 847-267-7000, 800-449-6439, cust_serv@cch.com, http://www.cch.com. Pub. Stacey Caywood.

354.5 351 USA ISSN 1945-9114
HD2763.A2
UTILITY SOURCING ADVISOR. Text in English. 200?. irreg.
Published by: I H S Global Insight (USA) Inc., 1000 Winter St, Waltham, MA 02451-1241. http://www.ihs.com.

351 SWE ISSN 1651-6885
UTREDNINGAR FRAAN RIKSDAGSFOERVALTNINGEN. Text in Swedish. 2003. irreg. back issues avail. **Document type:** *Government.*
Related titles: Online - full text ed.
Published by: Sveriges Riksdag/The Swedish Parliament, Stockholm, 10012, Sweden. TEL 46-8-7864000, FAX 46-8-7865871, rigsdagsinformation@riksdagen.se. **Dist. by:** Sveriges Riksdag, Tryckeriexpeditionen. ordermottagningen@riksdagen.se.

351 DEU ISSN 1437-997X
V B O B MAGAZIN. Text in German. 1951. 10/yr. free to members. adv. **Document type:** *Magazine, Trade.*
Formerly (until 1999): Die Bundesverwaltung (0007-5930)
Indexed: RASB.
Published by: Verband der Beschaeftigten der Obersten und Oberen Bundesbehoerden (Subsidiary of: Deutscher Beamtenbund), Dreizehnmorgenweg 36, Bonn, 53175, Germany. TEL 49-228-9579653, FAX 49-228-9579654, vbob@vbob.de. Ed. Franziska Schleyer. adv.: B&W page EUR 1,330, color page EUR 2,110. Circ: 15,000 (controlled).

VAASAN YLIOPISTO. JULKAISUJA. OPETUSJULKAISUJA/ UNIVERSITY OF VAASA. PROCEEDINGS. TEACHING AID SERIES. *see* BUSINESS AND ECONOMICS—Economic Systems And Theories, Economic History

351 FIN ISSN 0788-6675
VAASAN YLIOPISTO. JULKAISUJA. TUTKIMUKSIA. HALLINTOTIEDE/UNIVERSITY OF VAASA. PROCEEDINGS. RESEARCH PAPERS. ADMINISTRATIVE SCIENCE. Text in Multiple languages. 1982. irreg. price varies. back issues avail. **Document type:** *Monographic series, Academic/Scholarly.*
Formerly (until 1991): Vaasan Korkeakoulu. Julkaisuja. Tutkimuksia. Hallintotiede (0359-4750)
Related titles: ◆ Series of: Vaasan Yliopisto. Julkaisuja. Tutkimuksia. ISSN 0788-6667.
Published by: Vaasan Yliopisto/University of Vaasa, PO Box 700, Vaasa, 65101, Finland. TEL 358-6-3248111, FAX 358-6-3248187.

VAASAN YLIOPISTON JULKAISUJA. SELVITYKSIA JA RAPORTTEJA/UNIVERSITY OF VAASA. PROCEEDINGS. REPORTS. *see* BUSINESS AND ECONOMICS—Economic Systems And Theories, Economic History

351.41 GBR ISSN 1744-7178
JN500
VACHER'S QUARTERLY. Text in English. 1832. q. GBP 88 domestic; GBP 89 in Europe; GBP 95 elsewhere (effective 2009). back issues avail. **Document type:** *Directory, Bibliography.* **Description:** Provides details on all individuals and institutions within the political arena in both the UK and Europe.
Formerly (until 2004): Vacher's Parliamentary Companion (0958-0328)
Related titles: CD-ROM ed.; Microform ed.: (from PQC).
Published by: Vacher Dod Publishing Ltd., Westminster Tower, 3 Albert Emankment, London, SE1 7SP, United Kingdom. TEL 44-20-70917572, FAX 44-20-70917515, info@dodonline.co.uk, http://www.dodonline.co.uk.

368.4 362.6 BEL ISSN 1378-2622
VADE MECUM: BEGROTING VAN DE SOCIALE BESCHERMING (YEAR)/SOCIAL PROTECTION BUDGET. Text in Dutch. 1999. a., latest 2003. EUR 12.50 per issue (effective 2003). charts; stat. back issues avail. **Document type:** *Government.* **Description:** Surveys the Belgian social security budget, schemes for employed and self-employed persons, and general social assistance.
Formerly (until 2002): Vade Mecum: Begroting van de Sociale Zekerheid (1375-4440)
Related titles: French ed.: Vade Mecum: Budget de la Protection Sociale (Year). ISSN 1378-2614. EUR 7.50 per issue (effective 2003); ◆ Includes: Vade Mecum: Begrotingscontrole (Year). ISSN 1375-4394.

Published by: Ministere Federal des Affaires Sociales de la Sante Publique et de l'Environnement, Service des Publications/Federaal Ministerie van Sociale Zaken, Volksgezondheid en Leefmilieu, Publicaties Dienst, Rue de la Vierge Noire 3C, Zwarte Lievevrouwstraat 3C, Brussels, 1000, Belgium. TEL 32-2-509-8552, FAX 32-2-509-8016, roland.vanlaere@minisoc.fed.be, http://www.socialsecurity.fgov.be/bib/homehome.htm.

368.4 362.2 BEL ISSN 1375-4394
VADE MECUM: BEGROTINGSCONTROLE (YEAR)/BUDGET CONTROL. Text in Dutch. 1999. a. EUR 7.50 per issue (effective 2003). charts; stat. **Document type:** *Government.* **Description:** Surveys the Belgian social security budget, schemes for employed and self-employed persons, and general social assistance.
Related titles: French ed.: Vade Mecum: Controle Budetaire (Year). ISSN 1375-4408. EUR 7.50 per issue (effective 2003); ◆ Issued with: Vade Mecum: Begroting van de Sociale Bescherming (Year). ISSN 1378-2622.
Published by: Ministere Federal des Affaires Sociales de la Sante Publique et de l'Environnement, Service des Publications/Federaal Ministerie van Sociale Zaken, Volksgezondheid en Leefmilieu, Publicaties Dienst, Rue de la Vierge Noire 3C, Zwarte Lievevrouwstraat 3C, Brussels, 1000, Belgium. TEL 32-2-509-8552, FAX 32-2-509-8016, roland.vanlaere@minisoc.fed.be, http://www.socialsecurity.fgov.be/bib/homehome.htm.

VAELFAERD; SCB's tidskrift om arbetsliv, demografi och vaelfaerd. *see* PUBLIC ADMINISTRATION—Abstracting, Bibliographies, Statistics

351.492 NLD ISSN 1574-387X
VASTSTELLING VAN DE BEGROTINGSSTAAT VAN DE STATEN-GENERAAL IIA. Cover title: Rijksbegroting Staten-Generaal Begroting IIA. Text in Dutch. a.
Published by: (Tweede Kamer de Staten-Generaal), Sdu Uitgevers bv, Postbus 20025, The Hague, 2500 EA, Netherlands. TEL 31-70-3789911, FAX 31-70-3854321, sdu@sdu.nl, http://www.sdu.nl/.

351 NLD ISSN 1874-6152
VASTSTELLING VAN DE BEGROTINGSSTAAT VAN HET WADDENFONDS VOOR HET JAAR. Cover title: Rijksbegroting Waddenfonds. Text in Dutch. 2006. a.
Published by: (Netherlands. Ministerie van Financien, Ministerie van Volkshuisvesting, Ruimtelijke Ordening en Milieubeheer), Sdu Uitgevers bv, Postbus 20025, The Hague, 2500 EA, Netherlands. TEL 31-70-3789911, FAX 31-70-3854321, sdu@sdu.nl, http://www.sdu.nl/.

351 MDG
VAVOLOMBELONA. Text in Malagasy. 1985. w. **Document type:** *Newspaper.*
Published by: Fiangonan'i Jesoa Kristy eto Madagasikara/Eglise de Jesus Christ a Madagascar (Church of Jesus Christ in Madagascar), BP 271, Antananarivo, 101, Madagascar. TEL 302-53, FAX 263-72. Ed. Rev. Lala Rasendrahansina.

351 SVK ISSN 1337-0448
VEREJNA SPRAVA. Text in Slovak. 2006. m. EUR 4.81 newsstand/cover (effective 2009). **Document type:** *Magazine, Trade.*
Published by: Poradca s.r.o., Pri Celulozke 40, Zilina, 010 01, Slovakia. TEL 421-41-5652871, FAX 421-41-5652659, abos@i-poradca.sk, http://www.i-poradca.sk.

351.43 DEU ISSN 1612-5134
VERKEHRSPOLITIK IN FORSCHUNG UND PRAXIS. Text in German. 2003. irreg., latest vol.5, 2010. price varies. **Document type:** *Monographic series, Academic/Scholarly.*
Published by: Verlag Dr. Kovac, Leverkusenstr 13, Hamburg, 22761, Germany. TEL 49-40-3988800, FAX 49-40-39888055, info@verlagdrkovac.de.

VERMONT BAR JOURNAL. *see* LAW

351 347 USA ISSN 1071-3379
KFV36
VERMONT GOVERNMENT REGISTER. Text in English. 1991. m. adv. **Document type:** *Government.* **Description:** Covers executive orders of the Governor, Attorney General opinions, public laws enacted, banking and insurance agency information, public utility and environmental orders enacted, emergency rules, and gubernatorial appointments of state officials and board-commission members, notices of agency rulemaking.
Published by: LexisNexis (Subsidiary of: Reed Elsevier Group plc), 1016 W Ninth Ave, 1st Fl, King of Prussia, PA 19406. TEL 215 564-1788, 800 448-1515, customer.support@lexisnexis.com.

351.8 NLD ISSN 2210-9064
▼ **VERSLAG VAN HET TOEZICHT.** Text in Dutch. 2009. a.
Published by: Erfgoedinspectie, Postbus 16478, The Hague, 2500 BL, Netherlands. TEL 31-70-4124012, FAX 31-70-4124014, info@erfgoedinspectie.nl, http://www.erfgoedinspectie.nl.

351 FRA ISSN 2105-6420
VERT & BLEU. Text in French. 1998. q. **Document type:** *Magazine, Consumer.*
Formerly (until 2010): Communaute de Communes du Bassin de Marennes. Le Journal Communautaire (1624-477X)
Published by: Communaute de Communes du Bassin de Marennes, 10 Rue du Marechal Foch, BP 50028, Marennes, 17320, France. TEL 33-5-46859841, contact@bassin-de-marennes.com, http://www.bassin-de-marennes.com.

351 DEU ISSN 0042-4498
JA44
DIE VERWALTUNG; Zeitschrift fuer Verwaltungsrecht und Verwaltungswissenschaften. Text in German. 1968. q. EUR 124 combined subscription to individuals (print & online eds.); EUR 182 combined subscription to institutions (print & online eds.); EUR 36 newsstand/cover (effective 2012). adv. bk.rev. index. Supplement avail. **Document type:** *Journal, Academic/Scholarly.*
Related titles: Online - full text ed.: ISSN 1865-5211. 2008.
Indexed: A22, ABCPolSci, CA, DIP, FR, I13, IBR, IBSS, IBZ, P42, PAIS, PSA, RASB, SCOPUS, SociolAb, T02.
—IE, Infotrieve, INIST. **CCC.**
Published by: Duncker und Humblot GmbH, Carl-Heinrich-Becker-Weg 9, Berlin, 12165, Germany. TEL 49-30-7900060, FAX 49-30-79000631, info@duncker-humblot.de. Ed. J Masing. Circ: 500 (paid).

VERWALTUNGSARCHIV; Zeitschrift fuer Verwaltungslehre, Verwaltungsrecht und Verwaltungspolitik. *see* LAW

VERZEICHNIS RHEINLAND-PFAELZISCHER RECHT- UND VERWALTUNGSVORSCHRIFTEN. *see* LAW

VICROADS. ANNUAL REPORT. *see* TRANSPORTATION—Roads And Traffic

351 AUS ISSN 0819-5471
VICTORIA GOVERNMENT GAZETTE. GENERAL. Text in English. 1851. w.
Supersedes in part (in 1987): Victoria Government Gazette (0042-5095)
Published by: Craftsman Press, Locked Bag 255, Clayton South, VIC 3169, Australia. TEL 61-3-85146000, FAX 61-3-85146199, enquiries@craftpress.com.au, http://www.craftpress.com.au.

351 AUS ISSN 0819-5498
VICTORIA GOVERNMENT GAZETTE. PERIODICAL. Text in English. 1851. w.
Supersedes in part (in 1987): Victoria Government Gazette (0042-5095)
Published by: Craftsman Press, Locked Bag 255, Clayton South, VIC 3169, Australia. TEL 61-3-85146000, FAX 61-3-85146199, enquiries@craftpress.com.au, http://www.craftpress.com.au.

351 AUS ISSN 0819-548X
VICTORIA GOVERNMENT GAZETTE. SPECIAL. Text in English. 1851. w.
Supersedes in part (in 1987): Victoria Government Gazette (0042-5095)
Published by: Craftsman Press, Locked Bag 255, Clayton South, VIC 3169, Australia. TEL 61-3-85146000, FAX 61-3-85146199, enquiries@craftpress.com.au, http://www.craftpress.com.au.

VICTORIAN ADMINISTRATIVE LAW. *see* LAW—Constitutional Law

351 AUS ISSN 1449-8057
VICTORIAN AUDITOR-GENERAL'S OFFICE. ANNUAL PLAN. Text in English. 19??. a. free (effective 2009). **Document type:** *Government.*
Related titles: Online - full text ed.
Published by: Victorian Auditor-General's Office, Level 24, 35 Collins St, Melbourne, VIC 3000, Australia. TEL 61-3-86017000, FAX 61-3-86017010, comments@audit.vic.gov.au.

352.80994 AUS ISSN 1833-9689
HD3616.A84
VICTORIAN COMPETITION AND EFFICIENCY COMMISSION. ANNUAL REPORT. Text in English. 2005. a. free (effective 2009). back issues avail. **Document type:** *Government.*
Related titles: Online - full text ed.
Published by: Victorian Competition and Efficiency Commission, GPO Box 4379, Melbourne, VIC 3001, Australia. TEL 61-3-90925800, FAX 61-3-90925845, contact@vcec.vic.gov.au.

351.94 AUS ISSN 0158-1589
JQ5321
VICTORIAN GOVERNMENT DIRECTORY. Text in English. 1971. a. AUD 54.50 per issue; AUD 69.50 combined subscription per issue (print & CD-ROM eds.) (effective 2009). **Document type:** *Directory, Government.* **Description:** Guide to state government departments, agencies, and contact officers.
Formerly (until 1980): Victoria. Directory of Government Departments and Authorities (0155-5278)
Related titles: Diskette ed.
Published by: Information Victoria, 505 Little Collins St, Melbourne, VIC 3000, Australia. TEL 61-3-96038806, FAX 61-3-96039940. Circ: 3,000.

351 AUS ISSN 1326-429X
VICTORIAN PUBLIC SERVICE NOTICES. Text in English. 1995. bi-w.
Media: Online - full text.
Published by: Victoria, Office of the Public Service Commissioner, Level 3 1 Treasury Place, Melbourne, VIC 3002, Australia. TEL 61-3-93292266, FAX 61-3-93292899.

351 UKR ISSN 0320-7978
KKY7
VIDOMOSTI VERKHOVNOI RADY UKRAINY. Text in Ukrainian, Russian. 1941. w. UAK 84 domestic; USD 279 in United States (effective 2002). **Description:** Covers laws adopted by the Ukrainian Parliament.
Related titles: Online - full text ed.
Indexed: RASB.
—East View.
Published by: (Verkhovna Rada Ukrainy), Verkhovna Rada Ukrainy Vydavnytstvo/Parliamentary Publishing House, vul Nesterova 4, Kyiv, 03047, Ukraine. mail@golos.com.ua, http://uamedia.visti.net/golos. Ed. George Ganjurov. Circ: 15,000 (paid and controlled). **Dist. by:** East View Information Services, 10601 Wayzata Blvd, Minneapolis, MN 55305. TEL 952-252-1201, 800-477-1005, FAX 952-252-1202, info@eastview.com, http://www.eastview.com.

351 FRA ISSN 0042-5400
LA VIE COMMUNALE ET DEPARTEMENTALE; revue mensuelle de l'activite locale. Text in French. 1923. 11/yr. EUR 78.50 domestic; EUR 79.40 foreign (effective 2010). adv. bk.rev. bibl.; charts; illus.; stat.
Incorporates (1973-1984): Finances Communales et de Formation Permanente des Personnels Communaux. Revue (0294-8192); Which was formerly (1936-1973): Finances Communales. Revue (0035-208X); and (1924-1926): Le Mouvement Communal Francais (1146-8696); Which was formerly (1921-1923): La Quinzaine Urbaine (1146-870X)
Indexed: FR.
Published by: La Vie Communale et Departementale, 35 rue Marbeuf, Paris, 75008, France. TEL 43-59-27-41. Ed. Viviane d'Andigne.

351 LTU ISSN 1648-4541
➤ **VIESASIS ADMINISTRAVIMAS/PUBLIC ADMINISTRATION.** Text in Lithuanian, English. 2002. q. LTL 256 domestic; EUR 75 foreign (effective 2011). bk.rev. illus.; maps; stat. **Document type:** *Journal, Academic/Scholarly.* **Description:** Aims to present national achievements to foreign scientists, educators and civil servants at national and municipal level, i.e. for everybody who is interested in public administration theory and practice.
Indexed: A01, CA, P42.
Published by: Lietuvos Viesojo Administravimo Lavinimo Instituciju Asociacija/Lithuanian Public Administration Training Association, Birutes St 56, Vilnius, Lithuania. TEL 370-5-2724384, FAX 370-5-2721637, fmmc@fmmc.lt, http://www.fmmc.lt/VALA. Eds. Dr. Eugenijus Chlivickas, Dr. Habil B Melnikas. Circ: 200.

351 LTU ISSN 1648-2603
➤ **VIESOJI POLITIKA IR ADMINISTRAVIMAS/PUBLIC POLICY AND ADMINISTRATION.** Text in Lithuanian, English, German, Russian. 2002. q. LTL 200 domestic; LTL 240 foreign (effective 2011). back issues avail. **Document type:** *Journal, Academic/Scholarly.* **Description:** Aims to encourage scientific search of new theoretical and practical solutions to the formulation and implementation of public policy, to follow and analyze trends in public administration practice and suggest new modeling alternatives for decision making and implementation of public administration in the countries of Central and Eastern Europe.
Related titles: Online - full text ed.: ISSN 2029-2872.
Indexed: A01, CA.
Published by: Kauno Technologijos Universitetas/Kaunas University of Technology, K. Donelaicio g. 73, Kaunas, 44029, Lithuania. TEL 370-37-300000, FAX 370-37-324144, rastine@ktu.lt. Ed. Aleksandras Patapas.

351 GBR
VIEW (LONDON); focusing on members of the public and commercial services union. Variant title: P C S View. Text in English. 1922. m. GBP 1.80 per issue to non-members; free to members (effective 2009). adv. bk.rev.; music rev. back issues avail. **Document type:** *Magazine, Trade.* **Description:** Contains the latest news on pay and conditions, rights at work and campaigns.
Former titles (until 2001): P C S the Magazine; (until 1998): Red Tape (0034-2076)
Related titles: Online - full text ed.
Published by: Public and Commercial Services Union, 160 Falcon Rd, London, SW11 2LN, United Kingdom. TEL 44-20-79242727, FAX 44-20-79241847, membership@pcs.org.uk. Ed. Sharon Breen.

VILLE DE MONTREAL. ECONOMIC REPORT. *see* BUSINESS AND ECONOMICS

351 FRA ISSN 2108-1611
LES VILLES D'OYSE. Text in French. 2007. s-a. **Document type:** *Newsletter, Consumer.*
Published by: Communaute de Communes des Villes d'Oyse (C C V O), 16 Rue Albert Catalifaud, La Fere, 02800, France. TEL 33-3-23566222, FAX 33-3-23566223, ville.oyse@wanadoo.fr, http://www.cc-villesdoyse.org.

351.755 USA ISSN 1076-4577
VIRGINIA CAPITOLCONNECTIONS. Text in English. 1987. q. USD 20 (effective 2004). **Description:** Covers statewide issues from the inside. Figures in Virginia politics give you their side of current political issues.
Formerly (until 1994): Virginia Capital Connections
Published by: David Bailey Associates, 1001 East Broad St Ste 225, Richmond, VA 23219. TEL 804-643-5554, FAX 804-643-5927, http://www.dbava.com/index.html. Ed. Bonnie Atwood.

351 USA
VIRGINIA ISSUES & ANSWERS; a public policy forum. Text in English. s-a. back issues avail. **Document type:** *Journal, Academic/Scholarly.*
Related titles: Online - full text ed.
Published by: Virginia Polytechnic Institute and State University, 105 Media Bldg. (0109), Blacksburg, VA 24061. Pub. Lawrence G. Hincker. **Co-sponsor:** Virginia Polythecnic Institute and State University, Office of University Relations.

352.14 USA
JK3901
THE VIRGINIA NEWS LETTER (ONLINE). Text in English. 1924. bi-m. looseleaf. free (effective 2011). back issues avail. **Document type:** *Newsletter, Government.* **Description:** Focuses on specific public policy issues and their impact on state or local government in Virginia.
Former titles (until 2009): The Virginia News Letter (Print); (until 1997): University of Virginia. News Letter (0042-0271)
Media: Online - full text.
Indexed: P06, PAIS, RASB.
Published by: University of Virginia, Weldon Cooper Center for Public Service, PO Box 400206, Charlottesville, VA 22904. TEL 434-982-5522, coopercenter@virginia.edu.

343 BEL ISSN 1373-0509
VLAAMS TIJDSCHRIFT VOOR OVERHEIDSMANAGEMENT. Text in Dutch. 1996. q. EUR 85 (effective 2008). **Document type:** *Journal, Trade.*
Published by: Die Keure NV, Kleine Pathoekeweg 3, Bruges, 8000, Belgium. TEL 32-50-471272, FAX 32-50-335154, juridische.uitgaven@diekeure.be, http://www.diekeure.be.

352.68 USA
THE VOICE (AUSTIN). Text in English. q. free. **Document type:** *Newsletter.*
Media: Online - full content.
Published by: Texas Public Employees Association, 512 East 11th St, Ste 100, Austin, TX 78701. TEL 512-476-2691, 888-367-8732, FAX 512-476-1338, mail@tpea.org.

VOLKSHUISVESTINGSBELEID EN WONINGMARKT. *see* HOUSING AND URBAN PLANNING

351 BEL ISSN 1782-1851
W C O NEWS. (World Customs Organization) Text in English. 1983. s-a. free. **Document type:** *Magazine, Trade.* **Description:** Discusses issues relating to customs agencies worldwide.
Related titles: Online - full text ed.; ◆ Supplement(s): O M D Actualites. ISSN 1782-1843.
Published by: World Customs Organization (W C O)/Organisation Mondiale des Douanes (O M D), Rue du Marche 30, Brussels, 1210, Belgium. TEL 32-2-209-9211, FAX 32-2-209-9292, information@wcoomd.org.

351.492 NLD ISSN 2211-4769
▼ **W M O WETGEVING & RECHTSPRAAK.** (Wet Maatschappelijke Ondersteuning) Text in Dutch. 2011. s-a. EUR 26.10 per issue (effective 2011).
Published by: Kluwer B.V. (Subsidiary of: Wolters Kluwer N.V.), Postbus 23, Deventer, 7400 GA, Netherlands. TEL 31-570-673449, FAX 31-570-691555, info@kluwer.nl, http://www.kluwer.nl.

WAKE FOREST UNIVERSITY SCHOOL OF LAW. CONTINUING LEGAL EDUCATION. ANNUAL REVIEW, NORTH CAROLINA. *see* LAW

WASHINGTON (STATE). DEPARTMENT OF NATURAL RESOURCES. ANNUAL REPORT. *see* ENVIRONMENTAL STUDIES

WASHINGTON (STATE) LEGISLATURE. PICTORIAL DIRECTORY. *see* POLITICAL SCIENCE

WASHINGTON ADMINISTRATIVE LAW PRACTICE MANUAL. *see* LAW—Constitutional Law

351 USA ISSN 0250-6319
WASHINGTON. GENERAL SECRETARIAT ORGANIZATION OF AMERICAN STATES. SUMMARY OF THE DECISIONS TAKEN AT THE MEETINGS AND TEXTS OF THE RESOLUTIONS APPROVED. Text in English. 1948. irreg., latest 2001. **Document type:** *Trade.*
Formerly (until 1971): Organization of American States. Decisions Taken at the Meetings of the Council
Related titles: Spanish ed.: Sintesis de las Decisiones Tomadas en las Sesiones y Textos de las Resoluciones Aprobadas. ISSN 0250-6300.
Published by: Organization of American States, General Secretariat, 1889 F St, NW, Washington, DC 20006. TEL 202-458-3000, oaspress@oas.org, http://www.oas.org.

351.796 320 USA
WASHINGTON PUBLIC AFFAIRS DIGEST. Text in English. 1999. w. looseleaf. USD 62 (effective 2011). index. back issues avail. **Document type:** *Newsletter, Trade.*
Related titles: E-mail ed.
Published by: Ridenbaugh Press, PO Box 834, Carlton, OR 97111. TEL 503-852-0010, stapilus@ridenbaugh.com.

333.783 USA
WASHINGTON RECREATION AND PARK ASSOCIATION. SYLLABUS. Text in English. 1969. 10/yr. membership. adv. bk.rev. charts; illus. **Document type:** *Newsletter.*
Former titles: Washington Recreation and Park Association. Bulletin; Washington Recreation and Park Society. News (0042-9805)
Published by: Washington Recreation and Park Association, Inc., 4405 7th Ave SE, Ste. 202, Lacey, WA 98503-1055. TEL 206-874-1283, FAX 206-661-3929. Ed., R&P, Adv. contact Jim Webster. Circ: 1,050.

351 340 320 USA ISSN 0192-060X
JK1118
WASHINGTON REPRESENTATIVES. Variant title: Washington Representatives Directory. Text in English. 1977. s-a. USD 399; USD 799 combined subscription (print & online eds.); USD 269 per issue (effective 2011). **Document type:** *Directory, Trade.* **Description:** Compilation of over 18,000 Washington lobbyists, lawyers, government relations counselors, registered foreign agents, and other advocates, organized alphabetically by person and organization.
Formerly (until 1979): Directory of Washington Representatives of American Associations and Industry (0147-216X)
Related titles: Online - full text ed.
Published by: Columbia Books Inc., 8120 Woodmont Ave, Ste 110, Bethesda, MD 20814. TEL 202-464-1662, FAX 202-464-1775, 888-265-0600, info@columbiabooks.com, http://www.columbiabooks.com.

WASHINGTON STATE LABOR MARKET AND ECONOMIC REPORT (YEAR). *see* BUSINESS AND ECONOMICS—Labor And Industrial Relations

WASHINGTON UPDATE. *see* EDUCATION—Computer Applications

▼ **WATER ENVIRONMENT REGULATION WATCH (ONLINE).** *see* ENVIRONMENTAL STUDIES—Pollution

WAVENEY DISTRICT COUNCIL. PLANNING & BUILDING CONTROL. INFORMATION NOTES. *see* HOUSING AND URBAN PLANNING

351 CAN ISSN 1718-4886
THE WAY FORWARD NEWS/NOUVELLES SUR LES PROCHAINES ETAPES. Text in English. 2005. irreg., latest 2006, Dec. **Document type:** *Newsletter, Government.*
Media: Online - full text. **Related titles:** Print ed.: ISSN 1718-4908.
Published by: Public Works and Government Services Canada, Government Information Services Branch, 155 Queen St, 5th Flr, Ottawa, ON K1A 0S5, Canada. TEL 613-943-5130, FAX 613-947-1818, por-rop@pwgsc.gc.ca, http://www.pwgsc.gc.ca/por/text/rpt05-06-01-e.html.

WEEKLY LEGISLATIVE UPDATE. *see* PETROLEUM AND GAS

WEEKLY REGULATORY UPDATE. *see* PETROLEUM AND GAS

351.763 USA
WEEKLY REVIEW. Text in English. 1970. w. USD 200. **Description:** Review of Louisiana government and politics.
Related titles: Fax ed.; Online - full text ed.
Published by: Louisiana News Bureau, Inc., PO Box 44212, Baton Rouge, LA 70804. TEL 504-342-1240. Eds. Kevin Morgan, Michael Courtney.

WEGWIJZER WABO EN OMGEVINGSVERGUNNING. *see* ENVIRONMENTAL STUDIES

▼ **WEGWIJZER WET VEILIGHEIDSREGIO'S.** *see* PUBLIC HEALTH AND SAFETY

351.687355 ZAF
WES-KAAP. OFFISIELE KOERANT/WESTERN CAPE. OFFICIAL GAZETTE. Variant title: Province of the Cape of Good Hope Official Gazette. Text in Afrikaans, English. 1994 (no.4857). q. maps. **Document type:** *Government.*
Supersedes in part: Kaap die Goeie Hoop. Provinsiale Koerant - Cape of Good Hope. Provincial Gazette
Published by: Cape Provincial Administration, PO Box 659, Cape Town, 8000, South Africa.

353.7 IND ISSN 0049-7193
WEST BENGAL. Text in English. 1969. fortn. illus. **Document type:** *Journal, Government.*
Published by: Department of Information and Cultural Affairs, Writers' Bldgs, 3rd Fl, Kolkata, West Bengal 700 001, India. TEL 91-33-22544545, FAX 91-33-22141605, ica-dept@wb.gov.in.

WEST VIRGINIA. LEGISLATURE. COMMISSION ON SPECIAL INVESTIGATIONS. REPORT TO THE WEST VIRGINIA LEGISLATURE. *see* POLITICAL SCIENCE

WEST VIRGINIA RESEARCH LEAGUE. STATISTICAL HANDBOOK; a digest of selected data on state and local government in West Virginia. *see* PUBLIC ADMINISTRATION—Abstracting, Bibliographies, Statistics

351.747277 USA ISSN 0363-356X
HT167.5.W5 CODEN: YANTAE
WESTCHESTER PLANNING. Text in English. 1973. q. free. bk.rev. illus. **Description:** Covers planning and allied fields such as architecture, landscape architecture, law, political science, statistics and urban studies as they relate to Westchester.
Formerly: Westchester Planning Newsletter
Published by: Westchester County Department of Planning, 432 County Office Bldg, White Plains, NY 10601. TEL 914-682-2564. Ed. Mary R S Carlson. Circ: 2,000.

351.946 AUS ISSN 0043-3489
WESTERN AUSTRALIA. GOVERNMENT GAZETTE. Text in English. 1836. s-w. free (effective 2009). **Document type:** *Government.* **Description:** Publishes notices of a legal nature as required by acts of Parliament, and other official government notices.
Former titles (until 1990): Western Australia. Government Gazette of Western Australia; (until 1878): Western Australia. Western Australian Government Gazette
Related titles: Online - full text ed.
Published by: State Law Publisher, Ground Fl, 10 William St, Perth, W.A. 6000, Australia. TEL 61-8-93217688, FAX 61-8-93217536, sales@dpc.wa.gov.au.

351 AUS ISSN 1832-9411
WESTERN AUSTRALIA. OFFICE OF THE PUBLIC SECTOR STANDARDS COMMISSIONER. ANNUAL REPORT. Text in English. 1995. a. free (effective 2008). back issues avail. **Document type:** *Government.*
Formerly: Western Australia. Public Sector Standards Commission. Annual Report
Related titles: CD-ROM ed.: free to qualified personnel (effective 2008); Online - full text ed.: free (effective 2008).
Published by: Western Australia, Office of the Public Sector Standards Commissioner, GPO Box 2581, Perth, W.A. 6001, Australia. TEL 61-8-92606600, 800-676-607, FAX 61-8-92606611, phillip.torrisi@opssc.wa.gov.au, http://www.opssc.wa.gov.au/.

351 NLD ISSN 1574-4558
WET WERK EN BIJSTAND (DOETINCHEM). Cover title: W W B. Variant title: Tekstuitgave Wet Werk en Bijstand. Text in Dutch. a. EUR 35.38 (effective 2009).
Formerly (until 2004): Algemene Bijstandswet (1386-8217)
Published by: Reed Business bv (Subsidiary of: Reed Business), Postbus 4, Doetinchem, 7000 BA, Netherlands. TEL 31-314-349911, info@reedbusiness.nl, http://www.reedbusiness.nl.

WETTEKSTEN RUIMTELIJKE ORDENING EN BOUWEN. *see* HOUSING AND URBAN PLANNING

WHAT YOU CAN DO FOR YOUR COUNTRY. *see* SOCIAL SERVICES AND WELFARE

328.775 USA
WHEELER REPORT. Text in English. 1974. d. (during session; fortn. during interim). USD 900. **Description:** Reports on action taken in Wisconsin Legislature, including bill status information. Also covers attorney general opinion, agency appointments and interim committee activity.
Published by: Wheeler News Service, 121 E Main St, Ste 300, Madison, WI 53703-3315. TEL 608-257-2614. Ed. Richard Wheeler.

351.73 USA ISSN 0737-9218
E839.5
WHITE HOUSE WEEKLY. Text in English. 1981. 48/yr. USD 99 domestic; USD 145 foreign (effective 2006). 12 p./no.; **Document type:** *Newsletter.* **Description:** Covers the White House, including president and staff.
Related titles: Online - full text ed.: USD 99 (effective 2006).
Indexed: A26, E08, G08, I05, S09.
—CCC.
Published by: King Publishing Group, Inc., 1325 G St, N W, Ste 1003, Washington, DC 20005. TEL 202-662-9745, FAX 202-662-9719, lking@kingpublishing.com. Ed. Llewellyn King.

351 NLD ISSN 1574-6542
WIJZERWONEN. Text in Dutch. 1985. q.
Formerly (until 2004): Oud en Wijs (1381-8503)
Published by: Landelijke Vereniging Groepswonen van Ouderen, Herengracht 218, Amsterdam, 1016 BT, Netherlands. TEL 31-20-3200037, info@lvgo.nl, http://www.lvgo.nl.

348.025 USA
WISCONSIN ADMINISTRATIVE CODE. Text in English. base vol. plus irreg. updates. looseleaf. **Document type:** *Government.* **Description:** Contains all documents listing the administrative rules of state agencies.
Related titles: ◆ CD-ROM ed.: Wisconsin Administrative Code (CD-ROM); Supplement(s):.
Published by: Department of Administration, Document Sales and Distribution, 202 Thornton Ave, Box 7840, Madison, WI 53707. TEL 608-266-3358, docsales@mail.state.wi.us, http://www.legis.state.wi.us/.

348.025 USA
WISCONSIN ADMINISTRATIVE CODE (CD-ROM). Text in English. 19??. base vol. plus q. updates. price varies. **Document type:** *Journal, Trade.* **Description:** Covers the full text of every rule from 50-plus Wisconsin executive agencies. Rules are arranged alphabetically, simplifying and speeding your research.
Media: CD-ROM. **Related titles:** ◆ Print ed.: Wisconsin Administrative Code.
Published by: Thomson West (Subsidiary of: Thomson Reuters Corp.), 610 Opperman Dr, Eagan, MN 55123. TEL 651-687-7000, 800-344-5008, west.customer.service@thomson.com.

351.775 USA
WISCONSIN BLUE BOOK. Text in English. 1853. biennial. USD 8 (effective 2000). **Document type:** *Government.*
Indexed: SRI.
Published by: Department of Administration, Document Sales and Distribution, 202 Thornton Ave, Box 7840, Madison, WI 53707. TEL 608-266-3358. Ed. Lawrence Barish. R&P Allen Marty TEL 608-267-0713.

351.775 USA ISSN 0085-8226
WISCONSIN. DEPARTMENT OF ADMINISTRATION. ANNUAL FISCAL REPORT. Text in English. 1950. a. free.
Related titles: Microfiche ed.: (from CIS).
Indexed: SRI.
Published by: Department of Administration, Bureau of Financial Operations, PO Box 7864, Madison, WI 53707. TEL 608-266-1694. Ed. W J Raftery. Circ: 1,000.

WISCONSIN PUBLIC DOCUMENTS. *see* PUBLIC ADMINISTRATION—Abstracting, Bibliographies, Statistics

328.37 USA ISSN 0145-6628
KFW2425
WISCONSIN SESSION LAWS. Text in English. biennial. USD 32.30 (effective 2006).
Formerly (until 1911): Laws of Wisconsin
Indexed: P30.
Published by: Wisconsin State Legislature, Revisor of Statutes Bureau, 131 W Wilson St., Ste. 800, Madison, WI 53703-3261. TEL 608-266-2011, FAX 608-267-6978, http://www.legis.state.wi.us/rsb/.

WISCONSIN. STATE ELECTIONS BOARD. BIENNIAL REPORT. *see* POLITICAL SCIENCE

351.775 USA ISSN 0043-6720
HJ2441
THE WISCONSIN TAXPAYER. Text in English. 1933. m. USD 17.97; USD 3.50 per issue; free to qualified personnel (effective 2011). **Document type:** *Magazine, Government.* **Description:** Analyzes and comments on issues dealing with Wisconsin state and local government.
Indexed: P06.
Published by: Wisconsin Taxpayers Alliance, 401 N Lawn Ave, Madison, WI 53704. TEL 608-241-9789, FAX 608-241-5807, wistax@wistax.org.

WOMEN IN GOVERNMENT. *see* WOMEN'S INTERESTS

WOMEN IN PUBLIC SERVICE BULLETIN. *see* WOMEN'S INTERESTS

WOMEN'S POLICY JOURNAL OF HARVARD. *see* WOMEN'S STUDIES

WONINGWET EN VERWANTE WETGEVING. *see* HOUSING AND URBAN PLANNING

WORD FROM WASHINGTON (SAN ANTONIO). *see* BUSINESS AND ECONOMICS—Labor And Industrial Relations

352.68 USA ISSN 0886-9162
KFO342.A15
WORKERS' COMPENSATION JOURNAL OF OHIO. Abbreviated title: W C J O. Text in English. 1986. bi-m. (in 6 vols.). USD 535.56 (effective 2011). bk.rev. **Document type:** *Newsletter, Trade.* **Description:** Reviews judicial, legislative, and administrative developments in Ohio workers' compensation and intentional tort law.
Published by: Banks - Baldwin Law Publishing Co., PO Box 318063, Cleveland, OH 44131-8063. FAX 216-520-5655, http://www.bn.com. Ed. Jerald D Harris.

P

352.63 NZL ISSN 2230-3480
WORKING LIFE. Text in English. 1913. q. free to members (effective 2011). bk.rev.; rec.rev. back issues avail. **Document type:** *Journal, Consumer.* **Description:** Covers economic and social issues, international trade union news, personality profiles, health and safety, and PSA news.
Former titles (until 2010): Public Service Association. Journal (0110-6945); (until 1978): Public Service Journal; Which incorporated: New Zealand Public Service Association. Annual Report
Related titles: Online - full text ed.: ISSN 2230-3499.
Published by: New Zealand Public Service Association, 11 Aurora Terrace, PO Box 3817, Wellington, 6140, New Zealand. TEL 64-4-4957633, FAX 64-4-9172051, enquiries@psa.org.nz.

351 BEL
WORLD CUSTOMS ORGANIZATION. ANNUAL REPORT; the activities of the WCO. Text in English. a. free. charts; illus.; stat. **Document type:** *Corporate.* **Description:** Reviews the activities of the World Customs Organization for the previous fiscal year ended June.
Published by: World Customs Organization (W C O)/Organisation Mondiale des Douanes (O M D), Rue du Marche 30, Brussels, 1210, Belgium. TEL 32-2-209-9211, FAX 32-2-209-9292, information@wcoomd.org.

351 ZAF ISSN 1819-866X
WORLD JOURNAL OF PUBLIC ADMINISTRATION AND MANAGEMENT. Text in English. 2006. q. USD 120 in Africa to individuals; USD 180 elsewhere to individuals; USD 350 in Africa to institutions; USD 450 elsewhere to institutions; USD 85 in Africa to students; USD 100 elsewhere to students (effective 2007). **Description:** Provides in-depth analysis of developments in the organizational, administrative, and policy sciences as they apply to government and governance.
Published by: (World Research Organization), Isis Press, PO Box 1919, Cape Town, 8000, South Africa. TEL 27-21-4471574, FAX 27-86-6219999, orders@unwro.org, http://www.unwro.org/isispress.html.

351 USA ISSN 0894-1521
JF37
WORLDWIDE GOVERNMENT DIRECTORY. Variant title: Profiles of Worldwide Government Leaders. Worldwide Government Directory, with International Organizations. Text in English. 1981. a. USD 461 combined subscription (print & online eds.) (effective 2008). reprints avail. **Document type:** *Directory.* **Description:** Contains the names and addresses of government officials in every country in the world. Includes data on international organizations and foreign embassies abroad.
Formerly (until 19??): Lambert's Worldwide Government Directory (0276-900X)
Related titles: CD-ROM ed.; Online - full text ed.
—CCC.
Published by: C Q Press, Inc. (Subsidiary of: Sage Publications, Inc.), 2300 N St, NW, Ste 800, Washington, DC 20037. TEL 202-729-1900, 866-427-7737, FAX 800-380-3810, customerservice@cqpress.com. Ed. Linda Dziobek.

WYOMING. DEPARTMENT OF ADMINISTRATION AND INFORMATION. STATE LIBRARY. ANNUAL REPORT. *see* LIBRARY AND INFORMATION SCIENCES

351 347 USA
KFW4236
WYOMING GOVERNMENT REGISTER. Text in English. 1995. m. USD 914 (effective 2011). back issues avail. **Document type:** *Government.* **Description:** Covers executive orders of the Governor, Attorney General opinions, public laws enacted, public utility and environmental orders enacted, banking and insurance agency information, emergency rules, and gubernatorial appointments of state officials and board-commission members.

Formerly (until 2005): Weil's Wyoming Government Register (1083-0359)
Published by: LexisNexis (Subsidiary of: Reed Elsevier Group plc), 1016 W Ninth Ave, 1st Fl, King of Prussia, PA 19406. TEL 215 564-1788, 800 448-1515, customer.support@lexisnexis.com.

351.51 CHN ISSN 1007-0575
K28
XIANFAXUE, XINGZHENG FAXUE/STUDIES OF CONSTITUTIONS, STUDIES OF ADMINISTRATIVE LAW. Text in Chinese. 1996. m. USD 79 (effective 2009). 64 p./no.; **Document type:** *Journal, Academic/Scholarly.* **Description:** Contains reprints of articles on Chinese constitutional law, public administration and political system.
Published by: Zhongguo Renmin Daxue Shubao Ziliao Zhongxin/Renmin University of China, Information Center for Social Sciences, Dongcheng-qu, 3, Zhangzizhong Lu, Beijing, 100007, China. TEL 86-10-64039458, FAX 86-10-64015080, center@zlzx.org, http://www.zlzx.org/. **Dist. in US by:** China Publications Service, PO Box 49614, Chicago, IL 60649. TEL 312-288-3291, FAX 312-288-8570; **Dist. by:** China International Book Trading Corp, 35 Chegongzhuang Xilu, Haidian District, PO Box 399, Beijing 100044, China. TEL 86-10-68412045, FAX 86-10-68412023, cibtc@mail.cibtc.com.cn, http://www.cibtc.com.cn.

XIANGGANG (YEAR). *see* POPULATION STUDIES

351.5125 HKG
XIANGGANG TEBIE XINGZHENGQU ZHENGFU XIANBAO/ GOVERNMENT OF THE HONG KONG SPECIAL ADMINISTRATIVE REGION GAZETTE. (Supplements include Gazette Extraordinary and 6 specific supplements: No.1, Ordinances; no.2, Regulations and No.3 - Bills; no.4, Periodical lists of registered professionals, etc; no.5 Draft Bills, Executive Orders, Order of the State Council, etc; no.6, Public Notices.) Text in Chinese. 1853; N.S. 1997. w. Supplement avail. **Document type:** *Newspaper, Government.* **Description:** Contains statutory notices for appointment, departmental notices and public tenders.
Formerly (until 1997): Hong Kong Government Gazette
Related titles: Online - full content ed.
Published by: Xianggang Tebie Xingzhengqu. Zhengfu Wuliu Fuwushu/ Government of the Hong Kong Special Administrative Region. Government Logistics Department, 10/F, North Point Government Offices, 333 Java Rd, North Point, Hong Kong. TEL 852-2231-5105, FAX 852-2887-6591, info@gld.gov.hk. **Subscr. to:** Information Services Department, Publications Sales Unit, Rm 402, 4th Fl, Murray Bldg, Garden Rd, Hong Kong, Hong Kong. TEL 852-2537-1910, puborder@isd.gcn.gov.hk, http://www.info.gov.hk/isd/book_e.htm.

351 340 CHN ISSN 1005-0078
XINGZHENG FAXUE YANJIU/ADMINISTRATIVE LAW REVIEW. Text in Chinese. 1993. q. USD 26.80 (effective 2009). **Document type:** *Journal, Academic/Scholarly.*
Related titles: Online - full text ed.
Published by: Guojia Xingzheng Daxue, 6, Changchun Qiao Lu, Beijing, 100089, China. TEL 86-10-68929072.

351 CHN ISSN 1674-2710
XINJIANG WEIWUER ZIZHIQU RENMIN ZHENGFU GONGBAO. Text in Chinese. 2003. s-a. free. **Document type:** *Newspaper, Government.*
Formerly (until 2003): Xinjiang Zhengbao
Published by: Xinjiang Weiwuer Zizhiqu Renmin Zhengfu/Government of the Xinjiang Uygur Autonomous Region of China, 2, Zhongshan Er-Lu, Zizhiqu Renmin Zhengfu Bangong Dalou 11/F, Urumqi, 830041, China. TEL 86-991-2383234, FAX 86-991-2383232.

THE YALE JOURNAL ON REGULATION. *see* LAW

328.791 USA
YELLOW SHEET REPORT. Text in English. 1906. 3/w. (between legislative sessions). USD 195 per month (effective 2001). **Description:** Covers Arizona interim legislative committee activity and other state political and governmental news.
Published by: Arizona News Service, Inc. (Subsidiary of: Dolan Media Co.), 1835 W Adams, Phoenix, AZ 85007. TEL 602-258-7026, FAX 602-253-7636. Pub. Ned Creighton.

351.54 IND ISSN 0044-0515
DS401 CODEN: YOJAE5
YOJANA. Text in Hindi. 1957. m. INR 100 domestic; INR 530 in neighbouring countries; INR 730 elsewhere (effective 2011). adv. bk.rev. charts; illus.; stat. back issues avail. **Document type:** *Magazine, Government.* **Description:** Serves as an intellectual forum on the problems and achievements of the planning and development of India.
Related titles: Assamese ed.: INR 30; Bengali ed.: INR 30; English ed.: INR 60; Tamil ed.: INR 40; Telugu ed.: INR 40; Malayalam ed.: INR 30; Marathi ed.: INR 30; Gujarati ed.: INR 30.
Indexed: ARDT, BAS, EnvAb, EnvInd, F09, P30, PAA&I, RASB, SCOPUS, W09.
Published by: Ministry of Information & Broadcasting, Publications Division, Yojana Bhavan, Sansad Marg, New Delhi, 1100 01, India. TEL 91-11-23096738, http://publicationsdivision.nic.in/. **Subscr. in U.S. to:** InterCulture Associates; **Subscr. to:** I N S I O Scientific Books & Periodicals.

351 GBR ISSN 2046-9217
▼ **YOUR EAST RIDING (HOLDERNESS EDITION).** Text in English. 2011. q. free to qualified personnel (effective 2011). **Document type:** *Magazine, Trade.* **Description:** Features news and events from Holderness.
Supersedes in part (in 2011): East Riding News (1463-5577)
Related titles: Online - full text ed.: free (effective 2011).
Published by: East Riding of Yorkshire Council, Cross St, Beverley, HU17 9BA, United Kingdom. TEL 44-1482-887888, FAX 44-1482-393395, customer.services@eastriding.gov.uk. Ed. Lisa Mansell T.

351 GBR ISSN 2046-9241
▼ **YOUR EAST RIDING (MARKET WEIGHTON AND POCKLINGTON EDITION).** Text in English. 2011. q. free to qualified personnel (effective 2011). **Document type:** *Magazine, Trade.* **Description:** Features news and events from Market Weighton and Pocklington.
Supersedes in part (in 2011): East Riding News (1463-5577)
Related titles: Online - full text ed.: free (effective 2011).
Published by: East Riding of Yorkshire Council, Cross St, Beverley, HU17 9BA, United Kingdom. TEL 44-1482-887888, FAX 44-1482-393395, customer.services@eastriding.gov.uk. Ed. Lisa Mansell T.

328.71 CAN ISSN 0715-2213
THE YUKON GAZETTE. PARTS I AND II. Text in English, French. 1982. m. CAD 65; CAD 6 newsstand/cover (effective 2004).
Related titles: Online - full content ed.
Published by: Government of Yukon, Queen's Printer, Box 2703, Whitehorse, YT Y1A 2C6, Canada. TEL 867-667-5783, FAX 867-393-6210, queens.printer@gov.yk.ca.

320.951 CHN ISSN 1674-4012
YUNNAN ZHENGBAO. Text in Chinese. 1950. m. **Document type:** *Magazine, Government.*
Related titles: Online - full text ed.
Published by: Yunnan Sheng Renmin Zhengfu Bangongting, Wuhuashan Donglitang, Kunming, Yunnan 650021, China. TEL 86-871-3622913, FAX 86-871-3609815.

ZAMBIA. CENTRAL STATISTICAL OFFICE. FINANCIAL STATISTICS OF GOVERNMENT SECTOR (ECONOMIC AND FUNCTIONAL ANALYSIS). *see* PUBLIC ADMINISTRATION—Abstracting, Bibliographies, Statistics

ZAMBIA. CENTRAL STATISTICAL OFFICE. NATIONAL ACCOUNTS. *see* PUBLIC ADMINISTRATION—Abstracting, Bibliographies, Statistics

351.6894 ZMB
ZAMBIA. COMMISSION FOR INVESTIGATIONS. ANNUAL REPORT. Text in English. 1975. a. ZMK 10. **Document type:** *Government.*
Published by: Commission for Investigations, Old Bank of Bldg Ridgeway, PO Box 50494, Lusaka, 10101, Zambia. Circ: 500. **Dist. by:** Government Printer, PO Box 136, Lusaka, Zambia.

351 POL ISSN 1896-0200
JN6751.A1
➤ **ZARZADZANIE PUBLICZNE.** Text in Polish, English. 2005. s-a. **Document type:** *Journal, Academic/Scholarly.*
Related titles: Online - full text ed.
Published by: (Uniwersytet Jagiellonski, Instytut Spraw Publicznych), Wydawnictwo Uniwersytetu Jagiellonskiego/Jagiellonian University Press, ul Grodzka 26, Krakow, 31044, Poland. TEL 48-12-4312364, FAX 48-12-4301995, wydaw@if.uj.edu.pl. Ed. Aleksander Noworol.

351 UKR
ZBIRNYK URYADOVYKH NORMATYVNYKH AKTIV UKRAINY. Text in Ukrainian. 1997. m. USD 185 in United States (effective 2000).
Published by: Kabinet Ministriv Ukrainy, Ul Sadovaya 1, Kiev, Ukraine. TEL 229-16-92. **Dist. by:** East View Information Services, 10601 Wayzata Blvd, Minneapolis, MN 55305. TEL 952-252-1201, 800-477-1005, FAX 952-252-1202, info@eastview.com, http://www.eastview.com.

ZEITSCHRIFT FUER BEAMTENRECHT. *see* LAW

ZEITSCHRIFT FUER DEUTSCHES UND INTERNATIONALES BAU- UND VERGABERECHT. *see* LAW

351 DEU ISSN 0344-9777
➤ **ZEITSCHRIFT FUER OEFFENTLICHE UND GEMEINWIRTSCHAFTLICHE UNTERNEHMEN.** Text in German. 1978. q. EUR 124 (effective 2011). adv. bk.rev. stat. reprint service avail. from SCH. **Document type:** *Journal, Academic/Scholarly.*
Incorporates (in 1984): Oeffentliche Wirtschaft und Gemeinwirtschaft (0343-1479); Which was formerly (until 1973): Oeffentliche Wirtschaft (0029-8603)
Indexed: DIP, IBR, IBSS, IBZ, RASB, TM.
—CCC.
Published by: Nomos Verlagsgesellschaft mbH und Co. KG, Waldseestr 3-5, Baden-Baden, 76530, Germany. TEL 49-7221-21040, FAX 49-7221-210427, marketing@nomos.de, nomos@nomos.de, http://www.nomos.de. Ed. Frank Schulz-Nieswandt. Adv. contact Bettina Roos. Circ: 1,200 (paid and controlled).

➤ **ZEITSCHRIFT FUER PARLAMENTSFRAGEN.** *see* POLITICAL SCIENCE

351.43 AUT ISSN 2218-2977
ZEITSCHRIFT FUER VERGABERECHT. Variant title: R P A. Recht und Praxis der Oeffentlichen Auftragsvergabe. Text in German. 2001. bi-m. EUR 134; EUR 24 newsstand/cover (effective 2011). adv.
Former titles (until 2010): R P A Aktuell (2218-2969); (until 2003): Recht und Praxis der Oeffentlichen Auftragsvergabe (1680-8711)
Published by: Verlag Oesterreich GmbH, Baeckerstr 1, Vienna, 1010, Austria. TEL 43-1-610770, FAX 43-1-61077419, office@verlagoesterreich.at, http://www.jusline.at/verlagoesterreich/index.html.

352.14 AUT ISSN 1680-6492
ZEITSCHRIFT FUER VERGABERECHT UND BESCHAFFUNGSPRAXIS. Text in German. 2001. 11/yr. EUR 235; EUR 25.70 newsstand/cover (effective 2011). reprint service avail. from SCH. **Document type:** *Journal, Academic/Scholarly.*
Published by: Manz'sche Verlags- und Universitaetsbuchhandlung GmbH, Johannesgasse 23, Vienna, W 1010, Austria. TEL 43-1-531610, FAX 43-1-53161181, verlag@manz.at, http://www.manz.at. Eds. Johannes Schramm, Josef Aicher.

351 AUT ISSN 1017-3463
K30
ZEITSCHRIFT FUER VERWALTUNG. Text in German. 1976. bi-m. EUR 379; EUR 77 newsstand/cover (effective 2005). 148 p./no.; **Document type:** *Magazine, Trade.*
Published by: LexisNexis Verlag ARD Orac GmbH & Co. KG (Subsidiary of: LexisNexis Europe and Africa), Marxergasse 25, Vienna, W 1030, Austria. TEL 43-1-534520, FAX 43-1-53452141, verlag@orac.at, http://www.lexisnexis.at/. Ed. Heinz Peter Rill. Adv. contact Malgorzata Leitliner TEL 43-1-534521115. Circ: 1,100.

351 TWN ISSN 1681-3561
ZHENGCE YANJIU XUEBAO. Text in Chinese. 2001. m. **Document type:** *Journal, Academic/Scholarly.*
Related titles: Online - full text ed.
Published by: Nanhua Daxue, Gonggon Xingzheng Zhengce Yanjiuso/ Nanhua University, Institute of Public Administration and Policy, 32, Chung Keng Li, Dalin, Chiayi 62248, Taiwan. scho@mail.nhu.edu.tw, http://mail.nhu.edu.tw/~policy/.

351 CHN ISSN 1007-2004
ZHONGGUO GONGWUYUAN/CHINESE PUBLIC SERVANT. Text in Chinese. 1992. m. CNY 6 (effective 2006). **Document type:** *Journal, Academic/Scholarly.*
Formerly: Zhongguo Renshi (1003-4080)
Related titles: Online - full text ed.
Address: 5, Yuhui Li, Beijing, 100101, China.

351 CHN ISSN 2095-1507
▼ **ZHONGGUO JIGOU GAIGE YU GUANLI.** Text in Chinese. 2011. bi-m. **Document type:** *Journal, Government.*
Published by: Zhongguo Jigou Bianzhi Guanli Yanjiuhui, 85, Huan Si Nan Dajie, Dongcheng-qu, Beijing, 100703, China. TEL 86-10-52818583, FAX 86-10-52818585.

351.51 CHN ISSN 1006-0863
JQ1501.A1
ZHONGGUO XINGZHENG GUANLI/CHINESE PUBLIC ADMINISTRATION. Text in Chinese. 1985. m. USD 106.80 (effective 2009). **Document type:** *Academic/Scholarly.*
Related titles: Online - full text ed.
—East View.
Published by: Zhongguo Xingzheng Guanli Zazhishe, No 22 Xi'anmen Dajie, Beijing, 100017, China. TEL 86-1-6309-9102, FAX 86-1-6601-3279. Ed. Bao Jing. R&P Jing Bao.

351 CHN ISSN 1674-2028
ZHONGHUA RENMIN GONGHEGUO GUOJIA FAZHAN HE GAIGE WEIYUANHUI WENGAO/NATIONAL DEVELOPMENT AND REFORM COMMISSION OF THE PEOPLE'S REPUBLIC OF CHINA. GAZETTE. Text in Chinese. 2008. m. **Document type:** *Bulletin, Government.*
Published by: Zhonghua Renmin Gongheguo Guojia Fazhan he Gaige Weiyuanhui/National Development and Reform Commission of the People's Republic of China, 38, Yuetan Nan Jie, Beijing, 100824, China. ndrc@ndrc.gov.cn, http://www.ndrc.gov.cn/.

351.51 CHN ISSN 1004-3438
KNQ7
ZHONGHUA RENMIN GONGHEGUO GUOWUYUAN GONGBAO/ CHINA, PEOPLE'S REPUBLIC. STATE COUNCIL. GAZETTE. Text in Chinese. 1955. 3/m. USD 54 (effective 2009). **Document type:** *Newspaper, Government.*
Related titles: Online - full content ed.
—East View.
Published by: Zhonghua Renmin Gongheguo Guowuyuan/State Council of the People's Republic of China, 1741 Xinxiang, Beijing, 100017, China. TEL 86-10-66012399. **Dist. by:** China International Book Trading Corp, 35 Chegongzhuang Xilu, Haidian District, PO Box 399, Beijing 100044, China. TEL 86-10-68412045, FAX 86-10-68412023, cibtc@mail.cibtc.com.cn, http://www.cibtc.com.cn.

351 CHN ISSN 1000-0070
KNQ2514.A13
ZHONGHUA RENMIN GONGHEGUO QUANGUO RENMIN DAIBIAO DAHUI CHANGWU WEIYUANHUI GONGBAO/PEOPLE'S REPUBLIC OF CHINA. NATIONAL PEOPLE'S CONGRESS. STANDING COMMITTEE. GAZETTE. Text in Chinese. 1957. irreg. USD 30 (effective 2009). **Document type:** *Newspaper, Government.*
Related titles: Online - full text ed.
—East View.
Published by: Quanguoren Dachang Weihui Bangongting, Renmin Dahuitang, Beijing, 100805, China.

352.53 CHN ISSN 1001-067X
KNQ1572.A15
ZHONGHUA RENMIN GONGHEGUO. ZUIGAO RENMIN JIANCHAYUAN GONGBAO/CHINA, PEOPLE'S REPUBLIC. SUPREME PEOPLE'S PROCURATE POST. BULLETIN. Text in Chinese. 1989. bi-m. USD 21.60 (effective 2009). **Document type:** *Bulletin, Government.*
Published by: Zhonghua Renmin Gongheguo Zuigao Renmin Jianchayuan/Supreme People's Procuratorate of the People's Republic of China, 147, Heyan Dajie, Beijing, 100726, China. TEL 86-10-68630085. **Dist. by:** China International Book Trading Corp, 35 Chegongzhuang Xilu, Haidian District, PO Box 399, Beijing 100044, China. TEL 86-10-68412045, FAX 86-10-68412023, cibtc@mail.cibtc.com.cn, http://www.cibtc.com.cn.

ZHURNAL ISSLEDOVANII SOTSIAL'NOI POLITIKI/JOURNAL OF SOCIAL POLICY STUDIES. *see* SOCIAL SCIENCES: COMPREHENSIVE WORKS

351.6891 ZWE
ZIMBABWE GOVERNMENT GAZETTE. Text in English. w. (plus a. cumulation). USD 228. **Document type:** *Government.*
Published by: Department of Printing and Stationery, Causeway, PO Box 8062, Harare, Zimbabwe. TEL 706161.

351 DEU ISSN 0177-1965
ZIVILDIENST; Zeitschrift fuer die Zivildienst-Leistenden. Text in German. 1969. 10/yr. EUR 7 to non-members (effective 2009). bk.rev. reprints avail. **Document type:** *Magazine, Trade.*
Formerly (until 1970): Der Dienst (0177-1957)
—CCC.
Published by: Bundesamt fuer den Zivildienst, Sibille-Hartmann-Str 2-8, Cologne, 50964, Germany. TEL 49-221-36734060, FAX 49-221-36734281, info@baz.bund.de, http://www.zivildienst.de. Circ: 120,000.

351 CHN
ZUNYI TONGXUN. Text in Chinese. m. **Document type:** *Magazine, Consumer.*
Published by: (Zhong-Gong Ziyun Shi Wei), Zunyi Zazhishe/Zunyi Magazine House, Bldg.19, #8, Aomen Rd., Huichuan District, Zunyi, Guizhou 563000, China. TEL 86-852-8651682, FAX 86-852-8687029, zywb@sina.com. **Co-sponsors:** Zhong-Gong Ziyun Shi Wei Zhengce Yanjiushi; Zhong-Gong Ziyun Shi Wei Gongshi.

353.536 NZL ISSN 1177-2379
12 TO 24. Text in English. 1998. bi-m. **Document type:** *Newsletter.*
Former titles (until 2006): New Zealand. Ministry of Youth Development. Connect (1176-7111); (until 2004): New Zealand. Ministry of Youth Affairs. Connect (1176-0745); (until 2002): Infoyouthaffairs (1174-8451); Which was formed by the merger of (1997): Infoyouthaffairs.govt.nz (1174-068X); (1993-1997): Youth Workers Unplugged (1172-7888)
Related titles: Online - full text ed.: ISSN 1178-3370.
Published by: Ministry of Youth Development, Level 1, Charles Fergusson West Block, Bowen St, PO Box 1556, Wellington, 6001, New Zealand. TEL 64-4-9163300, FAX 64-4-9180091.

351 FRA ISSN 2105-6404
62, LE JOURNAL DU PAS-DE-CALAIS. Text in French. 1987. q. **Document type:** *Newspaper, Consumer.*
Formerly (until 2009): Pas-de-Calais (0989-5167)

Published by: Conseil General du Pas-de-Calais, Rue Ferdinand Buisson, Arras Cedex 9, 62018, France. TEL 33-3-21216262.

351.44 711.4 FRA ISSN 1268-8533
2001 PLUS. Variant title: Deux-Mille-Un Plus. Text in French. 1988. irreg., latest vol.62, 2003. **Document type:** *Monographic series, Government.*
Formerly (until 1993): UTH 2001 (1152-8559)
Indexed: IBSS.
—INIST.
Published by: Centre de Prospective et de Veille Scientifique, Tour Pascal B, La Defense, 92055 Cedex 04, France. TEL 33-1-40816323, FAX 33-1-40811444, CPVS.DRAST@equipement.gouv.fr.

PUBLIC ADMINISTRATION—Abstracting, Bibliographies, Statistics

016.351 AUS
Z7165.A8
A P A I S: AUSTRALIAN PUBLIC AFFAIRS INFORMATION SERVICE (ONLINE). (Part of Informit (formerly AUSTROM), the collection of databases) Text in English. 1978. base vol. plus s-m. updates. index. reprints avail. **Document type:** *Database, Abstract/Index.* **Description:** Indexes periodical literature in social sciences and humanities published in or relating to Australia.
Media: Online - full text. **Related titles:** CD-ROM ed.
Indexed: RASB.
Published by: National Library of Australia, Publications Section, Cultural and Educational Services Division, Canberra, ACT 2600, Australia. TEL 61-2-62621111, FAX 61-2-62571703, media@nla.gov.au.

352.021 SWE ISSN 0065-020X
AARSBOK FOER SVERIGES KOMMUNER/STATISTICAL YEARBOOK OF ADMINISTRATIVE DISTRICTS OF SWEDEN. Text in Swedish; Summaries in English. 1918. a. **Document type:** *Yearbook, Government.*
Related titles: Online - full text ed.
Published by: Statistiska Centralbyraan/Statistics Sweden, Karlawaegen 100, PO Box 24300, Stockholm, 10451, Sweden. TEL 46-8-50694000, FAX 46-8-50694899, scb@scb.se. Ed. Olle Storm. Circ: 3,500.

016.351 USA
ABSTRACTS OF PUBLIC ADMINISTRATION, DEVELOPMENT AND ENVIRONMENT. Text in English. 1988. a. USD 20 (effective 2000). back issues avail. **Document type:** *Abstract/Index.* **Description:** Abstracts of books published in English during the previous year on problems of development and developing countries.
Formerly: Abstracts of Development Studies
Published by: Indiana University, School of Public and Environmental Affairs, 1315 E Tenth St, Bloomington, IN 47405. Ed. Michael Parrish. Circ: 300.

351.021 UAE
ABU DHABI. DA'IRAT AT-TAKHTIT. AL-KITAB AL-IHSA'I AS-SANAWI/ ABU DHABI. DEPARTMENT OF PLANNING. STATISTICAL YEARBOOK. Text in Arabic. 1969. a. free. **Document type:** *Government.* **Description:** Includes statistics on climate, demographics, labor, industry, trade, transport and finance.
Formerly: Abu Dhabi. Department of Planning. Statistical Abstract and Yearbook
Published by: Department of Planning, Statistical Section, P O Box 12, Abu Dhabi, United Arab Emirates. TEL 971-2-727200, FAX 971-2-727749, TELEX 23194 PLANCO EM.

AGENT ORANGE REVIEW; for veterans who served in Vietnam. *see* ENVIRONMENTAL STUDIES—Toxicology And Environmental Safety

352.14021 USA ISSN 1935-5610
ALABAMA CITIES & COUNTIES GRAPHIC PERFORMANCE ANALYSIS. Variant title: Alabama Cities and Counties Graphic Performance Analysis. Text in English. 2006. a. USD 95 per issue (effective 2009). charts. **Document type:** *Monographic series, Trade.* **Description:** Provides comparisons in chart form, annual series of analytic charts, by peer group, within state. Each issue consist of 9 charts in each county peer group and each city peer group and 1 area chart per county. 100-200 graphs per state book.
Published by: Municipal Analysis Services, Inc., PO Box 13453, Austin, TX 78711. TEL 512-327-3328, munilysis@hotmail.com, http://sites.google.com/site/gregmichels.

016.351 CAN ISSN 1482-5864
ALBERTA. PUBLIC AFFAIRS BUREAU. CATALOGUE - ALBERTA. QUEEN'S PRINTER. Text in English. s-a. (plus a. cumulation). CAD 4.50 (effective 2000). **Document type:** *Government.*
Former titles (until 1996): Alberta. Public Affairs Bureau. Queen's Printer Bookstore Catalogue (1200-9830); (until 1995): Alberta. Public Affairs Bureau. List of Alberta Publications and Legilation (0837-7375); Which incorporated (in 1995): Alberta. Public Affairs Bureau. Government of Alberta Publications G A P Catalogue (1204-671X); Which was formerly (until 1994): Alberta. Public Affairs Bureau. Alberta Government Publications (0840-4976); (until 1987): Alberta. Public Affairs Bureau. Publications Catalogue, Alberta (0316-392X)
Published by: Alberta Public Affairs Bureau, Queen's Printer, 11510 Kingsway Ave, Edmonton, AB T5G 2Y5, Canada. TEL 780-427-4952, 780-422-2787, FAX 780-452-0668, http://www.qp.gov.ab.ca/index.cfm. Ed. Annie Re.

351.21 DEU ISSN 0721-7323
AMTLICHES ORTSVERZEICHNIS FUER BAYERN. Text in German. 1973. irreg. **Document type:** *Government.*
Published by: Bayerisches Landesamt fuer Statistik und Datenverarbeitung, Neuhauser Str 8, Munich, 80331, Germany. TEL 49-89-2119205, FAX 49-89-2119410, poststelle@statistik.bayern.de, http://www.statistik.bayern.de.

351.021 CAN ISSN 0383-4840
JS4.N6
ANNUAL REPORT OF MUNICIPAL STATISTICS. Text in English. a.
Published by: Nova Scotia. Government Publications, Box 637, Halifax, NS B3J 2T3, Canada. TEL 902-424-7580, FAX 902-424-7161, http://www.gov.ns.ca/snsmr.

352.13021 USA ISSN 1935-5459
ARKANSAS CITIES & COUNTIES GRAPHIC PERFORMANCE ANALYSIS. Text in English. 2006. a. USD 95 per issue (effective 2009). charts. **Document type:** *Monographic series, Trade.* **Description:** Provides comparisons in chart form, annual series of analytic charts, by peer group, within state. Each issue consist of 9 charts in each county peer group and each city peer group and 1 area chart per county. 100-200 graphs per state book.
Published by: Municipal Analysis Services, Inc., PO Box 13453, Austin, TX 78711. TEL 512-327-3328, munilysis@hotmail.com, http://sites.google.com/site/gregmichels. Ed. Greg Michels.

351.021 AUS
AUSTRALIA. BUREAU OF STATISTICS. A GUIDE TO MAJOR A.B.S. CLASSIFICATIONS (ONLINE). Text in English. 1990. irreg., latest 1998. free (effective 2009). **Document type:** *Government.* **Description:** Provides an overview of the major ABS classifications and assist users wishing to gain a broad understanding of these classifications.
Formerly: Australia. Bureau of Statistics. A Guide to Major A.B.S. Classifications (Print)
Media: Online - full text.
Published by: Australian Bureau of Statistics, Locked Bag 10, Belconnen, ACT 2616, Australia. TEL 61-2-62527037, 61-2-92684909, 300-135-070, FAX 61-2-62528103, client.services@abs.gov.au.

351.021 CHE
B F S AKTUELL/ACTUALITES O F S. Text in German, French. m. **Document type:** *Government.*
Published by: Bundesamt fuer Statistik, Espace de l'Europe 10, Neuchatel, 2010, Switzerland. TEL 41-32-7136011, FAX 41-32-7136012, information@bfs.admin.ch, http://www.bfs.admin.ch.

351.021 BRB
BARBADOS. REGISTRATION OFFICE. REPORT ON VITAL STATISTICS & REGISTRATIONS. Text in English. a., latest 1981. free. stat. **Document type:** *Government.*
Published by: Registration Office, Bridgetown, Barbados. Circ: 100.

351.12 DEU ISSN 1430-3175
BAYERISCHES LANDESAMT FUER STATISTIK UND DATENVERARBEITUNG. STATISTISCHE BERICHTE A: BEVOELKERUNG, GESUNDHEITSWESEN, GEBIET, ERWERBSTAETIGKEIT. Text in German. 195?. irreg. **Document type:** *Government.*
Formerly (until 1982): Bayerisches Statistisches Landesamt. Statistische Berichte A (1430-3000)
Published by: Bayerisches Landesamt fuer Statistik und Datenverarbeitung, Neuhauser Str 8, Munich, 80331, Germany. TEL 49-89-2119205, FAX 49-89-2119410, poststelle@statistik.bayern.de, http://www.statistik.bayern.de.

351.12 DEU ISSN 1430-3183
BAYERISCHES LANDESAMT FUER STATISTIK UND DATENVERARBEITUNG. STATISTISCHE BERICHTE B: BILDUNG, RECHTSPFLEGE, WAHLEN UND VOLKSENTSCHEIDE. Text in German. 1955. irreg. **Document type:** *Government.*
Formerly (until 1982): Bayerisches Statistisches Landesamt. Statistische Berichte B (1430-3019)
Related titles: Supplement(s): Landtagswahl von A bis Z. ISSN 0930-6889. 1978; Europawahl in Bayern. ISSN 0723-9327. 1979; Wahl zum Deutschen Bundestag in Bayern. ISSN 0932-7002. 1950.
Published by: Bayerisches Landesamt fuer Statistik und Datenverarbeitung, Neuhauser Str 8, Munich, 80331, Germany. TEL 49-89-2119205, FAX 49-89-2119410, poststelle@statistik.bayern.de, http://www.statistik.bayern.de.

351.21 DEU ISSN 0173-8070
BEITRAEGE ZUR STATISTIK BAYERNS. Text in German. 1850. a. EUR 20.50 (effective 2011). **Document type:** *Government.*
Related titles: Supplement(s): Amtliches Gemeindeverzeichnis fuer Bayern. ISSN 0721-7331. 1946.
Published by: Bayerisches Landesamt fuer Statistik und Datenverarbeitung, Neuhauser Str 8, Munich, 80331, Germany. TEL 49-89-2119205, FAX 49-89-2119410, poststelle@statistik.bayern.de, http://www.statistik.bayern.de.

351.021 BRA
BRAZIL. SERVICO SOCIAL DO COMERCIO. ANUARIO ESTATISTICO. Text in Portuguese. 1962. a. free. stat.
Published by: (Brazil. Assessoria de Divulgacao e Promocao Institucional), Servico Social do Comercio, Rua Voluntarios da Patria, 169 Andar 11, Rio De Janeiro, RJ 22270-000, Brazil.

352.13021 CAN
BRITISH COLUMBIA. MINISTRY OF MUNICIPAL AFFAIRS, RECREATION AND HOUSING. MUNICIPAL STATISTICS, INCLUDING REGIONAL DISTRICTS. Text in English. 1951. a. CAD 27. **Document type:** *Government.* **Description:** Contains financial and statistical information relating to municipalities and regional districts.
Former titles: British Columbia. Ministry of Municipal Affairs, Recreation and Culture. Municipal Statistics, Including Regional Districts; British Columbia. Ministry of Municipal Affairs. Municipal Statistics, Including Regional Districts (0702-6641); Which supersedes: British Columbia. Ministry of Municipal Affairs. Municipal Statistics (0521-0348)
Published by: Ministry of Municipal Affairs, Recreation and Housing, Victoria, BC, Canada. TEL 604-387-4063, FAX 604-387-1873. Circ: 1,250. **Subscr. to:** Crown Publications Inc. TEL 250-386-4636, FAX 250-386-0221.

352.13021 CAN ISSN 1712-1930
CA2PQBS11Q0108
BULLETIN STATISTIQUE REGIONAL. ABITIBI-TEMISCAMINGUE. Text in French. 2004. s-a. **Document type:** *Bulletin, Government.*
—CCC.
Published by: Institut de la Statistique du Quebec, 200 chemin Ste Foy, Quebec, PQ G1R 5T4, Canada. TEL 418-691-2401, 800-463-4090, FAX 418-643-4129, direction@stat.gouv.qc.ca, http://www.stat.gouv.qc.ca.

352.13021 CAN ISSN 1712-1949
CA2PQBS11Q0101
BULLETIN STATISTIQUE REGIONAL. BAS-SAINT-LAURENT. Text in French. 2004. s-a. **Document type:** *Bulletin, Government.*
—CCC.
Published by: Institut de la Statistique du Quebec, 200 chemin Ste Foy, Quebec, PQ G1R 5T4, Canada. TEL 418-691-2401, 800-463-4090, FAX 418-643-4129, direction@stat.gouv.qc.ca, http://www.stat.gouv.qc.ca.

352.13021 CAN ISSN 1712-1957
CA2PQBS11Q0103
BULLETIN STATISTIQUE REGIONAL. CAPITALE-NATIONALE. Text in French. 2004. s-a. **Document type:** *Bulletin, Government.*
—CCC.
Published by: Institut de la Statistique du Quebec, 200 chemin Ste Foy, Quebec, PQ G1R 5T4, Canada. TEL 418-691-2401, 800-463-4090, FAX 418-643-4129, direction@stat.gouv.qc.ca, http://www.stat.gouv.qc.ca.

352.13021 CAN ISSN 1712-1965
CA2PQBS11Q0117
BULLETIN STATISTIQUE REGIONAL. CENTRE-DU-QUEBEC. Text in French. 2004. s-a. **Document type:** *Bulletin, Government.*
—CCC.
Published by: Institut de la Statistique du Quebec, 200 chemin Ste Foy, Quebec, PQ G1R 5T4, Canada. TEL 418-691-2401, 800-463-4090, FAX 418-643-4129, direction@stat.gouv.qc.ca, http://www.stat.gouv.qc.ca.

352.13021 CAN ISSN 1712-1973
CA2PQBS11Q0112
BULLETIN STATISTIQUE REGIONAL. CHAUDIERE-APPALACHES. Text in French. 2004. s-a. **Document type:** *Bulletin, Government.*
—CCC.
Published by: Institut de la Statistique du Quebec, 200 chemin Ste Foy, Quebec, PQ G1R 5T4, Canada. TEL 418-691-2401, 800-463-4090, FAX 418-643-4129, direction@stat.gouv.qc.ca, http://www.stat.gouv.qc.ca.

352.13021 CAN ISSN 1712-1981
CA2PQBS11Q0109
BULLETIN STATISTIQUE REGIONAL. COTE-NORD. Text in French. 2004. s-a. **Document type:** *Bulletin, Government.*
—CCC.
Published by: Institut de la Statistique du Quebec, 200 chemin Ste Foy, Quebec, PQ G1R 5T4, Canada. TEL 418-691-2401, 800-463-4090, FAX 418-643-4129, direction@stat.gouv.qc.ca, http://www.stat.gouv.qc.ca.

352.13021 CAN ISSN 1712-199X
CA2PQBS11Q0105
BULLETIN STATISTIQUE REGIONAL. ESTRIE. Text in French. 2004. s-a. **Document type:** *Bulletin, Government.*
—CCC.
Published by: Institut de la Statistique du Quebec, 200 chemin Ste Foy, Quebec, PQ G1R 5T4, Canada. TEL 418-691-2401, 800-463-4090, FAX 418-643-4129, direction@stat.gouv.qc.ca, http://www.stat.gouv.qc.ca.

352.13021 CAN ISSN 1712-2007
CA2PQBS11Q0111
BULLETIN STATISTIQUE REGIONAL. GASPESIE-ILES-DE-LA-MADELEINE. Text in French. 2004. s-a. **Document type:** *Bulletin, Government.*
—CCC.
Published by: Institut de la Statistique du Quebec, 200 chemin Ste Foy, Quebec, PQ G1R 5T4, Canada. TEL 418-691-2401, 800-463-4090, FAX 418-643-4129, direction@stat.gouv.qc.ca, http://www.stat.gouv.qc.ca.

352.13021 CAN ISSN 1712-2015
CA2PQBS11Q0114
BULLETIN STATISTIQUE REGIONAL. LANAUDIERE. Text in French. 2004. s-a. **Document type:** *Bulletin, Government.*
—CCC.
Published by: Institut de la Statistique du Quebec, 200 chemin Ste Foy, Quebec, PQ G1R 5T4, Canada. TEL 418-691-2401, 800-463-4090, FAX 418-643-4129, direction@stat.gouv.qc.ca, http://www.stat.gouv.qc.ca.

352.13021 CAN ISSN 1712-2023
CA2PQBS11Q0115
BULLETIN STATISTIQUE REGIONAL. LAURENTIDES. Text in French. 2004. s-a. **Document type:** *Bulletin, Government.*
—CCC.
Published by: Institut de la Statistique du Quebec, 200 chemin Ste Foy, Quebec, PQ G1R 5T4, Canada. TEL 418-691-2401, 800-463-4090, FAX 418-643-4129, direction@stat.gouv.qc.ca, http://www.stat.gouv.qc.ca.

352.13021 CAN ISSN 1712-2031
CA2PQBS11Q0113
BULLETIN STATISTIQUE REGIONAL. LAVAL. Text in French. 2004. s-a. **Document type:** *Bulletin, Government.*
—CCC.
Published by: Institut de la Statistique du Quebec, 200 chemin Ste Foy, Quebec, PQ G1R 5T4, Canada. TEL 418-691-2401, 800-463-4090, FAX 418-643-4129, direction@stat.gouv.qc.ca, http://www.stat.gouv.qc.ca.

352.13021 CAN ISSN 1712-204X
CA2PQBS11Q0104
BULLETIN STATISTIQUE REGIONAL. MAURICIE. Text in French. 2004. s-a. **Document type:** *Bulletin, Government.*
—CCC.
Published by: Institut de la Statistique du Quebec, 200 chemin Ste Foy, Quebec, PQ G1R 5T4, Canada. TEL 418-691-2401, 800-463-4090, FAX 418-643-4129, direction@stat.gouv.qc.ca, http://www.stat.gouv.qc.ca.

352.13021 CAN ISSN 1712-2058
CA2PQBS11Q0116
BULLETIN STATISTIQUE REGIONAL. MONTEREGIE. Text in French. 2004. s-a. **Document type:** *Bulletin, Government.*
—CCC.
Published by: Institut de la Statistique du Quebec, 200 chemin Ste Foy, Quebec, PQ G1R 5T4, Canada. TEL 418-691-2401, 800-463-4090, FAX 418-643-4129, direction@stat.gouv.qc.ca, http://www.stat.gouv.qc.ca.

352.13021 CAN ISSN 1712-2066
CA2PQBS11Q0106
BULLETIN STATISTIQUE REGIONAL. MONTREAL. Text in French. 2004. s-a. **Document type:** *Bulletin, Government.*

P

—CCC.
Published by: Institut de la Statistique du Quebec, 200 chemin Ste Foy, Quebec, PQ G1R 5T4, Canada. TEL 418-691-2401, 800-463-4090, FAX 418-643-4129, direction@stat.gouv.qc.ca, http://www.stat.gouv.qc.ca.

352.13021 CAN ISSN 1712-2074
CA2PQBS11Q0110
BULLETIN STATISTIQUE REGIONAL. NORD-DU-QUEBEC. Text in French. 2004. s-a. **Document type:** *Bulletin, Government.*
—CCC.
Published by: Institut de la Statistique du Quebec, 200 chemin Ste Foy, Quebec, PQ G1R 5T4, Canada. TEL 418-691-2401, 800-463-4090, FAX 418-643-4129, direction@stat.gouv.qc.ca, http://www.stat.gouv.qc.ca.

352.13021 CAN ISSN 1712-2082
CA2PQBS11Q0107
BULLETIN STATISTIQUE REGIONAL. OUTAOUAIS. Text in French. 2004. s-a. **Document type:** *Bulletin, Government.*
—CCC.
Published by: Institut de la Statistique du Quebec, 200 chemin Ste Foy, Quebec, PQ G1R 5T4, Canada. TEL 418-691-2401, 800-463-4090, FAX 418-643-4129, direction@stat.gouv.qc.ca, http://www.stat.gouv.qc.ca.

352.13021 CAN ISSN 1712-2090
CA2PQBS11Q0102
BULLETIN STATISTIQUE REGIONAL. SAGUENAY-LAC-SAINT-JEAN. Text in French. 2004. s-a. **Document type:** *Bulletin, Government.*
—CCC.
Published by: Institut de la Statistique du Quebec, 200 chemin Ste Foy, Quebec, PQ G1R 5T4, Canada. TEL 418-691-2401, 800-463-4090, FAX 418-643-4129, direction@stat.gouv.qc.ca, http://www.stat.gouv.qc.ca.

351.021 CHE
BUNDESAMT FUER STATISTIK. INFO. Text in German. m. **Document type:** *Government.*
Published by: Bundesamt fuer Statistik, Espace de l'Europe 10, Neuchatel, 2010, Switzerland. TEL 41-32-7136011, FAX 41-32-7136012.

016.351 USA ISSN 0007-8514
C I S INDEX TO PUBLICATIONS OF THE UNITED STATES CONGRESS. Variant title: C I S Index. Text in English. 1970. a. abstr. index, cum.index: 1970-74; 1975-78; 1979-82; 1983-86; 1987-1990; 1991-1994. back issues avail. **Document type:** *Abstract/Index.* **Description:** Abstracts and indexes to information published by congressional committees.
Related titles: CD-ROM ed.: Congressional Masterfile 2. ISSN 1064-4679; Microform ed.: USD 26,170 domestic; USD 28,790 foreign (effective 2005); Online - full text ed.; ◆ Supplement(s): C I S Index Index.
—BLDSC (3267.637000).
Published by: Congressional Information Service, Inc. (Subsidiary of: ProQuest), 789 E Eisenhower Pky, PO Box 1346, Ann Arbor, MI 48106. TEL 734-761-4700, academicinfo@proquest.com, http://www.proquest.com.

016.351 USA ISSN 0749-4394
C O S S A WASHINGTON UPDATE. Text in English. 1981. s-w. looseleaf. USD 65 to individuals; USD 130 to institutions. index. back issues avail. **Document type:** *Newsletter.* **Description:** Discusses latest developments in congress and executive branch that affect funding for social and behavioral science research. Reports on current issues of federal policy such as regulations affecting research.
Formerly: C O S S A Legislative Report
Published by: Consortium of Social Science Associations, 1522 K St, N W, Ste 836, Washington, DC 20005. TEL 202-842-3525, FAX 202-842-2788. Ed. Michael Buckley.

016.351 USA ISSN 1542-9040
Z7161 CODEN: ABPSC
C S A POLITICAL SCIENCE & GOVERNMENT; a guide to periodical literature. (Cambridge Scientific Abstracts) Text in English. 1969. bi-m. (5/yr. (Feb., May, Aug., Oct. & Dec.), plus annual index in print & CD-ROM). USD 995 in North America (includes a. cum. index in print & on CD-ROM); USD 1,045 elsewhere (includes a. cum. index in print & on CD-ROM) (effective 2011). a. cum.index. reprints avail. **Document type:** *Abstract/Index.*
Formerly (until vol. 32, no. 6, 2000): A B C Pol Sci (0001-0456)
Related titles: ◆ Online - full text ed.: C S A Worldwide Political Science Abstracts.
Published by: ProQuest LLC (Bethesda) (Subsidiary of: Cambridge Information Group), 7200 Wisconsin Ave, Ste 715, Bethesda, MD 20814. TEL 301-961-6798, 800-843-7751, FAX 301-961-6799, journals@csa.com. Ed. Jill Blaemers.

352.13021 USA ISSN 1935-5793
CALIFORNIA CITIES & COUNTIES GRAPHIC PERFORMANCE ANALYSIS. Text in English. 2006. a. USD 95 per issue (effective 2009). charts. **Document type:** *Handbook/Manual/Guide, Trade.* **Description:** Provides comparisons in chart form, annual series of analytic charts, by peer group, within state. Each issue consist of 9 charts in each county peer group and each city peer group and 1 area chart per county. 100-200 graphs per state book.
Published by: Municipal Analysis Services, Inc., PO Box 13453, Austin, TX 78711. TEL 512-327-3328, munilysis@hotmail.com, http://sites.google.com/site/gregmichels. Ed. Greg Michels.

351.021 CMR ISSN 0258-0942
CAMEROON. DIRECTION DE LA STATISTIQUE ET DE LA COMPTABILITE NATIONALE. BULLETIN TRIMESTRIEL DE CONJONCTURE. Text in French. 1982. q. free.
Published by: Direction de la Statistique et de la Comptabilite Nationale/ Department of Statistics and National Accounts, BP 660, Yaounde, Cameroon. TEL 22-07-88.

351.021 CAN ISSN 1496-418X
CANADA. STATISTICS CANADA. CANADIAN CULTURE IN PERSPECTIVE: A STATISTICAL OVERVIEW/CANADA. STATISTIQUE CANADA. LE CANADA, SA CULTURE, SON PATRIMOINE ET SON IDENTITE: PERSPECTIVE STATISTIQUE. Text in English. 1985. biennial. CAD 23; USD 23 foreign. **Document type:** *Government.* **Description:** Contains survey highlights and statistical tables on government expenditures on culture, heritage activities, performing arts, literary arts, visual arts and crafts, broadcasting, film and video.
Former titles (until 2000): Canada. Statistics Canada. Canada's Culture, Heritage and Identity: a Statistical Perspective (1203-4533); (until 1995): Government Expenditures on Culture (1181-6651); (until 1989): Government Expenditures on Culture in Canada (0847-1258); (until 1988): Culture Statistics. Government Expenditures on Culture in Canada, Preliminary Statistics (0832-9486)
Related titles: Microform ed.: (from MML); Online - full text ed.: ISSN 1497-3472.
Published by: Statistics Canada, Operations and Integration Division (Subsidiary of: Statistics Canada/Statistique Canada), Circulation Management, 120 Parkdale Ave, Ottawa, ON K1A 0T6, Canada. TEL 613-951-7277, 800-267-6677, FAX 613-951-1584.

351.21 CAN ISSN 0317-5154
CA1BS13C211EXF
CANADA. STATISTICS CANADA. FIXED CAPITAL FLOWS AND STOCKS/CANADA. STATISTIQUE CANADA. FLUX ET STOCKS DE CAPITAL FIXE. Text in English, French. 1973. a.
Published by: (Statistics Canada, Construction Division), Statistics Canada/Statistique Canada, Publications Sales and Services, Ottawa, ON K1A 0T6, Canada. TEL 613-951-8116, infostats@statcan.ca, http://www.statcan.gc.ca.

352.6021 351.21 CAN ISSN 1484-5792
CA1BT22-63
CANADA. TREASURY BOARD. EMPLOYMENT STATISTICS FOR THE FEDERAL PUBLIC SERVICE. Text in English. 1994. a.
Related titles: Online - full text ed.: ISSN 1486-9993.
Published by: (Canada. Treasury Board), Treasury Board of Canada Secretariat, Corporate Communications/Secretariat du Conseil du Tresor du Canada, West Tower, Rm P-135, 300 Laurier Ave W, Ottawa, ON K1A 0R5, Canada. TEL 613-995-2855, FAX 613-996-0518, services-publications@tbs-sct.gc.ca, http://www.tbs-sct.gc.ca.

352.13021 USA ISSN 1935-5785
CAROLINAS CITIES & COUNTIES GRAPHIC PERFORMANCE ANALYSIS. Text in English. 2006. a. USD 95 per issue (effective 2009). charts. **Document type:** *Report, Trade.* **Description:** Provides comparisons in chart form, annual series of analytic charts, by peer group, within state. Each issue consist of 9 charts in each county peer group and each city peer group and 1 area chart per county. 100-200 graphs per state book.
Published by: Municipal Analysis Services, Inc., PO Box 13453, Austin, TX 78711. TEL 512-327-3328, munilysis@hotmail.com, http://sites.google.com/site/gregmichels. Ed. Greg Michels.

352.13021 USA
CENSUS OF GOVERNMENTS (ONLINE). Text in Chinese. 2003. irreg., latest 2007. free (effective 2009). **Document type:** *Government.* **Description:** Contains detailed Tables of the number of governments by type of government.
Media: Online - full text.
Published by: U.S. Census Bureau. Governments Division (Subsidiary of: U.S. Department of Commerce), 4600 Silver Hill Rd., Washington, DC 20233. TEL 800-242-2184, govs.cms.inquiry@census.gov.

351.021 GBR ISSN 0260-9762
HJ9041
CHARTERED INSTITUTE OF PUBLIC FINANCE AND ACCOUNTANCY. LOCAL GOVERNMENT COMPARATIVE STATISTICS. ESTIMATES. Text in English. 1981. a. GBP 150 per issue (effective 2009). back issues avail. **Document type:** *Report, Trade.* **Description:** Contains a selection of comparative financial and other statistics covering all aspects of local authority provision.
—CCC.
Published by: (Statistical Information Service), Chartered Institute of Public Finance and Accountancy, 3 Robert St, London, WC2N 6RL, United Kingdom. TEL 44-20-75435600, FAX 44-20-75435700, info@cipfa.org.uk, http://www.cipfa.org.uk.

016.351 USA
Z1223.5.N57
CHECKLIST OF OFFICIAL PUBLICATIONS OF THE STATE OF NEW YORK (ONLINE). Text in English. 1947. m. free (effective 2010). author index: vols.1-23. back issues avail. **Document type:** *Report, Government.* **Description:** Covers monthly compilation of New York State documents available via gopher, FTP or the web.
Formerly (until 2004): Checklist of Official Publications of the State of New York (Print) (0077-9296)
Media: Online - full text.
—Linda Hall.
Published by: (Collection, Acquisitions and Processing), New York State Library, Cultural Education Ctr, 222 Madison Ave, Albany, NY 12230. TEL 518-474-5355, FAX 518-474-5786, circ@mail.nysed.gov.

351.861021 COL
COLOMBIA. DEPARTAMENTO ADMINISTRATIVO NACIONAL DE ESTADISTICA. DIVISION POLITICO-ADMINISTRATIVA. Text in Spanish. 1953. irreg. illus.
Published by: Departamento Administrativo Nacional de Estadistica (D A N E), Bancos de Datos, Centro Administrativo Nacional (CAN), Avenida Eldorado, Apartado Aereo 80043, Bogota, CUND, Colombia.

352.13021 USA ISSN 1935-5777
COLORADO CITIES & COUNTIES GRAPHIC PERFORMANCE ANALYSIS. Text in English. 2006. a. USD 95 per issue (effective 2009). charts. **Document type:** *Report, Trade.* **Description:** Provides comparisons in chart form, annual series of analytic charts, by peer group, within state. Each issue consist of 9 charts in each county peer group and each city peer group and 1 area chart per county. 100-200 graphs per state book.
Published by: Municipal Analysis Services, Inc., PO Box 13453, Austin, TX 78711. TEL 512-327-3328, munilysis@hotmail.com, http://sites.google.com/site/gregmichels. Ed. Greg Michels.

352.13021 USA ISSN 1935-5769
CONNECTICUT CITIES & COUNTIES GRAPHIC PERFORMANCE ANALYSIS. Text in English. 2006. a. USD 95 per issue (effective 2009). charts. **Document type:** *Report, Trade.*
Published by: Municipal Analysis Services, Inc., PO Box 13453, Austin, TX 78711. TEL 512-327-3328, munilysis@hotmail.com, http://sites.google.com/site/gregmichels. Ed. Greg Michels.

351.021 CYP
CYPRUS. DEPARTMENT OF STATISTICS AND RESEARCH. FUNCTIONS AND SERVICES. Text in English. 1981. irreg. free. **Document type:** *Government.* **Description:** Provides information about the function and services of the Cyprus Department of Statistics and Research.
Published by: Ministry of Finance, Department of Statistics and Research, 13 Andreas Araouzos St, Nicosia, 1444, Cyprus. TEL 357-2-309318, FAX 357-2-374830.

351.021 USA
D L A P S. (Defense Logistics Agency Publishing System) Text in English. 1995. q. USD 92; USD 115 foreign. back issues avail. **Document type:** *Directory, Trade.* **Description:** Contains all D.L.A. regulatory publications and a selection of other Department of Defense titles.
Media: CD-ROM. **Related titles:** Online - full text ed.
Published by: U.S. Defense Logistics Agency, 8725 John J Kingman Rd, Ste 2533, Fort Belvoir, VA 22060-6221. **Subscr. to:** U.S. Government Printing Office, Superintendent of Documents.

016.351 IND ISSN 0377-7081
Z7164.A2
DOCUMENTATION IN PUBLIC ADMINISTRATION. Text in English. 1973. q. INR 150 domestic; USD 60 foreign (effective 2011). bibl. **Document type:** *Journal, Abstract/Index.*
Supersedes: Public Administration Abstracts and Index of Articles (0033-331X)
Published by: Indian Institute of Public Administration, Indraprastha Estate, Ring Rd, New Delhi, 110 002, India. TEL 91-11-23702400, FAX 91-11-23702440, diriipa@bol.net.in. Ed. S L Goel.

EMPLOYMENT AND PAYROLLS IN WASHINGTON STATE BY COUNTY AND INDUSTRY; industries covered by the Employment Security Act and federal employment covered by Title 5, U.S.C. 85. *see* BUSINESS AND ECONOMICS—Abstracting, Bibliographies, Statistics

EXCERPTA MEDICA. SECTION 36: HEALTH POLICY, ECONOMICS AND MANAGEMENT. *see* HEALTH FACILITIES AND ADMINISTRATION—Abstracting, Bibliographies, Statistics

016.351 AUS ISSN 1039-950X
KU12
FEDERAL STATUTES ANNOTATIONS. Text in English. a. AUD 654.50 (effective 2008). adv. **Document type:** *Abstract/Index.*
Former titles (until 1992): Federal Legislation Annotations (1036-3661); (until 1986): Annotations to the Acts and Regulations of the Australian Parliament; Commonwealth Statutes and Regulations Annotated
Related titles: CD-ROM ed.; Online - full text ed.: AUD 752.40 (effective 2008).
Published by: LexisNexis Butterworths (Subsidiary of: LexisNexis Asia Pacific), Level 9, Tower 2, 475-495 Victoria Ave, Locked Bag 2222, Chatswood Delivery Ctr, Chatswood, NSW 2067, Australia. TEL 61-2-94222174, FAX 61-2-94222405, customer.relations@lexisnexis.com.au.

352.13021 FIN ISSN 1239-7474
FINLAND. TILASTOKESKUS. ETELA-SUOMEN KATSAUS. Text in Finnish. 1997. a. **Document type:** *Government.*
Published by: Tilastokeskus/Statistics Finland, Tyopajakatu 13, Statistics Finland, Helsinki, 00022, Finland. TEL 358-9-17341, FAX 358-9-17342279, http://www.stat.fi.

352.13021 FIN ISSN 1239-7466
FINLAND. TILASTOKESKUS. ITA-SUOMEN KATSAUS. Text in Finnish. 1997. a. **Document type:** *Government.*
Published by: Tilastokeskus/Statistics Finland, Tyopajakatu 13, Statistics Finland, Helsinki, 00022, Finland. TEL 358-9-17341, FAX 358-9-17342279, http://www.stat.fi.

351.021 FIN ISSN 0787-7153
FINLAND. TILASTOKESKUS. KUNNALLISVAALIT/FINLAND. STATISTICS FINLAND. MUNICIPAL ELECTIONS/FINLAND. STATISTIKCENTRALEN. KOMMUNALVALEN. (Section XXIX B of Official Statistics of Finland) Text in English, Finnish, Swedish. 1909. irreg. **Document type:** *Government.*
Formerly (until 1985): Suomen Virallinen Tilasto. 29 B, Kunnallisvaalit (0355-2217); Which superseded in part (in 1931): Suomen virallinen tilasto. 29, Kunnallisvaalit (0430-5531)
Related titles: Online - full text ed.; ◆ Series of: Finland. Tilastokeskus. Suomen Virallinen Tilasto. ISSN 1795-5165.
Published by: Tilastokeskus/Statistics Finland, Tyopajakatu 13, Statistics Finland, Helsinki, 00022, Finland. TEL 358-9-17341, FAX 358-9-17342279.

352.13021 FIN ISSN 1238-2728
FINLAND. TILASTOKESKUS. KUNTAFAKTA. Text in Finnish. 1995. s-a. stat. **Document type:** *Government.*
Media: CD-ROM.
Published by: Tilastokeskus/Statistics Finland, Tyopajakatu 13, Statistics Finland, Helsinki, 00022, Finland. TEL 358-9-17341, FAX 358-9-17342279.

352.13021 FIN ISSN 1455-8696
FINLAND. TILASTOKESKUS. KUNTAKATSAUS. Text in Finnish. 1998. a. EUR 55 (effective 2005). stat. **Document type:** *Government.*
Published by: Tilastokeskus, Oulun Aluepalvelu/Statistics Finland. Oulu, Kirkkokatu 16, Oulu, 90100, Finland. TEL 358-8-5351410, FAX 358-8-5351430, oulu@stat.fi, http://www.stat.fi.

351.21 FIN ISSN 1238-4909
FINLAND. TILASTOKESKUS. KUNTAYHTYMIEN TALOUS/FINLAND. STATISTIKCENTRALEN. SAMKOMMUNERNAS EKONOMI. Text in Finnish, Swedish. 1972. a. EUR 18 (effective 2005). **Document type:** *Government.*
Formerly (until 1994): Finland. Tilastokeskus. Kuntainliittojen Talous (0784-9699); Which superseded in part (1982-1986): Tilastotiedotus - Tilastokeskus. J T, Julkisyhteisot (0359-081X)
Related titles: ◆ Series of: Finland. Tilastokeskus. Suomen Virallinen Tilasto. ISSN 1795-5165.
Published by: Tilastokeskus/Statistics Finland, Tyopajakatu 13, Statistics Finland, Helsinki, 00022, Finland. TEL 358-9-17341, FAX 358-9-17342279, http://www.stat.fi.

351.21 FIN ISSN 1236-6595
FINLAND. TILASTOKESKUS. KUNTAYHTYMIEN TALOUSARVIOT/FINLAND. STATISTIKCENTRALEN. SAMKOMMUNERNAS BUDGETER. Text in Finnish, Swedish. 1982. a. EUR 19 (effective 2008). **Document type:** *Government.*
Formerly (until 1993): Finland. Tilastokeskus. Kuntainliittojen Talousarviot (0784-9702); Which superseded in part (in 1986): Finland. Tilastokeskus. JT. Julkisyhteisot (0359-081X)
Related titles: Online - full text ed.; ◆ Series of: Finland. Tilastokeskus. Suomen Virallinen Tilasto. ISSN 1795-5165.

Published by: Tilastokeskus/Statistics Finland, Tyopajakatu 13, Statistics Finland, Helsinki, 00022, Finland. TEL 358-9-17341, FAX 358-9-17342279.

351.21 FIN ISSN 0784-9737
HJ55.3
FINLAND. TILASTOKESKUS. KUNTIEN TALOUSARVIOT/FINLAND. STATISTIKCENTRALEN. KOMMUNERNAS BUDGETER/ FINLAND.STATISTICS FINLAND. MUNICIPAL FINANCES. (Section XXXI of Official Statistics of Finland) Text in Finnish, Swedish; Summaries in English. 1968. a. EUR 19 (effective 2008). **Document type:** *Government.*
Former titles (until 1988): Finland. Tilastokeskus. Tilastotiedotus - Tilastokeskus. JT, Julkisyhteisot (0359-081X); (until 1982): Finland. Tilastokeskus. Kuntien Finanssitilasto (0430-5566)
Related titles: Online - full text ed.; ◆ Series of: Finland. Tilastokeskus. Suomen Virallinen Tilasto. ISSN 1795-5165.
Indexed: RASB.
Published by: Tilastokeskus/Statistics Finland, Tyopajakatu 13, Statistics Finland, Helsinki, 00022, Finland. TEL 358-9-17341, FAX 358-9-17342279.

351.21 FIN ISSN 1239-7482
FINLAND. TILASTOKESKUS. LANSI-SUOMEN KATSAUS. Text in Finnish. 1997. a. stat. **Document type:** *Government.*
Published by: Tilastokeskus/Statistics Finland, Tyopajakatu 13, Statistics Finland, Helsinki, 00022, Finland. TEL 358-9-17341, FAX 358-9-17342279.

352.13021 FIN ISSN 1238-9064
FINLAND. TILASTOKESKUS. OULUN ALUEPALVELU. POHJOIS-SUOMEN KATSAUS. Text in Finnish. 1989. a. stat. **Document type:** *Government.*
Formerly (until 1995): Finland. Tilastokeskus. Laanikatsaus. Oulun Laani (0788-1150)
Published by: Tilastokeskus, Oulun Aluepalvelu/Statistics Finland. Oulu, Kirkkokatu 16, Oulu, 90100, Finland. TEL 358-8-5351410, FAX 358-8-5351430, oulu@stat.fi, http://www.stat.fi.

352.13021 USA ISSN 1935-5858
FLORIDA CITIES & COUNTIES GRAPHIC PERFORMANCE ANALYSIS. Text in English. 2006. a. USD 95 per issue (effective 2009). charts. **Document type:** *Report, Trade.* **Description:** Provides comparisons in chart form, annual series of analytic charts, by peer group, within state. Each issue consist of 9 charts in each county peer group and each city peer group and 1 area chart per county. 100-200 graphs per state book.
Published by: Municipal Analysis Services, Inc., PO Box 13453, Austin, TX 78711. TEL 512-327-3328, munilysis@hotmail.com, http:// sites.google.com/site/gregmichels. Ed. Greg Michels.

351.021 DEU
GELSENKIRCHEN IM SPIEGEL DER STATISTIK. Text in German. 1982. s-a.
Published by: Stadt Gelsenkirchen, Amt fuer Informationsverarbeitung, Vattmannstr 11, Gelsenkirchen, 45877, Germany. TEL 0209-1692101. Circ: 350.

351.21 DEU ISSN 1862-7331
GEMEINDEFREIEN GEBIETE BAYERNS. Text in German. 1959. irreg. EUR 7.50 per issue (effective 2011). **Document type:** *Government.*
Supersedes in part (in 2005): Bayerisches Landesamt fuer Statistik und Datenverarbeitung. Statistische Berichte A: Bevoelkerung, Gesundheitswesen, Gebiet, Erwerbstaetigkeit (1430-3175); Which was formerly (until 1982): Bayerisches Statistisches Landesamt. Statistische Berichte A (1430-3000)
Published by: Bayerisches Landesamt fuer Statistik und Datenverarbeitung, Neuhauser Str 8, Munich, 80331, Germany. TEL 49-89-2119205, FAX 49-89-2119410, poststelle@statistik.bayern.de, http://www.statistik.bayern.de.

351.021 GRC
GEOGRAPHICAL CODE OF GREECE; by eparchy, municipality, commune and locality. Text in Greek. 1960. every 10 yrs. USD 8. back issues avail. **Document type:** *Government.* **Description:** Includes administrative changes and changes of geographical names.
Formerly (until 1990): Geographical Code of Greece, Eparchies, Municipalities, Communes and Localities
Published by: National Statistical Service of Greece, Statistical Information and Publications Division/Ethniki Statistiki Ypiresia tes Ellados, 14-16 Lykourgou St, Athens, 101 66, Greece. TEL 30-1-3289-397, FAX 30-1-3241-102.

352.13021 USA ISSN 1935-584X
GEORGIA CITIES & COUNTIES GRAPHIC PERFORMANCE ANALYSIS. Text in English. 2006. a. USD 95 per issue (effective 2009). charts. **Document type:** *Report, Trade.* **Description:** Provides comparisons in chart form, annual series of analytic charts, by peer group, within state. Each issue consist of 9 charts in each county peer group and each city peer group and 1 area chart per county. 100-200 graphs per state book.
Published by: Municipal Analysis Services, Inc., PO Box 13453, Austin, TX 78711. TEL 512-327-3328, munilysis@hotmail.com, http:// sites.google.com/site/gregmichels. Ed. Greg Michels.

351.021 DEU
GOETTINGER STATISTIK. Text in German. 1950. q.
Published by: Stadt Goettingen, Amt fuer Statistik und Stadtforschung, Postfach 3831, Goettingen, 37028, Germany. TEL 0551-4002353. Circ: 600.

352.14021 GBR ISSN 1758-1788
GREAT BRITAIN. DEPARTMENT OF COMMUNITIES AND LOCAL GOVERNMENT. LOCAL GOVERNMENT FINANCIAL STATISTICS: ENGLAND. Text in English. a. GBP 32 (effective 2010). stat. **Document type:** *Government.*
Supersedes in part (in 198?): Great Britain. Department of the Environment. Local Government Financial Statistics: England and Wales (0308-1745)
Related titles: Online - full text ed.: ISSN 1758-1796. 200?. free.
—CCC.
Published by: Great Britain. Department of Communities and Local Government, Eland House, Bressenden Pl, London, SW1E 5DU, United Kingdom. TEL 44-20-79444400, contactus@communities.gov.uk.

351.021 GBR
GREAT BRITAIN. H M TREASURY. CIVIL SERVICE STATISTICS (ONLINE). Text in English. 1971. a. free. **Document type:** *Government.* **Description:** Contains the latest civil Service employment statistics, providing key workforce statistics by department and agency whist the annual statistics provide regional analyses, diversity and earnings statistics.
Formerly (until 2001): Great Britain. H M Treasury. Civil Service Statistics (Print) (0267-095X)
Media: Online - full text.
Published by: (Great Britain. H.M. Treasury), Office for National Statistics, Rm 1.101, Government Bldgs, Cardiff Rd, Newport, S Wales NP10 8XG, United Kingdom. TEL 44-845-6013034, FAX 44-1633-652747, info@statistics.gsi.gov.uk, http:// www.statistics.gov.uk/default.asp.

016.351 USA ISSN 0092-3168
Z1223.Z7
GUIDE TO U S GOVERNMENT PUBLICATIONS. Variant title: Andriot. Text in English. 1962. a. USD 499 per issue (effective 2008). **Document type:** *Directory, Trade.* **Description:** A standard reference source in federal document collections.
Formerly (until 1973): Guide to U.S. Government Serials and Periodicals (0362-8132)
Published by: Gale (Subsidiary of: Cengage Learning), 27500 Drake Rd, Farmington Hills, MI 48331. TEL 248-699-4253, 800-877-4253, FAX 877-363-4253, gale.galeord@cengage.com.

352.13021 FIN ISSN 1455-7231
HA1450.5.Z9
HELSINGIN KAUPUNGIN TIETOKESKUS. TILASTOJA/CITY OF HELSINKI URBAN FACTS. STATISTICS/HELSINGFORS STADS FAKTACENTRAL. STATISTIK. Text in Multiple languages. 1990. irreg. **Document type:** *Monographic series, Government.*
Formerly (until 1998): Helsingin Kaupungin Tietokeskuksen Tilastoja (0788-0871)
Related titles: Online - full text ed.: ISSN 1796-721X. 2007.
Published by: Helsingin Kaupungin Tietokeskus/City of Helsinki Urban Facts, PO Box 5500, Helsinki, 00099, Finland. TEL 358-9-3101612, FAX 358-9-31036601, tietokeskus.kirjaamo@hel.fi, http://www.hel2.fi/ tietokeskus/kaupunkitilastot/index.html.

351.021 GBR ISSN 1759-7005
HV6208
HOME OFFICE. RESEARCH AND STATISTICS DIRECTORATE. STATISTICAL BULLETIN (ONLINE). Text in English. 1979. w. free (effective 2010). **Document type:** *Bulletin, Government.*
Supersedes in part (in 200?): Home Office. Research and Statistics Directorate. Statistical Bulletin (Print) (1358-510X); Which was formerly (until 1999): Home Office. Statistical Bulletin (0143-6384)
Media: Online - full text.
—BLDSC (8447.464650), IE. **CCC.**
Published by: Great Britain. Home Office, Direct Communications Unit, 2 Marsham St, London, SW1P 4DF, United Kingdom. TEL 44-20-70354848, FAX 44-20-70354745, public.enquiries@homeoffice.gsi.gov.uk.

352.13021 USA ISSN 1935-5823
ILLINOIS CITIES & COUNTIES GRAPHIC PERFORMANCE ANALYSIS. Text in English. 2006. a. USD 95 per issue (effective 2009). charts. **Document type:** *Report, Trade.* **Description:** Provides comparisons in chart form, annual series of analytic charts, by peer group, within state. Each issue consist of 9 charts in each county peer group and each city peer group and 1 area chart per county. 100-200 graphs per state book.
Published by: Municipal Analysis Services, Inc., PO Box 13453, Austin, TX 78711. TEL 512-327-3328, munilysis@hotmail.com, http:// sites.google.com/site/gregmichels. Ed. Greg Michels.

016.351 USA ISSN 0046-8908
INDEX TO CURRENT URBAN DOCUMENTS. Abbreviated title: I C U D. Text in English. 1972. q. (plus a. cumulation). Several purchase plans available - see http://www.urbdocs.com/order/index.asp. illus. index. back issues avail.; reprints avail. **Document type:** *Abstract/Index.* **Description:** Provides guidance on various reports and research that are generated by local government agencies, civic organizations, academic and research organizations, public libraries, and metropolitan and regional planning agencies in approximately 500 selected cities in the United States and Canada.
Related titles: CD-ROM ed.; Online - full content ed.
—Linda Hall.
Published by: Greenwood Publishing Group Inc. (Subsidiary of: A B C - C L I O), 88 Post Rd W, PO Box 5007, Westport, CT 06881. TEL 203-226-3571, 800-225-5800, FAX 877-231-6980, sales@greenwood.com, http://www.greenwood.com.

352.13021 USA ISSN 1935-5815
INDIANA CITIES & COUNTIES GRAPHIC PERFORMANCE ANALYSIS. Text in English. 2006. a. USD 95 per issue (effective 2009). charts. **Document type:** *Report, Trade.* **Description:** Provides comparisons in chart form, annual series of analytic charts, by peer group, within state. Each issue consist of 9 charts in each county peer group and each city peer group and 1 area chart per county. 100-200 graphs per state book.
Published by: Municipal Analysis Services, Inc., PO Box 13453, Austin, TX 78711. TEL 512-327-3328, munilysis@hotmail.com, http:// sites.google.com/site/gregmichels. Ed. Greg Michels.

352.77021 PRT ISSN 0872-1521
INQUERITO MENSAL DE CONJUNTURA A CONSTRUCAO E OBRAS PUBLICAS. Text in Portuguese. 1992. m.
Published by: Instituto Nacional de Estatistica, Av Antonio Jose de Almeida 2, Lisbon, 1000-043, Portugal. TEL 351-21-8426100, FAX 351-21-8426380, ine@ine.pt, http://www.ine.pt.

351.021 AGO ISSN 1010-4151
HA2211
INSTITUTO NACIONAL DE ESTADISTICA. BOLETIM MENSAL DE ESTADISTICA. Text in Spanish. 1969. m. **Document type:** *Bulletin, Government.*
Published by: Instituto Nacional de Estatistica, Caixa Postal 1215, Luanda, Angola.

INTEGRALE VEILIGHEIDSMONITOR. LANDELIJKE RAPPORTAGE. *see* LAW—Abstracting, Bibliographies, Statistics

352.13021 USA ISSN 1935-5831
IOWA CITIES & COUNTIES GRAPHIC PERFORMANCE ANALYSIS. Text in English. 2006. a. USD 95 per issue (effective 2009). charts. **Document type:** *Report, Trade.* **Description:** Provides comparisons in chart form, annual series of analytic charts, by peer group, within state. Each issue consist of 9 charts in each county peer group and each city peer group and 1 area chart per county. 100-200 graphs per state book.
Published by: Municipal Analysis Services, Inc., PO Box 13453, Austin, TX 78711. TEL 512-327-3328, munilysis@hotmail.com, http:// sites.google.com/site/gregmichels. Ed. Greg Michels.

351.021 USA
IOWA OFFICIAL REGISTER. Text in English. 1892. biennial. price varies. illus. **Document type:** *Directory, Government.*
Published by: Secretary of State of Iowa, Statehouse, Des Moines, IA 50319. TEL 515-281-8993, FAX 515-242-6235. Circ: 6,000. **Subscr. to:** Secretary of State Office, Statehouse, Des Moines, IA 50319.

351.021 ISR ISSN 0793-0275
GV132.5
ISRAEL. CENTRAL BUREAU OF STATISTICS. NATIONAL EXPENDITURE ON CULTURE, RECREATION AND SPORTS/HA-HOTSA'A HA-L'UMIT L'TARBUT, L'VIDDUR, U-L'SPORT. Text in English, Hebrew. 1992. irreg. ILS 43 per issue. **Document type:** *Government.*
Related titles: Diskette ed.
Published by: Central Bureau of Statistics/Ha-Lishka Ha-Merkazit L'Statistiqa, PO Box 13015, Jerusalem, 91130, Israel. TEL 972-2-6553400, FAX 972-2-6553325.

351.021 ITA ISSN 1721-9655
ITALY. ISTITUTO NAZIONALE DI STATISTICA. STATISTICHE DELLE AMMINISTRAZIONI PUBBLICHE (YEAR). Text in Italian. irreg., latest 1988-89 ed. **Document type:** *Government.*
Former titles (until 1998): Italy. Istituto Nazionale di Statistica. Statistiche sulla Amministrazione Pubblica (1971-4750); (until 1986): Italy. Istituto Nazionale di Statistica. Statistiche sulla Pubblica Amministrazione (1971-4769)
Published by: Istituto Nazionale di Statistica (I S T A T), Via Cesare Balbo 16, Rome, 00184, Italy. TEL 39-06-46731, http://www.istat.it.

016.351 ZAF
J8
JUTA - STATE LIBRARY INDEX TO THE GOVERNMENT GAZETTE. Text in English. 1979. base vol. plus q. updates. ZAR 725 base vol(s). per issue; ZAR 360 updates (effective 2001). back issues avail. **Document type:** *Journal, Abstract/Index.* **Description:** Alphabetical index of acts, proclamations, regulations, notices and legal advertisements in the Government Gazette of South Africa.
Formerly (until 1990): Government Gazette Index (0379-6078)
Related titles: CD-ROM ed.: Index to the Government Gazette of South Africa. ISSN 1024-2538. BRL 1,291.62 (effective 2001); Diskette ed.; Microfiche ed.; Online - full text ed.: Index to the Government Gazettes of South Africa. ISSN 1682-0630. ZAR 612 single user; ZAR 306 per additional user (effective 2007).
Published by: Juta & Company Ltd., Juta Law, PO Box 14373, Lansdowne, 7779, South Africa. TEL 27-21-7633500, FAX 27-11-8838169, cserv@juta.co.za, http://www.juta.co.za. Ed. Daphne Burger.

352.13021 USA ISSN 1935-6013
KANSAS CITIES & COUNTIES GRAPHIC PERFORMANCE ANALYSIS. Text in English. 2006. a. USD 95 per issue (effective 2009). charts. **Document type:** *Report, Trade.* **Description:** Provides comparisons in chart form, annual series of analytic charts, by peer group, within state. Each issue consist of 9 charts in each county peer group and each city peer group and 1 area chart per county. 100-200 graphs per state book.
Published by: Municipal Analysis Services, Inc., PO Box 13453, Austin, TX 78711. TEL 512-327-3328, munilysis@hotmail.com, http:// sites.google.com/site/gregmichels. Ed. Greg Michels.

351.021 CHE
KANTONE UND STAEDTE DER SCHWEIZ. STATISTISCHE UEBERSICHTEN/CANTONS ET VILLES SUISSES. DONNEES STATISTIQUES. Text in French, German. 1991. a. CHF 40 (effective 2001). **Document type:** *Government.*
Related titles: Diskette ed.
Published by: Bundesamt fuer Statistik, Espace de l'Europe 10, Neuchatel, 2010, Switzerland. TEL 41-32-7136011, FAX 41-32-7136012, information@bfs.admin.ch, http://www.admin.ch/bfs.

351.021 DEU ISSN 0451-4874
KASSELER STATISTIK. Text in German. 1970. q.
Published by: Stadt Kassel, Statistisches Amt und Wahlamt, Untere Karlsstr 8, Kassel, 34117, Germany. TEL 0561-7872299, FAX 0561-7872124.

352.13021 USA ISSN 1935-6005
KENTUCKY CITIES & COUNTIES GRAPHIC PERFORMANCE ANALYSIS. Text in English. 2006. a. USD 95 per issue (effective 2009). charts. **Document type:** *Report, Trade.* **Description:** Provides comparisons in chart form, annual series of analytic charts, by peer group, within state. Each issue consist of 9 charts in each county peer group and each city peer group and 1 area chart per county. 100-200 graphs per state book.
Published by: Municipal Analysis Services, Inc., PO Box 13453, Austin, TX 78711. TEL 512-327-3328, munilysis@hotmail.com, http:// sites.google.com/site/gregmichels. Ed. Greg Michels.

351.021 DEU ISSN 0933-632X
KOELNER STATISTISCHE NACHRICHTEN. SONDERHEFTE. Text in German. 1979. irreg. back issues avail. **Document type:** *Government.*
Published by: Stadt Koeln, Amt fuer Stadtentwicklung und Statistik, Athener Ring 4, Cologne, 50765, Germany. TEL 49-221-221-21887, FAX 49-221-22121900. Circ: 1,000.

351.021 DEU ISSN 1863-348X
KOMPENDIUM DER FINANZSTATISTIK. Text in German. 1953. a. stat. back issues avail. **Document type:** *Government.*
Former titles (until 2006): Handbuch der Finanzstatistik (0172-360X); (until 1979): Taschenbuch der Finanzstatistik fuer Rheinland-Pfalz (0172-3642); (until 1973): Taschenbuch der Finanz- und Steuerstatistik fuer Rheinland-Pfalz (0482-8909)

P

Published by: Statistisches Landesamt Rheinland-Pfalz, Mainzerstr 14-16, Bad Ems, 56130, Germany. TEL 49-2603-713240, FAX 49-2603-71193240, pressestelle@statistik.rlp.de, http://www.statistik.rlp.de.

016.351 CHE
LIST OF BOOKS AND ARTICLES CATALOGUED. Text in English. 1965. a. free. **Document type:** *Bibliography.* **Description:** Contains references to numerous books and articles from periodicals on all aspects of parliamentary or constitutional law received or purchased by the Library of the Inter-Parliamentary Union every year.
Published by: Inter-Parliamentary Union, 5, chemin du Pommier, Case postale 330, Geneva, 1218, Switzerland. TEL 41-22-9194150, FAX 41-22-9194160, TELEX 289784 IPUCH, postbox@mail.ipu.org, http://www.ipu.org.

016.35214 AUS ISSN 0727-7989
LOCAL GOVERNMENT INDEX NEW SOUTH WALES. Text in English. 1975. base vol. plus s-a. updates. looseleaf. AUD 608 (effective 2008). **Document type:** *Abstract/Index.* **Description:** An index to local government law, building law, environmental and planning law in New South Wales.
Published by: Lawbook Co. (Subsidiary of: Thomson Reuters (Professional) Australia Limited), PO Box 3502, Rozelle, NSW 2039, Australia. TEL 61-2-85877980, 300-304-195, FAX 61-2-85877981, 300-304-196, LTA.Service@thomsonreuters.com, http://www.thomson.com.au.

352.13021 USA ISSN 1935-5998
LOUISIANA CITIES & COUNTIES GRAPHIC PERFORMANCE ANALYSIS. Text in English. 2006. a. USD 95 per issue (effective 2009). charts. **Document type:** *Report, Trade.* **Description:** Provides comparisons in chart form, annual series of analytic charts, by peer group, within state. Each issue consist of 9 charts in each county peer group and each city peer group and 1 area chart per county. 100-200 graphs per state book.
Published by: Municipal Analysis Services, Inc., PO Box 13453, Austin, TX 78711. TEL 512-327-3328, munilysis@hotmail.com, http://sites.google.com/site/gregmichels. Ed. Greg Michels.

352.13021 USA ISSN 1935-5971
MAINE CITIES & COUNTIES GRAPHIC PERFORMANCE ANALYSIS. Text in English. 2006. a. USD 95 per issue (effective 2009). charts. **Document type:** *Report, Trade.* **Description:** Provides comparisons in chart form, annual series of analytic charts, by peer group, within state. Each issue consist of 9 charts in each county peer group and each city peer group and 1 area chart per county. 100-200 graphs per state book.
Published by: Municipal Analysis Services, Inc., PO Box 13453, Austin, TX 78711. TEL 512-327-3328, munilysis@hotmail.com, http://sites.google.com/site/gregmichels. Ed. Greg Michels.

016.3516897 MWI
MALAWI. GOVERNMENT PRINTER. CATALOGUE OF PUBLICATIONS. Text in English. 1974. q. **Document type:** *Government.*
Published by: Government Printer, PO Box 37, Zomba, Malawi.

351.021 MLT ISSN 0377-4503
MALTA. DEPARTMENT OF INFORMATION. REPORTS ON THE WORKING OF GOVERNMENT DEPARTMENTS. Text in English. 1905. a. USD 14. **Document type:** *Government.*
Published by: Department of Information, 3 Castille Place, Valletta, Malta. TEL 356-224901, FAX 356-237170, TELEX 1448 MW. Ed. Alfred D Baldacchino.

016.351 USA
Z1223.5.M3
MARYLAND. GENERAL ASSEMBLY. STATE DEPARTMENT OF LEGISLATIVE REFERENCE. LIBRARY AND INFORMATION SERVICES DIVISION. MARYLAND DOCUMENTS. Text in English. 1977. m. free to members (effective 2011). back issues avail. **Document type:** *Government.* **Description:** Lists all state and local publications catalogued by the state's Department of Legislative Services.
Formerly (until 19??): Maryland. General Assembly. State Department of Legislative Reference. Library Division. Maryland Documents (0195-3443)
Related titles: Online - full text ed.: free (effective 2011).
Published by: Department of Legislative Services, Legislative Sales, Legislative Services Bldg, 90 State Cir, Annapolis, MD 21401. TEL 410-946-5400, libr@mlis.state.md.us.

352.13021 USA ISSN 1935-598X
MASSACHUSETTS CITIES & COUNTIES GRAPHIC PERFORMANCE ANALYSIS. Text in English. 2006. a. USD 95 per issue (effective 2009). charts. **Document type:** *Report, Trade.* **Description:** Provides comparisons in chart form, annual series of analytic charts, by peer group, within state. Each issue consist of 9 charts in each county peer group and each city peer group and 1 area chart per county. 100-200 graphs per state book.
Published by: Municipal Analysis Services, Inc., PO Box 13453, Austin, TX 78711. TEL 512-327-3328, munilysis@hotmail.com, http://sites.google.com/site/gregmichels. Ed. Greg Michels.

351.021 USA
MASSACHUSETTS TAXPAYERS FOUNDATION. STATE BUDGET TRENDS. Text in English. 1973. a. USD 4. back issues avail. **Description:** Analysis of Governor's proposed budget, with 10-year comparisons.
Published by: Massachusetts Taxpayers Foundation Inc., 24 Province St, Boston, MA 02108. TEL 617-720-1000, FAX 617-720-0799. R&P Elizabeth Hogan.

352.13021 USA ISSN 1935-5947
MICHIGAN CITIES & COUNTIES GRAPHIC PERFORMANCE ANALYSIS. Text in English. 2006. a. USD 95 per issue (effective 2009). charts. **Document type:** *Report, Trade.* **Description:** Provides comparisons in chart form, annual series of analytic charts, by peer group, within state. Each issue consist of 9 charts in each county peer group and each city peer group and 1 area chart per county. 100-200 graphs per state book.
Published by: Municipal Analysis Services, Inc., PO Box 13453, Austin, TX 78711. TEL 512-327-3328, munilysis@hotmail.com, http://sites.google.com/site/gregmichels. Ed. Greg Michels.

352.13021 USA ISSN 1935-5955
MINNESOTA CITIES & COUNTIES GRAPHIC PERFORMANCE ANALYSIS. Text in English. 2006. a. USD 95 per issue (effective 2009). charts. **Document type:** *Report, Trade.* **Description:** Provides comparisons in chart form, annual series of analytic charts, by peer group, within state. Each issue consist of 9 charts in each county peer group and each city peer group and 1 area chart per county. 100-200 graphs per state book.
Published by: Municipal Analysis Services, Inc., PO Box 13453, Austin, TX 78711. TEL 512-327-3328, munilysis@hotmail.com, http://sites.google.com/site/gregmichels. Ed. Greg Michels.

352.13021 USA ISSN 1935-6056
MISSISSIPPI CITIES & COUNTIES GRAPHIC PERFORMANCE ANALYSIS. Text in English. 2006. a. USD 95 per issue (effective 2009). charts. **Document type:** *Report, Trade.* **Description:** Provides comparisons in chart form, annual series of analytic charts, by peer group, within state. Each issue consist of 9 charts in each county peer group and each city peer group and 1 area chart per county. 100-200 graphs per state book.
Published by: Municipal Analysis Services, Inc., PO Box 13453, Austin, TX 78711. TEL 512-327-3328, munilysis@hotmail.com, http://sites.google.com/site/gregmichels. Ed. Greg Michels.

352.13021 USA ISSN 1935-5963
MISSOURI CITIES & COUNTIES GRAPHIC PERFORMANCE ANALYSIS. Text in English. 2006. a. USD 95 per issue (effective 2009). charts. **Document type:** *Report, Trade.* **Description:** Provides comparisons in chart form, annual series of analytic charts, by peer group, within state. Each issue consist of 9 charts in each county peer group and each city peer group and 1 area chart per county. 100-200 graphs per state book.
Published by: Municipal Analysis Services, Inc., PO Box 13453, Austin, TX 78711. TEL 512-327-3328, munilysis@hotmail.com, http://sites.google.com/site/gregmichels. Ed. Greg Michels.

016.351 USA
MISSOURI STATE GOVERNMENT PUBLICATIONS. Text in English. 1972. m. USD 7; free to state residents (effective 2001). **Document type:** *Newsletter.*
Supersedes: Missouri State Government Documents
Related titles: Online - full text ed.
Published by: Missouri State Library, PO Box 387, Jefferson City, MO 65102. TEL 573-751-3615, FAX 573-751-3612. Circ: 2,500.

351.021 DEU ISSN 0173-8895
MUELHEIMER STATISTIK. Text in German. 1949. q. EUR 16 (effective 2005). **Document type:** *Bulletin, Government.*
Published by: Stadt Muelheim an der Ruhr, Amt fuer Statistik und Stadtforschung, Heinrich-Melzer-Str 1, Muelheim An Der Ruhr, 45468, Germany. TEL 49-208-4556800, FAX 49-208-4559999, info@stadt-mh.de, http://www.muelheim-ruhr.de.

352.13021 DEU
MUENCHNER STATISTIK. Text in German. 1975. q. EUR 5 (effective 2010). stat. back issues avail. **Document type:** *Bulletin, Government.*
Former titles: Muenchener Statistik. Monatsbericht (0171-5461); (until 1979): Statistischer Informationsdienst des Stadtentwicklungsreferates (0171-5453); (until 1976): Muenchener Statistik. Monatsbericht (0171-547X)
—CCC.
Published by: Statistisches Amt der Landeshauptstadt Muenchen, Schwanthalerstr 68, Munich, 80336, Germany. TEL 49-89-23328766, FAX 49-89-23325989, stat.amt@muenchen.de, http://www.muenchen.de/statamt.

016.35214 CAN
MUNICIPAL ACT AND INDEX TO LOCAL GOVERNMENT LEGISLATION MANUAL. Text in English. base vol. plus irreg. updates. looseleaf. CAD 37.50. **Description:** A consolidation of the Municipal Act and an Index to Local Government Legislation.
Published by: Ministry of Municipal Affairs, Recreation and Housing, Victoria, BC, Canada. **Subscr. to:** Crown Publications Inc. TEL 250-386-4636, FAX 250-386-0221, crown@pinc.com, http://www.crownpub.bc.ca.

351.021 CHE ISSN 1012-6325
JN8931
NATIONALRATSWAHLEN (YEAR)/ELECTIONS AU CONSEIL NATIONAL (YEAR); Uebersicht und Analyse. Text in French, German. 1943. every 4 yrs. CHF 23 (effective 2001). **Document type:** *Government.*
Published by: Bundesamt fuer Statistik, Espace de l'Europe 10, Neuchatel, 2010, Switzerland. TEL 41-32-7136011, FAX 41-32-7136012, information@bfs.admin.ch, http://www.admin.ch/bfs.

352.13021 USA ISSN 1935-6048
NEBRASKA CITIES & COUNTIES GRAPHIC PERFORMANCE ANALYSIS. Text in English. 2006. a. USD 95 per issue (effective 2009). charts. **Document type:** *Report, Trade.* **Description:** Provides comparisons in chart form, annual series of analytic charts, by peer group, within state. Each issue consist of 9 charts in each county peer group and each city peer group and 1 area chart per county. 100-200 graphs per state book.
Published by: Municipal Analysis Services, Inc., PO Box 13453, Austin, TX 78711. TEL 512-327-3328, munilysis@hotmail.com, http://sites.google.com/site/gregmichels. Ed. Greg Michels.

352.13021 USA ISSN 1935-603X
NEW JERSEY CITIES & COUNTIES GRAPHIC PERFORMANCE ANALYSIS. Text in English. 2006. a. USD 95 per issue (effective 2009). charts. **Document type:** *Report, Trade.* **Description:** Provides comparisons in chart form, annual series of analytic charts, by peer group, within state. Each issue consist of 9 charts in each county peer group and each city peer group and 1 area chart per county. 100-200 graphs per state book.
Published by: Municipal Analysis Services, Inc., PO Box 13453, Austin, TX 78711. TEL 512-327-3328, munilysis@hotmail.com, http://sites.google.com/site/gregmichels. Ed. Greg Michels.

016.35268 USA
NEW RESOURCES. Text in English. 1970. m. back issues avail. **Document type:** *Government.* **Description:** Lists recent state library acquisitions of interest to state employees.
Formerly (until 1988): New Resources for State Government and Agencies (0883-5853)
Published by: State Library, 1500 Senate St, PO Box 11469, Columbia, SC 29211. TEL 803-734-8666, FAX 803-734-8676, reference@statelibrary.sc.gov.

352.13021 USA ISSN 1935-5416
NEW YORK CITIES AND COUNTIES GRAPHIC PERFORMANCE ANALYSIS. Text in English. 2006. a. USD 95 per issue (effective 2009). charts. **Document type:** *Report, Trade.* **Description:** Provides comparisons in chart form, annual series of analytic charts, by peer group, within state. Each issue consist of 9 charts in each county peer group and each city peer group and 1 area chart per county. 100-200 graphs per state book.
Published by: Municipal Analysis Services, Inc., PO Box 13453, Austin, TX 78711. TEL 512-327-3328, munilysis@hotmail.com, http://sites.google.com/site/gregmichels. Ed. Greg Michels.

016.328 NZL
NEW ZEALAND. TABLES OF ACTS AND ORDINANCES AND STATUTORY REGULATIONS IN FORCE. Text in English. a. **Document type:** *Government.* **Description:** Used to locate Acts that are currently in force in New Zealand. It includes an alphabetical listing of all public, private and local Acts as well as any amending Acts.
Published by: New Zealand. House of Representatives, Parliament Buildings, Molesworth St, Wellington, 6160, New Zealand. TEL 64-4-4719999, FAX 64-4-4712551, http://www.parliament.nz/.

351.021 DEU ISSN 1863-9518
NORD REGIONAL. Text in German. 1998. a. **Document type:** *Government.*
Former titles (until 2006): Hamburg Regional (1619-3768); (until 2002): Hamburger Statistische Portraets (1433-7991)
Published by: Statistisches Amt fuer Hamburg und Schleswig-Holstein, Steckelhoern 12, Hamburg, 20457, Germany. TEL 49-40-428311766, FAX 49-40-428311700, poststelle@statistik-nord.de.

352.13021 USA ISSN 1935-6021
NORTH DAKOTA CITIES & COUNTIES GRAPHIC PERFORMANCE ANALYSIS. Text in English. 2006. a. USD 95 per issue (effective 2009). charts. **Document type:** *Report, Trade.* **Description:** Provides comparisons in chart form, annual series of analytic charts, by peer group, within state. Each issue consist of 9 charts in each county peer group and each city peer group and 1 area chart per county. 100-200 graphs per state book.
Published by: Municipal Analysis Services, Inc., PO Box 13453, Austin, TX 78711. TEL 512-327-3328, munilysis@hotmail.com, http://sites.google.com/site/gregmichels. Ed. Greg Michels.

352.13021 USA ISSN 1935-5750
NORTHEAST CITIES & COUNTIES GRAPHIC PERFORMANCE ANALYSIS. Text in English. 2006. a. USD 95 per issue (effective 2009). charts. **Document type:** *Report, Trade.* **Description:** Provides comparisons in chart form, annual series of analytic charts, by peer group, within state. Each issue consist of 9 charts in each county peer group and each city peer group and 1 area chart per county. 100-200 graphs per state book.
Published by: Municipal Analysis Services, Inc., PO Box 13453, Austin, TX 78711. TEL 512-327-3328, munilysis@hotmail.com, http://sites.google.com/site/gregmichels. Ed. Greg Michels.

352.13021 USA ISSN 1935-5432
NORTHWEST CITIES & COUNTIES GRAPHIC PERFORMANCE ANALYSIS. Text in English. 2006. a. USD 95 per issue (effective 2009). charts. **Document type:** *Report, Trade.* **Description:** Provides comparisons in chart form, annual series of analytic charts, by peer group, within state. Each issue consist of 9 charts in each county peer group and each city peer group and 1 area chart per county. 100-200 graphs per state book.
Published by: Municipal Analysis Services, Inc., PO Box 13453, Austin, TX 78711. TEL 512-327-3328, munilysis@hotmail.com, http://sites.google.com/site/gregmichels. Ed. Greg Michels.

352.13021 NOR ISSN 0332-8023
NORWAY. STATISTISK SENTRALBYRAA. KOMMUNESTYREVALGET/ STATISTICS NORWAY. MUNICIPAL AND COUNTY ELECTIONS. Text in English, Norwegian. 1902. quadrennial. NOK 75 (effective 1997); NOK 140 per issue (effective 2004). **Document type:** *Government.*
Formerly (until 1976): Norway. Statistisk Sentralbyraa. Kommunevalget (0333-0605)
Related titles: ◆ Series of: Norges Offisielle Statistikk. ISSN 0300-5585.
Published by: Statistisk Sentralbyraa/Statistics Norway, Kongensgate 6, P O Box 8131, Dep, Oslo, 0033, Norway. TEL 47-21-090000, FAX 47-21-094973, ssb@ssb.no, http://www.ssb.no.

351 NOR ISSN 0800-9783
HA1501
NORWAY. STATISTISK SENTRALBYRAA. KVARTALSVIS NASJONALREGNSKAP. Variant title: Kvartalsvis Nasjonalregnskap. Text in English, Norwegian. 1966. a. NOK 125 (effective 2000). **Document type:** *Government.*
Related titles: Online - full text ed.
Published by: Statistisk Sentralbyraa/Statistics Norway, Kongensgate 6, P O Box 8131, Dep, Oslo, 0033, Norway. TEL 47-21-090000, FAX 47-21-094973, ssb@ssb.no. Ed. Pia Tonjum TEL 47-21-094834.

351 NOR ISSN 0809-2001
NORWAY. STATISTISK SENTRALBYRAA. NASJONALREGNSKAPSSTATISTIKK. PRODUKSJON, ANVENDELSE OG SYSSELSETTING. Text in Norwegian. 1953. a.
Supersedes in part (in 1993): Norway. Statistisk Sentralbyraa. Nasjonalregnskapsstatistikk. (0808-5277); Which was formerly (until 1989): Norway. Statistisk Sentralbyraa. Nasjonalregnskap (0550-0494)
Related titles: Online - full text ed.
Published by: Statistisk Sentralbyraa/Statistics Norway, Kongensgate 6, P O Box 8131, Dep, Oslo, 0033, Norway. TEL 47-21-090000, FAX 47-21-094973, ssb@ssb.no.

351.021 NOR ISSN 0802-9067
HA1501
NORWAY. STATISTISK SENTRALBYRAA. STORTINGSVALGET/ STATISTICS NORWAY. PARLIAMENTARY ELECTIONS. Text in English, Norwegian. 1903. quadrennial. **Document type:** *Government.*
Supersedes in part (in 1986): Stortingsvalget. Hefte I (0800-921X); (in 1986): Stortingsvalget. Hefte II (0800-9228); Which was formerly (until 1981): Stortingsvalget (0800-9341); (until 1906): Statistik vedroerende Valgmandsvalgene og Stortingsvalgene
Related titles: Online - full text ed.; ◆ Series of: Norges Offisielle Statistikk. ISSN 0300-5585.

Published by: Statistisk Sentralbyraa/Statistics Norway, Kongensgate 6, P O Box 8131, Dep, Oslo, 0033, Norway. TEL 47-21-090000, FAX 47-21-094973, ssb@ssb.no. Circ: 1,800.

351.021 DEU ISSN 0944-1506
NUERNBERGER STATISTIK AKTUELL. Text in German. 1974. m. **Document type:** *Government.*
Published by: Stadt Nuernberg, Amt fuer Stadtforschung und Statistik, Unschlittplatz 7A, Nuernberg, 90403, Germany. TEL 49-911-2312843, FAX 49-911-2312844. Circ: 600.

351.021 GBR
OFFICE FOR NATIONAL STATISTICS. U.K. SERVICE SECTOR. Text in English. 1994. irreg., latest 2001. free (effective 2010). back issues avail. **Document type:** *Government.* **Description:** Provides economic and business statistics for the service sector industries derived from a wide range of official sources covering the period 1991-2000.
Formerly (until 200?): The U.K. Service Sector. Business Monitor SDQ11 (Print) (1360-4937)
Media: Online - full text.
—CCC.
Published by: Office for National Statistics, Rm 1.101, Government Bldgs, Cardiff Rd, Newport, S Wales NP10 8XG, United Kingdom. TEL 44-1633-653599, FAX 44-1633-652747, info@statistics.gov.uk, http://www.statistics.gov.uk/default.asp.

352.13021 USA ISSN 1935-553X
OHIO CITIES & COUNTIES GRAPHIC PERFORMANCE ANALYSIS. Text in English. 2006. a. USD 95 per issue (effective 2009). charts. **Document type:** *Report, Trade.* **Description:** Provides comparisons in chart form, annual series of analytic charts, by peer group, within state. Each issue consist of 9 charts in each county peer group and each city peer group and 1 area chart per county. 100-200 graphs per state book.
Published by: Municipal Analysis Services, Inc., PO Box 13453, Austin, TX 78711. TEL 512-327-3328, munilysis@hotmail.com, http://sites.google.com/site/gregmichels. Ed. Greg Michels.

352.13021 USA ISSN 1935-5521
OKLAHOMA CITIES & COUNTIES GRAPHIC PERFORMANCE ANALYSIS. Text in English. 2006. a. USD 95 per issue (effective 2009). charts. **Document type:** *Report, Trade.* **Description:** Provides comparisons in chart form, annual series of analytic charts, by peer group, within state. Each issue consist of 9 charts in each county peer group and each city peer group and 1 area chart per county. 100-200 graphs per state book.
Published by: Municipal Analysis Services, Inc., PO Box 13453, Austin, TX 78711. TEL 512-327-3328, munilysis@hotmail.com, http://sites.google.com/site/gregmichels. Ed. Greg Michels.

351.021 USA
HD2767.O7
OREGON. PUBLIC UTILITY COMMISSIONER. OREGON UTILITY STATISTICS. Text in English. 1970. a. free. stat.
Supersedes: Oregon Public Utility Commissioner. Statistics of Electric, Gas, Steam Heat, Telephone, Telegraph and Water Companies (0091-0546)
Indexed: SRI.
Published by: Public Utility Commissioner, 351 W Summer St, N E, Salem, OR 97310-0335. TEL 503-378-4373, FAX 503-373-7752. Circ: 350.

352.13021 USA ISSN 1935-5513
PENNSYLVANIA CITIES & COUNTIES GRAPHIC PERFORMANCE ANALYSIS. Text in English. 2006. a. USD 95 per issue (effective 2009). charts. **Document type:** *Report, Trade.* **Description:** Provides comparisons in chart form, annual series of analytic charts, by peer group, within state. Each issue consist of 9 charts in each county peer group and each city peer group and 1 area chart per county. 100-200 graphs per state book.
Published by: Municipal Analysis Services, Inc., PO Box 13453, Austin, TX 78711. TEL 512-327-3328, munilysis@hotmail.com, http://sites.google.com/site/gregmichels. Ed. Greg Michels.

351.021 DEU
PIRMASENS ZAHLEN UND FAKTEN: STATISTISCHE JAHRBUCH STADT PIRMASENS. Text in German. 1979. a. **Document type:** *Government.*
Published by: Stadtplanungsamt Pirmasens, Bahnhofstr 41, Pirmasens, 66953, Germany. TEL 06331-842433, FAX 06331-842540, TELEX 452286. Circ: 200.

351.21 PRT ISSN 1647-6166
▼ **O PORTAL DE ESTATISTICAS OFICIAIS.** Text in Portuguese. 2010. irreg. **Document type:** *Report, Government.*
Published by: Instituto Nacional de Estatistica, Av Antonio Jose de Almeida 2, Lisbon, 1000-043, Portugal. TEL 351-21-8426100, FAX 351-21-8426380, ine@ine.pt, http://www.ine.pt.

351.021 CAN
PROFILE OF ELECTORAL DISTRICTS (ONLINE EDITION). Text in English. irreg. free. **Description:** Provides detailed data on the 75 provincial electoral districts in B.C., based on the most recent Canadian Census data.
Formerly: Profile of Electoral Districts (Print Edition)
Media: Online - full text.
Published by: Ministry of Finance and Corporate Relations, B C Stats, PO Box 9410, Sta Prov Govt, Victoria, BC V8W 9V1, Canada. TEL 250-387-0359, FAX 250-387-0380, BC.Stats@gov.bc.ca.

016.75 USA
PUBLIC ADMINISTRATION ABSTRACTS. Text in English. 1974, base vol. plus s-m. updates. **Document type:** *Database, Abstract/Index.*
Formerly (until 2008): Sage Public Administration Abstracts (Online) (1940-2457)
Media: Online - full text.
Published by: EBSCO Publishing (Subsidiary of: EBSCO Industries, Inc.), 10 Estes St, PO Box 682, Ipswich, MA 01938. TEL 978-356-6500, 800-653-2726, FAX 978-356-6565, information@ebscohost.com, http://www.ebscohost.com.

016.351 USA
PUBLIC AFFAIRS INDEX. Text in English. base vol. plus w. updates. **Document type:** *Database, Abstract/Index.*
Media: Online - full text.
Published by: EBSCO Publishing (Subsidiary of: EBSCO Industries, Inc.), 10 Estes St, PO Box 682, Ipswich, MA 01938. TEL 978-356-6500, FAX 212-678-6619, information@ebscohost.com.

351.021 DEU ISSN 0174-2876
RHEINLAND-PFALZ HEUTE. Text in German. 1977. a. stat. back issues avail. **Document type:** *Government.*
Published by: Statistisches Landesamt Rheinland-Pfalz, Mainzerstr 14-16, Bad Ems, 56130, Germany. TEL 49-2603-713240, FAX 49-2603-71193240, pressestelle@statistik.rlp.de, http://www.statistik.rlp.de.

351.021 RWA
RWANDA. DIRECTION GENERALE DE LA STATISTIQUE. RAPPORT ANNUEL. Text in French. a.
Formerly: Rwanda. Direction Generale de la Documentation et de la Statistique. Rapport Annuel (0080-5033)
Published by: Direction Generale de la Statistique, BP 46, Kigali, Rwanda.

351.021 ZAF
SOUTH AFRICA. STATISTICS SOUTH AFRICA. FINAL SOCIAL ACCOUNTING MATRIX FOR SOUTH AFRICA. Text in English. irreg., latest 2002. **Document type:** *Government.*
Formerly (until Aug.1998): South Africa. Central Statistical Service. Final Social Accounting Matrix for South Africa
Related titles: Diskette ed.: ZAR 15 (effective 1999).
Published by: Statistics South Africa/Statistieke Suid-Afrika, Private Bag X44, Pretoria, 0001, South Africa. TEL 27-12-3108911, FAX 27-12-3108500, info@statssa.gov.za, http://www.statssa.gov.za.

016.35213 ZAF
SOUTH AFRICA. STATISTICS SOUTH AFRICA. LOCAL GOVERNMENT STATISTICS. Text in English. a., latest 1996. free. **Document type:** *Government.*
Former titles (until Aug1998): South Africa. Central Statistical Service. Local Government Statistics; South Africa. Department of Statistics. Local Government Statistics
Published by: Statistics South Africa/Statistieke Suid-Afrika, Private Bag X44, Pretoria, 0001, South Africa. TEL 27-12-3108911, FAX 27-12-3108500, info@statssa.gov.za, http://www.statssa.gov.za.

351.021 ZAF
SOUTH AFRICA. STATISTICS SOUTH AFRICA. STATISTICAL RELEASE. CENTRAL GOVERNMENT: REVENUE OF THE STATE REVENUE AND OTHER REVENUE ACCOUNTS. Text in English. a. **Document type:** *Government.*
Formerly (until Aug. 1998): South Africa. Central Statistical Service. Statistical Release. Central Government: Revenue of the State Revenue and Other Revenue Accounts
Published by: Statistics South Africa/Statistieke Suid-Afrika, Private Bag X44, Pretoria, 0001, South Africa. TEL 27-12-3108911, FAX 27-12-3108500, info@statssa.gov.za, http://www.statssa.gov.za.

351.021 ZAF
SOUTH AFRICA. STATISTICS SOUTH AFRICA. STATISTICAL RELEASE. FINANCIAL STATISTICS OF LOCAL AUTHORITIES AND REGIONAL SERVICES COUNCILS AND JOINT SERVICES BOARDS. Text in English. q. **Document type:** *Government.*
Formerly (until Aug. 1998): South Africa. Central Statistical Service. Statistical Release. Financial Statistics of Local Authorities and Regional Services Councils and Joint Services Boards
Published by: Statistics South Africa/Statistieke Suid-Afrika, Private Bag X44, Pretoria, 0001, South Africa. TEL 27-12-3108911, FAX 27-12-3108500, info@statssa.gov.za, http://www.statssa.gov.za.

352.13021 ZAF
SOUTH AFRICA. STATISTICS SOUTH AFRICA. STATISTICAL RELEASE. FINANCIAL STATISTICS OF LOCAL GOVERNMENTS (YEAR). Text in English. irreg., latest covers 1988-1989. **Document type:** *Government.*
Formerly (until Aug. 1998): South Africa. Central Statistical Service. Statistical Release. Financial Statistics of Local Governments (Year)
Published by: Statistics South Africa/Statistieke Suid-Afrika, Private Bag X44, Pretoria, 0001, South Africa. TEL 27-12-3108911, FAX 27-12-3108500, info@statssa.gov.za, http://www.statssa.gov.za.

351.021 ZAF
SOUTH AFRICA. STATISTICS SOUTH AFRICA. STATISTICAL RELEASE. NATIONAL GOVERNMENT EXPENDITURE. Text in English. a., latest 1994-1995. free. **Document type:** *Government.* **Description:** Economic and functional classification of the consolidated expenditure by the total general government sector.
Former titles: South Africa. Statistics South Africa. Statistical Release. Expenditure by the General Government; (until Aug. 1998): South Africa. Central Statistical Service. Statistical Release. Expenditure by the General Government
Published by: Statistics South Africa/Statistieke Suid-Afrika, Private Bag X44, Pretoria, 0001, South Africa. TEL 27-12-3108911, FAX 27-12-3108500, info@statssa.gov.za, http://www.statssa.gov.za.

352.13021 USA ISSN 1935-5505
SOUTH DAKOTA CITIES & COUNTIES GRAPHIC PERFORMANCE ANALYSIS. Text in English. 2006. a. USD 95 per issue (effective 2009). charts. **Document type:** *Report, Trade.* **Description:** Provides comparisons in chart form, annual series of analytic charts, by peer group, within state. Each issue consist of 9 charts in each county peer group and each city peer group and 1 area chart per county. 100-200 graphs per state book.
Published by: Municipal Analysis Services, Inc., PO Box 13453, Austin, TX 78711. TEL 512-327-3328, munilysis@hotmail.com, http://sites.google.com/site/gregmichels. Ed. Greg Michels.

351.021 SRB
SRBIJA I CRNA GORA ZAVOD ZA STATISTIKU. KOMUNALNI FONDOVI U GRADSKIM NASELJIMA. Text in Serbo-Croatian. irreg. **Document type:** *Government.*
Formerly: Yugoslavia. Savezni Zavod za Statistiku. Komunalni Fondovi u Gradskim Naseljima
Related titles: ◆ Series of: Srbija i Crna Gora. Zavod za Statistiku. Statisticki Bilten.
Published by: Srbija i Crna Gora Zavod za Statistiku/Serbia and Montenegro Statistical Office, Kneza Milosa 20, Postanski Fah 203, Belgrade, 11000. http://www.szs.sv.gov.yu.

351.021 DEU
STADT BOCHUM. AMT FUER STATISTIK UND STADTFORSCHUNG. BEITRAEGE ZUR STADTENTWICKLUNG. Text in German. 1969. irreg. EUR 13 (effective 2005). bibl.; charts. **Document type:** *Bulletin, Government.*
Published by: Stadt Bochum, Amt fuer Statistik und Stadtforschung, Willy-Brandt-Platz 2-8, Bochum, 44777, Germany. amt01@bochum.de, http://www.bochum.de/statistik/. Circ: 700.

351.021 DEU ISSN 0930-4274
STADT BOCHUM. AMT FUER STATISTIK UND STADTFORSCHUNG. SONDERBERICHTE. Text in German. 1954. 3/yr. EUR 5 (effective 2005). charts; illus. **Document type:** *Bulletin, Government.*
Published by: Stadt Bochum, Amt fuer Statistik und Stadtforschung, Willy-Brandt-Platz 2-8, Bochum, 44777, Germany. amt01@bochum.de, http://www.bochum.de/statistik/.

351.021 DEU ISSN 0067-9437
STADT BOCHUM. AMT FUER STATISTIK UND STADTFORSCHUNG. STATISTISCHES JAHRBUCH. Text in German. 1954. a. EUR 13 (effective 2005). charts. index. **Document type:** *Yearbook, Government.*
Published by: Stadt Bochum, Amt fuer Statistik und Stadtforschung, Willy-Brandt-Platz 2-8, Bochum, 44777, Germany. amt01@bochum.de, http://www.bochum.de/statistik/. Circ: 750.

351.021 DEU ISSN 0931-2900
STADT BOCHUM. AMT FUER STATISTIK UND STADTFORSCHUNG. VERWALTUNGSBERICHT. Text in German. 1912. a. index. **Document type:** *Bulletin, Government.*
Published by: Stadt Bochum, Amt fuer Statistik und Stadtforschung, Willy-Brandt-Platz 2-8, Bochum, 44777, Germany. amt01@bochum.de, http://www.bochum.de/statistik/. Circ: 115.

351.021 DEU ISSN 0939-463X
STADT BOCHUM. WAHLBUERO. WAHLEN IN BOCHUM. Text in German. 1946. irreg. price varies. charts; stat. **Document type:** *Bulletin, Government.* **Description:** Report and survey of general elections.
Former titles (until 1987): Stadt Bochum. Amt fuer Statistik und Stadtforschung. Einzelschrift (0931-5624); (until 1972): Stadt Bochum. Statistisches Amt. Einzelschriften (0523-7963)
Published by: Stadt Bochum, Wahlbuero, Willy-Brandt-Platz 2-6, Bochum, 44777, Germany. wahlbuero@bochum.de, http://www.bochum.de/wahlbuero/frame01.htm.

351.021 DEU ISSN 0940-9009
STADT DUISBURG. MATERIALEN ZUR STADTFORSCHUNG. Text in German. 1977. irreg., latest vol.20, 2006. price varies. charts; illus.; maps; stat. **Document type:** *Monographic series, Academic/Scholarly.* **Description:** Publishes sociological abstracts, bibliographies and statistics involving the city of Duisburg for urban researchers, planners and policy-makers.
Published by: Stadt Duisburg, Amt fuer Statistik, Stadtforschung und Europaangelegenheiten, Bismarckstr (Ndf) 150-158, Duisburg, 47049, Germany. TEL 49-203-2832181, FAX 49-203-2834404, amt12@stadt-duisburg.de, http://www.duisburg.de/vv/12/index.php. Circ: 300.

351.021 DEU ISSN 1431-0775
STADT DUISBURG. PROGRAMM-INFORMATIONS-DIENST. FOERDERPROGRAMME; Foederprogramme des Bundes, des Landes Nordrhein-Westfalen und der Europaeischen Union in Duisburg. Text in German. 1996. irreg. price varies. **Document type:** *Government.* **Description:** Publishes abstracts of interest to urban researchers, practitioners of regional planning, and policy-makers.
Published by: Stadt Duisburg, Amt fuer Statistik, Stadtforschung und Europaangelegenheiten, Bismarckstr (Ndf) 150-158, Duisburg, 47049, Germany. TEL 49-203-2832181, FAX 49-203-2834404, amt12@stadt-duisburg.de, http://www.duisburg.de/vv/12/index.php. Circ: 300.

351.021 DEU ISSN 0946-4883
STADT DUISBURG. WAHLEN (YEAR). Text in German. 1975. irreg., latest vol.103, 2005. free (effective 2008). charts; illus.; maps; stat. back issues avail. **Document type:** *Monographic series, Trade.*
Published by: Stadt Duisburg, Amt fuer Statistik, Stadtforschung und Europaangelegenheiten, Bismarckstr (Ndf) 150-158, Duisburg, 47049, Germany. TEL 49-203-2832181, FAX 49-203-2834404, amt12@stadt-duisburg.de, http://www.duisburg.de/vv/12/index.php. Circ: 500; 350 (controlled).

351.021 DEU
STADT FREIBURG IM BREISGAU. AMT FUER STATISTIK UND EINWOHNERWESEN. JAHRESHEFT. Text in German. 1977. a. stat. back issues avail. **Document type:** *Yearbook, Government.* **Description:** Studies the development of social and economic life within municipality of Freiburg.
Indexed: SpeleolAb.
Published by: Stadt Freiburg im Breisgau, Amt fuer Statistik und Einwohnerwesen, Wilhelmstr 20a, Freiburg Im Breisgau, 79098, Germany. TEL 49-761-2013200, FAX 49-761-2013299, statistik@stadt.freiburg.de. Circ: 400.

016.35213 DEU
STADT MANNHEIM. VIERTELJAHRESBERICHT. Text in German. 1972. q. back issues avail. **Document type:** *Government.*
Published by: Stadt Mannheim, Stabsstelle Stadtforschung, Postfach 103051, Mannheim, 68030, Germany. TEL 49-621-2939530, FAX 49-621-2939700. Ed. Werner Heidemann.

351.021 DEU ISSN 0934-5868
HT110
STADTFORSCHUNG UND STATISTIK; Zeitschrift des Verbandes Deutscher Staedtestatistiker. Text in German. 1987. s-a. EUR 14.32 (effective 2006). adv. **Document type:** *Journal, Corporate.*
Published by: Verband Deutscher Staedtestatistiker, c/o Stadt Oberhausen, Bereich Statistik und Wahlen, Oberhausen, 46042, Germany. TEL 49-208-8252387, FAX 49-208-8255120.

351.021 USA
STATISTICAL REVIEW OF GOVERNMENT IN UTAH. Text in English. 1958. a. USD 22 (effective 2000). **Description:** Contains most-used financial and statistical information about state and local governments in Utah.
Related titles: Microfiche ed.: (from CIS).
Indexed: SRI.
Published by: Utah Foundation, 10 W. Broadway., Ste. 307, Salt Lake Cty, UT 84101-2075. TEL 801-364-1837. Ed. Michael Christensen. Circ: 1,000.

352.13021 CAN ISSN 0702-0988
HJ9014.B7
STATISTICS RELATING TO REGIONAL AND MUNICIPAL GOVERNMENTS IN BRITISH COLUMBIA. Text in English. a. CAD 15.45. **Description:** Provides statistics on population, area of districts, incorporation dates and financial information.

Published by: Ministry of Municipal Affairs, Recreation and Housing, Victoria, BC, Canada. **Subscr. to:** Crown Publications Inc. TEL 250-386-4636, FAX 250-386-0221, crown@pinc.com, http://www.crownpub.bc.ca.

351.21 DEU ISSN 1433-2434
STATISTISCHE BERICHTE - BADEN-WUERTTEMBERG. A: BEVOELKERUNG, GESUNDHEITSWESEN, GEBIET UND ERWERBSTAETIGKEIT. Text in German. 1956. irreg. **Document type:** *Government.*
Formerly (until 1992): Statistisches Landesamt Baden-Wuerttemberg. Statistische Berichte A (1433-2256)
Published by: Statistisches Landesamt Baden-Wuerttemberg, Boeblinger Str 68, Stuttgart, 70199, Germany. TEL 49-711-6410, FAX 49-711-6412440, poststelle@stala.bwl.de, http://www.statistik.baden-wuerttemberg.de.

351.021 DEU ISSN 1433-2442
STATISTISCHE BERICHTE - BADEN-WUERTTEMBERG. B: BILDUNG, RECHTSPFLEGE, WAHLEN. Text in German. 1956. irreg. back issues avail. **Document type:** *Government.*
Formerly (until 1992): Statistisches Landesamt Baden-Wuerttemberg. Statistische Berichte B (1433-2264)
Published by: Statistisches Landesamt Baden-Wuerttemberg, Boeblinger Str 68, Stuttgart, 70199, Germany. TEL 49-711-6410, FAX 49-711-6412440, poststelle@stala.bwl.de, http://www.statistik.baden-wuerttemberg.de.

351.21 DEU ISSN 1430-5062
STATISTISCHE BERICHTE - RHEINLAND-PFALZ. B: BILDUNG, KULTUR, RECHTSPFLEGE, WAHLEN. Text in German. 1951. irreg. **Document type:** *Government.*
Formerly (until 1976): Statistisches Landesamt Rheinland-Pfalz. Statistische Berichte B (1430-4910); Which superseded in part (in 1956): Statistisches Landesamt Rheinland-Pfalz . Mitteilungen (0482-8887)
Published by: Statistisches Landesamt Rheinland-Pfalz, Mainzerstr 14-16, Bad Ems, 56130, Germany. TEL 49-2603-713240, FAX 49-2603-71193240, pressestelle@statistik.rlp.de.

351.21 DEU ISSN 1434-6486
STATISTISCHE BERICHTE - RHEINLAND-PFALZ. Z. Text in German. 1997. irreg. **Document type:** *Government.*
Published by: Statistisches Landesamt Rheinland-Pfalz, Mainzerstr 14-16, Bad Ems, 56130, Germany. TEL 49-2603-713240, FAX 49-2603-71193240, pressestelle@statistik.rlp.de.

351.021 CHE
STATISTISCHE INFORMATION/INFORMATIONS STATISTIQUES; Katalog der verfuegbaren Publikationen zur Bundestatistik. Text in French, German. 1985. a. free. **Document type:** *Government.*
Formerly: Publikationsverzeichnis
Related titles: German ed.
Published by: Bundesamt fuer Statistik, Espace de l'Europe 10, Neuchatel, 2010, Switzerland. TEL 41-32-7136011, FAX 41-32-7136012, information@bfs.admin.ch, http://www.admin.ch/bfs.

351.021 DEU ISSN 0944-1492
STATISTISCHE NACHRICHTEN DER STADT NUERNBERG. Text in German. 1946. q. back issues avail. **Document type:** *Government.* **Description:** Reports on population, housing, local economy, education and welfare.
Published by: Stadt Nuernberg, Amt fuer Stadtforschung und Statistik, Unschlittplatz 7A, Nuernberg, 90403, Germany. STA@stadt.nuernberg.de. Circ: 620.

352.13021 DEU ISSN 0930-3782
STATISTISCHER VIERTELJAHRESBERICHT HANNOVER. Text in German. 1896. q. adv. back issues avail. **Document type:** *Newsletter, Government.*
Published by: Landeshauptstadt Hannover, Abteilung Statistik, Rathaus, Trammplatz 2, Hannover, 30159, Germany. TEL 49-511-16842655, FAX 49-511-16845129, wahlen@hannover-stadt.de, http://www.hannover.de. Circ: 2,400.

352.21 DEU ISSN 1864-2594
STATISTISCHES AMT SAARLAND. STATISTISCHE BERICHTE A. Text in German. 19??. irreg. **Document type:** *Trade.*
Former titles (until 2007): Statistisches Landesamt Saarland. Statistische Berichte A (1430-1687); (until 1990): Statistisches Amt des Saarlandes. Statistische Berichte A (1430-1512); Which superseded in part (in 1960): Statistisches Amt des Saarlandes. Kurzbericht (0558-0846)
Published by: Statistisches Amt Saarland, Virchowstr 7, Saarbrucken, 66119, Germany. TEL 49-681-5015927, FAX 49-681-5015921, statistik@lzd.saarland.de, http://www.saarland.de/statistik.htm.

351.21 DEU ISSN 1864-2268
STATISTISCHES AMT SAARLAND. STATISTISCHE BERICHTE B. Text in German. 19??. irreg. **Document type:** *Trade.*
Former titles (until 2006): Statistisches Landesamt Saarland. Statistische Berichte B (1430-1695); (until 1990): Statistisches Amt des Saarlandes. Statistische Berichte B (1430-1520); Which superseded in part (in 1960): Statistisches Amt des Saarlandes. Kurzbericht (0558-0846)
Published by: Statistisches Amt Saarland, Virchowstr 7, Saarbrucken, 66119, Germany. TEL 49-681-5015927, FAX 49-681-5015921, statistik@lzd.saarland.de, http://www.saarland.de/statistik.htm.

351.21 DEU ISSN 1865-4126
STATISTISCHES AMT SAARLAND. STATISTISCHE BERICHTE C. Text in German. 19??. irreg. free (effective 2010). **Document type:** *Trade.*
Former titles (until 2007): Statistisches Landesamt Saarland. Statistische Berichte C (1430-1709); (until 1990): Statistisches Amt des Saarlandes. Statistische Berichte C (1430-1539); Which superseded in part (in 1960): Statistisches Amt des Saarlandes. Kurzbericht (0558-0846)
Published by: Statistisches Amt Saarland, Virchowstr 7, Saarbrucken, 66119, Germany. TEL 49-681-5015927, FAX 49-681-5015921, statistik@lzd.saarland.de, http://www.saarland.de/statistik.htm.

351.21 DEU ISSN 1864-8428
STATISTISCHES AMT SAARLAND. STATISTISCHE BERICHTE D. Text in German. 19??. irreg. free (effective 2010). **Document type:** *Trade.*
Former titles (until 2007): Statistisches Landesamt Saarland. Statistische Berichte D (1430-1717); (until 1990): Statistisches Amt des Saarlandes. Statistische Berichte D (1430-1547); Which superseded in part (in 1962): Statistisches Amt des Saarlandes. Kurzbericht (0558-0846)
Published by: Statistisches Amt Saarland, Virchowstr 7, Saarbrucken, 66119, Germany. TEL 49-681-5015927, FAX 49-681-5015921, statistik@lzd.saarland.de, http://www.saarland.de/statistik.htm.

351.21 DEU ISSN 1864-7464
STATISTISCHES AMT SAARLAND. STATISTISCHE BERICHTE E. Text in German. 19??. irreg. free (effective 2010). **Document type:** *Trade.*
Former titles (until 2006): Statistisches Landesamt Saarland. Statistische Berichte E (1430-1725); (until 1990): Statistisches Amt des Saarlandes. Statistische Berichte E (1430-1555); Which superseded in part (in 1960): Statistisches Amt des Saarlandes. Kurzbericht (0558-0846)
Published by: Statistisches Amt Saarland, Virchowstr 7, Saarbrucken, 66119, Germany. TEL 49-681-5015927, FAX 49-681-5015921, statistik@lzd.saarland.de, http://www.saarland.de/statistik.htm.

351.21 DEU ISSN 1864-2276
STATISTISCHES AMT SAARLAND. STATISTISCHE BERICHTE F. Text in German. 19??. irreg. free (effective 2010). **Document type:** *Trade.*
Former titles (until 2006): Statistisches Landesamt Saarland. Statistische Berichte F (1430-1733); (until 1990): Statistisches Amt des Saarlandes. Statistische Berichte F (1430-1563); Which superseded in part (in 1960): Statistisches Amt des Saarlandes. Kurzbericht (0558-0846)
Published by: Statistisches Amt Saarland, Virchowstr 7, Saarbrucken, 66119, Germany. TEL 49-681-5015927, FAX 49-681-5015921, statistik@lzd.saarland.de, http://www.saarland.de/statistik.htm.

351.21 DEU ISSN 1865-1631
STATISTISCHES AMT SAARLAND. STATISTISCHE BERICHTE G. Text in German. 19??. irreg. free (effective 2010). **Document type:** *Trade.*
Former titles (until 2006): Statistisches Landesamt Saarland. Statistische Berichte G (1430-1741); (until 1990): Statistisches Amt des Saarlandes. Statistische Berichte G (1430-1571); Which superseded in part (in 1960): Statistisches Amt des Saarlandes. Kurzbericht (0558-0846)
Published by: Statistisches Amt Saarland, Virchowstr 7, Saarbrucken, 66119, Germany. TEL 49-681-5015927, FAX 49-681-5015921, statistik@lzd.saarland.de, http://www.saarland.de/statistik.htm.

351.21 DEU ISSN 1865-4134
STATISTISCHES AMT SAARLAND. STATISTISCHE BERICHTE H. Text in German. 19??. irreg. free (effective 2010). **Document type:** *Trade.*
Former titles (until 2006): Statistisches Landesamt Saarland. Statistische Berichte H (1430-1784); (until 1990): Statistisches Amt des Saarlandes. Statistische Berichte H (1430-158X); Which superseded in part (in 1960): Statistisches Amt des Saarlandes. Kurzbericht (0558-0846)
Published by: Statistisches Amt Saarland, Virchowstr 7, Saarbrucken, 66119, Germany. TEL 49-681-5015927, FAX 49-681-5015921, statistik@lzd.saarland.de, http://www.saarland.de/statistik.htm.

351.21 DEU ISSN 1864-7456
STATISTISCHES AMT SAARLAND. STATISTISCHE BERICHTE K. Text in German. 19??. irreg. free (effective 2010). **Document type:** *Trade.*
Former titles (until 2006): Statistisches Landesamt Saarland. Statistische Berichte K (1430-1806); (until 1991): Statistisches Amt des Saarlandes. Statistische Berichte K (1430-1601); Which superseded in part (in 1963): Statistisches Amt des Saarlandes. Kurzbericht (0558-0846)
Published by: Statistisches Amt Saarland, Virchowstr 7, Saarbrucken, 66119, Germany. TEL 49-681-5015927, FAX 49-681-5015921, statistik@lzd.saarland.de, http://www.saarland.de/statistik.htm.

351.21 DEU ISSN 1864-2608
STATISTISCHES AMT SAARLAND. STATISTISCHE BERICHTE L. Text in German. 19??. irreg. free (effective 2010). **Document type:** *Trade.*
Former titles (until 2007): Statistisches Landesamt Saarland. Statistische Berichte L (1430-1814); (until 1990): Statistisches Amt des Saarlandes. Statistische Berichte L (1430-161X); Which superseded in part (in 1962): Statistisches Amt des Saarlandes. Kurzbericht (0558-0846)
Published by: Statistisches Amt Saarland, Virchowstr 7, Saarbrucken, 66119, Germany. TEL 49-681-5015927, FAX 49-681-5015921, statistik@lzd.saarland.de, http://www.saarland.de/statistik.htm.

351.21 DEU ISSN 1864-7367
STATISTISCHES AMT SAARLAND. STATISTISCHE BERICHTE M. Text in German. 19??. irreg. free (effective 2010). **Document type:** *Trade.*
Former titles (until 2006): Statistisches Landesamt Saarland. Statistische Berichte M (1430-1822); (until 1990): Statistisches Amt des Saarlandes. Statistische Berichte M (1430-1628); Which superseded in part (in 1960): Statistisches Amt des Saarlandes. Kurzbericht (0558-0846)
Published by: Statistisches Amt Saarland, Virchowstr 7, Saarbrucken, 66119, Germany. TEL 49-681-5015927, FAX 49-681-5015921, statistik@lzd.saarland.de, http://www.saarland.de/statistik.htm.

351.21 DEU ISSN 1865-4142
STATISTISCHES AMT SAARLAND. STATISTISCHE BERICHTE N. Text in German. 19??. irreg. free (effective 2010). **Document type:** *Trade.*
Former titles (until 2006): Statistisches Landesamt Saarland. Statistische Berichte N (1430-1830); (until 1990): Statistisches Amt des Saarlandes. Statistische Berichte N (1430-1652); Which superseded in part (in 1960): Statistisches Amt des Saarlandes. Kurzbericht (0558-0846)
Published by: Statistisches Amt Saarland, Virchowstr 7, Saarbrucken, 66119, Germany. TEL 49-681-5015927, FAX 49-681-5015921, statistik@lzd.saarland.de, http://www.saarland.de/statistik.htm.

351.21 DEU ISSN 1864-2616
STATISTISCHES AMT SAARLAND. STATISTISCHE BERICHTE P. Text in German. 19??. irreg. free (effective 2010). **Document type:** *Trade.*
Former titles (until 2006): Statistisches Landesamt Saarland. Statistische Berichte P (1430-1849); (until 1990): Statistisches Amt des Saarlandes. Statistische Berichte P (1430-1679); Which superseded in part (in 1960): Statistisches Amt des Saarlandes. Kurzbericht (0558-0846)
Published by: Statistisches Amt Saarland, Virchowstr 7, Saarbrucken, 66119, Germany. TEL 49-681-5015927, FAX 49-681-5015921, statistik@lzd.saarland.de, http://www.saarland.de/statistik.htm.

351.21 DEU ISSN 1438-3411
STATISTISCHES AMT SAARLAND. VEROEFFENTLICHUNGSVERZEICHNIS. Text in German. 1990. irreg. **Document type:** *Trade.*
Published by: Statistisches Amt Saarland, Virchowstr 7, Saarbrucken, 66119, Germany. TEL 49-681-5015927, FAX 49-681-5015921, statistik@lzd.saarland.de, http://www.saarland.de/statistik.htm.

352.13021 DEU ISSN 0178-160X
HA1330.C7
STATISTISCHES JAHRBUCH DER STADT KOELN. Text in German. 1911. a. **Document type:** *Yearbook, Government.*
—GNLM.
Published by: Stadt Koeln, Amt fuer Stadtentwicklung und Statistik, Athener Ring 4, Cologne, 50765, Germany. TEL 49-221-2211887, FAX 49-221-2211900.

351.021 DEU ISSN 0944-1514
STATISTISCHES JAHRBUCH DER STADT NUERNBERG. Text in German. 1977. a. stat. back issues avail. **Document type:** *Yearbook, Government.* **Description:** Contains tables on population, housing, local economy, education and welfare, plus selected data on the metropolitan area.
Published by: Stadt Nuernberg, Amt fuer Stadtforschung und Statistik, Unschlittplatz 7A, Nuernberg, 90403, Germany. TEL 49-911-2312840, FAX 49-911-2312844, STA@stadt.nuernberg.de, http://www.statistik.nuernberg.de. Circ: 750.

352.13021 DEU ISSN 0081-5349
HA1330.A1
STATISTISCHES JAHRBUCH DEUTSCHER GEMEINDEN. Text in German. 1890. a. EUR 65 (effective 2011). reprint service avail. from SCH. **Document type:** *Abstract/Index.* **Description:** Contains current data on area and population, economy, housing, transport, finances, taxes, etc. for cities and towns with over 10,000 inhabitants in Germany.
Published by: Deutscher Staedtetag, Im Klapperhof 23, Cologne, 50670, Germany. TEL 49-221-37710, FAX 49-221-3771128, staedtetag@staedtetag.de.

351.21 DEU ISSN 0930-5793
HA1261
STATISTISCHES JAHRBUCH FUER BAYERN. Text in German. 1894. a. EUR 39 (effective 2011). **Document type:** *Government.*
Incorporates (1972-2002): Bayerisches Landesamt fuer Statistik und Datenverarbeitung. Kreisdaten (0931-1599)
Related titles: CD-ROM ed.: ISSN 1437-0794. 1998. EUR 12 (effective 2010).
Published by: Bayerisches Landesamt fuer Statistik und Datenverarbeitung, Neuhauser Str 8, Munich, 80331, Germany. TEL 49-89-2119205, FAX 49-89-2119410, poststelle@statistik.bayern.de, http://www.statistik.bayern.de.

314 DEU ISSN 0943-5743
HA1232
STATISTISCHES JAHRBUCH FUER DIE BUNDESREPUBLIK DEUTSCHLAND. Text in German. 1952. a. EUR 71 (effective 2010). reprints avail. **Document type:** *Government.*
Formerly (until 1992): Statistisches Jahrbuch fuer das Vereinte Deutschland (0941-3774); Which was formed by the merger of (1952-1991): Statistisches Jahrbuch fuer die Bundesrepublik Deutschland (0081-5357); (1955-1990): Statistisches Jahrbuch der Deutschen Demokratischen Republik (0323-4258); Which incorporated (1961-1963): Statistisches Jahrbuch der Hauptstadt der Deutschen Demokratischen Republik Berlin (0435-6314)
Related titles: CD-ROM ed.; Microfiche ed.: (from PQC).
Indexed: GeoRef, RASB.
—GNLM. **CCC.**
Published by: Statistisches Bundesamt, Gustav-Stresemann-Ring 11, Wiesbaden, 65180, Germany. TEL 49-611-752405, FAX 49-611-753330, info@destatis.de, http://www.destatis.de.

352.021 DEU ISSN 1614-7510
HA1249.H3
STATISTISCHES JAHRBUCH HAMBURG. Text in German. 1967. a. **Document type:** *Yearbook, Government.*
Former titles (until 2004): Statistisches Landesamt Hamburg. Hamburger Statistisches Jahrbuch (1438-8480); (until 1999): Statistisches Landesamt Hamburg. Statistisches Taschenbuch (0170-7477); (until 1972): Freie und Hansestadt Hamburg. Statistisches Taschenbuch (0440-1557)
Related titles: Online - full text ed.: ISSN 1614-8053. 2004.
Published by: Statistisches Amt fuer Hamburg und Schleswig-Holstein, Steckelhoern 12, Hamburg, 20457, Germany. TEL 49-40-428311766, FAX 49-40-428311700, poststelle@statistik-nord.de.

352.13021 DEU ISSN 0720-3314
STATISTISCHES JAHRBUCH MUENCHEN. Text in German. a. EUR 15 (effective 2010). stat. back issues avail. **Document type:** *Yearbook, Academic/Scholarly.* **Description:** Contains official statistics of the city of Munich for the previous year.
Former titles (until 1980): Muenchener Statistik. Jahresbericht (0171-0583); (until 1976): Statistisches Jahrbuch der Landeshauptstadt Muenchen (0077-2062)
Published by: Statistisches Amt der Landeshauptstadt Muenchen, Schwanthalerstr 68, Munich, 80336, Germany. TEL 49-89-23328766, FAX 49-89-23325989, stat.amt@muenchen.de, http://www.muenchen.de/statamt.

352.021 DEU ISSN 1863-9100
HA1320
STATISTISCHES JAHRBUCH RHEINLAND-PFALZ. Text in German. 1948. a. back issues avail. **Document type:** *Government.*
Former titles (until 2006): Statistisches Landesamt Rheinland-Pfalz. Statistisches Taschenbuch (0948-5074); (until 1995): Statistisches Jahrbuch fuer Rheinland-Pfalz (0556-8358); (until 1959): Jahresergebnisse der Statistik in Rheinland-Pfalz (0930-5815)
Published by: Statistisches Landesamt Rheinland-Pfalz, Mainzerstr 14-16, Bad Ems, 56130, Germany. TEL 49-2603-713240, FAX 49-2603-71193240, pressestelle@statistik.rlp.de, http://www.statistik.rlp.de.

314 DEU ISSN 0487-6423
STATISTISCHES JAHRBUCH SCHLESWIG-HOLSTEIN. Text in German. 1952. a. charts; maps. index. **Document type:** *Government.* **Description:** Presents a statistical yearbook with comprehensive data on all topics.
Related titles: E-mail ed.
Published by: Statistisches Amt fuer Hamburg und Schleswig-Holstein, Steckelhoern 12, Hamburg, 20457, Germany. TEL 49-40-428311766, FAX 49-40-428311700, poststelle@statistik-nord.de. Circ: 950.

352.021 DEU
STATISTISCHES LANDESAMT HAMBURG. EIN STADTPORTRAET IN ZAHLEN. Text in German. 1977. a. **Document type:** *Government.*

Formerly (until 1996): Statistisches Landesamt Hamburg. Daten und Informationen Faltblatt
Related titles: English ed.: Hamburg State Bureau of Statistics. Facts and Figures.
Published by: Statistisches Amt fuer Hamburg und Schleswig-Holstein, Steckelhoern 12, Hamburg, 20457, Germany. TEL 49-40-428311766, FAX 49-40-428311700, poststelle@statistik-nord.de, http://www.statistik-nord.de.

351.21 DEU ISSN 0932-3740
STATISTISCHES LANDESAMT RHEINLAND-PFALZ. AMTLICHES GEMEINDEVERZEICHNIS. Text in German. 1946. irreg. **Document type:** *Government.*
Formerly (until 1981): Amtliches Gemeindeverzeichnis von Rheinland-Pfalz (0932-3732)
Published by: Statistisches Landesamt Rheinland-Pfalz, Mainzerstr 14-16, Bad Ems, 56130, Germany. TEL 49-2603-713240, FAX 49-2603-71193240, pressestelle@statistik.rlp.de, http://www.statistik.rlp.de.

351.21 DEU ISSN 1863-1371
STATISTISCHES LANDESAMT RHEINLAND-PFALZ. STATISTISCHE BAENDE. Text in German. 1949. irreg., latest vol.397, 2008. **Document type:** *Government.*
Former titles (until 2006): Rheinland-Pfalz (0174-6537); (until 1982): Statistik von Rheinland-Pfalz (0342-975X)
Published by: Statistisches Landesamt Rheinland-Pfalz, Mainzerstr 14-16, Bad Ems, 56130, Germany. TEL 49-2603-713240, FAX 49-2603-71193240, pressestelle@statistik.rlp.de.

352.13021 DEU
HA1248.R47
STATISTISCHES LANDESAMT RHEINLAND-PFALZ. STATISTISCHE MONATSHEFTE. Text in German. 1948. m. stat. back issues avail. **Document type:** *Government.*
Former titles (until 2004): Statistische Monatshefte Rheinland-Pfalz (0174-2914); (until 1958): Zahlenspiegel Rheinland-Pfalz (0174-2906); (until 1956): Wirtschaftszahlen Rheinland-Pfalz (0174-2892)
Published by: Statistisches Landesamt Rheinland-Pfalz, Mainzerstr 14-16, Bad Ems, 56130, Germany. TEL 49-2603-713240, FAX 49-2603-71193240, pressestelle@statistik.rlp.de.

351.021 DEU ISSN 0521-9973
STATISTISCHES TASCHENBUCH BADEN-WUERTTEMBERG. Text in German. 1963. a. **Document type:** *Government.*
Published by: Statistisches Landesamt Baden-Wuerttemberg, Boeblinger Str 68, Stuttgart, 70199, Germany. TEL 49-711-6410, FAX 49-711-6412440, poststelle@stala.bwl.de, http://www.statistik.baden-wuerttemberg.de. Circ: 2,000.

352.13021 DEU ISSN 0173-0029
STATISTISCHES TASCHENBUCH MUENCHEN. Text in German. 1980. a. EUR 5 (effective 2010). stat. back issues avail. **Document type:** *Yearbook, Government.* **Description:** Contains vital statistics for the city of Munich on a district by district basis.
Published by: Statistisches Amt der Landeshauptstadt Muenchen, Schwanthalerstr 68, Munich, 80336, Germany. TEL 49-89-23328766, FAX 49-89-23325989, stat.amt@muenchen.de, http://www.muenchen.de/statamt.

351.021 DEU
STRASSEN- UND GEBIETSVERZEICHNIS HAMBURG. Text in German. 1990. biennial. **Document type:** *Government.*
Formerly: Strassen- und Gebietsverzeichnis der Freien und Hansestadt Hamburg (0938-636X)
Published by: Statistisches Amt fuer Hamburg und Schleswig-Holstein, Steckelhoern 12, Hamburg, 20457, Germany. TEL 49-40-428311766, FAX 49-40-428311700, poststelle@statistik-nord.de.

016.351 DEU ISSN 0082-1829
DD15.5
TASCHENBUCH DES OEFFENTLICHEN LEBENS; Deutschland. Text in German. 1950. a. EUR 119.70 (effective 2010). adv. **Document type:** *Directory, Trade.*
Published by: Festland Verlag GmbH, Basteistr 88, Bonn, 53173, Germany. TEL 49-228-362021, FAX 49-228-351771, verlag@oeckl.de. Ed. Heinz Hey.

016.351 DEU ISSN 1433-9293
TASCHENBUCH DES OEFFENTLICHEN LEBENS. EUROPA UND INTERNATIONALE ZUSAMMENSCHLUESE. Text in English, German, French. 1996. a. EUR 91.50 per issue (effective 2009). adv. **Document type:** *Abstract/Index.* **Description:** Offers abstracts, bibliographies, and statistics in the field of public administration.
Related titles: CD-ROM ed.; Online - full text ed.
Published by: Festland Verlag GmbH, Basteistr 88, Bonn, 53173, Germany. TEL 49-228-362021, FAX 49-228-351771, verlag@oeckl.de. Ed. Heinz Hey.

352.13021 USA ISSN 1935-5491
TENNESSEE CITIES & COUNTIES GRAPHIC PERFORMANCE ANALYSIS. Text in English. 2006. a. USD 95 per issue (effective 2009). charts. **Document type:** *Report, Trade.* **Description:** Provides comparisons in chart form, annual series of analytic charts, by peer group, within state. Each issue consist of 9 charts in each county peer group and each city peer group and 1 area chart per county. 100-200 graphs per state book.
Published by: Municipal Analysis Services, Inc., PO Box 13453, Austin, TX 78711. TEL 512-327-3328, munilysis@hotmail.com, http://sites.google.com/site/gregmichels. Ed. Greg Michels.

352.13021 USA ISSN 1935-5440
TEXAS CITIES & COUNTIES GRAPHIC PERFORMANCE ANALYSIS. Text in English. 2006. a. USD 95 per issue (effective 2009). charts. **Document type:** *Report, Trade.* **Description:** Provides comparisons in chart form, annual series of analytic charts, by peer group, within state. Each issue consist of 9 charts in each county peer group and each city peer group and 1 area chart per county. 100-200 graphs per state book.
Published by: Municipal Analysis Services, Inc., PO Box 13453, Austin, TX 78711. TEL 512-327-3328. Ed. Greg Michels.

016.351 JPN ISSN 1348-9976
TOUKEI KENKYUU IHOU/RESEARCH MEMOIR OF OFFICIAL STATISTICS. Text in Japanese; Summaries in English. 1950. s-a. stat. **Document type:** *Report, Government.*
Formerly (until 2003): Tokeikyoku Kenkyu Iho/Research Memoir of the Statistics Bureau (0446-5849)
Published by: (Japan. Ministry of Internal Affairs and Communications. Statistical Research and Training Institute/Somucho. Tokeikenshujo), Japan. Ministry of Internal Affairs and Communications. Statistics Bureau/Somucho. Tokeikyoku, 19-1 Wakamatsu-cho, Shinjyuku-ku, Tokyo, 162-8668, Japan. TEL 81-3-5273-2020, http://www.stat.go.jp.

351.021 DEU ISSN 0948-2652
TRENDINFO. Text in German. 1947. m. EUR 30; EUR 3 per issue (effective 2008). charts; illus.; maps; stat. index. back issues avail. **Document type:** *Journal, Trade.* **Description:** Publishes articles of interest to urban researchers, practitioners, planners and policy makers in social and city planning.
Former titles (until 1995): Statistischer Monatsbericht (0945-2702); (until 1985): Duisburg. Amt fuer Statistik und Stadtforschung. Statistischer Monatsbericht (0173-8925); (until 1980): Duisburger Zahlenspiegel (0172-4592); (until 1947): Statistischer Monatsbericht der Stadt Duisburg (0172-4584)
Published by: Stadt Duisburg, Amt fuer Statistik, Stadtforschung und Europaangelegenheiten, Bismarckstr (Ndf) 150-158, Duisburg, 47049, Germany. TEL 49-203-2832181, FAX 49-203-2834404, amt12@stadt-duisburg.de, http://www.duisburg.de/vv/12/index.php. Circ: 500.

351.021 TUR ISSN 1300-1205
HJ9550.7
TURKEY. TURKIYE ISTATISTIK KURUMU. BUTCELER - BELEDIYELER, IL OZEL IDARLER VE KOYLER (YEAR)/TURKEY. TURKISH STATISTICAL INSTITUTE. BUDGETS - MUNICIPAL AND SPECIAL PROVINCIAL ADMINISTRATIONS AND VILLAGES (YEAR). Text in English, Turkish. 1931. a., latest 2006. TRY 10 per issue domestic; USD 20 per issue foreign (effective 2009). stat. 139 p./no.; **Document type:** *Government.* **Description:** Presents data on the budgets of municipalities and special provincial administrations and villages by revenue and expenditure on a provincial levels.
Related titles: CD-ROM ed.: TRY 5 per issue domestic; USD 10 per issue foreign (effective 2009).
Published by: T.C. Basbakanlik, Turkiye Istatistik Kurumu/Prime Ministry Republic of Turkey, Turkish Statistical Institute, Yucetepe Mah. Necatibey Cad No.114, Cankaya, Ankara, 06100, Turkey. TEL 90-312-4100410, FAX 90-312-4175886, ulka.unsal@tuik.gov.tr, http://www.tuik.gov.tr. Circ: 420.

351.021 TUR ISSN 1300-1221
TURKEY. TURKIYE ISTATISTIK KURUMU. KESIN HESAPLAR - BELEDIYELER VE IL OZEL IDARELERI (YEAR)/TURKEY. TURKISH STATISTICAL INSTITUTE. FINAL ACCOUNTS - MUNICIPALITIES AND SPECIAL PROVINCIAL ADMINISTRATIONS (YEAR). Text in Turkish, English. 1969. a., latest 2005. TRY 10 per issue domestic; USD 20 per issue foreign (effective 2009). stat. **Document type:** *Government.* **Description:** Presents data on the final accounts of municipalities and special provincial administrations by type of revenue and expenditure on a provincial level. It also represents data on total number workers in municipalities.
Related titles: CD-ROM ed.: TRY 5 per issue domestic; USD 10 per issue foreign (effective 2009).
Published by: T.C. Basbakanlik, Turkiye Istatistik Kurumu/Prime Ministry Republic of Turkey, Turkish Statistical Institute, Yucetepe Mah. Necatibey Cad No.114, Cankaya, Ankara, 06100, Turkey. TEL 90-312-4100410, FAX 90-312-4175886, ulka.unsal@tuik.gov.tr, http://www.tuik.gov.tr. Circ: 400.

351.021 TUR
TURKEY. TURKIYE ISTATISTIK KURUMU. MAHALLI IDARELER SECIMI/TURKEY. TURKISH STATISTICAL INSTITUTE. ELECTIONS OF LOCAL ADMINISTRATIONS. Text in English, Turkish. 1965. irreg. (election year). TRY 14 per issue domestic; USD 20 per issue foreign (effective 2009). stat. **Document type:** *Government.* **Description:** Includes results of elections for the general provincial assembly, members of municipal assemblies and mayor of major cities by municipality, province and district.
Related titles: CD-ROM ed.: TRY 7 per issue domestic; USD 10 per issue foreign (effective 2009).
Published by: T.C. Basbakanlik, Turkiye Istatistik Kurumu/Prime Ministry Republic of Turkey, Turkish Statistical Institute, Yucetepe Mah. Necatibey Cad No.114, Cankaya, Ankara, 06100, Turkey. TEL 90-312-4100410, FAX 90-312-4175886, ulka.unsal@tuik.gov.tr, http://www.tuik.gov.tr. Circ: 3,500.

016.351 USA ISSN 1936-6620
U.S. GENERAL ACCOUNTING OFFICE. OFFICE OF PUBLIC AFFAIRS. MONTH IN REVIEW (ONLINE). Text in English. 1967 (vol.18, no.10). m. free (effective 2011). bibl. back issues avail. **Document type:** *Report, Government.* **Description:** Includes legal decisions and opinions of the U.S. Comptroller General.
Former titles (until 2002): United States. General Accounting Office. Office of Public Affairs. Month in Review (Print); (until 1997): U.S. General Accounting Office. Office of Public Affairs. Reports and Testimony; (until 1986): U.S. General Accounting Office. Monthly List of G A O Reports (0364-8265); (until 1973): G A O Newsletter
Media: Online - full content.
Published by: United States Government Accountability Office, 441 G St, NW, Washington, DC 20548. TEL 202-512-3000, contact@gao.gov.

016.351 USA ISSN 0041-9443
UNIVERSITY OF CALIFORNIA. INSTITUTE OF GOVERNMENTAL STUDIES LIBRARY. ACCESSIONS LIST. Text in English. 1963. q. free. **Document type:** *Bibliography.*
Media: Online - full text.
Indexed: AIAP.
Published by: University of California, Berkeley, Institute of Governmental Studies, 109 Moses Hall #2370, Berkeley, CA 94720-2370. TEL 510-643-2370, FAX 510-643-0866, http://www.igs.berkeley.edu:8880/library/access.htm. Ed. Diana Neves.

351.021 SWE ISSN 1651-6710
HV338
VAELFAERD; SCB's tidskrift om arbetsliv, demografi och vaelfaerd. Text in Swedish. 1981. 4/yr. SEK 80 newsstand/cover (effective 2003). **Document type:** *Journal, Government.*
Formerly (until 2003): VaelfaerdsBulletinen (0280-1418)
Related titles: Online - full content ed.
Published by: Statistiska Centralbyraan/Statistics Sweden, Publishing Unit, Orebro, 70189, Sweden. TEL 46-19-176800, FAX 46-19-176444, scb@scb.se. Ed. Elisabeth Landgren Moeller.

352.13021 USA ISSN 1935-5483
VERMONT CITIES & COUNTIES GRAPHIC PERFORMANCE ANALYSIS. Text in English. 2006. a. USD 95 per issue (effective 2009). charts. **Document type:** *Report, Trade.* **Description:** Provides comparisons in chart form, annual series of analytic charts, by peer group, within state. Each issue consist of 9 charts in each county peer group and each city peer group and 1 area chart per county. 100-200 graphs per state book.
Published by: Municipal Analysis Services, Inc., PO Box 13453, Austin, TX 78711. TEL 512-327-3328, munilysis@hotmail.com, http://sites.google.com/site/gregmichels. Ed. Greg Michels.

352.13021 USA ISSN 1935-5645
VIRGINIA CITIES & COUNTIES GRAPHIC PERFORMANCE ANALYSIS. Text in English. 2006. a. USD 75 per issue (effective 2010). charts. **Document type:** *Report, Trade.* **Description:** Provides comparisons in chart form, annual series of analytic charts, by peer group, within state. Each issue consist of 9 charts in each county peer group and each city peer group and 1 area chart per county. 100-200 graphs per state book.
Related titles: Online - full text ed.
Published by: Municipal Analysis Services, Inc., PO Box 13453, Austin, TX 78711. TEL 512-327-3328, FAX 413-740-1294, munilysis@hotmail.com, http://sites.google.com/site/gregmichels.

328.73021 USA ISSN 0896-9469
JK1041
VITAL STATISTICS ON CONGRESS. Text in English. 1980. biennial. USD 29.95 per issue (effective 2010). back issues avail. **Document type:** *Trade.* **Description:** Contains the elements that define and describe Congress in the post-World War II era etc.
—CCC.
Published by: American Enterprise Institute for Public Policy Research, 1150 17th St NW, Washington, DC 20036. TEL 202-862-5800, FAX 202-862-7177.

351.12 DEU ISSN 0176-3407
VOLKSWIRTSCHAFTLICHE GESAMTRECHUNGEN FUER BAYERN. Text in German. 1982. irreg.
Formed by the merger of (1974-1982): Volkswirtschaftliche Gesamtrechnungen fuer Bayern. Teil 1: Entstehungsrechnung (0720-3357); (1974-1982): Volkswirtschaftliche Gesamtrechnungen fuer Bayern. Teil 2: Entstehung, Verteilung und Verwendung des Sozialprodukts (0720-3365); Both of which superseded in part (in 1978): Volkswirtschaftliche Gesamtrechnungen, VGR, und aktuelle Konjunkturdaten fuer Bayern (0720-3403)
Published by: Bayerisches Landesamt fuer Statistik und Datenverarbeitung, Neuhauser Str 8, Munich, 80331, Germany. TEL 49-89-2119205, FAX 49-89-2119410, poststelle@statistik.bayern.de, http://www.statistik.bayern.de.

P

351.21 DEU ISSN 0723-9351
WAHL ZUM BAYERISCHEN LANDTAG. Text in German. 1950. quinquennial. **Document type:** *Government.*
Published by: Bayerisches Landesamt fuer Statistik und Datenverarbeitung, Neuhauser Str 8, Munich, 80331, Germany. TEL 49-89-2119205, FAX 49-89-2119410, poststelle@statistik.bayern.de, http://www.statistik.bayern.de.

352.13021 USA ISSN 1935-5637
WASHINGTON CITIES & COUNTIES GRAPHIC PERFORMANCE ANALYSIS. Text in English. 2006. a. USD 75 per issue (effective 2010). charts. **Document type:** *Report, Trade.* **Description:** Provides comparisons in chart form, annual series of analytic charts, by peer group, within state. Each issue consist of 9 charts in each county peer group and each city peer group and 1 area chart per county. 100-200 graphs per state book.
Related titles: Online - full text ed.
Published by: Municipal Analysis Services, Inc., PO Box 13453, Austin, TX 78711. TEL 512-327-3328, FAX 413-740-1294, munilysis@hotmail.com, http://sites.google.com/site/gregmichels.

352.13021 GBR ISSN 0140-4482
HJ9041
WELSH LOCAL GOVERNMENT FINANCIAL STATISTICS. Text in English. 1977. a. free (effective 2009). **Document type:** *Government.* **Description:** Contains data relating to spending on local services, such as education, social services and highways, and the financing of this expenditure, including details of council tax levels in Wales.
—BLDSC (9294.660000).
Published by: Welsh Assembly Government, Statistical Directorate, Cathays Park, Cardiff, CF10 3NQ, United Kingdom. TEL 44-1443-845500, stats.info.desk@wales.gsi.gov.uk, http://wales.gov.uk/?lang=en.

352.13021 USA ISSN 1935-5602
THE WEST CITIES & COUNTIES GRAPHIC PERFORMANCE ANALYSIS. Text in English. 2006. a. USD 95 per issue (effective 2009). charts. **Document type:** *Report, Trade.* **Description:** Provides comparisons in chart form, annual series of analytic charts, by peer group, within state. Each issue consist of 9 charts in each county peer group and each city peer group and 1 area chart per county. 100-200 graphs per state book.
Published by: Municipal Analysis Services, Inc., PO Box 13453, Austin, TX 78711. TEL 512-327-3328, munilysis@hotmail.com, http://sites.google.com/site/gregmichels. Ed. Greg Michels.

352.13021 USA ISSN 1935-5424
WEST VIRGINIA CITIES & COUNTIES GRAPHIC PERFORMANCE ANALYSIS. Text in English. 2006. a. USD 75 per issue (effective 2010). charts. **Document type:** *Report, Trade.* **Description:** Provides comparisons in chart form, annual series of analytic charts, by peer group, within state. Each issue consist of 9 charts in each county peer group and each city peer group and 1 area chart per county. 100-200 graphs per state book.
Published by: Municipal Analysis Services, Inc., PO Box 13453, Austin, TX 78711. TEL 512-327-3328, FAX 413-740-1294, munilysis@hotmail.com, http://sites.google.com/site/gregmichels.

351.021 USA ISSN 0893-4568
HJ760
WEST VIRGINIA RESEARCH LEAGUE. STATISTICAL HANDBOOK; a digest of selected data on state and local government in West Virginia. Text in English. 1970. a. USD 15 (effective 2001). charts; stat. 94 p./no.;
Related titles: Microfiche ed.: (from CIS).
Indexed: SRI.

Published by: West Virginia Research League Inc., PO Box 11176, Charleston, WV 25339-1176. TEL 304-766-9495. Ed. Sarah F Roach.

352.13021 USA ISSN 1935-5629
WISCONSIN CITIES & COUNTIES GRAPHIC PERFORMANCE ANALYSIS. Text in English. 2006. a. USD 75 per issue (effective 2010). charts. **Document type:** *Report, Trade.* **Description:** Provides comparisons in chart form, annual series of analytic charts, by peer group, within state. Each issue consist of 9 charts in each county peer group and each city peer group and 1 area chart per county. 100-200 graphs per state book.
Published by: Municipal Analysis Services, Inc., PO Box 13453, Austin, TX 78711. TEL 512-327-3328, FAX 413-740-1294, munilysis@hotmail.com, http://sites.google.com/site/gregmichels.

016.351 USA ISSN 0364-507X
Z1223.5.W6
WISCONSIN PUBLIC DOCUMENTS. Text in English. 1916. q. free. index. **Document type:** *Government.*
Related titles: Microfiche ed.: (from BHP).
Published by: Wisconsin Historical Society, 816 State St, Madison, WI 53706. TEL 608-264-6527. Ed. Janet Monk. Circ: 500.

351.021 ZMB
ZAMBIA. CENTRAL STATISTICAL OFFICE. FINANCIAL STATISTICS OF GOVERNMENT SECTOR (ECONOMIC AND FUNCTIONAL ANALYSIS). Text in English. 1964. a. USD 4.50. **Document type:** *Government.*
Formerly: Zambia. Central Statistical Office. Government Sector Accounts (Economic and Functional Analysis) (0084-4527)
Published by: Central Statistical Office, PO Box 31908, Lusaka, Zambia. TEL 260-1-211231.

352.4021 ZMB
ZAMBIA. CENTRAL STATISTICAL OFFICE. NATIONAL ACCOUNTS. Text in English. 1965. a. ZMK 5. **Document type:** *Government.*
Published by: Central Statistical Office, PO Box 31908, Lusaka, Zambia. TEL 260-1-211231.

310 DEU ISSN 1864-5356
HA1330.B6
ZEITSCHRIFT FUER AMTLICHE STATISTIK BERLIN-BRANDENBURG. Text in German. 1947. m. bk.rev. charts; mkt.; stat. Supplement avail. **Document type:** *Bulletin, Trade.*
Former titles (until 2007): Berliner Statistik. Statistische Monatsschrift (1437-4196); (until 1998): Berliner Statistik. Monatsheft (0341-4531)
Indexed: P30, RASB.
Published by: Amt fuer Statistik Berlin-Brandenburg, Dortustr 46, Potsdam, 14467, Germany. TEL 49-331-39444, FAX 49-331-39418, info@statistik-bbb.de.

PUBLIC ADMINISTRATION—Computer Applications

351.0285 USA
ADMINISTRATORS' COMPUTER LETTER. Text in English. 1981. 12/yr. bk.rev.
Published by: American Newsfeatures Syndicate, 113 Wattenbarger Rd, Sweetwater, TN 37874-6135. TEL 800-484-4074, FAX 423-337-0222. Ed. Ray Burr. Circ: 123,701.

351.43 DEU ISSN 0944-6729
ANALOG UND DIGITAL. Text in German. 1992. 2/yr. free (effective 2008). **Document type:** *Journal, Trade.*
Published by: Staatsanzeiger fuer Baden-Wuerttemberg GmbH, Breitscheidstr 69, Stuttgart, 70176, Germany. TEL 49-711-666010, FAX 49-711-6660119, verlag@staatsanzeiger.de, http://www.staatsanzeiger-verlag.de.

351.0285 CAN ISSN 1703-0072
C I O GOVERNMENTS' REVIEW. (Chief Information Officer) Text in English. 1999. 8/yr. CAD 28 domestic; CAD 36 in United States; CAD 48 elsewhere (effective 2002). adv. **Document type:** *Magazine, Trade.* **Description:** Dedicated to covering the e-Government agenda cross-jurisdictionally.
Formerly (until 2001): Lac Carling Governments' Review (1490-5671)
Related titles: Online - full text ed.
Indexed: C03, CBCARef, P48, P49, PQC.
Published by: I T World Canada, Inc., No.302 - 55 Town Centre Court, Scarborough, ON M1P 4X4, Canada. TEL 416-290-0240, FAX 416-290-0238, general@itworldcanada.com.

351.0285 CHN ISSN 1672-7223
DIANZI ZHENGWU/E-GOVERNMENT. Text in Chinese. 2004. m. CNY 960; CNY 80 per issue (effective 2009). **Document type:** *Magazine, Government.*
Related titles: Online - full text ed.
Published by: Zhongguo Kexueyuan Guojia Kexue Tushuguan/Chinese Academy of Sciences, National Science Library, Zhongguancun Bei Si Huan Xi Lu #3, Beijing, 100190, China. TEL 86-10-82622546, FAX 86-10-62539144, http://www.las.ac.cn/.

351.0285 DEU ISSN 1860-2584
EGOVERNMENT COMPUTING. Text in German. 2001. 11/yr. EUR 64.20; EUR 9 per issue (effective 2010). adv. **Document type:** *Magazine, Trade.*
Formerly (until 2004): Government Computing (1618-3142)
Related titles: Online - full text ed.
Published by: Vogel IT-Medien GmbH, August-Wessels-Str 27, Augsburg, 86156, Germany. TEL 49-821-21770, FAX 49-821-2177150, zentrale@vogel-it.de, http://www.vogel-it.de. Ed. Gerald Viola. Pub. Werner Nieberle. adv.: B&W page EUR 7,100, color page EUR 8,900; trim 320 x 480. Circ: 20,865 (paid and controlled).

325 AUT ISSN 1997-4051
EGOVERNMENT REVIEW. Text in German. 2008. 2/yr. **Document type:** *Journal, Academic/Scholarly.*
Published by: Fachhochschule Kaernten, Studiengang Public Management, Europastr 4, Villach, 9524, Austria. TEL 43-5-905001201, FAX 43-5-905001210, puma@fh-kaernten.at. Ed. Elke Pototschnik. Pub. Wolfgang Eixelsberger.

351.0285 GBR ISSN 1740-7494
➤ **ELECTRONIC GOVERNMENT**; an international journal. Abbreviated title: E G. Text in English. 2004. 4/yr. EUR 494 to institutions (print or online ed.); EUR 672 combined subscription to institutions (print & online eds.) (effective 2012). abstr.; bibl.; charts; illus. back issues avail. **Document type:** *Journal, Academic/Scholarly.* **Description:** Dedicated to design, development, management, implementation, technology, and application issues in e-government.
Related titles: Online - full text ed.: ISSN 1740-7508 (from IngentaConnect).
Indexed: A26, A28, APA, B02, B15, B17, B18, BrCerAb, C&ISA, CA, CA/WCA, CIA, CerAb, CivEngAb, CorrAb, E&CAJ, E08, E11, EEA, EMA, ESPM, EnvEAb, ErgAb, G04, G08, H15, I05, Inspec, L04, LISTA, M&TEA, M09, MBF, METADEX, RiskAb, S09, SCOPUS, SolStAb, T02, T04, WAA.
—BLDSC (3702.254000), IE, Ingenta, Linda Hall. **CCC.**
Published by: Inderscience Publishers, PO Box 735, Olney, Bucks MK46 5WB, United Kingdom. TEL 44-1234-240519, FAX 44-1234-240515, editorial@inderscience.com. Ed. Dr. June Wei. **Subscr. to:** World Trade Centre Bldg, 29 Rte de Pre-Bois, Case Postale 856, Geneva 15 1215, Switzerland. subs@inderscience.com.

004 352.130 GBR ISSN 1369-9393
ELECTRONIC PUBLIC INFORMATION. Text in English. 1993. q. Subscr. rates varies. adv. Website rev.; bk.rev. back issues avail. **Document type:** *Journal, Trade.* **Description:** Focuses mainly on electronic public information systems run by local government and public sector organizations.
Formerly: E P I Today (1364-5692)
—BLDSC (3702.750500).
Published by: SPIN, 63a Hamilton Rd, Reading, Berks RG1 5RA, United Kingdom. TEL 44-118-961-2920. Ed. Mic Dover. Adv. contact Gwen Daly. Circ: 3,000.

351.0285 USA ISSN 1552-6976
FED TECH MAGAZINE. Text in English. 2004. q. free (effective 2011). **Document type:** *Magazine, Trade.* **Description:** Designed to assist IT decision makers and implementers who use technology to build a more effective federal government.
Published by: C D W Government, Inc, 200 N Milwaukee Ave, Vernon Hills, IL 60061. TEL 847-465-6000, http://www.cdwg.com. Ed. Ryan Petersen.

351.0285 USA ISSN 0893-052X
FEDERAL COMPUTER WEEK. Text in English. 1987. w. USD 100 domestic; USD 125 in Canada & Mexico; USD 165 elsewhere; free in US & Canada to qualified personnel (effective 2009). adv. bk.rev. 8 p./no. 3 cols./p.; back issues avail.; reprints avail. **Document type:** *Newspaper, Trade.* **Description:** Contains in-depth feature articles pertinent to the government information technology market.
Related titles: Online - full text ed.
Indexed: A15, A22, A26, ABIn, C10, CompD, CompLI, G08, GeoRef, I05, MicrocompInd, P17, P34, P48, P49, P51, P52, P53, P54, PQC, SoftBase, T02, TelAb.
—BLDSC (3901.873900).
Published by: 1105 Government Information Group (Subsidiary of: 1105 Media Inc.), 3141 Fairview Park Dr, Ste 777, Falls Church, VA 22042. TEL 703-876-5100, http://www.1105govinfo.com. Eds. John Stein Monroe TEL 703-876-5096, David Rapp TEL 703-876-5143.

351.0285 USA ISSN 0738-4300
TK7885.A1
G C N; the technology authority for government. (Government Computer News) Text in English. 1982. 30/yr. free domestic to qualified personnel; USD 125 in Canada & Mexico; USD 160 elsewhere (effective 2008). adv. bk.rev. back issues avail.; reprints avail. **Document type:** *Magazine, Trade.* **Description:** Focuses on how to buy, build and manage the technologies that run government by providing in-depth news, analysis and insight on how agencies are integrating, implementing and managing information technology.
Related titles: CD-ROM ed.: G C N (Year) Contracts Sourcing Guide; Microform ed.: (from PQC); Online - full text ed.
Indexed: A22, A26, B03, B11, CADCAM, CWI, CompD, CompLI, E08, G08, I05, M06, PCR2, PersLit, S09, S23, SoftBase, TelAb.
—BLDSC (4203.928000), CIS. **CCC.**
Published by: 1105 Government Information Group (Subsidiary of: 1105 Media Inc.), 3141 Fairview Park Dr, Ste 777, Falls Church, VA 22042. TEL 703-876-5100, http://www.1105govinfo.com. Ed. Wyatt Kash TEL 703-645-7861. Pub. Evilee Ebb TEL 703-876-5098. adv.: color page USD 16,135, B&W page USD 13,645. Circ: 90,000 (paid).

351.0285 USA
GOVERNMENT COMPUTER NEWS. CONTRACTS SOURCING GUIDE. Variant title: G C N Contracts Sourcing Guide. Text in English. a. adv. **Document type:** *Directory, Trade.* **Description:** Lists more than 2,500 leading providers of IT hardware, software, communication products, electronic commerce and electronic data interchange, and graphics and multimedia, sorted by 650 product categories. Enumerates many products available on GSA and IDIQ contracts.
Published by: 1105 Government Information Group (Subsidiary of: 1105 Media Inc.), 3141 Fairview Park Dr, Ste 777, Falls Church, VA 22042. TEL 703-876-5100, http://www.1105govinfo.com.

351.0285 USA
GOVERNMENT COMPUTER NEWS TECH EDITION. Text in English. q. software rev. charts; illus. back issues avail. **Document type:** *Magazine, Trade.* **Description:** Provides federal, state, and local government officials with LAB-based reviews and buying news of hardware, software, communications, and peripherals.
Formerly (until 2002): Government Computer News Shopper
Published by: 1105 Government Information Group (Subsidiary of: 1105 Media Inc.), 3141 Fairview Park Dr, Ste 777, Falls Church, VA 22042. TEL 703-876-5149, FAX 202-318-8968, gcnadproduction@1105media.com, http://www.1105govinfo.com.

351.0285 GBR ISSN 1462-2467
JN329.E4
GOVERNMENT COMPUTING. Text in English. 1987. m. GBP 75 domestic; GBP 85 foreign; free to qualified personnel (effective 2009). adv. bk.rev. back issues avail. **Document type:** *Magazine, Trade.* **Description:** Fosters debate between central and local government and computer industry professionals on the effective application and procurement of information technology, information services, information management, and communications in providing public services.
Incorporates (1994-2004): Business Continuity (1353-601X); Former titles (until 1998): Government Computing and Information Management; (until 1994): Government Computing (0951-7537)
—BLDSC (4203.935000), IE, Ingenta. **CCC.**
Published by: Kable Ltd., 20-24 Kirby St, London, EC1N 8TS, United Kingdom. claire.thomas@kable.co.uk. Ed. Mark Say TEL 44-20-33534886. Pub. Paul Smith. Adv. contact Roger Massey TEL 44-20-33532680. page GBP 3,520; trim 210 x 297.

GOVERNMENT HEALTH I T. *see* PUBLIC HEALTH AND SAFETY

GOVERNMENT INFORMATION AND IMAGING TECHNOLOGY. *see* COMMUNICATIONS—Video

351.0285 USA ISSN 1043-9668
JK2445.A8
GOVERNMENT TECHNOLOGY; solutions for state and local government in the information age. Text in English. 1987. m. free (effective 2008). adv. illus. Supplement avail.; back issues avail.; reprints avail. **Document type:** *Magazine, Trade.* **Description:** Provides top government executives with the applied knowledge and tailored solutions they need to shape the future of their agencies and departments.
Related titles: Online - full text ed.; ◆ Supplement(s): Mobile Government. ISSN 1543-3854.
Indexed: C10, CA, CompLI, P34, T02.
Published by: e.Republic, Inc., 100 Blue Ravine Rd, Folsom, CA 95630. TEL 916-932-1300, FAX 916-932-1470, getinfo@govtech.net, http://www.govtech.net/. Ed. Steve Towns TEL 916-932-1333. Pub. Don Pearson TEL 916-932-1312. adv.: page USD 16,950; trim 9 x 10.75. Circ: 78,219 (paid).

351.0285 USA
GOVERNMENT WINDOWS N T; the enterprise networking magazine from Government Computer News. Text in English. 1998. m. free to qualified personnel. adv. software rev. illus. **Document type:** *Newspaper, Trade.* **Description:** Discusses the use of Windows NT-based workstations in state and local government.
Published by: 1105 Government Information Group (Subsidiary of: 1105 Media Inc.), 3141 Fairview Park Dr, Ste 777, Falls Church, VA 22042. TEL 703-876-5100, http://www.1105govinfo.com. Circ: 70,000 (controlled).

I T TRENDS IN LOCAL GOVERNMENT. (Information Technology) *see* COMPUTERS—Information Science And Information Theory

351.0285 NLD ISSN 0928-9038
INFORMATIZATION DEVELOPMENTS AND THE PUBLIC SECTOR. Text in English. 1992. irreg., latest vol.9, 2005. price varies. back issues avail. **Document type:** *Monographic series, Academic/Scholarly.* **Description:** Covers developments in informatization policies and the effect of informatization on public administration.
—BLDSC (4496.691700). **CCC.**
Published by: I O S Press, Nieuwe Hemweg 6B, Amsterdam, 1013 BG, Netherlands. TEL 31-20-6883355, FAX 31-20-6870039, info@iospress.nl. **Subscr. to:** I O S Press, Inc, 4502 Rachael Manor Dr, Fairfax, VA 22032-3631. sales@iospress.com. **Dist. by:** Ohmsha Ltd. TEL 81-3-32330641, http://www.ohmsha.co.jp.

351.0285 USA ISSN 1558-2477
T14.5
➤ **INNOVATIONS (CAMBRIDGE)**; technology/governance/globalization. Text in English. 2006 (Jan.). q. USD 199 combined subscription in US & Canada to institutions (print & online eds.); USD 50 per issue in US & Canada to institutions (effective 2012). adv. back issues avail.; reprints avail. **Document type:** *Journal, Academic/Scholarly.* **Description:** Covers both policy challenges and proposed policy solutions, including the application of innovations in the global context.
Related titles: Online - full text ed.: ISSN 1558-2485. USD 172 in US & Canada to institutions (effective 2012).
Indexed: A22, A34, A35, A36, A38, AgBio, BA, CABA, E01, E12, F08, F12, GH, H16, I11, N02, P32, P37, PAIS, PGegResA, R12, S12, S13, S16, T05, TAR, VS, W11.
—BLDSC (4515.485830), IE.
Published by: (George Mason University, School of Public Policy, Harvard University, John F. Kennedy School of Government. Belfer Center for Science and International Affairs. Program on Intrastate Conflict), M I T Press, 55 Hayward St, Cambridge, MA 02142. TEL 617-253-2889, FAX 617-577-1545, journals-cs@mit.edu, http://mitpress.mit.edu. Eds. Iqbal Z Quadir, Philip E Auerswald TEL 703-993-3787. Pub. Nicholas Sullivan.

➤ **LANDESBEAUFTRAGTE FUER DATENSCHUTZ UND INFORMATIONSFREIHEIT NORDRHEIN-WESTFALEN. TAETIGKEITSBERICHT.** *see* COMPUTERS—Computer Security

351.0285 FRA ISSN 0768-9136
LETTRE INFORMATIQUE ET COLLECTIVITES LOCALES; un outil exclusif au service de l'infomatique territoriale. Text in French. 1985. bi-m. (22/yr). EUR 320 (effective 2009). **Document type:** *Newsletter, Trade.*
Published by: Groupe Moniteur, 17 rue d'Uzes, Paris, 75108, France. TEL 33-1-40133030, FAX 33-1-40135021, http://editionsdumoniteur.com. Ed. Catherine Barnasson. Circ: 800.

352.130285 USA
STATE & LOCAL GOVERNMENT COMPUTER NEWS. Text in English. 1995. m. software rev. charts; illus. back issues avail.; reprints avail. **Document type:** *Magazine, Trade.* **Description:** Provides information on computer products and applications in state, county and municipal government in the areas of public administration, law enforcement and safety, criminal justice and courts, and health and human services.
Formerly (until 2001): Government Computer News. State & Local (1080-1618)
Related titles: Online - full text ed.
Indexed: B03, B11, CompLI.
—CIS.
Published by: 1105 Government Information Group (Subsidiary of: 1105 Media Inc.), 3141 Fairview Park Dr, Ste 777, Falls Church, VA 22042. TEL 703-876-5149, FAX 202-318-8968, gcnadproduction@1105media.com, http://www.1105govinfo.com.

351 USA ISSN 1559-5277
STATE TECH. Text in English. 2001. q. free to qualified personnel (effective 2011). **Document type:** *Magazine, Trade.*
Published by: C D W Government, Inc, 200 N Milwaukee Ave, Vernon Hills, IL 60061. TEL 847-465-6000, http://www.cdwg.com.

351.0285 USA ISSN 1548-5668
T21.5.M53
TECH ALMANAC. Text in English. 1988. a. **Document type:** *Directory, Trade.* **Description:** Introduces government personnel to information technology companies in the Washington DC area and beyond.
Former titles (until 200?): Information Technology Almanac (1545-5076); (until 199?): Washington Technology Almanac (1077-6702); (until 1992): Mid - AtlanTech Almanac (1057-7297); (until 1990): Mid - AtlanTech Almanac of Area Technology (1057-7300)
Published by: 1105 Government Information Group (Subsidiary of: 1105 Media Inc.), 3141 Fairview Park Dr, Ste 777, Falls Church, VA 22042. TEL 703-876-5100, http://www.1105govinfo.com. Circ: 30,000 (controlled). **Subscr. to:** Washington Technology Service Center, PO Box 3238, Northbrook, IL 60065.

TECH CAPITAL; technology business and finance. *see* BUSINESS AND ECONOMICS—Banking And Finance—Computer Applications

351.0285 USA ISSN 1058-9163
WASHINGTON TECHNOLOGY; the national magazine for government contractors. Text in English. 1986. 22/yr. free to qualified personnel (effective 2008). adv. software rev. charts; illus. back issues avail.; reprints avail. **Document type:** *Magazine, Government.* **Description:** Provides in-depth news, analysis and insight on the business of delivering technology and services to government.
Related titles: Online - full text ed.: W T Online.
Indexed: A15, A28, ABIn, APA, B03, B11, BrCerAb, C&ISA, C10, CA/WCA, CIA, CerAb, CivEngAb, CorrAb, E&CAJ, E11, EEA, EMA, ESPM, EnvEAb, G06, G07, G08, H15, I05, M&TEA, M09, MBF, METADEX, MicrocompInd, P17, P29, P34, P48, P51, P53, P54, PQC, SolStAb, T02, T04, WAA.
—CIS, Linda Hall.
Published by: 1105 Government Information Group (Subsidiary of: 1105 Media Inc.), 3141 Fairview Park Dr, Ste 777, Falls Church, VA 22042. TEL 703-876-5100, http://www.1105govinfo.com. Ed. Nick Wakeman TEL 703-876-5087. Pub. Evilee Ebb TEL 703-876-5098. Circ: 40,100.

PUBLIC ADMINISTRATION—Municipal Government

see also HOUSING AND URBAN PLANNING ; SOCIAL SERVICES AND WELFARE

352.14 USA ISSN 1062-6514
A A C O G REGION. Text in English. 1974. q. free. illus. **Document type:** *Government.*
Supersedes: A A C O G Newsletter; Which was formerly: A A C O G Highlights
Published by: Alamo Area Council of Governments, 8700 Tesoro Dr., Ste. 700, San Antonio, TX 78217-6228. TEL 210-225-5201, FAX 210-225-5937. Ed. Vicki Arnold Curless. R&P Vicki Arnold Curless TEL 210-362-5204. Circ: 3,500.

352 GBR
A L G LONDON GOVERNMENT DIRECTORY (YEAR). Text in English. 19??. a., latest 2005. free (effective 2009). **Document type:** *Directory, Trade.* **Description:** Provides information on local government in London. Includes facts and statistics, plus contact information for local authorities in the capital and hundreds of other relevant organizations.
Published by: Association of London Government, 59 1/2 Southwark St, London, SE1 0AL, United Kingdom. TEL 44-20-79349999, info@londoncouncils.gov.uk, http://www.londoncouncils.gov.uk/.

352 GBR
A L G TRANSPORT AND ENVIRONMENT COMMITTEE ANNUAL REPORT (YEAR). Text in English. 19??. a. free (effective 2009). back issues avail. **Document type:** *Government.* **Description:** Contains a review of the work undertaken by the ALG in the past year.
Related titles: Online - full text ed.
Published by: Association of London Government, 59 1/2 Southwark St, London, SE1 0AL, United Kingdom. TEL 44-20-79349999, info@londoncouncils.gov.uk.

352.14 USA
A M C B O DIRECTORY OF BUILDING CODES AND REGULATIONS. Text in English. biennial. **Document type:** *Directory.*
Published by: Association of Major City Building Officials, 505 Huntmar Park Dr, Ste 210, Herndon, VA 22070. TEL 703-481-2038, FAX 703-481-3596, http://www.ncsbcs.org/newsite/AMCBO/amcbo_main_page.htm.

352.14 USA
A M C B O NEWSLETTER. Text in English. q. free (effective 2008). **Document type:** *Newsletter.* **Description:** Focuses on public safety and health and on vocational topics of value to building code officials.
Published by: Association of Major City Building Officials, 505 Huntmar Park Dr, Ste 210, Herndon, VA 22070. TEL 703-481-2038, FAX 703-481-3596, http://www.ncsbcs.org/newsite/AMCBO/amcbo_main_page.htm.

352 ITA ISSN 0393-3938
A N C I RIVISTA. (Associazione Nazionale dei Comuni Italiani) Text in Italian. 1957. 12/yr. adv. **Document type:** *Magazine, Trade.*
Published by: A N C I Servizi, Piazza Cola di Rienzo 69, Rome, 00192, Italy. TEL 39-06-36762300, FAX 39-06-36004686, info@anciservizi.it, http://www.anciservizi.it. Circ: 50,000.

A N J E C REPORT. *see* CONSERVATION

A R C ACTION. *see* HOUSING AND URBAN PLANNING

AARSBOK FOER SVERIGES KOMMUNER/STATISTICAL YEARBOOK OF ADMINISTRATIVE DISTRICTS OF SWEDEN. *see* PUBLIC ADMINISTRATION—Abstracting, Bibliographies, Statistics

352 ESP ISSN 2171-5009
ABOGACIA GENERAL DEL ESTADO. MEMORIA. Text in Spanish. 2003. a. back issues avail. **Document type:** *Report, Consumer.*
Formerly (until 2008): Abogacia General del Estado. Direccion del Servicio Juridico del Estado. Memoria (2171-3502)
Media: CD-ROM. **Related titles:** ◆ Supplement to: Spain. Ministerio de Justicia. Boletin de Informacion. ISSN 0211-4267.
Published by: Ministerio de Justicia, Centro de Publicaciones, San Bernardo 62, Planta Baja, Madrid, 28071, Spain. TEL 34-91-3904429, http://www.mju.es/publicaciones/.

352 FRA ISSN 1772-9173
ACHETEURS PUBLICS. Text in French. 2005. bi-m. **Document type:** *Magazine, Trade.*
Published by: Editialis, 13 Rue Louis Pasteur, Boulogne Billancourt, Cedex 92513, France. TEL 33-1-46999785.

THE ACHIEVER. *see* EDUCATION

352 USA
ACTIONLINES MAGAZINE. Text in English. 19??. 2/yr. USD 50 (effective 2010). adv. **Document type:** *Magazine, Government.* **Description:** Covers relevant, timely articles about issues affecting Indiana cities and towns and the municipal government.
Published by: Indiana Association of Cities and Towns, 200 S Meridian, Ste 340, Indianapolis, IN 46225. TEL 317-237-6200, FAX 317-237-6206. adv.: B&W page USD 735; 7 x 9.5. Circ: 4,500.

352 CAN ISSN 1914-0665
L'ACTUALITE MUNICIPALE. Text in French. 2007. q. **Document type:** *Newsletter, Government.*
Published by: Ville de Sept-Iles. Service de Communications, 546, Avenue De Quen, Sept-Iles, PQ G4R 2R4, Canada. TEL 418-962-2525, FAX 418-964-3213, http://www.ville.sept-iles.qc.ca.

352 ESP ISSN 1130-376X
ADMINISTRACION DE ANDALUCIA. Variant title: Revista Andaluza de Administracion Publica. Text in Spanish. 1990. q. **Document type:** *Magazine, Consumer.*
Published by: Junta de Andalucia, Instituto Andaluz de Administracion Publica, Ave. Ramon y Cajal No. 35, Sevilla, Andalucia 41004, Spain. TEL 34-955-042400, publicaciones.iapp@juntadeandalucia.es, http://www.juntadeandalucia.es/institutodeadministracionpublica/. Ed. Pedro Escribano Collado.

AGENDA (NEW BRUNSWICK). *see* COLLEGE AND ALUMNI

352 PRT ISSN 1645-8990
AGENDA MUNICIPAL DO SEIXAL. Text in Portuguese. 2004. irreg. **Document type:** *Magazine, Consumer.*
Published by: Camara Municipal do Seixal, Alameda dos Bomberos Volontarios, Seixal, 2844-001, Portugal. TEL 351-212-276700, FAX 351-212-276701, camara.geral@cm-seixal.pt, http://www.cm-seixal.pt.

ALABAMA CITIES & COUNTIES GRAPHIC PERFORMANCE ANALYSIS. *see* PUBLIC ADMINISTRATION—Abstracting, Bibliographies, Statistics

352.14 USA
ALABAMA. DEPARTMENT OF REVENUE. ANNUAL REPORT. Text in English. 1985. a. free. **Document type:** *Government.* **Description:** Provides a four-year compilation of state taxes and fees collected by the Revenue Dept.
Published by: Department of Revenue, Commissioner's Office, PO Box 327001, Montgomery, AL 36132-7001. TEL 334-242-1175, FAX 334-242-0550. Ed. Carla A Snellgrove. Circ: 1,000.

352.14 USA
ALABAMA. DEPARTMENT OF REVENUE. COUNTY LINES NEWSLETTER. Text in English. 1993. m. free. **Document type:** *Newsletter, Government.* **Description:** Standard features includes quarterly summary of local taxes collected the department; administrative rules and regulations, administrative rules public hearing notices, articles of interest to county licensing, collecting, and assessing officials.
Published by: Department of Revenue, Commissioner's Office, PO Box 327001, Montgomery, AL 36132-7001. TEL 334-242-1390, FAX 334-242-0550. Ed. Carla A Snellgrove. Circ: 1,000.

352.14 USA
ALABAMA. DEPARTMENT OF REVENUE. GENERAL SUMMARY OF STATE TAXES. Text in English. 1985. a. free. **Document type:** *Government.* **Description:** Provides a summary of state taxes and fees administered by the Revenue Department.
Published by: Department of Revenue, Research Division, PO Box 320001, Montgomery, AL 36132-0001. TEL 334-242-1380, FAX 334-242-0141. Ed. William E Crawford.

352.14 USA
ALABAMA. DEPARTMENT OF REVENUE. REVENUE REVIEW NEWSLETTER. Text in English. 1983. q. free. **Document type:** *Newsletter.* **Description:** Includes quarterly summary of taxes and fees collected by the department, administrative rules and regulations, articles of interest to tax professionals.
Published by: Department of Revenue, Commissioner's Office, PO Box 327001, Montgomery, AL 36132-7001. TEL 334-242-1390, FAX 334-242-0550. Ed. Carolyn Blackstock.

352.14 USA ISSN 0002-4309
ALABAMA MUNICIPAL JOURNAL. Text in English. 1935. m. USD 24; USD 2 per issue (effective 2010). illus. reprints avail. **Document type:** *Magazine, Trade.* **Description:** Features articles devoted to municipal government, its problems, solutions, trends, legal information as well as news of city and town governments statewide.
Formerly (until 1953): Alabama Local Government Journal
Related titles: Online - full text ed.: free (effective 2010).
Indexed: P06.
Published by: Alabama League of Municipalities, PO Box 1270, Montgomery, AL 36102. TEL 334-263-0200, FAX 334-262-2809, perryr@alalm.org. Ed. Carrie Banks. Circ: 4,500 (paid and controlled).

352 USA
ALASKA MUNICIPAL LEAGUE. Text in English. d.
Address: 217 Second St, Ste 200, Juneau, AK 99801. TEL 907-586-1325, 877-636-1325, FAX 907-463-5480, info@akml.org, http://www.akml.org.

352.14025 USA ISSN 0363-4167
JS451.A43
ALASKA MUNICIPAL OFFICIALS DIRECTORY. Text in English. 1958. a. USD 50. **Document type:** *Directory.* **Description:** Provides addresses, telephone and fax numbers, and names and titles of government officials for each of Alaska's incorporated municipalities. Other information for each municipality includes population, sales tax rate and type (if any), type and form of government, and municipality owned utilities.
Published by: Alaska Municipal League, 217 Second St, Ste 200, Juneau, AK 99801. http://www.akml.org. Ed. Kevin C Ritchie. Circ: 1,500.

352 CAN ISSN 0701-6522
ALBERTA. ALBERTA MUNICIPAL AFFAIRS. ANNUAL REPORT. Text in English. 19??. a.
Former titles (until 1972): Department of Municipal Affairs of the Province of Alberta. Annual Report (0701-6530); (until 1921): Department of Municipal Affairs of the Province of Alberta. Report
Published by: Alberta Municipal Affairs, Public Affairs Office (Subsidiary of: Alberta Municipal Affairs and Housing), 10155 102nd St, 18th Fl, Edmonton, AB T5J 4L4, Canada. TEL 403-427-8863, 780-427-8862, FAX 403-422-9105, 780-422-1419, http://www.municipalaffairs.gov.ab.ca/mahome/index.cfm.

352.14 IND ISSN 0024-5623
JS7001
ALL INDIA INSTITUTE OF LOCAL SELF GOVERNMENT. QUARTERLY JOURNAL. Text in English. 1930. q. free to members (effective 2011). bk.rev. charts. **Document type:** *Journal, Academic/Scholarly.*
Indexed: BAS, P06.
Published by: All India Institute of Local Self Government, M.N. Roy Human Development Campus, Plot No. 6, F-Block, Bandra Kurla complex, T.P.S. Rd No. 12, Bandra E, Mumbai, 400051, India. TEL 91-22-26571714, FAX 91-22-26572115, dgaiilsg@gmail.com, http://www.aiilsg.org/.

352 PRT ISSN 1645-9903
ALMADA. Text in Portuguese. 2000. irreg. **Document type:** *Magazine, Consumer.*
Published by: Camara Municipal de Almada, Largo Luis de Camoes, Almada, 2800-158, Portugal. TEL 351-212-724000, http://www.m-almada.pt.

352 PRT ISSN 1645-3026
ALMADA NA HISTORIA. Text in Portuguese. 2001. irreg. **Document type:** *Magazine, Consumer.*
Published by: Camara Municipal de Almada, Largo Luis de Camoes, Almada, 2800-158, Portugal. TEL 351-212-724000, http://www.m-almada.pt.

352 ESP ISSN 0211-4003
DP302.S31
ALTAMIRA. Text in Spanish. 1934. a. **Document type:** *Monographic series, Academic/Scholarly.*
Indexed: HistAb, MLA-IB.
Published by: Diputacion Regional de Cantabria, Gomez Orena, 5-3o, Santander, Cantabria 39003, Spain. http://www.gobcantabria.es/.

352 PRT ISSN 1647-8096
▼ **AMADORA SEMPRE EM MOVIMENTO.** Text in Portuguese. 2010. bi-m. **Document type:** *Magazine, Consumer.*
Published by: Camara Municipal da Amadora, Av Movimento das Forcas Armadas, Mina, 2700-595, Portugal. TEL 351-214-369000, FAX 351-214-922082, geral@cm-amadora.pt, http://www.cm-amadora.pt.

352 PRT ISSN 1646-0987
AMADORAEDUCA. Text in Portuguese. 200?. q. **Document type:** *Magazine, Consumer.*
Published by: Camara Municipal da Amadora, Av Movimento das Forcas Armadas, Mina, 2700-595, Portugal. TEL 351-214-369000, FAX 351-214-922082, geral@cm-amadora.pt, http://www.cm-amadora.pt.

352 PRT ISSN 1647-6085
▼ **AMARES.** Text in Portuguese. 2010. s-a. **Document type:** *Magazine, Consumer.*
Published by: Camara Municipal de Amares, Largo do Municipio, Amares, 4720-058, Portugal. TEL 531-253-993761, FAX 531-253-992643, http://www.cm-amares.pt.

352.14 USA ISSN 0149-337X
HT101 CODEN: ACCOD3
AMERICAN CITY & COUNTY. Text in English. 1909. m. USD 67 domestic; USD 87 foreign; USD 10 per issue; free to qualified personnel (effective 2011). adv. bk.rev. charts; illus.; mkt.; tr.lit. index. back issues avail.; reprints avail. **Document type:** *Magazine, Trade.* **Description:** Covers the issues, concepts and trends of local government and public works, including the activities and concerns of engineers and administrators of municipal, township, county and special district governments, consulting and sanitary engineers and private firms performing public services.
Formerly (until 1975): American City (0002-7936); Incorporates (1924-1991): American City & County Municipal Index (0077-2151)
Related titles: Microform ed.: ISSN 0364-9814 (from PQC); Online - full text ed.: ISSN 2161-9123. free (effective 2011).
Indexed: A01, A02, A03, A05, A08, A09, A10, A12, A13, A17, A20, A22, A23, A24, A25, A26, A32, ABIn, AIAP, AS&TA, AS&TI, ASFA, B01, B02, B04, B06, B07, B08, B09, B11, B13, B15, B17, B18, BRD, C10, C12, CBRI, ChemAb, E06, E08, ESPM, G04, G05, G06, G07, G08, HRIS, I05, I07, ISR, L09, M01, M02, M06, MASUSE, MagInd, P02, P06, P10, P13, P26, P27, P34, P53, P54, PAIS, PQC, R04, RASB, Repind, S02, S03, S04, S08, S09, S11, SCOPUS, SRI, SSAI, SSAb, SSI, T&II, T02, V02, V03, V04, W01, W02, W03, W05.
—BLDSC (0812.510000), IE, Ingenta, Linda Hall. **CCC.**
Published by: Penton Media, Inc., 6151 Powers Ferry Rd, Ste 200, Atlanta, GA 30339. TEL 770-955-2500, FAX 770-618-0204, http://www.penton.com. Ed. Bill Wolpin TEL 770-618-0112. Pub. Gregg Herring TEL 770-618-0333.

352.14 DEU
AMTLICHER SCHULANZEIGER FUER DEN REGIERUNGSBEZIRK UNTERFRANKEN; amtliches Mitteilungsblatt fuer die Volks-, Sonder- und Berufsschulen. Text in German. 1871. m. looseleaf. adv. bk.rev. back issues avail. **Document type:** *Government.*
Published by: Unterfranken Regierung, Peterplatz 9, Wuerzburg, 97070, Germany. TEL 49-931-3801307, FAX 49-931-3802307, franz.portscher@reg-ufr.bayern.de. Ed., R&P Franz Portscher. Circ: 1,000.

352.14 DEU ISSN 0003-2131
AMTLICHES KREISBLATT FUER DEN KREIS HERZOGTUM LAUENBURG. Text in German. 1883. w. EUR 1.12 per week (effective 2006). **Document type:** *Newspaper, Consumer.*
Published by: Luebecker Nachrichten GmbH, Herrenholz 10, Luebeck, 23556, Germany. TEL 49-451-1440.

352 DEU ISSN 1865-8288
AMTLICHES MITTEILUNGSBLATT DER GEMEINDE WASSERLOSEN; mit den Gemeindeteilen: Brebersdorf, Burghausen, Gressthal, Kaisten, Ruetschenhausen, Schwemmelsbach, Wasserlosen und Wuelfershausen. Text in German. 1981. w. EUR 26.40 (effective 2011). adv. **Document type:** *Newsletter, Trade.*

P

Published by: Revista Verlag GmbH, Am Oberen Marienbach 2 1/2, Schweinfurt, 97421, Germany. TEL 49-9721-387190, FAX 49-9721-3871938, post@revista.de.

352.14 DEU
AMTSBLATT DER GEMEINDE WILHELMSFELD. Text in German. 1960. w. back issues avail. **Document type:** *Newsletter, Trade.*
Published by: Gemeinde Wilhelmsfeld, Johann-Wilhelm-Str 61, Wilhelmsfeld, 69259, Germany. TEL 49-6220-5090, FAX 49-6220-50935, post@wilhelmsfeld.de, http://www.wilhelmsfeld.de/rathaus-einrichtungen/gemeindeverwaltung.html. Ed. Anke Flicker.

352.14 AUT ISSN 0038-8971
AMTSBLATT DER LANDESHAUPTSTADT LINZ. Text in German. 1921. s-m. EUR 36 (effective 2005). adv. bk.rev. illus.; stat. index. **Document type:** *Bulletin, Government.*
Former titles: Stadt Linz; Amtsblatt der Landeshauptstadt Linz
Published by: Landeshauptstadt Linz, Hauptplatz 1, Linz, O 4041, Austria. TEL 43-732-70701352, FAX 43-732-7070541352, info@mag.linz.at, http://www.linz.at. Ed., Adv. contact Edith Prass. Circ: 1,000.

352.14 DEU
AMTSBLATT DER LANDESHAUPTSTADT MUENCHEN. Text in German. 1952. 3/m. **Document type:** *Newsletter, Government.*
Published by: Landeshauptstadt Muenchen, Rathaus, Munich, 80313, Germany. TEL 49-89-23300, FAX 49-89-23326458, rathaus@muenchen.de, http://www.muenchen.de.

352.14 DEU ISSN 0172-2522
AMTSBLATT DER STADT KOELN. Text in German. 1970. w. back issues avail. **Document type:** *Government.* **Description:** Lists decisions and announcements of the town government concerning construction, planning and roads.
Related titles: CD-ROM ed.
Published by: Stadt Koeln, Presse und Informationsamt, Laurenzplatz 4, Cologne, 50667, Germany. TEL 49-221-22126456, FAX 49-221-22126486. Ed., R&P Henning von Borstell. Circ: 600.

352 AUT
AMTSBLATT DER STADT WIEN. Text in German. w. EUR 44; EUR 1.10 newsstand/cover (effective 2005). adv. **Document type:** *Newspaper, Government.*
Published by: N.J. Schmid Verlag, Leberstr 122, Vienna, 1110, Austria. TEL 43-1-74032735, FAX 43-1-74032750, g.milletich@schmid-verlag.at, http://www.schmid-verlag.at. Ed. Bettina Kutrovatz. Adv. contact Monika Steiner. page EUR 933.80; trim 176 x 252. Circ: 9,000 (paid and controlled).

352 DEU ISSN 1865-8008
AMTSBLATT DER VERWALTUNGSGEMEINSCHAFT EUERDORF; Mitteilungsblatt der Mitgliedsgemeinden. Text in German. 1990. w. EUR 26.40 (effective 2011). adv. **Document type:** *Newsletter, Trade.*
Published by: Revista Verlag GmbH, Am Oberen Marienbach 2 1/2, Schweinfurt, 97421, Germany. TEL 49-9721-387190, FAX 49-9721-3871938, post@revista.de.

352.14 DEU
AMTSBLATT DES KREISES WESEL; Amtliches Verkuendungsblatt. Text in German. 1975. m. free (effective 2011). **Document type:** *Bulletin, Trade.*
Published by: Kreis Wesel, Reeser Landstr 31, Wesel, 46483, Germany. TEL 49-281-2070, post@kreis-wesel.de, http://www.kreis-wesel.de.

352.14 DEU ISSN 0943-9064
AMTSBLATT FUER BERLIN. Text in German. 1951. w. EUR 81.80 (effective 2006). back issues avail. **Document type:** *Government.*
Formerly (until 1991): Amtsblatt fuer Berlin. Teil 1: Amtsblatt (0405-5039)
Related titles: Online - full text ed.
Published by: (Berlin. Senatsverwaltung fuer Inneres), Kulturbuch Verlag GmbH, Postfach 470449, Berlin, 12313, Germany. TEL 49-30-6618484, FAX 49-30-6617828, kbvinfo@kulturbuch-verlag.de, http://www.kulturbuch-verlag.de. Circ: 10,000.

352.14 AUT ISSN 0003-2271
AMTSBLATT FUER DAS LAND VORARLBERG. Text in German. 1946. w. bk.rev. **Document type:** *Bulletin, Government.*
Published by: Landesregierung Vorarlberg, Roemerstr 15, Bregenz, V 6901, Austria. TEL 43-5574-5110, FAX 43-5574-511920095, land@vorarlberg.at, http://www.vorarlberg.at. Ed., R&P Sandra Doppelmayer. Circ: 1,800.

352.14 DEU
AMTSBLATT FUER DEN LANDKREIS ROSENHEIM. Text in German. 1868. m.
Published by: Landratsamt Rosenheim, Wittelsbacherstr 53, Rosenheim, 83022, Germany. TEL 49-8031-39201, FAX 49-8031-3929001, poststelle@lra-rosenheim.de, http://www.landkreis-rosenheim.de. Circ: 400.

352.14 DEU
AMTSBLATT FUER SCHLESWIG-HOLSTEIN. Text in German. 1946. w. looseleaf. USD 40.
Published by: Innenministerium, Duesternbrooker Weg 92, Kiel, 24105, Germany. TEL 0431-5961, FAX 0431-596-3131. Circ: 4,000.

352.14 AUT
AMTSBLATT KAPFENBERG. Text in German. 1947. bi-m. free (effective 2011). **Document type:** *Newsletter, Consumer.*
Formerly: Amtsblatt der Stadt Kapfenberg (0003-2239)
Published by: Stadtgemeinde Kapfenberg, Koloman-Wallisch-Platz 1, Kapfenberg, 8605, Austria. TEL 43-3862-22501, FAX 43-3862-225012090, stadtgemeinde@kapfenberg.at.

352.14 DEU
AMTSBLATT - STADT AUGSBURG. Text in German. 1746. w. EUR 30; EUR 0.50 newsstand/cover (effective 2005). **Document type:** *Bulletin, Government.*
Published by: Stadt Augsburg, Amt fuer Oeffentlichkeitsarbeit, Maximilianstr 4, Augsburg, 86150, Germany. TEL 49-821-3249424, FAX 49-821-3249422, afoe.stadt@augsburg.de, http://www.augsburg.de. Circ: 730.

352 DEU ISSN 1865-8253
AMTSBLATT UND MITTEILUNGSBLATT FUER DEN MARKT OBERTHULBA. Text in German. 1974. w. EUR 26.40 (effective 2011). adv. **Document type:** *Newsletter, Trade.*
Published by: Revista Verlag GmbH, Am Oberen Marienbach 2 1/2, Schweinfurt, 97421, Germany. TEL 49-9721-387190, FAX 49-9721-3871938, post@revista.de.

352 DEU ISSN 1865-830X
AMTSBOTE DER GROSSGEMEINDE ROETHLEIN; mit den Gemeindenteilen Heidenfeld, Hirschfeld und Roethlein. Text in German. 1973. w. EUR 14.40 (effective 2011). adv. **Document type:** *Newsletter, Trade.*
Formerly (until 1985): Roethleiner Nachrichten
Published by: Revista Verlag GmbH, Am Oberen Marienbach 2 1/2, Schweinfurt, 97421, Germany. TEL 49-9721-387190, FAX 49-9721-3871938, post@revista.de.

352 PRT ISSN 1646-1037
ANADIA EM DIA. Text in Portuguese. 2000. q. **Document type:** *Magazine, Consumer.*
Published by: Camara Municipal de Anadia, Praca do Municipio, Anadia, 3780-909, Portugal. TEL 351-231-510730, FAX 351-231-510739, http://www.cm-anadia.pt.

354.71 CAN ISSN 0382-2486
HJ13
ANNUAL NORTHERN EXPENDITURE PLAN. Text in English. 1976. a.
Related titles: Online - full text ed.: ISSN 1494-2305.
Published by: Indian and Northern Affairs Canada, Advisory Committee on Northern Development, Terrasses de la Chaudiere, 10 Wellington N Tower, Hull, PQ K1A DH4, Canada. FAX 800-567-9604, infopubs@ainc-inac.gc.ca, http://www.ainc-inac.gc.ca/.

352.14 USA
ANTIEAU ON LOCAL GOVERNMENT LAW. Text in English. 1955. latest 2nd ed., 6 base vols. plus updates 3/yr. looseleaf. USD 1,661 base vol(s). (effective 2008). **Document type:** *Monographic series, Trade.* **Description:** Examines the local government law and provides a current perspective on municipal corporations as well as independent local government entities and counties, adding emerging topics such as telecommunications.
Related titles: Online - full text ed.
Published by: Matthew Bender & Co., Inc. (Subsidiary of: LexisNexis North America), 1275 Broadway, Albany, NY 12204. TEL 518-487-3000, 800-424-4200, FAX 518-487-3083, international@bender.com, http://bender.lexisnexis.com. Ed. Sandra Stevenson.

352 ESP ISSN 2172-6531
▼ **ANUARIO ARAGONES DE GOBIERNO LOCAL.** Text in Spanish. 2010. a. **Document type:** *Monographic series, Academic/Scholarly.*
Published by: Institucion Fernando el Catolico, Plaza de Espana 2, Zaragoza, 50071, Spain. TEL 34-976-288878, FAX 34-976-288869, ifc@dpz.es, http://ifc.dpz.es/.

352 ESP ISSN 1130-7625
DP402.B48
ANUARIO BRIGANTINO. Text in Spanish, English, Catalan. 1948. a. back issues avail. **Document type:** *Monographic series, Consumer.*
Related titles: Online - full text ed.
Published by: Ayuntamineto de Betanzos, Archivo Municipal, Emilio Romay, 1, Bentanzos, 15300, Spain. http://www.betanzos.net/.

ARTS & CULTURE FUNDING REPORT. *see* ART

352.14 MUS ISSN 0304-6451
JS7659.M3
ASSOCIATION OF URBAN AUTHORITIES. ANNUAL BULLETIN. Added title page title: Local Government in Mauritius. Text in English, French. 1962. a. **Document type:** *Bulletin.*
Published by: Association of Urban Authorities, City Hall, Port Louis, Mauritius. Circ: 200.

352 USA
ATASCADERO. Text in English. 2006 (May). 3/yr. Dist. free in some locations and inside Atascadero News. adv. **Document type:** *Magazine, Government.* **Description:** Encompasses all aspects of the City of Atascadero, including information relevant to the City, new City projects, travel, tourism, local business highlights, City Council, parks, planning, as well as the City's Recreation Guide.
Published by: City of Atascadero, 6907 El Camino Real, Atascadero, CA 93422. Ed. Jennifer Fanning TEL 805-461-5000 ext 3426. adv.: color page USD 1,300; 8.25 x 10.5.

ATLANTA REGIONAL COMMISSION. ANNUAL REPORT. *see* HOUSING AND URBAN PLANNING

352.14 AUS ISSN 1036-7055
THE AUSTRALIAN LOCAL GOVERNMENT GUIDE. Text in English. 1991. 3/yr. (Apr., Aug. & Dec.). AUD 479 domestic; AUD 435.45 foreign; AUD 749 combined subscription domestic (print & online eds.); AUD 680.91 combined subscription foreign (print & online eds.) (effective 2008). **Document type:** *Directory, Government.* **Description:** Contains detailed listing of local councils throughout Australia. included are contact details as well as a range of other useful information such as council expenditure/budgets, population, emergency services and regional industry.
Related titles: Online - full text ed.: AUD 529 domestic; AUD 480.91 foreign (effective 2008).
Published by: Crown Content, Level 2, 141 Capel St, North Melbourne, VIC 3051, Australia. TEL 61-3-93299800, FAX 61-3-93299698, online@crowncontent.com.au. Ed. Mr. Scott O'Halloran.

352.190 FRA ISSN 1775-2760
L'AVENIR ENSEMBLE. Text in French. 2002. irreg. **Document type:** *Bulletin, Consumer.*
Published by: Communaute de Communes de la Region de Molsheim-Mutzig, 2 route Ecospace, Molsheim, 67120, France. TEL 3-88498258, FAX 3-88493814.

AZIENDITALIA; mensile per gli enti locali e le loro aziende. *see* BUSINESS AND ECONOMICS—Management

AZIENDITALIA FINANZA E TRIBUTI. *see* BUSINESS AND ECONOMICS—Public Finance, Taxation

352.14 DEU ISSN 1437-9856
B B W MAGAZIN. (Beamtenbund Baden-Wuerttemberg) Text in German. 1961. 10/yr. EUR 15.90; EUR 2 newsstand/cover (effective 2009). adv. **Document type:** *Magazine, Trade.*
Former titles (until 1999): B B W Report (1435-2079); (until 1996): Der Beamte in Baden-Wuerttemberg (0172-0678)
Published by: D B B Verlag GmbH, Friedrichstr 165, Berlin, 10117, Germany. TEL 49-30-72619170, FAX 49-30-726191740, kontakt@dbbverlag.de, http://www.dbbverlag.de. Circ: 48,300 (controlled).

352.190 FRA ISSN 1776-1301
B S M INFO. (Bessin, Seulles et Mer) Text in French. 2004. s-a. **Document type:** *Bulletin, Government.*
Published by: Communaute de Communes Bessin, Seulles et Mer, 48 rue de la Mer, Courseulles-sur-Mer, France. TEL 33-2-31361759, contact@bessin-seulles-mer.fr, http://www.bessin-seulles-mer.fr.

352.14 UAE
BALADIAH RAS AL-KHAIMAH/RAS AL-KHAIMAH MUNICIPALITY. Text in Arabic. 1977. m. **Description:** News of municipal activities and other matters of local concern.
Published by: Municipal Government, P O Box 4, Ras Al Khaimah, United Arab Emirates. TEL 32422. Ed. Saud Bin Saghir Al Qusaimi. Circ: 3,000.

352 PRT ISSN 1645-3980
BARREIRO INFORMACAO MUNICIPAL. Text in Portuguese. 2002. bi-m. **Document type:** *Report, Consumer.*
Published by: Camara Municipal do Barreiro, R Miguel Lombarda, Barreiro, 2830-355, Portugal. TEL 351-21-2068000, FAX 351-21-2068001, geral@cm-barreiro.pt, http://www.cm-barreiro.pt.

352.14025 DEU ISSN 0174-8386
BAYERISCHES JAHRBUCH; das grosse Auskunfts- und Adressenwerk. Text in German. 1987. a. EUR 142 (effective 2009). adv. **Document type:** *Directory, Trade.* **Description:** Directory of Bavarian authorities.
Published by: De Gruyter Saur (Subsidiary of: Walter de Gruyter GmbH & Co. KG), Mies-van-der-Rohe-Str 1, Munich, 80807, Germany. TEL 49-89-769020, FAX 49-89-76902150, info@degruyter.com. Circ: 2,000.

352.14 DEU ISSN 1437-8337
BEHOERDEN SPIEGEL; unabhaengige Zeitung fuer den oeffentlichen Dienst. Text in German. 1984. m. EUR 38; EUR 1.50 newsstand/cover (effective 2011). adv. bk.rev. abstr.; bibl.; mkt. back issues avail. **Document type:** *Newspaper, Trade.* **Description:** Presents a special-interest publication for politicans and civil servants on public law and public procurement.
Related titles: ◆ Regional ed(s).: Berliner Behoerden Spiegel. ISSN 1437-8353.
Published by: ProPress Verlag GmbH, Am Buschhof 8, Bonn, 53227, Germany. TEL 49-228-970970, FAX 49-228-9709775. Circ: 98,181 (paid and controlled).

352 DEU ISSN 2192-2497
▼ **BEHOERDEN-SPIEGEL. VERWALTUNG KOMPAKT;** Der Newsletter fuer die oesterreichische Verwaltung. Text in German. 2011. fortn. **Document type:** *Newsletter, Trade.*
Published by: ProPress Verlag GmbH, Am Buschhof 8, Bonn, 53227, Germany. TEL 49-228-970970, FAX 49-228-9709775, verlag@behoerdenspiegel.de, http://www.behoerdenspiegel.de. Ed., Pub. R Uwe Proll. Adv. contact Frank de Meulenaer.

352 CHN ISSN 1002-3658
BEIJING NIANJIAN. Text in Chinese. 1990. a. **Document type:** *Yearbook, Government.*
Related titles: Online - full text ed.
Published by: Beijing Shi Difang Zhibianzuan Weiyuanhui, 19, Dong San Huan Nan Lu, Lianhe Guoji Dasha Yi-duan 13/F, Beijing, 100088, China. http://www.bjdfz.gov.cn/index.jsp.

352 DEU ISSN 1865-8229
BERGER NACHRICHTEN; amtliches Nachrichtenblatt der Gemeinde Bergrheinfeld. Text in German. 1970. w. EUR 23.64 (effective 2011). **Document type:** *Newsletter, Trade.*
Published by: Revista Verlag GmbH, Am Oberen Marienbach 2 1/2, Schweinfurt, 97421, Germany. TEL 49-9721-387190, FAX 49-9721-3871938, post@revista.de.

352.14 DEU
BERICHTE ZUR STADTENTWICKLUNG LUDWIGSHAFEN. Text in German. 1972. irreg. adv. **Document type:** *Government.*
Formerly: Informationen zur Stadtentwicklung Ludwigshafen
Published by: Stadt Ludwigshafen, Sparte Stadtentwicklung und Wirtschaftsfoerderung, Rathausplatz 20, Ludwigshafen Am Rhein, 67059, Germany. TEL 49-621-5042218, FAX 49-621-5043453, stadtentwicklung@ludwigshafen.she.de, harald.kuehne@ludwigshafen.de. Ed. Harald Kuehne. Adv. contact Volker Adam. Circ: 500.

352.14 DEU ISSN 1437-8353
BERLINER BEHOERDEN SPIEGEL; unabhaengige Zeitung fuer den oeffentlichen Dienst. Text in German. 1984. m. looseleaf. EUR 38; EUR 1.50 newsstand/cover (effective 2011). adv. bibl. back issues avail. **Document type:** *Newspaper, Trade.*
Related titles: ◆ Regional ed(s).: Behoerden Spiegel. ISSN 1437-8337.
Published by: ProPress Verlag GmbH, Am Buschhof 8, Bonn, 53227, Germany. TEL 49-228-970970, FAX 49-228-9709775.

352 DEU ISSN 1610-949X
BERLINER BEITRAEGE ZUR VERWALTUNGSPOLITIK. Text in German. 2002. irreg., latest vol.2, 2007. price varies. **Document type:** *Monographic series, Academic/Scholarly.*
Published by: Weissensee Verlag e.K., Simplonstr 59, Berlin, 10245, Germany. TEL 49-30-29049192, FAX 49-30-27574315, mail@weissensee-verlag.de.

352.14 DEU ISSN 0933-4343
BERLINFOERDERUNGSGESETZ. Text in German. 1973. base vol. plus irreg. updates. looseleaf. EUR 49.80 base vol(s). (effective 2009). **Document type:** *Monographic series, Trade.*
Published by: Erich Schmidt Verlag GmbH & Co. (Berlin), Genthiner Str 30 G, Berlin, 10785, Germany. TEL 49-30-2500850, FAX 49-30-250085305, vertrieb@esvmedien.de, http://www.erich-schmidt-verlag.de.

352.14 CHE
BERNISCHE STAATSPERSONAL ZEITUNG. Text in German. 11/yr.
Published by: Bernische Staatspersonal Verband, Postgasse 60, Bern, 3011, Switzerland. TEL 031-221166. Ed. Kurt Niklaus. Circ: 7,800.

352.14 DEU
BETRIFFT. Text in German. 1986. q. **Document type:** *Magazine, Government.*
Formerly: Wir Bei Der Stadt
Published by: Stadt Nuernberg, Presse- und Informationsamt, Rathaus, Rathausplatz 2, Nuernberg, 90317, Germany. TEL 49-911-2312372, FAX 49-911-2313660. Ed. Dr. Wolfgang Stoeckel. Circ: 15,000.

352 PRT ISSN 1646-0405
BIBLIOAMBIENTE. Text in Portuguese. 2004. q. **Document type:** *Magazine, Consumer.*

Published by: Camara Municipal de Viana do Castelo, Passeio das Mordomas da Romania, Viana do Castelo, Portugal. http://www.cm-viana-castelo.pt.

LES BIOGRAPHIES.COM. LE CONSEIL DE PARIS. *see* BIOGRAPHY

352.14 SWE ISSN 0281-5680
BLEKINGETINGET; personaltidning foer Landstinget Blekinge. Text in Swedish. 1968. bi-m.
Published by: Landstinget Blekinge, Karlskrona, 37181, Sweden.

352.14 ZAF ISSN 0006-4939
BLOEMFONTEIN NUUSBRIEF/BLOEMFONTEIN NEWSLETTER. Text in Afrikaans, English. 1965. m. free. illus.; stat.; tr.lit. index. **Document type:** *Newsletter.*
Published by: Public Relations Officer, PO Box 639, Bloemfontein, South Africa. Circ: 30,500.

352 CAN ISSN 1922-4826
▼ **BOARD OF DIRECTORS PROGRESS REPORT.** Text in English. 2009. s-a. free (effective 2010). back issues avail. **Document type:** *Report, Trade.*
Published by: Enterprise Saskatchewan, 303 Wicklow Ctr, 1133 - 4th St, Estevan, SK S4A 0W6, Canada. TEL 306-637-4505, FAX 306-637-4510, John.Slatnik@enterprisesask.ca.

352 CAN ISSN 1922-4834
▼ **BOARD OF DIRECTORS PROGRESS REPORT. HIGHLIGHTS.** Text in English. 2009. s-a. free (effective 2010). **Document type:** *Report, Trade.*
Published by: Enterprise Saskatchewan, 303 Wicklow Ctr, 1133 - 4th St, Estevan, SK S4A 0W6, Canada. TEL 306-637-4505, FAX 306-637-4510, John.Slatnik@enterprisesask.ca.

352 DEU ISSN 1617-4062
BOCHUMER VOLKSWIRTSCHAFTSLEHRE. Text in German. 2001. irreg., latest vol.2, 2004. price varies. **Document type:** *Monographic series, Academic/Scholarly.*
Published by: Bochumer Universitaetsverlag GmbH, Querenburger Hoehe 281, Bochum, 44801, Germany. TEL 49-234-9719780, FAX 49-234-9719786, bou@bou.de, http://bou.de.

352 PRT ISSN 1646-3196
BOLETIM CULTURAL DE VILA VERDE. Text in Portuguese. 2005. irreg. **Document type:** *Magazine, Consumer.*
Published by: Camara Municipal de Vila Verde, Praca do Municipio, Vila Verde, 4730-733, Portugal. TEL 351-253-310500, FAX 351-253-312036, geral@cm-vilaverde.pt, http://www.cm-vilaverde.pt.

352 ESP ISSN 2013-262X
BOLETIN DE ESTUDIOS AUTONOMICOS. Text in Spanish. 2005. 3/yr. back issues avail. **Document type:** *Bulletin, Consumer.*
Media: Online - full text. **Related titles:** ◆ Catalan ed.: Butleti d'Estudis Autonomics. ISSN 2013-0538; ◆ English ed.: I E A Newsletter. ISSN 2013-2700.
Published by: Generalitat de Catalunya, Institut d'Estudios Autonomics, Baixada de Sant Miquel, 8, Barcelona, 08002, Spain. TEL 34-93-3429821, FAX 34-93-3429801, iea.ri@gencat.cat, http://www.gencat.cat/.

352 ESP ISSN 1989-8959
▼ **BOLETIN OFICIAL DE CASTILLA Y LEON.** Text in Spanish. 2010. d. (Mon.-Fri.). back issues avail. **Document type:** *Bulletin, Government.*
Media: Online - full text.
Published by: Junta de Castilla y Leon, Consejeria de la Presidencia, C Santiago Alba 1, Valladolid, 47008, Spain. publicacionesbocy@jcyl.es, http://www.jcyl.es/.

352.14 USA ISSN 0006-7946
BOSTON CITY RECORD. Text in English. 1898. w. USD 50 (effective 2007). adv. charts. **Document type:** *Newsletter, Government.* **Description:** Presents municipal news, public notices and advertisements of invitations for sealed bids and proposals for all purchases of materials and services estimated to exceed $10,000 in value.
Published by: City of Boston, Boston City Hall, Rm. 206, Boston, MA 02201-1001. TEL 617-635-4000, FAX 617-635-3501, bob.malovich@ci.boston.ma.us, http://www.cityofboston.gov. Circ: 52.

352.14 AUT ISSN 0006-8225
BOTE FUER TIROL; Amtsblatt der Behoerden Aemter und Gerichte Tirols. Text in German. 1817. w. EUR 23 (effective 2005). index. **Document type:** *Government.*
Published by: Amt der Tiroler Landesregierung, Eduard-Wallnoefer-Platz 3, Innsbruck, T 6020, Austria. TEL 43-512-5082182, FAX 43-512-5082185, landeskanzleidirektion@tirol.gv.at, http://www.tirol.gv.at/organisation/landeskanzleidirektion.shtml. Ed. Alois Soraperra. Circ: 2,700.

352.14 FRA ISSN 1762-0589
DC14
BOTTIN DES COMMUNES ET DE L'INTERCOMMUNALITE. Text in French. 1978. a. **Document type:** *Monographic series, Trade.*
Former titles (until 2001): Bottin Communes (0406-8769)
Related titles: CD-ROM ed.: ISSN 1625-9572. 2000.
Published by: LexisNexis JurisClasseur, Relation Clients, 141 rue de Javel, Paris, Cedex 15 75747, France. TEL 33-1-45589200, FAX 33-1-45589400, relation.clients@lexisnexis.fr, http://www.lexisnexis.fr/lexisnexisjurisclasseur/juris_liste_revue.htm.

BRABANTS MEERJARENPROGRAMMA INFRASTRUCTUUR EN TRANSPORT. *see* TRANSPORTATION

352 NLD ISSN 1872-4019
BRABANTSTAD IN ONTWIKKELING. Text in Dutch. 200?. a.
Published by: Nederland in Ontwikkeling, Het Nieuwe Diep 33, Den Helder, 1781 AD, Netherlands. TEL 31-223-674080, FAX 31-223-674089, http://www.nederlandinontwikkeling.nl.

352 GBR ISSN 0305-8727
DA690.B8
BRISTOL RECORD SOCIETY. PUBLICATIONS. Text in English. 1930. a., latest vol.60, 2008. free to members (effective 2009). back issues avail. **Document type:** *Journal, Academic/Scholarly.* **Description:** Features Bristol charters and documents relating to trade, the port, ships, the traffic in slaves, the government of the city, ecclesiastical history, legal proceedings and social life in the city.
Indexed: PCI.
Published by: University of West England, Bristol Record Society, c/o Dr. Jonathan Harlow, St. Matthias Campus, Oldbury Ct Rd, Fishponds, Bristol, BS16 3JP, United Kingdom. TEL 44-1454-775731, Jonathan.Harlow@uwe.ac.uk, http://www.bris.ac.uk/Depts/History/bristolrecordsociety/index.htm. Ed. E S George.

BRITISH COLUMBIA DECISIONS - MUNICIPAL LAW CASES. *see* LAW

352.14 CAN
BRITISH COLUMBIA. MINISTRY OF MUNICIPAL AFFAIRS, RECREATION AND HOUSING. MUNICIPAL MANUAL. Text in English. base vol. plus irreg. updates. looseleaf. CAD 52. **Document type:** *Government.*
Formerly: British Columbia. Ministry of Municipal Affairs, Recreation and Culture. Municipal Manual
Published by: Ministry of Municipal Affairs, Recreation and Housing, Victoria, BC, Canada. **Subscr. to:** Crown Publications Inc. TEL 250-386-4636, FAX 250-386-0221, crown@pinc.com, http://www.crownpub.bc.ca.

BRITISH COLUMBIA. MINISTRY OF MUNICIPAL AFFAIRS, RECREATION AND HOUSING. MUNICIPAL STATISTICS, INCLUDING REGIONAL DISTRICTS. *see* PUBLIC ADMINISTRATION—Abstracting, Bibliographies, Statistics

352.8 CAN ISSN 1492-7152
JL429.5.O4
BRITISH COLUMBIA. OFFICE OF THE OMBUDSMAN. ANNUAL REPORT. Text in English. 1979. a.
Former titles (until 1999): Ombudsreport (1200-538X); (until 1993): British Columbia. Office of the Ombudsman. Annual Report of the Ombudsman (1195-3373); (until 1992): Province of British Columbia. Ombudsman. Annual Report to the Legislative Assembly (0835-5428); (until 1986): Legislative Assembly of British Columbia. Ombudsman. Annual Report of the Ombudsman to the Legislative Assembly of British Columbia (0713-2921); (until 1981): Annual Report of the Ombudsman to the Legislature of British Columbia (0226-8930)
Published by: Office of the Ombudsman, PO Box 9039, Stn Prov Govt, Victoria, BC V8W 9A5, Canada. TEL 250-387-5855, FAX 250-387-0198.

352 USA
THE BRONX REPORT; a message from Bronx Borough President. Text in English, Spanish. q. free. **Document type:** *Government.*
Published by: Office of Borough President Fernando Ferrer, The Bronx County Bldg, 851 Grand Concourse, Bronx, NY 10451. Ed. Clint Roswell.

BUCKS COUNTY PLANNING COMMISSION. PLANNING PROGRESS. *see* HOUSING AND URBAN PLANNING

352.14 DNK ISSN 1903-2684
BUDGETOVERSIGT. Text in Danish. 1980. a. back issues avail. **Document type:** *Trade.*
Supersedes in part (in 2006): Kommunal Budgetredegoerelse (0107-5098)
Related titles: Online - full text ed.: ISSN 1903-2692. 2001.
Published by: (Kommunernes Landsforening/National Association of Local Authorities in Denmark), Kommuneforlaget A/S (Subsidiary of: Kommuneinformation A/S), Holmens Kanal 7, Copenhagen K, 1060, Denmark. TEL 45-33-280300, FAX 45-33-280302, post@kommuneforlaget.dk, http://www.kommuneforlaget.dk. Ed. Lone Kjaer Knudsen.

BUILDING SAFETY JOURNAL; the professional journal of construction and fire safety. *see* BUILDING AND CONSTRUCTION

352 ESP ISSN 2013-0538
BUTLETI D'ESTUDIS AUTONOMICS. Text in Catalan. 2005. 3/yr. back issues avail. **Document type:** *Bulletin, Consumer.*
Media: Online - full text. **Related titles:** ◆ Spanish ed.: Boletin de Estudios Autonomicos. ISSN 2013-262X; ◆ English ed.: I E A Newsletter. ISSN 2013-2700.
Published by: Generalitat de Catalunya, Institut d'Estudios Autonomics, Baixada de Sant Miquel, 8, Barcelona, 08002, Spain. TEL 34-93-3429821, FAX 34-93-3429801, iea.ri@gencat.cat, http://www.gencat.cat/.

352 ESP ISSN 2013-2069
BUTLLETI PARTICIPACIO CIUTADANA. Text in Catalan. 2008. m. **Document type:** *Bulletin, Consumer.*
Media: Online - full text.
Published by: Generalitat de Catalunya, Direccio General de Participaio Ciutadana, Ave Diagonal, 409 4a., Barcelona, 08008, Spain. TEL 34-93-5526000, FAX 34-93-5526070, dgparticipacio.ri@gencat.cat, http://www10.gencat.cat/drep/AppJava/cat/ambits/participacio/index.jsp.

352 PRT ISSN 1646-9089
C E A M A REVISTA. (Centro de Estudos de Arquitectura Militar Almeida) Text in Portuguese. 2008. s-a. **Document type:** *Magazine, Consumer.*
Published by: Camata Municipal de Almeida, Praca da Liberdade, Almeida, 6350-130, Portugal. http://www.cm-almeida.pt.

352.14 FRA ISSN 0753-4418
LES CAHIERS DE LA FONCTION PUBLIQUE ET DE L'ADMINISTRATION. Text in French. 1982. m. EUR 138 (effective 2009). **Document type:** *Journal, Trade.*
Indexed: FR, IBSS.
Published by: Berger-Levrault Editions, 525 Rue Andre Ampere, Logistique Est, B P 79, Champigneulles, 54250, France. TEL 33-3-83388383, FAX 33-3-83388610, blc@berger-levrault.fr, http://www.berger-levrault.fr. Circ: 1,500.

352.14 IND ISSN 0008-0675
CALCUTTA MUNICIPAL GAZETTE. Text in Bengali, English. 1924. fortn.
Published by: Calcutta Municipal Corporation, Superintendent of Printing, 5 Surendranath Banarjee Rd, Kolkata, West Bengal 700 013, India. TEL 91-33-22861000, FAX 91-33-22861444, https://www.kmcgov.in.

342.09 USA ISSN 0743-0868
CALIFORNIA COUNTRY. Text in English. 1985. bi-m. USD 6 to non-members; free to members (effective 2005). adv. 52 p./no. 3 cols./p.; **Document type:** *Magazine, Government.* **Description:** Contains information on California county practices, public finance, social services, information technology, public works and economic development, administration of justice, environmental resources, and state and federal legislation.
Published by: California Farm Bureau Federation, 2300 River Plaza Dr, Sacramento, CA 95833-3293. TEL 916-561-5550, FAX 916-561-5695. Ed. Steve Adler. Pub. Ann Smith. Adv. contact Dennis Duncan. B&W page USD 1,700; trim 8.5 x 11. Circ: 7,300 (controlled).

342.09 USA
CALIFORNIA STATE ASSOCIATION OF COUNTIES LEGISLATIVE BULLETIN. Text in English. w. USD 30 to non-members; USD 10 to members. 36 p./no.; **Document type:** *Bulletin, Government.* **Description:** Offers current information on key legislation affecting counties. Reports on both state and federal legislative issues and also provides information on upcoming meetings.
Related titles: E-mail ed.; Fax ed.
Published by: California State Association of Counties, 1100 K St, Ste 101, Sacramento, CA 95814. TEL 916-327-7500, FAX 916-441-5507, http://www.csac.counties.org. Eds. Allison Smith, Susan Hyman.

352 PRT ISSN 1645-0701
CAMARA MUNICIPAL DA AMADORA. BALANCO SOCIAL. Text in Portuguese. 199?. irreg. **Document type:** *Report, Government.*
Published by: Camara Municipal da Amadora, Av Movimento das Forcas Armadas, Mina, 2700-595, Portugal. TEL 351-214-369000, FAX 351-214-922082, geral@cm-amadora.pt, http://www.cm-amadora.pt.

352 PRT ISSN 1646-5369
CAMARA MUNICIPAL DE CALHETA. BOLETIM INFORMATIVO. Text in Portuguese. 2002. s-a. **Document type:** *Magazine, Consumer.*
Published by: Camara Municipal de Calheta, Av Dom Manuel I, 46, Calheta, 9370-135, Portugal. camara@cm-calheta-madeira.com, http://www.cm-calheta-madeira.com.

352 PRT ISSN 1645-5053
CAMARA MUNICIPAL DE MELGACO. BOLETIM CULTURAL. Text in Portuguese. 2002. irreg. **Document type:** *Magazine, Consumer.*
Published by: Camara Municipal de Melgaco, Largo Hermenegildo Solheiro, Melgaco, 4960-551, Portugal. TEL 351-251-410100, FAX 351-251-402429, geral@cm-melgaco.pt, http://www.cm-melgaco.pt.

352 PRT ISSN 1645-7218
CAMARA MUNICIPAL DO MONTIJO. REVISTA. Text in Portuguese. 2008. q. **Document type:** *Magazine, Consumer.*
Formerly (until 200?): Boletim Municipal (1647-8479)
Published by: Camara Municipal do Montijo, Edificio dos Pacos do Concelho, Rua Manuel Neves Nunes de Almeida, Montijo, 2870-352, Portugal. TEL 351-21-2327600, FAX 351-21-2327608, geral@mun-montijo.pt, http://www.mun-montijo.pt.

P

352.9 AUS ISSN 1838-4501
▼ **CAMPAIGN ADVERTISING BY AUSTRALIAN GOVERNMENT DEPARTMENTS AND AGENCIES. FULL YEAR REPORT.** Text in English. 2009. a. free (effective 2011). back issues avail. **Document type:** *Report, Government.* **Description:** Covers the full financial year and provides data on both direct media placement expenditure and associated indirect campaign advertising expenditure.
Related titles: Online - full text ed.: ISSN 1838-451X. free (effective 2011).
Published by: Australian Government, Department of Finance and Deregulation, John Gorton Bldg, King Edward Terr, Parkes, ACT 2600, Australia. TEL 61-2-62152222, mediaenquiries@finance.gov.au.

352.14 USA ISSN 1086-1114
JS414
CARROLL'S COUNTY DIRECTORY. Text in English. 1984. s-a. USD 425 (effective 2011). **Document type:** *Directory, Government.* **Description:** Directory of over 42,000 county officials and administrators in approximately 3100 counties listed by state.
Formerly (until 1995): County Executive Directory (0742-1702)
Related titles: CD-ROM ed.: USD 630 (effective 1999); Online - full text ed.: ISSN 1944-3595.
Published by: Carroll Publishing, 4701 Sangamore Rd, Ste S 155, Bethesda, MD 20816. TEL 800-336-4240, 800-336-4240, FAX 301-263-9801, info@carrollpub.com.

352.14 USA ISSN 1083-933X
JS363
CARROLL'S MUNICIPAL DIRECTORY. Text in English. 1984. s-a. USD 425 (effective 2011). **Document type:** *Directory, Government.* **Description:** Directory of nearly 48,000 key officials in the municipal governments of the United States.
Formerly (until 1995): Municipal Executive Directory (0742-1710)
Related titles: CD-ROM ed.: ISSN 1521-317X; Online - full text ed.: ISSN 1944-3587. USD 630 (effective 1999).
Published by: Carroll Publishing, 4701 Sangamore Rd, Ste S 155, Bethesda, MD 20816. TEL 800-336-4240, FAX 301-263-9801, info@carrollpub.com.

352.14 USA
CARROLL'S MUNICIPAL DIRECTORY. ANNUAL. Text in English. a. USD 295 per issue (effective 2004). **Document type:** *Directory, Government.*
Published by: Carroll Publishing, 4701 Sangamore Rd, Ste S 155, Bethesda, MD 20816. TEL 800-336-4240, 800-336-4240, FAX 301-263-9801, info@carrollpub.com, http://www.carrollpub.com.

352.14025 USA ISSN 1082-1929
JK2482.E94
CARROLL'S STATE DIRECTORY. Text in English. 1980. 3/yr. USD 425 (effective 2011). **Document type:** *Directory, Government.* **Description:** Directory of more than 47,000 key officials in executive, legislative and judicial branches of state governments in the United States.
Formerly (until 1995): State Executive Directory (0276-7163)
Related titles: CD-ROM ed.: USD 530 (effective 1999); Online - full text ed.: ISSN 1944-3609.
Published by: Carroll Publishing, 4701 Sangamore Rd, Ste S 155, Bethesda, MD 20816. TEL 800-336-4240, FAX 301-263-9801, info@carrollpub.com.

352.14029 USA ISSN 1093-2070
JK2482.E94
CARROLL'S STATE DIRECTORY (YEAR) ANNUAL. Text in English. 1983. a. USD 295 per issue (effective 2004). **Document type:** *Directory, Government.* **Description:** Includes more than 43,000 contacts with name, office address and phone number in the executive, legislative, and judicial branches of state government.

Formerly (until 1995): State Executive Directory Annual (1056-7011); Which superseded in part (in 1991): Federal/State Executive Directory (0887-4727); Which was formerly (until 1984): Annual Federal/State Executive Directory (0734-4651)
Published by: Carroll Publishing, 4701 Sangamore Rd, Ste S 155, Bethesda, MD 20816. TEL 800-336-4240, 800-336-4240, FAX 301-263-9801, info@carrollpub.com, http://www.carrollpub.com.

352 NZL ISSN 1171-7467
CARTERTON DISTRICT COUNCIL. ANNUAL REPORT. Text in English. 1990. a.
Related titles: Online - full text ed.: ISSN 1177-9535.
Published by: Carterton District Council, Holloway St, PO Box 9, Carterton, New Zealand. TEL 64-6-3796626, FAX 64-6-3797832.

352.14 ITA
CASTEL BOLOGNESE NOTIZIE. Text in Italian. 1981. bi-m. free. 8 p./no. 4 cols./p.; back issues avail. **Document type:** *Newspaper, Consumer.* **Description:** Presents information on the local administration and its activities.
Formerly (until 2001): Castel Bolognese Notizie (Print)
Media: Online - full text.
Published by: Comune di Castel Bolognese, Piazza Bernardi 1, Castel Bolognese, RA 48014, Italy. http://www.comune.castelbolognese.ra.it. Ed., Adv. contact Maria Merenda. Circ: 3,500 (paid).

CAYMAN ISLANDS GAZETTE. *see* LAW

352 600 CHN ISSN 1008-2271
CHENGSHI GUANLI YU KEJI/MUNICIPAL ADMINISTRATION & TECHOLOGY. Text in Chinese. 1999. bi-m. USD 37.20 (effective 2009). **Document type:** *Journal, Academic/Scholarly.*
Related titles: Online - full text ed.
—East View.
Published by: Beijing Shi Shizheng Guanli Weiyuanhui, Xicheng-qu, 3, Sanlihe Beijiejia, Beijing, 100045, China. TEL 86-10-68529005. **Dist. by:** China International Book Trading Corp, 35 Chegongzhuang Xilu, Haidian District, PO Box 399, Beijing 100044, China. TEL 86-10-68412045, FAX 86-10-68412023, cibtc@mail.cibtc.com.cn, http://www.cibtc.com.cn.

352 NZL ISSN 1171-3224
CHRISTCHURCH CITY COUNCIL. ANNUAL REPORT. Text in English. a.
Formerly (until 1991): Christchurch City Council. Annual Financial Statement
Related titles: Online - full text ed.: ISSN 1177-9691.
Published by: Christchurch City Council, Civic Offices, 163-173 Tuam St, PO Box 237, Christchurch, 8011, New Zealand. TEL 64-3-9418999, FAX 64-3-9418786, info@ccc.govt.nz.

352 PRT ISSN 1646-169X
CIRA. Text in Portuguese. 1985. irreg. **Document type:** *Report, Consumer.*
Published by: Camara Municipal de Vila Franca de Xira, Praca Afonso de Albuquerque 2, Vila Franca de Xira, 2600-093, Portugal. TEL 351-263-285600.

352.14 GBR ISSN 0264-2751
HT119
➤ **CITIES**; the international journal of urban policy and planning. Text in English. 1983. bi-m. EUR 1,087 in Europe to institutions; JPY 144,200 in Japan to institutions; USD 1,215 elsewhere to institutions (effective 2012). adv. bk.rev. abstr.; illus. index. back issues avail.; reprints avail. **Document type:** *Journal, Academic/Scholarly.* **Description:** Focuses on the policies and technologies affecting urban environments and on the social, psychological and physical impact of planning policies.
Related titles: Microform ed.: (from PQC); Online - full text ed.: ISSN 1873-6084 (from IngentaConnect, ScienceDirect).
Indexed: A01, A03, A08, A20, A22, A26, AIAP, B01, B06, B07, B09, CA, CurCont, E04, E05, EIP, ESPM, EnvAb, EnvInd, GEOBASE, HPNRM, I05, IBSS, P30, P34, P42, PAIS, PCI, PSA, S02, S03, SCOPUS, SOPODA, SSA, SSCI, SSciA, SUSA, SociolAb, T02, W07.
—BLDSC (3267.792160), IE, Infotrieve, Ingenta. **CCC.**
Published by: Pergamon (Subsidiary of: Elsevier Science & Technology), The Blvd, Langford Ln, East Park, Kidlington, Oxford OX5 1GB, United Kingdom. TEL 44-1865-843434, FAX 44-1865-843970, JournalsCustomerServiceEMEA@elsevier.com. Ed. A Modarres. **Subscr. to:** Elsevier BV, Radarweg 29, PO Box 211, Amsterdam 1000 AE, Netherlands. TEL 31-20-4853757, FAX 31-20-4853432.

➤ **CITIES AND VILLAGES.** *see* HOUSING AND URBAN PLANNING

352.14 USA ISSN 1055-7814
CITIZEN PARTICIPATION. Text in English. 1957. q. **Document type:** *Magazine, Consumer.*
Former titles (until 1991): Greater Cleveland (1040-9122); (until 1987): The Citizens League of Greater Cleveland (0888-5435); (until 1985): The Citizens League's Greater Cleveland (0746-9209)
—CCC.
Published by: The Citizens League of Greater Cleveland, 1331 Euclid Ave, Cleveland, OH 44115. TEL 216-241-5340, FAX 216-736-7626, staff@citizensleague.org, http://www.citizensleague.org.

352.14 USA ISSN 0009-756X
CITIZENS' BUSINESS. Text in English. 1910. irreg. stat.
Published by: Economy League of Greater Philadelphia, 1700 Market St, Ste 3130, Philadelphia, PA 19103. TEL 215-563-3640, FAX 215-563-1566, http://www.economyleague.org. Circ: 3,000.

352.14 USA ISSN 0193-8371
JS303.A8
CITY & TOWN. Text in English. 1947. m. USD 20; USD 1.67 newsstand/cover (effective 2009). adv. bk.rev. illus. Index. 40 p./no. 2 cols./p.; reprints avail. **Document type:** *Magazine, Trade.* **Description:** Contains articles, information, documents, laws and other data about cities. Educates and informs municipal leaders, elected officials, supervisors about municipal affairs to help them govern, operate, and administer cities and towns effectively and efficiently.
Formerly: Arkansas Municipalities (0004-1866)
Published by: Arkansas Municipal League, PO Box 38, North Little Rock, AR 72115-0038. jkw@arml.org. Ed. Andrew Morgan. adv.: B&W page USD 375, color page USD 555. Circ: 6,800 (paid and free).

352.14 USA
CITY CLUB GADFLY. Text in English. 1959. m. free. bk.rev.
Formerly (until May 1978): City Club Comments (0009-7721)
Published by: City Club of New York, 17 Lexington Ave, PO Box F-2003, New York, NY 10010. TEL 212-207-3676, FAX 212-752-2934, cityclubofny@nycmail.com. Ed. Peter Rosenblatt. Circ: 2,500 (controlled).

352.14 USA ISSN 1936-0088
HJ9011
CITY FISCAL CONDITIONS IN (YEAR). Text in English. 1983. a. USD 30 (effective 2000). back issues avail. **Document type:** *Report, Trade.* **Description:** Contains survey of trends in city revenues and expenditures.
Former titles (until 1985): City Fiscal Conditions and Outlook for Fiscal (Year); (until 1983): City Fiscal Conditions in (Year)
Indexed: SRI.
Published by: National League of Cities, 1301 Pennsylvania Ave, N W, Ste 550, Washington, DC 20004. TEL 202-626-3150. R&P Mae Davis TEL 202-626-3000.

352.14 USA
CITY HALL. Text in English. 2006. 22/yr. USD 48 (effective 2009). **Document type:** *Newspaper, Consumer.* **Description:** Covers "the inner workings" of city and state government politics.
Published by: Manhattan Media, LLC, 63 W 38th St, Ste 206, New York, NY 10018. TEL 212-268-8600, FAX 212-268-9049, information@manhattanmedia.com. Circ: 21,000 (controlled).

352 NLD ISSN 1574-8782
CITY JOURNAL. Text in Dutch. 2005. 3/yr. free (effective 2010).
Published by: (Kenniscentrum Grote Steden), Netherlands Institute for City Innovation Studies, Postbus 90750, The Hague, 2509 LT, Netherlands. TEL 31-70-3440966, FAX 31-70-3440967, info@nicis.nl. Eds. Susanne Schippers, Nienke Ledegang. Circ: 6,200. **Co-publisher:** Kenniscentrum Grote Steden.

CITY MAYORS; running the world's cities. *see* POLITICAL SCIENCE

352.14 SWE
CITY OF STOCKHOLM. ANNUAL FINANCIAL REPORT (YEAR). Text in Swedish. a.
Published by: City of Stockholm Kammarkontor, City Hall, Stockholm, 10535, Sweden. TEL 46 8 785 91 83.

352.14 USA
CITY RECORD; official journal of the City of New York. Text in English. d. (Mon.-Fri.). USD 400 (effective 2006). charts; stat. **Document type:** *Newspaper, Government.* **Description:** Contains notices from New York City agencies on public hearings and meetings, court notices, property disposition, procurement solicitation and awards, agency rules, and special material which includes changes in personnel.
Published by: New York City Department of Citywide Administrative Services, 2208 Municipal Bldg., New York, NY 10007. TEL 212-639-9675. Ed., R&P Eli Blachman.

352.14 USA ISSN 1094-5784
JS451.N95
CITY SCAN (BISMARCK). Text in English. 1969. 10/yr. free to qualified personnel. adv. charts; illus. **Document type:** *Bulletin, Government.*
Formerly (until 1996): North Dakota League of Cities Bulletin (0279-800X)
Published by: North Dakota League of Cities, 410 E. Front Ave., Bismarck, ND 58504. TEL 701-223-3518, 800-472-2692, FAX 701-223-5174, http://www.ndlc.org/. Ed. Connie Sprynczynatyk. R&P, Adv. contact Jan Jordan. Circ: 2,850.

CITYSCAPE (DES MOINES). *see* HOUSING AND URBAN PLANNING

352.14 MEX ISSN 0187-8611
HT127.7
➤ **CIUDADES**; analisis de la coyuntura, teoria y historia urbana. Text in Spanish. 1989. q. MXN 70 domestic; USD 35 in the Americas; USD 45 elsewhere (effective 2006). adv. bk.rev. back issues avail. **Document type:** *Journal, Academic/Scholarly.*
Indexed: C01.
Published by: Red Nacional de Investigacion Urbana, Av. Maximino Avila Camacho 208, Puebla, 72000, Mexico. TEL 52-22-462832, FAX 52-22-324506. Ed., Adv. contact Elsa Patino Tovar. Circ: 2,000.

352 PRT ISSN 1647-0400
CLUBE SENIOR. Text in Portuguese. 2008. s-a. **Document type:** *Magazine, Consumer.*
Published by: Camara Municipal de Torres Vedras, Rua Santos Bernardes, Torres Vedras, Portugal. http://www.cm-tvedras.pt.

352 ESP ISSN 1889-9803
▼ **COLECCION BICENTENARIO 1808-2010.** Text in Spanish. 2009. irreg. back issues avail. **Document type:** *Monographic series, Government.*
Published by: Ayuntamiento de San Fernando, C Isaac Peral, 11 y 13, San Fernando, Andalucia 11100, Spain. TEL 34-956-944000, FAX 34-956-944458, oac@aytosanfernando.org, http://www.aytosanfernando.org/.

342.09 USA
COLORADO LAWS ENACTED AFFECTING MUNICIPAL GOVERNMENTS. Text in English. 19??. a. USD 40 to non-members; USD 20 to members (effective 2011). **Document type:** *Government.* **Description:** Presents selected laws of broad municipal interest that were enacted by the Colorado General Assembly.
Published by: Colorado Municipal League, 1144 Sherman St, Denver, CO 80203. TEL 303-831-6411, FAX 303-860-8175, cml@cml.org, http://www.cml.org.

352.14 USA ISSN 0010-1664
JS39
COLORADO MUNICIPALITIES. Text in English. 1925. bi-m. USD 150; USD 25 per issue (effective 2011). adv. bk.rev. illus. index, cum.index. **Document type:** *Magazine, Consumer.* **Description:** Presents articles on current interests and concerns of municipal officials, in Colorado, activities of Colorado municipalities and individuals involved in municipal government.
Indexed: P06.
—Ingenta.
Published by: Colorado Municipal League, 1144 Sherman St, Denver, CO 80203. TEL 303-831-6411, FAX 303-860-8175, cml@cml.org. Ed. Traci Stoffel TEL 303-831-6411. Adv. contact Lisa White.

352 NLD ISSN 1879-6176
▼ **COMBINATIEFUNCTIES.NL.** Text in Dutch. 2009. a. EUR 14.95 (effective 2010).
Related titles: Online - full text ed.: ISSN 1879-6184.
Published by: Vereniging Sport en Gemeenten, Postbus 103, Oosterbeek, 6860 AC, Netherlands. TEL 31-26-3396410, FAX 31-26-3396412, info@sportengemeenten.nl, http://www.sportengemeenten.nl.

352 CAN ISSN 1709-6235
COMMISSION MUNICIPALE DU QUEBEC. RAPPORT ANNUEL DE GESTION. Text in French. 1979. a.
Formerly (until 2001): Commission Municipale du Quebec. Rapport Annuel (0229-8139)
Published by: Commission Municipale du Quebec, Edifice Thais-Lacoste-Fremont, 10, rue Pierre-Olivier-Chauveau, Tour, 5e etage, Quebec, PQ G1R 4J3, Canada. TEL 418-691-2014, FAX 418-644-4676, cmq@mamm.gouv.qc.ca, http://www.cmq.gouv.qc.ca.

352 AUS ISSN 1836-0394
➤ **COMMONWEALTH JOURNAL OF LOCAL GOVERNANCE.** Text in English. 2008 (May). s-a. free (effective 2011). back issues avail. **Document type:** *Journal, Academic/Scholarly.* **Description:** Contains articles on local government ideas and practices within the sector, focusing on the themes of: Improving local governance and local government as an agent of development.
Media: Online - full text.
Indexed: A01, T02.
Published by: University of Technology, Sydney, Centre For Local Government, PO Box 123, Broadway, NSW 2007, Australia. TEL 61-2-95147884, FAX 61-2-95142274, http://www.clg.uts.edu.au/. Ed. Graham Sansom.

352.190 FRA ISSN 1775-0105
COMMUNAUTE DE COMMUNES DE LA HAUTE SEVRE. BULLETIN D'INFORMATION. Text in French. 1999. 3/yr. **Document type:** *Bulletin, Consumer.*
Published by: Communaute de Communes de la Haute Sevre, 1 rue du Minage, La Mothe Saint-Heray, 79800, France.

352.190 FRA ISSN 1775-7878
COMMUNAUTE DE COMMUNES DE L'ARENTELE, DURBION, PADOZEL. BULLETIN. Variant title: Bulletin d'Informations Communautaires. Text in French. 2005. a. **Document type:** *Bulletin, Consumer.*
Published by: Mairie de Gugnecourt, 411 Grande Rue, Gugnecourt, Girecourt-sur-Durbion, 88600, France.

352.190 FRA ISSN 1774-5462
COMMUNAUTE DE COMMUNES DU PAYS DE LUNEL. BULLETIN. Text in French. 1998. q. **Document type:** *Bulletin, Consumer.*
Formerly (until 2005): Pays de Lunel (1625-8266)
Published by: Mairie de Lunel, 386 av des Abrivados, Lunel, 34401 Cedex 1, France.

352.14 FRA ISSN 1142-5083
COMMUNES FORESTIERES DE FRANCE. Text in French. 1931. q. EUR 38 (effective 2009). adv. **Document type:** *Journal.*
Former titles (until 1974): Federation Nationale des Communes Forestieres de France. Bulletin Officiel (1142-5091); (until 1972): Federation des Communes Forestieres Francaises. Bulletin Officiel (1142-5105); (until 1959): Federation des Associations de Communes Forestieres Francaises. Bulletin Officiel (1142-5113)
Published by: Federation Nationale des Communes Forestieres de France, 13 rue du General Bertrand, Paris, 75007, France. TEL 33-1-45674798, FAX 33-1-45672599, info@fncofor.fr, http://portail.fncofor.fr. Ed. Brigitte Deshaires. Circ: 11,000.

354.75 FRA ISSN 1953-4884
LA COMMUNICATION DES COLLECTIVITES TERRITORIALES. Text in French. 2006. base vol. plus q. updates. looseleaf. EUR 127.96 base vol(s). (effective 2010). **Document type:** *Trade.*
Published by: Editions Dalian (Subsidiary of: Wolters Kluwer France), 1 Rue Eugene et Armand Peugeot, B P 720, Rueil Malmaison, 92856 Cedex, France. TEL 33-8-25080800, FAX 33-1-76734802, dalian@dalian.tm.fr, http://www.editions-dalian.fr/.

352 AUS ISSN 1838-3106
▼ **COMPLIANCE NEWS. INDEPENDENT NEWS FOR LOCAL GOVERNMENT.** Text in English. 2010. w. AUD 1,200 combined subscription (online & email eds.) (effective 2011). **Document type:** *Newsletter, Trade.* **Description:** Provides news and analysis impacting on the local government sector.
Media: Online - full text. **Related titles:** E-mail ed.
Published by: Thomson Reuters (Professional) Australia Limited (Subsidiary of: Thomson Reuters Corp.), PO Box 3502, Rozelle, NSW 2039, Australia. TEL 61-2-85877980, FAX 61-2-85877981, LTA.Service@thomsonreuters.com.

352 ITA ISSN 1724-207X
COMUNE DI SASSUOLO. Text in Italian. 1980. m. **Document type:** *Magazine, Consumer.*
Address: Via Fenuzzi 5, Sassuolo, MO 41049, Italy. TEL 39-0536-1844711, http://www.comune.sassuolo.mo.it.

352.14 ITA ISSN 0010-4973
COMUNI D'EUROPA. Text in Italian. 1952. m. free to qualified personnel. **Document type:** *Magazine, Consumer.*
Indexed: ELLIS.
Published by: Associazione Italiana del Consiglio dei Comuni e delle Regioni d'Europa (A I C C R E), Piazza di Trevi 86, Rome, 00187, Italy. TEL 39-06-69940461, FAX 39-06-6793275, http://www.aiccre.it. Circ: 8,000.

342.09 ITA ISSN 0394-8277
COMUNI D'ITALIA; rivista mensile di dottrina, giurisprudenza e tecnica amministrativa. Text in Italian. 1962. m. (10/yr.). EUR 108 (effective 2008). **Document type:** *Magazine, Trade.* **Description:** Addresses the most important facets of Municipal government; spanning from the problems of local officials to local finance, from environmental issues to an annotated representation of court decisions.
Indexed: DoGi.
Published by: Maggioli Editore, Via del Carpino 8/10, Santarcangelo di Romagna, RN 47822, Italy. TEL 39-0541-628111, FAX 39-0541-622020, editore@maggioli.it, http://www.maggioli.it. Ed. Tiziano Tessaro. Circ: 4,700.

352.14 ITA
CONFSERVIZI. ANNUARIO ASSOCIATI (YEAR). Text in Italian. 196?. a. stat. **Document type:** *Directory, Trade.*
Published by: Confederazione Nazionale dei Servizi (Confservizi), Via Cavour 179/a, Rome, 00184, Italy. TEL 39-06-478651, http://www.confservizi.net/.

352.14 ITA
CONFSERVIZI. COMPENDIO STATISTICO (YEAR); dati analitici delle imprese di servizio pubblico locale. Text in Italian. 1976. a. **Document type:** *Yearbook, Trade.*
Formerly (until 19??): Compendio Dati

Published by: Confederazione Nazionale dei Servizi (Confservizi), Via Cavour 179/a, Rome, 00184, Italy. TEL 39-06-478651, http://www.confservizi.net/.

352 USA
CONNECTICUT TOWN & CITY. Abbreviated title: C T & C. Text in English. 19??. bi-m. USD 18 to non-members; free to members (effective 2010). adv. **Document type:** *Newsletter, Government.* **Description:** Covers major intergovernmental issues, new ideas in municipal management and cost-saving measures by towns.
Published by: Connecticut Conference of Municipalities, 900 Chapel St, 9th Fl, New Haven, CT 06510. ccm@ccm-ct.org. adv.: B&W page USD 995; 7.5 x 9.75. Circ: 7,700.

352 USA
CONNECTION (PHOENIX). Text in English. 2003. m. free. **Document type:** *Newsletter, Trade.* **Description:** Aims to provide vital services and tools to all its members in the League of Arizona Cities and Towns, focusing principally on representing the interests of cities and towns before the legislature, and secondarily providing technical and legal assistance, coordinating shared services, and producing high quality conference and educational events.
Media: Online - full text.
Published by: League of Arizona Cities and Towns, 1820 West Washington St, Phoenix, AZ 85007. league@azleague.org. Ed. Mary Vinzant.

352 CAN ISSN 1912-5925
CONSEIL DES MONTREALAISES. RAPPORT D'ACTIVITE. Text in French. 2004. a. **Document type:** *Government.*
Published by: Conseil des Montrealaises, 800, boul. de Maisonneuve Est, 3e etage, Montreal, PQ H2L 4L8, Canada. TEL 514-872-9074, FAX 514-872-9848, conseildesmontrealaises@ville.montreal.qc.ca, http://www.ville.montreal.qc.ca/conseildesmontrealaises.

352.14.340 ESP ISSN 0210-2161
EL CONSULTOR DE LOS AYUNTAMIENTOS Y DE LOS JUZGADOS. Text in Spanish. 1852. 26/yr. EUR 539 (effective 2009). back issues avail. **Document type:** *Journal, Trade.*
Former titles (until 1945): El Consultor de los Ayuntamientos y de los Juzgados Municipales (1138-2244); (until 1869): El Consultor de los Ayuntamientos (1138-2236)
Related titles: Online - full text ed.
Published by: La Ley (Subsidiary of: Wolters Kluwer N.V.), Calle Collado Mediano 9, Las Rozas, Madrid 28230, Spain. TEL 34-902-420010, FAX 34-902-420012, clientes@laley.net, http://www.laley.net.

CORNWALL LOCAL TRANSPORT PLAN (YEAR). *see* TRANSPORTATION

352 USA
COUNCIL DIRECTIONS. Text in English. q. free. **Document type:** *Newsletter.*
Address: 230 E. Fifth St., St. Paul, MN 55101. TEL 651-602-1426, FAX 651-602-1464. Ed. Jim Martin.

352.14 FRA ISSN 0252-0699
COUNCIL OF EUROPE. STUDY SERIES: LOCAL AND REGIONAL AUTHORITIES IN EUROPE. Text in French. 1972. irreg. price varies. charts; stat.
Former titles: Council of Europe. Steering Committee on Regional and Municipal Matters. Study Series: Local and Regional Authorities in Europe; Council of Europe. Committee on Cooperation in Municipal and Regional Matters. Study Series: Local and Regional Authorities in Europe
Published by: Council of Europe/Conseil de l'Europe, Avenue de l'Europe, Strasbourg, 67075, France. TEL 33-3-88412581, FAX 33-3-88413910, publishing@coe.int, http://www.coe.int. **Dist. in U.S. by:** Manhattan Publishing Co., 468 Albany Post Rd, Croton On Hudson, NY 10520.

COUNTRY REVIEW. INDIA. *see* BUSINESS AND ECONOMICS—Economic Situation And Conditions

352.14 USA ISSN 0744-9798
COUNTY NEWS (WASHINGTON). Text in English. 1970 (vol.3). s-m. charts; illus.; stat. back issues avail.; reprints avail. **Document type:** *Newspaper, Consumer.*
Formerly (until 1973): N A C O News and Views (0027-5743)
Published by: National Association of Counties, 25 Massachusetts Ave, NW, Washington, DC 20001. TEL 202-393-6226, FAX 202-393-2630, http://www.naco.org.

352.14 FRA ISSN 1252-1574
LE COURRIER DES MAIRES ET DES ELUS LOCAUX. Text in French. 1993. m. (11/yr). EUR 76 combined subscription to individuals print & online eds.; EUR 120 combined subscription to institutions print & online eds. (effective 2009). adv. **Document type:** *Magazine, Trade.*
Formerly (until 1993): Le Courrier du Maire (1249-6936); Which was formed by the 1993 merger of: Lettre du Moniteur des Villes (1241-4751); (1990-1993): Moniteur des Villes (1156-6434)
Related titles: Online - full text ed.
Indexed: FR.
Published by: Groupe Moniteur, 17 rue d'Uzes, Paris, 75108, France. TEL 33-1-40133030, FAX 33-1-40135021, http://editionsdumoniteur.com. Ed. Alain Piffaretti. Adv. contact Pierre Dupont. Circ: 10,000.

330.9 USA
CREATING QUALITY CITIES. Text in English. 19??. 9/yr. free to members (effective 2010). adv. back issues avail. **Document type:** *Newsletter, Trade.* **Description:** Covers events important to Idaho cities as well as the various issues facing city government and Idaho citizens.
Formerly (until 199?): City Report
Related titles: Online - full text ed.: free (effective 2010).
Published by: Association of Idaho Cities, 3100 S Vista Ave, Ste 310, Boise, ID 83705. TEL 208-344-8594, FAX 208-344-8677. Ed., Pub., Adv. contact Ken Harward.

CRIMINAL LAW & JUSTICE WEEKLY. *see* LAW—Criminal Law

352.14 ITA ISSN 0394-6088
CROCEVIA; mensile di polizia municipale, stradale, amministrativa e sanitaria per i Vigili Urbani d'Italia. Text in Italian. 1946. m. (11/yr.). EUR 44 to individuals; EUR 118 to institutions (effective 2008). **Document type:** *Magazine, Trade.* **Description:** Informs municipal police on the recent changes in legal guidelines or technological innovations.
Indexed: IBR, IBZ.
Published by: Maggioli Editore, Via del Carpino 8/10, Santarcangelo di Romagna, RN 47822, Italy. TEL 39-0541-628111, FAX 39-0541-622020, editore@maggioli.it, http://www.maggioli.it. Circ: 6,450.

352.14 GBR
CROSS ON LOCAL GOVERNMENT LAW. Variant title: Local Government Law. Text in English. 1991. base vol. plus updates 3/yr. looseleaf. GBP 419 base vol(s). domestic; EUR 554 base vol(s). in Europe; USD 720 base vol(s). elsewhere (effective 2011). **Document type:** *Handbook/Manual/Guide, Trade.* **Description:** Provides a full and detailed account of local authorities' powers and duties in their many fields of operation.
Published by: Sweet & Maxwell Ltd. (Subsidiary of: Thomson Reuters Corp.), 100 Avenue Rd, London, NW3 3PF, United Kingdom. TEL 44-20-73937000, FAX 44-20-74491144, sweetandmaxwell.customer.services@thomson.com. Ed. Stephen Bailey. **Subscr. to:** PO Box 1000, Andover SP10 9AF, United Kingdom. TEL 44-20-73938051, sweetandmaxwell.international.queries@thomson.com.

352 ESP ISSN 0213-0475
DP302.A87
CUADERNOS ABULENSES. Text in Spanish. 1983. s-a. **Document type:** *Monographic series, Academic/Scholarly.*
Indexed: RILM.
Published by: Diputacion Provincial de Avila, Instituto Gran Duque de Alba, Paseo Dos de Mayo, 8, Avila, Castilla y Leon 05001, Spain. TEL 34-920-357116, FAX 34-920-352330, idga@diputacion.avitla.net, http://www.diputacionavila.es/.

352 ESP ISSN 1130-8133
DP302.C95
CUENCA. Text in Spanish. 1972. s-a. **Document type:** *Magazine, Government.*
Indexed: RILM.
Published by: Diputacion Provincial de Cuenca, Sargals, s-n, Cuenca, 16002, Spain. TEL 34-969-229570, FAX 34-969-230760, cultura@dipucuenca.es, http://www.dipucuenca.es/.

352.14 USA ISSN 0011-3727
CURRENT MUNICIPAL PROBLEMS. Text in English. 1959. 14 base vols. plus q. updates. bk.rev. charts. cum.index. 600 p./no.; **Document type:** *Journal, Trade.*
Related titles: Microfiche ed.: (from PQC); Cumulative ed(s).: ISSN 0161-5122. 1976.
Indexed: A22, A26, CLI, G08, LRI, LegCont. —Ingenta. **CCC.**
Published by: Thomson West (Subsidiary of: Thomson Reuters Corp.), 610 Opperman Dr, Eagan, MN 55123. TEL 651-687-7000, 800-344-5008, west.customer.service@thomson.com. Circ: 761.

352.14 USA ISSN 0740-1744
KFD1240
D.C. CODE UPDATER. (District of Columbia) Text in English. 1981. m. USD 300. charts. cum.index. back issues avail. **Description:** Lists current changes to District of Columbia code and rules and regulations.
Published by: David W. Lang, Ed. & Pub., P O Box 3107, Crofton, MD 21114. TEL 301-858-0127. Circ: 40 (paid).

352.14 351.485 SWE ISSN 1652-6511
DAGENS SAMHAELLE; kommunernas och landstingets tidning. Text in Swedish. 2004. 41/yr. SEK 655 (effective 2008). adv. bk.rev. illus. index. back issues avail. **Document type:** *Newspaper, Consumer.*
Formed by the merger of (1978-2004): Kommun-Aktuellt (0347-5484); (1914-2004): Landstingsvaerlden (0282-4485); Which was formerly (until 1985): Landstingens Tidskrift (0023-8074); (until 1966): Sveriges Landstings Tidskrift
Related titles: Online - full text ed.: 1996.
Published by: Dagens Samhaelle AB, Peter Myndes Backe 12, Stockholm, 11882, Sweden. TEL 46-8-4527300, FAX 46-8-6423013. Eds. Oerjan Bjoerklund TEL 46-8-4527307, Lena Hoerngren TEL 46-8-4527301. adv.: B&W page SEK 46,400, color page SEK 57,500; 231 x 485. Circ: 31,200.

352.14 ESP ISSN 0212-0585
DEBATS. Text in Spanish. 1982. 4/yr. EUR 30.05 domestic; EUR 39.07 in Europe; EUR 42.07 elsewhere (effective 2009). 150 p./no.; **Document type:** *Magazine, Consumer.* **Description:** Presents a panorama of current thought, centered under different headings.
Indexed: P09, PCI.
Published by: Diputacion Provincial de Valencia, Instituto Alfonso el Magnanimo, C. Quevedo 10, Valencia, 46001, Spain. TEL 34-96-3883733, FAX 34-96-388-3751. Ed. Josep Carles Lainez. Circ: 13,000. **Dist. by:** Asociacion de Revistas Culturales de Espana, C Covarruvias 9 2o. Derecha, Madrid 28010, Spain. TEL 34-91-3086066, FAX 34-91-3199267, info@arce.es, http://www.arce.es/.

352 ESP ISSN 2172-3265
▼ **DELIBERATION.** Text in Spanish. 2010. a. **Document type:** *Report, Consumer.*
Published by: Direccion General de Participacion Ciudadana, D. L., Paseo Maria Agustin, 36, Edif. Pignatelli, Zaragoza, 50071, Spain. TEL 34-976-714183, FAX 34-976-713218, http;//aragonparticipa.aragon.es/.

352.14 DEU ISSN 0948-2105
JS5431
DEMO; die Monatszeitschrift fuer Kommunalpolitik. Text in German. 1949. m. EUR 69; EUR 6.65 newsstand/cover (effective 2009). adv. bk.rev. abstr.; illus. index. **Document type:** *Magazine, Trade.*
Formerly (until 1994): Demokratische Gemeinde (0011-8303)
Related titles: Microform ed.: 1949; Online - full text ed.
Published by: Berliner Vorwaerts Verlagsgesellschaft mbH, Stresemannstr 30, Berlin, 10963, Germany. TEL 49-30-25594100, FAX 49-30-25594192, verlag@vorwaerts.de, http://www.vorwaerts.de. Ed. Stefan Groenebaum. Adv. contact Michael Blum. B&W page EUR 3,380, color page EUR 3,980. Circ: 12,539 (paid and controlled).

352.14 ECU
DESARROLLO LOCAL. Text in Spanish. 1987. irreg.
Published by: Centro de Capacitacion y Desarrollo de los Gobiernos Locales, Correo Central, Ave Diez de Agosto, 4612 y Juan Pablo Sanz, Apdo 1109, Quito, Pichincha, Ecuador. TEL 435205, TELEX 21026 IULA ED. Ed. Maria Arboleda.

352 PRT ISSN 1647-4473
DESCOBRIMENTOS. Text in Portuguese. 2004. irreg. **Document type:** *Magazine, Consumer.*
Published by: Camara Municipal de Lagos, Praca Gil Eanes, Lagos, 8600, Portugal. TEL 351-282-780900, http://www.cm-lagos.pt.

342.09 USA
DESKBOOK ENCYCLOPEDIA OF PUBLIC EMPLOYMENT LAW. Text in English. 1990. a. **Document type:** *Handbook/Manual/Guide, Trade.* **Description:** Provides an up-to-date compilation of summarized federal and state appellate court decisions that affect public employment.
Published by: Center for Education and Employment Law (Subsidiary of: Progressive Business Publications), PO BOX 3008, Malvern, PA 19355 . TEL 800-365-4900, FAX 610-647-8089, http://www.ceelonline.com/ceel/default.asp.

352.14 DEU ISSN 1617-8203
HT169.G4
DEUTSCHE ZEITSCHRIFT FUER KOMMUNALWISSENSCHAFTEN. Text in English, French, German. 1962. s-a. EUR 35 (effective 2009). adv. bk.rev. abstr.; charts; stat. index. **Document type:** *Journal, Academic/Scholarly.* **Description:** A forum for all disciplines related to urban studies.
Formerly (until 2001): Archiv fuer Kommunalwissenschaften (0003-9209)
Related titles: ◆ English ed.: German Journal of Urban Studies. ISSN 1861-0145.
Indexed: A22, ABCPolSci, DIP, FR, IBR, IBSS, IBZ, PAIS, PCI, SCOPUS. —IE. **CCC.**
Published by: Deutsches Institut fuer Urbanistik, Zimmerstr 13-15, Berlin, 10969, Germany. TEL 49-30-390010, FAX 49-30-39001100, difu@difu.de. Ed. Klaus-Dieter Beisswenger. adv.: page EUR 250; trim 155 x 225. Circ: 1,000.

351 DEU ISSN 1437-5745
DEUTSCHER STAEDTE- UND GEMEINDEBUND. SCHRIFTEN. Text in German. 1998. irreg., latest vol.2, 2001. price varies. **Document type:** *Monographic series, Academic/Scholarly.*
Published by: (Deutscher Staedte- und Gemeindebund), Erich Schmidt Verlag GmbH & Co. (Berlin), Genthiner Str 30 G, Berlin, 10785, Germany. TEL 49-30-2500850, FAX 49-30-250085305, vertrieb@esvmedien.de.

352 DEU ISSN 0179-8464
DEUTSCHER STAEDTETAG. MITTEILUNGEN. Text in German. 1946. 10/yr. adv. **Document type:** *Magazine, Trade.*
Published by: Deutscher Staedtetag, Im Klapperhof 23, Cologne, 50670, Germany. TEL 49-221-37710, FAX 49-221-3771128, staedtetag@staedtetag.de. Circ: 15,000 (paid and controlled).

352 DEU ISSN 0344-2446
DEUTSCHER STAEDTETAG. REIHE A: BEITRAEGE ZUR KOMMUNALPOLITIK. Variant title: D S T Beitraege zur Kommunalpolitik. Text in German. 1974. irreg., latest vol.31, 2003. price varies. **Document type:** *Monographic series, Academic/Scholarly.*
Published by: Deutscher Staedtetag, Im Klapperhof 23, Cologne, 50670, Germany. TEL 49-221-37710, FAX 49-221-3771128, staedtetag@staedtetag.de.

352 DEU ISSN 0344-2454
DEUTSCHER STAEDTETAG. REIHE B: BEITRAEGE ZUM KOMMUNALRECHT. Variant title: D S T Beitraege zum Kommunalrecht. Text in German. 1975. irreg., latest vol.6, 1991. price varies. **Document type:** *Monographic series, Academic/Scholarly.*
Published by: Deutscher Staedtetag, Im Klapperhof 23, Cologne, 50670, Germany. TEL 49-221-37710, FAX 49-221-3771128, staedtetag@staedtetag.de.

352 DEU ISSN 0344-2462
DEUTSCHER STAEDTETAG. REIHE C: BEITRAEGE ZUR BILDUNGSPOLITIK. Variant title: D S T Beitraege zur Bildungspolitik. Text in German. 1972. irreg., latest vol.27, 2002. price varies. **Document type:** *Monographic series, Academic/Scholarly.*
Published by: Deutscher Staedtetag, Im Klapperhof 23, Cologne, 50670, Germany. TEL 49-221-37710, FAX 49-221-3771128, staedtetag@staedtetag.de.

352 DEU ISSN 0344-2470
DEUTSCHER STAEDTETAG. REIHE D: BEITRAEGE ZUR SOZIALPOLITIK. Variant title: D S T Beitraege zur Sozialpolitik. Text in German. 1967. irreg., latest vol.30, 1999. price varies. **Document type:** *Monographic series, Academic/Scholarly.*
Published by: Deutscher Staedtetag, Im Klapperhof 23, Cologne, 50670, Germany. TEL 49-221-37710, FAX 49-221-3771128, staedtetag@staedtetag.de.

352 DEU ISSN 0344-2497
DEUTSCHER STAEDTETAG. REIHE F: BEITRAEGE ZUR WIRTSCHAFTS- UND VERKEHRSPOLITIK. Variant title: D S T Beitraege zur Wirtschafts- und Verkehrspolitik. Text in German. 1975. irreg., latest vol.15, 2008. price varies. **Document type:** *Monographic series, Academic/Scholarly.*
Published by: Deutscher Staedtetag, Im Klapperhof 23, Cologne, 50670, Germany. TEL 49-221-37710, FAX 49-221-3771128, staedtetag@staedtetag.de.

352 DEU ISSN 0344-2500
DEUTSCHER STAEDTETAG. REIHE G: BEITRAEGE ZUR FINANZPOLITIK. Variant title: D S T Beitraege zur Finanzpolitik. Text in German. 1973. irreg., latest vol.14, 2007. price varies. **Document type:** *Monographic series, Academic/Scholarly.*
Published by: Deutscher Staedtetag, Im Klapperhof 23, Cologne, 50670, Germany. TEL 49-221-37710, FAX 49-221-3771128, staedtetag@staedtetag.de.

352 DEU ISSN 0344-2519
DEUTSCHER STAEDTETAG. REIHE H: BEITRAEGE ZUR STATISTIK UND STADTFORSCHUNG. Variant title: D S T Beitraege zur Statistik und Stadtforschung. Text in German. 1972. irreg., latest vol.45, 2000. price varies. **Document type:** *Monographic series, Academic/Scholarly.*
Published by: Deutscher Staedtetag, Im Klapperhof 23, Cologne, 50670, Germany. TEL 49-221-37710, FAX 49-221-3771128, staedtetag@staedtetag.de.

P

352 DEU ISSN 0937-3888
DEUTSCHER STAEDTETAG. REIHE K: BEITRAEGE ZUR STAEDTISCHEN EUROPAARBEIT. Text in German. 1989. irreg. price varies. **Document type:** *Monographic series, Academic/ Scholarly.*
Published by: Deutscher Staedtetag, Im Klapperhof 23, Cologne, 50670, Germany. TEL 49-221-37710, FAX 49-221-3771128, staedtetag@staedtetag.de, http://www.staedtetag.de.

352 DEU ISSN 0946-8986
DEUTSCHER STAEDTETAG. REIHE L: BEITRAEGE ZUR FRAUENPOLITIK. Text in German. 1994. irreg., latest vol.6, 2000. price varies. **Document type:** *Monographic series, Academic/ Scholarly.*
Published by: Deutscher Staedtetag, Im Klapperhof 23, Cologne, 50670, Germany. TEL 49-221-37710, FAX 49-221-3771128, staedtetag@staedtetag.de, http://www.staedtetag.de.

352 DEU
DEUTSCHLAND KOMMUNAL. Text in German. a. EUR 22.50 per issue (effective 2009). adv. **Document type:** *Directory, Trade.*
Published by: Berliner Vorwaerts Verlagsgesellschaft mbH, Stresemannstr 30, Berlin, 10963, Germany. TEL 49-30-25594100, FAX 49-30-25594192, verlag@vorwaerts.de, http:// www.vorwaerts.de. adv.: color page EUR 2,200. Circ: 12,000 (controlled).

352.14 USA ISSN 0090-1989
JS451.N93
DIRECTORY: NORTH DAKOTA CITY OFFICIALS. Text in English. 1994 (35th ed.). biennial. USD 25 (effective 2006). adv. **Document type:** *Directory, Government.* **Description:** Lists city hall address and telephone, e-mail address, fax number, population, names of elected and appointed officials, and more.
Published by: North Dakota League of Cities, 410 E. Front Ave., Bismarck, ND 58504. TEL 701-223-3518, 800-472-2692, FAX 701-223-5174, http://www.ndlc.org/. Ed. Connie Sprynczynatyk. R&P, Adv. contact Jan Jordan.

352.14025 USA ISSN 1046-2686
JS39
DIRECTORY OF CITY POLICY OFFICIALS. Text in English. 1984. a. USD 40 (effective 2000). back issues avail. **Document type:** *Directory.* **Description:** Lists the names of mayors and council members in American cities of more than 30,000 people and league member cities. Includes city hall address and telephone number, population and form of government.
Published by: National League of Cities, 1301 Pennsylvania Ave, N W, Ste 550, Washington, DC 20004. TEL 202-636-3150. R&P Mae Davis TEL 202-626-3000.

352.14 USA
DIRECTORY OF GEORGIA MUNICIPAL OFFICERS AND ASSOCIATE MEMBERS. Text in English. a. USD 60 to non-members; free to members (effective 2006). adv. back issues avail. **Document type:** *Directory, Government.*
Published by: Georgia Municipal Association, 201 Pryor St, S W, Atlanta, GA 30303-3606. info@gmanet.com, http://www.gmanet.com. Ed. Charles Craig. Adv. contact Yolande Tanner.

352.14025 USA ISSN 0148-7442
JS303.M5
DIRECTORY OF MICHIGAN MUNICIPAL OFFICIALS. Text in English. s-a. USD 43 per issue. **Document type:** *Directory.*
Published by: Michigan Municipal League, 1675 Green Rd, Ann Arbor, MI 48106. TEL 313-662-3246, FAX 313-662-8083.

352.14025 USA ISSN 0890-1651
JS451.M65
DIRECTORY OF MINNESOTA CITY OFFICIALS. Text in English. 1986. a. USD 35. adv. **Document type:** *Directory, Government.*
Formerly: Directory of Minnesota Municipal Officials
Published by: League of Minnesota Cities, 145 University Ave W, St Paul, MN 55103-2044. TEL 612-281-1200, FAX 612-281-1299. Ed. Jodi Contreras. Adv. contact Gayle Brodt. Circ: 3,500.

352.14 USA
DIRECTORY OF NORTH CAROLINA MUNICIPAL OFFICIALS. Text in English. a. USD 40 (effective 2000). **Document type:** *Directory.*
Published by: North Carolina League of Municipalities, 215 N Dawson St, PO Box 3069, Raleigh, NC 27602. TEL 919-715-4000, FAX 919-733-9519. Ed. Margot F Christensen. Circ: 1,500.

352 USA
DIRECTORY OF TENNESSEE MUNICIPAL OFFICIALS. Text in English. a. USD 100 (effective 2006). **Document type:** *Directory.* **Description:** Lists Tennessee cities including personnel and municipal data, such as number of employees, population, charter form, size in square miles, and election date.
Published by: University of Tennessee at Knoxville, Municipal Technical Advisory Service, 600 Henley, Ste 120, Knoxville, TN 37996-4105. TEL 865-974-0411, FAX 865-974-0423.

352.14 BRA ISSN 0419-3911
DIRIGENTE MUNICIPAL. Text in Portuguese. 1966. m. USD 70. adv. bk.rev.
Published by: Editora Visao Ltda., Rua Alvaro de Carvalho, 354, Centro, Sao Paulo, SP 01050-070, Brazil. TEL 256-5011, FAX 258-1919. Ed. Hamilton Lucas de Oliveira. Circ: 15,600.

352 NZL ISSN 1177-6579
DISTRICT PLAN MONITORING SERIES. RESEARCH REPORT. Text in English. 2006. irreg.
Related titles: Online - full text ed.: ISSN 1177-6587. free.
Published by: Dunedin City Council, City Planning, PO Box 5045, Central City, Dunedin, New Zealand. TEL 64-3-4774000, FAX 64-3-4743366, cod.general@cityofdunedin.com, http:// www.cityofdunedin.com.

352 ESP ISSN 1889-9404
▼ **DISTRITO ESTE.** Text in Spanish. 2009. q. **Document type:** *Bulletin, Consumer.*
Published by: Agrupacion Socialista El Palo Pedregalejo, Calle Carlos Fontanura, 18, Malaga, Spain. TEL 34-952-298399, organizacion@psoepalop.com, http://www.psoepalop.com/.

352 NLD ISSN 1875-0117
DORPENKRANT. Text in Dutch. 2006. 3/yr.
Published by: PRIMO nh, Postbus 106, Purmerend, 1440 AC, Netherlands. TEL 31-299-418700, FAX 31-299-418799, info@primo-nh.nl, http://www.primo-nh.nl. Ed. Luc Overman. Circ: 2,000.

352.14 DEU ISSN 0012-7019
DUESSELDORFER AMTSBLATT. Text in German. 1946. w. EUR 30.60 (effective 2006). adv. bk.rev. **Document type:** *Government.*
Published by: Landeshauptstadt Duesseldorf, Amt fuer Kommunikation, Postfach 101120, Duesseldorf, 40002, Germany. TEL 49-211-8993131, FAX 49-211-8994179, presse@duesseldorf.de, http:// www.duesseldorf.de/presse. Circ: 4,200.

352 ESP ISSN 2013-1984
E-OBSERVATORI. Text in Catalan. 2008. w. **Document type:** *Bulletin, Consumer.*
Media: Online - full text.
Published by: Generalitat de Catalunya, Departament d'Interior, Relacions Institucionals i Participacio. Institut d'Estudis Autonomics/ Catalan Government. Ministry of Home Affairs, Institutional Relations and Participation. Institut d' Estudis Autonomics, Baixada de Sant Miquel, 8, Barcelona, 08002, Spain. TEL 34-93-3429800, FAX 34-93-3429801, http://www.gencat.cat/iea.

330 352 CAN ISSN 1708-5489
CA3PQMLE24
L'ECONOMIE METROPOLITAINE; bulletin d'information economique. Text in French. 2003. q. free. back issues avail. **Document type:** *Bulletin, Government.*
Related titles: Online - full text ed.: ISSN 1708-5497; ◆ English ed.: The Metropolitan Economy. ISSN 1708-5500.
Published by: Communaute Metropolitaine de Montreal, 1002 Rue Sherbrooke Ouest, Bureau 2400, Montreal, PQ H3A 3L6, Canada. TEL 514-350-2550, FAX 514-350-2599, info@cmm.qc.ca.

EDINBURGH COLLEGE OF ART - HERIOT-WATT UNIVERSITY. RESEARCH PAPER. see HOUSING AND URBAN PLANNING

352.14 USA
THE ELECTION BOOK. Text in English. 19??. biennial, latest 2007. USD 40 per issue to non-members; USD 20 per issue to members (effective 2011). **Document type:** *Government.* **Description:** Provides a checklist of actions required by the Municipal Election Code to be performed before, during and after elections.
Formerly (until 1999): Municipal Election Calendar
Published by: Colorado Municipal League, 1144 Sherman St, Denver, CO 80203. TEL 303-831-6411, FAX 303-860-8175, cml@cml.org, http://www.cml.org.

352.14 FRA ISSN 0181-2726
ELU D'AUJOURD'HUI; magazine de l'association nationale des elus communistes et republicains. Text in French. 1975. 11/yr. adv. **Document type:** *Magazine.*
Indexed: FR.
Address: 10 rue Parmentier, Montreuil-sous-Bois, 93100, France. TEL 33-1-48517878, FAX 33-1-48519262, elu@elunet.org. Ed. Emile Clet. Circ: 34,500.

352.14 CAN ISSN 1182-6274
JS1705
ENCYCLOPEDIA OF CANADIAN MUNICIPAL GOVERNMENTS. Text in English. 1990. a.
Published by: Municipal Publishers (Subsidiary of: Quaere Data Resources Inc.), 4583 Neville St, Burnaby, BC V5J 2G9, Canada. TEL 604-431-9808. Ed. Vian Andrews.

ENVIRONMENT WAIKATO. TECHNICAL REPORT. see ENVIRONMENTAL STUDIES

ENVIRONMENTAL AND URBAN ISSUES. see ENVIRONMENTAL STUDIES

352.14 ESP ISSN 1131-6381
EQUIPAMIENTO Y SERVICIOS MUNICIPALES. Text in Spanish. 1984. 6/yr. **Document type:** *Magazine, Trade.* **Description:** Covers equipment for municipal government: architectural, gardening, sanitation, and more.
Indexed: IECT.
Published by: Publiteca S.L., Jacinto Verdaguer, 25 2oB, Madrid, 28019, Spain. TEL 34-1-4713405, FAX 34-1-4713898. Circ: 5,000.

352 NLD ISSN 1878-9250
ERFGOEDBRIEF BREDA. Text in Dutch. 2004. s-a.
Published by: Gemeente Breda, Directie Ruimtelijke Ontwikkeling, Afdeling Stedenbouw en Erfgoed, Bureau Cultureel Erfgoed, Postbus 90156, Breda, 4800 RH, Netherlands. FAX 31-76-5293240, gemeentebreda@breda.nl, http://www.breda.nl. Eds. Gerard Otten, Johan Hendriks. Circ: 3,000.

354.35 GBR
ESSEX COUNTY COUNCIL. PLANNING. APPLICATIONS & DECISIONS (WASTE & MINERALS) (ONLINE). Text in English. q. free (effective 2009). back issues avail. **Document type:** *Bulletin, Government.*
Formerly: Essex County Council. Planning. Applications & Decisions (Waste & Minerals) (Print)
Media: Online - full content.
Published by: Essex County Council, County Planner, County Hall, Market Rd, Chelmsford, CM1 1LX, United Kingdom. TEL 44-845-7585592.

333.714 GBR
ESSEX GUIDE TO ENVIRONMENTAL ASSESSMENT. Text in English. 1992. base vol. plus irreg. updates. GBP 10; GBP 5 updates. **Document type:** *Bulletin.*
Published by: Essex County Council, County Planner, County Hall, Market Rd, Chelmsford, CM1 1LX, United Kingdom. TEL 44-1245-492211, FAX 44-1245-259353, http://www.essexcc.gov.uk/.

352.14 FRA ISSN 1265-3292
EUROPE LOCALE. Text in French. 1995. 4/yr. EUR 40 (effective 2008). **Document type:** *Magazine.* **Description:** Public administration in Europe and European policies and programs for local authorities.
Published by: Association Francaise du Conseil des Communes et Regions d'Europe, 30 rue d'Alsace Lorraine, Orleans, 45000, France. TEL 33-2-38778383, FAX 33-2-38772103, http://www.afccre.org. Ed. Ysabelle Roques.

352.14 FRA ISSN 0252-0990
EUROPEAN REGIONAL PLANNING STUDY SERIES. Text in English. 1977. irreg. price varies.
Related titles: French ed.: Amenagement du Territoire Europeen. Serie Etudes. ISSN 0252-0982.
Published by: Council of Europe/Conseil de l'Europe, Avenue de l'Europe, Strasbourg, 67075, France. TEL 33-3-88412581, FAX 33-3-88413910, publishing@coe.int, http://www.coe.int. **Dist. in U.S. by:** Manhattan Publishing Co., 468 Albany Post Rd, Croton On Hudson, NY 10520.

352 PRT ISSN 1647-273X
▼ **EVORA MOSAICO.** Text in Portuguese. 2009. q. **Document type:** *Magazine, Consumer.*
Published by: Camara Municipal de Evora, Praca de Sertorio, Evora, 7004-506, Portugal. TEL 351-266-777000, FAX 351-266-702950, http://cm-evora.pt.

352 ESP
FEDERACION ESPANOLA DE MUNICIPIOS Y PROVINCIAS. REVISTA. Text in Spanish. 1990. m. bk.rev. **Document type:** *Magazine, Government.*
Published by: Federacion Espanola de Municipios y Provincias, Nuncio, 8, Madrid, 28005, Spain. TEL 34-91-3643700, FAX 34-91-3655482, femp@femp.es, http://www.femp.es/. R&P Jesus Diaz Lobo. Adv. contact Pepa Nunez.

FEDERAL ELECTION CAMPAIGN FINANCING GUIDE. see BUSINESS AND ECONOMICS—Banking And Finance

352.14 USA ISSN 1080-5575
HJ275
FEDERAL GRANT DEADLINE CALENDAR. Text in English. 1995. s-a.
Related titles: ◆ Supplement to: Guide to Federal Funding for Governments and Nonprofits. ISSN 1055-596X.
Published by: Government Information Services (Subsidiary of: Thompson Publishing Group), 1725 K St, N W, 7th Fl, Washington, DC 20006. TEL 800-876-0226, FAX 202-759-9657, http:// www.thompson.com.

LA FINANZA LOCALE; rivista mensile di contabilita e tributi degli enti locali e delle regioni. see BUSINESS AND ECONOMICS—Public Finance, Taxation

351 DEU ISSN 1437-5702
FINANZWESEN DER GEMEINDEN. Text in German. 1992. irreg., latest vol.13, 2011. price varies. **Document type:** *Monographic series, Academic/Scholarly.*
Published by: Erich Schmidt Verlag GmbH & Co. (Berlin), Genthiner Str 30 G, Berlin, 10785, Germany. TEL 49-30-2500850, FAX 49-30-250085305, vertrieb@esvmedien.de.

352 ESP ISSN 2013-2387
FLAIX D'ACTUACIONS. Text in Spanish. 2007. m. back issues avail. **Document type:** *Bulletin, Consumer.*
Media: Online - full text.
Published by: Generalitat de Catalunya, Departament d'Innovacio, Universitats i Empresa, Pg de Gracia, 105, Barcelona, 08008, Spain. TEL 34-93-4849500, FAX 34-93-4849599, http://www.gencat.cat/ diue/departament/conseller/index.html.

352.14 USA
FLORIDA BAR. CITY COUNTY & LOCAL GOVERNMENT LAW SECTION AGENDA. Text in English. 19??. irreg. free to members (effective 2010). back issues avail. **Document type:** *Newsletter, Trade.*
Formerly: Florida Bar. Local Government Law Section Newsletter
Related titles: Online - full text ed.: free (effective 2010).
Published by: The Florida Bar, 651 E Jefferson St, Tallahassee, FL 32399. TEL 850-561-5600, 800-342-8060, FAX 850-561-9416, flabarwm@flabar.org, http://www.floridabar.org. Ed. Mary Helen Farris.

352 PRT ISSN 1647-2136
▼ **FONTINHA.** Text in Portuguese. 2009. irreg. **Document type:** *Magazine, Consumer.*
Published by: Camara Municipal de Torres Novas, Rua General Antonio Cesar de Vasconcelos Correia, Torres Novas, 2350-421, Portugal. TEL 351-249-839430, FAX 351-249-811780, http://www.cm-torresnovas.pt.

352 CAN
FORUM (OTTAWA). Text in English, French. s-a. CAD 26.75; CAD 4.50 newsstand/cover (effective 2000).
Published by: Federation of Canadian Municipalities, 24 Clarence St, Ottawa, ON K1P 5P3, Canada. TEL 613-244-6010, abaxter@fcm.ca, http://www.fcm.ca.

352.14 DEU ISSN 0721-1406
DIE FUNDSTELLE BADEN-WUERTTEMBERG. Text in German. 1948. s-m. EUR 298.20; EUR 226.80 to students (effective 2010). adv. back issues avail. **Document type:** *Bulletin, Trade.*
Published by: Richard Boorberg Verlag GmbH und Co. KG, Scharrstr 2, Stuttgart, 70563, Germany. TEL 49-711-73850, FAX 49-711-7385100, mail@boorberg.de. Ed. Wilfried Rump. Adv. contact Roland Schulz. Circ: 1,220 (paid and controlled).

352.14 DEU ISSN 0016-2779
DIE FUNDSTELLE BAYERN; Fachzeitschrift fuer die kommunale Praxis. Text in German. 1947. s-m. EUR 354.60; EUR 251.40 to students (effective 2010). adv. bk.rev. tr.lit. index. **Document type:** *Bulletin, Trade.*
—CCC.
Published by: Richard Boorberg Verlag GmbH und Co. KG, Scharrstr 2, Stuttgart, 70563, Germany. TEL 49-711-73850, FAX 49-711-7385100, mail@boorberg.de. Ed. Gerhard Ecker. Adv. contact Roland Schulz.

352.14 DEU ISSN 0721-135X
DIE FUNDSTELLE HESSEN; Fachzeitschrift fuer die kommunale Praxis. Text in German. 1948. 24/yr. EUR 325.80; EUR 240.60 to students (effective 2010). adv. **Document type:** *Bulletin, Trade.*
Published by: Richard Boorberg Verlag GmbH und Co. KG, Scharrstr 2, Stuttgart, 70563, Germany. TEL 49-711-73850, FAX 49-711-7385100, mail@boorberg.de. Ed. Michael Althaus.

352.14 DEU ISSN 0721-1376
DIE FUNDSTELLE NIEDERSACHSEN; Fachzeitschrift fuer die kommunale Praxis. Text in German. 1948. 2/m. EUR 325.80; EUR 230.40 to students (effective 2010). adv. **Document type:** *Bulletin, Trade.*
Published by: Richard Boorberg Verlag GmbH und Co. KG, Scharrstr 2, Stuttgart, 70563, Germany. TEL 49-711-73850, FAX 49-711-7385100, mail@boorberg.de. Ed. Hans-Juergen Krauss. Adv. contact Roland Schulz.

352.14 USA ISSN 1051-6964
G F O A NEWSLETTER. Text in English. 1932. s-m. looseleaf. USD 55 to non-members; free to members (effective 2011). bk.rev. tr.lit. back issues avail. **Document type:** *Newsletter, Trade.* **Description:** Provides information on legislative and regulatory issues, summarizes trends and events in the public finance field, lists current training seminars, and contains employment notices.
Former titles (until 1990): Government Finance Officers Association. Newsletter (1047-0247); (until 1984): Municipal Finance Officers Association of the United States and Canada. Newsletter; (until 1974): M F O A Newsletter; (until 1970): Municipal Finance Newsletter (0027-3481)
Related titles: Online - full text ed.
Indexed: ATI, BLI, P48, P53, P54, PQC.
Published by: Government Finance Officers Association, 203 N LaSalle St, Ste 2700, Chicago, IL 60601. TEL 312-977-9700, FAX 312-977-4806, publications@gfoa.org.

352.14 ZAF
GAFFNEYS LOCAL GOVERNMENT IN SOUTH AFRICA. Variant title: Official South African Local Government Yearbook. Text in English. 1909. a. ZAR 950 (effective 2005). adv. 1100 p./no. 2 cols./p.; **Document type:** *Directory, Government.* **Description:** Comprehensive information on local government in South Africa.
Former titles: Official South African Municipal Yearbook; Municipal Yearbook
Related titles: CD-ROM ed.
Published by: Gaffney Group, PO Box 812, Northlands, 2116, South Africa. TEL 27-11-8802114, FAX 27-11-8802116. Ed. Joy Leon. Pub. P C Gaffney. Adv. contact P.C. Gaffney. B&W page ZAR 15,000, color page ZAR 21,500. Circ: 3,000.

352 FRA ISSN 0769-3508
HC271
GAZETTE DES COMMUNES, DES DEPARTEMENTS, DES REGIONS. Text in French. 1980. w. (48/yr). EUR 111 to individuals; EUR 174 to institutions (effective 2009). adv. **Document type:** *Magazine, Trade.*
Formerly (until 1985): Gazette des Communes (0242-570X); Which was formed by the merger of (1934-1980): Gazette des Communes et du Personnel Communal (0242-5718); (1949-1980): L' Action Municipale (0001-7450)
Related titles: Online - full text ed.
Indexed: FR, SD.
Published by: Groupe Moniteur, 17 rue d'Uzes, Paris, 75108, France. TEL 33-1-40133030, FAX 33-1-40135021, http://editionsdumoniteur.com. Ed. Jean Dumonteil. Pub. Marc N Vigier. Circ: 27,092 (controlled).

352 DEU ISSN 1865-7982
GELDERSHEIMER NACHRICHTEN; Amtsblatt der Gemeinde Geldersheim. Text in German. 1979. w. adv. **Document type:** *Newsletter, Trade.*
Published by: Revista Verlag GmbH, Am Oberen Marienbach 2 1/2, Schweinfurt, 97421, Germany. TEL 49-9721-387190, FAX 49-9721-3871938, post@revista.de.

352.14 DEU ISSN 0340-3653
DIE GEMEINDE (COLOGNE); Zeitschrift fuer die kommunale Selbstverwaltung. Text in German. 1949. m. EUR 78.40; EUR 9.25 newsstand/cover (effective 2010). adv. **Document type:** *Journal, Trade.*
—CCC.
Published by: Schleswig-Holsteinischer Gemeindetag, Haus der Kommunalen Selbstverwaltung, Reventlouallee 6, Kiel, 24105, Germany. TEL 49-431-57005050, FAX 49-431-57005054, info@shgt.de, http://www.shgt.de. Circ: 1,681 (paid and controlled).

352 DEU ISSN 1865-8083
GEMEINDE NACHRICHTEN; amtliches Mitteilungsblatt der Gemeinde Oerlenbach. Text in German. 1972. w. EUR 26.40 (effective 2011). adv. **Document type:** *Newsletter, Trade.*
Published by: Revista Verlag GmbH, Am Oberen Marienbach 2 1/2, Schweinfurt, 97421, Germany. TEL 49-9721-387190, FAX 49-9721-3871938, post@revista.de.

352.14 DEU
GEMEINDE SCHOENAICH - RUECKSPIEGEL. Text in German. 1975. a. looseleaf. free. back issues avail. **Document type:** *Newsletter.*
Published by: Gemeinde Schoenaich, Buehlstr 10, Schoenaich, 71101, Germany. TEL 07031-6390, FAX 07031-63999. Ed. Hans Joerg Weinbrenner.

352 DEU ISSN 1865-8202
GEMEINDEBLATT; das amtliche Mitteilungsblatt der Gemeinde Euerbach. Text in German. 1973. w. EUR 26.40 (effective 2011). adv. **Document type:** *Newsletter, Trade.*
Published by: Revista Verlag GmbH, Am Oberen Marienbach 2 1/2, Schweinfurt, 97421, Germany. TEL 49-9721-387190, FAX 49-9721-3871938, post@revista.de.

352 DEU ISSN 1865-8016
GEMEINDEBLATT SCHONUNGEN; amtliche und sonstige Mitteilungen. Text in German. 2004. w. EUR 13.40 (effective 2011). adv. **Document type:** *Newsletter, Trade.*
Published by: Revista Verlag GmbH, Am Oberen Marienbach 2 1/2, Schweinfurt, 97421, Germany. TEL 49-9721-387190, FAX 49-9721-3871938, post@revista.de.

352.14 AUT ISSN 0016-609X
GEMEINDEBOTE. Text in German. 1963. irreg. (4-6/yr.). free. stat.
Published by: Marktgemeinde Hinterbruehl. Gemeindeamt, Hauptstrasse 66, Hinterbruehl, N 2371, Austria. Ed. G Tartarotti. Circ: 1,200.

352.14 DEU ISSN 0340-3645
DER GEMEINDEHAUSHALT. Text in German. 1900. m. EUR 140.90; EUR 16.50 per issue (effective 2010). adv. reprints avail. **Document type:** *Magazine, Trade.*
Indexed: IBR, IBZ.
—CCC.
Published by: W. Kohlhammer GmbH, Hessbruehlstr 69, Stuttgart, 70565, Germany. TEL 49-711-78630, FAX 49-711-78638204, kohlhammerkontakt@kohlhammer.de, http://www.kohlhammer.de. Ed. Johannes Werner Schmidt. adv.: B&W page EUR 850, color page EUR 2,320. Circ: 1,800 (paid and controlled).

352.14 DEU ISSN 0174-2612
DIE GEMEINDEKASSE BADEN-WUERTTEMBERG; Fachzeitschrift fuer das kommunale Finanzwesen. Text in German. 1955. m. EUR 199.80 (effective 2010). adv. **Document type:** *Bulletin, Trade.*
Published by: Richard Boorberg Verlag GmbH und Co. KG, Scharrstr 2, Stuttgart, 70563, Germany. TEL 49-711-73850, FAX 49-711-7385100, mail@boorberg.de.

352.14 DEU ISSN 0341-2245
DIE GEMEINDEKASSE BAYERN; Fachzeitschrift fuer das kommunale Finanzwesen. Text in German. 1950. 2/m. EUR 299.40 (effective 2010). adv. bk.rev. tr.lit. index. **Document type:** *Bulletin, Trade.*
Published by: Richard Boorberg Verlag GmbH und Co. KG, Scharrstr 2, Stuttgart, 70563, Germany. TEL 49-711-73850, FAX 49-711-7385100, mail@boorberg.de. Ed. Franz Koenigsperger.

352.14 DEU ISSN 1618-7679
DIE GEMEINDEKASSE HESSEN, NIEDERSACHSEN, NORDRHEIN-WESTFALEN, SCHLESWIG-HOLSTEIN; Fachzeitschrift fuer das kommunale Finanzwesen. Text in German. 1949. m. EUR 217.80 (effective 2010). adv. **Document type:** *Bulletin, Trade.*
Formerly (until 2000): Die Gemeindekasse. Ausgabe A (0174-2604)
Indexed: DIP, IBR, IBZ.
Published by: Richard Boorberg Verlag GmbH und Co. KG, Scharrstr 2, Stuttgart, 70563, Germany. TEL 49-711-73850, FAX 49-711-7385100, mail@boorberg.de.

352 DEU ISSN 1865-8164
GEMEINDENACHRICHTEN; amtliches Mitteilungsblatt der Gemeinde Kolitzheim. Text in German. 1978. w. EUR 17.40 (effective 2011). adv. **Document type:** *Newsletter, Trade.*
Published by: Revista Verlag GmbH, Am Oberen Marienbach 2 1/2, Schweinfurt, 97421, Germany. TEL 49-9721-387190, FAX 49-9721-3871938, post@revista.de.

352 DEU ISSN 0723-8274
DER GEMEINDERAT. Text in German. 1981. m. adv. **Document type:** *Magazine, Trade.*
Formed by the merger of (1977-1981): Der Gemeinderat. Ausgabe Baden-Wuerttemberg (0723-8223); (1980-1981): Der Gemeinderat. Ausgabe Bayern (0723-824X); (19??-1981): Der Gemeinderat. Ausgabe Hessen - Rheinland-Pfalz - Saarland (0723-8258); (1981-1981): Der Gemeinderat. Ausgabe Niedersachsen - Schleswig-Holstein (0723-8266)
Published by: Eppinger-Verlag OHG, Stauffenbergstr 18-20, Schwaebisch Hall, 74523, Germany. TEL 49-791-950610, FAX 49-791-9506141, info@eppinger-verlag.de, http://www.eppinger-verlag.de. Adv. contact Gertrud Gaertig. B&W page EUR 3,600, color page EUR 4,700; trim 185 x 270. Circ: 12,000 (controlled).

352.14 DEU ISSN 0016-6170
DIE GEMEINDEVERWALTUNG RHEINLAND-PFALZ; Fachzeitschrift fuer die kommunale Praxis. Text in German. 1957. s-m. EUR 255 (effective 2010). adv. **Document type:** *Bulletin, Trade.*
—CCC.
Published by: Richard Boorberg Verlag GmbH und Co. KG, Scharrstr 2, Stuttgart, 70563, Germany. TEL 49-711-73850, FAX 49-711-7385100, mail@boorberg.de. Ed. Michael Althaus. Adv. contact Roland Schulz.

352.14 DEU ISSN 1434-4025
GEMEINSAMES AMTSBLATT DES LANDES BADEN-WUERTTEMBERG. Text in German. 1953. irreg. (15-20/yr.). EUR 78; EUR 7.30 newsstand/cover (effective 2007). adv. bk.rev. index. **Document type:** *Magazine, Trade.*
Former titles (until 1998): Gemeinsames Amtsblatt des Innenministeriums, des Finanzministeriums, des Wirtschaftsministeriums, des Ministeriums fuer Laendlichen Raum, Ernaehrung, Landwirtschaft und Forsten, des Ministeriums fuer Arbeit, Gesundheit und Sozialordnung, des Umweltministeriums, des Verkehrsministeriums, des Ministeriums fuer Familie, Frauen, Weiterbildung und Kunst sowie der Regierungspraesidien des Landes Baden-W (1434-4017); (until 1992): Gemeinsames Amtsblatt des Innenministeriums, des Finanzministeriums, des Ministeriums fuer Wirtschaft, Mittelstand und Technologie, des Ministeriums fuer Laendlichen Raum, Ernaehrung, Landwirtschaft und Forsten, des Ministeriums fuer Arbeit, Gesundheit, Familie und Frauen, des Ministeriums fuer Umwelt, des Ministeriums fuer Bundes- und Europaangelegenheiten, des Verkehrsministeriums sowie der Regi (1434-4009); (until 1991): Gemeinsames Amtsblatt des Innenministeriums, des Finanzministeriums, des Ministeriums fuer Wirtschaft, Mittelstand und Technologie, des Ministeriums fuer Laendlichen Raum, Ernaehrung, Landwirtschaft und Forsten, des Ministeriums fuer Arbeit, Gesundheit, Familie und Sozialordnung, des Ministeriums fuer Umwelt sowie der Regierungspraesidien des Landes Baden-Wuerttemberg (0939-2726); (until 1988): Gemeinsames Amtsblatt des Innenministeriums, des Finanzministeriums, des Ministeriums fuer Wirtschaft, Mittelstand und Technologie, des Ministeriums fuer Laendlichen Raum, Landwirtschaft und Forsten, des Ministeriums fuer Arbeit, Gesundheit, Familie und Sozialordnung, des Ministeriums fuer Umwelt sowie der Regierungspraesidien des Landes Baden-Wuerttemberg (0935-1876); (until 1987): Gemeinsames Amtsblatt des Innenministeriums, des Finanzministeriums, des Ministeriums fuer Wirtschaft, Mittelstand und Technologie, des Ministeriums fuer Ernaehrung, Landwirtschaft, Umwelt und Forsten, des Ministeriums fuer Arbeit, Gesundheit, Familie und Sozialordnung sowie der Regierungspraesidien des Landes Baden-Wuerttemberg (0178-5389); (until 1984): Gemeinsames Amtsblatt des Innenministeriums, des Finanzministeriums, des Ministeriums fuer Wirtschaft, Mittelstand und Verkehr, des Ministeriums fuer Ernaehrung, Landwirtschaft und Umwelt, des Ministeriums fuer Arbeit, Gesundheit und Sozialordnung sowie der Regierungspraesidien des Landes Baden-Wuerttemberg (0016-6200); (until 1972): Gemeinsames Amtsblatt des Innenministeriums, des Finanzministeriums, des Wirtschaftsministeriums, des Ministeriums fuer Ernaehrung, Landwirtschaft, Weinbau und Forsten und der Regierungspraesidien des Landes Baden-Wuerttemberg. Ausgabe A (0341-308X); (until 1960): Gemeinsames Amtsblatt des Innenministeriums, des Finanzministeriums, des Ministeriums fuer Ernaehrung, Landwirtschaft und Forsten, des Ministeriums fuer Vertriebene, Fluechtlinge und Kriegsgeschaedigte und der Regierungspraesidien des Landes Baden-Wuerttemberg. Ausgabe A (0404-6021)
Indexed: DokStr, RASB.
Published by: (Schleswig-Holstein. Innenministerium), Staatsanzeiger fuer Baden-Wuerttemberg GmbH, Breitscheidstr 69, Stuttgart, 70176, Germany. TEL 49-711-666010, FAX 49-711-6660119, verlag@staatsanzeiger.de. adv.: B&W page EUR 725. Circ: 3,258 (paid and controlled).

352 ESP ISSN 0212-8195
GENERALITAT VALENCIANA. DIARI OFICIAL. Text in Catalan, Spanish. 1978. d. EUR 33.44 (effective 2009). back issues avail. **Document type:** *Bulletin, Consumer.*
Formerly (until 1982): Bulleti Oficial del Consell del Pais Valencia (0212-8209)
Related titles: CD-ROM ed.: ISSN 1139-0247. 1996; Microfiche ed.: ISSN 1139-2185.
Published by: Generalitat Valenciana, Conselleria de Cultura i Educacio, Plaza de Manise, 3, Valencia, 46003, Spain. TEL 34-96-3866170, FAX 34-96-3803478, infomacio@cult.gva.es, http://www.gva.es.

352.14 USA
JS39
GEORGIA'S CITIES. Text in English. 1951. m. (10/yr.). USD 36 (effective 2009). adv. bk.rev. **Document type:** *Newspaper, Consumer.* **Description:** Covers the activities of municipal government on Georgia, activities of the state and federal government affecting local governments, new trends in local government, and activities of the Georgia Municipal Association.
Former titles: Urban Georgia (0042-0875); Georgia Municipal Journal
Indexed: P06.
Published by: Georgia Municipal Association, 201 Pryor St, S W, Atlanta, GA 30303-3606. TEL 404-688-0472, FAX 404-577-6663, info@gmanet.com. Ed. Amy Henderson. Circ: 7,300 (free).

352.14 DEU ISSN 1861-0145
GERMAN JOURNAL OF URBAN STUDIES/DEUTSCHE ZEITSCHRIFT FUER KOMMUNALWISSENSCHAFTEN (ENGLISH EDITION). Text in English. s-a. free (effective 2011).
Media: Online - full text. **Related titles:** ◆ English ed.: Deutsche Zeitschrift fuer Kommunalwissenschaften. ISSN 1617-8203.
Indexed: CA, P42, PSA, S02, S03, SociolAb, T02.
—CCC.
Published by: Deutsches Institut fuer Urbanistik, Zimmerstr 13-15, Berlin, 10969, Germany. TEL 49-30-390010, FAX 49-30-39001100, difu@difu.de.

352.14 DEU ISSN 0342-3557
KKB4810
GESETZ- UND VERORDNUNGSBLATT FUER DAS LAND HESSEN. Text in German. 1945. irreg., latest vol.11, 2008. index. **Document type:** *Journal, Government.*
Indexed: DokStr.
Published by: (Luzern (Canton). Hessische Staatskanzlei), A. Bernecker Verlag, Unter dem Schoeneberg 1, Melsungen, 34212, Germany. TEL 49-5661-7310, FAX 49-5661-731111, info@bernecker.de, http://www.bernecke.de. Circ: 8,000.

352.14 DEU ISSN 0016-9129
KKC1710
GESETZ- UND VERORDNUNGSBLATT FUER SCHLESWIG-HOLSTEIN. Text in German. 1947. 27/yr.
Indexed: DokStr, RASB.
Published by: Innenministerium, Duesternbrooker Weg 92, Kiel, 24105, Germany. FAX 0431-596-3131. Circ: 4,000.

352 FRA ISSN 1957-6501
GESTION DU PERSONNEL TERRITORIAL AU QUOTIDIEN. Text in French. 2005. base vol. plus updates 3/yr. looseleaf. EUR 76 base vol(s).; EUR 15 updates per month (effective 2007).
Published by: Editions Weka, 249 Rue de Crimee, Paris, 75935 Cedex 19, France. TEL 33-1-53351717, FAX 33-1-53351701.

352.14 CHE
GESTION ET SERVICES PUBLICS. Text in French. 6/yr. **Document type:** *Trade.*
Published by: Verlag Forum Press AG, Ruetistr 22, Schlieren, 8952, Switzerland. TEL 41-1-7385260, FAX 41-1-7385261. Ed., R&P Christoph Bauer. Adv. contact Peter Wirth. Circ: 3,400.

352.14 ESP
GETAFE. AYUNTAMIENTO. BOLETIN INFORMATIVO. Text in Spanish. 12/yr.
Published by: Ayuntamiento de Getafe/Town Council, Plaza de la Constitucion, 1, Getafe, Madrid, 28901, Spain. TEL 34-91-2027911, http://www.getafe.es/. Ed. Pedro Castro Vazquez.

352 NLD
GIDS GEMEENTEBESTUREN. Text in Dutch. a. EUR 65.09 (effective 2009). adv. **Document type:** *Journal, Trade.*
Published by: Sdu Uitgevers bv, Postbus 20025, The Hague, 2500 EA, Netherlands. TEL 31-70-3789911, FAX 31-70-3854321, sdu@sdu.nl, http://www.sdu.nl/. adv.: B&W page EUR 1,795, color page EUR 2,695; 102 x 184. Circ: 4,000.

352 SRB ISSN 1451-3838
GLAS LOKALNE SAMOUPRAVE. Text in Serbian; Summaries in English, French, German. 2002. q. free. back issues avail. **Document type:** *Magazine, Government.* **Description:** Contains presentation of news, projects, expert opinions, international cooperation and interviews, covering various topics of interest to municipalitites and local self-government.
Published by: Stalna Konferencija Gradova i Opstina/Standing Conference of Towns and Municipalities, Makedonska 22, Belgrade, 11000. TEL 381-11-3223446, FAX 381-11-3221215, secretariat@skgo.org, http://www.skgo.org. Ed. Vojislav Krunic. Pub. Djordje Stanicic.

352.14 SWE ISSN 0280-8803
GOETEBORGS KOMMUNALKALENDER. Text in Swedish. 1929. a. SEK 190. **Document type:** *Government.*
Published by: Goeteborgs Stadskansli, Goeteborg, 40482, Sweden. TEL 46-31-611103, FAX 46-31-131248. Ed. Rolf Claesson. Circ: 3,000.

352.14 USA ISSN 0894-3842
JK2403
GOVERNING. Text in English. 1987. m. free to qualified personnel (effective 2011). adv. bk.rev. illus. index. back issues avail.; reprints avail. **Document type:** *Magazine, Government.* **Description:** Focuses on key management functions such as personnel, performance and leadership, as well as on the impact of changes in federalism, technology and regulation.
Incorporates: Public's Capital; (1984-1994): City & State (0885-940X)

P

Related titles: Online - full text ed.: ISSN 1930-6954.
Indexed: A22, A26, B04, BRD, G05, G06, G07, G08, HRIS, I05, M02, MagInd, P02, P10, P30, P34, P48, P53, P54, PAIS, PQC, R03, RGAb, RGPR, S02, S03, S11, T02, W03, W05.
—CIS, Ingenta. **CCC.**
Published by: C Q Press, Inc. (Subsidiary of: Sage Publications, Inc.), 2300 N St, NW, Ste 800, Washington, DC 20037. TEL 202-729-1900, FAX 800-380-3810, customerservice@cqpress.com, http://www.cqpress.com. Eds. Alan Ehrenhalt, Mark Stencel. Pub. Beth Bronder. Circ: 86,000 (paid and controlled).

352.14 USA ISSN 0883-8690
HC110.P63
GOVERNMENT ASSISTANCE ALMANAC. Text in English. 1985. a., latest 21st ed. USD 240 (effective 2008). stat. index. **Document type:** *Directory, Trade.* **Description:** Provides a data base of information on all 1,386 domestic financial and non-financial assistance programs, with a cross-referenced index, application guidelines, funding summary tables, and more than 3,000 addresses and telephone numbers for federal program headquarters and field offices.
Published by: Omnigraphics, Inc., PO Box 31-1640, Detroit, MI 48231. TEL 313-961-1340, 800-234-1340, FAX 313-961-1383, 800-875-1340, info@omnigraphics.com. Ed. J Robert Damouchel.

352.14 CAN ISSN 1185-0337
GOVERNMENT BUSINESS. Text in English. 1986. bi-m. CAD 18, USD 30. adv. bk.rev. back issues avail. **Document type:** *Journal, Trade.* **Description:** Examines trends, issues of government management, new products with specific government applications for administrators, facility managers and purchasers.
Formerly: Canadian Government Buyer (0829-8629)
Published by: Momentum Media Management, 4040 Creditview Rd, Unit 11, P O Box 1800, Mississauga, ON L5C 3Y8, Canada. TEL 905-813-7100, FAX 905-813-7117. Ed. Jay Barwell. Adv. contact Hugn Parkinson. B&W page CAD 2,535; trim 11 x 8. Circ: 19,000 (controlled).

352.14 ZAF
GOVERNMENT DIGEST. Abbreviated title: G D. Text in English. 1960. m. ZAR 171 (effective 2000). adv. bk.rev. illus. **Document type:** *Magazine, Trade.*
Former titles: Local Government Digest; Munisipale en Openbare Dienste (0024-5577)
Related titles: Supplement(s): Consulting Engineer Africa.
Indexed: ISAP.
Published by: Malnor (Pty) Ltd., Private Bag X20, Auckland Park, Johannesburg 2006, South Africa. TEL 27-11-7263081, FAX 27-11-7263017, malnor@iafrica.com. Ed. Donald Koch. R&P Ken Nortje. adv.: B&W page ZAR 5,020, color page ZAR 6,070; trim 210 x 297. Circ: 4,100.

352.14 USA
GOVERNMENTAL AFFAIRS REVIEW (ALBANY). Text in English. m.
Indexed: RehabLit.
Published by: Office of the State Comptroller, Division of Municipal Affairs, Smith State Office Bldg, Albany, NY 12236. TEL 518-474-5505.

352.14 HRV
GRAD KRIZEVCI. SLUZBENI VJESNIK. Text in Croatian. 1965. bi-m. **Document type:** *Government.*
Formerly: Sluzbeni Vjesnik Opcine Krizevci (0037-7163)
Published by: Grad Krizevci, Ivana Zakmardija Dijankoveckog 12, Krizevci, 48260, Croatia. Ed. Ana Lukacic Lojen. Pub. Grad Krizevci. Circ: 200.

352 DEU ISSN 1865-8261
GRAFENRHEINFELDER RUNDSCHAU; amtliches Nachrichtenblatt der Gemeinde Grafenrheinfeld. Text in German. 1974. w. EUR 13.20 (effective 2011). adv. **Document type:** *Newsletter, Trade.*
Published by: Revista Verlag GmbH, Am Oberen Marienbach 2 1/2, Schweinfurt, 97421, Germany. TEL 49-9721-387190, FAX 49-9721-3871938, post@revista.de.

352.73 USA ISSN 1544-516X
GRANTS FOR CITIES AND TOWNS (E-MAIL EDITION). Text in English. 2000. bi-w. USD 213; USD 8.87 per issue (effective 2008). **Document type:** *Newsletter, Trade.* **Description:** Provides timely information on new grant opportunities and funding programs for municipalities.
Media: E-mail.
Published by: Quinlan Publishing Group (Subsidiary of: Thomson West), 610 Opperman Dr, Eagan, MN 55123. TEL 651-687-7000, 800-937-8529, FAX 800-227-7097, bookstore@westgroup.com, http://west.thomson.com/quinlan.

GREAT BRITAIN. AUDIT COMMISSION. REPORT & ACCOUNTS (YEAR). *see* BUSINESS AND ECONOMICS—Banking And Finance

GREAT BRITAIN. AUDIT COMMISSION. REPORTS. *see* BUSINESS AND ECONOMICS—Banking And Finance

352 GBR
GREAT BRITAIN. DEPARTMENT OF COMMUNITIES AND LOCAL GOVERNMENT. LOCAL GOVERNMENT CONSULTATION PAPERS. Text in English. irreg. free. charts; stat. back issues avail. **Document type:** *Monographic series, Government.* **Description:** Discusses pertinent topics in all areas of municipal and regional public administration.
Formerly: Great Britain. Department of the Environment, Transport and the Regions. Local and Regional Government Consultation Papers (Print)
Related titles: Online - full content ed.
Published by: Great Britain. Department of Communities and Local Government, Eland House, Bressenden Pl, London, SW1E 5DU, United Kingdom. TEL 44-20-79444400, contactus@communities.gov.uk.

352 NLD
GREENPORT DUIN- EN BOLLENSTREEK. Text in Dutch. 2006. 4/yr. **Document type:** *Newsletter.*
Published by: Holland Rijnland, Postbus 558, Leiden, 2300 AN, Netherlands. TEL 31-71-5239090, FAX 31-71-5239099, secretariaat@hollandrijnland.net, http://www.hollandrijnland.net.

352.14 FRA ISSN 1271-7789
GREFFIER MUNICIPAL. Text in French. 4/yr. **Document type:** *Bulletin, Trade.*
Related titles: Online - full text ed.: free.
Published by: Syndicat General des Secretaires de Mairie Instituteurs, c/o Jacques Monnot, 15 Rue Jeanniot, Dijon, 21000, France. smi@syndicat-smi.fr. Ed. Marc Chabrier. Circ: 7,000.

352 DEU ISSN 1865-8172
GRETTSTADTER RUNDSCHAU. Text in German. 1978. w. EUR 26.40 (effective 2011). adv. **Document type:** *Newsletter, Trade.*
Published by: Revista Verlag GmbH, Am Oberen Marienbach 2 1/2, Schweinfurt, 97421, Germany. TEL 49-9721-387190, FAX 49-9721-3871938, post@revista.de.

352 FRA ISSN 0248-0573
JS4801
GROUPEMENT DE RECHERCHES COORDONNEES SUR L'ADMINISTRATION LOCALE. COLLECTION. Text in French. 1979. irreg. **Document type:** *Monographic series, Government.*
Published by: Centre National de la Recherche Scientifique, Campus Gerard-Megie, 3 Rue Michel-Ange, Paris, 75794, France. TEL 33-1-44964000, FAX 33-1-44965390, cnrseditions@cnrseditions.fr, http://www.cnrs.fr.

GROWTH AND CHANGE; a journal of urban and regional policy. *see* BUSINESS AND ECONOMICS—Production Of Goods And Services

352 PRT ISSN 1647-1083
GUARDA VIVA. Text in Portuguese. 2007. q. **Document type:** *Report, Government.*
Published by: Camara Municipal da Guarda, Praca do Municipio, Guarda, 6301-584, Portugal. geral@mu-guarda.pt, http://www.mun-guarda.pt.

352 FRA ISSN 1957-6250
GUIDE DE L'ACHETEUR PUBLIC. Text in French. 2004. base vol. plus updates 1/yr. looseleaf. EUR 92 base vol(s).; EUR 23 updates per month (effective 2007).
Published by: Editions Weka, 249 Rue de Crimee, Paris, 75935 Cedex 19, France. TEL 33-1-53351717, FAX 33-1-53351701.

352.14 USA ISSN 1055-596X
HJ275
GUIDE TO FEDERAL FUNDING FOR GOVERNMENTS AND NONPROFITS. Text in English. 1976. q. looseleaf. USD 339; includes supplement. **Description:** Details more than 360 federal aid programs available to state, county and municipal government, tribal governments and non-profit groups. Provides information on eligibility requirements, outlooks for funding, application deadlines, allowable uses of funds and program contacts (including telephone numbers).
Former titles (until 1990): Federal Funding Guide (0273-4435); (until 1980): Federal Funding Guide for Local Governments (0362-4285)
Related titles: ◆ Supplement(s): Federal Grant Deadline Calendar. ISSN 1080-5575.
—CCC.
Published by: Government Information Services (Subsidiary of: Thompson Publishing Group), 1725 K St, N W, 7th Fl, Washington, DC 20006. TEL 800-876-0226, FAX 202-739-9657. Ed. Charles Edwards.

352.14 AUT
GUMPOLDSKIRCHNER NACHRICHTEN. Text in German. 1982. q. **Document type:** *Newsletter, Government.*
Published by: Marktgemeinde Gumpoldskirchen, Gemeindeamt, Gumpoldskirchen, N 2352, Austria. TEL 43-2252-62101, FAX 43-2252-6210133. Circ: 1,500.

352.14 USA
HANDBOOK FOR ARKANSAS MUNICIPAL OFFICIALS. Text in English. irreg., latest 2007. USD 130 combined subscription per issue (print & CD-ROM eds.) (effective 2008). 1602 p./no.; **Document type:** *Handbook/Manual/Guide, Trade.* **Description:** Provide professionals with a practical reference tool of constitutional and statutory provisions governing the operation of cities and towns in Arkansas.
Related titles: CD-ROM ed.
Published by: Michie Company (Subsidiary of: LexisNexis North America), 701 E Water St, Charlottesville, VA 22902. TEL 434-972-7600, 800-446-3410, FAX 434-972-7677, customer.support@lexisnexis.com, http://www.michie.com.

352 NLD ISSN 1872-5856
DE HANDHAVINGSKRANT. Text in Dutch. 2005. a.
Published by: Ministerie van Justitie, Directie Handhaving, Postbus 20301, The Hague, 2500 EH, Netherlands. TEL 31-70-3707911, FAX 31-70-3707900, servicecentrum@minjus.nl.

352.14 USA ISSN 0073-1137
JK9349.O4
HAWAII. OFFICE OF THE OMBUDSMAN. REPORT. Text in English. 1971. a. free. stat. **Document type:** *Government.* **Description:** Annual report to the State Legislature; contains subject chapters, statistics, and case summaries.
Published by: Office of the Ombudsman, Kekuanaoa Bldg, 4th Fl, 465 S King St, Honolulu, HI 96813. TEL 808-587-0770, FAX 808-587-0773. Ed., R&P Robin K Matsunaga. Circ: (controlled).

352.14 DEU
HEIDELBERGER STADTBLATT. Text in German. 1946. w. **Document type:** *Newspaper, Consumer.*
Formerly (until 1993): Heidelberger Amtsanzeiger
Related titles: Online - full text ed.
Published by: Stadt Heidelberg, Amt fuer Oeffentlichkeitsarbeit, Marktplatz 10, Postfach 105520, Heidelberg, 69045, Germany. TEL 49-6221-5812000, FAX 49-6221-5812900, oeffentlichkeitsarbeit@heidelberg.de, http://www.heidelberg.de. Ed. Heike Diesselberg. Circ: 60,000.

352.14 DEU ISSN 0932-9757
DD901.D6
HEIMAT DORTMUND; Stadtgeschichte in Bildern und Berichten. Text in German. 1986. 3/yr. **Document type:** *Journal, Consumer.*
Published by: Klartext Verlag GmbH, Hesslerstr 37, Essen, 45329, Germany. TEL 49-201-8620631, FAX 49-201-8620622, info@klartext-verlag.de, http://www.klartext-verlag.de. Circ: 2,200.

HERNE IN ZAHLEN. JAHRBUCH (YEAR). *see* BUSINESS AND ECONOMICS—Abstracting, Bibliographies, Statistics

HERNE IN ZAHLEN. MONATSBERICHT. *see* BUSINESS AND ECONOMICS—Abstracting, Bibliographies, Statistics

HERNE IN ZAHLEN. VIERTELJAHRESBERICHTE. *see* BUSINESS AND ECONOMICS—Abstracting, Bibliographies, Statistics

352 NZL ISSN 1176-9750
HORIZONS REGIONAL COUNCIL. ANNUAL PLAN. Text in English. 1990. a.
Former titles (until 2003): Horizons.mw. Annual Plan (1176-9742); (until 1999): Manawatu-Wanganui Regional Council. Annual Plan (1172-4951); (until 1998): Manawatu-Wanganui Regional Council. Corporate Plan and Annual Plan (1171-7874); (until 1993): Manawatu Wanganui Regional Council. Corporate Plan (1170-3911)
Published by: Horizons Regional Council, 11-15 Victoria Ave, Private Bag 11025, Parmerston North, New Zealand. TEL 64-6-9522800, FAX 64-6-9522929, help@horizons.govt.nz.

352 NZL ISSN 1176-9548
HORIZONS REGIONAL COUNCIL. ANNUAL REPORT. Text in English. a.
Former titles (until 2002): Horizons.mw. Annual Report (1175-3722); (until 1998): Manawatu-Wanganui Regional Council. Annual Report (1172-0026); (until 1991): Manawatu-Wanganui Regional Council. Annual Financial Report
Published by: Horizons Regional Council, 11-15 Victoria Ave, Private Bag 11025, Parmerston North, New Zealand. TEL 64-6-9522800, FAX 64-6-9522929, help@horizons.govt.nz.

352.14 USA ISSN 0047-0651
JS344.C5
I C M A NEWSLETTER. Text in English. 19??. bi-w. free to members (effective 2011). adv. bk.rev. charts; tr.lit. back issues avail. **Document type:** *Newsletter, Trade.* **Description:** Covers the International City/County Management Association activities and local government position vacancies and appointments.
Formerly (until 1969): City Managers' Newsletter
Related titles: E-mail ed.: free to members (effective 2011).
Published by: International City/County Management Association, 777 N Capitol St NE, Ste 500, Washington, DC 20002. TEL 202-289-4262, 800-745-8780, FAX 202-962-3500, info@icma.org, http://icma.org/en/icma/home. Ed. Kathleen Karas.

352.14 USA
JS344.C5
I C M A PUBLIC MANAGEMENT MAGAZINE. (International City/County Management Association) Text in English. 1919. m. (11/yr.). USD 46 domestic to non-members; USD 62 foreign to non-members; free to members (effective 2011). adv. bk.rev. bibl.; illus. back issues avail.; reprints avail. **Document type:** *Magazine, Trade.* **Description:** Designed for quick and informative reading, articles deal with issues of common concern to local government managers.
Former titles (until 2007): Public Management (0033-3611); Which incorporated (in 1970): International City Management Association. Annual Conference. Proceedings; (until 1926): City Manager Magazine; (until 1923): City Manager Bulletin
Related titles: Microform ed.: (from MIM, PQC); Online - full text ed.
Indexed: A12, A13, A17, A22, A23, A25, A26, ABIn, ADPA, B01, B04, B06, B07, B08, B09, B13, BPI, BPIA, BRD, BusI, C12, CA, ChPerI, E08, FR, G05, G06, G07, G08, H09, H10, I05, I07, M01, M02, M06, MEA&I, MagInd, P02, P06, P10, P13, P27, P34, P48, P51, P53, P54, PAIS, PCI, PQC, PersLit, S02, S03, S05, S08, S09, S11, S23, SSAI, SSAb, SSI, T02, W01, W02, W03, W05.
—BLDSC (6967.700000), IE, Ingenta.
Published by: International City/County Management Association, 777 N Capitol St NE, Ste 500, Washington, DC 20002. TEL 202-289-4262, 800-745-8780, FAX 202-962-3500, info@icma.org, http://icma.org/en/icma/home. Ed. Beth Payne TEL 202-962-3619. Circ: 9,500.

352 ESP ISSN 2013-2700
I E A NEWSLETTER. (Institut d'Estudis Autonomics) Text in English. 2005. 3/yr. back issues avail. **Document type:** *Bulletin, Consumer.*
Media: Online - full text. **Related titles:** ◆ Spanish ed.: Boletin de Estudios Autonomicos. ISSN 2013-262X; ◆ Catalan ed.: Butleti d'Estudis Autonomics. ISSN 2013-0538.
Published by: Generalitat de Catalunya, Institut d'Estudios Autonomics, Baixada de Sant Miquel, 8, Barcelona, 08002, Spain. TEL 34-93-3429821, FAX 34-93-3429801, iea.ri@gencat.cat, http://www.gencat.cat/.

352.14 USA ISSN 0145-2290
JS42
I I M C NEWS DIGEST. Text in English. 1972. m. adv. tr.lit. back issues avail. **Document type:** *Newsletter, Trade.* **Description:** Provides educational information to municipal clerks and local government workers.
Published by: International Institute of Municipal Clerks, 8331 Utica Ave., Ste. 200, Rch Cucamonga, CA 91730-7600. TEL 909-592-4462, FAX 909-592-1555, hq@iimc.com. Ed., R&P, Adv. contact Chris Shalby. B&W page USD 695; trim 11 x 8.5. Circ: 10,400 (controlled).

352.14 USA ISSN 1541-8693
JS39
I Q REPORT. Variant title: Inquiry Report. Text in English. 1946. m. USD 149 to non-members; USD 119 to members (effective 2011). charts. back issues avail. **Document type:** *Report, Trade.* **Description:** Focuses on a single topic, offering comprehensive information, step-by-step solutions, and real-life examples of successful local government programs.
Former titles (until 2001): I Q Service Report (1541-8723); (until 1998): M I S Report (1541-8715); (until 1984): Management Information Service Report (0730-0239); (until 1969): Management Information Service (0047-5262)
Related titles: Online - full text ed.
Indexed: P06, PAIS, SPAA, UAA.
Published by: International City/County Management Association, 777 N Capitol St NE, Ste 500, Washington, DC 20002. TEL 202-289-4262, 800-745-8780, FAX 202-962-3500, info@icma.org, http://icma.org/en/icma/home. Ed. Mary Marik.

I T U. (Information Technology in Use) *see* COMPUTERS—Information Science And Information Theory

352.14 USA ISSN 1522-7928
IDAHO CITIES FOCUS. Text in English. 1964. q. USD 25 (effective 2000). adv. bk.rev. **Document type:** *Magazine, Trade.* **Description:** Promotes the activities and showcases the accomplishments of AIC member cities. It is sent to Idaho's State Legislators, state and federal government leaders, the Idaho Congressional delegation and Affiliate Members.
Formerly (until 199?): Idaho Cities (1095-9343); Supersedes: Gem City News (0300-8355)
Media: Duplicated (not offset).

Published by: Association of Idaho Cities, 3100 S Vista Ave, Ste 310, Boise, ID 83705. TEL 208-344-8594, FAX 208-344-8677. Ed. Ken Harward. R&P, Adv. contact Tondee P Clark. page USD 750; trim 11 x 8.5. Circ: 2,250 (controlled).

352 USA
THE IDAHO OBSERVER. Text in English. 1997. m. USD 25; USD 45 for 2 yrs.; USD 2 newsstand/cover (effective 2005). adv. **Document type:** *Newspaper.*
Published by: Don Harkens, PO Box 1353, Rathdrum, ID 83858-1353. Ed., Pub. Don Harkins. Adv. contact Ingri Cassei. page USD 400. Circ: 3,000 (paid).

352.14 USA ISSN 0019-2139
JS39
ILLINOIS MUNICIPAL REVIEW; the magazine of the municipalities. Text in English. 1922. m. USD 5 to qualified personnel (effective 2009). adv. illus. index. reprints avail. **Document type:** *Magazine, Trade.*
Indexed: P06.
Published by: Illinois Municipal League, PO Box 5180, Springfield, IL 62705-5180. TEL 217-525-1220, FAX 217-525-7438. Ed. Larry Frang. Circ: 13,500 (controlled).

352.14 CAN
IMPROVEMENT DISTRICT MANUAL. Text in English. base vol. plus irreg. updates. CAD 50.75. **Description:** Provides a comprehensive outline on some of the common procedures that are carried out under the Municipal Act.
Published by: Ministry of Municipal Affairs, Recreation and Housing, Victoria, BC, Canada. **Subscr. to:** Crown Publications Inc. TEL 250-386-4636, FAX 250-386-0221, crown@pinc.com, http://www.crownpub.bc.ca.

INDIANA L T A P NEWSLETTER. (Local Technical Assistance Program) *see* TRANSPORTATION—Roads And Traffic

352 ESP ISSN 1579-3451
INDICADOR DE RENTA DISPONIBLE BRUTA MUNICIPAL. Text in Spanish. 1997. a. free (effective 2008). **Document type:** *Bulletin, Consumer.*
Formerly (until 2001): Indicador de Renta Familiar Disponible Municipal (1139-5125)
Published by: Comunidad de Madrid, Instituto de Estadistica, Principe de Vargara 108, Madrid, 28002, Spain. TEL 34-91-5802540, FAX 34-91-5802664, jestadis@madrid.org, http://www.madrid.org/iestadis/index.htm.

352.021 ESP ISSN 1139-2908
INDICADORES MUNICIPALES. Text in Spanish. 1997. a. EUR 27.05 (effective 2003). back issues avail. **Document type:** *Bulletin, Consumer.*
Related titles: Online - full text ed.
Published by: Comunidad de Madrid, Instituto de Estadistica, Principe de Vargara 108, Madrid, 28002, Spain. TEL 34-91-5802540, FAX 34-91-5802664, jestadis@madrid.org, http://www.madrid.org/iestadis/index.htm.

352.14 DEU
INFORMATION FUER ORMESHEIM. Short title: I F O. Text in German. 1983. s-a. looseleaf. **Document type:** *Newsletter.*
Published by: Sozialdemokratische Partei Deutschlands (SPD), Ortsverein Ormesheim, Mozartstr 4, Mandelbachtal, 66399, Germany. TEL 49-6893-3996. Ed. Rainer Barth.

INFORMATIONEN ZUR MODERNEN STADTGESCHICHTE (I M S). *see* HOUSING AND URBAN PLANNING

INFORME ESTADISTICO DE LA SEGURIDAD SOCIAL. MUNICIPALIDAD CIUDAD CORDOBA. *see* SOCIAL SERVICES AND WELFARE

INFRASTRUCTURE (CHICAGO). *see* LAW

INTERNATIONAL CONFERENCE OF BUILDING OFFICIALS. BUILDING DEPARTMENT ADMINISTRATION. *see* BUILDING AND CONSTRUCTION

INTERNATIONAL CONFERENCE OF BUILDING OFFICIALS. CODE CHANGES COMMITTEE. ANNUAL REPORT. *see* BUILDING AND CONSTRUCTION

INTERNATIONAL CONFERENCE OF BUILDING OFFICIALS. EVALUATION REPORTS. *see* BUILDING AND CONSTRUCTION

INTERNATIONAL CONFERENCE OF BUILDING OFFICIALS. PLAN REVIEW MANUAL. *see* BUILDING AND CONSTRUCTION

352.14 USA ISSN 0892-3795
THE IOWA COUNTY. Text in English. 1972. m. USD 20 (effective 2005). adv. bk.rev. back issues avail. **Document type:** *Magazine, Trade.* **Description:** Promotes efficient and economically sound county government for the citizens of Iowa.
Formerly: County (Des Moines) (0199-7793)
Published by: Iowa State Association of Counties, 501 SW 7th St, Ste Q, Des Moines, IA 50309-4540. TEL 515-244-7181, FAX 515-244-6397. Adv. contact Denise Obrecht. page USD 462; 7 x 9.5. Circ: 2,000.

352.14 ITA ISSN 1126-7917
LE ISTITUZIONI DEL FEDERALISMO. Text in Italian. 1980. 5/yr. EUR 42 (effective 2008). **Document type:** *Magazine, Trade.* **Description:** Traces institutional changes in regional and local governments of Emilia-Romagna.
Formerly (until 1996): Regione e Governo Locale (0393-7437)
Indexed: DoGi.
Published by: Maggioli Editore, Via del Carpino 8/10, Santarcangelo di Romagna, RN 47822, Italy. TEL 39-0541-628111, FAX 39-0541-622020, http://www.maggioli.it. Circ: 5,000.

352 ITA ISSN 1828-468X
L'ITALIA DEI COMUNI. Text in Italian. 2005. m. **Document type:** *Magazine, Trade.*
Published by: A N C I Servizi, Piazza Cola di Rienzo 69, Rome, 00192, Italy. TEL 39-06-36762300, FAX 39-06-36004686, info@anciservizi.it, http://www.anciservizi.it.

352 PRT ISSN 1646-9852
ITINERENCIAS. Text in Portuguese. 2008. a. **Document type:** *Magazine, Consumer.*
Published by: Camara Municipal de Matosinhos, Avenida Dom Afonso Henriques, Matosinhos, 4454-510, Portugal. TEL 351-229-390900, FAX 351-229-351645, mail@cm-matosinhos.pt, http://www.cm-matosinhos.pt.

352.14 USA ISSN 1074-956X
J O B. (Job Opportunities Bulletin) Text in English. 1989. bi-w. adv. back issues avail. **Document type:** *Newsletter.* **Description:** Dedicated to the recruitment of the next generation of local government professionals, including minorities and women.
Related titles: Online - full text ed.: free to members (effective 2011).
Published by: International City/County Management Association, 777 N Capitol St NE, Ste 500, Washington, DC 20002. TEL 202-289-4262, 800-745-8780, FAX 202-962-3500, info@icma.org, http://icma.org/en/icma/home.

352.14 FRA ISSN 0021-8030
JOURNAL DES COMMUNES. Text in French. 1827. m. (8/yr). EUR 49 domestic to individuals; EUR 69 foreign to individuals; EUR 87 domestic to institutions; EUR 107 foreign to institutions (effective 2009). **Document type:** *Journal, Government.* **Description:** Contains information for municipalities on a monthly basis about taxes, new laws and regional activity.
Incorporates (1901-1998): Le Journal d'Administration des Communes Rurales (1157-0377)
Indexed: FR.
Published by: Victoires Editions, 38 rue Croix des Petits Champs, Paris, Cedex 01 75038, France. TEL 33-1-53459810, FAX 33-1-53459189.

352.14 FRA ISSN 0294-8095
JOURNAL DES MAIRES; et des conseillers municipaux. Text in French. 1857. m. (11/yr.). EUR 89 (effective 2009). adv. **Document type:** *Journal.*
Formerly (until 1863): Supplement Trimestriel du Secretaire de Mairie (1146-9099)
Indexed: FR.
Published by: SETAC, 22 rue Cambaceres, Paris, 75008, France. TEL 33-01-42655894, FAX 33-01-47428757, http://www.journaldemaires.com. Ed. Christophe Robert. Circ: 16,000.

352 GBR ISSN 1756-9583
▼ ➤ **JOURNAL OF TOWN & CITY MANAGEMENT.** Abbreviated title: J T C M. Text in English. 2010. q. GBP 180 combined subscription per vol. in the UK & Europe (print & online eds.) (effective 2012). adv. **Document type:** *Journal, Academic/Scholarly.* **Description:** Publishes briefings, reviews, applied research and opinion on all aspects of town and city management.
Related titles: Online - full text ed.: ISSN 1756-9591. 2010.
Published by: (Association of Town Centre Management, International Downtown Association USA), Henry Stewart Publications LLP, c/o Gwen Yates, Russell House, 28-30 Little Russell St, London, WC1A 2HN, United Kingdom. TEL 44-20-70923496, FAX 44-20-74042081, qweny@henrystewart.co.uk, http://www.henrystewart.com/default.aspx. Ed. Andres Coca-Stefaniak. Pub., Adv. contact Daryn Moody TEL 44-20-74043040. **Subscr. to:** Henry Stewart Publications, PO Box 361, Birmingham, AL 35201. TEL 205-995-1588, 800-633-4931, hsp@ebsco.com.

352.14 DNK ISSN 0903-6237
K C NYT. (Foreningen af Kommunale Chefer) Text in Danish. 1977. irreg. free membership. illus. **Document type:** *Newsletter, Consumer.*
Former titles (until 1987): F A K E Nyt (0906-8449); (until 1983): Foreningen af Kommunale Embedsmaend. Medlemsny (0906-8430); (until 1980): F A K E Nyt (0109-0925)
Related titles: Online - full text ed.
Published by: Foreningen af Kommunale Chefer, Niels Hemmingsens Gade 10, Copenhagen K, 1153, Denmark. TEL 45-33-768696, FAX 45-33-768697, kc@skaf-net.dk.

352.14 AUT ISSN 0022-7552
KAERNTNER GEMEINDEBLATT. Text in German. 1926. irreg. bk.rev. stat. index. **Document type:** *Newsletter, Consumer.*
Related titles: Microform ed.
Published by: (Kaernten. Amt der Kaerntner Landesregierung), Kaertner Druck- und Verlagsgesellschaft mbH, Viktringer Ring 28, Klagenfurt, K 9010, Austria. TEL 43-463-5866, FAX 43-463-5866321, info@kdruck.at, http://www.kaerntner-druckerei.at.

352.14 AUT ISSN 0022-7579
KAERNTNER LANDES-ZEITUNG. Text in German. 1949. w. EUR 34.98 domestic; EUR 69.77 foreign (effective 2005). **Document type:** *Newspaper, Consumer.*
Published by: Amt der Kaerntner Landesregierung, Arnulfplatz 1, Klagenfurt, K 9020, Austria. TEL 43-50-53622860, FAX 43-50-53622850, http://www.ktn.gv.at. Ed. Hildegard Tschuk.

352.14 USA ISSN 0022-8613
JS39
KANSAS GOVERNMENT JOURNAL. Text in English. 1914. m. USD 30 (effective 2009). adv. bk.rev. illus.; stat. index. reprints avail. **Document type:** *Magazine, Government.*
Indexed: P06.
Published by: League of Kansas Municipalities, 300 S W Eighth St, Topeka, KS 66603-3912. TEL 785-354-9565, FAX 785-354-4186, kgulley@lkm.org, http://www.lkm.org. Ed. Kimberly Winn. adv.: B&W page USD 325. Circ: 6,200 (paid).

342.09 USA ISSN 1087-7207
JK6830
KANSAS LEGISLATIVE HANDBOOK; a guide to the Kansas legislature and its members. Text in English. a. **Document type:** *Directory.* **Description:** Includes information on legislation organization, process, staff agencies and more. Provides biographical profiles on the legislators.
Formerly: Kansas Legislative Sourcebook
Published by: Government Research Service, PO Box 2067, Topeka, KS 66601-2067. TEL 785-232-7720, FAX 785-232-1615, grs@cjnetworks.com.

352.14 USA
JS39
KENTUCKY CITY MAGAZINE. Text in English. 1929. bi-m. adv. illus. 32 p./no.; **Document type:** *Magazine, Government.*
Former titles (until 2009): City Magazine; (until 199?): Kentucky City (0453-5677); (until 1968): Kentucky City Bulletin (0734-4996)
Published by: Kentucky League of Cities, 101 E Vine St, Ste 600, Lexington, KY 40507-3700. TEL 800-876-4552, FAX 859-977-3703, city@klc.org, http://www.klc.org. Ed. Terri Johnson. Circ: 27,100 (controlled).

KEY NOTE MARKET REVIEW: LOCAL GOVERNMENT SERVICES. *see* BUSINESS AND ECONOMICS—Production Of Goods And Services

352.14 AUT ISSN 0023-2017
KLAGENFURT; Mitteilungsblatt der Landeshauptstadt. Text in German. 1951. fortn. EUR 10 domestic; EUR 20 foreign (effective 2005). adv. bk.rev. bibl.; illus. index. **Document type:** *Newspaper, Government.*
Published by: Magistrat der Landeshauptstadt Klagenfurt, Neuer Platz 1, Klagenfurt, K 9010, Austria. TEL 43-463-5372271, FAX 43-463-516990, presse@klagenfurt.at. Ed. Veronika Meissnitzer. Adv. contact Ludmilla Dreier. Circ: 52,500 (controlled).

352 DNK ISSN 0900-1484
KOMMUNAL AARBOG. Text in Danish. 1930. a. DKK 790 (effective 2009). **Document type:** *Yearbook, Consumer.*
Related titles: Online - full text ed.
Address: Noerregade 18 A, Auning, 8963, Denmark. TEL 45-70-250095, FAX 45-70-250096. Ed. Tage Mikkelsen.

352 DEU
KOMMUNAL DIREKT. Text in German. bi-m. EUR 33; EUR 5.50 newsstand/cover (effective 2007). adv. **Document type:** *Magazine, Trade.*
Published by: V M Verlagsgruppe Macke GmbH, Eislebener Str 1, Erfurt, 99086, Germany. TEL 49-361-5662070, FAX 49-361-5662072, info@macke.net, http://www.macke.net. Ed. Ute Bosecker. Pub. Franz Huckewitz. Adv. contact Dieter Ulischberger TEL 49-361-5662070. B&W page EUR 2,960, color page EUR 3,990; trim 190 x 280. Circ: 23,070 (paid and controlled).

352.14 SWE ISSN 0282-0099
KOMMUNAL EKONOMI. Text in Swedish. 1969. 6/yr. SEK 350 (effective 2011). adv. 36 p./no.; **Document type:** *Journal, Trade.* **Description:** Contains information on the economics and finance of the local government.
Formerly (until 1982): Kommunalekonomen (0345-6315)
Related titles: Online - full text ed.
Published by: Foereningen Sveriges Kommunalekonomer, Drottninggatan 22, PO Box 6767, Gaevle, 80172, Sweden. TEL 46-26-128282, FAX 46-26-187672, http://www.kef.se. Ed. Thomas Pettersson TEL 46-31-130256. Adv. contact Tommy Flink. Circ: 3,700.

352 DEU ISSN 2190-1503
KOMMUNAL-KASSEN-ZEITSCHRIFT. Text in German. 1949. m. EUR 124 (effective 2011). **Document type:** *Journal, Trade.* **Description:** Serves as a guide or the municipal funds and enforcement practice. Contains practice-related articles and topics relevant law cases.
Related titles: Online - full text ed.
Published by: (Fachverband der Kommunalkassenverwalter e.V.), Verlag Reckinger & Co, Postfach 1754, Siegburg, 53707, Germany. TEL 49-2241-938340, FAX 49-2241-9383433.

352 DEU ISSN 1431-8253
KOMMUNALE ENTSORGUNG. Text in German. 19??. a. EUR 12 (effective 2006). adv. **Document type:** *Directory, Trade.*
Supersedes in part (in 1996): Kommunale Fahrzeuge und Entsorgung (1430-7073); Which was formerly (until 1993): Kommunale Fahrzeuge (1430-7065); (until 1984): Kommunale Land-, Luft- und Wasser-Fahrzeuge (0175-6745)
Published by: Kuhn Fachverlag GmbH & Co. KG, Bert-Brecht-Str 15-19, Villingen-Schwenningen, 78054, Germany. TEL 49-7720-3940, FAX 49-7720-394175, kataloge@kuhnverlag.de, http://www.kuhn-kataloge.de. Ed. Axel Bethge. Adv. contact Siegfried Girrbach. B&W page EUR 2,235, color page EUR 2,850. Circ: 5,103 (paid and controlled).

628 DEU ISSN 1432-038X
KOMMUNALE FAHRZEUGE. Text in German. 19??. a. EUR 12 (effective 2008). adv. **Document type:** *Directory, Trade.*
Supersedes in part (in 1996): Kommunale Fahrzeuge und Entsorgung (1430-7073); Which was formerly (until 1993): Kommunale Fahrzeuge (1430-7065); (until 1984): Kommunale Land-, Luft- und Wasser-Fahrzeuge (0175-6745)
Published by: Kuhn Fachverlag GmbH & Co. KG, Bert-Brecht-Str 15-19, Villingen-Schwenningen, 78054, Germany. TEL 49-7720-3940, FAX 49-7720-394175, katalog@kuhnverlag.de. Ed. Axel Bethge. Adv. contact Siegfried Girrbach. B&W page EUR 2,270, color page EUR 2,885; trim 180 x 254. Circ: 6,186 (paid and controlled).

352 DEU ISSN 1864-1490
KOMMUNALE FINANZEN IM FOKUS. Text in German. 2000. 4/yr. **Document type:** *Newsletter, Trade.*
Supersedes in part (in 2006): Kommunale Unternehmer im Fokus (1614-2012); Which was formerly (until 2004): NewsLetter. Kommunale Unternehmer im Fokus (1613-5016); (until 2003): NewsLetter. Oeffentliches Management (1610-7098)
Published by: Roedl und Partner GbR, Aeussere Sulzbacher Str 100, Nuernberg, 90491, Germany. TEL 49-911-91930, FAX 49-911-91931900, info@roedl.de.

352.14 CHE
KOMMUNALMAGAZIN. Text in German. 11/yr. **Document type:** *Consumer.*
Published by: Verlag Forum Press AG, Ruetistr 22, Schlieren, 8952, Switzerland. TEL 41-1-7385260, FAX 41-1-7385261. Ed. Werner Hochuli. R&P Christoph Bauer. Adv. contact Peter Wirth. Circ: 5,040.

352 DEU ISSN 0171-7510
KOMMUNALPRAXIS. AUSGABE BAYERN. Text in German. 1979. 11/yr. EUR 314.50; EUR 39 newsstand/cover (effective 2011). adv. **Document type:** *Journal, Academic/Scholarly.*
—CCC.
Published by: Carl Link Verlag (Subsidiary of: Wolters Kluwer Deutschland GmbH), Adolf-Kolping-Str 10, Kronach, 96317, Germany. TEL 49-9261-9694000, FAX 49-9261-9694111, info@wolters-kluwer.de, http://www.carllink.de. Adv. contact Marcus Kipp. Circ: 1,400 (paid and controlled).

352 DEU ISSN 1617-3759
KOMMUNALPRAXIS SPEZIAL. Text in German. 2001. 4/yr. EUR 89.90; EUR 30.50 newsstand/cover (effective 2011). adv. **Document type:** *Journal, Academic/Scholarly.*
Published by: Carl Link Verlag (Subsidiary of: Wolters Kluwer Deutschland GmbH), Adolf-Kolping-Str 10, Kronach, 96317, Germany. TEL 49-9261-9694000, FAX 49-9261-9694111, info@wolters-kluwer.de, http://www.carllink.de. Adv. contact Marcus Kipp. Circ: 1,000 (paid).

352.14 DEU ISSN 0942-5454
DIE KOMMUNALVERWALTUNG BRANDENBURG; Fachzeitschrift fuer die kommunale Praxis. Text in German. 1992. m. EUR 195 (effective 2010). adv. **Document type:** *Bulletin, Trade.*

P

Published by: Richard Boorberg Verlag GmbH und Co. KG, Scharrstr 2, Stuttgart, 70563, Germany. TEL 49-711-73850, FAX 49-711-7385100, mail@boorberg.de. Ed. Susanne Sonntag. Adv. contact Roland Schulz.

352.14 DEU ISSN 0949-0701
DIE KOMMUNALVERWALTUNG MECKLENBURG-VORPOMMERN; Fachzeitschrift fuer die kommunale Praxis. Text in German. 1995. m. EUR 195 (effective 2010). adv. **Document type:** *Bulletin, Trade.*
Published by: Richard Boorberg Verlag GmbH und Co. KG, Scharrstr 2, Stuttgart, 70563, Germany. TEL 49-711-73850, FAX 49-711-7385100, mail@boorberg.de. Ed. Susanne Sonntag. Adv. contact Roland Schulz.

352.14 DEU ISSN 0941-5815
DIE KOMMUNALVERWALTUNG SACHSEN; Fachzeitschrift fuer die kommunale Praxis. Text in German. 1990. m. EUR 195 (effective 2010). adv. **Document type:** *Bulletin, Trade.*
Published by: Richard Boorberg Verlag GmbH und Co. KG, Scharrstr 2, Stuttgart, 70563, Germany. TEL 49-711-73850, FAX 49-711-7385100, mail@boorberg.de. Ed. Susanne Sonntag. Adv. contact Roland Schulz.

352.14 DEU ISSN 0949-0698
DIE KOMMUNALVERWALTUNG SACHSEN-ANHALT; Fachzeitschrift fuer die kommunale Praxis. Text in German. 1995. m. EUR 195 (effective 2010). adv. **Document type:** *Bulletin, Trade.*
Published by: Richard Boorberg Verlag GmbH und Co. KG, Scharrstr 2, Stuttgart, 70563, Germany. TEL 49-711-73850, FAX 49-711-7385100, mail@boorberg.de. Ed. Susanne Sonntag. Adv. contact Roland Schulz.

352.14 DEU ISSN 0943-2434
DIE KOMMUNALVERWALTUNG THUERINGEN; Fachzeitschrift fuer die kommunale Praxis. Text in German. 1993. m. EUR 195 (effective 2010). adv. **Document type:** *Bulletin, Trade.*
Published by: Richard Boorberg Verlag GmbH und Co. KG, Scharrstr 2, Stuttgart, 70563, Germany. TEL 49-711-73850, FAX 49-711-7385100, mail@boorberg.de. Ed. Susanne Sonntag. Adv. contact Roland Schulz.

352.14 DNK ISSN 0903-0077
KOMMUNEN; information om dansk kommunalstyre: Danmarks kommunale efterretninger. Text in Danish. 1958. fortn. bk.rev. **Document type:** *Newspaper, Consumer.* **Description:** Publishes news about Danish municipal and regional government.
Published by: Altinget.dk, Gammel Strand 50, 2, Copenhagen K, 1202, Denmark. TEL 45-33-343540, adm@altinget.dk, http://www.altinget.dk. Eds. Claus Theilgaard, Rasmus Nielsen. Circ: 6,400. **Co-publisher:** dknyt.

352.21 DNK ISSN 1903-072X
KOMMUNERNES OEKONOMI. Text in Danish. 2007. a. back issues avail. **Document type:** *Trade.*
Supersedes in part (in 2007): Kommunal Butgetredegoerelse (0107-5098)
Published by: (Kommunernes Landsforening/National Association of Local Authorities in Denmark), Kommuneforlaget A/S (Subsidiary of: Kommuneinformation A/S), Holmens Kanal 7, Copenhagen K, 1060, Denmark. TEL 45-33-280300, FAX 45-33-280302, post@kommuneforlaget.dk, http://www.kommuneforlaget.dk.

352.14 CHE
KORRESPONDENZBLATT. Text in German. m.
Address: Matthof 18, Littau, 6014, Switzerland. TEL 041-574206. Ed. Plus Kost. Circ: 4,100.

352.14 SVN ISSN 1318-0746
KRANJCAN. Text in Slovenian. 1982. m. back issues avail.
Published by: Skupscina Obcine Kranj, Trg Revolucije 1, Kranj, 64000, Slovenia. TEL 064 25661. Circ: 6,700.

352.14 DEU
KREISAMTSBLATT DES LANDKREISES UND LANDRATSAMTES KRONACH. Text in German. 1900. w. looseleaf. EUR 6.25 per quarter (effective 2006). back issues avail. **Document type:** *Government.*
Formerly: Landkreis Kronach. Amtsblatt
Published by: Landratsamt Kronach, Gueterstr 18, Kronach, 96317, Germany. TEL 49-9261-6780, FAX 49-9261-678211, poststelle@lra-kc.bayern.de. Circ: 400.

352.14 DEU
KREISPOSTILLE. Text in German. 1967. q. free.
Published by: Kreis Neuss, Lindenstr 2-16, Grevenbroich, 41515, Germany. TEL 02181-6011130, FAX 02181-6012630. Circ: 6,000.

352.14 FIN ISSN 1236-0066
JS6291.A1
KUNTALEHTI. Text in Finnish. 1993. 21/yr. EUR 58 (effective 2005). adv. bk.rev. charts; illus.; stat. index. **Document type:** *Magazine, Trade.* **Description:** Covers municipal legislation, economy, local government, education, social welfare, cultural activities, the Parliament, and the European Community.
Formed by the merger of (1916-1993): Suomen Kunnallislehti (0039-5544); (1963-1993): Suomen Kunnat (0586-8971); Which incorporated (1963-1986): Suomen Kunnallisliiton Tiedotuslehti (0357-9271); Which was formerly (until 1979): Suomen Kunnallisliiton Tiedotuksia (0355-3760); (until 1969): Suomen Kunnallisliiton Tiedotuslehti
Related titles: Online - full text ed.
Published by: Suomen Kuntaliitto/Association of Finnish Local Authorities, Toinen Linja 14, Helsinki, 00530, Finland. TEL 358-9-7711, FAX 358-9-7712486. Ed. Olli Havu. Adv. contact Heikki Macklin. Circ: 17,800.

352 DEU ISSN 1864-1504
KURSBUCH STADTWERKE. Text in German. 2000. q. **Document type:** *Newsletter, Trade.*
Supersedes in part (in 2006): Kommunale Unternehmer im Fokus (1614-2012); Which was formerly (until 2004): NewsLetter. Kommunale Unternehmer im Fokus (1613-5016); (until 2003): NewsLetter. Oeffentliches Management (1610-7098)
Published by: Roedl und Partner GbR, Aeussere Sulzbacher Str 100, Nuernberg, 90491, Germany. TEL 49-911-91930, FAX 49-911-91931900, info@roedl.de.

352.14 IND ISSN 0023-5660
HN681
KURUKSHETRA (NEW DELHI). Text in Hindi, English. 1952. m. INR 100; INR 10 per issue (effective 2011). bk.rev. charts; illus. cum.index. **Document type:** *Journal, Government.* **Description:** Devoted to all aspects of rural reconstruction and village democracy. Features rural industrialisation, farm revolution, co-operative progress and problems of district and village administration.
Incorporates (1960-1970): Panchayati Raj (0553-0946); Which was formerly (until 1960): Gram Sevak
Related titles: English ed.
Indexed: P06, PAA&I.
—Ingenta.
Published by: Ministry of Information & Broadcasting, Publications Division, Soochna Bhawan, C.G.O Complex, Lodi Rd, New Delhi, 110 003, India. http://publicationsdivision.nic.in/. Ed. Kailash Chand Meena. **Subscr. in U.S. to:** InterCulture Associates; **Subscr. to:** I N S I O Scientific Books & Periodicals.

352.14 GBR ISSN 1472-2607
L A P V. LOCAL AUTHORITY PLANT & VEHICLES. Text in English. 1982. q. GBP 365 combined subscription to individuals (print & online eds.); GBP 1,490 combined subscription to institutions (print & online eds.); free to qualified personnel (effective 2009). adv. back issues avail. **Document type:** *Magazine, Trade.* **Description:** Directed to local authority and public utility executives responsible for specifying and purchasing plant vehicles and equipment.
Formerly (until 199?): Local Authority Plant & Vehicles (0263-9246)
Related titles: Online - full text ed.
Indexed: A26, E08, I05, S09.
Published by: Hemming Information Services Ltd. (Subsidiary of: Hemming Group Ltd.), 32 Vauxhall Bridge Rd, London, SW1V 2SS, United Kingdom. TEL 44-20-79736694, FAX 44-20-72335052, customer@hgluk.com, http://www.hemminginfo.co.uk. Ed. Ann Marie Knegt TEL 44-1935-374001. Pub. Matt Hobley TEL 44-20-79736642. Adv. contact Jo Langley TEL 44-20-76334503. B&W page GBP 800, color page GBP 1,200.

L A W R. (Local Authority Waste & Recycling) *see* ENVIRONMENTAL STUDIES—Waste Management

352 FRA ISSN 1773-4134
LAMY COLLECTIVITES TERRITORIALES RESPONSABILITES. Text in French. 2005. base vol. plus s-a. updates. looseleaf. EUR 995 base vol(s). per issue print & CD-ROM eds. (effective 2010). **Document type:** *Trade.*
Related titles: CD-ROM ed.: ISSN 1956-8096.
Published by: Lamy S.A. (Subsidiary of: Wolters Kluwer France), 1 Rue Eugene et Armand Peugeot, Rueil-Malmaison, 92856 Cedex, France. TEL 33-1-76733000, FAX 33-1-76734809, lamy@lamy.fr, http://www.wkf.fr.

352 FRA ISSN 1964-5899
LAMY FONCTION PUBLIQUE TERRITORIALE. Text in French. 2007. base vol. plus updates 2/yr. looseleaf. EUR 578 base vol(s). print & CD-ROM eds. (effective 2010). **Document type:** *Trade.*
Related titles: CD-ROM ed.: ISSN 1954-7536.
Published by: Lamy S.A. (Subsidiary of: Wolters Kluwer France), 1 Rue Eugene et Armand Peugeot, Rueil-Malmaison, 92856 Cedex, France. TEL 33-1-76733000, FAX 33-1-76734809.

LAND CONTAMINATION & RECLAMATION. *see* ENVIRONMENTAL STUDIES—Pollution

352.14 AUT ISSN 0023-7884
LANDESGESETZBLATT FUER DAS LAND SALZBURG. Text in German. 1945. irreg. looseleaf. index. **Document type:** *Government.*
Published by: Landesregierung Salzburg, Kaigasse 39, Salzburg, Sa 5010, Austria. TEL 43-662-80422035, FAX 43-662-80423070, buergerbuero@salzburg.gv.at, http://www.salzburg.gv.at. Circ: 2,000.

352 PRT ISSN 1647-211X
LANYOSO. Text in Portuguese. 2006. irreg. **Document type:** *Magazine, Consumer.*
Published by: Camara Municipal de Povoa do Lanhoso, Avenida Republica, Povoa de Lanhoso, 4830-513, Portugal. TEL 351-253-639700, FAX 351-253-639709, http://www.mun-planhoso.pt.

LAW AND ORDER MAGAZINE; the magazine for police management. *see* CRIMINOLOGY AND LAW ENFORCEMENT

342.066 CAN
THE LAW OF MUNICIPAL LIABILITY IN CANADA. Text in English. 1999. 3/yr. looseleaf. CAD 225 (effective 2007). **Document type:** *Handbook/Manual/Guide, Trade.*
Published by: LexisNexis Canada Inc. (Subsidiary of: LexisNexis North America), 123 Commerce Valley Dr E, Ste 700, Markham, ON L3T 7W8, Canada. TEL 905-479-2665, 800-668-6481, FAX 905-479-3758, 800-461-3275, info@lexisnexis.ca. Eds. David G Boghosian, J M Davison.

354.71 CAN ISSN 1180-2987
LEGISLATIVE ASSEMBLY OF ONTARIO. OFFICIAL REPORT OF DEBATES, HANSARD. Text in English, French. irreg.
Former titles (until 1990): Legislative Assembly of Ontario. Hansard, Official Report of Debates (0822-1278); (until 1983): Legislature of Ontario Debates. Official Report. Hansard (0701-7863)
Published by: Legislative Assembly/Assemblee Legislative, Legislative Library, 766 King St, P O Box 6000, Fredericton, NB E3B 5H1, Canada. TEL 506-453-2338, FAX 506-444-5889, jmcneil@gov.nb.ca.

352.14 ESP
LEON. BOLETIN DE INFORMACION MUNICIPAL. Text in Spanish. 1971. q.
Published by: Ayuntamiento de Leon, Julio del Campo, 7, Leon, 24002, Spain. TEL 34-987-101061, atencion-ciudadanos@aytoleon.com, http://www.aytoleon.com.

352 FRA ISSN 1771-2564
LA LETTRE DE L'INGENIERIE CULTURELLE; le mensuel d'information de la culture et des collectivites territoriales. Text in French. 2007. m. EUR 230 (effective 2009). **Document type:** *Newsletter, Trade.*
Published by: Editions Sorman, 13 rue d'Uzes, Paris, 75002, France. TEL 33-1-45084409, infos@editionssorman.com, http://www.internetmairie.com/publications/publications00.php3. Ed. Joy Sorman.

352.14 FRA ISSN 1165-9394
LA LETTRE DU CADRE TERRITORIAL. Text in French. 1984. m. EUR 60 combined subscription print & online eds. (effective 2011). back issues avail. **Document type:** *Magazine, Trade.*
Formerly (until 1987): La Lettre du Cadre Territorial de Claude Mauves (0767-0346)
Related titles: Online - full text ed.
Indexed: FR.
Published by: Reseau Territorial, BP 215, Voiron, Cedex 38506, France. TEL 33-4-76657136, FAX 33-4-76050163, info@territorial.fr, http://www.territorial.fr. Ed. Nicolas Braemer. Circ: 10,500.

352 FRA ISSN 1967-7529
LA LETTRE DU CONTENTIEUX; risques et responsabilites territoriales. Text in French. 2007. bi-w. (22/yr). EUR 399 (effective 2009). **Document type:** *Newsletter, Trade.*
Formerly (until 2008): Risques et Responsabilites Territoriales (1955-5490)
Published by: Editions Sorman, 13 rue d'Uzes, Paris, 75002, France. TEL 33-1-45084409, FAX 33-1-42337883, infos@editionssorman.com.

352 304.6 339 NLD ISSN 2211-9213
LEVEN IN NL. Text in Dutch. 2007. biennial. EUR 20 per issue (effective 2011).
Published by: (Vereniging van Nederlandse Gemeenten, Netherlands. Centraal Bureau voor de Statistiek), Sdu Uitgevers bv, Postbus 20025, The Hague, 2500 EA, Netherlands. TEL 31-70-3789911, FAX 31-70-3854321, sdu@sdu.nl, http://www.sdu.nl/.

352.14 GBR ISSN 1356-3696
LOCAL AUTHORITY BUILDING & MAINTENANCE. Text in English. 1985. m. (except Jul./Aug. combined). free to qualified personnel (effective 2009). adv. **Document type:** *Magazine, Trade.* **Description:** Providing a blend of news, views, product information and in-depth features on a variety of business topics relevant to the local authority building marketplace.
Related titles: Online - full text ed.
—CCC.
Published by: Hamerville Magazines Ltd., Regal House, Regal Way, Watford, Herts WD24 4YF, United Kingdom. TEL 44-1923-237799, FAX 44-1923-246901, office@hamerville.co.uk. Ed. Claire Clutten. Adv. contact Dave Jones. page GBP 2,500; trim 210 x 289. Circ: 17,500.

352 GBR
LOCAL AUTHORITY COMPANIES AND PARTNERSHIPS. Text in English. 1998. base vol. plus a. updates. looseleaf. GBP 300 (effective 2009). back issues avail. **Document type:** *Handbook/Manual/Guide, Trade.* **Description:** Covers both legislation and case law, follows law joint ventures, whether in the form of limited companies or various sorts of partnership.
Former titles (until 2010): Tottel's Local Authority Companies and Partnerships; (until 19??): Butterworths Local Authority Companies and Partnerships
Published by: Hann Barton Limited, Olive House, 54 Edward Rd. W., Bridgford, Nottingham NG2 5GB, United Kingdom. **Dist. by:** Marston Book Services Ltd., Box 269, Abingdon, Oxon OX14 4YN, United Kingdom. subscriptions@marston.co.uk.

352 620 IRL ISSN 1393-0397
LOCAL AUTHORITY NEWS. Cover title: L A N Local Authority News. Text in English. 1988. m. free to qualified personnel (effective 2005). adv. tr.lit. back issues avail. **Document type:** *Magazine, Government.* **Description:** Covers subjects of interest to local government and central government decision makers and contains positive coverage of positive projects.
Related titles: Online - full text ed.
Indexed: PADDI.
Published by: Nestron Ltd, 68 Middle Abbey St, Dublin, 1, Ireland. TEL 353-1-8720030, 353-1-8720084, FAX 353-1-8720856, nestron@indigo.ie. Ed. Annette O'Riordan. Pub., R&P, Adv. contact Frank Lambert.

352.14 GBR ISSN 0308-3594
JS3001
LOCAL COUNCIL REVIEW. Abbreviated title: L C R. Text in English. 1950. q. GBP 17 (effective 2009). adv. bk.rev. illus. **Document type:** *Magazine, Trade.*
Formerly (until 1973): Parish Councils Review (0031-2061)
Related titles: Online - full text ed.
Indexed: RICS.
Published by: National Association of Local Councils, 109 Great Russell St, London, WC1B 3LD, United Kingdom. TEL 44-20-76371865, FAX 44-20-74367451, nalc@nalc.gov.uk. Eds. Marie Dill, Alan Jones. Adv. contact Anthon Linton TEL 44-20-73060300 ext 228.

352.14 PAK
LOCAL GOVERNMENT. Text in English. 1974 (vol.5). m. PKR 25. adv. bk.rev.
Published by: Pakistan Group for the Study of Local Government, 14 Japan Mansion, Preedy St., Karachi, Pakistan. Ed. Malik M Siddiq.

026.34 AUS ISSN 1443-8631
LOCAL GOVERNMENT AND ENVIRONMENTAL LAW LIBRARY. Text in English. 1996. base vol. plus m. updates. AUD 5,970 for practices with up to 20 practitioners (effective 2004).
Formerly (until 2000): Local Government Law Library on CD-ROM (1327-1954)
Media: CD-ROM. **Related titles:** Online - full content ed.: AUD 2,115 (effective 2003).
Published by: Lawbook Co. (Subsidiary of: Thomson Reuters (Professional) Australia Limited), PO Box 3502, Rozelle, NSW 2039, Australia. TEL 61-2-85877980, 300-304-195, FAX 61-2-85877981, 300-304-196, LTA.Service@thomsonreuters.com, http://www.thomson.com.au.

352.14 AUS ISSN 1039-7213
KU2300.A57
LOCAL GOVERNMENT AND ENVIRONMENTAL REPORTS OF AUSTRALIA. Abbreviated title: L G E R A. Text in English. 1956. 4 parts/vol.; 5 vols./yr.), base vol. plus irreg. updates. AUD 3,913 bound vols. & parts (effective 2008). back issues avail. **Document type:** *Report, Trade.* **Description:** Contains reports and cases relating to environmental control, local government, valuation of land, compensation, town planning and powers and duties of statutory authorities from the high court and supreme courts of the states and territories of Australia.
Former titles (until 1993): Local Government Reports of Australia (0076-0242); (until 1956): The N S W Local Government Reports (1320-1603)
Related titles: CD-ROM ed.; Online - full text ed.

Published by: Lawbook Co. (Subsidiary of: Thomson Reuters (Professional) Australia Limited), PO Box 3502, Rozelle, NSW 2039, Australia. TEL 61-2-85877980, 300-304-195, FAX 61-2-85877981, 300-304-196, LTA.Service@thomsonreuters.com, http://www.thomson.com.au. Ed. Stefani White.

352.14 AUS ISSN 1326-9739
LOCAL GOVERNMENT AND PLANNING LAW GUIDE. Text in English. 1956. base vol. plus bi-m. updates. AUD 465 (effective 2008). back issues avail. **Document type:** *Handbook/Manual/Guide, Trade.* **Description:** Includes notes on cases on administration, building control, environment, local government, public health, town planning, and traffic and valuations.
Formerly (until 1995): Town Planning and Local Government Guide (0040-9995)
Published by: Lawbook Co. (Subsidiary of: Thomson Reuters (Professional) Australia Limited), PO Box 3502, Rozelle, NSW 2039, Australia. TEL 61-2-85877980, 300-304-195, FAX 61-2-85877981, 300-304-196, LTA.Service@thomsonreuters.com, http://www.thomson.com.au.

352.14 PHL ISSN 0024-5526
JS7301.A1
LOCAL GOVERNMENT BULLETIN. Text in English. 1966. bi-m. PHP 90, USD 15. bk.rev. illus.; stat.
Indexed: BAS, IPP, RASB.
Published by: University of the Philippines, College of Public Administration, Diliman, P.O. Box 198, Quezon City, Philippines. TEL 99-39-14. Eds. Alex Brillantes Jr., Vicente Mariano. Circ: 1,000.

352.14 GBR ISSN 0024-5534
JS3001
LOCAL GOVERNMENT CHRONICLE. Text in English. 1855. w. GBP 140 to individuals; GBP 220 to institutions (effective 2009). bk.rev. illus. index. reprints avail. **Document type:** *Magazine, Trade.* **Description:** Provides the latest local government news to council officers, councillors, MPs, ministers, and journalists. Includes in-depth analysis of issues as diverse as government policy developments, staff disputes, compulsory competitive tendering, public sector pay, Europe, finance, and housing.
Former titles (until 1955): Local Government Chronicle & Magisterial Reporter; (until 1928): Local Government Chronicle and Knight's Official Advertiser; (until 1872): Knight's Official Advertiser of Local Management in England and Wales
Related titles: Microform ed.: (from PQC); Online - full text ed.; Supplement(s): L G C Law and Administration. ISSN 1365-9812. 19??.
Indexed: ADPA, ELJI, LJI, RICS.
—BLDSC (5290.013000). **CCC.**
Published by: L G C Communications Ltd. (Subsidiary of: Emap Communications Ltd.), Greater London House, Hempstead Rd, London, NW1 7EJ, United Kingdom. TEL 44-20-77285000. Ed. Emma Maier TEL 44-20-77283772. Adv. contact David Bentley TEL 44-20-77283732. **Subscr. to:** CDS Global, Tower House, Sovereign Park, Market Harborough, Leics LE16 9EF, United Kingdom. TEL 44-1858-438804, subs@subscription.co.uk.

352.14 GBR ISSN 1472-3484
LOCAL GOVERNMENT EXECUTIVE. Abbreviated title: L G E. Text in English. 1993. bi-m. GBP 15 (effective 2009). adv. bk.rev. back issues avail.; reprints avail. **Document type:** *Magazine, Trade.* **Description:** Covers finance, communications, information technology, and news of conferences and exhibitions.
Former titles (until 2000): Local Government and Health Executive (1466-7975); (until 1999): Local Government Executive (1350-2719)
Related titles: Online - full text ed.
—CCC.
Published by: Excel Publishing, 127-129 Portland St, Manchester, M1 4PZ, United Kingdom. TEL 44-161-2362782, FAX 44-161-2362783, info@excelpublishing.co.uk, http://www.excelpublishing.co.uk/. adv.: color page GBP 1,495; trim 210 x 278. Circ: 4,200 (controlled).

352 GBR ISSN 1468-3024
LOCAL GOVERNMENT FIRST. Text in English. 1997. w. free to members (effective 2010). 16 p./no.; back issues avail. **Document type:** *Magazine, Government.* **Description:** Features news and views that matter on the LGA and local government.
Formerly (until 1999): Local Government Talkback (1368-5198)
Related titles: Audio cassette/tape ed.; Online - full text ed.: free (effective 2010).
—CCC.
Published by: Local Government Association, Local Government House, Smith Sq, London, SW1P 3HZ, United Kingdom. TEL 44-20-76643131, FAX 44-20-76643030, info@lga.gov.uk. Ed. Karen Thornton. Adv. contact Richard Mole.

352.14 AUS ISSN 0819-470X
LOCAL GOVERNMENT FOCUS (GREEN EDITION). Text in English. 1985. m. free. adv. back issues avail. **Document type:** *Newspaper.* **Description:** For states of Victoria, New South Wales and Tasmania. Promotes best practice and issues that have an impact on local government.
Incorporates (1996-2000): Local Government Focus (Gold Edition) (1326-3714)
Related titles: Online - full text ed.: 19??. free (effective 2009).
Published by: Eryl Morgan Publications Pty Ltd., 785 High St, Thornbury, VIC 3071, Australia. TEL 61-3-94169900, FAX 61-3-94169633. Ed. Corinne Morgan. Adv. contact Jan Morgan. Circ: 11,200.

LOCAL GOVERNMENT INDEX NEW SOUTH WALES. *see* PUBLIC ADMINISTRATION—Abstracting, Bibliographies, Statistics

352 GBR
LOCAL GOVERNMENT LAW. Text in English. 1998. 2 service issues & 1 quarterly bulletin per year), base vol. plus s-a. updates. looseleaf. GBP 354 base vol(s). (effective 2011). back issues avail. **Document type:** *Handbook/Manual/Guide, Trade.* **Description:** Provides vital information on local government powers organizations, finance and general principles of law and practice; addresses topical issues in education, housing and social services.
Former titles (until 2010): Tottel's Local Government Law; (until 2005): Butterworths Local Government Law
Published by: Bloomsbury Professional Ltd. (Subsidiary of: Bloomsbury Publishing plc), 41-43 Boltro Rd, Haywards Heath, West Sussex RH16 1BJ, United Kingdom. TEL 44-1444-416119, FAX 44-1444-440426, customerservices@bloomsburyprofessional.com. Eds. James Goudie, Justice Elias.

342.09 AUS ISSN 0727-7830
LOCAL GOVERNMENT LAW & PRACTICE NEW SOUTH WALES. Text in English. 1987. 3 base vols. plus q. updates. looseleaf. AUD 1,031 vols.1-3 (effective 2008). **Document type:** *Handbook/Manual/Guide, Trade.* **Description:** Includes the fully annotated Local Government Act 1993 (NSW) and a wide range of related legislation.
Related titles: CD-ROM ed.
Published by: Lawbook Co. (Subsidiary of: Thomson Reuters (Professional) Australia Limited), PO Box 3502, Rozelle, NSW 2039, Australia. TEL 61-2-85877980, 300-304-195, FAX 61-2-85877981, 300-304-196, LTA.Service@thomsonreuters.com, http://www.thomson.com.au.

342.09 USA ISSN 0362-5729
KFN7830.A15
LOCAL GOVERNMENT LAW BULLETIN. Text in English. 1975. irreg., latest no.122, 2009. price varies. back issues avail. **Document type:** *Bulletin, Academic/Scholarly.* **Description:** Addresses issues of interest to local and state government employees and officials.
Related titles: Online - full text ed.: free (effective 2010).
Published by: University of North Carolina at Chapel Hill, School of Government, Knapp-Sanders Bldg, Campus Box 3330, Chapel Hill, NC 27599. TEL 919-966-5381, FAX 919-962-0654, sales@sog.unc.edu, http://sog.unc.edu.

LOCAL GOVERNMENT LAW JOURNAL. *see* LAW

352.14 ZAF
LOCAL GOVERNMENT LIBRARY BULLETIN. Text in English. 1938. irreg. free. back issues avail. **Document type:** *Abstract/Index.* **Description:** Current-awareness information on local government and municipal services in South Africa and elsewhere.
Formerly (until 1992): Municipal Reference Library Bulletin - Bulletin van die Munisipale Naslaanbiblioteek
Published by: Greater Johannesburg Library Services, Central Johannesburg Library, Library Gardens, Market & Fraser Sts, Johannesburg, 2001, South Africa. TEL 27-11-836-3787, FAX 27-11-836-6607. Ed. C Wiltshire. Circ: 300.

352.14 AUS ISSN 1445-4335
LOCAL GOVERNMENT MANAGER. Abbreviated title: L G M. Text in English. 1957. bi-m. AUD 73 domestic; AUD 107 in New Zealand; AUD 127 elsewhere (effective 2009). adv. bk.rev. index. back issues avail. **Document type:** *Journal, Government.* **Description:** Provides articles in relation to new management technique applicable to local government senior managers.
Former titles (until 2001): Local Government Management (0819-1212); (until 1986): Local Government Administration (0024-5518)
Indexed: AusPAIS, PCI.
—Ingenta.
Published by: Local Government Managers Australia, Level 2, 153-161 Pk St, PO Box 5175, South Melbourne, VIC 3205, Australia. TEL 61-3-96829222, FAX 61-3-96828977, national@lgma.org.au, http://www.lgma.org.au. Ed. Jim Elvey TEL 61-3-96762755. Adv. contact David Fallick TEL 61-3-98246211. Circ: 5,000 (controlled).

352.14 GBR ISSN 0261-5185
LOCAL GOVERNMENT NEWS. Abbreviated title: L G N. Text in English. 1979. m. GBP 55 domestic; GBP 65 foreign; free to qualified personnel (effective 2009). adv. stat.; tr.lit. back issues avail. **Document type:** *Newspaper, Government.* **Description:** Covers news, legislative changes and central government policy for senior professional offices in local government.
—BLDSC (5290.019000). **CCC.**
Published by: Hemming Information Services Ltd. (Subsidiary of: Hemming Group Ltd.), 32 Vauxhall Bridge Rd, London, SW1V 2SS, United Kingdom. TEL 44-20-79736694, FAX 44-20-72335052, customer@hgluk.com, http://www.hemminginfo.co.uk. Ed. Laura Sharman TEL 44-20-79734644. Adv. contact Simon Ellicott TEL 44-20-79734735. color page GBP 2,750; trim 210 x 297.

352.14 AUS
LOCAL GOVERNMENT PLANNING & ENVIRONMENT N S W. (New South Wales) (Volume A: Local Government Act & Index; Volume B: Legislation & Acts; Volume C: Commentary) Text in English. 1992. 4-6 updates/yr. for each base vol.), 4 base vols. plus irreg. updates. looseleaf. AUD 2,031.70 (effective 2008). adv. **Description:** Provides a guide to local government, planning and environment law in New South Wales.
Related titles: CD-ROM ed.; Online - full text ed.: AUD 2,083.40 (effective 2008).
Published by: LexisNexis Butterworths (Subsidiary of: LexisNexis Asia Pacific), Level 9, Tower 2, 475-495 Victoria Ave, Locked Bag 2222, Chatswood Delivery Ctr, Chatswood, NSW 2067, Australia. TEL 61-2-94222174, FAX 61-2-94222405, academic@lexisnexis.com.au.

352.14 340 GBR
LOCAL GOVERNMENT PRECEDENTS AND PROCEDURES. Variant title: Harrison Local Government Precedents and Procedures. Text in English. 1996. 3 base vols. plus updates 2/yr. looseleaf. GBP 527 base vol(s). domestic; EUR 696 base vol(s). in Europe; USD 906 base vol(s). elsewhere (effective 2011). **Document type:** *Handbook/Manual/Guide, Trade.* **Description:** Covers tailor-made forms and precedents, procedures, drafting guidelines, checklists, specimen letters and legal summaries that support legal work across the entire range of local authority functions.
Published by: Sweet & Maxwell Ltd. (Subsidiary of: Thomson Reuters Corp.), 100 Avenue Rd, London, NW3 3PF, United Kingdom. TEL 44-20-79337000, FAX 44-20-74491144, sweetandmaxwell.customer.services@thomson.com. Eds. Alan Aisbett, Alan Harrison, Clive Grace. **Subscr. to:** PO Box 1000, Andover SP10 9AF, United Kingdom. TEL 44-20-73938051, sweetandmaxwell.international.queries@thomson.com.

352.14 AUS
LOCAL GOVERNMENT QUEENSLAND. Text in English. 1994. 2 base vols. plus updates 3/yr. looseleaf. AUD 846 base vol(s). (effective 2009). **Document type:** *Handbook/Manual/Guide, Trade.* **Description:** Includes the fully annotated Local Government Act 1993 and a wide range of related legislation.
Formerly (until 19??): Local Government Service Queensland
Published by: Lawbook Co. (Subsidiary of: Thomson Reuters (Professional) Australia Limited), PO Box 3502, Rozelle, NSW 2039, Australia. TEL 61-2-85877980, FAX 61-2-85877981, LTA.Service@thomsonreuters.com, http://www.thomson.com.au/legal/p_index.asp/. Ed. Paul Newman.

352.14 AUS
LOCAL GOVERNMENT REGULATIONS N S W. (New South Wales) Text in English. 1945. base vol. plus q. updates. looseleaf. AUD 448 (effective 2008). **Document type:** *Handbook/Manual/Guide, Trade.* **Description:** Includes all the regulations made under the Local Government Act 1993 (NSW).
Former titles: Local Government Regulations Services New South Wales; Local Government Ordinances Services (New South Wales) (0727-8004)
Related titles: CD-ROM ed.; Online - full text ed.
Published by: Lawbook Co. (Subsidiary of: Thomson Reuters (Professional) Australia Limited), PO Box 3502, Rozelle, NSW 2039, Australia. TEL 61-2-85877980, 300-304-195, FAX 61-2-85877981, 300-304-196, LTA.Service@thomsonreuters.com, http://www.thomson.com.au.

352.14 AUS
LOCAL GOVERNMENT SERVICE VICTORIA. Text in English. 1991. base vol. plus updates 4/yr. looseleaf. AUD 1,711 (effective 2008). **Document type:** *Handbook/Manual/Guide, Trade.* **Description:** Includes the Local Government Act 1989 (Vic.), related legislation and extensive commentary on local government.
Published by: Lawbook Co. (Subsidiary of: Thomson Reuters (Professional) Australia Limited), PO Box 3502, Rozelle, NSW 2039, Australia. TEL 61-2-85877980, 300-304-195, FAX 61-2-85877981, 300-304-196, LTA.Service@thomsonreuters.com, http://www.thomson.com.au.

352.14 GBR ISSN 0300-3930
JS40
➤ **LOCAL GOVERNMENT STUDIES.** Text in English. 1971. 5/yr. GBP 564 combined subscription in United Kingdom to institutions (print & online eds.); EUR 743, USD 933 combined subscription to institutions (print & online eds.) (effective 2012). adv. bk.rev. index. back issues avail.; reprint service avail. from PSC. **Document type:** *Journal, Academic/Scholarly.* **Description:** Covers the study of politics, and the management of local affairs.
Related titles: Online - full text ed.: ISSN 1743-9388. GBP 508 in United Kingdom to institutions; EUR 669, USD 839 to institutions (effective 2012) (from IngentaConnect).
Indexed: A20, A22, ADPA, ASCA, AmHI, BrHumI, CA, CurCont, DIP, E01, GEOBASE, H07, I02, I13, IBR, IBSS, IBZ, P02, P10, P34, P42, P47, P48, P53, P54, PAA&I, PQC, PSA, R02, S02, S03, S11, SCOPUS, SSCI, SociolAb, T02, W07.
—IE, Infotrieve, Ingenta. **CCC.**
Published by: Routledge (Subsidiary of: Taylor & Francis Group), 4 Park Sq, Milton Park, Abingdon, Oxon OX14 4RN, United Kingdom. TEL 44-20-70176000, FAX 44-20-70176336, subscriptions@tandf.co.uk, http://www.routledge.com. Eds. Colin Copus TEL 44-121-4144988, Philip Whiteman. Adv. contact Linda Hann TEL 44-1344-779945. **Subscr. to:** Taylor & Francis Ltd., Journals Customer Service, Sheepen Pl, Colchester, Essex CO3 3LP, United Kingdom.

352 NLD ISSN 0167-0980
LOKAAL BESTUUR. Text in Dutch. 1976. 11/yr. EUR 20 (effective 2008).
—IE.
Published by: Centrum voor Lokaal Bestuur, Postbus 1310, Amsterdam, 1000 BH, Netherlands. TEL 31-20-5512260, FAX 31-20-5512250, clb@pvda.nl. Ed. Jan de Roos.

336.2 BEL ISSN 1373-0460
LOKALE EN REGIONALE BELASTINGEN. Text in Dutch. 1997. q. EUR 122 (effective 2008). **Document type:** *Journal, Trade.*
Published by: Die Keure NV, Kleine Pathoekeweg 3, Bruges, 8000, Belgium. TEL 32-50-471272, FAX 32-50-335154, juridische.uitgaven@diekeure.be, http://www.diekeure.be.

352.14 USA ISSN 0164-3622
JS39
LOUISIANA MUNICIPAL REVIEW. Text in English. 1938. m. USD 12; USD 1.50 per issue (effective 2009). adv. bk.rev. **Document type:** *Magazine, Trade.* **Description:** Devoted to municipal government issues in Louisiana, the U.S., and intergovernmental relations.
Indexed: P06.
Published by: Louisiana Municipal Association, PO Box 4327, Baton Rouge, LA 70821. TEL 225-344-5001, 800-234-8274, FAX 225-344-3057, lamunicipalassociation@compuserve.com. Ed. Tom Ed McHugh. R&P, Adv. contact Thomas B Darensbourg Jr. Circ: 3,300 (paid and controlled).

352.14 CHE
LUZERNER KANTONSBLATT. Text in German. 1975. w. CHF 55. adv.
Published by: (Luzern (Canton). Hessische Staatskanzlei DEU), Raeber AG, Frankenstr 7-9, Lucerne, Switzerland. Circ: 7,050.

352 USA
M A CO NEWS. (Montana Association of Counties) Text in English. 1971. USD 25 (effective 2011). **Document type:** *Newsletter, Trade.* **Description:** News of all Montana counties.
Media: Online - full text.
Published by: Montana Association of Counties, 2715 Skyway Dr, Ste A, Helena, MT 59602. maco@mtcounties.org.

352.16 USA
M A G A ZINE (PHOENIX); a quarterly newsletter focusing on regional excellence. Text in English. 1995. q. adv. **Document type:** *Newsletter, Consumer.* **Description:** Highlights work being done by MAG and member agencies to improve the quality of life in the Maricopa region.
Related titles: Online - full text ed.
Published by: Maricopa Association of Governments, 302 N First Ave, Ste 300, Phoenix, AZ 85003. TEL 602-254-6300, FAX 602-254-6490. Ed. Keely Taft.

352.14 USA
M A P A REGIONAL DIRECTORY OF PUBLIC OFFICIALS. Text in English. 19??. a. USD 10 per issue (effective 2011). **Document type:** *Directory, Government.*
Published by: Omaha - Council Bluffs Metropolitan Area Planning Agency, 2222 Cuming St, Omaha, NE 68102. TEL 402-444-6866, FAX 402-342-0949, mapa@mapacog.org.

352.14 GBR
TD1
M J. Text in English. 1893. w. GBP 140 (effective 2009). film rev. charts; illus.; mkt.; stat. index. **Document type:** *Bulletin, Government.*

P

Former titles (until 2000): Municipal Journal (0143-4187); (until 1970): Municipal and Public Services Journal (0027-3430); (until 1966): Municipal Journal (0027-349X); (until 1961): Municipal Journal, Public Works Engineer and Contractors' Guide; (until 1952): Municipal Journal and Public Works Engineer; (until 1950): Municipal Journal; (until 1948): Municipal Journal, Local Government Administrator Contractors' Guide, and Public Works Engineers; Municipal Journal, Local Government Administrator, and Public Works Engineer; Municipal Journal and Public Works Engineer; (until 1937): The Municipal Journal and Public Works Engineer; (until 1924): Municipal Journal; (until 1905): Municipal Journal Established as London; (until 1900): Municipal Journal and London
Indexed: HRIS, P06, PAIS, RICS, SpeleolAb.
—BLDSC (5879.696000).
Published by: Municipal Journal Ltd., 32 Vauxhall Bridge Rd, London, SW1V 2SS, United Kingdom. TEL 44-1719-736400, FAX 44-1712-335051. Ed., Pub. Michael Burton TEL 44-20-79736623. Circ: 10,668.

352.14 ESP ISSN 1695-2995
M U F A C E. Text in Spanish. 1978. q. back issues avail. **Document type:** *Magazine, Trade.*
Related titles: Online - full text ed.: Muf@ce.
Published by: Mutualidad General de Funcionarios Civiles del Estado/ General Mutual Society of Civil Servants, Paseo Juan XXIII, 26, Madrid, 28071, Spain. TEL 34-91-2739500, FAX 34-91-2739882, http://www.map.es/muface. Eds. Elena Barrera, Catherine Mordos. Circ: 500,000 (controlled and free).

352 330 CAN ISSN 1911-4036
LE MAGAZINE LES ILES. Variant title: Les Iles. Text in French. 2006. q. free. **Document type:** *Magazine, Consumer.*
Published by: Les Iles, 380 Ch. Principal, Suite 201, Cap-aux-Meules, PQ G4T 1C9, Canada. TEL 418-986-2545, FAX 418-986-6126.

352.14 USA ISSN 0025-0791
JS39
MAINE TOWNSMAN. Text in English. 1939. m. USD 15 to non-members; free to members (effective 2005). adv. bk.rev. illus. Index. **Document type:** *Magazine, Trade.*
Published by: Maine Municipal Association, 60 Community Dr., Augusta, ME 04330-9486. FAX 207-626-5947. Ed., Adv. contact Michael L Starn. B&W page USD 392, color page USD 692. Circ: 4,400.

352.14 FRA
MAIRES DE FRANCE. Text in French. 1952. m. EUR 67 domestic; EUR 116.30 foreign (effective 2008). adv. bk.rev. abstr. index. **Document type:** *Magazine, Trade.*
Formerly: Departements et Communes (0045-9984)
Indexed: FR.
Published by: Association des Maires de France, 41 quai d'Orsay, Paris, Cedex 7 75343, France. TEL 33-1-44181414, FAX 33-1-44181416. Ed. Marie Therese Poitevin. Circ: 27,000.

MANAGEMENT IN GOVERNMENT. *see* BUSINESS AND ECONOMICS—Management

352 PRT ISSN 1647-1857
MARE CHEIA. Text in Portuguese. 2004. irreg. **Document type:** *Magazine, Consumer.*
Published by: Camara Municipal da Moita, Praca da Republica, Moita, 2864-007, Portugal. TEL 351-212-806714, FAX 351-212-894928, http://www.cm-moita.pt.

352 FRA ISSN 1262-1277
MARSEILLE. RECUEIL DES ACTES ADMINISTRATIFS. Text in French. 1894. s-m. EUR 0.85 per issue (effective 2010). **Document type:** *Bulletin, Government.*
Formerly (until 1994): Marseille. Bulletin Municipal (1279-3884)
Indexed: P30.
Published by: Ville de Marseille, Hotel de Ville, Place Villeneuve Bargeron, Marseille, 13233, France. http://www.mairie-marseille.fr.

352.14021 USA ISSN 0361-2090
JS451.M47
MASSACHUSETTS MUNICIPAL ASSOCIATION DIRECTORY. Text in English. 1964. a. USD 69 to non-members; USD 34 to members. adv. bk.rev. **Document type:** *Newsletter, Government.* **Description:** Lists local governments and officials in the commonwealth, including city and county governments and state professional organizations.
Related titles: ◆ Supplement(s): Municipal Advocate. ISSN 1046-2422.
Published by: Massachusetts Municipal Association, 60 Temple Place, Boston, MA 02111. TEL 617-426-7272, FAX 612-695-1314. Ed. John Ouellette. Circ: 4,200.

MASSACHUSETTS PRACTICE SERIES. MUNICIPAL LAW AND PRACTICE. *see* LAW

352 PRT
MATOSINHOS (ONLINE); revista municipal. Text in Portuguese. 2004. q. **Document type:** *Magazine, Consumer.*
Formerly (until 2011): Matosinhos (Print)
Media: Online - full text.
Published by: Camara Municipal de Matosinhos, Avenida Dom Afonso Henriques, Matosinhos, 4454-510, Portugal. TEL 351-229-390900, FAX 351-229-351645, mail@cm-matosinhos.pt, http://www.cm-matosinhos.pt.

352.2316 USA
THE MAYORS OF AMERICA'S PRINCIPAL CITIES. Text in English. s-a. USD 16 to non-members; USD 8 to members. **Document type:** *Directory.*
Published by: U.S. Conference of Mayors, Office of Public Affairs, 1620 Eye St, N W, Washington, DC 20006. TEL 202-293-7330. Ed. J Thomas Cochran. R&P Mike Brown.

MCQUILLIN MUNICIPAL LAW REPORT; a monthly review for lawyers, administrators and officials. *see* LAW

362.14 AUS ISSN 1833-7546
MEASURING COUNCIL PERFORMANCE IN TASMANIA. Text in English. 2000. a. free (effective 2009). back issues avail. **Document type:** *Government.* **Description:** Provides performance of councils reports of Tasmania.
Related titles: Online - full text ed.: ISSN 1833-7554.
Published by: Tasmania. Department of Premier and Cabinet, Local Government Office, GPO Box 123, Hobart, TAS 7001, Australia. TEL 61-3-62336758, FAX 61-3-62335602, lgo@dpac.tas.gov.au, http://www.dpac.tas.gov.au/divisions/lgo/.

352 FRA ISSN 1957-6307
MEMENTO DU SPORT. Text in French. 2005. base vol. plus updates 4/yr. looseleaf. EUR 109 base vol(s).; EUR 25 updates per month (effective 2009). **Document type:** *Trade.*
Published by: Editions Weka, 249 Rue de Crimee, Paris, 75935 Cedex 19, France. TEL 33-1-53351717, FAX 33-1-53351701.

352 PRT ISSN 1646-3420
MERTOLA INFORMACAO MUNICIPAL. Text in Portuguese. 2006. irreg. **Document type:** *Report, Consumer.*
Published by: Camara Municipal de Mertola, Largo Luis de Camoes, Mertola, 7750-329, Portugal. TEL 351-286-610100, FAX 351-286-610101, geral@cm-mertola.pt, http://www.cm-mertola.pt.

352 330 CAN ISSN 1708-5500
THE METROPOLITAN ECONOMY. Text in English. 2003. q. free. back issues avail. **Document type:** *Bulletin, Government.*
Related titles: Online - full text ed.: ISSN 1708-5519; ◆ French ed.: L' Economie Metropolitaine. ISSN 1708-5489.
Published by: Communaute Metropolitaine de Montreal, 1002 Rue Sherbrooke Ouest, Bureau 2400, Montreal, PQ H3A 3L6, Canada. TEL 514-350-2550, FAX 514-350-2599, info@cmm.qc.ca.

352.14 USA ISSN 0076-8014
K13
MICHIGAN MUNICIPAL LEAGUE. MUNICIPAL LEGAL BRIEFS. Text in English. 1961. bi-m. free to qualified personnel (effective 2006). reprints avail. **Document type:** *Magazine, Trade.*
Formerly: Municipal Attorneys' Newsletter Information Service
Published by: Michigan Municipal League, 1675 Green Rd, Ann Arbor, MI 48106. TEL 734-662-3246, 800-653-2483, FAX 734-662-8083, http://www.mml.org/. Circ: 700.

352 USA ISSN 1542-0957
MICHIGAN TOWNSHIP NEWS. Text in English. 1958. 11/yr.
Published by: Michigan Townships Association, 512 Westshire Dr., Lansing, MI 48908-0078. TEL 517-321-6467, FAX 517-321-8908. Ed. Debra N. McGuire. Pub. G. Lawrence Merrill. Adv. contact Ryan Knott.

352 FRA ISSN 1955-0146
MIDI-PYRENEES INFO. Text in French. 2006. bi-m. free. **Document type:** *Magazine, Consumer.*
Former titles (until 2006): Midi-Pyrenees Notre Region (1622-8839); (until 1997): Midi-Pyrenees Info (1270-0770)
Related titles: Online - full text ed.
Published by: Conseil Regional Midi-Pyrenees, 22 Bd du Marechal-Juin, Toulouse, Cedex 9 31406, France. TEL 33-5-61335050, FAX 33-5-61335266.

352.14 USA ISSN 0148-8546
JS39
MINNESOTA CITIES. Text in English. 1916. 10/yr. USD 43 (effective 2009). adv. bk.rev. charts; illus.; stat. index. **Document type:** *Magazine, Trade.* **Description:** Covers taxes, finances from the legislator's viewpoint, legislative programs, labor relations and court decisions.
Formerly (until 1976): Minnesota Municipalities (0026-5578)
Indexed: P06, PAIS.
Published by: League of Minnesota Cities, 145 University Ave W, St Paul, MN 55103-2044. TEL 651-281-1200, 800-925-1122, FAX 651-281-1299, webmaster@lmnc.org, http://www.lmnc.org. Ed. Claudia Hoffacker. adv.: B&W page USD 12,000; trim 7 x 10. Circ: 7,300 (controlled).

352 ESP ISSN 0213-2451
DP402.C54
MISCEL.LANIA CERVERINA. Text in Catalan. 1983. a. EUR 12 newsstand/cover (effective 2008). back issues avail.
Published by: Ajuntament de Cervera, Centre Municipal de Cultura, C. Major, 115 2nd, Cervera (Leida), 25200, Spain. TEL 34-973-530488, cultura@cmo-cervera.cat, http:/www.cmc.cervera.com/.

MISSISSIPPI CITIES & COUNTIES GRAPHIC PERFORMANCE ANALYSIS. *see* PUBLIC ADMINISTRATION—Abstracting, Bibliographies, Statistics

352.14 USA ISSN 0026-6337
JS303.M7
MISSISSIPPI MUNICIPALITIES. Text in English. 1955. q. adv. illus.; tr.lit. **Document type:** *Bulletin, Government.*
Indexed: P06.
Published by: Mississippi Municipal League, 600 E Amite St, Ste 104, Jackson, MS 39201-1906. TEL 601-353-5854, 800-325-7641, FAX 601-353-0435.

352.14 USA ISSN 0026-6647
JS39
MISSOURI MUNICIPAL REVIEW. Text in English. 1936. bi-m. USD 25; free to qualified personnel (effective 2010). adv. bk.rev. charts; illus. Index. 30 p./no.; back issues avail. **Document type:** *Magazine, Trade.* **Description:** Designed to meet the needs and interests of municipal officials in Missouri.
Published by: Missouri Municipal League, 1727 Southridge Dr, Jefferson City, MO 65109. TEL 573-635-9134, FAX 573-635-9009, info@mocities.com. Ed. Katie Bradley. adv.: B&W page USD 500, color page USD 550; trim 8.5 x 11. Circ: 6,400.

352.14 AUT
MITTEILUNGSBLATT DER STADT VILLACH. Text in German. 1947. s-m. USD 20 (effective 2000). adv. bk.rev. **Document type:** *Bulletin, Consumer.*
Published by: Magistrat der Stadt Villach, Pressestelle, Rathaus, Villach, K 9500, Austria. TEL 43-4242-2051700, FAX 43-4242-2051799, pressestelle@villach.at, http://www.villach.at. Ed. Andreas Kuchler. Circ: 29,550.

352.14 USA
MONITOR (RANCHO PALOS VERDE); we the people and our two cents worth. Text in English. 1988. q. USD 6; USD 10 foreign. **Document type:** *Newsletter.* **Description:** Contains investigative reporting on local government and court. Also analyzes present and future political events and environmental issues.
Published by: E T S Research Inc., 80 Narcissa Dr., Rancho Palos Verde, CA 90274. TEL 310-377-7608, FAX 310-377-2178. Ed., R&P Erica Stuart. Circ: 5,000.

352.14 USA ISSN 0026-9980
MONTANA LEAGUE OF CITIES & TOWNS. NEWSLETTER. Text in English. 1975 (no.139). irreg. (3-4/yr.). free. adv. illus. **Document type:** *Newsletter.*
Formerly: Montana Municipal League. Newsletter
Published by: Montana League of Cities & Towns, PO Box 1704, Helena, MT 59624. TEL 406-442-8768. Ed. Alec Hansen. Adv. contact Debbie Jones. Circ: 1,200.

352 PRT ISSN 1646-9844
MONTE MAYOR. Text in Portuguese. 2006. s-a. **Document type:** *Magazine, Consumer.*
Published by: Camara Municipal de Montemor-o-Velho, Praca da Republica, Montemor-o-Velho, 3140-258, Portugal. http://www.cm-montemorovelho.pt.

352.14 BEL
MOUVEMENT COMMUNAL. Text in French. 1918. 10/yr. EUR 40 to members; EUR 100 to non-members (effective 2005). adv. bk.rev. bibl.; illus. index. 64 p./no. 2 cols./p.; back issues avail. **Document type:** *Bulletin.* **Description:** Deals with issues relating to politics, public policy and public administration.
Published by: (Alliance Media), Union des Villes et Communes de Wallonie, rue de l'Etoile, 14, Namur, 5000, Belgium. TEL 32-81-240611, FAX 32-81-240610, commune@uvcw.be. Ed. Louise Marie Bataille. Pub. L M Bataille. R&P, Adv. contact Yves Kengen. Circ: 5,000.

MUNICIPAL ACT AND INDEX TO LOCAL GOVERNMENT LEGISLATION MANUAL. *see* PUBLIC ADMINISTRATION—Abstracting, Bibliographies, Statistics

352.14 USA ISSN 1046-2422
CODEN: BOISF6
MUNICIPAL ADVOCATE. Text in English. 1980. q. USD 49 to members; USD 99 to non-members (effective 2009). adv. **Document type:** *Magazine, Trade.* **Description:** Articles, news and information on municipal law, insurance, finance, public safety, land use and public works for mayors, town and city managers, finance committee chairmen, treasurers and other officials with purchasing authority.
Formerly (until 1988): Municipal Forum (1041-6021)
Related titles: ◆ Supplement to: Massachusetts Municipal Association Directory. ISSN 0361-2090.
Published by: Massachusetts Municipal Association, 60 Temple Place, Boston, MA 02111. TEL 617-426-7272, FAX 617-695-1314. Ed. John Ouellette. Circ: 4,525.

352.14 AUS ISSN 0077-2143
MUNICIPAL ASSOCIATION OF VICTORIA. MINUTES OF PROCEEDINGS OF ANNUAL SESSION. Text in English. 1879. a. index. **Document type:** *Proceedings.*
Published by: Municipal Association of Victoria, GPO Box 4326, Melbourne, VIC 3001, Australia. TEL 61-3-96675555, FAX 61-3-96675550, inquiries@mav.asn.au, http://www.mav.asn.au.

352 USA
MUNICIPAL BULLETIN. Text in English. 1941. bi-m. **Document type:** *Bulletin, Government.* **Description:** Covers NYCOM's activities and events, reports on legislative and other developments, analyses of special issues and other information on the municipal legal front.
Published by: New York Conference of Mayors and Municipal Officials, 119 Washington Ave, Albany, NY 12210. TEL 518-463-1185, FAX 518-463-1190, info@nycom.org. Ed. Jennifer Purcell. Circ: 7,000.

MUNICIPAL CONNECTION; product and news source for all your municipal needs. *see* BUSINESS AND ECONOMICS—Production Of Goods And Services

MUNICIPAL FINANCE JOURNAL. *see* BUSINESS AND ECONOMICS—Public Finance, Taxation

352 CAN ISSN 1180-5994
MUNICIPAL FINANCIAL INFORMATION. Text in Multiple languages. 1917. a. **Document type:** *Government.*
Former titles (until 1986): Local Government Finance in Ontario (0704-2906); (until 1974): Municipal Financial Information (0704-2892); (until 1972): Municipal Financial Report (0316-7690); (until 1970): Summary of Financial Reports of Municipalities (0316-7704); (until 1967): Annual Reports of Municipal Statistics (0316-7712); (until 1934): Municipal Statistics (0316-7720)
Published by: Ontario. Ministry of Municipal Affairs and Housing, 777 Bay St. 17th Fl, Toronto, ON M5G 2E5, Canada. TEL 416-585-7000, FAX 416-585-6470, mininfo@mah.gov.on.ca, http://www.mah.gov.on.ca.

MUNICIPAL LAWYER (BETHESDA). *see* LAW

352 CAN
MUNICIPAL LEADER. Text in English. q.
Published by: Association of Manitoba Municipalities, 1910 Saskatchewan Ave, W, Portage La Prairie, MB R1N 3B7, Canada. TEL 204-857-8666, FAX 204-239-0275. Ed. Terry Ross. Circ: 1,400.

MUNICIPAL LIABILITY RISK MANAGEMENT. *see* LAW

352.14 USA ISSN 0278-1301
KF5304.A75
MUNICIPAL LITIGATION REPORTER. Abbreviated title: M L R. Text in English. 1981. m. USD 497 (effective 2008). index. back issues avail.; reprints avail. **Document type:** *Newsletter, Trade.* **Description:** Covers full spectrum of litigation involving local government entities in all 50 states and U.S. territories and possessions.
Related titles: Online - full text ed.
—CIS.
Published by: Strafford Publications, Inc., 590 Dutch Valley Rd, N E, P O Drawer 13729, Atlanta, GA 30324. TEL 404-881-1141, FAX 404-881-0074, custserv@straffordpub.com. Pub. Richard C Ossoff.

352.14 USA ISSN 0196-9986
JS451.M37
MUNICIPAL MARYLAND. Text in English. 1948. 9/yr. USD 40 (effective 2009). adv. bk.rev. **Document type:** *Newsletter, Trade.* **Description:** Publishes articles on the economic, legislative, law-enforcement, and social issues that affect the state's cities and towns.
Formerly: Maryland Municipal News (0025-4304)
Published by: Maryland Municipal League, Inc., 1212 West St, Annapolis, MD 21401. TEL 410-268-7004. Ed. Karen Bohlen. Adv. contact Greg Napps TEL 410-267-1200. Circ: 2,000.

352.9 333 USA ISSN 1545-9500
MUNICIPAL PLANNING - LAND USE BULLETIN. Text in English. 2002 (Sept.). m. USD 139 (effective 2003). **Document type:** *Newsletter.*
Formerly (until 2003): Land Use Grants and Law Bulletin
Related titles: Online - full text ed.: ISSN 1545-9519.

Published by: Quinlan Publishing Group (Subsidiary of: Thomson West), 610 Opperman Dr, Eagan, MN 55123. TEL 651-687-7000, 800-937-8529, FAX 800-227-7097, bookstore@westgroup.com, http://west.thomson.com/quinlan. Ed. Patricia J. Lloyd. Pub. E Michael Quinlan.

332.6 CAN
HJ8514.B72
MUNICIPAL REDBOOK (BRITISH COLUMBIA & ALBERTA). Text in English. 1940. a. CAD 199 (effective 2000). adv. **Document type:** *Directory, Trade.* **Description:** Contains listings of British Columbia and Alberta municipalities, districts, hospitals and school districts.
Supersedes in part (in 1994): British Columbia Municipal Yearbook (Redbook) (0068-161X); Which was formerly (until 1949): Red Book of British Columbia Municipal Information (0317-4557)
Related titles: Diskette ed.
Published by: Journal of Commerce Ltd. (Subsidiary of: Construction Market Data Canada Inc.), 4285 Way, Burnaby, BC V5G 1H2, Canada. TEL 604-433-8164, 604-412-2250, 888-878-2121, FAX 604-433-9549, jofc@lynx.bc.ca, http://www.joconl.com. Ed. Anne Crittenden. Pub., R&P Judy Sirett TEL 604-412-2263. Adv. contact Dan Gnocato. B&W page CAD 1,449, color page CAD 2,208; trim 11 x 8.5. Circ: 1,643.

332.6 CAN ISSN 1489-6168
MUNICIPAL REDBOOK (BRITISH COLUMBIA). Key Title: B C Municipal Red Book. Text in English. 1949. a. CAD 111 (effective 2000). adv. **Document type:** *Directory, Trade.* **Description:** Contains listings of British Columbia municipalities, districts, hospitals and school districts.
Supersedes in part (in 1994): British Columbia Municipal Yearbook (Redbook) (0068-161X); Which was formerly (until 1949): Red Book of British Columbia Municipal Information (0317-4557)
Related titles: Diskette ed.
Published by: Journal of Commerce Ltd. (Subsidiary of: Construction Market Data Canada Inc.), 4285 Way, Burnaby, BC V5G 1H2, Canada. TEL 604-433-8164, 888-878-2121, FAX 604-433-9549, jofc@lynx.bc.ca, http://www.joconl.com. Ed. Anne Crittenden. Pub., R&P Judy Sirett TEL 604-412-2263. Adv. contact Dan Gnocato. B&W page CAD 1,449, color page CAD 2,208; trim 11 x 8.5.

352 USA
MUNICIPAL RESEARCH NEWS; resources for Washington cities and towns. Text in English. 1991. q. free to qualified personnel (effective 2011). **Document type:** *Magazine, Trade.*
Media: Online - full text.
Published by: Municipal Research Service Center, 2601 4th Ave, Ste 800, Seattle, WA 98121-1280. mrsc@mrsc.org. Ed. Connie Elliot.

352.14 CAN ISSN 0027-3589
JS39
MUNICIPAL WORLD. Text in English. 1891. m. CAD 55. adv. bk.rev. illus. index. **Document type:** *Magazine, Trade.* **Description:** Reviews management and planning strategies of municipalities, redistribution of jurisdictions and financial responsibilities between the province and municipal governments, energy conservation, environment, business development, roads and highways, housing, human rights, technology, role of the media in municipal reporting, heritage conservation, urban development, law enforcement, transportation, waste disposal, zoning, legal articles, opinions to municipal questions from readers.
Related titles: Microfiche ed.; Online - full text ed.
Indexed: C03, CBCARef, P06, P21, P48, PQC.
—CCC.
Published by: Municipal World Inc., P O Box 399, St Thomas, ON N5P 3V3, Canada. TEL 519-633-0031, FAX 519-633-1001. Ed. Susan Gardner. Pub. Michael Smither. Adv. contact Nicholas Smither. B&W page USD 1,771, color page USD 2,760. Circ: 6,500.

352 GBR ISSN 0305-5906
JS3003
MUNICIPAL YEAR BOOK. Abbreviated title: M Y B. Variant title: Municipal Yearbook. Text in English. 1897. a. (in 2 vols.). GBP 730 per issue to individuals; GBP 5,000 per issue to institutions (effective 2009). adv. **Document type:** *Directory, Government.* **Description:** Comprehensive guide to UK central and local government and public services.
Former titles (until 1973): The Municipal Year Book and Public Utilities Directory; (until 1949): The Municipal Year Book and Public Utilities Manual; (until 1935): The Municipal Year Book and Encyclopaedia of Local Government Administration; (until 1925): Municipal Year Book; (until 19??): Municipal Year Book of the United Kingdom for .
Related titles: Microfiche ed.: (from BHP); Online - full text ed.
—BLDSC (5985.415000).
Published by: Municipal Journal Ltd., 32 Vauxhall Bridge Rd, London, SW1V 2SS, United Kingdom. Circ: 7,000 (paid).

352.14 USA ISSN 0077-2186
JS344.C5
MUNICIPAL YEAR BOOK. Text in English. 1922. a. USD 156 per issue to non-members; USD 120 per issue to members (effective 2011). bk.rev. back issues avail. **Document type:** *Yearbook, Trade.* **Description:** Resource that combines important and timely analysis on current local government issues, survey-based research, best practices in local government, a review of local-state relations, congressional actions, and supreme court decisions, and exclusive salary survey results.
Formerly (until 1934): City Manager Yearbook
Related titles: CD-ROM ed.
Indexed: SRI.
—BLDSC (5985.412000).
Published by: International City/County Management Association, 777 N Capitol St NE, Ste 500, Washington, DC 20002. TEL 202-289-4262, 800-745-8780, FAX 202-962-3500, info@icma.org, http://icma.org/en/icma/home. Ed. Jane C Cotnoir.

352.14 USA ISSN 1054-4062
JS39
MUNICIPAL YELLOW BOOK; who's who in the leading city and county governments and local authorities. Text in English. 1991. s-a. USD 355 (effective 2008). illus. Index. **Document type:** *Directory, Trade.* **Description:** Contains contact and biographical information for city and county governments and local authorities.
Related titles: CD-ROM ed.; Online - full text ed.
—CCC.
Published by: Leadership Directories, Inc, 104 Fifth Ave, 2nd Fl, New York, NY 10011. TEL 212-627-4140, FAX 212-645-0931, info@leadershipdirectories.com. Ed. Brian Combs.

352.14 USA ISSN 0027-3597
JS39
THE MUNICIPALITY. Text in English. 1900. m. USD 18; USD 1.75 per issue (effective 2007). adv. bk.rev. charts; illus. index. reprints avail. **Document type:** *Magazine, Trade.* **Description:** Aims to assist municipal officials in their fields.
Formerly (until 1916): Wisconsin Municipality
Indexed: P06, PAIS.
—Ingenta.
Published by: League of Wisconsin Municipalities, 122 W Washington Ave, Ste 300, Madison, WI 53703. TEL 608-267-2380, FAX 608-267-0645, http://www.lwm-info.org. Ed. Jean Staral. Circ: 9,600 (paid and controlled).

352 PRT ISSN 1647-015X
MUNICIPIO DE COIMBRA. ANAIS. Key Title: Anais do Municipio de Coimbra. Text in Portuguese. 1937. irreg. **Document type:** *Report, Consumer.*
Published by: Camara Municipal de Coimbra, Praca 8 de Maio, Coimbra, 3000-300, Portugal. TEL 351-239-857500, FAX 351-239-820114, geral@cm-coimbra.pt, http://www.cm0coimbra.pt.

352 PRT ISSN 1646-9887
MUNICIPIO DE GAIA. Text in Portuguese. 2005. q. **Document type:** *Magazine, Consumer.*
Published by: Camara Municipal de Vila Nova de Gaia, Rua Alvares Cabral, Vila Nova de Gaia, 4400-017, Portugal. TEL 351-22-3742400, FAX 351-22-3742483, http://www.cm-gaia.pt.

352.14 DEU ISSN 1860-6695
N R W MAGAZIN. (Nordrhein-Westfalen) Text in German. 1972. 10/yr. EUR 15.90; EUR 2 newsstand/cover (effective 2009). adv. **Document type:** *Magazine, Trade.*
Former titles (until 2003): N W Magazin (1437-9848); (until 1998): Der Oeffentliche Dienst an Rhein und Ruhr (0172-0716)
Published by: D B B Verlag GmbH, Friedrichstr 165, Berlin, 10117, Germany. TEL 49-30-72619170, FAX 49-30-726191740, kontakt@dbbverlag.de, http://www.dbbverlag.de. Circ: 140,000 (controlled).

352.14 DEU ISSN 1615-0511
N S T - N. (Niedersaechsischer Staedtetag - Nachrichten) Text in German. 1972. m. EUR 48; EUR 4.50 newsstand/cover (effective 2010). adv. **Document type:** *Magazine, Trade.*
Former titles (until 1998): N S T - Nachrichten (1434-0372); (until 1997): Niedersaechsischer Staedtetag (0178-4226); (until 1984): Nachrichten fuer Staedte, Gemeinden, Samtgemeinden (0341-3551); (until 1975): Niedersaechsischer Staedteverband. Eilnachrichten (0341-3543)
Related titles: Online - full text ed.
Published by: Winkler & Stenzel GmbH, Schulze-Delitzsch-Str. 35, Burgwedel, 30938, Germany. TEL 49-5139-89990, FAX 49-5139-899950, info@winkler-stenzel.de, http://www.winkler-stenzel.de. Ed. Heiger Scholz. Adv. contact Kerstin Cordes. B&W page EUR 1,705, color page EUR 2,245; trim 180 x 262. Circ: 6,750 (paid and controlled).

352 DEU ISSN 1865-8067
NACHRICHTEN AUS DER GROSSGEMEINDE MASSBACH UND UMGEBUNG. Text in German. 1974. w. EUR 26.40 (effective 2011). adv. **Document type:** *Newsletter, Trade.*
Published by: Revista Verlag GmbH, Am Oberen Marienbach 2 1/2, Schweinfurt, 97421, Germany. TEL 49-9721-387190, FAX 49-9721-3871938, post@revista.de.

352 DEU ISSN 1865-8091
NACHRICHTEN AUS MOTTEN. Text in German. 2004. w. EUR 26.40 (effective 2011). **Document type:** *Newsletter, Trade.*
Published by: Revista Verlag GmbH, Am Oberen Marienbach 2 1/2, Schweinfurt, 97421, Germany. TEL 49-9721-387190, FAX 49-9721-3871938, post@revista.de.

352.14 AUT
NACHRICHTEN DER STADTGEMEINDE LIEZEN. Text in German. 1966. q. free. adv. **Document type:** *Newsletter.*
Published by: Stadtgemeinde Liezen, Rathaus, Liezen, St 8940, Austria. TEL 03612-22881, FAX 03612-22881-3. Ed. Herbert Waldeck. Adv. contact Rudolf Kaltenboeck. Circ: 3,500.

352.14 DEU
NACHRICHTENBLATT FUER DAS UNTERE HAERTSFELD. Text in German. 1961. w. looseleaf. EUR 25; EUR 48 outside of community (effective 2005). adv. back issues avail. **Document type:** *Newsletter, Consumer.*
Published by: Gemeinde Dischingen, Am Marktplatz, Dischingen, 89561, Germany. TEL 49-7327-8111, FAX 49-7327-8143, haussmann@dischingen.de. adv.: page EUR 255.

352.14 IND ISSN 0027-7584
JS7001
NAGARLOK; urban affairs quarterly. Text in English. 1969. q. INR 200 (effective 2011). bk.rev. bibl.; charts; stat. back issues avail. **Document type:** *Journal, Academic/Scholarly.*
Indexed: BAS, PAA&I.
—Ingenta.
Published by: (Centre for Urban Studies BGD), Indian Institute of Public Administration, Indraprastha Estate, Ring Rd, New Delhi, 110 002, India. TEL 91-11-23702400, FAX 91-11-23702440, diriipa@bol.net.in. Ed. Rakesh Hooja.

352.14 USA
HT392
NATIONAL ASSOCIATION OF REGIONAL COUNCILS. REGIONS. Text in English. 19??. q. free to members (effective 2011). back issues avail. **Document type:** *Newspaper, Trade.* **Description:** Covers issues in legislation, transportation, community and economic development, homeland security and the environment.
Former titles (until 2000): National Association of Regional Councils. Regional Reporter (1060-5029); (until 1989): National Association of Regional Councils. News and Notes (0897-1536); Which superseded (in 1986): Directors' News for Regional Council Executive Directors; Incorporates (1975-1989): National Association of Regional Councils. Washington Report (0196-4003); Which superseded: National Service to Regional Councils. Special Reports (0028-0135); Which incorporated: Regional Review Quarterly (0034-3382)
Related titles: Online - full text ed.: free (effective 2011).
Published by: National Association of Regional Councils, 777 N Capitol St NE, Ste 305, Washington, DC 20002. TEL 202-986-1032, FAX 202-986-1038, fred@narc.org.

352.14 USA ISSN 0027-9013
JS39
NATIONAL CIVIC REVIEW. Text in English. 1911. q. GBP 153 in United Kingdom to institutions; EUR 195 in Europe to institutions; USD 223 in United States to institutions; USD 263 in Canada & Mexico to institutions; USD 297 elsewhere to institutions; GBP 179 combined subscription in United Kingdom to institutions (print & online eds.); EUR 227 combined subscription in Europe to institutions (print & online eds.); USD 258 combined subscription in United States to institutions (print & online eds.); USD 298 combined subscription in Canada & Mexico to institutions (print & online eds.); USD 332 combined subscription elsewhere to institutions (print & online eds.) (effective 2012). adv. index. back issues avail.; reprint service avail. from PSC. **Document type:** *Journal, Academic/Scholarly.* **Description:** Brings together articles and essays from the people who are actively working on and thinking about the challenges facing America's cities and communities.
Formerly (until 1959): National Municipal Review (0190-3799); Which incorporated (1914-1932): Proportional Representation Review; (1911-1920): The Short Ballot Bulletin; (1914-1919): Equity; Which was formerly (until 1914): Equity Series
Related titles: Microfiche ed.: (from PMC, WSH); Microfilm ed.: (from WSH); Online - full text ed.: ISSN 1542-7811. GBP 115 in United Kingdom to institutions; EUR 147 in Europe to institutions; USD 223 elsewhere to institutions (effective 2012).
Indexed: A01, A02, A03, A08, A22, A23, A25, A26, ABCPolSci, AmH&L, B01, B04, B06, B07, B09, B13, BRD, CA, CBRI, CLI, E01, E06, E08, FutSurv, G06, G07, G08, H09, H10, I03, I05, I07, M01, M02, M06, N06, P02, P06, P10, P13, P27, P30, P34, P42, P48, P53, P54, PAIS, PCI, PQC, PSA, RASB, S02, S03, S05, S08, S09, S11, S23, SPAA, SPPI, SSAI, SSAb, SSI, SUSA, SociolAb, T02, W01, W02, W03, W05.
—IE, Ingenta.
Published by: (National Civic League, Inc.), Jossey-Bass Inc., Publishers (Subsidiary of: John Wiley & Sons, Inc.), 111 River St, Hoboken, NJ 07030. TEL 201-748-6000, FAX 201-748-6088, info@wiley.com. Ed. Michael McGrath.

352.14 USA ISSN 0164-5935
JS39
NATION'S CITIES WEEKLY. Text in English. 1978. w. USD 96 to non-members; free to members (effective 2009). adv. bk.rev. charts; illus. index. reprints avail. **Document type:** *Magazine, Trade.* **Description:** Discusses how national developments affect cities, with case studies on how local governments solve problems.
Formed by the merger of (1978-1978): City Weekly (0164-5595); (1963-1978): Nation's Cities (0028-0488)
Related titles: Microform ed.: (from PQC); Online - full text ed.
Indexed: A01, A02, A03, A08, A22, A26, AIAP, B02, B15, B17, B18, BusI, E07, G04, G05, G06, G07, G08, H09, HlthInd, I05, I07, L09, M01, M02, M06, MagInd, P02, P06, P07, P10, P34, P48, P53, P54, PQC, PSI, S05, S11, S23, SUSA, T&II, T02, UAA.
Published by: National League of Cities, 1301 Pennsylvania Ave, N W, Ste 550, Washington, DC 20004. TEL 202-626-3000, FAX 202-626-3043. Ed. Cindy Hogan. Circ: 30,000 (paid and free).

352.14 USA ISSN 0028-1905
JS39
NEBRASKA MUNICIPAL REVIEW. Text in English. 1930. m. USD 50; USD 5 per issue (effective 2009). adv. bk.rev. illus.; stat. **Document type:** *Magazine, Trade.* **Description:** Contains news and feature articles on local, state and federal government issues of interest to municipal officials.
Indexed: P06.
Published by: League of Nebraska Municipalities, 1335 L St, Lincoln, NE 68508. TEL 402-476-2829, FAX 402-476-7052, info@lonm.org. Ed., R&P Lynn Marienau. Adv. contact Tammy Sluka. Circ: 3,300.

352 NLD ISSN 1872-3594
NETHERLANDS. MINISTERIE VAN BINNENLANDSE ZAKEN EN KONINKRIJKSRELATIES. PERIODIEK ONDERHOUDSRAPPORT GEMEENTEFONDS. Text in Dutch. 199?. a.
Published by: Ministerie van Binnenlandse Zaken en Koninkrijksrelaties, Schedeldoekshaven 200, Postbus 20011, The Hague, 2500 EA, Netherlands. TEL 31-70-4266426, FAX 31-70-3639153, info@minbzk.nl, http://www.minbzk.nl.

330.9 USA ISSN 0749-016X
CODEN: NEJPFU
NEW ENGLAND JOURNAL OF PUBLIC POLICY. Short title: N E J P P. Text in English. 1985-2008; resumed 2010. s-a. back issues avail. **Document type:** *Journal, Academic/Scholarly.* **Description:** Offers policy analysts, academics, and the press in New England, the nation, and the world an arena in which they can define problems and develop approaches to solving them.
Related titles: Online - full text ed.
Indexed: A12, A17, ABIn, B01, B06, B07, B09, CA, H05, P30, P34, P48, P51, P53, P54, PQC, SOPODA, SociolAb, T02.
—BLDSC (6084.008000), Infotrieve.
Published by: John W. McCormack Graduate School of Policy Studies, University of Massachusetts at Boston, 100 Morrissey Blvd, Boston, MA 02125. TEL 617-287-5550, mccormack.gradschool@umb.edu.

NEW HAMPSHIRE GOVERNMENT REGISTER. *see* PUBLIC ADMINISTRATION

352.14 USA
NEW HAMPSHIRE MUNICIPAL PRACTICE SERIES: LAND USE, PLANNING AND ZONING (VOL. 15). Text in English. 1980. irreg. (in 1 vol.), latest vol.15. USD 84 base vol(s). (effective 2008). Supplement avail. **Document type:** *Monographic series, Trade.* **Description:** Covers nearly every issue public officials face on a daily basis, from zoning enforcement and subdivision control to historic district controls and wetlands protection.
Formerly: New Hampshire Municipal Practice Series: Land Use and Planning; Vol. 15
Published by: Michie Company (Subsidiary of: LexisNexis North America), 701 E Water St, Charlottesville, VA 22902. TEL 434-972-7600, 800-446-3410, FAX 434-972-7677, customer.support@lexisnexis.com, http://www.michie.com.

352.14 USA
NEW HAMPSHIRE PRACTICE SERIES: LOCAL GOVERNMENT LAW (VOLS. 13, 14 AND 14A). Text in English. 1990. irreg. (in 3 vols.), latest vol.14, 1995, 2nd ed. USD 217 base vol(s). (effective 2008). Supplement avail. **Document type:** *Monographic series, Trade.*
Description: Provides comprehensive coverage of the laws and practices relating to cities, towns, public officials, records and meetings, municipal power and liabilities, and elections.
Published by: Michie Company (Subsidiary of: LexisNexis North America), 701 E Water St, Charlottesville, VA 22902. TEL 434-972-7600, 800-446-3410, FAX 434-972-7677, customer.support@lexisnexis.com, http://www.michie.com. Ed. Peter J Loughlin.

352.14 USA
NEW HAMPSHIRE PRACTICE SERIES: MUNICIPAL FINANCE AND TAXATION (VOL. 16). Text in English. 1990. irreg., latest vol.16, 1993. USD 78 per vol. (effective 2008). Supplement avail. **Document type:** *Monographic series, Trade.* **Description:** Examines diverse road law topics, such as the definition, classification, regulation and maintenance of roadways, problem areas of highway discontinuance, Class IV highways, and paper streets.
Related titles: Online - full text ed.
Published by: Michie Company (Subsidiary of: LexisNexis North America), 701 E Water St, Charlottesville, VA 22902. TEL 434-972-7600, 800-446-3410, FAX 434-972-7677, customer.support@lexisnexis.com, http://www.michie.com. Ed. Peter J Loughlin.

352.14 USA ISSN 0028-5846
JS39
NEW JERSEY MUNICIPALITIES. Text in English. 1917. m. (Oct.-Jun.). USD 16 domestic to members; USD 25 foreign to members; USD 20 domestic to non-members (effective 2009). adv. bk.rev. illus. index. reprints avail. **Document type:** *Magazine, Trade.* **Description:** Discusses legislative and economic issues affecting New Jersey cities and towns, and contains articles on managing municipal affairs.
Indexed: P06.
Published by: New Jersey State League of Municipalities, 222 W State St, Trenton, NJ 08608. TEL 609-695-3481, FAX 609-695-0151. Ed. William G Dressel Jr. R&P Kyra Duran. Adv. contact Jean Howarth. Circ: 8,200.

352.14 USA
NEW JERSEY PRACTICE SERIES. LOCAL GOVERNMENT LAW. Text in English. 1993. 3 base vols. plus a. updates. USD 430 base vol(s). (effective 2010). **Document type:** *Journal, Trade.* **Description:** Provides essential information on planning boards, land use and environmental control, licensing, construction codes, tort liability, property taxes, and public contracts.
Published by: Thomson West (Subsidiary of: Thomson Reuters Corp.), 610 Opperman Dr, Eagan, MN 55123. TEL 651-687-7000, 800-344-5008, west.customer.service@thomson.com.

352.14 USA ISSN 0028-6257
NEW MEXICO MUNICIPAL LEAGUE. MUNICIPAL REPORTER. Text in English. 1959. m. free (effective 2010). bk.rev. back issues avail. **Document type:** *Newsletter, Trade.*
Related titles: Online - full text ed.: free (effective 2010).
Published by: New Mexico Municipal League, PO Box 846, Santa Fe, NM 87504. TEL 505-982-5573, 800-432-2036, FAX 505-984-1392. Ed. William F Fulginiti.

352 USA
NEW YORK (CITY). DEPARTMENT OF CITYWIDE ADMINISTRATIVE SERVICES. GREEN BOOK; official city directory. Text in English. a. USD 19.95 newsstand/cover (effective 2006). **Document type:** *Directory, Government.*
Published by: New York City Department of Citywide Administrative Services, 1 Centre St., Rm. 2223, New York, NY 10007. http://www.nyc.gov/html/dcas/html/home/home.shtml. R&P Denise Collins. Circ: 36,000.

352.14 USA ISSN 0094-7547
HJ9013.N5e
NEW YORK (CITY). SCHEDULES SUPPORTING THE EXECUTIVE BUDGET. Text in English. 1955. a.
Published by: Office of Management and Budget, 75 Park Pl, 6th Fl, New York, NY 10007. TEL 212-788-5807. Circ: 500.

352 USA
NEW YORK CITY REPORT. Text in English. 1976. s-m. looseleaf. USD 300 (effective 2000). adv. back issues avail. **Document type:** *Newsletter.* **Description:** Covers current New York City legislation, including new local laws.
Published by: New York Legislative Service, Inc., 15 Maiden Ln., Ste. 1000, New York, NY 10038-5117. TEL 212-962-2826, FAX 212-962-1420. Ed. Steve Harvey. R&P Laird M Ehlert. Adv. contact Laird Ehlert. Circ: 50 (paid).

352.14025 USA ISSN 0737-1314
JK3430
NEW YORK STATE DIRECTORY. Text in English. 1983. a. USD 129 per issue (effective 2005). **Document type:** *Directory.* **Description:** Provides access to more than 10,000 persons from the executive, legislative, and judicial branches of New York State Government, as well as local government officials and private sector experts concerned with New York State public policy issues.
Published by: Walker's Research, LLC, 1650 Borel Pl, Ste 130, San Mateo, CA 94402. TEL 650-341-1110, 800-258-5737, FAX 650-341-2351, http://www.walkersresearch.com.

352.14 USA
NEW YORK STATE MUNICIPAL BULLETIN. Text in English. 1934. bi-m. free to members. adv. **Document type:** *Bulletin, Government.* **Description:** Covers NYCOM activities, events, state and federal legislative developments, analysis of special issues, affiliate news, and information on the municipal legal front.
Published by: New York State Conference of Mayors and Municipal Officials, 119 Washington Ave, Albany, NY 12210. TEL 518-463-1185, FAX 518-463-1190, info@nycom.org, http://www.nycom.org/index.html. Circ: 7,000.

352.14 USA ISSN 0197-2472
NEW YORK STATE REGISTER. Text in English. 1928. w. USD 80 (effective 2006). adv. reprints avail. **Document type:** *Government.* **Description:** Publishes rule making notices, public hearings, executive orders, Attorney General opinions.
Formerly (until 1979): New York State Bulletin (0028-7555)
Related titles: Microfiche ed.: (from WSH); Microform ed.: (from PMC).
Indexed: P06.
Published by: Department of State, Office of Information Services, 41 State St, Albany, NY 12231. TEL 518-74-6785, adminrules@dos.state.ny.us. Circ: 2,000.

352.14 NZL ISSN 0028-8403
NEW ZEALAND LOCAL GOVERNMENT; the magazine for local authority decision makers. Text in English. 1964. m. NZD 100 (effective 2009). adv. bk.rev. illus. **Document type:** *Magazine, Trade.* **Description:** Provides independent news and feature coverage of the entire local government sector.
Formerly (until 1972): Local Body Review (0459-6587)
Indexed: GeoRef, INZP, SpeleolAb.
—Ingenta.
Published by: T P L. Media (Trade Publications), Newmarket, PO Box 9596, Auckland, 1149, New Zealand. TEL 64-9-5293027, FAX 64-9-5293001, info@tplmedia.co.nz, http://www.tplmedia.co.nz/. Ed. Don Kavanagh. Adv. contact Charles Fairburn. B&W page NZD 1,515, color page NZD 2,135. Circ: 1,947.

352.14025 NZL ISSN 1171-5588
NEW ZEALAND LOCAL GOVERNMENT DIRECTORY. Variant title: New Zealand Local Government Contacts Directory. Text in English. 1964. a. NZD 50 (effective 2009). adv. bk.rev. bibl.; illus. **Document type:** *Directory, Trade.* **Description:** Includes a complete listing of city and regional councils, local authority traders enterprises, area health boards, energy supply authorities, galleries and museums, libraries, licensing trusts and central government departments. Also includes a complete list of industry suppliers and a glossary of articles published annually in the NZ Local Government magazine.
Formerly: New Zealand Local Government Yearbook (0110-7763)
Published by: T P L. Media (Trade Publications), Newmarket, PO Box 9596, Auckland, 1149, New Zealand. TEL 64-9-5293027, FAX 64-9-5293001, info@tplmedia.co.nz, http://www.tplmedia.co.nz/. Ed. Malcolm Wall. Circ: 2,344.

NEW ZEALAND RESOURCE MANAGEMENT APPEALS. *see* HOUSING AND URBAN PLANNING

352 NZL ISSN 1176-8622
NGA PAE O TE MARAMATANGA. ANNUAL REPORT. Text in English. 2004. a.
Published by: Nga Pae o te Maramatanga/National Institute of Research Excellence for Maori Development and Advancement, Waipapa Marae Complex, Rehutai Bldg, 16 Wynyard St, University of Auckland, Private Bag 92019, Auckland, 1142, New Zealand. TEL 64-9-3737599 ext 84220, FAX 64-9-3737428, info@maramatanga.ac.nz.

352.14 DEU
NIEDERSACHSEN MAGAZIN. Text in German. 10/yr. EUR 19.90 to non-members (effective 2009). adv. **Document type:** *Magazine, Trade.*
Published by: Deutscher Beamtenbund, Landesbund Niedersachsen, Kurt-Schumacher-Str 29, Hannover, 30159, Germany. TEL 49-511-35398830, FAX 49-511-35398836, post@niedersachsen.dbb.de. adv.: B&W page EUR 1,440, color page EUR 2,340. Circ: 40,000 (controlled).

352.14 DEU ISSN 0028-9779
NIEDERSAECHSISCHE GEMEINDE; Monatsschrift fuer kommunale Selbstverwaltung. Text in German. 1949. bi-m. EUR 36; EUR 6 newsstand/cover (effective 2008). adv. bk.rev. stat. index. **Document type:** *Magazine, Trade.*
Published by: Niedersaechsischer Staedte- und Gemeindebund, Arnswaldtstr 28, Hannover, 30159, Germany. TEL 49-511-302850, FAX 49-511-3028530, nsgb@nsgb.de, http://www.nsgb.info. Ed. W Haack. adv.: B&W page EUR 1,500, color page EUR 3,600. Circ: 12,359 (controlled).

352.14 DEU ISSN 0946-7971
NIEDERSAECHSISCHE VERWALTUNGSBLAETTER; Zeitschrift fuer oeffentliches Recht und oeffentliche Verwaltung. Text in German. 1994. m. EUR 191.40; EUR 144.60 to students (effective 2010). adv. **Document type:** *Journal, Trade.*
Indexed: DIP, IBR, IBZ.
Published by: Richard Boorberg Verlag GmbH und Co. KG, Scharrstr 2, Stuttgart, 70563, Germany. TEL 49-711-73850, FAX 49-711-7385100, mail@boorberg.de.

352.14 DEU
NIEDERSAECHSISCHER STAEDTE- UND GEMEINDEBUND. SCHRIFTENREIHE. Text in German. irreg., latest vol.63. price varies. **Document type:** *Bulletin, Trade.*
Published by: Niedersaechsischer Staedte- und Gemeindebund, Arnswaldtstr 28, Hannover, 30159, Germany. TEL 49-511-302850, FAX 49-511-3028530, nsgb@nsgb.de, http://www.nsgb.info.

NORWAY. STATISTISK SENTRALBYRAA. KOMMUNESTYREVALGET/ STATISTICS NORWAY. MUNICIPAL AND COUNTY ELECTIONS. *see* PUBLIC ADMINISTRATION—Abstracting, Bibliographies, Statistics

352.14 DNK ISSN 1398-0440
NYHEDSMAGASINET DANSKE KOMMUNER. Text in Danish. 1970. w. (37/yr.). DKK 869 (effective 2009). adv. bk.rev. illus.; stat. index. **Document type:** *Magazine, Trade.*
Former titles (until 1997): Danske Kommuner (0107-3648); (until 1980): DK. Danske Kommuner (0011-6572); Which was formed by the merger of (1890-1970): Koebstadforeningens Tidsskrift (0907-5208); (1885-1970): Kommunal Tidende (0909-4199); Which was formerly (until 1968): Sogneraadstidende (0909-4180)
Related titles: CD-ROM ed.; Online - full text ed.
Published by: Kommunernes Landsforening/National Association of Local Authorities in Denmark, Weidekampsgade 10, PO Box 3370, Copenhagen S, 2300, Denmark. TEL 45-33-703370, FAX 45-33-703371, kl@kl.dk, http://www.kl.dk. Eds. Klaus Slanina Petersen, Tom Ekeroth TEL 45-33-703418. adv.: page DKK 17,600; 176 x 260. Circ: 5,938 (controlled).

O D. (Overheidsdocumentatie) *see* LIBRARY AND INFORMATION SCIENCES

352.14 DEU ISSN 0944-2316
JS7.G3
OBERBAYERISCHES AMTSBLATT. Text in German. 195?. m. EUR 67; EUR 2.90 per issue (effective 2011). **Document type:** *Journal, Government.*
Formerly (until 1993): Regierung von Oberbayern. Amtsblatt (0405-0665)
Published by: (Regierung von Oberbayern), Medienhaus Kastner AG, Schlosshof 2-6, Wolnzach, 85283, Germany. TEL 49-8442-92530, FAX 49-8442-2289, verlag@kastner.de, http://www.kastner.de.

352.14 SVN
ODLOCANJE/DECISION. Text in Slovenian. 1981. m. looseleaf. free. back issues avail.
Published by: Skupscina Obcine Ravne na Koroskem, Cecovje 12-a, Ravne na Koroskem, 62390, Slovenia. TEL 062 861-821. Circ: 1,200.

352.14 AUT
OE B Z; unabhaengige Fachzeitschrift fuer Oesterreichs Staedte und Gemeinden. Text in German. 1972 (vol.25). m. EUR 132 (effective 2005). bk.rev. illus. **Document type:** *Newspaper, Trade.*
Formerly: Oesterreichische Buergermeister Zeitung (0048-1424)
Address: Kutschkergasse42, Vienna, W 1180, Austria. TEL 43-1-47686, FAX 43-1-4768621, oebz@webway.at. Ed. Christine Pomberger. Pub. Gerd-Volker Weege. Adv. contact Alberta Zesewitz. Circ: 12,373.

DER OEFFENTLICHE DIENST. *see* LAW

352 PRT ISSN 1646-5970
OEIRAS EM REVISTA. Text in Portuguese. 1971. s-a. **Document type:** *Magazine, Consumer.*
Former titles (until 2006): Oeiras Municipal (1645-9571); (until 1987): Oeiras. Boletim Municipal (1647-838X)
Published by: Camara Municipal de Oeiras, Largo Marques de Pombal, Oeiras, 2784-501, Portugal. TEL 351-21-4408300, FAX 351-21-4408712, geral@cm-oeiras.pt, http://www.cm-oeiras.pt.

352.14 AUT ISSN 0029-912X
JS4501
OESTERREICHISCHE GEMEINDE-ZEITUNG. Text in German. 1934. m. EUR 35; EUR 4 newsstand/cover (effective 2005). adv. bk.rev. stat. **Document type:** *Newspaper, Trade.*
Published by: (Oesterreichischer Staedtebund), Ueberreuter Print - Und Digimedia GmbH, Industriestr 1, Korneuburg, N 2100, Austria. TEL 43-2262-7890, FAX 43-2262-789116, digimedia@ueberreuter.com. Ed. Adolf Pelinka. Circ: 6,000.

OFFICIAL (LOS ANGELES). *see* HEATING, PLUMBING AND REFRIGERATION

352 USA
OKLAHOMA CITIES & TOWNS NEWSLETTER. Text in English. 1970. m. USD 15 to members; USD 30 to non-members (effective 2009). **Document type:** *Newsletter, Government.*
Related titles: Online - full text ed.: 2004.
Published by: Oklahoma Municipal League, 201 NE 23d, Oklahoma City, OK 73105. TEL 405-528-7515, FAX 405-528-7560. Eds. Carolyn Stager, Jimi Layman.

353.39 CAN ISSN 0847-1746
ONTARIO BOARD OF PAROLE. ANNUAL REPORT. Variant title: Commission Ontarienne des Liberations Conditionnelles. Rapport Annuel. Text in English, French. 1989. a.
Published by: Ontario Parole and Earned Release Board, 415 Yonge St, Suite 1803, Toronto, ON M5B 2E7, Canada. TEL 416-325-4480, FAX 416-325-4485.

352 CAN ISSN 1206-7520
HD7305.O6
ONTARIO. MINISTRY OF MUNICIPAL AFFAIRS AND HOUSING. ANNUAL REPORT. Text in English. 1996. a., latest 2007. **Document type:** *Government.*
Formed by the merger of (1986-1996): Ontario. Ministry of Municipal Affairs. Annual Report (0833-1731); (1986-1996): Ontario. Ministry of Housing. Annual Report (0835-0213); Both of which superseded in part (1982-1986): Ontario Ministry of Municipal Affairs and Housing. Annual Report (0821-9079); Which was formerly (1974-1982): Ministry of Housing. Annual Report (0382-2729); Which incorporated (1966-1973): Ontario Housing Corporation. Annual Report (0078-4885); (1976-1978): Ontario Land Corporation. Annual Report (0706-7585)
Published by: Ontario. Ministry of Municipal Affairs and Housing, 777 Bay St. 17th Fl, Toronto, ON M5G 2E5, Canada. TEL 416-585-7000, FAX 416-585-6470, mininfo@mah.gov.on.ca.

352 PRT ISSN 1646-513X
OPPIDUM. Text in Portuguese. 2006. a. **Document type:** *Magazine, Consumer.*
Published by: Camara Municipal de Lousada, Pr Dr Francisco Sa Carneiro, Lousada, 4624-909, Portugal. TEL 351-255-820500, http://www.cm-lousada.pt.

352 DEU ISSN 1865-813X
ORTSSCHELLE BURKARDROTH; Amtsblatt des Marktes Burkardroth. Text in German. 1978. w. EUR 26.40 (effective 2011). **Document type:** *Newsletter, Trade.*
Published by: Revista Verlag GmbH, Am Oberen Marienbach 2 1/2, Schweinfurt, 97421, Germany. TEL 49-9721-387190, FAX 49-9721-3871938, post@revista.de.

352.14 USA
OUTREACH (COLLEGE PARK). Text in English. 1982. 5/yr. free. back issues avail. **Document type:** *Newsletter.*
Published by: Institute for Governmental Service, University of Maryland, 4511 Knox Rd, Ste 205, College Park, MD 20740. TEL 301-403-4610, FAX 301-403-4222. Ed. Elizabeth Watts. Circ: 1,130.

P A R ANALYSIS. (Public Affairs Research) *see* POLITICAL SCIENCE

352.14 340 GBR
THE P F I AND MAJOR STRATEGIC PROCUREMENT IN LOCAL GOVERNMENT. (Private Finance Initiative) Text in English. 1997. 2 base vols. plus updates 2/yr. looseleaf. GBP 548 base vol(s). domestic; EUR 724 base vol(s). in Europe; USD 942 base vol(s). elsewhere (effective 2011). **Document type:** *Handbook/Manual/Guide, Trade.* **Description:** Provides comprehensive coverage of every aspect of PFI work in the local government arena.
Published by: Sweet & Maxwell Ltd. (Subsidiary of: Thomson Reuters Corp.), 100 Avenue Rd, London, NW3 3PF, United Kingdom. TEL 44-20-73937000, sweetandmaxwell.customer.services@thomson.com. **Subscr. to:** PO Box 1000, Andover SP10 9AF, United Kingdom. TEL 44-20-73938051, sweetandmaxwell.international.queries@thomson.com.

P I R VILLE. CAHIERS. (Programme Interdisciplinaire de Recherche) *see* SOCIOLOGY

PARKING NEWS. *see* TRANSPORTATION—Roads And Traffic

352 ESP ISSN 2171-7001
PARLAMENTO DE CANTABRIA. BOLETIN OFICIAL (ONLINE). Text in Spanish. 1982. d. back issues avail. **Document type:** *Bulletin, Consumer.*
Media: Online - full text.
Published by: Parlamento de Cantabria, Servicios de Publicaciones, C Alta 31-33, Santander, Cantabria, 39008, Spain. TEL 34-942-241060, presidencia@parlamento-cantabria.es.

352 FRA ISSN 1951-896X
LA PAYE DANS LES COLLECTIVITES LOCALES ET LES ETABLISSEMENTS PUBLICS. Text in French. 1999. base vol. plus q. updates. looseleaf. EUR 127.96 base vol(s). (effective 2010). **Document type:** *Trade.*
Published by: Editions Dalian (Subsidiary of: Wolters Kluwer France), 1 Rue Eugene et Armand Peugeot, B P 720, Rueil Malmaison, 92856 Cedex, France. TEL 33-8-25080800, FAX 33-1-76734802, dalian@dalian.tm.fr, http://www.editions-dalian.fr/.

352.14 USA ISSN 1940-5774
JS39
PENNSYLVANIA BOROUGH NEWS. Text in English. 1962. m. USD 28 to non-members; USD 24 to members (effective 2008). adv. bk.rev. charts; illus. 68 p./no.; reprints avail. **Document type:** *Magazine, Trade.* **Description:** Articles, directories, indexes and announcements on governmental units at the borough and township level of the state, for governmental secretaries, administrators and clerks, county assessors, borough mayors and council members.
Former titles (until 2008): Borough News (1534-1895); (until 2001): Pennsylvanian (0031-4714)
Related titles: Microfilm ed.: (from PQC).
Indexed: A22, P06.
Published by: Pennsylvania State Association of Boroughs, Local Government Center, 2941 N Front St, Harrisburg, PA 17110. TEL 717-236-9526, FAX 717-236-8164, general@boroughs.org, http://www.boroughs.org. Ed. Courtney Accurti. Pub. Thomas A Klaum. Adv. contact Suzi Kalis. B&W page USD 590, color page USD 1,190; trim 7 x 10. Circ: 6,300 (paid); 400 (free). **Co-sponsors:** Assessors' Association of Pennsylvania; Pennsylvania Local Governmental Secretaries Association.

352.14 USA ISSN 0162-5160
PENNSYLVANIA TOWNSHIP NEWS. Text in English. 1948. m. USD 36 (effective 2011). adv. bk.rev. illus. reprints avail. **Document type:** *Magazine, Trade.* **Description:** Keeps township officials informed about new laws, legislation, rules and regulations, current issues, and the day-to-day operation of township government.
Published by: Pennsylvania State Association of Township Supervisors, 4855 Woodland Dr, Enola, PA 17025. TEL 717-763-0930, FAX 717-763-9732, psatsweb@psats.org. Ed., R&P, Adv. contact Ginni Linn. Pub. R Keith Hite. Circ: 10,000 (paid and free).

352.14 BRA ISSN 0100-8781
HA988.S2
PERFIL MUNICIPAL. Text in Portuguese. 1979. a.
Published by: Fundacao Sistema Estadual de Analise de Dados, Av Casper Libero, 464, Centro, Caixa Postal 8223, Sao Paulo, SP 01033-000, Brazil. TEL 229-2433, TELEX 011-31390 SEAD. Circ: 2,000.

304.6 352 CAN ISSN 1913-5343
PERSPECTIVE GRAND MONTREAL; bulletin d'analyse metropolitaine. Text in French. 2007. bi-m. free. back issues avail. **Document type:** *Bulletin, Government.*
Related titles: Online - full text ed.
Published by: Communaute Metropolitaine de Montreal, 1002 Rue Sherbrooke Ouest, Bureau 2400, Montreal, PQ H3A 3L6, Canada. TEL 514-350-2550, FAX 514-350-2599, info@cmm.qc.ca.

PLANNING & ZONING NEWS. *see* HOUSING AND URBAN PLANNING

PLANNING COMMISSIONERS JOURNAL; news & information for citizen planners. *see* HOUSING AND URBAN PLANNING

342.09 AUS
PLANNING LAW IN AUSTRALIA. Text in English. 1987. base vol. plus irreg. updates. looseleaf. AUD 2,430 (effective 2008). **Document type:** *Handbook/Manual/Guide, Trade.* **Description:** Explains the law and practice of environmental planning law in Australia, with a focus on the practice of planning, conservation of historical and natural places and new appeal structures to enforce planning law.
Formerly (until 1997): Town Planning Law and Practice
Related titles: Online - full text ed.
Published by: Lawbook Co. (Subsidiary of: Thomson Reuters (Professional) Australia Limited), PO Box 3502, Rozelle, NSW 2039, Australia. TEL 61-2-85877980, 300-304-195, FAX 61-2-85877981, 300-304-196, LTA.Service@thomsonreuters.com, http://www.thomson.com.au.

352.14 ESP
PLAZA DE LA CONSTITUCION. Text in Spanish. 1979. 22/yr. free. adv. bk.rev. **Document type:** *Government.*
Published by: Ayuntamiento de Getafe/Town Council, Plaza de la Constitucion, 1, Getafe, Madrid, 28901, Spain. TEL 34-91-2027911, http://www.getafe.es/. Ed. Luis Manuel Candil Martin. Adv. contact Pilar Buenache. Circ: 27,000 (paid); 22,000 (controlled).

PLUNKETT'S INFOTECH INDUSTRY ALMANAC. *see* COMPUTERS—Microcomputers

352 ESP ISSN 1133-7206
PONTENOVA; revista de novos investigadores. Text in Spanish. 1993. s-a. EUR 9. back issues avail. **Document type:** *Monographic series, Academic/Scholarly.*
Published by: Diputacion Provincial de Pontevedra, Ave. de Monte Rios, s-n, Pontevedra, 36071, Spain. TEL 34-986-804100, FAX 34-986-804124, editorial.revistas@depo.es, http://www.depontevedra.es/.

352 PRT ISSN 1646-382X
PONTES E VIRGULAS. Text in Portuguese. 2006. q. **Document type:** *Magazine, Consumer.*
Published by: Camara Municipal de Aveiro, Pacos do Conselho, Praca da Republica, Aveiro, 3810-156, Portugal. TEL 351-234-406300, FAX 351-234-406301, http://www.cm-aveiro.pt.

352 ESP ISSN 0211-5530
PONTEVEDRA; revista de estudios provinciais. Text in Spanish, Gallegan. 1980. s-a. EUR 12. back issues avail. **Document type:** *Monographic series, Academic/Scholarly.*
Published by: Diputacion Provincial de Pontevedra, Ave. de Monte Rios, s-n, Pontevedra, 36071, Spain. TEL 34-986-804100, FAX 34-986-804124, editorial.revistas@depo.es, http://www.depontevedra.es/.

352.14 NIC
POPOL-NA; revista para la promocion y el desarrollo municipal. Text in Spanish. 1992. q. NIC 40; USD 20 in Latin America; USD 25 elsewhere.
Published by: Fundacion Popol-Na para la Promocion y el Desarrollo Municipal, Plaza Espana 3 1/2 abajo, Apartado Postal 4611, Managua, Nicaragua. TEL 660605, FAX 660133.

352 MUS ISSN 1694-0369
PORT LOUIS FUND. ANNUAL REPORT. Text in English. 2005. a.
Published by: Port Louis Fund, 15th Flr, Air Mauritius Centre, 6, President John Kennedy St, Port Louis, Mauritius. http://www.portlouisfund.com.

352 ZAF ISSN 1729-9772
PORTFOLIO. MUNICIPALITIES IN SOUTH AFRICA. Text in English. 2004. a. ZAR 120 domestic; USD 43.90 foreign (effective 2007). adv.
Published by: Portfolio Business Publications (Pty) Ltd, PO Box 71707, Bryanston, 2021, South Africa. TEL 27-11-7870422, FAX 27-11-7870467, infojhb@portfolio.co.za, http://www.portfolio.co.za. adv.: page ZAR 32,620. Circ: 20,000.

352 DEU ISSN 1865-827X
POST AUS POPPENHAUSEN. Text in German. 1971. w. adv. **Document type:** *Newsletter, Trade.*
Published by: Revista Verlag GmbH, Am Oberen Marienbach 2 1/2, Schweinfurt, 97421, Germany. TEL 49-9721-387190, FAX 49-9721-3871938, post@revista.de.

352.14 320 FRA ISSN 0998-8289
POUVOIRS LOCAUX. Text in French. 1989. 4/yr. adv. bk.rev. **Document type:** *Journal, Consumer.* **Description:** Investigates topics on decentralization of government from various sources including elected officials, private experts and professors for the management of local government.
Indexed: FR, IBSS.
Published by: Institut de la Decentralisation, 28 Rue de Chateaudun, Paris, 75009, France. TEL 33-1-40827290, FAX 33-1-40827299, contact@idecentralisation.asso.fr. Ed. Frederic El Guedj. Pub. Jean Marc Ohnet. Adv. contact Frederic El-Guedj. Circ: 2,800; 2,200 (paid).

352.14 ESP
PREGONERO. Text in Spanish. 26/yr.
Published by: Ayuntamiento de Getafe/Town Council, Plaza de la Constitucion, 1, Getafe, Madrid, 28901, Spain. TEL 34-91-2027911, http://www.getafe.es/. Ed. R Rodriguez Aparicio. Circ: 120,000.

352 ITA ISSN 1120-351X
PRIME NOTE. Text in Italian. 1990. m. EUR 165.27 (effective 2006). **Document type:** *Journal, Trade.*
Related titles: Supplement(s): Prime Note. Zoom. ISSN 1123-4482. 1992.
Address: Via Confaloneri 2, Rome, 00195, Italy. segreteria@arial11.191.it, http://www.e-primenote.it. Ed. Dante Santucci.

354.71 CAN ISSN 0319-4973
PRINCE EDWARD ISLAND. LEGISLATIVE ASSEMBLY. JOURNAL. Key Title: Journal of the Legislative Assembly of the Province of Prince Edward Island. Text in English. 1894. d.
Published by: Prince Edward Island, Legislative Assembly, Province House, Richmond St, Charlottetown, PE C1A 7K7, Canada. TEL 902-368-5970, FAX 902-368-5175, htp://www.assembly.pe.ca/. Ed. Charles Mackay.

PRIVATIZATION WATCH. *see* POLITICAL SCIENCE

352 NLD ISSN 1569-1152
PROEFLOKAAL. Text in Dutch. 2001. q. EUR 20 (effective 2008).
Published by: Centrum voor Lokaal Bestuur, Postbus 1310, Amsterdam, 1000 BH, Netherlands. TEL 31-20-5512260, FAX 31-20-5512250, clb@pvda.nl. Ed. Jos Kuijs.

352 PRT ISSN 1647-0656
PROENCA EM REVISTA. Text in Portuguese. 2008. s-a. **Document type:** *Magazine, Consumer.*
Published by: Camara Municipal de Proenca-a-Nova, Avenida do Colegio, Proenca-a-Nova, 6150-401, Portugal. TEL 351-274-670000, FAX 351-274-672697, geral@cm-proencanova.pt, http://www.cm-proencanova.pt.

352 FRA ISSN 1959-111X
PROFESSION TERRITORIALE. Text in French. 1996. m. EUR 47 combined subscription to individuals (print & online eds.) (effective 2011). back issues avail. **Document type:** *Magazine, Trade.*
Former titles (until 2007): Femmes Territoriales (1763-3176); (until 2003): Secretaire Territoriale (1277-3220)
Related titles: Online - full text ed.
Published by: Reseau Territorial, BP 215, Voiron, Cedex 38506, France. TEL 33-4-76657136, FAX 33-4-76050163, info@territorial.fr.

352 ESP
PROVINCIA DE PONTEVEDRA. BOLETIN OFICIAL. Variant title: Boletin Oficial da Provincia de Pontevedra. Text in Spanish, Gallegan. d. **Document type:** *Bulletin, Government.*
Related titles: Online - full text ed.
Published by: Diputacion Provincial de Pontevedra, Ave. de Monte Rios, s-n, Pontevedra, 36071, Spain. TEL 34-986-804100, FAX 34-986-804124, editorial.revistas@depo.es, http://www.depontevedra.es/.

352 NLD ISSN 1879-4831
▼ **PROVINCIEWET - GEMEENTEWET.** Variant title: Wetteksten Provinciewet/Gemeentewet. Text in Dutch. 2009. a. EUR 16 (effective 2010).
Published by: Kluwer B.V. (Subsidiary of: Wolters Kluwer N.V.), Postbus 23, Deventer, 7400 GA, Netherlands. TEL 31-570-673449, FAX 31-570-691555, info@kluwer.nl, http://www.kluwer.nl.

352 FRA ISSN 1955-8082
PROXIMITES. Text in French. 2006. bi-m. EUR 38 (effective 2007). **Document type:** *Magazine, Consumer.*
Published by: Pedagofiche, Zac des Chataigniers, B P 40082, Chamalieres, Cedex 63408, France. TEL 33-4-73605993, FAX 33-4-73628876.

352.14 DEU ISSN 1433-4380
PS: HEIMATBRIEF. Text in German. 1937. a. free (effective 2010). **Document type:** *Government.*
Former titles (until 1997): Heimatbrief Pirmasens; (until 1996): Heimatbriefe der Stadt Pirmasens
Published by: Stadt Pirmasens, Postfach 2763, Pirmasens, 66933, Germany. TEL 49-6331-842222, FAX 49-6331-842286, presse@pirmasens.de.

352.14 CHE
DER PUB - IHRE ZEITUNG. Text in German. 1912. 20/yr. bk.rev. **Document type:** *Trade.* **Description:** Contains information for and about Swiss Federal employees and associations.
Formerly (until 1997): Schweizerische Beamten Zeitung
Published by: Personal Verband Bundesverwaltung, Bahnhofstr 20, Ostermundigen, 3072, Switzerland. TEL 41-31-9386061, FAX 41-31-9386065. Ed. Jean Pierre Metral. adv.: B&W page CHF 2,288; trim 440 x 290. Circ: 13,300 (controlled).

342.09 USA ISSN 0893-2573
KFM4225
PUBLIC AND LOCAL ACTS OF THE LEGISLATURE OF THE STATE OF MICHIGAN. Text in English. 1835. a. price varies. index. back issues avail. **Document type:** *Government.*
Published by: Legislative Council, Legislative Service Bureau, 124 W Allegan, MNT, 4th Fl, Box 30036, Lansing, MI 48909. TEL 517-373-0170, FAX 517-373-0171. Ed. Roger W Peters. Circ: 2,000.

352.4 GBR ISSN 1352-9250
HJ9701 CODEN: PUFIEK
PUBLIC FINANCE; the business weekly of the public sector. Text in English. 1896. w. GBP 100 domestic to non-members; GBP 130 foreign to non-members; free to members (effective 2010). adv. bk.rev. charts; illus.; stat. index. back issues avail. **Document type:** *Magazine, Trade.* **Description:** Provides the public servants up to date with the latest information that affects their work.
Former titles (until 1993): Public Finance and Accountancy (0305-9014); (until 1974): Local Government Finance (0024-5542)
Related titles: Microform ed.; Online - full text ed.
Indexed: A12, A22, ABIn, ADPA, ATI, B01, B02, B03, B06, B07, B08, B09, B11, B15, B16, B17, B18, BPIA, BusI, C12, CPM, Emerald, G04, G06, G07, G08, HlthInd, I05, Inspec, P06, P10, P34, P45, P48, P51, P53, P54, PAA&I, PQC, RICS, S02, S03, T&II.
—BLDSC (6963.399600), AskIEEE, IE, Infotrieve, Ingenta. **CCC.**
Published by: Chartered Institute of Public Finance and Accountancy, 3 Robert St, London, WC2N 6RL, United Kingdom. TEL 44-20-75435600, FAX 44-20-75435700, info@cipfa.org.uk, http://www.cipfa.org.uk. Ed. Mike Thatcher TEL 44-20-73242768. Adv. contact Leon Willoughby TEL 44-20-73242760. B&W page GBP 2,895, color page GBP 3,495; trim 210 x 297. Circ: 18,524.

352.14 GBR ISSN 1757-0743
PUBLIC SERVICE REVIEW. LOCAL GOVERNMENT AND THE REGIONS. Abbreviated title: Public Service Review. L G R. Text in English. 2000. s-a. GBP 50 (effective 2011). adv. back issues avail. **Document type:** *Magazine, Trade.* **Description:** Features the latest in finance, procurement, education, HR, civil contingency planning, the environment and other central issues on the local government agenda.
Former titles (until 2008): Public Service Review. Transport, Local Government and the Regions (1478-2200); (until 2002): Public Service Review. Department of Transport, Local Government and the Regions (1474-7677); (until 2001): Public Service Review. Department of the Environment, Transport and the Regions (1469-6827)
Related titles: Online - full text ed.: ISSN 2046-6161. free (effective 2011).
—**CCC.**
Published by: P S C A International Ltd., Ebenezer House, Rycroft, Newcastle-under-Lyme, Staffs ST5 2UB, United Kingdom. TEL 44-1782-630200, FAX 44-1782-625533, mailbox@publicservice.co.uk. Ed. Michael Thame. Adv. contact Gerrod Mellor TEL 44-1782-630200.

352.14 USA ISSN 0033-3840
TD1 CODEN: PUWOAH
PUBLIC WORKS; the voice of professionals serving America's communities. Text in English. 1896. m. free to qualified personnel (effective 2006). adv. bk.rev. abstr.; bibl.; charts; illus.; tr.lit. index. reprints avail. **Document type:** *Magazine, Trade.* **Description:** Serves industry professionals, consulting engineers, and contractors who design, construct, operate, maintain, and rehabilitate public works and infrastructure projects and programs in cities, counties, states, utilities, and special districts.
Formerly (until 1920): Municipal Journal & Public Works (0096-6169)
Related titles: Microform ed.: (from PMC, PQC); Online - full text ed.
Indexed: A05, A22, A23, A24, A28, A32, APA, AS&TA, AS&TI, B02, B04, B13, B15, B17, B18, BRD, BrCerAb, C&ISA, C10, CA/WCA, CIA, CerAb, ChemAb, CivEngAb, CorrAb, E&CAJ, E11, EEA, EMA, ESPM, EnerRev, EnvEAb, G04, G06, G07, G08, GeoRef, GeotechAb, H15, HRIS, I05, Inspec, M&TEA, M09, MBF, METADEX, P26, P48, P52, P54, PQC, RASB, Repind, S04, SCOPUS, SolStAb, SpeleolAb, T&II, T04, W03, W05, WAA.
—BLDSC (6969.780000), IE, Infotrieve, Ingenta, INIST, Linda Hall. **CCC.**
Published by: Public Works Journal Corporation (Subsidiary of: Hanley Wood, LLC), 426 South Westgate St, Addison, IL 60101. TEL 630-543-0870, FAX 630-543-3112. Ed. William D Palmer Jr. Pub. Pat Carroll TEL 630-705-2504. adv.: B&W page USD 6,820, color page USD 8,580; trim 7.75 x 10.75. Circ: 67,000 (controlled).

352.14 USA ISSN 0892-4171
JS39
QUALITY CITIES. Text in English. 1928. 6/yr. USD 10 to members; USD 20 to non-members (effective 2009). adv. bk.rev. illus. 64 p./no.; reprints avail. **Document type:** *Magazine, Trade.* **Description:** Covers subjects of interest to Florida municipal officials.
Formerly: Florida Municipal Record (0015-4164)
Indexed: P06.
Published by: Florida League of Cities, Inc., 301 S Bronough St, Ste 300, Tallahassee, FL 32301. TEL 850-222-9684, FAX 850-222-3806. Ed., R&P Beth Mulrennan. Pub. Michael Sittig. adv.: B&W page USD 500; 7.25 x 9.25. Circ: 4,700 (paid).

352.14 USA ISSN 0033-6483
QUILL (PRINCETON). Text in English. 1954. q. free. adv. **Document type:** *Newsletter.*
Media: Duplicated (not offset).

P

Published by: Municipal Clerks Association of N.J. Inc., Princeton Township, 11 Boxwood Terrace, Toms River, NJ 08755. TEL 609-924-5704, FAX 609-688-2031. Ed. Patricia C Shuss. Adv. contact L Manuel Hirshblond. Circ: 1,500.

352 NLD ISSN 1879-8616
R T M. Text in Dutch. 2002. q. free (effective 2010). **Document type:** *Magazine, Consumer.*
Formerly (until 2009): Rotterdam (1570-0895)
Published by: Gemeente Rotterdam, Postbus 70012, Rotterdam, 3000 KP, Netherlands. Eds. Afke Vermeer, Ronald Leer.

352.14 ITA ISSN 1723-9877
R U. RISORSE UMANE NELLA PUBBLICA AMMINISTRAZIONE. Text in Italian. 1987. 5/yr. EUR 166 (effective 2008); Includes online newsletter "RU Online". adv. **Document type:** *Magazine, Trade.*
Description: Intended for administrators and workers in the public sector; addresses the changing role of municipal and regional government from a legal, legislative and personal standpoint.
Formerly (until 2002): Rivista del Personale dell'Ente Locale (0394-8439)
Published by: Maggioli Editore, Via del Carpino 8/10, Santarcangelo di Romagna, RN 47822, Italy. TEL 39-0541-628111, FAX 39-0541-622020, editore@maggioli.it, http://www.maggioli.it. Ed. Renato Ruffini.

352 NLD ISSN 1570-3363
RAADSLEDEN NIEUWS. Text in Dutch. 2002. 6/yr. EUR 55 (effective 2009).
Published by: Sdu Uitgevers bv, Postbus 20025, The Hague, 2500 EA, Netherlands. TEL 31-70-3789911, FAX 31-70-3854321, sdu@sdu.nl, http://www.sdu.nl/. Eds. A M van Omme, Dr. H Koetje, Dr. H Tjalma-den Oudsten, Dr. E H A Willems.

352 NLD ISSN 1871-7233
RAADSLEDEN PAMFLET. Text in Dutch. 2005. q. price varies.
Published by: Sdu Uitgevers bv, Postbus 20025, The Hague, 2500 EA, Netherlands. TEL 31-70-3789911, FAX 31-70-3854321, sdu@sdu.nl, http://www.sdu.nl/.

352 PRT ISSN 1647-158X
RADIOGRAFIA. Text in Portuguese. 2008. s-a. **Document type:** *Magazine, Consumer.*
Published by: Camara Municipal de Alcobaca, Praca Joao de Deus Ramos, Alcobaca, 2461-501, Portugal. http://www.cm-alcobaca.pt.

352.14 DEU ISSN 0174-4984
DAS RATHAUS; Zeitschrift fuer Kommunalpolitik. Text in German. 1948. 6/yr. EUR 39.80; EUR 6.80 newsstand/cover (effective 2011). adv. **Document type:** *Magazine, Trade.*
Indexed: IBR, IBZ.
Published by: Max Schmidt-Roemhild KG, Mengstr 16, Luebeck, 23552, Germany. TEL 49-451-703101, FAX 49-451-7031253, info@schmidt-roemhild.de, http://www.beleke.de/unternehmen/verlage/schmidtroemhild/index.html. Ed. Lorenz Becker.

352.14 DEU ISSN 1619-3105
RATHAUS CONSULT. Text in German. 2003. q. EUR 15; EUR 4 newsstand/cover (effective 2008). adv. **Document type:** *Magazine, Trade.*
Published by: Union Betriebs GmbH, Egermannstr 2, Rheinbach, 53359, Germany. TEL 49-2226-8020, FAX 49-2226-802111, info@ubg-medienzentrum.de, http://www.ubg-medienzentrum.de. Ed. Andreas Oberholz. adv.: B&W page EUR 5,850; trim 185 x 247. Circ: 10,244 (paid and controlled).

351 AUT ISSN 1993-8098
RECHT UND FINANZEN FUER GEMEINDEN. Text in German. 2003. q. EUR 128.50; EUR 38.60 newsstand/cover (effective 2011). adv. reprint service avail. from SCH. **Document type:** *Journal, Academic/Scholarly.*
Formerly (until 2007): Rechts- und Finanzierungspraxis der Gemeinden (1727-0456)
Published by: Manz'sche Verlags- und Universitaetsbuchhandlung GmbH, Johannesgasse 23, Vienna, W 1010, Austria. TEL 43-1-531610, FAX 43-1-53161181, verlag@manz.at, http://www.manz.at. Eds. Markus Achatz, Peter Pilz.

352 NLD ISSN 1878-7983
DE RECHTSPOSITIE VAN GEMEENTELIJKE POLITIEKE AMBTSDRAGERS. BURGEMEESTERS EN WETHOUDERS. Text in Dutch. 2006. a. EUR 31.60 (effective 2011).
Published by: Sdu Uitgevers bv, Postbus 20025, The Hague, 2500 EA, Netherlands. TEL 31-70-3789911, FAX 31-70-3854321, sdu@sdu.nl, http://www.sdu.nl/.

352 NLD ISSN 1878-7835
DE RECHTSPOSITIE VAN GEMEENTELIJKE POLITIEKE AMBTSDRAGERS. RAADS- EN COMMISSIELEDEN. Text in Dutch. 2004. a. EUR 27.12 (effective 2011).
Published by: Sdu Uitgevers bv, Postbus 20025, The Hague, 2500 EA, Netherlands. TEL 31-70-3789911, FAX 31-70-3854321, sdu@sdu.nl, http://www.sdu.nl/.

352.14 DEU
REGIERUNGSBEZIRK OBERBAYERN. AMTLICHER SCHULANZEIGER. Text in German. m. EUR 30.20; EUR 2.80 newsstand/cover (effective 2007). **Document type:** *Bulletin, Trade.*
Published by: Regierungsbezirk Oberbayern, Maximilianstr 39, Munich, 80538, Germany. TEL 49-89-21760, FAX 49-89-21762914, poststelle@reg-ob.bayern.de, http://www.regierung.oberbayern.bayern.de.

352.14 CAN
REGIONAL DISTRICT LEGISLATION; a resource manual. Text in English. base vol. plus irreg. updates. looseleaf. CAD 37.80. back issues avail. **Description:** Assists regional district officials with the implementation of Bill 19.
Published by: Ministry of Municipal Affairs, Recreation and Housing, Victoria, BC, Canada. **Subscr. to:** Crown Publications Inc. TEL 250-386-4636, FAX 250-386-0221, crown@pinc.com, http://www.crownpub.bc.ca.

REGIONAL PLANNING NEWSBRIEFS; growing a great region together. *see* HOUSING AND URBAN PLANNING

352.14 USA ISSN 1941-532X
JS39
REVIEW (ANN ARBOR). Text in English. 1928. 10/yr. free to members. adv. bk.rev. charts; illus.; mkt. Index. reprints avail. **Document type:** *Magazine, Trade.*
Formerly (until 2008): Michigan Municipal Review (0026-2331)
Related titles: Microfilm ed.: (from PQC).
Indexed: A22, MMI, P06, PAIS.
Published by: Michigan Municipal League, 1675 Green Rd, Ann Arbor, MI 48106. TEL 734-662-3246, 800-653-2483, FAX 734-662-8083, http://www.mml.org/. Circ: 11,300 (controlled).

352.14 BRA ISSN 0034-7604
JS41
REVISTA DE ADMINISTRACAO MUNICIPAL. Text in Portuguese. 1954. q. adv. bk.rev. bibl.; illus.; stat. index, cum.index: 1965-1995. **Document type:** *Trade.*
Formerly (until 1960): Noticias Municipais (0101-1928)
Indexed: C01, IBR, IBZ, P30.
Published by: Instituto Brasileiro de Administracao Municipal, Largo IBAM 1, Rio De Janeiro, RJ 22271-070, Brazil. TEL 55-21-5377595, FAX 55-21-5371262. Ed. Francois E J de Bremaeker. Pub. Sandra Magon. Adv. contact Deoclides Jovino. Circ: 3,500.

352.14 ESP ISSN 1699-7476
REVISTA DE ESTUDIOS DE LA ADMINISTRACION LOCAL Y AUTONOMICA. Text in Spanish. 1942. 3/yr. EUR 28 domestic; EUR 31 elsewhere (effective 2010). bk.rev. bibl. index. **Document type:** *Journal, Government.*
Former titles (until 2004): Revista de Estudios de la Administracion Local (1578-4568); (until 2000): Revista de Estudios de Administracion Local y Autonomica (0213-4675); (until 1984): Revista de Estudios de la Vida Local (0034-8163)
Indexed: FR, IBR, IBZ, P30.
Published by: Instituto Nacional de Administracion Publica, Atocha 106, Madrid, 28012, Spain. TEL 34-91-2739100, FAX 34-91-2739270, publicaciones@inap.map.es.

352.14 ESP ISSN 1578-9241
REVISTA DE ESTUDIOS LOCALES. Text in Spanish. 1965. m. EUR 187 (effective 2009). **Document type:** *Journal, Trade.*
Former titles (until 1998): C U N A L. Cuerpos Nacionales de Administracion Local (1578-925X); (until 1973): Cuerpos Nacionales de Administracion Local. Boletin Informativo (1578-9144)
Published by: (Consejo General de Secretarios, Interventores y Tesoreros de la Administracion Local), Editorial Aranzadi S.A. (Subsidiary of: Thomson Reuters Corp.), Camino de Galar 15, Cizur Menor, Navarra 31190, Spain. TEL 34-948-297297, FAX 34-948-297200, clientes@aranzadi.es, http://www.aranzadi.es.

352 CHL ISSN 0718-8838
▼ **REVISTA IBEROAMERICANA DE ESTUDIOS MUNICIPALES.** Text in Spanish. 2010. s-a. back issues avail. **Document type:** *Magazine, Academic/Scholarly.*
Related titles: Online - full text ed.
Published by: Universidad Autonoma de Chile, Instituto Chileno de Estudios Municipales, Gaspar Banda, 3810, San Miguel, Santiago, Chile. TEL 56-2-8857743.

352 PRT ISSN 1647-1628
REVISTA MUNICIPAL DE SERNANCELHE. Text in Portuguese. 2008. q. **Document type:** *Magazine, Consumer.*
Published by: Camara Municipal de Sernancelhe, Edificio dos Pacos do Conselho, Sernancelhe, 3640-240, Portugal. TEL 351-254-598300, FAX 351-254-598318, geral@cm-sernancelhe.pt, http://www.cm-sernancelhe.pt.

352.14 ESP ISSN 0213-2206
HC387.V3
REVISTA VALENCIANA D'ESTUDIS AUTONOMICS. Text in Spanish. 1985. 3/yr. **Document type:** *Magazine, Government.*
Indexed: FR.
Address: Cabillers, 9, Valencia, 46003, Spain. TEL 34-6-3866157, FAX 34-6-3866137. Ed. Ramon Martin Mateo.

352.14 FRA ISSN 1779-577X
REVUE DES COLLECTIVITES LOCALES. Text in French. 1949. m. (11/yr.). adv. bk.rev. **Description:** Provides news from cities, departments and regions; surveys involving new products, new services, new jobs, new technologies that are important to the daily business of elected people.
Former titles (until 2004): Elus (1779-5761); (until 2003): Revue des Collectivites Locales et l'Equipement (0755-3269)
Indexed: FR.
—INIST.
Published by: Topix Medias, 5 rue Francois Ponsard, Paris, 75116, France. TEL 33-1-55746200, FAX 33-1-55746210, contact@topixmedias.fr. Circ: 16,000.

352 FRA ISSN 1770-1775
REVUE LAMY COLLECTIVITES TERRITORIALES. Text in French. 200?. m. EUR 359 combined subscription print & CD-ROM eds. (effective 2010). **Document type:** *Journal, Trade.*
Related titles: CD-ROM ed.: ISSN 1950-7860.
Published by: Lamy S.A. (Subsidiary of: Wolters Kluwer France), 1 Rue Eugene et Armand Peugeot, Rueil-Malmaison, 92856 Cedex, France. TEL 33-1-76733000, FAX 33-1-76734809, lamy@lamy.fr, http://www.wkf.fr.

352 PRT ISSN 1647-0494
RIO. Text in Portuguese. 2002. m. **Document type:** *Magazine, Consumer.*
Published by: Camara Municipal de Obidos, Edificio dos Pacos do Conselho, Largo de S Pedro, Obidos, 2510-086, Portugal. TEL 351-262-955505, FAX 351-262-955501, http://www.cm-obidos.pt.

RIVISTA GIURIDICA DI URBANISTICA. *see* HOUSING AND URBAN PLANNING

352.14 DEU
ROSDORFER MITTEILUNGEN; fuer die Gemeinde Rosdorf. Text in German. 1965. w. **Document type:** *Newspaper, Consumer.*
Published by: Gemeinde Rosdorf, Lange Str 12, Rosdorf, 37124, Germany. TEL 49-551-789010, FAX 49-551-7890155, gemeinde@rosdorf.de, http://www.rosdorf.de.

THE RURAL COUNCILLOR. *see* AGRICULTURE—Agricultural Economics

352.14 SWE ISSN 1400-7886
S E K O MAGASINET. (Service och Kommunikation) Text in Swedish. 1955. 11/yr. SEK 200 (effective 2001). adv. bk.rev. charts; illus.; tr.lit. **Document type:** *Magazine, Trade.*
Formerly (until 1995): Statsanstaelld (0039-0712)
Indexed: RILM.
Published by: S E K O, Box 1102, Stockholm, 11181, Sweden. TEL 46-8-7914100, FAX 46-8-211694. Ed., Pub. Bjoern Forsberg. adv.: B&W page SEK 20,700, color page SEK 29,100; trim 210 x 297. Circ: 210,941.

352.14 SWE ISSN 0280-6975
S K T F!TIDNINGEN. Text in Swedish. 1955. 20/yr. SEK 250 (effective 2001). adv. **Document type:** *Newspaper, Trade.*
Formerly (until 1982): Kommunaltjaenstemannen (0345-6323)
Published by: Sveriges Kommunaltjaenstemannafoerbund, Box 7825, Stockholm, 10397, Sweden. TEL 46-8-789-63-00, FAX 46-8-789-64-79. Ed., Pub. Kent Kaellqvist. Adv. contact Anita Wiklund. B&W page SEK 31,500, color page SEK 37,900; trim 227 x 296. Circ: 186,700.

352 DEU
SAARLAENDISCHE KOMMUNALZEITSCHRIFT. Text in German. 1950. m. EUR 24; EUR 2 newsstand/cover (effective 2008). adv. **Document type:** *Magazine, Trade.*
Published by: Saarlaendischer Staedte- und Gemeindetag, Talstr 9, Saarbruecken, 66119, Germany. TEL 49-681-926430, FAX 49-681-9264315, mail@ssgt.de, http://www.saarland-kommunal.de. Ed. Richard Nospers. adv.: B&W page EUR 590, color page EUR 870. Circ: 1,700 (paid and controlled).

352.14 DEU ISSN 0943-2442
SAECHSISCHE VERWALTUNGSBLAETTER; Zeitschrift fuer oeffentliches Recht und oeffentliche Verwaltung. Text in German. 1993. m. EUR 191.40; EUR 144.60 to students (effective 2010). adv. **Document type:** *Journal, Trade.*
Indexed: DIP, IBR, IBZ.
Published by: Richard Boorberg Verlag GmbH und Co. KG, Scharrstr 2, Stuttgart, 70563, Germany. TEL 49-711-73850, FAX 49-711-7385100, mail@boorberg.de.

SAFETYLINE. *see* CRIMINOLOGY AND LAW ENFORCEMENT

352 PRT ISSN 1646-6926
SAL. Text in Portuguese. 2007. irreg. **Document type:** *Magazine, Consumer.*
Published by: Camara Municipal de Aveiro, Pacos do Conselho, Praca da Republica, Aveiro, 3810-156, Portugal. TEL 351-234-406300, FAX 351-234-406301, http://www.cm-aveiro.pt.

352 ESP ISSN 0212-7105
SALAMANCA; revista provincial de estudios. Text in Spanish. 1982. q. back issues avail.
Formerly (until 1983): Provincia de Salamanca (0211-9730)
Published by: Diputacion Provincial de Salamanca, Felipe Espino, 1, Salamanca, 37002, Spain. TEL 34-923-293100, ediciones@dipsanet.es, http://www.dipsanet.es/. Ed. Jose Luis Martin.

352.14 ESP
SAN FERNANDO. Text in Spanish. 6/yr. **Document type:** *Government.*
Published by: Ayuntamiento de San Fernando de Henares, Plaza de Espana, s-m, San Fernando De Henares, Madrid 28830, Spain. TEL 34-91-6276700, informacion@ayto-sanfernando.com, http://www.ayto-sanfernando.com/ASFH/. Ed. A Martinez Escribano. Circ: 10,000.

352.14 AUT
ST. STEFANER GEMEINDENACHRICHTEN. Text in German. 1977. fortn. back issues avail. **Document type:** *Bulletin, Government.*
Published by: Gemeinde St. Stefan ob Leoben, Gemeindeamt, Dorfplatz 14, St. Stefan Ob Leoben, St 8713, Austria. TEL 43-3832-2250, FAX 43-3832-2250-7. Ed. Peter Pechan. Circ: 810.

352 PRT ISSN 0871-5726
SANTAREM. BOLETIM MUNICIPAL. Variant title: Boletim Municipal de Santarem. Text in Portuguese. 1976. irreg. **Document type:** *Bulletin, Consumer.*
Formerly (until 1998): Camara Municipal de Santarem. Boletim (1647-8355)
Published by: Camara Municipal de Santarem, Praca do Municipio, Santarem, 2005-245, Portugal. TEL 351-243-304200, FAX 351-243-304299, geral@cm-santarem.pt, http://www.cm-santarem.pt.

352 CAN ISSN 0845-6526
SASKATCHEWAN MUNICIPAL BOARD. ANNUAL REPORT. Text in English. a.
Formerly (until 1988): Saskatchewan Local Government Board. Annual Report (0708-4994)
Published by: Saskatchewan Municipal Board, 480-2151 Scarth St, Regina, SK S4P 3V7, Canada. TEL 306-787-6221, FAX 306-787-1610, info@smb.gov.sk.ca.

352.14 CAN ISSN 0581-8435
JS1721.S3
SASKATCHEWAN MUNICIPAL DIRECTORY. Text in English. 1909. a. CAD 10. **Document type:** *Directory.*
Published by: Saskatchewan Municipal Government, 1855 Victoria Ave, Regina, SK S4P 3V7, Canada. TEL 306-787-2635, FAX 306-787-4181. Ed. Jean Lazar. Circ: 5,000.

351 AUT
SCHRIFTENREIHE RECHT UND FINANZEN FUER GEMEINDEN. Variant title: Schriftenreihe R F G. Text in German. 2001. irreg., latest 2010. price varies. **Document type:** *Monographic series, Academic/Scholarly.*
Formerly (until 2007): Schriftenreihe Rechts- und Finanzierungspraxis der Gemeinden
Published by: Manz'sche Verlags- und Universitaetsbuchhandlung GmbH, Johannesgasse 23, Vienna, W 1010, Austria. TEL 43-1-531610, FAX 43-1-53161181, verlag@manz.at.

352 DEU ISSN 1865-8059
SCHWEBHEIMER AMTSBOTE. Text in German. 1977. w. EUR 26.40 (effective 2011). adv. **Document type:** *Newsletter, Trade.*
Published by: Revista Verlag GmbH, Am Oberen Marienbach 2 1/2, Schweinfurt, 97421, Germany. TEL 49-9721-387190, FAX 49-9721-3871938, post@revista.de.

352.14 CHE
DIE SCHWEIZER GEMEINDE. Text in German. 11/yr. **Document type:** *Bulletin.*
Published by: Schweizer Gemeinde, Solothurnstr 22, Schoenbuehl-Urtenen, 3322, Switzerland. TEL 41-31-8583116, FAX 41-31-8583115. Ed. Patrick Jacklin. Circ: 5,000.

352.1402571 CAN ISSN 1485-5518
SCOTT'S DIRECTORY OF CANADIAN MUNICIPALITIES. Text in English. 1998. a. CAD 239 per issue domestic; USD 239 per issue foreign (effective 2008). **Document type:** *Directory, Government.* **Description:** Contains 40,000 contacts and over 3,600 municipalities, cities, towns and villages across Canada.
Related titles: CD-ROM ed.: Canadian Municipalities Select; Online - full text ed.
Published by: Business Information Group, 12 Concorde Pl, Ste 800, Toronto, ON M3C 4J2, Canada. TEL 416-442-2122, 800-668-2374, FAX 416-442-2191, orders@businessinformationgroup.ca.

352.9 NLD ISSN 1871-5389
SDU WETTENVERZAMELING. ALGEMENE WET BESTUURSRECHT BESTUURS(PROCES)RECHT. Key Title: Sdu Wettenverzameling. Awb Bestuurs(proces)recht. Text in Dutch. 2005. a. EUR 34.86 (effective 2009).
Published by: Sdu Uitgevers bv, Postbus 20025, The Hague, 2500 EA, Netherlands. TEL 31-70-3789911, FAX 31-70-3854321, sdu@sdu.nl.

352 DEU ISSN 1865-8024
SENNFELDER NACHRICHTEN; amtliches Nachrichtenblatt der Gemeinde Sennfeld. Text in German. 1974. w. EUR 26.40 (effective 2011). adv. **Document type:** *Newsletter, Trade.*
Published by: Revista Verlag GmbH, Am Oberen Marienbach 2 1/2, Schweinfurt, 97421, Germany. TEL 49-9721-387190, FAX 49-9721-3871938, post@revista.de.

352 ZAF ISSN 1992-0164
SERVICE; leadership in local government. Text in English. 2002. bi-m. adv. **Document type:** *Magazine, Trade.*
Published by: Cape Media Corporation, Sanclare Bldg, 4th Flr, 21 Dreyer St, Claremont, Cape Town 7735, South Africa. TEL 27-21-6573800, FAX 27-21-6573866, info@capemedia.co.za. Ed. Michael Littlefield. adv.: page ZAR 23,800; trim 210 x 275. Circ: 10,000.

352.14 CHE
SERVICE ET COMMUNAUTE. Text in French, German, Italian. w.
Address: Hopfenweg 21, Bern, 3007, Switzerland. TEL 031-455562. Ed. Robert Andenmatten. Circ: 18,529.

352.14 CHE
SERVICES PUBLICS. Text in German. 23/yr. CHF 60; CHF 100 foreign. adv. **Document type:** *Newspaper.*
Address: Case Postale 1360, Lausanne, 1001, Switzerland. TEL 41-21-3238833, FAX 41-21-3209345. Ed. Doris Schuepp. R&P, Adv. contact Agostino Soldini. Circ: 12,000.

352.14 ITA ISSN 1825-8808
SERVIZI E SOCIETA. Text in Italian. 1969. bi-m. **Document type:** *Magazine, Trade.*
Former titles (until 1989): C I S P E L Lombardia (1825-8794); (until 1982): C R I P E L Lombardia (1825-8786)
Published by: Confederazione Nazionale dei Servizi (Confservizi), Via Cavour 179/a, Rome, 00184, Italy. TEL 39-06-478651, http://www.confservizi.net/.

352 ITA ISSN 1825-2729
SERVIZI POLIZIA MUNICIPALE. Text in Italian. 2003. w. EUR 90 (effective 2009). **Document type:** *Magazine, Trade.*
Media: Online - full text.
Published by: Noccioli Editore, Via Lucchese 84B, Osmannoro - Sesto Fiorentino, FI 50132, Italy. TEL 39-055-310316, FAX 39-055-310239, redazione@noccioli.it, http://www.noccioli.it.

352 PRT ISSN 1646-6640
SESIMBRA. BOLETIM MUNICIPAL. Text in Portuguese. 2007. m. **Document type:** *Bulletin, Consumer.*
Published by: Camara Municipal de Sesimbra, Rua da Republica 3, Sesimbra, 2970-741, Portugal. TEL 351-21-2288500, http://www.cm-sesimbra.pt.

352 GBR ISSN 1462-821X
SHAW'S LOCAL GOVERNMENT DIRECTORY. Text in English. 1996. a. GBP 39.50 (effective 2009). adv. index. **Document type:** *Directory, Trade.* **Description:** Lists the names, addresses, and telephone and fax numbers of all local authorities in the UK. Provides an extensive gazeteer of places.
Formerly (until 1999): Shaw's Directory of Local Authorities in the United Kingdom (1362-1181)
—CCC.
Published by: Shaw & Sons Ltd., Shaway House, 21 Bourne Park, Bourne Rd, Crayford, Kent DA1 4BZ, United Kingdom. TEL 44-1322-621100, FAX 44-1322-550553, sales@shaws.co.uk, http://www.shaws.co.uk.

352 PRT ISSN 1646-611X
SINTRA; revista municipal. Text in Portuguese. 2002. q. **Document type:** *Magazine, Consumer.*
Published by: Camara Municipal de Sintra, Largo Dr. Virgilio Horta 4, Sintra, 2714, Portugal. TEL 351-219-247000, http://www.cm-sintra.pt.

352.14 USA
SISTER CITY INTERNATIONAL QUARTERLY. Text in English. 1961. bi-m. free membership. adv. bk.rev. stat. back issues avail. **Document type:** *Newsletter.*
Former titles: Sister City News; T A A Newsletter (0300-6166)
Related titles: Online - full text ed.
Published by: Sister Cities International, 1301 Pennsylvania Ave, NW, Ste 850, Washington, DC 20004. TEL 202-347-8630, FAX 202-393-6524, http://www.sister-cities.org/. Circ: 30,000.

352.14 HRV ISSN 0037-7120
SLUZBENI GLASNIK OPCINE ROVINJ. Text in Croatian, Italian. 1964. irreg.
Published by: Skupstina Opcine Rovinj, Ul. Matteotti 1-1, Rovinj, Croatia. Ed. Marija Matosovic.

352 USA
SMALL COMMUNITY QUARTERLY. Text in English. 2001. q. free (effective 2005). **Document type:** *Journal, Government.* **Description:** Concentrates on issues of importance to small and rural towns. It features exclusive interviews with public policy and opinion leaders, articles on economic development, financial management, revenue generation, telecommunications, environmental concerns and more. It also includes helpful resources and updates on NCSC's publications and activities.
Published by: National Center for Small Communities, 444 N Capitol St., NW, Ste 397, Washington, DC 20001-1202. TEL 202-624-3550, FAX 202-624-3554, ncsc@sso.org. Ed. Faye Kann.

352 ITA ISSN 1128-7845
IL SOLE 24 ORE. GUIDE AGLI ENTI LOCALI. Text in Italian. 1997. w. **Document type:** *Magazine, Trade.*
Related titles: Online - full text ed.: ISSN 1828-0331.
Published by: Il Sole 24 Ore Business Media, Via Monte Rosa 91, Milan, 20149, Italy. TEL 39-02-30221, FAX 39-02-312055, info@ilsole24ore.com, http://www.gruppo24ore.com.

352.14 CHE
SOLOTHURNISCHE STAATSPERSONAL. Text in German. 1933. m. CHF 20; CHF 50 foreign (effective 2000). adv. bk.rev. **Document type:** *Government.*
Published by: Solothurnischer Staatspersonal Verband, Dammstr 21, Solothurn, 4500, Switzerland. TEL 41-32-6222277, FAX 41-32-6223211. Ed. P Bischof. Circ: 3,000.

SOUTH AFRICA. STATISTICS SOUTH AFRICA. LOCAL GOVERNMENT STATISTICS. *see* PUBLIC ADMINISTRATION—Abstracting, Bibliographies, Statistics

SOUTH AFRICA. STATISTICS SOUTH AFRICA. STATISTICAL RELEASE. FINANCIAL STATISTICS OF LOCAL GOVERNMENTS (YEAR). *see* PUBLIC ADMINISTRATION—Abstracting, Bibliographies, Statistics

352.14 USA ISSN 0300-6182
SOUTH DAKOTA MUNICIPALITIES. Abbreviated title: S D M L. Text in English. 1934. m. USD 30 to non-members; free to members (effective 2010). adv. bk.rev. 44 p./no. 2 cols./p.; back issues avail. **Document type:** *Magazine, Trade.* **Description:** Designed for the members of the South Dakota Municipal League in South Dakota's 300-plus incorporated cities and towns across the state, and many other organizations, associations and individuals.
Indexed: P06.
Published by: South Dakota Municipal League, 214 E Capitol Ave, Pierre, SD 57501. TEL 605-224-8654, FAX 605-224-8655. Ed. Carrie A Harer. adv.: page USD 279; 7 x 10. Circ: 3,000.

352.14 USA ISSN 0361-7130
JS39
SOUTHERN CITY. Text in English. m. USD 25 (effective 2000). adv. charts; illus. **Document type:** *Newspaper.*
Published by: North Carolina League of Municipalities, 215 N Dawson St, PO Box 3069, Raleigh, NC 27602. TEL 919-715-4000, FAX 919-733-9519. Ed. Margot F Christensen. Circ: 6,400.

352.14 DEU
SPEKTRUM (MAINZ); Veranstaltungs- und Kongressinformation der Landeshauptstadt Mainz. Text in German. 1973. q. free. **Document type:** *Journal, Trade.*
Published by: Congress Centrum Mainz GmbH, Rheinstr 66, Mainz, 55116, Germany. TEL 49-6131-2420, FAX 49-6131-242100, info@ccm.mainz.de, http://www.ccmainz.de. Circ: 10,000.

352.14 USA ISSN 0038-7711
SPOKANE, WASHINGTON. OFFICIAL GAZETTE. Text in English. 1910. w. USD 4.75. **Document type:** *Government.*
Indexed: P06.
Published by: City of Spokane, Washington, City Clerk, Municipal Bldg, 5th Fl, W 808 Spokane Falls Blvd, Spokane, WA 99201-3342. TEL 509-625-6354, FAX 509-625-6217. Ed. Terri L Pfister. Circ: 450.

352 NLD ISSN 1872-3918
DE STAAT VAN ROTTERDAM. Text in Dutch. 2003. a. EUR 20 (effective 2008).
Published by: Centrum voor Onderzoek en Statistiek, Gemeente Rotterdam, Gebouw "De Goudsesingel", 2e etage Goudsesingel 78, Rotterdam, 3011 KD, Netherlands. TEL 31-10-4899500, FAX 31-10-4899501, info@cos.rotterdam.nl, http://cos.rotterdam.nl.

352 AUT
DER STAATSBEAMTE. Text in German. q.
Published by: Staatsbeamte, Hiligenstaedterstrasse 131-1-3, Vienna, W 1190, Austria. TEL 01-372163, FAX 01-374117. Ed. F C Fetty.

352.14 AUT ISSN 0038-8939
STADLINGER POST. Text in German. 1952. q. adv. abstr.; stat. **Document type:** *Newsletter, Government.*
Published by: Gemeindeamt Stadl Paura, Marktplatz 1, Stadl-Paura, O 4651, Austria. TEL 43-7245-28011, FAX 43-7245-2801125, gemeinde@stadl-paura.ooe.gv.at, http://www.stadl-paura.at. Ed. Friedrich Urbanek. Circ: 900.

352.14 SWE ISSN 0038-8963
STADSBYGGNAD. Text in Swedish. 1935. bi-m. SEK 250 domestic; SEK 320 foreign; SEK 50 newsstand/cover (effective 2004). adv. illus.; mkt. index. **Document type:** *Magazine, Trade.*
Formerly (until 1958): Kommunalteknisk Tidskrift
Published by: Svenska Kommunal-Tekniska Foereningen/Swedish Association of Municipal Technicians, Maester Samuelsgatan 49, Stockholm, 11157, Sweden. TEL 46-8-201985, FAX 46-8-201509, info@skt.se. Ed., Pub. Martin Edman TEL 46-54-153292. Adv. contact Patrik Inmer TEL 46-8-7421008. B&W page SEK 5,900, color page SEK 8,900; trim 185 x 265. Circ: 12,000 (paid).

352.14 DEU
STADT BAMBERG. RATHAUS JOURNAL; Amtsblatt der Stadt Bamberg. Text in German. 1945. s-m. adv. **Document type:** *Journal, Government.*
Formerly (until 1998): Stadt Bamberg. Mitteilungsblatt
Published by: Stadt Bamberg, Rathaus Maxplatz, Bamberg, 96047, Germany. Ed. Steffen Schuetzwohl. Adv. contact Wolfgang Reiffert. Circ: 18,500.

352.14 DEU ISSN 1437-7330
STADT HERNE. ARBEITSMARKTBERICHT. Text in German. 1989. q. **Document type:** *Government.*
Published by: Stadt Herne, Amt fuer Informationsverarbeitung und Stadtforschung, Friedrich-Ebert-Platz 2, Postfach 101820, Herne, 44621, Germany. TEL 49-2323-16-0, FAX 49-2323-162311. Circ: 270.

STADT MANNHEIM. VIERTELJAHRESBERICHT. *see* PUBLIC ADMINISTRATION—Abstracting, Bibliographies, Statistics

352 DEU ISSN 1865-8199
STADTLAURINGER AMTSBOTE; Amtsblatt fuer den Markt Stadtlauringen. Text in German. 1978. w. EUR 26.40 (effective 2011). adv. **Document type:** *Newsletter, Trade.*
Published by: Revista Verlag GmbH, Am Oberen Marienbach 2 1/2, Schweinfurt, 97421, Germany. TEL 49-9721-387190, FAX 49-9721-3871938, post@revista.de.

352 DEU ISSN 0940-6212
STADTSPIEGEL EISENHUETTENSTADT. Text in German. 1961. m. adv. **Document type:** *Magazine, Consumer.*
Formerly (until 1991): Kulturspiegel Eisenhuettenstadt (0232-6523)
Published by: (Stadtverwaltung Eisenhuettenstadt), MultiMedia Frankfurt (Oder) GmbH, Friedrich-Ebert-Str 20, Frankfurt (Oder), 15234, Germany. TEL 49-335-555490, FAX 49-335-5554932, mmf@multimedia-ffo.de, http://www.multimedia-ffo.de. Eds. Juliane Fechner TEL 49-3364-566270, Maria Minew. adv.: page EUR 420. Circ: 5,000 (controlled).

352.14 DEU
STADTZEITUNG HEILBRONN. Text in German. 1945. fortn. looseleaf. adv. back issues avail. **Document type:** *Government.*
Formerly (until 1999): Amtsblatt fuer den Stadt- und Landkreis Heilbronn
Published by: Stadt Heilbronn Pressestelle, Rathaus, Postfach 3440, Heilbronn, 74024, Germany. TEL 49-7131-562288, FAX 49-7131-563169. Ed., R&P Klaus Koenninger. Adv. contact Margot Veigel. Circ: 50,000.

352.14 DEU ISSN 0038-9048
JS41
DER STAEDTETAG; Zeitschrift fuer Kommunalpolitik und kommunale Praxis. Text in German. 1948. bi-m. EUR 72; EUR 15 newsstand/cover (effective 2011). adv. bk.rev. charts; illus. index, cum.index. reprints avail. **Document type:** *Journal, Trade.*
Indexed: DokStr, IBR, IBZ, PAIS.
—CCC.
Published by: (Verband Kommunaler Abfallwirtschaft und Stadtreinigung e.V.), Carl Heymanns Verlag KG (Subsidiary of: Wolters Kluwer Deutschland GmbH), Luxemburger Str 449, Cologne, 50939, Germany. TEL 49-221-943730, FAX 49-221-94373901, marketing@heymanns.com, http://www.heymanns.com. Adv. contact Marcus Kipp. Circ: 1,200 (paid and controlled).

352.14 CHE
DER STAEDTISCHE. Text in German. m.
Published by: V P O D, Stauffacherstr 60, Zuerich, 8004, Switzerland. Circ: 7,500.

STATE & LOCAL GOVERNMENT COMPUTER NEWS. *see* PUBLIC ADMINISTRATION—Computer Applications

352.14 USA ISSN 0160-323X
JK2403
➤ **STATE AND LOCAL GOVERNMENT REVIEW**; a journal of research and viewpoints on state and local government issues. Text in English. 1968. 3/yr. USD 199, GBP 118 combined subscription to institutions (print & online eds.); USD 195, GBP 116 to institutions (effective 2011). bk.rev. illus. Index. back issues avail.; reprint service avail. from PSC. **Document type:** *Journal, Academic/Scholarly.*
Supersedes: Georgia Government Review (0016-8289)
Related titles: Online - full text ed.: ISSN 1943-3409. USD 179, GBP 106 to institutions (effective 2011).
Indexed: A22, ABCPolSci, CA, DIP, E01, I13, IBR, IBZ, P06, P34, P42, PAIS, PRA, PSA, SCOPUS, SPAA, SUSA, SociolAb, T02.
—BLDSC (8437.603000), IE, Ingenta. **CCC.**
Published by: (University of Georgia, Carl Vinson Institute of Government), Sage Publications, Inc., 2455 Teller Rd, Thousand Oaks, CA 91320. TEL 805-499-9774, FAX 805-499-0871, info@sagepub.com, http://www.sagepub.com/. Ed. Michael Scicchitano. Circ: 1,000. **Co-sponsor:** American Society for Public Administration, Section on Intergovernmental Administration and Management.

352.14 USA ISSN 1078-7356
KF5300
STATE & LOCAL LAW NEWS. Text in English. 1978. q. USD 44.95 to non-members; free to members (effective 2009). adv. 16 p./no.; back issues avail.; reprints avail. **Document type:** *Newsletter, Consumer.* **Description:** Provides information about current developments in the law of interest to state and local government lawyers.
Former titles (until 1994): Urban, State, and Local Law Newsletter (0195-7686); (until 1979): State, Local, and Urban Law Newsletter (0163-2922)
Indexed: A01, A26, CLI, G08, I05, LRI, P34.
—CCC.
Published by: (American Bar Association, The Section of State and Local Government Law), A B A Publishing, 750 N Lake Shore Dr, Chicago, IL 60611. TEL 312-988-5000, FAX 312-988-6081, service@abanet.org. Ed. Justina Cintron Perino. Circ: 6,000 (paid and controlled).

352.14 USA ISSN 0898-8374
STATE MUNICIPAL LEAGUE DIRECTORY. Text in English. a. USD 30 to non-members (effective 2000). **Document type:** *Directory.* **Description:** Guide to the operations and functions of state municipal associations.
Published by: National League of Cities, 1301 Pennsylvania Ave, N W, Ste 550, Washington, DC 20004. TEL 202-626-3150, FAX 202-626-3043, http://www.nlc.org. Ed. Mark Shapiro. R&P Mae Davis TEL 202-626-3000.

978.3 352 USA ISSN 0361-0292
STATE OF SOUTH DAKOTA. OFFICE OF THE ATTORNEY GENERAL. OFFICIAL OPINIONS. Variant title: Official Opinions. Text in English. 19??. irreg. **Document type:** *Government.*
Related titles: Online - full text ed.
Published by: South Dakota. Office of the Attorney General, 500 E Capitol Ave, Pierre, SD 57501-5070. TEL 605-773-3215, FAX 605-773-4106, atghelp@state.sd.us, http://www.state.sd.us/attorney/default.asp.

352.250993 NZL ISSN 1176-8304
STATE SERVICES COMMISSION. ANNUAL REPORT. Text in English. a. **Document type:** *Government.*
Former titles (until 1999): State Services Commission. Report (0545-7513); (until 1963): Public Service Commission. Report
Related titles: Online - full text ed.: ISSN 1177-7257.
Published by: State Services Commission, PO Box 329, Wellington, New Zealand. TEL 64-4-4956600, FAX 64-4-4956686, commission@ssc.govt.nz.

STATISTICS RELATING TO REGIONAL AND MUNICIPAL GOVERNMENTS IN BRITISH COLUMBIA. *see* PUBLIC ADMINISTRATION—Abstracting, Bibliographies, Statistics

STATISTISCHER VIERTELJAHRESBERICHT HANNOVER. *see* PUBLIC ADMINISTRATION—Abstracting, Bibliographies, Statistics

P

STATISTISCHES JAHRBUCH DER STADT KOELN. *see* PUBLIC ADMINISTRATION—Abstracting, Bibliographies, Statistics

STATISTISCHES JAHRBUCH DEUTSCHER GEMEINDEN. *see* PUBLIC ADMINISTRATION—Abstracting, Bibliographies, Statistics

STATISTISCHES JAHRBUCH HAMBURG. *see* PUBLIC ADMINISTRATION—Abstracting, Bibliographies, Statistics

STATISTISCHES LANDESAMT HAMBURG. EIN STADTPORTRAET IN ZAHLEN. *see* PUBLIC ADMINISTRATION—Abstracting, Bibliographies, Statistics

STATISTISCHES LANDESAMT RHEINLAND-PFALZ. STATISTISCHE MONATSHEFTE. *see* PUBLIC ADMINISTRATION—Abstracting, Bibliographies, Statistics

352 RUS
STAVROPOL'SKIE GUBERNSKIE VEDOMOSTI. Text in Russian. 3/w. USD 299 in United States.
Address: Ul Lenina 192, Stavropol, 355000, Russian Federation. TEL 7-8652-263367, FAX 7-8652-263365. Ed. A Emtsov. **Dist. by:** East View Information Services, 10601 Wayzata Blvd, Minneapolis, MN 55305. TEL 952-252-1201, 800-477-1005, FAX 952-252-1202, info@eastview.com, http://www.eastview.com.

352.14 GBR
STOCKTON NEWS. Text in English. 19??. bi-m. free (effective 2009). back issues avail. **Document type:** *Newsletter, Government.*
Description: Aims to provide news and information about the Council, its partner organizations and local community groups and businesses.
Related titles: Online - full text ed.
Published by: Stockton-on-Tees Borough Council, Municipal Bldgs, Church Rd, PO Box 11, Stockton-On-Tees, TS18 1LD, United Kingdom. TEL 44-1642-526164, FAX 44-1642-526166, communications@stockton.gov.uk. Ed. Vince Rutland.

352 ITA ISSN 1974-8663
STRUMENTARIO ENTI LOCALI. Text in Italian. 2006. m. **Document type:** *Directory, Trade.*
Published by: Dirittoitalia Editore, Piazza Principe Amedeo 31, Aversa, CE 81031, Italy. info@dirittoitalia.it, http://www.dirittoitalia.it.

352.14 USA ISSN 0743-2585
SUMMERVILLE POST. Text in English. 1976. q. USD 10. adv. illus. **Document type:** *Newsletter.* **Description:** Provides information about the activities of the association and about events affecting the neighborhood.
Published by: Summerville Neighborhood Association Inc., PO Box 12212, Augusta, GA 30914-2212. Circ: 2,365.

352 CAN ISSN 1924-0260
SUPPLEMENTARY ESTIMATES OF EXPENDITURE OF THE PROVINCE OF PRINCE EDWARD ISLAND IN SUPPORT OF THE SUPPLEMENTARY APPROPRIATION ACT. Text in English. 2004. irreg., latest 2010. free (effective 2010). **Document type:** *Government.*
Related titles: Online - full text ed.
Published by: Government of Prince Edward Island, Department of Finance and Municipal Affairs, Shaw Bldg, Second Fl S, 95 Rochford St, PO Box 2000, Charlottetown, PE C1A 7N8, Canada. TEL 902-368-4000, FAX 902-368-5544, jmdoherty@gov.pe.ca.

352.14 ISL ISSN 0255-8459
SVEITARSTJORNARMAL. Text in Icelandic. 1941. bi-m. adv.
Published by: Samband Islenskra Sveitarfelaga, Haaleitisbraut 11-13, Reykjavik, Iceland. TEL 354-581-3711. Circ: 4,800.

▼ **TAKING SIDES: CLASHING VIEWS ON STATE AND LOCAL GOVERNMENT ISSUES.** *see* PUBLIC ADMINISTRATION

332.02 GBR ISSN 1757-4013
TARGETJOBS CITY & FINANCE. Text in English. 1996. a. GBP 10.95 per issue (effective 2009). adv. **Document type:** *Journal, Trade.*
Description: Features articles and the opportunity for graduates to go more in depth researching finance careers.
Former titles (until 2008): Target City & Finance (1477-2337); (until 2001): City & Finance (1359-9410)
—CCC.
Published by: G T I Specialist Publishers, First Fl Offices, 75 Farringdon Rd, London, EC1M 3JY, United Kingdom. TEL 44-20-70611939, FAX 44-20-70611901.

352 368.4 NLD ISSN 2211-6532
TEKSTUITGAVE WETGEVING GEMEENTELIJKE SOCIALE ZEKERHEID. Variant title: Wetgeving Gemeentelijke Sociale Zekerheid. Text in Dutch. 2007. s-a. EUR 35.55 per issue (effective 2011).
Formerly (until 2011): Collectie Sociale Voorzieningen (2211-6567)
Published by: Kluwer B.V. (Subsidiary of: Wolters Kluwer N.V.), Postbus 23, Deventer, 7400 GA, Netherlands. TEL 31-570-673449, FAX 31-570-691555, info@kluwer.nl, http://www.kluwer.nl.

352.14025 USA
TENNESSEE GOVERNMENT OFFICIALS DIRECTORY; your all-inclusive guide to Tennessee state and local officials. Text in English. 1985. a. USD 102 combined subscription (print & online eds.) (effective 2008). **Document type:** *Directory, Trade.* **Description:** Lists all state, county, and city officials, including government officials and chambers of commerce, Tennessee colleges and universities, business and professional associations, lobbyists, Capitol Hill press corps and Tennessee newspapers, magazines, and radio and TV stations.
Related titles: Online - full text ed.
Published by: M. Lee Smith Publishers LLC, 5201 Virginia Way, PO Box 5094, Brentwood, TN 37024. TEL 615-661-0246, 800-274-6774, FAX 615-373-5183, custserv@mleesmith.com.

352.14 USA
TENNESSEE PUBLIC ACTS (YEAR); summaries of interest to municipal officials. Text in English. 1989. a. USD 20; USD 10 to qualified personnel (effective 2006). **Document type:** *Bulletin, Government.*
Description: Summarizes the year's public acts and provides date they become effective.
Former titles: Summary of Public Acts of Interest to Municipal Officials; Summary of New Laws, General Assembly (1049-605X)
Related titles: Online - full content ed.
Published by: University of Tennessee at Knoxville, Municipal Technical Advisory Service, 600 Henley, Ste 120, Knoxville, TN 37996-4105. TEL 865-974-0411, FAX 865-974-0423. Ed. Richard Stokes.

352.14 USA ISSN 0892-5380
HD3890.T2
TENNESSEE PUBLIC WORKS. Text in English. 1983. bi-m. USD 18.
Published by: Images Publications, PO Box 474, Loudon, TN 37774-0474. TEL 615-458-3560, FAX 615-458-4095. Ed. Frank Kirk. adv.: B&W page USD 500. Circ: 1,900.

352.14 USA ISSN 0040-3415
TENNESSEE TOWN AND CITY. Text in English. 1950. s-m. USD 6 to members (effective 2009). adv. bk.rev. charts; illus. Index. 6 p./no. 5 cols./p.; back issues avail. **Document type:** *Magazine, Trade.*
Description: Covers municipal and state government and politics.
Related titles: Online - full text ed.
Indexed: P06.
Published by: Tennessee Municipal League, 226 Capitol Blvd, Ste 710, Nashville, TN 37219-1894. TEL 615-255-6416, FAX 615-255-4752, gstahl@tml1.org, http://www.tml1.org. Ed. Carole Graves. Circ: 6,250 (controlled).

352.14 FRA ISSN 0991-2428
TERRITOIRES; la revue de la democratie locale. Text in French. 1958. 10/yr. EUR 55 domestic to individuals; EUR 75 foreign to individuals; EUR 75 domestic to institutions; EUR 95 foreign to institutions; EUR 35 domestic to students (effective 2008). adv. bk.rev. bibl. cum.index: 1968-1997. **Document type:** *Magazine.* **Description:** For elected officials, social workers and interested citizens.
Formerly (until 1988): Correspondance Municipale (0223-5951)
Related titles: Microfiche ed.
Indexed: FR.
—INIST.
Published by: Association pour la Democratie et l'Education Locale et Sociale (A D E L S), 24 Rue de l'Eglise, Paris, 75015, France. TEL 33-1-43554005, FAX 33-1-55283021. Ed. Sylvie Bamezet. R&P, Adv. contact Bernard Deljarie. Circ: 6,000.

352 NLD ISSN 1874-5253
THERMOMETER BINNENSTAD GRONINGEN. Text in Dutch. 2000. a. EUR 20 (effective 2010).
Published by: Stichting Intraval, Postbus 1781, Groningen, 9701 BT, Netherlands. TEL 31-50-3134052, FAX 31-50-3127526, info@intraval.nl, http://www.intraval.nl.

352.14 DEU ISSN 0941-7648
THUERINGER VERWALTUNGSBLAETTER; Zeitschrift fuer oeffentliches Recht und oeffentliche Verwaltung. Text in German. 1992. m. EUR 191.40; EUR 144.60 to students (effective 2010). adv. **Document type:** *Journal, Trade.*
Indexed: DIP, IBR, IBZ.
Published by: Richard Boorberg Verlag GmbH und Co. KG, Scharrstr 2, Stuttgart, 70563, Germany. TEL 49-711-73850, FAX 49-711-7385100, mail@boorberg.de.

352.14 BEL ISSN 0775-3217
TIJDSCHRIFT VOOR GEMEENTERECHT. Text in Dutch. 1987. bi-m. EUR 151.18 (effective 2003). **Document type:** *Trade.*
Published by: Kluwer Uitgevers (Subsidiary of: Wolters Kluwer Belgique), Ragheno Business Park, Motstraat 30, Mechelen, B-2800, Belgium. TEL 32-15-800-94571, info@kluwer.be, http://www.kluwer.be.

352.14 JPN ISSN 0916-7951
DS896
TOKYO METROPOLITAN NEWS. Text in Japanese. 1951. q. free to qualified personnel. charts; illus.; stat.
Formerly (until 1991): Tokyo Municipal News (0040-893X)
Related titles: Chinese ed.: Dongjing Dumin Tongxun. ISSN 0910-1020; Korean ed.: Tokyoto News. ISSN 1343-2079. 1988; French ed.: Tokyo Les Nouvelles Municipales. ISSN 1343-2060.
Indexed: BAS, P06, PAIS, RASB.
Published by: (Tokyo. Liaison and Protocol Section), Tokyo Metropolitan Government, Bureau of Citizens and Cultural Affairs, 8-1 Nishi-Shinjuku 2-chome, Shinjuku-ku, Tokyo, 160-0023, Japan. TEL 81-3-5388-3172, FAX 81-3-5388-1329, kokusai@keikatubunka.metro.tokyo.jp. Circ: 5,000.

352.14 USA ISSN 0040-9065
JS13
TOLEDO CITY JOURNAL. Text in English. 1916. w. USD 18 (effective 2000). **Document type:** *Newspaper, Government.*
Indexed: P06.
Published by: City of Toledo, One Government Ctr, Ste 2140, Toledo, OH 43604. TEL 419-245-1060. Ed. Michael J Beazley. Circ: 500.

352 PRT ISSN 2182-0589
TORRES VEDRAS. Variant title: Revista Municipal Torres Vedras. Text in Portuguese. 2008. bi-m. **Document type:** *Newsletter, Consumer.*
Formerly (until 2011): Um Concelho (1646-9917)
Published by: Camara Municipal de Torres Vedras, Rua Santos Bernardes, Torres Vedras, Portugal. http://www.cm-tvedras.pt.

352.14 JPN ISSN 0387-3382
HT101
TOSHI MONDAI/MUNICIPAL PROBLEMS. Text in Japanese. 1925. m. JPY 9,000 (effective 2001). adv. bk.rev. bibl. **Document type:** *Academic/Scholarly.*
Related titles: CD-ROM ed.: Index of Municipal Problems. JPY 3,000.
—Ingenta.
Published by: Tokyo Institute for Municipal Research, 1-3 Hibiyakoen, Chiyoda-ku, Tokyo, 100-0012, Japan. TEL 81-3-3591-1201, FAX 81-3-3591-1209. Pub. Shinichi Nomura. Adv. contacts Shinichi Nomura, Yosikatu Kono. Circ: 2,800.

352.14025 USA
THE TOUCHSTONE. Text in English. 19??. q. free to members (effective 2010). **Document type:** *Newsletter, Trade.* **Description:** Contains articles covering news and events of interest to AML membership.
Former titles (until 1991): Legislative Bulletin; (until 1984): Alaska Municipal League. Newsletter
Media: Online - full text.
Published by: Alaska Municipal League, 217 Second St, Ste 200, Juneau, AK 99801. TEL 907-586-1325, 877-636-1325, FAX 907-463-5480, info@akml.org. Ed. Jeremy Woodrow.

352.14 USA ISSN 1523-9055
TOWNSHIP PERSPECTIVE. Text in English. 1946. m. (11/yr.). USD 25 (effective 2006). adv. illus. 48 p./no. 3 cols./p.; back issues avail. **Document type:** *Magazine, Trade.* **Description:** Provides items of interest and general information for local government officials, particularly those representing townships.
Formerly (until 1999): Illinois County and Township Official (0019-1949)
Published by: Township Officials of Illinois, 408 S Fifth St, Springfield, IL 62701-1804. TEL 217-744-2212, FAX 217-744-7419. Ed. Bryan E Smith. Adv. contact Erin Valentine. page USD 550. Circ: 13,000 (paid).

352.14 CHE
U N SPECIAL. (United Nations) Text in English. m. **Document type:** *Bulletin.*
Published by: Publicite Generale, 34 rue de l Athenee, Postfach 145, Geneva 12, 1211, Switzerland. TEL 41-22-3473388, FAX 41-22-3462047. Circ: 10,000.

U.S. BUREAU OF THE CENSUS. GOVERNMENTS DIVISION. LOCAL GOVERNMENT EMPLOYMENT AND PAYROLL DATA. *see* BUSINESS AND ECONOMICS—Abstracting, Bibliographies, Statistics

352.14 USA ISSN 1049-2119
JS39
U S MAYOR. Text in English. 1934. s-m. USD 35 (effective 2010). adv. illus. back issues avail. **Document type:** *Newspaper.*
Former titles (until 1989): Mayor; (until 1971): United States Municipal News (0041-7955)
Related titles: Online - full text ed.: free (effective 2010).
Indexed: P06.
Published by: United States Conference of Mayors, 1620 Eye St, N W, Washington, DC 20006. TEL 202-861-6720, FAX 202-293-2352, info@usmayors.org. Ed. Tom Cochran. Adv. contact Doug Baj TEL 703-868-5206. B&W page USD 3,852, color page USD 5,008; 10 x 12. Circ: 9,000.

352 HUN ISSN 1416-1346
DB901
UJ DUNATAJ. Text in Hungarian. 1978. q.
Formerly (until 1996): Dunataj (0139-3324)
Indexed: RILM.
Published by: Tolna Megyei Onkormanyzati Hivatal, Szent Istvan ter 11-13, Szekszard, Hungary.

352.14 GBR ISSN 2046-6420
UKAUTHORITY REPORT. Text in English. 1993. bi-w. GBP 49 for public sector organisations; GBP 199 for commercial organisations (effective 2011). back issues avail. **Document type:** *Newsletter, Trade.* **Description:** Provides news, informed analysis, contracts won, new products and supplier news.
Former titles (until 2011): Tomorrow's Town Hall (2043-9733); (until 2009): Town Hall (1365-7186)
Related titles: Online - full text ed.
—CCC.
Published by: Informed Publications Ltd., PO Box 2087, Shoreham-by-Sea, West Sussex BN43 5RH, United Kingdom. TEL 44-1273-273941. Ed. Tim Hampson.

352.2316 USA
UNITED STATES CONFERENCE OF MAYORS. ANNUAL MEETING; official policy resolutions. Text in English. a. USD 10.
Published by: United States Conference of Mayors, 1620 Eye St, N W, Washington, DC 20006. TEL 202-293-7330.

352.2316 USA
UNITED STATES CONFERENCE OF MAYORS. PROJECTS AND SERVICES. Text in English. irreg. free to qualified personnel.
Description: Offers a variety of services, news and information covering a wide range of issues.
Published by: United States Conference of Mayors, 1620 Eye St, N W, Washington, DC 20006. TEL 202-293-7330.

352.14 USA
UNIVERSITY OF ILLINOIS. INSTITUTE OF GOVERNMENT AND PUBLIC AFFAIRS. WORKING PAPERS. Text in English. 1987. irreg. back issues avail. **Document type:** *Monographic series, Academic/Scholarly.*
Published by: University of Illinois at Urbana-Champaign, Institute of Government and Public Affairs, 1007 W Nevada St, MC-037, Urbana, IL 61801. TEL 217-333-3340, 866-794-3340, FAX 217-244-4817, http://www.igpa.uiuc.edu.

352.14 PHL
UNIVERSITY OF THE PHILIPPINES. COLLEGE OF PUBLIC ADMINISTRATION. LOCAL GOVERNMENT STUDIES. Text in English. 1962. irreg.
Published by: University of the Philippines, College of Public Administration, Diliman, P.O. Box 198, Quezon City, Philippines. TEL 95-13-65, TELEX CPAUP.

352.14 SVN
URADNI VESTNIK. Text in Slovenian. 1964. irreg. free.
Formerly: Uradni Vestnik Obcin Ormoz in Ptuj (0042-0778)
Published by: Radio-Tednik, Raiceva 6, Ptuj, Slovenia. FAX 386-062-771-223, nabiralnik@radio-tednik.si. Ed. Joze Smigoc. Circ: 11,000.

352.14 USA ISSN 0884-6421
KFU38
UTAH STATE DIGEST. Text in English. 1985. s-m. USD 48 (effective 2000). 1 cols./p.; **Document type:** *Bulletin, Government.*
Description: Contains the summary of the information found in the Utah State Bulletin.
Related titles: Online - full text ed.
Published by: Division of Administrative Rules, PO Box 141007, Salt Lake City, UT 84114-1007. TEL 801-538-3218, FAX 801-538-1773, asitmain.nlancast@email.state.ut.us. Ed. Nancy Lancaster. Circ: 150.

352 BEL ISSN 1378-9872
V F G - FORUM. (Vlaamse Federatie van Gemeentesecretarissen) Text in Dutch. 1998. 3/yr. EUR 75 (effective 2008). **Document type:** *Journal, Trade.*
Formerly (until 2002): Tijdschrift voor de Vlaamse Gemeentesecretaris (1373-9735)
Published by: Die Keure NV, Kleine Pathoekeweg 3, Bruges, 8000, Belgium. TEL 32-50-471272, FAX 32-50-335154, juridische.uitgaven@diekeure.be, http://www.diekeure.be.

352.14 NLD ISSN 1380-5398
V G S NIEUWSBRIEF. Text in Dutch. 1992. bi-m. EUR 71 (effective 2009). adv. **Document type:** *Newsletter, Trade.*
Published by: (Vereniging van Gemeentesecretarissen), Sdu Uitgevers bv, Postbus 20025, The Hague, 2500 EA, Netherlands. TEL 31-70-3789911, FAX 31-70-3854321, sdu@sdu.nl, http://www.sdu.nl/ . Ed. Ingrid de Bock. Pub. Dineke Sonderen.

352 USA
V L C T NEWS. (Vermont League of Cities & Townsm) Text in English. 2000. m. free to members; USD 60 to non-members (effective 2009). **Document type:** *Newsletter, Government.*
Related titles: Online - full text ed.: 2000.
Published by: Vermont League of Cities & Towns, 89 Main St, Ste 4, Montpelier, VT 05602-2948. info@vlct.org. Ed. Allyson Barrieau.

352.14 NLD ISSN 1566-1636
TD4
V N G-MAGAZINE. (Vereniging van Nederlandse Gemeenten) Text in Dutch. 1947. 24/yr. EUR 96; EUR 35 to students; EUR 8.25 newsstand/cover (effective 2008). adv. illus. **Document type:** *Trade.*
Former titles (until 1999): N G Magazine (0924-4816); (until 1990): Nederlandse Gemeente (0166-8927)
Indexed: A22, ELLIS, KES.
—IE, Infotrieve.
Published by: V N G Uitgeverij (Subsidiary of: Sdu Uitgevers bv), PO Box 30435, The Hague, 2500 GK, Netherlands. TEL 31-70-3738393, FAX 31-70-3469201, http://www.vnguitgeverij.nl. Eds. Inge Crul, Simon Kooistra. Pub. Dineke Sonderen. adv.: B&W page EUR 2,525, color page EUR 3,760; trim 210 x 297. Circ: 26,056.

352.14 CHE
V P O D ZEITUNG. Text in German. 21/yr. **Document type:** *Newspaper, Government.*
Formerly: V P O D Zeitung der Oeffentliche Dienst
Published by: Verband des Personals Oeffentlicher Dienste, Sonnenbergstr 83, Zuerich, 8030, Switzerland. TEL 41-1-2665252, FAX 41-1-2665253. Ed. Beatrice Kaestli Meier. Circ: 25,000.

352.14 DEU
VERBANDSGEMEINDE EDENKOBEN. AMTSBLATT. Text in German. 1980. w. free. adv. back issues avail.
Published by: Verbandsgemeinde Edenkoben, c/o Manfred Horn, Am Bachweg 3, Edenkoben, 67480, Germany. TEL 06323-80826, FAX 06323-80899. Circ: 8,000.

352.14 DEU ISSN 1617-1063
VERGABERECHT; Zeitschrift fuer oeffentliche und private Beschaffung. Text in German. 1991. bi-m. EUR 105; EUR 24 newsstand/cover (effective 2011). adv. **Document type:** *Magazine, Trade.*
Former titles: E C Public Contract Law (0948-2709); (until 1992): Europaeisches Vergaberecht (0939-4508)
Published by: Werner-Verlag GmbH (Subsidiary of: Wolters Kluwer Deutschland GmbH), Heddesdorfer Str 31, Neuwied, 56564, Germany. TEL 49-2631-8012222, FAX 49-2631-8012223, info@wolters-kluwer.de, http://www.werner-verlag.de. Adv. contact Marcus Kipp. Circ: 2,300 (paid).

352.14 DEU ISSN 0720-2407
VERWALTUNGSBLAETTER FUER BADEN-WUERTTEMBERG; Zeitschrift fuer oeffentliches Recht und oeffentliche Verwaltung. Text in German. 1980. m. EUR 239.40; EUR 183 to students (effective 2010). adv. **Document type:** *Journal, Trade.*
Indexed: DIP, IBR, IBZ.
Published by: Richard Boorberg Verlag GmbH und Co. KG, Scharrstr 2, Stuttgart, 70563, Germany. TEL 49-711-73850, FAX 49-711-7385100, mail@boorberg.de.

352 AUS
VICTORIA. AUDITOR-GENERAL. RESULTS OF FINANCIAL STATEMENT AND OTHER AUDITS (YEAR). Text in English. 1990. a. back issues avail. **Document type:** *Government.* **Description:** Contain the results of a number of special reviews and other investigations, and the results of financial statement audits for public sector agencies.
Supersedes in part (in 2005): Report on Public Sector Agencies (1446-2559); Which was formerly (until 2001): Victoria. Auditor-General. Report on Ministerial Portfolios (1033-2960)
Related titles: Online - full text ed.: free (effective 2009).
Published by: Victorian Auditor-General's Office, Level 24, 35 Collins St, Melbourne, VIC 3000, Australia. TEL 61-3-86017000, FAX 61-3-86017010, comments@audit.vic.gov.au, http://www.audit.vic.gov.au.

352 AUS
VICTORIA. AUDITOR GENERAL. RESULTS OF FINANCIAL STATEMENT AUDITS FOR AGENCIES WITH OTHER THAN (YEAR) BALANCE DATES, AND OTHER AUDITS. Text in English. 1990. a., latest 2008. AUD 25 per issue (effective 2009). back issues avail. **Document type:** *Government.*
Supersedes in part (in 2005): Report on Public Sector Agencies (1446-2559); Which was formerly (until 2001): Victoria. Auditor-General. Report on Ministerial Portfolios (1033-2960)
Related titles: Online - full text ed.: free (effective 2009).
Published by: Victorian Auditor-General's Office, Level 24, 35 Collins St, Melbourne, VIC 3000, Australia. TEL 61-3-86017000, FAX 61-3-86017010, comments@audit.vic.gov.au.

352 PRT ISSN 1647-1636
VILA DO CONDE EM REDE. Text in Portuguese. 2008. s-a. **Document type:** *Magazine, Consumer.*
Published by: Camara Municipal de Vila do Conde, Rua da Igreja, Vial do Conde, 4480754, Portugal. TEL 351-252-248400, FAX 351-252-641853.

352.14 USA ISSN 0732-9156
JS39
VIRGINIA REVIEW. Text in English. 1924. bi-m. USD 18 (effective 2011). adv. bk.rev. illus. 56 p./no. 3 cols./p.; reprints avail. **Document type:** *Magazine, Trade.* **Description:** For Virginia state and local government officials concerning management and practice issues of the day.
Formerly (until 1981): Virginia Municipal Review (0042-6660)
Related titles: Online - full text ed.
Indexed: P06.
Published by: JS Publications, Inc., 7307 Belmont Stakes Dr, Midlothian, VA 23112. Ed. James M Smith. Circ: 5,000 (paid and controlled).

352.14 USA ISSN 0042-6784
JS39
VIRGINIA TOWN & CITY. Text in English. 1966. m. free to members (effective 2010). bk.rev. charts; illus. **Document type:** *Magazine, Trade.* **Description:** Features include commentary and a marketplace, product and service guide, environmental counsel, a professional directory, and legal guidelines.
Published by: Virginia Municipal League, PO Box 12164, Richmond, VA 23241. TEL 804-649-8471, FAX 804-343-3758, e-mail@vml.org, http://www.vml.org/.

352 PRT ISSN 1647-6867
▼ **VIVA CAMARA DE LOBOS.** Text in Portuguese. 2010. q. **Document type:** *Magazine, Consumer.*
Published by: Camara Municipal de Camara de Lobos, Praca da Autonomia, Camara de Lobos, Madeira 9304-001, Portugal. http://www.cm-camaradelobos.pt.

352 USA
W A M NEWS. (Wyoming Association of Municipalities) Text in English. 19??. m. free to members. **Document type:** *Newsletter, Government.* **Description:** Serves as an exchange of ideas and information for officials of municipalities.
Former titles (until 1979): W A M News Bulletin; (until 1961): News Bulletin
Related titles: Online - full text ed.
Published by: Wyoming Association of Municipalities, 315 W 27th St, Cheyenne, WY 82001. Ed. Ginger Newman. Circ: 2,000.

352 NZL ISSN 1171-039X
WAIMAKARIRI DISTRICT COUNCIL. ANNUAL PLAN AND BUDGET. Text in English. 1991. a.
Related titles: Online - full text ed.: ISSN 1177-9748.
Published by: Waimakariri District Council, 215 High St, Private Bag 1005, Rangiora, New Zealand. TEL 64-3-3136136, FAX 64-3-3134432, office@wmk.govt.nz, http://www.wmk.govt.nz.

352.093 NZL
WAIMAKARIRI DISTRICT COUNCIL. LONG TERM COUNCIL COMMUNITY PLAN. Text in English. 1991. a.
Formerly: Waimakariri District Council. Draft Annual Plan and Budget (1170-5663)
Published by: Waimakariri District Council, 215 High St, Private Bag 1005, Rangiora, New Zealand. TEL 64-3-3136136, FAX 64-3-3134432, office@wmk.govt.nz, http://www.wmk.govt.nz.

352.14 USA
K14
WASHINGTON REPORT (WASHINGTON, 1977). Text in English. 1977. 10/yr. free. adv. illus. back issues avail.; reprints avail. **Document type:** *Newsletter.* **Description:** Provides timely information to town and township officials on the legislative, regulatory, funding, and policy decisions in Washington that could affect their communities.
Former titles: N A T A T's Reporter (Print) (0735-9691); N A T A T's National Community Reporter
Media: Online - full content.
Published by: National Association of Towns and Townships, 1130 Connecticut Ave, NW, Ste 300, Washington, DC 20036. TEL 202-454-3954, FAX 202-331-1598, info@natat.org. Ed. Jennifer J Imo. adv.: B&W page USD 1,035, color page USD 1,210. Circ: 15,000.

WELSH HOUSING QUARTERLY. *see* HOUSING AND URBAN PLANNING

WELSH LOCAL GOVERNMENT FINANCIAL STATISTICS. *see* PUBLIC ADMINISTRATION—Abstracting, Bibliographies, Statistics

352.14 USA ISSN 0279-5337
TD1
WESTERN CITY. Text in English. 1924. m. USD 39 domestic; USD 52 foreign; USD 26.50 to students (effective 2010). adv. bk.rev. illus. index. 48 p./no. 3 cols./p.; back issues avail.; reprints avail. **Document type:** *Magazine, Trade.* **Description:** Provides lively, interdisciplinary analyses of issues affecting local governance in a form and format suited for busy people.
Former titles (until 1976): Western City Magazine (0043-356X); (until 1960): Western City; (until 1930): Hydraulic Engineering (0097-6598); (until 1927): Modern Irrigation (0361-1876)
Related titles: Online - full text ed.
Indexed: CalPI, P06, UAA.
—Ingenta, Linda Hall.
Published by: League of California Cities, 1400 K St, 4th Floor, Sacramento, CA 95814. TEL 916-658-8200, FAX 916-658-8240, http://www.cacities.org. Ed. Jude Hudson TEL 916-658-8234. Adv. contact Pam Maxwell-Blodgett. B&W page USD 2,575, color page USD 3,875; trim 8.5 x 11. Circ: 9,466.

348.12 USA ISSN 0278-8004
KFW25
WEST'S WASHINGTON LEGISLATIVE SERVICE. Text in English. 19??. irreg. **Document type:** *Journal, Trade.*
Formerly (until 1980): Washington Legislative Service (0272-4227)
—CCC.
Published by: Thomson West (Subsidiary of: Thomson Reuters Corp.), 610 Opperman Dr, Eagan, MN 55123. TEL 651-687-8000, 800-344-5008, FAX 651-687-6674, west.support@thomson.com, http://west.thomson.com.

352.14 USA
WHAT'S HAPPENING FOR COMMUNITY LEADERS. Text in English. 1976. m. free (effective 2011). Supplement avail. **Document type:** *Newsletter, Government.* **Description:** Offers regional data, development and public interest news for Douglas, Sarpy and Washington counties in Nebraska, as well as Pottawattamie counties in Iowa.
Related titles: Online - full text ed.
Published by: Omaha - Council Bluffs Metropolitan Area Planning Agency, 2222 Cuming St, Omaha, NE 68102. TEL 402-444-6866, FAX 402-342-0949, mapa@mapacog.org.

352.14 POL ISSN 1234-1746
WIADOMOSCI RATUSZOWE; informator. Text in Polish. 1991. w. free. adv. **Document type:** *Newspaper.* **Description:** Presents official statements of the Cieszyn Municipal Government.
Published by: Urzad Miejski w Cieszynie, Rynek 1, Cieszyn, 43400, Poland. TEL 48-33-520701, FAX 48-33-511643. Ed. Jerzy Ruksza. Circ: 3,000 (controlled).

352 AUT
WIEN AKTUELL. Text in German. 18/yr. adv. **Document type:** *Magazine, Trade.*
Published by: N.J. Schmid Verlag, Leberstr 122, Vienna, 1110, Austria. TEL 43-1-74032735, FAX 43-1-74032750, g.milletich@schmid-verlag.at, http://www.schmid-verlag.at. Ed. Peter Enderle. Adv. contact Monika Steiner. color page EUR 3,100; trim 180 x 255. Circ: 150,000 (controlled).

352.14 AUT
WIENER NEUSTADT. AMTSBLATT DER STATUTARSTADT. Text in German. 1921. m. adv. **Document type:** *Government.* **Description:** Local government publication covering news and information, politics, education, commerce and industry, culture and sport. Includes reports and announcements of events and exhibitions.
Formerly: Wiener Neustadt. Amtsblatt der Stadt (0003-2255)
Published by: Magistrat, Rathaus, Wiener Neustadt, N 2700, Austria. TEL 43-2622-23531391. Ed. Franz Pinczolits. Circ: 24,180.

352.14 CHE
WIR STAEDTISCHEN. Text in German. 10/yr.
Address: Stauffacherstr 60, Zuerich, 8026, Switzerland. TEL 01-2412674. Circ: 7,500.

352.14 USA ISSN 0749-6818
WISCONSIN COUNTIES. Text in English. 1938. m. USD 24 (effective 2000). adv. **Document type:** *Government.*
Published by: Wisconsin Counties Association, 22 E. Mifflin St., Ste. 900, Madison, WI 53703-4247. TEL 608-224-5330, 800-922-1993, FAX 608-224-5325. Ed. Mark Rogacki. R&P Kelly Dempze. Adv. contact David Harried. B&W page USD 415. Circ: 3,450.

352.14 POL ISSN 0867-0935
JS6131.A1
WSPOLNOTA. Text in Polish. 1990. w. adv. **Document type:** *Newspaper.*
Related titles: Microfilm ed.: (from PQC).
Published by: Municipium S.A., Ul Marszalkowska 82, Warsaw, 00517, Poland. TEL 48-22-6287768, FAX 48-22-292633. Ed. Jozef Orzel. Circ: 20,000. **Co-publisher:** Bank Inicjatyw Gospodarczych S.A.

352.14 USA
YOUR REGION. Text in English. 1967. m. free. bk.rev. bibl. **Description:** Covers activities of the Council in the 16 county Dallas-Forth Worth region.
Formerly: Your Region in Action (0049-8432)
Published by: North Central Texas Council of Governments, P O Drawer COG, Arlington, TX 76005-5888. TEL 817-640-3300, FAX 817-640-7806. Ed. Edwina J Shires. Circ: 5,000.

352.14 CHE
Z V INFORMATION. (Zentralverband) Text in German. 1988. 10/yr. adv. **Document type:** *Journal, Trade.*
Published by: Zentralverband Staats- und Gemeindepersonal Schweiz, Langhaus 3, Postfach 1863, Baden, 5401, Switzerland. TEL 41-56-2040290, FAX 41-56-2040291, michael.merker@binderlegal.ch, http://www.zentral.ch. adv.: page CHF 1,800. Circ: 27,500 (controlled).

352.14 CHE
ZEITSCHRIFT FUER ZIVILSTANDSWESEN. Text in French, German, Italian. 11/yr.
Published by: Departem des Innern, Sektion Buergerrecht und Personenstand, Aarau, 5001, Switzerland. TEL 064-211561. Ed. W Heussler. Circ: 3,000.

352.14 DEU
ZUKUNFTSLAND HESSEN. Text in German. 1988. m. **Document type:** *Government.* **Description:** Covers living and working in Hesse; seeing and experiencing a land of culture and a past with a future.
Formerly (until 1997): Hessen - Report
Published by: Hessische Landesregierung, Bierstadter Str 2, Wiesbaden, 65189, Germany. TEL 49-611-323712, Ed. Klaus Peter Schmidt Degueller. Circ: 28,000.

352 FRA ISSN 2106-3168
360. Text in French. 2000. q. **Document type:** *Newsletter, Consumer.*
Formerly (until 2009): Notre Territoire (1775-2272)
Published by: La Communaute de Communes du Pays de Saint-Galmier, 1 Passage du Cloitre, Saint-Galmier, 42330, France. TEL 33-4-77949352, FAX 33-4-77949447, contact@ccpsg.fr, http://www.ccpsg.fr/index.php.

352.14 FRA ISSN 0245-3185
36000 COMMUNES. Text in French. 1971. 10/yr. **Description:** Providing a forum for the mayors of all the rural communities, the administrations and the ministries.
Related titles: Online - full text ed.: ISSN 2105-2980. 200?.
Indexed: FR.
Published by: Association des Maires Ruraux de France, 52 Av. Marechal Foch, Lyon, 69006, France. amrf@amrf.asso.fr. Ed. Helene Mira. Circ: 9,000.

PUBLIC FINANCE, TAXATION

see BUSINESS AND ECONOMICS—Public Finance, Taxation

PUBLIC HEALTH AND SAFETY

see also BIRTH CONTROL ; DRUG ABUSE AND ALCOHOLISM ; ENVIRONMENTAL STUDIES ; FIRE PREVENTION ; FUNERALS ; HEALTH FACILITIES AND ADMINISTRATION ; MEDICAL SCIENCES ; OCCUPATIONAL HEALTH AND SAFETY

362.1 PRT ISSN 1646-8201
A C E S S. DIRECTIVAS TECNICAS. (Administracao Central do Sistemas de Saude) Text in Portuguese. 2006. irreg. **Document type:** *Handbook/Manual/Guide, Trade.*
Published by: Administracao Central do Sistemas de Saude, Av Joao Crisostomo 11, Lisbon, 1000-177, Portugal. TEL 351-21-7925800, FAX 351-21-7925848, geral@acss.min-saude.pt, http://www.acss.min-saude.pt.

362.1 PRT ISSN 1646-8228
A C E S S. GUIAS. (Administracao Central do Sistemas de Saude) Text in Portuguese. 2006. irreg. **Document type:** *Handbook/Manual/Guide, Trade.*
Published by: Administracao Central do Sistemas de Saude, Av Joao Crisostomo 11, Lisbon, 1000-177, Portugal. TEL 351-21-7925800, FAX 351-21-7925848, geral@acss.min-saude.pt, http://www.acss.min-saude.pt.

A C P M HEADLINES (ONLINE). *see* MEDICAL SCIENCES

P

614 FRA ISSN 1771-7450
A D S P. (Actualite et Dossier en Sante Publique) Text in French. 1992. q. EUR 42.50 domestic; EUR 45.50 in Europe; EUR 46 DOM-TOM; EUR 47.30 elsewhere (effective 2009). **Document type:** *Journal, Government.*
Formerly (until 1998): Actualite et Dossier en Sante Publique (1243-275X)
Related titles: Online - full text ed.
Indexed: FR.
Published by: Haut Conseil de la Sante Publique, 14 Av. Duquesne, Paris, 07 75350 SP, France. TEL 33-1-40567980, FAX 33-1-40567949, hcsp-secr-general@sante.gouv.fr.

A F T E JOURNAL. *see* LAW—Criminal Law

A H C A NOTES. *see* SOCIAL SERVICES AND WELFARE

A H P JOURNAL. *see* SOCIAL SERVICES AND WELFARE

362.1 USA ISSN 1559-4068
A H R Q PUBLICATIONS CATALOG. (Agency for Healthcare Research and Quality) Text in English. 2001. s-a. **Document type:** *Catalog, Government.*
Media: Online - full text.
Published by: U.S. Department of Health and Human Services, Agency for Healthcare Research and Quality (A H R Q), 540 Gaither Rd, Ste 2000, Rockville, MD 20850. TEL 301-427-1104, info@ahrq.gov.

362.1 610 USA ISSN 1556-4193
A H R Q WEB M & M. (Agency for Healthcare Research and Quality Morbidity & Mortality) Text in English. 2003 (Feb.). m. free (effective 2011). **Document type:** *Journal, Government.* **Description:** Forum on patient safety and health care quality. This site features expert analysis of medical errors reported anonymously by the readers, interactive learning modules on patient safety, and forums for online discussion.
Media: Online - full text.
Published by: U.S. Department of Health and Human Services, Agency for Healthcare Research and Quality (A H R Q), 540 Gaither Rd, Ste 2000, Rockville, MD 20850. TEL 301-427-1104, info@ahrq.gov, http://www.ahrq.gov.

362.1 USA ISSN 1948-7479
A H S PULSE; the applied health science newsletter. (Applied Health Science) Text in English. 2000. s-a. free (effective 2009). back issues avail. **Document type:** *Newsletter, Trade.*
Related titles: Online - full text ed.
Published by: Indiana University, Department of Applied Health Science, 1025 E 7th St, HPER 116, Bloomington, IN 47405. TEL 812-855-3627, http://www.indiana.edu/~aphealth/index.shtml. Ed. Harriet Castrataro.

614.8 360 USA ISSN 0275-8407
CODEN: PCSREK
A M S STUDIES IN MODERN SOCIETY; political and social issues. (Abrahams Magazine Service) Text in English. 1982. irreg., latest vol.25, 2008. price varies. back issues avail.; reprints avail. **Document type:** *Monographic series, Academic/Scholarly.* **Description:** Monographs, reference works and bibliographies on contemporary social issues.
Indexed: E-psyche.
Published by: A M S Press, Inc., Brooklyn Navy Yard, 63 Flushing Ave, Bldg 292, Unit #221, Brooklyn, NY 11205. FAX 718-875-3800, queries@amspressinc.com.

362.1 CAN ISSN 1912-4864
A NOTRE SANTE. Text in French. 2005. irreg. **Document type:** *Monographic series, Consumer.*
Published by: Agence de la Sante et des Services Sociaux des Laurentide, 1000 Rue Labelle, Bur. 210, Saint-Jerome, PQ J7Z 5N6, Canada. TEL 450-436-8622, FAX 450-436-8622, information.rr15@ssss.gouv.qc.ca, http://www.rrsss15.gouv.qc.ca/index.htm.

A P C R I NEWSLETTER. *see* MEDICAL SCIENCES

A Q I S BULLETIN. *see* AGRICULTURE

A S D W A UPDATE. *see* WATER RESOURCES

362.1 USA ISSN 1930-6903
THE A S P E HIGHLIGHTER. (Assistant Secretary for Planning and Evaluation) Text in English. 2005. irreg. **Document type:** *Newsletter, Trade.* **Description:** About recently completed studies sponsored by ASPE.
Related titles: Online - full text ed.: ISSN 1930-6911.
Published by: U.S. Department of Health and Human Services, Assistant Secretary for Planning and Evaluation (A S P E), 200 Independence Ave SW, Washington, DC 20201. TEL 202-619-0257, FAX 877-696-6775, http://aspe.hhs.gov/index.shtml.

A W W A STREAMLINES; water news, advancement and practice. *see* WATER RESOURCES

614.8 AUS ISSN 1037-3403
ABORIGINAL AND ISLANDER HEALTH WORKER JOURNAL; a national resource journal for Aboriginal and Islander community education workers. Text in English. 1977. bi-m. AUD 38.50 domestic to individuals; AUD 44 domestic to institutions; AUD 22 domestic to students; AUD 49.50 foreign (effective 2008). adv. back issues avail. **Document type:** *Journal, Academic/Scholarly.* **Description:** Covers primary healthcare, community profiles, health promotion, best practice models and workforce issues facing aboriginal and Torres Strait Islanders.
Former titles (until 1991): Aboriginal and Islander Health Worker (1036-4102); (until 1989): Aboriginal Health Worker (0155-0357)
Indexed: A01, CA, P30, T02.
—Ingenta.
Published by: (Australia. Human Services and Health Department), Aboriginal and Islander Health Worker Journal, PO Box 502, Matraville, NSW 2036, Australia. TEL 61-2-93112593, FAX 61-2-93112814. Ed. Kathy Malera Bandjalan. R&P Donnaleen Campbell. Adv. contact Donna Daly. B&W page USD 500, color page USD 600; 210 x 302. Circ: 11,000.

614 658.3 USA ISSN 1538-0084
ABSOLUTE ADVANTAGE. Text in English. 2001. 10/yr. USD 89 (effective 2006). **Document type:** *Magazine, Trade.*
Published by: Wellness Councils of America, 9802 Nicholas St, Ste 315, Omaha, NE 68114-2106. TEL 402-827-3590, FAX 402-827-3594, wellworkplace@welcoa.org, http://www.welcoa.org.

ACADEMY OF HOSPITAL ADMINISTRATION. JOURNAL. *see* BUSINESS AND ECONOMICS—Management

362.1 ITA ISSN 0365-4109
R131.A1
ACCADEMIA DI STORIA DELL'ARTE SANITARIA. ATTI E MEMORIE. Text in Italian. 1921. bi-m. **Document type:** *Journal, Academic/Scholarly.*
Formerly (until 1934): Istituto Storico Italiano dell'Arte Sanitaria. Bollettino (0366-2292)
Indexed: P30.
Published by: Accademia di Storia dell'Arte Sanitaria, Lungotevere di Sassia 3, Rome, 00193, Italy. TEL 39-06-68352353, FAX 39-06-6833485.

614.8 GBR ISSN 0001-4575
HV675.A1 CODEN: AAPVB5
➤ **ACCIDENT ANALYSIS & PREVENTION.** Text in English. 1969. bi-m. EUR 1,880 in Europe to institutions; JPY 249,700 in Japan to institutions; USD 2,104 elsewhere to institutions (effective 2012). adv. bk.rev. charts; illus. Index. back issues avail.; reprints avail. **Document type:** *Journal, Academic/Scholarly.* **Description:** Provides wide coverage of the general areas relating to accidental injury and damage, including the pre-injury and immediate post-injury phases.
Related titles: Microform ed.: (from PQC); Online - full text ed.: ISSN 1879-2057 (from IngentaConnect, ScienceDirect).
Indexed: A01, A03, A08, A20, A22, A26, A28, AC&P, APA, ASCA, ASG, AddicA, B01, B06, B07, B09, B21, B25, BIOSIS Prev, BrCerAb, C&ISA, CA, CA/WCA, CIA, CIS, CISA, CPEI, CerAb, CivEngAb, CorrAb, CurCont, DIP, E&CAJ, E-psyche, E04, E05, E11, EEA, EMA, EMBASE, ESPM, EngInd, EnvEAb, ErgAb, ExcerpMed, FamI, H&SSA, H15, HRIS, I05, IAOP, IBR, IBZ, ICEA, INI, ISMEC, IndMed, M&TEA, M09, MBF, MEDLINE, METADEX, MycolAb, P03, P30, PEI, PsycInfo, PsycholAb, RASB, RefZh, RiskAb, S02, S03, SCOPUS, SSCI, SoftAbEng, SolStAb, T02, T04, W07, WAA.
—BLDSC (0573.130000), GNLM, IE, Infotrieve, Ingenta, INIST, Linda Hall. **CCC.**
Published by: (Association for the Advancement of Automotive Medicine USA), Elsevier Ltd (Subsidiary of: Elsevier Science & Technology), The Blvd, Langford Ln, Kidlington, Oxford, OX5 1GB, United Kingdom. TEL 44-1865-843434, FAX 44-1865-843970. Eds. K Kim, R Elvik. **Subscr. to:** Elsevier BV, Radarweg 29, PO Box 211, Amsterdam 1000 AE, Netherlands. JournalsCustomerServiceEMEA@elsevier.com, http://www.elsevier.nl.

362.1 NZL ISSN 1176-659X
ACROSS THE BOARD. Text in English. m. **Document type:** *Newsletter.*
Formerly (until 2004): Canterbury Healthline (1176-0427)
Related titles: Online - full text ed.: ISSN 1177-8660.
Published by: Canterbury District Health Board, Level 2, H Block, The Princess Margaret Hospital, Cashmere Rd, PO Box 1600, Christchurch, New Zealand. TEL 64-3-3644106, FAX 64-3-3644101.

ACTIVE TRAVEL CYMRU NEWS. *see* SPORTS AND GAMES—Bicycles And Motorcycles

ADMINISTRATION AND POLICY IN MENTAL HEALTH AND MENTAL HEALTH SERVICES RESEARCH. *see* MEDICAL SCIENCES

ADVANCED RESCUE TECHNOLOGY. *see* MEDICAL SCIENCES—Orthopedics And Traumatology

362.1 USA
ADVANCES (PRINCETON). Text in English. 1988. q. free. **Document type:** *Newsletter.* **Description:** Reports on the key work of the Foundation through articles and interviews, lists of recent grants, reports on closed grants, summaries of RWJF-funded research and other news from the Foundation.
Related titles: Online - full content ed.
Published by: Robert Wood Johnson Foundation, College Rd East and Rt 1, PO Box 2316, Princeton, NJ 08543-2316. TEL 888-631-9989. Ed. Paul Tarini.

▼ **ADVANCES IN EPIDEMIOLOGY.** *see* MEDICAL SCIENCES

ADVANCES IN THANATOLOGY. *see* PSYCHOLOGY

362.1 ESP ISSN 1578-3103
AGATHOS. Text in Spanish. 2001. q. EUR 31.93 (effective 2009). back issues avail. **Document type:** *Journal, Trade.*
Published by: Instituto de Servicios Sanitarios y Sociales, Diagonal 400, 5o., Barcelona, 08037, Spain. TEL 34-93-4591108, FAX 34-93-4593379. Ed. Dolores Colom.

AGENCE DE DEVELOPPEMENT DE RESEAUX LOCAUX DE SERVICES DE SANTE ET DE SERVICES SOCIAUX DE LA CAPITALE NATIONALE. RAPPORT ANNUEL DE GESTION. *see* SOCIAL SERVICES AND WELFARE

362.1 CAN ISSN 1719-8577
AGENCE DE DEVELOPPEMENT DE RESEAUX LOCAUX DE SERVICES DE SANTE ET DE SERVICES SOCIAUX DE LA COTE-NORD. RAPPORT ANNUEL. Text in French. 1973. a. **Document type:** *Government.*
Former titles (until 2004): Regie Regionale de la Sante et des Services Sociaux de la Cote-Nord. Rapport Annuel (1208-7661); (until 1993): C R S S S de la Cote-Nord. Rapport Annuel (0227-9134)
Published by: L' Agence de Developpement de Reseaux Locaux de Services de Sante et de Services Sociaux de la Cote-Nord, 691, rue Jalbert, Baie-Comeau, PQ G5C 2A1, Canada. TEL 418-589-9845, FAX 418-589-8574, Sandra_Morin@ssss.gouv.qc.ca, http://www.rrsss09.gouv.qc.ca/index.php.

362.1 CAN ISSN 1718-0120
AGENCE DE DEVELOPPEMENT DE RESEAUX LOCAUX DE SERVICES DE SANTE ET DE SERVICES SOCIAUX DE L'OUTAOUAIS. RAPPORT ANNUEL. Text in French. 1978. a. **Document type:** *Government.*
Former titles (until 2005): Agence de Developpement de Reseaux Locaux de Services de Sante et de Services Sociaux de l'Outaouais. Rapport Annuel de Gestion (1712-4921); (until 2004): Regie Regionale de la Sante et des Services Sociaux de l'Outaouais. Rapport Annuel (1195-2547); (until 1994): Conseil Regional de la Sante et des Services Sociaux de l'Outaouais. Rapport Annuel (0837-5496); (until 1986): Conseil de la Sante et des Services Sociaux de l'Outaouais. Rapport Annuel (0710-2569); (until 1985): Tournesol (0705-2898)
Published by: Agence de Developpement de Reseaux Locaux de Services de Sante et de Services Sociaux de l'Outaouais, 104, rue Lois, Gatineau, PQ J8Y 3R7, Canada. TEL 819-770-7747, FAX 819-771-8632, http://www.santeoutaouais.qc.ca, http://www.rrsss07.gouv.qc.ca/rrsss/RRSSS/index_f.aspx.

362.1 FRA ISSN 1761-5216
AGENCE FRANCAISE DE SECURITE SANITAIRE DES ALIMENTS. BULLETIN OFFICIEL. Text in French. 2002. s-a. EUR 76.30 (effective 2007). **Document type:** *Bulletin, Government.*
Published by: (Agence Francaise de Securite Sanitaire des Aliments (A F S S A)), Documentation Francaise, 29-31 Quai Voltaire, Paris, Cedex 7 75344, France. TEL 33-1-40157000, FAX 33-1-40157230.

362.1 USA ISSN 1932-1651
AGING TRENDS. Text in English. 2001. irreg. back issues avail. **Document type:** *Monographic series, Government.*
Media: Online - full text.
Published by: U.S. Department of Health and Human Services, Centers for Disease Control and Prevention. National Center for Health Statistics, 3311 Toledo Rd, Hyattsville, MD 20782. TEL 800-232-4636, cdcinfo@cdc.gov, http://www.cdc.gov/nchs.

AHA!. *see* CHILDREN AND YOUTH—For

362.1 USA ISSN 1932-2704
AIDS ACTION POLICY BRIEF. Text in English. 2001. irreg. **Document type:** *Bulletin, Consumer.*
Media: Online - full text. **Related titles:** Print ed.: ISSN 1932-2291.
Published by: AIDS Action, 1730 M Street NW, Ste 611, Washington, DC 20036. TEL 202-530-8030, FAX 202-530-8031, http://www.aidsaction.org.

AIDS BULLETIN. *see* MEDICAL SCIENCES—Communicable Diseases

362.1 USA ISSN 0899-9546
RA644.A25 CODEN: AEPREO
➤ **AIDS EDUCATION AND PREVENTION**; an interdisciplinary journal. (Acquired Immune Deficiency Syndrome) Text in English. 1989. bi-m. USD 90 combined subscription domestic to individuals (print & online eds.); USD 125 combined subscription foreign to individuals (print & online eds.); USD 435 combined subscription domestic to institutions (print & online eds.); USD 480 combined subscription foreign to institutions (print & online eds.) (effective 2011). adv. 96 p./no.; back issues avail.; reprints avail. **Document type:** *Journal, Academic/Scholarly.* **Description:** Provides information on prevention of AIDS geared towards all professionals: epidemiologists, physicians, health educators, psychologists, social workers, counselors and legislators.
Related titles: Online - full text ed.: ISSN 1943-2755.
Indexed: A01, A02, A03, A08, A20, A22, A29, A36, AIDS Ab, AIDS&CR, ASCA, AddicA, B20, B21, BRD, C06, C07, C08, C11, CA, CABA, CINAHL, CJPI, CPE, ChPerI, Chicano, CurCont, D01, E-psyche, E01, E02, E03, E04, E05, E09, EMBASE, ERA, ERI, ERIC, ESPM, EdA, EdI, ExcerpMed, FR, FamI, GH, H&SSA, H01, H04, I10, IBSS, IndMed, L01, L02, MEDLINE, N02, P03, P04, P10, P18, P19, P20, P21, P22, P24, P25, P26, P30, P33, P34, P39, P43, P46, P48, P50, P53, P54, PAIS, PQC, PsycInfo, PsycholAb, R10, R12, Reac, RiskAb, S02, S03, S21, SCOPUS, SFSA, SOPODA, SSA, SSCI, SWR&A, SociolAb, T02, T05, THA, ToxAb, ViroIAbstr, W03, W07, W09, W11.
—BLDSC (0773.083360), GNLM, IE, Infotrieve, Ingenta, INIST. **CCC.**
Published by: Guilford Publications, Inc., 72 Spring St, 4th Fl, New York, NY 10012. TEL 800-365-7006, FAX 212-966-6708, info@guilford.com. Ed. Dr. Francisco S Sy TEL 301-496-7074. R&P Kathy Kuehl. Adv. contact Marian Robinson. Circ: 1,000 (paid).

➤ **AIDS POLICY AND LAW**; biweekly newsletter on legislation, regulation and litigation. (Acquired Immune Deficiency Syndrome) *see* LAW

➤ **AIDS WEEKLY.** *see* MEDICAL SCIENCES—Communicable Diseases

➤ **AIR QUALITY, ATMOSPHERE AND HEALTH.** *see* ENVIRONMENTAL STUDIES—Pollution

614 DEU ISSN 0930-1364
AKADEMIE FUER OEFFENTLICHES GESUNDHEITSWESEN. BERICHTE UND MATERIALIEN. Text in German. 1983. irreg., latest vol.21, 2007. price varies. **Document type:** *Monographic series, Academic/Scholarly.*
Published by: Akademie fuer Oeffentliches Gesundheitswesen, Kanzlerstr 4, Duesseldorf, 40472, Germany. TEL 49-211-3109610, FAX 49-211-3109634, info@akademie-oegw.de, http://www.akademie-oegw.de.

614 DEU ISSN 0172-2131
RA264
AKADEMIE FUER OEFFENTLICHES GESUNDHEITSWESEN. SCHRIFTENREIHE. Text in German. 196?. irreg., latest vol.24, 2006. price varies. **Document type:** *Monographic series, Academic/Scholarly.*
Formerly (until 1974): Akademie fuer Staatsmedizin des Landes Nordrhein-Westfalen, Duesseldorf. Veroeffentlichungen (0172-2247)
Published by: Akademie fuer Oeffentliches Gesundheitswesen, Kanzlerstr 4, Duesseldorf, 40472, Germany. TEL 49-211-3109610, FAX 49-211-3109634, info@akademie-oegw.de, http://www.akademie-oegw.de.

614 AUT
AKTIV UND GESUND. Text in German. 1958. s-a. free. adv. charts; illus.; mkt.; stat. **Document type:** *Magazine, Consumer.*
Formerly: Merkur Magazin fuer Volksgesundheit (0026-010X)
Published by: Merkur Wechselseitige Versicherungsanstalt, Neutorgasse 57, Graz, St 8010, Austria. TEL 43-316-80340, FAX 43-316-80342534, merkur@merkur.at, http://www.merkur.at. Circ: 200,000.

614 ESP ISSN 2171-5750
▼ **AL DETALLE, SALUD PUBLICA.** Text in Spanish. 2010. bi-m. **Document type:** *Bulletin, Consumer.*
Published by: Distrito Sanitario Aljarafe, Unidad de Proteccion de la Salud, Ave Principe de Espana, s-n, Sanlucar la Mayor, Sevilla, 41800, Spain. TEL 34-955-007602, FAX 34-955-007607.

613 USA ISSN 0145-6857
ALABAMA'S HEALTH. Text in English. 1967. m. free. bk.rev. **Document type:** *Newsletter, Government.* **Description:** Describes events and topics of interest to public health professionals.

Published by: Alabama Department of Public Health, 0201 Monroe St, Montgomery, AL 36130-3017. TEL 334-206-5510, FAX 334-206-5534. Ed., R&P Arrol Sheehan. Pub. Dr. Jim McVay. Circ: 1,200 (controlled).

614 LBN ISSN 1990-3944
'ALAM AL-SIHHAT AL-'ARABI. Text in Arabic, English. 1985. 4/yr. USD 60. adv. bk.rev. **Document type:** *Journal, Trade.* **Description:** Covers articles of interest to importers and distributors of health care products and equipment, to hospital workers, and to ministries of health in the Middle East, Anglophone Africa and other countries.
Former titles (until 2006): Arab Health International (1015-8324); (until 1990): Arab Health (0257-3202)
Related titles: Online - full text ed.: Arab Health World. ISSN 1990-3987.
Published by: Chatila Publishing House, Chouran, P O Box 13-5121, Beirut, 1102-2802, Lebanon. TEL 961-1-352413, FAX 961-1-352419. Ed. Dr. Abdul Salam Chatila. Circ: 12,741.

362.1 CAN ISSN 1910-1570
ALBERTA CONSTRUCTION SAFETY ASSOCIATION INDUSTRIES. Text in English. 1998. a. **Document type:** *Government.*
Formerly (until 2003): Construction. Alberta Construction Safety Association industries (1494-0981)
Published by: Alberta Human Resources and Employment, 324 Legislature Bldg, 10800 - 97 Ave, Edmonton, AB T5K 2B6, Canada. TEL 780-415-4800, FAX 780-422-9556, ahre.communications@gov.ab.ca, http://www.hre.gov.ab.ca/cps/rde/xchg/hre/hs.xsl/563.html.

ALBERTA DOCTORS' DIGEST. *see* MEDICAL SCIENCES

362.1 CAN ISSN 1912-6093
ALBERTA HEALTH AND WELLNESS. ANNUAL REPORT. HIGHLIGHTS. Text in English. 2006. a. **Document type:** *Report, Trade.*
Published by: Alberta Health and Wellness, PO Box 1360, Station Main, Edmonton, AB T5J 2N3, Canada. TEL 780-427-1432, FAX 780-422-0102, http://www.health.gov.ab.ca.

ALERT; maandblad voor rampenbestrijding en crisisbeheersing. *see* CIVIL DEFENSE

ALERT (NEW YORK). *see* SOCIAL SERVICES AND WELFARE

362.1 EGY ISSN 1110-0036
ALEXANDRIA. HIGH INSTITUTE OF PUBLIC HEALTH. BULLETIN. Text in English. 1971. q. EGP 10 (effective 2004). **Document type:** *Bulletin, Academic/Scholarly.*
Published by: High Institute of Public Health, 165 El-Horreya Ave, El-Hadrah, Alexandria, Egypt. TEL 20-3-4215575. Ed. Dr. Moustafa I Morad.

614 IRL ISSN 2009-0234
ALL-IRELAND HEALTH DATA INVENTORY. PART 1: METADATA FOR KEY DATA SOURCES. Text in English. 2007. a.
Published by: Institute of Public Health in Ireland, 5th Flr, Bishop's Square, Redmond's Hill, Dublin, 2, Ireland. TEL 353-1-4786300, FAX 353-1-4786319, info@inispho.org, http://www.inispho.org.

362.1 JPN ISSN 0913-5146
AMAGASAKI SHIRITSU EISEI KENKYUJOHO/AMAGASAKI CITY INSTITUTE OF PUBLIC HEALTH. ANNUAL REPORT. Text in Japanese. 1971. a.
—BLDSC (1104.291000).
Published by: Amagasaki Shiritsu Eisei Kenkyujo/Amagasaki City Institute of Public Health, 4-4-8 Minamitsukaguchicho, Amagasaki-shi, Hyogo 661-0012, Japan. TEL 81-6-6426-6355, FAX 81-6-6428-2566.

AMBIENTE RISORSE SALUTE; scienza, tecnica e cultura per uno sviluppo di qualita. *see* ENVIRONMENTAL STUDIES

AMERICAN HEALTH CARE ASSOCIATION. PROVIDER. *see* SOCIAL SERVICES AND WELFARE

614 USA
AMERICAN HEALTH LINE. Abbreviated title: A H L. Text in English. d. USD 700 to individuals; USD 1,125 2-10 readers; USD 2,240 entire office (effective 2007). **Document type:** *Newsletter, Trade.* **Description:** Keeps readers up-to-date with the most important local and national news events that have a direct impact on health care.
Media: Online - full text. **Related titles:** E-mail ed.; Fax ed.
Indexed: NRN.
Published by: Advisory Board Company, 2445 M St NW, Washington, DC 20037-1435. TEL 202-266-5600, 800-717-3245, FAX 202-266-5700, website@advisory.com, http://www.advisoryboardcompany.com.

AMERICAN JOURNAL OF PREVENTIVE MEDICINE. *see* MEDICAL SCIENCES

614 USA ISSN 0090-0036
CODEN: AJHEAA
➤ **AMERICAN JOURNAL OF PUBLIC HEALTH.** Abbreviated title: A J P H. Text in English. 1911. m. USD 356 domestic to institutions; USD 400 foreign to institutions; USD 520 combined subscription domestic to institutions (print & online eds.); USD 562 combined subscription foreign to institutions (print & online eds.); USD 30 per issue domestic to institutions; USD 35 per issue foreign to institutions (effective 2010). adv. charts; illus. index. back issues avail.; reprints avail. **Document type:** *Journal, Academic/Scholarly.* **Description:** Contains reports of original research, demonstrations, evaluations, and other articles covering current aspects of public health.
Supersedes in part (in 1971): American Journal of Public Health and the Nation's Health (0002-9572); Which was formed by the merger of (1921-1928): Nation's Health (1076-0704); (until 1919): Interstate Medical Journal (1047-3491); (until 1899): Tristate Medical Journal and Practitioner; Interstate Medical Journal Incorporated (1881-1907): St. Louis Courier of Medicine (1079-9567); Which was formerly (1879-1881): Saint Louis Courier of Medicine and Collateral Sciences (1079-9559); (1912-1928): American Journal of Public Health (0271-4353); Which was formerly (until 1912): American Public Health Association. Journal (0273-1975); (until 1911): American Journal of Public Hygiene (0272-2313); (until 1907): American Journal of Public Hygiene and Journal of the Massachusetts Association of Boards of Health; (until 1904): Massachusetts Association of Boards of Health. Journal; American Journal of Public Health Incorporated (1873-1912): Public Health Papers and Reports (0737-8769)
Related titles: CD-ROM ed.; Microform ed.: (from PMC, PQC); Online - full text ed.: ISSN 1541-0048. USD 486 (effective 2010).
Indexed: A01, A02, A03, A08, A12, A13, A17, A20, A22, A25, A26, A29, A33, A34, A35, A36, A37, ABIn, ABS&EES, AHCMS, AIDS Ab, AIM, ASCA, ASG, AbAn, AcaI, AddicA, AgBio, AgeL, Agr, B01, B04, B06, B07, B08, B09, B20, B21, B25, BA, BDM&CN, BIOSIS Prev, BRD, BibAg, BiolDig, C06, C07, C08, C11, C12, C25, CA, CABA, CINAHL, CIS, CISA, CLFP, CTD, ChPerI, ChemAb, Chicano, CurCont, D01, DentAb, DentInd, DokArb, E-psyche, E02, E03, E04, E05, E07, E08, E12, EMBASE, ERA, ERI, ESPM, EdA, EdI, EnvAb, ExcerpMed, F09, FR, FS&TA, FamI, G03, G08, G10, GH, GSA, GSI, H&SSA, H01, H02, H04, H05, H09, H11, H12, H13, H17, HPNRM, HRA, HRIS, HlthInd, HospLI, I05, I12, INI, ISR, IndMed, Inpharma, JW, JW-EM, JW-P, JW-WH, Kidney, L01, L02, L09, LT, M01, M02, MCR, MEDLINE, MEDSOC, MS&D, MycolAb, N02, N03, NRN, O01, P02, P03, P04, P06, P10, P13, P15, P19, P20, P21, P22, P24, P25, P26, P27, P30, P32, P33, P34, P35, P39, P40, P42, P43, P48, P50, P51, P52, P53, P54, P56, PCI, PEI, PGegResA, PN&I, PQC, PRA, PollutAb, PopulInd, PsycInfo, PsycholAb, R08, R09, R10, R12, RA&MP, RILM, RM&VM, RRTA, Reac, RiskAb, S02, S03, S04, S05, S08, S09, S12, S13, S16, S20, S21, SAA, SCI, SCOPUS, SD, SFSA, SRI, SRRA, SSAI, SSAb, SSCI, SSI, SSciA, SWR&A, SWRA, T02, T05, THA, ToxAb, VS, VirolAbstr, W01, W02, W03, W05, W07, W09, W11.
—BLDSC (0835.900000), CASDDS, GNLM, IE, Infotrieve, Ingenta, INIST. **CCC.**
Published by: American Public Health Association, 800 I St, NW, Washington, DC 20001. TEL 202-777-2742, FAX 202-777-2534, comments@apha.org, http://www.apha.org. Ed. Mary E Northridge. Pub. Georges Benjamin. adv.: B&W page USD 1,800, color page USD 4,600; trim 8.25 x 10.875. Circ: 28,000.

➤ **AMERICAN MOSQUITO CONTROL ASSOCIATION. JOURNAL.** *see* BIOLOGY—Entomology

362.11 USA ISSN 1524-0835
AMERICAN PUBLIC HEALTH ASSOCIATION. ANNUAL MEETING. ABSTRACTS. Text in English. 1968. a. back issues avail. **Document type:** *Proceedings, Trade.*
Supersedes in part (in 1995): American Public Health Association. Meeting. Official Program (0892-3671); Which was formerly (until 1980): American Public Health Association. Meeting. Official Program and Abstracts (0892-368X); (until 1977): American Public Health Association. Meeting. Program and Abstracts (0892-3698); (until 197?): American Public Health Association and Related Organizations. Annual Meeting. Official Program & Abstracts; (until 1971): American Public Health Association. Annual Meeting. Abstracts (0362-3149)
—CCC.
Published by: American Public Health Association, 800 I St, NW, Washington, DC 20001. TEL 202-777-2742, FAX 202-777-2534, comments@apha.org.

362.11 USA ISSN 1524-0827
RA422
AMERICAN PUBLIC HEALTH ASSOCIATION. ANNUAL MEETING AND EXPOSITION. FINAL PROGRAM. Text in English. 1968. a. back issues avail. **Document type:** *Proceedings, Academic/Scholarly.*
Supersedes in part (in 1995): American Public Health Association. Meeting. Official Program (0892-3671); Which was formerly (until 1980): American Public Health Association. Meeting. Official Program and Abstracts (0892-368X); (until 1977): American Public Health Association. Meeting. Program and Abstracts (0892-3698); (until 197?): American Public Health Association and Related Organizations. Annual Meeting. Official Program & Abstracts; (until 1971): American Public Health Association. Annual Meeting. Abstracts (0362-3149)
—CCC.
Published by: American Public Health Association, 800 I St, NW, Washington, DC 20001. TEL 202-777-2742, FAX 202-777-2534, comments@apha.org.

658.31244 USA
AMERISURE SAFETY NEWS. Text in English. 1921. q. free to policyholders. adv. back issues avail. **Document type:** *Newsletter.* **Description:** Provides safety tips for use in the home, on the road and at the workplace.
Former titles: Michigan Mutual Safety News; Amerisure Companies Safety News; Shopman
Published by: Amerisure Insurance, 26777 Halstead, Farmington, MI 48331. TEL 278-615-9000. Ed., Adv. contact Jeff Marzolf. Circ: 7,000.
Co-sponsor: Amerisure Companies.

AMTSBLATT DES KREISES WESEL; Amtliches Verkuendungsblatt. *see* PUBLIC ADMINISTRATION—Municipal Government

362.1 ESP ISSN 1137-6627
R71 CODEN: ASSNFO
ANALES DEL SISTEMA SANITARIO DE NAVARRA. Text in Spanish. 1959-1984; resumed 1997. 3/yr. EUR 30 (effective 2009). back issues avail. **Document type:** *Monographic series, Government.*
Supersedes (1959-1984): Instituto Medico Beneficencia. Anales
Related titles: Online - full text ed.: free (effective 2011); ◆ Supplement(s): Anales del Sistema Sanitario de Navarra. Suplemento. ISSN 1137-814X.
Indexed: EMBASE, ExcerpMed, MEDLINE, P30, R10, Reac, SCI, SCOPUS, SSCI, W07.
—BLDSC (0884.770000). **CCC.**
Published by: (Gobierno de Navarra, Departamento de Salud), Gobierno de Navarra, Fondo de Publicaciones, Calle de la Navas de Tolosa 21, Pamplona, Navarra 31002, Spain. TEL 34-9848-427121, FAX 34-9848-427123, fondo.publicaciones@cfnavarra.es, http://www.navarra.es. Ed. Lluis Forge Llenas.

362.1 ESP ISSN 1137-814X
ANALES DEL SISTEMA SANITARIO DE NAVARRA. SUPLEMENTO. Text in Spanish. 1997. 3/yr. EUR 6 per issue (effective 2009). **Document type:** *Monographic series, Academic/Scholarly.*
Related titles: ◆ Supplement to: Anales del Sistema Sanitario de Navarra. ISSN 1137-6627.
—CCC.
Published by: Gobierno de Navarra, Fondo de Publicaciones, Calle de la Navas de Tolosa 21, Pamplona, Navarra 31002, Spain. TEL 34-9848-427121, FAX 34-9848-427123, fondo.publicaciones@cfnavarra.es, http://www.navarra.es.

614 ESP ISSN 1988-7418
ANDALUCIA ES SALUD. Text in Spanish. 2007. w.
Media: Online - full text.
Published by: Junta de Andalucia, Consejeria de Salud, Ave de la Innovacion s-n Edif. Arena 1, Sevilla, 41020, Spain. andaluciaessalud.csalud@juntadeandalucia.es, http://www.juntadeandalucia.es/salud/principal/. Ed. Monica Radial Espinosa.

ANDREWS LITIGATION REPORTER: DRUG RECALL. *see* LAW

344.04 USA ISSN 1553-0906
KF3875.A57
ANDREWS LITIGATION REPORTER: FOOD HEALTH & SAFETY. Text in English. 2004 (Sept). m. USD 590 (effective 2005). **Document type:** *Newsletter, Trade.*
—CCC.
Published by: Andrews Publications (Subsidiary of: Thomson West), 175 Strafford Ave, Bldg 4, Ste 140, Wayne, PA 19087. TEL 610-225-0510, 800-328-4880, FAX 610-225-0501, west.customer.service@thomson.com, http://west.thomson.com. Ed. Donna Higgins. Pub. Mary Ellen Fox.

613 AUS ISSN 1447-7483
ANEX BULLETIN. Text in English. 2002. q. **Document type:** *Bulletin, Trade.* **Description:** Provides a range of NSP-related issues and keeps harm reduction workers up to date with new information, research findings and emerging issues for the sector.
Related titles: Online - full content ed.
Published by: Association of Needle and Syringe Programs, Inc. (Anex), 600 Nicholson St, Ste 1 Level 2, Firtzroy North, VIC 3068, Australia. TEL 61-3-94866399, FAX 61-3-94867844, info@anex.org.au. Circ: 3,000.

614 ITA ISSN 0021-3071
CODEN: ADSAAB
ANNALI DELLA SANITA PUBBLICA. Text in Italian. 1970 (vol.23). 3/yr. bk.rev. **Document type:** *Journal, Academic/Scholarly.*
Related titles: Online - full text ed.: ISSN 1827-8094. 2004.
Indexed: ChemAb, P30.
—CASDDS, GNLM.
Published by: Ministero del Lavoro, della Salute e delle Politiche Sociali, Via Veneto 56, Rome, 00187, Italy. FAX 39-06-4821207, http://www.ministerosalute.it.

613 ITA ISSN 1120-9135
CODEN: NAIMAH
ANNALI DI IGIENE, MEDICINA PREVENTIVA E DI COMUNITA. Text in Italian; Summaries in English. 1895. bi-m. EUR 81.04 (effective 2008). adv. bk.rev. illus. index. **Document type:** *Journal, Academic/Scholarly.*
Former titles (until 1989): Nuovi Annali di Igiene e Microbiologia (0029-6287); (until 1950): Annali d'Igiene (0365-4842); (until 1916): Annali d'Igiene Sperimentale (0365-3161)
Related titles: Online - full text ed.
Indexed: A22, CISA, ChemAb, DentInd, EMBASE, ExcerpMed, FR, IndMed, MEDLINE, P30, R10, Reac, RefZh, SCOPUS.
—BLDSC (1014.180000), CASDDS, GNLM, IE, Infotrieve, Ingenta, INIST.
Published by: (Istituto di Igiene Giuseppe Sanarelli), Societa Editrice Universo, Via Giovanni Battista Morgagni 1, Rome, RM 00161, Italy. TEL 39-06-44231171, FAX 39-06-4402033, amministrazione@seu-roma.it, http://www.seuroma.com. Ed. G M Fara. Circ: 3,000.

614 USA ISSN 1047-2797
RA648.5 CODEN: ANNPE3
➤ **ANNALS OF EPIDEMIOLOGY.** Text in English. 1990. m. USD 802 in United States to institutions; USD 908 elsewhere to institutions (effective 2012). adv. back issues avail.; reprints avail. **Document type:** *Journal, Academic/Scholarly.* **Description:** Provides reports of original research in epidemiology of chronic and acute diseases of interest to clinical and public-health researchers.
Related titles: Microform ed.: (from PQC); Online - full text ed.: ISSN 1873-2585 (from IngentaConnect, ScienceDirect).
Indexed: A01, A03, A08, A20, A22, A26, A35, A36, ASFA, AgBio, B21, B25, BIOBASE, BIOSIS Prev, C06, C07, C08, CA, CABA, CINAHL, CIS, CTA, CurCont, D01, E12, EMBASE, ESPM, ExcerpMed, F08, F09, FR, FamI, G10, GH, H&SSA, H12, HPNRM, I05, IABS, ISR, IndMed, Inpharma, LT, MEDLINE, MS&D, MycolAb, N02, N03, NRN, NSA, P30, P33, P34, P35, P39, PollutAb, R08, R10, R12, RA&MP, RM&VM, RRTA, Reac, RiskAb, S01, S02, S03, S12, S13, S16, SCI, SCOPUS, SSciA, SoyAb, T02, T05, TAR, THA, ToxAb, VITIS, VS, VirolAbstr, W07, W09, W10, W11, WildRev.
—BLDSC (1040.470000), GNLM, IE, Infotrieve, Ingenta, INIST. **CCC.**
Published by: (American College of Epidemiology), Elsevier Inc. (Subsidiary of: Elsevier Science & Technology), 1600 John F Kennedy Blvd, Philadelphia, PA 19103. TEL 215-239-3900, FAX 215-238-7883, JournalCustomerService-usa@elsevier.com, http://www.elsevier.com. Ed. Dr. R Rothenberg. Adv. contact John Marmero Jr. TEL 212-633-3657.

➤ **ANNALS OF TROPICAL MEDICINE AND PUBLIC HEALTH.** *see* MEDICAL SCIENCES

353.9 354 USA ISSN 1545-9047
HV6432
ANNUAL EDITIONS: HOMELAND SECURITY. Text in English. 2003. a., latest 2nd ed. USD 22.25 per issue (effective 2010). back issues avail. **Document type:** *Journal, Academic/Scholarly.* **Description:** Provides a convenient, inexpensive, up-to-date collection of carefully selected articles from the most respected national and international magazines, newspapers, and journals.
Related titles: Online - full text ed.
Published by: McGraw-Hill, Contemporary Learning Series (Subsidiary of: McGraw-Hill Companies, Inc.), 1221 Ave of the Americas, New York, NY 10020. TEL 212-904-2000, FAX 212-512-2000, customer.service@mcgraw-hill.com, http://www.mhhe.com/cls/.

362.1 CAN ISSN 1487-1394
ANNUAL REPORT ON THE HEALTH OF THE POPULATION. Text in English. 1998. a. **Document type:** *Government.*
Related titles: French ed.: Rapport Annuel (Year) sur la Sante de la Population. ISSN 1485-5402.
Published by: Agence de Developpement de Reseaux Locaux de Sante et de Services Sociaux de Montreal, Direction de Sante Publique, Centre de documentation, a/s Sossee Zerdelian, 1301, rue Sherbrooke Est, Montreal, PQ H2L 1M3, Canada. TEL 514-528-2400, SZerdeli@santepub-mtl.qc.ca, http://www.santepub-mtl.qc.ca/.

P

614 USA ISSN 0163-7525
RA421 CODEN: AREHDT
➤ **ANNUAL REVIEW OF PUBLIC HEALTH.** Text in English. 1980. a. USD 251 combined subscription per issue to institutions (print & online eds.); USD 209 per issue to institutions (print or online ed.) (effective 2012). bibl.; charts; abstr. index, cum.index. back issues avail.; reprint service avail. from PSC. **Document type:** *Journal, Academic/Scholarly.* **Description:** Synthesizes and filters primary research to identify the principal contributions in the field of public health.
Related titles: Microfilm ed.: (from PQC); Online - full text ed.: ISSN 1545-2093.
Indexed: A01, A02, A03, A08, A20, A22, A26, A34, A35, A36, A38, AHCMS, AMHA, ASCA, AgBio, Agr, B20, B21, BIOSIS Prev, C06, C07, C11, CA, CABA, CIS, CurCont, DokArb, E08, E12, EMBASE, ESPM, ExcerpMed, FS&TA, Faml, GH, H&SSA, H04, H05, I05, I12, IBR, IBZ, ISR, IndMed, IndVet, Inpharma, LT, MEDLINE, MycolAb, N02, N03, P03, P10, P15, P19, P20, P21, P22, P24, P30, P33, P34, P42, P48, P50, P52, P53, P54, P56, PEI, PQC, PsycInfo, R10, R12, RM&VM, RRTA, Reac, S02, S03, S13, S16, SCI, SCOPUS, SSCI, SociolAb, SoyAb, T02, T05, THA, VS, W07, W11.
—BLDSC (1528.450000), CASDDS, GNLM, IE, Infotrieve, Ingenta, INIST. **CCC.**
Published by: Annual Reviews, PO Box 10139, Palo Alto, CA 94303. TEL 650-493-4400, FAX 650-424-0910, 800-523-8635, service@annualreviews.org. Eds. Jonathan E Fielding TEL 213-240-8117, Samuel Gubins.

➤ **ANNUAL SUMMARY OF OUTBREAKS IN NEW ZEALAND.** *see* MEDICAL SCIENCES—Communicable Diseases

362.1 ITA ISSN 1590-1157
ANNUARIO SANITA ITALIA. Text in Italian. 1954. a. EUR 220 combined subscription (print & online eds.) (effective 2009). adv. **Document type:** *Journal, Academic/Scholarly.* **Description:** Presents activities in Italy and at the Vatican.
Formerly (until 1990): Annali d'Italia (0391-5131)
Related titles: Online - full text ed.
Published by: Editoriale Publiaci, Via Tribuna di Tor de' Specchi 18a, Rome, Italy. TEL 39-06-69380070, FAX 39-06-233201318.

362.1 CHN ISSN 1671-4636
ANQUAN YU JIANKANG/SAFETY & HEALTH. Text in Chinese. 1986. m. **Document type:** *Journal, Academic/Scholarly.*
Formerly (until 2002): Laodong Anquan yu Jiankang (1006-3935)
Related titles: Online - full text ed.
Published by: Fujian Sheng Laodong Baohu Kexue Yanjiusuo, 45, Beihuan Zhong Lu, Fuzhou, 350003, China. TEL 86-591-87809643, FAX 86-591-87844574, http://www.fjsafety.com.

ANTI-INFECTIVES WEEK. *see* MEDICAL SCIENCES—Communicable Diseases

362.1 PRT ISSN 1646-8058
ANUARIO DA SAUDE. Text in Portuguese. 2001. a. **Document type:** *Report, Government.*
Published by: Ministerio da Saude, Avenida Joao Crisostomo 14, Lisbon 1, 1000-179, Portugal. TEL 351-217-984200, FAX 351-217-984220, http://www.min-saude.pt.

362.1 CAN ISSN 1912-4678
L'APPLICATION DE LA PROCEDURE D'EXAMEN DES PLAINTES ET L'AMELIORATION DE LA QUALITE DES SERVICES DES ETABLISSEMENTS DU RESEAU DE LA SANTE ET DES SERVICES SOCIAUX DE LA MONTEREGIE ET L'AGENCE DE LA SANTE ET DES SERVICES SOCIAUX DE LA MONTEREGIE. RAPPORT. Text in French. 1994. a. **Document type:** *Report, Trade.*
Former titles (until 2006): L' Application de la Procedure d'Examen des Plaintes des Etablissements du Reseau de la Sante et des Services Sociaux de la Monteregie et de l'Agence de Developpement de Reseaux Locaux de Services de Sante et de Services Sociaux-Monteregie. Rapport (1719-2773); (until 2004): L' Application de la Procedure d'Examen des Plaintes de la Regie Regionale de la Sante et des Services Sociaux de la Monteregie et des Etablissements du Reseau de Sante et des Services Sociaux de la Monteregie. Rapport (1719-2765)
Published by: Agence de la Sante et des Services Sociaux de la Monteregie, 1255, rue Beauregard, Longueuil, PQ J4K 2M3, Canada. TEL 450-928-6777, FAX 450-679-6443, agencemonteregie@ssss.gouv.qc.ca, http://www.rrsss16.gouv.qc.ca/index.html.

362.1 CAN ISSN 1912-466X
L'APPLICATION DE LA PROCEDURE D'EXAMEN DES PLAINTES ET L'AMELIORATION DE LA QUALITE DES SERVICES. RAPPORT ANNUEL. Text in French. 2005. a. **Document type:** *Report, Trade.*
Formerly (until 2006): Rapport des Plaintes (1912-4651)
Published by: Agence de la Sante et des Services Sociaux de Montreal, 3725, rue Saint-Denis, Montreal, PQ H2X 3L9, Canada. TEL 514-286-6500, FAX 514-286-5669, http://www.santemontreal.qc.ca/fr.

APPLIED HEALTH ECONOMICS AND HEALTH POLICY. *see* MEDICAL SCIENCES

362.1 DEU ISSN 0948-0935
ARBEIT UND GESUNDHEIT. SONDERAUSGABE VERKEHR. Text in German. 197?. a. **Document type:** *Magazine, Trade.*
Formerly (until 1994): Blickpunkt Arbeitssicherheit. Sondernummer (0930-9101)
Published by: Universum Verlagsanstalt GmbH KG, Taunusstr 54, Wiesbaden, 65183, Germany. TEL 49-611-9030-0, FAX 49-611-9030382, info@universum.de, http://www.universum.de.

613.62 DEU ISSN 0944-6052
CODEN: ASOUEO
ARBEITSMEDIZIN, SOZIALMEDIZIN, UMWELTMEDIZIN; Zeitschrift fuer Praxis, Klinik, Forschung, Begutachtung. Text in German. 1965. m. EUR 186 (effective 2010). adv. bk.rev. abstr.; charts; illus. index. **Document type:** *Journal, Academic/Scholarly.*
Former titles (until 1993): Arbeitsmedizin, Sozialmedizin, Praeventivmedizin (0300-581X); Arbeitsmedizin, Sozialmedizin, Arbeitshygiene (0003-7753)
Related titles: Supplement(s): A S U Protect. 2004.
Indexed: A20, A22, CISA, DIP, IBR, IBZ, P30, SCOPUS.
—BLDSC (1587.402750), GNLM, IE, Infotrieve, Ingenta, INIST. **CCC.**
Published by: (Deutsche Gesellschaft fuer Arbeitsmedizin und Umweltmedizin e.V.), Gentner Verlag Stuttgart, Forststr 131, Stuttgart, 70193, Germany. TEL 49-711-636720, FAX 49-711-63672747, gentner@gentnerverlag.de, http://www.gentnerverlag.de. Ed. Dr. Gerhard Triebig. Adv. contact Angela Gruessner. B&W page EUR 1,650, color page EUR 2,970; trim 206 x 291. Circ: 3,274 (paid and controlled). **Co-sponsor:** Oesterreichische Gesellschaft fuer Arbeitsmedizin.

ARBETE OCH HAELSA. *see* LABOR UNIONS

362.1 616 BEL ISSN 0778-7367
CODEN: ABMHAM
➤ **ARCHIVES OF PUBLIC HEALTH.** Text and summaries in English. 1938. bi-m. EUR 45 domestic; EUR 60 foreign (effective 2004). bk.rev. abstr.; bibl.; charts. index. 60 p./no.; **Document type:** *Academic/Scholarly.*
Former titles (until 1990): Archives Belges de Medecine Sociale, Hygiene, Medecine du Travail et Medecine (0003-9578); (until 1947): Archives Belges de Medecine Sociale et d'Hygiene (0365-4648); (until 1938); Revue de Pathologie et de Physiologie du Travail (0771-6192); (until 1931): Revue de Medecine et de Chirurgie des Accidents de Travail et des Maladies Professionnelles (0771-1301)
Related titles: Online - full text ed.: free (effective 2011).
Indexed: A35, A36, AgBio, C25, CABA, CISA, ChemAb, D01, E12, F08, F12, FR, FS&TA, GH, IndMed, LT, N02, P30, R12, RRTA, S13, S16, SCOPUS, T05, W10, W11.
—BLDSC (1640.530000), CASDDS, GNLM, IE, Infotrieve, INIST.
Published by: Institut Scientifique de Sante Publique/Scientific Institut of Public Health, Epidemiology, Rue Juliette Wytsmanstraat 14-16, Brussels, 1050, Belgium. TEL 32-02-642503, FAX 32-02-6425410. Ed. Herman Van Oyen. Circ: 600.

353.9 USA
RA21
ARIZONA HEALTH. Text in English. 1974. a. free. illus. **Document type:** *Government.*
Former titles (until 198?): Arizona. Department of Health Services. Annual Report (0362-1421); (until 1974): Arizona State Department of Health. Annual Report (0190-0633); Arizona State Department of Health. Biennial Report
Published by: Department of Health Services, 150 N 18th Ave, Phoenix,, AZ 85007. TEL 602-542-1001, FAX 602-542-0883, http://www.azdhs.gov/. Ed. Brad Christensen. Circ: 500 (controlled).

ARIZONA RADIATION REGULATORY AGENCY. ANNUAL REPORT. *see* ENERGY—Nuclear Energy

362.1 PRT ISSN 1646-172X
ARQUIVOS EGAS MONIZ. Text in Portuguese. 2005. s-a. **Document type:** *Report, Government.*
Published by: Centro Hospitalar de Lisboa Ocidental, Estrada do Forte do Alto do Duque, Lisbon, 1449-005, Portugal. TEL 351-21-0431000, FAX 351-21-0431589, http://www.chlo.min-saude.pt.

614 616.9 338.91 USA ISSN 1943-6742
R651
➤ **ARTICULATE;** undegraduate research applied to international development. Text in English. 2008. s-a. back issues avail. **Document type:** *Journal, Academic/Scholarly.* **Description:** Focuses on issues in international development, foreign aid, public health and health care in Africa.
Related titles: Online - full text ed.
Published by: Scoutbanana Publications, The Hill Bldg, Ste 3, 11704 Schram St, Grand Blanc, MI 48439. alex.h@scoutbanana.org.

➤ **ARZT IN NIEDEROESTERREICH.** *see* MEDICAL SCIENCES

362.1 USA ISSN 1010-5395
RA525
➤ **ASIA-PACIFIC JOURNAL OF PUBLIC HEALTH.** Abbreviated title: A P J P H. Text in English. 1986. bi-m. USD 376, GBP 221 to institutions; USD 384, GBP 226 combined subscription to institutions (print & online eds.) (effective 2012). adv. back issues avail.; reprint service avail. from PSC. **Document type:** *Journal, Academic/Scholarly.* **Description:** Focuses on health issues in the Asia-Pacific region.
Related titles: Online - full text ed.: ISSN 1941-2479. USD 346, GBP 203 to institutions (effective 2012).
Indexed: A22, A34, A36, B21, C06, C07, C25, CABA, D01, E01, E12, EMBASE, ESPM, ExcerpMed, F08, F09, GH, H&SSA, H16, H17, I14, LT, MEDLINE, N02, P03, P30, P33, P39, PN&I, PsycInfo, PsycholAb, R08, R10, R12, RA&MP, RRTA, Reac, RiskAb, S13, S16, SCI, SCOPUS, SSCI, SoyAb, T05, W07, W10, W11.
—BLDSC (1742.260900), IE, Infotrieve, Ingenta. **CCC.**
Published by: (The Asia-Pacific Academic Consortium for Public Health AUS), Sage Publications, Inc., 2455 Teller Rd, Thousand Oaks, CA 91320. TEL 800-818-7243, FAX 800-583-2665, info@sagepub.com, http://www.sagepub.com. Ed. Wah Yun Low.

➤ **ASIAN CONFERENCE ON DIARRHOEAL DISEASES AND NUTRITION.** *see* MEDICAL SCIENCES

➤ **ASIAN JOURNAL OF EPIDEMIOLOGY.** *see* MEDICAL SCIENCES

362.1 795 HKG ISSN 2218-7138
▼ ➤ **ASIAN JOURNAL OF GAMBLING ISSUES AND PUBLIC HEALTH.** Text in English. 2010 (Oct.). a. HKD 900, CNY 800, MOP 900, GBP 78, AUD 135, USD 120 combined subscription to institutions (print & online eds.) (effective 2011). back issues avail. **Document type:** *Journal, Academic/Scholarly.* **Description:** Contains research articles in gambling research, including legalization, technology, policies, addiction, financial markets, and treatment/recovery. Audience includes international scholars, experts and practitioners.
Related titles: Online - full text ed.: HKD 850, CNY 735, MOP 850, GBP 75, AUD 128, USD 115 to institutions (effective 2011).
Published by: Hong Kong Academy of Medicine Press, Rm.901, 9/F, HKAM Bldg., 99 Wong Hunk Hang Rd., Aberdeen, Hong Kong. TEL 852-28718807, FAX 852-25159061, hkampress@hkam.org.hk, http://www.hkampress.org. Eds. Larry Man Yum So, Xue Hong Wang.

➤ **ASIAN JOURNAL OF W T O & INTERNATIONAL HEALTH LAW AND POLICY.** *see* LAW—International Law

363.3481 617.72 USA
ASSOCIATION NEWS! (FORT COLLINS). Text in English. 1979. bi-m. USD 25 domestic to individuals; USD 40 foreign to individuals; free membership (effective 2006). adv. bk.rev. **Document type:** *Newspaper, Trade.* **Description:** Covers techniques, equipment and experiences pertinent to the job of public safety diver. For professional dive rescue specialists.
Former titles: Searchlines; Dive Rescue Specialist
Published by: International Association of Dive Rescue Specialists, 201 N Link Ln, Fort Collins, CO 80524. TEL 714-369-1660, 800-423-7791, FAX 970-482-0893, 714-369-1690, info@iadrs.org, http://www.iadrs.org. Ed. Steven J Linton. Circ: 3,000 (paid and free).

362.1 NZL ISSN 2230-2840
ASTHMA FOUNDATION. ANNUAL REPORT. Text in English. 1996. a. free (effective 2011). back issues avail. **Document type:** *Report, Trade.* **Description:** Features activities and work of the Asthma Foundation and its affiliated Asthma Societies.
Formerly (until 2009): Asthma and Respiratory Foundation of New Zealand. Annual Report (1178-2544)
Related titles: Online - full text ed.: ISSN 2230-2859.
Published by: Asthma Foundation, PO Box 1459, Wellington, 6140, New Zealand. TEL 64-4-4994592, FAX 64-4-4994594, info@asthmafoundation.org.nz, http://www.asthmanz.co.nz.

632.1 AUS
AUSTRALIA. DEPARTMENT OF HEALTH & AGEING. CHIEF MEDICAL OFFICER'S REPORT. Text in English. 1998. irreg. **Document type:** *Government.*
Published by: Australia. Department of Health and Ageing, GPO Box 9848, Canberra, ACT 2601, Australia. TEL 61-2-62891555, enquiries@health.gov.au.

362.1 AUS
AUSTRALIA. DEPARTMENT OF HEALTH & AGEING. OCCASIONAL PAPERS NEW SERIES. Text in English. 1997; N.S. (no.6). irreg., latest no.15, 2003. **Document type:** *Government.*
Former titles (until 2003): Australian Commonwealth Department of Health & Aged Care. Occasional Papers New Series; (until 1999): Australian Department of Health & Aged Care. Health and Aged Care Occasional Papers Series; (until 1998): H F S Occasional Papers Series (1329-4407)
Published by: Australia. Department of Health and Ageing, GPO Box 9848, Canberra, ACT 2601, Australia. TEL 61-2-62891555, enquiries@health.gov.au, http://www.health.gov.au/.

362.1 AUS
AUSTRALIA. DEPARTMENT OF THE TREASURY. ADVISORY PANEL ON THE MARKETING OF INFANT FORMULA. ANNUAL REPORT. Text in English. a. charts; stat. back issues avail. **Document type:** *Report, Trade.* **Description:** Reports on the efforts of the Australian Government to enforce the World Health Organization International Code of Marketing of Breast-Milk Substitutes.
Related titles: Online - full text ed.
Published by: (Australia. Advisory Panel on the Marketing in Australia of Infant Formula), Australian Government. Department of Health and Ageing. Office of Health Protection, GPO Box 9848, Canberra, ACT 2601, Australia. TEL 61-2-62891555, FAX 61-2-62816946, enquiries@health.gov.au, http://www.health.gov.au/internet/wcms/publishing.nsf/Content/ohp-about.htm.

616.9 AUS ISSN 1326-0200
RA553 CODEN: AZPHF6
➤ **AUSTRALIAN AND NEW ZEALAND JOURNAL OF PUBLIC HEALTH.** Text in English. 1977. bi-m. GBP 182 combined subscription in United Kingdom to institutions (print & online eds.); EUR 232 combined subscription in Europe to institutions (print & online eds.); USD 347 combined subscription in the Americas to institutions (print & online eds.); USD 355 combined subscription elsewhere to institutions (print & online eds.) (effective 2012). adv. bk.rev. 112 p./no.; back issues avail.; reprint service avail. from PSC. **Document type:** *Journal, Academic/Scholarly.* **Description:** Publishes research reports, reviews and letters on epidemiology, health policy, health services and health promotion.
Former titles: Australian Journal of Public Health (1035-7319); (until Dec. 1990): Community Health Studies (0314-9021)
Related titles: Microfilm ed.: (from PQC); Online - full text ed.: ISSN 1753-6405. GBP 157 in United Kingdom to institutions; EUR 202 in Europe to institutions; USD 302 in the Americas to institutions; USD 308 elsewhere to institutions (effective 2012) (from IngentaConnect).
Indexed: A12, A17, A20, A22, A26, A34, A36, ABIn, ASCA, AusPAIS, B01, B06, B07, B08, B09, B21, C06, C07, C08, C12, C25, C28, CA, CABA, CINAHL, CTA, CurCont, D01, DentInd, E01, E08, E12, EMBASE, ESPM, ExcerpMed, F08, F09, F12, Faml, G08, GH, H&SSA, H05, H11, H12, H13, H17, I05, INI, INZP, IndMed, IndVet, LT, MEDLINE, N02, N03, NRN, P10, P20, P24, P30, P33, P34, P37, P39, P48, P50, P51, P53, P54, PQC, R08, R10, R12, RA&MP, RM&VM, RRTA, Reac, S02, S03, S09, S12, S13, S16, SCI, SCOPUS, SD, SSCI, SoyAb, T02, T05, THA, VS, W07, W09, W11.
—BLDSC (1796.894000), GNLM, IE, Infotrieve, Ingenta, INIST. **CCC.**
Published by: (Public Health Association of Australia), Wiley-Blackwell Publishing Asia (Subsidiary of: Wiley-Blackwell Publishing Ltd.), 155 Cremorne St, Richmond, VIC 3121, Australia. TEL 61-3-92743100, FAX 61-3-92743101, subs@blackwellpublishingasia.com, http://www.wiley.com/WileyCDA/. Eds. Jeanne Daly, Judith Lumley. adv.: page AUD 902; 18.5 x 26. Circ: 2,500.

362.1 AUS
AUSTRALIAN DEPARTMENT OF HEALTH & AGED CARE. BUDGET PAPERS. Text in English. a. back issues avail. **Document type:** *Government.*
Related titles: Online - full content ed.
Published by: Australia. Department of Health and Ageing, GPO Box 9848, Canberra, ACT 2601, Australia. TEL 61-2-62891555, enquiries@health.gov.au.

632.1 AUS
AUSTRALIAN DEPARTMENT OF HEALTH & AGED CARE. CORPORATE PLAN. Text in English. a. back issues avail. **Document type:** *Government.*
Related titles: Online - full content ed.
Published by: Australia. Department of Health and Ageing, GPO Box 9848, Canberra, ACT 2601, Australia. TEL 61-2-62891555, enquiries@health.gov.au, http://www.health.gov.au/.

AUSTRALIAN FLUORIDATION NEWS. *see* WATER RESOURCES

613 AUS ISSN 1445-7253
RA553
➤ **AUSTRALIAN INDIGENOUS HEALTH BULLETIN.** Text in English. 1997. q. Website rev.; bk.rev. abstr.; bibl.; stat.; tr.lit. back issues avail. **Document type:** *Journal, Academic/Scholarly.* **Description:** Provides information about Australian Indigenous health.
Formerly (until Jul. 2001): Aboriginal and Torres Strait Islander Health Bulletin (1329-3362)

Media: Online - full content.
Published by: Australian Indigenous Health Info Net, c/o School of Indigenous Australian Studies, Edith Cowan University, Kurongkurl Katitjin Bldg, 2 Bradford St, Mount Lawley, W.A. 6050, Australia. TEL 61-8-93706336, FAX 61-8-93706022, healthinfonet@ecu.edu.au, http://www.healthinfonet.ecu.edu.au/. Ed. Neil Thomson.

➤ **THE AUSTRALIAN JOURNAL OF EMERGENCY MANAGEMENT.** *see* CIVIL DEFENSE

362.1042505 AUS ISSN 1038-5282
RA771.A1 CODEN: AJRHF6
➤ **AUSTRALIAN JOURNAL OF RURAL HEALTH.** Abbreviated title: A J R H. Text in English. 1992. bi-m. GBP 662 in United Kingdom to institutions; EUR 842 in Europe to institutions; USD 1,071 in the Americas to institutions; USD 1,298 elsewhere to institutions; GBP 762 combined subscription in United Kingdom to institutions (print & online eds.); EUR 968 combined subscription in Europe to institutions (print & online eds.); USD 1,232 combined subscription in the Americas to institutions (print & online eds.); USD 1,494 combined subscription elsewhere to institutions (print & online eds.) (effective 2012). adv. reprint service avail. from PSC. **Document type:** *Journal, Academic/Scholarly.* **Description:** Reports on all aspects of rural health from a variety of health and related disciplines.
Related titles: Online - full text ed.: ISSN 1440-1584. GBP 662 in United Kingdom to institutions; EUR 842 in Europe to institutions; USD 1,071 in the Americas to institutions; USD 1,298 elsewhere to institutions (effective 2012) (from IngentaConnect).
Indexed: A01, A02, A03, A08, A11, A22, A26, A36, A37, ASG, ASSIA, B21, C06, C07, C08, C11, CA, CABA, CINAHL, D01, E01, E12, EMBASE, ESPM, ExcerpMed, F09, GH, H&SSA, H04, H05, H12, INI, L11, LT, MEDLINE, N02, N03, P03, P30, P33, P34, P39, PAIS, PHN&I, PsycInfo, R08, R10, R12, RA&MP, RRTA, Reac, S02, S03, SCI, SCOPUS, SD, SOPODA, SSCI, SociolAb, T02, T05, W07, W11.
—BLDSC (1811.870000), IE, Infotrieve, Ingenta. **CCC.**
Published by: (National Rural Health Alliance, The Association for Australian Rural Nurses Inc., Australian College of Rural and Remote Medicine), Wiley-Blackwell Publishing Asia (Subsidiary of: Wiley-Blackwell Publishing Ltd.), 155 Cremorne St, Richmond, VIC 3121, Australia. TEL 61-3-92743100, FAX 61-3-92743101, subs@blackwellpublishingasia.com, http://www.wiley.com/WileyCDA/. Ed. James Dunbar TEL 61-3-55633315. adv.: B&W page AUD 1,012, color page AUD 2,057; trim 210 x 275. **Subscr. to:** Wiley-Blackwell Publishing Ltd.

➤ **AUSTRALIAN MEDICINE.** *see* MEDICAL SCIENCES

362.1 AUS
AUSTRALIAN RECALLS AND CANCELLATIONS BULLETIN. Text in English. 11/yr. AUD 75.90 domestic; AUD 79 foreign (effective 2008). back issues avail. **Document type:** *Bulletin, Government.*
Published by: Australian Government. Department of Health and Ageing. Therapeutic Goods Administration, PO Box 100, Woden, ACT 2606, Australia. TEL 61-2-62328610, FAX 61-2-62328605, info@health.gov.au.

362.1 AUS ISSN 1833-8976
AUSTRALIAN SPORTS ANTI-DOPING AUTHORITY. ANNUAL REPORT. Text in English. 1991. a. **Document type:** *Report, Trade.*
Formerly (until 2006): Australian Sports Drug Agency. Annual Report (1037-3780)
Media: Online - full text.
Published by: Australian Sports Anti-Doping Authority (A S A D A), PO Box 345, Curtin, ACT 2605, Australia. TEL 61-2-6206-0200, FAX 61-2-6206-0201, asada@asada.gov.au, http://www.asada.gov.au/index.htm.

613 NZL ISSN 2230-2972
▼ **AWARENESS TODAY.** Text in English. 2010. q. **Document type:** *Journal, Trade.*
Related titles: Online - full text ed.: ISSN 2230-2980.
Published by: A-Mark Publishing, 154 Armagh St, Christchurch, 8001, New Zealand. TEL 64-3-3797156.

THE B A P C O JOURNAL. *see* COMMUNICATIONS

B E L L E NEWSLETTER. (Biological Effects of Low Level Exposures) *see* ENVIRONMENTAL STUDIES—Toxicology And Environmental Safety

B M C HEALTH SERVICES RESEARCH. (BioMed Central) *see* MEDICAL SCIENCES

614 323 GBR ISSN 1472-698X
RA1 CODEN: BIHHBO
➤ **B M C INTERNATIONAL HEALTH AND HUMAN RIGHTS.** (BioMed Central) Text in English. 2001 (Jul.). irreg. free (effective 2011). adv. back issues avail.; reprints avail. **Document type:** *Journal, Academic/Scholarly.* **Description:** Features original research articles in health care in developing and transitional countries, and all issues relating to health and human rights.
Media: Online - full text.
Indexed: A01, A26, A35, A36, AgBio, BA, C06, C07, CA, CABA, CurCont, E12, EMBASE, ESPM, ExcerpMed, GH, H05, I05, N02, P20, P22, P30, P32, P33, P39, P40, PQC, R08, R12, S13, S16, SCOPUS, SSCI, T02, T05, TAR, W07, W11.
—Infotrieve. **CCC.**
Published by: BioMed Central Ltd. (Subsidiary of: Springer Science+Business Media), 236 Gray's Inn Rd, London, WC1X 8HB, United Kingdom. TEL 44-20-31922000, FAX 44-20-31922010, info@biomedcentral.com. Ed. Dr. Melissa Norton. Adv. contact Natasha Bailey TEL 44-20-31922231.

362.1 GBR ISSN 1471-2458
RA1 CODEN: BPHMAJ
➤ **B M C PUBLIC HEALTH.** (BioMed Central) Text in English. 2001 (Jan.). irreg. free (effective 2011). adv. back issues avail.; reprints avail. **Document type:** *Journal, Academic/Scholarly.* **Description:** Publishes original research articles in all aspects of epidemiology and public health medicine.
Media: Online - full text.
Indexed: A01, A02, A03, A08, A26, A34, A35, A36, A37, AgBio, AgrForAb, B23, BA, BP, C06, C07, C25, CA, CABA, CurCont, D01, E12, EMBASE, ESPM, ExcerpMed, F08, F09, F11, F12, FS&TA, GH, H05, H17, I05, IndVet, LT, MEDLINE, N02, N03, OR, P20, P22, P30, P32, P33, P34, P39, P40, P50, P54, PEI, PN&I, PQC, PollutAb, R07, R08, R10, R12, RA&MP, RM&VM, RRTA, Reac, RiskAb, S12, S13, S16, SCI, SCOPUS, SoyAb, T02, T05, VS, W07, W10, W11.
—Infotrieve. **CCC.**
Published by: BioMed Central Ltd. (Subsidiary of: Springer Science+Business Media), 236 Gray's Inn Rd, London, WC1X 8HB, United Kingdom. TEL 44-20-31922000, FAX 44-20-31922010, info@biomedcentral.com. Ed. Dr. Melissa Norton. Adv. contact Natasha Bailey TEL 44-20-31922231.

614 USA ISSN 1068-1213
KF3605.A15
B N A'S HEALTH CARE POLICY REPORT. (Bureau of National Affairs) Text in English. 1993. w. USD 1,593 (effective 2010 - 2011). s-a. index. 40 p./no.; back issues avail. **Document type:** *Report, Trade.* **Description:** Covers federal, state and private sector efforts to reform and manage the U.S. health care system.
Related titles: Online - full text ed.: ISSN 1521-5369. USD 1,577 (effective 2010 - 2011).
Indexed: H05, P34, S02, S03, SWR&A, T02.
—**CCC.**
Published by: The Bureau of National Affairs, Inc., 1801 S Bell St, Arlington, VA 22202. TEL 703-341-3000, 800-372-1033, FAX 703-341-4634, bnaplus@bna.com.

362.1 664 CHE ISSN 1662-131X
B V L - REPORTE. Text in German. 2007. 3/yr. EUR 75, USD 100 to institutions (effective 2010). reprint service avail. from PSC. **Document type:** *Journal, Academic/Scholarly.*
Related titles: Online - full text ed.: ISSN 1662-1352. 2007.
—**CCC.**
Published by: (Bundesamt fuer Verbraucherschutz und Lebensmittelsicherheit/Federal Office for Consumer Protection and Food Safety DEU), Birkhaeuser Verlag AG (Subsidiary of: Springer Science+Business Media), Viaduktstr 42, Postfach 133, Basel, 4051, Switzerland. TEL 41-61-2050707, FAX 41-61-2050799, info@birkhauser.ch, http://www.birkhauser.ch.

BAD TOELZ AKTUELL; Informationen und Veranstaltungen. *see* TRAVEL AND TOURISM

BAGIMLILIK DERGISI/JOURNAL OF DEPENDENCE. *see* DRUG ABUSE AND ALCOHOLISM

BAN NI TONGXING/COMPANION. *see* TRANSPORTATION—Roads And Traffic

363.192 GBR ISSN 1460-3136
BARBOUR INDEX FOOD SAFETY BRIEFING. Text in English. 1991. m. bk.rev. **Document type:** *Bulletin, Abstract/Index.* **Description:** Provides summaries of newly published U K and E C legislation, reports, and other authoritative and official publications on food safety and hygiene and related issues.
Formerly (until 1997): Food Safety Briefing (0964-9158)
Related titles: Diskette ed.; Online - full text ed.: ISSN 1743-2545. GBP 150.
Published by: Barbour (Subsidiary of: C M P Information Ltd.), Hinderton Pt, Lloyd Dr, Cheshire Oaks, Cheshire CH65 9HQ, United Kingdom. TEL 44-1344-899300, barbour-cmc@cmpi.biz, http://www.barbour-ehs.com.

BASIC BIEN-ETRE. *see* BEAUTY CULTURE

363.1799 BEL ISSN 0250-5010
QC795.32.S3 CODEN: ABVSDZ
BELGISCHE VERENIGING VOOR STRALINGSBESCHERMING. ANNALEN/ASSOCIATION BELGE DE RADIOPROTECTION. ANNALES. Text in Dutch, French. 1976. q. EUR 50 domestic; EUR 60 in the European Union; EUR 65 elsewhere (effective 2004).
Indexed: INIS AtomInd.
Published by: Belgische Vereniging voor Stalingsbescherming/Association Belge de Radioprotection, Wetenschappelijk Instituut Volksgezondheid Louis Pasteur, Juliette Wytsmanstraat 13, Brussels, 1050, Belgium. office@bvsabr.be, http://www.bvsabr.be.

613 NLD ISSN 2210-9722
▼ **BEM!.** Text in Dutch. 2010. 8/yr. EUR 29.50 (effective 2010). adv. **Document type:** *Magazine, Consumer.*
Published by: BEM! Publishers bv, Koopmanslaan 3, Doetinchem, 7005 BK, Netherlands. TEL 31-314-373680. Eds. Anneke van der Linden TEL 31-72-5280222, Roos Schreuder-van der Linden. Pub. Roos Schreuder-van der Linden. Adv. contact Anita Hoenderken TEL 31-314-373683.

362.2 NLD ISSN 1879-8721
HET BESLUIT. Text in Dutch. 1994. q. EUR 15 (effective 2010). **Document type:** *Bulletin.*
Formerly (until 2010): De Einder (1383-8083)
Published by: Stichting De Einder, Postbus 32, Son, 5690 AA, Netherlands. TEL 31-6-54350232, info@deeinder.nl.

613 NLD ISSN 2210-8513
DE BETEREWERELD. Text in Dutch. bi-m. adv. **Document type:** *Newspaper, Consumer.*
Published by: Stichting De Betere Wereld, Keizersgracht 253, Amsterdam, 1016 EB, Netherlands. TEL 31-20-5285093, FAX 31-20-5286959, http://www.debeterewereld.nl. Eds. Erwin Polderman, Nanny Schutte, Almar Fernhout. R&P Erwin Polderman. Adv. contact Minke de Kruijff. page EUR 9,995; 275 x 395.

362.1 613.7 AUS
BETTER HEALTH. Text in English. 1999. irreg. **Document type:** *Magazine, Consumer.*
Published by: Health Insurance Commission, PO Box 1001, Tuggeranong DC, ACT 2901, Australia. TEL 61-2-61246333, FAX 61-2-61246100, hic.info@hic.gov.au, http://www.hic.gov.au/.

363.7 POL ISSN 0867-4752
BEZPIECZENSTWO JADROWE I OCHRONA RADIOLOGICZNA. Text in Polish. 1989. q. free. **Document type:** *Bulletin.*
Published by: Panstwowa Agencja Atomistyki/National Atomic Energy Agency, ul. Konwaliowa 7A, Warsaw, 03194, Poland. TEL 48-22-6769120, FAX 48-22-6959815, tbia@paa.gov.pl. Ed. Leszek Mlynarczyk.

614 POL ISSN 1426-7918
BEZPIECZNA ZYWNOSC. Text in Polish. 1996. q.
Indexed: AgrLib.
Published by: Wydawnictwo Medyczne Borgis, ul Walbrzyska 3/5, Warsaw, 02739, Poland. wydawnictwo@borgis.pl. Circ: 5,000.

362.1 460 USA
BILINGUAL HANDBOOK FOR PUBLIC SAFETY PROFESSIONALS; a concise guide to fit into any memo book, pocket, briefcase. Text in English, Spanish. 1994. irreg. USD 23.95 includes audio cassette (effective 2000). **Document type:** *Handbook/Manual/Guide, Trade.* **Description:** Provides the means to communicate critical information on Spanish-speaking subjects in a variety of situations.
Published by: Gould Publications, Inc. (Subsidiary of: LexisNexis North America), 1333 North US Hwy 17-92, Longwood, FL 32750. TEL 800-533-1637, 877-374-2919, FAX 407-695-2906, criminaljustice@lexisnexis.com, http://www.gouldlaw.com.

363.32 303.625 364.1 USA ISSN 1558-6499
BIOSECURITY BULLETIN. Text in English. 1999. q. free (effective 2006).
Formerly (until Winter 2004): Biodefense Quarterly
Published by: University of Pittsbugh Medical Center, Center for Biosecurity, The Pier IV Bldg, 621 E Pratt St Ste 210, Baltimore, MD 21202. TEL 443-573-3304, FAX 443-573-3305.

363.34 USA ISSN 1559-7938
BIOTERRORISM AND OTHER PUBLIC HEALTH EMERGENCIES. Text in English. 2003. irreg., latest 2005. free (effective 2011). **Document type:** *Monographic series, Government.* **Description:** Proceedings from web conference call series designed to share the latest health services research findings, promising practices and other important information with State and local health officials and key health systems decisionmakers.
Published by: U.S. Department of Health and Human Services, Agency for Healthcare Research and Quality (A H R Q), 540 Gaither Rd, Ste 2000, Rockville, MD 20850. TEL 301-427-1104, info@ahrq.gov.

362.1 341.734 USA ISSN 1540-6164
BIOTERRORISM AND PUBLIC HEALTH; an internet resource guide. Text in English. 2002. a. USD 29.95 per issue (effective 2009). **Document type:** *Guide, Trade.* **Description:** Provides accurate sources of information on biological and chemical warfare.
Published by: Thomson P D R, Five Paragon Dr, Montvale, NJ 07645. TEL 888-227-6469, FAX 201-722-2680, TH.customerservice@thomson.com, http://www.pdr.net.

BIOTERRORISM WEEK. *see* POLITICAL SCIENCE—International Relations

614 CHE ISSN 0006-4629
BLAUES KREUZ. Variant title: Das Blaue Kreuz. Text in German. 1896. 10/yr. looseleaf. CHF 30 (effective 2006). bk.rev. illus. back issues avail. **Document type:** *Newsletter, Consumer.*
Related titles: Online - full text ed.
Published by: (Blue Cross of Switzerland), Blaukreuz Verlag, Lindenrain 5 A, PO Box 8957, Bern, 3001, Switzerland. TEL 41-31-3005863, FAX 41-31-3005865, verlag@blaueskreuz.ch, http://www.blaueskreuz.ch. Ed. Walter Liechti. Circ: 3,700.

614 DEU ISSN 0177-7165
BLICKPUNKT GESUNDHEITSAMT. Text in German. 1984. q. **Document type:** *Bulletin, Trade.*
Published by: Akademie fuer Oeffentliches Gesundheitswesen, Kanzlerstr 4, Duesseldorf, 40472, Germany. TEL 49-211-3109610, FAX 49-211-3109634, info@akademie-oegw.de.

344.04 USA ISSN 2150-3818
KF3821.A53
BLOOMBERG LAW REPORTS. HEALTH LAW. Text in English. 2008. m. USD 2,500 to non-members; free to members (effective 2009). **Document type:** *Report, Trade.*
Related titles: Online - full text ed.: ISSN 2152-9515.
Published by: Bloomberg Finance L.P., 499 Park Ave, New York, NY 10022. TEL 212-318-2200, FAX 212-980-4585, blaw_us@bloomberg.net, http://www.bloomberg.com. Ed. Jason M Brocks.

BO'GEON BOGJI PO'REOM/HEALTH AND WELFARE POLICY FORUM. *see* SOCIAL SERVICES AND WELFARE

362.1 KOR ISSN 1225-6315
BO'GEONHAG NONJIB/KOREAN JOURNAL OF PUBLIC HEALTH. Text in English, Korean. 1964. a. **Document type:** *Journal, Academic/Scholarly.*
Formerly (until 1977): Gonjun Bogen Jabji (0023-401X)
Published by: Daehan Bo'geon Hyeobhoe/Korean Public Health Association, Samseondong 2-ga, Seongbuk-gu, 42-12 Taegeuk Richibil # 201, Seoul, 136-043, Korea, S. TEL 82-2-9219520, FAX 82-2-9212035, kpha@khealth.org, http://khealth.org/.

614.49 BRA ISSN 1517-1159
RA644.A25
BOLETIM EPIDEMIOLOGICO AIDS. Text in Portuguese. 1969. s-m. free. stat.
Related titles: Online - full text ed.
Indexed: P30.
Published by: Ministerio da Saude, Esplanada dos Ministerios, Bloco G, Brasilia, DF 70058-900, Brazil. TEL 55-61-3211721, FAX 55-61-3213216, http://portal.saude.gov.br/saude/. Circ: 6,500.

614 VEN ISSN 1690-4648
RA644.M2
BOLETIN DE MALARIOLOGIA Y SALUD AMBIENTAL. Text in Spanish. 1961. s-a. **Document type:** *Journal, Academic/Scholarly.*
Formerly (until 2001): Direccion de Malariologia y Saneamiento Ambiental. Boletin (0304-5382)
Related titles: Online - full text ed.
Indexed: A34, A35, A36, A38, AgBio, AgrForAb, B23, BP, CABA, E12, F08, F12, GH, H16, H17, IndVet, LT, N02, OR, P33, P37, P39, PN&I, R08, R12, RA&MP, RRTA, S13, S16, SCI, T05, TAR, VS, W07, W11, Z01.
Published by: Instituto de Altos Estudios de Salud Publica, Direccion de Malariologia y Saneamiento Ambiental, Ave Bermudez Sur, Edif. Malariologia, Maracay, Aragua 2101, Venezuela. TEL 58-243-2325633, FAX 58-243-2326933. Ed. Evelyn Escalona de Yanes.

614 MEX ISSN 0366-1709
BOLETIN EPIDEMIOLOGICO. Text in Spanish. 1937. a. free. stat. **Document type:** *Bulletin, Trade.*
Published by: (Jefatura de Servicios de Medicina Preventiva), Instituto Mexicano del Seguro Social, Avenida Paseo de la Reforma 476, Col Juarez, Mexico City, DF 06600, Mexico.

P

614.4 USA ISSN 0255-6669
BOLETIN EPIDEMIOLOGICO. Text in Spanish, English. 1972. q. free (effective 2010). back issues avail. **Document type:** *Bulletin, Academic/Scholarly.* **Description:** Contains information about international resolutions and recommendations related with disease control, that support the countries in the formulation of their policies, carry out their programs and reinforce their infrastructure.
Formerly (until 1980): Boletin informativo sobre el dengue, la fiebre amarilla y el aedes aegypti en las Americas (0250-8451); Supersedes in part (in 1980): Informe Epidemiologico Semanal (1014-2959)
Related titles: Online - full text ed.; ◆ English ed.: Epidemiological Bulletin. ISSN 0256-1859.
Indexed: IBR, IBZ.
Published by: Pan American Health Organization/Organizacion Panamericana de la Salud (Subsidiary of: World Health Organization/ Organisation Mondiale de la Sante), 525 23rd St, NW, Washington, DC 20037. TEL 202-974-3000, FAX 202-974-3663, paho@pmds.com, http://www.paho.org.

362.1 ARG ISSN 1851-4014
BOLETIN EPIDEMIOLOGICO PERIODICO. Text in Spanish. 2002. m.
Published by: Ministerio de Salud y Ambiente de la Nacion, Direccion de Epidemiologia, Ave 6 de Julio 1025 8o. Piso, Buenos Aires, 1337, Argentina. http://www.direpi.vigia.org.ar/.

362.1 ESP ISSN 1135-6286
BOLETIN EPIDEMIOLOGICO SEMANAL. Text in Spanish. 1993. w. **Document type:** *Journal, Academic/Scholarly.*
Formerly (until 1994): Boletin Epidemiologico y Microbiologico (1133-8210); Which was formed by the merger of (1932-1993): Boletin Epidemiologico Semanal (0210-1653); (1979-1992): Boletin Microbiologico Semanal (1131-0367)
Related titles: Online - full text ed.
Indexed: A34, A35, A36, AgBio, CABA, E12, GH, H17, IndVet, LT, N02, N04, P33, P37, P39, PN&I, R08, R12, R13, RM&VM, RRTA, T05, TAR, VS.
—CCC.
Published by: Instituto de Salud Carlos III, Centro Nacional de Epidemiologia, Sinesio Delgado, 6, Madrid, 28029, Spain. TEL 34-91-3877802, FAX 34-91-3877816, otello@isciii.es.

614.4 616.9 CUB ISSN 1028-5083
BOLETIN EPIDEMIOLOGICO SEMANAL. Text in Spanish. 1991. w.
Related titles: Online - full text ed.: ISSN 1682-6914. 1997.
Published by: (Cuba. Ministerio de Salud Publica), Instituto "Pedro Kouri", Marianao 13, Apdo Postal 601, Havana, Cuba. TEL 53-7-22043, ciipk@ipk.sld.cu, http://www.sld.cu/instituciones/ipk.

614 USA ISSN 1086-4520
BORDER EPIDEMIOLOGICAL BULLETIN/BOLETIN EPIDEMIOLOGICO FRONTERIZO. Text in English, Spanish. 1975. bi-m. free. **Document type:** *Bulletin.* **Description:** Covers U.S.-Mexico border public health and epidemiology issues.
Published by: Pan American Health Organization, U.S. - Mexico Border Field Office, 5400 Suncrest Dr, Ste C-4, El Paso, TX 79912. TEL 915-845-5950, FAX 915-845-4361, mail@fep.paho.org. Ed. Dr. Joaquin Salcedo.

614.84 JPN ISSN 0006-7873
BOSAI/DISASTER PREVENTION. Text in Japanese. 1947. bi-m. adv. **Document type:** *Journal, Academic/Scholarly.*
Indexed: AJEE.
Published by: Tokyo Rengo Boka Kyokai/Tokyo Consolidated Fire Prevention Association, 1-3-5 Otemachi, Chiyoda-ku, Tokyo, 100-8141, Japan. TEL 81-3-32124010, FAX 81-3-32850460, renbou@atlas.plala.or.jp, http://business4.plala.or.jp/renbou/top.htm. Circ: 12,000.

BOSAI KAGAKU GIJUTSU KENKYUJO KENKYU HOKOKU. *see* EARTH SCIENCES

BOSAI KAGAKU GIJUTSU KENKYUJO KENKYU SHIRYO/NATIONAL RESEARCH INSTITUTE FOR EARTH SCIENCE AND DISASTER PREVENTION. TECHNICAL NOTE. *see* EARTH SCIENCES

BOSAI KAGAKU GIJUTSU KENKYUJO NENPO/NATIONAL RESEARCH INSTITUTE FOR EARTH SCIENCE AND DISASTER PREVENTION. ANNUAL REPORT. *see* EARTH SCIENCES

BOTSWANA. CENTRAL STATISTICS OFFICE. HEALTH STATISTICS REPORT. *see* MEDICAL SCIENCES—Abstracting, Bibliographies, Statistics

BRIEFINGS ON HOSPITAL SAFETY; the newsletter for hospital safety committees. *see* HEALTH FACILITIES AND ADMINISTRATION

362.1 USA ISSN 1545-4053
BRIEFINGS ON INFECTION CONTROL. Text in English. 1987. m. USD 349 combined subscription (print & online eds.) (effective 2011). **Document type:** *Newsletter, Trade.*
Related titles: Online - full text ed.: ISSN 1942-2954.
Indexed: A26, H11, I05, P21, P24, P48, P50, P52, P56, PQC.
—CCC.
Published by: H C Pro, Inc., 200 Hoods Ln, PO Box 1168, Marblehead, MA 01945. TEL 781-639-1872, 800-650-6787, FAX 781-639-7857, 800-639-8511, customerservice@hcpro.com, http://www.hcpro.com. Pub. Emily Sheahan.

BRIEFINGS ON PATIENT SAFETY. *see* HEALTH FACILITIES AND ADMINISTRATION

362.1 351 CAN ISSN 1499-4224
BRITISH COLUMBIA. LEGISLATIVE ASSEMBLY. SELECT STANDING COMMITTEE ON HEALTH. REPORT OF PROCEEDINGS (HANSARD). Text in English. 2001. irreg. **Document type:** *Proceedings, Trade.*
Published by: Legislative Assembly of British Columbia, Select Standing Committee on Health, Office of the Clerk of Committees, Rm 224, Parliament Bldgs, Victoria, BC, Canada. TEL 250-356-2933, 877-428-8337, FAX 250-356-8172, healthcommittee@leg.bc.ca, http://www.leg.bc.ca/cmt/38thparl/session-3/health/index.htm.

614.8 CAN ISSN 1499-0350
BRITISH COLUMBIA. MINISTRY OF HEALTH AND MINISTRY RESPONSIBLE FOR SENIORS. ANNUAL PERFORMANCE REPORT. Text in English. a. free. **Document type:** *Government.*
Former titles (until 2001): British Columbia. Ministry of Health and Ministry Responsible for Seniors. Annual Report (1203-6056); (until 1993): British Columbia. Ministry of Health and Ministry Responsible for Seniors. Ministry of Health Annual Report (1203-6099); (until 1990): British Columbia. Ministry of Health. Annual Report (0706-4810); (until 1977): British Columbia. Department of Health. Annual Report (0701-5372); Which was formed by the merger of (1949-1974): British Columbia Hospital Insurance Service. Annual Report (0701-5380); (1968-1975): Medical Services Commission of British Columbia. Annual Report (0317-7602); (1968-1974): Province of British Columbia. Mental Health Branch. Annual Report (0383-3526); Which was formerly (until 1968): Province of British Columbia. Mental Health Services Branch. Annual Report (0524-5486); (until 1959): Province of British Columbia. Mental Health Services. Annual Report (0407-2251); (until 1951): Province of British Columbia. Mental Hospitals. Annual Report
Published by: British Columbia, Ministry of Health, 1515 Blanshard St, 7th Fl, Victoria, BC V8W 3C8, Canada. TEL 604-387-2323. Circ: 4,000.

BRITISH COLUMBIA. MINISTRY OF PUBLIC SAFETY AND SOLICITOR GENERAL. GAMING POLICY AND ENFORCEMENT BRANCH. ANNUAL REPORT. *see* SPORTS AND GAMES—Outdoor Life

614 FRA ISSN 0245-7466
RA643.7.F8
BULLETIN EPIDEMIOLOGIQUE HEBDOMADAIRE. Abbreviated title: B E H. Text in French. w. EUR 62 (effective 2009). **Document type:** *Bulletin, Trade.* **Description:** For the practitioner; provides practical information, covers new diseases and recommendations for travelers.
Former titles: France. Ministere des la Sante et de la Famille. Bulletin Hebdomdaire d'Information Epidemiologique (0245-7474); France. Ministere des Affaires Sociales et de la Solidarite Nationale. Bulletin Epidemiologique; France. Ministere de la Sante et de la Famille. Bulletin Epidemiologique; France. Ministere de la Sante et de la Famille. Bulletin Epidemiologique
Related titles: Online - full text ed.: ISSN 1953-8030.
Indexed: A34, A35, A36, AgBio, BP, CABA, D01, E12, F08, FR, GH, H16, H17, IndVet, LT, N02, N03, P32, P33, P37, P39, P40, PN&I, R07, R08, R12, RM&VM, RRTA, S13, S16, SCOPUS, T05, VS, W10, W11.
—BLDSC (2853.440000), Infotrieve, INIST. **CCC.**
Published by: Institut de Veille Sanitaire, 12 Rue du Val d'Osne, Saint-Maurice, 94415 Cedex, France. TEL 33-1-41796700, FAX 33-1-41796767. Circ: 650.

614 DEU ISSN 1436-9990
RA421
➤ **BUNDESGESUNDHEITSBLATT - GESUNDHEITSFORSCHUNG - GESUNDHEITSSCHUTZ.** Text in German. 1886. m. EUR 132.71, USD 147 combined subscription to institutions (print & online eds.) (effective 2012). adv. bk.rev. bibl.; charts; stat. index. **Document type:** *Journal, Academic/Scholarly.* **Description:** Covers all aspects of public health care services and programs.
Former titles (until 1997): Bundesgesundheitsblatt (0007-5914); (until 1958): Reichsgesundheitsblatt (0370-4378); (until 1925): Veroeffentlichungen des Reichsgesundheitsamtes (0372-6541); (until 1919): Veroeffentlichungen des Kaiserlichen Gesundheitsamtes (0177-9575)
Related titles: Online - full text ed.: ISSN 1437-1588 (from IngentaConnect).
Indexed: A22, A26, CISA, DokArb, E01, EMBASE, ExcerpMed, F09, FS&TA, INIS AtomInd, IPackAb, MEDLINE, P&BA, P30, PST, R10, Reac, SCI, SCOPUS, W07.
—BLDSC (2930.200200), GNLM, IE, Infotrieve, Ingenta. **CCC.**
Published by: (Germany. Robert-Koch-Institut), Springer (Subsidiary of: Springer Science+Business Media), Tiergartenstr 17, Heidelberg, 69121, Germany. TEL 49-6221-4870, FAX 49-6221-345229. Ed. Heidemarie Rohdewohld. Adv. contact Stephan Kroeck TEL 49-30-827875739. Circ: 2,300. **Subscr. to:** Springer Distribution Center, Kundenservice Zeitschriften, Haberstr 7, Heidelberg 69126, Germany. TEL 49-6221-3454303, FAX 49-6221-3454229, subscriptions@springer.com; Springer New York LLC, Journal Fulfillment, PO Box 2485, Secaucus, NJ 07096. TEL 201-348-4033, 800-777-4643, FAX 201-348-4505, journals-ny@springer.com, http://www.springer.com. **Co-sponsors:** Bundesinstitut fuer Gesundheitlichen Verbraucherschutz und Veterinaermedizin; Institut fuer Wasser-, Boden- und Lufthygiene des Umweltbundesamtes; Bundesinstitut fuer Arzneimittel und Medizinprodukte.

362.1 CAN ISSN 1910-4006
BURNTWOOD REGIONAL HEALTH AUTHORITY. ANNUAL REPORT. Text in English. 199?. a., latest 2005. **Document type:** *Report, Trade.*
Published by: Burntwood Regional Health Authority, 867 Thompson Dr S, Thompson, MB R8N 1Z4, Canada. TEL 204-677-5350, FAX 204-677-5366, brha@brha.mb.ca, http://www.thompson.ca/dbs/brha/index.cfm.

363.78 USA
BUZZ WORDS. Text in English. bi-m. back issues avail. **Document type:** *Newsletter, Trade.*
Related titles: Online - full content ed.
Published by: Florida Mosquito Control Association, Inc., PO Box 358630, Gainesville, FL 32635-8630. TEL 352-281-3020, FAX 352-334-2286, http://www.floridamosquito.org/index.html. Ed. Roxane Connelly TEL 772-778-7200 x172.

C C E MAGAZINE. *see* HEALTH FACILITIES AND ADMINISTRATION

C D R WEEKLY (ONLINE). (Communicable Disease Report) *see* MEDICAL SCIENCES—Communicable Diseases

362.1 CAN ISSN 1914-4407
C-ENTERNET ANNUAL REPORT. Text in English. 2006. a. free (effective 2011). back issues avail. **Document type:** *Report, Government.*
Related titles: Online - full text ed.: ISSN 1924-7028. free (effective 2011); Ed.: ISSN 1924-701X. free (effective 2011).
Published by: Public Health Agency of Canada/Agence de Sante Publique du Canada, 1015, Arlington St, AL 6501H, Winnipeg, MB R3E 3R2, Canada. TEL 204-789-2000, FAX 204-789-7878.

362.1 CAN ISSN 1914-4415
C-ENTERNET RAPPORT ANNUEL. Text in French. 2006. a. free (effective 2011). **Document type:** *Report, Government.* **Description:** Examines changes in trends in human enteric diseases and levels of exposure to food borne pathogens, interpretations of laboratory data and data useful in epidemiological contexts of public health, water management and agribusiness.
Related titles: Online - full text ed.: ISSN 1924-701X. free (effective 2011).
Published by: Public Health Agency of Canada/Agence de Sante Publique du Canada, 1015, Arlington St, AL 6501H, Winnipeg, MB R3E 3R2, Canada. TEL 204-789-2000, FAX 204-789-7878, http://www.phac-aspc.gc.ca.

C F I A'S BIOTECHNOLOGY HIGHLIGHTS REPORT. *see* BIOLOGY—Biotechnology

362.1 CAN ISSN 1912-1431
C H E P A IN REVIEW. (Centre for Health Economics and Policy Analysis) Text in English. 2002. a. **Document type:** *Newsletter, Trade.*
Media: Online - full text.
Published by: McMaster University, Centre for Health Economics and Policy Analysis, Health Sciences Centre 3H1, 1200 Main St West, Hamilton, ON L8N 3Z5, Canada. TEL 905-525-9140 ext 22122, FAX 905-546-5211, chepa@mcmaster.ca.

613 CAN ISSN 1201-0383
C I H I DIRECTIONS. Text in English. 1990. 3/yr. (June, Oct. & Feb.). **Document type:** *Newsletter.*
Formerly (until 1994): Info M I S (1200-4669)
Published by: Canadian Institute for Health Information/Institut Canadien d'Information sur la Sante, 377 Dalhousie St, Ste 200, Ottawa, ON K1N 9N8, Canada. TEL 613-241-7860, FAX 613-241-8120, http://www.cihi.ca.

614.5 USA ISSN 1076-8025
LB3051
C L E A R EXAM REVIEW. Text in English. 1982. s-a. looseleaf. USD 30 (effective 2008). adv. bk.rev. back issues avail. **Document type:** *Guide, Trade.* **Description:** Testing issues for licensure of professional and occupational trends.
Published by: Council on Licensure, Enforcement and Regulation, 403 Marquis Ave, Ste 200, Lexington, KY 40502. TEL 859-269-1289, FAX 859-231-1943, aparfitt@mis.net. Circ: 600.

348.025 USA
C L E A R NEWS (ONLINE). Text in English. 1984. q. free to members (effective 2008). adv. back issues avail. **Document type:** *Newsletter.*
Formerly: C L E A R News (Print) (1076-8017)
Media: Online - full text.
Published by: Council on Licensure, Enforcement and Regulation, 403 Marquis Ave, Ste 200, Lexington, KY 40502. TEL 859-269-1289, FAX 859-231-1943, aparfitt@mis.net, http://www.clearhq.org. Ed. Lise Smith Peters.

616 USA ISSN 2151-1659
R11
▼ **C M I O;** information, evidence & effectiveness in medicine. Text in English. 2009. bi-m. free to qualified personnel (effective 2010). adv. back issues avail.; reprints avail. **Document type:** *Magazine, Consumer.* **Description:** Provides practical, tactical and progressive insight to exploit enterprise knowledge resources in today's competitive healthcare marketplace.
Related titles: Online - full text ed.: free (effective 2009).
Published by: Trimed Media Group, Inc., 235 Promenade St, Ste 455, Providence, RI 02908. TEL 401-383-5660, FAX 401-383-3896, sales@trimedmedia.com, http://www.trimedmedia.com. Pub. Jack Spears TEL 410-383-5660 ext 202. Adv. contact Michelle Tonner TEL 401-533-1062. B&W page USD 9,495, color page USD 10,395; trim 8.25 x 10.5. Circ: 10,000.

C O M A D E M INTERNATIONAL. PROCEEDINGS. (Condition Monitoring and Diagnostic Engineering Management) *see* TECHNOLOGY: COMPREHENSIVE WORKS

C O N C A W E REVIEW. (Conservation of Clean Air and Water in Europe) *see* ENVIRONMENTAL STUDIES

613.7 CAN ISSN 0703-5624
C P H A HEALTH DIGEST. Text in English. 1977. q. free to members. **Document type:** *Newsletter.*
Related titles: French ed.: A C S P Selection Sante.
Published by: Canadian Public Health Association, 1565 Carling Ave, Ste 400, Ottawa, ON K1Z 8R1, Canada. TEL 613-725-3769, FAX 613-725-9826. Ed. Gerald Dafoe. Circ: 3,000.

362.1 FRA ISSN 2107-6588
▼ **C R E A I P A C A ET CORSE. LA LETTRE.** (Centre Inter-Regional d'Etude, d'Action et d'Information Provence Alpes Cote d'Azur) Text in French. 2010. bi-m. **Document type:** *Newsletter, Consumer.*
Media: Online - full text.
Published by: Centre Inter-Regional d'Etude, d'Action et d'Information Provence Alpes Cote d'Azur et Corse, 6, Rue d'Arcole, Marseilles, 13006, France. TEL 33-4-96100660, FAX 33-4-96100669, contact@creai-pacacorse.com, http://www.creai-pacacorse.com/index.php.

362.1 TZA ISSN 0856-4043
C R H C S NEWS. (Commonwealth Regional Health Community Secretariat) Text in English. 1991. s-a. **Document type:** *Newsletter, Trade.*
Indexed: P30.
Published by: Commonwealth Regional Health Community for East, Central and Southern Africa (C R H C - E C S A), 3d Fl, Safari Business Centre, 46 Boma Rd, Arusha, Tanzania. TEL 255-27-2508362, FAX 255-27-2508292, info@crhcs.or.tz, http://www.crhcs.or.tz.

362.1 613.7 PRT ISSN 1647-0559
CADERNOS DE SAUDE. Text in Portuguese. 2008. s-a. **Document type:** *Journal, Academic/Scholarly.*
Published by: Universidade Catolica Portuguesa, Instituto de Ciencias da Saude, Edificio da Biblioteca Joao Paulo II, Palma de Cima, Lisbon, 1649-023, Portugal. TEL 351-21-7214147, FAX 351-21-269820, http://www.ics.lisboa.ucp.pt.

614 BRA ISSN 0102-311X
RA421 CODEN: CSAQEW
➤ **CADERNOS DE SAUDE PUBLICA/REPORTS IN PUBLIC HEALTH.** Text in Portuguese, Spanish, English. 1980. bi-m. BRL 75 domestic to individuals; USD 120 foreign to individuals; BRL 200 domestic to institutions; USD 200 foreign to institutions (effective 2005). adv. bk.rev.; software rev.; video rev.; Website rev. abstr.; illus.; maps. 300 p./no.; back issues avail. **Document type:** *Journal, Academic/Scholarly.* **Description:** Publishes original research reports and reviews on all aspects of public health, international health, preventive medicine, epidemiology, public health services, health policy and planning, and social sciences in health (including anthropology, sociology, and psychology).
Formed by the 1985 merger of: Cadernos de Saude Publica. Serie Ensaio (0101-2231); Cadernos de Saude Publica. Serie Pesquisa (0101-5729); Cadernos de Saude Publica. Serie Documento (0102-3128)
Related titles: Online - full text ed.: ISSN 1678-4464. free (effective 2011).
Indexed: A22, A34, A35, A36, A38, AgBio, B23, BA, C01, C25, CA, CABA, D01, E12, EMBASE, ExcerpMed, F08, F09, F11, F12, GH, H16, H17, IndMed, IndVet, LT, MEDLINE, MaizeAb, N02, N03, OR, P30, P33, P37, P38, P39, PAIS, PN&I, R07, R08, R10, R11, R12, RA&MP, RM&VM, RRTA, Reac, S02, S03, S12, S13, S16, SCI, SCOPUS, SOPODA, SSA, SSCI, SociolAb, SoyAb, T02, T05, TriticAb, VS, W07, W09, W10, W11.
—BLDSC (2947.170850), GNLM, IE, Infotrieve, Ingenta.
Published by: Escola Nacional de Saude Publica, Rua Leopoldo Bulhoes, 1480, Terreo, Bonsucesso, Rio De Janeiro, RJ 21041-210, Brazil. TEL 55-21-2598-2511, FAX 55-21-2598-2737. Eds. Carlos E A Coimbra Jr., Luis David Castiel. R&P, Adv. contact Maria Angela Cancado TEL 55-21-25982511. B&W page USD 450, color page USD 1,400; 180 x 250. Circ: 1,700 (paid); 300 (controlled).

614 344.440 FRA ISSN 1774-9832
LES CAHIERS DE DROIT DE LA SANTE DU SUD-EST; juridiques, historiques et prospectifs. Text in French. 2004. s-a. EUR 46; EUR 23 per issue (effective 2006). **Document type:** *Monographic series, Trade.*
Published by: Presses Universitaires d'Aix-Marseille, 3 av Robert Schuman, Aix-en-Provence, 13628, France.

CAHIERS DE SOCIOLOGIE ET DE DEMOGRAPHIE MEDICALES. *see* POPULATION STUDIES

CAHIERS D'ETUDES ET DE RECHERCHES FRANCOPHONES. SANTE. *see* MEDICAL SCIENCES

362.1 690 USA ISSN 1931-518X
KFC586.B8
CAL/O S H A CONSTRUCTION AND ELECTRICAL SAFETY ORDERS. (Occupational Safety and Health Administration) Text in English. 19??. irreg. USD 42.98 per issue (effective 2011). 288 p./no.; **Document type:** *Handbook/Manual/Guide, Trade.*
Related titles: CD-ROM ed.: USD 59.88 per issue (effective 2011).
Published by: Mangan Communications, Inc, 315 W 4th St, Davenport, IA 52801. TEL 563-323-6245, 877-626-2666, FAX 888-398-6245, safetyinfo@mancomm.com.

CALIFORNIA FIRE SERVICE. *see* FIRE PREVENTION

362.1 796.5 IRL ISSN 2009-1060
CALL OUT. Text in English. 2007. q. back issues avail. **Document type:** *Newsletter.*
Published by: Irish Mountain Rescue Association, 13 Joyce Way, Park West Business Park, Dublin, 12, Ireland. TEL 353-23-59822. Ed. Paul Whiting.

CAMBRIDGESHIRE COUNTY COUNCIL. ROAD SAFETY PLAN (YEAR). *see* TRANSPORTATION—Roads And Traffic

363 USA
CAMPUS SAFETY JOURNAL. Text in English. q. **Document type:** *Journal, Consumer.*
Published by: Bricepac, Inc., 12228 Venice Blvd, 541, PO Box 66515, Los Angeles, CA 90066. TEL 310-390-5277, FAX 310-390-4777, http://www.bricepac.com.

CAMPUS SECURITY REPORT (HORSHAM). *see* EDUCATION—School Organization And Administration

614 610 CAN ISSN 1188-4169
CODEN: CDWSE9
CANADA COMMUNICABLE DISEASE REPORT. Text in English, French. 1975. bi-m. CAD 110 domestic; USD 147 foreign (effective 2007). charts; illus.; stat. index. Supplement avail. **Document type:** *Newsletter, Trade.* **Description:** Provides information on infectious and other diseases for surveillance purposes.
Former titles (until 1992): Canada Diseases Weekly Report (0382-232X); Epidemiological Bulletin (0425-1474)
Related titles: Online - full text ed.: ISSN 1481-8531. free (effective 2004); ◆ French ed.: Releve des Maladies Transmissibles au Canada.
Indexed: A22, A34, A36, BioDAb, C03, C06, C07, CABA, CBCARef, D01, E12, EMBASE, ExcerpMed, GH, H17, IndMed, IndVet, LT, MEDLINE, N02, N03, N04, P30, P32, P33, P39, P40, P48, P50, P52, P56, PQC, R08, R10, R12, RM&VM, RRTA, Reac, SCOPUS, T05, VS, W11.
—BLDSC (3016.417400), GNLM, IE, Infotrieve, Ingenta. **CCC.**
Published by: (Canadian Medical Association/Association Medicale Canadienne, Canada. Department of National Health and Welfare, Laboratory Centre for Disease Control), Public Health Agency of Canada/Agence de Sante Publique du Canada, 0904A, Buock Claxton Bldg, Tunney's Pasture, Ottawa, ON K1A OK9, Canada. TEL 613-957-2991, FAX 613-941-5366, info@hc-sc.gc.ca, http://www.hc-sc.gc.ca. Ed., R&P Eleanor Paulson TEL 613-957-1788. Circ: 2,500.

613 CAN ISSN 1483-4618
CANADA EARTHSAVER. Text in English. 1990. bi-m. **Document type:** *Newsletter.*
Former titles (until 1995): E Q (1483-460X); (until 1994): Choices (Vancouver) (0846-3824)
Published by: EarthSave Canada, SPEC Bldg, 2150 Maple St, Vancouverb, BC V6J 3T3, Canada. TEL 604-731-5885, FAX 604-731-5805, office@earthsave.bc.ca. Ed. Nancy Callan.

CANADA. HEALTH CANADA. PERFORMANCE REPORT. *see* PUBLIC ADMINISTRATION

362.1 CAN ISSN 1719-3605
CANADA. NOVA SCOTIA DEPARTMENT OF HEALTH. MINISTERS' REPORT TO NOVA SCOTIANS. Text in English. 2004. a., latest 2005. **Document type:** *Government.*
Published by: Nova Scotia Department of Health, PO Box 488, Halifax, NS B3J 2R8, Canada. TEL 902-424-5818, 800-387-6665, FAX 902-424-0730, DOHWEB@gov.ns.ca, http://www.gov.ns.ca/health/default.htm.

362.1 CAN ISSN 1719-413X
CANADA. NOVA SCOTIA DEPARTMENT OF HEALTH. NOTIFIABLE DISEASES IN NOVA SCOTIA. SURVEILLANCE REPORT. Text in English. 2002. a., latest 2004. **Document type:** *Government.*
Formerly: Reportable Diseases in Nova Scotia. Surveillance Report (1713-4439)
Published by: Nova Scotia Department of Health, PO Box 488, Halifax, NS B3J 2R8, Canada. TEL 902-424-5818, 800-387-6665, FAX 902-424-0730, DOHWEB@gov.ns.ca, http://www.gov.ns.ca/health/default.htm.

362.1 CAN ISSN 1916-3991
CANADA. PUBLIC SAFETY CANADA. RESEARCH SUMMARY. Text in English. 1996. bi-m. back issues avail. **Document type:** *Monographic series, Trade.*
Former titles (until 2007): Canada. Public Safety and Emergency Preparedness Canada. Research Summary (1713-1499); (until 2004): Canada. Solicitor General Canada. Research Summary (1208-3119)
Related titles: Online - full text ed.: ISSN 1916-4009. free (effective 2011).
Published by: Public Safety Canada, 269 Laurier Ave W, Ottawa, ON K1A 0P8, Canada. TEL 613-944-4875, 800-830-3118, communications@ps.gc.ca.

362.1969792009 CAN ISSN 1491-5030
CANADA'S REPORT ON HIV/AIDS. Variant title: Strategic Approaches: Renewing the Response. Text in English. 1994. a. **Document type:** *Government.*
Formerly (until 1998): National AIDS Strategy, Phase II. Progress Report (1491-3259)
Related titles: Online - full content ed.
Published by: Public Health Agency of Canada/Agence de Sante Publique du Canada, 0904A, Buock Claxton Bldg, Tunney's Pasture, Ottawa, ON K1A OK9, Canada. TEL 613-957-2991, FAX 613-941-5366, info@hc-sc.gc.ca, http://www.hc-sc.gc.ca. **Dist. by:** Canadian HIV/AIDS Information Centre, 1565 Carling Ave, Ste 400, Ottawa, ON K1Z 8R1, Canada. TEL 613-725-3434, 877-999-7740, FAX 613-725-1205, aidssida@cpha.ca.

353.997 CAN ISSN 1487-2145
TX531
CANADIAN FOOD INSPECTION AGENCY. ANNUAL REPORT. Text in English. 1998. a.
Published by: Canadian Food Inspection Agency/Agence Canadienne d'Inspection des Aliments, 59 Camelot Dr, Ottawa, ON K1A 0Y9, Canada. TEL 613-225-2342, 800-442-2342, FAX 613-228-6125, cfiamaster@inspection.gc.ca.

610 CAN ISSN 1496-5372
CANADIAN HEALTH SERVICES RESEARCH FOUNDATION. LINKS. Text in English, French. 1997. q. **Document type:** *Journal, Trade.*
Formerly (until 2001): Quid Novi? (1488-9315)
—**CCC.**
Published by: Canadian Health Services Research Foundation/Fondation Canadienne de la Recherche sur les Services de Sante, 1565 Carling Ave, Ste 700, Ottawa, ON K1Z 8R1, Canada. TEL 613-728-2238, FAX 613-728-3527, http://www.chsrf.ca/home_e.php.

362.1 CAN ISSN 1910-8389
CANADIAN INSTITUTE FOR HEALTH INFORMATION. ANNUAL REPORT (ONLINE EDITION). Text in English. 200?. a. **Document type:** *Report, Trade.*
Media: Online - full text. **Related titles:** ◆ Print ed.: Canadian Institute for Health Information. Annual Report (Print Edition). ISSN 1719-1955; French ed.: ISSN 1910-8400.
Published by: Canadian Institute for Health Information/Institut Canadien d'Information sur la Sante, 377 Dalhousie St, Ste 200, Ottawa, ON K1N 9N8, Canada. TEL 613-241-7860, FAX 613-241-8120, nursing@cihi.ca, http://www.cihi.ca.

362.1 CAN ISSN 1719-1955
CANADIAN INSTITUTE FOR HEALTH INFORMATION. ANNUAL REPORT (PRINT EDITION). Text in English. 199?. a., latest 2006. **Document type:** *Government.*
Related titles: ◆ Online - full text ed.: Canadian Institute for Health Information. Annual Report (Online Edition). ISSN 1910-8389; French ed.: ISSN 1717-5607.
Published by: Canadian Institute for Health Information/Institut Canadien d'Information sur la Sante, 377 Dalhousie St, Ste 200, Ottawa, ON K1N 9N8, Canada. TEL 613-241-7860, FAX 613-241-8120, http://www.cihi.ca.

362.1 CAN ISSN 1709-0709
CANADIAN INSTITUTE FOR HEALTH INFORMATION. PRODUCTS AND SERVICES CATALOGUE. Text in English. 1997. a., latest 2006. **Document type:** *Catalog, Consumer.*
Formerly (until 2001): Canadian Institute for Health Information. Catalogue (1482-9231)
Related titles: Online - full text ed.: ISSN 1719-8402; ◆ French ed.: Institut Canadien d'Information sur la Sante. Catalogue des Produits et Services. ISSN 1709-0717.
Published by: Canadian Institute for Health Information/Institut Canadien d'Information sur la Sante, 377 Dalhousie St, Ste 200, Ottawa, ON K1N 9N8, Canada. TEL 613-241-7860, FAX 613-241-8120, http://www.cihi.ca.

CANADIAN JOURNAL OF COMMUNITY MENTAL HEALTH (ONLINE)/REVUE CANADIENNE DE SANTE MENTALE COMMUNAUTAIRE. *see* PSYCHOLOGY

614 CAN ISSN 0008-4263
RA421 CODEN: CJPEA4
➤ **CANADIAN JOURNAL OF PUBLIC HEALTH/REVUE CANADIENNE DE SANTE PUBLIQUE.** Text in English. 1910. bi-m. CAD 100.58 domestic; CAD 108.10 domestic in NF, NS & NB; CAD 121 in United States; CAD 156 elsewhere; CAD 20.33 per issue domestic; CAD 21.85 per issue domestic in NF, NS & NB; CAD 25 per issue in United States; CAD 30 per issue elsewhere (effective 2004). adv. bk.rev. charts; illus. Index. 80 p./no. 3 cols./p.; reprints avail. **Document type:** *Journal, Academic/Scholarly.* **Description:** Covers all aspects of public health, preventive medicine, health promotion, and public policy related to health.
Former titles (until 1942): Canadian Public Health Journal (0319-2652); (until 1928): Public Health Journal (0319-2660); Canadian Therapeutist and Sanitary Engineer
Related titles: Microform ed.: (from PMC, PQC); Online - full text ed.
Indexed: A20, A22, A26, A33, A34, A36, ASCA, ASFA, AbAn, AddicA, AgeL, B21, BDM&CN, BiolDig, C03, C06, C07, C08, C25, CA, CABA, CBCARef, CBPI, CINAHL, CPerI, CTA, ChemAb, ChemoAb, CurCont, D01, DentInd, DokArb, E08, E12, EMBASE, ESPM, ExcerpMed, F08, F09, F12, FR, FS&TA, FamI, G08, GH, H&SSA, H12, H13, H17, I05, INI, IndMed, IndVet, LT, MCR, MEDLINE, N02, N03, NRN, NSA, OR, P06, P10, P20, P21, P22, P24, P27, P30, P33, P34, P39, P45, P48, P50, P52, P53, P54, P56, PEI, PHN&I, PQC, PollutAb, R07, R08, R10, R12, RA&MP, RRTA, Reac, RiskAb, S02, S03, S09, S12, S13, S16, SAA, SCOPUS, SD, SSCI, SportS, T02, T05, THA, VS, VirolAbstr, W07, W09, W11.
—BLDSC (3035.000000), GNLM, IE, Infotrieve, Ingenta, INIST, Linda Hall. **CCC.**
Published by: Canadian Public Health Association, 1565 Carling Ave, Ste 400, Ottawa, ON K1Z 8R1, Canada. TEL 613-725-3769, FAX 613-725-9826. Adv. contact Karen Craven. Circ: 3,000.

➤ **CANADIAN MENTAL HEALTH ASSOCIATION. ANNUAL REPORT/ASSOCIATION CANADIENNE POUR LA SANTE MENTALE. RAPPORT ANNUEL.** *see* PSYCHOLOGY

362.1 CAN ISSN 1719-4903
CANADIAN PATIENT SAFETY INSTITUTE. ANNUAL REPORT. Text in English. 2005. a. **Document type:** *Report, Consumer.*
Related titles: French ed.: Institut Canadien pour la Securite des Patients. Rapport Annuel.
Published by: Canadian Patient Safety Institute/Institut Canadien pour la Securite des Patients, 100- 1730 St. Laurent Blvd., Ottawa, ON K1G 5L1, Canada. TEL 613-730-7322, FAX 613-730-7323, info@cpsi-icsp.ca, http://www.patientsafetyinstitute.ca/index.html.

362.1 CAN ISSN 1719-4067
LES CANADIENS ET LES CANADIENNES EN SANTE. Text in French. 2004. irreg. **Document type:** *Government.*
Media: Online - full text.
Published by: Health Canada/Sante Canada, 130, chemin Colonnade, IA 6501H, Ottawa, ON K1A 0K9, Canada. info@www.hc-sc.gc.ca, http://www.hc-sc.gc.ca.

CANCER CARE ONTARIO. ABORIGINAL CANCER CARE UNIT. NEWSLETTER. *see* MEDICAL SCIENCES—Oncology

362.1 NZL ISSN 1177-9659
CANCER CONTROL COUNCIL OF NEW ZEALAND. MAPPING PROGRESS. Text in English. 2007. a. **Document type:** *Journal, Trade.*
Related titles: Online - full text ed.: ISSN 1177-9675.
Published by: Cancer Control Council of New Zealand, PO Box 5013, Wellington, New Zealand. TEL 64-4-4700611, FAX 64-4-4962343, office@cancercontrolcouncil.govt.nz.

362.1 NZL ISSN 1177-9667
CANCER CONTROL COUNCIL OF NEW ZEALAND. SUMMARY MAPPING PROGRESS. Text in English. 2007. a. **Document type:** *Journal, Trade.*
Related titles: Online - full text ed.: ISSN 1178-1696.
Published by: Cancer Control Council of New Zealand, PO Box 5013, Wellington, New Zealand. TEL 64-4-4700611, FAX 64-4-4962343, office@cancercontrolcouncil.govt.nz.

CANTERBURY DISASTER SALVAGE TEAM. NEWSLETTER. *see* CIVIL DEFENSE

362.1 NZL ISSN 1176-3124
CANTERBURY DISTRICT HEALTH BOARD. DISTRICT ANNUAL PLAN. Text in English. 2003. a. **Document type:** *Government.*
Formerly: Canterbury District Health Board. Annual Plan (1176-1296)
Related titles: Online - full text ed.: ISSN 1177-9500.
Published by: Canterbury District Health Board, Level 2, H Block, The Princess Margaret Hospital, Cashmere Rd, PO Box 1600, Christchurch, New Zealand. TEL 64-3-3644103, FAX 64-3-3644101.

362.1 NZL ISSN 1176-2659
CANTERBURY DISTRICT HEALTH BOARD. STATEMENT OF INTENT. Text in English. 1996. a. **Document type:** *Government.* **Description:** Provides a high level focus on key financial and non-financial objectives and targets.
Formerly (until 2005): Canterbury Health. Statement of Intent (1172-7764)
Related titles: Online - full text ed.: ISSN 1177-9519.
Published by: Canterbury District Health Board, Level 2, H Block, The Princess Margaret Hospital, Cashmere Rd, PO Box 1600, Christchurch, New Zealand. TEL 64-3-3644106, FAX 64-3-3644101.

362.1 NZL ISSN 1176-0516
CANTERBURY DISTRICT HEALTH BOARD. STRATEGIC PLAN. Variant title: C D H B Strategic Plan. Text in English. 2002. triennial.
Related titles: Online - full text ed.: ISSN 1177-9527.
Published by: Canterbury District Health Board, Level 2, H Block, The Princess Margaret Hospital, Cashmere Rd, PO Box 1600, Christchurch, New Zealand. TEL 64-3-3644106, FAX 64-3-3644101.

362.1 NZL ISSN 1176-1288
CANTERBURY DISTRICT HEALTH BOARD. SUMMARY ANNUAL REPORT. Text in English. 2001. a. **Document type:** *Corporate.*
Related titles: Online - full text ed.: ISSN 1177-8202.
Published by: Canterbury District Health Board, Level 2, H Block, The Princess Margaret Hospital, Cashmere Rd, PO Box 1600, Christchurch, New Zealand. TEL 64-3-3644106, FAX 64-3-3644101.

362.1 NZL ISSN 1176-6883
CANTERBURY HEALTH NEEDS ASSESSMENT. Text in English. 2004. triennial. **Document type:** *Government.*
Related titles: Online - full text ed.

P

Published by: Canterbury District Health Board, Level 2, H Block, The Princess Margaret Hospital, Cashmere Rd, PO Box 1600, Christchurch, New Zealand. TEL 64-3-3644106, FAX 64-3-3644101.

362.1 NZL ISSN 1176-7669
CANTERBURY HEALTH NEEDS ASSESSMENT SUMMARY. Text in English. 2004. triennial. **Document type:** *Government.*
Related titles: Online - full text ed.
Published by: Canterbury District Health Board, Level 2, H Block, The Princess Margaret Hospital, Cashmere Rd, PO Box 1600, Christchurch, New Zealand. TEL 64-3-3644106, FAX 64-3-3644101.

362.1 ITA ISSN 1128-5524
CARE. COSTI DELL'ASSISTENZA E RISORSE ECONOMICHE. Text in Italian. 1999. q. **Document type:** *Journal, Trade.*
Related titles: Online - full text ed.: ISSN 2038-1794.
Published by: Il Pensiero Scientifico Editore, Via Panama 48, Rome, 00198, Italy. pensiero@pensiero.it, http://www.pensiero.it.

362.1 614.8 GBR ISSN 0045-5768
CARE ON THE ROAD. Text in English. 1972. bi-m. GBP 20 domestic to non-members; GBP 23.50 foreign to non-members; GBP 17.50 domestic to members; GBP 20.56 foreign to members (effective 2009). adv. bk.rev. illus.; stat. **Document type:** *Journal, Consumer.* **Description:** Covers road safety, relating to drivers, motorcyclists, cyclists and pedestrians.
Formerly (until 1972): Safety News (0036-2522); Incorporates: Road Accident Statistical Review; Driving Safety Bulletin; Drivers' Digest
Indexed: HRIS.
Published by: Royal Society for the Prevention of Accidents, Edgbaston Park, 353 Bristol Rd, Edgbaston, Birmingham, Worcs B5 7ST, United Kingdom. TEL 44-121-2482000, FAX 44-121-2482001, help@rospa.co.uk. Adv. contact Sue Philo TEL 44-1367-820949.

362.1 USA ISSN 1938-2790
CAROLINA PUBLIC HEALTH. Text in English. 1999. s-a. **Document type:** *Journal, Academic/Scholarly.* **Description:** Features news of faculty research, reports on partnerships with other schools, corporations and foundations, and accounts of the life of a public health professional, as well as updates on faculty, staff and student accomplishments.
Related titles: Online - full text ed.: ISSN 1938-2804. free (effective 2010).
Published by: University of North Carolina at Chapel Hill, School of Public Health, CB 7400, 135 Dauer Dr, Chapel Hill, NC 27599. TEL 919-966-3215, sphcomm@listserv.unc.edu. Ed. Linda Kastleman.

614 BRA ISSN 0103-4987
CASA DE OSWALDO CRUZ. CADERNOS. Text in Portuguese. 1990. a. **Document type:** *Monographic series, Academic/Scholarly.*
Indexed: P30.
Published by: Instituto Oswaldo Cruz, Av Brasil 4365, Rio de Janeiro, RJ 21040-360, Brazil. TEL 55-21-25984242, FAX 55-21-22805048, http://www.fiocruz.br.

362.1 USA ISSN 1943-0205
RA423.2
CASES IN PUBLIC HEALTH COMMUNICATION AND MARKETING. Text in English. 2007. a. free (effective 2010). back issues avail. **Document type:** *Journal, Academic/Scholarly.* **Description:** Aims to advance practice-oriented learning in the fields of public health communication and social marketing.
Media: Online - full text.
Published by: George Washington University, School of Public Health and Health Services, Ross Hall, 2300 Eye St, NW, Washington, DC 20037. TEL 202-994-2160, FAX 202-994-1850, pch@gwumc.edu, http://sphhs.gwumc.edu/.

614.88 GBR ISSN 0008-7580
CASUALTY SIMULATION; to simulate realism in first aid, nursing and rescue training. Text in English. 1946. q. free to members (effective 2009). adv. bk.rev. charts; illus. index, cum.index. 28 p./no.; back issues avail. **Document type:** *Journal, Trade.* **Description:** Includes information on medical conditions, acting, staging, make-up, planning and details of exercises.
Formerly (until 1958): Casualties Union. Journal
—BLDSC (3064.500000).
Published by: Casualties Union, c o Caroline Thomas, General Sec., PO Box 1942, London, E17 6YU, United Kingdom. TEL 44-8700-780590, hq@casualtiesunion.org.uk. Ed. Dougie Mac Eachran.

CATALYST (CAMBRIDGE). *see* ENERGY

362.1 USA ISSN 1930-4919
RM1
CENTERS FOR EDUCATION & RESEARCH ON THERAPEUTICS. ANNUAL REPORT. Text in English. 2000. a., latest 2006. free (effective 2011). **Document type:** *Report, Government.*
Related titles: Online - full text ed.: ISSN 1930-4927.
Published by: U.S. Department of Health and Human Services, Agency for Healthcare Research and Quality (A H R Q), 540 Gaither Rd, Ste 2000, Rockville, MD 20850. TEL 301-427-1104, info@ahrq.gov, http://www.ahrq.gov.

614.49 CZE ISSN 1210-7778
RA421 CODEN: CEJHEK
➤ **CENTRAL EUROPEAN JOURNAL OF PUBLIC HEALTH.** Text and summaries in English. 1956. q. CZK 492 domestic; EUR 166, USD 218 foreign (effective 2009). adv. bk.rev. bibl.; charts; illus. index. **Document type:** *Journal, Academic/Scholarly.* **Description:** Presents research papers on public health, health problems of the population and different population groups.
Formerly (until 1993): Journal of Hygiene, Epidemiology, Microbiology and Immunology (0022-1732)
Related titles: Online - full text ed.: ISSN 1803-1048.
Indexed: A01, A22, A36, B25, BIOSIS Prev, C06, C07, CA, CABA, CIN, CISA, ChemAb, ChemTitl, CurCont, D01, DBA, E12, EMBASE, ExcerpMed, F08, F12, FR, FS&TA, GH, H05, INIS AtomInd, IndMed, LT, MEDLINE, MycolAb, N02, N03, P20, P22, P24, P30, P33, P34, P37, P48, P50, P52, P54, P56, PHN&I, PQC, R08, R10, R12, RM&VM, RRTA, Reac, SCI, SCOPUS, SSCI, T02, T05, VS, W07, W11.
—BLDSC (3106.138200), CASDDS, GNLM, IE, Infotrieve, Ingenta, INIST. **CCC.**
Published by: (Statni Zdravotni Ustav/National Institute of Public Health), Tigis s. r. o., Havlovickeho 16, Prague 4, 152 00, Czech Republic. TEL 420-2-51813192, FAX 420-2-51681217, info@tigis.cz, http://www.tigis.cz. Ed. M Cerna. adv.: B&W page CZK 17,700, color page CZK 26,600; 260 x 176. Circ: 1,000.

362.1 CAN ISSN 1911-3374
CENTRAL L H I N ANNUAL REPORT. (Local Health Integration Network) Text in English. 2006. a. **Document type:** *Report, Trade.*
Published by: Local Health Integration Network/Reseaux Locaux d'Integration des Services de Sante, 140 Allstate Pkwy, Ste 210, Markham, ON L3R 5Y8, Canada. TEL 905-948-1872, 866-392-5446, FAX 905-948-8011, central@lhins.on.ca, http://www.lhins.on.ca.

362.1 AUS ISSN 1833-1424
CENTRAL NORTHERN ADELAIDE HEALTH SERVICE. ANNUAL REPORT. Text in English. 2005. a. free (effective 2008). back issues avail. **Document type:** *Report, Trade.* **Description:** Provides an overview of CNAHS developments and summary of the achievements for each financial year.
Related titles: Online - full text ed.: free (effective 2008).
Published by: Central Northern Adelaide Health Service, GPO Box 1898, Adelaides, SA 5001, Australia. TEL 61-8-82221400, FAX 61-8-82221402, cnahs@health.sa.gov.au, http://www.health.sa.gov.au/CNAHS/.

CENTRALFOERBUNDET FOER ALKOHOL- OCH NARKOTIKAUPPLYSNING. RAPPORT. *see* DRUG ABUSE AND ALCOHOLISM

362.1 CAN ISSN 1718-0228
CENTRE DE READAPTATION CONSTANCE-LETHBRIDGE. RAPPORT ANNUEL D'ACTIVITES/CONSTANCE-LETHBRIDGE REHABILITATION CENTRE. ANNUAL ACTIVITY REPORT. Text in English, French. 198?. a. **Document type:** *Report, Trade.*
Published by: (McGill University), Constance-Lethbridge Rehabilitation Centre/Centre de Readaptation Constance-Lethbridge, Communications CRCL, 7005, de Maisonneuve Blvd West, Montreal, PQ H4B 1T3, Canada. TEL 514-487-1770, FAX 514-487-0284, lharvey@ssss.gouv.qc.ca, http://www.clethbridge.qc.ca/home.php?&noflash=true.

362.1 CAN ISSN 1719-3915
CENTRE DE SANTE ET DE SERVICES SOCIAUX DE COTE-DES-NEIGES, METRO ET PARC-EXTENSION. RAPPORT ANNUEL D'ACTIVITES. Text in French. a. **Document type:** *Government.*
Formerly (until 2005): Centre Local de Services Communautaires Cote-des-Neiges. Rapport annuel d'Activites (1711-4896)
Published by: (McGill University), Centre de Sante et de Services Sociaux de Cote-des Neiges, Metro et Parc Extension, 5700, chemin de la Cote-des-Neiges, Montreal, PQ H3T 2A8, Canada. TEL 514-731-8531, FAX 514-731-9600, http://www.santemontreal.qc.ca/CSSS/delamontagne/fr/default.aspx.

362.1 CAN ISSN 1719-5780
CENTRE DE SANTE ET DE SERVICES SOCIAUX DE LA PETITE PATRIE ET VILLERAY. RAPPORT ANNUEL D'ACTIVITES. Text in French. 2005. a. **Document type:** *Report, Trade.*
Published by: Centre de Sante et de Services Sociaux de La Petite Patrie et Villeray, 1385, rue Jean-Talon Est, Montreal, PQ H2E 1S6, Canada. TEL 514-495-6767, FAX 514-495-6771, http://www.santemontreal.qc.ca/CSSS/petitepatrievilleray/fr/default.aspx.

362.1 CAN ISSN 1912-4066
CENTRE DE SANTE ET DE SERVICES SOCIAUX DE LA POINTE-DE-L'ISLE. RAPPORT ANNUEL DE GESTION. Text in French. 2005. a. **Document type:** *Report, Trade.*
Formerly (until 2006): Centre de Sante et de Services Sociaux de la Pointe-de-l'Isle. Rapport Annuel d'Activites (1719-4490)
Published by: Centre de Sante et de Services Sociaux de la Pointe-de-l'Isle, 9403, rue Sherbrooke Est, Montreal, PQ H1L 6P2, Canada. TEL 514-356-2572, FAX 514-356-2571.

362.1 CAN ISSN 1912-4120
CENTRE DE SANTE ET DE SERVICES SOCIAUX DE LAC-SAINT-JEAN-EST. RAPPORT ANNUEL DE GESTION. Text in French. 19??. a. **Document type:** *Report, Trade.*
Formerly (until 2005): Centre Le Jeannois. Rapport Annuel (1487-0312)
Published by: Centre de Sante et de Services Sociaux de Lac-Saint-Jean-Est, 300, boule. Champlain Sud Alma, Lac-Saint-Jean-Est, PQ G8B 5W3, Canada. TEL 418-669-2000, http://www.lejeannois.qc.ca.

362.1 360 CAN ISSN 1719-6434
CENTRE DE SANTE ET DE SERVICES SOCIAUX DE L'OUEST-DE-L'ILE. ANNUAL REPORT. Text in English. 2005. a. **Document type:** *Government.*
Related titles: French ed.: Centre de Sante et de Services Sociaux de l'Ouest-de-l'Ile. Rapport Annuel. ISSN 1719-6426.
Published by: Centre de Sante et de Services Sociaux de l'Ouest-de-l'Ile, 13800 blvd Gouin Ouest, Pierrefonds, PQ H8Z 3H6, Canada. TEL 514-626-2572, FAX 514-626-6514, http://www.santemontreal.qc.ca/CSSS/ouestdelile/fr/default.aspx.

613 CAN ISSN 1496-3612
RA778.A1 CODEN: CEWHAD
CENTRES OF EXCELLENCE FOR WOMEN'S HEALTH. RESEARCH BULLETIN. Variant title: Centres d'Excellence pour la Sante des Femmes. Bulletin de Recherche. Text in English. 2000. s-a.
Related titles: Online - full text ed.
Indexed: A26, AltPI, C03, C06, C07, C08, C11, CA, CBCARef, CINAHL, CPerI, GW, H12, I05, P48, P52, P56, PQC, T02, W09.
Published by: (Canada. Health Canada/Sante Canada, Canadian Women's Health Network/Reseau Canadien pour la Sante des Femmes), Centres of Excellence for Women's Health/Centres d'Excellence pour la Sant des Femmes, 419 Graham Ave, Suite 203, Winnipeg, MB R3C 0M3, Canada. TEL 888-818-9172, cwhn@cwhn.ca.

614 BRA ISSN 0009-0131
SF793
CENTRO PAN-AMERICANO DE FIEBRE AFTOSA. BOLETIN. Text in Portuguese. 1963. q. free. **Document type:** *Bulletin, Trade.* **Description:** Covers foot and mouth disease.
Formerly: Centro Pan-Americano de Febre Aftosa. Cuadernos
Indexed: A26, C01, I04, I05.
Published by: World Health Organization, Centro Pan Americano de Fiebre Aftosa, Av Presidente Kennedy 7778, Sao Bento - Duque de Caxias, Rio de Janeiro, RJ 25040-000, Brazil. TEL 55-21-36619000, FAX 55-21-36619001, e-mail@panaftosa.ops-oms.org, http://www.panaftosa.org.br. Circ: 1,500.

362.11 PRT ISSN 1645-8893
CENTROS DE SAUDE E HOSPITAIS. Text in Portuguese. 2004. irreg. **Document type:** *Report, Trade.*
Published by: Direccao Geral da Saude, Alameda Dom Afonso Henriques 45, Lisbon, 1049-005, Portugal. TEL 351-21-8430500, FAX 351-21-8430530, geral@dgs.pt, http://www.dgs.pt.

CERAM ENVIRONMENT BULLETIN (ONLINE). *see* ENVIRONMENTAL STUDIES

CEYLON JOURNAL OF MEDICAL SCIENCE. *see* MEDICAL SCIENCES

THE CHALLENGE. *see* MEDICAL SCIENCES—Respiratory Diseases

353.6 361 NLD
CHANGING WELFARE STATES. Text in English. irreg. price varies. **Document type:** *Monographic series.*
Published by: Amsterdam University Press, Herengracht 221, Amsterdam, 1016 BG, Netherlands. TEL 31-20-4200050, FAX 31-20-4203214, info@aup.nl, http://www.aup.nl.

CHARTERED INSTITUTE OF PUBLIC FINANCE AND ACCOUNTANCY. ENVIRONMENTAL HEALTH STATISTICS. ACTUALS. *see* PUBLIC HEALTH AND SAFETY—Abstracting, Bibliographies, Statistics

CHEMICAL REGULATION REPORTER: HAZARDOUS MATERIALS TRANSPORTATION. *see* TRANSPORTATION

CHEMIEKAARTEN; gegevens voor veilig werken met chemicalien. *see* CHEMISTRY

362.1 333.714 BLR ISSN 1026-2938
CHERNOBYL DIGEST; interdisciplinary bulletin of the Chernobyl problem information. Text in English, Russian; Summaries in English. 1991. a. BYB 200,000, USD 10. adv. bibl.; pat. back issues avail. **Document type:** *Bulletin.*
Related titles: Online - full text ed.: Chedibase.
Published by: (Natsiyanal'naya Akademiya Navuk Belarusi, Instytut Genetyki i Tsytalogii/National Academy of Sciences of Belarus, The Institute of Genetics and Cytology, UNESCO, Man and the Biosphere Programme, Chernobyl Ecological Sciences Network FRA), Vydavetstvo Belaruskaya Navuka/Publishing House Belaruskaya Navuka, ul F. Skaryny, 40, Minsk, 220141, Belarus. TEL 375-17-2633700, FAX 375-17-2637618, belnauka@infonet.by. Eds. Vladimir Prof. Sauchanka, Sergey Dromashko. adv.: page USD 340. Circ: 1,000 (paid).

CHILD ABUSE PREVENTION; national child protection clearing house newsletter. *see* SOCIAL SERVICES AND WELFARE

CHILD ABUSE PREVENTION ISSUES. *see* SOCIAL SERVICES AND WELFARE

CHILDLINKS. *see* CHILDREN AND YOUTH—About

CHILDREN'S BUREAU EXPRESS. *see* CHILDREN AND YOUTH—About

CHILDREN'S HEALTH & SAFETY. *see* CHILDREN AND YOUTH—About

614.427 USA ISSN 1041-5513
RA644.6
CHRONIC DISEASES NOTES & REPORTS. Abbreviated title: C D N R. Text in English. 1988. irreg. **Document type:** *Report, Government.* **Description:** Reports on activities of interest to health professionals involved with the myriad aspects of disease prevention and health promotion.
Related titles: Online - full text ed.: free (effective 2010); ◆ Supplement to: M M W R. ISSN 0149-2195.
Indexed: C06, C07, C08, CINAHL.
Published by: U.S. Department of Health and Human Services, Centers for Disease Control and Prevention, 1600 Clifton Rd, Atlanta, GA 30333. TEL 800-232-4636, cdcinfo@cdc.gov. **Subscr. to:** U.S. Government Printing Office, Superintendent of Documents.

362.1 BRA ISSN 1413-8123
RA463
CIENCIA & SAUDE COLETIVA. Text in Portuguese. 1996. s-a. **Document type:** *Journal, Academic/Scholarly.*
Related titles: Online - full text ed.: ISSN 1678-4561. 2001. free (effective 2011).
Indexed: A26, A34, A35, A36, AgBio, AgrForAb, C01, C25, C30, CA, CABA, D01, E12, EMBASE, ExcerpMed, F08, F12, G11, GH, H16, H17, I04, I05, I11, LT, MEDLINE, N02, N03, N04, O01, OR, P30, P32, P33, P37, P39, P42, PAIS, PHN&I, PSA, R07, R08, R12, R13, RA&MP, RRTA, S02, S03, S13, S16, SCOPUS, SSA, SSCI, SociolAb, SoyAb, T02, T05, TAR, VS, W07, W10, W11.
Published by: Associacao Brasileira de Pos - Graduacao em Saude Coletiva, Av Brasil 4036, Sala 700 Manguinhos, Rio de Janeiro, RJ 21040-361, Brazil. TEL 55-21-22904893.

615.952 AUS
CLEAN AIR UPDATE. Text in English. 1978. irreg., latest vol.57, 2008. free to members (effective 2009). bk.rev. back issues avail. **Document type:** *Newsletter, Trade.* **Description:** Contains feature articles on the various issues relevant to air pollution.
Former titles (until 2005): Non-Smokers' Update; (until 1994): Clean Air Clarion (0155-2899); (until 19??): Non-smokers' News; (until 1980): Non-smokers' Rights Movement Newsletter
Published by: Non-Smokers' Movement of Australia Inc., PO Box K860, Haymarket, NSW 1240, Australia. Ed., R&P Brian McBride.

CLEAN - SOIL, AIR, WATER (ONLINE). *see* WATER RESOURCES

CLEAN - SOIL, AIR, WATER (PRINT); a journal of sustainability and environmental safety. *see* WATER RESOURCES

CLEVELAND FOUNDATION. ANNUAL REPORT. *see* SOCIAL SERVICES AND WELFARE

CLINIC SURVEILLANCE OF SEXUALLY TRANSMITTED INFECTIONS IN NEW ZEALAND. *see* MEDICAL SCIENCES—Communicable Diseases

362.1 GBR ISSN 1179-2760
▼ **CLINICAL AUDIT.** Text in English. 2009. a. free (effective 2011). **Document type:** *Journal, Academic/Scholarly.*
Media: Online - full text.
—**CCC.**
Published by: Dove Medical Press Ltd., Beechfield House, Winterton Way, Macclesfield, SK11 0JL, United Kingdom. TEL 44-1625-509130, FAX 44-1625-617933. Ed. Marietta Stanton.

362.1 NZL ISSN 1179-5581
➤ **CLINICAL MEDICINE INSIGHTS: REPRODUCTIVE HEALTH.** Text in English. 2008. irreg. free (effective 2011). **Document type:** *Journal, Academic/Scholarly.* **Description:** Addresses all aspects of human reproductive health. Covers both male and female issues, from the physical to the psychological and the social.

Formerly (until 2010): Clinical Medicine: Reproductive Health (1178-6299)
Media: Online - full text.
Indexed: A01, C06, C07, T02.
—CCC.
Published by: Libertas Academica Ltd., PO Box 300-874, Mairangi Bay, Auckland, 0751, New Zealand. TEL 64-9-4763930, FAX 64-9-3531397, enquiries@la-press.com. Ed. Zeev Blumenfeld.

➤ **CLINICAL TOXICOLOGY.** *see* PHARMACY AND PHARMACOLOGY

362.1 CAN ISSN 1499-4313
CLINICUS. (Urgences Sante) Text in French. 2002. s-a. **Document type:** *Newsletter, Consumer.*
Related titles: Online - full text ed.: ISSN 1910-7609.
Published by: Corporation d' Urgences-Sante, 3232, rue Belanger, Montreal, PQ H1Y 3H5, Canada. TEL 514-723-5600, info@urgences-sante.qc.ca, http://www.urgences-sante.qc.ca/index.htm. Ed. Estelle Zehler.

614 NLD ISSN 1875-0508
COLLEGE VOOR ZORGVERZEKERINGEN. ZORGCIJFERS. Variant title: Zorgcijfers Kwartaalbericht. Text in Dutch. 2007. q.
Published by: College voor Zorgverzekeringen, Postbus 320, Diemen, 1110 AH, Netherlands. TEL 31-20-7978555, FAX 31-20-7978500, info@cvz.nl, http://www.cvz.nl.

363.12 388 USA ISSN 1934-8681
TL242
COLLISION (KIRKLAND); the international compendium for crash research. Text in English. 2006. s-a. USD 139 (effective 2007). adv. **Document type:** *Journal, Trade.* **Description:** Provides information on crash research, including crash test data, industry news and research, new safety technologies and conference proceedings.
Indexed: HRIS.
—BLDSC (3313.325000).
Published by: Collision Publishing, 118 Lake St S, Ste G, Kirkland, WA 98033. TEL 800-346-9571, FAX 425-284-2833, editor@collisionpublising.com. Ed. Sean Haight. adv.: page USD 760.

COMBUSTION SCIENCE AND TECHNOLOGY. *see* CHEMISTRY—Physical Chemistry

COMMON SENSE ABOUT AIDS. *see* MEDICAL SCIENCES—Communicable Diseases

614 GBR ISSN 1354-103X
COMMUNITY CARE MARKET NEWS. Abbreviated title: C C M N. Text in English. 1994. m. (except Aug./Sep. and Dec./Jan. combined). GBP 595 (print or online ed.); GBP 430 to qualified personnel (print or online ed.) (effective 2009). adv. back issues avail. **Document type:** *Newsletter, Trade.* **Description:** Provides news, comments and analysis to senior managers and decision makers within the rapidly changing community care market and its supporting services.
Related titles: Online - full text ed.
—CCC.
Published by: Laing & Buisson, 29 Angel Gate, City Rd, London, EC1V 2PT, United Kingdom. TEL 44-20-78339123, FAX 44-20-78339129, info@laingbuisson.co.uk, http://www.laingbuisson.co.uk. Ed. Justin Merritt TEL 44-20-78410049. Adv. contact Karen Ogilvie TEL 44-20-79235343.

COMMUNITY CARE REVIEW NEWSLETTER. *see* SOCIAL SERVICES AND WELFARE

COMMUNITY DENTISTRY AND ORAL EPIDEMIOLOGY (ONLINE). *see* MEDICAL SCIENCES—Dentistry

COMMUNITY DENTISTRY AND ORAL EPIDEMIOLOGY (PRINT). *see* MEDICAL SCIENCES—Dentistry

362.1 GBR
COMMUNITY HEALTH UK ACTION; journal of community health UK. Text in English. 1983. q. GBP 20 to individuals; GBP 80 to libraries; GBP 50 to institutions statutory; GBP 4 newsstand/cover (effective 2001). adv. bk.rev. **Document type:** *Journal, Trade.* **Description:** Aims to promote local community health initiatives and to publicize their work.
Formerly (until 199?): Community Health Action (1360-6115); Which was formed by the 1983 merger of: London Health News; Community Health Initiatives Resource Unit. Newsletter
Published by: Community Health UK, Freshford, PO Box 2977, Bath, BA2 7YR, United Kingdom. TEL 44-1225-723779, FAX 44-1225-722024, mail@chuk.org, http://www.chuk.org. Ed. Terry Drummond. R&P Linda Benn. Circ: 450 (paid).

613 CHL ISSN 0718-1515
COMPLEXUS. Variant title: Complejidad, Ciencia y Estetica. Text in Spanish. 2004. 3/yr. **Document type:** *Journal, Academic/Scholarly.*
Published by: Centro de Estudios en Teoria Relacional y Sistemas del Conocimiento, Las Dalias # 2893, Santiago, Chile. TEL 55-6-22236531, FAX 55-6-22091612, corporacion@sintesys.cl.

362.11068 352.8 USA ISSN 1546-1084
COMPLIANCE ASSESSMENT CHECKLIST FOR HOSPITALS. Text in English. 1999. a. **Document type:** *Trade.*
Former titles (until 2003): The Self-Assessment Checklist. Hospitals (1543-6942); (until 2001): The Hospital Survey Self-Assessment Checklist (1532-4028)
Published by: Joint Commission Resources, Inc. (Subsidiary of: Joint Commission on Accreditation of Healthcare Organizations), 1515 W 22nd St, Ste 1300W, Oak Brook, IL 60523. TEL 630-268-7400, jcrcustomerservice@pbd.com, http://www.jcrinc.com.

COMPREHENSIVE ACCREDITATION MANUAL FOR BEHAVIORAL HEALTH CARE. *see* SOCIAL SERVICES AND WELFARE

CONCERN NEWS. *see* SOCIAL SERVICES AND WELFARE

362.1 GBR ISSN 1752-1505
RA564.9.R43
➤ **CONFLICT AND HEALTH.** Text in English. 2007. irreg. free (effective 2011). adv. back issues avail. **Document type:** *Journal, Academic/Scholarly.* **Description:** Covers all aspects of the interrelationship between health and conflict.
Media: Online - full text.
Indexed: A01, A26, A36, CA, CABA, E12, GH, H12, H17, I05, P30, P33, P39, R08, R12, RA&MP, T02, T05.
—CCC.
Published by: BioMed Central Ltd. (Subsidiary of: Springer Science+Business Media), 236 Gray's Inn Rd, London, WC1X 8HB, United Kingdom. TEL 44-20-31922000, FAX 44-20-31922010, info@biomedcentral.com, http://www.biomedcentral.com. Eds. Edward Mills, Dr. Gregg Greenough, Sonal Singh.

362.1 CAN ISSN 1718-7419
CONSEIL ONTARIEN DE LA QUALITE DES SERVICES DE SANTE. RAPPORT ANNUEL. Text in French. 2006. a. **Document type:** *Report, Trade.*
Related titles: English ed.: Ontario Health Quality Council. Yearly Report. ISSN 1718-7397.
Published by: Ontario Health Quality Council/Conseil Ontarien de la Qualite des Services de Sante, 1075 Bay St, Ste 601, Toronto, ON M5S 2B1, Canada. TEL 416-323-6868, 866-623-6868, FAX 416-323-9261, ohqc@ohqc.ca, http://www.ohqc.ca/en/index.asp.

363 USA ISSN 1040-4376
➤ **CONTEMPORARY ISSUES IN RISK ANALYSIS.** Text in English. 1986. irreg., latest vol.5, 1992. price varies. back issues avail. **Document type:** *Proceedings, Academic/Scholarly.*
—CCC.
Published by: (Society for Risk Analysis), Springer New York LLC (Subsidiary of: Springer Science+Business Media), 233 Spring St, New York, NY 10013. TEL 212-460-1500, FAX 212-460-1575, service-ny@springer.com.

362.1 USA ISSN 1931-5635
CONTEXT (ATLANTA). Text in English. 2006. s-a. **Document type:** *Journal, Consumer.*
Media: Online - full text.
Published by: Health Students Taking Action Together, Inc., 1561 McLendon Ave, NE, Atlanta, GA 30307. Ed. Carmen Patrick Mohan.

362.1 AUS ISSN 1834-2221
CORONIAL COMMUNIQUE. Text in English. 2003. q. **Document type:** *Newsletter, Trade.* **Description:** Reports selected cases that have been reported to the State Coroner's Office.
Media: Online - full text.
Published by: Victorian Institute of Forensic Medicine, 57-83 Kavanagh St, Southbank, VIC 3006, Australia. TEL 61-3-96844444, FAX 61-3-96827353, assist@vifm.org.

362.1 USA ISSN 1948-6855
CORRECTCARE. Text in English. 1987. q. free to qualified personnel (effective 2009). adv. back issues avail. **Document type:** *Magazine, Trade.* **Description:** Features news, articles and commentary on timely and important topics of interest to correctional health care professionals.
Published by: National Commission on Correctional Health Care, 1145 W Diversey Pky, Chicago, IL 60614. TEL 773-880-1460, FAX 773-880-2424, info@ncchc.org. Ed. Jaime Shimkus. Adv. contact Lauren Bauer TEL 773-880-1460 ext 298. B&W page USD 1,750, color page USD 2,750; trim 8.5 x 11. Circ: 15,000.

362.1 GBR ISSN 0958-1596
RA421 CODEN: CPHRCD
➤ **CRITICAL PUBLIC HEALTH.** Text in English. 1979. q. GBP 384 combined subscription in United Kingdom to institutions (print & online eds.); EUR 503, USD 632 combined subscription to institutions (print & online eds.) (effective 2012). adv. back issues avail.; reprint service avail. from PSC. **Document type:** *Journal, Academic/Scholarly.* **Description:** Provides a multidisciplinary forum for those researching and developing public health practice. Addresses social and cultural implications of changes.
Formerly (until 1990): Radical Community Medicine (0265-0851)
Related titles: Online - full text ed.: ISSN 1469-3682. GBP 345 in United Kingdom to institutions; EUR 453, USD 569 to institutions (effective 2012) (from IngentaConnect).
Indexed: A01, A02, A03, A08, A22, A36, ASSIA, B21, C06, C07, C08, C11, CA, CABA, CINAHL, E01, E12, EMBASE, ESPM, ExcerpMed, GH, H&SSA, H04, H05, IBSS, LT, LeftInd, N02, N03, P03, P30, P34, P37, P42, P50, P52, P56, PAIS, PSA, PsycInfo, R10, R12, RRTA, Reac, RiskAb, S02, S03, SCOPUS, SSA, SociolAb, T02, T05, VS, W11.
—GNLM, IE, Infotrieve, Ingenta. **CCC.**
Published by: Routledge (Subsidiary of: Taylor & Francis Group), 4 Park Sq, Milton Park, Abingdon, Oxon OX14 4RN, United Kingdom. TEL 44-20-70176000, FAX 44-20-70176336, subscriptions@tandf.co.uk, http://www.routledge.com. Eds. David Evans, Paul Crawshaw. Adv. contact Linda Hann TEL 44-1344-779945. **Subscr. in N. America to:** Taylor & Francis Inc., Customer Services Dept, 325 Chestnut St, 8th Fl, Philadelphia, PA 19106. TEL 215-625-8900, 800-354-1420, FAX 215-625-2940, customerservice@taylorandfrancis.com; **Subscr. to:** Taylor & Francis Ltd., Journals Customer Service, Sheepen Pl, Colchester, Essex CO3 3LP, United Kingdom. TEL 44-20-70175544, FAX 44-20-70175198, tf.enquiries@tfinforma.com.

614 610 CUB ISSN 1013-2821
CUADERNOS DE HISTORIA DE LA SALUD PUBLICA. Text in Spanish. 1952. a. **Document type:** *Journal, Academic/Scholarly.*
Formerly (until 1961): Cuadernos de Historia Sanitaria (0045-9178)
Related titles: Online - full text ed.: ISSN 1561-2899. 1995.
Indexed: A01, C01, CA, P30, T02.
—Linda Hall.
Published by: (Centro Nacional de Informacion de Ciencias Medicas (C N I C M), Cuba. Oficina del Historiador de Salud Publica, Cuba. Ministerio de Salud Publica), Editorial Ciencias Medicas, Linea Esq 1, 10o, Vedado, Havana, 10400, Cuba. TEL 53-7-8323863. Ed. Jose Antonio Fidalgo. Circ: 1,300.

362.1 FRA ISSN 2106-3648
▼ **CULTURE PREVENTION.** Text in French. 2009. q. **Document type:** *Newsletter, Consumer.*
Published by: Institut Maritime de Prevention, 60, Av de la Perriere, Lorient, 56100, France. TEL 33-2-97350430, FAX 33-2-97350431, http://www.imp-lorient.fr.

CUSTOMER CIRCULAR. *see* OCCUPATIONAL HEALTH AND SAFETY

614.8 USA ISSN 1522-0389
D E S ACTION VOICE; a focus on diethylstilbestrol exposure. (Diethylstilbestrol) Text in English. 1979. q. USD 40 (effective 2006). bk.rev. abstr. back issues avail. **Document type:** *Newsletter.* **Description:** Covers the latest medical and legal information for D E S mothers, daughters and sons.
Published by: D E S Action USA, 158 S Stanwood Rd, Columbus, OH 43209. TEL 800-DES-9288, desaction@columbus.rr.com. Ed., R&P Pat Cody. Circ: 3,000 (paid).

D H S DAILY OPEN SOURCE INFRASTRUCTURE REPORT. *see* PUBLIC ADMINISTRATION

362.1 NOR ISSN 1501-4290
DAGENS MEDISIN. Text in Norwegian. 1998. 36/yr. NOK 699 (effective 2008). adv. **Document type:** *Newsletter, Trade.*
Related titles: Online - full text ed.: ISSN 1501-4304; ◆ Supplement(s): It:Helse. ISSN 1890-3177.
—CCC.
Address: PO Box 6970, St. Olavs Plass, Oslo, 0130, Norway. TEL 47-24-146870. Ed. Lottelise Folge. Adv. contact Per-Erik Nygaard TEL 47-24-146882. page NOK 40,000.

319.4 AUS ISSN 1833-1238
DATA LINKAGE SERIES. Text in English. 2005. irreg., latest vol.5, 2008. price varies. back issues avail. **Document type:** *Monographic series, Academic/Scholarly.* **Description:** Provides valuable information about the characteristics of people to those who are involved in child protection and juvenile justice data collection.
Related titles: Online - full text ed.: free (effective 2008).
Published by: Australian Institute of Health and Welfare, GPO Box 570, Canberra, ACT 2601, Australia. TEL 61-2-62441000, FAX 61-2-62441299, info@aihw.gov.au.

DEFENSE NUCLEAR FACILITIES SAFETY BOARD. REPORT TO CONGRESS ON ACQUISITIONS MADE FROM MANUFACTURER INSIDE AND OUTSIDE THE UNITED STATES, FISCAL YEAR (YEAR). *see* MILITARY

614 NLD ISSN 1873-8907
DEN HAAG TRANSMURAAL. Text in Dutch. q.
Published by: Stichting Transmurale Zorg Den Haag en Omstreken, Postbus 90603, The Hague, 2509 LP, Netherlands. TEL 31-70-3795093, info@transmuralezorg.nl, http://www.transmuralezorg.nl.

614.5 IND ISSN 1020-895X
DENGUE BULLETIN. Text in English. 19??. a. free (effective 2011). **Document type:** *Bulletin, Trade.*
Related titles: Online - full text ed.
Indexed: B25, BIOSIS Prev, EMBASE, ExcerpMed, MycolAb, R10, Reac, SCOPUS.
—BLDSC (3550.643600), IE, Ingenta.
Published by: World Health Organization, Regional Office for South-East Asia, World Health House, Indraprastha Estate, Mahatma Gandhi Marg, New Delhi, 110002, India. TEL 91-11-23370804, FAX 91-11-23370197, registry@searo.who.int.

DENMARK. DANMARKS STATISTIK. FAERDSELSUHELD/DENMARK. STATISTICS DENMARK. ROAD TRAFFIC ACCIDENTS. *see* POPULATION STUDIES—Abstracting, Bibliographies, Statistics

344.04 ESP ISSN 1133-7400
DERECHO Y SALUD. Abbreviated title: D S. Text in Spanish. 1993. s-a. **Document type:** *Journal, Trade.*
Published by: Asociacion Jurista de la Salud, Ave Romero Donallo, 21 3o. B, Santiago de Compostela, Coruna 15706, Spain. js@ajs.es, http://www.ajs.es/index.html.

362.1 610 ISR
DEREKH HAYYIM; monthly of health issues. Text in Hebrew. 1948. m. ILS 35, USD 17.50. adv. bk.rev. index. **Document type:** *Magazine, Consumer.*
Formerly (until 2005): Etanim (0334-3928)
Indexed: IHP.
Published by: Merkaz Kupat Holim, P O Box 16250, Tel Aviv, 62098, Israel. FAX 03-433500. Ed. David Taggar. Circ: 20,000.

614 USA ISSN 1564-0620
DESASTRES. PREPARATIVOS Y MITIGACION EN LAS AMERICAS. Text in Spanish. 1979. s-a. free to qualified personnel (effective 2010). back issues avail. **Document type:** *Newsletter, Trade.* **Description:** Focuses on the risks a financial crisis can pose to disaster management.
Formerly (until 1992): Preparacion para Casos de Desastre en las Americas (0251-4486)
Related titles: Online - full text ed.: ISSN 1564-0639; ◆ English ed.: Disasters. Preparedness and Mitigation in the Americas. ISSN 1564-0701.
—CCC.
Published by: Pan American Health Organization/Organizacion Panamericana de la Salud (Subsidiary of: World Health Organization/ Organisation Mondiale de la Sante), 525 23rd St, NW, Washington, DC 20037. TEL 202-974-3000, FAX 202-974-3663, paho@pmds.com.

613.62 DEU ISSN 1861-6577
DEUTSCHE GESELLSCHAFT FUER ARBEITSMEDIZIN UND UMWELTMEDIZIN. DOKUMENTATION. Text in German. 19??. a. **Document type:** *Monographic series, Academic/Scholarly.*
Former titles (until 2005): Deutsche Gesellschaft fuer Arbeitsmedizin und Umweltmedizin. Jahrestagung (1430-8754); (until 1994): Deutsche Gesellschaft fuer Arbeitsmedizin und Umweltmedizin. Bericht ueber die Jahrestagung (0947-8760); (until 1993): Deutsche Gesellschaft fuer Arbeitsmedizin. Bericht ueber die Jahrestagung (0931-8666)
—BLDSC (3615.569000). **CCC.**
Published by: Deutsche Gesellschaft fuer Arbeitsmedizin und Umweltmedizin e.V., Ratzeburger Allee 160, Luebeck, 23538, Germany. TEL 49-451-5003055, FAX 49-451-5003632, dgaum.mul@arbeitsmedizin.mu-luebeck.de, http://www-dgaum.med.uni-rostock.de.

DEUTSCHES AERZTEBLATT INTERNATIONAL. *see* MEDICAL SCIENCES

362.1 USA ISSN 1939-3431
DEVELOPMENTS IN GOVERNMENT POLICY, COMPLIANCE, LAB STRATEGY AND DIAGNOSTIC TESTING. Abbreviated title: D G P C. Text in English. 2007. q. USD 695 (effective 2008). **Document type:** *Newsletter, Trade.* **Description:** Presents the review all the key legislative changes, latest developments, mergers and acquisitions that affect the daily management of a lab, diagnostic testing and compliance programs.
Related titles: Online - full text ed.: USD 225 per issue (effective 2008).
—CCC.
Published by: Institute of Management & Administration, Inc., One Washington Park, Ste 1300, Newark, NJ 07102. TEL 973-718-4700, FAX 973-622-0595, subserve@ioma.com.

P

362 NLD ISSN 0927-4987
DEVELOPMENTS IN HEALTH ECONOMICS AND PUBLIC POLICY. Text in English. 1992. irreg., latest vol.9, 2005. price varies. back issues avail. **Document type:** *Monographic series, Academic/Scholarly.* **Description:** Publishes recent economic research and its applications to public policy problems of health and health services.
Indexed: EMBASE, ExcerpMed, MEDLINE, P30, R10, Reac, SCOPUS.
—BLDSC (3579.075100). **CCC.**
Published by: Springer Netherlands (Subsidiary of: Springer Science+Business Media), Van Godewijckstraat 30, Dordrecht, 3311 GX, Netherlands. TEL 31-78-6576050, FAX 31-78-6576474. Eds. H E Frech III, Peter Zweifel.

DEZINFEKTSIONNOE DELO. *see* MEDICAL SCIENCES—Communicable Diseases

DICKINSON'S F D A UPDATES. (Federal Drug Administration) *see* PUBLIC ADMINISTRATION

DIGITAL FORENSICS, SECURITY AND LAW. JOURNAL. *see* CRIMINOLOGY AND LAW ENFORCEMENT

DIGITAL SUNDHED; tillaeg om it i sundhedssektoren. *see* MEDICAL SCIENCES

362.1 CAN ISSN 1912-6298
DIRECTION DE LA LUTTE CONTRE LE CANCER. RAPPORT D'ACTIVITE. Text in French. 2006. a. **Document type:** *Report, Trade.*
Published by: Quebec, Ministere de la Sante et des Services Sociaux, 400, boul. Jean-Lesage, bureau 105, Quebec, PQ G1K 8W1, Canada. TEL 418-643-1344, 800-363-1363, http://www.msss.gouv.qc.ca/index.php.

613 USA ISSN 1549-8662
DIRECTIONS IN GLOBAL HEALTH. Text in English. 2004 (Jan.). 3/yr. free (effective 2010). back issues avail. **Document type:** *Newsletter, Trade.*
Related titles: Online - full text ed.: free (effective 2010).
Indexed: P50, P52, P56.
Published by: Program for Appropriate Technology in Health, PO Box 900922, Seattle, WA 98109. TEL 206-285-3500, FAX 206-285-6619, info@path.org.

362.1 USA ISSN 1935-7893
HV551.2
DISASTER MEDICINE AND PUBLIC HEALTH PREPAREDNESS. Abbreviated title: D M P H P. Text in English. 2007. q. USD 390 domestic to institutions; USD 488 in the Americas to institutions; EUR 394 in Europe to institutions; GBP 334 elsewhere to institutions (effective 2012). adv. back issues avail.; reprints avail. **Document type:** *Journal, Academic/Scholarly.* **Description:** Emphasizes public health preparedness and disaster response for all health care and public health professionals globally.
Related titles: Online - full text ed.: ISSN 1938-744X. 2007. free to members (effective 2012).
Indexed: A34, A36, C06, C07, CABA, CurCont, E12, EMBASE, ExcerpMed, F08, F12, GH, MEDLINE, N02, P30, P33, R08, R10, R12, Reac, S13, S16, SCI, SCOPUS, SSCI, T05, W07, W11.
—CCC.
Published by: American Medical Association, 515 N State St, Chicago, IL 60654. TEL 312-464-4200, 800-621-8335, FAX 312-464-4142, journalsales@ama-assn.org, http://www.ama-assn.org. Ed. Dr. James J James.

614 GBR ISSN 0965-3562
HV551.2 CODEN: DPMAEY
➤ **DISASTER PREVENTION AND MANAGEMENT**; an international journal. Abbreviated title: D P M. Text in English. 1992. 5/yr. EUR 8,839 combined subscription in Europe (print & online eds.); USD 9,869 combined subscription in the Americas (print & online eds.); GBP 5,959 combined subscription in the UK & elsewhere (print & online eds.); AUD 14,369 combined subscription in Australasia (print & online eds.) (effective 2012). reprint service avail. from PSC. **Document type:** *Journal, Academic/Scholarly.* **Description:** Advances available knowledge in the fields of disaster prevention and management; integrates extant methodologies and activities relating to disaster emergency and crisis management.
Incorporates: Disaster Management (0961-1428)
Related titles: Online - full text ed.: ISSN 1758-6100 (from IngentaConnect).
Indexed: A01, A03, A08, A12, A17, A22, A34, A37, ABIn, ASFA, B21, C25, CA, CABA, CurCont, E01, E04, E05, E12, ESPM, EmerIntel, Emerald, EnvEAb, ErgAb, F08, F12, GH, GeoRef, H&SSA, I11, IndVet, LT, N02, P10, P21, P37, P48, P50, P51, P52, P53, P54, P56, PQC, R12, RRTA, RefZh, RiskAb, S13, S16, SCOPUS, SOPODA, SSCI, SSciA, SWRA, T02, T05, TAR, VS, W07, W10, W11.
—BLDSC (3595.462000), IE, Infotrieve, Ingenta. **CCC.**
Published by: Emerald Group Publishing Ltd., Howard House, Wagon Ln, Bingley, W Yorks BD16 1WA, United Kingdom. TEL 44-1274-777700, FAX 44-1274-785201, information@emeraldinsight.com. Ed. Dr. Harry C Wilson. Pub. Nicola Codner.

362.1 USA ISSN 1537-2294
DISASTER SAFETY REVIEW. Text in English. 2002 (Fall). irreg.
Published by: Institute for Business & Home Safety, 4775 E. Fowler Ave., Tampa, FL 33617. TEL 813-286-3400, FAX 813-286-9960, info@ibhs.org, http://www.ibhs.org. Ed. Charlie Reese.

614 USA ISSN 1564-0701
HV553
DISASTERS. PREPAREDNESS AND MITIGATION IN THE AMERICAS; news and information for the international disaster community. Text in English. 1979. q. free (effective 2010). **Document type:** *Newsletter.* **Description:** Provides news about disaster preparedness activities in the countries of the Americas, and thus aims to encourage dialogue and the sharing of ideas among governments and agencies.
Formerly (until 1992): Disaster Preparedness in the Americas (0251-4494)
Related titles: Online - full content ed.: ISSN 1564-071X. 1997; ◆ Spanish ed.: Desastres. Preparativos y Mitigacion en las Americas. ISSN 1564-0620.
Indexed: A01, CA, EnvAb, I02, T02.
—CCC.
Published by: Pan American Health Organization/Organizacion Panamericana de la Salud (Subsidiary of: World Health Organization/Organisation Mondiale de la Sante), 525 23rd St, NW, Washington, DC 20037. TEL 202-974-3000, FAX 202-974-3663, paho@pmds.com. Circ: 26,000.

362.1 USA ISSN 1559-7490
R850.A1
DIVISION OF INTRAMURAL RESEARCH ANNUAL REPORT. Text in English. a. **Document type:** *Report, Trade.*
Formerly (until 1996): Annual Report of the Scientific Director
Media: Online - full text.
Published by: National Institute of Child Health and Human Development, Bldg 31 Room 2A32 MSC 2425, 31 Center Dr, Bethesda, MD 20892-2425. FAX 301-496-7101, 800-370-2943, http://www.nichd.nih.gov.

362.1 FRA ISSN 1622-9584
DOC STAT CHAMPAGNE-ARDENNE. Text in French. 2000. irreg. **Document type:** *Government.*
Related titles: Series: Les Formations aux Professions Sociales en Champagne-Ardenne en .. ISSN 2106-9514. 2000.
Published by: Direction Regionale des Affaires Sanitaires et Sociales d'Ile-de-France de Champagne-Ardenne (Subsidiary of: France. Direction Regionale des Affaires Sanitaires et Sociales d'Ile-de-France), 7 Bl Kennedy, Chalon en Champagne Cedex, 51037, France. TEL 33-3-26667878, FAX 33-3-26655746, http://www.champagne-ardenne.sante.gouv.fr.

614 HRV ISSN 1331-2499
DOKTOR U KUCI. Text in Croatian. 1998. m. **Document type:** *Magazine, Consumer.*
Published by: Europapress Holding d.o.o., Slavonska Avenija 4, Zagreb, 10000, Croatia. TEL 385-1-3642146, 385-1-3642145. Ed. Selma Mijatovic. Adv. contact Sanja Mlacak.

DRINKING WATER & BACKFLOW PREVENTION. *see* ENGINEERING—Civil Engineering

DROIT DE LA SANTE; lois et reglements annotes. *see* LAW

DRUG G M P REPORT. (Good Manufacturing Practices) *see* PHARMACY AND PHARMACOLOGY

362.1 AUS ISSN 1834-1918
DRUG-RELATED HOSPITAL STAYS IN AUSTRALIA. Text in English. 2006. a. **Document type:** *Journal, Trade.*
Media: Online - full text.
Published by: University of New South Wales, National Drug and Alcohol Research Centre, Faculty of Medicine, Sydney, NSW 2052, Australia. TEL 61-2-9385-8765, FAX 61-2-9385-1874, http://ndarc.med.unsw.edu.au.

DRUG SAFETY ADVISOR. *see* PHARMACY AND PHARMACOLOGY

DRUG SAFETY UPDATE. *see* PHARMACY AND PHARMACOLOGY

DRUGLINK. *see* PHARMACY AND PHARMACOLOGY

362.1 AUS ISSN 1833-5357
DRUGSPEAK. Text in English. q. **Document type:** *Newsletter, Consumer.*
Formerly (until 1999): Fish Called W A N A D A
Published by: Western Australian Network of Alcohol and Other Drug Agencies (W A N A D A), City West Lotteries House, 2 Delhi St., West Perth, W.A. 6005, Australia. TEL 61-8-9420-7236, FAX 61-8-9486-7988, drugspeak@wanada.org.au, http://www.wanada.org.au.

DU & JOBBET. *see* OCCUPATIONAL HEALTH AND SAFETY

DZIENNIK URZEDOWY MINISTRA ZDROWIA. *see* PUBLIC ADMINISTRATION

362.1 363.7 USA ISSN 1932-8109
E H S QUARTERLY REVIEW. (Environment, Health and Safety) Text in English. 2006. q. USD 75 per issue (effective 2010 - 2011). **Document type:** *Government.* **Description:** Provides an overview of key federal and state environmental and safety topics in one place.
Media: Online - full text.
—CCC.
Published by: The Bureau of National Affairs, Inc., 1801 S Bell St, Arlington, VA 22202. TEL 703-341-3000, 800-372-1033, FAX 703-341-4634, bnaplus@bna.com, http://www.bna.com.

628.5 USA
E M A NEWS. Text in English. q. USD 150 to members. adv. **Document type:** *Newsletter.*
Published by: Environmental Management Association, 1721 Pheasant Lane, Jeffersonville, PA 19403-3333. TEL 610-539-8588, FAX 610-539-9999. R&P Barry M Dressler. Adv. contact Slobodan Djurdjevic.

362.1 EGY ISSN 1020-0428
E M R O TECHNICAL PUBLICATIONS SERIES. (Regional Office for the Eastern Mediterranean) Text in English. 1978. irreg., latest 2008.
Formerly: E M R O Technical Publication (0250-8524)
Related titles: Arabic ed.: Al Mansurat Al-Tiqniyyat Li-Iqlim Sarq Al-Bahr Al-Mutawassit. ISSN 1014-9937. 1979.
—BLDSC (9311.904000).
Published by: World Health Organization, Regional Office for the Eastern Mediterranean, P O Box 1517, Alexandria, 21563, Egypt. TEL 20-3-48202234, FAX 20-3-48383916, khayat@who.sci.eg, http://www.emro.who.int/index.asp.

362.1 USA ISSN 1547-8459
E M S MANAGEMENT JOURNAL. (Emergency Medical Services) Text in English. 2004 (Jan.-Mar.). q. free (effective 2004).
Media: Online - full content.
Published by: HealthAnalytics, LLC, P. O. Box 2128, Lakeland, FL 38806. TEL 866-283-8765, FAX 617-812-8561, http://www.healthanalytics.net. Ed. Michael R. Gunderson. Pub. David M. Lindberg.

363 USA ISSN 1935-1445
E M S PRODUCT NEWS; the product resource for ems professionals. Abbreviated title: E M S P N. Text in English. 1993. bi-m. USD 56 domestic; USD 81 in Canada & Mexico; USD 114 elsewhere; free to qualified personnel (effective 2008). adv. **Document type:** *Magazine, Trade.* **Description:** Contains new product introductions, agency profiles, product applications, industry news, etc.
Former titles (until 2005): Emergency Medical Product News (1548-4645); (until 2004): Public Safety Product News (1085-8822)
Related titles: Online - full text ed.
Indexed: A15, ABIn, B02, B15, B17, B18, C06, C07, G04, G08, I05, P21, P24, P48, P50, P51, P52, P56, PQC, T02.
—CIS. **CCC.**
Published by: Cygnus Business Media, Inc., 1233 Janesville Ave, PO Box 803, Fort Atkinson, WI 53538. TEL 920-563-6388, 800-547-7377, FAX 920-563-1702, http://www.cygnusb2b.com. Eds. Nancy Perry TEL 800-547-7377 ext 1110, Ronnie Garrett TEL 800-547-7377 ext 1726. Pubs. Patrick Bernardo, Scott Cravens. Adv. contact Christi Frazer. B&W page USD 3,548, color page USD 4,398; trim 10.75 x 14.5. Circ: 25,000.

E P I VISION. (Epidemiologia) *see* MEDICAL SCIENCES

333.792 362.1 ITA ISSN 0392-3029
➤ **E S A R D A BULLETIN.** (European Safeguard Research and Development Association) Text in English. 1981. irreg. **Document type:** *Journal, Academic/Scholarly.* **Description:** Contains news of association activities and scientific and technical articles related to safeguards and verification.
Indexed: Inspec.
—BLDSC (3810.960000), IE, Ingenta, Linda Hall.
Published by: (European Commission, Directorate General - Research BEL), E S A R D A, c/o European Commission Joint Research Center, Bldg 36, TP361, Ispra, 21020, Italy. TEL 39-0332-785145, 39-0332-789306.

614 BRA ISSN 1809-0893
E S P CADERNOS. (Escola de Saude Publica Cadernos) Key Title: Cadernos ESP. Text in Portuguese. 2005. s-a. free (effective 2006). back issues avail. **Document type:** *Journal, Academic/Scholarly.*
Media: Online - full text.
Published by: Escola de Saude Publica, 3161 Meireles, Fortaleza, Ceara, 60165-090, Brazil. cadernos@esp.ce.gov.br. Ed. Erick Leite Maia de Messias.

362.1 TZA ISSN 0856-8960
RA552.T34
EAST AFRICA JOURNAL OF PUBLIC HEALTH. Text in English. 2006. irreg. free (effective 2011). **Document type:** *Journal, Academic/Scholarly.* **Description:** Publishes scientific research from a range of public health related disciplines including community medicine, epidemiology, nutrition, behavioral sciences, health promotion, health education, communicable and non-communicable diseases.
Media: Online - full text.
Indexed: A01, A36, B21, BP, CA, CABA, D01, E12, EMBASE, ESPM, ExcerpMed, F08, F11, GH, H&SSA, H05, H17, IIBP, LT, MEDLINE, N02, N03, P30, P33, P39, R08, R10, R12, RRTA, Reac, RiskAb, S12, SCOPUS, T02, T05, W11.
Published by: East African Public Health Association, PO Box 65015, Dar es Salaam, Tanzania. Ed. Kagoma S Mnyika.

614 EGY ISSN 1020-3397
RA541.N36 CODEN: EMHJAM
➤ **EASTERN MEDITERRANEAN HEALTH JOURNAL/AL-MAGALLAT AL-SIHHIYYAT LI-SARQ AL-MUTAWASSIT.** Text in English. 1995. m. USD 180 (effective 2012). back issues avail. **Document type:** *Journal, Academic/Scholarly.* **Description:** Provides a forum for the presentation and promotion of new policies and initiatives in health services and for the exchange of ideas, concepts, epidemiological data, research findings and other information, with special reference to the Eastern Mediterranean Region.
Related titles: Online - full text ed.: ISSN 1687-1634.
Indexed: A26, A34, A35, A36, A37, A38, AgBio, AgrForAb, B25, BIOSIS Prev, BP, C06, C07, C08, C25, C28, CA, CABA, CINAHL, D01, E12, EMBASE, ExcerpMed, F08, F09, GH, H12, H16, H17, I05, IIS, IndMed, IndVet, LT, M10, MEDLINE, MycolAb, N02, N03, P20, P22, P24, P30, P33, P37, P39, P48, P50, P54, PN&I, PQC, R08, R10, R12, R13, RA&MP, RM&VM, RRTA, Reac, S13, S16, SCOPUS, T02, T05, TAR, VS, W09, W11.
—BLDSC (3646.669520), IE, Ingenta. **CCC.**
Published by: World Health Organization, Regional Office for the Eastern Mediterranean, P O Box 1517, Alexandria, 21563, Egypt. TEL 20-3-48202234, FAX 20-3-48383916, khayat@who.sci.eg. Ed. Jane Nicholson.

614 CHL ISSN 0718-5294
ECONOMIA Y SALUD. Text in Spanish. 2007. q.
Published by: Ministerio de Salud, Departamento de Economia de la Salud, Mac Iver 154, Santiago, Chile. TEL 56-2-5740100, FAX 56-2-5740198, mtrebolledo@minsal.cl, http://163.247.51.38/desarrollo/css/desal/index.htm.

ECOTOXICOLOGY AND ENVIRONMENTAL SAFETY. *see* ENVIRONMENTAL STUDIES—Toxicology And Environmental Safety

ECUADOR. INSTITUTO NACIONAL DE ESTADISTICA Y CENSOS. CUENTAS NACIONALES DE LA SALUD. *see* PUBLIC HEALTH AND SAFETY—Abstracting, Bibliographies, Statistics

947.42 EST ISSN 0235-8026
EESTI ARST. Text in Estonian. 1958. bi-m. **Document type:** *Magazine, Trade.*
Formerly (until 1989): Noukogude Eesti Tervishoid (0134-2320)
Indexed: INIS AtomInd.
Published by: Eesti Arstide Liit, Pepleri 32, Tartu, 51010, Estonia. TEL 372-7-430029, FAX 372-7-430029. Ed. Vaino Sinisalu.

EGESZSEGFEJLESZTES; educatio sanitaria. *see* PHYSICAL FITNESS AND HYGIENE

362.1 EGY ISSN 1687-9546
▼ **EGYPTIAN JOURNAL OF HEALTH CARE/MAJALLAT AL-MISRIYYAT LIL-RI'AYYAT AL-SIHIYYAT.** Text in English; Summaries in Arabic. 2009. q. **Document type:** *Journal, Academic/Scholarly.*
Published by: Ain Shams University, Faculty of Nursing, Campus, Abassia, Egypt. http://nursing.shams.edu.eg/index.htm. Ed. Dr. Amira Elbeih.

614 IND ISSN 0973-8959
EHEALTH. Text in English. 2006. m. INR 900, USD 100 (effective 2011). adv. bk.rev. back issues avail. **Document type:** *Magazine, Trade.* **Description:** For healthcare service providers, medical professionals, researchers, policymakers and technology vendors involved in the business of healthcare IT and planning, service delivery, program management and application development.
Related titles: Online - full text ed.: free (effective 2011).
Indexed: I05.
Published by: Centre for Science, Development and Media Studies, G-4, Sector 39, Noida, Uttar Pradesh 201 301, India. TEL 91-120-2502180, FAX 91-120-2500060, http://www.csdms.in. Ed. Ravi Gupta.

362.1 AUS ISSN 1446-4381
R858.A1
EJOURNAL OF HEALTH INFORMATICS. Abbreviated title: e J H I. Text in English. 2001. q. free (effective 2011). **Description:** Dedicated to the advancement of health informatics and information technology in healthcare.
Media: Online - full text.
Indexed: A39, C27, C29, D03, D04, E13, R14, S14, S15, S18.
—CCC.
Published by: Health Informatics Society of Australia (H I S A) Ltd., 413 Lygon St, Brunswick East, VIC 3057, Australia. TEL 61-3-93880555, FAX 61-3-93882086, hisa@hisa.org.au, http://www.hisa.org.au.

ELEKTROMAGNETISCHE VELDEN/ELECTROMAGNETIC FIELDS. *see* PHYSICS—Electricity

ELELMISZERVIZSGALATI KOZLEMENYEK/JOURNAL OF FOOD INVESTIGATIONS. *see* FOOD AND FOOD INDUSTRIES

614 USA ISSN 1941-4110
THE EMANAGER; management strategies for improving health services. Text in English. 2008 (Mar.). s-a.
Media: Online - full text. **Related titles:** French ed.: ISSN 1942-4574; Spanish ed.: ISSN 1941-7403.
Published by: Management Sciences for Health, Inc., 748 Memorial Dr, Cambridge, MA 02139. TEL 617-250-9500, FAX 617-250-9090, communications@msh.org, http://www.msh.org.

363 USA ISSN 1534-0406
HV551.2
EMERGENCY, FIRE/RESCUE & POLICE PRODUCT REVIEW MAGAZINE. Abbreviated title: E F & P. Text in English. 2001. bi-m. USD 15 domestic; USD 40 foreign; free to qualified personnel (effective 2007). adv. **Document type:** *Magazine, Trade.*
Published by: W S M Media Group, 5808 Faringdon Pl, Ste 200, Raleigh, NC 27609-3930. adv.: B&W page USD 2,745, color page USD 3,030; trim 8.25 x 10.875. Circ: 45,170.

362.1 USA ISSN 1553-4995
HV551.3
EMERGENCY NUMBER PROFESSIONAL MAGAZINE; the voice of 9-1-1. Text in English. bi-m. free to members (effective 2005). adv. **Document type:** *Magazine, Trade.*
Former titles (until Jul. 2004): Emergency Number Operations (1552-3411); (until Feb. 2003): N E N A News
Published by: (National Emergency Number Association), Communication Technologies, Inc., 301 S. Main St. Ste. 1 W., Doylestown, PA 18901. TEL 215-230-9556, FAX 215-230-9601, info@ctipublishing.com. Pub. Philip McClurkin.

614.8 614.86 USA ISSN 1530-6666
T55.3.H3
EMERGENCY RESPONSE GUIDEBOOK. Text in English. irreg., latest 2008. free. **Document type:** *Government.* **Description:** Provides information for police and fire personnel on steps to be taken in the first critical minutes after a hazardous materials transportation accident.
Former titles (until 2000): North American Emergency Response Guidebook (1530-664X); (until 1996): Emergency Response Guidebook (0747-816X)
Related titles: Online - full content ed.
Published by: U.S. Department of Transportation, Pipeline and Hazardous Materials Safety Administration, Office of Hazardous Materials Safety, 1200 New Jersey Ave, SE East Bldg, 2nd Fl, Washington, DC 20590. training@dot.gov.

614 SWE ISSN 1752-8550
➤ **EMERGING HEALTH THREATS JOURNAL.** Text in English. 2008. q. free (effective 2011). back issues avail. **Document type:** *Journal, Academic/Scholarly.* **Description:** Publishes the latest international research on new and emerging threats to human health. Covers infectious diseases, hazardous chemicals and poisons, ionizing and non-ionizing radiation, natural and man-made disasters, emerging environmental hazards and emergency preparedness and response.
Related titles: Online - full text ed.: free (effective 2011).
Indexed: A01, A29, B&BAb, B19, B20, B21, CA, ESPM, H&SSA, I02, ImmunAb, RiskAb, SCOPUS, T02.
Published by: (Forum for Global Health Protection GBR), Co-Action Publishing, Ripvaegen 7, Jaerfaella, 17564, Sweden. TEL 46-18-4951150, FAX 46-18-4951138, info@co-action.net, http://www.co-action.net. Ed. Dr. Andrew Robertson.

362.1969 616.9 USA ISSN 1080-6059
➤ **EMERGING INFECTIOUS DISEASES (ONLINE).** Abbreviated title: E I D. Text in English. 1995. m. free (effective 2011). back issues avail. **Document type:** *Journal, Academic/Scholarly.* **Description:** Aims to promote the recognition of new and reemerging infectious diseases around the world and improve the understanding of factors involved in disease emergence, prevention, and elimination.
Media: Online - full text. **Related titles:** ◆ Print ed.: Emerging Infectious Diseases (Print). ISSN 1080-6040; French Translation; Esperanto Translation: Enfermedades Infecciosas Emergentes; Chinese Translation:.
Published by: U.S. Department of Health and Human Services, Centers for Disease Control and Prevention, 1600 Clifton Rd, Atlanta, GA 30333. TEL 404-639-1960, FAX 404-639-1954. Ed. D Peter Drotman.

362.1969 616.9 USA ISSN 1080-6040
RA648.5 CODEN: EIDIFA
➤ **EMERGING INFECTIOUS DISEASES (PRINT).** Text in English. 1995. m. free (effective 2010). bk.rev. illus.; abstr. 120 p./no.; back issues avail. **Document type:** *Journal, Academic/Scholarly.* **Description:** Reports on emerging infectious diseases worldwide, including reviews and analyses, epidemiologic and laboratory issues, and prevention strategies.
Related titles: ◆ Online - full text ed.: Emerging Infectious Diseases (Online). ISSN 1080-6059.
Indexed: A01, A02, A03, A08, A20, A22, A26, A29, A34, A35, A36, A38, ABS&EES, AIDS Ab, ASCA, AgBio, AgrForAb, B04, B20, B21, B25, BIOSIS Prev, BP, BRD, BiolDig, C06, C07, C11, C25, CA, CABA, CurCont, D01, DBA, E04, E05, E08, E12, EMBASE, ESPM, ExcerpMed, F08, F12, FS&TA, G03, G08, G11, GH, GSA, GSI, H11, H12, H16, H17, HPNRM, I05, ISR, IndMed, IndVet, Inpharma, JW-ID, LT, M01, M02, M05, M06, MEDLINE, MycolAb, N02, N03, N04, O01, P30, P32, P33, P34, P37, P39, PN&I, R07, R08, R10, R11, R12, R13, RA&MP, RM&VM, RRTA, Reac, RiskAb, S04, S06, S09, S12, S13, S16, SCI, SCOPUS, SSciA, T02, T05, TAR, VS, VirolAbstr, W03, W05, W07, W08, W11, WildRev, Z01.
—BLDSC (3733.426050), CASDDS, IE, Infotrieve, Ingenta.
Published by: U.S. Department of Health and Human Services, Centers for Disease Control and Prevention, 1600 Clifton Rd, Atlanta, GA 30333. TEL 404-639-1960, FAX 404-639-1954. Ed. D Peter Drotman.

362.1 GBR ISSN 1742-7622
RA648.5
➤ **EMERGING THEMES IN EPIDEMIOLOGY.** Text in English. 2004. irreg. free (effective 2011). adv. back issues avail. **Document type:** *Journal, Academic/Scholarly.* **Description:** Aims to promote debate and discussion on the theoretical and methodological aspects of epidemiology.
Media: Online - full text.
Indexed: A01, A26, A34, A36, C06, C07, CA, CABA, E12, EMBASE, ExcerpMed, GH, H05, H17, I05, IndVet, N02, N03, OGFA, P20, P24, P30, P32, P33, P52, P54, P56, PN&I, R08, R10, R12, Reac, SCOPUS, T02, T05, VS, VirolAbstr, W10, W11.
—CCC.
Published by: BioMed Central Ltd. (Subsidiary of: Springer Science+Business Media), 236 Gray's Inn Rd, London, WC1X 8HB, United Kingdom. TEL 44-20-31922000, FAX 44-20-31922010, info@biomedcentral.com, http://www.biomedcentral.com. Ed. Peter G Smith.

344.04 614 USA
END-OF-LIFE LAW DIGEST. Text in English. q. USD 200 (effective 2002).
Published by: Partnership for Caring, 1620 Eye Street NW, Ste 202, Washington, DC 20006. TEL 202-296-8071, 800-989-9455, FAX 202-296-8352, pfc@partnershipforcaring.org, http://www.partnershipforcaring.org.

ENVIRONMENT & ASSESSMENT. *see* ENVIRONMENTAL STUDIES

ENVIRONMENT, HEALTH & SAFETY BENCHMARKS. *see* ENVIRONMENTAL STUDIES

615.9 GBR ISSN 1758-3721
ENVIRONMENT IN BUSINESS. Abbreviated title: E I B. Text in English. 1991. m. GBP 239 (effective 2009). index. 16 p./no.; **Document type:** *Magazine, Trade.* **Description:** Covers a wide spectrum of subjects, including: enforcement activities; court cases; EU developments; environmental standards; official guidance; cleaner technology; industry sector initiatives; international trends; government policy and company practice.
Formerly (until 2008): Environment Information Bulletin (0964-5322)
Related titles: Online - full text ed.; ◆ Supplement to: Health and Safety Bulletin (Sutton). ISSN 1358-2208.
Indexed: RICS.
—BLDSC (3791.133500), IE, Infotrieve. **CCC.**
Published by: LexisNexis UK (Croydon Office), 2 Addiscombe Rd, Croydon, CR9 5AF, United Kingdom. TEL 44-20-86869141, FAX 44-20-86863155, customer.services@lexisnexis.co.uk, http://www.lexisnexis.co.uk. Ed. Paul Suff TEL 44-1273-698692. Adv. contact Shaun Bedford TEL 44-20-82121984.

ENVIRONMENT INTERNATIONAL. *see* ENVIRONMENTAL STUDIES

ENVIRONMENT OF CARE NEWS. *see* HEALTH FACILITIES AND ADMINISTRATION

ENVIRONMENTAL ALERT; the compliance guide for safety professionals. *see* ENVIRONMENTAL STUDIES—Waste Management

ENVIRONMENTAL AUDITING: F I F R A COMPLIANCE GUIDE. (Federal Insecticide, Fungicide, and Rodenticide Act) *see* ENVIRONMENTAL STUDIES—Toxicology And Environmental Safety

ENVIRONMENTAL HEALTH (ONLINE EDITION). *see* ENVIRONMENTAL STUDIES

363.7 GBR ISSN 1476-069X
RB1
➤ **ENVIRONMENTAL HEALTH: A GLOBAL ACCESS SCIENCE SOURCE.** Text in English. 2002 (Jul.). irreg. free (effective 2011). adv. back issues avail. **Document type:** *Journal, Academic/Scholarly.* **Description:** Includes all aspects of environmental and occupational medicine and related studies in toxicology and epidemiology.
Media: Online - full text.
Indexed: A01, A02, A03, A08, A10, A26, A34, A36, AgrForAb, BA, C06, C07, CA, CABA, CurCont, D01, E12, EMBASE, ExcerpMed, F08, F12, G02, G11, GH, H17, I05, I11, IndVet, LT, MEDLINE, MaizeAb, N02, N03, OR, P30, P32, P33, PN&I, R07, R08, R10, R12, R13, Reac, S12, S13, S16, SCI, SCOPUS, T02, T05, V03, VS, W07, W10, W11.
—CCC.
Published by: BioMed Central Ltd. (Subsidiary of: Springer Science+Business Media), 236 Gray's Inn Rd, London, WC1X 8HB, United Kingdom. TEL 44-20-31922000, FAX 44-20-31922010, info@biomedcentral.com, http://www.biomedcentral.com. Eds. David Ozonoff TEL 617-638-4620, Philippe Grandjean TEL 45-6550-3769.

➤ **ENVIRONMENTAL HEALTH AND PREVENTIVE MEDICINE.** *see* PHYSICAL FITNESS AND HYGIENE

➤ **ENVIRONMENTAL HEALTH CRITERIA.** *see* ENVIRONMENTAL STUDIES

362.1 NZL ISSN 1178-6302
➤ **ENVIRONMENTAL HEALTH INSIGHTS.** Text in English. 2008. irreg. free (effective 2011). **Document type:** *Journal, Academic/Scholarly.* **Description:** Looks at how environmental factors affect the health of individuals and societies.
Media: Online - full text.
Indexed: B21, C06, C07, E04, E05, ESPM, H&SSA, P30, PollutAb, SSciA, T02.
—CCC.
Published by: Libertas Academica Ltd., PO Box 302-624, North Harbour, Auckland, 1330, New Zealand. TEL 64-21-662617, FAX 64-21-740006, editorial@la-press.com. Ed. Timothy Kelley.

614 GBR ISSN 0969-9856
ENVIRONMENTAL HEALTH NEWS. Short title: E H N. Text in English. 1986. w. GBP 93 to non-members; free to members (effective 2009); includes Environmental Health Journal. adv. **Document type:** *Magazine, Academic/Scholarly.* **Description:** Covers environmental protection, food, health and safety, housing issues, and the new public health agenda.
—BLDSC (3791.498000). **CCC.**
Published by: Chartered Institute of Environmental Health, Chadwick Court, 15 Hatfields, London, SE1 8DJ, United Kingdom. TEL 44-20-79286006, FAX 44-20-78275883, 44-20-79285862, info@cieh.org. Ed. Will Hatchett TEL 44-20-78275908.

ENVIRONMENTAL HEALTH PERSPECTIVES. *see* ENVIRONMENTAL STUDIES

616.98 GBR ISSN 1752-3990
ENVIRONMENTAL HEALTH PRACTITIONER. Short title: E H P. Text in English. 1895. m. GBP 93 to non-members; free to members (effective 2009); includes Environmental Health News. adv. bk.rev. bibl.; charts; illus.; stat.; tr.lit. Index. reprints avail. **Document type:** *Magazine, Trade.* **Description:** Contains features that go into detail on food hygiene, health and safety, housing, pest control, pollution, waste disposal, noise and information technology.
Former titles (until 2005): Environmental Health Journal (1464-6862); (until 1998): Environmental Health (0013-9270); (until 1969): Public Health Inspector; (until 1964): The Sanitarian; (until 1932): The Sanitary Journal; (until 1902): Sanitary Inspectors Journal
Related titles: Microform ed.: (from PQC); Online - full text ed.
Indexed: A22, B28, CISA, E04, E05, EnvAb, FS&TA, H&TI, H06, RICS, T02, WasteInfo, WildRev.
—BLDSC (3791.499500), IE, Ingenta, INIST, Linda Hall. **CCC.**
Published by: Chartered Institute of Environmental Health, Chadwick Court, 15 Hatfields, London, SE1 8DJ, United Kingdom. TEL 44-20-79286006, FAX 44-20-79285862, info@cieh.org. Ed. Stuart Spear TEL 44-20-78275828.

363.72 CAN ISSN 0319-6771
➤ **ENVIRONMENTAL HEALTH REVIEW.** Text in English. 1956. q. CAD 30 domestic; CAD 38 in United States; CAD 45 overseas (effective 2002). adv. bk.rev. **Document type:** *Journal, Academic/Scholarly.*
Indexed: A22.
—GNLM.
Published by: D2 C3 Enterprises, White Rock Pastal Outlet, P O Box 75264, White Rock, BC V4B 5L4, Canada. TEL 604-543-0999, FAX 604-543-0904. Ed., Pub., R&P Domenic Losito. Adv. contact Debra Losito. Circ: 1,500.

➤ **ENVIRONMENTAL MANAGEMENT NEWS.** *see* ENVIRONMENTAL STUDIES

616.98 GBR ISSN 1357-9231
ENVIRONMENTAL PLANNING ISSUES. Text in English. 1993. irreg., latest no.27, 2006. price varies. back issues avail. **Document type:** *Monographic series, Consumer.*
Published by: International Institute for Environment and Development, 3 Endsleigh St, London, WC1H ODD, United Kingdom. TEL 44-20-73882117, FAX 44-20-73882826, info@iied.org, http://www.iied.org.

P

ENVIRONMENTAL RADIATION SURVEILLANCE IN WASHINGTON STATE. ANNUAL REPORT. *see* ENVIRONMENTAL STUDIES

ENVIRONMENTAL RADIOACTIVITY IN THE NETHERLANDS. *see* ENVIRONMENTAL STUDIES

614 CAN ISSN 1926-6197
▼ **ENVIRONMENTAL SCAN.** Text in English. 2009. irreg., latest vol.22, 2011. free (effective 2011). back issues avail. **Document type:** *Monographic series, Trade.* **Description:** Provides information to support health care decision-making and policy development in Canada.
Media: Online - full text.
Published by: Canadian Agency for Drugs and Technologies in Health, 600-865 Carling Ave, Ottawa, ON K1S 5S8, Canada. TEL 613-226-2553, FAX 613-226-5392, mediarequests@cadth.ca.

ENVIRONMENTAL TOXICOLOGY AND CHEMISTRY. *see* ENVIRONMENTAL STUDIES—Toxicology And Environmental Safety

ENVIRONNEMENT, RISQUES & SANTE. *see* ENVIRONMENTAL STUDIES

628 USA
EPI-GRAM. Text in English. m. **Document type:** *Government.*
Published by: Department of Human Services, Division of Disease Control, State House, Sta 11, Augusta, ME 04333. FAX 207-289-4172. Ed. Dr. Kathleen F Gensheiner.

362.1 USA ISSN 1930-0069
RA648.5
EPIDEMIOLOGIC INQUIRY. Text in English. 2006. w. **Document type:** *Newsletter, Consumer.*
Media: Online - full text.
Address: http://epidemiologic.blogspot.com.

362.1 GBR ISSN 1742-5573
RA651
➤ **EPIDEMIOLOGIC PERSPECTIVES & INNOVATIONS.** Text in English. 2004. irreg. free (effective 2011). adv. back issues avail. **Document type:** *Journal, Academic/Scholarly.* **Description:** Covers all aspects of epidemiologic research methods, applications, critical overviews, teaching tools, perspectives, and other analytic work.
Media: Online - full text.
Indexed: A01, A26, A36, CA, CABA, EMBASE, ExcerpMed, GH, H05, H17, I05, LT, N02, N03, P20, P30, P33, P52, P54, P56, R10, R11, R12, RRTA, Reac, SCOPUS, T02, T05, W11.
—CCC.
Published by: BioMed Central Ltd. (Subsidiary of: Springer Science+Business Media), 236 Gray's Inn Rd, London, WC1X 8HB, United Kingdom. TEL 44-20-31922000, FAX 44-20-31922010, info@biomedcentral.com, http://www.biomedcentral.com. Eds. Carl V Phillips, George Maldonado.

614.4 USA ISSN 0256-1859
RA650
EPIDEMIOLOGICAL BULLETIN. Text in English. 1942. q. free (effective 2009). **Document type:** *Bulletin, Academic/Scholarly.* **Description:** Includes information about international resolutions and recommendations related with disease control in the Americas.
Supersedes in part (in 1979): Informe Epidemiologico Semanal (1014-2959)
Related titles: ◆ Spanish ed.: Boletin Epidemiologico. ISSN 0255-6669.
Indexed: A22, CA, EMBASE, ExcerpMed, MEDLINE, P30, R10, Reac, SCOPUS, T02.
—BLDSC (3793.561000), IE, Ingenta. **CCC.**

Published by: Pan American Health Organization/Organizacion Panamericana de la Salud (Subsidiary of: World Health Organization/ Organisation Mondiale de la Sante), 525 23rd St, NW, Washington, DC 20037. TEL 202-974-3000, FAX 202-974-3663, paho@pmds.com. Circ: 4,000 (free).

614.4 USA ISSN 1044-3983
RA648.5 CODEN: EPIDEY

➤ **EPIDEMIOLOGY.** Text in English. 1990. bi-m. USD 822 domestic to institutions; USD 863 foreign to institutions (effective 2011). adv. back issues avail.; reprints avail. **Document type:** *Journal, Academic/ Scholarly.* **Description:** Covers articles and meta-analyses, novel hypotheses, descriptions and applications of new methods, and discussions of research theory or public health policy.
Related titles: Online - full text ed.: ISSN 1531-5487. USD 319 to individuals (effective 2011).
Indexed: A20, A22, A34, A36, A38, ASCA, ASFA, B21, BIOBASE, CA, CABA, CIS, CurCont, D01, E12, EMBASE, ESPM, ExcerpMed, F08, F09, F12, FR, FamI, GH, H&SSA, H16, I12, IABS, INI, ISR, IndMed, Inpharma, JW-ID, JW-WH, LT, MEDLINE, N02, N03, NRN, O01, P30, P33, P35, P37, P38, P39, PollutAb, R08, R10, R11, R12, RRTA, Reac, RiskAb, S13, S16, SCI, SCOPUS, SSCI, SoyAb, T05, THA, ToxAb, TriticAb, VS, W07, W10, W11.
—BLDSC (3793.574000), GNLM, IE, Infotrieve, Ingenta, INIST. **CCC.**
Published by: (International Society for Environmental Epidemiology, Epidemiology Resources Inc.), Lippincott Williams & Wilkins (Subsidiary of: Wolters Kluwer N.V.), Two Commerce Sq, 2001 Market St, Philadelphia, PA 19103. TEL 215-521-8300, FAX 215-521-8902, customerservice@lww.com, http://www.lww.com. Ed. Dr. Allen J Wilcox TEL 919-667-1688. Pub. Nancy Megley. Adv. contact Miriam Terron-Elder TEL 646-674-6538. Circ: 1,224.

614.4 616.8 GBR ISSN 2045-7960

➤ **EPIDEMIOLOGY AND PSYCHIATRIC SCIENCES.** Text in Italian. 1992. 4/yr. GBP 164, USD 270 to institutions; GBP 190, USD 313 combined subscription to institutions (print & online eds.) (effective 2012). adv. 80 p./no.; **Document type:** *Journal, Academic/Scholarly.* **Description:** Provides updated data and scientific information to epidemiologists, psychiatrists, psychologists, statisticians and other research and mental health workers primarily concerned with public health and epidemiological and social psychiatry.
Formerly (until 2011): Epidemiologia e Psichiatria Sociale (1121-189X)
Related titles: Online - full text ed.: ISSN 2045-7979. GBP 121, USD 200 to institutions (effective 2012); Supplement(s): Epidemiologia e Psichiatria Sociale. Monograph Supplement. ISSN 1827-4331. 1997.
Indexed: A20, A22, CurCont, E-psyche, EMBASE, ExcerpMed, IndMed, MEDLINE, P03, P30, PsycInfo, PsycholAb, R10, Reac, RefZh, SCOPUS, SOPODA, SSCI, W07.
—BLDSC (3793.537000), IE, Infotrieve, Ingenta. **CCC.**
Published by: Cambridge University Press, The Edinburgh Bldg, Shaftesbury Rd, Cambridge, CB2 8RU, United Kingdom. TEL 44-1223-326070, FAX 44-1223-325150, journals@cambridge.org. Ed. Michele Tansella. Circ: 800.

▼ ➤ **EPIDEMIOLOGY RESEARCH INTERNATIONAL.** *see* MEDICAL SCIENCES

➤ **EQUITY DIALOGUE.** *see* SOCIAL SERVICES AND WELFARE

362.1 ESP ISSN 0213-943X
Z6675.I5

ERGA. Text in Spanish. 1973. m. adv. bk.rev. index, cum.index: 1975-1988. **Document type:** *Government.*
Former titles (until 1988): Instituto Nacional de Seguridad e Higiene en el Trabajo. Boletin Bibliografico (0212-2359); (until 1981): Spain. Servicio Social de Higiene y Seguridad del Trabajo. Boletin Bibliografico (0210-069X)
Related titles: Online - full text ed.: Erga Online.
Published by: Ministerio de Trabajo y Asuntos Sociales, Instituto Nacional de Seguridad e Higiene en el Trabajo, Agustin de Bethencourt 4, Madrid, 28071, Spain. FAX 34-3-2803642, cnctinsht@mtas.es, http://www.mtas.es.

ERUUL MEND/HEALTH. *see* PHYSICAL FITNESS AND HYGIENE

614 BRA ISSN 1517-7130

ESPACO PARA A SAUDE. Text in Portuguese. 1999. s-a. free (effective 2006). back issues avail. **Document type:** *Journal, Academic/ Scholarly.*
Media: Online - full content.
Published by: Universidade Estadual de Londrina, Centro de Estudos em Saude Coletiva, Ave Robert Koch, 60, Londrina, PR 86038-440, Brazil. TEL 55-43-33375115, espacosaude@uel.br. Ed. Luiz Cordoni.

362.1 CAN ISSN 1912-1989

ESTIMATIONS PRELIMINAIRES DES DEPENSES DE SANTE DES GOUVERNEMENTS PROVINCIAUX ET TERRITORIAUX. Text in French. 2002. a. **Document type:** *Journal, Trade.*
Media: Online - full text. **Related titles:** English ed.: Preliminary Provincial and Territorial Government Health Expenditure Estimates. ISSN 1912-1970.
Published by: Canadian Institute for Health Information/Institut Canadien d'Information sur la Sante, 377 Dalhousie St, Ste 200, Ottawa, ON K1N 9N8, Canada. TEL 613-241-7860, FAX 613-241-8120, nursing@cihi.ca, http://www.cihi.ca.

614 362.1 ETH ISSN 1021-6790
RA755.E8

➤ **THE ETHIOPIAN JOURNAL OF HEALTH DEVELOPMENT.** Text in English. 1984. 3/yr. bk.rev. 80 p./no.; **Document type:** *Journal, Academic/Scholarly.* **Description:** Publishes analytical, descriptive, and methodological papers as well as original research on public health problems, management of health services, health care needs, and socio-economic and political factors related to health and development.
Related titles: Online - full text ed.: free (effective 2011).
Indexed: A34, A36, AbAn, BP, CABA, D01, E12, F08, GH, H16, H17, INIS AtomInd, IndVet, LT, N02, N03, P32, P33, P37, P39, P40, P50, P52, P56, PN&I, R08, R12, RA&MP, RM&VM, RRTA, S13, S16, SCI, SSCI, T05, TAR, VS, W07, W10, W11.
—BLDSC (3814.782000), GNLM, IE, Ingenta.
Published by: Ethiopian Public Health Association, Tikur Anbessa Hospital, PO Box 32812, Addis Ababa, Ethiopia. TEL 251-1-513628, FAX 251-1-517701, epha@telecom.net.et. Ed., R&P Yemane Berhane. Adv. contact Beki Asfaw. Circ: 1,000. **Co-sponsor:** Addis Ababa University.

616.009 305.8 GBR ISSN 1355-7858
RA448.4 CODEN: ETHEFR

➤ **ETHNICITY AND HEALTH.** Text in English. 1996. bi-m. GBP 708 combined subscription in United Kingdom to institutions (print & online eds.); EUR 937, USD 1,172 combined subscription to institutions (print & online eds.) (effective 2012). adv. back issues avail.; reprint service avail. from PSC. **Document type:** *Journal, Academic/ Scholarly.* **Description:** Publishes original papers from the full range of disciplines concerned with investigating the relationship between ethnicity and health, including medicine and nursing, public health, epidemiology, social sciences, population sciences, and statistics.
Related titles: Online - full text ed.: ISSN 1465-3419. GBP 638 in United Kingdom to institutions; EUR 843, USD 1,055 to institutions (effective 2012) (from IngentaConnect).
Indexed: A01, A02, A03, A08, A20, A22, A36, B21, C06, C07, C08, C11, CA, CABA, CINAHL, CurCont, E-psyche, E01, E12, EMBASE, ESPM, ExcerpMed, GEOBASE, GH, H&SSA, H04, H05, H13, IBSS, IndMed, LT, MEDLINE, N02, N03, OR, P03, P10, P20, P24, P25, P30, P33, P39, P42, P43, P46, P48, P50, P52, P53, P54, P56, PAIS, PEI, PQC, PSA, PsycInfo, PsycholAb, R08, R10, R12, RA&MP, RRTA, Reac, RiskAb, S02, S03, SCI, SCOPUS, SOPODA, SRRA, SSA, SSCI, SociolAb, T02, T05, W07, W11.
—IE, Infotrieve, Ingenta. **CCC.**
Published by: Routledge (Subsidiary of: Taylor & Francis Group), 4 Park Sq, Milton Park, Abingdon, Oxon OX14 4RN, United Kingdom. TEL 44-20-70176000, FAX 44-20-70176336, subscriptions@tandf.co.uk, http://www.routledge.com. Ed. Karl Atkin. Adv. contact Linda Hann TEL 44-1344-779945. **Subscr. in N. America to:** Taylor & Francis Inc., Customer Services Dept, 325 Chestnut St, 8th Fl, Philadelphia, PA 19106. TEL 215-625-8900, 800-354-1420, FAX 215-625-2940; **Subscr. to:** Taylor & Francis Ltd., Journals Customer Service, Sheepen Pl, Colchester, Essex CO3 3LP, United Kingdom. TEL 44-20-70175544, FAX 44-20-70175198.

614 688.8 NLD ISSN 1877-4148

ETIKETTERING VAN LEVENSMIDDELEN. Text in Dutch. 2002. biennial. EUR 47.12 (effective 2011).
Published by: Sdu Uitgevers bv, Postbus 20025, The Hague, 2500 EA, Netherlands. TEL 31-70-3789911, FAX 31-70-3854321, sdu@sdu.nl, http://www.sdu.nl/.

362.1 CHE ISSN 1020-7481

EURO OBSERVER. Variant title: European Observatory on Health Systems and Policies. Text in English. 1999. q. **Document type:** *Magazine, Consumer.*
Related titles: Online - full text ed.
—CCC.
Published by: (World Health Organization, European Centre for Health Policy BEL), World Health Organization/Organisation Mondiale de la Sante, Avenue Appia 20, Geneva 27, 1211, Switzerland. TEL 41-22-7912111, FAX 41-22-7913111, publications@who.int, http://www.who.int.

362.1 331 IRL ISSN 1830-7108
HD7260

EUROFOUND NEWS/FONDATION EUROPEENNE POUR L'AMELIORATION DES CONDITIONS DE VIE ET DE TRAVAIL. COMMUNIQUE. Text in Multiple languages. 1998. 10/yr. free. **Document type:** *Newsletter.* **Description:** Contains articles on current developments in Foundation research and activities as well as upcoming events and latest Foundation publications.
Formerly (until Jan.2007): European Foundation for the Improvement of Living and Working Conditions. Communique (1560-814X)
Related titles: E-mail ed.; Online - full text ed.
—BLDSC (3829.268470).
Published by: European Foundation for the Improvement of Living and Working Conditions/Fondation Europeenne pour l'Amelioration des Conditions de Vie et de Travail, Wyattville Rd, Loughlinstown, Co. Dublin 18, Ireland. TEL 353-1-2043100, FAX 353-1-2826456, information@eurofound.europa.eu. Circ: 15,500.

614 300 GBR ISSN 1356-1030

EUROHEALTH. Text in English. 1995. q. back issues avail. **Document type:** *Journal, Academic/Scholarly.* **Description:** Aims to bridge the gap between the scientific community and the policy-making community through evidence-based articles, debates, and discussions on contemporary health system and health policy issues.
Related titles: Online - full text ed.: free (effective 2010).
Indexed: A36, CABA, E12, GH, LT, N02, R12, RRTA, T05, TAR, W11.
—BLDSC (3829.268610), IE, Ingenta, INIST. **CCC.**
Published by: London School of Economics and Political Science, Houghton St, London, WC2A 2AE, United Kingdom. TEL 44-20-74057686, http://www.lse.ac.uk/. Ed. David McDaid TEL 44-20-79556381. **Co-sponsor:** European Health Policy Research Network.

362.1 DEU ISSN 1860-6636

EUROPAEISCHER INFORMATIONSBRIEF GESUNDHEIT. Text in German. 1994. bi-m. EUR 65 domestic; EUR 78 foreign (effective 2009). **Document type:** *Newsletter, Trade.* **Description:** Provides current and background information on European policies in the fields of health issues and consumer protection.
Formerly (until 2005): E U Informationsbrief Gesundheit (0948-2792)
Published by: Europa-Kontakt Informations- und Verlagsgesellschaft mbH, Karl-Liebknecht-Str 9, Berlin, 10178, Germany. TEL 49-30-28449090, FAX 49-30-284490915, eu.kontakt@t-online.de, http://www.europa-kontakt.de.

EUROPEAN JOURNAL OF EPIDEMIOLOGY. *see* MEDICAL SCIENCES

EUROPEAN JOURNAL OF HEALTH LAW. *see* MEDICAL SCIENCES

614 GBR ISSN 1101-1262
RA483 CODEN: EJPHF6

➤ **EUROPEAN JOURNAL OF PUBLIC HEALTH.** Abbreviated title: E J P H. Text in English. 1991. bi-m. GBP 400 in United Kingdom to institutions; EUR 602 in Europe to institutions; USD 803 in US & Canada to institutions; GBP 400 elsewhere to institutions; GBP 437 combined subscription in United Kingdom to institutions (print & online eds.); EUR 656 combined subscription in Europe to institutions (print & online eds.); USD 876 combined subscription in US & Canada to institutions (print & online eds.); GBP 437 combined subscription elsewhere to institutions (print & online eds.) (effective 2012). adv. bk.rev. back issues avail.; reprint service avail. from PSC. **Document type:** *Journal, Academic/Scholarly.* **Description:** Provides a forum for the discussion and debate of current public health issues in the European region.
Related titles: Online - full text ed.: ISSN 1464-360X. GBP 343 in United Kingdom to institutions; EUR 514 in Europe to institutions; USD 686 in US & Canada to institutions; GBP 343 elsewhere to institutions (effective 2012) (from IngentaConnect).
Indexed: A01, A02, A03, A08, A12, A20, A22, A34, A36, ABIn, AIDS Ab, ASG, AddicA, B21, C06, C07, C08, C25, CA, CABA, CINAHL, CurCont, D01, E01, E12, EMBASE, ERA, ESPM, ExcerpMed, F09, FR, FS&TA, FamI, GH, H&SSA, H04, H05, H13, H16, I14, ISR, Inpharma, LT, M12, MEDLINE, N02, N03, P03, P10, P20, P21, P22, P24, P25, P30, P33, P34, P37, P38, P39, P42, P48, P50, P51, P52, P53, P54, P56, PAIS, PHN&I, PQC, PSA, PollutAb, PsycInfo, PsycholAb, R08, R10, R12, RRTA, Reac, RiskAb, S02, S03, S13, S16, S19, S20, S21, SCI, SCOPUS, SOPODA, SSA, SSCI, SSciA, SociolAb, T02, T05, VS, W07, W10, W11.
—BLDSC (3829.738030), GNLM, IE, Infotrieve, Ingenta, INIST. **CCC.**
Published by: (European Public Health Association NLD), Oxford University Press, Great Clarendon St, Oxford, OX2 6DP, United Kingdom. TEL 44-1865-556767, FAX 44-1865-556646, enquiry@oup.co.uk, http://www.oup.co.uk/. Eds. Peter Allebeck, Johan P Mackenbach. adv.: B&W page GBP 720, B&W page USD 1,295; trim 210 x 296. Circ: 9,750.

362.1 DEU ISSN 1867-299X
K5

▼ ➤ **EUROPEAN JOURNAL OF RISK REGULATION.** Text in English. 2010. q. EUR 348; EUR 378 combined subscription (print & online eds.) (effective 2011). **Document type:** *Journal, Academic/Scholarly.* **Description:** Covers European law & policy regulating chemicals, nanomaterials, pharmaceuticals, pesticides, food and feed, cosmetics, industrial accidents and public health in general. Also includes discussion extends to other social sciences, such as regulation studies, risk analysis, safety science, political science and sociology.
Related titles: Online - full text ed.: ISSN 2190-8249. EUR 348 (effective 2011).
Indexed: I01, ILP, P10, P48, P53, P54, PQC, W03, W05.
—CCC.
Published by: Lexxion Verlagsgesellschaft mbH, Guentzelstr 63, Berlin, 10717, Germany. TEL 49-30-81450600, FAX 49-30-81450622, info@lexxion.de. Ed. Alberto Alemanno.

➤ **EVIDENCE REPORT - TECHNOLOGY ASSESSMENT (SUMMARY).** *see* MEDICAL SCIENCES

362.1 CAN ISSN 1710-2014

L'EVOLUTION DU CLIMAT ET VOTRE SANTE. Text in French. 2004. irreg. **Document type:** *Monographic series, Trade.*
Formerly (until 2006): Votre Sante et le Changement Climatique (1914-1335)
Media: Online - full text. **Related titles:** Ed.: Your Health and a Changing Climate. ISSN 1710-2006.
Published by: Health Canada/Sante Canada, Address Locator 0900C2, Ottawa, ON K1A OK9, Canada. TEL 613-957-2991, 866-225-0709, FAX 613-941-5366, info@www.hc-sc.gc.ca.

EXCHANGE ON HIV/AIDS, SEXUALITY AND GENDER. *see* MEDICAL SCIENCES—Communicable Diseases

363.78 USA

EXECUTIVE REPORTS. Cover title: Pest Control Executive Reports. Text in English. 1991. m. looseleaf. USD 69 domestic; USD 72 in Canada & Mexico; USD 80 elsewhere (effective 2001). bk.rev. charts; illus.; stat.; tr.lit. annual index. 6 p./no.; back issues avail. **Document type:** *Newsletter, Trade.* **Description:** Provides management information relating to pest control, for owners, managers and supervisors of pest control businesses.
Published by: Pinto & Associates, Inc., 29839 Oak Rd, Mechanicsville, MD 20659. TEL 301-884-3020, FAX 301-884-4068. Ed., R&P Sandra Kraft. Pub. Lawrence J Pinto. Circ: 350 (paid).

362.1 CAN ISSN 1718-9837

L'EXPRESS D R M G. (Departement Regional de Medecine Generale) Text in French. 2006. q. **Document type:** *Newsletter, Trade.*
Related titles: Online - full text ed.: ISSN 1718-9845.
Published by: Agence de la Sante et des Services Sociaux de Montreal, 3725, rue Saint-Denis, Montreal, PQ H2X 3L9, Canada. TEL 514-286-6500, FAX 514-286-5669, http://www.santemontreal.qc.ca/fr.

EYE TO EYE. *see* MEDICAL SCIENCES—Ophthalmology And Optometry

614 JPN ISSN 1349-6395

F B NEWS. (Firumu Badji) Variant title: Film Badge News. Text in Japanese. 1985. m. JPY 400 newsstand/cover (effective 2007). adv. **Document type:** *Corporate.*
Formerly (until 2001): Firumu Badji Nyusu (0917-3625)
Related titles: Online - full content ed.
Published by: Chiyoda Tekunoru Senryou Keisoku Jigyoubu/Chiyoda Technol Corp., 1-7-12 Yushima, Bunkyo-ku, Tokyo, 113-8681, Japan. TEL 81-3-38165210, FAX 81-3-58034890, ctc-master@c-technol.co.jp, http://www.c-technol.co.jp/index.html.

344.04 USA

F D A ENFORCEMENT MANUAL. (Food and Drug Administration) Text in English. 1993. m. looseleaf. USD 699 (print or online ed.) (effective 2008). reprints avail. **Document type:** *Handbook/Manual/Guide, Trade.* **Description:** For professionals in the drug, medical device, food and cosmetic industries who are responsible for compliance with FDA's tough enforcement strategies. Provides current information on FDA enforcement practices, and gives practical step-by-step guidance on enforcement options.
Related titles: Online - full text ed.: USD 799 (effective 2007).
Published by: Thompson Publishing Group, 805 15th St, N W, 3rd Floor, Washington, DC 20005. TEL 800-677-3789, FAX 202-872-4000, service@thompson.com. Ed. Arthur N Levine.

362.1 USA

F D A ENFORCEMENT REPORT (ONLINE EDITION). Text in English. w. free. **Document type:** *Government.* **Description:** Contains information on actions taken in connection with agency regulatory activities.
Media: Online - full text.
Published by: U.S. Department of Health and Human Services, Food and Drug Administration, 5600 Fishers Ln., Rockville, MD 20857. TEL 888-463-6332, FAX 301-443-9057.

F D A NEWS DRUG DAILY BULLETIN. (Federal Drug Administration) *see* PHARMACY AND PHARMACOLOGY

F D A NEWS NUTRACEUTICAL WEEKLY BULLETIN. (Federal Drug Administration) *see* PHARMACY AND PHARMACOLOGY

362.1 FRA ISSN 1771-2661
FACE AU RISQUES. L'HEBDO; la reference des acteurs de la maitrise des risques. Text in French. 2002. w. **Document type:** *Newsletter, Trade.*
Published by: Centre National de Prevention et de Protection, 48 Bd des Batignolles, Paris, 75017, France. TEL 33-1-44505772, FAX 33-1-44505799. **Subscr. to:** BP 2265, St. Marcel 27950, France. TEL 33-2-32536400.

FACTS AND ADVICE FOR AIRLINE PASSENGERS. *see* TRANSPORTATION—Air Transport

362.1 COL ISSN 0120-386X
RA467
FACULTAD NACIONAL DE SALUD PUBLICA. REVISTA. Abstracts in English; Text in Spanish. 1974. s-a. COP 36,000 domestic; USD 30 foreign (effective 2011). 110 p./no.; back issues avail. **Document type:** *Journal, Academic/Scholarly.*
Formerly (until 1979): Escuela Nacional de Salud Publica. Revista (0120-064X)
Related titles: Online - full text ed.: free (effective 2011) (from SciELO).
Indexed: C01.
Published by: Universidad de Antioquia, Facultad Nacional de Salud Publica, Apartado Postal 51922, Medellin, Colombia. TEL 57-4-510-6870, FAX 57-4-511-2506.

610 USA ISSN 0160-6379
RA421
➤ **FAMILY AND COMMUNITY HEALTH**; the journal of health promotion and maintenance. Abbreviated title: F C H. Text in English. 1978. q. USD 300.51 domestic to institutions; USD 474 foreign to institutions (effective 2011). adv. bk.rev. illus. back issues avail.; reprints avail. **Document type:** *Journal, Academic/Scholarly.* **Description:** Presents multidisciplinary perspectives and approaches for effective public and community health programs.
Related titles: Microform ed.: (from PQC); Online - full text ed.: ISSN 1550-5057.
Indexed: A20, A22, A26, A34, A36, ASCA, B21, C06, C07, C08, CA, CABA, CINAHL, CurCont, D01, E-psyche, E08, E12, EMBASE, ESPM, ExcerpMed, F09, FAMLI, Faml, G08, GH, H&SSA, H11, H12, H13, I05, I07, I11, IndVet, LT, M06, MEDLINE, N02, N03, N04, NRN, NurAb, P03, P10, P20, P24, P25, P30, P34, P48, P50, P53, P54, PEI, PQC, PsycInfo, PsycholAb, R10, R12, RRTA, Reac, RiskAb, S02, S03, S09, S13, S16, S23, SCOPUS, SOPODA, SSCI, SociolAb, T02, T05, TAR, VS, W07, W09, W11.
—BLDSC (3865.558000), GNLM, IE, Infotrieve, Ingenta. **CCC.**
Published by: Lippincott Williams & Wilkins (Subsidiary of: Wolters Kluwer N.V.), Two Commerce Sq, 2001 Market St, Philadelphia, PA 19103. TEL 215-521-8300, FAX 215-521-8902, customerservice@lww.com, http://www.lww.com. Ed. Jeanette Lancaster. Pub. Beth L Guthy. Adv. contact Caryn Ungashick TEL 816-214-5655. Circ: 600.

613 GBR
FAMILY PLANNING ASSOCIATION. REPORT AND ACCOUNTS. Text in English. 1939. a. free (effective 2009). **Document type:** *Journal, Trade.*
Former titles (until 1969): Family Planning Association. Annual Report and Accounts (0263-7731); (until 1968): Family Planning Association. Annual Report (0144-3119); (until 1967): Family Planning Association. Annual Report and Accounts (0263-7723); (until 1965): Family Planning Association. Annual Report
—CCC.
Published by: Family Planning Association, 50 Featherstone St, London, EC1Y 8QU, United Kingdom. TEL 44-20-76085240, FAX 44-845-1232349, fpadirect@fpa.org.uk, http://www.fpa.org.uk.

614.8 USA ISSN 0749-310X
TX150
FAMILY SAFETY & HEALTH. Text in English. 1942. q. USD 24.10 to non-members; USD 18.50 to members (effective 2009). illus. reprints avail. **Document type:** *Magazine, Consumer.* **Description:** Aims to prevent off-the-job injuries and to promote health and fitness through consumer education.
Former titles (until 1984): Family Safety (0014-7397); (until 1961): Home Safety Review
Related titles: Microform ed.: (from PQC); Online - full text ed.
Indexed: A01, A02, A03, A08, P34, T02.
—Ingenta.
Published by: National Safety Council, 1121 Spring Lake Dr, Itasca, IL 60143. TEL 630-775-2056, 800-621-7619, FAX 630-285-0797, customerservice@nsc.org, http://www.nsc.org.

362.1 CHN ISSN 1671-6310
FANGZAI BOLAN/OVERVIEW OF DISASTER PREVENTION. Text in Chinese. 1982. bi-m. CNY 60 (effective 2009). **Document type:** *Journal, Academic/Scholarly.*
Fomer titles (until 2002): Dizhen Keji Qingbao/Earthquake Information; (until 1988): Guowei Dizhen Keji Qingbao/Earthquake Information from Abroad
Related titles: Online - full text ed.
Published by: Zhongguo Dizhen Zaihai Fanyu Zhongxin, 9, Minzhuyuan Lu, Beijing, 100029, China.

614.094915 FRO
FAROE ISLANDS. LANDSLAEGEN PAA FAEROEERNE. MEDICINALBERETNING/CHIEF MEDICAL OFFICER IN THE FAROES. MEDICAL REPORT. Text mainly in Danish. 1982. a. stat. back issues avail. **Document type:** *Government.*
Formerly (until 1999): Landslaegen paa Faeroeerne. Aarsberetning (0903-7772)
Related titles: Online - full text ed.
Published by: Landslaeknin i Foeroyum/Chief Medical Officer in the Faroes, Sigmundargata 5, Torshavn, 110, Faeroe Islands. TEL 298-311832, FAX 298-317660, foe@sst.dk.

FEDERAL MOTOR CARRIER SAFETY ADMINISTRATION REGISTER; a daily summary of motor carrier applications and of decisions and notices. *see* TRANSPORTATION—Automobiles

614 USA ISSN 1070-9029
FEDERAL PHYSICIAN. Text in English. 1979. bi-m. USD 37.50 (effective 2000). adv. back issues avail. **Document type:** *Newsletter.* **Description:** Covers changes in federal physician pay and benefits, updates on changes affecting federal employees, news of federal health programs.
Published by: Federal Physicians Association, PO Box 45150, Washington, DC 20026. TEL 703-455-5947, FAX 703-455-8282. Ed. Dennis W Boyd. Adv. contact Nick Cordovana. Circ: 1,000 (controlled).

FEDERAL VETERINARIAN. *see* VETERINARY SCIENCE

344.04 FRA ISSN 1775-9196
FICHES PRATIQUES DU DROIT DE LA SANTE; edition permanente. Text in French. 2004. base vol. plus q. updates. looseleaf. EUR 174 base vol(s).; EUR 11 per month (effective 2009). **Document type:** *Catalog.*
Published by: Editions Weka, 249 Rue de Crimee, Paris, 75935 Cedex 19, France. TEL 33-1-53351717, FAX 33-1-53351701.

362.1 USA ISSN 1553-0302
FINDINGS BRIEF. Text in English. 1996. q. **Document type:** *Newsletter, Trade.*
Media: Online - full text.
Indexed: EMBASE, ExcerpMed, MEDLINE, P30, R10, Reac, SCOPUS.
Published by: AcademyHealth, 1801 K St, N W, Ste 701-L, Washington, DC 20006. TEL 202-292-6700, FAX 202-292-6800, info@academyhealth.org, http://academyhealth.org.

614 664 FIN ISSN 1796-4369
FINLAND. ELINTARVIKETURVALLISUUSVIRASTO EVIRA. JULKAISU. Text in Finnish. 2006. irreg. back issues avail. **Document type:** *Monographic series, Government.*
Formed by the merger of (2002-2006): Finland. Elainlaakinta- ja Elintarviketutkimuslaitos. Julkaisu (1458-6878); (1998-2006): Finland. Kasvintuotannon Tarkastuskeskus. Julkaisuja. B 2, Luomutuotanto (1455-4496); (2001-2006): Finland. Elintarvikevirasto. Julkaisu (1458-168X); Which was formed by the merger of (1998-2001): Finland. Elintarvikevirasto. Tutkimusraportteja (1455-3430); (1992-2001): Finland. Elintarvikevirasto. Tutkimuksia (1235-2764); (1992-2001): Valvonta (1235-2756); Which was formerly (until 1992): Finland. Elintarvikevirasto (0788-6039); Which superseded in part (in 1990): Finland. Kuluttaja-Asiain Osasto. Julkaisu (0784-7343)
Related titles: Online - full text ed.
Published by: Elintarviketurvallisuusvirasto/The Finnish Food Safety Authority, Mustialankatu 3, Helsinki, 00790, Finland. TEL 358-20-772003, FAX 358-20-7724350, info@evira.fi.

FINNISH INSTITUTE OF OCCUPATIONAL HEALTH. CURRENT RESEARCH PROJECTS. *see* HEALTH FACILITIES AND ADMINISTRATION

FIRE FOCUS. *see* FIRE PREVENTION

613 DEU
FIT!; D A K Magazin. Text in German. 1955. q. adv. **Document type:** *Magazine, Consumer.*
Published by: (Deutsche Angestellten Krankenkasse), G + J Corporate Editors GmbH (Subsidiary of: Gruner + Jahr AG & Co), Stubbenhuk 10, Hamburg, 20459, Germany. TEL 49-40-37030, FAX 49-40-37035010, info@corporate-editors.com, http://www.corporate-editors.com. Ed. Joachim Bokeloh. Adv. contact Heiko Hager.

362.1 616.97 CAN ISSN 1719-7449
LE FLASH HERBE A POUX. Text in French. 2000. irreg. **Document type:** *Bulletin, Consumer.*
Published by: Quebec, Agence de Sante et de Services Sociaux de la Monteregie, 1255, rue Beauregard, Longueuil, PQ J4K 2M3, Canada. TEL 450-928-6777 ext 4213, http://www.msss.gouv.qc.ca.

FLIGHT SAFETY. *see* AERONAUTICS AND SPACE FLIGHT

362.1 USA ISSN 2154-7084
FLORIDA MEDICAL MAGAZINE. Text in English. 200?. q. free to members (effective 2010). adv. back issues avail. **Document type:** *Magazine, Trade.* **Description:** Provides technical articles and features.
Related titles: Online - full text ed.: free (effective 2010).
Published by: Florida Medical Association, Inc., 123 S Adams St, Tallahassee, FL 32301. TEL 850-224-6496, 800-762-0233, FAX 850-224-6627, communications@medone.org. Ed. Karl M Altenburger. Adv. contact Shawn M Winship. color page USD 2,280; bleed 8.625 x 11.125.

FLUVIEW. *see* MEDICAL SCIENCES—Communicable Diseases

614 PHL ISSN 0046-4317
FOCUS ON MENTAL HEALTH. Text in English, Tagalog. 1951. q. USD 3.60 to individuals; USD 37 to institutions (effective 2000). charts; illus.; stat. **Document type:** *Newsletter.* **Description:** Covers public health and safety, community mental health, psychology and psychiatry, social work and social development.
Indexed: IPP.
Published by: Philippine Mental Health Association, 18 East Ave, PO Box 1040, Quezon City CPO, Quezon City Mm, 1100, Philippines. Ed. Regina G. De Jesus. Circ: 1,500.

614 CAN ISSN 0015-5195
FOCUS: SOCIAL AND PREVENTIVE MEDICINE. Text in English. 1964. 4/yr. adv. bk.rev. illus. **Document type:** *Newsletter.*
Related titles: Online - full content ed.
Published by: Community Health Services (Saskatoon) Association, 455 2nd Ave N, Saskatoon, SK S7K 2C2, Canada. TEL 306-652-0300, FAX 306-664-4120, healthinformationcentre@communityclinic.sk.ca. Ed., R&P Ingrid Larson. Adv. contact Ingrid Larsen. Circ: 5,300.

FOLIA ORTHICA. *see* NUTRITION AND DIETETICS

362.1 351 SWE ISSN 1402-0327
FOLKHAELSORAPPORT. Text in Swedish. 1993. irreg. **Document type:** *Monographic series, Government.*
Published by: Landstinget i Oestergoetland, Linkoeping, 581 91, Sweden. TEL 46-10-1030000, landstinget@lio.se, http://www.lio.se.

353.6 664 NZL ISSN 1177-4762
FOOD CONNECT. Text in English. 2006. q. back issues avail. **Document type:** *Newsletter, Trade.*
Formed by the merger of (1999-2005): Dairy Connection (1174-7846); (2000-2005): A P Bulletin (1174-4618); (2003-2004): Flourish (1176-3582)
Related titles: Online - full text ed.: ISSN 1177-8814.
Indexed: A34, A36, A37, A38, AgrForAb, B23, C25, CABA, E12, F08, F11, F12, FCA, G11, GH, H16, H17, IndVet, MaizeAb, N02, N03, N05, O01, OR, P32, P33, P37, P38, P39, P40, PGegResA, PN&I, R07, R08, R12, R13, S13, S16, S17, TAR, VS, W10, W11.
Published by: New Zealand Food Safety Authority, 68-86 Jervois Quay, PO Box 2835, Wellington, New Zealand. TEL 64-4-8942500, FAX 64-4-8942501, nzfsa.info@nzfsa.govt.nz.

FOOD FOCUS. *see* FOOD AND FOOD INDUSTRIES

362.1 GBR ISSN 1350-1879
FOOD FORUM. Text in English. 1992. q. GBP 74 (effective 2009). **Document type:** *Bulletin, Trade.* **Description:** Provides current information to persons responsible for food safety.
Indexed: FS&TA.
—CCC.
Published by: Chartered Institute of Environmental Health, Chadwick Court, 15 Hatfields, London, SE1 8DJ, United Kingdom. TEL 44-20-79286006, FAX 44-20-79285862, info@cieh.org, http://www.cieh.org.

FOOD INSIGHT. *see* FOOD AND FOOD INDUSTRIES

344.04 GBR
FOOD LAW. Text in English. 1990. irreg., latest no.3, 2009, Feb. GBP 95 per vol. (effective 2010). **Document type:** *Monographic series, Trade.* **Description:** Provides access to the legislation that affects practitioners on a daily basis.
Formerly (until 2004): Butterworths Food Law
Published by: Bloomsbury Professional Ltd. (Subsidiary of: Bloomsbury Publishing plc), 41-43 Boltro Rd, Haywards Heath, West Sussex RH16 1BJ, United Kingdom. TEL 44-1444-416119, FAX 44-1444-440426, customerservices@bloomsburyprofessional.com.

613 USA ISSN 0884-0806
CODEN: FPREEP
FOOD PROTECTION REPORT. Text in English. 1985. m. (11/yr.). bk.rev. back issues avail.; reprints avail. **Document type:** *Newsletter, Trade.* **Description:** Includes information on food safety news, concerns, and techniques for members of the food industry, the government, and academia.
—BLDSC (3981.865100).
Published by: Pike & Fischer, Inc. (Subsidiary of: The Bureau of National Affairs, Inc.), 1010 Wayne Ave, Ste 1400, Silver Spring, MD 20910. TEL 301-562-1530, 800-255-8131, FAX 301-562-1521, customercare@pf.com, http://www.pf.com. Ed. Ellen Morton. Pub., R&P U Joseph Hecker.

FOOD PROTECTION TRENDS; science and news from the International Association for Food Protection. *see* FOOD AND FOOD INDUSTRIES

614.3 636.089 NLD ISSN 1871-9295
FOOD SAFETY ASSURANCE AND VETERINARY PUBLIC HEALTH. Text in English. 2002. irreg., latest vol.5, 2009. price varies. **Document type:** *Monographic series, Academic/Scholarly.*
Published by: Wageningen Academic Publishers, PO Box 220, Wageningen, 6700 AE, Netherlands. TEL 31-317-476515, FAX 31-317-453417, info@wageningenacademic.com, http://www.wageningenacademic.com. Ed. Frans J M Smulders.

FOOD SAFETY HANDBOOK. *see* FOOD AND FOOD INDUSTRIES

THE FOOD SAFETY PROFESSIONAL. *see* FOOD AND FOOD INDUSTRIES

FOOD TALK; sanitation tips for food workers. *see* FOOD AND FOOD INDUSTRIES

363.1926 USA ISSN 1535-0150
FOOD TRACEABILITY REPORT. Text in English. 2001. m. USD 540 domestic; USD 615 foreign (effective 2011). **Document type:** *Newsletter, Trade.*
Related titles: Online - full text ed.
Indexed: B02, B15, B17, B18, G04, G06, G07, G08, I05.
Published by: Agra Informa U S A (Subsidiary of: C R C Press, LLC), 2200 Clarendon Blvd, Ste 1401, Arlington, VA 22201. TEL 703-527-1680, FAX 703-527-2401, cs@foodregulation.com, http://www.foodregulation.com.

613 NLD ISSN 1878-9943
FOOLCOLOR. Text in Dutch. 1998. bi-m. adv. **Document type:** *Magazine, Consumer.*
Formerly (until 2008): KlantenKrant (1389-2738)
Published by: FoolColor Mediaproducties, Johan van Oldenbarneveltlaan 15, Groningen, 9716 EA, Netherlands. TEL 31-50-5751390, redactie@foolcolormedia.nl. Ed. Henk Santing. Circ: 3,250.

362.1 330 USA ISSN 1558-9544
➤ **FORUM FOR HEALTH ECONOMICS & POLICY**; timely and evolving forums on important health care issues. Text in English. 1998. s-a. (1 issue in 2008). USD 485 to institutions; USD 1,455 to corporations (effective 2011). back issues avail. **Document type:** *Journal, Academic/Scholarly.* **Description:** Covers health economics and health policy. Each volume contains issue 1: Frontiers in Health Policy Research, and issue 2: Forums.
Incorporates (1998-2005): Frontiers in Health Policy Research (Online) (1537-2634)
Media: Online - full text.
Indexed: A36, B01, B06, B07, B09, C06, C07, CA, CABA, ESPM, EconLit, GH, H05, N02, N03, P30, P34, PAIS, RiskAb, T02, T05, W11.
—CCC.
Published by: Berkeley Electronic Press, 2809 Telegraph Ave, Ste 202, Berkeley, CA 94705. TEL 510-665-1200, FAX 510-665-1201, info@bepress.com.

614 FRA ISSN 0755-3374
RA407.5.F7
FRANCE. MINISTERE DE L'EMPLOI ET DE LA SOLIDARITE. ANNUAIRE DES STATISTIQUES SANITAIRES ET SOCIALES. Text in French. 1971. a., latest 1998. EUR 30.50 newsstand/cover (effective 2003). **Document type:** *Government.*
Supersedes: France. Ministere de la Sante et de la Securite Sociale. Tableaux Statistiques "Sante et Securite Sociale"; France. Ministere de la Sante. Tableaux Sante et Securite Sociale; France. Ministere de la Sante Publique et de la Securite Sociale. Annuaire Statistique de la Sante et de l'Action Sociale (0071-8866)
Published by: (France. Ministere du Travail, des Relations Sociales, de la Famille, de la Solidarite et de la Ville), Documentation Francaise, 29-31 Quai Voltaire, Paris, Cedex 7 75344, France. FAX 33-1-40157230.

614 DEU ISSN 1610-899X
FRANKFURTER SCHRIFTEN ZUR GESUNDHEITSPOLITIK UND ZUM GESUNDHEITSRECHT. Text in German. 2003. irreg., latest vol.11, 2010. price varies. **Document type:** *Monographic series, Academic/Scholarly.*

P

Published by: Peter Lang GmbH (Subsidiary of: Peter Lang Publishing Group), Eschborner Landstr 42-50, Frankfurt Am Main, 60489, Germany. TEL 49-69-7807050, FAX 49-69-78070550, zentrale.frankfurt@peterlang.com. Eds. Ingwer Ebsen, Thomas Gerlinger.

363.7 JPN ISSN 0918-9173
FUKUOKA-KEN HOKEN KANKYO KENKYUJO NENPO/FUKUOKA INSTITUTE OF HEALTH AND ENVIRONMENTAL SCIENCES. ANNUAL REPORT. Text in Japanese. 1974. a. free. back issues avail. **Document type:** *Academic/Scholarly.*
Formerly (until 1990): Fukuoka-ken Eisei Kogai Senta Nenpo/Fukuoka Environmental Research Center. Annual Report (0287-1254)
Published by: Fukuoka-ken Hoken Kankyo Kenkyujo/Fukuoka Institute of Health and Environmental Sciences, 39 Mukaizano, Dazaifu, Fukuoka, 818-0135, Japan. TEL 81-92-9219940, FAX 81-92-9281203, http://www.fihes.pref.fukuoka.jp/index.htm. Circ: 500.

362.1 USA
FUNDING WATCH. Text in English. 1990. m. free in state. **Document type:** *Newsletter, Government.* **Description:** Reports on public health-related funding to organizations in Texas.
Formerly (until July 1996): HIV Funding Watch
Published by: Texas Department of Health, Funding Information Center, 1100 W 49th St, Austin, TX 78756-3199. TEL 512-458-7684, FAX 512-458-7683. Ed. Darlene Murray. Circ: (controlled).

362.1 NLD
FUTURE HEALTH SCENARIOS. Text in English. 1987. irreg., latest vol.23, 1994. price varies. back issues avail. **Document type:** *Proceedings.* **Description:** Publishes studies on changes and projections in health care and health technology.
Published by: (Scenario Commission on Future Health Care Technology), Springer Netherlands (Subsidiary of: Springer Science+Business Media), Van Godewijckstraat 30, Dordrecht, 3311 GX, Netherlands. TEL 31-78-6576050, FAX 31-78-6576474.

THE FUTURE OF CHILDREN. *see* CHILDREN AND YOUTH—About

363.7 DEU ISSN 0932-6200
CODEN: GHBUEG
➤ **G I - GESUNDHEITS INGENIEUR**; Haustechnik - Bauphysik - Umwelttechnik. Text in German. 1877. bi-m. EUR 200; EUR 100 to students; EUR 38 newsstand/cover (effective 2011). adv. bk.rev. abstr.; bibl.; charts; illus.; pat. index. **Document type:** *Journal, Academic/Scholarly.*
Former titles (until 1985): Haustechnik, Bauphysik, Umwelttechnik (0172-8199); Gesundheits-Ingenieur (0016-9277)
Indexed: A22, ChemAb, IBR, IBZ, IBuildSA, IndMed, P30.
—CASDDS, GNLM, IE, Infotrieve, INIST, Linda Hall. **CCC.**
Published by: Oldenbourg Industrieverlag GmbH (Subsidiary of: Oldenbourg Wissenschaftsverlag GmbH), Rosenheimer Str 145, Munich, 81671, Germany. TEL 49-89-450510, FAX 49-89-45051207, oiv-info@oldenbourg.de. Ed. Klaus Usemann. Circ: 1,490 (paid and controlled).

362.1 DEU ISSN 1863-5245
RA969
➤ **G M S KRANKENHAUSHYGIENE INTERDISZIPLINAER.** (German Medical Science) Text in German, English. 2006. a. free (effective 2011). **Document type:** *Journal, Academic/Scholarly.* **Description:** Aims to foster understanding and practice in the emerging field of infection control.
Media: Online - full text.
Indexed: A01, P30, T02.
—CCC.
Published by: (Deutsche Gesellschaft fuer Krankenhaushygiene e.V.), German Medical Science (G M S), Ubierstr 20, Duesseldorf, 40223, Germany. TEL 49-211-312828, FAX 49-211-316819, info@egms.de.

362.1 CAN ISSN 1910-1872
G O L PUBLIC REPORT. (Government On-Line) Text in English. 2003. a., latest 2006. **Document type:** *Government.*
Media: Online - full text. **Related titles:** French ed.: G E D. Rapport Public. ISSN 1910-1880.
Published by: Health Canada/Sante Canada, Address Locator 0900C2, Ottawa, ON K1A OK9, Canada. TEL 613-957-2991, 866-225-0709, FAX 613-941-5366, info@www.hc-sc.gc.ca.

610 ESP ISSN 0213-9111
RA287
GACETA SANITARIA. Text in Spanish; Summaries in English. 1982. bi-m. EUR 93.44 combined subscription domestic print & online eds.; EUR 236.58 combined subscription foreign print & online eds. (effective 2009). bk.rev. bibl.; charts. back issues avail.; reprints avail. **Document type:** *Journal, Trade.*
Former titles (until 1986): Gaseta Sanitaria de Barcelona (0212-0542); (1888-1910): Gaceta Sanitaria de Barcelona (0212-2030)
Related titles: Online - full text ed.: ISSN 1578-1283. 1996. free (effective 2011) (from ScienceDirect).
Indexed: A22, A34, A36, A38, CABA, E12, EMBASE, ExcerpMed, F09, G11, GH, H17, IME, INI, IndMed, IndVet, LT, MEDLINE, N02, N03, P30, P33, P38, P39, R07, R08, R10, R11, R12, RRTA, Reac, S13, S16, SCI, SCOPUS, SSCI, SoyAb, T05, TAR, VS, W07, W10, W11.
—BLDSC (4066.169000), GNLM, IE, Infotrieve, Ingenta. **CCC.**
Published by: (Sociedad Espanola de Salud Publica y Administracion Sanitaria), Elsevier Doyma (Subsidiary of: Elsevier Health Sciences), Traversa de Gracia 17-21, Barcelona, 08021, Spain. TEL 34-932-418800, FAX 34-932-419020, editorial@elsevier.com. Ed. E. Fernandez Munoz. R&P Monica Barnes. Adv. contact Jose Antonio Hernandez. Circ: 3,700.

362.1 370 JPN ISSN 0386-9598
LB3414.J3
GAKKOU HOKEN KENKYUU/JAPANESE JOURNAL OF SCHOOL HEALTH. Text in Japanese. 1959. m. **Document type:** *Journal, Academic/Scholarly.*
—CCC.
Published by: Hoken Kenkyuusha/Japanese Association of School Health, Kagawa Medical University, Social Medicine, Hygiene and Public Health, 1750-1 Miki-cho, Kita-gun, Kagawa, 761-0793, Japan. TEL 81-87-8912433, FAX 81-87-8912134, s_health@med.kagawa-u.ac.jp.

614 ZAF ISSN 1818-9067
GEDAGTES; nuusbrief vir ondersteuners van die Suid-Afrikaanse Federasie vir Geestesgesondheid. Text in Afrikaans. 2006. 3/yr. **Document type:** *Newsletter.*
Related titles: ◆ English ed.: Thoughts. ISSN 1818-9059.
Published by: South African Federation for Mental Health/Suid-Afrikaanse Federasie vir Geestesgesondheid, Private Bag X 3053, Randburg, 2125, South Africa. TEL 27-11-7811852, FAX 27-11-3260625, safmh@sn.apc.org, http://www.safmh.org.za.

DE GEHEEL-ONTHOUDER; feiten en commentaren over alcohol en drugs. *see* DRUG ABUSE AND ALCOHOLISM

362.1 USA ISSN 1949-9248
GEN 7. Text in English. 2008. s-a. free to qualified personnel (effective 2009). **Document type:** *Journal, Consumer.* **Description:** Features stories about persons who are managing their diabetes.
Published by: U.S. Department of Health and Human Services, Indian Health Service, Diabetes Treatment and Prevention, The Reyes Bldg, 801 Thompson Ave, Ste 400, Rockville, MD 20852. TEL 505-248-4182, FAX 505-248-4188, diabetesprogram@ihs.gov, http://www.ihs.gov/MedicalPrograms/diabetes/.

362.1 NZL ISSN 1177-6773
GEOHEALTH. PROCEEDINGS. Text in English. 2002. biennial. **Document type:** *Government.* **Description:** Promotes the exchange of ideas and experiences in the application of health geographical information sciences and systems to public health research and practice.
Related titles: Online - full text ed.: ISSN 1177-6781.
Published by: Ministry of Health, Public Health Intelligence, PO Box 5013, Wellington, New Zealand. TEL 64-4-4962000, FAX 64-4-4952340, phi@moh.govt.nz, http://www.moh.govt.nz/phi.

362.1 AUS ISSN 1833-3656
GEORGE RESEARCH. Text in English. 2006. q. **Document type:** *Newsletter, Consumer.*
Media: Online - full text.
Published by: George Institute for International Health, PO Box M201, Missenden Rd, Sydney, NSW 2050, Australia. TEL 61-2-9993-4500, FAX 61-2-9993-4501, info@george.org.au.

614 AUT
GESUENDER LEBEN; Das Wohlfuehlmagazin. Text in German. 11/yr. EUR 20; EUR 2.60 newsstand/cover (effective 2007). adv. **Document type:** *Magazine, Consumer.*
Former titles: S - Gesuender Leben; S Kontakt
Published by: S P V Printmedien GmbH, Margaretenstr 22-2-9, Vienna, N 1040, Austria. TEL 43-1-5812890, FAX 43-1-581289023. Ed. Klaus Orthaber. Adv. contact Michael Hayek. Circ: 80,000.

628.2 JPN ISSN 0021-4639
TD511 CODEN: GSKSAQ
GESUIDO KYOKAISHI/JAPAN SEWAGE WORKS ASSOCIATION. JOURNAL. Text in Japanese. 1964. m. membership. adv. bibl.; charts; illus.; mkt.; tr.lit. Index. back issues avail. **Document type:** *Journal, Academic/Scholarly.*
Related titles: Online - full content ed.; ◆ Supplement(s): Gesuido Kyokaishi Ronbunshu. ISSN 0917-8252.
Indexed: ChemAb, INIS AtomInd.
—Linda Hall.
Published by: Nihon Gesuido Kyokai/Japan Sewage Works Association, Nihon Bldg., 2-6-2 Ote-machi, Chiyoda-ku, Tokyo, 100-0004, Japan. TEL 81-3-52000811, FAX 81-3-52000839, http://www.jswa.jp/. Circ: 12,000.

613 AUT
GESUNDE STADT. Text in German. q. adv. **Document type:** *Magazine, Consumer.*
Published by: D+R Verlagsgesellschaft mbH, Leberstr 122, Vienna, 1110, Austria. TEL 43-1-740770, FAX 43-1-74077841, office@d-r.at. Ed. Uschi Korda. Adv. contact Michael Scharnagl. B&W page EUR 2,180.19, color page EUR 2,906.91; trim 210 x 297. Circ: 20,000 (controlled).

362.1 DEU ISSN 1611-6321
GESUNDHEIT AKTUELL. Text in German. 1993. m. adv. **Document type:** *Magazine, Consumer.*
Published by: Intermed Verlagsgesellschaft mbH, Woerth Str 3, Fulda, 36037, Germany. TEL 49-661-94960, FAX 49-661-949630, info@intermedverlag.de. adv.: B&W page EUR 9,576, color page EUR 12,980. Circ: 393,260 (controlled).

362.1 DEU ISSN 0936-4056
GESUNDHEIT HEUTE; wellness & fitness. Text in German. 1988. bi-m. EUR 15; EUR 2.50 newsstand/cover (effective 2006). adv. **Document type:** *Magazine, Consumer.*
Formerly (until 1989): Diaet Aktuell (0933-1085)
Published by: Monrovia Verlag, Schuetzenstr 38, Wesel, 46487, Germany. TEL 49-2803-800534, FAX 49-2803-800536. adv.: B&W page EUR 2,975, color page EUR 4,075. Circ: 82,780 (paid and controlled).

614 AUT
GESUNDHEIT IM BRENNPUNKT. Text in German. 1989. irreg., latest vol.10, 2008. price varies. **Document type:** *Monographic series, Academic/Scholarly.*
Published by: Trauner Verlag und Buchservice GmbH, Koeglstr 14, Linz, 4020, Austria. TEL 43-732-778241212, FAX 43-732-778241400, office@trauner.at, http://www.trauner.at.

362.1 DEU
GESUNDHEIT KONKRET. Text in German. q. adv. **Document type:** *Magazine, Consumer.*
Published by: NewsWork Presse Agentur GmbH, Bahnhofstr 46, Sinzing, 93161, Germany. TEL 49-941-307410, FAX 49-941-3074110. adv.: page EUR 10,200. Circ: 960,000 (controlled).

362.1 DEU ISSN 1614-6441
GESUNDHEITSPOLITIK. Text in German. 1999. irreg., latest vol.4, 2009. price varies. **Document type:** *Monographic series, Academic/Scholarly.*
Published by: Ibidem Verlag, Melchiorstr 15, Stuttgart, 70439, Germany. TEL 49-711-9807954, FAX 49-711-9807952, ibidem@ibidem-verlag.de, http://www.ibidem-verlag.de.

614 DEU ISSN 1439-8893
GESUNDHEITSPOLITIK, MANAGEMENT, OEKONOMIE. Text in German. 1995. q. EUR 195 (effective 2007). adv. **Document type:** *Magazine, Trade.*
Incorporates (1999-2001): Krankenversicherungs- und Sozialrecht (1437-5230); Formerly (until 2000): Gesundheitspolitik (0948-3438)
—GNLM.
Published by: P M I Verlag AG, Oberfeldstr 29, Frankfurt Am Main, 60439, Germany. TEL 49-69-5480000, FAX 49-69-54800066, pmiverlag@t-online.de. adv.: B&W page EUR 750, color page EUR 1,465; 184 x 260. Circ: 1,500 (paid and controlled).

614 CHE ISSN 1420-5947
GESUNDHEITSPOLITISCHE INFORMATIONEN/POLITIQUE DE LA SANTE: INFORMATIONS. Short title: G P I. Text in Multiple languages. 1977. 4/yr. USD 60 (effective 2001). bk.rev.; Website rev. abstr.; bibl.; charts; stat. 46 p./no.; **Document type:** *Newsletter, Consumer.* **Description:** Examines health policies, health economics, medical sociology, patients' legal and human rights as well as related economic topics.
Published by: Schweizerische Gesellschaft fuer Gesundheitspolitik/Societe Suisse pour la Politique de la Sante (Swiss Society for Health Policy), Haldenweg 10 A, Muri B. Bern, 3074, Switzerland. TEL 41-31-9526655, FAX 41-31-952-6800, info@sggp.ch. Ed. Gerhard Kocher. Circ: 2,200.

614 DEU ISSN 1439-4421
DAS GESUNDHEITSWESEN (ONLINE). Text in German. 2000. m. EUR 299 to institutions (effective 2011).
Media: Online - full text. **Related titles:** Microform ed.: (from PQC); ◆ Print ed.: Das Gesundheitswesen (Print). ISSN 0941-3790; Supplement(s): Das Gesundheitswesen. Supplement (Online). ISSN 1615-5602. 2001.
—CCC.
Published by: Georg Thieme Verlag, Ruedigerstr 14, Stuttgart, 70469, Germany. TEL 49-711-8931421, FAX 49-711-8931410, leser.service@thieme.de, http://www.thieme.de.

614 DEU ISSN 0941-3790
RA421 CODEN: GHWNFX
➤ **DAS GESUNDHEITSWESEN (PRINT)**; Sozialmedizin, Gesundheits-System-Forschung, Public Health, Education, Oeffentlicher Gesundheitsdienst, Medizinischer Dienst. Text in German. 1939. 12/yr. EUR 229 to institutions; EUR 311 combined subscription to institutions (print & online eds.); EUR 36 newsstand/cover (effective 2011). adv. bk.rev. abstr.; charts; illus. index. reprints avail. **Document type:** *Journal, Academic/Scholarly.*
Former titles (until 1992): Oeffentliche Gesundheitswesen (0029-8573); (until 1967): Oeffentliche Gesundheitsdienst
Related titles: Microform ed.: (from PQC); ◆ Online - full text ed.: Das Gesundheitswesen (Online). ISSN 1439-4421; Supplement(s): Das Gesundheitswesen. Sonderheft. ISSN 0949-7013. 1993.
Indexed: A20, A22, CISA, CurCont, EMBASE, ExcerpMed, F09, FR, FS&TA, INI, IndMed, MEDLINE, P30, R10, Reac, S02, S03, SCOPUS, SSCI, W07.
—BLDSC (4165.078500), GNLM, IE, Infotrieve, Ingenta, INIST. **CCC.**
Published by: (Bundesverband der Aerzte des Oeffentlichen Gesundheitsdienstes e.V., Gesellschaft fuer Medizinische Ausbildung e.V.), Georg Thieme Verlag, Ruedigerstr 14, Stuttgart, 70469, Germany. TEL 49-711-8931421, FAX 49-711-8931410, kunden.service@thieme.de. Ed. Manfred Wildner. Adv. contact Andreas Schweiger TEL 49-711-8931245. Circ: 1,400 (paid and controlled). **Co-sponsors:** Berufsverband der Sozialversicherungsaerzte Deutschlands e.V.; Deutsche Gesellschaft fuer Public Health e.V.; Deutsche Gesellschaft fuer Sozialmedizin und Praevention.

614.2 NLD ISSN 1874-9631
GEZOND EN WEL. Key Title: Gezond&Wel. Text in Dutch. 2004. 3/yr. **Document type:** *Magazine, Consumer.*
Formerly (until 2006): Leef je Leven (1872-3217)
Published by: (Zorggroep Utrecht West), Axioma Communicatie BV/Axioma Communications BV (Subsidiary of: Springer Science+Business Media), Lt Gen Van Heutszlaan 4, Postbus 176, Baarn, 3740 AD, Netherlands. TEL 31-35-5488140, FAX 31-35-5425820, http://www.axioma.nl.

614 NLD ISSN 1874-1037
GEZONDGIDS. Text in Dutch. 1998. 10/yr. EUR 58 (effective 2009).
Formerly (until 2004): Gezond (1389-2215)
Published by: Consumentenbond, Enthovenplein 1, Postbus 1000, The Hague, 2500 BA, Netherlands. TEL 31-70-4454545, FAX 31-70-4454596, http://www.consumentenbond.nl.

344.04 NLD ISSN 1872-4205
GEZONDHEIDSWETGEVING IN DE PRAKTIJK. Variant title: Tekstuitgave Gezondheidswetgeving in de Praktijk. Text in Dutch. 2006. 4/yr. EUR 143.75 combined subscription (print & online eds.) (effective 2009).
Formerly (until 2006): Wetgeving Gezondheidszorg (1566-7243)
Related titles: Online - full text ed.: EUR 118 (effective 2009).
Published by: Bohn Stafleu van Loghum B.V. (Subsidiary of: Springer Science+Business Media), Postbus 246, Houten, 3990 GA, Netherlands. TEL 31-30-6383838, FAX 31-30-6383839, boekhandels@bsl.nl, http://www.bsl.nl. Eds. H E G M Hermans, J J M Linders, R N van Donk.

344.04 NLD ISSN 1574-4701
GEZONDHEIDSZORG JURISPRUDENTIE. Text in Dutch. 2004. m. EUR 178.50 combined subscription per quarter (print & online eds.) (effective 2009).
Related titles: Online - full text ed.
Published by: Sdu Uitgevers bv, Postbus 20025, The Hague, 2500 EA, Netherlands. TEL 31-70-3789911, FAX 31-70-3854321, sdu@sdu.nl, http://www.sdu.nl/.

614 659.2 NLD ISSN 1876-3030
GIDS PATIENTENINFORMATIE. Text in Dutch. 1990. a.
Published by: Nederlandse Patienten Consumenten Federatie, Postbus 1539, Utrecht, 3500 BM, Netherlands. TEL 31-30-2970303, FAX 31-30-2970606, npcf@npcf.nl, http://www.npcf.nl.

362.1 JPN ISSN 1340-2676
CODEN: GHKKEV
GIFU-KEN HOKEN KANKYO KENKYUJOHO. Text in Japanese. 1972. a. **Document type:** *Government.*
Formed by the merger of (1972-1992): Gifu-ken Eisei Kenkyujoho/Gifu Prefectural Institute of Public Health. Report (0385-1575); Which was formerly: Gifu-ken Eisei Kenkyujo Nenpo; (1970-1992): Gifu-ken Kogai Kenkyujo Nenpo (0385-1583)
—CASDDS.
Published by: Gifu-ken Hoken Kankyo Kenkyujo/Gifu Pref. Institute of Health & Environmental Sciences, 1-1, Naka-Fudogaoka, Kakamigahara, 504-0838, Japan. TEL 81-58-3802100, FAX 81-58-3715016, hokan@health.rd.pref.gifu.jp.

362.1 BGD ISSN 0253-7508
GLIMPSE. Text in English. 1979. bi-m. **Document type:** *Newsletter, Consumer.*
Related titles: Online - full text ed.
Indexed: P30, SCOPUS.
—BLDSC (4195.223000).
Published by: International Centre for Diarrhoeal Disease Research Bangladesh, GPO Box 128, Dhaka, 1000, Bangladesh. TEL 880-2-8811751, FAX 880-2-8823116, info@icddrb.org, http://www.icddrb.org.

614 USA ISSN 1937-514X
RA421
➤ **GLOBAL HEALTH**; an online journal for the digital age. Text in English. 2008. q. free (effective 2010). **Document type:** *Journal, Academic/Scholarly.* **Description:** For students preparing to enter careers in public health and health care worldwide.
Media: Online - full text.
Indexed: A01.
Published by: University of Findlay, College of Business, 1000 N Main St, Findlay, OH 45840. TEL 419-422-8313, 800-472-9502, FAX 419-434-4822, http://www.findlay.edu/academics/colleges/cobm/default.htm.

362.1 SGP ISSN 2010-0493
▼ **GLOBAL HEALTH DIPLOMACY.** Abbreviated title: G H D. Text in English. forthcoming 2011. irreg. **Document type:** *Monographic series, Academic/Scholarly.* **Description:** Focuses on negotiations that shape and manage the global policy environment for health in health and non-health fora.
Published by: World Scientific Publishing Co. Pte. Ltd., 5 Toh Tuck Link, Singapore, 596224, Singapore. TEL 65-6466-5775, FAX 65-6467-7667, wspc@wspc.com.sg, http://www.worldscientific.com. Eds. Ilona Kickbusch, Thomas E Novotny. **Dist. by:** World Scientific Publishing Co., Inc., 27 Warren St, Ste 401-402, Hackensack, NJ 07601. TEL 201-487-9655, 800-227-7562, FAX 201-487-9656, 888-977-2665, wspc@wspc.com; World Scientific Publishing Ltd., 57 Shelton St, London WC2H 9HE, United Kingdom. TEL 44-207-8360888, FAX 44-207-8362020, sales@wspc.co.uk.

362.1 USA ISSN 1939-2389
RA441
➤ **GLOBAL HEALTH GOVERNANCE**; the scholarly journal for the new health security paradigm. Text in English. 2007. s-a. free (effective 2011). back issues avail. **Document type:** *Journal, Academic/Scholarly.* **Description:** Provides a platform for academics and practitioners to explore global health issues and their implications for governance and security at national and international levels.
Media: Online - full text.
Published by: Seton Hall University, Center for Global Health Studies, 400 S Orange Ave, South Orange, NJ 07079. TEL 973-275-2515, FAX 973-275-2519, http://www.shu.edu/academics/diplomacy/global-health-studies/journal-global-health-governance.cfm. Ed. Yanzhong Huang.

600 GBR ISSN 1757-9759
RA427.8
➤ **GLOBAL HEALTH PROMOTION/PROMOTION ET EDUCATION.** Text in English, French, Spanish. 1982. q. USD 517, GBP 280 combined subscription to institutions (print & online eds.); USD 507, GBP 274 to institutions (effective 2011). adv. bibl.; charts; illus.; stat. biennial index. 48 p./no.; back issues avail.; reprint service avail. from PSC. **Document type:** *Journal, Academic/Scholarly.* **Description:** Presents theoretical research and practical papers on experiences, opinions and research leading to applications for health promotion and health education internationally.
Former titles (until Jul.2008): Promotion & Education (1025-3823); (until Mar.1994): Hygie (0751-7149); Which was formed by the merger of (1958-1982): International Journal of Health Education (0020-7306); (19??-1982): Revista Internacional de Educacion para la Salud (0254-4008); (1958-1982): Revue Internationale d'Education pour la Sante (0482-816X); Which was formerly (until 1972): Revue Internationale d'Education Sanitaire (1027-9288); (until 1968): Revue Internationale d'Education de la Sante (1027-927X)
Related titles: Microfilm ed.: (from PQC); Online - full text ed.: ISSN 1756-3976. USD 465, GBP 252 to institutions (effective 2011).
Indexed: A20, A22, A34, A36, AMHA, B29, C06, C07, C08, CA, CABA, CINAHL, CISA, CPE, D01, E01, E03, E09, EMBASE, ERI, ExcerpMed, F09, FAMLI, FR, GH, H05, IndMed, MEDLINE, N02, N03, NRN, P10, P18, P19, P20, P21, P22, P24, P30, P34, P48, P50, P53, P54, PAIS, PQC, R12, SCOPUS, T02, T05, TAR, W11.
—BLDSC (4195.418700), GNLM, IE, Infotrieve, Ingenta, INIST. **CCC.**
Published by: (Union Internationale de Promotion de la Sante et d'Education pour la Sante/International Union for Health Promotion and Education FRA), Sage Publications Ltd. (Subsidiary of: Sage Publications, Inc.), 1 Oliver's Yard, 55 City Rd, London, EC1Y 1SP, United Kingdom. TEL 44-20-73248500, FAX 44-20-73248600, info@sagepub.co.uk, http://www.uk.sagepub.com/home.nav. Ed. Maurice B Mittelmark. adv.: B&W page USD 11,500; 210 x 297. Circ: 4,000.

▼➤ **GLOBAL JOURNAL OF HEALTH SCIENCE.** *see* MEDICAL SCIENCES

➤ **GLOBAL PUBLIC HEALTH**; an international journal for research, policy and practice. *see* MEDICAL SCIENCES

362 610 USA ISSN 2151-9358
RA441
GLOBAL PULSE. Text in English. 2005. q. back issues avail. **Document type:** *Journal, Academic/Scholarly.* **Description:** Features articles addressing global health issues.
Media: Online - full content.
Published by: American Medical Student Association, 1902 Association Dr, Reston, VA 20191. TEL 703-620-6600, FAX 703-620-5873, amsa@amsa.org, http://www.amsa.org. Eds. Hana Akselrod, Julio Bracero.

362.1 320 GBR ISSN 1744-8603
RA441
➤ **GLOBALIZATION AND HEALTH.** Text in English. 2004. irreg. free (effective 2011). adv. back issues avail. **Document type:** *Journal, Academic/Scholarly.* **Description:** Provides a platform for research, knowledge sharing and debate on the topic of globalization and its effects on health, both positive and negative.
Media: Online - full text.
Indexed: A01, A26, A36, A39, C06, C07, C27, C29, CA, CABA, D01, D03, D04, E12, E13, EMBASE, ExcerpMed, GH, H05, I05, N02, N03, P30, P33, P39, R12, R14, S14, S15, S18, SCOPUS, T02, T05, TAR, W11.
—**CCC.**
Published by: BioMed Central Ltd. (Subsidiary of: Springer Science+Business Media), 236 Gray's Inn Rd, London, WC1X 8HB, United Kingdom. TEL 44-20-31922000, FAX 44-20-31922010, info@biomedcentral.com, http://www.biomedcentral.com. Eds. Emma Pitchforth, Greg Martin. Adv. contact Natasha Bailey TEL 44-20-31922231.

362.1 TWN
GONGAN HUANBAO BAODAO/SAFETY, HEALTH AND ENVIRONMENT TODAY. Text in Chinese. 2001. bi-m. **Document type:** *Government.*
Published by: Jingji Bu, Gongye Ju/Ministry of Economic Affairs, Industrial Development Bureau, 41-3, Hsin Yi Rd., Sec. 3, Taipei, Taiwan. TEL 886-2-27541255, FAX 886-2-27030160, http://www.moeaidb.gov.tw/.

GOOD PRACTICE IN HEALTH, SOCIAL CARE AND CRIMINAL JUSTICE. *see* SOCIAL SERVICES AND WELFARE

353.6 351.0285 USA ISSN 1559-2553
RA395.A3
GOVERNMENT HEALTH I T. Text in English. 2006 (Feb.). bi-m. free domestic; USD 125 in Canada & Mexico; USD 165 elsewhere (effective 2006). adv. **Document type:** *Magazine, Consumer.* **Description:** Reports on the emerging role for federal, state and local government in driving the use of technology in the public and private health care arenas in the United States and abroad.
Published by: F C W Media Group (Subsidiary of: 101Communications, Llc.), 3141 Fairview Park Dr, Ste 777, Falls Church, VA 22042. TEL 703-876-5100. Ed. John Stein Moore TEL 703-876-5096. Pub. Anne Armstrong TEL 703-876-5041. adv.: color page USD 7,500; trim 8.75 x 10.875. Circ: 30,000 (controlled).

614 GBR
RA241
GREAT BRITAIN. DEPARTMENT OF HEALTH. CHIEF MEDICAL OFFICER. ANNUAL REPORT. Variant title: Chief Medical Officer on the State of the Public Health. Text in English. 1921-1998; resumed 2001. a., latest 2003. price varies. reprints avail. **Document type:** *Government.*
Former titles (until 1997): Great Britain. Department of Health. On the State of the Public Health (0072-6087); Great Britain. Department of Health and Social Security. On the State of the Public Health (0260-3578)
Related titles: Audio cassette/tape ed.; Braille ed.; Diskette ed.; Online - full text ed.: free.
—**CCC.**
Published by: Great Britain. Department of Health, PO Box 777, London, SE1 6XH, United Kingdom. TEL 44-870-1555455, FAX 44-162-3724524, dh@prolog.uk.com.

614.3 GBR
GREAT BRITAIN. MEDICINES ACT 1968 ADVISORY BODIES. ANNUAL REPORT. Text in English. 1971. a. free (effective 2009). back issues avail. **Document type:** *Government.* **Description:** Contains the reports of the Medicines Commission, the Committee on Safety of Medicines, the Veterinary Products Committee, the British Pharmacopoeia Commission, and the Advisory Board on the Registration of Homeopathic Products.
Former titles (until 2007): Great Britain. Medicines Commission. Annual Report. (0309-2755); (until 19??): Great Britain. Committee on Safety of Medicines. Report
Related titles: Online - full text ed.
Published by: The Medicines and Healthcare Products Regulatory Agency, Department of Health, 10-2 Market Towers, 1 Nine Elms Ln, London, SW8 5NQ, United Kingdom. TEL 44-20-70842000, FAX 44-20-70842353, info@mhra.gsi.gov.uk, http://www.mhra.gov.uk. Ed. M Vallender.

THE GREY HOUSE TRANSPORTATION SECURITY DIRECTORY & HANDBOOK. *see* TRANSPORTATION

362.1 USA ISSN 1931-7050
GREY LITERATURE REPORT. Text in English. 1999. bi-m. free to qualified personnel (effective 2010). **Document type:** *Journal, Academic/Scholarly.* **Description:** Brings out health services research and selected public health topics.
Media: Online - full text.
Published by: New York Academy of Medicine, 1216 5th Ave, at 103rd St, New York, NY 10029. TEL 212-822-7200, library@nyam.org.

GRIP 4. *see* FIRE PREVENTION

362.1 FRA ISSN 2109-0947
▼ **GROUPEMENT DE COOPERATION SANITAIRE TELESANTE LORRAINE. LA LETTRE D'INFORMATION.** Text in French. 2010. s-a. **Document type:** *Newsletter, Consumer.*
Published by: G C S Telesante Lorraine, 6, Allee de Longchamp, Viller-les-Nancy, 54600, France. TEL 33-3-83971370, FAX 33-3-83971372, http://www.sante-lorraine.fr.

362.1 CAN ISSN 1910-1597
GUIDE TO HEALTH AUTHORITY ACCOUNTABILITY DOCUMENTS. Text in English. 1966. a. **Document type:** *Directory, Trade.*
Formerly (until 200?): Health Authority Business Plan and Annual Report Requirements (1480-3844)
Published by: Alberta Health and Wellness, PO Box 1360, Station Main, Edmonton, AB T5J 2N3, Canada. TEL 780-427-1432, FAX 780-422-0102, http://www.health.gov.ab.ca.

614 CHN ISSN 1001-1137
GUOWAI YIXUE (WEISHENG JINGJI FENCE)/FOREIGN MEDICAL SCIENCES (SANITATION ECONOMICS). Text in Chinese. 1984. q. USD 12 (effective 2009). **Document type:** *Journal, Academic/Scholarly.*
Related titles: Online - full text ed.
—East View.
Published by: Jiangsu Sheng Yixue Qingbao Yanjiusuo, 129, Hanzhong Lu, Nanjing, 210029, China. TEL 86-25-4706094. **Dist. by:** China International Book Trading Corp, 35 Chegongzhuang Xilu, Haidian District, PO Box 399, Beijing 100044, China. TEL 86-10-68412045, FAX 86-10-68412023, cibtc@mail.cibtc.com.cn, http://www.cibtc.com.cn.

GUTTMACHER POLICY REVIEW. *see* BIRTH CONTROL

614 PHL
H E A P JOURNAL. Text in English. 1961. q. PHP 2, USD 1.25. bk.rev.
Formerly: School Health Bulletin (0048-9417)
Published by: (Community-School Health Education Center), Philippine Normal College, Taft Ave, Manila, 2801, Philippines. Ed. Carmen F del Rosario. Circ: 100.

614.4 616.97 USA ISSN 1547-6375
H E P EXPRESS. (Hepatitis) Text in English. 2003 (Mar. 31). irreg., latest no.76, 2008. free (effective 2011). back issues avail. **Document type:** *Newsletter, Trade.* **Description:** Contains articles about new and important hepatitis A, B, and C information.
Media: Online - full text.
Published by: Immunization Action Coalition, 1573 Selby Ave, Ste 234, St. Paul, MN 55104. TEL 651-647-9009, FAX 651-647-9131, admin@immunize.org, http://www.immunize.org.

614.4 NZL ISSN 1178-9565
H R C NEWS. Text in English. 1991. q. free. **Document type:** *Newsletter, Trade.* **Description:** Includes articles about the full range of HRC-funded research, health research methods, funding news, research policy, research promotion.
Former titles: Health Research Council of New Zealand Newsletter (1170-4195); (until 1990): Medical Research Council of New Zealand. Information Bulletin; (until 1989): Medical Research Council of New Zealand, Newsletter
Related titles: Online - full text ed.: free.
Published by: Health Research Council of New Zealand, P.O. Box 5541, Auckland 1, New Zealand. TEL 64-9-3035200, FAX 64-9-3779988, info@hrc.govt.nz. Ed., Pub. Jenny Rankine. Circ: 2,000.

H S TODAY; insight & analysis for homeland security policy makers. *see* PUBLIC ADMINISTRATION

HAMMER. *see* MUSEUMS AND ART GALLERIES

HANDBOOK OF HEALTH ECONOMICS. *see* HEALTH FACILITIES AND ADMINISTRATION

362.1 GBR ISSN 1477-7517
RC566
➤ **HARM REDUCTION JOURNAL.** Text in English. 2004. irreg. free (effective 2011). adv. back issues avail. **Document type:** *Journal, Academic/Scholarly.* **Description:** Focuses on all aspects of minimizing the adverse effects of drugs.
Media: Online - full text.
Indexed: A01, A26, CA, CurCont, EMBASE, ExcerpMed, I05, P03, P30, PsycInfo, R10, Reac, SCOPUS, SSCI, T02, W07.
—**CCC.**
Published by: BioMed Central Ltd. (Subsidiary of: Springer Science+Business Media), 236 Gray's Inn Rd, London, WC1X 8HB, United Kingdom. TEL 44-20-31922000, FAX 44-20-31922010, info@biomedcentral.com, http://www.biomedcentral.com. Ed. Ernest Drucker. Adv. contact Natasha Bailey TEL 44-20-31922231.

344.04 368.014 USA ISSN 2155-6954
KF1297.P55
HARRISMARTIN'S CHINESE DRYWALL LITIGATION REPORT. Text in English. 200?. m. USD 995 combined subscription (print & online eds.) (effective 2010). **Document type:** *Report, Trade.* **Description:** Covers the field of litigation arising from defective, imported and domestic drywall.
Related titles: Online - full text ed.
Published by: HarrisMartin Publishing, 900 W Sproul Rd, Ste 101, Springfield, PA 19064. TEL 800-496-4319, FAX 610-647-5164, service@harrismartin.com.

616.98 USA
HARVARD MEDICAL SCHOOL. CENTER FOR HEALTH AND THE GLOBAL ENVIRONMENT. NEWSLETTER. Text in English. q. **Document type:** *Newsletter.* **Description:** Covers current research, news reports, events and debates concerning human health and the global environmental change.
Media: Online - full text.
Published by: Harvard Medical School, Center for Health and the Global Environment, 401 Park Dr, 2nd Fl, East Boston, MA 02215. TEL 617-384-8530, FAX 617-384-8585, chge@hms.harvard.edu.

614 AUS ISSN 1320-0593
HAZARD. Text in English. 1988. q. free (effective 2011). 20 p./no.; back issues avail. **Document type:** *Bulletin, Consumer.* **Description:** Contains information about injuries and their prevention.
Related titles: Online - full text ed.
Indexed: AusPAIS, SD.
Published by: Victorian Injury Surveillance Unit, Accident Research Centre, Bldg 70, Monash University, Clayton, VIC 3800, Australia. TEL 61-3-99051805, FAX 61-3-99051809, visu.enquire@muarc.monash.edu.au.

363.17 USA ISSN 0889-3454
HAZARDOUS MATERIALS NEWSLETTER. Text in English. 1980. bi-m. looseleaf. USD 55 in North America; USD 60 elsewhere (effective 2007). adv. bk.rev. abstr.; bibl.; tr.lit. 12 p./no.; back issues avail. **Document type:** *Newsletter, Trade.* **Description:** Addresses leak, fire, spill control for incident commanders and experienced responders. Covers incident causes, prevention, remedial action, chemical and biological agents.
Published by: Hazardous Materials Publishing, 89 Silver Circle, PO Box 204, Barre, VT 05641. TEL 802-479-2307. Ed., R&P John R Cashman. Adv. contact Maralyn Nolan. Circ: 419 (paid and free).

HAZARDOUS WASTE CONSULTANT. *see* ENVIRONMENTAL STUDIES—Waste Management

362.1 CAN ISSN 1712-1442
HD7659.B7
HAZARDS OF CONFINED SPACES. Text in English. 2003. irreg. **Document type:** *Handbook/Manual/Guide, Trade.*
Published by: Workers' Compensation Board of British Columbia, PO Box 5350, Stn Terminal, Vancouver, BC V6B 5L5, Canada. http://www.worksafebc.com/default.asp.

362.1 664 CAN ISSN 1712-1434
HD7659.B7
HAZARDS OF CONFINED SPACES FOR FOOD AND BEVERAGE INDUSTRIES. Text in English. 2004. irreg. **Document type:** *Handbook/Manual/Guide, Trade.*
Published by: Workers' Compensation Board of British Columbia, PO Box 5350, Stn Terminal, Vancouver, BC V6B 5L5, Canada. http://www.worksafebc.com/default.asp.

P

362.1 690 CAN ISSN 1712-1426
HD7659.B7
HAZARDS OF CONFINED SPACES FOR MUNICIPALITIES AND THE CONSTRUCTION INDUSTRY. Text in English. 2004. irreg.
Document type: *Handbook/Manual/Guide, Trade.*
Published by: Workers' Compensation Board of British Columbia, PO Box 5350, Stn Terminal, Vancouver, BC V6B 5L5, Canada. http://www.worksafebc.com/default.asp.

362.1 387 CAN ISSN 1708-6396
HD7659.B7
HAZARDS OF CONFINED SPACES FOR SHIPPING AND TRANSPORTATION INDUSTRIES. Text in English. 2004. irreg.
Document type: *Handbook/Manual/Guide, Trade.*
Published by: Workers' Compensation Board of British Columbia, PO Box 5350, Stn Terminal, Vancouver, BC V6B 5L5, Canada. http://www.worksafebc.com/default.asp.

HAZMAT TRANSPORTATION NEWS. see TRANSPORTATION

363.11 USA ISSN 1546-7309
HAZSAFETY TRAINING ADVISOR. Text in English. 2003. m. USD 189; free to qualified personnel (effective 2008). **Document type:** *Newsletter, Trade.* **Description:** Provides critical information on topics like labeling, placarding, handling flammables, emergency response, regulation changes and more.
Related titles: Online - full text ed.: ISSN 1546-7317.
—CCC.
Published by: J.J. Keller & Associates, Inc., 3003 W Breezewood Ln, PO Box 368, Neenah, WI 54957. TEL 877-564-2333, FAX 800-727-7516, kellersoft@jjkeller.com. Ed. Corrina C Peterson.

614 GBR ISSN 1363-4593
RA418
➤ **HEALTH**; an interdisciplinary journal for the social study of health, illness and medicine. Text in English. 1997. bi-m. USD 1,137, GBP 615 combined subscription to institutions (print & online eds.); USD 1,114, GBP 603 to institutions (effective 2011). adv. bk.rev. back issues avail.; reprint service avail. from PSC. **Document type:** *Journal, Academic/Scholarly.* **Description:** Focuses on the changing place of health matters in modern society.
Related titles: Online - full text ed.: ISSN 1461-7196. USD 1,023, GBP 554 to institutions (effective 2011).
Indexed: A01, A03, A08, A20, A22, B07, B28, C06, C07, C08, CA, CINAHL, CMM, CurCont, E-psyche, E01, EMBASE, ESPM, ExcerpMed, Faml, H04, H05, I14, IBSS, MEDLINE, P03, P30, PsycInfo, PsycholAb, R10, Reac, RiskAb, S02, S03, SCOPUS, SSA, SSCI, SociolAb, T02, V02, W07.
—BLDSC (4274.694140), IE, Infotrieve, Ingenta. **CCC.**
Published by: Sage Publications Ltd. (Subsidiary of: Sage Publications, Inc.), 1 Oliver's Yard, 55 City Rd, London, EC1Y 1SP, United Kingdom. TEL 44-20-73248500, FAX 44-20-73248600, info@sagepub.co.uk, http://www.uk.sagepub.com/home.nav. Ed. Michael Traynor. adv.: B&W page GBP 400; 140 x 210. **Subscr. in the Americas to:** Sage Publications, Inc., 2455 Teller Rd, Thousand Oaks, CA 91320. TEL 805-499-9774, FAX 805-499-0871, journals@sagepub.com.

610.5 CAN ISSN 1193-2295
HEALTH ACTION. Text in English. 1985. q. **Document type:** *Magazine, Consumer.* **Description:** Provides resources and information on the choices available to individuals in their quest for personal health and well-being.
Formerly (until 1992): Option (0832-0357)
Related titles: Online - full text ed.
Indexed: A04.
Published by: Health Action Network Society, 5262 Rumble St., No. 202, Burnaby, BC V5J 2B6, Canada. TEL 604-435-0512, FAX 604-435-1561, hans@hans.org, http://www.hans.org.

368.382 USA ISSN 0278-2715
➤ **HEALTH AFFAIRS**; the policy journal of the health sphere. Text in English. 1981. bi-m. USD 135 combined subscription in North America to individuals (print & online eds.); USD 185 combined subscription elsewhere to individuals (print & online eds.); USD 355 combined subscription in North America to institutions (print & online eds.); USD 405 combined subscription elsewhere to institutions (print & online eds.) (effective 2009). bk.rev. back issues avail.; reprints avail. **Document type:** *Journal, Academic/Scholarly.* **Description:** A health care policy and managed care journal that addresses health care system change from the perspectives of all its players, through data, analysis, policy proposals, and commentary.
Related titles: Microform ed.: (from PQC); Online - full text ed.: USD 335 to institutions (effective 2009).
Indexed: A01, A02, A03, A08, A12, A13, A17, A20, A22, A35, A36, ABIn, AHCMS, ASCA, ASG, AgBio, AgeL, B01, B06, B07, B08, B09, B21, B28, BPIA, Biostat, C06, C07, C08, C12, C28, CA, CABA, CINAHL, CurCont, E01, E12, EMBASE, ESPM, ExcerpMed, FR, Faml, GH, H&SSA, H01, H05, H13, H17, HRA, HospLI, I12, IBSS, INI, ISR, IndMed, Inpharma, LT, MEDLINE, ManagCont, N02, N03, P02, P10, P20, P21, P22, P24, P30, P32, P33, P34, P35, P39, P40, P42, P48, P50, P51, P52, P53, P54, P56, PAIS, PQC, PSA, PSI, R08, R10, R12, R13, Reac, S02, S03, S13, SCI, SCOPUS, SSA, SSCI, SWR&A, SociolAb, T02, T05, TAR, W07, W11.
—BLDSC (4274.710000), CIS, GNLM, IE, Infotrieve, Ingenta, INIST. **CCC.**
Published by: Project HOPE, 7500 Old Georgetown Rd, Ste 600, Bethesda, MD 20814-6133. TEL 301-656-7401, FAX 301-654-2845, hope@projecthope.org, http://www.projhope.org. Circ: 8,000 (paid). **Subscr. to:** Allen Press Inc., PO Box 1897, Lawrence, KS 66044. TEL 785-843-1234, FAX 785-843-1235.

362.1 USA ISSN 1544-5208
➤ **HEALTH AFFAIRS WEB EXCLUSIVES.** Text in English. 2001. w. free (effective 2010). **Document type:** *Journal, Academic/Scholarly.*
Media: Online - full text.
—CCC.
Published by: Project HOPE, 255 Carter Hall Ln, Millwood, VA 22646. TEL 800-544-4673, hope@projecthope.org, http://www.projhope.org.

362.1 USA ISSN 1079-0969
RA394 CODEN: HHRIF4
➤ **HEALTH AND HUMAN RIGHTS**; an international journal. Abbreviated title: H H R. Text in English; Summaries in English, French, Spanish. 1994. s-a. USD 39 domestic; USD 49 foreign (effective 2009). bk.rev. bibl. back issues avail. **Document type:** *Journal, Academic/Scholarly.* **Description:** Examines the impacts of health policies, programs, and practices on human rights and the effects of human rights violations on public health.
Related titles: Online - full text ed.: ISSN 2150-4113.
Indexed: A36, ASSIA, C06, C07, CA, CABA, EMBASE, ExcerpMed, Faml, GEOBASE, GH, IBSS, IndMed, MEDLINE, P05, P30, P34, P42, PAIS, PSA, Perlslam, R12, S02, S03, SCOPUS, SOPODA, SSA, SociolAb, T02, T05, W11.
—Infotrieve.
Published by: Harvard School for Public Health, Francois-Xavier Bagnoud Center for Health and Human Rights, 651 Huntington Ave, 7th Fl, Boston, MA 02115. TEL 617-432-0656, FAX 617-432-4310, fxbcenter@igc.org, http://www.hsph.harvard.edu. Ed. Paul Farmer. **Co-sponsor:** Association Francois-Xavier Bagnoud.

614 CHE ISSN 1684-1700
HEALTH AND HUMAN RIGHTS PUBLICATION SERIES. Text in English. 2002. irreg. **Document type:** *Monographic series, Academic/Scholarly.*
Published by: World Health Organization/Organisation Mondiale de la Sante, Avenue Appia 20, Geneva 27, 1211, Switzerland. TEL 41-22-7912111, FAX 41-22-7913111, publications@who.int, http://www.who.int.

HEALTH AND PERSONAL DEVELOPMENT LEARNING AREA MANUAL (YEAR). see EDUCATION

HEALTH & PLACE. see GEOGRAPHY

614 GBR ISSN 1477-7525
RA1
➤ **HEALTH AND QUALITY OF LIFE OUTCOMES.** Text in English. 2003. irreg. free (effective 2011). adv. back issues avail. **Document type:** *Journal, Academic/Scholarly.* **Description:** Covers papers on all aspects of health-related quality of life (HRQOL) assessment for the evaluation of medical therapies or psychosocial approaches and studies on psychometric properties of HRQOL measures, including cultural validation of instruments.
Media: Online - full text.
Indexed: A01, A02, A03, A08, A26, C06, C07, CA, CurCont, EMBASE, ExcerpMed, H05, H12, I05, MEDLINE, P20, P22, P30, P54, PQC, R10, Reac, SCI, SCOPUS, SSCI, T02, W07.
—CCC.
Published by: BioMed Central Ltd. (Subsidiary of: Springer Science+Business Media), 236 Gray's Inn Rd, London, WC1X 8HB, United Kingdom. TEL 44-20-31922000, FAX 44-20-31922010, info@biomedcentral.com, http://www.biomedcentral.com. Ed. Holger Schunemann. Adv. contact Natasha Bailey TEL 44-20-31922231.

➤ **HEALTH AND SAFETY BULLETIN (SUTTON).** see ENVIRONMENTAL STUDIES—Toxicology And Environmental Safety

353.96094105 GBR
HEALTH AND SAFETY EXECUTIVE ANNUAL REPORT AND ACCOUNTS. Variant title: House of Commons Papers. Health and Safety Executive Annual Report and Accounts. Text in English. 1974. a. free. back issues avail. **Document type:** *Government.*
Former titles (until 2009): Health and Safety Commission Annual Report and the Health and Safety Commission / Executive Accounts (1469-302X); (until 1999): Great Britain. Health and Safety Commission. Annual Report and Accounts (1462-0642); (until 1997): Great Britain. Health and Safety Commission. Annual Report (0954-2639); (until 1987): Health and Safety Commission. Report (0140-5969)
Related titles: Online - full text ed.: free (effective 2009).
—BLDSC (1502.194600). **CCC.**
Published by: (Great Britain. Health and Safety Executive), The Stationery Office, St Crispins, Duke St, Norwich, NR3 1PD, United Kingdom. TEL 44-1603-622211, FAX 44-870-6005533, customer.services@tso.co.uk, http://www.tso.co.uk.

HEALTH & SAFETY LAW REPORTER. see LAW

363.11094105 GBR ISSN 1751-7850
HEALTH AND SAFETY NEWSLETTER. Text in English. 1978. bi-m. GBP 20 (effective 2009). **Document type:** *Newsletter, Trade.* **Description:** Provides practical information which helps comply with the law and run a profitable, healthy and safe business.
Formerly (until Jun.2006): Health and Safety Commission. Newsletter (0144-5685)
—CCC.
Published by: Health and Safety Executive, Rose Court, 2 Southwark Bridge, London, SE1 9HS, United Kingdom. TEL 44-845-3450055, FAX 44-20-75562102, public.enquiries@hse.gov.uk. **Subscr. to:** H S E Books, PO Box 1999, Sudbury, Suffolk CO10 2WA, United Kingdom. TEL 44-1787-881165, FAX 44-1787-313995, hsesubs@prolog.uk.com, http://books.hse.gov.uk.

HEALTH AND SAFETY SCIENCE ABSTRACTS (ONLINE). see PUBLIC HEALTH AND SAFETY—Abstracting, Bibliographies, Statistics

362.1 363.1 GBR
HEALTH & SAFETY SPECIFIERS; health, safety and environmental safety. Text in English. 1974. 6/yr. GBP 24 (effective 2000). adv. bk.rev. **Document type:** *Handbook/Manual/Guide, Trade.*
Former titles: Health and Safety Specifications; Caution Magazine
Published by: Specifiers Journals Ltd, 32 Portland St, Cheltenham, Glos GL52 2PB, United Kingdom. TEL 44-1242-236336, FAX 44-1242-222331. Ed. Debbie Preece. R&P David Constantine. Adv. contact Peter Hebblethwaite. Circ: 14,433.

614 GBR ISSN 1365-2524
HV1
➤ **HEALTH AND SOCIAL CARE IN THE COMMUNITY (ONLINE).** Text in English. 1999. bi-m. GBP 647 in United Kingdom to institutions; EUR 821 in Europe to institutions; USD 1,195 in the Americas to institutions; USD 1,395 elsewhere to institutions (effective 2012). back issues avail. **Document type:** *Journal, Academic/Scholarly.* **Description:** Promotes interdisciplinary collaboration on policy and practice within health and social care in the community.
Media: Online - full text (from IngentaConnect). **Related titles:** Microform ed.: (from PQC); ◆ Print ed.: Health and Social Care in the Community (Print). ISSN 0966-0410.
—CCC.
Published by: Wiley-Blackwell Publishing Ltd. (Subsidiary of: John Wiley & Sons, Inc.), 9600 Garsington Rd, Oxford, OX4 2DQ, United Kingdom. TEL 44-1865-776868, 44-1865-776868, FAX 44-1865-714591, 44-1865-714591, customerservices@blackwellpublishing.com, customerservices@blackwellpublishing.com, http://www.wiley.com/WileyCDA/, http://www.wiley.com/.

614 GBR ISSN 0966-0410
HV1 CODEN: HSCCEL
➤ **HEALTH AND SOCIAL CARE IN THE COMMUNITY (PRINT).** Text in English. 1993. bi-m. GBP 647 in United Kingdom to institutions; EUR 821 in Europe to institutions; USD 1,195 in the Americas to institutions; USD 1,395 elsewhere to institutions; GBP 745 combined subscription in United Kingdom to institutions (print & online eds.); EUR 945 combined subscription in Europe to institutions (print & online eds.); USD 1,375 combined subscription in the Americas to institutions (print & online eds.); USD 1,605 combined subscription elsewhere to institutions (print & online eds.) (effective 2012). bk.rev. bibl. index. back issues avail.; reprint service avail. from PSC. **Document type:** *Journal, Academic/Scholarly.* **Description:** Promotes interdisciplinary collaboration on policy and practice within health and social care in the community.
Related titles: Microform ed.: (from PQC); ◆ Online - full text ed.: Health and Social Care in the Community (Online). ISSN 1365-2524.
Indexed: A01, A02, A03, A08, A20, A22, A26, A36, AMED, ASCA, ASG, ASSIA, AgeL, B28, C06, C07, C08, C11, C25, C28, CA, CABA, CINAHL, CurCont, E-psyche, E01, E12, EMBASE, ESPM, ExcerpMed, F09, Faml, GH, H04, H05, H12, LT, MEDLINE, N02, N03, OR, P03, P30, P34, P50, P52, P56, PAIS, PsycInfo, R10, R12, RA&MP, RRTA, Reac, RiskAb, S02, S03, SCOPUS, SSA, SSCI, SociolAb, T02, T05, TAR, W07, W11.
—BLDSC (4274.874000), GNLM, IE, Infotrieve, Ingenta. **CCC.**
Published by: Wiley-Blackwell Publishing Ltd. (Subsidiary of: John Wiley & Sons, Inc.), 9600 Garsington Rd, Oxford, OX4 2DQ, United Kingdom. TEL 44-1865-776868, FAX 44-1865-714591, customerservices@blackwellpublishing.com. Ed. Karen A Luker TEL 44-1613-060262.

362.1 GBR ISSN 1748-3654
RA986
THE HEALTH AND SOCIAL CARE YEARBOOK. Text in English. 1889. a. GBP 175 per issue to non-members; GBP 135 per issue to members (effective 2010). **Document type:** *Directory, Trade.* **Description:** Provides information about the NHS and related government organisations as well as independent hospitals and health services.
Former titles (until 2005): I H M Yearbook (1745-2597); (until 2000): I H S M Health & Social Services Yearbook (1366-8331); (until 1996): I H S M Health Services Year Book; (until 1995): Health Services Year Book.; (until 1994): Hospitals & Health Services Yearbook and Directory of Hospitals Suppliers (0300-5968); (until 1973): Hospitals Year Book and Directory of Hospital Suppliers (0300-8479); (until 1968): Hospitals Year-Book (0073-3474); (until 1931): Burdett's Hospitals and Charities; (until 1896): Burdett's Hospital and Charities Annual; (until 1894): Burdett's Hospital Annual and Year Book of Philanthropy
Related titles: CD-ROM ed.: I H S M Health and Social Services Database CD-ROM. GBP 250.
—CCC.
Published by: (Institute of Health Services Management), Beechwood House Publishing (Subsidiary of: Wilmington Group Plc), 2-3 Commercial Way, Christy Close, Southfields, Basildon, SS15 6EF, United Kingdom. TEL 44-1268-495600, FAX 44-1268-495601.

614 360 CAN ISSN 1184-650X
HEALTH AND SOCIAL SERVICE WORKFORCE IN ALBERTA. Text in English. 1979. a. back issues avail. **Description:** Contains data and information on the health and social services of employers and self-employed professionals.
Former titles (until 1990): Health and Social Service Personnel Working in Alberta (1184-6496); (until 1986): Survey of Health and Social Service Personnel Working in Alberta (1184-6488); (until 1984): Survey of Employers of Health and Social Service Personnel in Alberta (1184-647X); (until 1981): Survey of the Major Employers of Health and Social Service Personnel (1184-6461); (until 1980): Semi-Annual Surveys of the Major Employers of Health and Social Service Personnel (0225-9834)
Published by: Health and Social Service Disciplines Committee, Kensington Place, 5th Fl, 10011 109th St, Edmonton, AB T5J 3S8, Canada. TEL 403-427-2655.

HEALTH & SOCIAL WORK. see SOCIAL SERVICES AND WELFARE

362.13 USA ISSN 1553-3387
HEALTH BUSINESS WEEK. Text in English. 2004. w. USD 2,295 in US & Canada; USD 2,495 elsewhere; USD 2,525 combined subscription in US & Canada (print & online eds.); USD 2,755 combined subscription elsewhere (print & online eds.) (effective 2008). back issues avail. **Document type:** *Newsletter, Trade.*
Related titles: E-mail ed.; Online - full text ed.: ISSN 1553-3395. USD 2,295 combined subscription (online & email eds.); single user (effective 2008).
Indexed: A15, ABIn, B16, H13, P10, P20, P21, P48, P51, P53, P54, PQC.
Published by: NewsRx, 2727 Paces Ferry Rd SE, Ste 2-440, Atlanta, GA 30339. TEL 770-435-8286, 800-726-4550, FAX 770-435-6800, pressrelease@newsrx.com, http://www.newsrx.com. Pub. Susan Hasty TEL 770-507-7777.

362.296 CAN ISSN 1493-4388
HEALTH CANADA. TOBACCO CONTROL PROGRAMME. REPORT ON TOBACCO CONTROL. Text in English, French. 1999. a.
Published by: Health Canada, Tobacco Control Programme, P.L. 3507A1, Ottawa, ON K1A 0K9, Canada. TEL 866-318-1116, FAX 613-954-2284, TCP-PLT-questions@hc-sc.gc.ca.

338.43 362.1 USA
RA410.53
HEALTH CARE FINANCING REVIEW. MEDICARE AND MEDICAID STATISTICAL SUPPLEMENT. Variant title: Health Care Financing Review. Medicare and Medicaid Statistical Supplement. Text in English. 1979. a. back issues avail.; reprints avail. **Document type:** *Government.*

Former titles (until 2005): Health Care Financing Review. Statistical Supplement (1553-0930); (until 1995): Health Care Financing Review. Annual Supplement (1057-9389).
Related titles: Microfiche ed.: (from CIS); Online - full text ed.: free (effective 2011) (from PQC); ◆ Supplement to: Medicare & Medicaid Research Review.
Indexed: AHCMS, AmStI, EMBASE, ExcerpMed, HospLI, IUSGP, MCR, MEDLINE, MEDOC, P30, SCOPUS, SWR&A, WBSS.
Published by: Centers for Medicare & Medicaid Services (Subsidiary of: U.S. Department of Health and Human Services), 7500 Security Blvd, Baltimore, MD 21244. TEL 410-786-3000, 877-267-2323, FAX 410-786-6511, http://www.cms.gov/.

364.12 USA ISSN 1087-7835
KF3608.A4
HEALTH CARE FRAUD. Text in English. 19??. a. **Document type:** *Journal, Trade.*
—CCC.
Published by: American Bar Association, Center for Continuing Legal Education, 321 N Clark St, Chicago, IL 60610. TEL 312-988-5522, 800-285-2221, http://www.abanet.org/cle/.

HEALTH CARE NEWS. *see* MEDICAL SCIENCES

362.1 USA ISSN 1930-546X
RA399.A3
HEALTH CARE STAFFING SERVICES CERTIFICATION MANUAL. Text in English. 2005. a. USD 100 per issue (effective 2011). 100 p./no.; back issues avail. **Document type:** *Handbook/Manual/Guide, Trade.*
Published by: Joint Commission Resources, Inc. (Subsidiary of: Joint Commission on Accreditation of Healthcare Organizations), 1515 W 22nd St, Ste 1300W, Oak Brook, IL 60523. TEL 630-268-7400, jcrcustomerservice@pbd.com.

362.1 USA ISSN 1065-1403
RA407.3
HEALTH CARE STATE RANKINGS; health care in the 50 United States. Text in English. 1993. a. USD 75 per issue (effective 2011). 540 p./no.; **Document type:** *Report, Trade.* **Description:** Provides detailed, comparative statistical information on health care and health care finance in more than 500 categories for each of the 50 states.
—GNLM.
Published by: C Q Press, Inc. (Subsidiary of: Sage Publications, Inc.), 2300 N St, NW, Ste 800, Washington, DC 20037. TEL 202-729-1900, 866-427-7737, FAX 202-419-8749, 800-380-3810, customerservice@cqpress.com. Eds. Kathleen O'Leary Morgan, Scott Morgan.

338.47 GBR ISSN 0267-3223
RA410.55.G7
HEALTH CARE U K. Text in English. 1984. a. **Document type:** *Journal, Trade.*
Indexed: A22.
—CCC.
Published by: King's Fund, 11-13 Cavendish Sq, London, W1M 0AN, United Kingdom. TEL 44-20-73072400, FAX 44-20-73072801, publications@kingsfund.org.uk, http://www.kingsfund.org.uk/.

614.8 USA ISSN 1041-0236
CODEN: HECOER
➤ **HEALTH COMMUNICATION (PHILADELPHIA).** Text in English. 1989. 8/yr. GBP 779 combined subscription in United Kingdom to institutions (print & online eds.); EUR 1,041, USD 1,300 combined subscription to institutions (print & online eds.) (effective 2012). bk.rev. back issues avail.; reprint service avail. from PSC. **Document type:** *Journal, Academic/Scholarly.* **Description:** Features articles from scholars in communication, psychology, medicine, nursing and allied health fields.
Related titles: Online - full text ed.: ISSN 1532-7027. GBP 701 in United Kingdom to institutions; EUR 937, USD 1,170 to institutions (effective 2012).
Indexed: A01, A02, A03, A08, A20, A22, ASCA, ASG, ASSIA, B28, C06, C07, C08, CA, CINAHL, CMM, CommAb, CurCont, E-psyche, E01, EMBASE, ESPM, ExcerpMed, FS&TA, FamI, H05, H13, HPNRM, IndMed, L&LBA, MEDLINE, NRN, P02, P03, P10, P20, P24, P30, P34, P48, P52, P53, P54, P56, PAIS, PQC, PsycInfo, PsycholAb, S02, S03, SCOPUS, SOPODA, SSCI, SSciA, SociolAb, T02, W07.
—BLDSC (4274.953900), GNLM, IE, Infotrieve, Ingenta. **CCC.**
Published by: Routledge (Subsidiary of: Taylor & Francis Group), 325 Chestnut St, Ste 800, Philadelphia, PA 19106. TEL 800-354-1420, FAX 215-625-2940, journals@routledge.com, http://www.routledge.com. Ed. Teresa L Thompson. Adv. contact Linda Hann TEL 44-1344-779945.

362.1 USA ISSN 2155-3475
▼ **HEALTH E-NEWS.** Text in English. 2009. m. free (effective 2010). back issues avail. **Document type:** *Newsletter, Consumer.* **Description:** Provides medical and health related information.
Media: Online - full text.
Published by: Healthcare Outcome Strategies, LLC., 620 Meramec View Dr, Eureka, MO 63025. TEL 636-587-2742, http://healthcareoutcomestrategies.com/default.aspx.

HEALTH ECONOMICS, POLICY AND LAW. *see* MEDICAL SCIENCES

610 USA ISSN 1090-1981
RA440.A1 CODEN: HEDBFS
➤ **HEALTH EDUCATION & BEHAVIOR.** Text in English. 1957-1978; resumed 1980. bi-m. USD 1,187, GBP 698 combined subscription to institutions (print & online eds.) (effective 2011). adv. bk.rev. illus. Index. 130 p./no.; Supplement avail.; back issues avail.; reprint service avail. from PSC. **Document type:** *Journal, Academic/Scholarly.* **Description:** Discusses the promotion of public health by elevating the quality of health education, improving medical practice, and stimulating research.
Formerly (until vol.24, 1997): Health Education Quarterly (0195-8402); Which superseded (in 1980): Health Education Monographs (0073-1455)
Related titles: Microform ed.: (from PQC); Online - full text ed.: ISSN 1552-6127.
Indexed: A20, A22, A36, ASCA, ASSIA, Agr, B04, B07, B21, BRD, C06, C07, C08, CA, CABA, CINAHL, CMM, CPE, Chicano, CommAb, CurCont, D01, E-psyche, E01, E02, E03, E09, E12, EMBASE, ERI, ERIC, ESPM, EdA, EdI, ExcerpMed, FR, FamI, GH, H&SSA, H04, H13, INI, IndMed, LT, MEDLINE, N02, N03, NRN, P02, P03, P04, P10, P18, P20, P24, P25, P30, P33, P34, P48, P50, P52, P53, P54, P55, P56, PAIS, PEI, PQC, PsycInfo, PsycholAb, R08, R10, R12, RA&MP, RRTA, Reac, S02, S03, S13, S16, S21, SCOPUS, SD, SOPODA, SSCI, SWR&A, SociolAb, T02, T05, TAR, THA, V02, W03, W07, W11.
—BLDSC (4274.977000), GNLM, IE, Infotrieve, Ingenta, INIST. **CCC.**
Published by: (Society for Public Health Education), Sage Publications, Inc., 2455 Teller Rd, Thousand Oaks, CA 91320. TEL 805-499-9774, 800-818-7243, FAX 805-499-0871, 800-583-2665, info@sagepub.com. Ed. Mark Zimmerman. Circ: 3,000 (paid). **Subscr. outside the Americas to:** Sage Publications Ltd., 1 Oliver's Yard, 55 City Rd, London EC1Y 1SP, United Kingdom. TEL 44-207-3248701, FAX 44-207-3248733, subscription@sagepub.co.uk.

362.1 GBR ISSN 0017-8969
RA421
➤ **HEALTH EDUCATION JOURNAL.** Abbreviated title: H E J. Text in English. 19??. q. USD 611, GBP 330 combined subscription to institutions (print & online eds.); USD 599, GBP 323 to institutions (effective 2011). adv. bk.rev. index. back issues avail.; reprint service avail. from PSC. **Document type:** *Journal, Academic/Scholarly.* **Description:** Features papers on the major public health issues such as, HIV and AIDS, heart disease, cancers, smoking, sex education, alcohol, children's health, and health promotion policy and practice.
Formerly (until 1943): Health and Empire
Related titles: Microform ed.: (from PQC); Online - full text ed.: ISSN 1748-8176. USD 550, GBP 297 to institutions (effective 2011).
Indexed: A22, A26, A36, AEI, ASSIA, AddicA, B21, B28, BibAg, C06, C07, C08, CA, CABA, CINAHL, CPE, CurCont, E01, E12, EMBASE, ERIC, ESPM, ExcerpMed, FR, G08, GH, H&SSA, H11, H12, I05, IBSS, LT, N02, N03, P30, P50, P52, P56, PEI, R12, RRTA, S21, SCOPUS, SD, SSCI, T02, T05, W07, W11.
—BLDSC (4275.000000), GNLM, IE, Infotrieve, Ingenta. **CCC.**
Published by: Sage Publications Ltd. (Subsidiary of: Sage Publications, Inc.), 1 Oliver's Yard, 55 City Rd, London, EC1Y 1SP, United Kingdom. TEL 44-20-73248500, 44-20-73248701, FAX 44-20-73248733, 44-20-73248600, info@sagepub.co.uk, http://www.uk.sagepub.com/home.nav. adv.: B&W page GBP 400; 140 x 210. **Subscr. in the Americas to:** Sage Publications, Inc., 2455 Teller Rd, Thousand Oaks, CA 91320. TEL 805-499-9774, FAX 805-499-0871, journals@sagepub.com.

362.1 USA
➤ **THE HEALTH EDUCATOR.** Text in English. 1969. s-a. free to members (effective 2010). bk.rev. illus.; bibl.; charts. 2 cols./p.; back issues avail. **Document type:** *Journal, Academic/Scholarly.* **Description:** Publishes articles and research of interest to students in the national health education honor society. Includes health education research, service and teaching reports for all ages in all settings.
Formerly (until 1992): Eta Sigma Gamman (8756-5943)
Indexed: A26, C06, CA, E03, E07, ERI, ERIC, P30, T02.
Published by: Eta Sigma Gamma, 2000 University Ave, CL 325, Muncie, IN 47306. TEL 765-285-2258, 800-715-2559, FAX 765-285-3210, ESG@EtaSigmaGamma.org. Ed. Roberta J Ogletree TEL 618-453-2777.

614 GBR ISSN 1369-6513
RA1
➤ **HEALTH EXPECTATIONS**; an international journal of public participation in health care and health policy. Text in English. 1998. q. GBP 522 in United Kingdom to institutions; EUR 663 in Europe to institutions; USD 963 in the Americas to institutions; USD 1,122 elsewhere to institutions; GBP 600 combined subscription in United Kingdom to institutions (print & online eds.); EUR 763 combined subscription in Europe to institutions (print & online eds.); USD 1,108 combined subscription in the Americas to institutions (print & online eds.); USD 1,291 combined subscription elsewhere to institutions (print & online eds.) (effective 2012). adv. back issues avail.; reprint service avail. from PSC. **Document type:** *Journal, Academic/Scholarly.* **Description:** Aims to promote critical thinking and informed debate about all aspects of public participation in health care and health policy.
Related titles: Online - full text ed.: ISSN 1369-7625. GBP 522 in United Kingdom to institutions; EUR 663 in Europe to institutions; USD 963 in the Americas to institutions; USD 1,122 elsewhere to institutions (effective 2012) (from IngentaConnect).
Indexed: A01, A02, A03, A08, A22, A26, ASSIA, B21, B28, C06, C07, C08, C11, CA, CINAHL, CurCont, E01, EMBASE, ESPM, ExcerpMed, H&SSA, H04, H05, H12, MEDLINE, P03, P30, P34, PAIS, PsycInfo, PsycholAb, R10, Reac, RiskAb, S02, S03, SCI, SCOPUS, SSCI, SociolAb, T02, W07.
—BLDSC (4275.015545), IE, Infotrieve, Ingenta. **CCC.**
Published by: Wiley-Blackwell Publishing Ltd. (Subsidiary of: John Wiley & Sons, Inc.), 9600 Garsington Rd, Oxford, OX4 2DQ, United Kingdom. TEL 44-1865-776868, FAX 44-1865-714591, customerservices@blackwellpublishing.com. Ed. Vikki Entwistle TEL 44-1382-348658. Adv. contact Craig Pickett TEL 44-1865-476267.

613 USA ISSN 0749-4742
RA421 CODEN: PNMBAF
HEALTH FREEDOM NEWS. Text in English. 1955. q. USD 36 membership (effective 2006). adv. bk.rev. charts; illus.; stat. back issues avail. **Document type:** *Magazine, Consumer.* **Description:** Covers educational, legislative and legal topics related to health.
Former titles (until 1982): Public Scrutiny (0743-5053); National Health Federation. Bulletin (0027-9420)
—GNLM.
Published by: National Health Federation, PO Box 688, Monrovia, CA 91017-0688. contact-us@thenhf.com. Ed. Scott F Tips. Circ: 6,000 (paid).

344.04 USA ISSN 1531-6009
HEALTH INFORMATION COMPLIANCE INSIDER. Text in English. 2004. m. USD 249 combined subscription (print & online eds.) (effective 2011). **Document type:** *Newsletter, Trade.*
Related titles: Online - full text ed.: ISSN 1554-0448. USD 285 (effective 2004).
Indexed: A26, H11, I05, P21, P48, PQC.
—CCC.
Published by: H C Pro, Inc., 200 Hoods Ln, PO Box 1168, Marblehead, MA 01945. TEL 781-639-1872, 800-650-6787, FAX 781-639-7857, 800-639-8511, customerservice@hcpro.com, http://www.hcpro.com. Ed. Ilene MacDonald. Pub. Lauren McLeod. Circ: 2,000 (paid).

614.427 USA ISSN 0095-3539
RA783.5
HEALTH INFORMATION FOR INTERNATIONAL TRAVEL. Variant title: The Yellow Book. Text in English. 1974. biennial. back issues avail. **Document type:** *Government.* **Description:** Provides current information on vaccination, prophylaxis, and country entry requirements; U.S. Public Health Service recommendations; geographical distribution of potential health hazards; and how to avoid health problems while visiting foreign countries.
Related titles: Online - full text ed.: ISSN 1939-5574; ◆ Supplement to: M M W R. ISSN 0149-2195.
—GNLM.
Published by: U.S. Department of Health and Human Services, Centers for Disease Control and Prevention, 1600 Clifton Rd, Atlanta, GA 30333. TEL 800-232-4636, cdcinfo@cdc.gov. **Subscr. to:** U.S. Government Printing Office, Superintendent of Documents.

614 610 340 USA ISSN 0549-804X
HEALTH LAW BULLETIN. Text in English. 1958. irreg., latest no.91, 2009. bibl. back issues avail. **Document type:** *Bulletin, Academic/Scholarly.* **Description:** Provides guidance about several current issues in the application of North Carolina's childhood and adolescent immunization laws.
Formerly (until 1968): Public Health Bulletin (0546-4455)
Related titles: Online - full text ed.: free (effective 2010).
Published by: University of North Carolina at Chapel Hill, School of Government, Knapp-Sanders Bldg, Campus Box 3330, Chapel Hill, NC 27599. TEL 919-966-5381, FAX 919-962-0654, sales@sog.unc.edu, http://sog.unc.edu.

HEALTH LAW JOURNAL. *see* LAW

HEALTH LAW MATTERS. *see* LAW

HEALTH LAW UPDATE. *see* LAW

HEALTH LETTER (WASHINGTON). *see* MEDICAL SCIENCES

613 IRL ISSN 1649-7872
HEALTH LIVING & WELLBEING. Text in English. 2005. 10/yr. EUR 29.99 (effective 2006). adv. **Document type:** *Magazine, Consumer.* **Description:** Covers all aspects of a healthy lifestyle.
Published by: Proactive Publications, 88 Lower Baggot St, Dublin, 2, Ireland. TEL 353-1-6110840, FAX 353-1-6110941. Ed. Marie Loftus. adv.: color page EUR 2,200; trim 210 x 297.

613 614 NLD ISSN 1380-555X
HEALTH MANAGEMENT FORUM. Text in Dutch. 1984. q. EUR 50.88 (effective 2009). **Document type:** *Journal, Trade.*
Formerly (until 1995): S T G Bulletin (0169-135X)
Indexed: A22.
Published by: Stichting Toekomstscenarios Gezondheidszorg, Postbus 482, Leiden, 2300 AL, Netherlands. TEL 31-71-5181118, FAX 31-71-5181925, info@stg.nl.

614 613.7 USA ISSN 0735-9683
RA410.A1
➤ **HEALTH MARKETING QUARTERLY.** Abbreviated title: H M Q. Text in English. 1978. q. GBP 617 combined subscription in United Kingdom to institutions (print & online eds.); EUR 803, USD 799 combined subscription to institutions (print & online eds.) (effective 2012). adv. bk.rev. abstr.; bibl. back issues avail.; reprint service avail. from PSC. **Document type:** *Journal, Academic/Scholarly.* **Description:** Each issue is devoted to a select health service, and serves as a basic resource for marketing the selected service. Covers group practice marketing, mental health marketing, and long-term care marketing.
Former titles (until 1984): Topics in Strategic Planning for Health Care (0731-714X); Topics in Health Care; Health and Medical Care Services Review (0160-7618)
Related titles: Microfiche ed.: (from PQC); Microform ed.; Online - full text ed.: ISSN 1545-0864. GBP 555 in United Kingdom to institutions; EUR 723, USD 719 to institutions (effective 2012).
Indexed: A01, A03, A12, A13, A14, A17, A22, A26, ABIn, AHCMS, ASFA, ASG, B01, B02, B06, B07, B08, B09, B11, B15, B16, B17, B18, C06, C07, C12, CA, CMM, CPLI, CommAb, DIP, E01, E08, EMBASE, ESPM, EconLit, ExcerpMed, G04, G06, G07, G08, H05, H12, H13, HospAb, HospLI, I05, IBR, IBZ, JEL, M&MA, M02, MCR, MEDLINE, P03, P10, P20, P21, P24, P25, P30, P48, P50, P51, P52, P53, P54, P56, PQC, PsycInfo, PsycholAb, S09, SCOPUS, SOPODA, SWR&A, SociolAb, T02, ViroIAbstr.
—BLDSC (4275.052850), GNLM, IE, Infotrieve, Ingenta. **CCC.**
Published by: Routledge (Subsidiary of: Taylor & Francis Group), 325 Chestnut St, Ste 800, Philadelphia, PA 19106. TEL 215-625-8900, 800-354-1420, FAX 215-625-8914, journals@routledge.com, http://www.routledge.com. Eds. David L Louden, Robert E Stevens. adv.: B&W page USD 315, color page USD 550; trim 4.375 x 7.125. Circ: 294 (paid).

362.109147 351.8410915 IRL ISSN 1649-7996
HEALTH MATTERS. Variant title: H S E Health Matters. Text in English. 2005. q. **Document type:** *Newsletter.*
Published by: (Health Service Executive), Harmonia Ltd., Rosemount House, Dundrum Rd, Dublin, 14, Ireland. TEL 353-1-2405300, FAX 353-1-6619757, http://www.harmonia.ie.

HEALTH PATHWAYS. *see* MEDICAL SCIENCES

614 370 IRL ISSN 0168-8510
RA393
➤ **HEALTH POLICY.** Text in English. 1979. 15/yr. EUR 2,453 in Europe to institutions; JPY 326,100 in Japan to institutions; USD 2,745 elsewhere to institutions (effective 2012). Supplement avail.; back issues avail.; reprints avail. **Document type:** *Journal, Academic/Scholarly.* **Description:** Provides a forum for the discussion of health policy issues among health policy researchers, legislators, decision makers and other professionals.
Incorporates (in 1986): Effective Health Care (0167-871X); Formerly (until 1984): Health Policy and Education (0165-2281)
Related titles: Online - full text ed.: ISSN 1872-6054 (from IngentaConnect, ScienceDirect).

P

Indexed: A20, A22, A26, A35, A36, AHCMS, AMHA, ASCA, ASSIA, AbAn, AgBio, B01, B06, B07, B09, B21, BP, BPI, BRD, C06, C07, C08, CA, CABA, CINAHL, CPE, CurCont, D01, E12, EMBASE, ESPM, ExcerpMed, FR, FamI, GH, H&SSA, H05, H12, H17, HospAb, HospLI, I05, IBSS, INI, Inpharma, LT, MEDLINE, N02, N03, P03, P30, P33, P34, P39, PAIS, PsycInfo, PsycholAb, R08, R10, R12, RA&MP, RRTA, Reac, S02, S03, SCI, SCOPUS, SSCI, SociolAb, T02, T05, TAR, THA, VS, W01, W02, W03, W07, W11.
—BLDSC (4275.102700), GNLM, IE, Infotrieve, Ingenta, INIST. **CCC.**
Published by: (European Health Policy Forum), Elsevier Ireland Ltd (Subsidiary of: Elsevier Science & Technology), Elsevier House, Brookvale Plaza, E. Park, Shannon, Co. Clare, Ireland. TEL 353-61-709600, FAX 353-61-709100. Eds. Katrien Kesteloot, Mia Defever. **Subscr. to:** Elsevier BV, Radarweg 29, PO Box 211, Amsterdam 1000 AE, Netherlands. TEL 31-20-4853757, FAX 31-20-4853432, JournalsCustomerServiceEMEA@elsevier.com, http://www.elsevier.nl.

362.1 UGA ISSN 1728-6107
HEALTH POLICY AND DEVELOPMENT. Text in English. 2003. 3/yr. **Document type:** *Journal, Academic/Scholarly.* **Description:** It aims to widen access to relevant, scientifically rigorous and practically oriented information on public health policy, politics, planning and management.
Related titles: Online - full text ed.: free (effective 2011).
Published by: Uganda Martyrs University, PO Box 5498, Kampala, Uganda. TEL 256-038-410611, FAX 256-038-410100, umu@umu.ac.ug. Ed. Sam Agatre Okuonzi.

614 GBR ISSN 0268-1080
RA441.5
➤ **HEALTH POLICY AND PLANNING**; a journal on health in development. Text in English. 1986. bi-m. GBP 349 in United Kingdom to institutions; EUR 524 in Europe to institutions; USD 698 in US & Canada to institutions; GBP 349 elsewhere to institutions; GBP 381 combined subscription in United Kingdom to institutions (print & online eds.); EUR 572 combined subscription in Europe to institutions (print & online eds.); USD 760 combined subscription in US & Canada to institutions (print & online eds.); GBP 381 combined subscription elsewhere to institutions (print & online eds.) (effective 2012). adv. bk.rev. back issues avail.; reprint service avail. from PSC. **Document type:** *Journal, Academic/Scholarly.* **Description:** Covers issues in health policy, planning, management and evaluation in the developing world.
Related titles: Online - full text ed.: ISSN 1460-2237. 1997. GBP 263 in United Kingdom to institutions; EUR 395 in Europe to institutions; USD 526 in US & Canada to institutions; GBP 263 elsewhere to institutions (effective 2012) (from IngentaConnect).
Indexed: A12, A13, A17, A20, A22, A34, A36, ABIn, ASCA, ASSIA, B01, B06, B07, B09, B21, B28, C06, C07, CA, CABA, CurCont, D01, E-psyche, E01, E12, EMBASE, ESPM, ExcerpMed, F09, FS&TA, FamI, GH, H&SSA, H05, H13, H17, IBSS, IndVet, MEDLINE, MaizeAb, N02, N03, P03, P10, P20, P21, P22, P30, P33, P34, P37, P39, P42, P48, P50, P51, P52, P53, P54, P56, PAIS, PCI, PQC, PSA, PsycInfo, R08, R10, R12, Reac, RefugAb, S02, S03, S12, S13, S16, S21, SCI, SCOPUS, SOPODA, SSA, SSCI, SociolAb, T02, T05, VS, W07, W11.
—BLDSC (4275.103300), GNLM, IE, Infotrieve, Ingenta. **CCC.**
Published by: (London School of Hygiene and Tropical Medicine), Oxford University Press, Great Clarendon St, Oxford, OX2 6DP, United Kingdom. TEL 44-1865-556767, FAX 44-1865-556646, enquiry@oup.co.uk, http://www.oxfordjournals.org. Eds. Richard Coker, Sara Bennett. Pub. Mandy Sketch.

➤ **HEALTH POLICY RESEARCH.** *see* PUBLIC ADMINISTRATION

614 GBR ISSN 0957-4824
RA427.8 CODEN: HPINET
➤ **HEALTH PROMOTION INTERNATIONAL.** Text in English. 1986. q. GBP 425 in United Kingdom to institutions; EUR 638 in Europe to institutions; USD 850 in US & Canada to institutions; GBP 425 elsewhere to institutions; GBP 463 combined subscription in United Kingdom to institutions (print & online eds.); EUR 696 combined subscription in Europe to institutions (print & online eds.); USD 928 combined subscription in US & Canada to institutions (print & online eds.); GBP 463 combined subscription elsewhere to institutions (print & online eds.) (effective 2012). adv. bk.rev. back issues avail.; reprint service avail. from PSC. **Document type:** *Journal, Academic/Scholarly.* **Description:** Presents original articles, major reviews, and an editorial concerned with major health promotion themes.
Formerly (until 1990): Health Promotion (0268-1099)
Related titles: Online - full text ed.: ISSN 1460-2245. 1986. GBP 367 in United Kingdom to institutions; EUR 551 in Europe to institutions; USD 734 in US & Canada to institutions; GBP 367 elsewhere to institutions (effective 2012) (from IngentaConnect).
Indexed: A01, A03, A22, A36, ASCA, ASSIA, B04, B21, B28, BRD, C06, C07, C08, CA, CABA, CINAHL, CurCont, D01, E-psyche, E01, E12, EMBASE, ESPM, ExcerpMed, FR, FS&TA, FamI, G03, GH, GSA, GSI, H&SSA, H05, H16, HospAb, LT, MEDLINE, MRD, N02, N03, P03, P19, P20, P21, P22, P24, P25, P30, P33, P34, P39, P42, P48, P50, P52, P54, P56, PAIS, PCI, PEI, PHN&I, PQC, PSA, PsycInfo, PsycholAb, R10, R12, RRTA, Reac, S02, S03, S12, S13, S21, SCOPUS, SD, SOPODA, SSA, SSCI, SociolAb, T02, T05, TAR, W03, W05, W07, W11.
—BLDSC (4275.105183), GNLM, IE, Infotrieve, Ingenta. **CCC.**
Published by: (International Union for Health Promotion and Education FRA), Oxford University Press, Great Clarendon St, Oxford, OX2 6DP, United Kingdom. TEL 44-1865-556767, FAX 44-1865-556646, enquiry@oup.co.uk, http://www.oxfordjournals.org. Ed. John Catford. Pub. Mandy Sketch.

614 AUS ISSN 1036-1073
RA427.8
➤ **HEALTH PROMOTION JOURNAL OF AUSTRALIA.** Variant title: A H P A Journal. Text in English. 1991. 3/yr. free to members (effective 2008). adv. back issues avail. **Document type:** *Journal, Academic/Scholarly.* **Description:** Aims to facilitate communication between researchers, practitioners, and policymakers involved in health promotion activities.
Related titles: Online - full text ed.
Indexed: A11, ASSIA, C06, C07, C08, CA, CINAHL, EMBASE, ExcerpMed, H01, H05, MEDLINE, P20, P21, P22, P24, P30, P48, P50, P52, P54, P56, PAIS, PQC, R10, Reac, SCOPUS, SD, SSCI, T02, W07.
—BLDSC (4275.105184), IE, Ingenta.
Published by: Australian Health Promotion Association, c/o University of the Sunshine Coast, Maroochydore, QLD 4558, Australia. TEL 61-7-54302873, FAX 61-7-54301276, ahpa@usc.edu.au, http://www.healthpromotion.org.au. adv.: B&W page AUD 660; 17.5 x 26.

613 614 610 USA ISSN 1524-8399
RT90.3
➤ **HEALTH PROMOTION PRACTICE.** Text in English. 2000. q. USD 653, GBP 384 combined subscription to institutions (print & online eds.) (effective 2011). adv. back issues avail.; reprint service avail. from PSC. **Document type:** *Journal, Academic/Scholarly.* **Description:** Publishes authoritative, peer-reviewed articles devoted to the practical application of health promotion and education. Focuses on critical and strategic information for professionals engaged in the practice of developing, implementing and evaluating health promotion and disease prevention programs.
Related titles: Online - full text ed.: ISSN 1552-6372.
Indexed: A01, A03, A08, A22, A34, A36, ASSIA, C06, C07, C08, CA, CABA, CINAHL, CMM, CommAb, D01, E01, E12, EMBASE, ExcerpMed, FamI, GH, IndVet, LT, MEDLINE, N02, N03, N04, OR, P03, P30, P34, P37, PAIS, PEI, PsycInfo, R10, R12, RRTA, Reac, S02, S03, S13, S16, SCOPUS, SociolAb, T02, T05, VS, W11.
—BLDSC (4275.105187), IE, Infotrieve, Ingenta. **CCC.**
Published by: (Society for Public Health Education), Sage Publications, Inc., 2455 Teller Rd, Thousand Oaks, CA 91320. TEL 805-499-9774, 800-818-7243, FAX 805-499-0871, 800-583-2665, info@sagepub.com. Ed. Randy Schwartz. Circ: 2,540 (paid and free).

➤ **HEALTH PSYCHOLOGY.** *see* PSYCHOLOGY

613.194 CAN ISSN 1209-1367
HEALTH REPORTS (ONLINE). Text in English. 1996. q. free (effective 2011). **Document type:** *Journal, Government.*
Media: Online - full text. **Related titles:** ◆ Print ed.: Health Reports (Print). ISSN 0840-6529; Ed.: Rapports sur la Sante (Online). ISSN 1209-1375. 1996; ◆ Supplement(s): Life Tables, Canada, Provinces and Territories. ISSN 1910-3484; How Healthy Are Canadians?. ISSN 1708-7678. 1999.
—CCC.
Published by: Statistics Canada/Statistique Canada, Statistical Reference Centre, Rm. 1500, Main Bldg, Holland Ave, Ottawa, ON K1A 0T6, Canada. TEL 613-951-8116, 800-263-1136, FAX 877-287-4369, infostats@statcan.ca, http://www.statcan.gc.ca.

613.194 CAN ISSN 0840-6529
➤ **HEALTH REPORTS (PRINT).** Text in English. 1989. q. **Document type:** *Journal, Academic/Scholarly.* **Description:** Presents the most frequently requested health information in Canada.
Related titles: ◆ Online - full text ed.: Health Reports (Online). ISSN 1209-1367; French ed.: Rapports sur la Sante (Print). ISSN 1492-7128.
Indexed: C03, C04, C05, C11, CA, CBCARef, EMBASE, ExcerpMed, H04, H05, IndMed, MEDLINE, P19, P30, P48, P50, PQC, PopulInd, R10, Reac, SCOPUS, T02.
—BLDSC (4275.106250), GNLM, IE, Infotrieve, Ingenta. **CCC.**
Published by: Statistics Canada/Statistique Canada, Statistical Reference Centre, Rm. 1500, Main Bldg, Holland Ave, Ottawa, ON K1A 0T6, Canada. TEL 613-951-8116, 800-263-1136, FAX 877-287-4369, infostats@statcan.ca.

614 GBR ISSN 1478-4505
R1
➤ **HEALTH RESEARCH POLICY AND SYSTEMS.** Text in English. 2003. irreg. free (effective 2011). adv. back issues avail. **Document type:** *Journal, Academic/Scholarly.* **Description:** Covers papers about the use of electronic information and telecommunications technologies to support long distance clinical health care, patient and professional health-related education, public health and health administration.
Media: Online - full text.
Indexed: A01, A26, A35, A36, AgBio, B21, C06, C07, CA, CABA, E12, EMBASE, ESPM, ExcerpMed, GH, H&SSA, H05, I05, N02, N03, P20, P22, P30, P32, P33, P34, P39, P40, P50, P54, PN&I, PQC, R08, R12, SCOPUS, T02, T05, TAR, W11.
—CCC.
Published by: BioMed Central Ltd. (Subsidiary of: Springer Science+Business Media), 236 Gray's Inn Rd, London, WC1X 8HB, United Kingdom. TEL 44-20-31922000, FAX 44-20-31922010, info@biomedcentral.com, http://www.biomedcentral.com. Eds. Miguel Gonzalez Block, Stephen Hanney.

362.1 300 GBR ISSN 1369-8575
RA427.3 CODEN: HRSEAS
➤ **HEALTH, RISK & SOCIETY.** Text in English. 1999. bi-m. GBP 619 combined subscription in United Kingdom to institutions (print & online eds.); EUR 820, USD 1,029 combined subscription to institutions (print & online eds.) (effective 2012). adv. back issues avail.; reprint service avail. from PSC. **Document type:** *Journal, Academic/Scholarly.* **Description:** Aims to understand the social processes which influence the ways in which risks are taken, communicated, assessed and managed in relationship to health and health care.
Related titles: Online - full text ed.: ISSN 1469-8331. GBP 557 in United Kingdom to institutions; EUR 737, USD 926 to institutions (effective 2012) (from IngentaConnect).
Indexed: A01, A02, A03, A08, A22, A34, A35, A36, AgBio, B01, B06, B07, B09, B21, C06, C07, C08, C11, CA, CABA, CINAHL, CurCont, D01, E01, E04, E05, E12, EMBASE, ESPM, ErgAb, ExcerpMed, GH, H&SSA, H04, H17, IBSS, IndVet, L03, N02, N03, P03, P26, P30, P32, P33, P34, P37, P40, P50, P52, P54, P56, PAIS, PEI, PQC, PsycInfo, PsycholAb, R02, R10, R12, Reac, RiskAb, S02, S03, S12, S13, S16, SCOPUS, SSA, SSCI, SociolAb, T02, T05, VS, W07, W11.
—IE, Infotrieve, Ingenta, INIST. **CCC.**
Published by: Routledge (Subsidiary of: Taylor & Francis Group), 4 Park Sq, Milton Park, Abingdon, Oxon OX14 4RN, United Kingdom. TEL 44-20-70176000, FAX 44-20-70176336, subscriptions@tandf.co.uk, http://www.routledge.com. Ed. Dr. Andy Alaszewski. Adv. contact Linda Hann TEL 44-1344-779945. **Subscr. in N. America to:** Taylor & Francis Inc., Customer Services Dept, 325 Chestnut St, 8th Fl, Philadelphia, PA 19106. TEL 215-625-8900, 800-354-1420, FAX 215-625-2940, customerservice@taylorandfrancis.com; **Subscr. to:** Taylor & Francis Ltd., Journals Customer Service, Sheepen Pl, Colchester, Essex CO3 3LP, United Kingdom. TEL 44-20-70175544, FAX 44-20-70175198, tf.enquiries@tfinforma.com.

362.1 USA ISSN 1553-3409
HEALTH RISK FACTOR WEEK. Text in English. 2004. w. USD 2,295 in US & Canada; USD 2,495 elsewhere; USD 2,525 combined subscription in US & Canada (print & online eds.); USD 2,755 combined subscription elsewhere (print & online eds.) (effective 2008). back issues avail. **Document type:** *Newsletter, Trade.*
Related titles: E-mail ed.; Online - full text ed.: ISSN 1553-3417. USD 2,295 combined subscription (online & email eds.); single user (effective 2008).
Indexed: H13, P10, P19, P20, P48, P53, P54, PQC.
Published by: NewsRx, 2727 Paces Ferry Rd SE, Ste 2-440, Atlanta, GA 30339. TEL 770-435-8286, 800-726-4550, FAX 770-435-6800, pressrelease@newsrx.com, http://www.newsrx.com. Pub. Susan Hasty TEL 770-507-7777.

HEALTH SCIENCES REVIEW. *see* MEDICAL SCIENCES

HEALTH SERVICES AND OUTCOMES RESEARCH METHODOLOGY; an international journal devoted to quantitative methods for the study of the utilization, quality, cost and outcomes of health care. *see* MEDICAL SCIENCES

HEALTH SERVICES MANAGEMENT RESEARCH. *see* MEDICAL SCIENCES

HEALTH SERVICES RESEARCH; impacting health practice and policy through state-of-the- art research thinking. *see* HEALTH FACILITIES AND ADMINISTRATION

362.1 363.7 628.1 AUS
HEALTH STREAM NEWSLETTER; information and analysis for water and health professionals. Text in English. 1996. q. free (effective 2008). back issues avail. **Document type:** *Newsletter, Consumer.* **Description:** Provides conference reports, news items and information about the center on water quality and public health.
Related titles: Online - full text ed.: free (effective 2008).
Published by: C R C for Water Quality and Treatment, Private Mail Bag 3, Salisbury, SA 5108, Australia. TEL 61-8-82590326, FAX 61-8-82590228, crc@sawater.com.au. Ed. Martha Sinclair. Circ: 2,718.

614 USA
HEALTH WATCH (WASHINGTON D.C.). Text in English. 1996. m.
Media: Online - full content.
Published by: Health Care Financing Administration, 200 Independence Ave S W, Washington, DC 20201. http://www.hcfa.gov/publications/newsletters/healthwatch/.

614 360 CAN ISSN 1195-7506
RA410.9.C2
HEALTH WORKFORCE IN ALBERTA. ANNUAL REPORT. Text in English. 1977. a. free. **Document type:** *Government.* **Description:** Contains the results of the annual survey of health employers in Alberta concerning the number of personnel employed, their status, vacancy and turnover rates, and recruitment difficulties.
Formerly (until 1993): Alberta. Health and Social Services Disciplines Committee. Annual Report (0707-1434)
Published by: Alberta Health, Practitioner Services Division, 10025 Jasper Ave, 16th Fl, Edmonton, AB T5J 2N3, Canada. TEL 403-427-3276, FAX 403-422-2880. Ed. D Chesley. Circ: 500.

362.1 USA ISSN 1548-8268
HEALTHCARE DISPARITIES REPORT. Text in English. 2004 (Jan.). m. USD 229 (effective 2004). **Document type:** *Newsletter.*
Published by: C D Publications, Inc., 8204 Fenton St, Silver Spring, MD 20910. TEL 301-588-6380, 800-666-6380, FAX 301-588-6385, subscriptions@cdpublications.com, http://www.cdpublications.com. Ed. James S Byrne. Pub. Mike Gerecht.

HEALTHCARE INFECTION. *see* MEDICAL SCIENCES—Communicable Diseases

362.1 CAN ISSN 1485-7375
HEALTHCARE INFORMATION MANAGEMENT & COMMUNICATIONS CANADA. Text in English. 1987. q. CAD 50 (effective 2006). adv. back issues avail. **Document type:** *Magazine, Consumer.*
Formerly (until 1998): Healthcare Computing & Communications Canada (0842-5353)
Published by: Healthcare Computing & Communications Canada, Inc., 5782-172 St, Edmonton, AB T6M 1B4, Canada. TEL 780-489-4521, FAX 780-489-3290, healthcare@shaw.ca, http://www.hcccinc.com. Ed., Pub. Steven A Huesing. adv.: B&W page CAD 2,400, color page CAD 3,400; trim 8.125 x 10.875. Circ: 5,500 (paid and controlled).

362 USA ISSN 1551-8906
HEALTHCARE LEADERSHIP REPORT. Text in English. 2000. m. **Document type:** *Report, Trade.*
Formerly (until 2004): Healthcare Leadership & Management Report (1533-2292); Integrated Healthcare Report
Indexed: P30, SCOPUS.
Published by: American Governance & Leadership Group, 51 Evergreen Dr, Suite A, Bozeman, MT 59715-2458. TEL 406-556-0999, FAX 406-556-0998, Info@AmericanGovernance.com, http://www.AmericanGovernance.com.

HEALTHCARE LIFE SAFETY COMPLIANCE. *see* HEALTH FACILITIES AND ADMINISTRATION

HEALTHCARE MARKET NEWS. *see* HEALTH FACILITIES AND ADMINISTRATION

HEALTHCARE PARLIAMENTARY MONITOR (ONLINE). *see* MEDICAL SCIENCES

362.1 USA ISSN 1931-9754
RA395.A3
HEALTHCARE TRENDS & FORECASTS. Text in English. 200?. a., latest 2007. USD 107 per issue (effective 2007). **Document type:** *Report, Trade.*
Published by: Healthcare Intelligence Network, 1913 Atlantic Ave. Ste F4, Manasquan, NJ 08736. TEL 888-446-3530, FAX 732-292-3073, Info@hin.com, http://store.hin.com/index.html.

614 CAN ISSN 1488-917X
HEALTHCAREPAPERS. Text in English. q. CAD 140 domestic to individuals; USD 140 foreign to individuals; CAD 420 domestic to institutions; USD 420 foreign to institutions (effective 2005).
Related titles: Online - full text ed.
Indexed: C06, C07, C08, CINAHL, EMBASE, ExcerpMed, MEDLINE, P30, R10, Reac, SCOPUS.
—BLDSC (4275.247942), IE, Ingenta. **CCC.**

Published by: Longwoods Publishing Corp., 260 Adelaide St East, P.O. Box 8, Toronto, ON M5A 1N1, Canada. TEL 416-864-9667, FAX 416-368-6292, subscribe@longwoods.com. Ed. Peggy Leatt. Pub. Anton Hart.

362.1 IND ISSN 2229-337X
▼ **HEALTHLINE.** Text in English. 2010. s-a. **Document type:** *Journal, Academic/Scholarly.*
Related titles: Online - full text ed.: free (effective 2011).
Published by: Indian Association of Preventive & Social Medicine, Gujarat, Department of Community Medicine, Government Medical College, Bhavnagar, Gujarat, India.

362.1 GBR
HEALTHMATTERS (ONLINE). Text in English. irreg. free. **Document type:** *Magazine, Consumer.* **Description:** Covers topical issues of policy and practice in the fields of healthcare, social care and public health/health and wellbeing.
Media: Online - full text.
Address: s.iliffe@ucl.ac.uk. Ed. Steve Iliffe. Pub. Paul Walker.

613 613.2 NZL ISSN 1177-8113
HEALTHNEWS. Text in English. 2007. q. NZD 62 domestic; NZD 84 in Australian & South Pacific; NZD 90 elsewhere (effective 2008). **Document type:** *Magazine, Consumer.* **Description:** Each issue features an important health subject covering specific areas of traditional healthcare.
Published by: Healthy Options Ltd., 100 Grage Rd, PO Box 13209, Tauranga, New Zealand. TEL 64-7-5700560, FAX 64-7-5700360.

362.1 USA
HEALTHPOINT. Text in English. 1985. q. free. **Document type:** *Newsletter, Consumer.*
Published by: Mills-Peninsula Health Services, 1783 El Camino Real, Burlingame, CA 94010. TEL 650-696-5303, FAX 650-696-5374, http://www.mills-peninsula.org. Circ: 167,000 (free).

362.1 CAN ISSN 1714-3837
HEALTHY CANADIANS/CANADIENS EN SANTE. Text in English, French. 2002. irreg. **Document type:** *Government.*
Published by: Health Canada/Sante Canada, Address Locator 0900C2, Ottawa, ON K1A OK9, Canada. TEL 613-957-2991, 866-225-0709, FAX 613-941-5366, info@www.hc-sc.gc.ca.

362.1 AUS ISSN 1838-1308
▼ **HEALTHY COMMUNITIES NEWSLETTER.** Text in English. 2010. q. free (effective 2011). **Document type:** *Newsletter, Trade.* **Description:** Provides resources to health practitioners in NSW, keeps stakeholders informed of health reform developments and promotes best practice models in primary and community health.
Related titles: Online - full text ed.
Published by: New South Wales, Department of Health, Locked Mail Bag 961, North Sydney, NSW 2059, Australia. TEL 61-2-93919000, FAX 61-2-93919101, nswhealth@doh.health.nsw.gov.au.

362.1 USA
HEALTHY DIRECTIONS. Text in English. q. free. **Document type:** *Newsletter, Consumer.*
Published by: Mercy Hospital, 500 E Market St, Iowa City, IA 52245. TEL 319-339-0300, FAX 319-339-3831, http://www.mercyic.org. Ed. Denice Connell. Circ: 25,000 (free).

361 NOR
HELSENYTT.NO. Text in Norwegian. 1910. bi-m. adv. **Document type:** *Magazine, Consumer.* **Description:** Deals with medical issues in easy lay terms. Each issue has a main theme which is dealt with thoroughly.
Former titles (until 2006): Helsenytt for Alle (Print) (0333-2861); (until 1970): Helsenytt (0018-0157); (until 1963): Nasjonalforeningen mot Tuberkulosen for Folkehelsen (0333-287X)
Media: Online - full text.
—CCC.
Published by: Nasjonalforeningen for Folkehelsen, PO Box 7139, Majorstua, Oslo, 0307, Norway. TEL 47-23-120000, FAX 47-23-120001, post@nasjonalforeningen.no, http://www.nasjonalforeningen.no.

613 NOR ISSN 1890-2979
HELSEREVYEN ONLINE. Text in Norwegian. 2006. irreg. adv. **Document type:** *Magazine, Trade.*
Media: Online - full content.
Published by: Helserevyen AS, PO Box 170, Oernes, 8151, Norway. TEL 47-90-074056. Ed. Johan Votvik.

362.1 MEX ISSN 0437-4509
HIGIENE. Text in Spanish. 1948. 3/yr. free to members. **Document type:** *Magazine, Trade.*
Formerly (until 1950): Sociedad Mexicana de Higiene. Revista (0370-7385)
Published by: Sociedad Mexicana de Salud Publica, Herschel 109, Colonia Anzures, Delegacion Miguel Hidalgo, Mexico City, 11590, Mexico. TEL 52-52034291, FAX 52-52034229, http://www.smsp.org.mx.

614 ESP ISSN 1579-1734
HIGIENE Y SANIDAD AMBIENTAL. Text in Spanish. 2001. quadrennial. back issues avail. **Document type:** *Journal, Academic/Scholarly.*
Published by: Universidad de Granada, Departamento de Medicina Preventiva y Salud Publica, Campus Universitario de Cartuja, Granada, 18071, Spain. TEL 34-958-243169, FAX 34-958-249958, dpto-prev@ugr.es. Ed. Miguel Espigares Garcia.

362.1 CAN ISSN 1912-6344
RA643.86.C2
HIV/AIDS EPI UPDATES. (Human Immunodeficiency Virus - Acquired Immune Deficiency Syndrome) Text in English. 1998. a. **Document type:** *Journal, Trade.*
Related titles: Online - full text ed.: ISSN 1912-9378; French ed.: Actualites en Epidemiologie sur le VIH/Sida. ISSN 1912-6352.
Published by: Public Health Agency of Canada/Agence de Sante Publique du Canada, 0904A, Buock Claxton Bldg, Tunney's Pasture, Ottawa, ON K1A OK9, Canada. TEL 613-957-2991, FAX 613-941-5366, info@hc-sc.gc.ca, http://www.hc-sc.gc.ca.

362.196 323.4 USA
HIV POLICY WATCH. (Human Immunodeficiency Virus) Text in English. m. free. **Document type:** *Newsletter.* **Description:** Contains brief updates on ongoing HIV policy issues, such as HIV-related legislation and funding, state and federal HIV prevention reform efforts, needle exchange laws and policies, the status of various health care reform initiatives, housing advocacy, and the Ryan White CARE Act.
Related titles: Online - full text ed.
Published by: San Francisco AIDS Foundation, PO Box 426182, San Francisco, CA 94142. TEL 415-487-8060, FAX 415-487-8069.

362.1 JPN ISSN 0367-6110
CODEN: HOKBAQ
HOKEN BUTSURI/JAPANESE JOURNAL OF HEALTH PHYSICS. Text in Japanese. 1966. q. free to members (effective 2005). **Document type:** *Journal, Academic/Scholarly.*
Indexed: INIS AtomInd.
—BLDSC (4655.145000), IE, Ingenta. **CCC.**
Published by: Nihon Hoken Butsuri Kyogikai/Japan Health Physics Society, Level 3, Shinjuku Mitsui Building No. 2,, 3-3-11 Nishi-Shinjuku, Shinjuku-Ku, Tokyo, 160-0023, Japan. FAX 81-3-53397285, jhps@wwwsoc.nii.ac.jp.

362.1 JPN ISSN 0441-0793
RA532.H65 CODEN: HOEKAN
HOKKAIDORITSU EISEI KENKYUSHOHO/HOKKAIDO INSTITUTE OF PUBLIC HEALTH. REPORT. Text in Japanese. 1951. a. **Document type:** *Government.*
Indexed: A22, INIS AtomInd.
—BLDSC (7509.999000), IE, Ingenta.
Published by: Hokkaidoritsu Eisei Kenkyusho/Hokkaido Institute of Public Health, Kita 19, Nishi 12, Kita-ku, Sapporo, 060-0819, Japan. TEL 81-11-7472719, kikaku@iph.pref.hokkaido.jp.

362.1 613.7 JPN ISSN 0386-3530
CODEN: HKEGDK
HOKURIKU KOSHU EISEI GAKKAISHI/HOKURIKU JOURNAL OF PUBLIC HEALTH. Text in Japanese. 1974. s-a. **Document type:** *Journal, Academic/Scholarly.*
—BLDSC (4322.288400).
Published by: Hokuriku Koshu Eisei Gakkai, c/o Kanazawa Ika Daigaku Koshu Eiseigaku Kyositsu, 1-1 Daigaku, Uchinada-cho, Kahoku-gun, Ishikawa-ken, 920-0265, Japan.

362.1 USA ISSN 1093-7218
HOME & COMMUNITY HEALTH SPECIAL INTEREST SECTION QUARTERLY. Text in English. 1994. q. free to members. **Description:** Provides resources and support for occupational therapy professionals and students whose practice environment is in the home and community, including home health, adult day care, senior housing, wellness programs, community mental health centers, home modification and accessibility consultation.
Formerly (until 1997): Home & Community Health Special Interest Section Newsletter (1074-7737)
Indexed: C06, C07, C08, CINAHL, P24, P48, PQC.
—BLDSC (4325.429200). **CCC.**
Published by: American Occupational Therapy Association, Inc., 4720 Montgomery Ln, PO Box 31220, Bethesda, MD 20821-1220. TEL 301-652-2682, FAX 301-652-7711.

363 364.4 353.3 USA ISSN 1558-643X
UA927
➤ **HOMELAND SECURITY AFFAIRS.** Text in English. 2005. q. free (effective 2011). **Document type:** *Journal, Academic/Scholarly.*
Media: Online - full text.
Indexed: A39, C27, C29, D03, D04, E13, ESPM, I02, R14, RiskAb, S14, S15, S18, T02.
Published by: U.S. Naval Postgraduate School, Center for Homeland Defense and Security, I University Circle, Monterey, CA 93943-5001. TEL 831-656-2356, http://www.chds.us/.

➤ **HOMELAND SECURITY BRIEFING.** *see* CRIMINOLOGY AND LAW ENFORCEMENT

➤ **THE HOMELAND SECURITY REVIEW.** *see* PUBLIC ADMINISTRATION

➤ **HOPE HEALTH LETTER.** *see* PHYSICAL FITNESS AND HYGIENE

➤ **HOPITAUX MAGAZINE**; sante et societe. *see* HEALTH FACILITIES AND ADMINISTRATION

➤ **HOSPITAL MEDICINE ALERT.** *see* HEALTH FACILITIES AND ADMINISTRATION

➤ **HUANJING YU JIANKANG ZAZHI/JOURNAL OF ENVIRONMENT AND HEALTH.** *see* ENVIRONMENTAL STUDIES

➤ **HUMAN FACTORS AND AEROSPACE SAFETY**; an international journal. *see* AERONAUTICS AND SPACE FLIGHT

362.1 610.9 306.09 SWE ISSN 1403-8668
➤ **HYGIEA INTERNATIONALIS**; an interdisciplinary journal for the history of public health. Text in English. 1999. irreg. back issues avail. **Document type:** *Journal, Academic/Scholarly.* **Description:** Promotes, in the broadest sense, the study of the history of collective efforts for the improvement of the health of populations from antiquity to modernity with particular emphasis on the interdisciplinary analysis of the interaction between ideas on public health, organizations created to carry out these ideas, their implementation, and their social and demographic consequences.
Related titles: Online - full text ed.: ISSN 1404-4013. 1999. free (effective 2011).
Indexed: CA, HistAb, P34, SCOPUS, T02.
Published by: (International Network for the History of Public Health), Linkoeping University Electronic Press, Linkoeping Universitet, Linkoeping, 58183, Sweden. TEL 46-13-286609, FAX 46-13-284424, ep@ep.liu.se. Ed. Sam Willmer.

➤ **HYGIENES.** *see* HEALTH FACILITIES AND ADMINISTRATION

614.4 616.97 USA ISSN 1526-1786
I A C EXPRESS. (Immunization Action Coalition) Text in English. 1997. w. free (effective 2011). back issues avail. **Document type:** *Newsletter, Trade.*
Media: E-mail.
Published by: Immunization Action Coalition, 1573 Selby Ave, Ste 234, St. Paul, MN 55104. TEL 651-647-9009, FAX 651-647-9131, admin@immunize.org.

614 621.48 AUT ISSN 1020-525X
TK9152 CODEN: SSAEAW
I A E A SAFETY STANDARDS SERIES. (International Atomic Energy Agency) Text in English, French, Russian, Spanish, Arabic, Chinese. 1960. irreg. price varies. **Document type:** *Monographic series, Trade.*
Former titles (until 1996): International Atomic Energy Agency. Safety Series (1022-5420); I A E A Safety Series (0074-1892)
Related titles: CD-ROM ed.
Indexed: GeoRef, IMMAb, SpeleolAb.
—BLDSC (8069.150500), IE, INIST, Linda Hall.
Published by: International Atomic Energy Agency/Agence Internationale de l'Energie Atomique, Wagramer Str 5, Postfach 100, Vienna, W 1400, Austria. TEL 43-1-2600-0, FAX 43-1-2600-29302, sales.publications@iaea.org, http://www.iaea.org.

614.8 USA
I A E M BULLETIN. (International Association of Emergency Managers) Text in English. 1983. m. USD 115 (effective 2001). adv. **Document type:** *Bulletin, Trade.*
Formerly: N C C E M's Official Monthly Newsletter; N C C E M Bulletin (1063-9918)
Published by: International Association of Emergency Managers, 201 Park Washington Ct., Falls Church, VA 22046-4527. TEL 703-538-1795, FAX 703-241-5603. Ed. Karen Thompson. Circ: 1,800.

I A F C ON SCENE. (International Association of Fire Chiefs) *see* FIRE PREVENTION

613 USA ISSN 1093-1376
I C H F NEWSLETTER. Text in English. 1997. q. **Document type:** *Newsletter.*
Related titles: Online - full text ed.
Indexed: A04, C06, C07, C08, CA, CINAHL.
Published by: International Council for Health Freedom, 5580 La Jolla Blvd, B429, La Jolla, CA 92037. TEL 619-483-8569, FAX 619-581-6640. Ed. Michael L Culbert.

I C R U JOURNAL. (International Commission on Radiation Units and Measurements) *see* PHYSICS—Nuclear Physics

I N S E R M. COLLECTION GRANDES ENQUETES EN SANTE PUBLIQUE ET EPIDEMIOLOGIE. (Institut National de la Sante et de la Recherche Medicale) *see* MEDICAL SCIENCES

I S A B B JOURNAL OF HEALTH AND ENVIRONMENTAL SCIENCES. *see* ENVIRONMENTAL STUDIES

628 ITA ISSN 1972-2761
I S A INGEGNERIA SANITARIA AMBIENTALE. Text in Italian. N.S. 1952. 3/yr. adv. bk.rev. abstr.; bibl.; charts; illus. **Document type:** *Magazine, Trade.*
Former titles (until 2007): Ingegneria Sanitaria Ambientale (1125-9329); (until 1990): Ingegneria Sanitaria (0020-0980)
Indexed: ChemAb.
Published by: (Associazione Nazionale di Ingegneria Sanitaria (A N D I S)), T S A Editore, Via Andrea d'Isernia 28, Naples, 80122, Italy.

I S M P MEDICATION SAFETY ALERT! (ACUTE CARE EDITION). *see* PHARMACY AND PHARMACOLOGY

614 USA ISSN 1054-7053
I S S A TODAY. Text in English. 1975. 10/yr. USD 75 (effective 2000). adv. back issues avail. **Document type:** *Magazine, Trade.*
Related titles: Online - full text ed.
Published by: International Sanitary Supply Association, Inc., 7373 N Lincoln Ave, Lincolnwood, IL 60712-1799. TEL 800-225-4772, FAX 847-982-1012, info@issa.com. Ed. Lisa Veeck. R&P Bill Balek. Adv. contact Charlie Walden. Circ: 5,000 (controlled).

I Z A. *see* OCCUPATIONAL HEALTH AND SAFETY

I Z A MAGAZINE. *see* INSURANCE

628 ITA ISSN 1721-5366
IGIENE ALIMENTI. DISINFESTAZIONE & IGIENE AMBIENTALE. Text in Italian. 1984. bi-m. adv. **Document type:** *Magazine, Trade.* **Description:** Concerned with pest control.
Former titles (until 1996): Disinfestazione & Igiene Ambientale (1721-5358); (until 1993): Disinfestazione (1721-534X)
Published by: MO.ED.CO. Srl, Via San Martino 11C, Milan, 20122, Italy. TEL 39-02-58316074, FAX 39-02-58322564, info@moedco.it, http://www.moedco.it.

614 ITA ISSN 0019-1639
RA421 CODEN: ISPRA2
IGIENE E SANITA PUBBLICA. Text in Italian; Summaries in English, French, German, Italian. 1945. bi-m. EUR 70 domestic to institutions; EUR 75 foreign (effective 2009). adv. bk.rev. charts; illus. index. **Document type:** *Journal, Academic/Scholarly.*
Related titles: Microform ed.: (from PQC).
Indexed: ChemAb, EMBASE, ExcerpMed, MEDLINE, P30, SCOPUS.
—CASDDS, Linda Hall. **CCC.**
Published by: Nebo Sas Editore, Via Candia 101, Rome, 00192, Italy. TEL 39-06-39751674, FAX 39-06-39746586, redazione@igiene.org, http://www.igiene.org. Circ: 2,000.

362.1 ITA ISSN 1592-5633
IGIENE & SICUREZZA DEL LAVORO. Abbreviated title: I S L. Text in Italian. 1997. m. EUR 150 (print & online eds.) (effective 2008). **Document type:** *Journal, Trade.*
Related titles: CD-ROM ed.: ISSN 1592-5625; Online - full text ed.
Published by: IPSOA Editore (Subsidiary of: Wolters Kluwer Italia Srl), Strada 1, Palazzo F6, Milanofiori, Assago, MI 20090, Italy. TEL 39-02-82476888, FAX 39-02-82476436, http://www.ipsoa.it.

362.1 ITA ISSN 1129-5864
IGIENE E SICUREZZA DEL LAVORO. I CORSI. Text in Italian. 1999. m. EUR 100 combined subscription (print & online eds.) (effective 2008). **Document type:** *Magazine, Trade.*
Related titles: Online - full text ed.
Published by: IPSOA Editore (Subsidiary of: Wolters Kluwer Italia Srl), Strada 1, Palazzo F6, Milanofiori, Assago, MI 20090, Italy. TEL 39-02-82476888, FAX 39-02-82476436, http://www.ipsoa.it.

362.1 JPN ISSN 0914-5117
CODEN: IOKHEP
IKAGAKU OYO KENKYU ZAIDAN KENKYU HOKOKU/SUZUKEN MEMORIAL FOUNDATION. RESEARCH PAPERS. Text in English, Japanese; Summaries in English. 1982. a. **Document type:** *Corporate.* **Description:** Reports the pharmaceutical research and human health achievements supported by the foundation.
Indexed: ChemAb.
Published by: Ikagaku Oyo Kenkyu Zaidan/Suzuken Memorial Foundation, Suzuken Honsha, 8 Higashi-Kataha-Machi, Higashi-ku, Nagoya, Aichi 461-8701, Japan. TEL 81-52-9512139, FAX 81-52-9512166, http://www.suzukenzaidan.or.jp/. Pub. Ikagaku Oyo Kenkyu Zaidan.

614 CAN ISSN 1910-0035
IMMUNIZATION INITIATIVES/INITIATIVES EN IMMUNISATION. Text in English, French. 2001. irreg. **Document type:** *Newsletter, Consumer.*
Related titles: Online - full text ed.

P

Published by: (Canadian Public Health Association, Canadian International Immunization Initiative), Canadian Public Health Association, 1565 Carling Ave, Ste 400, Ottawa, ON K1Z 8R1, Canada. TEL 613-725-3769, FAX 613-725-9826, ciii@cpha.ca, http://www.cpha.ca.

362.1 CAN ISSN 1910-8931
IMPROVING THE HEALTH OF CANADIANS. SUMMARY REPORT. Text in English. 2004. biennial. CAD 25 per issue to non-profit organizations; CAD 35 per issue to institutions (effective 2006). **Document type:** *Report, Trade.*
Related titles: French ed.: Ameliorer la Sante des Canadiens. Rapport Sommaire. ISSN 1910-894X.
Published by: Canadian Institutes of Health Research (C I H R)/Instituts de Recherche en Sante au Canada (I R S C), 160 Elgin St, 9th Fl, Ottawa, ON K1A 0W9, Canada. TEL 613-941-2672, 888-603-4178, FAX 613-954-1800, info@cihr-irsc.gc.ca, http://www.cihr-irsc.gc.ca.

IN BRIEF. *see* BIRTH CONTROL

362.1 ESP ISSN 1132-1296
RA515
INDEX DE ENFERMERIA. Text in Spanish. 1992. q. EUR 45 domestic to individuals; EUR 65 foreign to individuals; EUR 65 domestic to institutions; EUR 150 foreign to institutions (effective 2009). **Document type:** *Journal, Academic/Scholarly.*
Related titles: Online - full text ed.: 2004. free (effective 2011).
Indexed: C06, CINAHL, SCOPUS.
Published by: Fundacion Index, Calle Horno de Marina 2, Granada, 18001, Spain. http://www.index-f.com/fundacion.php.

INDIAN JOURNAL OF PREVENTIVE AND SOCIAL MEDICINE. *see* MEDICAL SCIENCES

614 IND ISSN 0019-557X
RA421 CODEN: IPBHAH
INDIAN JOURNAL OF PUBLIC HEALTH. Text in English. 1957 (Sep.). q. INR 2,000 domestic to individuals; INR 600 domestic to institutions; USD 300 foreign to individuals; USD 100 foreign to institutions (effective 2011). adv. bk.rev. abstr.; charts; illus.; stat. index. back issues avail. **Document type:** *Journal, Academic/Scholarly.*
Description: Publishes publich health realted original articles, results of investigation and research, special articles, short communications, Articles on National health Program, Reports, Reviews, Notes and News as well as association matters.
Related titles: Online - full text ed.: ISSN 2229-7693. INR 500 domestic to individuals; INR 1,600 domestic to institutions; USD 80 foreign to individuals; USD 240 foreign to institutions (effective 2011).
Indexed: A22, A26, A36, C06, C07, ChemAb, EMBASE, ExcerpMed, F09, FR, FS&TA, H12, I05, INI, IndMed, MEDLINE, N03, P30, R10, Reac, S13, SAA, SCOPUS, T05, W09.
—BLDSC (4420.400000), GNLM, IE, Infotrieve, Ingenta, INIST.
Published by: (Indian Public Health Association), Medknow Publications and Media Pvt. Ltd., B-9, Kanara Business Ctr, Off Link Rd, Ghatkopar (E), Mumbai, Maharastra 400 075, India. TEL 91-22-66491818, FAX 91-22-66491817, publishing@medknow.com, http://www.medknow.com. Eds. Dr. Sanjay P Zodpey, Dr. Sandip K Ray.

THE INDIAN PRACTITIONER; a monthly journal of medicine, surgery & public health. *see* MEDICAL SCIENCES

614 IDN ISSN 0216-3527
INDONESIAN JOURNAL OF PUBLIC HEALTH/MAJALAH KESEHATAN MASYARAKAT INDONESIA. Text and summaries in English, Indonesian. 1969. m. IDR 3,500 per issue. adv. bk.rev. charts; illus.; stat. **Document type:** *Journal, Academic/Scholarly.*
Former titles: Indonesian Public Health Association. Journal; Indonesian Journal of Public Health
Published by: Ikatan Ahli Kesehatan Masyarakat Indonesia/Indonesian Public Health Association, d.a.: Pengurus Pusat IAKMI, Gedung Mochtar Lantai 2, cq. Bidang Pengembangan Keanggotaan IAKMI, Jalan Pegangsaan Timur No.16, Jakarta Pusat, 10320, Indonesia. syrl51@yahoo.com, http://www.iakmi.org/. Circ: 10,000.

613.5 USA ISSN 1600-0668
TD883.1
➤ **INDOOR AIR (ONLINE).** Text in English. 1991. bi-m. GBP 496 in United Kingdom to institutions; EUR 630 in Europe to institutions; USD 832 in the Americas to institutions; USD 970 elsewhere to institutions (effective 2012). **Document type:** *Journal, Academic/ Scholarly.*
Media: Online - full text (from IngentaConnect). **Related titles:** ◆ Print ed.: Indoor Air (Print). ISSN 0905-6947.
—CCC.
Published by: Wiley-Blackwell Publishing, Inc. (Subsidiary of: Wiley-Blackwell Publishing Ltd.), Commerce Pl, 350 Main St, Malden, MA 02148. TEL 781-388-8200, FAX 781-388-8210, info@wiley.com, http://www.wiley.com/WileyCDA/.

613.5 697 USA ISSN 0905-6947
TD883.1 CODEN: INAIE5
➤ **INDOOR AIR (PRINT)**; international journal of indoor air quality and climate. Text in English. 1991. bi-m. GBP 496 in United Kingdom to institutions; EUR 630 in Europe to institutions; USD 832 in the Americas to institutions; USD 970 elsewhere to institutions; GBP 571 combined subscription in United Kingdom to institutions (print & online eds.); EUR 726 combined subscription in Europe to institutions (print & online eds.); USD 957 combined subscription in the Americas to institutions (print & online eds.); USD 1,117 combined subscription elsewhere to institutions (print & online eds.) (effective 2012). adv. charts; illus. reprint service avail. from PSC. **Document type:** *Journal, Academic/Scholarly.* **Description:** Reports origional research on the indoor environment of non-industrial buildings.
Related titles: ◆ Online - full text ed.: Indoor Air (Online). ISSN 1600-0668; ◆ Supplement(s): Indoor Air. Supplement. ISSN 0908-5920.
Indexed: A01, A03, A08, A22, A26, A34, A36, A37, ASCA, AgrForAb, B21, BA, CA, CABA, CIN, ChemAb, ChemTitl, CurCont, D01, E01, E04, E05, E12, EMBASE, ESPM, ExcerpMed, F08, F11, F12, GH, H&SSA, H12, I10, IBuildSA, INIS AtomInd, ISR, IndMed, IndVet, LT, MEDLINE, N02, N03, P30, P32, P33, P37, P39, PollutAb, R07, R08, R12, RM&VM, S01, S13, S16, SCI, SCOPUS, T02, T05, ToxAb, VS, W07, W10.
—BLDSC (4438.046530), CASDDS, IE, Infotrieve, Ingenta, INIST. **CCC.**

Published by: (International Society of Indoor Air Quality and Climate DNK), Wiley-Blackwell Publishing, Inc. (Subsidiary of: Wiley-Blackwell Publishing Ltd.), Commerce Pl, 350 Main St, Malden, MA 02148. TEL 781-388-8200, FAX 781-388-8210, info@wiley.com, http://www.wiley.com/WileyCDA/. Eds. Jan Sundell, William Nazaroff. Adv. contact Claire Rogers.

613.5 USA ISSN 0908-5920
➤ **INDOOR AIR. SUPPLEMENT.** Text in English. 1993. irreg., latest vol.11, 2005. free with subscription to Indoor Air. **Document type:** *Monographic series, Academic/Scholarly.*
Related titles: Online - full text ed.: ISSN 1600-5554; ◆ Supplement to: Indoor Air (Print). ISSN 0905-6947.
Indexed: SCOPUS.
—INIST. **CCC.**
Published by: (International Society of Indoor Air Quality and Climate DNK), Wiley-Blackwell Publishing, Inc. (Subsidiary of: Wiley-Blackwell Publishing Ltd.), Commerce Pl, 350 Main St, Malden, MA 02148. TEL 781-388-8200, FAX 781-388-8210, info@wiley.com, http://www.wiley.com/WileyCDA/.

➤ **INDOOR ENVIRONMENT BUSINESS.** *see* ENVIRONMENTAL STUDIES

➤ **INDOOR ENVIRONMENT CONNECTIONS**; the newspaper for the iaq marketplace. *see* ENVIRONMENTAL STUDIES

➤ **INFECTION CONTROL WEEKLY MONITOR.** *see* HEALTH FACILITIES AND ADMINISTRATION

➤ **INFLUENZA SEASON SUMMARY.** *see* MEDICAL SCIENCES—Communicable Diseases

➤ **INFO.CA DE L'AGENCE.** *see* SOCIAL SERVICES AND WELFARE

362.1 AUS ISSN 1838-0557
▼ **INFOLINK**; focus on health. Text in English. 2010. s-a. free (effective 2011). back issues avail. **Document type:** *Magazine, Government.*
Formerly (until 2010): Disability Matters
Related titles: Online - full text ed.: free (effective 2011).
Published by: Disability SA, Barossa and Area Community Health Service, 29 N St, Angaston, SA 5353, Australia. TEL 61-8-85638544, FAX 61-8-85643434, disabilityinfo@dfc.sa.gov.au.

362.1 368.382 FRA ISSN 2108-1840
INFORMATION AUX PHARMACIENS. LETTRE. Text in French. 2006. irreg. **Document type:** *Newsletter, Trade.*
Formerly (until 2009): Pharmaciens. Lettre aux (1955-1304)
Published by: Caisse Nationale de l'Assurance Maladie des Travailleurs Salaries, 26-50, Av du Professeur Andre-Lemierre, Paris Cedex 20, 75986, France. TEL 33-1-72601000, http://www.ameli.fr/index.php.

201.7621 USA ISSN 1549-0971
INFORMATION PLUS REFERENCE SERIES. HEALTH AND WELLNESS; illness among Americans. Text in English. 1981. biennial, latest 2006. USD 49 per issue (effective 2008). **Document type:** *Monographic series, Academic/Scholarly.* **Description:** Provides a compilation of current and historical statistics, with analysis, on aspects of one contemporary social issue.
Supersedes in part (in 2001): Information Series on Current Topics. Health, A Concern for Every American (1534-1623)
Related titles: Online - full text ed.; ◆ Series of: Information Plus Reference Series.
Published by: Gale (Subsidiary of: Cengage Learning), 27500 Drake Rd, Farmington Hills, MI 48331. TEL 248-699-4253, 800-877-4253, FAX 877-363-4253, gale.customerservice@cengage.com, http://gale.cengage.com.

362.1 353.6 USA ISSN 1543-2556
RA395.A3
INFORMATION PLUS REFERENCE SERIES. THE HEALTH CARE SYSTEM; who benefits?. Text in English. 2003. biennial. USD 50 per issue (effective 2009). **Document type:** *Monographic series, Academic/Scholarly.* **Description:** Provides a clear and comprehensive summary of up-to-date research on the health care system and is interspersed with the statistical tables, charts, and graphs.
Supersedes in part (in 2001): Information Series on Current Topics. Health, a Concern for Every American (1534-1623)
Related titles: Online - full text ed.; ◆ Series of: Information Plus Reference Series.
Published by: Gale (Subsidiary of: Cengage Learning), 27500 Drake Rd, Farmington Hills, MI 48331. TEL 248-699-4253, 800-877-4253, FAX 248-699-8035, 877-363-4253, gale.customerservice@cengage.com, http://gale.cengage.com. Ed. Paula Kepos.

362.1 FRA ISSN 2106-6744
INFORMATIONS JURIDIQUES. Text in French. 2001. m. **Document type:** *Government.*
Published by: Institut National de Recherche et de Securite pour la Prevention des Accidents du Travail et des Maladies Professionnelles, 30 rue Olivier Noyer, Paris, 75680 Cedex 14, France. TEL 33-1-40443000, FAX 33-1-40443099, thanh@inrs.fr, http://www.inrs.fr.

614.8 CHE ISSN 1011-5706
INFORMATIONS PHARMACEUTIQUES O M S. (Organisation Mondiale de la Sante) Text in French. 1987. q. **Document type:** *Newsletter, Trade.*
Related titles: ◆ English ed.: W H O Drug Information. ISSN 1010-9609.
—INIST.
Published by: World Health Organization/Organisation Mondiale de la Sante, Avenue Appia 20, Geneva 27, 1211, Switzerland. TEL 41-22-7912111, FAX 41-22-7913111, publications@who.int, http://www.who.int.

INFORMAZIONE INNOVATIVA. *see* ENVIRONMENTAL STUDIES

362.1 ESP ISSN 1134-914X
INFORME DE SALUD PUBLICA. Text in Spanish; Summaries in Spanish. 1992. a.
Published by: Eusko Jaurlaritzaren Argitalpen-Zerbitzu Nagusia/Servicio Central de Publicaciones del Gobierno Vasco, Donostia-San Sebastian, 1, Vitoria-gasteiz, Alava 01010, Spain. TEL 34-945-018561, FAX 34-945-189709, hac-sabd@ej-gv.es, http://www.ej-gv.net/publicaciones.

362.1 CAN
INFRASTRUCTURE HEALTH AND SAFETY MAGAZINE (E-MAIL). Text in English. 1990. q. free (effective 2010). back issues avail. **Document type:** *Magazine, Trade.*
Former titles (until 2011): Infrastructure Health and Safety Magazine (Print) (1924-4177); (until 2010): Construction Safety Magazine (1485-7227); (until 1998): Construction Safety (1480-0683)
Media: E-mail.
Published by: Infrastructure Health and Safety Association, 5110 Creekbank Rd, Ste 400, Mississauga, ON L4W 0A1, Canada. TEL 905-625-0100, 800-263-5024, FAX 905-625-8998, info@ihsa.ca. Ed. John J Ihnat.

628 ITA ISSN 0394-5871
CODEN: IGEABH
INGEGNERIA AMBIENTALE. Abbreviated title: I A. Text in Italian; Summaries in English, Italian. 1972. 9/yr. EUR 119 combined subscription domestic (print & online eds.); EUR 210 combined subscription foreign (print & online eds.) (effective 2009). adv. bk.rev. Index. 70 p./no.; **Document type:** *Magazine, Trade.*
Formerly (until 1986): Ingegneria Ambientale Inquinamento e Depurazione (0302-7775)
Related titles: Online - full text ed.
Indexed: ASFA, CIN, ChemAb, ChemTitl, INIS AtomInd.
—BLDSC (4500.650000), CASDDS, IE, Ingenta, INIST.
Published by: (Centro di Ingegneria per la Protezione dell'Ambiente), C I P A Editore, Via Palladio 26, Milan, 20135, Italy. TEL 39-02.58301528, FAX 39-02.58301550, info@cipaeditore.it, http://www.cipaeditore.it. Circ: 1,300.

628 ITA
INGEGNERIA AMBIENTALE QUADERNI. Text in Italian; Summaries in English, Italian. 1984. 2/yr. **Document type:** *Monographic series, Trade.*
Formerly: Ingegneria Ambientale Inquinamento e Depurazione Quaderni
Indexed: ChemAb.
Published by: (Centro di Ingegneria per la Protezione dell'Ambiente), C I P A Editore, Via Palladio 26, Milan, 20135, Italy. TEL 39-02.58301528, FAX 39-02.58301550, info@cipaeditore.it, http://www.cipaeditore.it.

628 BRA ISSN 0446-2424
TD4
INGENIERIA SANITARIA. Text in English, French, Portuguese, Spanish. 1946. q. USD 16 (effective 2000). adv. bk.rev.
Indexed: Repind.
Published by: Interamerican Association of Sanitary and Environmental Engineering, Rua Nicolau Gagliardi, 354, Sao Paulo, SP 05429, Brazil. TEL 011-212-4080, FAX 011-814-2441, TELEX 11-81453. Eds. Osvaldo Rey, Luiz Augusto de Lima Pontes. Circ: 8,000.

INHALED PARTICLES. *see* HEALTH FACILITIES AND ADMINISTRATION

363.1 629.2042 USA
INJURY, COLLISION AND THEFT LOSSES. Text in English. a. **Document type:** *Report, Trade.*
Formerly (until 1992): H L D I Injury and Collision Loss Experience
Published by: Highway Loss Data Institute, 1005 N Glebe Rd, Ste 700, Arlington, VA 22201. TEL 703-247-1600, FAX 703-247-1595, publications@iihs.org.

614.8 USA ISSN 1538-5337
HA217
INJURY FACTS (YEAR). Text in English. 1921. a. USD 62.95 per issue to non-members; USD 43.95 per issue to members; USD 104.95 per issue to non-members (print & CD-ROM eds.); USD 73.95 per issue to members (print & CD-ROM eds.) (effective 2009). **Document type:** *Yearbook, Consumer.* **Description:** Contains statistical information pertinent to accidents.
Formerly (until 1999): Accident Facts (0148-6039)
Related titles: CD-ROM ed.: USD 62.95 per issue to non-members; USD 43.95 per issue to members (effective 2009); Microfiche ed.: (from CIS).
Indexed: SRI.
—Linda Hall.
Published by: (Statistics Department), National Safety Council, 1121 Spring Lake Dr, Itasca, IL 60143. TEL 630-775-2056, 800-621-7619, FAX 630-285-0797, customerservice@nsc.org, http://www.nsc.org.

INSIDE INFORMATION. *see* HEALTH FACILITIES AND ADMINISTRATION

362.1 CAN ISSN 1709-0717
INSTITUT CANADIEN D'INFORMATION SUR LA SANTE. CATALOGUE DES PRODUITS ET SERVICES. Text in French. 1997. a., latest 2006. **Document type:** *Catalog, Consumer.*
Formerly (until 2001): Institut Canadien d'Information sur la Sante. Catalogue (1484-7566)
Related titles: Online - full text ed.: ISSN 1719-8410; ◆ English ed.: Canadian Institute for Health Information. Products and Services Catalogue. ISSN 1709-0709.
Published by: Canadian Institute for Health Information/Institut Canadien d'Information sur la Sante, 377 Dalhousie St, Ste 200, Ottawa, ON K1N 9N8, Canada. TEL 613-241-7860, FAX 613-241-8120, http://www.cihi.ca.

362.1 CAN ISSN 1910-6300
INSTITUT NATIONAL DE SANTE PUBLIQUE DU QUEBEC. PROGRAMMATION. Text in French. 2005. triennial. **Document type:** *Government.*
Published by: Institut National de Sante Publique du Quebec, 945 Av Wolfe, Quebec, PQ G1V 5B3, Canada. TEL 418-650-5115 ext 5336, FAX 418-646-9328.

614 JPN
INSTITUTE OF PUBLIC HEALTH. ANNUAL REPORT/KOKURITSU KOSHU EISEI-IN NENPO. Text in Japanese. 1948. a.
Published by: National Institute of Public Health, 4-6-1 Shirokanedai, Minato-ku, Tokyo, 108-0071, Japan. Ed. Dr. Hidesuke Kobayashi.

INSTITUTION OF ENGINEERS (INDIA). ENVIRONMENTAL ENGINEERING DIVISION. JOURNAL. *see* ENVIRONMENTAL STUDIES

616.988 PRT ISSN 0303-7762
CODEN: AIHTDH
INSTITUTO DE HIGIENE E MEDICINA TROPICAL. ANAIS. Text and summaries in English, French, Portuguese. 1943. irreg., latest vol.10, 1984. bk.rev. **Document type:** *Trade.*
Former titles (until 1972): Lisbon. Escola Nacional de Saude de Medicina Tropical. Anais (0075-9767); (until 1966): Lisbon. Instituto de Medicina Tropical. Anais (0365-3307)
Indexed: ASFA, B21, ESPM, IndMed, P30, SCOPUS.

—GNLM, INIST.
Published by: Instituto de Higiene e Medicina Tropical, Servico de Documentacao e Informacao Cientifica, Rua Junqueira, 96, Lisboa, 1300-344, Portugal. TEL 351-1-3652600, FAX 351-1-3632105, biblio@ihmt.unl.pt, http://www.ihmt.unl.pt. Ed. Dr. Filomena Exposto. Circ: 1,000.

613 CHL ISSN 0716-1387
RA465 CODEN: BICHDZ
INSTITUTO DE SALUD PUBLICA DE CHILE. BOLETIN. Text in Spanish; Summaries in English. 1942. 2/yr. adv. bk.rev. bibl.; charts; illus.
Formerly: Instituto Bacteriologico de Chile. Boletin (0374-6224)
Indexed: ChemAb, IndMed.
—CASDDS.
Published by: Instituto de Salud Publica de Chile, Av Marathon 1000, Nunoa, Santiago, Chile. TEL 56-2-3507477, FAX 56-2-3507578, http://www.ispch.cl.

614 VEN ISSN 0798-0477
INSTITUTO NACIONAL DE HIGIENE RAFAEL RANGEL. REVISTA. Text in Spanish. 1968. q.
Indexed: C01.
Published by: Ministerio del Poder Popular para la Salud, Instituto Nacional de Higiene Rafael Rangel, Ciudad Universitaria de Caracas, Los Chaguaramos, Caracas, Venezuela. TEL 58-212-2191600, FAX 58-212-2191655, http://www.inhrr.gov.ve/index.htm.

614.86 USA ISSN 0018-988X
HE5614
INSURANCE INSTITUTE FOR HIGHWAY SAFETY. STATUS REPORT. Text in English. 1961. 10/yr. free. Index. reprints avail. **Document type:** *Newsletter, Consumer.* **Description:** Covers the varies research conducted by the Institute, as well as activities, proposals, news and related articles.
Formerly: I I H S Report
Related titles: Microform ed.: (from PQC); Online - full content ed.
Indexed: A22, ConsI, HRIS.
Published by: Insurance Institute for Highway Safety, 1005 North Glebe Rd, Arlington, VA 22201. TEL 703-247-1500, FAX 703-247-1588. Circ: 17,000.

362.1 SVK ISSN 1337-6853
INTERDISCIPLINARY TOXICOLOGY. Text in English. 2008. q. **Document type:** *Journal, Academic/Scholarly.*
Related titles: Online - full text ed.: ISSN 1337-9569. free (effective 2011).
Indexed: A34, A36, C25, D01, E12, F08, FCA, H16, N03, N04, P32, P33, R07, R08, S13, T05, W10.
Published by: Slovenska Akademia Vied, Ustav Experimentalnej Biologie Farmakologie a Toxicologie, Dubravska Cesta 9, Bratislava, 841 04, Slovakia. TEL 421-2-54773586, FAX 421-2-54775928, exfasekr@savba.sk, http://www.uef.sav.sk.

362.1 CAN ISSN 1718-3324
L'INTERFACE. Text in French. 2006. irreg. **Document type:** *Newsletter, Consumer.*
Published by: Centre de Sante et de Services Sociaux de Bordeaux-Cartierville-Saint-Laurent, 555, boule Gouin Ouest, Montreal, PQ H3L 1K5, Canada. TEL 514-331-3020, FAX 514-331-3358, http://www.santemontreal.qc.ca/CSSS/bordeauxcartiervillesaintlaurent/fr/default.aspx.

▼ **INTERNAL SECURITY.** *see* CRIMINOLOGY AND LAW ENFORCEMENT

THE INTERNATIONAL COMPARATIVE LEGAL GUIDE TO: PHARMACEUTICAL ADVERTISING (YEAR). *see* PHARMACY AND PHARMACOLOGY

THE INTERNATIONAL DIRECTORY OF SAFETY, SECURITY AND FIRE FIGHTING EQUIPMENT IMPORTERS. *see* BUSINESS AND ECONOMICS—Trade And Industrial Directories

INTERNATIONAL HEALTH NEWS. *see* MEDICAL SCIENCES

362.1 GBR ISSN 1475-9276
RA393
➤ **INTERNATIONAL JOURNAL FOR EQUITY IN HEALTH.** Text in English. 2002 (Apr.). irreg. free (effective 2011). adv. back issues avail.; reprints avail. **Document type:** *Journal, Academic/Scholarly.* **Description:** Aims to the state of knowledge about equity in health, defined as systematic and potentially remediable differences in health across populations and population groups defined socially, economically, demographically, or geographically.
Media: Online - full text.
Indexed: A01, A20, A26, A36, C06, C07, CA, CABA, CurCont, E12, EMBASE, ExcerpMed, GH, H05, H17, I05, LT, N02, N03, P20, P22, P30, P33, P39, PN&I, R08, R12, S13, S16, SCOPUS, SSCI, T02, T05, TAR, W07, W11.
—CCC.
Published by: BioMed Central Ltd. (Subsidiary of: Springer Science+Business Media), 236 Gray's Inn Rd, London, WC1X 8HB, United Kingdom. TEL 44-20-31922000, FAX 44-20-31922010, info@biomedcentral.com, http://www.biomedcentral.com. Ed. Barbara Starfield. Adv. contact Natasha Bailey TEL 44-20-31922231.

➤ **INTERNATIONAL JOURNAL OF C O M A D E M.** (Condition Monitoring and Diagnostic Engineering Management) *see* TECHNOLOGY: COMPREHENSIVE WORKS

➤ **INTERNATIONAL JOURNAL OF CIRCUMPOLAR HEALTH.** *see* MEDICAL SCIENCES

➤ **INTERNATIONAL JOURNAL OF CIRCUMPOLAR HEALTH. SUPPLEMENT.** *see* MEDICAL SCIENCES

362.1 610 BIH ISSN 1840-4529
R5
▼ ➤ **INTERNATIONAL JOURNAL OF COLLABORATIVE RESEARCH ON INTERNAL MEDICINE & PUBLIC HEALTH.** Text in English. 2009. q. free (effective 2011). **Document type:** *Journal, Academic/Scholarly.*
Media: Online - full text.
Indexed: A01, A26, A34, A36, CA, CABA, EMBASE, GH, H11, H12, I05, N02, N03, P33, P48, P50, PQC, R08, R12, SCOPUS, T02, T05.
Published by: (International Online Medical Council MYS), D R U N P P, Bolnicka bb, Sarajevo, 71000, Bosnia Herzegovina. Eds. Forouzan Bayat Nejad, Jaspreet S Brar.

➤ **INTERNATIONAL JOURNAL OF ENVIRONMENT AND HEALTH.** *see* ENVIRONMENTAL STUDIES

➤ **INTERNATIONAL JOURNAL OF ENVIRONMENTAL RESEARCH AND PUBLIC HEALTH.** *see* ENVIRONMENTAL STUDIES

➤ **INTERNATIONAL JOURNAL OF EPIDEMIOLOGY.** *see* MEDICAL SCIENCES

362.1 613.2 GBR ISSN 2042-5988
▼ **INTERNATIONAL JOURNAL OF FOOD, NUTRITION AND PUBLIC HEALTH.** Abbreviated title: I J F N P H. Text in English. 2010. q. back issues avail. **Document type:** *Journal, Trade.* **Description:** Aims to establish a channel of communication between food scientists, nutritionists, public health professionals, policy makers, governmental and non-governmental agencies, and others concerned the food, nutrition and public health dimensions.
Related titles: Online - full text ed.: ISSN 2042-5996. free (effective 2010).
Published by: World Association for Sustainable Development, PO Box 64607, London, SW8 9AT, United Kingdom. allam@worldsustainable.org. Eds. Allam Ahmed, Ihab Tewfik.

362.1 664 IND ISSN 0975-8712
▼ ➤ **INTERNATIONAL JOURNAL OF FOOD SAFETY, NUTRITION, PUBLIC HEALTH AND TECHNOLOGY.** Abbreviated title: I J F S N P H T. Text in English. 2009. free (effective 2011). **Document type:** *Journal, Academic/Scholarly.* **Description:** Contains research articles in the areas of food safety, nutrition, public health and technology.
Media: Online - full text.
Published by: A.Prabhu Britto, Ed. & Pub., 18A, Nataraja Thevar Colony, Ramanathapuram, Coimbatore, Tamil Nadu 641 045, India. britto@prabhubritto.org, prabhu.britto@gmail.com.

614.15 USA ISSN 1499-9013
RA1151
➤ **INTERNATIONAL JOURNAL OF FORENSIC MENTAL HEALTH.** Text in English. 2002. q. GBP 216 combined subscription in United Kingdom to institutions (print & online eds.); EUR 311, USD 388 combined subscription to institutions (print & online eds.) (effective 2012). reprint service avail. from PSC. **Document type:** *Journal, Consumer.* **Description:** Focuses on issues of criminal responsibility, competency or fitness to stand trial, risk assessment, family violence, and treatment of forensic clients.
Related titles: Online - full text ed.: ISSN 1932-9903. GBP 194 in United Kingdom to institutions; EUR 280, USD 349 to institutions (effective 2012).
Indexed: CA, CJA, P03, P52, P56, PsycInfo, PsycholAb, S02, S03, T02.
—BLDSC (4542.257300), IE, Ingenta. **CCC.**
Published by: (International Association of Forensic Mental Health Services CAN), Routledge (Subsidiary of: Taylor & Francis Group), 325 Chestnut St, Ste 800, Philadelphia, PA 19106. TEL 215-625-8900, 800-354-1420, FAX 215-625-2940, journals@routledge.com, http://www.routledge.com. Ed. Stephen D Hart.

362 368.384 USA ISSN 1389-6563
RA410.A1
INTERNATIONAL JOURNAL OF HEALTH CARE FINANCE AND ECONOMICS. Text in English. 2001. q. EUR 455, USD 475 combined subscription to institutions (print & online eds.) (effective 2012). adv. back issues avail.; reprint service avail. from PSC. **Document type:** *Journal, Academic/Scholarly.* **Description:** Addresses the problems of financing a health care system and financing's impact on health care performance.
Related titles: Online - full text ed.: ISSN 1573-6962 (from IngentaConnect).
Indexed: A12, A13, A22, A26, ABIn, BibLing, C06, C07, CA, CurCont, E01, EMBASE, ESPM, EconLit, ExcerpMed, H05, H12, JEL, MEDLINE, P20, P21, P22, P30, P48, P50, P51, P52, P53, P54, P56, PQC, RiskAb, SCOPUS, SSCI, T02, W07.
—BLDSC (4542.274700), IE, Infotrieve, Ingenta. **CCC.**
Published by: (International Health Economics Association CAN), Springer New York LLC (Subsidiary of: Springer Science+Business Media), 233 Spring St, New York, NY 10013. TEL 212-460-1500, FAX 212-460-1575, service-ny@springer.com. Eds. Mark Pauly, Pedro P Barros.

614 325 ITA ISSN 1824-8144
INTERNATIONAL JOURNAL OF HEALTH, CULTURE AND MIGRATION. Text in Multiple languages. 2005. 3/yr. **Document type:** *Journal, Trade.*
Published by: Societa Editrice Universo, Via Giovanni Battista Morgagni 1, Rome, RM 00161, Italy. TEL 39-06-44231171, FAX 39-06-4402033, amministrazione@seu-roma.it, http://www.seuroma.com.

362.1 910.285 GBR ISSN 1476-072X
RA1
➤ **INTERNATIONAL JOURNAL OF HEALTH GEOGRAPHICS.** Text in English. 2002 (Aug.). irreg. free (effective 2011). adv. back issues avail.; reprints avail. **Document type:** *Journal, Academic/Scholarly.* **Description:** Contains papers on the application of geographic information systems and science in public health, healthcare, health services, and health resources.
Media: Online - full text.
Indexed: A01, A02, A03, A08, A26, A34, A35, A36, A37, A38, AgBio, CA, CABA, CurCont, D01, E12, EMBASE, ExcerpMed, F08, F12, G11, GEOBASE, GH, H05, H16, H17, I05, IndVet, LT, MEDLINE, N02, N03, N04, OR, P20, P22, P30, P32, P33, P37, P39, P40, PN&I, PQC, PollutAb, R07, R08, R11, R12, RRTA, S13, S16, SCOPUS, SSCI, T02, T05, TAR, VS, W07, W10, W11, Z01.
—CCC.
Published by: BioMed Central Ltd. (Subsidiary of: Springer Science+Business Media), 236 Gray's Inn Rd, London, WC1X 8HB, United Kingdom. TEL 44-20-31922000, FAX 44-20-31922010, info@biomedcentral.com, http://www.biomedcentral.com. Ed. Maged N Kamel Boulos TEL 44-1752-586530. Adv. contact Natasha Bailey TEL 44-20-31922231.

614 USA ISSN 0020-7314
RA421 CODEN: IJUSC3
➤ **INTERNATIONAL JOURNAL OF HEALTH SERVICES.** Abbreviated title: I J H S. Text in English. 1971. q. USD 109 combined subscription to individuals (print & online eds.); USD 402 combined subscription to institutions (print & online eds.) (effective 2011). adv. bk.rev. abstr.; illus. back issues avail.; reprints avail. **Document type:** *Journal, Academic/Scholarly.* **Description:** Contains current and authoritative information on the development of the health care industry worldwide.
Related titles: Online - full text ed.: ISSN 1541-4469. USD 103 to individuals; USD 381 to institutions (effective 2011).
Indexed: A20, A22, A36, ABS&EES, AHCMS, ASCA, ASSIA, AbAn, AltPI, B21, C06, C07, C08, CA, CABA, CINAHL, CISA, Chicano, CurCont, DIP, E-psyche, E12, EMBASE, ERA, ESPM, ExcerpMed, F09, FR, FamI, G10, GEOBASE, GH, H&SSA, H01, H05, HospAb, HospLI, IBR, IBSS, IBZ, IndMed, LT, MCR, MEA&I, MEDLINE, N02, N03, P30, P34, P42, PAIS, PSA, R07, R10, R12, Reac, RefZh, RiskAb, S02, S03, S21, SCI, SCOPUS, SOPODA, SSA, SSCI, SociolAb, T02, T05, TAR, W07, W09, W10, W11.
—BLDSC (4542.278000), GNLM, IE, Infotrieve, Ingenta, INIST. **CCC.**
Published by: Baywood Publishing Co., Inc., 26 Austin Ave, PO Box 337, Amityville, NY 11701. TEL 631-691-1270, 800-638-7819, FAX 631-691-1770, Baywood@baywood.com. Ed. Vicente Navarro.

614.44 610 DEU ISSN 1438-4639
QR46 CODEN: IJEHFT
➤ **INTERNATIONAL JOURNAL OF HYGIENE AND ENVIRONMENTAL HEALTH.** Text in English. 1883. 6/yr. EUR 701 in Europe to institutions; EUR 688 to institutions in Germany, Austria and Switzerland; JPY 95,500 in Japan to institutions; USD 767 elsewhere to institutions (effective 2012). adv. **Document type:** *Journal, Academic/Scholarly.* **Description:** Covers the entire field of human activity influencing health, regarding both the private and public health services.
Incorporates (1996-2002): Environmental Epidemiology and Toxicology (1522-7987); Which was formerly (until 1999): Journal of Clean Technology, Environmental Toxicology and Occupational Medicine (1092-5732); Which was formed by the merger of (1991-1996): Journal of Clean Technology and Environmental Sciences (1052-1062); (1996-1996): International Journal of Occupational Medicine, Immunology and Toxicology (1089-0149); Former titles: Zentralblatt fuer Hygiene und Umweltmedizin (0934-8859); Which incorporated (1955-1991): Zeitschrift fuer die Gesamte Hygiene und Ihre Grenzgebiete (0049-8610); (until 1989): Zentralblatt fuer Bakteriologie, Mikrogiologie und Hygiene. Serie B, Umwelthygiene, Krankenhaushygiene, Arbeitshygiene, Praventive Medizin (0932-6073); (until 1985): Zentralblatt fuer Bakteriologie, Mikrobiologie und Hygiene.1 Abt. Originale B, Hygiene (0174-3015); (until 1980): Zentralblatt fuer Bakteriologie. 1 Abt. Originale B, Hygiene, Krankenhaushygiene, Betriebshygiene, Praventive Medizin (0172-5602); (until 1979): Zentralblatt fuer Bakteriologie, Parasitenkunde, Infektionskrankheiten und Hygiene. 1. Abteilung. Originale. Reihe B, Hygiene, Praventive Medizin (0300-9661); (until 1971): Archiv fuer Hygiene und Bakteriologie (0003-9144); (until 1929): Archiv fuer Hygiene (0365-2955)
Related titles: Microfilm ed.: (from PMC); Online - full text ed.: ISSN 1618-131X (from IngentaConnect, ScienceDirect).
Indexed: A01, A03, A08, A20, A22, A26, A34, A35, A36, A37, A38, ASCA, ASFA, AgBio, B21, B25, BA, BIOSIS Prev, BP, C06, C07, C25, CA, CABA, CIN, ChemTitl, CurCont, D01, DBA, DentInd, E01, E12, EMBASE, ESPM, ExcerpMed, F08, F11, F12, FR, FS&TA, GH, H&SSA, H16, H17, I05, I11, IBR, IBZ, ISR, IndMed, IndVet, Inpharma, LT, MEDLINE, MaizeAb, MycolAb, N02, N03, N05, OR, P30, P32, P33, P34, P39, PHN&I, PN&I, PollutAb, R07, R08, R10, R11, R12, R13, RA&MP, RM&VM, RRTA, Reac, RiskAb, S13, S16, SCI, SCOPUS, SWRA, SoyAb, T02, T05, ToxAb, VS, W07, W10, W11.
—BLDSC (4542.292000), CASDDS, GNLM, IE, Infotrieve, Ingenta, INIST. **CCC.**
Published by: (Gesellschaft fuer Hygiene, Umweltmedizin und Oeffentliche Gesundheit, International Society of Environmental Medicine/Internationale Gesellschaft fuer Umweltmedizin), Urban und Fischer Verlag (Subsidiary of: Elsevier GmbH), Loebdergraben 14a, Jena, 07743, Germany. TEL 49-3641-6263, FAX 49-3641-626443, info@urbanfischer.de, http://www.urbanundfischer.de. Ed. Dr. Michael Wilhem. Circ: 750 (paid and controlled). **Non-German speaking countries subscr. to:** Nature Publishing Group, Brunel Rd, Houndmills, Basingstoke, Hamps RG21 6XS, United Kingdom. TEL 44-1256-302629, FAX 44-1256-476117.

➤ **INTERNATIONAL JOURNAL OF INFECTIOUS DISEASES.** *see* MEDICAL SCIENCES—Communicable Diseases

➤ **INTERNATIONAL JOURNAL OF INJURY CONTROL AND SAFETY PROMOTION.** *see* CONSUMER EDUCATION AND PROTECTION

➤ **INTERNATIONAL JOURNAL OF LOW RADIATION.** *see* ENVIRONMENTAL STUDIES

610 362.1 615 IND ISSN 2230-8598
▼ ➤ **INTERNATIONAL JOURNAL OF MEDICINE AND PUBLIC HEALTH.** Abbreviated title: I J M P H. Text in English. 2011. q. free (effective 2011). adv. bk.rev. abstr. back issues avail. **Document type:** *Journal, Academic/Scholarly.* **Description:** Publishes articles in all fields of medicine and infectious diseases. It contains original articles, review articles, case reports, and letters to the editor.
Media: Online - full text.
Published by: (Scibiolmed.org), EManuscript Services, 1713, 41 A Cross, 1st Fl, 18 Main, Jayanagar 4 T Blk, Bangalore, Karnataka 560 041, India. TEL 91-7204242670, journals@emanuscript.in, http://www.emanuscript.in. Ed. Dr. S M Kadri TEL 91-9419010363. Pub., R&P Dr. Mueen Ahmed KK.

➤ **INTERNATIONAL JOURNAL OF MENTAL HEALTH.** *see* PSYCHOLOGY

➤ **INTERNATIONAL JOURNAL OF OCCUPATIONAL MEDICINE AND ENVIRONMENTAL HEALTH.** *see* OCCUPATIONAL HEALTH AND SAFETY

➤ **INTERNATIONAL JOURNAL OF PEST MANAGEMENT.** *see* AGRICULTURE—Crop Production And Soil

613 IRN ISSN 2008-7802
▼ **INTERNATIONAL JOURNAL OF PREVENTIVE MEDICINE.** Text in English. 2010. q. **Document type:** *Journal, Academic/Scholarly.*
Related titles: Online - full text ed.: ISSN 2008-8213. free (effective 2011).
Indexed: A01, P30.
Published by: Isfahan University of Medical Sciences, PO Box 81745-319, Isfahan, Iran. http://www.mui.ac.ir.

P

362.1 CHE ISSN 1661-8556
CODEN: SZPMAA

➤ **INTERNATIONAL JOURNAL OF PUBLIC HEALTH.** Text and summaries in English, French, German. 1934. bi-m. EUR 633, USD 737 combined subscription to institutions (print & online eds.) (effective 2012). adv. bk.rev. abstr.; bibl.; charts; illus. index. reprint service avail. from PSC. **Document type:** *Journal, Academic/Scholarly.* **Description:** Publishes original scientific papers and review articles in the field of epidemiology, preventive medicine, health services research, environmental health, medical sociology and industrial hygiene.
Former titles (until 2007): Sozial- und Praeventivmedizin / Social and Preventive Medicine (0303-8408); (until 1974): Praeventivmedizin (0301-0988); (until 1969): Zeitschrift fuer Praeventivmedizin (0044-3379); (until 1956): Gesundheit und Wohlfahrt (0367-4274)
Related titles: Online - full text ed.: ISSN 1661-8564 (from IngentaConnect).
Indexed: A20, A22, A26, A34, A36, ASCA, B25, BIOSIS Prev, C06, C07, CA, CABA, CIN, CISA, ChemAb, ChemTitl, CurCont, D01, E01, E08, E12, EMBASE, ExcerpMed, F09, FR, GH, H05, H12, H16, IBR, IBZ, INI, IndMed, Inpharma, LT, MEDLINE, MycolAb, N02, N03, P30, P33, R08, R12, RRTA, S02, S03, S09, S13, S16, SCI, SCOPUS, SSCI, T02, T05, W07, W11.
—CASDDS, GNLM, IE, Infotrieve, Ingenta, INIST. **CCC.**
Published by: (Schweizerische Gesellschaft fuer Praevention und Gesundheitswesen), Birkhaeuser Verlag AG (Subsidiary of: Springer Science+Business Media), Viaduktstr 42, Postfach 133, Basel, 4051, Switzerland. TEL 41-61-2050707, FAX 41-61-2050799, info@birkhauser.ch, http://www.birkhauser.ch/journals. Ed. Thomas Abel. **Subscr. in the Americas to:** Springer New York LLC, Journal Fulfillment, PO Box 2485, Secaucus, NJ 07096. TEL 201-348-4033, 800-777-4643, FAX 201-348-4505, journals@birkhauser.com; **Subscr. to:** Springer Distribution Center, Kundenservice Zeitschriften, Haberstr 7, Heidelberg 69126, Germany. TEL 49-6221-3454303, FAX 49-6221-3454229, birkhauser@springer.de.

362.1 323.4 IND

➤ **INTERNATIONAL JOURNAL OF PUBLIC HEALTH AND HUMAN RIGHTS.** Text in English. s-a. USD 425 (effective 2011). **Document type:** *Journal, Academic/Scholarly.* **Description:** Publishes articles related to public health and social sciences.
Related titles: Online - full text ed.: free (effective 2011).
Published by: Bioinfo Publications, 49/F-72, Vighnahar Complex, Front of Overseas Bank, Sector 12, Kharghar, Navi Mumbai, 410 210, India. TEL 91-22-27743967, FAX 91-22-66736413, editor@bioinfo.in, subscription@bioinfo.in.

362.1 USA ISSN 1942-9665

INTERNATIONAL JOURNAL OF SOCIAL HEALTH INFORMATION MANAGEMENT. Abbreviated title: I J S H I M. Text in English. 2008 (Jul.). s-a. USD 55; USD 90 combined subscription (print & CD-ROM eds.); USD 225 domestic to libraries; USD 255 foreign to libraries (effective 2009). back issues avail. **Document type:** *Journal, Academic/Scholarly.* **Description:** Provides intellectual frameworks for comprehensive and methodical research on the application of clinical care delivery, public health systems and information management in medicine.
Related titles: CD-ROM ed.: ISSN 1942-9673. USD 45 (effective 2009); Online - full text ed.: ISSN 2150-6760.
Published by: Intellectbase International Consortium, 1615 7th Ave N, Nashville, TN 37208. TEL 615-739-5124, FAX 615-739-5124, feedback@intellectbase.org, membership@intellectbase.org.

INTERNATIONAL JOURNAL OF TOXICOLOGY. *see* ENVIRONMENTAL STUDIES—Toxicology And Environmental Safety

INTERNATIONAL JOURNAL OF TROPICAL MEDICINE. *see* MEDICAL SCIENCES—Communicable Diseases

INTERNATIONAL NARCOTICS CONTROL BOARD. REPORT FOR (YEAR). *see* PHARMACY AND PHARMACOLOGY

362.1 USA ISSN 1947-4989
RA421

▼ ➤ **INTERNATIONAL PUBLIC HEALTH JOURNAL.** Text in English. 2009. q. USD 295 to institutions; USD 442 combined subscription to institutions (print & online eds.) (effective 2012). **Document type:** *Journal, Academic/Scholarly.* **Description:** Provides an international multidisciplinary forum with a holistic approach to public health issues, health and medicine, health and social policy, and epidemiology.
Related titles: Online - full text ed.: USD 295 (effective 2012).
Indexed: C06.
Published by: Nova Science Publishers, Inc., 400 Oser Ave, Ste 1600, Hauppauge, NY 11788. TEL 631-231-7269, FAX 631-231-8175, journals@novapublishers.com.

613 USA ISSN 0272-684X
RA440.A1 CODEN: IQCHBU

➤ **INTERNATIONAL QUARTERLY OF COMMUNITY HEALTH EDUCATION.** Text in English. 1981. q. USD 109 combined subscription to individuals (print & online eds.); USD 402 combined subscription to institutions (print & online eds.) (effective 2011). bk.rev. abstr.; illus. back issues avail.; reprints avail. **Document type:** *Journal, Academic/Scholarly.* **Description:** Focuses on the systematic application of social science and health education theory and methodology to public health problems.
Related titles: Online - full text ed.: ISSN 1541-3519. USD 103 to individuals; USD 381 to institutions (effective 2011).
Indexed: A22, A34, A36, AbAn, BAS, BP, C06, C07, C08, CA, CABA, CINAHL, CLFP, CPE, D01, DIP, E-psyche, E12, EMBASE, ERA, ExcerpMed, Faml, GH, H16, H17, IBR, IBZ, IndVet, LT, M12, MEDLINE, N02, N03, N04, NRN, P03, P20, P21, P24, P25, P30, P32, P33, P39, P48, P50, P52, P54, P56, PAIS, PN&I, PQC, PsycInfo, PsycholAb, R08, R10, R12, RILM, RRTA, Reac, S02, S03, S21, SCOPUS, SOPODA, SSA, SociolAb, T02, T05, TAR, VS, W11.
—BLDSC (4545.510000), IE, Infotrieve, Ingenta. **CCC.**
Published by: Baywood Publishing Co., Inc., 26 Austin Ave, PO Box 337, Amityville, NY 11701. TEL 631-691-1270, 800-638-7819, FAX 631-691-1770, Baywood@baywood.com. Ed. Dr. George P Cernada.

614.8 USA

INTERNATIONAL SYSTEM SAFETY CONFERENCE. PROCEEDINGS. Text in English. 1971. a. USD 105 per issue to non-members; USD 90 per issue to members (effective 2010). back issues avail. **Document type:** *Proceedings, Trade.* **Description:** Features technical papers on system and product safety.
Published by: System Safety Society, Inc., PO Box 70, Unionville, VA 22567. TEL 540-854-8630, systemsafety@system-safety.org, http://www.system-safety.org.

613.68 CHE ISSN 1020-0169
RA638

INTERNATIONAL TRAVEL AND HEALTH: VACCINATION REQUIREMENTS AND HEALTH ADVICE. Text in English. 1972. a. CHF 25 domestic; CHF 22.50 foreign (effective 2007). **Document type:** *Newsletter, Trade.* **Description:** Serves to alert physicians, health authorities and airline and shipping companies to changes in required and recommended vaccinations for travellers to every country in the world.
Former titles (until 1989): Vaccination Certificate Requirements and Health Advice for International Travel (0257-912X); (until 19??): Vaccination Certificate Requirements for International Travel and Health Advice to Travellers (0254-296X); (until 1981): Vaccination Certificate Requirements for International Travel (0512-3011)
Related titles: German ed.; French ed.: Voyages Internationaux et Sante. Vaccinations Exigees et Conseils d'Hygiene.
—GNLM, IE. **CCC.**
Published by: World Health Organization/Organisation Mondiale de la Sante, Avenue Appia 20, Geneva 27, 1211, Switzerland. TEL 41-22-7912111, FAX 41-22-7913111, publications@who.int. Circ: 15,000.

614 USA ISSN 1540-2614
RA648.5

➤ **THE INTERNET JOURNAL OF EPIDEMIOLOGY.** Text in English. 2002 (Jun.). s-a. free (effective 2011). adv. **Document type:** *Journal, Academic/Scholarly.*
Media: Online - full text.
Indexed: A01, A02, A03, A08, A26, C06, C07, CA, EMBASE, G08, H05, H11, H12, I05, SCOPUS, T02.
Published by: Internet Scientific Publications, Llc., 23 Rippling Creek Dr, Sugar Land, TX 77479. TEL 832-443-1193, FAX 281-240-1533, wenker@ispub.com. Ed. Florent Richy.

362.1 USA ISSN 1528-8315

➤ **THE INTERNET JOURNAL OF HEALTH.** Text in English. 2000. s-a. free (effective 2011). adv. bk.rev. back issues avail. **Document type:** *Journal, Academic/Scholarly.* **Description:** Provides information from the field of general health, disease prevention, fitness and nutrition; contains original articles, reviews, case reports, streaming slide shows, streaming videos, letters to the editor, press releases, and meeting information.
Media: Online - full text.
Indexed: A01, A02, A03, A08, A26, A39, C06, C07, C08, C27, C29, CA, CINAHL, D03, D04, E13, G08, H05, H11, H12, I05, R14, S06, S14, S15, S18, T02.
Published by: Internet Scientific Publications, Llc., 23 Rippling Creek Dr, Sugar Land, TX 77479. TEL 832-443-1193, FAX 281-240-1533, wenker@ispub.com. Ed. Mohamad Said Maani Takrouri.

362.1 USA ISSN 2155-6733

▼ ➤ **THE INTERNET JOURNAL OF PUBLIC HEALTH.** Text in English. 2010 (Sept.). s-a. free (effective 2011). **Document type:** *Journal, Trade.*
Media: Online - full text.
Indexed: A01.
Published by: Internet Scientific Publications, Llc., 23 Rippling Creek Dr, Sugar Land, TX 77479. TEL 832-443-1193, FAX 281-240-1533, wenker@ispub.com. Ed. Herbert Jelinek.

362.1 FRA ISSN 1437-9619

➤ **INTERNET JOURNAL OF PUBLIC HEALTH EDUCATION.** Text in English. 1999. irreg. back issues avail. **Document type:** *Journal, Academic/Scholarly.* **Description:** Pursues the systematic development and evaluation of public health and health sciences education and training.
Media: Online - full content.
Published by: Association of Schools of Public Health in the European Region, 9-11 Rue Benoit Malon, Surennes, 92150, France. office@aspher.org.

➤ **THE INTERNET JOURNAL OF THIRD WORLD MEDICINE.** *see* MEDICAL SCIENCES

614.4 USA ISSN 1540-269X

➤ **THE INTERNET JOURNAL OF WORLD HEALTH AND SOCIETAL POLITICS.** Text in English. 2002 (Jun.). s-a. free (effective 2011). adv. **Document type:** *Journal, Academic/Scholarly.*
Media: Online - full text.
Indexed: A01, A02, A03, A08, A26, A39, C27, C29, CA, D03, D04, E13, G08, H05, H11, H12, I05, P42, R14, S14, S15, S18, T02.
Published by: Internet Scientific Publications, Llc., 23 Rippling Creek Dr, Sugar Land, TX 77479. TEL 832-443-1193, FAX 281-240-1533, wenker@ispub.com. Ed. Dr. Bradley J. Phillips.

362.1 AUS ISSN 1833-8941

INTOUCH; the official magazine of Multiple Sclerosis N S W / V I C. Text in English. 2006. q. **Document type:** *Magazine, Consumer.*
Media: Online - full text.
Published by: Multiple Sclerosis Ltd., PO BOX 210, Lidcombe, NSW 2141, Australia. TEL 61-2-9646-0600, 800-287-367, FAX 61-2-9643-1486, msconnect@mssociety.com.au, http://www.msaustralia.org.au/index.htm. Ed. Lynn Guilhaus.

614 360 CAN
RA410.9.C2

INVENTORY OF HEALTH WORKFORCE IN ALBERTA. Text in English. 1978. a. free. back issues avail. **Document type:** *Government.* **Description:** Contains the results of the annual survey of professional associations in Alberta concerning information and statistical data on the number of personnel registered with each association.
Former titles (until 1992): Inventory of Health & Social Service Personnel (0848-7332); Health and Social Service Manpower in Alberta (0714-1904)
Published by: Alberta Health, Practitioner Services Division, 10025 Jasper Ave, 16th Fl, Edmonton, AB T5J 2N3, Canada. TEL 403-427-3276, FAX 403-422-2880. Ed. D Chesley. Circ: 500.

362.1 COL ISSN 0124-8146

INVESTIGACIONES ANDINA. Text in Spanish. 2000. s-a. **Document type:** *Journal, Academic/Scholarly.*
Related titles: Online - full text ed.: free (effective 2011) (from SciELO).
Indexed: F04.
Published by: Fundacion Universitaria del Area Andina, Calle 24 No 8-55, Pereira, Colombia. Ed. Jose William Martinez.

362.1 IRN ISSN 1735-1979

➤ **IRANIAN JOURNAL OF ENVIRONMENTAL HEALTH SCIENCE & ENGINEERING.** Text in English. 2004. q. **Document type:** *Journal, Academic/Scholarly.* **Description:** Publishes on all aspects of environmental health science, engineering and management.
Related titles: Online - full text ed.: ISSN 1735-2746. free (effective 2011).
Indexed: A34, A35, A36, A37, A38, AgrForAb, B21, B23, B25, BA, BIOSIS Prev, BioEngAb, C25, C30, CA, CABA, D01, E04, E05, E12, ESPM, F08, F11, F12, FCA, G11, GEOBASE, GH, H&SSA, H16, H17, I10, I11, IndVet, LT, MaizeAb, MycolAb, N02, N03, O01, OR, P32, P33, P37, P39, P40, P48, P50, PHN&I, PQC, PollutAb, R07, R08, R12, R13, RM&VM, S12, S13, S16, S17, SCI, SCOPUS, SoyAb, T02, T05, TAR, ToxAb, TriticAb, VS, W07, W10, W11.
—IE.
Published by: Tehran University of Medical Sciences Publications, Central Library & Documents Center, Poursina St, Tehran, 14174, Iran. TEL 98-21-6112743, FAX 98-21-6404377, http://diglib.tums.ac.ir/pub/journals.asp. Ed. S Nasseri.

614 IRN ISSN 2251-6085
CODEN: IJPHCD

➤ **IRANIAN JOURNAL OF PUBLIC HEALTH.** Text in English. 1971. q. IRR 60,000 domestic; USD 50 foreign (effective 2012). illus. index. back issues avail. **Document type:** *Journal, Academic/Scholarly.* **Description:** Publishes original papers, short communication, case report and letters to the editor on: Epidemiology, biostatistics, human ecology, occupational health, medical parasitology and mycology, environmental health and engineering (air, water and solid wastes, radiation), virology, immunology, bacteriology, nutrition and biochemistry, entomology, (lishmaniosis, malaria), human and medical genetics (community genetics, population genetics, cytogenetics, oncogenetics, molecular genetics and ethics), public health services (health education, health service management, mother & child health).
Formerly (until 2002): Majalle-Ye Behdasht-e Iran (0304-4556)
Related titles: Online - full text ed.: ISSN 2251-6093. free (effective 2011).
Indexed: A29, A34, A35, A36, A37, A38, AgBio, B20, B21, BA, BP, C06, C07, C25, CA, CABA, ChemAb, D01, E12, ESPM, ExtraMED, F08, F12, GH, H&SSA, H05, H16, H17, I11, IndVet, LT, N02, N03, P30, P32, P33, P37, P39, P40, P48, P50, PN&I, PQC, R08, R10, R11, R12, R13, RA&MP, RM&VM, RRTA, Reac, RiskAb, S13, S16, SCI, SCOPUS, SSCI, SoyAb, T02, T05, VS, ViroIAbstr, W07, W11.
—CASDDS, GNLM.
Published by: (Iranian Public Health Association), Danishgah-i Ulum-i Pizishki-i Tihran/Tehran University of Medical Sciences, Center for the Electronic Resources Provision & Journal Improvement, #7, Poursina Ave., Qods Ave., Enghelab Ave., PO Box 14155-5983, Tehran, Iran. TEL 98-21-88958195, FAX 98-21-88958196, journals@tums.ac.ir, http://journals.tums.ac.ir. Ed. Dariush D Farhud. Circ: 500.

➤ **IRISH CERVICAL SCREENING PROGRAMME. ANNUAL REPORT.** *see* MEDICAL SCIENCES—Obstetrics And Gynecology

362.1 JPN ISSN 1349-3809

IRYOU ANZEN. Text in Japanese. 2004. q. JPY 7,980 (effective 2006). **Document type:** *Journal, Academic/Scholarly.*
Published by: Elsevier Japan KK (Subsidiary of: Elsevier Science & Technology), 1-9-15 Higashi-Azabu, Minato-ku, Tokyo, 106-0044, Japan. info@elsevier.co.jp.

ISSUES DE LA GROSSESSE. *see* STATISTICS

ISSUES IN LAW AND MEDICINE. *see* MEDICAL SCIENCES

610 636.089 ITA ISSN 0021-2571
R61 CODEN: AISSAW

➤ **ISTITUTO SUPERIORE DI SANITA. ANNALI.** Text and summaries in English, Italian. 1938. q. EUR 57 domestic; EUR 67 foreign (effective 2011). bk.rev. abstr.; bibl.; illus.; charts; maps; stat. index, cum.index. 100 p./no.; back issues avail. **Document type:** *Journal, Academic/Scholarly.* **Description:** Original articles, monographs, reviews and technical notes on health issues in many areas of public health.
Former titles (until 1964): Istituto Superiore di Sanita. Rendiconti (0370-5811); (until 1941): Istituto di Sanita Pubblica. Rendiconti (0370-5803)
Related titles: Online - full text ed.: 2001. free (effective 2011).
Indexed: A22, A34, A35, A36, A38, AgBio, BP, CABA, CEABA, CIN, ChemAb, ChemTitl, D01, E12, EMBASE, ExcerpMed, F08, F12, FR, FS&TA, GH, H16, H17, I11, IndMed, IndVet, Inspec, LT, MEDLINE, N02, N03, N04, P30, P33, P37, P39, PHN&I, PN&I, R07, R08, R10, R12, RA&MP, RRTA, Reac, RefZh, S13, S16, SCI, SCOPUS, T05, VS, W07, W10, W11, Z01.
—BLDSC (1008.045000), AskIEEE, CASDDS, GNLM, IE, Infotrieve, Ingenta, INIST.
Published by: (Istituto Superiore di Sanita), Editrice Kurtis s.r.l., Via Luigi Zoja 30, Milan, 20153, Italy. TEL 39-02-48202740, FAX 39-02-48201219, info@kurtis.it, http://www.kurtis.it. Ed. Enrico Alleva. Circ: 1,000.

610 ITA ISSN 0393-5620

ISTITUTO SUPERIORE DI SANITA. CONGRESSI. Abbreviated title: I S T I S A N. Congressi. Text in Multiple languages. 1985. 5/yr. **Document type:** *Proceedings, Trade.*
Indexed: A34, A36, A38, BP, CABA, E12, GH, H16, IndVet, N02, N03, N04, N05, P33, R13, RA&MP, RM&VM, RefZh, S13, S16, VS, W10, W11.
Published by: Istituto Superiore di Sanita, Viale Regina Elena 299, Rome, 00161, Italy. TEL 39-06-4990, FAX 39-06-49387118, pubblicazioni@iss.it, http://www.iss.it.

610 ITA ISSN 0394-9303
RC109

ISTITUTO SUPERIORE DI SANITA. NOTIZIARIO. Text in Italian; Abstracts in English. 1988. m. looseleaf. free to qualified personnel. Website rev. bibl.; charts; illus.; stat.; abstr.; maps. cum.index: 1988-1994. 24 p./no.; back issues avail. **Document type:** *Newsletter, Trade.* **Description:** Presents activities of the institute, which is the scientific and technical body of the Italian national health service.
Related titles: Online - full text ed.: ISSN 1827-6296; Supplement(s): Strumenti di Riferimento.

Indexed: A34, A35, A36, A37, AgBio, BA, CABA, D01, E12, F08, GH, H16, IndVet, LT, N02, N03, N04, P33, P37, P39, PHN&I, PN&I, R08, R12, R13, RA&MP, RM&VM, RRTA, RefZh, S12, S13, S16, T05, TAR, VS, W10, W11.
Published by: Istituto Superiore di Sanita, Viale Regina Elena 299, Rome, 00161, Italy. TEL 39-06-4990, FAX 39-06-49387118, pubblicazioni@iss.it. Circ: 5,000 (controlled).

610 ITA ISSN 1123-3117
RC607.A26
ISTITUTO SUPERIORE DI SANITA. RAPPORTI. Abbreviated title: I S T I S A N. Rapporti. Text in Italian. 1994. 40/yr. **Document type:** *Monographic series, Trade.*
Indexed: A34, A35, A36, A37, A38, AgBio, B23, BA, BP, C25, C30, CABA, D01, E12, F08, FCA, GH, H16, H17, I11, IndVet, LT, MaizeAb, N02, N03, N04, O01, OR, P32, P33, P37, P39, P40, PGegResA, PHN&I, PN&I, R07, R08, R12, R13, RA&MP, RM&VM, RRTA, RefZh, S13, S16, S17, T05, TriticAb, VS, W10, W11.
—BLDSC (7289.305000), IE, Ingenta.
Published by: Istituto Superiore di Sanita, Viale Regina Elena 299, Rome, 00161, Italy. TEL 39-06-4990, FAX 39-06-49387118, pubblicazioni@iss.it, http://www.iss.it.

362.1 ITA ISSN 1723-7807
➤ **ITALIAN JOURNAL OF PUBLIC HEALTH/GIORNALE ITALIANO DI SALUTE PUBBLICA.** Text in Multiple languages. 2003. q. **Document type:** *Journal, Academic/Scholarly.* **Description:** Publishes original research and theoretical or methodological papers in the area of public health.
Related titles: Online - full text ed.: ISSN 1723-7815. free (effective 2011).
Indexed: SCOPUS.
Published by: Prex SpA, Via A Fava 25, Milan, 20125, Italy. TEL 39-02-679721. Ed. Giuseppe La Torre.

➤ **IT:HELSE.** *see* MEDICAL SCIENCES

362.1 FRA ISSN 1254-8472
J E T - JOURNAL EPIDEMIOLOGIE TERRAIN. Text in French. 19??. q. **Document type:** *Journal, Academic/Scholarly.*
Formerly (until 1994): Cablinfo (1243-8693)
—CCC.
Published by: Association pour le Developpement de l'Epidemiologie de Terrain, Chateau de Vacassy, 12, rue du Val d'Osne, Saint Maurice Cedex, 94415, France. TEL 33-1-42833554, FAX 33-1-55125335, epiter@epiter.org, http://www.epiter.org.

614 BGD ISSN 1012-8697
J O P S O M. (Journal of Preventive and Social Medicine) Text in Bengali. 1982. s-a. BDT 150 to individuals; BDT 200 to institutions. adv. back issues avail.
Indexed: P30.
Published by: National Institute of Preventive and Social Medicine, Mohakhali, Dhaka, 1212, Bangladesh. Ed. M Mobarak Ali. Circ: 500.

614 NLD ISSN 1876-6358
JAARBERICHT BEVOLKINGSONDERZOEK. Text in Dutch. 2006. a.
Published by: Gezondheidsraad/Health Council of the Netherlands, PO Box 16052, The Hague, 2500 BB, Netherlands. TEL 31-70-3407520, FAX 31-70-3407523, info@gr.nl, http://www.gr.nl.

614 539.2 NLD ISSN 1574-4191
JAARUITGAVE STRALINGSBESCHERMING. Text in Dutch. 2004. a. EUR 77.50 (effective 2009).
Published by: Sdu Uitgevers bv, Postbus 20025, The Hague, 2500 EA, Netherlands. TEL 31-70-3789911, FAX 31-70-3854321, sdu@sdu.nl, http://www.sdu.nl/. Ed. Carel Thijssen.

JAHRBUCH KRITISCHE MEDIZIN. *see* MEDICAL SCIENCES

353.6 TZA ISSN 0856-9517
JARIDA LA AFYA MOROGORO. Text in Swahili. 2003. bi-m.
Published by: Morogoro Health Project, PO Box 1193, Morogoro, Tanzania. TEL 255-23-2614002, FAX 255-23-2614148, morogorohealthproject@yahoo.com, http://project.jica.go.jp/tanzania/5481081E0/index.htm.

362.1 CHN
JIANKANG WENZHAI BAO/DIGEST OF HEALTH NEWSPAPER. Text in Chinese. 1991. w. CNY 31.20 (effective 2004). **Document type:** *Newspaper.*
Published by: Jiankang Baoshe, Dongzhimen Wai, 6, Xiaojiejia, Beijing, 100027, China. TEL 86-10-64620055. **Dist. by:** China International Book Trading Corp, 35 Chegongzhuang Xilu, Haidian District, PO Box 399, Beijing 100044, China. TEL 86-10-68412045, FAX 86-10-68412023, cibtc@mail.cibtc.com.cn, http://www.cibtc.com.cn.

JIBING JIANCE/DISEASE SURVEILLANCE. *see* MEDICAL SCIENCES—Communicable Diseases

JIYEOG SAHOE YEONG-YANG HAG-HOEJI/KOREAN JOURNAL OF COMMUNITY NUTRITION. *see* NUTRITION AND DIETETICS

301 USA ISSN 0197-5838
RC889
JOHNS HOPKINS UNIVERSITY. POPULATION INFORMATION PROGRAM. POPULATION REPORTS. SERIES L. ISSUES IN WORLD HEALTH. Text in Arabic, English, French, Portuguese, Spanish. 1979. irreg., latest vol.15, no.3, 2007. looseleaf. USD 2 per issue for developed countries; free in developing nations to qualified personnel (effective 2010). bibl.; charts; illus.; stat. cum.index. back issues avail. **Document type:** *Report, Consumer.*
Related titles: Online - full text ed.
Indexed: EMBASE, ExcerpMed, IndMed, MEDLINE, P30, PopulInd, SCOPUS.
Published by: Johns Hopkins University, Population Information Program, Bloomberg School of Public Health, 111 Market Pl, Ste 310, Baltimore, MD 21202. TEL 410-659-6300, FAX 410-659-6266, info@jhuccp.org, http://www.infoforhealth.org/. Ed. Ward Rinehart.

614.8 USA ISSN 1044-4017
JOINT COMMISSION PERSPECTIVES. Text in English. 1952. m. USD 319 combined subscription in North America (print & online eds.); USD 410 combined subscription (print & online eds.) (effective 2009). cum.index: 1983-1986. back issues avail.; reprints avail. **Document type:** *Newsletter, Trade.* **Description:** Contains details of changes made to accreditation and certification standards, requirements and joint commission initiatives, including the new scoring and decision process.
Incorporates (in 1989): Agenda for Change Update; Former titles (until 1987): J C A H Perspectives (0277-8327); (until 1981): Perspectives on Accreditation (0099-2402); Which was superseded (in 1971): Joint Commission on Accreditation of Hospitals.Bulletin (0449-1092)
Related titles: Online - full text ed.: USD 299 Single user (effective 2009) (from IngentaConnect).
Indexed: C06, C07, EMBASE, ExcerpMed, I12, INI, MEDLINE, P30, SCOPUS.
—BLDSC (4672.252490), Ingenta. **CCC.**
Published by: Joint Commission on Accreditation of Healthcare Organizations, 1 Renaissance Blvd, Oakbrook Terrace, IL 60181. TEL 630-792-5000, FAX 630-792-5005, customerservice@jointcommission.org, http://www.jointcommission.org/. Circ: 22,718.

614 USA ISSN 0449-122X
TX537
JOINT F A O - W H O CODEX ALIMENTARIUS COMMISSION. REPORT OF THE SESSION. Text in English. 1963. irreg. **Document type:** *Government.*
Related titles: Spanish ed.; French ed.
Published by: Food and Agriculture Organization of the United Nations, c/o Bernan Associates, 4501 Forbes Blvd, Ste 200, Lanham, MD 20706. TEL 301-459-7666, 800-865-3457, FAX 301-459-0056, 800-865-3450, customercare@bernan.com, http://www.fao.org.

JOURNAAL GGZ EN RECHT. *see* LAW

JOURNAL DE LA SANTE AUTOCHTONE. *see* NATIVE AMERICAN STUDIES

362.1 664 CHE ISSN 1661-5751
TX531
➤ **JOURNAL FUER VERBRAUCHERSCHUTZ UND LEBENSMITTELSICHERHEIT/JOURNAL FOR CONSUMER PROTECTION AND FOOD SAFETY.** Text in German. 2006. q. EUR 64, USD 77 combined subscription to institutions (print & online eds.) (effective 2012). reprint service avail. from PSC. **Document type:** *Journal, Academic/Scholarly.* **Description:** Publishes research articles, concise reviews, reports about administrative surveillance as well as announcements and reports of the German Federal Office for Consumer Protection and Food Safety. Carries developments and information on all fields of food and feed, crop protection coumpounds, veterinary drugs and gene technology.
Related titles: Online - full text ed.: ISSN 1661-5867 (from IngentaConnect).
Indexed: A22, A26, A34, A35, A36, A37, A38, AgBio, B21, B23, BA, BP, C25, C30, CABA, D01, E01, E12, ESPM, F08, F11, F12, FCA, FS&TA, G11, GH, H&SSA, H16, H17, I10, I11, IndVet, LT, MaizeAb, N02, N03, N04, O01, OR, P32, P33, P37, P38, P39, P40, PGegResA, PHN&I, PN&I, R07, R08, R11, R12, R13, RA&MP, RM&VM, RRTA, S12, S13, S16, S17, SCI, SCOPUS, SoyAb, T05, TAR, TriticAb, VS, W07, W10, W11.
—BLDSC (5072.309000), IE, Ingenta. **CCC.**
Published by: (Bundesamt fuer Verbraucherschutz und Lebensmittelsicherheit/Federal Office for Consumer Protection and Food Safety DEU), Birkhaeuser Verlag AG (Subsidiary of: Springer Science+Business Media), Viaduktstr 42, Postfach 133, Basel, 4051, Switzerland. TEL 41-61-2050707, FAX 41-61-2050799, info@birkhauser.ch, http://www.birkhauser.ch. Ed. Peter Brandt.

➤ **JOURNAL: NEWS OF THE BLOOD PROGRAMME IN CANADA.** *see* MEDICAL SCIENCES—Hematology

➤ **JOURNAL OF ABORIGINAL HEALTH.** *see* NATIVE AMERICAN STUDIES

➤ **JOURNAL OF AGRICULTURAL SAFETY AND HEALTH.** *see* AGRICULTURE

614 USA ISSN 0090-7421
R690
➤ **JOURNAL OF ALLIED HEALTH.** Text in English. 1972. q. USD 107 domestic; USD 126 foreign (effective 2010). bk.rev. abstr. back issues avail.; reprints avail. **Document type:** *Journal, Academic/Scholarly.* **Description:** Brings out scholarly works related to research and development, feature articles, research abstracts and book reviews.
Related titles: Microform ed.: (from MIM, PQC); Online - full text ed.: ISSN 1945-404X (from IngentaConnect).
Indexed: A22, AMED, C06, C07, C08, CA, CINAHL, DentInd, EMBASE, ExcerpMed, INI, IndMed, MEDLINE, P03, P16, P18, P20, P22, P24, P30, P48, P50, P52, P53, P54, P56, PQC, PsycInfo, PsycholAb, R10, Reac, SCOPUS, T02.
—BLDSC (4927.150000), GNLM, IE, Infotrieve, Ingenta. **CCC.**
Published by: Association of Schools of Allied Health Professions, 4400 Jenifer St, NW Ste 333, Washington, DC 20015. TEL 202-237-6481, FAX 202-237-6485, asahp@asahp.org. Ed. Thomas W Elwood. Adv. contact Mike Bokulich TEL 610-660-8097.

613 USA ISSN 1946-7079
RA776.9
➤ **JOURNAL OF BEHAVIOR ANALYSIS IN HEALTH, SPORTS, FITNESS AND MEDICINE**; an international scientific journal. Abbreviated title: J B A H S F M. Text in English. 2008. q. free (effective 2009). adv. back issues avail. **Document type:** *Journal, Consumer.* **Description:** Aims to foster a greater understanding of the impact of behavior analysis on health, sports, fitness, and behavioral medicine.
Media: Online - full content.
Indexed: SD, T02.
Published by: Behavior Analyst Online http://baojournal.com/. Ed. James Luiselli. Adv. contact Halina Dziewolska. page USD 200.

614.8 360 USA ISSN 1094-3412
CODEN: JBHRFT
➤ **JOURNAL OF BEHAVIORAL HEALTH SERVICES AND RESEARCH.** Abbreviated title: J B H S & R. Text in English. 1972. q. EUR 337, USD 411 combined subscription to institutions (print & online eds.) (effective 2012). adv. bk.rev. charts; illus.; stat.; abstr. index. back issues avail.; reprint service avail. from PSC. **Document type:** *Journal, Academic/Scholarly.* **Description:** Publishes original research on the organization, financing, delivery and outcomes of mental health services and substance abuse treatment services.
Formerly (until 1998): Journal of Mental Health Administration (0092-8623)
Related titles: Microfilm ed.: (from PQC); Online - full text ed.: ISSN 1556-3308 (from IngentaConnect).
Indexed: A01, A02, A03, A08, A12, A13, A17, A20, A22, A26, ABIn, ASSIA, B01, B06, B07, B08, B09, Biostat, C06, C07, C11, C12, CA, CJPI, CurCont, E-psyche, E01, E08, EMBASE, ExcerpMed, FamI, G08, H01, H02, H04, H05, H11, H12, H13, HospLI, I05, IBR, IBZ, INI, IndMed, MEDLINE, P02, P03, P10, P20, P21, P22, P24, P25, P26, P30, P34, P43, P48, P50, P51, P53, P54, PAIS, PQC, PsycInfo, PsycholAb, R10, Reac, S02, S03, S09, SCOPUS, SOPODA, SSCI, SWR&A, SociolAb, T02, V02, W07.
—BLDSC (4951.261000), GNLM, IE, Infotrieve, Ingenta. **CCC.**
Published by: (National Council for Community Behavioral Healthcare, Association of Behavioral Healthcare Management), Springer New York LLC (Subsidiary of: Springer Science+Business Media), 233 Spring St, New York, NY 10013. TEL 212-460-1500, FAX 212-460-1575, service-ny@springer.com. Ed. Bruce Lubotsky Levin. Circ: 2,000 (paid).

➤ **JOURNAL OF CLINICAL EPIDEMIOLOGY.** *see* MEDICAL SCIENCES

➤ **THE JOURNAL OF CLINICAL SLEEP MEDICINE.** *see* MEDICAL SCIENCES—Psychiatry And Neurology

➤ **JOURNAL OF COMMUNITY HEALTH**; the publication for health promotion and disease prevention. *see* MEDICAL SCIENCES

➤ **JOURNAL OF COMMUNITY MEDICINE AND PRIMARY HEALTH CARE.** *see* MEDICAL SCIENCES

362.1 USA ISSN 1543-5865
HV551.2
➤ **JOURNAL OF EMERGENCY MANAGEMENT.** Abbreviated title: J E M. Text in English. 2003 (Win.). bi-m. USD 203 to individuals; USD 278 to institutions (effective 2010). adv. bk.rev. reprints avail. **Document type:** *Journal, Academic/Scholarly.* **Description:** Serves the need of every emergency management director, emergency preparedness director, fire chief, police chief, town manager, and disaster management professionals at the city, county, state, and federal levels across the country.
Indexed: C06, C07.
—BLDSC (4977.200000), IE. **CCC.**
Published by: Weston Medical Publishing, LLC, 470 Boston Post Rd, Weston, MA 02493. TEL 781-899-2702, 800-743-7206, FAX 781-899-4900, brenda_devito@pnpco.com, subscription@pnpco.com, http://www.wmpllc.org. Ed. William L Waugh. Pub. Richard A DeVito Sr. TEL 781-899-2702 ext 107.

362.1 GBR ISSN 2046-4754
▼ **JOURNAL OF EMERGENT SCIENCE.** Text in English. 2011. s-a. GBP 30 to non-members; free to members (effective 2012). **Document type:** *Journal, Trade.* **Description:** Focuses on science (including health, technology and engineering) for young children from birth to 8 years of age.
Media: Online - full text.
Published by: Association for Science Education, College Ln, Hatfield, Herts AL10 9AA, United Kingdom. TEL 44-1707-283000, FAX 44-1707-266532, info@ase.org.uk. Eds. Jane Johnston, Sue Dale Tunnicliffe.

362.1 363.7 USA ISSN 1687-9805
➤ **JOURNAL OF ENVIRONMENTAL AND PUBLIC HEALTH.** Text in English. 2008. irreg. USD 195 (effective 2011). **Document type:** *Journal, Academic/Scholarly.* **Description:** Covers all areas of environmental and public health.
Related titles: Online - full text ed.: ISSN 1687-9813. free (effective 2011).
Indexed: A01, A34, A36, B21, B23, C06, C07, CA, CABA, D01, E12, ESPM, F08, F12, GH, H05, LT, N02, N03, P30, P33, P50, P52, PollutAb, R08, R12, R13, S13, S16, SCOPUS, T02, T05, W11.
Published by: Hindawi Publishing Corporation, 410 Park Ave, 15th Fl, PMB 287, New York, NY 10022. FAX 215-893-4392, 866-446-3294, hindawi@hindawi.com.

➤ **JOURNAL OF ENVIRONMENTAL HEALTH.** *see* ENVIRONMENTAL STUDIES

➤ **JOURNAL OF ENVIRONMENTAL HEALTH RESEARCH.** *see* ENVIRONMENTAL STUDIES

➤ **JOURNAL OF ENVIRONMENTAL PATHOLOGY, TOXICOLOGY AND ONCOLOGY.** *see* ENVIRONMENTAL STUDIES—Toxicology And Environmental Safety

363.72 IND
RA565.A1 CODEN: JESEAR
➤ **JOURNAL OF ENVIRONMENTAL SCIENCE & ENGINEERING.** Abbreviated title: J E S E. Text in English. 1958 (Nov.). q. INR 150 domestic to individuals; USD 40 foreign to individuals; INR 600 domestic to institutions; USD 200 foreign to institutions (effective 2011). bk.rev. bibl.; charts; illus.; tr.lit. Index. back issues avail.; reprints avail. **Document type:** *Journal, Academic/Scholarly.* **Description:** Covers environmental science and engineering and related areas. Publishes both review and research articles in the fields of environmental science and engineering.
Former titles (until 2004): Indian Journal of Environmental Health (0367-827X); (until 1971): Environmental Health (0013-9289); (until 1962): Central Public Health Engineering Research Institute. Bulletin (0366-2519)
Related titles: Online - full text ed.: free (effective 2011).
Indexed: A22, A29, A32, A34, A37, ASFA, AgrForAb, B20, B21, B25, BA, BIOSIS Prev, C25, C30, C33, CABA, CIN, CLL, ChemAb, ChemTitl, D01, E04, E05, E11, E12, ESPM, F08, F11, F12, FCA, FR, G11, GH, H16, I10, I11, IndMed, IndVet, MaizeAb, MycolAb, N02, N03, O01, OR, P30, P33, P38, PHN&I, PollutAb, R07, R08, R11, R12, RA&MP, S13, S16, S17, SCOPUS, SoyAb, T04, T05, TAR, VS, VirolAbstr, W10, W11.
—CASDDS, GNLM, IE, Infotrieve, Ingenta, INIST, Linda Hall.
Published by: National Environmental Engineering Research Institute, Nehru Marg, Nagpur, Maharashtra 440 020, India. TEL 91-712-2249885, FAX 91-712-2249900, director@neeri.res.in. Eds. Arindam Ghosh, S R Wate. **Subscr. to:** I N S I O Scientific Books & Periodicals.

➤ **JOURNAL OF ENVIRONMENTAL SCIENCE AND HEALTH. PART A: TOXIC HAZARDOUS SUBSTANCES AND ENVIRONMENTAL ENGINEERING.** *see* ENVIRONMENTAL STUDIES—Toxicology And Environmental Safety

➤ **JOURNAL OF ENVIRONMENTAL SCIENCE AND HEALTH. PART B: PESTICIDES, FOOD CONTAMINANTS, AND AGRICULTURAL WASTES.** *see* ENVIRONMENTAL STUDIES

P

➤ **JOURNAL OF EPIDEMIOLOGY & COMMUNITY HEALTH**; an international peer-reviewed journal for health professionals and researchers in all areas of epidemiology. *see* MEDICAL SCIENCES

➤ **JOURNAL OF FOOD PROTECTION.** *see* FOOD AND FOOD INDUSTRIES

614 IND ISSN 0973-1814
RA529
JOURNAL OF HEALTH AND DEVELOPMENT. Text in English. 2005. q. **Document type:** *Journal, Trade.* **Description:** Aims to highlight and encourage socially relevant theoretical and empirical work in the fields of health and related disciplines of development.
Published by: Jawaharlal Nehru University, Centre of Social Medicine and Community Health, New Mehrauli Rd, New Delhi, 110 067, India. TEL 91-11-26742676, FAX 91-11-26742580, http://www.jnu.ac.in/. Ed. K R Nayar. **Subscr. to:** Daanish Books, A-901, Taj Apartments, Gazipur, New Delhi 110 096, India.

JOURNAL OF HEALTH AND HUMAN SERVICES ADMINISTRATION. *see* HEALTH FACILITIES AND ADMINISTRATION

362.1 AUS ISSN 1837-5030
▼➤ **JOURNAL OF HEALTH & SAFETY, RESEARCH & PRACTICE.** Text in English. 2009. s-a. free to members. **Document type:** *Journal, Academic/Scholarly.*
Related titles: Online - full text ed.: free.
Published by: Safety Institute of Australia Inc., PO Box 2078, Gladstone Park, VIC 3043, Australia. TEL 61-3-83361995, 800-808-380, FAX 61-3-83361179. Ed. Steve Cowley.

➤ **JOURNAL OF HEALTH DISPARITIES RESEARCH AND PRACTICE.** *see* MEDICAL SCIENCES

➤ **JOURNAL OF HEALTH SCIENCE/EISEI KAGAKU.** *see* ENVIRONMENTAL STUDIES—Toxicology And Environmental Safety

614 362.1 GEO ISSN 1512-0651
JOURNAL OF HEALTH SCIENCES MANAGEMENT AND PUBLIC HEALTH; international journal. Text in English. 2000. q.
—East View.
Published by: (University of Scranton USA), Ministry of Health of Georgia, National Health Management Center, 51, Iv Javakhishvili St, Tbilisi, 380002, Georgia. TEL 995-32-956680, FAX 995-32-960300, nhmc@nilc.org.ge, http://www.aiha.com/english/partners/nhmc/nhmcpage.htm, http://www.aiha.com/english/partners/tbilscra.cfm?partID=44.

JOURNAL OF HEALTH SERVICES RESEARCH & POLICY. *see* MEDICAL SCIENCES

362.1 GBR ISSN 1179-3201
▼ **JOURNAL OF HEALTHCARE LEADERSHIP.** Text in English. 2010. irreg. free (effective 2011). **Document type:** *Journal, Academic/Scholarly.*
Media: Online - full text.
—CCC.
Published by: Dove Medical Press Ltd., Beechfield House, Winterton Way, Macclesfield, SK11 0JL, United Kingdom. TEL 44-1625-509130, FAX 44-1625-617933. Ed. Russell Taichman.

JOURNAL OF HEPATOLOGY, GASTROENTEROLOGY, INFECTIOUS DISEASES. *see* MEDICAL SCIENCES—Communicable Diseases

JOURNAL OF HIV - AIDS PREVENTION IN CHILDREN & YOUTH. *see* MEDICAL SCIENCES—Communicable Diseases

▼ **JOURNAL OF INFECTION AND PUBLIC HEALTH.** *see* MEDICAL SCIENCES—Communicable Diseases

JOURNAL OF OCCUPATIONAL AND ENVIRONMENTAL HYGIENE. *see* OCCUPATIONAL HEALTH AND SAFETY

JOURNAL OF OCCUPATIONAL AND ENVIRONMENTAL HYGIENE (ONLINE). *see* OCCUPATIONAL HEALTH AND SAFETY

362.1 USA ISSN 1549-8417
R729.8
JOURNAL OF PATIENT SAFETY. Text in English. 2005. q. USD 504 domestic to institutions; USD 583 foreign to institutions (effective 2011). adv. back issues avail.; reprints avail. **Document type:** *Journal, Academic/Scholarly.* **Description:** Presents research advances and field applications in every area of patient safety. Publishes articles describing near-miss opportunities, system modifications that are barriers to error, and the impact of regulatory changes on healthcare delivery.
Related titles: Online - full text ed.: ISSN 1549-8425.
Indexed: C06, C07, EMBASE, ExcerpMed, Inpharma, MEDLINE, P30, P35, PAIS, R10, Reac, SCOPUS.
—BLDSC (5030.008000), IE. **CCC.**
Published by: (National Patient Safety Foundation), Lippincott Williams & Wilkins (Subsidiary of: Wolters Kluwer N.V.), Two Commerce Sq, 2001 Market St, Philadelphia, PA 19103. TEL 215-521-8300, FAX 215-521-8902, customerservice@lww.com, http://www.lww.com. Ed. Nancy W Dickey. Pub. Nancy Megley. Adv. contact Sherry Reed TEL 410-528-4000 ext 8553. Circ: 610.

JOURNAL OF PESTICIDE SCIENCE. *see* ENGINEERING—Chemical Engineering

362.105 GBR ISSN 1741-3842
RA241 CODEN: JPHME9
➤ **JOURNAL OF PUBLIC HEALTH.** Text in English. 1979. q. GBP 286 in United Kingdom to institutions; EUR 430 in Europe to institutions; USD 573 in US & Canada to institutions; GBP 286 elsewhere to institutions; GBP 312 combined subscription in United Kingdom to institutions (print & online eds.); EUR 469 combined subscription in Europe to institutions (print & online eds.); USD 625 combined subscription in US & Canada to institutions (print & online eds.); GBP 312 combined subscription elsewhere to institutions (print & online eds.) (effective 2012). adv. bk.rev. index. back issues avail.; reprint service avail. from PSC. **Document type:** *Journal, Academic/Scholarly.* **Description:** Focuses on current theory and practice within the whole spectrum of public health. It looks in depth at the causes of disease and, in the light of this, how to prevent ill-health and promote good health.
Former titles (until 2004): Journal of Public Health Medicine (0957-4832); (until 1990): Community Medicine (0142-2456)
Related titles: Online - full text ed.: ISSN 1741-3850. GBP 250 in United Kingdom to institutions; EUR 375 in Europe to institutions; USD 500 in US & Canada to institutions; GBP 250 elsewhere to institutions (effective 2012) (from IngentaConnect).
Indexed: A01, A03, A08, A20, A22, A34, A35, A36, A38, ASCA, ASSIA, AddicA, AgBio, B21, BDM&CN, C06, C07, C08, CA, CABA, CINAHL, CurCont, D01, E01, E12, EMBASE, ESPM, ExcerpMed, FR, FS&TA, FamI, GH, H&SSA, H05, H13, H16, HospAb, IndMed, IndVet, Inpharma, LT, MCR, MEDLINE, N02, N03, P10, P20, P21, P22, P24, P30, P32, P33, P37, P38, P39, P40, P48, P50, P53, P54, PAIS, PN&I, PQC, R08, R10, R12, RM&VM, RRTA, Reac, RiskAb, S02, S03, S12, S13, S16, SCI, SCOPUS, SSCI, T02, T05, VS, VirolAbstr, W07, W11.
—BLDSC (5043.512000), GNLM, IE, Infotrieve, Ingenta, INIST. **CCC.**
Published by: (Faculty of Public Health), Oxford University Press, Great Clarendon St, Oxford, OX2 6DP, United Kingdom. TEL 44-1865-556767, FAX 44-1865-556646, enquiry@oup.co.uk, http://www.oxfordjournals.org. Eds. Gabriel Leung, Selena Gray. Pub. Mandy Sketch.

614 NGA
➤ **JOURNAL OF PUBLIC HEALTH AND EPIDEMIOLOGY.** Text in English. m. free (effective 2010). adv. **Document type:** *Journal, Academic/Scholarly.*
Media: Online - full text.
Published by: Academic Journals, PO Box 73023, Victoria Island, Lagos, Nigeria. service@academicjournals.org. Eds. Dr. Manish K Goel, Mostafa A Abolfotouh, Dr. Simon F Thomsen.

➤ **JOURNAL OF PUBLIC HEALTH DENTISTRY.** *see* MEDICAL SCIENCES—Dentistry

362.1 ITA ISSN 2038-9922
▼ **JOURNAL OF PUBLIC HEALTH IN AFRICA**; research and practice. Text in English. 2010. irreg. **Document type:** *Journal, Academic/Scholarly.*
Related titles: Online - full text ed.: ISSN 2038-9930. free (effective 2011).
Indexed: CABA, GH, T05.
Published by: Pagepress, Via Giuseppe Belli 4, Pavia, 27100, Italy. TEL 39-0382-1751762, FAX 39-0382-1750481, http://www.pagepress.org.

362.1 USA ISSN 1941-8337
▼➤ **JOURNAL OF PUBLIC HEALTH LEADERSHIP.** Text in English. 2009. q. ((bi-m. from 2010)). USD 100 combined subscription to individuals (print & online eds.); USD 350 combined subscription to institutions (print & online eds.) (effective 2009). **Document type:** *Journal, Academic/Scholarly.* **Description:** Aims to foster breakthroughs in health through academic discourse on non-traditional research methodologies, innovative teaching strategies, and ground-breaking practice efforts.
Related titles: Online - full text ed.: ISSN 1941-8345. 2009. USD 50 to individuals; USD 200 to institutions (effective 2009).
Published by: Charrette Publishing, 344 Gleneagle Cir, Irmo, SC 29063. TEL 803-467-4401, FAX 866-330-2654, info@cpub.org. Ed. Dr. Willie H Oglesby.

368.382 USA ISSN 1078-4659
RA395.A3
➤ **JOURNAL OF PUBLIC HEALTH MANAGEMENT AND PRACTICE.** Abbreviated title: J P H M P. Text in English. 1995. bi-m. USD 315.51 domestic to institutions; USD 450 foreign to institutions (effective 2011). adv. back issues avail.; reprints avail. **Document type:** *Journal, Academic/Scholarly.* **Description:** Addresses public health administration and profiles local programs and initiatives.
Related titles: Microform ed.: (from PQC); Online - full text ed.: ISSN 1550-5022.
Indexed: A22, A26, B02, B15, B17, B18, C06, C07, C08, CA, CINAHL, CurCont, E08, EMBASE, ExcerpMed, F09, G04, G08, H11, H12, I05, MEDLINE, P20, P21, P22, P24, P26, P30, P34, P48, P50, P52, P54, P56, PQC, R10, Reac, S09, SCOPUS, SSCI, T02, W07.
—BLDSC (5043.553000), IE, Infotrieve, Ingenta. **CCC.**
Published by: Lippincott Williams & Wilkins (Subsidiary of: Wolters Kluwer N.V.), 530 Walnut St, Philadelphia, PA 19106. TEL 215-521-8300, FAX 215-521-8902, customerservice@lww.com, http://www.lww.com. Ed. Lloyd F Novick. Pub. Beth Guthy. adv.: B&W page USD 1,165, color page USD 2,540; trim 7.75 x 10.75. Circ: 738.

362.1 GBR ISSN 0197-5897
RA421 CODEN: JPPODK
➤ **JOURNAL OF PUBLIC HEALTH POLICY.** Abbreviated title: J P H P. Text in English. 1979. q. USD 383 in North America to institutions; GBP 205 elsewhere to institutions (effective 2011). adv. bk.rev. back issues avail.; reprint service avail. from PSC. **Document type:** *Journal, Academic/Scholarly.* **Description:** Publishes contributions advancing the discussion of public health policy issues in the US and on an international level.
Related titles: Online - full text ed.: ISSN 1745-655X (from IngentaConnect).
Indexed: A01, A02, A03, A08, A20, A22, A26, A36, AHCMS, ASCA, ASSIA, B21, C06, C07, CA, CABA, CurCont, D01, DokArb, E01, E04, E05, E08, E12, EMBASE, ESPM, EnvAb, EnvInd, ExcerpMed, FR, FamI, GH, H&SSA, H05, H12, H13, HPNRM, I05, IndMed, LT, MEDLINE, N02, N03, NRN, P03, P10, P20, P21, P22, P30, P32, P34, P38, P40, P42, P48, P50, P52, P53, P54, P56, PAIS, PQC, PSA, PsycInfo, R10, R12, RRTA, Reac, S02, S03, S09, S13, S16, SCI, SCOPUS, SSA, SSCI, SSciA, SociolAb, T02, T05, THA, W07, W11.
—BLDSC (5043.570000), GNLM, IE, Infotrieve, Ingenta. **CCC.**
Published by: Palgrave Macmillan Ltd. (Subsidiary of: Macmillan Publishers Ltd.), Houndmills, Basingstoke, Hants RG21 6XS, United Kingdom. TEL 44-1256-329242, FAX 44-1256-479476, orders@palgrave.com, http://www.palgrave.com. Eds. Anthony Robbins, Phyllis Freeman. Pub. Neil Henderson TEL 44-1256-302959 ext 3116. Circ: 1,000. **Subscr. to:** Subscription Department, Brunel Rd, Houndmills, Basingstoke, Hants RG21 2XS, United Kingdom. TEL 44-1256-357893, FAX 44-1256-328339, subscriptions@palgrave.com.

362.1 616.8 GBR ISSN 1746-5729
➤ **JOURNAL OF PUBLIC MENTAL HEALTH**; the art, science and politics of creating a mentally healthy society. Text in English. 1999. q. EUR 689 combined subscription in Europe (print & online eds.); USD 889 combined subscription in the Americas (print & online eds.); GBP 529 combined subscription in the UK & elsewhere (print & online eds.); AUD 999 combined subscription in Australasia (print & online eds.) (effective 2012). adv. bk.rev. back issues avail. **Document type:** *Journal, Academic/Scholarly.* **Description:** Covers the research, policy and practice that put mental well-being at the heart of the public health agenda.
Former titles (until 2005): Journal of Mental Health Promotion (1475-9535); (until 2002): International Journal of Mental Health Promotion (1462-3730)
Related titles: Online - full text ed.: ISSN 2042-8731 (from IngentaConnect).
Indexed: B28, C06, C07, C08, CA, CINAHL, E-psyche, P20, P24, P25, P30, P34, P48, P50, P54, PQC, PsycInfo, PsycholAb, S02, S03, SWR&A.
—BLDSC (5043.635000), IE, Ingenta. **CCC.**
Published by: (Mental Health Foundation), Pier Professional Ltd. (Subsidiary of: Emerald Group Publishing Ltd.), Ste N4, The Old Market, Upper Market St, Hove, BN3 1AS, United Kingdom. TEL 44-1273-783720, FAX 44-1273-783723, info@pierprofessional.com. Ed. Woody Caan. Adv. contact Paul Somerville TEL 44-1273-783724. B&W page GBP 350; 150 x 255.

362.1 IRN ISSN 1682-2765
JOURNAL OF RESEARCH IN HEALTH SCIENCES. Key Title: Pizhuhish dar 'Ulum i Bihdashti. Text in English, Persian, Modern. 2001. s-a. **Document type:** *Journal, Academic/Scholarly.*
Related titles: Online - full text ed.: free (effective 2011).
Indexed: A36, A37, C06, C07, CABA, E12, EMBASE, ExcerpMed, GH, N02, N03, OR, P33, P39, PN&I, R08, R12, RA&MP, RM&VM, S13, S16, SCOPUS, T02, T05, TAR, W11.
Published by: Hamadan University of Medical Sciences, School of Public Health, PO Box 65175, Hamedan, 4171, Iran. TEL 98-811-8221722, FAX 98-811-8255301.

JOURNAL OF RURAL AND TROPICAL PUBLIC HEALTH. *see* ENVIRONMENTAL STUDIES

THE JOURNAL OF RURAL HEALTH. *see* MEDICAL SCIENCES

613 USA ISSN 0022-4391
LB3401 CODEN: JSHEA2
➤ **JOURNAL OF SCHOOL HEALTH.** Text in English. 1930. m. GBP 272 in United Kingdom to institutions; EUR 345 in Europe to institutions; USD 426 in the Americas to institutions; USD 532 elsewhere to institutions; GBP 313 combined subscription in United Kingdom to institutions (print & online eds.); EUR 397 combined subscription in Europe to institutions (print & online eds.); USD 490 combined subscription in the Americas to institutions (print & online eds.); USD 612 combined subscription elsewhere to institutions (print & online eds.) (effective 2012). adv. bk.rev. abstr.; bibl.; charts; stat. index, cum.index every 10 yrs. back issues avail.; reprints avail. **Document type:** *Journal, Academic/Scholarly.* **Description:** Addresses practice, theory, and research related to the health and well-being of school-aged youth.
Former titles (until 1937): School Physicians Bulletin; (until 1931): American Association of School Physicians. Bulletin
Related titles: Microform ed.: (from PQC); Online - full text ed.: ISSN 1746-1561. GBP 272 in United Kingdom to institutions; EUR 345 in Europe to institutions; USD 426 in the Americas to institutions; USD 532 elsewhere to institutions (effective 2012) (from IngentaConnect).
Indexed: A01, A02, A03, A08, A20, A22, A25, A26, A36, AMHA, ASCA, ASSIA, Acal, Agr, B04, B21, BRD, C06, C07, C08, C11, C12, C25, CA, CABA, CINAHL, CLFP, CPE, Chicano, CurCont, D01, DentInd, E01, E02, E03, E06, E07, E08, E12, ECER, EMBASE, ERI, ERIC, ESPM, EdA, EdI, ExcerpMed, F09, FCA, FamI, G05, G06, G07, G08, GH, H&SSA, H04, H05, H11, H12, H13, H16, HlthInd, I05, INI, IndMed, LT, M06, MEDLINE, MRD, N02, N03, NRN, NurAb, OR, P02, P04, P07, P10, P18, P20, P21, P22, P24, P30, P33, P34, P37, P39, P43, P48, P50, P52, P53, P54, P55, P56, PEI, PQC, PsycholAb, R08, R10, R12, RM&VM, RRTA, Reac, RiskAb, S02, S03, S04, S08, S09, S13, S16, S21, S23, SCI, SCOPUS, SD, SSCI, SoyAb, SportS, T02, T05, THA, W03, W05, W07, W11, WBA, WMB.
—BLDSC (5052.650000), GNLM, IE, Infotrieve, Ingenta, INIST. **CCC.**
Published by: (American School Health Association), Wiley-Blackwell Publishing, Inc. (Subsidiary of: Wiley-Blackwell Publishing Ltd.), 111 River St, Hoboken, NJ 07030. TEL 201-748-6000, FAX 201-748-6088, info@wiley.com. Ed. Kelli McCormack Brown. Adv. contact Kristin McCarthy TEL 201-748-7683.

➤ **JOURNAL OF SPORT AND HEALTH RESEARCH.** *see* SPORTS AND GAMES

➤ **JOURNAL OF SYSTEM SAFETY.** *see* ENGINEERING

➤ **JOURNAL OF TOXICOLOGY AND ENVIRONMENTAL HEALTH. PART A: CURRENT ISSUES.** *see* ENVIRONMENTAL STUDIES—Toxicology And Environmental Safety

➤ **JOURNAL OF TOXICOLOGY AND ENVIRONMENTAL HEALTH. PART B: CRITICAL REVIEWS.** *see* ENVIRONMENTAL STUDIES—Toxicology And Environmental Safety

614 NGA ISSN 2006-9820
▼➤ **JOURNAL OF TOXICOLOGY AND ENVIRONMENTAL HEALTH SCIENCES.** Text in English. 2009. m. free (effective 2010). adv. **Document type:** *Journal, Academic/Scholarly.*
Media: Online - full text.
Published by: Academic Journals, PO Box 73023, Victoria Island, Lagos, Nigeria. service@academicjournals.org. Eds. Dr. Jianbo Xiao, Dr. Seema Akbar.

➤ **JOURNAL OF TRAFFIC SAFETY EDUCATION.** *see* TRANSPORTATION—Automobiles

➤ **JOURNAL OF WATER AND HEALTH.** *see* WATER RESOURCES

614 CAN ISSN 1910-6335
JOURNEES ANNUELLES DE SANTE PUBLIQUE. Text in French. 1997. a. **Document type:** *Journal, Trade.*
Published by: Institut National de Sante Publique du Quebec, 945 Av Wolfe, Quebec, PQ G1V 5B3, Canada. TEL 418-650-5115 ext 5336, FAX 418-646-9328.

363.3 SWE ISSN 1652-2915
K B MS TEMASERIE. Text in Swedish. 2003. irreg. back issues avail. **Document type:** *Monographic series, Academic/Scholarly.*
Related titles: Online - full text ed.: ISSN 1653-7467.
Published by: Myndigheten foer Samhaellsskydd och Beredskap/ Swedish Civil Contingencies Agency, Karlstad, 65180, Sweden. TEL 46-771-240240, FAX 46-10-2405600, registrator@msb.se, http://www.msb.se.

KAGAWAKEN KANKYOU HOKEN KENKYUU SENTA SHOHOU/ KAGAWA PREFECTURAL RESEARCH INSTITUTE FOR ENVIRONMENTAL SCIENCES AND PUBLIC HEALTH. ANNUAL REPORT. *see* ENVIRONMENTAL STUDIES

614 664 NLD ISSN 1874-012X
KERNZAKEN. Text in Dutch. 2007. q. EUR 59 (effective 2008). adv.
Published by: Uitgeverij S W P, Postbus 257, Amsterdam, 1000 AG, Netherlands. TEL 31-20-3307200, FAX 31-20-3308040, http://www.swpbook.com. Ed. Rob Kooijmans. Pub. Paul Roosenstein. Circ: 13,500.

KIBARU. *see* ETHNIC INTERESTS

613 362.7 IRL ISSN 1649-9417
KIDS HEALTH. Text in English. 2007. bi-m. adv. **Document type:** *Magazine, Consumer.*
Published by: Proactive Publications, 88 Lower Baggot St, Dublin, 2, Ireland. TEL 353-1-6110840, FAX 353-1-6110941, http://www.hlaw.ie. Ed., Adv. contact Marie Loftus.

KIDSAFE. *see* CHILDREN AND YOUTH—About

362.1 DEU ISSN 1438-5066
KINDER, KINDER; sicher - gesund. Text in German. 1999. q. EUR 7.60 (effective 2007). adv. **Document type:** *Magazine, Trade.*
Published by: Universum Verlagsanstalt GmbH KG, Taunusstr 54, Wiesbaden, 65183, Germany. TEL 49-611-90300, FAX 49-611-9030183, info@universum.de. adv.: page EUR 1,840. Circ: 54,561 (paid).

KOKORO TO SHAKAI/MIND AND SOCIETY. *see* PSYCHOLOGY

614 JPN ISSN 1343-4292
RA421 CODEN: KISHFC
KOKURITSU IYAKUHIN SHOKUHIN EISEI KENKYUJO HOKOKU/ NATIONAL INSTITUTE OF HEALTH SCIENCES. BULLETIN. Text in Japanese; Summaries in English. 1886. a., latest 2005. free. adv. **Document type:** *Academic/Scholarly.* **Description:** Disseminates research activities of NIHS.
Formerly: Eisei Shinkenjo Hokoku (0077-4715)
Related titles: Online - full text ed.
Indexed: ChemAb, EMBASE, ExcerpMed, FS&TA, IndMed, MEDLINE, P30, R10, Reac, RefZh, SCOPUS.
—BLDSC (2640.170000), CASDDS, GNLM, INIST.
Published by: Kokuritsu Iyakuhin Shokuhin Eisei Kenkyujo/National Institute of Health Sciences, 1-18-1 Kamiyoga, Setagaya-ku, Tokyo, 158-8501, Japan. http://www.nihs.go.jp/index-j.html. Circ: 1,000.

614 DEU ISSN 0948-5228
KONTENRAHMEN FUER DIE TRAEGER DER GESETZLICHEN KRANKENVERSICHERUNG, KONTENRAHMEN FUER DIE TRAEGER DER SOZIALEN PFLEGEVERSICHERUNG UND DEN AUSGLEICHSFONDS. Text in German. 1981. base vol. plus updates 3/yr. looseleaf. EUR 78 base vol(s).; EUR 49.80 updates per issue (effective 2009). **Document type:** *Monographic series, Trade.*
Formerly (until 1995): Kontenrahmen fuer die Traeger der Gesetzlichen Krankenversicherung (0943-4100)
Published by: Erich Schmidt Verlag GmbH & Co. (Berlin), Genthiner Str 30 G, Berlin, 10785, Germany. TEL 49-30-2500850, FAX 49-30-250085305, vertrieb@esvmedien.de, http://www.erich-schmidt-verlag.de.

362.1021 360 JPN ISSN 0452-6104
HV411
KOSEI NO SHIHYO/JOURNAL OF HEALTH AND WELFARE STATISTICS. Text in Japanese. 1954. m. JPY 900 per issue (effective 2010). back issues avail. **Document type:** *Journal, Academic/ Scholarly.*
—BLDSC (5113.906060).
Published by: Kosei Tokei Kyokai/Health and Welfare Statistics Association, 5-13-14 Roppongi, Minato-ku, Tokyo, 106-0032, Japan. TEL 81-3-35863361, FAX 81-3-35844710.

628 JPN ISSN 0368-5187
KOSHU EISEI/JOURNAL OF PUBLIC HEALTH PRACTICE. Text in Japanese. 1946. m. JPY 28,200; JPY 36,700 combined subscription (print & online eds.) (effective 2010). **Document type:** *Journal, Academic/Scholarly.*
Related titles: Online - full text ed.: ISSN 1882-1170.
Published by: Igaku Shoin Ltd., 1-28-36 Hongo, Bunkyo-ku, Tokyo, 113-8719, Japan. TEL 81-3-3817-5600, FAX 81-3-3815-7791, info@igaku-shoin.co.jp. Circ: 3,500.

KOTSU SHINRIGAKU KENKYU/JAPANESE JOURNAL OF TRAFFIC PSYCHOLOGY. *see* TRANSPORTATION—Roads And Traffic

614 DEU ISSN 0936-076X
KRANKENVERSICHERUNG DER RENTNER. Text in German. 1982. base vol. plus updates 2/yr. looseleaf. EUR 49.80 base vol(s).; EUR 39.80 updates per issue (effective 2009). **Document type:** *Monographic series, Trade.*
Published by: Erich Schmidt Verlag GmbH & Co. (Berlin), Genthiner Str 30 G, Berlin, 10785, Germany. TEL 49-30-2500850, FAX 49-30-250085305, vertrieb@esvmedien.de, http://www.erich-schmidt-verlag.de.

614 697 JPN ISSN 0386-4081
TH6014
KUKI CHOWA EISEI KOGAKU/SOCIETY OF HEATING, AIR-CONDITIONING AND SANITARY ENGINEERING OF JAPAN. JOURNAL. Text in Japanese; Summaries in English, Japanese. 1917. m. membership. **Document type:** *Journal, Academic/Scholarly.*
Former titles (until 1962): Eisei Kogyo Kyokaishi (0386-4308); (until 1927): Danbo Reizo Kyokaishi
Indexed: INIS AtomInd, RefZh.
—Linda Hall. **CCC.**
Published by: Kuki Chowa Eisei Kogakkai/Society of Heating, Air-Conditioning and Sanitary Engineering of Japan, 1-8-1 Kita-Shinjuku, Shinjuku-ku, Tokyo, 169-0074, Japan. TEL 81-3-33638261, FAX 81-3-33638266, jigyou03@shase.or.jp, http://www.shasej.org/.

KUUKI CHOUWA, EISEI KOGAKKAI RONBUNSHUU/SOCIETY OF HEATING, AIR-CONDITIONING AND SANITARY ENGINEERS OF JAPAN. TRANSACTIONS. *see* HEATING, PLUMBING AND REFRIGERATION

614 616.8 NLD ISSN 1878-9633
KWALITEIT EN VEILIGHEID. Key Title: Kwaliteit & Veiligheid. Text in Dutch. 2008. a. EUR 14.95 (effective 2011).
Published by: Van der Hoeven Stichting, Willem Dreeslaan 2, Utrecht, 3500 AD, Netherlands. TEL 31-30-2758275, FAX 31-20-2758200, info@hoevenstichting.nl, http://www.hoevenstichting.nl.

614 JPN ISSN 0386-412X
TA495 CODEN: KDBKAW
KYOTO DAIGAKU BOSAI KENKYUJO NENPO/DISASTER PREVENTION RESEARCH INSTITUTE ANNUALS. Text in English, Japanese. 1957. a.
Indexed: GeoRef, INIS AtomInd.
—INIST.
Published by: Kyoto University, Disaster Prevention Research Institute/ Kyoto Daigaku Bosai Kenkyujo, Gokasho, Uji-shi, Kyoto-Fu 611-0011, Japan. TEL 81-774-383348, FAX 81-774-384030, http://www.dpri.kyoto-u.ac.jp/.

362.1 USA ,ISSN 1553-0671
L D I ISSUE BRIEF. (Leonard Davis Institute of Health Economics) Text in English. 1994. m. free (effective 2011). back issues avail. **Document type:** *Monographic series, Academic/Scholarly.* **Description:** Provides health care decision makers with the results of relevant health services research.
Media: Online - full text.
Indexed: EMBASE, ExcerpMed, MEDLINE, P30, R10, Reac, SCOPUS.
Published by: University of Pennsylvania, Leonard Davis Institute of Health Economics, Colonial Penn Center, 3641 Locust Walk, Philadelphia, PA 19104. TEL 215-898-5611, FAX 215-898-0229, asch@wharton.upenn.edu.

LABORATORY SURVEILLANCE OF CHLAMYDIA AND GONORRHOEA IN NEW ZEALAND. *see* MEDICAL SCIENCES—Communicable Diseases

613 CAN ISSN 1712-574X
LE LACTAZINE. Text in French. 2004. a., latest 2006. **Document type:** *Bulletin, Trade.*
Published by: Agence de la Sante et des Services Sociaux de la Capitale-Nationale, Direction Regionale de Sante Publique, 2400, avenue D'Estimauville, Beauport, PQ G1E 7G9, Canada. TEL 418-666-7000, FAX 418-666-2776.

LAERMBEKAEMPFUNG; Zeitschrift fuer Akustik, Schallschutz und Schwingungstechnik. *see* PHYSICS—Sound

614 340 FRA ISSN 1636-9726
LAMY DROIT DE LA SANTE. Text in French. 2002. 2 base vols. plus updates 2/yr. looseleaf. EUR 909 base vol(s). print & CD-ROM eds. (effective 2010). **Document type:** *Trade.*
Related titles: CD-ROM ed.; Online - full text ed.: EUR 154 (effective 2003).
Published by: Lamy S.A. (Subsidiary of: Wolters Kluwer France), 1 Rue Eugene et Armand Peugeot, Rueil-Malmaison, 92856 Cedex, France. TEL 33-1-76733000, FAX 33-1-76734809, lamy@lamy.fr.

LAMY HYGIENE ET SECURITE. *see* LAW

614 616 NLD ISSN 1874-8619
LANDELIJKE PREVALENTIEMETING ZORGPROBLEMEN. Text in Dutch. 1998. a.
Formerly (until 2005): Landelijke Prevalentie Onderzoek Decubitus (1571-8751)
Published by: Universiteit Maastricht, Sectie Verplegingswetenschap, Department of Health Care and Nursing Sciences, Postbus 616, Maastricht, 6200 MD, Netherlands. TEL 31-43-3881559.

614.83 USA ISSN 0277-9196
LAURISTON S. TAYLOR LECTURE SERIES. Variant title: Lauriston S. Taylor Lectures in Radiation Protection and Measurements. Text in English. 1977. a., latest vol.31. back issues avail. **Document type:** *Monographic series, Academic/Scholarly.*
Published by: National Council on Radiation Protection and Measurements, 7910 Woodmont Ave, Ste 400, Bethesda, MD 20814. TEL 301-657-2652, FAX 301-907-8768, NCRPpubs@NCRPonline.org.

363.7384 AUS ISSN 1324-6011
LEAD ACTION NEWS. Abbreviated title: L A N(LEAD Action News). Text in English. 1993. q. AUD 132 to institutions; free (effective 2009). bk.rev. bibl.; charts; illus.; maps; stat. back issues avail. **Document type:** *Newsletter, Trade.* **Description:** Contains latest information on the lead issues affecting the people.
Incorporates (in 1998): Lead Aware Times (1440-4966); Which was formerly (until 1997): Lead Advisory Service News (1440-0561)
Related titles: Online - full text ed.: free (effective 2009).
Published by: The LEAD Group Inc., PO Box 161, Summer Hill, NSW 2130, Australia. TEL 61-2-97160014, FAX 61-2-97169005. Eds. Elizabeth O'Brien, Tony Lennon.

362.11068 USA ISSN 1948-089X
RA971
LEADERSHIP (WESTCHESTER); breakthrough business management in health care. Text in English. 2008. s-a. free to members (effective 2009). adv. back issues avail. **Document type:** *Magazine, Trade.* **Description:** Provides analysis, case studies and practical strategies to help healthcare leaders stay ahead of the macro-trends and business challenges facing the entire healthcare community.
Published by: Healthcare Financial Management Association Learning Solutions, Inc. (Subsidiary of: Healthcare Financial Management Association), 2 Westbrook Corporate Ctr, Ste 700, Westchester, IL 60154. TEL 708-531-9600, 800-252-4362, FAX 708-531-0032. Adv. contact Dick Dudley TEL 847-615-2402. color page USD 13,125; trim 8.875 x 10.875. Circ: 75,000.

LEARNING IN HEALTH AND SOCIAL CARE. *see* MEDICAL SCIENCES

614 CHE
LEBEN UND GESUNDHEIT; monatlicher Ratgeber zur Foerderung einer naturgemaessen Lebensweise. Text in German. 1929. m. CHF 59 (effective 2000). adv. bk.rev. index. back issues avail. **Document type:** *Magazine, Consumer.*
Published by: Advent Verlag, Wylerhalde, Krattigen, 3704, Switzerland. TEL 41-33-6541065, FAX 41-33-6544431. Ed., Adv. contact Gunther Klenk. B&W page CHF 1,623, color page CHF 2,751. Circ: 15,000.

362.1 FRA ISSN 2108-6923
▼ **LA LETTRE DE L'I R T S.** (Institut Regional du Travail Social Nord - Pas de Calais) Text in French. 2010. q. **Document type:** *Newsletter, Trade.*
Media: Online - full text.
Published by: Institut Regional du Travail Social Nord - Pas de Calais, Rue Ambroise Pare, BP 71, Loos Cedex, 59373, France. TEL 33-3-20625370, FAX 33-3-20625377, http://www.irtsnpdc.fr.

614.8 GBR ISSN 1474-9211
LIFESAVERS MAGAZINE. Text in English. 1965. q. free to members (effective 2009). bk.rev. **Document type:** *Magazine, Trade.* **Description:** Provides up-to-date news, information and advise to those interested in life saving, lifeguarding and life support.
Former titles (until 2000): The Royal Life Saving Society U.K. Lifeguard (0968-7726); Royal Life Saving Society U.K. Lifesaver U.K.; Royal Life Saving Society - U.K. Quarterly Journal (0048-8704)
Indexed: SportS.
—**CCC.**
Published by: Royal Life Saving Society UK, River House, High St, Broom, Alcester, Warks B50 4HN, United Kingdom. TEL 44-1789-773994, FAX 44-1789-773995, http://www.lifesavers.org.uk/.

614 FIN ISSN 0355-6654
LIIKENNETURVA. REPORTS. Text in English. 1965. irreg., latest vol.19, 1977. back issues avail. **Document type:** *Monographic series, Academic/Scholarly.*
Formerly (until 1973): Reports from Talja
Related titles: Online - full text ed.; ◆ Finnish ed.: Liikenneturva. Tutkimuksia. ISSN 0782-2421.
—BLDSC (7534.980000).
Published by: Liikenneturva/Central Organization for Traffic Safety in Finland, Sitratie 7, PO Box 29, Helsinki, 00420, Finland. TEL 358-9-4174700. Circ: 200.

614 FIN ISSN 0782-2421
LIIKENNETURVA. TUTKIMUKSIA. Text in Finnish. 1965. irreg., latest vol.119, 2002. back issues avail. **Document type:** *Monographic series.*
Former titles (until 1986): Liikenneturva. Tutkimusosaston Julkaisuja (0357-9751); (until 1980): Liikenneturva. Tutkimuksia (0355-6646); (until 1973): Taljan Tutkimuksia
Related titles: Online - full text ed.; ◆ English ed.: Liikenneturva. Reports. ISSN 0355-6654.
Published by: Liikenneturva/Central Organization for Traffic Safety in Finland, Sitratie 7, PO Box 29, Helsinki, 00420, Finland. TEL 358-9-4174700.

▼ **LINK+.** *see* SOCIAL SERVICES AND WELFARE

614.8 CAN ISSN 0714-5896
LIVING SAFETY. Text in English. 1983. q. CAD 9.95 (effective 2000). **Document type:** *Journal, Consumer.*
Published by: Canada Safety Council, 1020 Thomas Spratt Pl, Ottawa, ON K1G 5L5, Canada. TEL 613-739-1535, FAX 613-739-1566. Ed. Jack A Smith. R&P Carole Deavey. Circ: 25,000.

362.1 CAN ISSN 1910-3514
LOI SUR L'ACCES A L'INFORMATION ET LA LOI SUR LA PROTECTION DES RENSEIGNEMENTS PERSONNELS (ANNEE). RAPPORT ANNUEL. Text in French. 1992. a., latest 2006. **Document type:** *Government.*
Former titles (until 2003): On the Administration of the Access to Information Act and the Privacy Act. Annual Reports (1207-0513); (until 1994): On the Administration of the Access to Information Act and the Privacy Act - Canada. Health and Welfare Canada. Annual Reports (1207-0505); Which was formed by the 1992 merger of: On the Administration of the Access to Information Act. Annual Report (1483-152X); On the Administration of the Privacy Act. Annual Report (1483-1538)
Media: Online - full text.
Published by: (Canada Public Service Agency/Agence de la Fonction Publique du Canada), Health Canada/Sante Canada, Address Locator 0900C2, Ottawa, ON K1A OK9, Canada. TEL 613-957-2991, 866-225-0709, FAX 613-941-5366, info@www.hc-sc.gc.ca.

362.1 GBR ISSN 1755-9146
LONDON JOURNAL OF PRIMARY CARE. Abbreviated title: L J P C. Text in English. 2008. s-a. GBP 150 per issue (effective 2011). back issues avail. **Document type:** *Journal, Trade.* **Description:** Covers the practice of primary care in London which continue to represent a beacon of modern service delivery.
Related titles: Online - full text ed.: ISSN 1755-9154. free (effective 2010).
Published by: International Medical Publishing Group, Frazer House, 32-38 Leman St, London, E1 8EW, United Kingdom. info@intmedpubgroup.com, http://www.intmedpubgroup.org. Ed. Paul Thomas.

614 USA ISSN 1535-363X
LONG-TERM CARE SURVEY ALERT. Text in English. 199?. m. USD 197 (effective 2009). back issues avail. **Document type:** *Newsletter, Trade.*
Related titles: Online - full text ed.: ISSN 1948-1055.
Indexed: H01, H05.
Published by: Eli Research, Inc., PO Box 90324, Washington, DC 20090. TEL 800-874-9180, FAX 800-789-3560, help@eliresearch.com, http://www.eliresearch.com. Eds. Karen Frazier Lusky TEL 615-708-8568, Mary Compton TEL 919-647-9569. **Subscr. to:** National Subscription Bureau, Inc., Dept 1380, Denver, CO 80291. TEL 800-472-0148, FAX 800-508-2592, subscribe@eliresearch.com.

362.1 USA ISSN 1531-5649
M E P S CHARTBOOK. (Medical Expenditure Panel Survey) Text in English. 1998. irreg., latest 2007. free (effective 2011). **Document type:** *Government.*
Related titles: Online - full text ed.: ISSN 1931-2946.
Published by: U.S. Department of Health and Human Services, Agency for Healthcare Research and Quality (A H R Q), 540 Gaither Rd, Ste 2000, Rockville, MD 20850. TEL 301-427-1104, 800-358-9295, info@ahrq.gov, http://www.ahrq.gov.

362.1 CAN ISSN 1718-3103
M E T I S S. CAHIERS. (Migrations et Ethnicite dans les Interventions de Sante et de Service Social) Text in French. 2006. 3/yr. **Document type:** *Journal, Trade.*
Published by: Centre de Sante et de Services Sociaux de la Montagne, 5700, chemin de la Cote-des-Neiges, Montreal, PQ H3T 2A8, Canada. TEL 514-731-8531, FAX 514-731-9600, http://www.santemontreal.qc.ca/CSSS/delamontagne/fr/default.aspx.

M I O S H A NEWS. (Michigan Occupational Safety and Health Act) *see* OCCUPATIONAL HEALTH AND SAFETY

614.4273 USA ISSN 0149-2195
RA407.3
M M W R. (Morbidity and Mortality Weekly Report) Variant title: Morbidity and Mortality Weekly Report. Text in English. 1951. w. USD 373 domestic; USD 522.20 foreign (effective 2010). stat.; illus. Index. back issues avail.; reprints avail. **Document type:** *Bulletin, Government.* **Description:** Provides information on communicable diseases, ranging from AIDS to malaria, on a state, regional, and national basis.
Formerly (until 1976): U.S. National Communicable Disease Center. Morbidity and Mortality (0091-0031)
Related titles: Microfiche ed.: (from CIS); Microform ed.: (from PQC); Online - full text ed.: ISSN 1545-861X. free (effective 2011); ◆ Supplement(s): Chronic Diseases Notes & Reports. ISSN 1041-5513; ◆ Health Information for International Travel. ISSN 0095-3539.
Indexed: A01, A02, A03, A08, A22, A26, A34, A35, A36, AIDS Ab, AgBio, AgrForAb, AmStI, B21, B25, BA, BIOSIS Prev, BP, BiolDig, C06, C07, C08, C11, CA, CABA, CINAHL, CJA, CLFP, CTD, CWI, ChPerI, D01, E08, E12, EMBASE, ESPM, EnvAb, ExcerpMed, F05, F06, F07, F08, F11, F12, FS&TA, G08, G11, GH, H&SSA, H01, H02, H04, H05, H11, H12, H13, H16, H17, HPNRM, HlthInd, I05, I12, IDIS, INI, IndMed, IndVet, Inpharma, JW, JW-EM, JW-ID, JW-WH, LT, M06, MEDLINE, MEDOC, MS&D, MycolAb, N02, N03, N04, NRN, OR, P02, P06, P10, P19, P20, P21, P22, P24, P27, P30, P32, P33, P34, P35, P37, P39, P40, P47, P48, P50, P52, P53, P54, P56, PEI, PHN&I, PN&I, PQC, R08, R10, R11, R12, R13, RA&MP, RM&VM, RRTA, Reac, RiskAb, S02, S03, S09, S13, S16, SCOPUS, SSciA, T02, T05, THA, TriticAb, VS, W10, W11.
—BLDSC (5966.650500), GNLM, IE, Infotrieve, Ingenta, INIST.
Published by: U.S. Department of Health and Human Services, Centers for Disease Control and Prevention, 1600 Clifton Rd, Atlanta, GA 30333. TEL 404-498-1150, 800-232-4636, FAX 404-498-2389. Ed. Frederic E Shaw TEL 404-498-6364. **Subscr. to:** U.S. Government Printing Office, Superintendent of Documents, U.S. Government Printing Office, Washington, DC 20401. TEL 202-512-1800.

MAINTAINING SAFE SCHOOLS. *see* EDUCATION—School Organization And Administration

614 610 IRN ISSN 1735-7586
➤ **MAJALLAH-I DANISHKADAH-I BIHDASHT VA ANSTITU TAHQIQAT-I BIHDASHTI/JOURNAL OF SCHOOL OF PUBLIC HEALTH AND INSTITUTE OF PUBLIC HEALTH RESEARCH.** Text in Persian, Modern; Abstracts in English. 2002. q. **Document type:** *Journal, Academic/Scholarly.* **Description:** Provides a forum for exchange of ideas and delates related to public health issues at the national and regional levels with a view to reaching appropriate solutions.
Related titles: Online - full text ed.: ISSN 1735-7543.
Indexed: A01, CA, H05, T02, VirolAbstr.
Published by: Danishgah-i Ulum-i Pizishki-i Tihran/Tehran University of Medical Sciences, PO Box 14155-6446, Tehran, Iran. TEL 98-21-88951402, FAX 98-21-88951397. Ed. Kourosh Holakouie Naieni.

➤ **MAJALLAH-I IPIDIMIYULUZHI-I IRAN/IRANIAN JOURNAL OF EPIDEMIOLOGY.** *see* MEDICAL SCIENCES—Communicable Diseases

362.1 IDN ISSN 1693-6728
MAKARA SERI KESEHATAN. Text in English, Indonesian. 1997. s-a. **Document type:** *Journal, Academic/Scholarly.*
Related titles: Online - full text ed.: free (effective 2011).
Published by: Universitas Indonesia, Kamous Universitas Indonesia, Depok, 16424, Indonesia. http://www.ui.ac.id. Ed. Dewi Susanna.

362.1 616.9 CAN ISSN 1912-6719
LES MALADIES INFECTIEUSES EN MONTEREGIE, INCLUANT LES MALADIES A DECLARATION OBLIGATOIRE (M A D O). RAPPORT ANNUEL. Text in French. 1998. a., latest 2004. **Document type:** *Government.*
Former titles (until 2005): Maladies a Declaration Obligatoire d'Origine Infectieuse. Rapport Annuel (1719-3885); (until 2004): Maladies a Declaration Obligatoire. Rapport Annuel (1491-6223)
Published by: Quebec, Agence de Sante et de Services Sociaux de la Monteregie, 1255, rue Beauregard, Longueuil, PQ J4K 2M3, Canada. TEL 450-928-6777 ext 4213, http://www.msss.gouv.qc.ca.

362.1 MYS ISSN 1675-1663
RA421
MALAYSIAN JOURNAL OF COMMUNITY HEALTH/JURNAL KESIHATAN MASYARAKAT MALAYSIA. Text in English, Malay. 2006. irreg. free (effective 2011). **Document type:** *Journal, Academic/Scholarly.*
Media: Online - full text.
Published by: Perbit Universiti Kebangsaan Malaysia/National University of Malaysia Press, Bangi, Selangor 43600, Malaysia. TEL 60-3-89215180, FAX 60-3-89254575, penerbit@ukm.my, http://pkukmweb.ukm.my/~penerbit/.

362.1 ROM ISSN 2068-7206
▼ ➤ **MANAGEMENT IN HEALTH.** Text in English. 2010. q. **Document type:** *Journal, Academic/Scholarly.*
Related titles: Online - full text ed.: ISSN 2067-7561. free (effective 2011); ◆ Romanian ed.: Management in Sanatate. ISSN 1453-4541.
Published by: Scoala Nationala de Sanatate Publica, Str Vaselor 31, Bucharest, 021253, Romania. TEL 40-21-2520425, FAX 40-21-2523014. Eds. Cristian Vladescu, Marius Ciutan.

362.1 ROM ISSN 1453-4541
➤ **MANAGEMENT IN SANATATE.** Text in Romanian. 1997. q. **Document type:** *Journal, Academic/Scholarly.*
Related titles: Online - full text ed.: ISSN 2067-757X; ◆ English ed.: Management in Health. ISSN 2068-7206.
Published by: Scoala Nationala de Sanatate Publica, Str Vaselor 31, Bucharest, 021253, Romania. TEL 40-21-2520425, FAX 40-21-2523014. Eds. Cristian Vladescu, Marius Ciutan.

361.3068 360 GBR ISSN 1360-936X
MANAGEMENT ISSUES IN SOCIAL CARE. Text in English. 1994. q. free. bk.rev. **Document type:** *Bulletin.* **Description:** Discusses management theory, good practice, welfare issues, and examples of innovation.
—BLDSC (5359.041800).
Published by: O L M Consulting, Howard House Commercial Centre, Howard St., North Shields, NE3 1AR, United Kingdom. TEL 44-191-296-5333, FAX 1344-884495. Ed. Gill Smith TEL 01344-882806. Circ: 750.

362.1 USA ISSN 1930-0298
RA394.9
MANAGEMENT SCIENCES FOR HEALTH. OCCASIONAL PAPERS. Text in English. 2005. irreg. **Document type:** *Monographic series, Trade.* **Description:** Publishes explorations of timely topics in the management of health programs.
Media: Online - full text.
Published by: Management Sciences for Health, Inc., 748 Memorial Dr, Cambridge, MA 02139. TEL 617-250-9500, FAX 617-250-9090, communications@msh.org.

362.1 NZL ISSN 1178-6191
MAORI HEALTH REVIEW. Text in English. 2007. m. free to qualified personnel (effective 2009). back issues avail. **Document type:** *Journal, Academic/Scholarly.*
Media: Online - full text.
Published by: Research Review Ltd., N Shore Mail Centre, PO Box 100116, Auckland, New Zealand. TEL 64-9-4102277, info@researchreview.co.nz.

362.1 ESP ISSN 1131-9240
MAR (MADRID, 1965). Text in Spanish. 1965. m. free. adv.
Formerly (until 1987): Hoja del Mar
Indexed: GeoRef, SpeleolAb.
Published by: Ministerio de Trabajo y Asuntos Sociales, Instituto Social de la Marina, Agustin de Bethencourt 4, Madrid, 28071, Spain. TEL 34-91-7006658, FAX 34-91-3199134, http://www.mtas.es.

363.12 797.1 USA ISSN 1542-5320
MARINE SAFETY UPDATE. Text in English. 1988 (Nov.). q. free to members (effective 2005). **Document type:** *Newsletter, Consumer.*
Related titles: Online - full text ed.: ISSN 1542-5444.
Published by: Alaska Marine Safety Education Association, 2924 Halibut Point Rd., Sitka, AK 99835-9668. amsea@alaska.com. Ed. Kristie Sherrodd.

MASS CYCLIST. *see* SPORTS AND GAMES—Bicycles And Motorcycles

614 NZL ISSN 1173-6437
MASSEY UNIVERSITY. CENTRE FOR PUBLIC HEALTH RESEARCH. MONITORING REPORT. Key Title: Quarterly Monitoring Report. Text in English. 2000. q. **Document type:** *Report, Academic/Scholarly.*
Former titles (until 2008): Massey University. Centre for Public Health Research. Quarterly Monitoring Report (1177-8822); (until 2004): New Zealand. National Cervical Screening Programme. Quarterly Report (1175-7094)
Related titles: Online - full text ed.: ISSN 1177-8830.
Published by: (New Zealand. National Cervical Screening Programme), Massey University, Centre for Public Health Research, Private Box 756, Wellington, New Zealand. TEL 64-4-3800602, FAX 64-4-3800600, cphr@massey.ac.nz, http://publichealth.massey.ac.nz.

362.1 614 SWE ISSN 1104-5701
MASTER OF PUBLIC HEALTH - THESIS. Text in Multiple languages. 1992. irreg., latest vol.7, 2011. SEK 150 per issue (effective 2011). back issues avail. **Document type:** *Monographic series, Academic/Scholarly.*
Related titles: Online - full text ed.
Published by: Nordiska Hoegskolan foer Folkhaelsovetenskap/The Nordic School of Public Health, Nya Varvat Byggnad 25, PO Box 12133, Goeteborg, 40242, Sweden. TEL 46-31-693900, FAX 46-31-691777, administration@nhv.se.

MATERIA SOCIO MEDICA. *see* MEDICAL SCIENCES

MATERNAL AND CHILD HEALTH JOURNAL. *see* MEDICAL SCIENCES—Obstetrics And Gynecology

MCMASTER UNIVERSITY. CENTRE FOR HEALTH ECONOMICS AND POLICY ANALYSIS. ANNUAL REPORT. *see* BUSINESS AND ECONOMICS

MEALEY'S LITIGATION REPORT: ANTIDEPRESSANT DRUGS. *see* LAW

MEALEY'S LITIGATION REPORT: ARTHRITIS DRUGS. *see* LAW—Civil Law

MEALEY'S LITIGATION REPORT: HORMONE REPLACEMENT THERAPY. *see* LAW

MEAT, POULTRY AND EGG PRODUCT INSPECTION DIRECTORY. *see* FOOD AND FOOD INDUSTRIES

MEDICAL CARE. *see* MEDICAL SCIENCES

MEDICAL ENVIRONMENT UPDATE. *see* HEALTH FACILITIES AND ADMINISTRATION

▼ **MEDICARE AND MEDICAID REIMBURSEMENT UPDATE.** *see* LAW

362.1 368.32 AUS ISSN 1838-2479
MEDICARE AUSTRALIA. ANNUAL REPORT. Text in English. 1975. a. back issues avail. **Document type:** *Report, Government.* **Description:** Provides members of parliament and senators with an accurate description of the activities of Medicare Australia.
Formerly (until 2006): Australia. Health Insurance Commission. Annual Report (0313-1041)
Related titles: Online - full text ed.: ISSN 1838-2460. free (effective 2011).
Published by: Medicare Australia, PO Box 1001, Tuggeranong, ACT 2901, Australia. TEL 61-2-61246333, FAX 61-2-61246222, info@medicareaustralia.gov.au.

MEDICARE COVERAGE ISSUES MANUAL. *see* INSURANCE

MEDICARE HOME HEALTH AGENCY MANUAL. *see* INSURANCE

MEDICARE. PART A. INTERMEDIARY MANUAL. PART 3. CLAIMS PROCESS. *see* INSURANCE

MEDICARE. PART B. CARRIER MANUAL. PART 3. CLAIMS PROCESS. *see* INSURANCE

MEDICARE PROVIDER REIMBURSEMENT MANUAL. *see* INSURANCE

MEDICARE SKILLED NURSING FACILITY MANUAL. *see* INSURANCE

614 ARG ISSN 0325-9552
MEDICINA Y SOCIEDAD. Text in Spanish. 1978. bi-m. back issues avail. **Document type:** *Journal, Academic/Scholarly.*
Related titles: Online - full text ed.
Indexed: C01.
Published by: Asociacion Civil Medicina y Sociedad, Sarmiento 1889 1o B, Buenos Aires, Argentina. TEL 54-11-43724019, FAX 54-11-43724042, info@medyscoc.org.ar. Ed. Alberto Cesar Manterola. Circ: 500.

614 ESP ISSN 1696-6007
EL MEDICO. ANUARIO DE LA SANIDAD Y DEL MEDICAMENTO EN ESPANA. Text in Spanish. 1994. a. **Document type:** *Yearbook, Consumer.*
Related titles: ◆ Supplement to: El Medico, Profesion y Humanidades. ISSN 0214-6363.
Published by: Grupo Saned, Capitan Haya 60, 1o, Madrid, 28028, Spain. TEL 34-91-7499500, FAX 34-91-7499501, saned@medynet.com, http://www.gruposaned.com.

362.1 KAZ
MEDITSINA. Text in Russian. 1923. m. USD 256 foreign (effective 2007). **Document type:** *Journal, Government.*
Formerly (until 2000): Zdravookhranenie Kazakhstana (0372-8277)
Indexed: P30, RASB.
—INIST.
Published by: Kazakhstan Respublinasynyn Densaulyk Ministrligi/ Ministry of Health of the Republic of Kazakhstan, Moskovskaya ul, 66, Astana, 010000, Kazakstan. TEL 317-2-317327, FAX 317-2-317327, zdrav@mz.gov.kz, http://www.mz.gov.kz. **Dist. by:** East View Information Services, 10601 Wayzata Blvd, Minneapolis, MN 55305. TEL 952-252-1201, 800-477-1005, FAX 952-252-1202, info@eastview.com, http://www.eastview.com.

614 658 BGR ISSN 1311-6770
➤ **MEDITSINSKI PREGLED. PRAKTICHESKA MEDITSINA.** Text in Bulgarian; Summaries in Bulgarian, English. 1970. q. BGL 14 domestic; USD 40 foreign (effective 2005). bk.rev. abstr.; bibl. index. 48 p./no.; back issues avail.; reprints avail. **Document type:** *Journal, Academic/Scholarly.* **Description:** Provides information about advances in Bulgarian medical science and practice, and methods adopted in management and administration of health care services.
Formerly: Iz Opita na Zdravnite Zavedeniia (0323-9233)
Indexed: ABSML.
Published by: Meditsinski Universitet - Sofia, Tsentralna Meditsinska Biblioteka, Tsentur za Informatsiia po Meditsina/Medical University - Sofia, Central Medical Library, Medical Information Center, 1 Sv Georgi Sofiiski ul, Sofia, 1431, Bulgaria. TEL 359-2-9522342, FAX 359-2-9522393, lydia@medun.acad.bg, http://www.medun.acad.bg/cmb_htm/cmb1_home_bg.htm. Ed. S Stoinov. R&P, Adv. contact Lydia Tacheva. Circ: 200.

613 DEU
MEDIZINSOZIOLOGIE UND GESUNDHEITSWISSENSCHAFTEN. Text in German. 2008. irreg., latest vol.2, 2010. price varies. **Document type:** *Monographic series, Academic/Scholarly.*
Published by: Lit Verlag, Grevener Str/Fresnostr 2, Muenster, 48159, Germany. TEL 49-251-6203222, FAX 49-251-231972, lit@lit-verlag.de.

MENTAL HEALTH IN FAMILY MEDICINE. *see* MEDICAL SCIENCES—Psychiatry And Neurology

614 150 GBR
MENTAL HEALTH REVIEW TRIBUNALS FOR ENGLAND AND WALES. ANNUAL REPORT. Text in English. a., latest 2002. **Document type:** *Government.*
Formed by the 1994 merger of: Mental Health Review Tribunal for England. Annual Report (Year); Mental Health Review Tribunal for Wales. Annual Report for (Year)
Indexed: E-psyche.
Published by: Great Britain. Department of Health, PO Box 777, London, SE1 6XH, United Kingdom. TEL 44-870-1555455, FAX 44-162-3724524, dh@prolog.uk.com, http://www.dh.gov.uk/.

MERGENT PUBLIC UTILITY & TRANSPORTATION MANUAL. *see* PUBLIC ADMINISTRATION

362.1 USA ISSN 1531-5673
RA410.53
METHODOLOGY REPORTS. Text in English. 19??. irreg., latest 2010. free (effective 2011). back issues avail. **Document type:** *Government.*
Formerly (until 2000): United States. Agency for Health Care Policy and Research. Methodology Report
Related titles: Online - full text ed.: ISSN 1931-2954.
Published by: U.S. Department of Health and Human Services, Agency for Healthcare Research and Quality (A H R Q), 540 Gaither Rd, Ste 2000, Rockville, MD 20850. TEL 301-427-1104, info@ahrq.gov, http://www.ahrq.gov.

362.1 USA ISSN 1937-2515
MICHIGAN JOURNAL OF PUBLIC HEALTH. Text in English. 2006. s-a. free (effective 2011). **Document type:** *Journal, Academic/Scholarly.* **Description:** Discusses issues relating to public health and welfare with particular emphasis on Michigan.
Media: Online - full text.
Published by: Michigan Public Health Association, PO Box 15306, Lansing, MI 48901. TEL 888-444-9295, koberst@mipha.org. Ed. Greg Cline.

614.8 537.534 USA ISSN 0275-6595
CODEN: MIWNE3
MICROWAVE NEWS; a report on non-ionizing radiation. Text in English. 1981. bi-m. USD 350 domestic; USD 375 foreign (effective 2005). adv. bk.rev. back issues avail.; reprints avail. **Document type:** *Newsletter, Trade.* **Description:** Health and safety issues related to electromagnetic fields and radiation with emphasis on power lines, cell phones, radar, radio and TV transmitters, appliances, etc.
—CASDDS. **CCC.**
Address: 155 East 77th St., Ste 3D, New York, NY 10021. TEL 212-517-2800, FAX 212-734-0316, mwn@pobox.com. Ed., Pub., R&P Louis Slesin.

614 UAE ISSN 1475-0805
MIDDLE EAST HEALTH. Text in English. 1977. bi-m. AED 200, USD 55 domestic; AED 250, USD 70 in GCC countries; AED 300, USD 85 elsewhere (effective 2007). adv. illus. back issues avail. **Document type:** *Magazine, Consumer.* **Description:** Publishes clinical and experimental articles on health issues worldwide.
Former titles (until 2001): Global Health (Middle East Edition) (1367-353X); (until 1996): Middle East Health (0263-1016); Which incorporated (in 1986): Middle East Dentistry; (until 1981): Middle East Health Supply and Services (0309-2003)

Indexed: P30.
Published by: Middle East Health Magazine, Ste 303, Office Land Building, Sheikh Rashid Rd, PO Box 825, Dubai, United Arab Emirates. TEL 971-4-3377274, FAX 971-4-3377297, editor@middleeastmagazine.com. Pub. Brian Wilkie. adv.: page USD 3,355; trim 210 x 297. Circ: 60,000.

MIELENTERVEYS/MENTAL HEALTH. *see* MEDICAL SCIENCES—Psychiatry And Neurology

THE MILBANK QUARTERLY; a journal of public health and health care policy . *see* POLITICAL SCIENCE

362.1 CAN ISSN 1718-4762
LE MILIEU. Text in French. 2005. m. **Document type:** *Magazine, Trade.*
Published by: Centre de Sante et de Services Sociaux d'Arthabaska-Erable, 100, rue de l'Ermitage, Victoriaville, PQ, Canada. TEL 819-758-7281.

MILJOE OCH HAELSA. *see* ENVIRONMENTAL STUDIES

362.1 ITA ISSN 2038-5293
▼ **MINISTERO DELLA SALUTE. QUADERNI.** Text in Multiple languages. 2010. bi-m. **Document type:** *Report, Government.*
Related titles: Online - full text ed.: ISSN 2038-5307.
Published by: Ministero della Salute, Lungotevere Ripa 1, Rome, 00153, Italy. TEL 39-06-59941, http://www.salute.gov.it.

362.1 CAN ISSN 1715-1813
MISE A JOUR SUR LES PESTICIDES A RISQUE REDUIT AU CANADA. Text in French. 2005. irreg., latest 2006. **Document type:** *Government.*
Related titles: Online - full text ed.: ISSN 1715-1821; English ed.: Update on Reduced-risk Pesticides in Canada. ISSN 1715-1791. 2005.
Published by: Health Canada, Pest Management Regulatory Agency/ Agence de Reglementation de la Lutte Antiparasitaire (Subsidiary of: Health Canada/Sante Canada), 2720 Riverside Dr, A.L. 6606D2, Ottawa, ON K1A 0K9, Canada. TEL 613-736-3799, 800-267-6315, FAX 613-736-3798, pmra_infoserv@hc-sc.gc.ca, http://www.pmra-arla.gc.ca/english/index-e.html.

MITIGATION AND ADAPTATION STRATEGIES FOR GLOBAL CHANGE; an international journal devoted to scientific, engineering, socio-economic and policy responses to environmental change. *see* ENVIRONMENTAL STUDIES

614 JPN ISSN 0917-3331
CODEN: MEKNEH
MIYAZAKIKEN EISEI KANKYO KENKYUJO NENPO/MIYAZAKI PREFECTURAL INSTITUTE FOR PUBLIC HEALTH AND ENVIRONMENT. ANNUAL REPORT. Text in Japanese; Summaries in English. 1991. a. **Document type:** *Journal, Academic/Scholarly.*
Formed by the merger of: Miyazakiken Kogai Senta Nenpo; Miyazakiken Eisei Kenkyujoho
—BLDSC (1355.370000), CASDDS.
Published by: Miyazakiken Eisei Kankyo Kenkyujo, 3-2 Gakuenkibanadai-Nishi 2-chome, Miyazaki-shi, 889-2155, Japan. TEL 81-985-581410, FAX 81-985-580930, http://www.pref.miyazaki.lg.jp/fukushi/ipe/.

THE MOBILITY FORUM; journal of the Air Mobility Command. *see* MILITARY

614.8 DEU ISSN 0544-7119
MODERNE UNFALLVERHUETUNG. Text in German. 1956. a. EUR 29.80 per issue (effective 2010). adv. bk.rev. back issues avail. **Document type:** *Trade.*
—GNLM, IE, Infotrieve.
Published by: Verlag Technik & Information e.K., Wohlfahrtstrasse 153, Bochum, 44799, Germany. TEL 49-234-943490, FAX 49-234-9434921, info@vti-bochum.de. Circ: 3,500.

613 615.5 POL ISSN 1231-3203
MOJE ZDROWIE; domowy poradnik medyczny. Text in Polish. 1992. m. **Document type:** *Magazine, Consumer.*
Published by: Wydawnictwo Kwadryga, ul Chelmska 19/21, Warsaw, 00724, Poland. TEL 48-22-8516668, FAX 48-22-5593565, gfarm@kwadryga.pl, http://www.kwadryga.pl.

362.1 USA ISSN 1535-3729
TH9041
MOLD REPORTER. Text in English. 2001. irreg. USD 36.50, USD 48.50 to individuals; USD 50, USD 62 to institutions (effective 2004). **Document type:** *Newsletter, Trade.*
—Linda Hall.
Published by: Abbey Publications, Inc., 7105 Geneva Dr, Austin, TX 78723-1510. TEL 512-929-3992, FAX 512-929-3995. Ed. Ellen R McCrady. Circ: 160 (paid); 35 (free).

MONASH UNIVERSITY ACCIDENT RESEARCH CENTRE. CONSULTANTS' REPORTS SERIES. *see* TRANSPORTATION—Roads And Traffic

MONASH UNIVERSITY ACCIDENT RESEARCH CENTRE. MINOR REPORTS SERIES. *see* TRANSPORTATION—Roads And Traffic

MONASH UNIVERSITY ACCIDENT RESEARCH CENTRE. OTHER REPORTS SERIES. *see* TRANSPORTATION—Roads And Traffic

362.1 USA
MONITOR (LYNCHBURG). Text in English. 1995. q. free to qualified personnel (effective 2006). **Document type:** *Newsletter.*
Published by: Centra Health, Inc., 1920 Atherholt Rd, Lynchburg, VA 24501. TEL 434-947-4731, FAX 434-947-4958, susan.brandt@centrahealth.com, http://www.centrahealth.com. Ed. Susan Brandt. Circ: 3,000 (free).

362.1 USA ISSN 1931-8669
HV5824.Y68
MONITORING THE FUTURE, NATIONAL RESULTS ON ADOLESCENT DRUG USE. OVERVIEW OF KEY FINDINGS. Text in English. 1999. a. free (effective 2011). back issues avail. **Document type:** *Monographic series, Government.*
Related titles: Online - full text ed.: ISSN 1931-8677.
Published by: U.S. Department of Health and Human Services, National Institute on Drug Abuse, 6001 Executive Blvd, Rm 5213, Bethesda, MD 20892. TEL 301-443-1124, information@nida.nih.gov, http://www.nida.nih.gov.

614.4 570 GBR ISSN 0740-0845
CODEN: MEBIEP
➤ **MONOGRAPHS IN EPIDEMIOLOGY AND BIOSTATISTICS.** Text in English. 1981. irreg., latest 2009. price varies. **Document type:** *Monographic series, Academic/Scholarly.*
Indexed: A22, CIS.
—BLDSC (5915.431000), IE, Ingenta. **CCC.**
Published by: Oxford University Press, Great Clarendon St, Oxford, OX2 6DP, United Kingdom. TEL 44-1865-556767, FAX 44-1865-556646, enquiry@oup.co.uk, http://www.oup-usa.org/catalogs/general/series/. **Orders in N. America to:** Oxford University Press, 2001 Evans Rd, Cary, NC 27513. TEL 919-677-0977 ext 5777, 800-852-7323, FAX 919-677-1714, jnlorders@oup-usa.org, http://www.us.oup.com.

353.6 TZA ISSN 0856-9525
MOROGORO HEALTH NEWSLETTER. Text in English. 2003. bi-m.
Published by: Morogoro Health Project, PO Box 1193, Morogoro, Tanzania. TEL 255-23-2614002, FAX 255-23-2614148, morogorohealthproject@yahoo.com, http://project.jica.go.jp/tanzania/5481081E0/index.htm.

614 GBR ISSN 1357-6275
HQ1073 CODEN: MORTF5
➤ **MORTALITY**; promoting the interdisciplinary study of death and dying. Text in English. 1996. q. GBP 464 combined subscription in United Kingdom to institutions (print & online eds.); EUR 613, USD 768 combined subscription to institutions (print & online eds.) (effective 2012). adv. bk.rev. illus. back issues avail.; reprint service avail. from PSC. **Document type:** *Journal, Academic/Scholarly.* **Description:** Features articles pertinent to academics in the fields of death studies anthropology, art, classics, history, literature, medicine, music, socio-legal studies, social policy, sociology, philosophy, psychology and religious studies.
Related titles: Online - full text ed.: ISSN 1469-9885. GBP 417 in United Kingdom to institutions; EUR 551, USD 691 to institutions (effective 2012) (from IngentaConnect).
Indexed: A01, A02, A03, A08, A22, AmHI, B21, BrHumI, C06, C07, C08, C11, CA, CINAHL, E01, E17, ESPM, H04, H05, H07, P03, P21, P24, P25, P48, P52, P56, PQC, PsycInfo, PsycholAb, S02, S03, S21, SCOPUS, SOPODA, SSA, SociolAb, T02.
—IE, Ingenta. **CCC.**
Published by: Routledge (Subsidiary of: Taylor & Francis Group), 4 Park Sq, Milton Park, Abingdon, Oxon OX14 4RN, United Kingdom. TEL 44-20-7017-6000, FAX 44-20-7017-6336, info@routledge.co.uk, http://www.routledge.com. Ed. Allan Kellehear. Adv. contact Linda Hann TEL 44-1344-779945. **Subscr. to:** Taylor & Francis Ltd., Journals Customer Service, Sheepen Pl, Colchester, Essex CO3 3LP, United Kingdom. TEL 44-20-70175544, FAX 44-20-70175198, tf.enquiries@tfinforma.com, subscriptions@tandf.co.uk, http://www.tandf.co.uk/journals.

614 595.7 USA ISSN 1554-4974
RA640
MOSQUITO AND VECTOR CONTROL ASSOCIATION OF CALIFORNIA. PROCEEDINGS AND PAPERS OF THE ANNUAL CONFERENCE. Text in English. 1930. a. USD 18 per issue (effective 2005); per vol. back issues avail.
Former titles (until 1996): California Mosquito and Vector Control Association. Proceedings and Papers of the Annual Conference (0160-6751); (until vol.45, 1977): California Mosquito Control Association. Proceedings and Papers of the Annual Meeting (0091-6501)
Indexed: Agr, P30.
—GNLM, Linda Hall.
Published by: Mosquito and Vector Control Association of California, 660 J St Ste 480, Sacramento, CA 95814. TEL 916-440-0826, FAX 916-442-4182, mvcac@mvcac.org, http://www.mvcac.org/index.htm. Circ: 800. **Co-sponsor:** American Mosquito Control Association.

362.1 CAN ISSN 1719-5918
MOTOR VEHICLE COLLISION INFORMATION. Text in English. 1992. a. **Document type:** *Government.*
Former titles (until 2003): Motor Vehicle Collision Statistics (1714-8081); (until 2001): Motor Vehicle Accident Statistics (1494-6378); (until 1997): Annual Traffic Safety Report (1483-1201); (until 1995): Traffic Safety Report (1483-118X); (until 1993): Nova Scotia Traffic Safety Report (1199-5866)
Published by: Nova Scotia, Department of Transportation and Public Works, PO Box 186, Halifax, NS B3J 2N2, Canada. TEL 902-424-2297, FAX 902-424-0532, tpwpaff@gov.ns.ca, http://www.gov.ns.ca/tran/default.asp.

353.6 CAN ISSN 1209-2053
MSCOMMUNIQUE. Text in English. 1996. irreg. (2-3/yr.).
Published by: British Columbia Medical Services Commission, PO Box 9480, Stn Prov Govt, Victoria, BC V8W 9E7, Canada. TEL 250-952-1059, 866-456-6950, FAX 250-952-3133.

628 DEU ISSN 0027-2957
CODEN: MUABD8
MUELL UND ABFALL; Fachzeitschrift fuer Abfall- und Ressourcenwirtschaft. Text in German. 1969. m. EUR 146.40; EUR 14.40 newsstand/cover (effective 2012). adv. bk.rev. **Document type:** *Newspaper, Trade.* **Description:** Emphasis is on sanitary engineering.
Related titles: Online - full text ed.: ISSN 1863-9763. 2007. EUR 146.40 (effective 2012).
Indexed: CIN, ChemAb, ChemTitl, GeoRef, IBR, IBZ, INIS AtomInd, Repind, SpeleolAb, TM, WasteInfo.
—BLDSC (5982.650000), CASDDS, IE, Infotrieve, Ingenta, Linda Hall. **CCC.**
Published by: Erich Schmidt Verlag GmbH & Co. (Berlin), Genthiner Str 30 G, Berlin, 10785, Germany. TEL 49-30-2500850, FAX 49-30-250085305, esv@esvmedien.de, http://www.esv.info. Ed. Klaus Fricke. Adv. contact Peter Taprogge. Circ: 2,400 (paid).

MUNAZZAMAT AL-SIHHAH AL-'ALAMIYYAH. SILSILAT AL-TAQARIR AL-FANNIYYAH. *see* MEDICAL SCIENCES

N A C A NEWS. *see* PETS

614.8 BEL ISSN 1780-7875
N A V B INFO. (Nationaal Actiecomite voor Veiligheid en Hygiene in het Bouwbedrijf) Text in Dutch. 1964. q. EUR 28; EUR 20 to qualified personnel (effective 2005). adv. bk.rev. illus.
Former titles (until 2004): Veilig Bouwen (1780-7220); (until 1978): Operatie Veiligheid (0771-2588); (until 1970): Let Op! Rood Licht (0771-9183)
Related titles: ◆ French ed.: C N A C Info. ISSN 1780-7867.
Published by: Nationaal Actiecomite voor Veiligheid en Hygiene in het Bouwbedrijf (NAVB)/Comite National d'Action pour la Securite et l'Hygiene dans la Construction (CNAC), Sint-Jansstraat 4, Brussel, 1000, Belgium. publications@navb.be. Ed. B Schoenmaekers. Circ: 27,000.

THE N A WAY MAGAZINE. (Narcotics Anonymous) *see* DRUG ABUSE AND ALCOHOLISM

614.8 USA ISSN 0890-3417
N C A H F NEWSLETTER; quality in the health marketplace. (National Council Against Health Fraud) Text in English. 1977. bi-m. looseleaf. USD 15 to individuals; USD 18 to libraries (effective 2007). bk.rev. index. 4 p./no. 3 cols./p.; back issues avail. **Document type:** *Newsletter.* **Description:** Focuses on health misinformation, fraud and quackery as public health problems. Contains summaries (with commentary) of current medical findings, reports on controversial health practices and other consumer health issues.
Formerly (until 2001): N C R H I Newsletter (National Council for Reliable Health Information, Inc.
Related titles: Microform ed.: (from PQC); Online - full text ed.
Indexed: A01, A02, A03, A04, A08, A15, A26, ABIn, CHNI, G08, H01, H02, H11, H12, HlthInd, I05, M01, M02, P05, P21, P24, P48, P51, P52, P56, PQC.
Published by: National Council Against Health Fraud, Inc., 119 Foster St, Building R, 2nd Fl, Peabody, MA 01960. TEL 978-532-9383, FAX 978-532-9450, ncahf.office@verizon.net, http://www.ncahf.com/. Ed. John M London. R&P Dr. Robert S Baratz. Circ: 2,000 (paid).

614.83 USA ISSN 0899-3416
RA569 CODEN: NCRCEG
N C R P COMMENTARY. Text in English. 1980. irreg., latest vol.20, 2007. price varies. back issues avail. **Document type:** *Monographic series, Academic/Scholarly.*
Related titles: Online - full text ed.
Published by: National Council on Radiation Protection and Measurements, 7910 Woodmont Ave, Ste 400, Bethesda, MD 20814. TEL 301-657-2652, FAX 301-907-8768, NCRPpubs@NCRPonline.org, http://www.ncrponline.org.

614.83 355.23 USA ISSN 0195-7740
CODEN: PNRME9
N C R P M PROCEEDINGS OF THE ANNUAL MEETING. Variant title: National Council on Radiation Protection and Measurements. Annual Meeting. Proceedings and Presentations. Text in English. 1979 (15th). a. USD 25 per issue (effective 2010). back issues avail. **Document type:** *Proceedings, Academic/Scholarly.*
Related titles: Online - full text ed.: USD 20 per issue (effective 2010).
Indexed: GeoRef, SpeleolAb.
—CASDDS, Linda Hall.
Published by: National Council on Radiation Protection and Measurements, 7910 Woodmont Ave, Ste 400, Bethesda, MD 20814. TEL 301-657-2652, FAX 301-907-8768, NCRPpubs@NCRPonline.org, http://www.ncrponline.org.

614.8 355.23 USA ISSN 0083-209X
CODEN: NCRDBG
N C R P REPORT. (National Council on Radiation Protection) Text in English. 1931. irreg., latest vol.163. price varies. back issues avail. **Document type:** *Monographic series, Academic/Scholarly.*
Related titles: Online - full text ed.
Indexed: A22, CIS, EIA, EMBASE, EnvAb, ExcerpMed, GeoRef, R10, Reac, SCOPUS, SpeleolAb.
—BLDSC (6067.817100), Linda Hall.
Published by: National Council on Radiation Protection and Measurements, 7910 Woodmont Ave, Ste 400, Bethesda, MD 20814. TEL 301-657-2652, FAX 301-907-8768, NCRPpubs@NCRPonline.org, http://www.ncrponline.org.

614.83 USA
N C R P SYMPOSIUM PROCEEDINGS. (National Council on Radiation Protection) Text in English. 1982. irreg., latest vol.3, 1996. USD 30 per issue (effective 2010). **Document type:** *Proceedings, Academic/Scholarly.*
Published by: National Council on Radiation Protection and Measurements, 7910 Woodmont Ave, Ste 400, Bethesda, MD 20814. TEL 301-657-2652, FAX 301-907-8768, NCRPpubs@NCRPonline.org, http://www.ncrponline.org.

N E C N P NEWSLETTER. *see* ENERGY

362.1 IND ISSN 1083-8678
RA407.5.I4
N F H S BULLETIN. (National Family Health Survey) Text in English. 1995. irreg. back issues avail. **Document type:** *Bulletin, Trade.*
Indexed: P30, SCOPUS.
Published by: International Institute for Population Sciences, Govandi Sta Rd, Deonar, Mumbai, Maharashtra 400 088, India. TEL 91-22-25562062, http://www.iipsindia.org.

614 GBR ISSN 1359-4443
RA412.5.G7
N H S MAGAZINE. (National Health Service) Text in English. 1995. 10/yr. free to qualified personnel. **Document type:** *Magazine, Consumer.* **Description:** Contains analysis and discussion of healthcare and health management issues and aims to engage people at the forefront of change and service modernisation locally.
—BLDSC (6109.523700).
Published by: National Health Service, Executive Communications Unit, Quarry House, Quarry Hill, Leeds, LS2 7UE, United Kingdom. TEL 44-113-254-5610, http://www.nhs.uk/. Ed. Stan Abbott. Pub. Peter Addison. Adv. contact John Wheelhouse.

614 GBR ISSN 1354-2362
N H S NEWS. (National Health Service) Text in English. m. adv. **Document type:** *Bulletin.*
Formerly (until 1994): N H S Management Executive News (0963-5688)
Published by: National Health Service, Executive Communications Unit, Quarry House, Quarry Hill, Leeds, LS2 7UE, United Kingdom. TEL 44-113-254-5610. Ed. Geoff Wilson. Adv. contact John Wheelhouse.

362.1 614 SWE ISSN 0283-1961
N H V-RAPPORT/N H V-REPORTS AND DOCTOR OF PUBLIC HEALTH-THESES. (Nordiska Hoegskolan foer Folkhaelsovetenskap) Text in English, Swedish. 1983. irreg., latest vol.5, no.3, 2011. SEK 150 per issue (effective 2011). back issues avail. **Document type:** *Monographic series, Academic/Scholarly.*
Formerly (until 1985): Rapport - N H V (0281-5966)
Related titles: Online - full text ed.

P

Published by: Nordiska Hoegskolan foer Folkhaelsovetenskap/The Nordic School of Public Health, Nya Varvat Byggnad 25, PO Box 12133, Goeteborg, 40242, Sweden. TEL 46-31-693900, FAX 46-31-691777, administration@nhv.se.

614 GBR ISSN 2043-0507
N I C E BULLETIN; an update for parliamentarians. Text in English. 19??. q. back issues avail. **Document type:** *Bulletin, Trade.* **Description:** Designed to update MPs and Lords in Westminster on recently issued NICE guidance as well as to alert readers to forthcoming recommendations and ensure they are familiar with NICE and their current work programme.
Former titles (until 2010): Health and Clinical Excellence (1747-4280); (until 2005): Parliamentary and Assembly Bulletin
Related titles: Online - full text ed.: ISSN 2043-0515. 2006. free (effective 2010).
Published by: National Institute for Health and Clinical Excellence, MidCity Pl, 71 High Holborn, London, WC1V 6NA, United Kingdom. TEL 44-845-0037780, FAX 44-845-0037784, nice@nice.org.uk.

353.6 USA ISSN 8756-601X
RA11
THE N I H ALMANAC. (National Institutes of Health) Text in English. 1965. a. **Document type:** *Government.*
Formerly (until 1978): The National Institutes of Health Almanac (0565-789X)
Related titles: Online - full text ed.: ISSN 1559-8691.
—Linda Hall.
Published by: U.S. Department of Health and Human Services, 200 Independence Ave, SW, Washington, DC 20201. TEL 877-696-6775, http://www.hhs.gov/.

362.1 USA ISSN 0893-4940
T55.3.H3
N I O S H CURRENT INTELLIGENCE BULLETIN. (National Institute for Occupational Safety and Health) Text in English. 1975. irreg. **Document type:** *Bulletin, Government.*
Related titles: Online - full text ed.: ISSN 1930-8817.
Published by: Centers for Disease Control & Prevention, National Institute for Occupational Safety and Health (Subsidiary of: U.S. Department of Health and Human Services), 1600 Clifton Rd, Atlanta, GA 30333. TEL 404-639-3311, http://www.cdc.gov/niosh/homepage.html.

362.1 USA
Z675.M4
N L M IN FOCUS. Text in English. w. free (effective 2010). back issues avail. **Document type:** *Newsletter, Government.*
Formerly (until 2005): N L M Newsline (Online) (1094-6004)
Media: Online - full text. **Related titles:** Microfilm ed.: (from PQC).
Published by: U.S. National Library of Medicine, 8600 Rockville Pike, Bethesda, MD 20894. TEL 301-594-5983, 888-346-3656, FAX 301-402-1384, custserv@nlm.nih.gov, http://www.nlm.nih.gov. Ed. Shana Potash TEL 301-496-6308.

362.1 USA
N R H A E NEWS. Text in English. 1978. fortn. free to members (effective 2005). adv. **Document type:** *Newsletter, Consumer.* **Description:** Information on rural health issues, policy and projects.
Former titles (until 2000): Rural Health F Y I (1083-6829); (until 1995): Rural Health Care
Media: Online - full content.
—CCC.
Published by: National Rural Health Association, 1 W Armour Blvd, Ste 203, Kansas City, MO 64111-2087. TEL 816-756-3140, FAX 816-756-3144, pubs@nrharural.org, http://www.nrharural.org. Ed., R&P Jeff Sullens. adv.: B&W page USD 325. Circ: 6,000 (controlled).

362.1 AUS ISSN 1034-7674
➤ **N S W PUBLIC HEALTH BULLETIN.** (New South Wales) Text in English. 1990. bi-m. free (effective 2012). adv. stat. cum.index: 1990-2000. 24 p./no.; back issues avail. **Document type:** *Bulletin, Government.* **Description:** Serves as an information vehicle for the whole public health community in New South Wales. Provides its readers with population health data as a means to motivate effective public health action.
Related titles: Online - full text ed.: ISSN 1834-8610. free (effective 2011); Supplement(s): N S W Public Health Bulletin. Supplement. ISSN 1835-8330.
Indexed: A34, A36, ASSIA, AusPAIS, B20, B21, C06, C07, CABA, D01, E12, EMBASE, ESPM, ExcerpMed, F08, F12, GH, H&SSA, IndVet, LT, MEDLINE, N02, N03, P30, P33, P39, R08, R10, RRTA, Reac, S13, S16, SCOPUS, SD, T05, VS, ViroIAbstr, W11.
—BLDSC (6180.590072).
Published by: (N S W Department of Health, Public Health Division), C S I R O Publishing, 150 Oxford St, PO Box 1139, Collingwood, VIC 3066, Australia. TEL 61-3-96627500, FAX 61-3-96627555, publishing@csiro.au, http://www.publish.csiro.au/home.htm. Ed. Lynne Madden TEL 61-2-93919956. R&P Carla Flores. Adv. contact Wendy Wild TEL 61-3-96627606.

353.6 664 NZL ISSN 1177-7109
N Z F S A BACKGROUND PAPER. Text in English. 2004. irreg., latest 2006. **Document type:** *Monographic series.*
Media: Online - full text.
Published by: New Zealand Food Safety Authority, 68-86 Jervois Quay, PO Box 2835, Wellington, New Zealand. TEL 64-4-8942500, FAX 64-4-8942501, nzfsa.info@nzfsa.govt.nz.

362.1 POL ISSN 1896-8546
NA RATUNEK. Text in Polish. 2007. q. PLZ 78 domestic (effective 2011). **Document type:** *Magazine, Trade.* **Description:** Aims to promote knowledge of the rescue; also presents the latest equipment and solutions used during the rescue activities, involvement in rescue training, promotion of the companies taking part in rescue operations, the integration of the environment through participation in national and international events such as competitions, fairs, conferences, seminars and training.
Related titles: Online - full text ed.
Published by: Wydawnictwo Elamed, Al Rozdzienskiego 188, Katowice, 40203, Poland. TEL 48-32-2580361, FAX 48-32-2039356, elamed@elamed.com.pl, http://www.elamed.com.pl. Ed. Malgorzata Podplomyk.

614.40715 JPN ISSN 0287-9549
NARA JOSHI DAIGAKU HOKEN KANRI SENTA NENPO/NARA WOMEN'S UNIVERSITY. HEALTH ADMINISTRATION CENTER. ARCHIVES OF HEALTH CARE. Text in Japanese; Contents page in English. 1978. a. charts. **Document type:** *Academic/Scholarly.*
Formerly (until 1983): Nara Joshi Daigaku Hoken Kanri Senta Kiyo (0286-505X)
Published by: Nara Joshi Daigaku, Hoken Kanri Senta/Nara Women's University, Health Administration Center, Kita-Uoyahigashi-Machi, Nara-shi, 630-8285, Japan. Ed. Kimihiro Yamamoto. Circ: 500.

613 HRV ISSN 0351-9384
NARODNI ZDRAVSTVENI LIST. Text in Croatian. 1958. m. **Document type:** *Magazine, Consumer.*
Published by: Zavod za Javno Zdravstvo Primorsko Goranske Zupanije, Kresimirova 52a, p.p. 382, Rijeka, 51000, Croatia. TEL 385-51-214359, FAX 385-51-213948. Ed. Vladimir Smesny.

362.1 CAN ISSN 1703-7697
NATIONAL ABORIGINAL HEALTH ORGANIZATION. ANNUAL REPORT. Text in English. 2002. a. **Document type:** *Report, Trade.*
Related titles: Online - full text ed.: ISSN 1912-2284. 2001; ◆ French ed.: Organisation Nationale de la Sante Autochtone. Rapport Annuel. ISSN 1703-7719; Inuktitut ed.: Arragutamat Titirarksimajuliunguvaktut. ISSN 1703-7700. 2002.
Published by: National Aboriginal Health Organization (N A H O)/Organisation Nationale de la Sante Autochtone (O N S A), 220 Laurier Ave W. Ste 1200, Ottawa, ON K1P 5Z9, Canada. TEL 613-237-9462, 877-602-4445, FAX 613-237-1810, naho@naho.ca, http://www.naho.ca/english.

364.4 362.8292 USA ISSN 1083-7310
NATIONAL BULLETIN ON DOMESTIC VIOLENCE PREVENTION. Text in English. 1995. m. USD 168; USD 14 per issue (effective 2008). **Document type:** *Newsletter, Trade.*
Related titles: Online - full text ed.: ISSN 1546-5306.
—CCC.
Published by: Quinlan Publishing Group (Subsidiary of: Thomson West), 610 Opperman Dr, Eagan, MN 55123. TEL 651-687-7000, 800-937-8529, FAX 800-227-7097, bookstore@westgroup.com, http://west.thomson.com/quinlan. Ed. Jeremy C. Fox.

362.1 610 ZAF ISSN 1816-3769
NATIONAL HEALTH LABORATORY SERVICE. ANNUAL REPORT. Variant title: N H L S Annual Report. Text in English. 2005. a.
Published by: National Health Laboratory Service, PO Box 1038, Johannesburg, 2000, South Africa. TEL 27-11-3866000, FAX 27-11-3866002.

614 JPN
RA421 CODEN: KEKHA7
NATIONAL INSTITUTE OF PUBLIC HEALTH. JOURNAL. Text in English, Japanese. 1952. q. free or exchange basis. abstr.; bibl.; charts; illus. index. **Document type:** *Bulletin.*
Former titles: Koshu Eisei Kenkyu - Institute of Public Health. Bulletin (0916-6823); (until 1990): Koshu Eiseiin Kenkyu Hokoku - Institute of Public Health. Bulletin (0020-3106)
Indexed: ChemAb, FR, P30.
—CASDDS, GNLM, INIST. **CCC.**
Published by: National Institute of Public Health, 4-6-1 Shirokanedai, Minato-ku, Tokyo, 108-0071, Japan. Ed. Dr. Toshiro Tango. Circ: 1,200.

362.1 IND ISSN 0976-3325
▼ **NATIONAL JOURNAL OF COMMUNITY MEDICINE.** Text in English. 2010. irreg. free (effective 2011). **Document type:** *Journal, Academic/Scholarly.*
Media: Online - full text.
Indexed: CABA, D01, GH, N02, N03, P33, R08, T05.
Address: Surat Municipal Institute of Medical Education & Research, Opposite Bombay Market, Umarwada, Surat, Gujarat 395 010, India. Ed. S L Kantharia.

614.8 AUS ISSN 1445-9922
NATIONAL SAFETY. Text in English. 1929. 11/yr. AUD 135 domestic to non-members; AUD 190 foreign to non-members; free to members (effective 2009). adv. bk.rev. charts; illus. index. **Document type:** *Magazine, Government.* **Description:** Provides information about the National Safety Council of Australia.
Incoporates (in 2004): C C H's Australian Occupational Health & Safety (1444-2280); Former titles (until 2001): N S C A's Australian Safety (1443-8429); (until 1999): Australian Safety News (1443-8410); (until 1986): Australian Health and Safety News (1443-8402); (until 1985): Australian Safety News (0005-0180)
Indexed: A22, ARI, CISA, CSNB, ErgAb, GeoRef, L12.
—BLDSC (6032.610000), IE, Ingenta.
Published by: National Safety Council of Australia, Bldg 4, Brandon Office Park, 540 Springvale Rd, Glen Waverley, VIC 3150, Australia. TEL 61-3-85621555, FAX 61-3-85621590, melbourne@nsca.org.au. Ed. Helen Borger TEL 61-2-89622600. adv.: page AUD 3,410; trim 210 x 297. Circ: 11,100 (controlled).

614.8 ZAF
NATIONAL SAFETY & OCCUPATIONAL HYGIENE/NASIONALE VEILIGHEID. Text mainly in English; Text occasionally in Afrikaans. 1938. bi-m. ZAR 145 domestic; ZAR 165 foreign (effective 2006). adv. bk.rev. illus.; stat.; tr.lit. **Document type:** *Journal, Trade.* **Description:** Aims to prevent accidents by promoting an awareness of accident situations as they exist in day-to-day living among members of the community.
Formerly: National Safety (0028-0097)
Indexed: B21, CISA, ESPM, H&SSA.
—IE.
Published by: (Southern African Protective Equipment Manufacturing Association, Institute of Safety Management), Safety First Association, PO Box 14402, Clubview, 0014, South Africa. TEL 27-12-6548349, FAX 27-12-6548358, raysaf@mweb.co.za. Ed. Debbie Myer. Circ: 3,200 (controlled).

362.1 USA ISSN 1945-3361
RA448.5.N4
➤ **NATIONAL SOCIETY OF ALLIED HEALTH. JOURNAL.** Text in English. 2003. a. adv. **Document type:** *Journal, Academic/Scholarly.* **Description:** Aims to improve the health care status of African Americans and at-risk populations including economically disadvantaged populations, through education, employment, community service and research.
Related titles: Online - full text ed.
Indexed: A26, C06, C07, CA, H11, H12, I05, P24, P48, PQC, T02.
Published by: National Society of Allied Health, 12138 Central Ave, Ste 562, Mitchellville, MD 20721. dcoverley@howard.edu. Ed. Rosemary Theriot.

362.1 USA ISSN 1559-4688
HV5825
NATIONAL SURVEY ON DRUG USE & HEALTH. RESULTS. Text in English. 2002. a. **Document type:** *Report, Trade.*
Formerly (until 2002): National Household Survey on Drug Abuse. Results
Related titles: Online - full text ed.: ISSN 1940-6738.
Published by: U.S. Department of Health and Human Services. Substance Abuse and Mental Health Services Administration, Office of Applied Studies, 1 Choke Cherry Rd, Rockville, MD 20857. TEL 240-276-1250, FAX 240-276-1260, http://oas.samhsa.gov/.

614 USA ISSN 0028-0496
THE NATION'S HEALTH. Abbreviated title: T N H. Text in English. 1911. 10/yr. USD 60 in US & Canada; USD 73 elsewhere (effective 2009). adv. bk.rev. charts; illus. back issues avail.; reprints avail. **Document type:** *Newspaper, Consumer.* **Description:** Covers public health policy, including legislative and other federal action.
Supersedes in part (in 1971): American Journal of Public Health and the Nation's Health (0002-9572); Which was formed by the 1927 merger of: American Journal of Public Health (0271-4353); Which was formerly (until 1912): American Public Health Association. Journal (0273-1975); (until 1911): American Journal of Public Hygiene (0272-2313); (until 1907): Massachusetts Association of Boards of Health. American Journal of Public Hygiene and Journal; (until 1904): Massachusetts Association of Boards of Health. Journal; Incorporates (1873-1912): Public Health Papers and Reports (0737-8769); Nation's Health (1076-0709)
Related titles: Microform ed.: (from PQC); Online - full text ed.: ISSN 2151-7584.
Indexed: A01, A02, A03, A08, A22, A23, A24, A26, B07, B13, BiolDig, C11, C12, G08, H01, H03, H04, H05, H11, H12, H13, HlthInd, I05, I07, M01, M02, MASUSE, MCR, P02, P10, P19, P20, P21, P27, P30, P34, P45, P48, P50, P53, P54, PQC, RehabLit, S02, S03, SCOPUS, T02, Telegen.
—INIST. **CCC.**
Published by: American Public Health Association, 800 I St, NW, Washington, DC 20001. TEL 202-777-2742, FAX 202-777-2534, comments@apha.org, http://www.apha.org. Adv. contact Ashell Alston TEL 202-777-2470. color page USD 4,600; trim 10.625 x 13.75. Circ: 28,000. **Subscr. to:** APHA.

NATURAL HAZARDS REVIEW. *see* ENVIRONMENTAL STUDIES

614.88 NLD ISSN 0925-6040
NEDERLANDS TIJDSCHRIFT VOOR E H B O EN REDDINGWEZEN. Text in Dutch. 1912. 6/yr. EUR 20.50; EUR 4.50 newsstand/cover (effective 2009). adv. bk.rev. bibl.; charts; illus.
Formerly (until 1991): Reddingwezen (0034-2114)
—IE, Infotrieve.
Published by: Koninklijke Nationale Bond voor Reddingwezen en Eerste Hulp bij Ongelukken "Het Oranje Kruis", Postbus 16462, The Hague, 2500 BL, Netherlands. TEL 31-70-3383232, FAX 31-70-3584151, ok@ehbo.nl, http://http://www.ehbo.nl/Oranjekruis. adv.: page EUR 1,090; trim 210 x 249. Circ: 6,500.

613 539.2 NLD ISSN 1879-9620
NEDERLANDS TIJDSCHRIFT VOOR STRALINGSBESCHERMING. Text in Dutch. 1976. q. EUR 40 (effective 2011). **Document type:** *Magazine, Trade.*
Formerly (until 2010): N V S Nieuws (1380-4499)
Published by: Nederlandse Vereniging voor Stralingshygiene, Postbus 342, Tiel, 4000 AH, Netherlands. TEL 31-344-786901, FAX 31-344-786906, administratie@nsv-straling.nl, http://www.nvs-straling.nl.

NEEDLE TIPS. *see* MEDICAL SCIENCES—Communicable Diseases

613 NLD ISSN 1871-3858
NETHERLANDS. INSPECTIE VOOR DE GEZONDHEIDSZORG. JAARBERICHT. Text in Dutch. 2005. a.
Published by: Inspectie voor de Gezondheidszorg, Postbus 16119, The Hague, 2500 BC, Netherlands. TEL 31-70-3407911, FAX 31-70-3407834, bestel@igz.nl.

614.2 NLD
NETWORK NEWSLETTER. Variant title: G-Raadmeter. Text in English. 2/yr. free (effective 2009).
Former titles: Graadmeter (0169-6211); Which incorporated (1987-1987): Meta (0920-8976); (until 1985): G R Bulletin
Related titles: English ed.: Network (The Hague). ISSN 1571-9618. 1987.
—IE.
Published by: Gezondheidsraad/Health Council of the Netherlands, PO Box 16052, The Hague, 2500 BB, Netherlands. TEL 31-70-3407520, FAX 31-70-3407523, info@gr.nl, http://www.healthcouncil.nl. Ed. A Wijbenga.

368.382 DEU
NEUE UNTERSUCHUNGS- UND BEHANDLUNGSMETHODEN. Text in German. 2 base vols. plus updates 4/yr. looseleaf. EUR 349 base vol(s).; EUR 105 updates (effective 2010). adv. **Document type:** *Trade.*
Related titles: CD-ROM ed.
Published by: Walhalla Fachverlag, Haus an der Eisernen Bruecke, Regensburg, 93042, Germany. TEL 49-941-56840, FAX 49-941-5684111, walhalla@walhalla.de. Ed. Werner Gerlach. adv.: B&W page EUR 300. Circ: 250 (controlled).

614 CAN ISSN 1499-4704
NEW BRUNSWICK. DEPARTMENT OF HEALTH AND WELLNESS. ANNUAL REPORT. Text in English, French. 1918. a. free. stat. **Document type:** *Government.*
Supersedes in part (in 2001): New Brunswick. Department of Health and Community Services. Annual Report (0838-3693); Which was formerly (until 1987): New Brunswick. Department of Health. Annual Report (0711-8376)
Published by: New Brunswick, Department of Health and Wellness, PO Box 5100, Fredericton, NB E3B 5G8, Canada. TEL 506-453-2536, FAX 506-444-4697, http://www.gnb.ca/0051/index-e.asp. Ed. Gerald Weseen. Circ: 700.

NEW BUSINESS HEALTHCARE MARKETING. *see* BUSINESS AND ECONOMICS—Marketing And Purchasing

NEW JERSEY STATE FIRE CODE. *see* FIRE PREVENTION

NEW SOLUTIONS; a journal of environmental and occupational health policy. *see* OCCUPATIONAL HEALTH AND SAFETY

614 USA ISSN 1077-1344
NEW YORK HEALTH LAW UPDATE. Text in English. 1994. m. USD 347 (effective 2008). back issues avail.; reprints avail. **Document type:** *Newsletter, Trade.* **Description:** Reports state-specific new public health laws that affect companies in New York.
Formerly (until 1994): New York Health Law Alert (1073-0443)
Related titles: Online - full text ed.
—CIS.
Published by: Strafford Publications, Inc., 590 Dutch Valley Rd, N E, P O Drawer 13729, Atlanta, GA 30324. TEL 404-881-1141, FAX 404-881-0074, custserv@straffordpub.com.

344.04 NZL ISSN 1176-631X
NEW ZEALAND. HEALTH AND DISABILITY COMMISSIONER. CASE NOTES. Text in English. 2006. biennial. NZD 29.75 (effective 2007). **Document type:** *Government.*
Published by: Office of the Health and Disability Commissioner, PO Box 1791, Auckland, New Zealand. TEL 64-9-3731060, FAX 64-9-3731061, hdc@hdc.org.nz.

362.1 NZL
NEW ZEALAND HEALTH AND DISABILITY SECTOR CONTACTS. Text in English. 1990. irreg.
Former titles (until 2005): New Zealand Health and Disability Sector Directory (Online); (until 2003): Health and Disability Sector in New Zealand (Online) (1174-7811); Which superseded in part (in 1998): Health Sector in New Zealand (1173-9398); Which was formerly (until 1995): Health Link (0114-9725)
Media: Online - full text.
Published by: New Zealand Ministry of Health, Box 5013, Wellington, New Zealand. TEL 64-4-4962000, FAX 64-4-4962340, emailmoh@moh.govt.nz, http://moh.govt.nz.

614 NZL ISSN 0112-0212
NEW ZEALAND JOURNAL OF ENVIRONMENTAL HEALTH. Text in English. 1952. q. NZD 45 (effective 2008). adv. bk.rev. charts; illus. **Document type:** *Journal, Academic/Scholarly.*
Former titles (until 1982): New Zealand Environmental Health Inspector (0110-4969); (until 1978): New Zealand Sanitarian (0048-0142)
—CCC.
Published by: New Zealand Institute of Environmental Health, PO Box 374, Paraparaumu, 5254, New Zealand. info@nzieh.org.nz, http://www.nzieh.org.nz.

NEW ZEALAND. LAND TRANSPORT SAFETY AUTHORITY. RULES. *see* TRANSPORTATION

NEW ZEALAND. MONTHLY SURVEILLANCE REPORT. *see* MEDICAL SCIENCES—Communicable Diseases

614 616.9 NZL ISSN 1176-2888
RA643.7.N45
NEW ZEALAND PUBLIC HEALTH SURVEILLANCE REPORT. Text in English. 2003 (Spr.). q. free. abstr.; charts; stat. 8 p./no.; back issues avail. **Document type:** *Bulletin, Trade.* **Description:** Contains surveillance, outbreak and research reports.
Formed by the merger of (1994-2003): Lablink (1173-1591); Which incorporated (1991-1994): Antimicrobial Newsletter (1170-8875); (1994-2003): New Zealand Public Health Report (1173-0250); Which was formerly (1991-1994): Communicable Disease New Zealand Weekly (1171-8064); Which superseded in part (1992-1992): C A B Current Awareness Bulletin (1171-722X)
Related titles: Online - full text ed.: free.
Indexed: C06, C07, C08, CINAHL, EMBASE, ExcerpMed, INZP, R10, Reac, SCOPUS.
—BLDSC (6096.835900). **CCC.**
Published by: Institute of Environmental Science & Research Ltd., Kenepuru Science Centre, 34 Kenepuru Dr, PO Box 50-348, Porirua, 5240, New Zealand. TEL 64-4-9140700, FAX 64-4-9140770, enquiries@esr.cri.nz, http://www.esr.cri.nz. Circ: 4,700.

NEW ZEALAND. STATISTICS NEW ZEALAND. DISTRICT HEALTH BOARD FINANCIAL STATISTICS. *see* BUSINESS AND ECONOMICS—Public Finance, Taxation

NICOTINE & TOBACCO RESEARCH. *see* TOBACCO

613 NLD ISSN 1876-8679
NIEUWSBRIEF M G M. (Meldpuntennetwerk Gezondheid en Milieu) Text in Dutch. 200?. s-a. EUR 20 membership (effective 2010).
Formerly (until 2007): Nieuwsbrief M N G M (1873-9547)
Published by: Meldpunt Gezondheid en Milieu, Regulierenring 9, Bunnik, 3981 LA, Netherlands. TEL 31-30-2430872, FAX 31-30-2430883, info@meldpuntgezondheidenmilieu.nl, http://www.meldpuntgezondheidenmilieu.nl.

NIHON HOUSHASEN ANZEN KANRI GAKKAISHI/JAPANESE JOURNAL OF RADIATION SAFETY MANAGEMENT. *see* PHYSICS—Nuclear Physics

614 JPN ISSN 0546-1766
CODEN: NKEZA4
NIHON KOSHU EISEI ZASSHI/JAPANESE JOURNAL OF PUBLIC HEALTH. Text in Japanese; Summaries in English, Japanese. 1954. m. adv. **Document type:** *Journal, Academic/Scholarly.*
Indexed: A22, ChemAb, EMBASE, ExcerpMed, F09, INI, INIS AtomInd, IndMed, JPI, MEDLINE, P30, R10, Reac, SCOPUS.
—BLDSC (4658.400000), CASDDS, GNLM, IE, Infotrieve, Ingenta.
Published by: Nihon Koshu Eisei Gakkai/Japanese Society of Public Health, 1-29-8, Shinjuku, Shinjuku-ku, Tokyo, 160-0022, Japan. TEL 81-3-33524338, FAX 81-3-33524605, http://www.jsph.jp/.

NIZHEGORODSKII MEDITSINSKII ZHURNAL. *see* MEDICAL SCIENCES

362.1 613 614 SWE
NORDISK HAELSA; ett nyhetsblad fraan nordiska haelsovaardshoegskolan. Text in Swedish. 1986. irreg. free. back issues avail. **Document type:** *Newsletter, Trade.*
Former titles (until 1996): N H V-Bulletinen (Print Edition) (1101-0924); (until 1990): Nordisk Haelsobulletin (1100-0430)
Media: Online - full content.
Published by: Nordiska Hoegskolan foer Folkhaelsovetenskap/The Nordic School of Public Health, Nya Varvat Byggnad 25, PO Box 12133, Goeteborg, 40242, Sweden. TEL 46-31-693900, FAX 46-31-691777, administration@nhv.se.

614 NOR ISSN 1504-3614
➤ **NORDISK TIDSKRIFT FOR HELSEFORSKNING.** Text in Danish, Norwegian, Swedish. 2005. s-a. NOK 300 to individuals; NOK 500 to institutions (effective 2010). bk.rev. **Document type:** *Journal, Academic/Scholarly.* **Description:** Nordic magazine for health research.
Related titles: Online - full text ed.: ISSN 1891-2982. 2009. free (effective 2011).
Published by: Hoegskolen i Bodoe, Enhet for Sykepleie- og Helsefag/ Bodoe University College, Nursing and Health, PO Box 1490, Bodoe, 8049, Norway. TEL 47-75-517200, FAX 47-75-517570, postmottak@hibo.no, http://www.hibo.no. Ed. Inger Lise Wang.

362.1 614 SWE ISSN 1404-904X
NORDISKA HOEGSKOLAN FOER FOLKHAELSOVETENSKAP. THESIS; master of science in public health. Text in Multiple languages. 2000. irreg., latest vol.1, 2010. SEK 150 per issue (effective 2011). back issues avail. **Document type:** *Monographic series, Academic/Scholarly.*
Related titles: Online - full text ed.: 2007.
Published by: Nordiska Hoegskolan foer Folkhaelsovetenskap/The Nordic School of Public Health, Nya Varvat Byggnad 25, PO Box 12133, Goeteborg, 40242, Sweden. TEL 46-31-693900, FAX 46-31-691777, administration@nhv.se.

614 NOR ISSN 0803-2491
NORSK EPIDEMIOLOGI/NORWEGIAN JOURNAL OF EPIDEMIOLOGY. Text in English, Norwegian. 1991. q. **Document type:** *Journal, Academic/Scholarly.*
Related titles: Online - full text ed.: ISSN 1891-5477. free (effective 2011).
Indexed: A01, A36, CA, CABA, D01, E12, EMBASE, ExcerpMed, GH, H05, LT, N02, N03, R10, Reac, S13, S16, SCOPUS, T02, T05, W11.
—BLDSC (6136.100000), IE. **CCC.**
Published by: Norsk Forening for Epidemiologi/Norwegian Epidemiological Society, c/o Competence Center for Clinical Research, AHH, Haukeland Hospital, Bergen, 5021, Norway. nofe@medisin.ntnu.no. Ed. Trond Flaten.

NORSK V V S. *see* HEATING, PLUMBING AND REFRIGERATION

362.1 USA ISSN 1536-9102
➤ **NORTHWEST PUBLIC HEALTH.** Text in English. 19??. s-a. back issues avail. **Document type:** *Journal, Academic/Scholarly.* **Description:** Provides information for public health practitioners, academicians, policy makers and others interested in creating the conditions that keep the public healthy.
Formerly (until 2001): Washington Public Health
Related titles: Online - full text ed.: ISSN 1536-9110. 2001. free (effective 2011).
Indexed: A34, A36, C06, C07, CABA, D01, E12, GH, H17, N02, N03, P33, P39, R08, R12, T05, W10, W11.
Published by: University of Washington, School of Public Health and Community Medicine, 1107 NE 45th St, Ste 400, Seattle, WA 98105. TEL 206-685-2617, FAX 206-543-9345, publichealth@uw.edu, http://sph.washington.edu/. Ed. Susan Allan.

➤ **NORWAY. JUSTISDEPARTEMENTET. DIREKTORATET FOR SAMFUNNSSIKKERHET OG BEREDSKAP. AARSBERETNING.** *see* FIRE PREVENTION

362.1 PRT ISSN 1647-3450
▼ **NOSSASAUDE.** Text in Portuguese. 2009. s-a. **Document type:** *Magazine, Consumer.*
Published by: Instituto de Administracao da Saude e Assuntos Sociais, Rua das Pretas 1, Funchal, Madeira 9004-515, Portugal. TEL 351-291-281421, http://iasaude.sras.gov-madeira.pt.

362.1 344.5 FRA ISSN 1770-1538
LE NOUVEAU GUIDE PRATIQUE DU RESPONSABLE DE LA SECURITE. Cover title: Le Responsable de la Securite. Text in French. 1994. 2 base vols. plus q. updates. looseleaf. EUR 196 base vol(s). (effective 2010). **Document type:** *Trade.*
Published by: Editions Dalian (Subsidiary of: Wolters Kluwer France), 1 Rue Eugene et Armand Peugeot, B P 720, Rueil Malmaison, 92856 Cedex, France. TEL 33-8-25080800, FAX 33-1-76734802, dalian@dalian.tm.fr, http://www.editions-dalian.fr/.

NUCLEAR PLANT JOURNAL. *see* ENERGY—Nuclear Energy

NUCLEAR TECHNOLOGY & RADIATION PROTECTION. *see* ENERGY—Nuclear Energy

614 DNK ISSN 1600-3373
NYHEDSBREV OM ULYKKESFORSKNING & FOREBYGGELSE. Text in Danish. 2000. 3/yr. free. back issues avail. **Document type:** *Newsletter, Consumer.*
Related titles: Online - full text ed.
Published by: Statens Institut for Folkesundhed, Syddansk Universitet/ National Institute of Public Health at Syddansk University (Subsidiary of: Syddansk Universitet/University of Southern Denmark), Oester Farimagsgade 5 A, Copenhagen K, 1399, Denmark. TEL 45-39-207777, FAX 45-39-208010, sif@si-folkesundhed.dk, http://www.si-folkesundhed.dk. Ed. Hanne Moeller. Circ: 800.

O E C D HEALTH WORKING PAPERS. (Organization for Economic Cooperation and Development) *see* MEDICAL SCIENCES

O E C D ILIBRARY: QUESTIONS SOCIALES/MIGRATIONS/SANTE. (Organisation for Economic Cooperation and Development) *see* SOCIAL SCIENCES: COMPREHENSIVE WORKS

O E C D SOCIAL ISSUES/MIGRATION/HEALTH ILIBRARY. (Organisation for Economic Cooperation and Development) *see* SOCIAL SCIENCES: COMPREHENSIVE WORKS

THE O E M REPORT. (Occupational and Environmental Medicine) *see* OCCUPATIONAL HEALTH AND SAFETY

O P I ISSUES NOTES. *see* SOCIAL SERVICES AND WELFARE

O P I POLICY BRIEFS. *see* SOCIAL SERVICES AND WELFARE

362.1 ESP ISSN 2013-2115
OBSERVATORI DE SEGURETAT VIARIA DE CATALUNYA. Text in Catalan. 2006. q. **Document type:** *Bulletin, Government.*
Published by: Generalitat de Catalunya, Observatori de Seguretat Viaria de Catalunya, Carrer de la Diputacion, 355, Barcelona, 08009, Spain. TEL 34-93-5512000, http://www.gencat.cat/.

OFFICE OF HEALTH ECONOMICS. ANNUAL LECTURE. *see* MEDICAL SCIENCES

362.2966 IRL ISSN 1649-9689
OFFICE OF TOBACCO CONTROL. ANNUAL REPORT/OIFIG UM RIALU TOBAC. TUARASCAIL BHLIANTUIL. Text in English, Gaelic. 2004. a.
Published by: Ireland. Office of Tobacco Control, Willow House, Millennium Park, Naas, Co Kildare, Ireland. TEL 353-45-852700, FAX 353-45-852799, info@otc.ie.

OFTALMOLOGIA SOCIALE; rivista di sanita pubblica. *see* HANDICAPPED—Visually Impaired

OKLAHOMA HEALTH STATISTICS. *see* PUBLIC HEALTH AND SAFETY—Abstracting, Bibliographies, Statistics

614 NLD ISSN 1871-7896
OMRING PLUS. Text in Dutch. 199?. 3/yr.
Formerly (until 2005): Thuiszorg Plus (Ed. De Omring) (1572-2821)
Published by: Zorgorganisatie Omring, Nieuwe Steen 36, Hoorn, 1625 HV, Netherlands. TEL 31-229-206706, http://www.omring.nl. Circ: 55,000.

ON SAFETY. *see* CONSUMER EDUCATION AND PROTECTION

362.18 796 USA ISSN 1556-956X
ON SCENE (LAKEWOOD); the journal of outdoor emergency care. Text in English. 2005 (Sum.). a. USD 25 per vol. domestic to non-members; USD 40 per vol. foreign to non-members; free to members (effective 2006). adv. **Document type:** *Magazine, Trade.*
Indexed: SD.
Published by: National Ski Patrol System, Inc., 133 S Van Gordon St Ste 100, Lakewood, CO 80228-1700. TEL 303-988-1111, FAX 303-988-3005, nsp@nsp.org, http://www.nsp.org. Ed. Wendy Schrupp. Adv. contact Mark Dorsey.

344.04 340 CAN ISSN 1910-3506
ON THE ACCESS TO INFORMATION ACT AND THE PRIVACY ACT. ANNUAL REPORT. Text in English. 1992. a. **Document type:** *Government.*
Former titles (until 2003): On the Administration of the Access to Information Act and the Privacy Act. Annual Reports (Print) (1207-0513); (until 1994): On the Administration of the Access to Information Act and the Privacy Act. Annual Reports (1207-0505); Which was formed by the 1992 merger of: On the Administration of the Access to Information Act. Annual Report (1483-152X); (1990-1992): On the Administration of the Privacy Act. Annual Report (1483-1538); Which superseded in part (in 1989): On the Administration of the Access to Information Act and the Privacy Act. Annual Report (1483-1511); Which was formerly (until 1987): On Access to Information and Protection of Privacy. Annual Report (1483-149X)
Media: Online - full text.
Published by: Health Canada/Sante Canada, Address Locator 0900C2, Ottawa, ON K1A OK9, Canada. TEL 613-957-2991, 866-225-0709, FAX 613-941-5366, info@www.hc-sc.gc.ca.

P

ON THE SAFETY PERFORMANCE OF THE CANADIAN NUCLEAR POWER INDUSTRY. ANNUAL C N S C STAFF REPORT FOR (YEAR). *see* ENERGY—Nuclear Energy

362.1 CAN ISSN 1713-3610
ONTARIO TRAUMA REGISTRY REPORT. INJURY DEATHS IN ONTARIO. Text in English. 1996. a. **Document type:** *Report, Trade.*
Former titles (until 1999): Injury Deaths in Ontario (1489-8969)
Related titles: Online - full text ed.: ISSN 1910-2097. 2002.
Published by: Canadian Institute for Health Information/Institut Canadien d'Information sur la Sante, 377 Dalhousie St, Ste 200, Ottawa, ON K1N 9N8, Canada. TEL 613-241-7860, FAX 613-241-8120, http://www.cihi.ca.

362.1 CAN ISSN 1490-8514
RD93.9.C2
ONTARIO TRAUMA REGISTRY REPORT. MAJOR INJURY IN ONTARIO. Text in English. 1998. a., latest 2004.
Related titles: Online - full text ed.: ISSN 1719-9344. 2002.
Published by: Canadian Institute for Health Information/Institut Canadien d'Information sur la Sante, 377 Dalhousie St, Ste 200, Ottawa, ON K1N 9N8, Canada. TEL 613-241-7860, FAX 613-241-8120, http://www.cihi.ca.

▼ **THE OPEN DRUG SAFETY JOURNAL.** *see* PHARMACY AND PHARMACOLOGY

614 NLD ISSN 1874-2971
RA648.5
➤ **THE OPEN EPIDEMIOLOGY JOURNAL.** Text in English. 2008. irreg. free (effective 2011). **Document type:** *Journal, Academic/Scholarly.* **Description:** Covers all areas of epidemiology related to preventive medicine and public health.
Media: Online - full text.
Indexed: A01, ESPM, NSA, P30, RiskAb, SCOPUS.
Published by: Bentham Open (Subsidiary of: Bentham Science Publishers Ltd.), PO Box 294, Bussum, AG 1400, Netherlands. TEL 31-35-6923800, FAX 31-35-6980150, subscriptions@bentham.org.

362.1 NLD ISSN 1874-9240
RA421
➤ **THE OPEN HEALTH SERVICES AND POLICY JOURNAL.** Text in English. 2008. irreg. free (effective 2011). **Document type:** *Journal, Academic/Scholarly.* **Description:** Covers the research, organization, planning, evaluation, management, financing, policy, and provision of health services and healthcare.
Media: Online - full text.
Indexed: ESPM, H05, P30, T02.
Published by: Bentham Open (Subsidiary of: Bentham Science Publishers Ltd.), PO Box 294, Bussum, AG 1400, Netherlands. TEL 31-35-6923800, FAX 31-35-6980150, subscriptions@bentham.org. Ed. Stephen S Coughlin.

613 USA ISSN 2162-2477
▼ ➤ **OPEN JOURNAL OF PREVENTIVE MEDICINE.** Abbreviated title: O J P M. Text in English. 2011. q. USD 156 (effective 2011). **Document type:** *Journal, Academic/Scholarly.* **Description:** Provides a platform for scientists and academicians all over the world to promote, share, and discuss various new issues and developments in different areas of preventive medicine.
Related titles: Online - full text ed.: ISSN 2162-2485. free (effective 2011).
Published by: Scientific Research Publishing, Inc., PO Box 54821, Irvine, CA 92619. service@scirp.org.

362.1 NLD ISSN 1876-2166
RC963
➤ **THE OPEN OCCUPATIONAL HEALTH & SAFETY JOURNAL.** Text in English. 2008. irreg. free (effective 2009). **Document type:** *Journal, Academic/Scholarly.* **Description:** Covers all areas of basic and applied research on occupational health and safety and work accidents prevention.
Media: Online - full text.
Indexed: ESPM.
Published by: Bentham Open (Subsidiary of: Bentham Science Publishers Ltd.), PO Box 294, Bussum, AG 1400, Netherlands. TEL 31-35-6923800, FAX 31-35-6980150, subscriptions@bentham.org. Ed. Pedro M Arezes.

362.1 NLD ISSN 1874-9445
RA421
➤ **THE OPEN PUBLIC HEALTH JOURNAL.** Text in English. 2008. irreg. free (effective 2011). **Document type:** *Journal, Academic/Scholarly.*
Media: Online - full text.
Indexed: A36, CABA, E12, ESPM, F08, F12, GH, H05, P30, P33, P39, R08, R12, T02, T05.
Published by: Bentham Open (Subsidiary of: Bentham Science Publishers Ltd.), PO Box 294, Bussum, AG 1400, Netherlands. TEL 31-35-6923800, FAX 31-35-6980150, subscriptions@bentham.org.

➤ **OPHTHALMIC EPIDEMIOLOGY.** *see* MEDICAL SCIENCES—Ophthalmology And Optometry

613 USA ISSN 2151-898X
ORAL HEALTH RESOURCE BULLETIN. Text in English. 1997. irreg. free (effective 2009). back issues avail. **Document type:** *Bulletin, Trade.*
Formerly (until 2003): M C H Program Interchange
Media: Online - full text. **Related titles:** Print ed.: ISSN 2151-8971.
Published by: Georgetown University, National Maternal and Child Oral Health Resource Center, PO Box 571272, Washington, DC 20057. TEL 202-784-9771, FAX 202-784-9777, OHRCinfo@georgetown.edu.

ORGANISATION MONDIALE DE LA SANTE. SERIE DE RAPPORTS TECHNIQUES. *see* MEDICAL SCIENCES

362.1 CAN ISSN 1703-7719
ORGANISATION NATIONALE DE LA SANTE AUTOCHTONE. RAPPORT ANNUEL. Text in French. 2002. a. **Document type:** *Report, Trade.*
Related titles: Online - full text ed.: ISSN 1912-2292. 2001; ◆ English ed.: National Aboriginal Health Organization. Annual Report. ISSN 1703-7697; Inuktitut ed.: Arragutamat Titirarksimajuliunguvaktut. ISSN 1703-7700. 2002.
Published by: National Aboriginal Health Organization (N A H O)/Organisation Nationale de la Sante Autochtone (O N S A), 220 Laurier Ave W. Ste 1200, Ottawa, ON K1P 5Z9, Canada. TEL 613-237-9462, 877-602-4445, FAX 613-237-1810, naho@naho.ca, http://www.naho.ca/english.

ORGANISATIONS CONCERNED WITH HEALTH AND SAFETY INFORMATION. *see* BUSINESS AND ECONOMICS—Trade And Industrial Directories

ORGANIZACION MUNDIAL DE LA SALUD. SERIE DE INFORMES TECNICOS. *see* MEDICAL SCIENCES

613 CAN ISSN 1715-9040
OUR HEALTH. Text in English. 2006. q. free (effective 2006). **Document type:** *Magazine, Consumer.* **Description:** Distributed in medical facilities and doctors' offices throughout Eastern Newfoundland.
Published by: (Eastern Health), Wanda Cuff Young, Inc., 842 Conception Bay Hwy, Ste 1, Conception Bay S, NF A1X 7T4, Canada. TEL 709-834-7977, 877-834-7977, FAX 709-834-4650, admin@wandacuffyoung.ca, http://www.wandacuffyoung.ca/ Index.asp. Ed. Susan Bonnell. Circ: 40,000.

613.9 USA ISSN 0737-3732
RG136.A1
OUTLOOK (SEATTLE); reproductive health. Text in English. 1983. q. free (effective 2010). back issues avail. **Document type:** *Newsletter, Academic/Scholarly.*
Related titles: Online - full text ed.: free (effective 2010); Spanish ed.; Portuguese ed.; Russian ed.; Chinese ed.; Indonesian ed.
Indexed: GW, P48, P50, P52, P56, PAIS, PQC.
Published by: Program for Appropriate Technology in Health, PO Box 900922, Seattle, WA 98109. TEL 206-285-3500, FAX 206-285-6619, info@path.org.

362.1 NZL ISSN 1177-2336
P H O YEARBOOK. (Public Health Organisation) Text in English. 2004. a.
Published by: New Zealand Ministry of Health, Box 5013, Wellington, New Zealand. TEL 64-4-4962000, FAX 64-4-4962340, emailmoh@moh.govt.nz, http://moh.govt.nz.

P P S ALERT FOR LONG TERM CARE; a journal tool for the MDS or RN coordinator. (Prospective Payment System) *see* HEALTH FACILITIES AND ADMINISTRATION

327.1747 USA
P S R MONITOR (ONLINE). Text in English. 1984. m. free to members. **Document type:** *Newsletter, Trade.*
Formerly: P S R Monitor (Print)
Media: E-mail.
Published by: Physicians for Social Responsibility, 1875 Connecticut Ave, NW, Ste 1012, Washington, DC 20009-5747. TEL 202-667-4260, FAX 202-667-4201, psrnatl@psr.org, http://www.psr.org. Ed. Meg Duskin. Circ: 5,000.

614.8 USA ISSN 0894-6264
R727
P S R REPORTS. Text in English. 1979. 4/yr. membership (effective 2005). adv. bk.rev. **Document type:** *Newsletter.* **Description:** Articles on the health and environmental impact of nuclear war, the nuclear arms race and military spending.
Formerly: P S R Newsletter
Published by: Physicians for Social Responsibility, 1875 Connecticut Ave, NW, Ste 1012, Washington, DC 20009-5747. psrnatl@psr.org. Ed. Meg Duskin. Circ: 25,000.

362.1 CZE ISSN 1804-7416
▼ **PACIENTSKE LISTY.** Text in Czech. 2009. m. CZK 180 (effective 2011). adv. **Document type:** *Magazine, Consumer.*
Published by: Mlada Fronta, Mezi Vodami 1952/9, Prague 4, 14300, Czech Republic. TEL 420-2-25276201, FAX 420-2-25276222, online@mf.cz, http://www.mf.cz. Ed. Dana Frantalova. Adv. contact Lenka Mihulkova.

PACIFIC DIET ADVISORY LEAFLET. *see* NUTRITION AND DIETETICS

362.1 610 COK ISSN 1015-7867
RA557
➤ **PACIFIC HEALTH DIALOG.** Text in English. 1994. s-a. (Mar. & Sep.). USD 69 (effective 2009). back issues avail. **Document type:** *Monographic series, Academic/Scholarly.* **Description:** Publishes original articles, brief communications, case reports, reviews, perspectives and other information and news relevant to community health and clinical medicine in the Pacific region. Audience include doctors, nurses, administrators, educators, and public health professionals.
Indexed: C06, C07, EMBASE, ExcerpMed, MEDLINE, P30, R10, Reac, SCOPUS.
—BLDSC (6329.438500), IE, Infotrieve, Ingenta. **CCC.**
Published by: Health Research Council of the Pacific Ltd., c/o Roro Daniel, Ministry of Health, PO Box 109, Rarotonga, Cook Isl. http://www.hrcp.org.fj/. Ed. Sitaleki A Finau. Circ: 1,500.

362.1 NZL ISSN 1178-6167
PACIFIC HEALTH REVIEW. Text in English. 2007. q. free to qualified personnel (effective 2009). back issues avail.
Media: Online - full text.
Published by: Research Review Ltd., N Shore Mail Centre, PO Box 100116, Auckland, New Zealand. TEL 64-9-4102277, info@researchreview.co.nz.

362.1 USA
PAINPATHWAYS; official magazine of the world institute of pain. Text in English. 2008. q. USD 20 (effective 2010). adv. illus. **Document type:** *Magazine, Consumer.* **Description:** For acute, chronic and cancer pain management. It's a resource for patients, caregivers and physicians seeking current research and therapies.
Address: 145 Kimel Park Dr, Ste 350, Winston-Salem, NC 27103. TEL 336-714-8389, info@painpathways.org. Ed. Richard L Rauck.

614 PAK ISSN 0030-9834
PAKISTAN JOURNAL OF HEALTH. Text in English. 1951. biennial. complementary. adv. bk.rev. charts; illus.; stat. **Document type:** *Journal, Academic/Scholarly.*
Related titles: CD-ROM ed.
Indexed: ChemAb, ExtraMED, P30.
Published by: College of Community Medicine, 6 Birdwood Rd., Lahore, Pakistan. TEL 92-42-7583945, FAX 92-42-7586395, jphpk@yahoo.com. Ed. Dr. Ilyas Ahmed Faridi. Circ: 1,000 (paid).

362.1 USA ISSN 1012-9685
PAN AMERICAN HEALTH ORGANIZATION. PROPOSED PROGRAM AND BUDGET ESTIMATES. Text in English. 19??. a. **Document type:** *Journal, Trade.*
Formerly (until 1959): Pan American Health Organization. Proposed Program and Budget of the Region of the Americas
—CCC.
Published by: Pan American Health Organization/Organizacion Panamericana de la Salud (Subsidiary of: World Health Organization/ Organisation Mondiale de la Sante), 525 23rd St, NW, Washington, DC 20037. TEL 202-974-3000, FAX 202-974-3663, paho@pmds.com, http://www.paho.org.

362.1 614 USA ISSN 1020-9492
PAN AMERICAN HEALTH ORGANIZATION. SCIENTIFIC AND TECHNICAL PUBLICATION. Text in English. 1953. irreg., latest vol.1, no.622, 2007. price varies. back issues avail. **Document type:** *Monographic series, Academic/Scholarly.*
Formerly: Pan American Health Organization. Scientific Publication (0555-8913)
Related titles: Online - full text ed.: free (effective 2010); Spanish ed.
—BLDSC (8176.909500), IE, Ingenta. **CCC.**
Published by: Pan American Health Organization/Organizacion Panamericana de la Salud (Subsidiary of: World Health Organization/ Organisation Mondiale de la Sante), 525 23rd St, NW, Washington, DC 20037. TEL 202-974-3000, FAX 202-974-3663, paho@pmds.com, http://www.paho.org.

PAN AMERICAN SANITARY BUREAU. ANNUAL REPORT OF THE DIRECTOR; promoting health, well-being and human security. *see* MEDICAL SCIENCES

614.4 POL ISSN 0035-7715
CODEN: RPZHAW
PANSTWOWY ZAKLAD HIGIENY. ROCZNIKI. Short title: Roczniki P Z H. Text in Polish; Summaries in English. 1950. q. USD 165 foreign (effective 2003). bk.rev. abstr.; charts; illus.; stat. index. **Document type:** *Journal, Academic/Scholarly.* **Description:** Covers hygiene, toxicology, food sciences, environment.
Indexed: A32, A34, A35, A36, A37, A38, AgBio, AgrAg, AgrForAb, AgrLib, B21, BA, C25, CABA, ChemAb, D01, DentInd, E12, EMBASE, ESPM, ExcerpMed, F08, F09, F12, FS&TA, GH, H&SSA, H16, I11, INIS AtomInd, IndMed, IndVet, LT, MEDLINE, MaizeAb, N02, N03, N04, O01, OR, P30, P33, P37, P38, P39, PHN&I, PN&I, PollutAb, R07, R08, R10, R11, R13, RA&MP, RM&VM, RRTA, Reac, S12, S13, S16, SCOPUS, SWRA, SoyAb, T05, TriticAb, VS, W10, W11.
—CASDDS, GNLM, INIST.
Published by: Panstwowy Zaklad Higieny/National Institute of Hygiene, Ul Chocimska 24, Warsaw, 00791, Poland. TEL 48-22-5421327. Ed. Kazimiera Cwiek Ludwicka. **Dist. by:** Ars Polona, Obroncow 25, Warsaw 03933, Poland. TEL 48-22-8261201, books119@arspolona.com.pl.

613 360 CAN ISSN 1719-5624
LE PARTENAIRE. Text in French. 2003. irreg. **Document type:** *Monographic series, Consumer.*
Media: Online - full text.
Published by: L' Agence de Developpement de Reseaux Locaux de Services de Sante et de Services Sociaux de l'Estrie, 300, rue King Est, bureau 300, Sherbrooke, PQ, Canada. TEL 819-566-7861.

614 IRL ISSN 0738-3991
R727.3
➤ **PATIENT EDUCATION AND COUNSELING.** Text in English. 1979. 15/yr. EUR 2,369 in Europe to institutions; JPY 314,200 in Japan to institutions; USD 2,648 elsewhere to institutions (effective 2012). bk.rev. back issues avail.; reprints avail. **Document type:** *Journal, Academic/Scholarly.* **Description:** For patient education researchers, managers, clinicians, and others involved in patient education and counseling services and administration.
Formerly (until 1983): Patient Counselling and Health Education (0190-2040); Incorporates (in 1986): Patient Education Reports; Which was formerly titled: Patient Education Newsletter
Related titles: Online - full text ed.: ISSN 1873-5134 (from IngentaConnect, ScienceDirect).
Indexed: A01, A03, A08, A20, A21, A22, A26, AHCMS, ASCA, ASG, ASSIA, C06, C07, C08, CA, CINAHL, CMM, CPE, CurCont, E-psyche, E03, E15, E16, EMBASE, ERA, ERI, ExcerpMed, F09, FAMLI, FamI, G10, H12, HospLI, I05, INI, IndMed, Inpharma, M12, MEDLINE, NRN, P03, P30, P34, PsycInfo, PsycholAb, R10, RI-1, RI-2, Reac, S19, S20, S21, SCI, SCOPUS, SSCI, T02, V05, W07, W09.
—BLDSC (6412.864600), GNLM, IE, Infotrieve, Ingenta, INIST. **CCC.**
Published by: Elsevier Ireland Ltd (Subsidiary of: Elsevier Science & Technology), Elsevier House, Brookvale Plaza, E. Park, Shannon, Co. Clare, Ireland. TEL 353-61-709600, FAX 353-61-709100. Eds. A Finset, Dr. L S Wissow. **Subscr. to:** Elsevier BV, Radarweg 29, PO Box 211, Amsterdam 1000 AE, Netherlands. TEL 31-20-4853757, FAX 31-20-4853432, JournalsCustomerServiceEMEA@elsevier.com, http://www.elsevier.nl.

362.1 GBR ISSN 1179-3198
▼ ➤ **PATIENT INTELLIGENCE.** Text in English. 2010. irreg. free (effective 2011). **Document type:** *Journal, Academic/Scholarly.*
Media: Online - full text.
—CCC.
Published by: Dove Medical Press Ltd., Beechfield House, Winterton Way, Macclesfield, SK11 0JL, United Kingdom. TEL 44-1625-509130, FAX 44-1625-617933. Ed. Madhu Davies.

362.1 GBR ISSN 1179-271X
▼ ➤ **PATIENT RELATED OUTCOME MEASURES.** Text in English. 2010. irreg. free (effective 2011). **Document type:** *Journal, Academic/Scholarly.*
Media: Online - full text.
—CCC.
Published by: Dove Medical Press Ltd., Beechfield House, Winterton Way, Macclesfield, SK11 0JL, United Kingdom. TEL 44-1625-509130, FAX 44-1625-617933. Ed. Robert H Howland.

➤ **PATIENT REPORTED OUTCOMES NEWSLETTER.** *see* MEDICAL SCIENCES

362.1 USA ISSN 1553-6637
PATIENT SAFETY & QUALITY HEALTHCARE. Text in English. 2004 (Jul/Sept). bi-m. free domestic to qualified personnel; USD 49.99; USD 10 per issue (effective 2005). adv. **Document type:** *Magazine, Trade.*
Published by: Lionheart Publishing, Inc., 506 Roswell St, Ste 220, Marietta, GA 30060. TEL 770-431-0867, FAX 770-432-6969, http://www.lionhrtpub.com. Ed. Susan Carr. Pub. John Llewellyn. Adv. contact Marvin Diamond TEL 770-431-0867 ext 208. B&W page USD 1,700; trim 8.375 x 10.875.

362.1 GBR ISSN 1754-9051
PATIENT SAFETY BULLETIN; emerging themes from reported incidents. Text in English. 2007. bi-m. **Document type:** *Bulletin, Trade.*
Related titles: Online - full text ed.: ISSN 1754-906X. free.
Published by: National Patient Saftey Agency, 4-8 Maple St, London, W1T 5HD, United Kingdom. TEL 44-20-79279500, FAX 44-20-79279501, enquiries@npsa.nhs.uk.

362.1 USA ISSN 1541-2938
PATIENT SAFETY MONITOR. Text in English. 2000 (Mar.). w. free. **Document type:** *Newsletter, Trade.*
Media: Online - full text.
Published by: H C Pro, Inc., 200 Hoods Ln, PO Box 1168, Marblehead, MA 01945. TEL 781-639-1872, FAX 781-639-7857, customerservice@hcpro.com.

614 610 IRN ISSN 1735-8132
PAYAVARD SALAMAT. Text in Persian, Modern; Abstracts in English, Persian, Modern. 2007. q. **Document type:** *Journal, Academic/ Scholarly.*
Related titles: Online - full text ed.: ISSN 2008-2665.
Published by: Danishgah-i Ulum-i Pizishki-i Tihran/Tehran University of Medical Sciences, Faculty of Allied Medical Sciences, No.13 Fare Danesh Alley, Ghods St., Keshavarz Blv., Tehran, Iran. TEL 98-21-88997052.

362.1 ITA ISSN 1970-8165
PEDIATRIA PREVENTIVA E SOCIALE. Text in Italian, English. 2006. q. EUR 77 in Europe (effective 2009). **Document type:** *Journal, Academic/Scholarly.*
Published by: (Societa Italiana di Pediatria Preventiva e Sociale (S I P P S)), Mattioli 1885 SpA, Via Coduro 1, Fidenza, PR 43036, Italy. TEL 39-0524-84547, FAX 39-0524-84751, http://www.mattioli1885.com. Ed. Guido Brusoni. Circ: 8,000.

362.11 USA ISSN 1941-7144
PENNSYLVANIA PATIENT SAFETY ADVISORY. Text in English. 2004. q. free (effective 2008).
Formerly: Patient Safety Advisory (1552-8596)
Media: Online - full content.
Indexed: C06, C07.
Published by: Pennsylvania Patient Safety Authority, PO Box 8410, Harrisburg, PA 17105. TEL 717-346-0469, FAX 717-346-1090, patientsafetyauthority@state.pa.us.

PERSONNEL DE LA C C S N SUR LE RENDEMENT EN MATIERE DE SURETE DES CENTRALES NUCLEAIRES AU CANADA. RAPPORT ANNUEL. (Commission Canadienne de Surete Nucleaire) *see* ENERGY—Nuclear Energy

628 MEX ISSN 0188-0012
PERSPECTIVAS EN SALUD PUBLICA. Text in English, Spanish. 1987. irreg. **Document type:** *Monographic series, Government.*

Published by: Instituto Nacional de Salud Publica, Av Universidad 655, Col Santa Maria Ahuacatitlan, Cerrada Los Pinos y Caminera, Cuernavaca, MORELOS 62100, Mexico. TEL 52-777-1012900, http://www.insp.mx.

614.4 USA ISSN 1020-5551
RA442
PERSPECTIVES IN HEALTH. Text in English. 1996. s-a. back issues avail. **Document type:** *Magazine, Consumer.*
Related titles: Online - full text ed.: ISSN 1564-0930; Spanish ed.: Perspectivas de Salud. ISSN 1020-556X.
Indexed: A26, G05, G06, G07, H12, I04, I05, P30.
—CCC.
Published by: Pan American Health Organization/Organizacion Panamericana de la Salud (Subsidiary of: World Health Organization/ Organisation Mondiale de la Sante), 525 23rd St, NW, Washington, DC 20037. TEL 202-974-3000, FAX 202-974-3663, paho@pmds.com.

PERSPECTIVES IN PUBLIC HEALTH. *see* SOCIAL SERVICES AND WELFARE

362.1 FRA ISSN 1481-9384
RC963.A1
PERSPECTIVES INTERDISCIPLINAIRES SUR LE TRAVAIL ET LA SANTE. Text in French. 1999. irreg. free (effective 2011). **Document type:** *Journal, Academic/Scholarly.*
Media: Online - full text.
Indexed: CA, P03, PsycInfo, S02, S03, SSA, SociolAb, T02.
—CCC.
Published by: Perspectives Interdisciplinaires sur le Travail et la Sante (PISTES), 30 Rue Olivier Noyer, Paris, 75680, France. TEL 33-1-40443119, FAX 33-1-40441414. Ed. Esther Coutier.

PEST CONTROL TECHNOLOGY. *see* ENGINEERING—Chemical Engineering

614 615.902 363.179 USA ISSN 0587-5943
PESTICIDE RESIDUES IN FOOD. Text in English. 1966. a. back issues avail. **Document type:** *Report, Trade.*
Formerly: Codex Committee on Pesticide Residues. Meeting. Report
Related titles: Online - full text ed.: free (effective 2011).
Published by: Food and Agriculture Organization of the United Nations, c/o Bernan Associates, 4501 Forbes Blvd, Ste 200, Lanham, MD 20706. TEL 301-459-7666, 800-865-3457, FAX 301-459-0056, 800-865-3450, customercare@bernan.com.

362.1 DEU
➤ **PFLEGE UND GESELLSCHAFT**; Zeitschrift fuer Pflegewissenschaft. Text in German. 2000. q. EUR 48; EUR 39.50 to students; EUR 14 newsstand/cover (effective 2011). adv. bk.rev. illus. 64 p./no.; back issues avail. **Document type:** *Journal, Academic/Scholarly.* **Description:** Covers all aspects of the health care industry.
Formerly: Pflegemagazin (1439-7420)
Published by: Juventa Verlag GmbH, Ehretstr 3, Weinheim, 69469, Germany. TEL 49-6201-90200, FAX 49-6201-902013, juventa@juventa.de, http://www.juventa.de. Ed. Juliane Falk. Adv. contact Annette Hopp. Circ: 1,600 (paid and controlled).

➤ **PFLEGE- UND KRANKENHAUSRECHT**; juristische Fachinformationen fuer Pflege und Krankenhausmanagement. *see* LAW—Civil Law

614 DEU ISSN 1618-0933
PHARMA BRIEF. Text in German. 1981. 10/yr. EUR 17 domestic; EUR 32 foreign (effective 2008). bk.rev. back issues avail. **Document type:** *Newsletter, Trade.* **Description:** Provides information on drug policy, rational use and prescribing of drugs in Germany and developing nations, and the marketing practices of German pharmaceutical manufacturers in developing countries.
Related titles: Online - full text ed.: ISSN 1618-4572.
Published by: B U K O Pharma-Kampagne, August-Bebel-Str 62, Bielefeld, 33602, Germany. TEL 49-9521-60550, FAX 49-9521-63789, info@bukopharma.de. Ed. Joerg Schaaber. Circ: 2,000.

PHYSICIANS' MEDICARE GUIDE. *see* INSURANCE

362.1 IRL ISSN 1649-8844
A PICTURE OF HEALTH. Text in English. 2003. a.
Published by: Health Research Board/Bord Taighde Slainte, 73 Lower Baggot St, Dublin, 2, Ireland. TEL 353-1-6761176, FAX 353-1-6612335, hrb@hrb.ie, http://www.hrb.ie.

362.1 CAN ISSN 1705-7841
➤ **PIMATISIWIN.** Text in English. 2003. s-a. free (effective 2011). **Document type:** *Journal, Academic/Scholarly.* **Description:** Aims to promote the sharing of knowledge and research experience between researchers, health professionals, and Aboriginal leaders and community members.
Media: Online - full text.
Indexed: A36, BNNA, CA, CABA, D01, E12, GH, LT, N02, N03, P30, RRTA, S13, S16, T02, T05, TAR.
—CCC.
Published by: Native Counselling Services of Alberta, 10975 124 St, Edmonton, AB T5M 0H9, Canada. TEL 780-451-4002, FAX 780-428-0187.

344.04 USA
PITTSBURGH JOURNAL OF ENVIRONMENTAL AND PUBLIC HEALTH LAW. Abbreviated title: P J E P H L. Text in English. 2007. a. USD 10 per vol. (effective 2010). **Document type:** *Journal, Academic/Scholarly.*
Related titles: Online - full text ed.
Published by: University of Pittsburgh, School of Law, 3900 Forbes Ave, Pittsburgh, PA 15260. TEL 412-648-1490, FAX 412-648-2648, deasy@pitt.edu, http://www.law.pitt.edu/. Ed. Theresa Miller-Sporrer.

362.1 CAN ISSN 1912-0591
PLAN DES ACTIVITES GENERALES. BILAN (ANNEE). Text in French. 200?. a. **Document type:** *Journal, Trade.*
Formerly (until 2005): Bilan des Activites (Annee) et Plan d'Activites (Annee) de l'Association pour la Sante Publique du Quebec (1716-2041)
Published by: Association pour la Sante Publique du Quebec, 4126, rue St-Denis - Bureau 200, Montreal, PQ H2W 2M5, Canada. TEL 514-528-5811, FAX 514-528-5590, info@aspq.org, http://www.aspq.org/index.php.

362.1 DEU ISSN 0930-7796
PLUSPUNKT; Sicherheit und Gesundheit in der Schule. Text in German. 1972. q. EUR 7.60 (effective 2008). adv. **Document type:** *Magazine, Trade.*
Formerly (until 1976): Gib Acht Spezial (0930-780X)
Published by: Universum Verlagsanstalt GmbH KG, Taunusstr 54, Wiesbaden, 65183, Germany. TEL 49-611-90300, FAX 49-611-9030183, info@universum.de, http://www.universum.de. adv.: page EUR 2,480. Circ: 65,500 (paid).

540 362.1 POL ISSN 1231-868X
➤ **PODSTAWY I METODY OCENY SRODOWISKA PRACY/ PRINCIPLES AND METHODS OF ASSESSING THE WORKING ENVIRONMENT.** Text in Polish; Summaries in English, Polish. 1985. q. PLZ 72; PLZ 18 per issue (effective 2003). charts; illus. index. 230 p./no. 1 cols./p.; back issues avail.; reprints avail. **Document type:** *Journal, Academic/Scholarly.* **Description:** Contains complete documentation on the harmful effects of definite chemical and physical agents on the human organism, together with the justification of MAC and MAI for these agents, adopted in Poland, and methods for their determination in the working environment. Helps to assess the hazards in the working environment and to establish appropriate medical prevention.
Published by: Centralny Instytut Ochrony Pracy/Central Institute for Labour Protection, Ul Czerniakowska 16, Warsaw, 00701, Poland. TEL 48-22-6234601, FAX 48-22-6233693, oinip@ciop.pl, http://www.ciop.pl. Ed. Danuta Koradecka. Circ: 280 (paid).

362.1 USA ISSN 1947-6752
D861
POLICY ANALYSIS BRIEF; innovative approaches to peace and security from the stanley foundation. Text in English. 200?. irreg. back issues avail. **Document type:** *Newsletter, Trade.* **Description:** Aims to connect people from different backgrounds, often producing clarifying insights and innovative solutions.
Supersedes in part (in 2005): Policy Bulletin
Related titles: Online - full text ed.: ISSN 1948-5700. free (effective 2009).
Published by: The Stanley Foundation, 209 Iowa Ave, Muscatine, IA 52761. TEL 563-264-1500, FAX 563-264-0864, info@stanleyfoundation.org.

POLITFOCUS GESUNDHEITSPOLITIK. *see* POLITICAL SCIENCE

362.1 ITA ISSN 2038-7717
POLITICHE E SERVIZI SOCIALI. Text in Italian. 1992. irreg. **Document type:** *Monographic series, Academic/Scholarly.*
Published by: Franco Angeli Edizioni, Viale Monza 106, Milan, 20127, Italy. TEL 39-02-2837141, FAX 39-02-26144793, redazioni@francoangeli.it, http://www.francoangeli.it.

362.1 ITA ISSN 1590-069X
➤ **POLITICHE SANITARIE**; economia organizzazione e valutazione dei servizi sanitari. Text in Italian; Summaries in English. 2000. q. USD 130 domestic to institutions; USD 200 foreign to institutions (effective 2009). adv. bk.rev. 56 p./no.; back issues avail. **Document type:** *Journal, Academic/Scholarly.*
Related titles: Online - full text ed.: ISSN 2038-1832.
Published by: Il Pensiero Scientifico Editore, Via Bradano 3-C, Rome, 00199, Italy. TEL 39-06-862821, FAX 39-06-86282250, pensiero@pensiero.it, http://www.pensiero.it. adv.: B&W page EUR 1,033, color page EUR 1,549; 21 x 28. Circ: 700 (paid).

➤ **POLSKA AKADEMIA NAUK. KOMITET GOSPODARKI WODNEJ. PRACE I STUDIA.** *see* WATER RESOURCES

614.4 GBR ISSN 1478-7954
RA407.A1
➤ **POPULATION HEALTH METRICS.** Text in English. 2003. irreg. free (effective 2011). adv. back issues avail. **Document type:** *Journal, Academic/Scholarly.* **Description:** Focuses on the measurement of the health of populations and addresses issues relating to concepts, methods, ethics, applications and results in the areas of health state measurement and valuation, summary measures of level of population health, and inequality in population health, descriptive epidemiology at the population level, burden of disease and injury analysis, disease and risk factor modelling for populations, and comparative assessment of risks to health at population level.
Media: Online - full text.
Indexed: A01, A26, A34, A36, C06, C07, CA, CABA, EMBASE, ExcerpMed, GH, H05, I05, IndVet, N02, N03, P20, P22, P30, P33, P39, PQC, R08, R10, R12, Reac, SCOPUS, T02, T05, VS, W11.
—CCC.
Published by: BioMed Central Ltd. (Subsidiary of: Springer Science+Business Media), 236 Gray's Inn Rd, London, WC1X 8HB, United Kingdom. TEL 44-20-31922000, FAX 44-20-31922010, info@biomedcentral.com, http://www.biomedcentral.com. Eds. Alan D Lopez, Christopher J L Murray.

362.1 CAN ISSN 1719-606X
POUR MIEUX COMPRENDRE LE MODE DE TARIFICATION AU TAUX PERSONNALISE. Text in French. a. **Document type:** *Government.*
Published by: Commission de la Sante et de la Securite du Travail, CP 6056, Montreal, PQ H3C 4E1, Canada. TEL 514-906-3060, FAX 514-906-3062, http://www.csst.qc.ca/portail/fr/index.htm.

POZ; health, hope & HIV. *see* MEDICAL SCIENCES—Communicable Diseases

362.1 305.896 USA ISSN 1940-5707
PRACTICAL PROMULGATION. Text in English. 2007. s-a. **Document type:** *Newsletter, Consumer.* **Description:** Examines the role of race in the spread of HIV and AIDS. Provides resources, stories andstatistics with the aim of educating and preventing the spread of HIV in the black community.
Published by: Black Freighter Productions, PO Box 374, Blue Island, IL 60406. http://www.blkfr8r.com. Ed. Solomohn Ennis.

362.1 DEU ISSN 0170-2602
PRAEVENTION; Zeitschrift fuer Gesundheitsfoerderung. Text in German. 1978. q. EUR 24.50; EUR 7.80 newsstand/cover (effective 2010). adv. **Document type:** *Magazine, Trade.*
Published by: Fachverlag Peter Sabo, Am Sonnenberg 17, Schwabenheim, 55270, Germany. TEL 49-6130-7760, FAX 49-6130-7971, info@sabo-buch.de, http://www.sabo-buch.de. Circ: 2,150 (paid and controlled).

362.1 DEU ISSN 1861-6755
RA1
PRAEVENTION UND GESUNDHEITSFOERDERUNG. Text in German. 2006. 4/yr. EUR 333, USD 433 combined subscription to institutions (print & online eds.) (effective 2012). adv. reprint service avail. from PSC. **Document type:** *Journal, Academic/Scholarly.*
Related titles: Online - full text ed.: ISSN 1861-6763 (from IngentaConnect).
Indexed: A22, A26, A36, CABA, D01, E01, E12, GH, LT, N02, N03, R12, RRTA, S13, S16, SCOPUS, T05, W11.
—IE, Ingenta. **CCC.**
Published by: Springer (Subsidiary of: Springer Science+Business Media), Tiergartenstr 17, Heidelberg, 69121, Germany. TEL 49-6221-4870, FAX 49-6221-345229, orders-hd-individuals@springer.com, http://www.springer.com. Ed. B Badura. Circ: 670 (paid and controlled).

PRAKTIKAN. *see* MEDICAL SCIENCES

PRATIQUE. *see* COMMUNICATIONS—Postal Affairs

PRAXIS UND RECHT. *see* BUSINESS AND ECONOMICS—Personnel Management

362.1 310 CAN ISSN 1712-4077
PREGNANCY OUTCOMES. Text in English. 2001. a. **Document type:** *Government.*
Media: Online - full text.
Published by: Statistics Canada/Statistique Canada, Communications Division, 3rd Fl, R H Coats Bldg, Ottawa, ON K1A 0A6, Canada. TEL 800-263-1136, infostats@statcan.ca, http://www.statcan.gc.ca.

362.1 NZL ISSN 1172-5648
PRESCRIBER UPDATE. Text in English. 1957. s-a. **Document type:** *Magazine, Trade.* **Description:** Designed for doctors, pharmacists and other health professionals who are interested in safer, more effective use of medicines and treatments.
Which was formerly (until 1992): Clinical Services Letter (0111-6258)
Related titles: Online - full text ed.: ISSN 1179-075X. 1993.
Indexed: Inpharma, P35, R10, Reac.
—CCC.
Published by: Medsafe, Level 6, Deloitte House, 10 Brandon St, PO Box 5013, Wellington, New Zealand. TEL 64-4-4962000, FAX 64-4-8196806, becci_slyfield@moh.govt.nz.

362 USA ISSN 1939-3687
THE PRESIDENT'S EMERGENCY PLAN FOR AIDS RELIEF. Text in English. 2005. a.
Media: Online - full content.
Published by: U.S. Department of State, Office of the Global AIDS Coordinator, 2100 Pennsylvania Ave, Ste 200, Washington, DC 20522. TEL 202-663-2708, FAX 202-663-2979, SGAC_Public_Affairs@state.gov.

614.8 ESP ISSN 0034-8732
PREVENCION; revista tecnica de seguridad y salud laborales. Text in Spanish. 1962. q. EUR 43.68 domestic (effective 2007). adv. bk.rev. **Document type:** *Journal, Academic/Scholarly.*
Formerly (until 1975): Revista de Prevencion (1132-3140)
Indexed: CISA.
—CCC.
Published by: Asociacion para la Prevencion de Accidentes, Camino Portuetxe 14, Edificio Ibaeta, San Sebastian, 20018, Spain. TEL 34-943-316201, FAX 34-943-316200, apa@apa.es, http://www.apa.es. Circ: 9,000.

371 USA
RE1
PREVENT BLINDNESS AMERICA. ANNUAL REPORT. Text in English. a. **Document type:** *Corporate.*
Former titles: National Society to Prevent Blindness. Annual Report (0270-4234); National Society for the Prevention of Blindness. Report
Published by: Prevent Blindness America, 500 E Remington Rd, Schaumburg, IL 60173. TEL 847-843-2020, FAX 847-843-8458. Ed. Jody Kenyon. R&P Joan Boyes.

362.41 USA
PREVENT BLINDNESS NEWS. Text in English. 1951. 3/yr. USD 12 to members (effective 2005). illus. **Document type:** *Newsletter, Consumer.*
Former titles: National Society to Prevent Blindness. Member News; Insight (Schaumburg); Prevent Blindness News (0032-8014); Incorporates: Wise Owl News (0043-6755)
Published by: Prevent Blindness America, 500 E Remington Rd, Schaumburg, IL 60173. TEL 800-331-2020, FAX 847-843-8458. Ed. Ken West. Circ: 25,000.

362.28 USA ISSN 1546-7376
HV6545
PREVENTING SUICIDE; the national journal. Text in English. 2002 (Oct.). 3/yr. free (effective 2004). **Document type:** *Journal, Academic/Scholarly.*
Published by: National Hopeline Network, 2001 N. Beauregard St., Ste. 1200, Alexandria, VA 22311-1724. info@hopeline.com. Ed. Paul G. Quinnett. Pub. H. Reese Butler II.

362.1 USA ISSN 0899-2614
RA421
PREVENTION REPORT. Text in English. m. **Document type:** *Government.*
Published by: U.S. Department of Health and Human Services, Public Health Service, 200 Independence Ave, S W, Washington, DC 20201. TEL 202-619-0257, 877-696-6775, http://www.os.dhhs.gov/.

PREVENTIVE MEDICINE. *see* MEDICAL SCIENCES

362.1 GBR ISSN 2043-8095
▼ **PRIMARY CARE SCOTLAND.** Text in English. 2010. bi-m. free to qualified personnel (effective 2011). adv. **Document type:** *Magazine, Trade.* **Description:** Publication for general practitioners and primary care teams in Scotland.
—CCC.
Published by: Connect Publications, Studio 2001, Mile End, Seedhill Rd, Paisley, Lewes PA1 1JS, United Kingdom. TEL 44-141-5610300, FAX 44-141-5610400, info@connectcommunications.co.uk. Ed. Bruce Oxley TEL 44-141-5603050. Adv. contact Ann Craib TEL 44-141-5603021.

P

362.10993 NZL ISSN 1177-424X
PRIMARY HEALTH & COMMUNITY SERVICES N Z. Text in English. 2006. a. NZD 30 per vol. (effective 2008). adv. **Document type:** *Directory, Trade.* **Description:** Draws together the health and well being services New Zealanders depend upon, providing an indispensable resource for health professionals, community workers, health administrators, social workers, probation officers, police, school counsellors, families shifting town, and anyone seeking specific health or community services.
Published by: Cervin Publishing Ltd., PO Box 68-450, Newton, Auckland, New Zealand. TEL 64-9-3608700, FAX 64-9-3608702, info@cervinpublishing.co.nz. Circ: 8,000.

362.1 NZL ISSN 1179-1748
➤ **PRIMARY PREVENTION INSIGHTS.** Text in English. 2008. irreg. free (effective 2011). **Document type:** *Journal, Academic/Scholarly.* **Description:** Covers all aspects of primary prevention of disease and mental disorders.
Media: Online - full text.
Indexed: C06.
—CCC.
Published by: Libertas Academica Ltd., PO Box 300-874, Mairangi Bay, Auckland, 0751, New Zealand. TEL 64-9-4763930, FAX 64-9-3531397, editorial@la-press.com. Ed. Dr. Jun Ma.

362.1 CAN ISSN 1719-6671
PRINCE ALBERT PARKLAND REGIONAL HEALTH AUTHORITY. ANNUAL REPORT. Text in English. 2003. a., latest 2005. **Document type:** *Government.*
Published by: Prince Albert Parkland Regional Health Authority, 1200-24th St West, Prince Albert, SK S6V 5T4, Canada. TEL 877-800-0002, http://www.paphr.sk.ca/menu_pg.asp.

354 614 CAN
PRINCE EDWARD ISLAND. DEPARTMENT OF HEALTH AND SOCIAL SERVICES. ANNUAL REPORT. Text in English. a. **Document type:** *Government.*
Formerly: Prince Edward Island. Department of Health. Annual Report (0317-4530)
Published by: Prince Edward Island, Department of Health and Social Services, P O Box 2000, Charlottetown, PE C1A 7N8, Canada. TEL 902-368-4900, FAX 902-368-4969. Circ: 500.

362.1 AUS ISSN 1833-8704
PRINCESS ALEXANDRA HOSPITAL MEDICAL RESEARCH. Text in English. 2006. triennial. **Document type:** *Journal, Consumer.*
Related titles: Online - full text ed.: ISSN 1833-8712.
Published by: Princess Alexandra Hospital, Centres for Health Research, GPO Box 48, Brisbane, QLD 4001, Australia. TEL 61-7-3234-0111, http://www.health.qld.gov.au/pahospital/research/publications.asp.

362.1 351 SWE ISSN 1650-8475
PRIORITERINGSCENTRUM. RAPPORT. Text in Swedish. 2001. 6/yr. back issues avail. **Document type:** *Monographic series, Government.* **Description:** Contains survey an analysis by the centre as commissioned by the National Board of Health and Welfare, covering the activities of local governments and assessing compliance with Sweden's Health and Medical Services Act and Riksdag's resolutions on priority setting.
Related titles: Online - full text ed.
Published by: Landstinget i Oestergoetland, PrioriteringsCentrum/Landstinget i Oestergoetland, The National Centre for Priority Setting in Health Care, Linkoeping, SE-581 91, Sweden. TEL 46-13-222000, FAX 46-13-227799, prioriteringscentrum@lio.se, http://e.lio.se/prioriteringscentrum/.

362.188 AUS ISSN 1448-9759
PRO UTILITATE. Text in English. 2003. q. free (effective 2009). **Document type:** *Newsletter, Consumer.*
Published by: St John Ambulance Australia Historical Society, PO Box 3895, Manuka, ACT 2600, Australia. TEL 61-2-62953777, enquiries@stjohn.org.au, http://www.stjohn.org.au.

614 RUS ISSN 0869-866X
PROBLEMY SOTSIALNOI GIGIENY, ZDRAVOOKHRANENIYA, I ISTORII MEDITSINY/PROBLEMS OF SOCIAL HYGIENE, HEALTH SERVICE AND HISTORY OF MEDICINE. Text in Russian; Summaries in English. 1942. bi-m. USD 278 foreign (effective 2005). adv. bk.rev. abstr.; bibl.; charts; illus.; stat. index. **Document type:** *Journal, Academic/Scholarly.* **Description:** Discusses theoretical problems of social hygiene and public health organization, the main trends in the development of health protection, scientific bases of planning, prognosticating and management in public health service.
Formerly: Sovetskoe Zdravookhranenie (0038-5239)
Indexed: CDSP, CISA, ChemAb, DentInd, EMBASE, ExcerpMed, F09, INI, IndMed, MEDLINE, P30, RASB, RefZh, S02, S03, SCOPUS, WBSS.
—BLDSC (0133.774330), East View, GNLM, INIST. **CCC.**
Published by: Izdatel'stvo Meditsina/Meditsina Publishers, ul B Pirogovskaya, d 2, str 5, Moscow, 119435, Russian Federation. TEL 7-095-2483324, meditsina@mtu-net.ru, http://www.medlit.ru. Ed. Oleg P Shchepin. Pub. A M Stochik. R&P T Scheglova. Adv. contact O A Fadeeva TEL 7-095-923-51-40. Circ: 500. **Dist. by:** East View Information Services, 10601 Wayzata Blvd, Minneapolis, MN 55305. TEL 952-252-1201, 800-477-1005, FAX 952-252-1202, info@eastview.com, http://www.eastview.com.

613 NZL ISSN 1176-9041
PROCARE PULSE. Variant title: Pulse. Text in English. 2002. q. adv. back issues avail. **Document type:** *Magazine, Consumer.* **Description:** Features health articles from prominent health professionals, a guide to ProCare services and special programmes, answers to important medical questions and much more.
Published by: (ProCare Health Limited), Ross Blake, Ed. & Pub., PO Box 36 285, Auckland, New Zealand. TEL 64-9-4808600.

643 USA ISSN 0092-7732
KF3945.A73
PRODUCT SAFETY AND LIABILITY REPORTER; a weekly review of consumer safety developments. Text in English. 1973. w. looseleaf. USD 2,321 (effective 2010 - 2011). index. back issues avail. **Document type:** *Report, Trade.* **Description:** Contains a notification and reference service providing coverage of current administrative, legislative, judicial, and industry developments relating to product safety and product liability.
Related titles: E-mail ed.; Online - full text ed.: ISSN 1522-5259. USD 2,090 (effective 2010 - 2011).
—CCC.
Published by: The Bureau of National Affairs, Inc., 1801 S Bell St, Arlington, VA 22202. TEL 703-341-3000, 800-372-1033, FAX 703-341-4634, bnaplus@bna.com.

600 USA ISSN 0098-7530
HC110.C63
PRODUCT SAFETY LETTER. Text in English. 1972. w. looseleaf. USD 997 in North America (effective 2005). bk.rev. charts. index. 4 p./no.; Supplement avail.; back issues avail. **Document type:** *Newsletter.* **Description:** Contains information for executives concerned with government regulation of consumer products.
—CCC.
Published by: Oberle Communications, 2573 Holly Manor Dr., Ste. 110, Falls Church, VA 22043-3909. TEL 703-289-9432, FAX 703-289-3909. Ed., Pub. Sean Oberle.

362.1 GBR ISSN 2046-5025
PROFESSIONAL PEST CONTROLLER. Abbreviated title: P P C. Text in English. 1992. q. free to qualified personnel (effective 2011). adv. bk.rev. charts; illus.; tr.lit. back issues avail. **Document type:** *Magazine, Trade.* **Description:** Aims to provide readers with an unbiased, high quality and professional magazine relevant to the pest control industry.
Related titles: Online - full text ed.: ISSN 2046-5033. free (effective 2011).
Published by: British Pest Control Association, 1 Gleneagles House, S St, Vernon Gate, Derby, DE1 1UP, United Kingdom. TEL 44-1332-294288, FAX 44-1332-225101, enquiry@bpca.org.uk, http://www.bpca.org.uk. Ed. Lorraine Norton. Adv. contact Sofi Halliday TEL 44-1332-225111. Circ: 3,000.

364.163 AUS ISSN 1324-9371
PROFESSIONAL SERVICES REVIEW. ANNUAL REPORT. Text in English. 1995. a. **Document type:** *Journal, Trade.*
—CCC.
Published by: Professional Services Review, PO Box 7152, Canberra Post Business Ctr, Fyshwick, ACT 2610, Australia. TEL 61-2-61209100, FAX 61-2-61209199, enquiries@psr.gov.au, http://www.psr.gov.au.

616.9 362.1 CAN ISSN 1913-3391
PROGRAMME DE SURVEILLANCE DE L'INFECTION PAR LE VIRUS DE L'IMMUNODEFICIENCE HUMAINE VIH AU QUEBEC. Text in French. 2005. a. **Document type:** *Government.*
Published by: Institut National de Sante Publique du Quebec, 945 Av Wolfe, Quebec, PQ G1V 5B3, Canada. TEL 418-650-5115 ext 5336, FAX 418-646-9328, http://www.inspq.qc.ca.

362.1 CAN ISSN 1910-0434
PROGRAMME DES SERVICES DE SANTE NON ASSURES. RAPPORT ANNUEL. Text in French. 200?. a., latest 2004. **Document type:** *Report, Trade.*
Media: Online - full text.
Published by: Health Canada/Sante Canada, Address Locator 0900C2, Ottawa, ON K1A OK9, Canada. TEL 613-957-2991, 866-225-0709, FAX 613-941-5366, info@www.hc-sc.gc.ca, http://www.hc-sc.gc.ca.

614 USA
PROJECT HOPE ALUMNI ASSOCIATION. THE BULLETIN. Text in English. 1963. 2/yr. free (effective 2010). adv. **Document type:** *Bulletin, Trade.*
Formerly: Hope News
Related titles: Online - full text ed.: free (effective 2010).
Published by: Project HOPE, 255 Carter Hall Ln, Millwood, VA 22646. TEL 800-544-4673, http://www.projhope.org. Ed. Laura Petrosian. R&P, Adv. contact Mary Stine. Circ: 100,000.

362.1 610 USA ISSN 1535-6191
HT167
PROJECTIONS (CAMBRIDGE). Text in English. 2000. a. back issues avail. **Document type:** *Journal, Academic/Scholarly.*
Related titles: Online - full text ed.: free (effective 2011).
—BLDSC (6924.907640).
Published by: Massachusetts Institute of Technology, Department of Urband Studies & Planning, 77 Massachusetts Ave, Rm 7-346, Cambridge, MA 02139. duspinfo@mit.edu.

362.1 AUS ISSN 1834-4917
PROSPECTIVE. Text in English. 2005. irreg. **Document type:** *Newsletter, Trade.*
Media: Online - full text.
Published by: South Australia, Department of Health. Population Research and Outcome Studies Unit, PO Box 287, Adelaide, SA 5000, Australia. TEL 618-8226-7042, FAX 618-8226-6244, PROS@health.sa.gov.au.

PROSPETTIVE SOCIALI E SANITARIE. *see* SOCIAL SERVICES AND WELFARE

613.7 DEU ISSN 1610-8507
PROVITA HEALTHCARE. Text in German. 2002. 4/yr. EUR 18; EUR 4.50 newsstand/cover (effective 2006). adv. **Document type:** *Magazine, Trade.*
Published by: Muehlen Verlag, Zum Wasserbaum 13, Salzhemmendorf, 31020, Germany. TEL 49-5153-5810, FAX 49-5153-5711, muehlen-verlag@t-online.de. adv.: B&W page EUR 2,200, color page EUR 3,520. Circ: 21,560 (paid and controlled).

614.49 POL ISSN 0033-2100
RA648.5
➤ **PRZEGLAD EPIDEMIOLOGICZNY.** Text in Polish; Summaries in English. 1947. q. EUR 162 foreign (effective 2006). adv. bk.rev. abstr.; charts; illus. index, cum.index. **Document type:** *Journal, Academic/Scholarly.* **Description:** Discusses epidemiology, bacteriology, parasitology, pathology and clinical aspects of infectious diseases.
Indexed: A22, A34, A36, A38, B23, BP, CABA, ChemAb, D01, DentInd, DokArb, E12, EMBASE, ExcerpMed, F08, F09, F11, F12, GH, H17, IndMed, IndVet, LT, MEDLINE, N02, N03, P30, P33, P37, P39, PN&I, R08, R10, R12, RA&MP, RM&VM, RRTA, Reac, S13, S16, SCOPUS, T05, VS, W11.
—BLDSC (6940.100000), GNLM, IE, Infotrieve, Ingenta, INIST.
Published by: Panstwowy Zaklad Higieny/National Institute of Hygiene, Ul Chocimska 24, Warsaw, 00791, Poland. TEL 48-22-5421327, azielinski@pzh.gov.pl, http://www.pzh.gov.pl. Ed., R&P Andrzej Zielinski. Circ: 750. **Dist. by:** Ars Polona, Obroncow 25, Warsaw 03933, Poland. TEL 48-22-5098609, FAX 48-22-5098610, arspolona@arspolona.com.pl, http://www.arspolona.com.pl. **Co-sponsor:** Polskie Towarzystwo Epidemiologow i Lekarzy Chorob Zakaznych - Polish Association of Epidemiologists and Infectionists.

➤ **PSICOLOGIA, SAUDE E DOCENCAS.** *see* PSYCHOLOGY

613 NLD ISSN 1878-4844
PSYCHOPRAKTIJK. Text in Dutch. 1999. bi-m. EUR 76 to individuals; EUR 152 to institutions (effective 2010). adv. **Document type:** *Journal, Academic/Scholarly.*
Formerly (until 2009): Psychopraxis (1566-6166)
Related titles: Online - full text ed.: ISSN 2210-7754.
—IE.
Published by: Bohn Stafleu van Loghum B.V. (Subsidiary of: Springer Science+Business Media), Postbus 246, Houten, 3990 GA, Netherlands. TEL 31-30-6383838, FAX 31-30-6383839, boekhandels@bsl.nl, http://www.bsl.nl. Eds. Ron van Deth, Sako Visser. Circ: 1,200.

PUBLIC ASSISTANCE & WELFARE TRENDS - STATE CAPITALS. *see* LAW

362.1 USA ISSN 1942-8812
PUBLIC HEALTH. Text in English. 2008 (Aug.). irreg., latest 2008. USD 49.95, GBP 34.95 per issue (effective 2010). back issues avail. **Document type:** *Monographic series, Academic/Scholarly.*
Published by: Praeger Publishers (Subsidiary of: Greenwood Publishing Group Inc.), 88 Post Rd W, Westport, CT 06881. TEL 800-368-6868, tech.support@greenwood.com, http://www.greenwood.com. Ed. Lawrence Cheskin.

PUBLIC HEALTH. *see* MEDICAL SCIENCES

614.49 NZL ISSN 1177-9934
PUBLIC HEALTH ADVICE; public health quarterly report. Variant title: Medical Officer of Health Public Health Advice. Text in English. 1995. q. **Document type:** *Bulletin, Trade.* **Description:** Presents the epidemiology of Auckland's notifiable diseases, articles on topical public health issues and advice from the Medical Officer of Health.
Related titles: Online - full text ed.: ISSN 1177-9942.
Published by: (Auckland District Health Board), Auckland Regional Public Health Service, Cornwall Complex, Floor 2, Bldg 15, Greenlane Clinical Ctr, Symonds St, Private Bag 92605, Auckland, 1150, New Zealand. TEL 64-9-6234600, arphs@adhb.govt.nz.

362.1 CAN ISSN 1912-4686
PUBLIC HEALTH AGENCY OF CANADA. REPORT ON PLANS AND PRIORITIES. Text in English. 2005. a. **Document type:** *Report, Trade.*
Published by: Public Health Agency of Canada/Agence de Sante Publique du Canada, 0904A, Buock Claxton Bldg, Tunney's Pasture, Ottawa, ON K1A OK9, Canada. TEL 613-957-2991, FAX 613-941-5366, info@hc-sc.gc.ca, http://www.hc-sc.gc.ca.

PUBLIC HEALTH AGENCY OF CANADA. SUSTAINABLE DEVELOPMENT STRATEGY/STRATEGIE DE DEVELOPPEMENT DURABLE. *see* BUSINESS AND ECONOMICS—Production Of Goods And Services

614 CAN ISSN 1181-960X
PUBLIC HEALTH & EPIDEMIOLOGY REPORT ONTARIO. Text in English. 1990. bi-w.
Published by: Ontario, Ministry of Health and Long-Term Care, Ste M1-57, Macdonald Block, 900 Bay St, Toronto, ON M7A 1N3, Canada. TEL 800-268-1154, FAX 416-314-8721.

362.1 AUS ISSN 1449-485X
PUBLIC HEALTH BULLETIN SOUTH AUSTRALIA. Text in English. 2004. q. **Document type:** *Bulletin, Consumer.*
Published by: South Australia, Department of Health, Citi Centre Bldg, 11 Hindmarsh Sq, Rundle Mall, PO Box 287, Adelaide, SA 5000, Australia. TEL 61-8-82266000, FAX 61-8-82266899, health.library@health.sa.gov.au, http://www.health.sa.gov.au.

362.1 GBR ISSN 1754-9973
➤ **PUBLIC HEALTH ETHICS.** Abbreviated title: P H E. Text in English. 2008. 3/yr. GBP 149 in United Kingdom to institutions; EUR 223 in Europe to institutions; USD 298 in US & Canada to institutions; GBP 149 elsewhere to institutions; GBP 162 combined subscription in United Kingdom to institutions (print & online eds.); EUR 244 combined subscription in Europe to institutions (print & online eds.); USD 325 combined subscription in US & Canada to institutions (print & online eds.); GBP 162 combined subscription elsewhere to institutions (print & online eds.) (effective 2012). adv. reprint service avail. from PSC. **Document type:** *Journal, Academic/Scholarly.* **Description:** Focuses on a systematic analysis of the moral problems in public health and preventive medicine.
Related titles: Online - full text ed.: ISSN 1754-9981. 2008. GBP 126 in United Kingdom to institutions; EUR 188 in Europe to institutions; USD 251 in US & Canada to institutions; GBP 126 elsewhere to institutions (effective 2012) (from IngentaConnect).
Indexed: A01, B21, EMBASE, ESPM, ExcerpMed, H&SSA, P30, PhilInd, SCOPUS, T02.
—IE. **CCC.**
Published by: Oxford University Press, Great Clarendon St, Oxford, OX2 6DP, United Kingdom. TEL 44-1865-556767, FAX 44-1865-556646, enquiry@oup.co.uk, http://www.oxfordjournals.org. Eds. Angus Dawson, Marcel Verweij.

614 362.1 DEU ISSN 0944-5587
RA421
PUBLIC HEALTH FORUM. Text in German. 1993. 4/yr. EUR 34 in Europe to institutions; EUR 34 to institutions in Germany, Austria and Switzerland; JPY 5,000 in Japan to institutions; USD 47 elsewhere to institutions (effective 2012). adv. **Document type:** *Journal, Academic/Scholarly.*
Related titles: Online - full text ed.: ISSN 1876-4851 (from ScienceDirect).
Indexed: CA, SCOPUS, T02.
—IE. **CCC.**

Published by: (Deutschen Gesellschaft fuer Public Health e.v., Deutsche Koordinierungsstelle fuer Gesundheitswissenschaften), Urban und Fischer Verlag (Subsidiary of: Elsevier GmbH), Loebdergraben 14a, Jena, 07743, Germany. TEL 49-3641-626430, FAX 49-3641-626432, journals@urbanfischer.de, http://www.urbanundfischer.de. Ed. Monika Huber. Adv. contact Eva Kraemer TEL 49-89-5383704. B&W page EUR 1,090, color page EUR 2,035. Circ: 1,450. **Non-German speaking countries subscr. to:** Nature Publishing Group, Brunel Rd, Houndmills, Basingstoke, Hamps RG21 6XS, United Kingdom. TEL 44-1256-302629, FAX 44-1256-476117

362.1 NZL ISSN 1177-3065
PUBLIC HEALTH INTELLIGENCE MONITORING REPORT. Text in English. 2006. irreg., latest vol.7, 2006. **Document type:** *Monographic series.*
Published by: New Zealand Ministry of Health, Box 5013, Wellington, New Zealand. TEL 64-4-4962000, FAX 64-4-4962340, emailmoh@moh.govt.nz, http://moh.govt.nz.

362.10993 NZL ISSN 1175-5164
PUBLIC HEALTH INTELLIGENCE OCCASIONAL BULLETIN. Text in English. 2001. irreg., latest vol.41, 2007. **Document type:** *Bulletin.*
Related titles: Online - full text ed.: ISSN 1177-7133.
Published by: New Zealand Ministry of Health, Box 5013, Wellington, New Zealand. TEL 64-4-4962000, FAX 64-4-4962340, emailmoh@moh.govt.nz, http://moh.govt.nz.

PUBLIC HEALTH LAW & POLICY JOURNAL. *see* LAW

614 GBR ISSN 1465-1505
➤ **PUBLIC HEALTH MEDICINE.** Text in English. 1999. 3/yr. GBP 45 per vol. domestic to individuals; GBP 60 per vol. foreign to individuals; GBP 60 per vol. domestic to institutions; GBP 90 per vol. foreign to institutions (effective 2009). back issues avail. **Document type:** *Journal, Academic/Scholarly.* **Description:** Provides articles on epidemiology, care groups, needs assessment, health service evaluation, clinical effectiveness and good practicea as well as a wide range of other public health topics.
Related titles: Online - full text ed.: GBP 30 per vol. (effective 2009).
Indexed: A36, CABA, D01, EMBASE, ExcerpMed, GH, N02, N03, R10, R12, Reac, SCOPUS, T05.
—BLDSC (6964.497000). **CCC.**
Published by: Rila Publications Ltd., 73 Newman St, London, W1A 4PG, United Kingdom. TEL 44-20-76311299, FAX 44-20-75807166, admin@rila.co.uk. Eds. Dr. Jennifer Bennett TEL 44-1273-485300, Salman Rawaf TEL 44-20-86874543.

➤ **PUBLIC HEALTH NURSING.** *see* MEDICAL SCIENCES—Nurses And Nursing

➤ **PUBLIC HEALTH NUTRITION.** *see* NUTRITION AND DIETETICS

614 USA ISSN 0033-3549
CODEN: HSRPAT
➤ **PUBLIC HEALTH REPORTS.** Abbreviated title: P H R. Text in English. 1878. bi-m. USD 63 to individuals (print or online ed.); USD 120 to institutions; USD 40 domestic to students; USD 70 combined subscription to individuals (print & online eds.); USD 20 per issue to individuals (print or online ed.) (effective 2010). adv. bk.rev. bibl.; charts; illus.; stat.; abstr. index. back issues avail.; reprints avail. **Document type:** *Journal, Academic/Scholarly.* **Description:** Covers research, policy, and commentary on public health issues.
Former titles (until 1974): Health Services Report (0090-2918); (until 1973): H S M H A Health Reports (0083-1204); (until 1971): Public Health Reports (0094-6214); (until 1896): Abstract of Sanitary Reports; (until 1890): Weekly Abstract of Sanitary Reports; (until 1887): United States. Marine Hospital Service.;Bulletins of the Public Health; Public Health Reports incorporated (1945-1951): Journal of Venereal Disease Information (0096-7025); Which was formerly (until 1945): Venereal Disease Information (0372-5421); (until 1922): Abstracts from Recent Medical and Public Health Papers; (1946-1951): C D C Bulletin (0270-3440)
Related titles: Microfiche ed.: (from CIS); Microform ed.: (from PMC, PQC); Online - full text ed.: ISSN 1468-2877.
Indexed: A01, A02, A03, A08, A20, A22, A23, A24, A25, A26, A34, A36, ABS&EES, AHCMS, AIDS Ab, AIM, ASCA, ASFA, Acal, Agr, AgrForAb, AmStI, B04, B13, BDM&CN, BP, BRD, BiolDig, C05, C06, C07, C08, C12, CA, CABA, CINAHL, CPerI, ChPerI, ChemAb, Chicano, CurCont, D01, DBA, DentAb, DokArb, E01, E08, E12, EMBASE, ESPM, ExcerpMed, F08, F09, FR, Faml, G03, G05, G06, G07, G08, G10, GH, GSA, GSI, H01, H02, H04, H05, H09, H11, H12, H13, H17, HPNRM, HRA, HlthInd, HospLI, I02, I05, I07, IHD, INI, ISR, IUSGP, IndMed, IndVet, Inpharma, LT, M01, M02, M06, MEA&I, MEDLINE, MagInd, N02, N04, NRN, OR, P02, P06, P10, P11, P13, P20, P21, P22, P24, P26, P27, P30, P33, P34, P35, P37, P39, P48, P50, P52, P53, P54, P56, PAIS, PHN&I, PN&I, PQC, PopulInd, R08, R10, R12, RASB, RM&VM, RRTA, Reac, S02, S03, S04, S05, S08, S09, S13, S16, S23, SCI, SCOPUS, SFSA, SPAA, SSAI, SSAb, SSCI, SSI, SSciA, SWR&A, SWRA, T02, T05, THA, VS, W01, W02, W03, W05, W07, W09, W11.
—BLDSC (6965.000000), CIS, GNLM, IE, Ingenta, INIST.
Published by: (U.S. Public Health Service), Association of Schools of Public Health, 1101 15th St, NW, Ste 910, Washington, DC 20005. TEL 202-296-1099, FAX 202-296-1252, info@asph.org, http://www.asph.org. Eds. Laurence Reed, Stella Lee TEL 202-296-1099 ext 146.

362.1 DEU ISSN 1616-6477
PUBLIC HEALTH RESEARCH AND PRACTICE. Text in English. 1999. a. **Document type:** *Journal, Trade.*
Published by: S. Roderer Verlag, In der Obern Au 12, Regensburg, 93055, Germany. TEL 49-941-7992270, FAX 49-941-795198, info@roderer-verlag.de, http://roderer-verlag.de.

362.1 FRA ISSN 2107-6952
▼ **PUBLIC HEALTH REVIEWS (ONLINE).** Text in English. 2010. s-a. free (effective 2011). **Document type:** *Journal, Academic/Scholarly.*
Media: Online - full text. **Related titles:** ◆ Print ed.: Public Health Reviews (Print). ISSN 0301-0422.
Indexed: A01, D01, P10, P27, P48, P50, P52, P53, P54, P56, PQC.
Published by: Ecole des Hautes Etudes en Sante Publique (E H E S P) Presses, Avenue du Professeur Leon Bernard, CS 74312, Rennes, 35043, France. TEL 33-2-99549098, FAX 33-2-99542284.

614 FRA ISSN 0301-0422
RA421 CODEN: PBHRAM
➤ **PUBLIC HEALTH REVIEWS (PRINT)**; an international quarterly. Text in English. 1972-2008; N.S. 2010. s-a. (q. until 2010). EUR 49 per issue (effective 2011). adv. bk.rev. abstr.; bibl.; illus.; stat. cum.index. back issues avail.; reprints avail. **Document type:** *Journal, Academic/Scholarly.* **Description:** Publishes review articles on public health topics, emphasizing the integration of current state of the art knowledge and translational issues, and interdisciplinary approaches, describing evidence-based policy and best practices, for the benefit of a wide audience, including SPH faculty and students, public health professionals, scientists, policy makers, and practitioners. Each issue is focused on one selected theme.
Related titles: ◆ Online - full text ed.: Public Health Reviews (Online). ISSN 2107-6952.
Indexed: A22, AIDS&CR, B21, C06, C07, C08, CINAHL, EIA, EMBASE, ESPM, EnerInd, ExcerpMed, FR, FS&TA, H&SSA, HospLI, IBR, IBZ, IndMed, MEDLINE, NRN, P30, R10, Reac, RiskAb, SCOPUS, ViroIAbstr.
—GNLM, IE, Infotrieve, Ingenta, INIST.
Published by: Ecole des Hautes Etudes en Sante Publique (E H E S P) Presses, Avenue du Professeur Leon Bernard, CS 74312, Rennes, 35043, France. TEL 33-2-99549098, FAX 33-2-99542284. Ed. Antoine Flahault. Pub. Denis Couet. R&P, Adv. contact ilana Levin TEL 33-17-9971593.

362.1 GBR ISSN 2043-6580
PUBLIC HEALTH TODAY. Text in English. 1990. q. free to members (effective 2010). back issues avail. **Document type:** *Magazine, Consumer.* **Description:** Features a range of articles from topical news items to interviews with key public health figures.
Former titles (until 2010): PH.Com (1472-7501); (until 1999): Public Health Physician (0960-3239)
Related titles: Online - full text ed.: free (effective 2010).
Published by: Faculty of Public Health, 4 St Andrews Pl, London, NW1 4LB, United Kingdom. TEL 44-20-79350243, FAX 44-20-72246973, enquiries@fph.org.uk. Ed. Alan Maryon-Davis.

PUBLIC POLICY FORUM. RESEARCH REPORTS. *see* PUBLIC ADMINISTRATION

363.1 USA ISSN 1526-1646
PUBLIC SAFETY COMMUNICATIONS. Text in English. 1935. m. free membership (effective 2004). adv. bk.rev. back issues avail. **Document type:** *Magazine, Trade.* **Description:** For persons who operate, maintain, install, design and manufacture the emergency communications systems used to answer the public's calls for police, fire and EMS services.
Formerly: A P C O Bulletin (0001-2165)
Published by: Association of Public-Safety Communications Officials International, Inc., 351 N Williamson Blvd, Daytona Beach, FL 32119-8437. TEL 386-322-2500, 888-272-6911, FAX 386-322-2501, apco@apco911.org, http://www.apco911.org. adv.: B&W page USD 2,207, color page USD 3,382. Circ: 13,892 (controlled).

362.1 USA
PUBLIC SAFETY FUNDING SOLUTION. Text in English. 2005. m. USD 379 (effective 2005). **Document type:** *Newsletter, Trade.* **Description:** Carries information on ways to obtain a portion of money set aside for training and equipment for the nation's public safety sector.
Published by: Cygnus Business Media, Inc., 1233 Janesville Ave, PO Box 803, Fort Atkinson, WI 53538. TEL 920-563-6388, FAX 920-563-1702, http://www.cygnusb2b.com.

353.60 GBR ISSN 2045-2357
PUBLIC SERVICE REVIEW. HEALTH AND SOCIAL CARE. Text in English. 2004. q. GBP 50 (effective 2011). adv. back issues avail. **Document type:** *Magazine, Trade.* **Description:** Designed for those involved in the provision of healthcare with a vital forum for discussing and debating new ideas and practices.
Formerly (until 2010): Public Service Review. Health (1742-2078)
Related titles: Online - full text ed.: ISSN 2046-6714. free (effective 2011).
—**CCC.**
Published by: P S C A International Ltd., Ebenezer House, Rycroft, Newcastle-under-Lyme, Staffs ST5 2UB, United Kingdom. TEL 44-1782-630200, FAX 44-1782-625533, mailbox@publicservice.co.uk. Ed. Caroline Pennington. Adv. contact Gerrod Mellor TEL 44-1782-630200.

628 ITA ISSN 0393-1072
PULIZIA INDUSTRIALE E SANIFICAZIONE. Text in Italian. 1968. m. adv. **Document type:** *Magazine, Trade.*
Published by: MO.ED.CO. Srl, Via San Martino 11C, Milan, 20122, Italy. TEL 39-02-58316074, FAX 39-02-58322564, info@moedco.it, http://www.moedco.it.

362.1 ITA ISSN 1971-7415
Q A (TORINO). (Quality Assurance) Text in Italian. 1990. q. **Document type:** *Magazine, Trade.*
Related titles: Online - full text ed.
Published by: (Societa Italiana per la Qualita dell'Assistenza Sanitaria), Centro Scientifico Editore, Via Borgone 57, Turin, 10139, Italy. TEL 39-011-3853656, FAX 39-011-3853244, cse@cse.it, http://www.cse.it. Ed. A Bonaldi.

362.1 USA ISSN 1932-040X
UB369
Q U E R I QUARTERLY. (Quality Enhancement Research Initiative) Text in English. 1999. q. **Document type:** *Newsletter, Government.*
Media: Online - full text.
Published by: U.S. Department of Veterans Affairs, Office of Research and Development, 810 Vermont Ave NW, Washington, DC 20420. TEL 202-745-8000, http://www.research.va.gov.

QICHE YU ANQUAN/AUTO & SAFETY. *see* TRANSPORTATION—Automobiles

QUADERNI DI COOPERAZIONE SANITARIA/CAHIERS DE COOPERATION MEDICALE/HEALTH COOPERATION PAPERS. *see* MEDICAL SCIENCES—Communicable Diseases

362.1 ITA ISSN 0393-9529
QUADERNI DI SANITA PUBBLICA. Text in Italian. 1978. q. EUR 39.50 (effective 2009). **Document type:** *Magazine, Trade.*
Published by: C I S Editore S.r.l., Via San Siro 1, Milan, 20149, Italy. TEL 39-02-4694542, FAX 39-02-48193584, http://www.ciseditore.it.

QUALITY ASSURANCE & FOOD SAFETY. *see* FOOD AND FOOD INDUSTRIES

362.1 ARG ISSN 1668-091X
RA1190
R E T E L. (Revista de Toxicologia en Linea) Text in English, Spanish, Portuguese. 2003. irreg. free (effective 2011). **Document type:** *Journal, Academic/Scholarly.*
Media: Online - full text.
Published by: Revista de Toxicologia en Linea

R F L. (Rundschau Fleischhygiene und Lebensmittelueberwachung) *see* FOOD AND FOOD INDUSTRIES

R S O MAGAZINE. (Radiation Safety Officer) *see* OCCUPATIONAL HEALTH AND SAFETY

R T E C S. (Registry of Toxic Effects of Chemical Substances) *see* ENVIRONMENTAL STUDIES—Toxicology And Environmental Safety

614.8 IND ISSN 0972-0464
➤ **RADIATION PROTECTION AND ENVIRONMENT.** Text in English. 1978. q. INR 2,000 domestic; USD 200 foreign (effective 2011). abstr.; bibl.; charts; illus.; maps; stat. Index. back issues avail.; reprints avail. **Document type:** *Journal, Academic/Scholarly.* **Description:** Covers radiation dosimetry, biological dosimetry, operational radiation protection, environmental radioactivity and radon/thoron measurements, development of instrumentation for radiation protection, nuclear and radiological emergency preparedness, radiation protection standards, radiological safety aspects in the application of radiation /radioisotopes in industry, medicine and research.
Formerly (until 1997): Bulletin of Radiation Protection (0253-6897)
Related titles: Online - full text ed.
Indexed: A22, INIS AtomInd.
—IE, Ingenta.
Published by: (Indian Association for Radiation Protection), Medknow Publications and Media Pvt. Ltd., B-9, Kanara Business Ctr, Off Link Rd, Ghatkopar (E), Mumbai, Maharastra 400 075, India. TEL 91-22-66491818, FAX 91-22-66491817, journals@medknow.com, http://www.medknow.com. Pub. Hemant Manjrekar.

➤ **RADIATION PROTECTION DOSIMETRY.** *see* PHYSICS—Nuclear Physics

363.1799 AUS ISSN 1444-2752
➤ **RADIATION PROTECTION IN AUSTRALASIA.** Abbreviated title: R P A. Text in English. 1979. q. free to members; AUD 50 to libraries (effective 2008). back issues avail. **Document type:** *Journal, Academic/Scholarly.* **Description:** Provides scientific articles, technical notes, discussion papers and comments on topics related to ionizing and non-ionizing radiation.
Formerly (until 1996): Radiation Protection in Australia (0729-7963)
Indexed: GeoRef, INIS AtomInd.
—BLDSC (7227.991950), IE, Ingenta.
Published by: Australasian Radiation Protection Society, PO Box 7108, Upper Fern Tree Gulley, VIC 3156, Australia. TEL 61-3-97560128, FAX 61-3-97536372, arps@21century.com.au. Ed. Cameron Jeffries TEL 61-8-81300708.

➤ **RADIATION PROTECTION MANAGEMENT**; the journal of applied health physics. *see* OCCUPATIONAL HEALTH AND SAFETY

➤ **RADIATION SAFETY MANAGEMENT.** *see* PHYSICS—Nuclear Physics

614 ESP ISSN 1133-1747
CODEN: RDPREY
RADIOPROTECCION. Text in Spanish. 1991. q. **Document type:** *Magazine, Trade.* **Description:** Publishes original articles, reviews, information and news related to the field of radiological safety.
Formerly (until 1993): Proteccion Radiologica (1131-916X)
Indexed: INIS AtomInd, Inspec.
Published by: Sociedad Espanola de Proteccion Radiologica, C/ Capitan Haya, 60, Madrid, 28020, Spain. TEL 34-917-499517, FAX 34-917-499503, secretaria.sociedades@medynet.com, http://www.sepr.es/.

362.1 ITA ISSN 1120-1762
RAGIUSAN; rassegna giuridica della sanita. Text in Italian. 1984. m. bk.rev. back issues avail. **Document type:** *Magazine, Trade.*
Indexed: DoGi.
Published by: Sipis Srl, Viale Parioli 77, Rome, 00197, Italy. TEL 39-06-8073336, FAX 39-06-8085817, sipis@tin.it.

RAUMPLANUNG UND UMWELTSCHUTZ IM KANTON ZURICH. *see* HOUSING AND URBAN PLANNING

363.1799 FRA ISSN 0397-9210
CODEN: RITMB3
RAYONNEMENTS IONISANTS. Text in French. 1971. q. EUR 26 (effective 2008). **Description:** Publishes articles concerning protection against radiation.
Indexed: FR, INIS AtomInd.
—INIST, Linda Hall. **CCC.**
Published by: Association pour les Techniques et les Sciences de Radioprotection, 47, rue Louis Pasteur, Leuville sur Orge, Montlhery, 91310, France. http://www.cc-pays-de-gex.fr/assoc/atsr-ri/atsr.htm. Ed. Gilles Hofmann.

362.1 PRT ISSN 1646-9933
RECOMENDACOES E ESPECIFICACOES TECNICAS DO EDIFICIO HOSPITALAR. Text in Portuguese. 2007. irreg. **Document type:** *Magazine, Trade.*
Published by: Administracao Central do Sistemas de Saude, Av Joao Crisostomo 11, Lisbon, 1000-177, Portugal. TEL 351-21-7925800, FAX 351-21-7925848, geral@acss.min-saude.pt, http://www.acss.min-saude.pt.

RECYCLING MAGAZIN; Trends, Analysen, Meinungen und Fakten zur Kreislaufwirtschaft. *see* TECHNOLOGY: COMPREHENSIVE WORKS

614.3 NLD ISSN 1574-4922
REGISTRATIE VAN VOEDSELINFECTIES EN -VERGIFTIGINGEN ONDERZOCHT DOOR G G D'S EN REGIONALE INSPECTIES GEZONDHEIDSBESCHERMING KEURINGSDIENSTEN VAN WAREN. Text in Dutch. 1998. a.
Published by: (Voedsel en Waren Autoriteit), Rijksinstituut voor Volksgezondheid en Milieu, Postbus 1, Bilthoven, 3720 BA, Netherlands. TEL 31-30-2749111, FAX 31-30-2742971, info@rivm.nl, http://www.rivm.nl.

P

REGULATORY UPDATE; government legislation and regulations related to plastics industry. *see* PLASTICS

362.1 CHN
RENMIN GONGAN BAO/PEOPLE'S PUBLIC SECURITY REVIEW. Text in Chinese. 1984. 6/w. CNY 273.96 (effective 2004). **Document type:** *Newspaper, Government.*
Published by: Renmin Gongan Baoshe, Fengtai-qu, 15, Fangzhuang Fangxingyuan, Beijing, 100078, China. **Dist. by:** China International Book Trading Corp, 35 Chegongzhuang Xilu, Haidian District, PO Box 399, Beijing 100044, China. TEL 86-10-68412045, FAX 86-10-68412023, cibtc@mail.cibtc.com.cn, http://www.cibtc.com.cn.

RENMIN GONGAN BAO. JIAOTONG ANQUAN ZHOUKAN. *see* TRANSPORTATION—Roads And Traffic

362.1 CHN
RENMIN GONGAN BAO. ZHIAN BAOWEI ZHOUKAN. Text in Chinese. w. CNY 28.80 (effective 2004). **Document type:** *Newspaper, Government.*
Related titles: Online - full content ed.
Published by: Renmin Gongan Baoshe, Fengtai-qu, 15, Fangzhuang Fangxingyuan, Beijing, 100078, China. **Dist. by:** China International Book Trading Corp, 35 Chegongzhuang Xilu, Haidian District, PO Box 399, Beijing 100044, China. TEL 86-10-68412045, FAX 86-10-68412023, cibtc@mail.cibtc.com.cn, http://www.cibtc.com.cn.

362.1 AUS ISSN 1832-9810
REPATRIATION GENERAL HOSPITAL. ANNUAL REPORT. Text in English. 199?. a., latest 2007. back issues avail. **Document type:** *Report, Trade.*
Related titles: Online - full text ed.: free (effective 2009).
Published by: Repatriation General Hospital, Daws Rd, Daws Park, SA 5041, Australia. TEL 61-8-82769666, 800-254-373, FAX 61-8-82779401, Celia.Painter@rgh.sa.gov.au.

362.1 FRA ISSN 2108-2367
▼ **REPERTOIRE DES CENTRES PERINATALS DE TYPE III ET DES RESEAUX DE PERINATALITE EN ILE-DE-FRANCE.** Text in French. 2010. a. **Document type:** *Report, Government.*
Published by: France. Direction Regionale des Affaires Sanitaires et Sociales d'Ile-de-France, 58-62, Rue de Mouzaia, Paris Cedex 19, 75935, France. TEL 33-1-44842222, dr75-direction@sante.gouv.fr, http: www.ile-de-france.sante.gouv.fr.

614 FRA ISSN 1761-1679
REPONSES A VOS QUESTIONS. Text in French. 2002. irreg., latest 2007. back issues avail. **Document type:** *Monographic series, Consumer.*
Published by: Editions Solar, 12 av. d'Italie, Paris, 75627 Cedex 13, France. edito@solar.tm.fr, contact@solar.tm.fr, http://www.solar.tm.fr.

616.89 150 GBR ISSN 0192-0812
RA790.A1
RESEARCH IN COMMUNITY AND MENTAL HEALTH. Text in English. 1979. irreg., latest vol.14, 2006. price varies. back issues avail. **Document type:** *Monographic series, Academic/Scholarly.*
Related titles: Online - full text ed.
Indexed: A22, ASSIA, CA, ChPerI, E-psyche, P30, PsycholAb, S02, S03, SCOPUS, SOPODA, SociolAb, T02.
—BLDSC (7736.700000), GNLM, IE, Infotrieve, Ingenta. **CCC.**
Published by: Emerald Group Publishing Ltd., Howard House, Wagon Ln, Bingley, W Yorks BD16 1WA, United Kingdom. TEL 44-1274-777700, FAX 44-1274-785201, emerald@emeraldinsight.com. Ed. William H Fischer. **Dist. by:** Turpin Distribution Services Ltd., Pegasus Dr, Stratton Business Park, Biggleswade, Bedfordshire SG18 8QB, United Kingdom. TEL 44-1767-604951, FAX 44-1767-601640, custserv@turpin-distribution.com, http://www.turpin-distribution.com/.

RESEARCH IN THE SOCIOLOGY OF HEALTH CARE. *see* MEDICAL SCIENCES

614 FRA ISSN 2105-7168
RESEAUX, SANTE & TERRITOIRE. Text in French. 1997. bi-m. EUR 110 (effective 2011).
Former titles (until 2009): Filieres & Reseaux 2 Sante (1774-6353); (until 2005): Filieres & Reseaux (1279-4538)
Published by: Editions de Sante, 49 Rue Galilee, Paris, 75116, France. TEL 33-1-40701615, FAX 33-1-40701614, editions.de.sante@wanadoo.fr.

362.1 CAN ISSN 1718-407X
RESILIENCE. Text in French. 2006. q. **Document type:** *Bulletin, Consumer.*
Published by: Quebec, Securite Publique/Quebec, Public Security, 2525, boul. Laurier, 5th floor, Tour du Saint-Laurent, Quebec, PQ G1V 2L2, Canada. TEL 418-644-6826, FAX 418-643-3194, infocom@msp.gouv.qc.ca, http://www.msp.gouv.qc.ca/index.asp.

362.1 USA
TH9402
RESPONDER SAFETY. Text in English. 2002 (Oct.). bi-m. free domestic to qualified personnel (effective 2011). adv. **Document type:** *Magazine, Trade.* **Description:** Contains articles and information on the response to civil emergency situations such as weather or terrorism; also covers government funding, regulations, training, studies and other related fields.
Former titles (until 2007): Homeland Response (1556-8121); (until 2004): Responder Safety (1542-5932)
Published by: Penton Media, Inc., 1300 E 9th St, Cleveland, OH 44114. TEL 216-696-7000, FAX 216-696-3432, information@penton.com, http://www.penton.com. Ed. Sandy Smith TEL 216-931-9464. Pub. John Di Paola TEL 216-931-9709. adv.: B&W page USD 5,000. Circ: 27,000.

344.04 FRA ISSN 1770-0914
RESPONSABLE SANTE; la lettre bimensuelle sur les risques en milieux hospitalier et medico-social. Text in French. 2004. s-m. (22/yr). EUR 503 (effective 2009). **Document type:** *Newsletter, Trade.*
Published by: Editions Sorman, 13 rue d'Uzes, Paris, 75002, France. TEL 33-1-45084409, infos@editionssorman.com, http://www.internetmairie.com/publications/publications00.php3.

362.1 CAN ISSN 1910-4405
RESSOURCES NATURELLES CANADA. DIVISION DE LA REGLEMENTATION DES EXPLOSIFS. RAPPORT AUX INTERVENANTS. Text in French. 2002. irreg., latest 2003. **Document type:** *Government.*
Media: Online - full text. **Related titles:** Print ed.: ISSN 1711-1390.
Published by: (Natural Resources Canada, Explosives Regulatory Division), Natural Resources Canada/Ressources Naturelles Canada, 601 Booth St, Ottawa, ON K1A 0E8, Canada. TEL 613-996-3919, FAX 613-943-8742, info-ottawa@gsc.nrcan.gc.ca, http://www.nrcan-rncan.gc.ca/com.

REVIEWS ON ENVIRONMENTAL HEALTH. *see* ENVIRONMENTAL STUDIES

614 ARG ISSN 1852-8724
▼ **REVISTA ARGENTINA DE SALUD PUBLICA.** Text in Spanish. 2009. q. **Document type:** *Magazine, Consumer.*
Published by: Ministerio de Salud, Ave 9 de Julio 1925, Buenos Aires, C1073ABA, Argentina. TEL 54-11-43799000, consultas@msal.gov.ar, http://www.msal.gov.ar/htm/site/default.asp.

614 ARG ISSN 1851-3638
REVISTA ARGENTINA DE ZOONOSIS Y ENFERMEDADES INFECCIOSAS EMERGENTES. Text in Spanish. 2003. q.
Published by: Asociacion Argentina de Zoonosis, Venezuela 550 P.B., Buenos Aires, Argentina. TEL 54-11-43313853, http://www.aazoonosis.org.ar/.

614 BRA ISSN 0100-0233
RA464.B33
REVISTA BAIANA DE SAUDE PUBLICA. Text in Portuguese; Summaries in English. 1974. s-a. bibl.; charts; stat. **Document type:** *Magazine, Consumer.*
Indexed: C01.
Published by: Secretaria da Saude do Estado da Bahia, Rua Conselheiro Pedro Luiz 171, Rio Vermelho, Salvador, BA 41950-610, Brazil. TEL 55-71-31165313, FAX 55-71-33342730, rbsp@saude.ba.gov.br, www.saude.ba.gov.br/rbsp.

362.1 BRA ISSN 1415-790X
RA650.55.B8
➤ **REVISTA BRASILEIRA DE EPIDEMIOLOGIA.** Text in English, Portuguese, Spanish. 2004. 3/yr. USD 25 to individuals; USD 40 to institutions (effective 2005). **Document type:** *Journal, Academic/Scholarly.* **Description:** Aims at publishing original articles, including critical reviews on specific themes, which may contribute to the development of epidemiology and related sciences.
Related titles: Online - full text ed.: ISSN 1980-5497. free (effective 2011).
Indexed: A36, C01, CABA, D01, E12, GH, H17, LT, MEDLINE, N02, N03, P30, P33, P39, R08, R12, S12, S13, SCOPUS, T05, TAR, W11.
Published by: Associacao Brasileira de Pos - Graduacao em Saude Coletiva, Av Brasil 4036, Sala 700 Manguinhos, Rio de Janeiro, RJ 21040-361, Brazil. TEL 55-21-22904893, revbrepi@edu.usp.br. Ed. Jose da Rocha Carvalheiro.

362.1 BRA ISSN 1518-2355
RA463
REVISTA BRASILEIRA DE SAUDE DA FAMILIA. Text in Portuguese. 1999. s-a. **Document type:** *Magazine, Consumer.*
Published by: Ministerio da Saude, Esplanada dos Ministerios, Bloco G, Brasilia, DF 70058-900, Brazil. TEL 55-61-3211721, FAX 55-61-3213216, http://portal.saude.gov.br/saude/.

371.71 BRA ISSN 1413-3415
REVISTA BRASILEIRA DE SAUDE ESCOLAR/BRAZILIAN JOURNAL OF SCHOOL HEALTH. Text in Portuguese. 199?. a. **Document type:** *Magazine, Trade.*
Published by: Associacao Brasileira de Saude Escolar, Praca Rubiao Vieira 61, Ciudade Universitaria, Sao Paulo, 05590-000, Brazil. Ed. Luzimar Teixeira.

362.1 BRA ISSN 2177-9910
▼ **REVISTA BRASILEIRA DE TERAPIAS E SAUDE.** Text in Portuguese. 2010. s-a. free (effective 2011). **Document type:** *Journal, Academic/Scholarly.*
Media: Online - full text.
Published by: Instituto Brasileiro de Therapias e Ensino, Rua Voluntarios da Patria 215, 2o Andar, Centro, Curitiba, PR 80020-000, Brazil. Eds. Naudimar di Pietro Simoes, Sandra Mara Silverio Lopes.

362.1 BRA ISSN 1807-8923
REVISTA BRASILEIRA DE VIGILANCIA SANITARIA/BRAZILIAN JOURNAL OF HEALTH SURVEILLANCE. Abbreviated title: R E V I S A. Text in Multiple languages. 2005. q. **Document type:** *Journal, Academic/Scholarly.*
Published by: Universidade de Sao Paulo, Faculdade de Saude Publica, Av Dr Arnaldo 715, Sao Paulo, 01246-904, Brazil.

362.1 BRA ISSN 1806-1222
REVISTA BRASILEIRA EM PROMOCAO DA SAUDE. Text in Portuguese. 1984. q. **Document type:** *Journal, Academic/Scholarly.*
Formerly (until 2002): Universidade de Fortaleza. Centro de Ciencias da Saude. Revista (0103-2828)
Related titles: Online - full text ed.: ISSN 1806-1230. 2003. free (effective 2011).
Indexed: CA, T02.
—IE.
Published by: Universidade de Fortaleza, Centro de Ciencias da Saude, Av Washington Soares 1321, Bairro Edson Queiroz, Fortaleza, CE 60811-955, Brazil. TEL 55-85-34773204. Ed. Carlos Antonio Bruno da Silva.

REVISTA CES MEDICINA. *see* MEDICAL SCIENCES

362.1 COL ISSN 2145-9932
▼ **REVISTA CES SALUD PUBLICA.** Text in Spanish. 2010. s-a. free (effective 2011). **Document type:** *Journal, Academic/Scholarly.*
Media: Online - full text.
Published by: Universidad CES, Calle 10 A, No 22, Medellin, Colombia. http://www.ces.edu.co.

362.1 CHL ISSN 0717-3652
REVISTA CHILENA DE SALUD PUBLICA. Text in Spanish. 1997. 3/yr. back issues avail. **Document type:** *Journal, Academic/Scholarly.*
Published by: Universidad de Chile, Facultad de Medicina, Escuela de Salud Publica, Independencia 1027, Santiago, Chile. http://www.med.uchile.cl.

614 CRI ISSN 1409-1429
REVISTA COSTARRICENSE DE SALUD PUBLICA. Text in Spanish. q. CRC 500 (effective 2010). back issues avail. **Document type:** *Journal, Academic/Scholarly.*
Related titles: Online - full text ed.: free (effective 2011) (from SciELO).
Published by: Asociacion Costarricense de Salud Publica, Apdo de Correos 4685, San Jose, 1000, Costa Rica. TEL 506-2338063, FAX 506-2338063. Ed. Darner Mora Alvarado.

614.4 CUB ISSN 0253-1151
RA648.5 CODEN: RCHEDF
REVISTA CUBANA DE HIGIENE Y EPIDEMIOLOGIA. Text in Spanish; Summaries in English, French, Spanish. 1963. q. CUP 6 domestic; USD 30 in North America; USD 32 in South America; USD 34 elsewhere (effective 2005). abstr.; bibl.; charts; illus. index. back issues avail. **Document type:** *Journal, Trade.* **Description:** Publishes articles on epidemiology, hygiene, food health and related subjects.
Formerly: Boletin de Higiene y Epidemiologia (0006-629X)
Related titles: Online - full text ed.: ISSN 1561-3003. 1995. free (effective 2011).
Indexed: A01, CA, ChemAb, ChemTitl, FR, IBR, IBZ, IndMed, Repind, SCOPUS, T02.
—CASDDS, INIST.
Published by: Centro Nacional de Informacion de Ciencias Medicas (C N I C M), Calle E No 454, El Vedado, Havana, 10400, Cuba. TEL 537-322004, FAX 537-333063, http://www.sld.cu. Circ: 1,400. **Co-sponsors:** Sociedad Cubana de Higiene y Epidemiologia; Instituto Nacional de Higiene, Epidemiologia y Microbiologia.

614 CUB ISSN 0864-3466
RA456.C7
REVISTA CUBANA DE SALUD PUBLICA. Text in Spanish; Summaries in English, Spanish. 1975. 3/yr. bibl.; charts; illus. index. **Document type:** *Journal, Academic/Scholarly.* **Description:** Covers the field of social medicine and organization and administration of the Cuban health system.
Incorporates (1987-2003): Revista Cubana de Nutricion y Alimentacion (0864-2133); Formerly (until 1998): Revista Cubana de Administracion de Salud (0252-1903)
Related titles: Online - full text ed.: ISSN 1561-3127. 1995. free (effective 2011).
Indexed: A01, A35, A36, AgBio, C01, CA, CABA, CIS, D01, E12, GH, H05, H16, H17, IBR, IBZ, IndMed, LT, N02, N03, P30, P33, P39, PopulInd, R08, R11, R12, RA&MP, RRTA, S13, S16, SCOPUS, SOPODA, SociolAb, T02, T05, TAR, VS, W11.
—INIST.
Published by: (Centro Nacional de Informacion de Ciencias Medicas (C N I C M), Cuba. Ministerio de Salud Publica), Editorial Ciencias Medicas, Linea Esq 1, 10o, Vedado, Havana, 10400, Cuba. TEL 53-7-8323863. Ed. Maria Julia Zamorano. **Co-sponsor:** Sociedad Cubana de Administracion de Salud.

614 ESP ISSN 1696-1641
RA395.S7
REVISTA DE ADMINISTRACION SANITARIA SIGLO XXI. Text in Spanish. 1997. q. back issues avail. **Document type:** *Journal, Academic/Scholarly.*
Formerly (until 2002): Administracion Sanitaria (1137-2966)
Related titles: Print ed.: ISSN 1988-3072. 2003.
Indexed: SCOPUS.
Published by: Elsevier Doyma (Subsidiary of: Elsevier Health Sciences), Traversa de Gracia 17-21, Barcelona, 08021, Spain. TEL 34-932-418800, FAX 34-932-419020, editorial@elsevier.com. Ed. Severiano Pena. Circ: 2,000.

362.1 BRA ISSN 1516-7704
REVISTA DE APS. (Atencao Primaria a Saude) Text in Portuguese. 1998. 3/yr. BRL 30 domestic; BRL 35 foreign (effective 2006). back issues avail. **Document type:** *Journal, Academic/Scholarly.*
Related titles: Online - full text ed.: ISSN 1809-8363. 1998.
Indexed: C06, C07, C08, CA, CINAHL, T02.
Published by: Universidade Federal de Juiz de Fora, Nucleo de Assesoria, Treinamento e Estudos em Saude, Campus UFJF Cidade Universitaria, Martelos, Juiz de Fora, 36036-900, Brazil. FAX 55-32-3293832, revista.aps@ufjf.edu.br. Circ: 2,500.

362.1 ESP ISSN 2173-1675
▼ **REVISTA DE COMUNICACION Y SALUD.** Text in Spanish, English. 2011. s-a. free (effective 2011). **Document type:** *Journal, Academic/Scholarly.*
Media: Online - full text.
Published by: Instituto Internacional de Comunicacion y Salud Ed. Aitor Ugarte.

362.1 610 ROM ISSN 1221-2520
RA523.R8 CODEN: IGIBA5
REVISTA DE IGIENA SI SANITATE PUBLICA. Text in Romanian; Summaries in English, French, German, Russian. 1951. 4/yr. adv. bk.rev. abstr.; bibl.; charts; illus. **Document type:** *Journal, Academic/Scholarly.*
Former titles (until 1990): Revista de Igiena, Bacteriologie, Virusologie, Parazitologie, Pneumoftiziologie. Igiena (1220-1146); (until 1989): Revista de Igiena, Bacteriologie, Virusologie, Parazitologie, Epidemiologie, Pneumoftiziologie. Serie Igiena (0303-8440); (until 1956): Revista de Igiena, Microbiologie si Epidemiologie (0367-8903)
Indexed: ChemAb.
Published by: Asociatia Medicala Romana/Romanian Medical Association, Str Ionel Perlea 10, Sector 1, Bucharest, 70754, Romania. amr@medica.ro, http://www.medica.ro. **Subscr. to:** ILEXIM, Str. 13 Decembrie 3, PO Box 136-137, Bucharest 70116, Romania.

REVISTA DE PSICOLOGIA DE LA SALUD/JOURNAL OF HEALTH PSYCHOLOGY. *see* PSYCHOLOGY

614 ESP ISSN 1577-9572
REVISTA DE SALUD AMBIENTAL. Text in Spanish. 1994. s-a. back issues avail. **Document type:** *Journal, Academic/Scholarly.*
Formerly (until 2001): Sociedad Espanola de Sanidad Ambiental. Boletin (1134-5314)
Related titles: Online - full text ed.: ISSN 1697-2791. 2001.
Published by: Sociedad Espanola de Sanidad Ambiental, C Londres 17, Madrid, 28028, Spain. TEL 34-91-3612600, FAX 34-91-3559208, sesa@tilesa.es, http://www.sanidadambiental.com/.

362.1 COL ISSN 0124-0064
RA467
➤ **REVISTA DE SALUD PUBLICA.** Text in English, Spanish, Portuguese. 1999. 3/yr. USD 30 in Latin America; USD 50 in US & Canada; USD 65 elsewhere (effective 2010). **Document type:** *Journal, Academic/Scholarly.* **Description:** Publishes original articles contributing to the study of public health and related disciplines and their use as tools for improving the population's quality of life.
Related titles: Online - full text ed.: free (effective 2011) (from SciELO).
Indexed: A26, A34, A35, A36, A37, AgBio, BA, C25, CA, CABA, D01, E12, EMBASE, ExcerpMed, F08, GH, H05, H17, I04, I05, IndVet, LT, MEDLINE, N02, N03, P30, P32, P33, P37, P39, P40, PN&I, R07, R08, R10, R12, RM&VM, RRTA, Reac, S13, S16, SCOPUS, T02, T05, TAR, VS, W11.
Published by: Universidad Nacional de Colombia, Facultad de Medicina, Instituto de Salud Publica, Oficina 318, Bogota, DC ZP 6A, Colombia. TEL 57-1-3165000.

614 ARG ISSN 1853-1180
REVISTA DE SALUD PUBLICA. Text in Spanish; Summaries in Spanish, Portuguese, English. 2004. s-a. back issues avail. **Document type:** *Journal, Academic/Scholarly.*
Related titles: Online - full text ed.: ISSN 1852-9429.
Published by: Universidad Nacional de Cordoba, Escuela de Salud Publica, Enrique Barros Esqq. Enfermera Gordillo Gomez, Ciudad Universitaria, Cordoba, 5000, Argentina. TEL 54-351-4333023, FAX 54-351-4334042, saludpublica@fcm-unc.edu.ar. Ed. Maria Cristina Cometto.

614 BRA ISSN 0103-4480
REVISTA DE SAUDE DO DISTRITO FEDERAL. Text in Portuguese. 1989. s-a. back issues avail.
Published by: Fundacao de Ensino e Pesquisa em Ciencias da Saude, SMHN - Quada 501 - Bloco A, Brasilia, D.F. 70710-904, Brazil. TEL 55-61-33254964, FAX 55-61-33260119, rsdf@saude.df.gov.br, http://www.fepecs.edu.br/revista/revistaantiga/index.htm#. Ed. Elza Maria De Souze.

614 BRA ISSN 0034-8910
RA421 CODEN: RSPUB9
➤ **REVISTA DE SAUDE PUBLICA.** Text in English, Portuguese, Spanish; Summaries in English, Portuguese. 1947. bi-m. BRL 34, USD 48 to individuals; BRL 38, USD 48 to institutions (effective 2003). bk.rev. bibl.; charts; illus. index. back issues avail. **Document type:** *Journal, Academic/Scholarly.* **Description:** Reflects scientific advances in the public health field through original research prepared by specialists, both domestic and foreign.
Formerly (until 1966): Universidade de Sao Paulo. Faculdade de Higiene e Saude Publica. Archivos (0365-2203)
Related titles: Online - full text ed.: ISSN 1518-8787. free (effective 2011).
Indexed: A20, A22, A29, A34, A35, A36, ASCA, ASFA, AgBio, B20, B21, B23, B25, BIOSIS Prev, C01, CA, CABA, CISA, CurCont, D01, DentInd, E12, EMBASE, ESPM, EntAb, ErgAb, ExcerpMed, F08, F09, F12, FR, GH, H&SSA, H16, H17, I10, IndMed, IndVet, LT, MEDLINE, MycolAb, N02, N03, OR, P30, P32, P33, P37, P39, PHN&I, PN&I, PollutAb, R07, R08, R10, R11, R12, R13, RA&MP, RM&VM, RRTA, Reac, RefZh, RiskAb, S12, S13, S16, SCI, SCOPUS, SSCI, SWRA, T02, T05, TAR, VS, ViroIAbstr, W07, W09, W10, W11, WildRev, Z01.
—BLDSC (7870.635000), CASDDS, GNLM, IE, Infotrieve, Ingenta, INIST.
Published by: Universidade de Sao Paulo, Faculdade de Saude Publica, Av Dr Arnaldo 715, Sao Paulo, 01246-904, Brazil. saudesoc@edu.usp.br. Ed. Dr. Oswaldo Paulo Forattini. Circ: 1,500.

614 ESP ISSN 1989-9882
▼ **REVISTA ESPANOLA DE COMUNICACION EN SALUD.** Text in Spanish. 2010. s-a. **Document type:** *Journal, Academic/Scholarly.*
Media: Online - full text.
Published by: Asociacion Espanola de Comunicacion Sanitaria, Calle Marquez de Larios, 10 - 2o. G, Malaga, 29005, Spain. TEL 34-952-224537, info@aecs.es. Ed. Maria Teresa Fuentes Hervias.

362.1 345 ESP ISSN 1696-9219
HV7041
REVISTA ESPANOLA DE INVESTIGACION CRIMINOLOGICA. Text in Spanish. 2003. a. free (effective 2011). **Document type:** *Journal, Academic/Scholarly.* **Description:** Covers all aspects of criminology.
Media: Online - full text.
—CCC.
Published by: Sociedad Espanola de Investigacion Criminologica, Universidad de Casilla-La Mancha, Facultad de Derecho de Albacete, Plaza Universidad 1, Albacete, 02071, Spain. maria.benitez@uclm.es, http://www.crimologia.net. Ed. Juanjo Medina Ariza.

614 ESP ISSN 1135-5727
REVISTA ESPANOLA DE SALUD PUBLICA. Text in Spanish; Summaries in English. 1926. 6/yr. bk.rev. abstr.; bibl.; charts; illus. **Document type:** *Journal, Government.* **Description:** Includes original papers on public health, sanitation and epidemiology.
Former titles (until 1995): Revista de Sanidad e Higiene Publica (0034-8899); (until 1931): Direccion General de Sanida. Boletin Tecnico (1576-2122)
Related titles: CD-ROM ed.: ISSN 1696-9820. 2001; Online - full text ed.: free (effective 2011).
Indexed: A22, A34, A35, A36, AgBio, C25, CABA, ChemAb, D01, E12, EMBASE, ExcerpMed, F08, GH, H16, H17, IBR, IBZ, IECT, IME, INI, IndMed, IndVet, LT, MEDLINE, N02, N03, P30, P32, P33, P37, P38, P39, P40, PHN&I, R08, R10, R12, RRTA, Reac, S13, S16, SCOPUS, SSCI, T05, TAR, VS, W07, W11.
—BLDSC (7854.315000), GNLM, IE, Infotrieve, Ingenta, INIST. **CCC.**
Published by: Ministerio de Sanidad, Politica Social e Igualdad, Paseo del Prado 18-20, P.B. Esq con Lope de Vega, Madrid, 28014, Spain. TEL 34-91-5964175, FAX 34-91-5964488, publicaciones@mpsi.es, http://www.msps.es/. Ed. Cristina Perez Andres.

REVISTA ESPANOLA DE SANIDAD PENITENCIARIA. *see* HEALTH FACILITIES AND ADMINISTRATION

362.1 PRT ISSN 1646-0332
REVISTA LUSOFONA DE CIENCIAS E TECNOLOGIAS DA SAUDE. Text in Portuguese. 2004. a. **Document type:** *Journal, Academic/Scholarly.*
Published by: Universidade Lusofona de Humanidades e Tecnologia, Edicoes Universitarias, Campo Grande 376, Lisbon, 1749-024, Portugal. TEL 351-217-515500, FAX 351-217-577006, http://ulusofona.pt.

614 MOZ ISSN 0254-5705
➤ **REVISTA MEDICA DE MOCAMBIQUE.** Text in Portuguese. 1982. 4/yr. adv. back issues avail. **Document type:** *Journal, Academic/Scholarly.*
Related titles: CD-ROM ed.
Indexed: ExtraMED, FR, P30.
—GNLM, INIST.
Published by: Ministerio da Saude, Instituto Nacional de Saude, Universidade Eduardo Mondlane, Faculdade de Medicina, C.P. 264, Maputo, Mozambique. TEL 258-1-431103, FAX 258-1-431103, mdgedge@malarins.uem.mz. Eds. Dr. Joao Schwalbach, Martinho Dgedge. Circ: 1,500.

362.1 610 BRA ISSN 1679-7140
➤ **REVISTA PANAMERICANA DE INFECTOLOGIA.** Text in Spanish, Portuguese. 1997. q. **Document type:** *Journal, Academic/Scholarly.* **Description:** Its aim is to develop the network of knowledge among specialists of infectious diseases in the Americas.
Related titles: Online - full text ed.: ISSN 1807-3352. 2004. free (effective 2011).
Published by: Asociacion Panamericana de Infectologia Ed. Sergio Cimerman.

614 USA ISSN 1680-5348
REVISTA PANAMERICANA DE SALUD PUBLICA (ONLINE). Abbreviated title: R P S P. Text in English. 1997. m. free (effective 2011). back issues avail. **Document type:** *Journal, Academic/Scholarly.* **Description:** Provides readers with a wealth of information regarding diabetes prevention and control, based on the just-released results of a binational research project conducted among the US-Mexico border population.
Media: Online - full text. **Related titles:** Microfiche ed.: (from CIS).
—CCC.
Published by: Pan American Health Organization/Organizacion Panamericana de la Salud (Subsidiary of: World Health Organization/Organisation Mondiale de la Sante), 525 23rd St, NW, Washington, DC 20037. TEL 202-974-3000, FAX 202-974-3663, paho@pmds.com, http://www.paho.org.

REVISTA PERUANA DE EPIDEMIOLOGIA. *see* MEDICAL SCIENCES—Communicable Diseases

REVISTA PERUANA DE MEDICINA EXPERIMENTAL Y SALUD PUBLICA. *see* MEDICAL SCIENCES—Experimental Medicine, Laboratory Technique

362.1 613.2 MEX ISSN 1870-0160
RA451
REVISTA SALUD PUBLICA Y NUTRICION. Text in Spanish. 2000. q. free (effective 2011). **Document type:** *Journal, Academic/Scholarly.* **Description:** Its goal is to publish the scientific works of the Faculty of Public Health and Nutricion of the University of Nuevo Leon.
Media: Online - full text.
Indexed: A34, A36, C01, C25, D01, E12, H16, N03, P33, R08, T05, W11.
Published by: Universidad Autonoma de Nuevo Leon, Facultad de Salud Publica y Nutricion, Ave Eduardo Aguirre Pequeno y Yuriria, Col Mitras Centro, Monterrey, NL 64460, Mexico. TEL 52-8-3484354, respyn@faspyn.uanl.mx. Ed. Pedro Cesar Cantu Martinez.

614 FRA ISSN 0398-7620
CODEN: RESPDF
➤ **REVUE D'EPIDEMIOLOGIE ET DE SANTE PUBLIQUE/ EPIDEMIOLOGY AND PUBLIC HEALTH.** Text in French; Summaries in English. 1953. 6/yr. EUR 413 in Europe to institutions; EUR 350.64 in France to institutions; JPY 63,700 in Japan to institutions; USD 537 elsewhere to institutions (effective 2012). bk.rev. illus. index. reprints avail. **Document type:** *Journal, Academic/Scholarly.* **Description:** Publishes work on contagious diseases, together with research on cardiovascular disease, cancer, suicide, and other topics that affect public health.
Former titles (until 1975): Revue d'Epidemiologie, Medecine Sociale et Sante Publique (0035-2438); (until 1970): Revue d'Hygiene et de Medecine Sociale (0484-8454)
Related titles: Microform ed.: (from PQC); Online - full text ed.: (from ScienceDirect).
Indexed: A20, A22, A29, A34, A35, A36, ASCA, ASFA, AgBio, B20, B21, B25, BDM&CN, BIOSIS Prev, BP, CABA, CISA, CurCont, D01, E12, EMBASE, ESPM, ExcerpMed, F09, FR, GH, H&SSA, H17, I10, IBR, IBZ, INI, INIS AtomInd, IndMed, Inpharma, LT, MCR, MEDLINE, MycolAb, N02, N03, P30, P33, P35, P37, P39, R08, R10, R12, RRTA, Reac, S13, S16, SCI, SCOPUS, T05, VS, ViroIAbstr, W07, W11.
—BLDSC (7900.109000), GNLM, IE, Infotrieve, Ingenta, INIST. **CCC.**
Published by: Elsevier Masson (Subsidiary of: Elsevier Health Sciences), 62 Rue Camille Desmoulins, Issy les Moulineaux, Cedex 92442, France. TEL 33-1-71165500, infos@elsevier-masson.fr, http://www.elsevier-masson.fr. Ed. Alfred Spira. Circ: 1,300.

614.094 FRA ISSN 1766-2389
➤ **REVUE DU SOIGNANT EN SANTE PUBLIQUE.** Text in French. 2004. 6/yr. EUR 119 in Europe to institutions; EUR 95 in France to institutions; JPY 15,700 in Japan to institutions; USD 146 elsewhere to institutions (effective 2010). **Document type:** *Journal, Academic/Scholarly.* **Description:** Provides all recent news on major prevention and health education themes for public heath nurses and staff.
Related titles: Online - full text ed.
Indexed: SCOPUS.
—CCC.
Published by: Elsevier Masson (Subsidiary of: Elsevier Health Sciences), 62 Rue Camille Desmoulins, Issy les Moulineaux, Cedex 92442, France. TEL 33-1-71165500, FAX 33-1-71165600, infos@elsevier-masson.fr. Ed. Yasmina Oouharzoune.

362.1 GBR ISSN 1179-1594
➤ **RISK MANAGEMENT AND HEALTHCARE POLICY.** Text in English. 2008. irreg. free (effective 2011). **Document type:** *Journal, Academic/Scholarly.* **Description:** Focuses on all aspects of public health, policy and preventative measures to promote good health and improve morbidity and mortality in the population.
Media: Online - full text.
Indexed: SCOPUS.
—CCC.
Published by: Dove Medical Press Ltd., Beechfield House, Winterton Way, Macclesfield, SK11 0JL, United Kingdom. TEL 44-1625-509130, FAX 44-1625-617933. Ed. Carole Baskin.

344 CAN ISSN 1718-4606
RISK MANAGEMENT FOR CAMPUS RECREATION. Text in English. 2006 (Mar.). q. USD 39.95; USD 15 per issue (effective 2006). **Document type:** *Newsletter, Trade.*
Published by: Ian McGregor & Associates, #502 -1790 Bayshore Dr, Vancouver, BC V6G 3G5, Canada. TEL 604-689-4833, FAX 778-371-8075, mcgregor@studentliferisk.com, http://www.studentliferisk.com/index.php.

362.1 USA ISSN 0091-3472
RA440.6
ROBERT WOOD JOHNSON FOUNDATION. ANNUAL REPORT. Text in English. 1971. a. free. illus. **Description:** Includes a message from our President and CEO, updates on major initiatives supported, a comprehensive list of grants awarded and a complete statement of financials.
Related titles: Online - full content ed.
Indexed: MCR.
Published by: Robert Wood Johnson Foundation, College Rd East and Rt 1, PO Box 2316, Princeton, NJ 08543-2316. TEL 888-631-9989. Ed. Jeanne Weber. Circ: 30,000.

362.1 CHN ISSN 1000-9876
ROUPIN WEISHENG/MEAT HYGIENE. Text in Chinese. 1983. m. **Document type:** *Journal, Academic/Scholarly.*
Related titles: Online - full text ed.
Indexed: B21, ESPM, FS&TA, I10.
Address: 73, Guangqumen Beili Jia, Beijing, 100062, China. TEL 86-10-51356217, FAX 86-10-51356216.

ROUTE. *see* TRANSPORTATION—Automobiles

362.1 CAN ISSN 1192-8808
RUPTURES (MONTREAL, 1994). Text in French. 1994. s-a. **Document type:** *Journal, Trade.*
—CCC.
Published by: Universite de Montreal, Groupe de Recherche Interdisciplinaire en Sante, CP 6128, Succursale Centre-Ville, Montreal, PQ H3C 3J7, Canada. TEL 514-343-6185, FAX 514-343-2207, gris@umontreal.ca, http://www.gris.umontreal.ca.

362.1 AUS ISSN 1445-6354
➤ **RURAL AND REMOTE HEALTH.** Text in English. 2001. irreg. free (effective 2011). **Document type:** *Journal, Academic/Scholarly.* **Description:** Provides an easily accessible, peer-reviewed, international evidence-base to inform improvement in health service delivery and health status in rural communities.
Media: Online - full content.
Indexed: A34, A36, AgrForAb, B21, C06, C07, C08, CA, CABA, CINAHL, CurCont, D01, E12, EMBASE, ESPM, ExcerpMed, F08, GH, H&SSA, H16, IndVet, LT, MEDLINE, N02, N03, P30, P33, P37, P39, PN&I, R08, R10, R12, RRTA, Reac, SCI, SCOPUS, SSCI, T02, T05, TAR, VS, W07, W11.
—CCC.
Published by: Australian Rural Health Education Network, PO Box 242, Deakin West, ACT 2600, Australia. TEL 61-2-62822166, FAX 61-2-62829166, eo@arhen.org.au, http://www.arhen.org.au. Ed. Paul Worley.

362.1 USA ISSN 2152-0267
RURAL POLICY BRIEF. Text in English. 19??. irreg. free (effective 2010). back issues avail. **Document type:** *Monographic series, Academic/Scholarly.*
Media: Online - full text.
Indexed: MEDLINE, P30.
Published by: University of Nebraska Medical Center, RUPRI Center for Rural Health Policy Analysis, 984350 Nebraska Medical Ctr, Omaha, NE 68198. TEL 402-559-5260, FAX 402-559-7259, healthpolicy@unmc.edu.

614 RWA
RWANDA. MINISTERE DE LA SANTE PUBLIQUE. RAPPORT ANNUEL. Text in French. a. **Document type:** *Government.*
Published by: Ministere de la Sante Publique/Ministry of Health, BP 84, Kigali, Rwanda. TEL 250-577458, FAX 250-576853, info@moh.gov.rw, http://www.moh.gov.rw.

S A H O NEWS. *see* HEALTH FACILITIES AND ADMINISTRATION

362.1 CAN ISSN 1195-907X
S.A.R. NEWS. Text in English. 1988. q. CAD 16. back issues avail. **Description:** Contains land search, rescue articles with sharing information.
Published by: Search and Rescue Society of British Columbia, P O Box 187, Victoria, BC V8W 2M6, Canada. TEL 604-384-6696, FAX 604-383-6849. Ed. Mike Doyle. Adv. contact Dave Houseman. B&W page USD 815, color page USD 1,223. Circ: 3,500.

363 CAN ISSN 1183-5036
S A R S C E N E. (Search and Rescue Scene) Text in English. 1991. q.
Published by: National Search and Rescue Secretariat, 400-275 Slater St, Ottawa, ON K1A 0K2, Canada. TEL 800-727-9414, FAX 613-996-3746.

S B Z - SANITAER, HEIZUNGS-, KLIMA- UND KLEMPNERTECHNIK. (Sanitar Blech Zentralheizung) *see* HEATING, PLUMBING AND REFRIGERATION

S I FS GROENLANDSSKRIFTER. (Statens Institut for Folkesundhed) *see* MEDICAL SCIENCES

614.4 SWE ISSN 1400-3473
S M I - TRYCK. (Smittskyddsinstitutet) Text in Swedish. 1986. irreg. price varies. **Document type:** *Monographic series, Academic/Scholarly.*
Formerly (until 1994): S B L Tryck (0283-328X)
Published by: Smittskyddsinstitutet/The Swedish Institute for Infectious Disease Control, Nobels Vaeg 18, Solna, 17182, Sweden. TEL 46-8-4572300, FAX 46-8-328330, smi@smi.ki.se.

362.28 NZL ISSN 1176-1644
S P I N Z NEWS. Text in English. 1999. 3/yr. **Document type:** *Newsletter, Trade.* **Description:** Aimed at people from a range of sectors, eg, health, education, community organisations, NGOs, academia etc, working within suicide prevention or who are interested in suicide prevention information. Articles focus on research, news, updates and sector developments specific to suicide prevention in New Zealand.
Related titles: Online - full text ed.: S P I N Z e-News.

P

Published by: Suicide Prevention Information New Zealand, PO Box 10051, Auckland, 1446, New Zealand. TEL 64-9-3007035, FAX 64-9-3007020, info@spinz.org.nz.

S T I LAB SURVEILLANCE. (Sexually Transmitted Infections) *see* MEDICAL SCIENCES—Communicable Diseases

SAFETY & HEALTH. *see* OCCUPATIONAL HEALTH AND SAFETY

614.8 GBR ISSN 0958-479X
CODEN: SAFPDZ

➤ **THE SAFETY & HEALTH PRACTITIONER.** Text in English. m. GBP 105 domestic; GBP 126 foreign (effective 2009). adv. bk.rev. **Document type:** *Magazine, Academic/Scholarly.*
Formerly: Safety Practitioner (0265-4792); Which superseded: Safety Surveyor and Protection
Related titles: Microform ed.: (from PQC); Online - full text ed.
Indexed: A12, A17, A26, ABIn, AESIS, B02, B11, B15, B17, B18, CISA, E08, ErgAb, G04, G06, G07, G08, GeoRef, H13, I05, Inspec, M&MA, P10, P20, P21, P26, P48, P50, P51, P52, P53, P54, P56, PQC, S09, WSCA.
—BLDSC (8065.716000), GNLM, IE, Infotrieve, Ingenta. **CCC.**
Published by: U B M Information Ltd. (Subsidiary of: United Business Media Limited), Ludgate House, 245 Blackfriars Rd, London, SE1 9UY, United Kingdom. TEL 44-20-79218060. Ed. Martina Weadick TEL 44-20-79218047. Pub. Adrian Newton TEL 44-20-79218546. adv.: page GBP 2,280; trim 215 x 285. Circ: 27,155.

➤ **SAFETY BRIEF.** *see* ENGINEERING—Mechanical Engineering

614.8 350.78 USA ISSN 0036-245X

SAFETY BRIEFS. Text in English. 1938. 4/yr. free. bk.rev. charts; stat. **Document type:** *Magazine, Trade.*
Published by: New Jersey State Safety Council, 6 Commerce Dr, Cranford, NJ 07016-3597. TEL 201-272-7712, FAX 201-276-6622. Ed. Carol Ann Giardelli. Circ: 10,000 (controlled).

614.862 CAN ISSN 0048-8968

SAFETY CANADA. Text in English. 1957. q. free. bk.rev. **Document type:** *Newsletter, Consumer.*
Formerly: Highway Safety News
Related titles: French ed.: Prevention au Canada.
Indexed: HRIS.
Published by: Canada Safety Council, 1020 Thomas Spratt Pl, Ottawa, ON K1G 5L5, Canada. TEL 613-739-1535, FAX 613-739-1566. Ed. Ethel Archard. Circ: 400 (controlled).

614.8 658 USA

SAFETY DIRECTOR'S REPORT YEARBOOK. Text in English. a. USD 224.95 print & online eds. (effective 2003). **Description:** Provides salary surveys for managers and staff, injury prevention strategies, effective environmental health and safety policies, best practices for department management, and new technology.
Related titles: Online - full text ed.: USD 219 (effective 2003).
Published by: Institute of Management & Administration, Inc., One Washington Park, Ste 1300, Newark, NJ 07102. TEL 973-718-4700, FAX 973-622-0595, subserve@ioma.com, http://www.ioma.com. Ed. Garett Seivold.

614 GBR ISSN 0459-2034

SAFETY EDUCATION. Text in English. 1966. 3/yr. GBP 15 domestic to non-members; GBP 17.63 foreign to non-members; GBP 12.50 domestic to members; GBP 14.69 foreign to members (effective 2009). adv. bk.rev. **Document type:** *Journal, Academic/Scholarly.* **Description:** Features news items, reviews, informational articles, case studies, and technical advice on instruction to children and young adults in the adoption of safety practices.
Formerly (until 1966): Child Training
Indexed: B29.
—BLDSC (8065.750000), IE, Ingenta. **CCC.**
Published by: Royal Society for the Prevention of Accidents, Edgbaston Park, 353 Bristol Rd, Edgbaston, Birmingham, Worcs B5 7ST, United Kingdom. TEL 44-121-2482000, FAX 44-121-2482001, help@rospa.co.uk. Adv. contact Sue Philo TEL 44-1367-820949.

SAFETY MEETING REPROS. *see* OCCUPATIONAL HEALTH AND SAFETY

614 CAN

SAFETY UPDATE. Text in English. 1961. q. free. **Document type:** *Report, Trade.*
Former titles (until 1978): Ontario Safety League. News (0700-9844); (until 1969): Safety News (0700-9836)
Published by: Ontario Safety League, 5045 Orbitor Dr., Bldg. 11, Suite 100, Mississauga, ON L4W 4Y4, Canada. TEL 905-625-0556, FAX 905-625-0677, info@osl.org, http://www.osl.org. Ed. Terry W Thompson. R&P Bert Killjan.

SAFETYEXCHANGE; railway safety is everyone's business. *see* TRANSPORTATION—Railroads

362.1 USA ISSN 1556-8849

SAFETYLIT INJURY PREVENTION LITERATURE UPDATE. Text in English. 2000. w. **Document type:** *Newsletter, Trade.*
Media: Online - full text.
Published by: San Diego State University, Graduate School of Public Health. Center for Injury Prevention Policy and Practice, 6475 Alvarado Rd. Ste 105, San Diego, CA 92120. TEL 619-594-3691, FAX 619-594-1995, http://www.cippp.org/index.htm. Ed., Pub. David Lawrence.

SAINT LOUIS UNIVERSITY JOURNAL OF HEALTH LAW & POLICY. *see* LAW

614 ARG ISSN 1669-2381
RA459

➤ **SALUD COLECTIVA.** Text in Spanish. 2005. q. ARS 60 domestic; USD 60 foreign; free to qualified personnel (effective 2011). adv. bk.rev. Index. back issues avail. **Document type:** *Journal, Academic/Scholarly.*
Related titles: Online - full text ed.: ISSN 1851-8265. 2005. free (effective 2011).
Indexed: C01, SCOPUS, SSCI, W07.
—IE, INIST.
Published by: Universidad Nacional de Lanus, 29 de Septiembre 3901, Lanus, Argentina. http://www.unla.edu.ar. Ed., Adv. contact Hugo Spinelli. Circ: 1,000.

614 VEN ISSN 1315-0138

SALUD DE LOS TRABADORES. Text in Spanish. 1993. s-a. back issues avail. **Document type:** *Journal, Academic/Scholarly.*
Related titles: Online - full text ed.
Indexed: A35, A36, AgBio, CABA, E12, F08, GH, P33, R12, RM&VM, T05.
Published by: Instituto de Altos Estudios de Salud Publica, Ave Bermudez Sur, Apdo Postal 2442, Maracay, 2101, Venezuela. TEL 58-243-2325633, FAX 58-243-2326933.

362.1 MEX ISSN 1405-2091

SALUD EN TABASCO. Text in Spanish. 1995. 3/yr. **Document type:** *Journal, Academic/Scholarly.*
Related titles: Online - full text ed.: free (effective 2011).
Indexed: C01.
Published by: Mexico. Estado de Tabasco. Secretaria de Salud, Avenida Paseo Tabasco 1504, Villahermosa, Tabasco 2000, Mexico. TEL 52-993-3163488.

614 ARG ISSN 1667-9024

SALUD PUBLICA. Text in Spanish. 2001. w. back issues avail. **Document type:** *Journal, Academic/Scholarly.*
Media: Online - full text.
Published by: Sociedad Iberoamericana de Informacion Cientifica (S I I C), Ave Belgrano 430, Buenos Aires, C1092AAR, Argentina. TEL 54-11-43424901, FAX 54-11-43313305, atencionallector@siicsalud.com, http://www.siicsalud.com. Ed. Rafael Beltran Castro.

614 MEX ISSN 0036-3634

➤ **SALUD PUBLICA DE MEXICO/PUBLIC HEALTH OF MEXICO.** Text in Spanish; Summaries in English, Spanish. 1959. bi-m. MXN 250 domestic; USD 75 in Latin America; USD 105 elsewhere (effective 2007). adv. bk.rev. bibl. back issues avail.; reprints avail. **Document type:** *Journal, Academic/Scholarly.* **Description:** Publishes results of public health research.
Incorporates (in 1977): Investigacion en Salud Publica
Related titles: CD-ROM ed.; Online - full text ed.: ISSN 1606-7916. free (effective 2011).
Indexed: A20, A22, A34, A35, A36, ASCA, AgBio, AgrForAb, Artemisa, B01, B07, B25, BIOSIS Prev, C01, C25, CA, CABA, CISA, CurCont, D01, E12, EMBASE, ExcerpMed, F08, GH, H05, INI, IndMed, IndVet, Inpharma, LT, MEDLINE, MaizeAb, MycolAb, N02, N03, P30, P33, P34, P37, P39, PAIS, PHN&I, PN&I, R08, R10, R11, R12, R13, RM&VM, RRTA, Reac, S02, S03, S12, S13, S16, SCOPUS, SSCI, SoyAb, T02, T05, TAR, TriticAb, VS, W07, W11.
—BLDSC (8071.800000), GNLM, IE, Infotrieve, Ingenta, INIST.
Published by: Instituto Nacional de Salud Publica, Av Universidad 655, Col Santa Maria Ahuacatitlan, Cerrada Los Pinos y Caminera, Cuernavaca, MORELOS 62100, Mexico. TEL 52-777-1012900. Ed., Pub., R&P Carlos Oropeza-Abundez. Adv. contact Monica Fuentes-Ramirez. Circ: 4,000.

614 362.1 COL ISSN 0120-5552
R21

➤ **SALUD UNINORTE.** Text in Spanish. 1984. s-a. **Document type:** *Journal, Academic/Scholarly.* **Description:** Publishes on topics of clinical medicine and biomedical sciences.
Related titles: Online - full text ed.: free (effective 2011).
Indexed: A36, C01, CABA, GH, I04, I05, N02, P33, SCOPUS, T02, T05.
Published by: Universidad del Norte, Division de Ciencias de la Salud, Comite Editorial, A.A. 1569, Barranquilla, Colombia. http://www.uninorte.edu.co. Ed. Carlo Vinicio Caballero Uribe.

362.1 360 VEN ISSN 1690-4419

➤ **SALUD & DESARROLLO SOCIAL**; revista de educacion para la salud y el desarrollo social. Text in Spanish, Portuguese; Summaries in English. 2003. 3/yr. **Document type:** *Journal, Academic/Scholarly.*
Published by: Centro de Investigacion y Reproduccion de Especies Silvestres, Apartado Postal 397, Merida, 5101, Venezuela. cires@ciens.ula.ve, http://www.ciens.ula.ve/~cires.

362.1 PRT ISSN 1647-0788

▼ **SALUTIS SCIENTIA.** Text in Portuguese. 2009. 3/yr. **Document type:** *Magazine, Trade.*
Published by: Cruz Vermelha Portugesa/Portuguese Red Cross, Palacio do Conde d'Obidos, Lisbon, Portugal. http://www.cruzvermelha.pt.

SANGYO IKA DAIGAKU ZASSHI. *see* OCCUPATIONAL HEALTH AND SAFETY

628 ITA ISSN 1722-7194

SANITA PUBBLICA E PRIVATA; bimestrale di diritto, economia e management in sanita. Text in Italian. 1981. m. (10/yr.). EUR 84 to individuals; EUR 136 to institutions (effective 2008). adv. **Document type:** *Magazine, Trade.* **Description:** Provides information on public health for both doctors and health administrators.
Formerly (until 2002): Sanita Pubblica (0393-4101)
Indexed: DoGi, P30.
—CCC.
Published by: Maggioli Editore, Via del Carpino 8/10, Santarcangelo di Romagna, RN 47822, Italy. TEL 39-0541-628111, FAX 39-0541-622020, editore@maggioli.it, http://www.maggioli.it.

SANITAER UND HEIZUNGS REPORT; das S H K Magazin. *see* HEATING, PLUMBING AND REFRIGERATION

614 CAN ISSN 1708-7694

LA SANTE DE LA POPULATION CANADIENNE. Text in French. 1999. a., latest 2005. **Document type:** *Government.*
Media: Online - full text. **Related titles:** Supplement to: Rapports sur la Sante (Online). ISSN 1209-1375. 1996.
Published by: Statistics Canada/Statistique Canada, Communications Division, 3rd Fl, R H Coats Bldg, Ottawa, ON K1A 0A6, Canada. TEL 800-263-1136, infostats@statcan.ca, http://www.statcan.gc.ca.

362.1 FRA ISSN 1958-9719

SANTE ENVIRONNEMENT. Variant title: Sante et Environnement. Text in French. 200?. irreg. **Document type:** *Newsletter.*
Published by: Institut de Veille Sanitaire, 12 Rue du Val d'Osne, Saint-Maurice, 94415 Cedex, France. TEL 33-1-41796700, FAX 33-1-41796767.

362.1 CAN ISSN 1203-3669

SANTE ET SERVICES SOCIAUX AU QUEBEC. Text in English. biennial. CAD 52.95 (effective 2000). **Document type:** *Directory.* **Description:** Contains listings of hospitals, health center, health associations, pharmaceutical companies, unions, research centers and pharmaceutical centers in Quebec.
Published by: Quebec dans le Monde, C P 8503, Sainte Foy, PQ G1V 4N5, Canada. TEL 418-659-5540, FAX 418-659-4143.

614 FRA ISSN 0995-3914
CODEN: SPBQA

SANTE PUBLIQUE. Text in French. 1988. bi-m. EUR 75 domestic to members; EUR 90 domestic to non-members; EUR 94 foreign to members; EUR 108 foreign to non-members (effective 2010). adv. bk.rev. **Document type:** *Journal, Academic/Scholarly.*
Formed by the 1988 merger of (1978-1988): Revue Francaise de la Sante Publique (0182-8819); (1987-1988): Ecole Nationale de la Sante Publique. Cahiers (0984-9289)
Indexed: EMBASE, ExcerpMed, F09, FR, IBSS, INI, IndMed, MEDLINE, P30, R10, Reac, SCI, SCOPUS, W07.
—BLDSC (8075.350100), GNLM, INIST. **CCC.**
Published by: Societe Francaise de Sante Publique, 2, av. du Doyen J. Parisot, B.P. 7, Vandoeuvre-les-Nancy, Cedex 54501, France. TEL 33-3-83448747, FAX 33-3-83443776, sfsp@cmp.u-nancy.fr.

362.1 CAN ISSN 1911-5784

SANTE PUBLIQUE. BULLETIN. Text in French. 1968. irreg., latest 2006, October. **Document type:** *Bulletin, Trade.*
Former titles (until 1989): Sante Publiqu'action (0843-0616); (until 1988): Sante Publiqu'ation (0843-0608); (until 1987): A S P Q. Bulletin (0826-9203); (until 1984): Association pour la Sante Publique du Quebec. Bulletin (0228-426X); (until 1980): Association pour la Sante Publique du Quebec. Bulletin Bimestriel (0227-6305)
Published by: Association pour la Sante Publique du Quebec, 4126, rue St-Denis - Bureau 200, Montreal, PQ H2W 2M5, Canada. TEL 514-528-5811, FAX 514-528-5590, info@aspq.org, http://www.aspq.org/index.php.

SANTE SECURITE AU TRAVAIL. FORMULAIRE COMMENTE. *see* LAW

362.1 658.3 FRA ISSN 1956-5488

SANTE TRAVAIL. Variant title: Sante et Travail. Text in French. 200?. irreg. **Document type:** *Newsletter.*
Published by: Institut de Veille Sanitaire, 12 Rue du Val d'Osne, Saint-Maurice, 94415 Cedex, France. TEL 33-1-41796700, FAX 33-1-41796767.

362.1 CAN ISSN 1719-783X

SASKATCHEWAN. VITAL STATISTICS. ANNUAL REPORT. Text in English. 1973. a., latest 2004.
Former titles (until 2002): Saskatchewan. Vital Statistics. Annual Statistical Report (1192-0742); (until 1989): Saskatchewan Health, Vital Statistics. Statistical Supplement (1182-2171); (until 1987): Saskatchewan Health. Vital Statistics. Annual Report (0710-670X); (until 1975): Saskatchewan Vital Statistics. Annual Report (0700-2572); Vital Statistics Division of the Department of Public Health. Province of Saskatchewan. Annual Report
Published by: Saskatchewan, Department of Health. Vital Statistics, 3475 Albert St, Regina, SK S4S 6X6, Canada. TEL 306-787-3251, 800-667-7551, FAX 306-787-8951.

362.1 BRA ISSN 1806-3365

SAUDE COLETIVA. Text in Multiple languages. 2004. q. **Document type:** *Journal, Academic/Scholarly.*
Related titles: Online - full text ed.: free (effective 2011).
Indexed: A34, A36, A37, C01, C06, C07, CABA, D01, E12, F08, F11, F12, GH, H16, H17, IndVet, LT, N02, N03, P33, P39, PN&I, R08, R12, RA&MP, RM&VM, RRTA, T05, TAR, VS, W11.
Published by: Editorial Bolina Brasil (Subsidiary of: Grupo Editorial Bolina), Alameda Pucurui 51-59 B, Tamporere - Barueri, Sao Paulo, 06460-100, Brazil. Ed. Fernando Gaio.

610 BRA ISSN 0104-1290
RA463

SAUDE E SOCIEDADE. Text in Portuguese. 1991. s-a. **Document type:** *Journal, Academic/Scholarly.* **Description:** Provides articles and notes on public health.
Related titles: Online - full text ed.: free (effective 2011).
Indexed: CA, S02, S03, SCOPUS, SSA, SSCI, SociolAb, T02, W07.
Published by: Universidade de Sao Paulo, Faculdade de Saude Publica, Av Dr Arnaldo 715, Sao Paulo, 01246-904, Brazil. Eds. Cleide Lavieri Martins, Helena Ribeiro. **Co-sponsor:** Associacao Paulista de Saude Publica.

362.1 PRT ISSN 1647-0583

SAUDE E TRABALHO. Text in Portuguese. 1995. s-a. **Document type:** *Magazine, Trade.*
Published by: Sociedade Portuguesa de Medicina do Trabalho, Av da Republica 34, Lisbon, 1050-193, Portugal. spmt@spmtrabalho.com, http://www.spmtrabalho.com.

362.1 301 BRA ISSN 2178-7085

▼ **SAUDE & TRANSFORMACAO SOCIAL.** Text in Portuguese, Spanish, English. 2010. 3/yr. free (effective 2011). **Document type:** *Journal, Academic/Scholarly.*
Media: Online - full text.
Published by: Universidade Federal de Santa Catarina, Centro de Ciencias da Saude, Campus Universitario, Trindade, Florianopolis, SC, Brazil. TEL 55-48-37219394, FAX 55-48-37219542, http://portalccs.ufsc.br. Ed. Rodrigo Otavio Moretti-Pires.

614 BRA ISSN 0103-1104

SAUDE EM DEBATE. Text in Portuguese. 1976. q. **Document type:** *Journal, Academic/Scholarly.*
Published by: Centro Brasileiro de Estudos de Saude, Ave Brasil 4036, Sala 1010 - 10 Andar, Rio de Janeiro, 21040-361, Brazil. TEL 55-21-38829140.

613 NLD ISSN 1878-8254

SCHELMENSTREEK. Text in Dutch. 2008. 3/yr. EUR 12.60 (effective 2010). adv.
Related titles: Online - full text ed.: ISSN 1878-8262.
Published by: K N M G, District Limburg, Akerstraat 81, Heerlen, 6417 BJ, Netherlands. info@knmglimburg.nl. Ed. Leo Baur. Circ: 4,500.

614 DEU ISSN 1863-7523

SCHREIBEN UND FORSCHEN; Lindauer Beitraege zu Pflege und Gesundheit. Text in German. 2007. irreg. price varies. **Document type:** *Monographic series, Academic/Scholarly.*
Published by: Logos Verlag Berlin, Comeniushof, Gubener Str 47, Berlin, 10243, Germany. TEL 49-30-42851090, FAX 49-30-42851092, redaktion@logos-verlag.de. Eds. Axel Olaf Kern, Birgit Vosseler.

362.1 DEU ISSN 1866-9611

DIE SCHWESTER - DER PFLEGER PLUS. Text in German. 1990. bi-m. **Document type:** *Journal, Trade.* **Description:** Contains information and advice on various types of home and hospice care.
Formerly (until 2008): Pflegen Ambulant (0937-0277)

Related titles: Online - full text ed.; ◆ Supplement to: Die Schwester - Der Pfleger. ISSN 0340-5303.
Published by: Bibliomed - Medizinische Verlagsgesellschaft mbH, Postfach 1150, Melsungen, 34201, Germany. TEL 49-5661-73440, FAX 49-5661-8360, info@bibliomed.de, http://www.bibliomed.de. Circ: 4,810 (paid and controlled).

600 FRA ISSN 0294-0337
CODEN: SSSAEC
➤ **SCIENCES SOCIALES ET SANTE.** Text in French. q. EUR 269 combined subscription domestic to institutions (print & online eds.); EUR 285 combined subscription in the European Union to institutions (print & online eds.); EUR 293 combined subscription elsewhere to institutions (print & online eds.) (effective 2011). **Document type:** *Journal, Academic/Scholarly.* **Description:** Serves as an information exchange between all health care fields.
Related titles: Online - full text ed.: ISSN 1777-5914.
Indexed: A20, A22, A36, ASCA, CA, CABA, CurCont, E12, FR, GH, IBSS, LT, N02, N03, P30, P33, P39, P42, PAIS, PSA, R08, R12, RRTA, S02, S03, S13, S16, SCOPUS, SOPODA, SSA, SSCI, SociolAb, T02, T05, TAR, W07, W11.
—GNLM, IE, Infotrieve, INIST.
Published by: John Libbey Eurotext, 127 Av. de la Republique, Montrouge, 92120, France. TEL 33-1-46730660, FAX 33-1-40840999, contact@jle.com, http://www.john-libbey-eurotext.fr. Ed. Doris Bonnet.

➤ **SCIPOLICY (ONLINE)**; science that matters. *see* MEDICAL SCIENCES

➤ **SDU WETTENVERZAMELING. GEZONDHEIDSRECHT.** *see* LAW

353.987 USA ISSN 1550-1434
SEA & SHORE. Text in English. 2004. q. free to qualified personnel (effective 2011). back issues avail. **Document type:** *Magazine, Government.*
Formed by the merger of (1969-2004): Fathom (0014-8822); (1999-2004): Ashore (1522-5755); Which was formerly (until 1999): Safetyline (1073-9335)
Related titles: Online - full text ed.: ISSN 1555-1601. free (effective 2011).
Indexed: G05, G06, G07, G08, I05.
—Ingenta.
Published by: Naval Safety Center (Subsidiary of: U.S. Department of the Navy), 375 A St, Norfolk, VA 23511. TEL 757-444-3520, safe-pao@navy.mil, http://www.safetycenter.navy.mil/.

363 USA ISSN 1544-7308
SEARCH AND RESCUE; the official publication of the National Association for Search and Rescue. Text in English. 2003 (May). 7/yr. USD 16.75 (effective 2003).
Related titles: Online - full text ed.: ISSN 1544-7316.
Published by: (National Association for Search and Rescue), W S M Media Group, 5808 Faringdon Pl, Ste 200, Raleigh, NC 27609-3930. Pub. Lesley A Castle.

362.1 USA ISSN 1932-2526
SEARCHLIGHT (W. HOLLYWOOD). Text in English. 1991. q. **Document type:** *Magazine, Consumer.*
Published by: AIDS Research Alliance, 621-A N. San Vicente Blvd., W. Hollywood, CA 90069. TEL 310-358-2423, FAX 310-358-2431, info@aidsresearch.org.

362.1 FRA ISSN 1962-4336
LA SECURITE POUR LES ETABLISSEMENTS RECEVANT DU PUBLIC. Text in French. 1997. 2 base vols. plus q. updates. EUR 192.42 base vol(s). (effective 2010).
Formerly (until 2008): Le Nouveau Guide Pratique de la Securite pour les Etablissements Recevant du Public (1776-6982)
Published by: Editions Dalian (Subsidiary of: Wolters Kluwer France), 1 Rue Eugene et Armand Peugeot, B P 720, Rueil Malmaison, 92856 Cedex, France. TEL 33-8-25080800, FAX 33-1-76734802, dalian@dalian.tm.fr, http://www.editions-dalian.fr/.

SECURITY SPECIFIER. *see* CRIMINOLOGY AND LAW ENFORCEMENT—Security

SEGURIDAD SOCIAL. *see* SOCIAL SERVICES AND WELFARE

▼ **LA SEGURIDAD SOCIAL ES NUESTRO DERECHO.** *see* SOCIAL SERVICES AND WELFARE

SEIKATSU TO KANKYO/LIFE AND ENVIRONMENT. *see* ENVIRONMENTAL STUDIES

614 JPN ISSN 0916-7226
CODEN: SEKEEM
SENDAI-SHI EISEI KENKYUJOHO/SENDAI MUNICIPAL INSTITUTE OF PUBLIC HEALTH. REPORT. Text in Japanese. 1966. a. **Document type:** *Government.*
Formerly (until 1988): Sendai-shi Eisei Shikenjoho (0387-9771)
—BLDSC (7604.578460).
Published by: Sendai-shi Eisei Kenkyujo/Sendai Municipal Institute of Public Health, Oroshimachi-Higashi 2-5-10, Wakabayashi-ku, Sendai, Miyagi 984-0002, Japan. TEL 81-22-2367722, FAX 81-22-2368601, fuk005610@city.sendai.jp, http://www.city.sendai.jp/kenkou/eisei-ken/hygiene/index.html.

613 NLD ISSN 1874-9763
SENECA, HET JOURNAAL. Text in Dutch. 2002. irreg.
Published by: (Seneca Congres), Axioma Communicatie BV/Axioma Communications BV (Subsidiary of: Springer Science+Business Media), Lt Gen Van Heutszlaan 4, Postbus 176, Baarn, 3740 AD, Netherlands. TEL 31-35-5488140, FAX 31-35-5425820, informatie@axioma.nl, http://www.axioma.nl.

362.1 CAN ISSN 1910-0345
SERVICES DE SANTE MENTALE EN MILIEU HOSPITALIER AU CANADA. Text in French. 2001. biennial.
Media: Online - full text. **Related titles:** Print ed.: ISSN 1912-7820; ◆ English ed.: Hospital Mental Health Services in Canada. ISSN 1910-0337.
Published by: Canadian Institute for Health Information/Institut Canadien d'Information sur la Sante, 377 Dalhousie St, Ste 200, Ottawa, ON K1N 9N8, Canada. TEL 613-241-7860, FAX 613-241-8120, nursing@cihi.ca, http://www.cihi.ca.

362.1 CAN ISSN 1911-5385
SERVICES DU LABORATOIRE DE SANTE PUBLIQUE DU QUEBEC. BOTTIN. Text in French. 2006. a. **Document type:** *Directory, Consumer.*
Published by: Institut National de Sante Publique du Quebec, 945 Av Wolfe, Quebec, PQ G1V 5B3, Canada. TEL 418-650-5115 ext 5336, FAX 418-646-9328, http://www.inspq.qc.ca.

SEX TALK; keeping members in touch with F P A. *see* BIRTH CONTROL

362.1 BRA ISSN 1984-6487
▼ ➤ **SEXUALIDAD, SALUD Y SOCIEDAD.** Text in Portuguese, Spanish, English. 2009. 3/yr. free (effective 2011). **Document type:** *Journal, Academic/Scholarly.*
Media: Online - full text.
Published by: Universidade do Estado do Rio de Janeiro, Instituto de Medicina Social, Rua Sao Francisco Xavier 524, Rio de Janeiro, 20550-900, Brazil. TEL 55-21-25877303, FAX 55-21-22641142, publicacoes@ims.uerj.br.

➤ **SEXUALLY TRANSMITTED INFECTIONS IN NEW ZEALAND.** *see* MEDICAL SCIENCES—Communicable Diseases

➤ **SHIJIE DIZHEN GONGCHENG/WORLD EARTHQUAKE ENGINEERING.** *see* ENGINEERING—Civil Engineering

➤ **SHOKUHIN EISEI KENKYU/FOOD SANITATION RESEARCH.** *see* FOOD AND FOOD INDUSTRIES

613.2 JPN ISSN 0015-6426
RA601 CODEN: SKEZAP
➤ **SHOKUHIN EISEIGAKU ZASSHI/FOOD HYGIENIC SOCIETY OF JAPAN. JOURNAL.** Text in English, Japanese. 1960. bi-m. free to members. adv. bk.rev. abstr.; charts; illus. Index. back issues avail. **Document type:** *Journal, Academic/Scholarly.*
Related titles: Online - full text ed.: ISSN 1882-1006.
Indexed: A22, A34, A35, A36, A38, AESIS, ASFA, AgBio, AgrForAb, ApicAb, B21, B25, BA, BIOSIS Prev, C25, CABA, CIN, ChemAb, ChemTitl, CurCont, D01, E12, EMBASE, ESPM, ExcerpMed, F08, F11, FCA, FS&TA, G11, GH, H&SSA, H16, H17, I10, INIS AtomInd, IndMed, IndVet, MEDLINE, MaizeAb, MycolAb, N02, N03, N04, O01, P30, P32, P33, P37, P38, P39, P40, PGrRegA, PHN&I, PN&I, R07, R08, R10, R11, R13, RA&MP, RM&VM, Reac, S12, S13, S16, SCI, SCOPUS, SoyAb, T05, TAR, TriticAb, VITIS, VS, W07, W10, W11.
—BLDSC (4754.400000), CASDDS, GNLM, IE, Infotrieve, Ingenta, INIST. **CCC.**
Published by: Nihon Shokuhin Eisei Gakkai/Food Hygienic Society of Japan, 2-6-1 Jingumae, Shibuya-Ku, Tokyo, 150-0001, Japan. TEL 81-3-34702933, FAX 81-3-34702975, http://www.shokuhineisei.jp/.

➤ **SHOKUHIN SHOSHA/FOOD IRRADIATION.** *see* FOOD AND FOOD INDUSTRIES

362.1 CHN ISSN 1673-7830
SHOUDU GONGGONG WEISHENG/CAPITAL JOURNAL OF PUBLIC HEALTH. Text in Chinese. 2007. bi-m. **Document type:** *Journal, Academic/Scholarly.*
Related titles: Online - full text ed.
Published by: Beijing Shi Jibeing Yufang Kongzhi Zhongxin/Beijing Center for Disease Prevention and Control, Dongcheng-qu, 16, Hepingli Zhongjie, Beijing, 100013, China. TEL 86-10-64407286, http://www.bjcdc.org.

SICHERHEIT ZUERST. *see* TRANSPORTATION—Railroads

614.8 HRV ISSN 0350-6886
SIGURNOST/SAFETY. Text in Croatian, English. 1959. 4/yr. adv. bk.rev. charts; illus. index, cum.index. **Document type:** *Journal, Academic/Scholarly.* **Description:** Covers safety issues in the work organization and living environment.
Formerly (until 1972): Sigurnost u Pogonu (0037-508X)
Related titles: Online - full text ed.: free (effective 2011).
Indexed: A01, A28, APA, B21, BrCerAb, C&ISA, CA, CA/WCA, CIA, CISA, CerAb, CivEngAb, CorrAb, E&CAJ, E11, EEA, EMA, ESPM, EnvEAb, H&SSA, H15, M&TEA, M09, MBF, METADEX, P52, P56, RiskAb, SCOPUS, SWRA, SolStAb, T02, T04, WAA, WatResAb.
—BLDSC (8276.480000), Linda Hall.
Published by: Zavod za Istrazivanje i Razvoj Sigurnosti/Institute of Safety Research and Development, Ul Grada Vukovara 68, Zagreb, 10000, Croatia. TEL 385-1-6111334, FAX 385-1-6119812, http://www.mzt.hr. Ed. Kresimir Telebec. Adv. contact Ljubica Dunaj Mutak. Circ: 1,000; 1,000 (paid). **Co-sponsor:** Ministarstvo Znanosti i Tehnologije Republike Hrvatske.

362.1 NOR ISSN 1890-064X
SIKKERT!. Text in Norwegian. 2006. irreg. **Document type:** *Newsletter, Consumer.*
Related titles: Online - full text ed.
Published by: Skadeforebyggende Forum/Norwegian Safety Forum, PO Box 2473, Solli, Oslo, 0202, Norway. TEL 47-23-284200, FAX 47-23-284422, post@skafor.org. Eds. Peter Koren, Johan Lund. Circ: 6,000 (controlled and free).

613 IRL ISSN 1393-483X
SLAINTE. Text in English. 1997. q. adv. **Document type:** *Magazine, Consumer.*
Published by: G P Communications, 108 Baggot St. Lower, Dublin, 2, Ireland. TEL 353-1-6629452, FAX 353-1-6789855. adv.: B&W page EUR 2,900, color page EUR 3,800. Circ: 15,000 (controlled).

362.1 USA ISSN 1528-6827
TD760
SMALL FLOWS QUARTERLY. Text in English. 1994. irreg.
Formed by the merger of: Small Flows Journal (1079-1531); Small Flows Newsletter
Indexed: A32, ASFA, B21, E11, E17, ESPM, PollutAb, T04.
—Ingenta.
Published by: The National Small Flows Clearinghouse (N S F C), West Virginia University, PO Box 6064, Morgantown, WV 26506. TEL 304-293-4191, 800-624-8301, FAX 304-293-3161.

614 616.9 SWE ISSN 1401-0690
SMITTSKYDD. Text in Swedish. 1985. bi-m. SEK 320 to individuals; SEK 150 to students (effective 2007). adv. back issues avail. **Document type:** *Magazine.*
Formerly (until 1995): E P I D Aktuellt
Published by: Smittskyddsinstitutet/The Swedish Institute for Infectious Disease Control, Nobels Vaeg 18, Solna, 17182, Sweden. TEL 46-8-4572300, FAX 46-8-328330, smi@smi.ki.se. Ed. Marco Morner TEL 46-8-4572314. Adv. contact Efva Bengtsson TEL 46-8-103920. B&W 1/2 page SEK 12,000, color page SEK 15,000; 180 x 235.

SOCIAL WORK IN HEALTH CARE. *see* SOCIAL SERVICES AND WELFARE

SOCIAL WORK IN PUBLIC HEALTH. *see* SOCIAL SERVICES AND WELFARE

614 NLD ISSN 1873-9970
SOCIALE KAART GEESTELIJKE GEZONDHEIDSZORG. Text in Dutch. 1981. a. EUR 74 (effective 2008).
Formerly (until 2006): Gids Geestelijke Gezondheidszorg (1386-5331)
Published by: Bohn Stafleu van Loghum B.V. (Subsidiary of: Springer Science+Business Media), Postbus 246, Houten, 3990 GA, Netherlands. TEL 31-30-6383872, FAX 31-30-6383991, boekhandels@bsl.nl, http://www.bsl.nl.

614 GBR ISSN 0037-8119
SOCIALISM AND HEALTH. Text in English. 1970. q. free (effective 2009). bk.rev. back issues avail. **Document type:** *Magazine, Trade.* **Description:** Promotes health and well-being and the eradication of inequalities through the application of socialist principles to society and government.
Published by: Socialist Health Association, 22 Blair Rd, E Chorlton, Manchester, M16 8NS, United Kingdom. TEL 44-870-0130065, admin@sochealth.co.uk. Ed. Gavin Ross TEL 44-1582-715399.

362.1 AUS ISSN 1833-0002
SOUTH AUSTRALIA. DEPARTMENT OF HEALTH. ANNUAL REPORT. Text in English. 2002. a. free (effective 2009). back issues avail. **Document type:** *Government.* **Description:** Provides achievements of South Australia, Department of Health for each financial year.
Supersedes in part (in 2005): South Australia. Department of Human Services. Annual Report (Online Edition) (1448-8728)
Media: Online - full text.
Published by: South Australia, Department of Health, Citi Centre Bldg, 11 Hindmarsh Sq, Rundle Mall, PO Box 287, Adelaide, SA 5000, Australia. TEL 61-8-82266070, FAX 61-8-82266677, health.library@health.sa.gov.au.

362.1 BGD ISSN 2220-9476
▼ ➤ **SOUTH EAST ASIA JOURNAL OF PUBLIC HEALTH.** Text in English. forthcoming 2011. 3/yr. **Document type:** *Journal, Academic/Scholarly.* **Description:** Publishes interdisciplinary studies on any aspect of public health research and practice from any categories of health professionals of the world. Topics include quality of health, health development, health prevention and prevention, community health, occupational health, health ethics, health economics, health care management, international health, mental health and health issues for aging population.
Related titles: Online - full text ed.: forthcoming.
Published by: Public Health Foundation, 85, South Bishil, Mirpur-1, Dhaka, 1216, Bangladesh. secretariat@phfbd.org. Pub., R&P Mahmuda Chowdhury.

➤ **SOUTHEAST ASIAN JOURNAL OF TROPICAL MEDICINE AND PUBLIC HEALTH.** *see* MEDICAL SCIENCES—Communicable Diseases

614 CHE
SOZIALE MEDIZIN. Text in German. 1974. 6/yr. CHF 79 to individuals; CHF 150 to institutions (effective 2006). adv. bk.rev. **Document type:** *Newspaper, Consumer.*
Address: Postfach, Basel, 4007, Switzerland. Ed. Ruedi Spoendlin. Adv. contact Fritz Wilechi. Circ: 2,500.

SOZIALGESETZBUCH: PFLEGEVERSICHERUNG. *see* LAW—Civil Law

SPACE SECURITY. *see* AERONAUTICS AND SPACE FLIGHT

613 NLD ISSN 1877-5845
RA648.5
▼ ➤ **SPATIAL AND SPATIO-TEMPORAL EPIDEMIOLOGY.** Text in English. 2009 (Sep.). 4/yr. EUR 223 in Europe to institutions; JPY 30,500 in Japan to institutions; USD 311 elsewhere to institutions (effective 2012). **Document type:** *Journal, Academic/Scholarly.* **Description:** Provides a forum for novel developments and advances in the area of geospatial health methodology.
Related titles: Online - full text ed.: ISSN 1877-5853 (from ScienceDirect).
Indexed: EMBASE, ExcerpMed, P30, SCOPUS, T02.
—**CCC.**
Published by: Elsevier BV (Subsidiary of: Elsevier Science & Technology), Radarweg 29, PO Box 211, Amsterdam, 1000 AE, Netherlands. TEL 31-20-4853911, FAX 31-20-4852457, JournalsCustomerServiceEMEA@elsevier.com, http://www.elsevier.nl. Ed. Andrew Lawson.

363.1 USA
SPEAKING OF SAFETY. Text in English. 3/yr. USD 20 domestic; USD 25 in Canada & Mexico; USD 30 foreign (effective 2000). **Document type:** *Newsletter.*
Published by: Laboratory Safety Institute, 192 Worcester Rd, Natick, MA 01760. TEL 508-647-1900, FAX 508-647-0062, labsafe@aol.com, http://www.labsafety.org. Ed. Patricia Hamn. Circ: 2,000 (paid).

SPEYERER SCHRIFTEN ZU GESUNDHEITSPOLITIK UND GESUNDHEITSRECHT. *see* LAW

362.1 DEU
STADT HAMBURG. INSTITUT FUER HYGIENE UND UMWELT. SCHRIFTENREIHE. Text in German. 2005. irreg., latest vol.5, 2010. price varies. **Document type:** *Monographic series, Academic/Scholarly.*
Published by: (Stadt Hamburg, Institut fuer Hygiene und Umwelt), Edition Temmen, Hohenlohestr 21, Bremen, 28209, Germany. TEL 49-421-348430, FAX 49-421-348094, info@edition-temmen.de, http://www.edition-temmen.de.

362.1 USA ISSN 1931-4183
RA645.D5
STANDARDS AND GUIDELINES FOR THE DIABETES PHYSICIAN RECOGNITION PROGRAM. Text in English. 19??. irreg., latest 2006. **Document type:** *Handbook/Manual/Guide, Trade.*
Published by: National Committee for Quality Assurance, 2000 L St. NW, Ste 500, Washington, DC 20036. TEL 202-955-3500, 888-275-7585, FAX 202-955-3599, http://www.ncqa.org.

STANDARDS FOR BEHAVIORAL HEALTH CARE. *see* SOCIAL SERVICES AND WELFARE

362.1 USA ISSN 1555-9890
STANDARDS FOR HOME HEALTH, PERSONAL CARE, SUPPORT SERVICES, AND HOSPICE. Text in English. 2007. biennial. USD 138 per issue to non-members; USD 110 per issue to members (effective 2011). **Document type:** *Handbook/Manual/Guide, Consumer.*

P

Formed by the merger of (2002-2007): Standards Manual for Home Health, Personal Care, Support Services (1531-2720); (2002-2007): Standards Manual for Hospice (1531-2712)
Published by: Joint Commission Resources, Inc. (Subsidiary of: Joint Commission on Accreditation of Healthcare Organizations), 1515 W 22nd St, Ste 1300W, Oak Brook, IL 60523. TEL 630-268-7400, jcrcustomerservice@pbd.com.

362.1 USA ISSN 1931-7077
RA1138
STANDARDS FOR RELATIONSHIP TESTING LABORATORIES. Text in English. 1990. biennial. USD 95 combined subscription per issue to non-members (print & CD-ROM eds.); USD 75 combined subscription per issue to members (print & CD-ROM eds.) (effective 2011). 58 p./no.; **Document type:** *Handbook/Manual/Guide, Trade.*
Formerly (until 2005): Standards for Parentage Testing Laboratories (1549-5507)
Related titles: CD-ROM ed.
Published by: American Association of Blood Banks, 8101 Glenbrook Rd, Bethesda, MD 20814. TEL 301-907-6977, FAX 301-907-6895, aabb@aabb.org.

613 DEU
START!. Text in German. q. adv. **Document type:** *Magazine, Consumer.*
Published by: (Deutsche Angestellten Krankenkasse), Journal International Verlags- und Werbegesellschaft mbH, Hanns-Seidel-Platz 5, Munich, 81737, Germany. TEL 49-89-6427970, FAX 49-89-64279777, info@journal-international.de, http://www.journal-international.de. Ed. Kristina Salaba. Adv. contact Andreas Wienert. color page EUR 10,680; trim 210 x 272. Circ: 760,000 (controlled).

614 USA
STATE HEALTH NOTES (ONLINE EDITION). Text in English. 1979. bi-w. USD 277 to private sector; USD 197 to government, non-profit & universities (effective 2000). charts; stat. back issues avail. **Document type:** *Newsletter, Government.* **Description:** Identifies and analyzes important health-related trends and innovations within state government.
Formerly: State Health Notes (Print Edition)
Published by: National Conference of State Legislatures, Forum For State Health Policy Leadership, 444 N Capitol St, N W, Ste 515, Washington, DC 20001. TEL 202-624-5400, FAX 202-737-1069, http://www.ncsl.org/programs/health/forum/. Ed. Christina Kent. Circ: 2,000.

351 USA ISSN 1074-4754
RA395.A3
STATE HEALTH WATCH. Text in English. 1994. m. USD 399 combined subscription (print & online eds.); USD 67 per issue (effective 2010). reprints avail. **Document type:** *Newsletter, Trade.* **Description:** Focuses on the latest and most significant developments in health policy at the state and county level.
Related titles: Online - full text ed.: ISSN 1945-1539.
Indexed: A01, A26, G08, H05, H11, H12, I05, P34, P50, S02, S03, SWR&A, T02.
—CCC.
Published by: A H C Media LLC (Subsidiary of: Thomson Corporation, Healthcare Information Group), 3525 Piedmont Rd, NE, Bldg 6, Ste 400, Atlanta, GA 30305. TEL 404-262-7436, 800-688-2421, FAX 404-262-7837, 800-284-3291, customerservice@ahcmedia.com, http://www.ahcmedia.com/. Pub. Brenda L Mooney TEL 404-262-5403. **Subscr. to:** PO Box 105109, Atlanta, GA 30348. TEL 404-262-5476, FAX 404-262-5560.

362.1 CAN ISSN 1719-5179
STATE OF SAFETY REPORT. Text in English. 2004. a. **Document type:** *Government.*
Published by: British Columbia Safety Authority, 400 - 88 6th St, New Westminster, BC V3L 5B3, Canada. TEL 604-660-6286, 866-566-7233, FAX 604-660-6215, info@safetyauthority.ca.

614 SWE ISSN 0346-1823
STATUS. Text in Swedish. 1938. 8/yr. membership. adv. bk.rev. **Document type:** *Journal, Academic/Scholarly.*
Published by: Riksfoerbundet foer Hjaert- och Lungsjuka/Swedish Heart and Lung Association, Fack 9090, Stockholm, 102 72, Sweden. TEL 46-8-55606208, FAX 46-8-6682385, info@hjart-lung.se. Circ: 32,000.

614 GBR ISSN 1354-2249
STAYING ALIVE; staying alive with water & leisure. Text in English. 1966. q. GBP 22 domestic to non-members; GBP 25.85 foreign to non-members; GBP 18 domestic to members; GBP 21.15 foreign to members (effective 2009). adv. bk.rev. charts; illus.; stat. **Document type:** *Bulletin, Consumer.* **Description:** Discusses issues relevant to safety in and around the home.
Former titles (until 1994): Care in the Home (0300-5909); (until 1972): Home Safety Journal (0018-4136); Incorporates: Water and Leisure Safety
Related titles: Online - full text ed.
Indexed: M01, M02.
—BLDSC (8459.501500), IE, Ingenta. **CCC.**
Published by: Royal Society for the Prevention of Accidents, Edgbaston Park, 353 Bristol Rd, Edgbaston, Birmingham, Worcs B5 7ST, United Kingdom. TEL 44-121-2482000, FAX 44-121-2482001, help@rospa.co.uk. Adv. contact Sue Philo TEL 44-1367-820949. Circ: 2,000 (paid).

614.48 AUS ISSN 0725-7066
STERILIZATION IN AUSTRALIA. Text in English. 1981. q. back issues avail. **Document type:** *Journal, Trade.* **Description:** Covers infection control, cleaning, disinfection, sterilization, new technologies in sterilization.
Related titles: Online - full content ed.: ISSN 1444-8467.
—Ingenta.
Published by: Sterilizing Research Advisory Council of Australia, PO Box 5212, Hughesdale, VIC 3166, Australia.

STICHTING ARBEIDSMARKT ZIEKENHUIZEN. NIEUWSBRIEF. *see* BUSINESS AND ECONOMICS—Labor And Industrial Relations

363.17 NOR ISSN 0806-895X
STRAALEVERNINFO. Variant title: N R P A Bulletin. Straalevernbulletin. Text in Norwegian. 1992. irreg. **Document type:** *Newsletter, Government.*
Formerly (until 1996): Straalevern-Nytt (0803-8988)
Related titles: Online - full text ed.: ISSN 1891-5191.
Indexed: INIS AtomInd.
Published by: Statens Straalevern/Norwegian Radiation Protection Authority, PO Box 55, Oesteraas, 1332, Norway. TEL 47-67162500, FAX 47-67147407, nrpa@nrpa.no.

363.7 NOR ISSN 0804-4910
STRAALEVERNRAPPORT/N R P A REPORT. Variant title: Norwegian Radiation Protection Authority Report. Text in Multiple languages. 1979. irreg. **Document type:** *Monographic series, Government.*
Former titles (until 1994): Statens Straalevern. Rapport (0804-2098); (until 1993): S I S Rapport (0800-4137)
Related titles: Online - full text ed.: ISSN 1891-5205.
Indexed: ASFA, B21.
—BLDSC (8470.450000).
Published by: Statens Straalevern/Norwegian Radiation Protection Authority, PO Box 55, Oesteraas, 1332, Norway. TEL 47-67162500, FAX 47-67147407, nrpa@nrpa.no.

STRAHLENTELEX MIT ELEKTROSMOG-REPORT; unabhaengiger Informationsdienst zu Radioaktivitaet, Strahlung und Gesundheit. *see* ENVIRONMENTAL STUDIES—Toxicology And Environmental Safety

353.6 USA ISSN 1542-2844
STRATEGIES FOR HEALTH CARE COMPLIANCE. Text in English. 1997. m. USD 349 combined subscription (print & online eds.) (effective 2011). **Document type:** *Newsletter, Trade.*
Related titles: Online - full text ed.: ISSN 1937-7363.
Indexed: A26, H11, I05, P21, P48, P50, P52, P56, PQC.
—CCC.
Published by: H C Pro, Inc., 200 Hoods Ln, PO Box 1168, Marblehead, MA 01945. TEL 781-639-1872, 800-650-6787, FAX 781-639-7857, 800-639-8511, customerservice@hcpro.com, http://www.hcpro.com. Ed. Ilene MacDonald. Pub. Lauren McLeod.

614 DEU ISSN 1864-7286
STUDIEN ZUR INTERNATIONALEN GESUNDHEITSFORSCHUNG. Text in German. 2007. irreg., latest vol.2, 2008. price varies. **Document type:** *Monographic series, Academic/Scholarly.*
Published by: Verlag Dr. Kovac, Leverkusenstr 13, Hamburg, 22761, Germany. TEL 49-40-3988800, FAX 49-40-39888055, info@verlagdrkovac.de. Ed. Petra Scheibler-Meissner.

613.7 362.1 USA ISSN 0891-849X
➤ **STUDIES IN HEALTH AND HUMAN SERVICES.** Text in English. 1983. irreg., latest vol.55, 2004. price varies. back issues avail. **Document type:** *Monographic series, Academic/Scholarly.*
—IE, Ingenta.
Published by: Edwin Mellen Press, 415 Ridge St, PO Box 450, Lewiston, NY 14092. TEL 716-754-2266, FAX 716-754-4056, cservice@mellenpress.com.

362.1 SDN ISSN 1990-7567
SUDANESE JOURNAL OF PUBLIC HEALTH/AL-MAJALLAT AL-SUDANIYYAT LI-L-SIHHAT AL'AMMAT. Text in Arabic, English. 2006. q. **Document type:** *Journal, Academic/Scholarly.*
Indexed: A34, A36, CABA, D01, E12, GH, N02, N03, N04, P33, R08, T05, W11.
Address: PO Box 303, Khartoum, Sudan. TEL 249-183-780446, FAX 249-183-771110, editor@sjph.net.sd, http://www.sjph.net.sd/main.htm. Ed. Dr. Elsheikh Elsiddig Badr.

THE SUSTAINABLE WORLD. *see* ENVIRONMENTAL STUDIES

SUSTAINABLE WORLD SERIES. *see* ENVIRONMENTAL STUDIES

613 SWE ISSN 1651-8624
SWEDEN. STATENS FOLKHAELSOINSTITUT. RAPPORT/SWEDEN. NATIONAL INSTITUTE OF PUBLIC HEALTH. REPORT. Variant title: Sweden. Statens Folkhaelsoinstitut. Rapport R . Text in Swedish. 1993. irreg. price varies. back issues avail. **Document type:** *Monographic series, Government.*
Formerly (until 2001): Folkhaelsoinstitutet. Rapport (1104-358X)
Related titles: Online - full text ed.
Indexed: A36, CABA, E12, GH, LT, N02, N03, W11.
Published by: Statens Folkhaelsoinstitut/National Institute of Public Health in Sweden, Forskarens Vaeg, Oestersund, 83140, Sweden. TEL 46-63-199600, FAX 46-63-199602, info@fhi.se.

T B & OUTBREAKS WEEK. (Tuberculosis) *see* MEDICAL SCIENCES—Communicable Diseases

T K AKTUELL. *see* INSURANCE

362.1 KOR ISSN 1738-3897
RA541.K6
TAEHAN POGON YONGU/KOREAN PUBLIC HEALTH RESEARCH. Text in Korean. 1975. s-a. **Document type:** *Journal, Academic/Scholarly.*
Formerly (until 2007): Daehan Bo'geon Hyeobhoeji/Korean Public Health Association. Journal (1225-6250)
Published by: Daehan Bo'geon Hyeobhoe/Korean Public Health Association, Samseondong 2-ga, Seongbuk-gu, 42-12 Taegeuk Richibil # 201, Seoul, 136-043, Korea, S. TEL 82-2-9219520, FAX 82-2-9212035, kpha@khealth.org, http://khealth.org/.

614 TWN
CODEN: ZGWXEQ
TAIWAN GONGGONG WEISHENG ZAZHI/TAIWAN JOURNAL OF PUBLIC HEALTH. Text in Chinese. 1982. bi-m. TWD 1,320; free to members (effective 2005). adv. **Document type:** *Journal, Academic/Scholarly.*
Former titles: Zhonghua Gonggong Weisheng Zazhi/Chinese Journal of Public Health (1023-2141); (until 1994): Zhonghua Minguo Gonggong Weisheng Xuehui Zazhi/National Public Health Association Republic of China. Journal (1011-6931)
Indexed: A29, B20, B21, CIN, ChemAb, ChemTitl, E17, ESPM, H&SSA, I10, RiskAb, SCOPUS, ViroIAbstr.
—BLDSC (8598.633800), CASDDS.
Published by: Taiwan Gonggong Weisheng Xuehui/Taiwan Public Health Association, Graduate Institutes of Epidemiology & Public Health, College of Public Health, National Taiwan University, No.1 Jen Ai Road Section 1, Taipei, 100, Taiwan. TEL 886-2-23919529, shcheng1@ha.mc.ntu.edu.tw. Ed. Lan Ji. adv.: B&W page USD 300, color page USD 500. Circ: 3,000. **Subscr. to:** Zhongzheng District, 19, Xuzhou Road, Taipei 100, Taiwan. TEL 886-2-23584341.

614 USA
RA776.9
TAKING SIDES: CLASHING VIEWS IN HEALTH AND SOCIETY. Text in English. 1993. irreg., latest 2010, 9th ed. illus. **Document type:** *Catalog, Academic/Scholarly.* **Description:** Presents current controversial issues in a debate-style format designed to stimulate student interest and develop critical thinking skills.
Formerly (until 2006): Taking Sides: Clashing Views on Controversial Issues in Health and Society (1094-7531)
Published by: McGraw-Hill, Contemporary Learning Series (Subsidiary of: McGraw-Hill Companies, Inc.), 1221 Ave of the Americas, New York, NY 10020. TEL 212-904-2000, 800-243-6532, FAX 212-512-2000, customer.service@mcgraw-hill.com, http://www.mhhe.com/cls/.

362.84994 616.1 NZL ISSN 1177-3820
TALA LELEI. Variant title: Health Promoting Churches' Newsletter. Pacific Islands Heartbeat. Newsletter. Text in English. 2006. q. back issues avail. **Document type:** *Newsletter, Consumer.*
Related titles: Online - full text ed.: ISSN 1177-567X.
Published by: (Pacific Islands Heartbeat), National Heart Foundation of New Zealand, PO Box 17160, Greenlane, Auckland, 1130, New Zealand. TEL 64-9—5719191, FAX 64-9-5719190, info@nhf.org.nz, http://www.nhf.org.nz.

362.1 GBR ISSN 2042-9053
▼ **TARGET RESEARCH.** Text in English. 2009. irreg. **Document type:** *Magazine, Consumer.*
Related titles: Online - full text ed.: free (effective 2010).
Published by: Muscular Dystrophy Campaign, 61 Southwark St, London, SE1 0HL, United Kingdom. TEL 44-20-78034800, FAX 44-20-78013495, info@muscular-dystrophy.org, http://www.muscular-dystrophy.org/.

363.72 USA ISSN 0883-8828
TECHLETTER; for pest control technicians. Text in English. 1985. bi-w. looseleaf. USD 49 domestic; USD 57 in Canada & Mexico; USD 70 elsewhere (effective 2001). bk.rev. illus.; tr.lit. annual index. 4 p./no.; back issues avail. **Document type:** *Newsletter, Trade.* **Description:** Training information for exterminators.
Published by: Pinto & Associates, Inc., 29839 Oak Rd, Mechanicsville, MD 20659. TEL 301-884-3020, FAX 301-884-4068. Ed., R&P Sandra Kraft. Pub. Lawrence J Pinto. Circ: 1,000 (paid).

TECHNIQUES HOSPITALIERES. *see* HEALTH FACILITIES AND ADMINISTRATION

362.1 PRT ISSN 1645-9431
TECNOHOSPITAL; revista de engenharia e gestao da saude. Text in Portuguese. 1998. 3/yr. **Document type:** *Magazine, Trade.*
Published by: (Associacao de Tecnicos de Engenharia Hospitalar Portugueses (A T E H P)), Publindustria Producao de Comunicacao, Praca da Corujeira 30, Oporto, 4300-144, Portugal. TEL 351-22-5899620, FAX 351-22-5899629, info@publindustria.pt, http://www.publindustria.pt.

344.04 NLD ISSN 1877-4490
▼ **TEKSTUITGAVE ZORG EN ZIEKTEKOSTEN.** Variant title: Zorg en Ziektekosten. Text in Dutch. 2009. s-a.
Published by: Kluwer B.V. (Subsidiary of: Wolters Kluwer N.V.), Postbus 23, Deventer, 7400 GA, Netherlands. TEL 31-570-673449, FAX 31-570-691555, info@kluwer.nl, http://www.kluwer.nl.

613 FIN ISSN 0789-8789
TERVE ELAMA. Text in Finnish. 1968. 4/yr. **Document type:** *Magazine, Consumer.*
Formerly (until 1990): Tee (0355-8622)
Related titles: Online - full text ed.: ISSN 1796-1688. 2000.
Published by: Juho Vainion Saatio/The Juho Vainion Foundation, Kalevankatu 17 A, Helsinki, 00100, Finland. TEL 358-9-6941220, FAX 358-9-6943462. Ed. Juha Silvanto.

614 BEL ISSN 1370-0650
TEST SANTE. Text in French. 1994. 6/yr. **Document type:** *Consumer.*
Related titles: Dutch ed.: Test Gezondheid. ISSN 1370-0847.
Published by: Association des Consommateurs/Verbruikersunie, Rue de Hollande 13, Bruxelles, 1060, Belgium. TEL 32-2-542-3555, FAX 32-2-5423250.

614 USA
TEXAS. DEPARTMENT OF HEALTH. ANNUAL REPORT. Text in English. 1987. irreg., latest 1995. free. **Document type:** *Government.*
Formerly: Texas. Department of Health Resources. Biennial Report (0163-1667)
Published by: Texas Department of State Health Services, 1100 West 49th St, Austin, TX 78756-3199. TEL 512-458-7111, 888-963-7111, http://www.dshs.state.tx.us.

TEXAS WATER UTILITIES JOURNAL. *see* WATER RESOURCES

▼ **THERAPEUTIC ADVANCES IN DRUG SAFETY.** *see* PHARMACY AND PHARMACOLOGY

614 ZAF ISSN 1818-9059
THOUGHTS; a newsletter for supporters of the South African Federation for Mental Health. Text in English. 2006. 3/yr. **Document type:** *Newsletter.*
Related titles: ◆ Afrikaans ed.: Gedagtes. ISSN 1818-9067.
Published by: South African Federation for Mental Health/Suid-Afrikaanse Federasie vir Geestesgesondheid, Private Bag X 3053, Randburg, 2125, South Africa. TEL 27-11-7811852, FAX 27-11-3260625, safmh@sn.apc.org, http://www.safmh.org.za.

344.04 NLD ISSN 2210-6596
▼ **TIJDSCHRIFT VOOR COMPLIANCE EN ZORG.** Text in Dutch. 2011. bi-m. EUR 295 (effective 2011). **Document type:** *Journal, Trade.*
Related titles: Online - full text ed.: ISSN 2210-660X.
Published by: Uitgeverij Den Hollander, Postbus 325, Deventer, 7400 AH, Netherlands. TEL 31-570-751225, FAX 31-570-751220, info@denhollander.info, http://www.denhollander.info.

344 NLD ISSN 0165-0874
CODEN: TGEZD
TIJDSCHRIFT VOOR GEZONDHEIDSRECHT. Text in Dutch. 1977. 8/yr. EUR 151, USD 226 combined subscription to institutions (print & online eds.) (effective 2009). adv. **Document type:** *Journal, Trade.*
Related titles: Online - full text ed.: ISSN 1875-6794.
Indexed: A22, E01, ELLIS.
—IE, Infotrieve.

Published by: Bohn Stafleu van Loghum B.V. (Subsidiary of: Springer Science+Business Media), Postbus 246, Houten, 3990 GA, Netherlands. TEL 31-30-6383872, FAX 31-30-6383991, boekhandels@bsl.nl, http://www.bsl.nl. Ed. J K M Gevers. Circ: 1,200 (paid).

TIJDSCHRIFT VOOR GEZONDHEIDSWETENSCHAPPEN. *see* MEDICAL SCIENCES

614.7 NLD ISSN 1872-5589
TOETS. Text in Dutch. 1994. bi-m. EUR 115; EUR 25 to students; EUR 21.50 newsstand/cover (effective 2008). adv. **Document type:** *Magazine, Trade.*
Formerly (until 2006): Kenmerken (0929-7537)
—IE.
Published by: Aeneas, Postbus 101, Boxtel, 5280 AC, Netherlands. TEL 31-411-650085, FAX 31-411-650080, mail@aeneas.nl. Eds. Emiel Bootsma, Diederik Bel.

TOKYO TORITSU EISEI KENKYUJO KENKYU NENPO/TOKYO METROPOLITAN RESEARCH LABORATORY OF PUBLIC HEALTH. ANNUAL REPORT. *see* MEDICAL SCIENCES

TRABALHO, EDUCACAO E SAUDE. *see* BUSINESS AND ECONOMICS—Labor And Industrial Relations

362.1 USA ISSN 1553-0787
TRACKING REPORT. Text in English. 2002. irreg., latest vol.14, 2006. **Document type:** *Bulletin, Trade.* **Description:** Follows key health care trends over time.
Media: Online - full content.
Indexed: EMBASE, ExcerpMed, MEDLINE, P30, SCOPUS.
Published by: Center for Studying Health System Change, 600 Maryland Ave, S W, Ste 550, Washington, DC 20024. TEL 202-484-5261, FAX 202-484-9258, hscinfo@hschange.org.

TRAFFIC INJURY PREVENTION. *see* ENGINEERING—Mechanical Engineering

614.8 380.5 USA ISSN 8756-4408
HE202.5
TRANSPORTATION SAFETY RECOMMENDATIONS. Text in English. 19??. m. back issues avail. **Document type:** *Report, Government.* **Description:** Provides reports on the board's safety oversight and accident information prevention activities and information on important transportation problems, issues, and other activities.
Published by: (U.S. Department of Transportation, National Transportation Safety Board, Bureau of Safety Programs), U.S. Department of Commerce, National Technical Information Service, 5301 Shawnee Rd, Alexandria, VA 22312. TEL 703-605-6000, 800-553-6847, info@ntis.gov, http://www.ntis.gov.

TRAUMA, VIOLENCE & ABUSE; a review journal. *see* MEDICAL SCIENCES—Orthopedics And Traumatology

613 NLD ISSN 1871-3467
TRENDRAPPORT BEWEGEN EN GEZONDHEID. Text in Dutch. 1997. biennial. EUR 25 (effective 2010).
Published by: (T N O, Preventie en Gezondheid), T N O, Kwaliteit van Leven, Wassenaarseweg 56, Postbus 56, Leiden, 2301 CE, Netherlands. TEL 31-71-5181817, FAX 31-71-5181903, info-arbeid@tno.nl, http://www.tno.nl/arbeid.

614 USA
TRENDS (WASHINGTON, 1969). Text in English. 1969. m. free to members (effective 2010). bk.rev. back issues avail. **Document type:** *Newsletter.*
Formerly: Allied Health Trends
Related titles: Online - full text ed.: free (effective 2010).
Published by: Association of Schools of Allied Health Professions, 4400 Jenifer St, NW Ste 333, Washington, DC 20015. TEL 202-237-6481, FAX 202-237-6485, asahp@asahp.org. Ed. Thomas W Elwood.

TRIODYNE SAFETY BULLETIN. *see* OCCUPATIONAL HEALTH AND SAFETY

TROPICAL MEDICINE & INTERNATIONAL HEALTH. *see* MEDICAL SCIENCES—Communicable Diseases

362.1 614 344.04 FRO ISSN 1604-3189
TRYGD & TRIVNI. Text in Faroese. 1988-2001; resumed 2005. irreg. adv. back issues avail. **Document type:** *Magazine, Trade.*
Related titles: Online - full text ed.
Published by: Arbeidsseftirlitid/Occupational Safety and Health Office, Falkavegur 6, Torshavn, 100, Faeroe Islands. TEL 298-357811, FAX 298-357810, arb@arb.fo. Ed. Aime Jacobsen.

TSUINFO ALERT. *see* EARTH SCIENCES—Geology

614 312 CAN ISSN 1487-9182
TUBERCULOSIS IN CANADA/CANADA. STATISTIQUE CANADA. LA STATISTIQUE DE LA TUBERCULOSE, VOLUME 2: INSTALLATIONS, SERVICES ET FINANCE DES ETABLISSEMENTS. (Catalog 83-207) Text in English, French. 1974. a. CAD 0.70, USD 0.85.
Former titles (until 1995): Canada. Statistics Canada. Tuberculosis Statistics (1195-4086); (until 1991): Canada. Statistics Canada. Health Reports. Supplement. Tuberculosis Statistics (1180-2413); (until 1987): Canada. Statistics Canada. Tuberculosis Statistics. Morbidity and Mortality (0708-4277); (until 1976): Canada. Statistics Canada. Tuberculosis Statistics. Morbidity and Mortality. Facilities and Services (0706-4365); Which was formed by the merger of (1937-1974): Canada. Statistics Canada. Volume 1: Tuberculosis Morbidity and Mortality (0381-887X); (1937-1974): Canada. Statistics Canada. Volume 2: Institutional Facilities, Services and Finances (0381-8845); Both of which superseded in part (in 1962): Canada. Bureau of Statistics. Tuberculosis Statistics (0381-8837); Which was formerly (until 1953): Canada. Bureau of Statistics. Tuberculosis Institutions (0381-8829); (until 1948): Canada. Bureau of Statistics. Annual Report of Tuberculosis Institutions (0381-8810)
—CCC.
Published by: Statistics Canada/Statistique Canada, Communications Division, 3rd Fl, R H Coats Bldg, Ottawa, ON K1A 0A6, Canada. http://www.statcan.gc.ca.

362.1 TUR
CODEN: THBDA2
TURK HIJIYEN VE DENEYSEL BIYOLOJI DERGISI/REVUE TURQUE D'HYGIENE ET DE BIOLOGIE EXPERIMENTALE/TURKISH BULLETIN OF HYGIENE AND EXPERIMENTAL BIOLOGY. Text in Turkish, English. 1938. 3/yr. bk.rev. bibl.; charts; illus. back issues avail. **Document type:** *Journal, Academic/Scholarly.*
Former titles (until 1982): Turk Hijiyen ve Tecrubi Biyoloji Dergisi (1016-3379); (until 1977): Turk Hijiyen ve Deneysel Biyoloji Dergisi (0377-9777); (until 1975): Turk Hijiyen ve Tecrubi Biyologi Dergisi (0049-4844); (until 1945): Turk Hifzissihha ve Tecruebi Biyoloji Mecmuasi (0371-7445)
Related titles: Online - full text ed.: free (effective 2011).
Indexed: A34, A35, A36, AgBio, B23, BP, CABA, ChemAb, D01, E12, F08, F11, F12, GH, H16, H17, IndMed, IndVet, N02, N03, N04, OR, P30, P32, P33, P39, P40, PGegResA, R08, R12, RA&MP, RM&VM, S13, S16, T05, VS, W11.
—BLDSC (9072.130000), GNLM, INIST.
Published by: Refik Saydam Hifzissihha Merkezi Baskanligi/Refik Saydam Hygiene Center, Cemal Gursel Cad., No:18 Sihhiye, Ankara, 06100, Turkey. TEL 90-312-4580000, FAX 90-312-4582408, bilgiedinme@rshm.gov.tr, http://www.rshm.gov.tr/. Ed. Dr. Aysegul Taylan Ozkan.

TURK SILAHLI KUVVETLER KORUYUCU HEKIMLIK BILGISI/T A F. PREVENTIVE MEDICINE BULLETIN. *see* MEDICAL SCIENCES

362.1 TKM
CODEN: ZDTUAB
TURKMENISTANYN LUKMANCYLYGY/TURKMENISTAN HEALTH CARE. Text in Turkmen, Russian, English. 1971. bi-m. USD 291 foreign (effective 2007). **Document type:** *Journal, Academic/Scholarly.*
Formerly (until 1992): Zdravookhranenie Turkmenistana (0513-8736)
Indexed: P30, RASB.
—CASDDS, East View, GNLM, INIST.
Published by: Ministry of Public Health, Ul Kerbabaeva 39-57, Ashgabat, 744004, Turkmenistan. TEL 993-12-391621. **Dist. by:** East View Information Services, 10601 Wayzata Blvd, Minneapolis, MN 55305. TEL 952-252-1201, 800-477-1005, FAX 952-252-1202, info@eastview.com, http://www.eastview.com.

362.1 USA ISSN 1559-4920
U R A C DIRECTORY OF ACCREDITED ORGANIZATIONS AND RESOURCE GUIDE. (Utilization Review Accreditation Commission) Text in English. 200?. a. **Document type:** *Directory, Consumer.*
Published by: U R A C, 1220 L St NW, Ste 400, Washington, DC 20005. TEL 202-216-9010, FAX 202-216-9006, directory@urac.org, http://www.urac.org.

614 USA
U S C HEALTH AFFAIRS. (University of Southern California) Text in English. 1976. a.
Published by: University of Southern California, Keck School of Medicine, Health Sciences Campus, University of Southern California, Los Angeles, CA 90033. TEL 323-442-1100, http://www.usc.edu/schools/medicine/ksom.html.

304.6 USA ISSN 1057-5987
RA407.3
U.S. CENTERS FOR DISEASE CONTROL AND PREVENTION. MORBIDITY AND MORTALITY WEEKLY REPORT. RECOMMENDATIONS AND REPORT. Text in English. 1982. irreg. USD 5 per issue domestic; USD 6.30 per issue foreign (effective 2010). back issues avail. **Document type:** *Report, Government.* **Description:** Contains articles that relay policy statements for prevention and treatment on all areas in Centers for Disease Control and Prevention scope of responsibility.
Formerly (until 1989): Morbidity and Mortality Weekly Report. Supplement
Related titles: Online - full text ed.: ISSN 1545-8601. free (effective 2011).
Indexed: A01, A02, A03, A08, C06, C07, C08, C11, CA, CINAHL, EMBASE, ExcerpMed, H01, H02, H04, Inpharma, MEDLINE, P30, P35, R10, Reac, SCOPUS, T02.
Published by: U.S. Department of Health and Human Services, Centers for Disease Control and Prevention, 1600 Clifton Rd, Atlanta, GA 30333. TEL 800-843-6356, 800-232-4636, cdcinfo@cdc.gov. Ed. Ron Moolenaar TEL 404-498-0576. **Subscr. to:** U.S. Government Printing Office, Superintendent of Documents.

614 USA ISSN 1930-8396
U.S. CENTERS FOR DISEASE CONTROL. SALMONELLA ANNUAL SUMMARY. Text in English. 1962. a., latest 2006. charts; stat. back issues avail. **Document type:** *Government.*
Formerly (until 199?): U.S. Centers for Disease Control. Salmonella Surveillance. Annual Summary
Media: Online - full text.
Published by: U.S. Department of Health and Human Services, Centers for Disease Control and Prevention, 1600 Clifton Rd, Atlanta, GA 30333. TEL 800-232-4636, cdcinfo@cdc.gov.

362.1 368.4 USA
U.S. DEPARTMENT OF HEALTH AND HUMAN SERVICES. CENTERS FOR MEDICARE & MEDICAID SERVICES. DATA COMPENDIUM (ONLINE). Text in English. a. **Document type:** *Government.*
Formerly (until 2002): U.S. Department of Health and Human Services. Centers for Medicare & Medicaid Services. Data Compendium (Print)
Media: Online - full content.
Published by: U.S. Department of Health and Human Services, Centers for Medicare & Medicaid Services, 7500 Security Blvd, Baltimore, MD 21244-1850. TEL 410-786-3000, 877-267-2323, http://www.cms.hhs.gov.

353 USA ISSN 0738-0372
RC261.A1
U.S. NATIONAL CANCER INSTITUTE. DIVISION OF EXTRAMURAL ACTIVITIES. ANNUAL REPORT. Text in English. a.
Published by: U.S. National Cancer Institute, Division of Extramural Activities, 6116 Executive Blvd, Rockville, MD 20852. http://deainfo.nci.nih.gov/.

362 USA
U.S. NATIONAL CENTER FOR HEALTH STATISTICS. VITAL AND HEALTH STATISTICS. SERIES 13. DATA ON HEALTH RESOURCES UTILIZATION. Text in English. 1966. irreg., latest vol.168, 2011. free (effective 2011). back issues avail. **Document type:** *Monographic series, Government.* **Description:** Contains statistics on the utilization of health manpower and facilities providing long-term care, ambulatory care, and family planning services.
Formerly (until 19??): U.S. National Center for Health Care Statistics. Vital and Health Statistics. Series 13. Data from the Hospital Discharge Survey (0083-2006); Which incorporated (1965-1974): U.S. National Center for Health Care Statistics. Vital and Health Statistics. Series 12. Data from the Institutional Population Surveys (0083-1964)
Related titles: Online - full text ed.
Indexed: CIS, EMBASE, ExcerpMed, IndMed, MEDLINE, P30, R10, Reac, SCOPUS.
—INIST.
Published by: U.S. National Center for Health Statistics, Data Dissemination Branch, Centers for Disease Control and Prevention, 3311 Toledo Rd, Rm 5407, Hyattsville, MD 20782. TEL 301-436-8500, 800-232-4636, FAX 301-436-4258, nchsed@cdc.gov.

353.0087 USA ISSN 1056-9030
KF2138
U.S. NUCLEAR REGULATORY COMMISSION. OFFICE OF ENFORCEMENT. SIGNIFICANT ENFORCEMENT ACTIONS. Text in English. 198?. s-a. **Document type:** *Government.*
Published by: (U.S. Nuclear Regulatory Commission, Office of Inspection and Enforcement), U.S. Nuclear Regulatory Commission, Washington, DC 20555. TEL 301-415-7000, 800-368-5642.

362.1 USA ISSN 0749-5005
U.S. REGULATORY REPORTER. Text in English. 198?. m. USD 395 in North America; USD 425 in Europe; USD 445 elsewhere (effective 2005). **Document type:** *Newsletter.* **Description:** Provides regulatory information for the pharmaceutical, medical, and allied industries.
—IE.
Published by: Barnett International, Rose Tree Corporate Ctr, 1400 N Providence Rd, Suite 2000, Media, PA 19063-2043. TEL 800-856-2556, FAX 610-565-5223, barnettinfo@parexel.com, http://www.barnettinternational.com.

613 IRL ISSN 1393-922X
ULTIMATE HEALTH. Text in English. 2000. bi-m. adv. **Document type:** *Magazine, Consumer.*
Address: Swan House, Leixlip, Co. Kildare, Ireland. TEL 353-1-6242827, FAX 353-1-6243272, info@ultimatehealth.ie. adv.: color page EUR 1,651. Circ: 18,000 (controlled).

628 AUT ISSN 0049-5131
UMWELTSCHUTZ. Text in German. 1963. 10/yr. EUR 56.60 domestic; EUR 75 foreign (effective 2004). adv. bk.rev. illus. **Document type:** *Magazine, Trade.*
Published by: Bohmann Druck und Verlag GmbH & Co. KG, Leberstr 122, Vienna, W 1110, Austria. TEL 43-1-740950, FAX 43-1-74095183, office.gl@bohmann.at, http://www.bohmann.at. Ed. Leopold Lukschanderl. Adv. contact Fiala Scheherezade. B&W page EUR 3,287, color page EUR 4,374; trim 185 x 250. Circ: 14,000.

UNIFORMED SERVICES UNIVERSITY OF THE HEALTH SCIENCES JOURNAL. *see* MILITARY

UNIT COSTS OF HEALTH & SOCIAL CARE. *see* SOCIAL SERVICES AND WELFARE

614 USA
UNITED STATES - MEXICO BORDER HEALTH ASSOCIATION. NEWS - NOTICIAS. Text in English, Spanish. 1976. q. USD 75 membership (effective 2007). **Document type:** *Newsletter, Trade.* **Description:** Reports on the activities of the association and its membership.
Published by: United States - Mexico Border Health Association, 5400 Suncrest Dr, Ste C-5, El Paso, TX 79912. TEL 915-833-6450, FAX 915-833-7840, mail@usmbha.org. Ed. Dr. Gerardo De Cosio. Circ: 800.

362.1 ARG ISSN 0327-3741
UNIVERSIDAD NACIONAL DE CORDOBA. FACULTAD DE CIENCIAS MEDICAS. ESCUELA DE SALUD PUBLICA. REVISTA. Text in Spanish. 1989. s-a. **Document type:** *Journal, Academic/Scholarly.*
Related titles: Online - full text ed.: free (effective 2011).
Indexed: C01.
Published by: Universidad Nacional de Cordoba, Facultad de Ciencias Medicas, Enrique Barros esq Enfermeria Gordillo Gomez, Ciudad Universitaria, Cordoba, 5000, Argentina. TEL 54-351-4333023, http://www.unc.edu.ar.

362.1 CAN ISSN 0830-890X
UNIVERSITE DE MONTREAL. GROUPE DE RECHERCHE INTERDISCIPLINAIRE EN SANTE. RAPPORT. Text in French. 1980. irreg. **Document type:** *Monographic series, Academic/Scholarly.*
Published by: Universite de Montreal, Groupe de Recherche Interdisciplinaire en Sante, CP 6128, Succursale Centre-Ville, Montreal, PQ H3C 3J7, Canada. TEL 514-343-6185, FAX 514-343-2207, gris@umontreal.ca, http://www.gris.umontreal.ca.

UNSCHEDULED EVENTS; research committee on disasters newsletter. *see* SOCIOLOGY

UNTER EINEM DACH. *see* INSURANCE

393.1 AUT ISSN 0042-0581
UNTERNEHMER; Magazin fuer Fuehrungskraefte der Wirtschaftskammern. Text in German. 1960. m. **Document type:** *Magazine, Trade.*
Published by: Wirtschaftskammer Oesterreich, Wiedner Hauptstr 63, Vienna, 1045, Austria. TEL 43-1-590900, FAX 43-1-590900250, callcenter@wko.at, http://wko.at. Circ: 14,333.

614 ZAF ISSN 1729-4991
URBAN HEALTH AND DEVELOPMENT BULLETIN. Text in English. 1989. q. free. **Document type:** *Bulletin, Trade.* **Description:** Contains information about urbanization and related health matters of interest to community health groups and organizations involved in urban policy formulation.
Formerly (until 1998): Urbanisation and Health Newsletter (1028-3315)
Indexed: ISAP, SCOPUS.
Published by: (National Urbanisation and Health Research Programme), Medical Research Council, PO Box 19070, Tygerberg, 7505, South Africa. TEL 27-21-938-0417, FAX 27-21-938-0342. Ed. Dr. John Seager. R&P Pam Cerff. Circ: 800.

UTAH MOSQUITO ABATEMENT ASSOCIATION. ANNUAL MEETING. PROCEEDINGS. *see* BIOLOGY—Entomology

V F D B; Zeitschrift fuer Forschung, Technik und Management im Brandschutz. (Vereinigung zur Foerderung des Deutschen Brandschutzes) *see* ENGINEERING—Chemical Engineering

P

VAASAN YLIOPISTO. JULKAISUJA. TUTKIMUKSIA. SOSIAALI- JA TERVEYSHALLINTO. *see* CRIMINOLOGY AND LAW ENFORCEMENT

614.4 616.97 USA ISSN 1525-7061
VACCINATE ADULTS. Text in English. 1997. s-a. free (effective 2011). back issues avail. **Document type:** *Newsletter, Trade.* **Description:** A magazine written for health professionals who provide services for adults.
Related titles: Online - full text ed.: ISSN 1526-1824.
Published by: Immunization Action Coalition, 1573 Selby Ave, Ste 234, St. Paul, MN 55104. TEL 651-647-9009, FAX 651-647-9131, admin@immunize.org. Ed. Dr. Deborah Wexler.

VACCINE WEEKLY. *see* PHARMACY AND PHARMACOLOGY

VEILIGHEID VOOROP. *see* TRANSPORTATION—Roads And Traffic

VERKEHRSPSYCHOLOGISCHER INFORMATIONSDIENST. *see* TRANSPORTATION—Roads And Traffic

362.1 AUS ISSN 1833-9042
VICMAP CATALOGUE. Text in English. 2003. a. free (effective 2010). **Document type:** *Catalog, Government.*
Formerly (until 2006): Vicmap Spatial Information Catalogue
Related titles: Online - full text ed.: ISSN 1833-9050. free (effective 2010).
Published by: State of Victoria, Department of Sustainability and Environment, PO Box 500, East Melbourne, VIC 3002, Australia. TEL 61-3-86362333, FAX 61-3-86362813, customer.service@dse.vic.gov.au.

362.1 AUS
VICTORIA. DEPARTMENT OF HUMAN SERVICES. ANNUAL REPORT (YEAR). Text in English. 1993. a. free (effective 2009). **Document type:** *Government.*
Formerly (until 1996): Victoria. Health and Community Services. Annual Report (1321-1471); Which was formed by the merger of (1990-1993): Victoria. Community Services Victoria. Annual Report (1037-4965); Which was formerly (1985-1989): Victoria. Department of Community Services. Report for the (Year) (0817-1343); (until 1985): Victoria. Department of Community Welfare Services. Annual Report (0726-8831); (until 1978): Victoria. Social Welfare Department. Annual Report for the (Year) (0726-9005); (1992-1993): Victoria. Health and Community Services. Health Annual Report (1322-4980); Which was formerly (1990-1992): Victoria. Department of Health. Annual Report (1030-8873); (until 1990): Victoria. Health Department Report (1322-4972); (1983-1985): Victoria. Health Comminion Report (1030-8865)
Related titles: Online - full text ed.
Published by: Victoria, Department of Human Services, 50 Lonsdale St, Melbourne, VIC 3000, Australia. TEL 61-3-90960000, 300-650-172, http://www.dhs.vic.gov.au/.

613 DEU
VIGO! UNILIFE BLEIBGESUND. Text in German. bi-m. free. adv. **Document type:** *Magazine, Consumer.*
Published by: (AOK-Bundesverband), W D V Gesellschaft fuer Medien & Kommunikation mbH & Co. OHG, Siemensstr 6, Bad Homburg, 61352, Germany. TEL 49-6172-6700, FAX 49-6172-670144, info@wdv.de, http://www.wdv.de. adv.: page EUR 4,000; trim 190 x 260. Circ: 268,837 (controlled).

614.8 USA ISSN 0199-1345
VIRGINIA'S HEALTH. Text in English. 1970. bi-m. free.
Supersedes (in 1979): Virginia Health Bulletin (0042-6547)
Published by: Virginia. Department of Health, Office of Health Education and Information, 109 Governor St, P.O. Box 2448, Richmond, VA 23218-2448. TEL 804-786-3552, FAX 804-371-6152, http://www.vdh.state.va.us. Ed. Dudley Olsson. Circ: 6,000.

616.9101 362.1 NZL ISSN 1179-903X
VIROLOGY WEEKLY REPORT (ONLINE). Text in English. 1994. w. free (effective 2010). back issues avail. **Document type:** *Report, Trade.*
Formerly (until 2010): Virology Weekly Report (Print) (1173-1680)
Media: Online - full text.
Published by: Institute of Environmental Science & Research Ltd., Kenepuru Science Centre, 34 Kenepuru Dr, PO Box 50-348, Porirua, 5240, New Zealand. TEL 64-4-9140700, FAX 64-4-9140770, enquiries@esr.cri.nz, http://www.esr.cri.nz. Eds. Judy Bocacao, Wendy Gunn.

362.1 LTU ISSN 1392-2696
VISUOMENES SVEIKATA/PUBLIC HEALTH. Text in Lithuanian, English. 1996. q. EUR 30 domestic; EUR 60 foreign (effective 2011). back issues avail. **Document type:** *Journal, Academic/Scholarly.* **Description:** Intended for researchers, public health managers and administrators, experts working in the field of epidemiology, biostatistics, occupational and environmental health as well as other readers interested in health status of population and factors affecting. Presents important health policy news, good practice examples, guidelines and recommendations.
Related titles: Online - full text ed.
Published by: Higienos Institutas/Institute of Hygiene, Dadzioji 22, Vilnius, 1128, Lithuania. TEL 370-52625479, FAX 370-52624663, institutas@hi.lt. Ed. Vytautas Jurkuvenas. Pub. Remigijus Jankauskas. Circ: 150.

355 USA
VITAL SIGNS (CAMBRIDGE). Text in English. 1988. 2/yr. USD 25 domestic; USD 35 foreign (effective 2000). bk.rev.; film rev. charts; illus. back issues avail. **Document type:** *Newsletter.* **Description:** Unites an international federation of 80 physicians' organizations worldwide practicing global social responsibility.
Related titles: Online - full text ed.
Published by: International Physicians for the Prevention of Nuclear War, 727 Massachusetts Ave, Cambridge, MA 02139-3323. TEL 617-868-5050, FAX 617-868-2560. Ed., R&P Lynn Martin. Circ: 30,000.

614 MEX ISSN 2007-0721
▼ **VIVA SALUD.** Text in Spanish. 2010. bi-m. **Document type:** *Bulletin, Government.*
Published by: Instituto Nacional de Salud Publica, Av Universidad 655, Col Santa Maria Ahuacatitlan, Cerrada Los Pinos y Caminera, Cuernavaca, MORELOS 62100, Mexico. TEL 52-777-1012900, mmorales@insp.mx, http://www.insp.mx.

628 RUS ISSN 0321-4044
CODEN: VSTEAO
VODOSNABZHENIE I SANITARNAYA TEKHNIKA. Text in Russian. 1913. m. USD 229 foreign (effective 2007). index. **Document type:** *Magazine, Trade.* **Description:** Covers construction of water-supply and sewage systems, water treatment and purification of sewage, heat supply, heating ventilation, environmental protection.
Indexed: CIN, CISA, ChemAb, ChemTitl, GeoRef, IBuildSA, RefZh, SpeleolAb.
—CASDDS, East View, INIST, Linda Hall. **CCC.**
Published by: Stroiizdat, Komsomol'skii pr-t 42, str. 2, Moscow, 119992, Russian Federation. Ed. V N Shvetsov. Circ: 17,000. **Dist. by:** East View Information Services, 10601 Wayzata Blvd, Minneapolis, MN 55305. TEL 952-252-1201, 800-477-1005, FAX 952-252-1202, info@eastview.com, http://www.eastview.com.

VOICES (WASHINGTON). *see* SOCIAL SERVICES AND WELFARE

614 361 DNK
VOKSNE (ONLINE). Text in Danish. irreg. DKK 800 (effective 2005). **Document type:** *Consumer.*
Media: Online - full text.
Published by: Jurainformation, Vesterbrogade 10, Copenhagen V, 1620, Denmark. TEL 45-70-230102, FAX 45-70-230103, post@jurainformation.dk, http://www.jurainformation.dk. Ed. Erik Voelund Mortensen.

614 NLD ISSN 1878-9455
VOOR U. Text in Dutch. 2003. q. **Document type:** *Magazine, Trade.*
Formerly (until 2007): B R U L Magazine (1571-9332); Which was formed by the 2003 merger of: Regio Bulletin. Eemland (1382-7456); Brandpost (1383-0724)
Published by: Veiligheidsregion Utrecht, Postbus 3154, Utrecht, 3502 GD, Netherlands. TEL 31-30-2404400, FAX 31-30-2404516, info@vru.nl.

614 DEU
VORDRUCKE FUER DIE VERTRAGSAERZTLICHE VERSORGUNG MIT ERLAEUTERUNGEN. Text in German. 1978. base vol. plus irreg. updates. looseleaf. price varies. **Document type:** *Monographic series, Academic/Scholarly.*
Formerly: Vordrucke fuer die Kassenaerztliche und Vertragsaerztliche Versorgung mit Erlaeuterungen (0934-8794)
Published by: Erich Schmidt Verlag GmbH & Co. (Berlin), Genthiner Str 30 G, Berlin, 10785, Germany. TEL 49-30-2500850, FAX 49-30-250085305, vertrieb@esvmedien.de, http://www.erich-schmidt-verlag.de.

362.1 NZL ISSN 1177-5157
VOYAGES. Text in English. 2006. s-a. **Document type:** *Newsletter, Trade.* **Description:** Aimed at those who are actively involved or have a strong interest in health issues relating to Pacific peoples.
Related titles: Online - full text ed.: ISSN 1177-5165.
Published by: Ministry of Health, Pacific Health Branch, PO Box 5013, Wellington, New Zealand. TEL 64-4-4962000, FAX 64-4-4962340, http://www.moh.govt.nz/pacific.

VSEMIRNAYA ORGANIZATSIYA ZDRAVOOKHRANENIYA. SERIYA TEKHNICHESKIKH DOKLADOV. *see* MEDICAL SCIENCES

VULNERABLE CHILDREN AND YOUTH STUDIES; an international interdisciplinary journal for research, policy and care. *see* CHILDREN AND YOUTH—About

614.8 CHE ISSN 1010-9609
RS189 CODEN: WDINE8
W H O DRUG INFORMATION. Text in English. 1987. q. CHF 112, USD 134.40 (effective 2012). **Document type:** *Journal, Academic/Scholarly.* **Description:** Communicates medicinal drug information that is either developed and issued by WHO or transmitted to WHO by research and regulatory agencies throughout the world.
Related titles: Online - full text ed.: ISSN 1996-8361. 200?; ◆ French ed.: Informations Pharmaceutiques O M S. ISSN 1011-5706.
Indexed: A01, A03, A08, A22, A26, A36, C06, C07, C08, C11, CA, CABA, CINAHL, E08, EMBASE, ExcerpMed, FR, G06, G07, G08, GH, H01, H04, H11, H12, I05, I12, IDIS, Inpharma, P10, P19, P21, P24, P27, P33, P34, P39, P48, P50, P52, P53, P54, P56, PQC, R12, S02, S03, S09, SCOPUS, T02, T05, TAR, W11.
—CASDDS, GNLM, IE, Infotrieve, Ingenta, INIST. **CCC.**
Published by: World Health Organization/Organisation Mondiale de la Sante, Avenue Appia 20, Geneva 27, 1211, Switzerland. TEL 41-22-7912111, FAX 41-22-7913111, publications@who.int. Circ: 1,848.

W H O TECHNICAL REPORT SERIES. *see* MEDICAL SCIENCES

362.1 THA ISSN 0125-1678
WARASAN SATHARANASUK SAT/JOURNAL OF PUBLIC HEALTH. Text in Thai. 1968. 3/yr. USD 20 (effective 2006). **Document type:** *Journal, Academic/Scholarly.*
Indexed: P30.
Published by: Mahidol University, Faculty of Public Health, 420/1 Rajvithi Rd., Rajchathevee, Bangkok, 10400, Thailand.

WASHINGTON HEALTHCARE SUMMIT. *see* LAW

362.1 USA ISSN 1934-6360
RA171
➤ **WASHINGTON STATE JOURNAL OF PUBLIC HEALTH PRACTICE.** Abbreviated title: W S J P H P. Text in English. 2008 (Oct.). q. free (effective 2010). bk.rev. back issues avail. **Document type:** *Journal, Academic/Scholarly.* **Description:** Focuses on public health, health education/promotion practice, teaching, research, and issues of interest to professionals in Washington and the Pacific Northwest.
Media: Online - full text.
Indexed: P30.
Published by: (Washington State Public Health Association), Central Washington University, 400 E 8th Ave, University Way, Ellensburg, WA 98926. TEL 509-963-1111, http://www.cwu.edu/. Ed. Melody S Madden.

➤ **WATER AND ENVIRONMENT JOURNAL.** *see* WATER RESOURCES

➤ **WATER SEWAGE AND EFFLUENT.** *see* WATER RESOURCES

614 CHE ISSN 0049-8114
RA651
WEEKLY EPIDEMIOLOGICAL RECORD. Text in English, French. 1926. w. CHF 346, USD 365.64 (effective 2012). bibl.; charts; illus.; stat. index. back issues avail. **Document type:** *Journal, Trade.* **Description:** Provides an essential instrument for the collation and dissemination of data, including global number of AIDS cases, useful in disease surveillance and control on a global level.
Related titles: Microfiche ed.: (from CIS); Online - full text ed.: ISSN 1996-8345. 200?. free (effective 2012).
Indexed: A01, A03, A08, A22, A26, A34, A35, A36, AIDS Ab, AgBio, BP, BRD, C06, C07, C08, C11, CA, CABA, CINAHL, D01, E08, E12, EMBASE, ExcerpMed, FR, G03, G08, GH, GSA, GSI, H01, H04, H05, H11, H12, H17, I05, IIS, INI, IndMed, IndVet, LT, MEDLINE, N02, N03, P19, P20, P21, P22, P24, P26, P30, P32, P33, P34, P37, P39, P40, P48, P50, P52, P54, P56, PN&I, PQC, R08, R10, R12, RM&VM, RRTA, Reac, S04, S06, S09, S13, S16, SCOPUS, T02, T05, VS, W03, W05, W11.
—BLDSC (9284.780000), GNLM, IE, Infotrieve, Ingenta, INIST. **CCC.**
Published by: World Health Organization/Organisation Mondiale de la Sante, Avenue Appia 20, Geneva 27, 1211, Switzerland. TEL 41-22-7912111, FAX 41-22-7913111, publications@who.int. Circ: 7,000.

344.04 328.37 NLD ISSN 2210-9382
▼ **WEGWIJZER WET VEILIGHEIDSREGIO'S.** Text in Dutch. 2010. a. EUR 29.75 (effective 2010).
Published by: Kluwer B.V. (Subsidiary of: Wolters Kluwer N.V.), Postbus 4, Alphen aan den Rijn, 2400 MA, Netherlands. TEL 31-172-466633, info@kluwer.nl, http://www.kluwer.nl.

WEISHENG JINGJI YANJIU/HEALTH ECONOMICS RESEARCH. *see* BUSINESS AND ECONOMICS

614 658.3 USA
THE WELL WORKPLACE NEWSLETTER. Text in English. 1986. m. free to members. bk.rev. back issues avail. **Document type:** *Newsletter.* **Description:** Provides a forum for corporate health promotion and wellness programs, cost-benefits of health promotion programs, information from the Wellness Council National Network, and the names of the healthiest companies in the U.S.
Formerly: Worksite Wellness Works (1053-492X)
Published by: Wellness Councils of America, 9802 Nicholas St, Ste 315, Omaha, NE 68114-2106. TEL 402-827-3590, FAX 402-827-3594, wellworkplace@welcoa.org. Ed., R&P Sandra Wendel. Circ: 3,000.

613 CAN ISSN 1496-1008
WELLNESSOPTIONS. Text in English. 2000. irreg. CAD 32 domestic for 6 issues; USD 38 in United States for 6 issues; USD 60 elsewhere for 6 issues (effective 2006). **Document type:** *Magazine, Consumer.*
Related titles: Online - full text ed.: USD 18.
Indexed: C03, CBCARef, P48, P52, P56, PQC, SD, T02.
Published by: WellnessOptions Publishing Inc., PO Box 160, Sta D, Toronto, ON M1R 5B5, Canada. TEL 416-502-9600, FAX 416-502-0699, info@wellnessoptions.ca, http://www.wellnessoptions.ca. Pub. Michael Y Chan.

613 614 NLD ISSN 2210-9226
WEMOS NIEUWSBRIEF. Text in Dutch. 2002. q.
Published by: Stichting Wemos, Postbus 1693, Amsterdam, 1000 BR, Netherlands. TEL 31-20-4352050, FAX 31-20-4686008, info@wemos.nl, http://www.wemos.nl.

362.1 CAN ISSN 1910-6319
WEST NILE VIRUS PROGRAM (YEAR): PLANNING DOCUMENT FOR MUNICIPALITIES. Text in English. 2005. a. **Document type:** *Handbook/Manual/Guide, Trade.*
Published by: Manitoba Health, 450 Broadway, Winnipeg, MB R3C 0V8, Canada. TEL 204-945-3744, 866-626-4862, FAX 204-945-4261, mgi@gov.mb.ca, http://www.gov.mb.ca/health/index.html.

362.1 PHL ISSN 2094-7321
▼ **WESTERN PACIFIC SURVEILLANCE AND RESPONSE.** Text in English, Chinese. 2010. **Document type:** *Journal, Academic/Scholarly.*
Related titles: Online - full text ed.: ISSN 2094-7313. free (effective 2011).
Published by: World Health Organization, Regional Office for the Western Pacific, PO Box 2932, Manila, 1000, Philippines. TEL 63-2-5288001, FAX 63-2-5211036.

344.04 NLD ISSN 1876-424X
WET MARKTORDENING GEZONDHEIDSZORG. Text in Dutch. 1988. m.
Formerly (until 2007): Wet Tarieven Gezondheidszorg (0922-3401)
Published by: Sdu Uitgevers bv, Postbus 20025, The Hague, 2500 EA, Netherlands. TEL 31-70-3789911, FAX 31-70-3854321, sdu@sdu.nl.

628 DEU ISSN 0342-5967
WOHNMEDIZIN. Text in German. 1962. bi-m. EUR 30.17 (effective 2005). bk.rev. back issues avail. **Document type:** *Journal, Academic/Scholarly.*
Formerly (until 1975): Wohnungsmedizin (0342-5959)
—GNLM.
Published by: Gesellschaft fuer Hygiene und Umweltmedizin, c/o Dr. Claudia Hornberg, Postfach 100131, Bielefeld, 33501, Germany. TEL 49-521-1064365, FAX 49-521-1066492, claudia.hornberg@uni-bielefeld.de, http://www.hygiene.ruhr-uni-bochum.de/ghu/Kontakt/kontakt.html.

363.348 CHE ISSN 0929-0850
HV553
WORLD DISASTERS REPORT. Text in English. 1993. a. EUR 22 (effective 2007). **Document type:** *Journal, Trade.*
Related titles: Arabic ed.; Spanish ed.; French ed.
—BLDSC (9354.235000).
Published by: International Federation of Red Cross and Red Crescent Societies, PO Box 372, Geneva 19, 1211, Switzerland. TEL 41-22-7304222, FAX 41-22-7330395, http://www.ifrc.org. **Dist. by:** Eurospan Group, 3 Henrietta St, Covent Garden, London WC2E 8LU, United Kingdom. TEL 44-20-7240-0856, FAX 44-20-7379-0609, orders@edspubs.co.uk, http://www.eurospangroup.com.

WORLD FEDERATION FOR MENTAL HEALTH. ANNUAL REPORT. *see* PSYCHOLOGY

WORLD FEDERATION FOR MENTAL HEALTH. NEWSLETTER. *see* PSYCHOLOGY

613 USA ISSN 1718-3340
WORLD HEALTH & POPULATION. Text in English. 1997. s-a. USD 206 combined subscription to individuals (print & online eds.) (effective 2010). **Document type:** *Journal, Academic/Scholarly.*
Formerly (until 2006): Journal of Health & Population in Developing Countries (1095-8940)
Related titles: Online - full text ed.: USD 42; USD 30 per issue (effective 2010).
Indexed: A36, BA, CABA, D01, E12, EMBASE, ESPM, GH, LT, MEDLINE, N02, N03, P30, P33, R08, SCOPUS, SSciA, T05, TAR, W11.
—Infotrieve, Ingenta.
Published by: University of North Carolina at Chapel Hill, Department of Health Policy and Administration, 1101 McGavran-Greenberg Bldg, 7411, Chapel Hill, NC 27599. TEL 919-966-7350, http://www.sph.unc.edu/hpaa/. Ed. John E Paul. Pub. W Anton Hart.

614 CHE
WORLD HEALTH ORGANIZATION. FACT SHEET. Text in English. 1977. m. **Document type:** *Bulletin, Trade.*
Related titles: Online - full text ed.: ISSN 1564-0949.
Published by: World Health Organization/Organisation Mondiale de la Sante, Avenue Appia 20, Geneva 27, 1211, Switzerland. TEL 41-22-7912111, FAX 41-22-7913111, publications@who.int, http://www.who.int.

614 CHE ISSN 0301-0740
RA8
WORLD HEALTH ORGANIZATION. HANDBOOK OF RESOLUTIONS AND DECISIONS OF THE WORLD HEALTH ASSEMBLY AND THE EXECUTIVE BOARD. Text in English. 1948. irreg., latest 1993. price varies. **Document type:** *Directory, Trade.*
Related titles: Arabic ed.: Munazzamat al-Sihhiyyah al-'Alamiyyah. Dalil Qararat Jam'iyyah al-Sihhiyyah wal-Majlis al-Tanfidhi. ISSN 1010-0202; Chinese ed.: Shijie Weisheng Dahui Ji Zhixing Weiyuanui Jueyi e Jueding Shouce. ISSN 1010-0245; Spanish ed.: Asamblea Mundial de la Salud y del Consejo Ejecutivo. Manual de Resoluciones y Decisiones. ISSN 1010-0210; Russian ed.: Vsemirnaya Assambleya Zdravookhraneniya i Ispolnitel'nogo Komiteta. Sbornik Rezolyutsii i Reshenii. ISSN 1010-0237; French ed.: Recueil des Resolutions et Decisions de l'Assemblee Mondiale de la Sante et du Conseil Executif. ISSN 1010-0229.
Published by: World Health Organization/Organisation Mondiale de la Sante, Avenue Appia 20, Geneva 27, 1211, Switzerland. TEL 41-22-7912111, FAX 41-22-7913111, publications@who.int, http://www.who.int. Circ: 8,000.

614 CHE
WORLD HEALTH ORGANIZATION. PRESS RELEASE. Text in English. 1997. m. **Document type:** *Bulletin, Trade.*
Related titles: Online - full text ed.: ISSN 1564-0965.
Published by: World Health Organization/Organisation Mondiale de la Sante, Avenue Appia 20, Geneva 27, 1211, Switzerland. TEL 41-22-7912111, FAX 41-22-7913111, publications@who.int, http://www.who.int.

614 EGY
WORLD HEALTH ORGANIZATION. REGIONAL OFFICE FOR THE EASTERN MEDITERRANEAN. ANNUAL REPORT OF THE REGIONAL DIRECTOR. Text in Arabic, English. 1950. a., latest 2007. free to qualified personnel. **Document type:** *Corporate.*
Former titles (until 1989): World Health Organization. Regional Office for the Eastern Mediterranean. Biennial Report of Regional Director; (until 1979): World Health Organization. Regional Office for the Eastern Mediterranean. Annual Report of the Regional Director (0512-3089)
Related titles: Microfiche ed.: (from CIS); Online - full text ed.
Indexed: IIS.
—GNLM.
Published by: World Health Organization, Regional Office for the Eastern Mediterranean, P O Box 1517, Alexandria, 21563, Egypt. FAX 20-3-4838916, TELEX 54028 WHO UN, http://www.emro.who.int/index.asp. Eds. Christopher Zielinski, Jane Nicholson. Circ: 3,000.

362.1 DNK ISSN 0378-2255
CODEN: WRPSDJ
WORLD HEALTH ORGANIZATION REGIONAL PUBLICATIONS. EUROPEAN SERIES. Text in English. 1976. 3/w. back issues avail. **Document type:** *Monographic series, Trade.*
Related titles: Online - full text ed.; Russian ed.: Regional'nye Publikacii Vsemirnaa Organizacia Zdravoohranenia. Evropejskaa Seria. ISSN 0258-4972; French ed.: Organisation Mondiale de la Sante. Publications Regionales. Serie Europeenne. ISSN 0250-8575.
Indexed: A22, A26, CWI, EMBASE, ExcerpMed, H11, H12, I05, MEDLINE, P30, R10, Reac, SCOPUS.
—IE, Infotrieve, Ingenta, INIST, Linda Hall. **CCC.**
Published by: World Health Organization, Regional Office for Europe, Scherfigsvej 8, Copenhagen OE, 2100, Denmark. TEL 45-39-171426, FAX 45-39-171818.

614 CHE ISSN 1020-3311
RA8
THE WORLD HEALTH REPORT. Text in English. 1948. a. CHF 40, USD 36 (effective 2007). **Document type:** *Journal, Academic/Scholarly.* **Description:** Reports on important diseases and assesses the impact of knowledge and technology on controlling them. Suggests needed actions and estimates their cost.
Formerly (until 1995): World Health Organization. Work of W H O (0509-2558)
Related titles: Microfiche ed.: (from CIS); Online - full text ed.: ISSN 1564-0809; French ed.: ISSN 1020-332X.
Indexed: A26, CWI, E08, G08, H11, H12, I05, IIS, P20, P48, P50, P54, PQC, RASB, S09.
—BLDSC (9356.048000), GNLM. **CCC.**
Published by: World Health Organization/Organisation Mondiale de la Sante, Avenue Appia 20, Geneva 27, 1211, Switzerland. TEL 41-22-7912111, FAX 41-22-7913111, publications@who.int, http://www.who.int. Circ: 8,000.

WORLD JOURNAL OF PLANNING AND DEVELOPMENT. *see* POLITICAL SCIENCE

614 ZAF ISSN 1991-1335
WORLD JOURNAL OF PUBLIC HEALTH. Text in English. 2006. q. USD 120 in Africa to individuals; USD 180 elsewhere to individuals; USD 350 in Africa to institutions; USD 450 elsewhere to institutions; USD 85 in Africa to students; USD 100 elsewhere to students (effective 2007).
Published by: (World Research Organization), Isis Press, PO Box 1919, Cape Town, 8000, South Africa. TEL 27-21-4471574, FAX 27-86-6219999, orders@unwro.org, http://www.unwro.org/isispress.html.

614 USA ISSN 2153-2028
▼ ➤ **WORLD MEDICAL & HEALTH POLICY.** Text in English. 2009. q. USD 485 to institutions; USD 1,455 to corporations (effective 2011). **Document type:** *Journal, Academic/Scholarly.* **Description:** Aims to encourage and promote interdisciplinary research at the intersection of public policy and medical practice.
Related titles: Online - full text ed.: ISSN 1948-4682. 2009.
—**CCC.**
Published by: Berkeley Electronic Press, 2809 Telegraph Ave, Ste 202, Berkeley, CA 94705. TEL 510-665-1200, FAX 510-665-1201, info@bepress.com. Eds. Otmar Kloiber, Tom Zimmerman.

➤ **WORLDWATCH READER.** *see* ENVIRONMENTAL STUDIES

362.1 USA
WYOMING. DEPARTMENT OF HEALTH. ANNUAL REPORT. Text in English. 1975. a. **Document type:** *Government.*
Formerly: Wyoming. Department of Health and Social Services. Annual Report (0098-6984)
Published by: Wyoming Department of Health, 401 Hathaway Bldg, Cheyenne, WY 82002. TEL 307-777-7656, 888-996-9104, http://wdh.state.wy.us. Circ: 500.

YALE JOURNAL OF HEALTH POLICY, LAW, AND ETHICS. *see* LAW

362.1 JPN ISSN 1348-8759
YAMAGUCHIKEN KANKYOU HOKEN KENKYUU SENTA SHOHOU. Text in Japanese. 2004. a. **Document type:** *Journal, Academic/Scholarly.*
Formed by the merger of (1999-2001): Yamaguchi-ken Kankyo Hoken Kenkyu Senta Nempo (1345-1936); Which was formerly (until 1998): Yamaguchi-ken Eisei Kogai Kenkyu Senta Nempo (0915-048X); Which was formed by the merger of (1958-1986): Yamaguchi-ken Eisei Kenkyujo Nenpo (0288-7436); (1975-1987): Yamaguchi-ken Kogai Senta Nenpo/Yamaguchi Prefectural Environmental Pollution Research Center. Annual Report (0914-031X); (1999-2003): Yamaguchi-ken Kankyo Hoken Kenkyu Senta Gyoseki Hokoku (1345-1944); Which was formerly (until 1989): Yamaguchi-ken Eisei Kogai Kenkyu Senta gyoseki Hokoku (0915-0498); (until 1986): Yamaguchi-ken Eisei Kenkyujo gyoseki Hokoku/Yamaguchi Prefectural Research Institute of Health. Annual Report (0513-4757)
Published by: Yamaguchiken Kankyou Hoken Kenkyuu Senta/Yamaguchi Prefectural Research Institute of Health, 535 Asada, Yamaguchi, 753-0871, Japan. TEL 81-83-9243670, FAX 81-83-9243673, http://kanpoken.pref.yamaguchi.lg.jp/.

628 JPN ISSN 0912-2826
YOKOHAMA CITY INSTITUTE OF HEALTH. ANNUAL REPORT. Text in Japanese; Summaries in English. 1962. a.
Published by: Yokohama-shi Eisei Kenkyujo/Yokohama City Institute of Health, 1-2-17 Takigashira, Isogo-ku, Yokohama, Kanagawa 235-0012, Japan. TEL 81-45-7549800, FAX 81-45-7542210, http://www.city.yokohama.jp/me/kenkou/eiken/. Circ: 300.

YOKOHAMA MEDICAL JOURNAL. *see* MEDICAL SCIENCES

362.1 CAN ISSN 1922-480X
YOUR DILICO. Text in English. 2007. q. back issues avail. **Document type:** *Newsletter, Trade.* **Description:** Provides information on new developments and initiatives happening within Dilico.
Related titles: Online - full text ed.: free (effective 2010).
Published by: Dilico Anishinabek Family Care, 200 Anemki Pl, Fort William First Nation, Thunder Bay, ON P7J 1L6, Canada. TEL 807-623-8511, 800-465-3985, FAX 807-626-7999.

362.1 AUS ISSN 1834-3015
YOUR HEALTH AND HUMAN SERVICES. Text in English. 2006. q. **Document type:** *Government.*
Media: Online - full text.
Published by: Tasmania, Department of Health and Human Services, GPO Box 125, Hobart, TAS 7001, Australia. TEL 61-3-6233-3185, 1300-135-513, http://www.dhhs.tas.gov.au/index.php.

614 USA
YOUR HEALTH TODAY. Text in English. 1997. d.
Media: Online - full content.
Published by: Jobson Publishing LLC, One Meadowlands Pl, Ste 1020, E Rutherford, NJ 07073.

613 614 NLD ISSN 1879-4084
▼ **Z-MAGAZINE.** Text in Dutch. 2009. q. **Document type:** *Magazine, Consumer.*
Published by: De Zorggroep, Postbus 694, Venlo, 5900 AR, Netherlands. TEL 31-77-3559520, communicatie@dezorggroep.nl, http://www.zorggroep-noord-limburg.nl.

614 RUS
ZAMESTITEL' GLAVNOGO VRACHA; lechebnaya rabota i meditsinskaya ekspertiza. Text in Russian. 2006. bi-m. RUR 2,191 domestic (effective 2007). **Document type:** *Journal, Trade.*
Published by: Mezhdunarodnyi Tsentr Finansovo-Ekonomicheskogo Razvitiya, ul Yaroslavskaya, dom 8, k 5, Moscow, 126106, Russian Federation. TEL 7-495-9379080, FAX 7-495-9379087, ap@mcfr.ru, http://www.zdrav.ru.

614 RUS ISSN 0044-1945
CODEN: ZDRVA4
ZDOROV'E. Text in Russian. 1955. m. USD 145 foreign (effective 2005). adv. bk.rev. bibl. index. back issues avail. **Document type:** *Magazine, Consumer.* **Description:** Focuses on healthy living and includes features on nutrition, beauty, travel, preventive medicine, new medical technologies, drug use, child care. Also includes reports from medical institutes.
Related titles: CD-ROM ed.; Diskette ed.; Fax ed.
Indexed: ChemAb.
—East View. **CCC.**
Published by: Izdatel'stvo Zdorov'e, Bumazhnyi pr 14, Moscow, 101454, Russian Federation. TEL 7-095-2573251, FAX 7-095-2505828. Ed. T Efimova. R&P T. Efimova TEL 7-05-2121403. adv.: color page USD 6,000. Circ: 185,000 (paid and controlled). **Dist. by:** East View Information Services, 10601 Wayzata Blvd, Minneapolis, MN 55305. TEL 952-252-1201, 800-477-1005, FAX 952-252-1202, info@eastview.com, http://www.eastview.com.

362.1 RUS
ZDOROV'E NASELENIYA I SREDA OBITANIYA. Text in Russian. 1993. m. USD 290 foreign (effective 2005). **Document type:** *Journal, Government.* **Description:** Contains information on the state of health of Russia's population related to the environment, materials of studies of group infections and mass diseases.
Published by: Gosudarstvennyi Komitet Sanitarno Epidemiologicheskogo Nadzora Rossiiskoi Federatsii, Vadkovskii per 18-20, Moscow, 103055, Russian Federation. TEL 7-095-9732671. **Dist. by:** East View Information Services, 10601 Wayzata Blvd, Minneapolis, MN 55305. TEL 952-252-1201, 800-477-1005, FAX 952-252-1202, info@eastview.com, http://www.eastview.com.

613 HRV ISSN 1330-6081
ZDRAVI ZIVOT. Text in Croatian. 1994. m. **Document type:** *Magazine, Consumer.*
Published by: Multigraf d.o.o., Maksimirska 50a, Zagreb, 10000, Croatia. TEL 385-1-2336666, FAX 385-1-212936. Ed. Vilko Tezak.

362.1 RUS ISSN 1028-9771
ZDRAVOOKHRANENIE; zhurnal dlia rukovoditelya i glavnogo bukhgaltera. Text in Russian. 1995. m. USD 349 foreign (effective 2007). **Document type:** *Magazine, Trade.* **Description:** Publishes regulatory documents, information about public health reform, regions, wages, labor protection, personnel service, accounting, taxation.
Indexed: RefZh.
—East View.
Published by: Mezhdunarodnyi Tsentr Finansovo-Ekonomicheskogo Razvitiya, ul Yaroslavskaya, dom 8, k 5, Moscow, 126106, Russian Federation. TEL 7-495-9379080, FAX 7-495-9379087, ap@mcfr.ru, http://www.zdrav.ru. **Dist. by:** East View Information Services, 10601 Wayzata Blvd, Minneapolis, MN 55305. TEL 952-252-1201, 800-477-1005, FAX 952-252-1202, info@eastview.com, http://www.eastview.com.

614 BLR ISSN 1027-7218
CODEN: ZDBEA9
ZDRAVOOKHRANENIE. Text in Russian. 1924-19??; resumed 1955. m. USD 238 foreign (effective 2005). adv. bk.rev. charts; illus.; stat. index. back issues avail. **Document type:** *Journal, Government.*
Former titles (until 1995): Zdravookhranenie Belorussii (0044-1961); (until 1941): Meditsinsky Zhurnal B.S.S.R.; (until 1938): Belorusskaya Meditsinskaya Mysl
Related titles: Fax ed.
Indexed: ChemAb, INIS AtomInd, MycolAb, P30, RASB.
—CASDDS, GNLM, INIST.
Published by: Ministerstvo Zdravookhraneniya/Ministry of Public Health, Vul Fabritsyusa 28, Minsk, 220001, Belarus. TEL 7-172-2262167. Ed. V Ulashchik. Pub. M Podgainy. R&P V. Ulashchik TEL 7-172-2221682. Adv. contact Myshkovskaya. B&W page USD 250, color page USD 450. Circ: 11,000. **Dist. by:** East View Information Services, 10601 Wayzata Blvd, Minneapolis, MN 55305. TEL 952-252-1201, 800-477-1005, FAX 952-252-1202, info@eastview.com, http://www.eastview.com.

570 RUS ISSN 0044-197X
RA412.5.R9
ZDRAVOOKHRANENIE ROSSIISKOI FEDERATSII/PUBLIC HEALTHCARE OF THE RUSSIAN FEDERATION. Text in Russian; Contents page in English. 1957. bi-m. USD 102 foreign (effective 2005). **Document type:** *Journal, Academic/Scholarly.* **Description:** Publishes scientific and practical materials on the health status of the population and on the development of public health services in autonomous republics, territories, regions and districts of the RSFSR.
Indexed: IndMed, P30, RASB.
—East View, GNLM, INIST. **CCC.**
Published by: Izdatel'stvo Meditsina/Meditsina Publishers, ul B Pirogovskaya, d 2, str 5, Moscow, 119435, Russian Federation. TEL 7-095-2483324, meditsina@mtu-net.ru, http://www.medlit.ru. Ed. Anatolii I Potapov. Pub. A M Stochik. R&P T Kurushina. Adv. contact O A Fadeeva TEL 7-095-923-51-40. Circ: 3,800. **Dist. by:** M K - Periodica, ul Gilyarovskogo 39, Moscow 129110, Russian Federation. TEL 7-095-2845008, FAX 7-095-2813798, info@periodicals.ru, http://www.mkniga.ru.

614 CZE ISSN 0044-1996
ZDRAVOTNICKE NOVINY; tydenik pracovniku ve zdravotnictvi. Text in Czech. 1955. w. CZK 590 (effective 2011). adv. **Document type:** *Magazine, Trade.*
Related titles: Online - full content ed.: CZK 500 (effective 2009).
—BLDSC (9438.870000).
Published by: Mlada Fronta, Mezi Vodami 1952/9, Prague 4, 14300, Czech Republic. TEL 420-2-25276201, FAX 420-2-25276222, online@mf.cz, http://www.mf.cz. Ed. Marketa Miksova TEL 420-2-25276295. Adv. contact Lenka Mihulkova. Circ: 35,000.

614 SVK ISSN 1335-4477
ZDRAVOTNICKE NOVINY. Text in Slovak. 1996. w. EUR 65.52 (effective 2009). adv. **Document type:** *Magazine, Trade.*
Published by: Sanoma Magazines Slovakia s.r.o., Kutlikova 17, Bratislava, 851 02, Slovakia. TEL 421-2-32150111, FAX 421-2-63830093, info@sanomaslovakia.sk. Ed. Ludovit Zarecky. Adv. contact Milos Inger. color page EUR 2,653; trim 210 x 297. Circ: 8,000 (paid and controlled).

614 POL ISSN 0044-2011
RA421
ZDROWIE PUBLICZNE/POLISH JOURNAL OF PUBLIC HEALTH. Text in Polish. 1885. m. bk.rev. abstr.; charts; illus.; stat. index. **Document type:** *Journal, Academic/Scholarly.* **Description:** Deals with social medicine, health care organization and health policy.
Formerly (until 1934): Zdrowie (0860-4525)
Related titles: Online - full text ed.: free (effective 2011).
Indexed: IndMed, P30.
—GNLM.

P

Published by: Akademia Medyczna w Lublinie, Al Raclawickie 1, Lublin, 20950, Poland. TEL 48-81-7478265, FAX 48-81-7478266. Ed. Miroslaw J Jarosz. Circ: 2,377. **Dist. by:** Ars Polona, Obroncow 25, Warsaw 03933, Poland. TEL 48-22-5098609, FAX 48-22-5098610, arspolona@arspolona.com.pl, http://www.arspolona.com.pl.

363.1 USA ISSN 1548-2197
ZEICHNER RISK ASSESSMENT. Text in English. 2002 (Aug.). w. USD 1,495 (effective 2004).
Related titles: E-mail ed.: ISSN 1548-2200.
Published by: Zeichner Risk Analytics, LLC, 3204 Juniper Ln., Falls Church, VA 22044. TEL 703-534-2001, FAX 703-534-2003, zra@zra.com, http://www.zra.com.

614 DEU ISSN 0943-1853
➤ **ZEITSCHRIFT FUER GESUNDHEITSWISSENSCHAFTEN/ JOURNAL OF PUBLIC HEALTH.** Text in English, German. 1993. bi-m. EUR 218, USD 278 combined subscription to institutions (print & online eds.) (effective 2012). adv. bk.rev. back issues avail.; reprint service avail. from PSC. **Document type:** *Journal, Academic/ Scholarly.*
Related titles: Online - full text ed.: ISSN 1613-2238 (from IngentaConnect).
Indexed: A22, A26, B21, BRD, C06, C07, CA, E01, E08, EMBASE, ESPM, ExcerpMed, G08, H&SSA, H05, H11, I05, IBR, IBZ, P03, P30, P50, P52, P56, PsycInfo, PsycholAb, R10, Reac, S02, S03, S09, SCOPUS, SSAI, SSAb, SSI, T02, W01, W02, W03, W05.
—BLDSC (5043.525000), GNLM, IE, Ingenta. **CCC.**
Published by: Springer (Subsidiary of: Springer Science+Business Media), Tiergartenstr 17, Heidelberg, 69121, Germany. TEL 49-6221-4870, FAX 49-6221-345229, subscriptions@springer.com, http://www.springer.com. Ed. W Kirch. adv.: color page EUR 1,830, B&W page EUR 790; trim 113 x 193. Circ: 720 (paid).

613 615 NLD ISSN 1878-8297
▼ **ZELFZORG ZAKEN.** Variant title: Z3. Text in Dutch. 2009. q. **Document type:** *Magazine, Consumer.*
Published by: (Neprofarm), Axioma Communicatie BV/Axioma Communications BV (Subsidiary of: Springer Science+Business Media), Lt Gen Van Heutszlaan 4, Postbus 176, Baarn, 3740 AD, Netherlands. TEL 31-35-5488140, FAX 31-35-5425820, informatie@axioma.nl, http://www.axioma.nl. Circ: 750.

362.1 POL ISSN 1731-7398
➤ **ZESZYTY NAUKOWE OCHRONY ZDROWIA. ZDROWIE PUBLICZNE I ZARZADZANIE.** Text in Polish, English. 2003. s-a. **Document type:** *Journal, Academic/Scholarly.*
Related titles: Online - full text ed.
Published by: (Uniwersytet Jagiellonski, Wydzial Nauk o Zdrowiu, Instytut Zdrowia Publicznego), Wydawnictwo Uniwersytetu Jagiellonskiego/Jagiellonian University Press, ul Grodzka 26, Krakow, 31044, Poland. TEL 48-12-4312364, FAX 48-12-4301995, wydaw@if.uj.edu.pl. Ed. W C Wlodarczyk.

614 CHN ISSN 1004-1257
➤ **ZHIYE YU JIANKANG/OCCUPATION AND HEALTH.** Text in Chinese. 1985. s-m. USD 86.40 (effective 2009). **Document type:** *Journal, Academic/Scholarly.* **Description:** Popular science magazine for medical workers and safety-control technicians in industrial companies.
Related titles: Online - full text ed.
Indexed: A34, A36, C25, D01, E12, N03, P33, R07, R08, S13, T05.
—BLDSC (9512.711000), East View.
Published by: Tianjin-shi Weisheng Fangbing Zhongxin/Tianjin Municipal Center of Health and Disease Prevention, 76, Hualong-dao, Hedong-qu, Tianjin, 300101, China. TEL 86-22-24333470, FAX 86-22-26023387. Circ: 100,000 (controlled). **Dist. by:** China International Book Trading Corp, 35 Chegongzhuang Xilu, Haidian District, PO Box 399, Beijing 100044, China. TEL 86-10-68412045, FAX 86-10-68412023, cibtc@mail.cibtc.com.cn, http://www.cibtc.com.cn.

362.1 CHN ISSN 1005-2720
ZHONGGUO BAOJIAN/CHINESE HEALTH CARE. Text in Chinese. 1993. 3/m. CNY 10 per issue (effective 2010). 48 p./no.; **Document type:** *Journal, Academic/Scholarly.*
Related titles: Online - full text ed.
—BLDSC (3180.279230), East View.
Published by: Zhongguo Baojian Zazhishe, 32, Baiziwan Lu, Pingguoshe-qu (Bei-qu), 2A-2116, Beijing, 100071, China. TEL 86-10-58263302, FAX 86-10-58263302, zgbaojian001@163.com, zgbj2116@163.com. **Dist. by:** China International Book Trading Corp, 35 Chegongzhuang Xilu, Haidian District, PO Box 399, Beijing 100044, China. TEL 86-10-68412045, FAX 86-10-68412023, cibtc@mail.cibtc.com.cn, http://www.cibtc.com.cn.

ZHONGGUO BINGYUAN SHENGWUXUE ZAZHI/CHINESE JOURNAL OF PATHOGEN BIOLOGY. *see* MEDICAL SCIENCES—Communicable Diseases

ZHONGGUO GETI FANGHU ZHUANGBEI/CHINA PERSONAL PROTECTION EQUIPMENT. *see* OCCUPATIONAL HEALTH AND SAFETY

614 CHN ISSN 1001-0580
ZHONGGUO GONGGONG WEISHENG/CHINESE JOURNAL OF PUBLIC HEALTH. Text in Chinese. 1985. m. USD 62.40 (effective 2009). adv.
Related titles: Online - full text ed.
Indexed: A22.
—BLDSC (3180.610000), East View, IE, Ingenta.
Published by: (Zhonghua Yufang Yixuehui/China Preventive Medicine Association), Zhongguo Gonggong Weisheng, Editorial department of China's Public Health, 42-1, Jixian Jie, Heping-qu, PO Box 292, Shenyang, Liaoning 110005, China. TEL 86-24-23388443, FAX 86-24-83380011. Ed. Dai Zhicheng. Adv. contact Xiying Li. B&W page USD 300, color page USD 500. Circ: 10,000. **Dist. overseas by:** China International Book Trading Corp, 35 Chegongzhuang Xilu, Haidian District, PO Box 399, Beijing 100044, China. TEL 86-10-68412045, FAX 86-10-68412023, cibtc@mail.cibtc.com.cn, http://www.cibtc.com.cn.

362.1 CHN ISSN 1001-9561
ZHONGGUO GONGGONG WEISHENG GUANLI/CHINESE JOURNAL OF PUBLIC HEALTH MANAGEMENT. Text in Chinese. 1985. bi-m. USD 31.20 (effective 2009). **Document type:** *Journal, Academic/ Scholarly.*
Former titles (until 1999): Zhongguo Gonggong Weisheng Xuebao/ Chinese Journal of Public Health (1001-0572); (until 1989): Zhongguo Gonggong Weisheng/China Public Health (1000-8497)
Related titles: Online - full text ed.
—East View.
Published by: Heilongjiang Sheng Jibing Yufang Kongzhi Zhongxinyuan, 40, Youfang Jie, Ha'erbin, 150030, China. TEL 86-451-55153630.

610 CHN ISSN 1672-0369
ZHONGGUO MINKANG YIXUE/MEDICAL JOURNAL OF CHINESE PEOPLE HEALTH. Text in Chinese. 1989. m. USD 98.40 (effective 2009). **Document type:** *Journal, Academic/Scholarly.*
Formerly (until 2003): Zhongguo Minzheng Yixue Zazhi/Medical Journal of Chinese Civil Administration (1002-4719)
Related titles: Online - full content ed.; Online - full text ed.
—BLDSC (5529.030000), East View.
Published by: Medical Journal Institution of Chinese People Health, A-2, Subdivision 9, He Ping Li, Jiang-Zhai Kou, Dong Cheng District, Beijing, 100013, China. Ed. Wei-Cai Tian. **Dist. by:** China International Book Trading Corp, 35 Chegongzhuang Xilu, Haidian District, PO Box 399, Beijing 100044, China. TEL 86-10-68412045, FAX 86-10-68412023, cibtc@mail.cibtc.com.cn, http:// www.cibtc.com.cn.

ZHONGGUO SHIPIN XUEBAO/CHINESE INSTITUTE OF FOOD SCIENCE AND TECHNOLOGY. JOURNAL. *see* FOOD AND FOOD INDUSTRIES

362.1 362 CHN ISSN 1674-9316
▼ **ZHONGGUO WEISHENG BIAOZHUN GUANLI/CHINA HEALTH STANDARD MANAGEMENT.** Text in Chinese. 2010. bi-m. **Document type:** *Journal, Academic/Scholarly.*
Related titles: Online - full text ed.
Published by: Zhongguo Weisheng Biaozhun Guanli Zazhieshe, 7/F, 30, Honglian Nan Lu, Xuanwu-qu, Beijing, 100055, China. TEL 86-10-63265066, FAX 86-10-63497683.

ZHONGGUO WEISHENG JINGJI/CHINESE HEALTH ECONOMICS. *see* BUSINESS AND ECONOMICS

362.1 CHN ISSN 1674-2982
ZHONGGUO WEISHENG ZHENGCE YANJIU/CHINESE JOURNAL OF HEALTH POLICY. Text in Chinese. 2008. m. CNY 180; CNY 15 per issue (effective 2010). **Document type:** *Journal, Academic/Scholarly.*
Related titles: Online - full text ed.
Published by: Zhongguo Yixue Kexueyuan/Chinese Academy of Medical Sciences, Zhaoyang-qu, 3, Yabao Lu, Beijing, 100020, China. TEL 86-10-52328667, FAX 86-10-52328670, http://www.imicams.ac.cn/.

362.1 CHN ISSN 1007-953X
ZHONGGUO WEISHENG ZIYUAN/CHINESE HEALTH RESOURCES. Text in Chinese. 1992. bi-m. CNY 5 newsstand/cover (effective 2006). **Document type:** *Journal, Academic/Scholarly.*
Related titles: Online - full text ed.
Address: 280, Changshu Lu, no.1 Lou, Shanghai, 200031, China. TEL 86-21-64710489, FAX 86-21-64313796.

ZHONGHUA JIBING KONGZHI ZAZHI/CHINESE JOURNAL OF DISEASE CONTROL & PREVENTION. *see* MEDICAL SCIENCES—Communicable Diseases

ZORG ANNO N U. (Nieuwe Unie) *see* MEDICAL SCIENCES—Nurses And Nursing

613 610.7365 NLD ISSN 1877-5659
ZORG EN ZEGGENSCHAP. Text in Dutch. 2008. 5/yr. EUR 45 (effective 2009). **Document type:** *Journal, Trade.*
Formed by the merger of (2007-2008): Client en Raad. Extramuraal (1875-2454); (2007-2008): Client en Raad. Intramuraal (1875-2462)
Published by: Landelijke Organisatie Clientenraden, Postbus 700, Utrecht, 3500 AS, Netherlands. TEL 31-30-2843200, FAX 31-30-2843201, loc@loc.nl. Ed. Melle Knuist. Circ: 7,000.

613 NLD ISSN 1568-427X
ZORGKRANT. Text in Dutch. 1998. w.
Formerly (until 2000): Care Net Holland. Nieuwsbrief (1389-4277)
Media: Online - full text.
Published by: ComboData B.V., Molenstraat 164, Monster, 2681 BW, Netherlands. TEL 31-6-22491219, info@combodata.nl, http:// www.combodata.nl.

ZORGMARKT. *see* BUSINESS AND ECONOMICS—Management

9-1-1 MAGAZINE. *see* COMMUNICATIONS

PUBLIC HEALTH AND SAFETY—Abstracting, Bibliographies, Statistics

310 USA
➤ **ADVANCES IN RISK ANALYSIS.** Text in English. 1983. irreg., latest vol.9, 1991. price varies. back issues avail. **Document type:** *Monographic series, Academic/Scholarly.*
Published by: (Society for Risk Analysis), Springer New York LLC (Subsidiary of: Springer Science+Business Media), 233 Spring St, New York, NY 10013. TEL 212-460-1500, FAX 212-460-1575, service-ny@springer.com.

➤ **AIDS & T B WEEKLY ABSTRACTS FROM CONFERENCE PROCEEDINGS.** (Tuberculosis) *see* MEDICAL SCIENCES—Abstracting, Bibliographies, Statistics

➤ **AIDS IN NEW YORK STATE.** *see* MEDICAL SCIENCES—Communicable Diseases

362.1021 AUS
AUSTRALIA. BUREAU OF STATISTICS. NATIONAL HEALTH SURVEY: HEALTH RISK FACTORS, AUSTRALIA (ONLINE). Text in English. 2001. irreg., latest 2001. free (effective 2009). **Document type:** *Government.* **Description:** Includes the interaction of socioeconomic, biomedical and environmental factors which contribute to illness and injury.
Media: Online - full text.
Published by: Australian Bureau of Statistics, Locked Bag 10, Belconnen, ACT 2616, Australia. TEL 61-2-92684909, 61-2-62527037, 300-135-070, FAX 61-2-62528103, client.services@abs.gov.au.

362.1021 AUS
AUSTRALIA. BUREAU OF STATISTICS. NATIONAL HEALTH SURVEY: INJURIES, AUSTRALIA (ONLINE). Text in English. 1990. irreg., latest 2001. free (effective 2009). back issues avail. **Document type:** *Government.* **Description:** Presents statistics and analysis of recent injuries reported from a four week period, as collected as part of the National Health Survey.
Media: Online - full text.
Published by: Australian Bureau of Statistics, Locked Bag 10, Belconnen, ACT 2616, Australia. TEL 61-2-92684909, 61-2-62527037, 300-135-070, FAX 61-2-62528103, client.services@abs.gov.au.

326.1021 AUS
AUSTRALIA. BUREAU OF STATISTICS. NATIONAL HEALTH SURVEY: SUMMARY OF RESULTS (ONLINE). Text in English. 1995. irreg., latest 2005. free (effective 2009). back issues avail. **Document type:** *Government.* **Description:** Contains a cross-section of survey results, including selected national statistics about long-term illnesses experienced; mental wellbeing; injuries; consultations with doctors and other health professionals.
Media: Online - full text.
Published by: Australian Bureau of Statistics, Locked Bag 10, Belconnen, ACT 2616, Australia. TEL 61-2-92684909, 61-2-62527037, 300-135-070, FAX 61-2-62528103, client.services@abs.gov.au.

362.1021 AUS
AUSTRALIA. BUREAU OF STATISTICS. NORTHERN TERRITORY OFFICE. NATIONAL HEALTH SURVEY: DARWIN-PALMERSTON AND ALICE SPRINGS (ONLINE). Text in English. 1995. irreg., latest 1995. free (effective 2009). **Document type:** *Catalog, Government.* **Description:** Provides a statistical overview of health related matters of the Northern Territory's urban centres of darwin-palmerston and alice springs.
Formerly: Australia. Bureau of Statistics. Northern Territory Office. National Health Survey: Darwin-Palmerston and Alice Springs (Print)
Media: Online - full text.
Published by: Australian Bureau of Statistics, Northern Territory Office, GPO BOX 3796, Darwin, N.T. 0801, Australia. TEL 61-2-92684909, 300-135-070.

362.1021 BEL
BELGIUM. MINISTERE DES AFFAIRES SOCIALES DE LA SANTE PUBLIQUE ET DE L'ENVIRONNEMENT. ADMINISTRATION DES SOINS DE SANTE. ANNUAIRE STATISTIQUE DES HOPITAUX/ BELGIUM. MINISTERIE VAN VOLKSGEZONDHEID EN LEEFMILIEU. BESTUUR VOOR DE VERZORGINGSINSTELLINGEN. STATISTISCH JAARBOEK VAN DE ZIEKENHUIZEN. (In 8 parts: Liste d'Adresses; Rapport Annuel; Activite dans les Hopitaux; Origine des Patients; Duree de Sejour Detaille; Activite des Medecins Hopitaliers; Personnel des Hopitaux; List d'Adresses des M R S) Text in Dutch, French. 1962. a. free. **Document type:** *Government.*
Former titles: Belgium. Ministere de la Sante Publique et de la Famille. Annuaire Statistique des Hopitaux; Belgium. Ministere de la Sante et de la Famille. Premiers et Principaux Resultats Statistiques de l'Enquete dans les Etablissements de Soins
Published by: Ministere des Affaires Sociales de la Sante Publique et de l'Environnement, Administration des Soins de Sante/Ministerie van Volksgezondheid en Leefmilieu, Bestuursafdeling voor de Verzorgingsinstellingen, Studiedienst, Cite Administrative de l'Etat, Quartier Vesale 502, Brussels, 1010, Belgium. TEL 32-2-210-45-11. Circ: 1,500.

614.86021 BEL ISSN 1378-1219
BELGIUM. NATIONAAL INSTITUUT VOOR DE STATISTIEK. GEZONDHEID. VERKEERSONGEVALLEN OP DE OPENBARE WEG MET DODEN EN GEWONDEN IN (YEAR). Key Title: Verkeersongevallen op de Openbare Weg met Doden of Gewonden. Text in Dutch. 1954. a. charts. **Document type:** *Government.* **Description:** Provides a statistical overview of deaths and injuries in traffic accidents on public highways.
Former titles (until 2000): Belgium. Nationaal Instituut voor de Statistiek. Verkeersongevallen op de Openbare Weg met Doden of Gewonden (0771-0577); (until 1973): Belgium. Nationaal Instituut voor de Statistiek. Statistiek van de Verkeersongevallen op de Openbare Weg (0522-7593)
Related titles: ◆ French ed.: Belgium. Institut National de Statistique. Sante. Accidents de la Circulation sur la Voie Publique avec Tues et Blesses en (Annee). ISSN 1378-1227.
Published by: Institut National de Statistique/Nationaal Instituut voor de Statistiek (Subsidiary of: Ministere des Affaires Economiques), Rue de Louvain 44, Brussels, 1000, Belgium. TEL 32-2-548-6211, FAX 32-2-548-6367.

304.6 CAN ISSN 1188-1437
HA747.B75
BRITISH COLUMBIA. DIVISION OF VITAL STATISTICS AGENCY. QUARTERLY DIGEST. Text in English. 1991. q. free. **Document type:** *Government.* **Description:** Presents current statistical data for selected health status indicators on a regional basis, and discusses public health issues affecting British Columbia.
Published by: Ministry of Health Services, British Columbia Vital Statistics Agency, 818 Fort St, Victoria, BC V8W 1H8, Canada. TEL 250-952-2558, FAX 250-952-2594. Ed. Julie M Macdonald.

363.1799021 CAN ISSN 1484-1169
RC965.R25
CANADA. HEALTH CANADA. REPORT ON OCCUPATIONAL RADIATION EXPOSURES IN CANADA. Text in English. 1978. a.
Formerly (until 1996): Occupational Radiation Exposures in Canada (0713-2298)
Related titles: Online - full text ed.: ISSN 1493-5651.
Published by: (Health Canada, Occupational Radiation Hazards Division), HECS Publishing, AL 0801A, Health Canada, Ottawa, ON K1A 0L2, Canada. TEL 613-954-0609, FAX 613-952-2551, http://www.hc-sc.gc.ca.

362.1021 CAN ISSN 1715-8141
CANCER SURVIVAL STATISTICS. Text in English. 1997. a. **Document type:** *Report, Trade.*
Media: Online - full text.
Published by: Statistics Canada, Health Division (Subsidiary of: Statistics Canada/Statistique Canada), R H Coats Bldg, 18th floor, Ottawa, ON K1A 0T6, Canada. TEL 613-951-8569.

016.3621 USA ISSN 0748-5093
RA407.3
CATALOG OF UNIVERSITY PRESENTATIONS. Text in English. 198?. a. back issues avail. **Document type:** *Catalog, Government.*
Description: NCHS collects, analyzes, and disseminates a wide range of health data, conducts methodological research, and supports the development and enhancement of statistical programs in US and around the world. The catalog provides brief descriptions of the topics offered by NCHS staff to the university community. Presentations cover the programs, surveys, activities, and data of NCHS.
Related titles: Online - full text ed.: ISSN 2159-9564. free (effective 2011).
Published by: U.S. Department of Health and Human Services, Centers for Disease Control and Prevention. National Center for Health Statistics, 3311 Toledo Rd, Hyattsville, MD 20782. TEL 800-232-4636, cdcinfo@cdc.gov.

614 GBR ISSN 0957-4956
RA630.G73
CHARTERED INSTITUTE OF PUBLIC FINANCE AND ACCOUNTANCY. CEMETERIES STATISTICS. ACTUALS. Text in English. 1989. a. GBP 120 per issue (effective 2009). back issues avail. **Document type:** *Report, Trade.* **Description:** Contains information of number and area of cemeteries; number of interments and new graves excavated; staff employed; revenue expenditure and income and fees and charges.
Supersedes in part (in 1989): Chartered Institute of Public Finance and Accountancy. Cemeteries and Crematoria Statistics. Actuals (0263-2969); Which was formed by the merger of (1956-1983): Chartered Institute of Public Finance and Accountancy. Crematoria Statistics (0534-2104); (1981-1983): Chartered Institute of Public Finance and Accountancy. Cemeteries Statistics. Actuals (0260-9959)
—**CCC.**
Published by: (Statistical Information Service), Chartered Institute of Public Finance and Accountancy, 3 Robert St, London, WC2N 6RL, United Kingdom. TEL 44-20-75435600, FAX 44-20-75435700, info@cipfa.org.uk, http://www.cipfa.org.uk.

614 GBR ISSN 0956-1439
RA630.G73
CHARTERED INSTITUTE OF PUBLIC FINANCE AND ACCOUNTANCY. CREMATORIA STATISTICS. ACTUALS. Text in English. 1989. a. GBP 120 per issue (effective 2009). back issues avail. **Document type:** *Report, Trade.* **Description:** Contains information of number and area of cemeteries; number of interments and new graves excavated; staff employed; revenue expenditure and income and fees and charges.
Supersedes in part (in 1989): Chartered Institute of Public Finance and Accountancy. Cemeteries and Crematoria Statistics. Actuals (0263-2969); Which was formed by the merger of (1956-1983): Chartered Institute of Public Finance and Accountancy. Crematoria Statistics. Actuals (0534-2104); (1981-1983): Chartered Institute of Public Finance and Accountancy. Cemeteries Statistics. Actuals (0260-9959)
—**CCC.**
Published by: (Statistical Information Service), Chartered Institute of Public Finance and Accountancy, 3 Robert St, London, WC2N 6RL, United Kingdom. TEL 44-20-75435600, FAX 44-20-75435700, info@cipfa.org.uk, http://www.cipfa.org.uk.

614.8 GBR ISSN 0266-9552
RA566.5.G7
CHARTERED INSTITUTE OF PUBLIC FINANCE AND ACCOUNTANCY. ENVIRONMENTAL HEALTH STATISTICS. ACTUALS. Text in English. 1984. a. GBP 120 per issue (effective 2009). back issues avail. **Document type:** *Report, Trade.* **Description:** Provides an analysis of revenue expenditure and income, including the net cost of individual core functions; the characteristics of each local authority area, including the numbers and type of dwelling stock; the hazards encountered; the number and type of premises subject to inspection.
—**CCC.**
Published by: (Statistical Information Service), Chartered Institute of Public Finance and Accountancy, 3 Robert St, London, WC2N 6RL, United Kingdom. TEL 44-20-75435600, FAX 44-20-75435700, info@cipfa.org.uk, http://www.cipfa.org.uk.

362.1021 CAN ISSN 1703-9363
COMPARABLE HEALTH INDICATORS, CANADA, PROVINCES AND TERRITORIES. Text in English. 2002. biennial. **Document type:** *Government.*
Media: Online - full text. **Related titles:** French ed.: Indicateurs de la Sante Comparables, Canada, Provinces et Territoires. ISSN 1703-9371.
Published by: Statistics Canada/Statistique Canada, Communications Division, 3rd Fl, R H Coats Bldg, Ottawa, ON K1A 0A6, Canada. TEL 800-263-1136, infostats@statcan.ca, http://www.statcan.gc.ca.

016.3621 USA
CURRENT ISSUES: HEALTH. Text in English. 2007. base vol. plus d. updates. USD 670 (effective 2011). **Document type:** *Database, Abstract/Index.*
Media: Online - full content.
Published by: H.W. Wilson, 950 University Ave, Bronx, NY 10452. TEL 718-588-8400, 800-367-6770, FAX 718-590-1617, 800-590-1617, custserv@hwwilson.com.

362.1021 CYP
CYPRUS. MINISTRY OF HEALTH. ANNUAL REPORT. Text in Greek. 1920. a. charts; stat. **Document type:** *Government.*
Supersedes (in 1991): Cyprus. Ministry of Health. Department of Medical and Public Health Services. Annual Report; And the reports of the other departments: Psychiatric Services, Dental Services, General State Laboratory, and Pharmaceutical Services
Published by: Ministry of Health, Nicosia, Cyprus. FAX 357-2-303498, TELEX 5734. Ed. Dr. G Malliotis. Circ: 200.

DOC STAT CHAMPAGNE-ARDENNE. *see* PUBLIC HEALTH AND SAFETY

362.1021 ECU
ECUADOR. INSTITUTO NACIONAL DE ESTADISTICA Y CENSOS. CUENTAS NACIONALES DE LA SALUD. Text in Spanish. irreg. **Document type:** *Government.*
Related titles: Diskette ed.
Published by: Instituto Nacional de Estadistica y Censos, Juan Larrea N15-36 y Jose Riofrio, Quito, Ecuador. TEL 593-2-529858, FAX 593-2-509836, inec1@ecnet.ec, http://www.inec.gov.ec.

ESTADISTICA DE ACCIDENTES DE TRABAJO. *see* BUSINESS AND ECONOMICS—Abstracting, Bibliographies, Statistics

016.614 NLD ISSN 0924-5723
CODEN: EMPHA
EXCERPTA MEDICA. SECTION 17: PUBLIC HEALTH, SOCIAL MEDICINE AND EPIDEMIOLOGY. Variant title: Public Health, Social Medicine and Epidemiology (Section 17 EMBASE). Text in English. 1955. 24/yr. EUR 7,360 in Europe to institutions; JPY 970,800 in Japan to institutions; USD 8,170 elsewhere to institutions (effective 2012). adv. index, cum.index. back issues avail. **Document type:** *Journal, Abstract/Index.* **Description:** Provides a comprehensive current-awareness service of trade and scholarly articles covering all facets of public health and social medicine, and includes health planning and education, epidemiology and prevention of communicable disease, public health aspects of risk populations, food and nutrition and environmental radiation, medical ethics, the influence of lifestyle on health, and the epidemiological aspects of water supply and purification.
Formerly: Excerpta Medica. Section 17: Public Health, Social Medicine and Hygiene (0014-4215)
Related titles: CD-ROM ed.; Online - full text ed.
—GNLM. **CCC.**
Published by: Excerpta Medica (Subsidiary of: Elsevier Health Sciences), Radarweg 29, Amsterdam, 1043 NX, Netherlands. TEL 31-20-4853975, FAX 31-20-4853188, excerptamedica@elsevier.com, http://www.excerptamedica.com.
Subscr. to: Elsevier BV, Radarweg 29, PO Box 211, Amsterdam 1000 AE, Netherlands. TEL 31-20-4853757, FAX 31-20-4853432, JournalsCustomerServiceEMEA@elsevier.com, http://www.elsevier.nl.

EXCERPTA MEDICA. SECTION 35: OCCUPATIONAL HEALTH AND INDUSTRIAL MEDICINE. *see* MEDICAL SCIENCES—Abstracting, Bibliographies, Statistics

016.3621 016.614 016.3526 GBR
GLOBAL HEALTH. Text in English. 2000. base vol. plus w. updates. **Document type:** *Database, Abstract/Index.* **Description:** Provides international coverage of all aspects of public health.
Media: Online - full text.
Published by: CABI (Subsidiary of: CAB International), Nosworthy Way, Wallingford, Oxfordshire OX10 8DE, United Kingdom. TEL 44-1491-832111, FAX 44-1491-829292, enquiries@cabi.org.

GREECE. NATIONAL STATISTICAL SERVICE. SOCIAL WELFARE AND HEALTH STATISTICS. *see* SOCIAL SERVICES AND WELFARE—Abstracting, Bibliographies, Statistics

016 363.11 USA ISSN 1555-662X
HD7260
HEALTH AND SAFETY SCIENCE ABSTRACTS (ONLINE). Text in English. 1981. base vol. plus m. updates. bk.rev. Index. back issues avail.; reprints avail. **Document type:** *Database, Abstract/Index.* **Description:** Abstracts journal on public health, occupational safety, and industrial hygiene.
Media: Online - full text.
—GNLM.
Published by: (Institute of Safety and Systems Management), ProQuest LLC (Bethesda) (Subsidiary of: Cambridge Information Group), 789 E Eisenhower Pky, Ann Arbor, MI 48103. TEL 734-761-4700, FAX 734-997-4222, info@proquest.com.

362.1021 CAN ISSN 1719-766X
HEPATITIS C. Text in English. 2003. a. **Document type:** *Government.*
Published by: Nova Scotia Department of Health, PO Box 488, Halifax, NS B3J 2R8, Canada. TEL 902-424-5818, 800-387-6665, FAX 902-424-0730, DOHWEB@gov.ns.ca, http://www.gov.ns.ca/health/default.htm.

362.1021 USA ISSN 0362-9279
HA331
IDAHO. DEPARTMENT OF HEALTH AND WELFARE. VITAL STATISTICS (YEAR). Key Title: Annual Summary of Vital Statistics (Boise). Cover title: Vital Statistics, Idaho. Text in English. 1946. a. USD 8 (effective 2000). illus.; stat. **Document type:** *Government.* **Description:** Covers statistics of Idaho. Includes population census, natality, mortality, marriages and divorces, induced abortions and more.
Related titles: Microfiche ed.: (from CIS).
Indexed: SRI.
Published by: Idaho Department of Health and Welfare, Center for Vital Statistics and Health Policy, 450 W State, 1st Fl, PO Box 83720, Boise, ID 83720-0036. TEL 208-334-5992, FAX 208-332-7261, http://www.healthandwelfare.idaho.gov. Ed. Janet Wick. Circ: 800.

ILLINOIS. DEPARTMENT OF HUMAN SERVICES. DIVISION OF DISABILITY AND BEHAVIORAL HEALTH SERVICES. ILLINOIS STATISTICS. *see* SOCIAL SERVICES AND WELFARE—Abstracting, Bibliographies, Statistics

614 016 USA
INDEX AND ABSTRACTS OF A P I HEALTH-RELATED RESEARCH (YEARS). Text in English. 1978. irreg., latest 13th ed. USD 73 per issue (effective 2008). **Document type:** *Abstract/Index.*
Former titles: American Petroleum Institute. Health and Environmental Sciences Department. Report and Other Publications, Index and Abstracts (1058-675X); American Petroleum Institute. Health and Environmental Sciences Department. Research Reports; American Petroleum Institute. Medicine and Biological Science Department. Medical Research Reports; American Petroleum Institute. Committee of Medicine and Environmental Health. Medical Research Reports
Indexed: APICat, APIH&E, APIOC, APIPR, APIPS, APITS.
Published by: American Petroleum Institute, Publications Section, 1220 L St, NW, Washington, DC 20005. TEL 202-682-8000, FAX 202-682-8408, apidata@api.org, http://www.api.org.

614 USA ISSN 1077-1212
HN51
(YEAR) INDEX OF SOCIAL HEALTH. Text in English. 1987. a. back issues avail. **Document type:** *Journal, Abstract/Index.* **Description:** Monitors the social well-being of American society.
Published by: Institute for Innovation in Social Policy, Vassar College, PO Box 529, Poughkeepsie, NY 12609. TEL 845-452-7332, FAX 845-452-7332, miringoff@vassar.edu.

362.1021 PRT ISSN 1646-4052
▼ **INQUERITO NACIONAL DE SAUDE.** Text in Portuguese. 2009. irreg. **Document type:** *Report, Government.*
Published by: Instituto Nacional de Estatistica, Av Antonio Jose de Almeida 2, Lisbon, 1000-043, Portugal. TEL 351-21-8426100, FAX 351-21-8426380, ine@ine.pt, http://www.ine.pt.

INTERNATIONAL NARCOTICS CONTROL BOARD. PSYCHOTROPIC SUBSTANCES; assessments of medical and scientific requirements. *see* PHARMACY AND PHARMACOLOGY—Abstracting, Bibliographies, Statistics

JOURNAL OF PREVENTION AND INTERVENTION IN THE COMMUNITY. *see* PSYCHOLOGY—Abstracting, Bibliographies, Statistics

614.1 USA
KENTUCKY ANNUAL VITAL STATISTICS REPORT. Text in English. 1911. a. back issues avail. **Document type:** *Government.*
Description: Presents birth, death, marriage, and divorce statistics in the state of Kentucky for the year.
Former titles: Kentucky. Cabinet for Health Services. Vital Statistics Report; Kentucky. Cabinet for Human Resources. Vital Statistics Report; Kentucky. Department for Human Resources. Selected Vital Statistics and Planning Data (0145-5990); Kentucky Vital Statistics (0098-6739); Kentucky Vital Statistics Report
Indexed: SRI.
Published by: Kentucky. Department for Public Health, 275 E Main St, Frankfort, KY 40621. TEL 502-564-2757, 800-372-2973, FAX 502-564-6533. Ed. George Robertson. Circ: 600.

KHIMICHESKAYA I BIOLOGICHESKAYA BEZOPASNOST'; informatsionno-analiticheskii zhurnal. *see* CHEMISTRY—Abstracting, Bibliographies, Statistics

362.1021 JPN ISSN 0911-8403
HV411
KOUSEIROUDOUSHOU. KOSEI TOKEI YORAN/JAPAN. MINISTRY OF HEALTH, LABOUR AND WELFARE. HANDBOOK OF HEALTH AND WELFARE STATISTICS. Text in Japanese. 1969. a. JPY 2,940. stat. **Document type:** *Government.*
Related titles: English ed.: Health and Welfare Statistics in Japan.
Published by: Kouseiroudoushou/Ministry of Health, Labour and Welfare, 7-3 Ichigaya-Honmura-cho, Shinjuku-ku, Tokyo, 1620845, Japan. http://www.mhlw.go.jp/.

614.021 JPN ISSN 0911-8497
RA643
KOUSEIROUDOUSHOU. SHOKUCHUDOKU TOKEI/JAPAN. MINISTRY OF HEALTH, LABOUR AND WELFARE. STATISTICAL REPORT ON FOOD POISONINGS. Text in English, Japanese. a. **Document type:** *Government.*
Supersedes in part (in 1981): Densenbyo Oyobi Shokuchudoku Tokei/Japan. Ministry of Health and Welfare. Statistics and Information Department. Statistical Report on Communicable Diseases and Food Poisonings (0448-3944)
Published by: Kouseiroudoushou/Ministry of Health, Labour and Welfare, 1-2-2 Kasumigaseki Chiyoda-ku, Tokyo, 100-8916, Japan. TEL 81-3-52531111, http://www.mhlw.go.jp/.

362.1021 CAN ISSN 1912-5879
LOST-TIME CLAIMS. YOUNG WORKERS. Text in English. 2005. a. **Document type:** *Government.*
Published by: Alberta Human Resources and Employment, 324 Legislature Bldg, 10800 - 97 Ave, Edmonton, AB T5K 2B6, Canada. TEL 780-415-4800, FAX 780-422-9556, ahre.communications@gov.ab.ca, http://www.hre.gov.ab.ca/cps/rde/xchg/hre/hs.xsl/563.html.

614 016 USA ISSN 1077-5587
RA410 CODEN: MCRRFH
➤ **MEDICAL CARE RESEARCH AND REVIEW.** Text in English. 1944. bi-m. USD 967, GBP 568 combined subscription to institutions (print & online eds.); USD 948, GBP 557 to institutions (effective 2011). bk.rev. bibl.; illus.; abstr. back issues avail.; reprint service avail. from PSC. **Document type:** *Journal, Academic/Scholarly.* **Description:** Analyzes, critiques, and synthesizes literature and research in the field of health care.
Former titles (until Mar. 1995): Medical Care Review (0025-7087); Public Health Economics and Medical Care Abstracts
Related titles: Microform ed.: (from PQC); Online - full text ed.: ISSN 1552-6801. USD 870, GBP 511 to institutions (effective 2011).
Indexed: A01, A02, A03, A08, A22, ASG, ASSIA, B07, C06, C07, C08, CA, CINAHL, CIS, CurCont, E-psyche, E01, EMBASE, ExcerpMed, H04, H05, H13, HRA, INI, ISR, IndMed, MEDLINE, P02, P03, P10, P20, P21, P24, P25, P30, P34, P48, P50, P52, P53, P54, P56, PAIS, PQC, PsycInfo, PsycholAb, R10, Reac, SCI, SCOPUS, SSCI, SociolAb, T02, V02, W07.
—BLDSC (5526.908000), GNLM, IE, Infotrieve, Ingenta, INIST. **CCC.**
Published by: (Foundation of the American College of Healthcare Executives), Sage Publications, Inc., 2455 Teller Rd, Thousand Oaks, CA 91320. TEL 805-499-9774, 800-818-7243, FAX 805-499-0871, 800-583-2665, info@sagepub.com. Ed. Gloria Bazzoli. Circ: 185 (paid).

362.1021 BGR ISSN 1312-0336
➤ **MEDITSINSKI PREGLED. MEDITSINSKI MENIDZHMENT I ZDRAVNA POLITIKA.** Text in Bulgarian. 1970. q. BGL 14 domestic; USD 40 foreign (effective 2005). adv. bk.rev. abstr.; bibl. index. 48 p./no.; **Document type:** *Journal, Academic/Scholarly.* **Description:** Contains original articles and abstracts of foreign publications in the field of public health planning and administration.
Formerly: Informatsiia za Rakovodni Kadri v Zdraveopazvaneto i Meditsinskata Nauka (0204-9791)
Published by: Meditsinski Universitet - Sofia, Tsentralna Meditsinska Biblioteka, Tsentur za Informatsiia po Meditsina/Medical University - Sofia, Central Medical Library, Medical Information Center, 1 Sv Georgi Sofiiski ul, Sofia, 1431, Bulgaria. TEL 359-2-9522342, FAX 359-2-9522393, lydia@medun.acad.bg, http://www.medun.acad.bg/cmb_htm/cmb1_home_bg.htm. Ed. Dr. V Borissovv. R&P, Adv. contact Lydia Tacheva. B&W page USD 50, color page USD 150; trim 160 x 110. Circ: 350.

362.1021 USA ISSN 0094-5641
RA407.4.M6
MINNESOTA HEALTH STATISTICS. Text in English. 1972. a. USD 10.95. **Document type:** *Government.*
Indexed: SRI.

P

Published by: Minnesota. Department of Health, Center for Health Statistics, P.O. Box 64975, St. Paul, MN 55164-0975. TEL 651-201-5000, 888-345-0823, http://www.health.state.mn.us. Ed. Linda Salkowicz. R&P Angie Sechler. Circ: 900. **Subscr. to:** Minnesota Bookstore, Print Communications Division, 117 University Ave., St. Paul, MN 55155.

362.021 USA ISSN 1941-4927
N C H S DATA BRIEF. (National Center for Health Statistics) Text in English. 2007. m. free (effective 2011). back issues avail. **Document type:** *Report, Government.* **Description:** Provides information about current public health topics.
Related titles: Online - full text ed.: ISSN 1941-4935.
Published by: U.S. Department of Health and Human Services, Centers for Disease Control and Prevention. National Center for Health Statistics, 3311 Toledo Rd, Hyattsville, MD 20782. TEL 800-232-4636, cdcinfo@cdc.gov, http://www.cdc.gov/nchs.

NARCOTIC DRUGS: ESTIMATED WORLD REQUIREMENTS FOR (YEAR). *see* PHARMACY AND PHARMACOLOGY—Abstracting, Bibliographies, Statistics

362.1021 AUS
NATIONAL HEALTH INFORMATION MODEL. VERSION 2 (ONLINE). Abbreviated title: N H I M V 2. Text in English. 1995. irreg., latest 2003. free (effective 2008). **Document type:** *Monographic series, Government.*
Former titles: National Health Information Model. Version 2 (Print); National Health Information Model
Media: Online - full text.
Published by: Australian Institute of Health and Welfare, GPO Box 570, Canberra, ACT 2601, Australia. TEL 61-2-62441000, FAX 61-2-62441299, info@aihw.gov.au.

362.1021 USA ISSN 1076-8084
RA407.3
NATIONAL HOSPITAL DISCHARGE SURVEY. Abbreviated title: N H D S. Text in English. 1990. a. free (effective 2011). **Document type:** *Report, Government.* **Description:** Designed to meet the need for information on characteristics of inpatients discharged from non-federal short-stay hospitals in the United States.
Related titles: Online - full text ed.
Published by: U.S. Department of Health and Human Services, Centers for Disease Control and Prevention. National Center for Health Statistics, 3311 Toledo Rd, Hyattsville, MD 20782. TEL 800-232-4636, cdcinfo@cdc.gov.

362.1021 NZL
NEW ZEALAND. STATISTICS NEW ZEALAND. HOUSEHOLD HEALTH SURVEY. Text in English. irreg., latest 1996-97. stat. **Document type:** *Government.* **Description:** Contains information about the health status of New Zealanders, their use and perception of health related behaviors such as smoking, alcohol consumption and exercise.
Related titles: Online - full content ed.
Published by: Statistics New Zealand/Te Tari Tatau, Statistics House, The Blvd, Harbour Quays, PO Box 2922, Wellington, 6140, New Zealand. TEL 64-4-9314600, FAX 64-4-9314610, info@stats.govt.nz, http://www.stats.govt.nz.

362.1021 NOR ISSN 0332-7906
HA1501
NORWAY. STATISTISK SENTRALBYRAA. HELSESTATISTIKK/ STATISTICS NORWAY. HEALTH STATISTICS. Text in Norwegian; Summaries in English. 18??. a. NOK 140 per issue (effective 2004). **Document type:** *Government.*
Former titles (until 1964): Norway. Statistisk Sentralbyraa. Sunnhetstilstanden og medisinalforholdene (0804-1865); (until 1906): Beretning om Sundhedstilstanden og Medicinalforholdene i Norge (0804-1636); Incorporated (in 1943): De Spedalske i Norge (0805-5971); Which was formerly (until 1902): Beretning om de Spedalske i Norge i Femaaret (0804-1628); (1861-1882): Tabeller over de Spedalske i Norge i Aaret (0804-1547)
Related titles: Online - full text ed.; ◆ Series of: Norges Offisielle Statistikk. ISSN 0300-5585.
Published by: Statistisk Sentralbyraa/Statistics Norway, Kongensgate 6, P O Box 8131, Dep, Oslo, 0033, Norway. TEL 47-21-090000, FAX 47-21-094973, ssb@ssb.no. Ed. Jens-Kristian Borgan TEL 47-21-094537.

OBZORNAYA INFORMATSIYA. PROBLEMY BEZOPASNOSTI I CHREZVYCHAINYKH SITUATSII. *see* CIVIL DEFENSE—Abstracting, Bibliographies, Statistics

362.1201 USA ISSN 0098-5651
OKLAHOMA HEALTH STATISTICS. Text in English. a. free (effective 2007). illus.
Formerly (1943-1971): Public Health Statistics, State of Oklahoma (0099-118X)
Published by: (Oklahoma. Public Health Statistics Division), Oklahoma. State Department of Health, 1000 Northeast Tenth St, Box 53551, Oklahoma City, OK 73117. TEL 405-271-5562, 405-271-5600, 800-522-0203, FAX 405-271-2899, derekp@health.ok.gov, http://www.health.state.ok.us.

362.1021 USA ISSN 1524-377X
RA407.4.O7
OREGON VITAL STATISTICS ANNUAL REPORT. Cover title: Oregon Health Division, Vital Statistics Annual Report. Variant title: Oregon Vital Statistics. Text in English. 1960. a. free. stat. **Document type:** *Government.* **Description:** Consists of Oregon health statistics collected from death, birth, marriage and divorce certificates, adolescent suicide attempt reports, and induced termination of pregnancy reports. Includes tables, graphs, and narrative.
Former titles (until 1990): Oregon Vital Statistics Report for Calendar Year; (until 1984): Oregon Public Health Statistics Report
Indexed: SRI.
Published by: Oregon Department of Human Services, Health Services, Center for Health Statistics, PO Box 14050, Portland, OR 97293-0050. TEL 971-673-1190, FAX 971-673-1201, dhs.info@state.or.us, http://oregon.gov/DHS/ph/chs/index.shtml. Circ: 2,000.

362.1021 USA ISSN 1524-3796
HA595
OREGON VITAL STATISTICS COUNTY DATA. Text in English. 1999. a. free. stat. **Document type:** *Government.* **Description:** Consists of Oregon Health Statistics collected from Death, Birth, Marriage and Divorce Certificates, Adolescent Suicide Attempt Reports, and Induced Termination of Pregnancy Reports. Includes tables of information for each Oregon County.
Published by: Oregon Department of Human Services, Health Services, Center for Health Statistics, PO Box 14050, Portland, OR 97293-0050. TEL 971-673-1190, FAX 971-673-1201, dhs.info@state.or.us, http://oregon.gov/DHS/ph/chs/index.shtml.

614 USA ISSN 1086-4539
RA407.5.M58
PERFILES DE SALUD DE LAS COMUNIDADES HERMANAS DE LA FRONTERA MEXICO - ESTADOS UNIDOS/SISTER COMMUNITIES HEALTH PROFILES OF THE U S - MEXICO BORDER. Text in English, Spanish. 1991. a. USD 75; USD 500 to corporations; includes all organization publications. **Document type:** *Monographic series.*
Published by: (United States Mexico Border Health Association), Pan American Health Organization, U.S. - Mexico Border Field Office, 5400 Suncrest Dr, Ste C-4, El Paso, TX 79912. TEL 915-845-5950, FAX 915-845-4361, mail@fep.paho.org. Ed. Dr. Hugo Vilchis Licon.

PROQUEST HEALTH MANAGEMENT. *see* HEALTH FACILITIES AND ADMINISTRATION—Abstracting, Bibliographies, Statistics

016.3621 USA
PROQUEST PUBLIC HEALTH. Text in English. base vol. plus updates. **Document type:** *Database, Abstract/Index.*
Media: Online - full text.
Published by: ProQuest (Subsidiary of: Cambridge Information Group), 789 E Eisenhower Pky, PO Box 1346, Ann Arbor, MI 48106. TEL 734-761-4700, 800-521-0600, FAX 734-997-4040, 888-241-5612, info@proquest.com.

REFERATIVNYI ZHURNAL. ORGANIZATSIYA I BEZOPASNOST' DOROZHNOGO DVIZHENIYA; otdel'nyi vypusk. *see* TRANSPORTATION—Abstracting, Bibliographies, Statistics

016.3621 RUS
REFERATIVNYI ZHURNAL. RISK I BEZOPASNOST'; otdel'nyi vypusk. Text in Russian. 1963. m. USD 249.60 foreign (effective 2011). **Document type:** *Journal, Abstract/Index.*
Former titles (until 1999): Referativnyi Zhurnal. Avariino-Spasatelnye Sluzhby (0204-3823); (until 1990): Risk i Bezopasnost'
Related titles: CD-ROM ed.; Online - full text ed.
—East View.
Published by: VINITI RAN, ul Usievicha 20, Moscow, 125190, Russian Federation. TEL 7-499-1526113, FAX 7-499-9430060, dir@viniti.ru, http://www.viniti.ru. **Dist. by:** Informnauka Ltd., Ul Usievicha 20, Moscow 125190, Russian Federation. alfimov@viniti.ru.

363.1021 USA ISSN 1084-3744
SAFETY ABSTRACTS. Text in English. 1995. irreg., latest vol.2, no.4, 1997. back issues avail. **Document type:** *Monographic series, Trade.*
Related titles: Online - full text ed.
Published by: Triodyne Inc., 450 Skokie Blvd, Northbrook, IL 60062. TEL 847-677-4730, FAX 847-647-2047, infoserv@triodyne.com.

SOUTH AFRICA. STATISTICS SOUTH AFRICA. STATISTICAL RELEASE. ROAD TRAFFIC COLLISIONS. *see* TRANSPORTATION—Abstracting, Bibliographies, Statistics

614.42 NCL ISSN 1018-0893
SOUTH PACIFIC EPIDEMIOLOGICAL AND HEALTH INFORMATION SERVICE ANNUAL REPORT. Text in English, French. 1972. a. **Document type:** *Monographic series.*
Published by: Secretariat of the Pacific Community, PO Box D5, Noumea, Cedex 98848, New Caledonia. TEL 687-262000, FAX 687-263818, spc@spc.int, http://www.spc.int.

362.1021 ITA ISSN 1121-1008
RA407.5.I8
STATISTICHE DELLA SANITA. Text in Italian. 1958. a. **Document type:** *Government.*
Supersedes in part (1958-1989): Statistiche Sanitarie (1121-0990); Which was formerly (until 1985): Annuario di Statistiche Sanitarie (0075-1758)
Published by: Istituto Nazionale di Statistica (I S T A T), Via Cesare Balbo 16, Rome, 00184, Italy. TEL 39-06-46731, http://www.istat.it.

SUMMARY HEALTH STATISTICS FOR THE U.S. POPULATION. *see* STATISTICS

362.1021 USA ISSN 1933-0138
RA407.3
SUMMARY HEALTH STATISTICS FOR U.S. ADULTS. Text in English. 1997. a. free (effective 2011). **Document type:** *Government.*
Supersedes in part (in 1997): Current Estimates from the National Health Interview Survey, United States
Related titles: Online - full text ed.: ISSN 1931-2962.
Published by: U.S. Department of Health and Human Services, Centers for Disease Control and Prevention. National Center for Health Statistics, 3311 Toledo Rd, Hyattsville, MD 20782. TEL 800-232-4636, cdcinfo@cdc.gov.

362.1021 USA ISSN 1931-2970
SUMMARY HEALTH STATISTICS FOR U.S. CHILDREN. Text in English. 1997. a. free (effective 2011). **Document type:** *Government.*
Supersedes in part (in 1997): Current Estimates from the National Health Interview Survey, United States
Media: Online - full text.
Published by: U.S. Department of Health and Human Services, Centers for Disease Control and Prevention. National Center for Health Statistics, 3311 Toledo Rd, Hyattsville, MD 20782. TEL 800-232-4636, cdcinfo@cdc.gov.

363.12021 CAN ISSN 1482-6992
TL553.53.C2
T S B STATISTICAL SUMMARY OF AVIATION OCCURRENCES. Variant title: Sommaire Statistique du B S T des Evenements Aeronautiques. Text in English, French. 1991. a.
Formerly (until 1994): T S B Statistical Summary. Air Occurrences (1196-3115)
Related titles: Online - full content ed.: ISSN 1701-6622.
Published by: Transportation Safety Board of Canada, 200 Promenade de Portage, Place du Centre 4th Fl, Gatineau, PQ KIA 1K8, Canada. TEL 819-994-3741, FAX 819-997-2239.

363.12021 CAN ISSN 1196-8702
T S B STATISTICAL SUMMARY, RAILWAY OCCURRENCES. (Transportation Safety Board) Text in English. a. **Document type:** *Report, Trade.*
Published by: Transportation Safety Board of Canada, 200 Promenade de Portage, Place du Centre 4th Fl, Gatineau, PQ KIA 1K8, Canada. TEL 819-994-3741, FAX 819-997-2239, http://www.tsb.gc.ca.

310 THA
THAILAND. NATIONAL STATISTICAL OFFICE. REPORT OF THE HEALTH AND WELFARE SURVEY (YEAR)/RAINGAN KANSAMRUAT KIEOKAP ANAMAI LAE SAWATDIKAN. Text in English, Thai. 1974. every 5 yrs. price varies. stat. **Document type:** *Government.* **Description:** Contains data on illness, public health, deformity, smoking, drinking and safety in driving.
Published by: Thailand. National Statistical Office. Statistical Forecasting Bureau, Larn Luang Rd, Bangkok, 10100, Thailand. TEL 66-2-2810333 ext 1410, 1411, FAX 66-2-2813814, binfopub@nso.go.th, http://www.nso.go.th/. Circ: 300.

U.S. DEPARTMENT OF HEALTH AND HUMAN SERVICES. INDIAN HEALTH SERVICE. TRENDS IN INDIAN HEALTH. *see* NATIVE AMERICAN STUDIES

304.6 USA
RA407.3 CODEN: NADADR
U.S. DEPARTMENT OF HEALTH AND HUMAN SERVICES. NATIONAL CENTER FOR HEALTH STATISTICS. NATIONAL HEALTH STATISTICS REPORTS. Text in English. 1976. irreg. free (effective 2011). **Document type:** *Report, Government.*
Formerly (until 2008): U.S. Department of Health and Human Services. National Center for Health Statistics. Advance Data from Vital and Health Statistics (0147-3956)
Related titles: Online - full text ed.; ◆ Supplement to: U.S. Department of Health and Human Services. National Center for Health Statistics. National Vital Statistics Reports. ISSN 1551-8922.
Indexed: FS&TA, P30, PopulInd, SCOPUS.
—GNLM, Infotrieve.
Published by: U.S. Department of Health and Human Services, Centers for Disease Control and Prevention. National Center for Health Statistics, 3311 Toledo Rd, Hyattsville, MD 20782. TEL 800-232-4636, cdcinfo@cdc.gov.

304.6021 USA ISSN 0083-2014
RA409
U.S. NATIONAL CENTER FOR HEALTH STATISTICS. VITAL AND HEALTH STATISTICS. SERIES 1. PROGRAMS AND COLLECTION PROCEDURES. Text in English. 1963. irreg., latest vol.53. free (effective 2011). **Document type:** *Monographic series, Government.*
Supersedes (in 1963): Health Statistics. Series A
Related titles: Online - full text ed.
Indexed: ChPerI, EMBASE, ExcerpMed, IndMed, MEDLINE, P30, SCOPUS.
—INIST.
Published by: U.S. Department of Health and Human Services, Centers for Disease Control and Prevention. National Center for Health Statistics, 3311 Toledo Rd, Hyattsville, MD 20782. TEL 800-232-4636, cdcinfo@cdc.gov.

614 USA ISSN 0083-1972
RA407.3
U.S. NATIONAL CENTER FOR HEALTH STATISTICS. VITAL AND HEALTH STATISTICS. SERIES 10. DATA FROM THE HEALTH INTERVIEW SURVEY. Text in English. 1963. irreg., latest vol.249, 2011. free (effective 2011). back issues avail. **Document type:** *Monographic series, Government.*
Formed by the merger of: Health Statistics from the U.S. National Health Survey. Series B; Health Statistics from the U.S. National Health Survey. Series C
Related titles: Online - full text ed.
Indexed: EMBASE, ExcerpMed, IndMed, MEDLINE, P30, R10, Reac, SCOPUS.
—Infotrieve, INIST.
Published by: (Data Dissemination Branch), U.S. National Center for Health Statistics, Metro IV Bldg, 3311 Toledo Rd, Hyattsville, MD 20782. TEL 301-458-4000, cdcinfo@cdc.gov.

614 USA
U.S. NATIONAL CENTER FOR HEALTH STATISTICS. VITAL AND HEALTH STATISTICS. SERIES 11. DATA FROM THE NATIONAL HEALTH EXAMINATION SURVEY, THE HEALTH AND NUTRITION EXAMINATION SURVEYS, AND THE HISPANIC HEALTH AND NUTRITION EXAMINATION SURVEY. Variant title: Data from the National Health Examination Survey and the National Health and Nutrition Examination Survey. Text in English. 1964. irreg., latest vol.250, 2010. free (effective 2011). back issues avail. **Document type:** *Monographic series, Government.* **Description:** Provides data from direct examination, testing, and measurement of national samples of the civilian noninstitutionalized population provide the basis for (1) estimates of the medically defined prevalence of specific diseases in the United States and the distribution of the population with respect to physical, physiological, and psychological characteristics and (2) analysis of relationships among the various measurements without reference to an explicit finite universe of persons.
Former titles (until 19??): U.S. National Center for Health Statistics. Vital and Health Statistics. Series 11. Data from the Health and Nutrition Examination Survey; U.S. National Center for Health Statistics. Vital and Health Statistics. Series 11. Data from the Health Examination Survey (0083-1980)
Related titles: Online - full text ed.
Indexed: EMBASE, ExcerpMed, IndMed, MEDLINE, P30, R10, Reac, SCOPUS.
—INIST.
Published by: U.S. National Center for Health Statistics, Data Dissemination Branch, Centers for Disease Control and Prevention, 3311 Toledo Rd, Rm 5407, Hyattsville, MD 20782. TEL 301-436-8500, 800-232-4636, FAX 301-436-4258, nchsed@cdc.gov.

614 USA
U.S. NATIONAL CENTER FOR HEALTH STATISTICS. VITAL AND HEALTH STATISTICS. SERIES 14. DATA ON HEALTH RESOURCES. Text in English. 1968. irreg., latest vol.34. free (effective 2011). back issues avail. **Document type:** *Monographic series, Government.* **Description:** Contains professional and facilities statistics on the number, geographic distribution, and characteristics of health professionals and facilities.

Formerly (until 1982): U.S. National Center for Health Statistics. Vital and Health Statistics. Series 14. Data on Health Resources: Manpower and Facilities (0083-1999)
Related titles: Online - full text ed.
Indexed: IndMed, P30.
—INIST.
Published by: U.S. National Center for Health Statistics, Data Dissemination Branch, Centers for Disease Control and Prevention, 3311 Toledo Rd, Rm 5407, Hyattsville, MD 20782. TEL 301-436-8500, 800-232-4636, FAX 301-436-4258, nchsed@cdc.gov.

304.6 USA ISSN 0083-2057
RA409 CODEN: VHSBA
U.S. NATIONAL CENTER FOR HEALTH STATISTICS. VITAL AND HEALTH STATISTICS. SERIES 2. DATA EVALUATION AND METHODS RESEARCH. Text in English. 19??. irreg., latest vol.152. free (effective 2011). back issues avail. **Document type:** *Monographic series, Government.*
Formerly (until 1963): Health Statistics from the U.S. National Health Survey. Series D
Related titles: Online - full text ed.
Indexed: CIS, EMBASE, ExcerpMed, IndMed, MEDLINE, P30, PopulInd, SCOPUS.
—Infotrieve, INIST.
Published by: U.S. Department of Health and Human Services, Centers for Disease Control and Prevention. National Center for Health Statistics, 3311 Toledo Rd, Hyattsville, MD 20782. TEL 800-232-4636, cdcinfo@cdc.gov.

304.6 USA ISSN 0083-2022
U.S. NATIONAL CENTER FOR HEALTH STATISTICS. VITAL AND HEALTH STATISTICS. SERIES 20. DATA ON MORTALITY. Text in English. 1965. irreg., latest vol.32, 2007. free (effective 2011). back issues avail. **Document type:** *Magazine, Government.* **Description:** Covers various statistics on mortality other than as included in regular annual or monthly reports.
Supersedes in part (in 1973): U.S. National Center for Health Statistics. Vital and Health Statistics. Series 22. Data on Natality and Mortality Surveys (0083-2049)
Related titles: Online - full text ed.
Indexed: EMBASE, ExcerpMed, IndMed, MEDLINE, P30.
—INIST.
Published by: (Data Dissemination Branch), U.S. National Center for Health Statistics, Data Dissemination Branch, Centers for Disease Control and Prevention, 3311 Toledo Rd, Rm 5407, Hyattsville, MD 20782. TEL 301-436-8500, 800-232-4636, FAX 301-436-4258, nchsed@cdc.gov.

304.6 USA ISSN 1057-7629
HA211
U.S. NATIONAL CENTER FOR HEALTH STATISTICS. VITAL AND HEALTH STATISTICS. SERIES 21. DATA ON NATALITY, MARRIAGE, AND DIVORCE. Key Title: Vital and Health Statistics. Series 21. Data on Natality, Marriage, and Divorce. Variant title: Data on Natality, Marriage, and Divorce. Text in English. 1964. irreg., latest vol.57, 2006. free (effective 2011). back issues avail. **Document type:** *Monographic series, Government.* **Description:** Reports of special indepth analysis of birth, marriage, and divorce data by numerous variables.
Formerly (until 1989): U.S. National Center for Health Statistics. Vital and Health Statistics. Series 21. Data from the National Vital Statistics System (0083-2030); Which incorporated in part (1965-1973): U.S. National Center for Health Statistics. Vital and Health Statistics. Series 22. Data on Natality and Mortality Surveys (0083-2049)
Related titles: Online - full text ed.
Indexed: EMBASE, ExcerpMed, IndMed, MEDLINE, P30, PopulInd, SCOPUS.
—INIST.
Published by: U.S. National Center for Health Statistics, Data Dissemination Branch, Centers for Disease Control and Prevention, 3311 Toledo Rd, Rm 5407, Hyattsville, MD 20782. TEL 301-436-8500, 800-232-4636, FAX 301-436-4258, nchsed@cdc.gov.

304.6 USA ISSN 0278-5234
U.S. NATIONAL CENTER FOR HEALTH STATISTICS. VITAL AND HEALTH STATISTICS. SERIES 23. DATA FROM THE NATIONAL SURVEY OF FAMILY GROWTH. Text in English. 1977. irreg., latest vol.30, 2011. free (effective 2011). back issues avail. **Document type:** *Monographic series, Government.*
Related titles: Online - full text ed.
Indexed: EMBASE, ExcerpMed, IndMed, MEDLINE, P30, PopulInd, SCOPUS.
—INIST.
Published by: U.S. National Center for Health Statistics, Data Dissemination Branch, Centers for Disease Control and Prevention, 3311 Toledo Rd, Rm 5407, Hyattsville, MD 20782. TEL 301-436-8500, 800-232-4636, FAX 301-436-4258, nchsed@cdc.gov.

304.6 USA
U.S. NATIONAL CENTER FOR HEALTH STATISTICS. VITAL AND HEALTH STATISTICS. SERIES 24. COMPILATIONS OF DATA ON NATALITY, MORTALITY, DIVORCE, AND INDUCED TERMINATIONS OF PREGNANCY. Text in English. 1989. irreg., latest vol.8. free (effective 2011). back issues avail. **Document type:** *Monographic series, Government.* **Description:** Reports on trends of births, deaths, marriages and divorces, along with abortions.
Related titles: Online - full text ed.
Published by: U.S. National Center for Health Statistics, Data Dissemination Branch, Centers for Disease Control and Prevention, 3311 Toledo Rd, Rm 5407, Hyattsville, MD 20782. TEL 301-436-8500, 800-232-4636, FAX 301-436-4258, nchsed@cdc.gov.

304.6 USA ISSN 0886-4691
U.S. NATIONAL CENTER FOR HEALTH STATISTICS. VITAL AND HEALTH STATISTICS. SERIES 3. ANALYTICAL AND EPIDEMIOLOGICAL STUDIES. Text in English. 1964. irreg., latest vol.34, 2011. free (effective 2011). **Document type:** *Monographic series, Government.*
Formerly (until 1983): U.S. National Center for Health Statistics. Vital and Health Statistics. Series 3. Analytical Studies (0083-2065)
Related titles: Online - full text ed.
Indexed: CIS, EMBASE, ExcerpMed, IndMed, MEDLINE, P30, R10, Reac, SCOPUS.
—INIST.
Published by: U.S. National Center for Health Statistics, Data Dissemination Branch, Centers for Disease Control and Prevention, 3311 Toledo Rd, Rm 5407, Hyattsville, MD 20782. TEL 301-436-8500, 800-232-4636, FAX 301-436-4258, nchsed@cdc.gov.

304.6021 USA ISSN 0083-2073
HA37
U.S. NATIONAL CENTER FOR HEALTH STATISTICS. VITAL AND HEALTH STATISTICS. SERIES 4. DOCUMENTS AND COMMITTEE REPORT. Text in English. 1965. irreg., latest vol.32. free (effective 2011). back issues avail. **Document type:** *Monographic series, Government.* **Description:** Contains reports of major committees concerned with vital and health statistics and documents such as recommended model vital registration laws and revised birth and death certificates.
Related titles: Online - full text ed.
Indexed: EMBASE, ExcerpMed, IndMed, MEDLINE, P30, SCOPUS.
—INIST.
Published by: U.S. National Center for Health Statistics, Data Dissemination Branch, Centers for Disease Control and Prevention, 3311 Toledo Rd, Rm 5407, Hyattsville, MD 20782. TEL 301-436-8500, 800-232-4636, FAX 301-436-4258, nchsed@cdc.gov.

304.6 USA ISSN 0892-8959
U.S. NATIONAL CENTER FOR HEALTH STATISTICS. VITAL AND HEALTH STATISTICS. SERIES 5. COMPARATIVE INTERNATIONAL VITAL AND HEALTH STATISTICS REPORTS. Text in English. 1984. irreg., latest vol.11. free (effective 2011). back issues avail. **Document type:** *Monographic series, Government.* **Description:** Comprises analytical and descriptive reports comparing U.S. vital and health statistics with those of other countries.
Related titles: Online - full text ed.
Indexed: CIS, EMBASE, ExcerpMed, IndMed, MEDLINE, P30, SCOPUS.
Published by: U.S. National Center for Health Statistics, Data Dissemination Branch, Centers for Disease Control and Prevention, 3311 Toledo Rd, Rm 5407, Hyattsville, MD 20782. TEL 301-436-8500, 800-232-4636, FAX 301-436-4258, nchsed@cdc.gov.

U.S. NATIONAL CENTER FOR HEALTH STATISTICS. VITAL AND HEALTH STATISTICS. SERIES 6. COGNITION AND SURVEY MEASUREMENT. *see* PSYCHOLOGY—Abstracting, Bibliographies, Statistics

614.109 USA ISSN 1931-2873
VITAL STATISTICS OF THE UNITED STATES. Text in English. 1937. a. price varies. back issues avail. **Document type:** *Report, Government.* **Description:** Presents detailed vital statistics data, including natality, mortality, marriage and divorce.
Formerly (until 1994): Vital Statistics of the United States (Print) (0083-6710); Which superseded in part (in 1937): Birth, Stillbirth, and Infant Mortality Statistics for the Continental United States, the Territory of Hawaii, the Virgin Islands. Annual Report; Mortality Statistics (1057-4328)
Media: Online - full text. **Related titles:** CD-ROM ed.
Indexed: A23, A24, B13, RASB.
—GNLM.
Published by: U.S. National Center for Health Statistics, Data Dissemination Branch, Centers for Disease Control and Prevention, 3311 Toledo Rd, Rm 5407, Hyattsville, MD 20782. TEL 301-436-8500, 800-232-4636, FAX 301-436-4258, nchsed@cdc.gov.

628 016 AUT ISSN 0083-761X
WASTE MANAGEMENT RESEARCH ABSTRACTS. Text in English. 1965. biennial. free. **Document type:** *Abstract/Index.*
Related titles: Online - full text ed.
Indexed: GeoRef, SpeleolAb.
Published by: International Atomic Energy Agency/Agence Internationale de l'Energie Atomique, Wagramer Str 5, Postfach 100, Vienna, W 1400, Austria. TEL 43-1-2600-0, FAX 43-1-2600-7, ron.shani@iaea.org, http://www.iaea.org/programmes/irais/. Circ: 2,100.

362.1021 RUS
ZDRAVOOKHRANENIE V ROSSII (YEAR). Text in Russian. a., latest 2005. RUR 330 per issue (effective 2005). **Document type:** *Government.*
Published by: Gosudarstvennyi Komitet Rossiiskoi Federatsii po Statistike/Federal State Statistics Office, ul Myasnitskaya 39, Moscow, 107450, Russian Federation. TEL 7-095-2074902, FAX 7-095-2074087, stat@gks.ru, http://www.gks.ru.

362.1021 CAN ISSN 1911-5520
ZOOM SANTE. Text in French. 2006. irreg. **Document type:** *Newsletter, Trade.*
Related titles: Online - full text ed.: ISSN 1911-5539.
Published by: Institut de la Statistique du Quebec, 200 chemin Ste Foy, Quebec, PQ G1R 5T4, Canada. TEL 418-691-2401, 800-463-4090, FAX 418-643-4129, direction@stat.gouv.qc.ca, http://www.stat.gouv.qc.ca.

PUBLISHING AND BOOK TRADE

see also BIBLIOGRAPHIES ; JOURNALISM ; LIBRARY AND INFORMATION SCIENCES ; PATENTS, TRADEMARKS AND COPYRIGHTS ; PRINTING

070.5 IND
A A B C NEWSLETTER. Text in English. 1992. q. looseleaf. free (effective 2011). adv. bk.rev. stat. 4 p./no. 3 cols./p.; back issues avail. **Document type:** *Newsletter, Trade.* **Description:** Reports activities and programmes of Afro-Asian Book Council, discusses issues in African and Asian Book Publishing, includes short-notices of books on books, reports conferences and seminars and other newsworthy items relating to authorship, publishing and printing, particularly in the Afro-Asian region.
Published by: Afro - Asian Book Council, 4835-24 Ansari Rd, New Delhi, 110 002, India. TEL 91-11-23261487, FAX 91-11-23267437, afro@aabcouncil.org.

070.5 700 USA
A A U P BOOK AND JACKET SHOW. Text in English. a. USD 10 newsstand/cover to non-members; free to members (effective 2005). **Document type:** *Journal, Trade.* **Description:** Features titles selected from annual AAUP-sponsored design competition.
Published by: Association of American University Presses, 71 W 23rd St., Suite 901, New York, NY 10010. TEL 212-989-1010, FAX 212-989-0275, http://aaupnet.org/index.html.

090 USA ISSN 1070-700X
Z479
THE A B A A NEWSLETTER. Text in English. 1989. q. USD 25; USD 30 in Canada & Mexico; USD 35 elsewhere. bk.rev. **Document type:** *Newsletter.* **Description:** Encourages interest in rare books and manuscripts and to maintain the highest standards in the antiquarian book trade.
Related titles: Online - full text ed.
Published by: Antiquarian Booksellers' Association of America, 400 Summit Ave., St. Paul, MN 55102-2662. http://www.clark.net/pub/rmharris/newsltr/newsltr.html. Ed. Robert Rulon Miller Jr. Circ: 800.

070.5 USA ISSN 0277-3104
Z475
A B A BOOK BUYER'S HANDBOOK (YEAR). Text in English. a. membership only. **Document type:** *Directory.* **Description:** Lists publishers, distributors and wholesalers of trade and professional books; includes addresses, telephone numbers, discount and payment policies, return policies, freight policies, sales representation.
Formerly: Book Buyer's Handbook
Related titles: Diskette ed.
Published by: American Booksellers Association, Inc., 828 S Broadway, Tarrytown, NY 10591. TEL 914-591-2665, 800-637-0037, FAX 914-591-2720. Ed. Linda Miller. Circ: 7,500; 7,500 (controlled).

070.5 USA ISSN 8756-0267
Z479
A B B W A JOURNAL; the trade publication of the Black book industry. (American Black Book Writers Association) Text in English. 1986. q. USD 30 domestic to individuals; USD 40 foreign to individuals; USD 50 domestic to institutions; USD 60 foreign to institutions. adv. bk.rev. back issues avail. **Document type:** *Journal, Trade.* **Description:** Covers Black books and reviews; Black writers; Black book publishing, and African-American literature.
—Ingenta.
Published by: American Black Book Writers Association, Inc., 4721 Coolidge Ave., Culver City, CA 90230-5116. TEL 213-822-5195. Ed. Toyomi Igus. Circ: 50,000.

P

A G I NORSK GRAFISK TIDSSKRIFT. *see* PRINTING

070.5 AUS
A P A MEMBERS DIRECTORY. Text in English. 1950. a., latest 2001-2002 Edition. AUD 11 per issue domestic to members; AUD 29.95 per issue domestic to non-members; AUD 35 per issue foreign (effective 2008). 136 p./no.; **Document type:** *Directory, Trade.* **Description:** Lists names, addresses and types of publishing activity carried out by the members of the association.
Former titles (until 2000): A P A Directory of Members; (until 1995): Australian Book Publishers Association. Directory of Members (1321-4640)
Published by: Australian Publishers Association, 60/89 Jones St, Ultimo, NSW 2007, Australia. TEL 61-2-92819788, FAX 61-2-92811073, apa@publishers.asn.au.

070.52 AUS
A S A NEWSLETTER. Text in English. 8/yr. free to members (effective 2008). adv. **Document type:** *Newsletter, Trade.*
Published by: Australian Society of Authors Ltd., PO Box 1566, Strawberry Hills, NSW 2012, Australia. TEL 61-2-93180877, FAX 61-2-93180530, asa@asauthors.org. adv.: page AUD 440; 180 x 270. Circ: 3,000.

070.5 USA
A S P I F NEWSLETTER. Text in English. 1983. s-a. USD 25 (effective 2000). **Document type:** *Newsletter.*
Published by: Association of Small Presses in Florida, 429 Hope St, Tarpon Springs, FL 34689. Ed., R&P John A Pyros. Circ: 100.

652.1 USA ISSN 1079-7025
A W P OFFICIAL GUIDE TO WRITING PROGRAMS. Text in English. 197?. irreg., latest 2005-2008 ed. USD 24.95 per issue (effective 2011). **Document type:** *Directory, Trade.* **Description:** Features extensive information on writing programs, colonies, conferences and centers throughout the United States, Canada and Europe. Indexed by region and subject.
Former titles (until 1991): A W P Catalogue of Writing Programs; (until 1980): Writers in Residence; (until 1976): Writers in Residence at Academic Institutions in the United States of America
Published by: (Association of Writers & Writing Programs), Dustbooks, PO Box 100, Paradise, CA 95967. TEL 530-877-6110, 800-477-6110, FAX 530-877-0222, publisher@dustbooks.com.

002 DNK ISSN 1903-3990
Z121
AARETS BEDSTE BOGARBEJDE/SELECTED BOOKS OF THE YEAR; den danske bogdesignpris. Text in Danish. 1941. a. price varies. illus. 34 p./no.; back issues avail. **Document type:** *Catalog, Consumer.*
Former titles (until 2008): Aarets Bogarbejde (0108-1810); (until 1981): Godt Bogarbejde (0107-2323); (until 1973): Aarets Bedste Bogproduktion (0107-2315)
Related titles: ◆ Issued with: Bogmarkedet. ISSN 0903-7195.
Published by: Forening for Boghaandvaerk/Association of Book Crafts, c/o Riget Consult, Hvedevaenget 5, Aalborg, 9000, Denmark. TEL 45-32-958515, 45-98-127933, boghaandvaerk@stofanet.dk. Circ: 2,000 (paid and controlled).

070.594 USA ISSN 1069-1219
Z1035
ACADEMIA; an online magazine & resource for academic librarians. Text in English. 1974; N.S. 1993. m. free (effective 2004). adv. bk.rev. illus. **Description:** News and information on developments in academic publishing, including bibliographic data for new and forthcoming titles available through Baker and Taylor.
Former titles (until 1993): Directions (Bridgewater) (0360-473X); Supersedes: Current Books for Academic Libraries (0011-3352)
Media: Online - full text.
Indexed: GeoRef, SpeleolAb.
—Ingenta.
Published by: Y B P Library Services (Subsidiary of: Baker & Taylor), 999 Maple St, Contoocook, NH 03229. TEL 603-746-3102, 800-258-3774, FAX 603-746-5628, academia@ybp.com, http://www.ybp.com/.

028.1 USA ISSN 0894-993X
Z1039.C65
ACADEMIC LIBRARY BOOK REVIEW. Text in English. 1985. q. USD 36 domestic; USD 44 foreign (effective 2003). adv. bk.rev. **Document type:** *Directory, Trade.*
Indexed: BRI, IBR, IBZ.
Address: 1-A Glenwood Ave, Lynbrook, NY 11563. TEL 516-593-1275, FAX 516-596-2911. Ed. Carol Hoffmann. Circ: 5,000.

028.1 NLD ISSN 1567-7842
➤ **DE ACADEMISCHE BOEKENGIDS.** Text in Dutch. 1995. bi-m. EUR 29.50 (effective 2008). adv. bk.rev. illus. back issues avail. **Document type:** *Journal, Academic/Scholarly.* **Description:** Reviews scholarly and academic books in all subject areas.
Supersedes (in 2000): Amsterdamse Boekengids (1381-6268)
Indexed: RILM.
Published by: Amsterdam University Press, Herengracht 221, Amsterdam, 1016 BG, Netherlands. TEL 31-20-4200050, FAX 31-20-4203214, info@aup.nl, http://www.aup.nl. Eds. Inge Klinkers, Shirley Haasnoot. adv.: page EUR 2,900; 224 x 176.

➤ **ACTA GRAPHICA**; journal of printing science and graphic communications. *see* TECHNOLOGY: COMPREHENSIVE WORKS

070.5 CAN ISSN 1182-3968
ACTIVE VOICE. Text in English. 1980. 6/yr. free to members. **Document type:** *Newsletter.*
Former titles (until 1990): Sic (0839-4636); (until 1987): Freelance Editors' Quarterly (0829-0830); (until 1980): Freelance Editors' Newsletter (0829-0822)
Published by: Editors' Association of Canada/Association Canadienne des Redacteurs - Reviseurs, 502-27 Carlton St, Toronto, ON M5B 1L2, Canada. TEL 416-975-1379, 866-226-3348, FAX 416-975-1637. Ed. Dawn Hunter. Pub. Rosemary Tanner. R&P Connie John.

ADMEDIA. *see* ADVERTISING AND PUBLIC RELATIONS

070.5 BEL
ADRES VOOR HET BOEKENVAK. Text in Dutch. 1929. a. USD 8. adv. index. **Document type:** *Directory, Trade.*
Former titles: Gids voor het Boekenvak in Vlaanderen; Lijstenboek
Published by: Vereniging ter Bevordering van het Vlaamse Boekwezen/ Flemish Book Trade Organisation, Hof ter Schrieklaan 17, Berchem-Antwerp, 2600, Belgium. TEL 32-3-2308923, FAX 32-3-2812240. Adv. contact Wim De Mont. Circ: 1,500.

381.45002 DEU ISSN 0065-2032
Z317
ADRESSBUCH FUER DEN DEUTSCHSPRACHIGEN BUCHHANDEL. Text in German. 1839. a. (in 3 vols.). EUR 135.30 (effective 2006). adv. **Document type:** *Directory, Trade.*
Indexed: RASB.
—GNLM.
Published by: M V B - Marketing- und Verlagsservice des Buchhandels GmbH, Postfach 100442, Frankfurt Am Main, 60004, Germany. TEL 49-69-13060, FAX 49-69-1306201, info@mvb-online.de. Circ: 4,500.

381.45002 DEU
ADRESSBUCH FUER DEN DEUTSCHSPRACHIGEN BUCHHANDEL CD-ROM. Text in German. s-a. EUR 141 per issue (effective 2006). **Document type:** *Directory, Trade.*
Media: CD-ROM.
Published by: M V B - Marketing- und Verlagsservice des Buchhandels GmbH, Postfach 100442, Frankfurt Am Main, 60004, Germany. TEL 49-69-13060, FAX 49-69-1306201, info@mvb-online.de, http://www.mvb-online.de.

070.5 SGP
ADVANCE BOOK INFORMATION. Text in English. m. free. **Document type:** *Bulletin, Trade.* **Description:** Provides information about books that World Scientific will be publishing and distributing in the near future.
Related titles: Online - full content ed.
Published by: World Scientific Publishing Co. Pte. Ltd., 5 Toh Tuck Link, Singapore, 596224, Singapore. TEL 65-6466-5775, FAX 65-6467-7667, wspc@wspc.com.sg, http://www.worldscientific.com.

070.5 CAN ISSN 0844-4404
ADVERTISER. Text in English. 1879. s-w. CAD 64.50 domestic; CAD 159.50 foreign. adv. back issues avail.
Related titles: Online - full text ed.
Published by: Kentville Publishing, P O Box 430, Kentville, NS B4N 3X4, Canada. TEL 902-678-2121. Ed. Paul Sparkes. Pub. Garnet Austen. Adv. contact Wayne Smith. Circ: 11,073.

070.5 800 ETH
AFRICA REVIEW OF BOOKS. Text in English. 2004. s-a. bk.rev. **Document type:** *Journal, Academic/Scholarly.*
Published by: Forum for Social Studies, Woreda 17 Kebele 25, House No.392, PO Box 25864, Addis Ababa, 1000, Ethiopia. TEL 251-1-6297888, FAX 251-1-6297889, fss@ethionet.et, http://www.fssethiopia.org.et/. **Co-sponsors:** Centre National de Recherche Scientifique et Technique en Anthropologie Sociale et Culturelle; Council for the Development of Social Science Research in Africa.

THE AFRICAN BOOK PUBLISHING RECORD. *see* PUBLISHING AND BOOK TRADE—Abstracting, Bibliographies, Statistics

070.5 ZWE ISSN 1019-5823
Z465
AFRICAN PUBLISHING REVIEW/REVISTA DAS EDICOES AFRICANAS/REVUE DE L'EDITION AFRICAINE. Text in English, French, Portuguese. 1992. bi-m. USD 30, GBP 20 in Africa to non-members; USD 50, GBP 35 elsewhere to non-members (effective 2000). adv. **Document type:** *Newsletter.* **Description:** Publishes news, analysis and perspectives on the African publishing industry, including country reports and discussion of development-related issues.
Indexed: PAIS.
Published by: African Publishers' Network (APNET), PO Box 3773, Harare, Zimbabwe. TEL 263-4-751202, FAX 263-4-751202. Eds. Jenny Waddington, Lesley Humphrey.

070.5 GBR
AFRICAN WRITERS' HANDBOOK. Text in English. 1984. irreg., latest 1999. GBP 36.95 per issue (effective 2009). **Description:** Part one consists of original contributions from major African writers, and two essays on African publishing. Part two consists of a resource covering such topics as how to choose a publisher and codes of conduct.
Published by: African Books Collective Ltd., PO Box 721, Oxford, OX1 9EN, United Kingdom. TEL 44-1869-349110, FAX 44-1869-349110, krisia.cook@africanbookscollective.com. Ed. James Gibbs.

002.075 SWE ISSN 1104-2974
ALLA TIDERS BOECKER; tidskrift foer bokelskare. Text in Swedish. 1993. q. adv. bk.rev. **Document type:** *Magazine, Trade.* **Description:** Book collecting, author profiles, reviews, large selection on small publishers with listings of new books.
Published by: Tryckerifoerlaget AB, Tumstocksvaegen 19, PO Box 7093, Taaby, 18707, Sweden. TEL 46-8-7567445, FAX 46-8-7560395. Ed. Leif Lindberg.

002.07 DEU ISSN 1611-4620
ALLES BUCH; Studien der Erlanger Buchwissenschaft. Text in German. 2003. irreg., latest vol.41, 2010. price varies. **Document type:** *Monographic series, Academic/Scholarly.*
Published by: Buchwissenschaft Universitaet Erlangen-Nuernberg, Katholischer Kirchenplatz 9, Erlangen, 91054, Germany. TEL 49-9131-8524743, FAX 49-9131-8524727, nikolaus.weichselbaumer@buchwiss.uni-erlangen.de, http://www.buchwiss.uni-erlangen.de. Eds. Ursula Rautenberg, Volker Titel.

070.5 GBR ISSN 1940-6355
THE ALTERNATIVE MEDIA HANDBOOK. Text in English. 2007. 3/yr. USD 37.95 per issue (effective 2009). illus. **Document type:** *Handbook/Manual/Guide, Consumer.* **Description:** Describes non-mainstream media forms that are independently run and community focussed, such as zines, pirate radio, online discussion boards, community run and owned broadcasting companies, and activist publications. Appeal to students studying media freedom, alternative media, media globalization and media production as well as anyone wishing to embark on a career in this field.
Related titles: Online - full text ed.: ISSN 1940-6363.
Published by: Routledge (Subsidiary of: Taylor & Francis Group), 2 Park Sq, Milton Park, Abingdon, Oxon OX14 4RN, United Kingdom. TEL 44-20-70176000, FAX 44-20-70176699, info@routledge.co.uk, http://www.routledge.com.

AMERICAN BOOK PRICES CURRENT. *see* PUBLISHING AND BOOK TRADE—Abstracting, Bibliographies, Statistics

AMERICAN BOOK PRICES CURRENT. FOUR YEAR INDEX. *see* PUBLISHING AND BOOK TRADE—Abstracting, Bibliographies, Statistics

017.8 USA ISSN 0002-7707
Z1201
AMERICAN BOOK PUBLISHING RECORD; arranged by Dewey Decimal Classification and indexed by author, title and subject. Short title: A B P R. Text in English. 1960. m. (a. edition avail.) (in 2 vols.). USD 550 annual ed. (effective 2011). index, cum.index. back issues avail. **Document type:** *Directory, Trade.* **Description:** Provides a catalog records. Contains 7 sections: Main Section - Dewey range 000-999; Adult Fiction; Juvenile Fiction; Mass Market; Author Index; Title Index; Subject Guide. Included in each entry: main entry, title (italics), subtitle, author statement, place of publication, publisher, publication date, collation, series statement, general note or contents note, LC call, LC card numbers, ISBN, price, binding, and subject tracings.
Indexed: ABIPC, BEL&L, RASB.
—BLDSC (0810.850000).
Published by: Grey House Publishing, 4919 Rte 22, PO Box 56, Amenia, NY 12501. TEL 518-789-8700, 800-562-2139, FAX 518-789-0556, books@greyhouse.com, customerservice@greyhouse.com, http://www.greyhouse.com/. Circ: 4,000.

381.45002 USA ISSN 0065-759X
Z475
AMERICAN BOOK TRADE DIRECTORY. Text in English. 1915. a. USD 349 (effective 2012). index. **Document type:** *Directory, Trade.* **Description:** Profiles 25,500 retail and antiquarian book dealers, as well as 1,200 book and magazine wholesalers, distributors and jobbers - in all 50 states and U.S. territories.
Formerly (until 1922): American Booktrade Manual
Related titles: Magnetic Tape ed.; Supplement(s): American Book Trade Directory. Updating Service. ISSN 0195-3303.
—BLDSC (0810.860000). **CCC.**
Published by: Information Today, Inc., 143 Old Marlton Pike, Medford, NJ 08055. TEL 609-654-6266, 800-300-9868, FAX 609-654-4309, custserv@infotoday.com, http://www.infotoday.com.

652.1 USA ISSN 1555-7448
PN147
THE AMERICAN DIRECTORY OF WRITER'S GUIDELINES. Text in English. 1997. irreg. USD 29.95 per issue domestic; USD 49.95 per issue in Canada (effective 2011). **Document type:** *Directory, Trade.* **Description:** A compilation of information for freelancers from more than 1,300 magazine editors and book publishers. Includes topics index plus detailed submission guidelines, editorial needs and extensive descriptions of each publisher's slant.
Published by: Quill Driver Books, 2006 S Mary, Fresno, CA 93721. TEL 559-233-6633, 800-345-4447, FAX 559-233-6933, Custserv@QuillDriverBooks.com.

090.75 USA ISSN 0887-8978
Z700.9
AMERICAN INSTITUTE FOR CONSERVATION OF HISTORIC AND ARTISTIC WORKS. BOOK & PAPER GROUP ANNUAL. Text in English. 1982. a. USD 30 to non-members; USD 20 to members (effective 2005). **Description:** Covers the conservation of books, documents and works of art on paper.
Indexed: A&ATA.
—Linda Hall.
Published by: American Institute for Conservation of Historic and Artistic Works, Book and Paper Group, 1717 K St, N.W., Ste 200, Washington, DC 20006. Ed. Robert Espinosa. Circ: 1,000.

017.8 USA ISSN 0065-9959
Z1035.1
AMERICAN REFERENCE BOOKS ANNUAL. Abbreviated title: A R B A. Text in English. 1970. a. USD 140 per issue (effective 2011). bk.rev. cum.index every 5 yrs. back issues avail. **Document type:** *Monographic series, Academic/Scholarly.* **Description:** Contains approximately 1,500 titles covering general reference, history, humanities, education, business, science and technology; features increased coverage of CD-Rom products.
Formerly: Preview (0024-4538)
Related titles: Online - full text ed.
Indexed: B14, BibLing, CBRI, ChPerI, Chicano, LIMI, RefSour.
—BLDSC (0853.540000), Linda Hall. **CCC.**
Published by: Libraries Unlimited, Inc. (Subsidiary of: A B C - C L I O), 130 Cremona Dr, PO Box 1911, Santa Barbara, CA 93116. TEL 800-368-6868, FAX 805-685-9685, 866-270-3856, lu-books@lu.com, http://www.lu.com.

AMERICAN SOCIETY OF BOOKPLATE COLLECTORS AND DESIGNERS. YEAR BOOK. *see* HOBBIES

AMERICAN WRITERS REVIEW; advice, tips and techniques from America's most successful writers & editors. *see* JOURNALISM

002 USA
AMERICANA EXCHANGE MONTHLY. Abbreviated title: A E. Text in English. m. **Description:** Online publishing venue for collectors, dealers, scholars, curators & anyone generally interested in the topics of American history as represented in the cultures of print and illustration. Includes feature articles, opinion pieces, guest columns, reviews of exhibitions, interviews with collectors, reports about auctions, and general news of interest to people who own, seek to own, seek to sell, want to research, or otherwise care about the genre of books that can be widely classified as Americanan.
Media: Online - full text.
Published by: Americana Exchange, Inc., 2723 Pacific Ave, San Francisco, CA 94115. TEL 415-563-5908, FAX 415-474-5962, editorial@americanaexchange.com, http://www.americanaexchange.com.

686.3 USA ISSN 0740-5804
Z116.A3
AMPERSAND. Text in English. 1980. q. USD 50 to institutional members (effective 2005). bk.rev. **Document type:** *Magazine, Trade.*
Indexed: ABM.
Published by: Pacific Center for the Book Arts, 300 De Haro St, San Francisco, CA 94103-5144. TEL 415-621-5744, ajpoltroon@aol.com. Ed. Alastair Johnston. R&P Jocelyn Bergen. Circ: 12,000 (free).

002 CAN ISSN 0003-200X
Z990
AMPHORA. Text in English. 1967. q. price varies. adv. bk.rev. illus. **Document type:** *Journal, Academic/Scholarly.* **Description:** Publishes articles on book art, book collecting, typography, private press publishing and related topics.
Related titles: Microfiche ed.
Indexed: BrArAb, CPerI, NumL.
Published by: Alcuin Society, P O Box 3216, Vancouver, BC V6B 3X8, Canada. TEL 604-888-9049, FAX 604-888-9052, deeddy@attglobal.net, http://www.alcuinsociety.com. R&P Jim Rainer. Adv. contact Doreen Eddy. Circ: 275 (paid).

070.5 USA
AMUSING YOURSELF TO DEATH; a guide to surfing the papernet. Text in English. 1997. irreg.
Related titles: Online - full text ed.
Address: PO Box 91934, Santa Barbara, CA 93190-1934. Ed. Ruel Gaviola.

ANALISIS POLITICO; revista de estudios politicos y relaciones internacionales. *see* POLITICAL SCIENCE

028.1 USA ISSN 0098-7379
Z3001
ANNUAL REVIEW OF ENGLISH BOOKS ON ASIA. Text in English. 1974. a.
Published by: Brigham Young University Press, 205 University Press Bldg, Provo, UT 84602. TEL 801-378-4636.

070.50688 AUT
Z2105
ANZEIGER; Die Zeitschrift fuer die oesterreichische Buchbranche. Text in German. 1866. m. EUR 100 (effective 2005). adv. bk.rev. charts; illus. index. **Document type:** *Magazine, Trade.*
Incorporates (1948-1996): Anzeiger des Verbandes der Antiquare Oesterreichs (0042-3610); Former titles: Buchanzeiger des Oesterreichischen Buchhandels; Anzeiger des Oesterreichischen Buchhandels (0003-6277); Anzeiger des Oesterreichischen Buch-, Kunst- und Musikalienhandels
Indexed: AIAP, RASB.
Published by: Hauptverband des Oesterreichischen Buchhandels, Gruenangergasse 4, Vienna, W 1010, Austria. TEL 43-1-5121535, FAX 43-1-5128482, hvb@buecher.at. R&P Inge Kralupper. Adv. contact Mirjam Reither. B&W page EUR 360, color page EUR 800; trim 210 x 297. Circ: 1,500 (paid and controlled).

APPRAISAL INSTITUTE RESOURCES CATALOG. *see* REAL ESTATE

686.3 DEU ISSN 1437-9406
ARBEITSKREIS BILD - DRUCK - PAPIER. Text in German. 1999. irreg., latest vol.15, 2011. price varies. **Document type:** *Monographic series, Academic/Scholarly.*
—BLDSC (1587.378000).
Published by: Waxmann Verlag GmbH, Steinfurter Str 555, Muenster, 48159, Germany. TEL 49-251-265040, FAX 49-251-2650426, info@waxmann.com. Eds. Christa Pieske, Irene Ziehe, Konrad Vanja.

ARBIDO. *see* LIBRARY AND INFORMATION SCIENCES

070.5 DEU ISSN 0066-6327
Z4
ARCHIV FUER GESCHICHTE DES BUCHWESENS. Text in German. 1956. s-a. **Document type:** *Journal, Academic/Scholarly.*
Indexed: BibInd, DIP, IBR, IBZ, MLA, MLA-IB, P30, PCI, RASB.
Published by: (Historische Kommission des Boersenvereins des Deutschen Buchhandels e.V.), M V B - Marketing- und Verlagsservice des Buchhandels GmbH, Postfach 100442, Frankfurt Am Main, 60004, Germany. TEL 49-69-1306-243, FAX 49-69-1306255, info@mvb-online.de, http://www.buchhaendler-vereinigung.de.

070.5 DEU
ARCHIV FUER GESCHICHTE DES BUCHWESENS. STUDIEN. Text in German. 1998. irreg., latest vol.8, 2010. price varies. **Document type:** *Monographic series, Academic/Scholarly.*
Published by: Walter de Gruyter GmbH & Co. KG, Genthiner Str 13, Berlin, 10785, Germany. TEL 49-30-26005176, 49-30-260050, info@degruyter.com, http://www.degruyter.de. Eds. Monika Estermann, Ursula Rautenberg.

002 FRA ISSN 0758-413X
Z116.A2
ART ET METIERS DU LIVRE. Text in French. 1891. bi-m. EUR 47 (effective 2009). adv. bk.rev. bibl.; charts; illus. index. back issues avail. **Document type:** *Magazine, Consumer.*

Formerly: Reluire (0034-4141)
Indexed: ABM, B24, SCOPUS.
—IE.
Published by: Editions Faton S.A., 25 Rue Berbisey, Dijon, 21000, France. TEL 33-1-80404104, http://www.faton.fr. Circ: 4,200.

070.5 JPN ISSN 0916-7838
Z448.7
ASIAN - PACIFIC BOOK DEVELOPMENT. Key Title: A B D Asian-Pacific Book Development. Text in English. 1969. q. USD 20. bk.rev. charts; illus.; stat. **Description:** Concerned with the situation and current events related to publishing and book promotion as well as with the common interests for the book-related personnel of the countries in Asia and the Pacific.
Former titles (until 1989): Asian Book Development (0388-5593); (until 1979): Tokyo Book Development Centre. Newsletter (0049-4046)
Indexed: BAS.
Published by: Asia-Pacific Cultural Centre for UNSECO, 6 Fukuro-Machi, Shinjuku-ku, Tokyo, 162-0828, Japan. TEL 81-3-3269-4435. Ed. Muneharu Kusaba. Circ: 2,500. **Dist. by:** International Marketing Corp., I.P.O. Box 5056, Tokyo 100-30, Japan. TEL 81-3-3661-7458, FAX 81-3-3667-9646.

070.5 USA ISSN 1557-6523
ASK THE BOOK SISTAH. Text in English. 2005. s-m. (2nd & 4th Tuesdays). free (effective 2007). **Document type:** *Newsletter, Consumer.* **Description:** Offers advice to writers about having their work be published.
Media: Online - full text.
Published by: The Book Sistah, 261 S. Main St. Ste. 319, Newtown, CT 06470. TEL 866-834-3942, info@thebooksistah.com, http://www.thebooksistah.com. Ed., Pub. Sophfronia Scott.

002.075 FRA ISSN 0220-388X
ASSOCIATION INTERNATIONALE DE BIBLIOPHILIE. NOUVELLES. Text in French. 1969.
Related titles: ◆ Supplement to: Bulletin du Bibliophile. ISSN 0399-9742.
Published by: Electre - Editions du Cercle de la Librairie, 35 rue Gregoire de Tours, Paris, 75006, France. TEL 33-1-44412805, FAX 33-1-43296895.

028.1 FRA ISSN 0242-035X
ASSOCIATION INTERNATIONALE DES CRITIQUES LITTERAIRES. REVUE. Text in French. 1969. s-a. adv. bk.rev. abstr.; bibl. **Document type:** *Proceedings, Academic/Scholarly.*
Formerly: International Association of Literary Critics. Bulletin
Indexed: MLA-IB.
Published by: Association Internationale des Critiques Litteraires, 3 Rue des Tanneurs, B.P. 4103, Tours, Cedex 1 37041, France. TEL 33-1-53101200, FAX 33-1-53101212, TELEX SCAM SGL 206963 F. Ed. Daniel Leuwers. Circ: 850.

070.5 USA ISSN 0276-5349
Z477
ASSOCIATION OF AMERICAN PUBLISHERS. ANNUAL REPORT. Text in English. a. **Document type:** *Corporate.* **Description:** Summary of the Association's activities for the previous year.
Published by: Association of American Publishers, Inc., 71 Fifth Ave, New York, NY 10003-3004. TEL 212-255-0200, FAX 212-255-7007. R&P Judith Platt TEL 202-232-3335.

070.5 USA ISSN 0748-8173
ASSOCIATION OF AMERICAN PUBLISHERS. MONTHLY REPORT. Cover title: A A P Monthly Report. Text in English. 1984. m. looseleaf. free to members (effective 2000). stat. back issues avail. **Document type:** *Newsletter.* **Description:** Discusses actions taken by the AAP over the past month and includes information on upcoming meetings and events.
—CCC.
Published by: Association of American Publishers, 50 F St N W No 400, Washington, DC 20001-1530. TEL 202-232-3335, FAX 202-745-0694. Ed. Judith Platt. Circ: 200 (controlled).

070.5 USA ISSN 0739-3024
Z475
ASSOCIATION OF AMERICAN UNIVERSITY PRESSES DIRECTORY. Text in English. 1961. a. USD 21 (effective 2008). index.
Published by: Association of American University Presses, 71 W 23rd St., Suite 901, New York, NY 10010. TEL 212-989-1010, FAX 212-989-0275, info@aaupnet.org, http://aaupnet.org/index.html. Circ: (controlled).

070.5 USA ISSN 1062-0036
Z473.R33
AT RANDOM; the magazine of Random House. Text in English. 1992. w. adv. bk.rev. **Document type:** *Magazine, Consumer.* **Description:** News, articles from the publishing world, including author interviews, photo essays and excerpts from forthcoming books.
Media: Online - full text.
Published by: Random House Inc. (Subsidiary of: W. Bertelsmann Verlag GmbH & Co. KG), 1745 Broadway, New York, NY 10019. TEL 212-782-9000, 800-733-3000, FAX 212-572-6066, ecustomerservice@randomhouse.com, http://www.randomhouse.com. Ed. Sean Abbott. Pub. Ann Godoff. Adv. contact Deborah Aiges.

028.1 CAN ISSN 1192-3652
ATLANTIC BOOKS TODAY. Text in English. 1974. q. CAD 14 (effective 2004). adv. bk.rev. back issues avail. **Document type:** *Magazine, Consumer.*
Formerly (until 1992): Atlantic Provinces Book Review (0316-5981)
Indexed: A26, C03, CBCARef, CBRI, CLitI, CPerI, G08, PQC.
Published by: Atlantic Publishers Marketing Association, 5502 Atlantic St, Halifax, NS B3H 1G4, Canada. TEL 902-423-4302, 902-420-0711, apma@dbis.ns.ca, http://www.atlanticpublishers.ca/. Circ: 30,000 (controlled).

070.5 USA ISSN 1946-0392
PN4784.C6 CODEN: CIRMEZ
AUDIENCE DEVELOPMENT. Abbreviated title: C M. Text in English. 1986. 4/yr. A supplement of FOLIO: and distributed with it four times a year. adv. bk.rev. illus. reprints avail. **Document type:** *Magazine, Trade.* **Description:** For circulation executives and publishers in the magazine and newsletter publishing industry. Covers management issues, subscriptions, renewals, controlled circulation, ABC, BPA, postal, fulfillment and more.
Formerly (until 2008): Circulation Management (0888-8191)
Related titles: Online - full text ed.; ◆ Supplement to: Folio:. ISSN 0046-4333.
Indexed: A28, APA, B01, B02, B03, B06, B07, B09, B11, B15, B17, B18, BPI, BRD, BrCerAb, C&ISA, CA/WCA, CIA, CerAb, CivEngAb, CorrAb, E&CAJ, E11, EEA, EMA, ESPM, EnvEAb, G04, G06, G07, G08, H15, I05, Inspec, L04, LISTA, M&TEA, M09, MBF, METADEX, SoftBase, SolStAb, T02, T04, W01, W02, W03, W05, WAA.
—AskIEEE, CIS, Linda Hall. **CCC.**
Published by: Red 7 Media, LLC, 10 Norden Pl, Norwalk, CT 06855. TEL 203-854-6730, FAX 203-854-6735, http://red7media.com. Pub. Tony Silber. adv.: B&W page USD 4,765, color page USD 6,210; trim 7.875 x 10.75. Circ: 10,000 (controlled).

070.5 USA
AUDIT BUREAU OF CIRCULATIONS. AUDIT REPORTS. Text in English. 19??. a. USD 550 for 3 yrs. (effective 2011). **Document type:** *Report, Corporate.* **Description:** Provides ABC-audited circulation figures for newspapers and periodicals.
Published by: Audit Bureau of Circulations, 48 W Seegers Rd, Arlington Heights, IL 60005. TEL 224-366-6939, FAX 224-366-6949, service@accessabc.com.

070.5 USA
AUDIT BUREAU OF CIRCULATIONS. BYLAWS AND RULES. Text in English. 19??. a. free to members (effective 2011). **Document type:** *Handbook/Manual/Guide, Trade.*
Related titles: French ed.
Published by: Audit Bureau of Circulations, 48 W Seegers Rd, Arlington Heights, IL 60005. TEL 224-366-6939, FAX 224-366-6949, service@accessabc.com.

090 DEU ISSN 0343-186X
Z1007
AUS DEM ANTIQUARIAT. Text in German. 1948. bi-m. EUR 84.50; EUR 25 to students; EUR 16.50 newsstand/cover (effective 2010). bk.rev. bibl.; illus. index. back issues avail. **Document type:** *Journal, Trade.*
Indexed: DIP, IBR, IBZ.
Published by: M V B - Marketing- und Verlagsservice des Buchhandels GmbH, Postfach 100442, Frankfurt Am Main, 60004, Germany. TEL 49-69-13060, FAX 49-69-1306201, info@mvb-online.de.

070.5 USA
AUSTIN BUSINESS JOURNAL BOOK OF LISTS. Text in English. 1986. a. USD 55 (effective 2008). adv. **Document type:** *Directory, Trade.* **Description:** Provides listings of hundreds of the hottest area companies in their fields, by ranking. It also provides the names of key decision makers, along with their titles and complete contact information.
Formerly: Austin Book of Lists
Related titles: CD-ROM ed.: USD 169.95 (effective 2008); Online - full text ed.: USD 169.95 (effective 2008).
Published by: Austin Business Journal, 111 Congress Ave, Ste 750, Austin, TX 78701-4043. TEL 512-494-2500, FAX 512-494-2525, austin@bizjournals.com, http://austin.bizjournals.com. Ed., R&P Beth Zacharias. Pub. Lisa Bormaster. Adv. contact Donna Sanagwin.

070.52 AUS ISSN 0045-026X
PN101
AUSTRALIAN AUTHOR; for writers and their readers. Text in English. 1969. 3/yr. AUD 26.40 domestic to individuals; AUD 38 foreign to individuals; AUD 35.20 domestic to institutions; AUD 50 foreign to institutions; free to members (effective 2008). adv. back issues avail. **Document type:** *Magazine, Trade.* **Description:** Provides up-to-date information about writing and publishing in Australia.
Indexed: AusPAIS, BEL&L, ChLitAb, RASB.
—Ingenta.
Published by: Australian Society of Authors Ltd., PO Box 1566, Strawberry Hills, NSW 2012, Australia. TEL 61-2-93180877, FAX 61-2-93180530, asa@asauthors.org. Ed. Angelo Loukakis. Adv. contact Tim Sinclair. page AUD 990; 210 x 280. Circ: 3,000.

AUSTRALIAN PRESS COUNCIL NEWS. *see* JOURNALISM

070.5 AUS ISSN 1327-340X
AUSTRALIAN WRITER. Text in English. 1965. bi-m. free to members (effective 2009). adv. back issues avail. **Document type:** *Magazine, Academic/Scholarly.* **Description:** Contains information about writing competitions, publishing opportunities, literary grants, national wards and writing courses, and also features interviews with writers, "how to" information, tips on how to sell your work, plus other valuable information.
Former titles (until 1996): Fellowship of Australian Writers. Victorian Section. Bulletin (1326-6195); (until 1973): Victorian Fellowship of Australian Writers. Newsletter (0311-8878)
Published by: Fellowship of Australian Writers (Victoria) Inc., PO Box 973, Eltham, VIC 3095, Australia. TEL 61-3-94315573, president@writers.asn.au. Ed., Adv. contact Renee Barber.

THE AUSTRALIAN WRITER'S MARKETPLACE. *see* BUSINESS AND ECONOMICS—Trade And Industrial Directories

070.5 PRT ISSN 1647-5623
AUTORES. Text in Portuguese. 1958. q. free. charts; illus. **Document type:** *Magazine, Trade.*
Published by: Sociedade Portuguesa de Autores, Av. Duque de Loule 31, Lisbon, 1069-153, Portugal. TEL 351-213-594400, FAX 351-213-530257, http://www.spautores.pt.

▼ **AVERAGE PRICES OF ACADEMIC BOOKS.** *see* LIBRARY AND INFORMATION SCIENCES

050 ITA ISSN 1128-6733
AZIENDA EDICOLA. Text in Italian. 1990. bi-m. **Document type:** *Magazine, Consumer.*
Published by: D E A - Iniziative Editoriali s.r.l., Via Chiossetto, 16, Milan, MI 20122, Italy. TEL 39-02-76014647, FAX 39-02-795028, deainedi@enter.it. Circ: 34,400.

B C BOOKWORLD. *see* LITERATURE

B U B; Forum fuer Bibliothek und Information. *see* LIBRARY AND INFORMATION SCIENCES

BACON'S MEDIA CALENDAR DIRECTORY. *see* BUSINESS AND ECONOMICS—Trade And Industrial Directories

BARRY R. LEVIN SCIENCE FICTION & FANTASY LITERATURE. *see* LITERATURE—Science Fiction, Fantasy, Horror

THE BATTERED SILICON DISPATCH BOX. *see* LITERATURE—Mystery And Detective

028.1 USA
➤ **THE BERKELEY REVIEW OF BOOKS.** Text in English. 1989-1990; resumed 1995. irreg. price varies. bk.rev. illus. back issues avail. **Document type:** *Monographic series, Academic/Scholarly.* **Description:** Contains fiction, essays, poetry and reviews.
Related titles: Special ed. of: The New Now Now New Millennium Turn-on Anthology 2001 to 3000 & Beyond. USD 35 (effective 2000).
Published by: Deserted X, 1731 Tenth St, Ste A, Berkeley, CA 94710. Ed. Harold David Moe.

➤ **BEST AMERICAN GAY FICTION.** *see* HOMOSEXUALITY

070.5083 GBR
BEST BOOK GUIDE. Text in English. 1995. a. free (effective 2010). bk.rev. back issues avail. **Document type:** *Handbook/Manual/Guide, Trade.* **Description:** Provides brief reviews of each title, along with bibliographic details and suggested reading level.
Formerly (until 2003): 100 Best Books (1460-7514)
Published by: Booktrust, Book House, 45 East Hill, London, SW18 2QZ, United Kingdom. TEL 44-20-85162977, FAX 44-20-85162978, query@booktrust.org.uk.

THE BEST CHILDREN'S BOOKS OF THE YEAR. *see* CHILDREN AND YOUTH—For

070.5 CHN ISSN 1001-4314
➤ **BIANJI XUEBAO/ACTA EDITOLOGICA.** Text in Chinese; Abstracts and contents page in English. 1989. bi-m. USD 150, CNY 130; CNY 22 per issue (effective 2009). adv. **Document type:** *Journal, Academic/Scholarly.* **Description:** Covers the science of editing sci-tech journals.
Related titles: Online - full text ed.
—East View.
Published by: (Zhongguo Kexue Jishu Qikan Bianji Xuehui/China Editology Society of Science Periodicals), Kexue Chubanshe/Science Press, 16 Donghuang Cheng Genbei Jie, Beijing, 100717, China. TEL 86-10-64000246, FAX 86-10-64030255, http://www.sciencep.com/. Ed. Haoyuan Chen. Circ: 3,500.

070.5 CHN ISSN 1007-3884
PN162
BIANJI XUEKAN/EDITORS BIMONTHLY. Text in Chinese. 1986. bi-m. **Document type:** *Magazine, Trade.*
Related titles: Online - full text ed.
Published by: Shanghai Shi Bianji Xuehui, no.11, 384 Ln., Jianguo W. St., Shanghai, 200031, China. TEL 86-21-64740475, FAX 86-21-64311015.

070.52 CHN ISSN 1003-6687
PN162
BIANJI ZHI YOU/EDITORS' FRIEND. Text in Chinese. 1985. bi-m. USD 62.40 (effective 2009). bk.rev. back issues avail. **Document type:** *Journal, Academic/Scholarly.* **Description:** Covers the fields of editing and publishing. Contains articles on editors' craft and techniques, researches laws in news and publishing, and comments on developments in China's publishing industry.
Formerly (until Jan. 1985): Editors' and Authors' Friend
Related titles: Online - full content ed.
Published by: Shanxi Renmin Chubanshe, 15, Jianshe Nanlu, 11/F, Chuban Dalou, Taiyuan, 030012, China. TEL 86-351-4922194, FAX 86-351-4922146. Circ: 9,300. **Dist. by:** China International Book Trading Corp, 35 Chegongzhuang Xilu, Haidian District, PO Box 399, Beijing 100044, China. TEL 86-10-68412045, FAX 86-10-68412023, cibtc@mail.cibtc.com.cn, http://www.cibtc.com.cn.

002 ITA ISSN 0006-0941
Z1007
LA BIBLIOFILIA; rivista di storia del libro e di bibliografia. Text in English, French, German, Italian. 1899. 3/yr. EUR 135 combined subscription foreign to institutions (print & online eds.) (effective 2012). adv. bk.rev. illus. reprints avail. **Document type:** *Journal, Academic/Scholarly.*
Related titles: Online - full text ed.: ISSN 2035-6110.
Indexed: A22, B24, DIP, HistAb, IBR, IBZ, L09, L11, L13, MLA, MLA-IB, P30, PCI, RASB, RILM.
—IE.
Published by: Casa Editrice Leo S. Olschki, Viuzzo del Pozzetto 8, Florence, 50126, Italy. TEL 39-055-6530684, FAX 39-055-6530214, celso@olschki.it, http://www.olschki.it. Ed. Edoardo Barbieri.

002.075 ITA ISSN 2036-069X
IL BIBLIOFILO. Text in Italian. 1996. irreg. **Document type:** *Monographic series, Academic/Scholarly.*
Published by: Gangemi Editore, Piazza San Pantaleo 4, Rome, Italy. TEL 39-06-6872774, FAX 39-06-68806189, info@gangemieditore.it, http://www.gangemi.com.

BIBLIOGRAFIA NAZIONALE ITALIANA. MONOGRAFIE. *see* PUBLISHING AND BOOK TRADE—Abstracting, Bibliographies, Statistics

028.1 USA ISSN 0006-128X
Z1008.B51
➤ **BIBLIOGRAPHICAL SOCIETY OF AMERICA. PAPERS.** Text in English. 1905. q. free to members (effective 2010). adv. bk.rev. illus. index. reprint service avail. from PSC. **Document type:** *Journal, Academic/Scholarly.*
Incorporates (1907-1912): Bibliographical Society of America. Bulletin; Formerly (1905-1909): Bibliographical Society of America. Proceedings and Papers (0272-5193)
Related titles: Online - full text ed.
Indexed: A01, A02, A03, A08, A20, A22, A26, AES, ASCA, AmH&L, AmHI, ArtHuCI, B04, B14, B24, BEL&L, BRD, BRI, CA, CBRI, CurCont, E08, FR, G08, H07, H08, H14, HAb, HistAb, HumInd, I05, IBR, IBRH, IBZ, L04, L07, L08, LISTA, LibLit, M01, M02, MLA-IB, P02, P10, P30, P48, P53, P54, PCI, PQC, RASB, RILM, S09, SCOPUS, T02, W03, W07.
—IE, Infotrieve, Ingenta, INIST, Linda Hall.
Published by: Bibliographical Society of America, PO Box 1537, Lenox Hill Station, New York, NY 10021. TEL 212-452-2710, FAX 212-452-2710, bsa@bibsocamer.org. Ed. T H Howard-Hill. Adv. contact Michele E Randall. page USD 300; 6 x 9.

➤ **BIBLIOGRAPHIE NATIONALE FRANCAISE. LIVRES (ONLINE EDITION).** *see* PUBLISHING AND BOOK TRADE—Abstracting, Bibliographies, Statistics

➤ **BIBLIOLOGIA**; elementa ad librorum studia pertinentia. *see* LIBRARY AND INFORMATION SCIENCES

P

028 PRT ISSN 1647-9114
BIBLIOTECA DE TEXTOS UNIVERSITARIOS. Text in Portuguese. 1972. irreg. **Document type:** *Monographic series, Academic/Scholarly.*
Published by: Editorial Presenca, Estrada das Palmeiras 59, Queiluz de Baixo, 2730-132, Portugal. TEL 351-21-4347000, FAX 351-21-4346502, info@editpresenca.pt, http://www.presenca.pt.

002.075 ITA ISSN 1723-4417
BIBLIOTECA DELLA RICERCA. BIBLIOGRAPHICA. Text in Italian. 2001. irreg. **Document type:** *Monographic series, Academic/Scholarly.*
Published by: Schena Editore, Viale Stazione 177, Fasano, BR 72015, Italy. TEL 39-080-4414681, FAX 39-080-4426690, info@schenaeditore.com, http://www.schenaeditore.com. Eds. Giovanni Dotoli, Vito Castiglione Minischetti.

070.5 686.2 ITA ISSN 1828-8693
BIBLIOTECA DI PARATESTO. Text in Italian. 2005. a. price varies. **Document type:** *Monographic series, Academic/Scholarly.* **Description:** Aims to study various aspects of publishing presentation and the use of text in its various forms, ranging from book to portal.
Published by: Fabrizio Serra Editore (Subsidiary of: Accademia Editoriale), c/o Accademia Editoriale, Via Santa Bibbiana 28, Pisa, 56127, Italy. TEL 39-050-542332, FAX 39-050-574888, accademiaeditoriale@accademiaeditoriale.it, http://www.libraweb.net.

BIBLIOTECA HISTORICA "MARQUES DE VALDECILLA". DOCUMENTOS DE TRABAJO. *see* HISTORY

BIBLIOTEKA TRADYCJI LITERACKICH/LITERARY TRADITION COLLECTION. *see* LITERATURE

090 HUN ISSN 0067-8007
BIBLIOTHECA HUNGARICA ANTIQUA. Text in Hungarian. 1960. irreg., latest vol.24, 1991. price varies.
Published by: Balassi Kiado, Muranyi u 61, Budapest, 1078, Hungary. TEL 36-1-3518575, FAX 36-1-3518565, balassi@mail.datanet.hu.

381.45002 FRA
BIBLIOTHEQUE(S). Text in French. 1907; N.S. 1956. bi-m. adv. bk.rev. bibl. **Document type:** *Bulletin.* **Description:** Offers practical advice and opinion for booksellers.
Formerly (until 2002): Association des Bibliothecaires Francais. Bulletin d'Informations (0004-5365)
Indexed: B04, L07, L08, L09, LibLit, RASB.
—IE, Ingenta, INIST. **CCC.**
Published by: Association des Bibliothecaires Francais, 31 rue de Chabrol, Paris, 75010, France. TEL 33-01-55331030, FAX 33-01-55331031, abf@abf.asso.fr. Ed. Jacqueline Gascuel. Pub., R&P Claudine Belayche. Adv. contact Caroline Paganucci. Circ: 5,400.

070.50688 SWE ISSN 1403-3313
Z4
BIBLIS. Variant title: Tidskriften Biblis. Text in Swedish. 1998. q. SEK 400 domestic; SEK 200 to students; SEK 475 in Europe; SEK 500 elsewhere (effective 2007). adv. bk.rev. bibl.; illus. index. back issues avail. **Document type:** *Journal, Academic/Scholarly.*
Formed by the merger of (1948-1998): Bokvaennen (0006-5846); (1957-1998): Biblis (Aarsbok) (0430-8417)
Related titles: Online - full text ed.
Indexed: B24, IBR, IBZ, MLA, MLA-IB, RILM.
Address: c/o Kungliga Biblioteket, PO Box 5039, Stockholm, 10422, Sweden. TEL 46-8-4634152, biblis@kb.se, http://www.kb.se/libris. Ed. Ingrid Svensson TEL 46-8-4634231. Circ: 2,000.

070.5 USA
BIG LITTLE TIMES. Text in English. 1981. bi-m. USD 15 membership; USD 3 newsstand/cover (effective 2006). adv. bk.rev. **Document type:** *Newsletter, Trade.* **Description:** Serves as a conduit among collectors and dealers interested in children's books that preceded the comic book format.
Published by: (Big Little Book Club of America), Educational Research and Applications Corporation, PO Box 1242, Danville, CA 94526. TEL 510-837-2086. Ed. Lawrence Lowery. Circ: 700.

070.5 USA
THE BIG PICTURE. Text in English. fortn. USD 120 (effective 2007). **Document type:** *Newsletter, Trade.* **Description:** Covers trends in digital content delivery to both retail and library markets. Provides insight, news, analysis and community in a fast-moving sector.
Published by: L J N Dawson.com

090 NLD ISSN 1879-3738
BIJDRAGEN TOT DE GESCHIEDENIS VAN DE NEDERLANDSE BOEKHANDEL/CONTRIBUTIONS TO THE HISTORY OF THE DUTCH BOOK TRADE. Text in Dutch. 1996. irreg., latest vol.11, 2011. price varies. **Document type:** *Monographic series, Academic/Scholarly.*
Published by: Uitgeversmaatschappij Walburg Pers BV, Postbus 4159, Zutphen, 7200 BD, Netherlands. TEL 31-575-510522, FAX 31-575-542289, info@walburgpers.nl, http://www.walburgpers.nl.

070.5 DEU ISSN 0342-3573
BINDEREPORT; Das Fachmagazin fuer Buchbinderei und Druckverarbeitung. Text in German. 1886. m. EUR 101 domestic; EUR 116 foreign; EUR 17 newsstand/cover (effective 2010). adv. bk.rev. charts; illus.; pat.; tr.lit. index. **Document type:** *Magazine, Trade.*
Former titles (until 1977): Allgemeiner Anzeiger fuer Buchbindereien (0002-5984); (until 1945): Nachrichtenblatt fuer das Deutsche Buchbinderhandwerk; (until 1944): Das Deutsche Buchbinderhandwerk
Indexed: DIP, IBR, IBZ, RefZh.
—**CCC.**
Published by: Schluetersche Verlagsgesellschaft mbH und Co. KG, Hans-Boeckler-Allee 7, Hannover, 30173, Germany. TEL 49-511-85500, FAX 49-511-85501100, info@schluetersche.de, http://www.schluetersche.de. Ed. Matthias Will. Adv. contact Susann Buglass. B&W page EUR 2,271, color page EUR 3,510; trim 188 x 272. Circ: 4,909 (paid and controlled).

686 USA ISSN 1075-1327
BINDERS' GUILD NEWSLETTER; a journal of hand bookbinding practice. Text in English. 1978. m. USD 39 domestic; USD 40 in Canada; USD 49 elsewhere (effective 2004). back issues avail. **Document type:** *Newsletter, Trade.* **Description:** Covers bookbinding and other related fields, including techniques, materials and advice.
Published by: Binders' Guild, 2925 Powell St, Eugene, OR 97405. TEL 541-485-6527, editor@bindersguild.org. Ed., Pub. Susan Lunas.

070.5 305.89607305 USA ISSN 1537-1484
BLACK BOOK NEWS. Text in English. 2001. m.
Address: PO Box 030064, Long Island, NY 11003. TEL 718-274-7040, blackbooknews@aol.com. Ed. Tyra Mason.

070.5 053 NLD ISSN 1574-2199
BOEK. Text in Dutch. 2004. 6/yr. EUR 34.50 domestic; EUR 39.50 in Belgium; EUR 49.50 in Europe; EUR 6.95 newsstand/cover (effective 2010). adv. **Document type:** *Magazine, Consumer.*
Published by: Ambo Anthos, Herengracht 499, Amsterdam, 1017 BT, Netherlands. TEL 31-20-5245411, FAX 31-20-4200422, info@amboanthos.nl, http://www.amboanthos.nl. Eds. Jacqueline de Jong, Jeroen Kans. Pub. Jeroen Kans. adv.: page EUR 1,500; trim 230 x 290.

070.5 BEL ISSN 1377-8714
BOEK.BEDRIJF - V B V B. (Vereniging ter Bevordering van het Vlaamse Boekwezen) Text in Dutch. 1929. m. adv. bibl. **Document type:** *Journal, Trade.*
Formerly (until 2002): Tijdingen (0778-1318)
Published by: Vereniging ter Bevordering van het Vlaamse Boekwezen/ Flemish Book Trade Organisation, Hof ter Schrieklaan 17, Berchem-Antwerp, 2600, Belgium. TEL 32-3-2308923, FAX 32-3-2812240. Ed., R&P, Adv. contact Wim De Mont. Circ: 2,000.

002.074 NLD ISSN 1568-2897
Z2435
BOEKBLAD MAGAZINE. Text in Dutch. 1834. 23/yr. EUR 259 combined subscription domestic (print & online eds.); EUR 345 combined subscription foreign (print & online eds.); EUR 119 combined subscription to students (print & online eds.) (effective 2009). adv. bk.rev. bibl.; illus.; stat. index. **Document type:** *Journal, Trade.* **Description:** Articles and news for the Dutch book trade.
Former titles (until 2001): Boekblad (0167-4765); (until 1980): Nieuwsblad voor de Boekhandel (0028-9965)
Related titles: Online - full text ed.
Indexed: A22, KES, RASB.
—IE, Infotrieve.
Published by: (Koninklijke Vereniging van het Boekenvak/Royal Association for the Booktrade), Media Business Press BV, Postbus 8632, Rotterdam, 3009 AP, Netherlands. TEL 31-10-2894078, FAX 31-10-2894076, info@mbp.nl, http://www.mbp.nl/. Ed. Lucie Th Vermij. Pub. Yvonne Joosten. adv.: color page EUR 2,553; trim 220 x 308. Circ: 2,526 (paid).

070.5 NLD ISSN 0928-4230
BOEKENPOST. Text in Dutch. 1992. bi-m. EUR 32 (effective 2008). adv. back issues avail. **Document type:** *Trade.*
Published by: C. Weghelaer Ed. & Pub., Jupiterstraat 101, Groningen, 9742 EV, Netherlands. TEL 31-50-5713966, FAX 31-50-5710389. Ed. J van der Veer. Adv. contact C Weghelaer.

002 NLD ISSN 0168-8391
DE BOEKENWERELD; tijdschrift voor boek & prent. Text in Dutch. 1984. 5/yr. EUR 34.90 domestic; EUR 47.50 foreign; EUR 27.50 to students (effective 2009). adv. bk.rev. bibl.; illus. index. **Document type:** *Magazine, Consumer.* **Description:** All about books and publishing, the history of the book trade, antiquarian books, book illustration and related topics.
Published by: Uitgeverij Vantilt, Postbus 1411, Nijmegen, 6501 BK, Netherlands. TEL 31-24-3602294, FAX 31-24-3600976, info@vantilt.nl. adv.: page EUR 280; 150 x 220.

381.45002 NLD ISSN 2211-6222
BOEKHANDELSBODE. Text in Dutch. 1971. m. **Document type:** *Bulletin, Trade.*
Former titles (until 2011): Boekhandelsbulletin (0167-9724); (until 1983): Nieuwsbulletin van en voor de Boekhandel (0165-7739)
Published by: (Koninklijke Boekverkopersbond), Boekenbon BV, Postbus 32, Bilthoven, 3720 AA, Netherlands. TEL 31-30-2287956, FAX 31-30-2284566, info@boekenbon.nl, http://www.boekenbon.nl.

028 NLD ISSN 1876-2050
BOEKVERKOPER (AMSTERDAM). Text in Dutch. 2008. q. EUR 36 to non-members; EUR 24 to members (effective 2008). adv. **Document type:** *Magazine, Trade.*
Published by: (Koninklijke Boekverkopersbond), Media Business Press BV, Naritaweg 14, Amsterdam, 1043 BZ, Netherlands. TEL 31-20-5141011, FAX 31-20-6220908, info@mbp.nl, http://www.mbp.nl/. Eds. Hannah Jansen, Lucie Vermij. Pub. Yvonne Joosten. Adv. contact Bas Hendirkse.

BOERN & BOEGER; tidsskrift for skolebiblioteker, skole- og kulturpolitik samt boerne- og ungdomskultur. *see* LIBRARY AND INFORMATION SCIENCES

070.50688 DEU ISSN 1611-4280
Z313
BOERSENBLATT. Text in German. 1991. w. EUR 450 to institutions; EUR 10 newsstand/cover (effective 2010). adv. bk.rev. index. **Document type:** *Journal, Trade.*
Formerly (until 2003): Boersenblatt fuer den Deutschen Buchhandel (0940-0044); Which was formed by the merger of (1945-1991): Boersenblatt fuer den Deutschen Buchhandel. Frankfurter Ausgabe (0340-7373); (1834-1991): Boersenblatt fuer den Deutschen Buchhandel. Leipziger Ausgabe (0006-5641)
Related titles: Online - full text ed.
Indexed: A22, BibCart, DIP, IBR, IBZ, L09, RASB.
—IE, Infotrieve. **CCC.**
Published by: (Boersenverein des Deutschen Buchhandels e.V.), M V B - Marketing- und Verlagsservice des Buchhandels GmbH, Postfach 100442, Frankfurt Am Main, 60004, Germany. TEL 49-69-13060, FAX 49-69-1306201, info@mvb-online.de, http://www.buchhaendler-vereinigung.de. Adv. contact Florian Boehler. Circ: 10,134 (paid and controlled).

028 DNK ISSN 1902-3286
BOGMAGASINET. Text in Danish. 2007-2008; resumed 2010. 5/yr. adv. bk.rev. back issues avail. **Document type:** *Magazine, Consumer.*
Related titles: Online - full text ed.: ISSN 1904-5409. 2010.
Published by: Arnold Busck, Koebmagergade 49, Copenhagen K, 1150d, Denmark. TEL 45-33-733500, FAX 45-33-733535, http://www.busck.dk. Ed. Andreas Nordkild Poulsen.

070.509489 DNK ISSN 0903-7195
Z2553
BOGMARKEDET. Text in Danish. 1855. 23/yr. DKK 950; DKK 495 to students; DKK 45 per issue (effective 2008). adv. bk.rev. illus.; stat. 3 cols./p.; back issues avail. **Document type:** *Magazine, Trade.*
Former titles (until 1988): Danske Bogmarked (0011-6556); (until 1948): Dansk Boghandlertidende (0903-4218); (until 1915): Nordisk Boghandlertidende (1396-4585); (until 1866): Dansk Boghandlertidende (1396-4941)
Related titles: Online - full text ed.; ◆ Includes: Aarets Bedste Bogarbejde. ISSN 1903-3990; Dansk Bogfortegnelse. Ugefortegnelse.
Indexed: RASB.
Published by: Danske Bogmarked I/S, Landemaerket 5, 3, Copenhagen K, 1119, Denmark. TEL 45-33-150844, FAX 45-33-156203, info@bogmarkedet.dk, http://www.bogmarkedet.dk. Ed. Nils Bjervig. Adv. contact Susan Bram. color page DKK 9,800; 150 x 212.
Co-sponsors: Danske Forlaeggerforening; Danske Boghandlerforening.

002.075 DNK ISSN 0006-5749
BOGVENNEN/BOOKLOVER. Text in Danish. 1893. a. DKK 450 to individual members; DKK 1,100 to institutional members; DKK 300 to students (effective 2009). bk.rev. illus. index. back issues avail. **Document type:** *Journal, Academic/Scholarly.* **Description:** Covers the function and aesthetics of books as well as the history and art of book production in the past, now, and in the future.
Formerly (until 1893): Forening for Boghaandvaerk. Aarsskrift
Indexed: MLA-IB.
Published by: Forening for Boghaandvaerk/Association of Book Crafts, c/o Riget Consult, Hvedevaenget 5, Aalborg, 9000, Denmark. TEL 45-32-958515, 45-98-127933, boghaandvaerk@stofanet.dk.

002 BGD ISSN 0006-5773
BOI. Text in Bengali. 1965. m. BDT 60, USD 2. adv. bk.rev. abstr.; charts; illus.; stat. index.
Published by: National Book Centre of Bangladesh, Grantha Bhaban 5, Bangabandhu Ave, Dhaka, 1000, Bangladesh. Ed. Fazle Rabbi. Circ: 5,000.

381.45002 NOR ISSN 0800-0778
Z398
BOK OG SAMFUNN. Text in Norwegian. 1981. 20/yr. NOK 995 domestic; NOK 1,100 foreign (effective 2011). adv. bk.rev. bibl. index. **Document type:** *Journal, Trade.* **Description:** Targets members of the Norwegian Booksellers Association as well as others working in the book trade.
Formed by the merger of (1976-1981): Bok og Samfunn. A-Utgave (0332-5946); (1976-1981): Bok og Samfunn. B-Utgave (0332-995X); Which both supersedes in part (1879-1976): Norske Bokhandlertidende (0029-1889)
Related titles: Online - full text ed.
Indexed: MLA-IB, RASB.
Published by: Norske Bokhandlerforening/Norwegian Booksellers' Association, Oevre Vollgate 15, Oslo, 0158, Norway. TEL 47-22-396800, FAX 47-22-396810, firmapost@bokhandlerforeningen.no, http://www.bokhandlerforeningen.no. Ed. Dag H Nestegaard TEL 47-22-404542. Adv. contact Pedera Oeyboe TEL 47-22-404541.

BOLETIN BIBLIOGRAFICO MEXICANO. *see* PUBLISHING AND BOOK TRADE—Abstracting, Bibliographies, Statistics

070.5 GBR ISSN 2042-8022
▼ ➤ **BOOK 2.0.** Text in English. forthcoming 2011. s-a. GBP 36, USD 68 to individuals; GBP 110, USD 154 to institutions (effective 2012). adv. **Document type:** *Journal, Academic/Scholarly.* **Description:** Aims to publish articles and reviews on developments in book creation and design (including the latest progressions in technology and software affecting illustration, design and book production).
Related titles: Online - full text ed.: ISSN 2042-8030. forthcoming. GBP 75, USD 105 (effective 2012).
Published by: Intellect Ltd., The Mill, Parnall Rd, Fishponds, Bristol, BS16 3JG, United Kingdom. TEL 44-117-9589910, FAX 44-117-9589911, info@intellectbooks.com, http://www.intellect-net.com/. Eds. Mick Gowar, Samantha J Rayner. Pub. Masoud Yazdani.

002.075 GBR ISSN 0952-8601
BOOK AND MAGAZINE COLLECTOR; thousands of books and magazines for sale and wanted. Text in English. 1984. m. GBP 42 domestic; GBP 46 in Europe; GBP 53 elsewhere; GBP 3.50 per issue (effective 2010). adv. bibl. cum.index. back issues avail. **Document type:** *Magazine, Trade.* **Description:** Covers a wide range of literature from the 18th Century to the present day. Lists thousands of titles for sale each month.
Indexed: ChLitAb.
Published by: Metropolis International Ltd, 140 Wales Farm Rd, London, W3 6UG, United Kingdom. TEL 44-20-87528181, FAX 44-20-87528185, metropolis@metropolis.co.uk, http://www.metropolis.co.uk/. Eds. Chris Peachment, David Shrimpton TEL 44-20-82538704.

686.3 CAN ISSN 1923-1776
▼ **BOOK ARTS CANADA.** Variant title: Book Arts du Livre Canada. Text in English. 2010. s-a. free to members (effective 2010). adv. bk.rev. illus. cum.index: 1983-1993. **Document type:** *Magazine, Academic/Scholarly.* **Description:** Showcases books from special collections in Canada, reviews books and exhibitions, and covers as many other subjects of interest to the CBBAG membership as space allows.
Formed by the merger of (1983-2010): Canadian Bookbinders & Book Artists Guild Newsletter (0822-9538); (2007-2010): Canadian Bookbinders & Book Artists Guild Journal (1916-2383)
Published by: Canadian Bookbinders & Book Artists Guild, 60 Atlantic Ave, Ste 112, Toronto, ON M6K 1X9, Canada. TEL 416-581-1071, FAX 416-581-1053, cbbag@cbbag.ca.

686.3 USA
THE BOOK ARTS CLASSIFIED. Text in English. 1993. q. USD 16 domestic; USD 22 foreign (effective 2004). adv. **Document type:** *Newspaper, Trade.* **Description:** Contains ads for an assortment of books, paper, equipment, and supplies; as well as listings for conferences, workshops, exhibitions, and calls for entry. Subscribers use their free classified ads and listings to buy, sell, trade, or just to communicate.
Published by: Book Arts Classified, PO Box 77167, Washington, DC 20013. TEL 301-220-2393, 800-821-6604, FAX 301-220-2394, pagetwo@bookarts.com. Pub. Tom Bannister. Circ: 5,000 (controlled).

BOOK ARTS NEWSLETTER. *see* ART

070.5 USA ISSN 1558-9889
Z284
BOOK BUSINESS. Text in English. 1998. 10/yr. free to qualified personnel (effective 2008). adv. back issues avail.; reprints avail. **Document type:** *Magazine, Trade.* **Description:** Contains strategies for improving book-publishing management and processes, cutting costs and reducing time to market for publishing companies of all sizes.
Formerly (until Jan. 2006): Booktech, the Magazine (1524-2293)
Related titles: Online - full text ed.: ISSN 1558-9978. free to qualified personnel (effective 2008).
Indexed: A15, ABIn, BPI, BRD, P48, P51, PQC, W01, W02, W03, W05.
—CIS. **CCC.**
Published by: North American Publishing Co., 1500 Spring Garden St., 12th Fl, Philadelphia, PA 19130. TEL 215-238-5300, FAX 215-238-5213, napcoinfo@napco.com, http://www.napco.com. Ed. Noelle Skodzinski. Pub. Mark S Hertzog TEL 215-238-5268. adv.: B&W page USD 4,400, color page USD 6,000; trim 7.75 x 10.5. Circ: 12,100.

002 USA ISSN 0006-7202
Z1008
BOOK CLUB OF CALIFORNIA. QUARTERLY NEWS-LETTER. Text in English. 1933. q. USD 55 to members (effective 2001). adv. bk.rev. cum.index. back issues avail. **Document type:** *Newsletter.* **Description:** Contains articles on the book arts, printing history, small presses, and western history.
Indexed: MLA-IB.
Published by: Book Club of California, 312 Sutter St, Ste 510, San Francisco, CA 94108. TEL 415-781-7532, FAX 415-781-7537. R&P, Adv. contact Ann Whipple. Circ: 1,000 (controlled).

002.075 GBR ISSN 0006-7237
Z990
THE BOOK COLLECTOR. Text in English. 1952. q. GBP 50 domestic; GBP 54 in Europe includes North America, South East Asia and Australasia (effective 2009). adv. bk.rev. bibl.; illus.; tr.lit. index. back issues avail.; reprint service avail. from PSC. **Document type:** *Journal, Academic/Scholarly.* **Description:** Contains news and reviews of auctions, publications and trade catalogues, bibliographies and checklists, private press books, exhibitions, appointments, departures and deaths.
Supersedes (in 1952): Book Handbook
Related titles: Microform ed.: (from PQC); Online - full text ed.
Indexed: A20, A21, A22, ASCA, AmHI, ArtHuCI, B04, B24, BEL&L, BRI, BrHumI, CBRI, CurCont, DIP, H07, IBR, IBRH, IBZ, L04, L07, L08, L09, L11, LISTA, LibLit, MLA, MLA-IB, P30, PCI, RASB, RI-1, RI-2, RILM, SCOPUS, T02, W07.
—BLDSC (2248.009500), IE, Infotrieve, Ingenta. **CCC.**
Published by: Collector Ltd., PO Box 12426, London, W11 3GW, United Kingdom. TEL 44-20-77923492, FAX 44-20-77923492, editor@thebookcollector.co.uk. Ed. Nicolas Barker. adv.: page GBP 240, page USD 390; 101 x 164. **Subscr. to:** 32 Swift Way, Thurlby, Nr Bourne, Lincolnshire PE10 0QA, United Kingdom. TEL 44-1778-338095, FAX 44-1778-338096.

381.45002 USA ISSN 1098-8521
BOOK DEALERS WORLD; direct mail marketplace for book dealers and self-publishers and writers. Text in English. 1980. q. USD 45 domestic; USD 60 foreign (effective 2007). adv. bk.rev. 32 p./no. 3 cols./p.; back issues avail. **Document type:** *Magazine, Trade.*
Published by: North American Bookdealers Exchange, PO Box 606, Cottage Grove, OR 97424. TEL 541-942-7455, FAX 541-942-7455, nabeajg@bookmarketingprofits.com. Ed., Adv. contact Al Galasso. page USD 400. Circ: 20,000 (paid and free).

028 NLD ISSN 1871-4242
BOOK-DELEN DOSSIER. Text in Dutch. 2006. s-a. EUR 13.12 (effective 2009).
Published by: Biblion Uitgeverij, Veursestraatweg 280, Leidschendam, 2265 CL, Netherlands. TEL 31-70-3377733, FAX 31-70-3377899, info@nbdbiblion.nl, http://www.nbdbiblion.nl/.

002.09 USA ISSN 1098-7371
Z4
➤ **BOOK HISTORY.** Text in English. 1998. a. USD 94 combined subscription per issue to institutions; USD 67 per issue to institutions (print or online ed.) (effective 2012). adv. bk.rev. illus. back issues avail.; reprint service avail. from PSC. **Document type:** *Journal, Academic/Scholarly.* **Description:** Covers all aspects of the history of the book, defined as the history of the creation, dissemination, and reception of script and print.
Related titles: Online - full text ed.: ISSN 1529-1499. USD 70 per issue to institutions (effective 2012).
Indexed: A01, A02, A03, A08, A22, AmH&L, AmHI, B04, BRD, CA, E01, H07, HistAb, L04, L05, L06, L07, L08, LISTA, LibLit, MLA-IB, T02, W03, W05.
—BLDSC (2248.103860), IE. **CCC.**
Published by: (Society for the History of Authorship, Reading, and Publishing), The Johns Hopkins University Press, 2715 N Charles St, Baltimore, MD 21218. TEL 410-516-6900, FAX 410-516-6968. Eds. Ezra Greenspan, Jonathan Rose. Pub. William M Breichner. **Subscr. to:** PO Box 19966, Baltimore, MD 21211. TEL 410-516-6987, 800-548-1784, FAX 410-516-3866, jrnlcirc@press.jhu.edu.

381.45002 USA ISSN 0160-970X
Z477
BOOK INDUSTRY TRENDS. Variant title: Book Industry Study Group. Research Report. Text in English. 1977. a. USD 100 to members; USD 750 to non-members (effective 2005). stat. back issues avail. **Document type:** *Monographic series, Trade.*
—BLDSC (2248.104000). **CCC.**
Published by: Book Industry Study Group, Inc., 19 W. 21st St., Rm. 905, New York, NY 10010-6848. TEL 212-929-1393, FAX 212-989-7542, bisg-info@bisg.org. R&P Frank Daly TEL 732-583-0066.

002 USA ISSN 1091-5540
Z1003.2
BOOK LOVERS. Cover title: BookLovers. Text in English. 1993. q. USD 10 (effective 1999). adv. bk.rev. back issues avail. **Document type:** *Magazine, Consumer.*
Address: PO Box 511396, Milwaukee, WI 53203-0241. TEL 414-384-2300, acth@execpc.com, booklove@execpc.com. Ed., R&P Tracy Walczak. Pub., Adv. contact Robert Jammer. page USD 14,350; trim 9.75 x 7.5. Circ: 5,500.

381.45002 USA ISSN 0891-8813
BOOK MARKETING UPDATE. Text in English. 1986. m. USD 60; USD 98 foreign. adv. bk.rev. bibl.; charts; illus.; stat. index. back issues avail. **Document type:** *Newsletter.* **Description:** Features ideas, tips, resources, case histories, and articles on book marketing, publicity, and promotions for large and small book publishers and authors.
—**CCC.**
Published by: Open Horizons Publishing, PO Box 205, Fairfield, IA 52556-0205. TEL 512-472-6130, FAX 515-472-1560. Ed., Pub., R&P John Kremer. Adv. contact Paula Fritchen. page USD 350; trim 11 x 8.5. Circ: 3,000 (paid).

070.5 USA
BOOK NEWS. Text in English. 1980. 10/yr. membership. **Document type:** *Newsletter.*
Published by: American Book Producers Association, 160 Fifth Ave, New York, NY 10010. TEL 212-645-2368, FAX 212-989-7542. Ed. David Rubel. Circ: 75.

028.1 USA ISSN 0006-730X
Z1007.B7166
BOOK-OF-THE-MONTH CLUB NEWS. Text in English. 1926. 17/yr. bk.rev. bibl.; illus. **Document type:** *Newsletter.*
Related titles: Online - full text ed.: B O M C Reading Room.
Published by: Book-Of-The-Month Club, Time & Life Bldg, 1271 Ave of the Americas, New York, NY 10020. TEL 212-522-4200, bomc_inquiries@bomc.com, http://www.bomc.com.

002 USA
BOOK PAGE. Text in English. 1988. m. USD 30 to individuals (effective 2009). adv. bk.rev. illus. 32 p./no.; back issues avail. **Document type:** *Newspaper, Consumer.* **Description:** Features book reviews, author interviews and news of the world of books.
Related titles: Online - full content ed.
Indexed: CBRI.
Published by: ProMotion, Inc., 2143 Belcourt Ave, Nashville, TN 37212. TEL 615-292-8926, FAX 615-292-8249, contact@bookpage.com. Ed. Lynn Green. Pub. Michael Zibart. Adv. contact Julia Steele. color page USD 9,995; 8.625 x 11.125. Circ: 450,000 (paid).

070.5 USA ISSN 1086-1319
CODEN: IPUNEW
BOOK PUBLISHING REPORT; weekly news and analysis of events shaping the book industry. Text in English. 1975. m. free in US & Canada to qualified personnel (effective 2008). adv. back issues avail. **Document type:** *Newsletter, Trade.* **Description:** Covers the deals, financials, bestsellers, legal developments, technological issues, distribution, retailing, people, etc.
Formerly (until 1995): B P Report on the Business of Book Publishing (0145-9457); Incorporates (1983-1989): International Publishing Newsletter (0740-7513); Audio Publishing Report (0888-4498)
Related titles: Online - full text ed.: USD 689 (effective 2005).
Indexed: A09, A10, B01, B06, B07, B08, B09, C12, PROMT, T02, V03, V04.
—CASDDS. **CCC.**
Published by: SIMBA Information (Subsidiary of: Market Research.Com), 11200 Rockville Pike, Ste 504, Rockville, MD 20852. TEL 240-747-3096, 888-297-4622, FAX 240-747-3004, customerservice@simbainformation.com, http://www.simbainformation.com. Ed. Michael Norris. Pub. Linda Kopp.

381.45002 USA
Z475
BOOK PUBLISHING RESOURCE GUIDE. Text in English. 1986. a. bibl. index. **Document type:** *Guide, Trade.* **Description:** Includes major wholesalers, bookstore chains, clubs, catalogues and over 2,000 media contacts.
Formerly: Book Marketing Opportunities: A Directory (0894-1785)
Related titles: Online - full text ed.
Published by: North American Publishing Co., 1500 Spring Garden St., 12th Fl, Philadelphia, PA 19130. TEL 215-238-5300, 800-777-8074, FAX 800-664-1533, http://www.napco.com. Circ: 2,000.

028.1 USA
THE BOOK READER. Text in English. bi-m. USD 20 (effective 1999). **Document type:** *Newspaper.*
Published by: Jay Bail, Ed. & Pub., 245 Mt Hermon Rd, Ste 256, Scotts Valley, CA 95066-4035. TEL 408-475-3412.

BOOK REVIEW INDEX: ANNUAL CUMULATION. *see* PUBLISHING AND BOOK TRADE—Abstracting, Bibliographies, Statistics

002.075 USA ISSN 1553-2690
BOOK SOURCE MAGAZINE. Text in English. bi-m. USD 20 domestic; USD 24 in Canada & Mexico; USD 40 elsewhere (effective 2004). adv.
Formerly (until 2002): Book Source Monthly (1047-9465)
Address: P O Box 567, Cazenovia, NY 13035. Ed., Pub. John C Huckans.

070.5 CAN ISSN 1484-9313
Z485
THE BOOK TRADE IN CANADA; your complete guide to the Canadian publishing marketplace. Text in English, French. 1975. a. CAD 125; CAD 150 foreign (effective 1999). adv. back issues avail. **Document type:** *Directory, Trade.* **Description:** Covers the Canadian book industry: information on publishers, booksellers, librarians, writers, media and suppliers.
Former titles (until 1998): Book Trade in Canada, with Who's Where (0836-8619); (until 1985): Book Trade in Canada (0700-5296); (until 1976): Book Publishers in Canada
—BLDSC (2248.280000).
Published by: Key Publishers Co. Ltd., 70 The Esplanade, 4th Fl, Toronto, ON M5E 1R2, Canada. TEL 416-360-0044, FAX 416-955-0794. Ed. Scott Anderson. Pub., R&P Sharon McAuley. Adv. contact June Dickenson. B&W page CAD 1,000, color page CAD 1,595; trim 10.88 x 8.38. Circ: 2,000 (paid).

028.1 810 USA ISSN 1937-5921
BOOKBROWSE PREVIEWS. Text in English. 2005. m. USD 34.95 (effective 2007). **Document type:** *Newsletter, Consumer.*
Media: Online - full content.
Published by: BookBrowse LLC, PO Box 2157, Saratoga, CA 95070. TEL 408-867-6500, info@bookbrowse.com, http://www.bookbrowse.com.

381.45002 GBR ISSN 1369-6572
BOOKDEALER; the monthly magazine for books, news and reviews. Text in English. 1971. m. GBP 29 domestic; GBP 41 in Europe; GBP 39 elsewhere (effective 2009). adv. bk.rev. **Document type:** *Journal, Trade.* **Description:** Features catalogue and book reviews, book chat, auction dates, notes from the underbidder and of course books wanted and books for sale.
Published by: Rare Books and Berry, Higherbourne, High St, Porlock, Somerset, TA24 8PU, United Kingdom. TEL 44-1643-863255. adv.: B&W page GBP 78, color page GBP 100; 123 x 193.

BOOKENDS (KUTZTOWN). *see* LIBRARY AND INFORMATION SCIENCES

028.1 USA ISSN 0006-7385
Z1035.A1
BOOKLIST. Text in English. 1969. bi-m. (22/yr.). USD 109.95 domestic; USD 126.95 foreign; USD 9 per issue (effective 2011); subscr. includes Book Links. adv. bk.rev. bibl.; illus. index, s-a. cum.index. back issues avail.; reprints avail. **Document type:** *Magazine, Trade.* **Description:** Contains reviews of recommended library materials for adults, young adults and children, both print and non-print.
Formerly (until 1969): The Booklist and Subscription Books Bulletin (0730-8957); Which was formed by the merger of (1930-1956): Subscription Books Bulletin; (1917-1956): The Booklist; Which was formerly (1905-1917): A L A Booklist
Related titles: CD-ROM ed.; Microform ed.: (from PQC); Online - full text ed.: 2006; ◆ Includes: Reference Books Bulletin. ISSN 8755-0962.
Indexed: A01, A02, A03, A08, A11, A22, A25, A26, A33, ABS&EES, AmHI, B04, B05, B14, BRI, C05, CBRI, CPerI, ChLitAb, ChPerI, Chicano, ConsI, E02, E03, E07, E08, ERI, EdA, EdI, G05, G06, G07, G08, G09, GardL, H07, I05, I07, L04, L05, L06, L07, L08, L09, LIMI, LISTA, LibLit, M01, M02, M06, M11, MASUSE, MEA&I, MLA-IB, MRD, MagInd, MicrocompInd, P02, P04, P06, P07, P10, P18, P34, P48, P53, P54, P55, PCR2, PQC, R06, RASB, RGAb, RGYP, RefSour, S08, S09, T02, TOM, U01, W03.
—BLDSC (2250.068000), IE, Infotrieve, Ingenta, Linda Hall. **CCC.**
Published by: American Library Association, 50 E Huron, Chicago, IL 60611. TEL 800-545-2433, FAX 312-440-9374, customerservice@ala.org, http://www.ala.org. Ed., Pub. Bill Ott. Adv. contact Linda Cohen TEL 914-944-0135. B&W page USD 5,950; trim 7.875 x 10.5. Circ: 20,200 (paid). **Subscr. to:** Kable Fulfillment Services, Inc., 308 E Hitt St, Mount Morris, IL 61504. TEL 888-350-0949, FAX 815-734-5858, blst@kable.com.

381.45002 BGD
BOOKMAN. Text in Bengali, English. 1979. q. BDT 10, USD 2 per issue. bibl. reprints avail.
Related titles: Microfilm ed.: (from PQC).
Published by: Bangladesh Books International Ltd., Ittefaq Bhaban, 1 Ramkrishna Mission Rd, PO Box 377, Dhaka, 3, Bangladesh. TEL 2-256071.

017.8 USA ISSN 0068-0133
BOOKMAN'S GUIDE TO AMERICANA. Text in English. 1956. irreg., latest vol.10, 1991. USD 82 per issue (effective 2009). **Document type:** *Directory, Bibliography.* **Description:** Presents an alphabetically arranged compilation of quotations transcribed from recent out-of-print booksellers' catalogs and a record of prices asked for out-of-print titles in American fiction and non-fiction.
Former titles (until 1971): J. Norman Heard Bookman's Guide to Americana; (until 1967): Bookman's Guide to Americana
Published by: Scarecrow Press, Inc. (Subsidiary of: Rowman & Littlefield Publishers, Inc.), 4501 Forbes Blvd, Ste 200, Lanham, MD 20706. TEL 301-459-3366, 800-462-6420, FAX 301-429-5748, 800-338-4550, custserv@rowman.com. Ed., Pub. Mr. Edward Kurdyla TEL 301-459-3366 ext 5604.

017.8 USA ISSN 0068-0141
Z1000
BOOKMAN'S PRICE INDEX; guide to the values of rare and other out-of-print books. Abbreviated title: B P I. Text in English. 1964. irreg., latest vol.90, 2009. USD 519 per vol. (effective 2009). back issues avail.; reprints avail. **Document type:** *Directory, Trade.* **Description:** Designed to be an index for rare and antiquarian books offered for sale in the catalogs of 100-200 book dealers in the United States, Canada, and the British Isles.
Published by: Gale (Subsidiary of: Cengage Learning), 27500 Drake Rd, Farmington Hills, MI 48331. TEL 248-699-4253, 800-877-4253, FAX 877-363-4253, gale.customerservice@cengage.com, http://gale.cengage.com. Ed. Daniel F McGrath.

070.5 USA ISSN 1546-0657
Z1003
BOOKMARKS; for everyone who hasn't read everything. Text in English. 2002 (Nov./Dec.). bi-m. USD 27.95 domestic; USD 37.95 in Canada; USD 57.95 elsewhere; USD 5.95 per issue (effective 2010). adv. illus. back issues avail. **Document type:** *Magazine, Consumer.* **Description:** Contains sections profiling classic authors, suggested reading, and a new books guide, which was created by researching all the major book reviews found in newspapers, magazines and the internet.
Indexed: A26, G05, G06, G07, I05.
Published by: Bookmarks Publishing LLC, 1818 MLK Blvd, Ste 181, Chapel Hill, NC 27514. TEL 888-488-6593, FAX 888-356-8107, letters@bookmarksmagazine.com. Ed., Pub. Jon Phillips. Adv. contact Laraine Stein TEL 415-751-5385.

015.9305 NZL ISSN 1176-8851
BOOKNOTES. Text in English. 1981. q. free to members (effective 2010). adv. bk.rev. back issues avail. **Document type:** *Magazine, Consumer.* **Description:** Publishes literary news, author interview, and reviews of recently published New Zealand and international books.
Related titles: Online - full text ed.: ISSN 1179-6022. free (effective 2010).
Published by: New Zealand Book Council, Level 7, Alan Burns Insurances House, 69-71 Boulcott St, Wellington, 6011, New Zealand. TEL 64-4-4991569, FAX 64-4-4991424, admin@bookcouncil.org.nz. Adv. contact Susanna Andrew.

P

769.52 929.6 GBR ISSN 0264-3693
Z993.A1
BOOKPLATE JOURNAL. Text in English. 1983. s-a. free to members (effective 2009). adv. bk.rev. illus. back issues avail.; reprints avail.
Document type: *Journal, Academic/Scholarly.* **Description:** Discusses all aspects of the history, making and collecting of bookplates.
Indexed: B24.
Published by: Bookplate Society, Yarkhill, Upper Bucklebury, Reading, RG7 6QH, United Kingdom. publications@bookplatesociety.org, http://www.bookplatesociety.org. Ed. Peter Youatt.

002.075 929 GBR ISSN 0309-7935
Z993.A1
BOOKPLATE SOCIETY NEWSLETTER. Text in English. 1972. s-a. free to members (effective 2009). **Document type:** *Newsletter.*
—**CCC.**
Published by: Bookplate Society, Yarkhill, Upper Bucklebury, Reading, RG7 6QH, United Kingdom. publications@bookplatesociety.org, http://www.bookplatesociety.org. Ed. Bryan J Welch.

070.5 NGA ISSN 0794-8603
Z468.N5
BOOKS. Text in English. 1987. q.
Published by: Booklinks Ltd., 15 Obafemi Awolowo Way, PO Box 2547, Ikeja, Lagos, Nigeria.

028.1 JPN
BOOKS AND ESSAYS/TOSHO. Text in Japanese. 1938. m. **Description:** To stimulate an interest in reading.
Published by: Iwanami Shoten, Publishers, 2-5-5 Hitotsubashi, Chiyoda-ku, Tokyo, 101-0003, Japan. TEL 81-3-3265-4111, FAX 81-3-239-9618, TELEX 39495. **Dist. overseas by:** Japan Publications Trading Co., Ltd., Book Export II Dept, PO Box 5030, Tokyo International, Tokyo 101-3191, Japan. TEL 81-3-32923753, FAX 81-3-32920410, infoserials@jptco.co.jp, http://www.jptco.co.jp.

070.5 CAN
BOOKS FOR EVERYBODY. Text in English. a. adv. **Document type:** *Catalog.*
Published by: Key Publishers Co. Ltd., 70 The Esplanade, 4th Fl, Toronto, ON M5E 1R2, Canada. TEL 416-360-0044, FAX 416-955-0794. Pub. Barbara Scott. adv.: color 1/2 page CAD 1,595. Circ: 300,000.

028.5 GBR ISSN 0143-909X
Z1037
BOOKS FOR KEEPS; the chidren's book magazine. Text in English. 1980. bi-m. GBP 26.50 domestic; GBP 29.50 in Europe; GBP 32.50 elsewhere (effective 2009). adv. bk.rev. bibl. index. back issues avail.
Document type: *Magazine, Consumer.* **Description:** Contains reviews, articles, and interviews on children's books.
Incorporates (1983-1988): British Book News Children's Books (0264-5637); School Bookshop News
Indexed: BRI, CBRI, ChLitAb.
—IE.
Published by: School Bookshop Association Ltd., 1 Effingham Rd, London, SE12 8NZ, United Kingdom. TEL 44-20-88524953, FAX 44-20-83187580, enquiries@booksforkeeps.co.uk. Ed. Rosemary Stones.

BOOKS FROM FINLAND. *see* PUBLISHING AND BOOK TRADE—Abstracting, Bibliographies, Statistics

BOOKS FROM KOREA. *see* PUBLISHING AND BOOK TRADE—Abstracting, Bibliographies, Statistics

002 BIH ISSN 0352-1044
PG1417.B6
BOOKS IN BOSNIA AND HERZEGOVINA. Text in English. 1982. a.
Document type: *Journal, Trade.*
Indexed: MLA-IB.
Published by: Association of Writers of Bosnia and Herzegovina, Ferhadija 19, Sarajevo, 71000, Bosnia Herzegovina.

070.5 IRL ISSN 0376-6039
Z331.7
BOOKS IRELAND. Text in English, Gaelic. 1976. 9/yr. USD 22. adv. bk.rev. tr.lit. index. **Document type:** *Journal, Trade.* **Description:** Provides bibliography listings and reviews of all Irish-interest and Irish-author books, with news of Irish publishing.
Related titles: Diskette ed.
Indexed: MLA-IB, RASB.
—BLDSC (2250.201000), IE, Ingenta.
Published by: Jeremy Addis Ltd., 11 Newgrove Ave, Dublin, 4, Ireland. TEL 353-1-2692185, FAX 353-1-2604927, booksi@eircom.net. Ed. Jeremy Addis. Circ: 3,180. **U.S. subscr. to:** Irish Books & Media, 1433 Franklin Ave E, Minneapolis, MN 55404-2135. TEL 612-871-3505.

BOOKS OF THE SOUTHWEST (ONLINE EDITION); a critical checklist of current Southwestern Americana. *see* PUBLISHING AND BOOK TRADE—Abstracting, Bibliographies, Statistics

028.1 CAN
BOOKS ON CANADA. Text in English, French. a. free. **Document type:** *Catalog.* **Description:** For academics and institutions interested in Canada and Canadian studies.
Related titles: Online - full text ed.
Published by: Association for the Export of Canadian Books, 504 1 Nicholas St, Ottawa, ON K1N 7B7, Canada. TEL 613-562-2324, FAX 613-562-2329. Ed. Catherine Montgomery. Circ: 11,000.

381.45002 GBR ISSN 0006-7539
Z2005
THE BOOKSELLER. Text in English. 1858. w. GBP 186 combined subscription domestic (print & online eds.); GBP 192 combined subscription in Europe (print & online eds.); GBP 264 combined subscription elsewhere (print & online eds.) (effective 2009). adv. bibl.; illus. back issues avail.; reprints avail. **Document type:** *Magazine, Trade.* **Description:** Covers all apects of the book trade industry.
Former titles (until 1933): The Publisher and Bookseller; (until 1928): The Bookseller; (until 1927): The Bookseller and the Stationery Trades' Journal; Which incorporated (in 1921): The Bookseller; Which was formerly: Bent's Literary Advertiser; Stationery Trades' Journal
Related titles: Online - full text ed.: GBP 186 (effective 2009).
Indexed: A09, A10, A22, A26, AmHI, B01, B06, B07, B09, BrHumI, ChLitAb, E08, G06, G07, G08, H07, I05, I06, I07, IBR, IBZ, ILD, L04, L05, L06, L09, LISTA, P06, P34, RefZh, S09, S23, SCOPUS, T02, U01, V03, V04.
—BLDSC (2250.220000), IE, Infotrieve, Ingenta. **CCC.**
Published by: Nielsen Entertainment Media UK Ltd, Endeavour House, 189 Shaftesbury Ave, London, WC2H 8TJ, United Kingdom. TEL 44-20-74206006, FAX 44-20-74206103. Ed. Neill Denny TEL 44-20-74206006 ext 6109. Adv. contact Nicola Chin TEL 44-20-74206006 ext 6124.

381.45002 USA
BOOKSELLER. Text in English. 1972. s-m. USD 36; USD 85 foreign (effective 1999). adv. bk.rev. tr.lit. **Document type:** *Newsletter, Trade.* **Description:** Trade paper for out-of-print bookdealers.
Indexed: ChLitAb.
Address: 14026 N. Ridgelawn Rd., Martinsuille, IL 62442. TEL 217-382-4502, FAX 217-382-4502. Ed., Pub., R&P Dwight Connelly. Adv. contact Carolyn Connelly. Circ: 1,000.

381.45002 PAK ISSN 0006-7547
BOOKSELLER. Text in English. 1968. m. PKR 90 domestic; USD 30 foreign. adv. bk.rev. **Document type:** *Newsletter, Trade.* **Description:** Covers book trade publishers.
Indexed: RASB.
Published by: Bookseller (International), P O Box 2387, Lahore, 54000, Pakistan. TEL 92-42-7232415, FAX 92-42-6360955. Ed., R&P Muhammad Saeed Shaikh. Adv. contact Muhammad Hamid Saeed. Circ: 24,000.

002.074 AUS ISSN 1833-5403
BOOKSELLER + PUBLISHER. Text in English. 1921. 9/yr. AUD 130 domestic; AUD 195 US, Canada & Europe; AUD 175 in Asia (effective 2010); Including B & P Book Buyer's Guide. adv. bk.rev. bibl.
Document type: *Magazine, Trade.* **Description:** Provides the most comprehensive and practical insights into the business of books.
Former titles (until 2006): Australian Bookseller and Publisher (0004-8763); Ideas
Related titles: Online - full text ed.; ◆ Supplement(s): Junior Bookseller + Publisher. ISSN 1833-5799; Innovation and Technology.
Indexed: AEI, ChLitAb, RASB.
—Ingenta. **CCC.**
Published by: Thorpe-Bowker (Subsidiary of: R.R. Bowker LLC), St Kilda Rd, PO Box 6509, Melbourne, VIC 8008, Australia. yoursay@thorpe.com.au. Ed. Matthia Dempsey TEL 61-3-85178351. Pub. Tim Coronel TEL 61-3-85178343. Adv. contact Xeverie Swee TEL 61-3-86450308. page AUD 2,825; bleed 220 x 307. Circ: 5,500 (paid).

381.45002 GBR ISSN 0952-1666
BOOKSELLERS ASSOCIATION. DIRECTORY OF MEMBERS (YEAR). Text in English. 19??. a. GBP 37 per issue domestic to non-members; GBP 42 per issue foreign to non-members; free to members (effective 2009). index. **Document type:** *Directory.* **Description:** Features details about members, including name contacts for each shop with details of subject specialization and special services offered.
Formerly (until 1986): Booksellers Association of Great Britain and Ireland. List of Members (0068-0249)
Related titles: Online - full text ed.
Published by: Booksellers Association of the United Kingdom & Ireland Ltd., 272 Vauhall Bridge Rd, London, SW1V 1BA, United Kingdom. TEL 44-20-78020802, FAX 44-20-78020803, mail@booksellers.org.uk.

381.45002 GBR ISSN 1745-3798
BOOKSELLING ESSENTIALS; essential for the business of bookselling. Text in English. 19??. q. free to members (effective 2009). back issues avail. **Document type:** *Newsletter, Trade.* **Description:** Covers areas of particular interest to booksellers and news on services to members.
Former titles (until 2003): Bookselling (0969-4862); (until 1993): Bookselling News (0268-246X)
Related titles: Online - full text ed.
Indexed: RASB.
—BLDSC (2250.242970).
Published by: Booksellers Association of the United Kingdom & Ireland Ltd., 272 Vauhall Bridge Rd, London, SW1V 1BA, United Kingdom. TEL 44-20-78020802, FAX 44-20-78020803, mail@booksellers.org.uk. Ed. Meryl Halls. Circ: 3,600.

381.45002 USA
BOOKSELLING THIS WEEK. Text in English. 1916. w. free (effective 2004). **Document type:** *Newsletter, Trade.*
Supersedes (in Apr. 1994): A B A Newswire; (in Feb. 1973): A B A Bulletin
Media: Online - full content.
Published by: American Booksellers Association, Inc., 828 S Broadway, Tarrytown, NY 10591. TEL 914-591-2665, 800-637-0037, FAX 914-591-2720. Ed. Rosemary Hawkins. Circ: 10,000 (free).

070.5 ITA ISSN 1972-8565
BOOKSHOP. Text in Italian. 2001. m. (10/yr.). EUR 15 (effective 2009).
Document type: *Magazine, Consumer.*
Published by: Editoriale Duesse SpA, Via Donatello 5b, Milan, 20131, Italy. TEL 39-02-277961, FAX 39-02-27796300, e-duesse@e-duesse.it, http://www.e-duesse.it.

028.1 GBR
BOOKSONLINE. Text in English. 1996 (Aug.). w. **Document type:** *Journal, Consumer.* **Description:** Reviews notable fiction and nonfiction books.
Media: Online - full text.
Published by: Telegraph Group Ltd, 3rd-4th Fl, Victory House, Meeting House Ln, Chatham, Kent, ME4 4TT, United Kingdom. TEL 44-1622-335030, 800-316-6977, customerservice@telegraph.co.uk.

070.5 USA ISSN 0000-1759
BOOKWIRE; the book industry resource. Text in English. 1999. irreg. (approx. m.). free (effective 2010). adv. charts; stat. **Document type:** *Journal, Trade.* **Description:** Offers coverage of all aspects of the book business for readers, writers, researchers, librarians, and publishers. Includes announcements of noteworthy events and features and lists from Publishers Weekly, Library Journal, and School Library Journal.
Media: Online - full text.
Published by: R.R. Bowker LLC (Subsidiary of: ProQuest), 630 Central Ave, New Providence, NJ 07974. TEL 908-286-1090, 800-526-9537, FAX 908-219-0098, info@bowker.com, http://www.bowker.com. Adv. contact Charlie Friscia.

070.48347 USA ISSN 0163-1128
Z477
BOOKWOMAN. Text in English. 1936. 3/yr. free to members. bk.rev.
Published by: Women's National Book Association, c/o Susannah Greenberg Public Relations, 2166 Broadway, #9-E, New York, NY 10024. TEL 212 208-4629, FAX 212 208-4629. Ed. Ellen Myrick. Circ: 1,200.

028.1 USA ISSN 1072-8317
THE BOSTON BOOK REVIEW. Text in English. 1993. 10/yr. USD 24; USD 3.25 newsstand/cover; USD 50 foreign (effective 1999). adv. bk.rev. illus. back issues avail.; reprints avail. **Document type:** *Journal, Consumer.* **Description:** Features poetry, fiction, interviews, art, and essays.
Related titles: Online - full text ed.
Indexed: BRI, CBRI.
Published by: Boston Book Review, 331 Harvard St., Ste 17, Cambridge, MA 02138. TEL 617-497-0344. Ed. Theoharis C Theoharis. Pub. Gregory Carr. R&P Kiril Alexandrov. Adv. contact Kiril Stefan Alexandrov. Circ: 10,000 (paid).

BRAILLE BOOK REVIEW. *see* HANDICAPPED—Visually Impaired

BRANDYWINE DOCUMENTS ON THE HISTORY OF BOOKS & PRINTING. *see* PRINTING

BRANDYWINE KEEPSAKE. *see* PRINTING

070.5 BEL
BREPOLS PUBLISHERS NEWSLETTER. Text in English, French. irreg., latest vol.33, 1997. free. **Document type:** *Newsletter.* **Description:** Provides news of recent and forthcoming scholarly publications from Brepols, including medieval studies, the arts, Latin literature, and religion.
Published by: Brepols Publishers, Begijnhof 67, Turnhout, 2300, Belgium. TEL 32-14-448020, FAX 32-14-428919, periodicals@brepols.net, http://www.brepols.net.

028.1 USA ISSN 1522-4511
BRIGHTLEAF; a Southern review of books. Text in English. 1997. q. USD 25 (effective 1999). adv. bk.rev. back issues avail. **Document type:** *Magazine, Consumer.* **Description:** Presents the best new writing from and about the literary South, including book reviews, features on Southern culture and Southern cities, and news of writers and theSouthern bookselling and publishing trades.
Indexed: AmHI.
Address: PO Box 11485, Raleigh, NC 27604. TEL 919-664-8650, FAX 919-664-8570. Ed., R&P David S Perkins. Adv. contact Debra Decamilis. Circ: 5,000.

700.942393 GBR ISSN 1750-3698
BRISTOL REVIEW OF BOOKS. Text in English. 2006. q. GBP 15 (effective 2009); free local bookshops, libraries and arts venues. back issues avail. **Document type:** *Magazine, Consumer.* **Description:** Covers local publishing. Includes reviews, comments, interviews, new poetry and fiction.
Published by: Bristol Books & Publishers, 84 Whiteladies Rd, Bristol, BS8 2QP, United Kingdom. maurice@bristolbooksandpublishers.co.uk, http://www.bristolbooksandpublishers.co.uk/.

070.5 GBR
THE BRITISH LIBRARY STUDIES IN THE HISTORY OF THE BOOK. Text in English. 1995. irreg., latest 2007. price varies. back issues avail. **Document type:** *Monographic series, Trade.* **Description:** Provides information about literary cultures.
Published by: British Library, St Pancras, 96 Euston Rd, London, NW1 2DB, United Kingdom. TEL 44-870-4441500, FAX 44-1937-546860, Customer-Services@bl.uk, http://www.bl.uk.

028.1 CHE
DAS BUCH - BUECHERPICK. Text in German. 1982. q. CHF 30 (effective 2004). adv. bk.rev. **Document type:** *Magazine, Trade.*
Formerly: Buecherpick (1016-9431)
Published by: Buecherpick Verlag AG, Gaemsenstr 2, Zurich, 8006, Switzerland. TEL 41-1-3669912, FAX 41-1-3669949, http://www.buecherpick.ch. Adv. contact Rene Frey TEL 41-1-3669947. Circ: 350,000.

070.5 DEU ISSN 1562-9279
BUCHFORSCHUNG; Beitraege zum Buchwesen. Text in German. 2000. irreg., latest vol.5, 2009. price varies. **Document type:** *Monographic series, Academic/Scholarly.*
Published by: Harrassowitz Verlag, Kreuzberger Ring 7b-d, Wiesbaden, 65205, Germany. TEL 49-611-5300, FAX 49-611-530560, verlag@harrassowitz.de, http://www.harrassowitz.de.

070.5 DEU ISSN 0524-8426
BUCHMARKT; das Ideenmagazin fuer den Fachhandel. Text in German. 1966. m. EUR 244; EUR 89 to students (effective 2009). adv.
Document type: *Magazine, Trade.*
Indexed: RASB.
Published by: BuchMarkt Verlag K. Werner GmbH, Sperberweg 4a, Meerbusch, 40668, Germany. TEL 49-2150-91910, FAX 49-2150-919191. Ed., Pub. Christian von Zittwitz. Adv. contact Kirsten Peters. B&W page EUR 1,115, color page EUR 1,529; trim 216 x 303. Circ: 4,700 (paid and controlled).

070.5 DEU
BUCHPROFILE; Medienempfehlungen fuer die Buechereiarbeit. Text in German. 1925. q. EUR 32 (effective 2009). bk.rev. cum.index.
Document type: *Bibliography.*
Formerly: Neue Buch (0028-3118)
Published by: Borromaeusverein e.V., Wittelsbacherring 7-9, Bonn, 53115, Germany. TEL 49-228-72580, FAX 49-228-7258189, info@borro.de, http://www.borro.de. Eds. Bettina Kraemer, Thomas Steinherr. Circ: 10,000.

070.5 800 DEU ISSN 1615-0732
BUCHREPORT EXPRESS. Text in German. 1970. w. EUR 420; EUR 8 newsstand/cover (effective 2007); subscr. includes 12 issues of Buchreport Magazin. adv. bk.rev. back issues avail. **Document type:** *Bulletin, Consumer.*
Supersedes in part (1970-1999): Buchreport (0176-8220)
Indexed: IBR, IBZ, RASB.
Published by: Harenberg Kommunikation Verlags und Medien GmbH & Co. KG, Koenigswall 21, Dortmund, 44137, Germany. TEL 49-231-90560, FAX 49-231-9056110, post@harenberg.de, http://www.harenberg.de. Ed. Thomas Wilking. Pub. Bodo Harenberg. Adv. contact Michael Janscheidt TEL 49-231-9056206. B&W page EUR 620, color page EUR 1,000. Circ: 4,500 (paid and controlled).

686.22 DEU ISSN 0724-7001
BUCHWISSENSCHAFTLICHE BEITRAEGE AUS DEM DEUTSCHEN BUCHARCHIV MUENCHEN. Text in German. 1950. irreg., latest vol.80, 2010. price varies. **Document type:** *Monographic series, Academic/Scholarly.*
Formerly: Buchwissenschaftliche Beitraege (0407-5439)
Published by: Harrassowitz Verlag, Kreuzberger Ring 7b-d, Wiesbaden, 65205, Germany. TEL 49-611-5300, FAX 49-611-530560, verlag@harrassowitz.de, http://www.harrassowitz.de.

070.5 DEU ISSN 1616-3613
BUCHWISSENSCHAFTLICHE FORSCHUNGEN. Text in German. 2000. irreg., latest vol.9, 2010. price varies. **Document type:** *Monographic series, Academic/Scholarly.*
Published by: Harrassowitz Verlag, Kreuzberger Ring 7b-d, Wiesbaden, 65205, Germany. TEL 49-611-5300, FAX 49-611-530560, verlag@harrassowitz.de, http://www.harrassowitz.de.

070.5 AUT
BUECHER AUS OESTERREICH. Text in German. 1947. 2/yr. adv. **Document type:** *Magazine, Trade.*
Formerly (until 1993): Oesterreichische Buch (0078-3455)
Published by: Hauptverband des Oesterreichischen Buchhandels, Gruenangergasse 4, Vienna, W 1010, Austria. hvb@buecher.at, http://www.buecher.at. R&P Inge Kralupper. Adv. contact Erna Laudenbach.

070.5 DEU
BUECHERGILDE-MAGAZIN. Text in German. 1924. q. free (effective 2009). bk.rev. illus. **Document type:** *Magazine, Trade.*
Formerly (until 1997): Buechergilde (0007-3032)
Published by: Buechergilde Gutenberg Verlagsgesellschaft mbH, Stuttgarter Str 25-29, Frankfurt am Main, 60329, Germany. TEL 49-69-2739080, FAX 49-69-27390826, service@buechergilde.de. Ed. Juergen Sander.

028 DEU
BUECHERMENSCHEN; das Hugendubel-Magazin fuer Leser. Text in German. 2002. 5/yr. free newsstand/cover (effective 2009). adv. **Document type:** *Magazine, Consumer.*
Published by: In Medias Res Marktkommunikation GmbH, Koenigstr 70, Nuerenberg, 90402, Germany. TEL 49-911-430530, FAX 49-911-4305344, info@imr.de, http://www.imr.de. Ed. Elisabeth Zeitler-Boos. Adv. contact Susanne Halfmann.

BUECHERSCHAU; Zeitschrift fuer Betriebs- und Gewerkschaftsbibliotheken. *see* LIBRARY AND INFORMATION SCIENCES

BULLDOG REPORTER'S BOOK MARKETING AND PUBLICITY; what's new and what's working to increase book sales. *see* ADVERTISING AND PUBLIC RELATIONS

BULLETIN CRITIQUE DU LIVRE EN FRANCAIS. *see* PUBLISHING AND BOOK TRADE—Abstracting, Bibliographies, Statistics

002.075 FRA ISSN 0399-9742
BULLETIN DU BIBLIOPHILE. Text in English, French, German. 1834. s-a. EUR 61 (effective 2009). adv. bk.rev. **Document type:** *Journal, Trade.*
Formed by the 1969 merger of: Bulletin du Bibliophile et du Bibliothecaire (0152-0571); Bibliophilie (0006-1603); Formerly: Librairie Ancienne et Moderne. Bulletin (0024-2128)
Related titles: ◆ Supplement(s): Association Internationale de Bibliophilie. Nouvelles. ISSN 0220-388X.
Indexed: B24, FR, MLA-IB, RASB.
—INIST. **CCC.**
Published by: (Association Internationale de Bibliophilie), Electre - Editions du Cercle de la Librairie, 35 rue Gregoire de Tours, Paris, 75006, France. TEL 33-1-44412805, FAX 33-1-44412819, http://www.editionsducercledelalibrairie.com. R&P, Adv. contact Martine Barruet.

BULLETIN JUGEND UND LITERATUR. *see* LIBRARY AND INFORMATION SCIENCES

BUREAU INTERNATIONAL DES SOCIETES GERANT LES DROITS D'ENREGISTREMENT ET DE REPRODUCTION MECANIQUE. BULLETIN. *see* PRINTING

BUSINESS BOOK REVIEW. *see* BUSINESS AND ECONOMICS

070.5 USA
BUSINESS OF CONSUMER BOOK PUBLISHING (YEAR). Text in English. irreg. USD 2,995 per issue; USD 2,795; USD 3,395 combined subscription (print & online eds.) (effective 2008). **Document type:** *Directory, Trade.* **Description:** Designed to be a market intelligence report for the U.S. trade book publishing industry.
Related titles: Online - full text ed.: USD 2,295 (effective 2005).
Published by: SIMBA Information (Subsidiary of: Market Research.Com), 11200 Rockville Pike, Ste 504, Rockville, MD 20852. TEL 240-747-3096, 888-297-4622, FAX 240-747-3004, customerservice@simbainformation.com. Pub. Linda Kopp.

070.5 USA ISSN 1555-6069
THE BUSINESS PUBLISHER. Text in English. 22/yr. USD 425 (effective 2009). **Document type:** *Newsletter, Trade.*
Related titles: Online - full text ed.: ISSN 1559-8209. 2006.
Indexed: B02, B15, B17, B18, G04, G06, G07, G08, I05.
Published by: J K Publishing, PO Box 71020, Milwaukee, WI 53211. TEL 414-332-1625, 414-803-3472, jkpubl@mac.com. Ed., Pub. Jack Kenney.

070.5 GBR ISSN 1473-740X
BUSINESS RATIO REPORT. BOOK PUBLISHERS. Text in English. 19??. a., latest no.31, 2008, Apr. GBP 365 per issue (effective 2010). charts; stat. **Document type:** *Report, Trade.* **Description:** Covers companies active as book publishers.
Former titles (until 2001): Business Ratio. Book Publishers (1470-689X); (until 2000): Business Ratio Plus: Book Publishers (1356-000X); (until 1994): Business Ratio Report: Book Publishers (0261-7463); Which superseded in part (in 1978): Business Ratio Report: Book and Periodical Publishers
Published by: Key Note Ltd. (Subsidiary of: Bonnier Business Information), Harlequin House, 5th Fl, 7 High St, Teddington, Richmond upon Thames, TW11 8EE, United Kingdom. TEL 44-845-5040452, FAX 44-845-5040453, sales@keynote.co.uk.

070.5 GBR ISSN 1474-9939
BUSINESS RATIO REPORT. PERIODICAL PUBLISHERS. Text in English. 19??. a. GBP 365 per issue (effective 2010). charts; stat. back issues avail. **Document type:** *Report, Trade.* **Description:** Covers companies active as periodical publishers.
Former titles (until 2001): Business Ratio. Periodical Publishers (1467-8918); (until 1999): Business Ratio Plus: Periodical Publishers (1356-0174); (until 1994): Business Ratio Report. Periodical Publishers (0261-9342); Which superseded in part (in 1978): Business Ratio Report: Book and Periodical Publishers
Published by: Key Note Ltd. (Subsidiary of: Bonnier Business Information), Harlequin House, 5th Fl, 7 High St, Teddington, Richmond upon Thames, TW11 8EE, United Kingdom. TEL 44-845-5040452, FAX 44-845-5040453, sales@keynote.co.uk.

381.45002 USA ISSN 0732-6599
Z475
BUY BOOKS WHERE, SELL BOOKS WHERE; a directory of out of print booksellers and collectors and their author and subject specialties. Text in English. 1978. irreg. (9th ed. 1994). USD 34.95 domestic; USD 31.45 domestic to libraries. adv. **Document type:** *Directory.* **Description:** Lists more than 2000 active dealers and collectors in the out of print book field in the U.S. and Canada, with names, addresses and pertinent information concerning the books they buy and/or sell.
Published by: Ruth E. Robinson Books, Rt 7, Box 162A, Morgantown, WV 26505. TEL 304-594-3140. Ed. Ruth E Robinson. Circ: 3,000.

381.45002 AUS
C B A A NEWS. Text in English. 1982. m. membership. adv. bk.rev. illus.; tr.lit. back issues avail. **Document type:** *Newsletter, Trade.*
Former titles (until 2008): Handbook & Newsletter; (until Jul.2007): C B A A News
Published by: Christian Bookselling Association of Australia Inc., PO Box 85, Bargo, NSW 2574, Australia. TEL 61-2-46841030, FAX 61-2-46843532, info@cbaa.com.au, http://www.cbaa.com.au. Circ: 350.

070.50688 USA ISSN 1941-9600
Z479
C B A RETAILERS + RESOURCES. (Christian Booksellers Association) Text in English. 1968. m. USD 49.95 to members; USD 59.95 to non-members (effective 2008). adv. bk.rev. illus. reprints avail. **Document type:** *Magazine, Trade.* **Description:** Trade magazine for the Christian retail industry. Provides articles on retail management, industry news, and product information.
Former titles (until 2007): Aspiring Retail (1934-4740); (until 2005): C B A Marketplace (1092-7239); (until 1997): Bookstore Journal (0006-7563)
Published by: (Christian Booksellers Association), C B A Service Corporation, PO Box 62000, Colorado Springs, CO 80962. TEL 719-265-9895, FAX 719-272-3510. Pub. Dorothy Gore. Circ: 6,500 (paid).

070.5 AUS
C B C A NEWS. (Children's Book Council of Australia) Text in English. 1984. 5/yr. **Document type:** *Newsletter, Academic/Scholarly.*
Former titles (until 2001): C B C News; (until 1989): Children's Book Council of Australia. Victorian Branch. Newsletter; Children's Book Council of Australia. Victorian Branch. Presidents Newsletter
Published by: The Children's Book Council of Australia, Victorian Branch, PO Box 81, Kew East, VIC 3102, Australia. TEL 300-360-436, office@cbc.org.au, http://www.cbc.org.au/.

028.5 USA
C B C FEATURES. (Children's Book Council) Text in English. 1945. s-a. free to members (effective 2011). bibl. index (July 1980-Feb. 1981) (Jan.-Aug. 1987) (Winter 1993-Fall 1997). **Document type:** *Newsletter, Trade.* **Description:** Lists of titles and materials, profiles of authors and publications, and feature articles pertaining to children's literature.
Formerly: Calendar (0008-0721)
Indexed: ChLitAb.
Published by: Children's Book Council, Inc., 54 W 39th St, 14 Fl, New York, NY 10018. cbc.info@cbcbooks.org, http://www.cbcbooks.org.

028.5 GBR
C B H S NEWSLETTER. Text in English. s-a. **Description:** Promotes an appreciation of children's books, and the study of their history, bibliography and literary content.
Indexed: ChLitAb.
Published by: Children's Books History Society, Carshalton Beeches, 2 Courtney Crescent, Carshalton, Surrey SM5 4LZ, United Kingdom.

028.5 CAN ISSN 0319-0080
PN1009.A1
➤ **C C L/LITTERATURE CANADIENNE POUR LA JEUNESSE.** (Canadian Children's Literature) Text in English, French. 1975. q. USD 29 in Canada to individuals; USD 39 in United States to individuals; USD 45 elsewhere to individuals; USD 36 in Canada to institutions; USD 46 in United States to institutions; USD 52 elsewhere to institutions (effective 2005). adv. bk.rev. bibl. back issues avail. **Document type:** *Journal, Academic/Scholarly.* **Description:** Presents reviews and criticism of Canadian books and other media for children and young adults. Examines the history of Canadian children's literature and contains in-depth reviews of recently published Canadian books and plays for young readers and ongoing interviews with writers and illustrators.
Indexed: A26, B14, C03, CA, CBCARef, CBPI, CBRI, CLitI, CPerl, ChLitAb, E08, G08, L05, L06, MLA-IB, P48, PQC, S09, T02.
—BLDSC (3019.405000), IE, Ingenta. **CCC.**
Published by: Canadian Children's Press, 4th Fl, MacKinnon Bldg, University of Guelph, Guelph, ON N1G 2W1, Canada. ccl@uoguelph.ca, http://www.uoguelph.ca/ccl/press. R&P, Adv. contact Gay Christofides TEL 519-824-4120 ext 3189. B&W page CAD 250. Circ: 900 (paid).

002 346.0482 CUB ISSN 1607-6087
C E N D A. Text in Spanish. 1999. s-a.
Media: Online - full text.
Published by: Centro Nacional de Derecho de Autor, Calle 15 No. 604 esq. B y C, Vedado, Havana, 10400, Cuba. TEL 53-78-323571, FAX 53-78-662030, cenda@cubarte.cult.cu, http://www.cenda.cult.cu/.

070.5 USA
C H L ANNUAL EQUIPMENT GUIDE AND C H L MONTHLY EQUIPMENT GUIDE. (Contractors Hot Line) Text in English. 1975. a. (plus m. updates). USD 175; USD 230 in Canada (effective 2000). adv. illus. **Document type:** *Guide, Trade.* **Description:** Buy-sell-trade publication for heavy construction.
Former titles: Contractors Hot Line Equipment Guide Annual and Monthly Updates; Hot Line Construction Equipment Monthly Update (1047-4382); Construction Equipment Guide (Fort Dodge); Supersedes: Equipment Estimator; (in 1980): American Contractor; Contractors Hot Line Quarterly
Published by: Heartland Construction Group, Inc., 1003 Central Ave, Fort Dodge, IA 50501. TEL 515-955-1600, 800-247-2000, FAX 515-574-2280, ceg@contractorshotline.com. Pub. Pamela Utley. Circ: 10,000.

028.5 ESP ISSN 0214-4123
C L I J. (Cuadernos de Literatura Infantil y Juvenil) Text in Spanish. 1988. 11/yr. EUR 70 (effective 2009). 86 p./no.; back issues avail. **Document type:** *Magazine, Consumer.* **Description:** Presents reviews of new children's books, news and events in the field, and research works on history, genres, authors and trends.
Related titles: Online - full text ed.
Indexed: BibInd, MLA-IB.
—**CCC.**
Published by: Torre de Papel S.L., Amigo 38, Barcelona, 08021, Spain. TEL 34-93-4141166, FAX 34-93-4144665. **Dist. by:** Asociacion de Revistas Culturales de Espana, C Covarruvias 9 2o. Derecha, Madrid 28010, Spain. TEL 34-91-3086066, FAX 34-91-3199267, info@arce.es, http://www.arce.es/.

028.1 CAN ISSN 1201-9364
C M MAGAZINE; Canadian review of materials . Text in English. 1971. w. free (effective 2010). bk.rev.; film rev. bibl.; illus. index. back issues avail.; reprints avail. **Document type:** *Magazine, Trade.* **Description:** Contains book reviews, media reviews, news, and author profiles of interest to teachers, librarians, parents and kids.
Former titles (until 1995): C M: Canadian Materials for Schools and Libraries (0821-1450); (until 1980): Canadian Materials (0317-4654)
Media: Online - full text.
Indexed: B05, BRI, C03, C05, CA, CBCARef, CBPI, CBRI, CPerl, G08, L04, LISTA, MRD, P48, PQC, T02.
—**CCC.**
Published by: Manitoba Library Association, 167 Houde Dr, Winnipeg, MB R3V 1C6, Canada. http://mla.mb.ca. Ed. Dave Jenkinson TEL 204-269-8840.

070.5 CAN
C M P A MEMBER NEWS. Text in English. 1981 (no.63). m. free membership (effective 2003). adv. **Document type:** *Newsletter.*
Media: Online - full content.
Published by: Canadian Magazine Publishers Association, 425 Adelaide St W, Ste 700, Toronto, ON M5V 3C1, Canada. ggarland@magazinescanada.com, http://www.cmpa.ca. Circ: 600.

017.8 MEX ISSN 0185-2493
KGF1572
C N I D A INFORMA; boletin bimestral de informacion autoral. (Centro Nacional de Informacion - Direccion General del Derecho de Autor) Text in Spanish. 1982. q. free. bk.rev.
Published by: Secretaria de Educacion Publica, Centro Nacional de Informacion - Direccion General del Derecho de Autor, Agencia Nacional ISBN, Mexico, MARIANO ESCOBEDO 438 Piso 3, Nueva Anzures, Mexico City, DF 11590, Mexico. TEL 203-16-38. Circ: 500.

800 TTO ISSN 1811-4873
Z1501
C R B. THE CARIBBEAN REVIEW OF BOOKS. Text in English. 1991-1994; resumed 2006. q. USD 40 in the Caribbean; USD 50 elsewhere (effective 2006);). adv. bk.rev. illus. back issues avail. **Document type:** *Journal, Academic/Scholarly.* **Description:** Presents the latest information on books published in, about or relevant to the Caribbean; includes information on authors, publishers and the book trade.
Formerly (until 1994): Caribbean Review of Books (1018-2926); Supersedes (in 1991): U W I P A Newsletter
Indexed: C32, L05, L06.
Published by: Media & Editorial Projects Ltd. (M E P), 6 Prospect Ave, Maraval, Port of Spain, Trinidad & Tobago. TEL 868-622-3821, FAX 868-628-0639, mep@wow.net, http://www.meppublishers.com. Ed. Nicholas Laughlin.

CABIRION: GAY BOOKS BULLETIN. *see* HOMOSEXUALITY

381.45002 FRA ISSN 1956-9327
LES CAHIERS DE LA LIBRAIRIE. Text in French. 1995. s-a.
Former titles (until 2006): Les Cahiers du S L F (1771-351X); (until 2004): La Voix des Libraires (1276-0471)
Related titles: Online - full text ed.: free.
Published by: Syndicat de la Librairie Francaise, Hotel de Massa, 38, rue du Faubourg Saint-Jacques, Paris, 75014, France. TEL 33-1-53622310, FAX 33-1-53621045, contact@syndicat-librairie.fr, http://www.syndicat-librairie.fr.

070.5 FRA ISSN 1951-3488
LES CAHIERS DU LIVRE. Text in French. 2006. irreg., latest 2008, November. EUR 20 per issue (effective 2009). **Document type:** *Monographic series, Academic/Scholarly.*
Published by: Presses Universitaires de Bordeaux, 3 Place de la Victoire, Bordeaux, 33000, France. TEL 33-5-54313314, FAX 33-5-56314694, http://pub.u-bordeaux3.fr.

CANADA. STATISTICS CANADA. PRINTING, PUBLISHING AND ALLIED INDUSTRIES/CANADA. STATISTIQUE CANADA. IMPRIMERIE, EDITION ET INDUSTRIES CONNEXES. *see* PUBLISHING AND BOOK TRADE—Abstracting, Bibliographies, Statistics

CANADIAN AUTHORS ASSOCIATION NATIONAL NEWSLINE. *see* LITERATURE

028.1 CAN ISSN 0383-770X
F1001
CANADIAN BOOK REVIEW ANNUAL. Text in English. 1975. a., latest vol.26. CAD 129.45 (effective 2001). bk.rev. **Description:** Original reviews of Canadian trade, scholarly, and reference titles published each year; full bibliographic information; comprehensive subject, author, title index; publishers directory.
Indexed: A26, B14, CBRI, CPerl, E08, G08, I05, S09.

P

Address: 44 Charles St W, Ste 3205, Toronto, ON M4Y 1R8, Canada. TEL 416-961-8537, FAX 416-961-1855, cbra@interlog.com, http://www.interlog.com/~cbra. Ed., Pub. Joyce M Wilson.

381.45002 CAN ISSN 0225-2392
CANADIAN BOOKSELLER; the magazine of book retailing. Text in English. 1978. 9/yr. CAD 22 domestic to non-members; USD 80 in United States to non-members; CAD 100 elsewhere to non-members; CAD 12 domestic to members; USD 45 in United States to members; CAD 65 elsewhere to members. adv. bk.rev. **Document type:** *Magazine, Trade.* **Description:** For owners, managers and staff of trade, college and independent bookstores.
Formerly: Net 30 (0225-6622)
Indexed: C03, CBCABus, CBPI, P48, PQC.
—**CCC.**
Published by: Canadian Booksellers Association, 789 Don Mills Rd, Ste 700, Toronto, ON H3C 1T5, Canada. TEL 416-467-7883, FAX 416-467-7886, editor@cbabook.org. Ed. Emily Sinkins. Adv. contact Rema Tatangelo. B&W page CAD 995, color page CAD 1,800; trim 10.75 x 8.13. Circ: 2,000 (paid).

028.5 CAN ISSN 1705-7809
CANADIAN CHILDREN'S BOOK NEWS. Text in English. 1979. 3/yr. CAD 19.50 (effective 2007). adv. bk.rev. illus. **Document type:** *Newsletter, Academic/Scholarly.*
Former titles (until 2002): Children's Book News (0705-0038); (until 1983): Book News Times; Book Times (0706-1064)
Indexed: B04, BRD, BRI, CBRI, I05, I07, L04, L07, L08, LISTA, LibLit, RGAb, W03, W05.
Published by: Canadian Children's Book Centre, 40 Orchard View Blvd, Ste 101, Toronto, ON M4R 1B9, Canada. TEL 416-975-0010, FAX 416-975-8970, info@bookcentre.ca. Ed., R&P Gillian O'Reilly. Adv. contact Hadley Dyer. Circ: 35,000.

CANADIAN HERITAGE. PUBLICATIONS ASSISTANCE PROGRAM. ACTIVITY REPORT. *see* PUBLIC ADMINISTRATION

070.5092 CAN ISSN 0008-4859
Z485
CANADIAN PUBLISHERS DIRECTORY. Text in English. 1935. 2/yr. Included with subscr. to Quill and Quire. adv. **Document type:** *Directory.*
Related titles: ◆ Supplement to: Quill and Quire. ISSN 0033-6491.
Published by: Key Publishers Co. Ltd., 70 The Esplanade, 4th Fl, Toronto, ON M5E 1R2, Canada. TEL 416-360-0044, FAX 416-955-0794. Ed. Scott Anderson. Pub., R&P Sharon McAuley. Adv. contact Alison Jones. Circ: 6,244.

070.5 ITA ISSN 1973-8323
IL CANTIERE BIBLIOTECA. Text in Italian. 1996. irreg. **Document type:** *Monographic series, Academic/Scholarly.*
Published by: Editrice Bibliografica SpA, Via Bergonzoli 1-5, Milan, MI 20127, Italy. TEL 39-02-28315996, FAX 39-02-28315906, bibliografica@bibliografica.it, http://www.bibliografica.it.

070.5 USA ISSN 0736-9077
CODEN: CCIREV
CAPELL'S CIRCULATION REPORT, INC.; the newsletter of magazine circulation. Text in English. 1982. 20/yr. USD 395 domestic; USD 445 foreign (effective 2007). adv. bk.rev. stat. 16 p./no.; back issues avail.; reprints avail. **Document type:** *Newsletter, Trade.* **Description:** Provides current information on what is happening in circulation trends, strategies, tactics and analyses.
Published by: Daniel Capell, Ed. & Pub., 2038 18th St, N W, Ste 403, Washington, DC 20009. TEL 202-332-6272, FAX 202-332-7428. Ed. E Daniel Capell. Adv. contact Kathy Capell TEL 800-567-7706. page USD 995. Circ: 500 (paid).

002.075 GBR ISSN 0142-1980
Y CASGLWR. Text in Welsh. 1923. 3/yr. free to members (effective 2009). **Document type:** *Bibliography.* **Description:** Covers all aspects of book collecting and bibliography.
Published by: Cymdeithdas Bob Owen, c/o Richard H. Lewis, 40 Maesceiro, Bow Street, Dyfed SY24 5BG, United Kingdom. Circ: 1,300.

CATALOGO COLECTIVO DE PUBLICACIONES PERIODICAS EXISTENTES EN BIBLIOTECAS CIENTIFICAS Y TECNICAS ARGENTINA. *see* PUBLISHING AND BOOK TRADE—Abstracting, Bibliographies, Statistics

017.8 ITA
CATALOGO DEGLI EDITORI ITALIANI. Text in Italian. a. price varies. **Document type:** *Directory, Trade.* **Description:** Lists Italian book publishers and distributors.
Published by: Editrice Bibliografica SpA, Via Bergonzoli 1-5, Milan, MI 20127, Italy. TEL 39-02-28315996, FAX 39-02-28315906, bibliografica@bibliografica.it, http://www.bibliografica.it. Circ: 2,000.

THE CATHOLIC. *see* RELIGIONS AND THEOLOGY—Roman Catholic

070.50282 USA ISSN 1077-6656
Z475
CATHOLIC BOOK PUBLISHERS ASSOCIATION DIRECTORY. Text in English. 1990. a. USD 35 (effective 2000). **Document type:** *Directory.* **Description:** Provides information about each publisher member of the Association for bookstore owners and managers.
Published by: Catholic Book Publishers Association, 8404 Jamesport Dr, Rockford, IL 61108. TEL 815-332-3245, FAX 815-332-3476, cpba3@aol.com. Ed., Adv. contact Terry A Wessel. Circ: 2,200 (controlled).

CENTER FOR CHILDREN'S BOOKS. BULLETIN. *see* CHILDREN AND YOUTH—About

015 FRA ISSN 1561-2082
CENTRE INTERNATIONAL DE RENCONTRES MATHEMATIQUES. PUBLICATIONS. Text in French. irreg.
—INIST.
Published by: Centre International de Rencontres Mathematiques, 163 Av de Luminy Case 916, Marseille, F-13288, France. TEL 33-4-9183-3000, FAX 33-4-9183-3005, http://www.cirm.univ-mrs.fr.

002 NLD ISSN 0069-1984
CENTRE NATIONAL D'ARCHEOLOGIE ET D'HISTOIRE DU LIVRE. PUBLICATIONS. Text in Dutch. 1965. irreg. price varies. **Document type:** *Monographic series, Bibliography.*
Published by: (Centre National d'Archeologie et d'Histoire du Livre BEL), Hes & De Graaf Publishers BV, Postbus 540, Houten, 3990 GH, Netherlands. TEL 31-30-6380071, FAX 31-30-6380099, info@hesdegraaf.com, http://www.hesdegraaf.com.

015 ITA ISSN 1972-005X
CENTRO PIO RAJNA. PUBBLICAZIONI. PERIODICI. Text in Italian. 1991. irreg. price varies. **Document type:** *Catalog, Bibliography.*
Published by: (Centro Pio Rajna), Salerno Editrice, Via Valadier 52, Rome, 00193, Italy. TEL 39-06-3608201, FAX 39-06-3223132, info@salernoeditrice.it, http://www.salernoeditrice.it.

015 ITA ISSN 1972-0041
CENTRO PIO RAJNA. PUBBLICAZIONI. SEZ.1. DOCUMENTI. Text in Italian. 1998. irreg. price varies. **Document type:** *Catalog, Bibliography.*
Published by: (Centro Pio Rajna), Salerno Editrice, Via Valadier 52, Rome, 00193, Italy. TEL 39-06-3608201, FAX 39-06-3223132, info@salernoeditrice.it, http://www.salernoeditrice.it.

015 ITA ISSN 1972-0033
CENTRO PIO RAJNA. PUBBLICAZIONI. SEZ.1. STUDI E SAGGI. Text in Italian. 1990. irreg. price varies. **Document type:** *Catalog, Bibliography.*
Published by: (Centro Pio Rajna), Salerno Editrice, Via Valadier 52, Rome, 00193, Italy. TEL 39-06-3608201, FAX 39-06-3223132, info@salernoeditrice.it, http://www.salernoeditrice.it.

015 USA ISSN 0361-7920
A CHECKLIST OF AMERICAN IMPRINTS. Text in English. 1830. irreg., latest 2001. price varies. back issues avail. **Document type:** *Monographic series, Trade.*
Published by: Scarecrow Press, Inc. (Subsidiary of: Rowman & Littlefield Publishers, Inc.), 4501 Forbes Blvd, Ste 200, Lanham, MD 20706. TEL 301-459-3366, 800-462-6420, FAX 301-429-5748, 800-338-4550, custserv@rowman.com, http://www.scarecrowpress.com. Ed., Pub. Mr. Edward Kurdyla TEL 301-459-3366 ext 5604. R&P Clare Cox TEL 212-529-3888 ext 308.

028.1 USA ISSN 1087-4925
CHICAGO BOOKS IN REVIEW. Text in English. 1996. q. USD 16; USD 25 foreign; free (effective 1998). adv. bk.rev. **Document type:** *Newspaper, Consumer.* **Description:** Promotes and chronicles books and equivalent media that are written by Chicagoans, about Chicago, or published in Chicago including Illinois.
Published by: Chicago Books in Review, Inc., 5840 N Kenmore Ave, Chicago, IL 60660-3721. TEL 773-561-6280, FAX 773-561-6280. Ed., Pub. Robert Remer. Circ: 55,000.

070.5 USA
➤ **CHICAGO GUIDES TO WRITING, EDITING, AND PUBLISHING.** Text in English. 1971. irreg., latest 1997. price varies. **Document type:** *Monographic series, Academic/Scholarly.*
Published by: University of Chicago, 5801 S Ellis Ave, Chicago, IL 60637. TEL 773-702-7899. Ed. Penelope Kaiserlian. R&P Perry Cartwright TEL 773-702-6096.

070.5083 USA ISSN 1525-4208
PN1009.A1
CHILDREN'S BOOK AND PLAY REVIEW. Text in English. 1980. bi-m. USD 15 domestic; USD 22 in Canada; USD 30 elsewhere; USD 3.50 newsstand/cover. play rev. index. **Document type:** *Journal, Consumer.* **Description:** Reviews fiction, non-fiction and plays written for young people. Includes 50-60 book reviews, 10-15 play reviews, and feature articles on children's literature and picture book illustrators.
Formerly (until 1995): Children's Book Review (0890-5746)
Related titles: ◆ Online - full content ed.: Children's Book and Play Review Online. ISSN 1525-4216.
Indexed: BRI, CBRI.
Address: c/o Marsha D Broadway, Harold B Lee Library, Brigham Young University, Provo, UT 84602-6887. TEL 801-378-6685, FAX 801-378-6708. R&P Marsha D Broadway.

070.5083 USA ISSN 1525-4216
CHILDREN'S BOOK AND PLAY REVIEW ONLINE. Text in English. bi-m. USD 5 (effective 2000). **Document type:** *Journal, Consumer.*
Media: Online - full content. **Related titles:** ◆ Print ed.: Children's Book and Play Review. ISSN 1525-4208.
Published by: Children's Book and Play Review, c/o Marsha D Broadway, Harold B Lee Library, Brigham Young University, Provo, UT 84602-6887. TEL 801-378-6685, FAX 801-378-6708, marsh_broadway@byu.edu.

028.5 USA ISSN 1073-7596
CHILDREN'S BOOK INSIDER; your monthly guide to children's writing success. Text in English. 1990. m. USD 29.95 domestic; USD 34.95 in Canada; USD 42.95 elsewhere (effective 2006). index. back issues avail. **Document type:** *Newsletter, Consumer.* **Description:** Provides market news, writing tips, articles on submission procedures and working with publishers, interviews with top authors, illustrators and editors in the children's book field.
Related titles: Online - full text ed.: USD 26.95 (effective 2006).
Address: 901 Columbia Rd., Ft. Collins, CO 80525. TEL 970-495-0056, FAX 800-807-1916. Ed. Jon Bard. Pub., R&P Laura Backes. Circ: 3,000 (paid).

028.5 GBR
CHILDREN'S BOOK NEWS MAGAZINE; for all those interested in children and what they read. Text in English. 1987. 3/yr. GBP 12 in United Kingdom; GBP 15 in Europe; GBP 18 elsewhere (effective 2001). **Document type:** *Newsletter.* **Description:** Presents information, reviews, and opinions on all matters concerning children and what they read.
Former titles (until 1999): Young Book Trust Newsletter; C B F News; C C B News (0266-4216)
Published by: Young Book Trust, Book House, 45 East Hill, London, SW18 2QZ, United Kingdom. TEL 44-20-8516-2977, FAX 44-20-8516-2978, booktrust@dial.pipex.com, http://www.booktrust.org.uk. Ed. Marsha Cawthorne.

028.5 USA ISSN 0897-9790
PN147.5
CHILDREN'S WRITER'S AND ILLUSTRATOR'S MARKET; where & how to sell your children's stories & illustrations. Text in English. 1995. a. USD 27.99 (effective 2009). illus. 448 p./no.; **Document type:** *Directory, Trade.* **Description:** Provides information on book publishing and magazine markets for both writers and illustrators of children's publishing. Contains advice to help market one's work.
Supersedes in part (in 1994): Guide to Literary Agents & Art/Photo Reps (1055-6087)
Published by: F + W Media Inc., 4700 E Galbraith Rd, Cincinnati, OH 45236. TEL 513-531-2690, 800-283-0963, FAX 513-531-0798, wds@fwpubs.com, http://www.fwpublications.com. Ed. Alice Pope.

CHILDREN'S WRITING UPDATE. *see* LITERATURE

CHINA MEDIA NEWSLETTER. *see* COMMUNICATIONS

070.5 CHN
CHINA PUBLISHING. Text in English. 2002. m. CNY 712 domestic; USD 88 foreign (effective 2008). adv. **Document type:** *Journal, Trade.*
Media: Online - full content.
Published by: C N P I E C Information Technology Co. Ltd., 16 Gongti East Rd, Beijing, China. TEL 86-10-65082324, FAX 86-10-65867006, e-journal@cnpeak.com. Ed., Pub. Wen Xiaofan. Adv. contact Zhao Chen.

028.1 USA ISSN 0009-4978
Z1035 CODEN: CHOIEZ
➤ **CHOICE**; current reviews for academic libraries. Text in English. 1963. m. USD 355 domestic; USD 475 in Canada & Mexico; USD 575 elsewhere (effective 2011). adv. bk.rev.; software rev. bibl.; illus. index. 200 p./no.; back issues avail.; reprints avail. **Document type:** *Journal, Academic/Scholarly.* **Description:** Each issue contains one or more bibliographic essays on selected topics, one or more feature pieces, and 600 reviews of new academic titles.
Related titles: CD-ROM ed.; Microfilm ed.: (from PQC); Online - full text ed.: ISSN 1943-5975.
Indexed: A25, A26, B04, B05, B14, BAS, BRI, CA, CBRI, ChPerl, Chicano, DIP, E02, E03, E07, E08, ERI, EdA, EdI, G08, G09, G10, I05, IBR, IBZ, L04, L07, L08, L09, LIMI, LISTA, LibLit, M06, MLA-IB, MRD, P02, P10, P13, P30, P34, P48, P53, P54, PQC, RASB, S02, S03, S08, S09, S23, T02, W03.
—BLDSC (3181.535000), Ingenta. **CCC.**
Published by: Association of College and Research Libraries (Subsidiary of: American Library Association), 50 E Huron St, Chicago, IL 60611 . TEL 312-280-2523, FAX 312-280-2520, acrl@ala.org. Ed., Pub. Irving E Rockwood TEL 860-347-6933. adv.: color page USD 3,585, B&W page USD 2,410; trim 7.25 x 9.25. Circ: 3,500 (paid).

028.1 USA
CHOICE REVIEWS ON CARDS. Text in English. m. USD 395 domestic; USD 445 in Canada & Mexico; USD 525 elsewhere; USD 40 per issue (effective 2009); Available subscribers of Choice or Choice Reviews Online. **Document type:** *Journal, Academic/Scholarly.* **Description:** Contains the complete set of reviews, and nothing but the reviews, from the corresponding issue of Choice magazine.
Related titles: ◆ Online - full content ed.: ChoiceReviews Online. ISSN 1523-8253.
Published by: Association of College and Research Libraries (Subsidiary of: American Library Association), 50 E Huron St, Chicago, IL 60611 . TEL 312-280-2523, 800-545-2433, FAX 312-280-2520, acrl@ala.org, http://www.ala.org/ala/mgrps/divs/acrl/index.cfm. Eds. Irving E Rockwood TEL 860-347-6933, Francine Graf. Pub. Irving E Rockwood TEL 860-347-6933. **Subscr. to:** PO Box 141, Annapolis Junction, MD 20701. TEL 240-646-7027, FAX 301-206-9789, subscriptions@ala-choice.org, choicesubscriptions@pmds.com.

028.1 USA ISSN 1523-8253
CHOICEREVIEWS ONLINE. Text in English. 1988. m. USD 425 (effective 2010). adv. back issues avail. **Document type:** *Journal, Academic/Scholarly.* **Description:** Provides access to the entire database of Choice (Middletown) reviews since Sep 1988.
Media: Online - full content. **Related titles:** ◆ Print ed.: Choice Reviews on Cards.
Published by: (Association of College and Research Libraries), American Library Association, 50 E Huron, Chicago, IL 60611. TEL 800-545-2433, FAX 312-440-9374, customerservice@ala.org, http://www.ala.org. Ed., Pub. Irvind E Rockwood. Adv. contact Pamela Marino. **Subscr. to:** PO Box 141, Annapolis Junction, MD 20701. TEL 40-646-7027, FAX 301-206-9789, choicesubscriptions@brightkey.net.

070.5 200 GBR ISSN 2045-6123
▼ **THE CHRISTIAN MARKETPLACE AT YOUR FINGERTIPS.** Text in English. 2010. bi-m. free to qualified personnel (effective 2010). adv. **Document type:** *Magazine, Consumer.* **Description:** The latest Christian book titles and resources available on the market.
Related titles: Online - full text ed.: free (effective 2010).
Published by: C C P Ltd, Broadway House, The Broadway, Crowborough, W Sussex TN6 1HQ, United Kingdom. TEL 44-1892-652472, subscriptions@premier.org.uk, http://www.ccpmagazines.co.uk. Ed. Clem Jackson.

070.50688 USA ISSN 0892-0281
CHRISTIAN RETAILING; the trade magazine of religious retailing. Text in English. 1955. 20/yr. USD 75 domestic; USD 97 in Canada; USD 110 elsewhere; free in US & Canada to qualified personnel (effective 2008). adv. bk.rev. back issues avail.; reprints avail. **Document type:** *Magazine, Trade.*
Former titles (until 198?): Christian Bookseller (0749-2510); (until 1983): Christian Bookseller & Librarian (0736-0649); (until 1982): Christian Bookseller (0009-5273)
Related titles: Online - full text ed.: USD 25 (effective 2008); Supplement(s); The Church Bookstore; Inspirational Gift Trends.
Published by: Strang Communications Co., 600 Rinehart Rd, Lake Mary, FL 32746. TEL 407-333-0600, FAX 407-333-7100, custsvc@strang.com, http://www.strang.com. Ed. Andy Butcher TEL 407-333-0600 ext 2680. Pub. David Condiff TEL 407-333-7110. Circ: 12,170.

CHRONICLE (RADFORD); S F, fantasy & horror's monthly trade journal. *see* LITERATURE—Science Fiction, Fantasy, Horror

070.5 CHN ISSN 1006-5784
CHUBAN CANKAO/PUBLISHING REFERENCE: NEW READINGS. Text in Chinese. 1988. m. USD 79.20 (effective 2009). **Document type:** *Journal, Academic/Scholarly.*
Related titles: Online - full text ed.
—East View.
Published by: Zhongguo Chuban Xiehui, Fengtai-qu, 97, Sanluju Lu, Beijing, 100073, China. TEL 86-10-51259172, FAX 86-10-51259162. **Dist. by:** China International Book Trading Corp, 35 Chegongzhuang Xilu, Haidian District, PO Box 399, Beijing 100044, China. TEL 86-10-68412045, FAX 86-10-68412023, cibtc@mail.cibtc.com.cn, http://www.cibtc.com.cn.

070.5 CHN ISSN 1001-9316
➤ **CHUBAN FAXING YANJIU/PUBLISHING RESEARCH.** Text in Chinese. 1985. bi-m. USD 62.40 (effective 2009). adv. **Document type:** *Academic/Scholarly.*
Related titles: Online - full text ed.
—East View.

Published by: (Zhongguo Chuban Kexue Yanjiusuo/Chinese Institute of Publishing Science), China Book Publishing House, No A-7 Xirongxian Hutong, Xicheng-qu, Beijing, 100031, China. TEL 86-10-6605-9539. Ed. Keming Wu. Adv. contact Zhang Li. Circ: 100,000 (paid).

070.5 CHN ISSN 1006-7000
CHUBAN GUANGJIAO/VAST VIEW ON PUBLISHING. Text in Chinese. 1995. m. **Document type:** *Magazine, Trade.*
Published by: Guangxi Chuban Zazhishe, 13, Wangyuan Lu, Nanning, 530022, China. TEL 86-771-5708350, FAX 86-771-5703775.
Co-sponsor: Guangxi Xinwen Chubanju.

070.509 CHN
CHUBAN SHILIAO/HISTORICAL MATERIAL ON PUBLISHING. Text in Chinese. 1982. q. USD 10. bk.rev.
Published by: Shanghai Chuban Gongzuozhe Xiehui/Shanghai Publishers Association, 5 Shaoxing Rd, Shanghai, 200020, China. TEL 4370176, FAX 86-21-433245. Eds. Song Yuanfang, Zhao Jiabi. Circ: 2,500.

▼ **CHUBAN YINGXIAO/MARKETING IN PUBLISHING.** *see* BUSINESS AND ECONOMICS—Marketing And Purchasing

070.5 658 TWN ISSN 1814-8859
CHUBAN YU GUANLI YANJIU/JOURNAL OF PUBLISHING AND MANAGEMENT. (vol.1 had 4 issues, vol.2 had 7 issues.) Text in Chinese. 2005. irreg. (5-7 issues/yr.). **Document type:** *Journal, Academic/Scholarly.*
Related titles: Online - full text ed.
Published by: Nanhua Daxue, Chuban Shiye Guanli Yanjiusuo/Nanhua University, Department of Publishing Organization Management, 32, Chung Keng Li, Dalin, Chiayi 62248, Taiwan. TEL 886-5-2721001 ext 2521, FAX 886-5-2427139, sally@mail.nhu.edu.tw, http://www.nhu.edu.tw/~publish/.

070.5 686.2 CHN ISSN 1007-1938
CHUBAN YU YINSHUA/PUBLISHING & PRINTING. Text in Chinese. 1990. q. CNY 5 newsstand/cover (effective 2006). **Document type:** *Journal, Academic/Scholarly.*
Related titles: Online - full text ed.
Published by: Shanghai Chuban Yinshua Gaodeng Zhuanke Xuexiao, 100, Shuifeng Lu, Shanghai, 200093, China. TEL 86-21-65671635, FAX 86-21-65674432.

070.5 CHN ISSN 1673-0119
CHUBANREN/CHINA PUBLISHERS. Text in Chinese. 2004. s-m. CNY 120 (effective 2009). **Document type:** *Magazine, Trade.*
Published by: Hunan Jiaoyu Chubanshe, Shaoshan Bei Lu, Changsha, 410007, China. TEL 86-731-85486727, 228411705@qq.com, http://www.shoulai.cn/09_index.aspx.

070.5 CHN ISSN 1674-4209
CHUBANYE/PUBLISHING INDUSTRY. Text in Chinese. 1978. m. CNY 108; CNY 9 per issue (effective 2011). bk.rev. **Document type:** *Journal, Academic/Scholarly.* **Description:** Reprints of articles on Chinese publishing industry, including policies and regulations.
Former titles (until 2009): Chuban Gongzuo/Publishing Work (1009-1645); (until 2000): Chuban Gongzuo, Tushu Pingjie (1001-2680)
Indexed: RASB.
Published by: Zhongguo Renmin Daxue Shubao Ziliao Zhongxin/Renmin University of China, Information Center for Social Sciences, 59, Zhongguancun Dajie, Haidian-qu, Beijing, 100872, China. TEL 86-10-64039458, FAX 86-10-64015080, center@zlzx.org. **Dist. in US by:** China Publications Service, PO Box 49614, Chicago, IL 60649. TEL 312-371-1761, FAX 312-288-8570.

070.5 KOR ISSN 1227-1985
Z464.K67
CH'ULPAN MOONWHA/KOREAN PUBLISHING JOURNAL. Text in Korean. 1948. m. adv. bk.rev. bibl. **Document type:** *Magazine, Trade.*
Published by: Korean Publishers Association/Daehan Chulpan Munhwa Hyeobhoe, 105-2, Sagan-dong, Jongno-gu, Seoul, 110-190, Korea, S. TEL 82-2-7352701, FAX 82-2-7385414, webmaster@kpa21.or.kr, http://www.kpa21.or.kr/main/index.htm. Circ: 2,000.

CLOVER INFORMATION INDEX. *see* PUBLISHING AND BOOK TRADE—Abstracting, Bibliographies, Statistics

090 ITA ISSN 1970-3937
CODICES MIRABILES. Text in Italian. 1985. irreg. **Document type:** *Monographic series, Academic/Scholarly.*
Published by: Salerno Editrice, Via Valadier 52, Rome, 00193, Italy. TEL 39-06-3608201, FAX 39-06-3223132, info@salernoeditrice.it, http://www.salernoeditrice.it.

COLE PAPERS; technology, journalism, publishing. *see* TECHNOLOGY: COMPREHENSIVE WORKS

COLLEGE PUBLISHING MARKET FORECAST (YEAR). *see* BUSINESS AND ECONOMICS—Economic Situation And Conditions

017.8 USA
COLORADO BOOK GUIDE; a directory of the Colorado book community. Text in English. 1991. biennial. USD 10.95 (effective 2000). adv. **Document type:** *Directory.* **Description:** Lists Colorado libraries, bookstores, publishers, literary agents, book manufacturers, writing and book organizations, and literacy programs.
Published by: Owaissa Communications Company, Inc., PO Box 8928, Denver, CO 80201. TEL 303-455-3123, FAX 303-455-2039. Pub. Tom Auer.

070.5 USA
COMPARABILITY UPDATE. Text in English. bi-m.
Published by: B P A International, 2 Corporate Dr., Ste 900, Shelton, CT 06484-6259. TEL 212-779-3200, FAX 212-752-1721.

COMPUTERITER; microcomputer news and views for the writer-editor. *see* COMPUTERS—Personal Computers

CONCATENATION. *see* LITERATURE—Science Fiction, Fantasy, Horror

CONTEMPORARY CANADIAN AUTHORS. *see* LITERATURE

CONTEMPORARY IMPRESSIONS. *see* ART

CONTENT PROVIDER MEDIA NEWSLETTER. *see* EDUCATION

070.5 USA
CONTENTWISE. Text in English. 1999. m. free to qualified personnel; USD 79 combined subscription (print & online eds.) (effective 2009). **Document type:** *Newsletter, Trade.* **Description:** Contains information for managers and marketers pursuing proven successful strategies for corporate and custom publishing.
Formerly (until 2008): Publications Management (1525-7444)
Related titles: Online - full text ed.
Indexed: A10, S22, V03.
Published by: McMurry, Inc., 1010 E Missouri Ave, Phoenix, AZ 85014. TEL 888 303-2373, FAX 602 427-0374, info@mcmurry.com, http://www.mcmurry.com. Ed. Wendalyn Nicholas.

070.5 GBR
CONTINUUM AND THE PUBLISHERS ASSOCIATION DIRECTORY OF PUBLISHING IN THE UNITED KINGDOM AND THE REPUBLIC OF IRELAND. Text in English. 1960. a. GBP 100 per issue (effective 2010). index. **Document type:** *Directory, Corporate.* **Description:** Contains contact details including addresses and websites- details of distribution and sales and marketing agents- key personnel- listing of main fields of activity- information on annual turnover, numbers of new titles and numbers of employees.
Former titles (until 2003): Continuum and the Publishers Association Directory of Publishing in the United Kingdom, Commonwealth and Overseas; (until 2000): Cassell and the Publishers Association Directory of Publishing (0268-0394); (until 1984): Cassell and Publishers Association Directory of Publishing in Great Britain, the Commonwealth, Ireland, South Africa and Pakistan (0143-2583); (until 1979): Cassell's Directory of Publishing in Great Britain, the Commonwealth, Ireland, South Africa and Pakistan (0308-7018); (until 1973): Cassell's Directory of Publishing in Great Britain, The Commonwealth, Ireland and South Africa (0069-097X); (until 1963): Cassell's Directory of Publishing in Great Britain, The Commonwealth and Ireland
—BLDSC (3062.800000).
Published by: Continuum International Publishing Group, The Tower Bldg, 11 York Rd, London, SE1 7NX, United Kingdom. TEL 44-20-79220880, FAX 44-20-79287894, info@continuumbooks.com.

CONTRAPUNCT. *see* JOURNALISM

COPYEDITING; because language matter. *see* JOURNALISM

070.50715 USA ISSN 0000-1821
CORPORATE TRAINING & DEVELOPMENT ADVISOR; news & analysis for professionals in the corporate training industry. Text in English. 1996. m. USD 625 (print or online ed.) (effective 2008). back issues avail.; reprints avail. **Document type:** *Newsletter, Trade.* **Description:** Delivers news and analysis on all aspects of the adult-education publishing industry.
Formerly (until May 2005): Lifelong Learning Market Report (1088-7512)
Related titles: Online - full text ed.: ISSN 0000-183X.
Indexed: A01, A02, A03, A08, A26, B01, B02, B06, B07, B09, B15, B17, B18, E03, E07, ERI, G04, G08, I05, T02.
Published by: SIMBA Information (Subsidiary of: Market Research.Com), 60 Long Ridge Rd., Ste 300, Stamford, CT 06902. TEL 203-325-8193, 800-307-2529, FAX 203-325-8915, info@simbanet.com. Eds. Sean Kilkelly, Stephanie Fagnani. Pub. Linda Kopp.

070.5 CRI
COSTA RICA Y LOS LIBROS. Text in Spanish. 199?. q. bibl.
Published by: Camara Costarricense del Libro, Apartado Postal 1571, San Jose, 1002, Costa Rica. TEL 34-9020, FAX 506-24-3607.

070.5 USA
CREATIVITY CONNECTION; a newsletter for writers. Text in English. 1990. q. USD 18 (effective 2000). bk.rev. tr.lit. back issues avail. **Document type:** *Newsletter.* **Description:** Contains how-to articles, personal profiles, publishing information, and listings of adult-education opportunities of interest to freelance writers and small press publishers.
Published by: University of Wisconsin at Madison, 500 Langdon St, Madison, WI 53706. http://www.wisc.edu. Ed., Pub. Marshall J Cook. Circ: 750.

CRITICAL REVIEW (PHILADELPHIA); a journal of politics and society. *see* LITERARY AND POLITICAL REVIEWS

028.1 FRA ISSN 0011-1600
Z1007
CRITIQUE; revue generale des publications francaises et etrangeres. Text in French. 1946. m. adv. bk.rev.; play rev. charts; illus. index. reprints avail. **Document type:** *Academic/Scholarly.*
Indexed: A20, A22, AmHI, ArtHuCI, B24, CA, CurCont, DIP, FR, H07, IBR, IBRH, IBSS, IBZ, IPB, MLA, MLA-IB, P42, PCI, PerIslam, RASB, RILM, S02, S03, SCOPUS, SOPODA, SociolAb, T02, W07.
—BLDSC (3487.490000), IE, Ingenta, INIST. **CCC.**
Address: 7 rue Bernard Palissy, Paris, 75006, France. TEL 33-1-45442316, FAX 33-1-45448236. Ed. Philippe Roger. Pub. Isabelle Chave.

017.8 CAN ISSN 0316-9448
Z1369
CURRENT CANADIAN BOOKS/LIVRES CANADIENS COURANTS. Text in English. 1971. m. CAD 48 (effective 1999). **Document type:** *Bibliography.* **Description:** Presents topical listings of bibliographic citations which represent new Canadian books, books published abroad which have association value, and books which must be ordered direct.
Formerly: Current Canadian Imprints Catalogued
Published by: John Coutts Library Services Ltd., 6900 Kinsmen, P O Box 1000, Niagara Falls, ON L2E 7E7, Canada. TEL 905-356-6382, FAX 905-356-5064. Ed. John R Grantier. Circ: 100 (controlled).

CURRENT JAPANESE PERIODICALS FOR (YEAR). *see* PUBLISHING AND BOOK TRADE—Abstracting, Bibliographies, Statistics

CUSTOMER MAGAZINES & CONTRACT PUBLISHING. *see* BUSINESS AND ECONOMICS—Production Of Goods And Services

D K NEWSLETTER; a journal of news and reviews of Indian publications in English. *see* BIBLIOGRAPHIES

070.50688 DEU ISSN 0343-5598
D N V. (Der Neue Vertrieb) Text in German. 1949. fortn. EUR 178 (effective 2007). adv. bk.rev. illus.; mkt.; tr.lit. **Document type:** *Magazine, Trade.* **Description:** Trade publication for paperback book, magazine, and newspaper businesses, featuring news, reports of events, and market information.
Formerly (until 1973): Der Neue Vertrieb (0170-0472)
Published by: Presse Fachverlag GmbH & Co. KG, Nebendahlstr 16, Hamburg, 22041, Germany. TEL 49-40-6090090, FAX 49-40-60900915, info@presse-fachverlag.de, http://www.presse-fachverlag.de. Ed. Ralf Deppe. Adv. contact Lars Luecke. B&W page EUR 2,095, color page EUR 2,950; trim 175 x 262. Circ: 1,789 (paid).

D P A MEMBERSHIP BOOK. *see* BUSINESS AND ECONOMICS—Trade And Industrial Directories

002 ITA ISSN 1828-9533
DA LIBRO A LIBRO; le biblioteche degli scrittori. Text in Italian. 1993. irreg. price varies. **Document type:** *Monographic series, Academic/Scholarly.*
Published by: De Luca Editori d'Arte, Via Ennio Quirino Visconti 11, Rome, 00193, Italy. TEL 39-06-32650712, FAX 39-06-32650715, libreria@delucaeditori.com, http://www.delucaeditori.com.

070.5 CHN ISSN 1006-7361
DAXUE CHUBAN/UNIVERSITY PUBLISHING. Text in Chinese. 1994. q. **Document type:** *Magazine, Trade.*
Related titles: Online - full text ed.
Published by: Zhongguo Daxue Chubaoshe Xiehui/China University Presses Association, Beijing Normal University Publishing Group, 19, Xinjie Kouwai Dajie, Beijing, 100875, China. TEL 86-10-58808284, FAX 86-10-58806196.

002 ESP ISSN 0214-2694
Z2685
DELIBROS; revista professional del libro. Text in Spanish. 1988. m. (11/yr.). EUR 150 domestic; EUR 170 foreign (effective 2009). adv. bk.rev. bibl.; illus. 64 p./no.; Supplement avail.; back issues avail. **Document type:** *Magazine, Consumer.* **Description:** Offers information and analysis on the world of books; reflects trends, includes articles of opinion, and contemplates national and international culture.
Related titles: Online - full text ed.
Indexed: IBR, IBZ.
Published by: Delibros S.A., C Eloy Gonzalo 27, 3o, Madrid, 28010, Spain. TEL 34-91-5914257, FAX 34-91-5943053. Ed. Jaime Brull. Adv. contact Eva Perez Nanclares. B&W page EUR 1,170, color page EUR 1,730; 270 x 265. Circ: 7,000. **Dist. by:** Asociacion de Revistas Culturales de Espana, C Covarruvias 9 2o. Derecha, Madrid 28010, Spain. TEL 34-91-3086066, FAX 34-91-3199267, info@arce.es, http://www.arce.es/.

070.5 DEU ISSN 0344-7278
KK7013
DEUTSCHER PRESSERAT. JAHRBUCH. Text in German. 1956. a. EUR 29 (effective 2011). adv. **Document type:** *Journal, Trade.*
Incorporates (2004-2004): Bericht zum Redaktionsdatenschutz (1612-8842); Formerly (until 1978): Deutscher Presserat. Taetigkeitsbericht (0418-9523)
Indexed: IBR, IBZ.
Published by: (Deutscher Presserat, Traegerverein), U V K Verlagsgesellschaft mbH, Schuetzenstr 24, Konstanz, 78462, Germany. TEL 49-7531-90530, FAX 49-7531-905398, nadine.ley@uvk.de. Circ: 4,000 (paid).

P

070.5 USA ISSN 2150-2196
Z286.E43
▼ **DIGITAL MAGAZINES.** Text in English. 2009. irreg. **Document type:** *Magazine, Trade.* **Description:** Offers publishers the unique opportunity to optimize their publications with video, audio and hyperlinks while saving the money traditionally spent on printing.
Published by: Nxtbook Media, 480 New Holland Ave, Ste 9000, Lancaster, PA 17602. TEL 717-735-9740.

002.075 USA ISSN 0012-2874
PS374.D5
DIME NOVEL ROUND-UP; a magazine devoted to the collecting, preservation and study of old-time dime and nickel novels, popular story papers, series books, and pulp magazines. Text in English. 1931 (Jan.). bi-m. USD 20; USD 4 per issue (effective 2005). adv. bk.rev. cum.index every 5 yrs. 36 p./no. 1 cols./p.; back issues avail. **Document type:** *Magazine, Consumer.*
Former titles (until Nov. 1953): Reckless Ralph's Dime Novel Round-Up; (until May 1931): Dime Novel Round-Up
Indexed: BibInd, MLA, MLA-IB.
Published by: J. Randolph Cox, Ed. & Pub., PO Box 226, Dundas, MN 55019-0226. TEL 507-645-5711. Ed., Pub., R&P J Randolph Cox. adv.: B&W page USD 25; trim 4 x 6. Circ: 200 (paid).

050 658.8 GBR
DIRECT DISTRIBUTION. Text in English. 2002. bi-m. adv. **Document type:** *Newsletter, Trade.* **Description:** Covers domestic and international distribution of magazines.
Published by: Complete Circulation and Marketing Ltd., Unit 8, Netherhall Yard, Mill Ln, Newick, E Sussex BN8 4JL, United Kingdom. TEL 44-1825-724623, FAX 44-1825-724623, http://www.completecircmktg.co.uk. Pub., Adv. contact Colin C Dann. color page GBP 483; trim 210 x 297. Circ: 2,000.

070.52 CAN ISSN 1702-3114
DIRECTORY OF EDITORS. Short title: E A C Directory of Editors. Text in English, French. 1980. a. adv. bk.rev. **Document type:** *Directory.*
Former titles (until 2002): E A C Membership List (1493-3683); (until 1999): Editors' Association of Canada. Directory of Editors (1196-8362); Freelance Editors' Association of Canada. Directory of Members (0226-9031)
Published by: Editors' Association of Canada/Association Canadienne des Redacteurs - Reviseurs, 502-27 Carlton St, Toronto, ON M5B 1L2, Canada. active_voice@editors.ca. Ed. Franklin Carter. Circ: 3,000.

070.5 JPN
DIRECTORY OF JAPANESE PUBLISHING INDUSTRY. Text in English. 1970. biennial. free. **Document type:** *Directory, Trade.*
Formerly: Guide to Publishers and Related Industries in Japan
Indexed: RASB.
Published by: Publishers' Association for Cultural Exchange Japan, 1-2-1 Sarugaku-cho, Chiyoda-ku, Tokyo, 101-0064, Japan. TEL 81-3-3291-5685, FAX 81-3-3233-3645, office@pace.or.jp, http://www.pace.or.jp. Ed. Hiroyasu Ochiai.

381.45002 USA
DIRECTORY OF MARKET COMPARABILITY PROGRAMS & MEMBERSHIP. Text in English. a. **Document type:** *Directory.* **Description:** Serves as a guide to BPA's Market Comparability Programs and Market Classifications.
Published by: B P A International, 2 Corporate Dr., Ste 900, Shelton, CT 06484-6259. TEL 212-779-3200, FAX 212-725-1721.

THE DIRECTORY OF POETRY PUBLISHERS. *see* LITERATURE—Poetry

050 USA ISSN 0277-1519
PN4820
DIRECTORY OF SMALL PRESS & MAGAZINE EDITORS & PUBLISHERS. Text in English. 1970. a. USD 25.95 per issue (effective 2011). **Document type:** *Directory, Trade.* **Description:** Lists editors and publishers of small presses and magazines with addresses and phone numbers.
Former titles (until 1981): Directory of Small Magazine - Press Editors and Publishers (0095-6414); (until 1971): Directory of Small Press / Mag Editors and Publishers
Related titles: CD-ROM ed.: USD 21 per issue (effective 2011).
Published by: Dustbooks, PO Box 100, Paradise, CA 95967. TEL 530-877-6110, 800-477-6110, FAX 530-877-0222, publisher@dustbooks.com. Ed. Len Fulton.

015.68 ZAF ISSN 1018-7626
Z674
DIRECTORY OF SOUTH AFRICAN PUBLISHERS; with addresses, ISBN identifiers, and other contact information. Text in Afrikaans, English. 1991. a. ZAR 96 (effective 1999). **Document type:** *Directory.*
Published by: National Library of South Africa, PO Box 496, Cape Town, 8000, South Africa. TEL 27-21-4246320, FAX 27-21-4233359, http://www.nlsa.ac.za.

070.5025 USA
DIRECTORY PUBLISHING: A PRACTICAL GUIDE. Text in English. irreg. USD 49.95 (effective 2000). **Document type:** *Directory.* **Description:** Covers nature and function of directories, editorial techniques, circulation marketing and production for directory publishers.
Published by: SIMBA Information (Subsidiary of: Market Research.Com), 11200 Rockville Pike, Ste 504, Rockville, MD 20852. TEL 240-747-3096, 888-297-4622, FAX 240-747-3004, info@simbanet.com, customerservice@simbainformation.com.

070.50688 DEU
DISTRIPRESS GAZETTE. Text in German. 3/yr. adv. **Document type:** *Magazine, Trade.* **Description:** Contains information for members of the Distripress organization of publishers and distributors.
Published by: (Distripress CHE), Presse Fachverlag GmbH & Co. KG, Nebendahlstr 16, Hamburg, 22041, Germany. TEL 49-40-57009-0, FAX 49-40-57009300, info@presse-fachverlag.de, http://www.presse-fachverlag.de. adv.: B&W page CHF 1,980, color page CHF 2,460; trim 237 x 330. Circ: 2,200 (controlled).

DONNEES STATISTIQUES SUR LE LIVRE BELGE DE LANGUE FRANCAISE. *see* PUBLISHING AND BOOK TRADE—Abstracting, Bibliographies, Statistics

070.5 USA
DOODY'S ELECTRONIC JOURNAL. Text in English. w. USD 395 (effective 2003). **Description:** Features 70,000 in print book and software titles including Doody's Reviews on 20,000 titles.
Media: Online - full text.
Published by: Doody Enterprises, Inc., 500 N. Michigan Ave., Ste. 1410, Chicago, IL 60611-3705. dan@doody.com.

DRAGON'S BREATH. *see* LITERARY AND POLITICAL REVIEWS

DRUK BELARUSI. *see* PUBLISHING AND BOOK TRADE—Abstracting, Bibliographies, Statistics

070.5 UKR
DRUKARSTVO; nauchno-prakticheskii zhurnal dlya spetsialistov isdatel'skogo dela, poligrafii i knigorasprostraneniya. Text in Ukrainian. 1994. bi-m. USD 95 in the Americas (effective 2000).
Published by: Blits Inform, Ul Kioto 25, Kiev, Ukraine. TEL 380-44-518-7551.

070.5 USA ISSN 1042-3737
CODEN: EPNWEE
E P S I G NEWS. Text in English. 1986. 4/yr. USD 50 or membership fee. bk.rev. **Document type:** *Newsletter.* **Description:** Covers new product announcements, user information, meeting announcements, and case studies from organizations and individuals using the Electronic Manuscript Standard for a variety of publishing ventures.
—CASDDS.
Published by: Electronic Publishing Special Interest Group, c/o GCARI, 100 Daingerfield Rd, Alexandria, VA 22314. TEL 703-519-8184, FAX 703-548-2867. Ed. Christopher Ziener. Circ: 300.

E S B NOTIZIE. (E.S.Burioni Ricerche Bibliografiche) *see* LIBRARY AND INFORMATION SCIENCES

002 USA ISSN 1525-6790
Z4
➤ **EARLY BOOK SOCIETY. JOURNAL**; for the study of manuscripts and printing history. Abbreviated title: J E B S. Text in English. 1997. a. USD 40 per issue (effective 2010). bk.rev. bibl.; illus. back issues avail. **Document type:** *Journal, Academic/Scholarly.* **Description:** Focuses on English and Continental works produced from 1350 to 1550 and also contains notes on manuscripts and early printed books, descriptive reviews of recent works in the field, and notes on libraries and collections.
Indexed: L04, L06, LISTA, MLA-IB, SCOPUS, T02.
Published by: (Early Book Society), Pace University Press, 41 Park Row, Rm 1510, New York, NY 10038. TEL 212-346-1405, FAX 212-346-1754, PaceUP@Pace.Edu. Ed. Martha W Driver.

028.1 AUT ISSN 1817-2709
EBENSOLCH; Rez-E-zine. Text in German. 2003. irreg., latest vol.19, 2005. **Document type:** *Trade.*
Media: Online - full content.
Address: Kaiserstr 67/2/32, Vienna, 1070, Austria. Ed., Pub. Sigrid Strohschneider-Laue.

028.1 USA ISSN 1084-1733
ECLECTIC BOOK REVIEWS. Text in English. 1993. 4/yr. USD 20 (effective 2000). adv. bk.rev. back issues avail. **Document type:** *Bibliography.* **Description:** Reviews new books from small publishers.
Published by: Library Research Associates Inc., 474 Dunderberg Rd, Monroe, NY 10950. TEL 914-783-1144. Ed. Dianne D McKinstrie. R&P, Adv. contact Matilda Gocek. B&W page USD 150; trim 11 x 8.5. Circ: 12,000.

015.44 BEL
LES EDITEURS BELGES DE LANGUE FRANCAISE. Text in French. 1960. a. free to qualified personnel. adv. **Document type:** *Directory.* **Description:** Lists information on French language publishers in Belgium, including senior personnel, overseas distributors and areas of specialization.
Former titles: Editeurs Belges de Langue Francaise et Leurs Livres; Livres Belges de Langue Francaise; Livres Belges
Published by: Association des Editeurs Belges (A D E B), Avenue Huart Hamoir 1/34, Brussels, 1030, Belgium. TEL 32-2-2416580, FAX 32-2167131 32-2/216 71 31, http://www.adeb.be. Circ: 4,000.

070.5 GBR ISSN 1748-0191
EDITING MATTERS; the magazine for editors and proofreaders. Text in English. 1989. bi-m. free to members; GBP 24 domestic to non-members; GBP 30 in Europe to non-members; GBP 36 elsewhere to non-members; GBP 4 per academic year (effective 2010). adv. back issues avail. **Document type:** *Magazine, Trade.* **Description:** For those who work with words for publication or are simply interested in learning about the world of editing and proofreading.
Former titles (until 2004): Copyright (1462-9275); (until 1998): Society of Freelance Editors and Proofreaders. Newsletter (0966-4416)
Related titles: Online - full text ed.
Published by: Society for Editors and Proofreaders, Erico House, 93-99 Upper Richmond Rd, Putney, London, SW15 2TG, United Kingdom. TEL 44-20-87855617, FAX 44-20-87855618, administration@sfep.org.uk. Ed. Hazel Reid.

070.5 USA ISSN 0193-7383
CODEN: EDEYDQ
THE EDITORIAL EYE; focusing on publications standards and practices. Text in English. 1978. m. USD 129 domestic; USD 139 in Canada; USD 149 elsewhere (effective 2008). bk.rev. illus. index. back issues avail.; reprints avail. **Document type:** *Newsletter, Trade.* **Description:** Covers editing, proofreading, publications management and language usage. Includes reviews of publishing and production techniques and technology.
Formerly: Eei
Indexed: GALA.
—CASDDS, Ingenta. **CCC.**
Published by: McMurry, Inc., 1010 E Missouri Ave, Phoenix, AZ 85014. TEL 602-395-5850, FAX 602-395-5853, info@mcmurry.com, http://www.mcmurry.com. Circ: 2,600 (paid).

EDITORIAL STRATEGIES; the art and science of creating great content. *see* JOURNALISM

070.5 NGA ISSN 0794-5655
EDITORS' FORUM; focusing on publications standards & practices. Text in English. 1986. q. NGN 50, USD 20. **Document type:** *Newsletter, Academic/Scholarly.*
Published by: Codat Publications, PO Box 9400, Ibadan, Oyo, Nigeria. TEL 234-22-314411. Ed., Pub. Clement O Adejuwon. Circ: 1,000.

015 CAN ISSN 1703-843X
EDMONTON'S MEDIA MAGAZINE. Text in English. 2002. s-a. USD 60 combined subscription print & online eds. (effective 2005). **Document type:** *Directory, Trade.* **Description:** Comprehensive directory of Edmonton's newspaper publishers, radio and television stations and multimedia designers of interest to publicists, fundraisers, public relations professionals, marketing and communications directors.
Related titles: Online - full content ed.
Address: 125, 11215 Jasper Ave, Edmonton, AB T5K 0L5, Canada. TEL 780-454-7936, FAX 780-454-9731, info@mediamag.ca.

EDPRESS MEMBERSHIP ROSTER AND FREE-LANCE DIRECTORY. *see* JOURNALISM

070.594 USA ISSN 0013-1806
EDUCATIONAL MARKETER; the educational publishing industry's voice of authority since 1968. Text in English. 1968. bi-w. USD 695 (print or online ed.) (effective 2008). adv. 8 p./no.; **Document type:** *Newsletter, Trade.* **Description:** Details readers on the changes in demographics, enrollment and funding and how they will affect sales of textbooks and technology products to schools and colleges.
Related titles: Online - full text ed.: USD 629 (effective 2005).
Indexed: A09, A10, A26, B01, B02, B06, B07, B08, B09, B15, B17, B18, C12, E03, E07, ERI, G04, G06, G07, G08, I05, T02, V03, V04.
—**CCC.**
Published by: SIMBA Information (Subsidiary of: Market Research.Com), 11200 Rockville Pike, Ste 504, Rockville, MD 20852. TEL 240-747-3096, 888-297-4622, FAX 240-747-3004, customerservice@simbainformation.com, http://www.simbainformation.com. Pub. Linda Kopp.

300 NLD ISSN 1873-653X
▼ **EGODOCUMENTS AND HISTORY SERIES.** Text in English. 2009. irreg., latest vol.4, 2011. **Document type:** *Monographic series, Academic/Scholarly.* **Description:** Covers cultural and social history based on egodocuments and the history of autobiographical writing within a cultural and social context.
Indexed: IZBG.
Published by: Brill, PO Box 9000, Leiden, 2300 PA, Netherlands. TEL 31-71-5353500, FAX 31-71-5317532, cs@brill.nl. Eds. Arianne Baggerman, Michael Mascuch, Rudolf Dekker.

686.3 ESP ISSN 1133-1860
ENCUADERNACION DE ARTE. Text in Spanish. 1993. s-a. EUR 77 domestic; EUR 100 foreign (effective 2009). **Document type:** *Bulletin, Trade.*
Published by: Asociacion para el Fomento de la Encuadernacion de Arte (A F E D A), Calle de Alcala 93, 2o-1, Madrid, 28009, Spain. TEL 34-91-4354226, FAX 34-91-5771994, info@afeda.org, http://www.afeda.org.

ENTERTAINMENT LAW REPORTER (ONLINE); movies, television, music, theater, publishing, multimedia, sports. *see* LAW

ENTERTAINMENT, PUBLISHING AND THE ARTS HANDBOOK. *see* COMMUNICATIONS—Television And Cable

070.5 DEU ISSN 0938-166X
EURO-KURIER. Text in German. 1990. m. adv. bk.rev. **Document type:** *Journal, Trade.*
Published by: Grabert Verlag, Am Apfelberg 18, Tuebingen, 72076, Germany. TEL 49-7071-40700, FAX 49-7071-407026, info@grabertverlag.de, http://www.grabert-verlag.de. Ed. Wigbert Grabert.

381.45002 GBR ISSN 0962-1997
EUROPEAN BOOK WORLD. Text in English. 1994. q. bibl. **Document type:** *Directory.* **Description:** Provides trade professionals with precise, up-to-date business contact details from listings of more than 25,000 publishing organizations, 75,000 libraries and 55,000 booksellers.
Related titles: CD-ROM ed.: GBP 1,292, EUR 2,030 (CDROM or online ed.) (effective 2009); Online - full text ed.
Published by: Anderson Rand Ltd., 10 Willow Walk, Cambridge, Cambs CB1 1LA, United Kingdom. TEL 44-1223-566640, FAX 44-1223-566643, arinfo@andrand.com, http://www.andrand.com/. Ed. Rand Anderson.

070.5 GBR ISSN 0258-3127
➤ **EUROPEAN SCIENCE EDITING.** Text in English. 1975. q. GBP 60 to non-members; free to members (effective 2011). adv. bk.rev.; software rev. back issues avail. **Document type:** *Journal, Academic/Scholarly.* **Description:** Publishes articles, reports meetings, announces new developments and forthcoming events, online resources, and highlights publications of interest to members.
Former titles (until 1986): Earth & Life Science Editing (0309-4715); (until 1977): Earth Science Editing (0950-1835)
Indexed: GeoRef, SCOPUS.
—BLDSC (3829.969000), IE, Infotrieve, INIST.
Published by: European Association of Science Editors, c/o Sheila Evered, Secretary, PO Box 6159, Reading, RG19 9DE, United Kingdom. TEL 44-118-9700322, FAX 44-118-9700322, secretary@ease.org.uk. Ed. Dr. Armen Yuri Gasparyan. Adv. contact Margaret Cooter. page GBP 940; bleed 210 x 297.

002.0277 DEU ISSN 0014-391X
EX LIBRIS; Aktueller Buchdienst fuer Studenten und Dozenten der Rechts, Wirtschafts, und Informatik. Text in German. 1963. s-a. bk.rev. bibl. **Document type:** *Journal, Trade.*
Published by: (Ex Libris), Felberg Verlag GmbH, An Gross St Martin 6, MBE-Fach 10, Cologne, 50667, Germany. TEL 49-221-4734896, FAX 49-221-2944796, felberg@felberg-verlag.de, http://www.felberg-verlag.de. Circ: 18,000 (controlled).

002.5083 FRA ISSN 0395-269X
Z994.F8
EX LIBRIS FRANCAIS. Text in French; Summaries in English, German. 1939. q. EUR 30 (effective 2008). adv. bk.rev. illus. **Document type:** *Bulletin, Trade.*
Published by: Association Francaise pour la Connaissance de l'Ex-Libris, Bibliotheque Municipale, 43 rue Stanislas, Nancy, Cedex 54042, France. exlibris.afcel@wanadoo.fr, http://pagesperso-orange.fr/exlibris.afcel. Ed. Louis Demezieres. R&P Germaine Meyer Noirel. Adv. contact Guy Vaucel. Circ: 325.

002.0277 DNK ISSN 0014-4681
EXLIBRIS-NYT. Text in Danish. 1960. 4/yr. DKK 300 to members (effective 2008). illus. **Document type:** *Magazine, Consumer.*
Published by: Dansk Exlibris Selskab/Danish Bookplate Society, c/o Frederikshavn Kunstmuseum, PO Box 47, Frederikshavn, 9900, Denmark. Ed. Klaus Roedel.

381.45002 GBR ISSN 1464-6463
F I P P WORLD MAGAZINE TRENDS. (Federation Internationale de la Presse Periodique) Text in English. 1994. a. GBP 299 per issue to non-members; GBP 199 per issue to members (effective 2010). abstr.; charts; mkt.; tr.lit.; illus.; pat.; tr.mk.; bibl.; maps; stat. back issues avail. **Document type:** *Directory, Trade.* **Description:** Provides a primary data source of worldwide magazine publishing trends in 66 countries.
Related titles: CD-ROM ed.; E-mail ed.; Online - full text ed.: GBP 80 to non-members; GBP 50 to members (effective 2009).
—**CCC.**
Published by: International Federation of the Periodical Press/Federation Internationale de la Presse Periodique, Queens House, 55-56 Lincoln's Inn Fields, London, WC2A 3LJ, United Kingdom. TEL 44-20-74044169, FAX 44-20-74044170, info@fipp.com.

070.5 USA
F P O. (For Publications Only) Text in English. 2007 (Sep.). q. USD 44 (effective 2007). **Document type:** *Magazine, Trade.* **Description:** Targets publishers, editors and designers who work in associations, corporate communications or small publishing businesses. Features profiles of influential publication designers and their process and products.
Published by: Auras Design, 8435 Georgia Ave, Silver Spring, MD 20910. TEL 301-587-4300, inforequest@auras.com, http://www.auras.com.

070.5 USA ISSN 1071-5916
F Y I FRANCE. Text in English. 1992. m. (except Aug.). USD 45 (effective 2001). adv. **Document type:** *Newsletter.* **Description:** Provides Internet, library, Minitel, and online digital information news from France and Europe for library and information professionals, researchers, book-dealers and publishers.
Media: Online - full text.
Address: PO Box 460668, San Francisco, CA 94146. TEL 415-282-4850, FAX 415-824-1072. Ed., Pub., R&P, Adv. contact Jack Kessler. Circ: 15,000.

002 HRV ISSN 1334-3327
FANTOM SLOBODE; knjizevni casopis. Text in Croatian. 2003. 3/yr.
Published by: Durieux d.o.o., Sulekova 23, Zagreb, 10000, Croatia. prodaja@durieux.hr, http://www.durieux.hr.

070.5 USA
FEDERAL PUBLISHERS COMMITTEE. SPECIAL REPORTS - TASK FORCE. Text in English. irreg. **Description:** Promotes the cost-effective management of the writing, editorial, and production of publishing in the U.S. federal government.
Published by: Federal Publishers Committee, c/o Glenn W King, Statistical Compendia Branch, U S Bureau of the Census, Washington, DC 20233. TEL 301-457-1171, FAX 301-457-4707. Ed. Glenn W King.

070.5 USA
FEDERAL PUBLISHERS. REPORTS OF MEETING; Guide to Federal Publishing. Text in English. m. **Document type:** *Government.* **Description:** Promotes the cost-effective management of the writing, editorial, and production aspects of publishing in the U.S. federal government.
Published by: Federal Publishers Committee, c/o Glenn W King, Statistical Compendia Branch, U S Bureau of the Census, Washington, DC 20233. TEL 301-457-1171, FAX 301-457-4707. Ed. Glenn W King.

305.4 USA ISSN 0741-6555
FEMINIST BOOKSTORE NEWS. Text in English. 1976. bi-m. USD 70 domestic; USD 93 foreign (effective 2000). adv. bk.rev. bibl.; stat.; tr.lit.; illus. Index. back issues avail.; reprints avail. **Document type:** *Magazine, Trade.* **Description:** Contains news briefs, feature articles, and reader correspondence pertaining to feminist bookselling and publishing. Reviews over 300 titles per issue.
Formerly: Feminist Bookstores Newsletter
Related titles: Microform ed.: (from PQC).
Indexed: FemPer.
—Ingenta.
Address: PO Box 882554, San Francisco, CA 94188. TEL 415-642-9993, FAX 415-642-9995. Ed., Pub., R&P Carol Seajay. Adv. contact Kathryn Werhane. Circ: 750 (paid).

015 FJI ISSN 0015-0916
FIJI. GOVERNMENT PRINTING DEPARTMENT. PUBLICATIONS BULLETIN. Text in English. s-a. free. **Document type:** *Government.*
Published by: Government Printing Department, PO Box 98, Suva, Fiji. Circ: 1,000.

FINANCIAL PRESS FACTS. *see* BUSINESS AND ECONOMICS—Trade And Industrial Directories

002.074 USA ISSN 1551-5001
Z284
FINE BOOKS & COLLECTIONS; magazines. Text in English. 2003. bi-m. USD 25 domestic; USD 32 in Canada & Mexico; USD 55 elsewhere (effective 2006). adv. illus. **Document type:** *Magazine, Consumer.*
Formerly: O P Magazine (1542-9962)
Address: 4905 Pine Cone Dr #2, Durham, NC 27707. TEL 919-489-1916, FAX 919-489-4767, subscriberservices@finebooksmagazine.com. Ed. Scott Brown.

070.5 USA ISSN 1099-7210
FIRST DRAFT. Text in English. 1992. m. USD 149 domestic; USD 179 foreign (effective 2011). **Document type:** *Newsletter, Trade.* **Description:** Contains clip art and articles for use in employee publications.
Related titles: Online - full text ed.: ISSN 1945-3523. free (effective 2011).
Published by: Lawrence Ragan Communications, Inc., 111 E Wacker Dr, Ste 500, Chicago, IL 60601. TEL 312-960-4100, 800-878-5331, FAX 312-861-3592, cservice@ragan.com, http://www.ragan.com. Pub. Mike King TEL 312-960-4133.

002.075 USA ISSN 1066-5471
Z1033.F53
FIRSTS; the book collector's magazine. Text in English. 1991. m. (10/yr.). USD 40 domestic; USD 60 in Canada; USD 95 elsewhere (effective 2010). adv. bk.rev. illus. Index. back issues avail.; reprints avail. **Document type:** *Magazine, Consumer.* **Description:** Designed for anyone who loves books and for collectors of first edition books.
Related titles: Online - full text ed.
Indexed: MLA-IB.
Published by: Firsts Magazine, Inc., PO Box 65166, Tucson, AZ 85728. TEL 520-529-1355.

686.2 CHE
FLASH. Text in French. 1998. 9/yr. **Document type:** *Newsletter, Trade.*
Formerly: S Z V Flash
Published by: Verband Schweizer Presse, Konradstr 14, Postfach 1202, Zurich, 8021, Switzerland. TEL 41-44-3186464, FAX 41-44-3186462, contact@schweizerpresse.ch. Circ: 2,000 (controlled).

070.5 USA
FLASH MARKET NEWS. Text in English. 1940. bi-m. USD 50 to non-members (effective 2000). **Document type:** *Bulletin.*
Published by: National Writers Association, 10940 S Parker Rd, #508, Parker, CO 80134-7440. TEL 303-751-7844, FAX 303-751-8593. Circ: 1,500.

028.1 NLD ISSN 0015-3540
DE FLEANENDE KRIE. Text in Frisian. 1954. 3/yr. EUR 21 domestic; EUR 28 foreign (effective 2008). adv. bk.rev. bibl.; illus.
Published by: Kristlik Fryske Folks Bibleteek, Jousterdyk 289, Aldehaske, 8465 PH, Netherlands. boekeklub.kffb@planet.nl, http://www.kffb.nl.

070.5 USA ISSN 0046-4333
PN4734 CODEN: FMMMD2
FOLIO:; the magazine for magazine management. Text in English. 1972. m. USD 96 domestic; USD 106 in Canada & Mexico; USD 116 elsewhere; USD 8 newsstand/cover (effective 2011). adv. bk.rev. illus. index. back issues avail.; reprints avail. **Document type:** *Magazine, Trade.* **Description:** Focuses on all aspects of the marketing, management and distribution of magazines.
Incorporates (in 1993): Folio's Publishing News (1053-4563); Which was formerly (until 1988): Publishing News (1043-8688)
Related titles: Microform ed.: (from PQC); Online - full text ed.; ◆ Supplement(s): Folio: SuperBook; ◆ Audience Development. ISSN 1946-0392.
Indexed: A09, A10, A12, A13, A14, A15, A17, A22, A25, A26, A28, ABIn, APA, B01, B02, B03, B04, B06, B07, B08, B09, B11, B15, B17, B18, BPI, BRD, BrCerAb, C&ISA, CA/WCA, CIA, CWI, CerAb, CivEngAb, CorrAb, E&CAJ, E08, E11, EEA, EMA, G04, G06, G07, G08, H14, H15, I05, Inpharma, M&TEA, M09, MBF, METADEX, MLA-IB, P02, P06, P10, P34, P48, P51, P53, P54, PQC, S08, S09, SRI, SoftBase, SolStAb, T&II, T02, T04, V03, V04, W01, W02, W03, W05, WAA.
—BLDSC (3974.395000), CASDDS, IE, Infotrieve, Ingenta, Linda Hall. **CCC.**
Published by: Red 7 Media, LLC, 10 Norden Pl, Norwalk, CT 06855. TEL 203-854-6730, FAX 203-854-6735, http://red7media.com. Pub. Tony Silber. adv.: B&W page USD 6,035, color page USD 7,835; 8.125 x 10.825. Circ: 10,959 (paid).

070.5 USA
FOLIO: SUPERBOOK. Text in English. 19??. a. free to qualified personnel (effective 2011). **Document type:** *Handbook/Manual/ Guide, Trade.* **Description:** Provides information on publishing resources and suppliers.
Former titles (until 2005): Folio. Special Source Book Issue for.. (1087-609X); (until 1993): Folio: Sourcebook
Related titles: Online - full text ed.: 2002; ◆ Supplement to: Folio:. ISSN 0046-4333.
Published by: Red 7 Media, LLC, 10 Norden Pl, Norwalk, CT 06855. TEL 203-854-6730, FAX 203-854-6735, mhughes@red7media.com, http://red7media.com.

070.5 ITA ISSN 1128-7284
FONDAZIONE GIANGIACOMO FELTRINELLI. QUADERNI. Text in Italian. 4/yr. **Document type:** *Journal, Academic/Scholarly.*
Published by: Fondazione Giangiacomo Feltrinelli, Via Gian Domenico Romagnosi 3, Milan, 20121, Italy. TEL 39-02-874175, FAX 39-02-86461855, fondazione@feltrinelli.it, http://www.feltrinelli.it.

FOOD WRITER. *see* JOURNALISM

FOOTPRINTS (TEMPE). *see* CLUBS

070.573 USA ISSN 0098-213X
FORECAST (CHARLOTTE). Text in English. 1975. m. adv. bk.rev. illus. **Document type:** *Magazine, Trade.* **Description:** Announcement journal of new and forthcoming adult and children's hardcover and trade paperback titles.
Formerly: New Books Preview Bulletin
Published by: Baker & Taylor, 2550 W Tyvola Rd, Ste 300, Charlotte, NC 28217. TEL 704-998-3100, 800-775-1800, btinfo@btol.com, http://www.btol.com. Adv. contact Brenda Larson TEL 908-541-7447. Circ: 50,000.

070.5 USA ISSN 1099-2642
FOREWORD; reviews of good books independently published. Text in English. 1998. bi-m. USD 40 domestic; USD 60 in Canada; USD 80 elsewhere; USD 10 newsstand/cover (effective 2008). adv. bk.rev. **Document type:** *Magazine, Trade.* **Description:** Provides reviews of independent and university press titles.
Indexed: A26, AmHI, H07, I05, L05, L06.
Published by: ForeWord Magazine, Inc., 129 1/2 E Front St, Traverse City, MI 49684. TEL 231-933-3699, FAX 231-933-3899. Ed. Alex Moore. Pub., R&P Victoria Sutherland. Adv. contact Maryann Batsakis. Circ: 15,000 (controlled).

028.1 USA
FOREWORD REVIEWS; good books independently published. Text in English. bi-m. USD 40 domestic; USD 60 in Canada; USD 80 elsewhere (effective 2011). **Document type:** *Magazine, Consumer.* **Description:** Features dozens of reviews on forthcoming titles, feature articles that preview category trends, and peer editorial and opinion pieces. It brings attention to the literary achievements of independent publishers and their authors.
Related titles: Online - full text ed.: USD 29.99 (effective 2011).
Address: 129 1/2 E Front St, Traverse City, MI 49684. TEL 231-933-3699, FAX 231-933-3899.

FREEDOM TO READ FOUNDATION NEWS. *see* LIBRARY AND INFORMATION SCIENCES

FREELANCE. *see* LITERATURE

070.5 AUS ISSN 1834-5026
FREELANCE REGISTER. Text in English. 1982. a. **Document type:** *Directory, Trade.*
Formerly (until 1993): Register of Freelance Publishing Services in Australia (0728-1544)
Related titles: Online - full text ed.: ISSN 1834-5034. 1998.
Published by: Society of Editors (Victoria) Inc., PO Box 176, Carlton South, VIC 3053, Australia. http://www.socedvic.org/cms/index.php.

FREELANCE WRITER'S REPORT. *see* JOURNALISM

070.5 USA ISSN 1094-4567
THE FREELANCER. Text in English. 1977. bi-m. looseleaf. USD 20 (effective 1999). adv. bk.rev. back issues avail. **Document type:** *Newsletter.*
Formerly: E F A Newsletter
Published by: Editorial Freelancers Association, Inc., 71 W 23rd St, Ste 1910, New York, NY 10010. TEL 212-929-5400, FAX 212-929-5439. Eds. Georgia Maas, Louise Weiss, Mary Ratcliffe TEL 212-787-3974. R&P, Adv. contact Mary Ratcliffe TEL 212-787-3974. Circ: 1,300.

028.5 BRA
FUNDACAO NACIONAL DO LIVRO INFANTIL E JUVENIL. NOTICIAS. Text in Portuguese. m. **Document type:** *Bulletin.* **Description:** Reports book publications, fairs and general information on children's and youth literature.
Published by: Fundacao Nacional do Livro Infantil e Juvenil, Rua da Imprensa, 16 Salas 1212 a 1215, Centro, Rio De Janeiro, RJ 20030-120, Brazil. TEL 55-21-2629130, FAX 55-21-2406649.

051 070.5 USA
FUNHOUSE. Text in English. 1995. irreg. USD 1 newsstand/cover (effective 2000).
Address: 11 Werner Rd, Greenville, PA 16125-9434. Ed. Brian Johnson.

741.64 USA ISSN 1068-7947
THE FUTURE IMAGE REPORT; the inside track in digital imaging. Text in English. 1993. 10/yr. USD 375; USD 390 in Canada & Mexico; USD 410 elsewhere. **Document type:** *Newsletter.* **Description:** Covers photography, digital imaging information, and new products.
Published by: Future Image, Inc., 520 S El Camino Real, Ste 206A, San Mateo, CA 94402. TEL 650-579-0493, 800-749-3572, FAX 650-579-0566. Ed. Alexis J Gerard. R&P R Freed.

050 NLD ISSN 1876-2476
G L COMPENDIUM; a quarterly news report on grey literature. (Grey Literature) Text in English. 2008. q. EUR 160 (effective 2008). **Document type:** *Journal, Trade.* **Description:** Covers the production, collection, access, and use of grey literature.
Indexed: LISTA.
Published by: Greynet - Grey Literature Network Service, Javastraat 194-HS, Amsterdam, 1095 CP, Netherlands. info@greynet.org. Ed., R&P Dominic John Farace.

GEKKAN MEDIA DEETA/MONTHLY MEDIA DATA. *see* BUSINESS AND ECONOMICS—Trade And Industrial Directories

070.5 DEU ISSN 0941-7877
GESCHICHTE DES BUCHHANDELS. Text in German. 1975. irreg., latest vol.8, 2003. price varies. **Document type:** *Monographic series, Academic/Scholarly.*
Published by: Harrassowitz Verlag, Kreuzberger Ring 7b-d, Wiesbaden, 65205, Germany. TEL 49-611-5300, FAX 49-611-530560, verlag@harrassowitz.de, http://www.harrassowitz.de.

070.5 USA
GILA QUEEN'S GUIDE TO THE MARKETS. Text in English. 1988. m. USD 24. **Description:** Provides news of the publishing marketplace, including book publishers, anthologies, magazines, and other information of interest to writers in all genres.
Published by: Kathryn Ptacek, Ed. & Pub., PO Box 97, Newton, NJ 07860-0097.

070.5 ITA ISSN 1124-9137
GIORNALE DELLA LIBRERIA. Text in Italian. 1888. m. EUR 68 domestic; EUR 115 foreign (effective 2008). adv. bk.rev. charts; stat.; illus. index. reprints avail. **Document type:** *Newspaper, Trade.* **Description:** Covers book publishing, book trade. Includes a bibliography of books published in Italy.
Former titles (until 1993): G D L. Giornale della Libreria (1124-9129); (until 1987): Giornale della Libreria (0017-0216); (until 1920): Giornale della Libreria, della Tipografia e delle Arti ed Industrie Affini (1124-9102)
Related titles: Online - full text ed.
Indexed: IBR, IBZ, MLA-IB, RASB.
Published by: (Associazione Italiana Editori (A I E)), Ediser Srl, Via delle Erbe 2, Milan, MI 20121, Italy. TEL 39-02-86915453, FAX 39-02-86993157, ediser@ediser.it, http://www.ediser.it. Circ: 5,000.

028.1 GBR ISSN 1472-2097
THE GOOD BOOK GUIDE. Text in English. 1977. m. GBP 27 domestic; GBP 33.75 in the European Union; GBP 38.25 elsewhere (effective 2009). adv. bk.rev. back issues avail. **Document type:** *Magazine, Consumer.* **Description:** An independent selection of books published in English, including fiction, biography, arts, travel, videos, CD-ROMS, and children's books accompanied by brief reviews.
Related titles: Online - full text ed.
Published by: Good Book Guide Ltd., Hamilton House, 6 Leconfield Estate, Cleator Moor, Cumbria, CA25 5QB, United Kingdom. TEL 44-1946-818150, FAX 44-1946-818131, enquiries@gbgdirect.com.

GORGIAS HISTORICAL CATALOGUES. *see* HISTORY—History Of Asia

DE GRAFISKE FAG. *see* PRINTING

070.5 CZE ISSN 1802-3320
GRAND BIBLIO. Text in Czech. 2007. m. CZK 216 (effective 2009). adv. **Document type:** *Magazine, Trade.*
Related titles: Online - full text ed.: ISSN 1802-4408.
Published by: Grand Princ s.r.o., Vinohradska 138, Prague 3, 130 00, Czech Republic. TEL 420-272-107111, FAX 420-272-107000, grandprinc@grandprinc.cz, http://www.grandprinc.cz. adv.: page CZK 48,500; trim 225 x 280. Circ: 50,000 (paid and controlled).

GRAPHIC COMMUNICATIONS WORLD; the bi-weekly briefing for senior management. *see* PRINTING

GRAPHIC NEWS. *see* PRINTING

381.45002 BRA
GUIA DAS LIVRARIAS E PONTOS DE VENDA DE LIVROS NO BRASIL. Text in Portuguese. 1976. irreg.
Published by: Sindicato Nacional dos Editores de Livros, Av Rio Branco, 37 Andar 15, Centro, Rio de Janeiro, 20090-003, Brazil.

GUIA DE LA DISTRIBUCION EN ESPANA; libros y publicaciones. *see* BUSINESS AND ECONOMICS—Trade And Industrial Directories

070.5 BRA
GUIA DOS EDITORES ASSOCIADOS. Text in Portuguese. 1978. irreg.
Formerly: Guia das Editoras Brasileiras
Published by: Sindicato Nacional dos Editores de Livros, Av Rio Branco, 37 Andar 15, Centro, Rio de Janeiro, 20090-003, Brazil. TEL 55-21-2336481, FAX 55-21-2538502.

070.5 FRA ISSN 1288-5533
GUIDE DU LIVRE ANCIEN ET DES LIBRAIRES. Text in French. 1930. a. free. **Document type:** *Directory.*
Whose former titles were (until 1998): Syndicat National de la Librairie Ancienne et Moderne. Repertoire des Membres (1142-4443); Guide a l'Usage des Amateurs de Livres (0224-6821); Which was formed by the merger of: Guide du Livre Ancien et du Livre d'Occasion (0294-8737); Syndicat National de la Librairie Ancienne et Moderne. Repertoire (0224-683X)
Published by: Syndicat National de la Librairie Ancienne et Moderne (S L A M), 4 Rue Git le Coeur, Paris, 75006, France. TEL 33-1-43294638, FAX 33-1-43254163, slam-livre@wanadoo.fr, http://www.slam-livre.fr.

070.52 USA ISSN 1078-6945
PN163
GUIDE TO LITERARY AGENTS; where and how to find the right agents to represent your work. Text in English. 1992. a. USD 27.99 (effective 2008). **Document type:** *Directory, Trade.* **Description:** Contains over 500 listings of literary and script agents in the U.S. and Canada.
Supersedes in part (in 1994): Guide to Literary Agents and Art - Photo Reps (1055-6087)
Published by: F + W Media Inc., 4700 E Galbraith Rd, Cincinnati, OH 45236. TEL 513-531-2690, 800-283-0963, FAX 513-531-0798, wds@fwpubs.com, http://www.fwpublications.com. Ed. Chuck Sambuchino.

GUIDE TO MICROFORMS IN PRINT. AUTHOR - TITLE. *see* LIBRARY AND INFORMATION SCIENCES

028.1 PRI
GUIDE TO REVIEWS OF BOOKS FROM AND ABOUT HISPANIC AMERICA/GUIA A LAS RESENAS DE LIBROS DE Y SOBRE HISPANOAMERICA. Text in English, Portuguese, Spanish. 1965. a. USD 165. bk.rev. back issues avail. **Document type:** *Bibliography.* **Description:** Contains summaries of reviews covering Latin America and the Caribbean. Includes coverage of Latin Americans in Canada, the U.S. and Great Britain. Fully indexed.
Published by: A M M Editions, PO Box 151, Sta 6, Ponce, 00732, Puerto Rico. Ed. Antonio Matos. Circ: 150.

686.3 USA ISSN 0434-9245
Z1008
GUILD OF BOOK WORKERS JOURNAL. Text in English. 1962. s-a. USD 40 (effective 2000). bk.rev.
Published by: Guild of Book Workers, Inc., 521 Fifth Ave, 17th Fl, New York, NY 10175. TEL 212-292-4444. Circ: 900.

070.5 USA ISSN 0730-3203
Z1008
GUILD OF BOOK WORKERS. NEWSLETTER. Text in English. 1975. bi-m. looseleaf. USD 40 (effective 2000). adv. bk.rev. back issues avail. **Document type:** *Newsletter.*
Published by: Guild of Book Workers, Inc., 521 Fifth Ave, 17th Fl, New York, NY 10175. TEL 212-292-4444. Ed. Margaret Johnson. Circ: 900.

070.5 BEL ISSN 0777-5067
➤ **DE GULDEN PASSER/COMPAS D'OR.** Text in Dutch, English, French, German. 1878. a. bk.rev. reprint service avail. from PSC. **Document type:** *Yearbook, Academic/Scholarly.* **Description:** Yearbook on the history of the book, especially in the Low Countries.

P

Formerly (until 1923): Maatschappij der Antwerpsche Bibliophilen. Uitgave (0777-4451)
Published by: Vereeniging der Antwerpsche Bibliophielen, Museum Plantin-Moretus, Vrijdamarkt 22, Antwerp, 2000, Belgium. TEL 32-3-2330294, FAX 32-3-2262516. Eds. Francine de Nave, Marcus De Schepper. Circ: 750.

➤ **GUTENBERG-GESELLSCHAFT. KLEINE DRUCKE.** *see* PRINTING

070.5 JPN
HAMBAI KAKUSHIN. Text in Japanese. 1963. m. JPY 31,000, USD 265 (effective 1999). back issues avail. **Document type:** *Trade.*
Published by: Shyogyokai Publishing Co. Ltd., 4-9 Azabudai 2-chome, Minato-ku, Tokyo, 106-0041, Japan. TEL 81-3-3224-7484, FAX 81-3-3589-1024. Ed. Tamiyo Uchiro. R&P Yasuhiko Matsui TEL 81-3-3224-7493. adv.: B&W page JPY 220,000, color page JPY 370,000; trim 282 x 210. Circ: 85,000.

686.3 686.2 NLD ISSN 1876-0848
HANDBOEKBINDEN. Text in Dutch. 2008. q. EUR 25 membership (effective 2008).
Formed by the merger of (1989-2008): Vouwbeen (0924-4832); (1989-2007): Stichting Boekbehoud. Bericht (1382-8118)
Published by: Stichting Handboekbinden, Postbus 50076, Almere, 1305 AB, Netherlands. TEL 31-35-5319471, info@stichting-handboekbinden.nl, http://www.stichting-handboekbinden.nl. Circ: 1,500.

070.5 USA
HANDBOOK OF CIRCULATION MANAGEMENT. Text in English. 19??. irreg., latest vol.2. **Document type:** *Handbook/Manual/Guide, Trade.*
Published by: Cowles Business Media (Subsidiary of: Cowles Media Company), 11 River Bend Dr, S,, PO Box 4949, Stamford, CT 06907. paul_mcdougall@cowlesbiz.com.

070.5 USA
HANDBOOK OF MAGAZINE PRODUCTION. Text in English. 19??. irreg., latest vol.2. **Document type:** *Handbook/Manual/Guide, Trade.*
Published by: Cowles Business Media (Subsidiary of: Cowles Media Company), 11 River Bend Dr, S,, PO Box 4949, Stamford, CT 06907. paul_mcdougall@cowlesbiz.com.

070.5 USA
HANDBOOK OF MAGAZINE PUBLISHING. Text in English. 19??. irreg., latest vol.3. **Document type:** *Handbook/Manual/Guide, Trade.*
Published by: Cowles Business Media (Subsidiary of: Cowles Media Company), 11 River Bend Dr, S,, PO Box 4949, Stamford, CT 06907. paul_mcdougall@cowlesbiz.com.

015.519 KOR ISSN 1227-1977
HANKUK CH'ULPAN YONGAM/KOREAN PUBLICATIONS YEARBOOK. Text in Korean. 1963. a. back issues avail. **Document type:** *Yearbook, Trade.*
Published by: Korean Publishers Association/Daehan Chulpan Munhwa Hyeobhoe, 105-2, Sagan-dong, Jongno-gu, Seoul, 110-190, Korea, S. TEL 82-2-7352701, FAX 82-2-7385414, webmaster@kpa21.or.kr, http://www.kpa21.or.kr/main/index.htm. Circ: 2,000.

HEARTLAND CRITIQUES. *see* LITERATURE—Adventure And Romance

HECATE'S AUSTRALIAN WOMEN'S BOOK REVIEW (ONLINE). *see* WOMEN'S STUDIES

381.45002 USA
HELEN HECKER'S HOTLINE; marketing strategies for publishers and entrepreneurs. Text in English. 1983. m. **Document type:** *Newsletter.*
Published by: Twin Peaks Press, PO Box 129, Vancouver, WA 98666-0129. TEL 360-694-2462, FAX 360-694-3210. Ed., Pub. Helen Hecker.

070.5 025.04 JPN
HENSHU KAIGI/WEB & PUBLISHING. Text in Japanese. 2001. m. JPY 10,560 (effective 2008). **Document type:** *Magazine, Trade.*
Published by: Sendenkaigi Co. Ltd., 3-13-16, Minami-Aoyama, Minato-ku, Tokyo, 107-8335, Japan. info@sendenkaigi.co.jp.

070.5 ESP ISSN 1577-3787
HIBRIS; revista de bibliofilia. Text in Spanish. 2001. bi-m. **Document type:** *Magazine, Consumer.*
Published by: Miseria & Cia, Tossal 24, Alicante, 03801, Spain. TEL 34-96-5544973.

017.8 USA ISSN 0894-2358
HISPANIC BOOKS BULLETIN; adult catalog. Text in English. 1987. a. free. **Description:** Catalog of English and Spanish language books and periodicals for adults.
Published by: Hispanic Books Distributors, Inc., 2555 N Coyote Dr, Ste 109, Tucson, AZ 85745-1235. TEL 520-690-0643, 800-624-2124, FAX 520-690-6574. Ed. Arnulfo D Trejo. Circ: 5,000.

028.1 GBR ISSN 1471-7492
HISTORICAL NOVELS REVIEW. Text in English. 1997. q. GBP 25 domestic membership; EUR 40 in Europe membership; USD 50 in United States membership; CAD 60 in Canada membership; AUD 65 in Australia membership; NZD 80 in New Zealand membership (effective 2009). bk.rev. back issues avail. **Document type:** *Magazine, Consumer.* **Description:** Contains reviews of all historical novels, including historical mysteries, fantasies, and family sagas, with occasional reviews of historical romance and nonfiction.
Indexed: MLA-IB.
Published by: Historical Novel Society, Marine Cottage, The Strand, Starcross, Devon, EX6 8NY, United Kingdom. TEL 44-2193-884898, richard@historicalnovelsociety.org. Pub. Richard Lee. Circ: 900 (paid and controlled).

HISTORY (WASHINGTON); reviews of new books. *see* HISTORY

028.1 USA ISSN 0018-2664
HISTORY BOOK CLUB REVIEW. Text in English. 1947. every 3 wks. membership. adv. bk.rev. illus. **Document type:** *Magazine, Consumer.*
Published by: History Book Club, Inc., 1225 S Market St, Mechanicsburg, PA 17055-4728. TEL 800-233-1066, customerservice@historybookclub.com, http://www.historybookclub.com. Circ: 110,000.

028 DEU
▼ **(HOER)BUECHER.** Text in German. 2011. bi-m. EUR 24.90; EUR 4.90 newsstand/cover (effective 2011). adv. **Document type:** *Magazine, Consumer.*
Formed by the merger of (2004-2011): Buecher (1860-8191); (2007-2011): Hoerbuecher (1866-3710)
Published by: Falkemedia, An der Halle 400, Kiel, 24149, Germany. TEL 49-431-2007660, FAX 49-431-20076650, info@falkemedia.de, http://www.falkemedia.de. Ed. Tina Schraml. Adv. contact Ines Heinrich.

002.2 DEU ISSN 1865-0031
HOERBUCH-NEWS VON DER HOEROTHEK. Text in German. 2001. irreg. **Document type:** *Newsletter, Trade.*
Formerly (until 2006): Hoerzliche News von der Hoerothek (1618-2804)
Media: Online - full content.
Published by: Rene R. Wagner - Neue Medien und Kommunikation, Sandkaul 1, Erkelenz-Keyenberg, 41812, Germany. TEL 49-2164-702500, FAX 49-2164-702544, redaktion@hoerothek.de.

002.2 DEU ISSN 1618-0453
DIE HOEROTHEK. Text in German. 2000. irreg. **Document type:** *Trade.*
Media: Online - full content.
Published by: Rene R. Wagner - Neue Medien und Kommunikation, Sandkaul 1, Erkelenz-Keyenberg, 41812, Germany. TEL 49-2164-702500, FAX 49-2164-702544. Ed., Pub., Adv. contact Rene Wagner.

HORA DE CIERRE. *see* JOURNALISM

028.5 USA ISSN 1044-405X
Z1037.A1
HORN BOOK GUIDE TO CHILDREN'S AND YOUNG ADULT BOOKS. Text in English. 1989. s-a. USD 60 domestic; USD 77 in Canada & Mexico; USD 81 elsewhere (effective 2011). adv. bk.rev. illus. Index. 250 p./no. 2 cols./p.; back issues avail.; reprints avail. **Document type:** *Magazine, Consumer.* **Description:** Contains reviews of over 2,000 titles-virtually every children's and young adult book published in the US.
Related titles: Online - full text ed.
Indexed: A26, BRI, CBRI, I05, P10, P18, P48, P53, P54, P55, PQC, S23.
—CCC.
Published by: Horn Book, Inc. (Subsidiary of: Media Source Incorporated), 56 Roland St, Ste 200, Boston, MA 02129. TEL 617-628-0225, 800-325-1170, FAX 617-628-0882, info@hbook.com. Ed. Roger Sutton. Pub. Ian Singer.

028.5 USA ISSN 0018-5078
Z1037.A1
THE HORN BOOK MAGAZINE; recommending books for children and young adults. Text in English. 1924. bi-m. USD 72 domestic to institutions; USD 89 in Canada to institutions (effective 2012); USD 93 elsewhere to institutions (effective 2011). adv. bk.rev. illus. Index. back issues avail.; reprints avail. **Document type:** *Magazine, Trade.* **Description:** Features interesting articles on children's and young adult literature.
Related titles: Microfiche ed.: (from NBI); Microform ed.: (from PQC); Online - full text ed.
Indexed: A01, A02, A03, A06, A08, A22, A25, A26, ABS&EES, ASIP, Acal, B04, B05, B14, BRD, BRI, C05, CBRI, CPerl, ChLitAb, ChPerl, Chicano, E02, E03, E07, E08, ERI, EdA, Edl, G05, G06, G07, G08, Gdlns, H14, I05, I07, L04, L05, L06, L07, L08, L09, LISTA, LibLit, M01, M02, MLA-IB, MRD, MagInd, P02, P04, P07, P10, P13, P18, P48, P53, P54, P55, PMR, PQC, R04, RGAb, RGYP, S08, S09, S23, SCOPUS, T02, W03, W05, WBA, WMB.
—BLDSC (4328.200000), IE, Ingenta. **CCC.**
Published by: Horn Book, Inc. (Subsidiary of: Media Source Incorporated), 56 Roland St, Ste 200, Boston, MA 02129. TEL 617-628-0225, 800-325-1170, FAX 617-628-0882, info@hbook.com. Ed. Roger Sutton. adv.: page USD 1,654; 5 x 8.

070.5 USA ISSN 0749-1255
HOTLINE (ARLINGTON). Text in English. bi-w. free to members. **Document type:** *Newsletter, Trade.*
Related titles: Online - full content ed.
Published by: Newsletter & Electronic Publishers Association, 1501 Wilson Blvd, Ste 509, Arlington, VA 22209. TEL 703-527-2333, 800-356-9302, FAX 703-841-0629, nepa@newsletters.org, http://www.newsletters.org/.

070.5 USA ISSN 0738-7415
HOW TO BE YOUR OWN PUBLISHER UPDATE. Text in English. 1988. a. looseleaf. USD 12.95 domestic; USD 15.95 in Canada; USD 19.95 elsewhere (effective 2007). adv. reprints avail. **Document type:** *Newsletter, Trade.* **Description:** A reference for self publishers. Covers areas of promotion, wholesale printing, and mailing approaches, publishing and book trade, advertising, public relations, business and the economics of small business. Provides resources for associations and organizations.
Published by: Prosperity & Profits Unlimited, PO Box 416, Denver, CO 80201. TEL 303-575-5676, FAX 303-575-1187, starsuccess@excite.com. Ed. A. Doyle. adv.: page USD 1,900. Circ: 10,000.

HUBEI FANGZHI. *see* JOURNALISM

070.5 USA
HUENEFELD REPORT; for managers and planners in modest-sized book publishing houses. Text in English. 1973. fortn. USD 88; USD 110 foreign (effective 1998). back issues avail. **Document type:** *Newsletter.* **Description:** Focuses on techniques and benchmarks for managers of book publishing houses with annual budgets under forty million dollars.
Published by: Huenefeld Company, Inc., PO Box 665, Bedford, MA 01730-0665. TEL 781-275-1070. Ed. John Huenefeld. Circ: 975.

I A P A NEWS. *see* JOURNALISM

070.594 AUT ISSN 0333-3620
Z286.S37
I A S P NEWSLETTER. Text in English. 1980. 4/yr. USD 60. **Document type:** *Newsletter.*
Indexed: RASB.
—CCC.
Published by: (International Association of Scholarly Publishers), Universitaetsverlag der Hochschuelerschaft an der Universitaet Wien GmbH, Berggasse 5, Vienna, W 1090, Austria. TEL 43-1-3105356, FAX 43-1-3197050. Ed. Michael Huter.

028.5 CHE
I B B Y CONGRESS PROCEEDINGS. Text in English. biennial. **Document type:** *Proceedings.*
Published by: International Board on Books for Young People, Nonnenweg 12, Postfach, Basel, 4003, Switzerland. TEL 41-61-2722917, FAX 41-61-2722757.

070.5 USA
I B P A INDEPENDENT. Text in English. 1982. m. USD 40 (effective 2009). adv. bk.rev. **Document type:** *Newsletter, Trade.* **Description:** Provides news of industry trends, publisher profiles and cooperative marketing ideas and information for small to medium-sized independent publishers.
Former titles: P M A Independent; P M A Newsletter (1058-4102)
Published by: Independent Book Publishers Association, 627 Aviation Way, Manhattan Beach, CA 90266. TEL 310-372-2732, FAX 310-374-3342, info@ibpa-online.org. Circ: 7,000 (paid and controlled).

I G F - JOURNAL; journal of the printing, bookbinding and paper workers in all countries. *see* PRINTING

070.5 USA ISSN 1542-0493
I O B A STANDARD. (Independent Online Booksellers Association) Text in English. 2000 (Apr.). q.
Media: Online - full content.
Published by: I O B A, P. O. Box 3881, Evergreen, CO 80437. editor@ioba.org, info@ioba.org. Ed. Shirley Bryant.

070.5 GBR
▼ **ILLUMINEA.** Text in English. 2010 (Jan.). q. **Document type:** *Magazine, Academic/Scholarly.* **Description:** Aims to keep academic librarians and information professionals up-to-date with the latest developments at OUP and across the publishing world.
Media: Online - full text. **Related titles:** Chinese ed.; Japanese ed.; Arabic ed.; Spanish ed.; French ed.
Published by: Oxford University Press, Great Clarendon St, Oxford, OX2 6DP, United Kingdom. TEL 44-1865-556767, FAX 44-1865-556646, enquiry@oup.co.uk, http://www.oxfordjournals.org. Ed. Kirsty Luff.

070.5 USA ISSN 1930-6016
IMAGINE (CAMBRIDGE). Text in English. 2000. m. USD 30 (effective 2007). adv. **Document type:** *Magazine, Consumer.* **Description:** Features information about media, publishing, music, theater and film in New England and the Northeast.
Formerly: iMMAgine
Published by: Imagine Publishing, 185 Mt Auburn St, Ste 3, Cambridge, MA 02138. TEL 617-576-0773, FAX 617-864-4923. Pub. Carol Patton.

070.5 FRA ISSN 0981-5309
IMPAC. Text in French. 1986. m. **Document type:** *Magazine, Trade.*
Published by: Filpac C G T, 263 rue de Paris, Montreuil, Cedex 93100, France. TEL 33-1-48188024, FAX 33-1-48519907, filpac@filpac-cgt.fr. Circ: 89,000.

IN-PLANT GRAPHICS. *see* PRINTING

070.5 USA
INDEPENDENT (ARLINGTON); a monthly notice of small press periodicals, books and ideas. Text in English. 1978. m. USD 10 to individuals; USD 12 to institutions. adv. bk.rev. reprints avail.
Supersedes (1975-1976): Butt
Related titles: Microfilm ed.: (from PQC).
Address: c/o Leonard J Andersen, 156 Pleasant St, Arlington, MA 02174. Circ: 800.

070.5 GBR ISSN 2043-6424
▼ **INDEPENDENT MAGAZINE PUBLISHER.** Text in English. 2010. bi-m. free to qualified personnel (effective 2010). adv. back issues avail. **Document type:** *Magazine, Trade.* **Description:** Helps publishing companies discover new products and services to increase their revenue, reduce costs and accelerate growth.
Related titles: Online - full text ed.: ISSN 2043-6432. free (effective 2010).
Published by: Econtra Publishing Ltd., 34 High St, Lenham, Kent ME17 2QD, United Kingdom. TEL 44-1622-851378. Ed., Pub. Jon Barrett. Adv. contact Charlotte Morgan.

381.45002 USA
Z231.5.L5
INDEPENDENT PUBLISHER (ONLINE). Text in English. 1983. bi-m. free (effective 2010). bk.rev. illus. reprints avail. **Document type:** *Journal, Trade.* **Description:** Provides information to the independent publishing industry through articles, excerpts, new title announcements and over 100 book reviews in each issue.
Former titles (until 2000): Independent Publisher (Print) (1098-5735); (until 1998): Small Press (0000-0485)
Media: Online - full text. **Related titles:** Microform ed.: (from PQC).
Indexed: A22, B04, B05, BRD, BRI, CBRI, GALA, L07, L08, LHTB, LibLit, W03, W05.
—Ingenta.
Published by: Jenkins Group, Inc., 1129 Woodmere Ave Ste B, Traverse City, MI 49686. TEL 231-933-0445, 800-706-4636, FAX 231-933-0448, publish@jenkinsgroupinc.com, http://www.jenkinsgroupinc.com. Ed. Jim Barnes.

017.8 USA ISSN 0192-6969
Z1035.1
INDEX TO AMERICAN REFERENCE BOOKS ANNUAL; a cumulative index to subjects, authors, and titles. Text in English. 1974. a. price varies. **Document type:** *Directory, Academic/Scholarly.*
Published by: Libraries Unlimited, Inc. (Subsidiary of: A B C - C L I O), 130 Cremona Dr, PO Box 1911, Santa Barbara, CA 93116. TEL 800-368-6868, FAX 805-685-9685, 866-270-3856, lu-books@lu.com, http://www.lu.com.

017 USA ISSN 1080-1154
Z5301
INDEX TO MARQUIS WHO'S WHO PUBLICATIONS. Text in English. 1974. a. USD 186.95 per issue in US & Canada; USD 214 per issue elsewhere (effective 2008). **Document type:** *Directory, Consumer.* **Description:** Provides a complete list of Who's Who names and the volume(s) in which they appear, such that the users can immediately pinpoint the correct volume.
Former titles (until 1994): Marquis Who's Who Index to Who's Who Books (0884-7118); (until 1985): arquis Who's Who Publications.Index to All Books (0148-3528)
Related titles: Magnetic Tape ed.
Published by: Marquis Who's Who LLC., 890 Mountain Ave, Ste 300, PO Box 10, New Providence, NJ 07974. TEL 908-673-1000, 800-473-7020, FAX 908-673-1189, sales@marquiswhoswho.com. Pub. James J Pfister.

070.5 GBR ISSN 0266-4860
INDEXERS AVAILABLE. Text in English. 1982. a. GBP 12.60 per issue (effective 2009). back issues avail. **Document type:** *Directory, Trade.* **Description:** Contains the directory of freelance indexers available for work.
Related titles: Online - full text ed.: free (effective 2009).
Published by: Society of Indexers, Woodbourn Business Ctr, 10 Jessell St, Sheffield, S9 3HY, United Kingdom. TEL 44-114-2449561, FAX 44-114-2449563, info@theindexer.org. Ed. Cath Topliff.

028.1 ITA ISSN 0393-3903
L'INDICE DEI LIBRI DEL MESE. Text in Italian. 1984. m. (except Aug.). EUR 51.50 domestic; EUR 72 in Europe; EUR 90 elsewhere (effective 2005). adv. bk.rev. back issues avail. **Document type:** *Magazine, Consumer.* **Description:** Reviews about 11000 books yearly, written by scholars and experts on subjects from literature and education, to politics and science. Also contains debates on cultural subject matter and announcements of cultural events.
Related titles: CD-ROM ed.; Online - full text ed.
Indexed: A22, RASB.
—Infotrieve.
Published by: L'Indice SpA, Via Madama Cristina 16, Turin, TO 10125, Italy. TEL 39-011-6693934, FAX 39-011-6699082.

070.5 DEU
INDUSTRIEGEWERKSCHAFT MEDIEN. SCHRIFTENREIHE FUER BETRIEBSRATE. Text in German. 1969. irreg. exchange basis. charts; illus. **Document type:** *Trade.*
Formerly: Industriegewerkschaft Druck und Papier. Schriftenreihe fuer Betriebsrate (0170-3463)
Published by: Vereinte Dienstleistungsgewerkschaft, Paula-Thiede-Ufer 10, Berlin, 10179, Germany. TEL 49-30-69560, FAX 49-30-69563141, info@verdi.de, http://www.verdi.de.

INFOPRESSE. *see* ADVERTISING AND PUBLIC RELATIONS

070.5 DEU ISSN 0723-4929
INFORMATION FUER DEN GMBH-GESCHAEFTSFUEHRER; Persoenliches - Beratung - Steuern - Recht - Geld. (Gesellschaft mit Beschraenkter Haftung) Text in German. 1982. w. EUR 62.25 (effective 2010). **Document type:** *Newsletter, Trade.*
Published by: Redmark.de (Subsidiary of: Rudolf Haufe Verlag GmbH & Co. KG), Fraunhoferstr 5, Planegg, 82152, Germany. TEL 49-180-5555690, FAX 49-89-89517250, service@redmark.de.

070.5 USA ISSN 1065-0393
HD9999.I493
INFORMATION MARKETPLACE DIRECTORY. Abbreviated title: I M D. Text in English. 1992. irreg. USD 295 (effective 2000). **Document type:** *Directory.* **Description:** Lists publishers (along with key personnel) of directories, databases, reference books, business newsletters, research reports, looseleaf publications and magazines.
Published by: SIMBA Information (Subsidiary of: Market Research.Com), 11200 Rockville Pike, Ste 504, Rockville, MD 20852. TEL 240-747-3096, 888-297-4622, FAX 240-747-3004, customerservice@simbainformation.com, http://www.simbainformation.com.

070.5 USA ISSN 1058-4730
Z479
INFORMATION PUBLISHING: BUSINESS - PROFESSIONAL MARKETS & MEDIA (YEAR). Text in English. 1991. irreg., latest vol.4, 1999. USD 1,995 (print or online ed.) (effective 2008). charts. **Document type:** *Handbook/Manual/Guide, Trade.* **Description:** Provides guidance on information publishing in 16 principal markets including advertising/marketing, business news, construction, credit, healthcare, scientific and 10 more.
Related titles: Online - full text ed.
—CCC.
Published by: SIMBA Information (Subsidiary of: Market Research.Com), 11200 Rockville Pike, Ste 504, Rockville, MD 20852. TEL 240-747-3096, 888-297-4622, FAX 240-747-3004, customerservice@simbainformation.com. Pub. Linda Kopp.

070.5 USA
INK (IDAHO SPRINGS). Text in English. m. free to members. adv. **Document type:** *Newsletter.* **Description:** Provides news on the free-paper publishing industry.
Published by: Association of Free Community Papers, 1634 Miner, PO Box 2020, Idaho Springs, CO 80452. TEL 877-203-2327, FAX 303-567-0520, afcp@pobox.com. Ed. Dave Neuharth. Adv. contact Vicki Fox. Circ: 2,200.

686.36 USA ISSN 0894-0479
Z271.3.M37
INK & GALL; the marbling journal. Text in English. 1987. 3/yr. USD 35; USD 40 foreign. adv. bk.rev. **Document type:** *Journal, Trade.* **Description:** Devoted to furthering the art of marbling; both traditional & modern techniques.
Indexed: ABIPC.
Published by: Dexter Ing, Pub., PO Box 1469, Taos, NM 87571. TEL 505-586-1607. Ed. Polly Fox. Circ: 1,500.

028 839.31 NLD ISSN 1877-8771
▼ **INKT!.** Text in Dutch. 2009. bi-m. EUR 29.75 (effective 2011). **Document type:** *Magazine, Consumer.*
Published by: Boekwinkeltjes, Diezestraat 32, Assen, 9406 RD, Netherlands. http://www.boekwinkeltjes.nl.

INNOVATION JOURNALISM. *see* COMMUNICATIONS

070.5 USA
INSIDE BORDERS. Text in English. m. free. adv. bk.rev. **Document type:** *Magazine, Consumer.* **Description:** Includes book excerpts, interviews with authors, and essays by authors whose books are carried by Borders bookstores.
Published by: Borders Group Inc, c/o Leslie Stainton, Ed, 100 Phoenix Dr, Ann Arbor, MI 48108. TEL 734-477-1100. Ed. Beth Fhaner. Adv. contact Carolyn Rice.

070.5 USA ISSN 1075-3281
INSIDE EXPORT; a guide to growing international markets for the U.S. publishing industry. Text in English. 1990. bi-m. USD 50. bk.rev. **Document type:** *Newsletter.* **Description:** News on developments in international book markets. Includes regional reports, intellectual property news, services, market opportunities, calendar of events.
Published by: (International Division), Association of American Publishers, Inc., 71 Fifth Ave, New York, NY 10003-3004. TEL 212-255-0200, FAX 212-255-7007. Ed. Fred Kobrak. Pub. Barbara J Meredith.

INSIDE REPORT ON NEW MEDIA. *see* COMPUTERS—Microcomputers

INTERMEDIOS DE LA COMUNICACION. *see* COMMUNICATIONS

090 GBR ISSN 0538-7159
INTERNATIONAL DIRECTORY OF ANTIQUARIAN BOOKSELLERS/ REPERTOIRE INTERNATIONAL DE LA LIBRAIRIE ANCIENNE. Text in English, French. 1951. irreg. price varies. adv. back issues avail. **Document type:** *Directory, Trade.*
Published by: International League of Antiquarian Booksellers/Ligue Internationale de la Librairie Ancienne, c/o Adrian Harrington, 64 A Kensington Church St, London, W8 4DB, United Kingdom. TEL 44-20-79371465, FAX 44-20-73680912, info@ilab.org, http://www.ilab-lila.com.

THE INTERNATIONAL DIRECTORY OF LITTLE MAGAZINES AND SMALL PRESSES. *see* PUBLISHING AND BOOK TRADE—Abstracting, Bibliographies, Statistics

070.5 GBR ISSN 0250-460X
INTERNATIONAL LEAGUE OF ANTIQUARIAN BOOKSELLERS. NEWSLETTER. Text in English, French. 1972. **Document type:** *Newsletter, Trade.*
Formerly (until 1974): Ligue Internationale de la Librairie Ancienne. Lettre (0250-4553)
Related titles: Online - full text ed.
Published by: International League of Antiquarian Booksellers/Ligue Internationale de la Librairie Ancienne, c/o Adrian Harrington, 64 A Kensington Church St, London, W8 4DB, United Kingdom. TEL 44-20-79371465, FAX 44-20-73680912, info@ilab.org, http://www.ilab-lila.com. Ed. Tom Congalton.

070.5 USA ISSN 0074-6827
Z291.5 CODEN: ILMPD3
INTERNATIONAL LITERARY MARKET PLACE; the directory of the international book publishing industry. Abbreviated title: I L M P. Text in English. 1965. a. USD 289 (effective 2011). index. 1650 p./no.; Supplement avail. **Document type:** *Directory, Trade.* **Description:** Contains profiles for more than 15,000 book-related concerns around the globe including 10,500 publishers and literary agents, 1,100 major booksellers and book clubs, and 1,500 major libraries and library associations.
Formerly (until 1970): International Literary Market Place. European Edition (0538-8562)
Related titles: Magnetic Tape ed.; ◆ Online - full text ed.: LiteraryMarketPlace.com.
—BLDSC (4543.020000), CASDDS. **CCC.**
Published by: Information Today, Inc., 143 Old Marlton Pike, Medford, NJ 08055. TEL 609-654-6266, 800-300-9868, FAX 609-654-4309, custserv@infotoday.com, http://www.infotoday.com. Ed. Karen Hallard.

070.5 CHE ISSN 0074-7556
INTERNATIONAL PUBLISHERS ASSOCIATION. PROCEEDINGS OF CONGRESS. Text in English. 1896. quadrennial. CHF 60, USD 54 (effective 2001). **Document type:** *Proceedings, Trade.* **Description:** Provides insights into the concerns of the international publishing community. Addresses such issues as copyright, piracy, censorship, world trends in education and electronic publishing.
Published by: International Publishers Association/Union Internationale des Editeurs (Internationale Verleger-Union), Ave Miremont 3, Geneva, 1206, Switzerland. TEL 41-22-3463018, FAX 41-22-3475717, secretariat@ipa-uie.org, http://www.ipa-uie.org. Ed., Pub., R&P, Adv. contact Benoit Mueller. Circ: 1,100.

070.5 GBR
INTERNATIONAL PUBLISHING HANDBOOK. Variant title: International Magazine Publishing Handbook. Text in English. 2005 (Jan.). biennial. GBP 135 per issue to non-members; GBP 95 per issue to members (effective 2010). **Document type:** *Handbook/Manual/ Guide, Trade.* **Description:** Provides the ideal introduction to publishing across borders from how to find the ideal partner to setting up the deal and including essential sample contracts.
Published by: International Federation of the Periodical Press/Federation Internationale de la Presse Periodique, Queens House, 55-56 Lincoln's Inn Fields, London, WC2A 3LJ, United Kingdom. TEL 44-20-74044169, FAX 44-20-74044170, info@fipp.com.

028 USA ISSN 1937-593X
INTERVIEW & READING GUIDE ROUNDUP. Text in English. 2005. m. USD 34.95 (effective 2007). **Document type:** *Newsletter, Consumer.*
Media: Online - full content.
Published by: BookBrowse LLC, PO Box 2157, Saratoga, CA 95070. TEL 408-867-6500, info@bookbrowse.com, http://www.bookbrowse.com.

070.5 AUS
AN INTRODUCTION TO AUSTRALIAN BOOK PUBLISHING. Text in English. irreg., latest 3rd Edition. AUD 16.50 per issue domestic to members; AUD 22 per issue domestic to non-members; AUD 25 per issue foreign (effective 2008). **Document type:** *Magazine, Consumer.* **Description:** Provides a "How It Works" guide to the book publishing industry.
Published by: Australian Publishers Association, 60/89 Jones St, Ultimo, NSW 2007, Australia. TEL 61-2-92819788, FAX 61-2-92811073, apa@publishers.asn.au.

028.1 800 IRL ISSN 1649-6981
IRISH BOOK REVIEW. Text in English. 2005. q. EUR 25 (effective 2006).
Published by: The Irish Book Review, Ashbrook House, 10 Main St, Raheny, Dublin, 5, Ireland. TEL 353-1-8511459, info@irishbookreview.com, http://www.irishbookreview.com.

381.45002 ISR ISSN 0333-6018
ISRAEL BOOK TRADE DIRECTORY; a guide to publishers, booksellers and the book trade in Israel. Text in English. 1967. biennial. USD 12 (effective 2001). adv. **Document type:** *Directory.* **Description:** Provides descriptions of each company, addresses, telephone and fax numbers for Israeli publishers, booksellers, agents and publishers' representatives, translators, archives, literary journals, etc.
Former titles: Israel Book Trades Directory: A Select List; Publishers and Printers of Israel: A Select List (0079-7820)
Address: P O Box 7705, Jerusalem, 91076, Israel. TEL 972-2-6432147, FAX 972-2-6437502, debasher@netvision.net.il. Ed., Adv. contact Asher Weill. page USD 240. Circ: 2,000.

070.5 RUS ISSN 0132-1889
IZDATEL'SKOE DELO. NAUCHNO-TEKHNICHESKII INFORMATSIONNYI SBORNIK. Text in Russian. bi-m.
Published by: Rossiiskaya Knizhnaya Palata/Book Chamber International, Ostozhenka 4, Moscow, 119034, Russian Federation. TEL 7-095-2911278, FAX 7-095-2919630, bookch@postman.ru, http://www.bookchamber.ru.

J B I A DIRECTORY. *see* BUSINESS AND ECONOMICS—Trade And Industrial Directories

070.5 JPN ISSN 0387-3927
J P G LETTER; news on English publishing in Japan and South-East Asia. Text in English. 1973. m. JPY 20,000, USD 200. adv. bk.rev. illus. **Description:** Lists new or updated publication titles in Japan and in Southeast/East Asian countries. Also includes comments on publishers and other information sources.
Supersedes: Asia Notebook (0004-4490)
—CCC.
Published by: Japan Publications Guide Service, 5-5-13 Matsushiro, Tsukuba-shi, Ibaraki-ken 305-0035, Japan. TEL 81-3-3661-7458, FAX 81-3-3667-9646. Ed. Warren E Ball. Circ: 600. **Subscr. to:** Intercontinental Marketing Corp., IPO Box 5056, Tokyo 100-30, Japan.

070.594 DEU ISSN 0075-2193
Z1000 CODEN: JABHBQ
JAHRBUCH DER AUKTIONSPREISE FUER BUECHER, HANDSCHRIFTEN UND AUTOGRAPHEN; Ergebnisse der Auktionen in Deutschland, den Niederlanden, Oesterreich und der Schweiz. Text in German. 1950. a. EUR 296 (effective 2009). adv. back issues avail.; reprints avail. **Document type:** *Catalog, Bibliography.*
Formerly: Jahrbuch der Auktionspreise
Related titles: CD-ROM ed.
Published by: Dr. Ernst Hauswedell und Co. Verlag, Haldenstr 30, Stuttgart, 70376, Germany. TEL 49-711-5499710, FAX 49-711-54997121, verlag@hauswedell.de, http://www.hauswedell.de. Circ: 1,700.

070.5 CAN ISSN 1493-2334
JANUARY MAGAZINE. Text in English. 1997. d. free (effective 2010). bk.rev. **Document type:** *Magazine, Consumer.* **Description:** Features interviews with authors from around the world as well as reviews of books written in all countries worldwide.
Media: Online - full text.
—CCC.
Published by: January Publishing Inc., 101-1001 W Broadway, Ste 192, Vancouver, BC V6H 4E4, Canada. Ed. Linda Richards.

070.5025 JPN ISSN 0287-9530
HD2429.J3
JAPAN DIRECTORY OF PROFESSIONAL ASSOCIATIONS. Text in English. 1984. irreg., latest vol.3, 1995. JPY 30,000 domestic; USD 300 foreign. adv. stat.; tr.lit. **Document type:** *Directory.* **Description:** Lists all types of associations, as well as selected institutes.
Related titles: Diskette ed.
—CCC.
Published by: Japan Publications Guide Service, 5-5-13 Matsushiro, Tsukuba-shi, Ibaraki-ken 305-0035, Japan. FAX 81-3-3667-9646. Ed. Warren E Ball. Circ: 2,000. **Subscr. to:** Intercontinental Marketing Corp., IPO Box 5056, Tokyo 100-30, Japan.

381.45002 JPN ISSN 0918-9580
Z3303
JAPANESE BOOK NEWS. Text in English. q. free to qualified personnel. **Document type:** *Newsletter, Trade.* **Description:** Contains the latest trends in Japanese publishing and selected new titles with brief descriptions of the content.
Related titles: Online - full text ed.
Published by: Japan Foundation, Arts and Culture Department, 4-4-1 Yotsuya, Shinjuku-ku, Tokyo, 160-0004, Japan. TEL 81-3-53696064, FAX 81-3-53696038. Ed., Pub. Susaki Masaru.

070.5 USA
Z475
JEFF HERMAN'S GUIDE TO BOOK PUBLISHERS, EDITORS, & LITERARY AGENTS. Text in English. 1991. a., latest 2008. USD 29.95 per issue (effective 2008). **Document type:** *Directory, Trade.*
Former titles (until 200?): Writer's Guide to Book Editors, Publishers, and Literary Agents (1089-3369); (until 1998): Insider's Guide to Book Editors, Publishers and Literary Agents (1064-5667); Insider's Guide to Book Editors and Publishers (1052-0120)
Published by: Three Dog Press, PO Box 1522, Stockbridge, MA 01262. http://www.jeffherman.com.

070.5 296 USA ISSN 1091-7977
JEWISH JOURNAL - NORTH OF BOSTON. Text in English. 1976. bi-w. (Fri.). USD 20 (effective 2001). adv. bk.rev.; film rev.; play rev. 5 cols./p.; **Document type:** *Newspaper, Newspaper-distributed.*
Former titles (until 1996): North Shore Jewish Press. Journal (1040-0095); (until 1986): North Shore Jewish Community. Journal (0746-0457)
Related titles: Online - full text ed.
Published by: North Shore Jewish Press Ltd., 201 Washington St, Ste 14, Box 555, Salem, MA 01970. TEL 978-745-4111, FAX 978-745-5333. Ed., Pub. Mark Arnold. Adv. contact Lois Kaplan. col. inch USD 14.95. Circ: 12,100 (paid). Wire service: JTA.

JOURNAL OF CHILDREN'S LITERATURE. *see* CHILDREN AND YOUTH—About

070.5 USA ISSN 1947-6574
▼ ➤ **JOURNAL OF MODERN PERIODICAL STUDIES.** Abbreviated title: J M P S. Text in English. 2010 (Apr.). s-a. USD 157 combined subscription to institutions (print & online eds.) (effective 2012). adv. reprint service avail. from PSC. **Document type:** *Journal, Academic/ Scholarly.*
Related titles: Online - full text ed.: ISSN 2152-9272. 2010 (Apr.). USD 112 to institutions (effective 2012).
Indexed: A22, E01.
—CCC.
Published by: Pennsylvania State University Press, 820 N University Dr, University Support Bldg 1, Ste C, University Park, PA 16802. TEL 814-865-1327, 800-326-9180, FAX 814-863-1408, info@psupress.org. Eds. Mark Morrisson, Sean Latham. Adv. contact Brian Beer TEL 814-863-5992. **Dist. by:** The Johns Hopkins University Press, PO Box 19966, Baltimore, MD 21211. TEL 410-516-6987, 800-548-1784, FAX 410-516-3866, jrnlcirc@press.jhu.edu, https://www.press.jhu.edu/.

P

028.1 USA ISSN 2150-8127
Z1003
JOURNAL OF REVIEWS INTERNATIONAL. Text in English. 200?. s-a. free (effective 2009). **Document type:** *Journal, Academic/Scholarly.*
Media: Online - full content.
Published by: Scientific Journals International (Subsidiary of: Global Commerce & Communication, Inc), 1407 33rd St S, Saint Cloud, MN 56301. TEL 320-217-6019, info@scientificjournals.org.

070.5 CAN ISSN 1198-9742
Z286.S37 CODEN: JSPUEQ
➤ **JOURNAL OF SCHOLARLY PUBLISHING.** Abbreviated title: J S P. Text in English. 1969. q. USD 110 in North America to institutions; USD 130 elsewhere to institutions; USD 135 combined subscription in North America to institutions (print & online eds.); USD 155 combined subscription elsewhere to institutions (print & online eds.) (effective 2011). adv. bk.rev. illus. index. 64 p./no.; back issues avail.; reprint service avail. from PSC. **Document type:** *Journal, Academic/Scholarly.* **Description:** Addresses the age-old problems in publishing as well as the new challenges resulting from changes in technology and funding.
Formerly (until 1994): Scholarly Publishing (0036-634X)
Related titles: Microfiche ed.: (from MML, PQC); Microform ed.: (from MML); Online - full text ed.: ISSN 1710-1166. USD 115 to institutions (effective 2011).
Indexed: A01, A03, A08, A20, A22, ASCA, AmH&L, ArtHuCI, B04, BAS, C03, C05, C10, CA, CBCARef, CBPI, CLI, CMM, CPE, CommAb, CurCont, DIP, E01, FR, GeoRef, HEA, HistAb, IBR, IBZ, ISTA, Inspec, L04, L07, L08, L09, LISTA, LibLit, MLA, MLA-IB, P48, PCI, PQC, SCOPUS, SSCI, SociolAb, T02, W04, W07.
—BLDSC (5052.640000), CIS, IE, Ingenta, INIST. **CCC.**
Published by: University of Toronto Press, Journals Division, 5201 Dufferin St, Toronto, ON M3H 5T8, Canada. TEL 416-667-7810, FAX 416-667-7881, journals@utpress.utoronto.ca. Ed. Tom Radko. R&P Jessica Shulist TEL 416-667-7777 ext 7849. Adv. contact Audrey Greenwood TEL 416-667-7777 ext 7766. Circ: 319.

070.5 USA ISSN 0737-7436
JOURNAL OF THE PRINT WORLD, INC. Text in English. 1978. q. USD 35 domestic to individuals; USD 48 foreign to individuals; USD 15 domestic to non-profit organizations (effective 2001). adv. bk.rev. illus. 56 p./no. 6 cols./p.; back issues avail. **Document type:** *Newspaper.*
—IE.
Published by: Journal of the Print World, PO Box 978, Meredith, NH 03253-0978. TEL 603-279-6479, FAX 603-279-1337. Ed. Charles Stuart Lane. Adv. contact Sophia Lane. Circ: 10,000.

028 NLD ISSN 2210-8416
K V B JAAROVERZICHT. Text in Dutch. 2006. a.
Formerly (until 2010): Jaaroverzicht Boekenvak (1874-5539)
Published by: Koninklijke Vereniging van het Boekenvak/Royal Association for the Booktrade, Postbus 15007, Amsterdam, 1001 MA, Netherlands. TEL 31-20-6240212, FAX 31-20-6208871, info@kvb.nl, http://www.kvb.nl.

KAGAN'S MEDIA TRENDS. *see* COMMUNICATIONS—Television And Cable

015 CHE ISSN 1661-9951
KARGER CATALOGUE. Text in English, German. a. **Document type:** *Catalog, Trade.*
Published by: S. Karger AG, Allschwilerstr 10, Basel, 4055, Switzerland. TEL 41-61-3061111, FAX 41-61-3061234, karger@karger.ch, http://www.karger.ch.

070.5 CHN ISSN 1005-0590
KEJI YU CHUBAN/SCIENCE TECHNOLOGY AND PUBLICATION. Text in Chinese. 1982. bi-m. USD 68.40 (effective 2009). **Document type:** *Journal, Academic/Scholarly.*
Formerly (until 1992): Keji Chuban/Science and Technology Publishing (1001-5272)
Related titles: Online - full text ed.
—East View.
Published by: Qinghua Daxue Chubanshe/Tsinghua University Press, Yan Dasha A, Beijing, 100084, China. TEL 86-10-62794475, FAX 86-10-62794474, http://www.tup.tsinghua.edu.cn/.

070.5 GBR
KEY NOTE MARKET ASSESSMENT. BOOK RETAILING ON THE INTERNET. Variant title: Book Retailing on the Internet Market Assessment. Text in English. 2001. irreg., latest 2007. GBP 880 per issue (effective 2010). back issues avail. **Document type:** *Report, Trade.* **Description:** Provides an overview of the book retailing on the internet, including industry structure, market size and trends, developments, prospects, and major company profiles.
Published by: Key Note Ltd. (Subsidiary of: Bonnier Business Information), Field House, 72 Oldfield Rd, Hampton, Mddx TW12 2HQ, United Kingdom. TEL 44-20-84818750, FAX 44-20-87830049, sales@keynote.co.uk.

KEY NOTE MARKET ASSESSMENT. CHILDREN'S PUBLISHING. *see* BUSINESS AND ECONOMICS—Marketing And Purchasing

KEY NOTE MARKET ASSESSMENT. LIFESTYLE MAGAZINES. *see* BUSINESS AND ECONOMICS—Production Of Goods And Services

070.5 338 GBR
KEY NOTE MARKET REPORT: BOOK PUBLISHING. Variant title: Book Publishing Market Report. Text in English. 19??. irreg., latest 2009, Oct. GBP 460 per issue (effective 2010). **Document type:** *Report, Trade.* **Description:** Provides an overview of a specific UK market segment and includes executive summary, market definition, market size, industry background, competitor analysis, current issues, forecasts, company profiles, and more.
Formerly (until 1995): Key Note Report: Book Publishing (0268-4446)
Related titles: CD-ROM ed.; Online - full text ed.
Published by: Key Note Ltd. (Subsidiary of: Bonnier Business Information), Harlequin House, 5th Fl, 7 High St, Teddington, Richmond upon Thames, TW11 8EE, United Kingdom. TEL 44-845-5040452, FAX 44-845-5040453, info@keynote.co.uk.

381.45002 GBR ISSN 1365-8204
KEY NOTE MARKET REPORT: BOOKSELLING. Variant title: Bookselling Market Report. Text in English. 198?. irreg., latest 2009, Feb. GBP 460 per issue (effective 2010). **Document type:** *Report, Trade.* **Description:** Provides an overview of a specific UK market segment and includes executive summary, market definition, market size, industry background, competitor analysis, current issues, forecasts, company profiles, and more.
Formerly (until 1996): Key Note Report: Bookselling (0957-7882)
Related titles: CD-ROM ed.; Online - full text ed.
Published by: Key Note Ltd. (Subsidiary of: Bonnier Business Information), Harlequin House, 5th Fl, 7 High St, Teddington, Richmond upon Thames, TW11 8EE, United Kingdom. TEL 44-845-5040452, FAX 44-845-5040453, info@keynote.co.uk.

KEY NOTE MARKET REPORT: CONSUMER MAGAZINES. *see* BUSINESS AND ECONOMICS—Production Of Goods And Services

KEY NOTE MARKET REPORT: NEWSPAPERS. *see* JOURNALISM

070.5 FIN ISSN 0047-343X
Z374.7
KIRJAKAUPPALEHTI. Text in Finnish. 1897. 7/yr. EUR 150 (effective 2004). bk.rev. illus. index. **Document type:** *Newspaper, Trade.* **Description:** Aims to inform, activate and educate booksellers and stationers as well as their personnel.
Formerly: Suomen Kirjakauppalehti - Finsk Bokhandelstidning
Indexed: RASB.
Published by: Kirjamedia Oy, Eerikinkatu 15-17D, Helsinki, 00100, Finland. TEL 358-9-6859910, FAX 358-9-68599119, http://www.kirjakauppaliitto.fi. Ed. Annike Aasvik. Circ: 2,000.

070.5 NOR ISSN 1503-0245
KLARTEKST. Text in Norwegian. 2000. 3/yr. back issues avail. **Document type:** *Magazine, Consumer.*
Related titles: Online - full text ed.: ISSN 1503-8343.
Published by: Universitetsforlaget AS/Scandinavian University Press (Subsidiary of: Aschehoug & Co.), Sehesteds Gate 3, P O Box 508, Sentrum, Oslo, 0105, Norway. TEL 47-24-147500, FAX 47-24-147501, post@universitetsforlaget.no.

070.5 RUS ISSN 0134-837X
Z8.R9
KNIGA ISSLEDOVANIYA. Text in Russian. 1959. 2/yr. bibl. cum.index every 2 yrs.
Indexed: IBR, IBZ.
Published by: Izdatel'stvo Kniga, Ul Gor'kogo 50, Moscow, 125047, Russian Federation.

070.5 RUS
KNIGA V PROSTRANSTVE KUL'TURY. Text in Russian. 2005. a. RUR 310 per issue domestic (effective 2010). **Document type:** *Journal, Trade.*
Related titles: ◆ Supplement to: Bibliotekovedenie. ISSN 0869-608X.
Published by: (Rossiiskaya Gosudarstvennaya Biblioteka/Russian State Library), Idatel'stvo Rossiiskoi Gosudarstvennoi Biblioteki Pashkov Dom/Pashkov Dom, Russian State Library Publishing House, Vozdizhenka 3/5, Moscow, 101000, Russian Federation. TEL 7-495-6955953, FAX 7-495-6955953, pashkov_dom@rsl.ru, http://www.rsl.ru/pub.asp. Circ: 500 (paid and controlled).

KNIGOIZDAVANE I PECHAT. *see* STATISTICS

070.5 CZE ISSN 1213-8231
KNIHOVNICKY ZPRAVODAJ VYSOCINA. Text in Czech. 2000. q. free. **Document type:** *Magazine, Trade.*
Media: Online - full content.
Published by: Krajska Knihovna Vysociny, Havlickovo namesti 87, Havlickuv Brod, 58002, Czech Republic. reditel@knihzdar.cz. Ed. Libuse Foberova. **Co-publisher:** Knihovna Mateje Josefa Sychry.

002 027 CZE ISSN 1210-8510
Z795.A1
KNIHY A DEJINY/BOOKS AND HISTORY. Text in Czech. 1994. s-a. back issues avail. **Document type:** *Journal, Academic/Scholarly.* **Description:** Covers the history of books, printing, and libraries in Bohemia to the middle of the twentieth century.
Related titles: Online - full text ed.
Published by: Akademie Ved Ceske Republiky, Knihovna, Narodni 3, Prague 1, 11522, Czech Republic. TEL 42-2-21403208, FAX 42-2-24240611, infoknav@lib.cas.cz. Ed. Anezka Badurova.

070.5 RUS ISSN 0132-1897
KNIZHNAYA TORGOVLYA. NAUCHNO-TEKHNICHESKII INFORMATSIONNYI SBORNIK. Text in Russian. 1992. bi-m. **Document type:** *Bibliography.*
Indexed: RASB.
Published by: Rossiiskaya Knizhnaya Palata/Book Chamber International, Ostozhenka 4, Moscow, 119034, Russian Federation. TEL 7-095-2911278, FAX 7-095-2919630, bookch@postman.ru, http://www.bookchamber.ru.

070.5 RUS ISSN 0869-6039
Z372
KNIZHNOE DELO. Text in Russian. 1992. bi-m. USD 72 foreign (effective 2003). adv. **Description:** News and trends of interest to publishers, booksellers and librarians.
Formerly: Knizhnoe Delo v Rossii
Indexed: RASB.
—East View.
Published by: Izdatel'stvo Progress, Ul Entuziastov 15, k 48, Moscow, 111024, Russian Federation. TEL 7-095-2731438. Ed. S S Nosov. Circ: 10,000. **Dist. by:** M K - Periodica, ul Gilyarovskogo 39, Moscow 129110, Russian Federation. TEL 7-095-2845008, FAX 7-095-2813798, info@periodicals.ru, http://www.mkniga.ru; East View Information Services, 10601 Wayzata Blvd, Minneapolis, MN 55305. TEL 952-252-1201, 800-477-1005, FAX 952-252-1202, info@eastview.com, http://www.eastview.com.

028.1 RUS ISSN 0023-2378
Z372
KNIZHNOE OBOZRENIE; review of newly published books. Text in Russian. 1966. w. USD 132 foreign (effective 2003).
Related titles: Microfiche ed.: (from EVP); Microfilm ed.: (from EVP).
Indexed: CDSP, RASB.
Published by: Ministerstvo Pechati i Informatsii Rossii, Sushchevskii Val ul 64, Moscow, 129272, Russian Federation. TEL 7-095-2816266, FAX 7-095-2816266. Ed. E S Averin. **Dist. by:** M K - Periodica, ul Gilyarovskogo 39, Moscow 129110, Russian Federation. TEL 7-095-2845008, FAX 7-095-2813798, info@periodicals.ru, http://www.mkniga.ru; East View Information Services, 10601 Wayzata Blvd, Minneapolis, MN 55305. TEL 952-252-1201, 800-477-1005, FAX 952-252-1202, info@eastview.com, http://www.eastview.com.

381.45002 RUS
KNIZHNYI BIZNES. Text in Russian. 1993. m. USD 188 foreign (effective 2005). bibl.; mkt.; stat.; tr.mk. 80 p./no.; reprints avail. **Document type:** *Magazine, Trade.* **Description:** Includes book market reports, book sale statistics, and publishing house ratings.
Published by: Informatsionno-Marketingovyi Tsentr Al'vis, B Ordynka 43, Moscow, 109017, Russian Federation. TEL 7-095-2317654, FAX 7-095-9529393. Ed. V M Drabkin TEL 7-095-9517213. Circ: 5,000. **Dist. by:** East View Information Services, 10601 Wayzata Blvd, Minneapolis, MN 55305. TEL 952-252-1201, 800-477-1005, FAX 952-252-1202, info@eastview.com, http://www.eastview.com.

070.5 SVK ISSN 1210-1982
Z1007
KNIZNA REVUE. Text in Slovak. 1991. bi-w. **Document type:** *Magazine, Trade.*
Related titles: Online - full content ed.: ISSN 1336-247X. 2002.
Published by: Redakcia Knizna Revue, Namestie SNP c12, Bratislava, 81224, Slovakia. TEL 421-7-59214185, FAX 421-7-52964563, krevue@litcentrum.sk.

070.5 SVK ISSN 1335-7026
KNIZNICA; zbornik o problemach a dejinach kniznej kultury. Text in Slovak; Summaries in English, German. 1974. m. EUR 32 (effective 2009). adv. **Document type:** *Journal, Trade.*
Related titles: Online - full text ed.: ISSN 1336-0965.
Indexed: L04, L13, LISTA, RASB.
Published by: Slovenska Narodna Kniznica, Martin, Nam J C Hronskeho 1, Martin, 03601, Slovakia. redakcia@snk.sk. Ed. Miroslava Domova. **Dist. by:** Slovart G.T.G. s.r.o., Krupinska 4, PO Box 152, Bratislava 85299, Slovakia. TEL 421-2-63839472, FAX 421-2-63839485, info@slovart-gtg.sk, http://www.slovart-gtg.sk.

028 SRB ISSN 0023-2416
KNJIZHEVNA NOVINE; list za knjizevnost i drushtvena pitania. Text in Serbo-Croatian. 1949. m. adv. bk.rev.; dance rev.; film rev.; music rev.; play rev. illus.; bibl. 24 p./no.; back issues avail. **Document type:** *Magazine, Consumer.*
Related titles: Online - full text ed.
Indexed: MLA, MLA-IB.
Published by: Udruzhen'e Knizhevnika Srbije/Association of Writers of Serbia, Frantsuska 7, Belgrade, 11000. TEL 381-11-2626081, FAX 381-11-2626278, uks@verat.net. adv.: page USD 250; 324 x 458. Circ: 10,000 (paid).

070.5 IND
KNOWLEDGESPEAK. Text in English. 2005. d. free (effective 2011). back issues avail. **Document type:** *Newsletter, Trade.* **Description:** Reports on all current and relevant developments within the STM (Scientific, Technical, Medical) publishing industry.
Media: E-mail. **Related titles:** Online - full text ed.
Published by: Scope e-Knowledge Center Pvt Ltd, II Fl, Temple Towers, Nandanam, 672 Anna Salai, Chennai, 600 035, India. TEL 91-44-24314201, FAX 91-44-24314206, scope@scopeknowledge.com, http://www.scopeknowledge.com. Ed. Sithara Chandran.

070.5 020 CAN ISSN 1499-1209
KNOWMAP; the knowledge management, auditing and mapping magazine. Text in English. m. USD 66; USD 10 newsstand/cover (effective 2003). **Document type:** *Magazine, Trade.*
Media: Online - full text.
Published by: Stanford Solutions Inc., 300-8120 Beddington Boulevard NW, Ste 325, Calgary, AB T3K 2A8, Canada. TEL 403-274-0564, editor@knowmap.com, http://www.knowmap.com.

070.5 011 UKR ISSN 2076-9326
Z8.U4
KNYZHKOVA PALATA UKRAINY. VISNYK. Variant title: Visnyk Knyzhkovoi Palaty. Text in Ukrainian. 1996. m. USD 321 foreign (effective 2010). **Document type:** *Journal, Academic/Scholarly.* **Description:** Contains information on science of bibliography, publishing, and statistical data on printed editions of Ukraine.
Related titles: Online - full text ed.: ISSN 2076-9555.
Published by: Knyzhkova Palata Ukrainy imeni Ivana Fedorova/Ivan Fedorov Book Chamber of Ukraine, Pr Gagarina 27, Kyiv, 02094, Ukraine. TEL 380-44-5520134, ukrbook@ukr.net, http://www.ukrbook.net. Ed. Mykola Senchenko. **Dist. by:** East View Information Services, 10601 Wayzata Blvd, Minneapolis, MN 55305. TEL 952-252-1201, 800-477-1005, FAX 952-252-1202, info@eastview.com, http://www.eastview.com.

070.5 KOR
KOREAN PUBLISHERS ASSOCIATION. DIRECTORY OF MEMBERS. Text in English. a. **Document type:** *Directory, Trade.* **Description:** Contains facts and figures of the Korean publishing industry, including listings of: Association members, copyright agencies, book importers and exporters, and publishing-related organizations.
Published by: Korean Publishers Association/Daehan Chulpan Munhwa Hyeobhoe, 105-2, Sagan-dong, Jongno-gu, Seoul, 110-190, Korea, S. TEL 82-2-7352701, FAX 82-2-7385414, webmaster@kpa21.or.kr, http://www.kpa21.or.kr/main/index.htm.

070.5 BEL
KREATIF JAARBOOK. Text in Flemish. a. **Description:** Covers free-lancing in Belgium for copywriters, artists, graphic designers, photographers and illustrators.
Published by: C E D Samsom (Subsidiary of: Wolters Samsom Belgie n.v.), Kouterveld 14, Diegem, 1831, Belgium. TEL 32-2-7231111.

KRESS REPORT. *see* COMMUNICATIONS

KRITIKA (BLOOMINGTON); explorations in Russian and Eurasian history. *see* HISTORY—History Of Europe

028.1 809 POL ISSN 1425-4808
KSIAZKI. Text in Polish. 1992. m.
Formerly (until 1995): Gazeta o Ksiazkach (1232-1699)
Related titles: ◆ Supplement to: Gazeta Wyborcza. ISSN 0860-908X.
Published by: Agora S.A., ul Czerska 8/10, Warsaw, 00732, Poland. TEL 48-22-6994301, FAX 48-22-6994603, http://www.agora.pl.

070.5 NLD ISSN 1574-3225
L I R A BULLETIN. (Literaire Rechten Auteurs) Text in Dutch. 2000. 3/yr.
Published by: Stichting LIRA, Postbus 3060, Hoofddorp, 2130 KB, Netherlands. TEL 31-23-7997807, FAX 31-23-7997700, lira@cedar.nl, http://www.lira.nl. Ed. Kees Holierhoek. Circ: 16,000.

015 FRA ISSN 1159-0947
L M A. PUBLICATIONS. (Laboratoire de Mecanique et d'Acoustique) Text in French. 194?. irreg. **Document type:** *Directory, Trade.*
Formerly (until 1990): Laboratoire de Mecanique et d'Acoustique. Note (0750-7356)
Indexed: RILM.
—INIST.

Published by: Centre National de la Recherche Scientifique, Campus Gerard-Megie, 3 Rue Michel-Ange, Paris, 75794, France. TEL 33-1-44964000, FAX 33-1-44965390, cnrseditions@cnrseditions.fr, http://www.cnrs.fr.

LAMBDA BOOK REPORT; a review of contemporary gay and lesbian literature. *see* HOMOSEXUALITY

070.5 USA
THE LATEST FROM M I N. (Media Industry Newsletter) Text in English. m. **Document type:** *Newsletter, Trade.* **Description:** Focuses on the top players and magazines in the media industry.
Media: E-mail.
Published by: Access Intelligence, LLC (Subsidiary of: Veronis, Suhler & Associates Inc.), 4 Choke Cherry Rd, 2nd Fl, Rockville, MD 20850. TEL 301-354-2000, clientservices@accessintel.com, http://www.accessintel.com. Adv. contact Amy Urban.

070.5 GBR ISSN 0953-1513
Z286.S37 CODEN: LEPUFJ
➤ **LEARNED PUBLISHING.** Text in English. 1977. q. GBP 100 combined subscription domestic to individuals (print & online eds.); EUR 145 combined subscription in Europe to individuals (print & online eds.); USD 210 combined subscription elsewhere to individuals (print & online eds.); USD 185 combined subscription domestic to institutions (print & online eds.); USD 275 combined subscription in Europe to institutions (print & online eds.); USD 365 combined subscription elsewhere to institutions (print & online eds.) (effective 2010). adv. bk.rev.; software rev. illus.; abstr. a.index. back issues avail.; reprints avail. **Document type:** *Journal, Academic/Scholarly.* **Description:** Provides the international scholarly community with information on academic publishing.
Formerly (until 1988): A L P S P Bulletin (0260-9428)
Related titles: Online - full text ed.: ISSN 1741-4857. GBP 78 domestic to individuals; EUR 115 in Europe to individuals; USD 150 elsewhere to individuals; GBP 145 domestic to institutions; EUR 210 in Europe to institutions; USD 280 elsewhere to institutions (effective 2010) (from IngentaConnect).
indexed: A20, A22, ASCA, C10, CA, CurCont, FR, ISTA, Inspec, L04, LISTA, P30, SCOPUS, SSCI, T02, W07.
—BLDSC (5179.325650), AskIEEE, IE, Infotrieve, Ingenta, INIST. **CCC.**
Published by: Association of Learned and Professional Society Publishers, 1-3 Ship St, Shoreham-by-Sea, West Sussex BN43 5DH, United Kingdom. Ed. Sally Morris TEL 44-1903-871286. Pub. Nick Evans TEL 44-20-87892394. adv.: B&W page GBP 450; 280 x 210. **Subscr. to:** Turpin Distribution Services Ltd., Pegasus Dr, Stratton Business Park, Biggleswade, Bedfordshire SG18 8QB, United Kingdom. TEL 44-1767-604800, FAX 44-1767-601640, custserv@turpin-distribution.com, http://www.turpin-distribution.com/.

028.1 USA ISSN 0732-8001
Z1039.M5
LECTOR (MOUNTAIN VIEW); the Hispanic book review online journal. Text in English. 1982. s-a. bk.rev. **Document type:** *Journal, Academic/Scholarly.* **Description:** Features English language reviews and information about Spanish language books published in Spain, Latin America and the US which are of interest to Hispanics in America.
Indexed: ChPerI, Chicano, MLA-IB.
Published by: Floricanto Press, 650 Castro St, Ste 120-331, Mountain View, CA 94041. TEL 415-552-1879, FAX 702-995-1410, info@floricantopress.com.

070.5 USA
LEE HOWARD NEWSLETTER; for small publishers and mail order book dealers. Text in English. 1979. q. adv. **Document type:** *Newsletter, Trade.* **Description:** Focuses on the self-publishing book market and mail-order book selling.
Formerly: Book Business Mart
Published by: Selective Books, Inc., PO Box 1140, Clearwater, FL 34617. Ed., Pub., R&P, Adv. contact Lee Howard. Circ: 5,500 (controlled).

070.5083 BEL
DE LEESWELP. Text in Dutch. 1959. 9/yr. EUR 42 (effective 2009). bk.rev. bibl.; illus. index.
Former titles (until 2004): Leesidee Jeugdliteratuur (1370-5962); (until 1995): Jeugdboekengids (0021-6054)
Published by: Vlaams Bibliografisch, Documentair en Dienstverlenend Centrum, Frankrijkiel 53-55, Antwerpen, 2000, Belgium. TEL 32-3-2261399, FAX 32-3-2326616, vlabin@bibliotheek.be, http://www.vlabinvbc.be. Ed. Jen de Groeve.

070.5 DEU ISSN 0940-1954
Z4
LEIPZIGER JAHRBUCH ZUR BUCHGESCHICHTE. Text in English, French, German. 1991. a. EUR 59 (effective 2011). adv. bk.rev. back issues avail. **Document type:** *Journal, Academic/Scholarly.*
Indexed: DIP, IBR, IBZ, MLA-IB.
Published by: Harrassowitz Verlag, Kreuzberger Ring 7b-d, Wiesbaden, 65205, Germany. TEL 49-611-5300, FAX 49-611-530560, verlag@harrassowitz.de, http://www.harrassowitz.de. Circ: 400 (paid).

LIBER; revista pentru bibliotecile pedagogice si scolare. *see* EDUCATION

002.075 CHE ISSN 0024-2152
Z990
LIBRARIUM. Text in English, French, German, Italian. 1958. 3/yr. CHF 150 membership (effective 2001). adv. bk.rev. illus. index. 72 p./no.; back issues avail. **Document type:** *Bulletin, Trade.* **Description:** Covers all aspects of collecting books, graphic art and autographs.
Indexed: DIP, IBR, IBZ, MLA, MLA-IB, RILM.
Published by: Schweizerische Bibliophilen-Gesellschaft, Fondation Martin Bodmer, 19-21 route du Guignard, Cologny-Geneva, CH-1223, Switzerland. TEL 41-22-7074433, FAX 41-22-7074430. Ed. Martin Bircher. adv.: page CHF 700. Circ: 750.

LIBRARY AND BOOK TRADE ALMANAC (YEAR); facts, figures, and reports. *see* LIBRARY AND INFORMATION SCIENCES

381.45002 USA ISSN 0024-2217
THE LIBRARY BOOKSELLER; books wanted by college and university libraries. Text in English. 1945. m. USD 50; USD 60 foreign (effective 1997). adv. **Document type:** *Journal, Trade.*
Published by: Danna D'Esopo Jackson, Ed. & Pub., PO Box 1818, Bloomington, IN 47402-1818. TEL 812-332-4440, FAX 812-332-2999. R&P, Adv. contact Danna D'Esopo Jackson. Circ: 150.

070.5 NLD ISSN 1874-4834
➤ **LIBRARY OF THE WRITTEN WORD.** Text in English. 2007. irreg., latest vol.7, 2008. price varies. **Document type:** *Monographic series, Academic/Scholarly.* **Description:** Covers the history of books, magazines and newspapers.
Related titles: Online - full text ed.: ISSN 1874-4842.
Indexed: IZBG.
Published by: Brill, PO Box 9000, Leiden, 2300 PA, Netherlands. TEL 31-71-5353500, FAX 31-71-5317532, cs@brill.nl.

028.1 ITA ISSN 0024-2683
Z2345
LIBRI E RIVISTE D'ITALIA. Text in Italian. 1950. bi-m. bk.rev. bibl. index. **Document type:** *Directory, Bibliography.*
Formerly (until 1958): Libri e Riviste (1122-6986)
Related titles: French ed.: Livres et Revues d'Italie. ISSN 1120-0863. EUR 26 domestic; EUR 44 foreign (effective 2004); English ed.: Italian Books and Periodicals. ISSN 0021-2881. 1958. EUR 26 domestic; EUR 44 foreign (effective 2004); Spanish ed.: Libros y Revistas de Italia. ISSN 1120-5490. EUR 22 domestic; EUR 44 foreign (effective 2004); German ed.: Bucher und Zeitschriften Italiens. ISSN 1120-5458. EUR 22 domestic; EUR 44 foreign (effective 2004).
Indexed: IBR, IBZ, MLA, MLA-IB, RASB.
Published by: (Italy. Ministero per i Beni e le Attivita Culturali), Istituto Poligrafico e Zecca dello Stato, Piazza Verdi 10, Rome, 00198, Italy. TEL 39-06-85082147, editoriale@ipzs.it, http://www.ipzs.it. Ed. Giuliano Vigini.

028.5 ITA ISSN 1120-4095
Z1037.4
LIBRI PER BAMBINI E RAGAZZI. Abbreviated title: Li B e R. Text in Italian. 1988. q. adv. bk.rev.; film rev.; tel.rev.; play rev.; Website rev. abstr.; bibl.; illus.; stat. index. 1121 p./no.; back issues avail. **Document type:** *Bulletin, Bibliography.* **Description:** Documents all the current Italian production in the field of children's books. Includes articles, comments, and reviews.
Related titles: CD-ROM ed.; Online - full text ed.; ◆ Supplement(s): Quaderni di Li B e R. ISSN 1121-3965.
Indexed: ChLitAb, IBR, IBZ.
Published by: Idest, Via Ombrone 1, Campi Bisenzio, FI 50013, Italy. TEL 39-055-8966577, FAX 39-055-8953344, liberweb@idest.net, http://www.idest.net. Circ: 3,000.

090 ITA
LIBRI RARI; collezione di ristampe con nuovi apparati. Text in Italian. 1977. irreg., latest 1997. price varies. **Document type:** *Monographic series, Academic/Scholarly.*
Published by: Edizioni Il Polifilo, Via Borgonuovo, 2, Milan, MI 20121, Italy. http://www.ilpolifilo.it.

381.45002 MEX ISSN 0186-2243
Z497
LIBROS DE MEXICO. Text in Spanish. 1985. q. USD 40 in the Americas; USD 50 elsewhere. adv. bibl.; illus. reprints avail. **Document type:** *Bibliography.* **Description:** Covers trade and industry in Mexico, as well as its history.
Indexed: C01, DIP, IBR, IBZ, RASB.
Published by: Camara Nacional de la Industria Editorial Mexicana, Holanda 13, Col. San Diego Churubusco, Coyoacan, DF 04120, Mexico. TEL 688-7122, FAX 604-3147, ciecprom@inetcorp.net.mx, http://www.libromex.com.mx. Ed., Adv. contact Federico Krafft Vera. Circ: 5,000.

070 GBR
LIBSITE NEWSLETTER. Text in English. 2004 (Sept.). q. free (effective 2009). back issues avail. **Document type:** *Newsletter, Trade.* **Description:** Brings you updates on initiatives at T&F, plus news on topical issues. Regular features will include: pricing options, new journals, bibliographic changes, administrator user guide and usage statistics.
Media: Online - full text.
Published by: Taylor & Francis Ltd. (Subsidiary of: Taylor & Francis Group), 4 Park Sq, Milton Park, Abingdon, Oxfordshire OX14 4RN, United Kingdom. TEL 44-20-70176000, FAX 44-20-70176336, subscriptions@tandf.co.uk, http://www.taylorandfrancis.com.

LINDEY ON ENTERTAINMENT, PUBLISHING AND THE ARTS. *see* LAW

028.1 DEU ISSN 0179-7417
LISTEN; Zeitschrift fuer Leserinnen und Leser. Text in German. 1985. irreg. adv. bk.rev. back issues avail. **Document type:** *Bibliography.*
Related titles: Online - full text ed.
Published by: Axel Dielmann Verlag, Schweizer Str 21, Frankfurt am Main, 60594, Germany. TEL 49-69-94359000, FAX 49-69-94359002, neugier@dielmann-verlag.de. Circ: 6,000.

070.5 USA ISSN 0000-1155
PN161 CODEN: LTYMA4
LITERARY MARKET PLACE; the directory of the American book publishing industry. Abbreviated title: L M P. Text in English. 1973. a. USD 339 (effective 2011). index. **Document type:** *Directory, Trade.* **Description:** Provides an insider's guide to the U.S. book publishing industry, covering various aspects of the business.
Formerly (until 1988): Literary Market Place with Names and Numbers (0161-2905); Which was formed by the merger of (1940-1973): Literary Market Place (0161-2891); (19??-1973): Names and Numbers (0075-9899); Which was formerly (until 1961): Book Industry Register (0000-1171)
Related titles: CD-ROM ed.; Magnetic Tape ed.; ◆ Online - full text ed.: LiteraryMarketPlace.com.
—BLDSC (5276.650000), CASDDS. **CCC.**
Published by: Information Today, Inc., 143 Old Marlton Pike, Medford, NJ 08055. TEL 609-654-6266, 800-300-9868, FAX 609-654-4309, custserv@infotoday.com, http://www.infotoday.com. Ed. Karen Hallard.

070.5 USA
LITERARYMARKETPLACE.COM; the world-wide resource for the book publishing industry. Text in English. 1998. w. USD 399 (effective 2010). **Document type:** *Directory, Trade.* **Description:** Featuring listings on more than 30,000 companies, books, periodicals, awards, courses or events in the book trade.
Supersedes (in 2000): Global L M P
Media: Online - full text. **Related titles:** CD-ROM ed.; Magnetic Tape ed.; ◆ Print ed.: International Literary Market Place. ISSN 0074-6827; ◆ Literary Market Place. ISSN 0000-1155.

Published by: Information Today, Inc., 143 Old Marlton Pike, Medford, NJ 08055. TEL 609-654-6266, 800-300-9868, FAX 609-654-4309, custserv@infotoday.com, http://www.infotoday.com.

070.5 RUS
LITERATURNYI BAZAR. Text in Russian. 1994. s-a. free. adv. back issues avail. **Document type:** *Newspaper, Consumer.* **Description:** Covers book trading, editing and designing.
Indexed: RASB.
Published by: Press - Invest Ltd., Kostyanskii per 13, Moscow, 103811, Russian Federation. TEL 7-095-2088257, FAX 7-095-2086319. Adv. contact Yana Gretsova. page USD 2,000; trim 250 x 375. Circ: 30,000. **Dist. by:** East View Information Services, 10601 Wayzata Blvd, Minneapolis, MN 55305. TEL 952-252-1201, 800-477-1005, FAX 952-252-1202, info@eastview.com, http://www.eastview.com.

LITERATUUR ZONDER LEEFTIJD; vaktijdschrift over jeugdliteratuur. *see* LITERATURE

017.8 PRT
LIVRARIA FIGUEIRINHAS CATALOGO. Text in Portuguese. 1898. a. free.
Published by: Editora Figueirinhas Lda., Rua Almada, 47, Porto, 4000, Portugal. FAX 325907. Circ: 5,000.

002 BEL ISSN 0024-533X
Z990
LE LIVRE ET L'ESTAMPE. Text in French. 1954. s-a. EUR 50 in the European Union; EUR 55 elsewhere (effective 2000). adv. bk.rev. bibl. cum.index: 1954-1985. **Document type:** *Bulletin.*
Indexed: IBR, IBZ, P30.
Published by: Societe Royale des Bibliophiles et Iconophiles de Belgique, Bd de l'Empereur 4, Brussels, 1000, Belgium. Ed. A Grisay. Circ: 350.

070.50688 FRA ISSN 0294-0019
LIVRES DE FRANCE. Text in French. 1982. 11/yr. EUR 88 domestic; EUR 105 foreign (effective 2003). adv. bk.rev. bibl.; illus.; stat. **Document type:** *Trade.*
Formed by the 1982 merger of: Livres de France (Edition avec Prix Cession de Base) (0223-4831); Livres de France (Edition Destine a l'Etranger) (0223-484X); Livres de France (Edition sans Prix) (0223-4823); All of which supersede in part (1959-1979): Bulletin du Livre (0007-456X); (1972-1979): Bibliographie de la France. Biblio (0335-5675); Which was formed by the merger of (1933-1971): Biblio (Mensuel) (1147-6710); (1814-1971): Bibliographie de la France (0006-1344); Which was formerly: Bibliographie de l'Empire Francais (1147-6680); (until 1811): Journal General de l'Imprimerie et de la Libraire (1147-6672); (1797-1810): Journal Typographique et Bibliographique (1147-6664)
Published by: Electre, 35 rue Gregoire de Tours, Paris, 75279 Cedex 06, France. TEL 33-01-44412862, FAX 33-01-44412864, commercial@electre.com. Ed. Jean Marie Doublet. Circ: 7,000.

381.45002 FRA ISSN 0294-0027
Z2165
LES LIVRES DU MOIS. Text in French. 1979. m. **Document type:** *Trade.*
Formed by the 1982 merger of: Livres du Mois (Edition avec Prix Cession de Base) (0223-498X); Livres du Mois (Edition Destine a l'Etranger) (0223-5005); Livres du Mois (Edition sans Prix) (0223-4998)
Related titles: ◆ Supplement to: Livres Hebdo. ISSN 0294-0000.
Indexed: A22, RASB.
—IE, Infotrieve, INIST.
Published by: Electre, 35 rue Gregoire de Tours, Paris, 75279 Cedex 06, France. TEL 33-01-44412862, FAX 33-01-44412864.

002.074 FRA ISSN 1957-1410
LIVRES EN VIE. Text in French. 2007. q. EUR 22 (effective 2009). **Document type:** *Magazine, Consumer.*
Address: Les Bruyeres du Mont Crepin, Frenes, 61800, France. http://www.livresenvie.com.

LIVRES HEBDO. *see* PUBLISHING AND BOOK TRADE—Abstracting, Bibliographies, Statistics

015.469 PRT ISSN 0870-5259
Z2715
LIVROS DE PORTUGAL. Text in Portuguese. 1940. m. USD 50. adv. bk.rev. bibl. **Document type:** *Bibliography.* **Description:** Covers news about the world book trade, includes interviews with publishers and book sellers, and lists a bibliography of new books and other printed materials from the previous month.
Indexed: IBR, IBZ, MLA-IB, RASB.
Published by: Associacao Portuguesa de Editores e Livreiros, Avenida dos Estados Unidos da America, 97 6o Esq, Lisbon, 1700, Portugal. TEL 351-1-8435180, FAX 351-1-8489377. Circ: 1,500. **Subscr. to:** Dinalivro, Travessa do Convento de Jesus, 15 r-c, Lisbon 1200, Portugal.

002 NLD ISSN 0957-9656
Z284 CODEN: LGOSEL
LOGOS; forum of the world book community. Text in English. 1990. 5/yr. EUR 256, USD 360 to institutions; EUR 280, USD 392 combined subscription to institutions (print & online eds.) (effective 2012). bk.rev. illus. back issues avail.; reprints avail. **Document type:** *Journal, Academic/Scholarly.* **Description:** Aims to deal in depth with issues which unite, divide, excite and concern the world of books.
Related titles: Online - full text ed.: ISSN 1878-4712. EUR 233, USD 327 to institutions (effective 2012) (from IngentaConnect).
Indexed: A22, A26, B04, BRD, BrHumI, CA, DIP, E01, G05, G06, G07, G08, I05, IBR, IBZ, Inspec, L04, L07, L08, L13, LISTA, LibLit, PAIS, RGAb, SOPODA, SociolAb, T02, W03, W05.
—BLDSC (5292.404000), IE, Infotrieve, Ingenta, Linda Hall. **CCC.**
Published by: (LOGOS International Publishing Education Foundation USA, Charles Levine, Ed. USA), Brill, PO Box 9000, Leiden, 2300 PA, Netherlands. TEL 31-71-5353500, FAX 31-71-5317532, http://www.brill.nl. Circ: 309 (paid). **Subscr. to:** LOGOS, c/o Gordon Graham, 5 Beechwood Dr, Marlow, Bucks SL7 2DH, United Kingdom. **Dist. by:** Turpin Distribution Services Ltd., Pegasus Dr, Stratton Business Park, Biggleswade, Bedfordshire SG18 8QB, United Kingdom. TEL 44-1767-604800, FAX 44-1767-601640, custserv@turpin-distribution.com, http://www.turpin-distribution.com/.

028.1 USA
LOS ANGELES TIMES BOOK REVIEW. Text in English. w. bk.rev. index. **Document type:** *Newspaper.*
Related titles: Microform ed.: (from PQC).
Indexed: CBRI, ChPerI.

P

Published by: Los Angeles Times Newspapers, Inc. (Subsidiary of: Tribune Company), 202 W 1st St, Los Angeles, CA 90012. TEL 213-237-5000, FAX 213-237-7679.

070.5 CHE ISSN 1423-6664
M. Text in German, French. 1998. 20/yr. CHF 60; CHF 70 foreign (effective 2000). **Document type:** *Journal, Trade.* **Description:** Contains information for journalists, booksellers and other related industry workers within the Swiss media unions.
Formed by the merger of (1858-1998): Helvetische Typographia (1420-9578); (1972-1998): S J U News (1423-6648); (1899-1998): Senefelder (1423-6680); (1996-1998): A S B Info (1423-6656); Which was formerly: Buchhaendlerin
Published by: Comedia die Mediengewerkschaft Schweiz, Monbijoustr 33, Bern, 3011, Switzerland. TEL 41-31-3906611, FAX 41-31-3906691, sekretariat@comedia.ch, http://www.comedia.ch. Circ: 1,900.

070.5 GBR
THE M D B MAGAZINE DIRECTORY. Text in English. 1985. s-a. USD 46; USD 24 per issue (effective 2010). adv. illus.; mkt.; stat. back issues avail. **Document type:** *Directory, Trade.* **Description:** Lists magazines and periodicals available for retail sale in the U.K.
Published by: B R A D Group (Subsidiary of: Emap Media Ltd.), Greater London House, Hampstead Rd, London, NW1 7EJ, United Kingdom. TEL 44-20-77284315, sales@bradinsight.com. Adv. contact Robert Garner TEL 44-20-77284316.

070.5 USA ISSN 1537-8462
Z480.P4
M I N MAGAZINE. (Media Industry Newsletter) Text in English. 199?. a. (Nov.). free to qualified personnel (effective 2009). adv. back issues avail.; reprints avail. **Document type:** *Magazine, Trade.* **Description:** Covers the magazine community's publishers, agencies and clients.
Related titles: Online - full text ed.: USD 1,690; free to qualified personnel (effective 2009).
Indexed: B02, B15, B17, B18, G04, G08, I05.
Published by: Access Intelligence, LLC (Subsidiary of: Veronis, Suhler & Associates Inc.), 4 Choke Cherry Rd, 2nd Fl, Rockville, MD 20850. TEL 301-354-2000, 800-777-5006, FAX 301-340-3819, clientservices@accessintel.com, http://www.accessintel.com. Ed. Mike Hammer. Pub., Adv. contact Debbie Vodenos TEL 301-354-1695. page USD 8,500; trim 7.875 x 10.75.

070.5 USA ISSN 1520-9830
M I N'S B2B. (Media Industry Newsletter) Text in English. 1998. w. includes with subscr. to Media Industry Newsletter. adv. **Document type:** *Newsletter, Trade.* **Description:** Covers news, analysis and strategies on business-to-business publishing.
Incorporates in part (in 2002): m i n's New Media Report
Media: E-mail. **Related titles:** Online - full text ed.
Indexed: A15, ABIn, B01, B07, P48, P51, PQC.
—CCC.
Published by: Access Intelligence, LLC (Subsidiary of: Veronis, Suhler & Associates Inc.), 4 Choke Cherry Rd, 2nd Fl, Rockville, MD 20850. TEL 301-354-2000, 800-777-5006, FAX 301-340-3819, clientservices@accessintel.com, http://www.accessintel.com. Ed. Steven Cohn TEL 212-621-4874.

M P A: SALES EDGE. *see* ADVERTISING AND PUBLIC RELATIONS

381.45002 USA
MAGA SCENE. Text in English. m. **Document type:** *Newsletter.* **Description:** Provides features on magazine merchandising, tips on improving the profitability of magazine programs, and industry trends.
Published by: Ingram Periodicals Inc., 1240 Heil Quaker Blvd, Box 7000, La Vergne, TN 37086.

070.5 USA
THE MAGAZINE; everything you need to know to make it in the magazine business. Text in English. 19??. irreg., latest vol.3. **Document type:** *Magazine, Trade.*
Published by: Cowles Business Media (Subsidiary of: Cowles Media Company), 11 River Bend Dr, S., PO Box 4949, Stamford, CT 06907. paul_mcdougall@cowlesbiz.com.

002 805 FRA ISSN 1955-592X
LE MAGAZINE DES LIVRES. Text in French. 2006. bi-m. EUR 47 for 2 yrs. (effective 2010). back issues avail. **Document type:** *Magazine, Consumer.*
Published by: Lafont Presse, 53 Rue du Chemin Vert, Boulogne-Billancourt, 92100, France. TEL 33-1-46102121, FAX 33-1-45792211.

070.5 USA ISSN 1074-7419
HF6105.U5
MAGAZINE DIMENSIONS. Abbreviated title: Mag.Dmens. Text in English. 1994. a. USD 535 per issue; USD 660 combined subscription per issue (effective 2011). adv. **Document type:** *Report, Trade.* **Description:** It covers ad size and the use of color,demographic,degree of ad clutter in issue,position in issue,product class.
Related titles: Online - full text ed.: USD 485 per issue (effective 2011).
Published by: Media Dynamics, Inc., 363 Centre St, Nutley, NJ 07110. TEL 973-542-8188, FAX 973-542-8190, info@mediadynamicsinc.com.

070.5 USA
MAGAZINE MERCHANDISING. Text in English. m. USD 300 (effective 2005).
Published by: Magazine Merchandising, Llc., 39-40 Broadway, Fair Lawn, NJ 07410. TEL 201-703-9808, FAX 201-703-9878, mkessler@magazinemerchandising.com, http://www.magazinemerchandising.com. Pub. Mike Kessler. Circ: 2,240.

070.5 USA
MAGAZINE PUBLISHERS ASSOCIATION. NEWSLETTER OF CIRCULATION. Text in English. q. **Document type:** *Newsletter.*
Published by: Magazine Publishers of America, 919 Third Ave, New York, NY 10022. TEL 212-872-3700.

070.5 USA
MAGAZINE PUBLISHERS OF AMERICA. Text in English. bi-m. **Document type:** *Newsletter.*
Address: 919 Third Ave, New York, NY 10022. TEL 212-872-3700.

070.5 USA
THE MAGAZINE RETAIL SALES EXPERIENCE. (Consists of 2 s-a. eds.: Performance Bulletins & Publisher's Notebooks) Text in English. 1997. q. USD 995 (effective 2003). **Document type:** *Journal, Trade.* **Description:** Contains critical analysis of trends in both magazine single copy sales and the structure of the mass market magazine distribution channel.
Published by: Harrington Associates, 12 Main St, Ste B, Norwalk, CT 06851. TEL 203-838-1701, FAX 203-838-1861, jharrington@nscopy.com.

381.45002 GBR ISSN 1359-1312
MAGAZINE WORLD; international review of changing markets and marketplaces. Text in English. 1994. q. free to members (effective 2009). adv. abstr.; tr.lit.; charts; mkt.; stat. back issues avail. **Document type:** *Magazine, Trade.* **Description:** Contains global news, international print and digital launches, regional focus, member profile, national association profile and suppliers directory.
Related titles: Online - full text ed.: free (effective 2009).
—CCC.
Published by: International Federation of the Periodical Press/Federation Internationale de la Presse Periodique, Queens House, 55-56 Lincoln's Inn Fields, London, WC2A 3LJ, United Kingdom. TEL 44-20-74044169, FAX 44-20-74044170, info@fipp.com. Ed. Amy Duffin. Pub. Christine Scott. Adv. contact Andrew Chidgey TEL 44-20-74047535. page GBP 4,000; trim 210 x 297. Circ: 7,300. **Dist. by:** Cradley Print.

MAGILL'S LITERARY ANNUAL. *see* LITERATURE

002 DEU ISSN 0946-090X
MAINZER STUDIEN ZUR BUCHWISSENSCHAFT. Text in German. 1995. irreg., latest vol.20, 2010. price varies. **Document type:** *Monographic series, Academic/Scholarly.*
Indexed: MSN.
Published by: Harrassowitz Verlag, Kreuzberger Ring 7b-d, Wiesbaden, 65205, Germany. TEL 49-611-5300, FAX 49-611-530560, verlag@harrassowitz.de, http://www.harrassowitz.de.

090 USA ISSN 1045-5388
Z1000
MANDEVILLE'S USED BOOK PRICE GUIDE. Text in English. 1962. triennial. USD 93. **Description:** Assists in the evaluation of rare, scarce, old, and used books. Provides the background for determining the current market value of books.
Formerly: Used Book Price Guide (0083-4807)
Published by: Price Guide Publishers, PO Box 82525, Kenmore, WA 98028-0525. TEL 206-783-7855. Ed., Pub., R&P Richard L Collins.

090 AUT
▼ **MANU SCRIPTA;** Editionen aus der Handschriftensammlung der Wienbibliothek. Text in German. 2009. irreg. price varies. **Document type:** *Monographic series, Academic/Scholarly.*
Published by: Boehlau Verlag GmbH & Co.KG., Wiesingerstr 1, Vienna, W 1010, Austria. TEL 43-1-3302427, FAX 43-1-3302432, boehlau@boehlau.at.

070.5 ITA ISSN 1971-226X
MANUALI UNIVERSITARI. Text in Italian. 2002. irreg. **Document type:** *Directory, Trade.*
Published by: Carocci Editore, Via Sardegna 50, Rome, 00187, Italy. TEL 39-06-42818417, FAX 39-06-42747931, clienti@carocci.it, http://www.carocci.it.

091 USA ISSN 0025-262X
Z41.A2
MANUSCRIPTS. Text in English. 1948. q. free to members (effective 2010). adv. illus.; mkt.; tr.lit. cum.index: vols.1-28, 29-40. back issues avail.; reprints avail. **Document type:** *Journal, Academic/Scholarly.* **Description:** For collectors, dealers, librarians, archivists, scholars and others with interest in original manuscripts.
Formerly (until 1953): Autograph collectors' Journal
Related titles: Microfilm ed.: (from PQC).
Indexed: A22, AmH&L, AmHI, CA, HistAb, MEA&I, MLA, MLA-IB, P30, T02.
—Ingenta.
Published by: Manuscript Society, 14003 Rampart Ct, Baton Rouge, LA 70810. TEL 908-459-0155, sands@manuscript.org. Ed. David R Chesnutt. Circ: 1,500.

MARKET GUIDE (NEW YORK). *see* BUSINESS AND ECONOMICS—Marketing And Purchasing

070.5 USA
MARKET INTELLIGENCE MONTHLY. Text in English. 2004. m. USD 795 (effective 2005). **Document type:** *Newsletter, Trade.* **Description:** Identifies joint ventures and new products announced in the publishing, information and training industries.
Published by: Whitestone Communications, Inc., 1350 Avenue of The Americas, Ste 1200, New York, NY 10019. TEL 212-957-7100, FAX 212-957-7508, ssevrens@whitestonecommunications.com, http://www.whitestonecommunications.com.

002 GBR ISSN 0261-3093
Z119
MATRIX (HEREFORDSHIRE); a review for printers and bibliophiles. Text in English. 1981. a. GBP 90 per issue (effective 2009). bk.rev. illus. reprints avail. **Document type:** *Journal, Academic/Scholarly.* **Description:** Articles on all aspects of 20th century fine printing, particularly private presses, wood-engraving, type design and rare book collections.
Indexed: ABM.
—CCC.
Published by: Whittington Press, Lower Marston Farm, Leominster, Herefords HR6 0NJ, United Kingdom. TEL 44-1885-400250, FAX 44-1885-400666, rose@whittingtonpress.plus.com, http://www.whittingtonpress.com.

MEDIA; Asia's media & marketing newspaper. *see* ADVERTISING AND PUBLIC RELATIONS

070.5 SGP ISSN 0129-6612
P92.A7
MEDIA ASIA; an Asian mass communication quarterly operations index. Text in English. 1974. q. SGD 50 in Singapore & Malaysia; SGD 60 in Asia; USD 60 elsewhere in Japan, Australia & New Zealand (effective 2004). bk.rev. illus. Index. 60 p./no.; back issues avail.; reprints avail. **Document type:** *Journal, Academic/Scholarly.* **Description:** Aims to meet the professional needs of communications personnel and administrators, scholars, and practitioners, as well as those of serious laypersons concerned with mass communication and society.
Related titles: Online - full text ed.
Indexed: A22, BAS, CMM, IBR, IBZ, IIFP, IITV, P14, P30, P48, P52, P53, P54, PAIS, PQC, RASB, REE&TA, SCOPUS.
—BLDSC (5525.253000), IE, Infotrieve, Ingenta. **CCC.**
Published by: Asian Media Information and Communication Centre, Publications Unit, PO Box 360, Jurong Point, 916412, Singapore. TEL 65-7927570, FAX 65-7927129, enquiries@amic.org.sg, http://www.amic.org.sg. Circ: 1,500.

070.5 AUS
MEDIA EXTRA. Variant title: M X. Text in English. w. ((Mon.), 49/yr.). AUD 225 for single user license (effective 2008). back issues avail. **Document type:** *Newsletter, Trade.*
Media: E-mail. **Related titles:** Online - full text ed.: AUD 250 domestic single user: (online or email ed.); AUD 227 foreign single user: (online or email ed.); AUD 200 domestic single user: (online or email ed.); AUD 181 foreign single user: (online or email ed.) (effective 2008); subscr. includes Weekly Book Newsletter.
Published by: Thorpe-Bowker (Subsidiary of: R.R. Bowker LLC), St Kilda Rd, PO Box 6509, Melbourne, VIC 8008, Australia. TEL 61-3-85178333, FAX 61-3-85178399, subscriptions@thorpe.com.au, http://www.thorpe.com.au. Adv. contact Xeverie Swee TEL 61-3-86450308.

070.5 NLD ISSN 1388-1930
MEDIA FACTS; vakblad over mediamanagement. Text in Dutch. 1998. bi-m. EUR 99 domestic; EUR 129 foreign; EUR 59 to students (effective 2009). adv. **Document type:** *Magazine, Trade.* **Description:** Covers all sectors of publishing, delivering news and information on the latest national and international developments.
Published by: Media Business Press BV, Postbus 8632, Rotterdam, 3009 AP, Netherlands. TEL 31-10-2894078, FAX 31-10-2894076, info@mbp.nl, http://www.mbp.nl/. Ed. Wim Verbei TEL 31-20-6632384. Pub. Yvonne Joosten. Adv. contact Alain Meijer. color page EUR 2,625; trim 230 x 300. Circ: 4,268 (paid and controlled).

070.5 USA
MEDIA GUIDE. Text in English. 1954. a. USD 40 newsstand/cover (effective 2001). **Document type:** *Directory, Trade.* **Description:** Directory of local print and broadcast media along with advice on accessing media.
Formerly: Publicity Guide
Published by: The Center for Community Solutions, 1226 Huron Rd, Ste 300, Cleveland, OH 44115. TEL 216-781-2944, FAX 216-781-2988, sbanks@CommunitySolutions.com, http://www.CommunitySolutions.com. Ed., R&P Sheryl McLean. Circ: 1,000.

MEDIA POCKET BOOK. *see* COMMUNICATIONS
MEDIAPERFORMANCE. *see* ADVERTISING AND PUBLIC RELATIONS

070.5 DEU ISSN 1431-9705
MEDIENGESCHICHTLICHE VEROEFFENTLICHUNGEN. Text in German. 1997. irreg., latest vol.4, 2006. price varies. **Document type:** *Monographic series, Academic/Scholarly.*
Published by: (Boersenverein des Deutschen Buchhandel e.V.), Harrassowitz Verlag, Kreuzberger Ring 7b-d, Wiesbaden, 65205, Germany. TEL 49-611-5300, FAX 49-611-530560, verlag@harrassowitz.de, http://www.harrassowitz.de.

MEDIENWISSENSCHAFT; Rezensionen - Reviews. *see* COMMUNICATIONS—Television And Cable

070 USA ISSN 1535-2927
Z490.4
MEDIOS; la revista para profesionales de la industria periodistica. Text in Spanish. 2000. m.
Related titles: Online - full text ed.: ISSN 1535-2935.
Published by: Leon Publications, PO Box 2000, Miami, FL 33233-1930. TEL 305-860-1314, FAX 305-860-5141, http://www.medios.com. Pub. Noel Leon.

METRO'S PLUS BUSINESS. *see* ADVERTISING AND PUBLIC RELATIONS

028.1 USA ISSN 0026-4377
MILWAUKEE READER. Text in English. 1942. m. USD 5. bk.rev. **Document type:** *Newsletter.*
Media: Duplicated (not offset).
Indexed: L09.
Published by: Milwaukee Public Library, 814 W Wisconsin Ave, Milwaukee, WI 53233. TEL 414-278-3031, FAX 414-278-2137. Ed. Lorelei Starck. Circ: 4,500.

790.13 099 USA ISSN 0894-5489
AS1
MINIATURE BOOK SOCIETY NEWSLETTER. Text in English. 1986. USD 30 membership (effective 2001). **Document type:** *Newsletter, Trade.*
Incorporates (in 200?): Miniature Book News (0026-5128)
Published by: Miniature Book Society, c/o Mark Palkovic, 620 Clinton Springs Ave, Cincinnati, OH 45229. mark.palkovic@uc.edu, http://membrane.com/books/.

070.5 DEU
MOHR KURIER; Theologie - Philosophie - Rechtswissenschaft - Wirtschaftswissenschaft. Text in German. 3/yr. free (effective 2011). **Document type:** *Catalog, Trade.*
Published by: Mohr Siebeck GmbH & Co. KG, Wilhelmstr 18, Tuebingen, 72074, Germany. TEL 49-7071-9230, FAX 49-7071-51104, info@mohr.de, http://www.mohr.de.

028.1 CAN ISSN 1480-2538
MONTREAL REVIEW OF BOOKS. Text in English. 1997. 3/yr. free (effective 2006). adv. bk.rev. **Document type:** *Journal, Academic/Scholarly.*
Indexed: C03, CBCARef, P48, PQC.

Published by: Association of English-Language Publishers of Quebec, 1200 Atwater Ave, Suite 3, Montreal, PQ H3Z 1X4, Canada. TEL 514-932-5633, FAX 514-932-5456, info@aelaq.org. Eds. Ian McGillis, Margaret Goldik. adv.: B&W page USD 1,075, color page USD 1,175; 10.25 x 13.5. Circ: 40,000.

070.5 USA ISSN 1531-0388
PS153.N5
MOSAIC LITERARY MAGAZINE. Text in English. 1998. q. USD 15; USD 6 per issue (effective 2008). adv. bk.rev. illus. back issues avail. **Document type:** *Magazine, Consumer.* **Description:** Covers all aspects of African American and Hispanic literature. Features interviews with some of today's top authors; previews adult and children's books, technology that makes the writer's life easier; profiles people in the publishing industry. Also includes a crossword puzzle, a look at a writer from our past, original fiction and poetry, and much more.
Related titles: Online - full text ed.
Indexed: ENW, IIBP, L06.
Address: 314 W 231st St, Ste 470, Bronx, NY 10463. TEL 718-432-1445, FAX 602-761-8150, http://www.mosaicbooks.com. Pub. Ron Kavanaugh. adv.: page USD 500; 8 x 10.5.

MULTICHANNEL MERCHANT. *see* ADVERTISING AND PUBLIC RELATIONS

070.5 USA
MULTICULTURAL PUBLISHING AND EDUCATION COUNCIL. NEWSLETTER. Text in English. 1989. bi-m. looseleaf. USD 48 (effective 1992). adv. bk.rev. tr.lit. back issues avail. **Document type:** *Newsletter.* **Description:** News of the minority publishing industry in the U.S., covering marketing and distribution issues, and news of book fairs.
Formerly: Multicultural Publishers Exchange Newsletter (1049-5428)
Related titles: Diskette ed.
Published by: Multicultural Publishing and Education Council, c/o Rennie Mau, President, 177 South Kihei Rd, Kihei, Maui, HI 96753. TEL 530-887-8033, FAX 530-888-0690. Adv. contact Rennie Mau. Circ: 1,500 (controlled).

MUSE (CLEVELAND). *see* LITERATURE

020.75 USA
PN162
MY BIG SOURCEBOOK. Text in English. 1981. a. USD 23.95. **Document type:** *Directory.* **Description:** Lists the best courses, books, periodicals, competitions, software, tools, and organizations for professional publications people.
Former titles (until 1993): Directory of Publications Resources (1062-8010); (until 1991): Directory of Editorial Resources (0731-4426)
Published by: E E I Press (Subsidiary of: E E I Communications Inc.), 66 Canal Center Plaza, Ste 200, Alexandria, VA 22314. TEL 703-663-0663, FAX 703-683-4915. Ed., R&P Linda B Jorgensen. Pub. Claire Kincaid.

N A P R A REVIEW; for retailers serving the body/mind/spirit marketplace. *see* NEW AGE PUBLICATIONS

N A P R BULLETIN. *see* ADVERTISING AND PUBLIC RELATIONS

381.45002 SGP ISSN 0129-9239
Z464.S55
N B D C S NEWS. Text in English. 1981. q. charts; illus. back issues avail. **Document type:** *Journal, Trade.* **Description:** Contains news of relevance to Singapore's book industry, as well as educational institutions and libraries.
Published by: National Book Development Council of Singapore, NBDCS Secretariat, Blk 162 Bukit Merah Central, Ste 05 3555, Singapore, 150162, Singapore. TEL 65-2732730. Ed. Vasantha Kumaree Siva. Circ: 4,000.

070.5 USA
THE N C B NEWS. Text in English. 1991. 3/yr. free to members (effective 2011). adv. **Document type:** *Newsletter.*
Formerly (until 1999): N C B Quarterly (1063-9365)
Related titles: Online - full text ed.
Published by: Nebraska Center for the Book, c/o Nebraska Library Commission, The Atrium, 1200 N Street, Ste 120, Lincoln, NE 68508-2023. TEL 402-471-3434, maryjo.ryan@nebraska.gov, http://centerforthebook.nebraska.gov. Ed. Mary Jo Ryan.

002.0277 USA ISSN 1932-8206
N H WRITER. (New Hampshire) Text in English. 1988. bi-m. USD 45 (effective 2007). adv. bk.rev. back issues avail. **Document type:** *Newsletter.* **Description:** Articles and network by and for New Hampshire writers and publishers. Includes listings, leads and calendars.
Formerly (until 2007): Ex Libris (Concord) (1042-6647)
Published by: New Hampshire Writers' Project, 2521 N. River Rd., Hooksett, NH 03106-1068. TEL 603-226-6649, FAX 603-226-0035. Ed. Martha Carlson Bradley. Circ: 750.

N O B S NEWSLETTER. *see* HOBBIES

N S K NEWS BULLETIN. (Nihon Shinbun Kyokai) *see* JOURNALISM

NANDE REKO; cuaderno de literatura popular. *see* LITERATURE

NASHR-I DANISH. *see* HUMANITIES: COMPREHENSIVE WORKS

NATIONAL BIBLIOGRAPHY OF BOTSWANA. *see* PUBLISHING AND BOOK TRADE—Abstracting, Bibliographies, Statistics

NATIONAL BRAILLE PRESS RELEASE. *see* HANDICAPPED—Visually Impaired

NATIONAL INFORMATION STANDARDS SERIES. *see* LIBRARY AND INFORMATION SCIENCES

NATIONAL NEWSAGENT; the journal of the Australian newsagency industry. *see* JOURNALISM

028.1 GBR
NAVAL & MILITARY PRESS. BOOKLIST. Text in English. 19??. m. back issues avail. **Description:** Contain information on majority of the current special offers and new titles.
Related titles: Online - full text ed.
Published by: The Naval & Military Press, Unit 10, Ridgewood Industrial Est, Ridgewood, Uckfield, East Sussex TN22 5QE, United Kingdom. TEL 44-1825-749494, FAX 44-1825-765701, order.dept@naval-military-press.com.

070.5 USA ISSN 1092-5279
PN4833
NET.JOURNAL DIRECTORY; the catalog of full text periodicals archived on the world wide web. Text in English. 1997. s-a. USD 240 domestic for two eds.; USD 242 in Canada for two eds.; USD 266 in United Kingdom for two eds.; USD 268 in Western Europe for two eds.; USD 276 elsewhere for two eds.; USD 135 newsstand/cover domestic (effective 2002). **Document type:** *Directory.* **Description:** Catalogs serial titles in their archives on the World Wide Web, serials whose full text may be read online or immediately downloaded. It includes 78,000 individual listings of over 20,000 titles from hundreds of verified individual Web sites and over two dozen fee-based Web-services and publisher Websites.
Related titles: Online - full text ed.: Net.Journal Finder.
Published by: Hermograph Press, PO Box 29023, Atlanta, GA 30359-0023. inquiries@hermograph.com, http://www.hermograph.com. Ed., Pub. Dr. Lawrence Krumenaker.

DIE NEUEN BUECHER; Das aktuelle Lesemagazin. *see* BIBLIOGRAPHIES

070.5 DEU ISSN 1432-6434
NEUMANN; Handbuch fuer den Pressevertrieb. Text in German. 1974. a. EUR 46; EUR 163 combined subscription print & CD-ROM eds. (effective 2005). **Document type:** *Directory, Trade.*
Former titles (until 1994): Neumann - Handbuch fuer den Pressevertrieb (0935-7866); (until 1986): Handbuch fuer den Pressevertrieb (0171-9300); (until 1978): Handbuch fuer den Zeitschriftenvertrieb (0171-9580)
Related titles: CD-ROM ed.: EUR 139 (effective 2005).
Published by: Presse Fachverlag GmbH & Co. KG, Nebendahlstr 16, Hamburg, 22041, Germany. TEL 49-40-6090090, FAX 49-40-60900915, info@presse-fachverlag.de, http://www.presse-fachverlag.de. Ed. Ralf Deppe. Circ: 3,000 (paid and controlled).

NEW AGE RETAILER; products for a better world, ideas for better business. *see* NEW AGE PUBLICATIONS

NEW AMERICAN REVIEW. *see* LITERATURE

686.3 GBR ISSN 0261-5363
Z267
➤ **THE NEW BOOKBINDER**; journal of designer bookbinders. Abbreviated title: T N B. Text in English. 1973. a. free to members (effective 2009). adv. bk.rev. illus. 96 p./no. 2 cols./p.; back issues avail. **Document type:** *Journal, Academic/Scholarly.* **Description:** Provides articles on contemporary and historical bookbinding and allied subjects as well as articles on techniques, structure and conservation.
Formerly (until 1981): Designer Bookbinders Review
Indexed: D05, SCOPUS.
—BLDSC (6082.280000).
Published by: Designer Bookbinders Publications Ltd., 6 Queen Sq, London, WC1N 3AR, United Kingdom. publications@designerbookbinders.org.uk.

➤ **NEW JERSEY MEDIA GUIDE.** *see* BUSINESS AND ECONOMICS—Trade And Industrial Directories

070.5 GBR ISSN 1368-5015
NEW JOURNAL NEWS. Text in English. 1982. s-a. free. adv. back issues avail. **Document type:** *Newsletter.* **Description:** Covers developments in international periodical publishing for libraries, publishers and CD-ROM manufacturers.
Former titles (until 1997): Blackwell's New Journal News; Readmore Newsletter
Published by: Swets Information Services, Hythe Bridge St, Oxford, OX1 2ET, United Kingdom. TEL 44-1865-792792, FAX 44-1865-790119, http://www.swetsblackwell.com. Ed., Adv. contact Paul Calow. R&P Jane Swift. B&W page GBP 500, B&W page USD 770; trim 11 x 8.5. Circ: 2,500 (controlled).

070.5 USA ISSN 0271-8197
Z477
NEW PAGES; alternatives in print & media. Text in English. 1979. 3/yr. adv. bk.rev. **Document type:** *Directory, Consumer.*
Related titles: Online - full text ed.
Indexed: BRI, CBRI.
—Ingenta.
Published by: New Pages Press, PO Box 1580, Bay City, MI 48706. TEL 908-671-0081, newpagesonline@hotmail.com, http://www.newpages.com. Ed. Denise Hill. Pub. Casey Hill. Circ: 5,000 (controlled).

070.5 USA ISSN 1521-1169
NEW SINGLE COPY; a newsletter about publishing. Text in English. 1996. 48/yr. USD 395 (effective 2005). adv. charts; illus.; stat. 2 p./no. 2 cols./p.; back issues avail. **Document type:** *Newsletter, Trade.* **Description:** Includes news itesm, statistics, and opinions about magazine and book publishing with an emphasis on distribution.
Related titles: E-mail ed.; Fax ed.
Published by: Harrington Associates, 12 Main St, Ste B, Norwalk, CT 06851. TEL 203-838-1701, FAX 203-838-1861, jharrington@nscopy.com. Ed., R&P, Adv. contact John Harrington. Circ: 300.

NEW YORK PRESS BOOKS & PUBLISHING. *see* LITERARY AND POLITICAL REVIEWS

028.1 USA ISSN 0028-7504
AP2
NEW YORK REVIEW OF BOOKS. Text in English. 1963. 20/yr. USD 69 domestic; USD 89 in Canada; USD 109 elsewhere; USD 5.95 newsstand/cover (effective 2009). adv. bk.rev. illus. 64 p./no.; back issues avail.; reprints avail. **Document type:** *Magazine, Consumer.* **Description:** Features commentary and opinion on politics, literature, science and culture by eminent writers.
Related titles: Microform ed.: (from PQC); Online - full text ed.: ISSN 1944-7744.
Indexed: A&ATA, A01, A02, A03, A08, A20, A21, A22, A25, A26, ABS&EES, ASCA, Acal, AmHI, ArtHuCI, B04, B05, B14, B24, BRD, BRI, CA, CBRI, CLitI, ChLitAb, CurCont, E08, FutSurv, G05, G06, G07, G08, G09, H07, I05, IAPV, IBR, IBRH, IBZ, IDP, IPARL, L04, LISTA, M01, M02, M06, MASUSE, MEA&I, MLA, MLA-IB, MagInd, MusicInd, P02, P10, P13, P30, P34, P48, P53, P54, PQC, PRA, R03, R04, R06, RASB, RGAb, RGPR, RI-1, RI-2, RILM, S07, S08, S09, SCOPUS, SOPODA, SociolAb, T02, W03, W07.
—BLDSC (6089.700000), IE, Infotrieve, Ingenta.
Published by: N Y R E V, Inc., 435 Hudson St, 3rd Fl, New York, NY 10014. TEL 212 757-8070, FAX 212 333-5374, web@nybooks.com. Ed. Robert Silvers. Pub. Rea S Hederman. Adv. contact Lara Frohlich Anderson. B&W page USD 13,175; 9.75 x 13.375. Circ: 135,109.

028.1 USA ISSN 0028-7806
AP2
NEW YORK TIMES BOOK REVIEW. Text in English. 1896. w. adv. bk.rev. bibl.; illus. Index. reprints avail. **Document type:** *Magazine, Consumer.* **Description:** Presents extended reviews of noteworthy books, short reviews, essays and articles on topics and trends in publishing, literature, culture and the arts. Includes lists of best sellers (hardcover and paperback).
Former titles (until 1923): New York Times Book Review and Magazine; (until 1920): New York Times Review of Books; (until 1911): New York Times Saturday Review of Books and Art; (until 1896): New York Times Saturday Book Review Supplement
Related titles: Diskette ed.; Microform ed.: (from PQC); Online - full text ed.: free to members (effective 2009); ◆ Supplement to: The New York Times. ISSN 0362-4331.
Indexed: A01, A02, A03, A08, A20, A21, A22, A25, A26, ABS&EES, ARG, ASCA, AmHI, ArtHuCI, B04, B05, B14, BEL&L, BRD, BRI, C12, CBRI, CLitI, ChLitAb, Chicano, CurCont, E08, G05, G06, G07, G08, G09, GardL, H07, I05, I07, IBRH, IDP, L04, L09, LISTA, M01, M02, MLA-IB, MagInd, MusicInd, N01, NewsAb, P02, P10, P13, P23, P48, P53, P54, PQC, R03, R04, R06, RGAb, RGPR, RI-1, RI-2, S07, S08, S09, SOPODA, SociolAb, T02, TOM, W03, W07.
—BLDSC (6089.766000), IE, Infotrieve, Ingenta.
Published by: New York Times Company, 620 8th Ave, New York, NY 10018. TEL 212-556-1234, FAX 212-556-7088, letters@nytimes.com. Pub. Arthur Ochs Sulzberger Jr. Adv. contact Denise Warren TEL 212-556-7894. color page USD 8,760.

028.1 USA
THE NEW YORK TIMES BOOK REVIEW. Text in English. 1922. w. Supplement avail.; back issues avail. **Document type:** *Newspaper, Consumer.*
Media: Microform.
Published by: (New York Times Company), ProQuest (Subsidiary of: Cambridge Information Group), 789 E Eisenhower Pky, PO Box 1346, Ann Arbor, MI 48106. TEL 734-761-4700, 800-521-0600, FAX 734-997-4040, 888-241-5612, info@proquest.com, http://www.proquest.com.

070.5 USA ISSN 1043-7452
PN4899.N42
NEWSINC.; The business of the newspaper business. Text in English. 1989. fortn. USD 425 (effective 1999). adv. bk.rev. back issues avail. **Document type:** *Newsletter.* **Description:** Covers financial aspects of the newspaper business.
Related titles: Online - full text ed.
Indexed: I05, PROMT.
—CCC.
Published by: The Cole Group, PO Box 719, Pacifica, CA 94044-0719. TEL 650-994-2100, FAX 650-994-2108. Ed. David M Cole.

070.5 CAN ISSN 1185-5088
NEWSLETTER TRENDS; a newsletter about newsletters. Text in English. 1991. bi-m. USD 55. adv. bk.rev. back issues avail. **Document type:** *Newsletter.* **Description:** Discusses newsletter writing, editing, design, production, photography, and management.
Published by: Collins Communications & Management Inc., 365 Bloor St E, Ste 1807, Toronto, ON M4W 3L4, Canada. TEL 416-968-7979, FAX 416-968-6818. Pub. Patricia Collins. Circ: 200.

070.5 CHN ISSN 1006-6691
AY39.C5
NIANJIAN XINXI YU YANJIU. Text in Chinese. 1991. bi-m. USD 31.20 (effective 2009). **Document type:** *Journal, Academic/Scholarly.*
Formelry (until 1995): Nianjian Gongzuo yu Yangiu (1005-7080)
Published by: Nianjian Xinxi yu Yanjiu Zazhishe, 45, Fuxingmen Nei Dajie, Beijing, 100801, China. TEL 86-10-66095540, FAX 86-10-66095089. **Dist. by:** China International Book Trading Corp, 35 Chegongzhuang Xilu, Haidian District, PO Box 399, Beijing 100044, China. TEL 86-10-68412045, FAX 86-10-68412023, cibtc@mail.cibtc.com.cn, http://www.cibtc.com.cn.

070.5 658.8 NLD ISSN 1879-9892
▼ **NIEUWSBRIEF VASTE BOEKENPRIJS.** Variant title: Vaste Boekenprijs. Text in Dutch. 2009. irreg.
Published by: Commissariaat voor de Media, Postbus 1426, Hilversum, 1200 BK, Netherlands. TEL 31-35-7737700, FAX 31-35-7737799, cvdm@cvdm.nl, http://www.cvdm.nl.

070.5 DEU
NIGELNAGELNEU. Text in German. s-a. adv. **Document type:** *Bibliography.*
Published by: K. Thienemanns Verlag, Blumenstr 36, Stuttgart, 70182, Germany. TEL 49-711-21055-0, FAX 49-711-21055-39. Adv. contact Jochen Kraeft.

002.0277 DNK ISSN 1604-8202
NORDISK EXLIBRIS TIDSSKRIFT. Short title: N E T. Text in Danish, English, German. 1946. 4/yr. DKK 300 to members (effective 2008). adv. bk.rev. illus. cum.index every 2 yrs. **Document type:** *Magazine, Consumer.* **Description:** Facts about book plates.
Former titles (until 2003): N E T. Nordisk Exlibris Tidsskrift (0900-2707); (until 1980): Nordisk Exlibris Tidsskrift (0029-1323)
Published by: Dansk Exlibris Selskab/Danish Bookplate Society, c/o Frederikshavn Kunstmuseum, PO Box 47, Frederikshavn, 9900, Denmark. Ed. Klaus Roedel.

NOTES AND QUERIES; for readers and writers, collectors and librarians. *see* LITERATURE

070.5 USA
NOTES FROM THE WINDOWSILL. Text in English. 1993. irreg. bk.rev. **Document type:** *Newsletter, Consumer.* **Description:** Covers books, particularly children's literature for parents, educators and children's literature enthusiasts.
Formerly: W E B online review (1072-6020)
Media: Online - full text.
Address: PO Box 401, Santa Cruz, CA 95061-0401. Ed. Wendy E Betts.

070.5 POL ISSN 1230-0624
Z365.7
NOTES WYDAWNICZY. Text in Polish. 1992. m. EUR 161 foreign (effective 2005).
Indexed: RILM.

P

Address: Grzybowska 37a p. IV, Warsaw, 00855, Poland. TEL 48-22-6203285. **Dist. by:** Ars Polona, Obroncow 25, Warsaw 03933, Poland. TEL 48-22-5098609, FAX 48-22-5098610, arspolona@arspolona.com.pl, http://www.arspolona.com.pl.

002.09 FRA ISSN 0335-752X
Z4
NOUVELLES DU LIVRE ANCIEN. Text in French. 1974. q. free to members. adv. bk.rev. bibl. **Document type:** *Newsletter.*
Description: Studies the history of books. Covers ancient works as well as works in progress.
Published by: Institut de Recherche et d'Histoire des Textes (Subsidiary of: Centre National de la Recherche Scientifique), 40 Avenue d'Iena, Paris, 75116, France. TEL 33-1-44439070, FAX 33-1-47238939, http://www.irht.cnrs.fr. Circ: 3,100. **Co-sponsor:** Bibliotheque Nationale de France.

070.5 BGR
NOVI KNIGI/NEW BOOKS. Text in Bulgarian. 1998. m. BGL 1.50 newsstand/cover (effective 2002). **Document type:** *Magazine.*
Description: Announces new and forthcoming books, literary magazines, and publishes excerpts from new books and a data-book of cultural events. Profiles translators, art-designers, literary agencies, etc. Publishes information on multimedia versions of fiction, educational and reference books.
Published by: Color Studio, Tzarigradsko Shosse 53, bl.2, 1st Fl, Sofia, 1504, Bulgaria. TEL 359-2-9441854. Ed. Raja Ivanova.

028.1 POL ISSN 0137-8562
Z2523
NOWE KSIAZKI. Text in Polish. 1949. m. EUR 40 foreign (effective 2005).
Published by: Biblioteka Narodowa, Al Niepodleglosci 213, Warsaw, 00973, Poland. TEL 48-22-6082374, FAX 48-22-6082488. **Dist. by:** Ars Polona, Obroncow 25, Warsaw 03933, Poland. TEL 48-22-5098609, FAX 48-22-5098610, arspolona@arspolona.com.pl, http://www.arspolona.com.pl.

002 DNK ISSN 0109-0208
NYT FOR BOGVENNER/NEWS FOR BOOKLOVERS. Text in Danish. 1980. q. membership. 8 p./no.; back issues avail. **Document type:** *Newsletter, Consumer.*
Related titles: Online - full text ed.
Published by: Forening for Boghaandvaerk/Association of Book Crafts, c/o Riget Consult, Hvedevaenget 5, Aalborg, 9000, Denmark. TEL 45-98-127933, 45-32-958515, boghaandvaerk@stofanet.dk. Eds. Bent Joergensen, Lilli Riget.

OESTERREICHISCHE BIBLIOGRAPHIE (ONLINE). *see* PUBLISHING AND BOOK TRADE—Abstracting, Bibliographies, Statistics

070.5 USA ISSN 1526-811X
OKLAHOMA PUBLISHER. Text in English. 1924. m. USD 12 (effective 2005). **Document type:** *Newspaper, Trade.*
Published by: Oklahoma Press Association, 3601 N Lincoln, Oklahoma City, OK 73105-5400. TEL 405-524-4421, FAX 405-524-2201. Pub. Mark Thomas. Adv. contact Tom Bradley. Circ: 1,200 (paid).

070.5 USA ISSN 2159-6158
▼ **THE OLD TOWN COMPASS.** Text in English. 2010. m. free (effective 2011). adv. **Document type:** *Magazine, Trade.* **Description:** Provides all the events going on in Old Town Compass community.
Related titles: Online - full text ed.: ISSN 2159-6166.
Published by: Master Media Group, 17 West Boscawen St, Winchester, VA 22601. TEL 540-662-0852, 888-662-1224, FAX 540-662-1021, info@mastermediagroup.com, http://www.mastermediagroup.com.

028.5 USA ISSN 1071-2526
ONCE UPON A TIME. Text in English. 1990. q. USD 27 domestic; USD 34 in Canada; USD 40 elsewhere; USD 7 newsstand/cover (effective 2007). adv. 32 p./no. 3 cols./p.; back issues avail.; reprints avail. **Document type:** *Magazine, Trade.* **Description:** Specialized for children's writers and illustrators and those interested in children's literature. Includes informative, nurturing, supportive, entertaining, and just plain helpful articles, writer-to-writer.
Published by: Audrey Baird, Ed. & Pub., 553 Winston Ct, St. Paul, MN 55118. TEL 651-457-6223. Ed., Pub., R&P, Adv. contact Audrey Baird. page USD 140. Circ: 1,000 (paid and controlled).

070.5 USA
ONLINE PUBLISHERS DIGEST. Text in English. m. **Document type:** *Magazine, Trade.*
Media: Online - full content.
Published by: Digest Publications, 29 Fostertown Rd, Medford, NJ 08055. TEL 609-953-4900, FAX 609-953-4905, http://www.limodigest.com. Ed. Don Truax.

070.5 USA ISSN 1559-3134
ONLINE PUBLISHING. Text in English. 199?. s-a. **Document type:** *Journal, Consumer.*
Related titles: Online - full text ed.: ISSN 1559-3142.
Published by: Atypon Systems, Inc, 5201 Great America Pkwy, Ste 510, Santa Clara, CA 95054. TEL 408-988-1240, FAX 408-988-1070, inquiries@atypon.com, http://www.atypon.com.

070.5 ROM ISSN 2066-740X
▼ **OPEN SOURCE SCIENCE JOURNAL.** Text in English. 2009. q. (s.a. until 2010). free. back issues avail. **Document type:** *Journal, Academic/Scholarly.* **Description:** Contains original papers include aspects concerning techniques, methods of open source development, ways of increasing and measuring open source quality, ways of use and legal aspects concerning development and use of open source.
Media: Online - full text.
Published by: Academia de Studii Economice din Bucuresti, Catedra de Informatica Economica/Academy of Economic Studies Bucharest,Computer Science Department, c/o Prof. Ion Ivan, Piata Romana no.6, sector 1, Bucuresti, 2413, Romania. Ed. Ion Ivan.

070.5 USA ISSN 0745-6379
OREGON PUBLISHER. Text in English. 1932. m. membership. adv. back issues avail. **Document type:** *Magazine, Trade.* **Description:** Covers industry news and issues of concern to newspaper publishers in Oregon.
Published by: Oregon Newspaper Publishers Association, 7150 S W Hampton St, Ste 111, Portland, OR 97223. TEL 503-624-6397, FAX 503-639-9009. Ed., R&P Lexi Witt. Pub. J Leroy Yorgason. Adv. contact Rose Stormer. Circ: 625 (controlled).

028.1 GBR
ORIGO. Text in English. 1979-1980; resumed 1995. q. bk.rev. illus. **Document type:** *Newsletter.* **Description:** Contains details of fine limited editions published by Genesis Publications, as well as related features. photos, guest celebrity columns, and reviews.
Published by: Genesis Publications Ltd., 2 Jenner Rd, Guildford, Surrey GU1 3PL, United Kingdom. TEL 44-1483-540973, FAX 44-1483-304709. Ed. Roman Milisic. Circ: 6,000 (controlled).

028.5 CAN ISSN 1192-2125
OUR CHOICE. Variant title: Memorable Canadian Books for Young People. Your Annual Guide to Canada's Best Children's Books. Text in English. 1978. s-a.
Former titles (until 1990): Our Choice/Your Choice (1185-2828); (until 1986): Our Choice (1185-281X)
Indexed: BRD, L04, L07, L08, LISTA, LibLit, W03, W05.
Published by: Canadian Children's Book Centre, 40 Orchard View Blvd, Ste 101, Toronto, ON M4R 1B9, Canada. TEL 416-975-0010, FAX 416-975-8970, info@bookcentre.ca.

028.1 USA
OUTCRY MAGAZINE. Text in English. q. free to qualified personnel (effective 2002).
Related titles: Online - full text ed.
Published by: Lara Publications, 12382 Trail Forest Ln, Florissant, MO 63033. TEL 314-653-0467, 800-599-7313, FAX 314-653-6543, outcrymagazine@yahoo.com, http://www.outcrybookreview.com.

070 GBR ISSN 0269-2147
OXBOW BOOK NEWS. Text in English. 1983. irreg., latest vol.77, 2009. **Document type:** *Newsletter, Trade.*
—CCC.
Published by: Oxbow Books, 10 Hythe Bridge St, Oxford, OX1 2EW, United Kingdom. TEL 44-1865-241249, FAX 44-1865-794449, oxbow@oxbowbooks.com, http://www.oxbowbooks.com.

028.1 GBR ISSN 2046-2808
THE OXONIAN REVIEW. Text in English. 2001. bi-w. free (effective 2011). **Document type:** *Journal, Trade.* **Description:** Features essays and reviews of recently published work in literature, politics, history, science and the arts.
Formerly (until 2009): The Oxonian Review of Books (1756-3917)
Media: Online - full text. **Related titles:** Print ed.
Published by: Graduate Members of the University of Oxford, c/o OUSU, Thomas Hull House, New Inn Hall St, Oxford, OX1 2DH, United Kingdom. Ed. William Kolkey.

070.5 GBR ISSN 0955-1360
P A NEWS UPDATE. (Publishers Association) Text in English. 197?. w. free (effective 2009). **Document type:** *Newsletter, Trade.*
Formerly (until 1988): P A News (0267-7733)
—CCC.
Published by: The Publishers Association, 29B Montague St, London, WC1B 5BW, United Kingdom. TEL 44-20-76919191, FAX 44-20-76919199, mail@publishers.org.uk, http://www.publishers.org.uk.

070.5 USA ISSN 0891-5229
P A S NEWSLETTER. Text in English. 1985. s-a. USD 35 (effective 2007). adv. 32 p./no.; **Document type:** *Newsletter, Trade.*
Related titles: Online - full text ed.
Published by: Publishers Association of the South, c/o Stephanie Williams, University Press of Florida, 15 NW 15th Street, Gainesville, FL 32611. info@pubsouth.org, http://www.pubsouth.org/ge. adv.: page USD 200; 7 x 10.

070.5 USA
P S P BULLETIN. (Professional Scholarly Publishing) Text in English. q. free to members. **Document type:** *Bulletin, Trade.*
Related titles: Online - full text ed.
Published by: Association of American Publishers, Inc., 71 Fifth Ave, New York, NY 10003-3004. TEL 212-255-0200, FAX 212-255-7007, spinto@publishers.org, http://www.publishers.org. Ed. Myer Kutz.

028 USA ISSN 1559-1468
P W BOOKLIFE; for the love of reading. (Publishers Weekly) Text in English. 2005 (Oct.-Nov.). bi-m. **Document type:** *Magazine, Consumer.*
Published by: Reed Business Information (Subsidiary of: Reed Business), 360 Park Ave S, New York, NY 10010. TEL 646-746-6400, FAX 646-746-7431, corporatecommunications@reedbusiness.com, http://www.reedbusiness.com.

070.5 USA
P W DAILY FOR BOOKSELLERS. (Publishers Weekly) Text in English. 1997. d. Included with subscr. to Publishers Weekly. back issues avail. **Document type:** *Newsletter, Trade.* **Description:** Gives booksellers useful information to help them sell more books, including books and authors that are receiving media and review attention, news stories about independent and chain booksellers, bestseller lists from around the country.
Media: E-mail.
Published by: Reed Business Information (Subsidiary of: Reed Business), PO Box 5669, Harlan, IA 51593. TEL 515-247-2984, 800-278-2991, FAX 712-733-8019, corporatecommunications@reedbusiness.com, http://www.reedbusiness.com.

070.5 USA
P W NEWSLINE. (Publishers Weekly) Text in English. d. Included with Publishers Weekly. **Document type:** *Newsletter, Trade.* **Description:** Delivers the latest news and analysis to the publishing business including industry trends, the latest job changes, technology shifts, seminars and events not to miss, and books and people creating buzz.
Media: E-mail.
Published by: Reed Business Information (Subsidiary of: Reed Business), 360 Park Ave S, New York, NY 10010. TEL 646-746-6400, FAX 646-746-7431, corporatecommunications@reedbusiness.com, http://www.reedbusiness.com.

070.5 USA ISSN 0000-1694
P W RELIGION BOOKLINE; the twice monthly source for religion professionals. (Publishers Weekly) Text in English. 1996. s-m. Included with subscr. to Publishers Weekly. adv. back issues avail.; reprints avail. **Document type:** *Newsletter, Trade.* **Description:** Contains information on religion and spiritual books and publishing.
Media: E-mail.
Published by: Reed Business Information (Subsidiary of: Reed Business), 360 Park Ave S, New York, NY 10010. TEL 646-746-6758, FAX 646-746-6631, corporatecommunications@reedbusiness.com, http://www.reedbusiness.com. Ed. Sara Nelson TEL 646-746-6751. Pub. Ronald Shank TEL 646-746-6548. Adv. contact Marisol Avalos TEL 646-746-6436.

PAGES (MARION); editorial and filler service for editors of company newsletters. *see* JOURNALISM

028.5 ITA
PAGINE GIOVANI. Text in Italian. 1977. q. free to members. bk.rev. **Document type:** *Bulletin, Consumer.* **Description:** Addresses topics concerning literature for youths. Promotes reading and literature. Includes activities of the association.
Published by: Gruppo di Servizio per la Letteratura Giovanile, Piazza Cardinal Ferrari 4, Rome, 00167, Italy. Circ: 2,000.

015.5491 PAK
PAKISTAN'S BOOKS & LIBRARIES; the only monthly magazine of its kind. Text in English. 1989. m. PKR 200, USD 25. adv. bk.rev. bibl. **Description:** Covers the book trade and libraries in Pakistan.
Published by: M. Nayeem Siddiqui Ed. & Pub., 305-15 F.B. Area, Karachi, 75950, Pakistan. TEL 21-685858, FAX 21-200678, TELEX 23898 CROWN PK. Circ: 2,000.

070.5 ESP ISSN 1135-6782
PANORAMICA DE LA EDICION ESPANOLA DE LIBROS. Text in Spanish. 1988. a. **Document type:** *Government.*
Published by: Ministerio de Educacion y Cultura, Direccion General del Libros, Archivos y Bibliotecas, Santiago Rusinol, 8, Madrid, 28040, Spain. TEL 34-91-544-8105, FAX 34-91-536-8822.

PANURGE. *see* LITERATURE

070.573 USA
PAPERBACK PARADE. Text in English. 1986. bi-m. USD 35 domestic for 5 issues; USD 55 foreign for 5 issues (effective 2001). adv. bk.rev. bibl.; illus. Index. 100 p./no.; back issues avail. **Document type:** *Magazine, Bibliography.* **Description:** Covers the hobby of collectible - rare paperbacks and books, authors, and artists.
Published by: Gryphon Books, PO Box 290, Brooklyn, NY 11228-0209. Adv. contact Gary Lovisi. Circ: 1,000.

PAPERBACK PREVIEWS. *see* LITERATURE

028.5 VEN
PARAPARA BOLETIN INFORMATIVO. Text in Spanish. 1980. 3/yr. **Description:** Contains information about personalities, prizes, seminars, congresses and fairs in the world of children's literature.
Supersedes in part (in 1990): Parapara
Published by: Banco del Libro, Apdo. 5893, Caracas, 1010-A, Venezuela. TEL 58-2-2661566, FAX 58-2-2663621. Circ: 300.

028.5 VEN ISSN 0798-1619
PARAPARA SELECCION DE LIBROS PARA NINOS Y JOVENES. Text in Spanish. 1980. 3/yr. bk.rev. **Description:** Offers a selection of books for children and young people, covering a different theme each issue.
Supersedes in part (in 1990): Parapara
Published by: Banco del Libro, Apdo. 5893, Caracas, 1010-A, Venezuela. TEL 58-2-2661566, FAX 58-2-2663621. Circ: 1,000.

070.5 686.2 ITA ISSN 1824-6249
P211
PARATESTO. Text in Italian. 2004. a. EUR 295 combined subscription domestic to institutions (print & online eds.); EUR 345 combined subscription foreign to institutions (print & online eds.) (effective 2009). **Document type:** *Journal, Academic/Scholarly.*
Related titles: Online - full text ed.: ISSN 1825-9537.
Published by: Fabrizio Serra Editore (Subsidiary of: Accademia Editoriale), c/o Accademia Editoriale, Via Santa Bibbiana 28, Pisa, 56127, Italy. TEL 39-050-542332, FAX 39-050-574888, accademiaeditoriale@accademiaeditoriale.it, http://www.libraweb.net.

070.5 ESP ISSN 1133-5556
PAUTAS/GUIDELINES. Text in Spanish. 1991. q. **Document type:** *Newsletter.* **Description:** Gathers new developments about culture and previews the content of associated magazines.
Published by: Asociacion de Revistas Culturales de Espana/Association of Cultural Magazines from Spain, Hortaleza, 75, Madrid, 28004, Spain. TEL 34-91-3086066, FAX 34-91-3199267. Ed. Enrique Helguera. Pub. Manuel Ortuno. R&P Paloma Valenciano.

070.5 ZAF ISSN 1815-3607
PEGBOARD. Text in English. 1994. q. ZAR 10 per issue (effective 2006). **Document type:** *Newsletter.*
Published by: Professional Editors' Group, PO Box 411684, Craighall, 2024, South Africa. peg@ananzi.co.za, http://www.editors.org.za.

070.5 USA
PENN STATE SERIES IN THE HISTORY OF THE BOOK. Text in English. 1996. irreg., latest 2009. price varies. back issues avail. **Document type:** *Monographic series, Academic/Scholarly.* **Description:** Contains topics such as professional authorship and the literary marketplace, the history of reading and book distribution, book-trade studies and publishing-house histories, and examinations of copyright and literary property.
Published by: Pennsylvania State University Press, 820 N University Dr, University Support Bldg 1, Ste C, University Park, PA 16802. TEL 814-865-1327, 800-326-9180, FAX 814-863-1408, info@psupress.org. Ed. James L W West III.

070.5 AUS ISSN 1323-5257
PHANTOM. Text in English. 1948. bi-m.
Published by: Frew Publications, 160 Castlereagh St, Ste 401 4th Fl, Sydney, NSW 2000, Australia. TEL 61-2-92618122, FAX 61-2-92679856, http://www.deepwoods.org/frew.html.

PIAZZA; lesen, leben, erleben. *see* WOMEN'S INTERESTS

POLIGRAFIST I IZDATEL'. *see* PRINTING

POLIGRAFIYA. *see* PRINTING

070.5 JPN
PRACTICAL GUIDE TO PUBLISHING IN JAPAN. Text in English. 1990. a. free. **Document type:** *Handbook/Manual/Guide, Trade.*
Published by: Publishers' Association for Cultural Exchange Japan, 1-2-1 Sarugaku-cho, Chiyoda-ku, Tokyo, 101-0064, Japan. TEL 81-3-3291-5685, FAX 81-3-3233-3645, office@pace.or.jp, http://www.pace.or.jp. Ed. Tanio Yokote.

PRESS (HARRISBURG). *see* JOURNALISM

PRESSE-PORTRAETS; das Angebot des Pressehandels. *see* BIBLIOGRAPHIES

070.50688 DEU ISSN 0341-8073
PRESSE REPORT; Magazin fuer den Einzelhandel. Short title: P R. Text in German. 1951. m. EUR 31.20 (effective 2008). adv. **Document type:** *Magazine, Trade.* **Description:** Provides content for the paperback book, magazine, and newspaper retail trades, featuring the latest news, sales strategies, businesses for sale, and new publications.
Former titles (until 1975): Informationsblatt fuer den Modernen Zeitungs- und Zeitschriftenhaendler (0176-6872); (until 1968): Zeitungs- und Zeitschriftenhandel (0044-3832); (until 1963): Zeitungs- und Zeitschriften-Haendler (0176-6899); (until 1960): Fachzeitschrift fuer den Zeitungs- und Zeitschriften-Einzelhandel (0176-6880)
Related titles: ◆ Supplement(s): Presse-Portraets. ISSN 0176-5248.
Published by: Presse Fachverlag GmbH & Co. KG, Nebendahlstr 16, Hamburg, 22041, Germany. TEL 49-40-6090090, FAX 49-40-60900915, info@presse-fachverlag.de, http://www.presse-fachverlag.de. Ed. Ralf Deppe. Adv. contact Manuela Busche. B&W page EUR 5,225; trim 175 x 262. Circ: 54,574 (paid).

070.5 AUT
PRESSEHANDBUCH (YEAR); Medien und Werbung in Oesterreich. Text in German. 1953. a. EUR 47 (effective 2005). adv. bk.rev. mkt.; tr.lit. index. **Document type:** *Directory, Trade.*
Formerly: Oesterreichs Presse, Werbung, Graphik (0030-0004)
Indexed: B03.
Published by: Verband Oesterreichischer Zeitungen, Wipplingerstr 15, Vienna, W 1013, Austria. TEL 43-1-53379790, FAX 43-1-5337979422, gs@voez.at, http://www.voez.at. Ed., R&P Robert Keilhauer. Adv. contact Barbara Kalab. Circ: 3,000.

070.5 USA ISSN 2150-2218
PN1009.A1
PREVIEW (NEW YORK). Text in English. 1999. s-a. **Document type:** *Magazine, Trade.*
Published by: Penguin Group (USA) Inc, 375 Hudson St, New York, NY 10014. http://us.penguingroup.com.

070.5 DEU ISSN 1612-8710
PRINT & MORE. Text in German. 2003. q. EUR 50 (effective 2010). adv. **Document type:** *Magazine, Trade.*
Published by: Verband Deutscher Zeitschriftenverleger e.V., Haus der Presse, Markgrafenstr 15, Berlin, 10969, Germany. TEL 49-30-7262980, FAX 49-30-726298103, info@vdz.de. Ed. Michael Geffken.

PRINT AND PRODUCTION MANUAL. *see* PRINTING

THE PRINT BUSINESS. *see* PRINTING

PRINT PUBLISHING FOR THE SCHOOL MARKET: (YEAR) REVIEW, TRENDS & FORECAST. *see* EDUCATION—Teaching Methods And Curriculum

PRINTING HISTORY. *see* PRINTING

070.5 GBR ISSN 1745-5944
PRINTMEDIA MANAGEMENT. Text in English. 2002. m. free (effective 2009). adv. back issues avail. **Document type:** *Magazine, Trade.* **Description:** Provides new innovations, company news, industry trends and new products and services in the print media industry.
Related titles: Online - full text ed.
—CCC.
Published by: First City Media Ltd., 28A Jubilee Trade Centre, Jubilee Rd, Letchworth, Herts SG6 1SP, United Kingdom. TEL 44-1462-678300, FAX 44-1462-481622. Eds. Andy Knaggs, Gareth Ward. Adv. contact Tom Vine.

THE PRIVATE LIBRARY. *see* LIBRARY AND INFORMATION SCIENCES

070.5 USA ISSN 1095-2187
Z477 CODEN: PRPRF9
PROFESSIONAL PUBLISHING REPORT. Text in English. 1997. s-m. USD 749 (print or online ed.) (effective 2008). **Document type:** *Newsletter, Trade.* **Description:** Provides details of revenue breakdowns by media and market; rankings of leading professional publishers by revenue; analysis of mergers and acquisitions; issues related to new technologies and much more.
Related titles: Online - full text ed.: USD 689 (effective 2005).
—CCC.
Published by: SIMBA Information (Subsidiary of: Market Research.Com), 11200 Rockville Pike, Ste 504, Rockville, MD 20852. TEL 240-747-3096, 888-297-4622, FAX 240-747-3004, customerservice@simbainformation.com. Pub. Linda Kopp.

PUB. *see* ADVERTISING AND PUBLIC RELATIONS

050 CUB ISSN 0864-3598
Z6954.C9
PUBLICACIONES SERIADAS CUBANAS. Text in Spanish. a.
Related titles: Online - full text ed.: ISSN 1682-0002.
Published by: Instituto Cubano del Libro, Palacio del Segundo Cabo, Calle 21, 459 esq. E y F, Havana, Cuba.

070.5 DEU
PUBLISH.DE. Text in German. 2/yr. EUR 4.50 newsstand/cover (effective 2008). adv. **Document type:** *Magazine, Trade.*
Published by: Deutscher Drucker Verlag GmbH, Postfach 4124, Ostfildern, 73744, Germany. TEL 49-711-448170, FAX 49-711-442099, info@publish.de, http://www.publish.de. Ed. Bernhard Niemela. Adv. contact Michael Bieber. color page EUR 4,300. Circ: 28,500 (paid and controlled).

070.5 NGA ISSN 0331-7714
Z468.N5
THE PUBLISHER. Text in English. 1985. a.?. NGN 150, USD 3.95. adv. back issues avail. **Document type:** *Journal, Trade.*
Published by: Nigerian Publishers' Association, Nue Bodija Estate, 14 Awosika Ave, GPO Box 2541, Ibadan, Oyo, Nigeria. TEL 234-22-411557. Ed. Damola Ifaturoti. Adv. contact Mgbechi F Ezeri. Circ: 2,000.

070.5 CAN ISSN 0380-8025
PUBLISHER. Text in English. 1919. 10/yr. CAD 40 (effective 2000). adv. bk.rev. **Document type:** *Journal, Trade.*
Supersedes: Canadian Community Publisher (0045-4583); Canadian Weekly Publisher (0008-5316)
Indexed: A12, A13, ABIn, C03, CBCABus, P48, P51, P53, P54, PQC.
Published by: Canadian Community Newspapers Association, 90 Eglinton Ave E Ste 206, Toronto, ON M4P 2Y3, Canada. TEL 416-482-1090, FAX 416-482-1908. Ed., R&P Robert Mackenzie. Pub. Michael Lavoie. Adv. contact Kim Magill. Circ: 2,200.

070.5 NZL ISSN 1177-6870
PUBLISHER (ONLINE). Text in English. 1977. bi-m. membership. adv. **Document type:** *Newsletter.* **Description:** Provides members with trade information, advertising, local and overseas book trade news and calendar events.
Former titles: Publisher (Print) (1173-048X); (until 1994): New Zealand Publishing News (0111-834X)
Media: Online - full text.
—CCC.
Published by: Book Publishers Association of New Zealand Inc., Private Bag 102902, North Shore, Auckland, 0745, New Zealand. TEL 64-9-4427426, FAX 64-9-4798536, bpanz@copyright.co.nz, http://www.bpanz.org.nz. Circ: 150 (paid).

PUBLISHER PLUG-IN. *see* COMPUTERS—Internet

017.8 USA ISSN 0742-0501
Z475
PUBLISHER'S DIRECTORY. Text in English. 1977. irreg., latest 33rd ed. USD 610 per vol. (effective 2009). **Document type:** *Directory, Trade.* **Description:** Provides details on approximately 30,000 U.S. and Canadian publishers, distributors and wholesalers.
Former titles (until 1984): Book Publishers Directory (0196-0903); Book Publishers of the U.S. and Canada
Related titles: Diskette ed.; Magnetic Tape ed.; Online - full text ed.
—BLDSC (7156.067900).
Published by: Gale (Subsidiary of: Cengage Learning), 27500 Drake Rd, Farmington Hills, MI 48331. TEL 248-699-4253, 800-877-4253, FAX 877-363-4253, gale.customerservice@cengage.com, http://gale.cengage.com. Ed. Wendy Van de Sande.

PUBLISHERS, DISTRIBUTORS & WHOLESALERS OF THE UNITED STATES; a directory of publishers, distributors, associations, wholesalers, software producers and manufacturers listing editorial and ordering addresses, and an ISBN publisher prefix index. *see* BUSINESS AND ECONOMICS—Trade And Industrial Directories

PUBLISHERS INFORMATION BUREAU REPORT; magazine advertising expenditures. *see* ADVERTISING AND PUBLIC RELATIONS

025.3 DEU ISSN 0939-1975
Z282 CODEN: PIIDE4
PUBLISHERS' INTERNATIONAL I S B N DIRECTORY (YEAR). (International Standard Book Number) Text in English, German. 1989. a. (in 4 vols.), latest vol.34, 2007. EUR 558 (effective 2009). adv. **Document type:** *Directory, Trade.* **Description:** Verified listings for publishers in 189 countries, indexed alphabetically, geographically, and numerically by ISBN. Includes microfilm, video and computer software publishers.
Formed by the merger of (1962-1989): Publishers' International Directory with I S B N Index (0939-1967); Which was formerly (until 1979): Internationales Verlagsadressbuch mit I S B N - Register (0074-9877); (1980-1989): Internationales I S B N Verlagsverzeichnis (0720-2768); Which was formerly (until 1980): Internationales I S B N Verlagsregister (0170-0103)
Related titles: CD-ROM ed.: EUR 558 (effective 2009).
—BLDSC (7156.069300).
Published by: (International ISBN Agency, Berlin), De Gruyter Saur (Subsidiary of: Walter de Gruyter GmbH & Co. KG), Mies-van-der-Rohe-Str 1, Munich, 80807, Germany. TEL 49-89-769020, FAX 49-89-76902150, info@degruyter.com.

025.7 DEU ISSN 0000-1716
Z282
PUBLISHERS' INTERNATIONAL I S B N DIRECTORY PLUS. (International Standard Book Number) Text in English, German. a., latest vol.12, 2008. EUR 558 (effective 2009). **Document type:** *Directory, Trade.* **Description:** Provides a reference for worldwide book ordering and full coverage of the international publishing community.
Media: CD-ROM.
Published by: De Gruyter Saur (Subsidiary of: Walter de Gruyter GmbH & Co. KG), Mies-van-der-Rohe-Str 1, Munich, 80807, Germany. TEL 49-89-769020, FAX 49-89-76902150, info@degruyter.com.

070.5 IND
PUBLISHERS' MONTHLY. Text in English, Hindi. 1959. m. INR 55 (effective 2011). bk.rev. bibl. **Document type:** *Magazine, Trade.*
Indexed: RASB.
Published by: S. Chand & Co. Ltd., 7361, Ram Nagar, Qutub Road, New Delhi, 110 055, India. TEL 91-11-23672080, FAX 91-11-23677446, info@schandgroup.com, http://www.schandgroup.com.

070.5 USA ISSN 0884-3090
PUBLISHER'S REPORT. Text in English. 1985. w. USD 40. bk.rev. **Document type:** *Newsletter.* **Description:** Furthers the visibility of independent publishing and provides a clearinghouse for information of interest to independent and self publishers.
Media: E-mail.
—CCC.
Published by: National Association of Independent Publishers, PO Box 430, Highland City, FL 33846-0430. TEL 863-648-4420, FAX 863-648-4420. Ed., Pub., R&P Betsy Lampe. Circ: 500.

070.5 USA ISSN 0000-0019
CODEN: PWEEAD
PUBLISHERS WEEKLY; the international news magazine of book publishing. Abbreviated title: P W(Publishers Weekly). Text in English. 1872. w. USD 249.99 domestic; USD 299.99 in Canada & Mexico; USD 399.99 elsewhere; free to qualified personnel (effective 2010). adv. bk.rev. bibl.; illus.; stat. Index. back issues avail.; reprints avail. **Document type:** *Magazine, Trade.* **Description:** Designed to serve all the segments involved in the creation, production, marketing and sale of the written word in book, audio, video and electronic formats.
Formerly (until 1873): Publishers' and Stationers' Weekly Trade Circular; Incorporates (in 1872): American Literary Gazette and Publishers' Circular; Which was formerly (until 1863): American Publishers' Circular and Literary Gazette; (until 1855): Norton's Literary Gazette and Publishers' Circular
Related titles: Fax ed.; Microfiche ed.: (from CIS); Microform ed.: (from PQC); Online - full text ed.: ISSN 2150-4008. USD 180 (effective 2009).
Indexed: A01, A02, A03, A06, A08, A09, A10, A11, A12, A13, A15, A17, A21, A22, A23, A24, A25, A26, ABIn, ABS&EES, Acal, B01, B02, B03, B04, B05, B06, B07, B08, B09, B11, B13, B14, B15, B17, B18, BAS, BPI, BRD, BRI, C05, C12, CA, CBRI, CLFP, CPerI, CWI, ChLitAb, ChPerI, Chicano, E02, E03, E06, E07, E08, ERI, EdA, EdI, F01, F02, G04, G05, G06, G07, G08, G09, GALA, GardL, HlthInd, I05, I07, IBR, IBZ, L04, L05, L06, L07, L08, L09, LHTB, LISTA, LibLit, M01, M02, M06, MASUSE, MEA&I, MLA-IB, MagInd, P02, P04, P06, P07, P10, P13, P34, P48, P51, P53, P54, PAIS, PMR, PQC, R03, R04, RASB, RGAb, RGPR, RI-1, RI-2, RILM, RefZh, S08, S09, S23, SRI, T&II, T02, V02, V03, V04, W01, W02, W03, W05.
—BLDSC (7156.080000), CASDDS, CIS, IE, Infotrieve, Ingenta, Linda Hall. **CCC.**
Published by: PWxyz, LLC, 71 West 23 St. #1608, New York, NY 10010. TEL 212-377-5500. Pub. Cevin Bryerman. adv.: B&W page USD 6,770, color page USD 9,000; trim 7.875 x 10.5. Circ: 738 (free); 18,640 (paid).

070.5 USA ISSN 1558-9641
Z284 CODEN: PPEXEP
PUBLISHING EXECUTIVE. Text in English. 1987. bi-m. free to qualified personnel (effective 2008). adv. back issues avail. **Document type:** *Magazine, Trade.* **Description:** Provides the latest magazine industry news and trends as well as in-depth interviews with leading publishing executives, thought-provoking blogs from Bob Sacks and Rob Yoegel and practical tips on all aspects of publishing in the "How-to Headquarters".
Former titles (until Jan. 2006): Print Media Magazine (1534-2115); (until 2000): Publishing & Production Executive (1048-3055); (until Nov. 1989): Publishing Technology (1040-9440)
Related titles: Online - full text ed.: ISSN 1558-996X. free to qualified personnel (effective 2008).
Indexed: A15, A22, ABIPC, ABIn, B02, B11, B15, B17, B18, BPI, BRD, CWI, EngInd, G04, G06, G07, G08, P48, P51, PQC, SCOPUS, SoftBase, W01, W02, W03, W05.
—BLDSC (7156.092900), Ingenta. **CCC.**
Published by: North American Publishing Co., 1500 Spring Garden St., 12th Fl, Philadelphia, PA 19130. TEL 215-238-5300, FAX 215-238-5213, magazinecs@napco.com, http://www.napco.com. Ed. Noelle Skodzinski TEL 215-238-5341. Pub. Mark S Hertzog TEL 215-238-5268. adv.: B&W page USD 5,520, color page USD 7,520; trim 7.75 x 10.5. Circ: 16,500.

P

070.5 USA ISSN 1539-1213
Z477
PUBLISHING FOR LIBRARY MARKETS (YEAR). Text in English. 1997. irreg., latest 2001. USD 1,995 per issue (print or online ed.) (effective 2008). **Description:** Evaluates library sales in different media including books, periodicals, online and CD-ROM/software to help formulate a business strategy and plan for the future of publishing business.
Related titles: Online - full text ed.
Published by: SIMBA Information (Subsidiary of: Market Research.Com), 11200 Rockville Pike, Ste 504, Rockville, MD 20852. TEL 240-747-3096, 888-297-4622, FAX 240-747-3004, customerservice@simbainformation.com. Pub. Linda Kopp.

070.5 USA ISSN 1523-7524
Z479
PUBLISHING FOR PROFESSIONAL MARKETS; review, trends & forecast. Text in English. 1996. a. USD 2,495 (print or online ed.) (effective 2008). **Document type:** *Directory, Trade.* **Description:** Helps professional publishers and suppliers create a profitable and strategic business plan.
Related titles: Online - full text ed.: USD 2,295 (effective 2005).
Published by: SIMBA Information (Subsidiary of: Market Research.Com), 60 Long Ridge Rd., Ste 300, Stamford, CT 06902. TEL 203-325-8193, FAX 203-325-8915, info@simbanet.com. Eds. Dan Strempel, Sean Kilkelly. Pub. Linda Kopp.

070.5 GBR ISSN 0309-2445
Z280
➤ **PUBLISHING HISTORY**; the social, economic and literary history of book, newspaper, and magazine publishing . Text in English. 1977. s-a. illus. back issues avail.; reprints avail. **Document type:** *Journal, Academic/Scholarly.* **Description:** Devoted to the socioeconomic and literary history of books, newspaper and magazine publishing.
Related titles: Online - full text ed.
Indexed: A20, A22, ASCA, AmH&L, AmHI, ArtHuCI, BEL&L, BrHumI, CA, ChLitAb, CurCont, H07, HistAb, IBR, IBZ, MLA-IB, PCI, RASB, T02, W07.
—BLDSC (7156.093000), IE, Ingenta. **CCC.**
Published by: ProQuest LLC, The Quorum, Barnwell Rd, Cambridge, CB5 8SW, United Kingdom. TEL 44-1223-215512, FAX 44-1223-215513, http://www.proquest.co.uk/. Ed. Simon Eliot. Circ: 200.

➤ **THE PUBLISHING INDUSTRY.** *see* BUSINESS AND ECONOMICS—Production Of Goods And Services

070.5 GBR
PUBLISHING MAGAZINE; magazines in the digital age. Text in English. 1991. 10/yr. GBP 25 domestic; GBP 45 foreign; GBP 2.50 newsstand/cover. adv. bk.rev.; software rev. back issues avail. **Document type:** *Magazine, Trade.* **Description:** Covers periodical publishing for directors and managers in the UK magazine and newspaper publishing industry.
Indexed: Inspec.
Published by: Forme Communications Ltd., 3 Percy St, London, W1P 9FA, United Kingdom. TEL 44-171-436-1671, FAX 44-171-436-1675. Ed. Harriet Marsh. Pub. Stephen Orr. Adv. contact Nicholas Friap. color page GBP 1,595; trim 297 x 210. Circ: 9,268.

070.5 GBR
PUBLISHING NEWS (ONLINE). Abbreviated title: P N Online. Text in English. 1979. w. bk.rev. illus. **Document type:** *Journal, Trade.*
Former titles (until 19??): Publishing News (Print) (0261-5398); Which incorporated: Paperback & Hardback Book Buyer; Book Buyer; Paperback Buyer
Media: Online - full text.
Indexed: RASB.
—CCC.
Published by: Publishing News Ltd., 39 Store St, London, WC1E 7DS, United Kingdom. TEL 44-203-0894460.

070.5 GBR
PUBLISHING PATHWAYS. Text in English. 1990. irreg., latest 2007. price varies. back issues avail. **Document type:** *Monographic series.*
Description: Features the work of leading specialists in book history including examples from the sixteenth to the twentieth century to covering some of the paths followed by books through the European network of print.
Published by: St Paul's Bibliographies, Ltd, 17 Greenbanks, Lyminge, Kent, CT18 8HG, United Kingdom. TEL 44-130-3862258, FAX 44-130-3862660, stpauls@stpaulsbib.com, http://www.oakknoll.com/okpstpauls.php. **Dist. by:** Oak Knoll Books, 310 Delaware St, New Castle, DE 19720. TEL 302-328-7232, 800-996-2556, FAX 302-328-7274, oakknoll@oakknoll.com, http://www.oakknoll.com.

070.5 USA
PUBLISHING PERSPECTIVES. Text in English. d. (Mon.-Fri.). adv. **Document type:** *Newsletter, Trade.*
Media: Online - full content.
Address: 1014 Fifth Ave, 4th Fl, New York, NY 10028. TEL 212-794-0116. Ed. Ed Nawotka. Adv. contact Erin Cox.

PUBLISHING POYNTERS; book and information marketing news and ideas from Dan Poynter. *see* BUSINESS AND ECONOMICS—Marketing And Purchasing

070.5 USA ISSN 1053-8801
Z1003 CODEN: PREQEI
➤ **PUBLISHING RESEARCH QUARTERLY.** Text in English. 1985. q. EUR 277, USD 382 combined subscription to institutions (print & online eds.) (effective 2012). bk.rev. illus. Index. back issues avail.; reprint service avail. from PSC. **Document type:** *Journal, Academic/Scholarly.* **Description:** Features research on or about books, the publishing and book distribution process, and the social, political, economic, and technological conditions that help shape this process.
Formerly (until 1991): Book Research Quarterly (0741-6148)
Related titles: Online - full text ed.: ISSN 1936-4792 (from IngentaConnect).
Indexed: A01, A02, A03, A08, A15, A20, A22, A26, ABIn, ASCA, AbAn, AmHI, C10, CA, CMM, ChLitAb, DIP, E01, E08, FR, G08, H07, H14, I05, IBR, IBZ, ISTA, L04, L05, L06, LISTA, M01, M02, MLA-IB, P10, P34, P48, P51, P53, P54, PAIS, PQC, RASB, S02, S03, S09, SCOPUS, SOPODA, SociolAb, T02.
—BLDSC (7156.094550), IE, Infotrieve, Ingenta, INIST. **CCC.**
Published by: Springer New York LLC (Subsidiary of: Springer Science+Business Media), 233 Spring St, New York, NY 10013. TEL 212-460-1500, FAX 212-460-1575, service-ny@springer.com. Ed. Robert E Baensch.

015.411 GBR
Z330.3.G7
PUBLISHING SCOTLAND YEARBOOK (YEAR). Text in English. 1988. a. GBP 9.99 per issue (effective 2009). bibl. **Document type:** *Directory, Trade.* **Description:** Provides information on Scottish publishers (with full page listings for over 100 Publishing Scotland publisher and network members); booksellers; literary festivals, prizes, awards and winners; Scottish library authorities; and a host of other organisations relevant to publishing.
Formerly (until 2008): Directory of Publishing in Scotland (0957-3615)
Published by: Scottish Publishers Association, 137 Dundee St, Edinburgh, Midlothian EH11 1BG, United Kingdom. TEL 44-131-2286866, FAX 44-131-2283220, info@scottishbooks.org.

070.5 ITA ISSN 1973-6061
PUBLISHING STUDIES. Text in Italian. 2007. irreg. **Document type:** *Monographic series, Trade.*
Related titles: Online - full text ed.: ISSN 1973-6053.
Published by: Polimetrica Publisher, Corso Milano 26, Monza, 20052, Italy. TEL 39-039-2301829, onlus@polimetrica.eu, http://www.polimetrica.eu.

070.5 IND
PUBLISHING TODAY (NEW DELHI, 2006). Text in English. 2006 (Dec.). m. free (effective 2011). **Document type:** *Newsletter, Trade.*
Description: Provides the news about the publishing industry and interviews a publishing personality every month.
Media: Online - full text.
Published by: Institute of Book Publishing, A-59, Okhla Industrial Area-II, New Delhi, 110 020, India. TEL 91-11-26387070, 91-11-26386165, mail@ibpindia.org.

070.5 NLD ISSN 2210-853X
▼ **PUBLISHR.NL MAGAZINE.** Text in Dutch. 2010. q. adv. **Document type:** *Magazine, Trade.*
Published by: Liones B.V., Postbus 1032, Rijswijk, 2280 CA, Netherlands. TEL 31-70-3191923, FAX 31-70-3193825, info@liones.nl, http://www.liones.nl.

070.5 ITA ISSN 1971-1042
Q G. (Quaderni Giornale) Variant title: Giornale della Libreria. Quaderni. Text in Italian. 2002. irreg. **Document type:** *Trade.*
Published by: Associazione Italiana Editori (A I E), Corso di Porta Romana 108, Milan, 20122, Italy. TEL 39-02-89280800, FAX 39-02-89280860, aie@aie.it, http://www.aie.it.

028.5 ITA ISSN 1121-3965
QUADERNI DI LI B E R. (Libri per Bambini e Ragazzi) Text in Italian. 1991. irreg. bk.rev. abstr.; bibl. **Document type:** *Monographic series, Bibliography.*
Related titles: ◆ Supplement to: Libri per Bambini e Ragazzi. ISSN 1120-4095.
Published by: Idest, Via Ombrone 1, Campi Bisenzio, FI 50013, Italy. TEL 39-055-8966577, FAX 39-055-8953344, liberweb@idest.net, http://www.idest.net.

002 NLD ISSN 0014-9527
Z1007
➤ **QUAERENDO**; a quarterly journal from the Low Countries devoted to manuscripts and printed books. Text mainly in English; Text occasionally in French, German. 1903. 4/yr. EUR 248, USD 347 to institutions; EUR 270, USD 378 combined subscription to institutions (print & online eds.) (effective 2012). adv. bk.rev. illus. index, cum.index: vols.1-26 (1971-1996). back issues avail.; reprint service avail. from PSC. **Document type:** *Journal, Academic/Scholarly.*
Former titles (until 1971): Het Boek (Antwerpen) (0774-9465); (until 1912): Tijdschrift voor Boek- en Bibliotheekwezen (0774-9457)
Related titles: Online - full text ed.: ISSN 1570-0690. EUR 225, USD 315 to institutions (effective 2012) (from IngentaConnect).
Indexed: A01, A03, A08, A22, AmHI, B24, BEL&L, CA, DIP, E01, FR, H07, HistAb, IBR, IBZ, IZBG, L04, L09, LISTA, MLA-IB, P30, PCI, SCOPUS, T02.
—IE, Infotrieve, Ingenta, INIST, Linda Hall. **CCC.**
Published by: Brill, PO Box 9000, Leiden, 2300 PA, Netherlands. TEL 31-71-5353500, FAX 31-71-5317532, cs@brill.nl. Ed. Croiset van Uchelen. Circ: 750. **Dist. by:** Turpin Distribution Services Ltd., Pegasus Dr, Stratton Business Park, Biggleswade, Bedfordshire SG18 8QB, United Kingdom. TEL 44-1767-604954, FAX 44-1767-601640, custserv@turpin-distribution.com, http://www.turpin-distribution.com/.

➤ **QUANGUO XINSHUMU/NATIONAL NEW BOOKS LIST.** *see* PUBLISHING AND BOOK TRADE—Abstracting, Bibliographies, Statistics

338.4707050941 GBR ISSN 1750-8347
QUARTERLY UPDATE. Variant title: B M L Quarterly Update. Text in English. 1991. q. GBP 140 combined subscription (print & online eds.) (effective 2009). back issues avail. **Document type:** *Magazine, Trade.* **Description:** Highlights many key consumer characteristics and trends, including data on the book market, both at home and overseas.
Former titles (until 2003): Quarterly Update. Book Marketing (1468-9219); (until 1998): Book Marketing Updates (0966-2936)
Related titles: Online - full text ed.
Published by: B M L, 39 Store St, London, WC1E 7DS, United Kingdom. TEL 44-870-8702345, johenry@publishingnews.co.uk.

686.3 AUS ISSN 1035-1817
QUEENSLAND BOOKBINDERS' GUILD. NEWSLETTER. Text in English. 1980. q. free to members (effective 2009). bk.rev. 12 p./no.; back issues avail. **Document type:** *Newsletter, Academic/Scholarly.*
Description: Contains topical news, reports of meetings and technical articles.
Published by: Queensland Bookbinders' Guild Inc., PO Box 3009, Tarragindi, QLD 4121, Australia. TEL 61-7-38483774.

028.1 CAN ISSN 0033-6491
Z487
QUILL AND QUIRE; Canada's magazine of book news and reviews. Abbreviated title: Q & Q. Text in English. 1935. 10/yr. CAD 59.95 domestic; CAD 95 foreign (effective 2010). adv. bk.rev. bibl.; illus.; stat. **Document type:** *Magazine, Trade.* **Description:** Provides agenda-setting editorial insights, useful analysis, and complete publishing news.
Incorporates (in 1989): Books for Young People (0835-8885)
Related titles: Microfiche ed.; Microfilm ed.: (from MML, MMP); Microform ed.: (from MML); Online - full text ed.; ◆ Supplement(s): Canadian Publishers Directory. ISSN 0008-4859.
Indexed: A26, A33, B05, C03, CBCARef, CBPI, CBRI, CLitI, CPerI, G08, MLA-IB, P48, PQC, RASB, SD, T02.
—CCC.
Published by: St. Joseph Media, 111 Queen St E, Ste 320, Toronto, ON M5C 1S2, Canada. TEL 416-364-3333, FAX 416-594-3374, communications@stjoseph.com, http://www.quillandquire.com/. Ed. Stuart Woods. Pub., Adv. contact Alison Jones. B&W page CAD 3,350, color page CAD 3,660; 8.25 x 10.75. Circ: 5,400 (paid).

028.1 USA ISSN 1061-6861
Z1035.A1
RAPPORT; the modern guide to books, music & more. Text in English. 1974. bi-m. USD 19.95. adv. bk.rev. illus. reprints avail. **Document type:** *Guide, Consumer.* **Description:** Extended reviews of current books and CDs, as well as articles and interviews with writers and musicians.
Formerly (until 1991): West Coast Review of Books (0095-3555)
Indexed: BRI, CBRI.
—Ingenta.
Published by: Rapport Publishing Co., Inc., 5265 Fountain Ave, Upper Terrace 6, Los Angeles, CA 90029. TEL 213-660-0433, 800-397-1266, FAX 213-660-0434. Ed. David Dreis. Adv. contact Glen Kenyon. Circ: 50,000.

741.6 ITA ISSN 1122-8148
ND2900
➤ **RARA VOLUMINA**; rivista di studi sull'editoria di pregio e il libro illustrato. Text in Italian; Abstracts in English. 1994. s-a. EUR 33.05 domestic; EUR 47.51 foreign (effective 2008). bk.rev. **Document type:** *Journal, Academic/Scholarly.* **Description:** Promotes specialized and interdisciplinary research on all aspects of bibliology, from codices and incunabula to modern books.
Published by: Maria Pacini Fazzi Editore, Via dell'Angelo Custode 33, Lucca, 55100, Italy. TEL 39-538-440188, FAX 39-538-464656, mpf@pacinifazzi.it. Circ: 1,000.

090 002.075 GBR ISSN 1746-7101
Z990
RARE BOOK REVIEW. Text in English. 1974. m. adv. bk.rev.; Website rev. bibl.; illus.; tr.lit.; mkt.; maps. 72 p./no.; back issues avail.; reprints avail. **Document type:** *Magazine, Bibliography.* **Description:** Features on antiquarian and rare books and literature pertaining and relevant to all those interested in literature.
Former titles (until 2004): Antiquarian Book Review (1477-4755); (until 2002): Antiquarian Book Monthly; (until 1993): Antiquarian Book Monthly Review (0306-7475)
Indexed: ChLitAb, SCOPUS.
—BLDSC (7291.797150), IE, Ingenta.
Published by: Countrywide Editions Ltd., 24 Maddox St, London, W1S 1PP, United Kingdom. TEL 44-20-75294220, subs@abmr.demon.co.uk. Adv. contact Wendy Rose.

028 NZL ISSN 1177-0562
READ ABOUT IT!. Variant title: Books in Homes Newsletter. Text in English. bi-m. **Document type:** *Newsletter.*
Published by: (Alan Duff Charitable Foundation), Books in Homes, PO Box 28-849, Remuera, Auckland, New Zealand. TEL 64-9-5790616, FAX 64-9-5790617, duffy@booksinhomes.org.nz.

070.5 GBR
THE RED BOOK; directory of publishers (year). Text in English. 1946. a. adv. **Document type:** *Directory, Trade.*
Incorporates (in 200?): Directory of UK and Irish Book Publishers; Former titles (until 200?): Whitaker's Red Book (1474-242X); (until 2000): Whitaker's Directory of Publishers (1362-1742); (until 1996): Whitaker's publishers in the United Kingdom and Their Addresses (0269-1043); (until 1990): Publishers in the United Kingdom and Their Addresses (0079-7839); (until 196?): Publishers and their Addresses
Published by: Nielsen BookData, 3rd Floor, Midas House, 62 Goldsworth Rd, Woking, GU21 6LQ, United Kingdom. TEL 44-870-7778710, FAX 44-870-7778711, sales@nielsenbookdata.co.uk, http://www.neilsenbookdata.com.

070.5 ARG ISSN 0325-1942
REDACCION; revista lider de opinion. Text in Spanish. m. (10/yr.). ARS 80, USD 100. illus.
Published by: Editorial Redaccion S.A., Bme. Mitre 1970, 2o piso, Buenos Aires, Argentina. TEL 54-114-9534355, FAX 54-114-9538455. Eds. Emiliana Lopez Saavedra, Hugo Gambini.

REDACTUEL. *see* JOURNALISM

REDAKTIONS ADRESS. *see* BUSINESS AND ECONOMICS—Trade And Industrial Directories

381.45002 CMR
REGIONAL CENTRE FOR BOOK PROMOTION IN AFRICA. BULLETIN OF INFORMATION/CENTRE REGIONAL DE PROMOTION DU LIVRE EN AFRIQUE. BULLETIN D'INFORMATION. Text in English, French. 1978. q.
Published by: Regional Centre for Book Promotion in Africa, BP 1646, Yaounde, Cameroon.

028.5 FRA ISSN 0398-8384
REVUE DES LIVRES POUR ENFANTS. Text in French. 1965. bi-m. EUR 54 domestic to individuals; EUR 60 in Europe to individuals; EUR 70 elsewhere to individuals; EUR 44 domestic to libraries; EUR 50 in Europe to libraries; EUR 57 elsewhere to libraries (effective 2009). adv. bk.rev. back issues avail. **Document type:** *Journal, Bibliography.*
Description: Reviews recently published children's books and publishes articles about children's literature and libraries.
Formerly: Bulletin d'Analyses de Livres pour Enfants
Indexed: ChLitAb.
Published by: (Centre National du Livre pour Enfants), Joie par les Livres, Quai Francois Mauriac, Paris, Cedex 13 75706, France. http://www.lajoieparleslivres.com. Ed. Annick Lorant-Jolly. Pub., Adv. contact Genevieve Patte. Circ: 5,000.

002 CHE ISSN 0037-9212
Z119
REVUE FRANCAISE D'HISTOIRE DU LIVRE. Text in French. 1931. a. EUR 70 to institutions (effective 2010). adv. bk.rev. bibl.; charts; illus. **Document type:** *Bibliography.* **Description:** Focuses on the history of books in France and abroad.
Formerly (until 1971): Societe des Bibliophiles de Guyenne. Bulletin (1142-463X)
Indexed: A22, B24, DIP, FR, IBR, IBZ, MLA-IB, P30.
—IE, INIST. **CCC.**
Published by: (Societe des Bibliophiles de Guyenne FRA), Librairie Droz S.A., 11 rue Firmin-Massot, Geneva 12, 1211, Switzerland. TEL 41-22-3466666, FAX 41-22-3472391, droz@droz.org, http://www.droz.org.

RIGHTS AND LIABILITIES OF PUBLISHERS, BROADCASTERS, AND REPORTERS. *see* LAW—Civil Law

070.5 CAN ISSN 1203-1887
RIGHTS CANADA. Text in English. 1976-198?; resumed 1990. s-a. adv. illus. **Document type:** *Catalog.* **Description:** A selected listing of Canadian titles for which foreign rights are available.
Related titles: Online - full text ed.
Published by: Association for the Export of Canadian Books, 504 1 Nicholas St, Ottawa, ON K1N 7B7, Canada. TEL 613-562-2324, FAX 613-562-2329, aecb@aecb.org, http://aecb.org. Ed. Nicolas Levesque. Adv. contact Catherine Montgomery. Circ: 2,600.

028.1 ITA ISSN 1124-4216
LA RIVISTA DEI LIBRI. Text in Italian. 1991. m. EUR 39 domestic; EUR 57.35 in Europe; EUR 82.35 Africa, America, Asia (effective 2009). adv. **Document type:** *Magazine, Consumer.*
Published by: New York Review of Books, Via de' Lamberti 1, Florence, FI 50123, Italy. TEL 39-055-219624, FAX 39-055-295427. Ed. Pietro Corsi. Adv. contact Flavio Biondi. Circ: 15,000.

ROMANCE WRITERS' REPORT. *see* LITERATURE—Adventure And Romance

ROMANTIC TIMES BOOK REVIEWS; the magazine for fiction lovers. *see* LITERATURE—Adventure And Romance

070.5 USA
ROUND TABLE (ANDERSON). Text in English. 1952. bi-m. free.
Published by: Protestant Church-Owned Publishers Association, 1200 E 5th St, Box 2499, Anderson, IN 46018. Ed. Richard Grant. Circ: 500.

RUCH WYDAWNICZY W LICZBACH/POLISH PUBLISHING IN FIGURES. *see* PUBLISHING AND BOOK TRADE—Abstracting, Bibliographies, Statistics

070.5 USA
RUSS VON HOELSCHER PUBLISHING REPORT. Text in English. 1980. 6/yr. USD 49 domestic; USD 59 foreign; USD 7.50 newsstand/cover (effective 2000). bk.rev. **Document type:** *Newsletter.* **Description:** Focuses on publishing and marketing ideas and strategies for non-fiction books.
Former titles (until 1992): Independent Publishing Report; (until 1984): Free Lance Writing and Publishing
Published by: Publishers Media, 1136 Broadway, Ste 3, Box 1295, El Cajon, CA 92022-1295. TEL 619-588-9103, FAX 619-588-9103, onlinemedia@access1.net. Ed. Russ A von Hoelscher. R&P Russ von Hoelscher. Circ: 3,900.

745.61 USA ISSN 1944-6306
PN147.5
S C B W I BULLETIN. Text in English. 1971. bi-m. free to members (effective 2009). bk.rev. **Document type:** *Bulletin, Trade.*
Description: Contains current information about the children's book market, articles on the craft of writing and illustrating for children, news and announcements, and a complete guide to SCBWI events around the world.
Formerly (until 1993): S C B W Bulletin
Related titles: Online - full text ed.: free (effective 2009).
Published by: Society of Children's Book Writers & Illustrators, 8271 Beverly Blvd, Los Angeles, CA 90048. TEL 323-782-1010, FAX 323-782-1892, scbwi@scbwi.org, http://www.scbwi.org. Eds. Lin Oliver, Stephen Mooser.

070.5 GBR
S F E P DIRECTORY (ONLINE). Text in English. 1990. a. 350 p./no.; **Document type:** *Directory.* **Description:** Provides contact information for more than 440 SfEP members plus details of the skills, subjects and services they offer.
Former titles (until 2005): S F E P Directory (Print) (1741-1459); (until 2003): Society of Freelance Editors and Proofreaders. Directory (0960-5533)
Media: Online - full text.
Published by: Society for Editors and Proofreaders, Erico House, 93-99 Upper Richmond Rd, Putney, London, SW15 2TG, United Kingdom. TEL 44-20-87855617, FAX 44-20-87855618, administration@sfep.org.uk. Circ: 2,000.

070.5 GBR ISSN 1073-1725
Z4
S H A R P NEWS. Text in English. 1992. q. free to members (effective 2010). bk.rev. bibl. back issues avail. **Document type:** *Newsletter, Academic/Scholarly.* **Description:** Discusses teaching programs, research projects, and course syllabi; lists conferences, lectures, fellowships, employment opportunities, and scholarly publications on the history of book publishing.
Related titles: Online - full text ed.: ISSN 2155-3491.
Indexed: MLA-IB.
Published by: (Wesleyan College USA), Society for the History of Authorship Reading and Publishing, c/o David Finkelstein Ed, Napier University,, Craighouse Campus, Craighouse Rd, Edinburgh, EH10 5LG, United Kingdom. members@sharpweb.org. Ed. Dr. Sydney Shep TEL 64-4-4635784.

070.5 PRT ISSN 0870-3124
B5
S O D I LIVROS. ANALISE. Text in Portuguese. 1984. q.
Published by: (Sociedade Distribuidora de Livros e Publicacoes), Editorial Fragmentos, Travessa de Estevao Pinto, 6-A, Lisbon, 1000, Portugal.

381.45002 USA ISSN 1087-2949
Z479
S P A N CONNECTION. Text in English. 1995. m. USD 115 in US & Canada (effective 2008). adv. index. 24 p./no. 3 cols./p.; back issues avail. **Document type:** *Newsletter, Trade.* **Description:** Journal of the small publishers association helping members to sell more books, increase profits and life their standing as an expert.
Published by: Small Publishers Association of North America, 1618 W Colorado Ave, Colorado Springs, CO 80904. TEL 719-475-1726, FAX 719-395-8374. Adv. contact Deb Ellis. page USD 970; trim 8.5 x 11. Circ: 3,500 (paid and controlled).

070.5 USA ISSN 0730-2223
S P E X. (Small-Publishers Exchange) Text in English. 1981. m. USD 40 to members. adv. bk.rev. **Document type:** *Newsletter.* **Description:** News, letters, notes, announcements, reviews, articles and book lists pertaining to the activities of independent authors, publishers, and printers.
Published by: Bay Area Independent Publishers Association, PO Box E, Corte Madera, CA 94976. TEL 415-257-8275. Ed. Margaret Speaker Yuan. Circ: 250.

070.5 USA
S S P BULLETIN. Text in English. bi-m. USD 65 (effective 1999). adv. **Document type:** *Newsletter.*
Former titles (until 1998): Scholarly Publishing Today (1062-0117); (until 1992): Society for Scholarly Publishing Newsletter
—CCC.
Published by: Society for Scholarly Publishing, 10200 W 44th Ave, Ste 304, Wheat Ridge, CO 80033. TEL 303-422-3914, FAX 303-422-8894. Ed. Greg Fagan. R&P, Adv. contact Michael Thompson.

070.5 USA ISSN 0000-1767
Z6951
SAMIR HUSNI'S GUIDE TO NEW CONSUMER MAGAZINES. Text in English. 1986. a. USD 49 (effective 2007). illus. **Document type:** *Directory, Trade.* **Description:** Covers new consumer magazines launched in the U.S. during the preceding year. Provides cover image and bibliographic data for each. Notable launches are reviewed and an annual winner named.
Formerly (until 1991): Samir Husni's Guide to New Magazines (0892-7170)
Related titles: Online - full text ed.
—CCC.
Published by: (University of Mississippi, Department of Journalism), Mr.Magazine, 231 Farley Hall, P O Box 2906, University, MS 38677. TEL 662-915-5502, FAX 662-915-7765, hsamir@olemiss.edu. Ed. Samir Husni TEL 662-915-5502.

028.1 USA
SANDIA REVIEW OF BOOKS. Text in English. 1986. m. USD 25. bk.rev. abstr.; illus. back issues avail. **Document type:** *Journal, Trade.*
Published by: (Lange Foundation), Sandia Communications, Inc., 1208 Nakomis Ave, N E, Ste B, Albuquerque, NM 87112-6053. TEL 505-299-5245. Circ: 12,500 (paid).

SAVAGE UNDERGROUND. *see* MOTION PICTURES

028 SRB ISSN 0354-3021
AP56
SAVREMENIK PLUS; knjizevni casopis. Text in Serbo-Croatian. 1955. 3/yr. bk.rev. **Document type:** *Magazine, Consumer.*
Formerly (until 1993): Savremenik (0036-519X)
Indexed: MLA, MLA-IB, RASB.
Published by: Apostrof, Francuska 7, Belgrade, 11000. Ed. Srba Ignatovich. Circ: 1,500.

070.5 DEU ISSN 0941-8504
DIE SCHOENSTEN DEUTSCHEN BUECHER. Text in German. 1991. a. EUR 11.99 (effective 2006). **Document type:** *Catalog, Bibliography.* **Description:** Report on the year's best books.
Formed by the merger of (1980-1991): Schoensten Buecher der Bundesrepublik Deutschland (0722-284X); Which was formerly (1971-1980): Fuenfzig Buecher (0344-1547); (1957-1971): Schoensten Deutschen Buecher (0558-8723); (1952-1957): Schoensten Buecher (0344-1652); (1968-1991): Schoensten Buecher der Deutschen Demokratischen Republik (0323-4959); Which was formerly (1955-1968): Spiegel Deutscher Buchkunst (0081-3702)
Published by: M V B - Marketing- und Verlagsservice des Buchhandels GmbH, Postfach 100442, Frankfurt Am Main, 60004, Germany. TEL 49-69-13060, FAX 49-69-1306201, info@mvb-online.de.

070.5 CHE ISSN 0080-6838
DIE SCHOENSTEN SCHWEIZER BUECHER/MOST BEAUTIFUL SWISS BOOKS/PIU BEI LIBRI SVIZZERA/PLUS BEAUX LIVRES SUISSES. Text in English, French, German, Italian. 1943. a. free. adv. bk.rev. **Document type:** *Bibliography.*
Published by: Eidgenoessisches Departement des Innern, Hallwylstr 15, Bern, 3003, Switzerland. TEL 41-31-3229267, FAX 41-31-3227834.

SCHOOL LIBRARY JOURNAL; the world's largest reviewer of books, multimedia, and technology for childrens and teens. *see* LIBRARY AND INFORMATION SCIENCES

028.1 AUT ISSN 1606-8092
BX2348.Z8
SCHRIFT/ZEICHEN; Literatur - Kunst - Religion. Text in German. 1947. q. EUR 20; EUR 5 newsstand/cover (effective 2005). **Document type:** *Magazine, Consumer.*
Formerly (until 2000): Die Zeit im Buch (0044-2089)
Published by: Literarisches Forum der Katholischen Aktion Oesterreichs, Waehringerstr 2-4, Vienna, 1090, Austria. TEL 43-1-317616531, FAX 43-1-317616517, ka.literarisches-forum@edw.or.at, http://www.literarisches-forum.at.

070.5 DEU ISSN 0942-4709
SCHRIFTEN UND ZEUGNISSE ZUR BUCHGESCHICHTE. Text in German. 1992. irreg., latest vol.18, 2006. price varies. **Document type:** *Monographic series, Academic/Scholarly.*
Published by: (Leipziger Arbeitskreis zur Geschichte des Buchwesens), Harrassowitz Verlag, Kreuzberger Ring 7b-d, Wiesbaden, 65205, Germany. TEL 49-611-5300, FAX 49-611-530560, verlag@harrassowitz.de, http://www.harrassowitz.de.

070.50688 CHE ISSN 0036-732X
Z2775
SCHWEIZER BUCH/LIBRO SVIZZERO/LIVRE SUISSE. Text in French, German, Italian, English. 1871. s-m. CHF 300 domestic; CHF 400 foreign; CHF 13 newsstand/cover (effective 2003). adv. bk.rev. bibl. index. 150 p./no. 2 cols./p.; back issues avail.; reprints avail. **Document type:** *Journal, Trade.*
Former titles (until 1942): Bibliographisches Bulletin der Schweizerischen Landesbibliothek (0257-6155); (until 1900): Bibliographie und Literarische Chronik der Schweiz (1022-5773); (until 1877): Bibliographie der Schweiz (0257-6147)
Related titles: Online - full text ed.: ISSN 1661-8211.
Indexed: RASB.
—Linda Hall.
Published by: (Schweizerischer Buchhaendler- und Verleger-Verband), Schweizerische Landesbibliothek/Bibliotheque Nationale Suisse, Hallwylstr 15, Bern, 3003, Switzerland. TEL 41-31-3228911, FAX 41-31-3228463, info@nb.admin.ch. R&P Elena Balzardi. Circ: 800.

070.50688 CHE ISSN 0036-7338
SCHWEIZER BUCHHANDEL/LIBRAIRIE SUISSE/LIBRERIA SVIZZERA. Text in German. 1943. 21/yr. CHF 148; CHF 198 foreign (effective 2000). adv. bk.rev. bibl.; charts. index. **Document type:** *Journal, Trade.* **Description:** Includes association news, reports of events, trade information, announcements of new publications, award presentations, list of events and exhibitions, letters from readers, list of advertisers, and positions available.
Indexed: KES, RASB.
Published by: Schweizerischer Buchhaendler- und Verleger-Verband, Alderstr 40, Zuerich, 8034, Switzerland. TEL 41-1-4212800, FAX 41-1-4212818, sbvv@swissbooks.ch. Eds. Carlo Bernasconi, Martin Walker. Circ: 3,000. **Subscr. to:** Fischer Druck AG, Muensingen 3110, Switzerland. TEL 41-31-7205111, FAX 41-31-7205212.

070.5 CHE ISSN 0080-7230
SCHWEIZER BUCHHANDELS-ADRESSBUCH. Text in German. 1966. a. CHF 74 (effective 2001). adv. **Document type:** *Directory, Trade.*
Published by: Schweizerischer Buchhaendler- und Verleger-Verband, Alderstr 40, Zuerich, 8034, Switzerland. TEL 41-1-4212800, FAX 41-1-4212818, sbvv@swissbooks.ch. Adv. contact Yolanda Canonica.

570 USA ISSN 1535-5365
Z286.S4
SCIENCE EDITOR. Text in English. 1978. bi-m. USD 46 to non-members; free to members (effective 2006). adv. bk.rev. **Document type:** *Newsletter.* **Description:** Forum for the exchange of information among authors, editors, and publishers in the life sciences.
Former titles (until 2000): C B E Views (0164-5609); (until 1978): Council of Biology Editors. Newsletter
Indexed: P30.
—Infotrieve.
Published by: Council of Science Editors, c/o Drohan Management Group, 12100 Sunset Hills Rd, Ste 130, Reston, VA 20190. TEL 703-437-4377, FAX 703-435-4390, CSE@CouncilScienceEditors.org, http://www.councilscienceeditors.org. Ed. Martha Tacker. Adv. contact Alison C Brown. Circ: 1,200.

002 AUS ISSN 1834-9013
➤ **SCRIPT & PRINT**; bulletin of the Bibliographical Society of Australia and New Zealand. Text in English. 1970. q. bk.rev. illus. 64 p./no.; back issues avail. **Document type:** *Journal, Academic/Scholarly.* **Description:** Covers book history, print cultures and bibliography: the history of printing, publishing, bookselling, typefounding, papermaking, bookbinding, palaeography and codicology, and textual bibliography.
Formerly (until 2004): Bibliographical Society of Australia and New Zealand. Bulletin (0084-7852)
Related titles: Online - full content ed.
Indexed: AEI, AusPAIS, MLA-IB, RILM, SCOPUS.
—Ingenta.
Published by: Bibliographical Society of Australia & New Zealand, c/o Archives, Special Collections & Grainger Museum, 3rd Fl, Baillieu Library, University of Melbourne, Melbourne, VIC 3010, Australia. TEL 61-3-8344-5366, FAX 61-3-9347-8627, morrison@umimelb.edu.au. Ed. Shef Rogers.

070.5 ITA ISSN 1970-0180
SCRIVERE; per la pagina, per lo schermo, per il lavoro. Text in Italian. 2006. w. (11/yr.). **Document type:** *Magazine, Consumer.*
Published by: De Agostini Editore, Via G da Verrazzano 15, Novara, 28100, Italy. TEL 39-0321-4241, FAX 39-0321-424305, info@deagostini.it, http://www.deagostini.it.

091 938 BEL ISSN 2037-0245
SEGNO E TESTO; international journal of manuscripts and text transmission. Text in English. 2003. a. EUR 72 (effective 2012). **Document type:** *Journal, Academic/Scholarly.* **Description:** Dedicated to the study of manuscripts and written culture.
Published by: (Universita degli Studi di Cassino ITA), Brepols Publishers, Begijnhof 67, Turnhout, 2300, Belgium. TEL 32-14-448020, FAX 32-14-428919, periodicals@brepols.net, http://www.brepols.net. Ed. Paolo De Paolis.

070.5 USA
SELECT (NEW YORK). Text in English. 1919. q. **Description:** Contains magazine industry news.
Formerly: S - M News
Published by: Select Magazine, 101 Park Ave, New York, NY 10178-0002. TEL 212-696-7300. Ed. Nancy Cooper. Circ: 2,000.

070.59305 GBR ISSN 1752-9433
THE SELF PUBLISHING MAGAZINE; helping you get the most from publishing your own book. Text in English. 2005. 3/yr. GBP 12 domestic (print or online ed.); GBP 16.50 in Europe (print or online ed.); GBP 24.50 elsewhere (print or online ed.); GBP 4.50 per issue domestic; GBP 7.50 per issue in Europe; GBP 10 per issue elsewhere (effective 2009). adv. bk.rev. **Document type:** *Magazine, Trade.* **Description:** Guides to anyone about to self publish their own book.
Formerly (until 2006): Readers' Review (1748-1422)
Related titles: Online - full text ed.
Published by: Troubador Publishing Ltd., 5 Weir Rd, Kibworth Beauchamp, Leicester, LE8 0LQ, United Kingdom. TEL 44-116-2792299, FAX 44-116-2792277. Ed. Jane Rowland. Pub. Jeremy Thompson. Adv. contact Wendy O Brien TEL 44-1392-873270. page GBP 180; 190 x 275.

070.5 USA
THE SELF-PUBLISHING MANUAL. Text in English. 19??. irreg. USD 14.95 per issue (effective 2011). **Document type:** *Handbook/Manual/Guide, Consumer.* **Description:** Covers copyright, book manufacturing, promotion, the Web, audio, video, CD-ROMs, magazine excerpting, foreign language editions and more. Includes how to write, print and sell your own book.
Published by: Dustbooks, PO Box 100, Paradise, CA 95967. TEL 530-877-6110, 800-477-6110, FAX 530-877-0222, info@dustbooks.com.

028.5 ITA ISSN 1120-253X
SFOGLIALIBRO; la biblioteca dei ragazzi. Text in Italian. 1988. 4/yr. adv. bk.rev. **Document type:** *Magazine, Consumer.* **Description:** Covers juvenile literature and children's libraries.
Related titles: ◆ Supplement to: Biblioteche Oggi. ISSN 0392-8586.
Published by: Editrice Bibliografica SpA, Via Bergonzoli 1-5, Milan, MI 20127, Italy. TEL 39-02-28315996, FAX 39-02-28315906, bibliografica@bibliografica.it, http://www.bibliografica.it. Circ: 3,000.

381.45002 GBR ISSN 0950-0715
Z327
SHEPPARD'S BOOK DEALERS IN BRITISH ISLES. Text in English. 1951. a., latest 28th ed. GBP 15 per issue (effective 2009). adv. **Document type:** *Directory, Trade.* **Description:** Lists antiquarian and second-hand book dealers in the British Isles, The Channel Islands, The Isle of Man and the Republic of Ireland.
Formerly (until 1986): Directory of Dealers in Secondhand and Antiquarian Books in the British Isles (0070-5411)
Published by: Richard Joseph Publishers Ltd., PO Box 15, Torrington, Devon EX38 8ZJ, United Kingdom. TEL 44-1805-625750, FAX 44-1805-625376, post@sheppardsworld.co.uk, http://www.sheppardsworld.co.uk. Ed. Richard Joseph. Adv. contact Claire Brumham.

381.45002 GBR ISSN 1361-9535
SHEPPARD'S BOOK DEALERS IN JAPAN. Text in English. 1994. irreg., latest 1994, 1st ed. GBP 24 per issue (effective 2009). **Document type:** *Directory, Trade.* **Description:** Lists antiquarian and secondhand book dealers in Japan. Includes Business Name, Proprietor, web sites, and book subject classification indexes.
Related titles: Online - full text ed.
Published by: Richard Joseph Publishers Ltd., PO Box 15, Torrington, Devon EX38 8ZJ, United Kingdom. TEL 44-1805-625750, FAX 44-1805-625376, post@sheppardsworld.co.uk. Ed. Richard Joseph. Adv. contact Claire Brumham.

381.45002 GBR ISSN 0962-2764
SHEPPARD'S BOOKDEALERS IN AUSTRALIA AND NEW ZEALAND. Text in English. 1991. triennial, latest 4th ed. GBP 30 per issue (effective 2008). adv. **Document type:** *Directory.* **Description:** Lists antiquarian and secondhand book dealers in Australia and New Zealand.
Related titles: Online - full text ed.
Published by: Richard Joseph Publishers Ltd., PO Box 15, Torrington, Devon EX38 8ZJ, United Kingdom. TEL 44-1805-625750, FAX 44-1805-625376, post@sheppardsworld.co.uk. Ed. Richard Joseph. Adv. contact Claire Brumham. Circ: 1,000.

381.45002 GBR ISSN 0269-1469
Z475
SHEPPARD'S BOOKDEALERS IN NORTH AMERICA. Text in English. 1954. biennial, latest 15th ed. GBP 30 per issue (effective 2009). adv. index. **Document type:** *Directory, Trade.*
Formerly (until 1986): Bookdealers in North America (0068-0109)
Related titles: Online - full text ed.
—BLDSC (8256.432100).
Published by: Richard Joseph Publishers Ltd., PO Box 15, Torrington, Devon EX38 8ZJ, United Kingdom. TEL 44-1805-625750, FAX 44-1805-625376, post@sheppardsworld.co.uk. Ed. Richard Joseph. Adv. contact Claire Brumham.

070.5 GBR
SHEPPARD'S INTERNATIONAL DIRECTORY OF EPHEMERA DEALERS. Text in English. 1994. irreg., latest 2nd ed. GBP 24 per issue (effective 2009). **Document type:** *Directory, Trade.* **Description:** Provides the details of ephemera dealers in twenty countries. Includes Business Name, Proprietor, web sites, and subject classification indexes.
Related titles: Online - full text ed.
Published by: Richard Joseph Publishers Ltd., PO Box 15, Torrington, Devon EX38 8ZJ, United Kingdom. TEL 44-1805-625750, FAX 44-1805-625376, post@sheppardsworld.co.uk. Ed. Richard Joseph. Adv. contact Claire Brumham.

070.5 GBR ISSN 0963-9721
SHEPPARD'S INTERNATIONAL DIRECTORY PRINT & MAP SELLERS. Text in English. 1987. irreg., latest 4th ed. GBP 27 per issue (effective 2009). **Document type:** *Directory, Trade.* **Description:** Lists print and map sellers in forty-two countries. Includes Business Name, Proprietor, web sites, and subject classification indexes - separate ones for maps and prints.
Related titles: Online - full text ed.
Published by: Richard Joseph Publishers Ltd., PO Box 15, Torrington, Devon EX38 8ZJ, United Kingdom. TEL 44-1805-625750, FAX 44-1805-625376, post@sheppardsworld.co.uk. Ed. Richard Joseph. Adv. contact Claire Brumham.

070.5 JPN ISSN 0037-3788
SHINKAN NEWS FOR READERS/SHINKAN NYUSU. Text in Japanese. 1959. m. JPY 2,232, USD 17. adv. bk.rev. bibl. **Description:** Covers forthcoming books.
Published by: Tokyo Shuppan Hanbai Co. Ltd., 6-24 Higashi-Goken-cho, Shinjuku-ku, Tokyo, 162-0813, Japan. FAX 03-3267-3781. Ed. Hiromasa Kohtaki. Circ: 150,000.

070.5 658 USA
SHORTRUNS; for publishers of books, journals, magazines and newsletters. Text in English. 1989. q. Website rev.; bk.rev.; software rev. abstr.; bibl.; charts; illus.; maps; mkt.; pat.; stat.; tr.lit. **Document type:** *Newsletter, Consumer.* **Description:** Caters to those publishers interested in pre-press and printing.
Related titles: Online - full text ed.
Published by: Marrakech Inc., 720 Wesley Ave, Tarpon Springs, FL 34689. TEL 727-942-2218, FAX 727-937-4758, print@marrak.com, http://www.marrak.com. Ed. Shirley Copperman. Pub., R&P Steen Sigmund TEL 727-942-2218. Circ: 18,500.

070.5 USA ISSN 2153-5825
SIGNATURE (MCLEAN). Text in English. 1965. bi-m. free to members (effective 2010). adv. back issues avail. **Document type:** *Magazine, Trade.* **Description:** Provides a first point of reference for best practices, reports, and applications.
Former titles (until 2010): Association Publishing (1055-2545); (until 1990): Snapshot; (until 19??): S N A P Bulletin
Published by: Association Media & Publishing, 8405 Greensboro Dr, No 800, McLean, VA 22102. TEL 703-506-3285, FAX 703-506-3266, info@associationmediaandpublishing.org. adv.: B&W page USD 726, color page USD 1,437; bleed 8.625 x 11.125.

SINDICATO NACIONAL DOS EDITORES DE LIVROS. INFORMATIVO BIBLIOGRAFICO. *see* BIBLIOGRAPHIES

070.5 BRA
SINDICATO NACIONAL DOS EDITORES DE LIVROS. JORNAL. Text in Portuguese. 1984. bi-m. **Document type:** *Journal, Corporate.*
Published by: Sindicato Nacional dos Editores de Livros, Av Rio Branco, 37 Andar 15, Centro, Rio de Janeiro, 20090-003, Brazil. TEL 55-21-2336481, FAX 55-21-2538502, snel@snel.org.br, http://www.snel.org.br.

070.5 SGP ISSN 0080-9659
Z464.S55
SINGAPORE BOOK WORLD. Text in Chinese, English, Malay. 1970. a. SGD 15. adv. bk.rev. back issues avail. **Document type:** *Journal, Trade.* **Description:** Features articles on book trade.
Indexed: BAS, L11.
—Ingenta.
Published by: National Book Development Council of Singapore, NBDCS Secretariat, Blk 162 Bukit Merah Central, Ste 05 3555, Singapore, 150162, Singapore. TEL 65-2732730. Ed. Hedwig Anuar. Circ: 3,000.

028.1 USA ISSN 1934-6557
Z1003
SIRREADALOT.ORG. Text in English. 2004. m. free (effective 2008). **Document type:** *Journal, Consumer.* **Description:** Features brief reviews of new books being published every month on a wide array of topics.
Address: 762 Martin Luther King Jr Blvd, Ste 500, Chapel Hill, NC 27514. TEL 919-929-2249, FAX 919-968-2557.

SKOLEBIBLIOTEKSAARBOG. *see* LIBRARY AND INFORMATION SCIENCES

SLOVO (MOSCOW). *see* LITERATURE

028.1 USA
Z1215
SMALL PRESS BOOK REVIEW (ONLINE). Text in English. 1985. q. domestic online only. bk.rev. **Document type:** *Journal, Trade.* **Description:** Contains brief descriptive, critical reviews of all types of books published by small presses and periodicals from independent presses. Includes a children's book section.
Formerly (until 1994): Small Press Book Review (Print) (8756-7202)
Media: Online - full content.
Indexed: BRI, CBRI.
Published by: Greenfield Press, PO Box 176, Southport, CT 06890. Ed., Pub. Henry Berry.

THE SMALL PRESS RECORD OF BOOKS IN PRINT (CD-ROM). *see* PUBLISHING AND BOOK TRADE—Abstracting, Bibliographies, Statistics

070.593 USA ISSN 1949-2731
SMALL PRESS REVIEW (ONLINE). Abbreviated title: S P R. Text in English. 1967. bi-m. USD 35 (effective 2011). adv. bk.rev. illus. back issues avail.; reprints avail. **Document type:** *Magazine, Trade.* **Description:** Includes two sections, one for books and one for magazines. Features include news and notes on editorial needs and contests, reviews, guest editorials, letters, listings in each issue of new publishers and their editorial slants, columns and the Free Sample Mart offering samples of 30 magazines and books.
Formerly (until 2009): Small Press Review (Print) (0037-7228); Which incorporated (1993-1994): Small Magazine Review (1068-7742)
Media: Online - full text. **Related titles:** ◆ Supplement to: The International Directory of Little Magazines and Small Presses. ISSN 0092-3974.
Indexed: AmHI, CBRI, H07, MLA-IB, NPI, T02.
Published by: Dustbooks, PO Box 100, Paradise, CA 95967. TEL 530-877-6110, 800-477-6110, FAX 530-877-0222, info@dustbooks.com. Ed. Len Fulton.

070.5 USA ISSN 1081-1133
SMALL PUBLISHER. Text in English. 1993. 6/yr. USD 15; USD 19.50 foreign (effective 1998). bk.rev. **Document type:** *Newspaper.* **Description:** Contains articles for persons at small companies publishing books, periodicals, and audio and video tapes. Also profiles successful self-publishers and small publishers.
Published by: Nigel Maxey, Ed. & Pub., PO Box 1620, Pineville, WV 24874-1620. TEL 304-732-8195. adv.: B&W page USD 200. Circ: 5,900.

028.1 GBR ISSN 1471-7484
SOLANDER. Text in English. 1997. s-a. GBP 25 domestic membership; EUR 40 in Europe membership; USD 50 in United States membership; CAD 60 in Canada membership; AUD 65 in Australia membership; NZD 80 in New Zealand membership (effective 2009). adv. back issues avail. **Document type:** *Magazine, Consumer.* **Description:** Contains interviews, articles, short fiction and commentary on historical fiction.
Indexed: MLA-IB.
Published by: Historical Novel Society, Marine Cottage, The Strand, Starcross, Devon, EX6 8NY, United Kingdom. TEL 44-2193-884898, richard@historicalnovelsociety.org. Pub. Richard Lee. Circ: 900 (paid and controlled).

SOUTHEAST - EAST ASIAN ENGLISH PUBLICATIONS IN PRINT. *see* PUBLISHING AND BOOK TRADE—Abstracting, Bibliographies, Statistics

SOUTHERN AFRICAN BOOKS IN PRINT. *see* BIBLIOGRAPHIES

028.1 USA ISSN 1559-971X
SOUTHERN REVIEW OF BOOKS. Text in English. 20??. m. free (effective 2011). back issues avail. **Document type:** *Newsletter, Consumer.*
Media: Online - full text.
Published by: Anvil Publishers, PO Box 2694, Tucker, GA 30085. TEL 770-938-0289, 800-500-3524, FAX 770-493-7232, custserv@anvilpub.com, http://www.anvilpub.com. Ed. Noel Griese.

SPANISH LANGUAGE BOOKS FOR CHILDREN & YOUNG ADULTS. *see* PUBLISHING AND BOOK TRADE—Abstracting, Bibliographies, Statistics

028.1 USA ISSN 0038-7606
SPIRITUAL BOOK NEWS. Text in English. 1958. 8/yr. bk.rev. **Document type:** *Newsletter.* **Description:** Contains feature reviews of book club selections, as well as notices and reviews of other current books available in the field of spiritual reading.
Published by: (Spiritual Book Associates), Ave Maria Press, P O Box 428, Notre Dame, IN 46556. TEL 219-287-2838, FAX 219-239-2904. Ed. Robert Hamma. Circ: 9,000.

SREDA; rossiisko-evropeiskii zhurnal o media. *see* COMMUNICATIONS

SRI LANKA NATIONAL BIBLIOGRAPHY. *see* PUBLISHING AND BOOK TRADE—Abstracting, Bibliographies, Statistics

028 371.9144 NLD ISSN 1872-5406
START!-KRANT. Text in Dutch. 2004. 10/yr. EUR 35 to individuals; EUR 60 to institutions (effective 2008).
Published by: Eenvoudig Communiceren, Postbus 10208, Amsterdam, 1001 EE, Netherlands. TEL 31-20-5206070, FAX 31-20-5206061, info@eenvoudigcommuniceren.nl, http://www.eenvoudigcommuniceren.nl.

070.5 USA ISSN 2154-7610
▼ **STRAT**; the newsletter of print and online magazine publishing strategy. Text in English. 2010. m. USD 89 (effective 2011). **Document type:** *Newsletter, Trade.* **Description:** News and information about print and online publishing.
Media: Online - full text.
Published by: William Dunkerley Publishing Consultants, 275 Batterson Dr, New Britain, CT 06053. TEL 860-881-2300 ext 91, wdpc@publishinghelp.com, http://www.publishinghelp.com.

070.5 USA
STRATEGIC PLANNING FOR MAGAZINE EXECUTIVES; how to take the guesswork out of magazine publishing decisions. Text in English. 19??. irreg., latest vol.2. **Document type:** *Handbook/Manual/Guide, Trade.*
Published by: Cowles Business Media (Subsidiary of: Cowles Media Company), 11 River Bend Dr, S,, PO Box 4949, Stamford, CT 06907. paul_mcdougall@cowlesbiz.com.

002 686.3 NLD ISSN 1570-2189
STUDIA BIBLIOTHECAE WITTOCKIANAE. Text in Multiple languages. 1984. irreg., latest vol.6, 2006. price varies. **Document type:** *Monographic series, Academic/Scholarly.*
Published by: Hes & De Graaf Publishers BV, Postbus 540, Houten, 3990 GH, Netherlands. TEL 31-30-6380071, FAX 31-30-6380099, info@hesdegraaf.com, http://www.hesdegraaf.com.

STUDIES IN BIBLIOGRAPHY. *see* BIBLIOGRAPHIES

070.5 CAN ISSN 1716-0626
STUDIES IN BOOK AND PRINT CULTURE. Text in English. 2001. irreg., latest 2002. price varies. **Document type:** *Monographic series, Academic/Scholarly.*
Published by: University of Toronto Press, 10 St Mary St, Ste 700, Toronto, ON M4Y 2W8, Canada. TEL 416-978-2239, FAX 416-978-4738, publishing@utpress.utoronto.ca, http://www.utppublishing.com. Ed. Leslie Howsam. **Subscr. to:** Order Fulfilment Division, 5201 Dufferin St, Toronto, ON M3H 5T8, Canada. TEL 416-667-7791, 800-565-9523, FAX 416-667-7832, 800-221-9985, utpbooks@utpress.utoronto.ca. **Dist. by:** Plymbridge Distributors Ltd, Estover Rd, Plymouth, Devon PL6 7PY, United Kingdom. TEL 44-1752-202300, FAX 44-1752-202330, enquiries@plymbridge.com, http://www.plymbridge.com.

070.5 USA ISSN 1077-1557
HF5415.126
SUBSCRIPTION MARKETING; what, why and how to test. Text in English. 1995. bi-m. USD 149 (effective 1999). back issues avail. **Document type:** *Newsletter, Trade.* **Description:** Shows and reveals the state of the direct-mail marketing industry. Reviews what works, what does not, and why.
Related titles: Online - full text ed.
Published by: Blue Dolphin Group, 31 Union Ave., Ste. 4, Sudbury, MA 01776-2269. TEL 508-378-7373, FAX 508-358-5795, http://www.subscriptionmarketing.com, http://www.bluedolphin.com. Ed. Mary van Doren. Pub. Donald L Nicholas. R&P Jesse Heinol. Circ: 375.

381.45002 GBR ISSN 1357-4426
SUBSCRIPTIONS STRATEGY; the direct marketing newsletter for publishers. Text in English. 1993. bi-m. adv. bk.rev. tr.lit. cum.index: 1993-1994. back issues avail. **Document type:** *Newsletter.* **Description:** Contains information on how to plan and execute a subscriptions marketing program, with reviews of the best current examples of publishers direct mail, page advertising and loose inserts.
Related titles: Online - full text ed.
Address: Polurrian Rd, Mullion, TR12 7HB, United Kingdom. Ed., Pub. Peter Hobday.

SUGAR NEEDLE. *see* FOOD AND FOOD INDUSTRIES—Bakers And Confectioners

070.5 SWE ISSN 0039-6451
Z407
SVENSK BOKHANDEL. Abbreviated title: SvB. Text in Swedish. 1952. 21/yr. SEK 590 domestic; SEK 1,390 foreign; SEK 350 to students (effective 2005). adv. index. back issues avail. **Document type:** *Magazine, Trade.*
Formed by the merger of (1863-1952): Svensk Bokhandelstidning; (1908-1952): Bokhandlaren; Which was formerly (until 1935): Bokhandlaren, Sortimentaren; (until 1927): Sortinaren
Related titles: Online - full text ed.
Indexed: ChLitAb, RASB.
Published by: Tidnings AB Svensk Bokhandel, Birkagatan 16C, Box 6888, Stockholm, 11386, Sweden. TEL 46-8-54541770, FAX 46-8-54541775. Ed. Lasse Winkler. Adv. contact Annika Lundmark TEL 46-8-54516066. B&W page SEK 4,500, color page SEK 7,900; 172 x 240. Circ: 4,300 (paid and controlled). **Co-sponsors:** Svenska Foerlaeggarefoereningen/Swedish Publishers Association; Svenska Bokhandlarefoereningen/Swedish Booksellers Association.

SWAZILAND NATIONAL BIBLIOGRAPHY. *see* PUBLISHING AND BOOK TRADE—Abstracting, Bibliographies, Statistics

SYDNEY STAR OBSERVER. *see* HOMOSEXUALITY

070.5 SWE ISSN 1403-3585
SYLWAN; den svenska pressens historia. Text in Swedish. 1998. irreg., latest 2006. price varies. back issues avail. **Document type:** *Monographic series, Academic/Scholarly.* **Description:** Monographs on Swedish media history.
Published by: N O R D I C O M A/S/Nordic Information Centre for Media and Communication Research, c/o University of Goeteborg, PO Box 713, Goeteborg, SE 40530, Sweden. TEL 46-31-7731000, FAX 46-31-7734655, info@nordicom.gu.se.

070.5 USA
T A R C WRITERS REPORT. Text in English. 1984. d. (w., m.). USD 60; USD 70 foreign. bk.rev. **Document type:** *Newsletter.* **Description:** Provides business and professional news of publishing industry and publishing trends for writers.
Related titles: Fax ed.
Published by: The Authors Resource Center, 4725 Ed Sunrise Dr, Ste 219, Tucson, AZ 85718-4534. TEL 520-577-7751, FAX 520-577-3994. Ed. Martha R Gore.

T L S; the Times literary supplement. (Times Literary Supplement) *see* LITERATURE

028.1 USA
TALKING BOOK REVIEW. Text in English. 1994. m. USD 30. **Document type:** *Newsletter.*
Address: 119 S Sumner St, Wheaton, IL 60187-5516. Ed. Kurt Luchs.

381.45002 USA
TARTAN BOOK SALES CATALOG. Text in English. 1940. 12/yr. free. adv. bk.rev. bibl.; illus. index. **Document type:** *Catalog.*
Supersedes: Tartan Book News; Book News (0006-7288)
Published by: Brodart Co., 500 Arch St, Williamsport, PA 17705. TEL 800-233-8467, FAX 717-326-6769. Ed. Guy McMullen. Circ: 8,000.

TASCHENBUCH DER FRAUENPRESSE. *see* WOMEN'S STUDIES

028 DEU
TASCHENBUCH MAGAZIN. Text in German. 1988. 3/yr. adv. **Document type:** *Magazine, Consumer.* **Description:** Contains information, articles and other features on books, authors and the publishing business for customers of bookstores.
Published by: Rossipaul Kommunikation GmbH, Menzinger Str 37, Munich, 80638, Germany. TEL 49-89-1791060, FAX 49-89-17910622, info@rossipaul.de. Adv. contact Ursula Rossipaul. Circ: 600,000 (controlled).

050 USA
TAYLOR TALK (ONLINE); the yearbook magazine. Text in English. 1960. s-a. free. illus. **Document type:** *Magazine, Trade.*
Formerly: Taylor Talk (Print) (0492-3901)
Published by: Taylor Publishing Co., 1550 W Mockingbird Ln, Dallas, TX 75235. TEL 800-677-2800, FAX 214-819-8131. Circ: 25,000.

002.075 GBR ISSN 1751-2034
Z987.5.G7
TEXTUALITIES. Text in English. 1987. a. bk.rev. back issues avail. **Document type:** *Journal, Consumer.* **Description:** Covers Scottish books, modern literature and trade profiles from a collector's and librarian's perspective.
Formerly (until 2006): Scottish Book Collector (0954-8769)
Related titles: Online - full text ed.: textualities.net. free (effective 2009).
Address: Main Point Books, 8 Lauriston St, Edinburgh, EH3 9DJ, United Kingdom. TEL 44-131-2284837, sales.dept@textualities.net.

070.5 DEU ISSN 0946-4077
DER THEMENPLAN. Text in German. 197?. a. (plus 1 update). EUR 190 (effective 2010). **Document type:** *Directory.*
Former titles (until 1993): Sonderthemen (0176-3032); (until 1984): Sonderveroeffentlichungen der Deutschen Medien (0173-3451); (until 1980): Sonderveroeffentlichungen der Deutschen Tages-, Publikums- und Fachpresse (0173-1025)
Related titles: CD-ROM ed.: EUR 154 (effective 2006); Online - full text ed.: EUR 168 (effective 2006).
Published by: Verlag Dieter Zimpel (Subsidiary of: Springer Fachmedien Wiesbaden GmbH), Abraham-Lincoln-Str 46, Wiesbaden, 65189, Germany. TEL 49-611-78780, FAX 49-611-7878200.

070.5 SWE ISSN 0284-6721
TIDNINGEN BOKEN; Nordens stoersta boktidning. Text in Swedish. 1987. 4/yr. (double volumes). SEK 199 to individuals; SEK 29 to institutions (effective 2000). adv. **Document type:** *Trade.*
Related titles: Audio cassette/tape ed.

Published by: AB Tidningsproduktion, Genarpsgatan 13, Fack 123, Malmo, 21228, Sweden. TEL 46-40-48-20-02, FAX 46-40-48-00-48. Ed. B Axelsson. Adv. contact Birgitta Olsson. **Subscr. to:** MediaService AB, Fack 5087, Kristianstad 29105, Sweden. TEL 46-44-10-10-22, FAX 46-44-10-67-60.

070.5 820 NLD ISSN 1386-5870
TIJDSCHRIFT VOOR TIJDSCHRIFTSTUDIES. Abbreviated title: T S. Text in Dutch. 1997. s-a. **Document type:** *Journal, Academic/ Scholarly.*
Related titles: Online - full text ed.: free (effective 2011).
Published by: Projectgroep Tijdschriftstudies, c/o Marloes Hulsken, Radboud Universiteit Nijmegen, afdeling Geschiedenis, Postbus 9103, Nijmegen, 6500 HD, Netherlands.

070.5 COL
TINTA FRESCA; revista informativa de la C C L. Text in Spanish. 1989. q. free. adv. bk.rev. abstr.; illus.; stat. **Document type:** *Trade.*
Formerly (until 1996): Correo Editorial (0121-1390)
Published by: Camara Colombiana del Libro, Carrera 17A No. 37-27, Bogota, CUND, Colombia. TEL 57-1-288-6188, FAX 57-1-287-3320. Ed. Miguel Laverde Espejo.

070.50688 DEU
DER TITELSCHUTZ ANZEIGER. Text in German. w. EUR 40; free to qualified personnel (effective 2005). adv. **Document type:** *Magazine, Trade.*
Related titles: ◆ Supplement(s): Der Titelschutz Anzeiger mit Software Titel.
Published by: Presse Fachverlag GmbH & Co. KG, Nebendahlstr 16, Hamburg, 22041, Germany. TEL 49-40-6090090, FAX 49-40-60900915, info@presse-fachverlag.de, http://www.presse-fachverlag.de. Adv. contact Angela Lautenschlaeger TEL 49-40-60900961. B&W page EUR 925; trim 175 x 262. Circ: 3,100 (controlled).

DER TITELSCHUTZ ANZEIGER MIT SOFTWARE TITEL. *see* COMPUTERS—Software

017.8 USA
Z649.F35
TITLES AND FEES. Text in English. 1978. s-a. **Document type:** *Catalog.*
Description: Directory of titles registered with the Copyright Clearance Center by participating publishers. Provides registered users with information needed to report photocopying activity.
Former titles: Catalog of Publisher Information (1065-7916); Publishers' Photocopy Fee Catalog (0887-2929); Permissions to Photocopy: Publishers' Fee List
Published by: Copyright Clearance Center, Inc., 222 Rosewood Dr, Danvers, MA 01923. TEL 978-750-8400, FAX 978-750-4744. Ed., R&P Tracey L Armstrong.

THE TOWERS CLUB U S A INFO MARKETING REPORT; money-making news for independent business persons and information merchants. *see* BUSINESS AND ECONOMICS—Marketing And Purchasing

381.45002 USA
TRADE BOOK PUBLISHING (YEAR): ANALYSIS BY CATEGORY. Text in English. 1994. irreg., latest 2001. USD 1,795 per issue (print or online ed.) (effective 2008). **Description:** Contains a five-year history and forecast of new title releases and revenue in more than 15 major categories.
Related titles: Online - full text ed.
Published by: SIMBA Information (Subsidiary of: Market Research.Com), 11200 Rockville Pike, Ste 504, Rockville, MD 20852. TEL 240-747-3096, 888-297-4622, FAX 240-747-3004, customerservice@simbainformation.com. Pub. Linda Kopp.

TRAVEL BOOKS WORLDWIDE; the travel book review. *see* TRAVEL AND TOURISM

070.5 CHE ISSN 0255-3570
CODEN: LDRPE6
TREFFPUNKT BIBLIOTHEK. Text in German. 1984. 4/yr. CHF 15 (effective 2001). bk.rev. **Document type:** *Bulletin, Government.*
Published by: Zentrum fuer Bibliotheksentwicklung Zuerich, Kantonale Bibliothekskommission, Hofwiesenstr 379, Zuerich, 8050, Switzerland. TEL 41-1-3101801, FAX 41-1-3101802, zentrum@kako-zh.ch, http://www.kako-zh.ch. Ed. Max Furrer. Circ: 2,000.

070.5 ITA ISSN 1828-4590
TUTTOLIBRI TEMPO LIBERO. Abbreviated title: T T L. Text in Italian. 1975. w. bk.rev. illus. **Document type:** *Newspaper, Consumer.*
Formerly (until 1999): Tuttolibri (0390-4873)
Related titles: ◆ Supplement to: La Stampa. ISSN 1122-1763.
Published by: Editrice la Stampa S.p.A, Via Carlo Marenco 32, Turin, TO 10126, Italy.

686.22 USA ISSN 1042-105X
TYPE & PRESS. Text in English. 1974. q. USD 5 domestic; USD 5.50 in Canada; USD 7.25 elsewhere. adv. bk.rev. back issues avail.
Published by: Press of the Golden Unicorn, 24667 Heather Court, Hayward, CA 94545. Ed. Fred C Williams. Circ: 1,000.

686.22 USA
TYPOGRAPHY DESIGN & USE. Text in English. 1992. q. looseleaf. USD 10 (effective 2005). bk.rev. **Document type:** *Newsletter.*
Description: Covers typography design, use, supplies, guidelines and trends.
Published by: Doron and Associates, 1213 Ridgecrest, Denton, TX 76205. TEL 940-483-0068, FAX 940-591-9586. Ed., Pub. Tom Doron. Circ: 6,100 (paid and controlled).

070.5 GBR
U K BOOK PUBLISHING INDUSTRY STATISTICS YEARBOOK (YEAR). (United Kingdom) Text in English. 2005. a. GBP 100 per issue (effective 2009). **Document type:** *Yearbook, Trade.* **Description:** Covers yearly news about the Publishers Association.
Formerly (until 2000): Book Trade Year Book (0950-4575)
Related titles: Online - full text ed.: GBP 75 per issue (effective 2009).
—CCC.
Published by: The Publishers Association, 29B Montague St, London, WC1B 5BW, United Kingdom. TEL 44-20-76919191, FAX 44-20-76919199, mail@publishers.org.uk, http://www.publishers.org.uk.

070.5 CUB
U P E C. Text in Spanish. bi-m. USD 10 in North America; USD 13 in South America; USD 15 in Europe; USD 21 elsewhere. illus.
Published by: (Union de Periodistas de Cuba), Ediciones Cubanas, Obispo 527, Havana, Cuba.

002 USA
U S B E BACK ISSUES SHELF LIST. (United States Book Exchange) Text in English. a. USD 150 to members.
Published by: United States Book Exchange, Periodicals and Serials Division, 2969 W 25th St, Cleveland, OH 44113. Ed. Jean Marie Zubal.

U S B E: FOR MEMBERS ONLY. (United States Book Exchange) *see* LIBRARY AND INFORMATION SCIENCES

070.5 USA
U.S. GOVERNMENT PRINTING OFFICE. STYLE MANUAL. Variant title: G P O Style Manual. Text in English. 1894. irreg., latest 2008, 30th ed. price varies. back issues avail. **Document type:** *Handbook/Manual/ Guide, Government.* **Description:** Covers the publishing style rules of the federal printer.
Related titles: CD-ROM ed.
Published by: U.S. Government Printing Office, 732 N Capitol St, NW, Washington, DC 20401. TEL 202-512-1800, 866-512-1800, FAX 202-512-2104, ContactCenter@gpo.gov, http://www.gpo.gov.

015 USA ISSN 0278-4912
U.S. NATIONAL CENTER FOR HEALTH STATISTICS. CATALOG OF PUBLICATIONS. Text in English. 19??. a. free (effective 2011). **Document type:** *Catalog, Government.*
Former titles (until 1980): U.S. National Center for Health Statistics. Current Listing and Topical Index to the Vital and Health Statistics Series (0092-7287); (until 1971): Current Listing of Vital and Health Statistics
Related titles: Online - full text ed.
Published by: U.S. National Center for Health Statistics, Metro IV Bldg, 3311 Toledo Rd, Hyattsville, MD 20782. TEL 301-458-4000, http://www.cdc.gov/nchs/.

070.5 NLD ISSN 2211-1891
UITGEVEN. Text in Dutch. 2008. a. EUR 39 (effective 2010).
Formerly (until 2009): Jaarboek Innovatief Uitgeven (2211-1883)
Published by: InCT, Postbus 33028, Rotterdam, 3005 EA, Netherlands. TEL 31-10-4520120, uitgever@inct.nl, http://www.inct.nl.

070.5 FRA ISSN 0398-5369
UNION PRESSE. Text in French. 11/yr. **Document type:** *Magazine, Trade.*
Address: 16 Place de la Republique, Paris, 75010, France. TEL 33-1-42402715, FAX 33-1-42404778. Ed. Isabelle Calabre. Circ: 35,000.

028.5 USA
UNITED STATES BOARD ON BOOKS FOR YOUNG PEOPLE. NEWSLETTER; building bridges of understanding through children's and young adult books. Variant title: U S B B Y Newsletter. Text in English. 1976. s-a. free to members (effective 2006). **Document type:** *Newsletter, Consumer.* **Description:** Source of information about books and related activities for children worldwide.
Formerly (until 1984): Friends of I B B Y Newsletter (International Board on Books for Young People)
Indexed: ChLitAb.
Published by: United States Board on Books for Young People, Inc., PO Box 1017, Honesdale, PA 18431-1017. TEL 414-229-4074, FAX 414-229-2812, jpaman@csd.uwm.edu, http://www.usbby.org. Circ: 1,250.

UNIVERSITA DEGLI STUDI DI GENOVA. ISTITUTO BOTANICO HANBURY. PUBBLICAZIONI. *see* BIOLOGY—Botany

015 ITA ISSN 1827-6636
UNIVERSITA DI CATANIA. FACOLTA DI SCIENZE POLITICHE. PUBBLICAZIONI. Text in Italian. 1998. irreg. **Document type:** *Magazine, Consumer.*
Published by: Universita degli Studi di Catania, Facolta di Scienze Politiche, Via Vittorio Emanuele 8, Catania, 95131, Italy. TEL 39-095-7465106, FAX 39-095-7465871, http://www.fscpo.unict.it.

015 ITA ISSN 0479-1320
UNIVERSITA DI PADOVA. FACOLTA DI SCIENZE POLITICHE. PUBBLICAZIONI. Text in Italian. 1954. irreg. **Document type:** *Bibliography.*
Published by: Universita degli Studi di Padova, Facolta di Scienze Politiche, Via del Santo 28, Padova, 35123, Italy. TEL 39-049-8274005, FAX 39-049-8274207, http://www.scipol.unipd.it.

070.5 NZL
UNIVERSITY OF OTAGO PRESS. NEWSLETTER. Text in English. m. **Document type:** *Newsletter.* **Description:** Contains articles and summaries of books published by the University Press.
Published by: University of Otago Press, Level 1, 398 Cumberland St, PO Box 56, Dunedin, New Zealand. TEL 64-3-4798807, FAX 64-3-4798385, university.press@otago.ac.nz.

090 USA
USED BOOK LOVER'S GUIDE SERIES. (Avail. in 7 regional eds.) Text in English. 1993. biennial. USD 20 online ed. (effective 2001); price varies for print editions. bk.rev. **Document type:** *Monographic series.*
Description: Lists 7,500 used, rare, and antiquarian book dealers in the United States and Canada. Includes specialty index with subject headings.
Formerly: Used Book Lover's Guide
Related titles: Online - full content ed.; Supplement(s):.
Published by: Book Hunter Press, PO Box 193, Yorktown Heights, NY 10598. TEL 914-245-6608, FAX 914-245-2630, bookhuntpr@aol.com, http://bookhunterpress.com. Ed., Pub. Susan Siegel.

070.5 NLD ISSN 0042-1367
UT DE SMIDTE FAN DE FRYSKE AKADEMY. Text in Frisian. 1966. q. free membership (effective 2009). bk.rev. charts; illus. **Document type:** *Newsletter.*
Published by: Fryske Akademy, Postbus 54, Ljouwert, 8900 AB, Netherlands. TEL 31-58-2131414, FAX 31-58-2131409, fa@fryske-akademy.nl, http://www.fryske-akademy.nl.

070.5 DEU ISSN 0947-4544
V D Z - EDITION. (Verband Deutscher Zeitschriftenverleger) Text in German. 1993. irreg. **Document type:** *Monographic series, Trade.*
Published by: Verband Deutscher Zeitschriftenverleger e.V., Haus der Presse, Markgrafenstr 15, Berlin, 10969, Germany. TEL 49-30-7262980, FAX 49-30-726298103, info@vdz.de, http://www.vdz.de.

070.5 DEU
V D Z - JAHRBUCH. (Verband Deutscher Zeitschriftenverleger) Text in German. 2003. a. EUR 49; EUR 29 to members (effective 2010). **Document type:** *Journal, Trade.*
Published by: Verband Deutscher Zeitschriftenverleger e.V., Haus der Presse, Markgrafenstr 15, Berlin, 10969, Germany. TEL 49-30-7262980, FAX 49-30-726298103, info@vdz.de, http://www.vdz.de.

070.5 NLD ISSN 1386-9027
VAKBLAD. Text in Dutch. 199?. 8/yr. EUR 40.25 (effective 2010). adv. **Document type:** *Magazine, Trade.*
Published by: (Groep Uitgevers voor Vak en Wetenschap), FolioDynamica B.V., Postbus 513, Zandvoort, 2040 EA, Netherlands. uitgever@foliodynamica.nl, http://www.foliodynamica.nl. Ed. Eric Ravestijn. Adv. contact Philippine Herkes. color page EUR 1,235; trim 210 x 297. Circ: 1,750.

VALORI. *see* PHILOSOPHY

070.5 DEU ISSN 1439-0736
Z317
VERLAGE; Deutschland - Oesterreich - Schweiz. Text in German. 1950. a. EUR 110 per issue (effective 2010). 1475 p./no.; **Document type:** *Directory, Trade.*
Former titles (until 2001): Deutschsprachige Verlage (0940-5593); (until 1991): Anschriften Deutscher Verlage und Auslaendischer Verlage mit Deutschen Auslieferungen (0066-4596)
Related titles: Online - full text ed.: ISSN 1862-1961.
Published by: Verlag der Schillerbuchhandlung Hans Banger, Guldenbachstr 1, Cologne, 50935, Germany. TEL 49-221-460140, FAX 49-221-4601427, banger@banger.de.

070.5 AUS
VICTORIAN WRITER. Text in English. 1991. m. free to members (effective 2008). **Document type:** *Newsletter, Academic/Scholarly.*
Description: Contains the latest industry information, courses, tips and advice on writing and publishing.
Former titles (until 2005): Write On (1039-5466); (until 1992): Centrefold (1037-0137)
Published by: Victorian Writers' Centre, 1st Fl, Nicholas Bldg, 37 Swanston St, Melbourne, VIC 3000, Australia. TEL 61-396549068, FAX 61-3-96544751, info@writers-centre.org. Eds. Naomi Morrison, Robyn Deed.

028.1 AUS ISSN 1039-2858
VIEWPOINT: ON BOOKS FOR YOUNG ADULTS. Text in English. 1993. q. bk.rev. back issues avail. **Document type:** *Journal, Academic/ Scholarly.* **Description:** Provides a forum for discussion of various issues and contrasting opinions about the books for young adult.
Related titles: Online - full content ed.
Published by: University of Melbourne, Department of Language and Literacy Education, PO Box 4286, Parkville, VIC 3052, Australia. TEL 61-3-83448617, FAX 61-3-83440025, http:// www.edfac.unimelb.edu.au/lale/. Ed. Pam Macintyre.

070.5 ITA ISSN 1972-6694
VIVAVERDI. Text in Italian. 1926. bi-m. free membership. **Document type:** *Magazine, Consumer.*
Former titles (until 2003): S I A E. Bollettino (1972-6708); (until 1993): Il Burcardo (1972-6872); (until 1993): Societa Italiana degli Autori ed Editori. Bollettino (1972-6880); (until 1943): Ente Italiano per il Diritto d'Autore. Bollettino (1972-6899); (until 1942): Societa Italiana degli Autori ed Editori. Bollettino (1972-6902); (until 1927): Societa Italiana degli Autori. Bollettino (1972-6910)
Published by: Societa Italiana degli Autori ed Editori (S I A E), Viale della Letteratura 30, Rome, 00144, Italy. TEL 39-06-59901, FAX 39-06-59647050, http://www.siae.it. Ed. Flaviano De Luca.

028.1 BGR ISSN 1310-4047
VSICHKO ZA KNIGATA. Text in Bulgarian. m. BGL 70 domestic; USD 70 foreign; BGL 6 newsstand/cover domestic (effective 2002). **Document type:** *Bulletin.* **Description:** Presents reliable information about Bulgarian books available on the book market.
Related titles: Online - full text ed.
Published by: Literature and Book House - Plovdiv, 10 Tsanko Lavrenov St., Plovdiv, 4000, Bulgaria. TEL 359-32-627238, FAX 359-32-632067, library@plovdiv.techno-link.com. Ed. Dimitrina Kovalakova.

070.5 USA
THE W I N INFORMER; the professional association for Christian writers. (Writers Information Network) Text in English. 1983. bi-m. USD 33; USD 37 foreign (effective 1999). bk.rev. back issues avail. **Document type:** *Newsletter, Trade.* **Description:** Covers news and trends in the writing profession and offers advice on the editing, ethical, and marketing aspects of writing.
Formerly: Writers Information Network
Published by: Elaine Wright Colvin, Ed. & Pub., 5359 Ruby Pl, N E, Box 11337, Bainbridge Island, WA 98110. TEL 206-842-9103, FAX 206-842-0536. Circ: 1,000 (paid).

070.5 USA
W P A NEWS - E-MAIL. Text in English. m. membership. adv. **Document type:** *Newsletter.*
Former titles: W P A News - Fax; W P A News; Issue
Related titles: Fax ed.
Published by: Western Publications Association, 823 Rim Crest Dr, Westlake Village, CA 91361. TEL 805-495-1863, FAX 805-497-1849. Ed., Pub., Adv. contact Jane Silbering. Circ: 1,000 (controlled).

830 AUT ISSN 1727-0561
WAGNIS. Text in German. 2003. 2/yr. EUR 34.20 for 2 yrs. (effective 2005). **Document type:** *Magazine, Trade.*
Published by: Wagner'sche Buchhandlung, Museumstr 4, Innsbruck, 6020, Austria. TEL 49-512-595050, FAX 49-512-5950538, marketing@wagnersche.at. Circ: 12,000 (controlled).

070.5 AUS
WEEKLY BOOK NEWSLETTER (ONLINE). Abbreviated title: W B N. Text in English. 2006. 49/yr. AUD 250 domestic single user: (online or email ed.); AUD 227 foreign single user: (online or email ed.) (effective 2008). adv. **Document type:** *Newsletter, Trade.*
Description: Provides the latest news coverage of the Australian book industry together with agency and personnel changes.
Media: Online - full text. **Related titles:** E-mail ed.
Published by: Thorpe-Bowker (Subsidiary of: R.R. Bowker LLC), St Kilda Rd, PO Box 6509, Melbourne, VIC 8008, Australia. TEL 61-3-85178333, FAX 61-3-85178399, yoursay@thorpe.com.au, http://www.thorpe.com.au. Adv. contact Xeverie Swee TEL 61-3-86450308. Circ: 50,000.

P

WENHUI DUSHU ZHOUBAO/WENHUI BOOK REVIEW. *see* LITERATURE

WHAT IS TO BE READ. *see* LITERATURE

070.5 USA ISSN 1554-7124
WHO'S BUYING WHOM. Text in English. a. USD 495 per issue (effective 2006). **Document type:** *Journal, Trade.* **Description:** Reports on acquisitions, divestitures, investments and joint ventures in the publishing, information and training industries.
Published by: Whitestone Communications, Inc., 1350 Avenue of The Americas, Ste 1200, New York, NY 10019. TEL 212-957-7100, FAX 212-957-7508, ssevrens@whitestonecommunications.com.

002.074 DEU ISSN 0170-7213
WHO'S WHO AT THE FRANKFURT BOOK FAIR; an international publishers' guide. Text in German. 1969. a. adv. **Document type:** *Directory, Trade.* **Description:** Includes up-to-date facts on 13,000 persons from 5,000 companies - publishers, managers, editors, heads of press and production departments, rights and license officers and publishers' representatives and agents.
Published by: Frankfurt Book Fair, Reineckstr 3, Frankfurt am Main, 60313, Germany. TEL 49-69-21020, FAX 49-69-2102227, info@book-fair.com, http://www.book-fair.com.

070.5 DEU ISSN 0341-2253
Z119
WOLFENBUETTELER NOTIZEN ZUR BUCHGESCHICHTE. Text in German. 1976. 2/yr. EUR 45 (effective 2011). **Document type:** *Journal, Academic/Scholarly.*
Indexed: BibInd, DIP, IBR, IBZ, MLA-IB, RASB.
—CCC.
Published by: (Wolfenbuetteler Arbeitskreis fuer Geschichte des Buchwesens), Harrassowitz Verlag, Kreuzberger Ring 7b-d, Wiesbaden, 65205, Germany. TEL 49-611-5300, FAX 49-611-530560, verlag@harrassowitz.de, http://www.harrassowitz.de. Eds. Erdmann Weyrauch, Werner Arnold. Circ: 750.

070.5 NLD
WOLTERS KLUWER JAARVERSLAG/WOLTERS KLUWER ANNUAL REPORT. Text in Dutch. a. free. **Document type:** *Corporate.* **Description:** Reports on activities of the company and its legal, medical, scientific and academic publishing subsidiaries in Belgium, France, Germany, Italy, The Netherlands, Spain, Sweden, the UK and the US.
Related titles: English ed.
Published by: Wolters Kluwer N.V., Zuidpoolsingel 2, PO Box 1030, Alphen aan den Rijn, 2400 BA, Netherlands. TEL 31-172-641400, FAX 31-172-474889, info@wolterskluwer.com, http://www.wolterskluwer.com.

070.5 GBR
WOMEN IN PUBLISHING AND THE BOOK TRADE IN AFRICA; an annotated directory. Text in English. 1997. irreg., latest 1997. GBP 23.95 per issue (effective 2010). **Document type:** *Directory, Trade.* **Description:** Focuses on how women are represented in the book world in Africa as well as the responsiveness of the publishing industry to gender issues. Also designed to serve as a networking tool. Includes details of women publishers in Africa, women in senior management positions in African publishing, and women in distribution and the retail book trade.
Published by: African Books Collective Ltd., PO Box 721, Oxford, OX1 9EN, United Kingdom. TEL 44-1869-349110, FAX 44-1869-349110, krisia.cook@africanbookscollective.com.

WORD WRAP. *see* LITERATURE

686.2244 DEU ISSN 1618-8381
WORLD OF PRINT. Text in German. 2002. m. **Document type:** *Magazine, Trade.*
Published by: C.A.T. Verlag Bloemer GmbH, Freiligrathring 18-20, Ratingen, 40878, Germany. TEL 49-2102-20270, FAX 49-2102-202790, worldofphoto@cat-verlag.de, http://www.cat-verlag.de. Circ: 9,548 (paid and controlled).

WRITE. *see* JOURNALISM

070.5 GBR ISSN 0084-2664
PN12
WRITERS' AND ARTISTS' YEARBOOK. Text in English. 1902. a. GBP 14.99 per issue (effective 2010). index. back issues avail. **Document type:** *Yearbook, Trade.* **Description:** Provides a reference for writers, artists, journalists, and publishers.
Formerly (until 1906): Writers' Year-Book
Related titles: Online - full text ed.
—BLDSC (9364.680000). **CCC.**
Published by: A. & C. Black (Publishers) Ltd., 36 Soho Sq, London, W1D 3QY, United Kingdom. TEL 44-20-77580200, publicity@acblack.com, http://www.acblack.com/.

070.52 USA ISSN 0084-2699
PS1
THE WRITERS DIRECTORY. Text in English. 1970. a. USD 281 (effective 2009). back issues avail. **Document type:** *Directory, Trade.* **Description:** Contains biographical, bibliographical, and contact information for more than 20,000 living authors with their professional addresses, pen names, genres, career information, and titles with publication dates.
Related titles: Online - full text ed.
—BLDSC (9364.701000).
Published by: Gale (Subsidiary of: Cengage Learning), 27500 Drake Rd, Farmington Hills, MI 48331. TEL 248-699-4253, 800-877-4253, FAX 877-363-4253, gale.customerservice@cengage.com, http://gale.cengage.com. Circ: 7,500.

070.5 CAN
WRITER'S GAZETTE. Text in English. 1994. bi-m. free (effective 2003); donations requested. adv. Website rev.; bk.rev.; play rev.; tel.rev. illus.; maps; tr.lit. back issues avail. **Document type:** *Newsletter, Consumer.* **Description:** Seeks to give writers information on best sellers, publishers and agents, a poetry corner, articles, classifieds, grants and scholarships.
Related titles: E-mail ed.; Fax ed.; Online - full text ed.; Large type ed. 16 pt.
Address: 7231 120th S, Ste #105, Delta, BC V4C-6P5, Canada. Ed. Krista Barrett. adv.: B&W page USD 1,200, color page USD 5,000; trim 10 x 8. Circ: 60,000.

070.52 USA
WRITERS INK. Text in English. 1975. irreg. (2-4/yr.). USD 18 domestic; USD 22 foreign (effective 2000). adv. bk.rev. illus. back issues avail. **Document type:** *Newsletter.* **Description:** Informs the public about the services this group offers.
Published by: (Writers Unlimited Agency, Inc.), Writers Ink Press, PO Box 2344, Selden, NY 11784-0749. TEL 631-451-0478, FAX 631-451-0478, axelrod@yahoo.com, http://www.poetrydoctor.com/. Ed., Pub. David B Axelrod. Adv. contact Daniel Axelrod. Circ: 1,500.

070.5 CAN ISSN 0225-610X
WRITER'S LIFELINE. Text in English. 1974. 3/yr. USD 18. adv. bk.rev.
Formerly: Lifeline (Cornwall) (0316-0602)
Address: P O Box 1641, Cornwall, ON K6H 5V6, Canada. TEL 613-932-2135, FAX 613-932-7735. Ed. Stephen Gill. Circ: 1,500.

381.45002 070.5 ITA ISSN 1974-8183
WRITERS MAGAZINE ITALIA. Text in Italian. 2005. bi-m. **Document type:** *Magazine, Trade.*
Published by: Associazione Delos Books, Via Torre Borromea 52, Casaletto Lodigiano, LO 26852, Italy. http://www.delosbooks.it.

070.5 USA ISSN 0084-2729
PN161
WRITER'S MARKET. Text in English. 1926. a. USD 29.99 (effective 2008). Index. back issues avail.; reprints avail. **Document type:** *Directory, Trade.* **Description:** Provides information on where to sell articles, books, fillers, greeting cards, novels, plays, scripts and short stories.
Related titles: CD-ROM ed.: ISSN 1086-7686. USD 39.99; Online - full content ed.
—BLDSC (9364.738000). **CCC.**
Published by: F + W Media Inc., 4700 E Galbraith Rd, Cincinnati, OH 45236. TEL 513-531-2690, 800-283-0963, FAX 513-531-0798, wds@fwpubs.com, http://www.fwpublications.com. Ed. Kirsten Holm.

686.22 USA ISSN 0895-898X
WRITER'S N W; news and reviews for the community of the printed word. Text in English. 1987. q. USD 10 domestic; USD 12 in Canada. adv. bk.rev. back issues avail. **Document type:** *Newspaper.* **Description:** Lists N.W. publishing and writing markets and events; includes articles on writing and publishing, author interviews, new books and software reviews.
Formerly: Writer's Northwest Newsletter
Published by: Media Weavers (Subsidiary of: Blue Heron Publishing, Inc.), 4140 SE 37th Ave., Apt. 10, Portland, OR 97202-3272. TEL 503-771-0428. Eds. Dennis Stovall, Linny Stovall. Circ: 75,000 (controlled).

070.5 USA ISSN 0896-7946
PN147
WRITER'S NORTHWEST HANDBOOK; comprehensive guide to writing and publishing in Oregon, Washington, Idaho, Montana, Alaska, and British Columbia. Text in English. 1986. biennial. USD 18.95. adv. **Document type:** *Directory.* **Description:** Lists 2,800 N.W. markets with editorial guidelines, and advertising resources, essays and interviews for writers and publishers.
Published by: Media Weavers (Subsidiary of: Blue Heron Publishing, Inc.), 4140 SE 37th Ave., Apt. 10, Portland, OR 97202-3272. TEL 503-771-0428. Eds. Dennis Stovall, Linny Stovall. Circ: 20,000.

070.5 USA ISSN 0084-2737
PN101
WRITER'S YEARBOOK. Text in English. 1930. a. USD 5.99 (effective 2009). adv. reprints avail. **Document type:** *Yearbook, Trade.* **Description:** Articles on how and where to sell writing.
Formerly: Writer's Year Book and Market Guide
Related titles: Microform ed.: (from PQC).
—CCC.
Published by: F + W Media Inc., 4700 E Galbraith Rd, Cincinnati, OH 45236. TEL 513-531-2690, 800-283-0963, wds@fwpubs.com, http://www.fwpublications.com. Circ: 50,000 (paid).

WRITING FOR MONEY (ONLINE EDITION); the Internet newsletter that shows you how to make money and live a great life as a freelance writer. *see* JOURNALISM

070.5 070 CHN ISSN 1673-3959
XIANDAI CHUBAN XUE - 21 SHIJI XINWEN YU CHUANBOXUE XILIE JIAOCAI/MODERN PUBLISHING - 21 CENTURY JOURNALISM & COMMUNICATION STUDIES. Text in Chinese. 2002. irreg. CNY 30 per issue (effective 2009). **Document type:** *Monographic series, Academic/Scholarly.*
Published by: Beijing Daxue Chubanshe/Peking University Press, 205, Chengfu Lu, Haidian-qu, Beijing, 100871, China. TEL 86-10-62752024, fd@pup.pku.edu.cn.

ZBORNIK MATICE SRPSKE ZA KNJIZEVNOST I JEZIK. *see* LINGUISTICS

070.5 CHN ISSN 1001-8859
Z462.7
ZHONGGUO CHUBAN NIANJIAN/CHINA PUBLISHERS' YEARBOOK. Text in Chinese. 1980. a. CNY 80. adv. **Document type:** *Directory.* **Description:** Contains articles on developments in China's publishing industry. Lists publishing companies and new publications; includes addresses, telephone and telegraph numbers, and personnel.
Published by: Publishers Association of China, 85 Dongsi Nan Dajie, Beijing, 100703, China. TEL 86-10-6523-6518. Ed. Julan Liu. Circ: 5,000.

070.5 CHN ISSN 1001-7143
ZHONGGUO KEJI QIKAN YANJIU/CHINESE JOURNAL OF SCIENTIFIC AND TECHNICAL PERIODICAL. Text in Chinese. 1990. bi-m. USD 53.40 (effective 2009). **Document type:** *Journal, Academic/Scholarly.*
Related titles: Online - full text ed.
—East View.
Published by: Zhongguo Kexueyuan Ziran Kexue Qikan Bianji Yanjiuhui/Chinese Academy of Sciences, Natural Science Periodicals Editing Society, c/o Institute of Microbiology, 13, Zhongguancun Beiyitiao, Beijing, 100080, China. TEL 86-10-62572403. Ed. Su Shisheng.

028.1 CHN ISSN 1002-235X
Z1035.A1
ZHONGGUO TUSHU PINGLUN/CHINA BOOK REVIEW. Text in Chinese. 1986. m. USD 46.80 (effective 2009). adv. bk.rev. **Document type:** *Journal, Academic/Scholarly.*
Related titles: Online - full text ed.
Published by: Liaoning Renmin Chubanshe, Tushu Pinglun Bianjibu/Liaoning People's Publishing House, 2, Heping Nandajie, Heping-qu, Shenyang, Liaoning 110001, China. TEL 86-24-23265976, FAX 86-10-64173406.

070.5 CHN
ZHONGGUO TUSHU SHANGBAO/CHINA BOOK BUSINESS REPORT. Text in Chinese. 1995. 2/w. CNY 99 (effective 2004). **Document type:** *Newspaper, Trade.*
Address: 19, Xisantuan Beilu, 3F, Waiyan Dasha, Beijing, 100089, China. TEL 86-10-68917687, FAX 86-10-68917657. **Dist. by:** China International Book Trading Corp, 35 Chegongzhuang Xilu, Haidian District, PO Box 399, Beijing 100044, China. TEL 86-10-68412045, FAX 86-10-68412023, cibtc@mail.cibtc.com.cn, http://www.cibtc.com.cn.

070.5 TWN ISSN 1013-087X
ZHONGHUA MINGUO CHUBAN NIANJIAN/PUBLICATIONS YEARBOOK, REPUBLIC OF CHINA. Cover title: Xingzhengyuan Xinwenju Chubanpin Mulu. Text in Chinese. 1977. a. TWD 1,000 newsstand/cover. **Document type:** *Directory, Government.*
Published by: Zhonghua Minguo (Taiwan) Xingzhengyuan Xinwenju/Republic of China (Taiwan), Government Information Office, 2 Tianjin St., Taipei, 100, Taiwan. TEL 886-2-23228888, http://info.gio.gov.tw/.

070.5 CHN ISSN 1000-6095
ZHONGWAI SHUZHAI/DIGEST OF CHINESE AND FOREIGN BOOKS. Text in Chinese. 1985. bi-m. USD 43.20 (effective 2009).
—East View.
Published by: Shanghai Renmin Chubanshe, Qikan Bu/Shanghai People's Publishing House, 54 Shaoxing Rd, Shanghai, 200020, China. TEL 021-4335250, FAX 021-4331665. Ed. Yu Chunde. Circ: 55,000.

070.5 USA ISSN 1537-6125
ZINE GUIDE; the ultimate independent press resource guide. Text in English. 1997. 2/yr. USD 12; USD 7.95 newsstand/cover (effective 2003). adv. **Document type:** *Magazine, Consumer.* **Description:** Provides reviews and listings of over a thousand independent magazines and publications,along with detailed indexes of bands, people, subjects and record labels.
Published by: Tail Spins Magazine, 908 N. Oakley, Ste 2, Chicago, IL 60622. TEL 773-269-2918, FAX 773-269-2584. Ed., Pub., R&P, Adv. contact Brent Ritzel. B&W page USD 350, color page USD 750. Circ: 12,000 (paid).

070.5 USA
ZINE WORLD; a reader's guide to the underground press. Text in English. 1996. q. USD 10 domestic; USD 14 in Canada & Mexico; USD 18 elsewhere; USD 3 per issue domestic; USD 4 per issue in Canada & Mexico; USD 5 per issue elsewhere (effective 2005). bk.rev. illus. **Document type:** *Magazine, Consumer.* **Description:** Devoted to coverage of small-scale amateur books and periodicals.
Related titles: Online - full text ed.
Published by: Jerianne Thompson, Ed. & Pub., PO Box 330156, Murfreesboro, TN 37113-0156. Ed. Jerianne Thompson.

028.1 USA
THE ZINE YEARBOOK. Text in English. a. USD 7 domestic; USD 9 foreign. **Document type:** *Magazine, Consumer.* **Description:** Seeks both to document small press writing efforts and to provide some much needed publicity and encouragement.
Published by: Become the Media, PO Box 20128, Toledo, OH 43610-0128.

070.5 DEU
ZWIEBEL. Text in German. 1965. a. free (effective 2011). **Document type:** *Catalog, Trade.*
Related titles: Online - full text ed.
Published by: Verlag Klaus Wagenbach, Emser Str 40-41, Berlin, 10719, Germany. TEL 49-30-2351510, FAX 49-30-2116140, mail@wagenbach.de.

PUBLISHING AND BOOK TRADE—Abstracting, Bibliographies, Statistics

015.6 DEU ISSN 0306-0322
Z465.7
THE AFRICAN BOOK PUBLISHING RECORD. Text in English; Text occasionally in French. 1975. q. EUR 412, USD 618 to institutions; EUR 475, USD 713 combined subscription to institutions (print & online eds.) (effective 2012). adv. bk.rev. bibl.; illus.; stat. back issues avail.; reprint service avail. from PSC. **Document type:** *Journal, Bibliography.* **Description:** Provides a current bibliography of African published materials. Includes features, articles, extensive book review section, reports and news about African publishing and book development.
Related titles: Online - full text ed.: ISSN 7865-8717. EUR 412, USD 618 to institutions (effective 2012).
Indexed: A22, ASD, BibInd, CCA, E01, IBR, IBZ, IIBP, L04, LISTA, MLA, MLA-IB, RASB, T02.
—BLDSC (0732.360000), IE. **CCC.**
Published by: De Gruyter Saur (Subsidiary of: Walter de Gruyter GmbH & Co. KG), Mies-van-der-Rohe-Str 1, Munich, 80807, Germany. TEL 49-89-769020, FAX 49-89-76902150, wdg-info@degruyter.com, http://www.saur.de/. Ed. Cecile Lomer. Circ: 500 (controlled).

015.73 USA ISSN 0091-9357
Z1000
AMERICAN BOOK PRICES CURRENT. Text in English. 1896. a., latest vol.107. USD 119.95 (effective 2001). adv.
Related titles: CD-ROM ed.: A B P C on C D - R O M. 1993. USD 150 (effective 2001).
Published by: Bancroft - Parkman, Inc., PO Box 1236, Washington, CT 06793. TEL 860-868-7408, FAX 860-868-0080, http://www.bookpricescurrent.com. Ed. Katherine Kyes Leab. R&P M Worth. Adv. contact M. Worth. Circ: 3,000 (paid).

015.71 USA
AMERICAN BOOK PRICES CURRENT. FOUR YEAR INDEX. Text in English. 1899. quadrennial. USD 495 (effective 2000). adv.
Formerly: American Book Prices Current. Five Year Index
Published by: Bancroft - Parkman, Inc., PO Box 1236, Washington, CT 06793. TEL 212-737-2715, FAX 860-868-0080. Ed. Katharine Kyes Leab.

016.002 NLD ISSN 0303-5964
Z117
ANNUAL BIBLIOGRAPHY OF THE HISTORY OF THE PRINTED BOOK AND LIBRARY. Key Title: A B H B. Text in English. 1973. biennial, latest vol.31, 2006. price varies. illus. reprints avail. **Document type:** *Bibliography.*
Indexed: RASB.
Published by: (International Federation of Library Associations and Institutions, Committee on Rare Books and Manuscripts), Springer Netherlands (Subsidiary of: Springer Science+Business Media), Van Godewijckstraat 30, Dordrecht, 3311 GX, Netherlands. TEL 31-78-6576050, FAX 31-78-6576474, http://www.springer.com.

070.5021 AUS
Z533.7
AUSTRALIA. BUREAU OF STATISTICS. BOOK PUBLISHERS, AUSTRALIA (ONLINE). Text in English. 1994. a. free (effective 2009). back issues avail. **Document type:** *Government.* **Description:** Presents data for businesses which had either book publishing as their main activity (book publishers) or generated $2m or more in income from book publishing, although this was not their main activity (other major contributors).
Formerly (until 2002): Australia. Bureau of Statistics. Book Publishers, Australia (Print) (1327-4643)
Media: Online - full text.
Published by: Australian Bureau of Statistics, Locked Bag 10, Belconnen, ACT 2616, Australia. TEL 61-2-92684909, 61-2-62527037, 300-135-070, FAX 61-2-62528103, client.services@abs.gov.au.

028.1021 AUS
AUSTRALIA. BUREAU OF STATISTICS. BOOK RETAILERS, AUSTRALIA (ONLINE). Text in English. 2000. irreg., latest 2004. free (effective 2009). **Document type:** *Government.* **Description:** Provides details on the number and value of books purchased and sold, as well as information on the book related operations of the four industries like newspaper, book and stationery retailing.
Formerly: Australia. Bureau of Statistics. Book Retailers, Australia (Print) (1832-7303)
Media: Online - full text.
Published by: Australian Bureau of Statistics, Locked Bag 10, Belconnen, ACT 2616, Australia. TEL 61-2-92684909, 300-135-070, FAX 61-2-92684654, client.services@abs.gov.au.

015.45 ITA ISSN 1125-0879
Z2341
BIBLIOGRAFIA NAZIONALE ITALIANA. MONOGRAFIE. Text in Italian. 1958. irreg. (plus a. cumulation). price varies. bk.rev. index. reprints avail. **Document type:** *Monographic series, Bibliography.*
Supersedes in part (in 1993): Bibliografia Nazionale Italiana (0006-1077)
Related titles: CD-ROM ed.; Microfilm ed.; Online - full text ed.: ISSN 1594-0403.
Indexed: RASB.
—Linda Hall.
Published by: (Biblioteca Nazionale Centrale di Firenze), Istituto Centrale per il Catalogo Unico delle Biblioteche Italiane e per le Informazioni Bibliografiche, Via Del Castro Pretorio, 105, Rome, RM 00185, Italy. TEL 39-06-4959217, FAX 39-06-4959302.

015.44 FRA ISSN 1626-0104
CODEN: BIFRA9
BIBLIOGRAPHIE NATIONALE FRANCAISE. LIVRES (ONLINE EDITION). Text in French. 1811. fortn. adv. bk.rev. index. reprints avail. **Document type:** *Bibliography.*
Former titles (until 2001): Bibliographie Nationale Francaise. Livres (Print Edition) (1142-3250); (until 1990): Bibliographie de la France. Livres (0150-1402); (until 1977): Bibliographie de la France. 1ere Partie, Bibliographie Officielle (0335-5667); Superseded in part (in 1979): Bibliographie de la France. Biblio (0335-5675); Which was formed by the merger of (1933-1971): Biblio (Mensuel) (1147-6710); (1814-1971): Bibliographie de la France (0006-1344); Which was formerly: Bibliographie de l'Empire Francais (1147-6680); (until 1811): Journal General de l'Imprimerie et de la Librairie (1147-6672); (1797-1810): Journal Typographique et Bibliographique (1147-6664)
Media: Online - full content. **Related titles:** Microfilm ed.: (from PMC).
Indexed: RASB.
—Linda Hall. **CCC.**
Published by: Bibliotheque Nationale de France, Site Francois Mitterand, Quai Francois Mauriac, Paris, 75706, France. TEL 33-1-53795950, FAX 33-1-53795045. Circ: 600. **Subscr. to:** Mereau, 175 bd. Anatole France, BP 189, Saint-Denis Cedex 93208, France. TEL 33-1-48133858, FAX 33-1-48130908.

015.72 MEX ISSN 0185-2027
Z1415
BOLETIN BIBLIOGRAFICO MEXICANO. Text in Spanish. 1940. bi-m. USD 15 (effective 1999). adv. bk.rev. bibl.; illus. reprints avail. **Document type:** *Bulletin, Bibliography.* **Description:** Lists books and other printed material.
Related titles: Microform ed.: (from PQC).
Indexed: L09, RASB.
Published by: Libreria de Porrua Hermanos y Cia., S.A., A. Rep. de Argentina, 15, 102 Piso, Mexico City, DF 06020, Mexico. TEL 52-5-7025467, FAX 52-5-7025474. Ed. Jose Antonio Perez Porrua. Circ: 25,000. **Subscr. to:** Apdo. M7990, Delegacion Cuauhtemoc, Mexico City, DF 06020, Mexico.

002.021 CAN ISSN 1911-317X
BOOK PUBLISHERS. DATA TABLES. Text in English. 2001. irreg. **Document type:** *Report, Trade.*
Formerly (until 2006): Book Publishers and Exclusive Agents. Data Tables (1708-8429)
Media: Online - full text. **Related titles:** French ed.: Les Editeurs de Livres. Tableaux de Donnees. ISSN 1911-3188.
Published by: Statistics Canada/Statistique Canada, Communications Division, 3rd Fl, R H Coats Bldg, Ottawa, ON K1A 0A6, Canada. TEL 800-263-1136, infostats@statcan.ca, http://www.statcan.gc.ca.

016.0281 USA
BOOK REVIEW INDEX. Text in English. base vol. plus d. updates. illus. Index. reprints avail. **Document type:** *Database, Abstract/Index.* **Description:** Provides quick access to reviews of books, periodicals, books on tape and electronic media representing a wide range of popular, academic and professional interests.
Media: Online - full text. **Related titles:** Print ed.: ISSN 0524-0581. 1965.
Published by: Gale (Subsidiary of: Cengage Learning), 27500 Drake Rd, Farmington Hills, MI 48331. TEL 248-699-4253, 800-877-4253, FAX 877-363-4253, gale.customerservice@cengage.com, http://www.galegroup.com. Ed. Beverly Baer. Circ: 3,000.

016.0281 USA
Z1035.A1
BOOK REVIEW INDEX: ANNUAL CUMULATION. Text in English. 1965. a. USD 427 (effective 2008). back issues avail. **Document type:** *Abstract/Index.* **Description:** Provides an annual compendium of book reviews from various periodicals.
Related titles: Online - full text ed.
Published by: Gale (Subsidiary of: Cengage Learning), 27500 Drake Rd, Farmington Hills, MI 48331. TEL 248-699-4253, 800-877-4253, FAX 877-363-4253, gale.customerservice@cengage.com, http://gale.cengage.com. Ed. Dana Ferguson.

016.0281 USA
BOOK REVIEW INDEX ONLINE PLUS. Text in English. base vol. plus d. updates. **Document type:** *Database, Abstract/Index.*
Media: Online - full text.
Published by: Gale (Subsidiary of: Cengage Learning), 27500 Drake Rd, Farmington Hills, MI 48331. TEL 248-699-4253, 800-877-4253, FAX 877-363-4253, gale.customerservice@cengage.com, http://gale.cengage.com.

800 015.4897 FIN ISSN 0006-7490
Z2520
➤ **BOOKS FROM FINLAND.** Text in English. 1967. q. EUR 20 domestic Finland and Scandinavia; EUR 27 elsewhere (effective 2005). adv. bk.rev. bibl.; illus. Index. 80 p./no.; back issues avail. **Document type:** *Journal, Academic/Scholarly.* **Description:** Covers modern and classic Finnish literature and writers.
Related titles: Online - full text ed.: ISSN 1455-9137. 1995.
Indexed: MLA, MLA-IB, RASB.
Published by: Suomalaisen Kirjallisuuden Seura/Finnish Literature Society, Hallituskatu 1, PO Box 259, Helsinki, 00171, Finland. TEL 358-9-131231, FAX 358-9-13123220, sks-fl@finlit.fi, http://www/finlit.fi. Ed. Kristina Carlson. Adv. contact Soila Lehtonen. B&W page EUR 600. Circ: 2,800.

015.519 KOR
BOOKS FROM KOREA. Text in English; Abstracts in English, Chinese. 1971. a. free. adv. bk.rev. **Document type:** *Directory, Trade.*
Published by: Korean Publishers Association/Daehan Chulpan Munhwa Hyeobhoe, 105-2, Sagan-dong, Jongno-gu, Seoul, 110-190, Korea, S. TEL 82-2-7352701, FAX 82-2-7385414, webmaster@kpa21.or.kr, http://www.kpa21.or.kr/main/index.htm. Circ: 2,000.

015.79 USA
Z1251.S8
BOOKS OF THE SOUTHWEST (ONLINE EDITION); a critical checklist of current Southwestern Americana. Text in English. 1957. q. free. bk.rev. bibl. **Document type:** *Abstract/Index.* **Description:** Publishes reviews of all books and other published items about the American Southwest and northern Mexico.
Formerly: Books of the Southwest (Print Edition) (0006-7520)
Published by: Books of the Southwest, 2508 Garner Field Rd, Uvalde, TX 78801-6265. TEL 830-278-8951. Ed. Rawlyn Richter. Circ: 400.

BRANDYWINE BIBLIOGRAPHY. *see* PRINTING—Abstracting, Bibliographies, Statistics

015.44 FRA ISSN 0007-4209
Z2165
BULLETIN CRITIQUE DU LIVRE EN FRANCAIS. Text in French. 1945. m. EUR 250 domestic; EUR 270 foreign (effective 2008). adv. bk.rev. abstr. index. back issues avail. **Document type:** *Bibliography.* **Description:** Analyses over 3500 titles each year.
Related titles: Diskette ed.
Indexed: RASB.
Published by: Association les Amis du Bulletin Critique du Livre Francais, 12 Rue de la Montagne Sainte Genevieve, Paris, 75005, France. TEL 33-1-46347777, FAX 33-1-43253467, bclf@infomedia.fr, http://www.celf.fr/bclf.htm. Ed. Pierre Parbel. Pub. Paul Thibault. Adv. contact Jean-Michel Vieillard. Circ: 5,000.

CALIFORNIA DIRECTORY OF ATTORNEYS. *see* LAW

686.2021 CAN ISSN 0575-9412
Z487
CANADA. STATISTICS CANADA. PRINTING, PUBLISHING AND ALLIED INDUSTRIES/CANADA. STATISTIQUE CANADA. IMPRIMERIE, EDITION ET INDUSTRIES CONNEXES. Text in English, French. 1920. a. CAD 40 domestic; USD 40 foreign (effective 1999). **Document type:** *Government.*
Related titles: Online - full text ed.
Published by: Statistics Canada, Operations and Integration Division (Subsidiary of: Statistics Canada/Statistique Canada), Circulation Management, 120 Parkdale Ave, Ottawa, ON K1A 0T6, Canada. TEL 613-951-7277, 800-267-6677, FAX 613-951-1584.

050 ARG
CATALOGO COLECTIVO DE PUBLICACIONES PERIODICAS EXISTENTES EN BIBLIOTECAS CIENTIFICAS Y TECNICAS ARGENTINA. Text in Spanish. 1942. irreg., latest 1981. Supplement avail. **Document type:** *Bibliography.*
Published by: Consejo Nacional de Investigaciones Cientificas y Tecnicas (C O N I C E T), Avda Rivadavia 1917, Buenos Aires, C1033AAJ, Argentina. TEL 54-11-49537230, conicet.gov.ar.

016.002 CHN ISSN 1005-0051
Z1033.B3
CHANGXIAO SHUZHAI/ABSTRACTS FROM BESTSELLERS. Text in Chinese. 1993. m. USD 36 (effective 2009). **Document type:** *Abstract/Index.* **Description:** Contains abstracts and list of Chinese books.
—East View.
Published by: Jiangsu Renmin Chubanshe/Jiangsu People's Publishing House, 165 Zhongyang Road, Nanjing, Jiangsu 210009, China. TEL 86-25-6634309, FAX 86-25-3379766, http://www.book-wind.com/. **Dist. by:** China International Book Trading Corp, 35 Chegongzhuang Xilu, Haidian District, PO Box 399, Beijing 100044, China. TEL 86-10-68412045, FAX 86-10-68412023, cibtc@mail.cibtc.com.cn, http://www.cibtc.com.cn.

016.0178 GBR ISSN 0140-1939
CLOVER INFORMATION INDEX. Text in English. 1974. q. GBP 58 domestic; GBP 69 foreign (effective 2000). **Document type:** *Abstract/Index.* **Description:** A subject guide to popular periodicals.
Related titles: CD-ROM ed.: GBP 119 (effective 2000); Online - full text ed.: GBP 125 (effective 2000).
Published by: Clover Publications, 32 Ickwell Rd, Northill, Biggleswade, Beds SG18 9AB, United Kingdom. TEL 44-1767-627363, FAX 44-1767-267004.

050 JPN
CURRENT JAPANESE PERIODICALS FOR (YEAR). Text in Japanese. a. **Description:** Lists both English- and Japanese-language periodicals that are available by subscription overseas, main title alpha list with U.S. dollar prices, index by category.
Published by: Japan Publications Inc., 2-1 Sarugaku-cho 1-chome, Chiyoda-ku, Tokyo, 101-0064, Japan. TEL 03-2958411, FAX 03-2958416. Ed. A Takeuchi.

016.05 SWE ISSN 0564-7568
DAGSPRESSENS DETALJSPRIDNING. Text in Swedish. 1968. a. looseleaf. SEK 2,195 (effective 2003). **Document type:** *Directory, Trade.* **Description:** Contains detailed analyses of the coverage of the Swedish daily press.
Published by: Tidningsstatistik AB, Linnegatan 87, Stockholm, 11478, Sweden. TEL 46-8-50742400, FAX 46-8-50742401, tidningsstatistik@ts.se, http://www.ts.se.

070.5021 BEL ISSN 0777-0006
DONNEES STATISTIQUES SUR LE LIVRE BELGE DE LANGUE FRANCAISE. Text in French. a., latest 1992, for the year 1990. free to qualified personnel. **Document type:** *Corporate.* **Description:** Statistical review of the state of French language publishing in Belgium.
Formerly (until 1983): Livre en Belgique en.. (0776-9997)
Published by: Association des Editeurs Belges (A D E B), Avenue Huart Hamoir 1/34, Brussels, 1030, Belgium. TEL 32-2-2416580, FAX 32-2167131 32-2/216 71 31, http://www.adeb.be.

015.478 BLR
DRUK BELARUSI. Text in Belorussian. 1976. a. **Description:** Contains information on all publications coming out in Belarus.
Former titles: Pechat' Belarusi; Pechat Belorusskoi S.S.R.
Published by: Natsiyanal'naya Knizhnaya Palata Belarusi/National Book Chamber of Belarus, Vul V Kharuzhai 31-a, Minsk, 220002, Belarus. Eds. A I Voronko, T G Rabushko. Circ: 300.

050 USA ISSN 0092-3974
Z6944.L5
THE INTERNATIONAL DIRECTORY OF LITTLE MAGAZINES AND SMALL PRESSES. Text in English. 1965. a. USD 37.95 per issue paper; USD 55 per issue cloth (effective 2011). **Document type:** *Directory, Trade.* **Description:** Lists 5,000 independent book and magazine publishers of everything from poetry and fiction to non-fiction of all kinds as well as photos, cartoons, essays, parts of novels, collages, plays and news items. Includes full editorial descriptions plus complete subject and regional indexes for quicker access.
Former titles (until 1974): Directory of Little Magazines and Small Presses (0363-2016); (until 1969): Directory of Little Magazines (0084-9979)
Related titles: CD-ROM ed.: USD 30 per issue (effective 2011); ♦ Supplement(s): Small Press Review (Online). ISSN 1949-2731.
Published by: Dustbooks, PO Box 100, Paradise, CA 95967. TEL 530-877-6110, 800-477-6110, FAX 530-877-0222, publisher@dustbooks.com. Ed. Len Fulton.

016.070 CHE ISSN 1424-4128
KATALOG DER SCHWEIZER PRESSE. PUBLIKUMSZEITSCHRIFTEN, SPEZIAL- UND HOBBYZEITSCHRIFTEN, FACHZEITSCHRIFTEN/CATALOGUE DE LA PRESSE SUISSE. PERIODIQUES S'ADRESSANT AU GRAND PUBLIC, JOURNAUX SPECIALISES LOISIRS ET PASSE-TEMPS, JOURNAUX PROFESSIONNELS. Text in German, French. 1912. a. CHF 30 (effective 2001). **Document type:** *Directory, Trade.* **Description:** Contains important information on over 1,700 newspapers, journals and other periodicals.
Former titles (until 2000): Katalog der Schweizer Presse. Fachzeitschriften (1422-6014); (until 1973): Katalog der Schweizer Presse. Zeitschriften, Fachblaetter (1422-609X); (until 1969): Zeitschriften- und Fachblaetterkatalog der Schweiz (1422-6081)
Published by: Verband Schweizerischer Werbegesellschaften/Association des Societes Suisses de Publicite, Av des Mousquines 4, Case Postale 339, Lausanne, 1001, Switzerland. TEL 41-21-2136141, FAX 41-21-3126709, dcl@vsw-assp.ch, http://www.vsw-assp.ch.

016.0705 RUS
KNIZHNAYA LETOPIS'. VSPOMOGATEL'NYE UKAZATELI. Text in Russian. q. **Document type:** *Bibliography.*
Indexed: RASB.
Published by: Rossiiskaya Knizhnaya Palata/Book Chamber International, Ostozhenka 4, Moscow, 119034, Russian Federation. TEL 7-095-2911278, FAX 7-095-2919630, bookch@postman.ru, http://www.bookchamber.ru.

016.0705 UKR ISSN 0130-9196
Z2519.6.A6
LITOPYS KNYH; derzhavnyi bibliografichnyi pokazhchyk Ukrainy. Text in Ukrainian. 1924. m. USD 366 foreign (effective 2005). **Document type:** *Bibliography.* **Description:** Bibliography of books published in Ukraine.
Indexed: RASB.
—East View.
Published by: (Ukraine. Ministerstvo Informatsii Ukrainy/Information Ministry of Ukraine), Knyzhkova Palata Ukrainy imeni Ivana Fedorova/Ivan Fedorov Book Chamber of Ukraine, Pr Gagarina 27, Kyiv, 02094, Ukraine. TEL 380-44-5520134, ukrbook@ukr.net, http://www.ukrbook.net. Ed. O B Zubareva. **Dist. by:** East View Information Services, 10601 Wayzata Blvd, Minneapolis, MN 55305. TEL 952-252-1201, 800-477-1005, FAX 952-252-1202, info@eastview.com, http://www.eastview.com.

016.0705 UKR
LITOPYS NOT. Text in Ukrainian. 1996. a. USD 68 per issue foreign (effective 2005). **Description:** Bibliography of all sheet music publications in Ukraine.

P

Published by: Knyzhkova Palata Ukrainy imeni Ivana Fedorova/Ivan Fedorov Book Chamber of Ukraine, Pr Gagarina 27, Kyiv, 02094, Ukraine. TEL 380-44-5520134, ukrbook@ukr.net, http://www.ukrbook.net. **Dist. by:** East View Information Services, 10601 Wayzata Blvd, Minneapolis, MN 55305. TEL 952-252-1201, 800-477-1005, FAX 952-252-1202, info@eastview.com, http://www.eastview.com.

016.0705 UKR ISSN 0136-0906
Z2514.U5
LITOPYS OBRAZOTVORCHYKH VYDAN'. Text in Ukrainian. 1996. a. USD 67 per issue foreign (effective 2005). **Document type:** *Bibliography.* **Description:** Bibliography of fine arts publications put out in Ukraine.
—East View.
Published by: Knyzhkova Palata Ukrainy imeni Ivana Fedorova/Ivan Fedorov Book Chamber of Ukraine, Pr Gagarina 27, Kyiv, 02094, Ukraine. TEL 380-44-5520134, ukrbook@ukr.net, http://www.ukrbook.net. **Dist. by:** East View Information Services, 10601 Wayzata Blvd, Minneapolis, MN 55305. TEL 952-252-1201, 800-477-1005, FAX 952-252-1202, info@eastview.com, http://www.eastview.com.

016.002 FRA ISSN 0294-0000
Z2165
LIVRES HEBDO. Text in French. 1982. 44/yr. EUR 320 domestic; EUR 387.50 foreign (effective 2003). adv. bk.rev. bibl.; illus.; stat. **Document type:** *Trade.*
Formed by the 1982 merger of: Livres Hebdo (Edition avec Prix Cession de Base) (0223-4807); Livres Hebdo (Edition Destine a l'Etranger) (0223-4815); Livres Hebdo (Edition sans Prix) (0223-4793); All of which supersede in part (1959-1979): Bulletin du Livre (0007-456X); (1972-1979): Bibliographie de la France. Biblio (0335-5675); Which was formed by the merger of (1933-1971): Biblio (Mensuel) (1147-6710); (1814-1971): Bibliographie de la France (0006-1344); Which was formerly: Bibliographie de l'Empire Francais (1147-6680); (until 1811): Journal General de l'Imprimerie et de la Libraire (1147-6672); (1797-1810): Journal Typographique et Bibliographique (1147-6664)
Related titles: ◆ Supplement(s): Service Ile-de-France. ISSN 1162-4469; ◆ Les Livres du Mois. ISSN 0294-0027.
Indexed: A22, RASB.
—IE, Infotrieve, INIST. **CCC.**
Published by: Electre, 35 rue Gregoire de Tours, Paris, 75279 Cedex 06, France. TEL 33-01-44412862, FAX 33-01-44412864, commercial@electre.com. Ed. Jean Marie Doublet. Circ: 9,000.

016.070 CHE
MEDIAPRINT. Text in German, French. 1999. 2/w. CHF 680 (effective 2001). **Document type:** *Directory, Trade.* **Description:** Presents updated information periodicals from throughout Switzerland.
Media: Online - full text.
Published by: Verband Schweizerischer Werbegesellschaften/Association des Societes Suisses de Publicite, Av des Mousquines 4, Case Postale 339, Lausanne, 1001, Switzerland. TEL 41-21-2136141, FAX 41-21-3126709, dcl@vsw-assp.ch, http://www.vsw-assp.ch.

015.6883 BWA ISSN 0027-8777
Z3559
NATIONAL BIBLIOGRAPHY OF BOTSWANA. Text in English. 1969. 3/yr. index. **Document type:** *Bibliography.* **Description:** Lists publications issued in Botswana and deposited at the National Library Service under terms of the legal deposit law.
Published by: National Library Service, Private Bag 0036, Gaborone, Botswana. TEL 267-352397, FAX 267-301149. Ed. Gertrude Kayaga Mulindwa. Pub. Basiamang Garebakwena. Circ: 300.

016.0705 JPN
NIHON KAGAKU GIJUTSU KANKEI CHIKUJI KANKOBUTSU SORAN (ONLINE)/DIRECTORY OF JAPANESE SCIENTIFIC PERIODICALS (ONLINE). Text in English, Japanese. 2001 (Oct.). irreg. **Document type:** *Directory, Academic/Scholarly.*
Media: Online - full content. **Related titles:** CD-ROM ed.: announced never published.
Published by: National Diet Library/Kokuritsu Kokkai Toshokan, Business, Science and Technology Division, 1-10-1 Nagata-cho, Chiyoda-ku, Tokyo, 100-0014, Japan. TEL 81-3-35812331, FAX 81-3-30541528, webmaster@ndl.go.jp, http://www.ndl.go.jp.

002.021 381.45002 NOR ISSN 1504-4203
NORMTALLSUNDERSOEKELSEN. Text in Norwegian. 19??. a. stat. back issues avail. **Document type:** *Report, Trade.*
Related titles: Online - full text ed.
Published by: Norske Bokhandlerforening/Norwegian Booksellers' Association, Oevre Vollgate 15, Oslo, 0158, Norway. TEL 47-22-396800, FAX 47-22-396810, firmapost@bokhandlerforeningen.no.

016.0705 UKR ISSN 0136-0922
NOVI VYDANNYA UKRAINY. Text in Ukrainian. 1996. 3/m. USD 436 foreign (effective 2005). **Document type:** *Bibliography.* **Description:** Bibliography of new books and brochures published in Ukraine.
—East View.
Published by: Knyzhkova Palata Ukrainy imeni Ivana Fedorova/Ivan Fedorov Book Chamber of Ukraine, Pr Gagarina 27, Kyiv, 02094, Ukraine. TEL 380-44-5520134, ukrbook@ukr.net, http://www.ukrbook.net. **Dist. by:** East View Information Services, 10601 Wayzata Blvd, Minneapolis, MN 55305. TEL 952-252-1201, 800-477-1005, FAX 952-252-1202, info@eastview.com, http://www.eastview.com.

016.0705 AUT ISSN 1726-4693
Z2105
OESTERREICHISCHE BIBLIOGRAPHIE (ONLINE). Text in German. 1946. fortn. index. cum.index: 1946-1972. **Document type:** *Bibliography.*
Formerly (until 2002): Oesterreichische Bibliographie. Reihe A: Verzeichnis der Oesterreichischen Neuerscheinungen (Print) (1023-1862); Which superseded in part (in 1983): Oesterreichische Bibliographie (0029-8913)
Media: Online - full text.
Indexed: RASB.
Published by: Oesterreichische Nationalsbibliothek, Josefsplatz 1, Vienna, 1015, Austria. TEL 43-1-53410, FAX 43-1-53410280, onb@onb.ac.at, http://www.onb.ac.at. Circ: 2,950.

015.51 CHN ISSN 0578-073X
Z3101 CODEN: NSAPEE
QUANGUO XINSHUMU/NATIONAL NEW BOOKS LIST. Text in Chinese. 1954. s-a. USD 105.60 (effective 2009). bibl. **Document type:** *Journal, Academic/Scholarly.* **Description:** Lists new books published in the People's Republic of China. Entries are arranged by subject, and include publisher, publication date, price, pages, and ISBN.
—East View.
Published by: Quanguo Xinshumu Zazhishe, 10, Xianxiaohutong, Beijing, 100005, China. TEL 86-10-65123403, FAX 86-10-65123410. **Dist. by:** China International Book Trading Corp, 35 Chegongzhuang Xilu, Haidian District, PO Box 399, Beijing 100044, China. TEL 86-10-68412045, FAX 86-10-68412023, cibtc@mail.cibtc.com.cn, http://www.cibtc.com.cn.

015.438 POL ISSN 0511-1196
RUCH WYDAWNICZY W LICZBACH/POLISH PUBLISHING IN FIGURES. Text in Polish. 1955. a., latest 1999. PLZ 22 domestic; USD 14.66 foreign (effective 2001). **Document type:** *Abstract/Index.* **Description:** Offers official statistical data concerning books and periodicals characterized by sheets, titles, copies, subject fields and publishers.
Published by: Biblioteka Narodowa, Instytut Bibliograficzny, Al Niepodleglosci 213, Warsaw, 02086, Poland. TEL 48-22-6082408, FAX 48-22-8255251, polonica@bn.org.pl, http://www.bn.org.pl. Ed. Krystyna Bankowska Bober. **Dist. by:** P.P. CHZ Ars Polona, Krakowskie Przedmiescie 7, Warsaw 00068, Poland.

016.070 CHE
SCHWEIZER PRESSE. ZEITUNGEN, AMTSBLAETTER, ANZEIGER, PUBLIKUMSZEITSCHRIFTEN/PRESSE SUISSE. JOURNAUX, FEUILLES OFFICIELLES, FEUILLES D'ANNONCES. PERIODIQUES S'ADRESSANT AU GRAND PUBLIC. Text in German, French. 1912. a. CHF 30 (effective 2001). **Document type:** *Directory, Trade.* **Description:** Contains information on over 800 newspapers classified by geographic zones.
Former titles: Katalog der Schweizer Presse. Zeitungen, Amtsblaetter, Anzeiger, Publikums-Zeitschriften (1422-5018); (until 1975): Katalog der Schweizer Presse. Zeitungen, Amtsblaetter, Anzeiger (0454-9783); (until 1969): Zeitungskatalog der Schweiz (1422-500X)
Published by: Verband Schweizerischer Werbegesellschaften/Association des Societes Suisses de Publicite, Av des Mousquines 4, Case Postale 339, Lausanne, 1001, Switzerland. TEL 41-21-2136141, FAX 41-21-3126709, dcl@vsw-assp.ch, http://www.vsw-assp.ch.

017.8 USA
Z1033.L73
THE SMALL PRESS RECORD OF BOOKS IN PRINT (CD-ROM). Text in English. 1969. a. USD 37.95 per issue (effective 2011). adv. **Document type:** *Bibliography.* **Description:** Lists some 50,000 books in print and available published by small, independent publishers world-wide. The volume is indexed by title, by author, by publisher and by subject for quick access.
Former titles (until 1997): The Small Press Record of Books in Print (Print) (0148-9720); (until 1975): Small Press Record of Books (0361-364X); (until 1972): Small Press Record of Non-periodical Publications (0081-0185)
Media: CD-ROM.
Published by: Dustbooks, PO Box 100, Paradise, CA 95967. TEL 530-877-6110, 800-477-6110, FAX 530-877-0222, publisher@dustbooks.com. Ed. Len Fulton.

017.8 JPN
SOUTHEAST - EAST ASIAN ENGLISH PUBLICATIONS IN PRINT. Text in English. 1987. irreg. JPY 25,000, USD 210. adv. **Document type:** *Directory.* **Description:** Covers the publications in Brunei, Burma, China, Hong Kong, Indonesia, Korea, Macao, Malaysia, Philippines, Singapore, Taiwan, Thailand and Vietnam.
Related titles: Diskette ed.
Published by: Japan Publications Guide Service, 5-5-13 Matsushiro, Tsukuba-shi, Ibaraki-ken 305-0035, Japan. FAX 81-3-3667-9646. Circ: 1,000. **Subscr. to:** Intercontinental Marketing Corp., IPO Box 5056, Tokyo 100-30, Japan.

016.0285 USA
SPANISH LANGUAGE BOOKS FOR CHILDREN & YOUNG ADULTS. Text in English. a. free. **Document type:** *Directory, Consumer.* **Description:** Catalog of Spanish and English language and bilingual books and periodicals for children.
Published by: Hispanic Books Distributors, Inc., 2555 N Coyote Dr, Ste 109, Tucson, AZ 85745-1235. TEL 520-690-0643, 800-624-2124, FAX 520-690-6574, hbdvsa@azstarnet.com. Ed. Arnulfo D Trejo. Circ: 5,000.

015.5493 LKA ISSN 0253-8229
Z3211
SRI LANKA NATIONAL BIBLIOGRAPHY. Text in English, Singhalese, Tamil. 1962. m. LKR 100 domestic; USD 50 foreign (effective 2001). 30 p./no. 2 cols./p.; **Document type:** *Bibliography.*
Formerly (until 1973): Ceylon National Bibliography (0009-0883)
Published by: National Library and Documentation Center, 14 Independence Ave., Colombo, 7, Sri Lanka. TEL 94-1-698847, FAX 94-1-685201. Circ: 500.

SVENSK ANNONSTAXA. *see* BIBLIOGRAPHIES

016.05 SWE
SVENSK ANNONSTAXA ONLINE. Text in Swedish. m. SEK 1,580 (effective 2001). **Document type:** *Directory, Trade.*
Media: Online - full content. **Related titles:** ◆ Print ed.: Svensk Annonstaxa. ISSN 0491-6522.
Published by: Tidningsstatistik AB, Linnegatan 87, Stockholm, 11478, Sweden. TEL 46-8-623-94-00, FAX 46-8-623-14-04, tidningsstatistik@ts.se, http://www.ts.se.

SVENSK REKLAMTAXA. *see* BIBLIOGRAPHIES

016.05 SWE
SVENSK REKLAMTAXA ONLINE. Text in Swedish. m. SEK 850 (effective 2001). **Document type:** *Directory, Trade.*
Media: Online - full content. **Related titles:** ◆ Print ed.: Svensk Reklamtaxa. ISSN 0282-0919.
Published by: Tidningsstatistik AB, Linnegatan 87, Stockholm, 11478, Sweden. TEL 46-8-623-94-00, FAX 46-8-623-14-04, tidningsstatistik@ts.se, http://www.ts.se.

015.6887 SWZ ISSN 0378-7710
Z3560
SWAZILAND NATIONAL BIBLIOGRAPHY. Text in English. 1974. a. SZL 52 domestic; USD 20 foreign (effective 1999). adv. back issues avail. **Document type:** *Bibliography.* **Description:** Lists publications issued in Swaziland or received at the University.
Published by: University of Swaziland, Library, Private Bag 4, Kwaluseni, Swaziland. TEL 268-85108, FAX 268-85276, TELEX 2087 WD. Ed. P Muswazi. R&P M R Mauuso. Adv. contact M.R. Mauuso. Circ: 100.

016.05 SWE ISSN 0281-7691
TS-BOKEN. Text in Swedish. 1942. a. looseleaf. SEK 2,975 (effective 2003). **Document type:** *Directory, Trade.* **Description:** Contains data on the spread and household coverage of the daily press, including comparisons of circulation with those of the preceding year.
Related titles: ◆ Online - full content ed.: TS-Boken Online.
Published by: Tidningsstatistik AB, Linnegatan 87, Stockholm, 11478, Sweden. TEL 46-8-623-94-00, FAX 46-8-623-14-04, tidningsstatistik@ts.se, http://www.ts.se.

016.05 SWE
TS-BOKEN ONLINE. Text in Swedish. m. SEK 2,690 (effective 2000). **Document type:** *Directory, Trade.*
Media: Online - full content. **Related titles:** ◆ Print ed.: TS-Boken. ISSN 0281-7691.
Published by: Tidningsstatistik AB, Linnegatan 87, Stockholm, 11478, Sweden. TEL 46-8-623-94-00, FAX 46-8-623-14-04, tidningsstatistik@ts.se, http://www.ts.se.

016.05 SWE ISSN 0346-3427
TS-TIDNINGEN. Text in Swedish. 1961. 4/yr. SEK 450 Vols. 1 and 3. Vols. 2 and 4 are free PDF files (effective 2001). **Document type:** *Directory, Trade.* **Description:** Presents the latest circulation figures for newspapers and periodicals.
Formerly (until 1972): TS-Aktuellt
Published by: Tidningsstatistik AB, Linnegatan 87, Stockholm, 11478, Sweden. TEL 46-8-50742400, FAX 46-8-50742401, tidningsstatistik@ts.se.

011 USA
ULRICHSWEB.COM. Text in English. 1999. w. Contact publisher. **Document type:** *Directory, Bibliography.* **Description:** Includes magazines, journals, newsletters, newspapers, annuals and irregular serials published worldwide. Entries include title, circulation, frequency, complete publisher address, telephone, fax, email and URL, description, subscription price, with subscription and distribution addresses, telephone, fax, email and URL information. Also includes bibliographic classification (LC, DDC and CODEN), abstracting and indexing information, document type notations, online and CD-ROM availability, document delivery service availability, advertising rates and contact name, among other data.
Media: Online - full text. **Related titles:** ◆ Print ed.: Ulrich's Periodicals Directory. ISSN 0000-2100.
Published by: Serials Solutions (Subsidiary of: ProQuest), 501 N 34th St, Ste 211, Seattle, WA 98103-8645. TEL 206-545-9056, 866-737-4257, FAX 206-525-9066, info@serialssolutions.com, http://www.serialssolutions.com. Ed. Laurie Kaplan TEL 908-219-0284.

PUBLISHING AND BOOK TRADE—Computer Applications

BEFORE & AFTER; how to design cool stuff. *see* COMPUTERS—Computer Graphics

070.50285 AUT ISSN 1028-771X
BUCH UND CO. Text in German. 1997. bi-m. **Document type:** *Magazine, Consumer.*
Published by: Buchkultur Verlagsgesellschaft mbH, Huetteldorferstr 26, Vienna, 1150, Austria. TEL 43-1-4794642-0, FAX 43-1-786338010, office@buchkultur.net, http://www.buchkultur.net.

620.00420285 070.5797 SWE ISSN 1104-1099
C A P & DESIGN. (Computer Assisted Publishing) Text in Swedish. 1985. 6/yr. SEK 799 (effective 2011). adv. **Document type:** *Magazine, Trade.* **Description:** Deals with all types of computer and pre-press systems from software and hardware to various available services.
Former titles (until 1993): C A P and D - Computer Assisted Publishing and Design (1102-8777); (until 1991): C A P - Computer Assisted Publishing (1100-0791); (until 1988): C W Focus (0282-8448)
Related titles: Online - full text ed.: ISSN 1402-4373.
Published by: I D G AB (Subsidiary of: I D G Communications Inc.), Karlbergsvaegen 77-81, Stockholm, 10678, Sweden. TEL 46-8-4536000, FAX 46-8-4536005, kundservice@idg.se, http://www.idg.se. Ed. Therese Jarnankar. Adv. contact Magnus Mu Ray. Circ: 10,000 (paid and controlled).

COMPUPRINT. *see* TECHNOLOGY: COMPREHENSIVE WORKS

070.5797 USA
COMPUTER PUBLISHING MARKET FORECAST (YEAR). Text in English. 1985. irreg., latest 2001, 16th ed. USD 2,195 per issue (print or online ed.) (effective 2008). adv. **Document type:** *Report, Trade.* **Description:** Covers the more than $3 billion market for computer books, magazines/periodicals, newsletters, journals, directories and online media.
Related titles: Online - full text ed.
Published by: SIMBA Information (Subsidiary of: Market Research.Com), 11200 Rockville Pike, Ste 504, Rockville, MD 20852. TEL 240-747-3096, 888-297-4622, FAX 240-747-3004, customerservice@simbainformation.com. Pub. Linda Kopp.

D T P TECHNIQUES. (Desktop Publishing) *see* COMPUTERS—Microcomputers

070.5797 NLD ISSN 1389-7888
D-ZONE. Text in Dutch. 1994. 6/yr. EUR 35 (effective 2009). adv. bk.rev.; software rev. illus.; mkt. back issues avail. **Document type:** *Consumer.*
Formed by the 1999 merger of: P S Magazine (Post Script) (1383-7222); WebMaster Magazine (1386-2375)
Published by: Hollandia Publishing BV, Postbus 341, Heerhugowaard, 1700 AH, Netherlands. TEL 31-72-5760500, FAX 31-72-5760505, hp@hollandia.nl, http://www.hollandia.nl. Eds. Jan Verberne, Hans Frederiks. Pub. Edwin Nunnink. Adv. contact Marten Mulder TEL 31-72-5760546.

686.22544416 AUS ISSN 1322-9230
DESKTOP. Text in English. 1986. m. AUD 74 domestic; AUD 120 foreign (effective 2008). adv. bk.rev. cum.index. back issues avail. **Document type:** *Magazine, Trade.* **Description:** Covers graphic design, prepress, publishing, multimedia and web design.
Former titles (until 1993): Desktop Magazine (1037-7603); (until 1991): Desktop Electronic Publishing and Graphics (1036-2207); (until 1990): Desktop Publishing and Graphics (1034-9200); (until 1989): Desktop Publishing (0818-111X)
Related titles: Online - full text ed.
Indexed: D05, SCOPUS.
Published by: Niche Media Pty Ltd (Subsidiary of: Waivcom Worldwide Ltd.), 170, Dorcas St, South Melbourne, VIC 3205, Australia. TEL 61-3-99484900, 800-804-160, FAX 61-3-99484999, subscriptions@niche.com.au. Ed. Jo Spurling. Adv. contact Chantelle Ford TEL 61-3-99484984. page AUD 3,990; trim 235 x 297. Circ: 10,000.

DESKTOP PUBLISHING. *see* COMPUTERS—Microcomputers

070.5797 DNK ISSN 1902-6757
DIGETALE MEDIER PROFESSIONEL. Text in Danish. 1991. 10/yr. DKK 500 (effective 2009). adv. **Document type:** *Magazine, Trade.* **Description:** News about desktop publishing techniques.
Former titles (until 2007): Digetale Medier (1604-6595); (until 2005): D T P Digetale Medier (1602-0545); (until 2001): D T P Grafiske Medier (1396-626X); (until 1996): Desktop Publishing (0906-5016)
Related titles: Online - full text ed.: ISSN 1902-4681.
Published by: Digitale Medier ApS, Soendre Strandvej 18, PO Box 18, Helsingoer, 3000, Denmark. TEL 45-49-265314, info@digitalemedier.dk. Ed. Henrik Malmgren. Adv. contact Mette Eilersen. color page DKK 44,880; 210 x 280. Circ: 7,500.

DIGITAL IMAGING & PUBLISHING. *see* COMPUTERS—Microcomputers

070.5797 USA
E-DOCUMENT NEWS. Text in English. 2004. 2/m. free. **Document type:** *Newsletter, Trade.* **Description:** Dedicated to covering all of the important industry news for the electronic document systems industry.
Media: E-mail.
Published by: Xplor International, 24238 Hawthorne Blvd, Torrance, CA 90505-6505. TEL 310-373-3633, 800-669-7567, FAX 310-375-4240, info@xplor.org, http://www.xplor.org. Ed. Paul LeTourneur.

070.5797 USA
THE ELECTRONIC PUBLISHING FORUM. Text in English. 1991. q. free. adv. back issues avail. **Description:** Contains articles, reviews and information on electronic publishing, writing, and literature.
Media: Diskette. **Related titles:** Online - full text ed.
Published by: Serendipity Systems, PO Box 140, San Simeon, CA 93452. TEL 805-927-5259. Ed. John Galuszka.

070.5797 NLD ISSN 1387-5256
ELECTRONIC PUBLISHING SERIES. Text in English. 1996. irreg., latest vol.7, 1997. price varies. **Document type:** *Monographic series, Academic/Scholarly.* **Description:** Covers the application of computers to the traditional areas of publishing such as creating documents, document design, document processing and printing.
Published by: Springer Netherlands (Subsidiary of: Springer Science+Business Media), Van Godewijckstraat 30, Dordrecht, 3311 GX, Netherlands. TEL 31-78-6576050, FAX 31-78-6576474. Ed. Eric van Herwijnen.

070.5797 USA
GOVERNMENT PUBLISHER. Text in English. 1981. a. USD 66. adv. bk.rev. **Document type:** *Handbook/Manual/Guide, Trade.* **Description:** Applications of electronic publishing by federal and state governments.
Published by: G P, Inc., PO Box 170, Salem, NH 03079. TEL 603-898-2822, FAX 603-898-3393. Ed. W Bunnell. Circ: 11,000.

I P ENEWS. (Interactive Publications) *see* LITERATURE

070.5797 ITA
ITALIA PUBLISHERS MAGAZINE; rivista professionale per DTP, pre press, digital printing, editoria elettronica, imaging. Text in Italian. 1987. 10/yr. adv. **Document type:** *Magazine, Trade.* **Description:** Details innovations and technological advances in the printing industry.
Related titles: Online - full text ed.
Published by: SunnyCom Publishing Srl, Via Stromboli 18, Milan, 20144, Italy. TEL 39-02-48516207, FAX 39-02-43400509. Circ: 12,000 (paid).

070.50285 USA ISSN 1080-2711
Z286.E43
➤ **THE JOURNAL OF ELECTRONIC PUBLISHING.** Abbreviated title: J E P. Text in English. 1995-2003; N.S. 2006 (Jan.). 3/yr. free (effective 2011). back issues avail. **Document type:** *Journal, Academic/Scholarly.* **Description:** Discusses all facets of publishing material in an electronic environment.
Media: Online - full text.
Indexed: A39, B04, BRD, C27, C29, CA, CMM, CommAb, D03, D04, E13, ISTA, Inspec, L04, L07, L08, L13, LISTA, LibLit, PAIS, R14, S14, S15, S18, SCOPUS, T02, W03, W05.
Published by: University of Michigan Library, Scholarly Publishing Office, 300 Hatcher N, 920 N University Ave, Ann Arbor, MI 48109. FAX 734-763-6850, lib.spo@umich.edu, http://www.lib.umich.edu/spo/. Ed. Judith Turner.

070.5797 USA ISSN 0196-4127
KLEPER REPORT ON DIGITAL PUBLISHING. Text in English. 1979. bi-m. USD 24.95 (effective 2001). adv. bk.rev.; software rev. back issues avail. **Document type:** *Newsletter.* **Description:** Covers all aspects of digital publishing, including print, web, electronic, and interactive media.
Former titles (until 1996): Personal Composition Report; Digest of Information on Phototypesetting
Related titles: E-mail ed.; Fax ed.; Online - full text ed.
Published by: Graphic Dimensions, 104 Eagle Pine Way, Rochester, NY 14623-5168. TEL 716-381-3428, FAX 716-385-9723. Ed., R&P, Adv. contact Michael Kleper.

070.5 BEL ISSN 1378-8957
M & C PUBLISHING. (Media et Communicatie) Text in Dutch. 2001. 5/yr. EUR 25 (effective 2010). adv. **Document type:** *Magazine, Trade.* **Description:** Provides comprehensive coverage of the entire electronic publishing workflow from data input to data output, including data processing and publishing.
Published by: Roularta Media Group, Research Park, Zellik, 1731, Belgium. TEL 32-2-4675611, FAX 32-2-4675757, communication@roularta.be. adv.: page EUR 2,300. Circ: 3,000 (paid and controlled).

MULTIMEDIA INFORMATION & TECHNOLOGY. *see* LIBRARY AND INFORMATION SCIENCES

070.5797 DNK ISSN 1904-335X
▼ **O J S PAA DANSK.** (Open Journal Systems) Text in Danish. 2010. irreg. **Document type:** *Consumer.*
Media: Online - full text.
Published by: Statsbiblioteket/State and University Library, Victor Albecks Vej 1, Aarhus C, 8000, Denmark. TEL 45-89-462022, FAX 45-89-462220, sb@statsbiblioteket.dk, http://www.statsbiblioteket.dk. Ed. Niels Erike Frederiksen.

O L M S OCCASIONAL PAPER. (Office of Leadership and Management Services) *see* LIBRARY AND INFORMATION SCIENCES—Computer Applications

070.5797 AUT ISSN 1609-2775
➤ **ONLINE PUBLISHING IN MEDICINE.** Text in English. 2000. q. USD 75 domestic; USD 115 foreign; USD 35 newsstand/cover (effective 2001). adv. back issues avail. **Document type:** *Journal, Academic/Scholarly.* **Description:** Publishes articles, case reports, reviews, and letters with the aim of improving communications in understanding the multidisciplinary field of modern online publishing involving basic science and clinical research in medicine and biomedicine.
Related titles: Online - full text ed.
Indexed: SCOPUS.
Published by: V I C E R Publishing, PO Box 14, Vienna, A-1097, Austria. TEL 43-676-9568085, FAX 43-676-9568086, vicer@vicer.org, http://www.vicer.org. Ed., R&P Roland Hofbauer. adv.: B&W page USD 1,700, color page USD 2,200. Circ: 1,000 (paid and controlled).

070.5797 USA
THE OVID OBSERVER. Text in English. q. **Document type:** *Newsletter.*
Published by: Ovid (Subsidiary of: Wolters Kluwer N.V.), 333 Seventh Ave, New York, NY 10001. sales@ovid.com. Ed. Christopher K Verdesi.

070.50285 AUT
P C UND CO; neue CD-ROMs - neue Buecher - neue Trends. (Personal Computer) Text in German. q. software rev. **Document type:** *Magazine, Trade.*
Published by: Buchkultur Verlagsgesellschaft mbH, Huetteldorferstr 26, Vienna, 1150, Austria. TEL 43-1-4794642-0, FAX 43-1-786338010, office@buchkultur.net, http://www.buchkultur.net. Ed. Enno Pigge.

686.2244 DEU
PREPRESS; world of print. Text in German. 1992. 10/yr. EUR 50 domestic; EUR 70 foreign; EUR 5 newsstand/cover (effective 2009). adv. **Document type:** *Magazine, Trade.*
Published by: C.A.T. Verlag Bloemer GmbH, Freiligrathring 18-20, Ratingen, 40878, Germany. TEL 49-2102-20270, FAX 49-2102-202790, worldofphoto@cat-verlag.de, http://www.cat-verlag.de. Ed. Daniela Bloemer. Adv. contact Oliver Goepfert. B&W page EUR 2,710, color page EUR 4,608. Circ: 11,346 (paid).

PUBLAW UPDATE. *see* LAW

070.5197 RUS ISSN 1560-5183
PUBLISH; dizain, verstka, pechat'. Text in Russian. 1996. 9/yr. RUR 621 (effective 2006). adv. **Document type:** *Magazine, Trade.*
Related titles: Online - full text ed.
Published by: Izdatel'stvo Otkrytye Sistemy/Open Systems Publications, ul Rustaveli, dom 12A, komn 117, Moscow, 127254, Russian Federation. TEL 7-095-2539206, FAX 7-095-2539204, info@osp.ru. adv.: B&W page USD 2,700, color page USD 4,500; 202 x 257. Circ: 10,000.

070.5797 BRA ISSN 0103-8869
PUBLISH. Text in Portuguese. 1991. bi-m. BRL 44.90 (effective 2002). adv. **Document type:** *Magazine, Trade.* **Description:** Presents up-to-date information on the desktop publishing and multimedia industries.
Related titles: Online - full text ed.
Published by: I D G Computerworld do Brasil, Rua Tabapua, 145-3 e 4 andar, Itaim Bibi, Sao Paulo, 04533-010, Brazil. TEL 55-11-3049-2000, FAX 55-11-3071-4022, negocios@idg.com.br, http://www.idg.com.br. adv.: B&W page BRL 8,400, color page BRL 10,700; trim 210 x 280. Circ: 15,000 (paid and controlled).

070.5797 BEL ISSN 1377-5685
PUBLISH & PRINT. Text in French. 1993. 10/yr. EUR 29 (effective 2006). adv. **Document type:** *Magazine, Trade.*
Former titles (until 2001): Publish (1374-0652); (until 1998): The Best of Mac News (1370-0065)
Published by: Best of Publishing, Rodenbachstraat 70, Brussels, 1190, Belgium. TEL 32-2-3493550, FAX 32-2-3493597, jp@best.be, http://www.computerworld.be. Pub. Jean-Paul De Clerk.

070.5197 PRT
PUBLISH PORTUGAL. Text in Portuguese. m. adv. **Document type:** *Magazine, Trade.* **Description:** Covers news related to electronic publishing, graphics works and printing, including new products, reviews, buyer's guide, feature stories, and case studies.
Published by: Edicoes Expansao Economica Lda., Rue Mario Castelhano, 40-1, Queluz de Baixo, Barcarena, 2749-502, Portugal. TEL 351-21-496-95-40, FAX 351-21-436-95-39, webmaster@expansao.iol.pt, http://www.expansao.iol.pt. adv.: color page USD 1,848; trim 205 x 275. Circ: 8,000 (paid and controlled).

070.5797 DEU ISSN 0948-1931
PUBLISHING PRAXIS; das Fachmagazin fuer digitalen workflow und electronic publishing. Text in German. 1995. 6/yr. EUR 62.45 domestic; EUR 75.70 foreign; EUR 10.20 newsstand/cover (effective 2009). adv. **Document type:** *Magazine, Trade.* **Description:** Trade publication for professional users involved in digital publishing.
Incorporates (1992-1995): Pablo (0942-4199)
Published by: Deutscher Drucker Verlag GmbH, Postfach 4124, Ostfildern, 73744, Germany. TEL 49-711-448170, FAX 49-711-442099, info@publish.de. Ed. Petra Ebeling. Adv. contact Michael Bieber. B&W page EUR 3,700, color page EUR 5,200; trim 210 x 297. Circ: 10,202 (paid).

686.22544416 USA ISSN 2160-6196
PUBLISHING TRENDS; news and opinion on the changing world of book publishing. Text in English. 1994. m. USD 245 in US & Canada; USD 295 elsewhere (effective 2011). back issues avail. **Document type:** *Newsletter, Trade.* **Description:** Provides news and opinion on the rapidly changing world of book publishing.
Related titles: Online - full text ed.: ISSN 2160-620X. USD 195 (effective 2011).
Published by: Market Partners International, Inc., 232 Madison Ave, Ste 1400, New York, NY 10016. TEL 212-447-0855, FAX 212-447-0785, info@mpi-us.com, http://www.marketpartnersinternational.com.

070.5797 006.6 USA ISSN 1536-1594
CODEN: SBSDE4
S B S DIGITAL DESIGN; the how-to newsletter for electronic designers. (Step by Step) Text in English. 1989. m. USD 90 domestic; USD 105.93 in Canada; USD 120 elsewhere (effective 2005). adv. bk.rev. charts; illus.; tr.lit. index. back issues avail. **Document type:** *Newsletter.* **Description:** Geared toward electronic designers and production professionals; contains how-to articles with step-by-step artwork for beginners as well as experienced desktop graphic designers.
Formerly (until 2001): Step-by-Step Electronic Design (1055-2774)
Related titles: Online - full text ed.
Indexed: ABIPC, P10, P16, P17, P48, P49, P52, P53, P54, PQC, S10, SoftBase.
Published by: Dynamic Graphics Group, PO Box 9007, Maple Shade, NJ 08052. TEL 856-380-4122, FAX 856-380-4101. Circ: 12,000.

070.50285 USA ISSN 1091-1898
SEYBOLD PUBLICATIONS. BULLETIN; Seybold news & views on electronic publishing. Text in English. 1995. w. USD 195 (effective 2004). **Document type:** *Bulletin, Trade.* **Description:** Covers the news on the publishing and Internet industries, including analysis of new technologies, previews of new products, insights on trends, flash highlights from trade shows and more.
Formerly (until 1996): Seybold Bulletin on Computer Publishing (1087-7975)
Media: E-mail.
Published by: Seybold Publications, 999 Oakmont Plaza Drive, Westmont, IL 60559. TEL 610-565-6864, 800-325-3830, FAX 610-565-1858.

P

070.50285 USA ISSN 1533-9211
Z286.E43 CODEN: SREEAB
THE SEYBOLD REPORT. Text in English. 1971. s-m. USD 499; USD 599 combined subscription (print & online eds.) (effective 2010). bk.rev.; software rev. charts; illus. cum.index. reprints avail. **Document type:** *Newsletter, Trade.* **Description:** Covers the developments in publishing technologies for print, web and e-book applications, including new products, case studies and significant trends.
Formed by the merger of (1982-2001): Seybold Report on Publishing Systems (0736-7260); Which was formerly (197?-1982): Seybold Report (0364-5517); (1996-2001): Seybold Report on Internet Publishing (1090-4808); Which was formerly (until 1996): Seybold Report on Desktop Publishing (0889-9762); Editing Technology (0046-1261)
Related titles: Online - full text ed.: ISSN 1945-340X.
Indexed: A01, A03, A08, A26, ABIPC, B01, B02, B03, B06, B07, B08, B09, B11, B15, B17, B18, C10, C12, C23, CompC, CompD, CompLI, EngInd, G01, G04, G06, G07, G08, GALA, I05, Inspec, M&MA, M01, M02, MicrocompInd, S01, SCOPUS, T02.
—BLDSC (8254.490000), AskIEEE, CASDDS, IE, Ingenta, INIST. **CCC.**
Published by: Seybold Publications, PO Box 4250, Frederick, MD 21705. TEL 240-629-3300. Ed., Pub. Molly Joss TEL 610-327-3958.

070.50285 USA ISSN 1538-845X
T R'S ONLINE CENSUS. (Telecommunications Reports) (Includes: Daily Multimedia Daily News Service) Text in English. 1991. q. USD 198 (effective 2011). bk.rev. index. back issues avail.; reprints avail. **Document type:** *Newsletter, Trade.* **Description:** Tracks major developments in the information industry, follows online services and interactive TV and video businesses, and reports targeting trends in these fast-changing markets. Alerts readers to new online services and the promotional strategies to market them.
Former titles: Interactive Services Report; Information and Interactive Services Report (1059-731X); Which was formed by the merger of (1987-1991): Electronic Shopping News (0893-0333); (1987-1991): Interactivity Report (0893-0325); Which was formed by the merger of (1980-1987): International Videotex Teletext News (0197-677X); (1982-1987): Teleservices Report (0730-0263)
Published by: Telecommunications Reports (Subsidiary of: Aspen Publishers, Inc.), 1333 H St, NW, Ste 100, Washington, DC 20005. TEL 202-312-6060, FAX 202-312-6111, customerservice@tr.com.

070.5797 CAN ISSN 1053-900X
Z52.2 CODEN: TTECEY
➤ **TEXT TECHNOLOGY**; the journal of computer text processing. Text in English, French. 1983. s-a. CAD 45 domestic to individuals; USD 45 in United States to individuals; USD 60 elsewhere to individuals; CAD 72 domestic to institutions; USD 72 in United States to institutions; USD 87 elsewhere to institutions. adv. bk.rev. bibl.; charts; illus.; stat. index. back issues avail. **Document type:** *Journal, Academic/Scholarly.* **Description:** contains articles and reviews of any computerized processing, analysis, or creating of textual materials. For academic and corporate researchers, writers, editors, and teachers.
Formerly (until 1990): Research in Word Processing Newsletter (0748-5484)
Indexed: CA, Inspec, MLA-IB, SCOPUS, SOPODA, SoftBase, T02.
—BLDSC (8800.628200), AskIEEE, IE, Ingenta.
Published by: (Wright State University - Lake Campus USA), McMaster University, Humanities Communications Centre, Togo Salmon Hall, Room 205A, McMaster University, 1280 Main St W, Hamilton, ON L8S 4M2, Canada. TEL 905-525-9140 ext 24650, FAX 905 577 6930. Eds. Arthur A Molitierno, Joanne Buckley. R&P Arthur A Molitierno. Adv. contact Joseph Cavanaugh. page USD 200; trim 7 x 4.5. Circ: 300.

070.5797 USA
X-RAY MAGAZINE (ONLINE); quark software workflow solutions and implementation. Text in English. 1995. bi-m. free. adv. **Document type:** *Magazine, Trade.* **Description:** Provides work flow practices, case studies, and new feature information about QuarkXPress, Quark Publishing System (QPS), Quark Dynamic Document Server (QuarkDDS), Quark Content Manager (QCM), and the customers and markets that Quark serves.
Formerly (until 2009): X-Ray Magazine (Print) (1092-9320)
Published by: The PowerXChange, LLC, PO Box 2049, Wheat Ridge, CO 80034. TEL 303-940-0600, FAX 303-565-5997. Ed. Cyndie Shaffstall. Adv. contact Mike Garard. page USD 10,000; trim 8.125 x 10.875. Circ: 300,000.

RADIO

see COMMUNICATIONS—Radio

RADIOLOGY AND NUCLEAR MEDICINE

see MEDICAL SCIENCES—Radiology And Nuclear Medicine

RAILROADS

see TRANSPORTATION—Railroads

REAL ESTATE

see also ARCHITECTURE ; BUILDING AND CONSTRUCTION ; BUSINESS AND ECONOMICS ; BUSINESS AND ECONOMICS—Investments ; HOUSING AND URBAN PLANNING ; LAW

333.33 DEU
A I Z - DAS IMMOBILIENMAGAZIN. Text in German. 2006. 10/yr. EUR 75; EUR 9.20 newsstand/cover (effective 2007). adv. **Document type:** *Magazine, Trade.*
Formed by the merger of (1964-2006): Der Grundbesitz (0722-6918); (1960-2006): A I Z - Allgemeine Immobilien-Zeitung (0001-1673); Which was formerly (1924-1960): Allgemeine Immobilien-Zeitung (0344-4902)
Published by: Immobilienverband Deutschland I V D Bundesverband e.V., Littenstr 10, Berlin, 10179, Germany. TEL 49-30-2757260, FAX 49-30-27572649, info@ivd.net, http://www.ivd.net. adv.: B&W page EUR 3,400, color page EUR 4,930. Circ: 10,000 (controlled).

333.33 AUS ISSN 1834-6529
A P I NATIONAL NEWSLETTER. Text in English. 2006. irreg. **Document type:** *Newsletter, Trade.*
Media: Online - full text.
Published by: Australian Property Institute, 6 Campion St, Deakin, ACT 2600, Australia. TEL 61-2-6282-2411, FAX 61-2-6285-2194, national@propertyinstitute.com.au, http://www.propertyinstitute.com.au.

333.33 GBR
A PLACE IN THE SUN. Text in English. 19??. 13/yr. GBP 32 domestic; GBP 55.99 in Europe; GBP 94.99 elsewhere (effective 2009). adv. back issues avail. **Document type:** *Magazine, Trade.*
Related titles: Online - full text ed.
Published by: A Place in the Sun, 2nd Fl, Rear W Office, 16 Winchester Walk, London, SE1 9AQ, United Kingdom. TEL 44-20-73572920, FAX 44-20-73579292, sarahn@apitsltd.com. Ed. Richard Way. adv.: page GBP 2,975; trim 213 x 278. Circ: 33,386.

346.043 USA
KF639
A PRACTICAL GUIDE TO DISPUTES BETWEEN ADJOINING LANDOWNERS - EASEMENTS. Text in English. 1989. 2 base vols. plus a. updates. looseleaf. USD 272 base vol(s). (effective 2008). **Document type:** *Handbook/Manual/Guide, Trade.* **Description:** Provides substantive and procedural guidance for a wide range of disputes between landowners.
Published by: Matthew Bender & Co., Inc. (Subsidiary of: LexisNexis North America), 1275 Broadway, Albany, NY 12204. TEL 518-487-3000, 800-424-4200, FAX 518-487-3083, international@bender.com, http://bender.lexisnexis.com.

333.33 USA
A R E S NEWSLETTER. Text in English. s-a. adv. back issues avail. **Document type:** *Newsletter.*
Published by: American Real Estate Society, c/o Diane Quarles, Clemson University, 424 Sirrine Hall, PO Box 341323, Clemson, SC 29634. TEL 216-687-4732, FAX 216-687-9331. Adv. contact James R Webb.

333.3 USA
A R E U E A NEWS BYTES. Text in English. s-m. free (effective 2008). **Document type:** *Newsletter.* **Description:** Provides announcements of upcoming meetings, past meeting highlights, member activities, placement announcements, industry notes, dissertation competitions and other current information.
Formerly: American Real Estate and Urban Economics Association Newsletter (Print)
Media: Online - full text.
Published by: American Real Estate and Urban Economics Association, PO Box 9958, Richmond, VA 23228. TEL 866-273-8321, FAX 877-273-8323, areuea@areuea.org.

333.33 USA ISSN 1547-7681
A S A PROFESSIONAL. (American Society of Appraisers) Text in English. 2004. q. USD 45 to non-members; USD 55 foreign; free to members (effective 2007).
Published by: American Society of Appraisers, 555 Herndon Pkwy. Ste. 125, Herndon, VA 20170. TEL 703-478-2228, 800-272-8258, FAX 703-742-8471, asainfo@appraisers.org, http://www.appraisers.org. Ed. Laurie Saunders.

333.33 USA ISSN 1946-9195
A Z R E; commercial real estate magazine. (Arizona Real Estate) Variant title: Arizona Commercial Real Estate. Text in English. 2005. bi-m. USD 30 (effective 2009). adv. back issues avail. **Document type:** *Magazine, Trade.* **Description:** Covers commercial development, brokerage, finance, construction, architecture, real estate law and property management.
Published by: A Z Big Media, 3101 N Central Ave, Ste 1070, Phoenix, AZ 85012. TEL 602-277-6045, FAX 602-650-0827. Ed. Janet Perez. adv.: color page USD 3,990; trim 8 x 10.875. Circ: 25,000.

333.77 IND
ACCOMMODATION TIMES; total newspaper for real estate. Text in English. 1986. fortn. INR 240; INR 10 per issue (effective 2011). adv. back issues avail. **Document type:** *Newsletter, Trade.*
Related titles: Online - full text ed.: free (effective 2011).
Published by: Accommodation Times Pvt. Ltd., Anmol Bldg, Ground Fl, 1st Ln, 7th Rd, Santacruz, Mumbai, Maharashtra 400 055, India. TEL 91-22-26114221. Ed. Murari Chaturvedi.

333.3 USA
ACQUISITION COLUMBUS. Text in English. m. USD 24. **Document type:** *Newspaper.* **Description:** For professionals in commercial and industrial real estate.
Address: 2910 Brookdown Dr, Columbus, OH 43235-2704. TEL 614-841-0085. Ed., Pub. Rufus Jones. Circ: (controlled).

ACTIVE ADULT. *see* GERONTOLOGY AND GERIATRICS

333.33 FRA ISSN 0764-5066
ACTIVITE IMMOBILIERE. Text in French. 1944. m. looseleaf. EUR 57 domestic; EUR 69 DOM-TOM; EUR 70 elsewhere (effective 2009). adv.
Formerly: Activite Immobiliere Commerciale et Industrielle
Published by: Groupe SOCAF, 26 av. de Suffren, Paris, 75015, France. TEL 33-1-44491950. Circ: 5,000.

L'ACTUALITE JURIDIQUE. DROIT ADMINISTRATIF. *see* LAW

L'ACTUALITE JURIDIQUE. DROIT IMMOBILIER. *see* LAW

333.33 IRL
ADDRESS. Text in English. 8/yr. adv. **Document type:** *Magazine, Trade.*
Published by: Sherry FitzGerald Group, Ormonde House, 12-13 Lower Leeson St., Dublin, 2, Ireland. TEL 353-1-6399273, FAX 353-1-6399259, http://www.sherryfitz.ie. adv.: color page EUR 2,539. Circ: 35,000 (controlled).

333.33 FRA ISSN 0767-9939
ADMINISTRER; la revue professionnelle de l'administrateur de biens. Text in French. 1971. m. adv. **Document type:** *Journal, Trade.*
Indexed: FR.
Address: 53 rue du Rocher, Paris, 75008, France. TEL 33-1-42936080, FAX 33-1-43870795, administrer@wanadoo.fr. Eds. Georges Duthil, Jean Robert Bouyeure. Circ: 4,000.

333.33 USA
ADVISOR (TRENTON). Text in English. 1977 (vol.15). q. free. **Document type:** *Newsletter, Government.*
Formerly: New Jersey Advisor
Published by: Real Estate Commission, Dept of Insurance, 20 W State St, CN 328, Trenton, NJ 08625. TEL 609-292-7053.

332.63 USA ISSN 1080-2177
HD7288.78.U5
AFFORDABLE HOUSING FINANCE. Key Title: Affordable Housing Finance, with the Tax Credit User's Resource Guide. Abbreviated title: A H F. Text in English. 1992. 8/yr. USD 119 domestic; USD 149 in Canada; USD 179 elsewhere; free to qualified personnel (effective 2011). adv. 92 p./no.; back issues avail.; reprints avail. **Document type:** *Magazine, Trade.* **Description:** Provides news, information and resources for developers, financing sources, professionals and service providers in the field of multifamily affordable housing.
Formerly: Affordable Housing Industry Information Service
Published by: Hanley Wood, LLC (Subsidiary of: J.P. Morgan Chase & Co.), 1 Thomas Cir, NW, Ste 600, Washington, DC 20005. TEL 202-452-0800, FAX 202-785-1974, fanton@hanleywood.com, http://www.hanleywood.com. Ed. John McManus. Pub. Robert M Britt.

333.33 USA
AGENCY LAW QUARTERLY/REAL ESTATE INTELLIGENCE REPORT. Text in English. 1989. q. **Document type:** *Magazine, Trade.* **Description:** Covers the news, trends and politics of the real estate business.
Related titles: E-mail ed.
Published by: Common Communications, Inc., P O Box 5702, Portsmouth, NH 03802. TEL 800-299-9961, irexec@reintel.com, http://www.reintel.com.

343.73 347.3 USA ISSN 1042-5845
KF6535
AGGRESSIVE TAX AVOIDANCE FOR REAL ESTATE INVESTORS. Text in English. 1981. a. USD 23.95 (effective 2000). **Document type:** *Monographic series.*
Published by: John T. Reed, Ed. & Pub., 342 Bryan Dr, Alamo, CA 94507. TEL 925-820-6292, FAX 925-820-1259. R&P John T Reed. Circ: 4,000 (paid).

346.04 USA
ALABAMA PROPERTY RIGHTS AND REMEDIES. Text in English. 1994. irreg., latest 3rd ed. USD 157 3rd ed. (effective 2008). Supplement avail. **Document type:** *Guide, Trade.* **Description:** Contains a comprehensive review of the statutory rights and remedies affecting real property in Alabama and guides through the procedural mechanics of property issues and litigation.
Published by: Michie Company (Subsidiary of: LexisNexis North America), 701 E Water St, Charlottesville, VA 22902. TEL 434-972-7600, 800-446-3410, FAX 434-972-7677, customer.support@lexisnexis.com, http://www.michie.com.

ALBERTA LINEAR PROPERTY ASSESSMENT MINISTER'S GUIDELINES. *see* BUSINESS AND ECONOMICS—Public Finance, Taxation

333.5 338.4791 NLD
ALL INN HOME MAGAZINE. Text in Dutch. 4/yr. EUR 22 (effective 2008). adv. **Document type:** *Magazine, Consumer.*
Published by: Mercurius Media Group, Nieuwe Fellenoord 54, PO Box 433, Eindhoven, 5600 AK, Netherlands. TEL 31-40-2364626, FAX 31-40-2364628, http://www.mercuriusmedia.nl. Ed. Doris Arns. Pub. Fatih Akkus. adv.: page EUR 895; 230 x 298. Circ: 30,000.

333.33 USA
AMERICA WEST FARM & RANCH. Text in English. 2002. 4/yr. USD 23.50; USD 5.95 newsstand/cover (effective 2005). adv. **Document type:** *Magazine, Consumer.* **Description:** Lists ranch properties in Washington, Oregon, California, Idaho, and Nevada.
Published by: Farm & Ranch Publishing, LLC, 50 Briar Hollow Ln., Ste. 650 E, Houston, TX 77027. TEL 713-334-9222, 800-580-7330, FAX 713-334-9977, info@farmandranch.com, http://www.farmandranch.com. Ed. Thelma Chewning. Adv. contact Vicki Jacobson. color page USD 4,490; trim 8.5 x 10.875. Circ: 40,000 (paid).

333.332 USA
AMERICAN SOCIETY OF APPRAISERS. NEWSLINE. Text in English. 1984. m. USD 20 (effective 2001). adv. 20 p./no.; back issues avail.; reprints avail. **Document type:** *Newsletter, Consumer.* **Description:** Provides information on appraisal-related issues and society activities.
Related titles: Online - full content ed.
Published by: American Society of Appraisers, PO Box 17265, Washington, DC 20041-0265. TEL 703-478-2228, FAX 703-742-8471, http://www.appraisers.org. Ed. Rebecca Maxey TEL 703-733-2103. R&P, Adv. contact Betty Snyder TEL 703-733-2107. page USD 800; 8.5 x 11. Circ: 7,000.

333.33 NLD ISSN 1871-5583
AMSTERDAM REAL ESTATE CITY BOOK. Text in English. 2004. biennial. EUR 45 (effective 2009). adv. **Document type:** *Journal, Trade.* **Description:** Contains extensive information about major real estate projects, top market players, and industry trends in and around Amsterdam.
Published by: Europe Real Estate Publishers B.V., North Sea Bldg, Gevers Deynootweg 93R, The Hague, 2586 BK, Netherlands. TEL 31-70-3528600, FAX 31-70-3527660, publishers@europe-re.com, http://www.europe-re.com. Pub. Ronald Elward. Adv. contact Michiel Foekens.

333.33 332 NLD ISSN 1879-5978
AMSTERDAM SCHOOL OF REAL ESTATE. BOEKENREEKS. Text in Dutch. 1992. irreg., latest vol.21, 2009. **Document type:** *Monographic series, Academic/Scholarly.*
Published by: Amsterdam School of Real Estate, Postbus 140, Amsterdam, 1000 AC, Netherlands. TEL 31-20-6681129, FAX 31-20-6680361, info@asre.uva.nl, http://www.asre.nl.

333.33 CAN ISSN 1912-2233
ANALYSE DU MARCHE DE LA REVENTE DU MONTREAL METROPOLITAIN. Text in French. 200?. q. **Document type:** *Report, Trade.*
Media: Online - full text. **Related titles:** English ed.: Analysis of the Resale Market. Montreal Metropolitan Area. ISSN 1912-2225.
Published by: Canada Mortgage and Housing Corporation/Societe Canadienne d'Hypotheques et de Logement, 700 Montreal Rd, Ottawa, ON K1A 0P7, Canada. TEL 613-748-2000, FAX 613-748-2098, chic@cmhc-schl.gc.ca, http://www.cmhc.ca.

333.33 CAN ISSN 1912-2705
ANALYSE DU MARCHE DE LA REVENTE. REGION METROPOLITAINE DE GATINEAU. Text in French. 200?. q. free (effective 2007). **Document type:** *Report, Trade.*
Media: Online - full text. **Related titles:** English ed.: Analysis of the Resale Market. Gatineau Metropolitan Area. ISSN 1912-2691.
Published by: Canada Mortgage and Housing Corporation/Societe Canadienne d'Hypotheques et de Logement, 700 Montreal Rd, Ottawa, ON K1A 0P7, Canada. TEL 613-748-2000, FAX 613-748-2098, chic@cmhc-schl.gc.ca, http://www.cmhc.ca.

333.33 CAN ISSN 1912-2322
ANALYSE DU MARCHE DE LA REVENTE. REGION METROPOLITAINE DE QUEBEC. Text in French. 199?. q. **Document type:** *Report, Trade.*
Formerly (until 2002): Analyse du Marche de la Revente du Quebec Metropolitain (Print Edition) (1700-2796)
Media: Online - full text. **Related titles:** English ed.: Analysis of the Resale Market. Quebec Metropolitan Area. ISSN 1912-2314.
Published by: Canada Mortgage and Housing Corporation/Societe Canadienne d'Hypotheques et de Logement, 700 Montreal Rd, Ottawa, ON K1A 0P7, Canada. TEL 613-748-2000, FAX 613-748-2098, chic@cmhc-schl.gc.ca, http://www.cmhc.ca.

333.33 340 USA ISSN 1554-7876
KFO112.A29
ANDERSON'S OHIO REAL ESTATE LAW HANDBOOK. Text in English. 1997. a., latest 2007. USD 75 per issue (effective 2008). **Document type:** *Handbook/Manual/Guide, Trade.*
Published by: LexisNexis (Subsidiary of: LexisNexis North America), 701 E Water St, PO Box 7587, Charlottesville, VA 22906. TEL 434-972-7600, 800-446-3410, FAX 800-643-1280, customer.support@lexisnexis.com, http://www.lexisnexis.com.

333.5 GBR ISSN 1473-3986
ANGLIA PROPERTY GUIDE. Text in English. 2001. m. GBP 30 (effective 2010). adv. back issues avail. **Document type:** *Magazine, Consumer.* **Description:** Contains properties for sale or rent via agents throughout East Anglia, England.
Published by: Fisher Marketing, Ventureforth House, South Denes Rd, Gt. Yarmouth, Norfolk, NR30 3PT, United Kingdom. TEL 44-1493-857002, FAX 44-1493-857003, enquiries@fisher-marketing.co.uk. Circ: 3,000 (paid); 3,000 (free).

346.04 CAN ISSN 1206-4831
ANNOTATED BRITISH COLUMBIA ASSESSMENT ACT. Text in English. base vol. plus s-a. updates. looseleaf. CAD 115 per vol. (effective 2005). charts. **Document type:** *Handbook/Manual/Guide, Trade.* **Description:** Provides the full text of the legislation and most relevant regulations, accompanied by section-by-section summaries and expert commentary.
Published by: Canada Law Book Inc., 240 Edward St, Aurora, ON L4G 3S9, Canada. TEL 905-841-6472, 800-263-3269, FAX 905-841-5085, b.loney@canadalawbook.ca, http://www.canadalawbook.ca. Ed. David Gill. R&P Nancy Nesbitt.

346.04 CAN
ANNOTATED BRITISH COLUMBIA OCCUPIERS LIABILITY ACT. Text in English. 1999. base vol. plus a. updates. looseleaf. CAD 95 per vol. (effective 2005). charts. **Document type:** *Handbook/Manual/Guide, Trade.* **Description:** Provides case-by-case annotations of cases relevant to the British Columbia Occupiers Liability Act, along with in-depth commentary.
Published by: Canada Law Book Inc., 240 Edward St, Aurora, ON L4G 3S9, Canada. TEL 905-841-6472, 800-263-3269, FAX 905-841-5085, b.loney@canadalawbook.ca, http://www.canadalawbook.ca. Ed. Eric Wagner. R&P Nancy Nesbitt.

333.33 340 CAN ISSN 1912-2519
ANNUAL REAL ESTATE FOR LAW CLERKS. Text in English, French. 2002. a. (5th ed.), latest 2006. CAD 70 per issue (effective 2007). **Document type:** *Journal, Trade.*

R

Published by: Law Society of Upper Canada/Barreau de Haut Canada, Osgoode Hall, 130 Queen St West, Toronto, ON M5H 2N6, Canada. TEL 416-947-3300, 800-668-7380, FAX 416-947-5263, lawsociety@lsuc.on.ca, http://www.lsuc.on.ca. Ed. Sylvana M D'Alimonte.

346.04 CAN ISSN 1719-8755
THE ANNUAL REAL ESTATE LAW SUMMIT. Text in English. 2004. a., latest 2006, 3rd. USD 100 per issue (effective 2006). **Document type:** *Proceedings, Trade.*
Published by: Law Society of Upper Canada/Barreau de Haut Canada, Osgoode Hall, 130 Queen St West, Toronto, ON M5H 2N6, Canada. TEL 416-947-3300, 800-668-7380, FAX 416-947-5263, lawsociety@lsuc.on.ca, http://www.lsuc.on.ca.

ANNUARIO DEGLI INTERMEDIARI IMMOBILIARI. *see* BUSINESS AND ECONOMICS—Banking And Finance

APARTMENT AGE; the voice of the industry. *see* HOUSING AND URBAN PLANNING

333.33 340 USA ISSN 1935-6137
APARTMENT BUILDING MANAGEMENT INSIDER. Text in English. 1986. m. looseleaf. USD 227 combined subscription (print & online eds.) (effective 2008). adv. Index. back issues avail.; reprints avail. **Document type:** *Newsletter, Trade.* **Description:** Provides how-to information on cutting operating costs; speeding rent collection from slow-pays; avoiding IAQ damages; winning disputes over operating expenses; attracting new tenants and retaining old ones; and making contractors perform at the right price.
Formerly (until 2007): Professional Apartment Management (0891-2599)
Related titles: Online - full text ed.: ISSN 1938-3061.
Indexed: A10, V03.
—CCC.
Published by: Vendome Group, LLC, 149 5th Ave, New York, NY 10010. TEL 212-812-8420, FAX 212-228-1308, customerservice@Vendomegrpsubs.com. Ed. Eric Yoo TEL 212-812-8435. Pub. Julie DiMauro. Circ: 6,000 (paid).

332.63 USA ISSN 1097-4059
APARTMENT FINANCE TODAY. Text in English. 1997. 9/yr. USD 39 domestic; USD 59 in Canada; USD 79 elsewhere; free to qualified personnel (effective 2011). adv. stat.; tr.lit. back issues avail. **Document type:** *Magazine, Trade.* **Description:** Covers financing and refinancing options for market-rate and affordable properties, including conventional lending sources, loan underwriting pricing trends, capital markets and rents, sales and acquisitions. For developers, owners, and asset managers of apartments.
Formerly (until 1998): Affordable Housing Today (1093-0795)
Related titles: Online - full text ed.
Published by: Hanley Wood, LLC (Subsidiary of: J.P. Morgan Chase & Co.), 1 Thomas Cir, NW, Ste 600, Washington, DC 20005. TEL 202-452-0800, FAX 202-785-1974, fanton@hanleywood.com, http://www.hanleywood.com. Ed. John McManus. Pub. Robert M Britt.

333.33 USA ISSN 0744-9143
APARTMENT MANAGEMENT NEWSLETTER; wealth building techniques for apartment owners & their managers. Text in English. 1975. m. USD 95 (effective 1999). bk.rev. charts; tr.lit. index. back issues avail. **Document type:** *Newsletter.*
Published by: Apartment Management Publishing Co., Inc., 16 West 32nd St, New York, NY 10001. TEL 212-273-0848. Ed. Helene Mandelbaum.

643.27 USA
APARTMENT MOVES; the moving planner. Text in English. 1996. bi-m. adv. **Document type:** *Magazine, Consumer.*
Published by: Conclave Group, LLC, 1748 Pierce St, Ste 2, Birmingham, MI 48009. TEL 800-765-4233, FAX 866-332-3430. adv.: color page USD 29,000; trim 8.375 x 10.875. Circ: 900,000.

333.33 USA
APARTMENT NEWS. Text in English. 1960. m. USD 50 (effective 2004). adv. bk.rev. charts; stat.; tr.lit. **Document type:** *Magazine, Trade.* **Description:** Covers rental, maintenance, marketing and legal issues affecting apartment building owners and managers.
Former titles: Orange County Apartment News (0747-3435); Orange County Apartment House News (0030-4247)
Published by: (Apartment Association of Orange County), Orange County Multi-Housing Service Corporation, 12822 Garden Grove Blvd, Ste D, Garden Grove, CA 92843. TEL 714-638-5550, FAX 714-638-6042. Ed. Romesh Joseph. Adv. contact Jeannie Aliss. Circ: 4,000.

333.33 USA ISSN 0191-8826
APARTMENT OWNER; San Fernando Valley - Ventura County - Santa Clarita - Antelope Valley. Text in English. 196?. m. USD 50 (effective 2000). adv. **Document type:** *Magazine, Trade.*
Published by: Apartment Association, 14550 Archwood St, Van Nuys, CA 91405. TEL 818-374-3240, FAX 818-787-6018. Ed. Shari Rosen. R&P, Adv. contact Arthur Aston Jr. B&W page USD 588. Circ: 3,000 (controlled).

APPARTEMENT EN EIGENAAR. *see* HOUSING AND URBAN PLANNING

333.332 CAN ISSN 0003-7079
APPRAISAL INSTITUTE DIGEST. Text in English. 1970 (vol.4). 4/yr. included in Canadian Appraiser. charts; illus.
Related titles: Microfilm ed.: (from MML).
Published by: Appraisal Institute of Canada, 403-200 Catherine St, Ottawa, ON K2P 2K9, Canada. TEL 204-783-2224, FAX 204-783-5575, info@aicanada.org, http://www.aicanada.org. Circ: 8,200.

017.8 USA
APPRAISAL INSTITUTE RESOURCES CATALOG. Text in English. 1950. a. free (effective 2003). adv. **Document type:** *Catalog.* **Description:** Lists education programs, books, periodicals, products and other services provided by the Appraisal Institute to its members as well as non-members.
Former titles (until 2001): Appraisal Institute Products and Services Catalogue; Appraisal Institute Publications Catalogue
Published by: Appraisal Institute, 550 W Van Buren St, Ste 1000, Chicago, IL 60607. info@appraisalinstitute.org, http://www.appraisalinstitute.org. Adv. contact Jennifer Pasiuk TEL 312-335-4478. page USD 1,500; 7.25 x 9.75.

333.332 USA ISSN 0003-7087
CODEN: APPJA5
➤ **THE APPRAISAL JOURNAL.** Text in English. 1932. q. USD 48 domestic to non-members; USD 90 foreign to non-members; USD 100 domestic to libraries; USD 140 foreign to libraries; USD 20 domestic to students; USD 60 foreign to students; free to members (effective 2010). adv. bk.rev. abstr.; charts; illus.; stat. index. 112 p./no. 2 cols./p.; back issues avail.; reprints avail. **Document type:** *Journal, Trade.* **Description:** Provides perspectives of professors, practitioners, and acknowledged authorities on all areas of real estate appraisal: residential, commercial, industrial, and rural.
Incorporates (in 1992): The Real Estate Appraiser (1061-8511); Which was formerly (until 1991): The Real Estate Appraiser and Analyst (0271-258X); (until 1978): The Real Estate Appraiser (0034-0677); (until 1963): The Residential Appraiser; (until 1956): Society of Real Estate Appraisers. Review; (until 1936): Residential Appraisers' Review; Formerly (until 1939): American Institute of Real Estate Appraisers of the National Association of Real Estate Boards. Journal
Related titles: Online - full text ed.
Indexed: A09, A10, A12, A13, A14, A17, A22, A23, A26, AAR, ABIn, ATI, B01, B02, B04, B06, B07, B08, B09, B11, B13, B15, B17, B18, BLI, BPI, BPIA, BRD, BusI, C12, CA, E08, G04, G06, G07, G08, H&TI, H06, I05, M01, M02, ManagCont, NPPA, P06, P30, P34, P48, P51, P53, P54, PAIS, PQC, RICS, S09, T&II, T02, V02, V03, V04, W01, W02, W03, W05.
—BLDSC (1580.130000), IE, Infotrieve, Ingenta.
Published by: Appraisal Institute, 550 W Van Buren St, Ste 1000, Chicago, IL 60607. TEL 312-335-4100, 888-756-4624, FAX 312-335-4400, info@appraisalinstitute.org. Ed. Nancy Bannon TEL 312-335-4445. Circ: 21,000.

333.33 USA ISSN 1942-8820
APPRAISAL PRESS. Text in English. 2008. m. free (effective 2008). **Document type:** *Magazine, Trade.*
Related titles: Online - full text ed.: ISSN 1942-8839.
Published by: A La Mode Inc., 3705 W Memorial Rd, Bldg 402, Oklahoma City, OK 73134. TEL 800-252-6633, info@alamode.com, http://www.alamode.com.

333.332 USA
APPRAISAL REVIEW. Text in English. q. membership. **Document type:** *Magazine, Trade.* **Description:** Subjects of interest to members of appraisal organizations.
Published by: National Association of Independent Fee Appraisers, 401 N. Michigan Ave., Ste. 2200, Chicago, IL 60611-4245. TEL 314-781-6688. Ed. Pierce Hollingsworth. Circ: 80,000.

333.33 USA
THE APPRAISAL TIMES. Text in English. m. USD 65 to non-members (effective 2001). adv. **Document type:** *Magazine, Trade.*
Former titles: National Association of Real Estate Appraisers Newsletter; N A R E A Real Estate Appraisal Newsletter
Published by: National Association of Real Estate Appraisers, 1224 N Nokomis N E, Alexandria, MN 56308-5072. TEL 320-763-7626, FAX 320-763-9290. Ed., Pub., Adv. contact Robert Johnson.

333.332 USA
APPRAISER GRAM. Text in English. 1966. m. looseleaf. **Document type:** *Newsletter.* **Description:** Information for members of the organization.
Published by: National Association of Independent Fee Appraisers, 401 N. Michigan Ave., Ste. 2200, Chicago, IL 60611-4245. TEL 314-781-6688. Ed. Donna Walter. Circ: 5,800.

333.332 USA
APPRAISER NEWS ONLINE. Text in English. irreg. **Document type:** *Magazine, Trade.* **Description:** Provides coverage of industry trends, legislative issues and regulatory developments affecting appraisers, as well as Appraisal Institute education, publication and membership offerings.
Media: Online - full content. **Related titles:** Fax ed.
Published by: Appraisal Institute, 550 W Van Buren St, Ste 1000, Chicago, IL 60607. TEL 312-335-4100, FAX 312-335-4400, info@appraisalinstitute.org.

333.332 USA
APPRAISER'S INFORMATION EXCHANGE (ONLINE EDITION). Text in English. q. **Document type:** *Journal, Trade.*
Media: Online - full text.
Published by: International Society of Appraisers, 1131 SW 7th St., Ste. 105, Renton, WA 98055-1229. TEL 206-241-0359, FAX 206-241-0436, isahq@isa-appraisers.org.

ARCHIVIO DELLE LOCAZIONI E DEL CONDOMINIO. *see* LAW

346.04 TZA ISSN 0856-9495
ARDHI NI UHAI. Text in Swahili. 2004. q.
Published by: Land Rights Research and Resources Institute, PO Box 75885, Dar Es Salaam, Tanzania. TEL 255-22-771360, FAX 255-22-771362, info@hakiardhi.org, http://hakiardhi.org.

ARIZONA BUSINESS MAGAZINE. *see* BUSINESS AND ECONOMICS—Office Equipment And Services

346.04 USA ISSN 1944-8546
KFA2480
ARIZONA REAL ESTATE LAW; Arizona constitution, statutes, and regulations with annotations and commentary. Text in English. 2007. a. USD 90 per issue (effective 2008). **Document type:** *Journal, Trade.* **Description:** Provides a comprehensive collection of laws and regulations governing real estate law in Arizona.
Published by: Thomson West (Subsidiary of: Thomson Reuters Corp.), 610 Opperman Dr, Eagan, MN 55123. TEL 651-687-7000, 800-344-5008, west.customer.service@thomson.com.

333.33 USA ISSN 0199-9206
HD266.A7
ARIZONA REALTOR DIGEST. Text in English. 1979. m. USD 6 (effective 2000). adv. **Document type:** *Magazine, Trade.*
Published by: Arizona Association of Realtors, 255 E Osborn Rd, 200, Phoenix, AZ 85012-2349. TEL 602-248-7787, FAX 602-351-2474. Ed., R&P, Adv. contact Diane Cole. Circ: 24,000.

333.33 USA
ASHLAND COUNTY PROPERTY MAGAZINE. Text in English. bi-m. free. **Document type:** *Magazine, Consumer.*
Published by: Ashland Publishing Co. LLC, 40 E. Second St., Ashland, OH 44805. TEL 419-281-0581, FAX 419-281-5591. Pub. Troy Dix. Adv. contact Jason Gwinnup. Circ: 9,000.

ASOCIACION NACIONAL DE PROMOTORES CONSTRUCTORES DE EDIFICIOS URBANOS. ANNUAL REPORT. *see* HOUSING AND URBAN PLANNING

ASOCIACION NACIONAL DE PROMOTORES CONSTRUCTORES DE EDIFICIOS URBANOS. PROMOCION. *see* HOUSING AND URBAN PLANNING

ASSET-BACKED ALERT. *see* BUSINESS AND ECONOMICS—Investments

346.04 USA ISSN 1947-2048
ASSISTED HOUSING ALERT. Text in English. 200?. m. USD 277 (effective 2009). back issues avail. **Document type:** *Guide, Trade.* **Description:** Provides essential information, how-to tips and business strategies for HUD, fair housing and ADA compliance.
Related titles: Online - full text ed.: ISSN 1947-2056.
Indexed: A10, V03.
Published by: Eli Research, Inc., PO Box 90324, Washington, DC 20090. TEL 800-874-9180, FAX 800-789-3560, help@eliresearch.com, http://www.eliresearch.com. **Subscr. to:** National Subscription Bureau, Inc., Dept 1380, Denver, CO 80291. TEL 800-472-0148, FAX 800-508-2592, subscribe@eliresearch.com.

ASSISTED HOUSING FINANCIAL MANAGEMENT INSIDER. *see* BUSINESS AND ECONOMICS—Accounting

333.33 340 USA ISSN 1072-009X
ASSISTED HOUSING MANAGEMENT INSIDER; the practical, plain-english newsletter for owners, managers, attorneys, and other real estate professionals. Text in English. 1993. m. USD 347 (print or online ed.); USD 520 combined subscription (print & online eds.) (effective 2008). adv. back issues avail.; reprints avail. **Document type:** *Newsletter, Trade.* **Description:** Provides advice and tips on how quickly and easily comply with even complex HUD rules and requirements.
Related titles: CD-ROM ed.: USD 297 (effective 2008); Online - full text ed.: ISSN 1938-310X. USD 357 (effective 2004).
Indexed: A10, V03.
—CCC.
Published by: Vendome Group, LLC, 149 5th Ave, New York, NY 10010. TEL 212-812-8420, FAX 212-228-1308, customerservice@Vendomegrpsubs.com, http://www.vendomegrp.com/. Ed. Janine Sagar. Pub. Julie DiMauro. Circ: 4,300 (paid).

333.33 ITA ISSN 1722-0637
ASTECASA. Text in Italian. 2001. m. **Document type:** *Magazine, Consumer.*
Published by: Terra Nova Editore, Viale Regina Margherita 269, Rome, 00198, Italy. TEL 39-0644080301, FAX 39-06-44080666, direzione@terranovaeditore.it, http://webtest.terranovaeditore.net.

333.33 BEL ISSN 1372-6420
ASTUCES & CONSEILS IMMOBILIER; lettre de conseils creatifs en matiere immobiliere. Text in French. 1997. bi-w. EUR 157 (effective 2007). **Document type:** *Newsletter, Trade.*
Published by: Indicator, Tiensesteenweg 306, Louvain, 3000, Belgium. TEL 32-16-359910, FAX 32-16-359935, service.clients@indicator.be.

333.33 USA ISSN 2154-2724
▼ **ATLANTA COMMERCIAL PROPERTIES E-NEWSLETTER.** Abbreviated title: A C P. Text in English. 2010. s-w. free (effective 2010). adv. **Document type:** *Newsletter, Trade.* **Description:** Covers the commercial real estate news in Atlanta.
Media: Online - full text.
Published by: France Publications, Inc., 3500 Piedmont Rd, Ste 415, Atlanta, GA 30305. TEL 404-832-8262, FAX 404-832-8260, scott@francepublications.com, http://www.francepublications.com. Pub., Adv. contact Scott France.

AUDIO ESTATE PLANNER. *see* LAW—Estate Planning

333.33 GBR ISSN 2040-7580
▼ **AUSTRALIA REAL ESTATE REPORT.** Text in English. 2009. q. EUR 850, USD 1,150 combined subscription (print & email eds.) (effective 2011). **Document type:** *Report, Trade.* **Description:** Provides industry professionals and strategists, sector analysts, business investors, trade associations and regulatory bodies with independent forecasts and competitive intelligence on the real estate and construction industry in Australia.
Related titles: E-mail ed.
Published by: Business Monitor International Ltd., Senator House, 85 Queen Victoria St, London, EC4V 4AB, United Kingdom. TEL 44-20-72480468, FAX 44-20-72480467, enquiry@businessmonitor.com.

333.33 AUS ISSN 1833-606X
THE AUSTRALIAN ACREAGE & PROPERTY REVIEW. Text in English. 1996. 11/yr. **Document type:** *Magazine, Trade.* **Description:** A property buyer's magazine.
Formerly (until 2006): The Australian Acreage Review (1442-097X)
Published by: The Western Weekender, PO Box 1900, Penrith, NSW 2751, Australia. TEL 61-2-47311310, FAX 61-2-47311267, info@westernweekender.com.au, http://weekender.trimedia.com.au.

333.33 AUS ISSN 1834-5662
AUSTRALIAN AND NEW ZEALAND PROPERTY JOURNAL. Text in English. 2007. q. AUD 88 domestic; AUD 120 foreign (effective 2007). **Document type:** *Journal, Academic/Scholarly.*
Formed by the merger of (1999-2007): Australian Property Journal (1441-4929); Which was formerly (until 1998): Valuer and Land Economist (1325-8672); (until 1991): Valuer (0042-241X); (until 1932): The New South Wales Valuer (0314-6170); (2001-2007): New Zealand Property Journal (1175-8171); Which was formerly (until 2000): New Zealand Valuers' Journal (0113-0315); (until 1986): New Zealand Valuer (0027-7282); (until 1946): New Zealand Valuers' Journal (0113-0366); (1941-1945): New Zealand Valuers' Bulletin (0113-0358)
Indexed: A26, G08, I05.
—BLDSC (1796.995000), IE.
Published by: Australian Property Institute, 6 Campion St, Deakin, ACT 2600, Australia. TEL 61-2-6282-2411, FAX 61-2-6285-2194, national@propertyinstitute.com.au, http://www.propertyinstitute.com.au. **Co-publisher:** Property Institute of New Zealand.

332.63 AUS ISSN 1449-7743
AUSTRALIAN BROKER. Text in English. 2004. m. AUD 120 domestic; AUD 156 foreign (effective 2009). adv. **Document type:** *Magazine, Consumer.* **Description:** A news magazine written for the Australian mortgage and finance broking industry.
Published by: Key Media Pty Ltd, Level 10, 1 Chandos St, St Leonards, NSW 2065, Australia. TEL 61-2-84374700, FAX 61-2-94394599, australia@keymedia.com.au, http://www.keymedia.com.au. Ed. Larry Schlesinger TEL 61-2-84374790. Adv. contact Simon Kerslake TEL 61-2-84374786.

332.63 AUS ISSN 1329-2447
AUSTRALIAN PROPERTY INVESTOR; for home buyers, investors, property professionals. Abbreviated title: A P I. Text in English. 1997. m. AUD 85 domestic; AUD 149 in Asia & the Pacific; AUD 189 elsewhere (effective 2008). back issues avail. **Document type:** *Magazine, Consumer.* **Description:** Covers news and interest trends to prospective buyers of both homes and investment properties in Australia.
Related titles: Online - full text ed.
Indexed: I05.
Published by: Australian Commercial Publishing Pty Ltd., Ste 902, Level 9, 9 Sherwood Rd, PO Box 1434, Toowong, QLD 4066, Australia. TEL 61-7-37209422, FAX 61-7-37209322. Eds. Eynas Brodie, Lane Boy. Adv. contacts Sandi Smith, Laurie O'Brien. Circ: 55,000.

333.33 AUS ISSN 1833-6299
AUSTRALIA'S UNIQUE HOMES MAGAZINE. Text in English. 2006. m. (11/yr.). adv. **Document type:** *Magazine, Trade.*
Formerly (until 2006): Victoria's Unique Homes Magazine (1833-0304)
Published by: Real Estate Media Pty Ltd, 117 Croydon Rd, Surrey Hills, VIC 3127, Australia. TEL 61-3-88092400, FAX 61-3-88092411, info@remg.com.au, http://www.remg.com.au/.

333.33 CAN
B C REAL ESTATE ASSOCIATION. BULLETIN (ONLINE EDITION). (British Columbia) Text in English. bi-m. **Document type:** *Newsletter.* **Description:** Features real estate news from a provincial perspective.
Media: Online - full text.
Published by: British Columbia Real Estate Association, 600-2695 Granville St, Vancouver, BC V6H 3H4, Canada. TEL 604-683-7702, FAX 604-683-8601, bcrea@bcrea.bc.ca.

B N A'S ENVIRONMENTAL DUE DILIGENCE GUIDE. (Bureau of National Affairs) *see* LAW

333.33 658 USA ISSN 0738-2170
TX980
B O M A EXPERIENCE EXCHANGE REPORT; income - expense analysis for office buildings. Text in English. 1920. a. USD 275 (effective 1998). back issues avail. **Document type:** *Report, Trade.* **Description:** Operating income and expense data for commercial real estate in North America.
Formerly (until vol.2, 1988): Trends (Washington, 1987)
Indexed: SRI.
Published by: Building Owners and Managers Association International, 1201 New York Ave, N W, Ste 300, Washington, DC 20005. TEL 202-408-2662, FAX 202-371-0181, info@boma.org, http://www.boma.org/. Eds. Ellen Ku, Matthew Bond. Circ: 3,500.

333.3 GBR ISSN 0265-0479
B S A DIRECTORY OF MEMBERS. Text in English. 19??. a. free (effective 2010). **Document type:** *Directory, Trade.* **Description:** Describes the association and its activities; lists member societies and their senior executives.
Formerly (until 1978): Building Societies Association. List of Members
—CCC.
Published by: Building Societies Association, 6th Fl, York House, 23 Kingsway, London, WC2B 6UJ, United Kingdom. TEL 44-20-75205900, FAX 44-20-72405290, information@bsa.org.uk, http://www.bsa.org.uk/.

BAALMAN & WELLS LAND TITLES OFFICE PRACTICE N S W. *see* LAW

333.33 GBR ISSN 2040-7831
▼ **BAHRAIN REAL ESTATE REPORT.** Text in English. 2009. q. EUR 850, USD 1,150 combined subscription (print & email eds.) (effective 2011). **Document type:** *Report, Trade.* **Description:** Provides industry professionals and strategists, sector analysts, business investors, trade associations and regulatory bodies with independent forecasts and competitive intelligence on the real estate and construction industry in Bahrain.
Related titles: E-mail ed.
Published by: Business Monitor International Ltd., Senator House, 85 Queen Victoria St, London, EC4V 4AB, United Kingdom. TEL 44-20-72480468, FAX 44-20-72480467, enquiry@businessmonitor.com.

333.33 332.1 USA ISSN 0005-5409
BANKER & TRADESMAN; the real estate, banking and commercial weekly for Massachusetts. Text in English. 1872. w. (Mon.). USD 278 (effective 2008). adv. bk.rev. back issues avail.; reprints avail. **Document type:** *Newspaper, Trade.*
Former titles (until 1896): Banker and Tradesman and Massachusetts Law Reporter; (until 1884): The Massachusetts Law Reporter
Related titles: Microform ed.: 1872 (from PQC); Online - full text ed.: USD 119 (effective 2008).
Indexed: A22.
Published by: The Warren Group, 280 Summer St, 8th Fl, Boston, MA 02210. TEL 617-428-5100, 800-356-8805, FAX 617-428-5119, publications@thewarrengroup.com, http://www.thewarrengroup.com/. Pub. Timothy M Warren Jr. Adv. contact Emily Torres. Circ: 8,006.

333.33 GBR ISSN 1754-713X
THE BARNSLEY PROPERTY AND LIVING GUIDE. Text in English. 2007. m. **Document type:** *Magazine, Consumer.* **Description:** Showcases and displays homes for sale and rent.
Published by: White Rabbit Publishing Ltd., 35 Croft Dr, Mapplewell, S Yorks S75 6AN, United Kingdom. TEL 44-870-6092651, FAX 44-1226-390243. Ed. Mark Stokes. Adv. contact Fraser Moody.

354.35 FRA ISSN 1959-920X
LES BAUX COMMERCIAUX. Text in French. 2000. base vol. plus s-a. updates. looseleaf. EUR 486 base vol(s). print & CD-ROM eds. (effective 2010). **Document type:** *Trade.*
Related titles: CD-ROM ed.: ISSN 1151-0080.
Published by: Lamy S.A. (Subsidiary of: Wolters Kluwer France), 1 Rue Eugene et Armand Peugeot, Rueil-Malmaison, 92856 Cedex, France. TEL 33-1-76733000, FAX 33-1-76734809, lamy@lamy.fr.

333.33 USA
BAY STATE APARTMENT OWNER. Text in English. 19??. q. free to members (effective 2009). adv. back issues avail.; reprints avail. **Document type:** *Magazine, Trade.* **Description:** Targets owners, property managers and vendors in the rental profession.
Published by: (Rental Housing Association), The Warren Group, 280 Summer St, 8th Fl, Boston, MA 02210. TEL 617-428-5100, 800-356-8805, FAX 617-428-5119, publications@thewarrengroup.com. Ed. Christina P O'Neill. Pub. Timothy M Warren Jr. Adv. contact Emily Torres. color page USD 2,395; trim 8.125 x 10.625.

333.33 DEU ISSN 1618-2405
BAYERISCHE HAUSBESITZER-ZEITUNG. Text in German. 1949. m. EUR 16.60; EUR 1.55 newsstand/cover (effective 2010). adv. **Document type:** *Newspaper, Trade.*
Published by: Haus- und Grundbesitzervereins Muenchen, Sonnenstr 13 III, Munich, 80331, Germany. TEL 49-89-551410, FAX 49-89-55141366, info@haus-und-grund-muenchen.de. adv.: B&W page EUR 1,386, color page EUR 1,766. Circ: 29,793 (paid and controlled).

BEACH HOUSES; for beach lovers everywhere!. *see* TRAVEL AND TOURISM

344.106434 GBR ISSN 0952-6064
BEDSIT BRIEFING. Text in English. 1987. bi-m. **Document type:** *Bulletin, Trade.*
—CCC.
Published by: Campaign for Bedsit Rights, 88 Old St, London, EC1V 9HU, United Kingdom. TEL 44-20-75051184, FAX 44-20-75052168, http://www.shelter.org.uk.

333.33 NLD ISSN 0165-2540
BEHEER EN ONDERHOUD. Text in Dutch. 1975. m. looseleaf. **Document type:** *Monographic series.* **Description:** Cost and management information for the management of real estate.
Published by: Reed Business bv (Subsidiary of: Reed Business), Hanzestraat 1, Doetinchem, 7006 RH, Netherlands. TEL 31-314-349911, FAX 31-314-343839, info@reedbusiness.nl, http://www.reedbusiness.nl.

333.33 NLD ISSN 1871-5591
BELGIUM REAL ESTATE YEARBOOK. Text in English. 2006. a. EUR 45 (effective 2009). adv. **Document type:** *Journal, Trade.* **Description:** Contains extensive information about major real estate projects, top market players, and industry trends in Belgium.
Published by: Europe Real Estate Publishers B.V., North Sea Bldg, Gevers Deynootweg 93R, The Hague, 2586 BK, Netherlands. TEL 31-70-3528600, FAX 31-70-3527660, publishers@europe-re.com, http://www.europe-re.com. Pub. Ronald Elward. Adv. contact Michiel Foekens. color page EUR 2,775; trim 175 x 255. Circ: 10,000 (paid and controlled).

333.33 DEU ISSN 0938-8893
BELLEVUE; Europas groesstes Immobilien-Magazin. Text in German. 1990. m. EUR 66.60; EUR 6.50 newsstand/cover (effective 2009). adv. **Document type:** *Magazine, Consumer.*
Related titles: Online - full text ed.
Published by: Bellevue and More AG, Dorotheenstr 64, Hamburg, 22301, Germany. TEL 49-40-6965950, FAX 49-40-696595199, impressum@bam-ag.de. Ed. Claus-Peter Haller. Adv. contact Jutta Meyer. page EUR 3,710; trim 210 x 280. Circ: 46,673 (paid and controlled). **Subscr. to:** Postfach 300, Offenburg 77649, Germany. TEL 49-1805-913170, abo@bellevue.de.

346.04 USA
BERGMAN ON NEW YORK MORTGAGE FORECLOSURES. Text in English. 1990. 3 base vols. plus s-a. updates. looseleaf. USD 592 base vol(s). (effective 2008). **Document type:** *Guide, Trade.* **Description:** Contains analysis of the law and provides guidance relating to residential and commercial property foreclosures in New York.
Related titles: CD-ROM ed.: USD 403 (effective 2002).
Published by: Matthew Bender & Co., Inc. (Subsidiary of: LexisNexis North America), 1275 Broadway, Albany, NY 12204. TEL 518-487-3000, 800-424-4200, FAX 518-487-3083, international@bender.com, http://bender.lexisnexis.com. Ed. Bruce J Bergman.

333.33 CHE
BERNER HAUSEIGENTUEMER. Text in German. 8/yr.
Address: Schwarzhallstr 31, Bern 14, 3000, Switzerland. TEL 031-256008. Ed. Daniel Rutsch. Circ: 8,000.

333.33 FRA ISSN 1246-225X
BERTRAND VACANCES. Variant title: Locations Vacances. Text in French. 198?. a. adv. bk.rev. **Document type:** *Consumer.* **Description:** Contains advertisements for the renting of vacation homes from private owners in France and elsewhere.
Formerly (until 1987): Bertrand Locations Vacances (0990-5944)
Published by: Editions Indicateur Bertrand, 43 bd. Barbes, Paris, 75018, France. TEL 33-1-49252627, FAX 33-1-49252600.

333.33 AUT ISSN 1605-5284
BESSER WOHNEN; die oesterreichische Wohnzeitschrift. Text in German. 1966. 12/yr. EUR 26 domestic; EUR 40 foreign (effective 2005). adv. **Document type:** *Magazine, Consumer.*
Published by: Verein Besser Wohnen, Stelzhamergasse 4/9, Vienna, W 1030, Austria. TEL 43-1-5350300, FAX 43-1-53503009. Ed., Pub., R&P Franz Klar. Adv. contact Claudia Fuchs. color page EUR 7,400; trim 185 x 265. Circ: 101,666.

332 CHE ISSN 1662-1565
BILANZ HOMES; Das Schweizer Immobilienmagazin. Text in German. 2007. 4/yr. CHF 30; CHF 12 newsstand/cover (effective 2011). adv. **Document type:** *Magazine, Consumer.*
Published by: Axel Springer Schweiz AG (Subsidiary of: Axel Springer Verlag AG), Foerrlibuckstr 70, Zuerich, 8005, Switzerland. TEL 41-43-4445111, FAX 41-43-4445091, info@axelspringer.ch, http://www.axelspringer.ch. Ed. Dirk Schuetz. Adv. contact Christine Lesnik. Circ: 60,000 (paid and controlled).

670.29 USA
BLACK'S GUIDE: ATLANTA INDUSTRIAL. Text in English. 1993. q. USD 1,185; USD 395 per issue (effective 2008). adv. charts; maps; mkt.; stat. back issues avail.; reprints avail. **Document type:** *Directory, Trade.*
Related titles: Online - full text ed.
Published by: Black's Guide, Inc, 5210 Chairman's Ct, Ste 2B, Frederick, MD 21703. TEL 800-385-9266, rbiese@blacksguide.com, http://www.blacksguide.com. Pub. Fran Piegari TEL 972-931-1299. Adv. contact John McCann TEL 800-500-2450 ext 35. color page USD 3,500, B&W page USD 2,225; trim 8.25 x 10.875.

333.33 USA
BLACK'S GUIDE: ATLANTA OFFICE. Text in English. 1993. q. USD 1,185; USD 395 per issue (effective 2008). adv. charts; maps; mkt.; stat. back issues avail.; reprints avail. **Document type:** *Directory, Trade.*
Formerly: Black's Office Leasing Guide: Atlanta
Related titles: Online - full text ed.
Published by: Black's Guide, Inc, 5210 Chairman's Ct, Ste 2B, Frederick, MD 21703. TEL 800-385-9266, rbiese@blacksguide.com, http://www.blacksguide.com. adv.: color page USD 4,615, B&W page USD 3,390; trim 8.25 x 10.875.

333.33 USA
BLACK'S GUIDE: BOSTON. Text in English. 1998. s-a. USD 359.95 domestic; USD 194.95 newsstand/cover (effective 2001). charts; maps; mkt.; stat. back issues avail. **Document type:** *Directory, Trade.*
Published by: Black's Guide, Inc, 5210 Chairman's Ct, Ste 2B, Frederick, MD 21703. TEL 800-385-9266, rbiese@blacksguide.com, http://www.blacksguide.com.

333.33 USA
BLACK'S GUIDE: CHICAGO. Text in English. 1993. s-a. USD 225 per issue (effective 2008). adv. charts; maps; mkt.; stat. back issues avail.; reprints avail. **Document type:** *Directory, Trade.*
Formerly: Black's Photo Guide: Chicago
Related titles: Online - full text ed.
Published by: Black's Guide, Inc, 5210 Chairman's Ct, Ste 2B, Frederick, MD 21703. TEL 800-385-9266, rbiese@blacksguide.com, http://www.blacksguide.com.

333.33 USA
BLACK'S GUIDE: CONNECTICUT - NEW YORK SUBURBS - OUTER BOROUGHS. Text in English. 1983. s-a. USD 225 per issue (effective 2008). adv. charts; maps; mkt.; stat. back issues avail.; reprints avail. **Document type:** *Directory, Trade.*
Former titles: Black's Office Leasing Guide: Connecticut - New York Suburbs; (until 1992): Black's Guide to the Office Space Market: Connecticut - New York Suburbs
Related titles: Online - full text ed.
Published by: Black's Guide, Inc, 5210 Chairman's Ct, Ste 2B, Frederick, MD 21703. TEL 800-385-9266, rbiese@blacksguide.com, http://www.blacksguide.com. adv.: color page USD 5,250, B&W page USD 4,475; trim 8.25 x 10.875.

670.29 USA
BLACK'S GUIDE: DALLAS - FORT WORTH INDUSTRIAL MARKET. Text in English. 1998. s-a. USD 379.95; USD 225 per issue (effective 2008). adv. mkt.; stat. back issues avail.; reprints avail. **Document type:** *Directory, Trade.*
Related titles: Online - full text ed.
Published by: Black's Guide, Inc, 5210 Chairman's Ct, Ste 2B, Frederick, MD 21703. TEL 800-385-9266, rbiese@blacksguide.com, http://www.blacksguide.com. Pub. Fran Piegari TEL 972-931-1299. adv.: color page USD 4,110, B&W page USD 2,650; trim 8.25 x 10.875.

333.33 USA
BLACK'S GUIDE: DALLAS - FORT WORTH OFFICE MARKET. Text in English. 1984. s-a. USD 379.95; USD 225 per issue (effective 2008). adv. charts; maps; mkt.; stat. back issues avail.; reprints avail. **Document type:** *Directory, Trade.*
Former titles: Black's Office Leasing Guide: Dallas - Fort Worth; (until 1985): Black's Guide to the Office Space Market: Dallas - Fort Worth
Related titles: Online - full text ed.
Published by: Black's Guide, Inc, 5210 Chairman's Ct, Ste 2B, Frederick, MD 21703. TEL 800-385-9266, rbiese@blacksguide.com, http://www.blacksguide.com. adv.: color page USD 6,335, B&W page USD 5,170; trim 8.25 x 10.875.

333.33 USA
BLACK'S GUIDE: DENVER. Text in English. 1982. s-a. USD 225 per issue (effective 2008). adv. charts; maps; mkt.; stat. back issues avail.; reprints avail. **Document type:** *Directory, Trade.*
Former titles: Black's Office Leasing Guide: Metro Denver - Boulder - Colorado Springs; Black's Guide to the Office Space Market: Denver (0733-2572)
Related titles: Online - full text ed.
Published by: Black's Guide, Inc, 5210 Chairman's Ct, Ste 2B, Frederick, MD 21703. TEL 800-385-9266, rbiese@blacksguide.com, http://www.blacksguide.com.

333.33 USA
BLACK'S GUIDE: GREATER BALTIMORE - ANNAPOLIS. Text in English. 1992. s-a. USD 194.95 newsstand/cover (effective 2001). charts; maps; mkt.; stat. back issues avail. **Document type:** *Directory, Trade.*
Formerly: Black's Broker Tenant Guide: The Greater Baltimore Area
Published by: Black's Guide, Inc, 5210 Chairman's Ct, Ste 2B, Frederick, MD 21703. TEL 800-385-9266, rbiese@blacksguide.com, http://www.blacksguide.com.

670.29 USA
BLACK'S GUIDE: GREATER PHILADELPHIA, SOUTH NEW JERSEY, DELAWARE & LEHIGH VALLEY INDUSTRIAL. Text in English. 1994. s-a. USD 359.95; USD 194.95 newsstand/cover (effective 2001). mkt.; stat. **Document type:** *Directory, Trade.*
Formerly (until 199?): Black's Guide: Greater Philadelphia Region and Lehigh Valley Industrial
Published by: Black's Guide, Inc, 5210 Chairman's Ct, Ste 2B, Frederick, MD 21703. TEL 800-385-9266, rbiese@blacksguide.com, http://www.blacksguide.com.

333.33 USA
BLACK'S GUIDE: GREATER PHILADELPHIA, SOUTH NEW JERSEY, DELAWARE & LEHIGH VALLEY OFFICE. Text in English. 1981. s-a. USD 359.95 domestic; USD 194.95 newsstand/cover (effective 2001). charts; maps; mkt.; stat. back issues avail. **Document type:** *Directory, Trade.*
Former titles (until 199?): Black's Guide: Greater Philadelphia Region and Lehigh Valley Office; Black's Guide to the Office Space Market: Philadelphia - South New Jersey - Delaware; (until 1986): Black's Guide to the Office Space Market: Philadelphia and Suburbs (0733-5040)

R

Published by: Black's Guide, Inc, 5210 Chairman's Ct, Ste 2B, Frederick, MD 21703. TEL 800-385-9266, rbiese@blacksguide.com, http://www.blacksguide.com.

333.33 USA
BLACK'S GUIDE: HOUSTON. Text in English. 1982. s-a. USD 379.95; USD 225 per issue (effective 2008). adv. charts; maps; mkt.; stat. back issues avail.; reprints avail. **Document type:** *Directory, Trade.*
Former titles: Black's Office and Industrial Guide: Houston; Black's Guide to the Office Space Market: Houston (0733-5059)
Related titles: Online - full text ed.
Published by: Black's Guide, Inc, 5210 Chairman's Ct, Ste 2B, Frederick, MD 21703. TEL 800-385-9266, rbiese@blacksguide.com, http://www.blacksguide.com. Pub. Becky Meyer TEL 281-304-8912. adv.: color page USD 5,975; trim 8.25 x 10.875.

333.33 USA
BLACK'S GUIDE: HOUSTON INDUSTRIAL. Text in English. 2000. s-a. USD 379.95; USD 225 per month (effective 2008). adv. mkt.; stat. back issues avail.; reprints avail. **Document type:** *Directory, Trade.*
Related titles: Online - full text ed.
Published by: Black's Guide, Inc, 5210 Chairman's Ct, Ste 2B, Frederick, MD 21703. TEL 800-385-9266, rbiese@blacksguide.com, http://www.blacksguide.com. Pub. Becky Meyer TEL 281-304-8912. adv.: color page USD 5,975; trim 8.25 x 10.875.

333.33 USA
BLACK'S GUIDE: LOS ANGELES - ORANGE COUNTY - INLAND EMPIRE. Text in English. 1982. s-a. USD 225 per issue (effective 2008). adv. charts; maps; mkt.; stat. back issues avail.; reprints avail. **Document type:** *Directory, Trade.*
Former titles: Black's Office Leasing Guide: The Greater Los Angeles Area; Black's Guide to the Office Space Market: Greater Los Angeles Area
Related titles: Online - full text ed.
Published by: Black's Guide, Inc, 5210 Chairman's Ct, Ste 2B, Frederick, MD 21703. TEL 800-385-9266, rbiese@blacksguide.com, http://www.blacksguide.com.

333.33 USA
BLACK'S GUIDE: METRO ORLANDO. Text in English. 1993. s-a. USD 379.95; USD 225 per issue (effective 2008). adv. charts; maps; mkt.; stat. back issues avail.; reprints avail. **Document type:** *Directory, Trade.*
Formerly: Black's Office Leasing Guide: Orlando - Central Florida
Related titles: Online - full text ed.
Published by: Black's Guide, Inc, 5210 Chairman's Ct, Ste 2B, Frederick, MD 21703. TEL 800-385-9266, rbiese@blacksguide.com, http://www.blacksguide.com. Pub. Rosemary Bidwell TEL 813-784-1176. adv.: color page USD 5,220; trim 8.25 x 10.875.

333.33 USA
BLACK'S GUIDE: MICHIGAN. Text in English. 1994. s-a. USD 225 per issue (effective 2008). adv. charts; maps; mkt.; stat. back issues avail.; reprints avail. **Document type:** *Directory, Trade.*
Formerly: Black's Guide: Metropolitan Detroit
Related titles: Online - full text ed.
Published by: Black's Guide, Inc, 5210 Chairman's Ct, Ste 2B, Frederick, MD 21703. TEL 800-385-9266, http://www.blacksguide.com. Pub. Arthur Tobani. Adv. contacts Carol Atkins TEL 847-441-2615, John McCann TEL 800-500-2450 ext 35.

670.29 USA
BLACK'S GUIDE: NEW JERSEY INDUSTRIAL MARKET. Text in English. 1994. s-a. USD 379.95; USD 225 per issue (effective 2008). adv. mkt.; stat. back issues avail.; reprints avail. **Document type:** *Directory, Trade.*
Related titles: Online - full text ed.
Published by: Black's Guide, Inc, 5210 Chairman's Ct, Ste 2B, Frederick, MD 21703. TEL 800-385-9266, rbiese@blacksguide.com, http://www.blacksguide.com. Pub. Arthur Tobani. Adv. contact John McCann TEL 800-500-2450 ext 35. B&W page USD 4,475, color page USD 5,250; trim 8.25 x 10.875.

333.33 USA
BLACK'S GUIDE: NEW JERSEY OFFICE MARKET. Text in English. 1976. s-a. USD 379.95; USD 225 per issue (effective 2008). adv. charts; maps; mkt.; stat. back issues avail.; reprints avail. **Document type:** *Directory, Trade.*
Former titles: Black's Office Leasing Guide: Northern New Jersey; Black's Guide to the Office Space Market: Northern New Jersey
Related titles: Online - full text ed.
Published by: Black's Guide, Inc, 5210 Chairman's Ct, Ste 2B, Frederick, MD 21703. TEL 800-385-9266, rbiese@blacksguide.com, http://www.blacksguide.com. Pub. Arthur Tobani. adv.: color page USD 5,250, B&W page USD 4,475; trim 8.25 x 10.875.

333.33 USA
BLACK'S GUIDE: SAN DIEGO. Text in English. 1995. a. USD 194.95 newsstand/cover (effective 2001). charts; maps; mkt.; stat. back issues avail. **Document type:** *Directory, Trade.*
Published by: Black's Guide, Inc, 5210 Chairman's Ct, Ste 2B, Frederick, MD 21703. TEL 800-385-9266, rbiese@blacksguide.com, http://www.blacksguide.com.

333.33 USA
BLACK'S GUIDE: SAN FRANCISCO BAY AREA. Text in English. 1984. a. USD 225 (effective 2008). adv. charts; maps; mkt.; stat. reprints avail. **Document type:** *Directory, Trade.*
Former titles: Black's Office Leasing Guide: San Francisco Bay Area - Sacramento; Black's Guide to the Office Space Market: San Francisco Bay Area
Related titles: Online - full text ed.
Published by: Black's Guide, Inc, 5210 Chairman's Ct, Ste 2B, Frederick, MD 21703. TEL 800-385-9266, rbiese@blacksguide.com, http://www.blacksguide.com. Adv. contact Monica Forthun TEL 323-634-1522.

670.29 USA
BLACK'S GUIDE: SOUTH FLORIDA FLEX - INDUSTRIAL MARKET. Text in English. 1996. quadrennial. USD 689.95; USD 225 per issue (effective 2008). adv. charts; maps; mkt.; stat. back issues avail.; reprints avail. **Document type:** *Directory, Trade.*
Related titles: Online - full text ed.
Published by: Black's Guide, Inc, 5210 Chairman's Ct, Ste 2B, Frederick, MD 21703. TEL 800-385-9266, rbiese@blacksguide.com, http://www.blacksguide.com. adv.: B&W page USD 4,925, color page USD 6,625; trim 8.25 x 10.875.

333.33 USA
BLACK'S GUIDE: SOUTH FLORIDA - OFFICE MARKET. Text in English. 1986. q. USD 689.95; USD 225 per issue (effective 2008). adv. charts; maps; mkt.; stat. back issues avail.; reprints avail. **Document type:** *Directory, Trade.*
Formerly: Black's Broker Tenant Guide: South Florida - Treasure Coast
Related titles: Online - full text ed.
Published by: Black's Guide, Inc, 5210 Chairman's Ct, Ste 2B, Frederick, MD 21703. TEL 800-385-9266, rbiese@blacksguide.com, http://www.blacksguide.com. adv.: color page USD 6,625, B&W page USD 4,925; trim 8.25 x 10.875.

333.33 USA
BLACK'S GUIDE: TAMPA BAY - SOUTHWEST FLORIDA. Text in English. 1986. s-a. USD 379.95; USD 225 per issue (effective 2008). adv. charts; maps; mkt.; stat. back issues avail.; reprints avail. **Document type:** *Directory, Trade.*
Formerly: Black's Broker Tenant Guide: Tampa Bay - Southwest Florida
Related titles: Online - full text ed.
Published by: Black's Guide, Inc, 5210 Chairman's Ct, Ste 2B, Frederick, MD 21703. TEL 800-385-9266, rbiese@blacksguide.com, http://www.blacksguide.com. Pub. Rosemary Bidwell TEL 813-784-1176. Adv. contact John McCann TEL 800-500-2450 ext 35. color page USD 6,720; trim 8.25 x 10.875.

333.33 USA
BLACK'S GUIDE: WASHINGTON D.C. METROPOLITAN AREA. Text in English. 1978. s-a. USD 359.95; USD 194.95 newsstand/cover (effective 2001). adv. charts; maps; mkt.; stat. back issues avail. **Document type:** *Directory, Trade.*
Former titles: Black's Washington Metropolitan Area Guide; (until 1992): Black's Broker - Tenant Guide: Washington - Baltimore; (until 1991): Black's Guide to the Office Space Market: Washington - Baltimore (0199-8145)
Published by: Black's Guide, Inc, 5210 Chairman's Ct, Ste 2B, Frederick, MD 21703. TEL 800-385-9266, rbiese@blacksguide.com, http://www.blacksguide.com.

333.33 USA
BLACK'S METRO RICHMOND GUIDE. Text in English. 1992. a. USD 194.95 (effective 2001). **Document type:** *Directory, Trade.*
Published by: Black's Guide, Inc, 5210 Chairman's Ct, Ste 2B, Frederick, MD 21703. TEL 800-385-9266, rbiese@blacksguide.com, http://www.blacksguide.com.

BLOOMBERG LAW REPORTS. REAL & PERSONAL PROPERTY. *see* LAW

333.33 ITA ISSN 2037-1578
▼ **BORSA IMMOBILIARE DI ROMA. LISTINO UFFICIALE.** Text in Italian. 2009. s-a. **Document type:** *Report, Trade.*
Related titles: Online - full text ed.: ISSN 2037-1586.
Published by: Tecnoborsa, Via Capitan Bavastro 116, Rome, 00154, Italy. http://www.tecnoborsa.com.

333.33 GBR ISSN 2040-7718
BOSNIA & HERZEGOVINA REAL ESTATE REPORT. Text in English. 200?. q. EUR 820, USD 1,150 combined subscription (print & email eds.) (effective 2010). **Document type:** *Report, Trade.* **Description:** Provides industry professionals and strategists, sector analysts, business investors, trade associations and regulatory bodies with independent forecasts and competitive intelligence on the real estate and construction industry in Bosnia-Herzegovina.
Related titles: E-mail ed.
Published by: Business Monitor International Ltd., Senator House, 85 Queen Victoria St, London, EC4V 4AB, United Kingdom. TEL 44-20-72480468, FAX 44-20-72480467, subs@businessmonitor.com.

333.33 USA
BOSTON OFFICE BUILDINGS. Text in English. 19??. a. **Document type:** *Magazine, Trade.* **Description:** Comprehensive review of Boston office buildings.
Published by: Yale Robbins, Inc., 31 E 28th St, New York, NY 10016. TEL 212-683-5700, FAX 212-497-0017, mrosupport@mrofficespace.com.

333.33 GBR ISSN 2040-753X
BRAZIL REAL ESTATE REPORT. Text in English. 200?. q. EUR 820, USD 1,150 combined subscription (print & email eds.) (effective 2010). **Document type:** *Report, Trade.* **Description:** Provides industry professionals and strategists, sector analysts, business investors, trade associations and regulatory bodies with independent forecasts and competitive intelligence on the real estate and construction industry in Brazil.
Related titles: E-mail ed.
Published by: Business Monitor International Ltd., Senator House, 85 Queen Victoria St, London, EC4V 4AB, United Kingdom. TEL 44-20-72480468, FAX 44-20-72480467, subs@businessmonitor.com.

346.04 GBR ISSN 2046-1119
BRIEFING FOR PLANNERS AND SURVEYORS (ONLINE). Text in English. 2008. m. **Document type:** *Journal, Trade.*
Formerly (until 2011): G E E Briefing for Planners and Surveyors (Print) (1757-5214)
Media: Online - full text.
Published by: Croner C C H Group Ltd. (Subsidiary of: Wolters Kluwer UK Ltd.), 145 London Rd, Kingston upon Thames, Surrey KT2 6SR, United Kingdom. TEL 44-20-85473333, FAX 44-20-85472638, info@croner.co.uk.

332.63 GBR ISSN 1473-1894
HD1361
➤ **BRIEFINGS IN REAL ESTATE FINANCE.** Text in English. 2001 (June). q. GBP 195 in United Kingdom to institutions; EUR 220 in Europe to institutions; USD 340 in the Americas to institutions; USD 340 elsewhere to institutions; GBP 215 combined subscription in United Kingdom to institutions (print & online eds.); EUR 242 combined subscription in Europe to institutions (print & online eds.); USD 374 combined subscription in the Americas to institutions (print & online eds.); USD 374 combined subscription elsewhere to institutions (print & online eds.) (effective 2009). adv. bk.rev. abstr.; charts; illus.; mkt.; stat. back issues avail.; reprint service avail. from PSC. **Document type:** *Journal, Academic/Scholarly.* **Description:** Dissemination of current and best practice, applied research and case studies in real estate finance.
Related titles: Online - full text ed.: ISSN 1555-0990. GBP 195 in United Kingdom to institutions; EUR 220 in Europe to institutions; USD 340 in the Americas to institutions; USD 340 elsewhere to institutions (effective 2009).
Indexed: A12, A15, A17, ABIn, B01, B06, B07, B09, BLI, CA, P48, P51, P53, P54, PQC, T02.
—BLDSC (2283.958378), IE, Ingenta. **CCC.**
Published by: John Wiley & Sons Ltd. (Subsidiary of: John Wiley & Sons, Inc.), 1-7 Oldlands Way, PO Box 808, Bognor Regis, West Sussex PO21 9FF, United Kingdom. TEL 44-1865-778315, FAX 44-1243-843232, cs-journals@wiley.com, http://eu.wiley.com/WileyCDA/. **Subscr. to:** 1-7 Oldlands Way, PO Box 809, Bognor Regis, West Sussex PO21 9FG, United Kingdom. TEL 44-1865-778054, cs-agency@wiley.com.

333.33 CAN ISSN 1910-071X
BRITISH COLUMBIA REAL ESTATE LAW DEVELOPMENTS. Text in English. bi-m. CAD 269 (effective 2008). **Document type:** *Newsletter, Trade.*
Media: Online - full text.
Published by: C C H Canadian Ltd. (Subsidiary of: Wolters Kluwer N.V.), 90 Sheppard Ave E, Ste 300, North York, ON M2N 6X1, Canada. TEL 416-224-2248, 800-268-4522, FAX 416-224-2243, 800-461-4131, cservice@cch.ca.

333.33 340 CAN
BRITISH COLUMBIA REAL ESTATE LAW GUIDE. Text in English. m. CAD 1,130 (effective 2008). **Document type:** *Handbook/Manual/Guide, Trade.* **Description:** Covers laws governing real estate transactions in B.C.
Related titles: CD-ROM ed.: CAD 1,130 (effective 2008); Online - full text ed.: CAD 1,130 (effective 2008).
Published by: C C H Canadian Ltd. (Subsidiary of: Wolters Kluwer N.V.), 90 Sheppard Ave E, Ste 300, North York, ON M2N 6X1, Canada. TEL 416-224-2248, 800-268-4522, FAX 416-224-2243, 800-461-4131, cservice@cch.ca.

333.33 340 CAN ISSN 1719-6582
BRITISH COLUMBIA REAL ESTATE PRACTICE MANUAL. Text in English. a. **Document type:** *Handbook/Manual/Guide, Trade.*
Published by: Continuing Legal Education Society of British Columbia, 300-845 Cambie St, Vancouver, BC V6B 5T2, Canada. TEL 604-669-3544, 800-663-0437, FAX 604-669-9260, http://www.cle.bc.ca/cle/default.htm.

333.33 USA ISSN 1935-1720
BROKERAGE PERFORMANCE REPORT. Text in English. 2003. a., latest 2007. USD 195 per issue (effective 2008). **Document type:** *Report, Trade.*
Related titles: Online - full text ed.: USD 175 per issue (effective 2008).
Published by: REAL Trends Inc., 6898 S University Blvd Ste 200, Littleton, CO 80122. TEL 303-741-1000, FAX 303-741-1070, realtrends@realtrends.com, http://www.realtrends.com/go/index.php.

333.33 CAN ISSN 1715-9636
BROKER'S LICENSING COURSE MANUAL. Text in English. 198?. a. **Document type:** *Handbook/Manual/Guide, Trade.*
Formerly (until 2006): Real Estate Agent's Pre-Licensing Course Manual (1198-8436)
Published by: (The University of British Columbia, Sauder School of Business, Real Estate Division), Real Estate Council of British Columbia, 900 - 750 W Pender St, Vancouver, BC V6C 2T8, Canada. TEL 604-683-9664, 877-683-9664, FAX 604-683-9017, info@recbc.ca, http://www.recbc.ca/index.htm.

333.33 USA
BRONX REALTOR NEWS. Text in English. 1927. bi-w. membership. adv. bk.rev. charts; illus.; stat.
Formerly (until 1980): Bronx Real Estate and Building News (0007-2265)
Published by: Bronx Board of Realtors, Inc., 1867 Williamsbridge Rd, Bronx, NY 10461-6205. Ed. Nunzio Delgreco. Circ: 1,000.

332.63 USA
BROOKFIELD PROPERTIES. ANNUAL REPORT. Text in English. a. **Document type:** *Corporate.*
Related titles: Online - full text ed.
Published by: Brookfield Properties, Three World Financial Center, New York, NY 10281. TEL 212-417-7000, FAX 212-417-7214, mcoley@brookfieldproperties.com, http://www.brookfieldproperties.com.

333.33 USA
THE BROWNSTONER. Text in English. q. USD 35; USD 25 renewals. adv. **Document type:** *Newsletter.*
Indexed: AIAP.
Published by: Brownstone Revival Committee, PO Box 577, New York, NY 10113. TEL 212-675-0560. Adv. contact Marvin Rock. Circ: 1,200.

333.33 USA ISSN 1934-4406
BUILDING. Text in English. 2007 (Jan.). m. USD 25 (effective 2007). **Document type:** *Magazine, Trade.* **Description:** Covers real estate development industry in the Spokane and North Idaho region.
Published by: ViVo Publications, 157 S. Howard, #11, Spokane, WA 99201. TEL 509-624-6300, FAX 509-624-6306, http://www.vivopub.com/. Ed. Linn Parish.

333.33 SGP
BUILDING AND ESTATE MANAGEMENT SOCIETY. PROCEEDINGS. Text in English. s-a.
Published by: Building and Estate Management Society, c/o Faculty of Architecture and Bldg, National University of Singapore, Kent Ridge, 0511, Singapore. TEL 7756666.

333.33 USA ISSN 1937-2930
BUILDING LONG ISLAND. Text in English. 2006. bi-m. USD 33 (effective 2007). **Document type:** *Magazine, Trade.* **Description:** Reports on the policies, projects and people that impact real estate development, architecture, construction and planning on Long Island.
Published by: D K H Communications, 30 Jericho Turnpike #271, Commack, NY 11725. TEL 631-543-0320, FAX 631-543-0344. Pub. Deborah Herman.

BUILDING SOCIETIES ASSOCIATION. ANNUAL REPORT. *see* BUILDING AND CONSTRUCTION

333.3 GBR
BUILDING SOCIETIES. YEARBOOK. Text in English. 1927. a. GBP 50 domestic to non-members; free to members (effective 2009). stat. **Document type:** *Yearbook, Trade.* **Description:** Provides addresses of building society members and a listing of surveyors.
Incorporates: Council of Mortgage Lenders. Yearbook

Published by: Building Societies Association, 6th Fl, York House, 23 Kingsway, London, WC2B 6UJ, United Kingdom. TEL 44-20-75205900, FAX 44-20-72405290, information@bsa.org.uk. **Co-sponsor:** Council of Mortgage Lenders.

333.3 GBR
BUILDING SOCIETY ANNUAL ACCOUNTS DATA. Text in English. 1995. a. GBP 90 per issue (effective 2010). stat. **Document type:** *Report, Trade.* **Description:** Features data drawn from the published reports and accounts of building societies.
Related titles: Diskette ed.: GBP 70 per issue (effective 2010).
Published by: Building Societies Association, 6th Fl, York House, 23 Kingsway, London, WC2B 6UJ, United Kingdom. TEL 44-20-75205900, FAX 44-20-72405290, information@bsa.org.uk, http://www.bsa.org.uk/.

BUILDING SOCIETY MORTGAGE ARREARS AND LOSSES REPORT. *see* BUSINESS AND ECONOMICS—Banking And Finance

333.33 GBR
BUILDING SOCIETY PEER GROUPS (FINANCIAL). Text in English. 19??. a. GBP 550 per issue (effective 2010). **Document type:** *Handbook/Manual/Guide, Trade.* **Description:** Provides comprehensive information, allowing for the comparison of the financial performance of each U.K. building society with its peers.
Published by: (Building Societies Association), The Data Ltd **Co-sponsor:** Council of Mortgage Lenders.

333.33 USA ISSN 0746-0023
HC101
BUSINESS FACILITIES; the location advisor. Text in English. 1968. m. USD 30 domestic; USD 63.75 foreign; free domestic to qualified personnel (effective 2008). adv. charts; illus.; stat.; tr.lit. back issues avail.; reprints avail. **Document type:** *Magazine, Trade.*
Formerly: A I P R (American Industrial Properties Report) (0193-7308)
Related titles: Online - full text ed.
Published by: Group C Communications, 44 Apple St, Ste 3, Tinton Falls, NJ 07724. TEL 732-842-7433, 800-524-0337, FAX 732-758-6634, tcoene@groupc.com, http://www.groupc.com. Ed. Karim Khan. Pub. Ted Coene. adv.: B&W page USD 6,200, color page USD 7,700. Circ: 43,500 (controlled and free).

333.33 FRA ISSN 1772-936X
BUSINESS IMMO; l'information de l'immobilier d'entreprise sur Internet et sur papier. Text in French. 2004. m. EUR 360 (effective 2009). **Document type:** *Magazine, Trade.*
Address: 20 Rue Laffitte, Paris, 75009, France. TEL 33-1-44838383, FAX 33-1-44838380, info@businessimmo.fr, http://www.businessimmo.fr.

333.33 FRA ISSN 1778-1655
BUSINESS IMMO. ANNUAIRE. Text in French. 1997. a. EUR 400 (effective 2009).
Formerly (until 2005): L' Annee Immobiliere (1291-5955)
Published by: Business Immo, 20 Rue Laffitte, Paris, 75009, France. TEL 33-1-44838383, FAX 33-1-44838380, info@businessimmo.fr, http://www.businessimmo.fr.

BUSINESS VALUATION REVIEW. *see* BUSINESS AND ECONOMICS—Banking And Finance

BUTTERWORTHS PROPERTY LAW SERVICE. *see* LAW

333.33 NZL ISSN 1177-0260
BUY A BUSINESS. Text in English. 2005. m. adv. **Document type:** *Magazine, Trade.* **Description:** Connects and informs buyers and sellers of business and franchise opportunities.
Published by: Paper Ventures Limited, 68 Volga St, Island Bay, Wellington, New Zealand. TEL 64-4-3839896. Ed. Willie Davenport TEL 64-4-3839896.

333.33 USA
C A A NEWS (SACRAMENTO, ONLINE). Text in English. 1959. m. free to members. **Document type:** *Newsletter, Trade.* **Description:** Designed to provide CAA members with timely CAA Network news briefs and information, as well as updates on member products, services and upcoming events.
Formerly: C A M M A News (Print)
Media: Online - full text.
Published by: California Apartment Association, 980 Ninth St, Ste 200, Sacramento, CA 95814-2721. TEL 916-447-7881, 800-967-4222, FAX 916-447-7903, http://www.caanet.org/. Ed. John Itzel. Circ: 12,500.

333.3 USA
C E A NEWS. Text in English. bi-m. adv. **Document type:** *Magazine, Trade.*
Published by: California Escrow Association, 2520 Venture Oaks Way, Ste. 150, Sacramento, CA 95833-4228. TEL 213-461-7383. Ed., R&P, Adv. contact Laura Bell. Circ: 2,000.

333.33 CAN ISSN 1495-5113
C M H C MORTGAGE MARKET TRENDS. Text in English. 1988. q. CAD 85 (effective 2003). **Document type:** *Government.*
Former titles (until 2000): Mortgage Market Trends (1493-6097); (until 1999): C M H C Mortgage Market Trends (1188-4215)
Published by: Canada Mortgage and Housing Corporation/Societe Canadienne d'Hypotheques et de Logement, 700 Montreal Rd, Ottawa, ON K1A 0P7, Canada. TEL 613-748-2000, FAX 613-748-2098, chic@cmhc-schl.gc.ca, http://www.cmhc.ca.

333.3 GBR
C M L ANNUAL REPORT. Text in English. 2001. a. back issues avail. **Document type:** *Report, Trade.* **Description:** Covers some of the most dramatic events ever seen in more than 150 years of UK mortgage lending.
Related titles: Online - full text ed.: free (effective 2009).
Published by: Council of Mortgage Lenders, Bush House, N W Wing, Aldwych, London, WC2B 4PJ, United Kingdom. TEL 44-845-3736771, FAX 44-845-3736778, events@cml.org.uk.

333.3 GBR
C M L DIRECTORY OF MEMBERS. Variant title: Directory of C M L Members and Associates. Text in English. 19??. irreg. free to members (effective 2009). **Document type:** *Directory, Trade.* **Description:** Describes the association and its activities; lists member organizations.
Related titles: Online - full text ed.
Published by: Council of Mortgage Lenders, Bush House, N W Wing, Aldwych, London, WC2B 4PJ, United Kingdom. TEL 44-845-3736771, FAX 44-845-3736778, events@cml.org.uk.

333.33 CAN
CALGARY REAL ESTATE NEWS. Text in English. w. (Thur.). free. **Document type:** *Newspaper, Consumer.* **Description:** Contains general interest feature articles, real estate advertisements and listings for Calgary and South-central Alberta for home buyers, including open houses and the most recent new MLS property listings.
Related titles: Online - full content ed.
Published by: Calgary Real Estate Board, 300 Manning Rd NE, Calgary, AB T2E 8K4, Canada. TEL 403-263-0530, FAX 403-218-3688, info@creb.com, http://www.creb.com/. Ed. Bruce Klippenstein.

333.33 USA ISSN 1058-8205
KFC811.A59
CALIFORNIA LAND USE LAW AND POLICY REPORTER. Text in English. 1991. 11/yr. USD 379.50 (effective 2005). 28 p./no.; back issues avail.; reprints avail. **Document type:** *Newsletter, Trade.*
Related titles: Online - full text ed.
Published by: Argent Communications Group, PO Box 1425, Foresthill, CA 95631-1425. TEL 530-367-3844, FAX 530-367-2613. Ed. Robert M. Schuster.

333.33 USA ISSN 0008-1450
HD251
CALIFORNIA REAL ESTATE. Text in English. 1920. 10/yr. USD 24 domestic; USD 44 foreign (effective 2005). adv. bk.rev. bibl.; charts; illus.; mkt.; stat. index. 56 p./no.; back issues avail.; reprints avail. **Document type:** *Magazine, Trade.* **Description:** Recognized for nearly 80 years as an authoritative source, featuring in-depth news and information focusing on California's real estate issues and trends.
Former titles (until 1975): California Real Estate Magazine (0732-2194); (until 1929): California Real Estate (0732-3832)
Related titles: Online - full text ed.; ◆ Supplement(s): Real Estate Technology.
Indexed: CalPI, P06.
Published by: California Association of Realtors, 525 S Virgil Ave, Los Angeles, CA 90020. TEL 213-739-8200, FAX 213-480-7724. Ed., Pub., R&P Anne Framroze TEL 213-739-8320. adv.: B&W page USD 4,895, color page USD 6,310. Circ: 100,000 (controlled).

333.33 USA
CALIFORNIA REAL ESTATE LAW AND PRACTICE. Text in English. 1973. 17 base vols. plus updates 3/yr. looseleaf. USD 2,625 base vol(s). (effective 2008). **Document type:** *Guide, Trade.* **Description:** Discusses every aspect of real estate litigation and business practice, complete with tax coverage of real estate transactions. Its extensive analysis of governing laws is complemented by (1) a one-volume, annotated compilation of significant California statutes and regulations, and (2) numerous practice-oriented features.
Related titles: CD-ROM ed.; Online - full text ed.
Published by: Matthew Bender & Co., Inc. (Subsidiary of: LexisNexis North America), 1275 Broadway, Albany, NY 12204. TEL 518-487-3000, 800-424-4200, FAX 518-487-3083, international@bender.com, http://bender.lexisnexis.com. Ed. Thomas M Dankert.

333.33 330 USA ISSN 1046-3844
KFC140
CALIFORNIA REAL ESTATE REPORTER. Text in English. 1986. m. looseleaf. USD 524 (effective 2008). **Document type:** *Magazine, Trade.* **Description:** Covers the latest California and federal real estate cases as well as significant statutory and regulatory developments affecting real property in California.
Related titles: CD-ROM ed.; Online - full text ed.
—CCC.
Published by: Matthew Bender & Co., Inc. (Subsidiary of: LexisNexis North America), 1275 Broadway, Albany, NY 12204. TEL 518-487-3000, 800-424-4200, FAX 518-487-3083, international@bender.com, http://bender.lexisnexis.com. Ed. David W Walters.

346.04 USA ISSN 1052-2921
K3
CALIFORNIA REAL PROPERTY JOURNAL. Text in English. 1982. q. USD 70 membership (effective 2008). **Description:** Contains information and announcements on current developments in real property law, in-depth articles on a range of topics, as well as news and information about the Section and its activities.
Related titles: Online - full text ed.
Indexed: A26, B04, CLI, FamI, G08, I01, I05, ILP, LRI.
Published by: State Bar of California, Real Property Law Section, 180 Howard St, San Francisco, CA 94105-1639. TEL 415-538-2564, FAX 415-538-2368. **Co-sponsor:** State Bar of California.

333.33 ESP
CAMBRA DE LA PROPIETAT URBANA DE BARCELONA. BUTLLETI. Text in Spanish, Catalan. q. back issues avail. **Document type:** *Bulletin, Consumer.*
Related titles: Online - full text ed.
Published by: Cambra de la Propietat Urbana de Barcelona, Via Laietana, 22, Barcelona, 08003, Spain. TEL 34-93-3192878, FAX 34-93-3192902.

333.33 GBR ISSN 2043-6912
CAMBRIDGE NEWS. HOMES NOW. Text in English. 1998. w. adv. **Document type:** *Newspaper, Trade.* **Description:** Provides property searches in and around the Cambridgeshire area.
Formerly (until 2010): Cambridge Evening News. Property News (1463-5399)
Published by: Cambridge Newspapers Ltd., Winship Rd, Milton, Cambridge, CB24 6PP, United Kingdom. TEL 44-1223-434434, newspapersales@cambridgenews.co.uk, http://www.cambridge-news.co.uk.

333.33 340 CAN
CANADIAN COMMERCIAL REAL ESTATE MANUAL. Text in English. 4/yr. looseleaf. CAD 722 domestic; USD 611.86 foreign (effective 2005). index. **Description:** Addresses the unique requirements of the commercial real estate industry. Covers the critical stages of development from acquisition through property management.
Published by: Carswell (Subsidiary of: Thomson Reuters Corp.), One Corporate Plz, 2075 Kennedy Rd, Toronto, ON M1T 3V4, Canada. TEL 416-609-8000, 800-387-5164, FAX 416-298-5094, carswell.customerrelations@thomson.com, http://www.carswell.com. Ed. Jim McDermott.

333.33 CAN ISSN 1717-4600
HD7305.A3
CANADIAN HOUSING OBSERVER. Text in English. 2003. a., latest 2005. free (effective 2006). **Document type:** *Bulletin, Trade.* **Description:** Provides an integrated and objective view of the housing challenges and changing needs of Canadians.
Related titles: Online - full text ed.: ISSN 1717-4619; ◆ French ed.: L' Observateur du Logement au Canada. ISSN 1717-4651.
Published by: Canada Mortgage and Housing Corporation/Societe Canadienne d'Hypotheques et de Logement, 700 Montreal Rd, Ottawa, ON K1A 0P7, Canada. TEL 613-748-2000, FAX 613-748-2098, http://www.cmhc.ca, http://www.schl.ca.

333.33 CAN
CANADIAN INDUSTRIAL PROPERTY GUIDE. Text in English, French. 1969. a. charts; illus.; mkt.; maps; tr.lit. back issues avail. **Document type:** *Handbook/Manual/Guide, Trade.*
Related titles: Online - full text ed.
Published by: R L P Publications, 5770 Hurontario St, Ste 200, Mississauga, ON L5R 3G5, Canada. TEL 905-501-6466, FAX 905-568-9444. Ed. Sheryl Davies. Pubs. Alex Strachan, Sheryl Davies. adv.: page CAD 5,039; trim 10.88 x 8.13. Circ: 40,000 (controlled).

333.5 CAN ISSN 0834-3357
CANADIAN PROPERTY MANAGEMENT. Text in English. 1986. 8/yr. CAD 53.45 (effective 2009). adv. **Document type:** *Magazine, Trade.* **Description:** Brings industry news along with technical articles and case law reports.
Published by: MediaEdge Communications, Llc, 5255 Yonge St, Ste 1000, Toronto, ON M2N 6P4, Canada. TEL 416-512-8186, 866-216-0860, FAX 416-512-8344, info@mediaedge.ca. Ed. Barbara Carss. Pub. Sean Foley. Circ: 12,500 (controlled).

333.33 CAN
CANADIAN PROPERTY VALUATION/EVALUATEUR CANADIEN. Text in Multiple languages. 1943; N.S. 1956. 4/yr. free to members. adv. bk.rev. **Document type:** *Journal.*
Former titles (until 2008): The Canadian Appraiser (0827-2697); (until 1984): A I M. Appraisal Institute Magazine (0383-6649); (until 1976): Appraisal Institute Magazine (0044-846X)
Related titles: Microfiche ed.: (from MML); Microform ed.: N.S. (from MML); Online - full text ed.; Supplement(s): Designated Members Source Guide. ISSN 1910-9636. 19??.
Indexed: A17, B06, B08, B09, CBPI, RICS.
—BLDSC (3044.078500), IE, Ingenta.
Published by: Appraisal Institute of Canada, 403-200 Catherine St, Ottawa, ON K2P 2K9, Canada. TEL 613-234-6533, FAX 613-234-7197, info@aicanada.org, http://www.aicanada.org. Adv. contact Cindy Robin. Circ: 6,000.

CANADIAN REAL ESTATE INCOME TAX GUIDE. *see* BUSINESS AND ECONOMICS—Public Finance, Taxation

333.33 CAN ISSN 1193-8021
CANADIAN REALTOR NEWS; official publication of organized real estate in Canada. Text in English, French. 1955. 10/yr. CAD 40. adv. bk.rev. charts; illus.; stat. index. reprints avail. **Document type:** *Newsletter, Trade.*
Formerly: Canadian Real Estate (0823-8197); Supersedes: C R E A Reporter (0315-3843); Canadian Realtor (0008-4905)
Related titles: Microfilm ed.: (from MML, PQC); Microform ed.: (from MML); French ed.
Indexed: CBPI, RICS.
Published by: Canadian Real Estate Association, 344 Slater St, Ste 1600, Building, Ottawa, ON K1R 7Y3, Canada. TEL 613-237-7111, FAX 613-234-2567, jmccarthy@crea.ca, info@crea.ca. Ed., R&P James B McCarthy. Adv. contact Lynn St Germain. B&W page USD 2,400. Circ: 70,000 (controlled).

CARLSONREPORT FOR SHOPPING CENTER MANAGEMENT. *see* BUSINESS AND ECONOMICS—Management

333.33 USA ISSN 1934-8142
CAROLINAS COMMERCIAL PROPERTIES. Text in English. 2006. bi-m. USD 51 (effective 2010). adv. **Document type:** *Magazine, Trade.* **Description:** Focuses on the incredible growth that is taking place in North and South Carolina and covers all the property types: office, retail, industrial, hospitality and multifamily.
Related titles: Online - full text ed.: Carolinas Commercial Properties E-Newsletter. ISSN 2154-2732. free (effective 2010).
Published by: France Publications, Inc., 3500 Piedmont Rd, Ste 415, Atlanta, GA 30305. TEL 404-832-8262, FAX 404-832-8260, scott@francepublications.com, http://www.francepublications.com. Ed. Lindsey Walker. Pub., Adv. contact Scott France.

333.33 PER ISSN 1605-3184
CASAS. Text in Spanish. m.
Related titles: Online - full text ed.: ISSN 1605-3176; ◆ Supplement to: Cosas. ISSN 1605-3168.
Published by: Editorial Letras e Imagenes, S.A., Recavarren, 111, Miraflores, Lima, 18, Peru. TEL 51-1-2411178, FAX 51-1-4473776, peru@cosas.com.

333.33 ITA ISSN 2036-2226
▼ **CASE STYLE.** Text in Multiple languages. 2009. q. **Document type:** *Magazine, Consumer.*
Related titles: Online - full text ed.: ISSN 2036-2269.
Published by: Publiword, Via Antonio Votto 3, Piacenza, 29100, Italy. TEL 39-0523-1996355.

333.33 USA
CHARLESTON METRO COMMERCE MAGAZINE. Text in English. 1987. q. USD 10 (effective 2000). adv. **Document type:** *Magazine, Trade.*
Former titles: Charleston Trident Commerce Magazine; Formerly: Charleston Real Estate Report
Published by: Atlantic Publication Group, Llc., Parkshore Center, One Poston Rd, Ste 190, Charleston, SC 29417-0007. TEL 843-747-0025, FAX 843-744-0816. Ed. Shannon Clark TEL 843-747-0025 ext 264. Pub. Marvin Jenkins. Adv. contact Andrew Sprague. B&W page USD 2,290, color page USD 4,020. Circ: 10,000.

333.33 FRA ISSN 1960-1549
CHATEAUX ET PROPRIETES. Text in French. 2007. q. EUR 64 for 2 yrs. (effective 2008). **Document type:** *Magazine, Consumer.*
Published by: Lafont Presse, 53 Rue du Chemin Vert, Boulogne-Billancourt, 92100, France. http://www.lafontpresse.fr.

R

333.33 690 CHN ISSN 1006-6659
CHENGSHI ZHUZHAI/CITY RESIDENCE. Text in Chinese. 1994. m. CNY 23 per issue domestic; CNY 8 per issue foreign (effective 2010). **Document type:** *Magazine, Trade.*
Related titles: Online - full text ed.
Published by: Zhongguo Jianzhu Sheji Yanjiuyuan/China Architecture Design & Research Group, 19, Chegongzhuang Jie, Rm.1443, 1418, Beijing, 100044, China. TEL 86-10-88371294, FAX 86-10-88327131, http://www.cadreg.com.cn/index.asp. **Co-sponsor:** Yatai Jianshe Keji Xinxi Yanjiusuo.

CHENGXIANG JIANSHE/URBAN AND RURAL CONSTRUCTION. *see* HOUSING AND URBAN PLANNING

333.33 USA
CHICAGO AGENT; for the well-informed real estate professional. Text in English. 2003. bi-w. USD 48 (effective 2009). adv. **Document type:** *Magazine, Trade.* **Description:** Contains industry trends and news, informing readers of the best practices of their peers as well as reliable advice from the experts.
Related titles: Online - full text ed.
Published by: Chicago Agent Publishing LLC, 2000 N Racine, Ste 3400, Chicago, IL 60614. TEL 773-296-6001, FAX 773-269-6103. Ed. Zipporah Porton. Pubs. Anne Brindle, Marci Sepulveda. Adv. contact Theresa Tellock. B&W page USD 910; trim 10.5 x 12.

333.33 USA ISSN 2154-901X
HG2040.5.U6
CHICAGO AREA COMMUNITY LENDING FACT BOOK. Text in English. 1984. a. **Document type:** *Journal, Consumer.* **Description:** Compiles mortgage lending data and aggregates it to the community level in the city of Chicago and regional area.
Formerly (until 2004): Community Lending Fact Book
Published by: Woodstock Institute, 407 S Dearborn, Chicago, IL 60605. TEL 312-368-0310.

333.33 GBR ISSN 2040-7548
▼ **CHILE REAL ESTATE REPORT.** Text in English. 2009. q. USD 975, EUR 695 combined subscription (print & email eds.) (effective 2011). **Document type:** *Report, Trade.* **Description:** Provides industry professionals and strategists, sector analysts, business investors, trade associations and regulatory bodies with independent forecasts and competitive intelligence on the real estate and construction industry in Chile.
Related titles: E-mail ed.
Published by: Business Monitor International Ltd., Senator House, 85 Queen Victoria St, London, EC4V 4AB, United Kingdom. TEL 44-20-72480468, FAX 44-20-72480467, subs@businessmonitor.com.

333.33 HKG ISSN 1021-6332
CHINA PROPERTY REVIEW. Text in Chinese, English. 1992. 10/yr. HKD 2,250, USD 295. adv. back issues avail. **Description:** Contains updates and comprehensive analysis of the real property market in P.R. China.
—CCC.
Published by: Asia Law & Practice Ltd. (Subsidiary of: Euromoney Institutional Investor Plc.), 5/F Printing House, 6 Duddell St, Central Hong Kong, Hong Kong. TEL 852-544-9918, FAX 852-543-7617. Ed. Chris Hunter. Adv. contact Wendy Foo. color page HKD 7,095; trim 210 x 280. Circ: 3,000.

333.33 GBR ISSN 2040-7599
▼ **CHINA REAL ESTATE REPORT.** Text in English. 2009. q. EUR 820, USD 1,150 combined subscription (print & email eds.) (effective 2011). back issues avail. **Document type:** *Report, Trade.* **Description:** Provides independent forecasts and competitive intelligence on the real estate and construction industry in China.
Related titles: E-mail ed.
Published by: Business Monitor International Ltd., Senator House, 85 Queen Victoria St, London, EC4V 4AB, United Kingdom. TEL 44-20-72480468, FAX 44-20-72480467, subs@businessmonitor.com.

333.33 USA ISSN 1098-0431
CHRISTIE'S GREAT ESTATES; the international showcase for distinctive properties. Text in English. 1995. q. USD 36 domestic; USD 60 in Canada; USD 68 elsewhere; USD 10 per issue (effective 2006). adv. **Document type:** *Magazine, Consumer.* **Description:** Showcases the world's finest luxury real estate on the market.
Published by: Christie's Great Estates, Inc. (Subsidiary of: Christie's), 125 Linclon, Ste 300, Santa Fe, NM 87501. TEL 505-983-8733, FAX 505-982-0348, info@christiesgreatestates.com, advertising@christiesgreatestates.com. Pub. Kay Coughlin. Adv. contact David Wilson. color page USD 6,850; trim 9.0625 x 10.875. Circ: 75,000 (paid).

333.33 340 GBR
COHABITATION: LAW AND PRECEDENTS. Text in English. 1999. base vol. plus updates 2/yr. looseleaf. GBP 372 base vol(s). domestic; EUR 492 base vol(s). in Europe; USD 640 base vol(s). elsewhere (effective 2011). **Document type:** *Handbook/Manual/Guide, Trade.* **Description:** Covers all aspects of law and procedure which relates to cohabitation from ownership of property to domestic violence, and from children to inheritance and succession.
Published by: Sweet & Maxwell Ltd. (Subsidiary of: Thomson Reuters Corp.), 100 Avenue Rd, London, NW3 3PF, United Kingdom. TEL 44-20-73937000, FAX 44-20-74491144, sweetandmaxwell.customer.services@thomson.com. Ed. Jane Craig. **Subscr. to:** PO Box 1000, Andover SP10 9AF, United Kingdom. TEL 44-20-73938051, sweetandmaxwell.international.queries@thomson.com.

COLLIER REAL ESTATE TRANSACTIONS AND THE BANKRUPTCY CODE. *see* BUSINESS AND ECONOMICS—Banking And Finance

333.33 USA
COLORADO REAL ESTATE FORMS. Text in English. 1988. latest 2nd ed., 3 base vols. plus irreg. updates. looseleaf. USD 533 base vol(s). includes diskette (effective 2008). Supplement avail. **Document type:** *Guide, Trade.* **Description:** Contains sample real estate forms and clause options to address all phases of the conveyancing process.
Related titles: Online - full text ed.
Published by: Michie Company (Subsidiary of: LexisNexis North America), 701 E Water St, Charlottesville, VA 22902. TEL 434-972-7600, 800-446-3410, FAX 434-972-7677, customer.support@lexisnexis.com, http://www.michie.com. Ed. Beverly J Quail.

333.33 USA ISSN 1060-4383
COLORADO REAL ESTATE JOURNAL. Text in English. 1992. s-m. USD 68; USD 3 newsstand/cover (effective 2005). adv. bk.rev. charts; mkt.; maps; stat.; tr.lit. 64 p./no. 5 cols./p.; back issues avail.; reprints avail. **Document type:** *Newspaper, Trade.* **Description:** Colorado's only commercial real estate trade publication.
Address: 1630 Welton St, Ste 300, Denver, CO 80202-4223. TEL 303-623-1148, FAX 303-623-2217. Ed. Kris Opperman Stern. Pub., R&P Jon Stern. Adv. contacts Jon Stern, Lori Golightly TEL 3036231148. page USD 1,295; trim 10.25 x 15.5. Circ: 4,000 (paid).

333.33 USA
COLORADO REALTOR. Text in English. 9/yr. **Document type:** *Newspaper.*
Formerly (until 2004): Colorado Realtor News
Published by: Colorado Association of Realtors, 309 Inverness Way, S., Englewood, CO 80112-5819. TEL 303-790-7099, FAX 303-790-7299. Ed. Tyrone Adams. Circ: 20,000 (paid).

333.33 USA ISSN 1061-138X
COMMERCIAL INC.; the magazine for commercial real estate. Text in English. 1987. m. USD 18 (effective 1998). adv. back issues avail. **Document type:** *Magazine, Trade.* **Description:** Covers the industrial and office real estate markets, provides updates on environmental laws, and publishes a directory of financial institutions serving the Michigan market.
Address: 28 W Huron St, Pontiac, MI 48342-2100. TEL 248-745-4794, FAX 248-332-3003. Ed. Robert Carr. Pub., R&P Bonnie M Taube. Adv. contact Dawn M Howard. Circ: 30,000.

333.33 332.6 USA ISSN 1524-3249
HD1361
COMMERCIAL INVESTMENT REAL ESTATE. Text in English. 1982. bi-m. USD 45 domestic to non-members; USD 55 in Canada & Mexico to non-members; free to members (effective 2010). adv. bk.rev. illus.; charts. index. 48 p./no. 3 cols./p.; back issues avail.; reprints avail. **Document type:** *Magazine, Trade.* **Description:** Provides practical information for professionals on all aspects of commercial real estate.
Former titles (until 1999): Commercial Investment Real Estate Journal (0887-4778); (until 1986): Commercial Investment Journal (0744-6446)
Related titles: Online - full text ed.
Indexed: A12, A13, A17, A22, ABIn, B01, B06, B07, B08, B09, B11, C12, CA, P48, P51, P53, P54, PQC, T02.
—BLDSC (3336.963640), IE, Ingenta.
Published by: (National Association of Realtors (Chicago)), C C I M Institute, 430 N Michigan Ave, Ste 800, Chicago, IL 60611. TEL 312-321-4460, 800-621-7027, FAX 312-321-4530, info@ccim.com, http://www.ccim.com. Pub. Jennifer Norbut TEL 312-321-4531. Adv. contact Kathleen Thomas TEL 202-721-1497. page USD 4,666; bleed 8.75 x 11. Circ: 20,546.

333.33 340 USA ISSN 0736-0517
KF593.C6
COMMERCIAL LEASE LAW INSIDER; the practical, plain-English, monthly newsletter for owners, managers, attorneys and other real estate professionals. Text in English. 1982. m. USD 337 (print or online ed.); USD 505 combined subscription (print & online eds.) (effective 2008). index. back issues avail.; reprints avail. **Document type:** *Newsletter, Trade.* **Description:** Presents tested commercial leasing strategies, techniques, and insights. Features include model lease clauses and checklists, as well as coverage of new court decisions affecting commercial leases.
Related titles: CD-ROM ed.; Online - full text ed.: ISSN 1938-3126.
Indexed: A10, V03.
—CCC.
Published by: Brownstone Publishers, Inc. (Subsidiary of: L R P Publications, Inc.), 655 Third Ave, 23rd Fl, New York, NY 10017. TEL 212-905-0550, 800-643-8095, FAX 212-473-8786, custserv@brownstone.com, http://www.brownstone.com/. Ed. Wendy Starr. Pub. John M Striker. R&P Mike Koplin. Circ: 3,700 (paid).

333.3 USA ISSN 0898-5634
KF593.C6
COMMERCIAL LEASING LAW AND STRATEGY. Text in English. 1988. m. looseleaf. USD 439 combined subscription (print & online eds.) (effective 2008). Index. back issues avail.; reprints avail. **Document type:** *Newsletter, Trade.* **Description:** Provides latest developments, strategies and techniques on the business and legal aspects of commercial leasing.
Related titles: Online - full text ed.: USD 419 (effective 2008).
Indexed: A26, B02, B15, B17, B18, G04, G08, I05.
—CCC.
Published by: Law Journal Newsletters (Subsidiary of: A L M), 1617 JFK Blvd, Ste 1750, Philadelphia, PA 19103. TEL 215-557-2300, 800-722-7670, customercare@incisivemedia.com, http://www.ljnonline.com. Ed. Stephanie McEvily.

332.63 USA ISSN 1520-3697
COMMERCIAL MORTGAGE ALERT. Text in English. 1993. 46/yr. USD 3,797 (effective 2011). adv. back issues avail. **Document type:** *Newsletter, Trade.* **Description:** Covers the commercial mortgage-backed securities (CMBS) market for issuers and investors, including information on real-estate investment trusts (REIT) and the traditional lending business.
Related titles: E-mail ed.: USD 2,497 (effective 2005); Online - full text ed.
Indexed: A15, ABIn, BLI, I05, P48, P51, P53, P54, PQC, PROMT.
Published by: Harrison Scott Publications, Inc., 5 Marine View Plz, Ste 301, Hoboken, NJ 07030. TEL 201-659-1700, FAX 201-659-4141, info@hspnews.com, http://www.hspnewsletters.com. Pub. Andrew Albert TEL 201-234-3960. Adv. contact Mary E Romano TEL 201-234-3968.

332 USA ISSN 1095-0729
COMMERCIAL MORTGAGE INSIGHT; the magazine for commercial mortgage finance. Text in English. 1997. m. USD 48 domestic (effective 2009). adv. back issues avail.; reprints avail. **Document type:** *Magazine, Trade.* **Description:** Designed for the top professionals in commercial mortgage finance - the mortgage bankers, brokers, life companies, pension funds, commercial banks and community/savings institutions involved with originating and servicing commercial and multi-family mortgages.
Published by: Zackin Publications Inc., 100 Willenbrock Rd, Oxford, CT 06478. TEL 203-262-4670, 800-325-6745, FAX 203-262-4680, info@zackin.com, http://www.zackin.com. Ed. Jessica Lillian. Pub. Paul Zackin TEL 800-325-6745 ext 223. Circ: 18,000.

333.33 340 GBR
COMMERCIAL PROPERTY DEVELOPMENT PRECEDENTS. Variant title: Heller Commercial Property Development Precedents. Text in English. 1994. 2 base vols. plus updates 2/yr. looseleaf. GBP 682 base vol(s). domestic; EUR 901 base vol(s). in Europe; USD 1,172 base vol(s). elsewhere (effective 2011). **Document type:** *Handbook/Manual/Guide, Trade.* **Description:** Provides all the documents needed for such agreements. It sets out carefully drafted contracts and clauses for funding of land acquisition; design and building construction, including project management; and the development of the property, including the agreement for sale.
Related titles: CD-ROM ed.: GBP 1,944 domestic to institutions; EUR 2,566.80 in Europe to institutions; USD 2,784 elsewhere to institutions (effective 2011).
Published by: Sweet & Maxwell Ltd. (Subsidiary of: Thomson Reuters Corp.), 100 Avenue Rd, London, NW3 3PF, United Kingdom. TEL 44-20-73937000, FAX 44-20-74491144, sweetandmaxwell.customer.services@thomson.com. **Subscr. to:** PO Box 1000, Andover SP10 9AF, United Kingdom. TEL 44-20-73938051, sweetandmaxwell.international.queries@thomson.com.

332.33 GBR
COMMERCIAL PROPERTY GUIDE. NORTH WEST. Text in English. 2000. a. GBP 35 per issue (effective 2009). adv. **Document type:** *Handbook/Manual/Guide, Trade.* **Description:** Contains rental information focusing on office, retail, industrial and investment markets that is extensively researched and published alongside key sub-regional economic facts and figures.
Published by: Newsco-Insider, Boulton House, 17-21 Chorlton St, Manchester, M1 3HY, United Kingdom. TEL 44-161-9079711, FAX 44-161-2369862, michelle.ferster@newsco.com, http://www.newsco.com/. Ed. Michael Taylor TEL 44-161-9079709. Adv. contact Lynn Barnett TEL 44-161-9079752. color page GBP 1,500. Circ: 12,000.

333.3387025429 GBR ISSN 1755-3997
COMMERCIAL PROPERTY GUIDE. WALES & SOUTH WEST. Variant title: Insider Commercial Property Guides. Wales & South West. Text in English. 2008. a. adv. **Document type:** *Directory, Trade.* **Description:** Contains updated figures on average rents in offices, industrial and retail property, transformational property projects and the progress made by urban regeneration companies, comprehensive listings of professional industry contacts from developers, lawyers and property lenders to surveyors, valuers, agents and architects in Wales and South West.
—CCC.
Published by: Newsco-Insider, Boulton House, 17-21 Chorlton St, Manchester, M1 3HY, United Kingdom. TEL 44-161-9079711, FAX 44-161-2369862, michelle.ferster@newsco.com, http://www.newsco.com/. Ed. Michael Taylor TEL 44-161-9079709. Adv. contact Steve Kane TEL 44-117-9065904.

COMMERCIAL PROPERTY MANAGEMENT INSIDER. *see* BUSINESS AND ECONOMICS—Management

333.33 GBR ISSN 1466-688X
COMMERCIAL PROPERTY MONTHLY. Text in English. 1979. bi-m. GBP 89 (effective 2009). adv. bk.rev. back issues avail. **Document type:** *Magazine, Trade.* **Description:** Covers real estate development and property management.
Related titles: Online - full text ed.
Published by: Belvedere Publishing Ltd., Challenge House, 616 Mitcham Rd, Croydon, CR9 3AU, United Kingdom. TEL 44-20-86836422, FAX 44-20-86836426. Ed. Lynda Bonney Doyle. adv.: B&W page GBP 985, color page GBP 1,570; trim 211 x 297. Circ: 20,000 (paid).

333.33 USA ISSN 1043-1675
CODEN: INPSE8
COMMERCIAL PROPERTY NEWS; the national newspaper for commercial property professionals. Abbreviated title: C P N. Text in English. 1987. m. USD 140 domestic; USD 185 in Canada; USD 341 elsewhere; free to qualified personnel (effective 2009). adv. Supplement avail.; back issues avail.; reprints avail. **Document type:** *Magazine, Trade.* **Description:** Provides news and information for for senior level executives in the commercial real estate market, including brokers, developers, investors, lenders, property managers, owners, and corporate real estate executives.
Formerly (until 1989): Real Estate Times (0893-1968)
Related titles: Online - full text ed.: USD 199 (effective 2009).
Indexed: A09, A10, A15, ABIn, B01, B02, B03, B06, B07, B09, B15, B17, B18, G04, G06, G07, G08, I05, M01, M02, P34, PQC, T02, V02, V03, V04.
—CIS. **CCC.**
Published by: Nielsen Business Publications (Subsidiary of: Nielsen Business Media, Inc.), 770 Broadway, New York, NY 10003. TEL 646-654-4500, FAX 646-654-4948, bmcomm@nielsen.com, http://www.nielsenbusinessmedia.com. Eds. Eugene Gilligan, Suzann D Silverman. Pub. Victoria Osorio. adv.: B&W page USD 10,885, color page USD 13,075; trim 9.75 x 13.75. Circ: 31,500 (controlled). **Subscr. to:** PO Box 16567, North Hollywood, CA 91615.

346.04 GBR
COMMERCIAL PROPERTY PRECEDENTS. Text in English. 19??. irreg. GBP 739.20 domestic; EUR 976.80 in Europe; USD 1,059 elsewhere (effective 2011). **Document type:** *Journal, Trade.*
Media: CD-ROM.
Published by: Sweet & Maxwell Ltd. (Subsidiary of: Thomson Reuters Corp.), 100 Avenue Rd, London, NW3 3PF, United Kingdom. TEL 44-20-73937000, FAX 44-20-74491144, sweetandmaxwell.customer.services@thomson.com, http://www.sweetandmaxwell.co.uk. **Subscr. to:** PO Box 1000, Andover SP10 9AF, United Kingdom. TEL 44-20-73938051, sweetandmaxwell.international.queries@thomson.com.

333.33 USA ISSN 1073-0370
COMMERCIAL REALTY REVIEW. Text in English. 1987. bi-m. USD 60 (effective 2002). adv. back issues avail. **Document type:** *Magazine, Trade.* **Description:** Covers the latest trends in commercial real estate investment, property management, renovation, development, and design in the Philadelphia region (Pennsylvania, New Jersey and Delaware).
Related titles: Online - full text ed.

Published by: J & C Publishing, Inc., 1528 Walnut St., Ste. 2008, Philadelphia, PA 19102-3613. Ed. Rebecca Zeiders. Pub. Henry J Stursberg. adv.: B&W page USD 2,900. Circ: 40,000.

333.33 340 USA ISSN 1933-5350
HD1286
THE COMMONS DIGEST. Text in English. 1986. q. free to members (effective 2011). back issues avail. **Document type:** *Journal, Academic/Scholarly.* **Description:** Devoted to understanding and improving the management of environmental resources that are used collectively by communities.
Formerly (until 2006): The Common Property Resource Digest (1062-5593)
Related titles: Online - full text ed.: ISSN 1933-5407. free (effective 2011).
Indexed: CABA, E12, S13, S16, W11.
Published by: International Association for the Study of the Commons, c/o Susan Buck, Environmental Studies Program, College of Arts & Science, University of North Carolina at Greensboro, PO Box 26170, Greensboro, NC 27402. TEL 336-256-0520, FAX 336-334-4315, iascp@indiana.edu. Ed. Alyne E Delaney TEL 45-98-942855.

333.33 332.6 330.9 USA ISSN 0893-9136
COMMONWEALTH LETTERS; for investors in single family homes. Text in English. 1978. m. looseleaf. USD 70; USD 82 foreign (effective 1998). adv. back issues avail. **Document type:** *Newsletter.* **Description:** A practical guide for small investors in income-producing houses with appropriate background data in tax-economics.
Formerly: Jack Miller's CommonWealth Letters
Published by: (National Capital Corporation), CommonWealth Press, Inc., PO Box 21172, Tampa, FL 33622. TEL 619-538-0151, FAX 619-484-7496. Ed., R&P, Adv. contact Chris Miller. Circ: 2,000.

333.33 346.04 USA
THE COMMUNICATOR (SAN DIEGO); the voice of our nation's appraisers and home inspectors. Text in English. 1994. q. USD 20 (effective 2003). adv. **Document type:** *Magazine, Trade.* **Description:** Reports on issues such as technology, industry trends, continuing education, state regulations and laws.
Published by: Frea, 4907 Morena Blvd, #1415, San Diego, CA 92117. TEL 800-882-4410, FAX 858-273-8026, frea@frea.com. Ed. Allison Iacopini TEL 858-483-2490. adv.: B&W page USD 2,800, color page USD 3,400; trim 8.5 x 10.875. Circ: 152,000.

333.33 USA ISSN 0199-9028
COMMUNIQUE (CHICAGO). Text in English. 1955. 8/yr. USD 25 to non-members. adv. bk.rev. tr.lit. index. **Document type:** *Magazine, Trade.* **Description:** Covers real estate sales techniques, management, finance and personal development.
Indexed: M&MA.
Published by: Women's Council of Realtors, 430 N Michigan Ave, Chicago, IL 60611. TEL 312-329-5967, FAX 312-329-3290. Ed., Adv. contact Kathy Greenholdt. Pub. Gary Krysler. Circ: 12,000; 12,000 (paid).

333.33 USA
COMMUNITIES MAGAZINE (ATLANTA). Text in English. 1978. bi-m. free (effective 2008). adv. **Document type:** *Magazine, Consumer.* **Description:** Gives a complete guide to all new home subdividisions and condominiums for the metropolitan Atlanta area.
Address: 2100 Powers Ferry Rd, N W Ste 400, Atlanta, GA 30339-5014. TEL 770-644-7575, FAX 770-644-7585. Ed., Adv. contact Laura Hearron. Pub., R&P Gib Dickey. Circ: 75,000.

333.33 USA ISSN 1553-068X
COMMUNITY ASSOCIATIONS INSTITUTE. COMMON GROUND; CA's magazine for condominium and homeowner associations. Text in English. 1984. bi-m. USD 65 to non-members; USD 39 to members (effective 2010). adv. bk.rev.; video rev.; Website rev. 54 p./no.; back issues avail.; reprints avail. **Document type:** *Magazine, Trade.* **Description:** Designed for volunteer board members, professional managers, accountants and attorneys who work with condominiums, townhouses and other forms of common interest ownership property.
Formerly (until 2004): Common Ground (0885-6133)
Related titles: Online - full text ed.
Indexed: P06, PAIS.
Published by: Community Associations Institute, 225 Reinekers Ln, Ste 300, Alexandria, VA 22314. TEL 703-548-8600, 888-224-4321, FAX 703-684-1581. Ed. Dori Meinert TEL 703-797-6249. Adv. contact Marc A Ingram TEL 703-797-6254.

333.33 CAN
CONDO LIFE MAGAZINE. Text in English. 1998. 5/yr. CAD 15. adv. **Document type:** *Magazine, Consumer.* **Description:** Presents a guide to Toronto's condominium real estate market.
Published by: Homes Publishing Group, 178 Main St, Unionville, ON L3R 2G9, Canada. TEL 905-479-4665, FAX 905-479-4482. Ed. Patrick Tivey. Pub. Michael Rosset. adv.: color page USD 4,600. Circ: 140,000.

CONNECTICUT COTTAGES & GARDENS. *see* GARDENING AND HORTICULTURE

333.33 USA
CONNECTICUT REAL ESTATE JOURNAL. Text in English. 1963. bi-m. **Document type:** *Newspaper, Trade.* **Description:** Includes articles and photos on real estate sales, mortgages and plans on commercial, industrial investment real estate.
Published by: East Coast Publications, Inc., PO Box 55, Accord, MA 02018. Pub. Lorraine Rayberg TEL 781-878-4540 ext 213.

333.33 USA
THE CONNECTICUT REALTOR. Text in English. 1977. q. free to members; USD 40 to non-members (effective 2001). adv. **Document type:** *Magazine, Trade.* **Description:** Covers legislative issues affecting industry, primarily association related materials, including general issues relating to real estate.
Related titles: Online - full text ed.
Published by: Connecticut Association of Realtors, 111 Founders Plaza, Ste 1101, East Hartford, CT 06108-3289. TEL 860-290-6601, FAX 860-290-6615. Pub. Lisa Governale. Adv. contact David Yosua. B&W page USD 1,000. Circ: 11,600 (controlled).

333.33 ITA ISSN 0010-7050
CONSULENTE IMMOBILIARE. Text in Italian. 1957. s-m. bk.rev. stat. index, cum.index. **Document type:** *Magazine, Trade.*
Published by: Il Sole 24 Ore Business Media, Via Monte Rosa 91, Milan, 20149, Italy. TEL 39-02-30221, FAX 39-02-312055, info@ilsole24ore.com, http://www.gruppo24ore.com.

340 GBR ISSN 0010-8200
K3
THE CONVEYANCER AND PROPERTY LAWYER. Text in English. 1915. bi-m. GBP 358, EUR 472, USD 616 (effective 2012). bk.rev. index. reprints avail. **Document type:** *Journal, Trade.* **Description:** Specialising in the law and practice of conveyancing and allied topics.
Formerly (until 1936): Conveyancer
Related titles: Online - full text ed.; Supplement(s): Bulletin for the Conveyancer. ISSN 0955-8004.
Indexed: A22, A26, B04, CLI, FamI, G08, I01, I03, I05, ILP, LJI, LRI, LegCont, PCI.
—IE, Ingenta. **CCC.**
Published by: Sweet & Maxwell Ltd. (Subsidiary of: Thomson Reuters Corp.), 100 Avenue Rd, London, NW3 3PF, United Kingdom. TEL 44-20-73937000, FAX 44-20-74491144, sweetandmaxwell.customer.services@thomson.com. Ed. Martin Dixon. **Subscr. to:** PO Box 1000, Andover SP10 9AF, United Kingdom. TEL 44-20-73938051, sweetandmaxwell.international.queries@thomson.com.

CONVEYANCERS' YEARBOOK. *see* LAW

CONVEYANCING AND PROPERTY LAW JOURNAL. *see* LAW

333.33 346.6 AUS
CONVEYANCING MANUAL NEW SOUTH WALES. Text in English. 1996. 2 base vols. plus q. updates. looseleaf. AUD 849 (effective 2008). **Document type:** *Handbook/Manual/Guide, Trade.* **Description:** Provide a step-by-step guide for your conveyancing business in New South Wales.
Related titles: CD-ROM ed.: AUD 525 for practices with up to 20 practitioners (effective 2003); Online - full content ed.: AUD 525 for practices with up to 20 practitioners (effective 2003).
Published by: Lawbook Co. (Subsidiary of: Thomson Reuters (Professional) Australia Limited), PO Box 3502, Rozelle, NSW 2039, Australia. TEL 61-2-85877980, 300-304-195, FAX 61-2-85877981, 300-304-196, LTA.Service@thomsonreuters.com, http://www.thomson.com.au.

333.33 346.6 AUS
CONVEYANCING MANUAL QUEENSLAND. Text in English. 1997. 2 base vols. plus q. updates. looseleaf. AUD 768 (effective 2008). **Document type:** *Handbook/Manual/Guide, Trade.* **Description:** Provides a core reference for conveyancing practitioners in Queensland.
Related titles: Online - full content ed.: AUD 500 for practices with up to 20 practitioners (effective 2003).
Published by: Lawbook Co. (Subsidiary of: Thomson Reuters (Professional) Australia Limited), PO Box 3502, Rozelle, NSW 2039, Australia. TEL 61-2-85877980, 300-304-195, FAX 61-2-85877981, 300-304-196, LTA.Service@thomsonreuters.com, http://www.thomson.com.au.

332 USA
THE COOPERATOR; the co-op & condo monthly. Text in English. m. free to members (effective 2011). **Document type:** *Newspaper, Trade.* **Description:** Serves the co-op and condo community with thousands of articles on management, finance, maintenance and more.
Related titles: Online - full text ed.: free (effective 2011).
Published by: Yale Robbins Publications, LLC, 102 Madison Ave, 5th Fl, New York, NY 10016. TEL 212-683-5700, FAX 646-405-9751, info@yrinc.com, http://marketing.yrpubs.com/. Pub. Yale Robbins. Adv. contact Henry Robbins.

333.33 382 USA ISSN 1524-508X
CORPORATE COMPASS. Text in English. q. adv. **Document type:** *Magazine, Trade.* **Description:** Reports on corporate expansion and location strategies in the Asia-Pacific region.
Published by: Asiamax, Inc., P O Box 922348, Norcross, GA 30092. TEL 404-681-4868, asiamax@corp-compass.com, 603-251-7973, http://www.corp-compass.com.

333.33 GBR ISSN 2043-9148
▼ ➤ **CORPORATE REAL ESTATE JOURNAL.** Abbreviated title: C R E J. Text in English. 2010. q. GBP 250 combined subscription per vol. in the UK & Europe (print & online eds.) (effective 2012). adv. **Document type:** *Journal, Academic/Scholarly.* **Description:** Publishes studies on new thinking, strategies and techniques in corporate real estate.
Related titles: Online - full text ed.: ISSN 2043-9156. 2010.
—**CCC.**
Published by: Henry Stewart Publications LLP, c/o Gwen Yates, Russell House, 28-30 Little Russell St, London, WC1A 2HN, United Kingdom. TEL 44-20-70923496, FAX 44-20-74042081, qweny@henrystewart.co.uk, http://www.henrystewart.com/default.aspx. Pub., Adv. contact Simon Beckett TEL 44-20-70923469. **Subscr. to:** Henry Stewart Publications, PO Box 361, Birmingham, AL 35201. TEL 205-995-1588, 800-633-4931, hsp@ebsco.com.

333.33 USA
COSTAR'S ATLANTA PROPERTY NEWS. Text in English. 2005. bi-m. adv. **Document type:** *Newsletter, Trade.*
Published by: CoStar Group, Inc., 2 Bethesda Metro Center, 10th Fl, Bethesda, MD 20814-5388. TEL 301-215-8300, 800-204-5960, FAX 301-718-2444, 800-613-1301, info@costar.com, http://www.costar.com/. Pub. Ben Johnson. adv.: color page USD 3,395; trim 10.4375 x 14.5. Circ: 15,000.

333.33 USA
COUNTRY'S BEST TOP SELLING HOME DESIGNS. Text in English. 1997. m. USD 3.99 per issue (effective 2004). **Document type:** *Magazine, Consumer.*
Formerly: Top Selling Home Plans
Published by: Cruz Bay Publishing (Subsidiary of: Active Interest Media), 300 Continental Blvd #650, El Segundo, CA 90245-5067. TEL 310-356-4100, FAX 310-356-4110, smcnamee@aimmedia.com, http://www.cruzbaypublishing.com. Ed. Steve Culpepper. Circ: 80,000 (paid).

COURRIER DES EMPLOYES D'IMMEUBLES. *see* BUSINESS AND ECONOMICS

333.33 USA ISSN 0194-7222
CREATIVE REAL ESTATE MAGAZINE; the real estate news observer. Text in English. 1972. m. USD 72 (effective 2000). adv. bk.rev. index. back issues avail. **Document type:** *Magazine, Trade.* **Description:** How-to journal for anyone who wants to make money in real estate.
Published by: Professional Publishers, Inc., Drawer L, Rancho Santa Fe, CA 92067. TEL 858-756-1441, FAX 858-756-1111. Ed. J.S. McNary. Pub., R&P A D Kessler. Adv. contact Jane Dent. page USD 600; trim 11 x 8.5. Circ: 77,000 (paid).

333.33 BEL
LE CRI. Text in French. 10/yr. free to members (effective 2005). **Document type:** *Newspaper, Consumer.*
Published by: Syndicat National des Proprietaires, Rue du Lombard 76, Bruxelles, 1000, Belgium. TEL 32-2-512-6287, FAX 32-2-512-4461, info@snp-aes.be, http://www.uipi.com/modules/wfchannel/index.php?pagenum=57. Ed. Bernard Robert.

CRITTENDEN GOLF INC. *see* SPORTS AND GAMES—Ball Games

333.33 USA ISSN 0888-9139
HD251
CRITTENDEN REAL ESTATE BUYERS. Text in English. 1984. w. Included with subscr. to Crittenden Directory of Real Estate Investors & Buyers. **Document type:** *Directory, Trade.* **Description:** Provides information on cap rates, target prices, IRRs and markets, what they will buy, motivations behind the deal and investments budgets.
Published by: Crittenden Publishing, Inc., PO Box 1150, Novato, CA 94948. TEL 415-382-2456, 800-421-3483, FAX 415-382-2416, czeineh@crittendennews.com.

387 332 USA ISSN 0736-0339
CRITTENDEN REPORT REAL ESTATE FINANCING. Text in English. 1975. w. USD 395 (effective 2000). index. back issues avail. **Document type:** *Newsletter.*
Published by: Crittenden Research, Inc., 45 Leveroni Court, Ste 204, PO Box 1150, Novato, CA 94948. donna@crittendennews.com, http://www.crittendenonline.com. Ed. John N Goodwin. Circ: 2,500.

333.33 GBR ISSN 2040-7734
CROATIA REAL ESTATE REPORT. Text in English. 200?. q. EUR 820, USD 1,150 combined subscription (print & email eds.) (effective 2010). **Document type:** *Report, Trade.* **Description:** Provides industry professionals and strategists, sector analysts, business investors, trade associations and regulatory bodies with independent forecasts and competitive intelligence on the real estate and construction industry in Croatia.
Related titles: E-mail ed.
Published by: Business Monitor International Ltd., Senator House, 85 Queen Victoria St, London, EC4V 4AB, United Kingdom. TEL 44-20-72480468, FAX 44-20-72480467, subs@businessmonitor.com.

658.23 GBR
CRONER'S PREMISES MANAGEMENT. Variant title: Croner's Premises Management Briefing. Premises Management. Text in English. 1992. base vol. plus updates 3/yr. looseleaf. GBP 499; GBP 710 combined subscription (print, online & CD-ROM eds.) (effective 2010). **Document type:** *Handbook/Manual/Guide, Trade.* **Description:** Provides essential information to guide through the day-to-day complexities of managing commercial or industrial premises.
Formerly: Premises Management Briefing (0965-2868)
Related titles: CD-ROM ed.: GBP 620 (effective 2010); Online - full text ed.
Published by: Croner C C H Group Ltd. (Subsidiary of: Wolters Kluwer UK Ltd.), 145 London Rd, Kingston upon Thames, Surrey KT2 6SR, United Kingdom. TEL 44-20-85473333, FAX 44-20-85472638, info@croner.co.uk.

333.33 ESP ISSN 1138-3488
CT. CATASTRO. Text in Spanish. 1989. 3/yr. back issues avail. **Document type:** *Magazine, Consumer.*
Formerly (until 1991): Catastro (0214-8404)
Published by: Ministerio de Economia y Hacienda, Direccion General del Catasro, Guzman el Bueno, 139, Madrid, 28003, Spain. TEL 34-91-5450797, FAX 34-91-5450777. Ed. Ignacio Duran Boo.

333 NLD
CURRENT ISSUES IN REAL ESTATE FINANCE & ECONOMICS. Text in English. 1988. irreg., latest vol.3, 1996. price varies. **Document type:** *Monographic series.*
Published by: Springer Netherlands (Subsidiary of: Springer Science+Business Media), Van Godewijckstraat 30, Dordrecht, 3311 GX, Netherlands. TEL 31-78-6576050, FAX 31-78-6576474.

346.047 USA
CURRENT LEASING LAW AND TECHNIQUES: FORMS. Text in English. 1982. 6 base vols. plus s-a. updates. looseleaf. USD 1,420 base vol(s). (effective 2008). **Document type:** *Handbook/Manual/Guide, Trade.* **Description:** Contains legal analysis, checklists, practice commentary and forms for various leasing transactions.
Published by: Matthew Bender & Co., Inc. (Subsidiary of: LexisNexis North America), 1275 Broadway, Albany, NY 12204. TEL 518-487-3000, 800-424-4200, FAX 518-487-3083, international@bender.com, http://bender.lexisnexis.com.

333.33 690.83 USA
CUSTOM BUILDERS AND THEIR COMMUNITIES. Text in English. 1995. a. USD 4.95 (effective 2001). adv. **Document type:** *Magazine, Consumer.* **Description:** Lists custom home builders in the over $300,000 price range in the Dallas/Ft. Worth area.
Published by: HPC Publications, Inc, 12001 N Central Expressway, Ste 640, Dallas, TX 75243. TEL 214-239-2399, FAX 214-239-7850. Ed. Maridee Boron. Adv. contact Pamela Stevens. color page USD 3,995; trim 8.38 x 5.25. Circ: 50,000 (controlled).

333.33 GBR ISSN 2040-7742
▼ **CZECH REPUBLIC REAL ESTATE REPORT.** Text in English. 2009. q. USD 975, EUR 695 combined subscription (print & online eds.) (effective 2011). **Document type:** *Report, Trade.* **Description:** Provides industry professionals and strategists, sector analysts, business investors, trade associations and regulatory bodies with independent forecasts and competitive intelligence on the real estate and construction industry in the Czech Republic.
Related titles: E-mail ed.
Published by: Business Monitor International Ltd., Senator House, 85 Queen Victoria St, London, EC4V 4AB, United Kingdom. TEL 44-20-72480468, FAX 44-20-72480467, subs@businessmonitor.com.

R

333.33 USA ISSN 0279-4195
DAILY COMMERCE. Text in English. 1917. d. (Mon.-Fri.). USD 264 (effective 2011). adv. bk.rev. **Document type:** *Newspaper, Trade.*
Former titles (until 1981): Los Angeles Daily Journal of Commerce; (until 1980): Journal of Commerce Review; (until 1976): Journal of Commerce and Independent Review (0021-9835)
Related titles: Microfilm ed.: (from LIB).
Published by: Daily Journal Corp., 915 E First St, Los Angeles, CA 90012. TEL 213-229-5300, FAX 213-229-5481, Circulation@dailyjournal.com. Ed. David Houston TEL 213-229-2452. Wire service: AP.

333.33 USA
DAILY TRANSCRIPT. Text in English. 1907. d. (Mon.-Fri.). **Document type:** *Newspaper, Consumer.*
Published by: Dolan Media Corp., 222 S, Ninth St, Ste 2300, Minneapolis, MN 55402. TEL 612-317-9420, FAX 612-321-0563, http://www.dolanmedia.com/.

333.77 USA ISSN 0894-0258
DALLAS - FORT WORTH HOME BUYER'S GUIDE. Text in English. 1972. bi-m. free. adv. bk.rev. charts; illus. **Document type:** *Guide, Consumer.* **Description:** New-home housing map-guide for the Dallas-Fort Worth Metroplex.
Former titles (until 1987): Living (Dallas - Fort Worth Edition) (0741-5494); (until 1983): Dallas - Fort Worth Living (0192-8546)
Published by: Home Buyer's Guide (Dallas), 12001 N Central Pky, Ste 640, Dallas, TX 75243. TEL 214-239-2399. Ed. Maridee Boron. Adv. contact Rhonda Denny. Circ: 75,000 (controlled).

333.33 USA
DALLAS / FORT WORTH NEW HOMES GUIDE. Text in English. 1972. m. free (effective 2005). adv. **Document type:** *Magazine, Consumer.*
Published by: H P C Publications, 3119 Campas Dr., Norcross, GA 30071. TEL 770-446-6580. Circ: 35,000 (free).

333.33 GBR ISSN 0011-5894
DALTONS WEEKLY; your perfect partner for buying and selling. Text in English. 1870. w. GBP 40; GBP 1 newsstand/cover (effective 1999). adv. illus. index. **Document type:** *Journal, Consumer.*
Address: Cl Tower, St George's Sq, New Malden, Surrey KT3 4JA, United Kingdom. TEL 44-181-949-6199, FAX 44-181-949-2718. Circ: 30,211 (paid). **Dist. by:** Seymour Distribution Ltd, 86 Newman St, London W1T 3EX, United Kingdom. FAX 44-207-396-8002, enquiries@seymour.co.uk.

333.33 USA
DAN'S HAMPTON STYLE. Variant title: Hampton Style. Text in English. 17/yr. free newsstand/cover. adv. **Document type:** *Magazine, Consumer.* **Description:** Covers all aspects of the people, houses, fashions, lifestyles and events in the Hamptons.
Published by: News Communications, Inc., 501 Madison Ave, 23rd Fl, New York, NY 10022-5608. TEL 212-689-2500, FAX 212-689-1998. Eds. Julia Nasser, Deborah Schoeneman. Adv. contact Kathy Rae. color page USD 4,820.

333.33 USA
THE DEAL MAKERS. Text in English. 1979. w. USD 274 (effective 2005). adv. bk.rev.; software rev.; Website rev. tr.lit. 36 p./no.; back issues avail.; reprints avail. **Document type:** *Newsletter, Trade.* **Description:** Covers retailers' expansion plans, developments planned and under way, current construction and rehabilitation of existing centers, and listings of property for sale, for retail real estate executives.
Formerly (until 1991): Retail Leasing Reporter
Related titles: E-mail ed.; Online - full content ed.
Published by: T K O Real Estate Advisory Group, PO Box 2630, Mercerville, NJ 08690. TEL 609-587-6200, 800-732-5856, FAX 609-587-3511, http://www.property.com. Ed., Pub., Adv. contact Ann O'Neal. R&P Ted Kraus. Circ: 6,000.

333.33 VNM
DELUXE PROPERTY. Text in Vietnamese. q. VND 70,000 (effective 2010). **Description:** Covers the high-end luxury residential and commercial properties in Vietnam, including luxury items such as cars, yachts, and interiors.
Published by: Oriental Media Company Ltd., 44C Cuu Long St., Tan Binh District, Hochiminh City, Viet Nam. TEL 84-8-38441612, FAX 84-8-38462296, info@oriental-ltd.com, http://www.oriental-ltd.com/. Pub. Jade Huynh.

659.1 720 FRA ISSN 0291-1191
DEMEURES ET CHATEAUX. Text in English, French. 1978. 8/yr. adv. bk.rev. illus.; tr.lit. **Document type:** *Journal, Consumer.* **Description:** Presents illustrated advertisements for castles, country seats and manors.
Formerly: Demeures et Chateaux en France (0180-3905)
Published by: Conseil Patrimoine, 52 Bd Victor Hugo, Nice, France. TEL 33-4-97030333, FAX 33-4-97030334, http://www.demeures-et-chateaux.com. Circ: 25,000.

333.33 USA
THE DESERT REAL ESTATE REPORT. Text in English. 19??. m. USD 450; USD 45 per issue; free to qualified personnel (effective 2009). back issues avail. **Document type:** *Newsletter, Consumer.* **Description:** Features homes, condos, country clubs, vacation homes, second homes, seasonal homes and investment property in Palm Springs, Palm Desert, Rancho Mirage, Cathedral City, Indian Wells, La Quinta, Indio and Desert Hot Springs.
Media: Online - full content.
Published by: Information Designs, 36101 Bob Hope Dr, Ste F2, Rancho Mirage, CA 92270. TEL 760-836-9139, 800-975-7720, rick@rereport.com, http://www.rereport.com.

333.37642812 USA
DESTINATION D F W. (Dallas Fort Worth) Text in English. 1990. a. USD 4.95 (effective 2001). adv. **Document type:** *Journal, Consumer.* **Description:** Serves as a relocation guide for people moving to the Dallas-Fort Worth area.
Published by: HPC Publications, Inc, 12001 N Central Expressway, Ste 640, Dallas, TX 75243. TEL 214-239-2399, FAX 214-239-7850. Ed. Maridee Boron. adv.: color page USD 6,475; trim 8 x 10.875. Circ: 70,000.

333.33 DEU ISSN 0724-6617
DEUTSCHE WOHNUNGSWIRTSCHAFT. Text in German. 1949. 10/yr. EUR 34; EUR 4.50 newsstand/cover (effective 2010). adv. bk.rev. charts; illus. index. reprints avail. **Document type:** *Magazine, Trade.*
Indexed: IBR, IBZ.
Published by: (Zentralverband der Deutschen Haus, Wohnungs und Grundeigentuemer e.V.), Haus und Grund Verlag und Service GmbH, Mohrenstr 33, Berlin, 10117, Germany. TEL 49-30-202160, FAX 49-30-2021-6555, zv@haus-und-grund.net, http://www.haus-und-grund.net. Ed. Kai Warnecke. Adv. contact Margret Boes. B&W page EUR 864, color page EUR 1,254; trim 170 x 265. Circ: 6,500 (paid and controlled). **Co-sponsor:** Haus und Grund Deutschland.

DEVELOPMENT (HERNDON). *see* BUILDING AND CONSTRUCTION

DEVELOPMENTS; news magazine for the resort-recreational real estate and community development industries. *see* HOUSING AND URBAN PLANNING

DICTIONNAIRE PERMANENT: GESTION IMMOBILIERE. *see* BUSINESS AND ECONOMICS—Management

346.440 FRA ISSN 1775-9234
DICTIONNAIRE PERMANENT TRANSACTIONS IMMOBILIERES. Text in French. 2004. base vol. plus m. updates. looseleaf. EUR 180 base vol(s).; EUR 20 per month (effective 2009).
Published by: Editions Legislatives, 80 ave de la Marne, Montrouge, Cedex 92546, France. TEL 33-1-40923636, FAX 33-1-40923663, http://www.editions-legislatives.fr. Ed. Jean-Jacques Veron.

333.33 FRA ISSN 1767-4328
DIMAG; le magazine du diagnostic immobilier. Text in French. 2004. bi-m. EUR 42.50; EUR 9.40 per issue (effective 2006). **Document type:** *Magazine, Consumer.*
Related titles: Supplement(s): Dimag - Hors-Serie. ISSN 1774-5365. 2005.
Published by: Cedille Editions, 27 rue Danielle-Casanova, Paris, 75001, France.

333.33 690 ESP ISSN 1133-7990
DIRECTIVOS CONSTRUCCION. Text in Spanish. 1986. 11/yr. EUR 317 domestic; EUR 332 in Europe; EUR 337 elsewhere (effective 2009). adv. Supplement avail.; back issues avail. **Document type:** *Magazine, Trade.*
Related titles: Online - full text ed.
Indexed: F04.
Published by: Wolters Kluwer Espana - Empresas (Subsidiary of: Wolters Kluwer N.V.), C Orense, 16 1a. Planta, Madrid, 28020, Spain. TEL 34-91-5566411, FAX 34-91-5554118, clientes@wkempresas.es, http://www.wkempresas.es. Ed. Salome Gonzalez Rubio. Circ: 7,000.

333 658.7 USA ISSN 0732-5983
HF5430.3
DIRECTORY OF MAJOR MALLS. Text in English. 1977. a. USD 599 (effective 2005). adv. maps. **Document type:** *Directory.* **Description:** Lists existing and planned shopping centers in the United States and Canada, over 250,000 sq.ft. of gross leasable area; includes portfolios of 48 leading owner-developers and over 250 top retailers seeking mall space. Computerized version, mailing labels, custom report services also available.
Related titles: CD-ROM ed.: 1977.
Published by: Directory of Major Malls, Inc., PO Box 837, Nyack, NY 10960-0837. TEL 914-426-0040, FAX 914-426-0802. Ed., Pub. Tama J Shor.

333.33029 USA
DIRECTORY OF PROFESSIONAL APPRAISERS. Text in English. a. USD 12.95 (effective 2001). adv. 175 p./no.; **Document type:** *Directory, Consumer.* **Description:** Lists appraisers accredited by ASA.
Former titles: Directory of Professional Appraisal Services (1051-1768); (until 1990): Professional Appraisal Services Directory (0196-4097)
Related titles: Online - full content ed.
Published by: American Society of Appraisers, PO Box 17265, Washington, DC 20041-0265. TEL 703-478-2228, FAX 703-742-8471, http://www.appraisers.org. Ed. Rebecca Maxey TEL 703-733-2103. R&P, Adv. contact Betty Snyder TEL 703-733-2107. page USD 1,000; 6.75 x 9.25. Circ: 5,000.

DISTRESSED BUSINESS AND REAL ESTATE NEWSLETTER. *see* LAW

DOLAN'S VIRGINIA BUSINESS OBSERVER. *see* LAW

333.33 658.1 USA
HF5430.3
DOLLARS & CENTS OF SHOPPING CENTERS / THE SCORE. Text in English. 2006. triennial. Supplement avail.; back issues avail.; reprints avail. **Document type:** *Report, Trade.*
Formed by the merger of (1961-2006): Dollars & Cents of Shopping Centers (0070-704X); (1992-2006): The SCORE (1076-0156); Which was formerly (until 1992): I C S C Shopping Center Operating Cost Analysis Report; (until 1987): I C S C Shopping Center Operating Cost Report
Indexed: SRI.
—CCC.
Published by: The Urban Land Institute, 1025 Thomas Jefferson St, NW, Ste 500 W, Washington, DC 20007. TEL 202-624-7000, FAX 202-624-7140, customerservice@uli.org.

333.33 USA ISSN 1943-7757
DOMUS. Text in English. 2008 (Oct.). m. USD 24 (effective 2008). **Document type:** *Magazine, Trade.*
Published by: Domus Media LLC, 1999 S Bascom Ave, Ste 1150, Campbell, CA 95008. http://www.odomus.com.

333.33 USA
DREAM HOMES INTERNATIONAL. Text in English. 19??. bi-m. USD 15; USD 6.75 newsstand/cover (effective 2011). **Document type:** *Magazine, Consumer.*
Related titles: Online - full text ed.: free (effective 2011).
Published by: Dream Communications, Inc., PO Box 3049, La Jolla, CA 92038. TEL 619-858-5365, subscriptions@dreamhomesmagazine.com. Pub. Michael Blassis. Adv. contact Andrew Dremak TEL 619-865-1440.

333.33 USA
DREAM HOMES LOS ANGELES. Text in English. 19??. m. **Document type:** *Magazine, Consumer.*
Published by: Dream Communications, Inc., PO Box 3049, La Jolla, CA 92038. TEL 619-858-5365, subscriptions@dreamhomesmagazine.com. Adv. contact Andrew Dremak TEL 619-865-1440.

333.33 USA
DREAM HOMES SAN DIEGO. Text in English. 19??. m. USD 25; USD 3.95 newsstand/cover (effective 2011). adv. **Document type:** *Magazine, Consumer.*
Related titles: Online - full text ed.: free (effective 2011).
Published by: Dream Communications, Inc., PO Box 3049, La Jolla, CA 92038. TEL 619-858-5365, subscriptions@dreamhomesmagazine.com. Pub. Michael Blassis. Adv. contact Andrew Dremak TEL 619-865-1440.

DROIT IMMOBILIER. CONSTRUCTION ET GESTION DE L'IMMEUBLE. FORMULAIRE COMMENTE. *see* LAW

DROIT IMMOBILIER. VENTE D'IMMEUBLE ET OPERATIONS D'AMENAGEMENT. FORMULAIRE COMMENTE. *see* LAW

333.33 USA ISSN 1091-6482
DUPONT REGISTRY: A BUYER'S GALLERY OF FINE HOMES. Text in English. 1995. m. USD 29.95 domestic; USD 49.95 in Canada; USD 89.95 elsewhere; USD 9.80 per issue domestic; USD 12.95 per issue in Canada; USD 14.95 per issue elsewhere (effective 2008). adv. illus. back issues avail. **Document type:** *Magazine, Consumer.* **Description:** Provides information about the luxury real estate, island property, mansions, ranches, estates, waterfront and mountain property and act as intermediary between luxury home sellers and buyers.
Related titles: Online - full text ed.
Published by: DuPont Publishing, Inc., 3051 Tech Dr, Saint Petersburg, FL 33716. TEL 727-573-9339, 800-233-1731, dcsupport@dupontregistry.com, http://www2.dupontregistry.com. Pub. Thomas L Dupont. Adv. contact Rick Parsons.

333.33 GBR
E G RETAIL. (Estates Gazette) Text in English. 2006. bi-m. Included with subscr. to: Estates Gazette. adv. back issues avail. **Document type:** *Magazine, Trade.* **Description:** Dedicated to retail property news and features which is mailed direct to senior retail property professionals and top retail executives across Europe.
Incorporates (2004-2005): Plaza
Related titles: Online - full text ed.
Published by: Estates Gazette Group (Subsidiary of: Reed Business Information Ltd.), 1 Procter St, Holborn, London, WC1V 6EU, United Kingdom. TEL 44-20-79111701, http://www.estatesgazettegroup.com/. Ed. Noella Pio Kivlehan TEL 44-20-79111820. Adv. contact Claire Hopkins TEL 44-20-79111751. page GBP 3,080; trim 210 x 297.

346.04 CZE ISSN 1803-7844
E-MAIL NOVINY BYTY A NEMOVITOSTI. Text in Czech. 200?. w. free. **Document type:** *Newsletter, Trade.*
Published by: Verlag Dashoefer s.r.o., Na Prikope 18, PO Box 756, Prague 1, 11121, Czech Republic. TEL 420-224-197333, FAX 420-224-197555, info@dashofer.cz, http://www.dashofer.cz.

333.33 USA
E. S. P.; Entertainment Specialty Projects. Text in English. 1999. m. USD 274 (effective 2005). adv. bk.rev. illus.; tr.lit. 28 p./no.; back issues avail.; reprints avail. **Document type:** *Newsletter, Trade.* **Description:** Covers all aspects of entertainment and specialty retailing, including downtown redevelopment.
Related titles: Online - full text ed.
Published by: T K O Real Estate Advisory Group, PO Box 2630, Mercerville, NJ 08690. TEL 609-587-6200, 800-732-5856, FAX 609-587-3511. Ed., Pub. Ann O'Neal. R&P Ted Kraus. adv.: B&W page USD 995, color page USD 2,295; trim 11 x 8.5. Circ: 6,000.

333.33 GBR
E S P C WEEKLY LIST. Text in English. 1982. w. adv. illus. **Document type:** *Newspaper.* **Description:** Covers the Edinburgh and Lothian real estate market.
Published by: Edinburgh Solicitors Property Centre, 85 George St, Edinburgh, EH2 3ES, United Kingdom. TEL 44-131-624-8888, FAX 44-131-624-8575, espc@espc.com. Ed., R&P Simon Fairclough. Adv. contact David Carson. Circ: 35,000.

ECO IMMOBILIER. *see* BUSINESS AND ECONOMICS

333.33 CHE
ECONOMIA FONDIARIA. Text in Italian. m.
Published by: Camera Ticinese dell'Economia Fondiaria, Via Dufour 1, Lugano, 6901, Switzerland. TEL 091-529171. Ed. Stelio Pesciallo. Circ: 15,000.

333.33 GBR ISSN 2040-784X
EGYPT REAL ESTATE REPORT. Text in English. 200?. q. EUR 820, USD 1,150 combined subscription (print & email eds.) (effective 2010). **Document type:** *Report, Trade.* **Description:** Provides industry professionals and strategists, sector analysts, business investors, trade associations and regulatory bodies with independent forecasts and competitive intelligence on the real estate and construction industry in Egypt.
Related titles: E-mail ed.
Published by: Business Monitor International Ltd., Senator House, 85 Queen Victoria St, London, EC4V 4AB, United Kingdom. TEL 44-20-72480468, FAX 44-20-72480467, subs@businessmonitor.com.

333.33 NOR ISSN 0803-7345
EIENDOMSMEGLEREN; organ for Norges eiendomsmeglerforbund. Text in Norwegian. 1938. m. adv. **Document type:** *Newsletter, Trade.*
Published by: Norges Eiendomsmeglerforbund/Norwegian Association of Real Estate Agensts, Hansteensgate 2, Oslo, 02583, Norway. TEL 47-22-542080, FAX 47-22-553106, firmapost@nef.no, http://www.nef.no. Ed. Finn Tueter. Adv. contact Lene Joensson.

332.63 DEU
DAS EIGENE HAUS. Text in German. m. EUR 19.20; EUR 1.60 newsstand/cover (effective 2006). adv. **Document type:** *Magazine, Consumer.*
Published by: Quoka Verlag GmbH, Sophienblatt 57, Kiel, 24114, Germany. TEL 49-431-9822919, FAX 49-431-9822955. adv.: B&W page EUR 1,600, color page EUR 1,650. Circ: 30,000 (controlled).

333.338 DNK ISSN 1903-2110
EJENDOM; magasin om byggeri, ejendom og investering. Text in Danish. 2008. 9/yr. DKK 685 (effective 2010). adv. back issues avail. **Document type:** *Magazine, Consumer.* **Description:** Covers real estate markets in Denmark and abroad.
Related titles: Online - full text ed.

Published by: S P Business Media ApS, Ndr Strandvej 119 C, Hellebaek, 3150, Denmark. TEL 45-49-253969, info@spbusinessmedia.dk, http://www.spbusinessmedia.dk. Ed. Kamilla Sevel TEL 45-42-760020. Adv. contact Nikolaja Pfeiffer TEL 45-29-387480. Circ: 3,500.

333.33 DNK ISSN 0013-2896
EJENDOMSMAEGLEREN. Text in Danish. 1934. 11/yr. DKK 1,125 (effective 2009). adv. bk.rev. abstr.; illus.; stat. **Document type:** *Magazine, Trade.*
Formerly (until 1949): Ejendomskommissionaeren; Incorporates (1985-1990): D E H Bladet (0900-8373); Which was formerly (1946-1985): Ejendomshandleren (0900-8276)
Related titles: Online - full text ed.: ISSN 1903-1726.
Published by: Dansk Ejendomsmaeglerforening/Danish Association of Chartered Real Estate Agents, Islands Brygge 43, Copenhagen S, 2300, Denmark. TEL 45-70-250999, FAX 45-32-644599, de@de.dk.

333.33 HKG
ELITE HOMES. Text in Chinese, English. a. HKD 45 per issue in Hong Kong & Macau; USD 11 per issue in Asia, excluding Japan; USD 12 per issue elsewhere (effective 2010). adv. **Document type:** *Magazine, Consumer.* **Description:** Covers the homes, apartments and new architectural projects in the luxury real estate market in Hong Kong, Asia and around the world.
Published by: Edipresse Asia Ltd., 6th Fl., Guardian House, 32 Oi Kwan Rd., Wanchai, Hong Kong. TEL 852-2547-7117, FAX 852-2858-2671, enquiry@edipresse.com.hk, http://www.edipresseasia.com/home.html. Ed. Albert Lo. Adv. contact May Lee. Circ: 45,900.

333.33 GBR ISSN 2042-7360
ENGAGED INVESTOR; the trustee magazine. Text in English. 2004. bi-m. free to qualified personnel (effective 2010). adv. back issues avail. **Document type:** *Magazine, Trade.* **Description:** Provides trustee training and education in all areas of pension fund management.
Related titles: Online - full text ed.: free (effective 2010).
Published by: Newsquest Specialist Media Ltd., 30 Cannon St, London, EC4M 6YJ, United Kingdom. TEL 44-20-76183456, info@newsquestspecialistmedia.com, http://www.newsquestspecialistmedia.com. Ed. Bob Campion TEL 44-20-76183485. Adv. contact Lucy Thomas TEL 44-20-76183435. color page GBP 5,402; trim 239 x 309.

333.33 FRA ISSN 1960-9434
ENTREPRENDRE IMMOBILIER. Text in French. 2007. bi-m. **Document type:** *Magazine, Consumer.*
Published by: Lafont Presse, 53 Rue du Chemin Vert, Boulogne-Billancourt, 92100, France. http://www.lafontpresse.fr.

ENVIRONMENTAL LAW IN REAL ESTATE AND BUSINESS TRANSACTIONS. *see* ENVIRONMENTAL STUDIES

EQUITABLE DISTRIBUTION OF PROPERTY. *see* LAW

333.33 DNK ISSN 1604-5602
ERHVERVSEJENDOM; magasinet for de professionelle erhvervs- og boligaktoerer. Text in Danish; Text occasionally in English. 1997. m. DKK 765 (effective 2009). adv. **Document type:** *Magazine, Trade.*
Formerly (until 2005): Markedsoversigten Erhvervsejendom (1399-0896)
Related titles: Online - full text ed.
Address: Dalgas Boulevard 48, Frederiksberg, 2000, Denmark. TEL 45-38-113477, FAX 45-38-113478. Ed. Carsten Lehrskov TEL 45-31-727472. Adv. contact Bjoern Larsen. page DKK 18,165; 188 x 264.

333.33 FRA ISSN 1955-6969
L'ESSENTIEL DE L'IMMOBILIER. Text in French. 2007. q. EUR 35 for 2 yrs. (effective 2010). **Document type:** *Magazine, Consumer.*
Published by: Lafont Presse, 53 Rue du Chemin Vert, Boulogne-Billancourt, 92100, France. TEL 33-1-46102121.

L'ESSENTIEL, DROIT DE L' IMMOBILIER ET URBANISME. *see* LAW

333.33 GBR ISSN 1366-4360
ESTATE AGENCY NEWS. Text in English. 1986 (Mar.). m. GBP 24.50 (effective 2009). adv. bk.rev. charts; illus. back issues avail. **Document type:** *Newspaper, Trade.* **Description:** Aims to serve residential real estate agents with news, views, and informed commentary.
Indexed: RICS.
—CCC.
Published by: Estates Press Ltd., Keenans Mill, Lord St, St Annes-on-Sea, Lancs FY8 2ER, United Kingdom. FAX 44-1253-783217. Ed. Tony Durkin TEL 44-1253-783215. Adv. contact Adrian Heywood TEL 44-1253-783206. Circ: 16,728.

333.33 GBR ISSN 0260-1001
THE ESTATE AGENT. Text in English. 19??. 10/yr. GBP 100 to non-members; free to members (effective 2009). bk.rev. **Document type:** *Magazine, Trade.* **Description:** Contains commercial and residential lettings and overseas property.
Formerly (until 1980): National Association of Estate Agents. News and Views
Indexed: ISAP, RICS.
Published by: National Association of Estate Agents, Arbon House, 6 Tournament Ct, Edgehill Dr, Warwick, Warwickshire CV34 6LG, United Kingdom. TEL 44-1926-496800, FAX 44-1926-417788, info@nfopp.co.uk, http://www.naea.co.uk.

333.33 AUS
ESTATE AGENT (CAMBERWELL). Abbreviated title: E A. Text in English. 1938. q. adv. bk.rev. abstr.; stat. index, cum.index. **Document type:** *Journal, Trade.* **Description:** Provides information about Real Estate Institute of Victoria.
Former titles (until 2002): Victorian Real Estate Journal (0815-3132); (until 1983): Real Estate and Stock Journal (0034-0669); (until 1938): Real Estate Journal (0815-3140)
Related titles: Online - full text ed.
Indexed: RICS.
Published by: Real Estate Institute of Victoria Ltd., 335 Camberwell Rdt, PO Box 443, Camberwell, VIC 3124, Australia. TEL 61-3-92056666, FAX 61-3-92056699, reiv@reiu.com.au, http://www.reiu.com.au/. adv.: page AUD 2,260; trim 210 x 280. Circ: 2,500 (controlled).

333.33 AUS
ESTATE AGENTS' PRACTICE MANUAL N S W. Text in English. 1991. 2-4/yr.), base vol. plus irreg. updates. looseleaf. AUD 802 (effective 2008). **Document type:** *Handbook/Manual/Guide, Trade.* **Description:** Covers how to conduct an estate agency business, including step-by-step guides to selling property and helps in understanding the practice and legal issues which arise for real estate agents.
Published by: Lawbook Co. (Subsidiary of: Thomson Reuters (Professional) Australia Limited), PO Box 3502, Rozelle, NSW 2039, Australia. TEL 61-2-85877980, 300-304-195, FAX 61-2-85877981, 300-304-196, LTA.Service@thomsonreuters.com, http://www.thomson.com.au.

333.33 USA
ESTATE AND PERSONAL FINANCIAL PLANNING. Text in English. 19??. 3 base vols. plus m. updates. looseleaf. USD 1,407.96 base vol(s). (effective 2010). **Document type:** *Journal, Trade.* **Description:** Covers the laws of wills, trusts, and the various taxes that affect lifetime and testamentary transfers, income of estates, trusts and others.
Published by: Thomson West (Subsidiary of: Thomson Reuters Corp.), 610 Opperman Dr, Eagan, MN 55123. TEL 651-687-7000, 800-344-5008, west.customer.service@thomson.com.

346.04 USA ISSN 2161-2463
K5
THE ESTATE PLANNING & COMMUNITY PROPERTY LAW JOURNAL. Abbreviated title: E P J. Text in English. 2007. s-a. USD 35 (effective 2011). **Document type:** *Journal, Trade.* **Description:** Contains scholarly articles written by national and international experts in the fields of estate planning, community property, and related legal topics.
Published by: Texas Tech University School of Law, MS0004, 1802 Hartford Ave, Lubbock, TX 79409. TEL 806-742-3793, FAX 806-742-1629, info.law@ttu.edu, http://www.law.ttu.edu/. Ed. Thuy B Thai.

333.33 332.04 GBR ISSN 0014-1240
ESTATES GAZETTE; devoted to land, commercial, industrial, residential and agricultural properties. Text in English. 1858. w. GBP 196 domestic; USD 850 foreign; GBP 4.30 newsstand/cover (effective 2009); subscr. includes E G Retail and Estates Gazette Directory. adv. mkt. index. back issues avail. **Document type:** *Magazine, Trade.* **Description:** Provides a comprehensive package of market information, industry news, a monthly directory, and coverage of legal, financial and professional developments.
Incorporates (in 2008): London Offices Market Analysis; Which was formerly: London Office Database. Market Analysis; Property Market Review and Auction Chronicle; Estates Journal
Related titles: Online - full text ed.; ◆ Supplement(s): Estates Gazette Directory.
Indexed: A09, A10, A15, ABIn, B01, B02, B03, B06, B07, B09, B15, B17, B18, BPI, BRD, ELJI, G04, G06, G07, G08, I05, LJI, P34, P48, P51, PQC, RICS, T02, V03, V04, W01, W02, W03, W05.
—BLDSC (3812.538000), CIS. **CCC.**
Published by: Estates Gazette Group (Subsidiary of: Reed Business Information Ltd.), 1 Procter St, Holborn, London, WC1V 6EU, United Kingdom. TEL 44-20-79111701. Ed. Fiona Harnett TEL 44-20-79111800. Adv. contact Claire Hopkins TEL 44-20-79111751. B&W page GBP 1,960, color page GBP 3,080; trim 210 x 297. Circ: 25,500.

333.33029 GBR
ESTATES GAZETTE DIRECTORY. Text in English. m. included with subscr. to: Estates Gazette. **Document type:** *Directory, Trade.* **Description:** Lists names, addresses, and phone numbers of real-estate agents, valuers, surveyors, auctioneers, and other purveyors of related services.
Related titles: ◆ Supplement to: Estates Gazette. ISSN 0014-1240.
Published by: Estates Gazette Group (Subsidiary of: Reed Business Information Ltd.), 1 Procter St, Holborn, London, WC1V 6EU, United Kingdom. TEL 44-20-79111701.

333.3 332.04 GBR ISSN 0951-9289
KD826.A2
ESTATES GAZETTE LAW REPORTS. Abbreviated title: E G L R. Text in English. 1985. 3/yr. GBP 115 per vol. (effective 2009). **Document type:** *Report, Trade.* **Description:** Contains reports on various aspects of real estate law.
Supersedes (in 1985): Estates Gazette Digest of Land and Property Cases (0071-1586)
—CCC.
Published by: Estates Gazette Group (Subsidiary of: Reed Business Information Ltd.), 1 Procter St, Holborn, London, WC1V 6EU, United Kingdom. TEL 44-20-79111701, http://www.estatesgazettegroup.com/. Ed. Hazel Marshall.

ESTATES WEST; the showcase for luxurious living. *see* INTERIOR DESIGN AND DECORATION

ESTATES WEST GOLF LIVING. *see* SPORTS AND GAMES—Ball Games

333.77 FRA ISSN 0183-5912
ETUDES FONCIERES. Text in French. 1978. bi-m. EUR 120 (effective 2008). **Document type:** *Journal, Trade.*
Indexed: FR.
—CCC.
Published by: Association des Etudes Foncieres, 7 av de la Republique, Paris, 75011, France. TEL 33-1-56982000, FAX 33-1-56982001, foncier@wanadoo.fr, http://www.foncier.org.

333.33 NLD ISSN 1871-4633
HD1393.58
EUROPE REAL ESTATE YEARBOOK. Text in English. 2004. a. EUR 65 (effective 2009). adv. **Document type:** *Journal, Trade.* **Description:** Presents analyses of European property funds, round table discussions with investors and developers, interviews with industry leaders, Who's Who and a European Index.
Related titles: CD-ROM ed.: EUR 30 (effective 2009).
Published by: Europe Real Estate Publishers B.V., North Sea Bldg, Gevers Deynootweg 93R, The Hague, 2586 BK, Netherlands. TEL 31-70-3528600, FAX 31-70-3527660, publishers@europe-re.com, http://www.europe-re.com. Pub. Ronald Elward. Adv. contact Michiel Foekens. color page EUR 5,075; trim 175 x 255. Circ: 10,000 (paid and controlled).

346.04 DEU ISSN 2190-8273
▼ **EUROPEAN PROPERTY LAW JOURNAL.** Text in English. forthcoming 2011. 4/yr. EUR 219, USD 329 to institutions; EUR 239, USD 359 combined subscription to institutions (print & online eds.) (effective 2012). **Document type:** *Journal, Academic/Scholarly.*
Related titles: Online - full text ed.: ISSN 2190-8362. forthcoming 2011. EUR 219, USD 329 to institutions (effective 2012).
Published by: Walter de Gruyter GmbH & Co. KG, Genthiner Str 13, Berlin, 10785, Germany. TEL 49-30-260050, FAX 49-30-26005251, info@degruyter.com, http://www.degruyter.de.

333.33 USA ISSN 1065-3635
EUROPEAN REAL ESTATE QUARTERLY. Text in English. 1991. q. free to qualified personnel; USD 65 per issue (effective 2008). adv. back issues avail.; reprints avail. **Document type:** *Newsletter, Trade.* **Description:** Seeks to familiarize institutional investors with the real estate opportunities in European property markets and to help explain the similarities and differences among the U.S. and European markets.
Related titles: ◆ Supplement to: The Institutional Real Estate Letter. ISSN 1044-1662.
Published by: Institutional Real Estate, Inc., 2274 Camino Ramon, San Ramon, CA 94583. TEL 925-244-0500, FAX 925-244-0520, irei@irei.com. Ed. Drew Campbell TEL 925-244-0500 ext 111. Pub. Geoffrey Dohrmann TEL 925-244-0500 ext 117. Adv. contact Brigite Thompson TEL 925-244-0500 ext 128.

333.33 GBR ISSN 0961-9712
EUROPROPERTY; the European property newsletter. Text in English. 1992. s-m. (22/yr.). GBP 795 (effective 2009). adv. **Document type:** *Magazine, Trade.* **Description:** Offers coverage of the pan-European commercial property market, including news and analysis, regional surveys, and profiles of leading property companies.
Formerly: Estates Europe (0967-1862)
Related titles: Online - full text ed.; Supplement(s): Estates Europe Directory.
Indexed: A09, A10, A15, ABIn, B01, B06, B07, B09, CA, P48, P51, PQC, RICS, T02, V03, V04.
—IE. **CCC.**
Published by: Estates Gazette Group (Subsidiary of: Reed Business Information Ltd.), 1 Procter St, Holborn, London, WC1V 6EU, United Kingdom. TEL 44-20-79111700, FAX 44-20-79111900. Ed. Berterik Tencate TEL 44-20-79111800. Adv. contact Claire Hopkins TEL 44-20-79111751. page GBP 2,495; trim 297 x 210.

333.5 336.2 USA ISSN 1945-8770
KF6377.Z9
EVERY LANDLORD'S TAX DEDUCTION GUIDE. Text in English. 2005. a. **Document type:** *Guide, Trade.*
Published by: Nolo Press, Inc., 950 Parker St, Berkeley, CA 94710. TEL 510-549-4660, 800-728-3555, FAX 510-859-0027, 800-645-0895, publicity@nolo.com, http://www.nolo.com.

333.33 USA ISSN 0896-0763
HD251 CODEN: NZSHER
EXECUTIVE GUIDE TO SPECIALISTS IN INDUSTRIAL AND OFFICE REAL ESTATE. Text in English. a. USD 70 (effective 2001). **Document type:** *Directory, Trade.* **Description:** For industrial and office real estate brokers worldwide.
Published by: Society of Industrial and Office Realtors, 1201 New York Ave NW, Ste. 350, Washington, DC 20005-6126. TEL 202-737-1150, lnasvaderani@mail.sior.com. Ed., R&P Linda Nasvaderani TEL 202-737-8783. Circ: 8,000.

333 USA ISSN 0191-2208
HD7287.67.U5
EXPENSE ANALYSIS: CONDOMINIUMS, COOPERATIVES AND PLANNED UNIT DEVELOPMENTS. Variant title: Expense Analysis. Text in English. 1978. a. USD 179.95 to members; USD 359.95 (print or online ed.) (effective 2008). **Document type:** *Journal, Trade.* **Description:** Reports median costs and operating data for condominiums throughout the US.
Supersedes in part (in 1977): Income - Expense Analysis: Apartments, Condominiums and Cooperatives (0161-5262); Which was formerly (until 1975): A Statistical Compilation and Analysis of Actual Income and Expenses Experienced in Apartment Building Operation (0271-4507)
Related titles: Online - full text ed.
Indexed: SRI.
Published by: Institute of Real Estate Management, 430 N Michigan Ave, Chicago, IL 60611. TEL 800-837-0706, FAX 312-661-0217, custserv@irem.org. Ed., R&P Matthew O'Hara.

333.33 USA
EXTRA EQUITY FOR HOMEBUYERS. Text in English. 1984. 3/yr. free (effective 2005). **Document type:** *Magazine, Consumer.* **Description:** Features promotional offers from national advertisers for persons buying a single-family home.
Published by: Smart Marketing Inc., 307 Greens Farms Rd, Greens Farms, CT 06436. TEL 203-254-1690, FAX 203-255-3707, info@smartmarketinginc.com, http://www.smartmarketinginc.com. Ed., Pub. William O'Brien. Adv. contact Bob Griswold. Circ: 235,000 (controlled).

333.33 FRA ISSN 0767-0192
F I A B C I PRESS. (International Real Estate Federation) Text in English. 1985. s-a. free. adv. bk.rev. **Document type:** *Newsletter, Trade.* **Description:** Provides news of the Federation.
Related titles: French ed.; Spanish ed.; German ed.
Published by: International Real Estate Federation (FIABCI), 17 Rue Dumont d'Urville, Paris, 75116, France. TEL 33-1-73795830, FAX 33-1-73795833, info@fiabci.org. Ed. Denis Cox. Adv. contact Laura Pyke. Circ: 5,000.

333.33 640.73 USA ISSN 0274-9882
F M O NEWS. Text in English. 1964. 8/yr. USD 12; USD 1.25 newsstand/cover (effective 2001). adv. **Document type:** *Magazine, Consumer.* **Description:** Reports on the federation's lobbying and legal efforts. Contains lifestyle-oriented information.
Published by: Federation of Manufactured Home Owners of Florida, 4020 Portsmouth Rd, Largo, FL 33771. TEL 727-530-7539, FAX 727-535-9427. Ed. Cheri Borman. Pub., R&P Charity Cicardo. Adv. contact Joyce Stanton TEL 727-530-7530. Circ: 87,000 (paid).

333.33 CHE ISSN 1660-5268
FACILITY MANAGEMENT SOLUTIONS. Text in German. 2003. q. CHF 60 (effective 2007). adv. **Document type:** *Journal, Trade.*
Published by: Robe Verlag AG, Bollackerweg 2, Kuettigen, 5024, Switzerland. TEL 41-62-8274500, FAX 41-62-8274501, info@robe-verlag.ch. adv.: B&W page CHF 2,950, color page CHF 4,270; trim 210 x 297. Circ: 5,520 (paid).

346.04 USA ISSN 1520-3093
FAIR HOUSING COACH. Text in English. 1998. m. USD 267 (effective 2010). **Document type:** *Newsletter, Trade.* **Description:** Provides clear, plain English explanations of the law and helpful case study examples for review and keep on hand.
Related titles: Online - full text ed.: ISSN 1938-3142.
Indexed: A10, V03.

R

—CCC.
Published by: Vendome Group, LLC, 149 5th Ave, New York, NY 10010. TEL 212-812-8420, 800-519-3692, info@vendomegrp.com.

333.33 USA ISSN 1933-2564
FAIRWAY LIVING. Text in English. 2006. q. USD 14.95; USD 5.95 newsstand/cover (effective 2007). adv. **Document type:** *Magazine, Consumer.* **Description:** Comprehensive information guide for people considering relocation, second home opportunities or retirement living.
Published by: Lifestyle Communication, 3102 Welcome Ln, Wilmington, NC 28409. TEL 910-792-5551, FAX 910-392-4551. Pub. Ben Hale. Adv. contact Kevin Miller TEL 888-311-7756. color page USD 10,995; trim 8.5 x 10.875. Circ: 50,000 (paid).

FAMILY HOME; bauen - wohnen - renovieren. *see* INTERIOR DESIGN AND DECORATION

333.33 CHN
FANGDICHAN BAO/REAL ESTATE DEVELOPMENT NEWS. Text in Chinese. 3/w. (Mon., Wed. & Thursday). CNY 222 (effective 2004). adv. **Document type:** *Newspaper, Trade.* **Description:** Covers the issues relating to real estate in the Shanghai regions.
Address: Shijingshan-qu Luguxiao-qu, 10, Liu-Heyuanjia, Beijing, 100040, China. TEL 86-10-68632057. **Dist. by:** China International Book Trading Corp, 35 Chegongzhuang Xilu, Haidian District, PO Box 399, Beijing 100044, China. TEL 86-10-68412045, FAX 86-10-68412023, cibtc@mail.cibtc.com.cn, http://www.cibtc.com.cn.

333.33 CHN ISSN 1009-4563
FANGDICHAN DAOKAN/REAL ESTATE GUIDE. Text in Chinese. 2000. bi-w. CNY 240 (effective 2009). **Document type:** *Magazine, Trade.*
Related titles: Online - full text ed.
Published by: (Guangzhou Shi Fangdichanye Xiehui), Fangdichan Daokan Chubanshe, 701, Dongfeng Dong Lu, Guangdong Gangao Zhongxin 508, Guangzhou, 510080, China. TEL 86-20-62625076, FAX 86-20-62625075. **Co-sponsor:** Zhongguo Fangdichan Xiehui.

333.33 SWE ISSN 0345-3278
FASTIGHETSMAEKLAREN/REAL ESTATE BROKER. Text in Swedish. 1942. q. SEK 25, USD 6. adv. **Document type:** *Trade.*
Published by: Maeklarsamfundet/Swedish Association of Real Estate Brokers, Fack 1487, Solna, 17128, Sweden. Ed. Anders Engstroem. Circ: 9,000 (controlled).

333.33 SWE ISSN 0348-5552
FASTIGHETSTIDNINGEN. Variant title: Svensk Fastighetstidning. Text in Swedish. 1909. 10/yr. SEK 470; SEK 34 per issue (effective 2004). adv. illus. index. back issues avail. **Document type:** *Magazine, Trade.* **Description:** Covers real estate management, financing, legal news and taxation, education, and product news.
Former titles (until 1978): Svensk Fastighetstidning (0346-2064); (until 1948): Sveriges Fastighetstidning; (until 1917): Byggnadsvaerlden. Uppl. B, Fastighetsaegartidningen; (until 1915): Byggnadsvaerlden; (until 1914): Nyhaeter fraan Byggnadsvaerlden
Related titles: Online - full text ed.
Published by: Fastighetsaegarna/Swedish Property Federation, Drottninggatan 33, PO Box 16132, Stockholm, 10323, Sweden. TEL 46-8-6135740, FAX 46-8-6135749, http://www.fastighetsagarna.se. Ed. Per-Yngve Bengtsson TEL 46-8-6135741. Adv. contact Jonas Hedqvist TEL 46-8-55040017. B&W page SEK 21,100, color page SEK 27,400; trim 185 x 270. Circ: 21,300 (controlled).

333.33 SWE ISSN 1102-0024
FASTIGHETSVAERLDEN. Text in Swedish. 1987. 11/yr. SEK 2,250 (effective 2004). adv. back issues avail. **Description:** News about the real estate market in Sweden.
Formerly (until 1988): Ekonomi och Marknad Fastighetsvaerlden (0284-9143)
Related titles: Online - full text ed.
Published by: Tidnings AB Fastighetsvaerlden, Djupdalsvaegen 1, PO Box 343, Stockholm, 19230, Sweden. TEL 46-8-6319020, FAX 46-8-6119515. Ed. Bjoern Rundquist. Adv. contact Jeannine Taengermark TEL 46-8-50325509. page SEK 16,900; 190 x 245. Circ: 2,500.

FEDERAL HOME LOAN BANK OF ATLANTA. ANNUAL REPORT. *see* BUSINESS AND ECONOMICS—Banking And Finance

333.33 USA
FEDERAL INCOME TAXATION OF REAL ESTATE. Text in English. base vol. plus s-a. updates. looseleaf. USD 295 base vol(s). (effective 2009). **Document type:** *Guide, Trade.* **Description:** Offers guidance in sheltering real estate income and creating tax savings for your clients.
Formerly: Robinson Federal Income Taxation of Real Estate
Related titles: Online - full text ed.: USD 525 (effective 2009).
Published by: W G & L Financial Reporting & Management Research (Subsidiary of: R I A), 395 Hudson St, New York, NY 10014. TEL 212-367-6300, 800-950-1216, FAX 212-337-4207, ria.customerservices@thomson.com, http://ria.thomson.com.

333.33 USA ISSN 0191-2704
HG2040.5.U5
FEDERAL NATIONAL MORTGAGE ASSOCIATION. ANNUAL REPORT. Text in English. 1949. a. back issues avail. **Document type:** *Report, Trade.*
Formerly (until 1968): Federal National Mortgage Association. Semi-Annual Report
Related titles: Online - full text ed.: free (effective 2010).
Published by: Federal National Mortgage Association (Fannie Mae), 3900 Wisconsin Ave, NW, Washington, DC 20016. TEL 800-732-6643.

333.33 336.2 USA
FEDERAL TAXES AFFECTING REAL ESTATE. Text in English. 1978. 2 base vols. plus s-a. updates. looseleaf. USD 397 base vol(s). (effective 2008). **Document type:** *Handbook/Manual/Guide, Trade.* **Description:** Fully explains and illustrates the most important federal tax principles applicable to real estate transactions. Comprehensive enough for the tax attorney or CPA, yet written clearly so that the non-tax professional can easily understand. Thourough coverage of the tax consequences of all types of real property transactions.
Related titles: Online - full text ed.
Published by: Matthew Bender & Co., Inc. (Subsidiary of: LexisNexis North America), 1275 Broadway, Albany, NY 12204. TEL 518-487-3000, 800-424-4200, FAX 518-487-3083, international@bender.com, http://bender.lexisnexis.com. Ed. L Rook.

333.33 GBR
FEDERATION OF PRIVATE RESIDENTS ASSOCIATIONS. NEWSLETTER. Text in English. 1973. q. free to members (effective 2009). back issues avail. **Document type:** *Newsletter, Trade.* **Description:** Provides member associations with legal, legislative and lobbying news, and to exchange information and experience.
Published by: Federation of Private Residents Associations, PO Box 10271, Epping, CM16 9DB, United Kingdom. TEL 44-871-2003324, info@fpra.org.uk. Ed. Amanda Gotham.

333.33 USA
THE FIRST-TIME HOME BUYER. Text in English. 2005. bi-m. USD 24 (effective 2007). adv. **Document type:** *Magazine, Consumer.* **Description:** Articles on the home buying process, mortgages, credit and financial fundamentals, helpful tips, and "buyer beware" information.
Related titles: Online - full text ed.: free.
Published by: EOTO Publishing, LLC, PO Box 271648, W Hartford, CT 06127. TEL 860-523-5982, FAX 860-523-5987, http://www.eotopublishing.com/. Ed. Siobhan Becker. Pub. Marton Lindsay. Adv. contact Joseph France. page USD 1,650; trim 8.375 x 10.875. Circ: 10,000 (free).

FLEET STREET REPORTS; cases on intellectual property law. *see* PATENTS, TRADEMARKS AND COPYRIGHTS

333.33 USA
HG2040.5.U5
FLEET'S GUIDE: DEBT & EQUITY SOURCEBOOK. Text in English. 1988. s-a. USD 375; USD 470 with diskette. adv. **Document type:** *Directory.* **Description:** Provides current information regarding sources of financing for income property.
Formerly: Fleet's Guide: Commercial Real Estate Financing Sourcebook (0899-9147)
Published by: KaraCo Publishing Group, 312 Marshall Ave, Laurel, MD 20707. TEL 301-279-6800. Ed. Robert K Hendel. Pub. Damiann Bilotta. adv.: B&W page USD 1,650.

FLORIDA COMMERCIAL LANDLORD - TENANT LAW. *see* LAW

333.33 USA ISSN 1936-8003
FLORIDA COMMERCIAL PROPERTIES. Text in English. 2007. bi-m. USD 52 (effective 2009). adv. **Document type:** *Magazine, Trade.* **Description:** Presents information, developments and opportunities in commercial real estate development in Florida.
Published by: France Publications, Inc., 3500 Piedmont Rd, Ste 415, Atlanta, GA 30305. TEL 404-832-8262, FAX 404-832-8260, scott@francepublications.com, http://www.francepublications.com. Ed. Stephanie Mayhew. Pubs. Jerry France TEL 404-832-8262 ext 111, Scott France. adv.: color page USD 1,300; trim 7.875 x 10.875. Circ: 9,000.

333.33 658 USA
FLORIDA COMMUNITY ASSOCIATION JOURNAL; journal for community association management. Text in English. 1987. m. USD 18 (effective 2005). adv. **Document type:** *Magazine, Trade.* **Description:** News and feature articles dealing with areas of interest to individuals responsible for the management and purchasing activities of condominium, homeowner and co-operative associations.
Formerly: Manager's Report
Published by: Advantage Publishing, 1000 Nix Rd, Little Rock, AR 72211. TEL 800-425-1314, FAX 501-280-9233, http://www.adpub.com. Ed. Terry McMurry. Circ: 22,000 (paid and controlled).

FLORIDA CONDOMINIUM LAW MANUAL. *see* LAW

FLORIDA MORTGAGE BROKER. *see* BUSINESS AND ECONOMICS—Banking And Finance

333.33 USA ISSN 0887-3208
FLORIDA REAL ESTATE AND DEVELOPMENT UPDATE; news and background information about Florida real estate, construction, development and building activities. Text in English. 1986. m. USD 100; USD 135 foreign. **Document type:** *Magazine.*
Published by: Mentor Communications, PO Box 290, Manhasset, NY 11030. TEL 516-741-8877, FAX 516-741-3131. Ed. H L Boerner. Pub. Hank Boerner. Circ: 3,000 (paid).

333.33 340 USA
FLORIDA REAL ESTATE TRANSACTIONS (CHARLOTTESVILLE). Text in English. 1982. 6 base vols. plus irreg. updates. looseleaf. USD 1,647 base vol(s). (effective 2008). **Document type:** *Report, Trade.* **Description:** Provides authoritative and comprehensive coverage of issues relevant to a real estate practice.
Related titles: Online - full text ed.
Published by: Michie Company (Subsidiary of: LexisNexis North America), 701 E Water St, Charlottesville, VA 22902. TEL 434-972-7600, 800-446-3410, FAX 434-972-7677, customer.support@lexisnexis.com, http://www.michie.com. Eds. Ralph E Boyer, William H Ryan.

333.33 USA
FLORIDA REAL ESTATE TRANSACTIONS (NEW YORK). Text in English. 1975. 6 base vols. plus irreg. updates. looseleaf. USD 1,647 base vol(s). (effective 2008). **Document type:** *Report, Trade.* **Description:** Covers issues on real estate practice including sales contracts, deeds, priorities and recording, special titles, mortgages, liens, landlord and tenant, zoning, cooperatives, condominiums, land use and environmental regulation.
Related titles: CD-ROM ed.
Published by: Matthew Bender & Co., Inc. (Subsidiary of: LexisNexis North America), 1275 Broadway, Albany, NY 12204. TEL 518-487-3000, 800-424-4200, FAX 518-487-3083, international@bender.com, http://bender.lexisnexis.com.

333.33 USA ISSN 0199-5839
FLORIDA REALTOR; the business magazine of Florida real estate. Text in English. 1925. m. (11/yr.). USD 19.95 domestic; USD 41 foreign (effective 2007). adv. software rev. charts; illus.; stat.; tr.lit. 64 p./no.; back issues avail. **Document type:** *Magazine, Trade.* **Description:** Provides real estate professionals with a useful combination of practical information, trend analysis and insights into the industry.
Related titles: Fax ed.; Online - full text ed.; Supplement(s): Real Estate Solutions Guide.
Published by: Florida Association of Realtors, PO Box 725025, Orlando, FL 32872-5025. TEL 407-438-1400, FAX 407-438-1411. Ed., R&P Doug Damerst. Pub. Jeffrey Zipper. Adv. contact Joe Bono. B&W page USD 3,740, color page USD 4,680. Circ: 150,000 (paid).

FLORIDA RESIDENTIAL LANDLORD - TENANT MANUAL. *see* LAW

333.33 346.04 USA ISSN 1942-6283
FORECLOSURESMASS MONTHLY. Text in English. 2004. m. USD 599.64 (effective 2008). **Document type:** *Newsletter, Trade.* **Description:** Features advice and tips about investing in the foreclosure market and updates in Massachusetts real estate law.
Published by: ForeclosuresMass Corp., 1257 Worchester Rd, #254, Framingham, MA 01701. http://www.foreclosuresmass.com. Ed. Jeremy Shapiro.

333.33 DEU ISSN 1439-7242
FORUM WOHNEIGENTUM. Text in German. 1946. bi-m. EUR 64 to non-members; EUR 14 newsstand/cover to non-members (effective 2009). bk.rev. stat. index. **Document type:** *Journal, Trade.*
Former titles (until 2000): I D - Informationsdienst und Mitteilungsblatt des V H W (0942-8437); Which incorporated (1984-1989): So Planen und Bauen (0177-0993); (until 1989): Deutsches Volksheimstaettenwerk. Informationsdienst (0178-7314)
Published by: V H W - Bundesverband fuer Wohnen und Stadtentwicklung e.V., Fritschestr 27-28, Berlin, 10585, Germany. TEL 49-30-3904730, FAX 49-30-390473190, bund@vhw.de. Circ: 4,800.

333.33 GBR ISSN 1751-6846
FRENCH PROPERTY NEWS. Text in English. 1989. m. GBP 32 (effective 2009). adv. bk.rev. stat.; tr.lit. back issues avail. **Document type:** *Magazine, Consumer.* **Description:** Matters relating to the purchase of property in France.
Published by: Archant Life Ltd (Subsidiary of: Archant Group), Archant House, Oriel Rd, Cheltenham, Glos GL50 1BB, United Kingdom. TEL 44-1242-216050, http://www.archantlife.co.uk. Ed. Karen Tait TEL 44-20-79783493. Adv. contact Justin Farnan TEL 44-1242-264760. page GBP 1,750; trim 210 x 297.

332.6 333.33 USA
HG5095
FREQUENTLY ASKED QUESTIONS ABOUT R E I TS. Text in English. 1974. irreg. USD 4 per issue (effective 2011). illus. **Document type:** *Handbook/Manual/Guide, Trade.* **Description:** Highlights the fundamentals of REIT investing, while providing industry information designed to introduce important concepts such as types of REITs, management structures and measures of financial performance.
Former titles R E I T Basic Facts; (until 1995): R E I T Fact Book (0095-1374)
Related titles: Online - full text ed.
Published by: National Association of Real Estate Investment Trusts, Inc., 1875 I St, NW, Ste 600, Washington, DC 20006. TEL 202-739-9400, FAX 202-739-9401.

333.33 SGP
FRONTIERS OF REAL ESTATE FINANCE. Text in English. 2003. irreg., latest vol.1, 2003. price varies. **Document type:** *Monographic series, Academic/Scholarly.*
Published by: World Scientific Publishing Co. Pte. Ltd., 5 Toh Tuck Link, Singapore, 596224, Singapore. TEL 65-6466-5775, FAX 65-6467-7667, wspc@wspc.com.sg, http://www.worldscientific.com. Ed. Mei J P. **Dist. by:** World Scientific Publishing Co., Inc., 27 Warren St, Ste 401-402, Hackensack, NJ 07601. TEL 201-487-9655, 800-227-7562, FAX 201-487-9656, 888-977-2665, wspc@wspc.com; World Scientific Publishing Ltd., 57 Shelton St, London WC2H 9HE, United Kingdom. TEL 44-207-8360888, FAX 44-207-8362020, sales@wspc.co.uk.

FRUGAL NEWS. *see* CONSUMER EDUCATION AND PROTECTION

332.63 USA ISSN 1947-4873
FUND TRACKER. Variant title: Institutional Real Estate Fund Tracker. Text in English. 2008. q. USD 1,200 (effective 2009). adv. back issues avail.; reprints avail. **Document type:** *Newsletter, Trade.* **Description:** Provides an overview of fund-raising activity in the private equity real estate arena.
Published by: Institutional Real Estate, Inc., 2274 Camino Ramon, San Ramon, CA 94583. TEL 925-244-0500, FAX 925-244-0520, irei@irei.com. Eds. Geoffrey Dohrmann TEL 925-244-0500 ext 117, Larry Gray TEL 925-244-0500 ext 119. Adv. contact Brigite Thompson TEL 925-244-0500 ext 128.

333.33 346.04 FRA ISSN 1957-6137
G F N P (ENGLISH EDITION). (Guide du Futur et Nouveau Proprietaire) Text in English. 2007. a. **Document type:** *Handbook/Manual/Guide, Trade.*
Published by: Guide du Futur et Nouveau Proprietaire (G F N P), 18 Rue Sainte Cecile, Toulouse, 31100, France. FAX 08-20300040.

346.04 333.33 FRA ISSN 1769-843X
G F N P (NATIONAL EDITION). (Guide du Futur et Nouveau Proprietaire) Text in French. 2004. a. EUR 12.90 (effective 2007). **Document type:** *Trade.*
Published by: Guide du Futur et Nouveau Proprietaire (G F N P), 18 Rue Sainte Cecile, Toulouse, 31100, France. FAX 08-20300040.

333.33 DEU ISSN 0945-9243
➤ **G U G AKTUELL.** (Grundstuecksmarkt und Grundstueckswert) Text in German. 1994. 6/yr. EUR 162; EUR 28 newsstand/cover (effective 2004). **Document type:** *Journal, Academic/Scholarly.*
Related titles: ◆ Supplement to: Grundstuecksmarkt und Grundstueckswert. ISSN 0938-0175.
Published by: Hermann Luchterhand Verlag GmbH (Subsidiary of: Wolters Kluwer Deutschland GmbH), Heddesdorfer Str 31, Neuwied, 56564, Germany. TEL 49-2631-8012222, FAX 49-2631-8012223, info@luchterhand.de, http://www.luchterhand.de.

333.33 USA ISSN 1934-8169
GEORGIA COMMERCIAL PROPERTIES. Text in English. 2006. bi-m. USD 50 (effective 2009). adv. **Document type:** *Magazine, Trade.* **Description:** Provides informarion on commercial real estate and shows who is doing what, when and where in Georgia.
Published by: France Publications, Inc., 3500 Piedmont Rd, Ste 415, Atlanta, GA 30305. TEL 404-832-8262, FAX 404-832-8260, scott@francepublications.com, http://www.francepublications.com. Ed. Kevin Jeselnik. Pubs. Jerry France TEL 404-832-8262 ext 111, Scott France.

346.043 USA
GEORGIA REAL ESTATE FORMS. Text in English. 1987. 3 base vols. plus irreg. updates. looseleaf. USD 514 base vol(s). (effective 2008). Supplement avail. **Document type:** *Handbook/Manual/Guide, Trade.* **Description:** Covers all eventualities of real estate law with detailed, point-by-point treatment of agreements relating to transfers of real property; deeds, leases and other instruments of conveyance; financing of real property; and miscellaneous forms.
Related titles: Diskette ed.
Published by: Michie Company (Subsidiary of: LexisNexis North America), 701 E Water St, Charlottesville, VA 22902. TEL 434-972-7600, 800-446-3410, FAX 434-972-7677, customer.support@lexisnexis.com, http://www.michie.com. Eds. Deborah E Glass, Russell S Grove Jr.

GEORGIA REAL ESTATE LAW LETTER; monthly updates on Georgia real estate law developments. *see* LAW

GEORGIA REAL ESTATE LICENSING AND APPRAISER LAWS AND REGULATIONS ANNOTATED. *see* LAW

333.1 USA ISSN 0433-6070
GEORGIA REALTOR. Text in English. m.
Published by: Georgia Association of Realtors, 3200 Presidential Drive, Atlanta, GA 30340-3981. TEL 770-451-1831, FAX 770-458-6992.

333.33 NLD ISSN 1872-7301
GERMANY REAL ESTATE YEARBOOK. Text in English. 2007. a. EUR 45 (effective 2008). adv.
Published by: Europe Real Estate Publishers B.V., North Sea Bldg, Gevers Deynootweg 93R, The Hague, 2586 BK, Netherlands. TEL 31-70-3528600, FAX 31-70-3527660, publishers@europe-re.com, http://www.europe-re.com. adv.: page EUR 2,700.

GIANT (OAK BROOK). *see* BUILDING AND CONSTRUCTION

333.33 USA
GLOBAL REAL ESTATE MONITOR. Text in English. 2006. m. free. **Document type:** *Newsletter, Trade.* **Description:** Focuses on U.S. and international commercial real estate industry topics, ranging from economic and market conditions and trends to discussions with global commercial real estate professionals.
Media: E-mail.
Published by: Penton Media, Inc., 6151 Powers Ferry Rd, Ste 200, Atlanta, GA 30339. TEL 770-955-2500, FAX 770-618-0204, information@penton.com, http://www.pentonmedia.com.

333.33 USA
HD1387
GLOBAL REAL ESTATE NEWS; the voice of the international real estate industry. Text in English. 1978. bi-m. USD 65 (effective 2002). adv. **Document type:** *Journal, Trade.*
Former titles: Appraisal Review and Mortgage Underwriting Journal (1041-1585); Appraisal Review Journal (0195-4407)
Published by: International Real Estate Institute, 1224 N Nokomis N E, Alexandria, MN 56308-5072. TEL 320-763-4648, FAX 320-763-9290. Ed., Pub., R&P, Adv. contact Robert Johnson. Circ: 10,000.

GODA GRANNAR. *see* BUILDING AND CONSTRUCTION

GOLF DEVELOPMENTS. *see* SPORTS AND GAMES—Ball Games

GOLF ESTATE; wonen & reizen. *see* SPORTS AND GAMES—Ball Games

333.33 USA
GORDON OFFICE MARKET REPORT. Text in English. q.
Published by: Edward S. Gordon Co., Inc., 200 Park Ave, New York, NY 10166. TEL 212-984-8000.

332.63 USA ISSN 2162-3007
▼ **GOVERNMENT DEAL FUNDING FOR REAL ESTATE INVESTORS AND DEVELOPERS.** Text in English. 2010. m. **Document type:** *Government.*
Published by: Government Deal Funding, Llc., 440B E Squantum St N, Quincy, MA 02171. TEL 617-275-4307, http://www.governmentdealfunding.com/.

333.33 SVK ISSN 1337-0758
GRAND. Text in Slovak. 2006. m. **Document type:** *Magazine, Trade.*
Published by: Argus Slovakia, s.r.o., Zadunajska Cesta 6, Bratislava 5, 851 01, Slovakia. TEL 421-2-63530312, FAX 421-2-63530314, argusslovakia@argusslovakia.sk, http://www.argusslovakia.sk.

332.85 SVK ISSN 1337-1061
GRAND REALITY. Text in Slovak. 2006. 16/yr. EUR 0.66 per issue domestic (effective 2009). **Document type:** *Magazine, Trade.*
Published by: Grand Princ Slovakia, s.r.o., Jozefska 19, Bratislava, 811 06, Slovakia. TEL 421-257-203050, FAX 421-257-203051, bratislava@grandprinc.sk, http://www.grandprinc.sk.

659 CZE
GRAND REALITY. Text in Czech. 2002. 16/yr. CZK 216 (effective 2009). adv. **Document type:** *Magazine, Trade.*
Related titles: Online - full text ed.: ISSN 1802-3401.
Published by: Grand Princ s.r.o., Vinohradska 138, Prague 3, 130 00, Czech Republic. TEL 420-272-107111, FAX 420-272-107000, grandprinc@grandprinc.cz, http://www.grandprinc.cz. adv.: page CZK 57,000; trim 225 x 280. Circ: 110,000 (paid and controlled).

333.3 SVK ISSN 1337-0766
GRAND RESIDENCE. Text in Slovak. 2006. bi-m. **Document type:** *Magazine, Trade.*
Published by: Argus Slovakia, s.r.o., Zadunajska Cesta 6, Bratislava 5, 851 01, Slovakia. TEL 421-2-63530312, FAX 421-2-63530314, argusslovakia@argusslovakia.sk, http://www.argusslovakia.sk.

333.3 917 USA ISSN 1935-7079
GREATER LOUISVILLE RELOCATION GUIDE. Text in English. 1989. a. free (effective 2007). adv. **Document type:** *Magazine, Consumer.* **Description:** Contains real estate, event, employment and business information for people relocating to or visiting Louisville, Kentucky.
Published by: Home Builders Association of Louisville, Inc., 1000 N Hurstbourne Pkwy, Louisville, KY 40223-6036. TEL 502-429-6000, FAX 502-429-6036, newhomes@hbal.com, http://www.hbal.com. Ed. Brian Miller.

333.33 USA
GREATER PHILADELPHIA, SOUTHERN NEW JERSEY AND DELAWARE OFFICE BUILDINGS. Text in English. 19??. a. **Document type:** *Magazine, Trade.* **Description:** Annual review of Greater Philadelphia, southern New Jersey and Delaware office buildings.
Formerly: Greater Philadelphia and Southern New Jersey Office Buildings
Published by: Yale Robbins, Inc., 31 E 28th St, New York, NY 10016. TEL 212-683-5700, FAX 212-497-0017, mrosupport@mrofficespace.com.

GREATER PHOENIX BLUE CHIP ECONOMIC FORECAST. *see* BUSINESS AND ECONOMICS—Economic Situation And Conditions

332.72 DEU ISSN 0941-5203
GRUND GENUG; lifestyle, people & real estate. Text in German. 1988. q. EUR 5 newsstand/cover (effective 2010). adv. **Document type:** *Magazine, Consumer.*
Published by: Grund Genug Verlag und Werbe GmbH, Stadthausbruecke 5, Hamburg, 20355, Germany. TEL 49-40-36131140, FAX 49-40-36131144. Ed. Michaela Rickmers. Pub. Christian Voelkers. Adv. contact Monika Schiffmann. Circ: 85,800 (paid and controlled).

DAS GRUNDEIGENTUM; Zeitschrift fuer die gesamte Grundstuecks-, Haus- und Wohnungswirtschaft. *see* HOUSING AND URBAN PLANNING

333.33 DEU ISSN 0938-0175
GRUNDSTUECKSMARKT UND GRUNDSTUECKSWERT; Zeitschrift fuer Immobilienwirtschaft, Bodenpolitik und Wertermittlung. Abbreviated title: G u G. Text in German. 1990. bi-m. EUR 194; EUR 44 newsstand/cover (effective 2011). adv. **Document type:** *Journal, Trade.*
Related titles: ◆ Supplement(s): G u G Aktuell. ISSN 0945-9243.
Indexed: IBR, IBZ.
Published by: Hermann Luchterhand Verlag GmbH (Subsidiary of: Wolters Kluwer Deutschland GmbH), Heddesdorfer Str 31, Neuwied, 56564, Germany. TEL 49-2631-8012222, FAX 49-2631-8012223, info@luchterhand.de, http://www.luchterhand.de. Adv. contact Marcus Kipp. Circ: 3,900 (paid and controlled).

333.33 USA
GUARANTOR (CHICAGO). Text in English. 1956. q. tr.lit. index. back issues avail. **Document type:** *Journal, Trade.*
Published by: Chicago Title and Trust Co., 171 N Clark St, Chicago, IL 60601. TEL 312-223-2000. Ed. Stephen Flanagan. Circ: 70,000.

333.33 ESP
GUIA DEL COMPRADOR DE CASAS. Text in Spanish. 1997. m. **Document type:** *Magazine, Consumer.* **Description:** Provides a full survey of the property market in highly detailed tables.
Published by: Editorial Moredi S.L., Hiedra no 2-C, Madrid, 28036, Spain. TEL 34-91-7339713, FAX 34-91-7339673, administrador@moredi.com, http://www.moredi.com. Ed. Marta Lopez. Pub. Ignacio de Lucas. Circ: 10,000 (paid and controlled).

333.33 ITA ISSN 1827-661X
GUIDA MUTUI. Text in Italian. 1999. m. **Document type:** *Magazine, Consumer.*
Published by: Terra Nova Editore, Viale Regina Margherita 269, Rome, 00198, Italy. TEL 39-0644080301, FAX 39-06-44080666, direzione@terranovaeditore.it, http://webtest.terranovaeditore.net.

346.04 FRA ISSN 1161-1790
LE GUIDE DU LOGEMENT ET DE L'HABITATION. Text in French. 1991. base vol. plus q. updates. EUR 125 base vol(s).; EUR 119 updates (effective 2009).
Published by: E S F Editeur (Subsidiary of: Reed Business Information France), 2 rue Maurice Hartmann, Issy-les-Moulineaux, 92133 Cedex, France. TEL 33-1-46294629, FAX 33-1-46294633, info@esf-editeur.fr.

332.63 346.052 NLD ISSN 2211-9590
▼ **GUIDE TO GLOBAL REAL ESTATE INVESTMENT TRUSTS.** Text in English. 2010. a. EUR 265 (effective 2011).
Published by: Kluwer Law International (Subsidiary of: Aspen Publishers, Inc.), PO Box 316, Alphen aan den Rijn, 2400 AH, Netherlands. TEL 31-172-641562, FAX 31-172-641555, sales@kluwerlaw.com, http://www.kluwerlaw.com.

GUIDE TO MARYLAND ZONING DECISIONS. *see* LAW

GULF COAST BUSINESS REVIEW. *see* BUSINESS AND ECONOMICS

333.33 USA
GULFSHORE HOMEBUYER. Text in English. q. adv. **Document type:** *Magazine, Consumer.* **Description:** Targets consumers who are seeking information about buying, building, remodeling, financing and furnishing homes in Florida.
Published by: Gulfshore Media, Inc. (Subsidiary of: CurtCo Robb Media LLC.), 9051 Tamiami Trail N, Ste. 202, Naples, FL 34108. TEL 239-449-4111, FAX 941-594-9986. adv.: B&W page USD 3,390, color page USD 4,240; trim 8.125 x 10.75.

333.33 CHN ISSN 1674-3695
GUOTU ZIYUAN XINXIHUA. Text in Chinese. 2001. bi-m. CNY 54 (effective 2004). **Document type:** *Magazine, Government.*
Related titles: Online - full text ed.
Published by: Zhonghua Renmin Gongheguo. Guotu Ziyuanbu Xinxi Zhongxin/P.R.C. Ministry of Land and Resources, 64, Funei Dajie, Beijing, 100812, China. TEL 86-10-66558621, FAX 86-10-66558621.

333.33 SVK ISSN 1335-8200
H N REALITY. (Hospodarske Noviny) Text in Slovak. 1999. m. adv. **Document type:** *Magazine, Trade.*
Published by: Ecopress, a.s., Seberiniho 1, Bratislava, 820 07, Slovakia. TEL 421-2-48238100, FAX 421-2-48238104, predplatne@ecopress.sk, http://ecopress.hnonline.sk. Pub. Milan Mokran. adv.: page EUR 3,286.20; trim 210 x 297.

333.33 USA ISSN 1079-7068
HABITAT (NEW YORK CITY EDITION). Text in English. 1982. 11/yr. USD 34.95 (effective 1998). adv. charts; illus.; stat. back issues avail. **Document type:** *Magazine, Trade.*
Formerly (until 1994): N Y Habitat (0745-0893); Incorporates: Loft Letter
Indexed: E04, E05, SUSA.
Published by: Carol Group Ltd., 928 Broadway, New York, NY 10010. TEL 212-505-2030, FAX 212-254-6795. Ed. Carol J Ott. Circ: 10,000 (controlled).

333.33 USA
HABITAT (REGIONAL EDITION). Text in English. 11/yr. USD 34.95 (effective 1998). back issues avail. **Document type:** *Magazine, Trade.*
Published by: Carol Group Ltd., 928 Broadway, New York, NY 10010. TEL 212-505-2030, FAX 212-254-6795. Ed. Carol J Ott. Circ: 8,000 (controlled).

HAMPTONS COTTAGES & GARDENS. *see* GARDENING AND HORTICULTURE

333.33 340 GBR
HANDBOOK OF DILAPIDATIONS. Text in English. 1992. base vol. plus updates 3/yr. looseleaf. GBP 532 base vol(s). domestic; EUR 703 base vol(s). in Europe; USD 915 base vol(s). elsewhere (effective 2011). **Document type:** *Handbook/Manual/Guide, Trade.* **Description:** Provides extensive coverage of the obligations and responsibilities for the repair of rented properties.
Published by: Sweet & Maxwell Ltd. (Subsidiary of: Thomson Reuters Corp.), 100 Avenue Rd, London, NW3 3PF, United Kingdom. TEL 44-20-73937000, FAX 44-20-74491144, sweetandmaxwell.customer.services@thomson.com. **Subscr. to:** PO Box 1000, Andover SP10 9AF, United Kingdom. TEL 44-20-73938051, sweetandmaxwell.international.queries@thomson.com.

333.33 340 GBR
HANDBOOK OF LAND COMPENSATION; law and valuation. Variant title: Hayward Handbook of Land Compensation. Text in English. 1995. base vol. plus updates 2/yr. looseleaf. GBP 530 base vol(s). domestic; EUR 700 base vol(s). in Europe; USD 911 base vol(s). elsewhere (effective 2011). **Document type:** *Handbook/Manual/Guide, Trade.* **Description:** Examines the law on all aspects of compensation in detail, with emphasis on the valuation issues.
Published by: Sweet & Maxwell Ltd. (Subsidiary of: Thomson Reuters Corp.), 100 Avenue Rd, London, NW3 3PF, United Kingdom. TEL 44-20-73937000, FAX 44-20-74491144, sweetandmaxwell.customer.services@thomson.com. **Subscr. to:** PO Box 1000, Andover SP10 9AF, United Kingdom. TEL 44-20-73938051, sweetandmaxwell.international.queries@thomson.com.

333.33 340 GBR
HANDBOOK OF RENT REVIEW. Text in English. 1981. base vol. plus updates 2/yr. looseleaf. GBP 573 base vol(s). domestic; EUR 757 base vol(s). in Europe; USD 985 base vol(s). elsewhere (effective 2011). **Document type:** *Handbook/Manual/Guide, Trade.* **Description:** Gives a complete guide to the relevant law and practice affecting rent review negotiations, arbitrations and determinations.
Related titles: CD-ROM ed.: GBP 1,833.60 domestic to institutions; EUR 2,018 in Europe to institutions; USD 2,626 elsewhere to institutions (effective 2011).
Published by: Sweet & Maxwell Ltd. (Subsidiary of: Thomson Reuters Corp.), 100 Avenue Rd, London, NW3 3PF, United Kingdom. TEL 44-20-73937000, FAX 44-20-74491144, sweetandmaxwell.customer.services@thomson.com. **Subscr. to:** PO Box 1000, Andover SP10 9AF, United Kingdom. TEL 44-20-73938051, sweetandmaxwell.international.queries@thomson.com.

333.33 340 GBR
HANDBOOK OF RESIDENTIAL TENANCIES. Text in English. 2001. base vol. plus updates 3/yr. looseleaf. GBP 433 base vol(s). domestic; EUR 572 base vol(s). in Europe; USD 745 base vol(s). elsewhere (effective 2011). **Document type:** *Handbook/Manual/Guide, Trade.* **Description:** Provides full coverage of the law and practice of residential tenancies, both long leases and rental tenancies, offering procedural guidance and "how-to" information to steer practitioners through all aspects of residential tenancy work.
Published by: Sweet & Maxwell Ltd. (Subsidiary of: Thomson Reuters Corp.), 100 Avenue Rd, London, NW3 3PF, United Kingdom. TEL 44-20-73937000, FAX 44-20-74491144, sweetandmaxwell.customer.services@thomson.com. Eds. Charles Boston, Del Williams, James Driscoll. **Subscr. to:** PO Box 1000, Andover SP10 9AF, United Kingdom. TEL 44-20-73938051, sweetandmaxwell.international.queries@thomson.com.

333.33 DEU
HAUS & GRUND (BADEN). Text in German. m. adv. **Document type:** *Magazine, Trade.*
Published by: Haus & Grund Baden, Lessingstrasse 10, Karlsruhe, 76135, Germany. TEL 49-721-8312810, FAX 49-721-8312812, info@haus-und-grund-baden.de, http://www.haus-und-grund-baden-esg.de. Ed. Anita Eulenbach. adv.: B&W page EUR 2,268, color page EUR 2,868.

333.33 DEU
HAUS & GRUND (BREMEN). Text in German. 1925. m. EUR 4.50 per issue to members; EUR 5.95 per issue to non-members (effective 2010). **Document type:** *Newspaper, Trade.*
Former titles (until 1995): Haus & Grund in Deutschland; (until 1993): Der Haus- und Grundeigentuemer; (until 1986): Bremische Hausbesitzerzeitung
Published by: Haus & Grund Landesverband Bremen e.V., Am Dobben 3, Bremen, 28203, Germany. TEL 49-421-368040, FAX 49-421-3680488, information@hug-hb.de. Ed. Bernd Richter TEL 49-421-3680410.

333.33 DEU
HAUS & GRUND (ESSEN); das Hauseigentuemer-Magazin im Ruhrgebiet. Text in German. m. EUR 3 newsstand/cover (effective 2010). adv. **Document type:** *Magazine, Trade.*
Formerly (until 2000): Westdeutscher Tuermer
Published by: Haus- Wohungs- und Grundeigentuemerverband Ruhr e.V., Huyssenallee 50, Essen, 45128, Germany. TEL 49-201-810660, FAX 49-201-8106644, gmbh@hug-essen.de. Ed. Christian Eissing. Adv. contact Anita Eulenbach. Circ: 32,632 (paid and controlled).

333.33 DEU
HAUS & GRUND (WESTFALEN). Text in German. 1976. 10/yr.
Former titles (until 1997): Haus & Grund (Ausgabe fuer Westfalen); (until 1997): Haus- und Grund in Deutschland (Ausgabe fuer Westfalen) (0944-2219); (until 1992): Haus- und Grundeigentuemer (0343-8821)
Published by: Haus & Grund Westfalen, Haldener Str 41, Hagen, 58095, Germany. TEL 49-2331-787180, FAX 49-2331-787172, ludger.baumeister@t-online.de. Ed. Ludger Baumeister.

333.33 AUT
HAUS UND EIGENTUM. Text in German. 1888. m. EUR 100 membership (effective 2005). **Document type:** *Newspaper, Consumer.*
Formerly: Hausbesitzer Zeitung
Published by: Zentralverband der Hausbesitzer Wiens und seiner Organisationen, Landesgerichtsstr 6, Vienna, W 1010, Austria. TEL 43-222-4063318, FAX 43-222-4065349, office@zvhausbesitzer.at, http://www.zvhausbesitzer.at. Ed. Friedrich Noszek. Circ: 12,000.

333.33 DEU ISSN 1860-8450
HAUS UND GRUND (AUSGABE HESSEN). Text in German. 1948. m. EUR 18; EUR 1.50 newsstand/cover (effective 2010). adv. 28 p./no. 4 cols./p.; **Document type:** *Magazine, Trade.*

R

Formerly (until 2005): Haus- und Grundbesitz (1430-7308)
Published by: (Landesverband der Hessischen Haus-, Wohnungs- und Grundeigentuemer e.V.), Haus und Grund Hessen e.V., Grueneburgweg 64, Frankfurt Am Main, 60322, Germany. TEL 49-69-729458, FAX 49-69-172635, hughessen@arcor.de, http://www.haus-und-grund-hessen.de. Ed. Guenther Belz. Adv. contact Christa Neidhoefer. B&W page EUR 1,381, color page EUR 1,993; 210 x 297. Circ: 20,567 (paid and controlled).

333.33 DEU
HAUS UND GRUND AKTUELL. Text in German. m. EUR 6 newsstand/cover (effective 2008). adv. **Document type:** *Magazine, Trade.*
Published by: Aktuell-Verlag Modrow GmbH, Martinistr 5, Herten-Westerholt, 45701, Germany. TEL 49-209-961920, FAX 49-209-9619220, info@aktuell-verlag-westerholt.de, http://www.aktuell-verlag-westerholt.de. Ed., Pub. Gerhard Modrow. adv.: B&W page EUR 1,400, color page EUR 2,150; trim 210 x 297. Circ: 9,604 (controlled).

333.5 DEU
HAUS UND GRUND NIEDERSACHSEN. Text in German. 1992. m. EUR 1.50 newsstand/cover (effective 2010). adv. **Document type:** *Newspaper, Consumer.*
Published by: Winkler & Stenzel GmbH, Schulze-Delitzsch-Str. 35, Burgwedel, 30938, Germany. TEL 49-5139-89990, FAX 49-5139-899950, info@winkler-stenzel.de, http://www.winkler-stenzel.de. adv.: B&W page EUR 4,810, color page EUR 6,160; trim 280 x 410. Circ: 40,000 (paid and controlled).

333.33 DEU
HAUS UND GRUND RHEINLAND-PFALZ. Text in German. 1915. m. adv. **Document type:** *Magazine, Trade.*
Published by: Haus und Grund Rheinland-Pfalz e.V., Kaiserstr 9, Mainz, 55116, Germany. TEL 49-6131-619720, FAX 49-6131-619868, info@haus-und-grund-rlp.de, http://www.haus-und-grund-rlp.de.

333.33 DEU
HAUS UND GRUND SAARLAND. Text in German. 1948. m. adv. **Document type:** *Magazine, Trade.*
Published by: Haus und Grund Saarland e.V., Bismarckstr 52, Saarbruecken, 66121, Germany. TEL 49-681-668370, FAX 49-681-68035, info@haus-und-grund-saarland.de, http://www.haus-und-grund-saarland.de.

333.33 CHE
HAUSBESITZER. Text in German. m. **Document type:** *Newspaper, Trade.*
Address: Leimenstr 3, Basel, 4051, Switzerland. TEL 41-61-2691616, FAX 41-61-2616255. Ed. Andreas Zappala. Circ: 18,000.

333.3 USA ISSN 0895-8556
HAWAII REALTOR JOURNAL. Text in English. m. USD 24 (effective 2000). adv. **Document type:** *Magazine, Trade.*
Published by: P M P Company, Ltd., 94-539 Puahi St., Waipahu, HI 96797-4208. TEL 808-621-8200, FAX 808-622-3025. Ed., R&P Jamie Kemp TEL 808-621-8200 ext 237. Pub. Peggi Murchison. Adv. contact Mark Zanetti. Circ: 7,000.

333.33 USA ISSN 1542-8311
HEARTLAND REAL ESTATE BUSINESS; the Midwest's real estate source. Text in English. 2002. m. USD 65 (effective 2009). adv. back issues avail.; reprints avail. **Document type:** *Magazine, Trade.* **Description:** Covers the latest news, developments and trends in commercial real estate in the Midwest. Features up-to-date information regarding ground-up projects and redevelopments, acquisitions and dispositions, financing, corporate real estate news and current events that are shaping the office, industrial, retail, hospitality, senior housing and multifamily sectors of real estate.
—CCC.
Published by: France Publications, Inc., 3500 Piedmont Rd, Ste 415, Atlanta, GA 30305. TEL 404-832-8262, FAX 404-832-8260, scott@francepublications.com, http://www.francepublications.com. Ed. Kevin Jeselnik. Pub. Jerry France TEL 404-832-8262 ext 111. Adv. contact Scott France.

HELIUM REPORT. *see* TRAVEL AND TOURISM

333.33 340 GBR
HILL & REDMAN'S LAW OF LANDLORD & TENANT. Variant title: Hill & Redman: Landlord & Tenant. Text in English. 1988. 6 base vols. plus updates 5/yr. looseleaf. GBP 689 base vol(s). (effective 2010); subscr. includes Hill & Redman's Law of Landlord & Tenant. Bulletins. **Document type:** *Handbook/Manual/Guide, Trade.* **Description:** Covers general law, business tenancies, the Rent Acts, public-sector residential tenancies, long leases and agricultural tenancies.
Related titles: Supplement(s): Hill & Redman's Law of Landlord & Tenant. Bulletins.
Published by: LexisNexis Butterworths, Halsbury House, 35 Chancery Ln, London, Mddx WC2A 1EL, United Kingdom. TEL 44-20-74002500, FAX 44-20-74002842, customer.services@lexisnexis.co.uk, http://www.lexisnexis.co.uk.

333.33 NLD ISSN 1572-820X
HOLLAND REAL ESTATE YEARBOOK. Text in English. 2000. a. EUR 45 (effective 2009). adv. **Document type:** *Journal, Trade.* **Description:** Provides extensive information about major real estate projects, market players, and industry trends in the Netherlands.
Published by: Europe Real Estate Publishers B.V., North Sea Bldg, Gevers Deynootweg 93R, The Hague, 2586 BK, Netherlands. TEL 31-70-3528600, FAX 31-70-3527660, publishers@europe-re.com, http://www.europe-re.com. Pub. Ronald Elward. Adv. contact Michiel Foekens. color page EUR 3,045; trim 175 x 255. Circ: 10,000 (paid and controlled).

HOME EQUITY NEWS. *see* BUSINESS AND ECONOMICS—Banking And Finance

HOME EQUITY STRATEGIES & ADVISE. *see* BUSINESS AND ECONOMICS—Banking And Finance

HOME OWNER BUILDING & IMPROVEMENTS BUYERS GUIDE. *see* BUILDING AND CONSTRUCTION

333.33 CAN
HOME TO HOME. Text in English. 2005 (Oct.). m. free. **Document type:** *Magazine, Consumer.* **Description:** Contains information for home buyers and real estate professionals, including directory of properties for sale.
Published by: Calgary Real Estate Board, 300 Manning Rd NE, Calgary, AB T2E 8K4, Canada. TEL 403-263-0530, FAX 403-218-3688, info@creb.com, http://www.creb.com/. Ed. Bruce Klippenstein. Circ: 20,000.

333.33 340 USA
HOMEOWNERS ASSOCIATION AND PLANNED UNIT DEVELOPMENT AND PRACTICE: FORMS. Text in English. 1977. 2/yr. USD 117 (effective 2008). **Document type:** *Journal, Trade.*
Published by: Matthew Bender & Co., Inc. (Subsidiary of: LexisNexis North America), 1275 Broadway, Albany, NY 12204. TEL 518-487-3000, 800-424-4200, FAX 518-487-3083, international@bender.com, http://bender.lexisnexis.com. Ed. Patrick J Rohan.

333.33 GBR ISSN 1750-0826
HOMES 24. Text in English. 2006. w. **Document type:** *Newspaper, Consumer.* **Description:** Designed to make it easy to search for property and homes for sale, and houses and flats for rent in local area.
Formed by the merger of (2005-2006): Homes and Property (1746-0379); (2004-2006): Homes and Property Post (1743-5269)
Published by: Archant Herts and Cambs (Subsidiary of: Archant Group), Bank House, Primett Rd, Stevenage, SG1 3EE, United Kingdom. TEL 44-1438-866000, http://www.archant.co.uk/regional_herts.aspx.

333.33 USA
HOMES & LAND MAGAZINE. Text in English. 1973. m. free. adv. **Document type:** *Magazine, Consumer.*
Published by: Homes & Land Affiliates, LLC, 1830 E Park Ave, Tallahassee, FL 32301. TEL 301-937-8547, FAX 301-937-8565. Adv. contact Paul Andrews. color page USD 235,000; trim 8.375 x 10.875.

333.33 GBR
HOMES OVERSEAS (ONLINE); the international homefinder. Text in English. 1965. bi-m. adv. bk.rev. illus.; mkt. **Document type:** *Magazine, Consumer.* **Description:** Serves as a guide for buying property abroad for investment, holidays or retirement.
Formerly (until 19??): Homes Overseas (Print) (0018-4241); Which incorporated: Time-Sharing Homes & Holidays
Media: Online - full text.
—CCC.
Published by: Trinity Mirror Digital Property Ltd, 10/11 Glademan Busines Quarter, Edison Ct, Wrexham Technology Park, Wrexham, LL13 7YT, United Kingdom. TEL 44-1978-315800, FAX 44-1978-315845, http://www.trinitymirror.com. Ed. Marc Da-Silva TEL 44-207-2932471. Circ: 12,000.

THE HOMESEEKER. *see* BUILDING AND CONSTRUCTION

333.33 HKG
HONG KONG PROPERTY REVIEW; a summary of completions, forecast completions, stock, vacancies, rentals and purchase prices. Text in Chinese, English. 1970. a. HKD 285 newsstand/cover (effective 2001). **Document type:** *Government.* **Description:** Comprehensively reviews the property market in Hong Kong in terms of completions, forecast completions, stock, vacancies, take up, average rentals and prices, and rental and price indices.
Formerly (until 1995): Property Review
Related titles: CD-ROM ed.
Published by: Rating and Valuation Department, 303 Cheung Sha Wan Rd, Cheung Sha Wan Government Offices, 13th Fl, Kowloon, Hong Kong. TEL 852-2150-8888, FAX 852-2152-0138, enquiries@rvd.gov.hk. Circ: 850. **Subscr. to:** Director of Information Services, Publications Sales Section, Information Services Department, 4th Fl, Murray Building, 22 Cotton Tree Dr, Central, Hong Kong, Hong Kong. TEL 852-2842-8844, FAX 852-2598-7482.

333.33 GBR ISSN 2040-7602
HONG KONG REAL ESTATE REPORT. Text in English. 200?. q. EUR 820, USD 1,150 combined subscription (print & email eds.) (effective 2010). **Document type:** *Report, Trade.* **Description:** Provides industry professionals and strategists, sector analysts, business investors, trade associations and regulatory bodies with independent forecasts and competitive intelligence on the real estate and construction industry in Hong Kong.
Related titles: E-mail ed.
Published by: Business Monitor International Ltd., Senator House, 85 Queen Victoria St, London, EC4V 4AB, United Kingdom. TEL 44-20-72480468, FAX 44-20-72480467, subs@businessmonitor.com.

333 USA
HOTEL JOURNAL; innside real estate. Text in English. 19??. m. free to qualified personnel (effective 2011). adv. back issues avail. **Document type:** *Journal, Trade.* **Description:** Focused on the transactions that impact the hotel marketplace and complements all of the hard-hitting news in Hotel Business with a look inside the deals.
Related titles: Online - full text ed.: USD 395; USD 20 per issue (effective 2011).
Published by: I C D Publications, Inc., 45 Research Way, Ste 106, East Setauket, NY 11733. TEL 847-913-8244, FAX 847-913-9202, http://www.homeworldbusiness.com/hw/. Ed. Dennis Nessler.

333.33 GBR ISSN 0018-6473
HOUSE BUYER. Text in English. 1955. m. GBP 25. adv. charts; illus.; mkt.; tr.lit. **Document type:** *Magazine, Consumer.*
Formerly: Houses and Estates
Published by: Brittain Publications, 137 George Ln, S Woodford, London, E18 1AJ, United Kingdom. TEL 081-530-7555, FAX 081-530-7609. Ed. Con Crowley.

333.33 USA
HOUSELAW. Text in English. m. USD 6,500 (effective 2001); Discount available to qualified subcribers. **Document type:** *Journal, Trade.* **Description:** Covers legal developments in housing finance and home equity lending.
Related titles: Online - full text ed.: USD 5,500 (effective 2001).
Published by: Consumer Credit Compliance Company, LLC, 971 Corporate Blvd, Ste 301, Linthicum, MD 21090. TEL 410-684-6800, 877-464-8326, FAX 410-684-6923, trohwedder@hudco.com, http://www.creditcompliance.com. Ed. Robert A. Cook.

HOUSING CHEAP OR ON A BUDGET NEWSLETTER. *see* CONSUMER EDUCATION AND PROTECTION

333.33 USA
HOUSING COURT REPORTER. Text in English. m. **Document type:** *Newsletter, Trade.*
Published by: Treiman Publications Corp., 2517 Owego Rd, Vestal, NY 13850. TEL 800-338-5262, FAX 607-748-4150, TreimanPub@aol.com, http://www.treimanpublication.com.

333.33 NZL ISSN 1179-8084
HOUSING FACTS (ONLINE). Variant title: Residential Housing Facts. Text in English. 1989. m. **Document type:** *Report, Trade.*
Formerly (until 2010): Housing Facts (Print) (1171-1620)
Media: Online - full text.
Published by: Real Estate Institute of New Zealand, PO Box 5663, Auckland, New Zealand. TEL 64-9-3561755, 800-473-469, FAX 64-9-3798471, reinz@reinz.co.nz.

333.3 GBR ISSN 0955-3800
HOUSING FINANCE. Text in English. 1975. q. stat. **Document type:** *Magazine, Trade.* **Description:** Publishes the latest developments in building and housing market activity, including savings and lending statistics.
Formerly (until 1989): B S A Bulletin (0261-6394)
Related titles: Online - full text ed.
Indexed: WBA.
—IE, Ingenta. **CCC.**
Published by: Council of Mortgage Lenders, Bush House, N W Wing, Aldwych, London, WC2B 4PJ, United Kingdom. TEL 44-845-3736771, FAX 44-845-3736778, events@cml.org.uk, http://www.cml.org.uk. Ed. Rob Pannell.

HOUSING FINANCE REVIEW. *see* BUILDING AND CONSTRUCTION

333.33 340 GBR
HOUSING LAW. Variant title: Arden Housing Law. Text in English. 1994. base vol. plus updates 2/yr. looseleaf. GBP 553 base vol(s). domestic; EUR 731 base vol(s). in Europe; USD 951 base vol(s). elsewhere (effective 2011). **Document type:** *Handbook/Manual/Guide, Trade.* **Description:** Provides a comprehensive treatment of the law that affects all accommodation and focuses on information relevant to the needs of all those advising on housing matters.
Published by: Sweet & Maxwell Ltd. (Subsidiary of: Thomson Reuters Corp.), 100 Avenue Rd, London, NW3 3PF, United Kingdom. TEL 44-20-73937000, FAX 44-20-74491144, sweetandmaxwell.customer.services@thomson.com. **Subscr. to:** PO Box 1000, Andover SP10 9AF, United Kingdom. TEL 44-20-73938051, sweetandmaxwell.international.queries@thomson.com.

333.33 340 GBR
HOUSING LAW & PRECEDENTS. Variant title: Driscoll Housing Law & Precedents. Text in English. 1994. base vol. plus updates 3/yr. looseleaf. GBP 426 base vol(s). domestic; EUR 563 base vol(s). in Europe; USD 732 base vol(s). elsewhere (effective 2011). **Document type:** *Handbook/Manual/Guide, Trade.* **Description:** Provides explanation and guidance on the law relating to residential landlord and tenant.
Published by: Sweet & Maxwell Ltd. (Subsidiary of: Thomson Reuters Corp.), 100 Avenue Rd, London, NW3 3PF, United Kingdom. TEL 44-20-73937000, FAX 44-20-74491144, sweetandmaxwell.customer.services@thomson.com. **Subscr. to:** PO Box 1000, Andover SP10 9AF, United Kingdom. TEL 44-20-73938051, sweetandmaxwell.international.queries@thomson.com.

333.33 CAN ISSN 1719-5381
HOUSING MARKET OUTLOOK. CALGARY (ONLINE). Text in English. 19??. q. **Document type:** *Newsletter, Trade.*
Former titles (until 2003): Housing Market Outlook. Calgary (Print Edition) (1706-2551); (until 1996): Calgary Housing Forecast (1207-9855)
Media: Online - full text.
Published by: Canada Mortgage and Housing Corporation/Societe Canadienne d'Hypotheques et de Logement, 700 Montreal Rd, Ottawa, ON K1A 0P7, Canada. TEL 613-748-2000, FAX 613-748-2098, chic@cmhc-schl.gc.ca, http://www.cmhc.ca.

333.33 CAN ISSN 1719-9123
HOUSING MARKET OUTLOOK. CANADA. Text in English. 2005. q. **Document type:** *Bulletin, Trade.*
Media: Online - full text.
Published by: Canada Mortgage and Housing Corporation/Societe Canadienne d'Hypotheques et de Logement, 700 Montreal Rd, Ottawa, ON K1A 0P7, Canada. TEL 613-748-2000, 800-668-2642, FAX 613-748-2098, chic@cmhc-schl.gc.ca, http://www.cmhc.ca.

333.33 CAN ISSN 1719-4571
HOUSING MARKET OUTLOOK. CHARLOTTETOWN (ONLINE). Text in English, French. 1991. s-a. CAD 40 (effective 2006). back issues avail. **Document type:** *Report, Trade.*
Former titles (until 1998): Housing Market Outlook. Charlottetown (Print) (1713-8183); (until 1996): Charlottetown Housing Forecast (1207-9219)
Media: Online - full text.
Published by: Canada Mortgage and Housing Corporation/Societe Canadienne d'Hypotheques et de Logement, 700 Montreal Rd, Ottawa, ON K1A 0P7, Canada. TEL 613-748-2000, FAX 613-748-2098, chic@cmhc-schl.gc.ca, http://www.cmhc.ca.

333.33 CAN ISSN 1719-5403
HOUSING MARKET OUTLOOK. EDMONTON. Text in English. 2002. q. **Document type:** *Newsletter, Government.*
Media: Online - full text.
Published by: Canada Mortgage and Housing Corporation/Societe Canadienne d'Hypotheques et de Logement, 700 Montreal Rd, Ottawa, ON K1A 0P7, Canada. TEL 613-748-2000, FAX 613-748-2098, chic@cmhc-schl.gc.ca, http://www.cmhc.ca.

333.33 CAN ISSN 1719-4652
HOUSING MARKET OUTLOOK. GATINEAU. Text in English. 2005. s-a. **Document type:** *Newsletter, Trade.*
Media: Online - full text.
Published by: Canada Mortgage and Housing Corporation/Societe Canadienne d'Hypotheques et de Logement, 700 Montreal Rd, Ottawa, ON K1A 0P7, Canada. TEL 613-748-2000, FAX 613-748-2098, chic@cmhc-schl.gc.ca, http://www.cmhc.ca.

333.33 CAN ISSN 1719-4679
HOUSING MARKET OUTLOOK. HAMILTON. Text in English. 2005. s-a. **Document type:** *Report, Trade.*
Media: Online - full text.
Published by: Canada Mortgage and Housing Corporation/Societe Canadienne d'Hypotheques et de Logement, 700 Montreal Rd, Ottawa, ON K1A 0P7, Canada. TEL 613-748-2000, FAX 613-748-2098, chic@cmhc-schl.gc.ca, http://www.cmhc.ca.

333.33 CAN ISSN 1719-4695
HOUSING MARKET OUTLOOK. KELOWNA. Text in English. 2002. s-a. **Document type:** *Newsletter, Trade.*
Media: Online - full text. **Related titles:** Print ed.: ISSN 1713-4099.
Published by: Canada Mortgage and Housing Corporation/Societe Canadienne d'Hypotheques et de Logement, 700 Montreal Rd, Ottawa, ON K1A 0P7, Canada. TEL 613-748-2000, FAX 613-748-2098, chic@cmhc-schl.gc.ca, http://www.cmhc.ca.

333.33 CAN ISSN 1719-4725
HOUSING MARKET OUTLOOK. KITCHENER C M A. (Census Metropolitan Areas) Text in English. q. **Document type:** *Bulletin, Government.*
Media: Online - full text.
Published by: Canada Mortgage and Housing Corporation/Societe Canadienne d'Hypotheques et de Logement, 700 Montreal Rd, Ottawa, ON K1A 0P7, Canada. TEL 613-748-2000, FAX 613-748-2098, chic@cmhc-schl.gc.ca, http://www.cmhc.ca.

333.33 CAN ISSN 1719-4741
HOUSING MARKET OUTLOOK. LONDON. Text in English. s-a. **Document type:** *Newsletter, Trade.*
Media: Online - full text.
Published by: Canada Mortgage and Housing Corporation/Societe Canadienne d'Hypotheques et de Logement, 700 Montreal Rd, Ottawa, ON K1A 0P7, Canada. TEL 613-748-2000, FAX 613-748-2098, chic@cmhc-schl.gc.ca, http://www.cmhc.ca.

333.33 CAN ISSN 1713-4129
HOUSING MARKET OUTLOOK. METRO VICTORIA. Text in English. q. **Document type:** *Bulletin, Trade.*
Formerly (until 2000): Housing Market Outlook. Victoria (1713-4110); (until 1996): Victoria Housing Forecast (1207-9995)
Related titles: Online - full text ed.: ISSN 1719-4768.
Published by: Canada Mortgage and Housing Corporation/Societe Canadienne d'Hypotheques et de Logement, 700 Montreal Rd, Ottawa, ON K1A 0P7, Canada. TEL 613-748-2000, FAX 613-748-2098, chic@cmhc-schl.gc.ca, http://www.cmhc.ca.

333.33 CAN ISSN 1719-542X
HOUSING MARKET OUTLOOK. MONTREAL (ONLINE). Text in English. 199?. q. **Document type:** *Bulletin, Trade.*
Former titles (until 2004): Housing Market Outlook. Montreal (Print) (1709-4704); (until 1996): Housing Forecast, Montreal Metropolitan Area (1207-5876)
Media: Online - full text. **Related titles:** ◆ French ed.: Perspectives du Marche de l'Habitation. Montreal. ISSN 1719-5446.
Published by: Canada Mortgage and Housing Corporation/Societe Canadienne d'Hypotheques et de Logement, 700 Montreal Rd, Ottawa, ON K1A 0P7, Canada. TEL 613-748-2000, FAX 613-748-2098, chic@cmhc-schl.gc.ca, http://www.cmhc.ca.

333.33 CAN ISSN 1719-5748
HOUSING MARKET OUTLOOK. NORTHERN ONTARIO. Text in English. 2005. s-a. **Document type:** *Bulletin, Consumer.*
Media: Online - full text.
Published by: Canada Mortgage and Housing Corporation/Societe Canadienne d'Hypotheques et de Logement, 700 Montreal Rd, Ottawa, ON K1A 0P7, Canada. TEL 613-748-2000, FAX 613-748-2098, chic@cmhc-schl.gc.ca, http://www.cmhc.ca.

333.33 CAN ISSN 1719-4792
HOUSING MARKET OUTLOOK. OSHAWA. Text in English. q. **Document type:** *Bulletin, Trade.*
Media: Online - full text.
Published by: Canada Mortgage and Housing Corporation/Societe Canadienne d'Hypotheques et de Logement, 700 Montreal Rd, Ottawa, ON K1A 0P7, Canada. TEL 613-748-2000, FAX 613-748-2098, chic@cmhc-schl.gc.ca, http://www.cmhc.ca.

333.33 CAN ISSN 1719-5454
HOUSING MARKET OUTLOOK. OTTAWA. Text in English. 2002. q. **Document type:** *Bulletin, Trade.*
Media: Online - full text.
Published by: Canada Mortgage and Housing Corporation/Societe Canadienne d'Hypotheques et de Logement, 700 Montreal Rd, Ottawa, ON K1A 0P7, Canada. TEL 613-748-2000, FAX 613-748-2098, chic@cmhc-schl.gc.ca, http://www.cmhc.ca.

333.33 CAN ISSN 1719-4814
HOUSING MARKET OUTLOOK. QUEBEC. Text in English. 2005. q. **Document type:** *Bulletin, Trade.*
Media: Online - full text.
Published by: Canada Mortgage and Housing Corporation/Societe Canadienne d'Hypotheques et de Logement, 700 Montreal Rd, Ottawa, ON K1A 0P7, Canada. TEL 613-748-2000, FAX 613-748-2098, chic@cmhc-schl.gc.ca, http://www.cmhc.ca.

333.33 CAN ISSN 1719-4830
HOUSING MARKET OUTLOOK. REGINA. Text in English. 2005. q. **Document type:** *Bulletin, Trade.*
Media: Online - full text.
Published by: Canada Mortgage and Housing Corporation/Societe Canadienne d'Hypotheques et de Logement, 700 Montreal Rd, Ottawa, ON K1A 0P7, Canada. TEL 613-748-2000, FAX 613-748-2098, chic@cmhc-schl.gc.ca, http://www.cmhc.ca.

333.33 CAN ISSN 1719-4857
HOUSING MARKET OUTLOOK. SAGUENAY. Text in English. 2005. q. **Document type:** *Bulletin, Trade.*
Media: Online - full text.
Published by: Canada Mortgage and Housing Corporation/Societe Canadienne d'Hypotheques et de Logement, 700 Montreal Rd, Ottawa, ON K1A 0P7, Canada. TEL 613-748-2000, FAX 613-748-2098, chic@cmhc-schl.gc.ca, http://www.cmhc.ca.

333.33 CAN ISSN 1719-5764
HOUSING MARKET OUTLOOK. SAINT JOHN, MONCTON AND FREDERICTON. Text in English. 2005. s-a. **Document type:** *Bulletin, Trade.*
Media: Online - full text.
Published by: Canada Mortgage and Housing Corporation/Societe Canadienne d'Hypotheques et de Logement, 700 Montreal Rd, Ottawa, ON K1A 0P7, Canada. TEL 613-748-2000, FAX 613-748-2098, chic@cmhc-schl.gc.ca, http://www.cmhc.ca.

333.33 CAN ISSN 1719-4873
HOUSING MARKET OUTLOOK. SASKATOON. Text in English. 2005. q. **Document type:** *Bulletin, Trade.*
Media: Online - full text.
Published by: Canada Mortgage and Housing Corporation/Societe Canadienne d'Hypotheques et de Logement, 700 Montreal Rd, Ottawa, ON K1A 0P7, Canada. TEL 613-748-2000, FAX 613-748-2098, chic@cmhc-schl.gc.ca, http://www.cmhc.ca.

333.33 CAN ISSN 1719-4911
HOUSING MARKET OUTLOOK. SHERBROOKE. Text in English. 2005. q. **Document type:** *Bulletin, Trade.*
Media: Online - full text.
Published by: Canada Mortgage and Housing Corporation/Societe Canadienne d'Hypotheques et de Logement, 700 Montreal Rd, Ottawa, ON K1A 0P7, Canada. TEL 613-748-2000, FAX 613-748-2098, chic@cmhc-schl.gc.ca, http://www.cmhc.ca.

333.33 CAN ISSN 1719-4938
HOUSING MARKET OUTLOOK. ST. CATHARINES - NIAGARA C M A. (Census Metropolitan Areas) Text in English. 2005. q. **Document type:** *Bulletin, Trade.*
Media: Online - full text.
Published by: Canada Mortgage and Housing Corporation/Societe Canadienne d'Hypotheques et de Logement, 700 Montreal Rd, Ottawa, ON K1A 0P7, Canada. TEL 613-748-2000, FAX 613-748-2098, chic@cmhc-schl.gc.ca, http://www.cmhc.ca.

333.33 CAN ISSN 1719-4962
HOUSING MARKET OUTLOOK. ST. JOHN'S (ONLINE). Text in English. 2005. q. **Document type:** *Bulletin, Trade.*
Formerly (until 1998): Housing Market Outlook. St. John's (Print Edition) (1713-8205); (until 1997): St. John's Housing Forecast (1207-9316)
Media: Online - full text.
Published by: Canada Mortgage and Housing Corporation/Societe Canadienne d'Hypotheques et de Logement, 700 Montreal Rd, Ottawa, ON K1A 0P7, Canada. TEL 613-748-2000, FAX 613-748-2098, chic@cmhc-schl.gc.ca, http://www.cmhc.ca.

333.33 CAN ISSN 1719-5489
HOUSING MARKET OUTLOOK. TORONTO. Text in English. 2002. q. **Document type:** *Bulletin, Trade.*
Media: Online - full text.
Published by: Canada Mortgage and Housing Corporation/Societe Canadienne d'Hypotheques et de Logement, 700 Montreal Rd, Ottawa, ON K1A 0P7, Canada. TEL 613-748-2000, FAX 613-748-2098, chic@cmhc-schl.gc.ca, http://www.cmhc.ca.

333.33 CAN ISSN 1719-4989
HOUSING MARKET OUTLOOK. TROIS-RIVIERES (ONLINE). Text in English. 1990. q. **Document type:** *Bulletin, Trade.*
Former titles: Housing Market Outlook. Trois-Rivieres (Print) (1714-3918); (until 1996): Housing Market Forecast for Trois-Rivieres Metropolitan Area (1209-0247); (until 1995): Housing Forecast, Trois-Rivieres Metropolitan Area (1209-0239)
Media: Online - full text.
Published by: Canada Mortgage and Housing Corporation/Societe Canadienne d'Hypotheques et de Logement, 700 Montreal Rd, Ottawa, ON K1A 0P7, Canada. TEL 613-748-2000, FAX 613-748-2098, chic@cmhc-schl.gc.ca, http://www.cmhc.ca.

333.33 CAN ISSN 1713-4102
HOUSING MARKET OUTLOOK. VANCOUVER. Text in English. q. **Document type:** *Bulletin, Trade.*
Formerly (until 1996): Vancouver Housing Forecast (1207-9987)
Related titles: Online - full text ed.: ISSN 1719-5004.
Published by: Canada Mortgage and Housing Corporation/Societe Canadienne d'Hypotheques et de Logement, 700 Montreal Rd, Ottawa, ON K1A 0P7, Canada. TEL 613-748-2000, FAX 613-748-2098, chic@cmhc-schl.gc.ca, http://www.cmhc.ca.

333.33 CAN ISSN 1719-5039
HOUSING MARKET OUTLOOK. WINDSOR (ONLINE). Text in English. q. **Document type:** *Bulletin, Trade.*
Former titles (until 1998): Housing Market Outlook. Windsor (Print Edition) (1713-0352); (until 1996): Windsor Housing Forecast (1207-9278)
Media: Online - full text.
Published by: Canada Mortgage and Housing Corporation/Societe Canadienne d'Hypotheques et de Logement, 700 Montreal Rd, Ottawa, ON K1A 0P7, Canada. TEL 613-748-2000, FAX 613-748-2098, chic@cmhc-schl.gc.ca, http://www.cmhc.ca.

333.33 CAN ISSN 1719-5055
HOUSING MARKET OUTLOOK. WINNIPEG. Text in English. 2005. q. **Document type:** *Bulletin, Trade.*
Media: Online - full text.
Published by: Canada Mortgage and Housing Corporation/Societe Canadienne d'Hypotheques et de Logement, 700 Montreal Rd, Ottawa, ON K1A 0P7, Canada. TEL 613-748-2000, FAX 613-748-2098, chic@cmhc-schl.gc.ca, http://www.cmhc.ca.

HOUSING NOW. HAMILTON. see HOUSING AND URBAN PLANNING

333.33 307.14 CAN ISSN 1495-3129
HOUSING NOW. METROPOLITAN LONDON. Text in English. 1998. q. **Document type:** *Bulletin, Trade.*
Related titles: Online - full text ed.: ISSN 1719-5101. 2002.
Published by: Canada Mortgage and Housing Corporation/Societe Canadienne d'Hypotheques et de Logement, 700 Montreal Rd, Ottawa, ON K1A 0P7, Canada. TEL 613-748-2000, FAX 613-748-2098, chic@cmhc-schl.gc.ca, http://www.cmhc.ca.

333.33 CAN ISSN 1495-3226
HOUSING NOW. METROPOLITAN WINDSOR. Text in English. 1998. q. **Document type:** *Bulletin, Trade.*
Related titles: Print ed.: Housing Now. Windsor. ISSN 1719-5144. 2002. free (effective 2006).
Published by: Canada Mortgage and Housing Corporation/Societe Canadienne d'Hypotheques et de Logement, 700 Montreal Rd, Ottawa, ON K1A 0P7, Canada. TEL 613-748-2000, FAX 613-748-2098, chic@cmhc-schl.gc.ca, http://www.cmhc.ca.

333.33 CAN ISSN 1719-5128
HOUSING NOW. NORTHERN ONTARIO. Text in English. 2002. q. **Document type:** *Bulletin, Trade.*
Media: Online - full text.
Published by: Canada Mortgage and Housing Corporation/Societe Canadienne d'Hypotheques et de Logement, 700 Montreal Rd, Ottawa, ON K1A 0P7, Canada. TEL 613-748-2000, FAX 613-748-2098, chic@cmhc-schl.gc.ca, http://www.cmhc.ca.

HOUSING POLICY DEBATE. see HOUSING AND URBAN PLANNING

HOUSINGWIRE MAGAZINE. see BUSINESS AND ECONOMICS—Banking And Finance

333.33 NZL
THE HUB. Text in English. 19??. 9/yr. adv. **Document type:** *Magazine, Trade.* **Description:** Covers the latest challenges and changes in the real estate industry.
Former titles (until 2010): R E (1176-9718); (until 2005): New Zealand Real Estate (0114-4618); (until 1977): Real Estate
Published by: Real Estate Institute of New Zealand, PO Box 5663, Auckland, New Zealand. TEL 64-9-3561755, FAX 64-9-3798471, reinz@reinz.co.nz, http://www.reinz.co.nz. Adv. contact Donna Peffers. Circ: 1,200.

333.33 NLD
HUIS. Text in Dutch. 1985. q. EUR 12.50 (effective 2010). adv. **Document type:** *Consumer.* **Description:** Covers all aspects of purchasing a house or apartment, from financing to furnishing and remodeling.
Published by: Service Productions, Spaarne 13, Haarlem, 2011 CC, Netherlands. TEL 31-23-5400223, FAX 31-23-5362545.

333.33 GBR ISSN 2040-7769
HUNGARY REAL ESTATE REPORT. Text in English. 200?. q. EUR 820, USD 1,150 combined subscription (print & email eds.) (effective 2010). **Document type:** *Report, Trade.* **Description:** Provides industry professionals and strategists, sector analysts, business investors, trade associations and regulatory bodies with independent forecasts and competitive intelligence on the real estate and construction industry in Hungary.
Related titles: E-mail ed.
Published by: Business Monitor International Ltd., Senator House, 85 Queen Victoria St, London, EC4V 4AB, United Kingdom. TEL 44-20-72480468, FAX 44-20-72480467, subs@businessmonitor.com.

332.63 ZAF ISSN 1816-3777
THE HUNT. Text in English. 2005. q.
Published by: Hunters, Shop 149, The Crescent, 1 Sunset Crescent, New Town Centre, Umhlanga Ridge, 4319, South Africa. TEL 27-31-5663656, info@thehunt.co.za, http://www.thehunt.co.za.

346.04 NLD ISSN 1380-6254
HUURRECHT (EINDHOVEN). Text in Dutch. 1994. bi-m. EUR 269 (effective 2009). **Document type:** *Newsletter, Trade.*
Published by: Euroforum Uitgeverij B.V., Postbus 125, Eindhoven, 5600 AC, Netherlands. TEL 31-40-2925950, FAX 31-40-2925955, info@euroforum-uitgeverij.nl, http://www.euroforum-uitgeverij.nl.

346.04 SWE ISSN 0018-8360
HYRESGAESTEN. Text in Swedish. 1962. 7/yr. free. illus.
Published by: Hyresgaestfoereningen/The Swedish Union of Tenants, PO Box 7514, Stockholm, 10392, Sweden. info@hyresgastforeningen.se, http://www.hyresgastforeningen.se. Ed. Peder Palmstierna. Circ: 23,000.

333.33 ITA ISSN 2039-0866
▼ **I B I RIVISTA.** (Immobili Brasile Italia) Text in Italian. 2010. q. **Document type:** *Journal, Trade.*
Published by: Immobili Brasile Italia (I B I), Via Aldo Moro 39, Padua, 35020, Italy. contatto@ibi-immobilibrasile.it, http://www.immobilibrasile.com.br.

332.632 GBR
I P D U K ANNUAL PROPERTY INDEX. (Investment Property Databank United Kingdom) Text in English. 1999. a. **Document type:** *Bulletin, Trade.* **Description:** Covers information on retail, office, industrial and other properties annually.
Formerly (until 2006): I P D U K Annual Index (1471-0951); Which was formed by the 1999 merger of: I P D Annual Index (1363-7711); I P D Annual Review (0959-1788)
—BLDSC (4567.282380).
Published by: Investment Property Databank Ltd., 1 St. John's Ln, London, EC1M 4BL, United Kingdom. TEL 44-20-73369200, FAX 44-20-73369399, enquiries@ipd.com.

352 USA
I R E I WEEKLY. Text in English. 1997. w. free. **Document type:** *Newsletter, Trade.* **Description:** Delivers news on people, events and trends taking place in the commercial real estate industry.
Formerly (until 200?): I R E I zine
Media: Online - full content.
Published by: Institutional Real Estate, Inc., 2274 Camino Ramon, San Ramon, CA 94583. TEL 925-244-0500, FAX 925-244-0520, circulation@irei.com, http://www.irei.com. Eds. Drew Campbell TEL 925-244-0500 ext 111, Sheila Hopkins TEL 925-244-0500 ext 115.

333.33 GBR ISSN 1361-1305
I R R V INSIGHT. Variant title: Insight Magazine. Text in English. 1928. m. GBP 60 to non-members; free to members (effective 2009). adv. bk.rev. abstr.; tr.lit. index. **Document type:** *Magazine, Trade.* **Description:** Features articles by some of the top practitioners including advice and information on new legislation, topical issues and best practice.
Former titles (1995): I R R V Journal (0961-804X); (until 1991): R R V Monthly (0959-6097); (until 1990): R V A Monthly (0959-4094); (until 1989): Rating and Valuation (0483-9889); (until 1960): Rating and Valuation Association. Journal
Indexed: RICS.
—CCC.
Published by: Institute of Revenues Rating and Valuation, 41 Doughty St, London, WC1N 2LF, United Kingdom. TEL 44-20-78313505, FAX 44-20-78312048. Ed. John Roberts.

333.33 USA
ILLINOIS REAL ESTATE FORMS. Text in English. 1989. 3 base vols. plus irreg. updates. looseleaf. USD 489 base vol(s). (effective 2008). Supplement avail. **Document type:** *Handbook/Manual/Guide, Trade.* **Description:** Contains purchase and sale agreements, and draft financing, land use and land trust documents, and more.
Related titles: Diskette ed.; Online - full text ed.
Published by: Michie Company (Subsidiary of: LexisNexis North America), 701 E Water St, Charlottesville, VA 22902. TEL 434-972-7600, 800-446-3410, FAX 434-972-7677, customer.support@lexisnexis.com, http://www.michie.com. Eds. Gregory W Hummel, Paul D Rudnick, Paul E Fisher.

R

333.33 USA
ILLINOIS REAL ESTATE JOURNAL. Text in English. 1998. bi-m. USD 29 (effective 2011). adv. 56 p./no.; back issues avail. **Document type:** *Journal, Trade.* **Description:** Covers commercial real estate news in Illinois.
Related titles: Online - full text ed.: free (effective 2011).
Published by: Real Estate Communications Group (Subsidiary of: Law Bulletin Publishing Co.), 415 N State St, Chicago, IL 60654. TEL 312-416-1860, FAX 312-416-1864, http://www.rejournals.com. Pub. Mark Menzies. Adv. contact John Mickey.

333.33 USA
ILLINOIS REAL ESTATE LEASING FORMS WITH PRACTICE COMMENTARY. Text in English. 1994. 2-3 updates/yr), 2 base vols. plus irreg. updates. looseleaf. USD 249.
Related titles: Diskette ed.: USD 75.
Published by: LexisNexis (Subsidiary of: LexisNexis North America), 701 E Water St, PO Box 7587, Charlottesville, VA 22906. TEL 434-972-7600, 800-446-3410, FAX 800-643-1280, customer.support@lexisnexis.com, http://www.lexisnexis.com/.

333.33 CHE
IMMOBILIA. Text in German. 1933. m. CHF 51 (effective 1997). **Document type:** *Bulletin.*
Published by: Schweizerische Verband der Immobilien-Treuhaender, Buchmattweg 4, Zuerich, 8057, Switzerland. Ed. Albert Petermann.

333.33 AUT
IMMOBILIEN BAZAAR. Text in German. w.
Address: Mayerhofgasse 1, Vienna, W 1040, Austria. TEL 01-501470, FAX 01-5056059.

333.33 DEU ISSN 0934-5639
IMMOBILIEN-BERATER; Handbuch fuer den wirtschaftlichen Erfolg mit Haus- und Wohnungsbesitz. Text in German. 1988. base vol. plus irreg. updates. looseleaf. EUR 49.80 base vol(s). (effective 2010). **Document type:** *Bulletin, Trade.*
Published by: V N R Verlag fuer die Deutsche Wirtschaft AG, Theodor-Heuss-Str 2-4, Bonn, 53095, Germany. TEL 49-228-9550555, FAX 49-228-3696001, info@vnr.de, http://www.vnr.de.

333.33 CHE
IMMOBILIEN GUIDE INTERNATIONAL. Text in German. bi-m. **Document type:** *Trade.*
Published by: Kretz AG, General Wille-Str 147, Postfach, Feldmeilen, 8706, Switzerland. TEL 41-1-9237656, FAX 41-1-9237657, info@kretzag.ch. Circ: 478,000 (controlled).

IMMOBILIEN MANAGER. *see* BUILDING AND CONSTRUCTION

333.33 DEU
IMMOBILIEN VERMIETEN UND VERWALTEN. Text in German. 1997. 10/yr. EUR 80 domestic; EUR 85 foreign; EUR 9 newsstand/cover (effective 2010). adv. 80 p./no.; **Document type:** *Newspaper, Consumer.*
Former titles (until 2008): Immobilien Vermieten; (until 2004): Der Vermieter (1434-9442)
Published by: Huss-Medien GmbH, Am Friedrichshain 22, Berlin, 10407, Germany. TEL 49-30-421510, FAX 49-30-42151232, verlag.wirtschaft@hussberlin.de, http://www.huss-medien.de. Ed. Peter-Michael Fritsch. Adv. contact Torsten Hanke. Circ: 11,787 (paid).

333.33 DEU ISSN 1435-7216
IMMOBILIEN VERTRAULICH. Text in German. 1998. 250/yr. EUR 475 (effective 2007). adv. **Document type:** *Magazine, Trade.*
Published by: Pulch Publishing GmbH, Kirchstr 9, Aarbergen, 65326, Germany. TEL 49-1805-785728, FAX 49-1805-785723, office@property-on.com. Ed., Pub. Bernd M. Pulch. adv.: page EUR 499. Circ: 9,000 (paid and controlled).

333.33 DEU ISSN 1433-7878
IMMOBILIEN ZEITUNG; Fachzeitung fuer die Immobilienwirtschaft. Text in German. 1989. w. EUR 189 domestic; EUR 269 foreign; EUR 4.40 newsstand/cover (effective 2005). adv. bk.rev.; software rev. charts; maps; mkt. 36 p./no. 5 cols./p.; back issues avail. **Document type:** *Newspaper, Trade.*
Related titles: Online - full text ed.
—CIS.
Published by: Immobilien Zeitung Verlagsgesellschaft mbH, Postfach 3420, Wiesbaden, 65024, Germany. TEL 49-611-973260, FAX 49-611-9732631. Ed. Thomas Porten. R&P Jan Mucha. Adv. contact Sabine Krewel TEL 49-611-9732626. Circ: 11,290 (paid and controlled).

333.33 DEU ISSN 1862-0930
DER IMMOBILIENBEWERTER. Text in German. 1978. bi-m. EUR 114.30 (effective 2009). adv. **Document type:** *Journal, Trade.*
Formerly (until 2006): Informationsdienst fuer Sachverstaendige
Published by: Bundesanzeiger Verlagsgesellschaft mbH, Amsterdamer Str 192, Cologne, 50735, Germany. TEL 49-221-976680, FAX 49-221-97668278, vertrieb@bundesanzeiger.de, http://www.bundesanzeiger.de. Adv. contact Melanie Sass. B&W page EUR 772; trim 186 x 260. Circ: 1,050 (paid and controlled).

333.33 DEU
DER IMMOBILIENMARKT. Text in German. bi-m. EUR 1.50 newsstand/cover (effective 2007). adv. **Document type:** *Magazine, Trade.*
Published by: Immobilienmarkt Verlagsgesellschaft mbH, Koenigsweg 1, Kiel, 24103, Germany. TEL 49-431-672701, FAX 49-431-678625. Ed. Peter Breiholdt. Adv. contact Eileen Goymann. B&W page EUR 1,700, color page EUR 2,520. Circ: 42,350 (controlled).

333.33 DEU ISSN 1431-9810
DER IMMOBILIENVERWALTER. Text in German. 1995. 7/yr. EUR 29; EUR 5.50 newsstand/cover (effective 2011). adv. **Document type:** *Magazine, Trade.*
Published by: Verlags-Marketing Stuttgart GmbH, Ludwigstr 26, Stuttgart, 70176, Germany. TEL 49-711-2388617, FAX 49-711-2388625, info@verlagsmarketing.de. Ed. Dieter Kuberski. adv.: B&W page EUR 4,000, color page EUR 5,440; trim 185 x 270. Circ: 10,294 (paid and controlled).

333.33 DEU ISSN 1614-7375
IMMOBILIENWIRTSCHAFT; Das Fachmagazin fuer Management, Recht und Praxis. Text in German. 1990. 10/yr. EUR 128; EUR 25.80 to students (effective 2010). adv. **Document type:** *Magazine, Trade.*
Former titles (until 2004): Immobilien, Wirtschaft und Recht (1614-1164); (until 2001): Immobilien, Praxis und Recht (1433-5166); (until 1997): P u R - Praxis und Recht fuer Immobilien-Verwaltung und -Management (1439-6173); (until 1995): P u R - Praxis und Recht fuer Immobilien-Marketing, -Verwaltung und -Management (0944-6036); (until 1993): P u R - Praxis und Recht der Grundstuecks- und Wohnungswirtschaft (0936-8434)
Published by: Rudolf Haufe Verlag GmbH & Co. KG, Hindenburgstr 64, Freiburg, 79102, Germany. TEL 49-761-36830, FAX 49-761-3683105, online@haufe.de, http://www.haufe.de. Ed. Dirk Labusch. Adv. contact Klaus Sturm. B&W page EUR 6,800, color page EUR 7,500; trim 210 x 280. Circ: 18,918 (paid and controlled).

IMMO!NVEST. *see* BUILDING AND CONSTRUCTION

332.8 CHE ISSN 1662-1557
IMMOSTREET. DEUTSCHSCHWEIZ. Text in German. 2007. m. **Document type:** *Magazine, Trade.*
Published by: ImmoStreet.ch SA, Rue St-Martin 9, Lausanne, 1003, Switzerland. info@immostreet.ch, http://www.immostreet.ch.

332.8 CHE ISSN 1662-1549
IMMOSTREET. ROMANDIE. Text in French. 2007. m. **Document type:** *Magazine, Trade.*
Published by: ImmoStreet.ch SA, Rue St-Martin 9, Lausanne, 1003, Switzerland. info@immostreet.ch, http://www.immostreet.ch.

690 333 USA ISSN 1046-8234
HD7287.6.U5
INCOME - EXPENSE ANALYSIS: CONVENTIONAL APARTMENTS. Variant title: Conventional Apartments. Text in English. 1954. a. USD 202.95 to members; USD 404.95 (print or online ed.) (effective 2008). **Document type:** *Journal, Trade.* **Description:** Detailed analysis of the financial operations of conventionally financed multi-family properties.
Supersedes in part (in 1985): Income - Expense Analysis: Apartments (0194-1941); Which superseded in part (in 1977): Income - Expense Analysis: Apartments, Condominiums and Cooperatives (0161-5262); Which was formerly (until 1975): A Statistical Compilation and Analysis of Actual Income and Expenses Experienced in Apartment Building Operation (0271-4507); (until 1973): Apartment Building Income - Expense Analysis (0084-6651)
Related titles: Online - full text ed.
Indexed: SRI.
Published by: Institute of Real Estate Management, 430 N Michigan Ave, Chicago, IL 60611. TEL 312-329-6025, 800-837-0706, FAX 312-661-0217, 800-338-4736, custserv@irem.org, http://www.irem.org. Ed., R&P Matthew O'Hara.

333.33 690 USA ISSN 1524-6426
HD7288.78.U5
INCOME - EXPENSE ANALYSIS: FEDERALLY ASSISTED APARTMENTS. Text in English. 1986. a. USD 359.95 per issue (print or online ed.); USD 179.95 per issue to members (effective 2008). **Document type:** *Journal, Trade.* **Description:** Summarizes the operating experience of apartment buildings across the US that receive subsidies under one of five federal programs, drawing on a sample of over 1500 buildings.
Supersedes in part (in 1985): Income/Expense Analysis. Apartments (0194-1941); Which superseded in part (in 1977): Income-Expense Analysis. Apartments, Condominiums & Cooperatives (0161-5262); Which was formerly (until 1975): A Statistical Compilation and Analysis of Actual Income and Expenses Experienced in Apartment Building Operation (0271-4507)
Related titles: Online - full text ed.
—CCC.
Published by: Institute of Real Estate Management, 430 N Michigan Ave, Chicago, IL 60611. TEL 312-329-6000, 312-410-7958, 800-837-0706, FAX 312-661-0217, 800-338-4736, custserv@irem.org.

333 USA
INCOME - EXPENSE ANALYSIS: OFFICE BUILDINGS, DOWNTOWN AND SUBURBAN. Text in English. 1976. a. USD 404.95 per issue to non-members; USD 202.95 per issue to members (effective 2008). **Document type:** *Journal, Trade.* **Description:** Analysis of office building revenues and expenses.
Former titles (until 1990): Expense Analysis: Office Buildings, Downtown and Suburban; (until 1981): Income - Expense Analysis: Suburban Office Buildings (0146-9630)
Related titles: Online - full text ed.
Indexed: SRI.
Published by: Institute of Real Estate Management, 430 N Michigan Ave, Chicago, IL 60611. TEL 800-837-0706, FAX 312-661-0217, 800-338-4736, custserv@irem.org.

333.33 690 USA ISSN 1524-6418
HF5430.3
INCOME - EXPENSE ANALYSIS: SHOPPING CENTERS, OPEN AND ENCLOSED. Text in English. 1991. a. USD 404.95 per issue to non-members; USD 202.95 per issue to members (effective 2008). **Document type:** *Journal, Trade.* **Description:** For real estate professionals. Provides income and expense data for open shopping centers and enclosed malls.
Related titles: Online - full text ed.
Published by: Institute of Real Estate Management, 430 N Michigan Ave, Chicago, IL 60611. TEL 312-329-6000, 312-410-7958, 800-837-0706, FAX 312-661-0217, 800-338-4736, custserv@irem.org.

332.63 BGR ISSN 1312-3122
INDEKS IMOTI/INDEX IMOTI. Text in Bulgarian. 2004. m. BGL 30 domestic; EUR 30 in Europe; USD 55 elsewhere (effective 2005). **Document type:** *Magazine, Trade.* **Description:** Aims to create a suitable and practical product which could be used both by professional participants of the real estate market and by final users. Covers trends and activities of the market and its particular segments.
Published by: Economedia, ul Ivan Vazov 20, et. 2, Sofia, Bulgaria. TEL 359-2-9376444, FAX 359-2-9376236.

332.63 IND ISSN 1937-7851
INDIA PROPERTY TIMES. Text in English. 2008. m. USD 10 (effective 2008). adv. **Document type:** *Magazine, Consumer.* **Description:** Provides news and expert opinions for potential buyers interested in investing in the Indian property market.
Address: No 94, T V H Beliciaa Towers, 10th Fl, Tower 2, M R C Nagar, Mandaveli, Chennai, Tamil Nadu 600 028, India. TEL 91-44-24631500, editor@indiapropertytimes.com. Ed. Abitha G. Pub. Murugavel Janakiraman.

333.33 GBR ISSN 2040-7610
INDIA REAL ESTATE REPORT. Text in English. 200?. q. EUR 820, USD 1,150 combined subscription (print & email eds.) (effective 2010). **Document type:** *Report, Trade.* **Description:** Provides industry professionals and strategists, sector analysts, business investors, trade associations and regulatory bodies with independent forecasts and competitive intelligence on the real estate and construction industry in India.
Related titles: E-mail ed.
Published by: Business Monitor International Ltd., Senator House, 85 Queen Victoria St, London, EC4V 4AB, United Kingdom. TEL 44-20-72480468, FAX 44-20-72480467, subs@businessmonitor.com.

INDIANAPOLIS AT HOME. *see* INTERIOR DESIGN AND DECORATION

333.33 FRA ISSN 0151-2943
INDICATEUR BERTRAND. Variant title: Indicateur Bertrand. Paris Banlieue. Text in French. 1971. s-m. EUR 90 (effective 2009). **Document type:** *Magazine, Consumer.* **Description:** Contains advertisements for the sale of houses and apartments in Paris and its suburbs.
Formerly (until 1973): Le Nouvel indicateur Bertrand. La Revue de la Construction (0150-5483); Which was formed by the merger of (1905-1971): Indicateur Bertrand (0019-6886); (1970-1971): Revue de la Construction et de l'Immobilier (0150-5475)
Published by: Editions Indicateur Bertrand, 43 bd. Barbes, Paris, 75018, France. TEL 33-1-49252627, FAX 33-1-49252600. Adv. contact Marc Ortalo. Circ: 25,000.

333.33 JPN ISSN 0073-7186
INDICES OF URBAN LAND PRICES AND CONSTRUCTION COST OF WOODEN HOUSES IN JAPAN. Text in Japanese. s-a. price varies.
Published by: Japan Real Estate Institute/Nihon Fudosan Kenkyusho, SVAX TS Bldg, 1-22-12 Toranomon, Minato-ku, Tokyo, 105-0001, Japan.

333.33 GBR ISSN 2040-7629
▼ **INDONESIA REAL ESTATE REPORT.** Text in English. 2009. q. USD 975, EUR 695 combined subscription (print & online eds.) (effective 2011). **Document type:** *Report, Trade.* **Description:** Provides industry professionals and strategists, sector analysts, business investors, trade associations and regulatory bodies with independent forecasts and competitive intelligence on the real estate and construction industry in Indonesia.
Related titles: E-mail ed.
Published by: Business Monitor International Ltd., Senator House, 85 Queen Victoria St, London, EC4V 4AB, United Kingdom. TEL 44-20-72480468, FAX 44-20-72480467, subs@businessmonitor.com.

333.33 CAN ISSN 1715-586X
INFO-LANDS/INFO-TERRES. Text in English. 2005. q. **Document type:** *Newsletter, Government.*
Published by: Indian and Northern Affairs Canada/Affaires Indiennes et du Nord Canada, Terrasses de la Chaudiere, 10 Wellington St, N Tower, Rm 1210, Gatineau, PQ K1A 0H4, Canada. TEL 800-567-9604, FAX 866-817-3977, infopubs@ainc-inac.gc.ca, http://www.ainc-inac.gc.ca.

333.33 FRA ISSN 0046-936X
L'INFORMATION IMMOBILIERE. Text in French. 1968. m. EUR 25 domestic; EUR 34 foreign (effective 2008). adv. bk.rev. 40 p./no.; **Document type:** *Magazine, Trade.*
Published by: Presse Immobiliere, 11 quai Anatole France, Paris, 75007, France. TEL 33-1-44113252, FAX 33-1-45560317. adv.: color page EUR 4,400; trim 210 x 297. Circ: 55,000.

333.33 FRA ISSN 0750-8042
INFORMATIONS RAPIDES DE LA COPROPRIETE. Text in French. 1963. m. back issues avail. **Document type:** *Magazine, Trade.* **Description:** Presents case laws and public regulations concerning joint ownership in real estate.
Formerly (until 1963): Informations Rapides des Cahiers de la Copropriete (0998-5719)
Published by: Groupe D P E - S A P, 9 Rue de l'Arbre Sec, Lyon, Cedex 01 69281, France. TEL 33-4-72982660, FAX 33-4-72982680, http://www.dpe-edition.com. Circ: 5,000.

333.33 ESP ISSN 1695-7415
INMOBILIARIA INDUSTRIAL Y LOGISTICA. Text in Spanish. 2002. m. **Document type:** *Magazine, Trade.*
Published by: Medios de Distribucion 2000 S.L., El Algabeno 53, Madrid, 28043, Spain. TEL 34-91-721895, FAX 34-91-721902, correo@logisticaytransporte.es, http://www.logisticaytransporte.es.

333.33 647.9 USA
INNSIDE ISSUES. Text in English. 1984. q. looseleaf. free. **Document type:** *Newsletter.* **Description:** Focuses on hotel and motel real estate investment and trends.
Published by: H M B A: America's Hotel Broker, 1420 N W Vivion Rd 111, Kansas City, MO 64118-4555. TEL 816-891-7070, 800-821-5191, FAX 816-891-7071. Ed., R&P Sharon Ralls Lemon. Pub. Robert Kralicek. Circ: 30,000.

333.33 332.7 USA ISSN 1932-9008
INSIDE ALTERNATIVE MORTGAGES. Text in English. 2005. bi-w. USD 725 (effective 2008). reprints avail. **Document type:** *Newsletter, Trade.*
Related titles: E-mail ed.
Published by: Inside Mortgage Finance Publications, 7910 Woodmont Ave, Ste 1000, Bethesda, MD 20814. TEL 301-951-1240, FAX 301-656-1709, http://www.imfpubs.com. Pub. Guy D Cecala TEL 301-951-1240 ext 314. Adv. contact Mark Macoit TEL 301-951-1240 ext 309.

INSIDE F H A LENDING. (Federal Housing Administration) *see* BUSINESS AND ECONOMICS—Banking And Finance

INSIDE M B S & A B S. (Mortgage Backed Securities & Asset Backed Securities) *see* BUSINESS AND ECONOMICS—Banking And Finance

332.33 GBR ISSN 2040-2104
INSIDER COMMERCIAL PROPERTY GUIDE. YORKSHIRE & HUMBER. Text in English. 200?. a. GBP 35 per issue (effective 2009). adv. **Document type:** *Directory, Trade.* **Description:** Contains rental information focusing on office, retail, industrial and investment markets.
Formerly (until 2007): Commercial Property Guide. Yorkshire & Humber (1479-635X)

—CCC.
Published by: Newsco-Insider, Boulton House, 17-21 Chorlton St, Manchester, M1 3HY, United Kingdom. TEL 44-161-9079711, FAX 44-161-2369862, michelle.ferster@newsco.com, http://www.newsco.com/. Ed. Michael Taylor TEL 44-161-9079709. Adv. contact Mark Webb TEL 44-113-2204411. page GBP 1,500. Circ: 10,000.

333.3387025424 GBR ISSN 1757-1421
INSIDER COMMERCIAL PROPERTY GUIDES. MIDLANDS. Variant title: Commercial Property Guide. Midlands. Text in English. 2007. a. GBP 40 per issue (effective 2010). adv. **Document type:** *Directory, Trade.* **Description:** Contains updated figures on average rents in offices, industrial and retail property, transformational property projects and the progress made by urban regeneration companies, comprehensive listings of professional industry contacts from developers, lawyers and property lenders to surveyors, valuers, agents and architects in Midlands.
Formed by the merger of (2004-2007): Commercial Property Guide. East Midlands (1744-0211); (200?-2007): Commercial Property Guide. West Midlands (1744-0238)
Related titles: Online - full text ed.
—CCC.
Published by: Newsco-Insider, Boulton House, 17-21 Chorlton St, Manchester, M1 3HY, United Kingdom. TEL 44-161-9079711, FAX 44-161-2369862, michelle.ferster@newsco.com, http://www.newsco.com/. Ed. Michael Taylor TEL 44-161-9079709. Adv. contact Adrian Simcox TEL 44-121-2041490. color page GBP 1,500. Circ: 12,000.

INSTITUTE ON PLANNING, ZONING AND EMINENT DOMAIN. PROCEEDINGS. *see* LAW

INSTITUTIONAL INVESTING IN INFRASTRUCTURE. *see* BUSINESS AND ECONOMICS—Investments

333.33 USA ISSN 1941-3858
INSTITUTIONAL REAL ESTATE DEALMAKERS. Text in English. 2008 (Apr.). 48/yr. USD 299 (effective 2008). **Document type:** *Newsletter, Trade.* **Description:** Presents a table of recent transactions, investor profiles, spotlights of prominent transactions, properties on the market, fund raising activity, capital markets reports and financing sources.
Media: Online - full content.
Published by: Institutional Real Estate, Inc., 2274 Camino Ramon, San Ramon, CA 94583. TEL 925-244-0500, FAX 925-244-0520, irei@irei.com.

333.33 USA ISSN 1044-1662
HD 1361
THE INSTITUTIONAL REAL ESTATE LETTER. Abbreviated title: T I R E L. Text in English. 1988. m. USD 2,495; USD 225 per issue (effective 2008). adv. charts. back issues avail.; reprints avail. **Document type:** *Newsletter, Trade.* **Description:** Features information on the people, issues, ideas and events driving the institutionalization and globalization of real estate.
Related titles: Online - full text ed.; ◆ Supplement(s): European Real Estate Quarterly. ISSN 1065-3635.
Published by: Institutional Real Estate, Inc., 2274 Camino Ramon, San Ramon, CA 94583. TEL 925-244-0500, FAX 925-244-0520, irei@irei.com. Ed. Rachel Speirs TEL 925-244-0500 ext 126. Pub. Geoffrey Dohrmann TEL 925-244-0500 ext 117. Adv. contact Sandy Terranova TEL 925-244-0500 ext 125. B&W page USD 4,150, color page USD 4,700; bleed 8.75 x 11.25.

352 USA
INSTITUTIONAL REAL ESTATE NEWSLINE. Abbreviated title: I R E N. Text in English. 199?. w. USD 795 (effective 2008). adv. back issues avail.; reprints avail. **Document type:** *Newsletter, Trade.* **Description:** Covers mergers, joint ventures, research, legislation, major property acquisitions, development, new business units, searches and offerings.
Media: E-mail. **Related titles:** Online - full text ed.: ISSN 1945-8622.
Published by: Institutional Real Estate, Inc., 2274 Camino Ramon, San Ramon, CA 94583. TEL 925-244-0500, FAX 925-244-0520, irei@irei.com. Ed. Ryan Garner TEL 925-244-0500 ext 105. Pub. Geoffrey Dohrmann TEL 925-244-0500 ext 117. Adv. contact Sandy Terranova TEL 925-244-0500 ext 125.

368.1 USA
INSURING REAL PROPERTY. Text in English. 1989. 3 base vols. plus irreg. updates. looseleaf. USD 597 base vol(s). (effective 2008). **Document type:** *Handbook/Manual/Guide, Trade.* **Description:** Covers various facets of real property insurance law and provides information that is needed to resolve insurance conflicts.
Related titles: CD-ROM ed.
Published by: Matthew Bender & Co., Inc. (Subsidiary of: LexisNexis North America), 1275 Broadway, Albany, NY 12204. TEL 518-487-3000, 800-424-4200, FAX 518-487-3083, international@bender.com, http://bender.lexisnexis.com. Ed. Stephen A Cozen.

INTEREST RATE RISK EXPOSURE REPORT. AREA: ASSETS > $1 BILLION. *see* BUSINESS AND ECONOMICS—Banking And Finance

INTEREST RATE RISK EXPOSURE REPORT. AREA: ASSETS LESS THAN ONE HUNDRED MILLION DOLLARS. *see* BUSINESS AND ECONOMICS—Banking And Finance

INTEREST RATE RISK EXPOSURE REPORT. AREA: ASSETS $100 MILLION - $1 BILLION. *see* BUSINESS AND ECONOMICS—Banking And Finance

INTEREST RATE RISK EXPOSURE REPORT. AREA: F H L B 11TH DISTRICT. (Federal Home Loan Bank) *see* BUSINESS AND ECONOMICS—Banking And Finance

INTEREST RATE RISK EXPOSURE REPORT. AREA: MIDWEST. *see* BUSINESS AND ECONOMICS—Banking And Finance

INTEREST RATE RISK EXPOSURE REPORT. AREA: NORTHEAST. *see* BUSINESS AND ECONOMICS—Banking And Finance

INTEREST RATE RISK EXPOSURE REPORT. AREA: OH. (Ohio) *see* BUSINESS AND ECONOMICS—Banking And Finance

INTEREST RATE RISK EXPOSURE REPORT. AREA: SOUTHEAST. *see* BUSINESS AND ECONOMICS—Banking And Finance

INTEREST RATE RISK EXPOSURE REPORT. AREA: U.S. TOTAL. *see* BUSINESS AND ECONOMICS—Banking And Finance

INTEREST RATE RISK EXPOSURE REPORT. AREA: WEST. *see* BUSINESS AND ECONOMICS—Banking And Finance

INTERNATIONAL ESTATE PLANNING. *see* LAW—Estate Planning

333.33 GBR
INTERNATIONAL HOMES LUXURY COLLECTION. Text in English. 1993. bi-m. GBP 18 (effective 2009). adv. back issues avail. **Document type:** *Magazine, Consumer.* **Description:** Lists information on international properties, houses, investments, mortgages, and auctions.
Former titles (until 200?): International Homes Investor (1756-2929); (until 2007): International Homes (1471-8715); (until 1999): International Property (1351-0746)
Published by: International Homes & Travel Ltd., 3 St Johns Ct, Moulsham St, Chelmsford, Essex CM2 0JD, United Kingdom. TEL 44-1245-358877, FAX 44-1245-357767, info@international-homes.com, http://www.international-homes.com/. Pub., Adv. contact Stuart Shield.

332.1 LTU ISSN 1648-715X
HD1361
INTERNATIONAL JOURNAL OF STRATEGIC PROPERTY MANAGEMENT. Text in English; Abstracts in Lithuanian, English. 1994. 4/yr. GBP 303 combined subscription in United Kingdom to institutions (print & online eds.); EUR 399, USD 499 combined subscription to institutions (print & online eds.) (effective 2012). **Document type:** *Journal, Academic/Scholarly.* **Description:** Provides a forum for discussion and debate relating to all areas of property management. Covers asset management, facilities management, property policy, budgeting and financial controls, enhancing residential property value, innovations in residential management, housing finance, etc.
Formerly (until 2003): Property Management (1648-0635)
Related titles: Online - full text ed.: ISSN 1648-9179. GBP 272 in United Kingdom to institutions; EUR 360, USD 449 to institutions (effective 2012).
Indexed: A12, A17, A26, A28, ABIn, APA, B01, B07, B16, BrCerAb, C&ISA, CA, CA/WCA, CIA, CerAb, CivEngAb, CorrAb, CurCont, E&CAJ, E11, EEA, EMA, H15, I05, Inspec, M&TEA, M09, MBF, METADEX, P10, P27, P48, P51, P53, P54, PQC, RefZh, SCOPUS, SSCI, SolStAb, T02, T04, W07, WAA.
—Linda Hall. **CCC.**
Published by: (Vilniaus Gedimino Technikos Universitetas, Publishing House "Technika"/Vilnius Gediminas Technical University), Vilniaus Gedimino Technikos Universitetas, Leidykla Technika, Sauletekio aleja 11, Vilnius, 10223, Lithuania. TEL 370-5-2745038, FAX 370-5-2370602, books@vgtu.lt, http://leidykla.vgtu.lt. Ed. E K Zavadskas.

▼ **INTERNATIONAL JOURNAL OF THE BUILT ENVIRONMENT AND ASSET MANAGEMENT.** *see* HOUSING AND URBAN PLANNING

333.33 USA ISSN 2154-8919
INTERNATIONAL REAL ESTATE REVIEW. Text in English. 199?. s-a. free (effective 2011). **Document type:** *Journal, Academic/Scholarly.* **Description:** Features theoretical and empirical academic research papers concerning the Asian real estate markets.
Formerly (until 1998): Journal of the Asian Real Estate Society (1029-6131)
Related titles: Online - full text ed.: free (effective 2011).
Indexed: IBR, IBZ.
Published by: Global Social Science Institute, 14 Eldwick Ct, Potomac, MD 20854. TEL 301-922-2341, sandy.wang@gssi.net, http://www.gssinst.org.

352 USA
INVESTMENT PROPERTY. Text in English. 1991. m. price varies. adv. back issues avail. **Document type:** *Monographic series, Trade.* **Description:** Provides a source of inside information on market activity and investment trends in commercial real estate.
Former titles (until 2000): Investment Property & Real Estate Capital Markets Report; (until 1998): Real Estate Capital Markets Report (1064-1491)
Published by: Institutional Real Estate, Inc., 2274 Camino Ramon, San Ramon, CA 94583. TEL 925-244-0500, FAX 925-244-0520, irei@irei.com. Ed. Sheila Hopkins TEL 925-244-0500 ext 115. Pub. Geoffrey Dohrmann TEL 925-244-0500 ext 117. Adv. contact Brigite Thompson TEL 925-244-0500 ext 128.

IRELAND'S ANTIQUES AND PERIOD PROPERTIES. *see* ANTIQUES

346.04 NLD ISSN 2210-8203
JAARBOEKJE ONROERENDE ZAKEN. Text in Dutch. a. EUR 29.95 (effective 2010).
Published by: (CMS Derks Star Busmann), Maklu BV, Koninginnelaan 96, Appeldoorn, 7301 EB, Netherlands. TEL 31-55-5220625, FAX 31-55-5225694, info@maklu.nl.

JACKSONVILLE HOMEBUYER. *see* LIFESTYLE

333.33 DEU
JAHRBUCH FUER HAUSEIGENTUEMER. Text in German. a. EUR 6 newsstand/cover (effective 2006). adv. **Document type:** *Magazine, Consumer.*
Published by: Haus und Grund Verlag und Service GmbH, Mohrenstr 33, Berlin, 10117, Germany. TEL 49-30-202160, FAX 49-30-2021-6555, zv@haus-und-grund.net, http://www.haus-und-grund.net. adv.: B&W page EUR 2,800, color page EUR 4,050. Circ: 70,000 (paid and controlled).

333.33 GBR ISSN 2044-4923
▼ **JAMAICA PROPERTY PAPER.** Text in English. 2010. q. free (effective 2011). adv. back issues avail. **Document type:** *Magazine, Trade.* **Description:** Features a wide range of properties and property related services in Jamaica.
Related titles: Online - full text ed.
Published by: Jamaica Property Paper Ltd., Ste 404, Albany House, 324/326 Regent St, London, W1B 3HH, United Kingdom. TEL 44-20-71176282, FAX 44-20-79006292.

333.33 GBR ISSN 2041-7101
JAPAN REAL ESTATE REPORT. Text in English. 200?. q. EUR 820, USD 1,150 combined subscription (print & email eds.) (effective 2010). **Document type:** *Report, Trade.* **Description:** Provides industry professionals and strategists, sector analysts, business investors, trade associations and regulatory bodies with independent forecasts and competitive intelligence on the real estate and construction industry in Japan.
Related titles: E-mail ed.
Published by: Business Monitor International Ltd., Senator House, 85 Queen Victoria St, London, EC4V 4AB, United Kingdom. TEL 44-20-72480468, FAX 44-20-72480467, subs@businessmonitor.com.

333.33 346.043 AUS
JESSUP'S LANDS TITLES OFFICE FORMS AND PRACTICE S A. Text in English. 1989. 3 base vols. plus s-a. updates. looseleaf. AUD 1,420 (effective 2008). **Document type:** *Handbook/Manual/Guide, Trade.* **Description:** Guides to the preparation of commonly-encountered conveyancing instruments and the official registration requirements demanded by the Registrar-General.
Formerly: Jessup's Lands Titles Office Practice S A
Published by: Lawbook Co. (Subsidiary of: Thomson Reuters (Professional) Australia Limited), PO Box 3502, Rozelle, NSW 2039, Australia. TEL 61-2-85877980, 300-304-195, FAX 61-2-85877981, 300-304-196, LTA.Service@thomsonreuters.com, http://www.thomson.com.au.

333.33 USA ISSN 0887-1922
JOHN T. REED'S REAL ESTATE INVESTOR'S MONTHLY. Text in English. 1986. m. looseleaf. USD 125 (effective 2000). bk.rev. charts; stat. 8 p./no.; back issues avail. **Document type:** *Newsletter.* **Description:** Includes articles on real estate investment and strategy, finance, management, tax laws, and other pertinent non-tax court decisions.
Published by: John T. Reed, Ed. & Pub., 342 Bryan Dr, Alamo, CA 94507. TEL 925-820-6292, FAX 925-820-1259. R&P John T Reed. Circ: 450 (paid); 71 (controlled).

333.33 GBR ISSN 2044-2068
THE JOURNAL HOMEMAKER.CO.UK. Text in English. 200?. w. adv. **Document type:** *Journal, Trade.* **Description:** Provides a platform for estate agents, letting agents and builders to reach even more home movers locally, regionally and nationally.
Formerly (until 200?): Homemaker (1758-8316)
Related titles: Online - full text ed.: free (effective 2010).
Published by: N C J Media Ltd., Groat Market, Newcastle Upon Tyne, NE1 1ED, United Kingdom. TEL 44-191-2327500, http://www.trinity-mirror-north-east.co.uk. Ed. Karen Overbury TEL 44-191-2016265.

332.63 GBR ISSN 1463-001X
HD1361
➤ **JOURNAL OF CORPORATE REAL ESTATE.** Abbreviated title: J C R E. Text in English. 1998. q. EUR 689 combined subscription in Europe (print & online eds.); USD 819 combined subscription in the Americas (print & online eds.); GBP 499 combined subscription in the UK & elsewhere (print & online eds.); AUD 1,289 combined subscription in Australasia (print & online eds.) (effective 2012). adv. back issues avail.; reprint service avail. from PSC. **Document type:** *Journal, Academic/Scholarly.* **Description:** Keeps CRE professionals in global corporations up to date with latest thinking and best practice in strategic management of corporate real estate.
Related titles: Online - full text ed.: ISSN 1479-1048 (from IngentaConnect).
Indexed: A12, A17, A22, ABIn, B01, B06, B07, B09, CA, E01, P48, P51, P53, P54, PQC, RICS, T02.
—BLDSC (4965.337800), IE, Ingenta. **CCC.**
Published by: Emerald Group Publishing Ltd., Howard House, Wagon Ln, Bingley, W Yorks BD16 1WA, United Kingdom. TEL 44-1274-777700, FAX 44-1274-785201, information@emeraldinsight.com. Ed. Dr. Clare Eriksson. Pub. Valerie Robillard. Circ: 1,500 (paid).

333.33 GBR ISSN 1753-9269
➤ **JOURNAL OF EUROPEAN REAL ESTATE RESEARCH.** Abbreviated title: J E R E R. Text in English. 2008. 3/yr. EUR 339 combined subscription in Europe (print & online eds.); USD 479 combined subscription in the Americas (print & online eds.); GBP 239 combined subscription in the UK & elsewhere (print & online eds.); AUD 639 combined subscription in Australasia (print & online eds.) (effective 2012). back issues avail.; reprint service avail. from PSC. **Document type:** *Journal, Academic/Scholarly.* **Description:** Aims to provide a European forum for the interchange of information and ideas relating to commercial and residential property.
Related titles: Online - full text ed.: (from IngentaConnect).
Indexed: A12, A17, ABIn, ESPM, EconLit, P48, P51, P53, P54, PQC, RiskAb.
—CCC.
Published by: (European Real Estate Society (E R E S) NLD), Emerald Group Publishing Ltd., Howard House, Wagon Ln, Bingley, W Yorks BD16 1WA, United Kingdom. TEL 44-1274-777700, FAX 44-1274-785201, information@emeraldinsight.com. Ed. Stanley McGreal. Pub. Rob Edwards.

333.33 690 GBR ISSN 1366-4387
➤ **JOURNAL OF FINANCIAL MANAGEMENT OF PROPERTY AND CONSTRUCTION.** Text in English. 1996. 3/yr. EUR 409 combined subscription in Europe (print & online eds.); USD 599 combined subscription in the Americas (print & online eds.); GBP 289 combined subscription in the UK & elsewhere (print & online eds.); AUD 619 combined subscription in Australasia (print & online eds.) (effective 2012). bk.rev. reprint service avail. from PSC. **Document type:** *Journal, Academic/Scholarly.* **Description:** Provides an international forum which brings together theoretical and practical based developments and new thinking in the financial management of property and construction throughout all its stages from initial conception, development investment, decision making, risk evaluation, site acquisition, planning, design, construction, maintenance and future life cycle valuation, financial return, change of use and possible demolition.
Related titles: Online - full text ed.: ISSN 1759-8443 (from IngentaConnect).
—IE. **CCC.**
Published by: (University of Ulster at Jordanstown, School of the Built Environment), Emerald Group Publishing Ltd., Howard House, Wagon Ln, Bingley, W Yorks BD16 1WA, United Kingdom. TEL 44-1274-777700, information@emeraldinsight.com. Eds. Akintola Akintoye TEL 44-141-3313626, Jim Birnie TEL 44-2890-366570. Pub. Valerie Robillard. **Subscr. to:** Emerald Group Publishing Limited, PO Box 1441, Fitzroy North, VIC 3068, Australia. TEL 61-3-90781748, FAX 61-3-90781748; Emerald Group Publishing Limited, One Mifflin Pl, Ste 400, Harvard Sq, Cambridge, MA 02138. TEL 617-576-5782, 888-309-7810, FAX 617-576-5883.

➤ **JOURNAL OF FINANCIAL SERVICES RESEARCH.** *see* BUSINESS AND ECONOMICS—Banking And Finance

R

333.33 USA ISSN 1931-1974
JOURNAL OF GOVERNMENT LEASING. Text in English. 2005. q. USD 200 (effective 2008). **Document type:** *Journal, Trade.*
Formerly (until 2008): Government Leasing News (1553-9571)
Published by: Government Leasing LLC, 13408 Glen Lea Way, Rockville, MD 20850. Ed. Dennis Eisen.

JOURNAL OF HOUSING RESEARCH. *see* HOUSING AND URBAN PLANNING

333.33 690 USA ISSN 2153-6813
▼ ➤ **JOURNAL OF INTERNATIONAL REAL ESTATE AND CONSTRUCTION STUDIES.** Text in English. 2010 (Mar.). s-a. USD 295 to institutions; USD 442 combined subscription to institutions (print & online eds.) (effective 2012). **Document type:** *Journal, Academic/Scholarly.* **Description:** Covers all facets of real estate and construction, including finance, dispute resolution, property rights, urban planning, health and safety.
Related titles: Online - full text ed.: USD 295 to institutions (effective 2012).
Published by: Nova Science Publishers, Inc., 400 Oser Ave, Ste 1600, Hauppauge, NY 11788. TEL 631-231-7269, FAX 631-231-8175, journals@novapublishers.com.

333.33 GBR ISSN 1463-578X
HD1387
➤ **JOURNAL OF PROPERTY INVESTMENT & FINANCE.** Abbreviated title: J P I F. Text in English. 1982. bi-m. EUR 6,009 combined subscription in Europe (print & online eds.); USD 7,119 combined subscription in the Americas (print & online eds.); GBP 4,239 combined subscription in the UK & elsewhere (print & online eds.); AUD 8,219 combined subscription in Australasia (print & online eds.) (effective 2012). bk.rev. reprint service avail. from PSC. **Document type:** *Journal, Academic/Scholarly.* **Description:** Forum for the interchange of information and ideas relating to property valuation and investment, property development, property mangement and decision making in all sectors of the property market.
Former titles (until 1999): Journal of Property Valuation and Investment (0960-2712); Which incorporated (1990-1997): Journal of Property Finance (0958-868X); (until 1990): Journal of Valuation (0263-7480)
Related titles: Online - full text ed.: ISSN 1470-2002 (from IngentaConnect).
Indexed: A12, A13, A17, A22, ABIn, ATI, B01, B06, B07, B09, CA, E01, ESPM, EmerIntel, Emerald, H&TI, P48, P51, P53, P54, PQC, RICS, RiskAb, SCOPUS, T02.
—BLDSC (5042.779000), IE, Infotrieve, Ingenta. **CCC.**
Published by: Emerald Group Publishing Ltd., Howard House, Wagon Ln, Bingley, W Yorks BD16 1WA, United Kingdom. TEL 44-1274-777700, FAX 44-1274-785201, information@emeraldinsight.com. Ed. Nick French. Pub. Valerie Robillard. **Subscr. in Australia to:** Emerald Group Publishing Limited, PO Box 1441, Fitzroy North, VIC 3068, Australia. TEL 61-3-90781748, FAX 61-3-90781748; **Subscr. in the Americas to:** Emerald Group Publishing Limited, One Mifflin Pl, Ste 400, Harvard Sq, Cambridge, MA 02138. TEL 617-576-5782, 888-309-7810, FAX 617-576-5883

333.33 USA ISSN 0022-3905
TX955
JOURNAL OF PROPERTY MANAGEMENT; the official publication of the Institute of Real Estate Management . Abbreviated title: J P M. Text in English. 1934. bi-m. USD 62.95 domestic; USD 72.32 in Canada; USD 100.99 elsewhere (effective 2009). adv. charts; illus.; tr.lit. Index. back issues avail.; reprints avail. **Document type:** *Journal, Trade.* **Description:** Provides a forum for sharing ideas and discussing new trends that affect the asset management of investment real estate. Articles may address the management of apartments, office buildings, shopping and strip centers, mixed use properties, office-industrial properties, condominiums, and special-purpose real estate.
Incorporates: Operating Techniques and Products Bulletin.; Former titles (until 1941): Journal of Certified Property Managers; (until 1938): Journal of Real Estate Management
Related titles: Online - full text ed.
Indexed: A10, A12, A13, A14, A17, A22, A23, A26, ABIn, B01, B02, B04, B06, B07, B08, B09, B13, B15, B17, B18, BPI, BPIA, BRD, BusI, C12, CA, E08, G04, G06, G07, G08, H&TI, HospI, I05, IBR, IBZ, ManagCont, P06, P34, P48, P51, P53, P54, PAIS, PQC, S09, SUSA, T&II, T02, V03, W01, W02, W03, W05.
—BLDSC (5042.780000), IE, Infotrieve, Ingenta. **CCC.**
Published by: Institute of Real Estate Management, 430 N Michigan Ave, Chicago, IL 60611. TEL 312-410-7958, 800-837-0706, FAX 312-661-0217, 800-338-4736, custserv@irem.org. R&P Amanda Drucker. Adv. contact Sheila Carter. B&W page USD 3,853, color page USD 5,053; trim 8.13 x 10.88. Circ: 23,750 (paid and free).

333.332 USA ISSN 1357-1419
➤ **JOURNAL OF PROPERTY TAX ASSESSMENT AND ADMINISTRATION.** Text in English. 19??. q. USD 245; free to members (effective 2011). adv. bk.rev. illus. Index. reprints avail. **Document type:** *Journal, Trade.* **Description:** Contains information on property tax assessment, law and policy, appraisal.
Formerly (until Jan. 2004): Assessment Journal (1073-8568); Which was formed by the merger of (1972-1993): Assessment and Valuation Legal Reporter (0090-6352); (1979-1993): Assessment Digest (0731-0277); (1987-1993): I A A O Update (0892-7154); Which was formerly (until 1987): International Association of Assessing Officers. News Bulletin (0741-4609); (1982-1993): Property Tax Journal (0731-0285); Which was formerly (1966-1981): Assessors Journal (0004-5071); International Assessor; I A A O Newsletter; Assessors News Letter - A N L (0004-508X)
Related titles: Online - full text ed.: ISSN 1548-3606.
Indexed: A01, A02, A03, A08, A10, A12, A13, A17, A22, ABIn, ATI, B01, B06, B07, B08, B09, C12, CA, H01, IPARL, P06, P34, P48, P51, P53, P54, PAIS, PQC, T02, V03.
—BLDSC (5042.781200), IE, Ingenta.
Published by: International Association of Assessing Officers, 314 W 10th St, Kansas City, MO 64105. TEL 816-701-8100, 800-616-I4226, FAX 816-701-8149. Circ: 7,800.

333.33 690 SGP
➤ **JOURNAL OF REAL ESTATE AND CONSTRUCTION.** Text in English. irreg. SGD 45; USD 50 foreign. **Document type:** *Journal, Academic/Scholarly.* **Description:** Publishes original papers relating to the built environment.
Published by: N U S Press Pte Ltd, National University of Singapore, 3 Arts Link, Singapore, 117569, Singapore. TEL 65-7761148, FAX 65-7740652, orders.nuspress@nus.edu.sg, http://www.nus.edu.sg/sup/cij. Ed. Paul Kratoska.

333.33 USA ISSN 0895-5638
HG2040 CODEN: JREEEI
➤ **JOURNAL OF REAL ESTATE FINANCE AND ECONOMICS.** Text in English. 1988. 8/yr. EUR 1,411, USD 1,470 combined subscription to institutions (print & online eds.) (effective 2012). adv. illus. back issues avail.; reprint service avail. from PSC. **Document type:** *Journal, Academic/Scholarly.* **Description:** Covers empirical and theoretical research in real estate finance and economics.
Related titles: Microform ed.: (from PQC); Online - full text ed.: ISSN 1573-045X (from IngentaConnect).
Indexed: A12, A22, A26, ABIn, ASCA, B01, B06, B07, B08, B09, BLI, BibLing, CA, CurCont, E01, ESPM, EconLit, FamI, H&TI, IBSS, JEL, P48, P51, P53, P54, PQC, RiskAb, SCOPUS, SSCI, SUSA, T02, W07.
—BLDSC (5047.750000), IE, Infotrieve, Ingenta. **CCC.**
Published by: Springer New York LLC (Subsidiary of: Springer Science+Business Media), 233 Spring St, New York, NY 10013. TEL 212-460-1500, FAX 212-460-1575, service-ny@springer.com. Eds. C F Sirmans, James B Kau, Steven R Grenadier. **Subscr. to:** Journal Fulfillment, PO Box 2485, Secaucus, NJ 07096. TEL 201-348-4033, FAX 201-348-4505, journals-ny@springer.com.

333.33 USA ISSN 0927-7544
HD1361
➤ **JOURNAL OF REAL ESTATE LITERATURE.** Abbreviated title: J P E L. Text in English. 1993. s-a. USD 200 to institutions (print or online ed.); USD 240 combined subscription to institutions (print & online eds.); free to members (effective 2010). bk.rev. abstr.; stat.; illus. Index. back issues avail.; reprints avail. **Document type:** *Journal, Academic/Scholarly.* **Description:** Covers research, dissertations, and works in progress, including information on software and data bases for the researcher; also presents case studies to support the classroom instruction of real estate.
Related titles: Microform ed.: (from PQC); Online - full text ed.: ISSN 1573-8809 (from IngentaConnect).
Indexed: A10, A12, A13, A17, A22, A26, ABIn, B01, B06, B07, B08, B09, BibInd, BibLing, CA, E01, EconLit, G09, H&TI, IBSS, JEL, P10, P48, P51, P53, P54, PQC, SCOPUS, T02, V03.
—BLDSC (5047.755000), IE, Infotrieve, Ingenta. **CCC.**
Published by: American Real Estate Society, c/o Diane Quarles, Clemson University, 424 Sirrine Hall, PO Box 341323, Clemson, SC 29634. TEL 864-656-1373, FAX 864-656-7519, equarle@clemson.edu, http://www.aresnet.org. Eds. John F McDonald, Karl L Gunterman.

333.33 USA ISSN 1083-5547
HD251
➤ **THE JOURNAL OF REAL ESTATE PORTFOLIO MANAGEMENT.** Abbreviated title: J R E P M. Text in English. 1995. q. USD 300 to institutions (print or online ed.); USD 340 combined subscription to institutions (print & online eds.); free to members (effective 2010). adv. illus. back issues avail.; reprints avail. **Document type:** *Journal, Academic/Scholarly.* **Description:** Covers research on the management of real-estate investments.
Related titles: Online - full text ed.
Indexed: A10, A12, A13, A17, A22, ABIn, B01, B06, B07, B08, B09, CA, EconLit, H&TI, IBSS, JEL, P48, P51, P53, P54, PQC, SCOPUS, T02, V03.
—BLDSC (5047.760000), IE, Ingenta. **CCC.**
Published by: American Real Estate Society, c/o Diane Quarles, Clemson University, 424 Sirrine Hall, PO Box 341323, Clemson, SC 29634. TEL 864-656-1373, FAX 864-656-7519, equarle@clemson.edu, http://www.aresnet.org. Eds. Glenn R Mueller, Ping Cheng, Randy I Anderson.

333.33 USA ISSN 1521-4842
JOURNAL OF REAL ESTATE PRACTICE AND EDUCATION. Text in English. 1998. a. USD 200 to individuals (print or online ed.); USD 240 combined subscription to individuals (print & online eds.); free to members (effective 2010). **Document type:** *Magazine, Trade.* **Description:** Encourages excellence in teaching and seeks to motivate research in real estate education and practice.
Related titles: Online - full text ed.: ISSN 1930-8914.
Indexed: A12, A13, A17, ABIn, ATI, CA, E09, EconLit, JEL, P10, P18, P48, P51, P53, P54, PQC, SCOPUS, T02.
—BLDSC (5047.765000), IE, Ingenta. **CCC.**
Published by: American Real Estate Society, c/o Diane Quarles, Clemson University, 424 Sirrine Hall, PO Box 341323, Clemson, SC 29634. TEL 864-656-1373, FAX 864-656-3748, equarle@clemson.edu. Eds. Kenneth H Johnson, William G Hardin III.

333.33 USA ISSN 0896-5803
CODEN: DOWLE8
➤ **JOURNAL OF REAL ESTATE RESEARCH.** Text in English. 1986. bi-m. free to members. adv. **Document type:** *Journal, Academic/Scholarly.*
Related titles: Online - full text ed.
Indexed: A10, A12, A13, A17, A22, ABIn, AIAP, B01, B06, B07, B08, B09, C12, CA, CurCont, EconLit, Emerald, H&TI, IBSS, JEL, P10, P48, P51, P53, P54, PQC, S02, S03, SCOPUS, SSCI, SUSA, T02, V03, W07.
—BLDSC (5047.770000), IE, Infotrieve, Ingenta. **CCC.**
Published by: American Real Estate Society, c/o Diane Quarles, Clemson University, 424 Sirrine Hall, PO Box 341323, Clemson, SC 29634. TEL 216-687-4732, FAX 216-687-9331, http://business.fullerton.edu/journal/. Ed. Ko Wang. R&P, Adv. contact James R Webb. Circ: 1,200.

333.33 GBR ISSN 1479-1110
HD1361
➤ **JOURNAL OF RETAIL & LEISURE PROPERTY.** Abbreviated title: R L P. Text in English. 2000. q. USD 534 in North America to institutions; GBP 287 elsewhere to institutions (effective 2011). adv. abstr.; bibl.; charts; illus.; stat. 96 p./no. 1 cols./p.; back issues avail.; reprints avail. **Document type:** *Journal, Academic/Scholarly.* **Description:** Publishes authoritative analysis and detailed briefings on new development and investment opportunities, as well as best practice case studies to demonstrate how to exploit them and extract maximum value from new and existing projects.
Formerly (until 2003): Journal of Leisure Property (1471-549X)
Related titles: Online - full text ed.: ISSN 1750-2098 (from IngentaConnect).
Indexed: A12, A17, A22, A26, ABIn, B01, B06, B07, B09, CA, E01, E08, H&TI, H06, I05, P03, P48, P51, P53, P54, PQC, PsycInfo, RICS, S09, SCOPUS, T02.
—BLDSC (5052.038750), IE, Ingenta. **CCC.**
Published by: Palgrave Macmillan Ltd. (Subsidiary of: Macmillan Publishers Ltd.), Houndmills, Basingstoke, Hants RG21 6XS, United Kingdom. TEL 44-1256-329242, FAX 44-1256-479476, orders@palgrave.com, http://www.palgrave.com. Pub. Helen Waller TEL 44-1256-303536. Circ: 400. **Subscr. to:** Subscription Department, Brunel Rd, Houndmills, Basingstoke, Hants RG21 2XS, United Kingdom. TEL 44-1256-357893, FAX 44-1256-328339, subscriptions@palgrave.com.

333.33 363.7 USA ISSN 1949-8276
TH880
▼ ➤ **JOURNAL OF SUSTAINABLE REAL ESTATE.** Text in English. 2009. a. USD 30 per issue (effective 2010). **Document type:** *Journal, Trade.* **Description:** Provides research on environmentally sustainable real estate development.
Related titles: Online - full text ed.: ISSN 1949-8284. 2009. free (effective 2010).
Indexed: EconLit.
—BLDSC (5067.734000), IE.
Published by: American Real Estate Society, c/o Diane Quarles, Clemson University, 424 Sirrine Hall, PO Box 341323, Clemson, SC 29634. equarle@clemson.edu, http://www.aresnet.org.

➤ **JURIS-CLASSEUR DES LOYERS ET DE LA PROPRIETE COMMERCIALE.** *see* LAW

346.04 LUX ISSN 1991-475X
JURISNEWS - REGARD SUR LE DROIT IMMOBILIER. Text in French. 2006. 8/yr. EUR 59 (effective 2008). **Document type:** *Newsletter, Trade.* **Description:** Deals with legal matters concerning real estate, property, co-ownership, etc.
Published by: Editions Promoculture, PO Box 1142, Luxembourg, L-1011, Luxembourg. TEL 352-480691, FAX 352-400950, info@promoculture.lu, http://www.promoculture.lu. Ed. Roy Reding. R&P Albert Daming. Circ: 300 (paid).

JURISPRUDENTIEWIJZER GRONDZAKEN, PACHT EN LANDELIJK GEBIED. *see* LAW

332.63 NLD ISSN 1874-0170
KANTOREN IN CIJFERS. Text in Dutch. 1999. a.
Formerly (until 2002): Kantorenatlas Nederland (1874-0189)
Related titles: ◆ Dutch ed.: Offices in Figures. ISSN 1872-468X.
Published by: CB Richard Ellis, Stadhouderskade 1, Amsterdam, 1054 ES, Netherlands. TEL 31-20-6262691, FAX 31-20-6246305, http://www.cbre.nl.

KEY NOTE MARKET ASSESSMENT. DIRECT MORTGAGES. *see* BUSINESS AND ECONOMICS—Banking And Finance

333.33 GBR ISSN 1475-6005
KEY NOTE MARKET ASSESSMENT. ESTATE AGENTS AND SERVICES. Variant title: Estate Agents & Services Market Assessment. Text in English. 2001. irreg., latest 2007, Sep. GBP 880 per issue (effective 2010). **Document type:** *Report, Trade.* **Description:** Provides an in-depth strategic analysis across a broad range of industries and contains an examination on the scope, dynamics and shape of key UK markets in the consumer, financial, lifestyle and business to business sectors.
Published by: Key Note Ltd. (Subsidiary of: Bonnier Business Information), Harlequin House, 5th Fl, 7 High St, Teddington, Richmond upon Thames, TW11 8EE, United Kingdom. TEL 44-845-5040452, FAX 44-845-5040453, sales@keynote.co.uk.

333.33 FIN ISSN 0782-7911
KIINTEISTO JA ISANNOITSIJA. Variant title: Kiinteisto ja Isannointi. Text in Finnish. 1986. m. EUR 52 (effective 2007). adv. **Document type:** *Magazine, Trade.*
Published by: (Suomen Isannoitsijaliitto/Finnish Real Estate Management Federation), Karprint Oy, Vanha Turunrie 371, Huhmari, 03150, Finland. TEL 358-9-41397300, FAX 358-9-41397405, http://www.karprint.fi. Ed. Eero Ahola. Adv. contact Arja Blom. page EUR 2,001. Circ: 13,000.

▼ **DE KLEINE GIDS HUURRECHT BEDRIJFSRUIMTE.** *see* LAW—Corporate Law

332.63 NLD ISSN 1878-8653
KLINKER. Text in Dutch. 2008. s-a. free (effective 2011). **Document type:** *Magazine, Consumer.* **Description:** Aims to keep investors informed about investment fund performance and new investment opportunities.
Published by: (Bouwfonds Real Estate Investment Management), Hemels BV, PO Box 369, Hilversum, 1200 AJ, Netherlands. TEL 31-35-6899900, FAX 31-35-6899999, info@hemels.com, http://www.hemels.com. Circ: 4,000 (controlled).

333.33 FIN ISSN 1796-2439
KOTONA; Sato-konsernin asiakaslehti. Text in Finnish. 1974. q. adv. **Document type:** *Magazine, Trade.*
Formerly (until 2006): Kurkihirsi (1236-4509)
Published by: Sanoma Magazines Finland Corporation, Lapinmaentie 1, Helsinki, 00350, Finland. TEL 358-9-1201, FAX 358-9-1205171, info@sanomamagazines.fi, http://www.sanomamagazines.fi. adv.: page EUR 2,500; 220 x 297. Circ: 32,000 (controlled).

333.33 GBR ISSN 2040-7866
▼ **KUWAIT REAL ESTATE REPORT.** Text in English. 2009. q. USD 975 (effective 2011). **Document type:** *Report, Trade.* **Description:** Features Business Monitor International (BMI)'s market assessment and independent 5-year forecasts to end-2015 of major construction projects in the residential and commercial real estate sectors, as well as property rental prices and yields in major cities.
Published by: Business Monitor International Ltd., Senator House, 85 Queen Victoria St, London, EC4V 4AB, United Kingdom. TEL 44-20-72480468, FAX 44-20-72480467, enquiry@businessmonitor.com.

333.33 USA ISSN 1933-141X
KF6397
L I H T C PROPERTY MANAGEMENT; reference materials and documentation for tax credit property managers. (Low-Income Housing Tax Credit) Text in English. irreg. USD 195 per issue (effective 2008). adv. **Document type:** *Handbook/Manual/Guide, Trade.* **Description:** Designed to provide up-to-date information on and to act as a navigational guide through the complex field of LIHTC compliance monitoring.
Published by: Novogradac & Co. LLP, 246 First St, 5th Flr, San Francisco, CA 94105. TEL 415-356-7960, FAX 415-356-8001, cpas@novoco.com. Adv. contact Junhee Byun TEL 415-356-8037.

333.33 HKG ISSN 1817-3853
L P LUXURY PROPERTIES/DI BIAO. Text in English. 2005. q. HKD 290 domestic; USD 60 in Indonesia, Philippines & China; MYR 70 in Malaysia; USD 38 in Singapore; THB 1,100 in Thailand; USD 120 elsewhere in Asia; USD 200 elsewhere (effective 2008). **Document type:** *Magazine, Consumer.*
Related titles: Online - full text ed.
Published by: Blu Inc Media (HK) Ltd. (Subsidiary of: S P H Magazines Pte Ltd.), Ste 2901, 29/F Universal Trade Centre, No. 3 Arbuthnot Rd, Central, Hong Kong. TEL 852-2165-2800, FAX 852-2868-1799, queries@bluincmedia.com, http://www.bluincmedia.com.hk/.

333.72 USA ISSN 1074-553X
LAKE HOME. Text in English. 1994. bi-m. USD 19.95; USD 4.95 newsstand/cover. **Document type:** *Magazine, Consumer.* **Description:** Combines the joy of lakeside living with a "lake ecology" point of view that addresses the environmental complexities and issues facing lakefront property owners.
Published by: Blue Water Communications, Inc., 137 N. Main St, West Bend, WI 53095. TEL 414-334-2501. Ed. David Rank. Pub. Frank Raimo. adv.: B&W page USD 1,696. Circ: 5,000.

333.33 346.043 FRA ISSN 1257-1709
LAMY DROIT IMMOBILIER. Text in French. 1994. 2 base vols. plus irreg. updates. looseleaf. EUR 673 base vol(s). print & CD-ROM eds. (effective 2010). **Document type:** *Trade.*
Related titles: CD-ROM ed.: ISSN 1284-1145; Online - full text ed.
Published by: Lamy S.A. (Subsidiary of: Wolters Kluwer France), 1 Rue Eugene et Armand Peugeot, Rueil-Malmaison, 92856 Cedex, France. TEL 33-1-76733000, FAX 33-1-76734809, lamy@lamy.fr.

333.33 USA ISSN 1059-9622
HD251
LAND (CHICAGO). Text in English. 1944. bi-m. USD 24 to non-members. adv. **Document type:** *Magazine, Trade.* **Description:** Focuses on land sales, brokerage management, and land development.
Former titles (until 1990): Realtors Land Institute (0888-5427); (until 1986): Farm and Land Realtor
—CCC.
Published by: Realtors Land Institute, 430 N Michigan Ave, Chicago, IL 60611. TEL 312-329-8440, FAX 312-329-8633. Ed. Paddy Buratto. Circ: 2,500.

333.33 GBR ISSN 1758-0250
LAND & BUSINESS. Text in English. 1907. m. free to members (effective 2009). adv. bk.rev. index. **Document type:** *Magazine, Trade.*
Former titles (until 2008): Country Landowner & Rural Business (1743-0232); (until 2001): Country Landowner (0011-0159); (until 1950): Central Landowners' Association. Journal
Indexed: RICS.
—BLDSC (5146.751000), IE, Ingenta.
Published by: Country Land & Business Association, 16 Belgrave Sq, London, SW1X 8PQ, United Kingdom. TEL 44-20-72350511, FAX 44-20-72354696, mail@cla.org.uk. Ed. Tom Quinn. Pub. Ollie Wilson. Adv. contact Mark Brown TEL 44-1242-259249.

323.4 GBR ISSN 0023-7574
HD591.A1
LAND & LIBERTY; putting people at the heart of economics. Text in English. 1894. q. GBP 2.50 newsstand/cover (effective 2009). bk.rev. charts. index. back issues avail. **Document type:** *Magazine, Consumer.* **Description:** Aims to explore how our common wealth should be used - and to demonstrate that this is the key to building the bridge of sustainability between private life, the public sector and our resources - between the individual, the community and the environment.
Related titles: Online - full text ed.: free (effective 2009).
Indexed: P06, RICS.
—BLDSC (5146.760000).
Published by: Henry George Foundation of Great Britain Ltd., 212 Piccadilly, London, W1J 9HG, United Kingdom. TEL 44-20-79171899, FAX 44-20-79171899, http://www.henrygeorgefoundation.org/. Ed. Peter Gibb.

333.33 USA ISSN 1943-9709
HD1395.5.U6
THE LAND REPORT. Text in English. 2007. q. USD 59.99 (effective 2009). adv. **Document type:** *Magazine, Consumer.*
Related titles: Online - full text ed.: ISSN 1943-9717.
Published by: The Land Report, 1 Perimeter Park S, Birmingham, AL 34243. TEL 205-970-6006, FAX 205-970-6300. Ed. Eric O'Keefe. Pub. Eddie Lee Rider Jr.

346.045 USA
LAND USE LAW. Text in English. 1993. irreg., latest 2003, 5th ed. USD 187 5th ed. (effective 2008). 734 p./no.; **Document type:** *Handbook/Manual/Guide, Trade.* **Description:** Includes information about zoning and subdivision controls, as well as innovative new controls such as growth management programs and environmental land use regulations.
Published by: Michie Company (Subsidiary of: LexisNexis North America), 701 E Water St, Charlottesville, VA 22902. TEL 434-972-7600, 800-446-3410, FAX 434-972-7677, customer.support@lexisnexis.com, http://www.michie.com. Ed. Daniel R Mandelker.

333.33 USA
LANDAMERICA QUARTERLY. Text in English. 1937. q. free. **Document type:** *Report, Trade.*
Formerly (until 1998): Lawyers Title News (0272-7161)
Published by: LandAmerica Financial Group, PO Box 27567, Richmond, VA 23261. TEL 804-281-6700, FAX 804-282-5453. Ed. Eleanor R Anders. Circ: 80,000.

333.73 NLD ISSN 0166-5839
DE LANDEIGENAAR; maandblad voor beheer van het buitengebied. Text in Dutch. 1953. bi-m. EUR 52.75 to non-members (effective 2009). adv. bk.rev. **Document type:** *Bulletin.* **Description:** Covers topics of interest to landowners, forest owners, and persons concerned with the economic and environmental aspects of land ownership.
Published by: Uitgeverij de Landeigenaar b.v., Postbus 870, Veenendaal, 3900 AW, Netherlands. TEL 31-318-578550, FAX 31-318-578558. Circ: 3,000. **Co-sponsor:** Federatie Particulier Grondbezit, Nederlandse Vereniging van Boseigenaren.

332.63 GBR ISSN 1757-7950
LANDLORD & BUY-TO-LET MAGAZINE. Text in English. 2007. bi-m. free to qualified personnel (effective 2009). adv. 64 p./no.; back issues avail. **Document type:** *Magazine, Trade.* **Description:** Designed for landlords and associated professionals of private residential sector.
Formerly (until 2008): Landlord (1753-2744)
Related titles: Online - full text ed.
Published by: Accession Exhibitions & Publishing Limited, 88 Lonsdale St, Stoke on Trent, ST4 4DP, United Kingdom. helpdesk@accession.uk.com. Ed. Oliver Romain. Adv. contact Warren Guirey. page GBP 1,695; 213 x 303. Circ: 25,000.

333.33 340 GBR
LANDLORD AND TENANT FACTBOOK. Text in English. 1992. base vol. plus updates 3/yr. looseleaf. GBP 451 base vol(s). domestic; EUR 596 base vol(s). in Europe; USD 775 base vol(s). elsewhere (effective 2011). **Document type:** *Handbook/Manual/Guide, Trade.* **Description:** Provides quick reference point on landlord and tenant law.
Published by: Sweet & Maxwell Ltd. (Subsidiary of: Thomson Reuters Corp.), 100 Avenue Rd, London, NW3 3PF, United Kingdom. TEL 44-20-73937000, FAX 44-20-74491144, sweetandmaxwell.customer.services@thomson.com. Eds. Matthew Marsh, Zia Bhaloo. **Subscr. to:** PO Box 1000, Andover SP10 9AF, United Kingdom. TEL 44-20-73938051, sweetandmaxwell.international.queries@thomson.com.

333.33 340 GBR ISSN 1365-8018
LANDLORD & TENANT LAW REVIEW. Variant title: Landlord & Tenant Review. Text in English. 1996. bi-m. GBP 324, EUR 427, USD 557 (effective 2012). **Document type:** *Journal, Academic/Scholarly.* **Description:** Provides specialist coverage of both commercial and residential landlord-and-tenant issues.
Published by: Sweet & Maxwell Ltd. (Subsidiary of: Thomson Reuters Corp.), 100 Avenue Rd, London, NW3 3PF, United Kingdom. TEL 44-20-73937000, FAX 44-20-74491144, sweetandmaxwell.customer.services@thomson.com. Ed. Mark Pawlowski. **Subscr. to:** PO Box 1000, Andover SP10 9AF, United Kingdom. TEL 44-20-73938051, sweetandmaxwell.international.queries@thomson.com.

333.33 340 GBR ISSN 1463-4473
LANDLORD AND TENANT REPORTS. Text in English. 1998. 3/yr. GBP 577, EUR 761, USD 992 (effective 2012). **Document type:** *Report, Trade.* **Description:** Presents reliable coverage of key decisions, helping the reader to carry out speedy research and assimilate the relevant information.
Published by: Sweet & Maxwell Ltd. (Subsidiary of: Thomson Reuters Corp.), 100 Avenue Rd, London, NW3 3PF, United Kingdom. TEL 44-20-73937000, FAX 44-20-74491144, sweetandmaxwell.customer.services@thomson.com. **Subscr. to:** PO Box 1000, Andover SP10 9AF, United Kingdom. TEL 44-20-73938051, sweetandmaxwell.international.queries@thomson.com.

333.33 340 GBR
LANDLORD AND TENANT SERVICE. Text in English. 1998. m. GBP 820 (effective 2009). **Description:** Contains the complete text of Woodfall: Landlord and Tenant, Property Legislation, and What's New, which updates readers on developments affecting landlord and tenant practice.
Media: CD-ROM.
Published by: Sweet & Maxwell Ltd. (Subsidiary of: Thomson Reuters Corp.), 100 Avenue Rd, London, NW3 3PF, United Kingdom. TEL 44-20-73937000, FAX 44-20-74491144, sweetandmaxwell.customer.services@thomson.com. **Subscr. to:** PO Box 1000, Andover SP10 9AF, United Kingdom. TEL 44-20-73938051, sweetandmaxwell.international.queries@thomson.com.

346.04 USA ISSN 1932-975X
LANDLORD TENANT. CALIFORNIA. Text in English. 2006. m. USD 213; USD 17.75 per issue (effective 2008). **Document type:** *Newsletter, Trade.* **Description:** Designed to help property owners and managers protect themselves against tenant issues that can carry serious legal consequences.
Related titles: Online - full text ed.: ISSN 1932-9768.
Published by: Quinlan Publishing Group (Subsidiary of: Thomson West), 610 Opperman Dr, Eagan, MN 55123. TEL 651-687-7000, 800-937-8529, FAX 800-227-7097, bookstore@westgroup.com, http://west.thomson.com/quinlan.

346.04 USA ISSN 1933-0286
LANDLORD TENANT. FLORIDA. Text in English. 2006. m. USD 213; USD 17.75 per issue (effective 2008). **Document type:** *Newsletter, Trade.* **Description:** Designed to help property owners and managers protect themselves against tenant issues that can carry serious legal consequences.
Related titles: Online - full text ed.: ISSN 1933-0294.
Published by: Quinlan Publishing Group (Subsidiary of: Thomson West), 610 Opperman Dr, Eagan, MN 55123. TEL 651-687-7000, 800-937-8529, FAX 800-227-7097, bookstore@westgroup.com, http://west.thomson.com/quinlan.

346.04 USA ISSN 1933-0308
LANDLORD TENANT. ILLINOIS. Text in English. 2006. m. USD 213; USD 17.75 per issue (effective 2008). **Document type:** *Newsletter, Trade.* **Description:** Designed to help property owners and managers protect themselves against tenant issues that can carry serious legal consequences.
Related titles: Online - full text ed.: ISSN 1933-0316.
Published by: Quinlan Publishing Group (Subsidiary of: Thomson West), 610 Opperman Dr, Eagan, MN 55123. TEL 651-687-7000, 800-937-8529, FAX 800-227-7097, bookstore@westgroup.com, http://west.thomson.com/quinlan.

340.5 USA ISSN 0271-5228
KF587.8
LANDLORD TENANT LAW BULLETIN. Text in English. 1979. m. USD 168; USD 14 per issue (effective 2008). index. back issues avail. **Document type:** *Newsletter, Trade.* **Description:** Designed to help property owners and managers address tenant issues that can carry serious legal consequences.
Related titles: Online - full text ed.: ISSN 1544-5046.
Indexed: A22.
—CCC.
Published by: Quinlan Publishing Group (Subsidiary of: Thomson West), 610 Opperman Dr, Eagan, MN 55123. TEL 651-687-7000, 800-937-8529, FAX 800-227-7097, bookstore@westgroup.com, http://west.thomson.com/quinlan.

333.33 USA
LANDLORD - TENANT MONTHLY. Text in English. m. **Document type:** *Newsletter, Trade.*
Published by: Treiman Publications Corp., 2517 Owego Rd, Vestal, NY 13850. TEL 800-338-5262, FAX 607-748-4150, TreimanPub@aol.com, http://www.treimanpublication.com.

346.04 USA ISSN 1932-9776
LANDLORD TENANT. NEW YORK. Text in English. 2006. m. USD 213; USD 17.75 per issue (effective 2008). **Document type:** *Newsletter, Trade.* **Description:** Designed to help property owners and managers protect themselves against tenant issues that can carry serious legal consequences.
Related titles: Online - full text ed.: ISSN 1932-9784.
Published by: Quinlan Publishing Group (Subsidiary of: Thomson West), 610 Opperman Dr, Eagan, MN 55123. TEL 800-937-8529, FAX 800-227-7097, http://west.thomson.com/quinlan.

346.04 USA ISSN 1932-9792
LANDLORD TENANT. OHIO. Text in English. 2006. m. USD 213; USD 17.75 per issue (effective 2008). **Document type:** *Newsletter, Trade.* **Description:** Designed to help property owners and managers protect themselves against tenant issues that can carry serious legal consequences.
Related titles: Online - full text ed.: ISSN 1932-9806.
Published by: Quinlan Publishing Group (Subsidiary of: Thomson West), 610 Opperman Dr, Eagan, MN 55123. TEL 651-687-7000, 800-937-8529, FAX 800-227-7097, bookstore@westgroup.com, http://west.thomson.com/quinlan.

346.011 USA ISSN 1932-9814
LANDLORD TENANT. PENNSYLVANIA. Text in English. 2006. m. USD 213; USD 17.75 per issue (effective 2008). **Document type:** *Newsletter, Trade.* **Description:** Designed to help property owners and managers protect themselves against tenant issues that can carry serious legal consequences.
Related titles: Online - full text ed.: ISSN 1932-9822.
Published by: Quinlan Publishing Group (Subsidiary of: Thomson West), 610 Opperman Dr, Eagan, MN 55123. TEL 651-687-7000, 800-937-8529, FAX 800-227-7097, bookstore@westgroup.com, http://west.thomson.com/quinlan.

346.04 USA ISSN 1542-5010
LANDLORD'S 'BOTTOM LINE' BULLETIN. Text in English. 1998. m. USD 213; USD 17.75 per issue (effective 2008). **Document type:** *Newsletter, Trade.* **Description:** Contains subletting, tenant disputes, multifamily dwellings, low-income housing issues, fair housing act regulations, drug busts and other criminal activities, and renting to students or multiple young couples.
Former titles (until 2002): Quinlan's Property Managers' Hotline (1529-7004); (until 199?): Quinlan's Property Managers' Insider (1523-2654)
Related titles: Online - full text ed.: ISSN 1545-925X.
Published by: Quinlan Publishing Group (Subsidiary of: Thomson West), 610 Opperman Dr, Eagan, MN 55123. TEL 651-687-7000, 800-937-8529, FAX 800-227-7097, bookstore@westgroup.com, http://west.thomson.com/quinlan. Ed. Annie Archaumbalt. Pub. Dennis Hofmaier.

R

333.33 USA ISSN 0163-951X
LANDOWNER. Text in English. 1979. s-m. USD 84 to individuals. **Description:** Provides information on the land market. Includes safe, creative ways to buy, sell or rent farm property. Also covers regional price trends and environmentally sound methods of farmland stewardship to enhance land productivity.
Published by: (Professional Farmers of America), Oster Communications, LLC, 219 Main St, Ste 200, Cedar Falls, IA 50613. TEL 319-277-1278, 800-635-3936, FAX 319-277-5803. Ed. Jerry Carlson.

333.33 USA
LAS VEGAS NEW HOMES GUIDE. Text in English. 2006. m. adv. **Document type:** *Magazine, Consumer.*
Published by: Stephens Media LLC, PO Box 70, Las Vegas, NV 89125-0070. TEL 702-383-1200, FAX 702-940-1096. Pub. Claire DeJesus TEL 702-871-6780 ext 356. adv.: color page USD 3,260; trim 6.5 x 10.5. Circ: 40,000 (free).

333.33 USA
THE LAS VEGAS REAL ESTATE REPORT. Text in English. 19??. m. USD 450; USD 45 per issue; free to qualified personnel (effective 2009). back issues avail. **Document type:** *Newsletter, Consumer.* **Description:** Features condos, single-family homes, gated communities, golf and tennis country clubs, high-rise luxury condos and estate properties in Las Vegas.
Media: Online - full content.
Published by: Information Designs, 921 American Pacific Dr, 305, Las Vegas, NV 89014. TEL 702-525-1888, rick@rereport.com, http://www.rereport.com.

LAW & PRACTICE OF REGISTERED CONVEYANCING. *see* LAW

346.04 USA ISSN 1940-3143
THE LEGAL DESCRIPTION; legislative and legal analysis for the real estate industry. Text in English. 2000. 24/yr. USD 575 combined subscription (print & online eds.) (effective 2008). adv. back issues avail. **Document type:** *Newsletter, Trade.* **Description:** Provides analysis of federal legislation and issues about title insurance and real estate settlement services.
Related titles: Online - full text ed.: ISSN 1940-5367.
Published by: October Research Corporation, PO Box 370, Richfield, OH 44286. TEL 330-659-6101, 877-662-8623, FAX 330-659-6102, contactus@thetitlereport.com, http://www.octoberresearch.com. Eds. Matthew Smith TEL 330-659-6101 ext 6144, Syndie Eardly.

346.04 USA
LEGALINES: PROPERTY KEYED TO THE BROWDER CASEBOOK. Text in English. irreg., latest vol.5. USD 21.95 per vol. **Document type:** *Monographic series, Trade.*
Published by: Gilbert Law Summaries (Subsidiary of: Thomson West), 610 Opperman Dr, Eagan, MN 55123. TEL 651-687-7000, 800-937-8529, bookstore@westgroup.com, http://west.thomson.com.

346.04 USA
LEGALINES: PROPERTY KEYED TO THE CRIBBET CASEBOOK. Text in English. irreg., latest 8th ed. USD 31.95 8th ed. (effective 2008). **Document type:** *Monographic series, Trade.* **Description:** Provides detailed explanation of the cases in the real property casebook by Cribbet.
Published by: Gilbert Law Summaries (Subsidiary of: Thomson West), 610 Opperman Dr, Eagan, MN 55123. TEL 651-687-7000, 800-937-8529, bookstore@westgroup.com.

346.04 USA
LEGALINES: PROPERTY KEYED TO THE DUKEMINIER CASEBOOK. Text in English. irreg., latest 6th ed. USD 30.95 6th ed. (effective 2008). **Document type:** *Monographic series, Trade.* **Description:** Provides detailed explanations of the cases in Dukeminier's real property casebook.
Published by: Gilbert Law Summaries (Subsidiary of: Thomson West), 610 Opperman Dr, Eagan, MN 55123. TEL 651-687-7000, 800-937-8529, bookstore@westgroup.com.

346.04 USA
LEGALINES: REAL PROPERTY KEYED TO THE RABIN CASEBOOK. Text in English. irreg., latest 3rd ed. USD 30.95 3rd ed. (effective 2008). **Document type:** *Monographic series, Trade.* **Description:** Provides detailed explanation of the cases in the real property casebook by Rabin.
Published by: Gilbert Law Summaries (Subsidiary of: Thomson West), 610 Opperman Dr, Eagan, MN 55123. TEL 651-687-7000, 800-937-8529, bookstore@westgroup.com.

333.33 332.63 FRA ISSN 0767-6379
LA LETTRE DE LA PIERRE. Text in French. 1985. 42/yr. EUR 728 (effective 2008). **Document type:** *Newsletter.* **Description:** Studies real estate trends and investment strategies.
Published by: Agence Innovapresse, 1 Place Boieldieu, Paris, 75002, France. TEL 33-1-42480907, FAX 33-1-42470076, abonnement@innovapresse.com. Ed. Anne Peyret.

333.33 USA ISSN 1555-7286
LEXISNEXIS ANSWERGUIDE NEW YORK REAL PROPERTY. Text in English. 2004. a. USD 125 per issue (effective 2008). **Document type:** *Handbook/Manual/Guide, Trade.* **Description:** Provides guidance for counsel representing purchasers, sellers, landlords and tenants and outlines methods for obtaining financing for both residential and commercial properties.
Related titles: Online - full text ed.: ISSN 1555-7294.
Published by: LexisNexis (Subsidiary of: LexisNexis North America), 701 E Water St, PO Box 7587, Charlottesville, VA 22906. TEL 434-972-7600, 800-446-3410, customer.support@lexisnexis.com, http://www.lexisnexis.com.

346.04 USA ISSN 1933-0553
KF566.A3
LEXISNEXIS REAL ESTATE REPORT. Text in English. 2006. m. USD 750 (effective 2007). **Description:** Covers real estate law. Presents case summaries, legislative and regulatory news, full-text court documents, and exclusive commentary articles on cases and issues in real estate litigation.
—CCC.
Published by: Mealey Publications & Conferences Group (Subsidiary of: LexisNexis North America), 217 W Church Rd, King of Prussia, PA 19406-0230. TEL 610-768-7800, 800-632-5397, FAX 610-768-0880, mealeyinfo@lexisnexis.com, http://www.mealeys.com.

728 333.33 BEL ISSN 1379-700X
LA LIBRE ESSENTIELLE IMMO. Text in French. 2002. m. back issues avail. **Document type:** *Magazine, Consumer.*
Published by: La Libre Belgique S.A., 79 Rue des Francs, Brussels, 1040, Belgium. TEL 32-2-7444444, FAX 32-2-2112832, llb.direction@saipm.com.

333.33 USA
LIVES OF REAL ESTATE; a brand of real trends. Cover title: lore. Text in English. 2004. bi-m. adv. **Document type:** *Magazine, Trade.* **Description:** Covers the personal stories of successful and distinct real estate professionals.
Published by: REAL Trends Inc., 6898 S University Blvd Ste 200, Littleton, CO 80122. TEL 303-741-1000, FAX 303-741-1070, realtrends@realtrends.com, http://www.realtrends.com/go/index.php. Ed. Steve Murray. Pub. Anne Randolph. adv.: page USD 6,000; trim 8.375 x 10.875.

LIVING FRANCE. *see* TRAVEL AND TOURISM

333.33 975.02 976.02 USA ISSN 1539-3208
LIVING SOUTHERN STYLE; featuring real estate opportunities throughout the South. Text in English. 2/yr. adv.
Published by: Realty Presentations, Inc., P.O. Box 374, Wilmington, NC 28402. TEL 910-763-2100, 800-713-4263, FAX 910-763-1461, info@livesouth.com, http://www.livesouth.com. Ed. Dave Robertson. Adv. contacts Daniel Cort, Daniel Keir.

333.5 RUS
LIZING REVIU/LEASING REVIEW. Text in Russian. 1997. bi-m. RUR 660 for 6 mos. (effective 2004). **Document type:** *Magazine, Trade.*
Related titles: Online - full text ed.
Published by: Izdatel'skii Dom Delovaya Pressa, Staromonetnyi per 10, Moscow, 109180, Russian Federation. TEL 7-095-9508360, sales@delpressa.ru. Ed. Aleksandr S Pronichkin.

333.33 910.09 USA
LOAN-A-HOME DIRECTORY. Text in English. 1968. s-a. looseleaf. USD 35. Supplement avail. **Document type:** *Directory.* **Description:** Residential listing service for members of the international academic, business and retired communities who need temporary long-term housing worldwide.
Published by: Muriel Gould, Ed.& Pub., 7 McGregor Rd, Woods Hole, MA 02543. TEL 508-548-4032.

333.33 USA ISSN 1943-4510
LOCAL REAL ESTATE DEALS MAGAZINE. Text in English. 2008. bi-m. adv. back issues avail. **Document type:** *Magazine, Consumer.* **Description:** Covers real estate trends around the country. Lists profiles of a succesful entrepreneurs and business leaders.
Published by: Home Team USA, Inc., 1612 Centerville Tpke, Ste 307, Virginia Beach, VA 23464. TEL 757-729-3124, 888-420-3560, FAX 757-275-2769. adv.: page USD 600; 7.75 x 10.

333.33 690 FIN ISSN 1455-7215
LOCUS. Text in Finnish. 1997. 8/yr. EUR 44 (effective 2006). adv. **Document type:** *Magazine, Trade.* **Description:** Magazine on management, dealing with the real estate business, construction and the management of companies operating in the real estate cluster.
Published by: Rakennustieto Oy/Building Information Ltd., Runeberginkatu 5, PO Box 1004, Helsinki, 00101, Finland. TEL 358-207-476400, FAX 358-207-476320, http://www.rakennustieto.fi. Ed. Saara Kerttula. Circ: 4,000.

333.33 GBR ISSN 2041-2037
▼ **LONDON PROPERTY (CENTRAL & SOUTH EDITION).** Text in English. 2009. m. GBP 3.95 newsstand/cover (effective 2010). adv. **Document type:** *Magazine, Trade.* **Description:** Covers the finest local properties on the market.
Published by: LTP Publications Ltd., Unit A1, Waterfront Studios, 1 Dock Rd, London, E16 1AG, United Kingdom. TEL 44-20-74742828. Adv. contact Steve Jessop TEL 44-7876-744900.

333.33 GBR ISSN 2041-1766
▼ **LONDON PROPERTY (ISLINGTON, CITY & DOCKLANDS EDITION).** Text in English. 2009. m. GBP 3.95 newsstand/cover (effective 2010). adv. **Document type:** *Magazine, Trade.* **Description:** Covers trends in the finest local properties on the market.
Published by: LTP Publications Ltd., Unit A1, Waterfront Studios, 1 Dock Rd, London, E16 1AG, United Kingdom. TEL 44-20-74742828. Adv. contact Mark Palmer TEL 44-7876-567900.

333.33 GBR ISSN 2041-1774
▼ **LONDON PROPERTY (NORTHWEST & CENTRAL EDITION).** Text in English. 2009. m. GBP 3.95 newsstand/cover (effective 2010). adv. **Document type:** *Magazine, Trade.* **Description:** Covers trends in the finest local properties on the market.
Published by: LTP Publications Ltd., Unit A1, Waterfront Studios, 1 Dock Rd, London, E16 1AG, United Kingdom. TEL 44-20-74742828. Adv. contact Kim Kenny TEL 44-7876-550900.

333.3 CAN
M R E ACTION. Text in English. 1980. m. looseleaf. free. charts; stat.
Published by: Manitoba Real Estate Association, 1240 Portage Ave, 2nd Fl, Winnipeg, MB R3G 0T6, Canada. TEL 204-772-0405, FAX 204-775-3781. Ed. Brian Collie. Circ: 2,100.

333.33 GBR
M - THE MAGAZINE FOR BRITANNIA MEMBERS. Text in English. 3/yr. free to members (effective 2009). adv. **Document type:** *Magazine, Consumer.* **Description:** Provides information on the Society and the benefits of remaining mutual to members.
Former titles: Britannia Home; Society
Related titles: Online - full text ed.
Published by: (Britannia Building Society), Redwood Publishing, 7 St Martin's Pl, London, WC2N 4HA, United Kingdom. TEL 44-20-77470700, FAX 44-20-77470701, info@redwoodgroup.net.

333.33 FRA ISSN 1969-1513
▼ **MAISONS & PROPRIETES.** Text in French. 2009. q. EUR 69 (effective 2010). **Document type:** *Magazine, Consumer.* **Description:** Specializes in exclusive listings of properties in France and abroad.
Published by: Lafont Presse, 53 Rue du Chemin Vert, Boulogne-Billancourt, 92100, France. TEL 33-1-46102121, FAX 33-1-45792211.

333.33 GBR ISSN 2040-7637
MALAYSIA REAL ESTATE REPORT. Text in English. 200?. q. EUR 820, USD 1,150 combined subscription (print & email eds.) (effective 2010). **Document type:** *Report, Trade.* **Description:** Provides industry professionals and strategists, sector analysts, business investors, trade associations and regulatory bodies with independent forecasts and competitive intelligence on the real estate and construction industry in Malaysia.
Related titles: E-mail ed.
Published by: Business Monitor International Ltd., Senator House, 85 Queen Victoria St, London, EC4V 4AB, United Kingdom. TEL 44-20-72480468, FAX 44-20-72480467, subs@businessmonitor.com.

333.33 USA
MANAGEMENT ISSUES & TRENDS. Abbreviated title: M I & T. Text in English. q. free to members (effective 2003). **Document type:** *Newsletter, Trade.* **Description:** Provides insights on critical business topics from industry leaders.
Published by: Council of Real Estate Brokerage Managers, 430 N Michigan Ave, Chicago, IL 60611. TEL 800-621-8738, FAX 312-329-8882, info@crb.com, http://www.crb.com.

MANAGING THE FLORIDA CONDOMINIUM. *see* LAW

333.33 336.2 DEU
MANDANTEN-INFORMATION FUER HAUS- UND GRUNDBESITZER. Text in German. 1993. m. EUR 1.91 per issue (effective 2011). **Document type:** *Journal, Trade.*
Formerly (until 2007): Steuer-Brief fuer Haus- und Grundbesitzer (0943-769X)
Published by: Deubner Verlag GmbH & Co. KG, Oststr 11, Cologne, 50996, Germany. TEL 49-221-9370180, FAX 49-221-93701890, kundenservice@deubner-verlag.de, http://www.vrp.de.

333.33 USA
MANN REPORT. Text in English. 10/yr. USD 49.95 domestic (effective 2005). adv. **Document type:** *Magazine, Trade.*
Formerly: Manhattan Report
Published by: Mann Publications, 1385 Broadway, Ste 1102, New York, NY 10018. TEL 212-840-6266, FAX 212-840-1954. Pub. Jeff Mann. adv.: page USD 3,000. Circ: 40,000 (paid).

333.340 USA ISSN 1938-6818
MANUFACTURED HOME LIVING. Text in English. 2007. q. free to members; USD 7.50 to non-members (effective 2007). **Document type:** *Newsletter, Consumer.* **Description:** Devoted to improving the health, safety, welfare and quality of life for owners of mobile homes by educating and promoting legislation that aids mobile home residents about laws pertaining to them.
Published by: Mobile Home Owners of America, 3421 Kitsap Way, Ste H, Bremerton, WA 98312. TEL 360-373-2436, mhoa2002@donobi.net, http://www.mhoa.net.

333.33 USA
THE MARIN REPORT; the Marin real estate newsletter. Text in English. m. free to qualified subscribers. **Document type:** *Newsletter, Consumer.* **Description:** Informs home buyers and sellers about the real estate process and the current market in Marin County, California.
Related titles: Online - full text ed.: 19??. USD 450; USD 45 per issue; free to qualified personnel (effective 2009).
Published by: Information Designs, 47E Tamal Vista Blvd, Corte Madera, CA 94925. TEL 415-297-9000. Pub. Rick Campbell.

333.33 USA
MARKET CYCLES. Text in English. 1983. q. **Document type:** *Newsletter.*
Published by: Center for Real Estate Studies, PO Box 3315, Palos Verde, CA 90274. TEL 310-265-0355. Ed. Eugene Vollucci. Circ: 3,200 (paid).

333.33 NLD ISSN 2210-4437
MARKETUPDATE. Text in Dutch. 2004. q. **Document type:** *Report, Consumer.*
Related titles: Online - full text ed.: ISSN 2210-4445; ◆ English Translation: MarketUpdate (English Edition). ISSN 2210-447X; ◆ German Translation: MarketUpdate (German Edition). ISSN 2210-4453.
Published by: Bouwfonds Real Estate Investment Management, De Beek 18, Hoevelaken, 3871 MS, Netherlands. TEL 31-33-7544630, FAX 31-33-7544656, researchbreim@bouwfonds.com, http://www.bouwfonds.com.

332.63 NLD ISSN 2210-447X
▼ **MARKETUPDATE (ENGLISH EDITION).** Text in English. 2010. q. **Document type:** *Report, Consumer.*
Related titles: Online - full text ed.: ISSN 2210-4488; ◆ Translation of: MarketUpdate. ISSN 2210-4437.
Published by: Bouwfonds Real Estate Investment Management, De Beek 18, Hoevelaken, 3871 MS, Netherlands. TEL 31-33-7504750, FAX 31-33-7504477, researchbreim@bouwfonds.com, http://www.bouwfonds.com.

332.63 NLD ISSN 2210-4453
MARKETUPDATE (GERMAN EDITION). Text in German. 2004. q. **Document type:** *Report, Consumer.*
Related titles: Online - full text ed.: ISSN 2210-4461; ◆ Translation of: MarketUpdate. ISSN 2210-4437.
Published by: Bouwfonds Real Estate Investment Management, De Beek 18, Hoevelaken, 3871 MS, Netherlands. TEL 31-33-7504750, FAX 31-33-7504477, researchbreim@bouwfonds.com, http://www.bouwfonds.com.

MARTIN BROWER'S ORANGE COUNTY REPORT. *see* BUSINESS AND ECONOMICS—Domestic Commerce

346.043 USA
MARYLAND LANDLORD - TENANT LAW: PRACTICE AND PROCEDURE. Text in English. 1994. irreg. (in 1 vol.), latest 2003, 3rd ed. USD 184 per vol. (effective 2008). 481 p./no.; **Document type:** *Monographic series, Trade.* **Description:** Covers all aspects of the landlord-tenant relationship.
Published by: Michie Company (Subsidiary of: LexisNexis North America), 701 E Water St, Charlottesville, VA 22902. TEL 434-972-7600, 800-446-3410, FAX 434-972-7677, custserv@michie.com, http://www.michie.com. Eds. Douglas M Bregman, Gary G Everngam.

346.043 USA
MARYLAND REAL ESTATE FORMS. Text in English. 1986. 2 base vols. plus irreg. updates. looseleaf. USD 303 base vol(s). includes diskette (effective 2006). **Document type:** *Handbook/Manual/Guide, Trade.* **Description:** Explanatory practice notes describe the source and purpose of the forms, and offer suggestions on how to modify them to best serve the client.
Related titles: Diskette ed.; Online - full text ed.
Published by: Michie Company (Subsidiary of: LexisNexis North America), 701 E Water St, Charlottesville, VA 22902. TEL 434-972-7600, 800-446-3410, FAX 434-972-7677, customer.support@lexisnexis.com, http://www.michie.com. Eds. Kevin L Shepherd, Russell R Reno Jr., Wilbur E Simmons Jr.

346.0437 USA
MASSACHUSETTS PRACTICE SERIES. REAL ESTATE LAW WITH FORMS. Text in English. 19??. 5 base vols. plus a. updates. USD 354 base vol(s). includes CD-ROM (effective 2010). **Document type:** *Journal, Trade.* **Description:** Provides detailed analysis of procedure and practice in the real estate area for buyers and sellers.
Related titles: Diskette ed.; ◆ Series of: Massachusetts Practice Series.
Published by: Thomson West (Subsidiary of: Thomson Reuters Corp.), 610 Opperman Dr, Eagan, MN 55123. TEL 651-687-7000, 800-344-5008, west.customer.service@thomson.com.

346.04 USA ISSN 2154-1841
MASSACHUSETTS REAL ESTATE LAW SOURCEBOOK & CITATOR. Text in English. 2003. a. USD 125 per issue (effective 2010). **Document type:** *Handbook/Manual/Guide, Trade.* **Description:** A compendium of essential resources for both commercial and residential real estate practitioners, combining the latest statutes, regulations, and judicial and administrative resources.
Formerly (until 2007): Massachusetts Real Estate Law Sourcebook (1553-4480)
Published by: Massachusetts Continuing Legal Education, Inc. (M C L E), 10 Winter Place, Boston, MA 02108. TEL 617-574-0300, http://www.mcle.org/MCLE_Web/ScriptContent/Index.cfm.

MASSACHUSETTS ZONING AND LAND USE LAW. *see* LAW

MATURE LIVING CHOICES. *see* GERONTOLOGY AND GERIATRICS

346.043 USA
MCDERMOTT'S HANDBOOK OF OHIO REAL ESTATE LAW. Text in English. 1980. irreg. (in 1 vol.). USD 20 (effective 2003). Supplement avail. **Description:** This reference covers virtually all Real Estate law topics in Ohio.

Published by: Michie Company (Subsidiary of: LexisNexis North America), 701 E Water St, Charlottesville, VA 22902. TEL 434-972-7600, 800-446-3410, FAX 434-972-7677, customer.support@lexisnexis.com, http://www.michie.com. Ed. Thomas J McDermott.

MEALEY'S LITIGATION REPORT: MORTGAGE LENDING. *see* LAW

THE MECKLENBURG TIMES. *see* BUSINESS AND ECONOMICS

333.33 USA ISSN 1931-8332
MEGA DREAM HOMES INTERNATIONAL. Text in English. 2006. m. adv. **Document type:** *Magazine, Consumer.*
Related titles: Online - full text ed.: free (effective 2011).
Published by: Dream Communications, Inc., PO Box 3049, La Jolla, CA 92038. TEL 619-858-5365, subscriptions@dreamhomesmagazine.com, http://www.dreamhomesmagazine.com. Pub. Michael Blassis. Adv. contact Andrew Dremak TEL 619-865-1440.

333.33 AUS ISSN 1832-4967
MELBOURNE LAND & HOMES. Text in English. 2005. q. **Document type:** *Magazine, Trade.* **Description:** Aims to provide the prospective buyer with information about all the leading house and land developments currently on offer around Melbourne.
Published by: Magnetwork Publishing (Subsidiary of: Hambledon Publishing), PO Box 23, Abbotsford, VIC 3067, Australia. TEL 61-3-94198947, http://www.melbournelandhomes.com.au/index.htm.

346.04 FRA ISSN 1779-6342
MEMENTO PRATIQUE FRANCIS LEFEBVRE. GESTION IMMOBILIERE. Text in French. 1997. a. EUR 97 newsstand/cover (effective 2008 & 2009).
Published by: Editions Francis Lefebvre, 42 rue de Villiers, Levallois-Perret, 92300, France. TEL 33-1-41052222.

346.04 FRA ISSN 1779-6334
MEMENTO PRATIQUE FRANCIS LEFEBVRE. URBANISME, CONSTRUCTION. Text in French. 1997. biennial. EUR 110 newsstand/cover (effective 2008 - 2009).
Published by: Editions Francis Lefebvre, 42 rue de Villiers, Levallois-Perret, 92300, France. TEL 33-1-41052222.

333.33 USA ISSN 0891-7698
MERCER COUNTY BOARD OF REALTORS. NEWSLINE. Text in English. 1986. 6/yr. USD 5. adv. **Document type:** *Newsletter, Trade.* **Description:** For realtors, realtor associates, and affiliate members of the Board. Covers real estate and related industries and association topics.
Published by: Mercer County Board of Realtors, 1428 Brunswick Avenue, Trenton, NJ 08638. TEL 609-392-3666, FAX 609-394-3939, info@mercerrealtors.com, http://www.mercerrealtors.com. Ed., Adv. contact Linda M Mottin TEL 856-424-9337. Circ: 1,900.

METRO CHICAGO OFFICE GUIDE. *see* BUSINESS AND ECONOMICS—Office Equipment And Services

333.33 USA ISSN 0893-0775
METRO CHICAGO REAL ESTATE. Text in English. 1913. bi-m. USD 40 (effective 2011). adv. bk.rev. back issues avail. **Document type:** *Magazine, Trade.*
Former titles (until 1987): Real Estate Magazine (0746-164X); (until 1983): Chicagoland's Real Estate Advertiser (0009-3769)
Related titles: Microfilm ed.
Published by: Real Estate Communications Group (Subsidiary of: Law Bulletin Publishing Co.), 415 N State St, Chicago, IL 60654. TEL 312-416-1860, FAX 312-416-1864, http://www.rejournals.com.

333.33 USA
METRO-CHICAGO RETAIL SPACE GUIDE. Text in English. 1989. s-a. free (effective 2011). adv. **Document type:** *Handbook/Manual/Guide, Trade.* **Description:** Contains a list of available retail space in and around the metropolitan Chicago market.
Related titles: Online - full text ed.
Published by: Law Bulletin Publishing Co., 415 N State St, Chicago, IL 60610. TEL 312-644-7800, FAX 312-753-7828, editor@lbpc.com, http://www.lawbulletin.com. Adv. contact Ernie Abood TEL 312-644-7119.

333.33 USA
METROHOUSE. Text in English. 2005 (Jun.). m. free. **Document type:** *Magazine, Consumer.* **Description:** Covers homeowner & home buying in the greater metropolitan areas north of New York City.
Published by: Luminary Publishing, Inc., 314 Wall St., Kingston, NY 12401. Ed. Jim Andrews.

333.33 CAN
METROTRENDS. Text in English. 1958. a. looseleaf. CAD 59.99. stat. **Document type:** *Journal, Trade.*
Formerly (until 1984): Real Estate Trends in Metropolitan Vancouver (0085-5405)
Published by: Real Estate Board of Greater Vancouver, 2433 Spruce St, Vancouver, BC V6H 4C8, Canada. TEL 604-736-4551, FAX 604-734-1778. Ed. Ray A Nelson. R&P Brad Scott. Circ: 1,000.

333.33 GBR ISSN 2040-7556
MEXICO REAL ESTATE REPORT. Text in English. 200?. q. EUR 820, USD 1,150 combined subscription (print & email eds.) (effective 2010). **Document type:** *Report, Trade.* **Description:** Provides industry professionals and strategists, sector analysts, business investors, trade associations and regulatory bodies with independent forecasts and competitive intelligence on the real estate and construction industry in Mexico.
Related titles: E-mail ed.
Published by: Business Monitor International Ltd., Senator House, 85 Queen Victoria St, London, EC4V 4AB, United Kingdom. TEL 44-20-72480468, FAX 44-20-72480467, subs@businessmonitor.com.

333.33 USA
MIAMI SKYLINE. Text in English. 2005. bi-m. **Document type:** *Magazine, Consumer.* **Description:** Focuses on the Miami-Dade, and Broward County condo market.
Address: 141 NE 3rd Ave. Ste. 303, Miami, FL 33132. TEL 305-377-2936, FAX 305-377-4402.

346.043 USA
MICHIGAN REAL ESTATE FORMS. Text in English. 1988. 3 base vols. plus irreg. updates. looseleaf. USD 398 base vol(s). (effective 2008). Supplement avail. **Document type:** *Monographic series, Trade.* **Description:** Covers every aspect of residential, commercial and construction transactions, leases, and condominiums.
Related titles: Diskette ed.: USD 75; Online - full text ed.
Published by: Michie Company (Subsidiary of: LexisNexis North America), 701 E Water St, Charlottesville, VA 22902. TEL 434-972-7600, 800-446-3410, FAX 434-972-7677, customer.support@lexisnexis.com, http://www.michie.com.

333.33 USA ISSN 1945-8053
MID ATLANTIC REAL ESTATE JOURNAL. Text in English. 2003. bi-w. USD 99 (effective 2009). adv. **Document type:** *Journal, Trade.* **Description:** Reports on the selling and leasing of commercial properties and also promotes services for real estate owners, developers, investors and brokers in Mid Atlantic states.
Formerly (until 200?): N J P A Real Estate Journal (1551-8655)
Address: PO Box 26, Accord, MA 02018. TEL 781-871-5298, 800-584-1062, FAX 781-871-5299, http://www.marejournal.com. Ed. Lindsay Hurley. Pub. Linda Christman. adv.: B&W page USD 1,295; trim 11 x 14.

333.33 USA ISSN 0893-2719
MIDWEST REAL ESTATE NEWS. Text in English. 1984. bi-m. USD 29 domestic; USD 75 foreign; USD 10 per issue (effective 2011). back issues avail.; reprints avail. **Document type:** *Magazine, Trade.* **Description:** Covers commercial and industrial real estate activity in 10 Midwestern states: Illinois, Indiana, Iowa, Kansas, Michigan, Minnesota, Missouri, Nebraska, Ohio, and Wisconsin.
Related titles: Microform ed.: (from PQC); Online - full text ed.: free (effective 2011).
Indexed: A22, B02, B15, B17, B18, G04, G06, G07, G08, I05.
—CCC.
Published by: Real Estate Communications Group (Subsidiary of: Law Bulletin Publishing Co.), 415 N State St, Chicago, IL 60654. TEL 312-416-1860, FAX 312-416-1864. Ed. Dan Rafter. Pub. Mark Menzies.

MIET- UND PACHTRECHT. *see* LAW—Civil Law

333.33 CHE
MIETEN UND WOHNEN. Short title: M & W. Text in German. 1992. 10/yr. CHF 25; CHF 35 foreign. **Document type:** *Newsletter.*
Published by: Schweizerischer Mieterinnen- und Mieterverband, Brauerstr 75, Zuerich, 8026, Switzerland. TEL 41-1-2910937, FAX 41-1-2910968. Ed. Elfie Schoepf. Adv. contact Edith Helfer.

333.33 DEU ISSN 0723-3418
MIETER MAGAZIN. Text in German. 1982. 10/yr. EUR 20; EUR 2 newsstand/cover (effective 2009). adv. **Document type:** *Magazine, Consumer.*
Published by: Berliner Mieterverein, Behrenstr 1C, Berlin, 10117, Germany. TEL 49-30-226260, FAX 49-30-22626162, bmv@berliner-mieterverein.de. adv.: B&W page EUR 1,500, color page EUR 2,400; trim 192 x 254. Circ: 110,000 (controlled).

333.33 CHE
MIETER ZEITUNG. Text in German. 11/yr.
Address: Postfach, Aarau, 5001, Switzerland. TEL 064-249449. Ed. Josef Beck. Circ: 56,000.

MIETRECHT KOMPAKT. *see* LAW—Civil Law

MIETRECHTLICHE ENTSCHEIDUNGEN. *see* LAW—Civil Law

333.33 USA ISSN 1086-4709
KFC140
MILLER & STARR CALIFORNIA REAL ESTATE. Text in English. 19??. irreg. looseleaf. price varies. **Document type:** *Monographic series, Trade.*
Media: CD-ROM. **Related titles:** Print ed.: 19??. USD 1,548 3rd ed. (effective 2008).
Published by: Thomson West (Subsidiary of: Thomson Reuters Corp.), 610 Opperman Dr, Eagan, MN 55123. TEL 651-687-7000, 800-344-5008, FAX 651-687-6674, west.support@thomson.com.

346.043 USA
MINNESOTA LEGAL FORMS: RESIDENTIAL REAL ESTATE. Text in English. 1981. base vol. plus irreg. updates. looseleaf. USD 129 base vol(s). (effective 2008). **Document type:** *Handbook/Manual/Guide, Trade.* **Description:** A guide for attorneys, closing agents, and other persons who draft real estate documents, this collection contains deeds, residential mortgage, affidavit and lien forms.
Related titles: Diskette ed.
Published by: Michie Company (Subsidiary of: LexisNexis North America), 701 E Water St, Charlottesville, VA 22902. TEL 434-972-7600, 800-446-3410, FAX 434-972-7677, customer.support@lexisnexis.com, http://www.michie.com.

346.04 USA ISSN 1931-9762
KFM5480
MINNESOTA PRACTICE SERIES. REAL ESTATE LAW. Text in English. 2003. a. USD 94 per issue (effective 2009). **Document type:** *Monographic series, Trade.* **Description:** Designed to be a resource for attorneys and real estate professionals at all levels of experience.
Published by: Thomson West (Subsidiary of: Thomson Reuters Corp.), 610 Opperman Dr, Eagan, MN 55123. TEL 651-687-7000, 800-344-5008, FAX 651-687-6674, west.support@thomson.com, http://west.thomson.com. Ed. Eileen Roberts.

333.3 USA ISSN 0893-2255
MINNESOTA REAL ESTATE JOURNAL. Text in English. 1985. m. USD 85 (effective 2011). back issues avail. **Document type:** *Journal, Trade.*
Related titles: Online - full text ed.: free (effective 2011).
Published by: Real Estate Communications Group (Subsidiary of: Law Bulletin Publishing Co.), 5353 Wayzata Blvd, Ste 307, Minneapolis, MN 55416. TEL 952-885-0815. Pub. Jeff Johnson.

333.33 USA
MINNESOTA REAL ESTATE JOURNAL LEASING GUIDE. Text in English. 1990. q. free with subsc. to Minnesota Real Estate Journal. adv. **Document type:** *Guide, Trade.* **Description:** Contains news coverage on office, industrial, retail, multi-housing, hotel, senior housing and development.
Published by: Law Bulletin Publishing Co., 415 N State St, Chicago, IL 60610. TEL 312-416-1860, FAX 312-753-7828, editor@lbpc.com, http://www.lawbulletin.com.

MINNESOTA RESIDENTIAL REAL ESTATE. *see* LAW—Civil Law

333.33 RUS
MIR I DOM. Text in Russian. m. USD 125 in United States.
Indexed: RASB.
Published by: Elita Publisher, A-ya 8, Moscow, 125252, Russian Federation. TEL 7-095-9435289, FAX 7-095-9435289. Ed. V M Gavrilov. **Dist. by:** East View Information Services, 10601 Wayzata Blvd, Minneapolis, MN 55305. TEL 952-252-1201, 800-477-1005, FAX 952-252-1202, info@eastview.com, http://www.eastview.com.

333.33 USA ISSN 1087-1128
MISSOURI REALTOR. Text in English. 1937. q. USD 15 (effective 2005). adv. **Document type:** *Magazine, Trade.* **Description:** Summarizes news of Missouri real estate and activities of the Missouri Association of Realtors.
Published by: Missouri Association of Realtors, 2601 Bernadette Pl, Box 1327, Columbia, MO 65205. TEL 573-445-8400, 800-403-0101, FAX 573-445-7865, http://www.missourirealtor.org/. Ed., R&P Susan Harper. Adv. contact Carma Reinhart. B&W page USD 600, color page USD 1,025. Circ: 23,000 (controlled).

333.33 CHE ISSN 1420-6994
MITTELALTER (BASEL)/MEDIOEVO/MOYEN AGE/TEMP MEDIEVAL; Zeitschrift des Schweizerischer Burgenvereins. Text in German, French. q. CHF 90 membership; CHF 12.50 newsstand/cover (effective 2008). charts; illus. **Document type:** *Journal, Academic/Scholarly.* **Description:** Covers medieval history, archeology, and castles in Switzerland.
Formerly (until 1996): Schweizerischer Burgenverein. Nachrichten (1420-9594)
Published by: Schweizerischer Burgenverein, Blochmonterstr 22, Basel, 4054, Switzerland. TEL 41-61-3612444, FAX 41-61-3639405, info@burgenverein.ch. Circ: 1,253 (paid).

333.33 USA
MOBILEHOME PARKS REPORT; the monthly report devoted to investment and ownership. Text in English. 1980. m. USD 135 (effective 2001). bk.rev. back issues avail. **Document type:** *Newsletter.* **Description:** Reports on legislation, issues and trends important to owners and developers of manufactured housing communities.
Formerly: Kerr Report (0273-2726)
Published by: Parks Publishing Company, 3807 Pasadena Ave, Ste 100, Sacramento, CA 95821. TEL 916-971-0489. Ed., Pub., R&P Thomas P Kerr. Circ: 300.

333.331 USA ISSN 0195-8194
HF5549.5.R47
MOBILITY (WASHINGTON). Text in English. 1980. 12/yr. USD 48; free to members (effective 2005). adv. bk.rev. index. **Description:** Examines industry issues and communicates association information to members.
Published by: Employee Relocation Council, 1717 Pennsylvania Ave NW, Ste. 800, Washington, DC 20006-4665. TEL 202-857-0857, FAX 202-467-4012. Pub. Jerry Holloman. Circ: 12,500.

MODERN ESTATE PLANNING. *see* BUSINESS AND ECONOMICS—Banking And Finance

346.04 GBR ISSN 1757-8116
MODERN STUDIES IN PROPERTY LAW. Text in English. 2001. a. GBP 75, USD 150 (effective 2011). **Document type:** *Journal, Academic/Scholarly.* **Description:** Covers a broad range of topics of immediate importance, not only in domestic law but also on a worldwide scale.
Published by: Hart Publishing Ltd., 16c Worchester Pl, Oxford, OX1 2JW, United Kingdom. TEL 44-1865-517530, FAX 44-1865-510710, mail@hartpub.co.uk, http://www.hartpub.co.uk. Ed. Susan Bright.

333.33 USA ISSN 1052-469X
MONTANA LAND MAGAZINE. Text in English. 1982. q. USD 20; USD 40 foreign. adv. back issues avail. **Document type:** *Magazine, Consumer.* **Description:** Lists real estate for sale throughout Montana and surrounding states.
Published by: Real Estate Publications, Inc. (Billings), PO Box 50999, Billings, MT 59105-0901. TEL 406-259-3534, FAX 406-259-1676. Ed. M Dangerfield.

332.63 USA ISSN 1541-8855
HG5095
MOODY'S CREDIT OPINIONS: REITS AND REAL ESTATE OPERATING COMPANIES. (Real Estate Investment Trusts) Text in English. q.
Published by: Moody's Investors Service, Inc. (Subsidiary of: Dun & Bradstreet Corporation), 99 Church St, New York, NY 10007. TEL 212-553-0300, http://www.moodys.com.

333.5 CZE ISSN 1212-5415
MORAVSKE REALITY. Variant title: Realtip. Text in Czech. 1999. m. CZK 180; CZK 17 newsstand/cover (effective 2010). adv. **Document type:** *Newspaper, Trade.*
Published by: Media-Press, spol. s r.o., Koblizna 24, Brno, 602 00, Czech Republic. TEL 420-533-339711, FAX 420-545-216347, denik@inzertexpres.cz, http://www.inzertexpres.cz.

333.33 USA ISSN 0047-813X
KF566.A3
MORTGAGE AND REAL ESTATE EXECUTIVES REPORT. Text in English. 1969. base vol. plus a. updates. USD 474 (effective 2008). charts; illus.; stat. **Document type:** *Newsletter, Trade.* **Description:** Provides analysis of recent developments and topics of discussion in the modern real estate market.
Incorporates (in Sep. 1976): Condominium Report; (in Jul. 1976): Real Estate Investors Report
Indexed: BLI, P48, P53, P54, PQC.
—CCC.
Published by: R I A (Subsidiary of: Thomson Reuters Corp.), PO Box 6159, Carol Stream, IL 60197. TEL 800-323-8724, ria.customerservices@thomson.com, http://ria.thomsonreuters.com. Circ: 5,000 (paid).

MORTGAGE & REAL ESTATE NEWS. *see* BUSINESS AND ECONOMICS—Banking And Finance

MORTGAGE BANKING; the magazine of real estate finance. *see* BUSINESS AND ECONOMICS—Banking And Finance

MORTGAGE FINANCE GAZETTE. *see* BUSINESS AND ECONOMICS—Banking And Finance

MORTGAGE LAW CENTRAL; legal and regulatory news and analysis for the mortgage industry. *see* BUSINESS AND ECONOMICS—Investments

MORTGAGE LENDING EXPERT. *see* BUSINESS AND ECONOMICS—Banking And Finance

R

332.63 AUS ISSN 1445-7970
MORTGAGE PROFESSIONAL AUSTRALIA. Text in English. 2003. m. AUD 60 domestic (effective 2008). **Document type:** *Magazine, Trade.*
Published by: Key Media Pty Ltd, Level 10, 1 Chandos St, St Leonards, NSW 2065, Australia. TEL 61-2-94394566, FAX 61-2-94394599, subscriptions@keymedia.com.au, http://www.keymedia.com.au. Ed. Larry Schlesinger TEL 61-2-84374790.

333.33 005.5 USA ISSN 1098-4038
MORTGAGE TECHNOLOGY. Abbreviated title: M T. Text in English. 1996. q. USD 89 domestic; USD 99 in Canada; USD 119 elsewhere (effective 2008). adv. back issues avail.; reprints avail. **Document type:** *Magazine, Trade.* **Description:** Contains the latest information on technology-related developments and their influences in the mortgage industry.
Related titles: Online - full text ed.
Indexed: B02, B03, B11, B15, B17, B18, BLI, G04, G06, G07, G08, I05, P48, P53, P54, PQC, T03.
—CCC.
Published by: SourceMedia, Inc., One State St Plz, 27th Fl, New York, NY 10004. TEL 212-803-8200, 800-221-1809, FAX 212-747-1154, custserv@sourcemedia.com, http://www.sourcemedia.com. Ed. Anthony Garritano TEL 212-803-8242. Circ: 12,000.

332.63 USA
MORTGAGEPULSE: NORTHEAST. Text in English. m. **Document type:** *Newsletter, Trade.* **Description:** Breaks down regional market data and reports back on the matters that affect the mortgage and real estate industry in the northeast.
Published by: Royal Media Group, 80 Broad St, Ste 1701, New York, NY 10004. TEL 212-564-8972, FAX 212-564-8973, info@royalmedia.com, http://www.royalmedia.com.

332.63 USA
MORTGAGEPULSE: SOUTHWEST. Text in English. m. **Document type:** *Newsletter, Trade.* **Description:** Breaks down regional market data and reports back on the matters that affect the mortgage and real estate industry in the southwest.
Published by: Royal Media Group, 80 Broad St, Ste 1701, New York, NY 10004. TEL 212-564-8972, FAX 212-564-8973, info@royalmedia.com, http://www.royalmedia.com.

332.63 USA
MORTGAGEPULSE: WEST. Text in English. m. **Document type:** *Newsletter, Trade.* **Description:** Breaks down regional market data and reports back on the matters that affect the mortgage and real estate industry in the west.
Published by: Royal Media Group, 80 Broad St, Ste 1701, New York, NY 10004. TEL 212-564-8972, FAX 212-564-8973, info@royalmedia.com, http://www.royalmedia.com.

333.33 USA ISSN 1930-3173
HT334.U5
MOVING & RELOCATION DIRECTORY. Text in English. 1992. a., latest 6th ed. USD 254 (effective 2008). **Document type:** *Directory, Trade.* **Description:** Reference guide which provides important contact information, statistical and demographic data, and other information to help people with relocation and moving. This edition covers 121 US cities, including large population centers as well as smaller cities that are popular relocation destinations.
Former titles (until 2001): Moving & Relocation Sourcebook and Directory (1540-9961); (until 1998): Moving and Relocation Sourcebook
Published by: Omnigraphics, Inc., PO Box 31-1640, Detroit, MI 48231. info@omnigraphics.com. Ed. Nancy Kriskern. Pub. Frederick G Ruffner Jr.

333.33 917 CAN ISSN 1495-9542
MOVING TO ALBERTA. Text in English. a. CAD 9.95 (effective 2000). adv. **Document type:** *Magazine, Consumer.* **Description:** Provides information and assistance to people relocating to the Alberta area.
Former titles (until 2001): Moving to & Around Alberta (0713-8369); (until 1982): Moving to Alberta (0702-9195)
Published by: Moving To Limited, 178 Main St, Unionville, ON L3R 2G9, Canada. TEL 905-479-4663, FAX 905-479-4482. Pub. Anita Wood. Adv. contact Linda Haines. color page CAD 8,600;.

333.33 CAN ISSN 1485-8304
MOVING TO MONTREAL/EMMENAGER A MONTREAL. Text in English, French. 1975. a. adv. **Document type:** *Magazine, Consumer.* **Description:** Provides information and guidance to those moving or relocating to the Montreal area.
Former titles (until 1998): Moving to Montreal Metropolitain (1483-5460); Moving to Montreal (0702-9225)
Published by: Moving To Limited, 178 Main St, Unionville, ON L3R 2G9, Canada. TEL 905-479-4663, FAX 905-479-4482. Pub. Anita Wood. Adv. contact Linda Haines. color page CAD 8,200;.

333.33 917.13 CAN ISSN 1709-4321
MOVING TO OTTAWA/EMMENAGER A OTTAWA - HULL. Text in English, French. 1977. a. adv. illus. **Document type:** *Magazine, Consumer.*
Former titles (until 2004): Moving to Ottawa - Outaouais (1481-7829); (until 2000): Moving to Ottawa - Hull (1484-6993); (until 1998): Moving to Metro Ottawa - Hull (1201-4265); (until 1995): Moving to Ottawa - Hull (0226-7837); (until 1978): Emanager a Ottawa - Hull (0702-9063)
Published by: (Moving Publications Ltd.), Moving To Limited, 178 Main St, Unionville, ON L3R 2G9, Canada. TEL 905-479-4663, FAX 905-479-4482. Pub. Anita Wood. Adv. contact Linda Haines. color page CAD 8,200;.

333.33 917.124 CAN ISSN 1496-5437
MOVING TO SASKATCHEWAN. Text in English. 1980. a. adv. illus. **Document type:** *Magazine, Consumer.* **Description:** Provides information and assistance to people relocating to the Saskatchewan region.
Former titles (until 200?): Moving to & Around Saskatchewan (0713-8385); (until 1983): Moving to Saskatchewan (0225-5383)
Published by: Moving To Limited, 178 Main St, Unionville, ON L3R 2G9, Canada. TEL 905-479-4663, FAX 905-479-4482. Pub. Anita Wood. Adv. contact Linda Haines. color page CAD 7,800;.

333.33 917 CAN ISSN 1495-995X
MOVING TO SOUTHWESTERN ONTARIO. Text in English. 1978. a. adv. **Document type:** *Magazine, Consumer.* **Description:** Provides relocation guidance and information on schools, neighborhoods, attractions, immigration, shopping, culture and housing costs in the southwestern Ontario region.
Former titles (until 199?): Moving to & Around Southwestern Ontario (0715-8114); (until 1984): Moving to Southwestern Ontario (0703-8496)
Published by: Moving To Limited, 178 Main St, Unionville, ON L3R 2G9, Canada. TEL 905-479-4663, FAX 905-479-4482, movingto@idirect.com, http://www.movingto.com. Pub. Anita Wood. Adv. contact Linda Haines. color page CAD 7,800;.

333.33 917.13 CAN ISSN 1496-5445
HC108.T68
MOVING TO TORONTO. Text in English. 1974. a. adv. **Document type:** *Magazine, Consumer.* **Description:** Provides relocation guidance and information on schools, neighborhoods, attractions, immigration, shopping, culture and housing costs in the greater Toronto area.
Former titles (until 2002): Moving to the Greater Toronto Area (1701-6479); (until 2001): Moving to & Around the Greater Toronto Area (1483-5487); (until 1997): Moving to and Around Metro Toronto and Area (1483-5479); (until 199?): Moving to and Around Toronto and Area (0713-8377); Moving to Toronto and Area (0226-7829); Moving to Toronto (0702-9179)
Published by: Moving To Limited, 178 Main St, Unionville, ON L3R 2G9, Canada. TEL 905-479-4663, FAX 905-479-4482. Pub. Anita Wood. Adv. contact Linda Haines. color page CAD 9,000;.

333.33 917.11 CAN ISSN 1495-9569
MOVING TO VANCOUVER & BRITISH COLUMBIA. Text in English. 1977. a. adv. illus. **Document type:** *Magazine, Consumer.* **Description:** Provides information and advice to people moving or relocating to the Vancouver area.
Former titles (until 2001): Moving to & Around Vancouver & B.C. (0713-8407); (until 1982): Moving to Vancouver and B.C. (0226-7276); (until 1980): Moving to Vancouver - Victoria (0702-9187)
Published by: Moving To Limited, 178 Main St, Unionville, ON L3R 2G9, Canada. TEL 905-479-4663, FAX 905-479-4482. Pub. Anita Wood. Adv. contact Linda Haines. color page CAD 8,600;.

333.33 917 CAN ISSN 1496-5453
MOVING TO WINNIPEG & MANITOBA. Text in English. 1976. a. adv. **Document type:** *Magazine, Consumer.* **Description:** Provides relocation information and guidance on schools, neighborhoods, attractions, immigration, shopping, culture and housing costs in the Winnipeg area.
Former titles (until 2002): Moving to & Around Winnipeg & Manitoba (0715-7053); (until 1984): Moving to Winnipeg (0702-9209)
Published by: Moving To Limited, 178 Main St, Unionville, ON L3R 2G9, Canada. TEL 905-479-4663, FAX 905-479-4482. Pub. Anita Wood. Adv. contact Linda Haines. color page CAD 7,800;.

333.33 USA
MR. LANDLORD; the survival newsletter for landlords and landladies. Text in English. 1985. m. looseleaf. USD 89 (effective 2005). adv. bk.rev. back issues avail.; reprints avail. **Document type:** *Newsletter.* **Description:** Aims to help landlords to attain and maintain maximum cashflow, control and gain cooperation from tenants, and to serve as a forum for rental owners nationwide to share ideas and concerns.
Published by: Mr Landlord, Inc., PO Box 64442, Virginia Beach, VA 23467. TEL 800-950-2250, FAX 757-436-2606. Ed. Jeffrey E Taylor. Circ: 15,000 (paid and controlled).

MULTI-HOUSING NEWS. *see* BUILDING AND CONSTRUCTION

333 USA ISSN 1931-9436
MULTIHOUSING PROFESSIONAL. Text in English. 1998. bi-m. free to qualified personnel. adv. **Document type:** *Magazine, Trade.* **Description:** Contains articles and features on educating multi-housing professionals, including items on human resources, customer service, legalities, and employment.
Former titles (until 200?): The Apartment Professional (1930-6334); Apartment Professionals' Resources & Services Guide (1530-2326)
Published by: The Apartment Professional, 26901 Agoura Rd Ste 150, Agoura Hills, CA 91301. TEL 888-577-7576, FAX 818-673-4747. adv.: color page USD 5,900, B&W page USD 5,500. Circ: 25,000 (paid and controlled).

333.332 USA
N A I F A CONVENTION. PROCEEDINGS. Text in English. a. **Document type:** *Proceedings.*
Published by: National Association of Independent Fee Appraisers, 401 N. Michigan Ave., Ste. 2200, Chicago, IL 60611-4245. TEL 314-781-6688.

333.33 USA
N A R E E NEWS. Text in English. 1947. bi-m. USD 150 to non-members (effective 2005). adv. bk.rev. bibl.; charts; illus.; stat. **Document type:** *Newsletter, Trade.* **Description:** Covers journalism, real estate, housing and urban planning and consumer education and protection.
Related titles: Online - full content ed.
Published by: National Association of Real Estate Editors, 1003 N W Sixth Terr, Boca Raton, FL 33486-3455. Ed. Mary Doyle-Kimball. Pub. David C. Kimball. adv.: page USD 700. Circ: 600.

333.33 332.6 USA
N A R E I T HANDBOOK. Text in English. 199?. a. adv. stat. **Document type:** *Directory, Trade.* **Description:** Contains a comprehensive, up-to-date listing of REIT's and real estate companies.
Related titles: Online - full text ed.: free to members (effective 2011).
Published by: National Association of Real Estate Investment Trusts, Inc., 1875 I St, NW, Ste 600, Washington, DC 20006. TEL 202-739-9400, FAX 202-739-9401, info@nareit.com.

333.33 NZL ISSN 1179-6103
N B R N Z PROPERTY INVESTOR. (National Business Review) Text in English. 1972. w. adv. bk.rev. charts; illus.; mkt.; stat. index. back issues avail. **Document type:** *Newsletter, Trade.* **Description:** Provides reports on all aspects of the commercial property market, including trends, market prices, legislation and industry groups. For property investors, developers and property professionals.
Former titles (until 2009): N Z Property Investor (1175-9909); (until 2009): Property Investor Weekly (1170-7623); (until 2008): New Zealand Property Investor (1173-3411); (until 1994): New Zealand Property (0113-4620); (until 1987): Property (0110-0793); (until 1976): N Z Property Investor
Related titles: Online - full text ed.
Published by: Liberty Holdings, Level 14 of the Citigroup Centre, 23 Customs St E, Auckland, New Zealand. customerservices@nbr.co.nz, http://www.nbr.co.nz.

333.33 USA ISSN 1530-3918
KFN5140.A15
N.Y. REAL PROPERTY LAW JOURNAL. Variant title: Real Property Law Journal. Text in English. 1973. 4/yr. free to members (effective 2008). adv. back issues avail.; reprints avail. **Document type:** *Journal, Trade.* **Description:** Features articles relating to the practice of real property law on various topics including property transactions, leases, zoning, disclosure, and cooperatives and condominiums.
Formerly (until 1995): New York State Bar Association. Real Property Law Section. Newsletter (0147-135X)
Related titles: Online - full text ed.: ISSN 1933-8465.
Published by: (Real Property Section), New York State Bar Association, 1 Elk St, Albany, NY 12207. TEL 518-463-3200, FAX 518-487-5517, newsletters@nysba.org. Eds. Marvin N Bagwell, William A Colavito, William P Johnson. Circ: 4,800 (controlled).

N Y REAL PROPERTY LAW SECTION JOURNAL. (New York) *see* LAW

333.33 NOR ISSN 0805-9837
NAERINGSEIENDOM. Text in Norwegian. 1989. 11/yr. NOK 450 (effective 2005). adv. **Document type:** *Magazine, Consumer.* **Description:** Commercial real estate in Norway.
Formerly (until 1990): Eiendomsboersen (0805-9845)
Published by: Mediehuset NaeringsEiendom AS, PO Box 2435, Solli, Oslo, 0201, Norway. TEL 47-23-115600, FAX 47-23-115601, post@ne.no, http://www.ne.no. Ed. Thor Arne Brun. Adv. contact Stig Basing. page NOK 27,080; 190 x 260. Circ: 47,695.

333.33 USA
NANTUCKET ISLAND LIVING; the source for real estate on Nantucket. Text in English. 2007. 7/yr. free. adv. **Document type:** *Magazine, Consumer.* **Description:** Contains comprehensive and extensive information for luxury real estate and life on Nantucket. Features include exclusive properties for sale, editorial content provides insight into real estate trends, dining, art galleries, and other people, places that make up this affluent destination.
Published by: Bresette + Co, Inc., 40 Congress St, Ste 500, Portsmouth, NH 03804. TEL 603-430-0770, FAX 603-430-9883, info@bresette.com, http://www.bresette.com. adv.: color page USD 2,245; trim 8.375 x 10.875. Circ: 25,000.

333.33 USA ISSN 1086-475X
HG2040.5.U5
NATIONAL MORTGAGE BROKER. Text in English. 1985. m. USD 59.95; USD 69.95 foreign. adv. bk.rev. charts; illus.; stat.; tr.lit. **Document type:** *Magazine, Trade.* **Description:** Covers developments and news affecting the mortgage brokering community, including legislative matters, industry automation, human resources, business management and other concerns.
Published by: National Association of Mortgage Brokers, 18206 N 19th Ave, Ste 2 A, Phoenix, AZ 85023. TEL 602-863-0700, FAX 602-863-2896. Ed., R&P Ron Wolf. Pub. Jon Ruzan. Adv. contact Pamela Martinez. Circ: 10,500 (paid).

333.33 USA ISSN 0027-9994
HD251
NATIONAL REAL ESTATE INVESTOR. Text in English. 1958. m. (plus a. Directory). USD 110 domestic; USD 121 in Canada; USD 130 elsewhere; free domestic to qualified personnel (effective 2011). adv. bk.rev. illus.; mkt.; stat.; tr.lit. Index. reprints avail. **Document type:** *Magazine, Trade.* **Description:** Covers the development, investment, financing and management of commercial real estate and its allied fields.
Related titles: Microfilm ed.: (from PQC); Online - full text ed.
Indexed: A09, A10, A12, A13, A14, A17, A22, A23, ABIn, AIAP, B01, B02, B04, B06, B07, B08, B09, B13, B15, B17, B18, BPI, BPIA, BRD, BusI, C12, G04, G06, G07, G08, H&TI, I05, M01, M02, P06, P34, P53, P54, PAIS, PQC, PSI, RICS, S22, T&II, T02, V03, V04, W01, W02, W03, W05.
—BLDSC (6030.030000), CIS, IE, Ingenta. **CCC.**
Published by: Penton Media, Inc., 6151 Powers Ferry Rd, Ste 200, Atlanta, GA 30339. TEL 770-955-2500, FAX 770-618-0204, information@penton.com, http://www.penton.com. Ed. Matt Valley TEL 770-618-0215. Circ: 33,708.

333.31029 USA ISSN 1075-1084
HD253
NATIONAL REFERRAL ROSTER; the nation's directory of real estate firms. Text in English. 1962. a. USD 95 to qualified personnel; USD 175 (effective 2004). adv. illus. **Document type:** *Directory.* **Description:** Lists thousands of U.S. real estate firms by state, city, and company.
Formerly (until 1994): National Roster of Realtors (0090-1741)
Related titles: Online - full text ed.
Published by: Stamats Business Media, Inc., 615 Fifth St, SE, Cedar Rapids, IA 52401. TEL 319-364-6167, 800-553-8878, FAX 319-369-0029, http://www.real-estate-roster.com. Ed. Candy Holub. Pub. Bill Stamats. Adv. contact Linda Thiesen. Circ: 15,000 (controlled).

333.33 USA ISSN 1079-0292
HD255
NATIONAL REVIEW OF REAL ESTATE MARKETS. Text in English. 1990. q. USD 929 (effective 1997 & 1998). 200 p./no.; back issues avail. **Document type:** *Bulletin.* **Description:** Review of economic and real estate conditions in 150 local markets across the US, with emphasis on economic growth, home prices, and foreclosing risk.
Former titles (until 1993): Cohane Rafferty's National Review of Real Estate Markets (1069-4986); (until 1992): Local Market Monitor (1056-0475)
Published by: Local Market Monitor, 70 Glen Rd, Wellesley, MA 02181. TEL 617-431-7151, FAX 617-431-0450. Ed. Ingo Winzer. Circ: 150 (paid).

NEBRASKA LEGAL FORMS: COMMERCIAL REAL ESTATE. *see* LAW

346.043 USA
NEBRASKA LEGAL FORMS: RESIDENTIAL REAL ESTATE. Text in English. 1982. 2-3/yr.), base vol. plus irreg. updates. looseleaf. USD 69.95 (effective 2003). **Description:** Covers Nebraska residential real estate proceedings; contains forms for purchasing, financing, developing, and foreclosing.
Related titles: Diskette ed.

Published by: Michie Company (Subsidiary of: LexisNexis North America), 701 E Water St, Charlottesville, VA 22902. TEL 434-972-7600, 800-446-3410, FAX 434-972-7677, customer.support@lexisnexis.com, http://www.michie.com.

333.33 RUS
NEDVIZHIMOST' ZA RUBEZHOM. Text in English, Russian. 1994. m. free. back issues avail. **Document type:** *Newspaper.*
Published by: Inter-Soyuz J.V., Pushkinskaya pl 5, Moscow, 103791, Russian Federation. TEL 7-095-2091694, FAX 7-095-2096132. Ed. Vladimir Olgin. adv.: page USD 2,600. Circ: 100,000.

333.33 GBR
NEGOTIATOR. Text in English. 1985. fortn. free to qualified personnel (effective 2009). adv. back issues avail. **Document type:** *Magazine, Trade.* **Description:** Covers all aspects of operating a residential real estate agency.
Published by: Ocean Media Group Ltd. (Subsidiary of: Trinity Mirror Plc.), 1 Canada Sq, 19th Fl, Canary Wharf, London, E14 5AP, United Kingdom. TEL 44-20-77728300, FAX 44-20-77728599, Pamela.McSweeney@oceanmedia.co.uk, http://www.oceanmedia.co.uk. Ed. Clare Bettelley TEL 44-20-77728310. Pub. Peter Sayer TEL 44-20-77728466. Adv. contact Mark Ferrell TEL 44-20-77728369. B&W page GBP 1,482; trim 230 x 300. Circ: 11,220.

NEIGHBORING PROPERTY OWNERS. *see* LAW—Civil Law

333.33 DEU
DAS NEUE MIETRECHT. Text in German. 1994. a. adv. **Document type:** *Magazine, Consumer.* **Description:** Presents tips and advice on renting properties.
Formerly: Mieter Dein Recht
Published by: Marken Verlag GmbH, Hansaring 97, Cologne, 50670, Germany. TEL 49-221-9574270, FAX 49-221-95742777, marken-info@markenverlag.de, http://www.markenverlag.de. Adv. contact Frank Krauthaeuser. B&W page EUR 5,900; trim 180 x 250. Circ: 150,000 (paid and controlled).

NEVADA JOURNAL (LAS VEGAS). *see* LAW

NEW ENGLAND CONDOMINIUM. *see* BUSINESS AND ECONOMICS—Cooperatives

333.3 USA ISSN 0028-4890
HD1379
NEW ENGLAND REAL ESTATE JOURNAL; the largest weekly commercial - investment newspaper in the world. Abbreviated title: N E R E J. Text in English. 1962. w. USD 139 (effective 2011). adv. bk.rev. **Document type:** *Newspaper, Trade.* **Description:** Covers commercial, industrial, and investment real estate.
Related titles: Online - full text ed.: free (effective 2011).
Published by: East Coast Publications, Inc., PO Box 55, Accord, MA 02081. TEL 781-878-4540, 800-654-4993, FAX 781-871-1853. Ed. Janet Donovan. Pub. Lorraine Rayberg TEL 781-878-4540 ext 213.

333.33 USA
NEW HAMPSHIRE LANDLORD AND TENANT LAW. Text in English. a. USD 48 (effective 2008). 344 p./no.; **Document type:** *Handbook/Manual/Guide, Trade.* **Description:** Contains a broad spectrum of topics including housing standards, fire regulations, warranties on prefabricated homes and more.
Published by: Michie Company (Subsidiary of: LexisNexis North America), 701 E Water St, Charlottesville, VA 22902. TEL 434-972-7600, 800-446-3410, FAX 434-972-7677, customer.support@lexisnexis.com, http://www.michie.com. Ed. George Harley.

333.33 GBR ISSN 1473-5016
NEW HOUSES IN NORTHERN IRELAND. Text in English. 2001. q. GBP 13 (effective 2010). adv. **Document type:** *Magazine, Consumer.* **Description:** Designed to provide house buyers with a comprehensive guide to new developments across the province.
Published by: Karen McAvoy Publishing Ltd., The Forge, 13b Lisburn Rd, Moira, BT67 OJR, United Kingdom. TEL 44-28-92612990, FAX 44-28-92612091, info@kmpltd.co.uk. Ed. Adam Hassin. adv.: color page GBP 1,045; trim 230 x 297.

NEW JERSEY & COMPANY. *see* BUSINESS AND ECONOMICS

333.33 USA
THE NEW JERSEY COOPERATOR; the condo, HOA & co-op monthly. Text in English. 2007. m. free to qualified personnel (effective 2011). **Document type:** *Newspaper, Trade.* **Description:** Addresses issues of importance to the cooperative and condominium community in New Jersey.
Related titles: Online - full text ed.: free (effective 2011).
Published by: Yale Robbins Publications, LLC, 102 Madison Ave, 5th Fl, New York, NY 10016. TEL 212-683-5700, FAX 212-545-0764, info@yrinc.com, http://marketing.yrpubs.com/.

333.33 USA
NEW JERSEY. DEPARTMENT OF THE TREASURY. LOCAL PROPERTY BRANCH NEWS. Text in English. 1953. 6/yr. (plus annual report). free. index. **Document type:** *Government.*
Formerly (until Dec. 1984): New Jersey. Department of the Treasury. Local Property and Public Utility Branch News
Published by: Department of the Treasury, Division of Taxation, Local Property Branch, 50 Barrack St, Trenton, NJ 08646. TEL 609-984-3276. Ed. Gary R Dal Corso. Circ: 2,300.

346.043 USA
NEW JERSEY REAL ESTATE FORMS. Text in English. 1992. 3 base vols. plus irreg. updates. looseleaf. USD 343 base vol(s). (effective 2008). Supplement avail. **Document type:** *Handbook/Manual/Guide, Trade.* **Description:** Covers residential, commercial and construction real estate transactions.
Related titles: Diskette ed.: USD 75; Online - full text ed.
Published by: Michie Company (Subsidiary of: LexisNexis North America), 701 E Water St, Charlottesville, VA 22902. TEL 434-972-7600, 800-446-3410, FAX 434-972-7677, custserv@michie.com, http://www.michie.com. Eds. Charles Applebaum, David S Gordon, Robert C Schachter.

333.33 USA ISSN 0028-5919
NEW JERSEY REALTOR. Text in English. 1970 (vol.12). m. USD 10. adv. illus. **Document type:** *Magazine, Trade.*
Published by: New Jersey Association of Realtors, 295 Pierson Ave, Edison, NJ 08837. TEL 732-494-5616, http://www.njar.com. Ed. Meredith Lavecchia. Pub. Walter T Backowski. Adv. contact Meredith Swanson. Circ: 38,000.

333.33 USA
NEW JERSEY STATE BAR ASSOCIATION. REAL PROPERTY, PROBATE AND TRUST LAW SECTION. NEWSLETTER. Text in English. 1966. irreg. bk.rev. back issues avail. **Document type:** *Newsletter, Trade.*
Published by: (Real Property, Probate and Trust Law Section), New Jersey State Bar Association, One Constitution Sq, New Brunswick, NJ 08901. TEL 732-249-5000, FAX 732 249-2815, info@njsba.com.

333.33 340 USA ISSN 0898-2961
KFX2022
NEW YORK APARTMENT LAW INSIDER; the how-to monthly for owners, M managers & real estate professionals. Text in English. 1979. m. looseleaf. USD 217 (print or online ed.); USD 325 combined subscription (print & online eds.) (effective 2008). adv. index. back issues avail.; reprints avail. **Document type:** *Newsletter, Trade.* **Description:** Features information on how to negotiate the ins and outs of rent stabilization, rent control, building maintenance requirements, correction of code violations and dealing with New York agencies.
Formerly (until 198?): The New York City Apartment Law Insider (0736-0495)
Related titles: CD-ROM ed.: USD 297 (effective 2008); Online - full text ed.: ISSN 1938-3134. USD 257 (effective 2004).
Indexed: A10, V03.
—CCC.
Published by: Vendome Group, LLC, 149 5th Ave, New York, NY 10010. TEL 212-812-8420, FAX 212-228-1308, customerservice@Vendomegrpsubs.com, http://www.vendomegrp.com/. Ed. Eric Yoo TEL 212-812-8435. Pub. Julie DiMauro. Circ: 4,200 (paid).

NEW YORK CITY. REAL PROPERTY TAX. ANNUAL REPORT. *see* BUSINESS AND ECONOMICS—Public Finance, Taxation

333.33 USA
NEW YORK HOUSE. Text in English. m. USD 36 (effective 2007). **Document type:** *Magazine, Trade.* **Description:** Contains property listings and editorial on progressive design and building practices and eco-friendly products and services.
Published by: ScheinMedia, 233 Fair St., Kingston, NY 12401. TEL 845-340-9600. Ed. Jim Andrews. Pub. Jonathan A. Schein.

333.33 340 USA ISSN 1938-3185
NEW YORK LANDLORD VS. TENANT; apartment law insider total decision service for landlords, managers, and attorneys. Text in English. 1985. m. USD 467 (print or online ed.); USD 700 combined subscription (print & online eds.) (effective 2008). adv. back issues avail.; reprints avail. **Document type:** *Newsletter, Trade.* **Description:** Features information on 80 real-life cases of landlord and tenant disputes.
Formerly (until 1993): Landlord vs. Tenant/NYC (0883-0746)
Related titles: Online - full text ed.: ISSN 1938-3118. USD 447 (effective 2004).
Indexed: A01, B02, B15, B17, B18, G04, G05, G06, G07, I05.
—CCC.
Published by: Vendome Group, LLC, 149 5th Ave, New York, NY 10010. TEL 212-812-8420, FAX 212-228-1308, customerservice@Vendomegrpsubs.com, http://www.vendomegrp.com/. Pub. Julie DiMauro.

363.5 USA ISSN 1080-1669
NEW YORK LIVING; the most comprehensive guide to residential properties in the metropolitan area. Text in English. 1995. 10/yr. USD 33 domestic; USD 73 foreign; USD 3.95 newsstand/cover domestic; USD 4.95 newsstand/cover in Canada (effective 2003). adv. illus. **Document type:** *Magazine, Consumer.* **Description:** Comprehensive source of residential properties in New York City, carries suburban listings, sales and mortgages, and rental buildings guide.
Published by: Chiba Publications, Inc., 3 East 48th Street, #2F, New York, NY 10017. TEL 212-980-8850, FAX 212-980-8858, chiba@newyorklivingmag.com. Ed., Pub. Akira Chiba. Adv. contact Brey C Brownlie. Circ: 10,000 (paid); 40,000 (controlled).

333.33 346.043 USA
NEW YORK PRACTICE GUIDE: REAL ESTATE. Text in English. 1986. 6 base vols. plus s-a. updates. looseleaf. USD 1,150 base vol(s). (effective 2008). **Document type:** *Handbook/Manual/Guide, Trade.* **Description:** Provides information for handling real estate transactions including in-depth analysis of the law, forms and checklists.
Related titles: CD-ROM ed.: USD 734 (effective 2008).
Published by: Matthew Bender & Co., Inc. (Subsidiary of: LexisNexis North America), 1275 Broadway, Albany, NY 12204. TEL 518-487-3000, 800-424-4200, FAX 518-487-3083, international@bender.com, http://bender.lexisnexis.com. Ed. Karl B Holtzschue.

333.3 USA ISSN 1057-2104
NEW YORK REAL ESTATE JOURNAL; the largest commercial - investment newspaper covering the state. Text in English. 1989. s-m. USD 99 (effective 2011). adv. bk.rev. back issues avail. **Document type:** *Newspaper, Trade.* **Description:** Comprehensive coverage of commercial, industrial, and investment real estate matters.
Related titles: Online - full text ed.: free (effective 2011).
Published by: East Coast Publications, Inc., PO Box 55, Accord, MA 02081. TEL 781-878-4540, 800-654-4993, FAX 781-871-1853. Eds. Heather Devaney, Jennifer Tempesa, Kristin Mattson.

NEW YORK REAL ESTATE LAW REPORTER. *see* LAW

333.33 346.043 USA
NEW YORK REAL PROPERTY. Text in English. 2005. irreg. looseleaf. USD 4,508 per issue (effective 2008). **Document type:** *Monographic series, Trade.* **Description:** Covers information on the New York real property.
Media: CD-ROM.
Published by: Matthew Bender & Co., Inc. (Subsidiary of: LexisNexis North America), 1275 Broadway, Albany, NY 12204. TEL 518-487-3000, 800-424-4200, FAX 518-487-3083, international@bender.com, http://bender.lexisnexis.com.

333.33 USA ISSN 1555-9343
NEW YORK STATE REALTOR. Text in English. 1970. bi-m. adv. charts; mkt.; stat.; tr.lit. back issues avail. **Document type:** *Magazine, Trade.* **Description:** Provides information about current events in the real estate industry and association activities and programs.
Former titles (until 2004): New York Report; Empire State Realtor (0279-6112)
Related titles: Online - full text ed.
Published by: New York State Association of Realtors, 130 Washington Ave, Albany, NY 12210-2200. TEL 518-463-0300, FAX 518-462-5474. Ed., R&P, Adv. contact Salvatore I Prividera. B&W page USD 2,999.50, color page USD 3,399.50. Circ: 55,000 (controlled).

333.33 NZL ISSN 1176-9947
NEW ZEALAND REAL ESTATE MARKET. SUMMARY REPORT. Text in English. s-a. **Document type:** *Report, Trade.*
Formerly (until 2004): Real Estate Market in New Zealand. Provisional Report (0112-3386)
Published by: Quotable Value Limited, PO Box 5098, Wellington, New Zealand. TEL 64-4-4738555, FAX 64-4-4738552, enquiries@qv.co.nz, http://www.qv.co.nz.

917 USA ISSN 1930-6296
F614.M6
NEWCOMER'S HANDBOOK FOR MOVING TO AND LIVING IN MINNEAPOLIS - ST. PAUL. Text in English. 1997. triennial, latest 2006, 3rd ed. USD 25.95 per issue (effective 2008). 456 p./no.;
Formerly (until 2006): Newcomer's Handbook for Minneapolis and Saint Paul (1087-8467)
Published by: First Books, 6750 SW Franklin St Ste A, Portland, OR 97223. TEL 503-968-6777, FAX 503-968-6779, https://www.firstbooks.com/index.php.

333.33 USA
NEWHOMES GUIDE - DALLAS FORT WORTH. Text in English. 1972. m. free. adv. maps. back issues avail. **Document type:** *Directory, Consumer.* **Description:** Comprehensive map guide to new home communities in Dallas/Fort Worth.
Formerly: HomeBuyer's Guide - Dallas Fort Worth
Related titles: Online - full text ed.
Published by: HPC Publications, Inc, 12001 N Central Expressway, Ste 640, Dallas, TX 75243. TEL 214-239-2399, FAX 214-239-7850. Ed. Maridee Boron. R&P Pamela Stevens. adv.: color page USD 2,315; trim 8 x 10.875. Circ: 35,000. **Dist. by:** Distributech. TEL 972-446-1590, FAX 972-446-2004.

647.920942105 GBR ISSN 1476-766X
NEWS ON THE BLOCK; help and advice for flat owners. Text in English. 2002. bi-m. GBP 49.99 combined subscription (print & online eds.); GBP 4.50 newsstand/cover (effective 2009). adv. **Document type:** *Magazine, Trade.* **Description:** Provides help and advice about flats.
Related titles: Online - full text ed.
—CCC.
Published by: Adrenaline Media Plc, 8 Canfield Pl, London, NW6 3BT, United Kingdom. TEL 44-845-6187746, FAX 44-845-6187749, info@adrenalinemedia.plc.uk, http://www.adrenalinemedia.plc.uk/. Ed. Jamie Reid. Adv. contact Tony Gold TEL 44-845-6187746.

333.33 USA
NEWSBREAK (NEWBURYPORT). Text in English. 1995. w. free. **Document type:** *Newsletter.* **Description:** Covers all topics pertaining to relocation real-estate economics. Includes late-breaking news and valuable advice.
Media: Online - full text. **Related titles:** Fax ed.
Published by: Mobility Services International, 124 High St, Newburyport, MA 01950. TEL 978-463-0348. Ed. Diane MacPherson.

333.33 POL ISSN 1506-2899
NIERUCHOMOSCI. Text in Polish. 1998. m. PLZ 299 domestic (effective 2005). **Document type:** *Journal, Trade.*
Published by: Wydawnictwo C.H. Beck, ul Gen. Zajaczka 9, Warsaw, 01518, Poland. TEL 48-22-3377600, FAX 48-22-3377601, redakcja@beck.pl, http://wydawnictwo.beck.pl.

333.33 POL ISSN 1506-5855
NIERUCHOMOSCI STOLECZNE. Text in Polish. 1998. w. PLZ 54 per month domestic; EUR 15 per month in Europe; USD 23 per month in North America (effective 2011). **Document type:** *Consumer.*
Related titles: ◆ Supplement to: Gazeta Wyborcza. ISSN 0860-908X.
Published by: Agora S.A., ul Czerska 8/10, Warsaw, 00732, Poland. TEL 48-22-5556000, FAX 48-22-5554850, prenumerata@gazeta.pl, http://www.agora.pl.

NIEUW COMMERCIEEL VASTGOED IN NEDERLAND. *see* BUSINESS AND ECONOMICS—Banking And Finance

333.33 DEU
NORDDEUTSCHE HAUSBESITZER-ZEITUNG. Text in German. 1898. m. EUR 20 (effective 2008). adv. **Document type:** *Magazine, Trade.*
Published by: Verband Schleswig-Holsteinischer Haus- Wohnungs- und Grundeigentuemer e.V., Sophienblatt 3, Kiel, 24103, Germany. TEL 49-431-6636110, FAX 49-431-6636188, info@haus-und-grund-sh.de, http://www.haus-und-grund-sh.de. adv.: color page EUR 9,397.65, B&W page EUR 6,063. Circ: 63,058 (paid and controlled).

333 USA
NORTH SHORE HOMES. Text in English. adv. **Document type:** *Newspaper.* **Description:** Covers local real estate; included as a supplement in 6 local papers.
Published by: Times - Beacon - Record Newspapers, PO Box 707, Setauket, NY 11733. TEL 516-571-7744. Ed. Leah D Dunaief. Pub. Leah S Dunaief. Adv. contact Kathryn Mandracchia.

333.33 USA ISSN 1554-0847
NORTHEAST REAL ESTATE BUSINESS. Text in English. 2004. m. USD 68 (effective 2009). adv. back issues avail.; reprints avail. **Document type:** *Magazine, Trade.* **Description:** Covers the latest news, developments and trends in commercial real estate in the northeastern states. Features up-to-date information regarding ground-up projects and redevelopments, acquisitions and dispositions, financing, corporate real estate news and current events that are shaping the office, industrial, retail, hospitality, senior housing and multifamily sectors of real estate.
—CCC.
Published by: France Publications, Inc., 3500 Piedmont Rd, Ste 415, Atlanta, GA 30305. TEL 404-832-8262, FAX 404-832-8260, scott@francepublications.com, http://www.francepublications.com. Ed. Stephanie Mayhew. Pub. Jerry France TEL 404-832-8262 ext 111. Adv. contact Scott France. B&W page USD 3,375; trim 10.8125 x 14. Circ: 20,053.

NORTHERN ARIZONA NEWCOMER'S GUIDE. *see* LIFESTYLE

R

333.33 USA
NORTHERN NEW ENGLAND REAL ESTATE JOURNAL. Variant title: New England Real Estate Journal. Text in English. 1973. w. USD 139 (effective 2011). adv. bk.rev. back issues avail. **Document type:** *Newspaper, Trade.* **Description:** Covers commercial, industrial, and investment real estate in Maine, New Hampshire, and Vermont.
Related titles: Online - full text ed.: free (effective 2011).
Published by: East Coast Publications, Inc., PO Box 55, Accord, MA 02081. TEL 781-878-4540, 800-654-4993, FAX 781-871-1853.

333.33 FRA ISSN 1960-1301
LE NOUVEL OBSERVATEUR. IMMOBILIER. Text in French. 200?. irreg. **Document type:** *Magazine, Consumer.*
Related titles: ◆ Supplement to: Le Nouvel Observateur. ISSN 0029-4713.
Published by: Nouvel Observateur, 12 Place de la Bourse, Paris, 75002, France. TEL 33-1-44883434, http://quotidien.nouvelobs.com.

333.33 CAN
NOVA SCOTIA REAL PROPERTY PRACTICE MANUAL. Text in English. base vol. plus updates 3/yr. looseleaf. CAD 405 base vol(s). (effective 2010). **Document type:** *Handbook/Manual/Guide, Trade.* **Description:** Provides an analysis of the practice and procedure of Nova Scotia real property law.
Published by: LexisNexis Canada Inc. (Subsidiary of: LexisNexis North America), 123 Commerce Valley Dr E, Ste 700, Markham, ON L3T 7W8, Canada. TEL 905-479-2665, 800-668-6481, FAX 905-479-3758, 800-461-3275, info@lexisnexis.ca. Ed. Charles W MacIntosh.

333.33 NLD ISSN 2210-2787
NVMAGAZINE. Variant title: Nederlandse Vereniging van Makelaars Magazine. Text in Dutch. 2007. bi-m. **Document type:** *Magazine, Trade.*
Published by: Nederlandse Vereniging van Makelaars in Onroerende Goederen (NVM), Postbus 2222, Nieuwegein, 3430 DC, Netherlands. TEL 31-30-6085185, FAX 31-20-6034003, info@nvm.nl, http://www.nvm.nl.

333.33 CAN ISSN 1717-4651
CA1NH2-1
L'OBSERVATEUR DU LOGEMENT AU CANADA. Text in French. 2003. a. **Document type:** *Bulletin, Trade.*
Related titles: Online - full text ed.: ISSN 1717-4627; ◆ English ed.: Canadian Housing Observer. ISSN 1717-4600.
Published by: Canada Mortgage and Housing Corporation/Societe Canadienne d'Hypotheques et de Logement, 700 Montreal Rd, Ottawa, ON K1A 0P7, Canada. TEL 613-748-2000, FAX 613-748-2098, http://www.cmhc.ca, http://www.schl.ca.

333.33 USA
OCEAN HOME; the luxury coastal lifestyle magazine. Text in English. 2006 (Sum.). bi-m. USD 25 domestic; USD 50 in Canada; USD 74 elsewhere; USD 5.99 per issue (effective 2011). adv. back issues avail. **Document type:** *Magazine, Consumer.* **Description:** Devoted to the enhanced real estate and lifestyle opportunities to be found only at the ocean's edge.
Related titles: Online - full text ed.: free (effective 2011).
Published by: R M S Media Group, Inc., 16 Haverhill St, Andover, MA 01810. TEL 978-623-8020, FAX 978-824-3975, info@rmsmg.com, http://rmsmg.com. Ed. Lindsay Lambert. Pub. Hugh Malone TEL 978-623-8020 ext 103.

333.33 AUT ISSN 0029-9189
OESTERREICHISCHE HAUSBESITZ. Text in German. 1926. 11/yr. EUR 85 membership (effective 2005). adv. bk.rev. **Document type:** *Journal, Trade.*
Published by: Reformverband Oesterreichischer Hausbesitzer, Boesendorferstr 2-13, Vienna, W 1010, Austria. TEL 43-1-5056177, FAX 43-1-5056171, rv-hausbesitzer@chello.at. Ed. Friedrich Ruttar.

333.33
OESTERREICHISCHE IMMOBILIEN-ZEITUNG. Text in German. 23/yr. EUR 104 domestic; EUR 123 foreign (effective 2005). adv. **Document type:** *Journal, Trade.*
Published by: (Landesinnung Wien der Immobilien- und Vermoegenstreuhaender), Verlag Lorenz, Ebendorferstr 10, Vienna, W 1010, Austria. TEL 43-1-40566950, FAX 43-1-4068693, office@verlag-lorenz.at. Ed. Ulrike Assem. Adv. contact Irene Esch. B&W page EUR 1,450, color page EUR 2,785; trim 180 x 244. Circ: 6,000.

332.63 AUT ISSN 2072-2230
▼ **OESTERREICHISCHE ZEITSCHRIFT FUER LIEGENSCHAFTSBEWERTUNG.** Variant title: Liegenschaftsbewertung. Text in German. 2009. bi-m. EUR 86 (effective 2011). reprint service avail. from SCH. **Document type:** *Journal, Trade.*
Published by: Manz'sche Verlags- und Universitaetsbuchhandlung GmbH, Johannesgasse 23, Vienna, W 1010, Austria. TEL 43-1-531610, FAX 43-1-53161181, verlag@manz.at, http://www.manz.at. Ed. Heimo Kranewitter.

333.33 USA ISSN 1548-4572
HD1393.58.U6
OFFICE BUILDINGS. Variant title: Office Building Magazine. Text in English. 199?. a. **Document type:** *Magazine, Trade.* **Description:** Published in 12 separate editions and contains individual building photographs to location maps. Plus, there are concise building descriptions that include such details as GBA, height, year of construction, floor-by-floor rentable floor sizes, and more.
Formed by the merger of (198?-199?): Manhattan Office Buildings. Midtown (0886-3725); (198?-199?): Manhattan Office Buildings. Midtown South (1046-8943); (198?-199?): Manhattan Office Buildings. Downtown (0886-2737); (19??-199?): New Jersey Office Buildings (1056-0165); Which was formed by the merger of: Central New Jersey Office Buildings; Northern New Jersey Office Buildings
Related titles: Regional ed(s).: Office Buildings (Manhattan Edition). USD 329 (effective 2008); Office Buildings (New Jersey Edition). USD 159 per issue (effective 2008); Office Buildings (Westchester/Connecticut Edition). USD 159 per issue (effective 2008); Office Buildings (Northeast Ohio Edition). USD 159 per issue (effective 2008); Office Buildings (Boston/Cambridge Edition). USD 159 per issue (effective 2008); Office Buildings (Suburban Boston Edition). USD 159 per issue (effective 2008); Office Buildings (Pittsburgh Edition). USD 159 per issue (effective 2008); Office Buildings (Greater Philadelphia Edition). USD 159 per issue (effective 2008).
Published by: Yale Robbins Publications, LLC, 102 Madison Ave, 5th Fl, New York, NY 10016. TEL 212-683-5700, FAX 212-497-0017, info@yrinc.com.

332.63 NLD ISSN 1872-468X
OFFICES IN FIGURES. Text in Dutch. 2002. a. **Description:** Provides insight into the structural and financial aspects of the Dutch office market.
Related titles: ◆ Dutch ed.: Kantoren in Cijfers. ISSN 1874-0170.
Published by: CB Richard Ellis, Stadhouderskade 1, Amsterdam, 1054 ES, Netherlands. TEL 31-20-6262691, FAX 31-20-6246305, http://www.cbre.nl.

346.043 USA
OHIO REAL PROPERTY, LAW AND PRACTICE. Text in English. 1996. latest 6th ed., 2 base vols. plus irreg. updates. looseleaf. USD 357 base vol(s). (effective 2008). **Document type:** *Handbook/Manual/Guide, Trade.* **Description:** Provides comprehensive information on real estate practice in Ohio. Contains forms, checklists, and analysis.
Related titles: Online - full text ed.
Published by: Michie Company (Subsidiary of: LexisNexis North America), 701 E Water St, Charlottesville, VA 22902. TEL 434-972-7600, 800-446-3410, FAX 434-972-7677, customer.support@lexisnexis.com, http://www.michie.com. Eds. James G. Durham, Robert M. Curry.

333.33 USA ISSN 1042-8119
OHIO REALTOR. Text in English. m. free to members (effective 2005). **Document type:** *Newspaper, Trade.*
Published by: Ohio Association of Realtors, 200 E Town St, Columbus, OH 43215. TEL 614-228-6675, FAX 614-228-2601, info@ohiorealtors.org. Ed. Nikki Gasbarro. Circ: 30,000 (free).

333.33 USA ISSN 1931-521X
KFO126.A15
OHIO RESIDENTIAL REAL ESTATE MANUAL. Text in English. 2005. a., latest 2007. USD 102 per issue (effective 2007). **Document type:** *Handbook/Manual/Guide, Trade.*
Published by: LexisNexis (Subsidiary of: LexisNexis North America), 701 E Water St, PO Box 7587, Charlottesville, VA 22906. TEL 434-972-7600, 800-446-3410, FAX 800-643-1280, customer.support@lexisnexis.com, http://www.lexisnexis.com.

346.043 USA
OKLAHOMA REAL ESTATE FORMS. Text in English. 1987. 3 base vols. plus irreg. updates. looseleaf. USD 528 base vol(s). includes diskette (effective 2008). Supplement avail. **Document type:** *Handbook/Manual/Guide, Trade.* **Description:** Covers every aspect of residential, commercial and construction transactions.
Related titles: Diskette ed.; Online - full text ed.
Published by: Michie Company (Subsidiary of: LexisNexis North America), 701 E Water St, Charlottesville, VA 22902. TEL 434-972-7600, 800-446-3410, FAX 434-972-7677, customer.support@lexisnexis.com, http://www.michie.com. Eds. Alan C Durbin, C Temple Bixler.

OLD-HOUSE JOURNAL. *see* BUILDING AND CONSTRUCTION

OLD-HOUSE JOURNAL RESTORATION DIRECTORY. *see* BUILDING AND CONSTRUCTION

333.33 CAN ISSN 0316-1471
ONTARIO HOMES BUYERS GUIDE. Text in English. 1974. 8/yr. USD 24 (effective 2000). adv. mkt.; maps. **Document type:** *Magazine, Consumer.* **Description:** Focuses on all areas of home ownership, including buying and selling, finance, design, decor, renovation and new-home buyers guide in the greater Toronto area.
Formerly (until 1975): Ontario Homes Magazines (0317-5197)
Published by: Homes Publishing Group, 178 Main St, Unionville, ON L3R 2G9, Canada. TEL 905-479-4663, FAX 905-479-4482, info@homesmag.com, http://www.homesmag.com. Ed. Patrick Tivy. Pub. Michael Rosset. Adv. contact Hope McLarnon. color page CAD 5,800. Circ: 100,000 (controlled).

ONTARIO REAL ESTATE LAW GUIDE. *see* LAW

333.33 USA
OPEN HOUSE (LAS VEGAS). Text in English. 1976. q. free (effective 2005). **Document type:** *Newsletter, Trade.*
Contact Owner: State of Nevada, Department of Business & Industry, Real Estate Div, 2501 E Sahara Ave, Ste 102, Las Vegas, NV 89104-4137. TEL 702-486-4033, FAX 702-486-4275, http://www.red.state.nv.us, realest@red.state.nv.us. Circ: 17,300 (controlled).

333.33 USA
OPEN HOUSE (MIAMI); a magazine of international design and architecture. Text in English. s-a. USD 21; USD 15 newsstand/cover (effective 2008). **Document type:** *Magazine, Consumer.*
Related titles: Online - full text ed.
Published by: Open House Magazine, P O Box 37610, Miami, FL 33137. openhouseinfo@aol.com. Ed. Sarah Miller Barothy. Pub. Patricia G Ernst. Adv. contact Mike Schadek.

346.04 FRA ISSN 1961-6597
OPERATIONS IMMOBILIERES; le bimedia juridique des professionnels de l'immobilier. Text in French. 2008. m. EUR 299 (effective 2008). **Document type:** *Magazine, Trade.*
Published by: Groupe Moniteur, 17 rue d'Uzes, Paris, 75108, France. TEL 33-1-40133030, FAX 33-1-40135021, http://editionsdumoniteur.com.

333.33 USA
THE ORANGE COUNTY REAL ESTATE REPORT. Text in English. 19??. m. USD 450; USD 45 per issue; free to qualified personnel (effective 2009). back issues avail. **Document type:** *Newsletter, Consumer.* **Description:** Contains average and median sales prices and trend charts for each of the cities in the Orange County.
Media: Online - full content.
Published by: Information Designs, 27742 Vista Del Lago, #1, Mission Viejo, CA 92692. TEL 949-939-2854, rick@rereport.com, http://www.rereport.com.

333.33 USA ISSN 1945-2179
ORANGE COUNTY REALTOR. Text in English. 2001. m. adv. **Document type:** *Newsletter, Trade.*
Published by: (Orange County Association of Realtors), Foley Publications Inc, 1720 S Bellaire St, Ste 601, Denver, CO 80222. TEL 303-758-7878, 800-628-6983, FAX 303-758-0020, http://www.foleypub.com. Circ: 11,600.

ORIGINATION NEWS. *see* BUSINESS AND ECONOMICS—Banking And Finance

333.33 USA
ORLANDO HOMEBUYER. Text in English. q. adv. **Document type:** *Magazine, Consumer.* **Description:** Offers a glossy showcase for the region's real estate industry and a comprehensive resource for consumers.
Published by: Gulfshore Media, Inc. (Subsidiary of: CurtCo Robb Media LLC.), 330 S Pineapple Ave, Ste 205, Sarasota, FL 34236-7032. TEL 941-643-3933, FAX 941-643-5017. adv.: B&W page USD 1,880, color page USD 2,350; trim 8.125 x 10.75.

332.63 NZL ISSN 1177-7265
OWN. Text in English. 2007. a. free (effective 2008). **Document type:** *Magazine, Consumer.*
Published by: (A S B Bank Limited USA), Jones Publishing, Victoria St W, PO Box 91344, Auckland, 1142, New Zealand. TEL 64-9-3606424, FAX 64-9-3587291, info@jonespublishing.co.nz, http://www.jonespublishing.co.nz/. Ed. Lucy Gilmore.

332.63 GBR
THE P E R E YEAR BOOK (YEAR). (Private Equity Real Estate) Text in English. 2006. a. USD 1,585 (effective 2010); subscr. includes PERE Magazine. **Document type:** *Yearbook, Trade.*
Published by: P E I Media, Sycamore House, Sycamore St, London, EC1Y 0SG, United Kingdom. TEL 44-20-75665444, subscriptions@peimedia.com, http://www.peimedia.com/.

P M A DIRECTORY. *see* BUSINESS AND ECONOMICS—Trade And Industrial Directories

PALM BEACH COTTAGES & GARDENS. *see* GARDENING AND HORTICULTURE

333.33 USA
PEOPLE TO KNOW (PHOENIX); Arizona commerical real estate. Text in English. 200?. a. USD 9.95 per issue (effective 2009). **Document type:** *Directory, Trade.* **Description:** Resource guide to the most influential people and companies in Arizona's commercial real estate industry.
Formerly (until 200?): A Z R E Directory (1946-9209)
Published by: A Z Big Media, 3101 N Central Ave, Ste 1070, Phoenix, AZ 85012. TEL 602-277-6045, FAX 602-650-0827. Ed. Janet Perez.

333.33 690 USA
PERSPECTIVE (INDIANAPOLIS). Text in English. 1985. bi-m. free to qualified personnel. adv. **Document type:** *Magazine, Trade.* **Description:** Reports on events and trends in the resort-condominium development, vacation-ownership, and or exchange and travel industries on an international, federal and state-wide basis.
Published by: Resort Condominiums International, PO Box 80229, Indianapolis, IN 46280-0229. TEL 317-871-9641, FAX 317-871-9507. Ed. Laurie Borman. Circ: 7,000 (controlled).

333.33 CAN ISSN 1719-9131
PERSPECTIVES DU MARCHE DE L'HABITATION. CANADA. Text in French. 2005. q. **Document type:** *Bulletin, Trade.*
Media: Online - full text.
Published by: Canada Mortgage and Housing Corporation/Societe Canadienne d'Hypotheques et de Logement, 700 Montreal Rd, Ottawa, ON K1A 0P7, Canada. TEL 613-748-2000, FAX 613-748-2098, http://www.schl.ca.

333.33 CAN ISSN 1719-5446
PERSPECTIVES DU MARCHE DE L'HABITATION. MONTREAL. Text in French. 2002. q. **Document type:** *Newsletter, Trade.*
Formerly (until 2005): Perspectives du Marche du Logement. Montreal (1719-5438)
Media: Online - full text. **Related titles:** ◆ English ed.: Housing Market Outlook. Montreal (Online). ISSN 1719-542X.
Published by: Canada Mortgage and Housing Corporation/Societe Canadienne d'Hypotheques et de Logement, 700 Montreal Rd, Ottawa, ON K1A 0P7, Canada. TEL 613-748-2000, FAX 613-748-2098, http://www.schl.ca.

333.33 307.14 CAN ISSN 1719-5756
PERSPECTIVES DU MARCHE DE L'HABITATION. NORD DE L'ONTARIO. Text in French. 2005. s-a. **Document type:** *Bulletin, Trade.*
Media: Online - full text.
Published by: Canada Mortgage and Housing Corporation/Societe Canadienne d'Hypotheques et de Logement, 700 Montreal Rd, Ottawa, ON K1A 0P7, Canada. TEL 613-748-2000, FAX 613-748-2098, http://www.schl.ca.

333.33 CAN ISSN 1719-5470
PERSPECTIVES DU MARCHE DE L'HABITATION. OTTAWA. Text in French. 2002. q. **Document type:** *Bulletin, Trade.*
Formerly (until 2005): Perspectives du Marche du Logement. Ottawa (1719-5462)
Media: Online - full text.
Published by: Canada Mortgage and Housing Corporation/Societe Canadienne d'Hypotheques et de Logement, 700 Montreal Rd, Ottawa, ON K1A 0P7, Canada. TEL 613-748-2000, FAX 613-748-2098, http://www.schl.ca.

333.33 CAN ISSN 1719-5500
PERSPECTIVES DU MARCHE DE L'HABITATION. TORONTO. Text in French. 2002. q. **Document type:** *Bulletin, Trade.*
Formerly (until 2005): Perspectives du Marche du Logement. Toronto (1719-5497)
Media: Online - full text.
Published by: Canada Mortgage and Housing Corporation/Societe Canadienne d'Hypotheques et de Logement, 700 Montreal Rd, Ottawa, ON K1A 0P7, Canada. TEL 613-748-2000, FAX 613-748-2098, http://www.schl.ca.

333.33 CAN ISSN 1719-539X
PERSPECTIVES DU MARCHE DU LOGEMENT. CALGARY. Text in French. 2002. q. **Document type:** *Bulletin, Trade.*
Media: Online - full text.
Published by: Canada Mortgage and Housing Corporation/Societe Canadienne d'Hypotheques et de Logement, 700 Montreal Rd, Ottawa, ON K1A 0P7, Canada. TEL 613-748-2000, FAX 613-748-2098, http://www.schl.ca.

333.33 CAN ISSN 1719-5411
PERSPECTIVES DU MARCHE DU LOGEMENT. EDMONTON. Text in French. 2002. q. **Document type:** *Bulletin, Trade.*
Media: Online - full text.

Published by: Canada Mortgage and Housing Corporation/Societe Canadienne d'Hypotheques et de Logement, 700 Montreal Rd, Ottawa, ON K1A 0P7, Canada. TEL 613-748-2000, FAX 613-748-2098, http://www.schl.ca.

333.33 CAN ISSN 1719-8240
PERSPECTIVES DU MARCHE DU LOGEMENT. SAINT JOHN, MONCTON ET FREDERICTON. Text in French. 2005. s-a. **Document type:** *Bulletin, Trade.*
Formerly (until 2005): Perspectives du Marche de l'Habitation. Saint John, Moncton et Fredericton (1719-5772)
Media: Online - full text.
Published by: Canada Mortgage and Housing Corporation/Societe Canadienne d'Hypotheques et de Logement, 700 Montreal Rd, Ottawa, ON K1A 0P7, Canada. TEL 613-748-2000, FAX 613-748-2098, http://www.schl.ca.

333.33 USA
PERSPECTIVES ON APARTMENT MANAGEMENT. Text in English. 2006. bi-m. USD 60; USD 12.95 newsstand/cover (effective 2007). adv. **Document type:** *Magazine, Trade.* **Description:** Provides up-to-date industry news, politics, issues, regulations, economics, and tips for better operations.
Published by: California Apartment Association, 980 Ninth St, Ste 200, Sacramento, CA 95814-2721. TEL 916-447-7881, 800-967-4222, FAX 916-447-7903. Adv. contact James Rutherford. B&W page USD 2,245, color page USD 2,695; trim 8.25 x 10.5. Circ: 19,000 (paid).

333.33 GBR ISSN 2040-7653
▼ **PHILIPPINES REAL ESTATE REPORT.** Text in English. 2009. q. EUR 850, USD 1,150 combined subscription (print & email eds.) (effective 2011). **Document type:** *Report, Trade.* **Description:** Provides industry professionals and strategists, sector analysts, business investors, trade associations and regulatory bodies with independent forecasts and competitive intelligence on the real estate and construction industry in Philippines.
Related titles: E-mail ed.
Published by: Business Monitor International Ltd., Senator House, 85 Queen Victoria St, London, EC4V 4AB, United Kingdom. TEL 44-20-72480468, FAX 44-20-72480467, enquiry@businessmonitor.com.

333.33 USA
PITTSBURGH OFFICE BUILDINGS. Text in English. 19??. a. **Document type:** *Magazine, Trade.* **Description:** Review of Pittsburgh office buildings.
Published by: Yale Robbins, Inc., 102 Madison Ave, New York, NY 10016. TEL 212-683-5700, FAX 212-497-0017, mrosupport@mrofficespace.com.

347.2 USA ISSN 1548-0755
K30
PLANNING & ENVIRONMENTAL LAW. Abbreviated title: P E L. Text in English. 1948. 11/yr. GBP 250 combined subscription in United Kingdom to institutions (print & online eds.); EUR 391, USD 489 combined subscription to institutions (print & online eds.) (effective 2012). adv. abstr. index. back issues avail.; reprints avail. **Document type:** *Journal, Academic/Scholarly.* **Description:** Covers information on land use case law and legislation.
Former titles (until 2004): Land Use Law and Zoning Digest (0094-7598); (until 1974): Zoning Digest (0084-5566)
Related titles: Microform ed.: (from PQC); Online - full text ed.: ISSN 1556-8601. GBP 225 in United Kingdom to institutions; EUR 352, USD 440 to institutions (effective 2012); ◆ Supplement(s): Zoning Practice. ISSN 1548-0135.
Indexed: A12, A15, A22, A26, ABIn, AIAP, CA, E01, E04, E05, E08, G02, G08, HRIS, I05, LRI, P06, P10, P45, P48, P51, P52, P53, P54, P56, PQC, S09, T02.
—IE, Ingenta. **CCC.**
Published by: (American Planning Association), Routledge (Subsidiary of: Taylor & Francis Group), 325 Chestnut St, Ste 800, Philadelphia, PA 19106. TEL 800-354-1420, FAX 215-625-2940, journals@routledge.com, http://www.routledge.com. Ed. Lora A Lucero TEL 505-247-0844. Adv. contact Linda Hann TEL 44-1344-779945.

PLANS DE MAISONS DU QUEBEC. *see* INTERIOR DESIGN AND DECORATION

333.33 USA ISSN 1553-3557
HD251
PLUNKETT'S REAL ESTATE & CONSTRUCTION INDUSTRY ALMANAC. Variant title: Real Estate & Construction Industry Almanac. Text in English. 2003. a. USD 299.99 combined subscription (print & CD-ROM eds.); USD 399.99 combined subscription (print,online & CD-ROM eds.) (effective 2009). **Document type:** *Directory, Trade.* **Description:** Covers major real estate development, brokerage, construction, management and investment sectors, trends and companies.
Related titles: CD-ROM ed.; Online - full text ed.: USD 299.99 (effective 2009).
Published by: Plunkett Research, Ltd, PO Drawer 541737, Houston, TX 77254. TEL 713-932-0000, FAX 713-932-7080, customersupport@plunkettresearch.com. Ed. Jack W Plunkett.

346.043 USA
POWELL ON REAL PROPERTY. Text in English. 1973. 17 base vols. plus q. updates. looseleaf. USD 3,203 base vol(s). (effective 2008). **Document type:** *Journal, Trade.* **Description:** Provides information about real property law and analyses pertinent case law, statutes and regulations.
Related titles: CD-ROM ed.: USD 3,509 (effective 2008).
Published by: Matthew Bender & Co., Inc. (Subsidiary of: LexisNexis North America), 1275 Broadway, Albany, NY 12204. TEL 518-487-3000, 800-424-4200, FAX 518-487-3083, international@bender.com, http://bender.lexisnexis.com. Eds. Michael Allan Wolf, Richard Powell.

333.33 346.045 USA
PRACTICAL GUIDE TO WINNING LAND USE APPROVALS AND PERMITS. Text in English. 1989. base vol. plus irreg. updates. looseleaf. USD 275 base vol(s). (effective 2008). **Document type:** *Handbook/Manual/Guide, Trade.* **Description:** Provides practical strategies and advice for obtaining and opposing the requisite approvals and permits and includes step-by-step case studies and more than 60 forms.
Related titles: CD-ROM ed.
Published by: Matthew Bender & Co., Inc. (Subsidiary of: LexisNexis North America), 1275 Broadway, Albany, NY 12204. TEL 518-487-3000, 800-424-4200, FAX 518-487-3083, international@bender.com, http://bender.lexisnexis.com.

346.04 GBR
PRACTICAL LEASE PRECEDENTS. Text in English. 1988. 3 base vols. plus updates 2/yr. looseleaf. GBP 489 base vol(s). domestic; EUR 646 base vol(s). in Europe; USD 841 base vol(s). elsewhere (effective 2011). **Document type:** *Handbook/Manual/Guide, Trade.* **Description:** Offers a definitive collection of lease documents that can be easily customized for precise needs.
Related titles: CD-ROM ed.: GBP 1,412.40 base vol(s). domestic to institutions; EUR 1,864.80 base vol(s). in Europe to institutions; USD 2,023 base vol(s). elsewhere to institutions (effective 2011).
Published by: Sweet & Maxwell Ltd. (Subsidiary of: Thomson Reuters Corp.), 100 Avenue Rd, London, NW3 3PF, United Kingdom. TEL 44-20-73937000, FAX 44-20-74491144, sweetandmaxwell.customer.services@thomson.com. **Subscr. to:** PO Box 1000, Andover SP10 9AF, United Kingdom. TEL 44-20-73938051, sweetandmaxwell.international.queries@thomson.com.

THE PRACTICAL REAL ESTATE LAWYER. *see* LAW

PRECEDENTS FOR THE CONVEYANCER. *see* LAW

333.33 340 USA
PREMISES LIABILITY LAW AND PRACTICE. Text in English. 1987. 3 base vols. plus irreg. updates. looseleaf. USD 933 base vol(s). (effective 2008). Supplement avail. **Document type:** *Handbook/Manual/Guide, Trade.* **Description:** Presents information on liability of a property owner for the criminal acts of third parties, premises liability in cooperatives and condominiums and liability of retail establishments.
Related titles: CD-ROM ed.
Published by: Matthew Bender & Co., Inc. (Subsidiary of: LexisNexis North America), 1275 Broadway, Albany, NY 12204. TEL 518-487-3000, 800-424-4200, FAX 518-487-3083, international@bender.com, http://bender.lexisnexis.com. Eds. Edward Martin, Norman Landau.

PRESCOTT AREA NEWCOMER'S GUIDE; a relocation guide for the communities of Prescott & Prescott Valley. *see* LIFESTYLE

332.63 GBR ISSN 1558-7177
HD1382.5
PRIVATE EQUITY REAL ESTATE; the global magazine for opportunity investing in real estate. Abbreviated title: P E R E. Text in English. 2005. 10/yr. USD 1,585 combined subscription (print & onlin eds.) (effective 2010); subscr. includes PERE Yearbook. adv. **Document type:** *Magazine, Trade.* **Description:** Designed to look beyond the deals to the strategies, markets and institutions shaping this global asset class. Combines news, features, special surveys and supplements.
Related titles: Online - full text ed.: 2006 (Sep.).
Published by: P E I Media, Sycamore House, Sycamore St, London, EC1Y 0SG, United Kingdom. TEL 44-20-75665444, subscriptions@peimedia.com. Ed. Philip Borel TEL 44-20-75665434. Adv. contact Alistair Robinson TEL 44-20-75665454.

333.33 DEU
DIE PRIVATE IMMOBILIENWIRTSCHAFT. Variant title: F W W - Die Private Immobilienwirtschaft. Text in German. 1946. 6/yr. EUR 45; EUR 8 newsstand/cover (effective 2009). adv. **Document type:** *Magazine, Trade.*
Formerly (until 2008): Die Freie Wohnungswirtschaft (0016-0784)
Indexed: SpeleolAb.
Published by: Bundesverband Freier Immobilien- und Wohnungsunternehmen e.V., Kurfuerstendamm 57, Berlin, 10707, Germany. TEL 49-30-327810, FAX 49-30-32781299, office@bfw-bund.de. Adv. contact Elke Heindrichs. B&W page EUR 1,485, color page EUR 2,145; trim 185 x 272. Circ: 3,500 (paid and controlled).

333.338 IRL ISSN 1649-9247
PRIVATE RESIDENTIAL TENANCIES BOARD. ANNUAL REPORT AND ACCOUNTS. Text in English. 2004. a.
Published by: Private Residential Tenancies Board, Canal House, Canal Rd, Dublin, 6, Ireland. TEL 353-1-8882960, prtb@prtb.ie.

333 DEU ISSN 0171-3523
PRIVATES EIGENTUM. Text in German. 1960. m. free to members. adv. bk.rev. **Document type:** *Magazine, Trade.* **Description:** Covers matters of housing and housing policy. Contains an extensive case law section with technical essays, book reviews, forthcoming events and club news.
Formerly (until 1974): Private Haus- und Grundbesitz (0171-3582)
Published by: Vereinigung der Haus-, Grund- und Wohnungseigentuemer Frankfurt am Main e.V., Niedenau 61, Frankfurt Am Main, 60325, Germany. TEL 49-69-7191370, FAX 49-69-71913720, zentrale@haus-grund.org, http://www.haus-grund.org. adv.: B&W page EUR 2,148, color page EUR 3,115. Circ: 17,580 (paid and controlled).

PROBATE & PROPERTY. *see* LAW—Estate Planning

333.33 CAN ISSN 1925-0061
PROFESSION BROKER. Text in English. 1982. q. adv. back issues avail. **Document type:** *Newsletter, Trade.* **Description:** Explains various subjects concerning the application of the real estate brokerage act, also deals with legal and ethical issues related to the practice of real estate brokerage.
Former titles (until 2010): Info-A C A I Q (English Edition) (1703-9800); (until 2002): A C A I Q Magazine (English Edition) (1205-8785); Which superseded in part (in 1996): A C A I Q Magazine (1198-8541); Which was formerly (until 1994): Contact (0838-018X)
Related titles: Online - full text ed.: free (effective 2011); French ed.: ISSN 1703-9797.
Published by: Organisme D'Autoreglementation du Courtage Immobilier du Quebec, 4905, boulevard Lapiniere, Bureau 2200, Brossard, PQ J4Z 0G2, Canada. TEL 450 676-4800, 800-440-5110, info@oaciq.com.

333.33 USA ISSN 1531-5975
PROFESSIONAL OFFICE BUILDING MANAGEMENT. Text in English. 1998. m. USD 257 (effective 2006). **Document type:** *Newsletter, Trade.* **Description:** Provides tested management techniques, legal insights, and how-to guidelines for managing an office building. Includes model notices and letters to tenants, sample forms, negotiation tips, and lease enforcement strategies. Also covers legal issues and recent court decisions.
—**CCC.**
Published by: Vendome Group, LLC, 149 5th Ave, New York, NY 10010. TEL 212-812-8420, FAX 212-228-1308, customerservice@Vendomegrpsubs.com, http://www.vendomegrp.com/.

333.33 USA
HD1361
PROFESSIONAL RELOCATION & REAL ESTATE DIRECTORY; directory of professional relocation services and real estate professionals. Text in English. 1980. a. USD 195 (effective 1999). adv. bk.rev. index. back issues avail. **Document type:** *Directory.*
Former titles: Professional Relocation and Real Estate Services; National Relocation and Real Estate Directory (1056-9723)
Published by: Relocation Information Service, Inc., 50 Water St, Norwalk, CT 06854-3061. TEL 203-855-1234. Ed. Peter S Featherston. Circ: 28,500.

333.33 CAN ISSN 1911-3951
PROFILES OF BUSINESS SUCCESS. BURLINGTON - OAKVILLE EDITION. Text in English. 2006. irreg. **Document type:** *Magazine, Trade.*
Published by: Profiles of Success Magazines Inc., 12-3610 Nashua Dr, Mississauga, ON L4V 1L2, Canada. TEL 905-362-0797, FAX 905-671-2130, production@ProfilesOfSuccess.ca, http://www.profilesofsuccess.ca/index.html.

333.33 658 CAN ISSN 1718-7591
PROFILES OF BUSINESS SUCCESS. HAMILTON - NIAGARA EDITION. Text in English. 2006. m. **Document type:** *Magazine, Trade.*
Published by: Profiles of Success Magazines Inc., 12-3610 Nashua Dr, Mississauga, ON L4V 1L2, Canada. TEL 905-362-0797, FAX 905-671-2130, production@ProfilesOfSuccess.ca, http://www.profilesofsuccess.ca/index.html.

333.33 658 CAN ISSN 1718-7605
PROFILES OF BUSINESS SUCCESS. ONTARIO NORTH EDITION. Text in English. 2006. irreg. **Document type:** *Magazine, Trade.*
Published by: Profiles of Success Magazines Inc., 12-3610 Nashua Dr, Mississauga, ON L4V 1L2, Canada. TEL 905-362-0797, FAX 905-671-2130, production@ProfilesOfSuccess.ca, http://www.profilesofsuccess.ca/index.html.

333.33 658 CAN ISSN 1718-7613
PROFILES OF BUSINESS SUCCESS. OTTAWA EDITION. Text in English. 2006. m. **Document type:** *Magazine, Trade.*
Published by: Profiles of Success Magazines Inc., 12-3610 Nashua Dr, Mississauga, ON L4V 1L2, Canada. TEL 905-362-0797, FAX 905-671-2130, production@ProfilesOfSuccess.ca, http://www.profilesofsuccess.ca/index.html.

333.33 658 CAN ISSN 1911-396X
PROFILES OF BUSINESS SUCCESS. SOUTHWESTERN ONTARIO EDITION. Text in English. 2006. irreg. **Document type:** *Magazine, Trade.*
Published by: Profiles of Success Magazines Inc., 12-3610 Nashua Dr, Mississauga, ON L4V 1L2, Canada. TEL 905-362-0797, FAX 905-671-2130, production@ProfilesOfSuccess.ca, http://www.profilesofsuccess.ca/index.html.

333.33 658 CAN ISSN 1718-7621
PROFILES OF BUSINESS SUCCESS. TORONTO EAST EDITION. Text in English. 2006. m. **Document type:** *Magazine, Trade.*
Published by: Profiles of Success Magazines Inc., 12-3610 Nashua Dr, Mississauga, ON L4V 1L2, Canada. TEL 905-362-0797, FAX 905-671-2130, production@ProfilesOfSuccess.ca, http://www.profilesofsuccess.ca/index.html.

333.33 658 CAN ISSN 1911-3978
PROFILES OF BUSINESS SUCCESS. TORONTO WEST, TORONTO NORTH EDITION. Text in English. 2006. irreg. **Document type:** *Magazine, Trade.*
Published by: Profiles of Success Magazines Inc., 12-3610 Nashua Dr, Mississauga, ON L4V 1L2, Canada. TEL 905-362-0797, FAX 905-671-2130, production@ProfilesOfSuccess.ca, http://www.profilesofsuccess.ca/index.html.

333.33 658 CAN ISSN 1718-763X
PROFILES OF BUSINESS SUCCESS. VANCOUVER EDITION. Text in English. 2006. m. **Document type:** *Magazine, Trade.*
Published by: Profiles of Success Magazines Inc., 12-3610 Nashua Dr, Mississauga, ON L4V 1L2, Canada. TEL 905-362-0797, FAX 905-671-2130, production@ProfilesOfSuccess.ca, http://www.profilesofsuccess.ca/index.html.

333.33 658 CAN ISSN 1911-4192
PROFILES OF BUSINESS SUCCESS. VANCOUVER WEST EDITION. Text in English. 2006. irreg. **Document type:** *Magazine, Trade.*
Published by: Profiles of Success Magazines Inc., 12-3610 Nashua Dr, Mississauga, ON L4V 1L2, Canada. TEL 905-362-0797, FAX 905-671-2130, production@ProfilesOfSuccess.ca, http://www.profilesofsuccess.ca/index.html.

333.33 CAN ISSN 1718-3863
PROFILES OF SUCCESS. MARITIMES EDITION. Text in English. 2006. irreg. **Document type:** *Magazine, Trade.*
Published by: Profiles of Success Magazines Inc., 12-3610 Nashua Dr, Mississauga, ON L4V 1L2, Canada. TEL 905-362-0797, production@ProfilesOfSuccess.ca, http://www.profilesofsuccess.ca/index.html.

333.33 FRA ISSN 1760-1436
PROMOTION IMMOBILIERE. Text in French. 1961. 3/yr. adv. bk.rev. bibl.; charts; illus.; stat. **Document type:** *Magazine, Trade.*
Former titles (until 2003): F N P C La Lettre (1629-3282); (until 2000): L' Immobilier Magazine (1255-6815); (until 1994): Promotion Immobiliere (0996-4134); Which incorporated (1962-1971): Hommes et Logements (0996-3529)
Published by: Federation Nationale des Promoteurs Constructeurs (F N P C), 106 Rue de l'Universite, Paris, 75007, France. TEL 33-1-47054436, FAX 33-1-47539273, contact@fpcfrance.fr, http://www.fnpc.fr.

333.33 USA ISSN 0033-1287
PROPERTIES (CLEVELAND). Text in English. 1937. m. USD 17.95 (effective 2001). bk.rev. charts; illus.; stat.; tr.lit. index. **Document type:** *Magazine, Trade.* **Description:** Serving the real estate and construction markets in northeast Ohio with industry news, profiles, personals, new products, literature, and helpful features.

R

Published by: Properties Magazine Inc., PO Box 112127, Cleveland, OH 44111-8127. TEL 216-251-0035, FAX 216-251-0064. Ed., Pub., Adv. contact Kenneth C Krych. Circ: 2,400 (paid and controlled).

333.33 USA ISSN 1545-6439
HD268.N5
PROPERTIES (NEW YORK). Text in English. 1999. 3/yr. USD 95 in US & Canada to individuals; USD 120 elsewhere to individuals; USD 195 in US & Canada to institutions; USD 220 elsewhere to institutions (effective 2004). charts; illus.; maps. back issues avail. **Document type:** *Journal, Trade.* **Description:** Focus on key development and investment issues facing New York real estate.
Published by: Baruch College, City University of New York, The Steven L. Newman Real Estate Institute, 137 East 22nd Street, New York, NY 10010. TEL 212-802-5940, FAX 212-802-5944, newman_institute@baruch.cuny.edu, baruch.cuny.edu/realestae. Ed. Henry Wollman.

333.33 GBR ISSN 1757-5508
▼ **PROPERTY & LIVING IN TURKEY.** Text in English. 2009. m. GBP 40.30 (effective 2010). adv. **Document type:** *Magazine, Trade.* **Description:** Focuses on promoting Turkey as a booming market to what it offers by way of retail, services, property and living standards with development and investment prospects amongst blue-chip companies, established developers and premier retail groups.
Published by: Silverstone Publishing, Ltd., 145-147 St John St, London, EC1V 4PY, United Kingdom. TEL 44-20-71930202, enquires@silverstonepublishing.com.

333.33 AUS ISSN 1327-449X
PROPERTY AUSTRALIA. Text in English. 1975. m. AUD 110 domestic; AUD 156 foreign (effective 2007). **Document type:** *Magazine, Trade.*
Former titles: Building Owner and Manager (0818-6162); (until 1986): B O M A (0815-2284); (until 198?): B O M A National News (0726-5727)
Related titles: Online - full text ed.
Published by: Property Council of Australia (Sydney), Level 26, Australia Square, 264-278 George St, Sydney, NSW 2000, Australia. TEL 61-2-9252-3111, FAX 61-2-9336-6901, info@propertyoz.com.au.

333.33 USA ISSN 1088-5811
PROPERTY DIGEST AND ECONOMIC DEVELOPMENT MAGAZINE. Text in English. 1991. 2/yr. USD 87.50 (effective 2001). adv. 48 p./no. 3 cols./p.; **Document type:** *Magazine, Trade.*
Formerly: Property Digest and Literature Review
Published by: Barry Inc., PO Box 551, Wilmington, MA 01887-0551. TEL 978-658-0441, FAX 978-657-8691. Adv. contact Therese Di Blasi TEL 978-658-0441. B&W page USD 2,410; trim 10.88 x 8. Circ: 7,800.

333.33 NZL ISSN 1177-9705
PROPERTY FOCUS. Text in English. 2006. m. free. back issues avail. **Document type:** *Journal, Trade.* **Description:** Assesses the state of the New Zealand real estate market.
Media: Online - full text.
Published by: National Bank of New Zealand, Level 7, 1 Victoria St, Wellington, 6011, New Zealand. TEL 64-4-8022000, FAX 64-4-4968639, treasury@nbnz.co.nz.

PROPERTY FORECAST (LONDON). *see* LAW

333.33 GBR ISSN 1749-9607
PROPERTY FRANCE. Variant title: World of Property & Property France Magazine. Text in English. 1989. bi-m. free to qualified personnel (effective 2009). adv. **Document type:** *Magazine, Consumer.* **Description:** Lists French real estate for sale, along with legal and financial services.
Formerly (until 2005): Focus on France (0957-5030)
Related titles: Online - full text ed.
Published by: Outbound Media & Exhibitions, 1 Commercial Rd, Eastbourne, E Sussex BN21 3XQ, United Kingdom. TEL 44-1323-726040, FAX 44-1323-649249.

PROPERTY LAW & PRACTICE IN QUEENSLAND; being a commentary on the Property Law Act 1974. *see* LAW

346.04 GBR ISSN 1461-0752
PROPERTY LAW JOURNAL. Text in English. 1998. 20/yr. GBP 192 (effective 2009). **Document type:** *Journal, Trade.* **Description:** Designed to give practical, up-to-date advice to property lawyers.
Published by: Legalease Ltd., Kensington Sq House, 12-14 Ansdell St, London, W8 5BN, United Kingdom. TEL 44-20-73969292, FAX 44-20-73969303, subscriptions@legalease.co.uk.

333.33 ZAF ISSN 1811-699X
THE PROPERTY MAGAZINE (GAUTENG EDITION). Text in English. 2004. m. ZAR 240 domestic; ZAR 940 foreign (effective 2007). adv. **Document type:** *Magazine, Consumer.*
Published by: Media Nova (Pty) Ltd, PO Box 785828, Sandton, 2146, South Africa. TEL 27-11-8842228, FAX 27-11-8842830, info@medianova.co.za, http://www.medianova.co.za. Pub. Tony Vaughan. Adv. contact Karen O'Moore.

333.33 ZAF ISSN 1811-7007
THE PROPERTY MAGAZINE (KWAZULU-NATAL EDITION). Text in English. 2004. m. ZAR 240 domestic; ZAR 940 foreign (effective 2007). adv. **Document type:** *Magazine, Consumer.*
Published by: Media Nova (Pty) Ltd, PO Box 785828, Sandton, 2146, South Africa. TEL 27-11-8842228, FAX 27-11-8842830, info@medianova.co.za, http://www.medianova.co.za. Pub. Tony Vaughan. Adv. contact Lucrisha Polton.

333.33 ZAF ISSN 1810-469X
THE PROPERTY MAGAZINE (WESTERN CAPE EDITION). Text in English. 2004. m. ZAR 240 domestic; ZAR 940 foreign (effective 2007). adv. **Document type:** *Magazine, Consumer.*
Published by: Media Nova (Pty) Ltd, PO Box 50601, The Waterfront, Cape Town, South Africa. TEL 27-21-4216868, FAX 27-21-4217891, info@medianova.co.za, http://www.medianova.co.za. Pub. Tony Vaughan. Adv. contact Maxine Vaughan.

333.33 GBR ISSN 0263-7472
HD1394.5.G7
➤ **PROPERTY MANAGEMENT.** Abbreviated title: P M. Text in English. 1982. 5/yr. EUR 6,919 combined subscription in Europe (print & online eds.); USD 8,079 combined subscription in the Americas (print & online eds.); GBP 4,869 combined subscription in the UK & elsewhere (print & online eds.); AUD 8,759 combined subscription in Australasia (print & online eds.) (effective 2012). bk.rev. back issues avail.; reprint service avail. from PSC. **Document type:** *Journal, Academic/Scholarly.* **Description:** Publishes articles to keep professionals in the field conversant with new thinking and research. Covers issues such as land use and development, marketing and leasing, maintenance and refurbishment.
Related titles: Online - full text ed.: ISSN 1758-731X (from IngentaConnect).
Indexed: A12, A17, A22, ABIn, B01, B06, B07, B09, CA, E01, ESPM, EmerIntel, Emerald, P48, P51, P53, P54, PQC, RICS, RiskAb, S02, S03, SCOPUS, T02.
—BLDSC (6927.309700), IE, Infotrieve, Ingenta. **CCC.**
Published by: Emerald Group Publishing Ltd., Howard House, Wagon Ln, Bingley, W Yorks BD16 1WA, United Kingdom. TEL 44-1274-777700, FAX 44-1274-785201, information@emeraldinsight.com. Ed. Frances Plimmer. Pub. Valerie Robillard.

333.33 658 USA
PROPERTY MANAGEMENT ASSOCIATION. BULLETIN. Text in English. 1975. m. USD 100 (effective 2000). adv. **Document type:** *Bulletin.* **Description:** Covers property management, association activities, and business management personnel.
Published by: Property Management Association, 7900 Wisconsin Ave, Ste 204, Bethesda, MD 20814-3601. TEL 301-587-6543. Ed. Thomas B Cohn. Pub. Eileen Francis. Adv. contact Sharla V Warren. Circ: 1,200.

333.33 CAN
PROPERTY MANAGEMENT REPORT. Text in English. 8/yr. **Document type:** *Magazine, Trade.* **Description:** Focuses on development and commercial real estate in the Greater Toronto Area, Hamilton and Niagara Region.
Published by: MediaEdge Communications, Llc, 5255 Yonge St, Ste 1000, Toronto, ON M2N 6P4, Canada. TEL 416-512-8186, 866-216-0860, FAX 416-512-8344, info@mediaedge.ca. Ed. Barbara Carss. Pub. Sean Foley. Circ: 12,500 (paid and controlled).

333.33 GBR ISSN 2044-5237
▼ **PROPERTY MANAGEMENT SELECT**; for owners and occupiers. Text in English. 2010. m. GBP 119 domestic; GBP 152 foreign; free to qualified personnel (effective 2011). adv. **Document type:** *Magazine, Trade.* **Description:** For everyone who is involved with or working in property management. Examines the latest trends in high performance buildings, energy efficient and management technologies, both technological and in terms of business practices.
Related titles: Online - full text ed.: ISSN 2044-5245. free (effective 2011).
Published by: Quartz Business Media Ltd., Westgate House, 120/130 Station Rd, Redhill, Surrey RH1 1ET, United Kingdom. TEL 44-1737-855000, FAX 44-1737-855475, info@quartzltd.com, http://www.quartzltd.co.uk/business. Ed. Peter MacLeod TEL 44-1737-855452. Pub. Martin Oliver TEL 44-1737-855205. Adv. contact Laurence Allen TEL 44-1737-855060. Circ: 100,000.

333.33 IRL ISSN 1649-7473
PROPERTY NATIONWIDE. Text in English. 2005. m. EUR 1.95 newsstand/cover (effective 2006). adv.
Published by: Pinacle Publishing, The Loft, Main St, Newcastle, Co. Dublin, Ireland. TEL 353-1-4580676, FAX 353-1-4580513. adv.: page EUR 1,250; trim 218 x 297.

333.33 GBR ISSN 1351-2781
PROPERTY NEWS MIDLANDS. Text in English. 1993. m. GBP 30 domestic; GBP 35 in Europe; GBP 40 elsewhere (effective 2010). adv. back issues avail. **Document type:** *Magazine, Trade.* **Description:** Designed for people who are actively involved, or are acting for companies, in the Midlands commercial property market.
Indexed: RICS.
—CCC.
Published by: Bennett Publishing Company, 2-3 The Centre, Weston-super-Mare, North Somerset BS23 1US, United Kingdom. TEL 44-1934-622000, FAX 44-1934-622123, enquiries@propnews.co.uk. adv.: color page GBP 1,365, B&W page GBP 1,145; 185 x 275. Circ: 8,102.

333.3387094227 GBR ISSN 1478-8225
PROPERTY NEWS SOUTH. Text in English. 2002. bi-m. GBP 30 domestic; GBP 35 in Europe; GBP 40 elsewhere (effective 2010). adv. **Document type:** *Magazine, Trade.* **Description:** Designed for people who are actively involved, or are acting for companies, in the South commercial property market.
—CCC.
Published by: Bennett Publishing Company, 2-3 The Centre, Weston-super-Mare, North Somerset BS23 1US, United Kingdom. TEL 44-1934-622000, FAX 44-1934-622123, enquiries@propnews.co.uk. adv.: B&W page GBP 1,045, color page GBP 1,285; 185 x 275.

333.33 GBR ISSN 0964-5209
PROPERTY NEWS SOUTH WEST AND SOUTH WALES. Text in English. 1991. m. GBP 30 domestic; GBP 35 in Europe; GBP 40 elsewhere (effective 2010). adv. back issues avail. **Document type:** *Magazine, Trade.* **Description:** Designed for people who are actively involved, or are acting for companies, in the South West and South Wales commercial property market.
—CCC.
Published by: Bennett Publishing Company, 2-3 The Centre, Weston-super-Mare, North Somerset BS23 1US, United Kingdom. TEL 44-1934-622000, FAX 44-1934-622123, enquiries@propnews.co.uk. adv.: B&W page GBP 1,045, color page GBP 1,285; 185 x 275. Circ: 7,106.

333.33 GBR ISSN 1743-4211
PROPERTY OBSERVER; your guide to property in West Kent. Variant title: West Kent Property Observer. Text in English. 2004. m. free (effective 2006). **Document type:** *Magazine, Consumer.*
Related titles: Online - full text ed.
Published by: K O S Media, Apple Hythe Rd, Smeeth, Ashford, Kent TN25 6SR, United Kingdom. TEL 44-1303-817000, FAX 44-1313-817001.

PROPERTY PEOPLE FOCUS (ONLINE). *see* HOUSING AND URBAN PLANNING

333.33 ZAF ISSN 1813-7806
PROPERTY POWER. Text in English. 2004. a. ZAR 54.95 (effective 2008). adv.
Media: CD-ROM. **Related titles:** Print ed.: ISSN 1994-5302. 2007.
Published by: Jeppessen Productions cc, PO Box 4772, La Lucia Ridge, 4019, South Africa. TEL 254-11-4527685, FAX 254-86-6178048. Circ: 32,000.

333.33 ZAF ISSN 1814-7232
THE PROPERTY PROFESSIONAL; the magazine for real estate sales and management. Text in English. 1992. m. (10/yr.). adv. illus. **Document type:** *Magazine, Trade.*
Published by: Future Publishing (Pty) Ltd., PO Box 3355, Rivonia, 2128, South Africa. TEL 27-11-8032040, FAX 27-11-8032022. adv.: color page ZAR 4,200; trim 210 x 297.

333 IRL ISSN 0790-1658
THE PROPERTY VALUER. Text in English. 1982. q. EUR 34 (effective 2005). adv. bk.rev. **Document type:** *Magazine, Trade.* **Description:** Contains national and international property news.
Published by: Irish Auctioneers and Valuers Institute (IAVI), 38 Merrion Sq. E., Dublin, 2, Ireland. TEL 353-1-6611794, FAX 353-1-6611797, info@iavi.ie. Ed., Adv. contact Valerie Bourke. color page EUR 1,140. Circ: 1,600.

333.33 AUS
PROPERTY VICTORIA. Text in English. 1984. m. free membership (effective 2009). adv. back issues avail. **Document type:** *Magazine, Trade.*
Former titles (until 2000): Victoria News; (until 1997): Property Victoria; (until 1996): B O M A Victoria. Newsletter; (until 1994): B O M A News (0816-0856)
Published by: Property Council of Australia (Victoria), 136 Exhibition St, Melbourne, VIC 3000, Australia. TEL 61-3-96508300, FAX 61-3-96508693, vic@propertyoz.com.au, http://www.propertyoz.com.au/VIC/Division/Default.aspx. Circ: 100.

333.33 GBR ISSN 1354-1471
PROPERTY WEEK; news, events and data from across the uk. Text in English. 1868. w. GBP 175 domestic; GBP 215 in Europe; GBP 329 elsewhere (effective 2010). adv. charts; illus. index. back issues avail.; reprints avail. **Document type:** *Magazine, Trade.*
Former titles (until Feb. 1994): C S W - The Property Week (0969-7594); (until 1992): Chartered Surveyor Weekly (0264-049X); (until 1982): Chartered Surveyor (0009-1936); Which was formed by the merger of (1868-1955): Royal Institution of Chartered Surveyors. Transactions (0309-6491); (1946-1955): Royal Institution of Chartered Surveyors. Journal; Which was formerly (until 1946): Chartered Surveyors Institution. Journal
Related titles: Microfilm ed.: (from PQC); Online - full text ed.: free (effective 2010).
Indexed: API, B02, B03, B11, B15, B17, B18, BibCart, BldManAb, G04, G06, G07, G08, I05, ICEA, IMMAb, LJI, RASB, RICS, SoftAbEng.
—BLDSC (6927.313350). **CCC.**
Published by: Builder Group plc. (Subsidiary of: C M P Information Ltd.), Ludgate House, 245 Blackfriars Rd, London, SE1 9UY, United Kingdom. TEL 44-20-79215000, FAX 44-20-75604404. Ed. Giles Barrie TEL 44-20-79218561. Pub. Chris Kilbee TEL 44-20-79218350. Adv. contact Mike Hartley TEL 44-20-79218345. B&W page GBP 1,880, color page GBP 3,080; trim 230 x 287. Circ: 23,146.

333.33 NLD ISSN 1875-242X
PROPERTYEU MAGAZINE. Text in English. 200?. 8/yr. EUR 495 (effective 2010). adv. **Document type:** *Magazine, Trade.* **Description:** Focuses on trends and developments in the international commercial property market, with an emphasis on Europe.
Published by: PropertyEuro, PO Box 75485, Amsterdam, 1070 AL, Netherlands. TEL 31-20-5753555, FAX 31-20-5753318. Ed. Judi Seebus. Pub. Henk Fleggen. adv.: page EUR 7,500; trim 215 x 280.

333.33 NLD ISSN 1572-3402
PROPERTYNL RETAIL FORECAST. (Netherlands) Text in Dutch. 2002. a.
Published by: PropertyNL, Postbus 75485, Amsterdam, 1070 AL, Netherlands. TEL 31-20-5753317, FAX 31-20-5753318, info@propertynl.com.

333.33 340 ESP ISSN 1889-2353
PROPIEDAD HORIZONTAL. Text in Spanish. 1982. m. free to qualified personnel. **Document type:** *Magazine, Trade.*
Former titles (until 2008): SepinNET Revista. Propiedad Horizontal (1886-9033); (until 2003): Propiedad Horizontal (1577-5739); (until 2000): Revista Juridica Sepin. Cuadernos Propiedad Horizontal (1575-4790); (until 1998): Revista Juridica Sepin (1575-4774); (until 1990): Sepin. Servicio Propiedad Inmobiliaria (1575-4766)
Published by: Sepin Editorial Juridica, Calle Mahon 8, Las Rozas, Madrid 28230, Spain. sac@sepin.es, http://www.sepin.es.

333.33 COL ISSN 1909-5384
PROPIEDADES. Text in Spanish. 2006. m.
Published by: El Colombiano S.A. y Cia., Carrera 48 No. 30 Sur 119, Envigado, Antioquia, Colombia. TEL 57-4-3359338, 57-4-3314849, http://www.elcolombiano.com/.

333.33 ESP ISSN 1575-1740
PROPIEDADES. Variant title: Propiedades en Espana. Text in Spanish. 1997. m. adv. **Document type:** *Magazine, Consumer.* **Description:** Presents houses, recreational properties, and homes for sale in tourist areas throughout Spain.
Published by: Globus Comunicacion (Subsidiary of: Bonnier AB), Covarrubias 1, Madrid, 28010, Spain. TEL 34-91-4471202, FAX 34-91-4471043, txhdez@globuscom.es. Ed. Pilar Lorente. Adv. contact Ramon Elias. color page EUR 1,374; trim 23 x 30.

333.33 ITA ISSN 0033-1422
PROPRIETA EDILIZIA LOMBARDA. Text in Italian. 1901. m. **Document type:** *Magazine, Trade.*
Former titles (until 1949): Notiziario per i Proprietari di Fabbricati (1825-8999); (until 1945): La Proprieta Edilizia (1825-9006)
Published by: Federazione Lombarda della Proprieta Edilizia, Via Meravigli 3, Milan, 20123, Italy. TEL 39-02-885591, http://www.assoedilizia.mi.it. Circ: 25,000.

333.33 CHE ISSN 1420-7613
PROPRIETE. Text in French. 1918. 10/yr. CHF 60 (effective 2001). adv. stat.; mkt. **Document type:** *Magazine, Consumer.* **Description:** Trade journal for real estate owners in the French section of Switzerland.
Formerly (until 1996): Bulletin Immobilier (0007-4675)
Published by: Federation Romande Immobiliere, Case Postale 2560, Lausanne, 1002, Switzerland. TEL 41-21-3414143, FAX 41-21-3414146, mail@fri.ch, http://www.fri.ch. Ed. Claudine Amstein. adv.: B&W page CHF 2,424, color page CHF 3,453; trim 195 x 276. Circ: 13,506.

333.33 FRA ISSN 0995-4708
PROPRIETES DE FRANCE. Text in French. bi-m. **Document type:** *Magazine, Consumer.* **Description:** Advertises luxury houses and apartments for sale or rent in France.
Published by: Editions Indicateur Bertrand, 43 bd. Barbes, Paris, 75018, France. TEL 33-1-49252627, FAX 33-1-49252600. Circ: 45,000.

PUBLIC LAND & RESOURCES LAW REVIEW. *see* LAW

346.04 NLD ISSN 2211-1786
PUBLIEKRECHT VOOR DE VASTGOEDSECTOR. Text in Dutch. 2007. a. EUR 37.69 (effective 2010).
Published by: Sdu Uitgevers bv, Postbus 20025, The Hague, 2500 EA, Netherlands. TEL 31-70-3789529, FAX 31-70-3854321, sdu@sdu.nl, http://www.sdu.nl/.

333.33 658.8 USA
PURPLE DOT MAGAZINE; personal marketing for today's real estate agent. Text in English. 2005 (Oct.). s-a. adv. **Document type:** *Magazine, Trade.* **Description:** Offers articles and advice for attracting clients, with an emphasis on the marketing and sales issues that affect real estate brokers and agents careers.
Published by: Purple Dot Group, 20 W 20th St, Ste 222, New York, NY 10011. TEL 212-822-8550, http://www.purpledotgroup.com. Pub. Marcus Schaller. adv.: color page USD 2,240; trim 8.5 x 11. Circ: 8,000 (controlled).

333.33 GBR ISSN 2040-7874
▼ **QATAR REAL ESTATE REPORT.** Text in English. 2009. q. USD 975, EUR 695 combined subscription (print & email eds.) (effective 2011). **Document type:** *Report, Trade.* **Description:** Provides industry professionals and strategists, sector analysts, business investors, trade associations and regulatory bodies with independent forecasts and competitive intelligence on the real estate and construction industry in Qatar.
Related titles: E-mail ed.
Published by: Business Monitor International Ltd., Senator House, 85 Queen Victoria St, London, EC4V 4AB, United Kingdom. TEL 44-20-72480468, FAX 44-20-72480467, subs@businessmonitor.com.

333.33 USA ISSN 2154-2716
▼ **R E BUSINESS ONLINE**; news, resources, directories. (Real Estate) Text in English. 2009. d. free (effective 2010). adv. **Document type:** *Newsletter, Trade.* **Description:** Covers the commercial real estate market.
Media: Online - full text.
Published by: France Publications, Inc., 3500 Piedmont Rd, Ste 415, Atlanta, GA 30305. TEL 404-832-8262, FAX 404-832-8260, scott@francepublications.com, http://www.francepublications.com. Ed. Cara Aliek. Pub. Jerrold France. Adv. contact Scott France.

333.33 USA
R E E ACTION. Text in English. q. looseleaf. adv. bk.rev. **Document type:** *Newsletter, Trade.* **Description:** Articles on real estate education. Includes association news.
Published by: Real Estate Educators Association, 19 Mantua Rd, Mount Royal, NJ 08061. TEL 856-423-3215, FAX 856-423-3420, info@reea.org, http://www.reea.org. Circ: 1,375.

333.33 AUS ISSN 1442-9683
R E I Q JOURNAL. Text in English. 1963. m. (11/yr.). free to members. adv. **Document type:** *Journal, Trade.*
Formerly: Real Estate Journal (Queensland) (0048-685X)
Published by: Real Estate Institute of Queensland, 21 Turbo Dr, PO Box 1555, Coorparoo, QLD 4151, Australia. Ed. E D Ross Elliott. Circ: 4,800.

333.3 USA
R E I T REVIEW. (Real Estate Investment Trust) Text in English. irreg.
Indexed: A13.
Published by: Locke Liddell & Sapp, 2200 Ross Avenue, Ste 2200, Dallas, TX 75201-6776.

352 USA
R E I T STREET. (Real Estate Investment Trust) Variant title: REITStreet. Text in English. 1996. m. **Document type:** *Magazine, Trade.* **Description:** Provides analysis and insight into institutional real estate securities and investments.
Formerly (until 2001): Institutional Real Estate Securities (1090-0551)
Published by: Institutional Real Estate, Inc., 2274 Camino Ramon, San Ramon, CA 94583. TEL 925-244-0500, FAX 925-244-0520, circulation@irei.com, http://www.irei.com.

333.33 USA
R E I T WATCH (ONLINE). (Real Estate Investment Trusts) Text in English. 1900. m. free (effective 2011). back issues avail. **Document type:** *Report, Trade.* **Description:** Constitutes a monthly statistical investment publication which details REIT industry performance for all property segments.
Formerly (until 1999): R E I T Watch (Print)
Media: Online - full text.
Published by: National Association of Real Estate Investment Trusts, Inc., 1875 I St, NW, Ste 600, Washington, DC 20006. TEL 202-739-9400, FAX 202-739-9401.

352 USA
R E I T WEEK. (Real Estate Investment Trust) Text in English. w. **Document type:** *Newsletter, Trade.* **Description:** Provides a source of information devoted to real estate investment trusts investing.
Media: Online - full content.
Published by: Institutional Real Estate, Inc., 2274 Camino Ramon, San Ramon, CA 94583. TEL 925-244-0500, FAX 925-244-0520, irei@irei.com, http://www.irei.com.

333.33 658 CAN ISSN 1201-1223
R E M: THE REAL ESTATE MAGAZINE. Text in English. 1989. m. CAD 26.75 (effective 2005). adv. charts; illus.; stat.; tr.lit. back issues avail. **Document type:** *Magazine, Trade.* **Description:** Trade magazine for real estate agents and brokers.
Formerly: R E M: Canada's Magazine for Real Estate Professionals
Indexed: I05.
Published by: House Magazines Inc., 808 Coxwell Ave, Toronto, ON M4C 3E4, Canada. TEL 416-425-3504, FAX 416-425-0040. Ed. Jim Adair. Pub. Heino Molls. Adv. contacts Heino Molls, Dennis Rock. page CAD 2,500. Circ: 37,000.

333.33 AUT
RAIFFEISEN WOHNWELT. Text in German. 3/yr. free. adv. **Document type:** *Magazine, Consumer.*
Former titles: Sparen - Bauen - Wohnen; Sparen - Planen - Bauen
Published by: (Raiffeisen Bausparkasse), Verlagsgruppe News Gesellschaft mbH (Subsidiary of: Gruner + Jahr AG & Co), Schlossgasse 10-12, Vienna, N 1050, Austria. TEL 43-1-5452577420, FAX 43-1-5452577421, anzeigen@orac-zeitschriften.at. Adv. contact Klaus Edelhofer. page EUR 11,530; trim 185 x 250. Circ: 910,000 (controlled).

333.33 CAN ISSN 1912-4805
RAPPORT SUR LE MARCHE LOCATIF. FAITS SAILLANTS. ALBERTA. Text in French. 2004. a. **Document type:** *Trade.*
Media: Online - full text. **Related titles:** English ed.: Rental Market Report. Alberta Highlights. ISSN 1912-4791.
Published by: Canada Mortgage and Housing Corporation/Societe Canadienne d'Hypotheques et de Logement, 700 Montreal Rd, Ottawa, ON K1A 0P7, Canada. TEL 613-748-2000, FAX 613-748-2098, chic@cmhc-schl.gc.ca, http://www.cmhc.ca.

333.33 CAN ISSN 1912-4821
RAPPORT SUR LE MARCHE LOCATIF. FAITS SAILLANTS. COLOMBIE-BRITANNIQUE. Text in French. 2004. a. **Document type:** *Report, Trade.*
Media: Online - full text. **Related titles:** English ed.: Rental Market Report. British Columbia Highlights. ISSN 1912-4813.
Published by: Canada Mortgage and Housing Corporation/Societe Canadienne d'Hypotheques et de Logement, 700 Montreal Rd, Ottawa, ON K1A 0P7, Canada. TEL 613-748-2000, FAX 613-748-2098, chic@cmhc-schl.gc.ca, http://www.cmhc.ca.

333.33 CAN ISSN 1912-3469
RAPPORT SUR LE MARCHE LOCATIF. FAITS SAILLANTS. ILE-DU-PRINCE-EDOUARD. Text in French. 200?. a. **Document type:** *Report, Trade.*
Media: Online - full text. **Related titles:** English ed.: Rental Market Report. Prince Edward Island Highlights. ISSN 1912-3450.
Published by: Canada Mortgage and Housing Corporation/Societe Canadienne d'Hypotheques et de Logement, 700 Montreal Rd, Ottawa, ON K1A 0P7, Canada. TEL 613-748-2000, FAX 613-748-2098, chic@cmhc-schl.gc.ca, http://www.cmhc.ca.

333.33 CAN ISSN 1912-340X
RAPPORT SUR LE MARCHE LOCATIF. FAITS SAILLANTS. MANITOBA. Text in French. 200?. a. **Document type:** *Newsletter, Trade.*
Published by: (Canada Mortgage and Housing Corporation/Societe Canadienne d'Hypotheques et de Logement, 700 Montreal Rd, Ottawa, ON K1A 0P7, Canada. TEL 613-748-2000, FAX 613-748-2098, chic@cmhc-schl.gc.ca, http://www.cmhc.ca.

333.33 CAN ISSN 1912-4899
RAPPORT SUR LE MARCHE LOCATIF. FAITS SAILLANTS. NOUVEAU-BRUNSWICK. Text in French. 2004. a. **Document type:** *Report, Trade.*
Media: Online - full text. **Related titles:** English ed.: Rental Market Report. New Brunswick Highlights. ISSN 1912-4880.
Published by: Canada Mortgage and Housing Corporation/Societe Canadienne d'Hypotheques et de Logement, 700 Montreal Rd, Ottawa, ON K1A 0P7, Canada. TEL 613-748-2000, FAX 613-748-2098, chic@cmhc-schl.gc.ca, http://www.cmhc.ca.

333.33 CAN ISSN 1912-3442
RAPPORT SUR LE MARCHE LOCATIF. FAITS SAILLANTS. NOUVELLE-ECOSSE. Text in French. 200?. a. **Document type:** *Bulletin, Trade.*
Media: Online - full text. **Related titles:** English ed.: Rental Market Report. Nova Scotia Highlights. ISSN 1912-3434.
Published by: Canada Mortgage and Housing Corporation/Societe Canadienne d'Hypotheques et de Logement, 700 Montreal Rd, Ottawa, ON K1A 0P7, Canada. TEL 613-748-2000, FAX 613-748-2098, chic@cmhc-schl.gc.ca, http://www.cmhc.ca.

333.33 CAN ISSN 1912-4848
RAPPORT SUR LE MARCHE LOCATIF. FAITS SAILLANTS. ONTARIO. Text in French. 2004. a. **Document type:** *Report, Trade.*
Media: Online - full text. **Related titles:** English ed.: Rental Market Report. Ontario Highlights. ISSN 1912-483X. 2004.
Published by: Canada Mortgage and Housing Corporation/Societe Canadienne d'Hypotheques et de Logement, 700 Montreal Rd, Ottawa, ON K1A 0P7, Canada. TEL 613-748-2000, FAX 613-748-2098, chic@cmhc-schl.gc.ca, http://www.cmhc.ca.

333.33 CAN ISSN 1912-4872
RAPPORT SUR LE MARCHE LOCATIF. FAITS SAILLANTS. QUEBEC. Text in French. 2004. a. **Document type:** *Report, Trade.*
Media: Online - full text. **Related titles:** English ed.: Rental Market Report. Quebec Highlights. ISSN 1912-4856.
Published by: Canada Mortgage and Housing Corporation/Societe Canadienne d'Hypotheques et de Logement, 700 Montreal Rd, Ottawa, ON K1A 0P7, Canada. TEL 613-748-2000, FAX 613-748-2098, chic@cmhc-schl.gc.ca, http://www.cmhc.ca.

333.33 CAN ISSN 1912-4961
RAPPORT SUR LE MARCHE LOCATIF. FAITS SAILLANTS. SASKATCHEWAN. Text in French. 2004. a. **Document type:** *Report, Trade.*
Media: Online - full text. **Related titles:** English ed.: Rental Market Report. Saskatchewan Highlights. ISSN 1912-4953.
Published by: Canada Mortgage and Housing Corporation/Societe Canadienne d'Hypotheques et de Logement, 700 Montreal Rd, Ottawa, ON K1A 0P7, Canada. TEL 613-748-2000, FAX 613-748-2098, chic@cmhc-schl.gc.ca, http://www.cmhc.ca.

333.33 CAN ISSN 1912-3426
RAPPORT SUR LE MARCHE LOCATIF. FAITS SAILLANTS. TERRE-NEUVE-ET-LABRADOR. Text in French. 200?. a. **Document type:** *Bulletin, Trade.*
Media: Online - full text. **Related titles:** English ed.: Rental Market Report. Newfoundland and Labrador Highlights. ISSN 1912-3418.
Published by: Canada Mortgage and Housing Corporation/Societe Canadienne d'Hypotheques et de Logement, 700 Montreal Rd, Ottawa, ON K1A 0P7, Canada. TEL 613-748-2000, FAX 613-748-2098, chic@cmhc-schl.gc.ca, http://www.cmhc.ca.

333.33 CAN ISSN 1912-4988
RAPPORT SUR LE MARCHE LOCATIF. FAITS SAILLANTS. YELLOWKNIFE. TERRITOIRES DU NORD-OUEST. Text in French. 2004. a. **Document type:** *Report, Trade.*
Media: Online - full text. **Related titles:** English ed.: Rental Market Report. Yellowknife, Northern Territories. Highlights. ISSN 1912-497X.
Published by: Canada Mortgage and Housing Corporation/Societe Canadienne d'Hypotheques et de Logement, 700 Montreal Rd, Ottawa, ON K1A 0P7, Canada. TEL 613-748-2000, FAX 613-748-2098, chic@cmhc-schl.gc.ca, http://www.cmhc.ca.

333.33 CAN ISSN 1912-5232
RAPPORT SUR LE MARCHE LOCATIF. GATINEAU. Text in French. 2001. a. **Document type:** *Report, Trade.*
Formerly (until 2004): Rapport sur les Logements Locatifs. Gatineau (1912-5224)
Media: Online - full text. **Related titles:** English ed.: Rental Market Report. Gatineau. ISSN 1912-5216. 199?.
Published by: Canada Mortgage and Housing Corporation/Societe Canadienne d'Hypotheques et de Logement, 700 Montreal Rd, Ottawa, ON K1A 0P7, Canada. TEL 613-748-2000, FAX 613-748-2098, chic@cmhc-schl.gc.ca, http://www.cmhc.ca.

333.33 CAN ISSN 1912-3477
RAPPORT SUR LE MARCHE LOCATIF. HALIFAX/RENTAL MARKET REPORTS. Text in French. 2001. a. **Document type:** *Bulletin, Trade.* **Description:** Presents the latest trends in vacancy rates, average rents and the rate of change at the sub-market level for buildings across Canada.
Formerly (until 2004): Rapport sur les Logements Locatifs. Halifax (1704-4316)
Media: Online - full text. **Related titles:** Print ed.: ISSN 1707-0945. 1999.
Published by: Canada Mortgage and Housing Corporation/Societe Canadienne d'Hypotheques et de Logement, 700 Montreal Rd, Ottawa, ON K1A 0P7, Canada. TEL 613-748-2000, FAX 613-748-2098, chic@cmhc-schl.gc.ca, http://www.cmhc.ca.

333.33 CAN ISSN 1912-5399
RAPPORT SUR LE MARCHE LOCATIF. KELOWNA. Text in French. 2001. a. **Document type:** *Report, Trade.*
Formerly (until 2004): Rapport sur les Logements Locatifs. Kelowna (1912-5380)
Media: Online - full text. **Related titles:** English ed.: Rental Market Report. Kelowna. ISSN 1912-5364.
Published by: Canada Mortgage and Housing Corporation/Societe Canadienne d'Hypotheques et de Logement, 700 Montreal Rd, Ottawa, ON K1A 0P7, Canada. TEL 613-748-2000, FAX 613-748-2098, chic@cmhc-schl.gc.ca, http://www.cmhc.ca.

333.33 CAN ISSN 1912-5437
RAPPORT SUR LE MARCHE LOCATIF. KITCHENER. Text in French. 2001. a. **Document type:** *Report, Trade.*
Formerly (until 2003): Rapport sur le Logements Locatifs. R M R de Kitchener (1912-5429)
Media: Online - full text. **Related titles:** English ed.: Rental Market Report. Kitchener C M A. ISSN 1912-5410.
Published by: Canada Mortgage and Housing Corporation/Societe Canadienne d'Hypotheques et de Logement, 700 Montreal Rd, Ottawa, ON K1A 0P7, Canada. TEL 613-748-2000, FAX 613-748-2098, chic@cmhc-schl.gc.ca, http://www.cmhc.ca.

333.33 CAN ISSN 1912-5461
RAPPORT SUR LE MARCHE LOCATIF. LONDON. Text in French. 2001. a. **Document type:** *Report, Trade.*
Formerly (until 2004): Rapport sur les Logements Locatifs. London (1912-5453)
Media: Online - full text. **Related titles:** English ed.: Rental Market Report. London. ISSN 1912-5445.
Published by: Canada Mortgage and Housing Corporation/Societe Canadienne d'Hypotheques et de Logement, 700 Montreal Rd, Ottawa, ON K1A 0P7, Canada. TEL 613-748-2000, FAX 613-748-2098, chic@cmhc-schl.gc.ca, http://www.cmhc.ca.

333.33 CAN ISSN 1912-5534
RAPPORT SUR LE MARCHE LOCATIF. MONTREAL. Text in French. 2001. a. **Document type:** *Report, Trade.*
Formerly (until 2004): Rapport sur les Logements Locatifs. Montreal (1912-5526)
Media: Online - full text. **Related titles:** English ed.: Rental Market Report. Montreal. ISSN 1912-5518.
Published by: Canada Mortgage and Housing Corporation/Societe Canadienne d'Hypotheques et de Logement, 700 Montreal Rd, Ottawa, ON K1A 0P7, Canada. TEL 613-748-2000, FAX 613-748-2098, chic@cmhc-schl.gc.ca, http://www.cmhc.ca.

333.33 CAN ISSN 1912-5550
RAPPORT SUR LE MARCHE LOCATIF. NORD DE L'ONTARIO. Text in French. 2002. a. **Document type:** *Report, Trade.*
Media: Online - full text. **Related titles:** ◆ English ed.: Rental Market Report. Northern Ontario (Print). ISSN 1709-3546.
Published by: Canada Mortgage and Housing Corporation/Societe Canadienne d'Hypotheques et de Logement, 700 Montreal Rd, Ottawa, ON K1A 0P7, Canada. TEL 613-748-2000, FAX 613-748-2098, chic@cmhc-schl.gc.ca, http://www.cmhc.ca.

333.33 CAN ISSN 1912-5682
RAPPORT SUR LE MARCHE LOCATIF. OSHAWA. Text in French. 2001. a. **Document type:** *Report, Trade.*
Formerly (until 2004): Rapport sur les Logements Locatifs. Oshawa (1912-5674)
Media: Online - full text. **Related titles:** English ed.: Rental Market Report. Oshawa. ISSN 1912-5666. 199?.
Published by: Canada Mortgage and Housing Corporation/Societe Canadienne d'Hypotheques et de Logement, 700 Montreal Rd, Ottawa, ON K1A 0P7, Canada. TEL 613-748-2000, FAX 613-748-2098, chic@cmhc-schl.gc.ca, http://www.cmhc.ca.

R

333.33 CAN ISSN 1912-5712
RAPPORT SUR LE MARCHE LOCATIF. OTTAWA (ONLINE). Text in French. 2001. a. **Document type:** *Report, Trade.*
Formerly (until 2004): Rapport sur les Logements Locatifs. Ottawa (Online) (1912-5704)
Media: Online - full text. **Related titles:** English ed.: Rental Market Report. Ottawa (Online). ISSN 1912-5690.
Published by: Canada Mortgage and Housing Corporation/Societe Canadienne d'Hypotheques et de Logement, 700 Montreal Rd, Ottawa, ON K1A 0P7, Canada. TEL 613-748-2000, FAX 613-748-2098, chic@cmhc-schl.gc.ca, http://www.cmhc.ca.

333.33 CAN ISSN 1912-5747
RAPPORT SUR LE MARCHE LOCATIF. QUEBEC. Text in French. 2001. a. **Document type:** *Report, Trade.*
Formerly (until 2004): Rapport sur les Logements Locatifs. Quebec (1912-5739)
Media: Online - full text. **Related titles:** Print ed.: Les Logements Locatifs. Quebec. Rapport. ISSN 1707-780X. 199?; Ed.: Rental Market Report. Quebec. ISSN 1912-5720. 2001.
Published by: Canada Mortgage and Housing Corporation/Societe Canadienne d'Hypotheques et de Logement, 700 Montreal Rd, Ottawa, ON K1A 0P7, Canada. TEL 613-748-2000, FAX 613-748-2098, chic@cmhc-schl.gc.ca, http://www.cmhc.ca.

333.33 CAN ISSN 1912-5054
RAPPORT SUR LE MARCHE LOCATIF. R M R DE CALGARY. (Region Metropolitaine de Recensement) Text in French. 2001. a. **Document type:** *Report, Trade.*
Formerly (until 2005): Rapport sur les Logements Locatifs. Calgary (1912-5046)
Media: Online - full text.
Published by: Canada Mortgage and Housing Corporation/Societe Canadienne d'Hypotheques et de Logement, 700 Montreal Rd, Ottawa, ON K1A 0P7, Canada. TEL 613-748-2000, FAX 613-748-2098, chic@cmhc-schl.gc.ca, http://www.cmhc.ca.

333.33 CAN ISSN 1912-5267
RAPPORT SUR LE MARCHE LOCATIF. R M R DE HAMILTON. (Region Metropolitaine de Recensement) Text in French. 2001. a. **Document type:** *Report, Trade.*
Formerly (until 2004): Rapport sur les Logements Locatifs. R M R de Hamilton (1912-5259)
Media: Online - full text. **Related titles:** English ed.: Rental Market Report. Hamilton C M A. ISSN 1912-5240. 2001.
Published by: Canada Mortgage and Housing Corporation/Societe Canadienne d'Hypotheques et de Logement, 700 Montreal Rd, Ottawa, ON K1A 0P7, Canada. TEL 613-748-2000, FAX 613-748-2098, chic@cmhc-schl.gc.ca, http://www.cmhc.ca.

333.33 CAN ISSN 1912-6158
RAPPORT SUR LE MARCHE LOCATIF. R M R DE REGINA. (Region Metropolitaine de Recensement) Text in French. 2001. a. **Document type:** *Report, Trade.*
Former titles (until 2005): Rapport sur les Logements Locatifs. Regina. (Online) (1912-614X)
Media: Online - full text. **Related titles:** English ed.: Rental Market Report. Regina. ISSN 1912-6131. 199?.
Published by: Canada Mortgage and Housing Corporation/Societe Canadienne d'Hypotheques et de Logement, 700 Montreal Rd, Ottawa, ON K1A 0P7, Canada. TEL 613-748-2000, FAX 613-748-2098, chic@cmhc-schl.gc.ca, http://www.cmhc.ca, http://www.schl.ca.

333.33 CAN ISSN 1912-6182
RAPPORT SUR LE MARCHE LOCATIF. R M R DE SASKATOON. Text in French. 2001. a. **Document type:** *Report, Trade.*
Former titles (until 2005): Rapport sur les Logements Locatifs. Saskatoon. (Online) (1912-6174)
Media: Online - full text. **Related titles:** English ed.: Rental Market Report. Saskatoon. ISSN 1912-6166.
Published by: Canada Mortgage and Housing Corporation/Societe Canadienne d'Hypotheques et de Logement, 700 Montreal Rd, Ottawa, ON K1A 0P7, Canada. TEL 613-748-2000, FAX 613-748-2098, chic@cmhc-schl.gc.ca, http://www.cmhc.ca, http://www.schl.ca.

333.33 CAN ISSN 1912-6387
RAPPORT SUR LE MARCHE LOCATIF. R M R DE TORONTO. (Region Metropolitaine de Recensement) Text in French. a. **Document type:** *Bulletin, Trade.*
Formerly (until 2004): Rapport sur les Logements Locatifs. R M R de Toronto. (1912-6379)
Media: Online - full text. **Related titles:** ◆ English ed.: Rental Market Report. Toronto C M A. ISSN 1912-6360.
Published by: Canada Mortgage and Housing Corporation/Societe Canadienne d'Hypotheques et de Logement, 700 Montreal Rd, Ottawa, ON K1A 0P7, Canada. TEL 613-748-2000, FAX 613-748-2098, chic@cmhc-schl.gc.ca, http://www.cmhc.ca, http://www.schl.ca.

333.33 CAN ISSN 1912-6743
RAPPORT SUR LE MARCHE LOCATIF. R M R DE WINNIPEG. (Region Metropolitaine de Recensement) Text in French. 2001. a. **Document type:** *Report, Trade.*
Formerly (until 2005): Rapport sur les Logements Locatifs. Winnipeg (Online) (1912-6735)
Media: Online - full text. **Related titles:** English ed.: Rental Market Report. Winnipeg. ISSN 1912-6727.
Published by: Canada Mortgage and Housing Corporation/Societe Canadienne d'Hypotheques et de Logement, 700 Montreal Rd, Ottawa, ON K1A 0P7, Canada. TEL 613-748-2000, FAX 613-748-2098, chic@cmhc-schl.gc.ca, http://www.cmhc.ca, http://www.schl.ca.

333.33 CAN ISSN 1912-5208
RAPPORT SUR LE MARCHE LOCATIF. R M R D'EDMONTON. (Region Metropolitaine de Recensement) Text in French. 2001. a. **Document type:** *Report, Trade.*
Formerly (until 2005): Rapport sur les Logements Locatifs. Edmonton (1912-5194)
Media: Online - full text. **Related titles:** Print ed.: Les Logements Locatifs. Edmonton. Rapport. ISSN 1707-5270; English ed.: Rental Market Report. Edmonton. ISSN 1912-5186. 199?.
Published by: Canada Mortgage and Housing Corporation/Societe Canadienne d'Hypotheques et de Logement, 700 Montreal Rd, Ottawa, ON K1A 0P7, Canada. TEL 613-748-2000, FAX 613-748-2098, chic@cmhc-schl.gc.ca, http://www.cmhc.ca.

333.33 CAN ISSN 1912-4929
RAPPORT SUR LE MARCHE LOCATIF. SAGUENAY. Text in French. 2003. a. **Document type:** *Report, Trade.*
Media: Online - full text. **Related titles:** English ed.: Rental Market Report. Saguenay. ISSN 1912-4902. 2003; Regional ed(s).: Rapport sur le Marche Locatif. Victoria. ISSN 1912-550X. 2001.
Published by: Canada Mortgage and Housing Corporation/Societe Canadienne d'Hypotheques et de Logement, 700 Montreal Rd, Ottawa, ON K1A 0P7, Canada. TEL 613-748-2000, FAX 613-748-2098, chic@cmhc-schl.gc.ca, http://www.cmhc.ca.

333.33 CAN ISSN 1912-5933
RAPPORT SUR LE MARCHE LOCATIF. SAINT JOHN. Text in French. 2001. a.
Formerly (until 2004): Rapport sur les Logements Locatifs. Saint John (1704-4359)
Media: Online - full text.
Published by: Canada Mortgage and Housing Corporation/Societe Canadienne d'Hypotheques et de Logement, 700 Montreal Rd, Ottawa, ON K1A 0P7, Canada. TEL 613-748-2000, FAX 613-748-2098, http://www.cmhc.ca, http://www.schl.ca.

333.33 CAN ISSN 1912-6247
RAPPORT SUR LE MARCHE LOCATIF. SHERBROOKE (ONLINE). Text in French. 2001. a. **Document type:** *Report, Trade.*
Formerly (until 2004): Rapport sur le Logements Locatifs. Sherbrooke (1912-6220)
Media: Online - full text. **Related titles:** Regional ed(s).: Rapport sur le Marche Locatif. St. John's. ISSN 1912-6336; Rapport sur le Marche Locatif. St. Catharines-Niagara. ISSN 1912-6328. 2001.
Published by: Canada Mortgage and Housing Corporation/Societe Canadienne d'Hypotheques et de Logement, 700 Montreal Rd, Ottawa, ON K1A 0P7, Canada. TEL 613-748-2000, FAX 613-748-2098, http://www.cmhc.ca, http://www.schl.ca.

333.33 CAN ISSN 1912-6638
RAPPORT SUR LE MARCHE LOCATIF. TROIS-RIVIERES. Text in French. 2001. a. **Document type:** *Report, Trade.*
Formerly (until 2004): Rapport sur les Logements Locatifs. Trois-Rivieres (1912-662X)
Media: Online - full text. **Related titles:** English ed.: Rental Market Report. Trois-Rivieres. ISSN 1912-6611. 1999.
Published by: Canada Mortgage and Housing Corporation/Societe Canadienne d'Hypotheques et de Logement, 700 Montreal Rd, Ottawa, ON K1A 0P7, Canada. TEL 613-748-2000, FAX 613-748-2098, http://www.cmhc.ca, http://www.schl.ca.

333.33 CAN ISSN 1912-6662
RAPPORT SUR LE MARCHE LOCATIF. VANCOUVER. Text in French. 2001. a. **Document type:** *Report, Trade.*
Formerly (until 2004): Rapport sur les Logements Locatifs. Vancouver (1912-6654)
Media: Online - full text. **Related titles:** ◆ English ed.: Rental Market Report. Vancouver (Online). ISSN 1912-6646.
Published by: Canada Mortgage and Housing Corporation/Societe Canadienne d'Hypotheques et de Logement, 700 Montreal Rd, Ottawa, ON K1A 0P7, Canada. TEL 613-748-2000, FAX 613-748-2098, http://www.cmhc.ca, http://www.schl.ca.

333.33 CAN ISSN 1912-6700
RAPPORT SUR LE MARCHE LOCATIF. WINDSOR. Text in French. 2001. a. **Document type:** *Report, Trade.*
Formerly (until 2004): Rapport sur les Logements Locatifs. Windsor (1912-6697)
Media: Online - full text. **Related titles:** English ed.: Rental Market Report. Windsor. ISSN 1912-6689. 199?.
Published by: Canada Mortgage and Housing Corporation/Societe Canadienne d'Hypotheques et de Logement, 700 Montreal Rd, Ottawa, ON K1A 0P7, Canada. TEL 613-748-2000, FAX 613-748-2098, http://www.schl.ca.

333.33 USA
THE REAL DEAL. Text in English. 2003. bi-w. USD 45 (effective 2004). adv. **Document type:** *Magazine, Trade.* **Description:** Contains current news, features and in-depth analysis for the savvy New York City real estate professional, from brokers to developers to appraisers.
Published by: The Real Deal, 36 E 23rd St, 2nd Fl, New York, NY 10010. TEL 212-592-4023. Ed. Stuart Elliott. Pub. Amir Korangy. Adv. contact Yoav Barilan TEL 646-279-8876. color page USD 3,640; trim 10.25 x 13.75.

REAL ESTATE. *see* LAW

332.63 USA ISSN 1520-3719
KF566.A15
REAL ESTATE ALERT. Text in English. 198?. 46/yr. USD 2,297 (effective 2011). adv. back issues avail. **Document type:** *Newsletter, Trade.* **Description:** Reports on future offerings of commercial properties, mortgage portfolios and real estate-owning companies, including real-estate investment trusts (REIT), pension funds and other big owners that are preparing to offer income-producing properties or mortgages.
Former titles (until 1996): Liquidation Alert; (until 1993): Thrift Liquidation Alert
Related titles: Fax ed.; Online - full text ed.
Indexed: A15, ABIn, BLI, I05, P48, P51, P53, P54, PQC, PROMT.
Published by: Harrison Scott Publications, Inc., 5 Marine View Plz, Ste 301, Hoboken, NJ 07030. TEL 201-659-1700, FAX 201-659-4141, info@hspnews.com, http://www.hspnewsletters.com. Pub. Andrew Albert TEL 201-234-3960. Adv. contact Mary E Romano TEL 201-234-3968.

333.33 USA ISSN 1945-8274
REAL ESTATE & INVESTMENT BUSINESS. Text in English. 2008. w. USD 2,295 in US & Canada; USD 2,495 elsewhere; USD 2,525 combined subscription in US & Canada (print & online eds.); USD 2,755 combined subscription elsewhere (print & online eds.) (effective 2011). adv. back issues avail. **Document type:** *Newsletter, Trade.* **Description:** Focuses on large equity and financial companies investing in real estate, reporting on their financial health, their investments and financial trends affecting markets.
Related titles: E-mail ed.; Online - full text ed.: ISSN 1945-8282. USD 2,295 combined subscription (online & e-mail eds.) (effective 2011).
Indexed: A15, ABIn, B02, B15, B17, B18, G04, I05, P16, P48, P51, P53, P54, PQC.
Published by: NewsRx, 2727 Paces Ferry Rd SE, Ste 2-440, Atlanta, GA 30339. TEL 770-435-8286, 800-726-4550, FAX 770-435-6800, pressrelease@newsrx.com, http://www.newsrx.com. Pub., Adv. contact Susan Hasty TEL 770-507-7777.

332.63 USA ISSN 1945-8290
REAL ESTATE & INVESTMENT WEEK. Text in English. 2008. w. USD 2,295 in US & Canada; USD 2,495 elsewhere; USD 2,525 combined subscription in US & Canada (print & online eds.); USD 2,755 combined subscription elsewhere (print & online eds.) (effective 2011). adv. back issues avail. **Document type:** *Newsletter, Trade.* **Description:** Provides the latest news and market analysis affecting real estate investments, as well as the latest business developments within the financial institutions that fund real estate markets.
Related titles: E-mail ed.; Online - full text ed.: ISSN 1945-8304. USD 2,295 combined subscription (online & e-mail eds.) (effective 2011).
Indexed: A15, ABIn, B02, B15, B17, B18, G04, I05, P16, P48, P51, P53, P54, PQC.
Published by: NewsRx, 2727 Paces Ferry Rd SE, Ste 2-440, Atlanta, GA 30339. TEL 770-435-8286, 800-726-4550, FAX 770-435-6800, pressrelease@newsrx.com, http://www.newsrx.com. Pub., Adv. contact Susan Hasty TEL 770-507-7777.

346.043 USA
REAL ESTATE BROKERAGE LAW AND PRACTICE. Text in English. 1985. 2 base vols. plus irreg. updates. looseleaf. USD 289 base vol(s). (effective 2008). **Document type:** *Handbook/Manual/Guide, Trade.* **Description:** Covers national real estate brokerage and provides information on legal analysis, practical guidance, checklists, case-winning strategies and annotated brokerage agreements, form letters and litigation documents.
Formerly: Real Estate Brokerage Law and Practice, Real Estate Transaction Series
Published by: Matthew Bender & Co., Inc. (Subsidiary of: LexisNexis North America), 1275 Broadway, Albany, NY 12204. TEL 518-487-3000, 800-424-4200, FAX 518-487-3083, international@bender.com, http://bender.lexisnexis.com. Ed. Rohan J Patrick.

333.33 USA ISSN 1086-2935
REAL ESTATE BROKER'S INSIDER; weekly newsletter. Text in English. 1968. s-m. USD 247 (effective 2008). bk.rev. charts; tr.lit. 8 p./no.; reprints avail. **Document type:** *Newsletter, Trade.* **Description:** Provides news and information to help the agency owner to increase profits.
Formerly (until 1996): Real Estate Insider (0034-0715)
Related titles: Online - full text ed.
—CCC.
Published by: Alexander Communications Group, Inc., 712 Main St, Ste 187B, Boonton, NJ 07005. TEL 973-265-2300, FAX 973-402-6056, info@alexcommgrp.com, http://www.alexcommgrp.com. Ed. Mary Klein. Pub. Margaret Dewitt. R&P Mary Dalessandro. Circ: 1,300 (controlled and free).

333.33 USA ISSN 0744-642X
HD1361
REAL ESTATE BUSINESS. Text in English. 1982. bi-m. USD 24.99 domestic to non-members; free domestic to members (effective 2005). adv. bk.rev.; software rev. stat.; tr.lit. back issues avail. **Document type:** *Magazine, Trade.* **Description:** Shares strategies to increase productivity and profitability, including new management and sales techniques to help you become a top-notch manager.
Related titles: Online - full text ed.
Published by: Council of Real Estate Brokerage Managers, 430 N Michigan Ave, Chicago, IL 60611. TEL 800-621-8738, FAX 312-329-8882, info@crb.com, http://www.crb.com. R&P Nancy Petersen. Adv. contact Mary C Newman. B&W page USD 2,380, color page USD 3,345; trim 10.75 x 8. Circ: 5,000 (controlled).

333.33 AUS ISSN 1839-0854
▼ **REAL ESTATE BUSINESS**; the monthly business magazine for Australia's real estate industry. Text in English. 2011. m. AUD 8.95 per issue; free to qualified personnel (effective 2011). adv. back issues avail. **Document type:** *Magazine, Trade.*
Related titles: Online - full text ed.: ISSN 1839-0862. free (effective 2011).
Published by: Stirling Publishing, Level 13, 132 Arthur St, N Sydney, NSW 2060, Australia. TEL 61-2-99223300, FAX 61-2-99226311, http://www.sterlingpublishing.com.au/. Ed. Simon Parker. Adv. contact Ben Hawley.

333.33 USA ISSN 1945-8312
REAL ESTATE BUSINESS JOURNAL. Text in English. 2008. w. USD 2,295 in US & Canada; USD 2,495 elsewhere; USD 2,525 combined subscription in US & Canada (print & online eds.); USD 2,755 combined subscription elsewhere (print & online eds.) (effective 2011). adv. back issues avail. **Document type:** *Newsletter, Trade.* **Description:** Monitors the financial health of the commercial and domestic real estate industry, as well as business developments affecting market trends and growth.
Related titles: E-mail ed.; Online - full text ed.: ISSN 1945-8320. USD 2,295 combined subscription (online & e-mail eds.) (effective 2011).
Indexed: A15, ABIn, B02, B15, B17, B18, G04, I05, P16, P48, P51, P53, P54, PQC.
Published by: NewsRx, 2727 Paces Ferry Rd SE, Ste 2-440, Atlanta, GA 30339. TEL 770-435-8286, 800-726-4550, FAX 770-435-6800, pressrelease@newsrx.com, http://www.newsrx.com. Pub., Adv. contact Susan Hasty TEL 770-507-7777.

333.33 USA
REAL ESTATE CONNECTION. Text in English. 2007. q. adv. **Document type:** *Magazine, Trade.* **Description:** Focuses exclusively on industry news affecting residential and commercial real estate professionals in Greater Boston.
Indexed: A10, V03.
Published by: The Warren Group, 280 Summer St, 8th Fl, Boston, MA 02210. TEL 617-428-5100, FAX 617-428-5119, info@thewarrengroup.com. Ed. Christina P O'Neill. adv.: color page USD 2,300; trim 8.125 x 10.625. Circ: 13,000 (paid).

REAL ESTATE DAILY: NORTH AMERICA EDITION. *see* BUSINESS AND ECONOMICS—Investments

333.3 USA
HD268.N5
REAL ESTATE DIRECTORY OF MANHATTAN. Text in English. a. USD 1,500 (effective 2001). back issues avail. **Document type:** *Directory.*

Former titles: First American Real Estate Solutions; Real Estate Directory of Manhattan (0098-8936); Real Estate Directory of the Borough of Manhattan
Published by: First American Real Estate Solutions, 1200 Harbor Blvd., 10th Fl., Weehawken, NJ 07087-6728. TEL 201-330-9600. Eds. Joe Eskenazi, Venice Kelly. Pub. George Livermore.

333.3 USA ISSN 1080-8620
HD251
➤ **REAL ESTATE ECONOMICS.** Text in English. 1973. q. GBP 383 in United Kingdom to institutions; EUR 485 in Europe to institutions; USD 514 in the Americas to institutions; USD 748 elsewhere to institutions; GBP 441 combined subscription in United Kingdom to institutions (print & online eds.); EUR 558 combined subscription in Europe to institutions (print & online eds.); USD 591 combined subscription in the Americas to institutions (print & online eds.); USD 860 combined subscription elsewhere to institutions (print & online eds.) (effective 2012). adv. bk.rev. illus. index, cum.index: 1973-1987. back issues avail.; reprints avail. **Document type:** *Journal, Academic/Scholarly.* **Description:** Publishes research and scholarly studies of current and emerging real estate issues.
Former titles (until 1995): American Real Estate and Urban Economics Association. Journal (1067-8433); (until 1988): A R E U A Journal (0270-0484); (until 1977): American Real Estate and Urban Economics Association. Journal (0092-914X)
Related titles: Microfiche ed.: (from PQC); Online - full text ed.: ISSN 1540-6229. GBP 383 in United Kingdom to institutions; EUR 485 in Europe to institutions; USD 514 in the Americas to institutions; USD 748 elsewhere to institutions (effective 2012) (from IngentaConnect).
Indexed: A10, A12, A13, A14, A17, A22, A23, A26, ABIn, ASCA, B01, B02, B06, B07, B08, B09, B13, B15, B16, B17, B18, BPI, BRD, C12, CA, CurCont, DIP, E01, E08, ESPM, EconLit, FamI, G04, G06, G07, G08, H&TI, I05, IBR, IBZ, JEL, P06, P10, P48, P51, P52, P53, P54, P56, PCI, PQC, RICS, RiskAb, S09, SCOPUS, SSCI, SUSA, T&II, T02, V03, W01, W02, W03, W05, W07.
—BLDSC (7303.280140), IE, Infotrieve, Ingenta. **CCC.**
Published by: (American Real Estate and Urban Economics Association), Wiley-Blackwell Publishing, Inc. (Subsidiary of: Wiley-Blackwell Publishing Ltd.), 111 River St, Hoboken, NJ 07030. TEL 201-748-6000, FAX 201-748-6088, info@wiley.com, http://www.wiley.com/WileyCDA/. Eds. Crocker H Liu, N Edward Coulson, Walter Torous.

333.33 USA
REAL ESTATE EDUCATORS ASSOCIATION. JOURNAL. Text in English. 1988. a. adv. **Description:** Articles on real estate education. Includes a membership directory.
Published by: Real Estate Educators Association, 19 Mantua Rd, Mount Royal, NJ 08061. TEL 856-423-3215, FAX 856-423-3420, info@reea.org, http://www.reea.org. Circ: 1,400.

333.33 USA
REAL ESTATE EDUCATORS ASSOCIATION. PROCEEDINGS. Text in English. 1985. a. USD 139 (effective 2008). back issues avail. **Document type:** *Proceedings, Trade.* **Description:** Contains academic research papers on a wide variety of real estate topics.
Formerly: Real Estate Educators Association. Proceedings (Print)
Media: CD-ROM.
Published by: Real Estate Educators Association, 19 Mantua Rd, Mount Royal, NJ 08061. TEL 856-423-3215, FAX 856-423-3420, info@reea.org, http://www.reea.org.

REAL ESTATE / ENVIRONMENTAL LIABILITY NEWS; the bi-weekly report on litigation, regulation, and industry practice. *see* LAW

333.33 330 USA
REAL ESTATE EXECUTIVE. Text in English. m. free to qualified personnel (effective 2009). adv. reprints avail. **Document type:** *Magazine, Trade.* **Description:** Features a prominent realty executive or an innovated agency within the real estate industry.
Published by: Sunshine Media, Inc., 8283 N Hayden Rd, Ste 220, Scottsdale, AZ 85258. TEL 480-522-2900, FAX 480-522-2901, info@sunshinemedia.com. Ed. Judith Tibbs. adv.: B&W page USD 1,055, color page USD 1,620; trim 8.5 x 11. Circ: 34,217.

333.33 USA ISSN 0748-318X
HD1361
REAL ESTATE FINANCE. Text in English. 1984. bi-m. USD 514; USD 103 per issue (effective 2011). bk.rev. illus. **Document type:** *Journal, Trade.* **Description:** Covers information on real estate investment and financing techniques.
Incorporates (1985-1989): Journal of Real Estate Development (0887-5812); (1984-198?): Real Estate Leasing Report (0748-3163); (1985-1986): Real Estate Finance Law Journal (0882-3413)
Related titles: Online - full text ed.
Indexed: A10, A12, A13, A17, A22, ABIn, AIAP, ATI, B01, B02, B04, B06, B07, B08, B09, B11, B15, B17, B18, BLI, BPI, BRD, C12, CA, G04, G08, I05, P53, P54, PQC, T02, V03, W01, W02, W03, W05.
—BLDSC (7303.280150), IE, Ingenta. **CCC.**
Published by: Aspen Publishers, Inc. (Subsidiary of: Wolters Kluwer N.V.), 76 Ninth Ave, 7th Fl, New York, NY 10011. TEL 212-771-0600, 800-317-3113, FAX 212-771-0885, ASPEN-CustomerService@wolterskluwer.com, https://www.aspenpublishers.com. Circ: 1,800. **Subscr. to:** 7201 McKinney Cir, Frederick, MD 21704. TEL 301-698-7100, FAX 301-695-7931.

333.33 332 USA ISSN 1529-6644
REAL ESTATE FINANCE AND INVESTMENT; the newsweekly of the commercial property and capital markets. Abbreviated title: R E F I. Text in English. 1995. w. EUR 2,350 combined subscription in Europe (print & online eds.); GBP 1,804 combined subscription in United Kingdom (print & online eds.); USD 2,825 combined subscription in US & elsewhere (print & online eds.) (effective 2011). adv. back issues avail.; reprints avail. **Document type:** *Newsletter, Trade.* **Description:** Presents news on all aspects of the commercial real estate property and capital markets with deals, key transactions, strategies and restructurings.
Related titles: Online - full text ed.
Indexed: A09, A10, A15, A26, ABIn, B02, B03, B15, B17, B18, BLI, G04, G06, G07, G08, P16, P48, P51, P53, P54, PQC.
—CIS. **CCC.**
Published by: Institutional Investor, Inc. (Subsidiary of: Euromoney Institutional Investor Plc.), 225 Park Ave S, New York, NY 10003. TEL 212-224-3800, 800-437-9997, FAX 212-224-3553, customerservice@iinews.com, http://www.institutionalinvestor.com. Ed. Steve Murray TEL 212-224-3603. Adv. contact Pat Bertucci TEL 212-224-3890.

330 USA ISSN 0898-0209
HD1361
REAL ESTATE FINANCE JOURNAL. Text in English. 1985. 23 base vols. plus q. updates. USD 351 (effective 2008). adv. illus. Index. reprints avail. **Document type:** *Journal, Trade.* **Description:** Examines the opportunities and pitfalls facing real estate owners, developers, investors and lenders.
Formerly (until 1993): Real Estate Finance Update (0891-9852)
Related titles: Online - full text ed.
Indexed: A12, A13, A17, A22, ABIn, AIAP, ATI, B01, B02, B06, B07, B08, B09, B11, B15, B17, B18, BLI, CA, G04, G06, G07, G08, H&TI, I05, P34, P48, P51, P53, P54, PQC, T02.
—BLDSC (7303.280180), IE, Ingenta. **CCC.**
Published by: R I A (Subsidiary of: Thomson Reuters Corp.), PO Box 6159, Carol Stream, IL 60197. TEL 800-323-8724, ria.customerservices@thomson.com, http://ria.thomsonreuters.com. Ed. Robert G. Koen. Circ: 2,500 (paid).

332.72 USA
REAL ESTATE FINANCING - TEXT, FORMS, TAX ANALYSIS. Text in English. 1973. 8 base vols. plus irreg. updates. looseleaf. USD 2,509 base vol(s). (effective 2008). **Document type:** *Handbook/Manual/Guide, Trade.* **Description:** Contains various types and facets of real estate financing.
Formerly: Real Estate Financing - Text, Forms, Tax Analysis, Real Estate Transaction Series
Related titles: CD-ROM ed.
Published by: Matthew Bender & Co., Inc. (Subsidiary of: LexisNexis North America), 1275 Broadway, Albany, NY 12204. TEL 518-487-3000, 800-424-4200, FAX 518-487-3083, international@bender.com, http://bender.lexisnexis.com. Ed. Rohan J Patrick.

333.33 USA ISSN 0034-0707
HD251
REAL ESTATE FORUM. Text in English. 1946. 8/yr. USD 129.95 domestic; USD 275 foreign (effective 2010). adv. bk.rev.; software rev. charts; illus.; stat.; tr.lit. back issues avail.; reprints avail. **Document type:** *Magazine, Trade.* **Description:** Provides analysis, market research studies and exclusive insights into corporate real estate, development asset management, investment, brokerage and financing.
Incorporates (2002-2004): Real Estate Mid-America (1547-4178)
Related titles: Online - full text ed.
Indexed: A16, ABIn, AIAP, B04, B12, B16, BPI, BRD, H&TI, P02, P10, P34, P48, P51, P53, P54, PQC, T02, W01, W02, W03.
Published by: A L M Real Estate Media Inc. (Subsidiary of: A L M), 120 Broadway, Fl 5, New York, NY 10271. TEL 212-457-9400, FAX 646-822-5358, http://www.remediainc.com. Ed. Sule Aygoren Carranza. Adv. contact Gregg W Christensen TEL 212-457-9664. color page USD 11,845; trim 7 x 10. **Subscr. to:** P O Box 3000, Denville, NJ 07834.

346.043 USA
REAL ESTATE HANDBOOK: LAND LAWS OF ALABAMA. Text in English. irreg., latest 8th ed. USD 156 8th ed. (effective 2008). Supplement avail. **Document type:** *Monographic series, Trade.* **Description:** Contains information on virtually every real estate statutes as well as current case law.
Related titles: Online - full text ed.
Published by: Michie Company (Subsidiary of: LexisNexis North America), 701 E Water St, Charlottesville, VA 22902. TEL 434-972-7600, 800-446-3410, FAX 434-972-7677, customer.support@lexisnexis.com, http://www.michie.com. Eds. Penny A Davis, Robert L McCurley Jr.

333.33 USA ISSN 1935-1747
REAL ESTATE INSIGHTS. Text in English. 1993. m. **Document type:** *Magazine, Trade.*
Formerly (until 2005): Real Estate Outlook (Print) (1935-1755); Which was formed by the 1993 merger of: Home Sales (1063-0511); Real Estate Outlook
Media: Online - full text.
Published by: National Association of Realtors (Chicago), 430 N Michigan Ave, Chicago, IL 60611. TEL 312-329-8458, 800-874-6500, FAX 312-329-5978, infocentral@realtors.org.

333.33 AUS ISSN 1443-0355
REAL ESTATE INSTITUTE OF NEW SOUTH WALES. JOURNAL. Text in English. 1923. m. free to members (effective 2009). adv. bk.rev. illus.; tr.lit.; mkt. index. back issues avail. **Document type:** *Journal, Trade.*
Former titles (until 1998): Real Estate Journal (1443-0347); (until 1946): Real Estate Institute of New South Wales. Quarterly Journal; (until 1941): Real Estate Institute of New South Wales. Monthly Journal; (until 1925): The Journal of the Real Estate Institute of New South Wales
Related titles: Online - full text ed.
Indexed: SD.
Published by: Real Estate Institute of New South Wales, PO Box A 624, Sydney South, NSW 2000, Australia. TEL 61-2-92642343, FAX 61-2-92679190, info@reinsw.com.au, http://www.rainsw.com.au. Ed. Roslyn Alderton. adv.: page AUD 2,799; 225 x 292.

333.33 AUS
REAL ESTATE INSTITUTE OF QUEENSLAND. ANNUAL REPORT. Text in English. 1981 (no.62). a. back issues avail. **Document type:** *Report, Trade.*
Related titles: Online - full text ed.
Published by: Real Estate Institute of Queensland, 21 Turbo Dr, PO Box 1555, Coorparoo, QLD 4151, Australia. TEL 61-7-32497347, FAX 61-7-32496211, reiq@reiq.com.au.

333.33 USA ISSN 2159-1849
REAL ESTATE INVESTMENT TODAY. Abbreviated title: R E I T. Text in English. 1981. bi-m. adv. bk.rev. back issues avail. **Document type:** *Magazine, Trade.* **Description:** Addresses a variety of public real estate, capital markets and real estate-related issues such as joint ventures, corporate government issues, insurance issues, the use of the internet amomg REIT and publicly traded real estate companies, the potential implications of tax reform on REIT's and investor relations issues.
Former titles (until 2010): Real Estate Portfolio (2159-1164); (until 1999): The R E I T Report (1082-815X); Which was formed by the 1981 merger of: R E I T Industry Monthly Review; R E I T Industry Investment Review; Trustee; What if?; N A R E I T Clippings
Related titles: Online - full text ed.: free (effective 2011).
Published by: National Association of Real Estate Investment Trusts, Inc., 1875 I St, NW, Ste 600, Washington, DC 20006. TEL 202-739-9400, FAX 202-739-9401.

333.33 USA
REAL ESTATE INVESTORS CLASSIFIED. Text in English. 1994. s-m. USD 239 (effective 2001). adv. bk.rev. 6 p./no.; **Document type:** *Newsletter.*
Formerly: For Sale by Fax
Related titles: Diskette ed.; E-mail ed.
Published by: T K O Real Estate Advisory Group, PO Box 2630, Mercerville, NJ 08690. TEL 609-587-6200, 800-732-5856, FAX 609-587-3511, dealmaker@dealmakers.net, http://www.property.com. Ed., Adv. contact Ann O'Neal. Pub., R&P Ted Kraus. Circ: 3,200.

333.33 USA ISSN 0146-0595
HD251
➤ **REAL ESTATE ISSUES.** Abbreviated title: R E I. Text in English. 1976. 3/yr. USD 48 domestic; USD 15 per issue (effective 2010). adv. bk.rev. charts; illus.; stat.; tr.lit. index. reprints avail. **Document type:** *Journal, Academic/Scholarly.* **Description:** Provides in-depth articles by leading authors on current industry issues and trends.
Related titles: Microform ed.: (from PQC); Online - full text ed.
Indexed: A09, A10, A12, A13, A17, A22, A26, ABIn, AIAP, B01, B02, B06, B07, B08, B09, B15, B17, B18, C12, E08, G04, G06, G07, G08, H&TI, I05, M01, M02, M06, P16, P48, P51, P53, P54, PQC, S09, S22, T02, V02, V03, V04.
—BLDSC (7303.280330), IE, Ingenta.
Published by: The Counselors of Real Estate, 430 N Michigan Ave, Chicago, IL 60611. TEL 312-329-8427, info@cre.org. Ed. Peter C Burley. adv.: page USD 600; trim 7 x 9.55.

333.33 JAM
REAL ESTATE JAMAICA. Text in English. 1985. bi-m. JMD 100, USD 2.50 per issue. adv. **Document type:** *Journal, Trade.*
Published by: Financial & Economic Resources Ltd., 12 Merrick Ave, Kingston, 10, Jamaica. TEL 809-929-2993, FAX 809-968-1188. Ed. John Jackson. Adv. contact Paul Anderson.

346.04 USA ISSN 1944-9453
REAL ESTATE LAW & INDUSTRY REPORT. Text in English. 2008 (Sep.). bi-w. USD 1,969 (print or online ed.) (effective 2010 - 2011). **Document type:** *Report, Trade.* **Description:** Brings you crucial updates on the wide-ranging issues that affect commercial real estate attorneys and professionals, including finance, equity and leasing, taxes, litigation, legislation, regulation, etc.
Related titles: Online - full text ed.: ISSN 1944-9461. 2008 (Sep.).
—**CCC.**
Published by: The Bureau of National Affairs, Inc., 1801 S Bell St, Arlington, VA 22202. TEL 703-341-3000, 800-372-1033, FAX 703-341-4634, bnaplus@bna.com.

346 333.33 USA ISSN 0548-7366
REAL ESTATE LAW & PRACTICE. Key Title: Real Estate Law and Practice Course Handbook Series. Text in English. 1968. irreg. (approx. 6/yr.). USD 455 (effective 1996). back issues avail. **Document type:** *Monographic series.*
Published by: Practising Law Institute, 810 Seventh Ave, 21st Fl, New York, NY 10019. TEL 212-824-5700, 800-260-4754, info@pli.edu, http://www.pli.edu.

REAL ESTATE LAW DIGEST. *see* LAW

REAL ESTATE LAW JOURNAL. *see* LAW

REAL ESTATE LAW REPORT. *see* LAW

R

333.33 346.043 USA ISSN 2150-0916
KF566.A3
REAL ESTATE LITIGATION. Text in English. 2000. q. free to members (effective 2009). back issues avail. **Document type:** *Newsletter.* **Description:** Features real estate disputes and their resolution, including issues of ownership, purchase and sale, title, casualty, and land use.
Published by: American Bar Association, 321 N Clark St, Chicago, IL 60654. TEL 312-988-5000, askaba@abanet.org. Ed. Veronica Jennings.

333.33 NLD ISSN 1388-3887
REAL ESTATE MAGAZINE. Text in Dutch. 1998. bi-m. EUR 130 (effective 2010). adv. illus. **Document type:** *Magazine, Trade.* **Description:** Contains management information for professionals working in real estate, covering such topics as strategy, portfolio planning, renovation, and urban planning.
Published by: WEKA Uitgeverij B.V., Postbus 61196, Amsterdam, 1005 HD, Netherlands. TEL 31-20-5826600, FAX 31-20-5826699, info@weka.nl, http://www.weka.nl. Eds. Peter Bekkering, Arie van der Ent. Adv. contact Jaap Kries. color page EUR 3,620; 175 x 248. Circ: 3,000.

333.33 CAN ISSN 1712-7246
REAL ESTATE MILLIONAIRE. Text in English. 2001. m. CAD 89 (effective 2006). **Document type:** *Newsletter, Trade.*
Related titles: Online - full text ed.: ISSN 1712-7254.
Published by: Lombardi Publishing Corp., 8555 Jane St, Concord, ON L4K 5N9, Canada. TEL 905-760-9929, FAX 905-264-9619, http://www.lombardipublishing.com.

333.33 CAN ISSN 0225-2783
REAL ESTATE NEWS. Text in English. 1970. w. (50/yr). free (effective 2004). adv. bk.rev. charts; illus.; stat. **Document type:** *Newspaper.* **Description:** Provides up-to-date information along with news and feature stories about trends and influences in the real estate market, mortgage rates, home security, home decorating and landscaping.
Formerly (until 1979): Toronto Real Estate (0225-2775); (until 1971): Toronto Homes for Sale (0225-2767)
Published by: Toronto Real Estate Board, 1400 Don Mills Rd, Toronto, ON M3B 3N1, Canada. TEL 416-443-8113, FAX 416-443-9185. Circ: 105,000.

333.3 USA ISSN 1072-9364
REAL ESTATE NEWS (BROOKLYN). Text in English. 1991. m.
Indexed: G08.
Published by: Landlord Tenant News, 92 E 98th St, Brooklyn, NY 11212-3827. TEL 718-953-5984.

333.33 USA
REAL ESTATE NEWS (CHICAGO). Text in English. 1927. q. USD 10 per issue; USD 40 (effective 2005). **Document type:** *Magazine, Trade.*

Published by: Real Estate News Publishing Corp., 3550 W Peterson, Ste 401, Chicago, IL 60659. TEL 773-866-9900, FAX 773-866-9881. Ed., Pub. Steven N. Polydoris. Circ: 5,000 (paid).

333.33 CAN
REAL ESTATE NEWS AND BUYERS GUIDE. Text in English. 1977. w. free. adv. back issues avail. **Document type:** *Newspaper, Trade.*
Published by: Conni Robinson, Pub., 333 Arvin Ave, Stoney Creek, ON L8E 2M6, Canada. TEL 416-523-5800, FAX 416-664-3102. Ed. Judi Pattison. Circ: 57,000.

333.3 USA ISSN 0749-8640
REAL ESTATE NEWSLINE. Text in English. 1984. q. free. index. 16 p./no.; **Document type:** *Newsletter.*
Published by: E & Y Kenneth Leventhal Real Estate Group, 2049 Century Park, Ste 1700, Los Angeles, CA 90067. TEL 310-277-0880, FAX 310-284-7970. Ed. Stan Ross. Circ: 35,000 (controlled).

333 USA
HD251
REAL ESTATE OUTLOOK: MARKET TRENDS & INSIGHTS. Text in English. 1976. m. looseleaf. USD 135 to non-members; USD 95 to members. **Document type:** *Newsletter.*
Formed by the 1993 merger of: Real Estate Outlook; Home Sales (1063-0511); Which was formerly titled: National Association of Realtors. Existing Home Sales (0161-5882); National Association of Realtors. Department of Economics and Research. Existing Home Sales Series, Annual Report
Related titles: Microfiche ed.: (from CIS).
Indexed: SRI.
Published by: National Association of Realtors, Research Group, 500 New Jersey Ave NW, Washington, DC 20001-2020. TEL 202-383-1137, FAX 202-383-7568. Ed. Kate Anderson. Circ: 1,400.

333.33 USA ISSN 0744-4516
THE REAL ESTATE PROFESSIONAL; the magazine for real estate sales and management. Text in English. 1977. bi-m. USD 39 in US & Canada; USD 72 rest of world (effective 2008). adv. back issues avail. **Document type:** *Magazine, Trade.* **Description:** Covers real estate sales and management.
Published by: Wellesley Publications, Inc., 1492 Highland Ave, Needham, MA 02492. TEL 781-444-4688, FAX 781-449-1112. Ed., Pub. Edward R DesRoches TEL 781-444-4688. Adv. contact Linc Murphy TEL 781-444-1977. B&W page USD 3,290; trim 8.125 x 10.875. Circ: 65,660 (paid and controlled).

333.33 336 USA
REAL ESTATE PROFESSIONAL'S TAX GUIDE. Text in English. 2005. base vol. plus s-a. updates. USD 553 base vol(s). (effective 2010). **Document type:** *Journal, Trade.* **Description:** Provides real estate professionals with clear explanations of complex real estate tax laws, and guidance on avoiding potential problems and tax traps. Includes worked-out examples and case studies illustrating the rules explained in the text.
Formerly: Real Estate Tax Guide
Published by: Thomson West (Subsidiary of: Thomson Reuters Corp.), 610 Opperman Dr, Eagan, MN 55123. TEL 651-687-7000, 800-344-5008, west.customer.service@thomson.com.

333.33 USA
REAL ESTATE RECORD. Text in English. 8/yr. incl. with subscr. to Real Estate Recording Guide. adv. **Document type:** *Newsletter, Trade.*
Indexed: AIAP.
Published by: Ernst Publishing Co., LLC, 1937 Delaware Turnpike, #B, PO Box 318, Clarksville, NY 12041. TEL 800-345-3822, FAX 800-252-0906, clientservice@ernstpublishing.com, http://www.ernstpublishing.com/. Ed., Pub. Carl R Ernst. R&P Carl Johnson. Adv. contact L Roberta Canier.

333.33
REAL ESTATE RECORDING GUIDE (ONLINE EDITION). Text in English. irreg. USD 795. **Document type:** *Directory, Trade.*
Media: Online - full content.
Published by: Ernst Publishing Co., LLC, 1937 Delaware Turnpike, #B, PO Box 318, Clarksville, NY 12041. TEL 800-345-3822, FAX 800-252-0906, clientservice@ernstpublishing.com, http://www.ernstpublishing.com/.

333 JPN ISSN 0532-7776
HD1361
REAL ESTATE RESEARCH/FUDOSAN KENKYU. Text in Japanese. 1959. q.
Published by: Japan Real Estate Institute/Nihon Fudosan Kenkyusho, SVAX TS Bldg, 1-22-12 Toranomon, Minato-ku, Tokyo, 105-0001, Japan.

333.33 NLD ISSN 1877-9700
REAL ESTATE RESEARCH QUARTERLY. Text in Dutch. 2002. q. EUR 25 (effective 2010).
Former titles (until 2009): Property Research Quarterly (1871-9120); (until 2005): PropertyNL Research Quarterly (1570-7814)
Published by: (Vereniging van Onroerend Goed Onderzoekers Nederland, Amsterdam School of Real Estate), PropertyNL, Postbus 75485, Amsterdam, 1070 AL, Netherlands. TEL 31-20-5753317, FAX 31-20-5753318, info@propertynl.com. **Co-publisher:** Vereniging van Onroerend Goed Onderzoekers Nederland.

333.33 USA ISSN 0034-0790
HD251
REAL ESTATE REVIEW. Text in English. 1971. 4 base vols. plus q. updates. USD 351.96 base vol(s). (effective 2010). adv. bk.rev. illus. Index. reprints avail. **Document type:** *Journal, Trade.* **Description:** Provides expert advice from the leaders of the real estate field who share the insights, opinions, and techniques that have made significant changes in the industry.
Related titles: Microform ed.: (from PQC); Online - full text ed.
Indexed: A09, A10, A12, A13, A14, A17, A20, A22, A23, A26, ABIn, ATI, B01, B02, B06, B07, B08, B09, B11, B13, B15, B16, B17, B18, BLI, BPI, BPIA, BRD, BusI, C12, CA, CLI, E08, G04, G06, G07, G08, I05, M01, M02, ManagCont, P10, P34, P48, P51, P53, P54, PAIS, PQC, RICS, S09, T&II, T02, V02, V03, V04, W01, W02, W03.
—BLDSC (7303.281500), IE, Ingenta.
Published by: (New York University, Real Estate Institute), Thomson West (Subsidiary of: Thomson Reuters Corp.), 610 Opperman Dr, Eagan, MN 55123. TEL 651-687-7000, 800-344-5008, west.customer.service@thomson.com. Circ: 7,000 (paid).

333.33 336.2 USA ISSN 1538-3792
HJ4181.A1
REAL ESTATE TAXATION. Text in English. 1973. base vol. plus q. updates. USD 275, USD 335; USD 435 combined subscription (print & online eds.) (effective 2008). adv. 48 p./no.; reprints avail. **Document type:** *Journal, Trade.* **Description:** Addresses a wide range of topics such as exchanges, partnerships, asset protection, REITs, etc.
Formerly (until 2001): Journal of Real Estate Taxation (0093-5107)
Related titles: Microform ed.: (from PQC); Online - full text ed.: 1991. USD 315 (effective 2008).
Indexed: A12, A13, A17, A20, A22, A26, ABIn, ASCA, ATI, B02, B15, B17, B18, BPIA, BusI, CA, CLI, FamI, G04, G06, G07, G08, I01, I05, ILP, L07, LRI, LegCont, P48, P51, P53, P54, PQC, PSI, SCOPUS.
—BLDSC (7303.281600), IE, Ingenta. **CCC.**
Published by: R I A (Subsidiary of: Thomson Reuters Corp.), PO Box 6159, Carol Stream, IL 60197. TEL 800-323-8724, ria@thomson.com, http://ria.thomsonreuters.com. Ed. Paul D Carman. Adv. contact Terry Storholm TEL 651-687-7327.

333.33 USA
REAL ESTATE TECHNOLOGY. Abbreviated title: R E T. Text in English. 1996. s-a. adv. bk.rev.; software rev.; Website rev. charts; illus.; stat.; tr.lit. 56 p./no.; **Document type:** *Magazine, Trade.* **Description:** Reports on how realtors can use technology in their profession.
Related titles: Online - full text ed.; ◆ Supplement to: California Real Estate. ISSN 0008-1450.
Published by: California Association of Realtors, 525 S Virgil Ave, Los Angeles, CA 90020. TEL 213-739-8200, FAX 213-480-7724. Ed. Anne Framroze TEL 213-739-8320. adv.: color page USD 10,800, B&W page USD 8,385; bleed 8.5 x 11. Circ: 200,000 (controlled).

333.33 HKG ISSN 1012-3253
REAL ESTATE TIMES/FANGDICHAN DAO BAO. Text in Chinese. m. HKD 172.
Address: 342 Hennessy Rd 10th Fl, Wanchai, Hong Kong, Hong Kong. TEL 852-573-8217, FAX 852-838-8304, TELEX 86990 EIA HXX.

333.33 CAN ISSN 1715-9652
REAL ESTATE TRADING SERVICES LICENSING COURSE MANUAL. Text in English. 1994. a. **Document type:** *Handbook/Manual/Guide, Trade.*
Formerly (until 2006): Real Estate Salesperson's and Sub-Mortgage Broker's Pre-Licensing Course Manual (1198-841X)
Published by: (Real Estate Council of British Columbia), The University of British Columbia, Sauder School of Business, Real Estate Division (Subsidiary of: University of British Columbia), PO Box 5380, Station Terminal, Vancouver, BC V6B 5N4, Canada. TEL 604-822-8444, 888-776-7733, FAX 604-822-8459, info@realestate.sauder.ubc.ca, http://www.sauder.ubc.ca/realestate/index.cfm.

REAL ESTATE TRANSACTIONS; tax planning and consequences. *see* BUSINESS AND ECONOMICS—Public Finance, Taxation

346.04 340 USA
REAL ESTATE TRANSACTIONS: CONDEMNATION PROCEDURE AND TECHNIQUES FORMS. Text in English. 1969. 6 base vols. plus irreg. updates. looseleaf. USD 2,017 base vol(s). (effective 2008). **Document type:** *Handbook/Manual/Guide, Trade.* **Description:** Provides techniques and guidelines for the handling of a condemnation case.
Published by: Matthew Bender & Co., Inc. (Subsidiary of: LexisNexis North America), 1275 Broadway, Albany, NY 12204. TEL 518-487-3000, 800-424-4200, FAX 518-487-3083, international@bender.com, http://bender.lexisnexis.com. Ed. Rohan J Patrick.

333.33 340 USA
REAL ESTATE TRANSACTIONS: CONDOMINIUM LAW AND PRACTICE FORMS. Text in English. 1965. 8 base vols. plus updates 3/yr. looseleaf. USD 2,149 base vol(s). (effective 2008). **Document type:** *Handbook/Manual/Guide, Trade.* **Description:** Provides guidance for handling condominium transactions including all aspects from creation to termination and addresses special problems.
Published by: Matthew Bender & Co., Inc. (Subsidiary of: LexisNexis North America), 1275 Broadway, Albany, NY 12204. TEL 518-487-3000, 800-424-4200, FAX 518-487-3083, international@bender.com, http://bender.lexisnexis.com. Eds. Melvin Riskin, Patrick J Rohan.

333.33 USA
REAL ESTATE TRANSACTIONS: PURCHASE AND SALE OF REAL PROPERTY. Text in English. 1987. 3 base vols. plus s-a. updates. looseleaf. **Description:** A transactional analysis of the purchase and sale of all types of property, covering issues arising from the pre-contract through the post-closing stages of a transaction.
Published by: Matthew Bender & Co., Inc. (Subsidiary of: LexisNexis North America), 1275 Broadway, Albany, NY 12204. TEL 518-487-3000, 800-424-4200, FAX 518-487-3083, international@bender.com, http://bender.lexisnexis.com.

333.33 USA
REAL ESTATE TRANSACTIONS SERIES. Text in English. a. looseleaf. USD 123 per issue. **Document type:** *Monographic series, Trade.*
Published by: Matthew Bender & Co., Inc. (Subsidiary of: LexisNexis North America), 1275 Broadway, Albany, NY 12204. TEL 518-487-3000, 800-424-4200, FAX 518-487-3083, international@bender.com, http://bender.lexisnexis.com.

333.33 USA
REAL ESTATE TRANSACTIONS: TAX PLANNING AND CONSEQUENCES. Text in English. 1973. base vol. plus a. updates. USD 234 base vol(s). (effective 2010). **Document type:** *Journal, Trade.* **Description:** Examines the tax consequences of real estate transactions, providing detailed examples from real-life situations, and offering cases, code provisions, rulings, regulations, checklists, and forms.
Published by: Thomson West (Subsidiary of: Thomson Reuters Corp.), 610 Opperman Dr, Eagan, MN 55123. TEL 651-687-7000, 800-344-5008, west.customer.service@thomson.com.

333.3 CAN
REAL ESTATE VICTORIA. Text in English. 1977. w. CAD 103 (effective 1999). adv. **Document type:** *Journal, Consumer.*
Address: Circulation Department, 818 Broughton St, Victoria, BC V8W 1E4, Canada. TEL 250-382-9171, FAX 250-382-9172. Pub. Glenda Turner. Circ: 20,000.

333.33 USA ISSN 1096-7214
REAL ESTATE WEEKLY. Text in English. 1952. w. (Wed.). USD 49; USD 72 for 2 yrs.; USD 108 for 3 yrs. (effective 2006). adv. **Document type:** *Newspaper, Trade.*
Related titles: Online - full text ed.
Indexed: G08, I05.
Published by: Hersom Acorn Newspapers, LLC, 135 Dreiser Loop, Bronx, NY 10475. Ed. Linda Barr. Pub. Christopher G Hagedorn. adv.: page USD 2,075. Circ: 9,383 (paid).

333.33 USA ISSN 1945-8339
REAL ESTATE WEEKLY NEWS. Text in English. 2008. w. USD 2,295 in US & Canada; USD 2,495 elsewhere; USD 2,525 combined subscription in US & Canada (print & online eds.); USD 2,755 combined subscription elsewhere (print & online eds.) (effective 2011). adv. back issues avail. **Document type:** *Newsletter, Trade.* **Description:** Provides comprehensive coverage of both the commercial and domestic real estate industries.
Related titles: E-mail ed.; Online - full text ed.: ISSN 1945-8347. USD 2,295 combined subscription (online & e-mail eds.) (effective 2011).
Indexed: A15, ABIn, I05, P16, P48, P51, P53, P54, PQC.
Published by: NewsRx, 2727 Paces Ferry Rd SE, Ste 2-440, Atlanta, GA 30339. TEL 770-435-8286, 800-726-4550, FAX 770-435-6800, pressrelease@newsrx.com, http://www.newsrx.com. Pub., Adv. contact Susan Hasty TEL 770-507-7777.

333.33 USA
REAL ESTATEMENT; what's new with the Idaho Real Estate Commission. Text in English. 1978. s-a. free. bk.rev. charts; stat. **Document type:** *Newsletter, Trade.*
Published by: Idaho Real Estate Commission, 633 N Fourth St, Boise, ID 83702. TEL 208-334-3285, FAX 208-334-2050. Ed., R&P Jill Randall. Circ: 8,000. **Subscr. to:** PO Box 83720, Boise, ID 83720-0077.

346.04 USA ISSN 1940-1655
REAL LAW CENTRAL; legal and regulatory news for the real estate industry. Text in English. 2007. 24/yr. USD 259 combined subscription (print & online eds.) (effective 2008). adv. back issues avail. **Document type:** *Newsletter, Trade.*
Related titles: Online - full text ed.: ISSN 1937-9935.
Published by: October Research Corporation, PO Box 370, Richfield, OH 44286. TEL 330-659-6101, 877-662-8623, FAX 330-659-6102, contactus@thetitlereport.com, http://www.octoberresearch.com. Eds. Jeremy Yohe TEL 330-659-6101 ext 6124, Matthew Smith TEL 330-659-6101 ext 6144.

333.33 USA ISSN 0445-4278
REAL PROPERTY. Text in English. 1955. q. looseleaf. **Document type:** *Newsletter, Trade.*
Published by: Illinois State Bar Association, Illinois Bar Center, 424 S Second St, Springfield, IL 62701. TEL 217-525-1760, 800-252-8908, FAX 217-525-9063, jfenski@isba.org, http://www.isba.org.

REAL PROPERTY INSTITUTE. *see* LAW

REAL PROPERTY LAW REPORTER. *see* LAW

333.33 USA ISSN 2152-2855
REAL PROPERTY POLICYSITE. Text in English. 199?. q. free (effective 2010). back issues avail. **Document type:** *Newsletter, Trade.* **Description:** Contains information and data that educate and promote improvements in real property asset management and the workplace.
Media: Online - full text.
Published by: U.S. General Services Administration, Office of Governmentwide Policy, Office of Real Property, 1800 F St, NW, Washington, DC 20405. TEL 202-501-8880, http://www.gsa.gov/Portal/gsa/ep/channelView.do?pageTypeId=8199&channelId=-24891. Ed. Stanley C Langfeld.

333.33 USA
REAL PROPERTY, PROBATE AND TRUST LAW NEWSLETTER. Text in English. 19??. s-a. free to members (effective 2011). **Document type:** *Newsletter, Trade.*
Published by: Pennsylvania Bar Association, 100 South St, Harrisburg, PA 17101. TEL 800-932-0311.

333.33 CAN ISSN 0703-4687
REAL PROPERTY REPORTS (3RD SERIES). Text in English. 1977. 2/yr. CAD 240 domestic; USD 203.39 foreign (effective 2005). adv. **Description:** Features all important decisions in real property law from all Canadian jurisdictions selected by experts in the field. Includes cases on Registry Acts and Land Titles legislation, agreements of purchase and sale, and damages for breach thereof.
Indexed: CLI, CPerI, G08, ICLPL, LRI.
—**CCC.**
Published by: Carswell (Subsidiary of: Thomson Reuters Corp.), One Corporate Plz, 2075 Kennedy Rd, Toronto, ON M1T 3V4, Canada. TEL 416-609-8000, 800-387-5164, FAX 416-298-5094, carswell.customerrelations@thomson.com, http://www.carswell.com. Eds. Jeffrey Lem, John Mascarin. Adv. contact Mariam Lalani TEL 416-298-5050.

333.33 CZE ISSN 1210-8308
REALIT. Text in Czech. 1994. m. CZK 531 (effective 2011). adv. **Document type:** *Magazine, Trade.*
Published by: Mlada Fronta, Mezi Vodami 1952/9, Prague 4, 14300, Czech Republic. TEL 420-2-25276201, FAX 420-2-25276222, online@mf.cz. Ed. Tomas Johanek. Adv. contact Marcela Conova.

333.33 USA
THE REALTOR (PORTLAND). Text in English. m. free to members (effective 2007). **Document type:** *Newspaper, Trade.*
Contact Owner: Pamplin Media Group, 6605 S E Lake Rd, Portland, OR 97222. Circ: 6,200 (paid).

333.33 USA ISSN 1522-0842
HD251
REALTOR MAGAZINE. Text in English. 1968. m. USD 56 domestic to non-members; USD 83 in Canada to non-members; USD 103 elsewhere to non-members; free to members (effective 2009). adv. bk.rev. charts; illus. index. 64 p./no. 3 cols./p.; back issues avail.; reprints avail. **Document type:** *Magazine, Trade.* **Description:** Serves as a forum of ideas, opinions, and practical applications among realtors and other real-estate agents in all areas of residential, commercial-investment, and brokerage-management real estate.
Former titles (until 1998): Today's Realtor (1086-8054); (until 1996): Real Estate Today (0034-0804); Which incorporated (in 1968): Realtor Reviews
Related titles: Microform ed.: (from PQC); Online - full text ed.

Indexed: A15, A22, A23, ABIn, B01, B02, B04, B06, B07, B08, B09, B11, B13, B15, B16, B17, B18, BPI, BRD, BusI, C12, G04, G05, G06, G07, G08, I05, M01, M02, MagInd, P02, P10, P48, P51, P53, P54, PQC, T&II, V02, W01, W02, W03.
—Ingenta.
Published by: National Association of Realtors (Chicago), 430 N Michigan Ave, Chicago, IL 60611. TEL 312-329-8458, 800-874-6500, FAX 312-329-5978. Ed. Stacey Moncrieff TEL 312-329-8496. Pub. Frank Sibley TEL 312-329-8599. adv.: B&W page USD 48,582, color page USD 58,879; trim 8 x 10.5.

333.33 USA ISSN 2152-789X
REALTOR REPORT. Text in English. 200?. m. **Document type:** *Newsletter, Trade.*
Published by: St. Louis Association of Realtors, 12777 Olive Blvd, St. Louis, MO 63141. TEL 314-576-0033, FAX 314-576-7143, http://www.stlrealtors.com.

333.33 USA ISSN 0034-1045
HG1
REALTY AND BUILDING. Text in English. 1888. bi-w. USD 54 (effective 2005). adv. bk.rev. illus.; mkt.; maps. 36 p./no. 3 cols./p.; back issues avail. **Document type:** *Magazine, Trade.* **Description:** Covers real estate ownership finance, construction, sale, and management, primarily in the greater Chicago metropolitan area.
Published by: Realty and Building, Inc., 5400 Lawrenceville Hwy NW, Lilburn, GA 30047-5927. TEL 312-467-1888, FAX 312-467-0225. Ed. Paul Pirhofer. R&P John C Cutler. Adv. contact Patricia Nebel TEL 312-467-1888. page USD 1,584; 7 x 10. Circ: 50,000 (paid).

333.33 USA
REALTY REPORT. Text in English. 1868. w. (& q.). USD 1,750 (effective 2001). back issues avail. **Document type:** *Directory.*
Former titles: T R W R E D I Property Data (1075-3664); (until 1993): R E D I Realty Report (1051-0737); Real Estate Record and Builder's Guide (0034-0774)
Published by: First American Real Estate Solutions, 1200 Harbor Blvd., 10th Fl., Weehawken, NJ 07087-6728. TEL 201-330-9600. Eds. Joe Eskenazi, Venice Kelly. Pub. George Livermore. R&P Joe Eskenazi. Circ: 1,500.

333.33 330 USA ISSN 1949-0798
▼ **REALTYSCORECARD.COM.** Abbreviated title: R S C. Text in English. 2009. w. free (effective 2009). **Document type:** *Newsletter, Trade.*
Media: Online - full content.
Published by: RealtyScoreCard.com, 57 W Timonium Rd, Ste 205, Timonium, MD 21093. TEL 410-941-2445, 866-766-9485.

RECHTSPFLEGER - STUDIENHEFTE. *see* LAW

346.04 NLD ISSN 1876-9934
RECHTSPRAAK VASTGOEDRECHT. Variant title: R V R. Text in Dutch. 2008. m. EUR 344.50; EUR 30.74 newsstand/cover (effective 2011). **Document type:** *Magazine, Trade.*
Published by: Kluwer B.V. (Subsidiary of: Wolters Kluwer N.V.), Postbus 23, Deventer, 7400 GA, Netherlands. TEL 31-570-673449, FAX 31-570-691555, info@kluwer.nl, http://www.kluwer.nl. Eds. E J Loos, G K Slagter.

333.33 USA ISSN 1082-8478
THE RECORD REPORTER. Text in English. 1918. d. (Mon - Fri). USD 165 (effective 2011). adv. **Document type:** *Newspaper, Trade.*
Formerly (until 1919): Tri-Court Record Reporter
Published by: Daily Journal Corp., 915 E, First St, Los Angeles, CA 90012. TEL 213-229-5300, FAX 213-229-5481.

333.33 USA
THE REGISTER. Text in English. 1993. m. free to qualified personnel (effective 2004). adv. back issues avail. **Document type:** *Magazine, Trade.* **Description:** Publishes information on new homes available for sale in the metropolitan Washington, D.C. area.
Formerly: New Homes Register
Published by: Bartow Communications, Inc., 7945 MacArthur Blvd, Ste 218, Cabin John, MD 20818. TEL 301-468-7001, FAX 301-468-7005, info@registermarketing.com, http://www.registermarketing.com. Ed., Pub., Adv. contact Randy Bartow. color page USD 1,595; trim 5.5 x 8.5. Circ: 25,516 (controlled).

333.33 USA ISSN 1067-0521
REGISTRY REVIEW. Text in English. 1978. w. USD 178 (effective 2006). adv. index. **Document type:** *Newspaper, Trade.* **Description:** Real estate and financial information for New Hampshire.
Published by: Real Data Corporation, 103 Bay St, Manchester, NH 03104-3007. TEL 603-669-3822, 800-578-1546, FAX 603-645-0072. Ed. Mary Lazzar. Pub. Irvin W Tolles. Circ: 3,500 (paid).

333.33 USA
THE RELO REPORT; relocation magazine. Text in English. 2007. 3/yr. adv. **Document type:** *Magazine, Consumer.*
Published by: Bartow Communications, Inc., 7945 MacArthur Blvd, Ste 218, Cabin John, MD 20818. TEL 301-468-7001, FAX 301-468-7005, info@registermarketing.com, http://www.registermarketing.com. Ed. Beth Dadisman. Pub., Adv. contact Randy Bartow. color page USD 1,095; trim 5.5 x 8.5. Circ: 20,310.

333.33 USA ISSN 1085-5289
RELOCATION JOURNAL & REAL ESTATE NEWS. Text in English. 1995. m. free. adv. bk.rev. back issues avail. **Document type:** *Newsletter.* **Description:** Discusses topics pertaining to relocation.
Formed by the merger of (1992-1995): Relocation Journal; (1927-1995): Real Estate News
Media: Online - full text.
Published by: Mobility Services International, 124 High St, Newburyport, MA 01950. TEL 978-463-0348. Ed. Diane MacPherson.

THE RELOCATION REPORT. *see* BUSINESS AND ECONOMICS—Personnel Management

333.33 CAN ISSN 1912-5038
RENTAL MARKET REPORT. CALGARY (ONLINE). Text in English. 1989. a. **Document type:** *Report, Trade.*
Former titles (until 2004): Rental Market Report. Calgary (Print) (1498-8488); (until 1996): Rental Market Report. Calgary C M A and Southern Alberta Centres (1207-1129)
Media: Online - full text.
Published by: Canada Mortgage and Housing Corporation/Societe Canadienne d'Hypotheques et de Logement, 700 Montreal Rd, Ottawa, ON K1A 0P7, Canada. TEL 613-748-2000, FAX 613-748-2098, chic@cmhc-schl.gc.ca, http://www.cmhc.ca.

333.33 CAN ISSN 1912-323X
RENTAL MARKET REPORT. MANITOBA HIGHLIGHTS. Text in English. 200?. a. **Document type:** *Bulletin, Trade.*
Media: Online - full text.
Published by: Canada Mortgage and Housing Corporation/Societe Canadienne d'Hypotheques et de Logement, 700 Montreal Rd, Ottawa, ON K1A 0P7, Canada. TEL 613-748-2000, FAX 613-748-2098, chic@cmhc-schl.gc.ca, http://www.cmhc.ca.

333.33 CAN ISSN 1912-5488
RENTAL MARKET REPORT. METRO VICTORIA. Text in English. 2001. a. **Document type:** *Report, Trade.*
Media: Online - full text. **Related titles:** Print ed.: ISSN 1713-529X. 199?.
Published by: Canada Mortgage and Housing Corporation/Societe Canadienne d'Hypotheques et de Logement, 700 Montreal Rd, Ottawa, ON K1A 0P7, Canada. TEL 613-748-2000, FAX 613-748-2098, chic@cmhc-schl.gc.ca, http://www.cmhc.ca.

333.5 CAN ISSN 1912-5542
RENTAL MARKET REPORT. NORTHERN ONTARIO (ONLINE). Text in English. 2002. a. **Document type:** *Government.*
Media: Online - full text. **Related titles:** ◆ Print ed.: Rental Market Report. Northern Ontario (Print). ISSN 1709-3546.
Published by: Canada Mortgage and Housing Corporation/Societe Canadienne d'Hypotheques et de Logement, 700 Montreal Rd, Ottawa, ON K1A 0P7, Canada. TEL 613-748-2000, FAX 613-748-2098, chic@cmhc-schl.gc.ca, http://www.cmhc.ca.

333.5 CAN ISSN 1709-3546
RENTAL MARKET REPORT. NORTHERN ONTARIO (PRINT). Text in English. 199?. a. **Document type:** *Government.*
Formerly (until 2002): Rental Market Report. Thunder Bay (1498-847X); (until 199?): Rental Market Survey. Thunder Bay C M A (1207-1293)
Related titles: ◆ Online - full text ed.: Rental Market Report. Northern Ontario (Online). ISSN 1912-5542; ◆ French ed.: Rapport sur le Marche Locatif. Nord de l'Ontario. ISSN 1912-5550.
Published by: Canada Mortgage and Housing Corporation/Societe Canadienne d'Hypotheques et de Logement, 700 Montreal Rd, Ottawa, ON K1A 0P7, Canada. TEL 613-748-2000, FAX 613-748-2098, chic@cmhc-schl.gc.ca, http://www.cmhc.ca.

333.33 CAN ISSN 1912-6212
RENTAL MARKET REPORT. SHERBROOKE (ONLINE). Text in English. 199?. a. **Document type:** *Report, Trade.*
Former titles (until 200?): Rental Market Report. Sherbrooke (Print Edition) (1707-7508); (until 1996): Rental Market Report. Sherbrooke Metropolitan Area and South of Quebec Census Agglomerations (1207-6481); (until 1995): Rental Market Report. Sherbrooke Metropolitan Area and Certain Centres with Populations of 10,000 or More in Estrie, Monteregie, Amiante and Coeur du Quebec (1207-6465)
Media: Online - full text.
Published by: Canada Mortgage and Housing Corporation/Societe Canadienne d'Hypotheques et de Logement, 700 Montreal Rd, Ottawa, ON K1A 0P7, Canada. TEL 613-748-2000, FAX 613-748-2098, chic@cmhc-schl.gc.ca, http://www.cmhc.ca, http://www.schl.ca.

333.33 CAN ISSN 1912-6263
RENTAL MARKET REPORT. ST. CATHARINES-NIAGARA. Text in English. 2001. a. **Document type:** *Report, Trade.*
Media: Online - full text. **Related titles:** Print ed.: ISSN 1707-0813. 199?.
Published by: Canada Mortgage and Housing Corporation/Societe Canadienne d'Hypotheques et de Logement, 700 Montreal Rd, Ottawa, ON K1A 0P7, Canada. TEL 613-748-2000, FAX 613-748-2098, chic@cmhc-schl.gc.ca, http://www.cmhc.ca, http://www.schl.ca.

333.33 CAN ISSN 1912-6360
RENTAL MARKET REPORT. TORONTO C M A. (Census Metropolitan Area) Text in English. 2001. a. **Document type:** *Bulletin, Trade.*
Media: Online - full text. **Related titles:** Print ed.: ISSN 1193-4794. 19??; ◆ French ed.: Rapport sur le Marche Locatif. R M R de Toronto. ISSN 1912-6387.
Published by: Canada Mortgage and Housing Corporation/Societe Canadienne d'Hypotheques et de Logement, 700 Montreal Rd, Ottawa, ON K1A 0P7, Canada. TEL 613-748-2000, FAX 613-748-2098, chic@cmhc-schl.gc.ca, http://www.cmhc.ca, http://www.schl.ca.

333.33 CAN ISSN 1912-6646
RENTAL MARKET REPORT. VANCOUVER (ONLINE). Text in English. 199?. a.
Media: Online - full text. **Related titles:** Print ed.: Rental Market Report. Vancouver (Print). ISSN 1713-6423. 199?; ◆ French ed.: Rapport sur le Marche Locatif. Vancouver. ISSN 1912-6662.
Published by: Canada Mortgage and Housing Corporation/Societe Canadienne d'Hypotheques et de Logement, 700 Montreal Rd, Ottawa, ON K1A 0P7, Canada. TEL 613-748-2000, FAX 613-748-2098, chic@cmhc-schl.gc.ca, http://www.cmhc.ca, http://www.schl.ca.

333.33 CAN
RENTERS NEWS. Text in English. w. **Document type:** *Magazine, Consumer.*
Address: 405 The West Mall, Toronto, ON M9C 5J1, Canada. TEL 416-784-3311, FAX 416-784-5300.

RES ET JURA IMMOBILIA. *see* LAW

333.33 AUS ISSN 1834-4593
RESEARCH. Text in English. 2006. q. **Document type:** *Monographic series, Trade.*
Media: Online - full text.
Published by: Urbis J H D, Level 21, 321 Kent St, Sydney, NSW 2000, Australia. TEL 612-8233-9900, FAX 612-8233-9966, info@urbisjhd.com.

333.33 NLD ISSN 1382-4848
➤ **RESEARCH ISSUES IN REAL ESTATE.** Text in English. 1994. irreg., latest vol.10, 2008. price varies. **Document type:** *Monographic series, Academic/Scholarly.*
Formerly: Real Estate Research Issues
—BLDSC (7741.569400).
Published by: (American Real Estate Society USA), Springer Netherlands (Subsidiary of: Springer Science+Business Media), Van Godewijckstraat 30, Dordrecht, 3311 GX, Netherlands. TEL 31-78-6576050, FAX 31-78-6576474. Ed. James Webb.

333.33 USA
RESIDENCE. Text in English. q. USD 5.95 newsstand/cover (effective 2005). adv. **Document type:** *Magazine, Consumer.*
Published by: Residence Publications Inc, 50 Briar Hollow Ln E, 6th Fl E, Houston, TX 77027. TEL 713-963-9050, 800-736-3134. Adv. contact Mitch Duffy. color page USD 6,000; trim 8.5 x 10.875. Circ: 8,059 (free); 68,941 (paid).

333.33 USA ISSN 1945-628X
RESIDENCE INTERNATIONAL. Text in English. 2003. q. USD 19.95 domestic; USD 39.95 in Canada; USD 59.95 elsewhere (effective 2008). **Document type:** *Magazine, Consumer.* **Description:** Showcases luxury real estate for sale regionally within the United States as well as abroad.
Published by: Regency Publishing Group, 50 Briar Hollow Ln, 6th Fl E, Houston, TX 77027. TEL 713-840-1176, http://rpghou.com.

332.63 AUS ISSN 1833-2889
RESIDENTIAL DEVELOPER MAGAZINE. Text in English. 2006. q. AUD 11.95 per issue (effective 2009). adv. **Document type:** *Magazine, Trade.* **Description:** A business magazine for those interested in residential development.
Published by: Property Council of Australia, Residential Development Council, Level 1, 11 Barrack St, Sydney, NSW 2000, Australia. TEL 61-02 90331900, FAX 61-02 90331991, info@propertyoz.com.au, http://propertycouncil.gravitymax.com.au/nat/page.asp?e_page=246178&category=. adv.: page AUD 3,300; trim 240 x 297.

333.33 USA ISSN 1541-7492
RESORT LIVING; a showcase of private retreats. Text in English. 2002. q. USD 41.94 (effective 2002). adv. **Description:** Covers the luxury real estate marketplace and other aspects of luxury home life.
Published by: Luxury Publishing, Inc., 3070 Rasmussen Rd., Ste. 130, Park City, UT 8409. TEL 435-940-1701, FAX 435-658-0630. Ed. Mark Nothaft TEL 480-966-1047.

333.5 658.8 NLD
RETAIL SPACE EUROPE YEARBOOK. Text in English. 2008. a. EUR 65 (effective 2009). **Document type:** *Journal, Trade.*
Published by: Europe Real Estate Publishers B.V., North Sea Bldg, Gevers Deynootweg 93R, The Hague, 2586 BK, Netherlands. TEL 31-70-3528600, FAX 31-70-3527660, publishers@europe-re.com, http://www.europe-re.com.

RETAIL TRAFFIC. *see* BUSINESS AND ECONOMICS—Marketing And Purchasing

REVISTA CRITICA DE DERECHO INMOBILIARIO. *see* LAW

333.33 340 FRA ISSN 1760-1630
LA REVUE BLEUE. Text in French. 1973. m. (10/yr). **Document type:** *Magazine, Trade.* **Description:** Informs on all aspects of real estate including the latest on laws, marketing, and information technology.
Former titles (until 2003): Revue d'Informations Juridiques et Pratiques (1295-0653); (until 1999): Federation Nationale des Agents Immobiliers. Informations (1153-2432)
Published by: Federation Nationale de l'Immobilier, 129 rue du Faubourg Saint-Honore, Paris, 75008, France. TEL 33-1-44207700, FAX 33-1-42258084, http://www.fnaim.fr. Ed. Yvan Frayssinhes. Pub. Philippe Audras.

333.33 FRA ISSN 0180-9849
REVUE DE DROIT IMMOBILIER. Text in French. 1979. q. EUR 195 (effective 2009). reprint service avail. from SCH. **Document type:** *Journal, Trade.*
Related titles: Online - full text ed.: ISSN 1760-7574.
Indexed: A22, FR.
—IE, Infotrieve. **CCC.**
Published by: Editions Dalloz, 31-35 rue Froidevaux, Paris, Cedex 14 75685, France. TEL 33-1-40645454, FAX 33-1-40645497, http://www.dalloz.fr. Ed. Philippe Malinvaud.

333.33 FRA ISSN 1954-9075
REVUE DE L'HABITAT. Text in French. 1959. m. EUR 52 (effective 2009). adv. stat. **Document type:** *Magazine.*
Formerly (until 2006): Revue de l'Habitat Francais (0048-7953)
Indexed: FR.
Published by: Societe Parisienne d'Editions et de Publications Immobilieres, 72-76 Rue de Longchamp, Paris, 75016, France. TEL 33-1-47053099, FAX 33-1-45561352. Ed. Jean Leveque. Circ: 24,630.

REVUE DES LOYERS, DE LA COPROPRIETE ET DES FERMAGES. *see* HOUSING AND URBAN PLANNING

333.33 USA ISSN 0035-5275
K22
RIGHT OF WAY; for the right of way professional. Text in English. 1954. bi-m. USD 30 domestic; USD 40 in Canada; USD 48 elsewhere (effective 2005). adv. bk.rev. charts; illus. cum.index: 1954-1984. **Document type:** *Magazine, Trade.* **Description:** Publishes technical articles covering subjects of interest to right-of-way professionals in acquisition management of real property rights for the public sector.
Indexed: EIA, EnvAb, HRIS.
Published by: International Right of Way Association, 19750 S Vermont Ave, Torrance, CA 90502-1144. TEL 310-538-0233, FAX 310-538-1471, info@irwaonline.org. Ed. David M Roman. R&P David Roman. Adv. contact Lorraine Calder. Circ: 9,500.

333.33 USA
ROBB REPORT COLLECTION. Text in English. 1999. m. USD 65 domestic; USD 75 in Canada; USD 105 elsewhere; USD 8.99 newsstand/cover (effective 2009). adv. back issues avail.; reprints avail. **Document type:** *Magazine, Consumer.* **Description:** Contains six issues focusing on premium automobiles and six issues highlighting exceptional real estate and home design that provide affluent buyers with the tools to make and execute major purchase decisions.
Former titles (until 2002): Robb Report's Showcase; (until 2001): Luxury Media's Showcase (1526-4807)
Published by: CurtCo Robb Media LLC., 29160 Heathercliff Rd, Ste 200, Malibu, CA 90265. TEL 310-589-7700, FAX 310-589-7723, support@robbreport.com, http://www.curtco.com. Ed. Erika Heet TEL 310-589-7662. Pub., Adv. contact Lincoln Jackson TEL 978-264-7550. page USD 18,100; bleed 8.375 x 11.063. Circ: 104,227.
Subscr. to: PO Box 558, Mount Morris, IL 61054. TEL 815-734-1216, 800-947-7472.

R

643.25 USA ISSN 1550-459X
ROBB REPORT VACATION HOMES. Text in English. 2004 (Fall). q. USD 19.97 domestic; USD 29.97 in Canada; USD 59.95 elsewhere (effective 2009). adv. back issues avail.; reprints avail. **Document type:** *Magazine, Consumer.* **Description:** Explores all the aspects of second, third and fourth home ownership that includes real estate investment opportunities, tax strategies, maintenance, home security and estate management.
Related titles: Online - full text ed.
Published by: CurtCo Robb Media LLC., 29160 Heathercliff Rd, Ste 200, Malibu, CA 90265. TEL 310-589-7700, FAX 310-589-7723, support@robbreport.com, http://www.curtco.com. Eds. Samantha Brooks TEL 310-589-7737, Adele Cygelman. Pub. Lincoln Jackson TEL 978-264-7550. Circ: 100,000.

333.33 USA
ROBSON COMMUNITY LIVING MAGAZINE. Text in English. 2004. q. adv. **Document type:** *Magazine, Consumer.*
Published by: Robson Communities, Inc., 9532 E Riggs Rd, Sun Lakes, AZ 85248. TEL 480-895-9200, FAX 480-895-0136, http://www.robson.com. Ed. Linda Robson TEL 480-895-4340. adv.: B&W page USD 3,400, color page USD 5,000; trim 8.375 x 10.875. Circ: 103,000.

333.33 USA
ROCKY MOUNTAIN FARM & RANCH. Text in English. 3/yr. USD 17.50; USD 5.95 newsstand/cover (effective 2005). adv. **Document type:** *Magazine, Consumer.* **Description:** Contains listings of ranch properties in Montana, Colorado, Wyoming and New Mexico.
Published by: Farm & Ranch Publishing, LLC, 50 Briar Hollow Ln., Ste. 650 E, Houston, TX 77027. TEL 713-334-9222, 800-580-7330, FAX 713-334-9977, info@farmandranch.com, http://www.farmandranch.com. Ed. Thelma Chewning. Adv. contact Mike Gammelgard. color page USD 4,490; trim 8.5 x 10.875. Circ: 40,000 (paid).

332.63 CZE ISSN 0231-679X
ROUBENKY. Text in Czech. 2006. q. CZK 35 newsstand/cover (effective 2010). **Document type:** *Magazine, Trade.*
Published by: Art Reality, s.r.o., Nadrazni 511, Navsi, 739 92, Czech Republic. TEL 420-737-900900, art-reality@art-reality.cz.

333.33 GBR ISSN 1754-9132
ROYAL INSTITUTION OF CHARTERED SURVEYORS. COMMERCIAL PROPERTY JOURNAL. Key Title: The Journal. R I C S Commercial Property. Text in English. 2006. bi-m. free to members (effective 2010). adv. back issues avail. **Document type:** *Journal, Trade.* **Description:** Focuses on specialist and technical issues, major changes in the legislation and regulatory issues, and the latest initiatives.
Related titles: Online - full text ed.: ISSN 1754-9140.
Published by: Royal Institution of Chartered Surveyors (R I C S), 12 Great George St, Parliament Sq, London, SW1P 3AD, United Kingdom. TEL 44-870-3331600, FAX 44-20-73343811, contactrics@rics.org. Ed. Ebuni Okolo TEL 44-207-6951533. Adv. contact Mei-Ling Mao TEL 44-20-74905632. B&W page GBP 1,680, color page GBP 1,945; 190 x 280. Circ: 56,000.

333.33850941 GBR ISSN 1754-9116
ROYAL INSTITUTION OF CHARTERED SURVEYORS. RESIDENTIAL PROPERTY JOURNAL. Key Title: The Journal. R I C S Residential Property Journal. Text in English. 2006. bi-m. free to members (effective 2010). adv. back issues avail. **Document type:** *Journal, Trade.* **Description:** Covers specialist and technical issues, major changes in law and regulations, and latest initiatives in the residential property market.
Related titles: Online - full text ed.: ISSN 1754-9124.
Published by: Royal Institution of Chartered Surveyors (R I C S), 12 Great George St, Parliament Sq, London, SW1P 3AD, United Kingdom. TEL 44-870-3331600, FAX 44-20-73343811, contactrics@rics.org. Ed. Roz Wrottesley TEL 44-207-6951632. Adv. contact Mei-Ling Mao TEL 44-20-74905632. B&W page GBP 1,470, color page GBP 1,735; 190 x 280. Circ: 22,000.

RPFLEGER. see LAW

333.33 USA
RURAL PROPERTY BULLETIN; national marketplace for rural property. Text in English. 1980. m. USD 16 (effective 2004). adv. bk.rev. 52 p./no. 3 cols./p.; **Document type:** *Catalog, Consumer.* **Description:** Lists all types of rural real estate and businesses for sale throughout the US.
Published by: R P B Media, Inc., 411A Highland Ave, Ste 406, Somerville, MA 02144. TEL 617-629-9790, 888-327-6289, steve@landandfarm.com, http://www.landandfarm.com. Ed., Pub., R&P, Adv. contact Sandy Benson. Circ: 18,000 (paid).

333.33 GBR ISSN 2040-7793
▼ **RUSSIA REAL ESTATE REPORT.** Text in English. 2009. q. EUR 850, USD 1,150 combined subscription (print & email eds.) (effective 2011). **Document type:** *Report, Trade.* **Description:** Provides industry professionals and strategists, sector analysts, business investors, trade associations and regulatory bodies with independent forecasts and competitive intelligence on the real estate and construction industry in Russia.
Related titles: E-mail ed.
Published by: Business Monitor International Ltd., Senator House, 85 Queen Victoria St, London, EC4V 4AB, United Kingdom. TEL 44-20-72480468, FAX 44-20-72480467, enquiry@businessmonitor.com.

333.33 ZAF
S A COMPLEX NEWS; your essential guide for modern living. (South Africa) Text in English. 2006. m. adv. **Document type:** *Magazine, Consumer.* **Description:** Covers residential complexes living, renovations, home loan, security, legal rights, and related issues.
Published by: Blue Planet Media, PO Box 1754, Houghton, JHB 2041, South Africa. TEL 27-11-6229889, FAX 27-84-135202020, enquiries@blueplanetmedia.net, http://www.blueplanetmedia.net/. Ed. Colin Farrelli. Pub. Jason Aarons. adv.: page ZAR 10,000; trim 210 x 297.

S N L REAL ESTATE SECURITIES WEEKLY. (Savings and Loans) see BUSINESS AND ECONOMICS—Investments

333.33 NZL ISSN 1177-3758
S Q M; Colliers International property magazine. (Square Metre) Text in English. 2005. q. adv. **Document type:** *Magazine, Consumer.* **Description:** Features articles on a range of commercial property people and projects from around New Zealand.
Published by: Colliers International, PO Box 1631, Auckland, New Zealand. TEL 64-9-3581888, FAX 64-9-3581999, info@colliersinternational.co.nz, http://www.colliers.com/Markets/NewZealand/. Ed. Sally Lindsay. Adv. contact Tony Nunns. page NZD 3,400; trim 225 x 275. Circ: 7,500.

333.33 DNK ISSN 1603-9661
SADOLIN & ALBAEK. NEWSLETTER; Erhvervsejendomme i Danmark og Udlandet. Text in Danish. 2000. 3/yr. back issues avail. **Document type:** *Magazine, Trade.* **Description:** Latest trends and market indicators in the Danish commercial property market.
Related titles: Online - full text ed.: ISSN 1901-3051; ◆ English ed.: Sadolin og Albaek. Newsletter (English Edition). ISSN 1603-967X.
Published by: Sadolin 0g Albaek A/S, Nikolaj Plads 26, Copenhagen K, 1067, Denmark. TEL 45-70-116655, FAX 45-33-327290, sa@sadolin-albaek.dk.

333.33 DNK ISSN 1603-967X
SADOLIN OG ALBAEK. NEWSLETTER (ENGLISH EDITION); commercial property in Denmark and abroad. Text in English. 2000. 3/yr. **Document type:** *Magazine, Trade.*
Related titles: Online - full text ed.: ISSN 1901-7960; ◆ Danish ed.: Sadolin & Albaek. Newsletter. ISSN 1603-9661.
Published by: Sadolin 0g Albaek A/S, Nikolaj Plads 26, Copenhagen K, 1067, Denmark. TEL 45-70-116655, FAX 45-33-327290, sa@sadolin-albaek.dk.

332.63 USA ISSN 2153-2141
▼ **SALT LAKE REALTOR.** Text in English. 2010. m. free to qualified personnel (effective 2010). adv. back issues avail. **Document type:** *Magazine, Consumer.* **Description:** Aims to inform realtors and their associates of present marketing happenings, encourage and support affirmative action in the local marketplace, and to educate them about trends in real estate.
Published by: Mills Publishing, Inc., 772 E 3300 St, Ste 200, Salt Lake City, UT 84106. TEL 801-467-9419, FAX 801-467-9571. Adv. contact Paula Bell. Circ: 7,000.

333.33 USA
THE SAN DIEGO COAST REAL ESTATE REPORT. Text in English. 19??. m. USD 450; USD 45 per issue; free to qualified personnel (effective 2009). back issues avail. **Document type:** *Newsletter, Consumer.* **Description:** Features sales and price trends, demographics and sale prices, school statistics and commentary on the towns North of San Diego from La Jolla to Encinitas.
Media: Online - full content.
Published by: Information Designs, 2835 Camino Del Rio South, Ste 345, San Diego, CA 92108. TEL 858-518-4924, rick@rereport.com, http://www.rereport.com.

333.33 USA ISSN 1063-5513
SAN DIEGO COMMERCE. Text in English. 1991. 3/w. (Tue, Wed, Fri). USD 66 (effective 2011). adv. **Document type:** *Newspaper, Trade.* **Description:** Covers news affecting the legal and real estate communities.
Published by: Daily Journal Corp., 915 E, First St, Los Angeles, CA 90012. TEL 213-229-5300, FAX 213-229-5481.

SAN JOSE POST-RECORD. see LAW

333.33 CHE
ST. GALLER HAUSEIGENTUEMER. Text in German. bi-m.
Address: Rosenbergstr 51, St. Gallen, 9000, Switzerland. TEL 071-231823, FAX 071-231846. Ed. Bert Gruendler. Circ: 12,500.

333.3 USA
SARASOTA - MANATEE HOMEBUYER. Text in English. a. adv. **Document type:** *Magazine, Consumer.*
Published by: Gulfshore Media, Inc. (Subsidiary of: CurtCo Robb Media LLC.), 330 S Pineapple Ave, Ste 205, Sarasota, FL 34236-7032. TEL 941-643-3933, FAX 941-643-5017. adv.: B&W page USD 3,035, color page USD 3,780.

333.33 GBR ISSN 2040-7882
SAUDI ARABIA REAL ESTATE REPORT. Text in English. 200?. q. EUR 820, USD 1,150 combined subscription (print & email eds.) (effective 2010). **Document type:** *Report, Trade.* **Description:** Provides industry professionals and strategists, sector analysts, business investors, trade associations and regulatory bodies with independent forecasts and competitive intelligence on the real estate and construction industry in Saudi Arabia.
Related titles: E-mail ed.
Published by: Business Monitor International Ltd., Senator House, 85 Queen Victoria St, London, EC4V 4AB, United Kingdom. TEL 44-20-72480468, FAX 44-20-72480467, subs@businessmonitor.com.

332.632 DNK ISSN 1904-2434
▼ **SCANDINAVIAN PROPERTY MAGAZINE;** construction, property and investments in the Oeresund region. Text in English. 2009. a. adv. **Document type:** *Magazine, Consumer.*
Related titles: Online - full text ed.
Published by: S P Business Media ApS, Ndr Strandvej 119 C, Hellebaek, 3150, Denmark. TEL 45-49-253969, info@spbusinessmedia.dk, http://www.spbusinessmedia.dk. Ed. Kamilla Sevel TEL 45-42-760020. Adv. contact Nikolaja Pfeiffer TEL 45-29-387480. page DKK 14,000.

690 DEU
SCHELLEKLOBBE. Text in German. 1973. s-a. **Document type:** *Magazine, Consumer.*
Published by: A B G Frankfurt Holding, Elbestr 48, Frankfurt Am Main, 60329, Germany. TEL 49-69-26080, FAX 49-69-2608277. Ed. Roland Frischkorn. Circ: 46,000.

333.33 CHE
SCHWEIZERISCHE HAUSEIGENTUEMER. Text in German. bi-w. **Document type:** *Newsletter.*
Published by: Schweizerischer Hauseigentuemerverband, Muehlebachstr 70, Zuerich, 8008, Switzerland.

333.33 340 GBR
SCOTTISH CONVEYANCING LEGISLATION. Text in English. 1998. base vol. plus updates 1/yr. looseleaf. GBP 597 base vol(s). domestic; EUR 789 base vol(s). in Europe; USD 1,026 base vol(s). elsewhere (effective 2011). **Document type:** *Handbook/Manual/Guide, Trade.* **Description:** Brings all statutes and statutory instruments which deal with or impinge upon Scottish conveyancing practice.
Published by: Sweet & Maxwell Ltd. (Subsidiary of: Thomson Reuters Corp.), 100 Avenue Rd, London, NW3 3PF, United Kingdom. TEL 44-20-73937000, FAX 44-20-74491144, sweetandmaxwell.customer.services@thomson.com. **Subscr. to:** PO Box 1000, Andover SP10 9AF, United Kingdom. TEL 44-20-73938051, sweetandmaxwell.international.queries@thomson.com.

333.33 340 GBR
SCOTTISH LANDLORD & TENANT LEGISLATION. Variant title: Brand Scottish Landlord & Tenant Legislation. Text in English. 1998. base vol. plus updates 1/yr. looseleaf. GBP 540 base vol(s). domestic; EUR 713 base vol(s). in Europe; USD 928 base vol(s). elsewhere (effective 2011). **Document type:** *Handbook/Manual/Guide, Trade.* **Description:** Provides consolidated legislation affecting this complex area of the law, along with expert annotations giving guidance on the interpretation of the primary legislation.
Published by: Sweet & Maxwell Ltd. (Subsidiary of: Thomson Reuters Corp.), 100 Avenue Road, London, NW3 3PF, United Kingdom. TEL 44-20-73937000, FAX 44-20-74491144, sweetandmaxwell.customer.services@thomson.com. Ed. David Brand. **Subscr. to:** PO Box 1000, Andover SP10 9AF, United Kingdom. TEL 44-20-73938051, sweetandmaxwell.international.queries@thomson.com.

333.33 340 GBR
SCOTTISH SURVEYOR'S FACTBOOK. Text in English. 1999. base vol. plus updates 2/yr. looseleaf. GBP 330 base vol(s). domestic; EUR 435.60 base vol(s). in Europe; USD 516 base vol(s). elsewhere (effective 2011). **Document type:** *Handbook/Manual/Guide, Trade.* **Description:** Fills a gap that exists in materials currently available to the Scottish property profession.
Related titles: Online - full text ed.
Published by: Sweet & Maxwell Ltd. (Subsidiary of: Thomson Reuters Corp.), 100 Avenue Road, London, NW3 3PF, United Kingdom. TEL 44-20-73937000, FAX 44-20-74491144, sweetandmaxwell.customer.services@thomson.com. **Subscr. to:** PO Box 1000, Andover SP10 9AF, United Kingdom. TEL 44-20-73938051, sweetandmaxwell.international.queries@thomson.com.

333.33 USA
THE SCOTTSDALE REAL ESTATE REPORT. Text in English. 19??. m. USD 450; USD 45 per issue; free to qualified personnel (effective 2009). back issues avail. **Document type:** *Newsletter, Consumer.* **Description:** Provides up-to-date, specific information about the Scottsdale real estate market and the negotiating strategies to use.
Media: Online - full content.
Published by: Information Designs, 21803 N Scottsdale Rd Ste 100, Scottsdale, AZ 85255. TEL 480-850-5000, FAX 480-850-5005, rick@rereport.com, http://www.rereport.com. Pub. Jeff Kalina.

▼ **SDU COMMENTAAR HUURRECHT.** see LAW—Corporate Law

333.33 USA
SEA SHELTERS. Text in English. 1982. 4/yr. free. adv.
Published by: Coastland Times, PO Box 500, Manteo, NC 27954. TEL 919-473-2105, FAX 919-473-1515. Ed. Darel Laprade. Circ: 20,000.

SEALES CAYMAN LETTER; an investment, economic and real estate review of the tax-free Cayman Islands. see BUSINESS AND ECONOMICS—Investments

333.33 USA
SECOND HOME. Text in English. 1999. q. USD 18.95; USD 3.95 newsstand/cover (effective 1999). **Document type:** *Magazine, Consumer.* **Description:** Explores second home options.
Published by: Wisner Publishing, LLC., 7009 S. Potomac, Englewood, CO 80112. TEL 800-264-2456.

332.63 USA ISSN 1530-0250
KF1079
SECURITIES LAW HANDBOOK SERIES. REAL ESTATE INVESTMENT TRUSTS HANDBOOK. Text in English. 1989. a. USD 483 (effective 2008). **Document type:** *Handbook/Manual/Guide, Trade.* **Description:** Provides information on the latest developments in taxable REIT subsidiaries.
Related titles: Online - full text ed.
Published by: Clark Boardman Callaghan (Subsidiary of: Thomson West), 610 Opperman Dr, Eagan, MN 55123. TEL 651-687-7000, 800-937-8529, FAX 651-687-7302, bookstore@westgroup.com.

333.33 USA ISSN 1073-4465
SELF-STORAGE LEGAL REVIEW. Text in English. 1994. bi-m. USD 135 (effective 2000). **Document type:** *Newsletter.* **Description:** Covers legal issues of interest to owners and operators of self-storage facilities.
Published by: D. Carlos Kaslow, Ed. & Pub., 2203 Los Angeles Ave, Berkeley, CA 94707. TEL 510-528-0630. Circ: 2,500 (paid).

LA SEMAINE JURIDIQUE. NOTARIALE ET IMMOBILIERE. see LAW

333.33 POL ISSN 1641-0785
SERWIS NIERUCHOMOSCI ADMINISTRACJI I ZARZADZANIA. Text in Polish. m. PLZ 60 (effective 2001).
Published by: Grupa Wydawnicza INFOR Sp. z o.o., Ul Okopowa 58/72, Warsaw, 01042, Poland. TEL 48-22-5304450, 48-22-5304208, bok@infor.pl. Ed. Andrzej Racinski. Adv. contact Waldemar Krakowiak.

333.33 CHN ISSN 1674-6996
SHANGYE JIAZHI/BUSINESS VALUE. Text in Chinese. 1987. m. CNY 240; CNY 20, HKD 40, USD 8 newsstand/cover (effective 2010). adv. **Document type:** *Magazine, Trade.* **Description:** Covers the real estate market, property management, and related policies and regulations in China.
Formerly (until 2009): Beijing Fangdichan/Beijing Real Estate (1002-2961)
Published by: Shangye Jiazhi Zazhishe (Subsidiary of: Beijing Beiguang Chuanmei Jituan/Beijing All Media and Culture Group), Chaoyang-qu, 41, Dong Si Huan Zhong Lu, Jiatai Guoji Dasha 1328, Beijing, 100025, China. TEL 86-10-85711956, FAX 86-10-80115555, http://www.bamc.com.cn/cn/. adv.: color page CNY 4,000. Circ: 10,000.

333.33 USA ISSN 1088-3339
HF5430.3
SHOPPING CENTER BUSINESS. Text in English. 1996. m. USD 79 (effective 2009). adv. back issues avail.; reprints avail. **Document type:** *Magazine, Trade.* **Description:** Focuses on company profiles, in-depth articles of current industry topics and activity reports from different geographic areas of the U.S. and abroad.
—CCC.
Published by: France Publications, Inc., 3500 Piedmont Rd, Ste 415, Atlanta, GA 30305. TEL 404-832-8262, FAX 404-832-8260, scott@francepublications.com, http://www.francepublications.com. Ed. Randall Shearin. Pub. Jerry France TEL 404-832-8262 ext 111. Adv. contact Scott France. Circ: 34,000.

333 658.7 USA ISSN 0885-209X
HF5429.7
SHOPPING CENTER DIGEST; the locations newsletter. Text in English. 1973. s-m. USD 309 domestic; USD 354 foreign (effective 2007). adv. tr.lit. 12 p./no. 3 cols./p.; back issues avail.; reprints avail. **Document type:** *Newsletter, Trade.* **Description:** Provides detailed information on new and expanding US and Canadian shopping centers, existing centers with space available, and expansion plans of retail chains.
Published by: Jomurpa Publishing Inc., 20 N Broadway, PO Box 837, Nyack, NY 10960-0837. TEL 845-348-7000, FAX 845-348-7011. Ed., Pub., R&P Murray Shor. adv.: B&W page USD 2,350, color page USD 3,550.

333.33 USA ISSN 0885-9841
HF5429.7
SHOPPING CENTERS TODAY. Abbreviated title: S C T. Text in English. 1957. m. USD 70 domestic to non-members; USD 99 foreign to non-members; USD 35 to members (effective 2011). adv. bk.rev. charts; illus.; stat. **Document type:** *Magazine, Trade.* **Description:** Trade magazine that covers all aspects of the shopping center industry.
Formerly: I C S C Newsletter
Related titles: Regional ed(s).: Shopping Centers Today Latinoamerica.
Indexed: B01, B07, P34.
Published by: International Council of Shopping Centers, 1221 Ave of the Americas, 41st Fl, New York, NY 10020. TEL 646-728-3800, FAX 732-694-1755, icsc@icsc.org. Ed. Edmund Mander. Adv. contact Vivian Levy. Circ: 60,000.

333.33 USA
SHORE HOMES. Text in English. 2004. q. adv. **Document type:** *Magazine, Trade.* **Description:** Contains information on new home construction and includes new communities, mortgage companies, lists of builders and active adult communities.
Published by: Shore Communcations, Inc., 16 Top Sail Village, Bethany Beach, DE 19930. TEL 301-468-7001, FAX 301-468-7005. adv.: color page USD 995; trim 5.25 x 7.25. Circ: 8,254.

333.33 USA
THE SILICON VALLEY REAL ESTATE REPORT. Text in English. m. USD 450; USD 45 per issue (effective 2009). **Document type:** *Newsletter, Consumer.* **Description:** Informs home buyers and sellers about the real estate process and the current market for the cities and neighborhoods in Santa Clara County, California.
Media: Online - full content.
Published by: Information Designs, 44-285 Russell Ln, Palm Desert, CA 92260. TEL 760-776-4056, rick@rereport.com, http://www.rereport.com.

333.33 GBR ISSN 2040-7661
▼ **SINGAPORE REAL ESTATE REPORT.** Text in English. 2009. q. EUR 820, USD 1,150 combined subscription (print & email eds.) (effective 2010). **Document type:** *Report, Trade.* **Description:** Provides industry professionals and strategists, sector analysts, business investors, trade associations and regulatory bodies with independent forecasts and competitive intelligence on the real estate and construction industry in Singapore.
Related titles: E-mail ed.
Published by: Business Monitor International Ltd., Senator House, 85 Queen Victoria St, London, EC4V 4AB, United Kingdom. TEL 44-20-72480468, FAX 44-20-72480467, subs@businessmonitor.com.

SNAKE RIVER BASIN & NORTH IDAHO ADJUDICATION DIGEST. *see* LAW

332.320941 GBR ISSN 1756-5928
SOCIETY MATTERS. Text in English. 2006. q. free to members (effective 2009). adv. back issues avail. **Document type:** *Magazine, Trade.* **Description:** Covers to get behind the headlines of the BSA's policies and offers readers the opportunity to hear from key people in the sector.
Related titles: Online - full text ed.: free (effective 2009).
Published by: Building Societies Association, 6th Fl, York House, 23 Kingsway, London, WC2B 6UJ, United Kingdom. TEL 44-20-75205900, FAX 44-20-72405290, information@bsa.org.uk. Ed. Rachel Le-Brocq. Adv. contact Charlotte Bell TEL 44-20-75205923.

333.33 USA
SOCIETY OF INDUSTRIAL AND OFFICE REALTORS. PROFESSIONAL REPORT. Text in English. 1991. q. USD 25 domestic; USD 45 foreign (effective 2000). **Document type:** *Report, Trade.* **Description:** Reports industry news in the fields of industrial and office real estate.
Formerly: Professional Report of Industrial and Office Real Estate (1067-4764)
Published by: Society of Industrial and Office Realtors, 1201 New York Ave NW, Ste. 350, Washington, DC 20005-6126. TEL 202-737-1150. Ed., Pub., R&P, Adv. contact Linda Nasvaderani TEL 202-737-8783. Circ: 3,500.

333.33 ITA ISSN 1827-6717
SOLOCASE. Text in Italian. 1994. w. free. **Document type:** *Magazine, Consumer.*
Published by: Terra Nova Editore, Viale Regina Margherita 269, Rome, 00198, Italy. TEL 39-0644080301, FAX 39-06-44080666, direzione@terranovaeditore.it, http://webtest.terranovaeditore.net.

SOUTH AFRICAN HOME OWNER. *see* ARCHITECTURE

332.63 ZAF ISSN 1995-655X
SOUTH AFRICAN REAL ESTATE INVESTOR MAGAZINE. Text in English. 2007. bi-m. ZAR 210 domestic; ZAR 833.33 foreign; ZAR 260 combined subscription domestic (print & online eds.); ZAR 877.19 combined subscription foreign (print & online eds.) (effective 2007). adv. **Document type:** *Magazine, Consumer.*
Related titles: Online - full text ed.
Published by: Real Estate Publishing Pty Ltd, Office 106, 1st Flr, Heritage House, 20 Dreyer St, Claremont, Cape Town, 7708, South Africa. TEL 27-21-6745026. Ed., Pub. Neale Petersen.

333 USA ISSN 1530-6097
SOUTHEAST REAL ESTATE BUSINESS. Text in English. 2000. m. USD 69 (effective 2009). adv. back issues avail.; reprints avail. **Document type:** *Magazine, Trade.* **Description:** Covers the latest news, developments and trends in commercial real estate in the southeast states. Features up-to-date information regarding ground-up projects and redevelopments, acquisitions and dispositions, financing, corporate real estate news and current events that are shaping the office, industrial, retail, hospitality, senior housing and multifamily sectors of real estate.
Published by: France Publications, Inc., 3500 Piedmont Rd, Ste 415, Atlanta, GA 30305. TEL 404-832-8262, FAX 404-832-8260, scott@francepublications.com, http://www.francepublications.com. Ed. Chris Thorn. Pub. Jerry France TEL 404-832-8262 ext 111. Adv. contact Scott France.

333.33 USA ISSN 1940-5766
SOUTHERN CALIFORNIA REAL ESTATE MAGAZINE. Text in English. 2008. m. free (effective 2008). adv. **Document type:** *Magazine, Consumer.*
Published by: Southwest Publishing Group Inc, 1171 S Robertson Blvd, Ste 166, Los Angeles, CA 90035. TEL 866-601-9824, FAX 310-388-0836, publisher@southwestpublishing.net, http://www.southwestpublishing.net. adv.: page USD 295. Circ: 50,000.

333.33 USA
SOUTHERN FARM & RANCH. Text in English. 4/yr. USD 23.50; USD 5.95 newsstand/cover (effective 2005). adv.
Published by: Farm & Ranch Publishing, LLC, 50 Briar Hollow Ln., Ste. 650 E, Houston, TX 77027. TEL 713-334-9222, 800-580-7330, FAX 713-334-9977, info@farmandranch.com, http://www.farmandranch.com. Ed. Thelma Chewning. adv.: color page USD 4,490; trim 8.5 x 10.875. Circ: 40,000 (paid).

332.63 GBR ISSN 1471-6607
SPANISH HOMES MAGAZINE. Text in English. 1991. bi-m. GBP 15 domestic; GBP 25 in Europe; GBP 35 elsewhere (effective 2004). adv. **Document type:** *Magazine, Consumer.* **Description:** Provides contact information and advice for those wishing to buy property in Spain as an investment, second home or to retire to.
Formerly (until 2000): Spanish Property News (1465-4687)
—CCC.
Published by: Future Publishing Ltd., Beauford Ct, 30 Monmouth St, Bath, Avon BA1 2BW, United Kingdom. TEL 44-1225-442244, FAX 44-1225-446019, customerservice@subscription.co.uk, http://www.futureplc.com. adv.: color page GBP 1,800; trim 188 x 275.

333.33 FRA ISSN 1961-6228
SPECIAL IMMOBILIER. Text in French. 2007. q. EUR 42 for 2 yrs. (effective 2008). **Document type:** *Magazine, Consumer.*
Published by: Lafont Presse, 53 Rue du Chemin Vert, Boulogne-Billancourt, 92100, France. http://www.lafontpresse.fr.

333.33 SVK ISSN 1337-6233
SPRAVA BUDOV. Text in Slovak. 2007. q. EUR 8 (effective 2011). adv. **Document type:** *Magazine, Trade.*
Published by: Jaga Group s.r.o., Imricha Karvasa 2, Bratislava, 811 07, Slovakia. TEL 421-2-52925989, FAX 421-2-50200210, knihkupectvo@jaga.sk, http://www.svetknih.sk. Ed. Katarina Vilkovska. Circ: 3,500 (paid).

333.5 USA
SQUARE FOOT MAGAZINE. Text in English. 1986. m. USD 59.46 (effective 2008). adv. back issues avail. **Document type:** *Magazine, Trade.* **Description:** Contains summary of lease and sales transactions involving office, retail, industrial, and apartment properties. Also includes review of market conditions affecting the value of those properties.
Formerly (until Aug.2007): Commercial Leasing Update
Address: 2741 W Palm Ln, Phoenix, AZ 85009. lross@squarefootmag.com. Ed. Kimberleyt McGhee TEL 602-288-8808. Adv. contact Lance Ross. color page USD 1,750; trim 8.5 x 11. Circ: 5,000.

STATE-BY-STATE MORTGAGE LENDING ALERT. EASTERN REGION. *see* BUSINESS AND ECONOMICS—Investments

STEDEBOUW & RUIMTELIJKE ORDENING. *see* HOUSING AND URBAN PLANNING

333.33 CAN ISSN 1715-8389
STRATA MANAGEMENT LICENSING COURSE MANUAL. Text in English. 2005. a. **Document type:** *Monographic series, Trade.*
Published by: (The University of British Columbia, Sauder School of Business, Real Estate Division), Real Estate Council of British Columbia, 900 - 750 W Pender St, Vancouver, BC V6C 2T8, Canada. TEL 604-683-9664, 877-683-9664, FAX 604-683-9017, info@recbc.ca, http://www.recbc.ca/index.htm.

STRATEGIC: HOUSING, FINANCIAL, COMMUNITY PARTNERS. *see* BUSINESS AND ECONOMICS—Banking And Finance

STRUCTURING FOREIGN INVESTMENT IN U.S. REAL ESTATE. *see* LAW

333.33 USA ISSN 2153-2915
▼ **STUDENT HOUSING BUSINESS**; the new voice of the student housing real estate industry. Text in English. 2009. bi-m. free to qualified personnel (effective 2010). adv. **Document type:** *Magazine, Trade.* **Description:** Covers news of student housing real estate industry.
Published by: France Publications, Inc., 3500 Piedmont Rd, Ste 415, Atlanta, GA 30305. TEL 404-832-8262, FAX 404-832-8260, scott@francepublications.com, http://www.francepublications.com. Pub. Jerrold France. Adv. contact Rich Kelley TEL 914-468-0818.

346.04 DEU ISSN 1868-0364
▼ **STUDIEN ZUM IMMOBILIENRECHT.** Text in German. 2009. irreg., latest vol.2, 2010. price varies. **Document type:** *Monographic series, Academic/Scholarly.*
Published by: Verlag Dr. Kovac, Leverkusenstr 13, Hamburg, 22761, Germany. TEL 49-40-3988800, FAX 49-40-39888055, info@verlagdrkovac.de.

333.33 USA
SUBURBAN LIFESTYLE. Text in English. 1990. q. adv. **Document type:** *Magazine, Consumer.*
Published by: Village Profile, 125 E Lake St, Ste 103, Bloomingdale, IL 60108. TEL 800-600-0134, http://www.villageprofile.com. Ed. Arley Harriman. adv.: B&W page USD 2,160, color page USD 2,560; trim 11 x 8.5. Circ: 48,500.

333.33 USA
SUBURBAN REAL ESTATE NEWS (MAINE). Text in English. 1980. m. back issues avail. **Document type:** *Newspaper, Trade.* **Description:** Covers real estate and related topics. Aimed at homeowners and buyers.
Published by: Suburban Publishing Company, 10 First Ave, PO Box 6039, Peabody, MA 01961. TEL 978-532-5880, 800-221-2078, FAX 978-532-4250, rayer@suburbanpublishing.com, http://www.suburbanpublishing.com. Ed. Bill Smith.

333.33 USA
SUBURBAN REAL ESTATE NEWS (NORTH OF BOSTON). Text in English. 1971. w. **Document type:** *Newsletter, Trade.* **Description:** Covers real estate and related topics. Aimed at home buyers, home sellers, realtors, and people who finance mortgages.
Published by: Suburban Publishing Company, 10 First Ave, PO Box 6039, Peabody, MA 01961. TEL 978-532-5880, 800-221-2078, FAX 978-532-4250, rayer@suburbanpublishing.com, http://www.suburbanpublishing.com. Ed. Bill Smith.

333.33 USA
SUBURBAN REAL ESTATE NEWS (SOUTH OF BOSTON). Text in English. 1971. w. **Document type:** *Newspaper, Trade.* **Description:** Covers real estate and related topics. Aimed at home buyers, home sellers, realtors, and people who finance mortgages.
Published by: Suburban Publishing Company, 10 First Ave, PO Box 6039, Peabody, MA 01961. TEL 978-532-5880, 800-221-2078, FAX 978-532-4250, rayer@suburbanpublishing.com, http://www.suburbanpublishing.com. Ed. Bill Smith.

333.33 USA
SUBURBAN REAL ESTATE NEWS (WEST OF BOSTON). Text in English. 1971. w. **Document type:** *Newspaper, Trade.* **Description:** Covers real estate and related topics. Aimed at home buyers, home sellers, realtors, and people who finance mortgages.
Published by: Suburban Publishing Company, 10 First Ave, PO Box 6039, Peabody, MA 01961. TEL 978-532-5880, 800-221-2078, FAX 978-532-4250, rayer@suburbanpublishing.com, http://www.suburbanpublishing.com. Ed. Bill Smith.

333.33 FRA ISSN 1957-2778
SUN RESIDENCES. Text in Multiple languages. 2007. irreg. **Document type:** *Magazine, Consumer.*
Published by: Reference Sud, 6 Rue Jean Daumas, Cannes, 06400, France. TEL 33-4-93680673, FAX 33-4-93687044.

SUPERINTENDENT OF INSURANCE ANNUAL REPORT. *see* INSURANCE

333 USA ISSN 1939-0262
HD1382.2
SURVEY REPORT ON COMPENSATION IN THE COMMERCIAL REAL ESTATE INDUSTRY. Text in English. 199?. a. USD 1,500 combined subscription (print & online eds.); Non-Participant; USD 2,100 combined subscription (print & online eds.) (effective 2009). **Document type:** *Report, Trade.* **Description:** Covers 85 jobs, representing a complete top-to-bottom hierarchy within the commercial real estate sector.
Related titles: Online - full text ed.: USD 1,900; USD 1,300 Non-Participant (effective 2009).
Published by: Watson Wyatt Data Services, 218 Rte 17 N, Rochelle Park, NJ 07662. TEL 201-843-1177, 877-906-8700, FAX 201-843-0101, survey.service@towerswatson.com, http://www.wwds.com.

658 333.33021 SWE ISSN 1102-9218
SVENSK FASTIGHETSINDIKATOR; fastighetsaegarens aarsbok. Text in Swedish. 1990. a. SEK 449 (effective 2004).
Related titles: Online - full text ed.
Published by: Tidnings AB Fastighetsvaerlden, Djupdalsvaegen 1, PO Box 343, Stockholm, 19230, Sweden. TEL 46-8-6319020, FAX 46-8-6119515.

333.33 340 GBR
SWEET & MAXWELL'S CONVEYANCING PRACTICE. Text in English. 1989. base vol. plus updates 3/yr. looseleaf. GBP 512 base vol(s). domestic; EUR 676 base vol(s). in Europe; USD 880 base vol(s). elsewhere (effective 2011). **Document type:** *Handbook/Manual/Guide, Trade.* **Description:** Provides a comprehensive guide to practical conveyancing.
Related titles: CD-ROM ed.: GBP 2,112 base vol(s). domestic to institutions; EUR 2,324 base vol(s). in Europe to institutions; USD 3,025 base vol(s). elsewhere to institutions (effective 2011).
Published by: Sweet & Maxwell Ltd. (Subsidiary of: Thomson Reuters Corp.), 100 Avenue Rd, London, NW3 3PF, United Kingdom. TEL 44-20-73937000, FAX 44-20-74491144, sweetandmaxwell.customer.services@thomson.com. Eds. Jill Alexander, Simon Spurgeon. **Subscr. to:** PO Box 1000, Andover SP10 9AF, United Kingdom. TEL 44-20-73938051, sweetandmaxwell.international.queries@thomson.com.

333.33 AUS
THE SYDNEY MORNING HERALD. HOME PRICE GUIDE. Text in English. 1989. irreg. **Document type:** *Directory, Newspaper-distributed.*
Formerly: Real Estate Price Guide (1033-3363)
Related titles: Online - full text ed.
Published by: (Australian Property Monitors), Sydney Morning Herald, GPO Box 506, Sydney, NSW 2001, Australia. TEL 800-817-616, FAX 61-2-85964928.

TABLE ROCK LAKE VACATION - SERVICE AND RELOCATION GUIDE. *see* TRAVEL AND TOURISM

TAX, ESTATE & FINANCIAL PLANNING FOR THE ELDERLY. *see* GERONTOLOGY AND GERIATRICS

TAX, ESTATE & FINANCIAL PLANNING FOR THE ELDERLY: FORMS AND PRACTICE. *see* GERONTOLOGY AND GERIATRICS

R

333.33 USA ISSN 8755-0628
KF6535.A15
TAX MANAGEMENT REAL ESTATE JOURNAL. Text in English. 1984. m. USD 777 (effective 2010 - 2011). index. back issues avail.; reprints avail. **Document type:** *Journal, Trade.* **Description:** Covers judicial, legislative, and administrative developments in the real estate area.
Related titles: Online - full text ed.: ISSN 1544-0796. 1999 (May). USD 453 (effective 2010 - 2011).
Indexed: A22, A26, ATI, B16, CLI, FamI, G08, I05, LRI, P10, P48, P53, P54, PQC.
—CCC.
Published by: Tax Management Inc. (Subsidiary of: The Bureau of National Affairs, Inc.), 1801 S Bell St, Arlington, VA 22202. TEL 703-341-5877, 800-372-1033, FAX 703-341-1623, bnaplus@bna.com.

346.04 NLD ISSN 1879-5773
TEKSTUITGAVE VASTGOED EN WONEN. Variant title: Vastgoed en Wonen. Text in Dutch. 2008. a. EUR 43 (effective 2010).
Formerly (until 2009): Tekstuitgave Wetgeving Wonen (1876-7567)
Published by: Kluwer B.V. (Subsidiary of: Wolters Kluwer N.V.), Postbus 4, Alphen aan den Rijn, 2400 MA, Netherlands. TEL 31-172-466633, info@kluwer.nl, http://www.kluwer.nl.

TELECOM REAL ESTATE ADVISER. *see* LAW

346.04 301.54 USA ISSN 0040-3083
TENANT/INQUILINO. Text in English, Spanish. 1971. m. (11/yr.). USD 2.50 newsstand/cover to individuals; USD 5 newsstand/cover to institutions (effective 2001). adv. bk.rev. charts; illus. **Document type:** *Newspaper, Consumer.*
Published by: Met Council, Inc., 339 Lafayette St., New York, NY 10012-2725. TEL 212-693-0550, FAX 212-693-0555, metcouncil@aol.com. Ed. Steve Wishnia. R&P Jenny Laurie TEL 212-693-0553. Circ: 3,500.

TENNESSEE REAL ESTATE LAW LETTER; expert coverage of trends in Tennessee real estate law. *see* LAW

346.04 USA ISSN 1931-6062
KFT1310.A29
TEXAS ANNOTATED PROPERTY CODE. Text in English. 200?. irreg., latest 2007. USD 102 per vol. (effective 2008). **Document type:** *Handbook/Manual/Guide, Trade.* **Description:** Covers full text of Texas property code and a number of real estate-related provisions from other codes.
Published by: LexisNexis (Subsidiary of: LexisNexis North America), 701 E Water St, PO Box 7587, Charlottesville, VA 22906. TEL 434-972-7600, 800-446-3410, FAX 800-643-1280, customer.support@lexisnexis.com, http://www.lexisnexis.com/.

333.33 USA ISSN 1939-0076
TEXAS APARTMENTS. Text in English. 2003. q. adv. **Document type:** *Magazine, Trade.* **Description:** Features articles on legal issues affecting the rental housing profession, property management topics, personal development, new TAA products and services, and legislative issues.
Related titles: Online - full text ed.: free (effective 2009).
Published by: (Texas Apartment Association), Naylor LLC, 5950 NW 1st Pl, Gainesville, FL 32607. TEL 352-332-1252, 800-369-6220, FAX 352-331-3525, http://www.naylor.com. Ed. Colleen Wooten. Pub. Kathleen Gardner. Adv. contact Jon Meurlott TEL 352-333-3379. B&W page USD 1,210; trim 8.375 x 10.875. Circ: 15,000.

333.33 USA
TEXAS FARM & RANCH. Text in English. 1993. 4/yr. USD 23.50; USD 5.95 newsstand/cover (effective 2005). adv. **Document type:** *Magazine, Consumer.* **Description:** Showcases Texas ranch properties and listings.
Published by: Farm & Ranch Publishing, LLC, 50 Briar Hollow Ln., Ste. 650 E, Houston, TX 77027. TEL 713-334-9222, 800-580-7330, FAX 713-334-9977, info@farmandranch.com, http://www.farmandranch.com. Ed. Thelma Chewning. Adv. contact Vicki Craig. color page USD 4,490; trim 8.5 x 10.875. Circ: 40,000 (paid).

346.04 332.04 USA
TEXAS FORECLOSURE: LAW AND PRACTICE. Text in English. 1984. latest 2001, 2nd ed., base vol. plus a. updates. USD 150 (effective 2008). Supplement avail. **Document type:** *Handbook/Manual/Guide, Trade.* **Description:** Covers such issues as bankruptcy considerations, sequestration, receivership, federal tax considerations, setoff, garnishment, sheriff's sales, landlord's liens, injunctions and property exemptions.
Published by: Thomson West (Subsidiary of: Thomson Reuters Corp.), 610 Opperman Dr, Eagan, MN 55123. TEL 651-687-7000, 800-344-5008, FAX 651-687-6674, west.support@thomson.com, http://west.thomson.com.

TEXAS MUNICIPAL ZONING LAW. *see* LAW

333.33 USA ISSN 1555-9173
TEXAS REAL ESTATE BUSINESS. Text in English. 2005 (Mar.). m. USD 64 (effective 2009). adv. reprints avail. **Document type:** *Magazine, Trade.* **Description:** Covers the latest news, developments and trends in commercial real estate in Texas. Features up-to-date information regarding ground-up projects and redevelopments, acquisitions and dispositions, financing, corporate real estate news and current events that are shaping the office, industrial, retail, hospitality, senior housing and multifamily sectors of real estate.
Related titles: Online - full text ed.: Texas Real Estate Business E-Newsletter. ISSN 2154-2740.
Published by: France Publications, Inc., 3500 Piedmont Rd, Ste 415, Atlanta, GA 30305. TEL 404-832-8262, FAX 404-832-8260, scott@francepublications.com, http://www.francepublications.com. Ed. Lindsey Walker. Pub. Jerry France TEL 404-832-8262 ext 111. Adv. contact Scott France. B&W page USD 2,900. Circ: 10,000.

333.33 USA ISSN 1068-1248
TEXAS REALTOR. Text in English. 1948. 10/yr. adv. **Document type:** *Magazine, Trade.*
Formerly (until 1968): Texas Landsman
Published by: Texas Association of Realtors, PO Box 2246, Austin, TX 78768-2246. Ed. Marty Kramer. adv.: B&W page USD 2,390; trim 10.88 x 8.25. Circ: 45,000.

346.045 USA
TEXAS ZONING AND LAND USE FORMS. Text in English. 1992. base vol. plus irreg. updates. looseleaf. USD 115.
Related titles: Diskette ed.: USD 50.
Published by: LexisNexis (Subsidiary of: LexisNexis North America), 701 E Water St, PO Box 7587, Charlottesville, VA 22906. TEL 434-972-7600, 800-446-3410, FAX 800-643-1280, customer.support@lexisnexis.com, http://www.lexisnexis.com/. Eds. Arthur J Anderson, William S Dahlstrom.

333.33 GBR ISSN 2040-7696
▼ **THAILAND REAL ESTATE REPORT.** Text in English. 2009. q. USD 975, EUR 695 combined subscription (print & email eds.) (effective 2011). **Document type:** *Report, Trade.* **Description:** Provides industry professionals and strategists, sector analysts, business investors, trade associations and regulatory bodies with independent forecasts and competitive intelligence on the real estate and construction industry in Thailand.
Related titles: E-mail ed.
Published by: Business Monitor International Ltd., Senator House, 85 Queen Victoria St, London, EC4V 4AB, United Kingdom. TEL 44-20-72480468, FAX 44-20-72480467, subs@businessmonitor.com.

333.33 CAN
THUNDER BAY REAL ESTATE NEWS. Text in English. 1983. w. CAD 100, USD 60. back issues avail. **Document type:** *Newsletter, Consumer.*
Published by: North Superior Publishing Inc., 1145 Barton St, Thunder Bay, ON P7B 5N3, Canada. TEL 807-623-2348, FAX 807-623-7515. Ed., Pub. Scott A Sumnr. Circ: 31,000.

333.33 SWE ISSN 1102-9137
TIDNINGEN FASTIGHETSFOERVALTAREN; en naturlig kontaktpunkt foer fastighetsbranschen. Variant title: Fastighetsfoervaltaren. Text in Swedish. 1990. 6/yr. adv. back issues avail. **Document type:** *Magazine, Trade.*
Related titles: Online - full text ed.
Published by: Hexanova Media Group, Fiskhamnsgatan 2, Goeteborg, 414588, Sweden. TEL 46-31-7190500, info@hexanova.se, http://www.hexanova.se. Ed., Pub. Urban Nilsson. adv.: color page SEK 31,500; trim 355 x 250. Circ: 24,000.

333.33 USA ISSN 1070-0234
TIERRA GRANDE. Text in English. 1978. q. USD 20; free to qualified personnel (effective 2007). illus. back issues avail.; reprints avail. **Document type:** *Magazine, Trade.* **Description:** Real estate research specific to Texas.
Former titles (until 1993): Real Estate Center Journal (0893-3332); (until 1987): Tierra Grande (0164-5781)
Published by: Texas A & M University, Real Estate Center, 2115 TAMU, College Station, TX 77843-2115. TEL 979-845-2031, FAX 979-845-0460. Pub. Gary Maler. Circ: 145,000 (controlled).

346.04 NLD ISSN 1573-9910
TIJDSCHRIFT AANBESTEDINGSRECHT. Text in Dutch. 2004. bi-m. EUR 126 (effective 2009). **Document type:** *Magazine, Trade.*
Related titles: Online - full text ed.: EUR 695 (effective 2009).
Indexed: T02.
Published by: Sdu Uitgevers bv, Postbus 20025, The Hague, 2500 EA, Netherlands. TEL 31-70-3789911, FAX 31-70-3854321, sdu@sdu.nl, http://www.sdu.nl/.

346.04 NLD ISSN 1879-6389
▼ **TIJDSCHRIFT HUURRECHT IN PRAKTIJK.** Variant title: H I P. Text in Dutch. 2009. 8/yr. EUR 199 (effective 2010). adv. **Document type:** *Magazine, Trade.*
Published by: Sdu Uitgevers bv, Postbus 20025, The Hague, 2500 EA, Netherlands. TEL 31-70-3789911, FAX 31-70-3854321, sdu@sdu.nl, http://www.sdu.nl/. Pub. Dr. G J G Schinkel.

333.5 346.04 NLD ISSN 1567-2913
TIJDSCHRIFT VOOR HUURRECHT BEDRIJFSRUIMTE. Text in Dutch. 2004. bi-m. EUR 331.75; EUR 49 to students (effective 2010). adv. **Document type:** *Magazine, Trade.*
Published by: Uitgeverij Den Hollander, Postbus 325, Deventer, 7400 AH, Netherlands. TEL 31-570-751225, FAX 31-570-751220, info@uitgeverijdenhollander.nl, http://www.denhollander.info. Ed. M T H de Gaay Fortman. adv.: B&W page EUR 1,040, color page EUR 1,940; trim 210 x 297. Circ: 1,500.

TITLE TOPICS. *see* INSURANCE

TOP MORTGAGE MARKET PLAYERS. *see* BUSINESS AND ECONOMICS—Trade And Industrial Directories

TORRENS SYSTEM IN NSW. *see* LAW

333.33 FRA ISSN 1958-136X
TRANSVERSALES IMMOBILIERES. Text in French. 199?. bi-m. EUR 60; EUR 15 per issue (effective 2008). **Document type:** *Magazine, Trade.*
Formerly (until 2007): U N I T. Le Journal (1258-8342)
Published by: Union Nationale de l'Immobilier (U N I T), 2 Rue de Seze, Paris, 75009, France. TEL 33-1-42937986, FAX 33-1-42937990, unit@unit.fr.

346.04 GBR ISSN 2046-3049
TRENDS & EVENTS. Text in English. 19??. a. free to members (effective 2011). **Document type:** *Newsletter, Trade.*
Formerly (until 2010): Review of Trends and Events
Related titles: Online - full text ed.: free (effective 2011).
Published by: I P Federation, Fifth Fl, 63-66 Hatton Garden, London, EC1N 8LE, United Kingdom. TEL 44-20-72423923, FAX 44-20-72423924, admin@ipfederation.com.

333.33 USA
TRIAD NEW HOME GUIDE. Text in English. q. USD 10. adv. back issues avail. **Document type:** *Magazine, Consumer.* **Description:** Describes and shows new homes and residential communities for prospective buyers in the Piedmont triad area.
Published by: Southern Trade Publications Co., PO Box 7344, Greensboro, NC 27417. TEL 336-454-3516, FAX 336-454-3649. Ed. Trudy Atkins. Pub., R&P, Adv. contact Day Atkins. color page USD 2,100; trim 11 x 8.5. Circ: 30,000.

333.33 USA
TRIANGLE REAL ESTATE. Text in English. 2007 (May). q. USD 48 (effective 2011). adv. **Document type:** *Magazine, Trade.* **Description:** Features profiles of Triangle real estate businesses and business leaders as well as feature stories and expert columns on architecture, construction, development, engineering, brokers, and property management, as well as, deals, transactions, announcements and development activity.
Published by: Business Leader Media, Dept 930, PO Box 1070, Charlotte, NC 28201. TEL 866-726-2887, http://www.businessleadermedia.com.

333.33 CAN
TRIZEC CANADA INC. ANNUAL REPORT. Text in English. 1996. a.
Formerly (until 2002): TrizecHahn Corporation. Annual Report (1483-0477); Which was formed by the merger of (1960-1995): Trizec Corporation Ltd. Annual Report (0707-4840); (1980-1995): Horsham Corporation. Annual Report (0849-7850); Which was formerly (until 1987): United Siscoe Mines Inc. Annual Report (0847-7299)
Published by: Trizec Canada Inc., BCE Pl., 181 Bay St., Ste. 3820, Box 800, Toronto, ON M5J 2T3, Canada. TEL 416-682-8600, 877-239-7200, FAX 416-364-5491, investor@trizeccanada.com.

TUCSON HOME MAGAZINE. *see* INTERIOR DESIGN AND DECORATION

333.33 GBR ISSN 2040-7815
▼ **TURKEY REAL ESTATE REPORT.** Text in English. 2009. q. EUR 850, USD 1,150 combined subscription (print & email eds.) (effective 2011). **Document type:** *Report, Trade.* **Description:** Provides industry professionals and strategists, sector analysts, business investors, trade associations and regulatory bodies with independent forecasts and competitive intelligence on the real estate and construction industry in Turkey.
Related titles: E-mail ed.
Published by: Business Monitor International Ltd., Senator House, 85 Queen Victoria St, London, EC4V 4AB, United Kingdom. TEL 44-20-72480468, FAX 44-20-72480467, enquiry@businessmonitor.com.

333.33 NLD ISSN 1873-989X
TURKEY REAL ESTATE YEARBOOK. Text in English. 2007. a. EUR 45 (effective 2009). **Document type:** *Journal, Trade.*
Published by: Europe Real Estate Publishers B.V., North Sea Bldg, Gevers Deynootweg 93R, The Hague, 2586 BK, Netherlands. TEL 31-70-3528600, FAX 31-70-3527660, publishers@europe-re.com, http://www.europe-re.com.

333.33 GBR ISSN 1363-2655
U K DIRECTORY OF PROPERTY DEVELOPERS, INVESTORS & FINANCIERS. (United Kingdom) Text in English. 1984. a. GBP 97.50 (effective 2001). **Document type:** *Directory, Corporate.* **Description:** Provides key information on the leading property developers, banks, building societies, finance houses, insurance companies, pension funds and property unit trusts included in the UK property market.
Formerly (until 1990): Directory of Property Developers, Investors & Financiers
Related titles: CD-ROM ed.; Online - full content ed.
Published by: Building Economics Bureau Ltd., Kings House, 32-40 Widmore Rd, Bromley, Kent BR1 1RY, United Kingdom. TEL 44-20-8464-5418, FAX 44-20-8313-3363. Eds. Geoff Parsons, Helen Speechly. Pub. Bernard Williams.

333.3387220941 GBR ISSN 1756-0659
U K PROPERTY; sector guide to investment & finance. Text in English. 2007. a. GBP 45 per issue (effective 2009). **Document type:** *Directory, Trade.* **Description:** Provides a unique region-by-region guide to key support organisations, the infrastructure of the region and key hot spots for economic activity.
—CCC.
Published by: Newsco-Insider, Boulton House, 17-21 Chorlton St, Manchester, M1 3HY, United Kingdom. TEL 44-161-9079711, FAX 44-161-2369862, michelle.ferster@newsco.com, http://www.newsco.com/. Ed. Michael Taylor TEL 44-161-9079709.

333.33 NOR
U S B L NYTT. (Ungdommens Selvbyggerlag) Text in Norwegian. 5/yr. adv. **Document type:** *Trade.* **Description:** USBL, a membership organization is devoted to finding housing for its members.
Published by: Ungdommens Selvbyggerlag, Storgaten 49, PO Box 4764, Sofienberg, Oslo, 0506, Norway. TEL 47-22-98-38-00, FAX 47-22-20-29-13. Circ: 22,000.

333.33 USA ISSN 8755-1608
HD1394
U S REAL ESTATE REGISTER. Text in English. 1967. a. USD 87.50 (effective 2001). adv. 400 p./no. 3 cols./p.; back issues avail. **Document type:** *Directory, Trade.* **Description:** Designed to help corporate real estate managers and all others in the real estate industry find the site, properties and services (appraisal, investment, construction, etc.) they need.
Formerly: Industrial-Commercial Real Estate Managers' Directory
Published by: Barry Inc., PO Box 551, Wilmington, MA 01887-0551. TEL 978-658-0441, FAX 978-657-8691. Ed. Joan L Carrns. Adv. contact Therese Diblasi TEL 978-658-0441. Circ: 15,000.

332.63 USA ISSN 1945-6565
HD251
U S RESIDENTIAL REAL ESTATE MARKET REPORT. Variant title: Market Report. Text in English. 200?. q. **Document type:** *Report, Trade.* **Description:** Aims to provide real estate investors with potential investment opportiies, market risk information and trends across real estate markets nationwide.
Related titles: CD-ROM ed.: ISSN 1945-7944; Online - full text ed.: ISSN 1945-8029.
Published by: PortReal LLC, PO Box 6061, Glen Allen, VA 23058. TEL 804-360-2701, sales@portreal.com.

333.5 651 USA
U.S. SITES AND DEVELOPMENT. Text in English. m. adv. **Document type:** *Magazine, Trade.* **Description:** Provides the latest information on moving or expanding companies, offering a wealth and variety of logistics solutions, geographic studies, and statistical information.
Published by: Grand View Media Group, Inc. (Subsidiary of: EBSCO Industries, Inc.), 200 Croft St, Ste 1, Birmingham, AL 35242. TEL 888-431-2877, FAX 205-408-3797, webmaster@grandviewmedia.com, http://www.gvmg.com. adv.: color page USD 5,500; trim 7.875 x 10.5.

333.5 651 USA
U.S. SITES AND DEVELOPMENT ANNUAL DIRECTORY. Text in English. a. **Document type:** *Directory, Trade.* **Description:** Provides a guide for the people and services needed for relocation, expansion or site selection.

Published by: Grand View Media Group, Inc. (Subsidiary of: EBSCO Industries, Inc.), 200 Croft St, Ste 1, Birmingham, AL 35242. TEL 888-431-2877, FAX 205-408-3797, webmaster@grandviewmedia.com, http://www.gvmg.com.

333.5 651 USA
U.S. SITES AND DEVELOPMENT RELOCATION JOURNAL. Variant title: Relocation Journal. Text in English. q. adv. **Document type:** *Magazine, Trade.* **Description:** Focuses on business recruiting and site development.
Published by: Grand View Media Group, Inc. (Subsidiary of: EBSCO Industries, Inc.), 200 Croft St, Ste 1, Birmingham, AL 35242. TEL 888-431-2877, FAX 205-408-3797, webmaster@grandviewmedia.com, http://www.gvmg.com.

333.33 USA
U.S. SITES MAGAZINE. Text in English. 1996. m. **Document type:** *Magazine, Trade.*
Published by: XpansionLab, Inc., 2700 Second Ave, Ste 3, Birmingham, AL 35233-2704. TEL 404-881-6420, FAX 404-881-6313, editor@acn.net, http://www.acn.net. Ed. Robert Pittman. Circ: 50,000 (controlled).

333.33 SGP ISSN 0129-3680
UNIBEAM. Text in English. a.
Published by: Building and Estate Management Society, c/o Faculty of Architecture and Bldg, National University of Singapore, Kent Ridge, 0511, Singapore. TEL 7756666.

333.33 USA
UNIFORM LAWS ANNOTATED. UNIFORM REAL PROPERTY ACTS. Text in English. a. USD 25 (effective 2003). **Document type:** *Journal, Trade.* **Description:** Provides complete text, prefatory notes, history, purposes, and provisions of each Uniform Real Property Act, including official comments, and an individual index for each section.
Published by: Thomson West (Subsidiary of: Thomson Reuters Corp.), 610 Opperman Dr, Eagan, MN 55123. TEL 651-687-7000, 800-344-5008, FAX 651-687-6674, west.support@thomson.com, http://west.thomson.com.

333.33 BEL
UNION DES PROFESSIONS IMMOBILIERES DE BELGIQUE. BULLETIN MENSUEL - MAANDBLAD. Text in French. m.
Published by: Union des Professions Immobilieres de Belgique, Av Albert I 29, Brussels, 1060, Belgium. TEL 3445768.

333.33 USA ISSN 0747-7465
HD1390.5
UNIQUE HOMES; the global resource of luxury real estate. Text in English. 1973. 6/yr. USD 46.97 domestic; USD 57.97 in Canada; USD 6.95 newsstand/cover (effective 2005). adv. back issues avail. **Document type:** *Magazine, Consumer.* **Description:** Presents some of the most exclusive homes and real estate available and provides information on the professionals who list and sell them.
Published by: Unique Homes, Inc., 327 Wall St, Princeton, NJ 08540. TEL 609-688-1110, FAX 609-688-0201. Ed. Kathleen Carlin Russell. Circ: 70,746.

333.33 USA
UNITEDLAND. Text in English. 1946. m. free.
Formerly: United Way
Published by: United Country Real Estate, 28250, Kansas City, MO 64188-0250. TEL 816-753-4212. Ed. Mike Podraza. Circ: 1,000.

333.33 USA ISSN 0068-5968
UNIVERSITY OF CALIFORNIA AT BERKELEY. FISHER CENTER FOR REAL ESTATE AND URBAN ECONOMICS. REPRINT SERIES. Text in English. 1948. irreg., latest vol.136, 2005. USD 5 per issue (effective 2010). back issues avail. **Document type:** *Monographic series, Academic/Scholarly.*
Published by: University of California, Berkeley, Fisher Center for Real Estate and Urban Economics, Gerson Bakar Faculty Bldg, F-602, Haas School of Business, MC#6105, Berkeley, CA 94720. TEL 510-643-6105, FAX 510-643-7357, creue@haas.berkeley.edu, http://groups.haas.berkeley.edu/RealEstate/.

333.3 USA
UNIVERSITY OF CALIFORNIA AT BERKELEY. FISHER CENTER FOR REAL ESTATE AND URBAN ECONOMICS. WORKING PAPER. Text in English. 1950. irreg. back issues avail. **Document type:** *Monographic series, Academic/Scholarly.*
Former titles: University of California, Berkeley. Center for Real Estate and Urban Economics. Research Report (0068-5976); (until 1963): University of California, Berkeley. Real Estate Research Program. Research Report
Related titles: Online - full text ed.: free (effective 2010).
Published by: University of California, Berkeley, Fisher Center for Real Estate and Urban Economics, Gerson Bakar Faculty Bldg, F-602, Haas School of Business, MC#6105, Berkeley, CA 94720. TEL 510-643-6105, FAX 510-643-7357, creue@haas.berkeley.edu.

333.33 USA ISSN 0589-381X
HD251
UNIVERSITY OF CONNECTICUT. CENTER FOR REAL ESTATE AND URBAN ECONOMIC STUDIES. ANNUAL REPORT. Text in English. 1966. a., latest 2007. **Document type:** *Journal, Academic/Scholarly.*
Published by: University of Connecticut, Center for Real Estate and Urban Economic Studies, 2100 Hillside Rd, Unit 4041, Storrs, CT 06269. TEL 860-486-3227, FAX 860-486-0349, recenter@business.uconn.edu, http://www.business.uconn.edu/cms/cms/p266.

333.33 GBR
UNIVERSITY OF ULSTER. SCHOOL OF THE BUILT ENVIRONMENT. REAL ESTATE STUDIES UNIT. OCCASIONAL PAPER. Text in English. irreg., latest vol.2, 1994. GBP 85. **Document type:** *Monographic series.*
Published by: (Real Estate Studies Unit), University of Ulster, School of the Built Environment, Coleraine, Londonderry BT52 1SA, United Kingdom.

333.3 USA ISSN 1088-8071
VACATION OWNERSHIP WORLD. Text in English. 1970. 9/yr. USD 65 domestic; USD 85 in Canada; USD 95 elsewhere (effective 2001). adv. back issues avail. **Document type:** *Magazine, Trade.* **Description:** For developers, marketers, sales, resort management executives and industry professionals.
Former titles: Resort Development and Operation (1088-808X); (until 1990): Resort Development (1040-5771); Resort Development Today (8750-1252); Resort Timesharing Today (0274-9327)
Indexed: H&TI, H06, Hospl, T02.
Published by: C H B Company, Inc., PO Box 5627, Bellingham, WA 98227-5627. TEL 360-676-4146, FAX 360-647-1311. Ed., Pub., R&P Scott Burlingame. Adv. contact Lynn Burlingame. Circ: 4,000.

333.33 USA ISSN 1087-0148
HD1387
VALUATION INSIGHTS AND PERSPECTIVES. Text in English. 1996. q. free to members (effective 2007). software rev.; Website rev. 48 p./no.; back issues avail.; reprints avail. **Document type:** *Magazine, Trade.* **Description:** Presents trends in real estate appraisal practice, topics of concern to the appraisal profession, information of use to appraisers to improve their business, and industry and institute news.
Related titles: Online - full text ed.
Indexed: A15, ABIn, B02, B15, B17, B18, G04, G06, G07, G08, I05, P48, P51, PQC, S22.
Published by: Appraisal Institute, 550 W Van Buren St, Ste 1000, Chicago, IL 60607. TEL 312-335-4100, FAX 312-335-4400, info@appraisalinstitute.org, http://www.appraisalinstitute.org. Ed. Emily Ruzeck. Adv. contact Jennifer Pasiuk TEL 312-335-4478. Circ: 80,000.

333.33 USA ISSN 1937-3864
VALUATION REVIEW; news and analysis for the real estate appraisal industry. Text in English. 2002. 24/yr. USD 294 combined subscription (print & online eds.) (effective 2008). adv. back issues avail. **Document type:** *Newsletter, Trade.* **Description:** Provides market intelligence, business news and state-by-state legal and regulatory information for the real estate services industry.
Related titles: Online - full text ed.: ISSN 1937-3872.
Published by: October Research Corporation, PO Box 370, Richfield, OH 44286. TEL 330-659-6101, 877-662-8623, FAX 330-659-6102, contactus@thetitlereport.com, http://www.octoberresearch.com. Eds. Jeremy Yohe TEL 330-659-6101 ext 6124, Matthew Smith TEL 330-659-6101 ext 6144.

333.33 NLD ISSN 0166-4204
VASTGOED; vakblad voor onroerend goed. Text in Dutch. 1926. m. (10/yr.). EUR 149 (effective 2010). adv. bk.rev. abstr.; charts; illus.; maps; stat.; tr.lit. index. **Document type:** *Magazine, Trade.* **Description:** For brokers and all others involved in real estate, such as financiers, project developers, municipalities, facility managers, architects and planners, building contractors, and investors.
Formerly (until 1973): Vaste Goederen (0042-286X)
Indexed: KES.
—IE, Infotrieve.
Published by: PSH Group, Kronenburgsingel 515, Arnhem, 6831 GM, Netherlands. TEL 31-26-7501800, FAX 31-26-7501801. Eds. Arie van Loopik, Roel Smit. adv.: B&W page EUR 1,995, color page EUR 3,075; trim 228 x 295. Circ: 7,250.

VASTGOEDMARKT. *see* BUILDING AND CONSTRUCTION

333.33 NLD ISSN 1877-5489
VASTGOEDPERSONALITY. Text in Dutch. 2008. s-a. EUR 6.95 newsstand/cover (effective 2011). adv. **Document type:** *Magazine, Trade.*
Address: Javastraat 74, Den Helder, 1782 DG, Netherlands. info@vastgoedpersonality.nl, http://www.vastgoedpersonality.nl. Pub. Erwin Asselman.

333.33 346.04 ITA
VENDITE GIUDIZIARIE. Text in Italian. 2003. m. **Document type:** *Directory, Trade.*
Published by: Edire, Via Estrafallaces 16, Lecce, 73100, Italy. TEL 39-0832-396996.

333.33 GBR ISSN 2040-7572
VENEZUELA REAL ESTATE REPORT. Text in English. 200?. q. EUR 820, USD 1,150 combined subscription (print & email eds.) (effective 2010). **Document type:** *Report, Trade.* **Description:** Provides industry professionals and strategists, sector analysts, business investors, trade associations and regulatory bodies with independent forecasts and competitive intelligence on the real estate and construction industry in Venezuela.
Related titles: E-mail ed.
Published by: Business Monitor International Ltd., Senator House, 85 Queen Victoria St, London, EC4V 4AB, United Kingdom. TEL 44-20-72480468, FAX 44-20-72480467, subs@businessmonitor.com.

333.33 340 DEU ISSN 0930-8369
VERBRAUCHER UND RECHT. Abbreviated title: V u R. Text in German. 1986. m. EUR 159 (effective 2011). adv. reprint service avail. from SCH. **Document type:** *Journal, Trade.*
Indexed: IBR, IBZ.
Published by: (Vereinigtes Institut fuer Europaeisches Wirtschafts- und Verbraucherrecht e.V.), Nomos Verlagsgesellschaft mbH und Co. KG, Waldseestr 3-5, Baden-Baden, 76530, Germany. TEL 49-7221-21040, FAX 49-7221-210427, nomos@nomos.de, http://www.nomos.de. Circ: 1,050 (paid and controlled).

346.04 DEU ISSN 1431-9055
DER VERMIETER-BRIEF. Text in German. 1996. m. EUR 265 (effective 2010). **Document type:** *Magazine, Trade.*
Incorporates (1999-2000): Werner Siepes Rendite-Brief (1439-247X)
Published by: Verlag fuer Vermieter und Immobilien-Wirtschaft (Subsidiary of: Wolters Kluwer Deutschland GmbH), Marlener Str 2, Offenburg, 77656, Germany. TEL 49-781-605303710, FAX 49-781-605303711, info@vdv-verlag.de, http://www.vdv-verlag.de. Ed. Heidi Schnurr.

346.04 DEU
VERMIETERTIPPS KONKRET!. Text in German. m. EUR 98 (effective 2010). **Document type:** *Magazine, Trade.*
Published by: Akademische Arbeitsgemeinschaft Verlag (Subsidiary of: Wolters Kluwer Deutschland GmbH), Janderstr 10, Mannheim, 68199, Germany. TEL 49-621-8626262, FAX 49-621-8626263, info@akademische.de, http://www.akademische.de.

VERMOGENSRECHTELIJKE ANNOTATIES. *see* LAW—Corporate Law

307.1 USA ISSN 1534-8377
KFV458 .A29
VERMONT PLANNING, DEVELOPMENT AND LAND USE LAWS ANNOTATED. Text in English. 199?. irreg. USD 49 per vol. (effective 2008). 417 p./no.; **Document type:** *Monographic series, Trade.* **Description:** Contains the Vermont planning and development act (Act 250), the laws governing state land use and development and related laws on development impact fees, building codes and the establishment of conservation commissions.
Published by: Michie Company (Subsidiary of: LexisNexis North America), 701 E Water St, Charlottesville, VA 22902. TEL 434-972-7600, 800-446-3410, FAX 434-972-7677, customer.support@lexisnexis.com, http://www.michie.com.

VERZAMELING WETGEVING VASTGOED EN MAKELAARDIJ. DEEL A: PRIVAATRECHT. *see* LAW—Corporate Law

VERZAMELING WETGEVING VASTGOED EN MAKELAARDIJ. DEEL B: FISCAAL RECHT. *see* LAW—Corporate Law

333.33 DNK ISSN 0900-2391
VI LEJERE. Text in Danish. 1968. q. membership. adv. **Document type:** *Magazine, Consumer.*
Formerly (until 1985): Bolignyt (0006-6524)
Related titles: Online - full text ed.: 2004.
Published by: Lejernes Landsorganisation, Reventlowsgade 14,4, Copenhagen V, 1651, Denmark. TEL 45-33-860910, FAX 45-33-860920. Ed. Keld Hammer. Circ: 93,000.

333.33 AUS ISSN 1834-2175
VICTORIAN PROPERTY SALES REPORT MEDIAN APARTMENT/UNIT PRICES. Text in English. 2006. q. AUD 9.99 (effective 2007). **Document type:** *Report, Trade.*
Media: Online - full text.
Published by: Victoria. Department of Sustainability and Environment, 8 Nicholson St, East Melbourne, VIC 3002, Australia. TEL 61-3-53325000, customer.service@dse.vic.gov.au, http://www.dse.vic.gov.au/dse/index.htm.

333.33 AUS ISSN 1834-2167
VICTORIAN PROPERTY SALES REPORT MEDIAN HOUSE PRICES. Text in English. 2006. q. AUD 9.99 (effective 2007). **Document type:** *Report, Trade.*
Media: Online - full text.
Published by: Victoria. Department of Sustainability and Environment, 8 Nicholson St, East Melbourne, VIC 3002, Australia. TEL 61-3-53325000, customer.service@dse.vic.gov.au, http://www.dse.vic.gov.au/dse/index.htm.

333.33 AUS ISSN 1834-2159
VICTORIAN PROPERTY SALES REPORT MEDIAN VACANT LAND PRICES. Text in English. 2006. q. AUD 9.99 (effective 2007). **Document type:** *Report, Trade.*
Media: Online - full text.
Published by: Victoria. Department of Sustainability and Environment, 8 Nicholson St, East Melbourne, VIC 3002, Australia. TEL 61-3-53325000, customer.service@dse.vic.gov.au, http://www.dse.vic.gov.au/dse/index.htm.

333.33 GBR ISSN 2040-770X
▼ **VIETNAM REAL ESTATE REPORT.** Text in English. 2009. q. EUR 850, USD 1,150 combined subscription (print & email eds.) (effective 2011). **Document type:** *Report, Trade.* **Description:** Provides industry professionals and strategists, sector analysts, business investors, trade associations and regulatory bodies with independent forecasts and competitive intelligence on the real estate and construction industry in Vietnam.
Related titles: E-mail ed.
Published by: Business Monitor International Ltd., Senator House, 85 Queen Victoria St, London, EC4V 4AB, United Kingdom. TEL 44-20-72480468, FAX 44-20-72480467, enquiry@businessmonitor.com.

346.04 728 690 SWE ISSN 0346-444X
VILLAAEGAREN. Text in Swedish. 1953. 5/yr. SEK 35 newsstand/cover to members. adv. 3 cols./p.; **Document type:** *Magazine, Consumer.*
Published by: Villaaegarnas Riksfoerbund, Box 7118, Sollentuna, 19207, Sweden. TEL 46-8-626-01-00, FAX 46-8-626-01-01, info@villariks.se, http://www.villariks.se. Ed. Roger Carlsson. Pub. Nils Schirren. Adv. contact Carina Vedin. B&W page SEK 27,000, color page SEK 32,200; trim 185 x 270. Circ: 184,000 (controlled).

VILLAGE COMMUNITIES OF AUSTRALIA. *see* SOCIAL SERVICES AND WELFARE

333.33 ITA ISSN 1121-8479
VILLE & CASALI; la prima rivista italiana del mercato immobiliare di prestigio. Text in Italian. 1990. m. EUR 35 (effective 2009). adv. illus. **Document type:** *Magazine, Consumer.*
Published by: Edizioni Living International SpA, Via Anton Giulio Bragaglia 33, Rome, 00123, Italy. TEL 39-06-30282, FAX 39-06-30282222, villeecasali@eli.it, http://www.villeecasali.com. Circ: 45,000.

353.55 USA
VIRGIN ISLANDS ZONING, BUILDING AND HOUSING LAWS AND REGULATIONS. Text in English. irreg., latest 2000. USD 31 (effective 2008). 256 p./no.; **Document type:** *Monographic series, Trade.* **Description:** Contains all laws classified to Title 29 of the Virgin islands code, the Virgin Islands rules and regulations relating to zoning and subdivision regulations, building codes and standards and housing codes and standards.
Related titles: Online - full text ed.
Published by: Michie Company (Subsidiary of: LexisNexis North America), 701 E Water St, Charlottesville, VA 22902. TEL 434-972-7600, 800-446-3410, FAX 434-972-7677, custserv@michie.com, http://www.michie.com.

346.043 USA
VIRGINIA LANDLORD - TENANT LAWS AND RULES ANNOTATED. Text in English. 1992. irreg., latest 1998. USD 35 per issue (effective 2008). 654 p./no.; **Document type:** *Handbook/Manual/Guide, Trade.* **Description:** Provides the real property professionals, land-owners, tenants, and attorneys specializing in real estate and real property law.
Formerly: Virginia Landlord - Tenant Law
Related titles: Online - full text ed.

R

Published by: Michie Company (Subsidiary of: LexisNexis North America), 701 E Water St, Charlottesville, VA 22902. TEL 434-972-7600, 800-446-3410, FAX 434-972-7677, customer.support@lexisnexis.com, http://www.michie.com.

346.043 USA
A VIRGINIA TITLE EXAMINER'S MANUAL. Text in English. 1992. irreg. (in 1 vol.), latest 3rd ed. USD 122 per vol. (effective 2008). 661 p./no.; **Description:** Provides overview of the many issues affecting titles to real property in Virginia.
Published by: Michie Company (Subsidiary of: LexisNexis North America), 701 E Water St, Charlottesville, VA 22902. TEL 434-972-7600, 800-446-3410, FAX 434-972-7677, customer.support@lexisnexis.com, http://www.michie.com.

333.33 USA ISSN 1092-9886
THE VOICE (INDIANAPOLIS). Text in English. 1920. m. USD 15 to non-members. adv. **Document type:** *Newsletter, Trade.* **Description:** For realtors and affiliate members of the trade association.
Formerly (until 1997): Realtor Voice (1057-4808); (until 1991): Metropolitan Indianapolis Realtor (0887-1620)
Published by: Metropolitan Indianapolis Board of Realtors, 1912 N Meridian St, Indianapolis, IN 46202. TEL 317-956-1912, FAX 317-956-5050. Eds. Bernie L Combs, Leslie Haney. Pub. Stephen J Sullivan. Adv. contact Julie Leahy. Circ: 5,000.

VOORRAADBEHEER EN WONINGMARKTONDERZOEK. *see* HOUSING AND URBAN PLANNING

346.04 NLD ISSN 1877-5128
▼ **VRAAGBAAK GRONDEXPLOITATIEWET.** Text in Dutch. 2009. a. EUR 55.65 (effective 2010).
Published by: Kluwer B.V. (Subsidiary of: Wolters Kluwer N.V.), Postbus 4, Alphen aan den Rijn, 2400 MA, Netherlands. TEL 31-172-466633, info@kluwer.nl, http://www.kluwer.nl.

346.04 NLD ISSN 1872-1761
VRAAGBAAK PLANSCHADE. Text in Dutch. 2003. a. EUR 51 (effective 2009).
Published by: Kluwer B.V. (Subsidiary of: Wolters Kluwer N.V.), Postbus 4, Alphen aan den Rijn, 2400 MA, Netherlands. TEL 31-172-466633, info@kluwer.nl, http://www.kluwer.nl.

346.0437 NLD ISSN 1381-6942
W R; tijdschrift voor huurrecht. (Woon Recht) Text in Dutch. 1982. 11/yr. looseleaf. EUR 135; EUR 200.44 combined subscription (print & online eds.); EUR 67.50 to students; EUR 16.40 newsstand/cover (effective 2009). back issues avail. **Document type:** *Academic/Scholarly.* **Description:** Covers all aspects of residential and business rental law.
Formerly (until 1995): Woonrecht (1380-281X)
Related titles: CD-ROM ed.; Online - full text ed.: EUR 164.40 (effective 2009).
Published by: Kluwer B.V. (Subsidiary of: Wolters Kluwer N.V.), Postbus 23, Deventer, 7400 GA, Netherlands. TEL 31-570-673555, FAX 31-570-691555, juridisch@kluwer.nl, http://www.kluwer.nl.

333.33 346.043 USA
WARREN'S WEED NEW YORK REAL PROPERTY. Text in English. 1938. latest 5th ed., 15 base vols. plus irreg. updates. looseleaf. USD 3,124 base vol(s). (effective 2008). Index. **Document type:** *Handbook/Manual/Guide, Trade.* **Description:** Discusses New York real estate law pertaining to attorney-in-fact and agency powers, brownfields law in NY, common ownership of real estate, corporations and other business entities, leasing and rent regulation, life estates and tenancy proceedings, mining of natural resources and mortgages.
Related titles: CD-ROM ed.: USD 2,397 (effective 2002).
Published by: Matthew Bender & Co., Inc. (Subsidiary of: LexisNexis North America), 1275 Broadway, Albany, NY 12204. TEL 518-487-3000, 800-424-4200, FAX 518-487-3083, international@bender.com, http://bender.lexisnexis.com. Ed. Oscar Warren.

333.33 USA
WASHINGTON STATE BAR ASSOCIATION. REAL PROPERTY, PROBATE AND TRUST SECTION. NEWSLETTER. Text in English. 1974. irreg. free to members (effective 2011). back issues avail. **Document type:** *Newsletter, Trade.*
Published by: Washington State Bar Association, 2101 Fourth Ave, Ste 400, Seattle, WA 98121-2330. questions@wsba.org, http://www.wsba.org.

346.043 340 USA
WEBSTER'S REAL ESTATE LAW IN NORTH CAROLINA. Text in English. 1994. irreg. (in 3 vols.), latest 1999, 5th ed. USD 237 5th ed. (effective 2008). Supplement avail. **Document type:** *Monographic series, Trade.* **Description:** Covers the fundamental principles of the law of real property as developed and defined by North Carolina legislation and judicial opinion.
Related titles: Online - full text ed.
Published by: Michie Company (Subsidiary of: LexisNexis North America), 701 E Water St, Charlottesville, VA 22902. TEL 434-972-7600, 800-446-3410, FAX 434-972-7677, customer.support@lexisnexis.com, http://www.michie.com.

333.33 690 ZAF
WEEKEND PROPERTY HOME FINDER. Text in English. 1974. w. free. adv. bk.rev.
Address: Devonshire Pl, PO Box 950, Durban, KwaZulu-Natal 4000, South Africa. TEL 305-7568. Ed. Colin Vineall. Circ: 63,000.

WEGWIJZER HYPOTHEEKVOORWAARDEN. *see* BUSINESS AND ECONOMICS—Banking And Finance

333.33 USA
WELCOME HOMEOWNER. Text in English. 1987. q. USD 12. adv. **Description:** Publication for all new homeowners in southern California within two weeks of escrow closing.
Published by: Welcome Homeowner, Inc., 12444 Victory Blvd., Ste. 316, N. Hollywood, CA 91606. TEL 818-508-1202. Ed. Ellen Tuck Meli. Circ: 200,000.

333.33 USA
WESTCHESTER - CONNECTICUT OFFICE BUILDINGS. Text in English. 19??. a. **Document type:** *Magazine, Trade.* **Description:** Annual review of Westchester County and Connecticut office buildings.
Formed by the merger of: Westchester Office Buildings; Connecticut Office Buildings
Published by: Yale Robbins, Inc., 31 E 28th St, New York, NY 10016. TEL 212-683-5700, FAX 212-497-0017, mrosupport@mrofficespace.com.

333.33 USA ISSN 0043-339X
WESTCHESTER REALTOR. Text in English. 1926. m. USD 10. adv. bk.rev. charts; illus.
Published by: Westchester County Board of Realtors, Inc., 59 S Broadway, White Plains, NY 10601. TEL 914-681-0833, FAX 914-681-6044. Ed. Glenn J Kalinoski. Circ: 4,500.

332.63 CAN
THE WESTERN INVESTOR; commercial real estate & business opportunities in Western Canada. Text in English. 1985. m. CAD 39; USD 39 in United States; CAD 99 elsewhere; CAD 2.95 newsstand/cover. adv. bk.rev. tr.lit. back issues avail. **Document type:** *Newspaper, Consumer.*
Published by: Westward Publications Ltd., 1155 West Pender St, No. 501, Vancouver, BC V6E 2P4, Canada. TEL 604-669-8500, FAX 604-669-2154. Ed. Anna Lilly. Pub. Cheryl Carter. Adv. contact Susan Plamondon. B&W page CAD 1,495; trim 15 x 10.25. Circ: 16,000.

333.33 USA ISSN 1547-965X
WESTERN REAL ESTATE BUSINESS. Text in English. 2003. m. USD 67 (effective 2009). adv. back issues avail.; reprints avail. **Document type:** *Magazine, Trade.* **Description:** Covers the latest news, developments and trends in commercial real estate in the western states. Features up-to-date information regarding ground-up projects and redevelopments, acquisitions and dispositions, financing, corporate real estate news and current events that are shaping the office, industrial, retail, hospitality, senior housing and multifamily sectors of real estate.
Published by: France Publications, Inc., 3500 Piedmont Rd, Ste 415, Atlanta, GA 30305. TEL 404-832-8262, FAX 404-832-8260, scott@francepublications.com, http://www.francepublications.com. Ed. Brian Lee. Pub. Jerry France TEL 404-832-8262 ext 111. Adv. contact Scott France. B&W page USD 3,375; trim 10.8125 x 14. Circ: 20,080.

333.33 USA ISSN 0043-4124
WESTERN REAL ESTATE NEWS. Text in English. 1964. s-m. USD 105 (effective 2006). adv. bk.rev. charts; illus. reprints avail. **Document type:** *Magazine, Trade.*
Related titles: Microform ed.: (from PQC).
Published by: (Business Extension Bureau), B E B Publications, 500 S Airport Blvd, San Francisco, CA 94080-9881. TEL 415-737-5700, FAX 415-737-9080. Ed. Maureen Chin. R&P, Adv. contact Gil Chin. Circ: 12,500.

333.33 GBR ISSN 0966-2219
WHAT HOUSE? (LONDON, 1992); the essential guide to new homes, interiors and gardens. Text in English. 1992. m. adv. **Document type:** *Magazine, Consumer.* **Description:** Provides details and tips on the essential aspects of househunting, homebuying, and interior and exterior maintenance.
—**CCC.**
Published by: Globespan Media Ltd., 1 East Poultry Ave, London, EC1A 9PT, United Kingdom. Ed. Rupert Bates.

WHERE TO RETIRE. *see* TRAVEL AND TOURISM

333.33 338.91 USA
WHO'S WHO IN INTERNATIONAL REAL ESTATE; certified international property specialists network membership directory. Text in English. a. membership. adv. **Document type:** *Directory.* **Description:** Membership directory for CIPS Network, the International Real Estate Specialists group of the National Association of Realtors. Offers a list of practitioners by country, language or business specialty.
Published by: Certified International Property Specialist Network, 430 N Michigan Ave, Chicago, IL 60611. TEL 312-324-8389, FAX 312-329-8358, narblobe@realtors.org, http://nar.realtor.com/intl/home.htm. Adv. contact Carol Weinrich. B&W page USD 1,200, color page USD 2,000; trim 11 x 8.5. Circ: 2,500 (paid).

346.04 GBR ISSN 1758-6178
WHO'S WHO LEGAL. REAL ESTATE. Text in English. 200?. biennial. USD 200 per issue (effective 2011). **Document type:** *Handbook/Manual/Guide, Trade.*
Published by: Law Business Research Ltd., 87 Lancaster Rd, London, W11 1QQ, United Kingdom. TEL 44-20-79081188, FAX 44-20-72296910, http://www.lbresearch.com/.

333.33 NLD ISSN 1875-2640
WINKELLOCATIEMARKT MAGAZINE. Text in Dutch. 200?. a. **Document type:** *Magazine, Trade.*
Published by: Management Producties, Postbus 82, Vlaardingen, 3130 AB, Netherlands. TEL 31-10-4350477, FAX 31-10-4357430, info@managementproducties.com, http://www.managementproducties.com. Circ: 2,500.

346.04 USA ISSN 1944-849X
KFW2526.A29
WISCONSIN REAL ESTATE AND CONSTRUCTION LAW STATUTES ANNOTATED. Text in English. irreg. USD 81 per issue (effective 2008). **Document type:** *Monographic series, Trade.*
Published by: Thomson West (Subsidiary of: Thomson Reuters Corp.), 610 Opperman Dr, Eagan, MN 55123. TEL 651-687-7000, 800-328-4880, FAX 651-687-7302, west.support@thomson.com, http://west.thomson.com.

333.33 CHE
WOHNEIGENTUM. Text in German. fortn. **Document type:** *Newsletter.*
Published by: Schweizerische Zentralstelle fuer Eigenheim- und Wohnbaufoerderung, Stampfenbachstr 69, Zuerich, 8035, Switzerland. TEL 01-3632240.

333.33 DEU
WOHNEN. Text in German. 1928. q. EUR 3.80; EUR 0.95 per issue (effective 2011). adv. **Document type:** *Magazine, Consumer.*
Formerly: Wohnen im Eigenen Heim
Published by: Verlag H M C Hamburg Media Company GmbH, Beim Strohhause 27, Hamburg, 20097, Germany. TEL 49-40-4136390, FAX 49-40-41363911, info@hmc.de, http://www.hmc.de. adv.: B&W page EUR 26,500, color page EUR 35,900; trim 210 x 280. Circ: 1,115,488 (controlled).

333.33 AUT
WOHNEN IN WIEN. Text in German. 6/yr.
Address: Falkestrasse 3, Vienna, W 1010, Austria. TEL 01-525360. Ed. Herbert Dobrovolny. Circ: 10,000.

DER WOHNUNGSEIGENTUEMER. *see* BUILDING AND CONSTRUCTION

333.33 DEU
WOHNUNGSEIGENTURM. Text in German. 1991. bi-m. looseleaf. EUR 128 (includes a CD-ROM) (effective 2010). **Document type:** *Trade.*
Related titles: CD-ROM ed.: EUR 79.
Published by: Redmark.de (Subsidiary of: Rudolf Haufe Verlag GmbH & Co. KG), Fraunhoferstr 5, Planegg, 82152, Germany. TEL 49-180-5555690, FAX 49-89-89517250, service@redmark.de.

333.33 DEU ISSN 1610-2207
WOHNUNGSPOLITISCHE INFORMATIONEN. Text in German. 1949. w. EUR 104 domestic; EUR 155 foreign; EUR 3.50 newsstand/cover (effective 2010). bk.rev. **Document type:** *Newspaper, Consumer.*
Formerly (until 1999): W I - Wohnungswirtschaftliche Informationen (0179-7948)
Indexed: BAS.
Published by: G d W Bundesverband Deutscher Wohnungs- und Immobilienunternehmen e.V., Mecklenburgische Str 57, Berlin, 14197, Germany. TEL 49-30-824030, FAX 49-30-82403199, mail@gdw.de, http://www.gdw.de.

333.33 DEU ISSN 0939-625X
HD9715.A1
DIE WOHNUNGSWIRTSCHAFT. Text in German. 1948. m. EUR 102; EUR 13.50 newsstand/cover (effective 2010). bk.rev. **Document type:** *Magazine, Trade.*
Former titles (until 1990): Gemeinnuetziges Wohnungswesen (0179-745X); (until 1949): Gemeinnuetzige Wohnungswirtschaft (0179-7468)
Indexed: EIP.
Published by: Hammonia-Verlag GmbH, Tangstedter Landstr 83, Hamburg, 33415, Germany. TEL 49-40-5201030, FAX 49-40-52010312, redaktion@hammonia.de, http://www.hammonia.de.

333.33 CHE
WOHNWIRTSCHAFT. Text in German. bi-m.
Published by: Aargauischen Hauseigentuemer Verband, Badstr 36, Baden, 5400, Switzerland. TEL 056-29683. Ed. Edwin Thoma.

333.33 340 GBR
WOODFALL: LANDLORD AND TENANT. Text in English. 1978. 5 base vols. plus updates 4/yr. looseleaf. GBP 982 base vol(s). domestic; EUR 1,297 base vol(s). in Europe; USD 1,688 base vol(s). elsewhere (effective 2011). **Document type:** *Handbook/Manual/Guide, Trade.* **Description:** Provides with a complete and definitive reference work covering residential, commercial and agricultural landlord and tenant law.
Related titles: CD-ROM ed.: GBP 1,996.80 base vol(s). domestic to institutions; EUR 2,197 base vol(s). in Europe to institutions; USD 2,860 base vol(s). elsewhere to institutions (effective 2011).
Published by: Sweet & Maxwell Ltd. (Subsidiary of: Thomson Reuters Corp.), 100 Avenue Rd, London, NW3 3PF, United Kingdom. TEL 44-20-73937000, FAX 44-20-74491144, sweetandmaxwell.customer.services@thomson.com. **Subscr. to:** PO Box 1000, Andover SP10 9AF, United Kingdom. TEL 44-20-73938051, sweetandmaxwell.international.queries@thomson.com.

333.33 GBR
WORLD OF PROPERTY (ONLINE). Text in English. 1986. q. free (effective 2009). adv. **Document type:** *Journal, Consumer.* **Description:** Lists property for sale and related services in Cyprus, Florida, Greece, Italy, Portugal, Spain, and other tourist regions throughout the world.
Formerly (until 2007): World of Property Magazine (Print) (1357-0269)
Media: Online - full text.
Published by: Outbound Media & Exhibitions, 1 Commercial Rd, Eastbourne, East Sussex BN21 3XQ, United Kingdom. TEL 44-1323-726040. Circ: 30,000.

333.33 CHN ISSN 1674-3431
XIN ZHIYE/NEW REAL ESTATE. Text in Chinese. 1988. bi-m. **Document type:** *Journal, Academic/Scholarly.*
Formerly (until 2008): Waimao yu Shang-jian/Foreign Trade & Commodity Inspection
Published by: Zhejiang Sheng Jikan Zongshe (Subsidiary of: Zhejiang Chuban Lianhe Jituan/Zhejiang Publishing United Group Co., Ltd), 347, tiyuchang Lu, Hangzhou, 310006, China.

333.33 ITA ISSN 1971-3614
YOUR HOUSE IN ITALY. Text in English. 2007. m. **Document type:** *Magazine, Consumer.*
Published by: Terra Nova Editore, Viale Regina Margherita 269, Rome, 00198, Italy. TEL 39-0644080301, FAX 39-06-44080666, direzione@terranovaeditore.it, http://webtest.terranovaeditore.net.

YOUR MONEY MAGAZINE; smarter saving, investing, spending and living. *see* BUSINESS AND ECONOMICS—Banking And Finance

333.33 GBR ISSN 2046-8172
YOUR PROPERTY NETWORK; the leading magazine for buy to let landlords and property investors. Text in English. 2008. m. GBP 4.95 per issue domestic; GBP 8.95 per issue in Europe; GBP 9.95 per issue elsewhere (effective 2011). **Document type:** *Magazine, Trade.* **Description:** Features articles relevant to the buy to let landlords and property investors.
Published by: Your Property Network Ltd., Green Park Offices, James St W, Bath, BA1 2BU, United Kingdom. TEL 44-1225-320849. Ed. Ant Lyons TEL 44-1225-320860.

333.33 DEU ISSN 0340-7497
ZEITSCHRIFT FUER MIET- UND RAUMRECHT. Text in German. 1948. m. EUR 210; EUR 24 newsstand/cover (effective 2011). adv. **Document type:** *Magazine, Trade.*
Indexed: IBR, IBZ.
—IE, Infotrieve. **CCC.**
Published by: Hermann Luchterhand Verlag GmbH (Subsidiary of: Wolters Kluwer Deutschland GmbH), Heddesdorfer Str 31, Neuwied, 56564, Germany. TEL 49-2631-8012222, FAX 49-2631-8012223, info@luchterhand.de, http://www.luchterhand.de. Adv. contact Marcus Kipp. Circ: 2,800 (paid and controlled).

690 DEU ISSN 1611-8650
ZEITSCHRIFT FUER WOHNUNGSEIGENTUMSRECHT; Begruendung, Verwaltung, Vermietung, Steuern, Verfahren. Abbreviated title: Z W E. Text in German. 2003. 10/yr. EUR 162; EUR 21 newsstand/cover (effective 2011). reprint service avail. from SCH. **Document type:** *Journal, Trade.*

Published by: Verlag C.H. Beck oHG, Wilhelmstr 9, Munich, 80801, Germany. TEL 49-89-381890, FAX 49-89-38189398, bestellung@beck.de, http://www.beck.de.

333.33 CHN ISSN 1002-8536
ZHONGGUO FANGDI XINXI/REAL ESTATE INFORMATION OF CHINA. Text in Chinese. 1987. m. USD 62.40 (effective 2009). **Document type:** *Journal, Academic/Scholarly.*
Related titles: Online - full text ed.
—East View.
Address: 22, Shatanhou Jie, Dongcheng-qu, Beijing, 100009, China. TEL 6013301, FAX 86-10-64021486.

333.33 CHN ISSN 1001-9138
ZHONGGUO FANGDICHAN/CHINA REAL ESTATE. Text in Chinese. 1980. m. USD 74.40 (effective 2009). adv. **Description:** Covers real estate policy and regulation, market, development, property management, design and real estate law in China.
Related titles: Online - full text ed.
Published by: Tianjin-shi Fangdichan Guanli-ju/Tianjin Municipal Administration of Real Estate, 6 Heanli Nanhai Lu, Heping-qu, Tianjin 300050, China. TEL 86-22-3399763, FAX 86-22-3303342. Ed. Jinze Wang. Circ: 20,000.

333.33 CHN
ZHONGGUO FANGDICHAN BAO/CHINA REAL ESTATE NEWS. Text in Chinese. 3/w. CNY 222 (effective 2004). **Document type:** *Newspaper, Consumer.*
Indexed: RASB.
Address: Shijingshan-qu Luguxiao-qu, 10, Liuheyuanjia, Beijing, 100040, China. TEL 86-10-68641682. **Dist. by:** China International Book Trading Corp, 35 Chegongzhuang Xilu, Haidian District, PO Box 399, Beijing 100044, China. TEL 86-10-68412045, FAX 86-10-68412023, cibtc@mail.cibtc.com.cn, http://www.cibtc.com.cn.

333.731 346.045 USA
ZONING AND LAND USE CONTROLS. Text in English. 1977. 10 base vols. plus irreg. updates. looseleaf. USD 2,247 base vol(s). (effective 2008). **Document type:** *Handbook/Manual/Guide, Trade.* **Description:** Covers issues in real estate law such as model ordinances, site plans, sample building permits and federal and state regulation.
Related titles: CD-ROM ed.: USD 2,441 (effective 2008).
Published by: Matthew Bender & Co., Inc. (Subsidiary of: LexisNexis North America), 1275 Broadway, Albany, NY 12204. TEL 518-487-3000, 800-424-4200, FAX 518-487-3083, international@bender.com, http://bender.lexisnexis.com. Eds. Eric Damian Kelly, Rohan J Patrick.

333.33 USA ISSN 0514-7905
KF5697
ZONING BULLETIN. Text in English. 1954. s-m. looseleaf. USD 1,352.64 (effective 2008). index. back issues avail. **Document type:** *Newsletter, Trade.* **Description:** Summarizes current cases addressing zoning issues for zoning administrators, enforcement officials and land developers.
Related titles: Microform ed.: (from PQC); Online - full text ed.: ISSN 1544-5836.
Indexed: A22.
—CCC.
Published by: Quinlan Publishing Group (Subsidiary of: Thomson West), 610 Opperman Dr, Eagan, MN 55123. TEL 651-687-7000, 800-937-8529, FAX 800-227-7097, info@quinlan.com, http://west.thomson.com/quinlan.

ZONING LAW AND PRACTICE. *see* LAW

ZONING PRACTICE. *see* HOUSING AND URBAN PLANNING

333.33 DEU
ZWEITE HAND IMMOBILIEN. Text in German. 1996. w. EUR 104; EUR 1.80 newsstand/cover (effective 2010). adv. **Document type:** *Magazine, Consumer.*
Published by: Zweite Hand Verlag, Askanischer Platz 3, Berlin, 10963, Germany. TEL 49-30-290210, FAX 49-30-2902199935, service@zweitehand.de, http://www.zweitehand.de. adv.: color page EUR 1,728. Circ: 13,800 (paid and controlled).

333.33 USA
2ND HOME JOURNAL. Text in English. 2004. q. USD 14.95 in US & Canada; USD 24.95 elsewhere (effective 2007). adv. **Document type:** *Magazine, Consumer.*
Related titles: Online - full text ed.
Published by: 2nd Home Association, 364 Railroad St, #4, St. Johnsbury, VT 05819. TEL 866-633-2882, FAX 802-748-0435, francis@2ndhome.net. Pub. Janet St. Onge. adv.: color page USD 3,925; trim 8.5 x 10.875. Circ: 50,032 (paid and controlled).

333.33 USA
2ND HOME SPECIALIST. Variant title: Second Home Specialist. Text in English. 2005. q. adv.
Published by: 2nd Home Association, 364 Railroad St, #4, St. Johnsbury, VT 05819. TEL 866-633-2882, FAX 802-748-0435, francis@2ndhome.net, http://www.2ndhome.net/. Pub. Janet St. Onge. adv.: color page USD 975; trim 8.5 x 10.875. Circ: 67,434.

333.33 USA
30 DAY NOTICE - TENANT TATTLER. Text in English. q. USD 3.
Published by: Seattle Tenants Union, 3902 D Ferdinand, c o Col Cong Church, Seattle, WA 98118-1740. TEL 206-722-6848. Ed. Bill Butler. Circ: 2,000.

REAL ESTATE—Abstracting, Bibliographies, Statistics

333.33 AUS
ADELAIDE CITYSCOPE. Text in English. 1999. 4/yr. looseleaf. AUD 1,690; AUD 2,365 combined subscription (print & CD-ROM eds.) (effective 2008). adv. illus.; maps. **Document type:** *Abstract/Index.* **Description:** Contains complete property index of all commercial buildings within the core section of the central business district of Adelaide, South Australia. Includes information, developments, ownership, prices, sales histories, exact boundaries and more.
Related titles: CD-ROM ed.: AUD 1,890 (effective 2008).
Published by: Cityscope Publications Pty. Ltd., Unit 2A, 19 Cotton St, PO Box 574, Nerang, QLD 4211, Australia. TEL 61-7-55964799, FAX 61-7-55963408, qld@cityscope.com.au. Ed. Neil Speirs.

304.6021 363.5021 AUS
AUSTRALIA. BUREAU OF STATISTICS. AUSTRALIAN CAPITAL TERRITORY'S YOUNG PEOPLE (ONLINE). Text in English. 1991. quinquennial, latest 1996. free (effective 2009). **Document type:** *Government.* **Description:** Provides a range of statistics on the Australian Capital Territory's young people. Compiled mainly from 1996 Census data, the profile includes sections on population, cultural diversity, living arrangements, education, working life and income.
Formerly (until 1996): Australia. Bureau of Statistics. Australian Capital Territory's Young People (Print)
Media: Online - full text.
Published by: Australian Bureau of Statistics, Locked Bag 10, Belconnen, ACT 2616, Australia. TEL 61-2-92684909, 300-135-070, FAX 61-2-92684654, client.services@abs.gov.au. **Co-sponsor:** National Youth Affairs Research Scheme.

AUSTRALIA. BUREAU OF STATISTICS. CHILDREN, AUSTRALIA: A SOCIAL REPORT (ONLINE). *see* CHILDREN AND YOUTH—Abstracting, Bibliographies, Statistics

333.33021 AUS
AUSTRALIA. BUREAU OF STATISTICS. HOUSE PRICE INDEXES: EIGHT CAPITAL CITIES (ONLINE). Text in English. 1989. q. free (effective 2009). back issues avail. **Document type:** *Government.* **Description:** Provides estimates of changes in housing prices for each of the eight capital cities of Australia.
Formerly (until 2003): Australia. Bureau of Statistics. House Price Indexes: Eight Capital Cities (Print) (1034-1897)
Media: Online - full text.
Published by: Australian Bureau of Statistics, Locked Bag 10, Belconnen, ACT 2616, Australia. TEL 61-2-62527037, FAX 61-2-92684654, client.services@abs.gov.au.

333.33021 AUS
AUSTRALIA. BUREAU OF STATISTICS. NEW SOUTH WALES OFFICE. NEW SOUTH WALES' YOUNG PEOPLE. Text in English. 1991. irreg. **Document type:** *Government.* **Description:** Provides a range of statistics on NSW's young people. Compiled mainly from 1996 Census data, the profile includes sections on population, cultural diversity, living arrangements, education, working life and income.
Published by: Australian Clearinghouse for Youth Studies, Private Bag 64, Hobart, TAS 7001, Australia. TEL 61-3-62262591, FAX 61-3-62262578, acys@educ.utas.edu.au, http://www.acys.info/. **Co-sponsor:** National Youth Affairs Research Scheme.

333.33021 AUS
AUSTRALIA. BUREAU OF STATISTICS. NORTHERN TERRITORY OFFICE. NORTHERN TERRITORY'S YOUNG PEOPLE (ONLINE). Text in English. 1991. irreg., latest 1996. free (effective 2009). back issues avail. **Document type:** *Catalog, Government.* **Description:** Provides a comprehensive range of statistics on young people aged in the Northern Territory.
Formerly: Australia. Bureau of Statistics. Northern Territory Office. Northern Territory's Young People (Print)
Media: Online - full text.
Published by: Australian Bureau of Statistics, Northern Territory Office, GPO BOX 3796, Darwin, N.T. 0801, Australia. TEL 61-2-92684909, 300-135-070. **Co-sponsor:** National Youth Affairs Research Scheme.

333.33021 AUS
AUSTRALIA. BUREAU OF STATISTICS. OCCASIONAL PAPER: MORTALITY OF INDIGENOUS AUSTRALIANS (ONLINE). Text in English. 1994. irreg., latest 1997. free (effective 2009). back issues avail. **Document type:** *Government.* **Description:** Describes the mortality of Indigenous Australians.
Formerly: Australia. Bureau of Statistics. Occasional Paper: Mortality of Indigenous Australians (Print)
Media: Online - full text.
Published by: Australian Bureau of Statistics, Locked Bag 10, Belconnen, ACT 2616, Australia. TEL 61-2-62527037, 61-2-92684909, 300-135-070, FAX 61-2-62528103, client.services@abs.gov.au.

333.33021 AUS
AUSTRALIA. BUREAU OF STATISTICS. QUEENSLAND OFFICE. QUEENSLAND'S YOUNG PEOPLE (ONLINE). Text in English. 1991. irreg. free (effective 2009). back issues avail. **Document type:** *Government.* **Description:** Provides a comprehensive range of statistics on young people aged 12-25 years in Queensland, using data from the latest Census of Population and Housing.
Formerly: Australia. Bureau of Statistics. Queensland Office. Queensland's Young People (Print)
Media: Online - full text.
Published by: Australian Bureau of Statistics, Queensland Office, GPO Box 9817, Brisbane, QLD 4001, Australia. TEL 61-2-92684909, 300-135-070, client.services@abs.gov.au. **Co-sponsor:** National Youth Affairs Research Scheme.

333.33021 AUS
AUSTRALIA. BUREAU OF STATISTICS. REAL ESTATE SERVICES, AUSTRALIA (ONLINE). Text in English. 1988. irreg., latest 2003. free (effective 2009). back issues avail. **Document type:** *Government.* **Description:** Contains information about real estate services in Australia, with selected characteristics about real estate agents.
Former titles: Australia. Bureau of Statistics. Real Estate Services, Australia (Print) (1444-0415); (until 1996): Australia. Bureau of Statistics. Real Estate Agents Industry, Australia
Media: Online - full text.
Published by: Australian Bureau of Statistics, Locked Bag 10, Belconnen, ACT 2616, Australia. TEL 61-2-92684909, 61-2-62527037, 300-135-070, FAX 61-2-62528103, client.services@abs.gov.au.

333.5021 AUS
AUSTRALIA. BUREAU OF STATISTICS. RENTERS IN AUSTRALIA (ONLINE). Text in English. 1994. irreg. free (effective 2009). **Document type:** *Government.* **Description:** Includes costs of renting, affordability, demand for public housing, as well as tenants' rental history.
Formerly: Australia. Bureau of Statistics. Renters in Australia (Print)
Media: Online - full text.
Published by: Australian Bureau of Statistics, Locked Bag 10, Belconnen, ACT 2616, Australia. TEL 61-2-62527037, 61-2-92684909, 300-135-070, FAX 61-2-62528103, client.services@abs.gov.au.

333.33021 AUS
AUSTRALIA. BUREAU OF STATISTICS. SOUTH AUSTRALIAN OFFICE. SOUTH AUSTRALIA'S YOUNG PEOPLE (ONLINE). Text in English. 1991. irreg., latest 1996. free (effective 2009). back issues avail. **Document type:** *Government.* **Description:** Provides a comprehensive range of statistics on young people aged 12-25 years in South Australia, using data from Census of Population and Housing.
Formerly: Australia. Bureau of Statistics. South Australian Office. South Australia's Young People (Print)
Media: Online - full text.
Published by: Australian Bureau of Statistics, South Australian Office, GPO Box 2272, Adelaide, SA 5001, Australia. TEL 61-2-92684909, 300-135-070, client.services@abs.gov.au. **Co-sponsor:** National Youth Affairs Research Scheme.

333.33021 AUS
AUSTRALIA. BUREAU OF STATISTICS. TASMANIAN OFFICE. TASMANIA'S YOUNG PEOPLE (ONLINE). Text in English. 1991. irreg., latest 1996. free (effective 2009). **Document type:** *Government.* **Description:** Provides a comprehensive range of statistics on young people aged 12-25 years in Tasmania, using data from the 1996 Census of Population and Housing.
Formerly (until 199?): Australia. Bureau of Statistics. Tasmanian Office. Tasmania's Young People (Print)
Media: Online - full text.
Published by: Australian Bureau of Statistics, Tasmanian Office, GPO Box 66A, Hobart, TAS 7001, Australia. TEL 61-2-92684909, 300-135-070, client.services@abs.gov.au. **Co-sponsor:** National Youth Affairs Research Scheme.

333.33021 AUS
AUSTRALIA. BUREAU OF STATISTICS. VICTORIAN OFFICE. VICTORIA'S YOUNG PEOPLE. Text in English. 1991. irreg., latest 1996. **Document type:** *Government.* **Description:** Provides a comprehensive range of statistics on young people aged 12-25 years in Victoria, using data from the 1996 census of population and housing.
Related titles: Online - full text ed.
Published by: Australian Bureau of Statistics, Victorian Office, GPO Box 2796Y, Melbourne, VIC 3001, Australia. TEL 61-2-62524909, 300-135-070, client.services@abs.gov.au. **Co-sponsor:** National Youth Affairs Research Scheme.

333.33021 AUS
AUSTRALIA. BUREAU OF STATISTICS. WESTERN AUSTRALIAN OFFICE. WESTERN AUSTRALIA'S YOUNG PEOPLE. Text in English. 1991. irreg., latest 1996. **Document type:** *Government.* **Description:** Provides a comprehensive range of statistics on young people aged 12-25 years in Western Australia, using data from the 1996 Census of Population and Housing.
Related titles: Online - full text ed.
Published by: Australian Bureau of Statistics, Western Australian Office, GPO Box K881, Perth, W.A. 6842, Australia. TEL 61-2-62524909, 300-135-070, client.services@abs.gov.au.

AUSTRALIA. BUREAU OF STATISTICS. YOUTH, AUSTRALIA: A SOCIAL REPORT (ONLINE). *see* CHILDREN AND YOUTH—Abstracting, Bibliographies, Statistics

333.33 AUS
BENCHMARKS (YEAR) (NEW SOUTH WALES SHOPPING CENTERS EDITION); survey of operating Costs. Text in English. 2005. a., latest 2008. AUD 250 per issue to non-members; AUD 180 per issue to members (effective 2009). **Document type:** *Abstract/Index.* **Description:** Provides information to owners and managers with a reliable tool for evaluating the performance of their assets and preparing operating budgets.
Related titles: Regional ed(s).: Benchmarks (Year) (Queensland Shopping Centers Edition). AUD 135 to non-members; AUD 90 to members (effective 2000); Benchmarks (Year) (Western Australia Shopping Centers Edition). AUD 135 to non-members; AUD 90 to members (effective 2000); Benchmarks (Year) (Victoria Shopping Centers Edition). AUD 150 to non-members; AUD 90 to members (effective 2000).
Published by: Property Council of Australia (Sydney), Level 1, 11 Barrack St, Sydney, NSW 2000, Australia. TEL 61-2-90331900, FAX 61-2-90331991, info@propertyoz.com.au.

333.33 AUS
BENCHMARKS (YEAR) (SYDNEY OFFICE BUILDINGS EDITION); survey of operating costs. Text in English. 2005. a., latest 2008. AUD 250 per issue to non-members; AUD 180 per issue to members (effective 2009). adv. charts; mkt.; stat. back issues avail. **Document type:** *Report, Trade.* **Description:** Provides information for property managers and property owners.
Related titles: Regional ed(s).: Benchmarks (Year) (Canberra Office Buildings Edition). AUD 150 per issue to non-members (effective 2000); Benchmarks (Year) (Brisbane Office Buildings Edition). AUD 135 to non-members; AUD 90 to members (effective 2000); Benchmarks (Year) (Perth Office Buildings Edition). AUD 135 per issue to non-members; AUD 90 per issue to members (effective 2000); Benchmarks (Year) (Melbourne Office Buildings Edition). AUD 150 per issue to non-members; AUD 100 per issue to members (effective 2000).
Published by: Property Council of Australia (Sydney), Level 1, 11 Barrack St, Sydney, NSW 2000, Australia. TEL 61-2-90331900, FAX 61-2-90331991, info@propertyoz.com.au. Adv. contact Patrick Cowie. B&W page AUD 2,000, color page AUD 3,000. Circ: 2,000.

333.33 AUS
BRISBANE CITYSCOPE. Text in English. 1986. 4/yr. looseleaf. AUD 1,615; AUD 2,270 combined subscription (print & CD-ROM eds.) (effective 2008). adv. maps. **Document type:** *Abstract/Index.* **Description:** Contains complete property index of all buildings within the Brisbane Central Business District. Includes descriptions, historical information developments, ownership, prices, sales histories, exact boundaries, and more.
Related titles: CD-ROM ed.: AUD 1,795 (effective 2008).
Published by: Cityscope Publications Pty. Ltd., Unit 2A, 19 Cotton St, PO Box 574, Nerang, QLD 4211, Australia. TEL 61-7-55964799, FAX 61-7-55963408, qld@cityscope.com.au. Ed. Neil Speirs.

R

333.33 AUS
BURKE ROAD CITYSCOPE. Text in English. 1988. 4/yr. AUD 785; AUD 1,240 combined subscription (print & CD-ROM eds.) (effective 2008). maps. **Document type:** *Abstract/Index.* **Description:** Contains complete property index of all buildings within the Camberwell Junction District Centre in eastern Melbourne. Includes descriptions, historical information, developments, ownership, tenancies, prices, sales history, exact boundaries, and more.
Related titles: CD-ROM ed.: AUD 900 (effective 2008).
Published by: Cityscope Publications Pty. Ltd., Level 1, 249 Pitt St, PO Box Q281, Sydney, NSW 1230, Australia. TEL 61-2-92676900, FAX 61-2-92675200, sydney@cityscope.com.au. Ed. Neil Speirs.

333.33021 CAN ISSN 1912-7057
C H S RENTAL MARKET SURVEY/STATISTIQUE DU LOGEMENT AU CANADA: ENQUETE SUR LE MARCHE LOCATIF. (Canadian Housing Statistics) Text in English, French. 2005. a. **Document type:** *Report, Trade.*
Media: Online - full text.
Published by: Canada Mortgage and Housing Corporation/Societe Canadienne d'Hypotheques et de Logement, 700 Montreal Rd, Ottawa, ON K1A 0P7, Canada. TEL 613-748-2000, FAX 613-748-2098, chic@cmhc-schl.gc.ca, http://www.cmhc.ca.

333.33 AUS
CANBERRA CITYSCOPE. Text in English. 1991. 4/yr. looseleaf. AUD 1,550; AUD 2,210 combined subscription (print & CD-ROM eds.) (effective 2008). adv. maps. **Document type:** *Abstract/Index.* **Description:** Contains a complete property index of all buildings within the Canberra City Centre, plus the outlying Town Centre districts of Woden, Belconnen and Tuggeranong. Includes descriptions, historical information, developments, ownership, prices, sales histories, exact boundaries, and more.
Related titles: CD-ROM ed.: AUD 1,735 (effective 2008).
Published by: Cityscope Publications Pty. Ltd., Level 1, 249 Pitt St, PO Box Q281, Sydney, NSW 1230, Australia. TEL 61-2-92676900, FAX 61-2-92675200, sydney@cityscope.com.au. Ed. Neil Speirs.

333.33 AUS
CHATSWOOD CITYSCOPE. Text in English. 1987. 4/yr. looseleaf. AUD 1,275; AUD 1,895 combined subscription (print & CD-ROM eds.) (effective 2008). adv. maps. **Document type:** *Abstract/Index.* **Description:** Contains complete property index of all commercial buildings within the Chatswood Central Business District and the Willoughby municipality in northern Sydney. Includes descriptions, historical information, developments, ownership, prices, sales histories, exact boundaries and more.
Related titles: CD-ROM ed.: AUD 1,420 (effective 2008).
Published by: Cityscope Publications Pty. Ltd., Unit 2A, 19 Cotton St, PO Box 574, Nerang, QLD 4211, Australia. TEL 61-7-55964799, FAX 61-7-55963408, qld@cityscope.com.au. Ed. Neil Speirs.

333.33 USA ISSN 1066-0933
HD1393.55
COMPARATIVE STATISTICS OF INDUSTRIAL OFFICE REAL ESTATE MARKETS. Text in English. 1980. a. USD 100 (effective 2001). stat. **Document type:** *Report, Trade.*
Former titles (until 1991): Guide to Industrial and Office Real Estate Markets (1048-2784); Industrial Real Estate Market Survey (0730-0131)
Media: Online - full content.
Indexed: SRI.
Published by: Society of Industrial and Office Realtors, 1201 New York Ave NW, Ste. 350, Washington, DC 20005-6126. TEL 202-737-1150. Ed., R&P Linda Nasvaderani TEL 202-737-8783. Circ: 3,500.

333.33 AUS
EASTERN SYDNEY CITYSCOPE. Text in English. 2002. 4/yr. looseleaf. AUD 1,275; AUD 1,895 combined subscription (print & CD-ROM eds.) (effective 2008). adv. maps. **Document type:** *Abstract/Index.* **Description:** Contains complete property index of all buildings within the Bondi Junction - Double Bay business districts in eastern Sydney, plus Oxford Street and part of William Street. Includes descriptions, historical information, developments, ownership, prices, sales histories, exact boundaries, and more.
Formerly: Bondi Junction Cityscope
Related titles: CD-ROM ed.: AUD 1,420 (effective 2008).
Published by: Cityscope Publications Pty. Ltd., Level 1, 249 Pitt St, PO Box Q281, Sydney, NSW 1230, Australia. TEL 61-2-92676900, FAX 61-2-92675200, sydney@cityscope.com.au. Ed. Neil Speirs.

333.33 AUS
GOLD COAST CITYSCOPE. Text in English. 1989. 4/yr. looseleaf. AUD 1,570; AUD 2,230 combined subscription (print & CD-ROM eds.) (effective 2008). adv. maps. **Document type:** *Abstract/Index.* **Description:** Contains a complete property index of the commercial centers of the Gold Coast towns in southern Queensland. Includes descriptions, historical information, developments, ownership, prices, sales histories, exact boundaries, and more.
Related titles: CD-ROM ed.
Published by: Cityscope Publications Pty. Ltd., Unit 2A, 19 Cotton St, PO Box 574, Nerang, QLD 4211, Australia. TEL 61-7-55964799, FAX 61-7-55963408, qld@cityscope.com.au. Ed. Neil Speirs.

IRELAND. CENTRAL STATISTICAL OFFICE. AGRICULTURAL LAND SALES. *see* AGRICULTURE—Abstracting, Bibliographies, Statistics

333.33 310 MAC
MACAO. DIRECCAO DOS SERVICOS DE ESTATISTICA E CENSOS. ESTATISTICAS DA CONSTRUCAO/MACAO. CENSUS AND STATISTICS DEPARTMENT. CONSTRUCTION STATISTICS. Text in Chinese, Portuguese. 1984. a. free. **Document type:** *Government.* **Description:** Provides a convenient source of information for those engaged in analyzing the housing market, including information on the structure and operating characteristics of all buildings.
Former titles: Macao. Direccao dos Servicos de Estatistica e Censos. Estatisticas de Construcao Civil e Operacoes sobre Imoveis; (until 1989): Macao. Direccao dos Servicos de Estatistica e Censos. Relatorio Anual da Construcao Civil - Construction in Macao (Annual Report)
Published by: Direccao dos Servicos de Estatistica e Censos, Alameda Dr Carlos d'Assumcao 411-417, Macao, Macau. TEL 853-3995311, FAX 853-307825, info@dsec.gov.mo, http://www.dsec.gov.mo.

333.33 MAC
MACAO. DIRECCAO DOS SERVICOS DE ESTATISTICA E CENSOS. ESTATISTICAS DAS SOCIEDADES/MACAO. CENSUS AND STATISTICS DEPARTMENT. STATISTICAL DATA CONCERNING COMPANIES. Text in Chinese, Portuguese. 1986. q. free. **Document type:** *Government.*
Supersedes in part (in 1994): Macao. Direccao dos Servicos de Estatistica e Censos. Indicadores Estatisticos - Operacoes sobre Imoveis e Sociedades
Published by: Direccao dos Servicos de Estatistica e Censos, Alameda Dr Carlos d'Assumcao 411-417, Macao, Macau. TEL 853-3995311, FAX 853-307825, info@dsec.gov.mo, http://www.dsec.gov.mo.

333.33 MAC
MACAO. DIRECCAO DOS SERVICOS DE ESTATISTICA E CENSOS. TRANSACCOES DE IMOVEIS/MACAO. CENSUS AND STATISTICS DEPARTMENT. TRANSACTIONS ON REAL ESTATE. Text in Chinese, Portuguese. 1986. q. free. **Document type:** *Government.*
Formerly: Macao. Direccao dos Servicos de Estatistica e Censos. Operacoes sobre Imoveis; Supersedes in part (in 1994): Macao. Direccao dos Servicos de Estatistica e Censos. Indicadores Estatisticos - Operacoes sobre Imoveis e Sociedades
Published by: Direccao dos Servicos de Estatistica e Censos, Alameda Dr Carlos d'Assumcao 411-417, Macao, Macau. TEL 853-3995311, FAX 853-307825, info@dsec.gov.mo, http://www.dsec.gov.mo.

333.33 AUS
MELBOURNE CITYSCOPE. Text in English. 1974. 4/yr. looseleaf. AUD 2,365; AUD 3,290 combined subscription (print & CD-ROM eds.) (effective 2008). adv. charts; illus.; maps. **Document type:** *Abstract/Index.* **Description:** Contains complete property index of all commercial buildings within the Melbourne Central Business District. Includes descriptions, historical information, developments, ownership, prices, sales histories, exact boundaries, and more.
Related titles: CD-ROM ed.
Published by: Cityscope Publications Pty. Ltd., Level 1, 249 Pitt St, PO Box Q281, Sydney, NSW 1230, Australia. TEL 61-2-92676900, FAX 61-2-92675200, sydney@cityscope.com.au. Ed. Neil Speirs.

333.33 AUS
MELBOURNE CITYSCOPE UNIT REPORT. Text in English. 1993. 4/yr. AUD 2,365; AUD 3,290 combined subscription (print & CD-ROM eds.) (effective 2008). adv. maps. **Document type:** *Abstract/Index.* **Description:** Contains a complete property index of all residential apartments within the Melbourne Central Business District. Includes descriptions, historical information, developments, ownership, prices, sales histories, exact boundaries, and more.
Related titles: CD-ROM ed.: AUD 2,650 (effective 2008).
Published by: Cityscope Publications Pty. Ltd., Level 1, 249 Pitt St, PO Box Q281, Sydney, NSW 1230, Australia. TEL 61-2-92676900, FAX 61-2-92675200, sydney@cityscope.com.au. Ed. Neil Speirs.

333.33 AUS
NORTH RYDE CITYSCOPE. Text in English. 1989. 4/yr. looseleaf. AUD 1,175; AUD 1,650 combined subscription (print & CD-ROM eds.) (effective 2008). adv. maps. **Document type:** *Abstract/Index.* **Description:** Contains complete index of all industrial properties within the Ryde municipality of Sydney. Includes descriptions, improvements, occupants, ownership, prices, sales histories, exact boundaries, zoning, and more.
Related titles: CD-ROM ed.: AUD 1,175 (effective 2008).
Published by: Cityscope Publications Pty. Ltd., Level 1, 249 Pitt St, PO Box Q281, Sydney, NSW 1230, Australia. TEL 61-2-92676900, FAX 61-2-92675200, sydney@cityscope.com.au. Ed. Neil Speirs.

333.33 AUS
NORTH SYDNEY CITYSCOPE. Text in English. 1980. 4/yr. looseleaf. AUD 1,900; AUD 2,775 combined subscription (print & CD-ROM eds.) (effective 2008). adv. charts; illus. **Document type:** *Abstract/Index.* **Description:** Contains complete property index of all commercial buildings within the North Sydney municipality. Includes descriptions, sales history, developments, ownership, historical information, prices, exact boundaries, and more.
Related titles: CD-ROM ed.: AUD 2,130 (effective 2008).
Published by: Cityscope Publications Pty. Ltd., Unit 2A, 19 Cotton St, PO Box 574, Nerang, QLD 4211, Australia. TEL 61-7-55964799, FAX 61-7-55963408, sydney@cityscope.com.au. Ed. Neil Speirs.

333.3021 NOR ISSN 0808-2154
HA1501
NORWAY. STATISTISK SENTRALBYRAA. STATISTIKK OVER EIENDOMSDRIFT, FORRETNINGSMESSIG TJENESTEYTING OG UTLEIERVIRKSOMHET/REAL ESTATE, RENTING AND BUSINESS ACTIVITIES STATISTICS. Text in English, Norwegian. 1981. a. **Document type:** *Government.*
Former titles (until 1996): Forretningsmessig Tjenesteyting (0804-4821); (until 1991): Tjenesteyting (0800-4056); (until 1982): Statistikk over Tjenesteyting (0804-5267)
Related titles: Online - full text ed.; ◆ Series of: Norges Offisielle Statistikk. ISSN 0300-5585.
Published by: Statistisk Sentralbyraa/Statistics Norway, Kongensgate 6, P O Box 8131, Dep, Oslo, 0033, Norway. TEL 47-21-090000, FAX 47-21-094973, ssb@ssb.no.

333.33 AUS
PARRAMATTA CITYSCOPE. Text in English. 1985. 4/yr. looseleaf. AUD 1,440; AUD 2,090 combined subscription (print & CD-ROM eds.) (effective 2008). adv. charts; illus.; maps. **Document type:** *Abstract/Index.* **Description:** Contains complete property index of all buildings within the Parramatta Central Business District in western Sydney. Includes descriptions, historical information, developments, ownership, prices, sales histories, exact boundaries, and more.
Related titles: CD-ROM ed.: AUD 1,615 (effective 2008).
Published by: Cityscope Publications Pty. Ltd., Level 1, 249 Pitt St, PO Box Q281, Sydney, NSW 1230, Australia. TEL 61-2-92676900, FAX 61-2-92675200, sydney@cityscope.com.au. Ed. Neil Speirs.

333.33 AUS
PERTH CITYSCOPE. Text in English. 1997. 4/yr. looseleaf. AUD 1,745; AUD 2,410 combined subscription (print & CD-ROM eds.) (effective 2008). **Document type:** *Abstract/Index.* **Description:** Contains complete property index of all commercial buildings within the Perth and West Perth Districts. Includes descriptions, historical information, developments, ownership, prices, sales histories, exact boundaries and more.
Related titles: CD-ROM ed.
Published by: Cityscope Publications Pty. Ltd., Unit 2A, 19 Cotton St, PO Box 574, Nerang, QLD 4211, Australia. TEL 61-7-55964799, FAX 61-7-55963408, qld@cityscope.com.au. Ed. Neil Speirs.

333.33021 CAN ISSN 1912-2365
RAPPORT STATISTIQUE A L'INTENTION DES AGENTS IMMOBILIERS. REGION METROPOLITAINE DE SAGUENAY. Text in French. 200?. q. **Document type:** *Newsletter, Trade.*
Media: Online - full text.
Published by: Canada Mortgage and Housing Corporation/Societe Canadienne d'Hypotheques et de Logement, 700 Montreal Rd, Ottawa, ON K1A 0P7, Canada. TEL 613-748-2000, FAX 613-748-2098, chic@cmhc-schl.gc.ca, http://www.cmhc.ca.

333.33021 CAN ISSN 1912-2381
RAPPORT STATISTIQUE A L'INTENTION DES AGENTS IMMOBILIERS. REGION METROPOLITAINE DE TROIS-RIVIERES, AGGLOMERATION DE SHAWINIGAN. Text in French. 200?. q. **Document type:** *Report, Trade.*
Media: Online - full text.
Published by: Canada Mortgage and Housing Corporation/Societe Canadienne d'Hypotheques et de Logement, 700 Montreal Rd, Ottawa, ON K1A 0P7, Canada. TEL 613-748-2000, FAX 613-748-2098, chic@cmhc-schl.gc.ca, http://www.cmhc.ca.

333.33 AUS
REAL ESTATE MARKET FACTS; a quarterly review of major residential property markets in Australia. Text in English. 1986. q. AUD 300 (effective 2009). back issues avail. **Document type:** *Bulletin, Trade.* **Description:** Features reports the state of residential property markets in major Australian cities.
Formerly (until 2004): Market Facts (0818-1152); Which was formed by the merger of (1981-1986): Market Facts (Geelong) (0811-3289); (1983-1986): Market Facts (Gold Coast) (0811-6148); (1977-1986): Market Facts (Brisbane) (0811-3564); (1977-1986): Market Facts (Adelaide) (0811-3513); (1977-1986): Market Facts (Melbourne) (0811-3556); (1977-1986): Market Facts (Perth) (0811-353X); (1984-1986): Market Facts (Hobart-Launceston) (0814-0189); (1977-1986): Market Facts (Canberra) (0811-3521); (1981-1986): Market Facts (Newcastle) (0811-3270); (1977-1986): Market Facts (Sydney) (0811-3548); Market Facts (Northern Territory: Darwin - Alice Springs)
Published by: Real Estate Institute of Australia, 16 Thesiger Ct, PO Box 234, Deakin West, ACT 2600, Australia. TEL 61-2-62824277, FAX 61-2-62852444, reia@reiaustralia.com.au. Circ: 1,000.

333.33 AUS
ST. KILDA ROAD CITYSCOPE. Text in English. 1984. 4/yr. looseleaf. AUD 1,280; AUD 1,895 combined subscription (print & CD-ROM eds.) (effective 2008). adv. charts; illus.; maps. **Document type:** *Abstract/Index.* **Description:** Contains complete property index of all commercial buildings. It includes descriptions, sales history, developments, ownership, historical information, prices, exact boundaries, and more.
Related titles: CD-ROM ed.: AUD 1,420 (effective 2008).
Published by: Cityscope Publications Pty. Ltd., Unit 2A, 19 Cotton St, PO Box 574, Nerang, QLD 4211, Australia. TEL 61-7-55964799, FAX 61-7-55963408, qld@cityscope.com.au, sydney@cityscope.com.au. Ed. Neil Speirs.

333.33 AUS
SHOPPING CENTRE DIRECTORY. NSW/ ACT (YEAR). Text in English. 2005. a., latest 2008. AUD 350 per issue domestic to non-members; AUD 362 per issue foreign to non-members; AUD 240 per issue domestic to members; AUD 252 per issue foreign to members (effective 2009). adv. stat. back issues avail. **Document type:** *Directory.* **Description:** Contains essential reference for shopping centre owners, managers, and retailers, providing a comprehensive listing of shopping centres in major cities and suburbs through out NSW & ACT. Information includes owner and management, tenancy and construction details, pedestrian estimates with indexes based on centre name, classification, owner, manager and locale.
Formerly (until 1992): Directory of Shopping Centres. New South Wales & Australian Capital Territory (Year)
Related titles: Regional ed(s).: Directory of Shopping Centres. Victoria (Year); Directory of Shopping Centres. South Australia (Year); Directory of Shopping Centres. Western Australia (Year); Directory of Shopping Centres. Queensland (Year).
Published by: Property Council of Australia (Sydney), Level 1, 11 Barrack St, Sydney, NSW 2000, Australia. TEL 61-2-90331900, FAX 61-2-90331991, info@propertyoz.com.au. Adv. contact Patrick Cowie. color page AUD 2,500; trim 275 x 210. Circ: 200.

333.33 316.8 ZAF
SOUTH AFRICA. STATISTICS SOUTH AFRICA. CENSUS OF ESTATE AGENCIES, RENT COLLECTORS, APPRAISERS AND VALUERS. Text in English. irreg., latest 1990. **Document type:** *Government.*
Formerly (until Aug. 1998): South Africa. Central Statistical Service. Census of Estate Agencies, Rent Collectors, Appraisers and Valuers
Published by: Statistics South Africa/Statistieke Suid-Afrika, Private Bag X44, Pretoria, 0001, South Africa. TEL 27-12-3108911, FAX 27-12-3108500, info@statssa.gov.za, http://www.statssa.gov.za.

333.33 ZAF
SOUTH AFRICA. STATISTICS SOUTH AFRICA. CENSUS OF LETTING OF OWN FIXED PROPERTY. Text in English. irreg., latest 1993. free. **Document type:** *Government.*
Formerly (until Aug. 1998): South Africa. Central Statistical Service. Census of Letting of Own Fixed Property
Published by: Statistics South Africa/Statistieke Suid-Afrika, Private Bag X44, Pretoria, 0001, South Africa. TEL 27-12-3108911, FAX 27-12-3108500, info@statssa.gov.za, http://www.statssa.gov.za.

333.33 316.8 ZAF
SOUTH AFRICA. STATISTICS SOUTH AFRICA. STATISTICAL RELEASE. CENSUS OF LETTING OF OWN FIXED PROPERTY (YEAR). Text in English. irreg., latest 1993. **Document type:** *Government.*
Formerly (until Aug. 1998): South Africa. Central Statistical Service. Statistical Release. Census of Letting of Own Fixed Property (Year)
Published by: Statistics South Africa/Statistieke Suid-Afrika, Private Bag X44, Pretoria, 0001, South Africa. TEL 27-12-3108911, FAX 27-12-3108500, info@statssa.gov.za, http://www.statssa.gov.za.

333.33 AUS
SOUTHBANK CITYSCOPE. Text in English. 1991. 4/yr. looseleaf. AUD 1,385; AUD 2,030 combined subscription (print & CD-ROM eds.) (effective 2008). adv. maps. **Document type:** *Abstract/Index.*
Description: Contains a complete property index of all buildings within the Southbank commercial area across the Yarra River from the City of Melbourne. Includes descriptions, historical information, developments, ownership, prices, sales histories, exact boundaries, and more.
Related titles: CD-ROM ed.: AUD 188,598 (effective 2008).
Published by: Cityscope Publications Pty. Ltd., Level 1, 249 Pitt St, PO Box Q281, Sydney, NSW 1230, Australia. TEL 61-2-92676900, FAX 61-2-92675200, sydney@cityscope.com.au. Ed. Neil Speirs.

333.33 AUS
SPRING HILL CITYSCOPE. Text in English. 1990. 4/yr. looseleaf. AUD 1,350; AUD 1,980 combined subscription (print & CD-ROM eds.) (effective 2008). adv. maps. **Document type:** *Abstract/Index.*
Description: Contains a complete property index of all buildings within the commercial centers of Spring Hill, Fortitude Valley and Coronation Drive, adjoining Brisbane city. Includes descriptions, historical information, developments, ownership, prices, sales histories, exact boundaries, and more.
Related titles: CD-ROM ed.: AUD 1,510 (effective 2008).
Published by: Cityscope Publications Pty. Ltd., Unit 2A, 19 Cotton St, PO Box 574, Nerang, QLD 4211, Australia. TEL 61-7-55964799, FAX 61-7-55963408, qld@cityscope.com.au. Ed. Neil Speirs.

333.33021 CAN ISSN 1912-2357
STATISTICAL REPORT FOR REAL ESTATE AGENTS. SAGUENAY METROPOLITAN AREA. Text in English. 200?. q. **Document type:** *Bulletin, Trade.*
Media: Online - full text.
Published by: Canada Mortgage and Housing Corporation/Societe Canadienne d'Hypotheques et de Logement, 700 Montreal Rd, Ottawa, ON K1A 0P7, Canada. TEL 613-748-2000, FAX 613-748-2098, chic@cmhc-schl.gc.ca, http://www.cmhc.ca.

333.33021 CAN ISSN 1912-2373
STATISTICAL REPORT FOR REAL ESTATE AGENTS. TROIS-RIVIERES CENSUS METROPOLITAN AREA. SHAWINIGAN CENSUS AGGLOMERATION. Text in English. 200?. q. **Document type:** *Report, Trade.*
Media: Online - full text.
Published by: Canada Mortgage and Housing Corporation/Societe Canadienne d'Hypotheques et de Logement, 700 Montreal Rd, Ottawa, ON K1A 0P7, Canada. TEL 613-748-2000, FAX 613-748-2098, chic@cmhc-schl.gc.ca, http://www.cmhc.ca.

SVENSK FASTIGHETSINDIKATOR; fastighetsaegarens aarsbok. *see* REAL ESTATE

333.33 AUS
SYDNEY CITYSCOPE. Text in English. 1973. 4/yr. looseleaf. AUD 2,385; AUD 3,310 combined subscription (print & CD-ROM eds.) (effective 2008). charts; illus.; maps. **Document type:** *Abstract/Index.*
Description: Contains complete property index of all commercial buildings within the Sydney Central Business District. Includes descriptions, historical information, developments, ownership, prices, sales histories, exact boundaries, and more.
Related titles: CD-ROM ed.: AUD 2,665 (effective 2008).
Published by: Cityscope Publications Pty. Ltd., Level 1, 249 Pitt St, PO Box Q281, Sydney, NSW 1230, Australia. TEL 61-2-92676900, FAX 61-2-92675200, sydney@cityscope.com.au. Ed. Neil Speirs.

333.33 AUS
SYDNEY CITYSCOPE UNIT REPORT. Text in English. 1989. 4/yr. adv. maps. **Document type:** *Abstract/Index.* **Description:** Contains a complete property index of all residential apartments within the Sydney Central Business District. Includes descriptions, historical information, developments, ownership, prices, sales histories, exact boundaries, and more.
Related titles: CD-ROM ed.
Published by: Cityscope Publications Pty. Ltd., Level 1, 249 Pitt St, PO Box Q281, Sydney, NSW 1230, Australia. TEL 61-2-92676900, FAX 61-2-92675200, http://www.cityscope.com.au. Ed. Neil Speirs.

REAL ESTATE—Computer Applications

333.33 USA ISSN 1521-5512
REAL ESTATE SOFTWARE GUIDE. Text in English. 1995. a. USD 4 domestic; USD 10 foreign (effective 2003). software rev. tr.lit. index. back issues avail. **Document type:** *Directory, Trade.* **Description:** Descriptions and reviews of software applications for realtors, investors, property managers, developers, attorneys, loan agents, appraisers, and anyone involved in real estate.
Related titles: Online - full text ed.
Published by: (Sherman & Company), Z-Law Software, Inc., PO Box 40602, Providence, RI 02940-0602. TEL 401-273-5588, 800-526-5588, FAX 401-421-5334. Ed., R&P Gary L Sherman TEL 401-331-3002. Pub. William H Sherman. Circ: 63,000 (paid).

333.330285 USA ISSN 1559-6249
REAL ESTATE TECHNOLOGY NEWS; the business journal of real estate technology and data. Abbreviated title: R E T N. Text in English. 2003. s-m. USD 297 (effective 2008). adv. back issues avail. **Document type:** *Journal, Trade.* **Description:** Designed for professionals whose livelihood depends upon keeping pace with state-of-the-art mortgage technology and the real estate data that powers these critical valuation and collateral risk systems.
Related titles: Online - full text ed.: ISSN 1934-659X.
Published by: October Research Corporation, PO Box 370, Richfield, OH 44286. TEL 330-659-6101, 877-662-8623, FAX 330-659-6102, http://www.octoberresearch.com. Eds. Jeremy Yohe TEL 330-659-6101 ext 6124, Matthew Smith TEL 330-659-6101 ext 6144.

RELIGIONS AND THEOLOGY

see also RELIGIONS AND THEOLOGY—Buddhist ; RELIGIONS AND THEOLOGY—Eastern Orthodox ; RELIGIONS AND THEOLOGY—Hindu ; RELIGIONS AND THEOLOGY—Islamic ; RELIGIONS AND THEOLOGY—Judaic ; RELIGIONS AND THEOLOGY—Other Denominations And Sects ; RELIGIONS AND THEOLOGY—Protestant ; RELIGIONS AND THEOLOGY—Roman Catholic

200 KEN
A A C C BULLETIN. Text in English, French. 1983. q. KES 36, USD 2.10. adv. bk.rev. **Document type:** *Bulletin.*
Formed by the 1983 merger of: A A C C Quarterly Bulletin; A A C C Newsletter
Indexed: HRIR.
Published by: All Africa Conference of Churches, Westlands, PO Box 14205, Nairobi, Kenya. TEL 254-2-441483, FAX 254-2-443241, TELEX 22175 AACC KE. Ed. Maxime V Rafransoa. Circ: 1,000.

200.71 USA ISSN 0277-1071
A A R ACADEMY SERIES. Text in English. 1974. irreg., latest 2008. price varies. back issues avail. **Document type:** *Monographic series, Trade.* **Description:** Monographs on a wide range of subjects within the academic study of religion.
Formerly (until 1981): A A R Dissertation Series (0145-272X)
Published by: American Academy of Religion, 825 Houston Mill Rd NE, Ste 300, Atlanta, GA 30329. TEL 404-727-3049, FAX 404-727-7959, aar@aarweb.org. Ed. Kimberly Rae Connor TEL 415-422-2869.

A C D A BULLETIN. *see* LIBRARY AND INFORMATION SCIENCES

230 GBR ISSN 2044-8635
A C E DISCUSSION PAPERS. Text in English. 19??. irreg. free to members (effective 2010). back issues avail. **Document type:** *Monographic series, Trade.*
Former titles (until 2009): Association of Christian Economists. Journal (0956-3067); (until 1989): A C E Journal
Published by: Association of Christian Economists, c/o Shirley Dex, Treasurer, Institute of Education, 20 Bedford Way, London, WC1H OAL, United Kingdom. S.Dex@ioe.ac.uk. Ed. Ian Smith.

200 USA
A C P NEWSLOG. Text in English. 1960; N.S. q. free to members (effective 2008). **Document type:** *Newsletter, Consumer.* **Description:** Covers association news, awards, management features, and member publication information.
Published by: Associated Church Press, P O Box 621001, Oviedo, FL 32762-1001. TEL 407-341-6615, FAX 407-386-3236, contactacp@aol.com, http://www.theacp.org. Ed. Joe Roos. Circ: 700.

230 GBR ISSN 0968-6045
A C T. Text in English. 1970. irreg. (1-2/yr.), latest no.24, 1985. **Document type:** *Monographic series, Consumer.* **Description:** Studies radical Christian discipleship, community living, Bible study.
Published by: Ashram Community Trust, 178 Abbeyfield Rd, Sheffield, S Yorks S4 7AY, United Kingdom. ashramcommunity@hotmail.com, http://www.ashram.org.uk/. Ed. Rev. John Vincent. Circ: 500.

A C W R NEWS. *see* LIBRARY AND INFORMATION SCIENCES

200 AUS ISSN 1031-8453
A.D. 2000; a journal of religious opinion. Variant title: A.D. Two Thousand. Text in English. 1988 (Apr.). 11/yr. AUD 50 combined subscription domestic (print & online eds.); AUD 65 combined subscription in New Zealand (print & online eds.); AUD 70 combined subscription in Asia & the Pacific (print & online eds.); AUD 75 combined subscription elsewhere (print & online eds.) (effective 2009). adv. bk.rev.; film rev. 20 p./no.; back issues avail. **Document type:** *Journal, Academic/Scholarly.* **Description:** Designed to help in reconstructing and consolidating a new culture of life and orthodox Christian faith in Australia.
Related titles: Online - full text ed.
Published by: Freedom Publishing Co., 582 Queensberry St, North Melbourne, VIC 3051, Australia. TEL 61-3-93265757, FAX 61-3-93282877. Ed., Adv. contact Michael Gilchrist. **Subscr. to:** PO Box 186, North Melbourne, VIC 3051, Australia. subs@ad2000.com.au.

200 USA ISSN 0300-7022
BL1
A D R I S NEWSLETTER. Text in English. 1971-1992; resumed 1995. q. free. bk.rev. abstr.; bibl. index. **Document type:** *Newsletter.* **Description:** Deals with religion and computer technology issues.
Indexed: CERDIC, RI-1, RI-2.
Published by: Association for the Development of Religious Information Services, PO Box 210735, Nashville, TN 37221-0735. TEL 615-662-5189, FAX 615-662-5251. Ed. Edward W Dodds. Circ: 125 (paid).

200 ITA ISSN 1825-893X
A E C. (Amicizia Ebraico-Cristiana) Text in Italian. 1951. q. free. bk.rev. bibl. **Document type:** *Magazine, Consumer.*
Former titles (until 2002): Amicizia Ebraico-Cristiana (1594-2465); (until 1989): Amicizia Ebraico-Cristiana di Firenze. Bollettino (1594-2457); (until 1965): Amicizia Ebraico-Cristiana (1128-1669)
Published by: Amicizia Ebraico-Cristiana di Firenze, Casella Postale 282, Florence, FI 50100, Italy. Circ: 500.

A F S NEWSLETTER. *see* PHILOSOPHY

266 276 USA ISSN 0884-6316
A I M INTERNATIONAL. (Africa Inland Mission) Text in English. 1896. q. free. bk.rev. illus. **Document type:** *Newsletter, Trade.* **Description:** Covers the mission's ministries, its personnel and the national church through which it serves.
Former titles: Inland Africa (0020-1464); (until 1916): Hearing and Doing
Related titles: Microfilm ed.
Published by: Africa Inland Mission International, PO Box 178, Pearl River, NY 10965. TEL 914-735-4014, FAX 914-735-1814. Ed., R&P Andy Hernberger. Pub. Ted Barnett. Circ: 30,000 (controlled).

230 AUS ISSN 1030-617X
A J L. (Australian Journal of Liturgy) Text in English. 1987. s-a. AUD 20; free to members (effective 2008). bk.rev. index. back issues avail. **Document type:** *Journal, Academic/Scholarly.* **Description:** Promotes the study of Christian liturgy at a scholarly level. Provides comments and information on liturgical matters with special reference to Australia.
Related titles: CD-ROM ed.; Online - full text ed.
Published by: Australian Academy of Liturgy, c/o Mrs. Elizabeth Harrington, Sec., C/- St Bernardine's Parish, 25 Verguide Rd, GPO Box 282, Brisbane, QLD 4001, Australia. TEL 61-7-33369442, FAX 61-7-32211705, jfh18111976@yahoo.com.au. Ed. Inari Thiel. Circ: 250.

266 USA ISSN 1545-6668
A M F NEWS. (American Missionary Fellowship) Text in English. 1974. triennial.
Published by: American Missionary Fellowship, P. O. Box 370, Villanova, PA 19085. TEL 610-527-4439, FAX 610-527-4720, http://www.americanmissionary.org. Ed. Holly M. Wismer.

200 USA ISSN 1059-7255
A M S STUDIES IN RELIGIOUS TRADITION. (Abrahams Magazine Service) Text in English. 1995. irreg., latest vol.2, 1994. **Document type:** *Monographic series, Academic/Scholarly.*
Published by: (Abrahams Magazine Service), A M S Press, Inc., Brooklyn Navy Yard, 63 Flushing Ave, Bldg 292, Unit #221, Brooklyn, NY 11205. TEL 718-875-8100, FAX 718-875-3800, editorial@amspressinc.com, queries@amspressinc.com, http://www.amspressinc.com.

200 USA
A P C E-NEWS. Text in English. 1998. 8/yr. free (effective 2009). back issues avail. **Document type:** *Newsletter, Trade.* **Description:** Designed to let members know what is current in chaplaincy and what the association is doing at national and state levels.
Media: Online - full text.
Published by: Association of Professional Chaplains, 1701 E Woodfield Rd, Ste 760, Schaumburg, IL 60173. TEL 847-240-1014, FAX 847-240-1015, info@professionalchaplains.org. Ed. Rita Kaufman.

200 KEN
A P S BULLETIN; a pan-African news and features service. (All Africa Press Service) Text in English. 1979. w. KES 600, USD 75. bk.rev. **Document type:** *Bulletin.* **Description:** Covers church and secular events with integrity, giving news an African perspective. Includes the continent's leading news and in-depth feature articles that probe behind the headlines in religion, socioeconomics, culture, political development, and environmental issues.
Indexed: E-psyche.
Published by: African Church Information Service, PO Box 14205, Nairobi, Kenya. TEL 254-2-44215, FAX 254-2-742352, TELEX 22175 NAIROBI KE. Circ: 350.

A S C A YEARBOOK. (Amsterdam School for Cultural Analysis) *see* PHILOSOPHY

200 USA
A T L A MONOGRAPH SERIES. Text in English. 1972. irreg., latest vol.48, 2002. price varies. back issues avail. **Document type:** *Monographic series, Trade.*
Published by: (American Theological Library Association), Scarecrow Press, Inc. (Subsidiary of: Rowman & Littlefield Publishers, Inc.), 4501 Forbes Blvd, Ste 200, Lanham, MD 20706. TEL 301-459-3366, 800-462-6420, FAX 301-429-5748, 800-338-4550, custserv@rowman.com. Ed. Kenneth E Rowe. Pub. Mr. Edward Kurdyla TEL 301-459-3366 ext 5604. R&P Clare Cox TEL 212-529-3888 ext 308.

A T L A RELIGION DATABASE. *see* RELIGIONS AND THEOLOGY—Abstracting, Bibliographies, Statistics

200 DNK ISSN 1603-015X
AABNE DOERE. Text in Danish. 2002. 11/yr. free. back issues avail. **Document type:** *Magazine, Consumer.*
Related titles: Online - full text ed.
Address: PO Box 1062, Holstebro, 7500, Denmark. TEL 45-97-407781, FAX 45-97-407783, denmark@opendoors.org. Ed. Joern Blohm Knudsen. Circ: 8,000.

AAN DE HAND. *see* EDUCATION

274.81 NOR ISSN 0400-227X
BX8037
AARBOK FOR DEN NORSKE KIRKE. Text in Norwegian. 1921. a. NOK 235 (effective 2011). adv. stat. index. **Document type:** *Report, Consumer.* **Description:** Events within the Church of Norway, with a full account of the clerical districts and church organizations and institutions.
Supersedes in part (in 1980): Norvegia Sacra (0801-7433)
—CCC.
Published by: Den Norske Kirke, Kirkeraadet/Church of Norway, PO Box 799, Sentrum, Oslo, 0106, Norway. TEL 47-23-081200, post.kirkeradet@kirken.no, http://www.kirken.no.

220 CHE ISSN 0567-5022
ABHANDLUNGEN ZUR THEOLOGIE DES ALTEN UND NEUEN TESTAMENTS. Text in German. 1944. irreg., latest vol.92, 2010. price varies. **Document type:** *Monographic series, Academic/Scholarly.*
Published by: Theologischer Verlag Zurich, Badenerstr 73, Zurich, 8026, Switzerland. TEL 41-44-2993355, FAX 41-44-2993358, tvz@ref.ch.

252 USA ISSN 1938-2235
BV4315
THE ABINGDON CHILDREN'S SERMON LIBRARY. Text in English. 2005. irreg., latest vol.3, 2008. back issues avail. **Document type:** *Handbook/Manual/Guide, Consumer.* **Description:** Offers preachers a ready resource of biblical-based children's sermons, which can be adapted for various age groups.
Published by: Abingdon Press, 201 Eighth Ave S, PO Box 801, Nashville, TN 37202. TEL 800-251-3320, FAX 800-836-7802, orders@abingdonpress.com. Ed. Brant D Baker.

ACADEMIA; Zeitschrift fuer Politik und Kultur. *see* LITERARY AND POLITICAL REVIEWS

220 NLD ISSN 1570-1980
➤ **ACADEMIA BIBLICA.** Text in English. 1972. irreg., latest vol.28, 2008. price varies. **Document type:** *Monographic series.*
Formerly (until 2003): Society of Biblical Literature. Disseration Series (0145-2770)
Indexed: IZBG.
Published by: (Society of Biblical Literature USA), Brill, PO Box 9000, Leiden, 2300 PA, Netherlands. TEL 31-71-5353500, FAX 31-71-5317532, cs@brill.nl.

➤ **ACADEMY OF SPIRITUALITY AND PARANORMAL STUDIES. PROCEEDINGS.** *see* PARAPSYCHOLOGY AND OCCULTISM

200 USA ISSN 1557-4326
ACCESS LEADER GUIDE. Text in English. 2000. q. price varies. back issues avail. **Document type:** *Magazine, Consumer.*
Formerly (until 2006): Family Bible Study. Access Leader Guide (1526-5218)
Published by: LifeWay Christian Resources, 1 Lifeway Plz, Nashville, TN 37234. TEL 615-251-2000, 800-458-2772, FAX 615-251-5933, customerservice@lifeway.com, http://www.lifeway.com.

200 USA ISSN 1557-3869
ACCESS LEADER PACK. Text in English. 2000. q. price varies. back issues avail. **Document type:** *Magazine, Consumer.*
Formerly (until 2006): Family Bible Study. Access Leader Pack (1526-8411)
Published by: LifeWay Christian Resources, 1 Lifeway Plz, Nashville, TN 37234. TEL 615-251-2000, 800-458-2772, FAX 615-251-5933, customerservice@lifeway.com, http://www.lifeway.com.

ACCION; revista paraguaya de reflexion y dialogo. *see* SOCIAL SCIENCES: COMPREHENSIVE WORKS

249 USA ISSN 0001-5083
ACT. Text in English. 1947. bi-m. looseleaf. USD 8 domestic; USD 10 foreign (effective 2000). bk.rev. **Document type:** *Newsletter.* **Description:** Covers topics of importance to families and has a Christian and social justice orientation.
Indexed: AmHI.
Published by: Christian Family Movement, 314 Sixth St, Rm 202, Box 272, Ames, IA 50010. TEL 515-232-7432, FAX 515-232-7432. Ed. Kathleen Miller. R&P Kay Aitchison. Circ: 2,500.

400 SVN ISSN 0351-2789
BX1520.S678
ACTA ECCLESIASTICA SLOVENIAE. Text in Slovenian. 1979. a.
Indexed: A01, HistAb, RILM.
Published by: Univerza v Ljubljani, Teoloska Fakultet, Poljanska 4, p p 2007, Ljubljana, 1000, Slovenia. TEL 386-1-4345810.

200 DNK ISSN 0106-0945
AS281
ACTA JUTLANDICA. TEOLOGISK SERIE/ACTA JUTLANDICA. THEOLOGY SERIES. Variant title: Teologisk Serie. Text in Multiple languages. 1935. irreg. price varies. back issues avail. **Document type:** *Monographic series, Academic/Scholarly.*
Related titles: ◆ Series of: Acta Jutlandica. ISSN 0065-1354.
Published by: (Det Laerde Selskab i Aarhus), Aarhus Universitetsforlag/ Aarhus University Press, Langelandsgade 177, Aarhus N, 8200, Denmark. TEL 45-89-425370, FAX 45-89-425380, unipress@au.dk.

200 NOR ISSN 1502-010X
ACTA THEOLOGICA. Text in Norwegian. 2000. irreg. **Document type:** *Monographic series, Academic/Scholarly.*
Published by: (Universitetet i Oslo, Teologiske Fakultet/University of Oslo, Faculty of Theology), Unipub Forlag AS, Kristan Ottosens Hus, PO Box 33, Blindern, Oslo, 0313, Norway. TEL 47-22-853300, FAX 47-22-853039, post@unipub.no, http://www.unipub.no.

200 ZAF ISSN 1015-8758
➤ **ACTA THEOLOGICA.** Text in English, Afrikaans; Summaries in English. 1980. 2/yr. bk.rev. abstr. back issues avail. **Document type:** *Journal, Academic/Scholarly.* **Description:** Publishes research articles on religion and theology intended for theologians, ministers and pastors.
Formerly (until 1989): Fax Teologica (1013-8072)
Related titles: Online - full text ed.: free (effective 2011).
Indexed: A01, A20, ArtHuCI, ISAP, IZBG, R&TA, SCOPUS, W07.
Published by: University of the Free State, Faculty of Theology/ Universiteit van die Vrystaat, Publications Office, Box 301, Bloemfontein, 9300, South Africa. TEL 27-51-4012351, FAX 27-51-4489203. Ed. Hermie Van Zyl.

200 001.3 SWE ISSN 0459-9969
ACTA UNIVERSITATIS LUNDENSIS. SECTIO 1. THEOLOGICA, JURIDICA, HUMANIORA. Text in Swedish. 1965. irreg.
Indexed: P30, PCI.
—INIST.
Published by: Almqvist & Wiksell International, Gamla Brogatan 26, Stockholm, 11285, Sweden.

ACTION NEWSLETTER. *see* COMMUNICATIONS

231.7652 USA ISSN 1094-8562
ACTS & FACTS. Text in English. 1972. m. free (effective 2011). bk.rev. 32 p./no.; back issues avail. **Document type:** *Magazine, Consumer.* **Description:** Contains articles and information of current interest dealing with creation, evolution, and related topics.
Formerly (until 1976): I C R Acts & Facts (0196-8068)
Related titles: Online - full text ed.
Indexed: CERDIC.
Published by: Institute for Creation Research, 1806 Royal Ln, PO Box 59029, Dallas, TX 75229. TEL 800-628-7640, subscriptions@icr.org.

ACTS OF WOMEN OF POWER. *see* WOMEN'S INTERESTS

ACTUALIDAD BIBLIOGRAFICA DE FILOSOFIA Y TEOLOGIA; selecciones de libros. *see* RELIGIONS AND THEOLOGY—Abstracting, Bibliographies, Statistics

220 CAN ISSN 1184-7204
ACTUALITES BIBLIQUES. Text in English. 1976. s-a. free. **Document type:** *Newsletter.*
Former titles (until 1990): Bulletin de Nouvelles Bibliques (0834-1842); (until 1984): Nouvelles Bibliques (0225-0489)
Related titles: ◆ English ed.: Our Bible Matters. ISSN 1486-5327.
Published by: Societe Biblique Canadienne/Canadian Bible Society, 10 Carnforth Rd, Toronto, ON M4A 2S4, Canada. TEL 416-757-4171, FAX 416-757-3376. Circ: 15,000.

230 340 DEU ISSN 0946-9176
ADNOTATIONES IN IUS CANONICUM. Text in German. 1995. irreg., latest vol.49, 2010. price varies. **Document type:** *Monographic series, Academic/Scholarly.*
Published by: Peter Lang GmbH (Subsidiary of: Peter Lang Publishing Group), Eschborner Landstr 42-50, Frankfurt Am Main, 60489, Germany. TEL 49-69-7807050, FAX 49-69-78070550, zentrale.frankfurt@peterlang.com. Eds. Elmar Guethoff, Karl-Heinz Selge.

230 USA ISSN 1940-3135
THE ADVENT TRUTH. Text in English. 2007. m. **Document type:** *Magazine, Consumer.* **Description:** Aims to help the Christians to have a deeper understanding of God's word, thus strengthening their relationship with their creator, redeemer and savior.
Published by: Advent Truth Ministries, PO Box 307, Forsyth, GA 31029. TEL 478-994-6110.

230 USA ISSN 1550-7378
ADVENTIST THEOLOGICAL SOCIETY. JOURNAL. Text in English. 1990. 2/yr. **Document type:** *Journal, Academic/Scholarly.*
Indexed: A21, GSS&RPL, OTA, R&TA, RI-1.
Published by: A T S Publications, P O Box 86, Berrien Springs, MI 49104.

268 USA ISSN 2151-0288
ADVENTURE GUIDE. Text in English. 2004. q. USD 3.99 per issue (effective 2009). **Document type:** *Magazine, Trade.* **Description:** Provides younger elementary students (grades 1-3) their very own Bible study guide, with exciting activities and features.
Formerly (until 2009): Explorer's Guide. Level 1 (1558-5492)
Published by: Randall House, 114 Bush Rd, PO Box 17306, Nashville, TN 37217. TEL 615-361-1221, 800-877-7030, FAX 615-367-0535.

268 USA ISSN 2151-0326
ADVENTURE KIDS DISCOVERY SHEETS FOR EARLY ELEMENTARY. Text in English. 2004. q. USD 3.99 per issue (effective 2009). **Document type:** *Guide, Trade.* **Description:** Contains thought-provoking in-class activities and study questions.
Formerly (until 2009): Discovery Sheets 1 for Early Elementary (1558-0725)
Published by: Randall House, 114 Bush Rd, PO Box 17306, Nashville, TN 37217. TEL 615-361-1221, 800-877-7030, FAX 615-367-0535.

268 USA ISSN 2151-0318
ADVENTURE KIDS TEACHING GUIDE FOR EARLY ELEMENTARY. Text in English. 2004. q. USD 6.99 per issue (effective 2009). **Document type:** *Guide, Trade.* **Description:** Includes teacher tips, reviews and reinforcement activities, bible memory resources and assistance (preparation checklist, devotionals, decor ideas).
Formerly (until 2009): CLEAR Teaching for Early Elementary (1558-0717)
Published by: Randall House, 114 Bush Rd, PO Box 17306, Nashville, TN 37217. TEL 615-361-1221, 800-877-7030, FAX 615-367-0535.

270 CHE ISSN 0522-4403
AENEAS-SILVIUS-STIFTUNG AN DER UNIVERSITAET BASEL. VORTRAEGE. Text in German. 1962. irreg., latest vol.45, 2009. price varies. **Document type:** *Monographic series, Academic/Scholarly.*
Published by: (Aeneas-Silvius-Stiftung an der Universitaet Basel), Schwabe und Co. AG, Steinentorstr 13, Basel, 4010, Switzerland. TEL 41-61-2789565, FAX 41-61-2789566, verlag@schwabe.ch, http://www.schwabe.ch.

230 USA ISSN 1088-6923
BX7990.L63
AFFIRMATION & CRITIQUE. Text in English. 1996. s-a. USD 20 domestic; USD 35 foreign (effective 2002).
Indexed: A21, RI-1.
Published by: Living Stream Ministry, PO Box 2121, Anaheim, CA 92814. TEL 714-991-4681, FAX 714-236-6054, books@lsm.org, http://www.lsm.org. Ed. Ron Kangas.

200 KEN
AFRICAN CHALLENGE BOOK SERIES. Text in English, French. q.
Former titles (until 1989): A A C C Magazine (1010-1071); (until 1982): A A C C Newsletter (1017-6977)
Indexed: HRIR.
Published by: All Africa Conference of Churches, Westlands, PO Box 14205, Nairobi, Kenya. TEL 254-2-441483, FAX 254-2-443241.

200 KEN
AFRICAN CHRISTIAN. Text in English. fortn. **Description:** Covers church news and developments in Africa.
Published by: African Church Information Service, PO Box 14205, Nairobi, Kenya. TEL 254-2-62974, TELEX 22175.

268 KEN
AFRIKA YA KESHO. Text in Swahili. 1961. m. adv. **Description:** A Christian magazine geared to older population, yet sold to the general public.
Formerly: Kesho (0023-0723)
Indexed: CERDIC.
Published by: (Africa Inland Church), Kesho Publications, PO Box 60, Kijabe, Kenya. Circ: 4,000.

266 NLD ISSN 1571-6635
AGAPE NIEUWS. Text in Dutch. 2003. 2/yr. **Document type:** *Magazine, Consumer.*
Formerly (until 2007): Agape Nieuws (1571-6635)
Published by: Stichting Agape, Postbus 271, Doorn, 3940 AG, Netherlands. TEL 31-343-415741, FAX 31-343-414161, info@agape.nl, http://www.agape.nl.

200 UKR
AHENTSII RELIHIINOI INFORMATSII. Text in Ukrainian. m. USD 80 foreign (effective 2000).
Published by: Radio Voskresinnya, Ozarkevycha 4, Lvov, 79016, Ukraine. TEL 380-322-742303, FAX 380-322-970875, rr@rr.lviv.ua. **Dist. by:** East View Information Services, 10601 Wayzata Blvd, Minneapolis, MN 55305. TEL 952-252-1201, 800-477-1005, FAX 952-252-1202, info@eastview.com, http://www.eastview.com.

200 GRC ISSN 1106-3076
AKTINES/BEAM. Text in Greek. 1937. m. **Description:** Promotes Christian civilization.
Indexed: PCI.
Published by: Christian Union, Karytsi St, Athens, 105 61, Greece. TEL 30-1-3235023. Circ: 10,000.

▼ **ALEPH OMEGA;** journal of spiritual neuroscience. *see* MEDICAL SCIENCES—Psychiatry And Neurology

ALFA; Bibelleseplan for barn 10-13 ar. *see* CHILDREN AND YOUTH—About

200 RUS ISSN 0203-3488
BS410
➤ **AL'FA I OMEGA.** Text in Russian. 1994. q. RUR 35, USD 1.40 newsstand/cover. **Document type:** *Journal, Academic/Scholarly.* **Description:** Addresses issues in Orthodox Christian theology, Biblical studies, Church history, patristics and church culture.
Published by: Obshchestvo po Rasprostraneniyu Sviashchennogo Pisaniya v Rossii, Ul Gertsena 44, str 2, Moscow, 121854, Russian Federation. TEL 7-095-2840558, FAX 7-095-2911595. Ed. Marina Zhurinskaya. Circ: 2,500. **Dist. by:** East View Information Services, 10601 Wayzata Blvd, Minneapolis, MN 55305. TEL 952-252-1201, 800-477-1005, FAX 952-252-1202, info@eastview.com, http://www.eastview.com.

266 KEN
ALL AFRICA CONFERENCE OF CHURCHES. REFUGEE DEPARTMENT. PROGRESS REPORT. Text in English. irreg., latest 1974.
Published by: All Africa Conference of Churches, Refugee Department, Pioneer House, Government Rd., PO Box 20301, Nairobi, Kenya.

266 KEN
ALL AFRICA CONFERENCE OF CHURCHES. REFUGEE DEPARTMENT. PROJECT LIST. Text in English. irreg., latest 1977.
Published by: All Africa Conference of Churches, Refugee Department, Pioneer House, Government Rd., PO Box 20301, Nairobi, Kenya.

207.2 MEX ISSN 0002-628X
ALMAS. Text in Spanish. 1950. m. USD 5. illus. **Document type:** *Newspaper.* **Description:** Covers missionary work overseas.
Published by: (Misioneros de Guadalupe), Editora Escalante, Cordoba 17, Apdo. 24-550, Mexico City 7, DF, Mexico. TEL 525-5731337. Ed. Jose Chavez Calderon. Circ: 225,000.

224 CHE ISSN 1662-1689
DAS ALTE TESTAMENT DIALOG. Text in German. 2007. irreg. price varies. **Document type:** *Monographic series, Academic/Scholarly.*
Published by: Peter Lang AG (Subsidiary of: Peter Lang Publishing Group), Hochfeldstr 32, Postfach 746, Bern 9, 3000, Switzerland. TEL 41-31-3061717, FAX 41-31-3061727, info@peterlang.com. Eds. M Fieger, S Hodel-Hoenes.

ALTER ORIENT UND ALTES TESTAMENT; Veroeffentlichungen zur Kultur und Geschichte des Alten Orients und des Alten Testamnets. *see* HISTORY—History Of The Near East

260 AUS ISSN 1441-9106
THE ALTERNATIVE (ONLINE). Text in English. 1995. q.
Formerly (until 1999): The Alternative (Print) (1323-4501)
Media: Online - full text.
Published by: Pastornet, PO Box 5148, Chisholm, ACT 2905, Australia. manager@pastornet.net.au, http://www.pastornet.net.au.

▼ **ALTERNATIVE SPIRITUALITY AND RELIGION REVIEW.** *see* NEW AGE PUBLICATIONS

200 ITA ISSN 2036-3729
ALTI STUDI DI STORIA DELLE RELIGIONI. Text in Multiple languages. 2007. irreg. **Document type:** *Monographic series, Academic/Scholarly.*
Published by: Societa Editrice Fiorentina, Via Aretina 298, Florence, 50136, Italy. TEL 39-055-5532924, FAX 39-055-5532085, redazione@sefeditrice.it, http://www.sefeditrice.it.

230 DEU ISSN 0341-2563
ALTOETTINGER LIEBFRAUENBOTE. Text in German. 1901. w. (Sun.). EUR 15.75 per quarter; EUR 1.25 newsstand/cover (effective 2008). adv. **Document type:** *Newspaper, Consumer.*
Published by: Altoettinger Liebfrauenbote Verlagsgesellschaft mbH, Neuoettingerstr 5, Altoetting, 84503, Germany. TEL 49-8671-12005, FAX 49-8671-13630, vertrieb@liebfrauenbote.de. Ed. Wolfgang Terhoerst. adv.: B&W page EUR 1,344, color page EUR 2,624; trim 224 x 320. Circ: 19,917 (controlled).

220 USA
AMAZING GRACE GOSPELLETTER. Text in English. 1997. m. **Document type:** *Newsletter, Consumer.*
Published by: Amazing Grace Publishing, 1401 Newcastle Ave., Westchester, IL 60154-3612. TEL 708-223-0070, FAX 708-223-0071, agrace@amazinggrace.org. Ed., R&P Rev. John Doonan. Adv. contact Barb Karcz.

200 USA
AMERICAN ACADEMY OF RELIGION. ANNUAL MEETING. Text in English. 19??. a. **Document type:** *Proceedings, Trade.* **Description:** Discusses events at the annual meeting of the American Academy of Religion and Society of Biblical Literature.
Published by: American Academy of Religion, 825 Houston Mill Rd NE, Ste 300, Atlanta, GA 30329. TEL 404-727-3049, FAX 404-727-7959, aar@aarweb.org.

200 USA ISSN 0002-7189
BV1460 .N23
➤ **AMERICAN ACADEMY OF RELIGION. JOURNAL.** Abbreviated title: J A A R. Text in English. 1933. q. GBP 140 in United Kingdom to institutions; EUR 199 in Europe to institutions; USD 209 in US & Canada to institutions; GBP 140 elsewhere to institutions; GBP 152 combined subscription in United Kingdom to institutions (print & online eds.); EUR 217 combined subscription in Europe to institutions (print & online eds.); USD 228 combined subscription in US & Canada to institutions (print & online eds.); GBP 152 combined subscription elsewhere to institutions (print & online eds.) (effective 2012). adv. bk.rev. bibl.; illus. index, cum.index: 1933-1979. back issues avail.; reprint service avail. from PSC. **Document type:** *Journal, Academic/Scholarly.* **Description:** Contains scholarly articles that cover the full range of world religious traditions alongwith provocative studies of the methodologies by which these traditions are explored.
Former titles (until 1967): Journal of Bible and Religion (0885-2758); (until 1937): National Association of Biblical Instructors. Journal (1549-9804); Which incorporated in part: Christian Education (1550-574X); Which was formerly (until 1919): American College. Bulletin
Related titles: Microfiche ed.; Microform ed.: (from PQC); Online - full text ed.: ISSN 1477-4585. 2002. GBP 127 in United Kingdom to institutions; EUR 181 in Europe to institutions; USD 190 in US & Canada to institutions; GBP 127 elsewhere to institutions (effective 2012) (from IngentaConnect).
Indexed: A01, A02, A03, A08, A20, A21, A22, A25, A26, ASCA, AmH&L, AmHI, ArtHuCI, B04, B05, B14, BAS, BRD, BRI, BrHuml, CA, CBRI, CERDIC, CurCont, DIP, E01, E08, FR, G08, H07, H08, H09, H10, H14, HAb, HistAb, Humlnd, I05, IBR, IBZ, M01, M02, MEA&I, MLA-IB, OTA, P02, P10, P30, P42, P48, P53, P54, PCI, PQC, PSA, Philind, R&TA, R05, RI-1, RI-2, RILM, S02, S03, S08, S09, SCOPUS, SSA, SociolAb, T02, W03, W07, W09.
—BLDSC (4683.740000), IE, Infotrieve, Ingenta, INIST. **CCC.**

Published by: (American Academy of Religion), Oxford University Press (Subsidiary of: Oxford University Press), 2001 Evans Rd, Cary, NC 27513. TEL 919-677-0977, FAX 919-677-1303, http://www.oxfordjournals.org. Ed. Charles Mathewes TEL 434-924-1398. Adv. contact Aislinn Jones TEL 404-727-8132. B&W page USD 650; 105 x 190. Circ: 11,000 (paid).

220 USA ISSN 0006-0801
BV2370
AMERICAN BIBLE SOCIETY RECORD. Text in English. 1818. 3/yr. adv. illus. index. 20 p./no.; back issues avail. **Document type:** *Magazine, Consumer.* **Description:** Contains news and articles concerning ABS' worldwide Bible mission.
Former titles (until 1970): Bible Society Record (1077-646X); (until 1843): American Bible Society. Extracts from the Correspondence (0276-1335); (until 1826): American Bible Society. Monthly Extracts from the Correspondence (0276-1327); (until 1821): American Bible Society. Quarterly Extracts
Related titles: Online - full text ed.: free (effective 2009).
Published by: American Bible Society, 1865 Broadway, New York, NY 10023. TEL 212-408-1200, FAX 212-408-1512, http://www.americanbible.org.

200 100 USA ISSN 0194-3448
BR1
➤ **AMERICAN JOURNAL OF THEOLOGY & PHILOSOPHY.** Abbreviated title: A J T P. Text in English. 1980. 3/yr. USD 110 combined subscription to institutions (print & online eds.) (effective 2012). adv. bk.rev. index. back issues avail. **Document type:** *Journal, Academic/Scholarly.* **Description:** Provides a forum for the discussion of issues in American theology and its dialogue with philosophy.
Related titles: Online - full text ed.: ISSN 2156-4795. USD 95 to institutions (effective 2012).
Indexed: A21, A22, E01, FR, H14, IBR, IBZ, P10, P28, P48, P53, P54, PCI, PQC, PhilInd, R&TA, RI-1, RI-2.
—BLDSC (0838.700000), IE, Ingenta, INIST.
Published by: (Highlands Institute for American Religious and Philosophical Thought), University of Illinois Press, 1325 S Oak St, Champaign, IL 61820. TEL 217-333-0950, FAX 217-244-8082, uipress@uillinois.edu. Ed. Michael L Raposa. Adv. contact Jeff McArdle TEL 217-244-0381. page USD 200.

➤ **AMERICAN LEPROSY MISSIONS ANNUAL REPORT.** *see* MEDICAL SCIENCES—Communicable Diseases

200 USA ISSN 1080-5389
AMERICAN LIBERAL RELIGIOUS THOUGHT. Text in English. 1995. irreg., latest vol.10, 2010. price varies. **Document type:** *Monographic series, Academic/Scholarly.*
Published by: Peter Lang Publishing, Inc. (Subsidiary of: Peter Lang Publishing Group), 29 Broadway, New York, NY 10006. TEL 212-647-7700, 800-770-5264, FAX 212-647-7707, customerservice@plang.com.

238 USA ISSN 1942-2709
BR1
AMERICAN THEOLOGICAL INQUIRY. Text in English. 2008. s-a. free (effective 2011). **Document type:** *Journal, Academic/Scholarly.* **Description:** Provides a forum for scholars who affirm the historic Ecumenical Creeds of Christendom to discuss contemporary developments, ideas, commentaries, and insights pertaining to theology, church, philosophy, culture and history, toward reforming American Christianity.
Related titles: Online - full text ed.: ISSN 1941-7624. free (effective 2011).
Indexed: A01, A21.
Published by: Wipf & Stock Publishers, 199 W 8th Ave, Ste 3, Eugene, OR 97401. TEL 541-344-1528, FAX 541-344-1506, Info@wipfandstock.com, http://wipfandstock.com/. Ed. Gannon Murphy.

202 USA ISSN 0740-0446
AMERICAN UNIVERSITY STUDIES. SERIES 7. THEOLOGY AND RELIGION. Text in English. 1984. irreg., latest vol.302, 2010. price varies. back issues avail. **Document type:** *Monographic series, Academic/Scholarly.* **Description:** Studies the theology and history of Christianity and other religions throughout the world.
—BLDSC (0858.078100), IE, Ingenta.
Published by: Peter Lang Publishing, Inc. (Subsidiary of: Peter Lang Publishing Group), 29 Broadway, New York, NY 10006. TEL 212-647-7700, 212-647-7706, 800-770-5264, FAX 212-647-7707, customerservice@plang.com.

AMICO DELL'ARTE CRISTIANA. *see* ART

200 FRA ISSN 1242-1472
AMITIES SPIRITUELLES. Text in French. 1919. q. EUR 8.50 domestic; EUR 9.50 foreign; EUR 2.50 newsstand/cover (effective 2002). bk.rev. **Document type:** *Bulletin, Consumer.* **Description:** Objective is to shed light on issues in Christianity and spirituality.
Former titles (until 1950): Amities Spirituelles. Bulletin (1242-1464); (until 1928): Les Amities Spirituelles (0003-1909)
Published by: Association des Amities Spirituelles, 14 Rue Campo-Formio, Paris, 75013, France. TEL 33-9-72976251, http://www.amities-spirituelles.fr. Ed. Jacques Sardin. Circ: 1,200.

230 HKG
AMITY NEWS SERVICE. Text in English. 1992. m. USD 20 (effective 2000). back issues avail. **Document type:** *Journal, Consumer.*
Published by: The Amity Foundation Hong kong Ltd., 4 Jordan Rd, Kowloon, Hong Kong. Eds. Ian Groves, Katrin Fiedler.

200 SWE ISSN 1650-7215
AMOS; magasinet foer livsfraagor och kristen tro. Text in Swedish. 2001. 6/yr. SEK 150 (effective 2006). adv. **Document type:** *Magazine, Consumer.*
Related titles: Online - full text ed.
Published by: (Svenska Kyrkan/Church of Sweden), Svenska Kyrkans Press AB, Goetgatan 22A, PO Box 15412, Stockholm, 10465, Sweden. TEL 46-8-4622800, FAX 46-8-6445604, info@svkpress.com, http://www.svkpress.com. Eds. Brita Hall, Kristin Lindh, Dag Tuvelius TEL 46-8-4622801. Adv. contact Thomas Grahl TEL 46-8-4622831. Circ: 660,000 (controlled and free).

230 DEU ISSN 1867-6421
AMOSINTERNATIONAL; Internationale Zeitschrift fuer christliche Sozialethik. Text in German. 1988. q. EUR 49.80; EUR 39.80 to students; EUR 12.80 newsstand/cover (effective 2011). **Document type:** *Journal, Academic/Scholarly.*
Former titles (until 2008): Amos (1864-5313); (until 2006): Gesellschaft im Test (0935-8404)
Published by: Aschendorff Verlag GmbH & Co. KG, Soester Str 13, Muenster, 48135, Germany. TEL 49-251-6900, FAX 49-251-6904570, buchverlag@aschendorff.de, http://www.aschendorff-buchverlag.de. Eds. Detlef Herbers, Richard Geisen.

220.07 NLD ISSN 1567-4649
AMSTERDAMSE CAHIERS VOOR EXEGESE VAN DE BIJBEL EN ZIJN TRADITIES. Text in Dutch. 1980. irreg., latest vol.22, 2005. EUR 14 per issue (effective 2011). **Document type:** *Monographic series, Academic/Scholarly.*
Formerly (until 1999): Amsterdamse Cahiers voor Exegese en Bijbelse Theologie (0169-250X)
Indexed: OTA.
Published by: Shaker Publishing BV, Postbus 3167, Maastricht, 6202 ND, Netherlands. TEL 31-43-3500424, FAX 31-43-3255090, info@shaker.nl, http://www.shaker.nl/.

200 USA
ANAHATA NADA/SOUNDLESS SOUND. Text in English. 1974. q. USD 1. bk.rev. illus.
Published by: (Sri Chinmoy Centre), AUM Publications, 85 42 160th St, Jamaica, NY 11432. TEL 718-523-1166. Ed. David Burke. **Subscr. to:** PO Box 32433, Jamaica, NY 11431.

271.71 AUT ISSN 0253-1593
➤ **ANALECTA CARTUSIANA**; review for Carthusian history and spirituality. Text in Multiple languages. 1970. irreg., latest vol.154, 2000. bk.rev. back issues avail. **Document type:** *Academic/Scholarly.*
Indexed: MLA.
Published by: Universitaet Salzburg, Institut fuer Anglistik und Amerikanistik, Akademiestrasse 24, Salzburg, Sa 5020, Austria. TEL 43-6217-7084. Ed., Pub., R&P James Hogg. Circ: 300 (paid).

909 230 USA ISSN 1935-6854
ANALECTA GORGIANA. Text in English. 2006. irreg., latest 2010. price varies. back issues avail. **Document type:** *Monographic series, Academic/Scholarly.* **Description:** Contains collection of obscure but commonly cited writings on religion and history primarily focusing on Christianity, theology and Biblical and Christian history.
Published by: Gorgias Press LLC, 954 River Rd, Piscataway, NJ 08854. TEL 732-885-8900, FAX 732-885-8908, helpdesk@gorgiaspress.com, http://www.gorgiaspress.com/bookshop/default.aspx.

271 940 BEL ISSN 0517-6735
BX3901
ANALECTA PRAEMONSTRATENSIA. Text in Dutch, English, French, German, Latin. 1925. 2/yr. EUR 30.40 domestic; EUR 35.08 in Europe; EUR 37.18 elsewhere (effective 2003). bk.rev. cum.index: 1925-1967. **Document type:** *Journal, Academic/Scholarly.* **Description:** Publishes studies relating to the history of the Norbertine Order.
Indexed: BibInd, CERDIC, FR, IBR, IBZ, MLA-IB, PCI.
—IE, INIST.
Published by: Praemonstratensia V.z.w., Abdij der Norbertijnen, Abdijstraat 1, Averbode, 3271, Belgium. TEL 32-13-780440, FAX 32-13-780439.

230 ESP ISSN 0304-4300
BX806.C3
ANALECTA SACRA TARRACONENSIA. Text in Spanish. 1925. a. EUR 22 (effective 2009). back issues avail. **Document type:** *Monographic series, Academic/Scholarly.*
Related titles: Online - full text ed.
Indexed: FR, IBR, IBZ, MLA-IB, P09, P30, PCI, RILM.
—INIST.
Published by: Fundacion Balmesiana, Calle Duran y Bas, 11, Barcelona, 08002, Spain. TEL 34-93-3026840, FAX 34-93-3170498, info@balmesiana.org, http:/www.balmesiana.org/. Ed. Pedro Suner.

200 CHL ISSN 0717-4152
ANALES DE TEOLOGIA. Text in Spanish. 1998. s-a. back issues avail. **Document type:** *Journal, Academic/Scholarly.*
Published by: Universidad Catolica de la Santisima Concepcion, Instituto de Teologia, Alfonso de Ribera, 2850, Concepcion, Chile. TEL 56-41-2735669. Ed. Patricio Merino Beas.

ANCIENT JUDAISM AND EARLY CHRISTIANITY. *see* RELIGIONS AND THEOLOGY—Judaic

230.0071 220.93 USA ISSN 0003-2980
BR1
➤ **ANDREWS UNIVERSITY SEMINARY STUDIES.** Text in English, French, German. 1963. s-a. USD 24 to individuals; USD 42 to institutions (effective 2011). bk.rev. charts; illus. index. 160 p./no. 1 cols./p.; back issues avail. **Document type:** *Journal, Academic/Scholarly.* **Description:** Contains articles on biblical studies; biblical archaeology; historical and theological studies; and research on applied theology.
Indexed: A21, A22, CERDIC, IZBG, MEA&I, OTA, R&TA, RI-1, RI-2.
—BLDSC (0900.420000), IE, Ingenta.
Address: Theological Seminary N136, Berrien Springs, MI 49104. TEL 269-471-6023, FAX 269-471-6202. Ed. John W Reeve.

200 FRA ISSN 0751-6460
ANGE GARDIEN. Text in French. 1891. 6/yr. free. **Document type:** *Bulletin.*
Published by: Association de l'Ange Gardien, 21 montee St. Laurent, Lyon, 69005, France. TEL 33-4-78380272. Ed. Louis Chauffour. Circ: 5,300.

202.15 USA ISSN 1082-3107
ANGELS ON EARTH. Text in English. 1995. bi-m. USD 19.95 domestic; USD 21.95 in Canada; USD 25.95 elsewhere (effective 2011). adv. 74 p./no. 2 cols./p.; back issues avail.; reprints avail. **Document type:** *Magazine, Consumer.* **Description:** Presents inspirational, true stories of persons who selflessly helped strangers in a time of need to bring out the best in all of us.
Indexed: M02, T02.
Published by: Guideposts, PO Box 5814, Harlan, LA 51593. TEL 800-431-2344, atyourservice@guideposts.org. Ed. Colleen Hughes.

200 BEL ISSN 2031-5929
BX1751.2
ANNALI DI SCIENZE RELIGIOSE. Text in Multiple languages. 2008. a. EUR 84 combined subscription (print & online eds.) (effective 2012). **Document type:** *Journal, Academic/Scholarly.* **Description:** International journal of religious scholarship with articles written in Italian, English, French, German and Arabic.
Related titles: Online - full text ed.
Published by: (Universita Cattolica del Sacro Cuore ITA), Brepols Publishers, Begijnhof 67, Turnhout, 2300, Belgium. TEL 32-14-448020, FAX 32-14-428919, periodicals@brepols.net, http://www.brepols.net.

261 CAN
THE ANNALS OF SAINT ANNE DE BEAUPRE. Text in English. 1885. m.
Published by: Redemptorist Fathers, Box 1000, St. Anne de Beaupre, PQ G0A 3C0, Canada. Ed. Fr. Roch Achard. Circ: 45,000.

200 USA ISSN 1546-251X
BL80.2
ANNUAL EDITIONS: WORLD RELIGIONS. Text in English. 2002 (Aug.). a. USD 22.25 per issue (effective 2010). **Document type:** *Journal, Academic/Scholarly.* **Description:** Addresses the foundations of religion, alternative paths, and religion in the modern world -including Hinduism, Buddhism, Christianity, and Judaism.
Related titles: Online - full text ed.
Published by: McGraw-Hill, Contemporary Learning Series (Subsidiary of: McGraw-Hill Companies, Inc.), 1221 Ave of the Americas, New York, NY 10020. customer.service@mcgraw-hill.com, http://www.dushkin.com.

▼ **ANNUAL REVIEW OF THE SOCIOLOGY OF RELIGION.** *see* SOCIOLOGY

209 DEU ISSN 0003-5157
BV710
ANNUARIUM HISTORIAE CONCILIORUM; Internationale Zeitschrift fuer Konziliengeschichtsforschung. Text in English, French, German, Italian, Spanish. 1969. s-a. EUR 98 (effective 2009). adv. bk.rev. reprints avail. **Document type:** *Journal, Academic/Scholarly.*
Indexed: A22, CERDIC, DIP, FR, IBR, IBZ, PCI.
—IE, Infotrieve, INIST. **CCC.**
Published by: Verlag Ferdinand Schoeningh GmbH, Postfach 2540, Paderborn, 33055, Germany. TEL 49-5251-1275, FAX 49-5251-127860, info@schoeningh.de, http://www.schoeningh.de. Ed. Walter Brandmueller.

ANNUARIUM STATISTICUM ECCLESIAE/STATISTICAL YEARBOOK OF THE CHURCH/STATISTIQUE DE L'EGLISE. *see* RELIGIONS AND THEOLOGY—Abstracting, Bibliographies, Statistics

230 305.896 305.4 USA ISSN 1559-3754
ANOINTED MAGAZINE. Text in English. 2006. bi-m. USD 12 (effective 2006). adv. **Document type:** *Magazine, Consumer.* **Description:** Promotes Christian values in fashion, music, careers, and relationships geared for African American women.
Published by: Exodus Media Group, PO BOX 52545, Philadelphia, PA 19115. TEL 800-683-9184, FAX 215-988-9316, info@exodusmediagroup.com, http://www.exodusmediagroup.com/index.html. adv.: page USD 1,250;.

ANPERE; anthropological perspectives on religion. *see* ANTHROPOLOGY

200 DEU ISSN 0003-519X
DIE ANREGUNG (NETTETAL); Seelsorglicher Dienst in der Welt von heute. Text in German. 1948. m. bk.rev. **Document type:** *Bulletin.*
Published by: Steyler Verlag, Bahnhofstr 9, Nettetal, 41334, Germany. TEL 49-2157-1202-20, FAX 49-2157-1202-22.

267.6 DEU
ANRUF. Text in German. 1896. q. EUR 9.95; EUR 2 newsstand/cover (effective 2009). adv. bk.rev. illus. **Document type:** *Magazine, Consumer.*
Formerly (until 1967): Die Jugend-Hilfe
Published by: (Deutscher Verband der Jugenbuende fuer Entschiedenes Christentum e.V.), Born-Verlag, Leuschnerstr 74, Kassel, 34134, Germany. TEL 49-561-4095107, FAX 49-561-4095112, info.born@ec-jugend.de, http://www.born-buch.de. Ed. Thomas Peters. Adv. contact Claudia Siebert. B&W page EUR 640, color page EUR 832; trim 186 x 266. Circ: 11,000 (controlled).

248.83 DEU ISSN 0721-2291
BV970
ANSAETZE; ESG-Nachrichten. Text in German. 1953. 3/yr. EUR 13 (effective 2009). bk.rev. abstr. back issues avail. **Document type:** *Newsletter, Consumer.* **Description:** Provides information on the activities of the German Student Christian Movement.
Formerly (until 1981): E S G - Nachrichten (0012-7981)
Published by: Evangelische StudentInnengemeinde in der Bundesrepublik Deutschland, Otto-Brenner-Str 9, Hannover, 30159, Germany. TEL 49-511-12150, FAX 49-511-1215299, esg@bundes-esg.de. Ed. Joern Moeller. **Co-sponsor:** Bundesministerium fuer Familie, Senioren, Frauen und Jugend.

207.11 DEU ISSN 0003-5270
BR4
ANSTOESSE; Zeitschrift der evangelischen Akademie Hofgeismar. Text in German. 1954. q. EUR 25 membership (effective 2009). bk.rev. index. **Document type:** *Newsletter, Consumer.*
Published by: Evangelische Akademie Hofgeismar, Postfach 1205, Hofgeismar, 34362, Germany. TEL 49-5671-8810, FAX 49-5671-881154, ev.akademie.hofgeismar@ekkw.de, http://www.akademie-hofgeismar.de.

223.7652100 USA ISSN 1930-3289
ANSWERS (HEBRON); building a biblical worldview. Text in English. 2006. q. USD 24 domestic; USD 27 in Australia includes Canada; GBP 14 in Europe; USD 39 elsewhere; USD 29.99 combined subscription domestic (print & online eds.); USD 32.99 combined subscription in Australia includes Canada (print & online eds.); USD 44.99 combined subscription elsewhere (print & online eds.) (effective 2010). adv. back issues avail. **Document type:** *Magazine, Consumer.* **Description:** Guides readers with practical answers to help them confidently communicate the gospel and biblical authority.
Related titles: Online - full text ed.: ISSN 1930-3297. USD 18 (effective 2010).
Published by: Answers in Genesis, PO Box 510, Hebron, KY 41048. TEL 859-727-2222, 800-778-3390, FAX 859-727-2299. Ed. Rick Barry. Adv. contact Dan Stelzer.

R

230 USA ISSN 1937-9056
BS651
➤ **ANSWERS RESEARCH JOURNAL.** Abbreviated title: A R J. Text in English. 2008. a. free (effective 2010). back issues avail. **Document type:** *Journal, Academic/Scholarly.* **Description:** Brings out scientific and other relevant research from the perspective of the recent creation and the flood within a biblical framework.
Media: Online - full text.
Published by: Answers in Genesis, PO Box 510, Hebron, KY 41048. TEL 859-727-2222, 800-778-3390, FAX 859-727-2299. Ed. Andrew A Snelling.

➤ **ANTHOLOGICA ANNUA.** *see* HISTORY

230 ESP ISSN 0214-7165
ANTIGUEDAD Y CRISTIANISMO; monografias historicas sobre la antiguedad tardia. Text in English, Spanish. 1984. a., latest vol.16, 1999. back issues avail. **Document type:** *Monographic series, Academic/Scholarly.* **Description:** Approaches subjects of history and material cultures of Late Antiquity.
Indexed: DIP, IBR, IBZ.
Published by: Universidad de Murcia, Servicio de Publicaciones, Edificio Saavedra Fajardo, C/ Actor Isidoro Maiquez 9, Murcia, 30007, Spain. TEL 34-968-363887, FAX 34-968-363414, http://www.um.es/publicaciones/.

ANUARIO DE DERECHO ECLESIASTICO DEL ESTADO. *see* LAW

200 ESP ISSN 1133-0104
BX940
ANUARIO DE HISTORIA DE LA IGLESIA. Text in Spanish. 1992. a. EUR 25 in the European Union; USD 30 elsewhere (effective 2009). **Document type:** *Journal, Academic/Scholarly.*
Related titles: Online - full text ed.: ISSN 2174-0887. 2003. free (effective 2011); ◆ Supplement(s): Centro de Documentacion y Estudios Josemaria Escriva de Balaguer. Cuadernos. ISSN 1139-5346.
Indexed: A01, A20, ArtHuCI, CA, CPL, SCOPUS, T02, W07.
—CCC.
Published by: (Universidad de Navarra, Facultad de Teologia), Universidad de Navarra, Servicio de Publicaciones, Campus Universitario, Pamplona, 31009, Spain. http://www.unav.es/publicaciones/.

278 CHL ISSN 0716-1662
BX1468.A1
ANUARIO DE LA HISTORIA DE LA IGLESIA EN CHILE. Text in Spanish. 1983. a.
Indexed: FR, IBR, IBZ.
—INIST.
Published by: Seminario Pontificio Mayor de Santiago Chile, Casilla 3-D, Walker Martinez, 2020, La Florida, Santiago, Chile. TEL 56-2-4883800, FAX 56-2-4883811, seminariopontificio@hotmail.com.

229 BEL ISSN 1155-3316
BS1700
APOCRYPHA. Text in French, English, German. 1990. a. EUR 98 combined subscription (print & online eds.) (effective 2012). back issues avail. **Document type:** *Journal, Academic/Scholarly.* **Description:** Publishes studies exploring aspects of apocryphal literature preserved in Christian and Jewish communities in Europe, Africa and Asia.
Related titles: Online - full text ed.
Indexed: A21, AIAP, API, FR, PCI, RI-1.
—INIST.
Published by: (Association pour l'Etude de la Litterature Apocryphe Chretienne), Brepols Publishers, Begijnhof 67, Turnhout, 2300, Belgium. TEL 32-14-448030, FAX 32-14-428919, periodicals@brepols.net, http://www.brepols.net.

200 BEL ISSN 1263-946X
APOCRYPHES. Text in French. 1993. irreg., latest vol.11, 2000. price varies. back issues avail. **Document type:** *Monographic series.* **Description:** Publishes French translations of apocryphal literature from European, Syriac, and Ethiopian sources.
Published by: Brepols Publishers, Begijnhof 67, Turnhout, 2300, Belgium. FAX 32-14-428919, periodicals@brepols.net. Eds. A Desreumaux, E Norelli.

266 FRA ISSN 1144-164X
L'APPEL DE L'AFRIQUE. Text in French. 1950. q. EUR 10 (effective 2009). **Document type:** *Bulletin.*
Formerly: Almanach Noir
Published by: Societe des Missions Africaines, 36 rue Miguel Hidalgo, Paris, 75019, France. TEL 33-1-42784215, FAX 33-1-42784676, sma.lyon@missions-africaines.org. Ed. Chataigne Paul. Circ: 24,000.

220 NLD ISSN 1477-8351
BS410
ARAMAIC STUDIES. Text in English. 1999. s-a. EUR 147, USD 207 to institutions; EUR 161, USD 225 combined subscription to institutions (print & online eds.) (effective 2012). adv. reprint service avail. from PSC. **Document type:** *Journal, Academic/Scholarly.* **Description:** Provides a common platform for all those engaged in research into the Aramaic versions of the Hebrew Bible, the Apocrypha and Pseudepigrapha and the New Testament.
Formerly: Journal for the Aramaic Bible (1462-3153)
Related titles: Online - full text ed.: ISSN 1745-5227. EUR 134, USD 188 to institutions (effective 2012) (from IngentaConnect).
Indexed: A01, A03, A08, A21, A22, AmHI, CA, DIP, E01, H07, IBR, IBZ, IZBG, OTA, SCOPUS, T02.
—IE, Ingenta. **CCC.**
Published by: (Universiteit Leiden, Faculty of Theology), Brill, PO Box 9000, Leiden, 2300 PA, Netherlands. TEL 31-71-5353500, FAX 31-71-5317532, cs@brill.nl. Eds. Bas ter Haar Romeny, Willem F Smelik.

299 AUT ISSN 1992-108X
ARBEITEN ZUR ANTIKEN RELIGIONSGESCHICHTE. Text in German. 1987. irreg., latest vol.4, 1994. price varies. **Document type:** *Monographic series, Academic/Scholarly.*
Published by: Verlag der Oesterreichischen Akademie der Wissenschaften, Postgasse 7/4, Vienna, W 1011, Austria. TEL 43-1-515813402, FAX 43-1-515813400, verlag@oeaw.ac.at.

200 DEU
➤ **ARBEITEN ZUR GESCHICHTE DES PIETISMUS.** Text in German. 1979. irreg., latest vol.55, 2010. price varies. **Document type:** *Monographic series, Academic/Scholarly.*
Published by: Vandenhoeck und Ruprecht, Theaterstr 13, Goettingen, 37073, Germany. TEL 49-551-508440, FAX 49-551-5084422.

230 DEU
ARBEITEN ZUR HISTORISCHEN RELIGIONSPAEDAGOGIK. Text in German. 2003. irreg., latest vol.9, 2011. price varies. **Document type:** *Monographic series, Academic/Scholarly.*
Published by: I K S Garamond, Leutragraben 1, Jena, 07743, Germany. TEL 49-3641-460850, FAX 49-3641-460855, garamond@iks-jena.de.

200 DEU ISSN 1861-5996
ARBEITEN ZUR KIRCHENGESCHICHTE. Text in German. 1925. irreg., latest vol.115, 2011. price varies. **Document type:** *Monographic series, Academic/Scholarly.*
Media: Large Type.
—CCC.
Published by: Walter de Gruyter GmbH & Co. KG, Genthiner Str 13, Berlin, 10785, Germany. TEL 49-30-260050, FAX 49-30-26005251, info@degruyter.com, http://www.degruyter.de. Eds. Christian Albrecht, Christoph Markschies.

200 DEU
ARBEITEN ZUR KIRCHLICHEN ZEITGESCHICHTE. REIHE A: QUELLEN. Text in German. 1985. irreg., latest vol.16, 2009. price varies. **Document type:** *Monographic series, Academic/Scholarly.*
Published by: Evangelische Arbeitsgemeinschaft fuer Kirchliche Zeitgeschichte, Geschwister-Scholl-Platz 1, Munich, 80539, Germany. TEL 49-89-21802828, FAX 49-89-21805339, karl-heinz.fix@evtheol.uni-muenchen.de, http://www.ekd.de/zeitgeschichte/index.html.

200 DEU
➤ **ARBEITEN ZUR KIRCHLICHEN ZEITGESCHICHTE. REIHE B: DARSTELLUNGEN.** Text in German. 1975. irreg., latest vol.51, 2010. price varies. **Document type:** *Monographic series, Academic/Scholarly.*
Published by: (Evangelische Arbeitsgemeinschaft fuer Kirchliche Zeitgeschichte), Vandenhoeck und Ruprecht, Theaterstr 13, Goettingen, 37073, Germany. TEL 49-551-508440, FAX 49-551-5084422, info@v-r.de.

225 DEU ISSN 0570-5509
➤ **ARBEITEN ZUR NEUTESTAMENTLICHEN TEXTFORSCHUNG.** Text in German. 1963. irreg., latest vol.43, 2010. price varies. **Document type:** *Monographic series, Academic/Scholarly.*
—CCC.
Published by: (Institut fuer Neutestamentlichen Textforschung), Walter de Gruyter GmbH & Co. KG, Genthiner Str 13, Berlin, 10785, Germany. TEL 49-30-260050, FAX 49-30-26005251, info@degruyter.com, http://www.degruyter.de.

200 DEU
➤ **ARBEITEN ZUR PASTORALTHEOLOGIE, LITURGIK UND HYMNOLOGIE.** Text in German. 1962. irreg., latest vol.56, 2008. price varies. **Document type:** *Monographic series, Academic/Scholarly.*
Formerly (until 2006): Arbeiten zur Pastoraltheologie (0570-5517)
Published by: Vandenhoeck und Ruprecht, Theaterstr 13, Goettingen, 37073, Germany. TEL 49-551-508440, FAX 49-551-5084422, info@v-r.de.

230 DEU ISSN 0949-3069
ARBEITEN ZUR RELIGION UND GESCHICHTE DES URCHRISTENTUMS. Text in German. 1995. irreg., latest vol.15, 2004. price varies. **Document type:** *Monographic series, Academic/Scholarly.*
Published by: Peter Lang GmbH (Subsidiary of: Peter Lang Publishing Group), Eschborner Landstr 42-50, Frankfurt Am Main, 60489, Germany. TEL 49-69-7807050, FAX 49-69-78070550, zentrale.frankfurt@peterlang.com. Ed. Gerd Luedemann.

372.82 DEU
ARBEITEN ZUR RELIGIONSPAEDAGOGIK. Text in German. 1982. irreg., latest vol.43, 2010. price varies. **Document type:** *Monographic series, Academic/Scholarly.*
Published by: V & R Unipress GmbH (Subsidiary of: Vandenhoeck und Ruprecht), Robert-Bosch-Breite 6, Goettingen, 37079, Germany. TEL 49-551-5084303, FAX 49-551-5084333, info@vr-unipress.de, http://www.v-r.de/en/publisher/unipress.

230 940 DEU
ARBEITEN ZUR SCHLESISCHEN KIRCHENGESCHICHTE. Text in German. 1988. irreg., latest vol.21, 2010. price varies. **Document type:** *Monographic series, Academic/Scholarly.*
Published by: Aschendorff Verlag GmbH & Co. KG, Soester Str 13, Muenster, 48135, Germany. TEL 49-251-6900, FAX 49-251-6904570, buchverlag@aschendorff.de, http://www.aschendorff-buchverlag.de.

221 DEU
ARBEITEN ZUR TEXT UND SPRACHE IM ALTEN TESTAMENT. Text in German. 1976. irreg., latest vol.91, 2010. price varies. **Document type:** *Monographic series, Academic/Scholarly.*
Published by: E O S Verlag, Erzabtei St. Ottilien, St.Ottilien, 86941, Germany. TEL 49-8193-71700, FAX 49-8193-71709, mail@eos-verlag.de.

200 CAN ISSN 0229-2807
BL1
ARC; the journal of the faculty of religious studies. Text in English. 1972. a. CAD 15; USD 15 foreign (effective 2000). adv. bk.rev. charts. back issues avail. **Document type:** *Journal, Academic/Scholarly.* **Description:** Covers the areas of comparative religions, interreligious dialogue, Christian theology, church history, biblical studies, philosophy of religion, and social ethics.
Incorporates (in 1998): Religious Traditions (0156-1650)
Indexed: A21, BAS, DIP, GSS&RPL, IBR, IBZ, R&TA, RI-1, RI-2.
Published by: McGill University, Faculty of Religious Studies, 3250 University St., Montreal, PQ H3A 2A7, Canada. TEL 514-398-4121, FAX 514-398-6665. Ed., Pub. James Mark Shields. Circ: 500.

ARCHAEOLOGY AND BIBLICAL STUDIES. *see* ARCHAEOLOGY

200 CHE ISSN 0066-6386
BX1970.A1
ARCHIV FUER LITURGIEWISSENSCHAFT; Internationale Fachzeitschrift fuer Liturgiewissenschaft. Text in English, French, German. 1921. 3/yr. CHF 190, EUR 130 (effective 2011). bk.rev. reprints avail. **Document type:** *Journal, Academic/Scholarly.*
Formerly (until 1941): Jahrbuch fuer Liturgiewissenschaft (0342-135X)
Indexed: A21, CERDIC, DIP, FR, IBR, IBZ, MLA-IB, PCI, RI-1, RI-2, RILM, SCOPUS.
—INIST. **CCC.**
Published by: (Abt-Herwegen-Institut Maria Laach e.V., Archiv fuer Liturgiewissenschaft), Academic Press Fribourg, Perolles 42, Fribourg, 1705, Switzerland. TEL 41-26-4264311, FAX 41-26-4264300, info@paulusedition.ch, http://www.paulusedition.ch/academic_press/. Ed. Stefan Langenbahn.

200 DEU ISSN 0066-6432
BR857.R5
ARCHIV FUER MITTELRHEINISCHE KIRCHENGESCHICHTE. Text in German. 1949. a. reprints avail. **Document type:** *Journal, Academic/Scholarly.*
Indexed: A21, B24, BibCart, DIP, FR, IBR, IBZ, RI-1, RI-2, RILM.
—INIST.
Published by: Gesellschaft fuer Mittelrheinische Kirchengeschichte, Jesuitenstr 13c, Trier, 54290, Germany. TEL 49-651-966270, FAX 49-651-9662720, petra.mattes@bgv-trier.de. Ed. Friedhelm Juergensmeier. Circ: 2,500.

270 DEU ISSN 0003-9381
BR300
ARCHIV FUER REFORMATIONSGESCHICHTE. AUFSATZBAND/ARCHIVE FOR REFORMATION HISTORY; Internationale Zeitschrift zur Erforschung der Reformation und ihrer Weltwirkungen. Text in English, German. 1904. a. EUR 89 per vol. (effective 2011). bk.rev. reprint service avail. from PSC. **Document type:** *Journal, Academic/Scholarly.* **Description:** Publishes articles relating to early modern European religious life and thought (magisterial Protestant, radical, and Catholic dimensions) and the extension of European theology and practice into the extra-European world from about 1450-1650.
Related titles: Microform ed.: (from PMC).
Indexed: A20, A21, A22, ASCA, ArtHuCI, B24, CA, CurCont, DIP, FR, HistAb, IBR, IBZ, MLA, MLA-IB, PCI, R&TA, RI-1, RI-2, SCOPUS, T02, W07.
—IE, Infotrieve, INIST. **CCC.**
Published by: (Verein fuer Reformationsgeschichte, Verein fuer Reformations Geschichte, Society for Reformation Research USA), Guetersloher Verlagshaus (Subsidiary of: Verlagsgruppe Random House GmbH), Carl-Miele-Str 214, Guetersloh, 33311, Germany. TEL 49-5241-74050, FAX 49-5241-740548, info@gtvh.de, http://www.gtvh.de. Eds. Anne Jacobson Schutte, Heinz Schilling, Susan C Karant-Nunn. Circ: 800 (paid and controlled). **Co-sponsor:** Society for Reformation Research.

270.6 DEU ISSN 0341-8375
Z7830
➤ **ARCHIV FUER REFORMATIONSGESCHICHTE. LITERATURBERICHT/ARCHIVE FOR REFORMATION HISTORY. LITERATURE REVIEW.** Text in German. 1907. a. EUR 89 per vol. (effective 2011). bk.rev. **Document type:** *Journal, Academic/Scholarly.* **Description:** Contains articles and reviews on the religious and church history of the Reformation era.
Indexed: A21, FR, IBR, IBZ, RASB, RI-1.
—INIST.
Published by: (Verein fuer Reformationsgeschichte, Society for Reformation Research USA), Guetersloher Verlagshaus (Subsidiary of: Verlagsgruppe Random House GmbH), Carl-Miele-Str 214, Guetersloh, 33311, Germany. TEL 49-5241-74050, FAX 49-5241-740548, info@gtvh.de, http://www.gtvh.de. Eds. Anne Jacobson Schutte, Heinz Schilling, Susan C Karant-Nunn. Circ: 480.

200 DEU ISSN 1436-3038
BL1.A1
ARCHIV FUER RELIGIONSGESCHICHTE. Text in German. 1999. a. EUR 198, USD 297 to institutions; EUR 229, USD 344 combined subscription to institutions (print & online eds.) (effective 2012). adv. reprint service avail. from SCH. **Document type:** *Journal, Academic/Scholarly.*
Related titles: Online - full text ed.: ISSN 1868-8888. EUR 198, USD 297 to institutions (effective 2012).
Indexed: A01, A26, DIP, IBR, IBZ, SCOPUS, T02.
Published by: Walter de Gruyter GmbH & Co. KG, Genthiner Str 13, Berlin, 10785, Germany. TEL 49-30-260050, FAX 49-30-26005251, info@degruyter.com.

200 150 NLD ISSN 0084-6724
BL53.A1
➤ **ARCHIV FUER RELIGIONSPSYCHOLOGIE/ARCHIVE FOR THE PSYCHOLOGY OF RELIGION.** Text mainly in English; Text occasionally in French, German. 1914. a. EUR 182, USD 254 to institutions; EUR 198, USD 277 combined subscription to institutions (print & online eds.) (effective 2012). back issues avail.; reprint service avail. from PSC. **Document type:** *Journal, Academic/Scholarly.* **Description:** Odest medium in the psychology of religion.
Related titles: Online - full text ed.: ISSN 1573-6121. EUR 165, USD 231 to institutions (effective 2012) (from IngentaConnect).
Indexed: A21, A22, ArtHuCI, CA, CurCont, DIP, E-psyche, E01, FR, IBR, IBZ, IZBG, P03, PCI, PsycInfo, RASB, RI-1, RI-2, SCOPUS, SSCI, T02, W07.
—IE, Ingenta, INIST. **CCC.**
Published by: (Internationale Gesellschaft fuer Religionspsychologie und Religionswissenschaft DEU), Brill, PO Box 9000, Leiden, 2300 PA, Netherlands. TEL 31-71-5353500, FAX 31-71-5317532, cs@brill.nl. Eds. Heinz Streib, James Day, Ralph W Hood Jr. **Dist. by:** Turpin Distribution Services Ltd., Pegasus Dr, Stratton Business Park, Biggleswade, Bedfordshire SG18 8QB, United Kingdom. TEL 44-1767-604954, FAX 44-1767-601640, custserv@turpin-distribution.com, http://www.turpin-distribution.com/.

200 DEU ISSN 0066-6491
BR857.S6
ARCHIV FUER SCHLESISCHE KIRCHENGESCHICHTE. Text in German. 1949. a. EUR 25 (effective 2010). reprints avail. **Document type:** *Journal, Academic/Scholarly.*
Indexed: B24, DIP, FR, IBR, IBZ, MLA-IB, NumL, RILM.
—BLDSC (1623.910000).
Published by: (Institut fuer Ostdeutsche Kirchen- und Kulturgeschichte), Aschendorff Verlag GmbH & Co. KG, Soester Str 13, Muenster, 48135, Germany. TEL 49-251-6900, FAX 49-251-6904570, buchverlag@aschendorff.de, http://www.aschendorff-buchverlag.de. Circ: 900.

200 FRA ISSN 0335-5985
BL60
ARCHIVES DE SCIENCES SOCIALES DES RELIGIONS. Text in English, French; Text occasionally in German, Spanish. 1956. 4/yr. bk.rev. abstr.; bibl.; charts; illus.; stat. **Document type:** *Journal, Academic/Scholarly.* **Description:** Articles can be grouped under various headings- methodology, epistemology, status of scientific approaches to religions, classics of the sociology of religions, new religious movements.
Formerly (until 1972): Archives de Sociologie des Religions (0003-9659)
Related titles: Online - full text ed.: ISSN 1777-5825. 2005.
Indexed: A20, A21, A22, AICP, AmH&L, BibInd, CA, FR, HistAb, I13, IBSS, P30, P42, PCI, PSA, PerIslam, R&TA, RASB, RI-1, RI-2, RILM, S02, S03, SCOPUS, SOPODA, SSA, SociolAb, T02.
—BLDSC (1643.110000), IE, Infotrieve, Ingenta, INIST. **CCC.**
Published by: (Groupe de Sociologie des Religions et de la Laicite, Archives des Sciences Sociales des Religions), College de France, Ecole des Hautes Etudes en Sciences Sociales (E H E S S), 96 Boulevard Raspail, Paris, 75006, France. TEL 33-1-53635658, FAX 33-1-49542428, editions@ehess.fr. Ed. Andre Mary. Circ: 1,200.

260 ITA ISSN 0066-6688
ARCHIVIO ITALIANO PER LA STORIA DELLA PIETA. 1951; N.S. 1970. a., latest vol.19, 2006. price varies. **Document type:** *Journal, Academic/Scholarly.*
Indexed: MLA-IB.
Published by: Edizioni di Storia e Letteratura, Via delle Fornaci 24, Rome, 00165, Italy. TEL 39-06-670307, FAX 39-06-671250, info@storiaeletteratura.it, http://www.storiaeletteratura.it.

200 HKG ISSN 1011-8101
AREOPAGUS; a living encounter with today's religious world. Text in Chinese. 1977. q. USD 24. adv. bk.rev. **Document type:** *Academic/Scholarly.* **Description:** Provides a forum for communication between the good news of Jesus Christ and the people of faith both in major world religions and new religious movements.
Former titles (until 1987): Update (Aarhus) (0108-7029); (until 1982): New Religious Movements Up-Date (0105-9998)
Related titles: Microfilm ed.: (from PQC).
Indexed: A21, GSS&RPL, RI-1, RI-2.
Published by: Tao Fang Shan Christian Centre, PO Box 33, Sha Tin, New Territories, Hong Kong. TEL 852-2691-1904, FAX 852-2695-9885. Ed. John G Lemond. Adv. contact Eric Bosell. Circ: 1,000.

230 NZL ISSN 1176-810X
ARISE SHINE; a magazine for Christians and those seeking the truth. Text in English. 2004. bi-m. adv. **Document type:** *Magazine, Consumer.*
Published by: Jesus First New Zealand, Triton Plaza, PO Box 305-063, North Shore City, Auckland, New Zealand. TEL 64-2-75443047, office@jesusfirst.org.nz, http://www.jesusfirst.org.nz.

207.114891 DNK ISSN 0107-363X
ARKEN. Text in Danish. 1979. bi-m. bk.rev. illus. **Document type:** *Magazine, Consumer.*
Formerly: Teologiske Fakultet. Bladet
Published by: (Koebenhavns Universitet, Teologiske Fakultet), Forlaget Arken, c/o Det Teologiske Fakultet, Koebenhavns Universitet, Koebmagergade 44-46, Copenhagen K, 1150, Denmark. TEL 45-35-323629. Ed. Stine Rothe.

ARMONIA DI VOCI. *see* MUSIC

ARMY CHAPLAINCY. *see* MILITARY

ARS DISPUTANDI; the online journal for philosophy of religion. *see* PHILOSOPHY

ARTE CRISTIANA; rivista internazionale di storia dell'arte e di arti liturgiche. *see* ART

ARTS (NEW BRIGHTON); the arts in religious and theological studies. *see* ART

200 ESP ISSN 1575-166X
BL7
ARYS. ANTIGUEDAD, RELIGIONES Y SOCIEDADES. Text in Spanish. 1998. a. **Document type:** *Journal, Academic/Scholarly.*
Published by: Universidad de Huelva, Servicio de Publicaciones, Campus el Carmen, Avenida de las Fuerzas Armadas s/n, Huelva, Andalucia 21071, Spain. TEL 34-95-9018000, publica@uhu.es, http://www.uhu.es/publicaciones/index.html.

200 ESP
ARZOBISPADO CASTRENSE DE ESPANA. BOLETIN OFICIAL ECLESIASTICO. Text in Spanish. 1950. bi-m. bk.rev. bibl. index. back issues avail. **Document type:** *Bulletin, Consumer.* **Description:** Contains documents of the Holy See, the Spanish Episcopal Conference, and the Military Archbishopric. Includes religious news and communiques, official military orders, and an obituary column.
Formerly (until Jan. 1986): Boletin Oficial de la Jurisdiccion Eclesiastica Castrense
Published by: Arzobispado Castrense de Orpana, Nuncio, 13, Madrid, 28005, Spain. TEL 34-1-366-8228, FAX 34-1-366-8225, arzcastrense@planalfa.es. Ed. Jose Martin Sanz. Circ: 700 (controlled).

200 USA ISSN 1044-6494
ASHLAND THEOLOGICAL JOURNAL. Text in English. 1968. a. bk.rev. back issues avail. **Document type:** *Journal, Academic/Scholarly.* **Description:** Articles of interest to seminary alumni in ministry and to the theological academic community.
Formerly (until 1981): Ashland Theological Bulletin (0888-2185)
Related titles: Online - full text ed.
Indexed: A21, OTA, R&TA, RI-1, RI-2, RILM.
—BLDSC (1742.057500).
Published by: Ashland Theological Seminary ats@ashland.edu, http://seminary.ashland.edu. Circ: 2,000.

200 SGP ISSN 0218-0812
ASIA JOURNAL OF THEOLOGY. Text in English. 1982. s-a. **Document type:** *Journal, Academic/Scholarly.*
Formerly (until 1986): East Asia Journal of Theology (0217-3859); Which was formed by the merger of (1968-1982): Northeast Asia Journal of Theology (0549-8899); (1960-1982): South East Asia Journal of Theology (0217-1244)
Related titles: Online - full text ed.
Indexed: A01, A03, A08, A21, CA, DIP, IBR, IBSS, IBZ, OTA, R&TA, RI-1, T02.
—BLDSC (1742.247000), Ingenta.
Published by: Association of Theological Education in South East Asia, 324 Onan Rd., Singapore, 1542, Singapore. atesea@info.com.ph, http://www.wocati.org/atesea.html.

THE ASIA PACIFIC ADVOCATE. *see* POLITICAL SCIENCE—Civil Rights

230 950 IND
ASIAN CHURCH TODAY. Text in English. 1984. q. back issues avail. **Document type:** *Magazine, Trade.*
Related titles: Online - full text ed.
Published by: Evangelical Fellowship of Asia, 805/92, Deepali Bldg, Nehru Pl, New Delhi, India. TEL 91-11-26431133, info@asiaevangelicals.org.

200 800 DNK ISSN 1901-6646
ASLAN (ONLINE). Text in Danish. 1990. irreg. bk.rev. **Document type:** *Newsletter, Consumer.* **Description:** Focuses on childrens' books with religious and ethical relevancy.
Formerly (until 200?): Aslan (Print) (0905-7749)
Media: Online - full content.
Published by: Aslan, Liljevej 8, Frederikssund, 3600, Denmark. TEL 45-47-313213. Ed. Gunhild Lindstroem.

ASOCIACION. *see* CHILDREN AND YOUTH—About

200 FRA ISSN 0991-8000
ASSEMBLEES DE DIEU DE FRANCE. ANNUAIRE. Text in French. 1958. a.
Formerly (until 1968): Viens et Vois. Annuaire (0083-6184)
Published by: Editions Viens et Vois, 1 Chemin de la Garde, Grezieu la Varenne, 69290, France.

200 USA ISSN 1091-3718
ASSEMBLY (NOTRE DAME). Text in English. 1978. bi-m. USD 15 domestic; USD 17 in Canada; USD 19 elsewhere (effective 2009). back issues avail. **Document type:** *Magazine, Consumer.* **Description:** Explores the relationship between Christian liturgy and Christian life.
Formerly (until 1978): Hucusque
Indexed: CPL.
Published by: (Notre Dame Center for Pastoral Liturgy), Liturgy Training Publications, 3949 South Racine Ave, Chicago, IL 60609. TEL 773-579-4900, 800-933-1800, http://www.ltp.org. Ed. David Fagerberg.

ASSOCIATION FOR PROFESSIONAL EDUCATION FOR MINISTRY. REPORT OF THE BIENNIAL MEETING. *see* EDUCATION—Higher Education

230 BEL ISSN 0587-1999
ASSOCIATION INTERNATIONALE D'ETUDES PATRISTIQUES. BULLETIN D'INFORMATION ET DE LIAISON. Text in English, French. 1968. irreg. (1-2/yr.). EUR 28 (effective 2012). bk.rev. bibl. **Document type:** *Journal, Academic/Scholarly.*
Published by: (Association Internationale d'Etudes Patristiques/ International Association for Patristic Studies ITA), Brepols Publishers, Begijnhof 67, Turnhout, 2300, Belgium. TEL 32-14-448020, FAX 32-14-428919, periodicals@brepols.net, http://www.brepols.net.

271.009 FRA ISSN 1774-5268
ASSOCIATION LES AMIS DE SAINT JACQUES. BULLETIN. Text in French. 1999. irreg. **Document type:** *Bulletin.*
Formerly (until 2005): Amis de Saint Jacques en Alsace. Le Bulletin (1625-211X)
Published by: Assocation Les Amis de Saint Jacques, 1 rue de la Chaine, Andlau, 67140, France.

ASSOCIATION OF BRITISH THEOLOGICAL AND PHILOSOPHICAL LIBRARIES. BULLETIN. *see* LIBRARY AND INFORMATION SCIENCES

ASSOCIATION OF GOSPEL RESCUE MISSIONS MEMBERSHIP DIRECTORY & RESOURCE GUIDE. *see* SOCIAL SERVICES AND WELFARE

268 USA ISSN 0362-1472
ASSOCIATION OF THEOLOGICAL SCHOOLS IN THE UNITED STATES AND CANADA. BULLETIN. Text in English. 19??. biennial. USD 10 per issue part 1: bylaws, procedures & policy statements; USD 10 per issue part 2: membership list; USD 5 per issue part 3: biennial meeting (effective 2010). adv. back issues avail.; reprints avail. **Document type:** *Bulletin, Academic/Scholarly.* **Description:** Covers association laws, procedures and policy statements, membership lists, meetings etc.
Incorporates: American Association of Theological Schools in the United States and Canada. Membership List; Formerly (until 1974): American Association of Theological Schools in the United States and Canada. Bulletin (0065-7360)
Related titles: Online - full text ed.
—CCC.
Published by: The Association of Theological Schools in the United States and Canada, 10 Summit Park Dr, Pittsburgh, PA 15275. TEL 412-788-6505, FAX 412-788-6510, ats@ats.edu.

200 USA ISSN 1932-698X
BR115.C8
@ THIS POINT. Text in English. 2006. s-a.
Media: Online - full text.
Published by: Columbia Theological Seminary, PO Box 520, Decatur, GA 30031. TEL 404-378-8821, http://www.ctsnet.edu.

200 POL ISSN 0208-9041
ATENEUM KAPLANSKIE. Text in Polish. 1909. bi-m. EUR 92 foreign (effective 2006).
Related titles: Online - full text ed.: ISSN 1689-0531. 1999.
Indexed: IBSS, IZBG.
Published by: Diecezja Wloclawska, ul Prymasa S Karnkowskiego 3, skr poczt 84, Wloclawek, 87800, Poland. TEL 48-54-2312395, FAX 48-54-2312655. Ed. Waldemar Karasinski. **Dist. by:** Ars Polona, Obroncow 25, Warsaw 03933, Poland. TEL 48-22-5098609, FAX 48-22-5098610, arspolona@arspolona.com.pl, http://www.arspolona.com.pl.

201.6 IDN
ATMA JAYA RESEARCH CENTRE. SOCIO-RELIGIOUS RESEARCH REPORT/PUSAT PENELITIAN ATMA JAYA. LAPORAN PENELITIAN KEAGAMAAN. Text in English. 1977. irreg. **Document type:** *Monographic series.*
Published by: Atma Jaya Research Centre/Pusat Penelitian Atma Jaya, Jalan Jenderal Sudirman 51, PO Box 2639, Jakarta, 10001, Indonesia. Ed. Paul W Kartono. Circ: (controlled).

967.5 200 BDI ISSN 0563-4245
AU COEUR DE L'AFRIQUE. Text in French. 1961. q. USD 40. adv. bk.rev. back issues avail. **Document type:** *Bulletin.* **Description:** Contains research on cultural, socio-political, theological and pastoral issues.
Formerly (until 1969): Theologie et Pastorale au Rwanda et au Burundi (0259-8892)
Indexed: CERDIC.
Published by: (Association des Conference des Ordinaires du Rwanda et Burundi), Presses Lavigerie, BP 1390, Bujumbura, Burundi. TEL 257-223263, FAX 257-223270. Ed. Diomede Mkurunziza. Circ: 1,000.

200 GBR ISSN 0004-7481
BV4485
AUDENSHAW PAPERS. Text in English. 1967. q. bk.rev. **Document type:** *Monographic series, Academic/Scholarly.*
Supersedes (1958-1968): Christian Comment (0144-9184)
Indexed: CERDIC.
—BLDSC (1787.750000).
Published by: Hinksey Network, 3 Thorne Park Rd, Torquay, Devon TQ2 6RX, United Kingdom. TEL 44-1803-690147, FAX 44-1803-690147, owenmary@onetel.net.uk. Ed. Adam Hood. Circ: 400.

267.6 DEU
AUFTRAG UND WEG. Text in German. 1915. q. bk.rev. **Document type:** *Magazine, Consumer.*
Published by: (Deutscher Verband der Jugenbuende fuer Entschiedenes Christentum e.V.), Born-Verlag, Leuschnerstr 74, Kassel, 34134, Germany. TEL 49-561-4095107, FAX 49-561-4095112, info.born@ec-jugend.de, http://www.born-buch.de. Ed. Klaus Matthiesen. Circ: 4,000.

200 DEU ISSN 1431-9845
AUFWAERTS (GIESSEN); die Zeitschrift mit den guten Nachrichten. Text in German. 1909. m. bk.rev. **Document type:** *Magazine, Consumer.*
Published by: Brunnen Verlag GmbH, Gottlieb-Daimler-Str 22, Giessen, 35398, Germany. TEL 49-641-60590, FAX 49-641-6059100, info@brunnen-verlag.de, http://www.brunnen-verlag.de. Ed. Ralf Tibusek.

299 SWE ISSN 2000-4419
AURA; tidskrift foer akademiska studier av nyreligiositet. Text in Swedish. 1996. a. SEK 150 membership (effective 2010). **Document type:** *Monographic series, Academic/Scholarly.* **Description:** Research and information on new religious movements.
Former titles (until 2009): Finyar (1653-6754); (until 2004): Finyar. Nyhetsbrev (1404-6571)
Published by: Foereningen Forskning och Information om Nya Religioesa Roerelser, c/o Religionshistoriska Institutionen, Stockholm Universitet, Stockholm, 10691, Sweden. TEL 46-8-162000, FAX 46-8-161227, info@finyar.se, http://www.finyar.se.

291 DEU ISSN 1860-8388
AUS RELIGION UND RECHT. Text in German. 2005. irreg., latest vol.15, 2010. price varies. **Document type:** *Monographic series, Academic/Scholarly.*
Published by: Frank und Timme GmbH, Wittelsbacherstr 27a, Berlin, 10707, Germany. TEL 49-30-88667911, FAX 49-30-86398731, info@frank-timme.de.

280.4 DEU
DIE AUSLESE; vierteljaehrliche Informationsschrift fuer Kirche und Friedhof. Text in German. 1958. 4/yr. EUR 2 newsstand/cover (effective 2007). adv. bk.rev. 30 p./no.; **Document type:** *Magazine, Trade.*
Published by: J.P. Bachem Verlag GmbH, Ursulaplatz 1, Cologne, 50668, Germany. TEL 49-221-16190, FAX 49-221-1619205, info@bachem-verlag.de, http://www.bachem-verlag.de. adv.: B&W page EUR 1,320, color page EUR 1,980; trim 180 x 261. Circ: 26,500 (controlled).

200 AUS ISSN 1022-3347
AUSTRALIAN BEACON. Text in English. 1968. m. AUD 30 domestic; AUD 35 in New Zealand; AUD 45 elsewhere (effective 2009); . adv. bk.rev. back issues avail. **Document type:** *Newspaper, Consumer.* **Description:** For Christians concerned with the state of the Church today.
Address: PO Box 642, Nanango, QLD 4615, Australia. TEL 61-7-41632160, nannews@burcom.com.au. Ed. Ray Smyth. Circ: 1,000 (paid).

220 AUS ISSN 0045-0308
➤ **AUSTRALIAN BIBLICAL REVIEW.** Abbreviated title: A B R. Text in English. 1951. a. AUD 16 in Australia & New Zealand; AUD 21 elsewhere (effective 2009). bk.rev. back issues avail. **Document type:** *Journal, Academic/Scholarly.* **Description:** Provides scholarly research on various Biblical topics.
Related titles: Online - full text ed.
Indexed: A11, A21, CA, CERDIC, IZBG, OTA, PCI, R&TA, RI-1, RI-2, T02.
—BLDSC (1797.800000).
Published by: The Fellowship for Biblical Studies Inc., 23 Gareth Dr, East Burwood, VIC 3151, Australia. bjincig@ccr.org.au. Eds. Anne Gardner, James S McLaren.

230 AUS
AUSTRALIAN CHRISTIAN (ONLINE). Text in English. 1898. m. adv. bk.rev. Index. 22 p./no.; back issues avail. **Document type:** *Newsletter, Consumer.*
Formerly (until 2005): Australian Christian (Print) (0004-8852); Which was formed by the merger of: Christian Pioneer; Australasian Christian Standard
Media: Online - full content.
Indexed: CERDIC.
Published by: Churches of Christ in Australia National Media and Communications, 1st Fl, 582 Heidelberg Rd, Fairfield, VIC 3078, Australia. TEL 61-3-94888800, FAX 61-3-94818543, cofcvictas@churchesofchrist.org.au, http://churchesofchrist.org.au, http://cofcaustralia.org. Ed. Craig Brown TEL 61-3-94888847. adv.: online banner AUD 120.

230 AUS
AUSTRALIAN CHRISTIAN WOMAN; inspired living. Abbreviated title: C W. Text in English. 1954. bi-m. AUD 29 domestic to senior citizens; AUD 37.95 in Australia & New Zealand; AUD 49 elsewhere; AUD 7.50 newsstand/cover (effective 2009). adv. **Document type:** *Magazine, Consumer.* **Description:** Covers topics related to christian women.

R

Published by: Media Incorporated Pty Ltd., PO Box 163, North Sydney, NSW 2059, Australia. TEL 61-2-84373541, FAX 61-2-99861431, enquiries@mediaincorp.com. Ed. Jenny Baxter. Pub. Matthew Danswan. Adv. contact Matthew Harvie TEL 61-2-90075373. color page AUD 1,200; 210 x 297.

990 200 AUS ISSN 1324-9436
AUSTRALIAN CHURCHES OF CHRIST HISTORICAL SOCIETY. DIGEST. Text in English. 1960. q. AUD 7 to non-members; free to members (effective 2008). **Document type:** *Magazine, Consumer.* **Description:** Offers information about the history of Churches and people.
Related titles: Online - full text ed.
Published by: Australian Churches of Christ Historical Society, c/o CCTC, 44 - 60 Jacksons Rd, PO Box 629, Mulgrave North, VIC 3170, Australia. TEL 61-3-97901000, FAX 61-3-97951688, admin@cctc.edu.au. Eds. Graeme Chapman TEL 61-3-97901000, Kerrie Handasyde TEL 61-3-97362704. Pub., R&P Graeme Chapman TEL 61-3-97901000. Circ: 50 (paid).

200 GBR ISSN 1031-2943
➤ **AUSTRALIAN RELIGION STUDIES REVIEW.** Abbreviated title: A R S R. Text in English. 1988. 3/yr. USD 300 combined subscription in North America to institutions (print & online eds.); GBP 185 combined subscription elsewhere to institutions (print & online eds.) (effective 2012). adv. back issues avail.; reprints avail. **Document type:** *Journal, Academic/Scholarly.* **Description:** Covers all aspects of the academic study of religion.
Related titles: Online - full text ed.: ISSN 1744-9014. USD 240 in North America to institutions; GBP 148 elsewhere to institutions (effective 2012).
Indexed: AusPAIS.
—IE. **CCC.**
Published by: (Australian Association for the Study of Religion AUS), Equinox Publishing Ltd., Unit S3, Kelham House, 3 Lancaster St, Sheffield, S6 3AF, United Kingdom. TEL 44-114-2725957, FAX 44-560-3459046, journals@equinoxpub.com, http://www.equinoxpub.com/. Eds. Jay Johnston, Paul Hedges. Adv. contact Val Hall.

➤ **AVIMO INFO.** *see* EDUCATION

200 SVK ISSN 1337-0626
AXIS MUNDI. Text in Slovak. 2006. s-a. **Document type:** *Journal, Academic/Scholarly.*
Published by: Slovenska Akademia Vied, Bratislava Slovenska Spolocnost pre Studium Nabozenstviev, Stefanikova 49, Bratislava, 814 38, Slovakia. TEL 421-2-52492751, FAX 421-2-52494391.

207.2 CAN
B C CHRISTIAN NEWS. Text in English. 1982. m. CAD 25 domestic; CAD 30 in United States; CAD 35 elsewhere (effective 1999). adv. bk.rev.; film rev.; play rev. back issues avail. **Document type:** *Newspaper.*
Former titles (until Oct. 1997): Christian Info News (0844-5699); (until 1989): Christian Info (0838-8547)
Published by: Christian Info (Vancouver - Lower Mainland) Society, Ste 200, 20316 56 Ave, Langley, BC V3A 3Y7, Canada. TEL 604-534-1444, FAX 604-534-2970. Ed. Flyn Ritchie. Pub., R&P Alan Stanchi. Adv. contact Peter Sawatsky. Circ: 33,000.

B C S P. (Bollettino del Centro Camuno di Studi Preistorici) *see* ARCHAEOLOGY

200 USA ISSN 2157-3123
BV4000
B T I MAGAZINE. Text in English. 2001. s-a. back issues avail. **Document type:** *Magazine, Consumer.* **Description:** Covers current events in the schools, new faculty publications, articles, announcements, issues in international mission and ecumenical relationships, as well as aspects in the interrelationship between science and religion.
Formerly (until 2009): Boston Theological Institute. Bulletin (1538-6597)
Related titles: Online - full text ed.: free (effective 2010).
Published by: Boston Theological Institute, 197 Herrick Rd, Newton Centre, MA 02459. TEL 617-527-4880, FAX 617-527-1073, mainoffice@bostontheological.org. Ed. Marian Gh Simion.

▼ **B-TWEENS**; ressurshefte for barneledere for tweens-grupper (10-13 ar). *see* CHILDREN AND YOUTH—About

BABEL UND BIBEL. *see* HISTORY—History Of The Near East

200 CAN ISSN 0708-5052
➤ **BAHA'I STUDIES.** Text in English. 1976. irreg. CAD 5 per issue. **Document type:** *Monographic series, Academic/Scholarly.*
Published by: Association for Baha'i Studies, 34 Copernicus St, Ottawa, ON K1N 7K4, Canada. TEL 613-233-1903. R&P Christine Zerbinis. Circ: 2,000.

200 DEU ISSN 0948-177X
BAMBERGER THEOLOGISCHE STUDIEN. Text in German. 1995. irreg., latest vol.34, 2008. price varies. **Document type:** *Monographic series, Academic/Scholarly.*
Published by: (Bamberger Theologische Studien e.V.), Peter Lang GmbH (Subsidiary of: Peter Lang Publishing Group), Eschborner Landstr 42-50, Frankfurt Am Main, 60489, Germany. TEL 49-69-7807050, FAX 49-69-78070550, zentrale.frankfurt@peterlang.com.

200 700 USA ISSN 0067-3129
BAMPTON LECTURES IN AMERICA. Text in English. 1949. irreg., latest 2008. price varies. back issues avail. **Document type:** *Monographic series, Academic/Scholarly.*
Published by: Columbia University Press, 61 W 62nd St, New York, NY 10023. TEL 212-459-0600, FAX 212-459-3678, orderentry@perseusbooks.com. Ed. Jennifer Crewe.

291.72 NLD ISSN 1877-2757
DE BAND. Text in Dutch. 1949. bi-m. **Document type:** *Magazine, Consumer.*
Formerly (until 2007): Band des Vredes (1380-4022); Which incorporated (1949-1989): Bijbellicht (0167-336X)
Published by: Filadelfia Zending, c/o R Kamp, Nieuwe Laan 41, Capelle aan den IJssel, 2902 BW, Netherlands. TEL 31-10-4516905, http://www.filadelfia-zending.nl. Ed. L Koster.

200 950 IND ISSN 0253-9365
BR118
➤ **BANGALORE THEOLOGICAL FORUM.** Abbreviated title: B T F. Text in English. 1967. q. INR 300 includes domestic and South Asia; USD 40 foreign to alumni (effective 2011). bk.rev. abstr. 200 p./no.; back issues avail. **Document type:** *Journal, Academic/Scholarly.*
Related titles: Microform ed.: (from PQC).
Indexed: A21, A22, OTA, R&TA, RI-1, RI-2.
—BLDSC (1861.608000).
Published by: United Theological College, 63, Millers Rd, Benson Town, PO Box 4613, Bangalore, Karnataka 560046, India. TEL 91-80-23333438, FAX 91-80-23330015, unitedtcb@gmail.com. Ed. K Jesurathnam.

230 USA
Z7755
BANGOR THEOLOGICAL SEMINARY. GENERAL THEOLOGICAL LIBRARY. BULLETIN. Text in English. 1908. q. USD 15. bk.rev. **Document type:** *Bulletin.* **Description:** Contains annotations and short reviews of 50-75 recently published books in the fields of theology and religion. Most issues include an article on a topic of current theological interest.
Former titles (until 1991): General Theological Center of Maine. Bulletin (1052-8202); (until 1988): General Theological Library. Bulletin (0361-0837)
Related titles: Online - full text ed.
Indexed: L09, MLA-IB.
Published by: Bangor Theological Seminary, 159 State St, Portland, ME 04101. TEL 207-874-2214. Ed. Clifton G Davis. Circ: 1,200.

BAPTIST QUARTERLY. *see* RELIGIONS AND THEOLOGY—Protestant

286 AUS ISSN 1323-4943
BAPTIST UNION OF VICTORIA. YEARBOOK. Text in English. 1971. a., latest 2000-2001. looseleaf. AUD 15 per issue (effective 2008). stat. **Document type:** *Yearbook, Consumer.* **Description:** Contains information about the activities, members, and statistics of Baptist Union of Victoria.
Formerly (until 1984): Baptist Union of Victoria. Handbook
Related titles: Online - full content ed.: 2001 (Oct.).
Published by: Baptist Union of Victoria, PO Box 377, Hawthorn, VIC 3122, Australia. TEL 61-3-98806100, FAX 61-3-98806123, info@buv.com.au.

BASIS; Christene School. *see* EDUCATION

200 CHE ISSN 0171-6840
BASLER UND BERNER STUDIEN ZUR HISTORISCHEN UND SYSTEMATISCHEN THEOLOGIE. Text in German. 1963. irreg., latest vol.72, 2004. price varies. **Document type:** *Monographic series, Academic/Scholarly.*
Formerly (until 1975): Basler Studien zur Historischen und Systematischen Theologie (0522-4594)
Published by: Peter Lang AG (Subsidiary of: Peter Lang Publishing Group), Hochfeldstr 32, Postfach 746, Bern 9, 3000, Switzerland. TEL 41-31-3061717, FAX 41-31-3061727, info@peterlang.com. Eds. Martin Sallmann, Martin Wallraff.

200 DEU ISSN 0005-6618
DAS BAUGERUEST; Mitarbeiterzeitschrift fuer ausserschul. Jugendbildung. Text in German. 1949. 4/yr. bk.rev. bibl.; tr.lit. index. **Document type:** *Bulletin.*
Published by: Verein zur Foerderung Evangelischer Jugendarbeit e.V., Hummelsteiner Weg 100, Nuernberg, 90459, Germany. TEL 49-911-4304-0, FAX 49-911-4304201. Ed. Rainer Brandt. Circ: 2,100.

BAUSTEINE KINDERGARTEN. RELIGIOESE ERZIEHUNG. *see* EDUCATION—Teaching Methods And Curriculum

220 DEU ISSN 0005-707X
DER BAYERISCHE KRIPPENFREUND. Text in German. 1917. q. EUR 12 (effective 2005). back issues avail. **Document type:** *Bulletin, Consumer.*
Published by: Verband Bayerischer Krippenfreunde, Gartenfeldstr 5, Kluesserath, 54340, Germany. TEL 49-6507-993056, FAX 49-6507-993057, vorstand@krippenverein.de, http://www.krippenfreunde-bayern.de. Circ: 5,000.

200 DEU ISSN 1867-5344
BAYREUTHER BEITRAEGE ZUR ERFORSCHUNG DER RELIGIOESEN GEGENWARTSKULTUR. Text in German. 2000. irreg. **Document type:** *Monographic series, Academic/Scholarly.*
Formerly (until 2008): Bayreuther Beitraege zur Religionsforschung (1617-0369)
Media: Online - full text.
Published by: Universitaet Bayreuth, Institut zur Erforschung der Religioesen Gegenwartskultur, Universitaetsstr, Kulturwissenschaftliche Fakultaet, Zi 1.25, Bayreuth, 95447, Germany. TEL 49-921-5541556, FAX 49-921-55844156, irg@uni-bayreuth.de, http://www.irg.uni-bayreuth.de.

THE BEACON (NEW YORK, 1922). *see* PHILOSOPHY

207.2 USA
BEADS OF TRUTH. Text in English. 1972. s-a. USD 10. adv. bk.rev. illus.
Published by: Three H O Foundation, 1620 Preuss Rd, Los Angeles, CA 90035. TEL 213-552-3416. Ed. S S Satsimran Kaur Khalsa. Circ: 3,000.

230 AUS
BEAUTY FOR ASHES; the beauty of ascended Christ Jesus. Text in English. 1998. q.
Media: Online - full text.
Published by: Endtime Ministries, PO Box 238, Landsborough, QLD, Australia. TEL 61-7-54941672, FAX 61-7-54948617, despatch@mail.cth.com.au, http://www.despatch.cth.com.au/Main/index.htm.

204.4 USA ISSN 1050-0332
BEFRIENDING CREATION. Text in English. 1985. bi-m. USD 20 (effective 1999). bk.rev. **Document type:** *Newsletter.* **Description:** Provides news and information to members about our spiritual relations with the environment.
Formerly (until 1988): Unity with Nature Newsletter
Related titles: Online - full text ed.
Published by: Friends Committee on Unity with Nature, 173B N Prospect St, Burlington, VT 05401-1607. TEL 802-658-0308, FAX 413-714-7011, fcun@fcun.org. Ed. Louis Cox. R&P Ruah Swennerfelt TEL 802-425-3377. Circ: 650.

BEHOLD (INVER GROVE HEIGHTS); arts for the church year. *see* ART

255.1 DEU
DIE BEIDEN TUERME; Rundbrief fuer die Freunde der Abtei Niederaltaich. Text in German. 1965. s-a. free (effective 2009). **Document type:** *Newsletter, Consumer.*
Published by: Benediktinerabtei Niederaltaich, Mauritiushof 1, Niederalteich, 94557, Germany. TEL 49-9901-2080, FAX 49-9901-208141, abtei@abtei-niederaltaich.de. Ed. Gerhard Voss. Circ: 4,550 (controlled).

230 CHE
BEITRAEGE ZU EINER THEOLOGIE DER RELIGIONEN. Text in German. 2005. irreg., latest vol.7, 2009. price varies. **Document type:** *Monographic series, Academic/Scholarly.*
Published by: Theologischer Verlag Zurich, Badenerstr 73, Zurich, 8026, Switzerland. TEL 41-44-2993355, FAX 41-44-2993358, tvz@ref.ch.

230 CHE
BEITRAEGE ZU THEOLOGIE, ETHIK UND KIRCHE. Text in German. 2006. irreg., latest vol.4, 2008. price varies. **Document type:** *Monographic series, Academic/Scholarly.*
Published by: Theologischer Verlag Zurich, Badenerstr 73, Zurich, 8026, Switzerland. TEL 41-44-2993355, FAX 41-44-2993358, tvz@ref.ch.

230 DEU ISSN 1438-0889
BEITRAEGE ZUR ALBERT-SCHWEITZER-FORSCHUNG. Text in German. 1990. irreg., latest vol.10, 2005. price varies. **Document type:** *Monographic series, Academic/Scholarly.*
Published by: Peter Lang GmbH (Subsidiary of: Peter Lang Publishing Group), Eschborner Landstr 42-50, Frankfurt Am Main, 60489, Germany. TEL 49-69-7807050, FAX 49-69-78070550, zentrale.frankfurt@peterlang.com.

220 DEU ISSN 0170-8716
BEITRAEGE ZUR BIBLISCHEN EXEGESE UND THEOLOGIE. Text in German. 1976. irreg., latest vol.30, 2002. price varies. **Document type:** *Monographic series, Academic/Scholarly.*
Published by: Peter Lang GmbH (Subsidiary of: Peter Lang Publishing Group), Eschborner Landstr 42-50, Frankfurt Am Main, 60489, Germany. TEL 49-69-7807050, FAX 49-69-78070550, zentrale.frankfurt@peterlang.com.

BEITRAEGE ZUR ERFORSCHUNG DER ANTIKEN MOABITIS (ARD EL-KERAK). *see* ARCHAEOLOGY

220 DEU ISSN 1430-063X
BEITRAEGE ZUR ERZIEHUNGSWISSENSCHAFT UND BIBLISCHEN BILDUNG. Text in German. 1997. irreg., latest vol.8, 2003. price varies. **Document type:** *Monographic series, Academic/Scholarly.*
Published by: Peter Lang GmbH (Subsidiary of: Peter Lang Publishing Group), Eschborner Landstr 42-50, Frankfurt Am Main, 60489, Germany. TEL 49-69-7807050, FAX 49-69-78070550, zentrale.frankfurt@peterlang.com. Ed. Hans-Theo Wrege.

BEITRAEGE ZUR GESCHICHTE DER PHILOSOPHIE UND THEOLOGIE DES MITTELALTERS. NEUE FOLGE. *see* PHILOSOPHY

200 DEU ISSN 0522-6619
BX1538.R37
BEITRAEGE ZUR GESCHICHTE DES BISTUMS REGENSBURG. Text in German. 1967. a. EUR 25 to members; EUR 12 student members (effective 2003). **Document type:** *Journal, Academic/Scholarly.*
Indexed: DIP, IBR, IBZ, RILM.
Published by: Verein fuer Regensburger Bistumsgeschichte e.V., St. Petersweg 11-13, Regensburg, 93047, Germany. TEL 49-941-595322520, FAX 49-941-595322521, archiv@bistum-regensburg.de, http://www.bistum-regensburg.de/archiv. Eds. Karl Hausberger, Paul Mai. Circ: 700.

200 DEU ISSN 0175-5323
BEITRAEGE ZUR GESCHICHTE UND LEHRE DER REFORMIERTEN KIRCHE. Text in German. 1937. irreg. price varies. **Document type:** *Monographic series, Academic/Scholarly.*
Published by: Neukirchener Verlag, Andreas-Braem-Str 18-20, Neukirchen-Vluyn, 47506, Germany. TEL 49-2845-392222, FAX 49-2845-33689, info@nvg-medien.de, http://www.nvg-medien.de.

200 DEU ISSN 1439-6491
BEITRAEGE ZUR HAGIOGRAPHIE. Text in German. 1999. irreg., latest vol.9, 2010. price varies. **Document type:** *Monographic series, Academic/Scholarly.*
Published by: Franz Steiner Verlag GmbH, Birkenwaldstr 44, Stuttgart, 70191, Germany. TEL 49-711-25820, FAX 49-711-2582290, service@steiner-verlag.de, http://www.steiner-verlag.de.

200 DEU ISSN 0340-6741
BEITRAEGE ZUR HISTORISCHEN THEOLOGIE. Text in German. 1929-1936; N.S. 1950. irreg., latest vol.157, 2011. price varies. **Document type:** *Monographic series, Academic/Scholarly.*
Published by: Mohr Siebeck GmbH & Co. KG, Wilhelmstr 18, Tuebingen, 72074, Germany. TEL 49-7071-9230, FAX 49-7071-51104, info@mohr.de.

230 DEU ISSN 0946-8803
BEITRAEGE ZUR KIRCHEN- UND KULTURGESCHICHTE. Text in German. 1994. irreg., latest vol.19, 2007. price varies. **Document type:** *Monographic series, Academic/Scholarly.*
Published by: Peter Lang GmbH (Subsidiary of: Peter Lang Publishing Group), Eschborner Landstr 42-50, Frankfurt Am Main, 60489, Germany. TEL 49-69-7807050, FAX 49-69-78070550, zentrale.frankfurt@peterlang.com. Ed. Christoph Weber.

230 CHE
BEITRAEGE ZUR PASTORALSOZIOLOGIE. Variant title: S P I - Reihe. Text in German. 1989. irreg., latest vol.13, 2009. price varies. **Document type:** *Monographic series, Academic/Scholarly.*
Formerly (until 2005): Schweizerisches Pastoralsoziologisches Institut. Publikationsreihe
Published by: Theologischer Verlag Zurich, Badenerstr 73, Zurich, 8026, Switzerland. TEL 41-44-2993355, FAX 41-44-2993358, tvz@ref.ch.

200 DEU ISSN 0943-4151
BEITRAEGE ZUR RATIONALEN THEOLOGIE. Text in German. 1993. irreg., latest vol.19, 2009. price varies. **Document type:** *Monographic series, Academic/Scholarly.*
Published by: Peter Lang GmbH (Subsidiary of: Peter Lang Publishing Group), Eschborner Landstr 42-50, Frankfurt Am Main, 60489, Germany. TEL 49-69-7807050, FAX 49-69-78070550, zentrale.frankfurt@peterlang.com. Eds. Joerg Dierken, Ulrich Barth.

200 DEU ISSN 0948-0277
BEITRAEGE ZUR THEOLOGISCHEN URTEILSBILDUNG. Text in German. 1996. irreg., latest vol.12, 2002. price varies. **Document type:** *Monographic series, Academic/Scholarly.*

Published by: Peter Lang GmbH (Subsidiary of: Peter Lang Publishing Group), Eschborner Landstr 42-50, Frankfurt Am Main, 60489, Germany. TEL 49-69-7807050, FAX 49-69-78070550, zentrale.frankfurt@peterlang.com. Ed. Gerhard Sauter.

220 DEU
BEITRAEGE ZUR WISSENSCHAFT VOM ALTEN UND NEUEN TESTAMENT. Text in German. irreg., latest vol.168, 2005. price varies. **Document type:** *Monographic series, Academic/Scholarly.*
Indexed: IZBG.
Published by: W. Kohlhammer GmbH, Hessbruehlstr 69, Stuttgart, 70565, Germany. TEL 49-711-78630, FAX 49-711-78638204, kohlhammerkontakt@kohlhammer.de, http://www.kohlhammer.de.

200 USA ISSN 1942-0617
D16.166
▼ **BELIEFS AND VALUES.** Text in English. 2009 (Mar.). s-a. USD 75 domestic to individuals; USD 95 foreign to individuals; USD 195 domestic to institutions; USD 220 foreign to institutions; USD 115 combined subscription domestic to individuals (print & online eds.); USD 145 combined subscription foreign to individuals (print & online eds.); USD 295 combined subscription domestic to institutions (print & online eds.); USD 330 combined subscription foreign to institutions (print & online eds.) (effective 2010). adv. back issues avail. **Document type:** *Journal, Academic/Scholarly.* **Description:** Examines the linkage between beliefs and values and the actions, policies, and practices of individuals, groups, organizations, governments, and societies around the world.
Related titles: Online - full text ed.: ISSN 1942-0625. 2009 (Mar.). USD 65 domestic to individuals; USD 85 foreign to individuals; USD 185 domestic to institutions; USD 210 foreign to institutions (effective 2010) (from IngentaConnect).
Indexed: CA, S02, S03, T02.
—CCC.
Published by: Springer Publishing Company, 11 W 42nd St, 15th Fl, New York, NY 10036. TEL 212-431-4370, 877-687-7476, FAX 212-941-7842, journals@springerpub.com. Ed. Craig N Shealy. Adv. contact Carrie Neff TEL 212-431-4370 ext 221. **Co-sponsor:** International Beliefs and Values Institute.

200 USA ISSN 2151-3538
THE BELL-RINGER. Text in English. 19??. bi-w. free (effective 2009). back issues avail. **Document type:** *Newsletter, Consumer.*
Formerly (until 1973): First Parish Church in Duxbury. Newsletter
Related titles: Online - full text ed.: free (effective 2009).
Published by: First Parish Church in Duxbury, PO Box 1764, Duxbury, MA 02331. TEL 781-934-6532, uuduxbury@verizon.net. Ed. Marge McLean.

THE BELTANE PAPERS; a journal of women's mysteries. *see* WOMEN'S INTERESTS

BENJAMIN; evangelische Monatszeitschrift fuer Maedchen und Jungen. *see* CHILDREN AND YOUTH—For

220 GBR
THE BEREAN EXPOSITOR. Text in English. 1909. bi-m. **Document type:** *Magazine, Academic/Scholarly.* **Description:** General Bible subjects for Bible students.
—BLDSC (1893.870000).
Published by: Berean Publishing Trust, Chapel of the Opened Book, 52a Wilson St, London, EC2A 2ER, United Kingdom. TEL 44-20-72471467, sales@bereanonline.org. Ed. Alan Carter. Circ: 600.

230 USA ISSN 0005-8890
THE BEREAN SEARCHLIGHT; studying God's word, rightly divided. Text in English. 1940. m. (except Jul). free (effective 2010). bk.rev. charts; illus. reprints avail. **Document type:** *Journal, Academic/Scholarly.* **Description:** Studies the Scriptures from a dispensational viewpoint, with a primary purpose to help readers study the Bible for themselves and strengthen their faith in God.
Related titles: Fax ed.; Microfilm ed.: (from PQC); Online - full text ed.
Published by: Berean Bible Society, PO Box 756, Germantown, WI 53022. TEL 262-255-4750, FAX 262-255-4195, berean@bereanbiblesociety.org. Ed. Ricky L Kurth. Circ: 20,000.

230 USA ISSN 1542-8559
BR1
THE BEST CHRISTIAN WRITING. Text in English. 2000. a., latest 2006. USD 17.95 per issue (effective 2010). back issues avail. **Document type:** *Monographic series, Trade.* **Description:** Contains accessible essays that provide an overview of the range and depth of Christian thinking and display the unity in diversity evident in today's leading Christian writers.
Published by: Jossey-Bass Inc., Publishers (Subsidiary of: John Wiley & Sons, Inc.), 111 River St, Hoboken, NJ 07030. TEL 201-748-6000, FAX 201-748-6088, info@wiley.com. Ed. John Wilson.

220 USA ISSN 1041-6382
BV4241
BEST SERMONS. Text in English. 1988. a. USD 17 per issue (effective 2011). **Document type:** *Trade.*
Published by: HarperCollins Publishers, Inc., 10 E 53rd St, New York, NY 10022. TEL 212-207-7000, orders@harpercollins.com, http://www.harpercollins.com.

230 CAN ISSN 1718-004X
BEYOND ORDINARY LIVING. Text in English. 2006. bi-m. CAD 18.50; CAD 4.95 newsstand/cover (effective 2006). **Document type:** *Magazine, Consumer.*
Address: 201 East River Rd., St. George, ON N0E 1N0, Canada. TEL 877-442-3449, FAX 519-442-4023, info@beyondordinaryliving.com, http://www.beyondordinaryliving.com. Ed., Pub. Ethel Rountree.

220 418.02 AUS
BEYOND WORDS. Text in English. 1986. q. free (effective 2009); donation solicited. bk.rev. back issues avail. **Document type:** *Magazine, Trade.*
Published by: Wycliffe Bible Translators Australia, 70 Graham Rd, Kangaroo Ground, VIC 3097, Australia. TEL 61-3-97122777, FAX 61-3-97122799, info_australia@wycliffe.org. Circ: 9,000 (controlled).

220 ITA ISSN 0006-0585
BS410
BIBBIA E ORIENTE; rivista per la conoscenza della Bibbia. Text in Italian, English, French. 1959. q. EUR 62 domestic; EUR 115 foreign (effective 2009). adv. bk.rev. illus.; bibl.; charts. index. Supplement avail. **Document type:** *Journal, Academic/Scholarly.*
Indexed: A21, DIP, FR, IBR, IBZ, OTA, PCI, RI-1, RI-2, RILM.
—INIST.
Published by: (Centro Studi Arti Grafiche), Sardini Editrice, Via della Pace 73, Bornato in Franciacorta, BS 25046, Italy. TEL 39-030-7750430, FAX 39-030-7254348, sardini@sardini.it. Ed. Fausto Sardini.

220 SWE ISSN 2000-7752
BIBEL. Text in Swedish. 1952. q. illus. **Document type:** *Magazine, Consumer.*
Former titles (until 2010): Bibelns Vaerld (1403-3550); (until 1998): Bibel-Journalen (0006-0607)
Related titles: Online - full text ed.: 2010.
Published by: Svenska Bibelsaellskapet/Swedish Bibel Society, PO Box 1235, Uppsala, 75142, Sweden. TEL 46-18-186330, FAX 46-18-186331, info@bibeln.se, http://www.bibeln.se. Ed. Torbjoern Stolpe.

220 CHE ISSN 1660-2641
BIBEL AKTUELL. Text in German. 1955. 4/yr. CHF 30; CHF 7.50 newsstand/cover (effective 2007). **Document type:** *Magazine, Consumer.*
Formerly (until 1991): Bibel-Nachrichten (1660-265X)
Related titles: French ed.: La Bible Aujourd'hui. ISSN 1661-9331. 1955.
Published by: Schweizerische Bibelgesellschaft/Societe Biblique Suisse, Spitalstr 12, Biel, 2501, Switzerland. TEL 41-32-3223858, FAX 41-32-3233957, info@die-bibel.ch. Circ: 10,500 (paid and controlled).

220 DEU
BIBEL IM JAHR. Text in German. 1964. a. EUR 9.80 (effective 2001). adv. bk.rev. illus. index. 144 p./no.; **Document type:** *Bulletin, Consumer.*
Published by: Katholisches Bibelwerk e.V., Silberburgstr 121, Stuttgart, 70176, Germany. TEL 49-711-6192050, FAX 49-711-6192077, bibelinfo@bibelwerk.de. Ed. Franz-Josef Ortkemper.

220 DNK ISSN 0900-6915
BIBEL OG HISTORIE; skrifter. Text in Danish. 1983. irreg., latest vol.25, 2003. price varies. back issues avail. **Document type:** *Monographic series, Academic/Scholarly.*
Published by: Aarhus Universitetsforlag/Aarhus University Press, Langelandsgade 177, Aarhus N, 8200, Denmark. TEL 45-89-425370, FAX 45-89-425380, unipress@au.dk.

220 AUT ISSN 0006-064X
BIBEL UND LITURGIE. Text in German. 1926. q. EUR 29.50; EUR 8 newsstand/cover (effective 2006). adv. bk.rev. abstr.; bibl.; tr.lit. index. **Document type:** *Bulletin, Academic/Scholarly.*
Indexed: CERDIC, DIP, IBR, IBZ, IZBG, OTA.
Published by: Oesterreichisches Katholisches Bibelwerk, Stiftsplatz 8, Klosterneuburg, 3400, Austria. TEL 43-2243-32938, FAX 43-2243-3293839, zeitschriften@bibelwerk.at, http://www.bibelwerk.at. Circ: 3,000.

220 DEU ISSN 0933-9949
BIBELREPORT. Text in German. 1968. q. EUR 3 (effective 2009). bk.rev. illus. back issues avail. **Document type:** *Bulletin, Consumer.* **Description:** Provides information to memebers of Bible societies in Germany and Austria.
Published by: Deutsche Bibelgesellschaft, Balinger Str 31, Stuttgart, 70567, Germany. TEL 49-711-71810, FAX 49-711-7181126, info@dbg.de. Ed. Veronika Ullmann.

200 USA ISSN 0746-0104
BIBLE ADVOCATE. Text in English. 1863. 10/yr. free. index. back issues avail. **Document type:** *Magazine, Consumer.* **Description:** Features articles on Bible doctrine, current issues in today's world, and other material intended to enrich the spiritual lives of those who seek to know about god.
Published by: (Church of God (Seventh Day), General Conference), Bible Advocate Press, PO Box 33677, Denver, CO 80233. TEL 303-452-7973, FAX 303-452-0657. Ed. Calvin Burrell. R&P Sherri Langton. Circ: 13,500.

220 AUS ISSN 1832-3391
BS410
➤ **THE BIBLE AND CRITICAL THEORY.** Text in English. 2004 (Dec.). 3/yr. free (effective 2011). back issues avail. **Document type:** *Journal, Academic/Scholarly.* **Description:** Publishes work by biblical critics as well as critical theorists interested in the questions the Bible and biblical studies pose for critical theory.
Media: Online - full text.
Indexed: A21, A26, CA, E08, I05, MLA-IB, S02, S03, S09, SociolAb, T02.
Published by: Monash University ePress, Bldg 4, Monash University, Wellington Rd, Clayton, VIC 3800, Australia. TEL 61-3-99050526, FAX 61-3 99058450, epress@lib.monash.edu.au, http://www.epress.monash.edu. Ed. Julie Kelso.

➤ **BIBLE AND SPADE.** *see* ARCHAEOLOGY

200 USA ISSN 1525-9846
BIBLE AND THEOLOGY IN AFRICA. Text in English. 2001. irreg., latest vol.11, 2010. price varies. **Document type:** *Monographic series, Academic/Scholarly.*
Published by: Peter Lang Publishing, Inc. (Subsidiary of: Peter Lang Publishing Group), 29 Broadway, New York, NY 10006. TEL 212-647-7700, 800-770-5264, FAX 212-647-7707, customerservice@plang.com.

220 CHE ISSN 1422-5972
LA BIBLE DANS L'HISTOIRE/BIBLE IN HISTORY. Text in French, English, German. 1996. irreg., latest vol.9, 2010. price varies. **Document type:** *Monographic series, Academic/Scholarly.*
Published by: Peter Lang AG (Subsidiary of: Peter Lang Publishing Group), Hochfeldstr 32, Postfach 746, Bern 9, 3000, Switzerland. TEL 41-31-3061717, FAX 41-31-3061727, info@peterlang.com. Ed. Joseph Alobaidi.

220 GBR
BIBLE EXPLORATION MATERIAL AND ANNUAL PROJECT. Text in English. a. GBP 9.95 (effective 2000). adv. **Document type:** *Bulletin.*
Former titles: Bible Exploration Material and Annual Scripture Project; Scripture Examination Material and Annual Scripture Project.
Published by: National Christian Education Council, 1020 Bristol Rd, Selly Oak, Birmingham, Worcs B29 6LB, United Kingdom. TEL 44-121-472-4242, FAX 44-121-472-7575, ncec@ncec.org.uk. Ed. Elizabeth Bruce. R&P Liam Purcell TEL 44-121-472-4242. Adv. contact Bernard Morgan. Circ: 2,000.

220 USA ISSN 0006-0739
BIBLE FRIEND; of Biblical faith and Christ's teaching. Text in English. 1903. m. USD 4. illus. **Document type:** *Newspaper.*
Published by: Osterhus Publishing House, Inc., 4500 W Broadway, Minneapolis, MN 55422. TEL 612-537-8335. Ed., R&P Ruth I Osterhus. Circ: 10,000.

220 NLD ISSN 1542-1295
THE BIBLE IN ANCIENT CHRISTIANITY. Text in English. 2006. irreg., latest vol.6, 2008. price varies. **Document type:** *Monographic series, Academic/Scholarly.*
Indexed: IZBG.
Published by: Brill, PO Box 9000, Leiden, 2300 PA, Netherlands. TEL 31-71-5353500, FAX 31-71-5317532, cs@brill.nl. Ed. D Jeffrey Bingham.

220 USA ISSN 0278-0259
BIBLE-IN-LIFE FRIENDS. Text in English. w. **Description:** Biblical themes aimed at children aged 6-8.
Published by: David C. Cook Publishing Co., 4050 Lee Vance View, Colorado Springs, CO 80918. TEL 708-741-2400. Ed. Ramona Warren.

220 004 USA ISSN 1943-9369
BIBLE IN TECHNOLOGY. Abbreviated title: B I T. Text in English. 2008 (Dec.). irreg., latest 2009. price varies. back issues avail. **Document type:** *Monographic series, Academic/Scholarly.* **Description:** Explores the intersection between biblical studies and computer technology.
Published by: Gorgias Press LLC, 954 River Rd, Piscataway, NJ 08854. TEL 732-885-8900, FAX 732-885-8908, helpdesk@gorgiaspress.com, http://www.gorgiaspress.com/bookshop/default.aspx.

220 GBR ISSN 0409-3151
THE BIBLE IN THE WORLD. Text in English. 1905. m. **Document type:** *Magazine, Consumer.*
—BLDSC (1947.833500).
Published by: British and Foreign Bible Society, Stonehill Green, Westlea, Swindon, SN5 7DG, United Kingdom. TEL 44-1793-418100, FAX 44-1793-418118, http://www.biblesociety.org.uk/.

230 USA ISSN 1945-5208
BIBLE LIGHT NEWSLETTER. Text in English. irreg. **Document type:** *Newsletter, Consumer.*
Published by: Bible Light International, PO Box 370, Ottawa, KS 66067. TEL 785-242-4150, FAX 785-242-8281, http://www.bible-light.com.

230 USA ISSN 1946-4207
BIBLE LIGHT ON THE NEWS. Text in English. 1994. m. free (effective 2009). back issues avail. **Document type:** *Newsletter, Trade.*
Published by: Bible Light International, PO Box 370, Ottawa, KS 66067. TEL 785-242-4150, FAX 785-242-8281, bli@bible-light.com, http://www.bible-light.com.

220 USA ISSN 2153-8808
BS410
▼ **BIBLE LITERACY LECTURES MONOGRAPH.** Text in English. 2010 (Apr.). a. USD 10 (effective 2011). **Document type:** *Monographic series, Consumer.*
Published by: Back to the Bible Publishing, 6400 Cornhusker Highway, Lincoln, NE 68501-2808. TEL 402-464-7200, info@backtothebible.org, http://www.backtothebible.org.

230 CAN
BIBLE MAGAZINE INTERNET EDITION. Text in English. q. **Description:** Includes articles on bible prophecy, church history and other bible based subjects.
Media: Online - full text.
Published by: Bible Magazine, 84 Lynden Rd, Box 21047, Brantford, ON N3R 6B0, Canada. TEL 519-449-3446. Ed. Paul Billington.

220 SWE ISSN 0347-2787
BIBLE RESEARCHER. Text in Arabic, English, French, German, Polish, Swedish; Summaries in English. 1975. m. SEK 120, USD 20. bk.rev. back issues avail. **Document type:** *Newsletter.*
Published by: European Human Rights, Marknadsvaegen 289, Taby, 18334, Sweden. TEL 08-768-1398. Ed. Ditlieb Felderer. Circ: 1,000.

261 USA ISSN 1556-8555
BIBLE STANDARD. Text in English. 1920. m. USD 12 (effective 2006). **Description:** Highlights doctrines, signs of the times.
Formerly (until 2004): Bible Standard and Herald of Christ's Kingdom (0006-081X)
Related titles: ◆ French ed.: L' Etendard de la Bible et Heraut du Royaume de Christ. ISSN 0245-9329; German ed.; Malay ed.; Tamil ed.; Ukrainian ed.; Danish ed.; Polish ed.
Indexed: CERDIC.
Published by: Laymen's Home Missionary Movement, 1156 Saint Matthews Rd., Chester Sprgs, PA 19425-2700. TEL 610-827-7665. Ed. Ralph Herzig. Circ: 6,000.

268 USA ISSN 1557-4334
BIBLE STUDIES FOR LIFE: HOLMAN CHRISTIAN STANDARD BIBLE ADVANCED BIBLE STUDY COMMENTARY. Variant title: Advanced Bible study commentary. Bible Studies for Life: Advanced Bible Study Commentary. Holman Christian Standard Bible Advanced Bible Study Commentary. Text in English. 2000. q. price varies. back issues avail. **Document type:** *Magazine, Consumer.* **Description:** Designed for teachers and learners who desire extensive commentary. It also includes explanations for key words and concepts, and bible background information.
Formerly (until 2006): F B S. Advanced Bible Study Commentary (1526-5285)
Published by: LifeWay Christian Resources, 1 Lifeway Plz, Nashville, TN 37234. TEL 615-251-2000, 800-458-2772, FAX 615-251-5933, customerservice@lifeway.com, http://www.lifeway.com.

268 USA ISSN 1557-4725
BIBLE STUDIES FOR LIFE: LIFE FOCUS ALL YOUTH LEARNER GUIDE HOLMAN C S B. (Christian Standard Bible) Text in English. 2003. q. price varies. back issues avail. **Document type:** *Magazine, Consumer.* **Description:** Contains teen-targeted articles and true-life testimonies.
Formerly (until 2006): F B S. All Youth Learner Guide H C S B (1541-5929)
Published by: LifeWay Christian Resources, 1 Lifeway Plz, Nashville, TN 37234. TEL 615-251-2000, 800-458-2772, FAX 615-251-5933, customerservice@lifeway.com, http://www.lifeway.com.

268 USA ISSN 1557-4717
BIBLE STUDIES FOR LIFE: LIFE FOCUS ALL YOUTH LEARNER GUIDE K J V. (King James Version) Text in English. 2000. q. price varies. back issues avail. **Document type:** *Magazine, Consumer.* **Description:** Contains teen-targeted articles and true-life testimonies and serves as the basis for in-class study and discussion.

R

Formerly (until 2006): Family Bible Study. All Youth Learner Guide K J V (1526-5307)
Published by: LifeWay Christian Resources, 1 Lifeway Plz, Nashville, TN 37234. TEL 615-251-2000, 800-458-2772, FAX 615-251-5933, customerservice@lifeway.com, http://www.lifeway.com.

268 USA ISSN 1557-4741
BIBLE STUDIES FOR LIFE: LIFE LESSONS LEARNER GUIDE. Text in English. 2003. q. price varies. back issues avail. **Document type:** *Magazine, Consumer.* **Description:** Designed to help adults discover and understand god's word for themselves.
Formerly (until 2006): F B S. Adult Learner Guide H C S B (1541-5945); (until 200?): F B S. Adult Learner Guide N I V
Published by: LifeWay Christian Resources, 1 Lifeway Plz, Nashville, TN 37234. TEL 615-251-2000, 800-458-2772, FAX 615-251-5933, customerservice@lifeway.com.

268 USA ISSN 1557-475X
BIBLE STUDIES FOR LIFE: LIFE TRUTHS LEADER GUIDE. Text in English. q. price varies. back issues avail. **Document type:** *Magazine, Consumer.* **Description:** Maintains a strong family focus by encouraging parents to discuss the struggles relative to their lives and continue their quest for god's truth in a world of many expectations.
Formerly (until 2006): Family Bible Studies: Life Truths Leader Guide (1526-5439)
Published by: LifeWay Christian Resources, 1 Lifeway Plz, Nashville, TN 37234. TEL 615-251-2000, 800-458-2772, FAX 615-251-5933, customerservice@lifeway.com, http://www.lifeway.com.

268 USA ISSN 1557-4954
BIBLE STUDIES FOR LIFE: LIFE WORDS K J V LEADER GUIDE. (King James Version) Text in English. 2000. q. price varies. back issues avail. **Document type:** *Magazine, Consumer.* **Description:** Focuses on the development of godly values, growth in biblical knowledge and understanding of a life of Christlike excellence.
Formerly (until 2006): F B S. Adult Leader Guide K J V (1526-5234)
Published by: LifeWay Christian Resources, 1 Lifeway Plz, Nashville, TN 37234. TEL 615-251-2000, 800-458-2772, FAX 615-251-5933, customerservice@lifeway.com, http://www.lifeway.com.

268 USA ISSN 1557-4148
BIBLE STUDIES FOR LIFE: LIFE WORDS K J V LEADER PACK. (King James Version) Text in English. 2006. q. price varies. back issues avail. **Document type:** *Magazine, Consumer.* **Description:** Helps teachers effectively guide adults of all ages in purposeful bible study.
Published by: LifeWay Christian Resources, 1 Lifeway Plz, Nashville, TN 37234. TEL 615-251-2000, 800-458-2772, FAX 615-251-5933, customerservice@lifeway.com, http://www.lifeway.com.

268 USA ISSN 1557-3850
BIBLE STUDIES FOR LIFE: LIFE2 YOUNGER YOUTH LEADER PACK. Text in English. 2003. q. **Document type:** *Guide, Consumer.* **Description:** For Grades 7-8.
Formerly (until 2006): Family Bible Study. Younger Youth Leader Pack (1542-9008)
Published by: LifeWay Christian Resources, 1 Lifeway Plz, Nashville, TN 37234. TEL 615-251-2000, 800-458-2772, customerservice@lifeway.com, http://www.lifeway.com.

268 USA ISSN 1557-3842
BIBLE STUDIES FOR LIFE: LIFEFX OLDER YOUTH LEADER PACK. Text in English. 2000. q. price varies. back issues avail. **Document type:** *Magazine, Consumer.*
Former titles (until 2006): Bible Studies for Life. Life Ventures Leader Pack (1557-4024); (until 2003): Family Bible Study. Ventures and Pathways Leader Pack (1526-8799)
Published by: LifeWay Christian Resources, 1 Lifeway Plz, Nashville, TN 37234. TEL 615-251-2000, 800-458-2772, FAX 615-251-5933, customerservice@lifeway.com, http://www.lifeway.com.

268 USA ISSN 1557-4938
BIBLE STUDIES FOR LIFE: LIFEFX OLDER YOUTH LEARNER. Text in English. 2000. q. **Document type:** *Guide, Consumer.*
Formerly (until 2006): F B S. Older Youth Learner Guide (1526-5560)
Published by: LifeWay Christian Resources, 1 Lifeway Plz, Nashville, TN 37234. TEL 615-251-2000, 800-458-2772, customerservice@lifeway.com, http://www.lifeway.com.

200 USA ISSN 1938-7814
BIBLE STUDIES FOR LIFE. LIFEMATTERS LEADER PACK. Text in English. 2008. q.
Published by: LifeWay Christian Resources, 1 Lifeway Plz, Nashville, TN 37234. TEL 615-251-2000, 800-458-2772, FAX 615-251-5933, customerservice@lifeway.com, http://www.lifeway.com.

268 USA
BIBLE STUDIES FOR LIFE: LIFEMATTERS LEARNER GUIDE. Text in English. 2000. q. USD 2.10 per issue (effective 2011). adv. back issues avail. **Document type:** *Magazine, Consumer.*
Former titles (until 2007): Bible Studies for Life: Lifematters (1938-4971); (until 200?): Bible Studies for Life: Life Answers Leader Guide (1557-4504); (until 2006): Family Bible Study: Life Answers Leader Guide (1526-5412)
Published by: LifeWay Christian Resources, 1 Lifeway Plz, Nashville, TN 37234. TEL 615-251-2000, 800-458-2772, FAX 615-251-5933, customerservice@lifeway.com. Ed. Laura Magness.

220 GBR
BIBLE STUDY MONTHLY. Text in English. 1924. bi-m. free (effective 2009). adv. bk.rev. back issues avail. **Document type:** *Journal, Academic/Scholarly.* **Description:** Covers Bible history, archaeology, prophecy, exposition, and devotion from a premillennial advent perspective.
Published by: Bible Fellowship Union, 4 Manor Gardens, Barnstone, Nottingham, NG13 9JL, United Kingdom.

220 USA
BIBLE TEACHER AND LEADER. Text in English. q. USD 7.99 per issue (effective 2008). **Document type:** *Magazine, Consumer.* **Description:** Contains lessons that features background, scripture exposition, pronunciation guides, illustrations and learning activities.
Published by: Standard Publishing, 8805 Governor's Hill Dr, Ste 400, Cincinnati, OH 45249. TEL 513-931-4050, 800-543-1353, FAX 877-867-5751, customerservice@standardpub.com, http://www.standardpub.com. Ed. Jonathan Underwood. R&P Mark A Taylor.

268 USA ISSN 1559-2146
BIBLE TEACHING FOR KIDS: 1S & 2S LEADER GUIDE. Text in English. 1970. q. price varies. back issues avail. **Document type:** *Magazine, Consumer.* **Description:** Designed for use in sunday school and extended teaching care programs and leaders can choose activities that best meet the learning style of their preschoolers.
Former titles (until 2006): Bible Teaching for 1's & 2's. Leader Guide (1522-0060); (until 1999): Preschool Bible Teacher. A. (0732-9431); (until 1982): Guide A for Preschool Teachers (0162-4474)
Published by: LifeWay Christian Resources, 1 Lifeway Plz, Nashville, TN 37234. TEL 615-251-2000, 800-458-2772, FAX 615-251-5933, customerservice@lifeway.com, http://www.lifeway.com.

268 USA ISSN 1559-2014
BIBLE TEACHING FOR KIDS: 1S & 2S LEADER PACK. Text in English. 19??. q. price varies. back issues avail. **Document type:** *Magazine, Consumer.* **Description:** Consists of colorful biblical illustrations and other ready-to-use teaching aids that will help teachers create a fun learning environment, while they explain the weekly bible truths.
Formerly (until 2006): Bible Teaching for 1's & 2's. Leader Pack (1522-5003); (until 19??): PreSchool Bible Teacher A. Resource kit (1090-1817)
Published by: LifeWay Christian Resources, 1 Lifeway Plz, Nashville, TN 37234. TEL 615-251-2000, 800-458-2772, FAX 615-251-5933, customerservice@lifeway.com, http://www.lifeway.com.

268 USA ISSN 1557-4393
BIBLE TEACHING FOR KIDS: 1ST & 2ND GRADERS LEADER GUIDE. Variant title: 1st and 2nd graders' leader guide. Text in English. 2000. q. price varies. back issues avail. **Document type:** *Magazine, Consumer.* **Description:** Contains a 4-step teaching plan that is easy to follow and helps leaders guide first and second graders through fun learning activities from the moment they arrive until they leave.
Formerly (until 2006): Family Bible Study: Bible Teaching for 1st and 2nd Graders' Leader Guide (1526-5366)
Published by: LifeWay Christian Resources, 1 Lifeway Plz, Nashville, TN 37234. TEL 615-251-2000, 800-458-2772, FAX 615-251-5933, customerservice@lifeway.com, http://www.lifeway.com.

268 USA ISSN 1557-3893
BIBLE TEACHING FOR KIDS: 1ST & 2ND GRADERS LEADER PACK. Text in English. 2000. q. price varies. back issues avail. **Document type:** *Magazine, Consumer.*
Former titles (until 2006): Family Bible Study: Bible Teaching for 1st and 2nd Graders. Leader Pack (1554-3838); (until 2005): Family Bible Study: 1st & 2nd Graders' Leader Pack (1526-8845)
Published by: LifeWay Christian Resources, 1 Lifeway Plz, Nashville, TN 37234. TEL 615-251-2000, 800-458-2772, FAX 615-251-5933, customerservice@lifeway.com, http://www.lifeway.com.

268 USA ISSN 1557-4385
BIBLE TEACHING FOR KIDS. 1ST AND 2ND GRADERS. LEARNER GUIDE. Text in English. 2000. q. USD 1.90 per issue (effective 2011). back issues avail. **Document type:** *Handbook/Manual/Guide, Consumer.* **Description:** Provides articles full of Bible stories, memory verses, and fun, engaging activities.
Formerly (until 2006): Family Bible Study. Bible Teaching for 1st and 2nd Graders. Learner Guide (1526-5374)
Published by: LifeWay Christian Resources, 1 Lifeway Plz, Nashville, TN 37234. TEL 615-251-2000, 800-458-2772, FAX 615-251-5933, customerservice@lifeway.com.

268 USA ISSN 1558-8270
BIBLE TEACHING FOR KIDS: 1ST AND 2ND GRADERS. TEACHING PICTURES. Text in English. 2000. q. price varies. back issues avail. **Document type:** *Magazine, Consumer.* **Description:** Contains 13 illustrated teaching pictures related to the weekly bible lessons.
Formerly (until 2006): Family Bible Study: Bible Teaching for 1st and 2nd Graders Teaching Pictures (1554-382X); (until 2005): Family Bible Study: 1st and 2nd Graders' Teaching Pictures (1526-8438)
Published by: LifeWay Christian Resources, 1 Lifeway Plz, Nashville, TN 37234. TEL 615-251-2000, 800-458-2772, FAX 615-251-5933, customerservice@lifeway.com, http://www.lifeway.com.

268 USA ISSN 1557-4377
BIBLE TEACHING FOR KIDS: 3RD AND 4TH GRADERS' LEADER GUIDE. Text in English. 2000. q. price varies. back issues avail. **Document type:** *Magazine, Consumer.* **Description:** Contains 4-step teaching plan that is easy to follow and helps leaders guide third and fourth graders through fun activities that teach them to apply biblical truth to everyday life situations.
Formerly (until 2006): Family Bible Study: Bible Teaching for 3rd and 4th Graders Leader Guide (1526-5668)
Published by: LifeWay Christian Resources, 1 Lifeway Plz, Nashville, TN 37234. TEL 615-251-2000, 800-458-2772, FAX 615-251-5933, customerservice@lifeway.com, http://www.lifeway.com.

268 USA ISSN 1557-3915
BIBLE TEACHING FOR KIDS: 3RD AND 4TH GRADERS. LEADER PACK. Text in English. 2000. q. price varies. back issues avail. **Document type:** *Magazine, Consumer.* **Description:** Designed to quickly transform the walls of the classroom into an exciting bible-learning environment and make preparing for class easy.
Former titles (until 2006): Family Bible Study. Bible Teaching for 3rd and 4th Graders. Leader Pack (1554-379X); (until 2005): Family Bible Study. 3rd and 4th Graders' Leader Pack (1526-8837)
Published by: LifeWay Christian Resources, 1 Lifeway Plz, Nashville, TN 37234. TEL 615-251-2000, 800-458-2772, FAX 615-251-5933, customerservice@lifeway.com, http://www.lifeway.com.

268 USA ISSN 1557-4318
BIBLE TEACHING FOR KIDS: 3RD AND 4TH GRADERS' LEARNER GUIDE. Variant title: 3rd and 4th graders' learner guide. Text in English. 2000. q. price varies. back issues avail. **Document type:** *Magazine, Consumer.*
Formerly (until 2006): Family Bible Study: Bible Teaching for 3rd and 4th Graders Learner Guide (1526-5676)
Published by: LifeWay Christian Resources, 1 Lifeway Plz, Nashville, TN 37234. TEL 615-251-2000, 800-458-2772, FAX 615-251-5933, customerservice@lifeway.com, http://www.lifeway.com.

268 USA ISSN 1558-8289
BIBLE TEACHING FOR KIDS: 3RD & 4TH GRADERS TEACHING PICTURES. Text in English. 2000. q. price varies. back issues avail. **Document type:** *Magazine, Consumer.* **Description:** Contains colorful teaching pictures that relates to one of the weekly bible lessons and is designed to help children understand the context of the bible story.
Former titles (until 2006): Family Bible Study: Bible Teaching for 3rd and 4th Graders. Teaching Pictures (1554-3781); (until 2005): Family Bible study: 3rd & 4th Graders' Teaching Pictures (1526-8470)
Published by: LifeWay Christian Resources, 1 Lifeway Plz, Nashville, TN 37234. TEL 615-251-2000, 800-458-2772, FAX 615-251-5933, customerservice@lifeway.com, http://www.lifeway.com.

268 USA ISSN 1559-2154
BIBLE TEACHING FOR KIDS: 3S-PRE-K. LEADER GUIDE. Text in English. 1969. q. price varies. back issues avail. **Document type:** *Magazine, Consumer.* **Description:** Designed for leaders to help preschoolers understand how to apply the bible lesson to their own lives.
Formerly (until 2006): Bible Teaching for 3's-Pre-K. Leader Guide (1522-0052); (until 1999): PreSchool Bible Teacher. B (0732-944X); (until 1982): Guide B for Preschool Teachers (0162-4482)
Published by: LifeWay Christian Resources, 1 Lifeway Plz, Nashville, TN 37234. TEL 615-251-2000, 800-458-2772, FAX 615-251-5933, customerservice@lifeway.com, http://www.lifeway.com.

268 USA ISSN 1559-1999
BIBLE TEACHING FOR KIDS: BABIES LEADER PACK. Text in English. 1999. q. price varies. back issues avail. **Document type:** *Magazine, Consumer.* **Description:** Designed to create a lively bible learning environment for babies up to twelve months of age.
Formerly (until 2006): Bible Teaching for Babies. Leader Pack (1522-4996)
Published by: LifeWay Christian Resources, 1 Lifeway Plz, Nashville, TN 37234. TEL 615-251-2000, 800-458-2772, FAX 615-251-5933, customerservice@lifeway.com, http://www.lifeway.com.

268 USA ISSN 1557-444X
BIBLE TEACHING FOR KIDS: GRADES 1-3 & 4-6 LEADER GUIDE. Variant title: Grades 1-3 and 4-6 Leader Guide. Text in English. 2000. q. price varies. back issues avail. **Document type:** *Magazine, Consumer.* **Description:** Provides a balanced approach to central bible concepts, essential bible skills and foundational bible stories for 1st-3rd, 4th-6th and 1st-6th grades.
Formerly (until 2006): Family Bible Study: Bible Teaching for Grades 1 to 3, 4 to 6 Leader Guide (1526-5404)
Published by: LifeWay Christian Resources, 1 Lifeway Plz, Nashville, TN 37234. TEL 615-251-2000, 800-458-2772, FAX 615-251-5933, customerservice@lifeway.com, http://www.lifeway.com.

268 USA ISSN 1557-3931
BIBLE TEACHING FOR KIDS: GRADES 1-3 & 4-6 LEADER PACK. Variant title: Bible Teaching for Kids: (Broadly) Grades 1-3 & 4-6 Leader Pack. Text in English. 2000. q. price varies. back issues avail. **Document type:** *Magazine, Consumer.* **Description:** Provides a balanced approach to central bible concepts, essential bible skills and foundational bible stories for 1st-3rd, 4th-6th and 1st-6th grades.
Former titles (until 2006): Family Bible Study: Bible Teaching for Grades 1 to 3 and 4 to 6. Leader Pack (1554-3846); (until 2005): Family Bible Study Leader Pack for Grades 1 to 3 and 4 to 6 (1526-8802)
Published by: LifeWay Christian Resources, 1 Lifeway Plz, Nashville, TN 37234. TEL 615-251-2000, 800-458-2772, FAX 615-251-5933, customerservice@lifeway.com, http://www.lifeway.com.

268 USA ISSN 1557-4490
BIBLE TEACHING FOR KIDS: KINDERGARTEN CONNECTION LEARNER GUIDE. Variant title: Kindergarten Connection Learner Guide. Text in English. 200?. q. price varies. back issues avail. **Document type:** *Magazine, Consumer.*
Formerly (until 2006): Family Bible Study: Kindergarten Connection Learner Guide (1555-3094)
Published by: LifeWay Christian Resources, 1 Lifeway Plz, Nashville, TN 37234. TEL 615-251-2000, 800-458-2772, FAX 615-251-5933, customerservice@lifeway.com, http://www.lifeway.com.

268 USA ISSN 1559-2022
BIBLE TEACHING FOR KIDS: KINDERGARTEN LEADER PACK. Text in English. 19??. q. price varies. back issues avail. **Document type:** *Magazine, Consumer.* **Description:** Provides a balanced approach to central bible concepts, essential bible skills and foundational bible stories for babies through preteens.
Former titles (until 2006): Bible Teaching for Kindergarten. Leader Pack (1522-502X); (until 1999): Preschool Bible Teacher C. Resource Kit (1090-168X)
Published by: LifeWay Christian Resources, 1 Lifeway Plz, Nashville, TN 37234. TEL 615-251-2000, 800-458-2772, FAX 615-251-5933, customerservice@lifeway.com, http://www.lifeway.com.

268 371.9 USA ISSN 1935-6242
BIBLE TEACHING FOR KIDS: SPECIAL BUDDIES GRADES 1-6. LEADER GUIDE. Text in English. 2007. q. USD 5.25 per issue (effective 2011). adv. back issues avail. **Document type:** *Handbook/Manual/Guide, Consumer.*
Published by: LifeWay Christian Resources, 1 Lifeway Plz, Nashville, TN 37234. TEL 615-251-2000, 800-458-2772, FAX 615-251-5933, customerservice@lifeway.com. Ed. Joy Kirkland Fisher.

268 USA ISSN 1935-6250
BIBLE TEACHING FOR KIDS: SPECIAL BUDDIES GRADES 1-6. LEARNER GUIDE. Text in English. 2007. q. USD 2.95 per issue (effective 2011). adv. back issues avail. **Document type:** *Handbook/Manual/Guide, Consumer.*
Published by: LifeWay Christian Resources, 1 Lifeway Plz, Nashville, TN 37234. TEL 615-251-2000, 800-458-2772, FAX 615-251-5933, customerservice@lifeway.com. Ed. Joy Kirkland Fisher.

268 USA ISSN 1949-4769
BIBLE TEACHING FOR PRETEENS. B T X. A BIBLE TEACHING EPERIENCE FOR PRETEENS. LEADER GUIDE. Variant title: Bible Teaching for Kids: B T X Preteen Leader Guide. Text in English. 200?. q. price varies. adv. **Document type:** *Guide, Consumer.* **Description:** Provides sunday school teaching plans designed just for preteens.
Former titles (until 2009): Bible Teaching for Kids. B T X. A Bible Teaching Experience for Preteens. Leader Guide (1936-8747); Which incorporated (2006-2007): Bible Teaching for Kids: Preteen Leader Guide (1557-4458); Which was formerly (until 2006): Family Bible Study: Bible Teaching for Preteens Leader Guide (1555-3213); (until 2005): Family Bible Study: Preteen Leader Guide (1526-5587)
Published by: LifeWay Christian Resources, 1 Lifeway Plz, Nashville, TN 37234. TEL 615-251-2000, 800-458-2772, FAX 615-251-5933, customerservice@lifeway.com, http://www.lifeway.com.

268 USA ISSN 1949-4750
BIBLE TEACHING FOR PRETEENS. B T X. A BIBLE TEACHING EXPERIENCE FOR PRETEENS. LEARNER GUIDE. Variant title: Bible Teaching for Kids: B T X Preteen Learner Guide. Text in English. 2000. q. price varies. back issues avail. **Document type:** *Magazine, Consumer.* **Description:** Provides a balanced approach to central bible concepts, essential bible skills and foundational bible stories for babies through preteens.
Former titles (until 2009): Bible Teaching for Kids. B T X. A Bible Teaching Experience for Preteens. Learner Guide (1936-8410); Which incorporated (2006-2007): Bible Teaching for Kids: Preteen Learner Guide (1557-4466); Which was formerly (until 2006): Family Bible Study: Preteen Learner Guide (1526-565X)
Published by: LifeWay Christian Resources, 1 Lifeway Plz, Nashville, TN 37234. TEL 615-251-2000, 800-458-2772, FAX 615-251-5933, customerservice@lifeway.com, http://www.lifeway.com.

268 USA ISSN 2150-7449
BIBLE TEACHING FOR PRETEENS. BTX. A BIBLE TEACHING EXPERIENCE FOR PRETEENS. LEADER PACK. Text in English. 2000. q. back issues avail. **Document type:** *Magazine, Consumer.* **Description:** Contains teaching aids needed for fifth- and sixth-grade sunday school classes.
Former titles (until 2009): Bible Teaching for Kids. B T X. A Bible Teaching Experience for Preteens. Leader Pack (1936-9093); (until 2007): Bible Teaching for Kids: Preteens. Leader Pack (1557-3982); (until 2006): Family Bible Study. Bible Teaching for Preteens. Leader Pack for Leaders of 5th and 6th Graders (1554-3811); (until 2005): Family Bible Study. Preteen Leader Pack (1526-8780)
Published by: LifeWay Christian Resources, 1 Lifeway Plz, Nashville, TN 37234. TEL 615-251-2000, 800-458-2772, FAX 615-251-5933, customerservice@lifeway.com, http://www.lifeway.com.

268 USA ISSN 2150-7457
BIBLE TEACHING FOR PRETEENS. BTX. A BIBLE TEACHING EXPERIENCE FOR PRETEENS. TEACHING PICTURES. Text in English. 2000. q. back issues avail. **Document type:** *Magazine, Consumer.*
Former titles (until 2009): Bible Teaching for Kids: BTX. Teaching Pictures. A Bible Teaching Experience for Preteens (1936-9107); (until 2007): Bible Teaching for Kids: Preteens. Teaching Pictures (1557-3990); (until 2006): Family Bible Study: Bible Teaching for Preteens. Teaching Pictures for Leaders of 5th and 6th Graders (1554-3803); (until 2005): Family Bible Study: Preteen Teaching Pictures (1526-8462)
Published by: LifeWay Christian Resources, 1 Lifeway Plz, Nashville, TN 37234. TEL 615-251-2000, 800-458-2772, FAX 615-251-5933, customerservice@lifeway.com, http://www.lifeway.com.

220 USA ISSN 0006-0836
BS410
THE BIBLE TODAY. Text in English. 1962. bi-m. USD 33 domestic; USD 47 foreign; USD 52 to libraries; USD 7 per issue (effective 2009). adv. bk.rev. illus. Index. reprints avail. **Document type:** *Magazine, Consumer.* **Description:** Explores scripture through illustrated articles and commentary that focus on a particular theme or book of the Bible and come from the most recent and best biblical scholarship.
Related titles: Microform ed.: (from PQC).
Indexed: A01, A22, CPL, OTA.
Published by: Liturgical Press, St John's Abbey, PO Box 7500, Collegeville, MN 56321. TEL 320-363-2213, 800-858-5450, FAX 320-363-3299, 800-445-5899, sales@litpress.org. Ed. Rev. Donald Senior. adv.: page USD 450; 4.5 x 7.5. Circ: 3,659.

THE BIBLE TRANSLATOR. PRACTICAL PAPERS. *see* LINGUISTICS

BIBLE TRANSLATOR. TECHNICAL PAPERS. *see* LINGUISTICS

207.2 USA
BIBLES FOR THE WORLD REPORT. Text in English. 1966. q. free to donors. bk.rev. **Document type:** *Newsletter.* **Description:** Focuses on bible distribution and follow-up ministry in the US and around the world.
Formerly: Bibles for the World News
Published by: Bibles for the World, Inc., PO Box 470, Colorado Springs, CO 80901. TEL 719-630-7733, FAX 719-630-1449. Eds. John L Pudaite, Rochunga Pudaite. Pub. Rochunga Pudaite. R&P John L Pudaite. Circ: 35,000.

230 FRA ISSN 1630-4977
BIBLIA. Text in French. 2001. m. EUR 58 domestic; EUR 58 DOM-TOM; EUR 58 in Belgium; EUR 65 elsewhere (effective 2009). back issues avail. **Document type:** *Magazine, Consumer.*
Published by: Editions du Cerf, 29 Boulevard La Tour Maubourg, Paris, 75340 Cedex 07, France. http://www.editionsducerf.fr.

220 DNK ISSN 1399-1361
BIBLIANA; tekst, kultur, historie. Text in Danish. 1999. s-a. DKK 180; DKK 160 to students (effective 2008). back issues avail. **Document type:** *Journal, Academic/Scholarly.* **Description:** Contains articles on the interpretation of biblical texts, culture in biblical times, and the relationship between history and Biblical scriptures.
Related titles: Online - full text ed.
Published by: Anis Forlaget, Frederiksberg Alle 10 A, Frederiksberg C, 1820, Denmark. TEL 45-33-249250, FAX 45-33-250607, info@anis.dk. Eds. Pernille Carstens, Allan Rosengren. **Dist. by:** International Specialized Book Services Inc.

BIBLICAL ARCHAEOLOGY REVIEW. *see* ARCHAEOLOGY

220 NLD ISSN 1874-3927
BIBLICAL ENCYCLOPEDIA. Text in English. irreg., latest vol.3, 2007. price varies. **Document type:** *Monographic series.*
Indexed: IZBG.
Published by: (Society of Biblical Literature USA), Brill, PO Box 9000, Leiden, 2300 PA, Netherlands. TEL 31-71-5353500, FAX 31-71-5317532, cs@brill.nl.

220 NLD ISSN 0927-2569
BS410
➤ **BIBLICAL INTERPRETATION**; a journal of contemporary approaches. Text in English. 1993. 5/yr. EUR 329, USD 461 to institutions; EUR 359, USD 503 combined subscription to institutions (print & online eds.) (effective 2012). bk.rev. back issues avail.; reprint service avail. from PSC. **Document type:** *Journal, Academic/Scholarly.* **Description:** Provides an interdisciplinary forum for fresh Biblical interpretation and critical analysis in a variety of styles, including post-structuralism, semiotics, feminism, liberation hermeneutics, and for theoretical discussions of such interpretations.
Related titles: Online - full text ed.: ISSN 1568-5152. EUR 299, USD 419 to institutions (effective 2012) (from IngentaConnect).
Indexed: A01, A02, A03, A08, A21, A22, AmHI, CA, DIP, E01, FamI, H07, IBR, IBZ, IZBG, J01, L05, L06, MLA-IB, OTA, PCI, R&TA, RI-1, RI-2, SCOPUS, T02.
—IE, Infotrieve, Ingenta. **CCC.**
Published by: Brill, PO Box 9000, Leiden, 2300 PA, Netherlands. TEL 31-71-5353500, FAX 31-71-5317532, cs@brill.nl. Ed. Hugh Pyper. **Dist. in N. America by:** Brill, PO Box 605, Herndon, VA 20172-0605. TEL 703-661-1585, 800-337-9255, FAX 703-661-1501, cs@brillusa.com; **Dist. by:** Turpin Distribution Services Ltd., Pegasus Dr, Stratton Business Park, Biggleswade, Bedfordshire SG18 8QB, United Kingdom. TEL 44-1767-604954, FAX 44-1767-601640, custserv@turpin-distribution.com, http://www.turpin-distribution.com/.

220.6 809.935 NLD ISSN 0928-0731
BS500
➤ **BIBLICAL INTERPRETATION SERIES.** Text in English. 1993. irreg., latest vol.109, 2011. price varies. back issues avail. **Document type:** *Monographic series, Academic/Scholarly.* **Description:** Publishes contemporary Biblical scholarship and studies of related issues in Biblical interpretation, providing a vehicle for experimental work from a whole range of newer perspectives, including feminist readings, semiotic and post-structuralist approaches, ecological, psychological and many other types of readings.
Indexed: IZBG.
Published by: Brill, PO Box 9000, Leiden, 2300 PA, Netherlands. TEL 31-71-5353500, FAX 31-71-5317532, cs@brill.nl. Eds. Paul Anderson, Yvonne Sherwood. **Dist. in N. America by:** Brill, PO Box 605, Herndon, VA 20172-0605. TEL 703-661-1585, 800-337-9255, FAX 703-661-1501, cs@brillusa.com; **Dist. by:** Turpin Distribution Services Ltd., Pegasus Dr, Stratton Business Park, Biggleswade, Bedfordshire SG18 8QB, United Kingdom. TEL 44-1767-604954, FAX 44-1767-601640, custserv@turpin-distribution.com, http://www.turpin-distribution.com/.

220 USA ISSN 1943-9377
BIBLICAL INTERSECTIONS. Text in English. 2008 (Dec.). irreg., latest 2010. price varies. back issues avail. **Document type:** *Monographic series, Academic/Scholarly.* **Description:** Promotes research that takes a comparative approach, seeking to understand the biblical texts in relation to cognate literature of the ancient world.
Published by: Gorgias Press LLC, 954 River Rd, Piscataway, NJ 08854. TEL 732-885-8900, FAX 732-885-8908, helpdesk@gorgiaspress.com, http://www.gorgiaspress.com/bookshop/default.aspx.

220 USA ISSN 1043-5522
BV4200
BIBLICAL PREACHING JOURNAL. Text in English. 1988. q. USD 35 domestic; USD 38 in Canada & Mexico; USD 50 elsewhere (effective 2005). back issues avail. **Document type:** *Journal, Trade.*
Published by: Deerhaven Press, PO Box 603, Versailles, KY 40383-0603. TEL 859-873-0550, 800-961-0015, FAX 859-873-5763, info@deerhaven.com, http://www.deerhaven.com.

230 USA ISSN 0277-0474
BIBLICAL SCHOLARSHIP IN NORTH AMERICA. Text in English. 1976. irreg., latest vol.22, 2006. price varies. back issues avail. **Document type:** *Monographic series, Trade.* **Description:** Monographs on important biblical scholars in the United States.
Published by: Society of Biblical Literature, The Luce Ctr, 825 Houston Mill Rd, Atlanta, GA 30329. TEL 404-727-3100, 866-727-9955, FAX 404-727-3101, sblexec@sbl-site.org. Ed. Bob Buller TEL 970-669-9900.

220 IRL ISSN 0006-0917
BIBLICAL THEOLOGY. Text in English. 1950. s-a. USD 3. bk.rev.
Published by: Donegal Democrat, Ballyshannon, Co. Donegal, Ireland. Eds. Rev. Dr J Thompson, Rev. R D Drysdale. Circ: 250.

220 GBR ISSN 0146-1079
BS410
➤ **BIBLICAL THEOLOGY BULLETIN.** Text in English. 1971. q. USD 235, GBP 127 combined subscription to institutions (print & online eds.); USD 230, GBP 124 to institutions (effective 2011). adv. bk.rev. bibl. index, cum.index. 50 p./no.; back issues avail.; reprint service avail. from PSC. **Document type:** *Journal, Academic/Scholarly.* **Description:** Covers Bible and theology for clergy, educators in religion and social sciences, college and seminary students, and libraries.
Related titles: Microfiche ed.: (from PQC, WMP); Online - full text ed.: ISSN 1945-7596. USD 212, GBP 114 to institutions (effective 2011).
Indexed: A01, A21, A22, A26, B14, BRI, CA, CBRI, CERDIC, CPL, DIP, E01, E08, G08, GSS&RPL, I05, IBR, IBZ, IZBG, OTA, PCI, R&TA, R05, RI-1, RI-2, S09, SCOPUS, T02.
—BLDSC (1947.856000), IE, Infotrieve, Ingenta. **CCC.**
Published by: (Biblical Theology Bulletin, Inc. USA), Sage Publications Ltd. (Subsidiary of: Sage Publications, Inc.), 1 Oliver's Yard, 55 City Rd, London, EC1Y 1SP, United Kingdom. TEL 44-20-73248500, FAX 44-20-73248600, info@sagepub.co.uk, http://www.uk.sagepub.com/home.nav. Ed. David M Bossman. adv.: B&W page USD 400; 8.5 x 11. Circ: 1,000 (paid).

220 SWE ISSN 0345-1453
BIBLICUM; tidskrift foer biblisk tro och forskning. Text in Swedish. 1937. q. SEK 150; SEK 99 to students (effective 2003). bk.rev. Index. Supplement avail.; back issues avail.
Formerly (until 1972): Foer Biblisk Tro (0015-5217)
Published by: Stiftelsen Biblicum, c/o Carl Peterson, Norra Stationsgatan 29, Traryd, 28772, Sweden. Ed. Alvar Svenson. Circ: 1,000.

220 HRV ISSN 1331-5757
BIBLIJA DANAS. Text in Croatian. 1996. q. **Document type:** *Journal, Academic/Scholarly.*
Indexed: A26.
Published by: Sveuciliste u Zagrebu, Katolicki Bogoslovni Fakultet, Institut za Biblijski Pastoral, Vlaska 38, Zagreb, 10001, Croatia. Ed. Tadej Vojnovic. **Co-publisher:** Hrvatska Franjevacka Provincija Sv. Cirila i Metoda.

200 ESP ISSN 1699-9088
BIBLIOTECA CONMEMORATIVA. Text in Spanish. 2000. irreg. **Document type:** *Monographic series, Academic/Scholarly.*
Published by: Editorail Libsa, S.A, C San Rafael No 4, Alcobendas, Madrid, 28108, Spain. TEL 34-91-6572580, FAX 34-91-6572583, libsa@libsa.es, http://www.libsa.es/.

200 ESP ISSN 1699-4450
BIBLIOTECA DE LAS RELIGIONES. Variant title: Religiones y Textos. Text in Spanish. 1999. irreg. **Document type:** *Monographic series, Academic/Scholarly.*
Published by: Ediciones del Orto, C San Maximo, 31 4o - 8 Edif. 2000, Madrid, 28041, Spain. TEL 34-91-5003174, FAX 34-91-5003185, ediclas@arrakis.es, http://www.edicionesclasicas.es/OrtoBibRelig.htm. Ed. Francisco Diez de Velasco.

200 ESP ISSN 0067-740X
BIBLIOTECA DE TEOLOGIA. Text in Spanish. 1962. irreg., latest vol.33, 2007. price varies. back issues avail. **Document type:** *Monographic series, Academic/Scholarly.*
Published by: (Universidad de Navarra, Facultad de Teologia), Universidad de Navarra, Servicio de Publicaciones, Campus Universitario, Pamplona, 31009, Spain.

200 ESP ISSN 2172-2269
BIBLIOTECA DE TEOLOGIA COMILLAS. Text in Spanish. 2000. a. **Document type:** *Monographic series, Academic/Scholarly.*
Published by: Universidad Pontificia de Comillas, C Alberto Aguilera 23, Madrid, 28015, Spain. TEL 34-91-5422800, FAX 34-91-5596569, oia@oia.upcomillas.es, http://www.upcomillas.es/.

200 ITA ISSN 1824-1387
BIBLIOTECA DI TEOLOGIA CONTEMPORANEA. Text in Italian. 1969. irreg. **Document type:** *Bibliography.*
Published by: Editrice Queriniana, Via Enrico Ferri 75, Brescia, BS 25123, Italy. TEL 39-030-2306925, FAX 39-030-2306932, http://www.queriniana.it.

230 PER ISSN 1609-9907
BIBLIOTECA ELECTRONICA CRISTIANA. Text in Spanish. 1999. irreg.
Media: Online - full text.
Published by: VE Multimedios, Ave Brasil 3029, Lima, 17, Peru. TEL 51-1-3410308, FAX 51-1-4344327, ve@multimedios.org, http://www.multimedios.org/.

200 SWE
BIBLIOTECA THEOLOGIAE PRACTICAE. Text in Swedish; Summaries in English, German. 1957. irreg., latest vol.61, 1999. price varies. back issues avail. **Document type:** *Monographic series.*
Published by: Arcus Foerlag, Fack 1026, Lund, 22104, Sweden. TEL 46-46-13-88-83, FAX 46-46-211-11-12.

268 POL ISSN 0208-7413
BIBLIOTEKA KAZNODZIEJSKA. Text in Polish. 1870. m. EUR 84 foreign (effective 2006).
Published by: (Kuria Metropolitalna w Poznaniu), Biblioteka Kaznodziejska, ul Chartowo 5, Poznan, 61245, Poland. TEL 48-61-8749268, FAX 48-61-8749226. **Dist. by:** Ars Polona, Obroncow 25, Warsaw 03933, Poland. TEL 48-22-5098609, FAX 48-22-5098610, arspolona@arspolona.com.pl, http://www.arspolona.com.pl.

BIBLIOTHECA DISSIDENTIUM. *see* BIBLIOGRAPHIES

200 BEL
BIBLIOTHECA EPHEMERIDUM THEOLOGICARUM LOVANIENSIUM. Text in French. 1954. irreg. (4-6/yr), latest vol.157, 2000. price varies. back issues avail. **Document type:** *Monographic series, Academic/Scholarly.*
Related titles: ◆ Supplement to: Ephemerides Theologicae Lovanienses. ISSN 0013-9513.
Indexed: IZBG, RI-2.
Published by: Leuven University Press, Blijde Inkomststraat 5, Leuven, 3000, Belgium. TEL 32-16-325345, FAX 32-16-325352, university.press@upers.kuleuven.ac.be, http://www.kuleuven.ac.be/upers.

200 NLD ISSN 1567-8385
BIBLIOTHECA HUMANISTICA & REFORMATORICA. Text in English, French, German. 1971. irreg., latest vol.60, 2004. price varies. **Document type:** *Monographic series, Academic/Scholarly.*
Published by: Hes & De Graaf Publishers BV, Postbus 540, Houten, 3990 GH, Netherlands. TEL 31-30-6380071, FAX 31-30-6380099, info@hesdegraaf.com, http://www.hesdegraaf.com.

BIBLIOTHECA VICTORINA; subsidia ad historiam canonicorum regularium investigandam. *see* HISTORY—History Of Europe

230 809 BEL ISSN 0996-4657
BIBLIOTHEQUE AUGUSTINIENNE. Text in French. 1933. irreg. price varies. **Document type:** *Monographic series, Academic/Scholarly.* **Description:** Provides its readers with a complete edition of the works of Saint Augustine in Latin along with a French translation.
Published by: (Institut d'Etudes Augustiniennes FRA), Brepols Publishers, Begijnhof 67, Turnhout, 2300, Belgium. TEL 32-14-448020, FAX 32-14-428919, periodicals@brepols.net, http://www.brepols.net. Ed. Jean Claude Fredouille.

281.72 BEL
BIBLIOTHEQUE COPTE DE NAG HAMMADI. SECTION CONCORDANCES. Text in French. 1992. irreg. price varies. **Document type:** *Monographic series, Academic/Scholarly.*
Published by: Peeters Publishers, Bondgenotenlaan 153, Leuven, 3000, Belgium. TEL 32-16-235170, FAX 32-16-228500, peeters@peeters-leuven.be, http://www.peeters-leuven.be.

281.72 BEL
➤ **BIBLIOTHEQUE COPTE DE NAG HAMMADI. SECTION ETUDES.** Text in French; Text occasionally in Multiple languages. 1983. irreg., latest vol.9, 1995. price varies. back issues avail. **Document type:** *Monographic series, Academic/Scholarly.*
Published by: Peeters Publishers, Bondgenotenlaan 153, Leuven, 3000, Belgium. TEL 32-16-235170, FAX 32-16-228500, http://www.peeters-leuven.be.

R

281.72 BEL ISSN 0824-9555
BT1390
➤ **BIBLIOTHEQUE COPTE DE NAG HAMMADI. SECTION TEXTES.** Text in Coptic, English, French. 1977. irreg., latest 2000. price varies. back issues avail. **Document type:** *Monographic series, Academic/Scholarly.* **Description:** Publishes studies on topics relating to gnosticism, early Christianity and the Coptic texts uncovered and Nag Hammadi, Egypt.
Published by: (Universite Laval, Faculte de Theologie et de Sciences Religieuses CAN), Peeters Publishers, Bondgenotenlaan 153, Leuven, 3000, Belgium. TEL 32-16-235170, FAX 32-16-228500, http://www.peeters-leuven.be. **Co-publisher:** Les Presses de l'Universite Laval.

291 FRA ISSN 1771-9518
BIBLIOTHEQUE DE CULTURE RELIGIEUSE. Text in French. 2004. irreg. back issues avail. **Document type:** *Monographic series.*
Published by: Librairie Fayard, 13 Rue du Montparnasse, Paris, 75006, France. TEL 33-1-45498200, FAX 33-1-42224017, http://www.editions-fayard.fr.

200 BEL
➤ **BIBLIOTHEQUE DE L'ECOLE DES HAUTES ETUDES SCIENCES RELIGIEUSES.** Text in French. 1889. irreg., latest vol.104, 1997. price varies. back issues avail. **Document type:** *Monographic series, Academic/Scholarly.*
Published by: (Ecole des Hautes Etudes Sciences Religieuses), Brepols Publishers, Begijnhof 67, Turnhout, 2300, Belgium. TEL 32-14-448020, FAX 32-14-428919, periodicals@brepols.net, http://www.brepols.net.

220 DEU ISSN 0930-4800
BIBLISCH-THEOLOGISCHE STUDIEN. Text in German. 1951. irreg., latest vol.73, 2005. price varies. **Document type:** *Monographic series, Academic/Scholarly.*
Formerly (until 1977): Biblische Studien (0520-0741)
Indexed: IZBG.
Published by: Neukirchener Verlag, Andreas-Braem-Str 18-20, Neukirchen-Vluyn, 47506, Germany. TEL 49-2845-392222, FAX 49-2845-33689, info@nvg-medien.de, http://www.nvg-medien.de.

220 CHE ISSN 0582-1673
BIBLISCHE BEITRAEGE. Text in German. 1961. irreg., latest vol.13, 1977. price varies. adv. illus. **Document type:** *Monographic series, Academic/Scholarly.*
Published by: Academic Press Fribourg, Perolles 42, Fribourg, 1705, Switzerland. TEL 41-26-4264311, FAX 41-26-264264300. Circ: 1,750.

220.7 DEU ISSN 0178-2967
BS514.2
BIBLISCHE NOTIZEN; Aktuelle Beitraege zur Exegese der Bibel und ihrer Welt. Text in German. 1976. q. EUR 96; EUR 25 newsstand/cover (effective 2010). **Document type:** *Journal, Academic/Scholarly.*
Indexed: A21, A22, FR, IZBG, OTA, RI-1.
—BLDSC (2020.765000), IE, Ingenta, INIST.
Published by: (Universitaet Salzburg, Bibelwissenschaft und Kirchengeschichte AUT), Verlag Herder GmbH, Hermann-Herder-Str 4, Freiburg Im Breisgau, 79104, Germany. TEL 49-761-27170, FAX 49-761-2717520, kundenservice@herder.de. Ed. Friedrich Reiterer.

220 DEU ISSN 0523-5154
BIBLISCHE UNTERSUCHUNGEN. Text in German. 1967. irreg., latest vol.30, 2001. price varies. **Document type:** *Monographic series, Academic/Scholarly.*
Published by: Verlag Friedrich Pustet, Gutenbergstr 8, Regensburg, 93051, Germany. TEL 49-941-920220, FAX 49-941-92022330, verlag@pustet.de, http://www.pustetverlag.de. Eds. Josef Hainz, Jost Eckert. Circ: 800.

220 DEU ISSN 0006-2014
BS410
BIBLISCHE ZEITSCHRIFT. Text in German. N.S. 1957. s-a. EUR 28 per issue (effective 2010). adv. bibl. index. reprints avail. **Document type:** *Journal, Academic/Scholarly.* **Description:** Collection of articles concerning the Old and the New Testament. Includes reviews and criticisms.
Related titles: Microform ed.: N.S. (from PQC).
Indexed: A20, A21, A22, ASCA, ArtHuCI, BibLing, CERDIC, CurCont, DIP, FR, IBR, IBZ, IZBG, OTA, PCI, R&TA, RI-1, RI-2, SCOPUS, W07.
—BLDSC (2020.800000), IE, Infotrieve, Ingenta, INIST. **CCC.**
Published by: Verlag Ferdinand Schoeningh GmbH, Postfach 2540, Paderborn, 33055, Germany. TEL 49-5251-1275, FAX 49-5251-127860, info@schoeningh.de.

200 ESP ISSN 2174-0593
▼ **BIDEGURUTZE.** Text in Spanish. 2011. s-a. back issues avail. **Document type:** *Magazine, Consumer.*
Media: Online - full text.
Published by: Instituto Diocesano de Teologia Pastoral, Plaza Nueva, 4 - 1o, Bilbao, 48005, Spain. TEL 34-944-795652, http://www.idtp.org/. Ed. Roberto Casas Andres.

BIJDRAGEN; international journal for philosophy and theology. *see* PHILOSOPHY

BILD - RAUM - FEIER. *see* ART

200 DEU
BILUM; fuer weltoffene Christennen. Text in German. 3/yr. EUR 15; EUR 7 newsstand/cover (effective 2011). **Document type:** *Journal, Trade.*
Published by: Steyler Missionare e.V., Bahnhofstr 9, Nettetal, 41334, Germany. TEL 49-2157-120200, FAX 49-2157-1202060, steyler@steyler.de. Ed. Christian Tauchner.

262.02 ESP
BISBAT DE TORTOSA. BUTLLETI OFICIAL/OBISPADO DE TORTOSA. BOLETIN OFICIAL. Text in Catalan. 1858. m. bk.rev. bibl. index. **Document type:** *Bulletin.*
Published by: Bisbat de Tortosa/Obispado de Tortosa, Cruera 5, Tortosa, Spain. TEL 34-977-440700, FAX 34-977-440378, bisbattortosa@planalfa.es.

200 GBR ISSN 1476-9948
BT82.7
BLACK THEOLOGY. Abbreviated title: B T. Text in English. 1998. 3/yr. USD 300 combined subscription in North America to institutions (print & online eds.); GBP 185 combined subscription elsewhere to institutions (print & online eds.) (effective 2012). adv. back issues avail.; reprints avail. **Document type:** *Journal, Academic/Scholarly.* **Description:** Provides a forum for the articulation and expression of issues of faith among Black people in the world.
Formerly (until 2002): Black Theology in Britain (1462-3161)
Related titles: Online - full text ed.: ISSN 1743-1670. USD 240 in North America to institutions; GBP 148 elsewhere to institutions (effective 2012).
Indexed: A01, A03, A08, A21, CA, R&TA, RI-1, SRRA, T02.
—IE. **CCC.**
Published by: (The Queens Foundation), Equinox Publishing Ltd., Unit S3, Kelham House, 3 Lancaster St, Sheffield, S6 3AF, United Kingdom. TEL 44-114-2725957, FAX 44-560-3459046, journals@equinoxpub.com, http://www.equinoxpub.com/. Ed. Dr. Anthony G Reddie. Adv. contact Val Hall.

270 940 DEU ISSN 0341-9479
BLAETTER FUER WUERTTEMBERGISCHE KIRCHENGESCHICHTE. Text in German. 1886. a. bk.rev. index. reprints avail. **Document type:** *Journal, Academic/Scholarly.*
Indexed: DIP, HistAb, IBR, IBZ, MLA-IB, P30, RILM.
Published by: Verein fuer Wuerttembergische Kirchengeschichte, Gaensheidestr 4, Stuttgart, 70184, Germany. TEL 49-711-2149212, FAX 49-711-2149236. Eds. Hermann Ehmer, Martin Brecht. Circ: 1,250.

200 CHE ISSN 0179-3012
BLAUES KREUZ. Text in German. 1897. m. EUR 2 per issue (effective 2009). **Document type:** *Magazine, Consumer.*
Published by: (Blaues Kreuz in Deutschland e.V.), Blaukreuz Verlag, Sonderfelder Weg 15, Luedenscheid, 58513, Germany. TEL 49-2351-4324943, FAX 49-2351-4324945, bkv@blaukreuz.de, http://www.blaukreuz.de. Circ: 5,400.

230 DEU
▼ **BLICKARTIST.** Text in German. 2010. irreg. price varies. **Document type:** *Monographic series, Academic/Scholarly.*
Published by: I K S Garamond, Leutragraben 1, Jena, 07743, Germany. TEL 49-3641-460850, FAX 49-3641-460855, garamond@iks-jena.de.

BOA SEMENTE. *see* CHILDREN AND YOUTH—For

220 PER
BOLETIN TEOLOGICO. Text in Spanish. 3/yr. USD 20 in Latin America; USD 35 elsewhere (effective 2004).
Indexed: OTA.
Published by: Fraternidad Teologica Latinoamericana/Latin American Theological Fraternity, Apartado 32, Lima, 43, Peru. TEL 51-1-3490023, FAX 51-1-3483225, fratela@terra.com.pe, http://www.fratela.org/.

BOLLINGEN SERIES. *see* PHILOSOPHY

220 DEU
BONNER BIBLISCHE BEITRAEGE. Text in German. 1950. irreg., latest vol.163, 2010. price varies. **Document type:** *Monographic series, Academic/Scholarly.*
Former titles: Athenaeums Monografien. Theologie (0938-3182); (until 1988): Bonner Biblische Beitraege (0520-5670)
Indexed: IZBG.
Published by: V & R Unipress GmbH (Subsidiary of: Vandenhoeck und Ruprecht), Robert-Bosch-Breite 6, Goettingen, 37079, Germany. TEL 49-551-5084303, FAX 49-551-5084333, info@vr-unipress.de, http://www.v-r.de/en/publisher/unipress.

200 300 DEU ISSN 1866-489X
BONNER ZENTRUM FUER RELIGION UND GESELLSCHAFT. STUDIEN. Text in German. 2006. irreg., latest vol.6, 2010. price varies. **Document type:** *Monographic series, Academic/Scholarly.*
Published by: Ergon Verlag, Keesburgstr 11, Wuerzburg, 97074, Germany. TEL 49-931-280084, FAX 49-931-282872, service@ergon-verlag.de.

264 DEU ISSN 0176-8573
BOTSCHAFT HEUTE. Text in German. 1975. 11/yr. looseleaf. EUR 114 (effective 2011). back issues avail. **Document type:** *Journal, Academic/Scholarly.* **Description:** Publication of interest to preachers. Features ideas for topics, songs, psalms, prayers, Bible excerpts, and liturgical texts for sermons on all Sundays and special celebrations.
Published by: Bergmoser und Hoeller Verlag GmbH, Karl-Friedrich-Str 76, Aachen, 52072, Germany. TEL 49-241-93888123, FAX 49-241-93888134, kontakt@buhv.de. Circ: 4,000 (paid and controlled).

BREAKAWAY. *see* CHILDREN AND YOUTH—For

230 USA ISSN 1930-5923
BREATH OF GOD. Text in English. 2006. bi-m. USD 18.95 (effective 2006). **Document type:** *Magazine, Consumer.* **Description:** Covers themes focused on modern Christian women, including topics such as marriage, parenting, singles, young adults/teens, workplace faith, health and fitness, recipes, up-to-date medical news, and spiritual gifts.
Published by: Lee Publishing, PO Box 77127, Atlanta, GA 30357-1127. customerservice@breathofgodmag.com.

220 DEU ISSN 0171-5666
BRENNPUNKT SEELSORGE; Beitraege zur biblischen Lebensberatung. Text in German. 1979. 4/yr. bk.rev. **Document type:** *Magazine, Consumer.*
Published by: Offensive Junger Christen e.V., Hel-Goettmann-Str, Reichelsheim, 64385, Germany. TEL 49-6164-93090, FAX 49-6164-930930, reichenberg@ojc.de, http://www.ojc.de.

289 USA ISSN 1071-4200
BX9675.A1
BRETHREN IN CHRIST HISTORY AND LIFE. Text in English. 1978. 3/yr. free (effective 2010). back issues avail. **Document type:** *Journal, Academic/Scholarly.* **Description:** Covers articles on the past and present life of the Brethren in Christ.
Indexed: A21, AmH&L, CA, ChrPI, HistAb, RI-1, T02.
Published by: Brethren in Christ, PO Box 3002, Grantham, PA 17027. GPierce@messiah.edu. Ed. Morris Sider TEL 717-766-7767.

200 USA ISSN 0006-9655
BX8551
BRETHREN JOURNAL. Text in English. 1902. m. USD 12 to individuals; USD 10 to institutions (effective 2008).
Published by: Unity of the Brethren in Texas, 6703 FM 2502, Brenham, TX 77833-9803. TEL 409-830-8762. Ed. Rev. Milton Maly.

200 USA
BRETHREN PEACE FELLOWSHIP NEWSLETTER. Text in English. 1968. bi-m. looseleaf. bk.rev. **Document type:** *Newsletter.* **Description:** Deals with issues of Christian peacemaking and resistance to war.
Published by: Brethren Peace Fellowship, PO Box 455, New Windsor, MD 21776. TEL 410-848-5631, braune@ccpl.carr.org. Ed. Kim McDowell. Circ: 750 (controlled).

BRIDGING REALITIES. *see* NEW AGE PUBLICATIONS

230 NLD ISSN 1871-6377
BRILL'S COMPANION TO THE CHRISTIAN TRADITION. Text in English. 2006. irreg., latest vol.31, 2011. price varies. **Document type:** *Monographic series, Academic/Scholarly.* **Description:** Covers persons, movements, schools and genres in medieval and early modern Christian life, thought and practice.
Indexed: IZBG.
—BLDSC (2284.110913).
Published by: Brill, PO Box 9000, Leiden, 2300 PA, Netherlands. TEL 31-71-5353500, FAX 31-71-5317532, cs@brill.nl.

220 NLD ISSN 1389-1170
BRILL'S READERS IN BIBLICAL STUDIES. Text in English. 1999. irreg., latest vol.6, 2000. price varies. **Document type:** *Monographic series, Academic/Scholarly.*
Indexed: IZBG.
Published by: Brill, PO Box 9000, Leiden, 2300 PA, Netherlands. TEL 31-71-5353500, FAX 31-71-5317532, cs@brill.nl.

270 NLD ISSN 1572-4107
➤ **BRILL'S SERIES IN CHURCH HISTORY.** Text in Dutch. 1970. irreg., latest vol.55, 2011. price varies. back issues avail. **Document type:** *Monographic series, Academic/Scholarly.*
Formerly (until 2004): Kerkhistorische Bijdragen (0169-8451)
Indexed: IZBG.
Published by: Brill, PO Box 9000, Leiden, 2300 PA, Netherlands. TEL 31-71-5353500, FAX 31-71-5317532, cs@brill.nl. Ed. Wim Janse. R&P Elizabeth Venekamp. **Dist. in N. America by:** Brill, PO Box 605, Herndon, VA 20172-0605. TEL 703-661-1585, 800-337-9255, FAX 703-661-1501, cs@brillusa.com; **Dist. by:** Turpin Distribution Services Ltd., Pegasus Dr, Stratton Business Park, Biggleswade, Bedfordshire SG18 8QB, United Kingdom. TEL 44-1767-604954, FAX 44-1767-601640, custserv@turpin-distribution.com, http://www.turpin-distribution.com/.

268 USA ISSN 2151-0261
▼ **THE BRINK.** Text in English. 2009. q. USD 6.99 per issue (effective 2009). **Document type:** *Magazine, Trade.* **Description:** Include interviews, stories, and opinion pieces about the topics twentysomethings care about.
Published by: Randall House, 114 Bush Rd, PO Box 17306, Nashville, TN 37217. TEL 615-361-1221, 800-877-7030, FAX 615-367-0535.

371.07 GBR ISSN 0141-6200
➤ **BRITISH JOURNAL OF RELIGIOUS EDUCATION.** Abbreviated title: B J R E. Text in English. 1934. 3/yr. GBP 226 combined subscription in United Kingdom to institutions (print & online eds.); EUR 298, USD 374 combined subscription to institutions (print & online eds.) (effective 2012). adv. bk.rev. charts. index. 80 p./no.; reprint service avail. from PSC. **Document type:** *Journal, Academic/Scholarly.* **Description:** Disseminates research on religion in education, presenting philosophical perspectives and exploring appropriate pedagogy.
Supersedes (in 1978): Learning for Living (0023-9704); Which was formerly (until 1961): Religion in Education
Related titles: Microform ed.: (from PQC); Online - full text ed.: ISSN 1740-7931. GBP 203 in United Kingdom to institutions; EUR 268, USD 337 to institutions (effective 2012) (from IngentaConnect).
Indexed: A01, A02, A03, A08, A20, A21, A22, AEI, AMR, ArtHuCI, B29, CA, CERDIC, CPE, E01, E03, ERI, ERIC, FamI, IBR, IBZ, P18, P48, P53, P54, PCI, PQC, RI-1, RI-2, SCOPUS, SSCI, T02, W07.
—IE, Ingenta. **CCC.**
Published by: (Christian Education, University of Warwick, Institute of Education), Routledge (Subsidiary of: Taylor & Francis Group), 4 Park Sq, Milton Park, Abingdon, Oxon OX14 4RN, United Kingdom. TEL 44-20-70176000, FAX 44-20-70176336, subscriptions@tandf.co.uk, http://www.routledge.com. Ed. Robert Jackson. Adv. contact Linda Hann TEL 44-1344-779945. Circ: 2,300. **Subscr. to:** Taylor & Francis Ltd., Journals Customer Service, Sheepen Pl, Colchester, Essex CO3 3LP, United Kingdom. TEL 44-20-70175544, FAX 44-20-70175198.

207 268.8 USA ISSN 0068-2721
BROADMAN COMMENTS; INTERNATIONAL SUNDAY SCHOOL LESSONS. Text in English. 1945. q. USD 4.99. **Description:** Supplementary reading on International Sunday School lessons for adults.
Published by: Broadman & Holman Publishing Group, 127 Ninth Ave N, Nashville, TN 37234. TEL 615-251-2533. Ed. Robert J Dean. Circ: 14,000.

230 NLD ISSN 1381-9518
BRON VAN CHRISTELIJKE GEEST. Text in Dutch. 1935. 56/yr. EUR 28.50 domestic; EUR 32 in Belgium (effective 2010).
Published by: Gooi en Sticht, Postbus 5018, Kampen, 8260 GA, Netherlands. TEL 31-38-3392556, FAX 31-38-3311776, gens@kok.nl, http://www.kok.nl.

266 USA ISSN 0007-2494
BV2000
BROWN GOLD. Text in English. 1943. m. illus. **Document type:** *Newsletter.*
Published by: New Tribes Mission Publications, 1000 E First St, Sanford, FL 32771-1487. TEL 407-323-3430, FAX 407-330-0376. Ed. Macon G Hare. Circ: 46,000.

BUDDHIST - CHRISTIAN STUDIES. *see* RELIGIONS AND THEOLOGY—Buddhist

268 USA ISSN 0745-1687
BUILDER (SCOTTDALE). Text in English. 1950. m. illus. **Document type:** *Magazine, Consumer.* **Description:** Directed to Christian educators and congregational leaders. Includes Sunday school teaching guides for each Sunday, following the Uniform Series outline.
Published by: Herald Press, 616 Walnut Ave, Scottdale, PA 15683-1999. TEL 724-887-8500, 800-245-7894, hp@mph.org, http://www.mph.org. Ed. David Hiebert. Circ: 5,300. **Co-publisher:** Faith & Life Press.

230 NGA ISSN 0795-9001
BUILDING THE BODY. Text in English. 2005. s-a.
Published by: Deeper Christian Life Ministry, PO Box 59, University of Lagos Post Office, Lagos, Nigeria. TEL 234-1-3110000, FAX 234-1-3113113, info@deeperlifeonline.org, http://www.dclm.org.

220 016.2 CHE ISSN 1421-2994
BULLETIN DE BIBLIOGRAPHIE BIBLIQUE. Text in French. 1991. 3/yr. CHF 35 to individuals; CHF 40 to institutions (effective 2004).
Indexed: OTA.
Published by: Universite de Lausanne, Institut Romand des Sciences Bibliques, Batiment Central, Lausanne-Dorigny, 1015, Switzerland. TEL 41-21-6922730, FAX 41-21-6922735, http://www2.unil.ch/irsb/.

255 FRA
BULLETIN DE LERINS. Text in French. 1930. q. EUR 15 domestic; EUR 18 foreign (effective 2008). **Document type:** *Bulletin, Trade.*
Former titles: Lerins (0767-9645); (until 1971): Congregation Cistercienne de Senaque et de la Pieuse Ligue Universelle pour les Ames de l'Abbaye de Lerins. (Publication) (0010-5813); (until 1966): Lerins (0767-9637); (until 1962): Congregation Cistercienne de Senanque. Bulletin (0767-9629)
Published by: Abbaye de Lerins, Ile St. Honorat, B P 157, Cannes, 06406, France. TEL 33-4-92995400, FAX 33-4-92995401, info@abbayedelerins.com, http://www.abbayedelerins.com/. Circ: 1,200.

200 GAB
BULLETIN EVANGELIQUE D'INFORMATION ET DE PRESSE. Text in French. m.
Address: BP 80, Libreville, Gabon.

220 USA ISSN 1065-223X
BS410
➤ **BULLETIN FOR BIBLICAL RESEARCH.** Abbreviated title: B B R. Text in English. 1991. q. USD 50 domestic to individuals; USD 65 foreign to individuals; USD 60 domestic to institutions; USD 75 foreign to institutions; free to members (effective 2010). bk.rev. 160 p./no.; back issues avail. **Document type:** *Journal, Academic/Scholarly.*
Indexed: A21, A22, IZBG, OTA, R&TA, RI-1.
—BLDSC (2834.523000), IE, Ingenta. **CCC.**
Published by: (Institute for Biblical Research), Eisenbrauns Inc., PO Box 275, Winona Lake, IN 46590. TEL 574-269-2011, FAX 574-269-6788, customerservice@eisenbrauns.com, http://www.eisenbrauns.com. Ed. Richard Hess.

221 NOR ISSN 1502-0827
BS410
➤ **BULLETIN FOR OLD TESTAMENT STUDIES IN AFRICA (ONLINE EDITION).** Variant title: B O T S A. Text in English. 1996. irreg. free. back issues avail. **Document type:** *Magazine, Academic/Scholarly.*
Formerly (until 2000): Newsletter on African Old Testament Scholarship (Online) (1500-7383)
Media: Online - full text.
—CCC.
Published by: Holter, Ed. & Pub., Knut, Misjonshoegskolen, Misjonsveien 34, Stavanger, 4024, Norway. TEL 47-51-516227, FAX 47-51-516225, knut.holter@mhs.no. Ed., Pub. Knut Holter.

200 GBR ISSN 2041-1863
BULLETIN FOR THE STUDY OF RELIGION. Abbreviated title: B S O R. Text in English. 1964. q. USD 135 combined subscription in North America to institutions (print & online eds.); GBP 80 combined subscription elsewhere to institutions (print & online eds.) (effective 2012). adv. back issues avail.; reprints avail. **Document type:** *Bulletin, Academic/Scholarly.* **Description:** Brings out articles that address religion in general, the history of the field of religious studies, method and theory in the study of religion, and pedagogical practices.
Formerly (until 2010): C S S R Bulletin (1060-1635); Which superseded in part (in 1988): Religious Study News (0885-0372); Which was formerly (until 1985): Council on the Study of Religion. Bulletin (0002-7170); (until 1970): American Academy of Religion. Bulletin (0569-2148)
Related titles: Online - full text ed.: ISSN 2041-1871. USD 110 in North America to institutions; GBP 65 elsewhere to institutions (effective 2012).
Indexed: A21, RI-1, RI-2.
—CCC.
Published by: Equinox Publishing Ltd., Unit S3, Kelham House, 3 Lancaster St, Sheffield, S6 3AF, United Kingdom. TEL 44-114-2725957, FAX 44-560-3459046, journals@equinoxpub.com, http://www.equinoxpub.com/. Ed. Craig Martin. Adv. contact Val Hall.

268 NLD ISSN 1873-510X
BULLETIN PASTORALE DIENSTVERLENING. Text in Dutch. 2004. s-a. EUR 1.50 newsstand/cover (effective 2009).
Published by: Bisdom Rotterdam, Pastorale Dienstverlening, Koningin Emmaplein 3, Rotterdam, 3016 AA, Netherlands. TEL 31-10-4148213, pastoraledienstverlening@bisdomrotterdam.nl, http://www.bisrotterdam.nl.

BUNYAN STUDIES. *see* LITERATURE

230.2 ESP ISSN 0521-8195
BR7
BURGENSE; collectanea scientifica. Text in French, Latin, Spanish. 1960. s-a. bk.rev. bibl. **Document type:** *Bulletin, Academic/Scholarly.*
Indexed: CERDIC, FR, OTA, P30.
—INIST.
Published by: Facultad de Teologia del Norte de Espana, Martinez del Campo, 10, Apartado 50, Burgos, 09003, Spain. TEL 34-947-700000, FAX 34-947-252025, teologiaburgos@planalfa.es, http://www.teologiaburgos.org/. Ed. Jaime Garcia Alvarez. Circ: 600 (paid).

BURIED HISTORY. *see* ARCHAEOLOGY

230 USA ISSN 0007-6309
THE BURNING BUSH. Text in English. 1902. q. USD 4 domestic; USD 4.50 foreign (effective 2002). 16 p./no.; back issues avail. **Document type:** *Newsletter, Trade.* **Description:** Contains sermons, editorials, seasonal poetry, religious articles, children's stories, and news from missions abroad.
Related titles: Online - full text ed.: Burning Bush Devotional.
Published by: Metropolitan Church Association, P O Box 156, Dundee, IL 60118-0156. TEL 262-248-6786. Circ: 730.

A BYTE OF GODLY COUNSEL. *see* BUSINESS AND ECONOMICS

BYZANZ, ISLAM UND CHRISTLICHER ORIENT. *see* HISTORY—History Of The Near East

230 USA ISSN 1089-5183
BX1404
THE C A R A REPORT. Text in English. 1995. q. USD 49 (effective 2005). back issues avail.
Indexed: CPL.
Published by: Center for Applied Research in the Apostolate, 2300 Wisconsin Ave, NW, Suite 400, Washington, DC 20007. TEL 202-687-8080, FAX 202-687-8083, cara@georgetown.edu.

C B M FREUNDESBRIEF. *see* SOCIAL SERVICES AND WELFARE

200 THA ISSN 0129-9891
C C A NEWS. Text in English. 1966. q. **Document type:** *Newsletter.*
Indexed: A21, RI-1.
Published by: Christian Conference of Asia, c/o Payap University, Muang, PO Box 183, Chiang Mai, 50000, Thailand. TEL 66-53-243906, FAX 66-53-247303, http://www.cca.org.hk/.

200 CHE
C C I A BACKGROUND INFORMATION. (Commission of the Churches on International Affairs) Text in English. 1975. irreg. (approx. 2/yr.). **Document type:** *Bulletin.*
Published by: (Commission of the Churches on International Affairs), World Council of Churches, 150 route de Ferney, PO Box 2100, Geneva 2, 1211, Switzerland. TEL 41-22-791-6111, FAX 41-22-791-0361. Ed. Dwain Epps. Circ: 2,000.

207 USA
C E A I NEWSLETTER. (Christian Educators Association International) Text in English. 1954. 9/yr. adv. **Document type:** *Newsletter, Trade.*
Related titles: Online - full text ed.
Published by: Christian Educators Association International, PO Box 41300, Pasadena, CA 91114. TEL 626-798-1124, FAX 626-798-2346. Ed. Denise Jones. Pub. Forrest Turpen.

C H I L D NEWSLETTER. *see* CHILDREN AND YOUTH—About

C P S NIEUWSBRIEF. *see* EDUCATION

215 USA ISSN 1933-0405
BL240.3
C S E R REVIEW. (Committee for the Scientific Examination of Religion) Text in English. 2006. q. USD 20 (effective 2007). bk.rev. **Document type:** *Magazine, Consumer.* **Description:** Covers membership news. Also features scholarly, scientific and critical examinations of religious beliefs, texts and practices in the interest of free inquiry and reason.
Published by: Center for Inquiry, PO Box 741, Amherst, NY 14226. TEL 716-636-4869, FAX 716-636-1733. Ed. Paul Kurtz.

200 500 USA ISSN 0889-8243
BL240.2
THE C T N S BULLETIN. Text in English. 19??. q. bk.rev. back issues avail. **Document type:** *Journal, Academic/Scholarly.*
Formerly (until 198?): C T N S Newsletter
Indexed: A21, RI-1.
—IE, Ingenta.
Published by: The Center for Theology and the Natural Sciences, 2400 Ridge Rd, Berkeley, CA 94709. TEL 510-848-8152, FAX 510-848-2535, ctnsinfo@ctns.org.

230 NLD ISSN 1566-9084
C V - KOERS. (Christen Vandaag) Text in Dutch. 11/yr. EUR 39 (effective 2009). adv. **Document type:** *Magazine, Consumer.*
Formed by the merger of (1970-1999): Koers (0167-2177); (1997-1999): Christen Vandaag (1387-5760)
Published by: EB Media, Postbus 2101, Deventer, 7420 AC, Netherlands. TEL 31-88-3263333, FAX 31-88-3263339, mail@ebmedia.nl, http://www.ebmedia.nl/. Eds. Bas Popkema, Sjoerd Wielenga, Ronald Westerbeek. adv.: color page EUR 1,158; trim 210 x 297. Circ: 11,590.

C W R MEMBERSHIP NEWSLETTER. *see* WOMEN'S STUDIES

200 LBN ISSN 1682-6574
CAHIERS DE L'ORIENT CHRETIEN. Text in French. 2003. irreg. **Document type:** *Academic/Scholarly.*
Published by: Universite Saint-Joseph, BP 16-6778, Beyrouth, 1100 2150, Lebanon. TEL 961-1-200-458, cedrac@usj.edu.lb, http://www.cedrac.usj.edu.lb/index.htm.

200 CAN ISSN 0710-4693
CAHIERS DE RECHERCHE ETHIQUE. Text in French. 1977. irreg. price varies.
Indexed: CERDIC.
Published by: Editions Bellarmin, 165 rue Deslauriers, St Laurent, PQ H4N 2S4, Canada. TEL 514-745-4290, FAX 514-745-4299.

200 FRA ISSN 1760-5776
CAHIERS D'ETUDES DU RELIGIEUX. Text in French. 2007. q. free (effective 2011). **Document type:** *Journal, Academic/Scholarly.*
Media: Online - full text.
Published by: Centre Interdisciplinaire d'Etudes du Religieux, Maison des Sciences de l'Homme de Montpellier, 17 Rue de l'Abbe de l'Epee, Montpellier, 34090, France. Eds. Anita Gonzalez-Raymond, Beatrice Bakhouche.

243 FRA ISSN 0222-9714
BS410
CAHIERS EVANGILE. Text in French. 1951. q. price varies. bk.rev. abstr. **Document type:** *Monographic series, Academic/Scholarly.*
Formerly: Cahiers Bibliques Trimestriels (0007-960X)
Indexed: OTA, PdeR.
—CCC.
Published by: (Service Biblique Evangile et Vie), Editions du Cerf, 29 Boulevard La Tour Maubourg, Paris, 75340 Cedex 07, France. http://www.editionsducerf.fr. Ed. Philippe Gruson. Circ: 16,000.

266 USA
CALL TO PRAYER. Text in English. 1919. 6/yr. free to qualified personnel. **Document type:** *Newsletter.* **Description:** Provides information to the constituency of the activities on the mission fields and in the home office so they can pray more intelligently for our work.
Published by: World Gospel Mission, 3783 State Rd 18 E, Box 948, Marion, IN 46952-0948. TEL 765-664-7331, FAX 765-671-7230. Ed. Jonathan Morgan. R&P Peggy Bushong TEL 765-671-7270. Circ: 33,000.

280.042 USA ISSN 1545-7311
BX1
CALL TO UNITY. Text in English. 1962. 2/yr. USD 10 domestic; USD 15 foreign; USD 5 to students; USD 6.50 newsstand/cover (effective 2008). adv. bk.rev. illus. reprints avail. **Document type:** *Magazine, Consumer.*
Formerly (until 2003): Mid-Stream (0544-0653); Which superseded in part (in 1973): Consultation on Church Union. Digest of the Proceedings of the Meeting (0589-4867)
Related titles: Microform ed.: (from PQC).
Indexed: A21, A22, R&TA, RI-1, RI-2, RILM.
Published by: Council on Christian Unity of the Christian Church, PO Box 1986, Indianapolis, IN 46206. TEL 317-635-3100, FAX 317-713-2588. Ed., Adv. contact Robert K Welsh. Circ: 500.

230 GBR
CAMBRIDGE STUDIES IN CHRISTIAN DOCTRINE. Text in English. 1999. irreg., latest 2008. price varies. back issues avail.; reprints avail. **Document type:** *Monographic series, Academic/Scholarly.* **Description:** Aims to engage critically with the traditional doctrines of Christianity, and at the same time to locate and make sense of them within a secular context.
Published by: Cambridge University Press, The Edinburgh Bldg, Shaftesbury Rd, Cambridge, CB2 8RU, United Kingdom. TEL 44-1223-312393, FAX 44-1223-315052, journals@cambridge.org, http://www.cambridge.org/uk. Ed. Daniel W Hardy. Adv. contact Rebecca Roberts TEL 44-1223-325083.

246.7 IRL ISSN 2009-0722
CAMFEST MAGAZINE. Text in English. 2007. q.
Published by: Christian Artists & Musicians, 28 Chestnut Grove, Termon Abbey, Drogheda, Ireland. TEL 353-41-872372365, http://www.camfest.org.

CAMPANIA SACRA; rivista di storia sociale e religiosa del Mezzogiorno. *see* HISTORY—History Of Europe

200 IND
CAMPUS LINK. Text in English. 1954. bi-m. bk.rev. maps. back issues avail. **Document type:** *Magazine, Consumer.* **Description:** Seeks to sensitize believing college students to reason out issues,and stand for Christ, creating an awareness of UESI ministry and leading them to maturity and involvement.
Former titles (until 1999): Our Link; (until 1977): Evangelical Student
Published by: Union of Evangelical Students of India, Publication Trust, 19 - 10 Millers Rd, Kilpauk, PO Box 1030, Chennai, Tamil Nadu 600 010, India. TEL 91-44-26421478, FAX 91-44-26433754, uesi54@eth.net, http://www.uesi.org.in/.

CAMSOC UPDATE. (Computer Aided Ministry Society) *see* COMPUTERS

200 USA
CAN NEWS. Text in English. 1997. m. USD 100 (effective 2002). back issues avail. **Document type:** *Newsletter, Consumer.* **Description:** Describes stories of reconciliation between families of different faiths, along with religious freedom updates.
Published by: Foundation for Religious Freedom, Cult Awareness Network Hotline and Information Service, 1680 N Vine St, Ste 415, Los Angeles, CA 90028. TEL 323-468-0567, 800-556-3055, FAX 323-468-0562, nancyo@telcocom.com, http://www.cultawarenessnetwork.org. Ed., Pub., R&P Nancy O'Meara TEL 323-468-0563. Circ: 2,000 (paid).

266.00971 CAN ISSN 0316-2907
CANADIAN GIDEON. Text in English, French. 1955. 5/yr. CAD 12 (effective 1999). bk.rev. illus. **Description:** Provides spiritual, theological comments.
Supersedes: Torch and Trumpet (0316-2915)
—CCC.
Published by: Gideons International in Canada, 501 Imperial Rd N, Guelph, ON N1H 7A2, Canada. TEL 519-823-1140, FAX 519-767-1913. Ed. Neil Bramble. Circ: 4,200.

200 CAN ISSN 0316-8743
CANADIAN RELIGIOUS CONFERENCE. BULLETIN. Text in English. 1955. q. CAD 18. adv. **Document type:** *Bulletin.*
Related titles: French ed.: Bulletin - Conference Religieuse Canadienne. ISSN 0316-8751.
Published by: Canadian Religious Conference, 4135 de Rouen St, 1st Fl, Montreal, PQ H1V 1G5, Canada. TEL 514-259-0856, FAX 514-259-0857, jocelyne@crcn.ca, http://www.crcn.ca. R&P Richard Renshaw. Adv. contact Marjolaine Tremblay.

220 USA ISSN 0068-970X
CANADIAN SOCIETY OF BIBLICAL STUDIES. BULLETIN/SOCIETE CANADIENNE DES ETUDES BIBLIQUES. BULLETIN. Text in English. 1935-1960; resumed 1964. a. CAD 10 domestic (effective 2001). **Document type:** *Bulletin.*
Published by: Canadian Society of Biblical Studies, c/o Dr John L McLaughlin, Ed, Wheeling Jesuit University, Wheeling, WV 26003. TEL 304-243-2310. Circ: 300.

200 ATG
CARIBBEAN GLOBAL. Text in English. 2005. bi-m. XEC 10, USD 5 newsstand/cover (effective 2005). **Document type:** *Magazine, Consumer.* **Description:** Provides a Christian perspective on global news & events.
Published by: Trinity Media Services, PO Box 1637, St. John's, Antigua. TEL 268-562-5284.

268 JAM ISSN 0253-066X
BR1
➤ **CARIBBEAN JOURNAL OF RELIGIOUS STUDIES.** Text in English. 1975. s-a. JMD 120, USD 12 domestic; USD 15 foreign (effective 2000). bk.rev. bibl. **Document type:** *Journal, Academic/Scholarly.* **Description:** Forum for discussion of religious and pastoral issues affecting the life of Caribbean people.
Indexed: A21, RI-1, RI-2.
—Ingenta.

R

Published by: United Theological College of the West Indies, Golding Ave., Mona, PO Box 136, Kingston, 7, Jamaica. TEL 809-927-2868, 809-927-1724, FAX 809-977-0812, unitheol@cwjamiaca.com, http://www.utcwi.edu.jm. Ed., R&P Howard K Gregory. Circ: 400 (paid).

200 USA ISSN 1087-4895
CARISMA Y VIDA CRISTIANA. Text in Spanish. 1983. bi-m. USD 12.95 domestic; USD 17.95 foreign; USD 2.50 newsstand/cover (effective 2007). adv. film rev.; video rev.; software rev.; bk.rev.; music rev. 80 p./no. 3 cols./p.; back issues avail. **Document type:** *Magazine, Trade.* **Description:** Brings news of what God is doing among the Hispanics.
Formerly (until 1995): Carisma Internacional (1079-9966)
Related titles: Magnetic Tape ed.
Published by: Strang Communications Co., 600 Rinehart Rd, Lake Mary, FL 32746. TEL 407-333-0600, FAX 407-333-7100, custsvc@strang.com, http://www.strang.com. Ed., R&P Lydia Morales. Pub. Stephen Strang. Adv. contact Brenda Rosa. Circ: 30,000.

260 DEU
CARITAS-KALENDER. Text in German. 1924. a. EUR 4.90 (effective 2006). adv. **Document type:** *Bulletin.*
Published by: (Deutscher Caritasverband e.V.), Lambertus-Verlag GmbH, Mitscherlichstr 56, Freiburg Im Breisgau, 79108, Germany. TEL 49-761-368250, FAX 49-761-3682533, info@lambertus.de, http://www.lambertus.de. Circ: 55,000.

CARL NEWELL JACKSON LECTURES. *see* FOLKLORE

230 USA ISSN 0008-672X
CAROLINA CHRISTIAN. Text in English. 1959. m. USD 10 (effective 1998). adv. bk.rev.
Published by: Carolina Christian Publications, Inc., PO Box 1369, Sta B, Yadkinville, NC 27055-1369. Ed. Dennis Conner. Circ: 1,600.

200 SLV
CARTAS A LA IGLESIA. Text in Spanish. s-m. SVC 65 domestic; USD 25 in Central America; USD 35 in North America; USD 45 in Europe; USD 50 elsewhere (effective 2005). **Document type:** *Bulletin, Academic/Scholarly.*
Published by: Universidad Centroamericana Jose Simeon Canas, U C A Editores, Apartado Postal 01-168, San Salvador, El Salvador. TEL 503-210-6600, FAX 503-210-6655, correo@www.uca.edu.sv, http://www.uca.edu.sv.

200 ESP ISSN 0213-4381
BR7
CARTHAGINENSIA; revista de estudios e investigacion. Text in Spanish, English. 1985. s-a. back issues avail. **Document type:** *Journal, Academic/Scholarly.*
Indexed: OTA.
Published by: (Universidad de Murcia, Instituto Teologico de Murcia O.F.M.), Universidad de Murcia, Servicio de Publicaciones, Edificio Saavedra Fajardo, C/ Actor Isidoro Maiquez 9, Murcia, 30007, Spain. TEL 34-968-363887, FAX 34-968-363414, http://www.um.es/publicaciones/.

240 ESP ISSN 0528-2772
CATEQUETICA. Text in Spanish. 1912. 4/yr. EUR 30 domestic; USD 47 foreign (effective 2009). **Document type:** *Magazine, Consumer.*
Former titles (until 1961): Sal Terrae. Parte Catequetica (0211-4577); (until 1960): Sal Terrae. Parte Practica (1138-1086); Which superseded in part (in 1954): Sal Terrae (0211-4569)
Related titles: Online - full text ed.: EUR 25 (effective 2009).
Published by: Editorial Sal Terrae, Poligono de Raos, Parcela 14-I, Maliano, Cantabria, 34600, Spain. TEL 34-942-369198, salterrae@salterrae.es, http://www.salterrae.es. Ed. Jose Luis Saborido.

230 CAN
CATHERINE; a Christian magazine for women. Text in English. 1945. 10/yr. CAD 12 domestic; USD 15 foreign (effective 2001). bk.rev. illus. **Document type:** *Magazine, Consumer.* **Description:** Covers women's issues, family concerns, overseas journal, recipes, crafts, profiles, human interest stories.
Former titles (until 1998): Sally Ann (0838-7397); (until 1988): Home Leaguer (0822-5079); Canadian Home Leaguer (0008-3771)
Published by: (Editorial Department), Salvation Army, Canada and Bermuda Territorial Headquarters, 2 Overlea Blvd, Toronto, ON M4H 1P4, Canada. TEL 416-422-6114, FAX 416-422-6120. Ed. Doreen Sturge. Circ: 13,000.

CATHOLIC ARCHIVES NEWSLETTER. *see* LIBRARY AND INFORMATION SCIENCES

222 USA ISSN 1044-6427
CATHOLIC BIBLE QUARTERLY MONOGRAPH SERIES. Abbreviated title: C B Q M S. Text in English. 1971. irreg., latest 45. price varies. back issues avail. **Document type:** *Monographic series, Academic/Scholarly.*
Indexed: CPL, IZBG, OTA, RI-1.
Published by: Catholic Biblical Association of America, 433 Caldwell Hall, The Catholic University of America, Washington, DC 20064. TEL 202-319-5519, cua-cathbib@cua.edu. Circ: 1,000.

268 ESP ISSN 1135-0814
CAUCES DE INTERCOMUNICACION. Text in Spanish. 1995. 3/yr. EUR 7 in Europe; USD 15 elsewhere (effective 2009). **Document type:** *Journal, Academic/Scholarly.*
Published by: (Universidad de Navarra, Facultad de Teologia), Universidad de Navarra, Servicio de Publicaciones, Campus Universitario, Pamplona, 31009, Spain. http://www.unav.es/publicaciones/.

200 LVA ISSN 1407-7841
BM376.L38
➤ **CELS/WAY.** Text in Latvian; Abstracts in English, Latvian. 1935. a. price varies. **Document type:** *Journal, Academic/Scholarly.* **Description:** Publishes articles on theology, religious studies, and cultural studies dedicated to the academic research of religion. It is not affiliated with any church.
Indexed: A01, T02.
Published by: (Latvijas Universitate, Teologijas Fakultate), Latvijas Universitate Akademiskais Apgads/University of Latvia Press, Baznicas Iela 5, Setas Korp. 3. Stava 351., 352. Kab., Riga, 1010, Latvia. Anna.Smite@lu.lv, http://www.lu.lv/apgads/index.html.

320 USA
CENTRAL AMERICA - MEXICO REPORT. Text in English. 1980. bi-m. USD 20 to individuals; USD 30 to institutions (effective 2000). bk.rev. illus. **Document type:** *Newspaper.* **Description:** Covers religious, political, social and economic developments in Central America, as well as relevant US policies on human rights issues.
Formerly (until 1996): Central America Report
Published by: Religious Task Force on Central America & Mexico, 3053 4th St, N E, Washington, DC 20017-1102. TEL 202-529-0441. Ed., R&P Margaret Swedish. Circ: 2,000.

200 378 CAN ISSN 1911-5474
CENTRE FOR STUDIES IN RELIGION & SOCIETY. Text in English. 1992. a. **Document type:** *Journal, Academic/Scholarly.*
Published by: University of Victoria, Centre for Studies in Religion and Society, Sedgewick B102, PO Box 1700, STN CSC, Victoria, BC V8W 2Y2, Canada. TEL 250-721-6325, FAX 250-721-6234, csrs@uvic.ca, http://www.csrs.uvic.ca.

CENTRO CAMUNO DI STUDI PREISTORICI. SYMPOSIA. *see* ART

248 ESP ISSN 1139-5346
CENTRO DE DOCUMENTACION Y ESTUDIOS JOSEMARIA ESCRIVA DE BALAGUER. CUADERNOS. Text in Spanish. 1997. a. EUR 6 in Europe; USD 7 elsewhere (effective 2009). **Document type:** *Journal, Academic/Scholarly.*
Related titles: ◆ Supplement to: Anuario de Historia de la Iglesia. ISSN 1133-0104.
Published by: (Universidad de Navarra, Facultad de Teologia), Universidad de Navarra, Servicio de Publicaciones, Campus Universitario, Pamplona, 31009, Spain. http://www.unav.es/publicaciones/.

200 ITA ISSN 1122-0384
CENTRO PRO UNIONE BULLETIN. Text in English. 1933. s-a. **Document type:** *Bulletin, Consumer.*
Indexed: A21, RI-1.
Published by: Centro Pro Unione, Frati Francescani dell'Atonement, Via S Maria dell'Anima 30, Rome, 00186, Italy. TEL 39-06-6879552, FAX 39-06-68133668, pro@pro.urbe.it, http://www.prounione.urbe.it.

200 ROM ISSN 1584-4196
➤ **CENTRULUI PENTRU DIALOG INTRE STIINTE SI TEOLOGIE. BULETINUL/CENTER FOR DIALOGUE BETWEEN SCIENCES AND THEOLOGY. BULLETIN.** Text in English, French, German, Italian, Romanian. 2004. s-a. ROL 41, EUR 10 (effective 2011). adv. **Document type:** *Journal, Academic/Scholarly.* **Description:** Contains interdisciplinary articles that covers: Theology, religious studies, philosophy of religions, ethics, philology, history, anthropology, political science, sociology, ecumenical dialogue and exact sciences. Audience includes professors and young researchers interested in the study of the dialogue between sciences and theology.
Related titles: Online - full text ed.
Published by: (Universitatea din Craiova, Centrului Pentru Dialog Intre Stiinte si Teologie/University of Craiova, Center for Dialogue between Sciences and Theology), Universitatea din Craiova, Editura Universitaria/University of Craiova, Universitaria Publishing House, Str. Brestei, nr.156A, Craiova, 200585, Romania. TEL 86-251-598054, FAX 86-251-412479, edituraunversitaria@yahoo.com, http://cis01.central.ucv.ro/edituraunversitaria/. Ed., R&P Calina Gelu. Pub. Nicoleta Calina. Circ: 500.

200 USA ISSN 2150-2730
▼ **CENTURION;** journal of first century social intelligence. Text in English. forthcoming 2011. q. **Document type:** *Journal, Academic/Scholarly.* **Description:** Publishes new analysis and research on understanding the evolution of social order in Western countries, specifically how social order was reorganized when polytheistic (Hellenistic/Roman) and monotheistic (Hebrew) cultures encountered each other in the first century Mediterranean world.
Media: Online - full content.
Published by: Kaiser Peer Publishing, PO Box 734, Churchville, NY 14428. TEL 585-393-1464, davidkaiser@spiritualneuroscience.org.

200 FRA ISSN 0411-5562
BR23
CERCLE ERNEST RENAN. CAHIERS. Text in French. 1954. q. EUR 40 domestic to members; EUR 55 DOM-TOM to members; EUR 55 in the European Union to members; EUR 62 elsewhere to members (effective 2008). bk.rev. bibl. **Document type:** *Academic/Scholarly.*
Incorporates: Cercle Ernest Renan. Bulletin
Indexed: CERDIC.
Published by: Cercle Ernest Renan, c/o Guy Rachet, 67 Bd Invalides, Paris, 75007, France. infos@cercleernestrenan.org. Ed. Pierre L Soisson. Circ: 1,000.

200 294.5 SWE ISSN 1652-0203
➤ **CHAKRA;** tidskrift foer indiske religioner. Text in Multiple languages. 2004. s-a. SEK 200 to individuals; SEK 250 to institutions; SEK 150 to students (effective 2010). **Document type:** *Journal, Academic/Scholarly.* **Description:** Covers religions in India.
Published by: Lunds Universitet, Centrum foer Teologi och Religionsvetenskap/Lund University, Department of Theology and Religious Studies, Allhelgma Kyrkogata 8, Lund, 22362, Sweden. TEL 46-46-2229040, FAX 46-46-2224426, http://www.teol.lu.se/. Eds. Katarina Plank, Kristina Myrvold.

322.1 USA ISSN 1053-9018
BT1211
CHALCEDON REPORT. Text in English. 1965. m. donation. back issues avail.; reprints avail. **Description:** For scholars and serious laymen, provides broad analysis of international social and cultural affairs from biblical perspectives.
Related titles: Microfiche ed.
Indexed: CCR.
Published by: Chalcedon, Inc., PO Box 158, Vallecito, CA 95251. TEL 209-728-4365, FAX 209-736-0536. Ed. Rev. Andrew Sandlin. Pub. Rev. Dr R J Rushdoony. Circ: 11,000.

207.2 GBR
CHANGING LONDON. Text in English. 1835. q. free (effective 2009). 12 p./no. 2 cols./p.; back issues avail. **Document type:** *Magazine, Consumer.*
Former titles (until 2005): Span; (until 1973): London City Mission Magazine (0047-5025)
Related titles: Online - full text ed.
Indexed: ApicAb, F&EA.
Published by: London City Mission, 175 Tower Bridge Rd, London, SE1 2AH, United Kingdom. TEL 44-20-74077585, FAX 44-20-74036711. Ed. Iain MacDonald.

LES CHANTIERS DU CARDINAL. *see* BUILDING AND CONSTRUCTION

200 DNK ISSN 0108-4453
BL6
➤ **CHAOS;** Skandinavisk tidsskrift for religionshistoriske studier. Text in Danish, Norwegian, Swedish. 1982. s-a. DKK 350 combined subscription (print & online eds.) (effective 2011). bk.rev. illus. **Document type:** *Journal, Academic/Scholarly.* **Description:** Articles, reviews, debates in the scientific study of the religions of the world.
Related titles: Online - full text ed.: ISSN 1901-9106. DKK 250 (effective 2011).
Indexed: CMCI, DIP, IBR, IBZ.
Published by: (Koebenhavns Universitet, Institut for Religionshistorie, Syddansk Universitet, Institut for Filosofi, Paedagogik og Religionsstudier/University of Southern Denmark, Institute of Philosophy, Education and the Study of Religions), Museum Tusculanum Press, c/o University of Copenhagen, Njalsgade 126, Copenhagen S, 2300, Denmark. TEL 45-35-329109, FAX 45-35-329113, info@mtp.dk, http://www.mtp.dk. Ed. Mikael Aktor. **Dist. in France by:** Editions Picard, Editions Picard, Paris 75006, France. TEL 33-1-43269778, FAX 33-1-43264264; **Dist. in UK by:** Gazelle Book Services Ltd., White Cross Mills, Hightown, Lancaster LA1 4UU, United Kingdom. TEL 44-1524-68765, FAX 44-1524-63232, sales@gazellebooks.co.uk, http://www.gazellebookservices.co.uk/; **Dist. in US & Canada by:** International Specialized Book Services Inc., 920 NE 58th Ave Ste 300, Portland, OR 97213. TEL 503-287-3093, 800-944-6190, FAX 503-280-8832, orders@isbs.com, http://www.isbs.com/. **Co-sponsor:** Religionshistorisk Forening.

200 USA ISSN 1099-9183
BV4375
➤ **CHAPLAINCY TODAY (SCHAUMBURG, 1999).** Text in English. 1936. s-a. adv. bk.rev. 56 p./no.; back issues avail. **Document type:** *Journal, Academic/Scholarly.* **Description:** Covers topics related to pastoral care.
Former titles (until 1998): CareGiver Journal (1077-842X); (until 1990): Care Giver (1077-8586); (until 1984): American Protestant Hospital Association. Bulletin (0003-0635)
Related titles: Online - full text ed.: USD 20 to individuals; USD 35 to institutions; free to members (effective 2009).
Indexed: A01, A21, CA, P30, R&TA, RI-1, RI-2, SCOPUS, T02.
—CCC.
Published by: Association of Professional Chaplains, 1701 E Woodfield Rd, Ste 760, Schaumburg, IL 60173. TEL 847-240-1014, FAX 847-240-1015, info@professionalchaplains.org. Ed. Rozann Allyn Shackleton. Adv. contact Jo Schrader.

200 USA ISSN 2156-7158
CHARISMA. Text in English. 1987. m. USD 24.97 (effective 2010). adv. bk.rev. back issues avail. **Document type:** *Magazine, Consumer.* **Description:** Provides information about Christanity.
Formerly (until 2010): Charisma & Christian Life (0895-156X); Which was formed by the merger of (19??-1987): Charisma (0279-0424); (1948-1987): Christian Life (0009-5427); Which incorporated (in 1961): Christian Parent; Which was formerly (until 1942): Magazine for the Christian Parent
Related titles: Online - full text ed.: free (effective 2010).
Indexed: A21, A22, ChrPI, GSS&RPL, RI-1.
Published by: Strang Communications Co., 600 Rinehart Rd, Lake Mary, FL 32746. TEL 407-333-0600, FAX 407-333-7100, magcustsvc@strang.com, http://www.strang.com. Ed. Marcus Yoars. Pub. Stephen Strang.

291 FRA ISSN 1952-0646
LES CHEMINS DU TEMPS. Text in French. 2006. irreg. **Document type:** *Monographic series, Consumer.*
Published by: Le Gout du Monde, Editeur, Conques, 12230, France. TEL 33-6-19800197, FAX 33-6-82923967, lgdm@legoutdumonde.com.

THE CHESTERTON REVIEW. *see* LITERATURE

200 USA ISSN 1549-0424
➤ **CHICAGO HISTORY OF AMERICAN RELIGION.** Text in English. 1973. irreg., latest 1990. price varies. adv. bk.rev. reprints avail. **Document type:** *Monographic series, Academic/Scholarly.*
Published by: University of Chicago, 5801 S Ellis Ave, Chicago, IL 60637. TEL 773-702-7899. Ed. Martin E Marty.

200 ITA ISSN 2038-4564
LA CHIESA NEL TEMPO; rivista quadrimestrale di vita e di cultura. Text in Italian. 1985. 3/yr. **Document type:** *Magazine, Consumer.*
Published by: Arcidiocesi di Reggio Calabria - Bova, Curia Metropolitana, Via Tommaso Campanella 63, Reggio Calabria, 89127, Italy. TEL 39-0965-385511, FAX 39-0965-330963, curia@reggiocalabria.chiesacattolica.it, http://www.webdiocesi.chiesacattolica.it/cci_new/vis_diocesi.jsp?idDiocesi=165.

248.845 USA
THE CHILDREN'S FRIEND. Text in English. 1937. q. free to qualified personnel (effective 2011). back issues avail. **Document type:** *Magazine, Consumer.* **Description:** Features character-building stories of courage, adventure, honesty, and kindness, as told from a Christian perspective, for children through age 12.
Media: Braille.
Published by: Christian Record Services, PO Box 6097, Lincoln, NE 68506. TEL 402-488-0981, FAX 402-488-7582, info@christianrecord.org, http://www.christianrecord.org.

CHILDREN'S MINISTRY. *see* CHILDREN AND YOUTH—About

CHILDWORLD. *see* CHILDREN AND YOUTH—About

200 DEU ISSN 0932-6855
CHINA HEUTE; Informationen ueber Religion und Christentum im Chinesischen Raum. Text in German. 1982. bi-m. EUR 25 (effective 2009). bk.rev. back issues avail. **Document type:** *Magazine, Consumer.*
Published by: China-Zentrum e.V., Arnold-Janssen-Str 22, Sankt Augustin, 53757, Germany. TEL 49-2241-237432, FAX 49-2241-205841, china-zentrum@china-zentrum.de. Ed. Katharina Wenzel-Teuber. Circ: 1,600.

200 GBR ISSN 0956-4314
BL1790
CHINA STUDY JOURNAL. Key Title: China Study Project Journal. Text in English. 1986. s-a. GBP 70 domestic to individuals (effective 2010). back issues avail. **Document type:** *Journal, Academic/Scholarly.* **Description:** Contains academic articles about religion in China by Chinese and European researchers, documentation of China source materials, and translations of Church documents.
Published by: Churches Together in Britain & Ireland, 39 Eccleston Sq, London, SW1V 1BX, United Kingdom. TEL 44 -207-9014890, FAX 44 -207-9014894, info@ctbi.org.uk.

230 USA ISSN 1554-3013
CHINESE LAW & RELIGION MONITOR. Text in English, Chinese. 2005. q. back issues avail. **Document type:** *Journal, Academic/Scholarly.*
Related titles: Online - full text ed.: ISSN 2160-2387.
Indexed: P10, P48, P53, P54, PQC.
Published by: China Aid Association, PO Box 8513, Midland, TX 79708. TEL 432-689-6985, 888-889-7757, FAX 432-686-8355, info@chinaaid.org, http://www.chinaaid.org.

200 USA ISSN 0896-7660
BR1
CHINESE THEOLOGICAL REVIEW. Text in English. 1985. a. **Document type:** *Journal, Academic/Scholarly.*
Indexed: A21, R&TA, RI-1, RI-2.
—BLDSC (3181.122200).
Published by: Foundation for Theological Education in Southeast Asia, 140 W Highland Ave, Philadelphia, PA 19118. TEL 215-381-0976, ftewilson@gmail.com. Ed. Janice Wickeri.

200 HKG ISSN 0009-4668
CHING FENG; a journal on Christianity and Chinese religion and culture. Text in English. 1957. q. USD 41 (effective 2000). adv. bk.rev. reprints avail. **Document type:** *Journal, Academic/Scholarly.*
Formerly (until 1964): Quarterly Notes on Christianity and Chinese Religion
Related titles: Microform ed.: (from NBI, PQC); Online - full text ed.
Indexed: A21, A22, BAS, HongKongiana, MLA-IB, R&TA, RASB, RI-1, RI-2.
Published by: Christian Study Centre on Chinese Religion & Culture Ltd., G/F., Theology Building, Chung Chi College, Chinese University of Hong Kong, Shatin, N.T., Hong Kong. TEL 852-2770-3310, FAX 852-2782-6869. Ed. Peter K H Lee. Circ: 1,200.

266 USA ISSN 0199-6487
CHINMAYA MISSION WEST NEWS. Text in English. bi-m. USD 7.
Published by: Chinmaya Mission, P O Box 129, Piercy, CA 95587. TEL 707-237-5321, FAX 707-247-3422, info-krishnalaya@chinmayamission.org, http://www.chinmaya.org.

200 CHE ISSN 0009-4994
CHOISIR; revue de reflexion chretienne. Text in French. 1959. 11/yr. CHF 80 domestic; CHF 85, EUR 53 foreign (effective 2001). adv. bk.rev. index. **Document type:** *Magazine, Academic/Scholarly.*
Published by: Revue Choisir, 18 Rue Jacques Dalphin, Carouge Ge, 1227, Switzerland. TEL 41-22-8274675, FAX 41-22-8274670, redaction@choisir.ch, http://www.choisir.ch. Circ: 3,000.

270 CHE ISSN 1662-0801
CHRESIS; Die Methode der Kirchenvaeter im Umgang mit der antiken Kultur. Text in German. 1984. irreg., latest vol.9, 2006. price varies. **Document type:** *Monographic series, Academic/Scholarly.*
Published by: Schwabe und Co. AG, Steinentorstr 13, Basel, 4010, Switzerland. TEL 41-61-2789565, FAX 41-61-2789566, verlag@schwabe.ch, http://www.schwabe.ch.

CHRETIENS ET SOCIETES XVIE-XXE SIECLES. *see* SOCIOLOGY

200 GBR ISSN 0964-0886
CHRISM. Text in English. 1965. s-a. GBP 7; GBP 3.50 per issue (effective 2009). bk.rev. back issues avail. **Document type:** *Journal, Academic/Scholarly.* **Description:** Features articles on different aspects of healing.
Formerly (until 1965): St. Raphael Quarterly
Published by: Guild of St. Raphael, c/o Organising Secretary, The Rectory, 3 Church Close, Hemsworth, Pontefract, WF9 4SJ, United Kingdom. TEL 44-151-2283193, FAX 44-151-2283193, office@guildofstraphael.org.uk. Ed. Helen Leathard TEL 44-1524-849495.

200 USA ISSN 0889-8901
CHRIST FOR THE NATIONS. Text in English. 1967. m. free. **Document type:** *Magazine, Consumer.*
Published by: Christ for the Nations, Inc., 3404 Conway St, Dallas, TX 75224. TEL 214-376-1711, FAX 214-302-6228. Ed. Freda Lindsay. R&P Patti Conn. **Subscr. to:** PO Box 769000, Dallas, TX 75376-9000.

220 GBR ISSN 0009-5117
THE CHRISTADELPHIAN; dedicated wholly to the hope of Israel. Text in English. 1864. m. GBP 33.60 domestic; GBP 34.80 foreign; USD 2.30 per issue (effective 2009). bk.rev. illus. index. back issues avail. **Document type:** *Magazine, Consumer.* **Description:** Promotes Bible study and a better understanding of Christadelphian beliefs.
Formerly (until 1870): The Ambassador of the Coming Age; Incorporates (18??-1870): Way
Related titles: Audio CD ed.: GBP 27 (effective 2009); Audio cassette/tape ed.: GBP 33 (effective 2009).
Published by: Christadelphian Magazine and Publishing Association Ltd., 404 Shaftmoor Ln, Hall Green, Birmingham, W Mids B28 8SZ, United Kingdom. TEL 44-121-7776328, FAX 44-121-7785024. Ed. Michael J Ashton. **Subscr. in Canada to:** The Christadelphian; **Subscr. in the US to:** The Christadelphian; **Subscr. to:** The Christadelphian.

200 DEU ISSN 0009-5184
DIE CHRISTENGEMEINSCHAFT; Monatsschrift zur religioesen Erneuerung. Text in German. 1924. m. EUR 50 (effective 2011). adv. bk.rev. index. **Document type:** *Magazine, Consumer.*
Indexed: CERDIC.
Published by: Verlag Urachhaus, Landhausstrasse 82, Stuttgart, 70190, Germany. TEL 49-711-2853201, FAX 49-711-2853211, info@urachhaus.com, http://www.urachhaus.com. Ed. Michael Heidenreich. Circ: 10,000.

230 CHE
CHRISTENTUM UND KULTUR; Basler Studien zu Theologie und Kulturwissenschaft des Christentums. Text in German. 2002. irreg., latest vol.11, 2009. price varies. **Document type:** *Monographic series, Academic/Scholarly.*
Published by: Theologischer Verlag Zurich, Badenerstr 73, Zurich, 8026, Switzerland. TEL 41-44-2993355, FAX 41-44-2993358, tvz@ref.ch.

CHRISTIAN ADVERTISING FORUM. *see* ADVERTISING AND PUBLIC RELATIONS

230 USA ISSN 1930-9074
CHRISTIAN APOLOGETICS JOURNAL. Text in English. 1998. 3/yr. **Document type:** *Journal, Consumer.*
Related titles: Online - full text ed.: ISSN 1930-9082.
Published by: Southern Evangelical Seminary, 3000 Tilley Morris Rd, Matthews, NC 28105. TEL 704-847-5600, 800-778-7884, FAX 704-845-1747, http://www.ses.edu/index.html. Ed. Dr. Norman L Geisler.

CHRISTIAN BIOETHICS; non-ecumenical studies in medical morality. *see* MEDICAL SCIENCES

CHRISTIAN BOOK READER. *see* LITERATURE

262 USA ISSN 0009-5281
BR1
THE CHRISTIAN CENTURY; thinking critically, living faithfully. Text in English. 1886. bi-w. USD 59 combined subscription (print & online eds.) (effective 2011). adv. bk.rev.; music rev.; film rev.; tel.rev. mkt.; stat.; illus. s-a. index. 48 p./no.; back issues avail.; reprints avail. **Document type:** *Magazine, Consumer.* **Description:** Publishes articles by theologians, historians and church leaders.
Incorporates (1918-1934): The World Tomorrow (0364-8583); (in 1926): The Christian Work; Which was formerly (until 1914): Christian Work and the Evangelist; Which superseded in part (in 1909): The Arena (1069-8272)
Related titles: CD-ROM ed.; Microfiche ed.: (from NBI, PQC); Online - full text ed.: USD 39 (effective 2011).
Indexed: A01, A02, A03, A08, A11, A21, A22, A25, A26, ABS&EES, Acal, AmHI, B04, B05, B14, BAS, BRD, BRI, C05, CBRI, CCR, CPerI, DIP, E06, E08, F01, F02, G05, G06, G07, G08, GSS&RPL, H07, H09, H14, HlthInd, I05, I07, IAPV, IBR, IBZ, L09, M01, M02, M06, MASUSE, MEA&I, MLA-IB, MRD, MagInd, P02, P10, P28, P30, P34, P48, P53, P54, PCI, PMR, PQC, PRA, R&TA, R03, R04, R05, R06, RASB, RGAb, RGPR, RI-1, RI-2, RILM, S02, S03, S08, S09, S23, SCOPUS, T02, TOM, U01, W03, W05, WBA, WMB.
—IE, Infotrieve, Ingenta. **CCC.**
Published by: Christian Century Foundation, 104 S Michigan Ave, Ste 700, Chicago, IL 60603. TEL 312-263-7510, FAX 312-263-7540. Ed., Pub. John M Buchanan.

CHRISTIAN CHIROPRACTOR. *see* MEDICAL SCIENCES—Chiropractic, Homeopathy, Osteopathy

CHRISTIAN CHIROPRACTORS ASSOCIATION JOURNAL. *see* MEDICAL SCIENCES—Chiropractic, Homeopathy, Osteopathy

200 USA
THE CHRISTIAN CHRONICLE; an international newspaper for members of Churches of Christ. Text in English. 1943. m. USD 20 (effective 2000). adv. bk.rev. illus. **Document type:** *Newspaper.* **Description:** National and international news, features, and announcements pertaining to the members and activities of the Churches of Christ.
Related titles: Microform ed.: (from PQC).
Published by: Oklahoma Christian University of Science and Arts, PO Box 11000, Oklahoma City, OK 73136-1100. TEL 405-425-5070, FAX 405-425-5076. Ed. Bailey McBride. R&P Lynn McMillan. Adv. contact Dale Jones. Circ: 100,000.

200 USA
CHRISTIAN CIVIC LEAGUE RECORD. Text in English. 1900. m. USD 10 (effective 1995). back issues avail. **Document type:** *Newsletter.*
Published by: Christian Civic League of Maine, 70 Sewall St, Box 5459, Augusta, ME 04332. TEL 207-622-7634, FAX 207-622-7635. Ed. Michael Heath. Circ: 5,500.

200 808 USA
THE CHRISTIAN COMMUNICATOR. Text in English. m. **Document type:** *Magazine, Trade.* **Description:** Source of news and encouragements to Christian writers and speakers.
Published by: A C W, 9731 N Fox Glen Dr, No 6F, Niles, IL 60714-5861. TEL 847-296-3964, FAX 847-296-0754, linjohnson@compuserve.com. Ed. Lin Johnson. Circ: 4,000 (paid).

CHRISTIAN COMPUTING MAGAZINE; applying tomorrow's technology to today's ministries. *see* COMPUTERS—Personal Computers

207.2 USA ISSN 0892-9300
CHRISTIAN CONQUEST. Text in English. 1969. m. USD 10 to institutions. illus.
Formerly (until 1987): New Wine (0194-438X)
Published by: Charles Simpson Ministries, Box 850067, Mobile, AL 36616. TEL 251-633-7900, FAX 251-639-1396, http://csmpublishing.org. Circ: 92,000.

230 155.67 GBR
CHRISTIAN COUNCIL ON AGEING. OCCASIONAL PAPER. Text in English. irreg. GBP 2 (effective 2002).
Published by: Christian Council on Ageing, Epworth House, Stuart Street, Derby, DE1 2EQ, United Kingdom.

253.5 USA ISSN 1076-9668
BV4012.2
CHRISTIAN COUNSELING TODAY. Text in English. 198?. q. USD 35 (effective 2005). **Document type:** *Magazine, Trade.* **Description:** Features articles on marriage and family counseling, spirituality, abuse, pastoral care, lay helping, sexual conflicts, the church as a healing community, and much more.
Former titles (until 1993): The Christian Journal of Psychology and Counseling (1051-9866); (until 1987): The Christian Counselor (0892-8614)
Indexed: A10, ChrPI, R&TA, V03.
Published by: American Association of Christian Counselors, PO Box 739, Forest, VA 24551. TEL 434-525-9470, 800-526-8673, FAX 434-525-9480, contactmemberservices@AACC.net. Ed. Archibald Hart.

200 USA ISSN 0195-265X
BV3750
CHRISTIAN CRUSADE; international Christian newspaper. Text in English. 1969. m. free. bk.rev. **Document type:** *Newspaper.* **Description:** Disseminates the church's missionary activities.
Formerly: Christian Crusade Weekly; Supersedes: Weekly Crusader (0509-9498)
Related titles: Microfilm ed.: (from PQC).
Indexed: A22.
Published by: Church of Christian Crusade, PO Box 977, Tulsa, OK 74102. TEL 417-451-4234, FAX 501-438-6054, bjhargis@aol.com. Ed. Keith Wilkerson. Pub. Dr. Billy James Hargis. Circ: 35,000 (controlled).

230 USA ISSN 1931-7107
CHRISTIAN EAR. Text in English. 2006. d. **Document type:** *Newsletter, Consumer.*
Media: Online - full text.
Published by: Gail Marvel http://christianear.blogspot.com.

200 USA ISSN 0739-8913
BV1460
CHRISTIAN EDUCATION JOURNAL. Abbreviated title: C E J. Text in English. 1980. s-a. USD 32 domestic; USD 40 foreign (effective 2011). bk.rev. back issues avail. **Document type:** *Journal, Academic/Scholarly.* **Description:** Promotes growth and advancement in Christian education.
Formerly (until 1983): Journal of Christian Education (0277-9935)
Related titles: Microfiche ed.: (from PQC); Microfilm ed.: (from PQC); Online - full text ed.
Indexed: A21, A22, A26, CA, CERDIC, ChrPI, E03, E07, ERI, G08, I05, P18, P28, P48, P53, P54, P55, PQC, R&TA, RI-1, RI-2, T02.
Published by: Biola University, Talbot School of Theology, 13800 Biola Ave, La Mirada, CA 90639. TEL 562-944-0351 ext 5321, 562-903-6000, http://www.talbot.edu.

268 USA
CHRISTIAN EDUCATORS JOURNAL. Text in English. 1961. q. USD 7.50 domestic to non-members; USD 11 foreign to non-members. adv. bk.rev. illus. back issues avail. **Document type:** *Magazine, Trade.*
Indexed: GSS&RPL.
Published by: Christian Educators Journal Association, c/o Peter Boogaart, 1628 Mayfair Dr NE, Grand Rapids, MI 49503. TEL 616-451-3274, FAX 616-459-0272. Ed. Lorna Van Gilst. Pub. Peter Boogaart. R&P Peter Boogart. Adv. contact Donald Oppewal. Circ: 4,500 (paid).

CHRISTIAN FAMILY CATALOG. *see* GIFTWARE AND TOYS

243 USA ISSN 1931-4728
CHRISTIAN FEMINISM TODAY. Text in English. 1980. q. USD 45 membership; USD 15 to students; free to members (effective 2006). bk.rev. back issues avail. **Document type:** *Newsletter.*
Former titles (until 2006): E E W C Update (1931-5104); (until 2000): Evangelical & Ecumenical Women's Caucus. Update (1064-0800); (until 1992): Evangelical Women's Caucus. Update
Published by: Ecumenical & Evangelical Women's Caucus, P.O. Box 78171, Indianapolis, IN 46278-6167. Ed., R&P Letha Dawson Scanzoni TEL 757-624-1776. Circ: 500 (paid).

200 MWI
CHRISTIAN FORUM. Text in English. q.
Indexed: ISAP.
Published by: Christian Council of Malawi, Lilongwe, Malawi. **Dist. by:** Christian Literature Association in Malawi, PO Box 503, Blantyre, Malawi.

230.0071 USA ISSN 1536-3759
LC368
➤ **CHRISTIAN HIGHER EDUCATION.** Text in English. 2002. 5/yr. GBP 212 combined subscription in United Kingdom to institutions (print & online eds.); EUR 281, USD 353 combined subscription to institutions (print & online eds.) (effective 2012). adv. reprint service avail. from PSC. **Document type:** *Journal, Academic/Scholarly.* **Description:** Features articles on developments being created and tested by those engaged in the study and practice of Christian higher education.
Related titles: Online - full text ed.: ISSN 1539-4107. GBP 191 in United Kingdom to institutions; EUR 253, USD 317 to institutions (effective 2012) (from IngentaConnect).
Indexed: A01, A02, A03, A08, A22, CA, CPE, ChrPI, E01, E03, ERI, ERIC, FamI, P18, P48, P53, P54, PQC, T02.
—IE, Ingenta. **CCC.**
Published by: Taylor & Francis Inc. (Subsidiary of: Taylor & Francis Group), 325 Chestnut St, Ste 800, Philadelphia, PA 19106. TEL 215-625-2940, 800-354-1420, orders@taylorandfrancis.com, http://www.taylorandfrancis.com. Ed. D Barry Lumsden.

➤ **CHRISTIAN HOME & SCHOOL.** *see* CHILDREN AND YOUTH—About

➤ **CHRISTIAN IRELAND TODAY.** *see* SOCIOLOGY

➤ **CHRISTIAN LIBRARY JOURNAL.** *see* LIBRARY AND INFORMATION SCIENCES

248 USA ISSN 0009-5435
CHRISTIAN LIVING; a magazine about family community and culture. Text in English. 1954. 8/yr. USD 23.95 (effective 2000). adv. bk.rev. illus. index. **Document type:** *Magazine, Consumer.*
Published by: Herald Press, 616 Walnut Ave, Scottdale, PA 15683-1999. TEL 724-887-8500, FAX 724-887-3111. Ed. Levi Miller. Circ: 4,000.

CHRISTIAN MANAGEMENT REPORT. *see* BUSINESS AND ECONOMICS—Management

▼ **THE CHRISTIAN MARKETPLACE AT YOUR FINGERTIPS.** *see* PUBLISHING AND BOOK TRADE

207.2 USA ISSN 0744-4052
CHRISTIAN MISSIONS IN MANY LANDS. Text in English. 1970 (vol.33). m. (11/yr.). free. bk.rev. illus.
Formerly: Fields (0015-0762)
Published by: Christian Missions in Many Lands, Inc., PO Box 13, Spring Lake, NJ 07762. TEL 908-449-8880. Circ: 14,000.

248 USA
CHRISTIAN MOTHER (PITTSBURGH). Text in English. 194?. q. USD 3 (effective 2000). **Document type:** *Newsletter.*
Published by: Archconfraternity of Christian Mothers, 220 37th St, Pittsburgh, PA 15201. TEL 412-683-2400. Ed. Rev. Bertin Roll. Circ: 30,000.

R

CHRISTIAN MOTORSPORTS ILLUSTRATED. *see* TRANSPORTATION—Automobiles

230 USA ISSN 0899-7292
CHRISTIAN*NEW AGE QUARTERLY; a bridge supporting dialogue. Text in English. 1989. q. USD 12.50 domestic; USD 18.50 foreign (effective 2011). adv. bk.rev. back issues avail. **Document type:** *Newsletter, Trade.* **Description:** Probes the common ground and distinctions of Christianity and the New Age movement - a forum for dialogue between the two ideologies.
Published by: Bethsheva's Concern AKA Christian*New Age Quarterly, PO Box 276, Clifton, NJ 07015.

230 USA
THE CHRISTIAN NEWS NETWORK. Text in English. m. **Description:** Features information on churches, ministries and Christian counseling.
Media: Online - full text.
Published by: Christian News Network

230 USA ISSN 1937-500X
CHRISTIAN ODYSSEY. Text in English. 2005. bi-m. free (effective 2007). **Document type:** *Magazine, Consumer.* **Description:** Contains articles and advice on Christian living and practice including Bible study, explanations of Christian beliefs, inspirational articles and book reviews.
Published by: Worldwide Church of God, PO Box 5005, Glendora, CA 91740. Ed. John Halford.

230 USA ISSN 1548-8233
THE CHRISTIAN POST. Text in English. 2004 (Mar.). w. **Document type:** *Newspaper.*
Published by: The Christian Post, 111 Pine St Ste 1725, San Francisco, CA 94111. TEL 415-986-2003, http://www.christianpost.com.

200 330 USA
CHRISTIAN PROFESSIONAL. Text in English. 2006. q. USD 16 (effective 2006). **Document type:** *Magazine, Consumer.* **Description:** Contains articles on Christian themed career, business and work relationships.
Published by: Christian Professional, LLC., 498 Town Center St. N. #243, Mooresville, IN 46158. Pub. Andrea Emerson.

230 USA
CHRISTIAN RANCHMAN. Text in English. 1976. m. bk.rev. back issues avail. **Document type:** *Newspaper.* **Description:** Outreach ministry to livestock industry. Provides testimonies of what God has done in livestock people's lives.
Published by: Cowboys for Christ, PO Box 7557, Ft. Worth, TX 76111. TEL 817-236-0023, FAX 817-256-0024. Ed. Ted K Pressley. R&P Estell McDonald. Circ: 38,000.

268 USA ISSN 0009-5575
CHRISTIAN RECORD. Text in English. 1900. q. free to qualified personnel (effective 2011). back issues avail. **Document type:** *Magazine, Consumer.* **Description:** Provides devotional and inspirational reading for adults with visual impairments.
Media: Braille.
Published by: Christian Record Services, PO Box 6097, Lincoln, NE 68506. TEL 402-488-0981, FAX 402-488-7582, info@christianrecord.org, http://www.christianrecord.org.

CHRISTIAN RETAILING; the trade magazine of religious retailing. *see* PUBLISHING AND BOOK TRADE

260 USA ISSN 0017-2251
BR1
➤ **CHRISTIAN SCHOLAR'S REVIEW**; a Christian quarterly of the arts and sciences. Text in English. 1955. q. USD 24 to individuals; USD 41 to institutions; USD 8 per issue (effective 2010). adv. bk.rev. abstr.; bibl. index, cum.index. back issues avail.; reprints avail. **Document type:** *Journal, Academic/Scholarly.* **Description:** Peer articles, essays, and publication reviews pertaining to Christian thought and the interrelationship between Christian thought and all areas of scientific, theological, philosophical, cultural, and social scholarly interest.
Formerly (until 1970): Gordon Review (0436-1644)
Related titles: Microfiche ed.; Microform ed.: (from PQC); Online - full text ed.
Indexed: A01, A21, A22, AES, BEL&L, CA, CERDIC, ChrPI, DIP, GSS&RPL, H14, IBR, IBZ, MEA&I, MLA, MLA-IB, OTA, P02, P10, P28, P30, P48, P53, P54, PCI, PQC, Phillnd, R&TA, RI-1, RI-2, T02.
—BLDSC (3181.920000), IE, Infotrieve, Ingenta.
Address: Hope College, PO Box 9000, Holland, MI 49422. TEL 616-395-7582, FAX 616-395-7490, steen@hope.cit.hope.edu. Ed. Don W King. Pub. David A Hoekema.

➤ **CHRISTIAN SCHOOL PRODUCTS.** *see* EDUCATION

200 MWI
CHRISTIAN SERVICE COMMITTEE OF THE CHURCHES IN MALAWI. ANNUAL REPORT. Text in English. a. free. **Document type:** *Corporate.* **Description:** Reports on activities of the organization, including agriculture, education, and social services.
Published by: Christian Service Committee of the Churches in Malawi, PO Box 51294, Limbe, Malawi. TEL 265-624977/13, FAX 265-624998, TELEX 44365 CSC MI, csc@malawi.net. Ed. Vincent Chibowa.

CHRISTIAN SINGLES; news and contacts. *see* SINGLES' INTERESTS AND LIFESTYLES

230 USA ISSN 1531-4057
CHRISTIAN SOCIAL THOUGHT SERIES. Text in English. 2001. irreg. USD 6 per issue (effective 2010). back issues avail. **Document type:** *Monographic series, Trade.*
Published by: Acton Institute for the Study of Religion and Liberty, 161 Ottawa Ave., NW, Ste 301, Grand Rapids, MI 49503. TEL 616-454-3080, FAX 616-454-9454, info@acton.org.

CHRISTIAN SOCIALIST. *see* POLITICAL SCIENCE

230 USA ISSN 0009-5656
CHRISTIAN STANDARD. Text in English. 1866. w. USD 26.99 (effective 2008). bk.rev. illus. index, cum.index: 1866-1966. 16 p./no.; **Document type:** *Magazine, Consumer.* **Description:** Designed for the leaders in christian churches and churches of christ : ministers, staff members, elders, deacons, committee chairpersons and teachers.
Incorporates: Christian Record; Disciple
Indexed: A22, ChrPI, GSS&RPL.
Published by: Standard Publishing, 8805 Governor's Hill Dr, Ste 400, Cincinnati, OH 45249. TEL 513-931-4050, 800-543-1353, FAX 877-867-5751, customerservice@standardpub.com, http://www.standardpub.com. Ed. Mark A Taylor. Circ: 50,000.

CHRISTIAN TEACHERS JOURNAL. *see* EDUCATION

230 USA
CHRISTIAN VANGUARD. Text in English. 1971. m. USD 25. back issues avail. **Document type:** *Newsletter.*
Published by: New Christian Crusade Church, PO Box 426, Metairie, LA 70004. TEL 504-279-5940.

248 USA ISSN 0009-5702
CHRISTIAN WOMAN. Text in English. 1933. 6/yr. USD 16.98 (effective 2005). adv. bk.rev. illus. index. **Document type:** *Magazine, Consumer.* **Description:** Features, poetry, fiction, lessons, and information on issues pertaining to contemporary family life, self-improvement, motivation, parenting, and marriage for the practicing female Christian, married or single, with advice and opinion columns.
Published by: Gospel Advocate Company, 1006 Elm Hill Pike, Nashville, TN 37210. TEL 615-254-8781, FAX 615-254-7411, http://www.gospeladvocate.com. Pub. Neil Anderson. Circ: 30,000.

267.4 AUS ISSN 1444-5603
CHRISTIAN WOMAN; inspired living. Text in English. 1954. bi-m. AUD 37.95 in Australia & New Zealand; AUD 49 elsewhere; AUD 29 domestic to senior citizens; AUD 7.50 per issue (effective 2008). adv. bk.rev. **Document type:** *Magazine, Trade.*
Incorporates (2004-2007): Joy Magazine (1176-7340)
Published by: Media Incorporated Pty Ltd., PO Box 163, North Sydney, NSW 2059, Australia. TEL 61-2-84373541, FAX 61-2-99861431, enquiries@mediaincorp.com. Ed. Jenny Baxter. Adv. contact Matthew Harvie TEL 61-2-90075373. color page AUD 1,200; 210 x 297. Circ: 7,500.

230 USA ISSN 1931-5090
CHRISTIAN WOMANHOOD. Text in English. 1975. m. USD 21 domestic; USD 26 foreign (effective 2007). **Document type:** *Magazine, Consumer.*
Published by: First Baptist Church of Hammond, Indiana, 8400 Burr St, Crown Point, IN 46307. TEL 219-365-3202, FAX 219-558-2610, requests@christianwomanhood.org.

200.82 CAN
CHRISTIAN WOMEN TODAY. Text in English. m. free. **Document type:** *Newsletter.* **Description:** Includes articles about prayer, sharing faith and growing closer to Jesus Christ.
Media: Online - full text.
Address: P O Box 300, Vancouver, BC V6C 2X3, Canada. TEL 604-514-2000. Ed. Ruthann Raycroft.

230 CHE ISSN 1424-8999
CHRISTIANISMES ANCIENS. Text in French. 2001. irreg., latest vol.2, 2003. price varies. **Document type:** *Monographic series, Academic/Scholarly.*
Published by: Peter Lang AG (Subsidiary of: Peter Lang Publishing Group), Hochfeldstr 32, Postfach 746, Bern 9, 3000, Switzerland. TEL 41-31-3061717, FAX 41-31-3061727, info@peterlang.com.

230 GBR ISSN 1747-7395
CHRISTIANITY; real life, real faith in the real world. Text in English. 2001. m. GBP 30 domestic; GBP 41 in Europe; GBP 43 elsewhere; GBP 3.20 newsstand/cover (effective 2009). adv. bk.rev.; music rev. back issues avail. **Document type:** *Magazine, Consumer.* **Description:** Aims to provide news and articles for christians and those interested in the christian faith from across the denominational spectrum.
Formerly (until 2004): Christianity + Renewal (1473-4745); Which was formed by the merger of (1966-2001): Renewal (Crowborough) (1351-4326); (1996-2001): Christianity (1365-3695); Which was formerly (until 1996): Alpha (0961-6950); Which was formed by the merger of (1987-1991): 21st Century Christian (0952-6269); Which was formerly (1965-1987): Buzz (0045-3692); (1989-1991): Today (New Malden) (0956-2648); Which was formerly (until Jan.1989): Leadership Today (0952-6277); (until 1987): Today (London) (0262-8023); (until 1982): Crusade (0011-2127)
Related titles: Online - full text ed.
Indexed: RASB.
Published by: C C P Ltd, PO Box 17911, London, SW1P 4YX, United Kingdom. Ed. John Buckeridge. Adv. contact Sue Bastin TEL 44-1892-652750. page GBP 1,950; bleed 216 x 303. Circ: 16,000.

CHRISTIANITY AND LITERATURE. *see* LITERARY AND POLITICAL REVIEWS

270 USA ISSN 1935-3863
CHRISTIANITY IN THE ISLAMIC WORLD. Text in English. 2006. irreg., latest 2008. price varies. back issues avail. **Document type:** *Monographic series, Academic/Scholarly.* **Description:** Highlights the historic and continuing relationship between Christianity and Islam.
Published by: Gorgias Press LLC, 954 River Rd, Piscataway, NJ 08854. TEL 732-885-8900, FAX 732-885-8908, helpdesk@gorgiaspress.com, http://www.gorgiaspress.com/bookshop/default.aspx.

261 USA ISSN 0009-5753
CHRISTIANITY TODAY; a magazine of evangelical conviction. Abbreviated title: C T. Text in English. 1956. m. USD 19.95 domestic; USD 32.95 foreign (effective 2010). adv. bk.rev.; film rev. bibl.; illus. index. back issues avail.; reprints avail. **Document type:** *Magazine, Consumer.* **Description:** Provides insightful christian perspective and thoughtful analysis on the relevant news, trends, and events of present days.
Incorporates (1997-200?): Christianity Online (1528-1876); Which incorporated (1997-1999): Computing Today (1092-9029)
Related titles: Microform ed.: (from PQC); Online - full text ed.: ISSN 1551-1855.
Indexed: A01, A02, A03, A08, A11, A21, A22, A25, A26, ABS&EES, Acal, B04, B05, B14, BAS, BRD, BRI, C05, C12, CBRI, CCR, CPerI, ChPerI, Chicano, ChrPI, E08, F01, F02, FamI, G05, G06, G07, G08, GSS&RPL, H14, I05, I07, M01, M02, M06, MASUSE, MEA&I, MLA-IB, MagInd, OTA, P02, P10, P28, P30, P34, P48, P53, P54, PMR, PQC, PRA, PerIslam, R&TA, R03, R04, R05, RASB, RGAb, RGPR, RI-1, RI-2, RILM, S02, S03, S08, S09, S23, SCOPUS, T02, U01, W03, W05, WBA, WMB.
—IE, Ingenta. **CCC.**
Published by: Christianity Today International, 465 Gundersen Dr, Carol Stream, IL 60188. TEL 630-260-6200, FAX 630-260-0114. Eds. David Neff, James I Packer, Harold B Smith. R&P Paulette De Paul. Adv. contact Frank Chihowski. B&W page USD 7,828, color page USD 8,328; trim 8 x 10.75. Circ: 140,000. **Subscr. to:** CDS, PO Box 37060, Boone, IA 50037-0060.

323.4 USA ISSN 1044-5846
CHRISTIANS IN CRISIS. Text in English. 1985. bi-m. free. **Document type:** *Newsletter.* **Description:** Covers religious freedom and church-state issues internationally.
Indexed: CCR.
Published by: Christian Forum Research Foundation, 1111 Fairgrounds Rd, Grand Rapids, MN 55744. TEL 218-326-2688, 800-286-5115, FAX 218-327-8905. Ed., R&P Sidney Reiners. Circ: 1,500 (controlled).

CHRISTLICHE DEUTSCHE AUTOREN DES 20. JAHRHUNDERTS. *see* LITERATURE

200 DEU ISSN 1619-2001
CHRISTLICHER DIGEST. Text in German. 2002. m. adv. **Document type:** *Magazine, Consumer.*
Formed by the merger of (1974-2002): Der Sonntagsbrief (0174-0350); (1951-2002): Evangelischer Digest (0177-185X); Which was formerly (until 1984): E D - Evangelischer Digest (0175-3797); Evangelischer Digest (0014-3537); (1946-2002): Katholischer Digest (1431-4932); Which was formerly (until 1986): Katholischer Digest. Ausgabe A (0177-2872); (until 1984): K D - Katholischer Digest. Ausgabe A (0724-0228); (until 1982): Katholischer Digest. Ausgabe A (0170-7868)
Published by: Verlag Christlicher Digest GmbH & Co. KG, Okenstrasse 23, Offenburg, 77652, Germany. TEL 49-781-289928420, FAX 49-781-289928500, verlag@christlicherdigest.de. Ed. Fred Heine. Adv. contact Dirk Keck. B&W page EUR 2,630, col. inch EUR 4,630. Circ: 32,000 (controlled).

CHRIST'S COLLEGE MAGAZINE. *see* EDUCATION—Higher Education

202 FRA ISSN 0009-5834
CHRISTUS; accompagner l'homme en quete de Dieu. Text in French. 1954. q. EUR 38 domestic; EUR 38 in Belgium; EUR 42 elsewhere (effective 2008). adv. **Document type:** *Journal, Consumer.*
Indexed: CERDIC, CPL, DIP, FR, IBR, IBZ, R&TA, RASB, RI-1, RI-2, RefugAb.
—**CCC.**
Published by: Assas Editions, 14 rue d'Assas, Paris, 75006, France. TEL 33-1-44394848, FAX 33-1-40490192. Ed. C Flipo. Circ: 6,000.

200 DEU ISSN 0009-5869
DIE CHRISTUS POST. Text in German. 1956. 5/yr. free (effective 2009). bk.rev. abstr.; bibl. **Document type:** *Newsletter, Consumer.*
Published by: Christliche Post- und Telekomvereinigung in Deutschland, Im Dorf 9a, Heeslingen, 27404, Germany. TEL 49-7158-63565, info@cptv-online.de, http://www.cptv-online.de. Ed. Karl-Heinz Bartscher. Circ: 1,200.

261 USA
CHRYSALIS READER. Text in English. 1985. a.
Address: R.R.1, Box 4510, Dillwyn, VA 23936. Ed. Susanna Van Rensselaer. Circ: 3,000.

322.1 USA ISSN 0009-6334
BR516
CHURCH & STATE. Text in English. 1948. 11/yr. USD 18 domestic; USD 25 foreign (effective 2005). bk.rev. illus. index. reprints avail. **Description:** Reviews church-state news and analysis. Promotes the concept of separation of church and state.
Formerly (until 1951): Church and State Newsletter
Related titles: Microform ed.: (from PQC); Online - full text ed.
Indexed: A01, A02, A03, A08, A21, A22, A26, CA, CERDIC, E03, E08, ERI, FamI, G06, G07, G08, H14, I05, I07, M02, MEA&I, P02, P05, P06, P10, P28, P34, P45, P48, P53, P54, PAIS, PQC, R05, RASB, RI-1, RI-2, S09, S11, S23, SCOPUS, T02.
—BLDSC (3189.733000), IE, Ingenta.
Published by: Americans United for Separation of Church and State, 518 C St, N E, Washington, DC 20002. TEL 202-466-3234, FAX 202-466-2587. Ed. Joseph L Conn. Pub. Barry W Lynn. R&P Susan Hansen. Circ: 30,000.

CHURCH & STATE; a magazine of Irish secularist opinion. *see* POLITICAL SCIENCE

254 USA ISSN 1531-8206
BV288
CHURCH & WORSHIP TECHNOLOGY. Text in English. m.
Published by: Workhorse Publications, P O Box 25310, Scottsdale, AZ 85255. TEL 480-585-0455.

200 CAN ISSN 1198-1156
CHURCH BUSINESS. PRODUCTS & TECHNOLOGY. Text in English. 1992. bi-m. CAD 18, USD 30. adv. bk.rev. **Document type:** *Journal, Trade.* **Description:** Covers the administration and facility management of Canadian churches for clergy, administration and property managers.
Former titles (until 1994): Church Business Magazine (1195-8642); Church Business (1183-2339)
Published by: Momentum Media Management, 4040 Creditview Rd, Unit 11, P O Box 1800, Mississauga, ON L5C 3Y8, Canada. TEL 905-813-7100, FAX 905-813-7117. Ed., R&P Jay Barwell. Adv. contact Hugh Parkinson. B&W page CAD 1,915, color page CAD 2,750; trim 11 x 8. Circ: 12,400 (controlled).

CHURCH EDUCATOR. *see* EDUCATION

CHURCH EXECUTIVE; the first source of information for business administrators of America's largest churches. *see* BUSINESS AND ECONOMICS—Management

230 336.2 USA
CHURCH FINANCE TODAY. Text in English. 1993. m. USD 59.95 (effective 2009). 4 p./no.; **Document type:** *Newsletter, Trade.* **Description:** Focuses on relevant IRS developments, court rulings, and legislation and provides examples and tips to help you navigate the requirements.
Formerly (until 2008): Church Treasurer Alert
Published by: Christianity Today International, 465 Gundersen Dr, Carol Stream, IL 60188. TEL 630-260-6200, FAX 630-260-0114, http://www.christianitytoday.com. Ed. Richard Hammar.

270 306 GBR ISSN 0009-6407
BR140
➤ **CHURCH HISTORY**; studies in Christianity and culture. Text in English. 1932. q. GBP 75, USD 149 to institutions; GBP 80, USD 162 combined subscription to institutions (print & online eds.) (effective 2012). adv. bk.rev. bibl.; illus. index, cum.index. 1 cols./p.; back issues avail.; reprint service avail. from PSC. **Document type:** *Journal, Academic/Scholarly.* **Description:** Coves all areas of the history of Christianity and its cultural contexts in all places and times, including its non-Western expressions.
Related titles: Microform ed.; Online - full text ed.: ISSN 1755-2613. GBP 69, USD 135 to institutions (effective 2012).
Indexed: A01, A02, A03, A08, A20, A21, A22, A26, ABS&EES, ASCA, AmH&L, AmHI, ArtHuCI, B04, B14, B24, BEL&L, BRD, BRI, CA, CBRI, CERDIC, ChrPI, CurCont, DIP, E01, E08, FR, FamI, G08, H05, H07, H08, H09, H10, H14, HAb, HistAb, HumInd, I05, IBR, IBZ, M01, M02, MLA-IB, OTA, P02, P10, P13, P28, P30, P48, P53, P54, PCI, PQC, R&TA, R05, RASB, RI-1, RI-2, RILM, S02, S03, S09, SCOPUS, SOPODA, SociolAb, T02, W03, W04, W05, W07.
—BLDSC (3189.768000), IE, Infotrieve, Ingenta, INIST. **CCC.**
Published by: (American Society of Church History USA), Cambridge University Press, The Edinburgh Bldg, Shaftesbury Rd, Cambridge, CB2 8RU, United Kingdom. TEL 44-1223-312393, FAX 44-1223-315052, journals@cambridge.org, http://www.cambridge.org/uk. Eds. Amanda Porterfield, John Corrigan. Adv. contact Rebecca Roberts TEL 44-1223-325083. page GBP 205, page USD 390. Circ: 3,400.

274 NLD ISSN 1871-241X
BR900
➤ **CHURCH HISTORY AND RELIGIOUS CULTURE.** Text in English. 1829. 4/yr. EUR 284, USD 398 to institutions; EUR 310, USD 434 combined subscription to institutions (print & online eds.) (effective 2012). bk.rev. bibl. reprint service avail. from PSC. **Document type:** *Journal, Academic/Scholarly.* **Description:** Explores church history in the Netherlands.
Former titles (until 2006): Nederlandsch Archief voor Kerkgeschiedenis (0028-2030); (until 1900): Archief voor Nederlandsche Kerkgeschiedenis (0166-9427)
Related titles: Online - full text ed.: ISSN 1871-2428. 200?. EUR 258, USD 362 to institutions (effective 2012) (from IngentaConnect).
Indexed: A01, A03, A08, A21, A22, AmH&L, AmHI, B24, CA, CERDIC, DIP, E01, H07, HistAb, IBR, IBZ, IZBG, MLA-IB, P30, PCI, RI-1, RI-2, T02, W04.
—BLDSC (3189.768200), IE, Infotrieve, Ingenta. **CCC.**
Published by: Brill, PO Box 9000, Leiden, 2300 PA, Netherlands. TEL 31-71-5353500, FAX 31-71-5317532, cs@brill.nl. Ed. Wim Janse.
Dist. by: Turpin Distribution Services Ltd., Pegasus Dr, Stratton Business Park, Biggleswade, Bedfordshire SG18 8QB, United Kingdom. TEL 44-1767-604954, FAX 44-1767-601640, custserv@turpin-distribution.com, http://www.turpin-distribution.com/.

340 200 336.2 USA
CHURCH LAW & TAX REPORT. Abbreviated title: C L & T R. Text in English. 1987. bi-m. USD 69; USD 99 combined subscription (print & online eds.) (effective 2008). adv. 32 p./no.; back issues avail. **Document type:** *Magazine, Consumer.* **Description:** Provides practical information to church leaders on important legal and tax developments that have a direct impact on ministry.
Related titles: Online - full text ed.
Published by: Christianity Today International, 465 Gundersen Dr, Carol Stream, IL 60188. TEL 630-260-6200, FAX 630-260-0114, http://www.christianitytoday.com. Ed. Richard Hammar. adv.: B&W page USD 1,995. Circ: 9,000.

200 NLD ISSN 1877-8720
▼ **CHURCH LIFE MAGAZINE.** Cover title: Church Life. Text in Dutch. 2009. q. EUR 17.50; EUR 4.95 newsstand/cover (effective 2010). adv. **Document type:** *Magazine, Consumer.*
Published by: Stichting Hij Leeft Zending, Postbus 7, Bilthoven, 3720 AA, Netherlands. TEL 31-30-6041970, http://www.hijleeft.nl. Ed. Hans Tims. Adv. contact Robbert Zwaan. Circ: 10,000.

THE CHURCH MUSIC REPORT. *see* MUSIC

268 GBR
CHURCH POCKET BOOK AND DIARY. Text in English. 19??. a. GBP 8.99 per issue (effective 2010). **Document type:** *Handbook/Manual/Guide, Consumer.* **Description:** Contains titles of Sundays and dates of festivals corresponding to the Common Worship Calendar and Lectionary and the Book of Common Prayer as well as includes space for weekly personal notes and space at the back for personal memoranda, addresses and telephone numbers.
Formerly: Churchman's Pocket Book and Diary (0069-4029)
Published by: Society for Promoting Christian Knowledge, 36 Causton St, London, SW1P 4ST, United Kingdom. TEL 44-20-75923900, spck@spck.org.uk, http://www.spck.org.uk/.

384 264 USA
CHURCH PRODUCTION MAGAZINE; an educational magazine for houses of worship covering: audio, video and lighting technologies. Text in English. bi-m. USD 44.95 (effective 2001); Free to qualified subscribers in U.S. and Canada. adv. **Document type:** *Magazine, Trade.* **Description:** Covers the application of audio, video and lighting as an educational tool in religious instruction and worship.
Address: 113 Winfair Dr, Cary, NC 27513. TEL 919-677-4000, FAX 919-677-4001, info@churchproduction.com, http://www.churchproduction.com. Ed. Brian Blackmore.

252 GBR ISSN 0069-4002
➤ **CHURCH PULPIT YEAR BOOK (YEAR).** Text in English. 1903. a., latest 2006. price varies. adv. index. back issues avail. **Document type:** *Yearbook, Academic/Scholarly.*
Published by: S C M - Canterbury Press Ltd., Religious and Moral Education Press, Saint Marys Works, St Marys Plain, Norwich, Norfolk NR3 3BH, United Kingdom. TEL 44-1603-612914, FAX 44-1603-624483, orders@norwichbooksandmusic.co.uk, http://www.scm-canterburypress.co.uk/rmep.asp. Ed. Joyce Critchlow.

230 USA ISSN 0009-6601
CHURCH WORLD. Text in English. 1930. w. (48/yr.). USD 27.50 domestic; USD 35 foreign; USD 0.75 per issue (effective 2005). adv. bk.rev.; film rev.; play rev. illus. 24 p./no. 5 cols./p.; back issues avail. **Document type:** *Newspaper, Consumer.*
Published by: Roman Catholic Diocese of Portland,ME, 510 Ocean Ave., Portland, ME 04103. TEL 207-773-6471, FAX 207-773-0182. Ed. Thomas J. Kardos. adv.: B&W page USD 562.50, color page USD 842.50; 5 x 15. Circ: 6,500. Wire service: CaNS.

200 301 BRA ISSN 1678-5274
BL7
➤ **CIENCIAS DA RELIGIAO.** Text in Portuguese; Abstracts in English, Portuguese. 2003. a. free (effective 2005). **Document type:** *Journal, Academic/Scholarly.*
Indexed: A01, C01, CA, F03, F04, T02.
Published by: Universidade Presbiteriana Mackenzie (Subsidiary of: Instituto Presbiteriano Mackenzie), Rua da Consolacao 896, Pr.2, Sao Paulo-SP, SP 01302-907, Brazil. TEL 55-11-32368666, FAX 55-11-32368302, http://www.mackenzie.com.br. Eds. Mrs. Marcia Costa Liberal, Mrs. Marcia Serra Viana, Mr. Ricardo Quadros Gouvea. R&P Mr. Fernando Santos Kerr.

271 USA ISSN 1062-6549
BX3401
➤ **CISTERCIAN STUDIES QUARTERLY.** Abbreviated title: C S Q. Text in English. 1966. q. USD 26 (effective 2010). adv. bk.rev. cum.index: 1966-2002. back issues avail. **Document type:** *Journal, Academic/Scholarly.* **Description:** Features review of the Christian monastic and contemplative spiritual tradition.
Formerly (until 1991): Cistercian Studies (0578-3224)
Related titles: Microform ed.: (from PQC); Online - full text ed.
Indexed: A01, A03, A08, A22, CA, CPL, DIP, IBR, IBZ, P28, P48, P53, P54, PCI, PQC, RILM, T02.
Published by: Order of the Cistercians of the Strict Observance, U S Region, 8400 Abbey Hill Rd, Dubuque, IA 52003. TEL 563-582-2595, FAX 563-582-5511, ocsoroma@ocso.org, http://www.ocso.org. Ed. Mark A Scott TEL 502-549-4417.

230 ESP ISSN 0210-3990
CISTERCIUM; revista monastica. Text in Spanish. 1927. 3/yr. **Document type:** *Magazine, Consumer.*
Supersedes (in 1949): La Voz del Cister (0210-4008)
Indexed: FR.
—INIST.
Published by: Monjes Cistercienses, Abadia de Sta. Ma. de Viaceli, Cobreces (Cantabria), 39320, Spain. TEL 34-942-725017, FAX 34-942-725086, revcistercium@planalfa.es, http://www3.planalfa.es/cistercienses/cister.htm.

200 700 ITA ISSN 0009-7632
BR5
CITTA DI VITA; bimestrale di religione arte e scienza. Text in Italian. 1946. bi-m. adv. bk.rev. bibl.; illus. index. **Document type:** *Magazine, Consumer.*
Indexed: MLA, MLA-IB.
Address: Piazza Santa Croce 16, Florence, FI 50122, Italy. info@cittadivita.org, http://www.cittadivita.org. Circ: 6,000.

200 900 BEL ISSN 0774-7241
CLAIRLIEU: TIJDSCHRIFT GEWIJD AAN DE GESCHIEDENIS DER KRUISHEREN. Text in Dutch. 1943. a. EUR 12.50 (effective Jan. 2002). bk.rev. **Document type:** *Bulletin.* **Description:** Covers history of the crosiers and spirituality.
Related titles: English ed.; German ed.; French ed.
Published by: Geschiedkundige Kring "Clairlieu", Pelserstraat 33, Maaseik, 3680, Belgium. TEL 003189566547, FAX 089566610. Ed. R. Janssen.

O CLARIM. *see* CHILDREN AND YOUTH—For

200 FRA ISSN 2108-5633
▼ **LES CLASSIQUES DE LA SPIRITUALITE.** Text in French. 2010. irreg. **Document type:** *Monographic series.*
Published by: Artege Editions, 11, Rue du Bastion Saint-Francois, Perpignan, 66000, France. http://www.editionsartege.fr.

CLEARFACTS. *see* POLITICAL SCIENCE

254 USA
BV652.A1
THE CLERGY JOURNAL; your practical guide to church leadership and personal growth. Text in English. 1924. 9/yr. USD 39.20 (effective 2005). adv. bk.rev. back issues avail. **Document type:** *Journal, Trade.*
Formerly (until 1993): Church Management (0009-6431); Incorporates (1881-1993): Record of Christian Work (0364-4855)
Related titles: Microfilm ed.: (from PQC); Online - full text ed.
Indexed: A22, CA, CCR, P28, P54.
Published by: Logos Productions Inc., 6160 Carmen Ave E, Inver Grove Heights, MN 55076. TEL 800-328-0200, FAX 651-457-4617, http://www.logosproductions.com. Pub. Pete Velander. R&P Sharilyn Figueroa. Adv. contact Steve Truran. B&W page USD 600, color page USD 1,200. Circ: 5,000 (paid).

240 USA
CLOSER WALK. Text in English. 1981. bi-m. USD 29.74 domestic; USD 36.95 in Canada; USD 60.95 elsewhere; USD 5.95 newsstand/cover (effective 2011). reprints avail. **Document type:** *Magazine, Trade.* **Description:** Provides insights from church leaders of the past. Aims to bring believers closer to God through the heritage of the saints.
Formerly: Timeless Insights
Published by: Walk Thru the Bible Ministries, Inc., 4201 N Peachtree Rd, Atlanta, GA 30341. TEL 800-361-6131, info@walkthru.org.

200.82 USA ISSN 0896-0038
CO-LABORER MAGAZINE. Text in English. 1961. bi-m. USD 8.75 (effective 1999). bk.rev. **Description:** Seeks to promote missions and deepen the spiritual life of women.
Published by: Women Nationally Active for Christ, PO Box 5002, Antioch, TN 37011-5002. TEL 615-731-6812, FAX 615-731-0771. Ed. Marjorie Workman. Circ: 11,000.

260 ESP ISSN 0213-6236
CODICE. Text in Spanish. 1985. s-a. back issues avail. **Document type:** *Magazine, Academic/Scholarly.*
Published by: Asociacion de Amigos del Archivo Historico Diocesano de la Catedral de Jaen, Plaza de Santa Maria, s-n, Jaen, Andalucia 23002, Spain. director@revista.codice.es, http://www.revistacodice.es/.

COLLABORATION; journal of the Integral Yoga of Sri Aurobindo and the Mother. *see* PHILOSOPHY

200 150 ITA ISSN 1828-0412
COLLANA DI PSICOLOGIA DELLA RELIGIONE. Text in Italian. 1999. irreg. price varies. **Document type:** *Monographic series, Academic/Scholarly.*
Published by: Centro Scientifico Editore, Via Borgone 57, Turin, 10139, Italy. TEL 39-011-3853656, FAX 39-011-3853244, cse@cse.it, http://www.cse.it.

200 BEL ISSN 0776-8354
COLLATIONES. VLAAMS TIJDSCHRIFT VOOR THEOLOGIE EN PASTORAAL. Text in Flemish. s-a. EUR 20; EUR 12 to students (effective 2003).
Indexed: IZBG, OTA.
—IE, Infotrieve, INIST.
Published by: Collationes, Biezekapelstraat 2, Gent, 9000, Belgium. http://www.theo.kuleuven.ac.be/nl/publ_coll.htm. Ed. Eric Vanden Berghe.

230 BEL ISSN 1158-7032
COLLECTION DES ETUDES AUGUSTINIENNES. SERIE ANTIQUITE. Text in French. 1954. irreg., latest vol.162, 2000. price varies. back issues avail. **Document type:** *Monographic series, Academic/Scholarly.*
Published by: (Institut d'Etudes Augustiniennes FRA), Brepols Publishers, Begijnhof 67, Turnhout, 2300, Belgium. TEL 32-14-448020, FAX 32-14-428919, periodicals@brepols.net, http://www.brepols.net. Ed. Jean Claude Fredouille.

230 BEL ISSN 1159-4888
COLLECTION DES ETUDES AUGUSTINIENNES. SERIE MOYEN AGE ET TEMPS MODERNES. Text in French. 1964. irreg., latest vol.35, 2000. price varies. back issues avail. **Document type:** *Monographic series, Academic/Scholarly.*
Published by: (Institut d'Etudes Augustiniennes FRA), Brepols Publishers, Begijnhof 67, Turnhout, 2300, Belgium. TEL 32-14-448020, FAX 32-14-428919, periodicals@brepols.net, http://www.brepols.net. Ed. Jean Claude Fredouille.

220 230 FRA ISSN 0259-5443
COLLECTION THEOLOGIQUE HOKHMA. Text in French. 1979. irreg. **Document type:** *Monographic series, Academic/Scholarly.*
Published by: Hokhma, 2 Rue du Brave Rondeau, La Rochelle, 17000, France. http://www.hokhma.org.

268 USA ISSN 1557-4474
COLLEGIATE+; dream more risk more be more. Variant title: Collegiate Plus. Text in English. 2000. q. USD 15.95; USD 2.95 per issue (effective 2008). adv. back issues avail. **Document type:** *Magazine, Consumer.* **Description:** Features in-depth bible studies, relevant articles and features, editorials and reviews of music, film and books.
Formerly (until 2006): F B S. Collegiate Learner Guide (1526-5358)
Published by: LifeWay Christian Resources, 1 Lifeway Plz, Nashville, TN 37234. TEL 615-251-2000, 800-458-2772, FAX 615-251-5933, customerservice@lifeway.com. Eds. Bop Bunn, Rhonda Delph. adv.: color page USD 1,524; trim 9.25 x 11.125. Circ: 23,078 (paid and controlled).

200 AUS ISSN 0588-3237
BR1
➤ **COLLOQUIUM.** Text in English. 1964. s-a. AUD 40 domestic to individuals; NZD 50 in New Zealand to individuals; NZD 55 elsewhere to individuals; AUD 50 domestic to institutions; NZD 65 foreign to institutions; AUD 20 domestic to students; NZD 22 in New Zealand to students (effective 2008). bk.rev. back issues avail. **Document type:** *Journal, Academic/Scholarly.* **Description:** Features issues in biblical studies, theology, ethics, and church history.
Formerly (until 1966): New Zealand Theological Review
Indexed: A11, A21, AusPAIS, CA, FamI, OTA, R&TA, RI-1, RI-2, RILM, T02.
—BLDSC (3315.319000), Ingenta. **CCC.**
Published by: Australian and New Zealand Society for Theological Studies, c/o Dr Mary J Marshall, Theology, Murdoch University, Murdoch, W.A. 6150, Australia. m.marshall@murdoch.edu.au, http://wwwsoc.murdoch.edu.au/anzsts/home.html. Eds. Nicola Hoggard Creegan, Tim Meadowcroft. Circ: 500.

➤ **COLLOQUIUM, MUSIC, WORSHIP, ARTS.** *see* MUSIC

230.007 USA
COLLOQUY (PITTSBURG). Text in English. 1999. s-a. free (effective 2010). adv. back issues avail.; reprints avail. **Document type:** *Newsletter, Consumer.*
Media: Online - full text.
Published by: The Association of Theological Schools in the United States and Canada, 10 Summit Park Dr, Pittsburgh, PA 15275. TEL 412-788-6505, FAX 412-788-6510, ats@ats.edu. Ed. Eliza Smith Brown.

COLUMBIA SERIES IN SCIENCE AND RELIGION. *see* SCIENCES: COMPREHENSIVE WORKS

220.6 CAN ISSN 0316-3040
COME AND SEE. Text in English. 1974. bi-m. free.
Published by: Nathanael Literature Distributors, 64 Hills Rd, Ajax, ON L1S 2W4, Canada. Ed. John van Dijk. Circ: 8,100.

220 GBR ISSN 0950-7191
COME LEARN BEGINNERS. Variant title: Come Learn God's Word. Text in English. 1978. 3/yr. GBP 2.20 per issue (effective 2010). back issues avail. **Document type:** *Magazine, Academic/Scholarly.* **Description:** Children's workbook for use with activity sheets to accompany the lessons for beginners.
Published by: Go Teach Publications Ltd., Unit 12 Paradise Mill, Park Lane, Macclesfield, SK11 6TJ, United Kingdom. TEL 44-1625-422279, FAX 44-1625-422272, editorial@goteach.org.uk.

220 375 GBR ISSN 0950-7213
COME LEARN JUNIORS. Variant title: Come Learn God's Word. Text in English. 1972. 3/yr. GBP 2.20 per issue (effective 2010). back issues avail. **Document type:** *Magazine, Academic/Scholarly.* **Description:** Children's workbook for use with activity sheets to accompany the lessons for juniors.
Published by: Go Teach Publications Ltd., Unit 12 Paradise Mill, Park Lane, Macclesfield, SK11 6TJ, United Kingdom. TEL 44-1625-422279, FAX 44-1625-422272, editorial@goteach.org.uk.

220 GBR ISSN 0950-7205
COME LEARN PRIMARIES. Variant title: Come Learn God's Word. Text in English. 1979. 3/yr. GBP 2.20 per issue (effective 2010). **Document type:** *Magazine, Academic/Scholarly.* **Description:** Children's workbook for use with activity sheets to accompany the lessons for primaries.
Published by: Go Teach Publications Ltd., Unit 12 Paradise Mill, Park Lane, Macclesfield, SK11 6TJ, United Kingdom. TEL 44-1625-422279, FAX 44-1625-422272, editorial@goteach.org.uk.

COMMAND; Christian perspectives on life in the military. *see* MILITARY

R

200 NLD ISSN 1874-8236
COMMENTARIA; sacred texts and their commentaries: Jewish, Christian and Islamic. Text in English. 2007. irreg., latest vol.3, 2009. price varies. **Document type:** *Monographic series, Academic/Scholarly.* **Description:** Addresses subjects within the general area of the interpretation of the sacred texts of Judaism, Christianity and Islam.
Indexed: IZBG.
Published by: Brill, PO Box 9000, Leiden, 2300 PA, Netherlands. TEL 31-71-5353500, FAX 31-71-5317532, cs@brill.nl. Eds. Grover A Zinn, Michael A Signer.

COMMON BOUNDARY; exploring spirituality, psychotherapy, and creativity. *see* PSYCHOLOGY

301.6 GBR ISSN 0010-325X
COMMON GROUND. Text in English. 1946. s-a. free to members (effective 2009). bk.rev. illus. back issues avail. **Document type:** *Magazine, Consumer.* **Description:** Deals with matters related to Christian-Jewish dialogue.
Related titles: Microform ed.: (from PQC); Online - full text ed.: free (effective 2009).
Indexed: CERDIC, IJP.
Published by: Council of Christians and Jews, Camelford House, 1st Fl, 87-89 Albert, Embankment, London, SE1 7TP, United Kingdom. TEL 44-20-78200090, FAX 44-20-78200504, cjrelations@ccj.org.uk. Ed. David Gifford.

230 USA ISSN 1547-9129
COMMON GROUND JOURNAL; perspectives on the church in the 21st century. Abbreviated title: C G J. Text in English. 2003. s-a. free (effective 2011). back issues avail. **Document type:** *Journal, Academic/Scholarly.* **Description:** Seeks to stimulate Christian Churches to thoughtful action to be the people of God in the world.
Media: Online - full text.
Indexed: A01, A39, C27, C29, D03, D04, E13, R14, S14, S15, S18, T02.
Address: c/o CanDoSpirit Network, 5250 Grand Ave, Ste 14-211, Gurnee, IL 60031. Ed. Soong-Chan Rah.

COMMUNAL COMPUTING NEWS. *see* COMPUTERS—Microcomputers

230.0071 AUS ISSN 0004-9662
COMMUNION; magazine of the liberal Catholic Church in Australia. Text in English. 1962. q. bk.rev. illus. 24 p./no.; back issues avail. **Document type:** *Magazine, Academic/Scholarly.* **Description:** Publishes articles on religious thought, poems, letters, church notices etc.
Formerly (until 1969): Australian Liberal Catholic (0572-1199)
Indexed: CERDIC.
Published by: Liberal Catholic Church in Australia, 23 St John s Ave, Gordon, NSW 2072, Australia. TEL 61-2-94181894, FAX 61-2-94985070, libcat@planetary.com.au.

200 USA ISSN 1052-1135
➤ **COMPARATIVE STUDIES IN RELIGION & SOCIETY.** Text in English. 1987. irreg., latest vol.4, 2010. price varies. back issues avail. **Document type:** *Monographic series, Academic/Scholarly.* **Description:** Discusses Eastern and Western religious traditions in various sociopolitical contexts.
—CCC.
Published by: University of California Press, Book Series, 2120 Berkeley Way, Berkeley, CA 94704. TEL 510-642-4247, FAX 510-643-7127, foundation@ucpress.edu. **Subscr. to:** California - Princeton Fulfillment Services, Inc., 1445 Lower Ferry Rd, Ewing, NJ 08618. TEL 609-883-1759, 800-777-4726, FAX 800-999-1958, orders@cpfsinc.com.

➤ **COMPASSION.** *see* WOMEN'S INTERESTS

230 ESP ISSN 0573-2018
COMPOSTELLANUM. Text in Spanish. 1956. s-a. back issues avail. **Document type:** *Magazine, Consumer.*
Indexed: OTA.
Published by: Arzobispado de Santiago de Compostela, Instituto de Estudios Jacobeos, Plaza de la Inmaculada, 1, Santiago de Compostela, 15704, Spain. web@archicompostela.org, http://www.archicompostela.org/.

200 GBR ISSN 0010-5236
➤ **CONCILIUM.** Text in English. 1965. 5/yr. GBP 40 domestic to individuals; GBP 60 foreign to individuals; GBP 55 domestic to institutions; GBP 75 foreign to institutions; GBP 11.50 per issue (effective 2009). adv. illus. back issues avail.; reprints avail. **Document type:** *Journal, Academic/Scholarly.* **Description:** Promotes theological discussion.
Related titles: Spanish ed.: ISSN 0210-1041. 1965.
Indexed: A20, A22, CERDIC, CLA, PCI, RI-2.
—IE. **CCC.**
Published by: S C M Press, 13-17 Long Ln, Londan, EC1A 9PN, United Kingdom. TEL 44-20-77767540, FAX 44-20-77767556, orders@scm-canterburypress.co.uk, http://www.scm-canterburypress.co.uk/.

200 ITA ISSN 1125-7164
CONCILIUM; rivista internazionale di teologia. Text in Italian. 1965. 5/yr. EUR 41.50 domestic; EUR 59.50 in Europe; EUR 72.50 elsewhere (effective 2009). adv. bk.rev. back issues avail. **Document type:** *Journal, Academic/Scholarly.*
Published by: Editrice Queriniana, Via Enrico Ferri 75, Brescia, BS 25123, Italy. TEL 39-030-2306925, FAX 39-030-2306932, redazione@queriniana.it.

200 DEU ISSN 0588-9804
CONCILIUM; Internationale Zeitschrift fuer Theologie. Text in German. 1964. 5/yr. EUR 49.80; EUR 39.80 to students; EUR 12.50 newsstand/cover (effective 2007). adv. back issues avail.; reprints avail. **Document type:** *Journal, Academic/Scholarly.*
Indexed: DIP, IBR, IBZ.
—CCC.
Published by: (Stichting Concilium NLD), Matthias-Gruenewald-Verlag GmbH (Subsidiary of: Schwabenverlag AG), Senefelderstr 12, Ostfildern, 73760, Germany. TEL 49-711-44060, FAX 49-711-4406177, mail@gruenewaldverlag.de, http://www.gruenewaldverlag.de. Ed. Norbert Reck. Adv. contact Nina Baab TEL 49-6131-928620. B&W page EUR 850; trim 120 x 200. Circ: 1,650 (paid and controlled).

230 BRA ISSN 1414-7327
CONCILIUM (BRAZILIAN EDITION); revista internacional de teologia. Text in Portuguese. 1965. 5/yr. BRL 85 domestic; USD 80 foreign (effective 2005). **Document type:** *Journal, Academic/Scholarly.* **Description:** Includes articles on ethics, Christian communities, faith and related issues.
Published by: Editora Vozes Ltda., Rua Mexico 174, Rio de Janeiro, RJ 20031 143, Brazil. TEL 55-21-22156386, FAX 55-21-25338358, vozes42@uol.com.br, http://www.editoravozes.com.br.

200 USA ISSN 0145-7233
BX8001
➤ **CONCORDIA JOURNAL.** Text in English. 1929. q. USD 15 domestic; USD 20 in Canada; USD 25 foreign (effective 2009). adv. bk.rev. back issues avail. **Document type:** *Journal, Academic/Scholarly.* **Description:** Features articles on a broad spectrum of theological topics as well as book reviews.
Supersedes (in 1975): C T M (0090-9823); Which was formerly (until 1973): Concordia Theological Monthly (0010-5279); Which was formed by the merger of (1855-1929): Lehre und Wehre (0360-6155); (1921-1929): Theological Monthly (0360-6201); (1877-1929): Pastoraltheologie (0360-6163)
Related titles: Microform ed.: (from PQC); Online - full content ed.
Indexed: A21, A22, BAS, CERDIC, ChrPI, MLA-IB, OTA, P30, R&TA, RI-1, RI-2.
—BLDSC (3399.477200), IE, Infotrieve, Ingenta.
Published by: Concordia Seminary, 801 Seminary Pl, St. Louis, MO 63105. TEL 314-505-7379, FAX 314-505-7380, communications@csl.edu. Ed. Travis J Scholl. Pub. Dale A Meyer.

230.0071 USA ISSN 0038-8610
BX8001
➤ **CONCORDIA THEOLOGICAL QUARTERLY.** Abbreviated title: C T Q. Text in English. N.S. 1938. q. USD 20 domestic; USD 25 in Canada; USD 40 elsewhere (effective 2010). bk.rev. cum.index: 1959-1964; 1977-2000. 96 p./no. 1 cols./p.; back issues avail. **Document type:** *Journal, Academic/Scholarly.* **Description:** Deals with classical studies and Protestant religion and theology.
Formerly (until 1977): The Springfielder (0884-2825)
Related titles: E-mail ed.: N.S. (from PQC); Online - full text ed.: N.S.
Indexed: A21, CERDIC, DIP, IBR, IBZ, OTA, P30, R&TA, RI-1, RI-2, RILM.
—BLDSC (3399.478300).
Published by: (Lutheran Church - Missouri Synod), Concordia Theological Seminary, 6600 N Clinton St, Fort Wayne, IN 46825. TEL 260-452-2100, info@ctsfw.edu. Ed. David P Scaer TEL 260-452-2134.

369.4 URY
CONFEDERACION LATINOAMERICANA DE ASOCIACIONES CRISTIANAS DE JOVENES. CARTA. Text in Spanish. irreg. free.
Formerly: Federacion Sudamericana de Asociaciones Cristianas de Jovenes. Noticias (0428-1039)
Related titles: English ed.
Published by: Confederacion Latinoamericana de Asociaciones Cristianas de Jovenes/Latin American Confederation of YMCAs, Colonia, 1884 Piso 1, Montevideo, 11205, Uruguay.

200 URY
CONFEDERACION LATINOAMERICANA DE ASOCIACIONES CRISTIANAS DE JOVENES. CONFEDERACION. Text in Spanish. 1982. q. free.
Published by: Confederacion Latinoamericana de Asociaciones Cristianas de Jovenes/Latin American Confederation of YMCAs, Colonia, 1884 Piso 1, Montevideo, 11205, Uruguay. Ed. Edgardo G Crovetto.

200 URY
CONFEDERACION LATINOAMERICANA DE ASOCIACIONES CRISTIANAS DE JOVENES. CONTACTO. Text in Spanish. 1982. m. free.
Published by: Confederacion Latinoamericana de Asociaciones Cristianas de Jovenes/Latin American Confederation of YMCAs, Colonia, 1884 Piso 1, Montevideo, 11205, Uruguay. Ed. Edgardo G Crovetto.

200 CAN ISSN 1180-0682
BX801
➤ **CONFRATERNITAS**; bulletin of the Society of Confraternity Studies. Text in English, French, Italian, Spanish. 1990. s-a. CAD 21.50 domestic; USD 21.50 foreign (effective 2007). bk.rev. bibl. back issues avail. **Document type:** *Journal, Academic/Scholarly.*
Indexed: AmHI, CA, H07, T02.
Published by: (Society of Confraternity Studies), University of Toronto, Victoria College, Centre for Reformation and Renaissance Studies, 71 Queen's Park Cresc East, Toronto, ON M5S 1K7, Canada. TEL 416-585-4465, FAX 416-585-4430, crss.publications@utoronto.ca, http://www.crrs.ca. Ed. Konrad Eisenbichler. Circ: 400 (paid).

➤ **CONGREGATIONAL LIBRARIES TODAY.** *see* LIBRARY AND INFORMATION SCIENCES

225 SWE ISSN 0069-8946
CONIECTANEA BIBLICA. NEW TESTAMENT SERIES. Text in English, French. 1966. irreg. price varies. back issues avail. **Document type:** *Monographic series, Academic/Scholarly.*
Former titles: Acta Seminarii Neotestamentici Upsaliensis; Coniectanea Neotestamentica
Indexed: FR.
—INIST.
Published by: Almqvist & Wiksell International, P O Box 7634, Stockholm, 10394, Sweden. FAX 46-8-24-25-43, info@city.akademibokhandeln.se, http://www.akademibokhandeln.se. Eds. Birger Olson, Rene Kieffer.

221 SWE ISSN 0069-8954
CONIECTANEA BIBLICA. OLD TESTAMENT SERIES. Text in Swedish. 1967. irreg. price varies. back issues avail. **Document type:** *Monographic series, Academic/Scholarly.*
Indexed: FR.
—INIST.
Published by: Almqvist & Wiksell International, P O Box 7634, Stockholm, 10394, Sweden. FAX 46-8-24-25-43. Eds. Stig Norin, Tryggve Mettinger.

230 FRA ISSN 0752-5346
CONNAISSANCE DES PERES DE L'EGLISE. Text in French. 1981. q. EUR 38 domestic; EUR 40 in the European Union; EUR 44 elsewhere (effective 2009). **Document type:** *Journal, Consumer.*
Indexed: FR.
—INIST.
Published by: Editions Nouvelle Cite, Domaine d'Arny, Bruyeres-le-Chatel, 91680, France. TEL 33-1-69171006, FAX 33-1-69171304, info@nouvellecite.fr, http://pagesperso-orange.fr/nouvelle.cite.

CONNECTIONS (WASHINGTON D.C.). *see* EDUCATION—Higher Education

200 AUS ISSN 1839-0129
▼ **CONNOR COURT QUARTERLY.** Abbreviated title: C C Q. Text in English. 2011. q. AUD 14.95 per issue (effective 2011). adv. **Document type:** *Magazine, Consumer.* **Description:** Focuses on the history, culture and religion in the western tradition.
Related titles: Online - full text ed.: ISSN 1839-0137. AUD 9.95 per issue (effective 2011).
Published by: Connor Court Publishing Pty Ltd., PO Box 1, Ballan, VIC 3342, Australia. TEL 61-3-90059167, FAX 61-3-53030960.

230.0071 028.5 USA ISSN 1075-7392
THE CONQUEROR. Text in English. 1957. bi-m. **Document type:** *Magazine, Consumer.*
Published by: United Pentecostal Church International, 8855 Dunn Rd., Hazelwood, MO 63042. TEL 314-837-7300, FAX 314-837-4503, gyouth8855@aol.com, http://www.upci.org/youth. Ed. Travis Miller. Circ: 6,000.

200 ITA ISSN 0035-600X
CONSACRAZIONE E SERVIZIO; rivista delle religiose. Text in Italian. 1952. m. bk.rev. index. **Document type:** *Magazine, Consumer.*
Formerly (until 1970): Rivista delle Religiose (1125-9744)
Indexed: DIP, IBR, IBZ.
Published by: Unione Superiore Maggiori d'Italia, Via Giuseppe Zanardelli, 32, Rome, RM 00186, Italy. TEL 39-6-68802336, FAX 39-6-68801935. Circ: 12,000.

200 ZAF ISSN 1996-8167
CONSPECTUS. Text in English. 2006. s-a.
Media: Online - full text.
Indexed: A01, CA, T02.
Published by: South African Theological Seminary, PO Box 258, Rivonia, 2128, South Africa. TEL 27-11-2344440, FAX 27-11-2344445, study@sats.edu.za, http://www.sats.edu.za.

230 COL ISSN 2011-3277
CONSTRUCTORES DE PAZ. Text in Spanish. 2007. q. **Document type:** *Magazine, Consumer.*
Published by: Corporacion Vallenpaz, Carrera 5 No. 11-68 Piso 5, Valle del Cauca, Cali, Colombia. TEL 57-2-8821933, FAX 57-2-8822573, vallenpaz@telesat.com.co, http://www.corporacionvallenpaz.com/.

268 USA ISSN 1521-9631
CONTACT (SIOUX CENTER). Text in English. 1988. q. USD 30 to members (effective 2007). **Document type:** *Newsletter, Trade.* **Description:** Publishes news from the International Association for the Promotion of Christian Higher Education, including conference and meeting information, association news from around the world, and activities of individual members and affiliate institutions.
Published by: International Association for the Promotion of Christian Higher Education, 498 4th Ave NE, Sioux Center, IA 51250. TEL 712-722-6346, FAX 712-722-6376, iapche@dordt.edu, http://www.iapche.org.

200 GBR
CONTACT (STOCKPORT); Covies, supporting children and youth. Text in English. m. **Document type:** *Newsletter.* **Description:** Provides information about Covies events, holidays, conferences, and personnel as well as prayer topics, advice, and letters.
Published by: (Covenanters), Covies, 11-13 Lower Hillgate, Stockport, Ches SK1 1JQ, United Kingdom. TEL 44-161-474-1262, FAX 44-161-474-1300. Ed. Paul Wilcox.

200 FRA ISSN 0045-8325
CONTACTS (PARIS, 1949); revue Francaise de l'Orthodoxie. Text in French. 1949. q. EUR 36 domestic; EUR 45 in the European Union; EUR 50 elsewhere (effective 2009). bk.rev. bibl. index. **Document type:** *Journal.*
Indexed: CERDIC, DIP, FR, IBR, IBZ.
—BLDSC (3425.025000), INIST.
Published by: Centre Ecumenique Enotikon, 14 Rue Victor Hugo, Courbevoie, 93400, France. TEL 33-1-43335248, FAX 33-1-43338672, postmaster@revue-contacts.com. Circ: 3,000.

CONTAGION; journal of violence, mimesis, and culture. *see* SOCIOLOGY

▼ **CONTEMPORARY REVIEW.** *see* BUSINESS AND ECONOMICS

230 100 DEU ISSN 1868-1336
▼ **CONTRIBUTIONES BONNENSES. REIHE 2: THEOLOGIE, PHILOSOPHIE.** Variant title: ContriBo 2. Text in German. 2009. irreg., latest vol.3, 2009. price varies. **Document type:** *Monographic series, Academic/Scholarly.*
Published by: Bernstein-Verlag GbR, Endenicher Str 97, Bonn, 53115, Germany. TEL 49-228-9658719, FAX 49-228-9658720, bernstein@bernstein-verlag.de.

220 BEL ISSN 0926-6097
➤ **CONTRIBUTIONS TO BIBLICAL EXEGESIS AND THEOLOGY.** Text in English, German. 1990. irreg., latest 2010. price varies. back issues avail. **Document type:** *Monographic series, Academic/Scholarly.* **Description:** Publishes scholarly monographs on Jewish and Christian theological issues.
Published by: Peeters Publishers, Bondgenotenlaan 153, Leuven, 3000, Belgium. TEL 32-16-235170, FAX 32-16-228500, http://www.peeters-leuven.be.

200 USA ISSN 8750-4812
CONVENTION HERALD. Text in English. 1955. bi-m. USD 5 (effective 2000 - 2001). adv. bk.rev.
Published by: Inter-Church Holiness Convention, 1817 26th St, Bedford, IN 47421. TEL 812-275-2119, FAX 812-277-9821. Ed., R&P Leonard Sankey. Circ: 12,500.

200 USA ISSN 1548-2057
BV4485
CONVERSATIONS; a forum for authentic transformation. Text in English. 2003. 2/yr. USD 15 domestic to individuals; USD 21 foreign to individuals; USD 45 worldwide to libraries (effective 2005). adv. **Document type:** *Magazine, Consumer.* **Description:** Aims to provide spiritual accompaniment and honest dialogue for those who long for radical transformation in Christ.
Indexed: CA, T02.

Published by: (Psychological Studies Institute), Lifesprings Resources, PO Box 9, Franklin Springs, GA 30639. TEL 888-924-6774 ext 399. adv.: B&W page USD 500. Circ: 4,000 (paid and controlled).

200 GBR ISSN 1479-2206
CONVERSATIONS IN RELIGION AND THEOLOGY. Abbreviated title: C R T. Text in English. 2003. s-a. includes with subscr. to Reviews in Religion and Theology. adv. back issues avail.; reprint service avail. from PSC. **Document type:** *Journal, Academic/Scholarly.* **Description:** Covers substantial reviews of the best writing in theology and religious studies, immediately followed by the author's reply.
Related titles: Online - full text ed.: ISSN 1479-2214 (from IngentaConnect).
Indexed: A01, A22, A26, CA, E01, P28, P48, P53, P54, PQC, PhilInd, T02.
—BLDSC (3463.582500), IE, Ingenta. **CCC.**
Published by: Wiley-Blackwell Publishing Ltd. (Subsidiary of: John Wiley & Sons, Inc.), 9600 Garsington Rd, Oxford, OX4 2DQ, United Kingdom. TEL 44-1865-776868, FAX 44-1865-714591, customerservices@blackwellpublishing.com. Ed. Kelton Cobb. Adv. contact Craig Pickett TEL 44-1865-476267.

200 USA ISSN 0273-3269
BX130
COPTIC CHURCH REVIEW. Text in English. 1980. q. bk.rev. Index. 32 p./no.; back issues avail. **Document type:** *Journal, Academic/ Scholarly.* **Description:** Covers Biblical studies with emphasis on spiritual exegesis, liturgical life of the Church, lives and writings of the Church Fathers, ascetic and mystic spirituality.
Related titles: Microfiche ed.; Microfilm ed.; Online - full text ed.
Indexed: A21, A22, R&TA, RI-1.
Published by: Society of Coptic Church Studies, PO Box 714, East Brunswick, NJ 08816. ralphyanney@hotmail.com.

CORPUS CHRISTIANORUM. LINGUA PATRUM. *see* LINGUISTICS

200 BEL ISSN 1781-5967
CORPUS CHRISTIANORUM. SERIES GRAECA. Text in Latin, Greek. 1977. irreg. (2-3/yr.), latest vol.42, 2000. back issues avail. **Document type:** *Monographic series, Academic/Scholarly.*
Published by: (Universite Catholique de Louvain, Instituut voor Vroegchristelijke en Byzantijnse Studies/Katholieke Universiteit Leuven), Brepols Publishers, Begijnhof 67, Turnhout, 2300, Belgium. FAX 32-14-428919, periodicals@brepols.net.

291 DEU
CORPUS ISLAMO-CHRISTIANUM. Text in German. 1987. irreg., latest vol.7, 2009. price varies. **Document type:** *Monographic series, Academic/Scholarly.*
Published by: Harrassowitz Verlag, Kreuzberger Ring 7b-d, Wiesbaden, 65205, Germany. TEL 49-611-5300, FAX 49-611-530560, verlag@harrassowitz.de, http://www.harrassowitz.de.

CORPUS SCRIPTORUM ECCLESIASTICORUM LATINORUM. *see* LITERATURE

264 870 SWE ISSN 1403-1515
CORPUS TROPORUM. Text in Multiple languages. 1975. irreg., latest vol.11, 2009. price varies. back issues avail. **Document type:** *Monographic series, Academic/Scholarly.*
Related titles: ◆ Series of: Acta Universitatis Stockholmiensis. ISSN 0346-6418.
Published by: (Stockholms Universitet, Institutionen foer Franska, Italienska och Klassiska Spraak/Stockholm University, Department of French, Italian and Classical Languages), Stockholms Universitet, Acta Universitatis Stockholmiensis, c/o Stockholms Universitetsbibliotek, Universitetsvaegen 10, Stockholm, 10691, Sweden. TEL 46-8-162800, FAX 46-8-157776, http://www.sub.su.se. Ed. Margaretha Fathli. **Dist. by:** Eddy.se AB, Norra Kyrkogatan 3, Visby 62155, Sweden. TEL 46-498-253900, FAX 46-498-249789, info@eddy.se, order@eddy.se, http://www.eddy.se, http:// acta.bokorder.se.

200 BRA ISSN 1677-2644
CORRELATIO. Text in Portuguese. 2002. irreg. **Document type:** *Monographic series, Academic/Scholarly.*
Media: Online - full text.
Published by: Universidade Metodista de Sao Paulo, Sociedade Paul Tillich do Brasil, Rua Alfeu Tavares, 149, Rudge Ramos, Sao Bernardo do Campo, SP 09641-000, Brazil. correlatio@hotmail.com, http://metodista.br/. Ed. Jaci Maraschin.

200 340 ITA ISSN 0394-2732
COSCIENZA E LIBERTA. Text in Italian. 1978. a. **Document type:** *Magazine, Consumer.*
Published by: Edizioni A D V, Via Chiantigiana, 30, Falciani, Impruneta, FI 50023, Italy. TEL 39-055-2326291, FAX 39-055-2326241, info@edizioniadv.it, http://www.edizioniadv.it.

COSMOS (EDINBURGH). *see* NEW AGE PUBLICATIONS

204.22 USA
COUNCIL OF THE MYSTIC ARTS. NEWSLETTER. Text in English. 12/yr. USD 24. illus.
Published by: Council of the Mystic Arts, Spectrum of the Seven Keys, 538 Hammond Ave, San Antonio, TX 78210.

COUNSELOR (WHEATON). *see* CHILDREN AND YOUTH—For

COUNTRY LIVING HOLIDAYS. *see* ARTS AND HANDICRAFTS

COURAGE IN THE STRUGGLE FOR JUSTICE AND PEACE. *see* SOCIOLOGY

COURTENAY LIBRARY OF REFORMATION CLASSICS. *see* HISTORY—History Of Europe

268 USA ISSN 1550-9575
CRAFT KINGDOM. Text in English. 1990. q. USD 3.19 per issue (effective 2009). back issues avail. **Document type:** *Magazine, Consumer.* **Description:** Covers Bible related paper craft activities for preschoolers and primaries.
Published by: Urban Ministries, Inc., Dept #4870, PO Box 87618, Chicago, IL 60680. TEL 708-868-7100, 800-860-8642, FAX 708-868-7105, customerservice@urbanministries.com.

202.4 GBR
CREATION. Text in English. 1971. q. free to members (effective 2009). bk.rev. back issues avail. **Document type:** *Journal, Academic/ Scholarly.* **Description:** Covers the scientific facts that are best explained by the Biblical account of creation.
Published by: Creation Science Movement, PO Box 888, Portsmouth, Hants PO6 2YD, United Kingdom. TEL 44-2392-293988, info@csm.org.uk, http://www.csm.org.uk. **Co-sponsor:** Evangelical Alliance.

213 500 AUS ISSN 0819-1530
CREATION; ex nihilo. Text in English. 1978. q. USD 25 (effective 2008). bk.rev. cum.index. 56 p./no.; back issues avail. **Document type:** *Magazine, Consumer.* **Description:** Presents scientific and biblical evidence for creationism and related subjects in a popular, easy-to-read format.
Formerly (until 1985): Ex Nihilo (0726-6782)
Indexed: ChrPI.
Published by: Creation Ministries International Ltd., PO Box 4545, Eight Mile Plains, QLD 4113, Australia. TEL 61-7-33409888, FAX 61-7-33409889, http://www.creationontheweb.com/. Circ: 50,000.

231.7652 500 USA ISSN 1094-6632
CREATION MATTERS. Text in English. 1996 (Jan.). bi-m. USD 38 domestic to non-members; USD 56 in Canada & Mexico to non-members; USD 73 elsewhere to non-members; free to members (effective 2010); subscr. includes Creation Research Society Quarterly. back issues avail.; reprints avail. **Document type:** *Newsletter, Academic/Scholarly.* **Description:** Contains both general news of interest to creationists as well as scientific news about creation and evolution.
Published by: Creation Research Society, PO Box 8263, St. Joseph, MO 64508. TEL 928-636-1153, contact@creationresearch.org.

CREATION RESEARCH SOCIETY QUARTERLY. *see* SCIENCES: COMPREHENSIVE WORKS

268 USA ISSN 2156-3098
CREATIVE CATECHIST; a religion teacher's journal. Text in English. 1967. bi-m. USD 23.95; USD 6.95 per issue (effective 2010). adv. abstr.; illus. index. back issues avail.; reprints avail. **Document type:** *Magazine, Consumer.* **Description:** Used as a training vehicle by pastors for laypersons working with them as church educators.
Formerly (until Sep.2010): Religion Teacher's Journal (0034-401X)
Related titles: Microform ed.: (from PQC).
Indexed: A22, CERDIC, CPL, MRD.
—CCC.
Published by: Bayard Inc. (Subsidiary of: Bayard Presse), PO Box 6015, New London, CT 06320. TEL 800-321-0411, FAX 800-572-0788, cservice@bayard-us.com, http://www.bayard-inc.com. Ed. Rosanne Coffey. Adv. contact Michelle Kopfmann. color page USD 3,265; 8.25 x 11. Circ: 30,000.

CREATOR; the bimonthly magazine of balanced music ministries. *see* MUSIC

THE CRESSET; a review of literature, the arts, and public affairs. *see* LITERARY AND POLITICAL REVIEWS

200 ITA ISSN 0393-3598
BR140
CRISTIANESIMO NELLA STORIA; ricerche storiche esegetiche teologiche. Text in English, French, German, Italian, Spanish; Summaries in English. 1980. 3/yr. EUR 47 domestic; EUR 62.20 in the European Union; EUR 65.60 elsewhere (effective 2008). bk.rev. bibl. index. back issues avail. **Document type:** *Journal, Academic/ Scholarly.*
Indexed: A21, CA, CERDIC, CLA, DIP, FR, HistAb, IBR, IBZ, IZBG, OTA, PCI, R&TA, RASB, RI-1, RI-2, T02.
—INIST.
Published by: (Istituto per le Scienze Religiose), Centro Editoriale Dehoniano, Via Scipione dal Ferro 4, Bologna, BO 40138, Italy. TEL 39-051-4290451, FAX 39-051-4290491, ced-amm@dehoniane.it, http://www.dehoniane.it. Ed. Giuseppe Alberigo. Circ: 1,700.

200 ECU ISSN 0011-1457
CRISTIANISMO Y SOCIEDAD. Text in Spanish. 1963. q. ARS 20,000, USD 15.
Indexed: A21, C01, H21, P08, R&TA, RASB, RI-1, RI-2.
Address: Apartado Postal 15067, Guayaquil, Guayas, Ecuador. Ed. Julio Barreiro.

200 GBR
CRISTION. Text in English. 1983. bi-m. GBP 5 domestic; GBP 6.50 foreign. adv. bk.rev. **Document type:** *Magazine, Consumer.* **Description:** Covers all aspects of religious life.
Published by: Cristion Publishing Company, 3 Maes Lowri, Aberystwyth, Dyfed SY23 2AU, United Kingdom. TEL 44-970-612925. Ed. Rev. E Ap Nefydd Roberts. adv.: page GBP 110. Circ: 2,250.

307 USA ISSN 0590-0980
CRITERION; a journal of conservative thought. Text in English. 1934. s-a. **Document type:** *Journal, Academic/Scholarly.*
Former titles (until 1961): Divinity School News (1074-1771); (until 1932): The Divinity Student (0190-5910)
Related titles: Online - full text ed.
Indexed: A21, P30, R&TA, RI-1.
—BLDSC (3487.388000).
Published by: University of Chicago, Divinity School, 1028 E 58th St, Chicago, IL 60637.

230 HRV ISSN 0350-7823
BX1609.C76
CROATICA CHRISTIANA PERIODICA. Text in Croatian. 1977. s-a. **Document type:** *Journal, Academic/Scholarly.*
Indexed: A26, FR, I05, R&TA, RILM.
—INIST.
Published by: Sveuciliste u Zagrebu, Katolicki Bogoslovni Fakultet, Institut za Crkvenu Povijest, Kontakova 1, Zagreb, 10000, Croatia. TEL 385-1-2392576, FAX 385-1-2336554. Ed. Franjo Sanjek.

301.6 FRA ISSN 1269-0104
CROIRE AUJOURD'HUI. Text in French. 1933. m. EUR 69 domestic; EUR 79 in Europe; EUR 79 DOM-TOM; EUR 84 elsewhere (effective 2009). index. reprints avail. **Document type:** *Magazine, Consumer.* **Description:** Produced by the Jesuits, it helps in understanding current problems, giving reference points, encouraging debate and reflection.
Former titles (until 1995): Cahiers pour Croire Aujourd'hui (0987-2213); (until 1987): Cahiers d'Action Religieuse et Sociale (0007-9669)
Indexed: CERDIC.
Published by: Bayard Presse, 3-5 rue Bayard, Paris, 75393 Cedex 08, France. TEL 33-1-44356060, FAX 33-1-44356161, redactions@bayard-presse.com, http://www.bayardpresse.com. Ed. Francois Boedec. Circ: 20,000.

230 USA
CROSS AND QUILL; the Christian writers newsletter. Text in English. 1976. bi-m. looseleaf. USD 20 domestic; USD 21 in Canada; USD 25 elsewhere (effective 2000). adv. bk.rev. index. **Document type:** *Newsletter.* **Description:** Information, writing tips and marketing news for writers of freelance material for the Christian market.
Incorporates (in Oct. 1989): Christian Writers Newsletter
Published by: Christian Writers Fellowship International, 1624 Jefferson Davis Rd, Clinton, SC 29325-6401. TEL 864-697-6035, http:// members.aol.com/cwfi/writers.htm. Ed., Pub., R&P, Adv. contact Sandy Brooks.

CROSS CURRENTS (NEW YORK). *see* EDUCATION—Higher Education

268 USA ISSN 1089-7720
CROSS FIRE YOUTH MINISTRY MAGAZINE. Text in English. 1995. w. (bi-w., & m.). **Document type:** *Magazine, Consumer.* **Description:** Focuses on the needs of Christian young people, youth ministers, and clergy involved in the good work of bringing the world's youth to Christ.
Media: Online - full text.
Address: 32 Eddy St, Ware, MA 01082-1351. david@crossfire.org, http://www.crossfire.org. Ed. David Pollette.

CROSSROADS; an interdisciplinary journal for the study of history, philosophy, religion and classics. *see* HISTORY

200 JPN ISSN 0911-7482
CROWNED WITH THORNS. Text in English. 1984. 3/yr. back issues avail. **Document type:** *Newsletter, Academic/Scholarly.*
Published by: United Church of Christ in Japan. Buraku Liberation Center/Nihon Kirisuto Kyodan, 2-16-14 Midorigaoka, Daito-shi, Osaka 574-0073, Japan. TEL 81-72-8758470, burakuliberation@mac.com, blc@nyc.odn.ne.jp, http:// www1.odn.ne.jp/burakuliberation/. Ed. Timothy D. Doyle.

200 CAN ISSN 0011-2186
BR1
CRUX (VANCOUVER); a quarterly journal of Christian thought and opinion. Text in English. 1966. q. CAD 14 domestic; USD 14 foreign; CAD 3.50 per issue (effective 2005). adv. bk.rev. bibl.; charts; illus.; stat. index, cum.index. back issues avail. **Document type:** *Journal, Academic/Scholarly.* **Description:** Goal is to relate the teachings of Scripture to a broad spectrum of academic, social and professional areas of interest, to integrate them and to apply the insights gained to corporate and personal Christian life.
Related titles: Microform ed.
Indexed: A21, A22, ChrPI, OTA, P30, R&TA, RASB, RI-1, RI-2, RILM.
—BLDSC (3490.132000), IE, Infotrieve, Ingenta. **CCC.**
Published by: Regent College, 5800 University Blvd, Vancouver, BC V6T 2E4, Canada. TEL 604-224-3245, FAX 604-224-3097. Ed. Donald M Lewis. R&P, Adv. contact Dal Schindell. Circ: 1,400 (paid).

282 USA ISSN 0591-2296
CRUX OF THE NEWS. Text in English. 1965. w. (Mon.). USD 79.50 (effective 2005). adv. bk.rev. **Document type:** *Newsletter, Consumer.*
Published by: Clarity Publishing, Inc., PO Box 758, Latham, NY 12110-0758. TEL 518-783-0058, FAX 518-783-7450. Ed., Pub. Richard A Dowd. Circ: 3,000 (paid and controlled).

CRUZADA EUCARISTICA. *see* CHILDREN AND YOUTH—For

200 ECU ISSN 0590-1731
CUADERNOS DE CRISTIANISMO Y SOCIEDAD. Text in Spanish. 1963. m. (except Jan. & Feb.).
Indexed: A21, RI-1.
Published by: Editorial Tierra Nueva S.R.L., Casilla 09-01-15067, Guayaquil, Buenos Aires, Ecuador.

CUADERNOS DE ESPIRITU. *see* PHILOSOPHY

200 ARG ISSN 0326-6737
BX8001
CUADERNOS DE TEOLOGIA. Text in Spanish. 1970. s-a. **Document type:** *Journal, Academic/Scholarly.*
Formed by the merger of (1950-1970): Cuadernos Teologicos (0328-9931); (1957-1970): Ekklesia (0328-1191)
Related titles: Online - full text ed.
Indexed: A21, I04, I05, RI-1.
Published by: Instituto Superior Evangelico de Estudios Teologicos, Camacua, 252, Buenos Aires, 1406, Argentina. TEL 54-11-46310224, info@isedet.edu.ar, http://www.isedet.edu.ar/. Circ: 1,200.

CUADERNOS PARA LA HISTORIA DE LA EVANGELIZACION EN AMERICA LATINA. *see* HISTORY—History Of North And South America

202 COL ISSN 0120-131X
CUESTIONES TEOLOGICAS Y FILOSOFICAS. Text in Spanish. 1974. q. **Document type:** *Journal, Academic/Scholarly.*
Indexed: C01, F04, T02.
Published by: Universidad Pontificia Bolivariana, Facultad de Teologia, Circular 1 No. 70-01, Laureles, Antioquia, Medellin, Colombia. TEL 57-4-4159050, FAX 57-4-4118560, teologia@upb.edu.co, http:// www.upb.edu.co/. Ed. Hernand Dario Cardona.

200 CHL ISSN 0718-5472
CULTURA Y RELIGION. Text in Spanish. 2007. s-a. **Document type:** *Journal, Academic/Scholarly.*
Related titles: Online - full text ed.: ISSN 0718-4727. 2007. free (effective 2011).
Published by: Universidad Arturo Prat, Instituto de Estudios Indigenas, Ave Arturo Pract 2120, Casilla 121, Iquique, Tarapaca, Chile. TEL 56-57-394344, isluga@unap.cl, http://www.unap.cl/.

200 GBR ISSN 1475-5610
BL1
➤ **CULTURE AND RELIGION.** Text in English. 1980. 3/yr. GBP 306 combined subscription in United Kingdom to institutions (print & online eds.); EUR 402, USD 506 combined subscription to institutions (print & online eds.) (effective 2012). adv. bk.rev. back issues avail.; reprint service avail. from PSC. **Document type:** *Journal, Academic/ Scholarly.* **Description:** Promotes critical investigation into all aspects of the study of religion and culture, particularly among scholars with an innovative and multidisciplinary focus.
Formerly (in May 2000): Scottish Journal of Religious Studies (0143-8301)
Related titles: Online - full text ed.: ISSN 1475-5629. GBP 276 in United Kingdom to institutions; EUR 362, USD 456 to institutions (effective 2012) (from IngentaConnect).

R

Indexed: A20, A21, A22, AICP, AmHI, AnthLit, BrHumI, CA, DIP, E01, H07, IBR, IBSS, IBZ, P48, P53, P54, PCI, PQC, R&TA, RI-1, RI-2, S02, S03, SCOPUS, SociolAb, T02.
—IE, Ingenta. **CCC.**
Published by: (University of Stirling, Department of Religious Studies), Routledge (Subsidiary of: Taylor & Francis Group), 4 Park Square, Milton Park, Abingdon, Oxon OX14 4RN, United Kingdom. subscriptions@tandf.co.uk, http://www.routledge.com. Ed. Malory Nye. Adv. contact Linda Hann TEL 44-1344-779945. Circ: 200. **Subscr. to:** Taylor & Francis Ltd., Journals Customer Service, Sheepen Pl, Colchester, Essex CO3 3LP, United Kingdom. TEL 44-20-70175544, FAX 44-20-70175198.

200 VAT ISSN 1022-8675
CULTURES AND FAITH. Text in English, French, Spanish, Italian. 1966. q. EUR 26 in Europe; USD 30 elsewhere (effective 2003). bk.rev. back issues avail. **Document type:** *Newsletter, Academic/Scholarly.* **Description:** Contains articles on modern atheism and religious indifference, dialogue between faith and culture, and science-faith relationships, with a greater emphasis on cultural issues. Includes worldwide news items and book notices.
Supersedes (in Sep. 1993): Atheism and Faith; Which was formerly: Atheism and Dialogue; Incorporates: Church and Cultures
Published by: Pontifical Council for Culture, Vatican City, 00120, Vatican City. TEL 39-06-69893811, FAX 39-06-69887368. Ed. Cardinal Paul Poupard. R&P B Ardura. Circ: 1,600.

200 CHE
CURRENT DIALOGUE. Text in English. a. **Document type:** *Bulletin.*
Formerly: Church and the Jewish People
Indexed: AMR.
Published by: (Office on Inter-Religious Relations), World Council of Churches, 150 route de Ferney, PO Box 2100, Geneva 2, 1211, Switzerland. TEL 41-22-791-6111, FAX 41-22-791-0361.

220 GBR ISSN 1476-993X
BS410 CODEN: FGOEAB
CURRENTS IN BIBLICAL RESEARCH. Abbreviated title: C B R. Text in English. 1993. 3/yr. USD 357, GBP 193 combined subscription to institutions (print & online eds.); USD 350, GBP 189 to institutions (effective 2011). adv. back issues avail.; reprint service avail. from PSC. **Document type:** *Journal, Academic/Scholarly.* **Description:** Summarizes the spectrum of recent research on particular topics or biblical books.
Formerly (until 2002): Currents in Research: Biblical Studies (0966-7377)
Related titles: Online - full text ed.: ISSN 1745-5200. USD 321, GBP 174 to institutions (effective 2011).
Indexed: A01, A03, A08, A21, A22, CA, DIP, E01, IBR, IBZ, IZBG, OTA, PCI, R&TA, RI-1, T02.
—BLDSC (3505.125000), IE, Ingenta. **CCC.**
Published by: Sage Publications Ltd. (Subsidiary of: Sage Publications, Inc.), 1 Oliver's Yard, 55 City Rd, London, EC1Y 1SP, United Kingdom. TEL 44-20-73248500, FAX 44-20-73248600, info@sagepub.co.uk, http://www.uk.sagepub.com/home.nav. Eds. Jonathan Klawens, Scot McKnight. **Subscr. in the Americas to:** Sage Publications, Inc., 2455 Teller Rd, Thousand Oaks, CA 91320. TEL 805-499-9774, FAX 805-499-0871, journals@sagepub.com.

200 NLD ISSN 0923-6201
➤ **CURRENTS OF ENCOUNTER**; studies on the contact between Christianity and other religions, beliefs, and cultures. Text in English. 1990. irreg., latest vol.36, 2008. price varies. adv. back issues avail. **Document type:** *Monographic series, Academic/Scholarly.* **Description:** Presents comparative studies on Christianity and other religions, beliefs, and cultures.
Indexed: AmHI, H07, T02.
Published by: Editions Rodopi B.V., Tijnmuiden 7, Amsterdam, 1046 AK, Netherlands. TEL 31-20-6114821, FAX 31-20-4472979, info@rodopi.nl. Eds. Henk Vroom, Henry Jansen, Jerald D Gort. **Dist in France by:** Nordeal, 30 rue de Verlinghem, BP 139, Lambersart 59832, France. TEL 33-3-20099060, FAX 33-3-20929495; **Dist in N America by:** Rodopi - USA, 606 Newark Ave, 2nd fl, Kenilworth, NJ 07033. TEL 908-497-9031, 800-225-3998, FAX 908-497-9035.

▼ ➤ **CURTANA**; sword of mercy. *see* MILITARY

202 USA
THE CUSAN. Text in English. 1948. s-a. free membership (effective 2005). bk.rev. 36 p./no. 1 cols./p.; **Document type:** *Magazine, Consumer.* **Description:** Features articles by and for members. Contains a focus which is spiritual, practical or humorous in nature.
Related titles: Braille ed.; Magnetic Tape ed.
Published by: CUSA - An Aposolate of the Sick or Disabled, 176 W Eighth St, Bayonne, NJ 07002. TEL 201-437-0412, ams4@juno.com, www.cusan.org. Ed. Lawrence Jadgfeld. R&P Anna Marie Sopko. Circ: 1,100.

200 DEU ISSN 0070-2234
CUSANUS-GESELLSCHAFT. BUCHREIHE. Text in German. 1964. irreg., latest vol.18, 2010. price varies. **Document type:** *Monographic series, Academic/Scholarly.*
Published by: (Cusanus-Gesellschaft), Aschendorff Verlag GmbH & Co. KG, Soester Str 13, Muenster, 48135, Germany. TEL 49-251-6900, FAX 49-251-6904570, buchverlag@aschendorff.de, http://www.aschendorff-buchverlag.de.

289.9 USA ISSN 1523-1216
BR1644
CYBERJOURNAL FOR PENTECOSTAL-CHARISMATIC RESEARCH. Text in Chinese, English. 1997. a. free (effective 2011). back issues avail. **Document type:** *Journal, Academic/Scholarly.*
Media: Online - full text.
Indexed: A21, A39, C27, C29, D03, D04, E13, R14, RI-1, S14, S15, S18.
Published by: Pentecostal Charismatic Theological Inquiry International http://www.pctii.org/index.html. Ed. Harold D Hunter.

220 ZAF
DAILY GUIDE; Bible reading notes for adults. Text in English. 1994. a. ZAR 7.95.
Published by: Scripture Union, PO Box 291, Rondebosch, Cape Town 7701, South Africa.

202.15 USA ISSN 0190-5457
BV4810
DAILY GUIDEPOSTS. Text in English. 1977. a. USD 16.15. **Description:** Presents an inspirational first-person story of human kindness and overcoming adversity for each day of the year.
Published by: Guideposts, 39 Seminary Hill Rd, Carmel, NY 10512. TEL 800-431-2344, FAX 845-288-2115.

220 ZAF
DAILY POWER; daily Bible reading notes for young people for the whole year. Text in English. 1994. a. ZAR 4.95.
Published by: Scripture Union, PO Box 291, Rondebosch, Cape Town 7701, South Africa.

200 340 ITA ISSN 2036-0754
DAIMON; annuario di diritto comparato delle religioni. Text in Italian. 2001. a. **Document type:** *Journal, Academic/Scholarly.*
Published by: Societa Editrice Il Mulino, Strada Maggiore 37, Bologna, 40125, Italy. TEL 39-051-256011, FAX 39-051-256034, riviste@mulino.it, http://www.mulino.it.

200 AUS
DAN CHUA MAGAZINE. Text in Vietnamese. 1977. m. **Document type:** *Bulletin, Consumer.*
Related titles: E-mail ed.; Fax ed.; Online - full content ed.
Address: 715 Sydney Rd, Brunswick, VIC 3056, Australia. danchua@donbosco.org.au, http://vietcatholic.net/danchua-uc/index.htm. Ed. Rev. A. Nguyen Quang.

200 RUS
DANILOVSKII BLAGOVESNIK. Text in Russian. 1991. q. USD 99 in the Americas (effective 2000).
Published by: Svyato-Danilov Monastyr', Danilovskii val., 22, Moscow, 113191, Russian Federation. TEL 7-095-9556736, FAX 7-095-9556779.

200 DNK ISSN 0901-3873
DANSK KIRKETIDENDE/DANISH CHURCH TIMES. Text in Danish. 1957. bi-w. DKK 350; DKK 175 to students (effective 2009). **Document type:** *Magazine, Consumer.*
Indexed: RILM.
Published by: Grundtvigsk Forum, Vartov, Farvergade 27, Copenhagen K, 1463, Denmark. TEL 45-33-732800, FAX 45-33-732806, vartov@vartov.dk. Ed. Birgitte Staklund Larsen.

225 DNK ISSN 0905-5371
DANSK KOMMENTAR TIL DET NYE TESTAMENTE. Variant title: D K N T. Text in Danish. 1989. irreg., latest vol.5, 2008. price varies. back issues avail. **Document type:** *Monographic series, Academic/Scholarly.*
Published by: Aarhus Universitetsforlag/Aarhus University Press, Langelandsgade 177, Aarhus N, 8200, Denmark. TEL 45-89-425370, FAX 45-89-425380, unipress@au.dk.

200 DNK ISSN 0105-3191
BR6
➤ **DANSK TEOLOGISK TIDSSKRIFT.** Text in Danish. 1884. 4/yr. DKK 270; DKK 200 to students (effective 2008). adv. bk.rev. back issues avail.; reprints avail. **Document type:** *Journal, Academic/Scholarly.*
Formerly (until 1938): Teologisk Tidsskrift for den Danske Folkekirke (0909-3265)
Related titles: Online - full text ed.: ISSN 1902-3898. 200?.
Indexed: A21, FR, IBR, IBZ, MLA-IB, OTA, PCI, R&TA, RASB, RI-1, RI-2, RILM.
—INIST.
Published by: Anis Forlaget, Frederiksberg Alle 10 A, Frederiksberg C, 1820, Denmark. TEL 45-33-249250, FAX 45-33-250607, info@anis.dk, http://www.anis.dk. Eds. Kirsten Nielsen, Niels Henrik Gregersen.

200 DNK ISSN 1903-6523
DANSK TIDSSKRIFT FOR TEOLOGI OG KIRKE. Text in Danish. 1974. q. DKK 250 domestic to individuals; DKK 300 foreign to individuals; DKK 350 domestic to institutions; DKK 400 foreign to institutions; DKK 150 domestic to students; DKK 200 foreign to students; DKK 100 per issue (effective 2009). back issues avail. **Document type:** *Magazine, Consumer.* **Description:** Students' magazine at Menighedsfakultetet.
Formerly (until 2008): Ichthys (0105-4791)
Indexed: IZBG, OTA.
Published by: Menighedsfakultetet/Lutheran School of Theology in Aarhus, Katrinebergvej 75, Aarhus N, 8200, Denmark. TEL 45-86-166300, FAX 45-86-166860, mf@teologi.dk, http://www.teologi.dk. Ed. Jeppe Nikolajsen.

220 DNK ISSN 1601-9407
DET DANSKE BIBELSELSKAB. AARBOG. Text in Danish. 1966. a. **Document type:** *Consumer.*
Former titles (until 2001): Det Danske Bibelselskabs Aarbog (0109-5846); Det Danske Bibelselskabs Aarsberetning
Published by: Det Danske Bibelselskab/The Danish Bible Society, Frederiksborggade 50, Copenhagen K, 1360, Denmark. TEL 45-33-127835, FAX 45-33-127850, bibelselskabet@bibelselskabet.dk, http://www.bibelselskabet.dk.

200 DEU ISSN 0948-4736
DARMSTAEDTER THEOLOGISCHE BEITRAEGE ZU GEGENWARTSFRAGEN. Text in German. 1997. irreg., latest vol.11, 2006. price varies. **Document type:** *Monographic series, Academic/Scholarly.*
Published by: Peter Lang GmbH (Subsidiary of: Peter Lang Publishing Group), Eschborner Landstr 42-50, Frankfurt Am Main, 60489, Germany. TEL 49-69-7807050, FAX 49-69-78070550, zentrale.frankfurt@peterlang.com.

200 ARG ISSN 1666-7832
BR7
DAVARLOGOS. Text in English, Portuguese, Spanish. 2002. s-a. ARS 25 domestic; USD 20 foreign (effective 2005). **Document type:** *Journal, Academic/Scholarly.*
Related titles: Online - full text ed.
Indexed: A01, CA, F03, F04, OTA, R&TA, T02.
Published by: Universidad Adventista del Plata, 25 de Mayo 99, Libertador San Martin, Entre Rios 3103, Argentina. TEL 54-343-4910010, FAX 54-343-4910300, informe@uap.edu.ar, http://www.uapar.edu. Eds. Fernando Aranda Fraga, Gerald A Klingbeil.

200 GBR
DAY ONE. Text in English. 1843. 3/yr. GBP 5 (effective 2001). adv. bk.rev. 24 p./no. 3 cols./p.; **Document type:** *Bulletin.* **Description:** Describes the work and covers all matters of the society.
Formerly: Joy and Light (0022-5703)
Published by: Lord's Day Observance Society, 3 Epsom Business Park, Kiln Ln, Epsom, Surrey KT17 1JF, United Kingdom. TEL 44-1372-728300, FAX 44-1372-722400, http://www.lordsday.co.uk. Ed. J G Roberts. Adv. contact Steve Devane. Circ: 10,000.

260 GBR
DAY ONE DIARY. Text in English. 1928. a. GBP 1.30 (effective 2000). adv. **Document type:** *Bulletin.* **Description:** Pocket diary with daily Bible verse based upon a theme.
Formerly: Happy Day Diary
Published by: Lord's Day Observance Society, 3 Epsom Business Park, Kiln Ln, Epsom, Surrey KT17 1JF, United Kingdom. Ed. J G Roberts. Adv. contact Steve Devane. Circ: 110,000.

200 NZL ISSN 1175-5245
DAYSTAR; New Zealand's evangelical monthly. Text in English. 2001. m. (except Feb.). NZD 34.95 domestic; NZD 60 foreign (effective 2008). adv. bk.rev.; music rev.; film rev. 20 p./no.; back issues avail. **Document type:** *Newsletter, Consumer.* **Description:** Provides news and features of interest to evangelical christians generally.
Published by: DayStar Publications Trust, Luckens Point, PO Box 180168, Auckland, 0663, New Zealand. TEL 0800-477-774, FAX 64-9-4797819, info@daystar.org.nz. Ed., R&P Julie Belding. Adv. contact Ray Curle. Circ: 5,000.

DE PROCESSIBUS MATRIMONIALIBUS. *see* LAW—Family And Matrimonial Law

DEAD SEA DISCOVERIES; a journal of current research on the scrolls and related literature. *see* RELIGIONS AND THEOLOGY—Judaic

235 USA ISSN 1939-4136
DEITIES AND ANGELS OF THE ANCIENT WORLD. Text in English. 2007 (Aug.). irreg. price varies. back issues avail. **Document type:** *Monographic series, Academic/Scholarly.* **Description:** Provides explorations into and possible explanations of those beings known as angels and deities in the ancient world that had some survival into the historic religions of the monotheistic tradition.
Published by: Gorgias Press LLC, 954 River Rd, Piscataway, NJ 08854. TEL 732-885-8900, FAX 732-885-8908, helpdesk@gorgiaspress.com, http://www.gorgiaspress.com/bookshop/default.aspx.

220 GRC ISSN 1012-2311
DELTION BIBLIKON MELETON/BULLETIN OF BIBLICAL STUDIES. Text in English, French, German, Greek. 1971; N.S. 1980. s-a. USD 20 foreign (effective 2000). bk.rev. **Document type:** *Journal, Academic/Scholarly.*
Indexed: IZBG, OTA.
—BLDSC (2834.526000).
Published by: (Philanthropic Institute "Artos Zoes"), Artos Zoes Publications, 28 Bouboulinas St, 2nd fl., Athens, 106 82, Greece. TEL 30-1-8824-547, FAX 30-1-8228-791, artos@otenet.gr. Ed. Savas Agouridis. Circ: 1,000.

230 CHE
DENKMAL; Standpunkte aus Theologie und Kirche. Text in German. 1998. irreg., latest vol.4, 2003. price varies. **Document type:** *Monographic series, Academic/Scholarly.*
Published by: Theologischer Verlag Zurich, Badenerstr 73, Zurich, 8026, Switzerland. TEL 41-44-2993355, FAX 41-44-2993358, tvz@ref.ch, http://www.tvz-verlag.ch.

220 DEU ISSN 1611-1257
DENNOCH; Klartext fuer junge Christen. Text in German. 1995. bi-m. EUR 24.40 (effective 2009). **Document type:** *Magazine, Consumer.*
Published by: Pulsmedien GmbH, Postfach 240105, Worms, 67527, Germany. TEL 49-6242-8209190, mail@pulsmedien.de, http://www.pulsmedien.de.

200 USA
DENVER JOURNAL; an online review of current biblical and theological studies. Text in English. 1998. irreg. free (effective 2011). **Document type:** *Journal, Consumer.*
Media: Online - full text.
Published by: Denver Seminary, PO Box 100000, Denver, CO 80250-0100. TEL 303-761-2482, 800-922-3040. Ed. Richard S Hess.

DERECHO Y RELIGION. *see* LAW

220 DEU ISSN 1865-1666
DEUTEROCANONICAL AND COGNATE LITERATURE STUDIES. Text in English. 2008. irreg., latest vol.12, 2011. price varies. **Document type:** *Monographic series, Academic/Scholarly.*
Published by: Walter de Gruyter GmbH & Co. KG, Genthiner Str 13, Berlin, 10785, Germany. TEL 49-30-260050, FAX 49-30-26005251, info@degruyter.com, http://www.degruyter.de. Ed. Friedrich Reiterer.

220 DEU ISSN 1614-3361
BS410
➤ **DEUTEROCANONICAL AND COGNATE LITERATURE YEARBOOK.** Text in English, German. 2004. a. EUR 115, USD 173 to institutions; EUR 130, USD 195 combined subscription to institutions (print & online eds.) (effective 2012). **Document type:** *Journal, Academic/Scholarly.*
Related titles: Online - full text ed.: ISSN 1614-337X. EUR 115, USD 173 to institutions (effective 2012).
Indexed: A01, A26, IBR, IBZ, T02.
—**CCC.**
Published by: Walter de Gruyter GmbH & Co. KG, Genthiner Str 13, Berlin, 10785, Germany. TEL 49-30-260050, FAX 49-30-26005251, info@degruyter.com. Ed. Friedrich Reiterer.

200 100 MYS ISSN 0012-1746
DHARMA; a quarterly devoted to universal religion, righteousness & culture. Text in English. 1949-1976; resumed 1977. q. MYR 6. bk.rev. illus. **Description:** Promotes the study of comparative theology and philosophy in its widest form. Promotes inter-cultural relations and spiritual values.
Indexed: PerIslam.
Published by: Pure Life Society/Persatuan, Batu 6 Jalan Puchong, Jalan Kelang Lama Post Office, Kuala Lumpur, 58200, Malaysia. TEL 03-792-9391, FAX 03-792-8303. Ed. Mother A Mangalam. Circ: 3,000.

230 410 FRA ISSN 0167-9554
DIA REGNO/DIVINE KINGDOM; Kristana Esperanto-Gazeto. Text in Esperanto. 1908. bi-m. EUR 16 (effective 2011). adv. bk.rev. back issues avail. **Document type:** *Newsletter, Consumer.* **Description:** Aims to spread the international language Esperanto among Christians, to strengthen ecumenism among Christian groups, and to spread the Christian message among Esperantists.
Indexed: MLA-IB.
Published by: Kristana Esperantista Ligo Internacia, 26 rue de Pre Ventnet, Nouaille-Maupertuis, 86340, France. TEL 33-549468021. Ed. Philippe Cousson.

230 DEU ISSN 1869-3261
▼ ➤ **DIACONIA**; journal for the study of christian social practice. Text in German. 2010. s-a. EUR 41 to individuals; EUR 82 to institutions; EUR 34.90 to students; EUR 22.90 newsstand/cover (effective 2011). **Document type:** *Journal, Academic/Scholarly.* **Description:** Aims to contribute new research and interpretations of Christian social practice with and among the marginalized.
Published by: Vandenhoeck und Ruprecht, Theaterstr 13, Goettingen, 37073, Germany. TEL 49-551-508440, FAX 49-551-5084422, info@v-r.de.

266 FIN ISSN 1796-5675
➤ **DIAKONIAN TUTKIMUS.** Text in Finnish. 2004. s-a. EUR 20 to individual members; EUR 100 to institutional members; EUR 10 to students (effective 2009). **Document type:** *Journal, Academic/ Scholarly.*
Related titles: Online - full text ed.: ISSN 1795-5270.
Published by: Diakonian Tutkimuksen Seura ry., c/o Kari Latvus, Jarvenpaantie 640, Jarvenpaa, 04400, Finland. TEL 358-400-979921. Ed. Kari Latvus.

261 268 DEU ISSN 1864-1628
DIAKONIE MAGAZIN. Text in German. 1947. q. free (effective 2009). adv. bk.rev. bibl.; charts; illus.; stat. **Document type:** *Magazine, Trade.*
Former titles (until 2007): Diakonie Report (0342-1643); (until 1975): Diakonische Werk (0012-1983)
Related titles: Regional ed(s).: Diakonie Report. Ausgabe Nordelbien, Hamburg. ISSN 0942-1483. 1990.
Indexed: IBR, IBZ.
Published by: Diakonisches Werk der Evangelischen Kirche in Deutschland e.V., Stafflenbergstr 76, Stuttgart, 70184, Germany. TEL 49-711-21590, FAX 49-711-2159288, diakonie@diakonie.de. Ed. Andreas Wagner. adv.: B&W page EUR 4,950; trim 210 x 280. Circ: 47,827 (controlled).

200 DEU
DIAKONIESCHWESTER. Text in German. 1898. m. bk.rev. back issues avail. **Document type:** *Newsletter, Consumer.*
Formerly (until 1950): Evangelischer Diakonieverein. Blaetter
Published by: Evangelischer Diakonieverein e.V., Glockenstr 8, Berlin, 14163, Germany. TEL 49-30-8099700, FAX 49-30-8022452, info@ev-diakonieverein.de, http://www.ev-diakonieverein.de. Circ: 3,500 (controlled).

200 SWE ISSN 1404-2924
DIAKONIVETENSKAPLIGA INSTITUTET. SKRIFTSERIE. Text mainly in Swedish; Text occasionally in English. 1999. irreg., latest vol.12, 2006. price varies. back issues avail. **Document type:** *Monographic series, Academic/Scholarly.*
Published by: Diakonivetenskapliga Institutet/Uppsala Institute for Diaconal and Social Studies, Samaritergraend 2, Uppsala, 75319, Sweden. TEL 46-18-564010, FAX 46-18-143144, dvi@svenskakyrkan.se.

200 SWE ISSN 1650-2523
DIAKONIVETENSKAPLIGA INSTITUTET. TEMABOK. Text in Swedish. 2000. irreg., latest vol.3, 2004. back issues avail. **Document type:** *Monographic series, Academic/Scholarly.*
Published by: Diakonivetenskapliga Institutet/Uppsala Institute for Diaconal and Social Studies, Samaritergraend 2, Uppsala, 75319, Sweden. TEL 46-18-564010, FAX 46-18-143144, dvi@svenskakyrkan.se, http://www.dvi.nu.

200 DEU
DIALOG (ONLINE). Text in German. 1973. irreg. free (effective 2009). bk.rev. **Document type:** *Newsletter, Consumer.*
Former titles (until 2007): Dialog (Print); (until 1992): D I A
Media: Online - full content.
Published by: Evangelisch - Lutherische Landeskirche Hannover, Informations- und Pressestelle, Archivstr 3, Hannover, 30169, Germany. TEL 49-511-1241399, FAX 49-511-1241820, ips.hannover@evlka.de, http://www.evlka.de. Circ: 19,500.

230 USA ISSN 0012-2033
BR1
➤ **DIALOG (ST PAUL)**; a journal of theology. Text in English. 1962. q. GBP 204 in United Kingdom to institutions; EUR 258 in Europe to institutions; USD 249 in the Americas to institutions; USD 398 elsewhere to institutions; GBP 235 combined subscription in United Kingdom to institutions (print & online eds.); EUR 297 combined subscription in Europe to institutions (print & online eds.); USD 287 combined subscription in the Americas to institutions (print & online eds.); USD 458 combined subscription elsewhere to institutions (print & online eds.) (effective 2012). adv. bk.rev. back issues avail.; reprint service avail. from PSC. **Document type:** *Journal, Academic/ Scholarly.* **Description:** Publishes a wide range of theological articles.
Related titles: Microform ed.: (from PQC); Online - full text ed.: ISSN 1540-6385. GBP 204 in United Kingdom to institutions; EUR 258 in Europe to institutions; USD 249 in the Americas to institutions; USD 398 elsewhere to institutions (effective 2012) (from IngentaConnect).
Indexed: A01, A02, A03, A08, A20, A21, A22, A26, ArtHuCI, CA, CERDIC, E01, Faml, H14, OTA, P02, P10, P28, P30, P48, P53, P54, PQC, R&TA, RI-1, RI-2, T02, W07.
—BLDSC (3579.730000), IE, Infotrieve, Ingenta. **CCC.**
Published by: (Pacific Lutheran Theological Seminary and Graduate Theological Union), Wiley-Blackwell Publishing, Inc. (Subsidiary of: Wiley-Blackwell Publishing Ltd.), 111 River St, Hoboken, NJ 07030. TEL 201-748-6000, FAX 201-748-6088, info@wiley.com. Ed. Kristin Johnston Largen TEL 717-334-6286 ext 2158. Adv. contact Kristin McCarthy TEL 201-748-7683.

200 USA
DIALOG (WILMINGTON). Text in English. 1966. w. USD 16. adv. bk.rev. **Document type:** *Newspaper.*
Published by: Diocese of Wilmington, 1925 Delaware Ave, Wilmington, DE 19806. TEL 302-573-3109, FAX 302-573-2397. Ed., R&P Gary Morton. Adv. contact William Lukowski. Circ: 48,000.

220 DEU ISSN 0937-1540
DIALOG DER KIRCHEN. Text in German. 1982. irreg., latest vol.14, 2008. price varies. **Document type:** *Monographic series, Academic/ Scholarly.*
Published by: Verlag Herder GmbH, Hermann-Herder-Str 4, Freiburg Im Breisgau, 79104, Germany. TEL 49-761-27170, FAX 49-761-2717520, kundenservice@herder.de, http://www.herder.de.

200 ESP ISSN 0210-2870
DIALOGO ECUMENICO; revista cuatrimestral de teologia ecumenica. Text in Spanish. 1966. 3/yr. USD 36 domestic; EUR 42 in Europe; EUR 50 elsewhere (effective 2008). adv. bk.rev. **Document type:** *Journal, Academic/Scholarly.*
Indexed: CERDIC, DIP, IBR, IBZ, RASB.
Published by: Universidad Pontificia de Salamanca, Servicio de Publicaciones, Calle Compania 5, Salamanca, 37002, Spain. TEL 34-923-277100.

261 LKA ISSN 0012-2181
DIALOGUE. Text in English. 1963. 3/yr. USD 10. adv. bk.rev.
Related titles: Online - full text ed.
Indexed: A21, RI-1, RI-2.
—BLDSC (3579.753000), IE, Ingenta.
Published by: Ecumenical Institute for Study and Dialogue, 490-5 Havelock Rd., Colombo, 6, Sri Lanka. Ed. Fr Aloysius Pieris. Circ: 1,000.

200 USA ISSN 0891-5881
BL1
➤ **DIALOGUE & ALLIANCE.** Text in English. 1987. s-a. USD 15 in the Americas to individuals; USD 20 in the Americas to institutions; USD 25 elsewhere; USD 10 per issue (effective 2011). bk.rev. back issues avail. **Document type:** *Journal, Academic/Scholarly.* **Description:** Aims to facilitate dialogue and alliance among the religious traditions of the world as a means of promoting peace.
Related titles: Microform ed.; Online - full text ed.
Indexed: A21, A22, GSS&RPL, Perlslam, R&TA, RI-1, RI-2.
—BLDSC (3579.775210), IE, Ingenta.
Published by: Inter-Religious Federation for World Peace, 4 W 43rd St, New York, NY 10036. TEL 212-869-6033, FAX 212-869-6424, info@irfwp.org. Ed. Dr. Frank F Kaufmann.

➤ **DIALOGUE ON CAMPUS**; linking the religious and the higher education systems. *see* EDUCATION—Higher Education

200 FRA
DICTIONNAIRE D'HISTOIRE ET DE GEOGRAPHIE ECCLESIASTIQUES. Text in French. irreg., latest vol.26, 1997. back issues avail. **Document type:** *Monographic series, Academic/ Scholarly.* **Description:** Discusses the geographical history of the Church and explores the lives of people who contributed to that history through their writings.
Published by: Letouzey et Ane Editeurs, 87 bd. Raspail, Paris, 75006, France. TEL 33-1-45488014, FAX 33-1-45490343. Ed. R Aubert. R&P Florence Letouzey.

221 DEU ISSN 1434-0631
DIELHEIMER BLAETTER ZUM ALTEN TESTAMENT UND SEINER REZEPTION IN DER ALTEN KIRCHE. Text in German. 1972. s-a. bk.rev. **Document type:** *Journal, Academic/Scholarly.*
Former titles (until 1984): D B A T - Dielheimer Blaetter zum Alten Testament (1434-0623); (until 1974): Dielheimer Blaetter zum Alten Testament (1434-0615)
Indexed: OTA.
Published by: Universitaet Heidelberg, Wissenschaftlich-Theologisches Seminar, Kisselgasse 1, Heidelberg, 69117, Germany. Eds. Bernd Jorg Diebner, Claudia Nauerth. Circ: 250.

DIELHEIMER BLAETTER ZUR ARCHAEOLOGIE UND TEXTUEBERLIEFERUNG DER ANTIKE UND SPAETANTIKE. *see* ARCHAEOLOGY

200 DEU ISSN 0720-9916
DIENST AM WORT - GEDANKEN ZUR SONNTAGSPREDIGT. Text in German. 1971. 8/yr. EUR 60; EUR 94 combined subscription print & online eds.; EUR 7.80 newsstand/cover (effective 2007). adv. **Document type:** *Magazine, Consumer.*
Formed by the merger of (1966-1971): Dienst am Wort (0419-1234); (194?-1971): Gedanken zur Sonntagspredigt (0720-9924); Which incorporated (1952-196?): Arbeitshefte der Religioesen Bildungsarbeit Stuttgart (0721-0124)
Related titles: Online - full text ed.: EUR 64 (effective 2007).
Published by: Schwabenverlag AG, Senefelderstr 12, Ostfildern, 73760, Germany. TEL 49-711-4406140, FAX 49-711-4406138, info@schwabenverlag.de, http://www.schwabenverlag.de. Ed. Anton Bauer. adv.: page EUR 550; trim 108 x 170. Circ: 3,700 (paid and controlled).

DIETRICH'S INDEX PHILOSOPHICUS. *see* RELIGIONS AND THEOLOGY—Abstracting, Bibliographies, Statistics

202 NOR ISSN 1501-9934
➤ **DIN**; tidsskrift for religion og kultur. Text in Norwegian. 1995. q. NOK 280 to individuals; NOK 500 to institutions (effective 2011). back issues avail. **Document type:** *Journal, Academic/Scholarly.*
Formerly (until 1999): Sic! (0806-7155)
Published by: Novus Forlag AS, Herman Foss Gate 19, Oslo, 0171, Norway. TEL 47-22-717450, FAX 47-22-718107, novus@novus.no. Ed. Bjoern Ola Tafjord.

268 USA ISSN 0890-3476
DIRECTION. STUDENT BOOK. Text in English. 1971. q. USD 3.69 per issue (effective 2008). back issues avail. **Document type:** *Magazine, Consumer.* **Description:** Contains weekly adult Bible lessons, including Scripture passages, a lesson focus and outline, historical and geographical backgrounds, discussions of the lesson text, study questions, a lesson project, and daily and weekly devotional readings.
Related titles: Large type ed.; Special ed(s).: Direction. Student Book (Large Print Edition). ISSN 1934-5658. USD 4.49 (effective 2008).
Published by: Urban Ministries, Inc., Dept #4870, PO Box 87618, Chicago, IL 60680. TEL 708-868-7100, 800-860-8642, FAX 708-868-7105, customerservice@urbanministries.com.

268 USA ISSN 1550-9141
DIRECTION. TEACHER GUIDE. Text in English. 1982. q. USD 5.59 per issue (effective 2008). back issues avail. **Document type:** *Magazine, Trade.* **Description:** Contains commentary on the International Uniform Lesson Series and teaching plans for adults.
Published by: Urban Ministries, Inc., Dept #4870, PO Box 87618, Chicago, IL 60680. TEL 708-868-7100, 800-860-8642, FAX 708-868-7105, customerservice@urbanministries.com.

200 USA
DIRECTORY OF DEPARTMENTS AND PROGRAMS OF RELIGIOUS STUDIES IN NORTH AMERICA. Text in English. 1978. a., latest 1999. USD 40 per vol. (effective 2003). adv. **Document type:** *Directory.* **Description:** Lists institutions that have a religious studies department or program.
Published by: Council of Societies for the Study of Religion, CSSR Executive Office, Rice University, MS-156, PO Box 1892, Houston, TX 77251. TEL 713-348-5721, 888-422-2777, FAX 713-348-5725, cssr@rice.edu, http://www.cssr.org. Ed., R&P David G Truemper. Adv. contact Ms. Pamela J Gleason. page USD 250; 6 x 9.

207.2 GBR ISSN 1466-6855
DIRECTORY OF ENGLISH - SPEAKING CHURCHES ABROAD. Text in English. 1966. a. GBP 4 per issue (effective 2009). illus.; maps. 112 p./no. 1 cols./p.; **Document type:** *Directory, Consumer.* **Description:** Lists English-speaking Protestant churches in over 80 countries where English is not the first language. It is designed to help those who travel internationally for work, on holiday, or to study, and for churches and Christian unions to help their members find fellowship abroad.
Published by: Intercontinental Church Society, 1 Athena Dr, Tachbrook Pk, Warwick, CV34 6NL, United Kingdom. TEL 44-1926-430347, FAX 44-1926-888092, enquiries@ics-uk.org.

DIRECTORY OF RELIGIOUS MEDIA. *see* BUSINESS AND ECONOMICS—Trade And Industrial Directories

DIRITTO E RELIGIONI. *see* LAW

262.9 340 ITA ISSN 1128-7772
IL DIRITTO ECCLESIASTICO. Text in Italian, Latin. 1890. q. EUR 245 combined subscription domestic to institutions (print & online eds.); EUR 295 combined subscription foreign to institutions (print & online eds.) (effective 2009). bk.rev. bibl. index, cum.index: 1890-1990. **Document type:** *Journal, Academic/Scholarly.* **Description:** Represents a culturally pluralistic perspective on legislations which involve the relationship between church and state.
Former titles (until 1989): Diritto Ecclesiastico e Rassegna di Diritto Matrimoniale (0391-2191); (until 1970): Diritto Ecclesiastico (0012-3455); (until 1943): Diritto Ecclesiastico e Rassegna di Diritto Matrimoniale (1120-0480); (until 1929): Diritto Ecclesiastico (1120-0472); (until 1923): Rivista di Diritto Ecclesiastico (1120-0464); (until 1922): Diritto Ecclesiastico Italiano (1120-0448); (until 1908): Rivista di Diritto Ecclesiastico (1120-043X)
Related titles: Online - full text ed.: ISSN 2035-3545.
Indexed: A22, CERDIC, CLA, DIP, IBR, IBZ.
—IE.
Published by: Fabrizio Serra Editore (Subsidiary of: Accademia Editoriale), c/o Accademia Editoriale, Via Santa Bibbiana 28, Pisa, 56127, Italy. TEL 39-050-542332, FAX 39-050-574888, accademiaeditoriale@accademiaeditoriale.it, http://www.libraweb.net.

200 100 GBR ISSN 1741-4164
➤ **DISCOURSE (HESLINGTON)**; learning and teaching in philosophical and religious studies. Text in English. 2001 (Aug.). s-a. free to qualified personnel (effective 2009). back issues avail. **Document type:** *Journal, Academic/Scholarly.* **Description:** Covers all aspects of developments in the scholarship of learning and teaching.
Formerly (until Aug.2003): The P R S - L T S N Journal (1474-2195)
Related titles: Online - full content ed.: ISSN 2040-3674. free (effective 2009).
Indexed: B29.
—BLDSC (3595.746500), IE, Ingenta.
Published by: Higher Education Academy, Subject Centre for Philosophical and Religious Studies, Department of Theology and Religious Studies, University of Leeds, Leeds, LS2 9JT, United Kingdom. TEL 44-113-3434184, FAX 44-113-3433654, enquiries@prs.heacademy.ac.uk, http://www.prs.heacademy.ac.uk. Ed. David J Mossley TEL 44-113-3436745.

➤ **DISCOVERIES IN THE JUDAEAN DESERT OF JORDAN.** *see* ARCHAEOLOGY

200 USA
DISTANT DRUMS. Text in English. 1979. irreg. (3-5/yr.), latest vol.16, 1995. looseleaf. USD 18 for 6 issues; USD 25 foreign for 6 issues. back issues avail. **Document type:** *Newsletter.* **Description:** Discusses syncretism in religion, education, and national and international affairs.
Address: 10205 Xeon St., N.W., Coon Rapids, IN 55433-4849. Ed. Ronald S Miller. Circ: 100.

230 100 ITA ISSN 0012-4257
B4
DIVUS THOMAS. Text in Italian. 1880. 3/yr. EUR 100 domestic; EUR 160 foreign (effective 2009). bk.rev. index. 200 p./no.; back issues avail.; reprints avail. **Document type:** *Magazine, Consumer.* **Description:** Offers scholarly study in theology and philosophy, chiefly in the field of Thomistic research.
Indexed: CERDIC, DIP, FR, IBR, IBZ, IPB, MLA, MLA-IB, OTA.
—INIST.
Published by: Edizioni Studio Domenicano, Via dell' Osservanza 72, Bologna, BO 40136, Italy. TEL 39-051-582034, FAX 39-051-331583, esd@alinet.it, http://www.esd-domenicani.it.

266 CIV
DJELIBA; le journal des jeunes chretiens. Text in French. 1974. 5/yr. XOF 3,000, USD 6 (effective 1998). adv. back issues avail. **Document type:** *Bulletin.*
Published by: Eglise Catholique en Cote d'Ivoire, 01 BP 1287, Abidjan, 01, Ivory Coast. TEL 21-69-79. Ed., R&P, Adv. contact Pierre Trichet. Pub. Archeveche d'Abidjan. Circ: 5,000.

220 BEL
➤ **DOCUMENTA Q.** Text in English. 1996. irreg., latest 1999. price varies. back issues avail. **Document type:** *Monographic series, Academic/ Scholarly.* **Description:** Provides scholarly commentary on a specific section of the Bible.
Published by: Peeters Publishers, Bondgenotenlaan 153, Leuven, 3000, Belgium. TEL 32-16-235170, FAX 32-16-228500, http://www.peeters-leuven.be.

200 ESP ISSN 1133-715X
DOCUMENTS D'ESGLESIA. Text in Catalan. 1966. fortn. **Document type:** *Journal, Consumer.*
Published by: Publicacions de l' Abadia de Montserrat, Ausias Marc 92-98, Barcelona, 08013, Spain. TEL 34-932-450303, FAX 34-932-473594, informacio@pamsa.com, http://www.pamsa.com. Ed. Bernabe Dalmau i Ribalta.

200 362.42 SWE ISSN 0345-2530
DOEVAS KYRKOBLAD; tidning foer Svenska kyrkans teckenspraakiga arbete. Text in Swedish. 1930. 6/yr. SEK 130 (effective 2006). **Document type:** *Magazine, Consumer.*

R

Formerly (until 1954): De Doevstummmas Kyrkoblad
Published by: (Svenska Kyrkan/Church of Sweden), Svenska Kyrkans Press AB, Goetgatan 22A, PO Box 15412, Stockholm, 10465, Sweden. TEL 46-8-4622800, FAX 46-8-6445604, http://www.svkpress.com. Ed. Anita Helloere.

230 DEU ISSN 1869-3962
▼ **DOGMATIK IN DER MODERNE.** Text in German. 2010. irreg. price varies. **Document type:** *Monographic series, Academic/Scholarly.*
Published by: Mohr Siebeck GmbH & Co. KG, Wilhelmstr 18, Tuebingen, 72074, Germany. TEL 49-7071-9230, FAX 49-7071-51104, info@mohr.de.

220 CHE ISSN 1022-193X
DOKIMION. Text in French, German. 1970. irreg., latest vol.35, 2011. price varies. **Document type:** *Monographic series, Academic/Scholarly.*
Published by: Academic Press Fribourg, Perolles 42, Fribourg, 1705, Switzerland. TEL 41-26-4264311, FAX 41-26-4264300, info@paulusedition.ch, http://www.paulusedition.ch/academic_press/.

DOODGEWOON (ONLINE); tijdschrift over de dood. *see* PHILOSOPHY

200 IND ISSN 0973-4678
DOON THEOLOGICAL JOURNAL. Text in English. 2004. s-a. INR 300 for 2 yrs. domestic; USD 40 for 2 yrs. in US & Canada; GBP 20, EUR 30 for 2 yrs. in Europe; USD 30 for 2 yrs. elsewhere (effective 2011). adv. **Document type:** *Journal, Academic/Scholarly.* **Description:** Promotes Christian theological learning, scholarly excellence, and thoughtful conversation between various Christian traditions in India.
Published by: Luther W. New Jr. Theological College, PO Kulhan, Sahastradhara Rd, Dehradun, Uttaranchal 248 001, India. TEL 91-135-2607260, FAX 91-135-2607617, info@ntcdoon.org, http://www.ntcdoon.org. Ed. Simon Samuel.

230 NLD ISSN 1572-8056
DOORGEEFBRIEF. Text in Dutch. 1992. 3/yr.
Published by: Gereformeerd Appel, Amazoneweg 90, Delft, 2622 DT, Netherlands. TEL 31-15-2565015, info@gereformeerdappel.nl.

DOUJIA AIXIN BAO/DORCAS LOVE MISSION POST. *see* SOCIAL SERVICES AND WELFARE

260 USA
DOVETAIL (DES MOINES). Text in English. 1977. q. looseleaf. USD 10. bk.rev. back issues avail. **Document type:** *Newsletter.* **Description:** Provides information on issues of conscience (conscientious objection to war, war tax resistance) and updates on peace efforts, especially in Iowa.
Formerly (until Sep. 1991): Dovetail - Peaces; Which was formed by the merger of: Peaces; Dovetail
Published by: Iowa Peace Network, 4211 Grand Ave, Des Moines, IA 50312. TEL 515-255-7114. Ed., R&P Susan Myers. Circ: 3,000.

DOVETAIL (ONLINE EDITION); a journal by and for Jewish/Christian families. *see* ETHNIC INTERESTS

242.72 USA ISSN 0748-4682
BX8201
➤ **DOXOLOGY.** Text in English. 1984. a. USD 10 per issue (effective 2010). **Document type:** *Journal, Academic/Scholarly.* **Description:** Offers a service to the academic world as well as those who are involved in the active practice of ministry in its many contexts.
Indexed: R&TA.
Published by: The Order of Saint Luke, 25 Tressel St, White Sulphur Springs, WV 24986. chancellor@saint-luke.org, http://www.saint-luke.net/. Ed. E Byron Anderson.

➤ **DREAMS & VISIONS**; new frontiers in Christian fiction. *see* LITERATURE

200 AUT ISSN 0012-6764
DRUZINA IN DOM. Text in Slovenian. m. **Document type:** *Magazine, Consumer.*
Published by: Druzba Sv. Mohorja, Viktringer Ring 26, Klagenfurt, K 9020, Austria. TEL 43-463-5651521, FAX 43-463-514189, office@mohorjeva.at.

230 SVN ISSN 1408-0931
DRUZINSKA KNJIZNICA. Text in Slovenian. 1975. irreg. **Document type:** *Monographic series, Academic/Scholarly.*
Published by: Mohorjeva Druzba, Presernova c 23, pp 150, Celje, 3001, Slovenia. TEL 386-3-4264800, FAX 386-3-4264810, info@mohorjeva-druzba-ce.si, http://www.mohorjeva.org.

200 SVN ISSN 1408-4287
DRUZINSKA PRATIKA. Text in Slovenian. 19??. a. EUR 4.80 newsstand/cover (effective 2010). **Document type:** *Magazine, Consumer.*
Published by: Mohorjeva Druzba, Presernova c 23, pp 150, Celje, 3001, Slovenia. TEL 386-3-4264800, FAX 386-3-4264810, info@mohorjeva-druzba-ce.si, http://www.mohorjeva.org.

200 NLD ISSN 1878-8106
▼ **DYNAMICS IN THE HISTORY OF RELIGIONS.** Text in English. 2010. irreg., latest vol.2, 2011. EUR 126, USD 179 per vol. (effective 2010). **Document type:** *Monographic series, Academic/Scholarly.* **Description:** Focuses on the crucial role of mutual encounters in the origins, development and internal differentiation of the major religious traditions.
Related titles: Online - full text ed.: ISSN 1878-8114.
Published by: Brill, PO Box 9000, Leiden, 2300 PA, Netherlands. TEL 31-71-5353500, FAX 31-71-5317532, cs@brill.nl. Ed. Volkhard Krech.

200 NGA ISSN 1117-1073
E C W A THEOLOGICAL SEMINARY. JOURNAL; journal of the faculty of ECWA Theological Seminary, Igbaja. (Evangelical Church of West Africa) Text in English. 1995. s-a. **Document type:** *Journal, Academic/Scholarly.*
Indexed: A21, RI-1.
Published by: Evangelical Church of West Africa, Zaria Road, Farin Gada, PO Box 5398, Jos, Plateau State, Nigeria. TEL 234-73-53574.

200 CHE ISSN 1606-4372
E E F - N E T. (Education and Ecumenical Formation) Text in English. 1999. 3/yr. **Document type:** *Newsletter, Academic/Scholarly.* **Description:** Provides a forum to share information across the many networks of ecumenical education around the world.
Related titles: Spanish ed.: ISSN 1606-4380. 1999; French ed.: ISSN 1609-1574. 2000.
Published by: Education and Ecumenical Formation (Subsidiary of: World Council of Churches), 150 route de Ferney, PO Box 2100, Geneva 2, 1211, Switzerland. TEL 41-22-791-61-13, FAX 41-22-791-03-61, ger@wcc-coe.org, http://www.wcc-coe.org/wcc/what/education/index-e.html. Ed. Gert Rueppell.

200 TUR ISSN 1309-5803
E - MAKALAT MEZHEP ARASTIRMALARI DERGISI. Text in Turkish, English. 2008. irreg. free (effective 2011). **Document type:** *Journal, Academic/Scholarly.*
Media: Online - full text.
Address: c/o Ahmet Ishak Denir, Ilahiyat Fakultesi, Rize Universitesi, Rize, 53100, Turkey. Ed. Ahmet Ishak Demir.

200 CHE ISSN 1420-4126
BX1
E N I BULLETIN. Text in English. 24/yr. CHF 95, USD 71.50 (effective 2000). **Document type:** *Bulletin, Consumer.*
Formerly (until 1994): Ecumenical Press Service (1023-4667)
Related titles: Online - full text ed.; French ed.: E N I Bulletin. Edition Francaise. ISSN 1421-3672. 1934.
Published by: Ecumenical News International, 150 route de Ferney, PO Box 2100, Geneva 2, 1211, Switzerland. TEL 41-22-7916087, FAX 41-22-7887244. Eds. Edmund Doogue, Stephen Brown. Circ: 2,300.

230 323.4 USA ISSN 1551-9325
BS680.S53
E-QUALITY. Text in English. 2002. q. free (effective 2010). back issues avail. **Document type:** *Journal, Academic/Scholarly.* **Description:** Provides practical information on biblical equality and justice for those who are exploring biblical equality.
Media: Online - full text.
Indexed: A01, CA, T02.
Published by: Christians for Biblical Equality, 122 W Franklin Ave, Ste 218, Minneapolis, MN 55404. TEL 612-872-6898, FAX 612-872-6891, cbe@cbeinternational.org. Ed. Jessica Colund. Pub. Mimi Haddad.

200 DEU ISSN 0344-9106
E Z W - TEXTE; Informationen - Impulse - Arbeitstexte. Text in German. 1970. irreg., latest vol.204, 2009. price varies. adv. back issues avail. **Document type:** *Monographic series, Academic/Scholarly.*
Published by: (Evangelische Kirche in Deutschland), Evangelische Zentralstelle fuer Weltanschauungsfragen, Auguststr 80, Berlin, 10117, Germany. TEL 49-30-28395211, FAX 49-30-28395212, info@ezw-berlin.de. Circ: 11,000.

230 DEU ISSN 1868-7032
▼ **EARLY CHRISTIANITY.** Text in English, German. 2010. 4/yr. EUR 49 to individuals; EUR 199 to institutions (effective 2012). **Document type:** *Journal, Academic/Scholarly.*
Related titles: Online - full text ed.: (from IngentaConnect).
Published by: Mohr Siebeck GmbH & Co. KG, Wilhelmstr 18, Tuebingen, 72074, Germany. TEL 49-7071-9230, FAX 49-7071-51104, info@mohr.de.

230 NLD ISSN 1878-4887
▼ **EARLY CHRISTIANITY AND ITS LITERATURE.** Variant title: E C I L. Text in English. 2009. irreg., latest vol.4, 2010. price varies. **Document type:** *Monographic series, Academic/Scholarly.*
Published by: (Society of Biblical Literature USA), Brill, PO Box 9000, Leiden, 2300 PA, Netherlands. TEL 31-71-5353500, FAX 31-71-5317532, cs@brill.nl. Ed. Gail R O'Day.

230 DEU ISSN 1862-197X
EARLY CHRISTIANITY IN THE CONTEXT OF ANTIQUITY. Text in German, English. 2006. irreg., latest vol.6, 2010. price varies. **Document type:** *Monographic series, Academic/Scholarly.*
Published by: Peter Lang GmbH (Subsidiary of: Peter Lang Publishing Group), Eschborner Landstr 42-50, Frankfurt Am Main, 60489, Germany. TEL 49-69-7807050, FAX 49-69-78070550, zentrale.frankfurt@peterlang.com. Ed. Joerg Ulrich.

202 USA ISSN 1050-0413
GF80
EARTHLIGHT; the magazine of spirituality ecology. Text in English. 1990. q. USD 24 domestic; USD 31 in Canada & Mexico; USD 45 elsewhere (effective 2005). adv. bk.rev.; music rev. back issues avail. **Document type:** *Magazine, Consumer.* **Description:** Addresses the environmental crisis from the perspective that it has its roots in the crisis of the human spirit.
Published by: Earthlight Magazine, 111 Fairmount Ave, Oakland, CA 94611. TEL 510-451-4926, FAX 510-451-3505. Ed., R&P K Lauren de Boer TEL 510-451-4976. Adv. contact Loretta A Peters TEL 510-451-4926. B&W page USD 350; trim 11 x 8.5. Circ: 3,000 (paid).

230 USA ISSN 1069-5664
EAST-WEST CHURCH & MINISTRY REPORT. Text in English. 1993. q. USD 53.95 in US & Canada to libraries; USD 63.95 elsewhere to libraries; USD 49.45 combined subscription in US & Canada to individuals (print & email eds.); USD 59.95 combined subscription elsewhere to individuals (print & email eds.) (effective 2011). film rev.; software rev.; Website rev.; bk.rev.; video rev. charts; stat.; bibl. Index. 16 p./no. 2 cols./p.; back issues avail.; reprints avail. **Document type:** *Report, Consumer.* **Description:** Encourages effective, culturally relevant and cooperative western Christian ministry in Central and Eastern Europe and the former Soviet Union.
Related titles: E-mail ed.: USD 22.95 (effective 2011).
Indexed: ABS&EES, ChrPI, DIP, IBR, IBZ, PAIS.
Published by: Global Center, Beeson Divinity School, Samford University, 800 Lakeshore Dr, Birmingham, AL 35229. TEL 205-726-2991, 800-888-8266, bdsinfo@samford.edu, http://www.beesondivinity.com. Ed. Dr. Mark R Elliott TEL 864-633-966.

281 USA ISSN 1539-1507
EASTERN CHRISTIAN STUDIES. Text in English. 2002. irreg., latest 2010. price varies. back issues avail. **Document type:** *Monographic series, Academic/Scholarly.* **Description:** Features collections of essays, texts and translations of the documents of Eastern Christianity, and studies of topics relevant to the unique world of historic Orthodoxy and early Christianity.
Published by: Gorgias Press LLC, 954 River Rd, Piscataway, NJ 08854. TEL 732-885-8900, FAX 732-885-8908, helpdesk@gorgiaspress.com, http://www.gorgiaspress.com/bookshop/default.aspx.

200 BEL
EASTERN CHRISTIAN TEXTS IN TRANSLATION. Text in English. 1996. irreg., latest 2000. price varies. bk.rev. back issues avail. **Document type:** *Monographic series, Academic/Scholarly.* **Description:** Presents translations of early Christian texts.
Published by: Peeters Publishers, Bondgenotenlaan 153, Leuven, 3000, Belgium. TEL 32-16-235170, FAX 32-16-228500, http://www.peeters-leuven.be. **Co-sponsor:** Catholic University of America.

230 GBR ISSN 1354-0580
EASTERN CHURCHES JOURNAL. Abbreviated title: E C J. Text in English. 1960. 3/yr. USD 40 in North America; USD 60 elsewhere (effective 2009). **Document type:** *Journal, Academic/Scholarly.* **Description:** Contains articles on the history, theology, liturgy, spirituality, and ecumenical dialogue of the Eastern Churches.
Incorporates (in 1994): Chrysostom (0529-5025)
Indexed: R&TA.
Published by: Society of St. John Chrysostom, 22 Binney St, London, W1Y 1YN, United Kingdom.

220 USA ISSN 0887-7165
EASTERN GREAT LAKES BIBLICAL SOCIETY. PROCEEDINGS. Text in English. 1981. a. **Document type:** *Proceedings.*
Indexed: A21, OTA, R&TA, RI-1.
Published by: Eastern Great Lakes Biblical Society, c/o Holly Toensing, Theology Dept, Xavier University, 3800 Victory Pkwy, Cincinnati, OH 45207. TEL 513-745-3796, toensing@xavier.edu, http://www.jcu.edu/bible/eglbs.

230 PRT ISSN 0872-3664
EBORENSIA. Variant title: Revista do Instituto Superior de Teologia de Evora. Text in Portuguese. 1988. irreg.
Indexed: OTA.
Published by: Instituto Superior de Teologia, Rua Vasco da Gama, 7, Apart. 2115, Evora, 7001-901, Portugal. TEL 351-266-746342, FAX 351-266-746341, istevora@mail.telepac.pt, http://www.diocese-evora.pt/html/iste.htm.

200 NLD
ECCLESIA. Text in Dutch. bi-w. EUR 22 (effective 2008).
Formerly (until 1989): Kerkblaadje (0166-705X)
Published by: Stichting Vrienden van Dr. H. F. Kohlbrugge, Baron Bentinckstr 51, Ommen, 7731 EK, Netherlands. TEL 31-529-456729, http://www.ecclesianet.nl. Eds. H Klink, L J Geluk.

330 282 POL ISSN 1895-1414
ECCLESIA. Text in Polish. 2006. bi-m. PLZ 64 domestic (effective 2011). **Description:** Designed for clergy, it covers the most important issues: finance, taxes, insurance, real estate administration, business and publishing in the parish.
Related titles: Online - full text ed.
Published by: Wydawnictwo Elamed, Al Rozdzienskiego 188, Katowice, 40203, Poland. TEL 48-32-2580361, FAX 48-32-2039356, elamed@elamed.com.pl, http://www.elamed.com.pl. Ed. Dorota Bartoszek.

200 NLD ISSN 1572-5022
ECCLESIA IN FASNA. Text in Dutch. 2005. q. **Document type:** *Magazine, Consumer.*
Media: Online - full text.
Published by: Wim Van 't Einde, Ed. & Pub. wimvanteinde@gmail.com, http://www.ecclesia-in-fasna.nl.

230 GBR ISSN 1759-6513
▼ **ECCLESIA REFORMANDA.** Text in English. 2009. s-a. GBP 15 domestic; GBP 18 in the European Union; GBP 20 elsewhere (effective 2010). back issues avail. **Document type:** *Magazine, Consumer.*
Address: PO Box 257, Lowestoft, NR32 9EU, United Kingdom. Ed. Matthew Mason.

230.071 NLD ISSN 1744-1366
BV593
➤ **ECCLESIOLOGY**; the journal for ministry, mission and unity. Text in English. 2004. 3/yr. EUR 191, USD 268 to institutions; EUR 209, USD 293 combined subscription to institutions (print & online eds.) (effective 2012). adv. reprint service avail. from PSC. **Document type:** *Journal, Academic/Scholarly.* **Description:** Designed to meet the growing demand for theological resources in the area of ecclesiology the scholarly study of the nature and purpose of the Christian Church.
Related titles: Online - full text ed.: ISSN 1745-5316. EUR 174, USD 244 to institutions (effective 2012) (from IngentaConnect).
Indexed: A01, A02, A03, A08, A22, CA, E01, IZBG, T02.
—IE. **CCC.**
Published by: (Centre for the Study of the Christian Church GBR), Brill, PO Box 9000, Leiden, 2300 PA, Netherlands. TEL 31-71-5353500, FAX 31-71-5317532, cs@brill.nl. Ed. Paul Avis. adv.: B&W page GBP 300; 130 x 200.

200 DEU
ECHO AUS AFRIKA UND ANDERN ERDTEILEN. Text in German. 1888. 10/yr. **Document type:** *Newsletter.*
Published by: St. Petrus Claver Sodalitaet, Billerstr 20, Augsburg, 86154, Germany. TEL 49-821-414077, FAX 49-821-426048. Circ: 26,000.

268 CHE
ECHOES; justice, peace and creation news. Text in English. 2/yr. **Document type:** *Bulletin.*
Published by: (J.P.C. Team), World Council of Churches, 150 route de Ferney, PO Box 2100, Geneva 2, 1211, Switzerland. TEL 41-22-791-6111, FAX 41-22-791-6409. Circ: 7,000.

202 USA
ECK SPIRITUALITY TODAY. Text in English. 1976. a. USD 5 (effective 2000). adv. 84 p./no.; **Document type:** *Journal, Consumer.* **Description:** Contains personal spiritual experiences that have changed people's lives, as well as a feature article by Sri Harold Klemp, the spiritual leader of Eckankar, exercises and approaches to experience the essence of God.
Former titles: Eckankar Journal; (until 1988): Eck Mata Journal; Eck News
Published by: Eckankar, PO Box 27300, Minneapolis, MN 55427-0300. TEL 612-544-3001, FAX 612-544-3754. Ed. Mary Carroll Moore. R&P John Kulick TEL 612-474-0700. Adv. contact Jon Goin. Circ: 12,000 (paid).

ECOLE PRATIQUE DES HAUTES ETUDES, SECTION DES SCIENCES RELIGIEUSES. ANNUAIRE. *see* SCIENCES: COMPREHENSIVE WORKS

200 FRA ISSN 0070-8860
ECRITS LIBRES. Text in French. 1955. irreg., latest 2010. price varies.
Published by: Librairie Fischbacher, 33 rue de Seine, Paris, 75006, France. TEL 33-1-43268487, FAX 33-1-43264887, http://www.librairiefischbacher.fr.

200 USA ISSN 0013-0761
ECUMENICAL COURIER. Text in English. 1941. irreg. (2-4/yr.). USD 15 donation (effective 2000). bk.rev. **Document type:** *Newsletter, Consumer.*
Published by: United States Conference for the World Council of Churches, 475 Riverside Dr, 915, New York, NY 10115. TEL 212-870-2533, FAX 212-870-2528. Ed., R&P Philip E Jenks TEL 212-870-3193. Pub. Jean S Stromberg. Circ: 5,000.

200 CHE
ECUMENICAL LETTER ON EVANGELISM. Text in English. 1956. irreg. (3-4/yr.). **Document type:** *Newsletter.*
Formerly (until 1994): Monthly Letter on Evangelism
Related titles: German ed.; French ed.
Indexed: CERDIC.
Published by: (Unit II - Team on Mission & Evangelism), World Council of Churches, 150 route de Ferney, PO Box 2100, Geneva 2, 1211, Switzerland. TEL 41-22-791-6111, FAX 41-22-791-0361. Ed. Ana Langeraki. Circ: 4,000.

200 GBR ISSN 0013-0796
BX1
THE ECUMENICAL REVIEW. Text in English. 19??. q. GBP 148 in United Kingdom to institutions; EUR 187 in Europe to institutions; USD 235 elsewhere to institutions; GBP 170 combined subscription in United Kingdom to institutions (print & online eds.); EUR 216 combined subscription in Europe to institutions (print & online eds.); USD 271 combined subscription elsewhere to institutions (print & online eds.) (effective 2012). adv. bk.rev. illus. index. back issues avail.; reprint service avail. from PSC. **Document type:** *Bulletin, Consumer.*
Description: Focuses on a theme of current importance to the movement for Christian unity, and each volume includes academic as well as practical analysis of significant moments in the quest for closer church fellowship and inter-religious dialogue.
Incorporates (1935-1948): Christendom (0190-4043); Which superseded (in 1935): Christian Union Quarterly
Related titles: Microfilm ed.: (from PQC); Online - full text ed.: ISSN 1758-6623. GBP 148 in United Kingdom to institutions; EUR 187 in Europe to institutions; USD 235 elsewhere to institutions (effective 2012).
Indexed: A01, A02, A03, A08, A20, A21, A22, A26, ASCA, AmHI, ArtHuCI, B04, B14, BRD, BRI, CA, CBRI, CERDIC, CurCont, DIP, E01, E08, FR, G06, G07, G08, H07, H08, H09, H10, H14, HAb, HumInd, I05, IBR, IBZ, MEA&I, MLA-IB, OTA, P02, P10, P13, P28, P30, P48, P53, P54, PCI, PQC, PRA, R&TA, R05, RI-1, RI-2, RILM, S05, S09, SCOPUS, T02, W03, W05, W07.
—BLDSC (3659.700000), IE, Infotrieve, Ingenta. **CCC.**
Published by: (World Council of Churches CHE), Wiley-Blackwell Publishing Ltd. (Subsidiary of: John Wiley & Sons, Inc.), 9600 Garsington Rd, Oxford, OX4 2DQ, United Kingdom. TEL 44-1865-776868, FAX 44-1865-714591, customer@wiley.co.uk. Ed. Theodore Gill.

200 USA ISSN 0360-9073
BX1
ECUMENICAL TRENDS. Text in English. 1972. m. USD 25 domestic; USD 27 foreign (effective 2010). bk.rev. reprints avail. **Document type:** *Journal, Academic/Scholarly.* **Description:** Provides news, opinion, documentation and features in the area of ecumenical and inter-religious activity. Directed toward persons involved in ecumenism and church leadership.
Related titles: Microform ed.: (from PQC).
Indexed: A21, A22, CPL, RI-1, RI-2.
—BLDSC (3659.702000), IE, Ingenta.
Published by: Franciscan Friars of the Atonement, 1350 Route 9, PO Box 306, Garrison, NY 10524. TEL 914-424-3671, 800-338-2620, FAX 845-424-2168.

200 CAN ISSN 0383-431X
ECUMENISM. Text in English. 1966. q. CAD 15, USD 17.50 (effective 2002). adv. bk.rev. 48 p./no. 2 cols./p.;
Related titles: Microfilm ed.: (from PQC); French ed.: Oecumenisme. ISSN 0383-4301.
Indexed: A21, A22, RI-1, RI-2, RILM.
Published by: Canadian Centre for Ecumenism/Oecumenisme, 2065 Sherbrooke St W, Montreal, PQ H3H 1G6, Canada. TEL 514-937-9176, FAX 514-937-4986, ccocce@total.net. Circ: 1,600 (paid).

261 CAN ISSN 0013-080X
BX1
THE ECUMENIST. Text in English. 1964. 4/yr. CAD 15 domestic; USD 15 in United States; USD 18 elsewhere (effective 2000). bk.rev. reprints avail.
Indexed: CERDIC, CPL, OTA, PQC.
—CCC.
Published by: Novalis, St Paul University, 223 Main St, Ottawa, ON K1S 1C4, Canada. TEL 613-236-1393, FAX 613-782-3004, http://www.novalis.ca. Ed. Gregory Baum. Circ: 5,300. **Subscr. to:** 49 Front St E, 2nd Fl, Toronto, ON M5E 1B3, Canada. TEL 800-387-7164, FAX 800-204-4140.

EDIFICATION; the journal of the Society for Christian Psychology. *see* PSYCHOLOGY

291 DEU ISSN 1866-427X
▼ **EDITION ISRAELOGIE.** Text in German. 2009. irreg., latest vol.3, 2010. price varies. **Document type:** *Monographic series, Academic/Scholarly.*
Published by: Peter Lang GmbH (Subsidiary of: Peter Lang Publishing Group), Eschborner Landstr 42-50, Frankfurt Am Main, 60489, Germany. TEL 49-69-7807050, FAX 49-69-78070550, zentrale.frankfurt@peterlang.com. Eds. Berthold Schwarz, Helge Stadelmann.

266 NLD ISSN 1871-8248
EEN WOORD UIT JERUZALEM. Text in Dutch. 2001. 5/yr.
Formerly (until 2005): Internationale Christelijke Ambassade Jeruzalem. Nieuwsbrief (1570-2227)
Published by: Internationale Christelijke Ambassade Jeruzalem, Nederlandse Afdeling/International Christian Embassy Jerusalem, Postbus 40180, Zwolle, 8004 DD, Netherlands. TEL 31-38-7501283, info@icej.nl.

230 NLD ISSN 0165-4268
DE EERSTE DAG. Text in Dutch. 1978. q. EUR 43; EUR 32.25 to students; EUR 14 newsstand/cover (effective 2008). adv.
Description: Ecumenical liturgical schedule with suggestions for psalms and hymns, exegetic study, and ideas for children in the church.
Published by: Boekencentrum Uitgevers, Goudstraat 50, Postbus 29, Zoetermeer, 2700 AA, Netherlands. TEL 31-79-3615481, FAX 31-79-3615489, info@boekencentrum.nl, http://www.boekencentrum.nl. adv.: page EUR 350; trim 210 x 297. Circ: 3,100.

200 CAN ISSN 0013-2322
L'EGLISE CANADIENNE; documents et informations. Text in French. 1968. m. (11/yr.). CAD 34.95 domestic; USD 42 in United States; CAD 65 elsewhere (effective 1999). adv. bk.rev. index. **Document type:** *Journal, Academic/Scholarly.* **Description:** Features studies and information on theological questions. Also covers life in the church in a general sense.
Indexed: CERDIC, PdeR.
Published by: Revue L'Eglise Canadienne, 6255 rue Hutchison, Bur 103, Montreal, PQ H2V 4C7, Canada. TEL 514-278-3025, 800-668-2547, FAX 514-278-3030. Ed., R&P Pierre Chouinard. Adv. contact Carmen Milette. Circ: 4,000.

291 150 DEU ISSN 1435-2435
EINBLICKE (FRANKFURT AM MAIN, 1998); Beitraege zur Religionspsychologie. Text in German. 1998. irreg., latest vol.4, 2002. price varies. **Document type:** *Monographic series, Academic/Scholarly.*
Published by: Peter Lang GmbH (Subsidiary of: Peter Lang Publishing Group), Eschborner Landstr 42-50, Frankfurt Am Main, 60489, Germany. TEL 49-69-7807050, FAX 49-69-78070550, zentrale.frankfurt@peterlang.com.

230 DEU ISSN 1865-8792
▼ **EKSTASIS**; religious experience from antiquity to the middle ages. Text in English. 2009. irreg., latest vol.3, 2011. price varies. **Document type:** *Monographic series, Academic/Scholarly.*
Published by: Walter de Gruyter GmbH & Co. KG, Genthiner Str 13, Berlin, 10785, Germany. TEL 49-30-26005220, FAX 49-30-26005251, info@degruyter.com, http://www.degruyter.de. Ed. John Levison.

200 ITA ISSN 1127-2554
EKUMENISMO; trimonata internacia gazeto pri ekumenaj temoj kaj aferoj. Text in Esperanto. 1985. q. **Document type:** *Newspaper, Consumer.*
Published by: Tutmonda Ekumena Ligo, Via Francesco Berni 9, Rome, RM 00185, Italy.

290 375.4 DEU ISSN 0724-4452
ELEMENTA THEOLOGIAE; Arbeiten zur Theologie und Religionspaedagogik. Text in German. 1984. irreg., latest vol.12, 2006. price varies. **Document type:** *Monographic series, Academic/Scholarly.*
Published by: Peter Lang GmbH (Subsidiary of: Peter Lang Publishing Group), Eschborner Landstr 42-50, Frankfurt Am Main, 60489, Germany. TEL 49-69-7807050, FAX 49-69-78070550, zentrale.frankfurt@peterlang.com. Ed. Roland Kollmann.

200 NLD ISSN 2211-5927
ELISABET. Text in Dutch. 1929. bi-w. EUR 34.95 domestic; EUR 68 in Europe; EUR 79 elsewhere (effective 2011). adv. **Document type:** *Magazine, Consumer.*
Formerly (until 2011): Elisabethbode (0013-6212)
Published by: Inspirit Media, Postbus 1577, Zwolle, 8001, Netherlands. TEL 31-88-3263330, http://www.inspiritmedia.nl. Eds. Marian Heek, Jeanet van der Linden. Circ: 66,920.

200 USA ISSN 8756-1336
ELISABETH ELLIOT NEWSLETTER. Text in English. 1982. bi-m. USD 7. bk.rev. back issues avail. **Document type:** *Newsletter.* **Description:** Publishes inspirational articles for a Christian audience.
Published by: (Servant Ministries), Servant Publications, PO Box 7711, Ann Arbor, MI 48107-7711. TEL 734-677-6490, FAX 734-677-6685. Ed., R&P Kathryn Deering TEL 734-677-1276. Circ: 18,000.

200 USA ISSN 2153-6120
▼ **EMAIL COMMUNIQUE OF THE SOCIETY OF KING CHARLES, THE MARTYR, AMERICAN REGION.** Text in English. 2009. m. free (effective 2010). back issues avail. **Document type:** *Journal, Academic/Scholarly.* **Description:** Provides information about the Society of King Charles and related theologies.
Media: Online - full text.
Published by: Society of King Charles the Martyr, Inc., 5500 Friendship Blvd, Ste 2009 N, Chevy Chase, MD 20815. http://www.skcm-usa.org/. Ed. Mark A Wuonola.

200 CAN ISSN 1481-4412
EMBRACE THE SPIRIT. Text in English. 1979. s-a. free to members. bk.rev. **Document type:** *Journal, Academic/Scholarly.* **Description:** Contains articles on ethical and moral issues, trends in religious education and the relationship between education and religious & moral issues.
Formerly (until 1999): Salt (0709-616X)
Related titles: Microfiche ed.: (from MML).
Indexed: C03, CEI, P48, PQC.
Published by: Alberta Teachers' Association, Religious Studies & Moral Education Council, 11010 142nd St NW, Edmonton, AB T5N 2R1, Canada. Ed. Rose Marie Hague. Circ: 242.

250 CAN
EMMAUS; a newsletter for friends of the C C C. Text in English. 1970. s-a. donation. bk.rev. **Document type:** *Newsletter, Consumer.*
Description: News and views from across Canada about the work of the CCC, its member churches, overseas partners and inter-church coalitions.
Former titles (until 199?): C C C Echo (1209-059X); (until 1995): Canadian Council of Churches. Entre - Nous (1184-0447); (until 1988): Canadian Council of Churches. News Bulletin (0835-8427); (until 1987): Canadian Council of Churches. Council Communicator (0045-4605)
Related titles: Microform ed.: 1970 (from MML); Online - full content ed.; French ed.: 1970.
Published by: Canadian Council of Churches, 47 Queen's Park Crescent East, Toronto, ON M5S 2C3, Canada. TEL 416-972-9494, 866-822-7645, FAX 416-927-0405, admin@ccc-cce.ca. Circ: 3,000.

207.2 USA ISSN 0194-5246
EMPHASIS ON FAITH AND LIVING. Text in English. 1969. bi-m. USD 15 foreign (effective 2001). adv. bk.rev. **Document type:** *Magazine, Trade.* **Description:** Communicates message and ministry of the Missionary Church.
Indexed: GSS&RPL.
Published by: Missionary Church, Inc., PO Box 9127, Ft. Wayne, IN 46899. TEL 219-747-2027, FAX 219-747-5331, mcdenomusa@aol.com. Ed. Robert L Ransom. R&P Robert Ransom. Circ: 13,000.

▼ **EMPIRICAL RESEARCH IN RELIGION AND HUMAN RIGHTS.** *see* POLITICAL SCIENCE

EMPIRICAL STUDIES IN THEOLOGY. *see* SOCIOLOGY

248.83 305.23 USA
ENCOUNTER (CINCINNATI). Text in English. 1951. w. USD 17.99 per issue (effective 2009). illus. 8 p./no.; back issues avail. **Document type:** *Magazine, Consumer.* **Description:** Contains articles graphically appealing, culturally relevant and biblically centered.
Formerly: Straight; Which was formed by the 1980 merger of: Glad; Now; Which was formerly (until 1977): Straight (0039-2081)
Related titles: CD-ROM ed.
Published by: Standard Publishing, 8805 Governor's Hill Dr, Ste 400, Cincinnati, OH 45249. TEL 513-931-4050, 800-543-1353, FAX 877-867-5751, customerservice@standardpub.com, http://www.standardpub.com. Ed. Kelly Carr. Pub., R&P Mark A Taylor. Circ: 50,000.

200 USA ISSN 0013-7081
BR1
ENCOUNTER (INDIANAPOLIS). Text in English. 1940. q. USD 18 (effective 2010). adv. bk.rev. index. reprints avail. **Document type:** *Journal, Academic/Scholarly.* **Description:** Discusses creative theological scholarship among believers in Christ and people of other faiths.
Formerly (until 1956): Shane Quarterly (0362-4609)
Related titles: Microfilm ed.: (from PQC); Online - full text ed.
Indexed: A21, A22, AmH&L, GSS&RPL, H09, H10, H14, HistAb, IZBG, MLA-IB, OTA, P02, P10, P28, P30, P48, P53, P54, PQC, PhilInd, RI-1, RI-2.
—BLDSC (3738.540000), IE, Infotrieve, Ingenta.
Published by: Christian Theological Seminary, 1000 W 42nd St, Indianapolis, IN 46208. TEL 317-924-1331, FAX 317-923-1961, ssemmler@cts.edu.

268 USA
ENCOUNTER (LINCOLN); for the blind. Text in English. q. free to qualified personnel (effective 2011). back issues avail. **Document type:** *Magazine, Consumer.* **Description:** Features sermons, answers to Bible questions, and in-depth guides to Bible doctrine for adults with visual impairments.
Media: Audio cassette/tape.
Published by: Christian Record Services, PO Box 6097, Lincoln, NE 68506. TEL 402-488-0981, FAX 402-488-7582, info@christianrecord.org, http://www.christianrecord.org.

230 ZAF
ENCOUNTER WITH GOD (SOUTH AFRICAN EDITION). Text in English. 1986. q. ZAR 8.50 per issue.
Formerly (until 1994): Daily Notes
Published by: Scripture Union, PO Box 291, Rondebosch, Cape Town 7701, South Africa. Ed. Tony Hobbs.

ENCOUNTERS; documents for Muslim Christian understanding. *see* RELIGIONS AND THEOLOGY—Islamic

230 ESP ISSN 1131-6519
➤ **ENCRUCILLADA**; revista galega de pensamento cristian. 1977. 5/yr. EUR 18; EUR 12 to students (effective 2008). bk.rev. illus. 94 p./no.; back issues avail. **Document type:** *Journal, Academic/Scholarly.*
Published by: Asociacion Encrucillada, Travesa de Vista Alegre 21, 1o. C, Santiago de Compostela, Spain. TEL 34-482-881978447, encrucillado@encrucillado.org.es, http://www.encrucillado.org.es/. Eds. Andres Torres, Xaime Manuel Gonzalez Ortega. Circ: 1,400.

200 USA ISSN 1066-1212
BL2525
ENCYCLOPEDIA OF AMERICAN RELIGIONS. Text in English. 1987. irreg., latest 2009, 8th ed. USD 362 per issue (effective 2009). **Document type:** *Monographic series, Academic/Scholarly.* **Description:** Details approximately 1,600 religious groups of North America, ranging from adventists to zen buddhists.
Related titles: Online - full text ed.
Published by: Gale (Subsidiary of: Cengage Learning), 27500 Drake Rd, Farmington Hills, MI 48331. TEL 248-699-4253, 800-877-4253, FAX 877-363-4253, gale.galeord@cengage.com. Ed. J Gordon Melton.

200 FRA ISSN 2100-1235
▼ **LES ENIGMES DU SACRE.** Text in French. 2009. q. EUR 8 newsstand/cover (effective 2011). **Document type:** *Magazine, Consumer.*
Published by: Export Press, 91 Rue de Turenne, Paris, 75003, France. TEL 33-1-40291451, FAX 33-1-42720743, dir@exportpress.com, http://www.exportpress.com.

200 FRA ISSN 2104-8134
▼ **LES ENIGMES DU SACRE. HORS-SERIE.** Text in French. 2009. a. EUR 12.50 newsstand/cover (effective 2011). **Document type:** *Magazine, Consumer.*
Published by: Export Press, 91 Rue de Turenne, Paris, 75003, France. TEL 33-1-40291451, FAX 33-1-42720743, dir@exportpress.com, http://www.exportpress.com.

204.2 USA ISSN 1946-0805
ENLIGHTENNEXT; the magazine for evolutionaries. Text in English. 1991. q. USD 23.95 domestic; USD 31.95 in Canada; USD 35.95 elsewhere; USD 7.50 per issue (effective 2009). adv. bk.rev. illus. 170 p./no.; back issues avail.; reprints avail. **Document type:** *Magazine, Consumer.* **Description:** Acts as forum for a penetrating investigation of important and challenging questions facing contemporary spiritual seekers.
Formerly (until 2008): What is Enlightenment? (1080-3432)
Related titles: Online - full text ed.: USD 19.95 (effective 2009).
Indexed: APW, T02.
—CCC.

R

Address: PO Box 2360, Lenox, MA 01240. TEL 413-637-6000, 800-376-3210, FAX 413-637-6015, info@EnlightenNext.org. Ed. Andrew Cohen. adv.: color page USD 1,795; trim 8.75 x 10.875. Circ: 75,000. **Subscr. to:** PO Box 9010, Maple Shade, NJ 08052. subscriptions@enlightennext.org.

230 ESP
ENSENANZA DE LA RELIGION. Text in Spanish. 1982. irreg., latest 2005. price varies.
Published by: (Universidad de Navarra, Facultad de Teologia), Universidad de Navarra, Servicio de Publicaciones, Campus Universitario, Pamplona, 31009, Spain. TEL 34-948-256850, FAX 34-948-256854, http://www.unav.es/publicaciones/.

262 ITA ISSN 0013-9505
EPHEMERIDES LITURGICAE; commentarium trimestre de re liturgica. Text in Multiple languages. 1887. q. EUR 28 domestic; EUR 40 in Europe; EUR 45 elsewhere (effective 2009). adv. bk.rev. 128 p./no.; reprints avail. **Document type:** *Journal, Academic/Scholarly.*
Indexed: A21, A22, CERDIC, CLA, DIP, FR, IBR, IBZ, MLA-IB, RI-1, RI-2, RILM.
—IE, Infotrieve, INIST.
Published by: (Centro Liturgico Vincenziano), C L V Edizioni Liturgiche, Via Pompeo Magno 21, Rome, 00192, Italy. TEL 39-06-3216114, FAX 39-06-3221078, http://www2.chiesacattolica.it/clv/. Circ: 1,500.

262 ITA
EPHEMERIDES LITURGICAE. BIBLIOTHECA. COLLECTIO SUBSIDIA. Text in Multiple languages. 1974. irreg., latest vol.115, 2001. price varies. **Document type:** *Monographic series, Academic/Scholarly.*
Indexed: RI-2.
Published by: (Centro Liturgico Vincenziano), C L V Edizioni Liturgiche, Via Pompeo Magno 21, Rome, 00192, Italy. TEL 39-06-3216114, FAX 39-06-3221078, http://www2.chiesacattolica.it/clv/.

200 ARG ISSN 0327-8514
BL51
EPIMELIA. Text in Spanish. 1992. s-a. ARS 25 domestic; USD 30 foreign (effective 2010). **Document type:** *Journal, Academic/Scholarly.*
Indexed: MLA-IB.
Published by: Universidad Argentina John F. Kennedy, Centro de Investigaciones en Filosofia e Historia de las Religiones, Bartolome Mitre, 1411, Buenos Aires, 1037, Argentina. TEL 54-11-43740730, info@kennedy.edu.ar, http://www.kennedy.edu.ar/. Circ: 500.

291 USA ISSN 1089-1307
EPIPHANY INTERNATIONAL. Text in English. 1995. a. **Document type:** *Journal, Academic/Scholarly.* **Description:** Aims to prepare scholars, teachers, and practitioners in the new field of formative spirituality.
Related titles: Online - full text ed.: USD 15 per issue (effective 2010).
Indexed: AmHI, CA, H07, R&TA, T02.
Published by: Epiphany Association, 820 Crane Ave, Pittsburgh, PA 15216. TEL 412-341-7494, 877-324-6873, FAX 412-341-7495, info@epiphanyassociation.org. Ed. Susan Muto.

200 901 USA ISSN 0149-3043
BL41
EPOCHE; journal of the history of religions at U.C.L.A. Text in English. 1972. a. USD 6. cum.index: 1972-82. back issues avail.
Formerly (until 1976): History of Religions Newsletter (0360-6147)
Indexed: A21, RI-1, RI-2.
Published by: University of California, Los Angeles, Graduate Students Association, 301 Kerckhoff Hall, 308 Westwood Plaza, Los Angeles, CA 90024. Ed. Rick Talbott. Circ: 850. **Subscr. to:** Department of History, UCLA, Los Angeles, CA 90024.

240 USA ISSN 1942-3306
EQUIPPING THE MAN IN THE MIRROR. Text in English. 2006. bi-m. USD 25 (effective 2008). **Document type:** *Magazine, Consumer.* **Description:** Features devotionals, scripture and stories to assist Christian male leaders in inspiring and helping others.
Formerly (until 200?): The Fourth Seed (1939-2885)
Published by: Man in the Mirror, 180 Wilshire Blvd., Casselberry, FL 32707. TEL 407-472-2100, 800-929-2536, FAX 407-331-7839.

ERASMUS OF ROTTERDAM SOCIETY YEARBOOK. *see* PHILOSOPHY

230 ZAF ISSN 1818-9342
DIE ERDEKRUIK/VESSEL. Text in Afrikaans, English. 1998. m. **Document type:** *Newspaper.*
Published by: Tydlose Nuus die Erdekruik cc, PO Box 18844, Pretoria North, 0116, South Africa. Circ: 30,000.

200 DEU ISSN 0172-1135
ERFAHRUNG UND THEOLOGIE; Schriften zur praktischen Theologie. Text in German. 1978. irreg., latest vol.37, 2010. price varies. **Document type:** *Monographic series, Academic/Scholarly.*
Published by: Peter Lang GmbH (Subsidiary of: Peter Lang Publishing Group), Eschborner Landstr 42-50, Frankfurt Am Main, 60489, Germany. TEL 49-69-7807050, FAX 49-69-78070550, zentrale.frankfurt@peterlang.com.

200 DEU ISSN 0014-0201
ERMLANDBRIEFE. Text in German. 1946. q. free to members. bk.rev. illus. back issues avail. **Document type:** *Newsletter, Consumer.*
Published by: Visitator Ermland, Ermlandweg 22, Muenster, 48159, Germany. TEL 49-251-211477, FAX 49-251-260517, ermlandhaus@visitator-ermland.de. Ed. Johannes Schwalke. Circ: 26,000.

200 ESP ISSN 1579-5276
ES POSIBLE. CONSTRUYAMOS OTRO MUNDO. Text in Spanish. 2002. bi-m. back issues avail. **Document type:** *Bulletin, Consumer.*
Published by: Caritas Espanola, San Bernardo, 99 bis 7a, Madrid, 28015, Spain. TEL 34-91-4441000, FAX 34-91-5934882, publicaciones@caritas-espa.org, http://www.caritas.es.

230 BRA ISSN 1807-2461
ESCOLA SUPERIOR DE TEOLOGIA. INSTITUTO ECUMENICO DE POS-GRADUACAO. SERIE ENSAIOS E MONOGRAFIAS. Key Title: Serie Ensaios e Monografias - IEPG. Text in Portuguese. 199?. a. **Document type:** *Monographic series, Academic/Scholarly.*
Indexed: A21, RI-1.
Published by: Escola Superior de Teologia, Instituto Ecumenico de Pos-Graduacao, Caixa Postal 14, Sao Leopoldo, RGS 93030-220, Brazil. TEL 55-51-21111400, FAX 55-51-21111411, est@est.com.br, http://www.est.com.br/. Ed. Wilhem Walchholz.

230 ESP ISSN 0210-3133
BR45
ESCRITOS DEL VEDAT. Text in Spanish. 1971. a. EUR 24.05 domestic; EUR 30.05 foreign.
Related titles: Online - full text ed.
Indexed: MLA-IB.
—CCC.
Published by: Seccion PP Dominicos. Facultad de Teologia de San Vicente Ferrer, C. Maestro Caphi, 50, Apdo. 136, Torrent, Valencia 46900, Spain. TEL 34-96-1551750, FAX 34-96-1564185, escritosvedat.ar@dominicos.org, http://www.dominicos.org/.

ESPIRITU. *see* PHILOSOPHY

200 FRA ISSN 0014-0775
BX802
ESPRIT ET VIE; revue catholique de formation permanente. Text in French. 1879. s-m. (22/yr). EUR 76 (effective 2009). bk.rev. bibl. index. **Document type:** *Magazine.* **Description:** Discusses readings, the Holy Scripture, theology, philosophy, liturgy, the history of literature, morals.
Formerly (until 1969): Ami du Clerge (1140-8243)
Indexed: CERDIC.
Published by: Editions du Cerf, 29 Boulevard La Tour Maubourg, Paris, 75340 Cedex 07, France. http://www.editionsducerf.fr. Circ: 5,000.

299 FRA ISSN 2116-9489
▼ **ESSENTIEL.** Text in French. 2011. bi-m. **Document type:** *Magazine, Consumer.*
Related titles: Online - full text ed.: ISSN 2115-2829.
Published by: Perle de Rosee, 1 Plan des Ecureuils, Sussargues, 34160, France. TEL 33-4-99634352, http://www.magazine-essentiel.com.

220 ESP ISSN 0014-1437
BS410
ESTUDIOS BIBLICOS. Text in English, French, German, Italian, Spanish. 1941. q. EUR 32 domestic; EUR 66 in Europe; USD 82.50 rest of world (effective 2009). bk.rev. bibl. back issues avail. **Document type:** *Journal, Academic/Scholarly.*
Indexed: A21, A22, DIP, FR, IBR, IBZ, MLA-IB, OTA, P09, PCI, RI-1.
—IE, Infotrieve, INIST.
Published by: Asociacion Biblica Espanola, Buen Suceso, 22, Madrid, 28008, Spain. TEL 34-91-4226265, abe@abe.org.es, http://www.abe.org.es/. Ed. Jose Cervantes Gabarron. Circ: 600.

200 ESP ISSN 0210-1610
BR7
ESTUDIOS ECLESIASTICOS; revista de teologia. Text in Spanish. 1922. q. EUR 33.50 domestic; EUR 44.70 in Europe; USD 65 in US & Canada; USD 60 in Latin America (effective 2008). bk.rev. bibl. **Document type:** *Academic/Scholarly.*
Indexed: A21, CERDIC, CLA, DIP, FR, IBR, IBZ, IZBG, OTA, RI-1, RI-2.
—INIST.
Published by: Universidad Pontificia Comillas de Madrid, Facultad de Teologia, C Universidad Comillas, 3, Madrid, 28049, Spain. TEL 34-91-7343950, FAX 34-91-7344570, revistas@pub.upco.es, http://www.upcomillas.es/.

200 ESP ISSN 0210-0363
ESTUDIOS TRINITARIOS. Text in Spanish. 1963. 3/yr. EUR 40 domestic; EUR 50 in Europe; USD 70 elsewhere (effective 2010). bk.rev. **Document type:** *Magazine, Consumer.*
Indexed: CERDIC.
Published by: Secretariado Trinitario Ediciones, Avda Filiberto Villalobos, 80, Salamanca, 37007, Spain. TEL 34-92-3235602, http://www.secretariadotrinitario.org/. Ed. P Nereo Silanes.

220 BRA ISSN 1676-4951
BS410
ESTUDOS BIBLICOS. Text in Portuguese. 1984. q. BRL 50 domestic; USD 50 foreign (effective 2005). **Document type:** *Journal, Academic/Scholarly.* **Description:** Analyses of the sacred scriptures.
Indexed: OTA.
Published by: Editora Vozes Ltda., Rua Mexico 174, Rio de Janeiro, RJ 20031 143, Brazil. TEL 55-21-22156386, FAX 55-21-25338358, vozes42@uol.com.br, http://www.editoravozes.com.br.

200 FRA ISSN 0245-9329
L'ETENDARD DE LA BIBLE ET HERAUT DU ROYAUME DE CHRIST. Text in French. 1957. bi-m. EUR 8 (effective 2009). **Document type:** *Bulletin.*
Related titles: ◆ English ed.: Bible Standard. ISSN 1556-8555; German ed.; Ukrainian ed.; Polish ed.; Tamil ed.; Danish ed.; Malay ed.
Published by: Mouvement Missionnaire Interieur Laique, c/o Gilbert Hermetz, 2 rue du Dr. Capiaux, Barlin, 62620, France. TEL 33-3-21259486, FAX 33-3-21272650. Ed. Bernard Hedman. Circ: 500.

ETHICS & POLICY. *see* SOCIOLOGY

ETHICS AND PUBLIC POLICY CENTER NEWSLETTER. *see* POLITICAL SCIENCE

200 305.896 USA ISSN 1948-7053
▼ ➤ **ETHIOPIAN JOURNAL OF RELIGIOUS STUDIES.** Text in English. 2010 (Jan.). a. USD 55 to individuals; USD 150 to institutions (effective 2011). **Document type:** *Journal, Academic/Scholarly.* **Description:** Covers topics in religious studies in Ethiopia.
Related titles: Online - full text ed.: ISSN 1948-7061. 2010 (Jan.).
Published by: African Academic Press (Subsidiary of: Tsehai Publishers and Distributors), PO Box 1881, Hollywood, CA 90078. TEL 323-533-7626, ewondimu@tsehaipublishers.com, http://tsehaipublishers.com/aap.

➤ **ETHISCHE PERSPECTIEVEN.** *see* PHILOSOPHY

220 CHE
ETHOS - DIE ZEITSCHRIFT FUER DIE GANZE FAMILIE. Text in German. 1983. m. CHF 62.10 (effective 2001). **Document type:** *Magazine, Consumer.* **Description:** Family oriented magazine of Bible study.
Published by: Schwengeler Verlag AG, Hinterburgstr 8, Berneck, 9442, Switzerland. TEL 41-71-7224358, FAX 41-71-7225665, info@schwengeler.ch, http://www.schwengeler.ch. Ed. Bruno Schwengeler. Circ: 30,000.

200 FRA ISSN 0992-6488
ETUDES D'HISTOIRE ET DE PHILOSOPHIE RELIGIEUSES. Text in French. 1922. irreg., latest 2008. **Document type:** *Journal, Academic/Scholarly.*
Indexed: PCI.
Published by: Presses Universitaires de France, 6 Avenue Reille, Paris, 75685, France. TEL 33-1-58103161, FAX 33-1-45897530, http://www.puf.com.

ETUDES GREGORIENNES; revue de musicologie religieuse. *see* MUSIC

200 060 FRA ISSN 0082-2612
ETUDES TEILHARDIENNES/TEILHARDIAN STUDIES. Text in French. 1969. irreg. price varies. **Document type:** *Monographic series, Academic/Scholarly.*
Indexed: RI-1.
—CCC.
Published by: Editions du Seuil, 27 Rue Jacob, Paris, 75006, France. TEL 33-1-40465050, FAX 33-1-40464300, contact@seuil.com, http://www.seuil.com. Ed. J P Demoulin.

EUROPA DOKUMENTARO. *see* HISTORY—History Of Europe

268 DEU ISSN 0721-3638
EUROPAEISCHE HOCHSCHULSCHRIFTEN. REIHE 33: RELIGIONSPAEDAGOGIK. Text in German. 1976. irreg., latest vol.20, 1999. price varies. **Document type:** *Monographic series, Academic/Scholarly.*
Published by: Peter Lang GmbH (Subsidiary of: Peter Lang Publishing Group), Eschborner Landstr 42-50, Frankfurt Am Main, 60489, Germany. TEL 49-69-7807050, FAX 49-69-78070550, zentrale.frankfurt@peterlang.com, http://www.peterlang.com.

200 DEU
EUROPAEISCHE RELIGIONSGESCHICHTE. Text in German. 2001. irreg., latest vol.2, 2003. price varies. **Document type:** *Monographic series, Academic/Scholarly.*
Published by: Diagonal Verlag, Alte Kasseler Str 43, Marburg, 35039, Germany. TEL 49-6421-681936, FAX 49-6421-681944, post@diagonal-verlag.de, http://www.diagonal-verlag.de.

230 DEU ISSN 1862-149X
EUROPAEISCHE WALLFAHRTSSTUDIEN. Text in German. 2006. irreg., latest vol.5, 2008. price varies. **Document type:** *Monographic series, Academic/Scholarly.*
Published by: Peter Lang GmbH (Subsidiary of: Peter Lang Publishing Group), Eschborner Landstr 42-50, Frankfurt Am Main, 60489, Germany. TEL 49-69-7807050, FAX 49-69-78070550, zentrale.frankfurt@peterlang.com.

207.2 USA
EUROPE TODAY. Text in English. 1971. q. free. adv. bk.rev. **Document type:** *Newsletter, Consumer.* **Description:** Reports the activities of GEM missionaries and national Christians to the mission's supporting constituency in North America.
Former titles: Christ to Europe; (until 1997): Europe Today (1084-3914); (until 1992): Europe Report (0274-8037); (until vol.18, no.5, 1988): G E M's Europe Report; Greater Europe Report
Related titles: Online - full text ed.
Published by: Greater Europe Mission, 18950 Base Camp Rd, Monument, CO 80132-8009. TEL 719-488-4114, FAX 719-488-8019. Ed., R&P Devere Curtiss. Circ: 25,000 (controlled).

200 305.4 BEL ISSN 1783-2454
➤ **EUROPEAN SOCIETY OF WOMEN IN THEOLOGICAL RESEARCH. JOURNAL/ASSOCIATION EUROPEENNE DES FEMMES POUR LA RECHERCHE THEOLOGIQUE. ANNUAIRE/EUROPAEISCHE GESELLSCHAFT FUER DIE THEOLOGISCHE FORSCHUNG VON FRAUEN. JAHRBUCH.** Text in English, French, German. 1992. a., latest vol.13, 2005. EUR 35 combined subscription (print & online eds.) (effective 2011). bk.rev. bibl. **Document type:** *Journal, Academic/Scholarly.* **Description:** Discusses issues relating to feminist theology and the current state of scholarship in Europe.
Formerly (until 2005): European Society of Women in Theological Research. Yearbook (1781-7846)
Related titles: Online - full text ed.: ISSN 1783-2446. 2003.
Indexed: RI-1.
—IE.
Published by: (European Society of Women in Theological Research), Peeters Publishers, Bondgenotenlaan 153, Leuven, 3000, Belgium. TEL 32-16-235170, FAX 32-16-228500, peeters@peeters-leuven.be, http://www.peeters-leuven.be. Ed. C Methuen.

200 ITA ISSN 1972-6163
Z7753
EUTIFRONE; bibliografia annuale di storia delle religioni. Text in Multiple languages. 2006. a. **Document type:** *Journal, Academic/Scholarly.*
Related titles: Online - full text ed.: ISSN 2039-2397.
Published by: (Universita degli Studi di Messina), Fabrizio Serra Editore (Subsidiary of: Accademia Editoriale), c/o Accademia Editoriale, Via Santa Bibbiana 28, Pisa, 56127, Italy. TEL 39-050-542332, FAX 39-050-574888, accademiaeditoriale@accademiaeditoriale.it, http://www.libraweb.net. Ed. Fabio Mora.

EVA (HILVERSUM). *see* WOMEN'S INTERESTS

200 974 USA ISSN 1529-4773
EVANGELICAL & REFORMED HISTORICAL SOCIETY NEWSLETTER. Text in English. 1970. s-a. USD 25 to members (effective 2000). bk.rev. back issues avail. **Document type:** *Newsletter.* **Description:** Contains news about society meetings, papers presented and members' activities.
Published by: Evangelical & Reformed Historical Society, Philip Schaff Library, Lancaster Theological Seminary, 555 W James St, Lancaster, PA 17603. TEL 717-290-8734, FAX 717-393-4254, erhs@lts.org, http://www.lts.org/erhs.htm. Ed., R&P John B Payne. Circ: 1,500 (paid).

200 USA ISSN 0741-1758
BR1
EVANGELICAL JOURNAL. Text in English. 1983. s-a.
Related titles: Online - full content ed.
Indexed: A21, OTA, R&TA, RI-1.
—BLDSC (3830.641400).
Published by: Evangelical School of Theology, 121 S College St, Myerstown, PA 17067. TEL 800-532-5775, info@evangelical.edu, http://www.evangelical.edu/.

266.5734 USA ISSN 0014-3359
BV2350
EVANGELICAL MISSIONS QUARTERLY. Text in English. 1964. q. USD 30.25 combined subscription print & online eds. (effective 2008). adv. bk.rev. index. **Document type:** *Magazine, Trade.* **Description:** Journal devoted to understanding evangelical Protestant missionary thought and practice.

Related titles: Online - full text ed.: ISSN 1945-0869.
Indexed: A21, A22, CCR, CERDIC, ChrPI, FamI, R&TA, RI-1, RI-2.
—CCC.
Published by: Evangelism and Missions Information Service, Wheaton College, 500 College SAve, Wheaton, IL 60187. TEL 630-752-7158, FAX 630-752-7155, http://www.gospelcom.net/emis. Ed. Scott Moreau. R&P Ken Gill. adv.: B&W page USD 650, color page USD 1,075. Circ: 7,000 (paid).

200 GBR ISSN 0144-8153
BR1
EVANGELICAL REVIEW OF THEOLOGY. Text in English. 1977. q. USD 63.30 to individuals (print or online ed.); USD 95 to institutions (print or online eds.); USD 76 combined subscription to individuals (print & online eds.); USD 114 combined subscription to institutions (print & online eds.) (effective 2010). bk.rev. reprints avail. **Document type:** *Journal, Academic/Scholarly.* **Description:** Interprets the Christian faith for contemporary living.
Related titles: Microform ed.: (from PQC); Online - full text ed.
Indexed: A01, A02, A03, A08, A21, A22, CA, CERDIC, ChrPI, DIP, FamI, IBR, IBZ, OTA, R&TA, RI-1, RI-2, T02.
—BLDSC (3830.702000), IE, Ingenta. **CCC.**
Published by: The Paternoster Press, c/o Aplhagraphics, 6 Angel Row, Nottingham, NG1 6HL, United Kingdom. TEL 44-115-8523614, FAX 44-115-8523601, periodicals@alphagraphics.co.uk, http://www.paternosterperiodicals.com.

207.2 DEU ISSN 0177-8706
BV2063
EVANGELIKALE MISSIOLOGIE. Text in German. 1984. q. EUR 17 (effective 2008). adv. bk.rev. index. back issues avail. **Document type:** *Magazine, Trade.* **Description:** Non-denominational publication covering information and discussions in all areas of mission work. Includes association news and events.
Related titles: Diskette ed.
Published by: Arbeitskreis fuer Evangelikale Missiologie, Rathenaustr 5-7, Giessenau, 35394, Germany. TEL 49-641-9797033, info@missiologie.org. Ed. Klaus Mueller. Circ: 1,000; 1,000 (paid).

200 DEU
EVANGELISCHE SAMMLUNG. Text in German. m.
Published by: Foerderverein Evangelische Sammlung Berlin e.V., Motzstr 52, Berlin, 10777, Germany. TEL 030-242252.

240 DEU ISSN 0014-3502
BR4
EVANGELISCHE THEOLOGIE. Text in German. 1923. bi-m. EUR 72 domestic; EUR 82.40 foreign; EUR 43.80 to students; EUR 15.60 newsstand/cover (effective 2011). adv. reprints avail. **Document type:** *Journal, Academic/Scholarly.*
Formerly (until 1934): Zwischen den Zeiten (1614-3477)
Related titles: Microform ed.: (from PQC); ◆ Supplement(s): Verkuendigung und Forschung. ISSN 0342-2410.
Indexed: A21, A22, CERDIC, DIP, FR, IBR, IBZ, IZBG, MLA-IB, OTA, PCI, R&TA, RI-1, RI-2, RILM.
—IE, Infotrieve, INIST. **CCC.**
Published by: Guetersloher Verlagshaus (Subsidiary of: Verlagsgruppe Random House GmbH), Carl-Miele-Str 214, Guetersloh, 33311, Germany. TEL 49-5241-740550, FAX 49-5241-740548, info@gtvh.de, http://www.gtvh.de. Ed. Michael Meyer-Blanck. Circ: 2,400. **Subscr. to:** VVA Zeitschriftenservice, Postfach 7777, Guetersloh 33310, Germany. TEL 49-5241-801969, FAX 49-5241-809620.

230 DEU ISSN 0174-3376
EVANGELISCHES SONNTAGSBLATT AUS BAYERN. Text in German. 1884. w. (Sun.). EUR 58 (effective 2010). adv. **Document type:** *Newspaper, Consumer.*
Published by: Gebr. Holstein GmbH und Co. KG, Erlbacherstr 104, Rothenburg ob der Tauber, 91541, Germany. TEL 49-9861-400384, FAX 49-9861-40079, info@rotabene.de, http://www.rotabene.de. Ed. Helmut Frank.

266 SWE ISSN 0280-6339
EVANGELISKA OESTASIENMISSIONEN. Text in Swedish. 1982. m. (9/yr.). bk.rev. illus.
Formed by the 1982 merger of (1952-1981): Missionstidningen Sinims Land (0345-7648); (1923-1981): Ljusglimtar (0024-5410)
Address: Regulatorvaegen 11, PO Box 4093, Huddinge, 14104, Sweden. TEL 46-8-608-96-49. Circ: 3,800.

200 DEU ISSN 0934-0769
EVANGELIUM UND WISSENSCHAFT; Beitraege zum interdisziplinaeren Gespraech. Text in German. 1980. 2/yr. EUR 3.50 newsstand/cover (effective 2010). **Document type:** *Journal, Academic/Scholarly.*
Related titles: Supplement(s): Evangelium und Wissenschaft. Beiheft. ISSN 0934-0777. 1986.
Indexed: IBR, IBZ.
Published by: Karl-Heim-Gesellschaft e.V., c/o Marion Schuetz-Schuffert, Reichweindamm 17, Berlin, 13627, Germany. TEL 49-30-60054997, info@karl-heim-gesellschaft.de, http://www.karl-heim-gesellschaft.de.

200 ITA
EVANGELIZZARE; mensile per animatori di catechesi. Text in Italian. 1974. m. (10/yr.). EUR 26 domestic; EUR 44.60 in the European Union; EUR 51.20 elsewhere (effective 2008). adv. bk.rev. **Document type:** *Magazine, Consumer.*
Published by: Centro Editoriale Dehoniano, Via Scipione dal Ferro 4, Bologna, BO 40138, Italy. TEL 39-051-4290451, FAX 39-051-4290491, ced-amm@dehoniane.it, http://www.dehoniane.it.

220.6 USA ISSN 0883-0053
BS543
EX AUDITU. Text in English. 1985. a. USD 20 per issue to individuals; USD 30 per issue to institutions; USD 12 per issue to students (effective 2010). back issues avail. **Document type:** *Journal, Academic/Scholarly.* **Description:** Contains the papers of the Fredrick Neumann Symposium of Princeton Theological Seminary.
Related titles: Online - full text ed.: USD 24 per issue (effective 2010).
Indexed: A21, IZBG, OTA, R&TA, RI-1.
—BLDSC (3834.471500).
Published by: (North Park Symposium on the Theological Interpretation of Scripture), Pickwick Publications, c/o Klyne Snodgrass, N Park Theological Seminary, 3225 . Foster Ave, Chicago, IL 60625. TEL 773-244-6243, FAX 773-244-6244. Ed. Klyne R Snodgrass.

200 NLD ISSN 0166-2740
BV2063
➤ **EXCHANGE**; journal of missiological and ecumenical research. Text in English. 1972. q. EUR 239, USD 333 to institutions; EUR 260, USD 364 combined subscription to institutions (print & online eds.) (effective 2012). back issues avail.; reprint service avail. from PSC. **Document type:** *Journal, Academic/Scholarly.* **Description:** Discusses issues in contemporary missiology and ecumenical relations between Christianity and other religions.
Related titles: Online - full text ed.: ISSN 1572-543X. EUR 217, USD 303 to institutions (effective 2012) (from IngentaConnect).
Indexed: A01, A03, A08, A21, A22, ASD, CA, E01, IZBG, PCI, R&TA, RI-1, RI-2, T02.
—BLDSC (3836.191000), IE, Ingenta. **CCC.**
Published by: (Interuniversitair Instituut voor Missiologie en Oecumenica, Leiden), Brill, PO Box 9000, Leiden, 2300 PA, Netherlands. TEL 31-71-5353500, FAX 31-71-5317532, cs@brill.nl. **Dist. by:** Turpin Distribution Services Ltd., Pegasus Dr, Stratton Business Park, Biggleswade, Bedfordshire SG18 8QB, United Kingdom. TEL 44-1767-604954, FAX 44-1767-601640, custserv@turpin-distribution.com, http://www.turpin-distribution.com/.

230 GBR ISSN 2041-2347
▼ **EXCORDE.** Text in English. 2009. a. **Document type:** *Monographic series, Trade.*
Published by: Franciscan International Study Centre, Giles Ln, Canterbury, Kent CT2 7NA, United Kingdom. TEL 44-1227-769349, FAX 44-1227-786648, info@franciscans.ac.uk.

280.4 658 USA ISSN 1943-099X
▼ **EXECUTIVE FOR CHRIST.** Text in English. 2009. q. USD 29.99 (effective 2009). **Document type:** *Magazine, Consumer.* **Description:** A guide for the ministry worker and faithbased executive.
Related titles: CD-ROM ed.: USD 9.99 (effective 2009); Online - full text ed.: ISSN 1943-1007. USD 4.99 (effective 2009).
Published by: Executive for Christ, Ltd., PO Box 551, Pickerington, OH 43147. TEL 614-592-2344, mraney@executiveforchrist.com.

230 ESP ISSN 1138-901X
EXODO. Text in Spanish. 1989. bi-m. EUR 25 (effective 2008). back issues avail. **Document type:** *Magazine, Consumer.*
Related titles: CD-ROM ed.: ISSN 1885-2556. 2004.
Published by: Centro Evangelio y Liberacion, Fernandez de los Rios, 2, 3o, Madrid, 28015, Spain. TEL 34-91-4472360, redaccion@exodo.org, http://www.oxodo.org/.

268 USA ISSN 2151-030X
EXPLORERS DISCOVERY SHEETS FOR UPPER ELEMENTARY. Text in English. 2004. q. USD 3.99 per issue (effective 2009). **Document type:** *Magazine, Trade.* **Description:** Provides thought-provoking in-class activities and study questions.
Formerly (until 2009): Discovery Sheets 2 for Upper Elementary (1558-5522)
Published by: Randall House, 114 Bush Rd, PO Box 17306, Nashville, TN 37217. TEL 615-361-1221, 800-877-7030, FAX 615-367-0535.

268 USA ISSN 2151-027X
EXPLORER'S GUIDE. Text in English. 2004. q. USD 3.99 per issue (effective 2009). **Document type:** *Magazine, Trade.* **Description:** Focuses on helping fourth through sixth grade students establish the important habit of spending daily time in God's word.
Formerly (until 2009): Explorer's Guide. Level 2 (1557-7511)
Published by: Randall House, 114 Bush Rd, PO Box 17306, Nashville, TN 37217. TEL 615-361-1221, 800-877-7030, FAX 615-367-0535.

268 USA ISSN 2151-0296
EXPLORERS TEACHING GUIDE FOR UPPER ELEMENTARY. Text in English. 2004. q. USD 6.99 per issue (effective 2009). **Document type:** *Guide, Trade.* **Description:** Includes teacher tips, review and reinforcement activities, bible memory resources and assistance (preparation checklists, devotionals, decor ideas).
Formerly (until 2009): CLEAR Teaching for Upper Elementary (1558-3015)
Published by: Randall House, 114 Bush Rd, PO Box 17306, Nashville, TN 37217. TEL 615-361-1221, 800-877-7030, FAX 615-367-0535.

268 USA ISSN 1527-7593
EXPLORING FAITH. MIDDLE ELEMENTARY. CLASS PAK. Text in English. 200?. q. back issues avail. **Document type:** *Magazine, Consumer.*
Published by: Cokesbury, 201 8th Ave, S, PO Box 801, Nashville, TN 37202. TEL 615-749-6000, cokes_serv@cokesbury.com, http://www.cokesbury.com.

268 USA ISSN 1527-7585
EXPLORING FAITH. MIDDLE ELEMENTARY. TEACHER. Text in English. 2001. q. USD 4 per issue (effective 2008). back issues avail. **Document type:** *Magazine, Consumer.*
Related titles: Online - full text ed.
Published by: Cokesbury, 201 8th Ave, S, PO Box 801, Nashville, TN 37202. TEL 615-749-6000, cokes_serv@cokesbury.com, http://www.cokesbury.com.

268 USA ISSN 1527-7623
EXPLORING FAITH. OLDER ELEMENTARY. CLASS PAK. Text in English. 200?. q. back issues avail. **Document type:** *Magazine, Consumer.*
Published by: Cokesbury, 201 8th Ave, S, PO Box 801, Nashville, TN 37202. TEL 615-749-6000, cokes_serv@cokesbury.com, http://www.cokesbury.com.

268 USA ISSN 1527-7615
EXPLORING FAITH. OLDER ELEMENTARY. TEACHER. Text in English. 200?. q. back issues avail. **Document type:** *Magazine, Consumer.*
Published by: Cokesbury, 201 8th Ave, S, PO Box 801, Nashville, TN 37202. TEL 615-749-6000, cokes_serv@cokesbury.com, http://www.cokesbury.com.

268 USA ISSN 1527-7534
EXPLORING FAITH. PRESCHOOL. CLASS PAK. Text in English. 2001. q. back issues avail. **Document type:** *Magazine, Consumer.*
Published by: Cokesbury, 201 8th Ave, S, PO Box 801, Nashville, TN 37202. TEL 615-749-6000, cokes_serv@cokesbury.com, http://www.cokesbury.com.

268 USA ISSN 1527-7526
EXPLORING FAITH. PRESCHOOL. TEACHER. Text in English. 200?. q. back issues avail. **Document type:** *Magazine, Consumer.*
Published by: Cokesbury, 201 8th Ave, S, PO Box 801, Nashville, TN 37202. TEL 615-749-6000, cokes_serv@cokesbury.com, http://www.cokesbury.com.

268 USA ISSN 1527-7607
EXPLORING FAITH. STUDENT. Text in English. 200?. q. back issues avail. **Document type:** *Magazine, Consumer.*
Published by: Cokesbury, 201 8th Ave, S, PO Box 801, Nashville, TN 37202. TEL 615-749-6000, cokes_serv@cokesbury.com, http://www.cokesbury.com.

268 USA ISSN 1527-7577
EXPLORING FAITH. STUDENT (MIDDLE ELEMENTARY EDITION). Text in English. 200?. q. back issues avail. **Document type:** *Magazine, Consumer.*
Published by: Cokesbury, 201 8th Ave, S, PO Box 801, Nashville, TN 37202. TEL 615-749-6000, cokes_serv@cokesbury.com, http://www.cokesbury.com.

200 GBR ISSN 0014-5246
BS410
EXPOSITORY TIMES; international journal of biblical studies, theology and ministry. Text in English. 1889. m. USD 351, GBP 190 combined subscription to institutions (print & online eds.); USD 344, GBP 186 to institutions (effective 2011). adv. bk.rev. index. 36 p./no.; back issues avail.; reprint service avail. from PSC. **Document type:** *Journal, Academic/Scholarly.* **Description:** Interdenominational articles, sermons and book reviews for ministers, scholars and theological students.
Related titles: Microfilm ed.: (from PQC, WMP); Online - full text ed.: ISSN 1745-5308. USD 316, GBP 171 to institutions (effective 2011).
Indexed: A01, A03, A08, A20, A21, A22, ASCA, ArtHuCI, CA, CurCont, DIP, E01, IBR, IBZ, IZBG, MLA-IB, OTA, P30, R&TA, RI-1, RI-2, SCOPUS, T02, W07.
—BLDSC (3843.370000), IE, Infotrieve, Ingenta. **CCC.**
Published by: Sage Publications Ltd. (Subsidiary of: Sage Publications, Inc.), 1 Oliver's Yard, 55 City Rd, London, EC1Y 1SP, United Kingdom. TEL 44-20-73248500, FAX 44-20-73248600, info@sagepub.co.uk, http://www.uk.sagepub.com/home.nav. Eds. John Riches, Karen Wenell, Paul Foster. adv.: B&W page GBP 350; 140 x 210. **Subscr. in the Americas to:** Sage Publications, Inc., 2455 Teller Rd, Thousand Oaks, CA 91320. TEL 805-499-9774, FAX 805-499-0871, journals@sagepub.com.

230.071 AUS ISSN 1835-4416
➤ **EYE OF THE HEART.** Text in English. 2008. 2/yr. free (effective 2008). back issues avail. **Document type:** *Journal, Academic/Scholarly.* **Description:** Addresses the inner meaning of philosophy and religion through elucidations of metaphysical, cosmological, and soteriological principles.
Related titles: Online - full text ed.
Published by: La Trobe University, Arts Program, PO Box 199, Bendigo, VIC 3552, Australia. TEL 61-3-54447243, FAX 61-3-54447970. Ed. Timothy Scott.

200 AUS
F A C T. (Faith and Atheism in Communist Territories) Text in English. 1979. m.
Published by: Voice of Peace Ltd. (Inc. in N.S.W.), PO Box 339, Cronulla, NSW 2230, Australia. TEL 61-2-95272387, FAX 61-2-95273335, http://www.voiceofpeace.org.au.

230.071 USA ISSN 1554-2270
BV4025
THE F T E GUIDE TO THEOLOGICAL EDUCATION. (Fund for Theological Education) Text in English. 2005. a. **Document type:** *Guide, Consumer.*
Published by: The Fund for Theological Education, 825 Houston Mill Rd., Ste 250, Atlanta, GA 30329. TEL 404-727-1450, FAX 404-727-1490.

FACT BOOK ON THEOLOGICAL EDUCATION. *see* RELIGIONS AND THEOLOGY—Abstracting, Bibliographies, Statistics

200 USA ISSN 1534-7176
FACTS FOR FAITH. Text in English. 2000. q. **Document type:** *Magazine, Consumer.*
Related titles: Online - full text ed.
Indexed: H14, P02, P10, P13, P48, P53, P54, PQC.
Published by: Reasons to Believe, PO Box 5978, Pasadena, CA 91117. TEL 626-335-1480, 800-482-7836, reasons@reasons.org, http://www.reasons.org.

230 AUS
FAIR DINKUM. Text in English. 1989. q. **Description:** Includes encouraging christian articles.
Media: Online - full content.
Address: 3 Kirk St, Elizabeth Park, SA, Australia. TEL 61-8-82547678, cu@cforu.net, http://www.cforu.net. Ed. Andrew Craig.

200 GBR ISSN 0014-701X
BR1
FAITH AND FREEDOM; a journal of progressive religion. Text in English. 1947. s-a. GBP 10, USD 20 (effective 1999 & 2000). adv. bk.rev. reprints avail. **Document type:** *Journal, Academic/Scholarly.*
Related titles: Microform ed.: (from PQC).
Indexed: A21, CERDIC, R&TA, RI-1, RI-2.
—BLDSC (3865.510600), IE, Ingenta.
Published by: (Harris Manchester College), Peter Godfrey Ed.& Pub., 41 Bradford Dr, Ewell, Epsom, Surrey KT19 0AQ, United Kingdom. TEL 44-181-393-8172, FAX 44-181-393-8172. R&P Rev. Peter Godfrey TEL 44-181-393-9122. Circ: 600.

200 CHE ISSN 0512-2589
FAITH AND ORDER PAPERS. Text in English. 1949. irreg., latest vol.182, 1998. price varies. cum.index: 1910-70. **Document type:** *Monographic series, Consumer.*
Indexed: RI-2.
Published by: (Publications Office), World Council of Churches, 150 route de Ferney, PO Box 2100, Geneva 2, 1211, Switzerland. TEL 41-22-791-6111, FAX 41-22-791-0361. **Dist. in U.S. by:** World Council of Churches, Distribution Center, Rt 222 & Sharadin Rd, Box 346, Kutztown, PA 19530-0346.

FAITH AND PHILOSOPHY. *see* PHILOSOPHY

230.05 USA ISSN 0098-5449
BR1
FAITH & REASON (FRONT ROYAL). Text in English. 1975. q. bk.rev. back issues avail. **Document type:** *Journal, Academic/Scholarly.*
Indexed: CERDIC, CPL, MLA-IB.

Published by: (Christendom College), Christendom Press, 134 Christendom Dr, Front Royal, VA 22630. TEL 800-877-5456, info@christendom.edu, http://www.christendom.edu. Circ: 500.

200 GBR ISSN 0309-1627
FAITH & WORSHIP. Text in English. 1976. a. free to members (effective 2009). bk.rev. back issues avail. **Document type:** *Magazine, Consumer.*
Related titles: Online - full text ed.: free (effective 2009).
Published by: Prayer Book Society, The Studio, Copyhold Farm, Lady Grove, Goring Heath, Reading, RG8 7RT, United Kingdom. TEL 44-118-9842582, pbs.admin@pbs.org.uk. **Subscr. to:** John Skinner.

202.2 USA
FAITH AT WORK. Text in English. 1947. q. bk.rev. **Document type:** *Magazine, Consumer.* **Description:** Edited for an inter-denominational group involved in personal and church renewal. Articles center on building relationships, discovering ministry, finding wholeness as persons and spiritual growth.
Published by: Faith At Work, Inc., 106 E Broad St, Ste B, Falls Curch, VA 22046-4501. TEL 703-237-3426, FAX 703-237-0157. Ed. Marjory Z Bankson. Circ: 20,000 (paid and free).

234.23 CAN
FAITH NEWS. Text in English. 1999. w. free. back issues avail. **Document type:** *Newsletter.* **Description:** Keeps readers up-to-date with news that touches upon faith matters, both Christian and the wider religions world.
Media: Online - full text.
Published by: Gogeco Cable Canada, Inc., Saint Main, P O Box 5076, Burlington, ON L7R 4S6, Canada. Ed. Darrell Buchanan.

200 ITA ISSN 0014-7095
FAMIGLIA CRISTIANA. Text in Italian. 1931. w. EUR 86 (effective 2008). adv. bk.rev.; film rev.; play rev. charts; illus.; stat. index, cum.index every 5 yrs. **Document type:** *Magazine, Consumer.*
Indexed: RASB.
Published by: Edizioni San Paolo, Piazza Soncino 5, Cinisello Balsamo, MI 20092, Italy. TEL 39-02-660751, FAX 39-02-66075211, sanpaoloedizioni@stpauls.it, http://www.edizionisanpaolo.it. Ed. Antonio Sciortino. Adv. contact Corrado Minnella. Circ: 863,314 (paid).

FAMILIA CRISTA; revista da paz e do amor - revista mensal para a familia. *see* SOCIOLOGY

FAMILIA Y SOCIEDAD. *see* SOCIOLOGY

200 DEU ISSN 0936-8043
FAMILIEN UND JUGEND - GOTTESDIENSTE. Text in German. 19??. 11/yr. looseleaf. EUR 114 (effective 2011). **Document type:** *Magazine, Consumer.* **Description:** For use in preparing Sunday services for children and youth.
Formerly (until 1989): Gottesdienste mit Kindern und Jugendlichen (0176-8581)
Published by: Bergmoser und Hoeller Verlag GmbH, Karl-Friedrich-Str 76, Aachen, 52072, Germany. TEL 49-241-93888123, FAX 49-241-93888134, kontakt@buhv.de. Ed. Willi Hoffsuemmer. Circ: 5,200 (controlled).

201.6 USA
FAMILY RADIO NEWS. Text in English. 1966. q. free. charts; illus. **Description:** Contains articles about the ministry of Family Radio as well as the program guide for the stations served.
Published by: Family Stations, Inc., 290 Hegenberger Rd, Oakland, CA 94621. TEL 800-543-1495, FAX 510-633-7983. Ed. Richard Homeres. Circ: 100,000.

200 USA ISSN 1553-9652
FAMILY REFORMATION. Text in English. 2004. q. USD 17.95; USD 5.95 newsstand/cover (effective 2004). **Document type:** *Magazine, Consumer.* **Description:** Covers the issues modern families face with Biblical references and answers.
Published by: Family Reformation, LLC., PO Box 436, Barker, TX 77413. TEL 281-579-0033, FAX 832-201-7620. Ed. Stacy McDonald. Pub. James McDonald.

207.2 USA
FAR EAST REPORTER. Text in English. 1976 (vol.22). bi-m. USD 5. illus.
Published by: Church of Houston Baptist International, Inc., PO Box 3333, Houston, TX 77253-3333. TEL 713-820-9111. Ed. Deanza Brock. Circ: 200,000.

200 CAN ISSN 1712-9168
➤ **FAREL. LA REVUE.** Text in French. 2006. a. CAD 10 (effective 2007). bk.rev. **Document type:** *Journal, Academic/Scholarly.*
Published by: Farel Reformed Theological Seminary/Farel Faculte de Theologie Reformee, 3407-A, av. du Musee, Montreal, PQ H3G 2C6, Canada. TEL 800-475-4482.

250 NOR ISSN 0014-8733
FAST GRUNN. Text in Norwegian. 1948. bi-m. NOK 250 (effective 1999). adv. bk.rev. illus. index. **Description:** Aimed at laymen leaders in the Church, the periodical features articles on theology, Church life, society and ethics; carries reviews of Church debate.
—CCC.
Published by: Lunde Forlag, Sinsenveien 25, Oslo, 0572, Norway. TEL 47-22-42-91-30, FAX 47-22-42-10-29. Ed. Jon Kvalbein. Pub. Lunde Forlag. R&P, Adv. contact Ove Eikje. Circ: 3,000.

220 DEU ISSN 2190-9849
▼ **FASZINATION BIBEL**; das Buch der Buecher lieben lernen. Text in German. 2010. 4/yr. EUR 19.80; EUR 6.50 newsstand/cover (effective 2011). adv. **Document type:** *Magazine, Consumer.*
Published by: Bundes Verlag GmbH, Bodenborn 43, Witten, 58452, Germany. TEL 49-2302-930930, FAX 49-2302-93093689, info@bundes-verlag.de, http://www.bundes-verlag.de. Pub. Ulrich Eggers. Adv. contact Ingo Rubbel. Circ: 15,000 (paid and controlled).

200 USA
FELLOWSHIP LIFE & LIFESTYLES. Text in English. 1975. q.
Published by: Fellowship of the Inner Light, 620 14 St, Virginia Beach, VA 23451. TEL 703-896-3673, FAX 804-428-6648. Ed. Stephen Haslam.

FEMINIST CRITICAL STUDIES IN RELIGION AND CULTURE. *see* WOMEN'S STUDIES

FEMINIST THEOLOGY. *see* WOMEN'S STUDIES

FIDES ET HISTORIA; the Journal of conference on faith and history. *see* HISTORY

200 GBR ISSN 1743-0615
➤ **FIELDWORK IN RELIGION.** Abbreviated title: F I R. Text in English. 2005. s-a. USD 220 combined subscription in North America to institutions (print & online eds.); GBP 135 combined subscription elsewhere to institutions (print & online eds.) (effective 2012). adv. back issues avail.; reprints avail. **Document type:** *Journal, Academic/Scholarly.* **Description:** Aims to publish articles, review essays, and book reviews relevant to the theoretical engagement with and practical undertaking of fieldwork in religion.
Related titles: Online - full text ed.: ISSN 1743-0623. USD 176 in North America to institutions; GBP 108 elsewhere to institutions (effective 2012).
—BLDSC (3925.427500), IE. **CCC.**
Published by: Equinox Publishing Ltd., Unit S3, Kelham House, 3 Lancaster St, Sheffield, S6 3AF, United Kingdom. TEL 44-114-2725957, FAX 44-560-3459046, journals@equinoxpub.com, http://www.equinoxpub.com/. Ed. Ron Geaves. Adv. contact Val Hall.

➤ **FILM UND THEOLOGIE.** *see* MOTION PICTURES

200 BEL ISSN 0777-074X
FILS D'ABRAHAM. Text in French. irreg., latest 2000. back issues avail. **Document type:** *Monographic series.* **Description:** Publishes studies of all religious groups that form the spiritual descendants of Abraham, including Samaritans, Jewish, Christian, Islamic and Mormon traditions.
Published by: Brepols Publishers, Begijnhof 67, Turnhout, 2300, Belgium. TEL 32-14-448020, FAX 32-14-428919, periodicals@brepols.net, http://www.brepols.net.

207.2 AUS ISSN 1443-4253
FIRST PRIORITY NOW. Text in English. 1971. q. AUD 8 to individuals (effective 2008). adv. bk.rev. back issues avail. **Document type:** *Magazine, Consumer.* **Description:** Publishes information regarding AGWM's activities.
Former titles (until 2000): Missions Update (1328-9519); (until 1997): World Missions Update (0158-6262); Garamut (0311-0362)
Published by: Assemblies of God World Missions, PO Box 254, Mitcham, VIC 3132, Australia. TEL 61-3-98724566, FAX 61-3-98723220, service@wm.acc.org.au. Ed. W Robert McQuillan. adv.: color page AUD 450. Circ: 13,000 (paid).

268 USA ISSN 2151-0253
FIRST STEPS TEACHING RESOURCES FOR INFANTS AND TODDLERS. Text in English. 2004. q. USD 6.99 per issue (effective 2009). **Document type:** *Guide, Trade.* **Description:** Includes ideas and suggestions to capture the attention of infants and toddlers and create a teaching nursery.
Formerly (until 2009): CLEAR Teaching Resources for Infants/Toddlers (1557-7503)
Published by: Randall House, 114 Bush Rd, PO Box 17306, Nashville, TN 37217. TEL 615-361-1221, 800-877-7030, FAX 615-367-0535.

260 USA ISSN 1047-5141
BL2525
FIRST THINGS; a monthly journal of religion and public life. Text in English. 1990. 10/yr. USD 39; USD 4.95 newsstand/cover (effective 2009). adv. bk.rev. Index. 80 p./no.; back issues avail.; reprints avail. **Document type:** *Journal, Academic/Scholarly.* **Description:** Examines issues arising at the crossroads of religion and public life today.
Related titles: Microfiche ed.; Microfilm ed.; Online - full text ed.
Indexed: A01, A02, A03, A08, A21, A22, A25, A26, AmHI, B04, BRD, CA, CCR, E08, G08, G10, H07, H08, H14, HAb, HumInd, I05, P02, P05, P10, P28, P30, P34, P48, P53, P54, PCI, PQC, R&TA, R05, RI-1, RI-2, RILM, S08, S09, SCOPUS, T02, W03, W05.
—BLDSC (3934.466700), IE, Infotrieve, Ingenta.
Published by: Institute on Religion and Public Life, 156 Fifth Ave, Ste 400, New York, NY 10010. TEL 212-627-1985, 800-783-4903, FAX 212-627-2184. Ed. Joseph Bottum. adv.: B&W page USD 1,850, color page USD 2,830; trim 8.12 x 10.87. Circ: 30,000 (paid). **Subscr. to:** Department FT, PO Box 401, Mt Morris, IL 61054.

THE FIT CHRISTIAN; a Christian health & fitness magazine. *see* PHYSICAL FITNESS AND HYGIENE

261 USA
THE FIVE STONES; newsletter for small churches. Text in English. q. USD 12.50 (effective 2001). bk.rev. 24 p./no.; **Document type:** *Journal, Academic/Scholarly.*
Published by: Five Stones, 69 Weymouth St, Providence, RI 02906. TEL 401-861-9405. Ed. Tony Pappas. Circ: 750.

FLAT EARTH NEWS; the last iconoclast. *see* HUMANITIES: COMPREHENSIVE WORKS

200 USA
FLOODTIDE; literature evangelism. Text in English. 1948. bi-m. free. bk.rev.
Published by: Christian Literature Crusade, Inc., PO Box 1449, Fort Washington, PA 19034. TEL 215-542-1242. Ed. Leona Hepburn. Circ: 6,500.

271 ITA ISSN 1123-573X
BX4705.J6
FLORENSIA. Text in Italian. 1987. a., latest vol.17, 2003. EUR 12 domestic; EUR 24 foreign (effective 2009). bk.rev. back issues avail. **Document type:** *Journal, Academic/Scholarly.* **Description:** Examines Gioacchino da Fiore and Gioachimism in the context of apocalyptic thought and the reform of Medieval Monacheism.
Indexed: IBR, IBZ, IPB, PCI.
Published by: (Centro Internazionale di Studi Gioachimiti), Edizioni Dedalo, Viale Luigi Jacobini 5, Bari, BA 70123, Italy. TEL 39-080-5311413, FAX 39-080-5311414, info@edizionidedalo.it, http://www.edizionidedalo.it. Ed. Cosimo Damiano Fonseca. Circ: 2,000.

914.606 200 ESP ISSN 1575-2836
FOC NOU; revista al servei dels Cristians. Text in Catalan. 1974. m. EUR 38 domestic; EUR 52.50 in Europe; EUR 59 elsewhere (effective 2009). adv. bk.rev. illus. back issues avail. **Document type:** *Magazine, Consumer.*
Published by: El Ciervo S.A., Calvet 56, Barcelona, 08021, Spain. TEL 34-93-2005145, FAX 34-93-2011015, http://www.elciervo.es. Ed. Roser Bofill Portabella. Circ: 3,000.

FOCUS (BELFAST). *see* SOCIAL SERVICES AND WELFARE

230 GBR
FOCUS (WELLESBOURNE). Text in English. 1975. q. GBP 0.30 (effective 1999). adv. bk.rev. **Document type:** *Newsletter.*
Formerly: Ascent
Published by: Christian Endeavour Union of Great Britain and Ireland, Wellesbourne House, Walton Rd, Wellesbourne, Warwick, CV35 9JB, United Kingdom. TEL 44-1789-470439, FAX 44-1789-470439. Ed. John Todd. Circ: 1,000.

250 USA ISSN 0894-3346
FOCUS ON THE FAMILY. Text in English. 1983. m. free (effective 2008). illus. reprints avail. **Document type:** *Magazine, Consumer.* **Description:** Addresses the challenges and joys of everyday life, relationships, parenting, marriage and faith.
Formerly: Focus on the Family Newsletter
Indexed: CCR, ChrPI, S02, S03.
Address: 8605 Explorer Dr, Colorado Springs, CO 80920. TEL 719-531-3400, 800-232-6459, FAX 719-531-3424, http://www.focusonthefamily.com. R&P Sarah Adams. Circ: 2,435,180 (controlled).

FOCUS ON THE FAMILY CLUBHOUSE. *see* CHILDREN AND YOUTH—For

FOCUS ON THE FAMILY CLUBHOUSE JR. *see* CHILDREN AND YOUTH—For

200 DNK ISSN 0105-3116
➤ **FOENIX.** Text in Multiple languages. 1977. q. DKK 300; DKK 200 to students; DKK 80 per issue (effective 2010). **Document type:** *Journal, Academic/Scholarly.*
Indexed: RILM.
Published by: Koebenhavns Universitet, Afdeling for Kirkehistorie/ University of Copenhagen. Department for Church History, Koebmagergade 44-46, Copenhagen K, 1150, Denmark. TEL 45-35-323961, FAX 45-35-323600, dtf@fak.teol.ku.dk, http://www.teol.ku.dk. Ed. Lene Matties.

254 SWE ISSN 1102-3821
FOER; organ foer Svenska kyrkans foersamlingsfoerbund. Text in Swedish. 1988. 6/yr. SEK 250 (effective 2006). adv. illus.; stat. **Document type:** *Magazine, Trade.* **Description:** Covers church administration.
Formerly (until 1991): Foersamlings- och Pastoratsvoervaltning (1100-8636)
Published by: Svenska Kyrkans Foersamlingsfoerbund, Medborgerplatsen 3-5, PO Box 4312, Stockholm, 10267, Sweden. TEL 46-8-7377000, FAX 46-8-7377145, forsamlingsforbundet@svenskakyrkan.se. Ed. Lars Lidstroem TEL 46-8-7377162. adv.: B&W page SEK 13,300, color page SEK 16,300; trim 185 x 270.

230 SWE ISSN 1650-0113
FOERBUNDET FOER KRISTEN HUMANISM OCH SAMHAELLSSYN. AARSBOK. Text in Swedish. 1939. a. SEK 190 membership (effective 2007). back issues avail. **Document type:** *Consumer.*
Formerly (until 1998): Aarsbok foer Kristen Humanism (0281-2800)
—INIST.
Published by: Foerbundet foer Kristen Humanism och Samhaellssyn, Samaritergraend 2, Uppsala, 75319, Sweden. TEL 46-18-101739, khs@swipnet.se, http://www.kristenhumanism.org.

200 054.1 FRA ISSN 0015-5357
FOI ET VIE. Text in French. 1898. 5/yr. adv. bk.rev. bibl.; charts; illus. index. **Description:** A religious and theological publication with protestant tendencies.
Indexed: A21, CERDIC, DIP, FR, IBR, IBZ, R&TA, RI-1, RI-2, RILM.
—BLDSC (3964.385000). **CCC.**
Published by: Association des Amis de la Revue Foi et Vie, 139 bd. du Montparnasse, Paris, 75006, France. Ed. Sylvain Dujancourt. R&P Francine Moussu TEL 33-1-43221599. Circ: 1,200.

220 418.2 SWE ISSN 1651-8365
FOLK & SPRAAK. Text in Swedish. 1977. bi-m. back issues avail. **Document type:** *Consumer.*
Former titles (until 2002): Wycliffe Rapport (0283-8273); (until 1985): Siluett
Published by: Wycliffe Bibeloeversaettare/Wycliffe Bible Translators, Sorterargatan 11, Vaellingby, 16250, Sweden. TEL 46-8-385530, FAX 46-8-385537, info@folk.se.

220 DEU ISSN 1861-602X
FONTES ET SUBSIDIA AD BIBLIAM PERTINENTES. Text in German. 2003. irreg., latest vol.5, 2008. price varies. **Document type:** *Monographic series, Academic/Scholarly.*
—CCC.
Published by: Walter de Gruyter GmbH & Co. KG, Genthiner Str 13, Berlin, 10785, Germany. TEL 49-30-26005220, FAX 49-30-26005251, info@degruyter.com, http://www.degruyter.de.

FOOTPRINTS (TEMPE). *see* CLUBS

220 DEU ISSN 0935-0764
FORSCHUNG ZUR BIBEL. Text in German. 1972. irreg., latest vol.123, 2010. price varies. **Document type:** *Monographic series, Academic/Scholarly.*
Indexed: IZBG.
Published by: Echter Verlag GmbH, Dominikanerplatz 8, Wuerzburg, 97070, Germany. TEL 49-931-660680, FAX 49-931-6606823, info@echter-verlag.de, http://www.echter.de.

200 DEU ISSN 0532-2081
FORSCHUNGEN UND QUELLEN ZUR KIRCHEN- UND KULTURGESCHICHTE OSTDEUTSCHLANDS. Text in German. 1964. irreg., latest vol.43, 2011. price varies. **Document type:** *Monographic series, Academic/Scholarly.*
Published by: (Institut fuer Ostdeutsche Kirchen- und Kulturgeschichte), Boehlau Verlag GmbH & Cie, Ursulaplatz 1, Cologne, 50668, Germany. TEL 49-221-913900, FAX 49-221-9139011, vertrieb@boehlau.de, http://www.boehlau.de.

221 DEU ISSN 0940-4155
FORSCHUNGEN ZUM ALTEN TESTAMENT. Text in German. 1991. irreg., latest vol.74, 2011. price varies. **Document type:** *Monographic series, Academic/Scholarly.* **Description:** Publishes research on all aspects of the Old Testament.
Indexed: IZBG.
Published by: Mohr Siebeck GmbH & Co. KG, Wilhelmstr 18, Tuebingen, 72074, Germany. TEL 49-7071-9230, FAX 49-7071-51104, info@mohr.de.

221 DEU ISSN 1611-4914
FORSCHUNGEN ZUM ALTEN TESTAMENT 2. REIHE. Text in German. 2003. irreg., latest vol.50, 2011. price varies. **Document type:** *Monographic series, Academic/Scholarly.*

Published by: Mohr Siebeck GmbH & Co. KG, Wilhelmstr 18, Tuebingen, 72074, Germany. TEL 49-7071-9230, FAX 49-7071-51104, info@mohr.de.

200 DEU ISSN 0341-8367
➤ **FORSCHUNGEN ZUR ANTHROPOLOGIE UND RELIGIONSGESCHICHTE.** Text in German, English. 1977. irreg., latest vol.42, 2008. price varies. **Document type:** *Monographic series, Academic/Scholarly.* **Description:** Covers all religions and their histories.
Published by: Ugarit-Verlag, Ricarda-Huch-Str 6, Muenster, 48161, Germany. TEL 49-251-8322661, FAX 49-251-8322662, verlag@ugarit-verlag.de. Eds. Manfred L.G. Dietrich, Oswald Loretz.

200 DEU
FORSCHUNGEN ZUR EUROPAEISCHEN GEISTESGESCHICHTE. Text in German. 1998. irreg., latest vol.9, 2008. price varies. **Document type:** *Monographic series, Academic/Scholarly.*
Published by: Verlag Herder GmbH, Hermann-Herder-Str 4, Freiburg Im Breisgau, 79104, Germany. TEL 49-761-27170, FAX 49-761-2717520, kundenservice@herder.de, http://www.herder.de.

200 DEU ISSN 0532-2154
➤ **FORSCHUNGEN ZUR KIRCHEN- UND DOGMENGESCHICHTE.** Text in German. 1954. irreg., latest vol.103, 2010. price varies. **Document type:** *Monographic series, Academic/Scholarly.*
Published by: Vandenhoeck und Ruprecht, Theaterstr 13, Goettingen, 37073, Germany. TEL 49-551-508440, FAX 49-551-5084422, info@v-r.de.

200 DEU ISSN 0176-7119
FORSCHUNGEN ZUR PRAKTISCHEN THEOLOGIE. Text in German. 1986. irreg., latest vol.18, 1999. price varies. **Document type:** *Monographic series, Academic/Scholarly.*
Published by: Peter Lang GmbH (Subsidiary of: Peter Lang Publishing Group), Eschborner Landstr 42-50, Frankfurt Am Main, 60489, Germany. TEL 49-69-7807050, FAX 49-69-78070550, zentrale.frankfurt@peterlang.com. Ed. Ulrich Nembach.

220 DEU
➤ **FORSCHUNGEN ZUR RELIGION UND LITERATUR DES ALTEN UND NEUEN TESTAMENTS.** Text in German. 1930. irreg., latest vol.234, 2010. price varies. **Document type:** *Monographic series, Academic/Scholarly.*
Indexed: IZBG.
Published by: Vandenhoeck und Ruprecht, Theaterstr 13, Goettingen, 37073, Germany. TEL 49-551-508440, FAX 49-551-5084422, info@v-r.de.

220 USA ISSN 0883-4970
BS410
➤ **FORUM (SANTA ROSA)**; foundations & facets. Text in English. 1985. s-a. USD 30 domestic; USD 35 foreign (effective 2010). back issues avail. **Document type:** *Journal, Academic/Scholarly.* **Description:** Brings out current research in biblical and cognate studies, including the historical Jesus, social phenomena of first- and second-century Palestine, and the myths manifested in American culture.
Indexed: A21, R&TA, RI-1, RI-2.
—BLDSC (4025.281500).
Published by: (Westar Institute), Polebridge Press, Willamette University, Westar Institute, 900 State St, Salem, OR 97301. TEL 503-375-5323, 877-523-3545, FAX 503-375-5324, orders@PolebridgePress.com.

260 CAN ISSN 1201-558X
FORUM FOCUS; a window on the global church. Text in English. 1991. s-a. CAD 10 (effective 2001). bk.rev. back issues avail. **Document type:** *Newsletter.*
Formerly (until 1991): Fish-Eye Lens (0835-6521)
Published by: Canadian Churches' Forum for Global Ministries, 230 St Clair Ave W, Toronto, ON M4V 1R5, Canada. TEL 416-924-9351, FAX 416-924-5356. Ed., R&P Robert Faris. Circ: 750.

200 DNK ISSN 0903-854X
FORUM FOR BIBELSK EKSEGESE. Text in Danish. 1988. irreg., latest vol.16, 2010. price varies. **Document type:** *Monographic series, Academic/Scholarly.* **Description:** Contains articles on biblical exegesis.
Indexed: OTA.
Published by: (Koebenhavns Universitet, Institut for Bibelsk Eksegese), Museum Tusculanum Press, c/o University of Copenhagen, Njalsgade 126, Copenhagen S, 2300, Denmark. TEL 45-35-329109, FAX 45-35-329113, info@mtp.dk, http://www.mtp.dk. Eds. Bodil Ejrnaes, Henrik Tronier, Lone Fatum, Mogens Muller, Niels Peter Lemche, Thomas L Thompson. **Dist. in France by:** Editions Picard, Editions Picard, Paris 75006, France. TEL 33-1-43269778, FAX 33-1-43264264; **Dist. in UK by:** Gazelle Book Services Ltd., White Cross Mills, Hightown, Lancaster LA1 4UU, United Kingdom. TEL 44-1524-68765, FAX 44-1524-63232, sales@gazellebooks.co.uk, http://www.gazellebookservices.co.uk/; **Dist. in US & Canada by:** International Specialized Book Services Inc., 920 NE 58th Ave Ste 300, Portland, OR 97213. TEL 503-287-3093, 800-944-6190, FAX 503-280-8832, orders@isbs.com, http://www.isbs.com/.

FORUM KIRCHENMUSIK. *see* MUSIC

230 CHE
FORUM PASTORAL. Text in German. 2003. irreg., latest vol.4, 2008. price varies. **Document type:** *Monographic series, Academic/Scholarly.*
Published by: Theologischer Verlag Zurich, Badenerstr 73, Zurich, 8026, Switzerland. TEL 41-44-2993355, FAX 41-44-2993358, tvz@ref.ch.

200 DEU ISSN 0343-7744
FORUM RELIGION; zur Praxis des Religionsunterrichtes. Text in German. 1975. q. EUR 24 in the European Union; EUR 27.80 elsewhere (effective 2007). adv. bk.rev. **Document type:** *Journal, Academic/Scholarly.*
Indexed: DIP, IBR, IBZ.
—CCC.
Published by: Kreuz Verlag GmbH & Co. KG, Postfach 800669, Stuttgart, 70506, Germany. TEL 49-711-788030, FAX 49-711-7880310, service@kreuzverlag.de, http://www.kreuzverlag.de. Ed. Bernhard Boettge. adv.: B&W page EUR 520. Circ: 2,000 (paid and controlled).

FORUM T T N. (Technik Theologie Naturwissenschaften) *see* SCIENCES: COMPREHENSIVE WORKS

200 100 POL ISSN 1641-1196
BX1564.A1
➤ **FORUM TEOLOGICZNE.** Text in Polish, German; Summaries in German. 2000. a. PLZ 20 domestic; USD 20 foreign (effective 2002 - 2003). abstr.; bibl. back issues avail. **Document type:** *Journal, Academic/Scholarly.* **Description:** Covers history of Church, philosophy, canon law; biblical, dogmatic, moral, pastoral and ecumenical theology.
Published by: (Uniwersytet Warminsko-Mazurski), Wydawnictwo Uniwersytetu Warminsko-Mazurskiego, ul J Heweliusza 14, Olsztyn, 10724, Poland. TEL 48-89-5233661, FAX 48-89-5233438, wydawca@uwm.edu.pl, http://www.uwm.edu.pl/wydawnictwo. Ed. Wladyslaw Nowak. Pub. Zofia Gawinek. Circ: 300 (paid and controlled).

202 GBR ISSN 0144-378X
➤ **FOUNDATIONS (READING).** Text in English. 1978. s-a. GBP 4 per issue domestic; GBP 5 per issue foreign (effective 2010). bk.rev. back issues avail. **Document type:** *Journal, Academic/Scholarly.* **Description:** Aims to cover contemporary theological issues by articles and reviews, taking in exegesis, biblical theology, church history and apologetics - and to indicate their relevance to pastoral ministry.
Related titles: Online - full text ed.
Indexed: A01, CA, T02.
—BLDSC (4025.280200).
Published by: Affinity (Partnership), 1st Fl, 52 New House Park, PO Box 246, Bridgend, CF31 9FD, United Kingdom. TEL 44-1656-640130, admin@affinity.org.uk. Circ: 900.

230 360 GBR ISSN 1461-2364
FOUNDATIONS (RUSHOLME); making connections for Christian social action. Text in English. 1998. q. GBP 14; GBP 20 foreign (effective 2001). adv. bk.rev. **Document type:** *Bulletin.* **Description:** Articles, news and reviews on issues of theology and the church's social engagement.
Published by: William Temple Foundation, Luther King House, Brighton Grove, Rusholme, Manc M14 5JP, United Kingdom. TEL 44-161-224-6404, FAX 44-161-248-9201. Ed. Christine Crosbie. Circ: 650 (paid).

FOUNDER'S SOUNDER. *see* MUSIC

299 USA
FOUR WINDS VILLAGE NEWS. Text in English. q. USD 12 (effective 2000). **Document type:** *Newspaper.*
Address: P.O. Box 112, Tiger, GA 30576. TEL 706-782-1964, fourwinds@rabun.net.

230 USA
THE FOURTH R (SANTA ROSA); an advocate for religious literacy. Text in English. 1987. bi-m. free to members (effective 2010). bk.rev. back issues avail. **Document type:** *Magazine, Consumer.* **Description:** Addresses a broad range of questions about the Christian religion, past and present.
Formerly (until 1989): Westar Magazine (0893-1658)
Published by: (Westar Institute), Polebridge Press, Willamette University, Westar Institute, 900 State St, Salem, OR 97301. TEL 503-375-5323, 877-523-3545, FAX 503-375-5324, orders@PolebridgePress.com.

230 943 DEU
FRAGMENTA MELANCHTHONIANA. Text in German. 2003. irreg., latest vol.4, 2009. price varies. **Document type:** *Monographic series, Academic/Scholarly.*
Published by: Verlag Regionalkultur, Bahnhofstr 2, Ubstadt-Weiher, 76698, Germany. TEL 49-7251-367030, FAX 49-7251-3670329, kontakt@verlag-regionalkultur.de, http://www.verlag-regionalkultur.de.

FRANCKESCHE STIFTUNGEN ZU HALLE. JAHRESPROGRAMM. *see* HISTORY—History Of Europe

271 NLD ISSN 1574-9193
FRATERS C M M. (Congregatie Mater Misericordiae) Text in Dutch. 1958. q.
Formerly (until 2005): Ontmoetingen (1567-9195)
Related titles: Indonesian Translation: Frater C M M. ISSN 1877-9719; English Translation: Brothers C M M. ISSN 1877-6256. 1993.
Published by: Congregatie van de Fraters van Onze Lieve Vrouw, Moeder van Barmhartigheid, Gasthuisring 54, Tilburg, 5041 DT, Netherlands. TEL 31-13-5432777, FAX 31-13-5441405, pbcmm@cmmbrothers.nl, http://www.cmmbrothers.nl. Ed. Jan Smits.

200 DEU ISSN 0722-8120
FRAU UND MUTTER; Ihre Zeitschrift fuer die ganze Familie. Text in German. 1918. m. looseleaf. EUR 16.20 in the European Union; EUR 18.60 elsewhere (effective 2005). **Document type:** *Bulletin, Consumer.*
Published by: (Arbeitsgemeinschaft Frau und Mutter), Kreuz Verlag GmbH & Co. KG, Postfach 800669, Stuttgart, 70506, Germany. TEL 49-711-788030, FAX 49-711-7880310, service@kreuzverlag.de, http://www.kreuzverlag.de. Circ: 42,000.

200 USA
FREE GRACE BROADCASTER. Text in English. 1989 (no.129). q. free.
Published by: (Mt. Zion Bible Church), Mt. Zion Publications, 2603 W Wright St, Pensacola, FL 32505. TEL 850-438-6666, FAX 850-438-0227. Ed. L R Shelton Jr.

323.442 USA
FREEDOM; investigative reporting in the public interest. Text in English. 1968. q. USD 22.50; USD 2.50 newsstand/cover (effective 2007). bk.rev. illus. 50 p./no.; **Document type:** *Magazine, Consumer.* **Description:** Covers various social and human rights issues structured with Scientology beliefs.
Related titles: Online - full text ed.; German ed.: Freiheit.
Published by: Church of Scientology International, 6331 Hollywood Blvd, Ste 1200, Los Angeles, CA 90028-6329. TEL 323-960-3500, FAX 323-960-3508. Ed. Thomas Whittle. Circ: 200,000.

THE FREETHINKER; the voice of atheism since 1881. *see* PHILOSOPHY

FREETHOUGHT TODAY. *see* PHILOSOPHY

FREIBURGER MEDIAEVISTISCHE VORTRAEGE. *see* PHILOSOPHY

282 DEU ISSN 0174-5875
FREIBURGER THEOLOGISCHE STUDIEN. Text in German. 1910. irreg., latest vol.175, 2010. price varies. **Document type:** *Monographic series, Academic/Scholarly.*
Published by: Verlag Herder GmbH, Hermann-Herder-Str 4, Freiburg Im Breisgau, 79104, Germany. TEL 49-761-27170, FAX 49-761-2717520, kundenservice@herder.de, http://www.herder.de.

230 DEU ISSN 0947-2320
FRIEDENSAUER SCHRIFTENREIHE. REIHE A: THEOLOGIE. Text in German. 1998. irreg., latest vol.10, 2008. price varies. **Document type:** *Monographic series, Academic/Scholarly.*
Published by: Peter Lang GmbH (Subsidiary of: Peter Lang Publishing Group), Eschborner Landstr 42-50, Frankfurt Am Main, 60489, Germany. TEL 49-69-7807050, FAX 49-69-78070550, zentrale.frankfurt@peterlang.com. Eds. Horst Rolly, Johann Gerhardt, Wolfgang Kabus.

FRIEDENSAUER SCHRIFTENREIHE. REIHE C: MUSIK - KIRCHE - KULTUR. *see* MUSIC

284.1 AUS ISSN 1037-2792
FRIENDS OF LUTHERAN ARCHIVES. JOURNAL. Text in English. 1991. a. free to members. **Document type:** *Magazine, Consumer.*
Published by: Friends of Lutheran Archives, 197 Archer St, North Adelaide, SA 5006, Australia. TEL 61-8-82677300, FAX 61-8-82677310, fola@lca.org.au, http://www.lca.org.au/lutherans/fola.cfm.

200 GBR ISSN 0016-1357
FRIENDS' QUARTERLY. Text in English. N.S. 1946. q. GBP 19 domestic; GBP 21 foreign (effective 2009). adv. bk.rev. cum.index every 3 yrs. back issues avail. **Document type:** *Magazine, Academic/Scholarly.* **Description:** Offers Quaker thoughts and concerns, peace, spirituality, theology and development.
Formerly (until 1946): Friends Quarterly Examiner (0144-9168)
Related titles: Microfilm ed.: (from WMP).
Indexed: BEL&L.
—BLDSC (4038.300000).
Published by: Friend Publications Ltd., 173 Euston Rd, London, NW1 2BJ, United Kingdom. TEL 44-20-76631010, FAX 44-20-76631182. Adv. contact George Penaluna TEL 44-1535-630230.

200 USA ISSN 1949-1115
▼ **FROM ANGELS TO YOU.** Text in English. forthcoming 2010. w. free (effective 2009). **Document type:** *Magazine, Consumer.* **Description:** Advice on connecting with angels.
Media: E-mail.
Published by: Paul Greblick, Ed. & Pub., 4327 S Hwy 27, No 250, Clermont, FL 34711. TEL 352-449-9891, paulgreblick@yahoo.com.

230 USA
FRONTIERSCAN. Text in English. m. USD 50 per 100 copies. back issues avail. **Document type:** *Bulletin.* **Description:** Condenses material published in Global Prayer Digest.
Published by: U S Center for World Mission, Frontier Fellowship, 1605 Elizabeth St, Pasadena, CA 91104. TEL 626-398-2249, FAX 626-398-2263. Ed. Roberta Winter. R&P Keith Carey TEL 626-398-2241. Circ: 16,000 (paid).

207.2 JPN ISSN 0910-7118
➤ **FUKUIN SENKYO.** Text in Japanese. 1947. m. JPY 6,000 domestic; JPY 6,500 foreign (effective 2003). adv. bk.rev.; Website rev. charts; illus. Index. 72 p./no.; back issues avail. **Document type:** *Journal, Academic/Scholarly.* **Description:** Provides theological and cultural articles on Japanese Christianity.
Supersedes in part (in 1985): Fukyo - Japan Missionary Bulletin (0021-4531)
Indexed: BAS.
—Ingenta.
Published by: Oriens Institute for Religious Research, 2-28-5 Matsubara, Setagaya-ku, Tokyo, 156-0043, Japan. TEL 81-3-33227601, FAX 81-3-33255322, http://www.oriens.or.jp. Ed., R&P M Matata. Adv. contact Ryu Suzuki. Circ: 2,100 (paid).

R

226 USA ISSN 0042-8264
FULL GOSPEL BUSINESS MEN'S VOICE. Text in English. 1953. bi-m. USD 10 to non-members; free to members (effective 2009). adv. 32 p./no. 2 cols./p.; back issues avail. **Document type:** *Magazine, Consumer.* **Description:** Designed to reach businessmen for Christ. Used by the organization's chapters and individuals as a witness tool.
Published by: Full Gospel Business Men's Fellowship International, 3 Holland, PO Box 19714, Irvine, CA 92618. TEL 949-461-0100, FAX 949-609-0344, international@fgbmfi.org. Ed. Bob Armstrong.

268 USA ISSN 1946-7656
FUSION (NASHVILLE); integrating truth, faith and life. Text in English. 2004. q. USD 28.99 (effective 2009). back issues avail. **Document type:** *Magazine, Consumer.* **Description:** Presents articles for adults to help readers integrate God's truth, the Christian faith, and everyday life. Also helps parents interact with their children around weekly biblical themes, which are the same for all age levels.
Formerly (until 2009): Clear Living Bible Study Magazine for Adults (1558-5166)
Published by: Randall House, 114 Bush Rd, PO Box 17306, Nashville, TN 37217. TEL 800-877-7030, FAX 615-367-0535. Eds. Jonathan Yandell, Danny Conn.

268 USA ISSN 1946-7648
FUSION TEACHING GUIDE. Text in English. 2004. q. USD 8.99 per issue (effective 2009). **Document type:** *Magazine, Consumer.* **Description:** Provides teachers of adult with an engaging study of the story of the Bible.
Formerly (until 2009): Clear Teaching for Adults (1558-5514)
Published by: Randall House, 114 Bush Rd, PO Box 17306, Nashville, TN 37217. TEL 800-877-7030, FAX 615-367-0535.

UN FUTURO PER L'UOMO. *see* SCIENCES: COMPREHENSIVE WORKS

GAY THEOLOGICAL JOURNAL; homosexual hermeneutics on religion & the Scriptures. *see* HOMOSEXUALITY

230 NLD ISSN 1878-8831
GEESTKRACHT; bulletin voor charismatische theologie. Text in Dutch. 1978. s-a. **Document type:** *Bulletin, Consumer.*
Formerly (until 2009): Bulletin voor Charismatische Theologie (0920-1378)
Published by: (Charismatische Werkgemeenschap Nederland), Ekklesia, Mosgroen 165, Zoetermeer, 2718 HJ, Netherlands. TEL 31-180-687333, FAX 31-180-687332, info@ekklesia.nl, http://www.ekklesia.nl.

201 DEU ISSN 0016-5921
BV5015
GEIST UND LEBEN. Text in German. 1927. bi-m. EUR 39; EUR 25.80 to students; EUR 7.80 newsstand/cover (effective 2010). adv. bk.rev. **Document type:** *Magazine, Consumer.*
Formerly (until 1947): Zeitschrift fuer Aszese und Mystik

Indexed: CERDIC, CPL, DIP, IBR, IBZ, MLA-IB.
Published by: Echter Verlag GmbH, Postfach 5560, Wuerzburg, 97005, Germany. info@echter-verlag.de, http://www.echter.de. Circ: 3,000 (paid).

291.72 NLD ISSN 2210-3139
GELOVEN ONDERWEG. Text in Dutch. 1965. q. EUR 25 (effective 2010).
Former titles (until 2010): Tijdschrift voor Geloof Onderweg (0920-2544); (until 1986): Tijdschrift voor het Gezin (0920-2994); (until 1981): Tijdschrift voor het Gezin de Rozenkrans (0920-3184)
Published by: Dominicanenklooster Huissen, Postbus 59, Huissen, 6851 AH, Netherlands. TEL 31-26-3264422, FAX 31-26-3254694, info@kloosterhuissen.nl, http://www.kloosterhuissen.nl.

291.72 NLD ISSN 1871-9694
GEMEENSCHAP VAN ZENDINGS-DIACONESSEN IN NEDERLAND. NIEUWSBRIEF. Text in Dutch. 2005. 4/yr.
Published by: Gemeenschap van Zendings-Diaconessen in Nederland, Jan van Zutphenweg 4, Amerongen, 3958 GE, Netherlands. TEL 31-343-459595, FAX 31-343-459575, amerongen@zdh.nl.

200 NLD ISSN 0016-6065
BX6195
GEMEENTELEVEN. Text in Dutch. 1956. 10/yr. adv. bk.rev.
Published by: Remonstrantse Gemeente Groningen, Postbus 1310, Groningen, 9701 BH, Netherlands. TEL 31-50-3130771, http://www.remonstranten.org. Ed. M A M de Jong. Circ: 250.

200 CAN ISSN 1183-3491
BL458
GENDER IN WORLD RELIGIONS. Text in English. 1990. a. USD 15. **Document type:** *Journal, Academic/Scholarly.* **Description:** Publishes scholarly articles bearing on the role of gender in world religions.
—CCC.
Published by: McGill University, Faculty of Religious Studies, 3250 University St., Montreal, PQ H3A 2A7, Canada. TEL 514-398-6138.

207.2 ITA ISSN 0016-6960
GENTES. Text in Italian. 1927. m. bk.rev. bibl.; illus.; stat. index. **Document type:** *Magazine, Consumer.*
Related titles: Online - full text ed.
Published by: Lega Missionaria Studenti, Via Massimiliano Massimo, 7, Rome, RM 00144, Italy. TEL 39-06-5439628, FAX 39-06-5910803. Circ: 3,000.

220 DEU
GESCHICHTE DER RELIGION IN DER NEUZEIT. Text in German. 2007. irreg., latest vol.3, 2010. price varies. **Document type:** *Monographic series, Academic/Scholarly.*
Published by: Wallstein Verlag GmbH, Geiststr 11, Goettingen, 37073, Germany. TEL 49-551-548980, FAX 49-551-5489833, info@wallstein-verlag.de, http://www.wallstein-verlag.de.

GESELLSCHAFT UND ETHIK. *see* PHILOSOPHY

230 DEU
GESTERN, HEUTE UND MORGEN. Text in German. 1929. 7/yr. EUR 16.80 (effective 2011). **Document type:** *Newsletter, Consumer.*
Published by: Guetersloher Verlagshaus (Subsidiary of: Verlagsgruppe Random House GmbH), Carl-Miele-Str 214, Guetersloh, 33311, Germany. TEL 49-5241-74050, FAX 49-5241-740548, info@gtvh.de, http://www.gtvh.de. Ed. Monika Hemkendreis.

207.2 610 DEU
GESUNDHEIT IN DER EINEN WELT; Nachrichten aus der Aerzlichen Mission. Text in German. 1950. q. free (effective 2009). bk.rev. illus. **Document type:** *Magazine, Trade.*
Formerly (until 1999): Nachrichen aus der Aerztlichen Mission (0027-7398)
Published by: Deutsches Institut fuer Aerztliche Mission e.V./German Institute for Medical Mission, Paul-Lechler-Str 24, Tuebingen, 72076, Germany. TEL 49-7071-206512, FAX 49-7071-206510, info@difaem.de, http://www.difaem.de. Ed. Rainward Bastian. Circ: 15,000.

GEWISSEN UND FREIHEIT. *see* POLITICAL SCIENCE—Civil Rights

200 100 USA ISSN 0732-7781
GIST. Text in English. 1975. q. 44 p./no. 2 cols./p.; back issues avail. **Document type:** *Magazine, Consumer.* **Description:** Expresses the theme of the absolute archetypal nature of humanity in first person, present tense, positive.
Published by: God Unlimited - University of Healing, 1101 Far Valley Rd, Campo, CA 91906. TEL 619-478-5111, 888-254-8793, unihealing@goduni.org, http://www.university-of-healing.edu.

200 DEU
GLAUBE HOFFNUNG LIEBE. Text in German. 1947. m. **Document type:** *Newsletter.*
Address: Weidenweg 21, Aachen, 52074, Germany. TEL 0241-872552, FAX 0241-875968. Ed., Pub. Horst Krueger. Circ: 3,100.

323.4 CHE ISSN 0254-4377
HX536
GLAUBE IN DER 2. WELT; Zeitschrift fuer Religionsfreiheit und Menschenrechte. Text in German. 1973. m. CHF 70 (effective 2000). back issues avail. **Document type:** *Magazine, Consumer.*
Indexed: PAIS, RASB.
Published by: Institut Glaube in der 2. Welt, Bergstr. 6, Postfach 9, Zollikon-Zurich, 8702, Switzerland. TEL 41-1-3913747, FAX 41-1-3914426. Ed. Erich Bryner.

230 DEU ISSN 0934-0785
GLAUBE UND DENKEN. Text in German. 1988. irreg., latest vol.24, 2009. price varies. **Document type:** *Monographic series, Academic/Scholarly.*
Indexed: IBR, IBZ.
Published by: (Karl-Heim-Gesellschaft e.V.), Peter Lang GmbH (Subsidiary of: Peter Lang Publishing Group), Eschborner Landstr 42-50, Frankfurt Am Main, 60489, Germany. TEL 49-69-7807050, FAX 49-69-78070550, zentrale.frankfurt@peterlang.com.

230 DEU ISSN 0935-8889
GLAUBE UND LEBEN; Kirchenzeitung fuer das Bistum Mainz. Text in German. 1947. w. (Sun.). EUR 6.55 per month (effective 2010). adv. **Document type:** *Newspaper, Consumer.*
Published by: Gesellschaft fuer kirchliche Publizistik Mainz GmbH, Erich-Dombrowski-Str 2, Mainz, 55127, Germany. TEL 49-6131-484150, FAX 49-6131-484158.

200 DEU ISSN 0179-3551
BR4
➤ **GLAUBE UND LERNEN**; Zeitschrift fuer theologische Urteilsbildung. Text in German. s-a. EUR 32; EUR 26 to students; EUR 18 newsstand/cover (effective 2009). adv. **Document type:** *Journal, Academic/Scholarly.*
Indexed: DIP, IBR, IBZ, IZBG, R&TA.
Published by: Vandenhoeck und Ruprecht, Theaterstr 13, Goettingen, 37073, Germany. TEL 49-551-508440, FAX 49-551-5084422, info@v-r.de, http://www.v-r.de. adv.: page EUR 460; trim 117 x 190. Circ: 1,000 (paid and controlled).

200 DEU
GLAUBEN LEBEN; Zeitschrift fuer Spiritualitaet im Alltag. Text in German. 1924. bi-m. EUR 31; EUR 6 newsstand/cover (effective 2009). adv. bk.rev. **Document type:** *Magazine, Consumer.*
Former titles (until 1995): Dienender Glaube (0012-2572); (until 1969): An Heiligen Quellen
Published by: Butzon und Bercker GmbH, Hoogeweg 71, Kevelaer, 47623, Germany. TEL 49-2832-9290, FAX 49-2832-929211, service@bube.de, http://www.butzonbercker.de. Ed. Dorothee Sandherr-Klemp. Circ: 2,900.

200 LKA
GLEANINGS. Text in English. 1982. q. LKR 16, USD 4.
Published by: Sioll School of Technology, Battaramulla, Sri Lanka. Ed. J F Newslan. Circ: 400. **Subscr. to:** Ecumenical Institute for Study and Dialogue, 490-5 Havelock Rd., Colombo 6, Sri Lanka.

200 USA ISSN 1521-6055
➤ **GLOBAL JOURNAL OF CLASSICAL THEOLOGY.** Text in English. 1998. 3/yr. free (effective 2010). **Document type:** *Journal, Academic/Scholarly.* **Description:** Dedicated to the enrichment and exchange of critical thought in the matters of theology, Christian thought, historiography, legal and apologetic issues, and the philosophical defense of the faith.
Media: Online - full text.
Indexed: R&TA.
Published by: (Patrick Henry College), Trinity College and Theological Seminary, 4233 Medwel Dr, Newburgh, IN 47630. TEL 812-853-0611, FAX 812-858-6403, contact@trinitysem.edu, http://www.trinitysem.edu. Ed. John Warwick Montgomery TEL 333-886-10882.

268 NLD ISSN 1570-1972
GLOBAL PERSPECTIVES ON BIBLICAL SCHOLARSHIP. Text in English. irreg., latest vol.9, 2005. price varies. **Document type:** *Monographic series, Academic/Scholarly.*
Indexed: IZBG.
Published by: (Society of Biblical Literature USA), Brill, PO Box 9000, Leiden, 2300 PA, Netherlands. TEL 31-71-5353500, FAX 31-71-5317532, cs@brill.nl.

207.2 USA ISSN 1045-9731
GLOBAL PRAYER DIGEST. Text in English, Portuguese, Spanish. 1982. m. USD 9; USD 18 foreign. index. back issues avail. **Document type:** *Newsletter.*
Published by: U S Center for World Mission, Frontier Fellowship, 1605 Elizabeth St, Pasadena, CA 91104. TEL 626-398-2249, FAX 626-398-2263. Ed., R&P Keith Carey TEL 626-398-2241. Circ: 10,000 (paid).

290 USA
GLOW INTERNATIONAL. Text in English. 1966. q. USD 150 in India; USD 26 elsewhere (effective 2003). adv. bk.rev. back issues avail. **Document type:** *Magazine, Consumer.*
Published by: The Meher Baba Work, 599 Edison Dr, E, Windsor, NJ 08520-5207. TEL 609-426-4345, zenocom@aol.com. Ed. Naosherwan Anzar. Circ: 1,000. **Subscr. to:** PO Box 10, New York, NY 10185.

200 DEU ISSN 0017-1409
GNADE UND HERRLICHKEIT. Text in German. 1949. bi-m. EUR 24 (effective 2005). **Document type:** *Bulletin.*
Indexed: CERDIC.
Published by: Paulus-Verlag Karl Geyer, Goethestr 38, Heilbronn, 74076, Germany. TEL 49-7131-172090, FAX 49-7131-953105, paulus-verlag@t-online.de, http://www.paulus-verlag.de.

220 GBR ISSN 0950-7221
GO TEACH BEGINNERS. Variant title: Go Teach God's Word to 3s-4s. Go Teach the Word of God to Beginners. Text in English. 1984. 3/yr. GBP 6.90 per issue (effective 2010). back issues avail. **Document type:** *Magazine, Academic/Scholarly.* **Description:** Teacher's book for teaching scripture lessons to 3-4 year olds.
Formerly (until 2000): Go Teach God's Word to Beginners
Published by: Go Teach Publications Ltd., Unit 12 Paradise Mill, Park Lane, Macclesfield, SK11 6TJ, United Kingdom. TEL 44-1625-422279, FAX 44-1625-422272, editorial@goteach.org.uk.

220 GBR ISSN 0950-7248
GO TEACH JUNIORS. Variant title: Go Teach God's Word to 8s-11s. Go Teach The Word of God to Juniors. Text in English. 1984. 3/yr. GBP 6.90 per issue (effective 2010). back issues avail. **Document type:** *Magazine, Academic/Scholarly.* **Description:** Teacher's book for teaching scripture lessons to 8-12 year olds.
Formerly (until 1999): Go Teach God's Word to Juniors
Published by: Go Teach Publications Ltd., Unit 12 Paradise Mill, Park Lane, Macclesfield, SK11 6TJ, United Kingdom. TEL 44-1625-422279, FAX 44-1625-422272, editorial@goteach.org.uk.

220 375 GBR ISSN 0950-723X
GO TEACH PRIMARIES. Variant title: Go Teach God's Word to 5s-7s. Go Teach The Word of God to Primaries. Text in English. 1984. 3/yr. GBP 6.90 per issue (effective 2010). illus. **Document type:** *Magazine, Academic/Scholarly.* **Description:** Teachers' book for teaching scripture lessons to 5-7 year olds.
Formerly (until 2001): Go Teach God's Word to 5s-8s
Published by: Go Teach Publications Ltd., Unit 12 Paradise Mill, Park Lane, Macclesfield, SK11 6TJ, United Kingdom. TEL 44-1625-422279, FAX 44-1625-422272, editorial@goteach.org.uk.

220 GBR ISSN 0950-7256
GO TEACH YOUNG TEENS. Variant title: Go Teach God's Word to 12s-14s. Go Teach The Word of God to Young Teens. Text in English. 1984. 3/yr. GBP 6.90 per issue (effective 2010). back issues avail. **Document type:** *Magazine, Academic/Scholarly.* **Description:** Teachers' book for teaching scripture lessons to over 12 year olds.
Formerly (until 2000): Go Teach God's Word to Young Teens
Published by: Go Teach Publications Ltd., Unit 12 Paradise Mill, Park Lane, Macclesfield, SK11 6TJ, United Kingdom. TEL 44-1625-422279, FAX 44-1625-422272, editorial@goteach.org.uk.

230 658 USA
GODLY COUNSEL. Text in English. m. USD 99 (effective 1998). **Document type:** *Newsletter.* **Description:** Contains articles on a wide range of business management topics, all based on Christian principles.
Related titles: Online - full text ed.: A Byte of Godley Counsel.
Published by: The C12 Group, 656 Flamingo Dr., Apollo Beach, FL 33572. Ed. Jim Peters.

200 BEL ISSN 1377-8323
GODS, HUMANS AND RELIGIONS/DIEUX, HOMMES ET RELIGIONS. Text in English, French. 2002. irreg., latest vol.18, 2009. price varies. **Document type:** *Monographic series, Academic/Scholarly.*
—BLDSC (4201.099164).
Published by: P I E - Peter Lang SA, 1 avenue Maurice, 6e etage, Brussels, 1050, Belgium. TEL 32-2-3477236, FAX 32-2-3477237, pie@peterlang.com, http://www.peterlang.net.

201.6 USA
GOD'S SPECIAL TIME; kairos of Colorado. Text in English. 1965. irreg. (3-4/yr.). USD 5. abstr.; bibl.; illus. **Document type:** *Newsletter, Consumer.* **Description:** Lists events and membership news.
Former titles: Colorado Kairos; (until 1982): Colorado Councillor (0010-1540); Rocky Mountain Churchman
Related titles: Online - full text ed.
Published by: Kairos of Colorado, Inc., P O Box 25004, Colorado Springs, CO 80936-5004. scenic_bye@yahoo.com. Circ: 2,000.

251 DEU ISSN 0340-6083
➤ **GOETTINGER PREDIGTMEDITATIONEN**; Evangelische Predigtmeditationen. Text in German. 1946. q. EUR 57 to individuals; EUR 114 to institutions; EUR 32.50 to students; EUR 18.90 newsstand/cover (effective 2011). adv. index. **Document type:** *Journal, Academic/Scholarly.*
Indexed: DIP, IBR, IBZ.
Published by: Vandenhoeck und Ruprecht, Theaterstr 13, Goettingen, 37073, Germany. TEL 49-551-508440, FAX 49-551-5084422, info@v-r.de. Ed. Martin Nicol. Circ: 2,000.

➤ **GOING ON FAITH**; the national newspaper for faith-based travel planners. *see* TRAVEL AND TOURISM

200 USA ISSN 1933-5385
GOLEM; journal of religion and monsters. Text in English. 2006. s-a. back issues avail. **Document type:** *Journal, Academic/Scholarly.*
Media: Online - full text.
Published by: Frances Flannery-Dailey http://www.golemjournal.org/index.htm.

266 ZAF ISSN 0017-2146
GOOD NEWS/GOEIE NUUS; the magazine with a message. Text in English. 1951. q. ZAR 10, USD 5.
Related titles: Afrikaans ed.
Published by: Good News Missionary Society, PO Box 7848, Johannesburg, 2000, South Africa. TEL 011-729-9581. Ed. Sean O'Sullivan. Circ: 5,000.

GORGIAS HANDBOOKS. *see* LINGUISTICS

GORGIAS HISTORICAL TEXTS. *see* HISTORY

203 USA ISSN 1937-3252
GORGIAS LITURGICAL STUDIES. Text in English. 2007. irreg., latest 2009. price varies. back issues avail. **Document type:** *Monographic series, Academic/Scholarly.* **Description:** Provides a venue for studies about liturgies as well as books containing various liturgies.
Published by: Gorgias Press LLC, 954 River Rd, Piscataway, NJ 08854. TEL 732-885-8900, FAX 732-885-8908, helpdesk@gorgiaspress.com, http://www.gorgiaspress.com/bookshop/default.aspx.

220 USA ISSN 1935-4398
GORGIAS OCCASIONAL HISTORICAL COMMENTARIES. Text mainly in English; Text occasionally in German, Hebrew. 2007. irreg., latest 2009. price varies. back issues avail. **Document type:** *Monographic series, Academic/Scholarly.* **Description:** Seeks to reprint historically important biblical commentaries.
Published by: Gorgias Press LLC, 954 River Rd, Piscataway, NJ 08854. TEL 732-885-8900, FAX 732-885-8908, helpdesk@gorgiaspress.com, http://www.gorgiaspress.com/bookshop/default.aspx.

200 USA ISSN 1937-3287
GORGIAS REFERENCE CLASSICS. Text in English. 2007. irreg., latest vol.2, 2009. price varies. back issues avail. **Document type:** *Monographic series, Academic/Scholarly.* **Description:** Covers the impact on historical understanding works from the nineteenth century and earlier in circulation.
Published by: Gorgias Press LLC, 954 River Rd, Piscataway, NJ 08854. TEL 732-885-8900, FAX 732-885-8908, helpdesk@gorgiaspress.com, http://www.gorgiaspress.com/bookshop/default.aspx.

GORGIAS STUDIES IN PHILOSOPHY AND THEOLOGY. *see* PHILOSOPHY

202 USA ISSN 1935-6935
GORGIAS THEOLOGICAL LIBRARY. Text in English. 2006. irreg., latest vol.2, 2010. price varies. back issues avail. **Document type:** *Monographic series, Academic/Scholarly.* **Description:** Presents core theological works for students of theology.
Published by: Gorgias Press LLC, 954 River Rd, Piscataway, NJ 08854. TEL 732-885-8900, FAX 732-885-8908, helpdesk@gorgiaspress.com, http://www.gorgiaspress.com/bookshop/default.aspx.

200 USA ISSN 0195-1297
GOSPEL ADVOCATE. Text in English. 1855. m. USD 16.98 (effective 2002). adv. index. **Document type:** *Magazine, Consumer.* **Description:** Devotional and educational material for church leaders and members.
Indexed: ChrPI.
Published by: Gospel Advocate Company, 1006 Elm Hill Pike, Nashville, TN 37210. TEL 615-254-8781, FAX 615-254-7411. Ed. Neil Anderson. Circ: 23,000. **Subscr. to:** PO Box 150, Nashville, TN 37202.

220 CAN ISSN 0829-4666
GOSPEL HERALD; for the promotion of New Testament Christianity. Text in English. 1936. m. CAD 14, USD 21 (effective 2001). adv. bk.rev.
Document type: *Newsletter, Consumer.* **Description:** Articles promoting New Testament Christianity, including teaching material for youth and women, and features history, news, and family life.
Published by: Gospel Herald Foundation, 4904 King St, Beamsville, ON L0R 1B6, Canada. TEL 905-563-7503, FAX 905-563-7503. Ed. Wayne Turner. R&P, Adv. contact Eugene C Perry. Circ: 1,325 (paid).

371.07 USA ISSN 0746-0880
THE GOSPEL HERALD AND SUNDAY SCHOOL TIMES. Text in English. 1902. q. free (effective 2007). **Document type:** *Newspaper, Consumer.*
Formerly: Sunday School Times and Gospel Herald (0039-5293)
Published by: Union Gospel Press, PO Box 6059, Cleveland, OH 44101. TEL 216-749-2100, 800-638-9988, FAX 216-749-2205, http://www.uniongospelpress.com/. Ed. Beryl C Bidlen. Circ: 50,000 (controlled).

THE GOSPEL MESSENGER. *see* HANDICAPPED—Visually Impaired

207.2 USA
GOSPEL OUTREACH. Text in English. 1949. q. free. **Document type:** *Newsletter.*
Formerly (until 1994): Worldwide Evangelist
Published by: Concordia Gospel Outreach, PO Box 201, Concordia, MO 63166-0201. TEL 314-268-1363, FAX 314-268-1329. Ed., R&P Annette Frank. Circ: 9,200 (controlled).

GOSPEL TODAY MAGAZINE; America's leading christian lifestyle magazine. *see* MUSIC

266 DEU
GOSSNER MISSION INFORMATION. Text in German. 1852. q. back issues avail. **Document type:** *Magazine, Consumer.*
Published by: Gossner Mission, Georgenkirchstr 69-70, Berlin, 10249, Germany. TEL 49-30-243445750, FAX 49-30-243445752, mail@gossner-mission.de, http://www.gossner-mission.de. Ed. Jutta Klimmt. Circ: 6,000 (controlled).

200 DEU ISSN 0017-2480
GOTTES WORT IM KIRCHENJAHR. Text in German. 1940. 3/yr. EUR 45 (effective 2010). adv. **Document type:** *Magazine, Consumer.*
Published by: Echter Verlag GmbH, Postfach 5560, Wuerzburg, 97005, Germany. info@echter-verlag.de, http://www.echter.de.

250 PRT
GRACAS DO PADRE CRUZ, S.J. Text in Portuguese. 1949. q. adv. bk.rev. **Document type:** *Magazine, Consumer.*
Formerly (until 1987): Gracas do Servo de Deus: Padre Cruz (0017-2758)
Published by: Vice Postulacao Causa Padre Cruz, Rua da Madalena 179, Lisbon, 1117-001, Portugal. TEL 351-21-8824590, FAX 351-21-8824599, causapadrecruz@padrecruz.org. Circ: 26,200.

230.071 USA
GRACE EVANGELICAL SOCIETY. JOURNAL. Text in English. 1988. s-a. USD 18.50 domestic; USD 21 in Canada & Mexico; USD 25 elsewhere (effective 2010). back issues avail. **Document type:** *Journal, Academic/Scholarly.*
Related titles: Online - full text ed.: free (effective 2010).
Indexed: GSS&RPL, R&TA.
Published by: Grace Evangelical Society, 100 W Oak St, Ste G, Denton, TX 76201. TEL 940-565-0000, ges@faithalone.org.

GRACE TIDINGS. *see* COLLEGE AND ALUMNI

230 BRA ISSN 0046-6271
GRANDE SINAL. Text in Portuguese. 1947. 6/yr. BRL 85 domestic; USD 80 foreign (effective 2005). bk.rev. abstr.; bibl.; illus.; stat. index.
Document type: *Journal, Academic/Scholarly.* **Description:** Texts and reflections about spirituality.
Published by: Editora Vozes Ltda., Rua Mexico 174, Rio de Janeiro, RJ 20031 143, Brazil. TEL 55-21-22156386, FAX 55-21-25338358, vozes42@uol.com.br, http://www.editoravozes.com.br. Ed. Nilo Agostini. Circ: 2,900.

GRANTS FOR RELIGION, RELIGIOUS WELFARE & RELIGIOUS EDUCATION (ONLINE). *see* EDUCATION—School Organization And Administration

220 808.80 FRA ISSN 1241-5286
BS410
➤ **GRAPHE.** Text in French. 1992. a. bk.rev. back issues avail.
Document type: *Journal, Academic/Scholarly.* **Description:** Explores the influence of the Bible on literature and the arts in the Judeo-Christian world.
Indexed: MLA-IB.
Published by: Universite de Lille III (Charles de Gaulle), S E G E S, B P 149, Villeneuve d'Ascq, Cedex 59653, France. TEL 33-3-20416497, FAX 33-3-20416191. Ed. Jacques Sys. Circ: 250.

200 USA
GRAVITAS; a journal of religion and theology. Text in English. 1999. a.
Media: Online - full content.
Indexed: CPerI.
Published by: Graduate Theological Union Library, 2400 Ridge Rd, Berkeley, CA 94709. TEL 510-649-2501, FAX 510-649-2508, gravitas@gtu.edu. Ed. Jay Feist.

230 USA ISSN 1947-5837
BV652.25
GREAT COMMISSION RESEARCH JOURNAL. Text in English. s-a. USD 30 domestic; USD 38 foreign (effective 2009). **Document type:** *Journal, Academic/Scholarly.* **Description:** Communicates recent thinking and research related to the American Society for Church Growth.
Formerly (until 2009): American Society for Church Growth. Journal (1091-2711)
Indexed: A21, ChrPI, R&TA, RI-1.
Published by: Biola University, Cook School of Intercultural Studies, 13800 Biola Ave, La Mirada, CA 90639. TEL 562-903-4727, joy.bergk@biola.edu, http://cook.biola.edu/grad/.

200 DEU ISSN 1439-1708
GREIFSWALDER THEOLOGISCHE FORSCHUNGEN. Text in German. 2001. irreg., latest vol.20, 2010. price varies. **Document type:** *Monographic series, Academic/Scholarly.*
Published by: Peter Lang GmbH (Subsidiary of: Peter Lang Publishing Group), Eschborner Landstr 42-50, Frankfurt Am Main, 60489, Germany. TEL 49-69-7807050, FAX 49-69-78070550, zentrale.frankfurt@peterlang.com. Ed. Christfried Boettrich.

268 GBR ISSN 1743-2308
THE GRID. Text in English. 198?. q. GBP 2 per issue (effective 2010). illus. 84 p./no.; **Document type:** *Magazine, Consumer.* **Description:** Presents church curriculum for young people ages 11 to 13.
Former titles (until 2004): The S A L T Programme for 11 to 13 (Sharing and Learning Together) (0968-5391); (until 1993): Learning Together with 11-14's (0963-486X); (until 198?): Teaching 10-13's (0308-356X); Which seperseded in part (in 1975): Teaching Teenagers 11-14's (0040-067X)
Related titles: CD-ROM ed.: free to members (effective 2010).
—**CCC.**
Published by: Scripture Union, 207-209 Queensway, Bletchley, Milton Keynes, Bucks MK2 2EB, United Kingdom. TEL 44-1908-856000, FAX 44-1908-856111, info@scriptureunion.org.uk.

200 400 DEU ISSN 0232-2900
GRIECHISCHEN CHRISTLICHEN SCHRIFTSTELLER DER ERSTEN JAHRHUNDERTE. Text in English, German, Greek, Latin. 1953. irreg., latest vol.15, 2007. price varies. **Document type:** *Monographic series, Academic/Scholarly.*
Related titles: Microfiche ed.: (from IDC).
Published by: Walter de Gruyter GmbH & Co. KG, Genthiner Str 13, Berlin, 10785, Germany. TEL 49-30-260050, FAX 49-30-26005251, info@degruyter.com, http://www.degruyter.de.

GROUP (LOVELAND); the youth ministry magazine. *see* CHILDREN AND YOUTH—About

200 GBR ISSN 0144-171X
GROVE PASTORAL SERIES. Text in English. 1972. q. GBP 10; GBP 3.50 per issue (print or online ed.) (effective 2009). back issues avail.
Document type: *Monographic series, Trade.* **Description:** Provides clear and concise explorations of pastoral ministry.
Supersedes in part (in 1980): Grove Booklet on Ministry and Worship (0305-3067)
Related titles: Online - full text ed.
—BLDSC (4220.570000), IE, Ingenta. **CCC.**
Published by: Grove Books Ltd., Ridley Hall Rd, Cambridge, CB3 9HU, United Kingdom. TEL 44-1223-464748, FAX 44-1223-464849, sales@grovebooks.co.uk.

200 GBR ISSN 0262-799X
GROVE SPIRITUALITY SERIES. Text in English. 1982. q. GBP 10; GBP 3.50 per issue (print or online ed.) (effective 2009). back issues avail.
Document type: *Monographic series, Trade.* **Description:** Provides clear and concise explorations of the spiritual and devotional life.
Related titles: Online - full text ed.
—BLDSC (4220.580000), IE, Ingenta. **CCC.**
Published by: Grove Books Ltd., Ridley Hall Rd, Cambridge, CB3 9HU, United Kingdom. TEL 44-1223-464748, FAX 44-1223-464849, sales@grovebooks.co.uk.

230 CAN ISSN 1920-8677
GROWING TOGETHER (ECUMENICAL EDITION, ONLINE). Text in English. 1993. a. free (effective 2011). back issues avail. **Document type:** *Bulletin, Academic/Scholarly.*
Formerly: Growing Together (Ecumenical Edition, Print) (1481-9465)
Media: Online - full text.
Published by: Prairie Centre for Ecumenism, 600-45th St W, Saskatoon, SK S7L 5W9, Canada. TEL 306-653-1633, FAX 306-653-1821, pce@ecumenism.net, http://ecumenism.net/pce/.

200 DEU ISSN 1610-7764
GRUNDSCHULE RELIGION. Text in German. 2002. q. EUR 52; EUR 20 newsstand/cover (effective 2011). adv. **Document type:** *Journal, Academic/Scholarly.*
Published by: Erhard Friedrich Verlag GmbH, Im Brande 17, Seelze, 30926, Germany. TEL 49-511-400040, FAX 49-511-40004170, info@friedrich-verlag.de. Adv. contact Bianca Kraft. Circ: 5,000 (paid and controlled).

200 DEU
GRUSS DER GROSSHEPPACHER SCHWESTERNSCHAFT; Kind und Schwester. Text in German. s-a. **Document type:** *Newsletter.*
Published by: Stiftung Grossheppacher Schwesternschaft, Postfach 1124, Weinstadt, 71365, Germany. TEL 49-7151-9934-0, FAX 49-7151-993450. Ed. Willi Duerring. Circ: 6,000.

GUIDE TO SOCIAL SCIENCE AND RELIGION. *see* RELIGIONS AND THEOLOGY—Abstracting, Bibliographies, Statistics

202.15 USA ISSN 0017-5331
BV4800
GUIDEPOSTS; true stories of hope and inspiration. Text in English. 1945. m. (11/yr.). USD 9.97 domestic; USD 13.97 in Canada; USD 24.97 elsewhere (effective 2010). adv. illus. Index. 64 p./no.; reprints avail.
Document type: *Magazine, Consumer.* **Description:** Presents true first-person narratives that inspire successful and happy living.
Related titles: Audio cassette/tape ed.; Large type ed. 18 pt.: USD 16.97 domestic; USD 19.97 in Canada; USD 28.97 elsewhere (effective 2009).
Indexed: CCR, M02, T02.
Address: 39 Seminary Hill Rd, Carmel, NY 10512. TEL 845-225-3681, FAX 845-228-2143, http://www.guideposts.org. Ed. Edward Grinnan. Circ: 300,000.

GUIDEPOSTS SWEET 16. *see* CHILDREN AND YOUTH—For

200 DEU
GUTE BESSERUNG. Text in German. 1977. m. EUR 162 (effective 2011).
Document type: *Magazine, Consumer.* **Description:** Publication concerned with giving strength and information to those who are ill, by means of religion and humor.
Published by: Bergmoser und Hoeller Verlag GmbH, Karl-Friedrich-Str 76, Aachen, 52072, Germany. TEL 49-241-93888123, FAX 49-241-93888134, kontakt@buhv.de. Ed. Johannes Zitterer. Circ: 50,000.

H M MAGAZINE; the hard music magazine. (Hard Music) *see* MUSIC

291.72 362.5 NLD ISSN 1877-5519
H MAGAZINE. Text in Dutch. 2005. bi-m.
Formerly (until 2008): Stichting Hulp Oost-Europe. Nieuwsbrief (1872-1796)
Published by: Stichting Hulp Oost-Europe, Postbus 455, Barneveld, 3770 AL, Netherlands. TEL 31-342-420554, FAX 31-342-420553, info@hulpoosteuropa.nl.

230 TZA ISSN 0856-938X
HABARI NJEMA. Text in English. 2004. w.
Published by: Good News for All Trust Fund, Kijitonyama Plot No. 729, Box 32414, Dar Es Salaam, Tanzania.

200 USA ISSN 1072-1053
HAIWAI XIAOYUAN/OVERSEAS CAMPUS. Text in English. 1992. bi-m. back issues avail. **Document type:** *Magazine, Academic/Scholarly.*
Description: Covers evangelistic topics for Chinese scholars and students overseas.
Published by: Campus Evangelical Fellowship, Inc., 1753 Cabrillo Ave, Torrance, CA 90501. TEL 310-328-8200, FAX 310-328-8207, info@oc.org.

HALLESCHE QUELLENPUBLIKATIONEN UND REPERTORIEN. *see* HISTORY—History Of Europe

268 USA ISSN 0072-9787
HANDBOOK OF DENOMINATIONS IN THE U S. (United States) Text in English. quinquennial. **Document type:** *Handbook/Manual/Guide, Consumer.* **Description:** Reference describing many religious bodies in the US, with information on their historical background and doctrines.
Published by: Abingdon Press, 201 Eighth Ave S, PO Box 801, Nashville, TN 37202. TEL 800-251-3320, FAX 800-836-7802, orders@abingdonpress.com.

225 DEU ISSN 0932-9706
HANDBUCH ZUM NEUEN TESTAMENT. Text in German. 1974. irreg. price varies. **Document type:** *Monographic series, Academic/Scholarly.*
Published by: Mohr Siebeck GmbH & Co. KG, Wilhelmstr 18, Tuebingen, 72074, Germany. TEL 49-7071-9230, FAX 49-7071-51104, info@mohr.de.

250 NLD ISSN 1876-8024
BV1
HANDELINGEN; tijdschrift voor praktische theologie. Text in Dutch. 1967. q. EUR 40.50 domestic; EUR 48 foreign; EUR 20.50 to students; EUR 13.50 newsstand/cover (effective 2010). **Document type:** *Journal, Trade.*
Former titles (until 2008): Praktische Theologie (0165-6511); (until 1973): Ministerium (0026-5306)
—Infotrieve, INIST.
Published by: (Stichting Praktische Theologie), Waanders Uitgevers, Postbus 1129, Zwolle, 8001 BC, Netherlands. TEL 31-38-4673400, FAX 31-38-4673401, info@waanders.nl, http://www.waanders.nl. Ed. Evert R Jonker.

200 DEU ISSN 1861-6011
HANS-LIETZMANN-VORLESUNGEN. Text in German. 1996. irreg., latest vol.10, 2009. price varies. **Document type:** *Monographic series, Academic/Scholarly.*
Published by: Walter de Gruyter GmbH & Co. KG, Genthiner Str 13, Berlin, 10785, Germany. TEL 49-30-26005220, FAX 49-30-26005251, info@degruyter.com, http://www.degruyter.de.

HAPPENINGS. *see* SOCIAL SERVICES AND WELFARE

HARMONY (SAN FRANCISCO); voices for a just future. *see* POLITICAL SCIENCE—Civil Rights

200 USA ISSN 1932-7595
HARUAH: BREATH OF HEAVEN. Text in English. 2006. m. **Document type:** *Magazine, Consumer.*
Related titles: Online - full text ed.: ISSN 1932-7609.
Published by: Double-Edged Publishing, Inc., 9618 Misty Brook Cove, Cordova, TN 38016. http://www.doubleedgedpublishing.com.

200 USA ISSN 1550-2465
BV4070
➤ **HARVARD DIVINITY BULLETIN.** Abbreviated title: H D B. Text in English. 2001. 3/yr. free to qualified personnel (effective 2010). adv. bk.rev. illus. Index. back issues avail.; reprints avail. **Document type:** *Magazine, Academic/Scholarly.* **Description:** Contains articles, reviews, and opinion pieces on religion and contemporary life, religion and the arts, religious history, and the study of religion.
Formerly (until Sum./Fall 2001): Harvard Divinity Bulletin, Religion & Values in Public Life (1550-2457); Which was formed by the merger of (1992-2001): Religion & Values in Public Life (1084-3949); (1959-2001): Harvard Divinity Bulletin (0017-8047); Which was formerly (1936-1959): Harvard Divinity School Bulletin (0362-5117)
Related titles: Microfiche ed.; Online - full text ed.: 2001. free (effective 2007).
Indexed: A21, RI-1, RI-2.
—BLDSC (4265.886400).
Published by: Harvard Divinity School, 45 Francis Ave, Cambridge, MA 02138. TEL 617-496-1813, kathryn_dodgson@harvard.edu. Ed. Wendy S McDowell. Adv. contact Charlie Roth TEL 516-729-3509. Circ: 22,000.

➤ **HARVARD SEMITIC MONOGRAPHS.** *see* LINGUISTICS

200 GBR ISSN 0017-8160
BR1
➤ **HARVARD THEOLOGICAL REVIEW.** Abbreviated title: H T R. Text in English. 1908. q. GBP 124, USD 206 to institutions; GBP 137, USD 227 combined subscription to institutions (print & online eds.) (effective 2012). adv. bk.rev. charts; illus. Index. 128 p./no.; back issues avail.; reprints avail. **Document type:** *Journal, Academic/Scholarly.* **Description:** Contains scholarly articles in the field of religious studies.
Related titles: Microfiche ed.; Online - full text ed.: ISSN 1475-4517. GBP 114, USD 190 to institutions (effective 2012).
Indexed: A01, A02, A03, A08, A20, A21, A22, A26, ASCA, AmH&L, AmHI, ArtHuCI, B04, BRD, CA, CERDIC, CurCont, DIP, E01, E08, FR, G08, H07, H08, H09, H10, H14, HAb, HistAb, HumInd, I05, I07, IBR, IBZ, IZBG, LID&ISL, M01, M02, MLA, MLA-IB, OTA, P02, P10, P28, P30, P48, P53, P54, PCI, PQC, PhilInd, R&TA, R05, RASB, RI-1, RI-2, S05, S09, S23, SCOPUS, T02, W03, W05, W07.
—BLDSC (4270.690000), IE, Infotrieve, Ingenta. **CCC.**

R

Published by: Cambridge University Press, The Edinburgh Bldg, Shaftesbury Rd, Cambridge, CB2 8RU, United Kingdom. TEL 44-1223-312393, FAX 44-1223-315052, journals@cambridge.org, http://www.cambridge.org/uk. Ed. Francois Bovon. R&P Linda Nicol TEL 44-1223-325702. Adv. contact Rebecca Roberts TEL 44-1223-325083. page GBP 345, page USD 655. Circ: 1,600. **Subscr. to:** Cambridge University Press, 32 Ave of the Americas, New York, NY 10013. TEL 212-337-5000, FAX 212-691-3239, journals_subscriptions@cup.org. **Dist. by:** Cambridge University Press Distribution Center.

201 USA ISSN 0073-0726
HARVARD THEOLOGICAL STUDIES. Abbreviated title: H T S. Text in English. 1916. irreg., latest vol.64, 2010. price varies. back issues avail.; reprints avail. **Document type:** *Monographic series, Academic/Scholarly.* **Description:** Brings out dissertations and monograph by either a Harvard Divinity School or Harvard University Study of Religion doctoral student.
Published by: Harvard Divinity School, 45 Francis Ave, Cambridge, MA 02138. TEL 617-495-5786, FAX 617-496-9402, kathryn_dodgson@harvard.edu. Eds. Francois Bovon, Peter B Machinist TEL 617-495-0333. **Dist. by:** Harvard University Press.

200 USA
HARVEST (WHEATON); reaching the unreached. Text in English. 1997. q. free. **Document type:** *Newsletter, Trade.*
Published by: Mission to the Americas, 2715 Welton St., Denver, CO 80205-2913. rmiller@mtta.org, http://www.mtta.org. Ed. Rick Miller. Circ: 30,000 (controlled and free).

202 GBR ISSN 1752-038X
THE HEALER. Text in English. 1953. bi-m. donation. adv. illus. index. back issues avail. **Document type:** *Magazine, Consumer.* **Description:** Features articles on spiritual healing and simple philosophy.
Formerly (until 2006): The Spiritual Healer (0038-7622)
Related titles: Online - full text ed.: free (effective 2009).
Published by: Harry Edwards Healing Sanctuary, Burrows Lea, Hook Ln, Shere, Guildford, Surrey GU5 9QG, United Kingdom. TEL 44-1483-202054, FAX 44-1483-205613, info@burrowslea.org.uk. Ed. Gary Waugh.

207.2 GBR ISSN 0017-8829
HEALING HAND. Text in English. 18??. 3/yr. free (effective 2009). bk.rev. back issues avail. **Document type:** *Magazine, Consumer.* **Description:** Provides news of activities of the society as well as articles on medical missions.
Former titles (until 1966): Edinburgh Medical Missionary Society. Quarterly Paper (0307-3416); (until 1871): Edinburgh Medical Missionary Society. Occasional Papers
Published by: Emmanuel Healthcare, 7 Washington Ln, Edinburgh, EH11 2HA, United Kingdom. TEL 44-131-3133828, FAX 44-131-3134662, info@emms.org.

200 USA ISSN 1087-1586
➤ **HEALING MINISTRY.** Text in English. 1994. q. USD 84 domestic to individuals; USD 104 in Canada to individuals; USD 136 elsewhere to individuals; USD 147 domestic to institutions; USD 169 in Canada to institutions; USD 238 elsewhere to institutions (effective 2010). adv. 48 p./no.; reprints avail. **Document type:** *Journal, Academic/Scholarly.* **Description:** Provides lay people and clergy of all denominations a professional focus on a variety of issues concerning spiritual caregiving and bereavement support.
Indexed: C06, C07.
—CCC.
Published by: Weston Medical Publishing, LLC, 470 Boston Post Rd, Weston, MA 02493. TEL 781-899-2702, 800-743-7206, FAX 781-899-4900, brenda_devito@pnpco.com, subscription@pnpco.com, http://www.wmpllc.org. Pub. Richard A DeVito Sr. TEL 781-899-2702 ext 107.

200 USA ISSN 1943-6556
HEALING SPIRIT. Text in English. 19??. s-a. USD 15 domestic to non-members; USD 18 foreign to non-members; free to members (effective 2009). adv. back issues avail. **Document type:** *Magazine, Trade.* **Description:** Provides the commitment to advocacy for the profession of chaplaincy, promoting quality care for all who are in need.
Former titles (until 2006): The A P C News (1526-2790); (until 1998): Tie (Schaumburg) (1077-8403)
Related titles: Online - full text ed.: free (effective 2009).
Published by: Association of Professional Chaplains, 1701 E Woodfield Rd, Ste 760, Schaumburg, IL 60173. TEL 847-240-1014, FAX 847-240-1015, info@professionalchaplains.org. Ed. Rita Kaufman.

260 GBR ISSN 1748-8028
HE@LTHYCHURCH.MAG.UK. Text in English. 1979. q. back issues avail. **Document type:** *Magazine, Trade.* **Description:** Designed to improve the health and growth potential of local church.
Formerly (until 2003): Church Growth Digest (0268-7658)
Related titles: Online - full text ed.
Published by: Healthy Church UK, PO Box 100, Sandy, SG19 1ZR, United Kingdom. TEL 44-1767-692938, FAX 44-871-2771249, philip@healthychurch.co.uk.

HEARTBEAT : FM103.2 NEWSLETTER. *see* COMMUNICATIONS—Radio

200 AUT ISSN 0017-9620
HEILIGER DIENST. Text in German. 1947. q. EUR 20; EUR 5.50 newsstand/cover (effective 2005). bk.rev. **Document type:** *Bulletin, Consumer.* **Description:** Covers liturgy and liturgical practice.
Indexed: CERDIC, DIP, IBR, IBZ, IZBG, RILM.
Published by: (Oesterreichisches Liturgisches Institut), Verlag St. Peter, Postfach 113, Salzburg, Sa 5010, Austria. TEL 43-662-84457684, FAX 43-662-84457680, oeli@liturgie.at. Ed. P Winfried Bachler. Circ: 900.

230 DEU
HEINRICHSBLATT. Text in German. 1893. w. (Sun.). EUR 5.50 per month (effective 2010). adv. **Document type:** *Newspaper, Consumer.*
Published by: (Erzbischoefliches Ordinariat Bamberg), Heinrichs Verlag GmbH, Heinrichsdamm 32, Bamberg, 96047, Germany. TEL 49-951-51920, FAX 49-951-519215, ramer@heinrichs-verlag.de. Ed. Andreas Kuschbert.

200 CHE
HELVETIA SACRA. Text in German, French. 1972. irreg., latest vol.10, 2007. price varies. **Document type:** *Monographic series, Academic/Scholarly.*
Published by: Schwabe und Co. AG, Steinentorstr 13, Basel, 4010, Switzerland. TEL 41-61-2789565, FAX 41-61-2789566, verlag@schwabe.ch, http://www.schwabe.ch.

200 SWE ISSN 0018-0335
HEMMETS VAEN; den alkristna rikstidning. Text in Swedish. 1897. w. SEK 329, USD 40 (effective 1990). adv. bk.rev. illus.
Supersedes: Missionsblad foer Kronobergs Laen
Published by: Evangeliipress, Fack 1712, Orebro, 70117, Sweden. Ed. Stig Hallzon. Circ: 45,000.

230 USA ISSN 0895-7622
HENCEFORTH. Text in English. 1972. 3/yr. **Document type:** *Journal, Academic/Scholarly.*
Indexed: R&TA.
Published by: Berkshire Christian College, College Campus, Lenox, MA 01240. TEL 800-218-3067.

200 NLD ISSN 0929-7154
HERADEMING; tijdschrift voor spiritualiteit en mystiek. Text in Dutch. 1993. q. EUR 31.50 domestic; EUR 37.50 in Belgium; EUR 8.95 newsstand/cover (effective 2009). adv. illus. **Document type:** *Bulletin.* **Description:** Discusses topics pertaining to spirituality and mysticism.
Published by: Kok Tijdschriften, Postbus 5018, Kampen, 8260 GA, Netherlands. TEL 31-38-3392555, http://www.kok.nl. Circ: 2,650.

240 USA
HERALD OF HIS COMING. Text in English. 1941. m. free. back issues avail. **Document type:** *Newspaper, Consumer.* **Description:** Articles on practical examples of living out and putting into practice Bible teaching, with prayers and scripture.
Published by: Gospel Revivals, Inc., PO Box 279, Seelyville, IN 47878-0279. TEL 812-442-6200, FAX 812-442-6201, gospelrevivals@cs.com. Ed., R&P Lois J Stucky. Pub. Rich Carmichael. Circ: 90,000.

HERDERS BIBLIOTHEK DER PHILOSOPHIE DES MITTELALTERS. *see* PHILOSOPHY

200 ITA ISSN 1590-6833
BR5
HERMENEUTICA. Text in Italian. 1981. a. EUR 23 domestic; EUR 25 foreign (effective 2009). **Document type:** *Monographic series, Academic/Scholarly.*
Indexed: A01, OTA, PhilInd, R&TA, T02.
Published by: (Universita degli Studi di Urbino, Istituto Superiore di Scienze Religiose), Editrice Morcelliana SpA, Via Gabriele Rosa 71, Brescia, BS 25121, Italy. TEL 39-030-46451, FAX 39-030-2400605, http://www.morcelliana.it.

220 100 BRA ISSN 1518-9724
BX6154
HERMENEUTICA. Text in Portuguese. 2000. a. **Document type:** *Journal, Academic/Scholarly.*
Indexed: IZBG, OTA.
Published by: Seminario Adventista Latino Americano de Teologia, C P 18, Cachoeira, BA 44300-000, Brazil. TEL 55-75-4258035, FAX 55-75-4258106, salt@iaene.br.

220 CHE ISSN 1660-5403
HERMENEUTISCHE BLAETTER. Text in German. 1995. 2/yr. **Document type:** *Journal, Academic/Scholarly.*
Former titles (until 2002): TheoLogica (1660-542X); (until 1998): Hermeneutische Blaetter (1660-539X)
Related titles: Online - full text ed.: ISSN 1660-5578.
Published by: Universitaet Zuerich, Institut fuer Hermeneutik und Religionsphilosophie, Kirchgasse 9, Zuerich, 8001, Switzerland. TEL 41-44-6344711, FAX 41-44-6344991, hermes@theol.unizh.ch, http://www.unizh.ch/hermes/ihr_willkommen.html. Ed. Philipp Stoellger.

200 DEU ISSN 0440-7180
HERMENEUTISCHE UNTERSUCHUNGEN ZUR THEOLOGIE. Text in English, German. 1962. irreg., latest vol.57, 2010. price varies. **Document type:** *Monographic series, Academic/Scholarly.*
Published by: Mohr Siebeck GmbH & Co. KG, Wilhelmstr 18, Tuebingen, 72074, Germany. TEL 49-7071-9230, FAX 49-7071-51104, info@mohr.de.

200 USA ISSN 1932-6718
HERMIT KINGDOM STUDIES IN CHRISTIANITY AND JUDAISM. Text in English. 2005. irreg. **Document type:** *Monographic series, Consumer.*
Published by: Hermit Kingdom Press, 12325 Imperial Hwy, Ste 156, Norwalk, CA 90650. info@TheHermitKingdomPress.com, http://www.thehermitkingdompress.com/index.htm.

200 USA ISSN 1932-6696
HERMIT KINGDOM STUDIES IN HISTORY AND RELIGION. Text in English. 2006. irreg. **Document type:** *Monographic series, Consumer.*
Published by: Hermit Kingdom Press, 12325 Imperial Hwy, Ste 156, Norwalk, CA 90650. info@TheHermitKingdomPress.com, http://www.thehermitkingdompress.com/index.htm.

268 GBR ISSN 2044-0154
▼ **HEROES OF THE FAITH**; inspiring insights from men and women who proved god. Text in English. 2010. q. GBP 14 domestic; GBP 27 foreign; GBP 3.50 per issue (effective 2010). adv. back issues avail. **Document type:** *Magazine, Consumer.* **Description:** Contains articles and interviews to inspire and inform anyone who has an interest in Christian heritage.
Published by: New Life Publishing Co., PO Box 777, Nottingham, NG11 6ZZ, United Kingdom. TEL 44-115-8240777, info@newlife.co.uk. adv.: page GBP 350.

207.2 DEU ISSN 0942-5489
HERRNHUTER BOTE. Text in German. 1949. m. EUR 24; EUR 12 to students (effective 2009). adv. bk.rev. illus. **Document type:** *Newsletter, Consumer.* **Description:** Contains articles on a wide variety of subjects involving the Moravian Church.
Formerly (until 1992): Bruederbote (0724-4533)
Published by: Evangelische Brueder-Unitaet, Zittauer Str 20, Herrnhut, 02747, Germany. TEL 49-35873-4870, FAX 49-35873-48799, info@ebu.de, http://www.ebu.de. Ed. Thomas Przyluski. Circ: 1,650.

200 ZAF ISSN 0259-9422
BR9.A34
➤ **HERVORMDE TEOLOGIESE STUDIES.** Abbreviated title: H T S. Text in Afrikaans, Dutch, English, German; Summaries in English. 1942. irreg. adv. bk.rev. Supplement avail. **Document type:** *Journal, Academic/Scholarly.* **Description:** Features articles on topics in all the theological disciplines including Bible study.
Related titles: Online - full text ed.: ISSN 2072-8050. free (effective 2011).
Indexed: A01, A20, A21, A22, ArtHuCI, DIP, IBR, IBZ, IIBP, ISAP, IZBG, OTA, R&TA, RI-1, RI-2, SCOPUS, T02, W07.
—BLDSC (4300.390000), IE, Ingenta.
Published by: University of Pretoria, Faculty of Theology/Universiteit van Pretoria, Fakulteit Teologie, Lynwood Rd, Pretoria, 0002, South Africa. TEL 27-12-420-3806, FAX 27-12-420-2887, vanaarde@ccnet.up.ac.za.

100 200 GBR ISSN 0018-1196
BX801
➤ **THE HEYTHROP JOURNAL**; a bi-monthly review of philosophy and theology. Text in English. 1960. bi-m. GBP 291 in United Kingdom to institutions; EUR 369 in Europe to institutions; USD 521 in the Americas to institutions; USD 609 elsewhere to institutions; GBP 335 combined subscription in United Kingdom to institutions (print & online eds.); EUR 426 combined subscription in Europe to institutions (print & online eds.); USD 599 combined subscription in the Americas to institutions (print & online eds.); USD 701 combined subscription elsewhere to institutions (print & online eds.) (effective 2012). adv. bk.rev. bibl.; charts; illus. index. back issues avail.; reprint service avail. from PSC. **Document type:** *Journal, Academic/Scholarly.* **Description:** Features on contemporary philosophical and theological issues, including the bible, ecclesiastical history and the sociology of religion.
Related titles: Microform ed.: (from PQC); Online - full text ed.: ISSN 1468-2265. GBP 291 in United Kingdom to institutions; EUR 369 in Europe to institutions; USD 521 in the Americas to institutions; USD 609 elsewhere to institutions (effective 2012) (from IngentaConnect).
Indexed: A01, A03, A08, A20, A21, A22, A26, ASCA, AmHI, ArtHuCI, CA, CERDIC, CLA, CPL, CurCont, DIP, E01, FR, H07, IBR, IBZ, IPB, MLA-IB, OTA, PCI, PhilInd, R&TA, RI-1, RI-2, SCOPUS, T02, W07.
—BLDSC (4303.100000), IE, Infotrieve, Ingenta, INIST. **CCC.**
Published by: Wiley-Blackwell Publishing Ltd. (Subsidiary of: John Wiley & Sons, Inc.), 9600 Garsington Rd, Oxford, OX4 2DQ, United Kingdom. TEL 44-1865-776868, FAX 44-1865-714591, customerservices@blackwellpublishing.com. Ed. Patrick Madigan. Adv. contact Craig Pickett TEL 44-1865-476267. **Co-sponsor:** University of London, Heythrop College.

268 USA ISSN 1540-9384
HIGH SCHOOL SPIRIT STUDENT GUIDES. Text in English. 19??. q. USD 3.99 per issue (effective 2009). **Document type:** *Magazine, Consumer.*
Former titles (until 2002): High School Spirit Study Guides (1093-1589); (until 1997): High School Spirit Magazine (1080-9767); (until 1995): Hi-Teen Student Guide (1059-3365); (until 1992): Hi-Teen Student (0190-3810)
Published by: Gospel Publishing House, 1445 N Boonville Ave, Springfield, MO 65802. TEL 800-641-4310, FAX 417-862-5881, 800-328-0294, CustSrvReps@ag.org, http://www.gospelpublishing.com/.

274 ESP ISSN 0018-215X
BR1020
HISPANIA SACRA. Text in Spanish. 1945. s-a. EUR 50.99 domestic; EUR 63.92 foreign (effective 2009). adv. bk.rev. illus. back issues avail.; reprints avail. **Document type:** *Journal, Academic/Scholarly.* **Description:** Presents documents of Church history in Spain and Europe and the occidental culture.
Related titles: Microfilm ed.; Online - full text ed.: ISSN 1988-4265. free (effective 2011).
Indexed: A20, A21, A22, ArtHuCI, BibInd, CA, FR, H21, HistAb, IBR, IBZ, MLA-IB, P08, P09, P30, PCI, R&TA, RI-1, RI-2, RILM, SCOPUS, T02, W07.
—BLDSC (4315.765000), IE, Infotrieve, Ingenta, INIST.
Published by: (Consejo Superior de Investigaciones Cientificas (C S I C), Centro de Estudios Historicos), Consejo Superior de Investigaciones Cientificas (C S I C), Departamento de Publicaciones, Vitruvio 8, Madrid, 28006, Spain. publ@csic.es, http://www.publicaciones.csic.es. Ed. Jose Andres-Gallego. Circ: 800.

200 FRA ISSN 2106-3486
▼ **HISTOIRE DES MYTHOLOGIES & RELIGIONS.** Text in French. 2010. q. EUR 8 (effective 2011). **Document type:** *Magazine, Consumer.*
Published by: Export Press, 91 Rue de Turenne, Paris, 75003, France. TEL 33-1-40291451, FAX 33-1-42720743, dir@exportpress.com, http://www.exportpress.com.

HISTORIA; journal of the Historical Society of Israel. *see* HISTORY

200 DEU ISSN 1861-5678
HISTORIA HERMENEUTICA. Text in German. 2005. irreg., latest vol.10, 2011. price varies. **Document type:** *Monographic series, Academic/Scholarly.* **Description:** Dedicated to the study of hermeneutics and its theory in the Early Modern Era (1500-1850).
—CCC.
Published by: Walter de Gruyter GmbH & Co. KG, Genthiner Str 13, Berlin, 10785, Germany. TEL 49-30-260050, FAX 49-30-26005251, info@degruyter.com, http://www.degruyter.de. Ed. Lutz Danneberg.

200 SWE ISSN 0439-2132
HISTORIA RELIGIONUM. Text in Multiple languages. 1961. irreg., latest vol.21, 2002. price varies. back issues avail. **Document type:** *Monographic series, Academic/Scholarly.*
Related titles: ◆ Series of: Acta Universitatis Upsaliensis. ISSN 0346-5462.
Published by: Uppsala Universitet, Acta Universitatis Upsaliensis/University Publications from Uppsala, PO Box 256, Uppsala, 75105, Sweden. TEL 46-18-4716804, FAX 46-18-4716804, acta@ub.uu.se, http://www.ub.uu.se/upu/auu/index.html. Ed. Bengt Landgren. **Dist. by:** Almqvist & Wiksell International.

200 ITA ISSN 2035-5572
BL41
▼ **HISTORIA RELIGIONUM.** Text in Multiple languages. 2009. a. EUR 115 combined subscription (print & online eds.) (effective 2010). **Document type:** *Journal, Academic/Scholarly.*
Related titles: Online - full text ed.: ISSN 2035-6455.

Published by: Fabrizio Serra Editore (Subsidiary of: Accademia Editoriale), c/o Accademia Editoriale, Via Santa Bibbiana 28, Pisa, 56127, Italy. TEL 39-050-542332, FAX 39-050-574888, accademiaeditoriale@accademiaeditoriale.it, http://www.libraweb.net. Ed. Giovanni Filoramo.

220 BEL
HISTORICAL COMMENTARY ON THE OLD TESTAMENT. Text in English. 1994. irreg., latest 1999. price varies. back issues avail. **Document type:** *Monographic series, Academic/Scholarly.* **Description:** Publishes studies in the Christian exegetical tradition with a historical approach to the texts.
Published by: Peeters Publishers, Bondgenotenlaan 153, Leuven, 3000, Belgium. TEL 32-16-235170, FAX 32-16-228500, peeters@peeters-leuven.be, http://www.peeters-leuven.be.

220.6 NLD ISSN 1382-4465
➤ **HISTORY OF BIBLICAL INTERPRETATION SERIES.** Text in English. 1995. irreg., latest vol.1, 1995. price varies. **Document type:** *Monographic series, Academic/Scholarly.*
Indexed: IZBG.
Published by: Brill, PO Box 9000, Leiden, 2300 PA, Netherlands. TEL 31-71-5353500, FAX 31-71-5317532, cs@brill.nl, http://www.brill.nl. Ed. Robert Morgan. **Dist. in N. America by:** Brill, PO Box 605, Herndon, VA 20172-0605. TEL 703-661-1585, 800-337-9255, FAX 703-661-1501, cs@brillusa.com; **Dist. by:** Turpin Distribution Services Ltd., Pegasus Dr, Stratton Business Park, Biggleswade, Bedfordshire SG18 8QB, United Kingdom. TEL 44-1767-604954, FAX 44-1767-601640, custserv@turpin-distribution.com, http://www.turpin-distribution.com/.

220 NLD ISSN 1874-3935
HISTORY OF BIBLICAL STUDIES. Text in English. 2008. irreg. **Document type:** *Monographic series, Academic/Scholarly.*
Indexed: IZBG.
Published by: (Society of Biblical Literature USA), Brill, PO Box 9000, Leiden, 2300 PA, Netherlands. TEL 31-71-5353500, FAX 31-71-5317532, cs@brill.nl.

291 230 297 NLD ISSN 1570-7350
THE HISTORY OF CHRISTIAN-MUSLIM RELATIONS. Text in English. 2003. irreg., latest vol.10, 2008. price varies. **Document type:** *Monographic series, Academic/Scholarly.*
Indexed: IZBG.
Published by: Brill, PO Box 9000, Leiden, 2300 PA, Netherlands. TEL 31-71-5353500, FAX 31-71-5317532, cs@brill.nl. Eds. David Thomas, Gerrit Reinink, Tarif Khalidi.

200 USA ISSN 0018-2710
BL1
➤ **HISTORY OF RELIGIONS.** Abbreviated title: H R. Text in English. 1961. q. USD 213 combined subscription to institutions (print & online eds.) (effective 2012). adv. bk.rev. illus. Index. 96 p./no.; back issues avail.; reprint service avail. from PSC. **Document type:** *Journal, Academic/Scholarly.* **Description:** Studies religious phenomena from prehistory to modern times, both within particular traditions and across cultural boundaries.
Related titles: Online - full text ed.: ISSN 1545-6935. USD 181 to institutions (effective 2012).
Indexed: A01, A02, A03, A08, A20, A21, A22, A25, A26, AICP, ASCA, AbAn, AmH&L, AmHI, ArtHuCI, B04, BAS, BRD, CA, CERDIC, CurCont, DIP, E08, EI, FR, G05, G06, G07, G08, GSS&RPL, H05, H07, H08, H09, H10, H14, HAb, HistAb, Humlnd, I05, I07, IBR, IBZ, L05, L06, MEA&I, MLA-IB, OTA, P02, P10, P28, P30, P48, P53, P54, PCI, PQC, Perlslam, Philind, R&TA, R05, RASB, RI-1, RI-2, RILM, S02, S03, S08, S09, S23, SCOPUS, T02, W03, W04, W07.
—BLDSC (4318.420000), IE, Infotrieve, Ingenta, INIST. **CCC.**
Published by: (University of Chicago), University of Chicago Press, 1427 E 60th St, Chicago, IL 60637. TEL 773-702-7600, FAX 773-702-0694, subscriptions@press.uchicago.edu. Eds. Bruce Lincoln, Matthew Kapstein, Wendy Doniger. **Subscr. to:** PO Box 370050, Chicago, IL 60637. TEL 773-753-3347, 877-705-1878, FAX 773-753-0811, 877-705-1879.

200 USA ISSN 1941-871X
THE HISTORY OF THE HOLY MAR MA'IN. Text in English, Syriac. 2008. irreg., latest 2009. USD 51.04 per issue (effective 2010). **Document type:** *Monographic series, Academic/Scholarly.*
Published by: Gorgias Press LLC, 954 River Rd, Piscataway, NJ 08854. TEL 732-885-8900, FAX 732-885-8908, helpdesk@gorgiaspress.com, http://www.gorgiaspress.com/bookshop/default.aspx.

HODOS; Wege bildungsbezogener Ethikforschung in Philosophie und Theologie. *see* PHILOSOPHY

220 230 FRA ISSN 0379-7465
BR3
HOKHMA. Text in French. 1976. 3/yr. **Document type:** *Journal, Academic/Scholarly.*
Indexed: IZBG, OTA.
Address: 2 Rue du Brave Rondeau, La Rochelle, 17000, France. http://www.hokhma.org.

HOLIDAYS, FESTIVALS AND CELEBRATIONS OF THE WORLD DICTIONARY; detailing 2,500 observances from all 50 States and more than 100 nations. *see* ANTHROPOLOGY

HOLLYWOOD JESUS REVIEWS. *see* MOTION PICTURES

200 GBR ISSN 1474-9475
DS101
➤ **HOLY LAND STUDIES**; a multidisciplinary journal. Abbreviated title: H L S. Text in English. 2002. s-a. GBP 101 domestic to institutions; USD 204 in North America to institutions; GBP 112 elsewhere to institutions; GBP 126 combined subscription domestic to institutions (print & online eds.); USD 255 combined subscription in North America to institutions (print & online eds.); GBP 140 combined subscription elsewhere to institutions (print & online eds.) (effective 2012). back issues avail.; reprints avail. **Document type:** *Journal, Academic/Scholarly.* **Description:** Features fresh and stimulating ideas, with special attention to issues that have contemporary relevance and general public interest.
Related titles: Online - full text ed.: ISSN 1750-0125. 2006. USD 166 in North America to institutions; GBP 91 elsewhere to institutions (effective 2012).
Indexed: A01, A02, A03, A08, A22, CA, DIP, E01, I02, IBR, IBZ, J01, M10, T02.
—IE. **CCC.**

Published by: Edinburgh University Press, 22 George Sq, Edinburgh, Scotland EH8 9LF, United Kingdom. TEL 44-131-6504218, FAX 44-131-6503286, journals@eup.ed.ac.uk. Ed. Dr. Nur Masalha. Adv. contact Ruth Allison TEL 44-131-6504220.

200 USA
HOME TIMES; a good little newspaper for God and country. Text in English. 1988. m. **Document type:** *Newspaper, Consumer.* **Description:** Contains news and analysis of world, national and local issues, people features, and much more. All with a Biblical perspective and family values.
Published by: Neighbor News Inc., 3676 Collin Dr, Ste. 16, West Palm Beach, FL 33406-4719. TEL 561-439-3509, FAX 561-968-1758. Pub. Dennis Lombard. Circ: 6,000 (paid).

270.092 USA ISSN 1542-6637
ML3187.5
HOMECOMING MAGAZINE. Text in English. 2003. bi-m. USD 21.95 domestic; USD 26.95 in Canada; USD 30.95 elsewhere (effective 2009). adv. **Document type:** *Magazine, Consumer.* **Description:** Features behind-the-scenes news from the Homecoming family, interviews with intriguing people of faith and inspirational reflections from best-loved artists.
Published by: Salem Publishing, 104 Woodmont Blvd, Ste 300, Nashville, TN 37205. TEL 615-386-3011, 800-527-5226, FAX 615-312-4266, customerservice@salempublishing.com, http://www.salempublishing.com. Adv. contact Dede Donatelli-Tarrant TEL 805-987-5072.

251 ESP ISSN 0439-4208
HOMILETICA; revista de predicacion liturgica. Text in Spanish. 1912. 6/yr. EUR 42 domestic; USD 60 foreign (effective 2009). **Document type:** *Magazine, Consumer.*
Supersedes in part (in 1960): Sal Terrae. Parte Practica (1138-1086); Which superseded in part (in 1954): Sal Terrae (0211-4569)
Related titles: Online - full text ed.: EUR 34 (effective 2009).
Published by: Editorial Sal Terrae, Poligono de Raos, Parcela 14-I, Maliano, Cantabria, 34600, Spain. TEL 34-942-369198, http://www.salterrae.es. Ed. Juan Francisco Herrero Garcia.

251 DEU ISSN 0018-4276
BV1
➤ **HOMILETISCHE MONATSHEFTE**; fuer Predigt - Katechese - Gottesdienst. Text in German. 1925. m. EUR 69 to individuals; EUR 138 to institutions; EUR 46 to students; EUR 9.30 newsstand/cover (effective 2011). adv. bk.rev. index. **Document type:** *Journal, Academic/Scholarly.*
Indexed: DIP, IBR, IBZ.
—**CCC.**
Published by: Vandenhoeck und Ruprecht, Theaterstr 13, Goettingen, 37073, Germany. TEL 49-551-508440, FAX 49-551-5084422, info@v-r.de. Ed. Wolf Dietrich Berner. Circ: 2,200 (paid and controlled).

200 USA
HOMILY HELPS. Text in English. 1981. w. looseleaf. USD 35 domestic; USD 43 in Canada; USD 51 elsewhere (effective 2011). adv. back issues avail. **Document type:** *Newsletter, Trade.* **Description:** Aid to preaching for Catholic clergy.
Related titles: E-mail ed.: USD 35 (effective 2011).
Published by: St. Anthony Messenger Press, 28 W Liberty St, Cincinnati, OH 45202. TEL 513-241-5615, 800-488-0488, FAX 513-241-0399, stanthony@americancatholic.org, http://www.americancatholic.org.

252 USA ISSN 0732-1872
BV4200
HOMILY SERVICE; an ecumenical resource for sharing the word. Text in English. 1968. q. USD 136, GBP 81, EUR 108 combined subscription to institutions (print & online eds.) (effective 2010). adv. reprint service avail. from PSC. **Document type:** *Journal, Academic/Scholarly.* **Description:** Ecumenical resource for sharing scripture. Includes exegetical analysis of scriptural readings.
Related titles: Online - full text ed.: ISSN 1547-3562. USD 128, GBP 77, EUR 102 to institutions (effective 2010) (from IngentaConnect).
Indexed: A22, CA, E01, T02.
—IE, Ingenta. **CCC.**
Published by: (Liturgical Conference, Inc.), Taylor & Francis Inc. (Subsidiary of: Taylor & Francis Group), 325 Chestnut St, Ste 800, Philadelphia, PA 19106. TEL 215-625-2940, 800-354-1420, orders@taylorandfrancis.com, http://www.taylorandfrancis.com. Ed. Sarah Webb Phillips. Adv. contact Linda Hann TEL 44-1344-779945.

200 FRA ISSN 0018-4322
L'HOMME NOUVEAU. Text in French. 1946. bi-m. EUR 70 (effective 2009). bk.rev. **Document type:** *Newspaper, Consumer.* **Description:** Analyzes the news in the light of the Gospel.
Published by: Homme Nouveau, 10 rue Rosenwald, Paris, 75015, France. TEL 33-1-53689977, FAX 33-1-45321084. Ed. Philippe Maxence. Pub. Marcel Clement. Circ: 40,000.

944 200 BEL ISSN 1258-2697
HOMMES DE DIEU ET REVOLUTION. Text in French. 1993. irreg., latest vol.3, 1995. back issues avail. **Document type:** *Monographic series.* **Description:** Publishes studies on religion and revolution in France.
Published by: Brepols Publishers, Begijnhof 67, Turnhout, 2300, Belgium. FAX 32-14-428919, periodicals@brepols.net. Ed. B Plongeron.

200 USA
HONOR THE PROMISE. Text in English. 1979. irreg. USD 5. **Document type:** *Newsletter.*
Published by: National Christian Leadership Conference for Israel, 134 E 39th St, New York, NY 10016. TEL 212-213-8636, FAX 212-683-3475. Eds. Nancy G. Carroll, Rose Thering. Circ: 10,000.

230 615.5 USA ISSN 1547-6669
HOPEKEEPERS; joyfully serving the chronically ill. Text in English. 2004. q. USD 17.97 (effective 2007). 64 p./no.; **Document type:** *Magazine, Consumer.* **Description:** Provides a Christian perspective of the issues involved with chronic illness, including spiritual struggles, family challenges, alternative medicine, devotionals, caregiving, doctor's advice, and profiles of celebrities and national HopeKeepers groups.
Published by: Rest Ministries, Inc., PO Box 502928, San Diego, CA 92150. TEL 888-751-7378, rest@restministries.org, http://www.restministries.org. Ed. Lisa Copen. Circ: 2,000 (paid); 10,000.

200 CAN ISSN 1923-8185
▼ **HOPE'S REASON**; a journal of apologetics. Text in English. 2010. irreg. **Document type:** *Journal, Academic/Scholarly.*
Related titles: Online - full text ed.: ISSN 1923-8193. free (effective 2011).
Address: editor@apologeticsjournal.com. Ed. Stephen J Bedard.

268 USA ISSN 1042-8461
HORIZON (CHICAGO). Text in English. 1975. q. USD 27 domestic to non-members; USD 34 foreign to non-members; free to members (effective 2010). adv. back issues avail. **Document type:** *Journal, Academic/Scholarly.* **Description:** Provides articles relating to vocation ministry and research on religious life.
Formerly (until 1989): Call to Growth, Ministry (0883-6280)
Indexed: CPL.
Published by: National Religious Vocation Conference, 5401 S Cornell Ave, Ste 207, Chicago, IL 60615. TEL 773-363-5454, FAX 773-363-5530, nrvc@nrvc.net, http://www.nrvc.net.

220 NLD ISSN 0195-9085
BS543.A1
➤ **HORIZONS IN BIBLICAL THEOLOGY.** Text in English. 1979. s-a. EUR 123, USD 173 to institutions; EUR 134, USD 188 combined subscription to institutions (print & online eds.) (effective 2012). adv. bk.rev. back issues avail.; reprint service avail. from PSC. **Document type:** *Journal, Academic/Scholarly.*
Related titles: Online - full text ed.: ISSN 1871-2207. EUR 112, USD 157 to institutions (effective 2012) (from IngentaConnect).
Indexed: A21, A22, CA, DIP, E01, IBR, IBZ, IZBG, OTA, PCI, R&TA, RI-1, RI-2, T02.
—BLDSC (4326.794500), IE, Ingenta. **CCC.**
Published by: (Pittsburgh Theological Seminary USA), Brill, PO Box 9000, Leiden, 2300 PA, Netherlands. TEL 31-71-5353500, FAX 31-71-5317532, cs@brill.nl. Ed. Lewis Donelson. Circ: 500. **Dist. by:** Turpin Distribution Services Ltd., Pegasus Dr, Stratton Business Park, Biggleswade, Bedfordshire SG18 8QB, United Kingdom. TEL 44-1767-604954, FAX 44-1767-601640, custserv@turpin-distribution.com, http://www.turpin-distribution.com/.

200 BRA ISSN 1679-9615
BR7
HORIZONTE; revista de estudos de teologia e ciencias da religiao. Text in Portuguese. 1997. s-a. **Document type:** *Journal, Academic/Scholarly.*
Related titles: Online - full text ed.: ISSN 2175-5841. free (effective 2011).
Indexed: C01.
Published by: Editora P U C Minas, Rua Padre Pedro Evangelista 377, Belo Horizonte, 30535-490, Brazil. TEL 55-31-33758189, FAX 55-31-33766498, editora@pucminas.br, http://www.pucminas.br/editora/.

200 ESP ISSN 2172-2080
HORIZONTES DEL ESPIRITU. Text in Spanish. 199?. irreg. **Document type:** *Monographic series, Academic/Scholarly.*
Published by: Ediciones Robinbook, S.L., Industria 11, Barcelona, 08329, Spain. TEL 34-93-551411, FAX 34-93-5404092, http://www.robinbook.com/.

266 ESP
HUELLAS DOMINICANAS; boletin informativo de los dominicos de la Provincia del Rosario. Text in Spanish. 1970. q. **Document type:** *Bulletin, Consumer.*
Published by: Secretariado de Misiones Dominicanas, Apado. 10, Avila, 05003, Spain.

200 NLD ISSN 0018-7119
HUIZER KERKBLAD. Text in Dutch. 1935. w. EUR 15.75 for 6 mos. (effective 2009). adv. bk.rev.
Published by: J. Bout en Zoon, Ceintuurbaan 32-34, Huizen, 1271 BJ, Netherlands. TEL 31-35-5253293, FAX 31-35-5241150, info@boutdruk.nl, http://www.boutdruk.nl.

201.6 USA
HUMAN KINDNESS FOUNDATION NEWSLETTER; a little good news. Text in English. 1974. q. looseleaf. free. **Document type:** *Newsletter.*
Formerly: Prison - Ashram Project Newsletter
Published by: Human Kindness Foundation, Rt 1, Box 201 N, Durham, NC 27705. TEL 919-942-2138. Ed. Bo Lozoff. Circ: 21,000.

HUMANISMUS AKTUELL; Zeitschrift fuer Kultur und Weltanschauung. *see* SOCIAL SCIENCES: COMPREHENSIVE WORKS

200 PRT ISSN 0870-080X
BR7
HUMANISTICA E TEOLOGIA. Text in Portuguese. 1980. 3/yr. EUR 12.50 domestic; EUR 27.50 foreign (effective 2004).
Indexed: OTA.
Published by: Universidade Catolica Portuguesa, Faculdade de Teologia, Rua Diogo Botelho, 1327, Porto, 4169-005, Portugal. TEL 351-22-6196284, 351-22-6196271, FAX 351-22-6196291, dirft@porto-ucp.pt, http://www.porto.ucp.pt/faculda/teologia/teolog.htm.

230 100 DEU
HUMANISTISCHE RUNDSCHAU. Text in German. 1990. q. free to members (effective 2010). bk.rev.; music rev. bibl.; illus. back issues avail. **Document type:** *Newsletter, Consumer.*
Formerly: Freireligioese Rundschau
Published by: Die Humanisten Wuerttemberg, K.d.oe.R. Freireligioese Landesgemeinde, Moerikestr 14, Stuttgart, 70178, Germany. TEL 49-711-6493780, FAX 49-711-6493886, andreas.henschel@dhuw.de. Eds. Andreas Henschel, Walter Tannert.

HUMANITAS; revista de antropologia y cultura cristiana. *see* ANTHROPOLOGY

211 USA ISSN 1945-8592
HUUMANISTS NEWS. Text in English. 200?. a. **Document type:** *Newsletter, Consumer.*
Related titles: Online - full text ed.
Published by: Huumanists, PO Box 185202, Hamden, CT 06518. TEL 203-281-6232. Ed. David E Schafer.

THE HYMN; a journal of congregational song. *see* MUSIC

THE HYMNOLOGY ANNUAL. *see* MUSIC

I C S A NEWSLETTER. *see* EDUCATION—Higher Education

R

261 301 NLD
I C S CAHIERS. Text in Dutch. s-a. EUR 25; EUR 15 to students (effective 2009).
Published by: (ICS, Forum voor Geloof, Wetenschap en Samenleving), Boekencentrum Uitgevers, Goudstraat 50, Postbus 29, Zoetermeer, 2700 AA, Netherlands. TEL 31-79-3615481, info@boekencentrum.nl, http://www.boekencentrum.nl. Eds. Dr. Anja Vrijmoeth, Dr. Govert J Buijs.

207.2 GBR ISSN 1755-294X
I C S NEWS AND PRAYER DIARY. Text in English. 2006. q. back issues avail. **Document type:** *Newsletter, Trade.*
Formed by the merger of (1999-2006): I C S News (1469-1361); Which was formerly (until 1999): Going Places (1353-8101); (until 1994): Intercon (0264-0961); (until 1982): Intercom (0020-5265); (1999-2006): I C S Prayer Diary (1469-1973); Which was formerly (until 1999): Monthly Prayer Diary
Related titles: Online - full text ed.: free (effective 2008).
Published by: Intercontinental Church Society, 1 Athena Dr, Tachbrook Pk, Warwick, CV34 6NL, United Kingdom. TEL 44-1926-430347, FAX 44-1926-888092, enquiries@ics-uk.org, http://www.ics-uk.org. Ed. David Healey TEL 44-1926-430347.

I C S NEWSLETTER. *see* ART

200 BEL ISSN 1370-6020
➤ **I N T A M S REVIEW**; journal for the study of marriage and spirituality. (International Academy for Marital Spirituality) Text in English, French, German, Italian, Spanish. 1995. s-a. EUR 50 combined subscription (print & online eds.) (effective 2011). **Document type:** *Journal, Academic/Scholarly.*
Related titles: Online - full text ed.: ISSN 1783-1474.
Indexed: A22, F09, Faml.
—IE.
Published by: (International Academy for Marital Spirituality (I N T A M S)), Peeters Publishers, Bondgenotenlaan 153, Leuven, 3000, Belgium. TEL 32-16-235170, FAX 32-16-228500, peeters@peeters-leuven.be, http://www.peeters-leuven.be. Ed. T Knieps-Port Le Roi.

200 VEN ISSN 0798-1236
I T E R REVISTA DE TEOLOGIA. Text in Spanish. 1990. s-a.
Indexed: C01, FR, OTA.
—INIST.
Published by: Instituto de Teologia para Religiosos, 3o Avda. con 6ta Transversal, Altamira, Apdo 68865, Caracas, DF 1060, Venezuela. TEL 39-2-2650505, FAX 39-2-2653264.

200 600 USA ISSN 1073-5976
I T E S T BULLETIN. Text in English. 1969. q. free to members (effective 2010). bk.rev. 18 p./no.; back issues avail. **Document type:** *Bulletin, Academic/Scholarly.* **Description:** Contains articles pertaining to theology/faith, and science and technology.
Published by: Institute for Theological Encounter with Science and Technology, Cardinal Rigali Ctr, 20 Archbishop May Dr, Ste 3400A, St Louis, MO 63119. TEL 314-792-7220, ITEST-Info@faithscience.org. Ed. Sister Marianne Postiglione.

200 600 USA
I T E S T CONFERENCE PROCEEDINGS. Text in English. 1970. a. free to members (effective 2010). back issues avail. **Document type:** *Proceedings, Academic/Scholarly.* **Description:** Contains edited versions of meetings on topics such as artificial intelligence, bio-technology, law, the environment, Christian and Jewish perspectives on creation, sci-tech education in Church-related colleges and universities, the human genome project, population issues, and Christianity and the environmental ethos, evolution and creation.
Published by: Institute for Theological Encounter with Science and Technology, Cardinal Rigali Ctr, 20 Archbishop May Dr, Ste 3400A, St Louis, MO 63119. TEL 314-792-7220, ITEST-Info@faithscience.org, http://www.faithscience.org/.

266 ZMB
ICENGELO; Christian magazine in Bemba. Text in Bemba. 1970. m. ZMK 200; USD 20 foreign. **Document type:** *Newspaper.* **Description:** Covers religious, social and health topics.
Published by: Mission Press, PO Box 71581, Ndola, Zambia. TEL 260-2-680456, FAX 260-2-680464. Ed. Rev. Miha Drevenzek. Circ: 30,000.

268 ESP
ICONO PERPETUO SOCORRO. Text in Spanish. 1899. m. EUR 13, USD 40 (effective 2009). adv. bk.rev. illus. **Document type:** *Newspaper, Consumer.*
Formerly: P S
Published by: Editorial Perpetuo Socorro, Covarrubias, 19, Madrid, 28010, Spain. TEL 34-91-4455126, FAX 34-91-4455127, perso@pseditorial.com, http://www.pseditorial.com/. Ed. Paulino Sutil. Circ: 11,000 (controlled).

ICONOGRAPHY OF RELIGIONS. *see* ART

ICONOGRAPHY OF RELIGIONS. SECTION 2, NEW ZEALAND. *see* ART

ICONOGRAPHY OF RELIGIONS. SECTION 24, CHRISTIANITY. *see* ART

ICONOGRAPHY OF RELIGIONS. SUPPLEMENTS. *see* ART

261 USA ISSN 1937-3856
BV630.3
IF MY PEOPLE. Text in English. 2007. q. USD 23.95 domestic; USD 34.95 in Canada; USD 47 elsewhere (effective 2008). adv. **Document type:** *Magazine, Consumer.* **Description:** Provides Christian perspective and guidance on current events, morality, culture and lifestyle.
Published by: Faithful Stewardship, Inc, 6336 N Oracle Rd #326-331, Tucson, AZ 85704. TEL 520-797-8200, FAX 570-307-1608.

200 ESP ISSN 1135-4712
BL7
➤ **'ILU**; revista de ciencias de las religiones. Text in Spanish. 1995. a., latest vol.15, 2010. EUR 18 domestic; EUR 24 in Europe; EUR 28 elsewhere (effective 2011). bk.rev. back issues avail. **Document type:** *Journal, Academic/Scholarly.* **Description:** Publishes articles about the history of religion. Emphasizes Roman Catholic, Judaic and Islam religions on the Iberian Peninsula.
Related titles: CD-ROM ed.: ISSN 1698-1014; Online - full text ed.: ISSN 1988-3269. free; ◆ Supplement(s): 'Ilu. Monografias. ISSN 1138-4972; ◆ 'Ilu. Cuadernos. ISSN 1139-1529.
Indexed: A21, FR, H21, I14, MLA-IB, OTA, P08, P28, P48, P53, P54, PQC, R&TA, RI-1, S02, S03, SociolAb, T02.
—INIST.
Published by: (Universidad Complutense de Madrid, Facultad de Filologia), Universidad Complutense de Madrid, Servicio de Publicaciones, C/ Obispo Trejo 2, Ciudad Universitaria, Madrid, 28040, Spain. TEL 34-91-3941127, FAX 34-91-3941126, servicio.publicaciones@rect.ucm.es, http://www.ucm.es/publicaciones. Ed. Guadalupe Seijas de los Rios-Zarzosa.

200 ESP ISSN 1578-1305
'ILU. ANEJOS; revista de ciencias de las religiones. Text in Spanish. 2001. irreg. price varies. **Document type:** *Monographic series, Academic/Scholarly.*
Formed by the merger of (1998-2000): 'Ilu. Cuadernos (1139-1529); (1998-2000): 'Ilu. Monografias (1138-4972)
Indexed: FR.
—INIST.
Published by: Universidad Complutense de Madrid, Servicio de Publicaciones, C/ Obispo Trejo 2, Ciudad Universitaria, Madrid, 28040, Spain. TEL 34-91-3941127, FAX 34-91-3941126, servicio.publicaciones@rect.ucm.es, http://www.ucm.es/publicaciones.

200 DEU ISSN 0019-2597
BV2354
IM LANDE DER BIBEL. Text in German. 1955. 3/yr. free (effective 2009). bk.rev. bibl.; illus. **Document type:** *Magazine, Consumer.*
Published by: (Jerusalemsverein), Berliner Missionswerk, Georgenkirchstr 69-70, Berlin, 10249, Germany. TEL 49-30-24344123, FAX 49-30-24344124, bmw@berliner-missionswerk.de. Ed. Almut Nothnagle. Circ: 15,000.

200 DEU ISSN 0176-8565
IMAGE (AACHEN); Arbeitshilfe fuer Pfarrdienste. Text in German. 1970. 11/yr. looseleaf. EUR 150 (effective 2011). back issues avail. **Document type:** *Magazine, Trade.*
Published by: Bergmoser und Hoeller Verlag GmbH, Karl-Friedrich-Str 76, Aachen, 52072, Germany. TEL 49-241-93888123, FAX 49-241-93888134, kontakt@buhv.de. Circ: 7,000.

200 051 USA ISSN 1087-3503
IMAGE (SEATTLE); a journal of the arts & religion. Text in English. 1989. q. USD 39.95 domestic; USD 49.95 foreign (effective 2010). adv. bk.rev. 136 p./no.; **Document type:** *Journal, Consumer.* **Description:** Features fiction, poetry and art as well as documents and analyzes contemporary artists working with religious themes and imagery.
Indexed: A21, A30, A31, AmHI, ChrPI, H07, IAPV, MLA-IB, R&TA, RI-1, RI-2, RILM, T02.
Published by: Center for Religious Humanism, 3307 Third Ave W, Seattle, WA 98119. TEL 206-281-2988, FAX 206-281-2979. Ed., Pub. Gregory Wolfe. adv.: page USD 600; 5.5 x 8.5. **Subscr. to:** PO Box 3000, Denville, NJ 07834. TEL 866-481-0688.

202.2 ESP ISSN 0211-5441
IMAGENES DE LA FE. Text in Spanish. 1963. m. EUR 48.50 domestic; EUR 51 foreign (effective 2010). **Document type:** *Magazine, Consumer.*
Published by: PPC Editorial, Agastia 80, Madrid, 28043, Spain. TEL 34-91-744-4550, FAX 31-91-7444891, vidanvev@ppc.editorial.com. Ed. Rosario Marin Malave. Circ: 10,000.

IMPACT; Asian magazine for human transformation. *see* SOCIAL SCIENCES: COMPREHENSIVE WORKS

230 AUS
IMPACT (SYDNEY). Text in English. 1990. q. **Document type:** *Magazine, Consumer.*
Media: Online - full content.
Published by: Wesley Mission, PO Box A5555, Sydney South, NSW 1235, Australia. TEL 61-2-92635555, FAX 61-2-92644681, wesleymission@wesleymission.org.au.

200 GBR ISSN 1463-9955
BL624
➤ **IMPLICIT RELIGION.** Text in English. 1998. q. USD 440 combined subscription in North America to institutions (print & online eds.); GBP 246 combined subscription elsewhere to institutions (print & online eds.) (effective 2012). adv. back issues avail.; reprints avail. **Document type:** *Journal, Academic/Scholarly.* **Description:** Contains papers on theory and evidence in the study of religion and secularity, and those which explore the relationship between the context and dynamism of religious and secular phenomena.
Related titles: Online - full text ed.: ISSN 1743-1697. USD 352 in North America to institutions; GBP 196 elsewhere to institutions (effective 2012).
Indexed: A01, CA, R&TA, RILM, S02, S03, SCOPUS, SSA, SociolAb, T02.
—IE. CCC.
Published by: (Centre for the Study of Implicit Religion & Contemporary Spirituality), Equinox Publishing Ltd., Unit S3, Kelham House, 3 Lancaster St, Sheffield, S3 8AF, United Kingdom. TEL 44-114-2725957, FAX 44-560-3459046, journals@equinoxpub.com, http://www.equinoxpub.com/. Ed. Edward Bailey. Adv. contact Val Hall.

266 DEU
IMPULSE (GIESSEN); fuer missionarisches christsein. Text in German. 1978. q. EUR 1.70 newsstand/cover (effective 2009). adv. bk.rev. **Document type:** *Magazine, Consumer.*
Published by: Campus fuer Christus, Am Unteren Rain 2, Giessen, 35394, Germany. TEL 49-641-975180, FAX 49-641-9751840, info@campus-d.de. Ed. Lucia Ewald. Adv. contact Monika Moehlmann. page EUR 1,061; trim 210 x 297. Circ: 17,000 (controlled).

266 DEU
IN DIE WELT - FUER DIE WELT; Magazin fuer Mission und Partnerschaft. Text in German. bi-m. EUR 6.50 (effective 2010). 32 p./no.; **Document type:** *Magazine, Consumer.*
Published by: Vereinte Evangelische Mission, Rudolfstrasse 137, Wuppertal, 42285, Germany. TEL 49-202-890040, FAX 49-202-8900479, uem@vemission.org, http://www.vemission.org. Ed. Thomas Sandner.

240 USA ISSN 1942-1397
IN HIS PRESENCE MAGAZINE. Text in English. 2008. q. USD 15 (effective 2009). **Document type:** *Magazine, Consumer.* **Description:** Provides information about God's presence and anointing.
Published by: Christian Outreach Publications, 5309 Baltimore Ave, Hyattsville, MD 20740. TEL 240-764-5217, FAX 240-764-5225, christianpublications@comcast.net.

200 DEU ISSN 1434-2251
:IN RELIGION. Text in German. 1997. 9/yr. EUR 94.50; EUR 15 newsstand/cover (effective 2011). **Document type:** *Journal, Academic/Scholarly.*
Published by: Bergmoser und Hoeller Verlag GmbH, Karl-Friedrich-Str 76, Aachen, 52072, Germany. TEL 49-241-93888123, FAX 49-241-93888134, kontakt@buhv.de.

200 GBR ISSN 0019-3283
IN TOUCH (PINNER); with the grail. Text in English. 1969. q. bk.rev.; play rev. illus. 12 p./no. 3 cols./p.; back issues avail. **Document type:** *Newsletter, Consumer.*
Formerly: Mosaic
Indexed: BrArAb.
Published by: (Grail), The Grail, 125 Waxwell Ln, Pinner, Mddx HA5 3ER, United Kingdom. TEL 44-208-8660505, FAX 44-208-8661408, publications@grailsociety.org.uk.

200 USA ISSN 1065-9307
BV4025
IN TRUST. Text in English. 1989. q. USD 20 (effective 2002). adv. illus.
Address: 2611 Columbia Pike., Arlington, VA 22204-4409. http://www.intrust.org. Ed. William R MacKaye.

200 PER ISSN 1024-8862
BX1425.A1
INCULTURACION. Text in Spanish. 1995. s-a. PEN 30 domestic; USD 18 in United States; USD 20 in Europe; PEN 15 newsstand/cover (effective 2001).
Published by: Instituto de Estudios Aymaras, Apdo Postal 295, Puno, Peru. **Co-publisher:** Centro de Estudios y Publicaciones.

220 USA
INDEPENDENT LESSON SERMON QUARTERLY. Text in English. q. USD 10 domestic; USD 17 foreign (effective 2000).
Published by: Plainfield Christian Science Church (Independent), 905 Prospect Ave, Box 5619, Plainfield, NJ 07060. TEL 908-756-4669.

200 NLD ISSN 1876-6641
INDEX TO THE STUDY OF RELIGIONS. Variant title: I S R. Text in English. 2008. base vol. plus a. updates. EUR 680, USD 920 (effective 2010). **Document type:** *Database, Abstract/Index.*
Media: Online - full text.
Published by: Brill, PO Box 9000, Leiden, 2300 PA, Netherlands. TEL 31-71-5353500, FAX 31-71-5317532, cs@brill.nl.

230.09 IND ISSN 0019-4530
BR1150
INDIAN CHURCH HISTORY REVIEW. Abbreviated title: I C H R. Text in English. s-a. INR 150 domestic to individuals; USD 15, EUR 14 foreign to individuals (effective 2011). bk.rev. index. back issues avail. **Document type:** *Magazine, Consumer.*
Formerly (until 1967): Church History Association of India. Bulletin
Indexed: A21, A22, BAS, R&TA, RI-1, RI-2.
—IE, Ingenta.
Published by: Church History Association of India, c/o. Dharmaram College, Hosur Rd, Bangalore, Karnataka 560 029, India. chai1935@rediffmail.com. Circ: 500.

230 IND ISSN 0019-5685
BR1 CODEN: JPSRB8
➤ **INDIAN JOURNAL OF THEOLOGY.** Text in English. 1952. s-a. INR 100 India, Asia, Africa & Latin America; GBP 6 UK, Australia & New Zealand; DEM 15 European countries; USD 10 USA, Canada & Japan (effective 2011). adv. bk.rev. bibl. index. back issues avail. **Document type:** *Journal, Academic/Scholarly.* **Description:** Encourages efforts to reinterpret Christian theology. Serves as a link between the East and West theological thinking.
Indexed: A21, FR, OTA, R&TA, RI-1, RI-2.
Published by: Serampore College, Theology Department, Serampore Post, Hooghly District, West Bengal 712 201, India. TEL 91-33-26521067, FAX 91-33-26623816, sertheo@vsnl.com, principal@seramporecollege.org. Eds. Dr. K P Aleaz, Dr. Pratap C Gine. Circ: 500. **Subscr. to:** I N S I O Scientific Books & Periodicals, PO Box 7234, Indraprastha HPO, New Delhi 110 002, India. iihm@ap.nic.in, http://iihm.ap.nic.in/.

220 USA
INDIANA STUDIES IN BIBLICAL LITERATURE. Text in English. 1985. irreg., latest 2004. price varies. back issues avail. **Document type:** *Monographic series, Academic/Scholarly.*
Published by: Indiana University Press, 601 N Morton St, Bloomington, IN 47404. TEL 812-855-8817, 800-842-6796, FAX 812-855-7931, journals@indiana.edu, http://iupress.indiana.edu.

200 FRA ISSN 1953-2245
LES INDISPENSABLES DE LA SPIRITUALITE. Text in French. 2006. irreg. back issues avail. **Document type:** *Monographic series, Consumer.*
Published by: Librairie Fayard, 13 Rue du Montparnasse, Paris, 75006, France. TEL 33-1-45498200, FAX 33-1-42224017, http://www.editions-fayard.fr.

200 FRA ISSN 2108-2472
▼ **INFO' A E E.** (Association pour l'Evangelisation des Enfants) Text in French. 2010. irreg. **Document type:** *Newsletter, Consumer.*
Published by: Association pour l'Evangelisation des Enfants, BP 48, Wissous, 91322, France. TEL 33-1-60117577, aeef@club-internet.fr, http://www.aeefrance.org.

230 CHE ISSN 0942-4822
BR735
INFORMATIONES THEOLOGIAE EUROPAE; Internationales oekumenisches Jahrbuch fuer Theologie. Text in English, French, German. 1992. a. CHF 57 domestic; EUR 44 in Germany; EUR 41 in Europe; GBP 36, USD 57 (effective 2011). back issues avail. **Document type:** *Yearbook, Academic/Scholarly.*
Indexed: DIP, IBR, IBZ.

Published by: Peter Lang AG (Subsidiary of: Peter Lang Publishing Group), Hochfeldstr 32, Postfach 746, Bern 9, 3000, Switzerland. TEL 41-31-3061717, FAX 41-31-3061727, info@peterlang.com, http://www.peterlang.ch. Ed. Ulrich Nembach.

230 274 NLD ISSN 1574-9886
INFORUM. Text in Dutch. 1986. q. EUR 15 (effective 2009).
Formerly (until 2004): Apropos (0920-7910)
Published by: ICS, Forum voor Geloof, Wetenschap en Samenleving, Zonnehof 23, Amersfoort, 3811 ND, Netherlands. TEL 31-6-51257908, info@icsnet.nl, http://www.icsnet.nl.

200 SWE ISSN 1401-8616
INGAANG. Text in Swedish. 2001. q. SEK 140 domestic; SEK 180 foreign (effective 2006). back issues avail. **Document type:** *Monographic series, Academic/Scholarly.*
Published by: Johannelunds Teologiska Hoegskola/Johannelund Theological College, Heidenstamsgatan 75, Uppsala, 75427, Sweden. TEL 46-18-169900, FAX 46-18-169910, johannelund@efs.svenskakyrkan.se, http://www.johanelund.nu.

INNER PATHS; a magazine of eastern and western spiritual teaching. *see* NEW AGE PUBLICATIONS

230 USA ISSN 1942-2989
BV652.1
INNER RESOURCES FOR LEADERS. Text in English. 2008. 3/yr. free (effective 2011). back issues avail. **Document type:** *Journal, Academic/Scholarly.*
Media: Online - full text.
Published by: Regent University, School of Global Leadership & Entrepreneurship, 1333 Regent University Dr, Virginia Beach, VA 23464. TEL 757-352-4550, FAX 757-352-4823. Eds. Corne J Bekker, Doris Gomez.

200 GBR ISSN 0020-1723
INQUIRER. Text in English. 1842. fortn. GBP 17.50 in United Kingdom; GBP 25 in United States. adv. bk.rev. illus.
Related titles: Microfilm ed.: (from PQC, WMP); Microform ed.: (from PQC).
Published by: Inquirer Publishing Co. Ltd., 1-6 Essex St, London, WC2R 3AA, United Kingdom. Ed. Rev. K Gilley. Circ: 2,500.

261 USA
INSIDE JOURNAL; the hometown newspaper of America's prisoners. Text in English. 1990. bi-m.
Published by: Prison Fellowship Ministries, Box 17429, Washington, DC 20041-0429. Ed. Jeff Peck. Circ: 400,000.

200 USA
INSIGHT (LOVES PARK). Text in English. 1971. m. charts; illus. **Document type:** *Newsletter.*
Incorporates (1993-1994): Reflections (Loves Park); Former titles (until 1993): Breakthrough; Which incorporated (1927-1989): EuroVision Advance; Which was formerly: Slavic Gospel News (0049-0709)
Published by: Slavic Gospel Association, 6151 Commonwealth Dr, Loves Park, IL 61111. TEL 815-282-8900, FAX 815-282-8901. Ed. Robert W Lovell. R&P Janet Pauley. Circ: 60,000.

200 USA
INSIGHTS FOR PREACHERS; a publication for parish pastors providing sermon resources on common lectionary texts. Text in English. 1973. q. USD 22 (effective 2001). bk.rev. back issues avail. **Document type:** *Journal, Trade.*
Former titles: Insights into Preaching; Insights (Springfield) (0164-7709); Incorporates (1981-1985): Kerygma
Published by: King Publications, 5697 Applebutter Hill Rd, Coopersburg, PA 18036-9560. TEL 610-967-3901, FAX 610-967-2128. Ed., Pub., R&P Richard H Stough Sr. Circ: 1,000 (paid).

230 GBR
INSPIRE (WORTHING). Text in English. 2006. m. GBP 12 to individuals; free to churches (effective 2009). adv. **Document type:** *Magazine, Consumer.* **Description:** Contains articles of encouragement, stories, and practical ideas for your church plus fun items, recommended websites, puzzles and great giveaways.
Published by: Christian Publishing and Outreach Ltd., Garcia Estate, Canterbury Rd, Worthing, West Sussex BN13 1BW, United Kingdom. TEL 44-1903-264556, FAX 44-1903-830066, sales@cpo.org.uk, http://www.cpo-online.org.uk/. Ed. Russ Bravo. Adv. contact Paula Taylor TEL 44-1903-604342. color page GBP 1,250; bleed 171 x 246. Circ: 85,000 (controlled).

INSTRUMENTA LEXICOLOGIA LATINA. *see* CLASSICAL STUDIES

200 BEL ISSN 1379-9878
INSTRUMENTA PATRISTICA ET MEDIAEVALIA. Text in Multiple languages. 1959. irreg., latest vol.43, 2002. price varies. back issues avail. **Document type:** *Monographic series, Academic/Scholarly.* **Description:** Scholarly monographs on early and modern Christian theology, history and texts.
Formerly (until 2001): Instrumenta Patristica (0534-4255)
Published by: (St. Pietersabdij, Steenbrugge), Brepols Publishers, Begijnhof 67, Turnhout, 2300, Belgium. FAX 32-14-428919, periodicals@brepols.net.

268 USA ISSN 1550-9354
INTEEN. TEACHER. Text in English. 1982. q. USD 5.59 per issue (effective 2008). back issues avail. **Document type:** *Magazine, Consumer.* **Description:** Contains commentary and background on the international uniform lessons series and teaching plans geared toward teens 15-17.
Published by: Urban Ministries, Inc., Dept #4870, PO Box 87618, Chicago, IL 60680. TEL 708-868-7100, 800-860-8642, FAX 708-868-7105, customerservice@urbanministries.com.

200 BEL ISSN 0776-2488
INTER-PRESSE; relations internationales dialogue interreligieux. Text in French. 1984. q. adv. bk.rev. **Description:** Focuses on all interreligious themes worldwide. Celebrates the universality of religion and addresses human rights.
Formerly (until 1988): Dialogue Interreligieux (0775-5325)
Published by: Centre d'Inter-Action Culturelle, Rue de la Procession 4, Rosieres, 1331, Belgium. TEL 32-2-653-53-24, FAX 32-2-654-19-08. Ed. Pierre Houart.

200 HKG
INTER-RELIGIO; a network of Christian organizations for interreligious encounter in east Asia. Text in English. 1982. s-a. USD 12 (effective 2001). bk.rev. index. back issues avail. **Document type:** *Newsletter.* **Description:** Contains articles on inter-religious dialogues, news events and publications.
Published by: Christian Study Centre on Chinese Religion & Culture Ltd., 6-F Kiu Kin Mansion, 556 Nathan Rd, Kowloon, Hong Kong. TEL 852-2770-3310, FAX 852-26035224, csccrc@yahoo.com.hk, blawless@hkstar.com, http://www.ic.nanzan-u.ac.jp/SHUBUNKEN/inter-re.html. Ed. Brian Lawless. Circ: 700.

267 JAM ISSN 0020-5087
INTER-SCHOOL & INTER-VARSITY CHRISTIAN FELLOWSHIP; for prayer and praise. Text in English. m. free. bk.rev.
Formerly: Inter-School and Inter-Varsity Christian Fellowship of the West Indies
Media: Duplicated (not offset).
Published by: Students Christian Fellowship and Scripture Union, 22 Hagley Park Plaza, PO Box 281, Kingston, 10, Jamaica. Ed. Sam McCook. Circ: 800.

200 BRA ISSN 1809-8479
INTERACOES: CULTURA E COMUNIDADE. Text in Portuguese. 2006. a. **Document type:** *Journal, Academic/Scholarly.*
Related titles: Online - full text ed.: ISSN 1983-2478. free (effective 2011).
Published by: Faculdade Catolica de Uberlandia, Rua Padre Pio 300, Bairro Osvaldo Rezende, Uberlandia, MG 38400-386, Brazil. Ed. Vani Terezinha De Rezende.

207.2 GBR
INTERACT. Text in English, Polish. 1943. 3/yr. free (effective 2009). adv. illus. back issues avail. **Document type:** *Magazine, Consumer.* **Description:** Contains news and features on a Christian charity that produces free Bible resources for people all around the world.
Former titles: S G M News; S G M News Digest (0048-9859)
Published by: S G M Lifewords, 5 Eccleston St, London, SW1W 9LZ, United Kingdom. TEL 44-20-77302155, FAX 44-20-77300240, uk@sgmlifewords.com.

200 401 USA
THE INTERCESSOR. Text in English. 19??. bi-m. free (effective 2011). **Document type:** *Newsletter, Consumer.* **Description:** A prayer newsletter focusing on corporate needs and translation work issues.
Related titles: Online - full text ed.
Published by: Wycliffe Bible Translators, Inc., PO Box 628200, Orlando, FL 32862. TEL 407-852-3600, 800-992-5433, FAX 407-852-3601, Info_USA@wycliffe.org.

INTERCESSOR. *see* ADVERTISING AND PUBLIC RELATIONS

291.72 DEU
INTERCULTURA; missions- und kulturgeschichtliche Forschungen. Text in English, German. 2002. irreg., latest vol.9, 2009. price varies. **Document type:** *Monographic series, Academic/Scholarly.*
Published by: Ruediger Koeppe Verlag, Wendelinstr 73-75, Cologne, 50933, Germany. TEL 49-221-4911236, FAX 49-221-4994336, info@koeppe.de.

201.6 NLD ISSN 1872-4477
INTERCULTURAL THEOLOGY AND STUDY OF RELIGIONS/ THEOLOGIE INTERKULTURELL UND STUDIUM DER RELIGIONEN. Text in English. 2006 (Jul.). irreg., latest vol.2, 2007. price varies. **Document type:** *Monographic series, Academic/ Scholarly.*
Indexed: A01, T02.
Published by: (International Society for Intercultural Theology and Study of Religion), Editions Rodopi B.V., Tijnmuiden 7, Amsterdam, 1046 AK, Netherlands. TEL 31-20-6114821, FAX 31-20-4472979, info@rodopi.nl. Eds. Dr. Chibueze Udeani, Claude Ozankom, Friedrich Reiterer, Klaus Zaptoczky.

230.05 USA ISSN 0092-6558
BR1
INTERDENOMINATIONAL THEOLOGICAL CENTER. JOURNAL. Text in English. 1973. s-a. bk.rev. charts; illus.; maps; stat. 250 p./no.; back issues avail. **Document type:** *Journal, Academic/Scholarly.* **Description:** Publishes information dedicated to the advancement of theological education with a special emphasis on the African-American perspective.
Related titles: Microform ed.: (from PQC).
Indexed: A21, CERDIC, R&TA, RI-1, RI-2, RILM.
—BLDSC (4802.064000).
Published by: Interdenominational Theological Center, 700 Martin Luther King Jr Dr, SW, Atlanta, GA 30314. TEL 404-527-7700, http://www.itc.edu.

200 USA ISSN 1556-3723
BL1.A2
➤ **INTERDISCIPLINARY JOURNAL OF RESEARCH ON RELIGION.** Text in English. 2005 (Jan.). a. free (effective 2010). back issues avail. **Document type:** *Journal, Academic/Scholarly.*
Media: Online - full text.
Indexed: A01, CA, P42, PSA, S02, S03, SociolAb, T02.
Published by: Institute for Studies of Religion, Baylor University, One Bear Pl 97236, Waco, TX 76798. TEL 254-710-7555, FAX 254-710-1428, ISR@baylor.edu, http://www.isreligion.org.

266 DEU ISSN 1867-5492
INTERKULTURELLE THEOLOGIE. Text in German. 1975. q. EUR 24 (effective 2011). adv. bk.rev. index. **Document type:** *Journal, Academic/Scholarly.*
Former titles (until 2008): Zeitschrift fuer Mission (0342-9423); (until 1974): Evangelische Missionszeitschrift (0014-3472)
Indexed: A21, CERDIC, DIP, FR, IBR, IBZ, RI-1, RI-2.
Published by: Verlag Otto Lembeck, Gaertnerweg 16, Frankfurt Am Main, 60322, Germany. TEL 49-69-5970988, FAX 49-69-5975742, verlag@lembeck.de. Circ: 1,000.

200 USA ISSN 2155-1723
▼ **INTERMOUNTAIN WEST JOURNAL OF RELIGIOUS STUDIES.** Text in English. 2009. s-a. free (effective 2011). **Document type:** *Journal, Consumer.* **Description:** Designed to promote the academic study of religion at the graduate and undergraduate levels.
Media: Online - full text.
Published by: Utah State University, 1400 Old Main Hill, Logan, UT 84322. TEL 435-797-1000, helpdesk@usu.edu. Eds. Christopher James Blythe, Jay A Burton.

206.5 USA
INTERNATIONAL ASSOCIATION OF LIBERAL RELIGIOUS WOMEN. NEWSLETTER. Text in English. 1949. a. membership. **Document type:** *Newsletter.*
Former titles: International Union of Liberal Christian Women. Newsletter; International League of Liberal Christian Women. Newsletter (0074-6746)
Published by: International Association of Liberal Religious Women, c/o Tina Jas, 935 Bridge Rd, Eastham, MA 02642-1203. TEL 508-247-9063.

200 DEU ISSN 1864-757X
INTERNATIONAL BONHOEFFER INTERPRETATIONS. Text in English. 2008. irreg., latest vol.3, 2010. price varies. **Document type:** *Monographic series, Academic/Scholarly.*
—BLDSC (4537.335525).
Published by: Peter Lang GmbH (Subsidiary of: Peter Lang Publishing Group), Eschborner Landstr 42-50, Frankfurt Am Main, 60489, Germany. TEL 49-69-7807050, FAX 49-69-78070550, zentrale.frankfurt@peterlang.com.

200 GBR ISSN 1472-2089
BX7101
INTERNATIONAL CONGREGATIONAL JOURNAL. Text in English. 2001. s-a. free to members (effective 2010). adv. back issues avail. **Document type:** *Journal, Academic/Scholarly.* **Description:** Features articles that reflect the theology, scholarship, liturgy and history of Congregationalism, and provide a lively intellectual forum for institutions, fellowships and individuals.
Related titles: Online - full text ed.
Indexed: A01, A02, A03, A08, CA, T02.
—**CCC.**
Published by: International Congregational Fellowship, ICF Communications, 4 Clarence St, Market Harborough, LE16 7NE, United Kingdom.

230 USA ISSN 1559-9191
INTERNATIONAL DELIVERANCE MAGAZINE. Text in English. 2005. q. **Document type:** *Magazine, Consumer.*
Published by: International Deliverance Ministries (I D M), PO Box 23826, Detroit, MI 48223-0826. TEL 313-583-1335, info@indel.org, http://www.indel.org.

230.071 NLD ISSN 1874-0049
INTERNATIONAL HANDBOOKS OF RELIGION AND EDUCATION. Text in English. 2006. a. **Document type:** *Monographic series, Academic/ Scholarly.*
Related titles: Online - full text ed.: ISSN 1874-0057.
—IE.
Published by: Springer Netherlands (Subsidiary of: Springer Science+Business Media), Van Godewijckstraat 30, Dordrecht, 3311 GX, Netherlands. TEL 31-78-6576050, FAX 31-78-6576474.

201 NLD ISSN 0020-7047
BL51 CODEN: IJPREB
➤ **INTERNATIONAL JOURNAL FOR PHILOSOPHY OF RELIGION.** Text in English. 1970. bi-m. (in 2 vols., 3 nos./vol.). EUR 707, USD 740 combined subscription to institutions (print & online eds.) (effective 2012). adv. bk.rev. bibl.; illus. Index. back issues avail.; reprint service avail. from PSC. **Document type:** *Journal, Academic/ Scholarly.* **Description:** Provides a non-sectarian and independent forum for the exposition, development and criticism of philosophical insights and theories relevant to religion in any of its varied forms.
Related titles: Microform ed.: (from PQC); Online - full text ed.: ISSN 1572-8684 (from IngentaConnect).
Indexed: A01, A02, A03, A08, A20, A21, A22, A26, ASCA, AmHI, ArtHuCI, B04, BRD, BibLing, CA, CurCont, DIP, E01, E08, FR, G08, H07, H08, H09, H10, H14, HAb, HumInd, I05, IBR, IBSS, IBZ, MEA&I, P02, P10, P28, P48, P53, P54, PCI, PQC, PhilInd, R&TA, R05, RASB, RI-1, RI-2, S09, SCOPUS, T02, W03, W05, W07.
—BLDSC (4542.455000), IE, Infotrieve, Ingenta, INIST. **CCC.**
Published by: Springer Netherlands (Subsidiary of: Springer Science+Business Media), Van Godewijckstraat 30, Dordrecht, 3311 GX, Netherlands. TEL 31-78-6576050, FAX 31-78-6576474, http://www.springer.com. Ed. Eugene Thomas Long.

R

200 150 USA ISSN 1050-8619
BL53.A1 CODEN: IPRLEB
➤ **THE INTERNATIONAL JOURNAL FOR THE PSYCHOLOGY OF RELIGION.** Abbreviated title: I J P R. Text in English. 1991. q. GBP 391 combined subscription in United Kingdom to institutions (print & online eds.); EUR 520, USD 654 combined subscription to institutions (print & online eds.) (effective 2012). adv. bk.rev. illus. back issues avail.; reprint service avail. from PSC. **Document type:** *Journal, Academic/Scholarly.* **Description:** Presents articles covering a variety of important topics, such as the social psychology of religion, religious development, conversion, religious experience, religion and social attitudes and behavior, religion and mental health, and psychoanalytic and other theoretical interpretations of religion.
Related titles: Online - full text ed.: ISSN 1532-7582. GBP 352 in United Kingdom to institutions; EUR 468, USD 589 to institutions (effective 2012).
Indexed: A01, A02, A03, A08, A20, A21, A22, ASSIA, ArtHuCI, CA, CurCont, E-psyche, E01, FamI, I14, P03, P28, P30, P43, P48, P53, P54, PCI, PQC, PsycInfo, PsycholAb, R&TA, RI-1, RI-2, S02, S03, SCOPUS, SOPODA, SSCI, SociolAb, T02, W07.
—BLDSC (4542.506200), IE, Infotrieve, Ingenta. **CCC.**
Published by: Routledge (Subsidiary of: Taylor & Francis Group), 325 Chestnut St, Ste 800, Philadelphia, PA 19106. TEL 800-354-1420, FAX 215-625-2940, journals@routledge.com, http://www.routledge.com. Ed. Raymond F Paloutzian. Adv. contact Linda Hann TEL 44-1344-779945.

200 GBR ISSN 2041-9511
▼ ➤ **INTERNATIONAL JOURNAL FOR THE STUDY OF NEW RELIGIONS.** Abbreviated title: I J S N R. Text in English. 2010. s-a. USD 220 combined subscription in North America to institutions (print & online eds.); GBP 135 combined subscription elsewhere to institutions (print & online eds.) (effective 2012). adv. back issues avail.; reprints avail. **Document type:** *Journal, Academic/Scholarly.*
Related titles: Online - full text ed.: ISSN 2041-952X. USD 176 in North America to institutions; GBP 108 elsewhere to institutions (effective 2012).
—**CCC.**

Published by: (International Society for the Study of New Religions), Equinox Publishing Ltd., Unit S3, Kelham House, 3 Lancaster St, Sheffield, S6 3AF, United Kingdom. TEL 44-114-2725957, FAX 44-560-3459046, journals@equinoxpub.com, http://www.equinoxpub.com/. Eds. Carole Cusack, Liselotte Frisk. Adv. contact Val Hall.

260.9 GBR ISSN 1474-225X
BR140
➤ **INTERNATIONAL JOURNAL FOR THE STUDY OF THE CHRISTIAN CHURCH.** Abbreviated title: I J S C C. Text in English. 2001. q. GBP 201 combined subscription in United Kingdom to institutions (print & online eds.); EUR 263, USD 332 combined subscription to institutions (print & online eds.) (effective 2012). adv. back issues avail.; reprint service avail. from PSC. **Document type:** *Journal, Academic/Scholarly.* **Description:** Seeks to promote ecumenical exchange of research and scholarship over a wide geographical area.
Related titles: Online - full text ed.: ISSN 1747-0234. GBP 181 in United Kingdom to institutions; EUR 237, USD 298 to institutions (effective 2012).
Indexed: A01, A03, A08, A22, CA, DIP, E01, IBR, IBZ, P48, P53, P54, PQC, R&TA, T02.
—IE, Ingenta. **CCC.**
Published by: Routledge (Subsidiary of: Taylor & Francis Group), 4 Park Sq, Milton Park, Abingdon, Oxon OX14 4RN, United Kingdom. TEL 44-20-70176000, FAX 44-20-70176336, subscriptions@tandf.co.uk, http://www.routledge.com. Eds. Christine Hall, Geoffrey Rowell. Adv. contact Linda Hann TEL 44-1344-779945. **Subscr. to:** Taylor & Francis Ltd., Journals Customer Service, Sheepen Pl, Colchester, Essex CO3 3LP, United Kingdom. TEL 44-20-70175544, FAX 44-20-70175198.

➤ **INTERNATIONAL JOURNAL OF CHILDREN'S SPIRITUALITY.** *see* PSYCHOLOGY

➤ **INTERNATIONAL JOURNAL OF CULTIC STUDIES.** *see* SOCIOLOGY

266 USA ISSN 2161-3354
INTERNATIONAL JOURNAL OF FRONTIER MISSIOLOGY. Abbreviated title: I J F M. Text in English. 1984. q. USD 18; USD 4 per issue (effective 2011). back issues avail. **Document type:** *Journal, Academic/Scholarly.*
Formerly (until 2007): International Journal of Frontier Missions (0743-2429)
Related titles: Online - full text ed.: free (effective 2011).
Indexed: A21, RI-1.
Published by: International Student Leaders Coalition for Frontier Missions, 1605 E Elizabeth St, Pasadena, CA 91104. TEL 626-398-2119, FAX 626-398-2337. Ed., Pub. Brad Gill.

200 DEU ISSN 1430-6921
➤ **INTERNATIONAL JOURNAL OF PRACTICAL THEOLOGY.** Text in English, German. 1997. s-a. EUR 138, USD 207 to institutions; EUR 159, USD 239 combined subscription to institutions (print & online eds.) (effective 2012). adv. reprint service avail. from PSC. **Document type:** *Journal, Academic/Scholarly.* **Description:** Provides information and dialogue on the current state of affairs of interdisciplinary and international research on religion.
Related titles: CD-ROM ed.; Online - full text ed.: ISSN 1612-9768. EUR 138, USD 207 to institutions (effective 2012).
Indexed: A01, A02, A03, A08, A21, A22, A26, CA, E01, I05, IBR, IBZ, P02, P28, P48, P53, P54, PQC, R&TA, RI-1, SCOPUS, T02.
—BLDSC (4542.481700), IE, Ingenta. **CCC.**
Published by: Walter de Gruyter GmbH & Co. KG, Genthiner Str 13, Berlin, 10785, Germany. TEL 49-30-260050, FAX 49-30-26005251, info@degruyter.com. Eds. Richard Osmer, Wilhelm Graeb. adv.: page EUR 100; trim 112 x 181. Circ: 280 (paid and controlled).

200 NLD ISSN 1872-5171
INTERNATIONAL JOURNAL OF PUBLIC THEOLOGY. Text in English. 2007. 4/yr. EUR 213, USD 299 to institutions; EUR 233, USD 326 combined subscription to institutions (print & online eds.) (effective 2012). reprint service avail. from PSC. **Document type:** *Journal, Academic/Scholarly.* **Description:** Seeks to promote dialogue within different academic disciplines such as politics, economics, cultural studies, religious studies, as well as with spirituality, globalization and society in general.
Related titles: Online - full text ed.: ISSN 1569-7320. EUR 194, USD 272 to institutions (effective 2012) (from IngentaConnect).
Indexed: A01, A21, A22, CA, E01, IZBG, P34, T02.
—BLDSC (4542.509255), IE. **CCC.**
Published by: Brill, PO Box 9000, Leiden, 2300 PA, Netherlands. TEL 31-71-5353500, FAX 31-71-5317532, cs@brill.nl. Ed. S Kim.

INTERNATIONAL JOURNAL OF RELIGION AND SOCIETY. *see* SOCIOLOGY

200 USA ISSN 2154-8633
▼ ➤ **THE INTERNATIONAL JOURNAL OF RELIGION AND SPIRITUALITY IN SOCIETY.** Text in English. 2010. q. **Document type:** *Journal, Academic/Scholarly.* **Description:** Features research on religious philosophies and their contexts throughout history in the world, places of worship, on the streets, and in communities.
Related titles: Online - full text ed.: ISSN 2154-8641. 2010. USD 300 to institutions (effective 2010).
Published by: Common Ground Publishing, University of Illinois Research Park, 60 Hazelwood Dr, Ste 226, Champaign, IL 61820. TEL 217-328-0405, kathryn@commongroundpublishing.com, http://www.commongroundpublishing.com.

▼ ➤ **INTERNATIONAL JOURNAL OF RELIGION AND SPORT.** *see* SPORTS AND GAMES

➤ **INTERNATIONAL JOURNAL OF SERVANT-LEADERSHIP.** *see* PHILOSOPHY

200 GBR ISSN 1463-1652
BR1
➤ **INTERNATIONAL JOURNAL OF SYSTEMATIC THEOLOGY.** Abbreviated title: I J S T. Text in English. 1999. q. GBP 377 in United Kingdom to institutions; EUR 477 in Europe to institutions; USD 631 in the Americas to institutions; USD 737 elsewhere to institutions; GBP 434 combined subscription in United Kingdom to institutions (print & online eds.); EUR 550 combined subscription in Europe to institutions (print & online eds.); USD 727 combined subscription in the Americas to institutions (print & online eds.); USD 848 combined subscription elsewhere to institutions (print & online eds.) (effective 2012). adv. back issues avail.; reprint service avail. from PSC. **Document type:** *Journal, Academic/Scholarly.* **Description:** Contains academic articles on systematic theology and for substantial reviews of major new works of scholarship.
Related titles: Online - full text ed.: ISSN 1468-2400. GBP 377 in United Kingdom to institutions; EUR 477 in Europe to institutions; USD 631 in the Americas to institutions; USD 737 elsewhere to institutions (effective 2012) (from IngentaConnect).
Indexed: A01, A03, A08, A20, A21, A22, A26, ArtHuCI, CA, CurCont, DIP, E01, IBR, IBZ, OTA, RI-1, SCOPUS, T02, W07.
—BLDSC (4542.690500), IE, Infotrieve, Ingenta. **CCC.**
Published by: Wiley-Blackwell Publishing Ltd. (Subsidiary of: John Wiley & Sons, Inc.), 9600 Garsington Rd, Oxford, OX4 2DQ, United Kingdom. TEL 44-1865-776868, FAX 44-1865-714591, customerservices@blackwellpublishing.com. Adv. contact Craig Pickett TEL 44-1865-476267. B&W page GBP 445, B&W page USD 823; 112 x 190. Circ: 450.

➤ **INTERNATIONAL JOURNAL OF TRANSPERSONAL STUDIES.** *see* PSYCHOLOGY

➤ **INTERNATIONAL RECONCILIATION.** *see* POLITICAL SCIENCE—Civil Rights

➤ **INTERNATIONAL REVIEW OF BIBLICAL STUDIES/INTERNATIONALE ZEITSCHRIFTENSCHAU FUER BIBELWISSENSCHAFT UND GRENZGEBIETE.** *see* RELIGIONS AND THEOLOGY—Abstracting, Bibliographies, Statistics

266 GBR ISSN 0020-8582
BV2351
INTERNATIONAL REVIEW OF MISSION. Text in English. 1911. bi-m. GBP 148 in United Kingdom to institutions; EUR 187 in Europe to institutions; USD 235 elsewhere to institutions; GBP 170 combined subscription in United Kingdom to institutions (print & online eds.); EUR 216 combined subscription in Europe to institutions (print & online eds.); USD 271 combined subscription elsewhere to institutions (print & online eds.) (effective 2012). adv. bk.rev. bibl.; illus. index; cum.index: 1912-1990. reprint service avail. from PSC. **Document type:** *Bulletin, Consumer.* **Description:** Provides information on christianity.
Related titles: Microform ed.: (from PQC); Online - full text ed.: ISSN 1758-6631. GBP 148 in United Kingdom to institutions; EUR 187 in Europe to institutions; USD 235 elsewhere to institutions (effective 2012) (from IngentaConnect).
Indexed: A01, A02, A03, A06, A08, A21, A22, A26, AICP, AMR, AmHI, B04, BAS, BRD, CA, CERDIC, Chicano, ChrPI, E01, E06, E08, FR, G06, G07, G08, H07, H08, H09, H10, H14, HAb, HumInd, I05, IBR, IBZ, M01, M02, MEA&I, MLA-IB, P02, P10, P28, P30, P48, P53, P54, PCI, PQC, R&TA, R05, RI-1, RI-2, S05, S09, SPPI, T02, W03.
—BLDSC (4547.380000), IE, Infotrieve, Ingenta. **CCC.**
Published by: (World Council of Churches CHE, CWME - Unit II: Churches in Mission CHE), Wiley-Blackwell Publishing Ltd. (Subsidiary of: John Wiley & Sons, Inc.), 9600 Garsington Rd, Oxford, OX4 2DQ, United Kingdom. TEL 44-1865-776868, FAX 44-1865-714591, customer@wiley.co.uk, http://www.wiley.com/. Eds. Jacques Matthey, Dr. Jooseop Keum.

210 NLD ISSN 0925-4153
INTERNATIONAL SERIES IN THE PSYCHOLOGY OF RELIGION. Text in English, German. 1990. irreg., latest vol.14, 2005. price varies. back issues avail. **Document type:** *Monographic series, Academic/Scholarly.* **Description:** Examines religion from a psychological perspective.
Indexed: A01, E-psyche, T02.
—BLDSC (4549.270500), IE, Ingenta.
Published by: Editions Rodopi B.V., Tijnmuiden 7, Amsterdam, 1046 AK, Netherlands. TEL 31-20-6114821, FAX 31-20-4472979, info@rodopi.nl. Ed. Dr. Jaap A Belzen. **Dist in France by:** Nordeal, 30 rue de Verlinghem, BP 139, Lambersart 59832, France. TEL 33-3-20099060, FAX 33-3-20929495; **Dist in N America by:** Rodopi - USA, 606 Newark Ave, 2nd fl, Kenilworth, NJ 07033. TEL 908-497-9031, 800-225-3998, FAX 908-497-9035.

201.6 CAN
INTERNATIONAL SOCIETY FOR THE SOCIOLOGY OF RELIGION. DIRECTORY. Text in English. 1948. biennial. bk.rev. **Document type:** *Newsletter.*
Formerly: International Conference for the Sociology of Religion. Directory (0074-297X)
Published by: International Society for the Sociology of Religion, Universite Sainte-Anne, Nouvelle-Ecosse, Pointe-de-l'eglise, NS BOW 1MO, Canada. TEL 902-769-2114, FAX 902-769-2930.

201.6 CAN
INTERNATIONAL SOCIETY FOR THE SOCIOLOGY OF RELIGION. NEWSLETTER - BULLETIN. Text in English. s-a. CAD 70. **Document type:** *Bulletin.*
Published by: International Society for the Sociology of Religion, Universite Sainte-Anne, Nouvelle-Ecosse, Pointe-de-l'eglise, NS BOW 1MO, Canada. TEL 902-769-2114, FAX 902-769-2930.

INTERNATIONAL STUDIES IN RELIGION AND SOCIETY. *see* SOCIOLOGY

200 USA ISSN 1949-8411
▼ **INTERNATIONAL VOICES IN BIBLICAL STUDIES.** Text in English. 2009. irreg. free (effective 2009). **Document type:** *Monographic series, Academic/Scholarly.* **Description:** Features books on biblical studies from scholars around the world.
Media: Online - full content.
Published by: Society of Biblical Literature, The Luce Ctr, 825 Houston Mill Rd, Atlanta, GA 30329. TEL 404-727-3100, FAX 404-727-3101, sblexec@sbl-site.org, http://www.sbl-site.org.

200 DEU ISSN 0934-7259
INTERNATIONALE CARDINAL-NEWMAN-STUDIEN. Text in German. 1994. irreg., latest vol.19, 2006. price varies. **Document type:** *Monographic series, Academic/Scholarly.*
Published by: Peter Lang GmbH (Subsidiary of: Peter Lang Publishing Group), Eschborner Landstr 42-50, Frankfurt Am Main, 60489, Germany. TEL 49-69-7807050, FAX 49-69-78070550, zentrale.frankfurt@peterlang.com. Ed. Guenter Biemer.

200 CHE ISSN 0020-9252
BX4751
INTERNATIONALE KIRCHLICHE ZEITSCHRIFT. Text in German. 1911. q. CHF 76 domestic; CHF 82 foreign (effective 2011). bk.rev. bibl. index. **Document type:** *Bulletin, Consumer.*
Indexed: A21, CERDIC, DIP, FR, IBR, IBZ, IZBG, OTA, RI-1, RI-2.
—INIST. **CCC.**
Published by: Staempfli Verlag AG (Subsidiary of: LexisNexis Europe and Africa), Woelflistr 1, Bern, 3001, Switzerland. TEL 41-31-3006666, FAX 41-31-3006688, verlag@staempfli.com, http://www.staempfli.com. Ed. Urs von Arx. Circ: 555 (paid).

200 DEU ISSN 0949-6068
INTERNATIONALE THEOLOGIE/INTERNATIONAL THEOLOGY. Text in English, German. 1996. irreg., latest vol.13, 2009. price varies. **Document type:** *Monographic series, Academic/Scholarly.*
Published by: Peter Lang GmbH (Subsidiary of: Peter Lang Publishing Group), Eschborner Landstr 42-50, Frankfurt Am Main, 60489, Germany. TEL 49-69-7807050, FAX 49-69-78070550, zentrale.frankfurt@peterlang.com.

200 DEU ISSN 1990-4231
INTERNATIONALES JAHRBUCH FUER DIE TILLICH-FORSCHUNG/INTERNATIONAL YEARBOOK FOR TILLICH RESEARCH. Text in German. 2005. a. EUR 63, USD 95 to institutions; EUR 73, USD 110 combined subscription to institutions (print & online eds.) (effective 2012). **Document type:** *Journal, Academic/Scholarly.*
Related titles: Online - full text ed.: EUR 63, USD 95 to institutions (effective 2012); Print ed.: ISSN 2190-7455.
Published by: Walter de Gruyter GmbH & Co. KG, Genthiner Str 13, Berlin, 10785, Germany. TEL 49-30-260050, FAX 49-30-26005251, info@degruyter.com.

220 NLD ISSN 0929-015X
INTERPRETATIE; tijdschrift voor bijbelse theologie. Text in Dutch. 1993. 8/yr. EUR 59; EUR 44.25 to students (effective 2008). adv. **Document type:** *Academic/Scholarly.* **Description:** Provides a forum for interpretation of the Bible.
Incorporates (in 1978): Ter Herkenning (Zoetermeer) (0165-2397)
Published by: Boekencentrum Uitgevers, Goudstraat 50, Postbus 29, Zoetermeer, 2700 AA, Netherlands. TEL 31-79-3615481, FAX 31-79-3615489, info@boekencentrum.nl, http://www.boekencentrum.nl. Ed. M van Veldhuizen. adv.: page EUR 300; trim 210 x 297. Circ: 1,100.

220 230 USA ISSN 0020-9643
BR1
➤ **INTERPRETATION (RICHMOND)**; a journal of bible and theology. Text in English. 1889. q. USD 193, GBP 127 to institutions; USD 198, GBP 130 combined subscription to institutions (print & online eds.) (effective 2012). adv. bk.rev. bibl.; illus. index, cum.index: 1947-1995. back issues avail.; reprints avail. **Document type:** *Journal, Academic/Scholarly.* **Description:** Contains articles and essays of biblical and theological interpretation for scholars, clergy, and laity of all denominations.
Former titles (until 1947): The Union Seminary Review (0362-904X); (until 1913): Union Seminary Magazine
Related titles: Microform ed.: (from PQC); Online - full text ed.: ISSN 2159-340X. USD 178, GBP 117 to institutions (effective 2012).
Indexed: A01, A02, A03, A08, A20, A21, A22, A25, A26, AmHI, ArtHuCI, B04, B14, BRD, BRI, CA, CBRI, ChrPI, CurCont, DIP, E08, FR, G05, G06, G07, G08, GSS&RPL, H07, H08, H09, H10, H14, HAb, HumInd, I05, I07, IAJS, IBR, IBZ, IZBG, M01, M02, OTA, P02, P10, P13, P28, P42, P45, P48, P53, P54, PCI, PQC, R&TA, R05, RASB, RI-1, RI-2, S05, S08, S09, S23, SCOPUS, T02, W03, W05, W07.
—BLDSC (4557.347000), IE, Infotrieve, Ingenta, INIST.
Published by: (Union Theological Seminary), Sage Publications Ltd. (Subsidiary of: Sage Publications, Inc.), 1 Oliver's Yard, 55 City Rd, London, EC1Y 1SP, United Kingdom. TEL 44-20-73248500, FAX 44-20-73248600, info@sagepub.co.uk, http://www.uk.sagepub.com/home.nav. Ed. Samuel E Balentine. **Co-publisher:** Presbyterian School of Christian Education.

200 DEU ISSN 2191-2114
▼ **INTERRELIGIOESE UND INTERKULTURELLE BILDUNG IM KINDESALTER.** Text in German. 2010. irreg. price varies. **Document type:** *Monographic series, Academic/Scholarly.*
Media: Large Type.
Published by: Waxmann Verlag GmbH, Steinfurter Str 555, Muenster, 48159, Germany. TEL 49-251-265040, FAX 49-251-2650426, info@waxmann.com.

200 GBR ISSN 1742-1888
BL410
INTERRELIGIOUS INSIGHT; a journal of dialogue and engagement. Text in English. 1980. q. GBP 24 to non-members; free to members (effective 2009). adv. bk.rev. 64 p./no.; back issues avail. **Document type:** *Magazine, Academic/Scholarly.* **Description:** Covers historical and contemporary questions of inter-faith dialogue and cooperation between religions and ideologies.
Former titles (until 2003): World Faiths Encounter (0968-7718); (until 1992): World Faiths Insight (0273-1266); Which was formed by the merger of (1976-1980): Insight (0148-3935); (1961-1980): World Faiths
Indexed: ChrPI.
—BLDSC (4557.441270), IE.
Published by: World Congress of Faiths, London Inter Faith Ctr, 125 Salusbury Rd, London, NW6 6RG, United Kingdom. TEL 44-20-89593129, FAX 44-20-76043052, enquires@worldfaith.org. Eds. Alan Race, Jim Kenney, K L S Rao.

200 USA ISSN 1542-9695
INTERSECTION; interfaith insights on faith & politics. Text in English. 2000. q.
Formerly (until 2002): Interfaith Insights (1532-1355)
Published by: The Interfaith Alliance Foundation, 1331 H St. NW 11th Fl., Washington, DC 20005. TEL 202-639-6370, FAX 202-639-6375, tia@interfaithalliance.org, http://www.interfaithalliance.org.

200 USA ISSN 1092-5708
INTO THE LIGHT. Text in English. 1906. s-a. membership. adv. bk.rev. **Document type:** *Newsletter.* **Description:** Updates on Waldensian ministry in Italy, Argentina and Uruguay, and ministry exchanges between Waldensian and US churches.
Former titles: American Waldensian Society. Newsletter (0894-9999); American Waldensian Aid Society. Newsletter (0517-5798)
Related titles: Online - full text ed.
Published by: American Waldensian Society, P O Box 20241, Lehigh Valley, PA 18002-0241. TEL 610-432-9569, FAX 610-432-9518. Eds. Rev. Edward Santana-Grace, Rev. Ruth Santana-Grace. Pubs. Revs Edward, Ruth Santana Grace. R&P Edward Santana Grace. Adv. contact Rev. Edward Santana-Grace. Circ: 2,500.

255 BEL ISSN 0021-0978
BX1
IRENIKON. Text in Dutch. 1926. q. EUR 39.75 in Europe; EUR 42.25 elsewhere (effective 2005). adv. bk.rev. bibl. index. back issues avail. **Document type:** *Academic/Scholarly.*
Indexed: A21, A22, CERDIC, DIP, FR, IBR, IBZ, IndMed, MLA-IB, PCI, RI-1, RI-2.
—IE, Infotrieve, INIST.
Published by: Monastere de l'Exaltation de la Sainte Croix, Rue du monastere 65, Chevetogne, 5590, Belgium. TEL 32-83-211763, FAX 32-83-216045, abbaye@monasterechevetogne.com. Ed., R&P Thaddee Barnas. Pub. Luc Vanderheyden. Circ: 1,600.

200 IRL ISSN 0332-4427
IRISH BIBLICAL ASSOCIATION. PROCEEDINGS. Text in English. 1976. a. adv. bk.rev. back issues avail. **Document type:** *Proceedings.* **Description:** Presents academic papers on Scripture studies with a particular interest in Hiberno-Latin studies.
Indexed: OTA, PCI, R&TA.
—BLDSC (6740.700000). **CCC.**
Published by: Irish Biblical Association, c/o Anthony O'Leary, Milltown Institute, Milltown Park, Dublin, 6, Ireland. http://www.theology.ie/iba/. Ed. Kieran O'Mahony. Circ: 250.

221 GBR ISSN 0268-6112
BS543
➤ **IRISH BIBLICAL STUDIES.** Text in English. 1979. q. GBP 9 to individuals; GBP 19, EUR 35, USD 40 to institutions (effective 2009). bk.rev. back issues avail. **Document type:** *Journal, Academic/Scholarly.* **Description:** Covers the Old and New Testaments and related material.
Indexed: DIP, IBR, IBZ, IZBG, OTA, R&TA.
—BLDSC (4570.400000), IE, Ingenta.
Published by: Union Theological College, 108 Botanic Ave, Belfast, BT7 1JT, United Kingdom. TEL 44-28-90205080, FAX 44-28-90205099, admin@union.ac.uk. Ed. J C McCullough.

200 GBR ISSN 0021-1400
BX801
➤ **IRISH THEOLOGICAL QUARTERLY.** Abbreviated title: I T Q. Text in English. 1906. q. GBP 204, USD 377 to institutions; GBP 208, USD 385 combined subscription to institutions (print & online eds.) (effective 2012). bk.rev. index. 96 p./no.; back issues avail.; reprint service avail. from PSC. **Document type:** *Journal, Academic/Scholarly.* **Description:** Publishes constructive and critical scholarship in the areas of systematic, moral, and historical theology as well as sacred scripture.
Related titles: Microform ed.: (from PQC); Online - full text ed.: ISSN 1752-4989. GBP 187, USD 347 to institutions (effective 2012).
Indexed: A21, A22, CLA, CPL, DIP, E01, FR, IBR, IBZ, IZBG, MLA-IB, OTA, P30, PCI, PhilInd, R&TA, RI-1, RI-2, SCOPUS.
—BLDSC (4574.870000), IE, Infotrieve, Ingenta, INIST. **CCC.**
Published by: (Pontifical University, St. Patrick's College IRL), Sage Publications Ltd. (Subsidiary of: Sage Publications, Inc.), 1 Oliver's Yard, 55 City Rd, London, EC1Y 1SP, United Kingdom. TEL 44-20-73248701, 44-20-73248500, FAX 44-20-73248600, info@sagepub.co.uk, http://www.uk.sagepub.com/home.nav. Ed. Michael A Conway.

200 ITA ISSN 0392-7288
BP172
ISLAMOCHRISTIANA/DIRASAT ISLAMIYYA MASIHIYYA. Text in Arabic, English, French. 1975. a. bk.rev. **Document type:** *Journal, Academic/Scholarly.* **Description:** Publishes articles, documents and materials concerned with the theoretical and practical aspects, past and present, of the Muslim-Christian dialogue.
Indexed: A21, FR, I14, MLA-IB, PCI, RI-1, RI-2.
—INIST.
Published by: Pontificio Istituto di Studi Arabi e d'Islamistica (P I S A I), Viale di Trastevere 89, Rome, 00153, Italy. TEL 39-06-58392611, FAX 39-06-5882595, info@pisai.org, http://www.pisai.it.

200 DEU
ISRAEL HEUTE. Text in German. 1978. m. EUR 48 (effective 2011). adv. **Document type:** *Magazine, Consumer.*
Related titles: ◆ Dutch ed.: Israel Today. ISSN 1875-256X.
Published by: Bundes Verlag GmbH, Bodenborn 43, Witten, 58452, Germany. TEL 49-2302-930930, FAX 49-2302-93093689, info@bundes-verlag.de, http://www.bundes-verlag.de. Ed. Michael Schneider. Adv. contact Juergen Bublitz. Circ: 18,000 (paid and controlled).

ISSUES IN CHRISTIAN EDUCATION. *see* EDUCATION

200 USA ISSN 1081-9479
ISSUES IN SYSTEMATIC THEOLOGY. Text in English. 1997. irreg., latest vol.15, 2007. price varies. **Document type:** *Monographic series, Academic/Scholarly.* **Description:** Seeks to explore such issues as the relation of reason and revelation, experience and doctrine, the meaning of revelation, method in theology, Trinitarian Theology, the doctrine of God, Christology, sacraments and the Church.
Published by: Peter Lang Publishing, Inc. (Subsidiary of: Peter Lang Publishing Group), 29 Broadway, New York, NY 10006. TEL 212-647-7700, 800-770-5264, FAX 212-647-7707, customerservice@plang.com, http://www.peterlangusa.com. Ed. Paul D Molnar.

281 FRA ISSN 0021-2423
BX1781
ISTINA. Text in French. 1954. q. bk.rev. index. back issues avail.; reprints avail. **Document type:** *Academic/Scholarly.*
Related titles: Microfilm ed.: (from PQC).
Indexed: A21, CERDIC, DIP, FR, IBR, IBSS, IBZ, MLA-IB, RI-1, RI-2.
—INIST.
Published by: Centre d'Etudes Istina, 45 rue de la Glaciere, Paris, 75013, France. TEL 33-1-42174560, FAX 33-1-42174562. Ed. Bernard Dupuy. Circ: 1,100.

ISTITUTO UNIVERSITARIO ORIENTALE. ANNALI; rivista del Dipartimento di Studi Asiatici e del Dipartimento di Studi e Ricerche su Africa e Paesi Arabi. *see* HUMANITIES: COMPREHENSIVE WORKS

200 301 570 ITA ISSN 1127-3216
ITINERARIUM; rivista multidisciplinare dell'Istituto Teologico "S. Tommaso" Messina. Text in Italian; Summaries in English, French. 1993. 3/yr. EUR 30 domestic; EUR 40 foreign (effective 2008). adv. bk.rev. **Document type:** *Monographic series, Academic/Scholarly.*
Indexed: OTA.
Published by: Istituto Teologico San Tommaso, Via del Pozzo 43, Messina, 98121, Italy. TEL 39-090-3691111, FAX 39-090-3691520, http://www.itst.it.

262.9 340 ESP ISSN 0021-325X
K9
➤ **IUS CANONICUM.** Text in Spanish; Summaries in English, Latin. 1961. s-a. EUR 52 in Europe; EUR 96 elsewhere (effective 2009). bk.rev. back issues avail. **Document type:** *Journal, Academic/Scholarly.* **Description:** Discusses canon law.
Related titles: Online - full text ed.
Indexed: A01, A26, CA, CERDIC, CLA, DIP, F03, F04, FR, I04, I05, IBR, IBZ, P09, PCI, R&TA, S02, S03, T02.
—INIST. **CCC.**
Published by: (Universidad de Navarra, Facultad de Derecho Canonico - Instituto Martin de Azpilicueta), Universidad de Navarra, Servicio de Publicaciones, Campus Universitario, Pamplona, 31009, Spain. http://www.unav.es/publicaciones/. Circ: 1,000.

211.6 ITA ISSN 0021-3268
K9
IUSTITIA. Text in Italian. 1948. q. EUR 50 in the European Union; EUR 75 elsewhere (effective 2008). adv. bk.rev. index. **Document type:** *Journal, Academic/Scholarly.* **Description:** Provides an intersection of Catholic legislative doctrine and secular thought on the grounds of promoting civil and political freedom.
Indexed: CERDIC, DoGi, IBR, IBZ, PAIS.
—IE.
Published by: (Unione Giuristi Cattolici Italiani), Casa Editrice Dott. A. Giuffre (Subsidiary of: LexisNexis Europe and Africa), Via Busto Arsizio, 40, Milan, MI 20151, Italy. TEL 39-02-380891, FAX 39-02-38009582, giuffre@giuffre.it, http://www.giuffre.it. Ed. Benito Perrone. Circ: 1,300.

200 305.4 NOR ISSN 1504-1573
J K; magasin for jenter i alle aldre. (Jesuskvinner) Text in Norwegian. bi-m. NOK 229 (effective 2006). **Document type:** *Magazine, Consumer.*
Published by: Jesuskvinner, PO Box 1058, Oslo, 0104, Norway. TEL 47-22-472046, info@jesuskvinner.no, http://www.jesuskvinner.no.

J O Y; investigating the philosophy, science, and spirituality of yoga. (Journal of Yoga) *see* NEW AGE PUBLICATIONS

200 DEU ISSN 0342-6505
JA. Text in German. 1969. bi-m. EUR 37.80 (effective 2010). bk.rev. **Document type:** *Magazine, Consumer.*
Published by: Frick Verlag GmbH, Bernhardstr 40, Pforzheim, 75177, Germany. TEL 49-7231-102842, FAX 49-7231-357744, info@frickverlag.de, http://www.frickverlag.de.

200 DEU ISSN 0342-6513
JA, DAS WORT FUER ALLE. Text in German. 1982. m. looseleaf. EUR 17.40 (effective 2005). **Document type:** *Bulletin, Consumer.*
Published by: (Berliner Stadtmission), Kreuz Verlag GmbH & Co. KG, Postfach 800669, Stuttgart, 70506, Germany. TEL 49-711-788030, FAX 49-711-7880310, service@kreuzverlag.de, http://www.kreuzverlag.de. Ed. Bettina Kopps. Circ: 12,000.

261.26 SWE ISSN 0283-3484
JABBOK. Variant title: Tidskriften Jabbok. Text in Swedish. 1985. q. SEK 160 domestic (effective 2003). adv. bk.rev. **Description:** Aims at creating mutual trust between Jews and Christians and promoting a friendly attitude to the country of Israel and its people.
Published by: Stiftelsen Jabbok, Skarpnaecks Alle 58, PO Box 2017, Skarpnack, 12821, Sweden. TEL 46-8-60425897. Ed. Ben Benson.

200 DEU ISSN 0341-9126
BR857.H4
JAHRBUCH DER HESSISCHEN KIRCHENGESCHICHTLICHEN VEREINIGUNG. Text in German. 1949. a. EUR 25 to non-members; EUR 20 to members (effective 2005). index. back issues avail. **Document type:** *Academic/Scholarly.*
Indexed: DIP, IBR, IBZ.
Published by: Hessische Kirchengeschichtliche Vereinigung, Ahastr 5A, Darmstadt, 64285, Germany. TEL 49-6151-366383, FAX 49-6151-366394, hkv@ekhn-kv.de. Circ: 700.

200 DEU ISSN 0178-3629
JAHRBUCH DER RELIGIONSPAEDAGOGIK. Text in German. 1985. a. EUR 26.90 (effective 2005). **Document type:** *Journal, Academic/Scholarly.*
Indexed: DIP, IBR, IBZ, PCI.
Published by: Neukirchener Verlag, Andreas-Braem-Str 18-20, Neukirchen-Vluyn, 47506, Germany. TEL 49-2845-392222, FAX 49-2845-33689, info@nvg-medien.de, http://www.nvg-medien.de.

200 DEU ISSN 0075-2541
BR128.A2
JAHRBUCH FUER ANTIKE UND CHRISTENTUM. Text in German. 1958. a. EUR 74 (effective 2010). bk.rev. **Document type:** *Journal, Academic/Scholarly.*
Related titles: Supplement(s): Jahrbuch fuer Antike und Christentum. Ergaenzungsband. ISSN 0448-1488. 1964.
Indexed: A01, A21, B24, BrArAb, DIP, FR, IBR, IBZ, MLA-IB, P30, PCI, RASB, RI-1, RI-2, RILM, SCOPUS, T02.
—IE, INIST. **CCC.**
Published by: (Universitaet Bonn, Franz Joseph Doelger-Institut), Aschendorff Verlag GmbH & Co. KG, Soester Str 13, Muenster, 48135, Germany. TEL 49-251-6900, FAX 49-251-6904570, buchverlag@aschendorff.de, http://www.aschendorff-buchverlag.de.

200 DEU ISSN 0075-2568
BR857.B8
JAHRBUCH FUER BERLIN-BRANDENBURGISCHE KIRCHENGESCHICHTE. Text in German. 1963. a. EUR 17.50 per issue (effective 2010). **Document type:** *Yearbook.*
Supersedes: Jahrbuch fuer Brandenburgische Kirchengeschichte
Indexed: DIP, IBR, IBZ, MLA-IB.
—BLDSC (4630.380000).
Published by: (Arbeitsgemeinschaft fuer Berlin-Brandenburgische Kirchengeschichte), Wichern Verlag GmbH, Georgenkirchstr 69-70, Berlin, 10249, Germany. TEL 49-30-28874811, FAX 49-30-28874820, info@wichern.de, http://www.wichern.de. Circ: 850.

220 DEU ISSN 0935-9338
BS543.A1
JAHRBUCH FUER BIBLISCHE THEOLOGIE. Text in German. 1986. a. EUR 39.90 (effective 2004). back issues avail.
Indexed: IBR, IBZ, IZBG, MLA-IB, OTA, PCI.
—**CCC.**
Published by: Neukirchener Verlag, Andreas-Braem-Str 18-20, Neukirchen-Vluyn, 47506, Germany. TEL 49-2845-392222, FAX 49-2845-33689, http://www.nvg-medien.de.

JAHRBUCH FUER CHRISTLICHE SOZIALWISSENSCHAFTEN. *see* SOCIOLOGY

JAHRBUCH FUER RELIGIONSPHILOSOPHIE. *see* PHILOSOPHY

JAHRBUCH FUER WESTFAELISCHE KIRCHENGESCHICHTE. *see* HISTORY—History Of Europe

266 DEU ISSN 0931-248X
JAHRBUCH MISSION. Text in German. 1969. a. EUR 5 (effective 2001). adv. bk.rev. **Document type:** *Yearbook, Academic/Scholarly.*
Formerly: Evangelische Mission Jahrbuch (0531-4798)
Indexed: DIP, IBR, IBZ.
Published by: (Verband Evangelischer Missionskonferenzen), Missionshilfe Verlag, Normannenweg 17-21, Hamburg, 20537, Germany. TEL 49-40-25456143, FAX 49-40-2542987, demh@emw-d.de, http://www.emw-d.de. Ed. Frank Kuerschner-Pelkmann. Pub. Martin Keiper. R&P Klaus Schaefer. Adv. contact Elke Rahn. Circ: 8,000.

280.042 JPN ISSN 0021-4353
BR1300
JAPAN CHRISTIAN ACTIVITY NEWS. Text in English. 1952. s-a. (q. until 2004). bk.rev. illus. **Document type:** *Newsletter, Consumer.* **Description:** Covers the activities of Christians in Japan including: the peace movement in Japan, the homeless, prisons, social outcasts, the role of women in the Church, Christian identity in Japan, inter-religious dialog, Protestant/Catholic cooperation, and more.
Media: Duplicated (not offset).
Indexed: ICUIS.
Published by: National Christian Council in Japan, Rm 24, 2-3-18 Nishi-Waseda, Shinjuku-ku, Tokyo, 169-0051, Japan. TEL 81-3-32030372, FAX 81-3-32049495, general@ncc-j.org. Ed. Rev. Claudia Genung Yamamoto. Circ: 600.

270.82 GBR ISSN 1474-8797
JAPAN CHRISTIAN LINK NEWS; serving Christ among the Japanese worldwide. Variant title: JCL News. Text in English. 1965. s-a. free donations (effective 2009). 8 p./no.; back issues avail. **Document type:** *Bulletin, Consumer.* **Description:** Features news and comment about trends in Japan and the work of Japan Christian Link.
Former titles (until 2001): Japan News (0307-3033); (until 1968): Japan Evangelistic Band Magazine
Related titles: Online - full text ed.: free (effective 2009).
Published by: Japan Christian Link, PO Box 68, Sevenoaks, Kent TN13 2ZY, United Kingdom. info@jclglobal.org.

207.2 JPN ISSN 1344-7297
➤ **JAPAN MISSION JOURNAL.** Text and summaries in English. 1947. q. USD 35 (effective 2007). adv. bk.rev. back issues avail. **Document type:** *Journal, Academic/Scholarly.* **Description:** Provides apublication dealing exclusively with the evangelization and acculturation of Christianity to Japan.
Supersedes in part (in 1984): Fukyo (0021-4531)
—Ingenta.
Published by: Oriens Institute for Religious Research, 2-28-5 Matsubara, Setagaya-ku, Tokyo, 156-0043, Japan. TEL 81-3-33227601, FAX 81-3-33255322, http://www.oriens.or.jp. Ed., R&P, Adv. contact M Matata. Circ: 1,000 (paid).

220 JPN ISSN 0912-9243
BS410
JAPANESE BIBLICAL INSTITUTE. ANNUAL. Text in English, Japanese. 1975. a. **Document type:** *Journal, Academic/Scholarly.*
Indexed: IZBG, OTA.
Published by: (Nihon Seishogaku Kenkyujo/Japanese Biblical Institute), Yamamoto Shoten Ltd., 2-7, Kanda, Jimbocho, Chiyoda-ku, Tokyo, 101-0051, Japan. TEL 81-3-3261-0847, FAX 81-3-3261-6276, http://www.book-kanda.or.jp/kosyo/1083/index.asp.

299.56 JPN ISSN 0448-8954
BL2202
JAPANESE RELIGIONS. Text in English. 1959. s-a. USD 220 combined subscription in North America to institutions (print & online eds.); USD 135 combined subscription elsewhere to institutions (print & online eds.) (effective 2012). adv. bk.rev. back issues avail.; reprints avail. **Document type:** *Journal, Academic/Scholarly.*
Related titles: Online - full text ed.: ISSN 2046-908X. USD 176 in North America to institutions; USD 108 elsewhere to institutions (effective 2012).
Indexed: A21, A22, BAS, FR, R&TA, RI-1, RI-2.
—BLDSC (4661.600000), IE, Infotrieve, Ingenta, INIST.
Published by: (National Christian Council of Japan, Center for the Study of Japanese Religions), Equinox Publishing Ltd., Unit S3, Kelham House, 3 Lancaster St, Sheffield, S6 3AF, United Kingdom. TEL 44-114-2725957, FAX 44-560-3459046, journals@equinoxpub.com. Ed. Elizabeth Tinsley. Adv. contact Val Hall.

200 DEU ISSN 1439-4634
JERUSALEMER THEOLOGISCHES FORUM. Text in German. 2000. irreg., latest vol.15, 2010. price varies. **Document type:** *Monographic series, Academic/Scholarly.*
Indexed: IZBG.
Published by: Aschendorff Verlag GmbH & Co. KG, Soester Str 13, Muenster, 48135, Germany. TEL 49-251-6900, FAX 49-251-6904570, buchverlag@aschendorff.de, http://www.aschendorff-buchverlag.de.

232 ITA ISSN 1123-055X
JESUS. Text in Italian. 1979. m. EUR 31 (effective 2008). adv. **Document type:** *Magazine, Consumer.*
Indexed: RASB.
Published by: Edizioni San Paolo, Piazza Soncino 5, Cinisello Balsamo, MI 20092, Italy. TEL 39-02-660751, FAX 39-02-66075211, sanpaoloedizioni@stpauls.it, http://www.edizionisanpaolo.it. Ed. D Stefano Andreatta.

268 USA ISSN 1550-9540
JESUS AND ME. STUDENT MAGAZINE. Abbreviated title: J A M Student Magazine. Text in English. 1998. q. USD 3.49 per issue (effective 2008). back issues avail. **Document type:** *Magazine, Consumer.* **Description:** Contains Bible lessons for ages 12-14, with special features such as Gospel Jams, Locker Room, and Reality Check.
Published by: Urban Ministries, Inc., Dept #4870, PO Box 87618, Chicago, IL 60680. TEL 708-868-7100, 800-860-8642, FAX 708-868-7105, customerservice@urbanministries.com.

268 USA ISSN 1550-9559
JESUS AND ME. TEACHER GUIDE. Abbreviated title: J A M. Teacher Guide. Text in English. 1998. q. USD 5.59 per issue (effective 2008). back issues avail. **Document type:** *Magazine, Consumer.* **Description:** Contains biblical background and commentary, plus teaching plans for ages 12-14 and other resources.
Published by: Urban Ministries, Inc., Dept #4870, PO Box 87618, Chicago, IL 60680. TEL 708-868-7100, 800-860-8642, FAX 708-868-7105, customerservice@urbanministries.com.

JESUS MAESTRO. *see* CHILDREN AND YOUTH—For

291 NLD ISSN 1388-2074
JEWISH AND CHRISTIAN PERSPECTIVES SERIES. Text in English. 1998. irreg., latest vol.17, 2008. price varies. **Document type:** *Monographic series, Academic/Scholarly.*
Indexed: IZBG.
Published by: Brill, PO Box 9000, Leiden, 2300 PA, Netherlands. TEL 31-71-5353500, FAX 31-71-5317532, cs@brill.nl.

230 HKG ISSN 1023-8727
JIANDAO XUEKAN; a journal of Bible & theology. Text in Chinese. 1994. s-a. (Jan. & Jul.). HKD 160 domestic; USD 35 in SE Asia; USD 40 elsewhere (effective 2005). **Description:** Covers religion and society, including politics, China, modern issues and theology.
Related titles: Supplement(s): Jiandao Zhuankan. ISSN 1024-0101.
Indexed: A21, ChrPI, OTA, R&TA, RI-1.
Published by: Jiandao Shenxueyuan/Alliance Bible Seminary, 22, Peak Road, Cheung Chau, Hong Kong. TEL 852-29810345, FAX 852-29819777, abspo@abs.edu.

230 CAN
JIDU JIAOSIXIANG PINGLUN/REGENT REVIEW OF CHRISTIAN THOUGHTS. Text in Chinese. s-a. USD 22.50 newsstand/cover foreign (effective 2007). **Document type:** *Journal, Academic/Scholarly.*
Published by: Regent College, Chinese Studies Program, 5800 University Blvd, Vancouver, BC V6T 2E4, Canada. TEL 604-224-3245, FAX 604-224-3097, chinese.studies@regent-college.edu, http://www.regentcsp.org/.

JIIPEE; paper for boys and girls. *see* CHILDREN AND YOUTH—For

JINBUN KAGAKU KENKYU/HUMANITIES: CHRISTIANITY AND CULTURE. *see* HUMANITIES: COMPREHENSIVE WORKS

JINGSHEN WENMING DAOKAN/GUIDE TO SPIRITUAL CIVILIZATION. *see* PHILOSOPHY

200 GBR ISSN 1758-8456
➤ **JOINT LITURGICAL STUDIES.** (Subscr. includes: Liturgical Studies (3 issues per year) and Collection (1 issue per year).) Text in English. 1975. s-a. free per issue to members (effective 2009). bk.rev. back issues avail. **Document type:** *Monographic series, Academic/Scholarly.* **Description:** Contains articles concerned with the scholarly study of the liturgy of the Christian churches, especially the churches of the Anglican communion.
Former titles (until 1995): Alcuin / G R O W Liturgical Study (0951-2667); (until 1975): Grove Liturgical Studies (0306-0608)
—BLDSC (4672.337000). **CCC.**
Published by: Alcuin Club, 5 Saffron Str, Royston, SG8 9TR, United Kingdom. TEL 44-1763-248676, alcuinclub@gmail.com.

➤ **JORNADAS INTERDISCIPLINARIAS RELIGION Y CULTURA.** *see* ETHNIC INTERESTS

255 USA ISSN 0021-7603
BX1407.N4
JOSEPHITE HARVEST. Text in English. 1888. q. USD 5; donation. **Description:** Sent to all benefactors of Josephite Fathers to promote interest in missionary work.
Published by: St. Joseph's Society of the Sacred Heart, 1130 N Calvert St, Baltimore, MD 21202. TEL 410-727-3386, FAX 410-752-8571. Ed. Joseph C Verrett. Circ: 90,000 (controlled).

JOTTINGS. *see* HANDICAPPED—Visually Impaired

230 306 USA ISSN 1530-5228
➤ **THE JOURNAL FOR CULTURAL AND RELIGIOUS THEORY.** Text in English. 1999. 3/yr. free (effective 2011). bk.rev.; film rev. back issues avail. **Document type:** *Journal, Academic/Scholarly.* **Description:** Devoted to both disciplinary and interdisciplinary scholarship of a cutting-edge nature that deals broadly with the phenomenon of religion and cultural theory.
Media: Online - full text.
Indexed: A21, A39, C27, C29, D03, D04, E13, R14, S14, S15, S18.
Published by: The Whitestone Foundation, 2075 S University Blvd, Ste 262, Denver, CO 80210. http://www.whitestonefoundation.org/.

291 ZAF ISSN 1834-3627
BL1
➤ **JOURNAL FOR THE RENEWAL OF RELIGION AND THEOLOGY.** Text in English. 2006. irreg. **Document type:** *Journal, Academic/Scholarly.*
Media: Online - full text.
Indexed: A01, A39, C27, C29, CA, D03, D04, E13, R14, S14, S15, S18, T02.

200 500 USA ISSN 0021-8294
BL1 CODEN: JSSRBT
➤ **JOURNAL FOR THE SCIENTIFIC STUDY OF RELIGION.** Text in English. 1961. q. GBP 137 in United Kingdom to institutions; EUR 174 in Europe to institutions; USD 180 in the Americas to institutions; USD 268 elsewhere to institutions; GBP 158 combined subscription in United Kingdom to institutions (print & online eds.); EUR 201 combined subscription in Europe to institutions (print & online eds.); USD 207 combined subscription in the Americas to institutions (print & online eds.); USD 308 combined subscription elsewhere to institutions (print & online eds.) (effective 2012). adv. bk.rev. charts; stat.; illus. index, cum.index: 1961-1981. reprint service avail. from PSC. **Document type:** *Journal, Academic/Scholarly.* **Description:** Stimulates and communicates important scientific research on religious institutions and experiences.
Related titles: Microform ed.: (from PQC); Online - full text ed.: ISSN 1468-5906. GBP 137 in United Kingdom to institutions; EUR 174 in Europe to institutions; USD 180 in the Americas to institutions; USD 268 elsewhere to institutions (effective 2012) (from IngentaConnect).
Indexed: A01, A02, A03, A08, A20, A21, A22, A25, A26, ABS&EES, ASCA, AbAn, AmH&L, AmHI, ArtHuCI, B04, BAS, BNNA, BRD, CA, CERDIC, ChPerI, CurCont, DIP, E-psyche, E01, E08, FR, FamI, G08, G10, GSS&RPL, H07, H08, H09, H10, H14, HAb, HumInd, I05, IBR, IBSS, IBZ, IJP, ISAP, J01, MEA&I, MLA-IB, OTA, P02, P03, P10, P13, P28, P30, P34, P42, P43, P48, P53, P54, PCI, PQC, PRA, PSA, PSI, PhilInd, PsycInfo, PsycholAb, R&TA, R05, RASB, RI-1, RI-2, S02, S03, S08, S09, SCOPUS, SOPODA, SSA, SSCI, SociolAb, T02, W03, W05, W07, W09.
—BLDSC (5061.500000), IE, Infotrieve, Ingenta, INIST. **CCC.**
Published by: (Society for the Scientific Study of Religion), Wiley-Blackwell Publishing, Inc. (Subsidiary of: Wiley-Blackwell Publishing Ltd.), 111 River St, Hoboken, NJ 07030. TEL 201-748-6000, FAX 201-748-6088, info@wiley.com, http://www.wiley.com/WileyCDA/. Ed. Marie Cornwall TEL 801-422-3115. Adv. contact Kristin McCarthy TEL 201-748-7683.

➤ **JOURNAL FOR THE STUDY OF JUDAISM. SUPPLEMENT.** *see* RELIGIONS AND THEOLOGY—Judaic

200 ZAF ISSN 1011-7601
BL2463
➤ **JOURNAL FOR THE STUDY OF RELIGION.** Text in English. 1980; N.S. 1988. s-a. ZAR 100 in Africa; USD 50 elsewhere (effective 2001). adv. bk.rev. abstr.; bibl.; charts; stat. biennial index. 150 p./no. 1 cols./p.; back issues avail. **Document type:** *Journal, Academic/Scholarly.* **Description:** Forum for scholarly contributions on topics of contemporary significance in the academic study of religion.
Formerly (until 1988): Religion in Southern Africa (0258-3224)
Related titles: Online - full text ed.
Indexed: A21, IIBP, ISAP, PerIslam, R&TA, RI-1, RI-2.
—BLDSC (5066.928000), IE, Ingenta.
Published by: Association for the Study of Religion in Southern Africa, c/o Dept of Religious Studies, University of Cape Town, Privage Bag, Rondebosch, KwaZulu-Natal 7701, South Africa. TEL 27-331-2605571. Ed., Adv. contact A I Tayob TEL 021-6503399. Circ: 240.

205 GBR ISSN 1749-4907
BT695.5
JOURNAL FOR THE STUDY OF RELIGION, NATURE AND CULTURE. Abbreviated title: J S R N C. Text in English. 1992. q. USD 440 combined subscription in North America to institutions (print & online eds.); GBP 246 combined subscription elsewhere to institutions (print & online eds.) (effective 2012). adv. bk.rev. back issues avail.; reprints avail. **Document type:** *Journal, Academic/Scholarly.* **Description:** Provides forum for constructive and normative studies on the relationship between religion and ecology.
Former titles (until 2007): Ecotheology (1363-7320); (until 1996): Theology in Green (0966-7814)
Related titles: Online - full text ed.: ISSN 1749-4915. 2004. USD 352 in North America to institutions; GBP 196 elsewhere to institutions (effective 2012).
Indexed: A01, A03, A08, A21, A22, CA, DIP, E04, E05, G02, IBR, IBZ, RI-1, T02.
—BLDSC (5066.928500), IE, Ingenta. **CCC.**
Published by: (The International Society for the Study of Religion, Nature & Culture USA), Equinox Publishing Ltd. journals@equinoxpub.com, http://www.equinoxpub.com/. Ed. Bron Taylor. Adv. contact Val Hall.

200 ROM ISSN 1583-0039
BL85
➤ **JOURNAL FOR THE STUDY OF RELIGIOUS AND IDEOLOGIES.** Short title: J S R I. Abstracts in English; Text in Romanian, English. 2002. 3/yr. free (effective 2011). **Document type:** *Journal, Academic/Scholarly.* **Description:** Encourages interdisciplinary approaches engaging the following domains: interreligious dialogue, philosophy of religions, political philosophy and political science, ethics, religious studies, anthropology, sociology, educational science and communications theory.
Media: Online - full text.
Indexed: A20, A26, AmHI, ArtHuCI, CA, CurCont, E08, H07, I05, P28, P48, P53, P54, PQC, SCOPUS, T02, W07.
Published by: Universitatea "Babes-Bolyai", Catedra de Filosofie Sistematica, Mihail Kogalniceanu nr. 1, Cluj-Napoca, RO-3400, Romania. TEL 40-264-405300, FAX 40-264-191.906, http://www.ubbcluj.ro. Ed. Sandu Frunza.

200 GBR ISSN 2044-0243
▼ ➤ **JOURNAL FOR THE STUDY OF SPIRITUALITY.** Abbreviated title: J S S. Text in English. 2011. s-a. USD 220 combined subscription in North America to institutions (print & online eds.); GBP 135 combined subscription elsewhere to institutions (print & online eds.) (effective 2012). adv. back issues avail.; reprints avail. **Document type:** *Journal, Academic/Scholarly.*
Related titles: Online - full text ed.: ISSN 2044-0251. 2011. USD 176 in North America to institutions; GBP 108 elsewhere to institutions (effective 2012).
—**CCC.**
Published by: (British Association for the Study of Spirituality), Equinox Publishing Ltd., Unit S3, Kelham House, 3 Lancaster St, Sheffield, S6 3AF, United Kingdom. TEL 44-114-2725957, FAX 44-560-3459046, journals@equinoxpub.com, http://www.equinoxpub.com/. Ed. Cheryl Hunt. Adv. contact Val Hall.

225 NLD ISSN 1476-8690
BT301.3
➤ **JOURNAL FOR THE STUDY OF THE HISTORICAL JESUS.** Text in English. 2003. s-a. EUR 234, USD 328 to institutions; EUR 255, USD 357 combined subscription to institutions (print & online eds.) (effective 2012). adv. reprint service avail. from PSC. **Document type:** *Journal, Academic/Scholarly.* **Description:** Provides a forum for academic discussion of Jesus within the context of first-century Palestine, but accessible to the very wide non-scholarly readership interested in the way this topic, so vital for most Christians, is and has been investigated and presented.
Related titles: Online - full text ed.: ISSN 1745-5197. EUR 213, USD 298 to institutions (effective 2012) (from IngentaConnect).
Indexed: A01, A03, A08, A22, CA, DIP, E01, IBR, IBZ, IZBG, SCOPUS, T02.
—IE. **CCC.**
Published by: Brill, PO Box 9000, Leiden, 2300 PA, Netherlands. TEL 31-71-5353500, FAX 31-71-5317532, cs@brill.nl. Ed. Robert L Webb. adv.: B&W page GBP 300; 130 x 200.

225 GBR ISSN 0142-064X
BS410
➤ **JOURNAL FOR THE STUDY OF THE NEW TESTAMENT.** Text in English. 1978. 5/yr. GBP 335, USD 621 to institutions; GBP 342, USD 634 combined subscription to institutions (print & online eds.) (effective 2012). bk.rev. illus. Index. back issues avail.; reprint service avail. from PSC. **Document type:** *Journal, Academic/Scholarly.* **Description:** Aims to present cutting-edge work for a readership of scholars, teachers in the field of new testament, postgraduate students and advanced undergraduates.
Related titles: Online - full text ed.: ISSN 1745-5294. GBP 308, USD 571 to institutions (effective 2012).
Indexed: A01, A02, A03, A08, A21, A22, BibLing, CA, DIP, E01, FR, IBR, IBZ, IZBG, PCI, R&TA, RI-1, RI-2, RILM, SCOPUS, T02.
—BLDSC (5066.917000), IE, Ingenta, INIST. **CCC.**
Published by: Sage Publications Ltd. (Subsidiary of: Sage Publications, Inc.), 1 Oliver's Yard, 55 City Rd, London, EC1Y 1SP, United Kingdom. TEL 44-20-73248500, FAX 44-20-73248600, info@sagepub.co.uk, http://www.uk.sagepub.com/home.nav. Ed. Simon Gathercole. **Subscr. in the Americas to:** Sage Publications, Inc., 2455 Teller Rd, Thousand Oaks, CA 91320. TEL 805-499-9774, FAX 805-499-0871, journals@sagepub.com.

221 GBR ISSN 0309-0892
BS410
➤ **JOURNAL FOR THE STUDY OF THE OLD TESTAMENT.** Text in English. 1976. 5/yr. GBP 335, USD 621 to institutions; GBP 342, USD 634 combined subscription to institutions (print & online eds.) (effective 2012). illus. back issues avail.; reprint service avail. from PSC. **Document type:** *Journal, Academic/Scholarly.* **Description:** Provides wide range of critical approaches, plays a vital role in the field of biblical studies.
Related titles: Online - full text ed.: ISSN 1476-6728. GBP 308, USD 571 to institutions (effective 2012).
Indexed: A01, A02, A03, A08, A21, A22, BibLing, CA, DIP, E01, FR, IBR, IBZ, IZBG, JewAb, M10, MLA-IB, OTA, PCI, R&TA, RI-1, RI-2, SCOPUS, T02.
—BLDSC (5066.920000), IE, Infotrieve, Ingenta, INIST. **CCC.**
Published by: Sage Publications Ltd. (Subsidiary of: Sage Publications, Inc.), 1 Oliver's Yard, 55 City Rd, London, EC1Y 1SP, United Kingdom. TEL 44-20-73248500, FAX 44-20-73248600, info@sagepub.co.uk, http://www.uk.sagepub.com/home.nav. Eds. John Jarick, Keith Whitelam. **Subscr. in the Americas to:** Sage Publications, Inc., 2455 Teller Rd, Thousand Oaks, CA 91320. TEL 805-499-9774, FAX 805-499-0871, journals@sagepub.com.

200 GBR ISSN 0951-8207
BS1700
JOURNAL FOR THE STUDY OF THE PSEUDEPIGRAPHA. Abbreviated title: J S P. Text in English. 1987. q. GBP 353, USD 654 to institutions; GBP 360, USD 667 combined subscription to institutions (print & online eds.) (effective 2011). bk.rev. back issues avail.; reprint service avail. from PSC. **Document type:** *Journal, Academic/Scholarly.* **Description:** Provides a forum for scholars to discuss and review most recent developments in this burgeoning field in the academy.
Related titles: Online - full text ed.: ISSN 1745-5286. GBP 324, USD 600 to institutions (effective 2012); ◆ Supplement(s): Library of Second Temple Studies.
Indexed: A01, A03, A08, A21, A22, CA, DIP, E01, IBR, IBZ, IZBG, OTA, PCI, R&TA, RI-1, RI-2, SCOPUS, T02.
—BLDSC (5066.925000), IE. **CCC.**
Published by: Sage Publications Ltd. (Subsidiary of: Sage Publications, Inc.), 1 Oliver's Yard, 55 City Rd, London, EC1Y 1SP, United Kingdom. TEL 44-20-73248500, FAX 44-20-73248600, info@sagepub.co.uk, http://www.uk.sagepub.com/home.nav. Eds. James Mueller, Loren Stuckenbruck, Robert Hayward. **Subscr. in the Americas to:** Sage Publications, Inc., 2455 Teller Rd, Thousand Oaks, CA 91320. TEL 805-499-9774, FAX 805-499-0871, journals@sagepub.com.

200 370 GBR ISSN 1740-7141
BV4019
➤ **JOURNAL OF ADULT THEOLOGICAL EDUCATION.** Abbreviated title: J A T E. Text in English. 1988. s-a. USD 220 combined subscription in North America to institutions (print & online eds.); GBP 135 combined subscription elsewhere to institutions (print & online eds.) (effective 2012). adv. back issues avail.; reprints avail. **Document type:** *Journal, Academic/Scholarly.* **Description:** Promotes dialogue amongst those involved in adult theological education.
Formerly (until 2004): British Journal of Theological Education (1352-741X)
Related titles: Online - full text ed.: ISSN 1743-1654. USD 176 in North America to institutions; GBP 108 elsewhere to institutions (effective 2012).
Indexed: A01, A02, A03, A08, CA, E03, ERI, T02.
—BLDSC (4918.945500), IE. **CCC.**
Published by: (Cambridge Theological Federation), Equinox Publishing Ltd., Unit S3, Kelham House, 3 Lancaster St, Sheffield, S6 3AF, United Kingdom. TEL 44-114-2725957, FAX 44-560-3459046, journals@equinoxpub.com, http://www.equinoxpub.com/. Ed. Nigel Rooms. Adv. contact Val Hall. **Co-sponsor:** The Association of Centres of Adult Theological Education.

200 GHA ISSN 0855-3262
BR1359
JOURNAL OF AFRICAN CHRISTIAN THOUGHT. Text in English. 1998. s-a. **Document type:** *Journal, Academic/Scholarly.*
Indexed: A21, RI-1.
Published by: Akrofi - Christaller Memorial Centre, PO Box 76, Akropong-Akuapem, Ghana. TEL 233-27-556718, acmc@libr.ug.edu.gh, http://www.acmcghana.org.

JOURNAL OF AFRICAN CULTURES AND RELIGION. *see* SOCIOLOGY

210 UGA ISSN 1018-8592
JOURNAL OF AFRICAN RELIGION AND PHILOSOPHY; a journal of religion and philosophy in Africa. Text in English. 1988. 2/yr. GBP 12 per issue. adv. bk.rev. **Document type:** *Journal, Academic/Scholarly.* **Description:** Publishes comparative studies on African religions, and related theological, sociological, and philosophical issues.
Formerly (until 1989): African Mind
Indexed: ASD, PLESA.
Published by: Sun Publishers, PO Box 16144, Kampala, Wandegeya, Uganda. Ed. L Njinya Mujinya. Circ: 5,000.

253 USA ISSN 1933-3978
➤ **JOURNAL OF APPLIED CHRISTIAN LEADERSHIP.** Text in English. 2006. s-a. USD 35 (effective 2010). **Document type:** *Journal, Academic/Scholarly.* **Description:** Provides a forum for communication between academics, practitioners and Christian leaders in the field of applied leadership theory.
Related titles: Print ed.: ISSN 1933-3986.
Indexed: A01, P28, P48, P51, P53, P54, PQC.
Published by: Andrews University, Christian Leadership Center, Seminary Hall, Berrien Springs, MI 49104. TEL 269-471-8332, FAX 269-471-6202, clc@andrews.edu. Ed. Yvonna Applewhite.

200 USA ISSN 1085-3286
BR1
JOURNAL OF ASIAN AND ASIAN AMERICAN THEOLOGY. Text in English. 1996. a. **Document type:** *Journal, Academic/Scholarly.* **Description:** Covers a critical study of the challenges and the contributions of third world feminist theologians to the theological discipline.
Indexed: A21, R&TA, RI-1.
Published by: Center for Asian Studies, Claremont Institute, 937 W Foothill Blvd., Ste E, Claremont, CA 91711. TEL 909-621-6825, FAX 909-626-8724, info@claremont.org, http://www.claremont.org.

200 PHL ISSN 0119-3228
BV3151
JOURNAL OF ASIAN MISSION. Text in English. 1999. s-a. PHP 300 domestic; USD 15 in Asia; USD 20 elsewhere (effective 2003). adv. bk.rev. cum.index every 5 yrs.; first index in vol.6, no.1 (Mar. 2004). 150 p./no.; back issues avail. **Document type:** *Journal, Consumer.* **Description:** Provides a forum to assess theories and practices in mission applied specially in Asia.
Published by: Asia Graduate School of Theology, PO Box 377, Baguio City, 2600, Philippines. TEL 63-74-442-2779, FAX 63-74-442-6378, juliema@mozcom.com, http://www.apts.edu/jam. Ed. Julie C Ma. adv.: page USD 50; trim 15 x 22. Circ: 320.

200 CAN ISSN 0838-0430
➤ **JOURNAL OF BAHA'I STUDIES.** Text in English. 1988. q. CAD 20 domestic to individuals; USD 20 foreign to individuals; USD 30 foreign to institutions; CAD 6 newsstand/cover (effective 2000). bk.rev. index. back issues avail. **Document type:** *Journal, Academic/Scholarly.*
Indexed: A21, C03, CA, CBCARef, FR, MLA-IB, P28, P48, P53, P54, PQC, RI-1, RI-2, T02.
—INIST.
Published by: Association for Baha'i Studies, 34 Copernicus St, Ottawa, ON K1N 7K4, Canada. TEL 613-233-1903, FAX 613-233-3644, AS929@freenet.carleton.ca, http://www.bahai-studies.ca/~absnam. R&P Christine Zerbinis. Circ: 2,300.

➤ **JOURNAL OF BELIEFS AND VALUES**; studies in religion & education. *see* EDUCATION

220 USA ISSN 1944-107X
▼ ➤ **JOURNAL OF BIBLICAL AND PNEUMATOLOGICAL RESEARCH.** Text in English. 2009. a. USD 20 per issue (effective 2009). **Document type:** *Journal, Academic/Scholarly.* **Description:** Dedicated to research on the narratively and rhetorically minded exegesis of biblical and related texts.
Indexed: A01, T02.
Published by: Wipf & Stock Publishers, 199 W 8th Ave, Ste 3, Eugene, OR 97401. TEL 541-344-1528, FAX 541-344-1506, Info@wipfandstock.com.

220 USA ISSN 0021-9231
BS410
➤ **JOURNAL OF BIBLICAL LITERATURE.** Abbreviated title: J B L. Text in English. 1881. q. USD 180 domestic to non-members; USD 198 in Canada & Mexico to non-members; USD 203 elsewhere to non-members; USD 40 domestic to members; USD 58 in Canada & Mexico to members; USD 63 elsewhere to members; USD 195 combined subscription domestic to institutions (print & online eds.); USD 213 combined subscription in Canada & Mexico to institutions (print & online eds.); USD 218 combined subscription elsewhere to institutions (print & online eds.) (effective 2009). adv. bk.rev. illus. index. 200 p./no.; back issues avail.; reprints avail. **Document type:** *Journal, Academic/Scholarly.* **Description:** Promotes critical and academic biblical scholarship and reflects the full range of methods, models, and interests used by members of the SBL.
Formerly (until 1890): Society of Biblical Literature and Exegesis. Journal (1069-8337)
Related titles: Microfiche ed.; Microfilm ed.: (from PMC, PQC); Online - full text ed.: ISSN 1934-3876. USD 155 to non-members; free to members (effective 2009).
Indexed: A01, A02, A03, A08, A20, A21, A22, A26, ASCA, AmHI, ArtHuCI, B04, BRD, BibLing, CA, CBRI, CERDIC, CurCont, DIP, E08, G08, GSS&RPL, H07, H08, H09, H10, H14, HAb, HumInd, I05, IBR, IBZ, IJP, IZBG, J01, JewAb, L05, L06, LIFT, M01, M02, M10, MEA&I, MLA-IB, OTA, P02, P10, P28, P48, P53, P54, PCI, PQC, R&TA, R05, RASB, RI-1, RI-2, S05, S09, SCOPUS, T02, W03, W05, W07.
—BLDSC (4951.550000), IE, Infotrieve, Ingenta. **CCC.**
Published by: Society of Biblical Literature, The Luce Ctr, 825 Houston Mill Rd, Atlanta, GA 30329. TEL 404-727-3100, 866-727-9955, FAX 404-727-3101, sblexec@sbl-site.org. Ed. James C VanderKam. Adv. contact Phillip Stokes TEL 404-727-3096. page USD 600; trim 6 x 9. Circ: 4,200.

261 258 USA ISSN 1941-4692
JOURNAL OF BIBLICAL PERSPECTIVES IN LEADERSHIP. Abbreviated title: J B P L. Text in English. 2006. s-a. free (effective 2011). back issues avail. **Document type:** *Journal, Academic/ Scholarly.*
Media: Online - full text.
Published by: Regent University, School of Global Leadership & Entrepreneurship, 1333 Regent University Dr, Virginia Beach, VA 23464. TEL 757-352-4550, FAX 757-352-4823. Ed. Corne J Bekker.

220 USA ISSN 1075-0347
THE JOURNAL OF BIBLICAL STORYTELLING. Text in English. 1989. a. USD 9 per issue; USD 7 per issue to libraries (effective 2007). bk.rev. **Document type:** *Journal, Academic/Scholarly.*
Indexed: R&TA.
Published by: Network of Biblical Storytellers, 1000 W 42nd St, Indianapolis, IN 46208-3301. TEL 317-931-2352, 800-355-nobs, nobsint@nobs.org. Pub. Pam Faro.

200 USA ISSN 1534-3057
BS491.3
➤ **JOURNAL OF BIBLICAL STUDIES.** Text in English. 2001. irreg., latest vol.6, no.2, 2006. bk.rev. back issues avail. **Document type:** *Journal, Academic/Scholarly.* **Description:** Covers all aspects in the field of Biblical Studies in general, including, archaeology, linguistics, exegesis, history, and textual issues.
Media: Online - full text.
Published by: Brian Tucker, Ed. & Pub. Ed. Brian Tucker.

▼ ➤ **JOURNAL OF CHILDHOOD AND RELIGION.** *see* CHILDREN AND YOUTH—About

371.07 AUS ISSN 0021-9657
BV1460
➤ **JOURNAL OF CHRISTIAN EDUCATION**; faith shaping leadership, teaching and learning. Text in English. 1958. 3/yr. AUD 60 domestic to individuals; USD 55 in United States to individuals; GBP 24 in United Kingdom to individuals; AUD 55 elsewhere to individuals; AUD 77 domestic to institutions; USD 70 in United States to institutions; GBP 30 in United Kingdom to institutions; AUD 70 elsewhere to institutions (effective 2009). bk.rev. bibl. Index. 64 p./no.; back issues avail. **Document type:** *Journal, Academic/Scholarly.* **Description:** Analyzes the implications of the Christian faith on education and examines its contribution, particularly to educational policy making, leadership, teaching and learning, curriculum and resources, and teacher development.
Related titles: Online - full text ed.
Indexed: A21, A22, AEI, CPE, ChrPI, DIP, ERO, IBR, IBZ, PCI, R&TA, RI-1, RI-2, SCOPUS.
—BLDSC (4958.270000), IE, Ingenta.
Published by: Australian Christian Forum on Education Inc., PO Box 602, Epping, NSW 1710, Australia. TEL 61-2-98686644, FAX 61-2-98686644, business@acfe.org.au. Eds. Grant Maple, Ian Lambert. R&P Austin Hukins. Circ: 500 (paid and controlled).

➤ **JOURNAL OF CHRISTIAN NURSING.** *see* MEDICAL SCIENCES—Nurses And Nursing

230 USA ISSN 0360-1420
BR1
JOURNAL OF CHRISTIAN RECONSTRUCTION. Text in English. 1974. s-a. USD 18 to individuals; USD 20.50 foreign to individuals; USD 16 to libraries; USD 18.50 foreign to libraries. reprints avail. **Description:** Scholarly and lay articles on the revitalization of the intellectual and cultural heritage of Christians in terms of standards set in the Old and New Testaments.
Related titles: Microfilm ed.: (from PQC).
Indexed: A21, ChrPI, RI-1, RI-2.
Published by: Chalcedon, Inc., PO Box 158, Vallecito, CA 95251. TEL 209-728-4365, FAX 209-736-0536. Ed. Rev. Andrew Sandlin. Pub. Rev. Dr R J Rushdoony. Circ: 2,000.

JOURNAL OF CHRISTIANITY AND FOREIGN LANGUAGES. *see* LINGUISTICS

322.1 USA ISSN 0021-969X
BV630.A1
➤ **JOURNAL OF CHURCH AND STATE.** Abbreviated title: J C S. Text in English. 1959. q. GBP 96 in United Kingdom to institutions; EUR 138 in Europe to institutions; USD 144 in US & Canada to institutions; GBP 96 elsewhere to institutions; GBP 104 combined subscription in United Kingdom to institutions (print & online eds.); EUR 150 combined subscription in Europe to institutions (print & online eds.); USD 156 combined subscription in US & Canada to institutions (print & online eds.); GBP 104 combined subscription elsewhere to institutions (print & online eds.) (effective 2012). adv. bk.rev. index. back issues avail.; reprint service avail. from PSC,WSH. **Document type:** *Journal, Academic/Scholarly.* **Description:** Discusses issues relating to the separation of church and state, as espoused in the US constitution.
Related titles: Microfiche ed.: (from WSH); Microfilm ed.: (from PMC, WSH); Microform ed.: (from PQC, WSH); Online - full text ed.: ISSN 2040-4867. GBP 86 in United Kingdom to institutions; EUR 125 in Europe to institutions; USD 130 in US & Canada to institutions; GBP 86 elsewhere to institutions (effective 2012) (from IngentaConnect).
Indexed: A01, A02, A03, A08, A20, A21, A22, A25, A26, ABRCLP, ABS&EES, ASCA, AmH&L, AmHI, ArtHuCI, B04, B14, BAS, BRD, BRI, CA, CBRI, CCME, CERDIC, CLI, ChrPI, CurCont, DIP, E07, E08, EAA, FamI, G05, G06, G07, G08, H07, H08, H14, HAb, HistAb, HumInd, I05, I07, IBR, IBSS, IBZ, L03, LRI, M01, M02, MEA&I, P02, P06, P10, P28, P30, P34, P42, P45, P48, P53, P54, PAIS, PCI, PQC, PSA, PerIslam, R&TA, R05, RI-1, RI-2, S02, S03, S08, S09, S23, SCOPUS, SociolAb, T02, W03, W05, W07.
—BLDSC (4958.365000), IE, Infotrieve, Ingenta. **CCC.**
Published by: (Baylor University, J M Dawson Institute of Church-State Studies), Oxford University Press (Subsidiary of: Oxford University Press), 2001 Evans Rd, Cary, NC 27513. TEL 919-677-0977, 800-445-9714, FAX 919-677-1303, http://www.us.oup.com. Ed. Christopher Marsh.

200 USA ISSN 0894-2838
BV4319
THE JOURNAL OF COMMUNICATION AND RELIGION. Text in English. 1985. s-a. USD 25 domestic to individuals; USD 35 foreign to individuals; USD 50 domestic to institutions; USD 60 foreign to institutions; USD 12.50 domestic to students; USD 22.50 foreign to students (effective 2005). bk.rev. **Description:** Publishes articles that advance theory and research about communication in religious contexts.
Formerly (until 1986): Religious Communication Today
Related titles: Online - full text ed.
Indexed: A21, AmHI, CA, CMM, CommAb, E03, ERI, FamI, H07, IJCS, L06, R&TA, RI-1, S02, S03, T02.
Published by: The Religious Communication Association, c/o Michael E Eidenmuller, Dept of Communication, University of Texas, 3900 University Blvd, Tyler, TX 75799. TEL 903-566-7093, FAX 903-566-7287, eiden@cox.net. Ed. Sterk Helen. Circ: 675.

200 GBR ISSN 1353-7903
BL1 CODEN: JCRLFY
➤ **JOURNAL OF CONTEMPORARY RELIGION.** Text in English. 1984. 3/yr. GBP 472 combined subscription in United Kingdom to institutions (print & online eds.); EUR 624, USD 784 combined subscription to institutions (print & online eds.) (effective 2012). adv. bk.rev. back issues avail.; reprint service avail. from PSC. **Document type:** *Journal, Academic/Scholarly.* **Description:** Provides a forum for discussion and analysis of new religions and trends and developments within mainstream churches.
Formerly (until 1995): Religion Today (0267-1700)
Related titles: Online - full text ed.: ISSN 1469-9419. GBP 425 in United Kingdom to institutions; EUR 562, USD 706 to institutions (effective 2012) (from IngentaConnect).
Indexed: A01, A02, A03, A08, A21, A22, AICP, ASSIA, BrHumI, CA, E01, IBSS, P42, P48, P53, P54, PQC, PSA, PerIslam, R&TA, S02, S03, SCOPUS, SOPODA, SociolAb, T02.
—IE, Infotrieve, Ingenta. **CCC.**
Published by: (Centre for New Religious Movements), Routledge (Subsidiary of: Taylor & Francis Group), 4 Park Sq, Milton Park, Abingdon, Oxon OX14 4RN, United Kingdom. TEL 44-20-70176000, FAX 44-20-70176336, subscriptions@tandf.co.uk, http://www.routledge.com. Eds. Elisabeth Arweck, Peter B Clarke. Adv. contact Linda Hann TEL 44-1344-779945. Circ: 500. **Subscr. to:** Taylor & Francis Ltd., Journals Customer Service, Sheepen Pl, Colchester, Essex CO3 3LP, United Kingdom. TEL 44-20-70175544, FAX 44-20-70175198.

200 500 AUS ISSN 1833-6213
➤ **JOURNAL OF CREATION.** Text in English. 1984. 3/yr. USD 39 (effective 2008). bk.rev. abstr.; charts; illus. 128 p./no.; back issues avail. **Document type:** *Journal, Academic/Scholarly.* **Description:** Technical study of the sciences as they relate to the study of biblical creation and Noah's flood.
Former titles (until 2006): T J (1446-2648); (until 2001): Creation ex Nihilo Technical Journal (1036-2916); (until 1991): Ex Nihilo Technical Journal (0814-6764)
Indexed: ChrPI.
Published by: Creation Ministries International Ltd., PO Box 4545, Eight Mile Plains, QLD 4113, Australia. TEL 61-7-33409888, FAX 61-7-33409889. Ed. Pierre Gunnar Jerlstrom. Circ: 2,000.

200 IND ISSN 0253-7222
BL1
➤ **JOURNAL OF DHARMA**; an international quarterly of world religions. Text in English. 1975. q. bk.rev. 180 p./no.; reprints avail. **Document type:** *Journal, Academic/Scholarly.* **Description:** Serves as a forum for the exchange of ideas and experience regarding the approaches and methods to the problems related to man's religious quest.
Related titles: E-mail ed.; Fax ed.; Microfilm ed.: (from PQC).
Indexed: A20, A21, A22, ASCA, ArtHuCI, BAS, CurCont, DIP, IBR, IBZ, PhilInd, R&TA, RASB, RI-1, RI-2, SCOPUS, W07.
—BLDSC (4969.403000), IE, Infotrieve, Ingenta.
Published by: (Dharma Research Association), Dharmaram College, Centre for the Study of World Religions, c/o Fr. Rector, Bangalore, Karnataka 560 029, India. TEL 91-80-41116300, FAX 91-80-41116000, registrar@dvk.in. Ed. Jose Nandhikkara.

270 GBR ISSN 0022-0469
BR140
➤ **JOURNAL OF ECCLESIASTICAL HISTORY.** Text in English. 1950. q. GBP 299, USD 517 to institutions; GBP 328, USD 565 combined subscription to institutions (print & online eds.) (effective 2012). adv. bk.rev. bibl.; illus. index. back issues avail.; reprint service avail. from PSC. **Document type:** *Journal, Academic/Scholarly.* **Description:** Contains material on the history of the Christian Church as an institution and its relations with other religions and society.
Related titles: Microform ed.: (from PQC); Online - full text ed.: ISSN 1469-7637. GBP 277, USD 477 to institutions (effective 2012).
Indexed: A01, A02, A03, A08, A20, A21, A22, A26, ASCA, AmH&L, AmHI, ArtHuCI, B04, B24, BRD, BrArAb, CA, CERDIC, CurCont, E01, E08, FR, G08, GSS&RPL, H07, H08, H09, H10, H14, HAb, HistAb, HumInd, I05, MLA-IB, NumL, P02, P10, P28, P30, P48, P53, P54, PCI, PQC, R&TA, R05, RASB, RI-1, RI-2, S02, S03, S09, SCOPUS, SOPODA, SociolAb, T02, W03, W07, W09.
—BLDSC (4971.700000), IE, Infotrieve, Ingenta, INIST. **CCC.**
Published by: Cambridge University Press, The Edinburgh Bldg, Shaftesbury Rd, Cambridge, CB2 8RU, United Kingdom. TEL 44-1223-312393, FAX 44-1223-315052, journals@cambridge.org, http://www.cambridge.org/uk. Eds. Diarmaid MacCulloch, James Carleton Paget. R&P Linda Nicol TEL 44-1223-325702. **Subscr. to:** Cambridge University Press, 32 Ave of the Americas, New York, NY 10013. TEL 212-337-5000, FAX 212-691-3239, journals_subscriptions@cup.org.

260 USA ISSN 0022-0558
BX1
➤ **JOURNAL OF ECUMENICAL STUDIES.** Text in English. 1957. q. USD 45 domestic to individuals; USD 50 foreign to individuals; USD 105 domestic to institutions; USD 110 foreign to institutions (effective 2011). bk.rev. abstr.; illus. index. back issues avail.; reprints avail. **Document type:** *Journal, Academic/Scholarly.* **Description:** Features scholarly articles in the field of dialogue across lines of religious difference.
Incorporates (in 1968): College Theology Notes; Which was formerly (until Oct.1968): Sacred Doctrine Notes; (until 1966): Magister

R

Related titles: Microfiche ed.: (from WSH); Microfilm ed.: (from PMC, WSH); Microform ed.: (from WSH); Online - full text ed.: ISSN 2162-3937. USD 40 to individuals; USD 100 to institutions (effective 2008).
Indexed: A01, A02, A03, A08, A20, A21, A22, A25, A26, ABS&EES, ASCA, AmH&L, AmHI, B04, BAS, BRD, BRM, CA, CERDIC, CLI, CPL, DIP, E08, FR, G08, GSS&RPL, H07, H08, H09, H10, H14, HAb, HistAb, HumInd, I05, IBR, IBZ, IJP, J01, MEA&I, OTA, P02, P10, P13, P30, P48, P53, P54, PCI, PQC, R&TA, R05, RI-1, RI-2, S08, S09, T02, W03, W05.
—BLDSC (4973.096000), IE, Infotrieve, Ingenta, INIST.
Published by: Duquesne University Press, 600 Forbes Ave, Pittsburgh, PA 15282. TEL 412-396-6610, 800-666-2211, FAX 412-396-5984, http://www.dupress.duq.edu.

268 GBR ISSN 1366-5456
LC368
➤ **JOURNAL OF EDUCATION & CHRISTIAN BELIEF.** Text in English. 1970. s-a. bk.rev. illus. cum.index: vols.1-6. back issues avail. **Document type:** *Journal, Academic/Scholarly.* **Description:** Provides a Christian viewpoint on education in both maintained and private-sector schools and colleges.
Formerly (until 1997): Spectrum (0305-7917)
Related titles: Online - full text ed.
Indexed: A01, A03, A08, A21, AES, CA, CERDIC, CPE, ERA, MLA-IB, R&TA, RI-1, S21, T02.
—BLDSC (4973.123000), IE, Ingenta.
Published by: (The Association of Christian Teachers), The Paternoster Press, c/o Aplhagraphics, 6 Angel Row, Nottingham, NG1 6HL, United Kingdom. TEL 44-115-8523614, FAX 44-115-8523601, periodicals@alphagraphics.co.uk, http://www.paternosterperiodicals.com. Ed. John Shortt. **Dist. in U.S. & Canada by:** The Paternoster Press, P O Box 11127, Birmingham, AL 35201-1127.

230 NLD ISSN 0922-2936
➤ **JOURNAL OF EMPIRICAL THEOLOGY.** Abbreviated title: J E T. Text in English. 1988. s-a. EUR 139, USD 194 to institutions; EUR 151, USD 211 combined subscription to institutions (print & online eds.) (effective 2012). bk.rev. Index. reprint service avail. from PSC. **Document type:** *Journal, Academic/Scholarly.* **Description:** Publishes theological articles which are directly or indirectly based on empirical research and empirical methodology, and which contribute to a deeper understanding of religion in modern times, in relation to the Christian tradition.
Incorporates (2000-2004): International Journal of Education and Religion (1389-9791)
Related titles: Online - full text ed.: ISSN 1570-9256. EUR 126, USD 176 to institutions (effective 2012) (from IngentaConnect).
Indexed: A01, A02, A03, A08, A21, A22, CA, E01, E03, ERI, IBR, IBZ, IZBG, P04, R&TA, RI-1, RI-2, T02.
—IE, Ingenta. **CCC.**
Published by: (Katholieke Universiteit Nijmegen, Theologisch Institut BEL), Brill, PO Box 9000, Leiden, 2300 PA, Netherlands. TEL 31-71-5353500, FAX 31-71-5317532, cs@brill.nl. **Dist. in N. America by:** Brill, PO Box 605, Herndon, VA 20172-0605. TEL 703-661-1585, 800-337-9255, FAX 703-661-1501, cs@brillusa.com; **Dist. by:** Turpin Distribution Services Ltd., Pegasus Dr, Stratton Business Park, Biggleswade, Bedfordshire SG18 8QB, United Kingdom. TEL 44-1767-604954, FAX 44-1767-601640, custserv@turpin-distribution.com, http://www.turpin-distribution.com/.

➤ **JOURNAL OF EUROPEAN STUDIES.** *see* HISTORY—History Of Europe

269 USA ISSN 1543-4680
JOURNAL OF EVANGELISM AND MISSIONS. Abbreviated title: J E M. Text in English. 2001. a. USD 10 per issue (effective 2010). **Document type:** *Journal, Academic/Scholarly.*
Published by: Mid-America Baptist Theological Seminary, 2095 Appling Rd, Cordova, TN 38016. TEL 901-751-8453, 800-968-4508, FAX 901-751-8454. Ed. Steve Wilkes.

268 USA ISSN 1949-2235
JOURNAL OF FAITH AND THE ACADEMY. Text in English. 2008. s-a.
Published by: Faulkner University, Institute of Faith and the Academy, 5345 Atlanta Hwy, Montgomery, AL 36109. TEL 334-272-5820, 800-879-9816, myoung@faulkner.edu, http://www.faulkner.edu/academics/scholarscouncil/faithandacademy.asp.

200 355 USA ISSN 2154-8315
▼ **JOURNAL OF FAITH AND WAR.** Text in English. 2009. irreg. free (effective 2010). **Document type:** *Journal, Academic/Scholarly.* **Description:** Features essays, treatises, reviews and commentaries that relate directly to the integration of faith with national security decisions and actions, and with the leadership of military forces and security agencies.
Media: Online - full text.
Published by: Association for Christian Conferences, Teaching and Service, 7220 W Jefferson St, Ste 335, Lakewood, CO 80235. TEL 800-487-8108, accts@accts.org, http://www.accts.org.

200 305.4 USA ISSN 8755-4178
HQ1393
➤ **JOURNAL OF FEMINIST STUDIES IN RELIGION.** Abbreviated title: J F S R. Text in English. 1985. s-a. USD 89.50 combined subscription to institutions (print & online eds.) (effective 2012). adv. illus. 140 p./no.; back issues avail.; reprint service avail. from PSC. **Document type:** *Journal, Academic/Scholarly.* **Description:** Provides a forum for discussion among women and men of differing feminist perspectives as well as highlighting feminist scholarship in religion.
Related titles: Online - full text ed.: ISSN 1553-3913. USD 59 to institutions (effective 2012).
Indexed: A01, A02, A03, A08, A20, A21, A22, A26, ASCA, AmHI, ArtHuCI, B04, BRD, CA, CurCont, DIP, E01, E08, FamI, FemPer, G08, GSS&RPL, H07, H08, HAb, HumInd, I05, IBR, IBZ, M01, M02, MLA-IB, P02, P10, P28, P48, P53, P54, PCI, PQC, R&TA, R05, RI-1, RI-2, S09, SCOPUS, T02, W03, W05, W06, W07, W09, WSA.
—BLDSC (4983.940000), IE, Infotrieve, Ingenta. **CCC.**
Published by: Indiana University Press, 601 N Morton St, Bloomington, IN 47404. TEL 812-855-8817, 800-842-6796, FAX 812-855-7931, journals@indiana.edu, http://iupress.indiana.edu. Eds. Elisabeth Schussler Fiorenza, Melanie Johnson-DeBaufre, Stephanie May. Circ: 950 (paid).

➤ **JOURNAL OF HEALTH CARE CHAPLAINCY.** *see* PHYSICAL FITNESS AND HYGIENE

➤ **JOURNAL OF HELLENIC RELIGION;** studies on ancient Greek religion. *see* CLASSICAL STUDIES

➤ **JOURNAL OF LAW AND RELIGION.** *see* LAW

➤ **JOURNAL OF MANAGEMENT, SPIRITUALITY & RELIGION;** an international blind refereed journal. *see* BUSINESS AND ECONOMICS—Management

➤ **JOURNAL OF MEDIA AND RELIGION.** *see* COMMUNICATIONS

204.22 800 USA ISSN 1947-6566
BV5080
➤ **JOURNAL OF MEDIEVAL RELIGIOUS CULTURES.** Abbreviated title: J M R C. Text occasionally in French; Text in English. 1974. s-a. USD 157 combined subscription to institutions (print & online eds.) (effective 2012). adv. bk.rev. bibl. Index. 60 p./no.; back issues avail.; reprint service avail. from PSC. **Document type:** *Journal, Academic/Scholarly.* **Description:** Publishes literary and historic research on mysticism, particularly that of medieval England and the rest of Europe, along with associated texts.
Former titles (until 2010): Mystics Quarterly (0742-5503); (until 1984): Fourteenth Century English Mystics Newsletter (0737-5840)
Related titles: Online - full text ed.: ISSN 2153-9650. USD 112 to institutions (effective 2012).
Indexed: A01, A03, A08, A21, A22, AmHI, BibInd, CA, E01, H07, MLA, MLA-IB, R&TA, RI-1, RI-2, RILM, T02.
—BLDSC (5017.577000), IE, Ingenta. **CCC.**
Published by: Pennsylvania State University Press, 820 N University Dr, University Support Bldg 1, Ste C, University Park, PA 16802. TEL 814-865-1327, 800-326-9180, FAX 814-863-1408, info@psupress.org. Eds. Christine F Cooper-Rompato, Ezra Greenspan, Kendra Boileau. **Dist. by:** The Johns Hopkins University Press, PO Box 19966, Baltimore, MD 21211. TEL 410-516-6987, 800-548-1784, FAX 410-516-3866, jrnlcirc@press.jhu.edu, https://www.press.jhu.edu/.

200 305.31 NZL ISSN 1177-2484
HQ1088
➤ **JOURNAL OF MEN, MASCULINITIES AND SPIRITUALITY.** Text in English. 2007. s-a. free (effective 2011). bk.rev. **Document type:** *Journal, Academic/Scholarly.* **Description:** Addresses not only monotheistic religions and spiritualities but also Eastern, indigenous, new religious movements and other spiritualities which resist categorization.
Media: Online - full text.
Indexed: A01, A26, A39, C27, C29, CA, D03, D04, E13, I05, S15, S18, SCOPUS, T02.
Address: http://www.jmmsweb.org/?q=user/2.

230.071 USA ISSN 1092-9525
JOURNAL OF MINISTRY & THEOLOGY. Text in English. 1997. s-a. USD 16 domestic; USD 21 foreign; USD 9 per issue (effective 2011). **Document type:** *Journal, Academic/Scholarly.* **Description:** Provides a forum for faculty, students, and friends of BBS to apply theology in ministry for the benefit of local church and parachurch organizations. Regular features of The Journal include articles on biblical exegesis; pastoral, biblical, and systematic theology; ethics; church history; missions; and ministry issues.
Indexed: A01, T02.
Published by: Baptist Bible Seminary, 538 Venard Rd, Clarks Summit, PA 18411. TEL 570-586-2400. Ed. Gary Gromacki TEL 570-585-9395.

250 USA ISSN 1542-3050
BV4000 CODEN: JPACA8
JOURNAL OF PASTORAL CARE & COUNSELING. Abbreviated title: J P C & C. Text in English. 1947. q. USD 60 to individuals; USD 100 to institutions; USD 60 combined subscription to students (print & online eds.) (effective 2010). adv. bk.rev. index. reprints avail. **Document type:** *Journal, Academic/Scholarly.* **Description:** Includes articles that reflect the cutting edges of clinical pastoral education and the pastoral counseling movements.
Formerly (until 2002): The Journal of Pastoral Care (0022-3409); Which incorporated (1947-1949): Journal of Clinical Pastoral Work (2156-6682)
Related titles: Microfilm ed.: (from PQC); Online - full text ed.: USD 40 to individuals; USD 100 to institutions; USD 25 to students (effective 2010).
Indexed: A21, A22, ASSIA, CCR, CERDIC, E-psyche, EMBASE, ExcerpMed, F09, FamI, INI, MEA&I, MEDLINE, P30, PC&CA, PsycholAb, R&TA, RI-1, RI-2, SCOPUS, SWR&A.
—BLDSC (5029.550000), IE, Ingenta. **CCC.**
Published by: Journal of Pastoral Care Publications, Inc., c/o Sheilah Hawk, 1549 Clairmont Rd, Ste 103, Decatur, GA 30033. TEL 404-320-0195, FAX 404-835-5096, jpcp@jpcp.org.

268 USA ISSN 0449-508X
THE JOURNAL OF PASTORAL COUNSELING. Text in English. 1966. s-a. USD 25 in North America to individuals; USD 35 elsewhere to individuals; USD 40 in North America to institutions; USD 50 elsewhere to institutions (effective 2007). 100 p./no. 1 cols./p.; **Document type:** *Magazine, Consumer.* **Description:** Publishes articles written from the various perspectives of psychoanalysis, psychiatry, psychology, social work, counseling and guidance, clinical sociology, cultural anthropology, pastoral ministry, theology, etc.
Related titles: Online - full text ed.
Indexed: A01, A02, A03, A08, A21, A22, A26, CA, E08, G08, I05, P28, P48, P53, P54, PQC, R&TA, R05, RI-1, S09, T02.
—BLDSC (5029.700000).
Published by: Iona College, Graduate Department of Pastoral and Family Counseling, 715 North Ave, New Rochelle, NY 10801. TEL 914-633-2418, rburns@iona.edu. Ed. Kevin Barry. Circ: 800 (controlled).

253 USA ISSN 1064-9867
BV4000
JOURNAL OF PASTORAL THEOLOGY. Text in English. 1991. s-a. USD 40 to individuals; USD 80 to institutions (effective 2011). adv. bk.rev. back issues avail. **Document type:** *Journal, Academic/Scholarly.*
Related titles: Online - full text ed.: ISSN 2161-4504.
Indexed: A21, FamI, R&TA, RI-1.
Published by: Society for Pastoral Theology, c/o ACPE, Inc.,, 1549 Clairmont Rd, Ste 103, Decatur, GA 30033. TEL 404-320-1472, FAX 404-320-0849, societyforpastoraltheology@yahoo.com, http://www.societyforpastoraltheology.com. Ed. Pamela Cooper-White.

210 USA ISSN 1555-5100
BL51
➤ **JOURNAL OF PHILOSOPHY & SCRIPTURE.** Text in English. 2003 (Fall). a. free (effective 2011). back issues avail. **Document type:** *Journal, Academic/Scholarly.* **Description:** Dedicated to reading scripture in light of philosophy and to examining philosophy in light of scripture.
Media: Online - full text.
Indexed: A39, C27, C29, D03, D04, E13, R14, S14, S15, S18.
Published by: Villanova University, Department of Philosophy, St Augustine Center for the Liberal Arts - Rm 105, 800 Lancaster Ave, Villanova, VA 19085. TEL 610-519-4600, FAX 610-519-7249, kathryn.szumanski@villanova.edu, http://www.villanova.edu/artsci/philosophy/.

➤ **JOURNAL OF PREHISTORIC RELIGION.** *see* ARCHAEOLOGY

➤ **JOURNAL OF PSYCHOLOGY AND CHRISTIANITY.** *see* PSYCHOLOGY

➤ **JOURNAL OF PSYCHOLOGY AND THEOLOGY;** an evangelical forum for the integration of psychology and theology. *see* PSYCHOLOGY

▼ ➤ **JOURNAL OF RACE, ETHNICITY, AND RELIGION.** *see* ETHNIC INTERESTS

220 NLD ISSN 1872-5163
BX9401
➤ **JOURNAL OF REFORMED THEOLOGY.** Text in English. 2007. 3/yr. EUR 153, USD 215 to institutions; EUR 167, USD 234 combined subscription to institutions (print & online eds.) (effective 2012). reprint service avail. from PSC. **Document type:** *Journal, Academic/Scholarly.* **Description:** Provides a forum for debate on classical and contemporary theological issues and offers an update on new theological and biblical literature.
Related titles: Online - full text ed.: ISSN 1569-7312. EUR 139, USD 195 to institutions (effective 2012) (from IngentaConnect).
Indexed: A01, A21, A22, CA, E01, IZBG, T02.
—IE. **CCC.**
Published by: Brill, PO Box 9000, Leiden, 2300 PA, Netherlands. TEL 31-71-5353500, FAX 31-71-5317532, cs@brill.nl. Ed. Eddy Van der Borght.

200 USA ISSN 0022-4189
BR1
➤ **THE JOURNAL OF RELIGION.** Text in English. 1921. q. USD 200 combined subscription to institutions (print & online eds.) (effective 2012). adv. bk.rev. illus. Index. back issues avail.; reprint service avail. from PSC. **Document type:** *Journal, Academic/Scholarly.* **Description:** Promotes critical and systematic inquiry into the meaning and import of religion. Also embraces literary, social, psychological, and philosophical studies of religion.
Formed by the merger of (1897-1921): American Journal of Theology (1550-3283); (1893-1921): The Biblical World (0190-3578); Which was formerly (until 1893): The Old and New Testament Student (0190-5937); (until 1889): The Old Testament Student (0190-5945); (until 1883): The Hebrew Student (0190-5953)
Related titles: Microform ed.: (from MIM, PMC, PQC); Online - full text ed.: ISSN 1549-6538. USD 170 to institutions (effective 2012).
Indexed: A01, A02, A03, A08, A20, A21, A22, A25, A26, ASCA, AcaI, AmHI, ArtHuCI, B04, B05, B14, BAS, BEL&L, BRD, BRI, CA, CBRI, CurCont, E08, FR, FamI, G05, G06, G07, G08, G10, GSS&RPL, H07, H08, H09, H10, H14, HAb, HumInd, I05, I06, I07, IBR, IBZ, IPB, M01, M02, MEA&I, MLA-IB, OTA, P02, P10, P13, P28, P30, P48, P53, P54, PCI, PQC, PerIslam, PhilInd, R&TA, R04, R05, RASB, RI-1, RI-2, S02, S03, S05, S08, S09, S23, SCOPUS, SOPODA, SociolAb, T02, W03, W07, W09.
—BLDSC (5049.200000), IE, Infotrieve, Ingenta, INIST. **CCC.**
Published by: (University of Chicago), University of Chicago Press, 1427 E 60th St, Chicago, IL 60637. TEL 773-702-7600, FAX 773-702-0694, subscriptions@press.uchicago.edu. Eds. Jean Bethke Elshtain, Willemien Otten. Adv. contact Cheryl Jones TEL 773-702-7361. **Subscr. to:** PO Box 370050, Chicago, IL 60637. TEL 773-753-3347, 877-705-1878, FAX 773-753-0811, 877-705-1879.

200 330 174 USA ISSN 2153-0319
HF5387
▼ ➤ **JOURNAL OF RELIGION AND BUSINESS ETHICS.** Text in English. 2010. s-a. free (effective 2010). **Document type:** *Journal, Academic/Scholarly.* **Description:** Examines the ethical and religious issues that arise in the modern business setting, such as corporate governance, accounting practices, employee/employer relationships, the environment, advanced technology, power relationships, and the role of government in the economy.
Media: Online - full text.
Indexed: B01, T02.
Published by: DePaul University, 2331 N Racine Ave, Chicago, IL 60614. TEL 773-988-9972, tobrien8@depaul.edu, http://www.depaul.edu/.

➤ **JOURNAL OF RELIGION AND FILM.** *see* MOTION PICTURES

200 150 USA ISSN 0022-4197
RC321 CODEN: JRHEAT
➤ **JOURNAL OF RELIGION AND HEALTH.** Text in English. 1961. q. EUR 950, USD 996 combined subscription to institutions (print & online eds.) (effective 2012). adv. bk.rev. charts; illus. Index. back issues avail.; reprint service avail. from PSC. **Document type:** *Journal, Academic/Scholarly.* **Description:** Explores contemporary modes of religious thought with emphasis on its relevance to current medical and psychological research.
Related titles: Microform ed.: (from PQC); Online - full text ed.: ISSN 1573-6571 (from IngentaConnect).
Indexed: A01, A03, A08, A20, A21, A22, A26, ASCA, ArtHuCI, BibLing, C06, C07, CA, CurCont, E01, EMBASE, ExcerpMed, FamI, GSS&RPL, H13, IJP, MEA&I, MEDLINE, P02, P03, P10, P20, P22, P28, P30, P48, P50, P53, P54, PC&CA, PQC, PsycInfo, PsycholAb, R&TA, R10, RI-1, RI-2, Reac, S02, S03, SCOPUS, SSCI, T02, W07.
—BLDSC (5049.350000), IE, Infotrieve, Ingenta. **CCC.**
Published by: Springer New York LLC (Subsidiary of: Springer Science+Business Media), 233 Spring St, New York, NY 10013. TEL 212-460-1500, FAX 212-460-1575, service-ny@springer.com. Ed. Donald R Ferrell TEL 802-867-4469.

200 CAN ISSN 1703-289X
BL65.C8
➤ **JOURNAL OF RELIGION AND POPULAR CULTURE.** Text in English. irreg. free (effective 2011). bk.rev. **Document type:** *Journal, Academic/Scholarly.* **Description:** Explores the interrelations and interactions between religion and religious expression and popular culture.
Media: Online - full text.
Indexed: A21, A26, A39, AmHI, C03, C27, C29, CA, CBCARef, CPerI, D03, D04, E08, E13, G08, H07, I05, MLA-IB, P10, P28, P48, P53, P54, PQC, R14, S09, S14, S15, S18, S23, T02.
—CCC.
Address: University of Saskatchewan, St Tomas More College, 1437 College Dr, Room 131, Saskatoon, SK S7N 0W6, Canada. Ed. Mary Ann Beavis TEL 306-966-8948.

230 USA ISSN 1522-5658
BL1
➤ **JOURNAL OF RELIGION AND SOCIETY.** Abbreviated title: J R S. Text in English. 1999. irreg., latest vol.12, 2010. free (effective 2011). back issues avail. **Document type:** *Journal, Academic/Scholarly.* **Description:** Promotes the cross-disciplinary study of religion and its diverse social dimension through the publications of research articles, discussions and critical notes.
Media: Online - full text. **Related titles:** Supplement to: Journal of Religion and Society. Supplement Series. ISSN 1941-8450.
Indexed: A21, PAIS, R&TA, RI-1, SociolAb.
Published by: Creighton University, Center for the Study of Religion and Society, 2500 California Plz, Omaha, NE 68178. TEL 402-280-2700, http://moses.creighton.edu/kripke/index.html. Ed. Ronald A Simkins.

➤ **JOURNAL OF RELIGION AND SPIRITUALITY IN SOCIAL WORK**; social thought. *see* SOCIAL SERVICES AND WELFARE

200 792 USA ISSN 1544-8762
➤ **THE JOURNAL OF RELIGION AND THEATRE.** Text in English. 2002 (Fall). irreg. free (effective 2011). **Document type:** *Journal, Academic/Scholarly.* **Description:** It aims to provide descriptive and analytical articles examining the spirituality of world cultures in all disciplines of the theatre, performance studies in sacred rituals of all cultures, themes of transcendence in text, on stage, in theatre history, the analysis of dramatic literature, and other topics relating to the relationship between religion and theatre.
Media: Online - full text.
Indexed: MLA-IB.
Published by: Association for Theatre in Higher Education, Religion and Theater Focus Group, PO Box 1290, Boulder, CO 80306. TEL 303-530-2167, 888-284-3737, FAX 303-530-2168, http://www.fa.mtu.edu/~dlbruch/rt/journal.html. Ed. Heather A Beasley.

200 362.4 USA ISSN 1522-8967
BV4460 CODEN: JRDRFJ
➤ **JOURNAL OF RELIGION, DISABILITY & HEALTH**; bridging clinical practice and spiritual supports. Abbreviated title: J R D H. Text in English. 1993. q. GBP 318 combined subscription in United Kingdom to institutions (print & online eds.); EUR 415, USD 420 combined subscription to institutions (print & online eds.) (effective 2012). adv. bk.rev. 120 p./no. 1 cols./p.; back issues avail.; reprint service avail. from PSC. **Document type:** *Journal, Academic/Scholarly.* **Description:** Provides an interfaith, interdisciplinary forum that will reflect and support the growing dialogue between religious/spiritual perspectives and clinical/scientific perspectives in supporting people with disabilities and their families.
Formerly (until 1998): Journal of Religion in Disability and Rehabilitation (1059-9258)
Related titles: Microfiche ed.; Microform ed.; Online - full text ed.: ISSN 1522-9122. GBP 286 in United Kingdom to institutions; EUR 373, USD 379 to institutions (effective 2012).
Indexed: A01, A03, A22, AMED, ASSIA, AbAn, B21, C06, C07, C08, CA, CINAHL, CPE, DIP, E01, E17, ESPM, F09, FamI, IBR, IBZ, M02, PC&CA, PerIslam, R&TA, S02, S03, SCOPUS, SOPODA, SWR&A, SociolAb, T02.
—BLDSC (5049.352100), IE, Ingenta. **CCC.**
Published by: Routledge (Subsidiary of: Taylor & Francis Group), 325 Chestnut St, Ste 800, Philadelphia, PA 19106. TEL 215-625-8900, 800-354-1420, FAX 215-625-8914, journals@routledge.com, http://www.routledge.com. Ed. William C Gaventa. adv.: B&W page USD 315, color page USD 550; trim 4.375 x 7.125. Circ: 227 (paid).

200 NLD ISSN 1874-8910
BL689
➤ **JOURNAL OF RELIGION IN EUROPE.** Text in English. 2008. 3/yr. EUR 229, USD 320 to institutions; EUR 249, USD 349 combined subscription to institutions (print & online eds.) (effective 2012). reprint service avail. from PSC. **Document type:** *Journal, Academic/Scholarly.* **Description:** Provides a forum for multi-disciplinary research into the complex dynamics of religious discourses and practices in Europe, historical and contemporary.
Related titles: Online - full text ed.: ISSN 1874-8929. EUR 208, USD 291 to institutions (effective 2012) (from IngentaConnect).
Indexed: A22, AmHI, CA, E01, H07, IZBG, SCOPUS, T02.
—IE. **CCC.**
Published by: Brill, PO Box 9000, Leiden, 2300 PA, Netherlands. TEL 31-71-5353500, FAX 31-71-5317532, cs@brill.nl, http://www.brill.nl. Eds. Hans G Kippenberg, Max Weber Kolleg.

200 NLD ISSN 2211-8330
▼ **JOURNAL OF RELIGION IN JAPAN.** Text in English. forthcoming 2012. 3/yr. EUR 198, USD 277 to institutions; EUR 216, USD 302 combined subscription to institutions (print & online eds.) (effective 2012). **Document type:** *Journal, Academic/Scholarly.*
Related titles: Online - full text ed.: ISSN 2211-8349. forthcoming 2012. EUR 180, USD 252 to institutions (effective 2012).
Published by: Brill, PO Box 9000, Leiden, 2300 PA, Netherlands. TEL 31-71-5353500, FAX 31-71-5317532, cs@brill.nl, http://www.brill.nl.

JOURNAL OF RELIGION, SPIRITUALITY & AGING; the interdisciplinary journal of practice, theory & applied research. *see* GERONTOLOGY AND GERIATRICS

202 USA ISSN 1047-7845
Z7753 CODEN: JRTIE3
➤ **JOURNAL OF RELIGIOUS & THEOLOGICAL INFORMATION.** Abbreviated title: J R T I. Text in English. 1993. q. GBP 136 combined subscription in United Kingdom to institutions (print & online eds.); EUR 197, USD 167 combined subscription to institutions (print & online eds.) (effective 2012). adv. 120 p./no. 1 cols./p.; back issues avail.; reprint service avail. from PSC. **Document type:** *Journal, Academic/Scholarly.* **Description:** Presents articles pertaining to the production, dissemination, preservation, and bibliography of religious and theological information.
Related titles: Microform ed.: (from PQC); Online - full text ed.: ISSN 1528-6924. GBP 123 in United Kingdom to institutions; EUR 177, USD 151 to institutions (effective 2012).
Indexed: A01, A03, A21, A22, AbAn, AmH&L, CA, DIP, E01, GSS&RPL, H14, HistAb, IBR, IBZ, ISTA, Inspec, J01, L04, L13, LISTA, M02, P02, P10, P28, P48, P53, P54, PC&CA, PQC, PerIslam, R&TA, RI-1, RI-2, RILM, RefZh, SCOPUS, T02.
—BLDSC (5049.352700), AskIEEE, IE, Ingenta. **CCC.**
Published by: Routledge (Subsidiary of: Taylor & Francis Group), 270 Madison Ave, New York, NY 10016. TEL 212-216-7800, FAX 212-244-1563, journals@routledge.com, http://www.routledge.com. Ed. Mark Stover.

200 USA ISSN 0384-9694
BJ1
➤ **JOURNAL OF RELIGIOUS ETHICS.** Text in English. 1973. q. GBP 202 combined subscription in United Kingdom to institutions (print & online eds.); EUR 243 combined subscription in Europe to institutions (print & online eds.); USD 252 combined subscription in the Americas to institutions (print & online eds.); USD 393 combined subscription elsewhere to institutions (print & online eds.) (effective 2012). adv. bk.rev. illus. back issues avail.; reprint service avail. from PSC. **Document type:** *Journal, Academic/Scholarly.* **Description:** Explores various aspects of religious ethics.
Related titles: Microform ed.: (from PQC); Online - full text ed.: ISSN 1467-9795. GBP 184 in United Kingdom to institutions; EUR 233 in Europe to institutions; USD 229 in the Americas to institutions; USD 359 elsewhere to institutions (effective 2012) (from IngentaConnect); Supplement(s): J R E Studies in Religious Ethics. ISSN 0145-2797.
Indexed: A01, A02, A03, A08, A20, A21, A22, A26, ABS&EES, ASCA, AmHI, ArtHuCI, B04, BRD, CA, CERDIC, CurCont, E-psyche, E01, E08, FamI, G08, H07, H08, H09, H10, H14, HAb, HumInd, I05, MLA-IB, OTA, P02, P10, P28, P30, P48, P53, P54, PCI, PQC, PerIslam, PhilInd, R&TA, R05, RI-1, RI-2, S02, S03, S09, SCOPUS, T02, W03, W07.
—BLDSC (5049.353000), IE, Infotrieve, Ingenta. **CCC.**
Published by: Wiley-Blackwell Publishing, Inc. (Subsidiary of: Wiley-Blackwell Publishing Ltd.), 111 River St, Hoboken, NJ 07030. TEL 201-748-6000, FAX 201-748-6088, info@wiley.com, http://www.wiley.com/WileyCDA/. Eds. John Kelsay TEL 850-644-2154, Sumner B Twiss. Adv. contact Kristin McCarthy TEL 201-748-7683.

200 AUS ISSN 0022-4227
BR140
➤ **JOURNAL OF RELIGIOUS HISTORY.** Text in English. 1960. q. GBP 335 in United Kingdom to institutions; EUR 427 in Europe to institutions; USD 486 in the Americas to institutions; USD 659 elsewhere to institutions; GBP 386 combined subscription in United Kingdom to institutions (print & online eds.); EUR 491 combined subscription in Europe to institutions (print & online eds.); USD 559 combined subscription in the Americas to institutions (print & online eds.); USD 758 combined subscription elsewhere to institutions (print & online eds.) (effective 2012). bk.rev. bibl. cum.index every 2 yrs. back issues avail.; reprint service avail. from PSC. **Document type:** *Journal, Academic/Scholarly.* **Description:** Publishes articles and reviews current work in the history of religions and their relationship with all aspects of human experience.
Related titles: Microform ed.: (from PQC); Online - full text ed.: ISSN 1467-9809. GBP 335 in United Kingdom to institutions; EUR 427 in Europe to institutions; USD 486 in the Americas to institutions; USD 659 elsewhere to institutions (effective 2012) (from IngentaConnect).
Indexed: A01, A02, A03, A08, A20, A21, A22, A26, ASCA, AmH&L, AmHI, ArtHuCI, AusPAIS, CA, CERDIC, CurCont, E01, E08, FR, G06, G07, G08, H05, H07, H14, HistAb, I05, MEA&I, MLA-IB, P02, P10, P28, P30, P48, P53, P54, PCI, PQC, R&TA, R05, RASB, RI-1, RI-2, S02, S03, S09, SCOPUS, SociolAb, T02, W07.
—BLDSC (5049.355000), IE, Infotrieve, Ingenta, INIST. **CCC.**
Published by: (Association for the Journal of Religious History), Wiley-Blackwell Publishing Asia (Subsidiary of: Wiley-Blackwell Publishing Ltd.), 155 Cremorne St, Richmond, VIC 3121, Australia. TEL 61-3-92743100, FAX 61-3-92743101, subs@blackwellpublishingasia.com, http://www.wiley.com/WileyCDA/. Eds. Carole Cusack, Christopher Hartney. Adv. contact Yasemin Caglar TEL 61-3-83591071. Circ: 700. **Co-sponsor:** Religious History Society.

200 USA ISSN 1935-6943
BV652.1
➤ **JOURNAL OF RELIGIOUS LEADERSHIP.** Abbreviated title: J R L. Text in English. 2002. s-a. USD 115 to institutions; free to members (effective 2010). back issues avail. **Document type:** *Journal, Academic/Scholarly.*
Related titles: Online - full text ed.: ISSN 1935-7060.
Indexed: A21.
Published by: Academy of Religious Leadership, Inc., c/o David Forney, PO Box 520, Decatur, GA 30031. contact@arl-jrl.org, http://www.arl-jrl.org/. Ed. David G Forney.

200 CAN ISSN 1183-3262
BL2015
JOURNAL OF RELIGIOUS PLURALISM. Text in English. 1991. a. USD 15. **Description:** Provides a forum for the discussion of religious pluralism as represented by plurality of religious traditions, a plurality of methods of studying religions, and a plurality of new religious movements.
Indexed: GSS&RPL.
—CCC.
Published by: McGill University, Faculty of Religious Studies, 3250 University St., Montreal, PQ H3A 2A7, Canada. TEL 514-398-6138. Eds. Arvind Sharma, Kathleen M Dugan.

200 USA ISSN 0193-3604
BL1
JOURNAL OF RELIGIOUS STUDIES. Text in English. 1972. s-a. USD 4. adv. bk.rev. illus. back issues avail.
Formerly: Ohio Journal of Religious Studies (0094-5668)
Indexed: A21, CERDIC, MLA-IB, PhilInd, RASB, RI-1, RI-2.
Published by: Cleveland State University, Department of Religion, 2121 Euclid Ave, Cleveland, OH 44115. Ed. Frederick Holck. Circ: 1,200.

200 IND ISSN 0047-2735
BL1
THE JOURNAL OF RELIGIOUS STUDIES. Text in English. 1969. s-a. INR 50 per issue (effective 2011). bk.rev. 200 p./no. 1 cols./p.; back issues avail.; reprints avail. **Document type:** *Journal, Academic/Scholarly.* **Description:** Covers religion, theology, comparative religion, philosophy and allied subjects.
Indexed: RI-1.
—Ingenta.
Published by: Punjabi University Patiala, Department of Religious Studies, Patiala, Punjab 147 002, India. TEL 91-175-3046533, http://punjabiuniversity.ac.in.

200 USA ISSN 0022-4235
BR1
➤ **THE JOURNAL OF RELIGIOUS THOUGHT.** Text in English. 1943. s-a. USD 20, USD 30 domestic (effective 2010). bk.rev. bibl.; illus. cum.index. reprints avail. **Document type:** *Journal, Academic/Scholarly.* **Description:** Contains articles from persons of varied theological and ethnic backgrounds.
Related titles: Microform ed.: (from PQC); Online - full text ed.
Indexed: A01, A02, A03, A08, A21, A22, A26, AbAn, AmHI, B04, BAS, BRD, CA, DIP, E08, FR, G08, H07, H08, H14, HAb, HumInd, I05, IBR, IBZ, IIBP, M01, M02, MEA&I, MLA-IB, P02, P10, P28, P48, P53, P54, PCI, PQC, PhilInd, R&TA, R05, RI-1, RI-2, RILM, S09, T02, W03, W04.
—BLDSC (5049.360000), IE, Ingenta, INIST.
Published by: Howard University, School of Divinity, 1400 Shepherd St, NE, Washington, DC 20017. TEL 202-806-0500, FAX 202-806-0711, http://divinity.howard.edu/. Ed. Cain Hope Felder.

➤ **JOURNAL OF RESEARCH ON CHRISTIAN EDUCATION.** *see* EDUCATION

➤ **JOURNAL OF RITUAL STUDIES.** *see* ANTHROPOLOGY

200 USA ISSN 1551-3432
BL41
JOURNAL OF SCRIPTURAL REASONING. Text in English. 2001. irreg. (1-3/yr.). free (effective 2011). back issues avail. **Document type:** *Journal, Academic/Scholarly.*
Media: Online - full text.
Published by: Society of Scriptural Reasoning http://www.depts.drew.edu/ssr/nationalssr/. Ed. Jacob Goodson.

200 951 USA ISSN 2153-0114
DS721
▼ ➤ **JOURNAL OF SINO-WESTERN COMMUNICATIONS.** Variant title: J S W C. Text in English. 2009 (Dec.). s-a. free (effective 2009). **Document type:** *Journal, Academic/Scholarly.* **Description:** Articles on the interaction between the Bible and China and contemporary interactions between the Chinese and the western culture from a historical perspective.
Related titles: Online - full text ed.: ISSN 1946-6188.
Indexed: A01.
Published by: Institute of Sino-Western Communication, 1160 Regent St, Ste B, Alameda, CA 94501. TEL 510-862-7487, journalswc@gmail.com.

200 USA ISSN 1094-5253
➤ **JOURNAL OF SOUTHERN RELIGION.** Text in English. 2002. irreg. free (effective 2011). back issues avail. **Document type:** *Journal, Academic/Scholarly.*
Media: Online - full text.
Indexed: A21, R&TA, RI-1.
Published by: Association for the Study of Southern Religion, c/o Rodger M. Payne, Editor, Department of Philosophy and Religious Studies, Louisiana State University, Baton Rouge, LA 70803. Eds. Luke E Harlow, Michael Pasquier.

248 USA ISSN 1939-7909
BR100
➤ **JOURNAL OF SPIRITUAL FORMATION AND SOUL CARE.** Text in English. 2008 (May). s-a. USD 30 domestic; USD 38 foreign (effective 2011). back issues avail. **Document type:** *Journal, Academic/Scholarly.* **Description:** Advances the discussion of the theory and practice of Christian formation and soul care for the sake of the educational ministries of the church, Christian education and other para-church organizations through scholarly publications that are rooted in biblical exegesis, systematic theology, the history of Christian spirituality, philosophical analysis, psychological theory/research, spiritual theology, and Christian experience.
Indexed: A01, A21, A26, CA, I05, T02.
Published by: Biola University, Institute for Spiritual Formation, 13800 Biola Ave, La Mirada, CA 90639. TEL 562-777-4005, 562-944-0351 ext 5321, FAX 562-777-4024, spiritualformation@biola.edu, http://www.biola.edu/spiritualformation. Ed. John Coe.

➤ **JOURNAL OF SPIRITUALITY AND PARANORMAL STUDIES.** *see* PARAPSYCHOLOGY AND OCCULTISM

➤ **JOURNAL OF SPIRITUALITY IN MENTAL HEALTH.** *see* PSYCHOLOGY

➤ **JOURNAL OF SPIRITUALITY, LEADERSHIP AND MANAGEMENT.** *see* BUSINESS AND ECONOMICS—Management

▼ ➤ **JOURNAL OF THE ARCHAEOLOGY OF RELIGION.** *see* ARCHAEOLOGY

200 150 CAN ISSN 1192-3830
JOURNAL OF THE PSYCHOLOGY OF RELIGION. Text in English. 1992. a. CAD 15. **Document type:** *Journal, Academic/Scholarly.* **Description:** Forum for drawing impartially on all branches of psychology to shed light on religious phenomena to overcome current compartmentalizations.
Indexed: E-psyche, R&TA.
Published by: McGill University, Faculty of Religious Studies, 3250 University St., Montreal, PQ H3A 2A7, Canada. TEL 514-398-6138. Eds. Arvind Sharma, Kaisa Puhakka.

R

220 USA ISSN 1936-0843
BS543.A1
JOURNAL OF THEOLOGICAL INTERPRETATION. Text in English. 2007 (Apr.). s-a. USD 30 domestic to individuals; USD 35 foreign to individuals; USD 40 domestic to institutions; USD 45 foreign to institutions (effective 2010). back issues avail. **Document type:** *Journal, Academic/Scholarly.*
—CCC.
Published by: Eisenbrauns Inc., PO Box 275, Winona Lake, IN 46590. TEL 574-269-2011, FAX 574-269-6788, customerservice@eisenbrauns.com, http://www.eisenbrauns.com. Ed. Joel B Green.

220 GBR ISSN 0022-5185
BR1
➤ **JOURNAL OF THEOLOGICAL STUDIES.** Text in English. 1899. s-a. GBP 240 in United Kingdom to institutions; EUR 361 in Europe to institutions; USD 431 in US & Canada to institutions; GBP 240 elsewhere to institutions; GBP 262 combined subscription in United Kingdom to institutions (print & online eds.); EUR 394 combined subscription in Europe to institutions (print & online eds.); USD 470 combined subscription in US & Canada to institutions (print & online eds.); GBP 262 combined subscription elsewhere to institutions (print & online eds.) (effective 2012). adv. bk.rev. abstr.; bibl.; charts; illus. index. back issues avail.; reprint service avail. from PSC. **Document type:** *Journal, Academic/Scholarly.* **Description:** Covers the entire range of theological research, scholarship, and interpretation. Reproduces ancient and modern texts, inscriptions, and documents that have not before appeared in type.
Related titles: Microform ed.: (from PQC); Online - full text ed.: ISSN 1477-4607. GBP 218 in United Kingdom to institutions; EUR 328 in Europe to institutions; USD 392 in US & Canada to institutions; GBP 218 elsewhere to institutions (effective 2012) (from IngentaConnect).
Indexed: A01, A02, A03, A08, A20, A21, A22, A26, ASCA, AmHI, ArtHuCI, B04, B24, BRD, BibLing, BrHumI, CA, CERDIC, CurCont, DIP, E01, E08, FR, FamI, G08, H07, H08, H14, HAb, HumInd, I05, IBR, IBZ, IZBG, MLA, MLA-IB, OTA, P02, P10, P28, P48, P53, P54, PCI, PQC, R&TA, R05, RASB, RI-1, RI-2, S02, S03, S09, SCOPUS, T02, W03, W05, W07.
—BLDSC (5069.070000), IE, Infotrieve, Ingenta, INIST. **CCC.**
Published by: Oxford University Press, Great Clarendon St, Oxford, OX2 6DP, United Kingdom. TEL 44-1865-556767, FAX 44-1865-556646, enquiry@oup.co.uk, http://www.oxfordjournals.org. Eds. Graham Gould, John Barton. Adv. contact Linda Hann TEL 44-1344-779945.

260 ZAF ISSN 0047-2867
BR1
➤ **JOURNAL OF THEOLOGY FOR SOUTHERN AFRICA.** Text in English. 3/yr. ZAR 50 in Africa to individuals; USD 50 elsewhere to individuals; ZAR 75 in Africa to institutions; USD 75 elsewhere to institutions (effective 2004). adv. bk.rev. abstr. index. 112 p./no.; back issues avail. **Document type:** *Journal, Academic/Scholarly.*
Formerly (until 1972): Mente et Manu
Related titles: Microfilm ed.: (from PQC, WMP); Online - full text ed.: 1972.
Indexed: A21, A22, AbAn, CERDIC, IIBP, ISAP, OTA, P28, P30, P48, P53, P54, PQC, R&TA, RI-1, RI-2.
—BLDSC (5069.074000), IE, Infotrieve, Ingenta.
Published by: University of KwaZulu-Natal, School of Theology & Religion, Private Bag X01, Scottsville, Pietermaritzburg, KwaZulu-Natal 3209, South Africa. TEL 27-33-2606106, FAX 27-33-2605858, http://www.ricsa.ora.za. Circ: 600.

200 USA ISSN 1947-2390
▼ ➤ **THE JOURNAL OF TRADITIONS AND BELIEFS.** Text in English. 2009. a. USD 20 per issue (effective 2009). **Document type:** *Journal, Academic/Scholarly.* **Description:** Features research on religion and spirituality in the history of Africa and the Diaspora.
Published by: (Cleveland State University), The Initiative for the Study of Religion and Spirituality in the History of Africa in the Diaspora, 2121 Euclid Ave, RT 1915, Cleveland, OH 44115. TEL 216-523-7182, r.williams@csuohio.edu.

200 150 USA ISSN 1945-5445
BF1045.A48
▼ **JOURNAL OF TRANCE RESEARCH.** Text in English. 2009 (Jan.). s-a. USD 25; free to qualified personnel (effective 2010). **Document type:** *Journal, Academic/Scholarly.* **Description:** Promotes dialog about the theoretical foundations and professional practice of trance analysis.
Formerly announced as: Journal of Trance Theory and Practice
Related titles: Online - full text ed.
Published by: Trance Research Foundation, PO Box 84, Laytonville, CA 95454. TEL 707-984-8186, info@trance.edu, http://trance.edu. Ed. Dennis Wier.

230 USA ISSN 1943-1538
THE JOURNAL OF WORLD CHRISTIANITY; bringing together scholars in a variety of fields who study christianity in global, local, and comparative contexts. Text in English. 2008. q. back issues avail. **Document type:** *Journal, Academic/Scholarly.*
Media: Online - full text.
Published by: New York Theological Seminary, 475 Riverside Dr, Ste 500, New York, NY 10115. TEL 212-870-1211, FAX 212-870-1236, online@nyts.edu, http://www.nyts.edu. Eds. Dale T Irvin, Patrick Provost-Smith.

230 DEU ISSN 1931-8235
➤ **JOURNAL OF WORLD CHRISTIANITY (ONLINE).** Text in English. 2007. irreg. **Document type:** *Journal, Academic/Scholarly.* **Description:** Contains comparative studies of both local forms of Christianity in the areas in which it has historically existed or presently exists, and with the place of Christianity in inter-religious dialogue, the history of interactions between Christianity and persons of other faiths, and interactions between Christian groups separated by confessional, ecclesiastical, geographical, or geo-political divides.
Formerly (until 200?): Journal of World Christianity (Print) (1931-7999)
Published by: Walter de Gruyter GmbH & Co. KG, Genthiner Str 13, Berlin, 10785, Germany. TEL 49-30-260050, FAX 49-30-26005251, info@degruyter.com, http://www.degruyter.de. Eds. Dale T Irvin, Patrick Provost-Smith.

220 ZAF ISSN 1992-1993
JOY! MAGAZINE. Text in English. 2006. bi-m. ZAR 199.90 for 2 yrs. domestic; ZAR 499.90 for 2 yrs. foreign (effective 2006). adv. **Document type:** *Magazine, Consumer.*
Published by: Independent Christian Media (Pty) Ltd., PO Box 2990, Somerset West, 7129, South Africa. TEL 27-21-8524061, FAX 27-21-8525781. Ed. Erin Georgiou. Adv. contact Jenny-Lee Robinson. color page ZAR 8,450; trim 210 x 276.

291 CHE ISSN 0171-676X
JUDAICA ET CHRISTIANA. Text in German. 1976. irreg., latest vol.24, 2009. price varies. **Document type:** *Monographic series, Academic/Scholarly.*
Published by: Peter Lang AG (Subsidiary of: Peter Lang Publishing Group), Hochfeldstr 32, Postfach 746, Bern 9, 3000, Switzerland. TEL 41-31-3061717, FAX 41-31-3061727, info@peterlang.com. Eds. Clemens Thoma, Simon Lauer.

JUDAICA IBEROAMERICANA. *see* ETHNIC INTERESTS

291 DEU ISSN 1866-4873
JUDENTUM - CHRISTENTUM - ISLAM. Variant title: Christentum und Islam. Text in German. 2002. irreg., latest vol.9, 2011. price varies. **Document type:** *Monographic series, Academic/Scholarly.*
Published by: Ergon Verlag, Keesburgstr 11, Wuerzburg, 97074, Germany. TEL 49-931-280084, FAX 49-931-282872, service@ergon-verlag.de.

200.711 DEU ISSN 1430-2667
JUGEND - RELIGION - UNTERRICHT; Beitraege zu einer dialogischen Religionspaedagogik. Text in German. 1996. irreg., latest vol.12, 2009. price varies. **Document type:** *Monographic series, Academic/Scholarly.*
Published by: Waxmann Verlag GmbH, Steinfurter Str 555, Muenster, 48159, Germany. TEL 49-251-265040, FAX 49-251-2650426, info@waxmann.com. Ed. Wolfram Weisse.

200 100 BIH ISSN 0350-6398
BX3645.B54
JUKIC; zbornik radova. Text in Croatian. 1971. a. USD 7 (effective 2003). back issues avail. **Document type:** *Academic/Scholarly.*
Indexed: RASB.
Published by: Zbor Franjevackih Bogoslova "Jukic", Aleja Bosne Srebrene 111, Sarajevo, 71000, Bosnia Herzegovina. TEL 387-33-453266, FAX 387-33-460507, tajnteol@bih.net.ba. Ed. Mile Babic. Circ: 1,000.

200 DEU ISSN 1867-2213
JULIUS-WELLHAUSEN-VORLESUNG. Text in German. 2008. irreg., latest vol.3, 2011. price varies. **Document type:** *Monographic series, Academic/Scholarly.*
Published by: Walter de Gruyter GmbH & Co. KG, Genthiner Str 13, Berlin, 10785, Germany. TEL 49-30-26005220, FAX 49-30-26005251, info@degruyter.com, http://www.degruyter.de. Eds. Reinhard Kratz, Rudolf Smend.

200 USA ISSN 1535-2676
JUMU/BEHOLD. Text in Chinese. 2001. bi-m. back issues avail. **Document type:** *Magazine, Consumer.* **Description:** Covers christianity related topics.
Published by: Campus Evangelical Fellowship, Inc., 1753 Cabrillo Ave, Torrance, CA 90501. TEL 310-328-8200, FAX 310-328-8207, info@oc.org.

201.6 DEU
BX8001
JUNGE KIRCHE; Unterwegs fuer Gerechtigkeit, Frieden und Bewahrung der Schoepfung. Text in German. 1933. q. EUR 26; EUR 6.50 newsstand/cover (effective 2011). adv. bk.rev. index. **Document type:** *Journal, Academic/Scholarly.* **Description:** Christian socialist publication with articles about religion, politics, ecumenical issues, justice, peace and the integrity of creation.
Incorporated (1969-1974): Akid (0171-5151)
Indexed: CERDIC, DIP, RASB.
Published by: Verlag Junge Kirche, Luisenstr 54, Uelzen, 29525, Germany. TEL 49-581-77666, FAX 49-581-77666, verlag@jungekirche.de. Ed. Gerard Minnaard. Pub. Hans-Juergen Benedict. adv.: color page EUR 1,000, B&W page EUR 675. Circ: 4,000 (paid and controlled).

268 DEU ISSN 1438-2741
JUNGSCHARHELFER; Mitarbeiterhilfe fuer Jungen- und Maedchenarbeit. Text in German. 1954. q. EUR 27.20; EUR 6.80 newsstand/cover (effective 2009). bk.rev. **Document type:** *Magazine, Consumer.*
Former titles (until 1996): Jungscharhelfer. Ausgabe A (0721-054X); (until 1969): Jungscharhelfer (0022-6467)
—CCC.
Published by: (Gemeindejugendwerk), Oncken Verlag GmbH, Muendener Str 13, Kassel, 34123, Germany. TEL 49-561-520050, FAX 49-561-5200550, zeitschriften@oncken.de, http://www.oncken.de. Ed. Kay Moritz. Circ: 1,600.

268 USA ISSN 1550-8870
JUNIORWAY BIBLE ACTIVITIES. Abbreviated title: J B A. Text in English. 1993. q. USD 3.19 per issue (effective 2008). back issues avail. **Document type:** *Magazine, Consumer.* **Description:** Provides learning activities to reinforce Christian education.
Published by: Urban Ministries, Inc., Dept #4870, PO Box 87618, Chicago, IL 60680. TEL 708-868-7100, 800-860-8642, FAX 708-868-7105, customerservice@urbanministries.com.

268 USA ISSN 1550-915X
JUNIORWAY. STUDENT MAGAZINE. Text in English. 198?. q. USD 3.49 per issue (effective 2009). back issues avail. **Document type:** *Magazine, Consumer.* **Description:** Contains contemporary stories, scripture passages, games and other activities, reader contributions, and suggestion for practical implementation.
Published by: Urban Ministries, Inc., Dept #4870, PO Box 87618, Chicago, IL 60680. TEL 708-868-7100, 800-860-8642, FAX 708-868-7105, customerservice@urbanministries.com.

268 USA ISSN 1550-9168
JUNIORWAY. TEACHER GUIDE. Text in English. 1982. q. USD 5.59 per issue (effective 2008). back issues avail. **Document type:** *Magazine, Consumer.* **Description:** Contains Bible background, sunday school teaching plans for ages 9-11.
Published by: Urban Ministries, Inc., Dept #4870, PO Box 87618, Chicago, IL 60680. TEL 708-868-7100, 800-860-8642, FAX 708-868-7105, customerservice@urbanministries.com.

200 340 DEU ISSN 0449-4393
JUS ECCLESIASTICUM; Beitraege zum evangelischen Kirchenrecht und zum Staatskirchenrecht. Text in German. 1965. irreg., latest vol.94, 2011. price varies. **Document type:** *Monographic series, Academic/Scholarly.*
Indexed: FR.
Published by: Mohr Siebeck GmbH & Co. KG, Wilhelmstr 18, Tuebingen, 72074, Germany. TEL 49-7071-9230, FAX 49-7071-51104, info@mohr.de.

▼ **JUST WOMEN.** *see* WOMEN'S INTERESTS

327.172 GBR ISSN 0306-7645
JUSTPEACE; journal of Pax Christi. Text in English. 1936. bi-m. free to members (effective 2009). adv. bk.rev. 4 p./no.; back issues avail. **Document type:** *Newsletter, Trade.* **Description:** Contains news items, letters, and calendar of events pertaining to Christian pacifism and the activities and members of the international Catholic peace movement.
Formerly: Pax Bulletin (0031-3319)
Related titles: Online - full text ed.: free (effective 2009).
Published by: Pax Christi, Christian Peace Education Ctr, St Joseph's, Watford Way, Hendon, London, NW4 4TY, United Kingdom. TEL 44-20-82034884, FAX 44-20-82035234, info@paxchristi.org.uk.

K F U K-K F U M - MAGASINET. (Kristelig Forening for Unge Kvinner, Kristelig Forening for Unge Menn) *see* CHILDREN AND YOUTH—For

200 NOR ISSN 0807-7525
K I F O PERSPEKTIV; forskning i kirke, religion, samfunn. (Kirkeforskning) Variant title: Kirkeforskning Perspektiv. Text in Norwegian. 1996. irreg., latest vol.21, 2010. price varies. back issues avail. **Document type:** *Monographic series, Academic/Scholarly.*
Published by: (Stiftelsen Kirkeforskning/Centre for Church Research), Tapir Akademisk Forlag A/S, Nardoveien 14, Trondheim, 7005, Norway. TEL 47-73-593210, FAX 47-73-593204, post@tapirforag.no, http://www.tapirforlag.no.

267 SWE ISSN 2000-4125
K R I S S; tidskrift om tro, hopp och kaerlek. Text in Swedish. 19??. s-a. SEK 100 (effective 2010). back issues avail. **Document type:** *Magazine, Consumer.*
Former titles (until 2009): KRISSaren; (until 2001): In Spe (1400-8637); (until 1994): Krissaren (1100-8563); (until 1988): KRISS Informerar
Related titles: Online - full text ed.
Published by: Kristna Studentroerelsen i Sverige/Student Christian Movement in Sweden, c/o Klas Corbelius, Baeckgatan 30, Norrkoeping, 60347, Sweden. TEL 46-73-3385863, exp@kriss.se. Ed. Jennie Wadman. Circ: 500.

230 SWE ISSN 1653-2856
K R I S S. SKRIFTSERIE. (Kristna Studentroerelsen i Sverige) Text in Swedish. 1969. irreg. back issues avail. **Document type:** *Monographic series, Consumer.*
Formerly (until 2005): K R I S S-Serien (0347-8017)
Published by: Kristna Studentroerelsen i Sverige/Student Christian Movement in Sweden, c/o Klas Corbelius, Baeckgatan 30, Norrkoeping, 60347, Sweden. TEL 46-73-3385863, exp@kriss.se.

200 DEU ISSN 1611-5015
K U - PRAXIS. (Konfirmandenunterricht) Text in German. 1973. irreg., latest vol.54, 2008. price varies. **Document type:** *Monographic series, Academic/Scholarly.*
Published by: Guetersloher Verlagshaus (Subsidiary of: Verlagsgruppe Random House GmbH), Carl-Miele-Str 214, Guetersloh, 33311, Germany. TEL 49-5241-74050, FAX 49-5241-740548, info@gtvh.de, http://www.gtvh.de.

200 MWI ISSN 1025-0956
KACHERE TEXTS. Text in English. 1979-1993; N.S. 1995. irreg. price varies. **Document type:** *Monographic series.*
Former titles (until 1995): Religion in Malawi (1025-0948); (until 1987): Sources for the Study of Religion in Malawi; (until 1980): Chancellor College. Department of Religious Studies. Staff Seminar Paper
Indexed: RILM.
Published by: Kachere Series, P O B 1037, Zomba, Malawi. Circ: 500 (controlled).

KACIC. *see* HISTORY—History Of Europe

230 GTM ISSN 1014-9341
BS543.A1
KAIROS. Text in Spanish. 1986. s-a. **Document type:** *Journal, Academic/Scholarly.*
Indexed: A01, A21, CA, F03, F04, RI-1, T02.
Published by: Seminario Teologico Centroamericano, Apdo Postal 213, Guatemala City, 01901, Guatemala. TEL 502-24710573, FAX 502-24735957, seteca@seteca.edu, http://www.seteca.edu/.

200 HRV ISSN 1846-4599
KAIROS (ENGLISH EDITION). Text in English. 2007. s-a. **Document type:** *Journal, Academic/Scholarly.*
Related titles: Online - full text ed.: free (effective 2011); Croatian ed.: ISSN 1846-4580.
Published by: Biblijski Institut, Kuslanova 21, Zagreb, Croatia. kairos@bizg.hr, http://www.bizg.hr.

200 DEU ISSN 0022-779X
KAISERSWERTHER MITTEILUNGEN. Text in German. 1836. 3/yr. free. bk.rev. illus. **Document type:** *Newsletter.*
Published by: Kaiserswerther Diakonie, Alte Landstr 179, Duesseldorf, 40489, Germany. TEL 49-211-4093551, FAX 49-211-4093554, http://www.kaiserswerther-diakonie.de. Eds. Cornelia Coenen Marx, Martin Klaemmt. Circ: 26,000.

200 IND ISSN 0022-8028
KALYAN. Text in Hindi. 1927. m. adv. back issues avail. **Document type:** *Magazine, Consumer.*
Published by: Gita Press, Sagdesh Psesad Jalan, Gorakhpur, Uttar Pradesh, India. admin@gitapress.orgg.

KANON. *see* LAW

262.981 340 ITA
KANONIKA. Text in English, French, German, Greek, Italian. 1992. irreg., latest vol.8, 1997. price varies. **Document type:** *Monographic series, Academic/Scholarly.* **Description:** Covers the law of the Eastern Churches.

Published by: (Pontificio Istituto Orientale/Pontificum Institutum Studiorum Orientalium), Edizioni Orientalia Cristiana (Subsidiary of: Pontificio Istituto Orientale/Pontificum Institutum Studiorum Orientalium), Piazza Santa Maria Maggiore 7, Rome, 00185, Italy. TEL 39-06-447417104, FAX 39-06-4465576, http://www.pio.urbe.it. Ed. George Nedungatt S J. Circ: 1,000.

348 DEU ISSN 0929-0680
KANONISTISCHE STUDIEN UND TEXTE. Text in German. 1963. irreg., latest vol.54, 2008. price varies. **Document type:** *Monographic series, Academic/Scholarly.*
Published by: Duncker und Humblot GmbH, Carl-Heinrich-Becker-Weg 9, Berlin, 12165, Germany. TEL 49-30-7900060, FAX 49-30-79000631, info@duncker-humblot.de.

272 726 NLD ISSN 1875-1644
KAPELLEN EN KRUISEN. Text in Dutch. 1992. q.
Formerly (until 2007): Stichting Kruisen en Kapellen in Limburg. Nieuwsbrief (2211-5080)
Related titles: Online - full text ed.: ISSN 1875-1652.
Published by: Stichting Kruisen en Kapellen in Limburg, Postbus 470, Roermond, 6040 AL, Netherlands. TEL 31-475-386781, FAX 31-475-331944, skkl@bisdom-roermond.nl, http://www.kruisenenkapellenlimburg.nl.

253.5 150 USA ISSN 1937-1667
BV4012.2
KARDIAGRAM. Text in English. 2007. q. free (effective 2011). back issues avail. **Document type:** *Journal, Academic/Scholarly.*
Description: A forum for sharing counseling and pastoral care news, information and ideas for clergy and laypeople in religious organizations.
Media: Online - full text.
Published by: Methodist Counseling & Consultation Services, The Terry Bldg, 1801 E 5th St, Ste 110, Charlotte, NC 28204. TEL 704-375-5354, FAX 704-375-3069, mccsc@bellsouth.net, http://www.mccsvs.org/MCCS/welcome.html.

200 DEU ISSN 0022-9245
KASSELER SONNTAGSBLATT; christliches Familienblatt fuer Deutschland. Text in German. 1879. w. EUR 1.70 newsstand/cover (effective 2007). adv. bk.rev. illus.; mkt. **Document type:** *Newspaper, Consumer.*
Published by: Kasseler Sonntagsblatt Verlagsgesellschaft mbH, Werner-Heisenberg-Str 7, Kassel, 34123, Germany. TEL 49-561-959250, FAX 49-561-9592514. Ed. Rolf Schwarz. Adv. contact Helmut Wiegand TEL 49-561-894499. B&W page EUR 1,728, color page EUR 3,024; trim 205 x 270. Circ: 11,928 (paid and controlled).

KATALOGE DER FRANCKESCHEN STIFTUNGEN. *see* HISTORY—History Of Europe

200 NLD ISSN 1573-5699
KEN UZELVE. Text in Dutch. 1938. m. adv. bk.rev. illus. **Description:** Masonic review of the Netherlands.
Formerly (until 2003): Algemeen Maconniek Tijdschrift (0002-5267)
Published by: Orde van Vrijmetselaren onder het Grootoosten der Nederlanden/Grand East of the Netherlands, Postbus 11525, The Hague, 2505 AM, Netherlands. TEL 31-70-3460046, FAX 31-70-3615919, orde@vrijmetselarij.nl, http://www.vrijmetselarij.nl. Ed. Willem Verstraaten.

200 952 JPN ISSN 0917-818X
KENKYUJOHO. Variant title: Nanzan Shukyo Bunka Kenkyujo Kenkyujoho. Text in Japanese. 1991. a. free. **Document type:** *Academic/Scholarly.*
Published by: Nanzan Institute for Religion and Culture, 18 Yamazato-cho, Showa-ku, Nagoya, 466-8673, Japan. TEL 81-52-8323111, FAX 81-52-8336157, nirc@ic.nanzan-u.ac.jp, http://www.nanzan-u.ac.jp/SHUBUNKEN/index.htm.

200 NLD ISSN 0165-2346
KERK EN THEOLOGIE. Text in Dutch. 1950. q. EUR 54 to individuals; EUR 66 to institutions; EUR 40.50 to students; EUR 16.60 newsstand/cover (effective 2008). adv. **Document type:** *Academic/Scholarly.* **Description:** Publishes articles on exegesis, hermeneutics, theological praxis and related topics.
Formerly: Onder Eigen Vaandel
Published by: Boekencentrum Uitgevers, Goudstraat 50, Postbus 29, Zoetermeer, 2700 AA, Netherlands. TEL 31-79-3615481, FAX 31-79-3615489, info@boekencentrum.nl, http://www.boekencentrum.nl. adv.: page EUR 205; 120 x 200. Circ: 600.

200 NLD ISSN 0023-0685
KERUGMA. Text in Dutch. 1957. q. EUR 37.50 domestic; EUR 39 in Belgium; EUR 11 newsstand/cover (effective 2009).
Indexed: CERDIC.
Published by: Gooi en Sticht, Postbus 5018, Kampen, 8260 GA, Netherlands. TEL 31-38-3392556, gens@kok.nl.

220 USA ISSN 0888-3513
KERUX; a journal of biblical - theological preaching. Text in English. 1986. 3/yr. USD 15 in North America; USD 20 elsewhere (effective 2000). bk.rev. back issues avail. **Document type:** *Journal, Academic/Scholarly.* **Description:** Intended for ministers, seminary students and Christian laypersons.
Media: Online - full text.
Indexed: A21, OTA, R&TA, RI-1.
Published by: Kerux Inc, 1131 Whispering Highlands Dr, Escondido, CA 92027. Ed. James T Dennison.

200 DEU ISSN 0023-0707
BR4
➤ **KERYGMA UND DOGMA**; Zeitschrift fuer theologische Forschung und kirchliche Lehre. Text in German. 1955. q. EUR 55 to individuals; EUR 110 to institutions; EUR 33 to students; EUR 17.90 newsstand/cover (effective 2011). adv. bk.rev. index. **Document type:** *Journal, Academic/Scholarly.*
Indexed: A21, A22, CERDIC, DIP, FR, IBR, IBZ, IZBG, OTA, R&TA, RI-1, RI-2.
—BLDSC (5090.370000), IE, Infotrieve, INIST. **CCC.**
Published by: Vandenhoeck und Ruprecht, Theaterstr 13, Goettingen, 37073, Germany. TEL 49-551-508440, FAX 49-551-5084422, info@v-r.de. Ed. Gunther Wenz. Circ: 900 (paid and controlled).

➤ **KEXUE YU WUSHENLUN/SCIENCE AND ATHEISM.** *see* SCIENCES: COMPREHENSIVE WORKS

➤ **KIDZ CHAT**; a magazine for God's kids. *see* CHILDREN AND YOUTH—For

➤ **KIERKEGAARD STUDIES.** *see* PHILOSOPHY

➤ **KIERKEGAARD STUDIES MONOGRAPH SERIES.** *see* PHILOSOPHY

268 NLD ISSN 0928-821X
KIND OP MAANDAG. Text in Dutch. 1982. 7/yr. EUR 395 to institutions (effective 2010). **Document type:** *Magazine, Trade.*
Incorporates (1989-1992): Kind aan Huis (0924-0292)
Published by: Vereniging N Z V, Postbus 1492, Amersfoort, 3800 BL, Netherlands. TEL 31-33-4606011, FAX 31-33-4606020, info@nzv.nl, http://www.nzv.nl.

268 NLD
KIND OP ZONDAG. Text in Dutch. 1930. 7/yr. EUR 89.90 (effective 2010). adv. bk.rev. 60 p./no.; **Document type:** *Magazine.* **Description:** Religious education for children.
Formerly (until 1997): Kind en Zondag (0023-1444)
Published by: Vereniging N Z V, Postbus 1492, Amersfoort, 3800 BL, Netherlands. TEL 31-33-4606011, FAX 31-33-4606020, info@nzv.nl, http://www.nzv.nl.

200 DEU
KINDERERLEBEN - KINDERTHEOLOGIE. Abbreviated title: KET. Text in German. 2006. irreg., latest vol.4, 2010. price varies. **Document type:** *Monographic series, Academic/Scholarly.*
Published by: I K S Garamond, Leutragraben 1, Jena, 07743, Germany. TEL 49-3641-460850, FAX 49-3641-460855, garamond@iks-jena.de.

200 DEU ISSN 1436-6657
DER KINDERGOTTESDIENST. Text in German. 1982. q. EUR 19.80 (effective 2011). **Document type:** *Magazine, Consumer.*
Formerly (until 1995): Kindergottesdienst - Lass Mich Hoeren (0177-056X); Which was formed by the merger of (1963-1982): Kindergottesdienst (0341-7190); (1950-1982): Lass Mich Hoeren (0177-0578)
Published by: Guetersloher Verlagshaus (Subsidiary of: Verlagsgruppe Random House GmbH), Carl-Miele-Str 214, Guetersloh, 33311, Germany. TEL 49-5241-74050, FAX 49-5241-740548, info@gtvh.de, http://www.gtvh.de. Ed. Bernd Schlueter.

KINSHIP. *see* SOCIAL SERVICES AND WELFARE

200 TZA
KIPALAPALA LEO. Text in English, Swahili. 1989 (vol.29). a. USD 1. **Document type:** *Magazine, Academic/Scholarly.* **Description:** Offers scholarly commentary on the African Synod in Tanzania.
Indexed: PLESA.
Published by: St. Paul's Senior Seminary, PO Box 325, Tabora, Tanzania. TEL 255-51-2532. Ed. Deac John Tenamwenye.

200 AUT
KIRCHE BUNT. Text in German. 1946. w. bk.rev. **Document type:** *Newsletter, Consumer.*
Former titles (until 1971): St. Poeltner Kirchenzeitung (0036-3170); (until 1960): Christophorus; (until 1959): Dioezese
Published by: Dioezese St. Poelten, Klostergasse 15, St. Poelten, N 3100, Austria. TEL 43-2742-3243390, FAX 43-2742-3243396, presse.stpoelten@kirche.at, http://www.dsp.at.

284 DEU
KIRCHE IN MARBURG; Mitteilungen der evangelischen und Katholischen Gemeinden. Text in German. 1936. m. free (effective 2005). adv. bk.rev. illus. **Document type:** *Newspaper, Consumer.*
Formerly: Gemeindebote (0016-6103)
Published by: Gesamtverband der Evangelischen Kirchengemeinden in Marburg, Barfuessertor 34, Marburg, 35037, Germany. TEL 49-6421-91120, FAX 49-6421-911230, redaktion@ekmr.de, http://www.ekmr.de. Circ: 26,600 (controlled). **Co-sponsor:** Katholische Pfarrgemeinde in Marburg-Stadt.

200 DEU
➤ **KIRCHE - KONFESSION - RELIGION.** Text in German. 1962. irreg., latest vol.55, 2009. price varies. **Document type:** *Monographic series, Academic/Scholarly.*
Formerly (until 2001): Kirche und Konfession (0453-929X)
Published by: (Konfessionskundliches Institut des Evangelischen Bundes), V & R Unipress GmbH (Subsidiary of: Vandenhoeck und Ruprecht), Robert-Bosch-Breite 6, Goettingen, 37079, Germany. TEL 49-551-5084303, FAX 49-551-5084333, info@vr-unipress.de, http://www.v-r.de/en/publisher/unipress.

➤ **KIRCHE UND RECHT.** *see* LAW

➤ **KIRCHE UND RECHT**; Zeitschrift fuer die kirchliche und staatliche Praxis. *see* LAW

➤ **KIRCHEN IM LAENDLICHEN RAUM.** *see* ARCHITECTURE

➤ **KIRCHENMUSIKALISCHE NACHRICHTEN.** *see* MUSIC

230 DEU ISSN 1862-5142
KIRCHLICHE ORGANISATIONEN ERFOLGREICH FUEHREN. Text in German. 2006. irreg. **Document type:** *Trade.*
Published by: Bergmoser und Hoeller Verlag GmbH, Karl-Friedrich-Str 76, Aachen, 52072, Germany. TEL 49-241-93888123, FAX 49-241-93888134, kontakt@buhv.de, http://www.buhv.de.

KIRCHLICHE ZEITGESCHICHTE; Internationale Halbjahresschrift fuer Theologie und Geschichtswissenschaft. *see* HISTORY—History Of Europe

200 DEU ISSN 1866-8771
KIRCHLICHE ZEITGESCHICHTE. MITTEILUNGEN. Text in German. 1978. a. EUR 12 (effective 2009). **Document type:** *Journal, Academic/Scholarly.*
Formerly (until 2007): Evangelische Arbeitsgemeinschaft fuer Kirchliche Zeitgeschichte. Mitteilungen (0949-5908)
Published by: Evangelische Arbeitsgemeinschaft fuer Kirchliche Zeitgeschichte, Geschwister-Scholl-Platz 1, Munich, 80539, Germany. TEL 49-89-21802828, FAX 49-89-21805339, karl-heinz.fix@evtheol.uni-muenchen.de, http://www.ekd.de/zeitgeschichte/index.html.

200 DEU ISSN 0023-1827
KIRCHLICHES AMTSBLATT FUER DAS BISTUM ESSEN. Text in German. 1958. s-m. looseleaf. index. **Document type:** *Newsletter, Consumer.*
Published by: Bischoefliches Generalvikariat Essen, Zwoelfling 16, Essen, 45127, Germany. TEL 49-201-2204266, FAX 49-201-2204507, presse@bistum-essen.de, http://www.bistum-essen.de. Circ: 2,200.

262.3 DEU
KIRCHLICHES AMTSBLATT FUER DAS BISTUM TRIER. Text in German. 1853. m. index. back issues avail. **Document type:** *Newsletter, Consumer.* **Description:** Provides official documentation of diocesan regulations, laws and news.
Formerly (until 1965): Kirchlicher Amtsanzeiger fuer die Dioezese Trier
Published by: Bischoefliches Generalvikariat Trier, Hinter dem Dom 6, Trier, 54290, Germany. TEL 49-651-71050, FAX 49-651-7105498, bistum-trier@bistum-trier.de, http://www.bistum-trier.de. Circ: 2,700 (controlled).

200 JPN ISSN 0288-6138
KIRISUTOKYO RONSO/INSTITUTE FOR RESEARCH OF CHRISTIAN CULTURE. BULLETIN. Text in Japanese. 1959. a. **Document type:** *Bulletin, Academic/Scholarly.*
Supersedes in part (in 1967): Shoin Joshi Gakuin Daigaku. Kenkyu Kiyo (0288-612X); Which was formerly (until 1966): Shoin Tanki Daigaku. Kenkyu Kiyo (0288-6111)
Published by: Kobe Shoin Joshi Gakuin Daigaku, Kobe Shoin Joshi Gakuin Tanki Daigaku, Gakujutsu Kenkyukai/Kobe Shoin Women's University and College, Society for Academic Research, 1-2-1, Shinohara-Obanoyama- cho, Nada-ku, Kobe, 657-0015, Japan. TEL 81-78-8826125, FAX 81-78-8822656, http://ksw.shoin.ac.jp/research/index.html.

058.82 NOR ISSN 0023-186X
AP45
KIRKE OG KULTUR. Text in Norwegian. 1894. 4/yr. NOK 385 to individuals; NOK 698 to institutions; NOK 310 to students (effective 2010). bk.rev. index. back issues avail. **Document type:** *Journal, Academic/Scholarly.* **Description:** Presents essays and debate on topics within culture, ethics, religion, philosophy and society.
Formerly (until 1919): For Kirke og Kultur (0801-8456); Which incorporates (1877-1893): Luthersk Ugeskrift (0805-6668); (1896-1917): Excelsior (0805-6641)
Related titles: Online - full text ed.: ISSN 1504-3002. 2004. NOK 798 (effective 2010).
Indexed: BEL&L, DIP, IBR, IBZ, MLA, MLA-IB, NAA.
Published by: Universitetsforlaget AS/Scandinavian University Press (Subsidiary of: Aschehoug & Co.), Sehesteds Gate 3, P O Box 508, Sentrum, Oslo, 0105, Norway. TEL 47-24-147500, FAX 47-24-147501, post@universitetsforlaget.no. Eds. Inge Loenning, Kjetil Hafstad. Circ: 900.

274.81 NOR ISSN 0800-4102
KIRKEAKTUELT. Text in Norwegian. 1977. q. NOK 110 (effective 2011). adv. **Document type:** *Magazine, Consumer.*
Related titles: CD-ROM ed.: ISSN 0809-8441. 2006; Print ed.: ISSN 1890-9205. 2005.
Published by: Den Norske Kirke, Kirkeraadet/Church of Norway, PO Box 799, Sentrum, Oslo, 0106, Norway. TEL 47-23-081200, post.kirkeradet@kirken.no. Ed. Siv Thompsen. Circ: 17,800.

270 DNK ISSN 0450-3171
BR980
KIRKEHISTORISKE SAMLINGER. Text in Multiple languages. 1849. a. DKK 220; DKK 140 to students (effective 2009). cum.index: 1849-2006. back issues avail. **Document type:** *Monographic series, Academic/Scholarly.*
Indexed: MLA-IB, PCI, RASB.
—INIST.
Published by: Selskabet for Danmarks Kirkehistorie, c/o Afdeling for Kirkehistorie, Koebmagergade 44-46, Copenhagen V, 1150, Denmark. csj@teol.ku.dk, http://www.teol.ku/afd/akh.

200 DNK ISSN 1601-8230
KIRKEN I DAG/NEWS FROM KIRKEFONDET. Text in Danish. 1990. q. DKK 195; DKK 60 per issue (effective 2009). adv. back issues avail. **Document type:** *Magazine, Consumer.* **Description:** Matters concerning church life, church and society, lithurgy, church art and architecture, organisation of the church.
Formerly (until 2002): Nyt fra Kirkefondet
Published by: Kirkefondet, Peter Bangs Vej 1 F, Frederiksberg, 2000, Denmark. TEL 45-33-730033, FAX 45-33-730030, kirkefondet@kirkefondet.dk. Circ: 3,000.

268 DNK ISSN 1602-2785
KIRKEN UNDERVISER. Text in Danish. 1961. 4/yr. DKK 235 (effective 2009). adv. bk.rev. **Document type:** *Magazine, Academic/Scholarly.*
Former titles (until 2000): Kirkens Undervisning (0900-1433); (until 1985): Religionspaedagogisk Orientering, Episkopet (0901-425X); (until 1976): Episkopet (0105-6867)
Related titles: Online - full text ed.
Published by: Kirkefaglig Videreuddannelse, Peter Bangs Vej 1, Frederiksberg, 2000, Denmark. TEL 45-38-384120, FAX 45-38-111259, kirkefaglig-videreuddannelse@kirkefaglig-videreuddannelse.dk, http://www.kirkefaglig-videreuddannelse.dk. Ed. Helle Marie Danielsen. Circ: 1,000.

200 FIN ISSN 1459-2681
KIRKON TUTKIMUSKESKUS. JULKAISUJA. Text in Finnish. 1969. irreg. back issues avail. **Document type:** *Monographic series, Academic/Scholarly.*
Former titles (until 2003): Kirkon Tutkimuskeskus. Sarja A (0781-898X); (until 1985): Kirkon Tutkimuslaitos. Sarja A (0355-1423)
Related titles: Online - full text ed.: ISSN 1459-2703. 2003; ◆ Series: Research Institute of the Lutheran Church in Finland. Publications. ISSN 0355-144X.
Published by: Kirkon Tutkimuskeskus/Research Institute of the Lutheren Church of Finland, PO Box 239, Tampere, 33101, Finland. TEL 358-3-31233400, FAX 358-3-31233450, ktk@evl.fi, http://www.evl.fi/kkh/ktk/index.htm.

KLASSE, DIE EVANGELISCHE SCHULE. *see* EDUCATION

▼ **KLEINE LEUTE - GROSSER GOTT**; 20 Stundenentwuerfe fuer 3- bis 6-Jaehrige. *see* CHILDREN AND YOUTH—About

200 DEU
KLEINE TEXTE DER FRANCKESCHEN STIFTUNGEN. Text in German. 1995. irreg., latest vol.13, 2009. price varies. **Document type:** *Monographic series, Academic/Scholarly.*
Published by: Franckesche Stiftungen zu Halle, Franckeplatz 1, Haus 37, Halle, 06110, Germany. TEL 49-345-2127499, FAX 49-345-2127433, verlag@francke-halle.de, http://www.francke-halle.de.

R

268 USA ISSN 1939-0742
KNOWN. Text in English. 2008. q. USD 4.50 per issue (effective 2009). back issues avail. **Document type:** *Handbook/Manual/Guide, Trade.* **Description:** Bible study with a holistic approach to spiritual development.
Related titles: Online - full text ed.
Published by: LifeWay Christian Resources, 1 Lifeway Plz, Nashville, TN 37234. TEL 615-251-2000, 800-458-2772, FAX 615-251-5933, customerservice@lifeway.com.

268 USA ISSN 1943-6017
KNOWN E-LEADER GUIDE. Text in English. 2008. q. USD 6.50 per issue (effective 2009). back issues avail. **Document type:** *Handbook/Manual/Guide, Trade.* **Description:** Designed to provide a holistic approach to student spiritual development helping students know God, own their faith, and make their faith known.
Media: Online - full content.
Published by: LifeWay Christian Resources, 1 Lifeway Plz, Nashville, TN 37234. TEL 615-251-2000, 800-233-1123, FAX 615-251-5933, customerservice@lifeway.com, http://www.lifeway.com.

268 USA ISSN 1939-0734
KNOWN LEADER. Text in English. 2008. q. USD 6.50 per issue (effective 2009). **Document type:** *Journal, Trade.*
Related titles: Online - full text ed.
Published by: LifeWay Christian Resources, 1 Lifeway Plz, Nashville, TN 37234. TEL 615-251-2000, 800-458-2772, FAX 615-251-5933, customerservice@lifeway.com.

268 USA ISSN 1943-6033
KNOWN MID-WEEK EVENT. Text in English. 2008. q. USD 29.95 per issue (effective 2009). **Document type:** *Magazine, Trade.* **Description:** Provides a holistic approach to student spiritual development by helping the students to know god, own their faith, and make their faith known.
Media: Online - full content.
Published by: LifeWay Christian Resources, 1 Lifeway Plz, Nashville, TN 37234. TEL 615-251-2000, 800-233-1123, 800-458-2772, FAX 615-251-5933, customerservice@lifeway.com, http://www.lifeway.com.

268 USA ISSN 1943-605X
KNOWN QUARTERLY BUNDLE. Text in English. 2008. q. USD 149.95 per issue (effective 2009). back issues avail. **Document type:** *Journal, Trade.* **Description:** Designed to provide a holistic approach to student spiritual development helping students know God, own their faith, and make their faith known.
Media: Online - full content.
Published by: LifeWay Christian Resources, 1 Lifeway Plz, Nashville, TN 37234. TEL 615-251-2000, 800-233-1123, FAX 615-251-5933, customerservice@lifeway.com, http://www.lifeway.com.

KOELNER VEROEFFENTLICHUNGEN ZUR RELIGIONSGESCHICHTE. *see* HISTORY—History Of Europe

230 DEU ISSN 1864-886X
KOMMENTARE ZU SCHRIFTEN LUTHERS. Text in German. 2007. irreg., latest vol.2, 2009. price varies. **Document type:** *Monographic series, Academic/Scholarly.*
Published by: Mohr Siebeck GmbH & Co. KG, Wilhelmstr 18, Tuebingen, 72074, Germany. TEL 49-7071-9230, FAX 49-7071-51104, info@mohr.de.

220 DEU
▼ **KOMMENTARE ZUR APOKRYPHEN LITERATUR.** Text in German. 2010. irreg. price varies. **Document type:** *Monographic series, Academic/Scholarly.*
Published by: Vandenhoeck und Ruprecht, Theaterstr 13, Goettingen, 37073, Germany. TEL 49-551-508440, FAX 49-551-5084422, info@v-r.de.

268 USA ISSN 1945-0117
KONTAGIOUS. Text in English. 2008. q. USD 3 per issue (effective 2008). adv. **Document type:** *Magazine, Consumer.*
Related titles: Online - full text ed.: ISSN 1945-0125.
Published by: DaRon Publishing, PO Box 29484, Charlotte, NC 28229. TEL 866-471-8805, info@kontagiousmagazine.com.

200 DEU ISSN 0949-7277
KONTAKTE (TUEBINGEN); Beitraege zum religioesen Zeitgespraech. Text in German. 1995. irreg., latest vol.12, 2003. price varies. back issues avail. **Document type:** *Monographic series, Academic/Scholarly.* **Description:** Studies various contemporary theological topics.
Published by: A. Francke Verlag GmbH, Dischinger Weg 5, Tuebingen, 72070, Germany. TEL 49-7071-97970, FAX 49-7071-979711, info@francke.de, http://www.francke.de.

200 DEU ISSN 0724-6366
KONTEXTE; Neue Beitraege zur historischen und systematischen Theologie. Text in German. 1983. irreg., latest vol.37, 2004. price varies. **Document type:** *Monographic series, Academic/Scholarly.*
Published by: Peter Lang GmbH (Subsidiary of: Peter Lang Publishing Group), Eschborner Landstr 42-50, Frankfurt Am Main, 60489, Germany. TEL 49-69-7807050, FAX 49-69-78070550, zentrale.frankfurt@peterlang.com.

200 POL ISSN 1233-9261
KOSCIOL WSPOLCZESNY, ALTERNATYWA DLA CHRZESCIJANSTWA; miesiecznik religijny. Text in Polish. 1995. m. PLZ 1.80 newsstand/cover. back issues avail.
Published by: Faktor Sp. z o.o., ul Ksiecia Wladyslawa Opolskiego 3 a, Kety, 32650, Poland. TEL 48-33-453888. Ed. Jozef Gaweda. Circ: 5,000.

299.93 DNK ISSN 0107-7902
KOSMOS (DANISH EDITION). Text in Danish. 1967. 10/yr. DKK 420 (effective 2009). adv. bk.rev. **Document type:** *Magazine, Consumer.* **Description:** Includes articles on spiritual science based on the work of the Danish writer, Martinus.
Formerly: Kontakt med Martinus Instituttet
Related titles: Online - full text ed.; Esperanto ed.: ISSN 1600-4116. 1994; Swedish ed.: ISSN 0107-7910. 1958. SEK 490 (effective 2009); Spanish ed.: ISSN 1398-3563; English ed.: ISSN 0107-7929. 1978; German ed.: ISSN 0107-7937. 19??.
Indexed: ChemAb.
Published by: Martinus Institut, Mariendalsvej 94, Frederiksberg, 2000, Denmark. TEL 45-38-346280, FAX 45-33-346180, info@martinus.dk, http://www.martinus.dk.

200 CZE ISSN 0023-4613
KRESTANSKA REVUE. Text in Czech. 1927-1939; resumed 1946. 6/yr. CZK 250 domestic; EUR 30 in Europe; USD 35 elsewhere (effective 2009). bk.rev. **Document type:** *Magazine, Consumer.*
Indexed: CERDIC.
Published by: Oikumene Akademicka Y M C A, Cerna 9, Prague 1, 11555, Czech Republic. predplatne@krestanskarevue.cz. Circ: 1,800 (paid).

260 DNK ISSN 1901-7766
KRISTENT PERSPEKTIV. Text in Danish. 1997. q. DKK 100 (effective 2009). **Document type:** *Magazine, Consumer.* **Description:** Current religious and ethical problems from a conservative Christian point of view.
Published by: Perspektiv Bibelskole, Ahornsvej 36, Odense SV, 5250, Denmark. TEL 45-66-175888. Ed. Carsten Thomsem.

200 DNK ISSN 0106-6749
KRITISK FORUM FOR PRAKTISK TEOLOGI. Text in Danish. 1980. q. DKK 275; DKK 225 to students (effective 2008). back issues avail. **Document type:** *Monographic series, Academic/Scholarly.* **Description:** Theme-based quarterly aimed at ministers and theologians in the Christian faith.
Related titles: Online - full text ed.
Indexed: RILM.
Published by: Anis Forlaget, Frederiksberg Alle 10 A, Frederiksberg C, 1820, Denmark. TEL 45-33-249250, FAX 45-33-250607, info@anis.dk. Ed. Jesper Stange.

220 SWE ISSN 1104-4969
KROENIKA; bibeln till alla. Text in Swedish. 1993. q.
Published by: Bibeln till Alla (BTA), Siktgatan 10, Vallingby, 16226, Sweden.

270 NLD ISSN 2210-5719
KRONIEK SINT AGATHA. Text in Dutch. 2003. q.
Former titles (until 2010): Kroniek Sint Aegten (1872-5260); (until 2006): Kroniek Sint Agatha (1571-6856)
Published by: (Stichting Sint Aegten), Stichting Erfgoedcentrum Nederlands Kloosterleven, Kloosterlaan 24, Sint Agatha, 5435 XD, Netherlands. TEL 31-485-311007, info@erfgoedkloosterleven.nl.

KRUT; kritisk utbildningstidskrift. *see* EDUCATION

322.1 DEU
KURIER (LIESBORN); der christlichen Mitte. Text in German. 1988. m. bk.rev. 4 p./no.; **Document type:** *Newsletter, Consumer.*
Published by: Christliche Mitte, Lippstaedter Str 42, Liesborn, 59329, Germany. TEL 49-2523-8388, FAX 49-2523-6138, info@christliche-mitte.de. Ed. Adelgunde Mertensacker. Circ: 20,000.

KVINNOR & FUNDAMENTALISM. *see* WOMEN'S INTERESTS

284.1 SWE ISSN 1651-405X
KYRKANS TIDNING. Text in Swedish. 1982. 46/yr. SEK 620 (effective 2006). adv. bk.rev. illus. 12 p./no. 6 cols./p.; **Document type:** *Newspaper, Consumer.*
Formerly (until 2002): Svenska Kyrkans Tidning (0280-4603); Which was formed by the merger of (1942-1982): Vaar Kyrka (0042-2673); (1971-1982): M E D (0012-1940); (1973-1982): Aktuellt; (1966-1982): Foersamlings- och Pastoratfoervaltning (0015-5284)
Related titles: Audio cassette/tape ed.; Includes: Mission (Uppsala). ISSN 1402-8298. 1961. free (effective 2004).
Indexed: RILM.
Published by: (Svenska Kyrkan/Church of Sweden), Svenska Kyrkans Press AB, Goetgatan 22A, PO Box 15412, Stockholm, 10465, Sweden. TEL 46-8-4622800, FAX 46-8-6445604, info@svkpress.com, http://www.svkpress.com. Eds. Elisabeth Sandlund TEL 46-8-4622802, Morgan Ahlberg TEL 46-8-4622803, Dag Tuvelius TEL 46-8-4622801. adv.: page SEK 44,200; trim 250 x 370. Circ: 45,700.

209 SWE ISSN 0085-2619
BR140
KYRKOHISTORISK AARSSKRIFT. Text in English, Swedish; Summaries in English, French, German. 1900. a. SEK 175 membership; SEK 125 to students; SEK 195 per issue (effective 2007). adv. bk.rev. cum index: 1900-2000. back issues avail. **Document type:** *Journal, Consumer.*
Related titles: ◆ Series of: Svenska Kyrkohistoriska Foereningen. Skrifter II, Ny Foeljd. ISSN 0491-6786.
Indexed: A21, BAS, CA, DIP, HistAb, IBR, IBZ, MLA-IB, NAA, P30, RASB, RI-1, RI-2, T02.
Published by: Svenska Kyrkohistoriska Foereningen/Swedish Society of Church History, PO Box 511, Uppsala, 75126, Sweden. Ed. Anders Jarlert. Circ: 1,000.

KYRKOMUSIKERNAS TIDNING. *see* MUSIC

266.2 SWE ISSN 1402-3563
L M F. Text in Danish, Norwegian, Swedish. 1902. bi-m. SEK 60 (effective 1997). bk.rev. illus.
Formerly (until 1996): Meddelande till L M F (0345-7842)
Published by: Laerarnas Missionsfoerening, Chapmansgatan 6, Goeteborg, 41454, Sweden. TEL 46-31-12-54-40, FAX 46-31-12-54-40. Eds. Margareta Burgen, Margareta Hoverstam. Circ: 2,000.

200 GTM ISSN 1012-2982
BR1642.L29
LATIN AMERICAN PASTORAL ISSUES. Text in Spanish. 1988. a. USD 6 (effective 1997). bk.rev.
Published by: Centro Evangelico Latinoamericano de Estudios Pastorales, Apdo 1710, Guatemala City, 01901, Guatemala. FAX 502-2323455. Ed. Dennis A Smith. **Subscr. to:** 8424 N W 56th St, PO Box GUA 629, Miami, FL 33166.

LAVAL THEOLOGIQUE ET PHILOSOPHIQUE. *see* PHILOSOPHY

LAW & JUSTICE; the Christian law review. *see* LAW

207.2 UGA ISSN 0047-424X
LEADERSHIP; a magazine for Christian leaders in Africa. Text in English. 1956. bi-m. USD 3.50; USD 18 in Africa; USD 24 elsewhere. bk.rev. illus.; stat. **Document type:** *Newspaper.* **Description:** Examines social, moral and religious issues for the purposes of forming and informing Christian youth and adults.
Published by: (Comboni Missionaries), Leadership Publications, PO Box 2522, Kampala, Uganda. TEL 256-41-221358, FAX 256-41-222407. Ed., R&P Rev. Raphael Dellagiacoma. Circ: 5,200 (paid).

LEADERSHIP. *see* BUSINESS AND ECONOMICS—Management

280 USA ISSN 0199-7661
BV4000
LEADERSHIP (CAROL STREAM); a practical journal for church leaders. Text in English. 1980. q. USD 22 domestic; USD 35 foreign (effective 2008). adv. bibl.; illus. back issues avail. **Document type:** *Magazine, Consumer.* **Description:** Provides leaders with insight and inspiration from ministry innovators, visionaries, sages and scholars - those who know and understand the role of a leader.
Related titles: Microfiche ed.; Online - full text ed.: ISSN 1551-1804.
Indexed: A21, A22, A26, CCR, ChrPI, E08, G06, G07, G08, I05, R&TA, R05, RI-1, RI-2, RILM, S09.
—CCC.
Published by: Christianity Today International, 465 Gundersen Dr, Carol Stream, IL 60188. TEL 630-260-6200, FAX 630-260-0114. Eds. Marshall Shelley, Harold B Smith. R&P Dawn Zemke. Adv. contact Brian Ondracek TEL 630-260-6202. B&W page USD 4,797, color page USD 5,330; trim 8 x 10.75. Circ: 48,000. **Subscr. to:** CDS, PO Box 37060, Boone, IA 50037-0060.

200 CHE
LEBEN; Monatszeitschrift der Fokolar-Bewegung in der Schweiz. Text in German. 1974. m. back issues avail. **Document type:** *Magazine, Consumer.*
Published by: (Fokolar-Bewegung Schweiz), Verlag Neue Stadt, Verenastr 7, Zuerich, 8038, Switzerland. TEL 41-44-4826011, FAX 41-44-4826017, verlag@neuestadt.ch, http://www.neuestadt.ch.

230 USA ISSN 1554-8759
BX9401
LEBEN; a journal of reformed life. Text in English. 2005. q. USD 9.95 (effective 2006). adv. **Document type:** *Journal, Consumer.* **Description:** Contains Christian history and biography, told through lives of reformers and patriots, missionaries and martyrs.
Published by: City Seminary Press, 2150 River Plaza Dr, Ste 150, Sacramento, CA 95833. TEL 916-473-8866 ext 6, editor@leben.us, http://www.cityseminary.org/. Ed. Wayne Johnson. adv.: color page USD 500; trim 7.375 x 9.625.

220 DEU ISSN 1435-6465
LEBENS- UND GLAUBENSWELTEN. Text in German. 1998. irreg., latest 2009. price varies. **Document type:** *Monographic series, Academic/Scholarly.*
Published by: Shaker Verlag GmbH, Kaiserstr 100, Herzogenrath, 52134, Germany. TEL 49-2407-95960, FAX 49-2407-95969, info@shaker.de.

▼ **LEBENSLUST**; Menschen, Leben, Glauben. *see* GENERAL INTEREST PERIODICALS—Germany

LECTIO DIFFICILIOR. *see* WOMEN'S INTERESTS

200 225 FRA ISSN 0750-1919
LECTIO DIVINA. Text in French. 1946. irreg. **Document type:** *Journal, Academic/Scholarly.*
Indexed: IZBG.
Published by: Editions du Cerf, 29 Boulevard La Tour Maubourg, Paris, 75340 Cedex 07, France. http://www.editionsducerf.fr.

252 USA ISSN 1938-5552
LECTIONARY PREACHING WORKBOOK. Text in English. 1984. a. **Document type:** *Handbook/Manual/Guide, Trade.* **Description:** Provides lectionary texts, Biblical commentary, theological reflections and creative preaching ideas to assist busy pastors starting points in developing weekly church sermons.
Published by: C S S Publishing Co., 517 S Main St, Lima, OH 45804. TEL 419-227-1818, 800-241-4056, FAX 419-228-9184, info@csspub.com, http://www.csspub.com.

252 USA ISSN 1938-7377
LECTIONARY TALES FOR THE PULPIT. Text in English. 1994. a. price varies. back issues avail. **Document type:** *Monographic series, Trade.* **Description:** Includes inspirational stories and homilies to provide spiritual enrichment and assist in sermon development.
Related titles: Online - full text ed.
Published by: C S S Publishing Co., 517 S Main St, Lima, OH 45804. TEL 419-227-1818, 800-241-4056, FAX 419-228-9184, info@csspub.com, http://www.csspub.com. Pub. Wesley T Runk.

252 USA ISSN 1940-8730
LECTIONARY WORSHIP AIDS. Text in English. 1984. a. price varies. back issues avail. **Document type:** *Monographic series.* **Description:** Features several prayers relating to the assigned scriptural passages for every Sunday and major observance in Cycle C of the revised common lectionary.
Related titles: Online - full text ed.
Published by: C S S Publishing Co., 517 S Main St, Lima, OH 45804. TEL 419-227-1818, 800-241-4056, FAX 419-228-9184, info@csspub.com, http://www.csspub.com. Pub. Wesley T Runk.

252 USA ISSN 1938-5560
LECTIONARY WORSHIP WORKBOOK. Text in English. 1988. a. price varies. back issues avail. **Document type:** *Monographic series, Trade.*
Related titles: Online - full text ed.
Published by: C S S Publishing Co., 517 S Main St, Lima, OH 45804. TEL 419-227-1818, 800-241-4056, FAX 419-228-9184, info@csspub.com, http://www.csspub.com. Pub. Wesley T Runk.

200 LSO
LESELINYANA LA LESOTHO/LESOTHO CHRISTIAN NEWSPAPER. Text occasionally in English. 1863. fortn. adv. bk.rev. **Document type:** *Newspaper.*
Published by: Lesotho Evangelical Church, PO Box 7, Morija, 190, Lesotho. TEL 266-360244, FAX 266-360005. Ed., Adv. contact Aaron B Thoahlane. Circ: 7,500.

230 USA
LETTER FROM PLYMOUTH ROCK. Text in English. 1980. bi-m. looseleaf. bk.rev. charts; illus.; stat. back issues avail. **Document type:** *Newsletter.* **Description:** Looks at life from a biblical perspective.
Published by: Plymouth Rock Foundation, 1120 Long Pond Rd, Plymouth, MA 02360. TEL 603-876-4685, 800-210-1620, FAX 603-876-4128, info@plymrock.org, http://plymrock.org. Ed. Rus Walton. Circ: 15,000.

266 FRA ISSN 1247-0287
LE LEVANT (FRENCH EDITION). Text in French. 1923. q. bk.rev. illus. **Document type:** *Newsletter.* **Description:** Contains news on partner churches in the Middle East (Lebanon, Syria, Egypt, Iran, Algeria, Armenia) and on Christian - Muslim relations.

Related titles: German ed.: Le Levant (German Edition). ISSN 1247-0279.
Published by: Action Chretienne en Orient, 7 rue du General Offenstein, Strasbourg, 67100, France. TEL 33-3-88391155, FAX 33-3-88402798, aco@media-net.fr. Ed. Ernest Reichert. Circ: 10,000 (paid).

266 NLD ISSN 1871-5958
LEVEN.NU. Variant title: Leven Punt Nu. Text in Dutch. 1997. s-a. **Document type:** *Magazine, Consumer.*
Formerly (until 2003): Ongeloooflijk! (1387-9901)
Published by: Uitgeverij H. Medema, Postbus 113, Vaassen, 8170 AC, Netherlands. TEL 31-578-574995, FAX 31-578-573099, info@medema.nl, http://www.medema.nl.

230 USA
BR1
➤ **LEXINGTON THEOLOGICAL QUARTERLY (ONLINE).** Text in English. 1909. q. bk.rev. **Document type:** *Journal, Academic/Scholarly.* **Description:** Contains lectures and sermons delivered within the Seminary community and scholarly papers prepared by the faculty, other scholars and students.
Formerly: Lexington Theological Quarterly (Print) (0024-1628); Which superseded (in 1966): The College of the Bible Quarterly (0160-8770)
Related titles: E-mail ed.: free to qualified personnel (effective 2011) (from PQC).
Indexed: A21, A22, CERDIC, MLA-IB, OTA, R&TA, RI-1, RI-2.
—BLDSC (5185.720000), IE, Ingenta.
Published by: Lexington Theological Seminary, 631 S Limestone St, Lexington, KY 40508. TEL 859-252-0361, 866-296-6087, sway@lextheo.edu.

230 GBR ISSN 0953-7805
LIBERTARIAN ALLIANCE. RELIGIOUS NOTES. Text in English. 1990. irreg., latest 1999. back issues avail. **Document type:** *Monographic series, Trade.*
Related titles: Online - full text ed.: ISSN 2042-2792. free (effective 2009).
Published by: Libertarian Alliance, 2 Lansdowne Row, Ste 35, London, W1J 6HL, United Kingdom. TEL 44-7956-472199. Ed. Nigel Meek.

261 USA ISSN 0024-2055
BX6101
LIBERTY (HAGERSTOWN); a magazine of religious freedom. Text in English. 1906. bi-m. USD 7.95 (effective 2008). adv. bk.rev. illus. index, cum.index. reprints avail. **Document type:** *Magazine, Consumer.*
Related titles: Microform ed.: (from PQC); Online - full text ed.
Indexed: A22, CCR, HRIR, P06.
—Ingenta.
Published by: (International Religious Liberty Association (I R L A)/Asociacion Internacional de Libertad Religiosa), Review and Herald Publishing Association, 55 W Oak Ridge Dr, Hagerstown, MD 21740. TEL 301-393-4037, info@rhpa.org, http://www.rhpa.org. Ed. Lincoln Steed. Circ: 200,000.

LIBERTY UNIVERSITY LAW REVIEW. *see* LAW

LIBRARY LINES. *see* LIBRARY AND INFORMATION SCIENCES

221 GBR
THE LIBRARY OF HEBREW BIBLE/OLD TESTAMENT STUDIES. Text in English. 1976. irreg., latest vol.484, 2010. price varies. back issues avail. **Document type:** *Monographic series, Academic/Scholarly.* **Description:** Covers cutting-edge international scholarship in biblical studies and has attracted leading authors and editors in the field.
Formerly (until 2005): Journal for the Study of the Old Testament. Supplement Series (0309-0787)
Indexed: A22, IZBG, OTA, RI-2.
—IE, Ingenta. **CCC.**
Published by: Continuum International Publishing Group, The Tower Bldg, 11 York Rd, London, SE1 7NX, United Kingdom. TEL 44-20-79220880, FAX 44-20-79287894, info@continuumbooks.com. Eds. Andrew Mein, Claudia Camp.

225 GBR
THE LIBRARY OF NEW TESTAMENT STUDIES. Text in English. 1980. irreg., latest vol.370, 2010. price varies. back issues avail. **Document type:** *Monographic series, Academic/Scholarly.* **Description:** Aims to aspects of new testament study including historical perspectives, social-scientific and literary theory, and theological, cultural and contextual approaches.
Formerly (until 2007): Journal for the Study of the New Testament. Supplement Series (0143-5108)
Indexed: A22, IZBG, PCI, RI-2.
—IE, Ingenta. **CCC.**
Published by: Continuum International Publishing Group, The Tower Bldg, 11 York Rd, London, SE1 7NX, United Kingdom. TEL 44-20-79220880, FAX 44-20-79287894, info@continuumbooks.com.

LIBRARY OF PHILOSOPHY AND RELIGION. *see* PHILOSOPHY

200 GBR
LIBRARY OF SECOND TEMPLE STUDIES. Text in English. 1988. irreg. **Document type:** *Monographic series, Academic/Scholarly.*
Formerly (until 2004): Journal for the Study of the Pseudepigrapha. Supplement Series (0951-8215)
Related titles: ◆ Supplement to: Journal for the Study of the Pseudepigrapha. ISSN 0951-8207.
Indexed: IZBG.
—IE, Ingenta.
Published by: T & T Clark Ltd. (Subsidiary of: Continuum International Publishing Group), 59 George St, Edinburgh, EH2 2LQ, United Kingdom. TEL 44-131-2254703, FAX 44-131-2204260, mailbox@tandtclark.co.uk, http://www.tandtclark.com.

230 ESP ISSN 0211-4011
LICEO FRANCISCANO; revista de estudio e investigacion. Text in Spanish. 1930. 3/yr. **Document type:** *Magazine, Consumer.*
Published by: Convento de San Francisco, Campillo de San Francisco, 3, Santiago de Compostela, Galicia 15080, Spain. http://www.sanfrancisco.es.org/.

266 DEU ISSN 0945-4179
LICHT IM OSTEN. Text in German. 1920. bi-m. free. bk.rev. bibl.; illus. **Document type:** *Newsletter.*
Formerly: Dein Reich Komme (0011-7692)
Published by: Licht im Osten Missionsbund, Zuffenhauserstr 37, Korntal-Muenchingen, 70825, Germany. TEL 49-711-839908-0, FAX 49-711-8399084. Ed., Pub. Erwin Damson. Circ: 27,900.

200 USA ISSN 1099-2650
LIFE AT WORK. Text in English. 1998. bi-m. USD 14.95; USD 19.95 in Canada; USD 29.95 elsewhere (effective 1999). adv. **Document type:** *Magazine, Consumer.*
Published by: Life at Work Company, 2086 N Bridgeton Ct, Fayetteville, AR 72701-2992. TEL 479-444-0664. Ed. Stephen Caldwell. Adv. contact DeDe Donatelli-Tarrant.

242 USA
LIFEGLOW; a large print magazine. Text in English. 1983. bi-m. free to qualified personnel (effective 2011). **Document type:** *Magazine, Consumer.* **Description:** Features inspirational, devotional articles and a variety of stories from a Christian perspective for adults with visual impairments.
Related titles: Online - full text ed.: free (effective 2011).
Published by: Christian Record Services, PO Box 6097, Lincoln, NE 68506. TEL 402-488-0981, FAX 402-488-7582, info@christianrecord.org, http://www.christianrecord.org.

200 GBR ISSN 0308-3624
LIFELINE. Text in English. 1976. m. (except Jan. & July). 12 p./no.; back issues avail. **Document type:** *Magazine, Consumer.* **Description:** Deals with religious topics, news of the church and other matters of interest to members and friends.
Formerly (until 1976): New Church Herald
Related titles: Online - full text ed.: free (effective 2010).
Indexed: CCR.
Published by: General Conference of the New Church, 20 Bloomsbury Way, London, WC1A 2TH, United Kingdom. http://www.generalconference.org.uk. Ed. Alan Misson TEL 44-20-87775098. **Subscr. to:** New Church House.

220 USA ISSN 1939-0831
LIFEWALK; through the Bible every year devotional. Text in English. 2007. m. USD 24.95; USD 3.50 per issue (effective 2011). adv. back issues avail. **Document type:** *Magazine, Consumer.*
Published by: LifeWay Christian Resources, 1 Lifeway Plz, Nashville, TN 37234. TEL 615-251-2000, 800-458-2772, FAX 615-251-5933, customerservice@lifeway.com. Ed. Woody Parker.

230 USA ISSN 1932-9326
LIFTED MAGAZINE. Text in English. 2005. bi-m. **Document type:** *Magazine, Consumer.* **Description:** For young adults between the ages of 18 and 34.
Media: Online - full text.
Published by: Lifted Magazine, Inc., 14781 Memorial Dr, Ste 1747, Houston, TX 77079. TEL 800-653-8592, tiffany@liftedmag.com, http://liftedmagazine.com/index.asp.

264.005 GBR ISSN 1753-9870
LIGHT FOR THE LECTIONARY. Text in English. 2004. q. GBP 5.99 per issue (effective 2010). **Document type:** *Magazine, Consumer.* **Description:** Contains 15 all-age service outlines with nine or ten elements organised under the headings of 'Bible', 'Prayer' and 'Helpful Extras'.
Formerly (until 2007): Light Years (1743-2324)
—CCC.
Published by: Scripture Union, 207-209 Queensway, Bletchley, Milton Keynes, Bucks MK2 2EB, United Kingdom. TEL 44-1908-856000, FAX 44-1908-856111, info@scriptureunion.org.uk. **Subscr. to:** Mail Order, PO Box 5148, Milton Keynes MLO, Bucks MK2 2YZ, United Kingdom. TEL 44-1908-856006, FAX 44-1908-856020, mailorder@scriptureunion.org.uk.

200 GBR ISSN 0047-4657
LIGHT ON A NEW WORLD. Text in English. 1967. bi-m. free (effective 2009). **Document type:** *Magazine, Consumer.*
Related titles: Microform ed.; Online - full text ed.
—BLDSC (5212.350000).
Published by: (Bexley Christadelphians Ecclesia (Dawn Fellowship)), Light Bible Publications, PO Box 760, Bexley, Kent DA5 1UB, United Kingdom. Ed. Colin Dryland. Circ: 5,000.

200 USA ISSN 2153-2834
▼ **LIGHTHOUSE CHRISTIAN LITERARY MAGAZINE.** Text in English. 2009. s-a. back issues avail. **Document type:** *Magazine, Consumer.* **Description:** Provides information about Christianity.
Media: Online - full text.
Published by: Tonya Latrice Wilson, Ed. & Pub. Ed., Pub. Tonya Latrice Wilson.

220 NLD ISSN 1877-7554
▼ **LINGUISTIC BIBLICAL STUDIES.** Text in English. 2009. irreg., latest vol.4, 2010. price varies. **Document type:** *Monographic series, Academic/Scholarly.* **Description:** Aims to develop and promote the linguistically informed study of the Bible in its original languages.
Published by: Brill, PO Box 9000, Leiden, 2300 PA, Netherlands. TEL 31-71-5353500, FAX 31-71-5317532, cs@brill.nl. Ed. Stanley E Porter.

230.0071 028.5 USA
LISTEN MAGAZINE; celebrating positive choices. Text in English. 1948. 9/yr. USD 19 domestic; USD 26 foreign; USD 27.95 domestic includes Teaching Guide; USD 34.95 foreign includes Teaching Guide (effective 2009). back issues avail.; reprints avail. **Document type:** *Magazine, Consumer.* **Description:** Teaches kids about the consequences of drugs, offers help to those already involved and promotes the benefits of healthy living.
Related titles: Online - full text ed.
Published by: Review and Herald Publishing Association, 55 W Oak Ridge Dr, Hagerstown, MD 21740. TEL 301-393-3000, FAX 301-393-4055, info@rhpa.org, http://www.rhpa.org. Ed. Celeste Perrino-Walker. Circ: 40,000.

LISTENING; journal of religion and culture. *see* SOCIOLOGY

200 800 USA ISSN 0732-1929
PN49
➤ **LITERATURE AND BELIEF.** Text in English. 1981. s-a. USD 10 domestic; USD 14 foreign (effective 2011). adv. bk.rev. back issues avail. **Document type:** *Journal, Trade.* **Description:** Focuses on the moral-religious aspects of literature through scholarly critical articles, interviews, reviews and poetry.
Related titles: Microfiche ed.
Indexed: AES, AmHI, H07, LCR, MLA, MLA-IB, PhilInd.
—BLDSC (5276.712750). **CCC.**
Published by: Brigham Young University, College of Humanities, Center, Study of Christian Values in Literature, 3076F Jesse Knight Bldg, Provo, UT 84604-9989. TEL 801-422-8150, FAX 801-378-8724, http://humanities.byu.edu/.

➤ **LITERATURE AND THEOLOGY;** an international journal of religion, theory and culture. *see* LITERATURE

▼ ➤ **LITTERAE ET THEOLOGIA.** *see* LITERATURE

▼ ➤ **THE LITTLE CHRISTIAN.** *see* CHILDREN AND YOUTH—For

264 BEL ISSN 1381-2041
➤ **LITURGIA CONDENDA.** Text in Dutch, English. 1993. irreg. (approx. 2/yr), latest 2010. price varies. back issues avail. **Document type:** *Monographic series, Academic/Scholarly.* **Description:** Publishes current scholarship in liturgical research, with particular emphasis on innovation in methods, and explorations of new questions.
Published by: (Universiteit van Tilburg, Liturgisch Instituut/Tilburg University, Liturgical Institute NLD), Peeters Publishers, Bondgenotenlaan 153, Leuven, 3000, Belgium. TEL 32-16-235170, FAX 32-16-228500, http://www.peeters-leuven.be.

200 782.5 POL ISSN 1234-4214
LITURGIA SACRA; przeglad liturgiczno-muzyczny. Text in Polish. 1995. q. EUR 33 foreign (effective 2006). **Document type:** *Journal, Academic/Scholarly.*
Published by: (Uniwersytet Opolski, Wydzial Teologiczny), Wydawnictwo Uniwersytetu Opolskiego, ul Sienkiewicza 33, Opole, 45037, Poland. TEL 48-77-4410878, wydawnictwo@uni.opole.pl. **Dist. by:** Ars Polona, Obronców 25, Warsaw 03933, Poland. TEL 48-22-5098609, FAX 48-22-5098610, arspolona@arspolona.com.pl, http://www.arspolona.com.pl.

200 DEU ISSN 0344-9092
LITURGIE KONKRET. Text in German. 1977. m. EUR 32; EUR 4.90 newsstand/cover (effective 2010). adv. **Document type:** *Journal, Academic/Scholarly.*
Related titles: CD-ROM ed.: ISSN 1434-8799. 1998. EUR 99 (effective 2010); Online - full text ed.: EUR 99 (effective 2010).
Published by: Verlag Friedrich Pustet, Gutenbergstr 8, Regensburg, 93051, Germany. TEL 49-941-920220, FAX 49-941-92022330, verlag@pustet.de, http://www.pustetverlag.de. Ed. Guido Fuchs. Circ: 5,600 (paid).

200 DEU ISSN 0076-0048
LITURGIEWISSENSCHAFTLICHE QUELLEN UND FORSCHUNGEN. Text in German. 1919. irreg., latest vol.97, 2008. price varies. **Document type:** *Monographic series, Academic/Scholarly.*
Published by: Aschendorff Verlag GmbH & Co. KG, Soester Str 13, Muenster, 48135, Germany. TEL 49-251-6900, FAX 49-251-6904570, buchverlag@aschendorff.de, http://www.aschendorff-buchverlag.de. Ed. W Heckenbach. R&P Dirk F Passmann. Adv. contact Petra Landsknecht.

200 NLD ISSN 1879-7008
LITURGISCHE HANDREIKING VOOR DE WEEKDAGEN. Text in Dutch. 1978. q. EUR 156.25 (effective 2010).
Published by: (Abdij van Berne, Werkgroep voor Liturgie), Uitgeverij Abdij van Berne, Postbus 60, Heeswijk, 5473 ZH, Netherlands. TEL 31-413-299299, FAX 31-413-299288, info@abdijvanberne.nl, http://www.uitgeverijberne.nl.

264 DEU ISSN 0024-5100
LITURGISCHES JAHRBUCH; Vierteljahreshefte fuer Fragen des Gottesdienstes. Text in German. 1951. q. EUR 39.90; EUR 31.90 to students; EUR 12.80 newsstand/cover (effective 2011). adv. bk.rev. index. **Document type:** *Journal, Academic/Scholarly.*
Indexed: A01, A21, A22, DIP, FR, IBR, IBZ, R&TA, RI-1, RI-2, RILM, T02.
—IE, Infotrieve, INIST. **CCC.**
Published by: (Deutsches Liturgisches Institut Trier), Aschendorff Verlag GmbH & Co. KG, Soester Str 13, Muenster, 48135, Germany. TEL 49-251-6900, FAX 49-251-6904570, buchverlag@aschendorff.de, http://www.aschendorff-buchverlag.de. Ed. Andreas Heinz. Circ: 950 (paid and controlled).

264 USA ISSN 0458-063X
BV169
➤ **LITURGY.** Text in English. 1956; N.S. 1980. q. GBP 73 combined subscription in United Kingdom to institutions (print & online eds.); EUR 98, USD 122 combined subscription to institutions (print & online eds.) (effective 2012). adv. bk.rev. bibl. back issues avail.; reprint service avail. from PSC. **Document type:** *Journal, Academic/Scholarly.* **Description:** Provides parish leaders with essays, guidelines, rituals, prayers that help to promote liturgical renewal and ecumenism.
Related titles: Microfilm ed.: N.S. (from PQC); Online - full text ed.: ISSN 1557-3001. GBP 66 in United Kingdom to institutions; EUR 88, USD 110 to institutions (effective 2012) (from IngentaConnect).
Indexed: A01, A03, A08, A22, CA, CERDIC, CPL, E01, P48, P53, P54, PQC, RILM, T02.
—IE, Ingenta. **CCC.**
Published by: Liturgical Conference, Inc., PO Box 31, Evanston, IL 60204. TEL 847-866-3875, Ron-Anderson@garrett.edu, http://www.liturgicalconference.org. Eds. L Edward Phillips, Sara Webb Phillips. **Subscr. to:** Taylor & Francis Inc., Customer Services Dept, 325 Chestnut St, 8th Fl, Philadelphia, PA 19106. TEL 215-625-8900, 800-354-1420, FAX 215-625-8914, customerservice@taylorandfrancis.com.

264.36 USA ISSN 1084-0842
LITURGY OF THE WORD. Text in English. 1996. a. USD 8.95 per issue (effective 2011). **Document type:** *Magazine, Trade.* **Description:** Contains all of the readings, psalms, and antiphons for Sundays and holy days; a complete order of Mass; devotional prayers; the entrance and communion songs.
Published by: World Library Publications, Inc. (Subsidiary of: J.S. Paluch Co., Inc.), 3708 River Rd, Ste 400, Franklin Park, IL 60131. TEL 847-233-2752, 800-621-5197, FAX 847-233-2762, 888-957-3291, wlpcs@jspaluch.com.

LIVE WIRE; connecting kids to christ. *see* CHILDREN AND YOUTH—For

200 USA ISSN 0193-5968
BX809.F6
LIVING CITY. Text in English. 1967. m. USD 25 in US & Canada; USD 40 in Central America; USD 50 in Europe & South America; USD 60 (effective 2000). back issues avail. **Description:** News of a world striving for unity.

R

Published by: Focolare Movement, Inc., Women's Branch, 179 Robinson Ave, Bronx, NY 10465. TEL 718-828-2932, FAX 718-892-0419, http://www.livingcity.com, http://www.focolare.org. Ed. Sharry Silvi. Circ: 8,000. **Subscr. to:** PO Box 837, Bronx, NY 10465.

261 CAN ISSN 1487-9557
LIVING LIGHT NEWS. Text in English. 1995. bi-m.
Published by: Living Light Ministries, 5304 89th St #200, Edmonton, AB T6E 5P9, Canada. Ed. Jeff Caporale. Circ: 20,000.

200 USA ISSN 1059-2733
BV4200
THE LIVING PULPIT; dedicated to the art of the sermon. Text in English. 1992. q. USD 39 (effective 2009). back issues avail. **Document type:** *Journal, Consumer.* **Description:** Dedicated to the art of the sermon.
Related titles: Online - full text ed.: ISSN 1946-1771.
Indexed: A21, RI-1.
Published by: The Living Pulpit, Inc., 475 Riverside Dr, Ste 500, New York, NY 10115. TEL 212-870-1299. Ed. Keith A Russell. Pub. Douglas S Stivison.

242 NOR ISSN 1500-533X
LOGOS; bibelleseplan for voksne. Text in Norwegian. 1959. q. NOK 280 (effective 2011). **Document type:** *Magazine, Trade.*
Formerly (until 1998): Bibelnokkelen (0800-0417)
Published by: Bibelleseringen i Norge, Postboks 9285, Oslo, 0134, Norway. TEL 47-22-992969, kontor@bibelleseringen.no, http://www.bibelleseringen.no.

LONERGAN STUDIES NEWSLETTER. *see* PHILOSOPHY

LOOKOUT (NEW YORK). *see* SOCIAL SERVICES AND WELFARE

200 BEL
➤ **LOUVAIN THEOLOGICAL AND PASTORAL MONOGRAPHS.** Text in English. 1990. irreg., latest 2010. price varies. back issues avail. **Document type:** *Monographic series, Academic/Scholarly.*
Published by: (Universite Catholique de Louvain, Faculte de Theologie et de Droit Canonique), Peeters Publishers, Bondgenotenlaan 153, Leuven, 3000, Belgium. TEL 32-16-235170, FAX 32-16-228500, http://www.peeters-leuven.be.

200 USA
LUIS PALAU LETTER. Text in English. 1964. m. **Document type:** *Newsletter.* **Description:** Shares ministry vision and results with supporters.
Published by: Luis Palau Evangelistic Association, PO Box 1173, Portland, OR 97207. TEL 503-614-1500, FAX 503-614-1599, lpea@palau.org, http://www.gospelcom.net/lpea. Ed., R&P David Sanford.

220 264 FRA ISSN 0024-7359
BR3
LUMIERE ET VIE; revue de formation et de reflexion theologiques. Text in French. 1951. q. adv. bk.rev. bibl. index. back issues avail. **Document type:** *Journal.*
Indexed: A21, CERDIC, CPL, FR, IBR, IBZ, IZBG, OTA, PCI, RI-1, RI-2.
—CCC.
Published by: Association Lumiere et Vie, 2 place Gailleton, Lyon, 69002, France. TEL 33-4-78426683, FAX 33-4-78372382. Ed. Christian Duquoc. Adv. contact Gabriele Nolte. Circ: 5,000.

230.0071 SWE ISSN 1102-769X
LUND STUDIES IN ETHICS AND THEOLOGY. Text in English, Swedish. 1992. irreg. price varies. **Document type:** *Monographic series, Academic/Scholarly.*
Published by: Lunds Universitet, Centrum foer Teologi och Religionsvetenskap/Lund University, Department of Theology and Religious Studies, Allhelgma Kyrkogata 8, Lund, 22362, Sweden.

200.19 SWE ISSN 1103-5757
LUND STUDIES IN PSYCHOLOGY OF RELIGION. Text in English. 1993. irreg., latest vol.8, 2006. price varies. **Document type:** *Monographic series, Academic/Scholarly.*
Indexed: E-psyche.
Published by: Lunds Universitet, Centrum foer Teologi och Religionsvetenskap/Lund University, Department of Theology and Religious Studies, Allhelgma Kyrkogata 8, Lund, 22362, Sweden. TEL 46-46-2229040, FAX 46-46-2224426, teol@teol.lu.se, http://www.teol.lu.se/.

200.9 PRT ISSN 0076-1508
BR910
➤ **LUSITANIA SACRA.** Text in Portuguese; Abstracts in English. 1956. a., latest vol.14, 2002. EUR 20 domestic; EUR 30 in Europe; EUR 50 elsewhere (effective 2005). adv. bk.rev. back issues avail. **Document type:** *Monographic series, Academic/Scholarly.*
Indexed: CA, FR, HistAb, T02.
—INIST.
Published by: Universidade Catolica Portuguesa, Centro de Estudos de Historia Religiosa, Caminho de Palma de Cima, Lisbon, 1649-023, Portugal. TEL 351-21-7214130, FAX 351-21-7270256, secretariado@cehr.ucp.pt, http://www.ucp.pt/cehr. Ed. Manuel Clemente. Pub., R&P Paulo Fontes. Adv. contact Isabel Costa.

220 ITA
LUX BIBLICA; rivista teologica. Text in Italian. 1990. s-a. bk.rev. 200 p./no.; back issues avail. **Document type:** *Monographic series, Academic/Scholarly.* **Description:** Consists of one monographic issue and one theological journal issue per year. Brings the Bible to bear on issues of importance for the Christian faith and ministry.
Published by: Istituto Biblico Evangelico Italiano, Via del Casale Corvio 50, Rome, 00132, Italy. TEL 39-06-20762293, FAX 39-06-2070151, http://www.ibei.it.

266 USA ISSN 0740-6460
M A R C NEWSLETTER; that everyone may hear. Text in English. q. free. adv. **Document type:** *Newsletter.* **Description:** News and articles on strategic planning for world evangelization by Christian mission agencies.
Indexed: CERDIC.
Published by: (Mission Advanced Research & Communication Center), M A R C (Subsidiary of: World Vision International), 800 W Chestnut Ave, Monrovia, CA 91016-3198. TEL 626-303-8811, 800-777-7752, FAX 626-301-7786. Ed. John A Kenyon. Pub. Bryant Myers. Adv. contact Steve Singley.

200 USA ISSN 1049-152X
M A R GOSPEL MINISTRIES NEWSLETTER. (Middle Atlantic Regional) Text in English. 1989. s-a. free. bk.rev. **Document type:** *Newsletter.* **Description:** Covers African American church and current events of M A R Gospel Ministries.
Published by: (Middle Atlantic Regional Gospel Ministries), Middle Atlantic Regional Press, PO Box 6021, Washington, DC 20005. TEL 202-265-7609. Ed. E Myron Noble.

M E T E M - INTERNATIONAL SOCIETY OF TORONTO FOR HUNGARIAN CHURCH HISTORY. NEWSLETTER/M E T E M. HIREK. (Magyar Egyhaztorteneti Enciklopedia Munkakozossege) *see* HISTORY—History Of Europe

200 DNK ISSN 1604-911X
M F BLADET; fra menighedsfakultetet. (Menighedsfakultetet) Text in Danish. 1971. 10/yr. free (effective 2004). **Document type:** *Magazine, Trade.*
Former titles (until 2005): Menighedsfakultetets Venneblad (1604-0899); (until 2004): Vennebladet (1396-2531); (until 1996): Menighedsfakultetes Venneblad (0108-1373); (until 1982): M F (0108-304X); (until 1975): Menighedsfakultetet (0108-3058)
Related titles: Online - full text ed.: ISSN 1604-9500.
Published by: Menighedsfakultetet/Lutheran School of Theology in Aarhus, Katrinebergvej 75, Aarhus N, 8200, Denmark. TEL 45-86-166300, FAX 45-86-166860, mf@teologi.dk.

200 KOR ISSN 1738-3196
BR9.K6
MA'DANG: JOURNAL OF CONTEXTUAL THEOLOGY IN EAST ASIA. Text in English. 2004. s-a. USD 20 to individuals in Europe, N.America, Australia, New Zealand, East Asia; USD 10 elsewhere to individuals; USD 30 to institutions in Europe, N.America, Australia, New Zealand, East Asia; USD 20 elsewhere to institutions (effective 2009). **Document type:** *Journal, Academic/Scholarly.* **Description:** Contains articles on Minjung theology, feminist theology, human rights, peace, religious and ecological concerns in the context of globalization.
Published by: Korea Association of Progressive Theologians, c/o Micah Eun-Kyu, Kim, Sungkonghoe University, Institute for the Study of Theology, 1-1, Hang-dong, Kuro-Ku, Seoul, 152-716, Korea, S. TEL 82-2-26104343, FAX 82-2-26104764. Ed. Yong-Bock Kim.

210 SWE ISSN 1654-5788
MAGASINET EXISTERA. Variant title: Existera. Text in Swedish. 2007. q. SEK 147 (effective 2007). **Document type:** *Magazine, Consumer.*
Published by: Svenska Kyrkans Press AB, Goetgatan 22A, PO Box 15412, Stockholm, 10465, Sweden. TEL 46-8-4622800, FAX 46-8-6445604, info@svkpress.com, http://www.svkpress.com. Eds. Brita Hall, Dag Tuvelius TEL 46-8-4622801. Pub. Dag Tuvelius TEL 46-8-4622801. Adv. contact Johnny Thelin.

MAGISTRA; a journal of woman's spirituality in history. *see* WOMEN'S STUDIES

268 PRT ISSN 0874-4998
CODEN: M
MAGNIFICANT. Text in Portuguese. 1948. m. EUR 7 domestic; EUR 13 in Europe; EUR 15 elsewhere (effective 2005). **Document type:** *Magazine, Consumer.*
Published by: Editorial/AO, Lago das Teresinhas, 5, Braga, 4714-509, Portugal. TEL 351-253-201220, FAX 351-253-201221, http://www.ppcj.pt/AO/AO.html. Ed. Heitor Morais da Silva. Circ: 5,300.

200 DEU ISSN 1254-7697
MAGNIFICAT; Das Stundenbuch. Text in German. 1994. m. EUR 48; EUR 5 newsstand/cover (effective 2009). **Document type:** *Magazine, Consumer.*
Published by: Butzon und Bercker GmbH, Hoogeweg 71, Kevelaer, 47623, Germany. TEL 49-2832-9290, FAX 49-2832-929211, service@bube.de, http://www.butzonbercker.de. Ed. Johannes Bernhard Uphus.

MAGYAR EGYHAZTORTENETI VAZLATOK/ESSAYS IN CHURCH HISTORY IN HUNGARY. *see* HISTORY—History Of Europe

MAINZER HYMNOLOGISCHE STUDIEN. *see* MUSIC

200 FRA ISSN 0025-0937
BX1970.A1
LA MAISON - DIEU; revue de science liturgique. Text in French. 1945. q. EUR 50.40 domestic; EUR 60 foreign (effective 2004). adv. bk.rev. index. **Document type:** *Journal, Academic/Scholarly.*
Indexed: A22, CERDIC, DIP, FR, IBR, IBZ, PCI.
—IE, Infotrieve, INIST.
Published by: (Centre National de Pastorale Liturgique), Editions du Cerf, 29 Boulevard La Tour Maubourg, Paris, 75340 Cedex 07, France. http://www.editionsducerf.fr. Ed. Paul De Clerck. Circ: 2,600.

266 CAN ISSN 0225-7068
MANDATE. Text in English. 1969. q. (includes special ed.). CAD 8.50; CAD 14.50 foreign (effective 1999). adv. **Document type:** *Journal, Consumer.* **Description:** Covers mission and justice work in Canada and overseas.
Published by: United Church of Canada, 3250 Bloor St W, Ste 300, Etobicoke, ON M8X 2Y4, Canada. TEL 416-231-5931, FAX 416-231-3103. Ed., Adv. contact Rebekah Chevalier. R&P R Chevalier. Circ: 12,500.

MANICHAEAN STUDIES. *see* RELIGIONS AND THEOLOGY—Other Denominations And Sects

200 ZAF ISSN 1817-4108
MANNA. Text in Afrikaans. 2006. q. ZAR 20 domestic; ZAR 45 foreign (effective 2006).
Published by: Groot is U Trou, PO Box 21, Montana Park, Pretoria, 0159, South Africa. TEL 27-12-9976331, admin@grootisutrou.co.za, http://www.grootisutrou.co.za.

200 ESP ISSN 0214-2457
MANRESA; espiritualidad ignaciana. Text in Spanish. 1925. q. EUR 29 domestic; EUR 48 in Europe; EUR 55 in Latin America and Africa; EUR 58 in US & Canada; EUR 66 in Asia (effective 2003). adv. bk.rev. 102 p./no.; **Document type:** *Monographic series, Bibliography.*
Indexed: CERDIC, IBR, IBZ, P09, PCI.
Published by: Compania de Jesus, Centro Loyola de Estudios y Comunicacion Social, Pablo Aranda 3, Madrid, 28006, Spain. TEL 34-91-5624930, FAX 34-91-5634073. Ed., R&P Jose Antonio Garcia Rodriguez. Circ: 1,000.

220 FRA ISSN 1952-2339
MANUELS DU TRADUCTEUR. Text in French. 1997. irreg. **Document type:** *Monographic series.*
Published by: Alliance Biblique Universelle/United Bible Societies, c/o French Bible Society, 5 Av. des Erables, BP 47, Villiers-le-Bel, 95400, France. TEL 33-1-39945051, FAX 33-1-39905351.

220 NLD ISSN 1573-997X
MARANATHA. Text in Dutch. 1917. a. EUR 12.50 (effective 2009).
Formerly (until 2003): Maranatha Kalender (1573-9961)
Published by: Uitgeverij Kok, Postbus 5018, Kampen, 8260 GA, Netherlands. TEL 31-38-3392555, http://www.kok.nl.

200 DEU ISSN 1612-2941
BL4
MARBURG JOURNAL OF RELIGION. Text in English. 1996. irreg. free (effective 2011). **Document type:** *Journal, Academic/Scholarly.* **Description:** Publishs empirical and theoretical studies of religion.
Media: Online - full text.
—CCC.
Address: http://www.uni-marburg.de/fb03/religionswissenschaft/journal/mjr/. Ed. Edith Franke.

200 DEU ISSN 1867-7592
MARBURGER BEITRAEGE ZUR KIRCHLICHEN ZEITGESCHICHTE. Text in German. 2007. irreg., latest vol.2, 2008. price varies. **Document type:** *Monographic series, Academic/Scholarly.*
Published by: Tectum Wissenschaftsverlag Marburg, Biegenstr 4, Marburg, 35037, Germany. TEL 49-6421-481523, FAX 49-6421-43470, email@tectum-verlag.de. Ed. Jochen-Christoph Kaiser.

200 DEU ISSN 0542-657X
MARBURGER THEOLOGISCHE STUDIEN. Text in German. 1963. irreg., latest vol.63, 2000. price varies. **Document type:** *Monographic series.*
Published by: N.G. Elwert Verlag, Reitgasse 7-9, Marburg, 35037, Germany. TEL 49-6421-17090, FAX 49-6421-15487, elwertmail@elwert.de, http://www.elwert.de.

266 232 AUT ISSN 0025-3022
MARIANNHILL. Text in German. bi-m. EUR 6.40 (effective 2005). bk.rev. **Document type:** *Magazine, Consumer.*
Published by: Missionare von Mariannhill, Schloss Riedegg, Riedegg 1, Gallneukirchen, O 4210, Austria. TEL 43-7235-62224, prokura@mariannhill.at, http://www.mariannhill.at. Eds. Br Franziskus Puehringer, P A Balling. Circ: 45,000.

282 USA
MARKINGS. Text in English. 1971. m. (11/yr.). USD 37.95. **Document type:** *Journal, Trade.* **Description:** Homily service for priests.
Published by: Thomas More Association, 205 W Monroe St, 6th Fl, Chicago, IL 60606. TEL 312-609-8880. Circ: 3,000.

MARS HILL REVIEW. *see* LITERATURE

291.2 170 DEU ISSN 1610-7241
MARTIN BUCER SEMINAR. JAHRBUCH. Text in German. 2001. a. EUR 16 per issue (effective 2010). **Document type:** *Yearbook, Academic/Scholarly.*
Published by: (Evangelical Theological University), Verlag fuer Kultur und Wissenschaft/Culture and Science Publishers, Friedrichstr 38, Bonn, 53111, Germany. TEL 49-228-9650381, FAX 49-228-9650389, info@vkwonline.de, http://www.vkwonline.de. Ed. Dr. Thomas P Schirrmacher.

200 DEU ISSN 0580-2091
MARTIN-GRABMANN-FORSCHUNGSINSTITUT. VEROEFFENTLICHUNGEN. Text in German. 1958. irreg., latest vol.50, 2005. price varies. **Document type:** *Monographic series, Academic/Scholarly.*
Formerly (until 1967): Grabmann-Institut der Universitaet Muenchen. Mitteilungen (0580-2083)
Published by: Ludwig-Maximilians-Universitaet Muenchen, Martin-Grabmann-Forschungsinstitut, Geschwister-Scholl-Platz 1, Munich, 80539, Germany. TEL 49-89-21802479, FAX 49-89-21802480, Grabmann-Institut@KathTheol.Uni-Muenchen.de, http://www.kaththeol.uni-muenchen.de/grabmann/.

200 USA ISSN 1052-181X
MARTIN LUTHER KING, JR. MEMORIAL STUDIES IN RELIGION, CULTURE AND SOCIAL DEVELOPMENT. Text in English. 1992. irreg., latest vol.10, 2006. price varies. **Document type:** *Monographic series, Academic/Scholarly.* **Description:** Promotes scholarly research and writing in areas that reflect the interrelatedness of religion and social-cultural-political development both in American society and in the world.
Published by: Peter Lang Publishing, Inc. (Subsidiary of: Peter Lang Publishing Group), 29 Broadway, New York, NY 10006. TEL 212-647-7706, 212-647-7700, 800-770-5264, FAX 212-647-7707, customerservice@plang.com. Ed. Mozella G Mitchell.

230 IND
MASIHI SEVAK. Text and summaries in English. 1975. 3/yr. INR 150 domestic; USD 25 foreign (effective 2011). **Document type:** *Journal, Academic/Scholarly.* **Description:** Describes articles, sermons and reports about Christian Ministry for publication.
Published by: United Theological College, 63, Millers Rd, Benson Town, PO Box 4613, Bangalore, Karnataka 560046, India. TEL 91-80-23333438, FAX 91-80-23330015, unitedtcb@gmail.com, http://www.utcbangalore.in/. Ed. Peniel Rufus Jesudasan.

230 NZL ISSN 1179-7312
MASSAH. Text in English. 1996. s-a. free (effective 2010). back issues avail. **Document type:** *Journal, Trade.*
Published by: New Zealand Council of Christians and Jews, 80 Webb St, Wellington, New Zealand. TEL 64-27-2202202. Ed. Tony Stroobant.

207.2 GBR
MASTER AND THE MULTITUDE. Text in English. 1853. q. free to members (effective 2009). illus. **Document type:** *Newsletter.* **Description:** Mission work in the British Isles.
Published by: Open-Air Mission, 4 Harrier Ct, Woodside Rd, Slip End, Luton, LU1 4DQ, United Kingdom. TEL 44-1582-841141, FAX 44-1582-841145, oamission@btinternet.com.

200 USA
MASTERING LIFE. Text in English. 1990. q. free. bk.rev. illus. back issues avail. **Document type:** *Newsletter, Consumer.* **Description:** Covers Christianity and sexuality in terms of Christian ethics with topics such as child abuse and homosexuality.
Related titles: Online - full content ed.

Published by: Mastering Life Ministries, PO Box 351149, Jacksonville, FL 32235-1149. Staff@MasteringLife.org. Ed., Pub., R&P David Kyle Foster. Circ: 1,000 (controlled).

200 GBR ISSN 1743-2200
N72.R4
➤ **MATERIAL RELIGION**; the journal of objects, art & belief. Text in English. 2005 (Mar.). 3/yr. USD 415 combined subscription in US & Canada to institutions (print & online eds.); GBP 213 combined subscription elsewhere to institutions (print & online eds.) (effective 2011). adv. illus. reprint service avail. from PSC. **Document type:** *Journal, Academic/Scholarly.* **Description:** Seeks to explore how religion happens in material culture - images, devotional and liturgical objects, architecture and sacred space, works of art and mass-produced artifacts.
Related titles: Online - full text ed.: ISSN 1751-8342. USD 353 in US & Canada to institutions; GBP 181 elsewhere to institutions (effective 2011) (from IngentaConnect).
Indexed: A01, A02, A03, A07, A08, A20, A21, A26, A30, A31, AA, ABM, AICP, ArtHuCI, ArtInd, B04, BRD, BrHumI, CA, CurCont, D05, I05, I14, IBR, IBSS, IBZ, MLA-IB, S02, S03, SCOPUS, SociolAb, T02, W03, W05, W07.
—BLDSC (5393.530000), IE, Ingenta. **CCC.**
Published by: Berg Publishers (Subsidiary of: Oxford International Publishers Ltd.), 1st Fl Angel Ct, 81 St Clements St, Oxford, Berks OX4 1AW, United Kingdom. TEL 44-1865-245104, FAX 44-1865-791165, enquiry@bergpublishers.com. Eds. Birgit Meyer, Crispin Paine, S Brent Plate. **Dist. addr.:** Turpin Distribution Services Ltd., Pegasus Dr, Stratton Business Park, Biggleswade, Bedfordshire SG18 8QB, United Kingdom. TEL 44-1767-604800, FAX 44-1767-601640, custserv@turpin-distribution.com, http://www.turpin-distribution.com/.

200 DEU ISSN 0721-2402
BL4
MATERIALDIENST. Text in German. 1937. m. EUR 30; EUR 2.50 newsstand/cover (effective 2009). adv. **Document type:** *Magazine, Trade.*
Indexed: DIP, IBR, IBZ.
Published by: Evangelische Zentralstelle fuer Weltanschauungsfragen, Auguststr 80, Berlin, 10117, Germany. TEL 49-30-28395211, FAX 49-30-28395212, info@ezw-berlin.de. adv.: B&W page EUR 285. Circ: 3,800 (paid).

280.4 DEU
MATHILDE-ZIMMER-STIFTUNG. BLAETTER. Text in German. 1906. bi-m. adv. bk.rev. **Document type:** *Newsletter, Consumer.*
Published by: Mathilde-Zimmer-Stiftung e.V., Bayerische Str 31, Berlin, 10707, Germany. TEL 49-30-8892660, FAX 49-30-88926626, mzstev@t-online.de. Circ: 2,000.

▼ **MATURE SPIRITUALLY MAGAZINE.** *see* LIFESTYLE

230 CAN ISSN 1481-0794
BR118
THE MCMASTER JOURNAL OF THEOLOGY AND MINISTRY (ONLINE). Text in English, French. 1979-1993; N.S. 1998. a. (s.a. until 1993). free. bk.rev. **Document type:** *Journal, Academic/ Scholarly.* **Description:** Seeks to provide pastors, educators and interested laypersons with the fruits of theological, biblical and professional studies in a readable form.
Former titles (until 1993): McMaster Journal of Theology (Print) (0849-0899); Theodolite (0225-7270); McMaster Theological Bulletin
Media: Online - full content.
Indexed: A01, A21, CA, CERDIC, RI-1, RI-2, T02.
Published by: McMaster Divinity College, 1280 Main St W, Hamilton, ON L8S 4K1, Canada. http://www.macdiv.ca/home.php. Ed. John Rook. Circ: 1,000.

MEDIA DEVELOPMENT. *see* COMMUNICATIONS

MEDICINE, RELIGION TOGETHER. *see* MEDICAL SCIENCES

200 GBR ISSN 2046-5726
➤ **MEDIEVAL MYSTICAL THEOLOGY**; the journal of the eckhart society. Text in English. 1992. s-a. USD 220 combined subscription in North America to institutions (print & online eds.); USD 135 combined subscription elsewhere to institutions (print & online eds.) (effective 2012). adv. **Document type:** *Journal, Academic/Scholarly.* **Description:** Focuses the influence of Neo-Platonism, Aristotelianism, Patristics, Judaism and Islam on Christian medieval mystical theology, as well as interpretations of the tradition for today.
Formerly (until 2010): The Eckhart review (0969-3661)
Related titles: Online - full text ed.: ISSN 2046-5734. USD 176 in North America to institutions; USD 108 elsewhere to institutions (effective 2012).
Published by: Equinox Publishing Ltd., Unit S3, Kelham House, 3 Lancaster St, Sheffield, S6 3AF, United Kingdom. TEL 44-114-2725957, FAX 44-560-3459046, journals@equinoxpub.com. Ed. Duane Williams. Adv. contact Val Hall.

➤ **MEDIEVAL SERMON STUDIES.** *see* LITERATURE

200 DEU ISSN 0171-3841
MEDITATION; Zeitschrift fuer christliche Spiritualitaet und Lebensgestaltung. Text in German. 1974. q. EUR 20.50; EUR 6.20 newsstand/cover (effective 2008). adv. bk.rev. bibl.; illus. index. back issues avail. **Document type:** *Magazine, Consumer.* **Description:** Reflections and reports about spirituality.
Published by: Matthias-Gruenewald-Verlag GmbH (Subsidiary of: Schwabenverlag AG), Senefelderstr 12, Ostfildern, 73760, Germany. TEL 49-711-44060, FAX 49-711-4406177, mail@gruenewaldverlag.de. Ed. Mechthild Hamburger. Adv. contact Nina Baab TEL 49-6131-928620. B&W page EUR 750; trim 120 x 200. Circ: 1,200 (paid).

MEDITERRANEAN STUDIES. *see* HISTORY—History Of The Near East

MEELEVEN; kwartaalblad over verslaving en kerk. *see* DRUG ABUSE AND ALCOHOLISM

221 ISR ISSN 0334-8814
BS410
MEGADIM. Text in Hebrew. 1986. 2/yr. ILS 110 (effective 2008). bk.rev. **Document type:** *Academic/Scholarly.*
Indexed: IHP.
Published by: Yaakov Herzog College, Alon Shvut, Gush Etzion, 90433, Israel. TEL 972-2-993-7333, FAX 972-2-993-2796, herzog@herzog.ac.il. Circ: 1,500.

200 USA ISSN 0194-7826
BX9998
MEGIDDO MESSAGE. Text in English. 1914. 10/yr. looseleaf. USD 10 (effective 2000). adv. index, cum.index: 1915-1998. reprints avail. **Description:** Seeks to encourage Bible study and application and to promote and uphold Christian Morals and values.
Indexed: A22.
Published by: Megiddo Church, 481 Thurston Rd, Rochester, NY 14619-1697. TEL 716-235-4150, FAX 716-436-3627. Ed. Ruth E Sisson. Adv. contact Donna Mathias. Circ: 17,500.

230 DEU
MEINE WELT. Text in German. 1948. m. EUR 13.80 (effective 2011). **Document type:** *Magazine, Consumer.*
Formerly (until 1972): Der Kinderbote
Published by: Guetersloher Verlagshaus (Subsidiary of: Verlagsgruppe Random House GmbH), Carl-Miele-Str 214, Guetersloh, 33311, Germany. TEL 49-5241-74050, FAX 49-5241-740548, info@gtvh.de, http://www.gtvh.de. Ed. Heidrun Viehweg. **Subscr. to:** VVA Zeitschriftenservice, Postfach 7777, Guetersloh 33310, Germany. TEL 49-5241-801969, FAX 49-5241-809620.

230 100 DEU
MELANCHTHON-SCHRIFTEN DER STADT BRETTEN. Text in German. 1988. irreg., latest vol.10, 2006. price varies. **Document type:** *Monographic series, Academic/Scholarly.*
Published by: Frommann-Holzboog Verlag e.K., Koenig-Karl-Str 27, Stuttgart, 70372, Germany. TEL 49-711-9559690, FAX 49-711-9559691, info@frommann-holzboog.de, http://www.frommann-holzboog.de.

283 GBR
MELANESIA NEWS. Text in English. 1977. s-a. **Document type:** *Newsletter.* **Description:** Contains news from the Church of the Province of Melanesia (Anglican).
Published by: Melanesian Mission, Harpsden Rectory, 2 Harpsden Way, Henley-on-Thames, Oxon RG9 1NL, United Kingdom. TEL 44-1491-573401, FAX 44-1491-579871. Ed. Angelique Fox. R&P Peter J Fox. Circ: 1,200.

200 PNG ISSN 0256-856X
BR1
MELANESIAN JOURNAL OF THEOLOGY. Text in English. 1985. 2/yr. USD 26 in developing nations (effective 2005). bk.rev. back issues avail. **Document type:** *Journal, Academic/Scholarly.* **Description:** Aims to stimulate the writing of theology by Melanesians for Melanesians.
Indexed: A21, R&TA, RI-1, RI-2, RILM, SPPI.
Published by: Melanesian Association of Theological Schools, c/o Christian Leaders Training College, PO Box 382, Mt. Hagen, WHP, Papua New Guinea. TEL 675-5461001, FAX 675-5461009, dhanson@cltc.ac.pg. Ed., R&P Doug Hanson. Circ: 140 (paid).

200 212.5 MLT ISSN 1012-9588
BX804
MELITA THEOLOGICA. Text in English, French, Italian. 1947. 2/yr. USD 27. adv. bk.rev. index. Supplement avail. **Document type:** *Journal, Academic/Scholarly.* **Description:** Contains articles in dogmatic and moral theology, fundamental theology, holy scripture, canon law, spiritual theology, liturgy, patrology, ecclesiastical history, Christian archaeology, philosophy and sociology.
Indexed: OTA, P30, R&TA.
—BLDSC (5544.700000), IE, Infotrieve, Ingenta.
Published by: Theology Students' Association, University of Malta, Msida, MSD 04, Malta. TEL 356-333998. Ed. Rev. Dr Anthony Abela. Circ: 600. **Subscr. to:** Foundation for Theological Studies, Tal Virtu, Rabat RBT 09, Malta. TEL 356-455497. **Co-sponsor:** University of Malta, Faculty of Theology.

200 MLT
➤ **MELITA THEOLOGICA SUPPLEMENTARY SERIES.** Text in English. 1991. irreg. (approx. a.), latest vol.2, 1992. price varies. back issues avail. **Document type:** *Monographic series, Academic/Scholarly.* **Description:** Publishes monographic studies and collections of essays on topics in theology and related issues.
Published by: Theology Students' Association, University of Malta, Msida, MSD 04, Malta. TEL 356-333998. **Subscr. to:** Foundation for Theological Studies, Tal Virtu, Rabat RBT 09, Malta. TEL 356-455497. **Co-sponsor:** University of Malta, Faculty of Theology.

➤ **MEMORIE DOMENICANE.** *see* HISTORY

248.8 305.31 USA ISSN 1524-1122
MEN OF INTEGRITY. Abbreviated title: M O I. Text in English. 1998. bi-m. USD 17.95; USD 25.95 in Canada (effective 2008). adv. back issues avail. **Document type:** *Magazine, Consumer.* **Description:** Provides biblical based easy devotionals and biblical answers to the challenges men face.
Related titles: Online - full text ed.: ISSN 1551-2134.
Published by: Christianity Today International, 465 Gundersen Dr, Carol Stream, IL 60188. TEL 630-260-6200, FAX 630-260-0114. Ed. Harold B Smith. adv.: color page USD 1,260; trim 8 x 10.75. Circ: 60,000.

230 USA ISSN 2155-3564
▼ **MEN OF VALOR.** Text in English. 2009. a. **Document type:** *Journal, Consumer.*
Published by: Redeemed Christian Church of God, North America, c/o Pastor K. B. Sanusi, Restoration Chapel, 13406 Beechnut St, Houston, TX 77083. TEL 832-721-4199, hq@rccgna.org.

268 NLD ISSN 0165-5116
MENIGERLEI GENADE; prekenserie. Text in Dutch. 1911. q. EUR 37.50 domestic; EUR 42 in Belgium (effective 2009). **Description:** Publishes sermons.
Published by: Kok Tijdschriften, Postbus 5018, Kampen, 8260 GA, Netherlands. TEL 31-38-3392555, http://www.kok.nl. Eds. A Jobsen, P Schelling.

200 DNK ISSN 0907-3272
MENIGHEDSFAKULTETET. VIDENSKABELIGE SERIE. Text in Danish. 1992. irreg. price varies. back issues avail. **Document type:** *Monographic series, Academic/Scholarly.*
Published by: (Menighedsfakultetet/Lutheran School of Theology in Aarhus), Forlagsgruppen Lohse, Korskaervej 25, Fredericia, 7000, Denmark. TEL 45-75-934455, FAX 45-75-924275, info@lohse, http://www.lohse.dk.

254.041489 DNK ISSN 0904-8545
MENIGHEDSRAADENES BLAD. Text in Danish. 1922. 10/yr. DKK 650 (effective 2009). **Document type:** *Newsletter, Consumer.* **Description:** Contains articles and information of interest to the members of the association of local Danish church councils.
Published by: Landsforeningen af Menighedsraadsmedlemmer, Damvej 17-19, Sabro, 8471, Denmark. TEL 45-87-322133, FAX 45-87-198040, kontor@menighesraad.dk, http://www.menighedsraad.dk. Ed. Niels Erik Kjaer Larsen. Adv. contact Louise Beck Boegholm.

268 PRT ISSN 0874-4955
MENSAGEIRO DO CORACAO DE JESUS. Text in Portuguese. 1874. m. EUR 12.50 domestic; EUR 20 in Europe; USD 34 in the Americas; EUR 26 elsewhere (effective 2005). **Document type:** *Magazine, Consumer.*
Published by: Editorial/AO, Lago das Teresinhas, 5, Braga, 4714-509, Portugal. TEL 351-253-201220, FAX 351-253-201221, http://www.ppcj.pt/AO/AO.html. Ed. Dario S.J. Pedroso.

200 ESP ISSN 0211-6561
MENSAJERO; del corazon de Jesus. Text in Spanish. 1866. m. EUR 29.50 (effective 2009). adv. bk.rev. illus. back issues avail. **Document type:** *Magazine, Consumer.* **Description:** Covers religious and family subjects. Includes some political, social and cultural issues.
Related titles: Online - full text ed.
Indexed: I04, I05.
Published by: Ediciones Mensajero, Sancho de Azpeitia 2, Bajo, Bilbao, 48014, Spain. TEL 34-94-4470358, FAX 34-94-4472630, mensajero@mensajero.com. Ed. Juan Antonio Irazabal. Circ: 19,500.

MENSCHEN UND KULTUREN. *see* HISTORY

291.72 NLD ISSN 2211-6559
MENSEN MET EEN MISSIE. NIEUWSBRIEF. Text in Dutch. q. **Document type:** *Newsletter, Consumer.*
Published by: Mensen met een Missie, Postbus 16442, The Hague, 2500 BK, Netherlands. TEL 31-70-3136700, FAX 31-70-3136777, http://www.mensenmeteenmissie.nl.

MENTAL HEALTH, RELIGION & CULTURE. *see* PSYCHOLOGY

200 HUN ISSN 0026-0126
MERLEG; folyoiratok es konyvek szemleje. Text in Hungarian; Summaries in English, German. 1965. q. HUF 1,000 (effective 2000). adv. bk.rev. abstr.; bibl. index. **Document type:** *Academic/Scholarly.*
Indexed: OTA.
Published by: Merleg Egyesuelet, Varsanyi Iren 4 I/4, Budapest, 1027, Hungary. Ed., R&P Janos Boor. Circ: 3,500. **Dist. by:** Moha u 16, Agard 2484, Hungary. TEL 36-22-371793, FAX 36-22-371763.

MERTON ANNUAL: STUDIES IN THOMAS MERTON, RELIGION, CULTURE, LITERATURE, AND SOCIAL CONCERNS. *see* LITERATURE

200 800 USA ISSN 0899-4927
CODEN: BIOGEP
THE MERTON SEASONAL; a quarterly review. Text in English. 1976. q. looseleaf. free to members (effective 2010). bk.rev. bibl.; illus. **Document type:** *Journal, Academic/Scholarly.* **Description:** Contains articles, book reviews and other information of interest to members of Thomas Merton Society.
Formerly: Merton Seasonal
Published by: (Bellarmine University), Thomas Merton Center, 5129 Penn Ave, Pittsburgh, PA 15224. TEL 412-301-3022, FAX 412-361-0540, info@thomasmertoncenter.org, http://www.thomasmertoncenter.org/. Ed. Patrick F O'Connell. **Co-sponsor:** International Thomas Merton Society.

R

200 USA ISSN 0026-0231
BX6101
MESSAGE (HAGERSTOWN); the magazine for virtuous living. Text in English. 1898. bi-m. USD 26 (effective 2009). adv. bk.rev.; rec.rev. illus. index. back issues avail. **Document type:** *Magazine, Consumer.* **Description:** Presents the Bible-based gospel of Jesus Christ to effect positive life-change and virtuous living for today and eternity.
Former titles (until 1978): The Message Magazine (0162-6019); (until 1935): Gospel Herald
Indexed: CCR.
Published by: Review and Herald Publishing Association, 55 W Oak Ridge Dr, Hagerstown, MD 21740. TEL 301-393-3000, info@rhpa.org, http://www.rhpa.org. Ed. Washington Johnson TEL 301-393-4100. Adv. contact Genia Blumenberg TEL 301-393-3170. B&W page USD 2,060, color page USD 2,540; trim 8.125 x 10.625. Circ: 69,000.

200 USA ISSN 0746-0635
MESSAGE OF THE CROSS. Text in English. 1950. q. free. adv. bk.rev. **Description:** Christian living and world missions.
Published by: Bethany Fellowship Inc., 6820 Auto Club Rd, Minneapolis, MN 55438. TEL 612-829-2492, FAX 612-829-2767. Ed., R&P George R Foster.

220 USA ISSN 0889-4159
MESSAGE OF THE OPEN BIBLE. Text in English. 1920. bi-m. USD 9.75 domestic; USD 17 foreign (effective 2000). **Description:** Informs, inspires and educates members of the denomination.
Published by: Open Bible Standard Churches, Open Bible Publishers, 2020 Bell Ave, Des Moines, IA 50315-1096. TEL 515-288-6761, FAX 515-288-2510. Ed. Jeff Farmer. R&P Andrea Johnson. Circ: 4,000 (paid).

230 NLD ISSN 0168-1869
MET ANDERE WOORDEN. Text in Dutch. 1982. q. **Document type:** *Magazine, Consumer.*
Related titles: Online - full text ed.: ISSN 1879-9612.
Published by: Nederlands Bijbelgenootschap, Postbus 620, Haarlem, 2003 RP, Netherlands. TEL 31-23-5146146, FAX 31-23-5342095, info@bijbelgenootschap.nl.

200 NLD ISSN 0943-3058
BL1
➤ **METHOD & THEORY IN THE STUDY OF RELIGION.** Text in Dutch. 1988. q. EUR 286, USD 400 to institutions; EUR 312, USD 437 combined subscription to institutions (print & online eds.) (effective 2012). bk.rev. back issues avail.; reprint service avail. from PSC. **Document type:** *Journal, Academic/Scholarly.* **Description:** Addresses the problems of methodology and theory in the academic study of religion.
Related titles: Online - full text ed.: ISSN 1570-0682. EUR 260, USD 364 to institutions (effective 2012) (from IngentaConnect).

Indexed: A01, A03, A08, A20, A21, A22, ArtHuCI, CA, DIP, E01, IBR, IBZ, IZBG, OTA, PCI, R&TA, RI-1, RI-2, SCOPUS, T02, W07.
—BLDSC (5745.620000), IE, Infotrieve, Ingenta. **CCC.**
Published by: (North American Association for the Study of Religion), Brill, PO Box 9000, Leiden, 2300 PA, Netherlands. TEL 31-71-5353500, FAX 31-71-5317532, cs@brill.nl. Ed. Matthew Day. **Dist. by:** Turpin Distribution Services Ltd., Pegasus Dr, Stratton Business Park, Biggleswade, Bedfordshire SG18 8QB, United Kingdom. TEL 44-1767-604954, FAX 44-1767-601640, custserv@turpin-distribution.com, http://www.turpin-distribution.com/.

➤ **METHOD: JOURNAL OF LONERGAN STUDIES.** *see* PHILOSOPHY

▼➤ **METTERDAAD MAGAZINE.** *see* BUSINESS AND ECONOMICS—International Development And Assistance

205 USA ISSN 0887-1760
BR1
MID-AMERICA JOURNAL OF THEOLOGY. Text in English. 1985. a. **Document type:** *Journal, Academic/Scholarly.* **Description:** Publishes articles on topics of exegetical and theological interest.
Indexed: A21, OTA, R&TA, RI-1.
Published by: Mid-America Reformed Seminary, 229 Seminary Dr, Dyer, IN 46311. TEL 219-864-2400, 800-440-6277, FAX 219-864-2410, info@midamerica.edu, http://www.midamerica.edu.

200 NLD ISSN 0165-3121
MIDDERNACHTSROEP. Text in Dutch. m. EUR 17.40 (effective 2009). **Document type:** *Magazine, Consumer.*
Published by: Middernachtsroep Nederland, Postbus 193, Doorn, 3940 AD, Netherlands. TEL 31-343-477288, FAX 31-343-477447, info@middernachtsroep.nl, http://www.middernachtsroep.nl.

MIGRANTI-PRESS; settimanale di informazione sulla mobilita umana. *see* POPULATION STUDIES

202 DEU ISSN 0047-7362
MILITAERSEELSORGE. Text in German. 1965. q. free. bk.rev. Supplement avail. **Document type:** *Bulletin.* **Description:** Catholic publication with articles devoted to the spiritual care of people in the military.
Published by: Katholisches Militaerbischofsamt, Postfach 190199, Bonn, 53037, Germany. TEL 0228-9121-0, FAX 0228-9121-105. Ed. Ernst Niermann.

THE MILITARY CHAPLAIN. *see* MILITARY

200 USA ISSN 1083-4761
BT875.A1
MILLENNIAL PROPHECY REPORT. Text in English. 1993. q. USD 60 to individuals; USD 90 to institutions. back issues avail. **Document type:** *Newsletter.* **Description:** Provides objective reporting on millenarian ideas and activities in the US and the rest of the world, including persons or groups discussing sudden global changes (environmental, social, political or religious).
Related titles: Online - full text ed.
Published by: Millennium Watch Institute, 4429 Larchwood Ave., Philadelphia, PA 19104-3915. TEL 800-666-4694. Ed. Ted Daniels.

MINDFLIGHTS. *see* LITERATURE—Science Fiction, Fantasy, Horror

267 270 ZMB
MINDOLO WORLD. Text in English. 1961. s-a. ZMK 3,000, USD 5 (effective 1999). adv. **Document type:** *Newsletter.* **Description:** Features articles which analyze the theological, educational, and developmental issues that have a bearing on the Mindolo Ecumenical Foundation.
Formerly: Mindolo News Letter (0076-8901)
Published by: Mindolo Ecumenical Foundation, PO Box 21493, Kitwe, Zambia. TEL 260-2-214572, FAX 260-2-211001. Ed., R&P Chris Akufuna. Circ: 500.

200 CHE ISSN 0255-8777
BV4019
MINISTERIAL FORMATION. Text in English. 1978. q. USD 15. **Document type:** *Newsletter, Academic/Scholarly.* **Description:** Aims to encourage sharing and cooperation among all working for the renewal of the churches through programs of ministerial formation.
Indexed: A21, RI-1, RI-2.
Published by: Education and Ecumenical Formation (Subsidiary of: World Council of Churches), 150 route de Ferney, PO Box 2100, Geneva 2, 1211, Switzerland. TEL 41-22-791-61-13, FAX 41-22-791-03-61, ger@wcc-coe.org, http://www.wcc-coe.org/wcc/what/education/index-e.html. Circ: 1,600.

251 USA ISSN 0894-3966
MINISTER'S MANUAL (YEAR); preaching and worship planning. Text in English. a. USD 28.95 (effective 2000).
Published by: Logos Productions, 6160 Carmen Ave E, Inver Grove Heights, MN 55076-4422. Ed. Sharilyn A Figueroa. Pub. Pete Velander.

200 DEU ISSN 0937-9886
MINISTRANTENPOST; Die Zeitschrift fuer Ministrantinnen und Ministranten. Key Title: Minipost. Text in German. 1984. m. EUR 17.50; EUR 2 newsstand/cover (effective 2009). **Document type:** *Magazine, Consumer.*
Formerly (until 1989): Ministranten-Post (0176-2710)
Published by: Butzon und Bercker GmbH, Hoogeweg 71, Kevelaer, 47623, Germany. TEL 49-2832-9290, FAX 49-2832-929211, service@bube.de, http://www.butzonbercker.de. Ed. Heidi Rose.

253 USA ISSN 0891-5725
BV4000
MINISTRIES TODAY; the magazine for Christian leaders. Text in English. 1983. bi-m. USD 14.97 domestic; USD 19.97 in Canada; USD 24.97 elsewhere (effective 2008). adv. 92 p./no. 3 cols./p.; back issues avail.; reprints avail. **Document type:** *Magazine, Consumer.* **Description:** Profiles pastors and other Christian leaders and covers all aspects of church leadership.
Formerly (until 1986): Ministries (0739-3997); Incorporates: Buckingham Report
Related titles: Online - full text ed.: free (effective 2008).
Indexed: A22, CCR, CPL, GSS&RPL.
Published by: Strang Communications Co., 600 Rinehart Rd, Lake Mary, FL 32746. TEL 407-333-0600, FAX 407-333-7100, custsvc@strang.com, http://www.strang.com. Ed. Marcus Yoars. Pub. Stephen Strang. Circ: 30,000.

200 USA ISSN 2159-4198
MINISTRY & LEADERSHIP. Text in English. 1965. q. **Document type:** *Magazine, Trade.* **Description:** Promotes Reformed Theological Seminary through articles designed to edify readers through solid biblical instruction, and through reports that focus primarily on the national and global impact of RTS students, faculty and alumni.
Former titles (until 2008): Reformed Quarterly; (until 2007): R T S Reformed Quarterly; (until 19??): R T S Ministry; (until 1988): R T S Bulletin; (until 1982): Reformed Theological Seminary. Bulletin (0145-9201)
Related titles: Online - full text ed.: free (effective 2011).
Published by: Reformed Theological Seminary, 5422 Clinton Blvd, Jackson, MS 39209. TEL 601-923-1600, FAX 601-923-1654. Ed. Lyn Perez.

264 USA ISSN 1520-6211
BV169
MINISTRY & LITURGY. Abbreviated title: M L. Text in English. 1973. 10/yr. USD 50 (print or online ed.) (effective 2010). adv. bk.rev. 40 p./no.; back issues avail.; reprints avail. **Document type:** *Magazine, Trade.* **Description:** Features articles on topics of interest to the entire parish team-rites, music, faith formation, Scripture, art and architecture, hospitality.
Former titles (until 1999): Modern Liturgy (0363-504X); (until 1976): Folk Mass and Modern Liturgy (0094-775X)
Related titles: Microform ed.: (from PQC); Online - full text ed.: ISSN 2153-5582.
Indexed: A21, A22, CERDIC, CPL, MAG, MusicInd, RI-1, RI-2, RILM.
Published by: Resource Publications, Inc., 160 E Virginia St, Ste 290, San Jose, CA 95112. TEL 408-286-8505, 888-273-7782, FAX 408-287-8748, info@rpinet.com. adv.: B&W page USD 1,326; 7.25 x 10. Circ: 30,000 (paid and free).

200 USA ISSN 1938-1921
THE MINISTRY OF THE WORD. Text in English. 1997. m. back issues avail.
Formerly (until 2008): The Ministry Magazine (1096-7966)
Published by: Living Stream Ministry, PO Box 2121, Anaheim, CA 92814. TEL 714-991-4681, office@lsm.org, http://www.lsm.org.

261 USA ISSN 1074-1739
MINNESOTA CHRISTIAN CHRONICLE. Text in English. 1978. bi-w.
Published by: Beard Communications, 623 Lilac Dr N., # A, Minneapolis, MN 55422-4609. Ed. Doug Trouten. Circ: 8,000.

220 RUS ISSN 1562-1413
MIR BIBLII/WORLD OF THE BIBLE. Text in Russian. 1993. s-a. USD 87 to institutions (effective 2003). illus. back issues avail. **Document type:** *Academic/Scholarly.* **Description:** Examines biblical scholarship, focusing on translation and interpretation. Seeks to promote biblical knowledge in Russia, cooperation between scholars, and to provide materials for related schools. Also looks to introduce contemporary issues to Russian orthodox thought. Includes articles on history, philology, archeology. Aimed at a wide audience.
Indexed: RASB.
Published by: Bibleisko-Bogoslovskii Institut Svyatogo Apostola Andreya/St. Andrew's Biblical Theological College, ul Ierusalimskaya, d.3, Moscow, 109316, Russian Federation. standrews@standrews.ru, http://www.standrews.ru. Ed. A Bodrov. R&P A Pospelov. Circ: 2,000. **Dist. by:** East View Information Services, 10601 Wayzata Blvd, Minneapolis, MN 55305. TEL 952-252-1201, 800-477-1005, FAX 952-252-1202, info@eastview.com, http://www.eastview.com.

204 USA ISSN 0026-5802
MIRACULOUS MEDAL. Text in English. 1928. q. free. illus. **Document type:** *Newsletter.* **Description:** Devotional magazine.
Published by: Central Association of the Miraculous Medal, 475 E Chelten Ave, Philadelphia, PA 19144. TEL 215-848-1010. Ed. Rev. William J O'Brien. Circ: 340,000 (controlled).

202 ESP ISSN 0210-9522
BX880
MISCELANEA COMILLAS; revista de teologia y ciencias humanas. Text in Spanish. 1943. s-a. EUR 40 domestic; EUR 74.80 elsewhere (effective 2009). adv. bk.rev. **Document type:** *Journal, Academic/Scholarly.* **Description:** Contains papers and scholarly research by faculty members in the areas of dogmatic and fundamental theology, sacred scripture, pastoral theology, history, philosophy, psychology, spirituality, bioethics and other related fields.
Indexed: A21, CERDIC, DIP, IBR, IBZ, IPB, MLA-IB, OTA, P09, PCI, RI-1, RI-2.
—BLDSC (5811.840000), INIST.
Published by: Universidad Pontificia Comillas de Madrid, Facultades de Filosofia y Letras y Teologia, Madrid, 28049, Spain. TEL 34-91-7343950, FAX 34-91-7344570.

261.26 USA ISSN 0792-0474
BV2619
➤ **MISHKAN.** Text in English. 1984. q. USD 40 domestic; USD 36 in Israel; USD 12 per issue (effective 2011). bk.rev. back issues avail. **Document type:** *Journal, Academic/Scholarly.* **Description:** Covers Biblical and theological debate on issues relating to Jewish evangelism, Hebrew-Christian and Messianic-Jewish identity, and Jewish-Christian relations.
Related titles: Online - full text ed.: USD 25 (effective 2011).
Indexed: R&TA.
Published by: Pasche Institute of Jewish Studies, 4010 Gaston Ave, Dallas, TX 75246. jimsibley@pascheinstitute.org, http://www.pascheinstitute.org. **Co-sponsor:** Caspari Center for Biblical and Jewish Studies.

266 ESP
MISIONEROS JAVERIANOS. Text in Spanish. 1963. m. free. illus. **Document type:** *Magazine, Consumer.*
Address: Monserrat, 9, Madrid, 28008, Spain. Circ: 48,000.

230 NOR ISSN 0809-8999
MISJONSHOEGSKOLEN. DISSERTATION SERIES/SCHOOL OF MISSION AND THEOLOGY. DISSERTATION SERIES. Text in English. 2006. irreg. **Document type:** *Monographic series, Academic/Scholarly.*
Published by: Misjonshoegskolens Forlag/School of Mission and Theology, Misjonsveien 34, Stavanger, 4024, Norway. TEL 47-51-516210, FAX 47-51-516225, http://www.mhs.no.

230.071 NOR ISSN 1504-1204
MISJONSHOEGSKOLEN. RESSURSSERIE. Text in Norwegian. 2004. irreg., latest vol.1, 2004. **Document type:** *Monographic series, Academic/Scholarly.*
Published by: Misjonshoegskolens Forlag/School of Mission and Theology, Misjonsveien 34, Stavanger, 4024, Norway. TEL 47-51-516210, FAX 47-51-516225, http://www.mhs.no.

230 NLD ISSN 1574-9754
MISKOTTE NIEUWSBRIEF. Text in Dutch. 1995. irreg. free (effective 2010).
Published by: (Dr. K. H. Miskotte Stichting), Skandalon Mediale Projecten, Postbus 138, Vught, 5260 AC, Netherlands. TEL 31-30-2218250, FAX 31-84-7186782, info@skandalon.nl, http://www.skandalon.nl. Ed. Jan de Vlieger.

291.72 NLD ISSN 1874-5873
MISSIO WERELDWIJD. Text in Dutch. 1946. bi-m. EUR 10 (effective 2009).
Former titles (until 2007): Missieinteractie (1567-178X); (until 2000): Missie in Aktie (0167-2916); (until 1984): Missie-Actie (1382-046X)
Published by: Missio Nederland, Postbus 93140, The Hague, 2509 AC, Netherlands. TEL 31-70-3047444, FAX 31-70-3818355, missio@missio.nl, http://www.missio.nl.

200 DEU
MISSION. Text in German. 1908. 3/yr. free (effective 2009). **Document type:** *Magazine, Consumer.*
Former titles (until 1975): Der Ruf; (until 1949): Berliner Missionsberichte
Published by: Berliner Missionswerk, Georgenkirchstr 69-70, Berlin, 10249, Germany. TEL 49-30-24344123, FAX 49-30-24344124, bmw@berliner-missionswerk.de. Circ: 28,000 (controlled).

207.2 USA
MISSION. Text in English. q. USD 3. **Document type:** *Newsletter.* **Description:** Provides information about the activities of the congregation which is dedicated to the interracial apostolate in the U.S. and Haiti.
Published by: Sisters of the Blessed Sacrament, 1663 Bristol Pike, Bensalem, PA 19020-8502. TEL 215-244-9900. Ed. Christa McGill. Circ: 4,000.

207.2 CAN ISSN 1198-0400
BV2130
MISSION; journal of mission studies. Text in English, French. 1967. s-a. CAD 25.68 domestic; USD 25 foreign. bk.rev. **Document type:** *Journal, Academic/Scholarly.*
Formerly (until 1994): Kerygma (0023-0693)
Indexed: A21, DIP, FR, IBR, IBZ, RI-1, RI-2.
—INIST.
Published by: Saint Paul University, Institute of Mission Studies (Subsidiary of: Saint Paul University/Universite Saint-Paul), 223 Main St, Ottawa, ON K1S 1C4, Canada. TEL 613-236-1393, FAX 613-782-3005. Ed. Martin Roberge. Circ: 250.

200 USA ISSN 2156-440X
MISSION FRIENDS AT HOME. Text in English. 19??. q. USD 25.99 (effective 2010). **Document type:** *Journal, Consumer.* **Description:** Contains songs, games, activities, and note to parents.
Former titles (until 2010): Share (1095-4309); (until 1998): Mission Friends Share (0888-8922)
Published by: Woman's Missionary Union, 100 Missionary Ridge, PO Box 830010, Birmingham, AL 35283. TEL 205-991-8100, 800-968-7301, FAX 205-995-4840, customer_service@wmu.org, http://www.wmu.com.

291.72 USA ISSN 2156-4337
MISSION FRIENDS LEADER. Text in English. 1970. q. USD 21.99 (effective 2010). **Document type:** *Journal, Consumer.* **Description:** Covers session plans and weekly activities in interest areas such as music, art, blocks, nature, homeliving, and more.
Formerly (until 2010): Start (0162-6841)
Published by: Woman's Missionary Union, 100 Missionary Ridge, PO Box 830010, Birmingham, AL 35283. TEL 205-991-8100, 800-968-7301, FAX 205-995-4840, customer_service@wmu.org, http://www.wmu.com.

207.2 USA ISSN 0889-9436
MISSION FRONTIERS. Text in English. 1979. bi-m. USD 18 domestic; USD 26 foreign (effective 2004). adv. bk.rev. back issues avail. **Document type:** *Bulletin, Consumer.*
Indexed: CCR, DIP, GSS&RPL, IBR, IBZ.
Published by: U S Center for World Mission, 1605 Elizabeth St, Pasadena, CA 91104-2721. TEL 626-797-1111, FAX 626-398-2263, http://www.uscwm.org. Eds. Darrell Dorr, Ralph Winter. adv.: page USD 1,800. Circ: 120,000.

291.72 NLD ISSN 0168-9789
BV2000
➤ **MISSION STUDIES.** Text in Multiple languages. 1973. s-a. EUR 129, USD 179 to institutions; EUR 140, USD 196 combined subscription to institutions (print & online eds.) (effective 2012). bk.rev. back issues avail.; reprint service avail. from PSC. **Document type:** *Journal, Academic/Scholarly.* **Description:** Aims to better enable the International Association for Mission Studies to expand its services as a forum for the scholarly study of biblical, theological, historical and practical questions related to mission.
Formerly (until 1983): I A M S News Letter (0166-2848)
Related titles: Online - full text ed.: ISSN 1573-3831. EUR 117, USD 163 to institutions (effective 2012) (from IngentaConnect).
Indexed: A01, A02, A03, A08, A21, A22, CA, E01, IZBG, R&TA, RI-1, SCOPUS, T02.
—IE, Ingenta. **CCC.**
Published by: (International Association for Mission Studies (I A M S)), Brill, PO Box 9000, Leiden, 2300 PA, Netherlands. TEL 31-71-5353500, FAX 31-71-5317532, cs@brill.nl. Eds. Catherine Rae Ross, J Jayakiran Sebastian, Lalsangkima Pachuau, Susan Smith. **Dist. by:** Turpin Distribution Services Ltd., Pegasus Dr, Stratton Business Park, Biggleswade, Bedfordshire SG18 8QB, United Kingdom. TEL 44-1767-604954, FAX 44-1767-601640, custserv@turpin-distribution.com, http://www.turpin-distribution.com/.

291.72 DEU
MISSION UND GEGENWART/MISSION - PAT AND PRESENT. Text in German. 2008. irreg., latest vol.4, 2010. price varies. **Document type:** *Monographic series, Academic/Scholarly.*
Published by: Ruediger Koeppe Verlag, Wendelinstr 73-75, Cologne, 50933, Germany. TEL 49-221-4911236, FAX 49-221-4994336, info@koeppe.de.

207.2 CAN ISSN 0026-6116
MISSIONS-ETRANGERES. Text in French. 1941. 5/yr. CAD 10 domestic; USD 10 foreign (effective 2002). charts; illus.; stat. back issues avail. **Document type:** *Newsletter.* **Description:** Covers the works of the Roman Catholic Missionary Society in Asia, South America and Africa.
Published by: Societe des Missions Etrangeres, 160 Place Juge Desnoyers, Pont Viau, Ville de Laval, PQ H7G 1A4, Canada. TEL 450-667-4190, FAX 450-667-3006. Ed. Renaude Gregoire. Circ: 24,000 (paid).

DIE MITARBEITERIN; Werkheft fuer Frauenbildung und Frauenseelsorge. *see* WOMEN'S INTERESTS

MITEINANDER GOTT ENTDECKEN. *see* EDUCATION

200 DEU ISSN 0939-9186
BL256
➤ **MITTEILUNGEN FUER ANTHROPOLOGIE UND RELIGIONSGESCHICHTE.** Text in English, French, German, Italian, Spanish. 1969. irreg., latest vol.19, 2008. price varies. adv. bk.rev. **Document type:** *Monographic series, Academic/Scholarly.*
Formerly (until 1991): Jahrbuch fuer Anthropologie und Religionsgeschichte (0341-0684)
Indexed: AICP.
Published by: Ugarit-Verlag, Ricarda-Huch-Str 6, Muenster, 48161, Germany. TEL 49-251-8322661, FAX 49-251-8322662, verlag@ugarit-verlag.de. Eds. A. Haeussling, Manfred L.G. Dietrich, W Dupre.

200 TZA ISSN 0047-7583
MLEZI/EDUCATOR; a journal for preaching and teaching religion. Text in Swahili. 1970. bi-m. TZS 360, USD 18 (effective 1994). adv. bk.rev. illus. **Document type:** *Academic/Scholarly.* **Description:** Covers research on problems facing those teaching in the church.
Published by: Peramiho Publications, PO Box 41, Peramiho, Tanzania. TEL 255-1-580-8236, TELEX 21540. Ed. Vitus Ndunguru. Circ: 18,000 (paid).

200 GBR ISSN 1353-1425
BX5011
MODERN BELIEVING. Text in English. 1911. q. GBP 8.75 per issue domestic to non-members; GBP 10.50 per issue foreign to non-members; free to members (effective 2009). adv. bk.rev. index. back issues avail. **Document type:** *Journal, Academic/Scholarly.* **Description:** Explores the current thinking and trends within Christian doctrine, ecclesiology, contextual, social and pastoral theology, all within the milieu of the modern world.
Formerly (until 1994): Modern Churchman (0026-7597)
Related titles: Microfilm ed.: (from PQC); Online - full text ed.
Indexed: A21, CERDIC, DIP, IBR, IBZ, MEA&I, P30, R&TA, RI-1, RI-2.
Published by: Modern Churchpeople's Union, 9 Westward View, Liverpool, L17 7EE, United Kingdom. TEL 44-845-3451909, office@modchurchunion.org. Ed. Paul Badham.

200 GBR
MODERN CHURCHPEOPLE'S UNION. OCCASIONAL PAPERS. Text in English. 19??. irreg., latest 2007, Oct. free to members.
Related titles: Online - full text ed.: free (effective 2009).
Published by: Modern Churchpeople's Union, 9 Westward View, Liverpool, L17 7EE, United Kingdom. TEL 44-845-3451909, office@modchurchunion.org. Ed. Jonathan Clatworthy.

200 GBR ISSN 0266-7177
BR1
➤ **MODERN THEOLOGY.** Text in English. 1984. q. GBP 459 in United Kingdom to institutions; EUR 583 in Europe to institutions; USD 759 in the Americas to institutions; USD 1,033 elsewhere to institutions; GBP 528 combined subscription in United Kingdom to institutions (print & online eds.); EUR 671 combined subscription in Europe to institutions (print & online eds.); USD 874 combined subscription in the Americas to institutions (print & online eds.); USD 1,189 combined subscription elsewhere to institutions (print & online eds.) (effective 2012). adv. bk.rev. back issues avail.; reprint service avail. from PSC. **Document type:** *Journal, Academic/Scholarly.* **Description:** Publishes scholarly articles addressing issues specific to the discipline of theology and wider issues from a theological perspective.
Related titles: Microform ed.; Online - full text ed.: ISSN 1468-0025. GBP 459 in United Kingdom to institutions; EUR 583 in Europe to institutions; USD 759 in the Americas to institutions; USD 1,033 elsewhere to institutions (effective 2012) (from IngentaConnect).
Indexed: A01, A02, A03, A08, A21, A22, A26, AmHI, B04, BRD, BrHumI, CA, E01, E08, FamI, G08, H07, H08, H14, HAb, HumInd, I05, P02, P10, P28, P48, P53, P54, PCI, PQC, PhilInd, R&TA, R05, RASB, RI-1, RI-2, S09, SCOPUS, T02, W03.
—BLDSC (5898.210000), IE, Infotrieve, Ingenta. **CCC.**
Published by: Wiley-Blackwell Publishing Ltd. (Subsidiary of: John Wiley & Sons, Inc.), 9600 Garsington Rd, Oxford, OX4 2DQ, United Kingdom. TEL 44-1865-776868, FAX 44-1865-714591, customerservices@blackwellpublishing.com. Eds. Jim Fodor TEL 716-375-2399, William T Cavanaugh TEL 651-962-5335. adv.: B&W page GBP 445, B&W page USD 823; 112 x 190. Circ: 700.

➤ **LE MONDE DE LA BIBLE**; histoire art archeologie. *see* ARCHAEOLOGY

230 ESP ISSN 2172-203X
MONUMENTA REGNI GRANATENSIS HISTORICA. EPISTULAE. Text in Catalan. 2006. a. **Document type:** *Monographic series, Academic/Scholarly.*
Published by: Universidad de Granada, Cuesta del Hospicio s/n, Granada, 18071, Spain. TEL 34-958-243025, FAX 34-958-243066, informa@ugr.es, http://www.ugr.es.

200 USA
MOODY STUDENT. Text in English. 1935. fortn. USD 9. adv.
Published by: Moody Bible Institute, 820 N. LaSalle Blvd., Chicago, IL 60610. TEL 312-329-4000, FAX 312-329-2149, www.moody.edu. Ed. Wendy Cameron. Circ: 2,100.

200 170 BEL ISSN 0928-2742
➤ **MORALITY AND THE MEANING OF LIFE.** Text in English, German. 1992. irreg. (approx a.), latest 2007. price varies. back issues avail. **Document type:** *Monographic series, Academic/Scholarly.*
Published by: Peeters Publishers, Bondgenotenlaan 153, Leuven, 3000, Belgium. TEL 32-16-235170, FAX 32-16-228500, http://www.peeters-leuven.be.

➤ **MOREANA.** *see* HISTORY—History Of Europe

➤ **MOUNTAIN IDEALS.** *see* GENERAL INTEREST PERIODICALS—United States

➤ **MOUNTAIN PATH.** *see* PHILOSOPHY

200 DEU
MUENCHENER THEOLOGISCHE FORSCHUNGEN. Text in German. 2003. irreg., latest vol.2, 2004. price varies. **Document type:** *Monographic series, Academic/Scholarly.*
Published by: V & R Unipress GmbH (Subsidiary of: Vandenhoeck und Ruprecht), Robert-Bosch-Breite 6, Goettingen, 37079, Germany. TEL 49-551-5084303, FAX 49-551-5084333, info@vr-unipress.de, http://www.v-r.de/en/publisher/unipress.

200 DEU
MUENCHNER THEOLOGISCHE BEITRAEGE. Text in German. 1999. irreg., latest vol.14, 2010. price varies. **Document type:** *Monographic series, Academic/Scholarly.*
Published by: Herbert Utz Verlag GmbH, Adalbertstr 57, Munich, 80799, Germany. TEL 49-89-27779100, FAX 49-89-27779101, utz@utzverlag.com. Ed. Nikolaus Knoepffler.

206.57 USA ISSN 1524-251X
BX5971.O73
MUNDI MEDICINA. Text in English. 1989. 3/yr. free. bk.rev. **Document type:** *Newsletter.* **Description:** Provides news of the monastic community of Holy Cross Monastery.
Published by: (Order of the Holy Cross), Holy Cross Monastery, PO Box 99, West Park, NY 12493. TEL 845-384-6660, http://www.holycrossmonastery.com. Ed. Bro. Paul Littlefield. R&P Br Paul Littlefield. Circ: 6,500 (controlled).

207 ESP ISSN 1134-7074
MUNDO NEGRO; revista misional africana. Text in Spanish. 1960. m. adv. bk.rev. bibl.; illus.; maps; stat.; tr.lit. index. back issues avail. **Document type:** *Magazine, Consumer.* **Description:** Contains general information about the African continent (politics, economics, religion) and about Blacks in America.
Related titles: Online - full text ed.
Indexed: MLA-IB.
Published by: Misioneros Combonianos, Congregacion Misionera, Arturo Soria, 101, Madrid, 28043, Spain. TEL 34-91-4152412, FAX 34-91-5192550, mundonegro@planalfa.es, http://www3.planalfa.es/mcombonianos. Circ: 100,000 (controlled).

200 UGA
MUNNO. Text in Luganda. 1911. m. UGX 1,200. adv. **Document type:** *Newspaper.*
Formerly: Musizi (0541-4385)
Address: PO Box 4027, Kampala, Uganda. Ed. J Kayondo. Circ: 6,500.

LE MUSEON; revue d'etudes orientales. *see* ASIAN STUDIES

226 PAK ISSN 0254-7856
AL-MUSHIR/COUNSELOR. Text in English, Urdu. 1959. q. PKR 75, USD 18. bk.rev. **Document type:** *Journal, Academic/Scholarly.* **Description:** Discusses Christian-Muslim relations; Islamic, Christian theology and cultural, social issues in the context of Pakistan.
Indexed: I14.
Published by: Christian Study Centre, 126-B Murree Rd., P O Box 579, Rawalpindi, Pakistan. TEL 92-51-567412, FAX 92-51-584594. Ed. Charles Amjad Ali. Circ: 650.

MUSIK UND KIRCHE. *see* MUSIC

MUSIK UND MESSAGE. *see* MUSIC

230 USA ISSN 1533-2470
BS680.S53
MUTUALITY. Text in English. 1994. q. USD 40 to non-members; USD 6 per issue to non-members; free to members (effective 2010); subscr. includes with Priscilla Papers. adv. back issues avail. **Document type:** *Magazine, Consumer.* **Description:** Provides inspiration, encouragement, and information on topics related to a biblical view of mutuality between men and women in the home, church, and world.
Indexed: A01, CA, T02.
Published by: Christians for Biblical Equality, 122 W Franklin Ave, Ste 218, Minneapolis, MN 55404. TEL 612-872-6898, FAX 612-872-6891, cbe@cbeinternational.org. Ed. Megan Greulich. Pub. Mimi Haddad.

MUZIEK EN LITURGIE. *see* MUSIC

MUZIEKBODE. *see* MUSIC

MY OPINIONS; incest and illegitimacy. *see* PHILOSOPHY

200 COL ISSN 0027-5638
BX1751A1
MYSTERIUM. Text in Spanish. 1946. q. COP 50. bk.rev. bibl. index.
Published by: Provincia Occidental Claretianos de Colombia, Apartado Aereo 51 841, Medellin, ANT, Colombia.

230 DEU
MYSTIK IN GESCHICHTE UND GEGENWART; Texte und Untersuchungen. Text in German. 1985. irreg., latest vol.19, 2005. price varies. **Document type:** *Monographic series, Academic/Scholarly.*
Published by: Frommann-Holzboog Verlag e.K., Koenig-Karl-Str 27, Stuttgart, 70372, Germany. TEL 49-711-9559690, FAX 49-711-9559691, info@frommann-holzboog.de, http://www.frommann-holzboog.de.

200 FRA ISSN 1765-8071
MYTHES, IMAGINAIRES, RELIGIONS. Text in French. 2004. irreg., latest 2008. back issues avail. **Document type:** *Monographic series, Academic/Scholarly.*
Published by: Presses Universitaires du Septentrion, Rue du Barreau, BP 30199, Villeneuve d'Ascq, Cedex 59654, France. TEL 33-3-20416680, FAX 33-3-20416690, septentrion@septentrion.com, http://www.septentrion.com.

200 ITA ISSN 1972-2516
BL5
MYTHOS; rivista di storia delle religioni. Text in Multiple languages. 1989. a. **Document type:** *Journal, Academic/Scholarly.*
Related titles: Online - full text ed.: ISSN 2037-7746. 2006.
Published by: Universita degli Studi di Palermo, Facolta di Lettere e Filosofia, Viale delle Scienze 12, Palermo, 90128, Italy. TEL 39-091-6560225, FAX 39-091-427366, http://www.unipa.it.

N C R V GIDS. *see* COMMUNICATIONS—Radio

N C R V MAGAZINE. *see* COMMUNICATIONS—Radio

N E A R I NEWSLETTER. *see* LIBRARY AND INFORMATION SCIENCES

200 RUS ISSN 1810-1623
N G RELIGII. Text in Russian. 1997. s-m. USD 141 foreign (effective 2005). **Document type:** *Magazine, Consumer.* **Description:** Covers problems or religion and policy with regard to religion in today's Russia. Presents materials on Orthodox Christianity, Islam, Judaism and other religions, denominations and sects active in Russia.
Related titles: Online - full content ed.: ISSN 1810-1631; ♦ Supplement to: Nezavisimaya Gazeta. ISSN 1560-1005.
Published by: Nezavisimaya Gazeta, Myasnitskaya 13, Moscow, 101000, Russian Federation. TEL 7-095-9255543, info@ng.ru, http://www.ng.ru. **Dist. by:** East View Information Services, 10601 Wayzata Blvd, Minneapolis, MN 55305. TEL 952-252-1201, 800-477-1005, FAX 952-252-1202, info@eastview.com, http://www.eastview.com.

N R B MAGAZINE. (National Religious Broadcasters) *see* COMMUNICATIONS—Television And Cable

200 952 JPN ISSN 0386-720X
NANZAN INSTITUTE FOR RELIGION AND CULTURE. BULLETIN. Text in English. 1977. a. free. back issues avail. **Document type:** *Bulletin.*
Indexed: BAS, FR, RASB.
—BLDSC (2629.105000), INIST.
Published by: Nanzan Institute for Religion and Culture, 18 Yamazato-cho, Showa-ku, Nagoya, 466-8673, Japan. TEL 81-52-8323111, FAX 81-52-8336157, nirc@ic.nanzan-u.ac.jp, http://www.nanzan-u.ac.jp/SHUBUNKEN/index.htm. Circ: 1,200.

200 JPN ISSN 0387-3730
NANZAN JOURNAL OF THEOLOGICAL STUDIES. Text in Japanese. 1978. a. free.
Published by: (Ecclesiastical Faculty of Theology), Nanzan University, 18 Yamazato-cho, Showa-ku, Nagoya-shi, Aichi-ken 466-8673, Japan. TEL 81-52-832-3111, FAX 81-52-835-1444.

230 PHL
NATIONAL RENEWAL; our rebirth in Christ. Text and summaries in English. 1993. m. PHP 420; USD 36 foreign. adv. back issues avail. **Document type:** *Consumer.* **Description:** Presents fresh Christian perspective on Philippines' national concerns and relevant issues affecting every Filipino.
Related titles: CD-ROM ed.
Indexed: IPP.
Published by: Seedtime Publishing, Inc., 51 10th St, Rolling Hills Village, New Manila, Quezon City, 1112, Philippines. TEL 63-2-7222621, FAX 63-2-7218723. Ed. Coylee Gamboa. Pub. Didi Maranon. Adv. contact Raul Lanting. B&W page PHP 9,000, color page PHP 13,500. Circ: 7,000.

202 USA
BF1001
THE NATIONAL SPIRITUALIST SUMMIT. Text in English. 1919. m. bibl.; illus. back issues avail. **Document type:** *Magazine, Consumer.* **Description:** Deals with spiritual - religious issues, from an inspirational point of view.
Former titles (until 1981): National Spiritualist Summit of Spiritual Understanding; (until 1979): National Spiritualist (0882-1275); (until 1974): Summit of Spiritual Understanding; (until 1963): National Spiritualist
Published by: National Spiritualist Association of Churches, 13 Cottage Row, PO Box 6089, Lily Dale, AZ 85376. TEL 623-975-0596, FAX 623-975-0596, secretary@nsac.org. Ed. Laura Lee Perkins.

230 ESP ISSN 0470-3790
NATURALEZA Y GRACIA; revista cuatrimestral de ciencias eclesiasticas. Text in Spanish. 1954. 3/yr. USD 44 foreign. **Document type:** *Magazine, Consumer.*
Indexed: IPB.
Published by: Hermanos Menores Capuchinos de Castilla, C. Ramon y Cajal, 5-7, Salamanca, 37002, Spain. TEL 34-923-214653. Ed. Alejandro Villalmonte.

200 RUS ISSN 0028-1239
NAUKA I RELIGIYA. Text in Russian. 1959. m. USD 114 foreign (effective 2003). bk.rev. bibl.; illus.; stat.
Related titles: Microfiche ed.: (from EVP); Microfilm ed.: (from PQC).
Indexed: CDSP, CERDIC, RASB.
Published by: Vsesoyuznoe Obshchestvo "Znanie", Tovarishchevskii per 8, Moscow, 109004, Russian Federation. TEL 7-095-9110126. Ed. V F Pravotorov. Circ: 285,000. **Dist. by:** M K - Periodica, ul Gilyarovskogo 39, Moscow 129110, Russian Federation. TEL 7-095-2845008, FAX 7-095-2813798, info@periodicals.ru, http://www.mkniga.ru; East View Information Services, 10601 Wayzata Blvd, Minneapolis, MN 55305. TEL 952-252-1201, 800-477-1005, FAX 952-252-1202, info@eastview.com, http://www.eastview.com.

NAVY CHAPLAIN. *see* MILITARY

NEAR EASTERN ARCHAEOLOGY. *see* ARCHAEOLOGY

230 NLD ISSN 0028-212X
BR2
NEDERLANDS THEOLOGISCH TIJDSCHRIFT. Text in Dutch. 1818. q. EUR 53 to individuals; EUR 65 to institutions; EUR 39.75 to students; EUR 16.35 newsstand/cover (effective 2008). adv. bk.rev. bibl. index. **Document type:** *Journal, Academic/Scholarly.*
Supersedes (in 1946): Nieuwe Theologische Studien (1872-9355)
Indexed: A21, A22, CERDIC, FR, IPB, MLA-IB, OTA, PCI, R&TA, RI-1, RI-2.
—BLDSC (6071.380000), IE, Infotrieve, Ingenta, INIST.
Published by: Boekencentrum Uitgevers, Goudstraat 50, Postbus 29, Zoetermeer, 2700 AA, Netherlands. TEL 31-79-3615481, FAX 31-79-3615489, info@boekencentrum.nl, http://www.boekencentrum.nl. Ed. E P Schaafsma. adv.: page EUR 205; trim 160 x 245. Circ: 550.

225 ZAF ISSN 0254-8356
➤ **NEOTESTAMENTICA.** Text in English. 1967. s-a. ZAR 80 in Africa; USD 45 elsewhere (effective 2004). adv. bk.rev. reprints avail. **Document type:** *Journal, Academic/Scholarly.* **Description:** Contains literary, historical and theological reflections on New Testament texts.
Related titles: Microfiche ed.
Indexed: A21, DIP, FR, IBR, IBZ, ISAP, IZBG, PCI, R&TA, RI-1.
—BLDSC (6075.655000), IE, Ingenta, INIST. **CCC.**

R

Published by: New Testament Society of South Africa/Nuwe Testamentiese Werkgemeenskap van Suid-Afrika, c/o Dept of New Testament, University of the Orange Free State, PO Box 339, Bloemfontein, 9300, South Africa. TEL 27-51-4012667, FAX 27-51-489203. Ed. H C van Zyl. Circ: 430.

➤ **NESHAMA**; encouraging the exploration of women's spirituality in Judaism. *see* WOMEN'S STUDIES

266 GBR
NET WORK. Variant title: Fishermen's Mission's Network Magazine. Text in English. 1886. 2/yr. free. adv. charts; illus. **Document type:** *Newsletter.*
Formerly (until 1995): Toilers of the Deep (0040-8824)
Related titles: Online - full text ed.
—BLDSC (6076.631700).
Published by: Royal National Mission to Deep Sea Fishermen, Fishermen's Mission Head Office, Mather House, 4400 Parkway, Solent Business Park, Whiteley, Hamps PO15 7FJ, United Kingdom. TEL 44-1489-566910, enquiries@rnmdsf.org.uk. Circ: 40,000.

207.2 USA
NETWORK (ATLANTA). Text in English. 1983. q. bk.rev. illus.; stat. **Description:** Covers foreign mission work of the church.
Supersedes (1957-1983): W P M Newsletter (World Presbyterian Missions) (0042-9783)
Media: Duplicated (not offset).
Published by: Presbyterian Church in America, Mission to the World, PO Box 29765, Atlanta, GA 30359. TEL 404-320-3373, FAX 404-325-5974. Ed. Marc Kyle. Circ: 88,000 (controlled).

200 DEU ISSN 2190-7331
NEUE HALLESCHE BERICHTE; Quellen und Studien zur Geschichte und Gegenwart Suedindiens. Text in German. 1999. irreg., latest vol.9, 2010. price varies. **Document type:** *Monographic series, Academic/Scholarly.*
Published by: Franckesche Stiftungen zu Halle, Franckeplatz 1, Haus 37, Halle, 06110, Germany. TEL 49-345-2127499, FAX 49-345-2127433, verlag@francke-halle.de, http://www.francke-halle.de.

200 DEU ISSN 0344-7022
NEUE STADT. Text in German. 1957. 10/yr. EUR 32 (effective 2011). adv. back issues avail. **Document type:** *Journal, Academic/Scholarly.*
Indexed: AIAP.
Published by: Verlag Neue Stadt, Muenchener Str 2, Oberpframmern, 85667, Germany. TEL 49-8093-2091, FAX 49-8093-2096, verlag@neuestadt.com, http://www.neuestadt.com. Circ: 20,000.

200 DEU ISSN 0340-6806
NEUE THEOLOGISCHE GRUNDRISSE. Text in German. 1948. irreg. price varies. **Document type:** *Monographic series, Academic/Scholarly.*
Published by: Mohr Siebeck GmbH & Co. KG, Wilhelmstr 18, Tuebingen, 72074, Germany. TEL 49-7071-9230, FAX 49-7071-51104, info@mohr.de.

201 DEU ISSN 0028-3517
BR4
NEUE ZEITSCHRIFT FUER SYSTEMATISCHE THEOLOGIE UND RELIGIONSPHILOSOPHIE. Text in German, English. 1923. q. EUR 194, USD 291 to institutions; EUR 223, USD 335 combined subscription to institutions (print & online eds.) (effective 2012). adv. bk.rev. bibl. index. reprint service avail. from SCH. **Document type:** *Journal, Academic/Scholarly.* **Description:** Seeks to keep open a forum of responsible thought in the controversial issue of contemporary theology, and offers a variety of ways to formulate questions.
Former titles (until 1962): Neue Zeitschrift fur Systematische Theologie (0179-6127); (until 1957): Zeitschrift fur Systematische Theologie (0179-6135)
Related titles: Online - full text ed.: ISSN 1612-9520. EUR 194, USD 291 to institutions (effective 2012).
Indexed: A01, A20, A21, A22, A26, ASCA, ArtHuCI, BAS, CERDIC, CurCont, DIP, E01, FR, H14, I05, IBR, IBZ, IPB, MLA-IB, P02, P10, P28, P48, P53, P54, PCI, PQC, R&TA, RASB, RI-1, RI-2, SCOPUS, T02, W07.
—IE, Infotrieve, INIST. **CCC.**
Published by: Walter de Gruyter GmbH & Co. KG, Genthiner Str 13, Berlin, 10785, Germany. TEL 49-30-260050, FAX 49-30-26005251, info@degruyter.com, http://www.degruyter.de. Ed. Oswald Bayer. Adv. contact Dietlind Makswitat TEL 49-30-260050. page EUR 200; trim 112 x 181. Circ: 550 (paid and controlled).

200 DEU ISSN 0028-3665
NEUES LEBEN. Text in German. 1956. 10/yr. EUR 27; EUR 2.70 newsstand/cover (effective 2007). adv. bk.rev. illus. **Document type:** *Magazine, Consumer.* **Description:** Contains information on the practical aspects of Christian life.
Indexed: E-psyche.
Published by: Neues Leben Medien e.V, Koelnerstr 23, Altenkirchen, 57610, Germany. TEL 49-2681-941250, FAX 49-2681-941100, peter.schulte@neuesleben.com. Ed. Rainer Schacke. Pubs. Peter Schulte, Wilfried Schulte. Adv. contact Joerg Wuerz. B&W page EUR 1,064, color page EUR 1,381; trim 186 x 257. Circ: 16,000 (paid); 4,000 (controlled).

200 DEU
NEUES LEBEN - SINGLE LEBEN; Die christliche Zeitschrift fuer Alleinstehende. Text in German. q. EUR 10.80; EUR 2.70 newsstand/cover (effective 2007). **Document type:** *Magazine, Consumer.*
Published by: Neues Leben Medien e.V, Koelnerstr 23, Altenkirchen, 57610, Germany. TEL 49-2681-941250, FAX 49-2681-941100, peter.schulte@neuesleben.com, http://www.neuesleben.com.

225 DEU ISSN 1862-2666
NEUTESTAMENTLICHE ENTWUERFE ZUR THEOLOGIE. Text in German. 2001. irreg., latest vol.16, 2010. price varies. **Document type:** *Monographic series, Academic/Scholarly.*
Published by: A. Francke Verlag GmbH, Dischinger Weg 5, Tuebingen, 72070, Germany. TEL 49-7071-97970, FAX 49-7071-979711, info@francke.de, http://www.francke.de.

NEW ATHENAEUM/NEUES ATHENAEUM. *see* PHILOSOPHY

200 UGA
NEW CENTURY. Text in English. 1959. m. USD 20. adv. bk.rev.; play rev. **Document type:** *Newspaper.*
Formerly: New Day (0028-4556)
Published by: Church of Uganda, PO Box 14123, Mengo, Uganda. TEL 256-270218, FAX 256-250922. Ed. James E Mutumba. Circ: 5,000.

200 PHL ISSN 0118-0673
NEW CITY. Text in English. 1966. m. PHP 300; USD 30 foreign (effective 1999). adv. **Document type:** *Magazine, Trade.*
Indexed: AIAP.
Published by: (Focolare Movement for Men), New City Press, PO Box 332, Manila, Philippines. TEL 2-714-2947, FAX 2-7160092. Ed. Carlo Maria Gentile. Circ: 6,200 (controlled).

200 GBR ISSN 0142-7725
NEW CITY (LONDON). Text in English. 1970. 11/yr. GBP 16.50 domestic; GBP 20 foreign (effective 2002). bk.rev. 20 p./no.; back issues avail. **Document type:** *Newsletter.* **Description:** Examines religion and theology via the Focolare Movement.
Published by: Mariapolis Ltd. Focolare Movement, 57 Twyford Ave, London, W3 9PZ, United Kingdom. TEL 44-20-8992-7666. Ed. Frank Johnson. R&P Rumold van Geffen. Circ: 1,200.

202 GBR ISSN 0140-7457
NEW CITY SPECIALS. Text in English. 1977. irreg. price varies. **Document type:** *Monographic series, Academic/Scholarly.*
—**CCC.**
Published by: Urban Theology Unit, 210 Abbeyfield Rd, Sheffield, S Yorks S4 7AZ, United Kingdom. TEL 44-114-2435342, FAX 44-114-2435356, office@utusheffield.fsnet.co.uk, http://www.utusheffield.org.uk.

260 USA ISSN 0360-0181
BV600
NEW CONVERSATIONS. Text in English. 1975. 3/yr. USD 10. bk.rev.
Indexed: A21, RI-1, RI-2.
Published by: United Church Board for Homeland Ministries, 700 Prospect Ave, Cleveland, OH 44115-1100. TEL 216-736-3277, FAX 216-736-3263. Ed. Nanette M Roberts. Circ: 1,500 (controlled).

NEW CRUCIBLE; a magazine about man and his environment. *see* PSYCHOLOGY

207.2 GBR
NEW DAY. Text in English. 1896. 2/yr. free. **Document type:** *Bulletin.*
Former titles (until 1973): The Leprosy Mission In Action; (until 1972): Without the Camp (0043-7018)
—BLDSC (6083.020000).
Published by: Leprosy Mission, Goldhay Way, Orton Goldhay, Peterborough, PE2 5GZ, United Kingdom. TEL 44-1733-370505, FAX 44-1733-404880, post@tlmew.org.uk, http://www.leprosymission.org.uk. Ed. Claire Tuck. Circ: 165,000.

NEW HORIZONS. *see* BUSINESS AND ECONOMICS—International Development And Assistance

230 USA ISSN 1946-5920
▼ **NEW IDENTITY MAGAZINE**; God in focus. World in scope. Text in English. 2009. q. USD 8.80 per issue (effective 2009). adv. back issues avail. **Document type:** *Magazine, Consumer.* **Description:** Presents topics, issues and opinions into the ways you view the world as Christians and how Christians are viewed by the world.
Related titles: Online - full text ed.: ISSN 1946-5939.
Address: PO Box 375, Torrance, CA 90508. TEL 310-947-8707, feedback@newidentitymagazine.com. Ed., Pub. Cailin Briody Henson.

268 USA ISSN 1084-872X
BV1560
THE NEW INTERNATIONAL LESSON ANNUAL. Text in English. 1956. a. **Document type:** *Consumer.* **Description:** Detailed explanations of the Bible for every Sunday session.
Formerly (until 199?): The International Lesson Annual (0074-6770)
Published by: Abingdon Press, 201 Eighth Ave S, PO Box 801, Nashville, TN 37202. TEL 800-251-3320, FAX 800-836-7802, orders@abingdonpress.com, http://www.abingdonpress.com/.

THE NEW LIBERATOR. *see* PHILOSOPHY

200 305.31 USA
HQ1090.3
NEW MAN (ONLINE); the magazine about becoming men of integrity. Text in English. 1994. m. free (effective 2009). bk.rev. illus. back issues avail.; reprints avail. **Document type:** *Magazine, Consumer.* **Description:** Features fresh, timely and often hilarious articles designed to refresh guys while challenging them to be better leaders at work, at church and at home.
Formerly (until 2007): New Man (Print) (1077-3959)
Media: Online - full text.
Indexed: CCR, ChrPI.
—Ingenta.
Published by: Strang Communications Co., 600 Rinehart Rd, Lake Mary, FL 32746. TEL 407-333-0600, FAX 407-333-7100, custsvc@strang.com, http://www.strang.com. Ed. Robert Andrescik. Pub. Stephen Strang. Adv. contact David Condiff TEL 407-333-7110. Circ: 215,000 (paid).

230 USA ISSN 0895-7460
BX9571
THE NEW MERCERSBURG REVIEW. Text in English. 1985. 2/yr. **Document type:** *Proceedings.* **Description:** Contains proceedings of the annual convocation as well as other articles on subjects pertinent to the aims and interests of the Society.
Indexed: R&TA.
Published by: The Mercersburg Society, 1811 Lincoln Way E, Chambersburg, PA 17201-3309. TEL 717-263-8593, FAX 717-263-9010, stjohns@cyn.net, lindendb@aol.com. Ed. Rev. Linden DeBie.

201.6 968.320 ZAF ISSN 0038-2523
DT1701
NEW SOUTH AFRICAN OUTLOOK; an ecumencial magazine for thinkers and decision makers. Text in English. 1870. q. ZAR 44 domestic; USD 30 foreign (effective 2004). adv. bk.rev. index. **Document type:** *Magazine, Consumer.*
Former titles (until 1998): Outlook; (until 1922): Christian Express; (until 1876): Kaffir Express
Related titles: Microfilm ed.: (from WMP).
Indexed: ASD, CERDIC, HRIR, ISAP.
Published by: Outlook Publications (Pty) Ltd., Rondebosch, PO Box 245, Cape Town, Cape Town 7700, South Africa. TEL 27-21-4481334, FAX 27-21-4478183, fionasouthafrica@hotmail.com. Ed., R&P James R Cochrane. Pub. Fiona Burtt. Circ: 500.

230 170 GBR
NEW STUDIES IN CHRISTIAN ETHICS. Text in English. 1992. irreg., latest 2009. price varies. back issues avail.; reprints avail. **Document type:** *Monographic series, Academic/Scholarly.* **Description:** Aims to engage centrally with the secular moral debate at the highest possible intellectual level and to demonstrate that Christian ethics can make a distinctive contribution to this debate.
Published by: Cambridge University Press, The Edinburgh Bldg, Shaftesbury Rd, Cambridge, CB2 8RU, United Kingdom. TEL 44-1223-312393, FAX 44-1223-315052, journals@cambridge.org, http://www.cambridge.org/uk. Eds. Robin Gill, Stanley Hauerwas, Stephen R L Clark.

NEW TESTAMENT ABSTRACTS (ONLINE). *see* RELIGIONS AND THEOLOGY—Abstracting, Bibliographies, Statistics

NEW TESTAMENT ABSTRACTS (PRINT); a record of current literature. *see* RELIGIONS AND THEOLOGY—Abstracting, Bibliographies, Statistics

225 220 NLD ISSN 2210-6685
▼ **THE NEW TESTAMENT GOSPELS IN THEIR JUDAIC CONTEXTS.** Text in English. 2010. irreg., latest vol.1, 2010. **Document type:** *Monographic series, Academic/Scholarly.*
Published by: Brill, PO Box 9000, Leiden, 2300 PA, Netherlands. TEL 31-71-5353500, FAX 31-71-5317532, cs@brill.nl. Ed. Bruce Clinton.

225 GBR ISSN 0028-6885
➤ **NEW TESTAMENT STUDIES.** Text in English, French, German. 1950. q. GBP 149, USD 266 to institutions; GBP 160, USD 289 combined subscription to institutions (print & online eds.) (effective 2012). adv. bk.rev. back issues avail.; reprint service avail. from PSC. **Document type:** *Journal, Academic/Scholarly.* **Description:** Covers all aspects of the text and theology of the New Testament.
Formerly (until 1954): Society for New Testament Studies. Bulletin
Related titles: Microform ed.: (from PQC); Online - full text ed.: ISSN 1469-8145. GBP 146, USD 260 to institutions (effective 2012).
Indexed: A01, A02, A03, A08, A20, A21, A22, A26, ASCA, AmHI, ArtHuCI, B04, BRD, BibLing, CA, CERDIC, CPL, ChrPI, CurCont, DIP, E01, E08, FR, G08, H07, H08, H09, H10, H14, HAb, HumInd, I05, IBR, IBZ, IZBG, M01, M02, MLA-IB, P02, P10, P28, P48, P53, P54, PCI, PQC, R&TA, R05, RASB, RI-1, RI-2, S09, SCOPUS, T02, W03, W07.
—BLDSC (6088.862000), IE, Infotrieve, Ingenta, INIST. **CCC.**
Published by: (Studiorum Novi Testamenti Societas), Cambridge University Press, The Edinburgh Bldg, Shaftesbury Rd, Cambridge, CB2 8RU, United Kingdom. TEL 44-1223-312393, FAX 44-1223-315052, journals@cambridge.org, http://www.cambridge.org/uk. Ed. John Barclay. R&P Linda Nicol TEL 44-1223-325702. Adv. contact Rebecca Roberts TEL 44-1223-325083. page GBP 470, page USD 895. Circ: 2,400. **Subscr. to:** Cambridge University Press, 32 Ave of the Americas, New York, NY 10013. TEL 212-337-5000, FAX 212-691-3239, journals_subscriptions@cup.org.

225 DEU ISSN 1616-816X
NEW TESTAMENT STUDIES IN CONTEXTUAL EXEGESIS/ NEUTESTAMENTLICHE STUDIEN ZUR KONTEXTUELLEN EXEGESE. Text in English, German. 2005. irreg., latest vol.5, 2009. price varies. **Document type:** *Monographic series, Academic/Scholarly.*
Published by: Peter Lang GmbH (Subsidiary of: Peter Lang Publishing Group), Eschborner Landstr 42-50, Frankfurt Am Main, 60489, Germany. TEL 49-69-7807050, FAX 49-69-78070550, zentrale.frankfurt@peterlang.com, http://www.peterlang.com.

225 NLD
NEW TESTAMENT TOOLS, STUDIES AND DOCUMENTS. Text in Dutch. N.S. 2007. irreg., latest vol.37, 2007. price varies. **Document type:** *Monographic series, Academic/Scholarly.* **Description:** Presents studies of the New Testament, and bibliographies of research and commentary relevant to further study.
Formed by the merger of (1960-2007): New Testament Tools and Studies (0077-8842); (1935-2007): Studies and Documents
Indexed: IZBG.
Published by: Brill, PO Box 9000, Leiden, 2300 PA, Netherlands. TEL 31-71-5353500, FAX 31-71-5317532, cs@brill.nl. Eds. Bart D Ehrman, Eldon J Epp. R&P Elizabeth Venekamp. **Dist. by:** Turpin Distribution Services Ltd., Pegasus Dr, Stratton Business Park, Biggleswade, Bedfordshire SG18 8QB, United Kingdom. TEL 44-1767-604954, FAX 44-1767-601640, custserv@turpin-distribution.com, http://www.turpin-distribution.com/.

200 GBR ISSN 1471-4043
NEW VISION. Text in English. 1921. bi-m. free to members (effective 2009). bk.rev. 16 p./no. 1 cols./p.; back issues avail. **Document type:** *Magazine, Trade.* **Description:** Devoted to the spiritual life.
Formerly (until 1999): Science of Thought Review (1460-2660)
Published by: (The Hamblin Trust), The Hamblin Vision (Subsidiary of: The Hamblin Trust), The Secretary, Bosham House, Main Rd, Bosham, Chichester, PO18 8PJ, United Kingdom. TEL 44-1243-572109, FAX 44-1243-572109, office@thehamblinvision.org.uk. Ed. Elizabeth Medler.

250 USA ISSN 1043-2221
BV676
NEW WOMEN, NEW CHURCH. Text in English. 1978. bi-m.
Published by: Women's Ordination Conference, Box 2693, Fairfax, VA 22031-0693. TEL 703-352-1006, woc@womenordination.org, http://www.womenordination.org/.

287.6 USA ISSN 0043-8812
BV2550
NEW WORLD OUTLOOK; United Methodist missions. Text in English. 1911; N.S. 1941. bi-m. USD 15 (effective 1999). adv. bk.rev. illus. index. **Description:** Covers United Methodist Mission work and around the world.
Formerly: World Outlook
Indexed: CERDIC, MEA&I.
Published by: United Methodist Church, General Board of Global Ministries, 475 Riverside Dr, Rm 1476, New York, NY 10115. TEL 212-870-3765, FAX 212-870-3940. Ed., R&P Alma Graham. Pub. Randolph Nugent. Adv. contact Ruth Kurtz. Circ: 30,000 (paid).

220 USA
NEW YORK CHRISTIAN TIMES; good news for a change!. Text in English. 1990. bi-w. USD 36.
Published by: Harvest Press, 1061 Atlantic Ave, Brooklyn, NY 11238. TEL 718-638-6397, FAX 718-638-1810. Circ: 28,000.

NEW YORK PEARL. *see* POLITICAL SCIENCE

200 RUS
NG-RELIGII. Text in Russian. bi-m. adv.
Published by: Hezavicilaya Gazeta, Ul. Myasnitskaya, 13, Moscow, 101000, Russian Federation. TEL 7-095-928-4850, FAX 7-095-925-3180, ngr@ng.ru. Pub. Vitalii Tretyakov. Circ: 2,450 (paid).

200 NLD ISSN 2210-2248
NIEUWSBRIEF THEOLOGIE EN LEVENSBESCHOUWING. Text in Dutch. 200?. s-a.
Published by: Christelijke Hogeschool Windesheim, Afdeling Theologie en Levensbeschouwing, Campus 2-6, Zwolle, 8017 CA, Netherlands. TEL 31-38-4699911, http://www.windesheim.nl.

291.72 NLD ISSN 2211-209X
NIEUWSBRIEF ZENDING. Text in Dutch. 2002. 4/yr. **Document type:** *Newsletter, Consumer.*
Published by: Kerk in Actie, Postbus 456, Utrecht, 3500 AL, Netherlands. TEL 31-30-8801456, servicedesk@kerkinactie.nl, http://www.kerkinactie.nl.

230 NGA ISSN 0029-005X
BR1463.N5 CODEN: REGSAT
NIGERIAN CHRISTIAN. Text in English. 1967-1982; N.S. 1984. m. USD 36. adv. bk.rev. illus. **Document type:** *Journal, Academic/Scholarly.* **Description:** Reports on matters of importance to Nigerian national life with critical references to Christianity in the region.
Indexed: CERDIC.
Published by: (Christian Council of Nigeria), Daystar Press, PO Box 1261, Ibadan, Oyo, Nigeria. TEL 234-2-810-2670. Ed. Phillip Ladokun. Circ: 2,000.

207.2 ITA ISSN 0029-0173
BV3500
NIGRIZIA; il mensile dell'Africa e del mondo nero. Text in Italian. 1883. m. (11/yr.). EUR 28 domestic; EUR 50 in Europe; EUR 58 elsewhere (effective 2009). bk.rev. illus.; stat. index. **Document type:** *Magazine, Consumer.*
Related titles: Online - full text ed.
Indexed: AICP, CCA, CERDIC, MLA-IB.
Published by: Missionari Comboniani, Vicolo Pozzo 1, Verona, 37129, Italy. redazione@nigrizia.it, http://www.comboni.org. Eds. Gino Barsella, Renato Sesana Kizito. Circ: 25,000.

200 NOR ISSN 0809-7291
➤ **NORDIC JOURNAL OF RELIGION AND SOCIETY.** Variant title: N J R S. Text in English. 1988. s-a. NOK 250 domestic to individuals (print ed.); NOK 312 domestic to individuals (online ed.); NOK 562 combined subscription domestic to individuals (print & online eds.); NOK 350 foreign to individuals (print or online ed.); NOK 550 combined subscription foreign to individuals (print & online eds.); NOK 400 domestic to institutions (print ed.); NOK 500 domestic to institutions (online ed.); NOK 750 combined subscription domestic to institutions (print & online eds.); NOK 500 foreign to institutions (print ed.); NOK 400 foreign to institutions (online ed.); NOK 600 combined subscription foreign to institutions (print & online eds.) (effective 2011). back issues avail. **Document type:** *Journal, Academic/Scholarly.*
Formerly (until 2005): Tidsskrift for Kirke, Religion, Samfunn (0802-0167)
Related titles: Online - full text ed.: ISSN 1890-7008. 2008.
Indexed: A01, ArtHuCI, CurCont, T02, W07.
—BLDSC (6117.927090).
Published by: (Stiftelsen Kirkeforskning/Centre for Church Research), Tapir Akademisk Forlag A/S, Nardoveien 14, Trondheim, 7005, Norway. TEL 47-73-593210, FAX 47-73-593204, post@tapirforag.no. Eds. Paal Repstad, Inger Furseth. Circ: 250.

230 DNK ISSN 1901-2888
➤ **NORDISK TEOLOGI.** Text in Danish, Norwegian, Swedish. 2006. a. back issues avail. **Document type:** *Journal, Academic/Scholarly.*
Media: Online - full content.
Published by: Dansk Bibel Institut/Copenhagen Lutheran School of Theology, Frederiksborggade 1 B 1, Copenhagen K, 1360, Denmark. TEL 45-33-135500, FAX 45-33-136989, dbi@dbi.edu, http://www.dbi.edu. Ed. Flemming Poulsen.

230 NOR ISSN 0029-2176
BR6
NORSK TEOLOGISK TIDSSKRIFT/NORWEGIAN THEOLOGICAL JOURNAL. Text in Norwegian; Summaries in English. 1900. q. NOK 478 to individuals; NOK 755 to institutions; NOK 280 to students (effective 2010). bk.rev. abstr. index. **Document type:** *Journal, Academic/Scholarly.*
Related titles: Online - full text ed.: ISSN 1504-2979. NOK 855 (effective 2010).
Indexed: A21, BAS, CERDIC, DIP, FR, HistAb, IBR, IBZ, OTA, P30, PCI, R&TA, RI-1, RI-2.
—Infotrieve, INIST. **CCC.**
Published by: (Universitetet i Oslo, Teologiske Fakultet/University of Oslo, Faculty of Theology), Universitetsforlaget AS/Scandinavian University Press (Subsidiary of: Aschehoug & Co.), Sehesteds Gate 3, P O Box 508, Sentrum, Oslo, 0105, Norway. TEL 47-24-147500, FAX 47-24-147501, post@universitetsforlaget.no. Ed. Tarald Rasmussen. Circ: 500.

266 NOR ISSN 1504-6605
➤ **NORSK TIDSSKRIFT FOR MISJONSVITENSKAP/NORWEGIAN JOURNAL OF MISSION AND MISSIONARY QUESTIONS.** Text in Norwegian. 1947. q. NOK 300 domestic to individuals; NOK 400 domestic to institutions; NOK 500 elsewhere (effective 2011). bk.rev. index. back issues avail. **Document type:** *Magazine, Academic/Scholarly.* **Description:** Norwegian journal of missiology.
Former titles (until 2007): Norsk Tidsskrift for Misjon (0029-2214); (until 1948): Norsk Misjonstidsskrift (0801-1540)
Indexed: CERDIC, DIP, IBR, IBZ.
Published by: (Egede Instituttet), Tapir Akademisk Forlag A/S, Nardoveien 14, Trondheim, 7005, Norway. TEL 47-73-593210, FAX 47-73-593204, post@tapirforag.no, http://www.tapirforlag.no. Eds. Kristin Norseth, Tormod Engelsviken. Circ: 250.

250 IND
THE NORTH INDIA CHURCH REVIEW. Abbreviated title: N I C R. Text in English. 1890. m. INR 15 per issue domestic; INR 150 domestic; USD 30, EUR 20 foreign; USD 30 in Europe; USD 30 in Australia & New Zealand (effective 2011). adv. bk.rev. 28 p./no. 2 cols./p.; back issues avail. **Document type:** *Magazine, Consumer.*
Former titles (until 1994): North India Churchman; (until 1970): The United Church Review; (until 1929): The Indian Standard
Related titles: Online - full text ed.: free (effective 2011).
Published by: Church of North India Synod, Department of Communications, c/o Mr. Alwan Masih, CNI Bhawan, 16 Pandit Pant Marg, New Delhi, 110 001, India. TEL 91-11-23731079, FAX 91-11-23716901, cnisynod@nda.vsnl.net.in. Ed. Alwan Masih.

THE NORTH STAR (ROCHESTER); a journal of African American religious history. *see* ETHNIC INTERESTS

NORTHERN NEVADA FAMILY LIFE. *see* CHILDREN AND YOUTH—About

230 NOR ISSN 1503-4380
NOTAT. Variant title: K I F O Notat. Text in Norwegian. 2003. irreg., latest 2011. back issues avail. **Document type:** *Monographic series, Consumer.*
Related titles: Online - full text ed.: 2007.
Published by: Stiftelsen Kirkeforskning/Centre for Church Research, PO Box 45, Vinderen, Oslo, 0319, Norway. TEL 47-23-334720, FAX 47-23-334729, kifo@kifo.no.

200 301 PER
NOTICIAS ALIADAS. Text in Spanish. w. USD 55 Latin America and Caribbean; USD 65 to individuals; USD 110 to institutions (effective 2000). back issues avail. **Document type:** *Bulletin.* **Description:** Focuses on issues involving the church, women's rights, grassroots organizations, indigenous issues, the environment and neoliberal economic programs in Latin America.
Related titles: E-mail ed.; Online - full text ed.; ◆ English ed.: Latinamerica Press. ISSN 0254-203X.
Indexed: HRIR, RASB.
Address: Apdo Postal 18 0964, Miraflores, Lima 18, Peru. TEL 511-261-9469, FAX 511-261-4753. Ed. Elsa Chanduvi Jana. Pub. Barbara J Fraser. Circ: 1,650.

230 809 BEL ISSN 1248-7848
NOUVELLE BIBLIOTHEQUE AUGUSTINIENNE. Text in French. 1992. irreg. price varies. **Document type:** *Monographic series, Academic/Scholarly.*
Published by: (Institut d'Etudes Augustiniennes FRA), Brepols Publishers, Begijnhof 67, Turnhout, 2300, Belgium. periodicals@brepols.net, http://www.brepols.net.

NOUVELLE BIBLIOTHEQUE INITIATIQUE. *see* HISTORY—History Of Europe

230 BEL ISSN 0029-4845
BX802
NOUVELLE REVUE THEOLOGIQUE. Text in French. 1868. q. EUR 39 domestic; EUR 55 in US & Canada; EUR 55 in Japan; EUR 47 in Europe; EUR 42 elsewhere (effective 2004). bk.rev. bibl. index. 176 p./no.; back issues avail. **Document type:** *Academic/Scholarly.*
Indexed: A21, A22, CERDIC, CLA, CPL, DIP, FR, IBR, IBZ, IPB, IZBG, MLA-IB, OTA, R&TA, RASB, RI-1, RI-2.
—BLDSC (6176.845000), IE, Infotrieve, Ingenta, INIST.
Address: Bd St Michel 24, Brussels, 1040, Belgium. TEL 32-2-7393480, FAX 32-2-7393481. Ed., R&P Bernard Pottier. Circ: 3,000.

200 USA ISSN 1542-7315
BR1
➤ **NOVA ET VETERA (ENGLISH EDITION).** Text in English. 2003. 2/yr. **Document type:** *Journal, Academic/Scholarly.* **Description:** International forum for theological and philosophical studies from a contemporary thomistic perspective.
Related titles: ◆ French ed.: Nova et Vetera (French Edition). ISSN 0029-5027.
Indexed: A01, R&TA, T02.
—BLDSC (6178.220000).
Published by: The Augustine Institute, 3001 S Federal Bldg, Denver, CO 80236. FAX 303-438-2933, http://www.augustineinstitute.org.

200 ITA ISSN 1827-6784
NOVECENTO TEOLOGICO. Text in Italian. 1999. irreg. price varies. **Document type:** *Monographic series, Academic/Scholarly.*
Published by: Editrice Morcelliana SpA, Via Gabriele Rosa 71, Brescia, BS 25121, Italy. TEL 39-030-46451, FAX 39-030-2400605, http://www.morcelliana.it.

225 NLD ISSN 0048-1009
BS410
➤ **NOVUM TESTAMENTUM**; an international quarterly for New Testament and related studies. Text in English, French, German. 1956. q. EUR 284, USD 397 to institutions; EUR 309, USD 433 combined subscription to institutions (print & online eds.) (effective 2012). cum.index: vols.1-35. back issues avail.; reprint service avail. from PSC. **Document type:** *Journal, Academic/Scholarly.* **Description:** International coverage of New Testament studies, including literary and textual criticism, critical interpretation, theology and the historical and literary background of the New Testament and early Christian literature. Includes a bibliographic section, Bibliographia Gnostica.
Related titles: Microform ed.: (from SWZ); Online - full text ed.: ISSN 1568-5365. EUR 258, USD 361 to institutions (effective 2012) (from IngentaConnect); ◆ Supplement(s): Novum Testamentum. Supplements. ISSN 0167-9732.
Indexed: A01, A02, A03, A08, A20, A21, A22, ASCA, AmHI, ArtHuCI, BibLing, CA, CERDIC, CurCont, DIP, E01, FR, H07, IBR, IBZ, IZBG, MLA-IB, PCI, R&TA, RASB, RI-1, RI-2, SCOPUS, T02, W07.
—IE, Infotrieve, Ingenta, INIST. **CCC.**
Published by: Brill, PO Box 9000, Leiden, 2300 PA, Netherlands. TEL 31-71-5353500, FAX 31-71-5317532, cs@brill.nl. **Dist. by:** Turpin Distribution Services Ltd., Pegasus Dr, Stratton Business Park, Biggleswade, Bedfordshire SG18 8QB, United Kingdom. TEL 44-1767-604954, FAX 44-1767-601640, custserv@turpin-distribution.com, http://www.turpin-distribution.com/.

225 DEU
NOVUM TESTAMENTUM ET ORBIS ANTIQUUS - STUDIEN ZUR UMWELT DES NEUEN TESTAMENTS. Text in German, French. 2003. irreg., latest vol.86, 2010. price varies. **Document type:** *Monographic series, Academic/Scholarly.*
Formed by the merger of (1986-2003): Novum Testamentum et Orbis Antiquus (1420-4592); (1962-2003): Studien zur Umwelt des Neuen Testaments
Published by: Vandenhoeck und Ruprecht, Theaterstr 13, Goettingen, 37073, Germany. TEL 49-551-508440, FAX 49-551-5084422, info@v-r.de.

225 NLD ISSN 0167-9732
➤ **NOVUM TESTAMENTUM. SUPPLEMENTS.** Text in Dutch. 1958. irreg., latest vol.130, 2008. price varies. back issues avail. **Document type:** *Monographic series, Academic/Scholarly.* **Description:** Scholarly studies on topics pertaining to the history of early Christianity and studies in the New Testament.
Related titles: ◆ Supplement to: Novum Testamentum. ISSN 0048-1009.
Indexed: IZBG, RI-1.
—BLDSC (6180.445200), IE, Ingenta.
Published by: Brill, PO Box 9000, Leiden, 2300 PA, Netherlands. TEL 31-71-5353500, FAX 31-71-5317532, cs@brill.nl, http://www.brill.nl. Eds. David Moessner, Margaret Mitchell. R&P Elizabeth Venekamp. **Dist. by:** Turpin Distribution Services Ltd., Pegasus Dr, Stratton Business Park, Biggleswade, Bedfordshire SG18 8QB, United Kingdom. TEL 44-1767-604954, FAX 44-1767-601640, custserv@turpin-distribution.com, http://www.turpin-distribution.com/.

200 338 AUS
NOYCE PUBLISHING. RELIGION AND DEVELOPMENT SERIES. Text in English. 1972. irreg., latest vol.8, 1998. **Document type:** *Monographic series, Academic/Scholarly.* **Description:** Explores the interaction of religion and economic development.
Formerly (until 1985): Librarians for Social Change (0305-165X)
Published by: Noyce Publishing, GPO Box 2222 T, Melbourne, VIC 3001, Australia. noycepublishing@hotmail.com.

200 ARG ISSN 0327-7097
NUEVO MUNDO. Text in Spanish. 1971. s-a. USD 40 (effective 1999). **Document type:** *Academic/Scholarly.*
Indexed: IBR, IBZ, OTA.
Published by: Ediciones Castaneda, Centenario, 1399, San Antonio De Padua, Buenos Aires 1718, Argentina. Ed. Oscar Blanco. Pub. Eduardo Bierzychudek.

200.9 NLD ISSN 0029-5973
BL1
➤ **NUMEN**; international review for the history of religions. Text in English, French, German, Italian. 1954. 5/yr. EUR 389, USD 546 to institutions; EUR 425, USD 595 combined subscription to institutions (print & online eds.) (effective 2012). bk.rev. bibl. back issues avail.; reprint service avail. from PSC. **Document type:** *Journal, Academic/Scholarly.* **Description:** Publishes original, international contributions reporting the results of investigations carried out in the history of religions.
Related titles: Microform ed.: (from SWZ); Online - full text ed.: ISSN 1568-5276. EUR 354, USD 496 to institutions (effective 2012) (from IngentaConnect); ◆ Supplement(s): Numen Book Series. ISSN 1570-9434.
Indexed: A01, A03, A08, A20, A21, A22, AICP, AmH&L, AmHI, ArtHuCI, BAS, BibInd, CA, CERDIC, CurCont, DIP, E01, FR, H07, HistAb, IBR, IBSS, IBZ, IZBG, MEA&I, MLA-IB, PCI, PhilInd, R&TA, RASB, RI-1, RI-2, T02, W07.
—BLDSC (6184.650000), IE, Infotrieve, Ingenta, INIST. **CCC.**
Published by: (International Association for the History of Religions), Brill, PO Box 9000, Leiden, 2300 PA, Netherlands. TEL 31-71-5353500, FAX 31-71-5317532, cs@brill.nl. Eds. Einar Thomassen, Gustavo Benavides. R&P Elizabeth Venekamp. **Dist. by:** Turpin Distribution Services Ltd. custserv@turpin-distribution.com, http://www.turpin-distribution.com/.

201.69 NLD ISSN 1570-9434
➤ **NUMEN BOOK SERIES**; studies in the history of religions. Text in Dutch. 1954. irreg., latest vol.121, 2008. price varies. back issues avail. **Document type:** *Monographic series, Academic/Scholarly.* **Description:** Publishes scholarly studies on topics in the history of specific ancient and modern religions throughout the world, comparative studies, and proceedings of conferences.
Formerly (until 1999): Studies in the History of Religions (0169-8834); Supersedes: Numen Supplements, Altera Series (0169-8885)
Related titles: ◆ Supplement to: Numen. ISSN 0029-5973.
Indexed: IZBG, PCI, RI-2.
—BLDSC (8490.676000), IE, Ingenta. **CCC.**
Published by: (International Association for the History of Religions), Brill, PO Box 9000, Leiden, 2300 PA, Netherlands. TEL 31-71-5353500, FAX 31-71-5317532, cs@brill.nl, http://www.brill.nl. R&P Elizabeth Venekamp. **Dist. by:** Turpin Distribution Services Ltd., Pegasus Dr, Stratton Business Park, Biggleswade, Bedfordshire SG18 8QB, United Kingdom. TEL 44-1767-604954, FAX 44-1767-601640, custserv@turpin-distribution.com, http://www.turpin-distribution.com/.

200 ITA
NUOVA BIBLIOTECA DI SCIENZE RELIGIOSE. Text in Italian. 197?. irreg. price varies. **Document type:** *Monographic series, Academic/Scholarly.*
Formerly (until 200?): Biblioteca di Scienze Religiose (1970-7770)
Published by: Universita Pontificia Salesiana, Editrice L A S, Piazza dell'Ateneo Salesiano 1, Rome, 00139, Italy. TEL 39-06-87290626, FAX 39-06-87240629, las@ups.urbe.it, http://las.ups.urbe.it.

230 ITA ISSN 1127-8722
BR735
LA NUOVA EUROPA; rivista internazionale di cultura. Text in Italian. 1960. bi-m. EUR 30 domestic; EUR 36.15 foreign (effective 2009). adv. bk.rev. bibl.; illus.; maps. index. back issues avail. **Document type:** *Magazine, Consumer.* **Description:** Deals with art, literature, culture and theology of Russia.
Former titles (until 1992): Altra Europa (1120-0685); (until 1985): Centro Studi Russia Cristiana. Rivista (0391-2795); (until 1976): Russia Cristiana (0485-7348); (until 1965): Russia Cristiana Ieri e Oggi (1120-0693)
Related titles: Online - full text ed.
Indexed: CERDIC, DIP, IBR, IBZ, RASB.
Published by: (Fondazione Russia Cristiana), La Nuova Europa, Via Tasca 36, Seriate, BG 24068, Italy. TEL 39-035-294021, FAX 39-035-293064, rcedizr@tin.it, http://www.russiacristiana.org. Circ: 2,000.

NURTURE; journal for home and school. *see* EDUCATION

200 200.21 SWE ISSN 1651-0755
NYCKELN TILL SVENSKA KYRKAN/KEY TO THE CHURCH OF SWEDEN; verksamhet och ekonomi. Text in Swedish. 2001. a., latest 2004. stat. **Document type:** *Yearbook.*
Formed by the merger of (1991-2000): Ekonomisk Redogoerelse foer Kyrkokommuner (1101-8410); (1994-2000): Nyckeln till Svenska Kyrkans Verksamhet och Finanser (1104-5795)

R

Published by: (Svenska Kyrkans Foersamlingsfoerbund, Sweden. Statistiska Centralbyraan/Statistics Sweden), Svenska Kyrkan/ Church of Sweden, Kyrkans Hus, Sysslomansgatan 4, Uppsala, 75170, Sweden. TEL 46-18-169600, FAX 46-18-169707, info@svenskakyrkan.se. **Dist. by:** Statistiska Centralbyraan, Publishing Unit, Orebro 70189, Sweden. TEL 46-19-176800, FAX 46-19-176444, scb@scb.se, http://www.scb.se.

DEN NYE DIALOG. *see* PHILOSOPHY

220 DNK ISSN 1902-4746
NYT FRA BIBELSELSKABET. Text in Danish. 1982. q. free. illus. back issues avail. **Document type:** *Newsletter, Consumer.*
Former titles (until 2007): Nyt fra det Dansk Bibelselskab (1600-5643); (until 1999): Nyt fra Bibelselskabet (0108-898X); Danske Bibelselskab. Medlemsbrev
Related titles: Online - full text ed.
Published by: Det Danske Bibelselskab/The Danish Bible Society, Frederiksborggade 50, Copenhagen K, 1360, Denmark. TEL 45-33-127835, FAX 45-33-127850, bibelselskabet@bibelselskabet.dk, http://www.bibelselskabet.dk. Eds. Soeren Moesgaard Moeller, Tine Lindhardt.

207.2 DNK ISSN 1603-6689
NYT FRA DANSKE SOEMANDS- OG UDLANDSKIRKER. Text in Danish. 2004. bi-m. DKK 100 (effective 2008). adv. **Document type:** *Newsletter, Consumer.* **Description:** Brings the latest news of the Danish churches outside Denmark.
Formed by the merger of (1871-2004): Havnen (0902-9591); (1927-2004): Dansk Kirkehilsen (0105-7383); Which was formerly (until 1976): Dansk Kirke i Udlandet (0105-7375)
Related titles: Online - full text ed.
Published by: Danske Soemands- og Udlandskirker/The Danish Church Abroad/Danish Seamen's Church, Smallegade 47, Frederiksberg, 2000, Denmark. TEL 45-70-261828, FAX 45-70-261824, kontor@dsuk.dk. Eds. Torben Elmbaek Joergensen, Margith Pedersen. Adv. contact Frank Graven-Nielsen. Circ: 7,500.

200 NOR ISSN 0802-9504
NYTT NORSK KIRKEBLAD; for teologi og praksis. Text in Norwegian. 1973. m. NOK 220; NOK 110 to students (effective 2005). back issues avail. **Document type:** *Journal.*
Formerly (until 1990): Teologi for Menigheden (0800-1642); Supersedes in part (in 1990): Dynamis (0332-8961)
Published by: Praktisk-Teologiske Seminar, PO Box 1075, Blindern, Oslo, 0316, Norway. TEL 47-22-850310, praktikum@teologi.uio.no, 47-22-850301.

230 NLD ISSN 2210-7339
OASE MAGAZINE. Text in Dutch. 2008. 5/yr. EUR 42.50 (effective 2010). **Document type:** *Magazine, Consumer.*
Published by: Oase Media b.v., Postbus 204, Nijkerk, 3860 AE, Netherlands. TEL 31-33-2570439, FAX 31-33-2536447, info@oasemedia.nl, http://www.oaasemedia.nl.

200 CAN ISSN 1922-2424
OBLATE SPIRIT. Text in English. q. free (effective 2010). back issues avail. **Document type:** *Newsletter, Trade.*
Formerly (until 2009): Oblate Mission (1914-0924)
Published by: Oblate Mission Office, c/o AMMI Lacombe, 601 Taylor St, W, Saskatoon, SK S7M 0C9, Canada. TEL 306-653-6453, 866-432-6264, FAX 306-652-1133, lacombemami@sasktel.net.

280 DEU ISSN 0029-8654
OEKUMENISCHE RUNDSCHAU. Text in German. 1952. q. EUR 36; EUR 25 to students; EUR 10 per issue (effective 2011). adv. bk.rev. index. **Document type:** *Journal, Academic/Scholarly.*
Indexed: A21, CERDIC, DIP, FR, IBR, IBZ, RI-1, RI-2, RILM.
Published by: (Deutscher Oekumenischer Studienausschuss), Verlag Otto Lembeck, Gaertnerweg 16, Frankfurt Am Main, 60322, Germany. TEL 49-69-5970988, FAX 49-69-5975742, verlag@lembeck.de. Ed. Barbara Rudolf. Circ: 1,000.

200 DEU ISSN 0179-9959
OEKUMENISCHER INFORMATIONSDIENST. Text in German. 1982. q. adv. bk.rev. back issues avail. **Document type:** *Newsletter, Consumer.*
Published by: Oekumenische Gesellschaft fuer G F S, Postfach 500113, Frankfurt Am Main, 60391, Germany. ecunet@t-online.de, http://www.ecunet.de. Ed. Ulrich Schmitthenner. Adv. contact Philipp Mertens. Circ: 3,000.

DIE OESTERREICHISCHE HOEHERE SCHULE. *see* EDUCATION—Higher Education

OESTERREICHISCHES ARCHIV FUER RECHT & RELIGION. *see* LAW

207.2 DEU ISSN 0030-011X
OFFENE TUEREN. Text in German. 1907. bi-m. adv. bk.rev. illus. **Document type:** *Newsletter.* **Description:** Focuses on the work of German missionaries in various countries.
Published by: Missionshaus Bibelschule Wiedenest e.V., Olper Str 10, Bergneustadt, 51702, Germany. TEL 49-2261-406135, FAX 49-2261-406155. Ed. Thomas Meyerhoefer. Adv. contact Klaus Brinkmann. Circ: 11,000.

282 279 AUS ISSN 1321-4764
OFFICIAL DIRECTORY OF THE CATHOLIC CHURCH IN AUSTRALIA. Text in English. 1914. a. (Apr.). AUD 82.50 (print or online ed.); AUD 132 combined subscription (print & online eds.) (effective 2009). adv. 680 p./no.; **Document type:** *Directory, Trade.* **Description:** Contains a directory listing of the Catholic church in Australia. Listings include: People - bishops, religious leaders, priests, deacons, pastoral associates, school principals, diocesan personnel; locations - parishes, Mass centers, convents, religious houses, schools, welfare organizations, hospitals, retirement and nursing homes, retreat centers; contact details - addresses, phone and fax numbers, websites, E-mail Addresses.
Former titles (until 1981): Official Directory of the Catholic Church in Australia and New Zealand (1321-4756); (until 1976): Official Directory of the Catholic Church of Australia and Papua-New Guinea, New Zealand and the Pacific Islands (0078-3919); (until 1973): Catholic Church of Australia & Papua-New Guinea, New Zealand & the Pacific Islands. Year Book; (until 1969): Catholic Church of Australia, New Zealand and Oceania. Year Book; (until 1962): Catholic Church of Australasia. Year Book; (until 1961): Australasian Catholic Directory
Related titles: Online - full text ed.

Published by: National Council of Priests, PO Box 295, Belmont, NSW 3216, Australia. TEL 61-3-52443680, FAX 61-3-52444762, national.office@ncp.catholic.org.au.

OLD TESTAMENT ABSTRACTS. *see* RELIGIONS AND THEOLOGY—Abstracting, Bibliographies, Statistics

221 ZAF ISSN 1010-9919
BS410
➤ **OLD TESTAMENT ESSAYS.** Text mainly in English; Text occasionally in Afrikaans, Dutch, German; Notes in French. 1983-1987; N.S. 1988. 3/yr. ZAR 150, USD 100 (effective 2005). adv. bk.rev. back issues avail. **Document type:** *Journal, Academic/Scholarly.* **Description:** Publishes articles on all aspects of Old Testament literature, theology, archaeology and society.
Related titles: Online - full text ed.
Indexed: ISAP, IZBG, OTA, R&TA.
Published by: Old Testament Society of South Africa, Department of Ancient Languages, University of Pretoria, Pretoria, 0002, South Africa. TEL 27-12-4202685, FAX 27-12-4204008, bothapj@libarts.up.ac.za. Ed., R&P P J Botha. Circ: 400.

230 296 ESP ISSN 0211-5514
BM535
EL OLIVO; documentacion y estudios para el dialogo entre judios y cristianos. Text in Spanish. 1977. s-a. back issues avail. **Document type:** *Journal, Academic/Scholarly.*
Indexed: IBR, IBZ.
Published by: Centro de Estudios Judeo-Cristianos, Hilarion Eslava 50, 6o, Madrid, 28015, Spain.

261 USA ISSN 1099-6877
ON MISSION; helping you share christ in the real world. Abbreviated title: O M. Text in English. 1930. q. free (effective 2011). adv. back issues avail. **Document type:** *Magazine, Consumer.* **Description:** Provides content which better helps Southern Baptists better share Christ, evangelize, start new churches, participate in short and long-term mission trips, and support missionary efforts throughout North America.
Former titles (until 1998): Missions USA (0279-5345); (until 1981): Home Missions (0018-408X); (until 1954): Southern Baptist Home Missions
Related titles: Online - full text ed.
Published by: North American Mission Board, 4200 N Point Pky, Alpharetta, GA 30022. TEL 770-410-6000, 800-634-2462, FAX 770-410-6082, http://www.namb.net/. Ed. Carol Pipes TEL 770-410-6382.

230 USA
ONE-TO-ONE (COLORADO SPRINGS); ministry review. Text in English. 10/yr. **Document type:** *Magazine, Consumer.*
Related titles: Online - full content ed.
Published by: Navigators, 3820 N 30th St, Colorado Springs, CO 80904. TEL 719-598-1212, FAX 719-260-0479, info@navigators.org. Ed. Dean Ridings.

ONLINE NOETIC NETWORK. *see* NEW AGE PUBLICATIONS

230 940 BEL ISSN 0774-2827
BX806.D8
➤ **ONS GEESTELIJK ERF**; tijdschrift voor de geschiedenis van de vroomheid in de Nederlanden. Text in Dutch. 1927. q. EUR 55 combined subscription (print & online eds.) (effective 2011). back issues avail. **Document type:** *Journal, Academic/Scholarly.* **Description:** Publishes contributions on the history of piety in the Netherlands, and related topics in religion and medieval studies.
Related titles: Online - full text ed.: ISSN 1783-1652.
Indexed: A22, BibInd, FR, IBR, IBZ, MLA-IB, PCI, SCOPUS.
—IE, INIST.
Published by: (Universitaire Faculteiten Sint Ignatius te Antwerpen/ Ruusbroecgenootschap), Peeters Publishers, Bondgenotenlaan 153, Leuven, 3000, Belgium. TEL 32-16-235170, FAX 32-16-228500, peeters@peeters-leuven.be, http://www.peeters-leuven.be. Ed. Th Mertens.

291.72 NLD ISSN 1878-4534
ONZE KRANT. Text in Dutch. 1960. 3/yr. **Document type:** *Newspaper, Consumer.*
Published by: Societeit voor Afrikaanse Missien, Postbus 49, Cadier en Keer, 6267 AC, Netherlands. TEL 31-43-4077373, FAX 31-43-4077374.

200 JPN ISSN 0030-3259
OOMOTO. Text in English. 1956. bi-m. JPY 1,200, USD 5. bk.rev. illus.
Indexed: MLA-IB.
Published by: Oomoto International, Kameoka-shi, Kyoto-Fu 621, Japan. TEL 07712-2-5561. Circ: 5,000.

THE OPEN SOCIETY; serving New Zealand's non-religious community since 1927. *see* PHILOSOPHY

282 USA ISSN 1059-3144
OPUS DEI AWARENESS NETWORK. Short title: O D A N. Text in English. 1991. USD 15 domestic; USD 20 foreign (effective 2003). bk.rev. back issues avail. **Document type:** *Newsletter.* **Description:** Provides a forum for the discussion of adverse experiences of former members, participants, individuals and families involved in the religious group, Opus Dei.
Related titles: Online - full text ed.
Published by: Opus Dei Awareness Network, Inc., PO Box 4333, Pittsfield, MA 01202. TEL 413-499-7168, FAX 413-499-7860. Ed. Dianne Dinicola. Circ: 650 (paid); (controlled).

291.72 NLD ISSN 0929-4783
OPWEKKING MAGAZINE. Text in Dutch. 1966. m. (11/yr.). EUR 15; EUR 1.50 newsstand/cover (effective 2010). adv. **Document type:** *Magazine, Consumer.*
Formerly (until 1991): Opwekking (0167-3017)
Published by: Stichting Opwekking, Ruitenbeek 16, Putten, 3881 LW, Netherlands. TEL 31-341-352641, FAX 31-341-352189, info@opwekking.nl, http://www.opwekking.nl. adv.: B&W page EUR 1,012; trim 210 x 297. Circ: 10,000.

ORACAO E VIDA. *see* CHILDREN AND YOUTH—For

ORACLE (SIERRA MADRE). *see* PARAPSYCHOLOGY AND OCCULTISM

200 BRA ISSN 1807-8222
ORACULA. Text in Portuguese. 2004. s-a. free (effective 2011). **Document type:** *Journal, Academic/Scholarly.*
Media: Online - full text.
Indexed: T02.

Published by: Universidade Metodista de Sao Paulo, Faculdade de Filosofia e Ciencias da Religiao, Rua do Sacramento 230, Rudge Ramos, Sao Bernardo do Campo, SP 09600000, Brazil. TEL 55-11-43665808, FAX 55-11-43665815, posreligiao@metodista.br, http://www.oracula.com.br/index.htm. Ed. Paulo Augusto de Souza Nogueira.

200 DEU ISSN 0340-6407
BR4
ORIENS CHRISTIANUS; Hefte fuer die Kunde des christlichen Orients. Text in English, French, German. 1911. a. EUR 78 per vol. (effective 2011). adv. bk.rev. back issues avail.; reprints avail. **Document type:** *Journal, Academic/Scholarly.*
Indexed: A21, A22, BibLing, DIP, FR, IBR, IBZ, MLA-IB, PCI, RASB, RI-1, RI-2.
—IE, INIST.
Published by: Harrassowitz Verlag, Kreuzberger Ring 7b-c, Wiesbaden, 65205, Germany. TEL 49-611-5300, FAX 49-611-530560, verlag@harrassowitz.de, http://www.harrassowitz.de. Ed. Hubert Kaufhold. Circ: 400.

296 956 USA ISSN 1942-1281
ORIENTALIA, JUDAICA, CHRISTIANA. Text in English. 2008 (May). irreg., latest 2009. price varies. back issues avail. **Document type:** *Monographic series, Academic/Scholarly.* **Description:** Dedicated to Jewish Second Temple and non-Talmudic traditions that survived within the Christian Orient.
Published by: Gorgias Press LLC, 954 River Rd, Piscataway, NJ 08854. TEL 732-885-8900, FAX 732-885-8908, helpdesk@gorgiaspress.com, http://www.gorgiaspress.com/ bookshop/default.aspx.

ORIGINS DESIGN. *see* SCIENCES: COMPREHENSIVE WORKS

200 NGA ISSN 0030-5596
BL80.2
ORITA; Ibadan journal of religious studies. Text in English. 1967. s-a. USD 20 (effective 2002). adv. bk.rev. illus. cum.index. **Document type:** *Journal, Academic/Scholarly.* **Description:** Offers a mirror of Nigerian thinking on religion.
Indexed: A22, ASD, DIP, IBR, IBSS, IBZ, MEA&I, MLA-IB, OTA, PerIslam, RASB, RILM.
—IE.
Published by: University of Ibadan, Department of Religious Studies, Ibadan, Oyo, Nigeria. Ed. S O Abogunrin. Circ: 500 (controlled).

200 DEU
OSNABRUECKER DOGMATISCHE STUDIEN. Text in German. 1999. irreg., latest vol.2, 2000. price varies. **Document type:** *Monographic series, Academic/Scholarly.*
Published by: V & R Unipress GmbH (Subsidiary of: Vandenhoeck und Ruprecht), Robert-Bosch-Breite 6, Goettingen, 37079, Germany. TEL 49-551-5084303, FAX 49-551-5084333, info@vr-unipress.de, http://www.v-r.de/en/publisher/unipress. Ed. Erwin Dirscherl.

220 DEU
OSNABRUECKER STUDIEN ZUR JUEDISCHEN UND CHRISTLICHEN BIBEL. Text in German. 2000. irreg., latest vol.2, 2001. price varies. **Document type:** *Monographic series, Academic/Scholarly.*
Published by: V & R Unipress GmbH (Subsidiary of: Vandenhoeck und Ruprecht), Robert-Bosch-Breite 6, Goettingen, 37079, Germany. TEL 49-551-5084303, FAX 49-551-5084333, info@vr-unipress.de, http://www.v-r.de/en/publisher/unipress. Eds. Christoph Dohmen, Helmut Merkel.

200 USA ISSN 1933-7957
BR115.C8
THE OTHER JOURNAL.COM; an intersection of theology and culture. Text in English. 2002. q. **Document type:** *Magazine, Trade.*
Media: Online - full text.
Published by: Mars Hill Graduate School, 2501 Elliott Ave, Seattle, WA 98121. TEL 206-876-6100, 888-977-2002, FAX 206-876-6195, info@mhgs.edu, http://www.mhgs.edu/index.asp. Ed. Chris Keller.

200 NLD ISSN 0030-6746
OUDE PADEN. Text in Dutch. 1937. q. EUR 24.50 domestic; EUR 32.25 in Belgium; EUR 7 newsstand/cover (effective 2009).
Published by: Kok Tijdschriften, Postbus 5018, Kampen, 8260 GA, Netherlands. TEL 31-38-3392555, http://www.kok.nl. Eds. Dr. H Florijn, J P Neven, J Mastenbroek.

230 NLD ISSN 0166-2392
OUDERLINGENBLAD; maandblad voor ouderlingen en andere pastorale werkers. Text in Dutch. 1922. 11/yr. EUR 23.50 domestic; EUR 34.25 in Belgium; EUR 3.99 newsstand/cover (effective 2009). **Document type:** *Bulletin.* **Description:** Gives support to all people who work in or for the church.
Related titles: Audio cassette/tape ed.; Talking Book ed.
Published by: Kok Tijdschriften, Postbus 5018, Kampen, 8260 GA, Netherlands. TEL 31-38-3392555, http://www.kok.nl.

OUDTESTAMENTISCHE STUDIEN. *see* RELIGIONS AND THEOLOGY—Judaic

200 NLD ISSN 1877-2846
OUDVADERS. Text in Dutch. 2005. bi-m. EUR 39.50 domestic; EUR 44 in Belgium (effective 2010). **Document type:** *Magazine, Trade.*
Published by: Uitgeverij de Groot Goudriaan, Postbus 5018, Kampen, 8260 GA, Netherlands. TEL 31-38-3392555, http://www.kok.nl. Eds. L J van Valen, R Bisschop, W J van Asselt.

220 CAN ISSN 1486-5327
OUR BIBLE MATTERS. Text in English. 1960. 3/yr. free. **Document type:** *Newsletter.* **Description:** Demonstrates how the society translates, publishes and distributes the word of God to those in need.
Former titles (until 1998): Canadian Bible Society Newsletter (1192-6805); (until 1992): Canadian Bible Society Quarterly Newsletter (0832-1590)
Related titles: ◆ English ed.: Actualites Bibliques. ISSN 1184-7204.
Published by: Canadian Bible Society/Societe Biblique Canadienne, 10 Carnforth Rd, Toronto, ON M4A 2S4, Canada. TEL 416-757-4171, FAX 416-757-3376. Ed. Connie Stamp. Circ: 134,000.

OUR DAILY BREAD. *see* HANDICAPPED—Visually Impaired

200 NGA ISSN 1597-376X
OUR DAILY MANNA. Text in English. 2004. q. USD 10 newsstand/cover (effective 2007).
Published by: Chapel of Liberty Inc., PO Box 7049, Surulere, Lagos, Nigeria. TEL 234-802-3154316. Ed. Sr. Ladi Achoba.

OVERHEID-PARTICULIER INITIATIEF REEKS. *see* LAW

220 781.7 NLD ISSN 1877-7996
OVERZICHT VAN DE GEZANGEN. Text in Dutch. 1969. s-a. EUR 10 per vol. (effective 2011).
Published by: (Abdij van Berne, Werkgroep voor Liturgie), Uitgeverij Abdij van Berne, Postbus 60, Heeswijk, 5473 ZH, Netherlands. TEL 31-413-299299, FAX 31-413-299288, info@abdijvanberne.nl, http://www.uitgeverijberne.nl.

283 GBR
THE OXFORD DIOCESAN YEAR BOOK. Text in English. 1857. a. GBP 10.50 per issue domestic; GBP 15 per issue foreign (effective 2009). **Document type:** *Directory, Trade.* **Description:** Contains Parish and office-holder information including contact details for the Oxford diocese.
Published by: Oxford Diocesan Publications Ltd., Diocesan Church House, North Hinksey, Oxford, Oxon OX2 0NB, United Kingdom. TEL 44-1865-208200, FAX 44-1865-790470.

▼ **OXFORD JOURNAL OF LAW AND RELIGION.** *see* LAW

207.2 GBR
OXFORD MISSION NEWS. Text in English. 1894. 2/yr. (May, Nov.). bk.rev.; music rev. 52 p./no. 1 cols./p.; back issues avail. **Document type:** *Newsletter, Consumer.* **Description:** Contains letters from the superiors of the Oxford Mission stations in India and Bangladesh, describing their activities. Includes other articles of interest to mission supporters.
Formerly: Oxford Mission (0048-2579)
Media: Duplicated (not offset). **Related titles:** Print ed.
Published by: Oxford Mission, c/o Mrs. Gillian Wilson, Ed., 10 Chesil St, Winchester, Hants SO23 OHU, United Kingdom. TEL 44-1962-865824, FAX 44-1962-853109. Ed. Mrs. Gillian Wilson. Circ: 1,800.

201 GBR ISSN 0078-7272
OXFORD THEOLOGICAL MONOGRAPHS. Text in English. 1958. irreg., latest 2009. price varies. back issues avail. **Document type:** *Monographic series, Academic/Scholarly.*
Published by: Oxford University Press, Great Clarendon St, Oxford, OX2 6DP, United Kingdom. TEL 44-1865-556767, FAX 44-1865-556646, enquiry@oup.co.uk, http://www.oup-usa.org/catalogs/general/series/.

226 365 USA
P F I WORLD REPORT. Text in English, French, Spanish. 1981. bi-m. free. **Document type:** *Newsletter.* **Description:** Covers the worldwide activities of the Prison Fellowship ministries, with stories on the impact of ministry activities on prisoners' lives.
Former titles (until Oct. 1993): Jubilee International; (until 1991): Fellowship Communique (0738-1530); (until 1983): Jubilee International (0736-9662)
Published by: Prison Fellowship International, PO Box 17434, Washington, DC 20041. TEL 703-481-0000, FAX 703-481-0003. Ed. Christopher P Nicholson. Circ: 6,500 (controlled).

P L I M REPORT. (Power Latent in Man) *see* PARAPSYCHOLOGY AND OCCULTISM

200.7 USA ISSN 0889-8936
BL2525
P R R C: EMERGING TRENDS. Text in English. 1979. m. looseleaf. USD 38 in North America; USD 45 elsewhere. **Document type:** *Newsletter.* **Description:** Presents the results of recent surveys on religious beliefs and practices, with commentary, based on studies by Gallup and other polling organizations.
Related titles: Microfiche ed.: (from CIS).
Indexed: CCR, SRI.
Published by: Princeton Religion Research Center, 502 Carnegie Ctr., Ste. 300, Princeton, NJ 08540-6289. TEL 609-921-8112, FAX 609-924-0028. Circ: 1,900.

P W RELIGION BOOKLINE; the twice monthly source for religion professionals. (Publishers Weekly) *see* PUBLISHING AND BOOK TRADE

207.2 USA
PACIFIC CHRISTIAN COLLEGE BULLETIN. Text in English. 1928. 4/yr. **Document type:** *Bulletin.* **Description:** Articles and faculty information for students and constituency of Pacific Christian College.
Published by: Pacific Christian College, 2500 E Nutwood Ave, Fullerton, CA 92631. TEL 714-879-3901, FAX 714-526-0231. Ed. Becky Ahlberg.

200 FJI ISSN 1027-037X
BR9.P22
PACIFIC JOURNAL OF THEOLOGY. Text in English. 1988. s-a. **Document type:** *Journal, Academic/Scholarly.*
Indexed: A21, OTA, R&TA, RI-1.
Published by: South Pacific Association of Theological Schools, 30 Gardiner St Nasese, PO Box 2426, Suva, Fiji. TEL 679-3301942.

200 294.54 AUS ISSN 1030-570X
BX1
➤ **PACIFICA**; Australasian theological studies. Text in English. 1988. 3/yr. AUD 50 domestic to individuals; AUD 66.50 to individuals in USA & Europe; AUD 61 in Asia & the Pacific to individuals; AUD 65 domestic to institutions; AUD 81.50 to institutions in USA & Europe; AUD 76 in Asia & the Pacific to institutions; AUD 35 domestic to students; AUD 51.50 to students in USA & Europe; AUD 46 in Asia & the Pacific to students (effective 2009). adv. bk.rev. index. back issues avail. **Document type:** *Journal, Academic/Scholarly.* **Description:** Covers all areas of theology, with emphasis on theological work in Australasia and Pacific Region.
Related titles: Diskette ed.; Online - full text ed.
Indexed: A01, A11, A21, CA, CPL, DIP, FR, GSS&RPL, IBR, IBZ, OTA, P28, P30, P48, P53, P54, PQC, PhilInd, RI-1, RI-2, T02.
—BLDSC (6331.815000), IE, Infotrieve, Ingenta, INIST.
Published by: Pacifica Theological Studies Association Inc., PO Box 271, Brunswick East, VIC 3057, Australia. TEL 61-3-93415898, FAX 61-3-93476371. Ed. Brendan Byrne TEL 61-3-93415800. Circ: 500 (paid). **Co-sponsor:** Melbourne College of Divinity.

200 DEU ISSN 0343-7280
PADERBORNER THEOLOGISCHE STUDIEN. Text in German. 1974. irreg., latest vol.50, 2009. **Document type:** *Monographic series, Academic/Scholarly.*
Published by: (Theologische Fakultaet Paderborn), Verlag Ferdinand Schoeningh GmbH, Postfach 2540, Paderborn, 33055, Germany. TEL 49-5251-1275, FAX 49-5251-127860, info@schoeningh.de, http://www.schoeningh.de. Eds. Herbert Haslinger, Josef Meyer, Maria Neubrand.

255 248 ITA ISSN 0030-9214
PADRE SANTO; periodico dei Cappuccini liguri. Text in Italian. 1912. m. **Document type:** *Magazine, Consumer.*
Published by: Frati Minori Cappuccini, Provincia di Genova/Ordo Fratrum Minorum Capuccinorum, Piazza Cappuccini 1, Genoa, GE 16122, Italy.

200 USA ISSN 0475-4816
LA PALABRA DIARIA. Text in Spanish. 1955. m. USD 10.95 domestic; USD 17.95 foreign (effective 2003). **Document type:** *Magazine, Consumer.* **Description:** Contains daily devotional readings, with poetry and articles on spiritual inspiration, human relations, and everyday living.
Related titles: ◆ English ed.: Daily Word. ISSN 0011-5525.
Published by: Unity School of Christianity, 1901 NW Blue Pkwy, Unity Village, MO 64065-0001. TEL 816-524-3550, FAX 816-251-3553, http://www.unityworldhq.org. Ed. Colleen Zuck. Pub. Lynne Brown. R&P Elaine Meyer TEL 816-524-3550 ext 6585.

203.8 USA ISSN 1541-8138
PALABRAS PASTORALES. Text in Spanish. 2002. q. USD 9.95 domestic; USD 21.50 foreign (effective 2005). **Description:** Liturgy planning resource in Spanish.
Related titles: ◆ English ed.: Pastoral Patterns. ISSN 1079-4751.
Published by: World Library Publications, Inc. (Subsidiary of: J.S. Paluch Co., Inc.), 3708 River Rd, Ste 400, Franklin Park, IL 60131. TEL 800-621-5197, wlpcs@jspaluch.com, http://www.wlp.jspaluch.com/. Ed. Mr. Eduardo Rivera. R&P Ms. Rita Larkin.

PALAESTINA ANTIQUA. *see* ARCHAEOLOGY

PALESTINE EXPLORATION QUARTERLY. *see* ARCHAEOLOGY

207.2 DEU ISSN 1439-6580
PALLOTTIS WERK; daheim und draussen. Text in German. 1949. q. free (effective 2011). bk.rev. **Document type:** *Bulletin.* **Description:** Catholic publication covering missionary work in Germany and abroad, especially Third World countries.
Published by: Herz-Jesu-Provinz der Pallottiner, Vinzenz-Pallotti-Str 14, Friedberg, 86316, Germany. TEL 49-821-600520, FAX 49-821-60052252, info@pallottiner.org. Circ: 60,000.

200 FRA ISSN 0299-6898
PANORAMA; France chretienne. Text in French. 1968. m. (11/yr.). EUR 44 domestic (effective 2009 & 2010). adv. bk.rev.; film rev. illus. **Document type:** *Magazine, Consumer.* **Description:** Helps Christians to find a focus in their lives through their religion.
Incorporates (1977-1993): Foi Aujourd'hui (0152-139X); Formerly (until 1986): Panorama Aujourd'hui (0048-2838); Which was formed by the merger of (193?-1968): Chretiens d' Aujourd'hui (1150-1154); Which was formerly (until 1963): Mon Village (1150-1197); (1950-1968): Panorama Chretien (0479-4273); Which was formerly (until 1957): Familial (1149-2929); (until 1954): Familial Digest (1149-2910)
Indexed: PdeR.
Published by: Bayard Presse, 3-5 rue Bayard, Paris, 75393 Cedex 08, France. TEL 33-1-44356060, FAX 33-1-44356161, redactions@bayard-presse.com, http://www.bayardpresse.com. Ed. Bertrand Revillion. Circ: 50,000.

PARABOLA; where spiritual traditions meet. *see* FOLKLORE

THE PARISH POST. *see* RELIGIONS AND THEOLOGY—Protestant

PARMARTH. *see* PHILOSOPHY

200 LBN ISSN 0258-8331
PAROLE DE L'ORIENT. Text in English, French. 1970. s-a. USD 35 domestic; USD 45 foreign (effective 2001). adv. bk.rev. 400 p./no. 1 cols./p.; back issues avail. **Document type:** *Journal, Academic/Scholarly.* **Description:** Examines the theology, exegeses, patrology, liturgy and history of churches in the Near and Middle East.
Indexed: BibLing, CA, HistAb, IPB, MLA-IB, RILM, T02.
—INIST.
Published by: Universite Saint Esprit, Kaslik, P O Box 446, Jounieh, Lebanon. TEL 961-9-640664, FAX 961-9-642333, melto@cyberia.net.lb. Ed., R&P, Adv. contact Rev. P Elie Khalife-Hachem TEL 961.9.263703. Circ: 1,000.

230 USA ISSN 1932-9571
BR118
PARTICIPATIO. Text in English. 2007. a. free (effective 2010). **Document type:** *Journal, Academic/Scholarly.* **Description:** Designed apprehend the significance of Thomas F.Torrance's work and to advance his evangelical and scientific theology for the benefit of the Church, academy, and society.
Media: Online - full text.
Published by: Thomas F. Torrance Theological Fellowship Ed. Todd Speidell.

200 300 DEU ISSN 1432-3265
PASSAGEN & TRANSZENDENZEN; Studien zur materialen Religions- und Kultursoziologie. Text in German. 1997. irreg., latest vol.11, 2002. price varies. **Document type:** *Monographic series, Academic/Scholarly.*
Published by: U V K Verlagsgesellschaft mbH, Schuetzenstr 24, Konstanz, 78462, Germany. TEL 49-7531-90530, FAX 49-7531-905398, nadine.ley@uvk.de, http://www.uvk.de. Ed. Michael Ebertz.

250 DEU ISSN 0031-2681
PASSAUER BISTUMSBLATT; Kirchenzeitung der Dioezese Passau. Text in German. 1936. w. EUR 3.50 per month (effective 2009). adv. bk.rev.; film rev. abstr.; illus. **Document type:** *Newspaper, Consumer.*
Published by: (Diozese Passau), Verlag Passauer Bistumsblatt GmbH, Domplatz 3, Passau, 94032, Germany. TEL 49-851-3931320, FAX 49-851-31893. Ed. Wolfgang Krinninger. Adv. contact Paul Hickl. B&W page EUR 980; trim 195 x 302. Circ: 19,009 (paid and controlled).

PASTORAL PSYCHOLOGY. *see* PSYCHOLOGY

230 USA ISSN 1098-3562
PASTORAL THEOLOGY. Text in English. 2000. irreg., latest vol.4, 2003. price varies. back issues avail. **Document type:** *Monographic series, Academic/Scholarly.* **Description:** Encourages the theological exploration of Christianity's commitment to action, the relationship between ecclesiology and ethics, and between doctrine and practice.
Published by: Peter Lang Publishing, Inc. (Subsidiary of: Peter Lang Publishing Group), 29 Broadway, New York, NY 10006. TEL 212-647-7700, 800-770-5264, FAX 212-647-7707, customerservice@plang.com, http://www.peterlangusa.com. Ed. Iain Torrance.

250 DEU ISSN 0031-2800
PASTORALBLAETTER; Predigt und Seelsorge in der Praxis. Text in German. 1860. m. EUR 48 (effective 2005). adv. **Document type:** *Bulletin, Consumer.*
Indexed: IBR, IBZ.
—CCC.
Published by: Kreuz Verlag GmbH & Co. KG, Postfach 800669, Stuttgart, 70506, Germany. TEL 49-711-788030, FAX 49-711-7880310, service@kreuzverlag.de, http://www.kreuzverlag.de. Ed. Gerhard Engelsberger. Circ: 4,500.

230 DEU ISSN 1862-0442
PASTORALE REFLEXIONEN. Text in German. 2006. irreg. price varies. **Document type:** *Monographic series, Academic/Scholarly.*
Published by: Shaker Verlag GmbH, Kaiserstr 100, Herzogenrath, 52134, Germany. TEL 49-2407-95960, FAX 49-2407-95969, info@shaker.de, http://www.shaker.de.

253 340 NLD ISSN 1875-0850
PASTORALE VERKENNINGEN. EXTERN KATERN. Text in Dutch. 2006. s-a.
Published by: Ministerie van Justitie, Dienst Justitiele Inrichtingen, Postbus 30132, The Hague, 2500 GC, Netherlands. TEL 31-70-3704961, FAX 31-70-3702921, http://www.dji.nl. Ed. C Donner.

200 GTM
PASTORALIA. Text in Spanish. 1974. a. USD 6 in the Americas; USD 7 elsewhere. bk.rev.
Supersedes (in 1977, vol.4, nos.1-2): C E L E P Ensayos Ocasionales
Published by: Centro Evangelico Latinoamericano de Estudios Pastorales, Apdo 1710, Guatemala City, 01901, Guatemala. FAX 502-2323455. Ed. Dennis A Smith.

200 DEU ISSN 1437-6679
PASTORALPSYCHOLOGIE UND SPIRITUALITAET. Text in German. 1999. irreg., latest vol.13, 2009. price varies. **Document type:** *Monographic series, Academic/Scholarly.*
Published by: Peter Lang GmbH (Subsidiary of: Peter Lang Publishing Group), Eschborner Landstr 42-50, Frankfurt Am Main, 60489, Germany. TEL 49-69-7807050, FAX 49-69-78070550, zentrale.frankfurt@peterlang.com.

250 DEU ISSN 0720-6259
BV4000
➤ **PASTORALTHEOLOGIE**; Monatsschrift fuer Wissenschaft und Praxis in Kirche und Gesellschaft. Text in German. 1904. m. EUR 62 to individuals; EUR 124 to institutions; EUR 47 to students; EUR 14.90 newsstand/cover (effective 2011). adv. bk.rev. index. **Document type:** *Journal, Academic/Scholarly.*
Former titles (until 1981): Wissenschaft und Praxis in Kirche und Gesellschaft (0031-2827); (until 1970): Pastoraltheologie (0174-9927); (until 1966): Monatsschrift fuer Pastoraltheologie (0174-9870)
Indexed: CERDIC, DIP, IBR, IBZ, RILM.
—CCC.
Published by: Vandenhoeck und Ruprecht, Theaterstr 13, Goettingen, 37073, Germany. TEL 49-551-508440, FAX 49-551-5084422, info@v-r.de. Ed. Eberhard Hauschildt. Circ: 2,000 (paid and controlled).

204.32 ZAF ISSN 0031-2932
PATH OF TRUTH. Text in English. 1937. m. free. **Description:** Contains daily reading, meditations, and metaphysics lectures.
Related titles: Afrikaans ed.: Huis van Geluk.
Published by: School of Truth Ltd., Cape House, 5th Fl., Cnr. MacLaren & Fox Sts, Johannesburg, 2001, South Africa. TEL 011-838-6954, FAX 011-833-1802. Ed. Wille Martin. Circ: 10,450. **Subscr. to:** PO Box 6116, Johannesburg 2000, South Africa.

200 100 IND ISSN 0971-927X
BL1
PATHWAY TO GOD; one God, one world, one humanity. Text in English. 1966. q. bk.rev. 64 p./no. 1 cols./p.; back issues avail.; reprints avail. **Document type:** *Journal, Academic/Scholarly.* **Description:** Covers topics on religous philosophy, teachings of Indian Sages and Saints, mysticism and science of yoga in comparison with today's world of social sciences and scientific progress.
Published by: Academy of Comparative Philosophy and Religion Belgaum, Gurudeo Mandir, Hindwadi, Belgaum, Karnataka 590 011, India. TEL 91-831-467231, info@racprbgm.org.

225 880 BEL
➤ **PATRISTIC STUDIES.** Text in Dutch, English, German. 1990. irreg., latest 2010. price varies. illus. back issues avail. **Document type:** *Monographic series, Academic/Scholarly.* **Description:** Studies New Testament Biblical texts.
Published by: Peeters Publishers, Bondgenotenlaan 153, Leuven, 3000, Belgium. TEL 32-16-235170, FAX 32-16-228500, http://www.peeters-leuven.be.

230 USA ISSN 1094-6217
PATRISTIC STUDIES. Text in English. 2000. irreg., latest vol.9, 2008. price varies. back issues avail. **Document type:** *Monographic series, Academic/Scholarly.* **Description:** Provides access to research at the cutting-edge of current Patristic Studies.
—BLDSC (6412.976100).
Published by: Peter Lang Publishing, Inc. (Subsidiary of: Peter Lang Publishing Group), 29 Broadway, New York, NY 10006. TEL 212-647-7700, 800-770-5264, FAX 212-647-7707, customerservice@plang.com, http://www.peterlangusa.com. Ed. Gerald Bray.

200 DEU ISSN 0553-4003
➤ **PATRISTISCHE TEXTE UND STUDIEN.** Text in German; Text occasionally in English. 1963. irreg., latest vol.66, 2011. price varies. back issues avail. **Document type:** *Monographic series, Academic/Scholarly.*
—CCC.
Published by: Walter de Gruyter GmbH & Co. KG, Genthiner Str 13, Berlin, 10785, Germany. TEL 49-30-260050, FAX 49-30-26005251, info@degruyter.com, http://www.degruyter.de. Ed. Ekkehard Muehlenberg.

200 DEU ISSN 0940-4015
PATROLOGIA; Beitraege zum Studium der Kirchenvaeter. Text in German. 1991. irreg., latest vol.23, 2010. price varies. **Document type:** *Monographic series, Academic/Scholarly.*

R

Published by: Peter Lang GmbH (Subsidiary of: Peter Lang Publishing Group), Eschborner Landstr 42-50, Frankfurt Am Main, 60489, Germany. TEL 49-69-7807050, FAX 49-69-78070550, zentrale.frankfurt@peterlang.com.

PAUL-GERHARDT-GESELLSCHAFT. BEITRAEGE. *see* LITERATURE—Poetry

225 NLD ISSN 1572-4913
PAULINE STUDIES. Text in English. 2004. irreg., latest vol.4, 2008. price varies. **Document type:** *Monographic series, Academic/Scholarly.*
Indexed: IZBG.
Published by: Brill, PO Box 9000, Leiden, 2300 PA, Netherlands. TEL 31-71-5353500, FAX 31-71-5317532, cs@brill.nl. Ed. Stanley E Porter.

202 USA ISSN 1059-2350
BP605.S73
PEARLS OF WISDOM. Text in English. 1958. w. USD 45 (effective 2000). back issues avail. **Description:** Disseminates the teachings and progressive revelation from the Ascended Masters delivered through their messengers, Mark L. and Elizabeth Clare Prophet, with insights and techniques to accelerate one's spiritual growth.
Related titles: Microfiche ed.
Published by: (Church Universal and Triumphant), The Summit Lighthouse, P O Box 5000, Corwin Springs, MT 59030. TEL 406-848-9500, FAX 406-848-9555. Ed. Elizabeth Clare Prophet. Circ: (controlled).

200 FRA ISSN 1765-4866
PELERIN. Text in French. 1873. w. EUR 74.90 (effective 2008). bk.rev.; film rev.; play rev. bibl.; illus.; mkt. **Document type:** *Magazine, Consumer.* **Description:** France's leading Catholic weekly, it presents world news from a Christian perspective, as well as columns on health, law, education, leisure.
Former titles (until 2004): Pelerin Magazine (0764-4663); (until 1984): Pelerin (0399-5755); (until 1976): Pelerin du Vingtieme Siecle (0031-4145); (until 1963): Pelerin (0399-5747)
Published by: Bayard Presse, 3-5 rue Bayard, Paris, 75393 Cedex 08, France. TEL 33-1-44356060, FAX 33-1-44356161, redactions@bayard-presse.com, http://www.bayardpresse.com. Ed. Renee Poujol. Pub. Bernard Porte. Circ: 338,000 (paid).

202 USA ISSN 0031-4250
➤ **PENDLE HILL PAMPHLETS.** Text in English. 1934. irreg., latest no.406, 2010. price varies. back issues avail. **Document type:** *Monographic series, Academic/Scholarly.* **Description:** Articles focus on spiritual formation and active social witness for peace and justice.
Related titles: Microfilm ed.: (from PQC); Online - full text ed.
Published by: (Pendle Hill, a Quaker Center for Study and Contemplation), Pendle Hill Publications, 338 Plush Mill Rd, Wallingford, PA 19086. TEL 610-566-4507, 800-742-3150, FAX 610-566-3679, info@pendlehill.org.

230 GBR ISSN 2041-3599
▼ **PENTECOSTUDIES**; an interdisciplinary journal for research on the pentecostal and charismatic movements. Text in English. 2010. s-a. USD 220 combined subscription in North America to institutions (print & online eds.); GBP 135 combined subscription elsewhere to institutions (print & online eds.) (effective 2012). adv. back issues avail.; reprints avail. **Document type:** *Journal, Academic/Scholarly.* **Description:** Provides the study of Pentecostal and Charismatic Christianity. It also invites work that attends to historical, contemporary and regional studies.
Related titles: Online - full text ed.: ISSN 1871-7691. USD 176 in North America to institutions; GBP 108 elsewhere to institutions (effective 2012).
Published by: (European Research Network on Global Pentecostalism), Equinox Publishing Ltd., Unit S3, Kelham House, 3 Lancaster St, Sheffield, S6 3AF, United Kingdom. TEL 44-114-2725957, FAX 44-560-3459046, journals@equinoxpub.com, http://www.equinoxpub.com/. Ed. Mark J Cartledge. Adv. contact Val Hall.

202 GBR ISSN 0967-6147
PEOPLE'S BIBLE STUDIES. Text in English. 1992. irreg. price varies. **Document type:** *Monographic series, Academic/Scholarly.*
—CCC.
Published by: Urban Theology Unit, 210 Abbeyfield Rd, Sheffield, S Yorks S4 7AZ, United Kingdom. TEL 44-114-2435342, FAX 44-114-2435356, office@utusheffield.fsnet.co.uk, http://www.utusheffield.org.uk.

200 USA
PERE MARQUETTE THEOLOGY LECTURE SERIES. Text in English. 1969. irreg. price varies. **Document type:** *Monographic series, Academic/Scholarly.* **Description:** Documents annual public lectures by theologians.
Published by: Marquette University, Memorial Library, Rm 164, P O Box 3141, Milwaukee, WI 53201. TEL 414-288-1564, FAX 414-288-7813, http://www.mu.edu/mupress. **Subscr. to:** Book Masters, Standing Order Dept, 1444 U S Rt 2, Mansfield, OH 44903.

230 BEL ISSN 0180-7439
LES PERES DANS LA FOI. Text in French. 1977. irreg., latest vol.56, 1994. price varies. **Document type:** *Monographic series.* **Description:** Publishes studies of historical figures, doctrines and practices of the early Christian church.
Published by: (Association Jacques Paul Migne), Brepols Publishers, Begijnhof 67, Turnhout, 2300, Belgium. FAX 32-14-428919.

200 NLD ISSN 1568-3443
PERICOPE. Text in English. 2000. irreg., latest vol.6, 2007. price varies. **Document type:** *Monographic series, Academic/Scholarly.*
Indexed: IZBG.
Published by: Brill, PO Box 9000, Leiden, 2300 PA, Netherlands. TEL 31-71-5353500, FAX 31-71-5317532, cs@brill.nl.

PERSONA Y SOCIEDAD. *see* SOCIAL SCIENCES: COMPREHENSIVE WORKS

200 BRA ISSN 0102-4469
PERSPECTIVA TEOLOGICA (BELO HORIZONTE). Text in Portuguese. 1969. 3/yr.
Indexed: C01, CPL, OTA.
Published by: Centro de Estudos Superiores da Companhia de Jesus, Faculdade de Teologia, Caixa Postal 5024, Belo Horizonte, MG 31611-970, Brazil. cespublicacoe@cesjesuit.br.

PERSPECTIVE (TORONTO, 1967). *see* PHILOSOPHY

215 USA ISSN 0892-2675
BL240.2
➤ **PERSPECTIVES ON SCIENCE AND CHRISTIAN FAITH.** Text in English. 1949. q. USD 40 to individuals; USD 65 to institutions (effective 2011). adv. bk.rev. abstr. 72 p./no.; back issues avail. **Document type:** *Journal, Academic/Scholarly.* **Description:** Academic articles related to issues involving the interaction of science and Christian faith.
Formerly (until 1987): American Scientific Affiliation. Journal: Evangelical Perspectives on Science and Christian Faith (0003-0988)
Related titles: Microform ed.: (from PQC).
Indexed: A01, A21, A22, A26, CA, CERDIC, ChrPI, GSS&RPL, I05, P30, R&TA, RI-1, RI-2, S06, SWR&A, T02.
—IE, Ingenta. **CCC.**
Published by: American Scientific Affiliation, PO Box 668, Ipswich, MA 01938. TEL 978-356-5656, FAX 978-356-5656, asa@asa3.org, http://asa3online.org. Ed. Arie Leegwater TEL leeg@calvin.edu.

221 222 NLD ISSN 0169-9008
➤ **PESHITTA INSTITUTE, LEIDEN. MONOGRAPHS.** Text in Dutch. 1972. irreg., latest vol.17, 2008. price varies. back issues avail. **Document type:** *Monographic series, Academic/Scholarly.* **Description:** Scholarly studies on the Syriac translations of the Old and New Testaments.
Indexed: IZBG.
Published by: (Peshitta Institute, Leiden), Brill, PO Box 9000, Leiden, 2300 PA, Netherlands. TEL 31-71-5353500, FAX 31-71-5317532, cs@brill.nl, http://www.brill.nl. R&P Elizabeth Venekamp. **Dist. in N. America by:** Brill, PO Box 605, Herndon, VA 20172-0605. TEL 703-661-1585, 800-337-9255, FAX 703-661-1501, cs@brillusa.com; **Dist. by:** Turpin Distribution Services Ltd., Pegasus Dr, Stratton Business Park, Biggleswade, Bedfordshire SG18 8QB, United Kingdom. TEL 44-1767-604954, FAX 44-1767-601640, custserv@turpin-distribution.com, http://www.turpin-distribution.com/.

291 FRA ISSN 1951-5626
PETITE BIBLIOTHEQUE DES SPIRITUALITES. Text in French. 2006. irreg. back issues avail. **Document type:** *Monographic series, Consumer.*
Published by: Editions Plon, 76 rue Bonaparte, Paris, 75284 Cedex 06, France. TEL 33-1-44413500, FAX 33-1-44413053, http://www.plon.fr.

200 SWE ISSN 1652-1390
PETRUS; ett maanedsmagasin om kristen tro fraan Dagen. Text in Swedish. 1999. 11/yr. adv.
Formerly (until 2003): Petrus/Nya Dagens Helgmagasin
Published by: Dagengruppen AB, L M Ericssons Vaeg 4-8, Stockholm, 10536, Sweden. TEL 46-8-6192400, FAX 46-8-6566051, info@dagen.com. Ed. Miriam Arrebaeck TEL 46-8-6192480. Adv. contact Aake Lindh TEL 46-8-6192450. page SEK 17,000; 176 x 256.

PHILIPPINE STUDIES. *see* HUMANITIES: COMPREHENSIVE WORKS

200 PHL ISSN 0115-9577
PHILIPPINIANA SACRA. Text in English, Spanish. 1966. 3/yr. PHP 550, USD 40; USD 15 newsstand/cover (effective 2001). bk.rev. By Authors, by Articles and by Book Review. 200 p./no.; back issues avail. **Document type:** *Journal, Academic/Scholarly.* **Description:** Contains scholarly research in the fields of ecclesiastical disciplines; comments on kindred matters; contributions to the doctrinal and anthropological heritage of the Phils; critical studies of the diverse problems assailing spiritual and cultural growth of communities in the Far East.
Indexed: A01, BAS, CLA, FR, IPP, T02.
—INIST.
Published by: University of Santo Tomas, Ecclesiastical Faculties, Ecclesiastical Publications Office, Espana St, Manila, 1008, Philippines. TEL 731-3522, 731-3101, FAX 731-3522, publishing@ust.edu.ph, http://www.ust.edu.ph. Eds. Angel Aparicio, Javier Gonzalez, Jose Ma Tinoko, Roberto Pinto. Circ: 500.

PHILOSOPHIA CHRISTI. SERIES 2. *see* PHILOSOPHY

▼ **PHILOSOPHICAL STUDIES IN SCIENCE AND RELIGION.** *see* PHILOSOPHY

100 200 NLD
PHILOSOPHY AND RELIGION (AMSTERDAM). Text in English. 2001. irreg. price varies. **Document type:** *Monographic series, Academic/Scholarly.* **Description:** Publishes critical studies on religious attitudes, values and beliefs.
Related titles: ◆ Series of: Value Inquiry Book Series. ISSN 0929-8436.
Published by: Editions Rodopi B.V., Tijnmuiden 7, Amsterdam, 1046 AK, Netherlands. TEL 31-20-6114821, FAX 31-20-4472979, info@rodopi.nl. Ed. Kenneth A Bryson. **Dist. by:** Rodopi - USA, 606 Newark Ave, 2nd fl, Kenilworth, NJ 07033. TEL 908-497-9031, FAX 908-497-9035.

PHILOSOPHY AND RELIGION (LEIDEN); a comparative yearbook. *see* PHILOSOPHY

PHILOSOPHY & THEOLOGY. *see* PHILOSOPHY

200 NLD ISSN 2210-481X
▼ **PHILOSOPHY OF RELIGION.** Text in English. 2010. irreg., latest vol.1, 2010. EUR 103, USD 146 per vol. (effective 2010). **Document type:** *Monographic series, Academic/Scholarly.*
Related titles: Online - full text ed.: ISSN 2210-4828.
Published by: Brill, PO Box 9000, Leiden, 2300 PA, Netherlands. TEL 31-71-5353500, FAX 31-71-5317532, cs@brill.nl. Ed. Jerome Gellman.

249 GRC ISSN 0031-8396
PHONI TOU EVANGELIOU/VOICE OF THE GOSPEL. Text in Greek. 1944. m. USD 15. bk.rev. abstr.; bibl.; illus. index. **Document type:** *Journal, Academic/Scholarly.* **Description:** Family-oriented Christian magazine.
Published by: A M G International, 14 Souri St, Pireas, 185 47, Greece. TEL 30-1-3623-495, FAX 30-1-6548-506, http://www.amgpublishers.com/www, http://www.amg.gr. Ed. Spiros Zodhiates. R&P Argyris Petrou. Circ: 6,500.

266 ITA ISSN 0031-9600
IL PICCOLO MISSONARIO. Short title: P M. Text in Italian. 1927. m. EUR 22 domestic; EUR 44 in Europe; EUR 50 elsewhere (effective 2009). adv. film rev.; bk.rev.; music rev.; Website rev. **Document type:** *Magazine, Consumer.*
Related titles: Online - full text ed.
Published by: Missionari Comboniani, Vicolo Pozzo 1, Verona, 37129, Italy. TEL 39-045-8003534, FAX 39-045-8001737. Circ: 25,000.

230 028.5 DEU
PICO; Kinderzeitschrift der Steyler Missionare. Text in German. 1990. m. EUR 1.90 newsstand/cover (effective 2011). **Document type:** *Magazine, Consumer.*
Published by: Steyler Missionare e.V., Bahnhofstr 9, Nettetal, 41334, Germany. TEL 49-2157-120200, FAX 49-2157-1202060, steyler@steyler.de, http://www.steyler.at. Ed. P E Schoppert. Circ: 40,000 (paid and controlled).

200 DEU ISSN 1862-2690
PIETAS LITURGICA. Text in German. 1983. irreg., latest vol.14, 2004. price varies. **Document type:** *Monographic series, Academic/Scholarly.*
Published by: A. Francke Verlag GmbH, Dischinger Weg 5, Tuebingen, 72070, Germany. TEL 49-7071-97970, FAX 49-7071-979711, info@francke.de, http://www.francke.de.

200 DEU ISSN 1862-2704
PIETAS LITURGICA. STUDIA. Text in German. 1985. irreg., latest vol.21, 2010. price varies. **Document type:** *Monographic series, Academic/Scholarly.*
Published by: A. Francke Verlag GmbH, Dischinger Weg 5, Tuebingen, 72070, Germany. TEL 49-7071-97970, FAX 49-7071-979711, info@francke.de, http://www.francke.de.

200 ZAF ISSN 0031-9805
PILGRIM/PELGRIM. Text in Afrikaans, English. 1930. bi-m. ZAR 25 domestic; ZAR 30 foreign (effective 2004). bk.rev. illus. **Description:** Deals mainly with practical issues.
Indexed: CERDIC.
Published by: Africa Evangelistic Band/Afrika Evangeliese Bond, PO Box 77, Constantia, 7848, South Africa. mwhhm3@mweb.co.za. Ed. G A Till. R&P G.A. Till. Circ: 4,000.

200 RUS
PILGRIM. Text in Russian. s-a. USD 69 in United States.
Address: Kronshtadskii bulv 12-b, Moscow, 125212, Russian Federation. TEL 7-095-4521918, FAX 7-095-4521918. Ed. O V Lysenskii. **Dist. by:** East View Information Services, 10601 Wayzata Blvd, Minneapolis, MN 55305. TEL 952-252-1201, 800-477-1005, FAX 952-252-1202, info@eastview.com, http://www.eastview.com.

200 SWE
PILGRIM. Text in Swedish. 1966. q. SEK 260 (effective 2001). **Document type:** *Magazine, Consumer.*
Published by: Bokfoerlaget Cordia AB, Box 11175, Goeteborg, 40424, Sweden. TEL 46-31-774-03-33, FAX 46-31-774-03-32, johan.kjork@cordia.se. Ed. Peter Halldorf. R&P Goeran Rask. Adv. contact Johan Kjoerk. **Subscr. to:** Trots Allt, Kundtjaenst Verbum, Fack 15169, Stockholm 10123, Sweden. TEL 46-8-743-65-80, FAX 46-8-644-46-67.

200 GBR
PILGRIM POST. Text in English. 1990. bi-m. GBP 13 (effective 2000). adv. bk.rev. **Document type:** *Bulletin.* **Description:** Examines ecumenical Christianity.
Formerly: Vision One
Published by: Churches Together in England, 27 Tavistock Sq, London, WC1H 9HH, United Kingdom. TEL 44-20-75298131, FAX 44-20-75298134, office@cte.org.uk, http://www.churches-together.net/. Ed., R&P Rev. Roger Nunn TEL 44-123-551-1622. Circ: 2,500.

110 USA ISSN 0361-0802
CODEN: PILGDR
PILGRIMAGE. Text in English. 1972. 3/yr. USD 22 domestic; USD 32 in Canada & Mexico; USD 40 elsewhere (effective 2010). bk.rev. back issues avail. **Document type:** *Journal, Academic/Scholarly.* **Description:** Seeks to understand and celebrate the human journey through personal and experiential writing.
Related titles: Microform ed.: (from PQC).
Indexed: A21, A22, RI-1, RI-2.
—CCC.
Published by: Pilgrimage Press, Inc., PO Box 9110, Pueblo, CO 81008. Ed., Pub. Maria Melendez. Circ: 1,000 (paid).

200 USA ISSN 2156-5066
THE PIONEER (NORTHAMPTON). Text in English. 1966. m. free membership (effective 2010). back issues avail. **Document type:** *Newsletter, Academic/Scholarly.* **Description:** Provides information about the Unitarian Society of Northampton and Florence.
Related titles: Online - full text ed.: free (effective 2010).
Published by: Unitarian Society of Northampton and Florence, 220 Main St, Northampton, MA 01060. TEL 413-584-1390, admin@uunorthampton.org.

200 USA ISSN 1949-9078
BR1
▼ ➤ **PITTSBURGH THEOLOGICAL JOURNAL.** Text in English. 2009. s-a. USD 15 to individuals; USD 25 to institutions (effective 2009). **Document type:** *Journal, Academic/Scholarly.* **Description:** Contains research, dissertation abstracts, book reviews and sermons by the Pittsburgh Theological Seminary community.
Published by: Pittsburgh Theological Seminary, 616 N Highland Ave, Pittsburgh, PA 15206. TEL 412-362-5610, FAX 412-363-3260.

230 USA
PLAINS FAITH. Text in English. 2004 (Sep.). q. USD 10 (effective 2004). **Document type:** *Magazine, Consumer.* **Description:** Covers nondenominational Christian topics which focuses on the High Plains region, including Southwestern Kansas, the Oklahoma Panhandle, Eastern New Mexico, the Texas Panhandle and the South Plains region.
Address: PO Box 52407, Amarillo, TX 79159. Ed., Pub. Debra Wells. Circ: 7,500.

PLANET WALK. *see* LITERATURE

PLUGGED IN (COLORADO SPRINGS). *see* CHILDREN AND YOUTH—About

268 FRA ISSN 0751-6010
POINTS DE REPERE. Text in French. 1973. 6/yr. EUR 39 domestic; EUR 42 DOM-TOM; EUR 42 in the European Union; EUR 48 elsewhere (effective 2009 & 2010). Supplement avail. **Document type:** *Magazine, Consumer.* **Description:** The magazine for catechists. It offers a variety of questions to reflect on, practical advice to use in catechism classes and essential pointers to help one communicate one's faith.
Formerly: Catechistes d'Aujourd'hui (0008-7742)

Published by: (Centre National de l'Enseignement Religieux (C N E R)), Bayard Presse, 3-5 rue Bayard, Paris, 75393 Cedex 08, France. TEL 33-1-44356060, FAX 33-1-44356161, redactions@bayard-presse.com, http://www.bayardpresse.com. Eds. Annick Poullain, Catherine Faucher. Circ: 44,000.

207 268.8 USA ISSN 0079-2543
POINTS FOR EMPHASIS; INTERNATIONAL SUNDAY SCHOOL LESSONS IN POCKET SIZE. Text in English. 1917. a. USD 3.50. **Document type:** *Magazine, Consumer.* **Description:** Supplementary reading to international Sunday school lessons for adults.
Published by: Broadman & Holman Publishing Group, 127 Ninth Ave N, Nashville, TN 37234. TEL 615-251-2533. Ed. Frent C Butler. Circ: 33,000.

253 SWE ISSN 1653-2600
POLANCO; tidskrift foer ignatiansk andlighet. Text in Swedish. 2005. a. SEK 300 membership (effective 2011). **Document type:** *Yearbook, Consumer.*
Published by: Foereningen Kompass, c/o Ingrid Larsson, Loegen 138, Lysekil, 45391, Sweden. info@foreningenkompass.se. Ed. Mikael Loewegren.

POLIFEMO; rivista di storia delle religioni e storia antica. *see* HISTORY

322.1 GBR ISSN 1462-317X
BT83.59
POLITICAL THEOLOGY. Text in English. 1999. bi-m. USD 590 combined subscription in North America to institutions (print & online eds.); GBP 365 combined subscription elsewhere to institutions (print & online eds.) (effective 2012). adv. back issues avail.; reprints avail. **Document type:** *Journal, Academic/Scholarly.* **Description:** Aims to promote theological engagement with mainstream British political life.
Related titles: Online - full text ed.: ISSN 1743-1719. USD 472 in North America to institutions; GBP 292 elsewhere to institutions (effective 2012).
Indexed: A01, A03, A08, A21, CA, P42, PSA, R&TA, S02, S03, SCOPUS, SociolAb, T02.
—BLDSC (6543.925500), IE, Ingenta. **CCC.**
Published by: Equinox Publishing Ltd., Unit S3, Kelham House, 3 Lancaster St, Sheffield, S6 3AF, United Kingdom. TEL 44-114-2725957, FAX 44-560-3459046, journals@equinoxpub.com, http://www.equinoxpub.com/. Eds. David True, Graeme Smith, Timothy F Simpson.

POLITICS AND RELIGION. *see* POLITICAL SCIENCE

POLITICS, RELIGION & IDEOLOGY. *see* POLITICAL SCIENCE—International Relations

POLKA; Polish women's quarterly magazine. *see* WOMEN'S INTERESTS

299.94 GBR ISSN 1528-0268
BF1571
➤ **THE POMEGRANATE**; the international journal of pagan studies. Text in English. 1997. s-a. USD 220 combined subscription in North America to institutions (print & online eds.); GBP 135 combined subscription elsewhere to institutions (print & online eds.) (effective 2012). adv. back issues avail.; reprints avail. **Document type:** *Journal, Academic/Scholarly.* **Description:** Provides a forum for papers, essays and symposia on both ancient and contemporary Pagan religious practices.
Related titles: Online - full text ed.: ISSN 1743-1735. USD 176 in North America to institutions; GBP 108 elsewhere to institutions (effective 2012).
Indexed: A01, A20, A21, ArtHuCI, CA, CurCont, SCOPUS, T02, W07.
—BLDSC (6549.197500), IE. **CCC.**
Published by: Equinox Publishing Ltd., Unit S3, Kelham House, 3 Lancaster St, Sheffield, S6 3AF, United Kingdom. TEL 44-114-2725957, FAX 44-560-3459046, journals@equinoxpub.com, http://www.equinoxpub.com/. Ed. Chas Clifton. Adv. contact Val Hall.

200 DEU ISSN 0032-4132
POMHAJ BOH. Text in German. 1950. m. EUR 8 (effective 2009). illus. **Document type:** *Magazine, Consumer.*
Published by: Domowina Verlag GmbH, Tuchmacherstr 27, Bautzen, 02625, Germany. TEL 49-3591-5770, FAX 49-3591-577207, domowinaverlag@t-online.de, http://www.domowinaverlag.de.

230 DEU
▼ **POPULAERE KULTUR UND THEOLOGIE.** Variant title: POPKULT. Reihe Populaere Kultur und Theologie. Text in German. 2009. irreg., latest vol.9, 2011. price varies. **Document type:** *Monographic series, Academic/Scholarly.*
Published by: I K S Garamond, Leutragraben 1, Jena, 07743, Germany. TEL 49-3641-460850, FAX 49-3641-460855, garamond@iks-jena.de.

200 USA ISSN 2157-8419
BR563.N4
THE POSITIVE COMMUNITY; good news from the church and community. Text in English. 1999. m. (11/yr.). USD 20 (effective 2010). **Document type:** *Magazine, Trade.* **Description:** Provides information about the church and the community.
Formerly (until 200?): The Positive Community News
Related titles: Online - full text ed.: ISSN 2157-8427. free (effective 2010).
Published by: The Positive Community Corp., 133 Glenridge Ave, Montclair, NJ 07042. TEL 973-233-9200, FAX 973-233-9201, positive.corp@verizon.net. Ed. Jean Nash Wells. Pub. Adrian A Council.

202.15 USA ISSN 1083-0650
POSITIVE LIVING. Text in English. bi-m. USD 15.95; USD 22.95 foreign (effective 1998). **Description:** Devoted to helping readers live their best through inspirational stories of acts of human kindness and by applying spiritual values in everyday life.
Indexed: SCOPUS.
Published by: Guideposts, 39 Seminary Hill Rd, Carmel, NY 10512. TEL 800-431-2344, FAX 845-228-2151.

200 GBR ISSN 1743-887X
➤ **POSTSCRIPTS**; the journal of sacred texts and contemporary worlds. Text in English. 2004. 3/yr. USD 300 combined subscription in North America to institutions (print & online eds.); GBP 185 combined subscription elsewhere to institutions (print & online eds.) (effective 2012). adv. back issues avail.; reprints avail. **Document type:** *Journal, Academic/Scholarly.* **Description:** Devoted to the academic study of scripture around the globe.
Related titles: Online - full text ed.: ISSN 1743-8888. USD 240 in North America to institutions; GBP 148 elsewhere to institutions (effective 2012).
Indexed: A21.
—IE. **CCC.**
Published by: Equinox Publishing Ltd., Unit S3, Kelham House, 3 Lancaster St, Sheffield, S6 3AF, United Kingdom. TEL 44-114-2725957, FAX 44-560-3459046, journals@equinoxpub.com, http://www.equinoxpub.com/. Ed. Elizabeth Castelli. Adv. contact Val Hall.

➤ **POTCHEFSTROOM UNIVERSITY FOR CHRISTIAN HIGHER EDUCATION. WETENSKAPLIKE BYDRAES. REEKS B: NATUURWETENSKAPPE. SERIES.** *see* EDUCATION—Higher Education

➤ **POTCHEFSTROOM UNIVERSITY FOR CHRISTIAN HIGHER EDUCATION. WETENSKAPLIKE BYDRAES. REEKS H: INOUGURELE REDES.** *see* EDUCATION—Higher Education

242 USA ISSN 0032-6003
POWER FOR LIVING. Text in English. 1942. q. illus.
Indexed: CCR.
Published by: Scripture Press Publications, Inc., 4050 Lee Vance View, Colorado Springs, CO 80918-7102. TEL 719-536-0100, 800-708-5550. Ed. Don H Alban Jr.

230 USA ISSN 0032-6011
POWER FOR TODAY. Text in English. 1955. q. USD 7.95. adv. reprints avail.
Media: Duplicated (not offset). **Related titles:** Microfilm ed.: (from PQC).
Published by: 20th Century Christian Foundation, 2809 Granny White Pike, Nashville, TN 37204. TEL 615-383-3842. Eds. Emily Y Lemley, Steven S. Circ: 50,000.

200 USA ISSN 2155-2355
BL600
▼ **PRACTICAL MATTERS.** Text in English. 2009. s-a. free (effective 2011). **Document type:** *Journal, Academic/Scholarly.* **Description:** Features transdisciplinary multimedia research on religious practices and practical theology.
Media: Online - full text.
Published by: Emory University, Candler School of Theology, 1531 Dickey Dr, Atlanta, GA 30322. TEL 404-727-6326, candler@emory.edu, http://www.candler.emory.edu/.

200 USA ISSN 1947-6248
▼ **PRACTICAL THEOLOGY.** Text in English. 2010. irreg. price varies. **Document type:** *Monographic series, Academic/Scholarly.* **Description:** A book series on practical theology and religion.
Published by: Peter Lang Publishing, Inc. (Subsidiary of: Peter Lang Publishing Group), 29 Broadway, New York, NY 10006. TEL 212-647-7700, FAX 212-647-7707, customerservice@plang.com.

300 GBR ISSN 1756-073X
PRACTICAL THEOLOGY. Text in English. 1960. 3/yr. USD 300 combined subscription in North America to institutions (print & online eds.); GBP 185 combined subscription elsewhere to institutions (print & online eds.) (effective 2012). adv. back issues avail.; reprint service avail. from PSC. **Document type:** *Journal, Academic/Scholarly.* **Description:** Designed for the development of pastoral studies and practical theology by publishing creative articles which report good practice, and which offer fresh theoretical and practical insights in this area.
Formerly (until 2008): Contact (1352-0806)
Related titles: Online - full text ed.: ISSN 1756-0748. 2008. USD 240 in North America to institutions; GBP 148 elsewhere to institutions (effective 2012).
Indexed: A21, AMED, RI-1.
—BLDSC (6596.225000), IE, Ingenta. **CCC.**
Published by: (The British & Irish Association for Practical Theology), Equinox Publishing Ltd., Unit S3, Kelham House, 3 Lancaster St, Sheffield, S6 3AF, United Kingdom. TEL 44-114-2725957, FAX 44-560-3459046, journals@equinoxpub.com, http://www.equinoxpub.com/. Ed. Eric Stoddart. Adv. contact Val Hall.

220 ZAF ISSN 1010-8017
PRACTICAL THEOLOGY IN SOUTH AFRICA. Key Title: Praktiese Teologie in S.A. Text in English, Afrikaans. 1986. s-a. back issues avail. **Document type:** *Journal, Academic/Scholarly.*
Related titles: Online - full text ed.
Indexed: A21, ISAP, RI-1.
Address: PO Box 12549, Hatfield, 0028, South Africa. Ed. Nel Malan.

240 DEU ISSN 0936-403X
PRAEDICA VERBUM; Zeitschrift im Dienste der Glaubensverkuendigung. Text in German. 1955. bi-m. EUR 33; EUR 6 newsstand/cover (effective 2008). adv. **Document type:** *Journal, Trade.*
Published by: (Paedagogische Stiftung Cassianeum), Schwabenverlag AG, Senefelderstr 12, Ostfildern, 73760, Germany. TEL 49-711-4406140, FAX 49-711-4406138, info@schwabenverlag.de. Ed. Peter Neuhauser. adv.: page EUR 550. Circ: 2,000 (paid and controlled).

207.2 AUS
PRAISE & PRAYER CALENDAR. Text in English. 19??. bi-m. includes subscr. with SkyWaves. back issues avail. **Document type:** *Magazine, Consumer.* **Description:** Features significant prayer points that includes prayer for missionaries across the world and prayer for the various countries such as India, Cambodia, Russia etc.
Published by: Far East Broadcasting Co., PO Box 183, Caringbah, NSW 1495, Australia. TEL 61-2-95256460, FAX 61-2-95261250, febcoz@tpg.com.au, http://www.febc.org.au. Circ: 8,500.

240 DEU ISSN 0946-3518
BV1
PRAKTISCHE THEOLOGIE; Zeitschrift fuer Praxis in Kirche, Gesellschaft und Kultur. Text in German. 1966. q. EUR 88 domestic; EUR 98.50 foreign; EUR 57.40 to students; EUR 27.25 newsstand/cover (effective 2011). adv. bk.rev. index. **Document type:** *Journal, Academic/Scholarly.*
Former titles (until 1993): Theologia Practica (0938-5320); (until 1988): Themen der Praktischen Theologie - Theologia Practica (0720-9525); (until 1981): Theologia Practica (0049-3643)
Indexed: A22, CERDIC, DIP, FR, IBR, IBZ, PCI, RILM.
—IE, Infotrieve. **CCC.**
Published by: Guetersloher Verlagshaus (Subsidiary of: Verlagsgruppe Random House GmbH), Carl-Miele-Str 214, Guetersloh, 33311, Germany. TEL 49-5241-74050, FAX 49-5241-740548, info@gtvh.de, http://www.gtvh.de. Ed. Jan Hermelink. Circ: 1,000. **Subscr. to:** VVA Zeitschriftenservice, Postfach 7777, Guetersloh 33310, Germany. TEL 49-5241-801969, FAX 49-5241-809620.

282 CHE ISSN 1422-4410
PRAKTISCHE THEOLOGIE IM DIALOG. Text in German. 1987. irreg., latest vol.32, 2008. price varies. **Document type:** *Monographic series, Academic/Scholarly.*
Published by: Academic Press Fribourg, Perolles 42, Fribourg, 1705, Switzerland. TEL 41-26-4264311, FAX 41-26-4264300, info@paulusedition.ch, http://www.paulusedition.ch/academic_press/.

230 DEU ISSN 1865-1658
PRAKTISCHE THEOLOGIE IM WISSENSCHAFTSDISKURS/ PRACTICAL THEOLOGY IN THE DISCOURSE OF THE HUMANITIES. Text in German. 2007. irreg., latest vol.10, 2011. price varies. **Document type:** *Monographic series, Academic/Scholarly.*
Published by: Walter de Gruyter GmbH & Co. KG, Genthiner Str 13, Berlin, 10785, Germany. TEL 49-30-260050, FAX 49-30-26005251, info@degruyter.de, http://www.degruyter.de.

230 DEU ISSN 1862-8958
PRAKTISCHE THEOLOGIE IN GESCHICHTE UND GEGENWART. Text in German. 2006. irreg., latest vol.9, 2011. price varies. **Document type:** *Monographic series, Academic/Scholarly.*
Published by: Mohr Siebeck GmbH & Co. KG, Wilhelmstr 18, Tuebingen, 72074, Germany. TEL 49-7071-9230, FAX 49-7071-51104, info@mohr.de.

200 GBR ISSN 1748-2348
PRAXIS NEWS OF WORSHIP. Text in English. 2004. q. looseleaf. free to members (effective 2009). bk.rev. back issues avail. **Document type:** *Newsletter, Trade.* **Description:** Contains news and articles relating to worship, liturgy and music - particularly in the Church of England, but with an eye to other provinces and denominations from time to time.
Formed by the merger of (1975-2004): News of Liturgy (0263-7170); (1982-2004): News of Hymnody (0263-2306); (19??-2004): Praxis News
—CCC.
Published by: (Praxis), Grove Books Ltd., Ridley Hall Rd, Cambridge, CB3 9HU, United Kingdom. TEL 44-1223-464748, FAX 44-1223-464849, sales@grovebooks.co.uk, http://www.grovebooks.co.uk. Ed. Gilly Myers.

230 GBR ISSN 1479-215X
PRAYER BOOK SOCIETY JOURNAL. Text in English. 1975. s-a. free to members (effective 2009). bk.rev. back issues avail. **Document type:** *Journal, Consumer.* **Description:** Emphasizes traditionalism in the Church of England and, in particular, for the 1662 Book of Common Prayer.
Incorporates (1976-2000): Faith and Heritage (0140-0266)
Related titles: Online - full text ed.: free (effective 2009).
Published by: Prayer Book Society, The Studio, Copyhold Farm, Lady Grove, Goring Heath, Reading, RG8 7RT, United Kingdom. TEL 44-118-9842582, pbs.admin@pbs.org.uk. Adv. contact Ian Woodhead TEL 44-1380-870384.

200 CAN ISSN 1911-0391
PRAYERLINE. Text in English. 1993. m. **Document type:** *Magazine, Consumer.*
Related titles: Online - full text ed.
Published by: Christian Aid Mission, 201 Stanton St, Fort Erie, ON L2A 3N8, Canada. TEL 905-871-1773, 800-871-0882, FAX 905-871-5165, friends@christianaid.ca, http://www.christianaid.ca/index.htm.

251 USA ISSN 0274-600X
PRAYERS FOR WORSHIP. Text in English. 1978. q. looseleaf. USD 45.95; USD 17.23 per issue; USD 54.95 combined subscription (print & CD-ROM eds.) (effective 2011). adv. **Document type:** *Handbook/ Manual/Guide, Trade.*
Related titles: CD-ROM ed.: USD 39.95; USD 14.98 per issue (effective 2011); Online - full text ed.: USD 29.95; USD 11.23 per issue (effective 2011).
Published by: Liturgical Publications Inc., 2875 South James Dr, New Berlin, WI 53151. TEL 800-950-9952, CustomerService@LPiResourceCenter.comCustomerService@LPiResourceCenter.com, http://www.4lpi.com.

291.61 251 USA ISSN 1544-3914
PREACH. Text in English. 2003. bi-m. **Document type:** *Magazine, Trade.* **Description:** Helps preachers develop the art of preaching.
Published by: World Library Publications, Inc. (Subsidiary of: J.S. Paluch Co., Inc.), 3708 River Rd, Ste 400, Franklin Park, IL 60131. TEL 847-233-2752, 800-621-5197, FAX 847-233-2762, 888-957-3291, wlpcs@jspaluch.com, http://www.wlp.jspaluch.com/.

251 USA ISSN 0882-7036
PREACHING. Text in English. 1985. bi-m. USD 39.95 domestic; USD 46.95 in Canada; USD 54.95 elsewhere (effective 2009). adv. bk.rev.; software rev. back issues avail. **Document type:** *Magazine, Trade.* **Description:** Features practical articles on preaching, sermon manuscripts and homiletic helps.
Indexed: A21, CCR, RI-1, RI-2.
—CCC.
Published by: Salem Publishing, 104 Woodmont Blvd, Ste 300, Nashville, TN 37205. TEL 615-312-4250, 800-527-5226, FAX 615-385-4112, customerservice@salempublishing.com, http://www.salempublishing.com. Adv. contact Dede Donatelli-Tarrant TEL 805-987-5072.

251 USA ISSN 1940-8749
PREACHING THE MIRACLES. Text in English. 1984. a. price varies. back issues avail. **Document type:** *Monographic series, Trade.* **Description:** Contains five sections devoted to each of the nine miracles in cycle C of the revised common lectionary.
Related titles: Online - full text ed.
Published by: C S S Publishing Co., 517 S Main St, Lima, OH 45804. TEL 419-227-1818, 800-241-4056, FAX 419-228-9184, info@csspub.com, http://www.csspub.com. Pub. Wesley T Runk.

R

252 USA ISSN 1938-5579
PREACHING THE PARABLES. Text in English. 1987. a. price varies. back issues avail. **Document type:** *Monographic series, Trade.* **Description:** Provides a gold mine of background material on each of the eighteen parables appearing in Cycle C of the Revised Common Lectionary.
Related titles: Online - full text ed.
Published by: C S S Publishing Co., 517 S Main St, Lima, OH 45804. TEL 419-227-1818, 800-241-4056, FAX 419-228-9184, info@csspub.com, http://www.csspub.com. Pub. Wesley T Runk.

200 DEU ISSN 0079-4961
PREDIGTSTUDIEN. Text in German. 1968. s-a. EUR 24.90 per issue (effective 2005). **Document type:** *Bulletin.*
Published by: Kreuz Verlag GmbH & Co. KG, Postfach 800669, Stuttgart, 70506, Germany. TEL 49-711-788030, FAX 49-711-7880310, service@kreuzverlag.de, http://www.kreuzverlag.de. Circ: 7,000.

200 RUS
➤ **PREDSTAVITEL'NAYA VLAST' - XXI VEK**; zakonodatel'stvo, kommentarii, problemy. Text in Russian. 1994. bi-m. USD 163 in United States (effective 2007). **Document type:** *Journal, Academic/Scholarly.* **Description:** The analytical legal research and practical publication comprises the essays on authority, comments on and evaluation of laws and bills, practice of law and other statutory acts enforcement; deals with the issues of finances, taxation, science and education, civil society, etc.
Published by: Gosudarstvennaya Duma Federal'nogo Sobraniya Rossiiskoi Federatsii, Komitet po Delam Obshchestvennykh Ob'edinenii i Religioznykh Organizatsii, ul Okhotnyi ryad, dom 1, Moscow, 103265, Russian Federation. Ed. A P Lyubimov. **Dist. by:** East View Information Services, 10601 Wayzata Blvd, Minneapolis, MN 55305. TEL 952-252-1201, 800-477-1005, FAX 952-252-1202, info@eastview.com, http://www.eastview.com.

268 USA ISSN 1550-9362
PRESCHOOL PLAYHOUSE. STUDENT FOLDER. Text in English. 1980. q. USD 3.49 per issue (effective 2009). back issues avail. **Document type:** *Magazine, Consumer.* **Description:** Contains Bible lesson worksheet and it a Bible story and a contemporary story to illustrate and apply the Bible lesson for ages 2-5.
Published by: Urban Ministries, Inc., Dept #4870, PO Box 87618, Chicago, IL 60680. TEL 708-868-7100, 800-860-8642, FAX 708-868-7105, customerservice@urbanministries.com.

268 USA ISSN 1550-9370
PRESCHOOL PLAYHOUSE. TEACHER GUIDE. Text in English. 1980. q. USD 5.59 per issue (effective 2008). back issues avail. **Document type:** *Magazine, Consumer.* **Description:** Contains Bible background and teaching plans for ages 2-5.
Published by: Urban Ministries, Inc., Dept #4870, PO Box 87618, Chicago, IL 60680. TEL 708-868-7100, 800-860-8642, FAX 708-868-7105, customerservice@urbanministries.com.

200 CAN ISSN 1188-5580
BV4000C652
PRESENCE MAGAZINE. Text in English. 1962. 8/yr. CAD 35 domestic; CAD 65 foreign (effective 2002 - 2003). adv. bk.rev. bibl. back issues avail. **Document type:** *Magazine, Consumer.* **Description:** Contains information and reflection in a Christian perspective, on events and tendencies of actual society. Includes main paper on current events, public personality interviews, chronicles on spirituality, church and media, national and international news.
Former titles (until 1992): Nouveau Magazine Communaute Chretienne; Communaute Chretienne (0010-3454)
Related titles: CD-ROM ed.: Repere.
Indexed: CERDIC, PdeR.
Published by: Presence Magazine Inc., 2715 chemin Cote Ste Catherine, Montreal, PQ H3T 1B6, Canada. TEL 514-739-9797, FAX 514-739-1664, presence@presencemag.qc.ca. Ed. Jean Claude Breton. R&P Marie Therese Guilbault. Adv. contact Madeleine Lanthier. B&W page CAD 450; trim 10 x 7.5. Circ: 3,000.

200 COL
PRESENCIA. Text in Spanish. 1950. m. USD 14. adv. abstr.; bibl.
Published by: Editorial Presencia Ltda., Calle 23, 24-20, Bogota, DE, Colombia. Ed. Maria Carrizosa de Umana. Circ: 15,000.

230 VEN ISSN 0798-0256
BR115.C8
PRESENCIA ECUMENICA. Text in Spanish. 1985. q. USD 16 in North America; USD 20 elsewhere. adv. cum.index: 1985-1995 in no.36. back issues avail. **Document type:** *Bulletin.* **Description:** Discusses issues relating to Latin American ecumenical movement and gives information about developments in religious and theological fields.
Indexed: C01.
Published by: Accion Ecumenica, La Pastora, C. Norte 10, San Vicente a Medina 139, Apdo. Postal 6314, Carmelitas, Caracas, 1010-A, Venezuela. TEL 58-2-811548, FAX 58-2-8611196. Ed. Manuel Larreal. Pub. Alexander Campos. Adv. contact Ligia Gonzalez. Circ: 1,500.

261 USA ISSN 1098-3775
PRESERVING CHRISTIAN HOMES. Text in English. 1970. bi-m.
Published by: General Youth Division, 8855 Dunn Rd, Hazelwood, MO 63042. Ed. Todd Gaddy. Circ: 4,500.

PRESS ON. *see* CHILDREN AND YOUTH—For

200 FRA ISSN 0181-6578
PRIER; l'aventure spirituelle. Text in French. 1978. 10/yr. EUR 29 domestic (effective 2010). **Document type:** *Magazine, Consumer.* **Description:** A review of modern prayer and contemplation.
Address: 80 Boulevard Auguste Blanqui, Paris, 75707, France. TEL 33-1-48884600. Circ: 85,000.

268 USA ISSN 0032-8278
PRIMARY DAYS; makes Bible truths live. Text in English. 1939 (vol.5). q. charts; illus. **Description:** Presents the teachings of the Bible for children ages 6-8.
Published by: Scripture Press Publications, Inc., 4050 Lee Vance View, Colorado Springs, CO 80918-7102. TEL 719-536-0100, 800-708-5550, http://www.cookministries.com. Ed. Janice K Briton.

268 USA ISSN 1550-8854
PRIMARY STREET. STUDENT FOLDER. Text in English. 1975. q. USD 3.49 per issue (effective 2008). back issues avail. **Document type:** *Magazine, Consumer.* **Description:** Contains 13 Bible lesson folders for children 6-8; each folder includes: a Bible story written for beginner, intermediate, and advanced readers and related activities designed for the same three reading levels.
Published by: Urban Ministries, Inc., Dept #4870, PO Box 87618, Chicago, IL 60680. TEL 708-868-7100, 800-860-8642, FAX 708-868-7105, customerservice@urbanministries.com.

268 USA ISSN 1550-8862
PRIMARY STREET. TEACHER GUIDE. Text in English. 1975. q. USD 5.59 per issue (effective 2009). back issues avail. **Document type:** *Magazine, Consumer.* **Description:** Contains Bible background and commentary on the Sunday School lessons for ages 6-8, plus teaching plans and other aids.
Published by: Urban Ministries, Inc., Dept #4870, PO Box 87618, Chicago, IL 60680. TEL 708-868-7100, 800-860-8642, FAX 708-868-7105, customerservice@urbanministries.com.

200 RUS ISSN 0201-4793
BR1644.5.R8
PRIMIRITEL'. Text in Russian. 1991. q. USD 85 in North America (effective 2000).
Indexed: RASB.
Address: Ul Orenburgskaya 10a, Moscow, 111621, Russian Federation. TEL 7-095-7004244. **Dist. by:** East View Information Services, 10601 Wayzata Blvd, Minneapolis, MN 55305. TEL 952-252-1201, 800-477-1005, FAX 952-252-1202, info@eastview.com, http://www.eastview.com.

200 USA
PRINCETON READINGS IN RELIGIONS. Text in English. 1995. irreg., latest 2009. price varies. illus. back issues avail. **Document type:** *Monographic series, Academic/Scholarly.* **Description:** Designed for students, specialists discover a wealth of unfamiliar and valuable material. Explores and analyzes the scriptures and other writings of the world's religions.
Published by: Princeton University Press, 41 William St, Princeton, NJ 08540. TEL 609-258-4900, 800-777-4726, FAX 609-258-6305, cpriday@pupress.co.uk. **Subscr. addr. in US:** California - Princeton Fulfillment Services, Inc., 1445 Lower Ferry Rd, Ewing, NJ 08618. TEL 609-883-1759, 800-777-4726, FAX 609-883-7413, 800-999-1958, orders@cpfsinc.com. **Dist. addr. in Canada:** University Press Group.; **Dist. addr. in UK:** John Wiley & Sons Ltd.

220 USA ISSN 0898-753X
BS680.S53
PRISCILLA PAPERS. Text in English. 1987. q. USD 40 to non-members; USD 8 per issue to non-members; free to members (effective 2010); subscr. includes with Mutuality Magazine. back issues avail. **Document type:** *Journal, Academic/Scholarly.* **Description:** Addresses biblical interpretation, church history, and other academic disciplines as they relate to men and women offering mutual service in the Christian community and family.
Indexed: A01, CA, ChrPI, R&TA, T02.
Published by: Christians for Biblical Equality, 122 W Franklin Ave, Ste 218, Minneapolis, MN 55404. TEL 612-872-6898, FAX 612-872-6891, cbe@cbeinternational.org. Ed. William David Spencer. Pub. Mimi Haddad.

238 USA ISSN 1079-6479
HN30
PRISM (WYNNEWOOD). Text in English. 1988. bi-m. USD 25 domestic; USD 35 in Canada & Mexico; USD 55 elsewhere (effective 2005). adv. bk.rev. **Document type:** *Magazine, Consumer.*
Formerly (until 1993): E S A Advocate (1063-9152)
Indexed: R&TA, RI-1, RI-2.
Published by: Evangelicals for Social Action, 10 E Lancaster Ave, Wynnewood, PA 19096-3495. TEL 610-645-9390, 800-650-6600, FAX 610-649-8090, esa@esa.mhs.compuserve.com, http://www.esa-online.org. Ed., R&P Dwight Ozard TEL 610-645-9391. Pub. Ronald J Sider. Circ: 10,000.

200 DEU ISSN 0935-9168
DAS PRISMA; Beitraege zu Pastoral, Katechese & Theologie. Text in German. 1988. s-a. EUR 12 (effective 2011). **Document type:** *Journal, Academic/Scholarly.*
Published by: (Fokolar-Bewegung), Verlag Neue Stadt, Muenchener Str 2, Oberpframmern, 85667, Germany. TEL 49-8093-2091, FAX 49-8093-2096, verlag@neuestadt.com, http://www.neuestadt.com.

PRISMET; pedagogisk tidsskrift. *see* EDUCATION

291.72 USA ISSN 1930-8159
PRISON LIVING MAGAZINE. Text in English. 2006. q. USD 16 (effective 2007). **Document type:** *Magazine, Consumer.*
Related titles: Online - full text ed.: ISSN 1930-8167.
Published by: Total Life Ministries, Inc., 10645 N Tatum Blvd, Ste 200-661, Scottsdale, AZ 85254. TEL 602-296-3420, 800-419-2891, FAX 480-626-5857, http://www.totallifeministries.com/index.html.

282 289.9 USA ISSN 1063-8512
BR1
PRO ECCLESIA. Text in English. 1992. q. USD 30 (effective 2005).
Related titles: Online - full text ed.
Indexed: A21, RI-1.
—Ingenta. **CCC.**
Published by: Center for Catholic and Evangelical Theology, c/o Carl E Braaten, Editor, 16005 Huron Dr, Sun City W, AZ 85375. TEL 623-214-5977, carlebraat@aol.com, http://www.e-ccet.org/.

PROCESS PERSPECTIVES. *see* PHILOSOPHY

200 704.948 NLD ISSN 1877-3370
PROF. DR. G. VAN DER LEEUW-STICHTING. NWSBRF. Text in Dutch. 2008. s-a. EUR 17.50 membership (effective 2011). **Document type:** *Newsletter, Consumer.*
Published by: (Prof. Dr. G. van der Leeuw Stichting), Skandalon Mediale Projecten, Postbus 138, Vught, 5260 AC, Netherlands. TEL 31-30-2218250, FAX 31-84-7186782, info@skandalon.nl, http://www.skandalon.nl. Eds. Abe van der Werff, Dr. Anne M Spijkerboer, Frank Petter.

269.20715 USA
PROFILE (WHEATON). Text in English. 1967. 3/yr. free. **Document type:** *Newsletter.*
Formerly: Teacher Training Profile
Published by: Evangelical Training Association, 327, Wheaton, IL 60189-0327. TEL 630-668-6400, FAX 630-668-8437. Ed. Jonathan Thigpen. R&P Linda Sorenson. Circ: 35,000.

282.477 CAN ISSN 0033-054X
PROGRESS/POSTUP. Text in English, Ukrainian. 1959. bi-w. CAD 30 domestic; CAD 50 foreign; CAD 1.25 newsstand/cover (effective 2000). adv. bk.rev.; film rev.; play rev. illus. 16 p./no. 5 cols./p.; **Document type:** *Newspaper.* **Description:** Provides teachings of the Ukrainian Catholic Church Hierarchy. Presents parish life and activities of Ukrainian Catholic families in Winnipeg. Reports on events in other parts of Canada, in Ukraine and in other countries.
Related titles: Ukrainian ed.
Published by: (Ukrainian Catholic Archeparchy of Winnipeg), Progress Printing & Publishing Co. Ltd., 233 Scotia St, Winnipeg, MB R2V 1V7, Canada. TEL 204-334-4826, FAX 204-339-4006, postup@mts.net. Ed. Fr. Michael Winn. R&P, Adv. contact Lidiya Firman. Circ: 25,000.

170 USA
PROGRESS (MEDFORD). Text in English. 1895. m. USD 2. bk.rev. back issues avail. **Document type:** *Newsletter.*
Published by: International Reform Federation, 888, Alloway, NJ 08001-0888. TEL 609-985-7724. Ed. Lawrence L Dunn. Circ: 2,500.

204 ITA ISSN 0394-5936
PROGRESSIO (ENGLISH EDITION); Ignatian spirituality for laypeople. Text in English. 1924. 4/yr. illus. index, cum.index every 10 yrs. Supplement avail.; back issues avail. **Document type:** *Magazine, Consumer.*
Supersedes in part (in 1970): Progressio (0033-0728); Which was formerly (until 1967): Acies Ordinata (0394-5707)
Published by: Christian Life Community/Comunita di Vita Cristiana, Borgo Santo Spirito 8, Casella Postale 6139, Rome, 00195, Italy. TEL 39-06-6868079, FAX 39-06-68132497.

204 ITA ISSN 0394-591X
PROGRESSIO (FRENCH EDITION). Text in French. 1924. 4/yr. **Document type:** *Magazine, Consumer.*
Supersedes in part (in 1970): Progressio (0033-0728); Which was formerly (until 1967): Acies Ordinata (0394-5707)
Published by: Christian Life Community/Comunita di Vita Cristiana, Borgo Santo Spirito 8, Casella Postale 6139, Rome, 00195, Italy. TEL 39-06-6868079, FAX 39-06-68132497.

204 ITA ISSN 0394-5928
PROGRESSIO (SPANISH EDITION). Text in Spanish. 1924. 4/yr. **Document type:** *Magazine, Consumer.*
Supersedes in part (in 1970): Progressio (0033-0728); Which was formerly (until 1967): Acies Ordinata (0394-5707)
Published by: Christian Life Community/Comunita di Vita Cristiana, Borgo Santo Spirito 8, Casella Postale 6139, Rome, 00195, Italy. TEL 39-06-6868079, FAX 39-06-68132497.

220 CAN ISSN 0048-5578
PROPHETIC EXPOSITOR. Text in English. 1964. m. membership. adv. bk.rev. abstr.; bibl.; charts; illus.; stat. index. **Document type:** *Bulletin.*
Media: Duplicated (not offset).
Published by: British Israel World Federation (Canada) Inc., 313 Sherbourne St, Toronto, ON M5A 2S3, Canada. TEL 416-921-5996. Ed., Pub. D.C. Nesbit. Circ: 1,600.

220.15 USA ISSN 0033-1341
PROPHETIC NEWSLETTER; the news in the light of the Bible. Text in English. 1959. m. per issue contribution. illus. **Document type:** *Newsletter.*
Published by: World Prophetic Ministry, Inc., P O Drawer 907, Colton, CA 92324. TEL 909-825-2767. Ed. David Breese. Circ: 25,000.

200.92 USA
PROPHETIC OBSERVER. Text in English. 1938. m. USD 20. reprints avail.
Formerly (since 1993): Gospel Truths (0017-2383); Supersedes (in 1990): Torch (Oklahoma City) (0195-1823)
Related titles: Microform ed.: (from PQC).
Published by: Southwest Radio Church, PO Box 100, Bethany, OK 73008-0100. TEL 405-235-5396, FAX 405-236-4634. Ed. N W Hutchings. Circ: 35,000.

200 GBR ISSN 1470-6288
PROPHETIC WITNESS. Text in English. 1918. m. GBP 22 domestic; GBP 28 foreign (effective 2009). adv. bk.rev. illus. 24 p./no.; back issues avail. **Document type:** *Magazine, Consumer.* **Description:** Contains prophetic news, Israel in the Scriptures, biblical exposition, comment and current affairs.
Former titles (until 1999): Your Tomorrow (0951-5178); (until 1987): Prophetic Witness (0033-135X); Which incorporated (1879-19??): Prophetic News and Israel's Watchman (0033-1333)
Indexed: CERDIC.
Published by: Prophetic Witness Movement International, PO Box 109, Leyland, Lancashire PR25 1 WB, United Kingdom. TEL 44-1772-452846, FAX 44-1772-452846, info@pwmi.org. Ed. Rev. Glyn L Taylor.

220 AUT
PROTOKOLLE ZUR BIBEL. Text in German. 1992. s-a. EUR 10.50 (effective 2004).
Indexed: IZBG, OTA.
Published by: (Arbeitsgemeinschaft der Assistentinnen und Assistenten an Bibelwissenschaftlichen Instituten in Oesterreich), Aleph-Omega Verlag, Institut fuer Alt- und Neutestamentliche Wissenschaft, Universitaetsplatz 1, Salzburg, 5020, Austria. christine.hofer_ranftl@sbg.ac.at, http://www.sbg.ac.at/anw/verlag_home.htm. Eds. Johannes Schiller, Konrad Huber, Ursula Rapp.

200 ESP ISSN 0478-6378
BX805
PROYECCION; teologia y mundo actual. Text in Spanish. 1954. q. USD 19 (effective 2001). adv. bk.rev. back issues avail. **Document type:** *Magazine, Academic/Scholarly.*
Indexed: DIP, IBR, IBZ, OTA.
Published by: Facultad de Teologia de Granada, Campus Universitario de Cantuja s/n, Granada, 18080, Spain. TEL 34-958-185252, FAX 34-958-162559, info@eol-granada.com, http://www.teol.granada.com/. Ed., Pub., Adv. contact Juan M Rufo. Circ: 2,100.

200 POL ISSN 1230-4379
➤ **PRZEGLAD RELIGIOZNAWCZY.** Text in English, Polish, Russian; Summaries in English, Russian. 1957. q. PLZ 100 domestic; USD 25 foreign; PLZ 28 newsstand/cover (effective 1999). bk.rev. bibl.; illus. index. **Document type:** *Journal, Academic/Scholarly.* **Description:** Presents sociological research for an academic audience.
Formerly (until 1992): Euhemer (0014-2298)
Indexed: FR, IBR, IBSS, IBZ, MLA-IB, RASB.
—INIST.
Published by: Polskie Towarzystwo Religioznawcze, Ul Jaracza 1, lok. 6, PO Box 151, Warsaw, 00959, Poland. TEL 48-22-6252642. Ed. Zbigniew Stachowski. Circ: 2,000.

220.48 NLD ISSN 0079-7197
➤ **PSEUDEPIGRAPHA VETERIS TESTAMENTI GRAECE.** Text in Dutch. 1964. irreg., latest vol.6, 2005. price varies. back issues avail. **Document type:** *Monographic series, Academic/Scholarly.*
Indexed: IZBG.
Published by: (Universiteit Leiden), Brill, PO Box 9000, Leiden, 2300 PA, Netherlands. TEL 31-71-5353500, FAX 31-71-5317532, cs@brill.nl, http://www.brill.nl. R&P Elizabeth Venekamp. **Dist. by:** Turpin Distribution Services Ltd., Pegasus Dr, Stratton Business Park, Biggleswade, Bedfordshire SG18 8QB, United Kingdom. TEL 44-1767-604954, FAX 44-1767-601640, custserv@turpin-distribution.com, http://www.turpin-distribution.com/.

➤ **PSICOANALISI RELIGIOSA.** *see* PSYCHOLOGY

200 SWE ISSN 0283-149X
PSYCHOLOGIA ET SOCIOLOGIA RELIGIONUM. Text in Multiple languages. 1987. irreg., latest vol.16, 2002. price varies. back issues avail. **Document type:** *Monographic series, Academic/Scholarly.*
Formerly (until 1984): Psychologia Religionum (0346-6094)
Related titles: ◆ Series of: Acta Universitatis Upsaliensis. ISSN 0346-5462.
Published by: Uppsala Universitet, Acta Universitatis Upsaliensis/ University Publications from Uppsala, PO Box 256, Uppsala, 75105, Sweden. TEL 46-18-4716804, FAX 46-18-4716804, acta@ub.uu.se, http://www.ub.uu.se/upu/auu/index.html. Ed. Bengt Landgren. **Dist. by:** Almqvist & Wiksell International.

▼ **PSYCHOLOGY OF RELIGION AND SPIRITUALITY.** *see* PSYCHOLOGY

PSYCHOTHERAPIE UND SEELSORGE; Magazin fuer Psychotherapie und Seelsorge. *see* PSYCHOLOGY

PUBBLICAZIONI DI DIRITTO ECCLESIASTICO. *see* LAW

PUBLIC JUSTICE REPORT (ONLINE). *see* POLITICAL SCIENCE—International Relations

201.6 DEU ISSN 0343-1401
PUBLIK-FORUM; Zeitung kritischer Christen. Text in German. 1968. fortn. EUR 85.60; EUR 3.80 newsstand/cover (effective 2007). adv. bk.rev. **Document type:** *Newspaper, Consumer.*
Formerly (until 1972): Publik (0033-3956)
Published by: (Leserinitiative Publik e.V.), Publik Forum Verlagsgesellschaft mbH, Postfach 2010, Oberursel, 61410, Germany. TEL 49-6171-70030, FAX 49-6171-700340. Eds. Peter Rosien, Wolfgang Kessler. adv.: B&W page EUR 2,681, color page EUR 3,888. Circ: 43,662.

200 USA
PULPIT HELPS; for preaching, teaching & living God's word. Text in English. 1975. m. USD 22.99 (effective 2002). adv. bk.rev. illus. back issues avail. **Document type:** *Newspaper.*
Former titles: Pulpit and Bible Study; (until 1992): Pulpit Helps (0193-3914)
Indexed: CCR.
Published by: Advancing the Ministries of the Gospel International, 6815 Shallowford Rd, Chattanooga, TN 37421-1755. TEL 423-894-6060, 800-251-7206, FAX 423-510-8074. Ed., Pub. Bob Dasal. R&P Ted Kyle. Adv. contact Carlton Dunn. B&W page USD 2,776, color page USD 3,226. Circ: 15,000 (paid); 60,000 (controlled).

251 USA ISSN 0195-1548
PULPIT RESOURCE. Text in English. 1973. q. USD 44.95 domestic to individuals; USD 54.96 in Canada to individuals; USD 75.90 domestic to institutions; USD 81.90 foreign to institutions. back issues avail. **Document type:** *Journal, Trade.* **Description:** Resource and illustrative material for preparation of sermons for ministers, priests, rabbis and lay speakers.
Related titles: Diskette ed.
Published by: Logos Productions, 6160 Carmen Ave E, Inver Grove Heights, MN 55076-4422. TEL 612-451-9945, FAX 612-457-4617. Ed. William H Willimon. Circ: 8,000.

230 BOL ISSN 1608-1579
PUNTO DE ENCUENTRO. Text in Spanish. 1999. q.
Related titles: Online - full text ed.: ISSN 1608-1722.
Published by: Editorial Verbo Divino, Ave. Juan de la Rosa O-2216, Cochabamba, Bolivia. TEL 591-4-4286297, FAX 591-4-4420733, http://verbodivino-bo.com/.

200 LKA
PUTHIYA ULAHAM. Text in Tamil. 1976. 6/yr.
Published by: Centre for Better Society, 115, 4th Cross St., Jaffna, Sri Lanka. TEL 21-22627. Ed. Rev. S J Emmanuel. Circ: 1,500.

QUADERNI DI DIRITTO E POLITICA ECCLESIASTICA. *see* LAW

200 ITA ISSN 1827-6601
QUADERNI DI STUDI ECUMENICI. Text in Italian. 2000. s-a. price varies. **Document type:** *Monographic series, Academic/Scholarly.*
Published by: Pontificio Ateneo Antonianum, Istituto di Studi Ecumenici San Bernardino, Castello 2786, Venice, 30122, Italy. info@isevenezia.it, http://www.isevenezia.it.

200 933 ISR
QUADERNI DI TERRA SANTA. Text in Multiple languages. 1963. irreg., latest 1991. back issues avail. **Document type:** *Monographic series, Academic/Scholarly.*
Published by: Franciscan Printing Press, PO Box 14064, Jerusalem, 91140, Israel. TEL 972-2-6266592, FAX 972-2-6272274, fpp@bezeqint.net, http://198.62.75.1/www1/ofm/fpp/FPPmain.html.

220 DEU ISSN 0943-478X
QUAESTIONES DISPUTATAE. Text in German. 1993. irreg., latest vol.238, 2010. price varies. **Document type:** *Monographic series, Academic/Scholarly.*
Indexed: IZBG.
Published by: Verlag Herder GmbH, Hermann-Herder-Str 4, Freiburg Im Breisgau, 79104, Germany. TEL 49-761-27170, FAX 49-761-2717520, kundenservice@herder.de, http://www.herder.de.

202 USA ISSN 0033-5061
BX7601
QUAKER LIFE; informing and equipping friends - a publication of friends united meeting. Text in English. 1960. 10/yr. USD 24; USD 2 newsstand/cover (effective 1999). adv. bk.rev. illus. index. back issues avail. **Description:** Publishes religious news and articles to inform and equip Friends.
Formed by the merger of: American Friend; Quaker Action
Indexed: CERDIC.
Published by: Friends United Meeting (Quakers), 101 Quaker Hill Dr, Richmond, IN 47374-1980. TEL 765-962-7573, FAX 765-966-1293. Ed. Johan Maurer. Pub., R&P Ben Richmond. Adv. contact Norma Cox. B&W page USD 475, color page USD 575; trim 10.75 x 8.25. Circ: 8,200.

266 USA ISSN 0033-6017
QUEEN OF ALL HEARTS; the true devotion magazine. Text in English. 1950. bi-m. USD 20; USD 23 foreign (effective 1999). bk.rev. illus. back issues avail. **Description:** Religious forum covering Christianity and missionaries.
Published by: Montfort Missionaries, 26 S Saxon Ave, Bay Shore, NY 11706. TEL 516-665-0726, FAX 516-665-4349. Ed. J Patrick Gaffney S M M. R&P Roger Charest. Circ: 3,500 (paid).

220 AUS ISSN 1449-6372
QUEENSLAND SOWER. Text in English. 2004. q. free to qualified personnel (effective 2009). **Document type:** *Magazine, Consumer.*
Published by: The Bible Society in Australia (Queensland), GPO Box 1228, Brisbane, QLD 4000, Australia. TEL 61-7-32215683, FAX 61-7-32290063, biblesq@bible.org.au, http://www.biblesociety.com.au.

200 DEU ISSN 0480-7480
QUELLEN UND ABHANDLUNGEN ZUR MITTELRHEINISCHEN KIRCHENGESCHICHTE. Text in German. 1954. irreg., latest vol.92, 1998. **Document type:** *Monographic series, Academic/Scholarly.*
Published by: Gesellschaft fuer Mittelrheinische Kirchengeschichte, Jesuitenstr 13c, Trier, 54290, Germany. petra.mattes@bgv-trier.de, http://mittelrheinische-kirchengeschichte.de.

QUELLEN UND STUDIEN ZU GESCHICHTE UND KUNST IM BISTUM HILDESHEIM. *see* HISTORY—History Of Europe

230 DEU
QUELLEN UND STUDIEN ZUR NEUEREN THEOLOGIEGESCHICHTE. Text in German. 1996. irreg., latest vol.8, 2009. price varies. **Document type:** *Monographic series, Academic/Scholarly.*
Published by: Verlag Friedrich Pustet, Gutenbergstr 8, Regensburg, 93051, Germany. TEL 49-941-920220, FAX 49-941-92022330, verlag@pustet.de, http://www.pustetverlag.de.

230 378 HKG ISSN 1684-6206
BR1060
➤ **QUEST**; an interdisciplinary journal for Asian Christian scholars. Text in English. 2002 (Nov.). s-a. USD 24 per academic year to individuals outside of Hong Kong; USD 40 per academic year to institutions outside of Hong Kong (effective 2005). **Document type:** *Journal, Academic/Scholarly.*
Indexed: MLA-IB.
Published by: Zhongwen Daxue Chubanshe/Chinese University Press, The Chinese University of Hong Kong, Shatin, New Territories, Hong Kong. TEL 852-2609-6508. Ed. Mr. Suh K S David. Pub. Mr. Luk Steven. R&P, Adv. contact Mr. Chan Wendy.

200 USA ISSN 1070-244X
QUEST (BOSTON); a monthly for religious liberals. Text in English. 1945. m. membership. bk.rev. **Document type:** *Newsletter.*
Related titles: Audio cassette/tape ed.
Published by: Unitarian Universalist, Church of the Larger Fellowship, 25 Beacon St, Boston, MA 02108-2823. TEL 617-742-2100, FAX 617-523-4123, afisher@uua.org, clf@uua.org, http://www.uua.orgf. Eds. Jane Rzepka, Noreen Kimball. R&P Amy Fisher. Circ: 3,000 (controlled).

QUESTION DE. *see* PARAPSYCHOLOGY AND OCCULTISM

200 ESP ISSN 0214-7769
QUESTIONS DE VIDA CRISTIANA. Text in Catalan. 4/yr. **Document type:** *Magazine, Consumer.*
Published by: Publicacions de l' Abadia de Montserrat, Ausias Marc 92-98, Barcelona, 08013, Spain. TEL 34-932-450303, FAX 34-932-473594, informacio@pamsa.com, http://www.pamsa.com. Ed. Andreu Marques.

230 BEL ISSN 0774-5524
➤ **QUESTIONS LITURGIQUES**; studies on liturgy. Text in French, English. 1910. q. EUR 50 combined subscription (print & online eds.) (effective 2011). Index. 300 p./no.; **Document type:** *Journal, Academic/Scholarly.* **Description:** Reviews liturgical scholarship.
Former titles (until 1971): Questions Liturgiques et Paroissiales (0774-5532); (until 1914): Questions Liturgiques (0779-2050)
Related titles: Online - full text ed.: ISSN 1783-1709.
Indexed: A21, FR, MLA-IB, RI-1.
—IE, INIST.
Published by: (Universite Catholique de Louvain, Faculte de Theologie et de Droit Canonique), Peeters Publishers, Bondgenotenlaan 153, Leuven, 3000, Belgium. TEL 32-16-235170, FAX 32-16-228500, peeters@peeters-leuven.be, http://www.peeters-leuven.be. Ed. L Leijssen. **Co-sponsor:** Abbaye du Mont Cesar.

261 USA
THE QUIET HOUR. Text in English. q.
Published by: Cook Communications Ministries, 4050 Lee Vance View, Colorado Springs, CO 80918. TEL 719-536-0100, http://www.cookministries.com.

220 USA ISSN 0744-4796
QUIET MIRACLE. Text in English. 1923. q. adv.
Formerly: B L I Crusader
Published by: Bible Literature International, 477, Columbus, OH 43216-0477. TEL 614-267-3116, FAX 614-267-7110. Ed. Annette Vasulka. Circ: 20,000 (controlled).

220 USA
QUIET WALK. Text in English. 1988. m. free (effective 2011). **Document type:** *Magazine, Trade.* **Description:** Provides devotional insights into the Bible's key chapters along with scripture based prayers. Includes portions of scripture from the Psalms with the aim of stimulating worship and confession.
Related titles: E-mail ed.
Published by: Walk Thru the Bible Ministries, Inc., 4201 N Peachtree Rd, Atlanta, GA 30341. TEL 800-361-6131, info@walkthru.org.

▼ **QUNTRES**; an online journal for the history, culture, and art of the Jewish book. *see* LINGUISTICS

R C C COUNSELOR. *see* ADVERTISING AND PUBLIC RELATIONS

323.442 USA ISSN 2150-0274
R C D A NEWSLETTER. (Religion in Communist Dominated Areas) Text in English. 1962. q. bk.rev. illus. index. back issues avail. **Document type:** *Newsletter.* **Description:** Covers issues pertaining to religion and human rights.
Former titles (until 2008): R C D A (1061-656X); (until 1991): Religion in Communist Dominated Areas (0034-3978)
Indexed: A21, ABS&EES, MEA&I, PerIslam, RI-1, RI-2.
—Ingenta.
Published by: Research Center for Religion & Human Rights in Closed Societies, Ltd., 475 Riverside Dr, Ste 448, New York, NY 10115. TEL 212-870-2481, FAX 212-663-6771.

R E TODAY. (Religious Education) *see* EDUCATION

200 BRA ISSN 1677-1222
BL7
R E V E R. REVISTA DE ESTUDOS DA RELIGIAO. Text in Multiple languages. 2001. q. free (effective 2011). **Document type:** *Journal, Academic/Scholarly.*
Media: Online - full text.
Indexed: CA, T02.
Published by: Pontificia Universidade Catolica de Sao Paulo, Programa de Estudos Pos-Graduados em Ciencias da Religiao Eds. Edenio Valle, Maria Jose Rosado Nunes.

200 USA
R I A L UPDATE. Text in English. 1949. q. free. charts; illus.; stat. **Document type:** *Newsletter.* **Description:** Provides general information on strengthening congregation from an inter-faith perspective.
Formerly: R I A L News
Published by: Religion in American Life, 2 Queenston Pl, Rm 200, Princeton, NJ 08540. TEL 609-921-3639, FAX 609-921-0551. Ed. Nicholas van Dyck. Circ: 4,000 (controlled).

R N A NEWSLETTER. *see* JOURNALISM

RADIO NIEUWS. *see* COMMUNICATIONS—Radio

201.6 USA ISSN 0275-0147
BR1.A2
RADIX. Text in English. 1969. q. USD 15 domestic; USD 20 foreign (effective 2010). bk.rev.; music rev.; video rev. illus. back issues avail. **Document type:** *Magazine, Consumer.* **Description:** Includes interviews with people who influence church and society, feature articles, reviews and editorials dealing with the interface of Christian faith and culture.
Formerly (until 1976): Right On
Related titles: Microfilm ed.
Indexed: A21, RI-1, RI-2.
Published by: Radix Magazine, Inc., PO Box 4307, Berkeley, CA 94704. TEL 510-548-5329. Ed. Sharon Gallagher.

RAGIONE & FEDE. *see* PHILOSOPHY

230 100 DEU
RATIO FIDEI; Beitraege zur philosophischen Rechenschaft der Theologie. Text in German. 1998. irreg., latest vol.43, 2010. price varies. **Document type:** *Monographic series, Academic/Scholarly.*
Published by: Verlag Friedrich Pustet, Gutenbergstr 8, Regensburg, 93051, Germany. TEL 49-941-920220, FAX 49-941-92022330, verlag@pustet.de, http://www.pustetverlag.de.

REACH (NEW HAVEN). *see* EDUCATION

REAL ACADEMIA DE CIENCIAS MORALES Y POLITICAS. ANALES. *see* POLITICAL SCIENCE

REAL ACADEMIA DE CIENCIAS POLITICAS Y MORALES. PUBLICACIONES. *see* POLITICAL SCIENCE

248.4804 NZL ISSN 1172-9236
REALITY; Christian reflections on today's world. Text in English. 1923. bi-m. adv. bk.rev.; film rev.; music rev.; software rev. **Document type:** *Magazine, Consumer.* **Description:** Interdenominational, evangelical articles of topical and spiritual interest. Also news of the Bible College of New Zealand and its graduates.
Formerly (until vol.75, no.6): Reaper (0034-107X)
—CCC.
Published by: Bible College of New Zealand Inc., Henderson, Auckland, 1231, New Zealand. TEL 64-9-8374209. Ed. Diane Benge. R&P Amanda Sachtleben TEL 64-9-836-7810. Adv. contact Russell Ford. B&W page NZD 500; trim 180 x 275. Circ: 5,000.

200 DEU
REALLEXIKON FUER ANTIKE UND CHRISTENTUM. Text in German. 1950. irreg., latest vol.23, 2010. price varies. **Document type:** *Monographic series, Academic/Scholarly.*
Published by: Anton Hiersemann Verlag, Haldenstr 30, Stuttgart, 70376, Germany. TEL 49-711-5499710, FAX 49-711-54997121, info@hiersemann.de, http://www.hiersemann.de.

230 189 BEL ISSN 1775-8696
BR65.A62
RECHERCHES AUGUSTINIENNES ET PATRISTIQUES. Text in French. 1958. irreg., latest vol.31, 1999. price varies. back issues avail. **Document type:** *Monographic series, Academic/Scholarly.*
Formerly (until 2003): Recherches Augustiniennes (0484-0887)
Indexed: A21, MLA-IB, PCI, RI-1, RI-2, RILM.
—CCC.
Published by: (Institut d'Etudes Augustiniennes FRA), Brepols Publishers, Begijnhof 67, Turnhout, 2300, Belgium. TEL 32-14-448020, FAX 32-14-428919, periodicals@brepols.net, http://www.brepols.net.

R

220 BEL ISSN 1370-7493
BX800.A1
➤ **RECHERCHES DE THEOLOGIE ET PHILOSOPHIE MEDIEVALES/ FORSCHUNGEN ZUR THEOLOGIE UND PHILOSOPHIE DER MITTELALTERS**; a journal of ancient and medieval Christian literature. Text in English, French, German. 1929. s-a. EUR 95 combined subscription (print & online eds.) (effective 2011). adv. bk.rev. bibl. index. back issues avail. **Document type:** *Journal, Academic/Scholarly.* **Description:** Publishes research in medieval theology and philosophy.
Formerly (until vol.64, 1997): Recherches de Theologie Ancienne et Medievale (0034-1266); Incorporates (1929-1997): Bulletin de Theologie Ancienne et Medievale (0007-442X)
Related titles: Online - full text ed.: ISSN 1783-1717.
Indexed: A20, A21, A22, ArtHuCI, CERDIC, CurCont, DIP, FR, IBR, IBZ, IPB, MLA, MLA-IB, PCI, R&TA, SCOPUS, W07.
—IE, INIST.
Published by: (Abbaye du Mont Cesar), Peeters Publishers, Bondgenotenlaan 153, Leuven, 3000, Belgium. TEL 32-16-235170, FAX 32-16-228500, peeters@peeters-leuven.be, http://www.peeters-leuven.be. Ed. C Steel. **Co-sponsor:** Universite Catholique de Louvain, Faculte de Philosophie et Lettres.

262.9 340 FRA
RECHERCHES INSTITUTIONNELLES. Text in French. irreg., latest vol.22, 1995. illus. **Document type:** *Monographic series.*
Related titles: ◆ Series: Recherches Institutionnelles. Droit et Eglises. ISSN 0220-7818; ◆ Recherches Institutionnelles. Recherche Documentaire. ISSN 0244-6936; ◆ Recherches Institutionnelles. Culture et Religion. ISSN 0154-0416; ◆ Recherches Institutionnelles. Institutions et Histoire. ISSN 0243-2412.
Published by: CERDIC Publications, 11 rue Jean Sturn, Nordheim, 67520, France. TEL 33-1-88877107, FAX 33-1-88877125. Eds. J Schlick, M Zimmerman. Circ: 2,000.

262.9 FRA ISSN 0154-0416
RECHERCHES INSTITUTIONNELLES. CULTURE ET RELIGION. Text in French. 1978.
Related titles: ◆ Series of: Recherches Institutionnelles.
Published by: CERDIC Publications, 11 rue Jean Sturn, Nordheim, 67520, France. TEL 33-1-88877107, FAX 33-1-88877125.

262.9 FRA ISSN 0220-7818
RECHERCHES INSTITUTIONNELLES. DROIT ET EGLISES. Text in French. 1978.
Related titles: ◆ Series of: Recherches Institutionnelles.
Published by: CERDIC Publications, 11 rue Jean Sturn, Nordheim, 67520, France. TEL 33-1-88877107, FAX 33-1-88877125.

262.9 FRA ISSN 0243-2412
RECHERCHES INSTITUTIONNELLES. INSTITUTIONS ET HISTOIRE. Text in French. 1980.
Related titles: ◆ Series of: Recherches Institutionnelles.
Published by: CERDIC Publications, 11 rue Jean Sturn, Nordheim, 67520, France. TEL 33-1-88877107, FAX 33-1-88877125.

262.9 FRA ISSN 0244-6936
RECHERCHES INSTITUTIONNELLES. RECHERCHE DOCUMENTAIRE. Text in French. 1979.
Related titles: ◆ Series of: Recherches Institutionnelles.
Published by: CERDIC Publications, 11 rue Jean Sturn, Nordheim, 67520, France. TEL 33-1-88877107, FAX 33-1-88877125.

RECORD (NEW YORK, 1976). *see* HOMOSEXUALITY

200 USA
REFLECTION AND THEORY IN THE STUDY OF RELIGION. Text in English. 1970. irreg., latest 2009. price varies. back issues avail. **Document type:** *Monographic series, Trade.* **Description:** Monographs on a wide variety of topics in the academic study of religion.
Formerly: A A R Studies in Religion (0084-6287)
—CCC.
Published by: American Academy of Religion, 825 Houston Mill Rd NE, Ste 300, Atlanta, GA 30329. TEL 404-727-3049, FAX 404-727-7959, aar@aarweb.org. Ed. Theodore Vial TEL 303-765-3166.

200 USA ISSN 0362-0611
BR1
REFLECTIONS (NEW HAVEN). Text in English. 1904. s-a. free (effective 2011). **Document type:** *Journal, Academic/Scholarly.*
Former titles (until 1966): Yale Divinity News (0364-8613); (until 192?): Yale Divinity Quarterly
Related titles: Microfilm ed.: 1965.
Indexed: A21, RI-1.
Published by: Yale University, Divinity School, 409 Prospect St, New Haven, CT 06511. TEL 203-432-5033, http://www.yale.edu/divinity/. **Co-sponsors:** Institute of Sacred Music; Berkeley Divinity School.

200 GBR ISSN 1462-2459
BR300
➤ **REFORMATION AND RENAISSANCE REVIEW.** Abbreviated title: R R R. Text in English. 1999. 3/yr. USD 300 combined subscription in North America to institutions (print & online eds.); GBP 185 combined subscription elsewhere to institutions (print & online eds.) (effective 2012). adv. back issues avail.; reprints avail. **Document type:** *Journal, Academic/Scholarly.* **Description:** Provides a platform for scholars to publish papers on theology and spirituality, both Protestant and Catholic, of the 15th through the 17th centuries.
Related titles: Online - full text ed.: ISSN 1743-1727. USD 240 in North America to institutions; GBP 148 elsewhere to institutions (effective 2012).
Indexed: A01, A03, A08, A21, CA, H05, IBR, IBZ, R&TA, RI-1, T02.
—BLDSC (7332.505000), IE. **CCC.**
Published by: (Society of Reformation Studies), Equinox Publishing Ltd., Unit S3, Kelham House, 3 Lancaster St, Sheffield, S6 3AF, United Kingdom. TEL 44-114-2725957, FAX 44-560-3459046, journals@equinoxpub.com, http://www.equinoxpub.com/. Ed. Ian Hazlett. Adv. contact Val Hall.

230 AUS ISSN 0034-3072
BX9401
REFORMED THEOLOGICAL REVIEW. Text in English. 1942. 3/yr. bk.rev. biennial index, cum.index: 1942-1992. **Document type:** *Journal, Academic/Scholarly.* **Description:** Contains biblical and theological articles.
Indexed: A21, A22, CERDIC, FR, IZBG, OTA, R&TA, RI-1, RI-2.
—BLDSC (7332.530000), IE, Ingenta, INIST. **CCC.**
Address: PO Box 635, Doncaster, VIC 3108, Australia. reftheol@ozemail.com.au.

248.82 AUT
REGENBOGEN; katholische Kinderzeitschrift fuer Maedchen und Buben. Text in German. 1946. 40/yr. looseleaf. EUR 20; EUR 0.50 newsstand/cover (effective 2005). adv. bk.rev. illus. **Document type:** *Newspaper, Consumer.*
Formerly (until 1977): Gotteskinder (0017-2510)
Published by: Katholische Kirche in Kaernten, Dioezese Gurk, Tarviser Str 30, Klagenfurt, 9020, Austria. TEL 43-463-58772551, FAX 43-463-58772559, info@kath-kirche-kaernten.at, http://www.kath-kirche-kaernten.at. Circ: 60,000.

200 DEU ISSN 0170-9151
REGENSBURGER STUDIEN ZUR THEOLOGIE. Text in German. 1976. irreg., latest vol.68, 2009. price varies. **Document type:** *Monographic series, Academic/Scholarly.*
Published by: Peter Lang GmbH (Subsidiary of: Peter Lang Publishing Group), Eschborner Landstr 42-50, Frankfurt Am Main, 60489, Germany. TEL 49-69-7807050, FAX 49-69-78070550, zentrale.frankfurt@peterlang.com.

200 DEU
REGULAE BENEDICTI STUDIA. TRADITIO ET RECEPTIO. Text in German. 1974. irreg., latest vol.22, 2009. price varies. **Document type:** *Monographic series, Academic/Scholarly.*
Formerly (until 2009): Regulae Benedicti Studia. Supplementa (0174-0105)
Published by: E O S Verlag, Erzabtei St. Ottilien, St.Ottilien, 86941, Germany. TEL 49-8193-71700, FAX 49-8193-71709, mail@eos-verlag.de.

REIHE KIRCHENBAU. *see* ARCHITECTURE

264 DEU
REIHE RELIGIONSWISSENSCHAFTEN. Text in German. 1975. irreg., latest vol.10, 1995. price varies. **Document type:** *Monographic series, Academic/Scholarly.*
Published by: Herbert Utz Verlag GmbH, Adalbertstr 57, Munich, 80799, Germany. TEL 49-89-27779100, FAX 49-89-27779101, utz@utzverlag.com, http://www.utzverlag.de.

051 USA ISSN 1543-317X
RELEVANT. Text in English. 2003. bi-m. USD 12 domestic; USD 18 in Canada; USD 24 elsewhere; USD 3.95 newsstand/cover (effective 2006). adv. **Document type:** *Magazine, Consumer.* **Description:** Contains articles and features covering God, life and progressive culture.
Published by: Relevant Media Group, Inc., 600 Rinehart Rd, Lake Mary, FL 32771. TEL 407-333-7152, FAX 407-333-7153, info@relevantmediagroup.com, http://www.relevantmediagroup.com. Ed. Cara Baker. Pub. Cameron Strang.

268 CHE ISSN 1662-8861
RELI.; Zeitschrift fuer Religionsunterricht und Lebenskunde. Text in German. 1972. q. CHF 42.50; CHF 14 newsstand/cover (effective 2010). **Document type:** *Journal, Academic/Scholarly.*
Formerly (until 2008): R L - Zeitschrift fuer Religionsunterricht und Lebenskunde (1660-0622)
Indexed: IBR, IBZ.
Published by: Theologischer Verlag Zurich, Badenerstr 73, Zurich, 8026, Switzerland. TEL 41-44-2993355, FAX 41-44-2993358, tvz@ref.ch, http://www.tvz-verlag.ch. Eds. Friedemann Stenger, Matthias Kuhl.

200 NLD ISSN 1571-0815
RELIC. Variant title: Studies in Dutch Religious History. Text in English. 2002. irreg., latest vol.3, 2005. price varies. **Document type:** *Monographic series, Academic/Scholarly.*
Published by: (ReLiC, Centre for Dutch Religious History), Uitgeverij Verloren, Torenlaan 25, Hilversum, 1211 JA, Netherlands. TEL 31-35-6859856, FAX 31-35-6836557, info@verloren.nl, http://www.verloren.nl.

200 BRA ISSN 0100-8587
HN39.L3
RELIGIAO & SOCIEDADE. Text in Portuguese. 1977. s-a. **Document type:** *Journal, Academic/Scholarly.*
Related titles: Online - full text ed.: free (effective 2011).
Indexed: C01, CA, F04, IBR, IBZ, S02, S03, SociolAb, T02.
Published by: Instituto de Estudos da Religiao, Rua do Russel 76, Rio de Janeiro, 22210-010, Brazil. TEL 55-21-25553782, FAX 55-21-25583764, iser@iser.org.br, http://www.iser.org.br/. Ed. Patricia Birman.

230 NLD ISSN 1872-3497
RELIGIE & SAMENLEVING. Text in Dutch. 2006. 3/yr. EUR 20 (effective 2009).
Published by: Eburon Academic Publishers, PO Box 2867, Delft, 2601 CW, Netherlands. TEL 31-15-2131484, FAX 31-15-2146888. Pubs. Maarten Fraanje, Wiebe de Jager.

200 CZE ISSN 1210-3640
➤ **RELIGIO**; revue pro religionistiku. Variant title: Study of Religions. Text in Multiple languages. 1993. s-a. USD 30 foreign (effective 2009). **Document type:** *Journal, Academic/Scholarly.* **Description:** Publishes articles, commentaries, discussions, documents, translations, reports and reviews related to a wide spectrum of topics connected to the academic study of religions.
Published by: (Ceska Spolecnost pro Studium Nabozenstvi/Czech Society for the Study of Religions), Masarykova Univerzita, Filozoficka Fakulta/Masaryk University, Faculty of Arts, Arna Novaka 1, Brno, 60200, Czech Republic. TEL 420-549-491111, FAX 420-549-491520.

200 CAN ISSN 1180-0135
BL3R45
➤ **RELIGIOLOGIQUES.** Text in French. 1990. s-a. CAD 34 to individuals; CAD 38 to institutions; CAD 20 to students (effective 2008). **Document type:** *Journal, Academic/Scholarly.*
Indexed: A21, FR, MLA-IB, RI-1.
—INIST.
Published by: Universite du Quebec a Montreal, Departement des Sciences Religieuses, CP 8888, succ. Centre-Ville, Montreal, PQ H3C 3P8, Canada. TEL 514-987-4497, FAX 514-987-7856. **Subscr. to:** Presses de l'Universite du Quebec, Le Delta I, 2875 boul. Laurier, bureau 450, Ste Foy, PQ G1V 2M2, Canada.

200 GBR ISSN 0048-721X
BL1
➤ **RELIGION.** Text in English. 1971. q. GBP 291 combined subscription in United Kingdom to institutions (print & online eds.); EUR 349, USD 465 combined subscription to institutions (print & online eds.) (effective 2012). adv. bk.rev. illus. back issues avail.; reprint service avail. from PSC. **Document type:** *Journal, Academic/Scholarly.* **Description:** Covers interdisciplinary and cross-cultural research in religious studies, including descriptive, explanatory, methodological, and critical studies about religion and the study of religion, with relevant contributions from the disciplines of anthropology, archaeology, history, philosophy of science, political theory, psychology, and sociology.
Related titles: Online - full text ed.: ISSN 1096-1151. GBP 261 in United Kingdom to institutions; EUR 313, USD 418 to institutions (effective 2012) (from IngentaConnect).
Indexed: A01, A02, A03, A08, A20, A21, A22, A26, AmHI, ArtHuCI, B04, BAS, BRD, BrHumI, CA, CERDIC, CurCont, DIP, E01, E08, FR, FamI, G08, H07, H08, H14, HAb, HumInd, I05, IBR, IBSS, IBZ, M01, M02, MEA&I, OTA, P02, P10, P48, P53, P54, PCI, PQC, R05, RASB, RI-1, RI-2, S02, S03, S09, SCOPUS, T02, W03, W07.
—BLDSC (7356.435000), IE, Infotrieve, Ingenta, INIST. **CCC.**
Published by: Taylor & Francis Ltd. (Subsidiary of: Taylor & Francis Group), 4 Park Sq, Milton Park, Abingdon, Oxfordshire OX14 4RN, United Kingdom. TEL 44-1235-828600, FAX 44-1235-829000, info@tandf.co.uk, http://www.tandf.co.uk/journals. Eds. Michael Stausberg, Steven Engler.

230.071 DEU ISSN 2191-8066
▼ **RELIGION.** Variant title: Religion 5-10. Text in German. 2011. q. EUR 80 (effective 2011). **Document type:** *Journal, Trade.*
Related titles: Special ed(s).: Religion (Ausgabe mit Materialpaket). ISSN 2191-8058. 2011.
Published by: Erhard Friedrich Verlag GmbH, Im Brande 17, Seelze, 30926, Germany. TEL 49-511-400040, FAX 49-511-40004170, info@friedrich-verlag.de.

371.07 DNK ISSN 0108-4488
RELIGION; tidsskrift for religionslaererforenigen for gymnasiet og hk. Text in Danish. 1973. q. DKK 200; DKK 380 membership; DKK 65 per issue (effective 2009). adv. **Document type:** *Magazine, Trade.*
Published by: Religionslaererforeningen for Gymnasiet og H F, c/o Marie-Louise Ebert Lauritsen, Krum Om 8, Toender, 6270, Denmark. marielouiseebertlauritsen@gmail.dk, http://www.emu.dk/gym/fag/re/foreningen/index.html. Ed. Signe Elise Bro. adv.: page DKK 1,800.

200 DEU ISSN 1861-4329
RELIGION - AESTHETIK - MEDIEN. Text in German. 2006. irreg., latest vol.2, 2007. price varies. **Document type:** *Monographic series, Academic/Scholarly.*
Published by: Peter Lang GmbH (Subsidiary of: Peter Lang Publishing Group), Eschborner Landstr 42-50, Frankfurt Am Main, 60489, Germany. TEL 49-69-7807050, FAX 49-69-78070550, zentrale.frankfurt@peterlang.com, http://www.peterlang.com. Ed. Wilhelm Graeb.

201.6 USA ISSN 1052-1151
BL65.C8
➤ **RELIGION AND AMERICAN CULTURE**; a journal of interpretation. Abbreviated title: R A C. Text in English. 1991. s-a. USD 147 combined subscription to institutions (print & online eds.) (effective 2012). adv. illus. back issues avail.; reprint service avail. from PSC. **Document type:** *Journal, Academic/Scholarly.* **Description:** Explores the interplay between religion and other spheres of American culture.
Related titles: Microfilm ed.: USD 67.50 to institutions (effective 2002 - 2003); Online - full text ed.: ISSN 1533-8568. USD 111 to institutions (effective 2012).
Indexed: A01, A02, A03, A08, A20, A21, A22, A26, ASCA, AmH&L, AmHI, ArtHuCI, B04, BRD, BrHumI, CA, ChrPI, CurCont, DIP, E-psyche, E01, E08, G08, H07, H08, HAb, HumInd, I05, IBR, IBZ, MLA-IB, P10, P28, P42, P46, P48, P53, P54, PCI, PQC, PSA, R&TA, R05, RI-1, RI-2, S02, S03, S09, S11, SCOPUS, SSA, SociolAb, T02, W03, W07.
—IE, Infotrieve, Ingenta. **CCC.**
Published by: (Indiana University - Purdue University Indianapolis, Center for the Study of Religion and American Culture), University of California Press, Journals Division, 2000 Ctr St, Ste 303, Berkeley, CA 94704. TEL 510-643-7154, 877-262-4226, FAX 510-642-9917, customerservice@ucpressjournals.com. Adv. contact Jennifer Rogers TEL 510-642-6188. Circ: 575. **Subscr. to:** 149 5th Ave, 8th Fl, New York, NY 10010. participation@jstor.org.

➤ **RELIGION & EDUCATION.** *see* EDUCATION

▼ ➤ **RELIGION AND GENDER.** *see* SOCIOLOGY

200 323.4 NLD ISSN 1871-031X
K18
➤ **RELIGION AND HUMAN RIGHTS**; an international journal. Text in English. 2006. 3/yr. EUR 178, USD 250 to institutions; EUR 194, USD 272 combined subscription to institutions (print & online eds.) (effective 2012). bk.rev. back issues avail.; reprint service avail. from PSC. **Document type:** *Journal, Academic/Scholarly.* **Description:** Provides a forum for the discussion of issues which are of crucial importance and which have global reach. It covers the points of contact, interactions, conflicts and reconciliations inherent to the relationship between teachings, principles, laws and practice of religions or beliefs on the one hand, and modern international and regional systems for the promotion and protection of human rights on the other hand.
Related titles: Online - full text ed.: ISSN 1871-0328. EUR 162, USD 227 to institutions (effective 2012) (from IngentaConnect).
Indexed: A22, CA, E01, IZBG, P42, SCOPUS, T02.
—BLDSC (7356.438600), IE, Ingenta. **CCC.**
Published by: Martinus Nijhoff (Subsidiary of: Brill), PO Box 9000, Leiden, 2300 PA, Netherlands. TEL 31-71-5353500, FAX 31-71-5317532, marketing@brill.nl.

➤ **RELIGION AND LITERATURE.** *see* LITERATURE

290 100 DEU ISSN 0080-0848
➤ **RELIGION AND REASON**; method and theory in the study and interpretation of religion. Text in German. 1972. irreg., latest vol.49, 2010. price varies. back issues avail. **Document type:** *Monographic series, Academic/Scholarly.*
—BLDSC (7356.453000).

Published by: Walter de Gruyter GmbH & Co. KG, Genthiner Str 13, Berlin, 10785, Germany. TEL 49-30-260050, FAX 49-30-26005251, info@degruyter.com, http://www.degruyter.de.

200 327 USA ISSN 1945-3256
RELIGION AND SECURITY MONOGRAPH SERIES. Text in English. 2008 (Oct.). irreg., latest 2008. USD 10 per issue (effective 2011). **Document type:** *Monographic series, Academic/Scholarly.*
Related titles: Online - full text ed.: free (effective 2011).
Published by: Institute for Global Engagement, PO Box 12205, Arlington, VA 22219. TEL 703-527-3100, info@globalengage.org.

200 USA ISSN 2150-9298
BL60
▼ ➤ **RELIGION AND SOCIETY**; advances in research. Text in English. 2010 (Oct.). a. GBP 111 combined subscription in United Kingdom to institutions (print & online eds.); EUR 140 combined subscription in Europe to institutions (print & online eds.); USD 189 combined subscription elsewhere to institutions (print & online eds.) (effective 2011). adv. **Document type:** *Journal, Academic/Scholarly.*
Description: Responds to the need for a rigorous, in-depth review of current work in the expanding sub-discipline of the anthropology of religion.
Related titles: Online - full text ed.: ISSN 2150-9301. GBP 100 in United Kingdom to institutions; EUR 126 in Europe to institutions; USD 170 elsewhere to institutions (effective 2011).
—CCC.
Published by: Berghahn Books Inc., 150 Broadway, Ste 812, New York, NY 10038. TEL 212-233-6004, FAX 212-233-6007, journals@berghahnbooks.com, http://www.berghahnbooks.com. Eds. Ramon Sarro, Simon Coleman.

290 100 DEU ISSN 1437-5370
➤ **RELIGION AND SOCIETY.** Text in German. 1976. irreg., latest vol.52, 2011. price varies. back issues avail. **Document type:** *Monographic series, Academic/Scholarly.*
Indexed: NAA, RASB.
—CCC.
Published by: Walter de Gruyter GmbH & Co. KG, Genthiner Str 13, Berlin, 10785, Germany. TEL 49-30-260050, FAX 49-30-26005251, info@degruyter.com, http://www.degruyter.de. Eds. Gustavo Benavides, Kocku von Stuckrad.

200 USA ISSN 1553-9962
BL53.A1
RELIGION AND SOCIETY IN CENTRAL AND EASTERN EUROPE. Text in English. 2005. a. **Document type:** *Journal, Academic/Scholarly.*
Media: Online - full text.
Indexed: CA, T02.
Published by: (International Study of Religion in Eastern and Central Europe Association), West Virginia University, Religious Studies Program, PO Box 6286, Morgantown, WV 26506. http://religiousstudies.wvu.edu/. Ed. Peter Torok.

220 DEU ISSN 1437-4641
RELIGION AND SOCIETY IN TRANSITION. Text in German, English. 1999. irreg., latest vol.8, 2008. price varies. **Document type:** *Monographic series, Academic/Scholarly.*
Published by: Waxmann Verlag GmbH, Steinfurter Str 555, Muenster, 48159, Germany. TEL 49-251-265040, FAX 49-251-2650426, info@waxmann.com. Ed. Wolfram Weisse.

200 NLD ISSN 1079-9265
BL65.C8
➤ **RELIGION AND THE ARTS.** Text in Dutch. 1997. 5/yr. EUR 364, USD 509 to institutions; EUR 397, USD 556 combined subscription to institutions (print & online eds.) (effective 2012). bk.rev. back issues avail.; reprint service avail. from PSC. **Document type:** *Journal, Academic/Scholarly.* **Description:** An international forum for the scholarly discussion on the expression of religious sentiments in art.
Related titles: Online - full text ed.: ISSN 1568-5292. EUR 331, USD 463 to institutions (effective 2012) (from IngentaConnect).
Indexed: A01, A02, A03, A08, A21, A22, A30, A31, ABM, AmHI, B24, BrHumI, CA, E01, H07, I14, IBR, IBZ, IZBG, MLA-IB, RI-1, SCOPUS, T02.
—BLDSC (7356.436500), IE, Ingenta. **CCC.**
Published by: (Boston College USA), Brill, PO Box 9000, Leiden, 2300 PA, Netherlands. TEL 31-71-5353500, FAX 31-71-5317532, cs@brill.nl. **Dist. by:** Turpin Distribution Services Ltd., Pegasus Dr, Stratton Business Park, Biggleswade, Bedfordshire SG18 8QB, United Kingdom. TEL 44-1767-604954, FAX 44-1767-601640, custserv@turpin-distribution.com, http://www.turpin-distribution.com/.

200 NLD ISSN 1061-5210
BL60
RELIGION AND THE SOCIAL ORDER. Text in English. 1991. irreg., latest vol.16, 2008. price varies. back issues avail. **Document type:** *Monographic series, Academic/Scholarly.*
Indexed: A22, CA, IZBG, PCI, S02, S03, SCOPUS, SSA, SociolAb, T02.
—BLDSC (7356.453500), IE, Ingenta. **CCC.**
Published by: Brill, PO Box 9000, Leiden, 2300 PA, Netherlands. TEL 31-71-5353500, FAX 31-71-5317532, cs@brill.nl. Ed. William H Swatos.

200 NLD ISSN 1023-0807
BR1
➤ **RELIGION AND THEOLOGY**; a journal of contemporary religious discourse. Text in English. 1968; N.S. 1994. s-a. EUR 213, USD 299 to institutions; EUR 233, USD 326 combined subscription to institutions (print & online eds.) (effective 2012). adv. bk.rev. back issues avail.; reprint service avail. from PSC. **Document type:** *Journal, Academic/Scholarly.* **Description:** For contemporary religious discourse with an emphasis on new ways of understanding our multifaceted religious heritage.
Formerly (until 1994): Theologia Evangelica (0255-8858)
Related titles: Microfilm ed.: N.S. (from PQC); Online - full text ed.: ISSN 1574-3012. N.S. EUR 194, USD 272 to institutions (effective 2012) (from IngentaConnect).
Indexed: A01, A03, A08, A21, A22, CA, E01, ISAP, IZBG, OTA, PCI, R&TA, RI-1, RI-2, S02, S03, T02.
—BLDSC (7356.456100), IE, Ingenta. **CCC.**

Published by: (University of South Africa, School of Humanities, Social Sciences and Theology ZAF), Brill, PO Box 9000, Leiden, 2300 PA, Netherlands. TEL 31-71-5353500, FAX 31-71-5317532, cs@brill.nl. Circ: 700. **Dist. by:** Turpin Distribution Services Ltd., Pegasus Dr, Stratton Business Park, Biggleswade, Bedfordshire SG18 8QB, United Kingdom. TEL 44-1767-604954, FAX 44-1767-601640, custserv@turpin-distribution.com, http://www.turpin-distribution.com/.

200 DEU ISSN 0936-5141
RELIGION BETRIFFT UNS. Text in German. 1990. bi-m. EUR 63; EUR 15 newsstand/cover (effective 2011). **Document type:** *Journal, Academic/Scholarly.*
Published by: Bergmoser und Hoeller Verlag GmbH, Karl-Friedrich-Str 76, Aachen, 52072, Germany. TEL 49-241-93888123, FAX 49-241-93888134, kontakt@buhv.de.

200 150 GBR ISSN 2153-599X
▼ ➤ **RELIGION, BRAIN & BEHAVIOR.** Text in English. forthcoming 2011 (Mar.). 3/yr. GBP 274 combined subscription in United Kingdom to institutions (print & online eds.); EUR 361, USD 451 combined subscription to institutions (print & online eds.) (effective 2012). **Document type:** *Journal, Academic/Scholarly.*
Related titles: Online - full text ed.: ISSN 2153-5981. forthcoming 2011 (Mar.). GBP 249 in United Kingdom to institutions; EUR 328, USD 411 to institutions (effective 2012).
—CCC.
Published by: Taylor & Francis Ltd. (Subsidiary of: Taylor & Francis Group), 4 Park Sq, Milton Park, Abingdon, Oxfordshire OX14 4RN, United Kingdom. TEL 44-20-70176000, FAX 44-20-70176336, info@tandf.co.uk, http://www.tandf.co.uk/journals.

291 GBR ISSN 1749-8171
BL1
➤ **RELIGION COMPASS.** Text in English. 2007. bi-m. GBP 561 in United Kingdom to institutions; EUR 714 in Europe to institutions; USD 445 in the Americas to institutions; USD 1,100 elsewhere to institutions (effective 2012). back issues avail. **Document type:** *Journal, Academic/Scholarly.* **Description:** Surveys current research within all disciplines of religious studies.
Media: Online - full content.
Indexed: A01, A21, BrHumI.
—IE, Ingenta. **CCC.**
Published by: Wiley-Blackwell Publishing Ltd. (Subsidiary of: John Wiley & Sons, Inc.), 9600 Garsington Rd, Oxford, OX4 2DQ, United Kingdom. TEL 44-1865-776868, FAX 44-1865-714591, customerservices@blackwellpublishing.com, http://www.wiley.com/. Eds. Scott Noegel, Tamara Sonn.

200 USA ISSN 1539-2430
BL1.A1
RELIGION EAST & WEST. Text in English. 2001. a. USD 12 per issue in North America to individuals; USD 18 per issue in North America to institutions; USD 20 per issue elsewhere (effective 2011). back issues avail. **Document type:** *Journal, Academic/Scholarly.* **Description:** Includes doctrine, practice, ethics, history, biography and the relation of religion to other aspects of life.
Related titles: Online - full text ed.: free (effective 2011).
Indexed: A01, A02, A03, A08, A21, CA, RI-1, T02.
Published by: Institute for World Religions, 2245 McKinley Ave, Ste B, Berkeley, CA 94703. TEL 510-666-1176, FAX 510-548-4551. Ed. David Rounds.

391.56242 USA ISSN 1027-9369
RELIGION FOR PEACE; newsletter on inter-religious dialogue and action for peace. Text in English. 1974. 3/yr. USD 25. back issues avail. **Document type:** *Newsletter.* **Description:** Includes youth page and reports from various committees of the conference.
Indexed: PerIslam.
Published by: World Conference on Religion and Peace, International Division, 777 United Nations Plaza, New York, NY 10017. TEL 212-687-2163, FAX 212-983-0566. Ed. William F Vendley. Circ: 4,000.

200 299 USA ISSN 1556-262X
RELIGION, HEALTH, AND HEALING. Text in English. 2006. irreg., latest 2010. price varies. back issues avail. **Document type:** *Monographic series, Academic/Scholarly.*
Published by: Praeger Publishers (Subsidiary of: Greenwood Publishing Group Inc.), 88 Post Rd W, Westport, CT 06881. TEL 800-368-6868, tech.support@greenwood.com, http://www.greenwood.com. Eds. Linda Barnes, Susan Sered.

204 810 USA ISSN 1556-4843
RELIGION IN AMERICA (CARY). Text in English. 1991. irreg., latest 2008. price varies. illus.; maps. back issues avail. **Document type:** *Monographic series, Academic/Scholarly.* **Description:** Covers topics in religion in America through literature.
Indexed: RI-1.
Published by: Oxford University Press (Subsidiary of: Oxford University Press), 2001 Evans Rd, Cary, NC 27513. TEL 919-677-0977, FAX 919-677-1303, orders.us@oup.com.

201.6 951 NLD ISSN 1877-6264
▼ **RELIGION IN CHINESE SOCIETIES.** Text in English. 2011. irreg., latest vol.2, 2011. price varies. **Document type:** *Monographic series, Academic/Scholarly.* **Description:** Covers religious practices in all Chinese societies, including Mainland China, Hong Kong and Macau, Taiwan, and overseas Chinese communities throughout Southeast Asia and elsewhere.
Published by: Brill, PO Box 9000, Leiden, 2300 PA, Netherlands. TEL 31-71-5353500, FAX 31-71-5317532, cs@brill.nl.

201.69 DEU ISSN 1439-8753
RELIGION IN DER GESCHICHTE. Text in German. 1993. irreg., latest vol.18, 2009. price varies. **Document type:** *Monographic series, Academic/Scholarly.*
Published by: Verlag fuer Regionalgeschichte, Windelsbleicher Str 13, Guetersloh, 33335, Germany. TEL 49-5209-980266, FAX 49-5209-980277, regionalgeschichte@t-online.de, http://www.regionalgeschichte.de.

201.6 DEU ISSN 1432-0304
RELIGION IN DER GESELLSCHAFT. Text in German. 1995. irreg., latest vol.25, 2009. price varies. **Document type:** *Monographic series, Academic/Scholarly.*
Published by: Ergon Verlag, Keesburgstr 11, Wuerzburg, 97074, Germany. TEL 49-931-280084, FAX 49-931-282872, service@ergon-verlag.de.

200 DEU ISSN 0721-4022
RELIGION IN DER OEFFENTLICHKEIT. Text in German. 1996. irreg., latest vol.10, 2008. price varies. **Document type:** *Monographic series, Academic/Scholarly.*
Published by: Peter Lang GmbH (Subsidiary of: Peter Lang Publishing Group), Eschborner Landstr 42-50, Frankfurt Am Main, 60489, Germany. TEL 49-69-7807050, FAX 49-69-78070550, zentrale.frankfurt@peterlang.com, http://www.peterlang.com. Ed. Juergen Heumann.

200 947 USA ISSN 1069-4781
BR738.6
RELIGION IN EASTERN EUROPE. Abbreviated title: R E E. Text in English. 1981. bi-m. looseleaf. bk.rev. back issues avail. **Document type:** *Journal, Academic/Scholarly.*
Formerly (until 1993): Occasional Papers on Religion in Eastern Europe (0731-5465)
Related titles: Microfilm ed.; Online - full text ed.
Indexed: A01, A03, A08, A21, ABS&EES, CA, PerIslam, RI-1, RI-2, T02.
—Ingenta.
Published by: Christians Associated for Relationships with Eastern Europe, c/o Associated Mennonite Biblical Seminary, 3003 Benham Ave, Elkhart, IN 46517. TEL 574-296-6209, FAX 574-295-0092, http://www.caree.info. Eds. Paul Mojzes, Walter Sawatsky.

200 900 DEU ISSN 0942-8941
RELIGION IN GESCHICHTE UND GEGENWART. Text in German. 1993. irreg., latest vol.2, 1993. price varies. **Document type:** *Monographic series, Academic/Scholarly.*
Published by: Centaurus Verlag & Media KG, Kaiser-Joseph-Str 267, Freiburg, 79098, Germany. TEL 49-761-1525861, FAX 49-761-1525868, info@centaurus-verlag.de.

200 MWI
RELIGION IN MALAWI. Text in English. 1987. a. MWK 5. bk.rev. back issues avail. **Document type:** *Journal, Academic/Scholarly.*
Description: Covers information and discussions in all fields of religion in Malawi.
Related titles: Diskette ed.
Published by: (Department of Theology and Religious Studies), University of Malawi, Chancellor College, PO Box 280, Zomba, Malawi. TEL 265-50-522549, FAX 265-50-522046. Ed. Joseph Chakanza. Circ: 500 (paid).

200 100 DEU ISSN 1616-346X
RELIGION IN PHILOSOPHY AND THEOLOGY. Text in English, German. 2000. irreg., latest vol.54, 2011. price varies. **Document type:** *Monographic series, Academic/Scholarly.*
Published by: Mohr Siebeck GmbH & Co. KG, Wilhelmstr 18, Tuebingen, 72074, Germany. TEL 49-7071-9230, FAX 49-7071-51104, info@mohr.de.

270 USA ISSN 1947-444X
B802
▼ ➤ **RELIGION IN THE AGE OF ENLIGHTENMENT.** Text in English. 2010 (Feb.). a. USD 125 each vol. (effective 2011). **Document type:** *Journal, Academic/Scholarly.* **Description:** Presents research on religion and religious attitudes and practices during the age of Enlightenment in the fields of history, theology, literature, philosophy, the sciences, economics, and the law.
Indexed: MLA-IB.
Published by: A M S Press, Inc., 63 Flushing Ave, Unit 221, Bldg 292, Ste 417, Brooklyn, NY 11205. TEL 718-875-8100, FAX 718-875-3800, editorial@amspressinc.com. Ed. Brett C McInelly.

200 NLD ISSN 1542-1279
RELIGION IN THE AMERICAS SERIES. Text in English. 2002. irreg., latest vol.8, 2008. price varies. **Document type:** *Monographic series.*
Description: Explores the complex theologies, philosophies, and interaction of different forms of Christianity with the societies, politics, religions and cultures of the variety of people in the Americas.
Indexed: IZBG.
Published by: Brill, PO Box 9000, Leiden, 2300 PA, Netherlands. TEL 31-71-5353500, FAX 31-71-5317532, cs@brill.nl. Ed. Henri Gooren.

RELIGION IN THE NEWS. *see* JOURNALISM

200 340 DEU ISSN 1611-938X
RELIGION - KULTUR - RECHT. Text in German. 2003. irreg., latest vol.11, 2009. price varies. **Document type:** *Monographic series, Academic/Scholarly.*
Published by: Peter Lang GmbH (Subsidiary of: Peter Lang Publishing Group), Eschborner Landstr 42-50, Frankfurt Am Main, 60489, Germany. TEL 49-69-7807050, FAX 49-69-78070550, zentrale.frankfurt@peterlang.com, http://www.peterlang.com.

RELIGION & LIVSFRAAGOR (ROL). *see* EDUCATION

200 NLD ISSN 1875-4511
RELIGION PAST AND PRESENT. Text in English. 2007. irreg. EUR 990, USD 1,350 (effective 2010). **Document type:** *Monographic series, Academic/Scholarly.*
Media: Online - full text.
Published by: Brill, PO Box 9000, Leiden, 2300 PA, Netherlands. TEL 31-71-5353500, FAX 31-71-5317532, cs@brill.nl. Eds. Don S Browning, Eberhard Juengel, Hans D Betz.

RELIGION, POLITICS, AND PUBLIC LIFE. *see* POLITICAL SCIENCE

200 CHE ISSN 1422-4429
RELIGION - POLITIK - GESELLSCHAFT IN DER SCHWEIZ. Text in German. 1987. irreg., latest vol.55, 2011. price varies. **Document type:** *Monographic series, Academic/Scholarly.*
Published by: Academic Press Fribourg, Perolles 42, Fribourg, 1705, Switzerland. TEL 41-26-4264311, FAX 41-26-4264300, info@paulusedition.ch, http://www.paulusedition.ch/academic_press/.

200 DEU ISSN 1438-955X
RELIGION - STAAT - GESELLSCHAFT; Zeitschrift fuer Glaubensformen und Weltanschauungen. Text in English, German. 2000. 2/yr. adv. **Document type:** *Journal, Academic/Scholarly.* **Description:** Attempts to analyze the influence of religion on the cultural, political and economical development of society.
Related titles: Online - full text ed.
Indexed: CA, DIP, IBR, IBSS, IBZ, P42, PSA, S02, S03, SCOPUS, SociolAb, T02.
Published by: Lit Verlag, Grevener Str/Fresnostr 2, Muenster, 48159, Germany. TEL 49-251-235091, FAX 49-251-231972, lit@lit-verlag.de, http://www.lit-verlag.de. Eds. Gerhard Besier, Hubert Seiwert. adv.: B&W page EUR 500; trim 115 x 180. Circ: 450 (paid and controlled).

R

200 335 GBR ISSN 0963-7494
BR738.6 CODEN: RSSOFA
➤ **RELIGION, STATE AND SOCIETY**; the Keston journal. Text in English. 1973. q. GBP 664 combined subscription in United Kingdom to institutions (print & online eds.); EUR 916, USD 1,151 combined subscription to institutions (print & online eds.) (effective 2012). adv. bk.rev. bibl. index. reprint service avail. from PSC. **Document type:** *Journal, Academic/Scholarly.* **Description:** Presents articles on religious communities in communist and formerly communist countries, and social, cultural, ethical and religious issues influencing the emergence of the new Europe.
Formerly (until 1992): Religion in Communist Lands (0307-5974)
Related titles: Microform ed.: (from PQC); Online - full text ed.: ISSN 1465-3974. GBP 597 in United Kingdom to institutions; EUR 825, USD 1,036 to institutions (effective 2012) (from IngentaConnect).
Indexed: A01, A03, A08, A21, A22, AMR, B21, CA, CERDIC, DIP, E01, E17, ESPM, HRIR, I02, I13, IBR, IBSS, IBZ, P28, P34, P42, P45, P46, P48, P53, P54, PCI, PQC, PSA, R&TA, R02, RI-1, S02, S03, SCOPUS, SOPODA, SSA, SociolAb, T02.
—IE, Infotrieve, Ingenta. **CCC.**
Published by: (Keston Institute), Routledge (Subsidiary of: Taylor & Francis Group), 4 Park Sq, Milton Park, Abingdon, Oxon OX14 4RN, United Kingdom. TEL 44-20-70176000, FAX 44-20-70176336, subscriptions@tandf.co.uk, http://www.routledge.com. Ed. Dr. Philip Walters. Adv. contact Linda Hann TEL 44-1344-779945. **Subscr. to:** Taylor & Francis Ltd., Journals Customer Service, Sheepen Pl, Colchester, Essex CO3 3LP, United Kingdom. TEL 44-20-70175544, FAX 44-20-70175198, tf.enquiries@tfinforma.com.

200 100 DEU ISSN 1436-2600
RELIGION UND AUFKLAERUNG. Text in German. 1998. irreg., latest vol.20, 2011. price varies. **Document type:** *Monographic series, Academic/Scholarly.*
Published by: Mohr Siebeck GmbH & Co. KG, Wilhelmstr 18, Tuebingen, 72074, Germany. TEL 49-7071-9230, FAX 49-7071-51104, info@mohr.de.

200 USA ISSN 0886-2141
BL1
RELIGION WATCH; a newsletter monitoring trends in contemporary religion. Text in English. 1985. m. (11/yr.). USD 25; USD 27 foreign (effective 1999). bk.rev. **Document type:** *Newsletter.*
Indexed: CCR, PerIslam.
Address: PO Box 652, North Bellmore, NY 11710. TEL 516-781-0835, FAX 516-781-0835. Ed., Pub., R&P Richard P Cimino.

200 DEU ISSN 1867-7487
RELIGIONEN AKTUELL. Text in German. 2007. irreg., latest vol.5, 2009. price varies. **Document type:** *Monographic series, Academic/Scholarly.*
Published by: Tectum Wissenschaftsverlag Marburg, Biegenstr 4, Marburg, 35037, Germany. TEL 49-6421-481523, FAX 49-6421-43470, email@tectum-verlag.de. Ed. Bertram Schmitz.

230 DEU ISSN 1867-1292
RELIGIONEN IM DIALOG. Text in German. 2008. irreg., latest vol.4, 2011. price varies. **Document type:** *Monographic series, Academic/Scholarly.*
Published by: Waxmann Verlag GmbH, Steinfurter Str 555, Muenster, 48159, Germany. TEL 49-251-265040, FAX 49-251-2650426, info@waxmann.com.

200 300 DEU ISSN 1866-5977
RELIGIONEN IN KULTUR UND GESELLSCHAFT. Text in German. 2008. irreg., latest vol.2, 2009. price varies. **Document type:** *Monographic series, Academic/Scholarly.*
—BLDSC (7356.477690).
Published by: Weissensee Verlag e.K., Simplonstr 59, Berlin, 10245, Germany. TEL 49-30-29049192, FAX 49-30-27574315, mail@weissensee-verlag.de.

291.175 ITA ISSN 0394-9397
BL60
RELIGIONI E SOCIETA; rivista di scienze sociali della religione. Text in Italian; Abstracts in English. 1986. 3/yr. adv. cum.index:1986-2002. **Document type:** *Journal, Academic/Scholarly.* **Description:** Religious forum covering theology, philosophy and sociology of religions.
Related titles: Online - full text ed.: ISSN 1722-4705. 2003. free (effective 2008).
Indexed: CA, DIP, IBR, IBZ, P42, PSA, S02, S03, SCOPUS, SOPODA, SSA, SociolAb, T02.
Published by: (Associazione per lo Studio del Fenomeno Religioso), Fabrizio Serra Editore (Subsidiary of: Accademia Editoriale), c/o Accademia Editoriale, Via Santa Bibbiana 28, Pisa, 56127, Italy. TEL 39-050-542332, FAX 39-050-574888, accademiaeditoriale@accademiaeditoriale.it, http://www.libraweb.net. Circ: 320 (controlled).

200 ITA ISSN 2036-3710
RELIGIONI, IDENTITA, CULTURE. Text in Italian. 2007. irreg. price varies. **Document type:** *Monographic series, Academic/Scholarly.*
Published by: Societa Editrice Fiorentina, Via Aretina 298, Florence, 50136, Italy. TEL 39-055-5532924, FAX 39-055-5532085, redazione@sefeditrice.it, http://www.sefeditrice.it. Ed. Federico Squarcini.

200 CHE ISSN 2077-1444
▼ ➤ **RELIGIONS.** Text in English. 2010. q. free (effective 2011). **Document type:** *Journal, Academic/Scholarly.* **Description:** Publishes regular research papers, reviews, communications and reports on research projects on religious thought and practice.
Media: Online - full text.
Published by: M D P I AG, Postfach, Basel, 4005, Switzerland. TEL 41-61-6837734, FAX 41-61-3028918, http://www.mdpi.org/. Ed. Peter I. Kaufman TEL 804-289-8003.

200 CAN
RELIGIONS AND BELIEFS/RELIGIONS ET CROYANCES. Text in English, French. 1993. irreg. price varies. **Document type:** *Monographic series, Consumer.* **Description:** Studies on various aspects of religion: the religions of America, religion in relation with ethics and the Bible and culture.
Published by: University of Ottawa Press/Presses de l'Universite d'Ottawa, 542 King Edward, Ottawa, ON K1N 6N5, Canada. TEL 613-562-5246, FAX 613-562-5247. Ed. Robert Choquette.

820 GBR ISSN 1422-8998
RELIGIONS AND DISCOURSE. Text in English. 1999. irreg., latest vol.49, 2011. price varies. **Document type:** *Monographic series, Academic/Scholarly.*
Published by: Peter Lang Ltd. (Subsidiary of: Peter Lang Publishing Group), Evenlode Ct, Main Rd, Long Hanborough, Oxfordshire OX29 8SZ, United Kingdom. TEL 44-1993-880088, FAX 44-1993-882040, info@peterlang.com. Ed. James Francis.

306.4 200 FRA ISSN 1778-3453
RELIGIONS CONTEMPORAINES. Text in French. 2005. irreg. back issues avail. **Document type:** *Monographic series.*
Published by: Editions Karthala, 22-24 Boulevard Arago, Paris, 75013, France. TEL 33-1-43311559, FAX 33-1-45352705, karthala@orange.fr, http://www.karthala.com.

200 FRA ISSN 1772-7200
RELIGIONS & HISTOIRE. Text in French. 2005. bi-m. EUR 54 (effective 2009). back issues avail. **Document type:** *Magazine, Consumer.*
Published by: Editions Faton S.A., 25 Rue Berbisey, Dijon, 21000, France. TEL 33-3-80404104, http://www.faton.fr.

292 937 NLD ISSN 0927-7633
➤ **RELIGIONS IN THE GRAECO-ROMAN WORLD.** Text in Dutch. 1961. irreg., latest vol.166, 2008. price varies. back issues avail. **Document type:** *Monographic series, Academic/Scholarly.* **Description:** Scholarly monographs on historical, bibliographical and archaeological aspects of Egyptian, Mithraic and Oriental religions in all parts of the Roman Empire and the Graeco-Roman world.
Formerly (until vol.114, 1992): Etudes Preliminaires aux Religions Orientales dans l'Empire Romain (0531-1950)
Indexed: IZBG, RI-2.
—BLDSC (7356.477630).
Published by: Brill, PO Box 9000, Leiden, 2300 PA, Netherlands. TEL 31-71-5353500, FAX 31-71-5317532, cs@brill.nl, http://www.brill.nl. R&P Elizabeth Venekamp. **Dist. by:** Turpin Distribution Services Ltd., Pegasus Dr, Stratton Business Park, Biggleswade, Bedfordshire SG18 8QB, United Kingdom. TEL 44-1767-604954, FAX 44-1767-601640, custserv@turpin-distribution.com, http://www.turpin-distribution.com/.

290 DEU ISSN 0939-2580
➤ **RELIGIONSGESCHICHTLICHE VERSUCHE UND VORARBEITEN.** Text in German. 1903. irreg., latest vol.58, 2011. price varies. **Document type:** *Monographic series, Academic/Scholarly.*
Published by: Walter de Gruyter GmbH & Co. KG, Genthiner Str 13, Berlin, 10785, Germany. TEL 49-30-260050, FAX 49-30-26005251, info@degruyter.com, http://www.degruyter.de. Eds. Fritz Graf, Guenter Abel.

371.07 DNK ISSN 0108-559X
RELIGIONSLAEREREN; tidsskrift for religionsundervisning i Danmark. Text in Danish. 1950. 5/yr. DKK 325 to individual members; DKK 375 to institutional members; DKK 225 to students (effective 2009). adv. **Document type:** *Magazine, Trade.*
Formerly: Meddelelser fra og med Religionslaererforeningen
Indexed: AMR.
Published by: Religionslaererforeningen, c/o John Rydahl, Religionspaedagogiske Center, Frederiksberg Alle 10 A, Frederiksberg C, 1820, Denmark. TEL 45-26-136996, john.rydahl@skolekom.dk, http://www.religionslaererforeningen.dk. Ed. Karsten Braeuner.

230 DEU
RELIGIONSPAEDAGOGIK IM DISKURS. Variant title: Reihe Religionspaedagogik im Diskurs. Text in German. 2005. irreg., latest vol.10, 2010. price varies. **Document type:** *Monographic series, Academic/Scholarly.*
Published by: I K S Garamond, Leutragraben 1, Jena, 07743, Germany. TEL 49-3641-460850, FAX 49-3641-460855, garamond@iks-jena.de.

268 DEU
RELIGIONSPAEDAGOGIK IN EINER MULTIKULTURELLEN GESELLSCHAFT. Text in German. 1997. irreg., latest vol.4, 2002. price varies. **Document type:** *Monographic series, Academic/Scholarly.*
Published by: Waxmann Verlag GmbH, Steinfurter Str 555, Muenster, 48159, Germany. TEL 49-251-265040, FAX 49-251-2650426, info@waxmann.com. Ed. Wolfram Weisse.

268 DEU
RELIGIONSPAEDAGOGIK IN PLURALER GESELLSCHAFT. Text in German. 2002. irreg., latest vol.15, 2010. price varies. **Document type:** *Monographic series, Academic/Scholarly.*
Published by: Verlag Herder GmbH, Hermann-Herder-Str 4, Freiburg Im Breisgau, 79104, Germany. TEL 49-761-27170, FAX 49-761-2717520, kundenservice@herder.de, http://www.herder.de.

291 DEU
▼ **RELIGIONSPAEDAGOGISCHE GESPRAECHE ZWISCHEN JUDEN, CHRISTEN UND MUSLIMEN.** Text in German. 2009. irreg. price varies. **Document type:** *Monographic series, Academic/Scholarly.*
Published by: Frank und Timme GmbH, Wittelsbacherstr 27a, Berlin, 10707, Germany. TEL 49-30-88667911, FAX 49-30-86398731, info@frank-timme.de.

200 SWE ISSN 1652-7895
RELIGIONSVETENSKAPLIGA STUDIER FRAAN GAEVLE. Text in Swedish. 2005. irreg., latest vol.1, 2005. **Document type:** *Monographic series, Academic/Scholarly.*
Published by: Swedish Science Press, PO Box 118, Uppsala, 75104, Sweden. TEL 46-18-365566, FAX 46-18-365277, info@ssp.nu, http://www.ssp.nu.

200 DNK ISSN 0108-1993
BL9.D36
➤ **RELIGIONSVIDENSKABELIGT TIDSSKRIFT.** Text in Danish; Summaries in English. 1982. s-a. DKK 168 (effective 2010). adv. bk.rev. back issues avail. **Document type:** *Journal, Academic/Scholarly.*
Related titles: Online - full text ed.: ISSN 1904-8181.
Published by: Aarhus Universitet, Det Teologiske Fakultet. Afdeling for Religionsvidenskab/University of Aarhus, Faculty of Theology, Department of the Study of Religion, Taasingegade 3, Aarhus C, 8000, Denmark. TEL 45-89-421111, FAX 45-86-130490, teo@au.dk, http://www.teo.au.dk. Ed. Anders Klostergaard Petersen. **Dist. by:** Aarhus Universitetsforlag, Langelandsgade 177, Aarhus N 8200, Denmark. TEL 45-89-425370, FAX 45-89-425380, unipress@au.dk, http://www.unipress.dk.

200 DEU ISSN 0931-122X
RELIGIONSWISSENSCHAFT. Text in German. 1987. irreg., latest vol.15, 2008. price varies. **Document type:** *Monographic series, Academic/Scholarly.*
Published by: Peter Lang GmbH (Subsidiary of: Peter Lang Publishing Group), Eschborner Landstr 42-50, Frankfurt Am Main, 60489, Germany. TEL 49-69-7807050, FAX 49-69-78070550, zentrale.frankfurt@peterlang.com, http://www.peterlang.com.

200 DEU ISSN 0934-2192
RELIGIONSWISSENSCHAFTLICHE REIHE. Text in German. 1988. irreg., latest vol.27, 2008. price varies. **Document type:** *Monographic series, Academic/Scholarly.*
Published by: Diagonal Verlag, Alte Kasseler Str 43, Marburg, 35039, Germany. TEL 49-6421-681936, FAX 49-6421-681944, post@diagonal-verlag.de. Pub. Thomas Schweer.

200 DEU ISSN 0179-9215
RELIGIONSWISSENSCHAFTLICHE TEXTE UND STUDIEN. Text in German. 1986. irreg., latest vol.14, 2007. price varies. **Document type:** *Monographic series, Academic/Scholarly.*
Published by: Georg Olms Verlag, Hagentorwall 7, Hildesheim, 31134, Germany. TEL 49-5121-15010, FAX 49-5121-150150, info@olms.de.

RELIGIOUS & THEOLOGICAL ABSTRACTS. *see* RELIGIONS AND THEOLOGY—Abstracting, Bibliographies, Statistics

200 658 USA ISSN 1050-2742
RELIGIOUS CONFERENCE MANAGER. Text in English. 1972. 8/yr. free domestic to members (effective 2011). adv. **Document type:** *Magazine, Trade.* **Description:** Provides religious planners with information to help them in arranging for and conducting meetings and conventions.
Related titles: Online - full text ed.
Indexed: A09, A10, A26, B02, B07, B15, B17, B18, BPI, BRD, E08, G04, G05, G06, G07, G08, I05, R05, S09, T02, V03, V04, W01, W02, W03, W05.
—CCC.
Published by: (Religious Conference Management Association), Penton Media, Inc., 11 River Bend Dr South, PO Box 4949, Stamford, CT 06907-0949. TEL 203-358-9900, FAX 203-358-5823, information@penton.com, http://www.pentonmedia.com. Ed. Larry Keltto TEL 507-455-2136. adv.: B&W page USD 2,530, color page USD 3,830; trim 10.75 x 8. Circ: 3,600.

200.071 DEU ISSN 1862-9547
RELIGIOUS DIVERSITY AND EDUCATION IN EUROPE. Text in English, German. 2006. irreg., latest vol.20, 2010. price varies. **Document type:** *Monographic series, Academic/Scholarly.* **Description:** Examines the changing roles of religion and education in Europe.
—BLDSC (7356.496500).
Published by: Waxmann Verlag GmbH, Steinfurter Str 555, Muenster, 48159, Germany. TEL 49-251-265040, FAX 49-251-2650426, info@waxmann.com.

200 371.07 USA ISSN 0034-4087
BV1460 CODEN: RLEDAN
➤ **RELIGIOUS EDUCATION**; a platform for the free discussion of issues in the field of religion and their bearing on education. Text in English. 1906. 5/yr. GBP 118 combined subscription in United Kingdom to institutions (print & online eds.); EUR 156, USD 197 combined subscription to institutions (print & online eds.) (effective 2012). adv. bk.rev. index. reprint service avail. from PSC. **Document type:** *Journal, Academic/Scholarly.* **Description:** Offers an interfaith forum for exploring religious identity, formation, and education in faith communities, academic disciplines and institutions, and public life and the global community.
Incorporates (19??-1906): Religious Education Association. Annual Convention. Proceedings
Related titles: Microform ed.: (from PMC, PQC); Online - full text ed.: ISSN 1547-3201. GBP 106 in United Kingdom to institutions; EUR 140, USD 177 to institutions (effective 2012) (from IngentaConnect).
Indexed: A01, A02, A03, A08, A20, A21, A22, ABS&EES, ASCA, AmHI, ArtHuCI, B04, B05, BRD, BRI, CA, CBRI, CERDIC, CPE, CurCont, E01, E02, E03, E06, ERI, ERIC, EdA, EdI, FR, FamI, GSS&RPL, H07, H09, H10, IJP, J01, P04, P18, P28, P30, P43, P48, P53, P54, P55, PCI, PQC, PhilInd, PsycholAb, R&TA, RI-1, RI-2, S02, S03, S05, SCOPUS, T02, W03, W07.
—IE, Infotrieve, Ingenta, INIST. **CCC.**
Published by: (Religious Education Association), Taylor & Francis Inc. (Subsidiary of: Taylor & Francis Group), 325 Chestnut St, Ste 800, Philadelphia, PA 19106. TEL 215-625-2940, 800-354-1420, orders@taylorandfrancis.com, http://www.taylorandfrancis.com. Ed. Dr. Jack Seymour. Adv. contact Linda Hann TEL 44-1344-779945.

➤ **RELIGIOUS FUNDING RESOURCE GUIDE.** *see* SOCIAL SERVICES AND WELFARE

201.6 NLD
▼ ➤ **RELIGIOUS HISTORY AND CULTURE SERIES.** Text in English. 2009. irreg. **Document type:** *Monographic series, Academic/Scholarly.* **Description:** Provides a forum to advance the study of the history of religion and religious culture.
Published by: Brill, PO Box 9000, Leiden, 2300 PA, Netherlands. TEL 31-71-5353500, FAX 31-71-5317532, cs@brill.nl. Eds. Fred van Lieburg, Joris van Eijnatten.

➤ **RELIGIOUS PRODUCT NEWS.** *see* BUSINESS AND ECONOMICS—Office Equipment And Services

➤ **RELIGIOUS SOCIALISM.** *see* POLITICAL SCIENCE

200 GBR ISSN 0034-4125
BL1
➤ **RELIGIOUS STUDIES**; an international journal for the philosophy of religion. Text in English. 1965. q. GBP 237, USD 407 to institutions; GBP 246, USD 425 combined subscription to institutions (print & online eds.) (effective 2012). adv. bk.rev. illus. index. back issues avail.; reprint service avail. from PSC. **Document type:** *Journal, Academic/Scholarly.* **Description:** Covers primarily the philosophy and history of religion.
Related titles: Microform ed.: (from PQC); Online - full text ed.: ISSN 1469-901X. GBP 219, USD 383 to institutions (effective 2012).
Indexed: A20, A21, A22, A25, A26, ASCA, AmHI, ArtHuCI, B14, BAS, BRD, BRI, BrHumI, CA, CBRI, CERDIC, CurCont, DIP, E01, E08, FR, G06, G07, G08, H07, H08, H09, H10, H14, HAb, HumInd, I05, I07, IBR, IBZ, IJP, IPB, MEA&I, MLA-IB, P02, P10, P28, P48, P53, P54, PCI, PQC, PerIslam, PhilInd, R&TA, R05, RASB, RI-1, RI-2, S08, S09, S23, SCOPUS, SOPODA, SociolAb, T02, W03, W07.

—BLDSC (7356.550000), IE, Infotrieve, Ingenta, INIST. **CCC.**
Published by: Cambridge University Press, The Edinburgh Bldg, Shaftesbury Rd, Cambridge, CB2 8RU, United Kingdom. TEL 44-1223-312393, FAX 44-1223-315052, journals@cambridge.org, http://www.cambridge.org/uk. Ed. P A Byrne. R&P Linda Nicol TEL 44-1223-325702. Adv. contact Rebecca Roberts TEL 44-1223-325083. page GBP 460, page USD 875. Circ: 1,200. **Subscr. to:** Cambridge University Press, 32 Ave of the Americas, New York, NY 10013. TEL 212-337-5000, FAX 212-691-3239, journals_subscriptions@cup.org.

200 GBR ISSN 0829-2922
➤ **RELIGIOUS STUDIES AND THEOLOGY.** Abbreviated title: R S T. Text in English. 1981. s-a. USD 220 combined subscription in North America to institutions (print & online eds.); GBP 135 combined subscription elsewhere to institutions (print & online eds.) (effective 2012). adv. bk.rev. index. back issues avail.; reprints avail. **Document type:** *Journal, Academic/Scholarly.* **Description:** Presents fresh scholarship in both theology and religious studies, particularly those that use the resources of the world's religious traditions.
Formerly (until 1985): Religious Studies Bulletin (0710-0655)
Related titles: Online - full text ed.: ISSN 1747-5414. USD 176 in North America to institutions; GBP 108 elsewhere to institutions (effective 2012).
Indexed: A21, C03, CBCARef, CERDIC, P28, P48, P53, P54, PQC, R&TA, RI-1, RI-2.
—BLDSC (7356.550500), IE, Ingenta. **CCC.**
Published by: Equinox Publishing Ltd., Unit S3, Kelham House, 3 Lancaster St, Sheffield, S6 3AF, United Kingdom. TEL 44-114-2725957, FAX 44-560-3459046, journals@equinoxpub.com, http://www.equinoxpub.com/. Ed. Earle Waugh. Adv. contact Val Hall.

200 PHL ISSN 0115-6349
BR1
RELIGIOUS STUDIES JOURNAL. Text in English. 1978. a. PHP 30, USD 3.20. adv. bk.rev. **Document type:** *Journal, Academic/Scholarly.* **Description:** Publishes scholarly articles reflecting significant quantitative or qualitative research. Includes speeches, research reports, and "state of the art" papers.
Indexed: IPP.
Published by: De La Salle University, Religious Studies Department, 2401 Taft Ave, Manila, Philippines. TEL 63-2-524-46-11, FAX 63-2-521-9094. Circ: 300.

200 USA
BL1
RELIGIOUS STUDIES NEWS (ONLINE). Abbreviated title: R S N. Text in English. 1964. q. USD 47.25 to institutions (effective 2010). adv. bk.rev. back issues avail. **Document type:** *Newspaper, Trade.* **Description:** Provides a medium to communicate important events, announcements, dates, and issues to persons involved in the academic study of religon.
Former titles (until 2010): Religious Studies News (Print) (0885-0372); (until 1985): Council on Study of Religion. Bulletin (0002-7170); (until 1970): American Academy of Religion. Bulletin (0569-2148)
Media: Online - full text.
Indexed: A22, OTA, RI-1, RI-2.
Published by: (Society of Biblical Literature), American Academy of Religion, 825 Houston Mill Rd NE, Ste 300, Atlanta, GA 30329. TEL 404-727-3049, FAX 404-727-7959, aar@aarweb.org. Ed. Stephanie Gray. Circ: 10,000.

RELIGIOUS STUDIES REVIEW; a quarterly review of publications in the field of religion and related disciplines. *see* RELIGIONS AND THEOLOGY—Abstracting, Bibliographies, Statistics

200 GEO
RELIGIYA. Text in Russian. m. USD 129 in United States.
Address: Ul M Kostava 14, Tbilisi, 380096, Georgia. TEL 995-32-998737. Ed. Viktor Rtskhiladze. **Dist. by:** East View Information Services, 10601 Wayzata Blvd, Minneapolis, MN 55305. TEL 952-252-1201, 800-477-1005, FAX 952-252-1202, info@eastview.com, http://www.eastview.com.

RESEARCH IN MINISTRY (ONLINE); an index to Doctor of Ministry project reports and theses. *see* RELIGIONS AND THEOLOGY—Abstracting, Bibliographies, Statistics

305.896073 USA ISSN 1055-1158
RESEARCH IN RELIGION AND FAMILY: BLACK PERSPECTIVES. Text in English. 199?. irreg., latest vol.6, 2005. price varies. **Document type:** *Monographic series, Academic/Scholarly.* **Description:** Examines the goals of family and religion within the black tradition.
Indexed: IIBP.
Published by: Peter Lang Publishing, Inc. (Subsidiary of: Peter Lang Publishing Group), 29 Broadway, New York, NY 10006. TEL 212-647-7706, 212-647-7700, 800-770-5264, FAX 212-647-7707, customerservice@plang.com, http://www.peterlang.com. Ed. Noel Leo Erskine.

200 NLD ISSN 1046-8064
BL60
➤ **RESEARCH IN THE SOCIAL SCIENTIFIC STUDY OF RELIGION.** Text in English. 1989. irreg., latest vol.19, 2008. price varies. back issues avail. **Document type:** *Monographic series, Academic/Scholarly.* **Description:** Contains international articles examining religion and religious organizations from a variety of social science perspectives.
Indexed: A21, A22, CA, IZBG, P03, PsycInfo, RI-1, RI-2, S02, S03, SCOPUS, SSA, SociolAb, T02.
—BLDSC (7770.600000), IE, Ingenta. **CCC.**
Published by: Brill, PO Box 9000, Leiden, 2300 PA, Netherlands. TEL 31-71-5353500, FAX 31-71-5317532, cs@brill.nl. Eds. Andrew Village, Ralph Piedmont.

200 FIN ISSN 0355-144X
RESEARCH INSTITUTE OF THE LUTHERAN CHURCH IN FINLAND. PUBLICATIONS. Text in English. 1971. irreg. price varies. back issues avail. **Document type:** *Monographic series, Academic/Scholarly.*
Related titles: Online - full text ed.: ISSN 1459-2711; ◆ Series of: Kirkon Tutkimuskeskus. Julkaisuja. ISSN 1459-2681.
Published by: Kirkon Tutkimuskeskus/Research Institute of the Lutheren Church of Finland, PO Box 239, Tampere, 33101, Finland. TEL 358-3-31233400, FAX 358-3-31233450, ktk@evl.fi, http://www.evl.fi/kkh/ktk/index.htm.

RESEARCH NEWS & OPPORTUNITIES IN SCIENCE AND THEOLOGY. *see* SCIENCES: COMPREHENSIVE WORKS

230.071 DEU
▼ **RESEARCH ON RELIGIOUS AND SPIRITUAL EDUCATION.** Text in English. 2011. irreg., latest vol.3, 2011. price varies. **Document type:** *Monographic series, Academic/Scholarly.* **Description:** Focuses on schools, families and communities as contexts of religious and spiritual learning and instruction.
Published by: Waxmann Verlag GmbH, Steinfurter Str 555, Muenster, 48159, Germany. TEL 49-251-265040, FAX 49-251-2650426, info@waxmann.com. Eds. Kirsi Tirri, Theo van der Zee, Ulrich Riegel.

200 SWE ISSN 1654-7322
RESEARCH PAPER SERIES. Text in English, Swedish. 2007. irreg. **Document type:** *Monographic series, Academic/Scholarly.*
Published by: Teologiska Hoegskolan/Stockholm School of Theology, Aakeshovsvaegen 29, Bromma, 16839, Sweden. TEL 46-8-56435700, FAX 46-8-56435706, ths@ths.se, http://www.ths.se.

220 ESP ISSN 1134-5233
RESENA BIBLICA. Text in Spanish. 1994. q. EUR 26.78 domestic; EUR 40.05 in Europe; EUR 39.56 elsewhere (effective 2009). **Document type:** *Monographic series, Academic/Scholarly.*
Published by: Asociacion Biblica Espanola, Buen Suceso, 22, Madrid, 28008, Spain. TEL 34-91-4226265, abe@abe.org.es, http://www.abe.org.es/. Ed. Jose Cervantes Gabarron.

THE RESHAPING OF PSYCHOANALYSIS; from Sigmund Freud to Ernest Becker. *see* PSYCHOLOGY

207 GBR ISSN 0143-2710
RESOURCE. Text in English. 1978. 3/yr. free to members (effective 2009). bk.rev. 32 p./no. 2 cols./p.; **Document type:** *Magazine, Academic/Scholarly.* **Description:** Contains 24 pages of reflection on, the nature of religious education, contemporary issues within the faith communities, classroom practice at all levels, the politics of religious education, worldwide perspectives, etc.
—**CCC.**
Published by: (Professional Council for Religious Education), R E Today Services (Subsidiary of: Christian Education), 1020 Bristol Rd, Selly Oak, Birmingham, B29 6LB, United Kingdom. TEL 44-121-4724242, FAX 44-121-4727575, admin@retoday.org.uk. Ed. Bill Gent.

200 CAN ISSN 0708-2177
RESTORATION. Text in English. 1947. 10/yr. CAD 6 (effective 1999). reprints avail. **Document type:** *Newspaper.*
Related titles: Microform ed.: (from PQC).
Published by: Madonna House, Inc., 2888 Dafoe Rd, Combermere, ON K0J 1L0, Canada. TEL 613-756-3713, http://www.mv.igs.net/~madonnah/. Ed., R&P Paulette Curran. Circ: 7,200 (paid).

200 USA ISSN 0034-5830
RESTORATION HERALD. Text in English. 1925. m. USD 8. adv. bk.rev. illus.
Related titles: Audio cassette/tape ed.
Published by: Christian Restoration Association, 7133 Central Parke Blvd., Mason, OH 45040-7451. TEL 513-385-0461. Ed. Thomas D Thurman. Circ: 4,500 (controlled).

230 USA ISSN 0486-5642
BX7075.A1
➤ **RESTORATION QUARTERLY.** Text in English. 1957. q. adv. bk.rev. back issues avail. **Document type:** *Journal, Academic/Scholarly.* **Description:** Devoted to advancing knowledge and understanding of New Testament Christianity, its backgrounds, its history, and its implications for the present age.
Indexed: A21, A22, CERDIC, DIP, FamI, IBR, IBZ, OTA, P30, R&TA, RI-1, RI-2.
—BLDSC (7777.850000), IE, Infotrieve, Ingenta.
Published by: Restoration Quarterly Corporation, ACU Station, Box 28227, Abilene, TX 79699. Ed. James W Thompson TEL 915-674-3730.

207.2 GBR ISSN 1747-454X
RETHINKING MISSION (ONLINE). Text in English. 1974. q. free (effective 2010). **Document type:** *Journal, Consumer.* **Description:** Covers theological reflections on mission.
Former titles (until 2006): Rethinking Mission (Print) (1479-7984); (until 2003): Thinking Mission (0143-8514)
Media: Online - full text.
Published by: United Society for the Propagation of the Gospel, 200 Great Dover St, London, SE1 4YB, United Kingdom. TEL 44-20-73785678, FAX 44-20-73785650, enquiries@uspg.org.uk, http://www.uspg.org.uk/. Ed. Joshva Raja.

230 USA ISSN 1527-781X
REV. Text in English. 1997. bi-m. USD 29.95 domestic; USD 36.95 foreign (effective 2009). adv. back issues avail. **Document type:** *Magazine, Trade.* **Description:** Provides information about pastor-oriented resources.
Formerly (until 1999): Vital Ministry (1094-7981)
Indexed: CCR.
Published by: Group Publishing, Inc., PO Box 481, Loveland, CO 80539. TEL 970-669-3836, 800-447-1070, FAX 970-292-4373, info@group.com, http://www.group.com. Adv. contact Linda Davis. page USD 2,518; trim 8 x 10.75.

REVIEW (NEW YORK, 1976). *see* HOMOSEXUALITY

220 USA ISSN 1099-0321
BS410
REVIEW OF BIBLICAL LITERATURE. Text in English. 1998. free (effective 2011). adv. **Document type:** *Journal, Academic/Scholarly.* **Description:** Includes reviews of various topical studies, multi-author volumes, reference works, commentaries, dictionaries, bible translations, software, and other resources for the classroom and research. Multiple and contrasting reviews are often presented. The material reviewed and reviewers come from varied academic, social, and religious perspectives.
Media: Online - full text. **Related titles:** ◆ Cumulative ed(s).: Review of Biblical Literature (Cumulative Edition). ISSN 1099-0046.
Published by: Society of Biblical Literature, The Luce Ctr, 825 Houston Mill Rd, Atlanta, GA 30329. TEL 404-727-3100, 866-727-9955, FAX 404-727-3101, sblexec@sbl-site.org, http://www.sbl-site.org.

220 USA ISSN 1099-0046
BS410
REVIEW OF BIBLICAL LITERATURE (CUMULATIVE EDITION). Abbreviated title: R B L. Text in English. 1998. a. USD 100 per issue domestic to non-members; USD 112 per issue in Canada & Mexico to non-members; USD 115 per issue elsewhere to non-members; USD 35 per issue domestic to members; USD 47 per issue in Canada & Mexico to members; USD 50 per issue elsewhere to members (effective 2009). adv. **Description:** Covers reference works, commentaries, dictionaries, multiauthor volumes, biblical translations, and reviews of a title in several languages.
Related titles: Online - full text ed.; ◆ Cumulative ed. of: Review of Biblical Literature. ISSN 1099-0321.
Indexed: A01, A02, A03, A08, A21, AmHI, CA, DIP, H07, IBR, IBZ, IZBG, L05, L06, RI-1, T02.
Published by: Society of Biblical Literature, The Luce Ctr, 825 Houston Mill Rd, Atlanta, GA 30329. TEL 404-727-3100, 866-727-9955, FAX 404-727-3101, sblexec@sbl-site.org, http://www.sbl-site.org. Adv. contact Phillip Stokes TEL 404-727-3096.

200 327 USA ISSN 1557-0274
BR115.I7
THE REVIEW OF FAITH & INTERNATIONAL AFFAIRS. Text in English. 2003 (Spr.). 4/yr. GBP 179 combined subscription in United Kingdom to institutions (print & online eds.); EUR 236, USD 295 combined subscription to institutions (print & online eds.) (effective 2012). adv. reprint service avail. from PSC. **Document type:** *Journal, Academic/Scholarly.* **Description:** Examines the relation of religion to international relations.
Formerly (until 2005): The Brandywine Review of Faith & International Affairs (1543-5725)
Related titles: Online - full text ed.: ISSN 1931-7743. GBP 161 in United Kingdom to institutions; EUR 212, USD 266 to institutions (effective 2012).
Indexed: A01, A20, ArtHuCI, CurCont, GSS&RPL, PAIS, T02, W07.
—**CCC.**
Published by: Institute for Global Engagement, Council on Faith & International Affairs, PO Box 12205, Arlington, VA 22219-2205. TEL 703-527-3100, FAX 703-527-5965, info@RFIAonline.org, https://www.rfiaonline.org. Ed., Adv. contact Dennis R. Hoover. page USD 300; trim 7 x 10.

200 330 USA ISSN 2153-6716
▼ **REVIEW OF RELIGION, ECONOMICS, & CULTURE.** Text in English. 2010 (June). irreg. price varies. **Document type:** *Journal, Academic/Scholarly.*
Related titles: Online - full text ed.: ISSN 2153-6708. 2010 (June). free.
Published by: St. George Seminary Press, PO Box 2723, Huntsville, AL 35801. metropolitan@southwestdiocese.org, http://www.southwestdiocese.org. Ed. John Vornholt.

200 GBR ISSN 1350-7303
BL1
REVIEWS IN RELIGION AND THEOLOGY. Abbreviated title: R R T. Text in English. 1994. q. GBP 304 in United Kingdom to institutions; EUR 384 in Europe to institutions; USD 509 in the Americas to institutions; USD 592 elsewhere to institutions; GBP 349 combined subscription in United Kingdom to institutions (print & online eds.); EUR 443 combined subscription in Europe to institutions (print & online eds.); USD 586 combined subscription in the Americas to institutions (print & online eds.); USD 681 combined subscription elsewhere to institutions (print & online eds.) (effective 2012). adv. bk.rev. back issues avail.; reprint service avail. from PSC. **Document type:** *Journal, Academic/Scholarly.* **Description:** Promotes awareness of new theological writing.
Related titles: Online - full text ed.: ISSN 1467-9418. GBP 304 in United Kingdom to institutions; EUR 384 in Europe to institutions; USD 509 in the Americas to institutions; USD 592 elsewhere to institutions (effective 2012) (from IngentaConnect).
Indexed: A01, A03, A08, A22, A26, CA, E01, T02.
—BLDSC (7794.192950), IE, Infotrieve, Ingenta. **CCC.**
Published by: Wiley-Blackwell Publishing Ltd. (Subsidiary of: John Wiley & Sons, Inc.), 9600 Garsington Rd, Oxford, OX4 2DQ, United Kingdom. TEL 44-1865-776868, FAX 44-1865-714591, customerservices@blackwellpublishing.com. Ed. Uriah Kim. Adv. contact Craig Pickett TEL 44-1865-476267.

200 BRA ISSN 0104-0529
BR7
REVISTA DE CULTURA TEOLOGICA. Text in Portuguese. 1961. q. BRL 35 (effective 2004).
Indexed: OTA.
Published by: Pontificia Faculdade de Teologia Nossa Senhora da Assuncao, Av. Nazare, 993, Sao Paulo, 04263-100, Brazil.

200 ESP ISSN 0034-8147
BX805
REVISTA DE ESPIRITUALIDAD. Text in Spanish. 1941. q. adv. bk.rev. bibl. index. **Document type:** *Magazine, Consumer.*
Indexed: FR.
—INIST.
Published by: Padres Carmelitas Descalzos, Triana, 9, Madrid, 28016, Spain. FAX 34-91-3591661. Circ: 1,200.

220 BRA ISSN 1676-3394
BT83.57
REVISTA DE INTERPRETACION BIBLICA LATINO - AMERICANO. Short title: R I B L A. Text in Portuguese. 1988. 3/yr. BRL 55 domestic; USD 50 foreign (effective 2005). **Document type:** *Journal, Academic/Scholarly.*
Related titles: Portuguese ed.
Indexed: OTA, RI-1.
Published by: Editora Vozes Ltda., Rua Mexico 174, Rio de Janeiro, RJ 20031 143, Brazil. TEL 55-21-22156386, FAX 55-21-25338358, vozes42@uol.com.br, http://www.editoravozes.com.br.

200 BRA ISSN 0101-8434
REVISTA ECLESIASTICA BRASILEIRA. Text in Portuguese. 1941. q. BRL 100 domestic; USD 199 foreign (effective 2005). adv. bk.rev. bibl. **Document type:** *Journal, Academic/Scholarly.* **Description:** About the mission of the Church in Brazil and the world.
Indexed: CPL, IZBG, OTA, R&TA.
Published by: Editora Vozes Ltda., Rua Mexico 174, Rio de Janeiro, RJ 20031 143, Brazil. TEL 55-21-22156386, FAX 55-21-25338358, vozes42@uol.com.br, http://www.editoravozes.com.br. Ed. Eloi Dionisio Piva. Circ: 3,000.

R

200 BRA ISSN 2177-952X
▼ **REVISTA ELECTRONICA ESPACO TEOLOGICO.** Text in Portuguese. 2010. s-a. free (effective 2011). **Document type:** *Journal, Academic/Scholarly.*
Media: Online - full text.
Published by: Pontificia Universidade Catolica de Sao Paulo, Faculdade de Teologia, Av Nazare 993, Ipiranga, Sao Paulo, 04263-100, Brazil. Ed. Cezar Teixeira.

200 ESP ISSN 0210-7112
BR7
REVISTA ESPANOLA DE TEOLOGIA. Text in Spanish. 1940. q. EUR 33 domestic; EUR 69 in Europe; USD 95 rest of world (effective 2008). bk.rev. bibl. **Document type:** *Journal, Academic/Scholarly.*
Indexed: A21, DIP, FR, IBR, IBZ, MLA-IB, OTA, P09, PCI, RI-1, RI-2.
—INIST.
Published by: Facultad de Teologia "San Damaso", C Jerte 10, Madrid, 28005, Spain. TEL 34-91-3644010. Circ: 400.

200 BRA ISSN 1678-7307
BL2592.U513
REVISTA ESPIRITUAL DE UMBANDA. Text in Portuguese. 2003. m. BRL 5.90 newsstand/cover (effective 2006). **Document type:** *Magazine, Consumer.*
Published by: Editora Escala Ltda., Av Prof Ida Kolb, 551, Casa Verde, Sao Paulo, 02518-000, Brazil. TEL 55-11-38552100, FAX 55-11-38579643, escala@escala.com.br, http://www.escala.com.br.

200 800 100 ESP ISSN 0210-0525
REVISTA ESTUDIOS; revista trimestral publicada por los frailes de la orden de la merced. Text in Spanish. 1945. q. USD 60. adv. bk.rev. Supplement avail. **Document type:** *Academic/Scholarly.*
Indexed: IBR, IBZ, MLA-IB, P09, P30, PCI.
Published by: Provincia de la Merced de Castilla, Belisana, 2, Madrid, 28043, Spain. TEL 34-1-3002972, FAX 34-1-3002994. Ed. Luis Vazquez Fernandez. Adv. contact Jose Amable Suarez. Circ: 500.

200 MEX
REVISTA IBEROAMERICANA DE TEOLOGIA. Text in Spanish. 2005. s-a. back issues avail. **Document type:** *Journal, Academic/Scholarly.*
Related titles: Online - full text ed.
Published by: Universidad Iberoamericana, Departamento de Ciencias Religiosas, Av. Prol. Paseo de la Reforma 880. Edif. J Nivel 1, Col. Lomas de Santa Fe, Mexico, D.F., 01210, Mexico. TEL 52-55-59504035, FAX 52-55-59504256, dcr@uia.mx, http://www.uia.mx/web/site/tpl-Nivel2.php?menu=mgAcademia&seccion=acReligiosas.

200 SLV ISSN 0259-9872
BT30.L37
REVISTA LATINOAMERICANA DE TEOLOGIA. Text in Spanish. 1984. 3/yr. SVC 70 domestic; USD 20 in Central America; USD 30 in North America; USD 35 in Europe; USD 40 elsewhere (effective 2005). **Document type:** *Journal, Academic/Scholarly.*
Related titles: Online - full content ed.
Indexed: C01, IBR, IBZ, OTA.
Published by: Universidad Centroamericana Jose Simeon Canas, U C A Editores, Apartado Postal 01-168, San Salvador, El Salvador. TEL 503-210-6600, FAX 503-210-6655, correo@www.uca.edu.sv.

200 PRT ISSN 1646-1630
REVISTA LUSOFONA DE CIENCIA DAS RELIGIOES. Text in Portuguese. 2002. s-a. **Document type:** *Journal, Academic/Scholarly.*
Formerly (until 2006): Revista Portuguesa de Ciencia das Religioes (1645-5584)
Published by: Universidade Lusofona de Humanidades e Tecnologia, Edicoes Universitarias, Campo Grande 376, Lisbon, 1749-024, Portugal. TEL 351-217-515500, FAX 351-217-577006, http://ulusofona.pt. Ed. Alfredo Teixeira.

200 ECU
REVISTA MENSAJERO. Text in Spanish. 1884. m. (10/yr.). ECS 2,500, USD 13. **Description:** Examines the concerns and issues of present-day Catholics living in Ecuador.
Published by: Ediciones Mensajero, Apdo 17 01 4100, Quito, Pichincha, Ecuador. Circ: 5,000.

220 FRA ISSN 0035-0907
BS410
REVUE BIBLIQUE. Text in French. 1892. q. EUR 180 (effective 2010). bk.rev. bibl.; charts; illus. index, cum.index: 1892-1972; 1973-1993. **Document type:** *Journal, Academic/Scholarly.*
Former titles (until 1945): Vivre et Penser (1240-3040); (until 1940): Revue Biblique (1240-3032)
Related titles: Microfiche ed.: (from IDC); Supplement(s): Cahiers de la Revue Biblique. ISSN 0575-0741.
Indexed: A20, A21, A22, ASCA, ArtHuCI, BibLing, CERDIC, CurCont, DIP, FR, IBR, IBZ, IZBG, MLA-IB, OTA, PCI, R&TA, RASB, RI-1, RI-2, SCOPUS, W07.
—BLDSC (7892.820000), IE, Infotrieve, Ingenta, INIST. **CCC.**
Published by: (Ecole Biblique et Archeologique de Jerusalem ISR), J. Gabalda et Cie, 69 Rue du Petit Pende, Pende, 80230, France. editions@gabalda.com. Ed. R P de Tarragon. Pub. J P Gabalda.

281 809 BEL ISSN 1768-9260
BX2901
REVUE D' ETUDES AUGUSTINIENNES ET PATRISTIQUES. Text in Multiple languages; Summaries in English, French. 1935. s-a. EUR 81.20 (effective 2011). bk.rev. bibl.; illus. index. **Document type:** *Journal, Academic/Scholarly.* **Description:** Publishes original scholarship in the areas concerning early Christianity and the High Middle Ages, including history, literature, philology, exegesis, philosophy and archaeology, as well as other related disciplines. Also publishes an annual systematic review of studies on Augustine.
Former titles (until 2004): Revue des Etudes Augustiniennes (0035-2012); (until 1955): Annee Theologique (0994-592X); (until 1940): Sens Chretien (0994-5911); (until 1939): Les Essais Catholiques (0994-5903)
Indexed: A22, BibInd, CERDIC, DIP, FR, IPB, MLA, MLA-IB, PCI, PhilInd, R&TA, SCOPUS.
—IE, Infotrieve, INIST.
Published by: (Institut d'Etudes Augustiniennes FRA), Brepols Publishers, Begijnhof 67, Turnhout, 2300, Belgium. TEL 32-14-448030, FAX 32-14-428919, periodicals@brepols.net, http://www.brepols.net. Ed. Jean Claude Fredouille.

200 FRA ISSN 0035-1423
BL3
REVUE DE L'HISTOIRE DES RELIGIONS; histoire comparee des religions, histoire religieuse. Text in French. 1880. q. EUR 59 combined subscription domestic to individuals (print & online eds.); EUR 69 combined subscription foreign to individuals (print & online eds.); EUR 83 combined subscription domestic to institutions (print & online eds.); EUR 93 combined subscription foreign to institutions (print & online eds.) (effective 2008). bk.rev. q. index. reprint service avail. from SCH. **Document type:** *Journal, Academic/Scholarly.* **Description:** Encompasses the general history of religions as well as a more in depth focus on particular aspects of a different religion each issue.
Related titles: Microfilm ed.: (from BHP); Online - full text ed.: ISSN 2105-2573. 2004.
Indexed: A20, A21, A22, ASCA, AmH&L, ArtHuCI, BAS, CA, CurCont, DIP, FR, H09, H10, HistAb, I14, IBR, IBZ, IZBG, MLA-IB, P30, PCI, RASB, RI-1, RI-2, S05, SCOPUS, T02, W07.
—IE, Infotrieve, INIST. **CCC.**
Published by: (College de France), Armand Colin, 21 Rue du Montparnasse, Paris, 75283 Cedex 06, France. TEL 33-1-44395447, FAX 33-1-44394343, infos@armand-colin.fr.

221 296.155 FRA ISSN 0035-1725
BM487.A62
➤ **REVUE DE QUMRAN.** Text in English, French, German, Italian, Latin, Spanish. 1958. s-a. EUR 130 (effective 2010). bk.rev. **Document type:** *Journal, Academic/Scholarly.* **Description:** Examines the Dead Sea Scrolls.
Indexed: A21, A22, BibLing, DIP, FR, IBR, IBZ, IZBG, L09, OTA, PCI, R&TA, RASB, RI-1, RI-2, SCOPUS.
—IE, Infotrieve, INIST. **CCC.**
Published by: J. Gabalda et Cie, 69 Rue du Petit Pende, Pende, 80230, France. editions@gabalda.com. Ed. Emile Puech. Circ: 1,000.

200 100 CHE ISSN 0035-1784
BR3
REVUE DE THEOLOGIE ET DE PHILOSOPHIE. Text in French. 1868. q. CHF 59 domestic to individuals; CHF 63 foreign to individuals; CHF 75 domestic to institutions; CHF 80 foreign to institutions (effective 2008); effective 1996 & 1997. bk.rev. index. **Document type:** *Journal, Academic/Scholarly.*
Former titles (until 1911): Revue de Theologie et de Philosophie et Compte-rendu des Principales Publications Scientifiques (1010-3864); (until 1872): Theologie et Philosophie (0259-7152)
Related titles: Microfilm ed.: (from BHP).
Indexed: A21, CERDIC, DIP, FR, IBR, IBZ, IPB, IZBG, MLA-IB, OTA, PCI, PhilInd, RI-1, RI-2, RILM, SCOPUS.
—BLDSC (7956.070000), INIST.
Published by: Cahiers de la Revue de Theologie et de Philosophie, 7 ch des Cedres, Lausanne, 1004, Switzerland.

200 100 CHE ISSN 0250-6971
REVUE DE THEOLOGIE ET DE PHILOSOPHIE. CAHIERS. Text in French. 1977. irreg., latest vol.23, 2009. **Document type:** *Monographic series, Academic/Scholarly.*
Indexed: A21, PCI, RI-1, RI-2.
Published by: Librairie Droz S.A., 11 rue Firmin-Massot, Geneva 12, 1211, Switzerland. TEL 41-22-3466666, FAX 41-22-3472391, droz@droz.org, http://www.droz.org.

205 FRA ISSN 1266-0078
BJ2
REVUE D'ETHIQUE ET DE THEOLOGIE MORALE. Text in French. 1947. 4/yr. price varies. **Document type:** *Monographic series, Academic/Scholarly.* **Description:** Forum for exchange between theologians and theosophists.
Formerly (until 1994): Le Supplement (0750-1455)
Indexed: A21, CERDIC, CPL, FR, IBSS, RI-1, RI-2.
—INIST.
Published by: Editions du Cerf, 29 Boulevard La Tour Maubourg, Paris, 75340 Cedex 07, France. http://www.editionsducerf.fr. Ed. Nicolas Jean Sed. Circ: 3,000.

274 BEL ISSN 0300-9505
BR840
REVUE D'HISTOIRE DE L'EGLISE DE FRANCE. Text in French; Summaries in English, German. 1910. s-a. EUR 84 combined subscription (print & online eds.) (effective 2012). bk.rev. back issues avail.; reprints avail. **Document type:** *Journal, Academic/Scholarly.*
Related titles: Online - full text ed.
Indexed: A20, A22, AmH&L, CA, CERDIC, DIP, FR, HistAb, IBR, IBZ, MLA-IB, P30, PCI, T02.
—IE, Infotrieve, INIST.
Published by: (Societe d'Histoire Religieuse de la France FRA), Brepols Publishers, Begijnhof 67, Turnhout, 2300, Belgium. TEL 32-14-448030, FAX 32-14-428919, periodicals@brepols.net, http://www.brepols.net. Ed. Philippe Boutry.

200 BEL ISSN 0035-2381
BX940
REVUE D'HISTOIRE ECCLESIASTIQUE. Text in French. 1900. q. USD 227 combined subscription (print & online eds.) (effective 2012). adv. bk.rev. bibl.; charts. index, cum.index every 15-20 yrs. reprints avail. **Document type:** *Journal, Academic/Scholarly.*
Related titles: Microfiche ed.: (from IDC); Online - full text ed.
Indexed: A20, A21, A22, ASCA, ArtHuCI, BibInd, CurCont, DIP, FR, HistAb, IBR, IBZ, IPB, MLA, MLA-IB, P30, PCI, R&TA, RASB, RI-1, RI-2, RILM, SCOPUS, W07.
—IE, Infotrieve, Ingenta, INIST.
Published by: (Universite Catholique de Louvain, Bureau de la Revue d'Histoire Ecclesiastique), Brepols Publishers, Begijnhof 67, Turnhout, 2300, Belgium. TEL 32-14-448020, FAX 32-14-428919, periodicals@brepols.net, http://www.brepols.net.

200 FRA ISSN 0035-2403
BR3
REVUE D'HISTOIRE ET DE PHILOSOPHIE RELIGIEUSES. Text in French; Summaries in English. 1921. q. EUR 30 domestic; EUR 33 in the European Union; EUR 36 elsewhere; EUR 20 domestic to students; EUR 22 in the European Union to students; EUR 24 elsewhere to students (effective 2010). adv. bk.rev. charts; illus. index, cum.index: 1920-1945, 1946-1974. back issues avail.; reprints avail. **Document type:** *Journal, Academic/Scholarly.* **Description:** Provides a scientific study of various biblical, historical, philosophical and dogmatic problems posed by the development of Christian theological thought and its links with non-Christian thought. Also involves the study of inter-testamentary Judaism and the history of the Reformation.
Incorporates (in 1920): Annales de Bibliographie Theologique (1245-7183); (in 1962): Eglise & Theologie (1245-7205); Supersedes in part (in 1869): Revue de Theologie (1245-7175); Which was formerly (until 1862): Nouvelle Revue de Theologie (1245-7167); (until 1957): Revue de Theologie et de Philosophie Chretienne (1245-7159)
Related titles: Microfilm ed.: (from PQC).
Indexed: A20, A21, A22, BibLing, CA, CERDIC, DIP, FR, HistAb, IBR, IBZ, IPB, IZBG, MLA-IB, P30, PCI, R&TA, RASB, RI-1, RI-2, SPPI, T02.
—IE, Infotrieve, INIST. **CCC.**
Published by: Universite de Strasbourg, Faculte de Theologie Protestante, 9, place de l'Universite, Strasbourg, 67084, France. FAX 33-3-88140137, http://www.premiumorange.com/theologie.protestante/index.php. Circ: 1,000.

200 CAN ISSN 0700-6500
REVUE NOTRE DAME DU CAP. Text in French. 1892. 10/yr. CAD 11.50 (effective 2000). adv. bk.rev. **Document type:** *Magazine, Consumer.*
Published by: Corporation Revue Notre-Dame du Cap, 626 rue Notre Dame, Cap De La Madeleine, PQ G8T 4G9, Canada. TEL 819-374-2441, FAX 819-374-2441. Ed., R&P Jerome Martineau. Pub. Paul Arsenault. Adv. contact Leo Paul Nobert. Circ: 75,000 (paid).

200 CAN ISSN 1495-9313
REVUE SCRIPTURA, NOUVELLE SERIE. Text in French. s-a. CAD 20 to individuals; CAD 30 to institutions (effective 2005). **Document type:** *Journal, Academic/Scholarly.*
Former titles (until 1999): Scriptura, Nouvelle Serie (1489-2421); (until 199?): Revue Scriptura (0847-3420); (until 1989): Scriptura (0849-1445)
Indexed: OTA.
Published by: Universite de Montreal, Faculte de Theologie, C.P. 6128 succ. Centre-ville, Montreal, PQ H3C 3J7, Canada. TEL 514-343-7080, FAX 514-343-5738.

200 FRA ISSN 0035-4295
BX802
REVUE THOMISTE; revue doctrinale de theologie et de philosophie. Text in French. 1893. q. EUR 67 domestic; EUR 80 in the European Union; EUR 84 elsewhere (effective 2009). adv. bk.rev. index. reprint service avail. from PSC. **Document type:** *Journal, Academic/Scholarly.* **Description:** Aims to promote theological wisdom and Christian humanism to today's culture.
Related titles: Microfilm ed.: (from BHP).
Indexed: A22, BibInd, CERDIC, DIP, FR, IBR, IBZ, IPB, IZBG, MLA, MLA-IB, PCI, PhilInd, R&TA, RASB.
—IE, Infotrieve, INIST. **CCC.**
Published by: Dominicains de la Province de Toulouse, Impasse Lacordaire, Toulouse, Cedex 4 31078, France. TEL 33-5-62173126, FAX 33-5-62173117. Ed. Pere Serge Thomas Bonino. R&P Serge Thomas Bonino. Circ: 1,100.

230 DEU
RHOEN BRIEF. Text in German. q. free (effective 2009). **Document type:** *Newsletter, Consumer.*
Published by: Christliche Tagungsstaette Hohe Rhoen e.V., Fischzucht 1-5, Bischofsheim, 97653, Germany. TEL 49-9772-93040, FAX 49-9772-930419, info@hohe-rhoen.org, http://www.hohe-rhoen.org. Ed. Fritz Schroth.

RICERCHE DI STORIA SOCIALE E RELIGIOSA. *see* SOCIOLOGY

282 ITA ISSN 0391-8424
RICERCHE PER LA STORIA RELIGIOSA DI ROMA. Text in Italian. 1977. irreg., latest vol.10, 1999. price varies. **Document type:** *Monographic series, Academic/Scholarly.*
Indexed: PCI.
Published by: Edizioni di Storia e Letteratura, Via delle Fornaci 24, Rome, 00165, Italy. TEL 39-06-670307, FAX 39-06-671250, info@storiaeletteratura.it, http://www.storiaeletteratura.it.

200 ITA ISSN 1120-8333
RICERCHE TEOLOGICHE. Text in Italian. 1990. s-a. EUR 39.60 domestic; EUR 53.70 in the European Union; EUR 55.90 elsewhere (effective 2008). **Document type:** *Magazine, Consumer.*
Indexed: OTA.
Published by: (Societa Italiana per la Ricerca Teologica), Centro Editoriale Dehoniano, Via Scipione dal Ferro 4, Bologna, BO 40138, Italy. TEL 39-051-4290451, FAX 39-051-4290491, ced-amm@dehoniane.it, http://www.dehoniane.it.

RIGHT TO HOUSING REPORT. *see* HOUSING AND URBAN PLANNING

RIGHTEOUS NURSE MAGAZINE. *see* MEDICAL SCIENCES—Nurses And Nursing

200 CHE ISSN 0254-3966
RISK BOOK SERIES. Text in English. 1965. q. CHF 47.50, USD 35 (effective 1999). **Document type:** *Monographic series, Academic/Scholarly.*
Formerly (until 1978): Risk (0035-5585)
Indexed: A21, CERDIC, RI-1.
—BLDSC (7972.585000).
Published by: World Council of Churches, 150 route de Ferney, PO Box 2100, Geneva 2, 1211, Switzerland. TEL 41-22-791-6111, FAX 41-22-791-0361. Circ: 4,000.

RITES EGYPTIENS. *see* ARCHAEOLOGY

220 ITA ISSN 0035-5798
RIVISTA BIBLICA. Text in Italian. 1953. q. EUR 40.50 domestic; EUR 50.80 in the European Union; EUR 56 elsewhere (effective 2008). bk.rev. **Document type:** *Magazine, Consumer.*
Indexed: A21, A22, FR, OTA, RI-1.
—BLDSC (7981.800000), IE, Infotrieve, Ingenta, INIST.

Published by: (Associazione Biblica Italiana), Centro Editoriale Dehoniano, Via Scipione dal Ferro 4, Bologna, BO 40138, Italy. TEL 39-051-4290451, FAX 39-051-4290491, ced-amm@dehoniane.it, http://www.dehoniane.it.

264 ITA ISSN 0035-6395
RIVISTA DI PASTORALE LITURGICA. Text in Italian. 1962. bi-m. EUR 26.50 domestic; EUR 45.50 in Europe; EUR 61.50 elsewhere (effective 2009). adv. **Document type:** *Magazine, Consumer.*
Published by: Editrice Queriniana, Via Enrico Ferri 75, Brescia, BS 25123, Italy. TEL 39-030-2306925, FAX 39-030-2306932, redazione@queriniana.it, http://www.queriniana.it. Ed. Daniele Piazzi.

200 ITA
RIVISTA DI SCIENZE RELIGIOSE. Text in Italian. s-a. EUR 25 domestic; EUR 29 foreign (effective 2009). **Document type:** *Magazine, Consumer.*
Indexed: OTA.
Published by: Facolta Teologica Pugliese, Largo San sabino 1, Bari, 70122, Italy. http://www.facoltateologica.it. Ed. Salvatore Palese.

200 ITA ISSN 1827-7365
RIVISTA DI STORIA DEL CRISTIANESIMO. Text in Italian. 2004. s-a. EUR 37 domestic; EUR 40 foreign (effective 2009). **Document type:** *Journal, Academic/Scholarly.*
Indexed: T02.
Published by: Editrice Morcelliana SpA, Via Gabriele Rosa 71, Brescia, BS 25121, Italy. TEL 39-030-46451, FAX 39-030-2400605, http://www.morcelliana.it.

274 900 ITA ISSN 0035-6557
BR870 CODEN: QJRMAM
RIVISTA DI STORIA DELLA CHIESA IN ITALIA. Text in English, French, German, Italian, Latin, Spanish. 1947. s-a. EUR 75 domestic to institutions; EUR 130 foreign to institutions (effective 2009). bk.rev. bibl.; charts; stat.; tr.lit. index. back issues avail. **Document type:** *Journal, Academic/Scholarly.*
Related titles: Online - full text ed.
Indexed: A22, BibInd, CA, DIP, FR, HistAb, IBR, IBZ, MLA-IB, P30, PCI, RASB, T02.
—IE, Infotrieve, INIST.
Published by: Vita e Pensiero (Subsidiary of: Universita Cattolica del Sacro Cuore), Largo Gemelli 1, Milan, 20123, Italy. TEL 39-02-72342335, FAX 39-02-72342260, redazione.vp@mi.unicatt.it. Ed. Agostino Paravicini Bagliani. Circ: 1,000.

209 ITA ISSN 0035-6573
BR140
RIVISTA DI STORIA E LETTERATURA RELIGIOSA. Text in English, French, German, Italian. 1965. 3/yr. EUR 140 combined subscription foreign to institutions (print & online eds.) (effective 2012). adv. bk.rev. **Document type:** *Journal, Academic/Scholarly.*
Related titles: Online - full text ed.: ISSN 2035-7583.
Indexed: A20, A21, A22, ASCA, ArtHuCI, CA, CERDIC, CurCont, DIP, FR, HistAb, IBR, IBZ, MLA, MLA-IB, PCI, RI-1, RI-2, SCOPUS, T02, W07.
—IE, Infotrieve, INIST.
Published by: (Universita degli Studi di Torino), Casa Editrice Leo S. Olschki, Viuzzo del Pozzetto 8, Florence, 50126, Italy. TEL 39-055-6530684, FAX 39-055-6530214, celso@olschki.it, http://www.olschki.it. Eds. Carlo Ossola, Giorgio Cracco, Mario Rosa. Circ: 1,000.

209 ITA ISSN 1122-4274
RIVISTA DI STORIA E LETTERATURA RELIGIOSA. BIBLIOTECA. STUDI. Text in Italian. 1990. irreg., latest vol.13, 2001. price varies. **Document type:** *Monographic series, Academic/Scholarly.*
Published by: Casa Editrice Leo S. Olschki, Viuzzo del Pozzetto 8, Florence, 50126, Italy. TEL 39-055-6530684, FAX 39-055-6530214, celso@olschki.it, http://www.olschki.it.

209 ITA ISSN 0392-016X
RIVISTA DI STORIA E LETTERATURA RELIGIOSA. BIBLIOTECA. TESTI E DOCUMENTI. Text in Italian. 1967. irreg., latest vol.16, 1996. price varies. **Document type:** *Monographic series, Academic/Scholarly.*
Published by: Casa Editrice Leo S. Olschki, Viuzzo del Pozzetto 8, Florence, 50126, Italy. TEL 39-055-6530684, FAX 39-055-6530214, celso@olschki.it, http://www.olschki.it.

202 ITA ISSN 0035-6638
RIVISTA DI VITA SPIRITUALE. Text in Italian. 1947. bi-m. EUR 26 domestic; EUR 28 in Europe; EUR 40 elsewhere (effective 2009). bk.rev. bibl. index. **Document type:** *Magazine, Consumer.* **Description:** For priests, monks, nuns, and the laity.
Published by: (Centro Interprovinciale O.C.D.), Edizioni O.C.D., Via Anagnina 662-B, Rome, 00040, Italy. TEL 39-06-7989081, FAX 39-06-79890840, info@ocd.it, http://www.edizioniocd.it. Circ: 2,000.

282 209 NLD ISSN 1871-4579
RKKERK.NL KERKELIJKE DOCUMENTATIE. Text in Dutch. 1970. 10/yr. looseleaf. EUR 56.50; EUR 44.50 to students (effective 2010). bibl. index.
Former titles (until 2003): Kerkelijke Documentatie 121 (0923-3849); (until 1989): Informatiebulletin 121. Kerkelijke Documentatie (0922-3517); (until 1988): Archief van de Kerken (0022-9342); Which incorporated: Katholiek Archief
Indexed: CERDIC.
Published by: Rooms-Katholiek Kerkgenootschap in Nederland Secretariaat, Afdeling Pers en Communicatie, Biltstraat 121, Postbus 13049, Utrecht, 3507 LA, Netherlands. TEL 31-30-2326911, FAX 31-30-2334601, media@rkk.nl, http://www.katholieknederland.nl/rkkerk. Eds. Michel Bronzwaer, Dr. Bert Elbertse.

200 USA ISSN 1544-4856
ROAD TO EMMAUS; a journal of Orthodox faith and culture. Text in Russian. 2000. q. USD 25 domestic; USD 30 in Canada; USD 40 elsewhere (effective 2007). illus. **Document type:** *Journal.*
Published by: Road To Emmaus, PO Box 16021, Portland, OR 97292-0021. TEL 866-783-6628. Ed., Pub. Richard Betts. Circ: 750.

200 USA
THE ROCK (ELGIN). Text in English. q. **Document type:** *Newsletter, Consumer.* **Description:** Helps junior high students in Sunday school to develop a Christian perspective on life through faith in Jesus Christ.
Former titles: Sprint (Elgin) (0277-0377); (until 1983): Looking Ahead (Elgin) (0162-9549)
Published by: Cook Communications Ministries, 4050 Lee Vance View, Colorado Springs, CO 80918. TEL 719-536-0100, http://www.cookministries.com.

ROCK & SLING. *see* LITERATURE

ROEMISCHE HISTORISCHE MITTEILUNGEN. *see* HISTORY—History Of Europe

ROTTENBURGER JAHRBUCH FUER KIRCHENGESCHICHTE. *see* HISTORY—History Of Europe

268 USA ISSN 2151-0342
ROUND 2 TAKE 'N TALK SHEETS FOR 4S & 5S. Text in English. 2004. q. USD 3.99 per issue (effective 2009). **Document type:** *Handbook/Manual/Guide, Trade.* **Description:** Provides meaningful activities for the class and home. Offers ideas for family interaction related to the lesson's theme and focus.
Formerly (until 2009): Take 'n Talk for 4s & 5s (1558-0369)
Published by: Randall House, 114 Bush Rd, PO Box 17306, Nashville, TN 37217. TEL 615-361-1221, 800-877-7030, FAX 615-367-0535.

268 USA ISSN 2151-0334
ROUND 2 TEACHING GUIDE FOR 4S & 5S. Text in English. 2004. q. USD 6.99 per issue (effective 2009). **Document type:** *Handbook/Manual/Guide, Trade.* **Description:** Provides teachers with the necessary tools and information to most effectively teach 4- and 5-year olds and help connect God's word to their lives.
Formerly (until 2009): CLEAR Teaching for 4s & 5s (1558-3007)
Published by: Randall House, 114 Bush Rd, PO Box 17306, Nashville, TN 37217. TEL 615-361-1221, 800-877-7030, FAX 615-367-0535.

200 USA
ROUNDTABLE REPORT. Text in English. 1980. bi-m. USD 25.
Formerly: Religious Round Table
Address: 3295 Popular Ave, Box 11467, Memphis, TN 38111. TEL 901-458-3795. Ed. Donna Mooshian Striegel.

200 307.1412 GBR ISSN 1470-4994
RURAL THEOLOGY; international, ecumenical and interdisciplinary perspectives. Text in English. 198?. s-a. USD 220 combined subscription in North America to institutions (print & online eds.); GBP 135 combined subscription elsewhere to institutions (print & online eds.) (effective 2012). adv. back issues avail.; reprints avail. **Document type:** *Journal, Academic/Scholarly.* **Description:** Aims to promote theological reflection on matters of rural concern, to enhance the ministry and mission of rural churches, and to bring rural issues to the forefront of church and government agenda.
Formerly (until 1999): Better Country (0968-8781)
Related titles: Online - full text ed.: ISSN 2042-1273. USD 176 in North America to institutions; GBP 108 elsewhere to institutions (effective 2012).
Published by: Equinox Publishing Ltd., Unit S3, Kelham House, 3 Lancaster St, Sheffield, S6 3AF, United Kingdom. TEL 44-114-2725957, FAX 44-560-3459046, journals@equinoxpub.com, http://www.equinoxpub.com/. Ed. Leslie Francis. Adv. contact Val Hall.

RUTGERS JOURNAL OF LAW AND RELIGION. *see* LAW

220 AUS ISSN 1832-5092
S A AND N T SOWER. (South Australia and Northern Territory) Text in English. 2005. q. **Document type:** *Magazine, Consumer.*
Formerly (until 2005): South Australia Sower (1449-6097)
Published by: The Bible Society in Australia (South Australia), 770 South Rd, Glandore, SA 5037, Australia. TEL 61-8-82924888, FAX 61-8-82924899, infosa@bible.com.au, http://www.biblesociety.com.au.

220 USA ISSN 1555-7278
BS411
➤ **THE S B L FORUM.** (Society of Biblical Literature) Text in English. 2003. m. free (effective 2009). **Document type:** *Journal, Academic/Scholarly.* **Description:** Provides short, useful articles to inform, educate, and address the professional needs of biblical scholars, as well as those interested in biblical studies.
Media: Online - full content.
—CCC.
Published by: Society of Biblical Literature, The Luce Ctr, 825 Houston Mill Rd, Atlanta, GA 30329. TEL 404-727-3100, 866-727-9955, FAX 404-727-3101, sblexec@sbl-site.org. Ed. Leonard Greenspoon.

299.93 USA ISSN 0883-1300
CODEN: AACHBY
S C P JOURNAL. Text in English. 1973. q. donation. bk.rev. back issues avail. **Document type:** *Journal, Academic/Scholarly.* **Description:** Offers top-quality award-winning analysis and commentary on the inside workings of spiritual trends, cults, and new religions.
Formerly (until 1977): Spiritual Counterfeits Project. Journal
Indexed: ChrPI.
Published by: Spiritual Counterfeits Project, Inc, PO Box 4308, Berkeley, CA 94704. TEL 510-540-0300, FAX 510-540-1107, scp@scp-inc.org.

200 USA ISSN 0883-1319
S C P NEWSLETTER. Text in English. 1975. q. donation. bk.rev.; film rev. 16 p./no. 3 cols./p.; back issues avail. **Document type:** *Newsletter, Trade.* **Description:** Offers critical insight from a Christian perspective on social, cultural, and spiritual trends, including the New Age movement, the occult, cults, and UFOs.
Formerly (until 1980): Spiritual Counterfeits Project. Newsletter
Published by: Spiritual Counterfeits Project, Inc, PO Box 4308, Berkeley, CA 94704. TEL 510-540-0300, FAX 510-540-1107, scp@scp-inc.org.

200 BRA ISSN 0036-1267
S E D O C. (Servicio de Documentacao) Text in Portuguese. 1968. 6/yr. BRL 85 domestic; USD 80 foreign (effective 2005). **Document type:** *Magazine, Consumer.*
Published by: Editora Vozes Ltda., Rua Mexico 174, Rio de Janeiro, RJ 20031 143, Brazil. TEL 55-21-22156386, FAX 55-21-25338358, vozes42@uol.com.br, http://www.editoravozes.com.br. Ed. Volnei Beroken Brock. Circ: 2,400.

207.2 CAN ISSN 0711-6683
BV3500
S I M NOW. (Society for International Ministries) Text in English. 1958. q. free in Canada and U.S. bk.rev. reprints avail. **Description:** To inform of SIM activities and create interest in missions.
Formerly (until Jan. 1982): Africa Now (0044-6513)
Indexed: CCA, RASB.
Published by: S I M International, 10 Huntingdale Blvd, Scarborough, ON M1W 2S5, Canada. TEL 416-497-2424, FAX 416-497-2444. Ed., R&P David W Fuller. Circ: 125,000.

200 RUS
S NAMI BOG. Text in Russian. 1992. bi-m. USD 95 in United States (effective 2000).
Address: Ul Domodedovskaya 5 korp 3 kv 361, Moscow, 115551, Russian Federation. TEL 7-095-3915058. Ed. E A Likhacheva. **Dist. by:** East View Information Services, 10601 Wayzata Blvd, Minneapolis, MN 55305. TEL 952-252-1201, 800-477-1005, FAX 952-252-1202, info@eastview.com, http://www.eastview.com.

230 GBR
S P C K INTERNATIONAL STUDY GUIDE. Text in English. 19??. irreg. price varies. back issues avail. **Document type:** *Monographic series, Consumer.*
Published by: Society for Promoting Christian Knowledge, 36 Causton St, London, SW1P 4ST, United Kingdom. TEL 44-20-75923900, spck@spck.org.uk, http://www.spck.org.uk/.

200 SWE ISSN 0039-6699
BX8001
S P T: SVENSK PASTORALTIDSKRIFT; kyrkligt forum. Variant title: Svensk Pastoraltidskrift. Text in Swedish. 1959. bi-w. SEK 575 domestic; SEK 445 to students; SEK 875 elsewhere; SEK 25 per issue (effective 2007). bk.rev. Index. **Document type:** *Magazine, Academic/Scholarly.* **Description:** Scholarly articles, book reviews, ecclesiopolitical comments, bible analysis for sermons and other information relating to the Church of Sweden.
Related titles: E-mail ed.; Fax ed.
Published by: Stiftelsen Kyrkligt Forum, PO Box 2085, Uppsala, 75002, Sweden. Ed. Erik Petren TEL 46-26-612531. Pub. Yngve Kalin. Adv. contact Bo Carlsson.

200 DEU ISSN 0936-6423
SAARBRUECKER THEOLOGISCHE FORSCHUNGEN. Text in German. 1989. irreg., latest vol.10, 2007. price varies. **Document type:** *Monographic series, Academic/Scholarly.*
Published by: Peter Lang GmbH (Subsidiary of: Peter Lang Publishing Group), Eschborner Landstr 42-50, Frankfurt Am Main, 60489, Germany. TEL 49-69-7807050, FAX 49-69-78070550, zentrale.frankfurt@peterlang.com. Ed. Gotthold Hasenhuettl.

200 100 ITA ISSN 1594-7068
SACRA DOCTRINA. Text in Italian. 1956. bi-m. EUR 100 domestic; EUR 160 foreign (effective 2009). bk.rev. bibl. index. 120 p./no.; back issues avail.; reprints avail. **Document type:** *Journal, Academic/Scholarly.*
Indexed: CERDIC, DIP.
Published by: Edizioni Studio Domenicano, Via dell' Osservanza 72, Bologna, BO 40136, Italy. TEL 39-051-582034, FAX 39-051-331583, esd@alinet.it, http://www.esd-domenicani.it. Circ: 1,500.

230 USA
SACRA DOCTRINA; Christian theology for a postmodern age. Text in English. 1998. irreg., latest 2010. price varies. back issues avail. **Document type:** *Monographic series, Academic/Scholarly.* **Description:** Covers Christian theology in context of post modern culture intended for pastors, educated lay-people, theological students, and scholars.
Published by: (Christian Theological Research Fellowship), William B. Eerdmans Publishing Co., 2140 Oak Industrial Dr NE, Grand Rapids, MI 49505. TEL 616-459-4591, 800-253-7521, FAX 616-459-6540, info@eerdmans.com. Ed. Alan G Padgett.

R

SACRED DANCE GUILD JOURNAL. *see* DANCE

202 USA ISSN 1096-5939
SACRED JOURNEY; the journal of fellowship in prayer. Text in English. 1949. bi-m. USD 18 domestic; USD 26 foreign (effective 2007). bk.rev. 48 p./no.; back issues avail.; reprints avail. **Document type:** *Journal, Consumer.* **Description:** Interfaith journal of prayers, poetry and personal experience stories with some interviews of spiritual leaders.
Formerly: Fellowship in Prayer (0014-9837)
Related titles: Online - full content ed.
Published by: Fellowship in Prayer, Inc., 291 Witherspoon St, Princeton, NJ 08542-3269. TEL 609-924-6863, FAX 609-924-6910, editorial@sacredjourney.org. Ed. Lisa M. Calyton. Circ: 10,000.

230 AUS ISSN 1449-048X
SACRED SPACE; the prayer book. Text in English. 2004. a. AUD 32.95 per issue (effective 2009). **Description:** Contains devotional articles on prayers and short sections from scripture with detailed explanations.
Related titles: Online - full text ed.
Published by: (Jesuit Communication Center IRL), Michelle Anderson Publishing Pty Ltd, Chapel St N, PO Box 6032, South Yarra, VIC 3141, Australia. TEL 61-3-98269028, FAX 61-3-98268552, mapubl@bigpond.net.au.

230 BEL ISSN 0771-7776
BX800.A1
SACRIS ERUDIRI. Text in Multiple languages. 1948. a., latest vol.44, 2005. EUR 137 combined subscription (print & online eds.) (effective 2012). back issues avail. **Document type:** *Journal, Academic/Scholarly.*
Related titles: Online - full text ed.
Indexed: A21, DIP, FR, IBR, IBZ, IPB, MLA-IB, OTA, PCI, RILM, SCOPUS.
—IE, INIST.
Published by: (Sint-Pietersabdij, Steenbrugge), Brepols Publishers, Begijnhof 67, Turnhout, 2300, Belgium. TEL 32-14-448030, FAX 32-14-428919, periodicals@brepols.net, http://www.brepols.net.

220 ESP
SAGRADA BIBLIA. Text in Spanish. 1976. irreg., latest 1997. price varies.
Published by: (Universidad de Navarra, Facultad de Teologia), Universidad de Navarra, Servicio de Publicaciones, Campus Universitario, Pamplona, 31009, Spain. TEL 34-948-256850, FAX 34-948-256854, http://www.unav.es/publicaciones/.

230 USA ISSN 1545-3367
B765.A84
➤ **THE SAINT ANSELM JOURNAL.** Text in English, French, German. 2003. s-a. free (effective 2011). back issues avail. **Document type:** *Journal, Academic/Scholarly.* **Description:** Covers the life, thought, teachings and spirituality of Saint Anselm.

Media: Online - full text.
Indexed: A01, A39, C27, C29, CA, D03, D04, E13, Philind, R14, S14, S15, S18, T02.
Published by: Saint Anselm College, 100 Saint Anselm Dr, Manchester, NH 03102. TEL 603-641-7000, FAX 603-641-7340, busoffice@anselm.edu. Ed. Duane Bruce TEL 603-518-3991.

230 AUS ISSN 0036-3103
ST. MARK'S REVIEW; a journal of Christian thought and opinion. Text in English. 1955. q. AUD 30 domestic to individuals; AUD 45 foreign to individuals; AUD 70 domestic to institutions; AUD 90 foreign to institutions; AUD 10 per issue domestic to individuals; AUD 15 per issue foreign to individuals; AUD 25 per issue domestic to institutions; AUD 30 per issue foreign to institutions (effective 2009). adv. bk.rev. cum.index. 48 p./no.; back issues avail.; reprints avail. **Document type:** *Journal, Academic/Scholarly.* **Description:** Discusses of matters that of importance to the christian community in Australia and for the life of our society.
Related titles: Microform ed.: (from PQC).
Indexed: A21, AusPAIS, CERDIC, RI-1, RI-2, RILM.
—BLDSC (8070.191000), IE, Ingenta. **CCC.**
Published by: St. Mark's National Theological Centre, 15 Blackall St, Barton, ACT 2600, Australia. TEL 61-2-62726252, FAX 61-2-62734067, stmarksadmin@csu.edu.au. Ed. Scott Cowdell. Circ: 700 (paid).

200 USA ISSN 0038-8815
BX5971
ST. PAUL'S PRINTER. Text in English. 1958. q. donation. bk.rev. illus.; stat. **Document type:** *Newsletter.*
Published by: Society of St. Paul (Palm Desert), PO Box 14350, Palm Desert, CA 92255-4350. TEL 760-568-2200, FAX 760-568-2525. Ed. Rev. Andrew Rank. Circ: 5,000.

200 AUS ISSN 0816-0031
SALT. Text in English. 1985. s-a. free (effective 2008). bk.rev. illus.; tr.lit. **Document type:** *Magazine, Consumer.* **Description:** Provides prayer information on tertiary campus in Australia, while addressing issues relevant to students on those campuses. Topical issues are addressed in feature articles.
Related titles: Online - full text ed.: free (effective 2008).
Published by: Australian Fellowship of Evangelical Students Inc., PO Box 684, Kingsford, NSW 2032, Australia. TEL 61-2-96970313, FAX 61-2-96979265, national@afes.org.au. Eds. Mark Barry, Rebecca Jee. Circ: 3,500.

200 330.9 POL ISSN 1425-5081
SAMARITAN. Text in English, Russian. 1995. q. PLZ 12 in Europe; USD 25 elsewhere. back issues avail. **Document type:** *Newsletter, Consumer.* **Description:** Presents difficult social problems in the former communist countries of Eastern and Central Europe; social and diaconal activities of churches in Eastern Europe; shows the solutions in critical situations; introduces religious and cultural diversity of these countries.
Related titles: Diskette ed.; E-mail ed.; Fax ed.
Published by: Swiatowa Rada Kosciolow, Deaprtament IV - Biuro do Spraw Europy Wschodniej/World Council of Churches, Programme Unit IV - Eastern Europe Office, Ul Skladowa 9, Bialystok, 15399, Poland. TEL 48-85-7421857, FAX 48-85-7428719. Ed. Anna Radziukiewicz. R&P Grazyna Nazaruk. Circ: 1,500.

200 DEU ISSN 0342-1465
BX1
UNA SANCTA; Zeitschrift fuer oekumenische Begegung. Text in German. 1946. q. EUR 20.50 (effective 2003). index. back issues avail. **Document type:** *Magazine, Academic/Scholarly.* **Description:** Provides a forum for worldwide ecumenical contacts and promotes interreligious dialogue.
Indexed: DIP, FR, IBR, IBZ, IZBG.
Published by: Kyrios Verlag GmbH, Postfach 1125, Meitingen, 86400, Germany. TEL 49-8271-8080, FAX 49-8271-80865. Ed. Gerhard Voss. Circ: 1,000.

250 AUT ISSN 0036-3162
ST. POELTNER DIOEZESANBLATT. Text in German. 1785. irreg. (approx. 12/yr.). bk.rev. bibl.; charts. **Document type:** *Newsletter, Consumer.*
Published by: Bischoefliches Ordinariat St. Poelten, Domplatz 1, St. Poelten, N 3100, Austria. TEL 43-2742-324, FAX 43-2742-324309, bo.stpoelten@kirche.at, http://www.kirche.at/stpoelten/. Ed. Heinrich Fasching. Circ: 800.

371.07 BRA ISSN 0036-4614
SANTUARIO DE APARECIDA. Text in Portuguese. 1900. w. USD 6.42 domestic; USD 45.50 foreign. adv. bk.rev. illus.
Published by: (Congregacao do Santissimo Redentor), Editora Santuario, RUA PADRE CLARO MONTEIRO, 342, Aparecida, SP 12570-000, Brazil. TEL 0125-362140, FAX 0125-362141, TELEX 125659 CSRE BR. Ed. Manoel Jose Paixao. Circ: 40,000.

SAPIENZA; rivista internazionale di filosofia e di teologia. *see* PHILOSOPHY

201.6 CAN ISSN 0315-7970
LE SAUVEUR. Text in English. 1926. 6/yr. CAD 8.
Published by: Sanctuaire de la Reparation au Sacre-Coeur, 3650 bd de la Rousseliere, Montreal, PQ H1A 2X9, Canada. TEL 514-642-5391, FAX 514-642-5033. Ed. Yves Deschenes. Circ: 10,000.

225 DNK ISSN 1904-2159
▼ ➤ **SCANDINAVIAN EVANGELICAL E-JOURNAL FOR NEW TESTAMENT STUDIES.** Text in English. 2010. irreg. **Document type:** *Journal, Academic/Scholarly.*
Media: Online - full text.
Indexed: A01.
Published by: Dansk Bibel Institut/Copenhagen Lutheran School of Theology, Frederiksborggade 1 B 1, Copenhagen K, 1360, Denmark. TEL 45-33-135500, FAX 45-33-136989, dbi@dbi.edu, http://www.dbi.edu. Ed. Nicolai Techow.

221 NOR ISSN 0901-8328
SCANDINAVIAN JOURNAL OF THE OLD TESTAMENT. Text in Norwegian. s-a. GBP 106 combined subscription in United Kingdom to institutions (print & online eds.); EUR 141, USD 177 combined subscription to institutions (print & online eds.) (effective 2012). reprint service avail. from PSC. **Document type:** *Journal, Academic/Scholarly.* **Description:** Devoted to international Old Testament scholarship, with particular emphasis on Scandinavian scholarship.
Related titles: Online - full text ed.: ISSN 1502-7244. 2000. GBP 96 in United Kingdom to institutions; EUR 127, USD 159 to institutions (effective 2012) (from IngentaConnect).
Indexed: A01, A02, A03, A08, A20, A21, A22, ArtHuCI, CA, E01, IZBG, OTA, P48, P53, P54, PQC, R&TA, RI-1, RI-2, SCOPUS, T02, W07.
—BLDSC (8087.517700), IE, Infotrieve, Ingenta. **CCC.**
Published by: Taylor & Francis A S (Subsidiary of: Taylor & Francis Group), Biskop Gunnerusgate 14A, PO Box 12 Posthuset, Oslo, 0051, Norway. TEL 47-23-103460, FAX 47-23-103461, journals@tandf.no. Ed. Niels Peter Lemche. **Subscr. to:** Taylor & Francis Ltd., Journals Customer Service, Sheepen Pl, Colchester, Essex CO3 3LP, United Kingdom. TEL 44-20-70175544, FAX 44-20-70175198, tf.enquiries@tfinforma.com.

207.2 CAN ISSN 0700-6802
SCARBORO MISSIONS. Text in English. 1919. 7/yr. CAD 8 (effective 2000). adv. bk.rev. back issues avail. **Description:** Presents a global vision of faith; one which promotes within the Canadian church a dialogue and understanding of the faiths, cultures and struggles of the people among whom missionaries work.
Published by: Scarboro Foreign Mission Society, 2685 Kingston Rd, Scarborough, ON M1M 1M4, Canada. TEL 416-261-7135, sfms@scarboromissions.caweb.net. Ed., R&P Rev. Gerald Curry. Circ: 17,000.

220 NLD ISSN 1879-9078
▼ **DE SCHEURBIJBEL.** Text in Dutch. 2009. a. EUR 14.95 (effective 2010).
Published by: Uitgeverij Van Gennep, Nieuwezijds Voorburgwal 330, Amsterdam, 1012 RW, Netherlands. TEL 31-20-6247033, FAX 31-20-6247035, info@vangennep-boeken.nl, http://www.vangennep-boeken.nl. Pub. Chris ten Kate.

SCHLANGENBRUT; Streitschrift fuer feministisch und religioes interessierte Frauen. *see* WOMEN'S STUDIES

200 100 DEU ISSN 1861-6038
SCHLEIERMACHER-ARCHIV. Text in German. 1985. irreg., latest vol.24, 2011. price varies. **Document type:** *Monographic series, Academic/Scholarly.*
Published by: Walter de Gruyter GmbH & Co. KG, Genthiner Str 13, Berlin, 10785, Germany. TEL 49-30-260050, FAX 49-30-26005251, info@degruyter.com, http://www.degruyter.de.

200 USA
SCHLEIERMACHER STUDIES AND TRANSLATIONS. Text in English. 1990. irreg., latest vol.26, 2009. price varies. back issues avail. **Document type:** *Monographic series, Academic/Scholarly.*
Published by: Edwin Mellen Press, 415 Ridge St, PO Box 450, Lewiston, NY 14092. TEL 716-754-2266, FAX 716-754-4056, cservice@mellenpress.com.

SCHOLARS' CHOICE; significant current theological literature from abroad. *see* RELIGIONS AND THEOLOGY—Abstracting, Bibliographies, Statistics

230 DEU
▼ **SCHRIFTEN DER PHILOSOPHISCH-THEOLOGISCHE HOCHSCHULE ST. POELTEN.** Text in German. 2010. irreg. price varies. **Document type:** *Monographic series, Academic/Scholarly.*
Published by: (Philosophisch-Theologische Hochschule der Dioezese St. Poelten AUT), Verlag Friedrich Pustet, Gutenbergstr 8, Regensburg, 93051, Germany. TEL 49-941-920220, FAX 49-941-92022330, verlag@pustet.de, http://www.pustetverlag.de.

200 CHE
SCHRIFTEN OEKUMENISCHES INSTITUT LUZERN. Text in German. 2004. irreg., latest vol.8, 2009. price varies. **Document type:** *Monographic series, Academic/Scholarly.*
Published by: (Universitaet Luzern, Oekumenisches Institut Luzern), Theologischer Verlag Zurich, Badenerstr 73, Zurich, 8026, Switzerland. TEL 41-44-2993355, FAX 41-44-2993358, tvz@ref.ch.

SCHRIFTEN ZUM STAATSKIRCHENRECHT. *see* LAW

291 DEU ISSN 1610-6954
SCHRIFTEN ZUR PRAKTISCHEN THEOLOGIE. Text in German. 2002. irreg., latest vol.11, 2009. price varies. **Document type:** *Monographic series, Academic/Scholarly.*
Published by: Verlag Dr. Kovac, Leverkusenstr 13, Hamburg, 22761, Germany. TEL 49-40-3988800, FAX 49-40-39888055, info@verlagdrkovac.de.

200 DEU ISSN 0944-0542
SCHRIFTENREIHE ZUR RELIGIOESEN KULTUR. Text in German. 1993. irreg., latest vol.7, 2006. price varies. **Document type:** *Monographic series, Academic/Scholarly.*
Published by: Ardey-Verlag GmbH, An den Speichern 6, Muenster, 48157, Germany. TEL 49-251-41320, FAX 49-251-413220, grabowsky@ardey-verlag.de.

THE SCHWARZ REPORT. *see* POLITICAL SCIENCE

209 CHE ISSN 1661-3880
SCHWEIZERISCHE ZEITSCHRIFT FUER RELIGIONS- UND KULTURGESCHICHTE/REVUE D'HISTOIRE ECCLESIASTIQUE SUISSE. Text in French, German. 1907. a. CHF 70, EUR 45 (effective 2011). bk.rev. bibl. reprints avail. **Document type:** *Journal, Academic/Scholarly.*
Formerly (until 2004): Zeitschrift fuer Schweizerische Kirchengeschichte (0044-3484)
Related titles: Microfiche ed.: (from IDC).
Indexed: CERDIC, DIP, FR, IBR, IBZ, MLA-IB.
—INIST.
Published by: (Vereinigung fuer Schweizerische Kirchengeschichte), Editions Saint-Paul Fribourg, Perolles 42, Fribourg, 1700, Switzerland. TEL 41-26-4264331, FAX 41-26-4264330, info@paulusedition.ch, http://www.paulusedition.ch.

215 GBR ISSN 0954-4194
AS122
SCIENCE AND CHRISTIAN BELIEF. Text in English. 1866. s-a. USD 50.20 to individuals (print or online ed.); USD 100.40 to institutions (print or online ed.); USD 60.20 combined subscription to individuals (print & online eds.); USD 120.50 combined subscription to institutions (print & online eds.) (effective 2010). bk.rev. bibl. index, cum.index every 5 yrs. **Document type:** *Journal, Academic/Scholarly.* **Description:** Provides information about Christian religional belief.
Formed by the merger of (1985-1989): Science and Faith (0268-2885); (1958-1989): Faith and Thought. Victoria Institute. Journal (0014-7028); Which was formerly (until 1958): Victoria Institute or Philosophical Society of Great Britain. Journal of the Transactions
Related titles: Online - full text ed.
Indexed: A01, A03, A08, A21, CA, CERDIC, FR, P30, R&TA, RI-1, RI-2, T02.
—BLDSC (8131.830000), IE, Ingenta. **CCC.**
Published by: The Paternoster Press, c/o Aplhagraphics, 6 Angel Row, Nottingham, NG1 6HL, United Kingdom. TEL 44-115-8523614, FAX 44-115-8523601, periodicals@alphagraphics.co.uk, http://www.paternosterperiodicals.com.

SCIENCE ET ESPRIT. *see* PHILOSOPHY

SCIENCE OF RELIGION; abstracts and index of recent articles. *see* RELIGIONS AND THEOLOGY—Abstracting, Bibliographies, Statistics

202.2 ZAF ISSN 0036-8466
SCIENCE OF THE SOUL. Text in English. 1963. q. ZAR 28, USD 24 (effective 1999). adv. bk.rev. back issues avail. **Description:** Concerns the practice of meditation taught by a living meditation master.
Published by: Radha Soami Satsang Beas, PO Box 41355, Craighall, Gauteng 2024, South Africa. TEL 27-11-7889152, FAX 27-11-7889152. R&P Matthew Seal. Circ: 3,000 (paid).

291 FRA ISSN 1621-3440
SCIENCES DES RELIGIONS (PARIS). Text in French. 2000. irreg. back issues avail. **Document type:** *Monographic series, Consumer.*
Published by: (Ecole Pratique des Hautes Etudes, Section des Sciences Religieuses), Editions Albin Michel, 22 rue Huyghens, Paris, 75014, France. TEL 33-1-42791000, FAX 33-1-43272158, http://www.albin-michel.fr.

200 FRA ISSN 1778-4913
SCIENCES DES RELIGIONS (RENNES). Text in French. 2005. irreg., latest 2007. price varies. **Document type:** *Monographic series, Academic/Scholarly.*
Published by: Presses Universitaires de Rennes, Campus de la Harpe, 2 Rue du Doyen Denis-Leroy, Rennes, Cedex 35044, France. TEL 33-2-99141401, FAX 33-2-99141407, pur@uhb.fr.

SCIENTIA ET RELIGIO. *see* PHILOSOPHY

▼ **SCIENTIFIC GOD JOURNAL.** *see* SCIENCES: COMPREHENSIVE WORKS

274 GBR ISSN 0264-5572
➤ **SCOTTISH CHURCH HISTORY SOCIETY. RECORDS.** Text in English. 1923. a. GBP 15, USD 32 (effective 2010). bk.rev. bibl. index. back issues avail. **Document type:** *Monographic series, Academic/Scholarly.* **Description:** Provides papers on history of church in Scotland including links abroad.
Indexed: PCI.
—BLDSC (7325.120000), IE, Ingenta.
Published by: Scottish Church History Society, c/o Miss Virginia Russell, Hon, Secretary, 16 Murrayburn Park, Edinburgh, EH14 2PX, United Kingdom. TEL 44-131-4423772, virginia.russell@btopenworld.com, http://www.schs.org.uk/. Ed. James Kirk. Circ: 280.

207.2 GBR ISSN 0048-9778
BV2100
SCOTTISH INSTITUTE OF MISSIONARY STUDIES BULLETIN. Text in English. 1967. s-a. GBP 2, USD 5. bk.rev. reprints avail.
Media: Duplicated (not offset). **Related titles:** Microform ed.: (from PQC).
Indexed: CERDIC, RASB.
Published by: Scottish Institute of Missionary Studies, Department of Religious Studies, University of Aberdeen, King's College, Aberdeen, Aberdeenshire AB9 2UB, United Kingdom. Ed. A F Walls. Circ: 500.

230 GBR ISSN 0036-9306
BR1
➤ **SCOTTISH JOURNAL OF THEOLOGY.** Text in English. 1948. q. GBP 129, USD 236 to institutions; GBP 134, USD 243 combined subscription to institutions (print & online eds.) (effective 2012). adv. bk.rev. illus. index. back issues avail.; reprint service avail. from PSC. **Document type:** *Journal, Academic/Scholarly.* **Description:** Publishes contributions of major theological and philosophical interest from the world's leading scholars. Includes articles on biblical and applied theology intended to help the preacher and teacher.
Related titles: Online - full text ed.: ISSN 1475-3065. GBP 125, USD 226 to institutions (effective 2012).
Indexed: A20, A21, A22, A26, ASCA, AmHI, ArtHuCI, B04, BRD, CA, CERDIC, CurCont, E01, E08, FR, G08, H07, H08, H14, HAb, HumInd, I05, IZBG, MLA-IB, OTA, P02, P10, P28, P48, P53, P54, PCI, PQC, Philind, R&TA, R05, RI-1, RI-2, RILM, S09, SCOPUS, T02, W03, W07.
—BLDSC (8210.630000), IE, Infotrieve, Ingenta, INIST. **CCC.**
Published by: Cambridge University Press, The Edinburgh Bldg, Shaftesbury Rd, Cambridge, CB2 8RU, United Kingdom. TEL 44-1223-312393, FAX 44-1223-315052, journals@cambridge.org, http://www.cambridge.org/uk. Eds. Bryan Spinks, Ian Torrance. Adv. contact Rebecca Roberts TEL 44-1223-325083. page GBP 460, page USD 875. Circ: 1,200. **Subscr. to:** Cambridge University Press, 32 Ave of the Americas, New York, NY 10013. TEL 212-337-5000, FAX 212-691-3239, journals_subscriptions@cup.org.

➤ **SCRIPTA HUMANISTICA.** *see* HISTORY—History Of Europe

200 FIN ISSN 0582-3226
SCRIPTA INSTITUTI DONNERIANI ABOENSIS. Text in English, French, German. 1967. triennial. EUR 28 (effective 2003). back issues avail.; reprints avail. **Document type:** *Monographic series, Academic/Scholarly.* **Description:** Deals with history of religions, comparative religion, phenomenology of religion.
Related titles: Online - full text ed.
Published by: Donner Institute for Research in Religious and Cultural History, Steiner Memorial Library, PO Box 70, Aabo, 20501, Finland. TEL 358-2-2154315, FAX 358-2-2311290, donner.institute@abo.fi, http://web.abo.fi/instut/di. Ed. Tore Ahlbaeck. Circ: 376. **Dist. by:** Almqvist & Wiksell International.

200 ESP ISSN 0036-9764
BR7
➤ **SCRIPTA THEOLOGICA.** Text in Spanish. 1969. 3/yr. EUR 48 in Europe; EUR 75 elsewhere (effective 2009). bk.rev. **Document type:** *Journal, Academic/Scholarly.*
Related titles: Online - full text ed.

Indexed: A01, A21, A26, CA, DIP, F03, F04, FR, I04, I05, IBR, IBZ, OTA, R&TA, RI-1, RI-2, T02.
—INIST. **CCC.**
Published by: (Universidad de Navarra, Facultad de Teología), Universidad de Navarra, Servicio de Publicaciones, Campus Universitario, Pamplona, 31009, Spain. http://www.unav.es/publicaciones/. Ed. Lucas F Mateo-Seco.

268 USA ISSN 1520-4308
SCRIPTURE STUDIES. Text in English. 1994. 10/yr. **Document type:** *Newsletter.* **Description:** Dedicated to the study and exposition of the Bible.
Related titles: Online - full text ed.
Published by: Scripture Studies Inc., 20010 Via Natalie., Yorba Linda, CA 92887-3152. Ed., R&P Scott Sperling TEL 949-581-4844.

220 ITA ISSN 1824-6559
LA SCRITTURA E L'INTERPRETAZIONE. Text in Italian. 1991. irreg. price varies. **Document type:** *Monographic series, Academic/Scholarly.*
Published by: G.B. Palumbo & C. Editore SpA, Via Ricasoli 59, Palermo, 90139, Italy. TEL 39-091-588850, FAX 39-091-6111848, http://www.palumboeditore.it.

200 028.5 ITA ISSN 0036-9950
SE VUOI. Text in Italian. 1960. bi-m. EUR 18 domestic; EUR 26 in Europe (effective 2009). bk.rev. **Document type:** *Magazine, Consumer.* **Description:** Magazine for young people in search of God and the vocation.
Published by: Istituto Regina degli Apostoli, Via Mole, 3, Castel Gandolfo, RM 00040, Italy. TEL 39-06-932-0356, FAX 39-06-936-0700, apsevuoi@tiscalinet.it. Circ: 9,000.

215 USA ISSN 1943-1848
BL240.2
SEARCH (WASHINGTON DC); science, religion, culture. Text in English. 1990. bi-m. adv. back issues avail. **Document type:** *Magazine, Consumer.* **Description:** Explores life's complexities by encouraging a robust, reflective, integrated conversation about how science affects the human spirit.
Former titles (until 2008): Science & Spirit (1086-9808); (until 1995): Science & Religion News (1048-8642)
Related titles: Online - full text ed.: ISSN 1943-1856.
Indexed: A01, A03, A08, A26, CA, GSS&RPL, I05, P28, P48, P53, P54, PQC, T02.
—CCC.
Published by: Heldref Publications, c/o Taylor & Francis, 325 Chestnut St, Ste 800, Philadelphia, PA 19106. TEL 215-625-8900, heldref@subscriptionoffice.com, http://www.heldref.org. Ed. Peter Manseau. **Subscr. to:** PO Box 830350, Birmingham, AL 35283. TEL 866-802-7059, FAX 205-995-1588.

220 NGA ISSN 0795-8994
SEARCH THE SCRIPTURES. Text in English. 2005. irreg.
Published by: Deeper Christian Life Ministry, PO Box 59, University of Lagos Post Office, Lagos, Nigeria. TEL 234-1-3110000, FAX 234-1-3113113, info@deeperlifeonline.org, http://www.dclm.org.

211.6 USA ISSN 1063-2611
BL2700
SECULAR HUMANIST BULLETIN. Text in English. 1984. q. USD 20 (effective 1999). **Document type:** *Newsletter.* **Description:** Promotes the philosophy of Secular Humanism while critically examining supernatural claims. Contains news, opinions and items of humor.
Related titles: Microform ed.: (from PQC); ◆ Supplement to: Free Inquiry. ISSN 0272-0701.
Indexed: RASB.
Published by: CODESH, Inc., PO Box 664, Amherst, NY 14226. TEL 716-636-7571, FAX 716-636-1733. Ed., R&P Matt Cherry. Circ: 5,000.

221 DNK ISSN 1603-6565
➤ **SEE-J. HIPHIL OLD TESTAMENT.** (Scandinavian Evangelical E-Journal. Hebrew Bible Theory, Interpretation, Poetics, History, Interacti) Variant title: H I P H I L Old Testament. Text in English. 2004. a. back issues avail. **Document type:** *Journal, Academic/Scholarly.* **Description:** Old Testament Hebrew bible theology, interpretation, poetics, history, interactivity, and linguistics with particular emphasis on bridging the gap between the ancient authors and modern readers.
Media: Online - full content.
Published by: Dansk Bibel Institut/Copenhagen Lutheran School of Theology, Frederiksborggade 1 B 1, Copenhagen K, 1360, Denmark. TEL 45-33-135500, FAX 45-33-136989, dbi@dbi.edu, http://www.dbi.edu. Ed. Jens Bruun Kofoed.

268 296.68 USA
SEEK; the abundant life. Text in English. 1970. w. USD 16.99 per issue (effective 2009). back issues avail. **Document type:** *Magazine, Consumer.* **Description:** Features articles and stories related to each week's lesson, questions that help students apply the lesson to their lives, daily bible readings and lesson Scripture.
Published by: Standard Publishing, 8805 Governor's Hill Dr, Ste 400, Cincinnati, OH 45249. TEL 513-931-4050, 800-543-1353, FAX 877-867-5751, customerservice@standardpub.com, http://www.standardpub.com. Ed. Garry Allen. Pub., R&P Mark A Taylor. Circ: 72,000.

201 ITA ISSN 0394-364X
SEGNI DEI TEMPI; rivista trimestrale per un cristianesimo migliore. Text in Italian. 1921. q. EUR 9 (effective 2009). index. **Document type:** *Magazine, Consumer.*
Published by: Edizioni A D V, Via Chiantigiana, 30, Falciani, Impruneta, FI 50023, Italy. TEL 39-055-2326291, FAX 39-055-2326241, info@edizioniadv.it, http://www.edizioniadv.it. Circ: 12,000.

200 FRA ISSN 2105-6323
LE SEIGNEUR EST PROCHE. Text in French. 200?. a. **Document type:** *Consumer.*
Published by: Bibles et Publications Chretiennes, 30 Rue Chateauvert, BP 335, Valence, 26003, France. TEL 33-4-75781275, FAX 33-4-75428155, info@bpcbs.com, http://www.bpcbs.com.

230 ESP ISSN 0037-119X
SELECCIONES DE TEOLOGIA. Text in Spanish. 1962. q. EUR 28 domestic; USD 34 foreign (effective 2009). adv. index. **Document type:** *Monographic series, Academic/Scholarly.*
Related titles: Print ed.
Indexed: CERDIC.
Published by: Instituto de Teologia Fundamental, Facultad de Teologia de Catalunya, Roger de Lluria, 13, Barcelona, 08010, Spain. TEL 34-93-3172338, FAX 34-93-3171094. Ed. Josep Gimenez. Circ: 4,500.

200 NLD ISSN 1567-200X
BS410
➤ **SEMEIA STUDIES.** Text in English, Greek, Hebrew. 1974. irreg., latest vol.64, 2008. price varies. bk.rev. bibl.; charts; illus. cum.index. 200 p./no.; back issues avail.; reprints avail. **Document type:** *Monographic series, Academic/Scholarly.* **Description:** Formely published as a journal, this book series presents academic papers on biblical criticism.
Formerly (until Jun. 2003): Semeia (0095-571X)
Related titles: Microfiche ed.; Online - full content ed.: free to members (effective 2002); Online - full text ed.
Indexed: A01, A03, A08, A20, A21, A22, A26, ASCA, AmHI, CA, CERDIC, E08, G08, H07, I05, IZBG, MLA-IB, OTA, P28, P48, P53, P54, PCI, PQC, R05, RI-1, RI-2, S09, SCOPUS.
—IE, Ingenta. **CCC.**
Published by: (Society of Biblical Literature USA), Brill, PO Box 9000, Leiden, 2300 PA, Netherlands. TEL 31-71-5353500, FAX 31-71-5317532, cs@brill.nl.

200 DNK ISSN 1398-7763
SEMIKOLON; undervisningsnoter o.l. fra menighedsfakultetet. Text in Danish. 1999. irreg., latest vol.6, 2007. price varies. back issues avail. **Document type:** *Monographic series, Academic/Scholarly.*
Published by: (Menighedsfakultetet/Lutheran School of Theology in Aarhus), Forlagsgruppen Lohse, Korskaervej 25, Fredericia, 7000, Denmark. TEL 45-75-934455, FAX 45-75-924275, info@lohse, http://www.lohse.dk.

220 410 FRA ISSN 0154-6902
BS410
➤ **SEMIOTIQUE ET BIBLE.** Text in French. 1975. q. adv. bk.rev. **Document type:** *Journal, Academic/Scholarly.*
Indexed: CERDIC, FR.
—INIST. **CCC.**
Published by: Centre pour l'Analyse du Discours Religieux, 25 rue du Plat, Lyon, Cedex 2 69288, France. TEL 33-4-72325030, FAX 33-4-72325151, http://www.univ-catholyon.fr.

220 NLD ISSN 1044-6761
SEPTUAGINT AND COGNATE STUDIES SERIES. Text in English. irreg., latest vol.54, 2006. price varies. **Document type:** *Monographic series.*
Formerly: Septuagint and Cognate Studies (0145-2754)
Indexed: IZBG.
Published by: (Society of Biblical Literature USA), Brill, PO Box 9000, Leiden, 2300 PA, Netherlands. TEL 31-71-5353500, FAX 31-71-5317532, cs@brill.nl.

220 NLD ISSN 1572-3755
SEPTUAGINT COMMENTARY SERIES. Text in English. 2005. irreg., latest vol.5, 2008. price varies. **Document type:** *Monographic series.*
Indexed: IZBG.
Published by: Brill, PO Box 9000, Leiden, 2300 PA, Netherlands. TEL 31-71-5353500, FAX 31-71-5317532, cs@brill.nl.

252 USA ISSN 1937-1446
SERMONS ON THE FIRST READINGS. Text in English. 2002. a. price varies. back issues avail. **Document type:** *Monographic series, Consumer.* **Description:** Features sermons for each Sunday and major celebration throughout the church year.
Related titles: Online - full text ed.
Published by: C S S Publishing Co., 517 S Main St, Lima, OH 45804. TEL 419-227-1818, 800-241-4056, FAX 419-228-9184, info@csspub.com, http://www.csspub.com. Pub. Wesley T Runk.

252 USA ISSN 1937-1330
SERMONS ON THE GOSPEL READINGS. Text in English. 2002. a. price varies. back issues avail. **Document type:** *Monographic series, Consumer.* **Description:** Provides a treasure trove of creative homiletic ideas and practical, scripture-based wisdom in messages based on Gospel texts from Cycle C of the Revised Common Lectionary.
Related titles: Online - full text ed.
Published by: C S S Publishing Co., 517 S Main St, Lima, OH 45804. TEL 419-227-1818, 800-241-4056, FAX 419-228-9184, info@csspub.com, http://www.csspub.com. Pub. Wesley T Runk.

252 USA ISSN 1937-1454
SERMONS ON THE SECOND READINGS. Text in English. 2002. a. price varies. back issues avail. **Document type:** *Monographic series, Consumer.* **Description:** Designed to be an extensive anthology of enlightening sermons based on the Second Readings from Cycle C of the Revised Common Lectionary.
Related titles: Online - full text ed.
Published by: C S S Publishing Co., 517 S Main St, Lima, OH 45804. TEL 800-241-4056, FAX 419-228-9184, info@csspub.com, http://www.csspub.com.

230 ARG ISSN 0326-6702
SERVICIO DE INFORMACIONES RELIGIOSAS. Text in Spanish. 1977. m. **Document type:** *Bulletin, Academic/Scholarly.*
Indexed: A21, RI-1, RILM.
Published by: Instituto Superior Evangelico de Estudios Teologicos, Camacua, 252, Buenos Aires, 1406, Argentina. TEL 54-11-46310224, info@isedet.edu.ar, http://www.isedet.edu.ar/.

200 ITA ISSN 0037-2773
SERVIZIO DELLA PAROLA. Text in Italian. 1968. 10/yr. EUR 40.50 domestic; EUR 71 in Europe; EUR 91 elsewhere (effective 2009). **Document type:** *Magazine, Consumer.*
Published by: Editrice Queriniana, Via Enrico Ferri 75, Brescia, BS 25123, Italy. TEL 39-030-2306925, FAX 39-030-2306932, redazione@queriniana.it, http://www.queriniana.it. Ed. Chino Biscontin.

260 FIN ISSN 1797-4119
SETLEMENTTI; liike on ihmisen muotoinen. Text in Finnish. 1928. q. EUR 30 (effective 2008). **Document type:** *Magazine, Consumer.*
Formerly (until 2008): Yhdysside (0357-3184)
Published by: Suomen Setlementtiliitto ry/Finnish Federation of Settlements, Lantinen Brahenkatu 2, Helsinki, 00510, Finland. TEL 358-10-8375500, FAX 358-9-2722012, http://www.setlementtiliitto.fi.

260 FIN ISSN 1456-2936
SETLEMENTTIJULKAISUJA/SETTLEMENT PUBLICATIONS. Text mainly in Finnish; Text occasionally in English. 1998. irreg. **Document type:** *Monographic series, Consumer.*
Published by: Suomen Setlementtiliitto ry/Finnish Federation of Settlements, Lantinen Brahenkatu 2, Helsinki, 00510, Finland. TEL 358-10-8375500, FAX 358-9-2722012.

200 ITA ISSN 1590-4601
SETTE E RELIGIONI. Text in Italian. 1991. q. back issues avail. **Document type:** *Monographic series, Academic/Scholarly.*
Published by: Edizioni Studio Domenicano, Via dell' Osservanza 72, Bologna, BO 40136, Italy. TEL 39-051-582034, FAX 39-051-331583, esd@alinet.it, http://www.esd-domenicani.it.

SHAMAN; journal of the International Society for Shamanistic Research. *see* ALTERNATIVE MEDICINE

SHAMBHALA SUN; buddhism culture meditation life. *see* RELIGIONS AND THEOLOGY—Buddhist

200 HKG ISSN 1812-366X
SHANDAO QIKAN/HILL ROAD. Text in Chinese. s-a. HKD 50 newsstand/cover (effective 2006). **Document type:** *Journal, Academic/Scholarly.*
Indexed: A21, RI-1.
Published by: Xianggang Jinxinhui Shenxueyuan/Hong Kong Baptist Theological Seminary, 1, Nin Ming Rd., Sai O, Sai Kung (North), New Territories, Hong Kong. TEL 852-27159511, FAX 852-27610868, inquiry@hkbts.edu.hk.

207.2 GBR ISSN 1367-6741
SHARE (BIRMINGHAM). Text in English. 1963. q. bk.rev.; video rev. 16 p./no. 4 cols./p.; back issues avail. **Document type:** *Magazine, Consumer.* **Description:** Designed for the members of the South American Mission Society.
Formerly (until 1975): Sent (0037-2269)
Related titles: Online - full text ed.: free (effective 2009); Supplement(s): Partners' News.
Indexed: CERDIC.
Published by: South American Mission Society, Allen Gardiner Cottage, Pembury Rd, Tunbridge Wells, Kent, TN2 3QU, United Kingdom. TEL 44-1892-538647, FAX 44-1892-525797, finsec@samsgb.org. Ed. Robert Lunt.

200 USA ISSN 0193-8274
BV4000
SHARING THE PRACTICE. Text in English. 1971. q. USD 7.50 newsstand/cover to non-members; free to members (effective 2010). adv. bk.rev. back issues avail. **Document type:** *Journal, Academic/Scholarly.* **Description:** For members of the clergy to share their interests and experiences.
Incorporates (1976-1978): Academy of Parish Clergy. News and Views (0361-2406); Which was formerly (until 1976): Academy of Parish Clergy. Journal (0044-5835)
Related titles: Microform ed.: 1978 (from PQC).
Indexed: A22, CCR.
Published by: Academy of Parish Clergy, Inc., 2249 Florinda St, Sarasota, FL 34231. pjbinder2@juno.com, http://www.apclergy.org. Ed. Dr. Robert Cornwall. Circ: 350.

230 808.81 USA ISSN 0745-1245
SHARING THE VICTORY. Text in English. 1982. m. USD 19.95 domestic; USD 36 foreign (effective 2007). adv. bk.rev. back issues avail. **Document type:** *Magazine, Consumer.* **Description:** Christian publication aimed at individuals involved in athletics at any level.
Formerly (until 1982): Christian Athlete (0744-0227)
Published by: Fellowship of Christian Athletes, 8701 Leeds Rd, Kansas City, MO 64129. TEL 800-289-0909, FAX 816-921-8755, http://www.fca.org. Ed. Jill Ewert. Pub. Les Steckel. Adv. contact Jocelyn Godfrey. Circ: 60,000 (paid).

200 CHN ISSN 1007-6255
SHIJIE ZONGJIAO WENHUA/WORLD RELIGIOUS CULTURE. Variant title: Religious Cultures in the World. Text in Chinese. 1980. q. USD 12 (effective 2009). **Document type:** *Journal, Academic/Scholarly.*
Formerly (until 1994): Shijie Zongjiao Ziliao (1000-4505)
Related titles: Online - full text ed.
—East View.
Published by: Zhongguo Shehui Kexueyuan, Shijie Zhongjiao Yanjiusuo/Chinese Academy of Social Sciences, Institution of World Religions, 5, Jiangnei Dajie, Beijing, 100732, China. TEL 86-10-65137744 ext 5486. **Dist. by:** China International Book Trading Corp, 35 Chegongzhuang Xilu, Haidian District, PO Box 399, Beijing 100044, China. TEL 86-10-68412045, FAX 86-10-68412023, cibtc@mail.cibtc.com.cn, http://www.cibtc.com.cn.

200 TWN ISSN 1728-645X
SHIJIE ZONGJIAO XUEKAN/JOURNAL OF WORLD RELIGIONS. Text in Chinese. 2003. s-a. **Document type:** *Journal, Academic/Scholarly.*
Related titles: Online - full text ed.
Published by: Nanhua Daxue, Zongjiaoxue Yanjiuso/Nanhua University, Graduate Institute of Religious Studies, 32, Chung Keng Li, Dalin, Chiayi 62248, Taiwan. TEL 886-5-2721001 ext 2161, ijhsieh@mail.nhu.edu.tw, http://www.nhu.edu.tw/~compare/.

200 CHN ISSN 1000-4289
BL9.C4
SHIJIE ZONGJIAO YANJIU/STUDIES ON WORLD RELIGION. Text in Chinese. 1979. q. USD 20.80 (effective 2009). **Document type:** *Journal, Academic/Scholarly.*
Related titles: Online - full text ed.
Indexed: RILM.
—East View.
Published by: Zhongguo Shehui Kexueyuan, Zhexue Yanjiusuo/Chinese Academy of Social Sciences, Institute of Philosophy, 5 Jianguomennei Dajie, Beijing, 10000732, China. TEL 86-10-65138393. **Dist. by:** China International Book Trading Corp, 35 Chegongzhuang Xilu, Haidian District, PO Box 399, Beijing 100044, China. TEL 86-10-68412045, FAX 86-10-68412023, cibtc@mail.cibtc.com.cn, http://www.cibtc.com.cn.

SHINE; fashion - style - excellence - hope. *see* WOMEN'S INTERESTS

200 919.306 PER ISSN 0254-2021
F3429
SHUPIHUI. Text in Spanish. 1976. q. USD 18. bk.rev.
Indexed: IBR, IBZ.

R

Published by: Centro de Estudios Teologicos de la Amazonia, Putmayo, 355, Iquitos, Peru. TEL 233552, FAX 23-31-90. Ed. Joaquin Garcia Sanchez. Circ: 1,000.

242 NOR ISSN 0809-5027
SIESTA. Text in Norwegian. 1967. q. **Document type:** *Magazine, Trade.*
Formerly (until 1995): Tenningsnokkelen (0800-0409)
Published by: Bibelleseringen i Norge, Postboks 9285, Oslo, 0134, Norway. TEL 47-22-992969, kontor@bibelleseringen.no, http://www.bibelleseringen.no.

268 USA ISSN 1944-6330
SIGNIFICANT LIVING; celebrating life & faith - midlife & beyond. Abbreviated title: S L. Text in English. 2007. bi-m. USD 19.95 (effective 2009). adv. **Document type:** *Magazine, Consumer.* **Description:** Designed to help adults approaching midlife and beyond discover a life of significance from a faith based perspective.
Published by: Total Living International, 2880 Vision Ct, Aurora, IL 60506. TEL 800-443-0227. Ed. Peg Short TEL 630-801-3692. Adv. contacts Dathel Grosshart TEL 623-979-5482, Pam Barnett TEL 231-386-1186. color page USD 2,537, B&W page USD 2,233; bleed 8.25 x 11.

200 PER ISSN 1022-789X
SIGNOS; para los nuevos tiempos. Text in Spanish. 1980. s-m. USD 50 in Latin America; USD 94 elsewhere (effective 2001). **Document type:** *Newsletter.*
Published by: Centro de Estudios y Publicaciones, Camilo Carrillo 479, Jesus Maria, Apdo Postal 11 0107, Lima, 11, Peru. TEL 51-14-4336453, FAX 51-14-4331078, cepu@amauta.rcp.net.pe, http://www.cep.com.pe. Ed. Rosa Alayza. **Co-sponsor:** Instituto Bartolome de Las Casas - Rimac.

SIGNS. *see* MUSIC

200 GBR
SIGNS OF THE TIMES. Text in English. 19??. q. free to members (effective 2009). back issues avail. **Document type:** *Magazine, Trade.* **Description:** Contains articles about the different issues that impact on the church, society and culture.
Published by: Modern Churchpeople's Union, 9 Westward View, Liverpool, L17 7EE, United Kingdom. TEL 44-845-3451909, office@modchurchunion.org. Ed. Anthony Woollard.

220 JPN ISSN 0037-5055
SIGNS OF THE TIMES. Text in Japanese. 1899. m. JPY 5,980, USD 58 (effective 2001). adv. **Document type:** *Trade.* **Description:** Contains Bible stories and discusses health, education and family issues.
Published by: (Seventh-day Adventist Church USA), Fukuinsha, 1966 Kami-Kawai-cho, Asahi-ku, Yokohama-shi, Kanagawa-ken 241-0802, Japan. TEL 81-45-921-1414, FAX 81-45-921-4349. Ed., Pub., R&P, Adv. contact Tetsuya Yamamoto. Circ: 40,000.

294.6 IND ISSN 0037-5128
BL2017
➤ **THE SIKH REVIEW.** Text in English. 1953. m. INR 250 domestic; USD 40 in US & Canada; GBP 20 in Europe; INR 25 newsstand/cover (effective 2011). adv. bk.rev. abstr. **Document type:** *Journal, Academic/Scholarly.* **Description:** A theological and socio-cultural journal of Sikhism in global setting.
Indexed: BAS, RASB.
Published by: Sikh Cultural Centre, 116 Karnani Mansion, 25 A Park St, Kolkata, West Bengal 700 016, India. TEL 91-33-2299656, FAX 91-33-4757092, sikhreview@vsnl.com. Ed. Saran Singh. Pub., Adv. contact Narinder Pal Singh. Circ: 5,000.

➤ **SINO-WESTERN CULTURAL RELATIONS JOURNAL.** *see* HISTORY

200 ZAF
SKOTAVILLE BLACK THEOLOGY SERIES. Text in English. irreg., latest vol.6. **Document type:** *Monographic series.*
Published by: Skotaville Publishers, PO Box 32483, Braamfontein, Johannesburg 2017, South Africa. **Dist. outside Africa by:** African Books Collective Ltd., The Jam Factory, 27 Park End St, Oxford, Oxon OX1 1HU, United Kingdom. TEL 0865-726686, FAX 0865-793298.

201.7 AUS
SKYWAVES. Text in English. 19??. bi-m. free (effective 2009). back issues avail. **Document type:** *Magazine, Consumer.* **Description:** Provides information about the founding and development of FEBC.
Published by: Far East Broadcasting Co., PO Box 183, Caringbah, NSW 1495, Australia. TEL 61-2-95256460, 300-720-017, FAX 61-2-95261250, febcoz@tpg.com.au. Circ: 8,500.

261 BLR
SLOVO; Khristianskaya gazeta. Text in Russian. d. adv.
Published by: Pramen Nazdei, Ul Pushkina 41, Minsk, 220082, Belarus. TEL 375-172-553821, 375-172-531924, FAX 375-172-535241. Eds. Elena Azarina, Ruslan Klyuchnik.

260 HRV ISSN 0037-7074
SLUZBA BOZJA; liturgijsko-pastoralna revija. Text in Croatian. 1961. q. USD 20. adv. bk.rev. index.
Published by: Franjevacka Visoka Bogoslovija Makarska/Franciscan High School for Theology at Makarska, Zrtava Fasizma 1, Makarska, 58300, Croatia. TEL 059 612-259. Ed. Marko Babic. Circ: 1,400.

220 028.5 GBR ISSN 1463-5550
SNAPSHOTS; Bible reading for children. Text in English. 1999. q. GBP 11; GBP 3 per issue (effective 2010). bk.rev. charts; illus.; maps. back issues avail. **Document type:** *Magazine, Consumer.* **Description:** Covers Bible reading for children 8 to 10 years old.
Related titles: Online - full text ed.
—CCC.
Published by: Scripture Union, 207-209 Queensway, Bletchley, Milton Keynes, Bucks MK2 2EB, United Kingdom. TEL 44-1908-856000, FAX 44-1908-856111, info@scriptureunion.org.uk. Ed. Lizzie Green. **Subscr. to:** Mail Order, PO Box 5148, Milton Keynes MLO, Bucks MK2 2YZ, United Kingdom. TEL 44-1908-856006, FAX 44-1908-856020, mailorder@scriptureunion.org.uk.

SOCIAL COMPASS; international review of sociology of religion. *see* SOCIOLOGY

266 NLD ISSN 1874-8937
BV2000
➤ **SOCIAL SCIENCES AND MISSIONS.** Text in English, French. 1995. 2/yr. EUR 144, USD 201 to institutions; EUR 157, USD 220 combined subscription to institutions (print & online eds.) (effective 2012). reprint service avail. from PSC. **Document type:** *Journal, Academic/Scholarly.*
Formerly (until 2007): Le Fait Missionnaire (1420-2018)
Related titles: Online - full text ed.: ISSN 1874-8945. EUR 131, USD 183 to institutions (effective 2012) (from IngentaConnect).
Indexed: A01, A21, A22, CA, E01, FR, IZBG, P42, S02, S03, SociolAb, T02.
—BLDSC (8318.186225), IE, INIST. **CCC.**
Published by: (Universite de Lausanne, Observatoire des Religions en Suisse CHE), Brill, PO Box 9000, Leiden, 2300 PA, Netherlands. TEL 31-71-5353500, FAX 31-71-5317532, cs@brill.nl. Eds. Didier Peclard, Eric Morier-Genoud.

230 USA ISSN 0737-5778
HV530
➤ **SOCIAL WORK AND CHRISTIANITY.** Text in English. 1974. q. USD 98 domestic to institutions; USD 105 in Canada to institutions; USD 113 elsewhere to institutions; free to members (effective 2010). bk.rev. back issues avail. **Document type:** *Journal, Academic/Scholarly.* **Description:** Brings out articles, contributions, book reviews, and letters which deal with issues related to the integration of faith and professional social work practice and other professional concerns which have relevance to Christianity.
Formerly (until 1979): The Paraclete
Related titles: Online - full text ed.: ISSN 1944-7779.
Indexed: CA, ChrPI, GSS&RPL, P03, P27, P28, P45, P48, P53, P54, PQC, PsycInfo, S02, S03, SCOPUS, SSA, SWR&A, SociolAb, T02.
—BLDSC (8318.223200). **CCC.**
Published by: North American Association of Christians in Social Work, PO Box 121, Botsford, CT 06404. TEL 888-426-4712, FAX 888-426-4712, info@nacsw.org. Ed. David Sherwood.

200 ARG ISSN 0326-9795
BR115.W6
SOCIEDAD Y RELIGION. Text in Spanish. 1985. s-a. **Document type:** *Journal, Academic/Scholarly.*
Published by: Centro de Investigaciones y Estudios Laborales, Programa de Investigaciones Economicas sobre Tecnologia, Trabajo y Empleo, Saavedra 15 PB y 4o Piso, Buenos Aires, C1083ACA, Argentina. TEL 54-11-49527440, FAX 54-11-49537651, postmaster@ceil-piette.gov.ar. Ed. Floreal Forni. Circ: 500.

200 USA ISSN 1934-080X
SOCIETY FOR BUDDHIST-CHRISTIAN STUDIES. NEWSLETTER. Text in English. 1988. s-a. **Document type:** *Newsletter, Consumer.*
Published by: Society for Buddhist-Christian Studies, c/o Frances Adeney, Louisville Seminary, 1044 Alta Vista Rd, Louisville, KY 40205. fadeney@lpts.edufadeney@lpts.edu, http://www.society-buddhist-christian-studies.org.

200 500 USA
SOCIETY FOR COMMON INSIGHTS. JOURNAL. Text in English. 1976. s-a. USD 5 to individuals; USD 6 to institutions. bk.rev. charts; illus. back issues avail.
Indexed: CERDIC.
Published by: Society for Common Insights, c/o Kurt Johnson, Department of Biology, City University of New York, Convent Ave and 138th St, New York, NY 10031. Eds. Eric L Quinter, Kurt Johnson.

225 GBR ISSN 0081-1432
SOCIETY FOR NEW TESTAMENT STUDIES. MONOGRAPH SERIES. Text in English. 1965. irreg., latest 2010. price varies. index. back issues avail.; reprints avail. **Document type:** *Monographic series, Academic/Scholarly.* **Description:** Presents specialised research into all aspects of New Testament textual and historical culture, taking a range of approaches.
Indexed: IZBG.
—BLDSC (5917.125000).
Published by: (Society for New Testament Studies), Cambridge University Press, The Edinburgh Bldg, Shaftesbury Rd, Cambridge, CB2 8RU, United Kingdom. TEL 44-1223-312393, FAX 44-1223-315052, journals@cambridge.org, http://www.cambridge.org/uk. Ed. John M Court. R&P Linda Nicol TEL 44-1223-325702.

SOCIETY FOR OLD TESTAMENT STUDY. BOOK LIST. *see* RELIGIONS AND THEOLOGY—Abstracting, Bibliographies, Statistics

207.2092 AUS
SOCIETY MATTERS. Text in English. 1990. 3/yr. illus.; tr.lit. back issues avail. **Document type:** *Newsletter.* **Description:** Contains stories from the mission field: stories of new postulants and novices of where they come from, how they were attracted to missionary life and their training and education; a column written by our congregational leader.
Published by: Divine Word Missionaries, 199 Epping Rd, Marsfield, NSW 2121, Australia. TEL 61-2-98692666, FAX 61-2-98681010, fundraising@divineword.org.au, http://www.divineword.com.au.

220 NLD ISSN 1569-3627
SOCIETY OF BIBLICAL LITERATURE. SYMPOSIUM SERIES. Text in English. 1996. irreg., latest vol.45, 2008. price varies. **Document type:** *Monographic series.*
Indexed: IZBG.
Published by: (Society of Biblical Literature USA), Brill, PO Box 9000, Leiden, 2300 PA, Netherlands. TEL 31-71-5353500, FAX 31-71-5317532, cs@brill.nl.

230 USA ISSN 1540-7942
BJ1188.5
➤ **SOCIETY OF CHRISTIAN ETHICS. JOURNAL.** Abbreviated title: J S C E. Text in English. 1975. s-a. bk.rev. back issues avail. **Document type:** *Journal, Academic/Scholarly.* **Description:** Designed for students, faculty, and scholars in search of the latest developments and issues in the world of Christian and religious ethics.
Former titles (until 2002): Society of Christian Ethics. Annual (0732-4928); (until 1981): Selected Papers From the Annual Meeting (0278-4645); (until 1980): American Society of Christian Ethics. Selected Papers. Annual Meeting (0146-5821)
Related titles: Microfiche ed.; Online - full text ed.
Indexed: A20, A21, A22, ASCA, ArtHuCI, CurCont, P30, PhilInd, R&TA, RI-1, RI-2, SCOPUS, W07.
—BLDSC (4883.150000), IE, Ingenta. **CCC.**
Published by: (Society of Christian Ethics), Georgetown University Press, PO Box 5126, St. Cloud, MN 56302. TEL 320-253-5407, FAX 320-252-6984, gupress@georgetown.edu, http://www.press.georgetown.edu. Eds. Mary Jo Iozzio, Patricia Beattie Jung. **Dist by:** Hopkins Fulfillment Service.

230 658 170 BEL ISSN 1015-8693
SOCIO-ECONOMIC PAPERS. Text in English. 198?. irreg. back issues avail. **Document type:** *Monographic series, Trade.* **Description:** Reflects on the role of Christian ethics in society, the economy, and the work place.
Related titles: German ed.; French ed.
Published by: International Christian Union of Business Executives/ Union Internationale Chretienne des Dirigeants d'Entreprises, 2 Pl des Barricades, Brussels, 1000, Belgium. TEL 32-2-218-3114, FAX 32-2-219-7037. Ed. Alexandre Schramme. Pub. Josef M Mertes.

SOCIOLOGY OF RELIGION; a quarterly review. *see* SOCIOLOGY

202 USA ISSN 1550-1140
BR115.W6
SOJOURNERS MAGAZINE; faith, politics, culture. Text in English. 1971. m. (11/yr.). USD 39.95 domestic; USD 49.95 in Canada; USD 59.95 elsewhere (effective 2009). adv. bk.rev. illus. back issues avail.; reprints avail. **Document type:** *Magazine, Consumer.* **Description:** Covers theological, social, cultural and political topics, and provides resources for spiritual discussion, study and renewal.
Former titles (until 2001): Sojourners (0364-2097); (until 1976): Post American (0361-2422)
Related titles: Microfiche ed.; Online - full text ed.
Indexed: A01, A03, A08, A21, A22, A25, A26, AltPI, AmHI, B04, BRD, CA, CCR, CERDIC, ChPerI, Chicano, ChrPI, E07, E08, G06, G07, G08, GSS&RPL, H07, H08, H14, HAb, HRIR, HumInd, I05, I07, MRD, P07, P10, P28, P30, P34, P48, P53, P54, PQC, PRA, R05, RI-1, RI-2, S08, S09, S23, SCOPUS, T02, W03, W05.
—Ingenta. **CCC.**
Published by: Sojourners, 3333 14th St, NW, Ste 200, Washington, DC 20010. TEL 202-328-8842, 800-714-7474, FAX 202-328-8757, sojourners@sojo.net. Eds. Jim Rice, Jim Wallis. Adv. contact Larisa Friesen, page USD 2,055; trim 8.1875 x 10.875.

200 URY
SOLERIANA. Text in Spanish. 1974. s-a. USD 30 (effective 1999). bk.rev. **Document type:** *Academic/Scholarly.* **Description:** Contains articles on philosophy and theology. Covers conferences.
Formerly (until no.18, 1994): Instituto Teologico del Uruguay Monsenor Mariano Soler. Libro Anual
Indexed: OTA.
Published by: Facultad Teologica del Uruguay "Mons. Mariano Soler", San Fructuoso, 1019, Montevideo, 11800, Uruguay. TEL 598-2-2085808, FAX 598-2-2000289, bibeo@ucu.edu.uy. Ed. Roberto Russo. Circ: 500.

230 CHE ISSN 0067-4907
SONDERBAENDE ZUR THEOLOGISCHEN ZEITSCHRIFT. Text in German. 1966. irreg. price varies. **Document type:** *Academic/Scholarly.*
Formerly: Beihefte zur Theologischen Zeitschrift
Published by: Friedrich Reinhardt Verlag, Missionsstr 36, Basel, 4012, Switzerland. Ed. Bo Reicke. Circ: 1,000. **Dist. by:** Albert J. Phiebig Books, PO Box 352, White Plains, NY 10602.

200 100 NLD ISSN 0038-1527
BL1
➤ **SOPHIA**; international journal for philosophy of religion, metaphysical theology and ethics. Text in English. 1962. 4/yr. EUR 294, USD 357 combined subscription to institutions (print & online eds.) (effective 2012). adv. bk.rev. tr.lit. 176 p./no.; reprint service avail. from PSC. **Document type:** *Journal, Academic/Scholarly.* **Description:** Covers the broad spectrum of philosophy of religion, including cross-cultural issues, feminist theology, ethics, indigenous justice and eco-theology.
Related titles: Microform ed.: (from PQC); Online - full text ed.: ISSN 1873-930X (from IngentaConnect); Regional ed(s).: ISSN 1088-8357.
Indexed: A20, A21, A22, A26, ArtHuCI, AusPAIS, CERDIC, E01, FR, I05, MLA, MLA-IB, P28, P48, P53, P54, PCI, PQC, PhilInd, RI-1, RI-2, SCOPUS, W07.
—BLDSC (8328.180000), IE, Ingenta, INIST. **CCC.**
Published by: (Society for Philosophy of Religion and Philosophical Theology AUS), Springer Netherlands (Subsidiary of: Springer Science+Business Media), Van Godewijckstraat 30, Dordrecht, 3311 GX, Netherlands. TEL 31-78-6576050, FAX 31-78-6576474, http://www.springer.com. Ed. Purushottama Bilimoria. **Subscr. to:** Springer Distribution Center, Kundenservice Zeitschriften, Haberstr 7, Heidelberg 69126, Germany. TEL 49-6221-3454303, FAX 49-6221-3454229, subscriptions@springer.com.

200 100 USA ISSN 1521-1231
BL1
SOPHIA (VIRGINIA); the journal of traditional studies. Text in English. 1995. s-a. USD 35 domestic; USD 42 in Canada & Mexico; USD 54 elsewhere; USD 18 per issue domestic; USD 22 per issue in Canada & Mexico; USD 28 per issue elsewhere (effective 2010). video rev.; Website rev.; bk.rev. 250 p./no. 1 cols./p.; back issues avail. **Document type:** *Journal, Academic/Scholarly.* **Description:** Explores particular religious traditions from around the world.
Published by: Foundation for Traditional Studies, PO Box 370, Oakton, VA 22124. TEL 703-476-8837, FAX 703-476-5218, customerservice@traditional-studies.org, http://www.traditional-studies.org.

200 NLD ISSN 2211-4408
▼ **SOPHIE.** Text and summaries in Dutch. 2011. bi-m. EUR 30 domestic; EUR 40 foreign; EUR 15 foreign to students; EUR 6 newsstand/cover foreign (effective 2011). adv. **Document type:** *Magazine, Consumer.*
Formed by the merger of (1973-2011): Beweging (0167-1766); (1975-2011): Ellips (1570-2057); Which was formerly (until 2002): Bijbel en Wetenschap (0167-2258)
Published by: (Stichting voor Christelijke Filosofie), Buijten en Schipperheijn B.V., Postbus 22708, Amsterdam, 1100 DE, Netherlands. TEL 31-20-5241010, FAX 31-20-5241011, http://www.buijten.nl, info@buijten.nl. Eds. A Deddens, J Hoogland.

200 100 LTU ISSN 1392-7450
SOTER. Text in Multiple languages. 1924. s-a. **Document type:** *Journal, Academic/Scholarly.*
Related titles: Online - full text ed.: free (effective 2011).
Indexed: PhilInd.
Published by: Vytauto Didziojo Universitetas, Faculty of Theology/ Vytautas Magnus University, Gimnazijos g 7, Kaunas, 44260, Lithuania. TEL 370-37-205489, FAX 370-37-323477, info@adm.vdu.lt.

200 AUS ISSN 1833-7465
SOUL PURPOSE MAGAZINE; people connecting people. Text in English. 2006. q. adv. **Document type:** *Magazine, Consumer.* **Description:** Provides of various learnings, attitudes and ways of life.
Media: Online - full text. **Related titles:** Print ed.: ISSN 1833-7457.
Published by: Kindred Spirit Enterprises, PO Box 2562, Sunbury, VIC 3429, Australia. TEL 61-3-97409667, FAX 61-3-97407349, kse@kindredspirit.com.au, http://www.kindredspirit.com.au. Ed. Leanne Synan.

201.6 USA ISSN 0744-8333
BR560.S6
SOURCE (SEATTLE). Text in English. 1960. m. USD 20 (effective 2000). adv. bk.rev. **Document type:** *Newspaper.*
Supersedes (in 1980): Church Council of Greater Seattle Occasional News (0010-9924); Formerly: Council in Action
Published by: Church Council of Greater Seattle, 4759 15 Ave, N E, 3rd Fl, Seattle, WA 98105-4404. TEL 206-525-1213, FAX 206-525-1218. Ed., R&P Leanne Skooglund Hofford. Adv. contact Grant Angle. Circ: 6,000.

291.8 FRA ISSN 0750-1978
SOURCES CHRETIENNES. Text in French. 1941. irreg., latest vol.479, 2003. price varies. **Document type:** *Monographic series.*
Published by: (Institut des Sources Chretiennes), Editions du Cerf, 29 Boulevard La Tour Maubourg, Paris, 75340 Cedex 07, France. http://www.editionsducerf.fr.

220 USA ISSN 1931-0943
➤ **SOURCES FOR BIBLICAL AND THEOLOGICAL STUDY.** Abbreviated title: S B T S. Text in English. 19??. irreg., latest vol.10, 2005. price varies. 500 p./no.; back issues avail. **Document type:** *Monographic series, Academic/Scholarly.*
Published by: Eisenbrauns Inc., PO Box 275, Winona Lake, IN 46590. TEL 574-269-2011, FAX 574-269-6788, customerservice@eisenbrauns.com, http://www.eisenbrauns.com.

268 301 USA ISSN 1529-6024
SOUTHERN CHRISTIAN FAMILY; keeping the family together through Christian values. Text in English. 2000. m. USD 15; USD 1 newsstand/cover (effective 2001). adv. **Document type:** *Magazine, Consumer.*
Address: 111 Camille St., Senatobia, MS 38668-2506. southernchristian@aol.com. Ed. Jeff Thigpen.

200 286 USA ISSN 0038-4828
BX6201
➤ **SOUTHWESTERN JOURNAL OF THEOLOGY.** Text in English. 1958. s-a. USD 27 domestic; USD 32 foreign (effective 2010). bk.rev. back issues avail.; reprints avail. **Document type:** *Journal, Academic/Scholarly.* **Description:** Contains theological information.
Related titles: Microform ed.: (from PQC).
Indexed: A21, A22, CERDIC, ChrPI, IZBG, OTA, R&TA, RI-1, RI-2, SBPI.
—BLDSC (8357.210000), IE, Ingenta.
Published by: Southwestern Baptist Theological Seminary, Box 22000, Fort Worth, TX 76122. TEL 817-923-1921, registrar@swbts.edu, http://www.swbts.edu.

200 ZAF ISSN 0038-5980
THE SOWER. Text in English. 1957. q. free. illus.
Related titles: Microfiche ed.
Indexed: IPP.
Published by: Bible Society of South Africa, PO Box 6215, Roggebaai, Cape Town 8012, South Africa. FAX 27-21-419-4846. Ed. Rev. N N Turley. Circ: 68,000 (controlled).

SPAETMITTELALTER, HUMANISMUS, REFORMATION. *see* HISTORY—History Of Europe

200 KEN
SPEARHEAD. Text in English. 1969. 5/yr. KES 900; USD 62 in Africa; USD 92 in Europe & Asia; USD 99 in the Americas (effective 2003). back issues avail. **Document type:** *Monographic series, Academic/Scholarly.*
Formerly (until 1977): Gaba Pastoral Papers
Indexed: CERDIC.
Published by: (Amecea Pastoral Institute), AMECEA Gaba Publications, PO Box 4002, Eldoret, Kenya. TEL 254-321-61218. Circ: 2,500.

230 DEU ISSN 0947-0735
SPEE-JAHRBUCH. Text in German. 1994. a. **Document type:** *Journal, Academic/Scholarly.*
Published by: (Friedrich-Spee-Gesellschaft e.V.), Paulinus Verlag GmbH, Maximineracht 11c, Trier, 54295, Germany. TEL 49-651-46080, FAX 49-651-4608221, verlag@paulinus.de.

200 255 NLD ISSN 0038-7320
SPELING. Text in Dutch. 1948. q. EUR 23.35; EUR 8.30 newsstand/cover (effective 2009). bk.rev.; play rev. illus. **Document type:** *Magazine, Consumer.*
Formerly (until 1968): Carmel (1879-4181)
Indexed: CERDIC.
—IE, Infotrieve.
Published by: H. Gianotten B.V., Postbus 9228, Tilburg, 5000 HE, Netherlands. TEL 31-13-5425050, FAX 31-13-5359175, info@drukkerijgianotten.nl, http://www.drukkerijgianotten.nl. Ed. Loet Swart. Circ: 8,000.

230.071 028.5 USA ISSN 1040-3868
SPIRIT (ST. PAUL); lectionary-based weekly for Catholic teens. Text in English. 1981. 28/yr. USD 25 (effective 2005). **Document type:** *Magazine, Consumer.* **Description:** Centers on the Sunday gospel and explores Catholic doctrine as it applies to teenagers.
Published by: Good Ground Press, 1884 Randolph Ave, St Paul, MN 55105-1700. TEL 651-690-7010, FAX 651-690-7039, sales@goodgroundpress.com, jmcsj9@mail.idt.net. Ed. Joan Mitchell. Circ: 26,000 (paid).

230 USA ISSN 2160-9640
▼ **SPIRIT ALIVE MAGAZINE.** Text in English. 2011. 13/yr. adv. **Document type:** *Magazine, Consumer.*
Related titles: Online - full text ed.: ISSN 2160-9675. free (effective 2011).
Published by: Jus Being Real Productions, 839-B Hwy 163, Calhoun, TN 37309. Ed., Adv. contact Lila Robinson. Pub. Gary Robinson.

220 USA ISSN 1948-0857
SPIRIT OF THE PLAINS MAGAZINE; a Christian magazine for the Northern plains. Text in English. 2005. q. USD 12 (effective 2009). adv. back issues avail. **Document type:** *Magazine, Consumer.* **Description:** Provides spiritual articles on Christianity for the Northern Plains.
Published by: Prairie Hearth Publishing, LLC, 231 Broadway Ave, Ste #6, PO Box 569, Yankton, SD 57078. TEL 605-260-2487, 866-567-7959, FAX 605-665-5303, http://www.prairiehearthpub.com. Pubs. Alan Sorensen, Loretta Sorensen. Adv. contact Rodger Wenzlaff.

200 DEU
SPIRITA (ONLINE); Zeitschrift fuer Religionswissenschaft. Text in German. 1987. irreg. back issues avail. **Document type:** *Journal, Academic/Scholarly.*
Formerly (until 2001): Spirita (Print Edition) (0933-8985)
Media: Online - full content.
Indexed: DIP, IBR, IBZ.
Published by: Diagonal Verlag, Alte Kasseler Str 43, Marburg, 35039, Germany. TEL 49-6421-681936, FAX 49-6421-681944, post@diagonal-verlag.de, http://www.diagonal-verlag.de. Eds. Steffen Rink, Thomas Schweer.

200 USA
BL625.7
SPIRITLED WOMAN (ONLINE); empowered for purpose. Text in English. 1998. bi-m. USD 17.95 domestic; USD 22.95 in Canada (effective 2007). adv. back issues avail. **Document type:** *Magazine, Trade.* **Description:** Aims to call women into intimate fellowship with God to empower women to fulfull God's purpose in their lives.
Formerly (until 2008): SpiritLed Woman (Print) (1098-349X)
Media: Online - full text. **Related titles:** Fax ed.
Published by: Strang Communications Co., 600 Rinehart Rd, Lake Mary, FL 32746. TEL 407-333-0600, FAX 407-333-7100, custsvc@strang.com, http://www.strang.com. Ed. Lee J Grady. Pub. Joy Strang. adv.: B&W page USD 3,495, color page USD 4,125; trim 5.38 x 8.88. Circ: 100,000 (paid).

SPIRITUAL INFORMATION BULLETIN. *see* PARAPSYCHOLOGY AND OCCULTISM

202 USA ISSN 0038-7630
BX2350.A1
SPIRITUAL LIFE; a quarterly of contemporary spirituality. Text in English. 1955. q. USD 20 domestic; USD 25 foreign (effective 2007). bk.rev. bibl. 64 p./no.; back issues avail.; reprints avail. **Document type:** *Magazine, Consumer.* **Description:** Discusses contemporary spirituality.
Related titles: Microform ed.: (from PQC); Online - full text ed.
Indexed: A22, CERDIC, CPL, P28, P48, P53, P54, PQC.
Published by: Washington Province of Discalced Carmelite Friars, Inc., 2131 Lincoln Rd, N E, Washington, DC 20002. TEL 202-832-8489, 800-832-8489, FAX 202-832-8967. Ed., R&P Edward O'Donnell. Pub. Fr. Jude Peters. Circ: 10,000.

291 USA ISSN 1938-1875
SPIRITUAL LIVING DIGEST. Text in English. 2007. m. free (effective 2009). **Document type:** *Magazine, Consumer.* **Description:** Contains articles, tips and quotes to support readers' spiritual practices and to help readers live in accordance with their spiritual principles and values.
Media: Online - full content.
Published by: Rhoberta Shaler Ed. & Pub., 525-42 W El Norte Pkwy, Escondido, CA 92026. TEL 760-735-8686, info@SpiritualLivingNetwork.com.

200 ITA ISSN 1825-3563
SPIRITUALITA. Text in Italian. 1974. irreg. **Document type:** *Magazine, Consumer.*
Published by: Editrice Queriniana, Via Enrico Ferri 75, Brescia, BS 25123, Italy. TEL 39-030-2306925, FAX 39-030-2306932, redazione@queriniana.it, http://www.queriniana.it.

200 ITA
LA SPIRITUALITA CRISTIANA. Text in Italian. 1981. irreg., latest vol.20. price varies. **Document type:** *Monographic series, Academic/Scholarly.*
Published by: Edizioni Studium, Via Cassiodoro 14, Rome, 00193, Italy. TEL 39-06-6865846, FAX 39-06-6875456, info@edizionistudium.it, http://www.edizionistudium.it.

SPIRITUALITY & HEALTH; the soul body connection. *see* ALTERNATIVE MEDICINE

200 USA
SPIRITUALITY FOR TODAY. Text in English. 1995. m. back issues avail. **Description:** Dedicated to a variety of current themes and questions concerning the Christian faith.
Media: Online - full text.
Address: PO Box 7466, Greenwich, CT 06836. Ed. Rev. Mark Connolly.

230 USA ISSN 1533-1709
BV4501.3
SPIRITUS; a journal of Christian spirituality. Text in English. N.S. 199?(Mar.). s-a. USD 115 to institutions (print or online ed.); USD 161 combined subscription to institutions (print & online eds.); USD 69 per issue to institutions (effective 2011). adv. back issues avail.; reprint service avail. from PSC. **Document type:** *Journal, Academic/Scholarly.* **Description:** Covers a wide range of disciplines within the field of religious studies: history, philosophy, theology, and psychology.
Formerly (until 2001): Christian Spirituality Bulletin (1082-9008)
Related titles: Online - full text ed.: ISSN 1535-3117.
Indexed: A20, A21, A22, ArtHuCI, ChrPI, DIP, E01, GSS&RPL, IBR, IBZ, MLA-IB, P28, P48, P53, P54, PQC, RILM, SCOPUS, W07.
—BLDSC (8415.440000), IE. **CCC.**
Published by: (Society for the Study of Christian Spirituality), The Johns Hopkins University Press, 2715 N Charles St, Baltimore, MD 21218. TEL 410-516-6900, FAX 410-516-6968, bjs@press.jhu.edu. Ed. Douglas Burton-Christie. Pub. William M Breichner. Circ: 712. **Subscr. to:** PO Box 19966, Baltimore, MD 21211. TEL 410-516-6987, 800-548-1784, FAX 410-516-3866, jrnlcirc@press.jhu.edu.

266 FRA ISSN 0038-7665
SPIRITUS; experience et recherche missionnaires. Text in French. 1959. q. bk.rev. abstr.; bibl. index. **Document type:** *Journal.* **Description:** Aims to advance the missionary vocation and improve communication among diverse churches.
Related titles: Online - full text ed.
Indexed: CERDIC, FR.
—**CCC.**
Published by: Association de la Revue Spiritus, c/o Seminaire des Missions, 12 Rue du Pere Mazurie, Chevilly-Larue, Cedex 94669, France. TEL 33-1-46867030, FAX 33-1-46867274, http://www.spiritains.org/pub/spiritus/spiritus.htm. Ed. Alese Gillet. Circ: 2,500.

200 HRV ISSN 0042-7659
SPLITSKO-MAKARSKA NADBISKUPIJA. VJESNIK. Text in Croatian. 1948-1991; resumed 2002. q. free. bk.rev.
Former titles (until 1969): Biskupija Splitska i Makarska. Vjesnik (1332-022X); (until 1965): Biskupija Splitska i Makarska. Sluzbeni Vjesnik (1332-0211); (until 1964): Mjesecna Okruznica (1332-0203)
Published by: Splitsko-Makarska Nadbiskupija, Poljana Kneza Trpimira, 7, Split, 21000, Croatia. TEL 385-21-407555, FAX 385-21-407538, http://split.hbk.hr. Ed. Marijan Ivan Bodrozic. Circ: 400.

261 USA ISSN 1075-3125
SPORTS SPECTRUM. Text in English. 1987. 6/yr.
Published by: Discovery House Publishers (Subsidiary of: R B C Ministries), PO Box 3566, Grand Rapids, MI 49501. TEL 616-942-9218, FAX 616-957-5741. Ed. Dave Branon. Circ: 50,000.

268 USA ISSN 2151-0369
SQUARE 1 TAKE 'N TALK SHEETS FOR 2S & 3S. Text in English. 2004. q. USD 3.99 per issue (effective 2009). **Document type:** *Handbook/Manual/Guide, Trade.* **Description:** Provides meaningful activities for the class and home. Offers ideas for family interaction related to the lesson's theme and focus.
Formerly (until 2009): Take 'n Talk for 2s & 3s (1557-749X)
Published by: Randall House, 114 Bush Rd, PO Box 17306, Nashville, TN 37217. TEL 615-361-1221, 800-877-7030, FAX 615-367-0535.

268 USA ISSN 2151-0350
SQUARE 1 TEACHING GUIDE FOR 2S & 3S. Text in English. 2004. q. USD 6.99 per issue (effective 2009). **Document type:** *Handbook/Manual/Guide, Trade.* **Description:** Provides teachers with the necessary tools and information to most effectively teach 2 and 3 year olds and helps connect God's word to their lives.
Formerly (until 2009): CLEAR Teaching for 2s & 3s (1558-5190)
Published by: Randall House, 114 Bush Rd, PO Box 17306, Nashville, TN 37217. TEL 615-361-1221, 800-877-7030, FAX 615-367-0535.

STAATSKIRCHENRECHTLICHE ABHANDLUNGEN. *see* LAW—Constitutional Law

207.2 DEU
STADT GOTTES; Illustrierte Familienzeitschrift. Text in German. 1878. m. EUR 22.20 (effective 2011). **Document type:** *Magazine, Consumer.*
Published by: Steyler Missionare e.V., Bahnhofstr 9, Nettetal, 41334, Germany. TEL 49-2157-120200, FAX 49-2157-1202060, steyler@steyler.de. Ed. Christian Tauchner.

268.8 230.00715 USA
STANDARD LESSON COMMENTARY KING JAMES VERSION; international Sunday school lessons. Text in English. 1954. w. USD 19.99 per issue (effective 2009). back issues avail. **Document type:** *Magazine, Consumer.* **Description:** Contains a verse-by-verse explanation of the bible text, detailed lesson background, discussion questions, study helps and pronunciation guides.
Former titles: King James Version Standard Lesson Commentary; Standard Lesson Commentary (0081-4245)
Published by: Standard Publishing, 8805 Governor's Hill Dr, Ste 400, Cincinnati, OH 45249. TEL 513-931-4050, 800-543-1353, FAX 877-867-5751, customerservice@standardpub.com, http://www.standardpub.com. Ed. Jonathan Underwood. R&P Mark A Taylor. Circ: 200,000.

230 DEU
▼ **STANDORTE IN ANTIKE UND CHRISTENTUM.** Text in German. 2010. irreg., latest vol.3, 2010. price varies. **Document type:** *Monographic series, Academic/Scholarly.*
Published by: Anton Hiersemann Verlag, Haldenstr 30, Stuttgart, 70376, Germany. TEL 49-711-5499710, FAX 49-711-54997121, info@hiersemann.de, http://www.hiersemann.de.

200 USA
STARTHROWERS. Text in English. 1977. m. USD 5.
Formerly (until 1985): Agape (Franklin)
Address: 615 Throwbridge, Box 192, Franklin, LA 70538.

266 DEU ISSN 1862-2542
STEFANUS; aktiv in Kirche und Welt. Text in German. 1949. 6/yr. EUR 25 (effective 2010). illus. **Document type:** *Newsletter, Consumer.*
Published by: Stefanuswerk e.V., Am Muenster 11, Heiligkreuztal, 88499, Germany. TEL 49-7371-18646, FAX 49-7371-18643, kloster-heiligkreuztal@stefanus.de. Ed. Andrea Kotter.

200 NLD ISSN 1877-5527
STEM VAN VERVOLGDE CHRISTENEN. Text in Dutch. 1978. bi-m. **Document type:** *Magazine, Consumer.*
Former titles (until 2009): Stem der Martelaren (0169-8893); (until 1985): Stichting "de Ondergrondse Kerk" (0167-272X)
Published by: Stichting De Ondergrondse Kerk, Postbus 705, Gorinchem, 4200 AS, Netherlands. TEL 31-183-561186, FAX 31-183-561229, info@sdok.org, http://www.sdok.nl.

207.2 DEU ISSN 0722-6942
STEYLER MISSIONSCHRONIK. Text in German. 1959. a. **Document type:** *Bulletin.*
Published by: (Steyler Missionswissenschaftliches Institut), Steyler Verlag, Bahnhofstr 9, Nettetal, 41334, Germany. TEL 49-2157-1202-20, FAX 49-2157-1202-22.

291.72 NLD ISSN 1875-3027
STICHTING KOM OVER EN HELP. NIEUWSBRIEF. Text in Dutch. 197?. 7/yr.
Formerly (until 2005): Stichting Kom Over en Help. Informatiebulletin (0928-0553)
Published by: Stichting Kom Over en Help, Watergoorweg 75a, Postbus 138, Nijkerk, 3860 AC, Netherlands. TEL 31-33-2463208, FAX 31-33-2462807, info@komoverenhelp.nl, http://www.komoverenhelp.nl.

200 NLD ISSN 2211-7725
STICHTING WERKGROEP KERK EN DIER. NIEUWSBRIEF. Text in Dutch. 200?. a. **Document type:** *Newsletter, Consumer.*
Published by: Stichting Werkgroep Kerk en Dier, Juliana van Stolberglaan 4A, Naarden, 1412 BG, Netherlands. info@kerkendier.nl, http://www.kerkendier.nl.

R

268 028.5 DNK ISSN 1601-1708
STIFINDER; en bibellaeseplan for juniorer. Text in Danish. 1985. q. DKK 150 (effective 2008). illus. **Document type:** *Magazine, Consumer.*
Former titles (until 2001): Nu Paa Vej; (until 1986): Paa Vej (0900-3355)
Published by: Bibellaeser-Ringen, Korskaervej 25, Fredericia, 7000, Denmark. TEL 45-82-271337, info@blr.dk, http://www.blr.dk.

207.2 DEU ISSN 1618-4114
STIMME DER MAERTYRER. Text in German. 1993. m. EUR 6 (effective 2010). 12 p./no. 3 cols./p.; back issues avail. **Document type:** *Magazine, Consumer.* **Description:** Devoted to information about the the persecution of Christians around the world as well as aid and support for them.
Formerly (until 2000): Stimme der Maertyrer - H M K Kurier (0949-9105); Which was formed by the merger of (1969-1993): Stimme der Maertyrer; (1985-1993): H M K Kurier
Published by: Hilfsaktion Maertyrerkirche e.V., Tuefinger Str 3, Uhldingen-Muehlhofen, 88690, Germany. TEL 49-7556-92110, FAX 49-7556-921140, h-m-k@h-m-k.org, http://www.h-m-k.org.

200 NZL ISSN 1171-7920
STIMULUS; the New Zealand journal of Christian thought and practice. Text in English. q. NZD 48 domestic; NZD 66 in Australia & Pacific; NZD 70 in North America, Asia, PNG; NZD 74 in Europe; NZD 78 elsewhere (effective 2008). back issues avail. **Document type:** *Journal, Academic/Scholarly.* **Description:** Provides provocative and challenging material for thoughtful readers.
Related titles: Online - full content ed.; Online - full text ed.
Indexed: A01, A02, A03, A08, A21, CA, RI-1, T02.
Address: PO Box 306, Masterton, New Zealand. TEL 64-6-3789699, FAX 64-6-3775117, dgnz@xtra.co.nz. Pub. Douglas Maclachlan.

291 SWE ISSN 0562-1070
STOCKHOLM STUDIES IN COMPARATIVE RELIGION. Text in Multiple languages. 1961. irreg., latest vol.35, 2010. price varies. back issues avail. **Document type:** *Monographic series, Academic/Scholarly.*
Related titles: ◆ Series of: Acta Universitatis Stockholmiensis. ISSN 0346-6418.
Published by: Stockholms Universitet, Acta Universitatis Stockholmiensis, c/o Stockholms Universitetsbibliotek, Universitetsvaegen 10, Stockholm, 10691, Sweden. TEL 46-8-162800, FAX 46-8-157776, http://www.sub.su.se. Ed. Margaretha Fathli. **Dist. by:** Eddy.se AB, Norra Kyrkogatan 3, Visby 62155, Sweden. TEL 46-498-253900, FAX 46-498-249789, info@eddy.se, order@eddy.se, http://www.eddy.se, http://acta.bokorder.se.

200 ITA ISSN 2039-3652
STORIA DELLE RELIGIONI. Text in Italian. 1985. irreg., latest vol.13, 1997. price varies. **Document type:** *Monographic series, Academic/Scholarly.*
Published by: L' Erma di Bretschneider, Via Cassiodoro 19, Rome, 00193, Italy. TEL 39-06-6874127, FAX 39-06-6874129, lerma@lerma.it, http://www.lerma.it. Eds. Enrico Montanari, Guilia Piccaluga, Ugo Bianchi.

200 DEU
STORMARNSPIEGEL. Text in German. 1973. irreg. (6-8/yr.). bk.rev. back issues avail.
Published by: Kirchenkreis Stormarn, Kirchenkreisvorstand, Rockenhof 1, Hamburg, 22359, Germany. TEL 040-603-143-28. Circ: 1,320.

200 DEU
STREIFLICHTER (KRAICHTAL). Text in German. bi-m. EUR 8 (effective 2009). back issues avail. **Document type:** *Magazine, Consumer.*
Published by: C V J M Landesverband Baden, Muehlweg 10, Kraichtal, 76703, Germany. TEL 49-7251-9824610, FAX 49-7251-9824619, http://www.cvjmbaden.de. Ed. Peter Bauer. Circ: 3,000.

200 SWE ISSN 0346-1890
STRIDSROPET. Text in Swedish. 1883. 24/yr. SEK 395 in Scandinavia; SEK 695 elsewhere; SEK 20 per issue (effective 2004). adv. **Document type:** *Consumer.*
Related titles: Audio cassette/tape ed.
Published by: Svenska Fraelsningsarmen/Swedish Salvation Army, c/o Goeran Andresasson, Bruksuddevaegen 22, Alingsaas, 144191, Sweden. TEL 46-8-56228200, FAX 46-8-56228397, info@fralsningsarmen.se. Ed. Eva Kleman. Adv. contact Ethel Forsell TEL 46-8-56228273. color page SEK 12,000; 195 x 265. Circ: 12,000.

STROMATA; antigua ciencia y fe. *see* PHILOSOPHY

220 USA ISSN 0039-2677
THE STUDENT (LINCOLN). Text in English. 1927. m. free to qualified personnel (effective 2011). back issues avail. **Document type:** *Consumer.* **Description:** Provides daily helps for the serious adult Bible student with a visual impairment.
Media: Braille.
Published by: Christian Record Services, PO Box 6097, Lincoln, NE 68506. TEL 402-488-0981, FAX 402-488-7582, info@christianrecord.org, http://www.christianrecord.org.

270.092 USA ISSN 1073-8487
STUDENT LEADERSHIP JOURNAL. Text in English. 1988. q. USD 4 per issue to non-members. bk.rev. back issues avail. **Description:** A practical journal on Biblical leadership for Christian students on secular college campuses.
Indexed: CCR.
Published by: Inter-Varsity Christian Fellowship of the United States of America, 6400 Schroeder Rd, Box 7895, Madison, WI 53707-7895. TEL 608-274-9001, FAX 608-274-7882. Ed. Jeff Yourison. Circ: 8,000.

200 ITA ISSN 0393-8417
BL5
STUDI E MATERIALI DI STORIA DELLE RELIGIONI. Text in Italian; Text occasionally in English, French, German. 1925. s-a. bk.rev. **Document type:** *Journal, Academic/Scholarly.*
Former titles (until 1982): Studi Storico-Religiosi (0393-4128); (until 1976): Religioni e Civilta (0393-8409); (until 1969): Studi e Materiali di Storia delle Religioni (0036-1690)
Indexed: DIP, FR, IBR, IBZ, MLA-IB, PCI, T02.
—INIST.
Published by: Universita degli Studi di Roma "La Sapienza", Dipartimento di Studi Storico-Religiosi, Citta Universitaria, Rome, RM 00185, Italy. TEL 06-4957308, FAX 06-4453753. Ed. Alberto Camplani.

270 ITA ISSN 1122-0694
STUDI E TESTI PER LA STORIA RELIGIOSA DEL CINQUECENTO. Text in Italian. 1986. irreg., latest vol.11, 2000. price varies. **Document type:** *Monographic series, Academic/Scholarly.*
Published by: Casa Editrice Leo S. Olschki, Viuzzo del Pozzetto 8, Florence, 50126, Italy. TEL 39-055-6530684, FAX 39-055-6530214, celso@olschki.it, http://www.olschki.it.

200 ITA ISSN 0393-3687
STUDI ECUMENICI. Text in Italian; Summaries in English. 1983. q. bk.rev. bibl. index. back issues avail. **Document type:** *Journal, Academic/Scholarly.* **Description:** An ecumenical formation's review, an instrument for search, proposal and dialogue between various church's theologies.
Indexed: A21, OTA, RI-1, RI-2.
Published by: Pontificio Ateneo Antonianum, Istituto di Studi Ecumenici San Bernardino, Castello 2786, Venice, 30122, Italy. info@isevenezia.it, http://www.isevenezia.it.

220 ITA ISSN 1970-545X
STUDIA BIBLICA (ROME). Text in Latin. 2004. irreg. **Document type:** *Monographic series, Academic/Scholarly.*
Published by: Citta Nuova Editrice, Via Pieve Torina 55, Rome, 00156, Italy. TEL 39-06-3216212, FAX 39-06-3207185, comm.editrice@cittanuova.it, http://www.cittanuova.it.

200 SWE ISSN 1101-878X
➤ **STUDIA BIBLICA UPSALIENSIA.** Text in Multiple languages. 1991. irreg., latest vol.1, 1991. price varies. **Document type:** *Monographic series, Academic/Scholarly.*
Related titles: ◆ Series of: Acta Universitatis Upsaliensis. ISSN 0346-5462.
Published by: Uppsala Universitet, Acta Universitatis Upsaliensis/ University Publications from Uppsala, PO Box 256, Uppsala, 75105, Sweden. TEL 46-18-4716804, acta@ub.uu.se, http://www.ub.uu.se/upu/auu/index.html. Ed. Bengt Landgren. **Dist. by:** Almqvist & Wiksell International.

220 CHE ISSN 1015-3497
STUDIA FRIBURGENSIA. Text in French, German. 1924. irreg., latest vol.110, 2011. price varies. **Document type:** *Monographic series, Academic/Scholarly.*
Indexed: FR.
—INIST.
Published by: Academic Press Fribourg, Perolles 42, Fribourg, 1705, Switzerland. TEL 41-26-4264311, FAX 41-26-4264300, info@paulusedition.ch, http://www.paulusedition.ch/academic_press/.

200 ZAF ISSN 1017-0499
BR1450
STUDIA HISTORIAE ECCLESIASTICAE; journal of the Church History Society of Southern Africa. Text in Multiple languages. 1973. s-a. USD 34.02 foreign (effective 2005). **Document type:** *Journal, Academic/Scholarly.*
Indexed: A21, ISAP, R&TA, RI-1.
Published by: School of Ecclesiastical Sciences, PO Box 20004, Noordbrug, 2522, South Africa. TEL 27-12-4204111, FAX 27-12-3625168.

200 SWE ISSN 0562-2751
STUDIA HISTORICO-ECCLESIASTICA UPSALIENSIA. Text in Swedish. 1961. irreg., latest vol.40, 1998. price varies. back issues avail. **Document type:** *Monographic series, Academic/Scholarly.*
Related titles: ◆ Series of: Acta Universitatis Upsaliensis. ISSN 0346-5462.
Published by: Uppsala Universitet, Acta Universitatis Upsaliensis/ University Publications from Uppsala, PO Box 256, Uppsala, 75105, Sweden. TEL 46-18-4716804, FAX 46-18-4716804, acta@ub.uu.se, http://www.ub.uu.se/upu/auu/index.html. Ed. Bengt Landgren. **Dist. by:** Almqvist & Wiksell International.

220 NLD ISSN 0169-8125
BS1700
➤ **STUDIA IN VETERIS TESTAMENTI PSEUDEPIGRAPHA.** Text in Dutch. 1970. irreg., latest vol.22, 2008. price varies. back issues avail. **Document type:** *Monographic series, Academic/Scholarly.* **Description:** Publishes texts, translations and critical studies on Old Testament pseudepigrapha and apocrypha.
Indexed: CCMJ, IZBG, MathR.
Published by: Brill, PO Box 9000, Leiden, 2300 PA, Netherlands. TEL 31-71-5353500, FAX 31-71-5317532, cs@brill.nl, http://www.brill.nl. R&P Elizabeth Venekamp. **Dist. by:** Turpin Distribution Services Ltd., Pegasus Dr, Stratton Business Park, Biggleswade, Bedfordshire SG18 8QB, United Kingdom. TEL 44-1767-604954, FAX 44-1767-601640, custserv@turpin-distribution.com, http://www.turpin-distribution.com/.

230 USA ISSN 0039-3207
BV170
➤ **STUDIA LITURGICA.** Text in English. 1962. q. free to members (effective 2010). bk.rev. 128 p./no.; back issues avail. **Document type:** *Journal, Academic/Scholarly.*
Indexed: A21, A22, CERDIC, DIP, FR, IBR, IBZ, PCI, RASB, RI-1, RI-2, RILM, SCOPUS.
—BLDSC (8482.973000), IE, Infotrieve, Ingenta, INIST. **CCC.**
Published by: Societas Liturgica, c/o Karen Westerfield Tucker, Boston University, School of Technology, 745 Commonwealth Ave, Boston, MA 02215. president@societas-liturgica.org. Ed. Karen Westerfield Tucker.

240 ITA ISSN 0081-6736
➤ **STUDIA MORALIA.** Text in English, French, German, Italian, Spanish; Summaries in English, Spanish. 1963. s-a. EUR 40 domestic; EUR 48 foreign (effective 2011). bk.rev. index. 300 p./no.; back issues avail. **Document type:** *Journal, Academic/Scholarly.* **Description:** Contains research articles on ethical issues from a theological perspective.
Indexed: CERDIC, DIP, IBR, IBZ, PCI, PhilInd.
Published by: Editiones Academiae Alfonsianae, Via Merulana 31, Rome, 00185, Italy. TEL 39-06-494901, FAX 39-06-4465887, segreteria@alfonsiana.edu. Ed. Luciano Panella.

200 POL ISSN 1643-2762
STUDIA OECUMENICA. Text in Polish. 2001. a., latest vol.2, 2002. price varies. **Document type:** *Journal, Academic/Scholarly.*
Published by: (Uniwersytet Opolski, Wydzial Teologiczny, Uniwersytet Opolski, Wydzial Teologiczny, Instytut Ekumenizmu i Badan nad Integracja), Wydawnictwo Uniwersytetu Opolskiego, ul Sienkiewicza 33, Opole, 45037, Poland. TEL 48-77-4410878, wydawnictwo@uni.opole.pl.

200 956 ISR ISSN 0585-5403
STUDIA ORIENTALIA CHRISTIANA. Text in Arabic, Coptic, English, French, Italian. 1956. a., latest vol.40, 2007. EUR 111 combined subscription (print & online eds.) (effective 2012); price varies. illus. back issues avail. **Document type:** *Monographic series, Academic/Scholarly.* **Description:** Publishes scholarly articles on theological, historical, ethnological, and linguistic topics relating to Christianity in the Middle East.
Related titles: Online - full text ed.
Indexed: RILM.
Published by: (Franciscan Centre of Christian Oriental Studies in Cairo EGY), Franciscan Printing Press, PO Box 14064, Jerusalem, 91140, Israel. TEL 972-2-6286594, FAX 972-2-6284717, fpp@bezeqint.net, http://198.62.75.5/opt/xampp/custodia/tsancta/00fpp.php. **Dist. by:** Brepols Publishers.

200 956 ISR
STUDIA ORIENTALIA CHRISTIANA. MONOGRAPHIAE. Text in Arabic, Coptic, English, French, German, Italian, Latin. 1955. irreg., latest vol.8, 1998. price varies. illus. **Document type:** *Monographic series.* **Description:** Publishes scholarly studies of theological, historical, ethnological, and linguistic topics relating to Christianity in the Middle East.
Published by: (Franciscan Centre of Christian Oriental Studies in Cairo EGY), Franciscan Printing Press, PO Box 14064, Jerusalem, 91140, Israel. TEL 972-2-6286594, FAX 972-2-6284717, fpp@bezeqint.net, http://198.62.75.5/opt/xampp/custodia/tsancta/00fpp.php.

210 100 ITA ISSN 0039-3304
B4
STUDIA PATAVINA; rivista di scienze religiose. Text in Italian; Abstracts in English. 1954. 4/yr. EUR 39 domestic; EUR 47 foreign (effective 2009). adv. bk.rev. index. 250 p./no. 1 cols./p.; back issues avail. **Document type:** *Journal, Academic/Scholarly.* **Description:** Emphasizes the promotion of the study of all religious disciplines; organizes meetings from many cultural institutions.
Indexed: CERDIC, FR, IPB, MLA-IB, OTA.
—INIST.
Published by: Facolta Teologica del Triveneto, Via del Seminario 29, Padua, 35122, Italy. TEL 39-049-657099, FAX 39-049-8761934, studiapatavina@iol.it, http://www.fttr.it. Circ: 1,800.

225 281 888 BEL
➤ **STUDIA PATRISTICA.** Text in English, French, German. 1954. irreg., latest 2010. price varies. back issues avail. **Document type:** *Monographic series, Academic/Scholarly.*
Published by: (University of Oxford, The Faculty of Law GBR), Peeters Publishers, Bondgenotenlaan 153, Leuven, 3000, Belgium. TEL 32-16-235170, FAX 32-16-228500, http://www.peeters-leuven.be.

➤ **STUDIA PHILOSOPHIAE RELIGIONIS.** *see* PHILOSOPHY

200 CHE ISSN 1424-7607
STUDIA RELIGIOSA HELVETICA. Text in French, German, English. 1982. irreg., latest vol.9, 2004. price varies. **Document type:** *Monographic series, Academic/Scholarly.*
Indexed: IBR, IBZ.
Published by: Peter Lang AG (Subsidiary of: Peter Lang Publishing Group), Hochfeldstr 32, Postfach 746, Bern 9, 3000, Switzerland. TEL 41-31-3061717, FAX 41-31-3061727.

200 CHE ISSN 1424-7593
STUDIA RELIGIOSA HELVETICA. SERIES ALTERA. Text in English, French, German. 1995. irreg., latest vol.9, 2003. price varies. **Document type:** *Monographic series, Academic/Scholarly.*
Published by: Peter Lang AG (Subsidiary of: Peter Lang Publishing Group), Hochfeldstr 32, Postfach 746, Bern 9, 3000, Switzerland. TEL 41-31-3061717, FAX 41-31-3061727, info@peterlang.com.

200 943.8 POL ISSN 0137-3420
BR9.P6
STUDIA TEOLOGICZNO-HISTORYCZNE SLASKA OPOLSKIEGO. Text in Polish. 1973. irreg., latest vol.22, 2002. price varies. **Document type:** *Monographic series, Academic/Scholarly.*
Published by: (Uniwersytet Opolski, Wydzial Teologiczny), Wydawnictwo Uniwersytetu Opolskiego, ul Sienkiewicza 33, Opole, 45037, Poland. TEL 48-77-4410878, wydawnictwo@uni.opole.pl, http://www.wydawnictwo.uni.opole.pl/.

230 GBR ISSN 0039-338X
BR1
➤ **STUDIA THEOLOGICA**; Scandinavian journal of theology. Text in English, German. 1947. s-a. GBP 82 combined subscription in United Kingdom to institutions (print & online eds.); EUR 107, USD 135 combined subscription to institutions (print & online eds.) (effective 2012). bk.rev. bibl. index, cum.index every 10 yrs. back issues avail.; reprint service avail. from PSC. **Document type:** *Journal, Academic/Scholarly.* **Description:** Presents Scandinavian contributions to the field of international theology.
Related titles: Microform ed.: (from PQC); Online - full text ed.: ISSN 1502-7791. GBP 74 in United Kingdom to institutions; EUR 97, USD 122 to institutions (effective 2012) (from IngentaConnect).
Indexed: A01, A03, A08, A20, A21, A22, AmHI, BibLing, CA, CERDIC, DIP, E01, FR, H07, IBR, IBZ, MLA, MLA-IB, PCI, R&TA, RASB, RI-1, RI-2, RILM, T02.
—BLDSC (8483.227000), IE, Infotrieve, Ingenta, INIST. **CCC.**
Published by: Routledge (Subsidiary of: Taylor & Francis Group), 4 Park Sq, Milton Park, Abingdon, Oxon OX14 4RN, United Kingdom. TEL 44-20-70176000, FAX 44-20-70176336, subscriptions@tandf.co.uk, http://www.routledge.com. Ed. Jan-Olav Henriksen. Adv. contact Linda Hann TEL 44-1344-779945. **Subscr. to:** Taylor & Francis Ltd., Journals Customer Service, Sheepen Pl, Colchester, Essex CO3 3LP, United Kingdom. TEL 44-20-70175544, FAX 44-20-70175198, tf.enquiries@tfinforma.com.

230 SWE ISSN 1401-1557
STUDIA THEOLOGICA HOLMIENSIA. Text in Swedish. 1996. irreg., latest vol.17, 2008. **Document type:** *Monographic series, Academic/Scholarly.*
Published by: Teologiska Hoegskolan/Stockholm School of Theology, Aakeshovsvaegen 29, Bromma, 16839, Sweden. TEL 46-8-56435700, FAX 46-8-56435706, ths@ths.se.

230 SWE ISSN 0491-2853
STUDIA THEOLOGICA LUNDENSIA. Text in English, German, Swedish. 1952. irreg., latest vol.52, 1997. price varies. **Document type:** *Journal, Academic/Scholarly.*
Published by: Lunds Universitet, Centrum foer Teologi och Religionsvetenskap/Lund University, Department of Theology and Religious Studies, Allhelgma Kyrkogata 8, Lund, 22362, Sweden.

220 NLD ISSN 1876-4096
STUDIEBIJBEL MAGAZINE. Text in Dutch. 2007. q. EUR 22.50; EUR 6.50 newsstand/cover (effective 2008).
Published by: Centrum voor Bijbelonderzoek, Postbus 503, Veenendaal, 3900 AM, Netherlands. TEL 31-318-503098, FAX 31-318-503163, info@studiebijbel.nl.

200 100 DEU
STUDIEN FUER RELIGION, WISSENSCHAFT UND KUNST. Text in German. 2002. irreg. price varies. **Document type:** *Monographic series, Academic/Scholarly.*
Published by: Universitaetsverlag Winter GmbH, Dossenheimer Landstr 13, Heidelberg, 69121, Germany. TEL 49-6221-770260, FAX 49-6221-770269, info@winter-verlag-hd.de, http://www.winter-verlag-hd.de.

200 900 DEU ISSN 1436-3003
STUDIEN UND TEXTE ZU ANTIKE UND CHRISTENTUM. Text in German. 1998. irreg., latest vol.60, 2011. price varies. **Document type:** *Monographic series, Academic/Scholarly.*
Published by: Mohr Siebeck GmbH & Co. KG, Wilhelmstr 18, Tuebingen, 72074, Germany. TEL 49-7071-9230, FAX 49-7071-51104, info@mohr.de.

200 DEU ISSN 0949-3077
STUDIEN UND TEXTE ZUR RELIGIONSGESCHICHTLICHEN SCHULE. Text in German. 1996. irreg., latest vol.6, 2001. price varies. **Document type:** *Monographic series, Academic/Scholarly.*
Published by: Peter Lang GmbH (Subsidiary of: Peter Lang Publishing Group), Eschborner Landstr 42-50, Frankfurt Am Main, 60489, Germany. TEL 49-69-7807050, FAX 49-69-78070550, zentrale.frankfurt@peterlang.com. Ed. Gerd Luedemann.

STUDIEN ZU KIRCHE UND KUNST. *see* ART

200 DEU ISSN 1860-0700
STUDIEN ZUM INTERRELIGIOESEN DIALOG. Text in German. 1997. irreg., latest vol.10, 2011. price varies. **Document type:** *Monographic series, Academic/Scholarly.*
Published by: Waxmann Verlag GmbH, Steinfurter Str 555, Muenster, 48159, Germany. TEL 49-251-265040, FAX 49-251-2650426, info@waxmann.com. Eds. Andre Ritter, Hans-Christoph Gossmann.

225 AUT ISSN 1027-3360
STUDIEN ZUM NEUEN TESTAMENT UND SEINER UMWELT. SERIE A. Text in German. 1976. irreg. **Document type:** *Monographic series, Academic/Scholarly.*
Indexed: DIP, IBR, IBZ, IZBG.
Published by: Katholisch-Theologische Privatuniversitaet Linz, Institut fuer Bibelwissenschaft des Neuen Testamentes, Bethlehemstr 20, Linz, Austria. TEL 43-70-7842934160, FAX 43-70-7842934155, a.fuchs@ktu-linz.ac.at, http://www.kth-linz.ac.at/institute/nt/index.htm.

230 DEU ISSN 1611-0080
STUDIEN ZUR AUSSEREUROPAEISCHEN CHRISTENTUMSGESCHICHTE/STUDIES IN THE HISTORY OF CHRISTIANITY IN THE NON-WESTERN WORLD; Asien, Afrika, Lateinamerika. Text in English, German. 1998. irreg., latest vol.16, 2010. price varies. **Document type:** *Monographic series, Academic/Scholarly.*
Published by: Harrassowitz Verlag, Kreuzberger Ring 7b-d, Wiesbaden, 65205, Germany. TEL 49-611-5300, FAX 49-611-530560, verlag@harrassowitz.de, http://www.harrassowitz.de.

STUDIEN ZUR CHRISTLICHEN KUNST. *see* ART

230 CHE
STUDIEN ZUR CHRISTLICHEN RELIGIONS- UND KULTURGESCHICHTE. Text in German. 2003. irreg., latest vol.15, 2011. price varies. **Document type:** *Monographic series, Academic/Scholarly.*
Published by: Academic Press Fribourg, Perolles 42, Fribourg, 1705, Switzerland. TEL 41-26-4264311, FAX 41-26-4264300, info@paulusedition.ch, http://www.paulusedition.ch/academic_press/.

STUDIEN ZUR GERMANIA SACRA. *see* HISTORY—History Of Europe

200 DEU ISSN 0938-5924
➤ **STUDIEN ZUR KIRCHENGESCHICHTE NIEDERSACHSENS.** Text in German. 1919. irreg., latest vol.42, 2009. price varies. **Document type:** *Monographic series, Academic/Scholarly.*
Published by: V & R Unipress GmbH (Subsidiary of: Vandenhoeck und Ruprecht), Robert-Bosch-Breite 6, Goettingen, 37079, Germany. TEL 49-551-5084303, FAX 49-551-5084333, info@vr-unipress.de, http://www.v-r.de/en/publisher/unipress. Ed. Inge Mager.

230 DEU
▼ **STUDIEN ZUR RELIGIONSPAEDAGOGIK UND PRAKTISCHEN THEOLOGIE.** Text in German. 2010. irreg., latest vol.3, 2011. price varies. **Document type:** *Monographic series, Academic/Scholarly.*
Published by: I K S Garamond, Leutragraben 1, Jena, 07743, Germany. TEL 49-3641-460850, FAX 49-3641-460855, garamond@iks-jena.de.

230 DEU
▼ **STUDIEN ZUR SPIRITUALITAET UND SEELSORGE.** Text in German. 2010. irreg. price varies. **Document type:** *Monographic series, Academic/Scholarly.*
Published by: Verlag Friedrich Pustet, Gutenbergstr 8, Regensburg, 93051, Germany. TEL 49-941-920220, FAX 49-941-92022330, verlag@pustet.de, http://www.pustetverlag.de.

200 CHE ISSN 0379-2366
STUDIEN ZUR THEOLOGISCHEN ETHIK. Text in German. 1977. irreg., latest vol.131, 2011. price varies. **Document type:** *Monographic series, Academic/Scholarly.*
Published by: Academic Press Fribourg, Perolles 42, Fribourg, 1705, Switzerland. TEL 41-26-4264311, FAX 41-26-4264300, info@paulusedition.ch, http://www.paulusedition.ch/academic_press/.

200 SWE ISSN 1650-8718
STUDIER AV INTER-RELIGIOESA RELATIONER/STUDIES ON INTER-RELIGIOUS RELATIONS. Text mainly in Swedish; Text occasionally in English. 2001. irreg. price varies. back issues avail. **Document type:** *Monographic series, Academic/Scholarly.*
Published by: Makadam Foerlag & Bokproduktion AB, Egmontgatan 6, Goeteborg, 41270, Sweden. TEL 46-31-409899, FAX 46-31-7334363, info@makadambok.se, http://www.makadambok.se.

200.71 USA ISSN 1083-2378
➤ **STUDIES IN AMERICAN RELIGION.** Text in English. 1981. irreg., latest vol.80, 2004. price varies. bibl. index. back issues avail. **Document type:** *Monographic series, Academic/Scholarly.*
Published by: Edwin Mellen Press, 415 Ridge St, PO Box 450, Lewiston, NY 14092. TEL 716-754-2266, FAX 716-754-4056, cservice@mellenpress.com. Ed. Herbert Richardson.

➤ **STUDIES IN ART AND RELIGIOUS INTERPRETATION.** *see* ART

220 USA ISSN 0894-6361
➤ **STUDIES IN BIBLE AND EARLY CHRISTIANITY.** Text in English. 1981. irreg., latest vol.67, 2009. price varies. back issues avail. **Document type:** *Monographic series, Academic/Scholarly.*
Published by: Edwin Mellen Press, 415 Ridge St, PO Box 450, Lewiston, NY 14092. TEL 716-754-2266, FAX 716-754-4056, cservice@mellenpress.com.

➤ **STUDIES IN BIBLICAL GREEK.** *see* LINGUISTICS

➤ **STUDIES IN BIBLICAL HEBREW.** *see* LINGUISTICS

200 800 USA ISSN 1570-1999
STUDIES IN BIBLICAL LITERATURE (ATLANTA). Text in English. 1946. irreg., latest vol.18, 2007. price varies. back issues avail. **Document type:** *Monographic series, Academic/Scholarly.* **Description:** Focus on biblical or theological themes, literary aspects of the biblical literature, the social world of the biblical writings, historical issues, or other comparable areas of study.
Former titles (until 2002): Society of Biblical Literature. Monograph Series (0145-269X); (until 1971): Journal of Biblical Literature. Monograph Series (0075-4153)
Indexed: IZBG.
Published by: Society of Biblical Literature, The Luce Ctr, 825 Houston Mill Rd, Atlanta, GA 30329. TEL 404-727-3100, 866-727-9955, FAX 404-727-3101, sblexec@sbl-site.org. Ed. Bob Buller TEL 970-669-9900.

220 USA ISSN 1089-0645
STUDIES IN BIBLICAL LITERATURE (NEW YORK). Text in English. 1998. irreg., latest vol.132, 2010. price varies. back issues avail. **Document type:** *Monographic series, Academic/Scholarly.* **Description:** Seeks to make available studies which will make a significant contribution to the ongoing biblical discourse.
Published by: Peter Lang Publishing, Inc. (Subsidiary of: Peter Lang Publishing Group), 29 Broadway, New York, NY 10006. TEL 212-647-7700, 800-770-5264, FAX 212-647-7707, customerservice@plang.com, http://www.peterlangusa.com. Ed. Hemchand Gossai.

230 170 GBR ISSN 0953-9468
BJ1188.5
➤ **STUDIES IN CHRISTIAN ETHICS.** Abbreviated title: S C E. Text in English. 1988. q. USD 549, GBP 297 combined subscription to institutions (print & online eds.); USD 538, GBP 291 to institutions (effective 2011). adv. bk.rev. back issues avail.; reprint service avail. from PSC. **Document type:** *Journal, Academic/Scholarly.* **Description:** Each issue examines an important theme in contemporary Christian ethics with contributions from major moral theologians.
Related titles: Online - full text ed.: ISSN 1745-5235. USD 494, GBP 267 to institutions (effective 2011).
Indexed: A01, A03, A08, A22, CA, DIP, E01, IBR, IBZ, P30, R&TA, RI-1, RI-2, SCOPUS, T02.
—BLDSC (8489.904000), IE, Infotrieve, Ingenta. **CCC.**
Published by: (Society for the Study of Christian Ethics), Sage Publications Ltd. (Subsidiary of: Sage Publications, Inc.), 1 Oliver's Yard, 55 City Rd, London, EC1Y 1SP, United Kingdom. TEL 44-20-73248500, FAX 44-20-73248600, info@sagepub.co.uk, http://www.uk.sagepub.com/home.nav. Ed. Susan F Parsons. adv.: B&W page GBP 450; 130 x 205. **Subscr. in the Americas to:** Sage Publications, Inc., 2455 Teller Rd, Thousand Oaks, CA 91320. TEL 805-499-9774, FAX 805-499-0871, journals@sagepub.com.

261 296.3 291 USA ISSN 1930-3777
BM535
➤ **STUDIES IN CHRISTIAN-JEWISH RELATIONS.** Text in English. 2005. a. free (effective 2011). back issues avail. **Document type:** *Journal, Academic/Scholarly.*
Media: Online - full text.
Indexed: A01.
Published by: (Council of Centers on Jewish-Christian Relations), Boston College, Center for Christian-Jewish Learning, 140 Commonwealth Ave, Chestnut Hill, MA 02467. cjlearning@bc.edu, http://www.bc.edu/research/cjl/. Eds. Kevin Spicer, Ruth Langer.

207.2 NLD ISSN 0924-9389
➤ **STUDIES IN CHRISTIAN MISSION.** Text in Dutch. 1990. irreg., latest vol.35, 2008. price varies. back issues avail. **Document type:** *Monographic series, Academic/Scholarly.* **Description:** Scholarly monographs on the history of Christian missionary activities and related theological issues.
Indexed: IZBG.
—BLDSC (8489.909000), IE, Ingenta.
Published by: Brill, PO Box 9000, Leiden, 2300 PA, Netherlands. TEL 31-71-5353500, FAX 31-71-5317532, cs@brill.nl, http://www.brill.nl. Eds. Heleen L Murre-van den Berg, Marc R Spindler. R&P Elizabeth Venekamp. **Dist. in N. America by:** Brill, PO Box 605, Herndon, VA 20172-0605. TEL 703-661-1585, 800-337-9255, FAX 703-661-1501, cs@brillusa.com; **Dist. by:** Turpin Distribution Services Ltd., Pegasus Dr, Stratton Business Park, Biggleswade, Bedfordshire SG18 8QB, United Kingdom. TEL 44-1767-604954, FAX 44-1767-601640, custserv@turpin-distribution.com, http://www.turpin-distribution.com/.

322.1 USA
➤ **STUDIES IN CHURCH AND STATE.** Text in English. 1988. irreg., latest 1991. price varies. back issues avail. **Document type:** *Monographic series, Academic/Scholarly.* **Description:** Examines the interplay of religion and politics in various cultures worldwide.
Published by: Princeton University Press, 41 William St, Princeton, NJ 08540. TEL 609-258-4900, 800-777-4726, FAX 609-258-6305, cpriday@pupress.co.uk. Ed. John F Wilson. **Subscr. addr. in US:** California - Princeton Fulfillment Services, Inc., 1445 Lower Ferry Rd, Ewing, NJ 08618. TEL 609-883-1759, 800-777-4726, FAX 609-883-7413, 800-999-1958, orders@cpfsinc.com. **Dist. addr. in Canada:** University Press Group.; **Dist. addr. in UK:** John Wiley & Sons Ltd.

260 USA ISSN 1074-6749
STUDIES IN CHURCH HISTORY. Text in English. 1994. irreg., latest vol.12, 2010. price varies. **Document type:** *Monographic series, Academic/Scholarly.*
Published by: Peter Lang Publishing, Inc. (Subsidiary of: Peter Lang Publishing Group), 29 Broadway, New York, NY 10006. TEL 212-647-7700, 800-770-5264, FAX 212-647-7707, customerservice@plang.com, http://www.peterlangusa.com. Ed. William Fox.

270 GBR ISSN 0424-2084
BR141
STUDIES IN CHURCH HISTORY. Text in English. 1964. a. USD 90, GBP 45 per vol. (effective 2010). back issues avail. **Document type:** *Monographic series, Academic/Scholarly.* **Description:** Contain a wide range of papers on major themes in ecclesiastical history, viewed from a wide historical context and in a broad inter-disciplinary relationship.
Indexed: A22, MLA-IB, PCI, RI-1.
—BLDSC (8489.930000), IE, Ingenta. **CCC.**
Published by: (Ecclesiastical History Society), Boydell & Brewer Ltd., Whitwell House, St Audrys Park Rd, Melton, Woodbridge, IP12 1SY, United Kingdom. TEL 44-1394-610600, FAX 44-1394-610316, trading@boydell.co.uk, http://www.boydell.co.uk.

207.2 USA
➤ **STUDIES IN COMPARATIVE RELIGION.** Text in English. 1987. irreg., latest vol.6, 1996. price varies. back issues avail. **Document type:** *Monographic series, Academic/Scholarly.*
Published by: Edwin Mellen Press, 415 Ridge St, PO Box 450, Lewiston, NY 14092. TEL 716-754-2266, FAX 716-754-4056, cservice@mellenpress.com.

200 NLD ISSN 1877-2129
▼ ➤ **STUDIES IN CRITICAL RESEARCH ON RELIGION.** Text in English. 2010. irreg. **Document type:** *Monographic series, Academic/Scholarly.* **Description:** Provides a venue for scholars engaged in critical research on religion.
Published by: Brill, PO Box 9000, Leiden, 2300 PA, Netherlands. TEL 31-71-5353500, FAX 31-71-5317532, cs@brill.nl. Ed. Warren S Goldstein.

200 USA ISSN 1527-8247
STUDIES IN EDUCATION AND SPIRITUALITY. Text in English. 2001. irreg., latest vol.9, 2005. price varies. back issues avail. **Document type:** *Monographic series, Academic/Scholarly.* **Description:** Presents the reader with the most recent thinking about the role of religion and spirituality in higher education. It includes a wide variety of perspectives, including students, faculty, administrators, religious life and student life professionals, and representatives of related educational and religious institutions.
Published by: Peter Lang Publishing, Inc. (Subsidiary of: Peter Lang Publishing Group), 29 Broadway, New York, NY 10006. TEL 212-647-7700, 800-770-5264, FAX 212-647-7707, customerservice@plang.com, http://www.peterlangusa.com. Eds. Peter Laurence, Victor Kazanjian.

200 BEL ISSN 0926-2326
BL410
➤ **STUDIES IN INTERRELIGIOUS DIALOGUE.** Text in English. 1990. 2/yr. EUR 40 combined subscription (print & online eds.) (effective 2011). adv. bk.rev. Index. **Document type:** *Journal, Academic/Scholarly.* **Description:** Provides a forum for academic discussion and comparative study of religious beliefs and philosophies of life, systematic and practical issues concerning interreligious relations, and other matters related to the modern situation of a pluralist culture.
Related titles: Online - full text ed.: ISSN 1783-1806.
Indexed: A21, PCI, RI-1.
—BLDSC (8490.775600), IE, Ingenta.
Published by: (Free University, Faculty of Theology NLD), Peeters Publishers, Bondgenotenlaan 153, Leuven, 3000, Belgium. TEL 32-16-235170, FAX 32-16-228500, peeters@peeters-leuven.be, http://www.peeters-leuven.be. Ed. A Camps. **Orders in the US:** Orbis Books, Dept WEB, PO Box 302, Maryknoll, NY 10545. TEL 914-941-7636 ext 2477, 914-941-7636 ext 2576, 800-258-5838, FAX 914-941-7005, orbisbooks@maryknoll.org, http://www.maryknoll.org/MALL/ORBIS. **Co-publisher:** Orbis Books.

200 301 NLD ISSN 1573-4188
➤ **STUDIES IN MEDIEVAL AND REFORMATION TRADITIONS**; culture, beliefs and tradition. Text in English. 2004. irreg., latest vol.137, 2008. price varies. **Document type:** *Monographic series, Academic/Scholarly.* **Description:** Provides a forum for monographs and text editions on subjects pertaining to the watershed between the Middle Ages and the Reformation.
Formed by the merger of (1966-2004): Studies in Medieval and Reformation Thought (0585-6914); (1995-2004): Culture, Beliefs and Tradition (1382-5364)
Indexed: IZBG.
Published by: Brill, PO Box 9000, Leiden, 2300 PA, Netherlands. TEL 31-71-5353500, FAX 31-71-5317532, cs@brill.nl. Ed. Andrew Colin Gow. **Dist. in N. America by:** Brill, PO Box 605, Herndon, VA 20172-0605. TEL 703-661-1585, 800-337-9255, FAX 703-661-1501, cs@brillusa.com; **Dist. by:** Turpin Distribution Services Ltd., Pegasus Dr, Stratton Business Park, Biggleswade, Bedfordshire SG18 8QB, United Kingdom. TEL 44-1767-604954, FAX 44-1767-601640, custserv@turpin-distribution.com, http://www.turpin-distribution.com/.

230 190 BEL ISSN 1381-2025
➤ **STUDIES IN PHILOSOPHICAL THEOLOGY.** Text in English, French, German. 1988. irreg. (approx. 3/yr), latest 2009. price varies. back issues avail. **Document type:** *Monographic series, Academic/Scholarly.* **Description:** Publishes scholarly studies on philosophical issues in contemporary Christian theology.
Published by: Peeters Publishers, Bondgenotenlaan 153, Leuven, 3000, Belgium. TEL 32-16-235170, FAX 32-16-228500, http://www.peeters-leuven.be.

➤ **STUDIES IN PHILOSOPHY AND RELIGION.** *see* PHILOSOPHY

R

200 USA ISSN 0008-4298
STUDIES IN RELIGION/SCIENCES RELIGIEUSES. Text in English, French. 1955. q. USD 334, GBP 180 combined subscription to institutions (print & online eds.); USD 327, GBP 176 to institutions (effective 2011). adv. bk.rev. charts. index. reprint service avail. from PSC. **Document type:** *Journal, Academic/Scholarly.* **Description:** Offers articles covering the field of religious and theological studies as well as reviews and critical notes on recent publications.
Formerly (until 1970): Canadian Journal of Theology (0576-5579)
Related titles: Online - full text ed.: ISSN 2042-0587. USD 301, GBP 162 to institutions (effective 2011).
Indexed: A20, A21, A22, ABS&EES, ASCA, ArtHuCI, BAS, C03, CBCARef, CERDIC, CurCont, DIP, E01, FR, IBR, IBZ, IZBG, MEA&I, MLA, MLA-IB, OTA, P30, P48, PCI, PQC, PhilInd, R&TA, RI-1, RI-2, SCOPUS, W07.
—BLDSC (8491.430000), IE, Infotrieve, Ingenta, INIST. **CCC.**
Published by: (Canadian Corporation for Studies in Religion CAN), Sage Publications, Inc., 2455 Teller Rd, Thousand Oaks, CA 91320. TEL 805-499-9774, 800-818-7243, FAX 805-499-0871, info@sagepub.com, http://www.sagepub.com. Eds. Alain Bouchard, Francis Landy. Circ: 1,350.

200 USA ISSN 0894-7082
➤ **STUDIES IN RELIGION AND SOCIETY.** Text in English. 1981. irreg., latest vol.70, 2010. price varies. back issues avail. **Document type:** *Monographic series, Academic/Scholarly.*
Indexed: RI-2.
Published by: Edwin Mellen Press, 415 Ridge St, PO Box 450, Lewiston, NY 14092. TEL 716-754-2266, FAX 716-754-4056, cservice@mellenpress.com.

200 700 NLD ISSN 1877-3192
▼ **STUDIES IN RELIGION AND THE ARTS.** Text in English. 2009. irreg., latest vol.3, 2010. price varies. **Document type:** *Monographic series, Academic/Scholarly.*
Published by: Brill, PO Box 9000, Leiden, 2300 PA, Netherlands. TEL 31-71-5353500, FAX 31-71-5317532, cs@brill.nl. Eds. Eric Ziolkowski, James Najarian.

322.1 USA ISSN 1087-8459
STUDIES IN RELIGION, POLITICS, AND PUBLIC LIFE. Text in English. 1999. irreg., latest vol.2, 1999. price varies. back issues avail. **Document type:** *Monographic series, Academic/Scholarly.* **Description:** Publishes studies on the role of religion and religiously motivated convictions in politics and public life.
Published by: Peter Lang Publishing, Inc. (Subsidiary of: Peter Lang Publishing Group), 29 Broadway, New York, NY 10006. TEL 212-647-7700, 800-770-5264, FAX 212-647-7707, customerservice@plang.com, http://www.peterlangusa.com. Ed. Gabriel Palmer-Fernandez.

STUDIES IN RELIGION, SECULAR BELIEFS AND HUMAN RIGHTS. *see* POLITICAL SCIENCE

220 FIN ISSN 1797-3449
STUDIES IN REWRITTEN BIBLE. Text in Multiple languages. 2008. irreg. **Document type:** *Monographic series, Academic/Scholarly.*
Published by: Aabo Akademi, Teologiska Fakulteten/Aabo Academy. Faculty of Theology, Biskopgatan 16, Aabo, 20500, Finland. TEL 358-2-21531, FAX 358-2-2154835. Ed. Antti Laato. **Dist. by:** Eisenbrauns Inc.

200 BEL ISSN 0926-6453
BL624
➤ **STUDIES IN SPIRITUALITY.** Text in English, French, German, Spanish. 1990. a., latest vol.15, 2005. EUR 65 combined subscription (print & online eds.) (effective 2011). adv. Index. 300 p./no.; **Document type:** *Journal, Academic/Scholarly.* **Description:** Publishes multidisciplinary articles on spirituality and mysticism, including theoretical questions, fundamental aspects and phenomena of spiritual transformation, with the main focus on the Judeo-Christian tradition.
Related titles: Online - full text ed.: ISSN 1783-1814; ◆ Supplement(s): Studies in Spirituality Supplements. ISSN 1572-6649.
Indexed: MLA-IB.
—IE.
Published by: Peeters Publishers, Bondgenotenlaan 153, Leuven, 3000, Belgium. TEL 32-16-235170, FAX 32-16-228500, peeters@peeters-leuven.be, http://www.peeters-leuven.be. Ed. Kees Waaijman.

200 BEL ISSN 1572-6649
➤ **STUDIES IN SPIRITUALITY SUPPLEMENTS.** Text in English, Spanish. 1991. irreg., latest 2010. price varies. back issues avail. **Document type:** *Monographic series, Academic/Scholarly.* **Description:** Takes an interdisciplinary approach to the study of spirituality in all its facets.
Related titles: ◆ Supplement to: Studies in Spirituality. ISSN 0926-6453.
Published by: Peeters Publishers, Bondgenotenlaan 153, Leuven, 3000, Belgium. TEL 32-16-235170, FAX 32-16-228500, http://www.peeters-leuven.be.

200 NLD ISSN 1876-1518
▼ **STUDIES IN SYSTEMATIC THEOLOGY.** Text in English. 2009. irreg., latest vol.5, 2010. price varies. **Document type:** *Monographic series, Academic/Scholarly.*
Published by: Brill, PO Box 9000, Leiden, 2300 PA, Netherlands. TEL 31-71-5353500, FAX 31-71-5317532, cs@brill.nl. Eds. Miikka Ruokanen, Stephen Bevans.

230 NLD ISSN 1573-5664
➤ **STUDIES IN THE HISTORY OF CHRISTIAN TRADITIONS.** Text in Dutch. 1966. irreg., latest vol.141, 2008. price varies. back issues avail. **Document type:** *Monographic series, Academic/Scholarly.* **Description:** Covers topics in Christian theology.
Formerly (until 2004): Studies in the History of Christian Thought (0081-8607)
Indexed: IZBG.
—BLDSC (8490.656500), IE, Ingenta.
Published by: Brill, PO Box 9000, Leiden, 2300 PA, Netherlands. TEL 31-71-5353500, FAX 31-71-5317532, cs@brill.nl, http://www.brill.nl. Ed. Robert J Bast. R&P Elizabeth Venekamp. **Dist. by:** Turpin Distribution Services Ltd., Pegasus Dr, Stratton Business Park, Biggleswade, Bedfordshire SG18 8QB, United Kingdom. TEL 44-1767-604954, FAX 44-1767-601640, custserv@turpin-distribution.com, http://www.turpin-distribution.com/.

➤ **STUDIES IN THE HISTORY OF MEDIEVAL RELIGION.** *see* HISTORY—History Of Europe

207.2 USA
➤ **STUDIES IN THE HISTORY OF MISSIONS.** Text in English. 1989. irreg., latest vol.24, 2003. price varies. back issues avail. **Document type:** *Monographic series, Academic/Scholarly.*
Published by: Edwin Mellen Press, 415 Ridge St, PO Box 450, Lewiston, NY 14092. TEL 716-754-2266, FAX 716-754-4056, cservice@mellenpress.com.

200 GBR ISSN 1661-1985
STUDIES IN THE HISTORY OF RELIGIOUS AND POLITICAL PLURALISM. Text in English. 2006. irreg., latest vol.4, 2009. price varies. back issues avail. **Document type:** *Monographic series, Academic/Scholarly.* **Description:** Covers studies in the history of religious and political pluralism.
Published by: Peter Lang Ltd. (Subsidiary of: Peter Lang Publishing Group), Evenlode Ct, Main Rd, Long Hanborough, Oxfordshire OX29 8SZ, United Kingdom. TEL 44-1993-880088, FAX 44-1993-882040, info@peterlang.com. Ed. Richard Bonney.

200.19 USA
➤ **STUDIES IN THE PSYCHOLOGY OF RELIGION.** Text in English. 1987. irreg., latest vol.7, 1995. price varies. back issues avail. **Document type:** *Monographic series, Academic/Scholarly.*
Indexed: E-psyche.
Published by: Edwin Mellen Press, 415 Ridge St, PO Box 450, Lewiston, NY 14092. TEL 716-754-2266, FAX 716-754-4056, cservice@mellenpress.com.

200 NLD ISSN 1566-208X
STUDIES IN THEOLOGY AND RELIGION. Text in English. 1999. irreg., latest vol.13, 2009. price varies. **Document type:** *Monographic series, Academic/Scholarly.*
Indexed: IZBG.
Published by: Brill, PO Box 9000, Leiden, 2300 PA, Netherlands. TEL 31-71-5353500, FAX 31-71-5317532, cs@brill.nl, http://www.brill.nl. Ed. Jan Willem van Henten.

200 GBR ISSN 1662-9930
▼ **STUDIES IN THEOLOGY, SOCIETY AND CULTURE.** Text in English. 2009. irreg., latest vol.2, 2009. price varies. **Document type:** *Monographic series, Academic/Scholarly.*
Published by: Peter Lang Ltd. (Subsidiary of: Peter Lang Publishing Group), Evenlode Ct, Main Rd, Long Hanborough, Oxfordshire OX29 8SZ, United Kingdom. TEL 44-1993-880088, FAX 44-1993-882040, info@peterlang.com.

200.82 USA
➤ **STUDIES IN WOMEN AND RELIGION.** Text in English. 1979. irreg., latest vol.44, 2005. price varies. back issues avail. **Document type:** *Monographic series, Academic/Scholarly.*
Published by: Edwin Mellen Press, 415 Ridge St, PO Box 450, Lewiston, NY 14092. TEL 716-754-2266, FAX 716-754-4056, cservice@mellenpress.com.

230 GBR ISSN 1354-9901
BR115.C8
STUDIES IN WORLD CHRISTIANITY; the Edinburgh review of theology and religion. Abbreviated title: S W C. Text in English. 1995. 3/yr. GBP 148 domestic to institutions; USD 295 in North America to institutions; GBP 162 elsewhere to institutions; GBP 184 combined subscription domestic to institutions (print & online eds.); USD 368 combined subscription in North America to institutions (print & online eds.); GBP 202 combined subscription elsewhere to institutions (print & online eds.) (effective 2012). bk.rev. illus. back issues avail.; reprints avail. **Document type:** *Journal, Academic/Scholarly.* **Description:** Explores the new challenges and opportunities faced by every branch of Christian theology and studies.
Formerly (until 1995): Edinburgh Review of Theology and Religion
Related titles: Online - full text ed.: ISSN 1750-0230. 2006. USD 242 in North America to institutions; GBP 133 elsewhere to institutions (effective 2012).
Indexed: A01, A03, A08, A20, A21, A22, AmHI, ArtHuCI, CA, CurCont, H07, R&TA, RI-1, RILM, T02, W07.
—BLDSC (8492.007530), IE. **CCC.**
Published by: Edinburgh University Press, 22 George Sq, Edinburgh, Scotland EH8 9LF, United Kingdom. TEL 44-131-6504218, FAX 44-131-6503286, journals@eup.ed.ac.uk. Ed. Brian Stanley. Adv. contact Ruth Allison TEL 44-131-6504220.

230 NLD ISSN 1873-9229
STUDIES IN WORLD CHRISTIANITY AND INTERRELIGIOUS RELATIONS. Text in English, French. 1988. irreg., latest vol.45, 2007. price varies. back issues avail. **Document type:** *Monographic series, Academic/Scholarly.* **Description:** Aims to stimulate scholarly studies of church practices and theological reflections within the contexts of their surrounding cultures, religions, socio-economic systems and political institutions.
Formerly (until 2007): Kerk en Theologie in Context (0922-9086)
Related titles: Online - full text ed.: (from IngentaConnect).
Indexed: A01, I02, P02, P10, P28, P48, P53, P54, PQC, T02.
—Ingenta.
Published by: Editions Rodopi B.V., Tijnmuiden 7, Amsterdam, 1046 AK, Netherlands. TEL 31-20-6114821, FAX 31-20-4472979, info@rodopi.nl. Ed. Frans Wijsen.

STUDIES OF CLASSICAL INDIA. *see* PHILOSOPHY

200 NLD ISSN 2210-4720
▼ **STUDIES ON THE CHILDREN OF ABRAHAM.** Text in English. 2010. irreg. EUR 108 per vol. domestic; EUR 154 per vol. foreign (effective 2011). **Document type:** *Monographic series, Academic/Scholarly.*
Related titles: Online - full text ed.: ISSN 2210-4739.
Published by: Brill, PO Box 9000, Leiden, 2300 PA, Netherlands. TEL 31-71-5353500, FAX 31-71-5317532, cs@brill.nl. Eds. Antti Laato, Dr. Camilla Adang, David Thomas.

STUDIES ON THE TEXTS OF THE DESERT OF JUDAH. *see* RELIGIONS AND THEOLOGY—Judaic

200 ROM ISSN 1011-8845
BX690
STUDII TEOLOGICE. Text in Romanian. 1929. q. **Document type:** *Journal, Academic/Scholarly.*
Indexed: A21, RI-1, T02.
Published by: Institutul Biblic si de Misiune al Bisericii Ortodoxe Romane, Intr Miron Cristea 6, Sector 4, Bucharest, Romania. TEL 40-021-4067194, FAX 40-021-3360059, http://www.edituripatriarhiei.ro.

STUDIO (ALBURY); a journal of Christians writing. *see* LITERATURE

225 BEL
➤ **STUDIORUM NOVI TESTAMENTI AUXILIA.** Text in English, French, German. 1965. irreg. price varies. **Document type:** *Monographic series, Academic/Scholarly.* **Description:** Publishes New Testament studies research.
Published by: (Universite Catholique de Louvain, Faculte de Theologie et de Droit Canonique), Leuven University Press, Blijde Inkomststraat 5, Leuven, 3000, Belgium. TEL 32-16-325345, FAX 32-16-325352, http://www.kuleuven.ac.be/upers.

230 ESP ISSN 0585-766X
STUDIUM (MADRID); revista de filosofia y teologia. Text in Spanish. 1961. 3/yr. **Document type:** *Journal, Academic/Scholarly.*
Indexed: FR, IPB, P09, PCI, PhilInd.
—INIST.
Published by: Institutos Pontificios de Filosofia y Teologia "Santo Tomas", Apdo 61.150, Madrid, 28080, Spain. TEL 34-91-3024246, FAX 34-91-7665584, jgvalles@idecnet.com.

200 ESP ISSN 0211-0741
AS302.O9
STUDIUM OVETENSE. Text in Spanish. 1973. a., latest vol.33, 2006. **Document type:** *Monographic series, Academic/Scholarly.*
Indexed: CLA, MLA-IB, OTA, RILM.
—CCC.
Published by: Seminario Metropolitano de Oviedo, Apartado 157, Oviedo, 33080, Spain. TEL 34-985-220897, seoviedo@las.es.

200 IDN ISSN 0854-9176
STULOS. Text in English. 1993. s-a. **Document type:** *Journal, Academic/Scholarly.*
Indexed: A21, R&TA, RI-1.
Published by: Bandung Theological Seminary, Bandung, 40173, Indonesia.

220 DEU
STUTTGARTER BIBELSTUDIEN. Text in German. 1973. irreg., latest vol.198, 2003. price varies. **Document type:** *Monographic series, Academic/Scholarly.*
Indexed: IZBG.
Published by: Katholisches Bibelwerk e.V., Silberburgstr 121, Stuttgart, 70176, Germany. TEL 49-711-6192050, FAX 49-711-6192077, bibelinfo@bibelwerk.de, http://www.bibelwerk.de.

220 DEU ISSN 0935-7106
STUTTGARTER BIBLISCHE AUFSATZBAENDE. Text in German. 1988. irreg., latest vol.42, 2006. price varies. **Document type:** *Monographic series, Academic/Scholarly.*
Indexed: IZBG.
Published by: Katholisches Bibelwerk e.V., Silberburgstr 121, Stuttgart, 70176, Germany. TEL 49-711-6192050, FAX 49-711-6192077, bibelinfo@bibelwerk.de, http://www.bibelwerk.de.

220 DEU ISSN 0935-7297
STUTTGARTER BIBLISCHE BEITRAEGE. Text in German. 1976. irreg., latest vol.57, 2006. price varies. **Document type:** *Monographic series, Academic/Scholarly.*
Indexed: IZBG.
Published by: Katholisches Bibelwerk e.V., Silberburgstr 121, Stuttgart, 70176, Germany. TEL 49-711-6192050, FAX 49-711-6192077, bibelinfo@bibelwerk.de, http://www.bibelwerk.de.

371.07 GBR ISSN 1753-9919
SUBMERGE. Text in English. 1947. bi-m. GBP 13.50; GBP 2.50 per issue (effective 2010). music rev.; bk.rev. charts; illus. **Document type:** *Magazine, Consumer.* **Description:** Bible reading guide for ages 11 - 14.
Formerly (until 2007): One Up (1360-3051)
Related titles: Online - full text ed.
Indexed: RASB.
—CCC.
Published by: Scripture Union, 207-209 Queensway, Bletchley, Milton Keynes, Bucks MK2 2EB, United Kingdom. TEL 44-1908-856000, FAX 44-1908-856111, info@scriptureunion.org.uk.

220 ITA ISSN 1027-3441
SUBSIDIA BIBLICA. Text in Italian, English, French, Spanish. 1972. irreg., latest vol.21, 2001. price varies. **Document type:** *Monographic series, Academic/Scholarly.* **Description:** Contains various Biblical studies.
—BLDSC (8503.370000).
Published by: Pontificio Istituto Biblico/Pontifical Biblical Institute, Via della Pilotta 25, Rome, 00187, Italy. TEL 39-06-695261, FAX 39-06-695266211, http://www.biblico.it. Ed. James Swetnam.

231 USA ISSN 1557-9751
BL65 .S85
SUFFERING; Stauros notebook. Text in English. 1982. q. USD 20 (effective 2007). **Document type:** *Magazine, Consumer.* **Description:** Contains articles and stories on themes of religious healing and spirituality.
Formerly (until 2005): Stauros Notebook (1543-8716)
Related titles: CD-ROM ed.: ISSN 1557-9778; Online - full text ed.: ISSN 1557-976X.
Published by: Stauros U.S.A., 5700 N Harlem, Chicago, IL 60631. TEL 773-484-0581, FAX 773-631-8059, stauros@stauros.org. Ed. Stephen A Schmidt.

200 TUR ISSN 1300-9672
BP1
➤ **SULEYMAN DEMIREL UNIVERSITESI. ILAHIYAT FAKULTESI DERGISI/S D U FACULTY OF THEOLOGY. JOURNAL.** Text in Turkish. 1993. s-a. **Document type:** *Journal, Academic/Scholarly.*
Related titles: Online - full text ed.: free (effective 2009).
Indexed: I14, MLA-IB.
Published by: Suleyman Demirel Universitesi, Ilahiyat Fakultesi, Faculty of Theology, Isparta, 32260, Turkey. TEL 90-246-2371061, FAX 90-246-2371058. Ed. Necdet Durak.

200 USA ISSN 0039-5161
SUNDAY; the magazine for the Lord's Day Alliance. Text in English. 1913. 4/yr. USD 12 to members (effective 2002). adv. bk.rev.; rec.rev. bibl.; charts; illus. **Document type:** *Magazine, Consumer.*
Indexed: CERDIC.
Published by: Lord's Day Alliance of the U.S., 2930 Flowers Rd S, Atlanta, GA 30341. TEL 770-936-5376, FAX 770-936-5385. Ed., R&P, Adv. contact Tim Norton. Circ: 12,000.

200 USA ISSN 0039-5188
SUNDAY DIGEST; selected reading for Christian adults. Text in English. 1886. q. USD 3.50 (effective 1999). bk.rev. illus.
Indexed: AIPP.
Published by: David C. Cook Publishing Co., 4050 Lee Vance View, Colorado Springs, CO 80918. TEL 719-536-0100. Ed. Judy Couchman. Circ: 125,000.

230 USA ISSN 2152-4122
SUNDAY MORNING PRELUDE. Text in English. 2004. q.
Related titles: Online - full text ed.: ISSN 2152-4149.
Published by: Remnant Christian Assembly, PO Box 2706, Southfield, MI 48037. TEL 248-352-0599, http://www.remnant.us.

200 FIN ISSN 0356-9349
SUOMALAINEN TEOLOGINEN KIRJALLISUUSSEURA. JULKAIAU. Text in Finnish. 1905. irreg., latest vol.245, 2005. back issues avail. **Document type:** *Monographic series, Academic/Scholarly.*
Published by: Suomalainen Teologinen Kirjallisuusseura, PO Box 33, Helsinki, 00014, Finland. TEL 358-9-19122076, FAX 358-9-19123033, stksj@pro.tvs.fi.

200 FIN ISSN 0356-0759
➤ **SUOMEN KIORIALLISEN SEURA. TOIMITUKSIA.** Text in Multiple languages; Summaries in English, German. 1895. irreg. price varies. back issues avail. **Document type:** *Monographic series, Academic/ Scholarly.*
—BLDSC (3929.590000).
Published by: Suomen Kirkkohistoriallinen Seura/Finnish Society of Ecclesiastical History, c/o Dept of Church History, University of Helsinki, PO Box 33, Aleksanterinkatu 7, Helsinki, 00014, Finland. TEL 358-9-19123040, FAX 358-9-19123033, http://www.skhs.fi.

948 200 FIN ISSN 0356-0767
SUOMEN KIRKKOHISTORIALLINEN SEURA. VUOSIKIRJA/FINSKA KYRKOHISTORISKA SAMFUNDET. AARSKRIFT. Text in Finnish, Swedish; Summaries in English. 1911. a. EUR 20 membership (effective 2005). **Document type:** *Yearbook, Academic/Scholarly.*
Published by: Suomen Kirkkohistoriallinen Seura/Finnish Society of Ecclesiastical History, c/o Dept of Church History, University of Helsinki, PO Box 33, Aleksanterinkatu 7, Helsinki, 00014, Finland. TEL 358-9-19123040, FAX 358-9-19123033, http://www.skhs.fi.

220 FRA
SUPPLEMENT AU DICTIONNAIRE DE LA BIBLE. Text in French. irreg., latest vol.12, 1997. back issues avail. **Document type:** *Monographic series, Academic/Scholarly.* **Description:** Publishes articles and research papers exploring different interpretations of the Bible.
Published by: Letouzey et Ane Editeurs, 87 bd. Raspail, Paris, 75006, France. TEL 33-1-45488014, FAX 33-1-45490343. R&P Florence Letouzey.

200 USA ISSN 2151-8726
▼ **SUSIE**; a global sisterhood for teen girls. Text in English. 2009. m. USD 36 combined subscription (print & online eds.) (effective 2009). back issues avail. **Document type:** *Magazine, Consumer.* **Description:** Designed to lead girls into intimacy with Christ, guide them in developing healthy relationships, showcase positive entertainment choices, provide healthy role models and teach positive self-image.
Related titles: Online - full text ed.: ISSN 2151-8734.
Published by: Premier Studios Publishing, 10000 Marshall Dr, Lenexa, KS 66215. TEL 913-438-1004, FAX 913-438-1006, info@premierstudios.com, http://www.premierstudios.com. Ed. Susie Shellenberger.

220 SWE ISSN 1100-2298
BS410
➤ **SVENSK EXEGETISK AARSBOK.** Text in Multiple languages; Summaries in English. 1936. a. SEK 200 domestic membership; SEK 300 elsewhere membership; SEK 100 to students (effective 2011). bk.rev. illus. cum index: 1936-1995, 1996-2000, 2001-2003. back issues avail. **Document type:** *Yearbook, Academic/Scholarly.*
Indexed: A21, DIP, FR, IBR, IBZ, IZBG, MLA-IB, OTA, PCI, R&TA, RI-1, RI-2.
—INIST.
Published by: Svenska Exegetiska Saellskap, c/o Stig Norin, Teologiska Institionen, Uppsala Universitet, PO Box 511, Uppsala, 75120, Sweden. stig.norin@teol.uu.se.

200 SWE ISSN 0283-0302
BL10
SVENSK RELIGIONSHISTORISK AARSSKRIFT. Text in Swedish. 1985. a. SEK 250 membership; SEK 125 to students (effective 2007). **Document type:** *Yearbook, Academic/Scholarly.*
Published by: Svenska Samfundet foer Religionshistorisk Forskning, c/o Susanne Olsson, Soedertoerns Hoegskola, Huddinge, 14189, Sweden. susanne.olsson@sh.se, http://www.finyar.se/ssrfs%20hemsida/ettan.htm. Ed. Marja-Liisa Keinaenen.

230 SWE ISSN 0039-6761
BR6
SVENSK TEOLOGISK KVARTALSKRIFT. Abbreviated title: S T K. Text in Swedish, English, German. 1925. q. SEK 220 domestic; SEK 125 domestic to students; SEK 260 in Europe; SEK 300 elsewhere; SEK 55 per issue (effective 2007). adv. bk.rev. abstr.; bibl. index, cum.index every 10 yrs. back issues avail. **Document type:** *Journal, Academic/Scholarly.* **Description:** Concentrates on systematic theology involving all religions.
Indexed: A21, BibLing, CERDIC, FR, IBR, IBZ, MLA-IB, OTA, PCI, R&TA, RASB, RI-1, RI-2.
Address: c/o Centrum foer Teologi och Religionsvetenskap, Allhelgona Kyrkogata 8, Lunds Universitet, Lund, 22362, Sweden. TEL 46-46-2223765, FAX 46-46-2224426, hannelore.stein@teol.lu.se. Ed. Jesper Svartnik. Circ: 1,000.

200 SWE
SVENSKA KYRKAN. BESTAEMMELSER (ONLINE). Text in Swedish. 1983. irreg. free. **Document type:** *Monographic series.*
Former titles (until 2004): Svenska Kyrkan. Bestaemmelser (Print) (1650-0776); (until 2000): Svenska Kyrkan. Foerfattningssamling (0281-6938)
Media: Online - full content.
Published by: Svenska Kyrkan/Church of Sweden, Kyrkans Hus, Sysslomansgatan 4, Uppsala, 75170, Sweden. TEL 46-18-169600, FAX 46-18-169707, info@svenskakyrkan.se.

200 SWE ISSN 0491-6786
SVENSKA KYRKOHISTORISKA FOERENINGEN. SKRIFTER II, NY FOELJD/SWEDISH SOCIETY OF CHURCH HISTORY. PUBLICATIONS II, NEW SERIES. Text in Swedish, English. 1900. irreg., latest vol.58, 2005. back issues avail. **Document type:** *Monographic series, Academic/Scholarly.*
Formerly (until 1950): Svenska Kyrkohistoriska Foereningen. Skrifter (1101-3362)
Related titles: ◆ Series: Kyrkohistorisk Aarsskrift. ISSN 0085-2619.
Published by: Svenska Kyrkohistoriska Foereningen/Swedish Society of Church History, PO Box 511, Uppsala, 75126, Sweden.

200 GBR
SWEDENBORG SOCIETY JOURNAL. Text in English. 1986. irreg., latest vol.5, 2007. GBP 9.50 per issue (effective 2009). bk.rev. back issues avail. **Document type:** *Journal, Academic/Scholarly.* **Description:** Contains articles about Emanuel Swedenborg and his ideas.
Formerly (until 2001): Swedenborg Society Magazine
Published by: Swedenborg Society, 20-21 Bloomsbury Way, London, WC1A 2TH, United Kingdom. TEL 44-20-74057986, FAX 44-20-78315848, sales@swedenborg.org.uk, http://www.swedenborg.co.uk. Ed. Stephen McNeilly.

200 USA ISSN 0039-7547
BV3750
SWORD OF THE LORD; America's foremost christian publication. Text in English. 1934. bi-w. USD 15 (effective 1999). adv. bk.rev. index. **Description:** Features sermons, Bible studies, and reports of growing churches, as well as columns for women, children, and teens.
Published by: Sword of the Lord Foundation, 224 Bridge Ave, PO Box 1099, Murfreesboro, TN 37133. TEL 615-893-6700, FAX 615-895-7447. Ed. Shelton Smith. Circ: 100,000.

200 FRA ISSN 1814-5825
LE SYCOMORE. Text in French. 1996. irreg. **Document type:** *Magazine, Consumer.*
Indexed: R&TA.
Published by: Alliance Biblique Universelle/United Bible Societies, c/o French Bible Society, 5 Av. des Erables, BP 47, Villiers-le-Bel, 95400, France. TEL 33-1-39945051, FAX 33-1-39905351.

SYMPOSION; a journal of Russian thought. *see* PHILOSOPHY

230 DEU ISSN 0939-5199
T A N Z. (Texte und Arbeiten zum Neutestamentlichen Zeitalter) Text in German. 1989. irreg., latest vol.50, 2010. price varies. **Document type:** *Monographic series, Academic/Scholarly.* **Description:** Studies the literature and theology reflected in the literature of the New Testament times.
Published by: A. Francke Verlag GmbH, Dischinger Weg 5, Tuebingen, 72070, Germany. TEL 49-7071-97970, FAX 49-7071-979711, info@francke.de, http://www.francke.de.

220 USA ISSN 1089-7747
BS471
➤ **T C**; a journal of biblical textual criticism. (Textual Criticism) Text in English. 1996. irreg., latest vol.15, 2010. free (effective 2011). bk.rev. **Document type:** *Journal, Academic/Scholarly.* **Description:** Dedicated to the study of the Jewish and Christian biblical texts.
Media: Online - full text.
Indexed: A01, A03, A08, A21, AmHI, CA, H07, J01, L05, L06, R&TA, RI-1, T02.
Published by: James R. Adair, Jr, Ed. & Pub., 486 Castleaire Dr, Stone Mountain, GA 30087. TEL 770-931-4285, FAX 770-935-1663, jadair@emory.edu. Ed. Jan L H Krans TEL 31-20-5986621.

202 NGA ISSN 0794-7046
T C N N RESEARCH BULLETIN. Text in English. 1978. s-a. USD 25 for 2 yrs. adv. bk.rev. back issues avail. **Document type:** *Bulletin, Academic/Scholarly.*
Published by: Theological College of Northern Nigeria, PO Box 64, Bukuru, Plateau State, Nigeria. Ed., Adv. contact Timothy Palmer. Circ: 400.

207.2 USA ISSN 0163-3422
T E A M HORIZONS. Text in English. 1925. 3/yr. free. illus. **Document type:** *Magazine, Consumer.* **Description:** Contains stories and articles for supporters of TEAM missionaries and anyone else interested in missions work.
Published by: Evangelical Alliance Mission, PO Box 969, Wheaton, IL 60189-0969. TEL 630-653-5300, FAX 630-653-1826. Ed. Beth Kalopisis. Circ: 42,000 (controlled).

230 ZAF
T F M MONITOR. (Training for Ministries) Text in English. 1992. irreg. (approx. q.). **Document type:** *Newsletter.*
Published by: Church of the Province of South Africa, Department of Training for Ministries, Pretoria Diocese, PO Box 1032, Pretoria, 0001, South Africa.

T F W M NEWSLETTER. *see* TECHNOLOGY: COMPREHENSIVE WORKS

200 BEL ISSN 1370-6691
T G L. TIJDSCHRIFT VOOR GEESTELIJK LEVEN. Text in Dutch. 1990. bi-m. EUR 18.75 domestic; EUR 18.75 in Netherlands; EUR 31.75 foreign (effective 2007).
Formed by the merger of (1945-1989): Tijdschrift voor Geestelijk Leven (1572-7890); (1971-1989): Relief (0167-1316)
Published by: TGL, Guimardstr 1, Brussel, 1040, Belgium. TEL 32-2-5099672, FAX 32-2-5099704, info@tgl.be, http://www.tgl.be. Ed. Ignace D'hert.

200 800 DEU ISSN 0941-0570
T H L I. (Textwissenschaft Theologie Hermeneutik Literaturanalyse Informatik) Text in German. 1991. irreg., latest vol.9, 1994. price varies. **Document type:** *Monographic series, Academic/Scholarly.*
Published by: A. Francke Verlag GmbH, Dischinger Weg 5, Tuebingen, 72070, Germany. TEL 49-7071-97970, FAX 49-7071-979711, info@francke.de, http://www.francke.de.

371.07 CAN ISSN 1196-6777
T R A C E NEWS. Text in English. 1976. 2/yr. CAD 15 (effective 2000). **Document type:** *Newsletter.*
Former titles (until 1991): T R A C E Teachers of Religion and Christian Ethics (1196-6769); (until 1979): T R A C E S Teachers of Religion and Christian Ethics in Saskatchewan (0704-6421); (until 1977): T R A C E Newsletter (0701-192X)
Published by: (Teachers of Religion and Christian Ethics), Saskatchewan Teachers' Federation, 2317 Arlington Ave., Saskatoon, SK S7J 2H8, Canada. stf@stf.sk.ca. Ed. Miles Myers.

T T N - AKZENTE. (Technik Theologie Naturwissenschaften) *see* SCIENCES: COMPREHENSIVE WORKS

▼ **T Y J MAGAZINE**; encouraging the souls & enriching the minds of our christian youth. (Team Youth Journal) *see* LIFESTYLE

TA ETHIKA. *see* PHILOSOPHY

200 GBR ISSN 0039-8837
AP4
THE TABLET. Text in English. 19??. w. GBP 72 domestic; USD 124 in US & Canada; AUD 185 in Australia & New Zealand (effective 2009). adv. bk.rev.; film rev. index. back issues avail.; reprints avail. **Document type:** *Newspaper, Consumer.* **Description:** Covers religion, politics, society, ethics and the arts.
Formerly (until 1840): True Tablet
Related titles: Microform ed.: (from PQC).
Indexed: A22, CERDIC, CPL, RASB.
—BLDSC (8597.450000), IE, Infotrieve, Ingenta. **CCC.**
Published by: Tablet Publishing Co. Ltd., 1 King St Cloisters, Clifton Walk, London, W6 0QZ, United Kingdom. TEL 44-20-87488484, FAX 44-20-87481550, tablet@subscription.co.uk. Ed. Catherine Pepinster. Pub. Ignatius Kusiak. Adv. contact San Gow TEL 44-20-78806217.

200 TWN ISSN 0251-4788
BR118
TAIWAN SHENXUE LUKAN/TAIWAN JOURNAL OF THEOLOGY. Text in Chinese. 1979. a. **Document type:** *Journal, Academic/Scholarly.*
Indexed: A21, RI-1.
Published by: Taiwan Shengxueyuan, 20 Lane 2, Section 2, Yang Teh Ta Road, Shihlin District, Taipei, 11106, Taiwan. TEL 886-2-28822370, http://www.taitheo.org.tw/.

200 TWN
TAIWAN SHENXUEYUAN YUANXUN. Text in Chinese. 1981. bi-m. **Document type:** *Journal, Academic/Scholarly.*
Related titles: Online - full text ed.
Published by: Taiwan Shengxueyuan, 20 Lane 2, Section 2, Yang Teh Ta Road, Shihlin District, Taipei, 11106, Taiwan. TEL 886-2-28822370, http://www.taitheo.org.tw/.

200 USA ISSN 1541-8448
BL1
TAKING SIDES: CLASHING VIEWS ON CONTROVERSIAL ISSUES IN RELIGION. Text in English. 2003 (Nov.). irreg., latest 2003, 1st ed. **Document type:** *Catalog, Academic/Scholarly.* **Description:** Covers controversial issues in religion through paired pro and con articles on such issues as the existence of evil, the doctrine of salvation, abortion and cloning, the theory of evolution, justifications for war, and the sanctity of the family.
Published by: McGraw-Hill, Contemporary Learning Series (Subsidiary of: McGraw-Hill Companies, Inc.), 1221 Ave of the Americas, New York, NY 10020. TEL 212-904-2000, 800-243-6532, FAX 212-512-2000, customer.service@mcgraw-hill.com, http://www.mhhe.com/cls/.

200 USA
TANTRA: THE MAGAZINE. Text in English. 1991. q. USD 18. adv. bk.rev. illus. **Document type:** *Magazine, Consumer.* **Description:** Devoted to tantric practices found throughout the world, including history, philosophy, rituals and life-styles.
Address: PO Box 2187, Ranchos De Taos, NM 87557. Ed. Ananda Hubert. Pub. Alan Verdegraal. Circ: 13,000.

220 USA
TAPESTRY. Text in English. 1994. m. USD 29.74 domestic; USD 36.95 in Canada; USD 60.95 elsewhere; USD 3.95 newsstand/cover (effective 2011). **Document type:** *Magazine, Trade.* **Description:** Devotional magazine designed for women.
Published by: Walk Thru the Bible Ministries, Inc., 4201 N Peachtree Rd, Atlanta, GA 30341. TEL 800-361-6131, info@walkthru.org.

268.8 USA ISSN 0082-1713
TARBELL'S TEACHER'S GUIDE; to the International Sunday School Lessons. Text in English. 1905. a. USD 7.95 (effective 1999). **Description:** Bible commentary using KJV and RSV for Sunday School teachers.
Published by: David C. Cook Publishing Co., 4050 Lee Vance View, Colorado Springs, CO 80918. TEL 719-536-0100. Ed. William P Barker. Circ: 2,300.

200 KEN
TARGET. Text in English. 1964. bi-m.
Address: PO Box 72839, Nairobi, Kenya. Ed. Rebeka Njau. Circ: 17,000.

250 USA ISSN 1047-4250
TAWAGOTO. Text in English. 1975. 3/yr. USD 30 domestic; USD 35 foreign (effective 2002). adv. bk.rev.; film rev.; music rev. back issues avail. **Document type:** *Newsletter, Consumer.* **Description:** Reflects the communication and teaching work of Lee Lozowick, and chronicles the process of spiritual growth of the members of Hohm Sahaj Mandir.
Incorporated (1988-1989): Divine Slave Gita (0733-5369); Formerly: At Hohm Newsletter
Published by: (Hohm Sahaj Mandir), Hohm Press, PO Box 4272, Prescott, AZ 86302. TEL 928-778-9189, FAX 928-717-1779, staff@hohmpress.com, http://www.hohmpress.com. Ed. Angelon Young. R&P, Adv. contact Dasya Zuccarello. Circ: 250.

270.092 USA
TEACHERS OF VISION. Text in English. 1953. bi-m. free to members (effective 2004). adv. bk.rev. 16 p./no.; **Document type:** *Newsletter, Consumer.* **Description:** Articles of interest to Christians serving in public schools.
Formerly (until 2000): Vision (Pasadena) (0882-6609)
Published by: Christian Educators Association International, PO Box 41300, Pasadena, CA 91114. TEL 626-798-1124, FAX 626-798-2346. Ed. Forrest Turpen. R&P, Adv. contact Judy Turpen. Circ: 8,000 (paid and controlled).

R

200.71 GBR ISSN 1368-4868
BL41
➤ **TEACHING THEOLOGY AND RELIGION.** Text in English. 1998. q. GBP 306 in United Kingdom to institutions; EUR 387 in Europe to institutions; USD 515 in the Americas to institutions; USD 596 elsewhere to institutions; GBP 352 combined subscription in United Kingdom to institutions (print & online eds.); EUR 446 combined subscription in Europe to institutions (print & online eds.); USD 592 combined subscription in the Americas to institutions (print & online eds.); USD 686 combined subscription elsewhere to institutions (print & online eds.) (effective 2012). bk.rev.; film rev.; software rev. reprint service avail. from PSC. **Document type:** *Journal, Academic/ Scholarly.* **Description:** Includes articles on: the philosophy and theology of teaching, assessment in theology and religion, the relation between teaching church history and theology, objectivity and advocacy in teaching, and other issues in teaching and learning in theology and religion.
Related titles: Online - full text ed.: ISSN 1467-9647. GBP 306 in United Kingdom to institutions; EUR 387 in Europe to institutions; USD 515 in the Americas to institutions; USD 596 elsewhere to institutions (effective 2012) (from IngentaConnect).
Indexed: A01, A03, A08, A21, A22, A26, AmHI, B29, CA, CPE, E01, E03, E07, ERI, H07, P02, P18, P28, P48, P53, P54, PQC, RI-1, S21, SCOPUS, T02.
—BLDSC (8614.349500), IE, Infotrieve, Ingenta. **CCC.**
Published by: (American Academy of Religion USA, The Association of Theological Schools in the United States and Canada USA), Wiley-Blackwell Publishing Ltd. (Subsidiary of: John Wiley & Sons, Inc.), 9600 Garsington Rd, Oxford, OX4 2DQ, United Kingdom. TEL 44-1865-776868, FAX 44-1865-714591, customerservices@blackwellpublishing.com, http://www.wiley.com/ WileyCDA/. Ed. Patricia Killen. Adv. contact Kristin McCarthy. **Co-sponsors:** Wabash Center for Teaching and Learning in Theology and Religion; Society for Biblical Literature.

➤ **TEACHING WITH COMPASSION, COMPETENCE, COMMITMENT.** *see* EDUCATION

➤ **TEAM N Y I MAGAZINE**; resourcing Nazarene youth workers. *see* EDUCATION

➤ **TECHNOLOGIES FOR WORSHIP.** *see* TECHNOLOGY: COMPREHENSIVE WORKS

220 375 GBR ISSN 0261-2860
TEEN-SEARCH. Text in English. 1981. 3/yr. GBP 2.20 per issue (effective 2010). illus. back issues avail. **Document type:** *Magazine, Academic/ Scholarly.* **Description:** Contains questions, puzzles and other activities to get young teens to recall and think through what they have learned in the lesson, referring to the bible passage and other texts.
Published by: Go Teach Publications Ltd., Unit 12 Paradise Mill, Park Lane, Macclesfield, SK11 6TJ, United Kingdom. TEL 44-1625-422279, FAX 44-1625-422272, editorial@goteach.org.uk.

TEILHARD AUJOURD'HUI. *see* PHILOSOPHY

200 USA ISSN 0741-4250
B2430.T374
TEILHARD PERSPECTIVES. Text in English. 1983. s-a. USD 2 per issue to non-members; free to members (effective 2010). back issues avail. **Document type:** *Newsletter, Academic/Scholarly.* **Description:** Provides fresh perspectives on Teilhard de Chardin's remarkable evolutionary vision often in ways that directly relate to an ecologically and spiritually sustainable earth community.
Related titles: Online - full text ed.: free (effective 2010).
Published by: American Teilhard Association, c o John Grim, PO Box 280, Lewisburg, PA 17837. TEL 570-577-1205, grim@religionandecology.org, http://www.teilharddechardin.org/ association.html. Ed. Arthur Fabel.

200 USA ISSN 0739-2303
B2430.T374
TEILHARD STUDIES. Text in English. 1978. s-a. USD 4 per issue to non-members; free to members (effective 2010). back issues avail. **Document type:** *Monographic series, Academic/Scholarly.*
Related titles: Online - full text ed.: free (effective 2010).
Indexed: A21, AmHI, CA, H07, RI-1, T02.
Published by: American Teilhard Association, c o John Grim, PO Box 280, Lewisburg, PA 17837. TEL 570-577-1205, grim@religionandecology.org, http://www.teilharddechardin.org/ association.html. Ed. Kathleen Duffy.

220 DNK ISSN 0904-4868
➤ **TEKST OG TOLKNING.** Text in Danish. 1970. irreg., latest vol.12, 2000. price varies. **Document type:** *Monographic series, Academic/ Scholarly.*
Published by: (Koebenhavns Universitet, Institut for Bibelsk Eksegese), Museum Tusculanum Press, c/o University of Copenhagen, Njalsgade 126, Copenhagen S, 2300, Denmark. TEL 45-35-329109, FAX 45-35-329113, info@mtp.dk, http://www.mtp.dk. **Dist. in France by:** Editions Picard, Editions Picard, Paris 75006, France. TEL 33-1-43269778, FAX 33-1-43264264; **Dist. in UK by:** Gazelle Book Services Ltd., White Cross Mills, Hightown, Lancaster LA1 4UU, United Kingdom. TEL 44-1524-68765, FAX 44-1524-63232, sales@gazellebooks.co.uk, http://www.gazellebookservices.co.uk/; **Dist. in US & Canada by:** International Specialized Book Services Inc., 920 NE 58th Ave Ste 300, Portland, OR 97213. TEL 503-287-3093, FAX 503-280-8832, orders@isbs.com, http://www.isbs.com/.

200 USA
TELLING THE TRUTH. Text in English. m. adv.
Published by: Triple T Ministries, 12814 U S Hwy 41 N, Evansville, IN 47711. TEL 812-867-2418. Ed. George Dooms. Circ: 2,000.

200 FIN ISSN 0497-1817
BL1.A1
➤ **TEMENOS**; studies in comparative religion presented by scholars in Denmark, Finland, Norway and Sweden. Text in English. 1965. s-a. price varies. bk.rev. **Document type:** *Journal, Academic/Scholarly.* **Description:** Devoted to history of religions, comparative religion, phenomenology of religion.
Indexed: A20, A21, AICP, ASCA, ArtHuCI, BAS, FR, IBR, IBZ, MLA-IB, OTA, PCI, RASB, RI-1, RI-2, RILM, SCOPUS, W07.
—BLDSC (8789.760000), IE, Ingenta, INIST.
Published by: Finnish Society for the Study of Comparative Religion, c/o Nils G. Holm, Aabo Akademi University, Aabo, 20500, Finland. TEL 358-2-2154398, FAX 358-2-2154902. Eds. Nils G. Holm, Veikko Anttonen. Circ: 350. **Dist. by:** Academic Bookstore, PO Box 128, Helsinki 00101, Finland.

200 ITA ISSN 1124-0431
TEMI DI PREDICAZIONE - OMELIE. Text in Italian. 1957. m. adv. **Document type:** *Magazine, Consumer.*
Indexed: CERDIC.
Published by: Editrice Domenicana Italiana, Via G Marotta 12, Naples, 80133, Italy. http://www.edi.na.it.

TEMOIGNAGE CHRETIEN. *see* LITERARY AND POLITICAL REVIEWS

271.7913 AUS ISSN 1328-9187
TEMPLER RECORD. Text and summaries in English, German. 1946. m. free to members (effective 2009). adv. 40 p./no.; **Document type:** *Newsletter, Trade.* **Description:** Aims to promote Templer Christian thinking.
Related titles: Online - full content ed.
Published by: Temple Society Australia, 152 Tucker Rd, Bentleigh, VIC 3204, Australia. TEL 61-3-95576713, FAX 61-3-95577943, tsa@templesociety.org.au. Ed. Mrs. Herta Uhlherr. Circ: 600.

200 ITA ISSN 1120-267X
BR5
TEOLOGIA. Text in Multiple languages. 1976. q. EUR 36.50 per issue (effective 2009). **Document type:** *Journal, Academic/Scholarly.*
Indexed: CERDIC, OTA.
Published by: (Facolta Teologica dell'Italia Settentrionale), Libreria Editrice Glossa, Piazza Paolo VI 6, Milan, 20121, Italy. TEL 39-02-877609, FAX 39-02-72003162, http://www.glossaeditrice.it.

200 ARG ISSN 0328-1396
TEOLOGIA. Text in Spanish. 1962. q. ARS 70 (effective 2010). back issues avail. **Document type:** *Journal, Academic/Scholarly.*
Related titles: Online - full text ed.
Indexed: CA, F04, T02.
Published by: Pontificia Universidad Catolica Argentina, Facultad de Teologia, Concordia 4422, Buenos Aires, C1419AOH, Argentina. TEL 54-11-45016748, FAX 54-11-45016428, teologia@uca.edu.ar, http://www2.uca.edu.ar/esp/sec-fteologia/esp/page.php?subsec= nfacultad. Circ: 600.

230 ESP ISSN 0495-1549
BX2350.65
TEOLOGIA ESPIRITUAL. Text in Spanish. 1958. 3/yr. bk.rev. index. **Document type:** *Bulletin, Consumer.*
Indexed: BibInd, DIP, IBR, IBZ, MLA-IB.
Published by: Facultad de Teologia "San Vicente Ferrer", Seccion Dominicos, Cirilo Amaros, 54, Valencia, 46004, Spain. TEL 34-96-3517750, FAX 34-96-3526805, facteologiavlc.ar@dominicos.org, http://www.dominicos.org/. Circ: 600.

230 VEN
TEOLOGIA I U S I. Text in Spanish. a.
Indexed: OTA.
Published by: Instituto Universitario Seminario Interdiocesano Santa Rosa de Lima, Apdo 129, Caracas, DF 1010-A, Venezuela. FAX 58-2-813567.

200 ESP ISSN 0212-1964
TEOLOGIA Y CATEQUESIS. Text in Spanish. 1982. q. EUR 32 domestic; EUR 66 in Europe; USD 82.50 rest of world (effective 2008). bk.rev. bibl. back issues avail. **Document type:** *Journal, Academic/Scholarly.*
Published by: Facultad de Teologia "San Damaso", C Jerte 10, Madrid, 28005, Spain. TEL 34-91-3644010. Circ: 400.

230 FIN ISSN 0040-3555
➤ **TEOLOGINEN AIKAKAUSKIRJA/TEOLOGISK TIDSKRIFT.** Text in Swedish, Finnish; Summaries in English. 1896. 6/yr. EUR 38 domestic; EUR 44 in Europe; EUR 48 elsewhere (effective 2005). adv. bk.rev. charts; illus. index, cum.index. 100 p./no. 6 cols./p.; back issues avail. **Document type:** *Magazine, Academic/Scholarly.*
Indexed: IZBG.
Published by: Teologinen Julkaisuseura r.y., PO Box 33, Helsinki, 00014, Finland. TEL 358-9-174527, FAX 358-9-19123033, toimitus@tatt.fi, http://www.tatt.fi. Ed. Marti Nissinen TEL 358-9-3892979. Circ: 2,500.

200 DNK ISSN 1603-337X
AARHUS UNIVERSITET. DET TEOLOGISKE FACULTET. AARSSKRIFT. Text in Danish. 2003. a. back issues avail. **Document type:** *Yearbook, Consumer.*
Related titles: Online - full text ed.
Published by: Aarhus Universitet, Det Teologiske Fakultet/University of Aarhus, Faculty of Theology, Taasingegade 3, Aarhus C, 8000, Denmark. TEL 45-89-421111, FAX 45-89-130490, teo@au.dk. Ed. Ulrik Vosgerau.

TESTIFY SISTER MAGAZINE. *see* WOMEN'S INTERESTS

200.19 ITA
TESTIMONI; quindicinale di informazione e aggiornamento per istituti di vita consacrata. Text in Italian. 1978. fortn. EUR 32.90 domestic; EUR 52 in the European Union; EUR 59.70 elsewhere (effective 2008). adv. bk.rev. **Document type:** *Magazine, Consumer.* **Description:** Informs consecrated men and women on psychology and spiritual life.
Published by: Centro Editoriale Dehoniano, Via Scipione dal Ferro 4, Bologna, BO 40138, Italy. TEL 39-051-4290451, FAX 39-051-4290491, ced-amm@dehoniane.it, http://www.dehoniane.it. Circ: 11,000.

TESTIMONIANZE. *see* LITERARY AND POLITICAL REVIEWS

207.8 GBR
TESTIMONY MAGAZINE; for the study and defence of the holy scripture. Text in English; Alternating issues in Acholi, Multiple languages. 1931. m. GBP 12.15 domestic; AUD 46 in Australia; CAD 39 in Canada; NZD 53 in New Zealand; USD 33 in United States; GBP 22 elsewhere (effective 2009). bk.rev.; software rev.; Website rev. charts; illus.; maps. index. 36 p./no. 2 cols./p.; back issues avail. **Document type:** *Magazine, Consumer.* **Description:** Designed for the study and defence of the Holy Scripture.
Published by: Testimony Magazine Promoting Committee, The Pines, Ling Common Rd, Castle Rising, King's Lynn, United Kingdom. info@testimony-magazine.org. Ed. Eric Marshall.

220 NLD ISSN 1569-3619
TEXT-CRITICAL STUDIES. Cover title: S B L Text-Critical Studies. Text in English. 2002. irreg. price varies. **Document type:** *Monographic series.* **Description:** Publishes textual criticism of the Hebrew Bible/Old Testament or New Testament.
Indexed: IZBG.
Published by: (Society of Biblical Literature USA), Brill, PO Box 9000, Leiden, 2300 PA, Netherlands. TEL 31-71-5353500, FAX 31-71-5317532, cs@brill.nl.

220 DEU ISSN 0170-1096
TEXTE & KONTEXTE. Text in German. 1978. q. EUR 17 (effective 2008). back issues avail. **Document type:** *Journal, Academic/Scholarly.*
Indexed: IZBG, OTA.
Published by: Verein fuer Politische und Theologische Bildung Lehrhaus e.V., Nervierstr 12, Dortmund, 44263, Germany. Ed. Andreas Bedenbender.

230 DEU
▼ **TEXTE UND STUDIEN ZUR EUROPAEISCHEN GEISTESGESCHICHTE. REIHE A.** Text in German. 2011. irreg. price varies. **Document type:** *Monographic series, Academic/Scholarly.*
Published by: Aschendorff Verlag GmbH & Co. KG, Soester Str 13, Muenster, 48135, Germany. TEL 49-251-6900, FAX 49-251-6904570, buchverlag@aschendorff.de, http://www.aschendorff-buchverlag.de. Eds. Harald Schwaetzer, Jorge Machetta, Klaus Reinhardt.

230 DEU
▼ **TEXTE UND STUDIEN ZUR EUROPAEISCHEN GEISTESGESCHICHTE. REIHE B.** Text in German. 2011. irreg. price varies. **Document type:** *Monographic series, Academic/Scholarly.*
Published by: Aschendorff Verlag GmbH & Co. KG, Soester Str 13, Muenster, 48135, Germany. TEL 49-251-6900, FAX 49-251-6904570, buchverlag@aschendorff.de, http://www.aschendorff-buchverlag.de. Eds. Harald Schwaetzer, Inigo Bocken, Marc de Mey, Wolfgang Christian Schneider.

200 465 DEU ISSN 0082-3589
BR45
TEXTE UND UNTERSUCHUNGEN ZUR GESCHICHTE DER ALTCHRISTLICHEN LITERATUR. Text in German. 1952. irreg., latest vol.167, 2011. price varies. **Document type:** *Monographic series, Academic/Scholarly.*
Related titles: Microfiche ed.: (from IDC).
Indexed: PCI.
Published by: Walter de Gruyter GmbH & Co. KG, Genthiner Str 13, Berlin, 10785, Germany. TEL 49-30-260050, FAX 49-30-26005251, info@degruyter.com, http://www.degruyter.de. Ed. Christoph Markschies.

230 BEL
➤ **TEXTES ET ETUDES LITURGIQUES/STUDIES IN LITURGY.** Text in French, English. 1953 (No 2). irreg., latest 2010. price varies. back issues avail. **Document type:** *Monographic series, Academic/ Scholarly.* **Description:** Studies Christian liturgical texts.
Published by: Peeters Publishers, Bondgenotenlaan 153, Leuven, 3000, Belgium. TEL 32-16-235170, FAX 32-16-228500, http://www.peeters-leuven.be.

200 LBN ISSN 1682-8615
TEXTES ET ETUDES SUR L'ORIENT CHRETIEN/MUSUS WA-DIRASAT FI AL-SHARQ AL-MASIHI. Text in French, Arabic. 1986. irreg. **Document type:** *Academic/Scholarly.*
Published by: Universite Saint-Joseph, BP 16-6778, Beyrouth, 1100 2150, Lebanon. TEL 961-1-200-458, cedrac@usj.edu.lb, http:// www.cedrac.usj.edu.lb/index.htm.

222 CHE
TEXTPRAGMATISCHE STUDIEN ZUR LITERATUR- UND KULTURGESCHICHTE DER HEBRAEISCHEN BIBEL. Text in German. 2003. irreg., latest vol.3, 2006. price varies. **Document type:** *Monographic series, Academic/Scholarly.*
Published by: Theologischer Verlag Zurich, Badenerstr 73, Zurich, 8026, Switzerland. TEL 41-44-2993355, FAX 41-44-2993358, tvz@ref.ch.

225 NLD ISSN 1574-7085
TEXTS AND EDITIONS FOR NEW TESTAMENT STUDY. Text in English. 2005. irreg., latest vol.3, 2007. price varies. **Document type:** *Monographic series, Academic/Scholarly.* **Description:** Publishes texts and editions, with commentary and comment, of important sources for the study of the New Testament and its world.
Indexed: IZBG.
—CCC.
Published by: Brill, PO Box 9000, Leiden, 2300 PA, Netherlands. TEL 31-71-5353500, FAX 31-71-5317532, cs@brill.nl. Eds. Stanley E Porter, Wendy J Porter.

220 USA ISSN 1935-6927
TEXTS AND STUDIES. Text in English. 2004. irreg., latest 2009. price varies. back issues avail. **Document type:** *Monographic series, Academic/Scholarly.* **Description:** Covers critical editions, studies of primary sources, and analyses of textual traditions.
Published by: Gorgias Press LLC, 954 River Rd, Piscataway, NJ 08854. TEL 732-885-8900, FAX 732-885-8908, helpdesk@gorgiaspress.com, http://www.gorgiaspress.com/ bookshop/default.aspx.

200 USA
➤ **TEXTS AND STUDIES IN RELIGION.** Text in English. 1977. irreg., latest vol.109, 2005. price varies. back issues avail.; reprints avail. **Document type:** *Monographic series, Academic/Scholarly.*
Published by: Edwin Mellen Press, 415 Ridge St, PO Box 450, Lewiston, NY 14092. TEL 716-754-2266, FAX 716-754-4056, cservice@mellenpress.com.

270.2 909 USA ISSN 1935-6846
TEXTS FROM CHRISTIAN LATE ANTIQUITY. Text mainly in English; Text occasionally in Syriac. 2006. irreg., latest 2009. price varies. back issues avail. **Document type:** *Monographic series, Academic/ Scholarly.* **Description:** Features letters and other writings from Christian figures from late antiquity, as well as modern scholarly commentary.
Published by: Gorgias Press LLC, 954 River Rd, Piscataway, NJ 08854. TEL 732-885-8900, FAX 732-885-8908, helpdesk@gorgiaspress.com, http://www.gorgiaspress.com/ bookshop/default.aspx.

220 ISR ISSN 0082-3767
BS410
TEXTUS; studies of the Hebrew University. Text in English; Summaries in Hebrew. 1960. a., latest vol.24, 2008. USD 53.30 per issue to non-members; USD 48 per issue to members (effective 2008). back issues avail. **Document type:** *Monographic series, Academic/Scholarly.*
Indexed: A22, DIP, IBR, IBZ, MLA-IB, OTA, PCI.
—BLDSC (8813.785000), IE, Ingenta.
Published by: (Hebrew University of Jerusalem), Magnes Press (Subsidiary of: Hebrew University of Jerusalem), Hebrew University, Jerusalem, The Sherman Building for Research Management, PO Box 39099, Jerusalem, 91390, Israel. TEL 972-2-658-6660, FAX 972-2-563-3370, hubp@h2.hum.juhi.ac.il, http://www.magnespress.co.il/website_en/index.asp?action=show_covers&covers_mode=home_page. Ed. Dr. Alexander Rofe. **Dist. by:** Eisenbrauns Inc., PO Box 275, Winona Lake, IN 46590.

THAT'S THE SPIRIT MAGAZINE. *see* PARAPSYCHOLOGY AND OCCULTISM

200 DEU ISSN 0943-9587
THEION; Studien zur Religionskultur - studies in religious culture. Text in German. 1993. irreg., latest vol.24, 2009. price varies. **Document type:** *Monographic series, Academic/Scholarly.*
Published by: Peter Lang GmbH (Subsidiary of: Peter Lang Publishing Group), Eschborner Landstr 42-50, Frankfurt Am Main, 60489, Germany. TEL 49-69-7807050, FAX 49-69-78070550, zentrale.frankfurt@peterlang.com, http://www.peterlang.com. Eds. Edmund Weber, Wilhelm-Ludwig Federlin.

230.0711 GBR ISSN 0307-8388
BR1.A1
THEMELIOS. Text in English. 1976. 3/yr. GBP 10 domestic to individuals; GBP 13 foreign to individuals; USD 16 domestic to individuals; USD 20 foreign to individuals; GBP 15 domestic to institutions; GBP 18 foreign to institutions; USD 23 domestic to institutions; USD 28 foreign to institutions (effective 2009). bk.rev. bibl. back issues avail. **Document type:** *Journal, Academic/Scholarly.* **Description:** Provides cutting edge articles on a wide range of issues relevant to students of theology and RS.
Indexed: A21, A22, OTA, R&TA, RI-1, RI-2.
—BLDSC (8814.477000), IE, Ingenta. **CCC.**
Published by: Universities and Colleges Christian Fellowship, 38 De Montfort St, Leicster, LE1 7GP, United Kingdom. TEL 44-116-2551700, FAX 44-116-2555672, email@uccf.org.uk. **Co-sponsor:** International Fellowship of Evangelical Students.

200 DEU ISSN 1862-8028
THEMENHEFTE GEMEINDE. Text in German. 1972. 9/yr. EUR 108; EUR 15 newsstand/cover (effective 2011). **Document type:** *Journal, Trade.*
Former titles (until 2006): Themenhefte Gemeindearbeit (0937-8766); (until 1990): Forum (0722-7647); (until 1982): Forum fuer Pfarrgemeinderate (0722-7639)
Published by: Bergmoser und Hoeller Verlag GmbH, Karl-Friedrich-Str 76, Aachen, 52072, Germany. TEL 49-241-93888123, FAX 49-241-93888134, kontakt@buhv.de. Circ: 3,700.

220 NLD ISSN 1388-3909
THEMES IN BIBLICAL NARRATIVE. Text in English. 1998. irreg., latest vol.12, 2008. price varies. **Document type:** *Monographic series, Academic/Scholarly.*
Indexed: IZBG.
—CCC.
Published by: Brill, PO Box 9000, Leiden, 2300 PA, Netherlands. TEL 31-71-5353500, FAX 31-71-5317532, cs@brill.nl.

200 370 DEU ISSN 1863-0502
BL41
THEO-WEB. ZEITSCHRIFT FUER RELIGIONPAEDAGOGIK. Text in German. 2002. s-a. free (effective 2011). **Document type:** *Journal, Academic/Scholarly.*
Media: Online - full text.
Indexed: A39, C27, C29, D03, D04, E13, R14, S14, S15, S18.
—CCC.
Published by: Theo-Web, c/o Martin Rothgangel, Platz der Goettinger Sieben 2, Goettingen, 37073, Germany. TEL 49-551-397119, martin@rothgangel.de. Ed., Pub. Martin Rothgangel.

260 CAN ISSN 1495-7922
THEOFORUM. Text in English, French. 1970. 3/yr. CAD 46.80, USD 43 domestic; CAD 60 foreign (effective 2000). adv. bk.rev. index. reprints avail. **Document type:** *Journal, Academic/Scholarly.*
Formerly: Eglise et Theologie (0013-2349)
Related titles: Microform ed.: (from PQC).
Indexed: A21, A22, CERDIC, CLA, DIP, FR, IBR, IBZ, MLA-IB, OTA, R&TA, RI-1, RI-2.
—BLDSC (8814.502750), IE, Ingenta, INIST. **CCC.**
Published by: Saint Paul University, Faculty of Theology (Subsidiary of: Saint Paul University/Universite Saint-Paul), 223 Main St, Ottawa, ON K1S 1C4, Canada. TEL 613-236-1393, FAX 613-751-4028. Ed., R&P, Adv. contact Leo Laberge.

230 SWE ISSN 1652-9480
THEOLOGIA; tidskrift foer kyrklig teologi. Text in Swedish. 2005. 3/yr. SEK 240 domestic; SEK 320 in Scandinavia; SEK 70 per issue (effective 2006). **Document type:** *Magazine, Consumer.*
Published by: Artos & Norma Bokfoerlag AB, Kyrkstadsvaegen 6, Skellefteaa, 93133, Sweden. TEL 46-910-779102, FAX 46-910779155, info@artos.se, http://www.artos.se. Ed. Bro. Johannes Sandgren. Pub. Per Aakerlund.

200 HUN ISSN 0133-7599
BR9.H8
THEOLOGIAI SZEMLE. Text in Hungarian. 1925. 6/yr. bk.rev. **Document type:** *Academic/Scholarly.*
Indexed: HistAb, P30, RILM.
Published by: Magyarorszagi Egyhazak Okumenikus Tanacsa/ Ecumenical Council of Churches in Hungary, Magyar tudosok krt. 3, Budapest, 1117, Hungary. TEL 36-1-3712690, FAX 36-1-3712691. Ed., R&P Tibor Gorog. Circ: 1,000.

200 900 ITA ISSN 1973-6193
THEOLOGICA ET HISTORICA. Key Title: Theologica & Historica. Text in Italian. 1992. a. **Document type:** *Journal, Academic/Scholarly.*
Formerly (until 1994): Theologica (1973-6185)
Published by: (Pontificia Facolta Teologica della Sardegna), Edizioni Piemme SpA, Via Galeotto del Carretto 10, Casale Monferrato, AL 15033, Italy. TEL 39-0142-3361, FAX 39-0142-74223, http://piemme3.bluestudio.it.

200 GBR ISSN 0954-2191
THEOLOGICAL BOOK REVIEW. Text in English. 1988. 3/yr. GBP 18, USD 36. adv. bk.rev. **Document type:** *Catalog.* **Description:** For theological librarians and educators to aid them in current book selections.
Published by: Feed the Minds, Albany House, 67 Sydenham Rd, Guildford, Surrey GU1 3RY, United Kingdom. TEL 44-1483-888580, FAX 44-1483-888581. Ed. Ian Markham. R&P D Olga Davies. Adv. contact D O Davies. Circ: 600.

230.007 371.07 USA ISSN 0040-5620
BV4019
➤ **THEOLOGICAL EDUCATION.** Text in English. 1964. s-a. USD 15, USD 10 to individuals (effective 2010). adv. stat. index. back issues avail.; reprints avail. **Document type:** *Journal, Academic/Scholarly.*
Related titles: Microform ed.: (from PQC); Online - full text ed.
Indexed: A21, A22, CERDIC, FamI, GSS&RPL, R&TA, RI-1, RI-2.
—CCC.
Published by: The Association of Theological Schools in the United States and Canada, 10 Summit Park Dr, Pittsburgh, PA 15275. TEL 412-788-6505, FAX 412-788-6510, ats@ats.edu.

➤ **THEOLOGICAL LIBRARIANSHIP.** *see* LIBRARY AND INFORMATION SCIENCES

200 LBN ISSN 0379-9557
BR1
THEOLOGICAL REVIEW. Text in English. 1978. s-a.
Formerly: Near East School of Theology. Quarterly
Related titles: Online - full text ed.: ISSN 2076-4723.
Indexed: A01, A03, A08, A21, A22, CA, I14, IZBG, OTA, R&TA, RI-1, T02.
—BLDSC (8814.523690), IE, Ingenta.
Published by: Near East School of Theology, NEST, Sourati St, Chouron, P O Box 13-5780, Beirut, 1102-2070, Lebanon. TEL 961-1-346708, FAX 961-1-347129, nest.adm@inco.com.lb, http://www.reformiert-online.net.

230 USA ISSN 0040-5639
BX801
➤ **THEOLOGICAL STUDIES**; a jesuit-sponsored journal of theology. Abbreviated title: T S. Text in English. 1940. q. USD 28 domestic to individuals; USD 40 foreign to individuals; USD 55 foreign to institutions (school/library); USD 12 per issue domestic; USD 16 per issue foreign (effective 2009). bk.rev. illus. index, cum.index: vols.1-40. back issues avail.; reprints avail. **Document type:** *Journal, Academic/Scholarly.* **Description:** Publishes scholarly articles, bulletins, and notes on religions, ethics, history, and spirituality.
Related titles: Microform ed.: (from PQC); Online - full text ed.
Indexed: A01, A02, A03, A08, A20, A21, A22, A26, ASCA, AmHI, ArtHuCI, B04, B14, BRD, BRI, CA, CBRI, CERDIC, CLA, CPL, CurCont, DIP, E08, FR, G08, H07, H08, H09, H10, H14, HAb, HumInd, I05, IBR, IBZ, IZBG, M01, M02, MLA-IB, OTA, P02, P10, P28, P30, P34, P48, P53, P54, PCI, PQC, PhilInd, R&TA, R05, RI-1, RI-2, RefSour, S02, S03, S09, SCOPUS, T02, W03, W05, W07.
—BLDSC (8814.524000), IE, Infotrieve, Ingenta, INIST. **CCC.**
Published by: Theological Studies, Inc., c/o David G Schultenover, Ed, Marquette University, 100 Coughlin Hall, Box 1881, Milwaukee, WI 53201. TEL 414-288-3164. Ed. David G Schultenover.

266 DEU ISSN 0930-0341
THEOLOGIE DER DRITTEN WELT. Text in German. 1981. irreg., latest vol.39, 2010. price varies. **Document type:** *Monographic series, Academic/Scholarly.*
Published by: Verlag Herder GmbH, Hermann-Herder-Str 4, Freiburg Im Breisgau, 79104, Germany. TEL 49-761-27170, FAX 49-761-2717520, kundenservice@herder.de, http://www.herder.de.

200 DEU ISSN 0342-1457
BR4
THEOLOGIE DER GEGENWART. Text in German. 1957. q. EUR 30; EUR 10 newsstand/cover (effective 2009). bk.rev. **Document type:** *Magazine, Consumer.*
Indexed: DIP, IBR, IBZ.
—IE.
Published by: Butzon und Bercker GmbH, Hoogeweg 71, Kevelaer, 47623, Germany. TEL 49-2832-9290, FAX 49-2832-929211, service@bube.de, http://www.butzonbercker.de. Circ: 1,350.

200 DEU ISSN 1862-1678
BR4
THEOLOGIE.GESCHICHTE; Zeitschrift fuer Theologie und Kulturgeschichte. Text in English, German, French. 2006. irreg. free (effective 2011). **Document type:** *Journal, Academic/Scholarly.*
Media: Online - full text.
Address: c/o Lucia Scherzberg, Institut fuer Katholische Theologie, Gebaeude A4 2, Postfach 151150, Saarbruecken, 66041, Germany. TEL 49-681-3022348, FAX 49-681-3022954. Eds. August Leugers-Scherzberg, Lucia Scherzberg.

220 DEU ISSN 1862-6157
THEOLOGIE - RELIGIONSWISSENSCHAFT. Text in German. 2005. irreg., latest vol.8, 2009. price varies. **Document type:** *Monographic series, Academic/Scholarly.*
Published by: Frank und Timme GmbH, Wittelsbacherstr 27a, Berlin, 10707, Germany. TEL 49-30-88667911, FAX 49-30-86398731, info@frank-timme.de.

230 DEU
THEOLOGIE UND DIENST. Text in German. 1973. irreg., latest vol.30. price varies. **Document type:** *Bulletin, Academic/Scholarly.*
Published by: (Pilgermission St. Chrischona CHE), Brunnen Verlag GmbH, Gottlieb-Daimler-Str 22, Giessen, 35398, Germany. TEL 49-641-60590, FAX 49-641-6059100, info@brunnen-verlag.de, http://www.brunnen-verlag.de. Circ: 3,000.

200 DEU ISSN 0170-9461
THEOLOGIE UND WIRKLICHKEIT. Text in German. 1974. irreg., latest vol.11, 1981. price varies. **Document type:** *Monographic series, Academic/Scholarly.*
Published by: Peter Lang GmbH (Subsidiary of: Peter Lang Publishing Group), Eschborner Landstr 42-50, Frankfurt Am Main, 60489, Germany. TEL 49-69-7807050, FAX 49-69-78070550, zentrale.frankfurt@peterlang.com, http://www.peterlang.com.

220 PER ISSN 1022-5390
THEOLOGIKA; revista biblico - teologica. Text in Spanish. 1983. s-a. **Document type:** *Journal, Academic/Scholarly.*
Indexed: A21, C01, IZBG, OTA, RI-1.
Published by: Universidad Peruana Union, Facultad de Teologia, Carretera Central km 19.0 Nana, Lima, Peru. TEL 51-1-3590094, FAX 51-1-3590063, http://www.upeu.edu.pe.

200 CAN ISSN 1188-7109
BR3T54
THEOLOGIQUES. Text in French. 1993. s-a. CAD 31 domestic to individuals; CAD 40 foreign to individuals; CAD 47 domestic to institutions; CAD 50 foreign to institutions (effective 2005).
Related titles: Online - full content ed.
Indexed: CPL, FR, IBSS.
—INIST.
Published by: Universite de Montreal, Faculte de Theologie, C.P. 6128 succ. Centre-ville, Montreal, PQ H3C 3J7, Canada. TEL 514-343-7080, FAX 514-343-5738.

200 NLD ISSN 1572-5057
THEOLOGISCH DEBAT. Text in Dutch. 2004. q. EUR 40 domestic; EUR 45 in Belgium (effective 2009).
—IE.
Published by: Uitgeverij Kok, Postbus 5018, Kampen, 8260 GA, Netherlands. TEL 31-38-3392555, FAX 31-38-3328912, http://www.kok.nl.

230 CHE
THEOLOGISCH-EKKLESIOLOGISCHE BEITRAEGE AARGAU. Text in German. 2005. irreg., latest vol.5, 2009. price varies. **Document type:** *Monographic series, Academic/Scholarly.*
Published by: Theologischer Verlag Zurich, Badenerstr 73, Zurich, 8026, Switzerland. TEL 41-44-2993355, FAX 41-44-2993358, tvz@ref.ch.

200 DEU ISSN 0040-5663
THEOLOGISCH-PRAKTISCHE QUARTALSCHRIFT. Text in German. 1848. q. EUR 35; EUR 10 newsstand/cover (effective 2010). adv. bk.rev. 112 p./no.; **Document type:** *Journal, Academic/Scholarly.*
Indexed: CERDIC, CLA, DIP, FR, IBR, IBZ, OTA.
—INIST.
Published by: (Katholisch-Theologische Privatuniversitaet Linz AUT), Verlag Friedrich Pustet, Gutenbergstr 8, Regensburg, 93051, Germany. TEL 49-941-920220, FAX 49-941-92022330, verlag@pustet.de, http://www.pustetverlag.de. Ed. Franz Gruber.

207.2 DEU ISSN 0342-2372
THEOLOGISCHE BEITRAEGE. Text in German. 1970. bi-m. EUR 27.90; EUR 5.10 newsstand/cover (effective 2011). adv. bk.rev. **Document type:** *Journal, Academic/Scholarly.* **Description:** Non-denominational publication containing essays on religion, ethics, and evangelism.
Indexed: CERDIC, DIP, IBR, IBZ, IZBG, OTA.
Published by: Theologischer Verlag R. Brockhaus, Bodenborn 43, Witten, 58452, Germany. TEL 49-2302-93093800, FAX 49-2302-93093801, info@brockhaus-verlag.de, http://fuenf.scm-digital.net/show.sxp/7380.html. Ed. Birgitta Zeihe-Muenstermann. Circ: 3,400 (controlled).

200 DEU ISSN 0563-4288
➤ **THEOLOGISCHE BIBLIOTHEK TOEPELMANN.** Text in German. 1952. irreg., latest vol.155, 2011. price varies. **Document type:** *Monographic series, Academic/Scholarly.*
—CCC.
Published by: Walter de Gruyter GmbH & Co. KG, Genthiner Str 13, Berlin, 10785, Germany. TEL 49-30-260050, FAX 49-30-26005251, info@degruyter.com, http://www.degruyter.de.

230 CHE ISSN 0082-3902
THEOLOGISCHE DISSERTATIONEN. Summaries in English, German. 1969. irreg. price varies. **Document type:** *Monographic series, Academic/Scholarly.*
Related titles: German ed.; English ed.
Published by: (Universitaet Basel, Theologische Fakultaet), Friedrich Reinhardt Verlag, Missionsstr 36, Basel, 4012, Switzerland. Ed. Bo Reicke. **Dist. by:** Albert J. Phiebig Books, PO Box 352, White Plains, NY 10602.

220 CHE
THEOLOGISCHE HOCHSCHULE CHUR. SCHRIFTENREIHE. Variant title: Schriftenreihe der Theologischen Hochschule Chur. Text in German. 2002. irreg., latest vol.7, 2006. price varies. **Document type:** *Monographic series, Academic/Scholarly.*
Published by: (Theologische Hochschule Chur), Academic Press Fribourg, Perolles 42, Fribourg, 1705, Switzerland. TEL 41-26-4264311, FAX 41-26-4264300, info@paulusedition.ch, http://www.paulusedition.ch/academic_press/.

200 DEU ISSN 0040-5671
Z7753
THEOLOGISCHE LITERATURZEITUNG; Monatsschrift fuer das gesamte Gebiet der Theologie und Religionswissenschaft. Text in German. 1876. m. EUR 136 domestic to individuals; EUR 169 foreign to individuals; EUR 168 domestic to institutions; EUR 198 foreign to institutions (effective 2009). adv. bk.rev. index. 56 p./no.; back issues avail. **Document type:** *Journal, Academic/Scholarly.*
Incorporates (1880-1943): Theologisches Literaturblatt (0323-6285)
Indexed: A21, A22, BibInd, BibLing, CERDIC, DIP, FR, IBR, IBZ, MLA-IB, OTA, PCI, R&TA, RASB, RI-1, RI-2, SCOPUS.
—IE, Infotrieve, INIST.
Published by: Evangelische Verlagsanstalt GmbH, Blumenstr 76, Leipzig, 04155, Germany. TEL 49-341-7114115, FAX 49-341-7114150, info@eva-leipzig.de, http://www.eva-leipzig.de. Ed. Dr. Annette Weidhas. Adv. contact Christine Herrmann TEL 49-341-7114122. page EUR 680; trim 175 x 255. Circ: 1,300 (paid).

230 DEU ISSN 0040-5698
BR4
THEOLOGISCHE RUNDSCHAU. Text in German. 1929. q. EUR 84 to individuals; EUR 179 to institutions; EUR 44 to students (effective 2012). adv. bk.rev. index. reprint service avail. from SCH. **Document type:** *Journal, Academic/Scholarly.* **Description:** Reports and reviews of problems and developments in all theological fields.
Related titles: Online - full text ed.: ISSN 1868-727X. 2009 (from IngentaConnect).
Indexed: A21, A22, BibLing, CERDIC, DIP, FR, IBR, IBZ, IPB, IZBG, MLA-IB, OTA, PCI, R&TA, RASB, RI-1, RI-2, RILM, SCOPUS.
—IE, Infotrieve, INIST. **CCC.**

R

Published by: Mohr Siebeck GmbH & Co. KG, Wilhelmstr 18, Tuebingen, 72074, Germany. TEL 49-7071-9230, FAX 49-7071-51104, info@mohr.de. Adv. contact Tilman Gaebler. Circ: 950 (paid and controlled).

200 DEU ISSN 1433-4534
THEOLOGISCHE STUDIEN. Text in German. 1997. irreg., latest 2008. price varies. **Document type:** *Monographic series, Academic/Scholarly.*
Published by: Shaker Verlag GmbH, Kaiserstr 100, Herzogenrath, 52134, Germany. TEL 49-2407-95960, FAX 49-2407-95969, info@shaker.de.

200 DEU ISSN 0941-8717
THEOLOGISCHE TEXTE UND STUDIEN. Text in German. 1992. irreg., latest vol.14, 2009. price varies. **Document type:** *Monographic series, Academic/Scholarly.*
Published by: Georg Olms Verlag, Hagentorwall 7, Hildesheim, 31134, Germany. TEL 49-5121-15010, FAX 49-5121-150150, info@olms.de.

200 DEU ISSN 1613-5261
THEOLOGISCHE TRENDS. Text in German. 1988. irreg., latest vol.15, 2006. price varies. **Document type:** *Monographic series, Academic/Scholarly.*
Published by: Peter Lang GmbH (Subsidiary of: Peter Lang Publishing Group), Eschborner Landstr 42-50, Frankfurt Am Main, 60489, Germany. TEL 49-69-7807050, FAX 49-69-78070550, zentrale.frankfurt@peterlang.com, http://www.peterlang.com.

200 CHE ISSN 0040-5701
BR4
THEOLOGISCHE ZEITSCHRIFT. Text in German. 1945. q. CHF 32 newsstand/cover (effective 2008). adv. bk.rev. abstr.; bibl. cum.index. **Document type:** *Journal, Academic/Scholarly.*
Indexed: A21, A22, BAS, BibLing, CERDIC, DIP, FR, IBR, IBZ, IPB, IZBG, MLA-IB, OTA, PCI, Philind, R&TA, RI-1, RI-2.
—IE, Infotrieve, INIST.
Published by: (Universitaet Basel, Theologische Fakultaet), Friedrich Reinhardt Verlag, Missionsstr 36, Basel, 4012, Switzerland. TEL 41-61-2646450, FAX 41-61-2646488, verlag@reinhardt.ch, http://www.reinhardt.ch. Ed. K Seybold. Circ: 750.

220 DEU ISSN 1431-200X
THEOLOGISCHES GESPRAECH; Freikirchliche Beitraege zur Theologie. Text in German. 1977. 4/yr. EUR 24; EUR 6.50 newsstand/cover (effective 2009). **Document type:** *Journal, Academic/Scholarly.*
Published by: Oncken Verlag GmbH, Muendener Str 13, Kassel, 34123, Germany. TEL 49-561-520050, FAX 49-561-5200550, zeitschriften@oncken.de, http://www.oncken.de. Ed. Michael Rohde.

200 SVK ISSN 1335-5570
➤ **THEOLOGOS.** Text in Slovak, English, Italian, German. 1999. s-a. **Document type:** *Journal, Academic/Scholarly.*
Related titles: Online - full text ed.: E-Theologos. ISSN 1338-1350 (from Versita).
Published by: Presovska Univerzita, Greckokatolicka Teologicka Fakulta, Ulica Biskupa Gojdica 2, Presov080 01, Slovakia. TEL 421-51-7725166, FAX 421-51-7733840, http://www.unipo.sk. Ed. Peter Sturak.

200 GBR ISSN 0040-571X
BR1
THEOLOGY. Text in English. 1920. bi-m. USD 333, GBP 180 combined subscription to institutions (print & online eds.); USD 326, GBP 176 to institutions (effective 2011). bk.rev. index. back issues avail.; reprint service avail. from PSC. **Document type:** *Journal, Academic/Scholarly.* **Description:** Designed for those who want to broaden their knowledge of contemporary theological studies including latest thinking in biblical studies, historical theology, systematic theology, pastoral theology and ethics.
Related titles: CD-ROM ed.; Microform ed.; Online - full text ed.: ISSN 2044-2696. USD 300, GBP 162 to institutions (effective 2011).
Indexed: A21, A22, A26, AmHI, B04, BAS, BRD, BrHumI, CA, DIP, E08, G08, H07, H08, HAb, HumInd, I05, IBR, IBZ, IZBG, LID&ISL, MLA-IB, PCI, R&TA, R05, RI-1, RI-2, RILM, S09, SCOPUS, T02, W03.
—BLDSC (8814.541000), IE, Ingenta. **CCC.**
Published by: (Society for Promoting Christian Knowledge), Sage Publications Ltd. (Subsidiary of: Sage Publications, Inc.), 1 Oliver's Yard, 55 City Rd, London, EC1Y 1SP, United Kingdom. TEL 44-20-73248500, FAX 44-20-73248600, info@sagepub.co.uk, http://www.uk.sagepub.com/home.nav. Ed. Rev. Stephen Plant.

201.6 USA
THEOLOGY AND CULTURE NEWSLETTER. Text in English. 1967. a. free. bk.rev. back issues avail. **Document type:** *Newsletter.* **Description:** Trends in theology, church renewal - for clergy and active laity.
Published by: Andover Newton Theological School, 210 Herrick Rd, Newton, MA 02159. TEL 617-964-1100, FAX 617-965-9756. Ed. Dorothy Fackre. Circ: 3,400 (controlled).

200 174.2 NLD ISSN 0928-8783
➤ **THEOLOGY AND MEDICINE.** Text in English. 1992. irreg., latest vol.9, 1997. price varies. back issues avail. **Document type:** *Monographic series, Academic/Scholarly.*
—BLDSC (8814.541220).
Published by: Springer Netherlands (Subsidiary of: Springer Science+Business Media), Van Godewijckstraat 30, Dordrecht, 3311 GX, Netherlands. TEL 31-78-6576050, FAX 31-78-6576474. Ed. Earl E Shelp.

200 500 GBR ISSN 1474-6700
BL240.3
➤ **THEOLOGY AND SCIENCE.** Text in English. 2003. q. GBP 425 combined subscription in United Kingdom to institutions (print & online eds.); EUR 569, USD 710 combined subscription to institutions (print & online eds.) (effective 2012). adv. back issues avail.; reprint service avail. from PSC. **Document type:** *Journal, Academic/Scholarly.* **Description:** Publishes critically reviewed articles that promote the creative mutual interaction between the natural sciences and theology.
Related titles: Online - full text ed.: ISSN 1474-6719. 2003. GBP 383 in United Kingdom to institutions; EUR 512, USD 640 to institutions (effective 2012) (from IngentaConnect).
Indexed: A01, A03, A08, A22, BrHumI, CA, E01, FamI, IBR, IBZ, PQC, T02.
—IE, Ingenta. **CCC.**
Published by: (The Center for Theology and the Natural Sciences USA), Routledge (Subsidiary of: Taylor & Francis Group), 4 Park Sq, Milton Park, Abingdon, Oxon OX14 4RN, United Kingdom. TEL 44-20-70176000, FAX 44-20-70176336, subscriptions@tandf.co.uk, http://www.routledge.com. Adv. contact Linda Hann TEL 44-1344-779945. **Subscr. to:** Taylor & Francis Ltd., Journals Customer Service, Sheepen Pl, Colchester, Essex CO3 3LP, United Kingdom. TEL 44-20-70175544, FAX 44-20-70175198, tf.enquiries@tfinforma.com.

201.6 GBR ISSN 1355-8358
BT708
➤ **THEOLOGY AND SEXUALITY.** Text in English. 1994. 3/yr. USD 425 combined subscription in North America to institutions (print & online eds.); GBP 246 combined subscription elsewhere to institutions (print & online eds.) (effective 2012). adv. bk.rev. back issues avail.; reprints avail. **Document type:** *Journal, Academic/Scholarly.* **Description:** Provides a forum for publication of new theological work on issues of sexuality and gender.
Related titles: Online - full text ed.: ISSN 1745-5170. 1994. USD 340 in North America to institutions; GBP 196 elsewhere to institutions (effective 2012).
Indexed: A01, A03, A08, A21, CA, DIP, G10, IBR, IBZ, L01, L02, R&TA, RI-1, S02, S03, T02, W09.
—BLDSC (8814.541350), IE, Ingenta. **CCC.**
Published by: (Institute for the Study of Christianity and Sexuality), Equinox Publishing Ltd., Unit S3, Kelham House, 3 Lancaster St, Sheffield, S6 3AF, United Kingdom. TEL 44-114-2725957, FAX 44-560-3459046, journals@equinoxpub.com, http://www.equinoxpub.com/. Eds. Elizabeth Stuart, George Loughlin. Adv. contact Val Hall.

230 USA ISSN 0040-5736
BR1
➤ **THEOLOGY TODAY.** Text in English. 1944. q. USD 305, GBP 165 combined subscription to institutions (print & online eds.); USD 299, GBP 162 to institutions (effective 2011). adv. bk.rev. illus.; abstr. index, cum.index every 10 yrs. back issues avail.; reprint service avail. from PSC. **Document type:** *Journal, Academic/Scholarly.* **Description:** Publishes articles on a wide range of classical and contemporary theological issues.
Related titles: Microform ed.: (from MIM, PQC); Online - full text ed.: ISSN 2044-2556. USD 275, GBP 149 to institutions (effective 2011).
Indexed: A01, A02, A03, A07, A08, A20, A21, A22, A25, A26, A30, A31, AA, ASCA, AmHI, ArtHuCI, ArtInd, B04, B14, BRD, BRI, BRM, CA, CBRI, CCR, CERDIC, CurCont, DIP, E08, FR, G08, GSS&RPL, H07, H08, H09, H10, H14, HAb, HumInd, I05, IBR, IBZ, M01, M02, MEA&I, MLA-IB, OTA, P02, P10, P28, P30, P48, P53, P54, PCI, PQC, Philind, R&TA, R05, RASB, RI-1, RI-2, RILM, S05, S08, S09, SCOPUS, T02, W03, W05, W07.
—BLDSC (8814.545000), IE, Infotrieve, Ingenta. **CCC.**
Published by: (Princeton Theological Seminary), Sage Publications, Inc., 2455 Teller Rd, Thousand Oaks, CA 91320. TEL 805-499-9774, FAX 805-499-0871, info@sagepub.com. Ed. Gordon S Mikoski.

200 100 CHE
THEOPHIL; Zuercher Beitraege zu Religion und Philosophie. Text in German. 1995. irreg., latest vol.10, 2006. price varies. **Document type:** *Monographic series, Academic/Scholarly.*
Published by: Theologischer Verlag Zurich, Badenerstr 73, Zurich, 8026, Switzerland. TEL 41-44-2993355, FAX 41-44-2993358, tvz@ref.ch.

200 BRA ISSN 1676-1332
THEOPHILOS; revista de teologia e filosofia. Text in Portuguese. 2001. s-a. back issues avail. **Document type:** *Journal, Academic/Scholarly.*
Related titles: Online - full text ed.
Published by: Universidade Luterana do Brasil, Apartado Postal 92420-280, Canoas RS, 124, Brazil. info@luther.ulbra.tche.br, editora@ulbra.br.

200 CHE ISSN 1664-0136
▼ **THEOREMES**; enjeux des approches empiriques des religions. Text in French, English. 2010. s-a. free (effective 2011). **Document type:** *Journal, Academic/Scholarly.*
Media: Online - full text.
Published by: Universite de Geneve, Institut Romand de Systematique et d'Ethique, 5 Rue de Candolle, Genva, 1211, Switzerland. Ed. Yann Schmitt.

THEORIE UND PRAXIS DER SOZIALPAEDAGOGIK. *see* CHILDREN AND YOUTH—About

220 DEU ISSN 1435-6864
THEOS; Studienreihe Theologische Forschungsergebnisse. Text in German. 1991. irreg., latest vol.88, 2010. price varies. **Document type:** *Monographic series, Academic/Scholarly.*
Published by: Verlag Dr. Kovac, Leverkusenstr 13, Hamburg, 22761, Germany. TEL 49-40-3988800, FAX 49-40-39888055, info@verlagdrkovac.de.

200 USA ISSN 8756-4785
BL1
➤ **THETA ALPHA KAPPA. JOURNAL.** Text in English. 1978 (Spr.). s-a. free to members (effective 2010). **Document type:** *Journal, Academic/Scholarly.* **Description:** Covers student academic work in religious studies or theology.
Published by: Theta Alpha Kappa, c/o David Grant, Dept of Religion, Texas Christian University, TCU Box 298100, 2800 South University Dr, Fort Worth, TX 76129. TEL 817-257-6447, FAX 817-257-7495, dgrant@tcu.edu. Ed. Leo H Madden.

200 GBR ISSN 0309-3492
THIRD WAY (HARROW); christian comment on culture. Text in English. 1977. 10/yr. GBP 30 (effective 2009). adv. music rev.; film rev.; play rev.; bk.rev. charts; illus. 32 p./no.; back issues avail. **Document type:** *Magazine, Academic/Scholarly.*
—BLDSC (8820.144000), IE, Ingenta.
Published by: Third Way Trust Ltd., 13-17 Long Ln, Barbican, London, EC1A 9PN, United Kingdom. TEL 44-20-77761082, ads@thirdway.org.uk. adv.: page GBP 375; 186 x 273.

230 121 180 BEL
➤ **THOMAS INSTITUUT UTRECHT SERIES.** Text in English. 1993. irreg., latest 2009. price varies. back issues avail. **Document type:** *Monographic series, Academic/Scholarly.* **Description:** Examines the philosophical and theological writings and teachings of Saint Thomas Aquinas (1225-1274).
Published by: (Katholieke Theologische Universiteit te Utrecht NLD, Thomas Instituut te Utrecht NLD), Peeters Publishers, Bondgenotenlaan 153, Leuven, 3000, Belgium. TEL 32-16-235170, FAX 32-16-228500, http://www.peeters-leuven.be.

291 DNK ISSN 1902-5823
TIDSSKRIFT OM ISLAM & KRISTENDOM. Text in Danish. 1997. s-a. DKK 300 to individual members; DKK 200 to students (effective 2009). **Document type:** *Magazine, Consumer.*
Formerly (until 2007): Nyhedsbrev om Islam og Kristendom (1398-2362)
Published by: Islamisk-Kristent Studiecenter/Islamic-Christian Study Centre, Noerregade 32.1, Copenhagen N, 2200, Denmark. TEL 45-35-373526, iks@ikstudiecenter.dk, http://www.ikstudiecenter.dk.

▼ **TIJDSCHRIFT VOOR RELIGIE, RECHT EN BELEID.** *see* LAW

266 SWE ISSN 1402-1838
TILL LIV; evangelisk luthersk missionstidning. Text in Swedish. 1912. m. SEK 350; SEK 350 to students (effective 2008). adv. bk.rev. index. **Document type:** *Magazine, Consumer.*
Formerly: Bibeltrogna Vaenners Missionstidning (0006-0658)
Published by: Missionssaellskapet Bibeltrogna Vaenner, Smala Graend 5, Stockholm, 11139, Sweden. TEL 46-8-55923104, FAX 46-8-225922, http://www.elmbv.se. Ed. Eva Andersson TEL 46-46-399365.

200 100 DEU ISSN 2192-1938
▼ **TILLICH-FORSCHUNGEN/RECHERCHES SUR TILLICH/TILLICH RESEARCH.** Text in German. 2011. irreg., latest vol.2, 2011. price varies. **Document type:** *Monographic series, Academic/Scholarly.*
Published by: Walter de Gruyter GmbH & Co. KG, Genthiner Str 13, Berlin, 10785, Germany. TEL 49-30-260050, FAX 49-30-26005251, info@degruyter.com, http://www.degruyter.de.

230 100 DEU
TILLICH PREVIEW. Text in German. 2007. irreg., latest vol.3, 2010. price varies. **Document type:** *Monographic series, Academic/Scholarly.*
Published by: Lit Verlag, Grevener Str/Fresnostr 2, Muenster, 48159, Germany. TEL 49-251-235091, FAX 49-251-231972, lit@lit-verlag.de.

230 100 DEU
TILLICH-STUDIEN. Text in German. 1999. irreg., latest vol.23, 2010. price varies. **Document type:** *Monographic series, Academic/Scholarly.*
Published by: Lit Verlag, Grevener Str/Fresnostr 2, Muenster, 48159, Germany. TEL 49-251-235091, FAX 49-251-231972, lit@lit-verlag.de. Eds. Erdmann Sturm, Werner Schuessler.

TIME OF SINGING; a magazine of Christian poetry. *see* LITERATURE—Poetry

240 USA ISSN 0740-9680
TIMES OF RESTORATION. Text in English. 1949. bi-m. free. bk.rev. **Document type:** *Monographic series.* **Description:** Presents articles encouraging Christian belief and practice.
Former titles (until 1985): Restoration Tidings; (until 1984): Standard (0038-9404)
Published by: K C M Publications, PO Box 445, Dublin, NH 03444-0445. TEL 603-563-8492, FAX 603-563-8138. Ed., R&P Timothy F Murray TEL 603-563-7152. Circ: 500 (paid and controlled). **Subscr. to:** Kingdom Press, 105 Chestnut Hill Rd, Amherst, NH 03031.

TODAY'S CHRISTIAN DOCTOR. *see* MEDICAL SCIENCES

230.0071 028.5 371.071 USA ISSN 1537-0135
TODAY'S CHRISTIAN TEEN; college prep guide. Text in English. 1990. a. free domestic to students (effective 2007). 40 p./no.; **Document type:** *Magazine, Consumer.*
Published by: Right Ideas, Inc., Box 100, Morgantown, PA 19543. TEL 610-856-6830, FAX 610-856-6831, tcpubs@mkpt.com. Ed. Mr. Jerry Thacker. R&P Mrs. Elaine Williams. Circ: 100,000.

TODAY'S SINGLE; serving the singles of America. *see* SINGLES' INTERESTS AND LIFESTYLES

TOER REEKS. *see* EDUCATION

230 NOR ISSN 1891-8832
▼ **TOERST.** Text in Multiple languages. 2021. s-a. free. adv. **Document type:** *Magazine, Consumer.*
Related titles: Online - full text ed.: ISSN 1891-8840.
Published by: Areopagos, PO Box 6763, St Olavs Pl, Oslo, 0130, Norway. TEL 47-23-331710, FAX 47-23-331729, areopagos@areopagos.org. Ed. Ann Kristin van Zijp Nilsen. Circ: 3,000.

230 USA ISSN 1937-4992
TOGETHER (GLENDORA); Worldwide Church of God news. Text in English. 2005. bi-m. **Document type:** *Magazine, Consumer.*
Published by: Worldwide Church of God, PO Box 5005, Glendora, CA 91740.

261 USA
TOGETHER (GROTTOES). Text in English. 1987. q.
Published by: Shalom Publishers, Route 2, Box 656, Grottoes, VA 24441. Ed. Melodie M Davis. Circ: 150,000.

299.5 JPN ISSN 0495-7180
BL1899
TOHO SHUKYO/JOURNAL OF EASTERN RELIGIONS. Text in Japanese. 1951. s-a. **Document type:** *Journal, Academic/Scholarly.*
Published by: Nippon Dokyo Gakkai/Japan Society of Taoistic Research, University of Tsukuba, Graduate School of Humanities & Society Sciences, 1-1-1 Tennodai, Tsukuba, 305-8571, Japan. dokyo@wwwsoc.nii.ac.jp, http://wwwsoc.nii.ac.jp/dokyo/.

TOPICS IN RELIGION: A BIBLIOGRAPHIC SERIES. *see* RELIGIONS AND THEOLOGY—Abstracting, Bibliographies, Statistics

220 DEU ISSN 2191-7426
▼ **TOPOI BIBLISCHER THEOLOGIE/TOPICS OF BIBLICAL THEOLOGY.** Text in German. 2011. irreg. price varies. **Document type:** *Monographic series, Academic/Scholarly.*
Published by: Mohr Siebeck GmbH & Co. KG, Wilhelmstr 18, Tuebingen, 72074, Germany. TEL 49-7071-9230, FAX 49-7071-51104, info@mohr.de.

200 CAN ISSN 0826-9831
BR1
➤ **TORONTO JOURNAL OF THEOLOGY.** Abbreviated title: T J T. Text in English. 1985. s-a. USD 95 domestic to institutions; USD 115 foreign to institutions (effective 2011). bk.rev. index. **Document type:** *Journal, Academic/Scholarly.* **Description:** Covers historical, philosophical and systematic theology, ethics, biblical and pastoral studies, the history of Christianity, Christianity and culture, interreligious dialogue and related subjects.

Related titles: Online - full text ed.: ISSN 1918-6371. USD 75 to institutions (effective 2011).
Indexed: A01, A21, C03, CA, CBCARef, OTA, P30, P48, PCI, PQC, R&TA, RI-1, RI-2, T02.
—BLDSC (8868.760000), IE, Infotrieve, Ingenta. **CCC.**
Published by: (Wilfrid Laurier University Press), University of Toronto Press, Journals Division, 5201 Dufferin St, Toronto, ON M3H 5T8, Canada. TEL 416-667-7810, FAX 416-667-7881, journals@utpress.utoronto.ca, http://www.utpress.utoronto.ca.

200 USA ISSN 8756-7385
TORONTO STUDIES IN RELIGION. Text in English. 1987. irreg., latest vol.30, 2010. price varies. back issues avail. **Document type:** *Monographic series, Academic/Scholarly.* **Description:** Contributes to the scholarly and academic understanding of religion.
—BLDSC (8868.785000), IE, Ingenta.
Published by: Peter Lang Publishing, Inc. (Subsidiary of: Peter Lang Publishing Group), 29 Broadway, New York, NY 10006. TEL 212-647-7700, 212-647-7706, 800-770-5264, FAX 212-647-7707, customerservice@plang.com, http://www.peterlang.com. Ed. Donald Wiebe.

200 USA
➤ **TORONTO STUDIES IN THEOLOGY.** Text in English. 1978. irreg., latest vol.98, 2009. price varies. back issues avail. **Document type:** *Monographic series, Academic/Scholarly.*
Published by: Edwin Mellen Press, 415 Ridge St, PO Box 450, Lewiston, NY 14092. TEL 716-754-2266, FAX 716-754-4056, cservice@mellenpress.com.

200.22 ITA ISSN 1974-4706
TOTEM. Text in Italian. 2008. m. **Document type:** *Magazine, Consumer.*
Published by: Acacia Edizioni, Via Copernico 3, Binasco, MI 20082, Italy. http://www.acaciaedizioni.com.

200 700 ITA ISSN 1970-3465
TRA ARTE E TEOLOGIA. Text in Italian. 2001. irreg. **Document type:** *Monographic series, Academic/Scholarly.*
Published by: Editrice Ancora, Via G Battista Niccolini 8, Milan, 20154, Italy. TEL 39-02-3456081, FAX 39-02-34560866, editrice@ancora-libri.it, http://www.ancora-libri.it.

200 ITA ISSN 1128-9333
TRACCE. LITTERAE COMMUNIONIS. Text in Multiple languages. 1974. m. adv. bk.rev. **Document type:** *Magazine, Consumer.* **Description:** Contains articles and editorials regarding the activities of and relationship between the church and state.
Former titles (until 1993): C.L. Litterae Communionis (1120-1010); (until 1976): C.L. Comunione e Liberazione (1120-1029)
Related titles: French ed.: Traces (Paris). ISSN 1632-4439. 2000; Portuguese ed.: Passos. ISSN 1518-8647. 1999; Spanish ed.: Huellas. ISSN 1695-5137. 1996; Italian ed.: Traces. ISSN 1828-6763. 1999.
Published by: (Gruppi di Comunione e Liberazione), Cooperativa Editoriale Nuovo Mondo, Via Nicola Antonio Porpora 127, Milan, MI 20131, Italy. TEL 39-02-28174420, FAX 39-02-26149340, cltracce@comunioneliberazione.org, http://www.comunioneliberazione.org/tracce. Ed. Alberto Savorana. Adv. contact Laura Penazzo.

267 NLD ISSN 1574-7697
TRACK 7. Text in Dutch. 1963. q.
Formerly (until 2004): Rechte Sporen (0167-1723)
Published by: Bond van Gereformeerde Ouderverenigingen, c/o AJGM Mostermans, Melrose 44, Duiven, 6992 BD, Netherlands. TEL 31-316-266672, bgj-bgo-mostermans@hetnet.nl.

230 CHE ISSN 0172-1372
TRADITIO CHRISTIANA; themes et documents patristiques. Text in French. 1969. irreg., latest vol.14, 2006. price varies. **Document type:** *Monographic series, Academic/Scholarly.*
Published by: Peter Lang AG (Subsidiary of: Peter Lang Publishing Group), Hochfeldstr 32, Postfach 746, Bern 9, 3000, Switzerland. TEL 41-31-3061717, FAX 41-31-3061727, info@peterlang.com, http://www.peterlang.com. Ed. Willy Rordorf.

225 BEL
➤ **TRADITIO EXEGETICA GRAECA.** Text in English, French, German, Greek. 1991. irreg., latest 2010. price varies. back issues avail. **Document type:** *Monographic series, Academic/Scholarly.*
Published by: (Universite Catholique de Louvain, Departement d'Etudes Greques, Latines et Orientales), Peeters Publishers, Bondgenotenlaan 153, Leuven, 3000, Belgium. TEL 32-16-235170, FAX 32-16-228500, http://www.peeters-leuven.be.

230 DEU ISSN 1434-5277
TRADITION, REFORM, INNOVATION; Studien zur Modernitaet des Mittelalters. Text in German. 1999. irreg., latest vol.14, 2007. price varies. **Document type:** *Monographic series, Academic/Scholarly.*
Published by: Peter Lang GmbH (Subsidiary of: Peter Lang Publishing Group), Eschborner Landstr 42-50, Frankfurt Am Main, 60489, Germany. TEL 49-69-7807050, FAX 49-69-78070550, zentrale.frankfurt@peterlang.com, http://www.peterlang.com. Ed. Nikolaus Staubach.

201.66 USA
TRANS WORLD RADIO. Text in English. 1980. q. free. **Document type:** *Magazine, Trade.* **Description:** Missionary broadcasting magazine, concentrating on TWR's worldwide ministry.
Former titles: T W Radio (1071-3468); Trans World Radio (0274-9831)
Address: PO Box 8700, Cary, NC 27512-8700. TEL 919-460-3700, FAX 919-460-3702. Ed. Elizatheth Boocks. R&P Marion L Tunis TEL 919-460-3779. Circ: 40,000 (controlled).

TRANSFIGURATION; Nordisk tidsskrift for kunst og kristendom. *see* ART

230 GBR ISSN 0265-3788
➤ **TRANSFORMATION**; an international journal of holistic mission studies. Text in English. 1984. q. USD 399, GBP 215 combined subscription to institutions (print & online eds.); USD 391, GBP 211 to institutions (effective 2011). back issues avail.; reprint service avail. from PSC. **Document type:** *Journal, Academic/Scholarly.* **Description:** Provides a forum for discussion on economics, development, violence, family life and other ethical issues, with a focus on Christian social ethics.
Related titles: Online - full text ed.: ISSN 1759-8931. USD 359, GBP 194 to institutions (effective 2011).
Indexed: A01, A03, A08, A21, A22, AmHI, CA, ChrPI, E01, H07, ISAP, R&TA, RI-1, RI-2, T02.
—BLDSC (9020.593000), IE, Ingenta. **CCC.**
Published by: (Oxford Centre for Mission Studies), Sage Publications Ltd. (Subsidiary of: Sage Publications, Inc.), 1 Oliver's Yard, 55 City Rd, London, EC1Y 1SP, United Kingdom. TEL 44-20-73248500, FAX 44-20-73248600, info@sagepub.co.uk, http://www.uk.sagepub.com/home.nav. Ed. David Emmanuel Singh. Circ: 1,800.

220 DEU ISSN 1618-2480
TRANSFORMATIONEN (BAD WALDSEE). Text in German. 2001. 2/yr. **Document type:** *Journal, Academic/Scholarly.*
Published by: Deutsche Gesellschaft fuer Pastoralpsychologie e.V., St-Leonhard-Str 24/1, Bad Waldsee, 88339, Germany. TEL 49-7524-905211, info@pastoralpsychologie.de.

261 144 ROM ISSN 0255-0539
DR201
TRANSILVANIA. Text in Romanian. 1868. 4/yr. USD 20 in Europe; USD 30 elsewhere. adv. bk.rev. **Document type:** *Academic/Scholarly.* **Description:** Presents issues on themes of the theology, anthropology, and philosophy of culture. Interested in humanism.
Indexed: MLA-IB, SCOPUS.
Published by: Casa de Presa si Editura Cultura Nationala, Str. Dr. Ion Ratiu 2, Sibiu, 2400, Romania. TEL 40-24-69213377. Ed. Ion Mircea. Adv. contact Ioan Metiu. Circ: 1,000 (controlled).

283 GBR ISSN 0967-926X
TRANSMISSION. Text in English. 1992. q. free (effective 2010). **Document type:** *Newspaper.* **Description:** Features Anglicans in world mission.
Related titles: Online - full text ed.
Published by: United Society for the Propagation of the Gospel, 200 Great Dover St, London, SE1 4YB, United Kingdom. TEL 44-20-73785678, FAX 44-20-73785650, enquiries@uspg.org.uk. Ed. Mike Brooks.

230 DEU ISSN 1865-5629
TRIA CORDA; Jenaer Vorlesungen zu Judentum, Antike und Christentum. Text in German. 2007. irreg., latest vol.6, 2010. price varies. **Document type:** *Monographic series, Academic/Scholarly.*
Published by: Mohr Siebeck GmbH & Co. KG, Wilhelmstr 18, Tuebingen, 72074, Germany. TEL 49-7071-9230, FAX 49-7071-51104, info@mohr.de.

230 DEU ISSN 0041-2945
BR4
TRIERER THEOLOGISCHE ZEITSCHRIFT. Text in German. 1947. q. EUR 33.50; EUR 15.50 to students; EUR 9.50 newsstand/cover (effective 2011). adv. bk.rev. index. **Document type:** *Journal, Academic/Scholarly.*
Indexed: CLA, DIP, FR, IBR, IBZ, IZBG, MLA-IB, OTA.
—BLDSC (9050.610300), INIST. **CCC.**
Published by: (Theologische Fakultaet Trier), Paulinus Verlag GmbH, Maximineracht 11c, Trier, 54295, Germany. TEL 49-651-46080, FAX 49-651-4608221, verlag@paulinus.de. **Co-sponsor:** Katholisch-Theologischer Fachbereich der Universitaet Mainz.

289 USA ISSN 0360-3032
BR1
➤ **TRINITY JOURNAL.** Text in English. 1971-1978; N.S. 1980. s-a. (in 1 vol., 2 nos./vol.). USD 18 domestic; USD 26 in Canada; USD 32 elsewhere (effective 2010). adv. bk.rev. back issues avail. **Document type:** *Journal, Academic/Scholarly.* **Description:** Deals with classic biblical, historical, and theological issues.
Formerly (until 1974): Trinity Studies (0360-2915)
Related titles: CD-ROM ed.: Theological Journal Library CD. USD 99.95 New & Updated CD (effective 2004); Microfilm ed.: N.S. (from PQC); Online - full text ed.
Indexed: A21, A22, BRI, BRM, CBRC, CBRI, CCR, ChrPI, FR, GSS&RPL, IZBG, OTA, P28, P48, P53, P54, PQC, R&TA, RI-1, RI-2.
—BLDSC (9050.662400), IE, Ingenta, INIST.
Published by: Trinity Evangelical Divinity School, 2065 Half Day Rd, Deerfield, IL 60015. TEL 800-345-8337, tedsadm@tiu.edu. Ed. Dana M Harris.

200 SGP
TRINITY THEOLOGICAL JOURNAL. Text in Chinese, English. a. **Document type:** *Journal, Academic/Scholarly.*
Indexed: OTA.
Published by: Trinity Theological College, 490 Upper Bukit Timah Rd, Singapore, 678093, Singapore. TEL 65-676-76677, FAX 65-676-76477, info@ttc.edu.sg.

200 001.3 USA ISSN 1092-3632
TRIUMPH OF THE PAST. Text in English. 1996. m. USD 22 (effective 2000). bk.rev. back issues avail. **Document type:** *Newsletter.* **Description:** Recommends, investigates and develops the principles embodied in Christianity which direct society to serve the individuals who compose it. Encompasses literature, history, politics, economics and religion.
Address: PO Box 29535, Columbus, OH 43229. TEL 614-261-1300. Ed., Pub. Michael Stephen Lane. Circ: 1,000 (paid).

230 DEU ISSN 1866-9638
TROELTSCH-STUDIEN. Text in German. 1982; N.S. 2006. irreg., latest vol.4, 2011. price varies. **Document type:** *Monographic series, Academic/Scholarly.*
Published by: Walter de Gruyter GmbH & Co. KG, Genthiner Str 13, Berlin, 10785, Germany. TEL 49-30-260050, FAX 49-30-26005251, info@degruyter.com, http://www.degruyter.de. Ed. Friedrich Wilhelm Graf.

285 AUS ISSN 0813-796X
TROWEL AND SWORD. Text in English. 1954. m. (11/yr.). AUD 35 domestic; NZD 50 in New Zealand; AUD 92.50 elsewhere; AUD 5 newsstand/cover (effective 2009). adv. bk.rev. back issues avail. **Document type:** *Magazine, Trade.* **Description:** Provides for the edification and defense of the Reformed and Presbyterian faith and life in Australasia.
Related titles: Online - full content ed.
Published by: Reformed Churches Publishing House, c/o Geoff van Schie, 6 Preston Rd,, Langford, W.A. 6147, Australia. TEL 61-8-92585374. Ed. Geoff Van Schie. Adv. contact John Hughes TEL 61-8-94442020.

290 DEU ISSN 0942-3761
TUEBINGER BEITRAEGE ZUR RELIGIONSWISSENSCHAFT. Text in German. 1995. irreg., latest vol.6, 2008. price varies. **Document type:** *Monographic series, Academic/Scholarly.*
Published by: Peter Lang GmbH (Subsidiary of: Peter Lang Publishing Group), Eschborner Landstr 42-50, Frankfurt Am Main, 60489, Germany. TEL 49-69-7807050, FAX 49-69-78070550, zentrale.frankfurt@peterlang.com. Eds. Burkhard Gladigow, Guenter Kehrer.

121 DEU ISSN 1432-4709
TUEBINGER STUDIEN ZUR THEOLOGIE UND PHILOSOPHIE. Text in German. 1991. irreg., latest vol.24, 2006. price varies. **Document type:** *Monographic series, Academic/Scholarly.* **Description:** Contains research and scholarly articles on various aspects of faith and philosophy.
—BLDSC (9068.278250).
Published by: A. Francke Verlag GmbH, Dischinger Weg 5, Tuebingen, 72070, Germany. TEL 49-7071-97970, FAX 49-7071-979711, info@francke.de, http://www.francke.de.

230 USA ISSN 1930-1324
TURNING POINT CHRISTIAN WORLDVIEW SERIES. Text in English. 1987. irreg. **Document type:** *Monographic series, Consumer.*
Published by: Crossway Books, 1300 Crescent St, Wheaton, IL 60187. TEL 630-682-4300, 800-543-1659, FAX 630-682-4785, info@gnpcb.org, http://www.gnpcb.org.

207 GBR ISSN 0082-7118
BS543.A1
TYNDALE BULLETIN. Text in English. 1956. s-a. GBP 16.90 domestic; GBP 23.90 elsewhere (effective 2009). abstr. back issues avail. **Document type:** *Journal, Consumer.* **Description:** Covers articles which make an original contribution to biblical and theological research.
Formerly (until 1966): The Tyndale House Bulletin (1757-0514)
Indexed: A20, A21, A22, ArtHuCI, CurCont, IZBG, OTA, R&TA, RI-1, RI-2, W07.
—BLDSC (9077.455000), IE, Ingenta. **CCC.**
Published by: Tyndale House, 36 Selwyn Gardens, Cambridge, CB3 9BA, United Kingdom. TEL 44-1223-566601, FAX 44-1223-566608.

U C E A. (Ubi Caritas et Amor) *see* HOMOSEXUALITY

280.4 GBR ISSN 1742-4623
U S P G PRAYER DIARY. Text in English. 1990. q. free (effective 2009). **Document type:** *Bulletin.* **Description:** Includes prayer and liturgical material.
Formerly (until 2004): Encounter (0958-2797)
Published by: United Society for the Propagation of the Gospel, 200 Great Dover St, London, SE1 4YB, United Kingdom. TEL 44-20-73785678, FAX 44-20-73785650, enquiries@uspg.org.uk, http://www.uspg.org.uk/.

U S P S JOURNAL. *see* PARAPSYCHOLOGY AND OCCULTISM

200 DEU ISSN 0340-7225
U T B. (Uni-Taschenbuecher) Text in German. 1971. irreg. price varies. **Document type:** *Monographic series, Academic/Scholarly.*
Indexed: GeoRef.
Published by: Boehlau Verlag GmbH & Cie, Ursulaplatz 1, Cologne, 50668, Germany. TEL 49-221-913900, FAX 49-221-9139011, vertrieb@boehlau.de, http://www.boehlau.de.

UGARIT-FORSCHUNGEN; internationales Jahrbuch fuer die Altertumskunde Syrien-Palaestinas. *see* HISTORY—History Of The Near East

220 DEU ISSN 0948-1125
UGARITSCH-BIBLISCHE LITERATUR. Text in German. 1984. irreg. price varies. **Document type:** *Monographic series, Academic/Scholarly.*
Published by: Ugarit-Verlag, Ricarda-Huch-Str 6, Muenster, 48161, Germany. TEL 49-251-8322661, FAX 49-251-8322662, verlag@ugarit-verlag.de, http://www.ugarit-verlag.de.

269 NLD ISSN 0166-4166
UITDAGING. Text in Dutch. 1973. m. (11/yr.). EUR 21.65 (effective 2009). adv.
Incorporates (1991-1998): Agape Bulletin (0927-8591)
Published by: EB Media, Postbus 2101, Deventer, 7420 AC, Netherlands. TEL 31-88-3263333, FAX 31-88-3263339, mail@ebmedia.nl, http://www.ebmedia.nl/. Eds. Jan Kees Nentjes, Ronald Koops. Pub. Leendert de Jong. Adv. contact Eddy Morren. color page EUR 1,120; trim 286 x 420. Circ: 9,000.

200 HUN ISSN 0133-1205
UJ EMBER. Text in Hungarian. 1945. w. USD 97.
Related titles: Microfilm ed.: (from PQC).
Indexed: RASB.
Address: Kossuth Lajos utca 1, Budapest, 1053, Hungary. TEL 117-3933, FAX 117-3471. Ed. Laszlo Lukacs. Circ: 100,000.

ULTIMATE REALITY AND MEANING; interdisciplinary studies in the philosophy of understanding. *see* PHILOSOPHY

200 BRA ISSN 1415-899X
➤ **ULTIMO ANDAR**; cadernos de pesquisa em ciencias da religiao. Text in Portuguese; Summaries in English, Portuguese. 1998. a. BRL 15 newsstand/cover domestic; USD 5 newsstand/cover foreign (effective 2003). bk.rev. back issues avail. **Document type:** *Academic/Scholarly.* **Description:** Contains articles written by graduate students of religion on their thesis topics.
Published by: (Mestrado em Ciencias da Religiao), Pontificia Universidade Catolica de Sao Paulo, Faculdade de Fonoaudiologia, Rua Monte Alegre, 984, Perdizes, Sao Paulo, SP 05014-001, Brazil. TEL 55-11-3870-8529, FAX 55-11-3870-8529, Procres@exatas.pucsp.br. Eds. Maria Jose Rosado Nunes, Waldecy Tenorio. Circ: 500.

200 TUR ISSN 1301-3394
ULUDAG UNIVERSITESI. ILAHIYAT FAKULTESI. DERGISI/REVIEW OF THE FACULTY OF THEOLOGY OF ULUDUG UNIVERSITY. Text in English, Turkish. 1986. a. **Document type:** *Journal, Academic/Scholarly.*
Related titles: Online - full text ed.: free evening (effective 2011).
Published by: Uludag Universitesi, Ilahyat Fakultesi/Uludag University, Faculty of Theology, Fethiye Mh Kirlangic Sk 2, Nilufer, Bursa, 16140, Turkey.

266 ZAF ISSN 0041-6274
UMAFRIKA; the Zulu weekly. Text in Zulu. 1911. w. ZAR 60. adv. bk.rev. charts; illus. **Description:** Aims to offer a Christian-based perspective on contemporary society. Functions as an instrument of communication leading to reconciliation mainly among the Zulu-speaking population of South Africa.

R

Related titles: Microfilm ed.
Published by: Mariannhill Mission Institute, The Monastery, PO Box 11002, Mariannhill, 3601, South Africa. TEL 031-7002720, FAX 031-7003707. Ed. Cyril Madlada. Circ: 80,000.

200 DEU ISSN 0041-6444
UNAUSFORSCHLICHER REICHTUM; Zweimonatsschrift fuer Gott und sein Wort. Text in German. 1932. bi-m. EUR 10, CHF 20 (effective 2005). adv. bk.rev. index, cum.index: 1932-1993. **Document type:** *Bulletin.*
Published by: (Freunde Konkordanter Wortvekuendigung e.V. Pforzheim), Konkordanter Verlag Pforzheim, Leipziger Str 11, Birkenfeld, 75217, Germany. TEL 49-7231-485620, FAX 49-7231-485529, info@konkordanterverlag.de, http://www.konkordanterverlag.de. Circ: 1,000.

200 GBR ISSN 1744-5833
UNDERSTANDING FAITH. Text in English. 2003. irreg., latest 2009. GBP 9.95 per issue (effective 2009). back issues avail. **Document type:** *Monographic series, Academic/Scholarly.* **Description:** Helps to interested person wishing to know how the GOD faith began, what it teaches and how its followers have tried to practise and spread their faith through the centuries.
Published by: Dunedin Academic Press Ltd., 8 Albany St, Hudson House, Edinburgh, EH1 3QB, United Kingdom. TEL 44-131-4732397, FAX 44-1250-870920.

287 USA ISSN 1946-648X
UNFINISHED. Text in English. 19??. q. free (effective 2009). back issues avail. **Document type:** *Magazine, Consumer.* **Description:** Contains information about the missionaries, ministries, and worldwide mission trends and issues.
Formerly (until 2006): Heartbeat
Related titles: Online - full text ed.
Published by: The Mission Society, 6234 Crooked Creek Rd, Norcross, GA 30092. TEL 770-446-1381, 800-478-8963, FAX 770-446-3044, info@themissionsociety.org. Ed. Ruth A Burgner TEL 678-542-9038. Pub. Philip R Granger.

200 DEU ISSN 0932-0180
BX9801
UNITARISCHE BLAETTER; fuer ganzheitliche Religion und Kultur. Text in German. 1948. bi-m. EUR 33 domestic; EUR 36 foreign; EUR 5.25 per issue (effective 2011). adv. bk.rev. illus. index. 48 p./no. 2 cols./p.; back issues avail. **Document type:** *Bulletin, Consumer.*
Formerly: Glaube und Tat (0017-1123)
Published by: (Religionsgemeinschaft Deutsche Unitarier e.V.), Verlag Deutsche Unitarier, Birkenstr 4, Ravensburg, 88214, Germany. TEL 49-751-62596, FAX 49-751-67201, verlag@unitarier.de, http://www.unitarier.de. Ed. Wiebke Muensterberg. Pub. Micha Ramm. Circ: 1,400 (paid).

268 FRA ISSN 1248-9646
UNITE DES CHRETIENS; revue de formation et d'information oecumenique. Text in French. 1971. q. back issues avail.
Indexed: CERDIC.
Published by: Association pour l'Unite des Chretiens, 80 rue de l'Abbe Carton, Paris, 75014, France. TEL 1-45-42-00-39, FAX 1-45-42-03-07. Ed. Guy Lourmande. Circ: 3,500.

266 AUS
UNITING WORLD. Text in English. 2006 (Dec.). q. **Document type:** *Magazine, Consumer.*
Formed by the merger of (2002-2006): Overseas Aid News; (2000-2006): Mission Partners (1445-9361); Which was formerly (1989-2000): World Mission Partners (1033-2243); (until 1989): World Mission Update
Published by: Uniting International Mission, PO Box A2266, Sydney South, NSW 1235, Australia. TEL 61-2-82674267, FAX 61-2-92627936, uim@nat.uca.org.au. Ed. Rev. John Barr.

UNIVERSIDAD ACADEMIA HUMANISMO CRISTIANO. REVISTA. *see* HUMANITIES: COMPREHENSIVE WORKS

262.9 ESP ISSN 0069-505X
UNIVERSIDAD DE NAVARRA. COLECCION CANONICA. Text in Spanish. 1959. irreg. price varies. **Document type:** *Monographic series, Academic/Scholarly.* **Description:** Discusses canon law.
Former titles (until 1965): Universidad de Navarra. Facultad de Derecho Canonico. Publicaciones; (until 1963): Estudio General de Navarra. Coleccion Canonica (0475-526X)
Published by: (Universidad de Navarra, Facultad de Derecho Canonico - Instituto Martin de Azpilicueta), Universidad de Navarra, Servicio de Publicaciones, Campus Universitario, Pamplona, 31009, Spain. TEL 34-948-256850, FAX 34-948-256854, http://www.unav.es/publicaciones/.

200 ESP ISSN 0078-8759
UNIVERSIDAD DE NAVARRA. COLECCION CANONICA. MANUALES. Text in Spanish. 1973. irreg., latest vol.7, 1988. price varies. **Document type:** *Monographic series, Academic/Scholarly.*
Published by: (Universidad de Navarra, Facultad de Derecho Canonico - Instituto Martin de Azpilicueta), Universidad de Navarra, Servicio de Publicaciones, Campus Universitario, Pamplona, 31009, Spain. TEL 34-948-256850, FAX 34-948-256854, http://www.unav.es/publicaciones/.

200.71 COL
UNIVERSIDAD JAVERIANA. FACULTAD DE TEOLOGIA. COLECCION TEOLOGIA HOY. Text in Spanish. irreg. price varies. **Document type:** *Monographic series.*
Supersedes (in 1994): Universidad Javeriana. Facultad de Teologia. Coleccion Profesores
Published by: Pontificia Universidad Javeriana, Facultad de Teologia, Carrera 10 No. 65-48, Apartado Aereo 54953, Bogota, DE, Colombia. TEL 57-1-2124846, FAX 57-1-2123360. Ed. Silvio Cajiao.

230 AUT ISSN 0579-7780
UNIVERSITAET INNSBRUCK. THEOLOGISCHE FAKULTAET. STUDIEN UND ARBEITEN. Text in German. 1968. irreg., latest vol.10, 1974. price varies. **Document type:** *Monographic series, Academic/Scholarly.*
Related titles: Series of: Universitaet Innsbruck. Veroeffentlichungen.
Published by: Universitaet Innsbruck, Theologische Fakultaet, Karl-Rahner-Platz 1, Innsbruck, 6020, Austria. TEL 43-512-50796130, FAX 43-512-5072959, Theologie@uibk.ac.at, http://www.uibk.ac.at/theol/.

UNIVERSITE CATHOLIQUE DE LOUVAIN. INSTITUT ORIENTALISTE. PUBLICATIONS. *see* HISTORY—History Of Asia

UNIVERSITE SAINT-JOSEPH. FACULTE DES LETTRES ET DES SCIENCES HUMAINES. RECHERCHES. SERIE B: ORIENT CHRETIEN. *see* ASIAN STUDIES

UNIVERSITY OF HEALING. SYLLABUS. *see* EDUCATION

UNIVERSITY OF ST. THOMAS MAGAZINE. *see* COLLEGE AND ALUMNI

200 POL ISSN 0137-2432
BL9.P6
UNIWERSYTET JAGIELLONSKI. ZESZYTY NAUKOWE. STUDIA RELIGIOLOGICA/UNIVERSITAS IAGELLONICA. ACTA SCIENTIARUM LITTERARUMQUE. STUDIA RELIGIOLOGICA. Text in Polish. 1977. a. price varies. **Document type:** *Journal, Academic/Scholarly.*
Indexed: FR, IBSS.
Published by: (Uniwersytet Jagiellonski, Instytut Religioznawstwa), Wydawnictwo Uniwersytetu Jagiellonskiego/Jagiellonian University Press, ul Grodzka 26, Krakow, 31044, Poland. TEL 48-12-4312364, FAX 48-12-4301995, wydaw@if.uj.edu.pl. Ed. Jan Drabina.

200 POL ISSN 1425-7998
UNIWERSYTET OPOLSKI. WYDZIAL TEOLOGICZNY. PRZEGLAD PISMIENNICTWA TEOLOGICZNEGO. Text in Polish. 1995. s-a. PLZ 13 per issue (effective 2004). **Document type:** *Journal, Academic/Scholarly.*
Published by: (Uniwersytet Opolski, Wydzial Teologiczny), Wydawnictwo Uniwersytetu Opolskiego, ul Sienkiewicza 33, Opole, 45037, Poland. TEL 48-77-4410878, wydawnictwo@uni.opole.pl.

220 POL ISSN 1428-7218
UNIWERSYTET OPOLSKI. WYDZIAL TEOLOGICZNY. STUDIA BIBLIJNE. SCRIPTURA SACRA. Text in Polish. 1997. irreg., latest vol.5, 2001. **Document type:** *Monographic series, Academic/Scholarly.*
Indexed: IZBG.
Published by: (Uniwersytet Opolski, Wydzial Teologiczny), Wydawnictwo Uniwersytetu Opolskiego, ul Sienkiewicza 33, Opole, 45037, Poland. TEL 48-77-4410878, wydawnictwo@uni.opole.pl.

220 USA ISSN 0042-0476
BS491
UNSEARCHABLE RICHES. Text in English. 1909. bi-m. USD 1 (effective 2010). index, cum.index every 10 yrs. back issues avail. **Document type:** *Magazine, Consumer.* **Description:** Contains expositions and commentary pertaining to scripture.
Related titles: Online - full text ed.
Published by: Concordant Publishing Concern, 15570 Knochaven Rd, Santa Clarita, CA 91387. TEL 661-252-2112, email@concordant.org.

230 DEU ISSN 1617-335X
UNTERSUCHUNGEN ZUM CHRISTLICHEN GLAUBEN IN EINER SAEKULAREN WELT. Text in German. 2001. irreg., latest vol.5, 2009. price varies. **Document type:** *Monographic series, Academic/Scholarly.*
Published by: Peter Lang GmbH (Subsidiary of: Peter Lang Publishing Group), Eschborner Landstr 42-50, Frankfurt Am Main, 60489, Germany. TEL 49-69-7807050, FAX 49-69-78070550, zentrale.frankfurt@peterlang.com, http://www.peterlang.com.

200 DEU ISSN 0930-1313
UNTERWEGS (MUNICH). Text in German. 1983. q. free to members (effective 2009). bk.rev. **Document type:** *Newsletter, Consumer.*
Published by: Deutscher Katecheten-Verein e.V., Preysingstr 83C, Munich, 81667, Germany. TEL 49-89-480921242, FAX 49-89-480921237, info@katecheten-verein.de, http://www.katecheten-verein.de. Circ: 11,000.

231.76 GBR
UP BEAT; leaders guide. Text in English. 1985. q. free to qualified personnel. adv. bk.rev. **Description:** For leaders of "Under 12's," groups affiliated with Covies churches. Offers advice on planning and preparation, drama, worship, discipline, safety and security, and resource materials.
Supersedes (in 1997): Leader; Which was formerly: Leaders' Digest. Covenanter and Juco Leader
Published by: Covies, 11-13 Lower Hillgate, Stockport, Ches SK1 1JQ, United Kingdom. TEL 44-161-474-1262, FAX 44-161-474-1300. R&P Dorothy Mason. Circ: 2,000 (controlled).

291.72 NLD ISSN 2210-9609
▼ **UPDATE (RHENEN).** Text in Dutch. 2010. q. EUR 10 (effective 2011).
Related titles: Online - full text ed.: ISSN 2210-9617.
Published by: Stichting Osteuropa Mission, Postbus 167, Rhenen, 3910 AD, Netherlands. TEL 31-317-712466, http://www.osteuropamission.nl.

266 SWE ISSN 2001-0087
UPPDRAG MISSION. Text in Swedish. 1846. 5/yr. adv. bk.rev. **Document type:** *Magazine, Consumer.*
Former titles (until 2011): Hela Jorden (1102-0105); (until 1991): Missionsorientering (0345-8059); (until 1972): Evangeliska Missionen; (until 1921): Lunds Missions-tidning
Related titles: Online - full text ed.
Published by: Lunds Missionssaellskap, Stiftskansliet, PO Box 32, Lund, 22100, Sweden. styrelsen@lundsmissionssallskap.se, http://www.lundsmissionssallskap.se. Ed. Marie Bosund Hedberg. Circ: 2,000.

200 SWE ISSN 1102-7878
UPPSALA STUDIES IN FAITH AND IDEOLOGIES. Text in Multiple languages. 1964. irreg., latest vol.11, 2002. price varies. back issues avail. **Document type:** *Monographic series, Academic/Scholarly.*
Formerly (until 1991): Studia Doctrinae Christianae Upsaliensia (0585-508X)
Related titles: ◆ Series of: Acta Universitatis Upsaliensis. ISSN 0346-5462.
Published by: Uppsala Universitet, Acta Universitatis Upsaliensis/University Publications from Uppsala, PO Box 256, Uppsala, 75105, Sweden. TEL 46-18-4716804, FAX 46-18-4716804, acta@ub.uu.se, http://www.ub.uu.se/upu/auu/index.html. Ed. Bengt Landgren. **Dist. by:** Almqvist & Wiksell International.

268 USA
UPWARD QUEST NEWSLETTER; a treasure of ideas promoting a happy, peaceful, prosperous, unlimited way of life. Text in English. 1974. m. 4 p./no.; back issues avail. **Document type:** *Newsletter, Consumer.* **Description:** Publishes on spiritual themes for people who are seeking to live healthier, more positive and prosperous lives.
Published by: Golden Key Ministry - Unity, PO Box 13356, Scottsdale, AZ 85267-3356. TEL 602-789-7127, qkm@amug.org. Ed., Pub. John W Adams.

URBAN FAMILY; the magazine of hope and progress. *see* ETHNIC INTERESTS

200 RWA ISSN 1019-8768
URUNANA. Text in French. 1967. 3/yr. USD 5; USD 11 in Africa; USD 30 elsewhere. bk.rev. **Document type:** *Bulletin.* **Description:** Publishes theological and philosophical papers. Reflects on the intellectual activities of the seminary.
Published by: Grand Seminaire de Nyakibanda, BP 85, Butare, Rwanda. TEL 250-30-793. Ed. Alexandre Kabera. Pub. Thomas Nahimana. Circ: 800.

200 GBR ISSN 1757-8949
BX1970.A1
▼ **USUS ANTIQUIOR**; a journal dedicated to the sacred liturgy. Text in English. 2010 (Jul.). s-a. GBP 100 combined subscription to institutions (print & online eds.); USD 159 combined subscription in United States to institutions (print & online eds.) (effective 2012). **Document type:** *Journal, Academic/Scholarly.* **Description:** Committed to the study and promotion of the historical, philosophical, theological and pastoral aspects of the Roman rite as developed in tradition.
Related titles: Online - full text ed.: ISSN 2041-0999. GBP 91 to institutions; USD 145 in United States to institutions (effective 2012) (from IngentaConnect).
—CCC.
Published by: (The Society of St. Catherine of Siena), Maney Publishing, Ste 1C, Joseph's Well, Hanover Walk, Leeds, W Yorks LS3 1AB, United Kingdom. TEL 44-113-2432800, FAX 44-113-3868178, maney@maney.co.uk, http://www.maney.co.uk. Eds. Alcuin Reid, Laurence Paul Hemming. **Subscr. in N. America to:** Maney Publishing, 875 Massachusetts Ave, 7th Fl, Cambridge, MA 02139. TEL 866-297-5154, FAX 617-354-6875, maney@maneyusa.com.

V E BULLETIN. (Voluntary Euthanasia) *see* PHILOSOPHY

V R B - INFORMATIE. *see* LIBRARY AND INFORMATION SCIENCES

200 SWE ISSN 0042-2010
VAAR FANA. Text in Swedish. 1905. m. illus. **Document type:** *Bulletin, Consumer.*
Formerly (until vol.41, 1945): Svenska Fraelsningsarmens Tidning
Published by: Svenska Fraelsningsarmen/Swedish Salvation Army, c/o Goeran Andresasson, Bruksuddevaegen 22, Alingsaas, 144191, Sweden. goran.andreasson@missionskyrkan.se. Ed. Margaret Abrahmsson.

268 USA
VANTAGE POINT (LINCOLN); for the blind. Text in English. 1955. q. free to qualified personnel (effective 2011). back issues avail. **Document type:** *Magazine, Consumer.* **Description:** Features nature, adventure, and informative interviews, all told from a Christian perspective, geared toward adults with visual handicaps.
Formerly (until 2007): Christian Record Talking Magazine (0009-5583)
Media: Audio cassette/tape.
Published by: Christian Record Services, PO Box 6097, Lincoln, NE 68506. TEL 402-488-0981, FAX 402-488-7582, info@christianrecord.org, http://www.christianrecord.org.

200 RUS
VERA I MUZHESTVO. Text in Russian. q.
Indexed: RASB.
Published by: Assotsiatsiya Khristian-Voennosluzhashchikh, Altuf'evskoe shosse 82, kv 353, Moscow, 127562, Russian Federation. TEL 7-095-9084324. **Dist. by:** East View Information Services, 10601 Wayzata Blvd, Minneapolis, MN 55305. TEL 952-252-1201, 800-477-1005, FAX 952-252-1202, info@eastview.com, http://www.eastview.com.

200 930 ITA ISSN 0391-8564
VERBA SENIORUM; collana di testi e studi patristici. Text in Italian. irreg., latest vol.12. price varies. **Document type:** *Monographic series, Academic/Scholarly.*
Published by: Edizioni Studium, Via Cassiodoro 14, Rome, 00193, Italy.

200 ZAF ISSN 1609-9982
BV1
➤ **VERBUM ET ECCLESIA.** Text in Afrikaans. 1980. 2/yr. bk.rev. back issues avail. **Document type:** *Journal, Academic/Scholarly.* **Description:** Stimulates theological debate through the publication of original articles in all theological disciplines.
Formerly (until 2001): Skrif en Kerk (0257-8891)
Related titles: Online - full text ed.: ISSN 2074-7705. free (effective 2011).
Indexed: A01, A21, DIP, IBR, IBZ, ISAP, IZBG, OTA, RI-1, RI-2, T02.
Published by: University of Pretoria, Faculty of Theology/Universiteit van Pretoria, Fakulteit Teologie, Lynwood Rd, Pretoria, 0002, South Africa. TEL 27-12-420-2358, FAX 27-12-4204016. Ed. Dirk J Human.

230 DEU
VEREIN FUER RHEINISCHE KIRCHENGESCHICHTE. SCHRIFTENREIHE. Text in German. 1953. irreg., latest vol.177, 2010. price varies. **Document type:** *Monographic series, Academic/Scholarly.*
Published by: (Verein fuer Rheinische Kirchengeschichte), Dr. Rudolf Habelt GmbH, Am Buchenhang 1, Bonn, 53115, Germany. TEL 49-228-923830, FAX 49-228-923836, info@habelt.de, http://www.habelt.de.

266 DEU ISSN 0342-2410
BR4
VERKUENDIGUNG UND FORSCHUNG. Text in German. 2/yr. EUR 48; EUR 29.70 newsstand/cover (effective 2011). reprints avail. **Document type:** *Journal, Academic/Scholarly.*
Related titles: ◆ Supplement to: Evangelische Theologie. ISSN 0014-3502.
Indexed: CERDIC, DIP, FR, IBR, IBZ, IZBG, OTA.
—INIST. CCC.
Published by: Guetersloher Verlagshaus (Subsidiary of: Verlagsgruppe Random House GmbH), Carl-Miele-Str 214, Guetersloh, 33311, Germany. TEL 49-5241-74050, FAX 49-5241-740548, info@gtvh.de, http://www.gtvh.de. Ed. Henning Theissen. Circ: 1,500. **Subscr. to:** VVA Zeitschriftenservice, Postfach 7777, Guetersloh 33310, Germany. TEL 49-5241-801969, FAX 49-5241-809620.

220 CHE ISSN 0939-6233
BS410
VESTIGIA BIBLIAE. Text in German. 1979. a. CHF 90 (effective 2011). adv. bk.rev. **Document type:** *Journal, Academic/Scholarly.*
Indexed: IBR, IBZ.
Published by: (Deutsche Bibelarchiv), Peter Lang AG (Subsidiary of: Peter Lang Publishing Group), Hochfeldstr 32, Postfach 746, Bern 9, 3000, Switzerland. TEL 41-31-3061717, FAX 41-31-3061727, info@peterlang.com, http://www.peterlang.com. Ed. Bruno Reudenbach.

VETERA CHRISTIANORUM. *see* ARCHAEOLOGY

220 DEU ISSN 0571-9070
VETUS LATINA; Aus der Geschichte der lateinischen Bibel. Text in German. 1957. irreg., latest vol.39, 2010. price varies. **Document type:** *Monographic series, Academic/Scholarly.*
Published by: Verlag Herder GmbH, Hermann-Herder-Str 4, Freiburg Im Breisgau, 79104, Germany. TEL 49-761-27170, FAX 49-761-2717520, kundenservice@herder.de, http://www.herder.de.

VETUS TESTAMENTUM. *see* RELIGIONS AND THEOLOGY—Judaic

VETUS TESTAMENTUM. SUPPLEMENTS. *see* RELIGIONS AND THEOLOGY—Judaic

230 USA
VICTORY NEWS. Variant title: Success Stories. Text in English. 1983 (Mar.). q. USD 285 domestic; USD 320 foreign; USD 80 per issue domestic; USD 92 per issue foreign (effective 2010). back issues avail. **Document type:** *Magazine, Academic/Scholarly.* **Description:** Contains positive essays and poetry about important events in life.
Published by: Franklin Publishing Company, 2723 Steamboat Cir, Arlington, TX 76006. TEL 817-548-1124, FAX 817-369-2689. Pub. Dr. Ludwig Otto.

268 PRT ISSN 0874-4971
VIDA EM TESTEMUNHO. Variant title: Boletim da Liga Eucaristica. Text in Portuguese. 1972. m. EUR 2 domestic; EUR 7.50 foreign (effective 2005). **Document type:** *Magazine, Consumer.*
Published by: Editorial/AO, Lago das Teresinhas, 5, Braga, 4714-509, Portugal. TEL 351-253-201220, FAX 351-253-201221, http://www.ppcj.pt/AO/AO.html. Ed. Manuel P Morais.

200 BRA ISSN 0507-7184
VIDA PASTORAL. Text in Portuguese. 1960. bi-m. free. adv. bk.rev. bibl.; illus.
Former titles: Pastoral Popular; Vida Pastoral (0042-5265)
Published by: (Pia Sociedade de Sao Paulo), Edicoes Paulinas, Rua Dr Pinto Ferraz, 183, VI Mariana, Sao Paulo, SP 04117-040, Brazil. Ed. Angelo Songego. Circ: 25,000.

200 BEL ISSN 0771-6842
➤ **VIE CONSACREE.** Text in French. 1925. bi-m. bk.rev. bibl. index. **Document type:** *Monographic series, Academic/Scholarly.*
Formerly (until 1965): Revue des Communautes Religieuses
Indexed: CERDIC, CLA, FR.
Published by: Centre de Documentation et de Recherche Religieuses, Rue de Bruxelles 61, Namur, 5000, Belgium. fidelite@fundp.ac.be, http://www.fundp.ac.be/. Ed., Pub. Jean Burton. Adv. contact Jean Hanotte. Circ: 2,500. **Dist. by:** Fidelite. TEL 32-81-221551, FAX 32-81-221551.

202 FRA ISSN 0042-5613
BX2350.2
VIE SPIRITUELLE. Text in French. 1919. 4/yr. price varies. bk.rev. bibl. **Document type:** *Monographic series, Academic/Scholarly.*
Formerly (until 1945): La Vie Spirituelle, Ascetique et Mystique (0988-2480)
Indexed: CERDIC, CPL, MLA-IB, OTA, RASB.
—CCC.
Published by: Editions du Cerf, 29 Boulevard La Tour Maubourg, Paris, 75340 Cedex 07, France. Circ: 3,500.

200 DEU ISSN 1618-0100
VIELE CHARISMEN, EIN LEIB. Text in German. 1989. q. EUR 14 (effective 2011). **Document type:** *Journal, Academic/Scholarly.*
Formerly (until 2000): Charisma (0936-2681)
Published by: Verlag Neue Stadt, Muenchener Str 2, Oberpframmern, 85667, Germany. TEL 49-8093-2091, FAX 49-8093-2096, verlag@neuestadt.com, http://www.neuestadt.com.

200 NLD ISSN 1571-4942
VIEREN. Text in Dutch. 1892; N.S. 1946; N.S. 2003. q. EUR 13; EUR 3.50 newsstand/cover (effective 2009). bk.rev. illus. index. **Document type:** *Bulletin.*
Formed by the 2003 merger of: Rond de Tafel (0035-8169); Which was formerly: Offer; Inzet (1381-7744)
Indexed: CERDIC.
Published by: (Abdij van Berne, Werkgroep voor Liturgie), Grafische Bedrijven Berne B.V., Postbus 27, Heeswijk, 5473 ZG, Netherlands. TEL 33-413-291330, FAX 33-413-292270, http://www.uitgeverijberne.nl.

281.9 NLD ISSN 0042-6032
➤ **VIGILIAE CHRISTIANAE**; a review of early Christian life and languages. Text in Multiple languages. 1947. 5/yr. EUR 353, USD 494 to institutions; EUR 385, USD 539 combined subscription to institutions (print & online eds.) (effective 2012). adv. bk.rev. index. back issues avail.; reprint service avail. from PSC. **Document type:** *Journal, Academic/Scholarly.* **Description:** Publishes articles and short notes of a cultural, historical, linguistic or philological nature on early Christian literature written after the New Testament, as well as on Christian epigraphy and archaeology.
Related titles: Microform ed.: (from RPI, SWZ); Online - full text ed.: ISSN 1570-0720. EUR 321, USD 449 to institutions (effective 2012) (from IngentaConnect); ◆ Supplement(s): Vigiliae Christianae. Supplement. ISSN 0920-623X.
Indexed: A01, A02, A03, A08, A20, A21, A22, ASCA, AmHI, ArtHuCI, B24, BibInd, BibLing, CA, CurCont, DIP, E01, FR, H07, IBR, IBZ, IPB, IZBG, MLA, MLA-IB, PCI, R&TA, RASB, RI-1, RI-2, RILM, SCOPUS, T02, W07.
—BLDSC (9236.080000), IE, Infotrieve, Ingenta, INIST. **CCC.**
Published by: Brill, PO Box 9000, Leiden, 2300 PA, Netherlands. TEL 31-71-5353500, FAX 31-71-5317532, cs@brill.nl. Eds. J C M van Winden, J den Boeft, Johannes van Oort. **Dist. by:** Turpin Distribution Services Ltd., Pegasus Dr, Stratton Business Park, Biggleswade, Bedfordshire SG18 8QB, United Kingdom. TEL 44-1767-604954, FAX 44-1767-601640, custserv@turpin-distribution.com, http://www.turpin-distribution.com/.

209 NLD ISSN 0920-623X
➤ **VIGILIAE CHRISTIANAE. SUPPLEMENT.** Text in English, French, German. 1987. irreg., latest vol.93, 2008. price varies. back issues avail. **Document type:** *Monographic series, Academic/Scholarly.* **Description:** Scholarly translations, commentary and critical studies of texts and issues relating to early Christianity.
Related titles: ◆ Supplement to: Vigiliae Christianae. ISSN 0042-6032.
Indexed: IZBG, PCI.
—BLDSC (9236.081000), IE, Ingenta. **CCC.**
Published by: Brill, PO Box 9000, Leiden, 2300 PA, Netherlands. TEL 31-71-5353500, FAX 31-71-5317532, cs@brill.nl, http://www.brill.nl. R&P Elizabeth Venekamp. **Dist. in N. America by:** Brill, PO Box 605, Herndon, VA 20172-0605. TEL 703-661-1585, 800-337-9255, FAX 703-661-1501, cs@brillusa.com; **Dist. by:** Turpin Distribution Services Ltd., Pegasus Dr, Stratton Business Park, Biggleswade, Bedfordshire SG18 8QB, United Kingdom. TEL 44-1767-604954, FAX 44-1767-601640, custserv@turpin-distribution.com, http://www.turpin-distribution.com/.

200 NLD ISSN 0169-5606
BL1
➤ **VISIBLE RELIGION**; annual for religious iconography. Text in English, French, German. 1982. irreg., latest vol.7, 1990. price varies. illus. back issues avail. **Document type:** *Monographic series, Academic/Scholarly.*
Indexed: AICP, IZBG.
—CCC.
Published by: (Rijksuniversiteit Groningen/University of Groningen, Institute for Religious Iconography), Brill, PO Box 9000, Leiden, 2300 PA, Netherlands. TEL 31-71-5353500, FAX 31-71-5317532, cs@brill.nl, http://www.brill.nl. Ed. Hans G Kippenberg. R&P Elizabeth Venekamp. **Dist. by:** Turpin Distribution Services Ltd., Pegasus Dr, Stratton Business Park, Biggleswade, Bedfordshire SG18 8QB, United Kingdom. TEL 44-1767-604954, FAX 44-1767-601640, custserv@turpin-distribution.com, http://www.turpin-distribution.com/.

268 USA ISSN 1083-0804
BX2380
VISION (CHICAGO); catholic religious vocation discernment guide. Text in English. 1992. a. free to qualified personnel (effective 2011). adv. **Document type:** *Guide, Consumer.* **Description:** Designed for a young adult audience. Provides writing on prayer and discernment, religious life, women religious, priests, brothers, missionaries, and celibacy.
Related titles: Online - full text ed.: free (effective 2011).
Published by: National Religious Vocation Conference, 5401 S Cornell Ave, Ste 207, Chicago, IL 60615. TEL 773-363-5454, FAX 773-363-5530, nrvc@nrvc.net, http://www.nrvc.net. Pubs. Daniel Grippo, Patrice J Tuohy.

226 USA
VISION (COSTA MESA). Text in English. 19??. irreg. **Description:** Covers the work of the fellowship around the world.
Published by: Full Gospel Business Men's Fellowship International, 3 Holland, PO Box 19714, Irvine, CA 92618. TEL 949-461-0100, FAX 949-609-0344, international@fgbmfi.org, http://www.fgbmfi.org.

200 DEU ISSN 1434-1921
VISIONEN; das Magazin fuer ganzheitliches Leben. Text in German. 1985. m. EUR 43; EUR 4.20 newsstand/cover (effective 2007). adv. bk.rev.; music rev. 80 p./no. 3 cols./p.; back issues avail. **Document type:** *Magazine, Consumer.* **Description:** Comparative study of religions.
Former titles (until 1997): Wege und Visionen (0944-4963); (until 1993): Vision (0941-8784); (until 1992): Universale Religion (0179-0617)
—CCC.
Published by: Sandila Import-Export Handels GmbH, Saegestr 37, Herrischried, 79737, Germany. TEL 49-7764-93970, FAX 49-7764-939739, info@sandila.de, http://www.sandila.de. Ed. Gerlinde Gloeckner. Adv. contact Bernd Gloeckner. B&W page EUR 2,700, color page EUR 2,950. Circ: 6,800 (paid and controlled).

207.2 USA
VISITOR. Variant title: Columbia Union Visitor. Text in English. 1895. m. USD 18 to non-members; free to members (effective 2009). adv. bk.rev. back issues avail.; reprints avail. **Document type:** *Magazine, Trade.* **Description:** Provides administrative leadership, governance, and support services to conferences, ministries, healthcare institutions, elementary and secondary schools and colleges.
Formerly (until 1908): Welcome Visitor
Related titles: Online - full text ed.
Published by: (Columbia Union Conference of Seventh-Day Adventists), Review and Herald Publishing Association, 55 W Oak Ridge Dr, Hagerstown, MD 21740. TEL 301-393-3000, FAX 301-393-4055, info@rhpa.org, http://www.rhpa.org. Ed. Celeste Ryan Blyden. Adv. contact Beth Michaels TEL 301-596-0800 ext 574. B&W page USD 1,500, color page USD 2,200; trim 8.125 x 10.625. Circ: 44,500.

200 USA
VISTA (INDIANAPOLIS); journal for holy living. Text in English. 1907. q. USD 3.59 newsstand/cover (effective 2007). bk.rev. **Document type:** *Magazine, Consumer.* **Description:** Designed for adults who want the challenge of a deep Christian commitment and practical holy living. Provides articles and fiction on current Christian concerns and issues.
Published by: Wesleyan Publishing House, PO Box 50434, Indianapolis, IN 46250-0434. TEL 317-570-5191, 800-493-7539, FAX 317-570-5290, submissions@wesleyan.org, http://www.wesleyan.org. Ed., R&P Kelly Trennepohl. Pub. Nathan Birky. Circ: 95,000.

240 ITA ISSN 0042-7330
VITA CONSACRATA; rivista per istituti religiosi e secolari. Text in Italian. 1964. bi-m. adv. bk.rev. bibl. index. **Document type:** *Magazine, Consumer.*
Formerly: Vita Religiosa
Indexed: CLA.
Published by: Editrice Ancora, Via G Battista Niccolini 8, Milan, 20154, Italy. TEL 39-02-3456081, FAX 39-02-34560866, editrice@ancora-libri.it, http://www.ancora-libri.it. Circ: 1,200.

200 ITA
VITA PASTORALE. Text in Italian. 1912. m. (11/yr.). EUR 26 (effective 2008). **Document type:** *Magazine, Consumer.*
Published by: Edizioni San Paolo, Piazza Soncino 5, Cinisello Balsamo, MI 20092, Italy. TEL 39-02-660751, FAX 39-02-66075211, http://www.edizionisanpaolo.it. Ed. Giuseppe Soro. Circ: 36,000.

322.1 NLD ISSN 1574-7247
VIZIER. Text in Dutch. 2004. q.
Published by: S G P - ChristenUnie Zuid-Holland, Postbus 90602, The Hague, 2509 LP, Netherlands. TEL 31-70-4417051, http://www.zuidholland.christenunie.nl. Eds. Andries van Dijk, Rudy Ligtenberg, Suzan Sierksma. Circ: 8,000.

200 BRA ISSN 1809-9076
VOCE EM PAZ. Text in Portuguese. 2006. bi-m. BRL 12.90 newsstand/cover (effective 2007). **Document type:** *Magazine, Consumer.*
Published by: Digerati Comunicacao e Tecnologia Ltda., Rua Haddock Lobo 347, 12o andar, Sao Paulo, 01414-001, Brazil. TEL 55-11-32172600, FAX 55-11-32172617, http://www.digerati.com.br.

200 GTM
VOCES DEL TIEMPO; revista de religion y sociedad. Text in Spanish. 1992. q. GTQ 30; (Latin America $10; elsewhere $15).
Published by: Sociedad para el Estudio de la Religion en Guatemala, 11 Calle, 9-44, 2o Nivel, Zona 1, Guatemala City, Guatemala. TEL 29440.

220 USA ISSN 0049-6669
BX7990.I53
VOICE (GRANDVILLE). Text in English. 1930. 6/yr. USD 7.50. adv. bk.rev. illus. **Description:** Discusses personal growth, clergy development, biblical exegesis (textual and topical), and current themes.
Published by: Independent Fundamental Churches of America, PO Box 810, Grandville, MI 49468. TEL 616-457-5920. Ed. Paul J Dollaske. Circ: 11,500.

VOICE OF REASON. *see* POLITICAL SCIENCE—Civil Rights

272.9 USA
VOICE OF THE MARTYRS. Text in English. 1967. m. free domestic (effective 2009). bk.rev. illus. 16 p./no.; **Document type:** *Newsletter, Consumer.* **Description:** Contains news on atrocities against and persecution of Christians and their families in communist countries, former communist nations and Muslim areas.
Related titles: Multiple languages ed.
Published by: Voice of the Martyrs, Inc., PO Box 443, Bartlesville, OK 74005. TEL 877-337-0302, FAX 918-338-0189, http://www.persecution.com.

248 IRL ISSN 1649-6159
THE VOICE TODAY. Text in English. 2004. w. EUR 83.20 domestic; EUR 119.60 in United Kingdom; EUR 125 elsewhere (effective 2007). adv.
Published by: Benedicta Communications, 11 Merrion Square, Dublin, 2, Ireland. TEL 353-1-6475750. Ed. Simon Rowe.

266 FRA ISSN 0293-9932
VOIX D'AFRIQUE (PARIS). Text in French, German. 1923. 4/yr. EUR 10 (effective 2008). **Document type:** *Magazine, Consumer.* **Description:** Tries to give objective information about the country and news of White Fathers missionaries doing work in Africa.
Indexed: MLA-IB.
Published by: Peres Blancs Missionnaires d'Afrique, 20 rue du Printemps, Paris, 75017, France. TEL 33-1-42278179, FAX 33-1-42255017, voix.afrique@wanadoo.fr, http://peres-blancs.cef.fr. Circ: 9,500.

VOIX NOUVELLES; chants litugiques et musiques sacrees. *see* MUSIC

200 NLD ISSN 1571-4004
VOLZIN. Text in Dutch. 2002. fortn. EUR 85.55 domestic; EUR 136.50 foreign (effective 2009). adv. bk.rev. illus. **Document type:** *Newspaper, Consumer.* **Description:** Covers Church issues and their context in society.
Formed by the merger of (1912-2002): De Bazuin (0005-7312); (1983-2002): H N-Magazine (0168-8693); Which was formerly (1958-1983): Hervormd Nederland (0018-0939); Which incorporated (1997-1998): Loopgraven (1387-0920); (1969-1987): Voorlopig (0166-3380)
Related titles: Microfiche ed.: (from IDC).
Indexed: CERDIC.
Published by: Koninklijke BDU Uitgeverij BV, Postbus 67, Barneveld, 3770 AB, Netherlands. TEL 31-342-494911, FAX 31-342-413141, http://www.bdunet.nl. Ed. Jan van Hooydonk. adv.: B&W page EUR 874, color page EUR 1,458; trim 210 x 297. Circ: 11,000.

200 BRA ISSN 0104-0073
BR1
VOX SCRIPTURAE; revista teologica brasileira. Text in Portuguese. 1991. s-a. **Document type:** *Journal, Academic/Scholarly.*
Indexed: A21, IZBG, OTA, R&TA, RI-1.
Published by: Igreja de Nova Vida, Rua Cincinnato Braga 286, Sao Paulo, Brazil. TEL 55-11-32512144, http://www.novavida.com.br.

230 NLD ISSN 1574-9916
VPWINFO.NL. Text in Dutch. 1986. q.
Former titles (until 2004): Federatie V P W Nederland. Kontaktblad (1386-7814); (until 1987): Landelijk Beraad 7 V P W's. Kontaktblad (1386-8438)
Published by: Federatie V P W Nederland, Palestrinastr 1 b, Utrecht, 3533 EH, Netherlands. TEL 31-30-2933315.

268 NLD ISSN 0167-2770
VREDE OVER ISRAEL. Text in Dutch. 5/yr.
Published by: Christelijke Gereformeerde Kerken in Nederland, Deputaten Kerk en Israel, Postbus 334, Veenendaal, 3900 AH, Netherlands. TEL 31-318-582350, FAX 31-318-582351, info@kerkenisrael.nl. Ed. C J van den Boogert.

327 NLD ISSN 1574-2725
VREDESSPIRAAL. Text in Dutch. 1999. 3/yr. EUR 15 (effective 2009). adv. bk.rev. abstr. **Document type:** *Magazine, Consumer.* **Description:** Discusses theological aspects of nonviolence through the subjects of social justice, confession, conscientious objection and peace education.
Former titles (until 2005): Vonk (1572-7521); (until 2003): Vier in Een (1566-8347); Which was formed by the merger of (1989-1999): OecuMenens (0924-1299); (1980-1999): Uittocht (1383-1062); (1983-1999): Kerk en Vrede (0924-5596); Which was formerly (1946-1983): Militia Christi (0026-4156)
Indexed: CERDIC.
Published by: Kerk en Vrede, Postbus 1528, Utrecht, 3500 BM, Netherlands. TEL 31-30-2316666, FAX 31-30-2714759, secretariaat@kerkenvrede.nl. Ed. Jan Schaake.

DE VRIJDENKER. *see* PHILOSOPHY

230 CHE
W C C FOCUS. Text in English. s-a. **Document type:** *Newsletter.*

R

Published by: (Programme Unit II), World Council of Churches, 150 route de Ferney, PO Box 2100, Geneva 2, 1211, Switzerland. TEL 41-22-791-6111, FAX 41-22-7981346.

200 CHE
W C C NEWS. (World Council of Churches) Text in English. 4/yr. **Document type:** *Newsletter, Consumer.* **Description:** Contains stories about the activities of the Council and the fellowship of member churches around the world.
Related titles: German ed.: Oe R K Nachrichten; Spanish ed.: C M I. Noticias; French ed.: C O E. Nouvelles.
Published by: World Council of Churches, 150 route de Ferney, PO Box 2100, Geneva 2, 1211, Switzerland. TEL 41-22-791-6111, FAX 41-22-7981346, http://www.oikoumene.org/. Ed. Kristine Greenaway.

230 CHE
W C C PUBLICATIONS; new and forthcoming resources from the World Council of Churches. Text in English. s-a. **Document type:** *Newsletter, Consumer.*
Published by: World Council of Churches, 150 route de Ferney, PO Box 2100, Geneva 2, 1211, Switzerland. TEL 41-22-7916379, FAX 41-22-7981346, http://www.oikoumene.org/.

202 AUS ISSN 0260-3705
➤ **W E A THEOLOGICAL NEWS.** (World Evangelical Alliance) Text in English. 1969-1994; resumed 1995. q. free to qualified personnel (effective 2009). adv. software rev.; Website rev.; bk.rev. 4 p./no.; back issues avail. **Document type:** *Newsletter, Academic/Scholarly.* **Description:** Provides news of interest to evangelical theologians and theological educators. Contains information about seminaries, consultations, seminars theological news & developments, and other worldwide activities.
Former titles (until 2002): W E F Theological News; (until 2001): Theological News; Incorporates (in Feb.1982): Theological Education Today
Related titles: CD-ROM ed.; Online - full text ed.: free (effective 2009).
Published by: World Evangelical Alliance, Theological Commission, 17 Disraeli St, Indooroopilly, QLD 4068, Australia. TEL 61-7-38783178, tc@worldevangelicalalliance.com, http://www.worldevangelicalalliance.com/commissions/tc. Ed. David Parker. Circ: 1,000.

268 330.9 CAN ISSN 0821-1248
W R F COMMENT. Text in English. 1982. q. free. adv. bk.rev. back issues avail. **Document type:** *Bulletin.* **Description:** Promotes a Christian perspective of work, economics and industrial relations.
Published by: Work Research Foundation, 5920 Atlantic Dr, Mississauga, ON, Canada. TEL 905-670-7386, FAX 905-670-8416. Ed. Pypker.

200 DEU ISSN 1867-0644
WALDENSER-MAGAZIN. Text in German. 193?. q. EUR 23 membership (effective 2009). **Document type:** *Magazine, Consumer.*
Formerly (until 2006): Deutsche Waldenser (0174-786X)
Published by: Deutsche Waldenservereinigung, Henri-Arnaud-Haus, Oetisheim-Schoenenberg, 75443, Germany. TEL 49-7041-7436, FAX 49-7041-863677, info@waldenser.de, http://www.waldenser.com. Circ: 1,500.

200 NLD ISSN 0167-1871
WAPENVELD. Text in Dutch. 1950. 6/yr. EUR 23; EUR 18 to students; EUR 5.50 newsstand/cover (effective 2008).
Published by: Boekencentrum Uitgevers, Goudstraat 50, Postbus 29, Zoetermeer, 2700 AA, Netherlands. TEL 31-79-3615481, FAX 31-79-3615489, info@boekencentrum.nl, http://www.boekencentrum.nl. Eds. H G Schaaf, B T Wallet.

200 AUS
WARCRY. Text in English. 1883. w. AUD 63 (effective 2009). film rev.; play rev. illus. back issues avail. **Document type:** *Magazine, Consumer.*
Published by: Salvation Army, Australia Eastern Territory Territorial Headquarters, PO Box 479, Blackburn, VIC 3130, Australia. TEL 61-3-88782303, FAX 61-3-88784816, http://www.salvos.org.au. Adv. contact Sarah John.

200 DEU ISSN 0341-7158
WAS UND WIE?; Arbeitshilfen zur religioesen Erzeihen der 3 bis 7 jahrigen. Text in German. 1972. q. EUR 36.80; EUR 29.80 to students; EUR 11.95 newsstand/cover (effective 2011). **Document type:** *Journal, Academic/Scholarly.*
Published by: Guetersloher Verlagshaus (Subsidiary of: Verlagsgruppe Random House GmbH), Carl-Miele-Str 214, Guetersloh, 33311, Germany. TEL 49-5241-74050, FAX 49-5241-740548, info@gtvh.de, http://www.gtvh.de. Ed. Susanne Buescher. Circ: 5,300. **Subscr. to:** VVA Zeitschriftenservice, Postfach 7777, Guetersloh 33310, Germany. TEL 49-5241-801969, FAX 49-5241-809620.

200 320 USA ISSN 2151-7010
▼ **WASHINGTON COLLEGE STUDIES IN RELIGION, POLITICS AND CULTURE.** Text in English. forthcoming 2011 (Aug.). irreg. **Document type:** *Monographic series, Academic/Scholarly.* **Description:** Explores the role of religious belief in political and cultural life around the world.
Published by: (Washington College, Institute for Religion, Politics and Culture), Peter Lang Publishing, Inc. (Subsidiary of: Peter Lang Publishing Group), 29 Broadway, New York, NY 10006. TEL 212-647-7700, FAX 212-647-7707, customerservice@plang.com, http://www.peterlang.com.

WATERWHEEL. see WOMEN'S STUDIES

230 GBR ISSN 0043-1575
BX2350.A1
➤ **THE WAY**; a journal of contemporary spirituality. Text in English. 1961. q. GBP 33 domestic to individuals; EUR 54 in Europe to individuals; USD 62 in United States to individuals; GBP 36 elsewhere to individuals; GBP 52 domestic to institutions; EUR 84 in Europe to institutions; USD 95 in United States to institutions; GBP 54 elsewhere to institutions; GBP 10 per issue to institutions (effective 2009). adv. bk.rev. back issues avail. **Document type:** *Journal, Academic/Scholarly.* **Description:** Covers contemporary Christian spirituality and the Ignation spiritual tradition.
Related titles: Microform ed.: (from PQC); Online - full text ed.: GBP 22 domestic to individuals; EUR 33 in Europe to individuals; USD 38 in United States to individuals (effective 2009).
Indexed: A22, CERDIC, CPL, OTA, PCI, RI-1, RI-2.
—BLDSC (9280.780000), IE, Ingenta.
Published by: (Society of Jesus AUS), The Way, Campion Hall, Oxford, OX1 1QS, United Kingdom. TEL 44-1865-286117, FAX 44-1865-286117. Ed. Paul Nicholson. **Distr. addr.:** Turpin Distribution Services Ltd., Pegasus Dr, Stratton Business Park, Biggleswade, Bedfordshire SG18 8QB, United Kingdom. TEL 44-1767-604954, 44-1767-604951, custserv@turpin-distribution.com, http://www.turpin-distribution.com/.

202 USA
THE WAY FOURTH. Text in English. 1979. q. USD 13. bk.rev. **Document type:** *Newsletter.* **Description:** Dedicated to the teachings of this spiritual tradition, with emphasis on meditation.
Formerly: Ganymede
Published by: (Tayu Center), Tayu Press, PO Box 11554, Santa Rosa, CA 95406. TEL 707-829-9579. Ed. Stuart E Goodnick. Circ: 400.

200 GBR ISSN 0043-1605
WAY OF LIFE; the church's ministry of healing. Text in English. 1911. q. GBP 8 (effective 2009). bk.rev. index. **Document type:** *Magazine, Consumer.* **Description:** Provides news of guild activities and also offers thought provoking articles related to wholeness, sermons, addresses, prayers and poems.
Former titles: For Health; Healing
Indexed: CERDIC.
Published by: Guild of Health, c/o St Marylebone Church, 17, Marylebone Rd, London, NW1 5LT, United Kingdom. TEL 44-20-75631389, guildofhealth@stmarylebone.org. Ed. Steve Press TEL 44-1303-277399.

268 USA
WEEKLY BIBLE READER. Text in English. 1965. q. USD 16.99 per issue (effective 2009). back issues avail. **Document type:** *Magazine, Consumer.* **Description:** Designed to help kids take the lessons home to share with their family and includes activities, stories, family fun activities and daily devotional readings.
Published by: Standard Publishing, 8805 Governor's Hill Dr, Ste 400, Cincinnati, OH 45249. TEL 513-931-4050, 800-543-1353, FAX 877-867-5751, customerservice@standardpub.com, http://www.standardpub.com. Pub., R&P Mark A Taylor. Circ: 104,000.

220 NLD ISSN 2210-2167
▼ **WEET MAGAZINE.** Text in Dutch. 2010. bi-m. EUR 25 (effective 2010). adv. **Document type:** *Magazine, Consumer.*
Published by: Christelijke Tijdschriften BV, Postbus 223, Utrecht, 3500 AE, Netherlands. TEL 31-30-2303508, http://www.christelijketijdschriftenbv.nl. adv.: color page EUR 1,200; trim 210 x 297. Circ: 12,000.

250 DEU
WEG UND ZIEL. Text in German. 1948. w. EUR 62.40 (effective 2011). adv. bk.rev. back issues avail. **Document type:** *Newspaper, Consumer.* **Description:** Information about the Johannische Church and related regional news.
Published by: (Johannische Kirche), Verlag Weg und Ziel, Am Glauer Hof 5, Glau, 14959, Germany. TEL 49-337-3180042, FAX 49-337-3113116, jpd-online@web.de, http://www.johannische-kirche.de. Ed. Rainer Gerhardt TEL 49-33731-13115. Circ: 2,000.

200 DEU ISSN 0043-2040
➤ **WEGE ZUM MENSCHEN**; Zeitschrift fuer Seelsorge und Beratung, heilendes und soziales Handeln. Text in German. 1949. 6/yr. EUR 69 to individuals; EUR 138 to institutions; EUR 42 to students; EUR 18.90 newsstand/cover (effective 2011). adv. index. **Document type:** *Journal, Academic/Scholarly.*
Indexed: CERDIC, DIP, IBR, IBZ, RILM.
—CCC.
Published by: Vandenhoeck und Ruprecht, Theaterstr 13, Goettingen, 37073, Germany. TEL 49-551-508440, FAX 49-551-5084422, info@v-r.de. Circ: 2,000 (paid and controlled).

200 028.5 DEU
WEITE WELT. Text in German. 1921. m. EUR 16.50; EUR 1.50 newsstand/cover (effective 2011). **Document type:** *Magazine, Consumer.*
Published by: Steyler Missionare e.V., Bahnhofstr 9, Nettetal, 41334, Germany. TEL 49-2157-120200, FAX 49-2157-1202060, steyler@steyler.de. Ed. Wolfgang Wagerer.

WELT-SICHTEN. see POLITICAL SCIENCE—International Relations

220 220.93 DEU ISSN 1431-2379
BS635.3
WELT UND UMWELT DER BIBEL. Text in German. 1996. q. EUR 36; EUR 28 to students (effective 2010). 64 p./no.; **Document type:** *Journal, Academic/Scholarly.*
Indexed: DIP, IBR, IBZ, IZBG.
Published by: Katholisches Bibelwerk e.V., Silberburgstr 121, Stuttgart, 70176, Germany. TEL 49-711-6192050, FAX 49-711-6192077, bibelinfo@bibelwerk.de, http://www.bibelwerk.de.

207.2 NLD ISSN 0165-988X
BV3000
WERELD EN ZENDING; oecumenisch tijdschrift voor missiologie en missionaire praktijk. Text in Dutch. 1948. 4/yr. EUR 32.50 domestic; EUR 34 in Belgium; EUR 39 foreign; EUR 8.75 newsstand/cover (effective 2009). adv. bk.rev. index. **Description:** Covers Protestant and Roman Catholic mission activities of interest to readers in the Netherlands and the Flemish portion of Belgium.
Formed by the 1972 merger of: Heerbaan (0017-9531); Het Messiewerk (0169-8249)
Indexed: BAS, CERDIC, P30.
—IE.
Published by: Uitgeverij Kok, Postbus 5018, Kampen, 8260 GA, Netherlands. TEL 31-38-3392555, FAX 31-38-3328912, http://www.kok.nl. Ed. Dr. Thessa Ploos. **Co-sponsors:** Nederlandse Missieraad; Comite van de Missionerende Instituten, BE; Verenigde Protestantse Kerk in Belgie; Nederlandse Zendingsraad.

WERELDWIJD; tijdschrift over evangelizatie en ontwikkeling. see POLITICAL SCIENCE—International Relations

266 USA ISSN 0739-0440
WESLEYAN WORLD. Text in English. 1968. q. donation. 32 p./no.; back issues avail. **Document type:** *Magazine, Consumer.* **Description:** Informs and motivates on behalf of overseas Wesleyan World Missions.
Published by: Wesleyan World Missions, 50434, Indianapolis, IN 46250-0434. TEL 317-595-4172, FAX 317-841-1125. Eds. Joy Bray, Wayne Derr TEL 317-570-5172. R&P Wayne Derr TEL 317-570-5172. Circ: 48,000 (controlled).

270 NGA ISSN 0083-8187
BL2465
WEST AFRICAN RELIGION. Text in English. 1963. s-a. NGN 3, USD 8 per issue. adv. bk.rev. **Document type:** *Journal, Academic/Scholarly.*
Indexed: A21, CERDIC, MLA-IB, RI-1, RI-2.
Published by: University of Nigeria, Department of Religion, Nsukka, Enugu State, Nigeria. Ed. O U Kalu. Circ: 1,000.

230 USA
WESTAR INSTITUTE. SEMINAR PAPERS. Text in English. 19??. s-a. USD 45 domestic; USD 50 foreign (effective 2010). **Document type:** *Proceedings, Academic/Scholarly.* **Description:** Working papers of institute seminars, including the Jesus Seminar.
Related titles: E-mail ed.: USD 25 (effective 2010).
Published by: (Westar Institute), Polebridge Press, Willamette University, Westar Institute, 900 State St, Salem, OR 97301. TEL 503-375-5323, 877-523-3545, FAX 503-375-5324, orders@PolebridgePress.com.

230 DEU
WESTFALIA SACRA; Quellen und Forschungen zur Kirchengeschichte Westfalens. Text in German. 1948. irreg., latest vol.14, 2005. price varies. **Document type:** *Monographic series, Academic/Scholarly.*
Published by: Aschendorff Verlag GmbH & Co. KG, Soester Str 13, Muenster, 48135, Germany. TEL 49-251-6900, FAX 49-251-6904570, buchverlag@aschendorff.de, http://www.aschendorff-buchverlag.de. R&P Dirk F Passmann. Adv. contact Petra Landsknecht.

704.948 200 USA ISSN 1079-5723
THE WESTMINSTER COLLEGE LIBRARY OF BIBLICAL SYMBOLISM. Text in English. 1998. irreg., latest 1998. price varies. **Document type:** *Monographic series, Academic/Scholarly.* **Description:** Encourages works of scholarship which explore the artistic and theological depths of biblical symbols.
Published by: Peter Lang Publishing, Inc. (Subsidiary of: Peter Lang Publishing Group), 29 Broadway, New York, NY 10006. TEL 212-647-7706, 800-770-5264, FAX 212-647-7707, customerservice@plang.com. Ed. Macky Peter W.

THE WESTMINSTER TANNER-MCMURRIN LECTURES ON THE HISTORY AND PHILOSOPHY OF RELIGION AT WESTMINSTER COLLEGE. see EDUCATION

230 USA ISSN 0043-4388
BR1
THE WESTMINSTER THEOLOGICAL JOURNAL. Abbreviated title: W T J. Text in English. 1938. s-a. USD 20 to individuals; USD 35 to institutions; USD 15 to students (effective 2011). bk.rev. index, cum.index. back issues avail. **Document type:** *Journal, Academic/Scholarly.* **Description:** Advances Christian theological scholarship, with emphasis on biblical studies and Reformed theology.
Related titles: CD-ROM ed.: Theological Journal Library CD. USD 99.95 New & Updated CD (effective 2004); Microform ed.: (from PQC); Online - full text ed.
Indexed: A01, A03, A08, A21, A22, CA, CERDIC, ChrPI, DIP, FR, IBR, IBZ, IZBG, MLA-IB, OTA, R&TA, RI-1, RI-2, T02.
—BLDSC (9304.800000), IE, Ingenta, INIST.
Published by: Westminster Theological Seminary, PO Box 27009, Philadelphia, PA 19118. TEL 215-887-5511, 800-373-0119, FAX 215-887-5404, communications@wts.edu. Ed. Vern S Poythress.

WHITE CRANE; a journal of gay wisdom & culture. see HOMOSEXUALITY

200 USA ISSN 0043-5007
WHITE WING MESSENGER. Text in English. 1923. bi-w. USD 10. bk.rev. illus. **Document type:** *Newsletter.*
Published by: (Church of God of Prophecy), White Wing Publishing House, PO Box 3000, Cleveland, TN 37311. TEL 615-476-8536, FAX 615-559-5133. Ed., R&P Billy D Murray. Pub. John Pace. Circ: 16,000.

200 305.4 CAN ISSN 1209-465X
THE WICK. Text in English. 1973. q. CAD 10 (effective 1999). adv. bk.rev. back issues avail. **Document type:** *Newsletter.* **Description:** Publishes news and features relating to women's concerns, human rights, spiritual development and ecumenism; the four aspects of the Women's Inter-Church Council of Canada.
Former titles (until 1995): Women's Inter-Church Council of Canada. Newsletter (0822-2061); (until 1981): Hi There (0826-3078)
Related titles: Fax ed.; Online - full text ed.
Published by: Women's Inter-Church Council of Canada, 602 60th St Clair Ave E, Toronto, ON M4T 1N5, Canada. TEL 416-929-5184, FAX 416-929-4064. Ed., R&P, Adv. contact Sara Stratton. Circ: 3,500 (paid).

221 DEU ISSN 1435-9618
WIENER ALTTESTAMENTLICHE STUDIEN. Text in German. 1999. irreg., latest vol.6, 2009. price varies. **Document type:** *Monographic series, Academic/Scholarly.*
Published by: Peter Lang GmbH (Subsidiary of: Peter Lang Publishing Group), Eschborner Landstr 42-50, Frankfurt Am Main, 60489, Germany. TEL 49-69-7807050, FAX 49-69-78070550, zentrale.frankfurt@peterlang.com, http://www.peterlang.com. Ed. James Alfred Loader.

DER WIENER STEPHANSDOM - FORSCHUNGEN UND MATERIALIEN. see ARCHITECTURE

200 DEU
WILLOWNETZ; reaching seekers - building believers. Text in German. 1999. q. EUR 12; EUR 3 newsstand/cover (effective 2011). adv. **Document type:** *Magazine, Consumer.*
Published by: Bundes Verlag GmbH, Bodenborn 43, Witten, 58452, Germany. TEL 49-2302-930930, FAX 49-2302-93093689, info@bundes-verlag.de, http://www.bundes-verlag.de. Ed. Gotthard Westhoff. Adv. contact Ingo Rubbel. Circ: 31,000 (paid).

230 DEU ISSN 1611-454X
WISSENSCHAFT UND RELIGION. Text in German. 2003. irreg., latest vol.22, 2009. price varies. **Document type:** *Monographic series, Academic/Scholarly.*
Published by: Peter Lang GmbH (Subsidiary of: Peter Lang Publishing Group), Eschborner Landstr 42-50, Frankfurt Am Main, 60489, Germany. TEL 49-69-7807050, FAX 49-69-78070550, zentrale.frankfurt@peterlang.com, http://www.peterlang.com. Eds. Alfred Rinnerthaler, Hans Paarhammer.

200 DEU ISSN 1867-7711
WISSENSCHAFTLICHE BEITRAEGE AUS DEM TECTUM-VERLAG. REIHE RELIGIONSWISSENSCHAFTEN. Text in German. 2008. irreg., latest vol.3, 2010. price varies. **Document type:** *Monographic series, Academic/Scholarly.*
Published by: Tectum Wissenschaftsverlag Marburg, Biegenstr 4, Marburg, 35037, Germany. TEL 49-6421-481523, FAX 49-6421-43470, email@tectum-verlag.de.

200 DEU ISSN 1861-6836
WISSENSCHAFTLICHE BEITRAEGE AUS DEM TECTUM-VERLAG. REIHE THEOLOGIE. Text in German. 1999. irreg., latest vol.5, 2009. price varies. **Document type:** *Monographic series, Academic/Scholarly.*
Published by: Tectum Wissenschaftsverlag Marburg, Biegenstr 4, Marburg, 35037, Germany. TEL 49-6421-481523, FAX 49-6421-43470, email@tectum-verlag.de.

220 DEU ISSN 0512-1582
WISSENSCHAFTLICHE MONOGRAPHIEN ZUM ALTEN UND NEUEN TESTAMENT. Text in German. 1959. irreg., latest vol.115, 2007. price varies. **Document type:** *Monographic series, Academic/Scholarly.*
Indexed: IZBG.
Published by: Neukirchener Verlag, Andreas-Braem-Str 18-20, Neukirchen-Vluyn, 47506, Germany. TEL 49-2845-392222, FAX 49-2845-33689, info@nvg-medien.de, http://www.nvg-medien.de.

225 DEU ISSN 0512-1604
WISSENSCHAFTLICHE UNTERSUCHUNGEN ZUM NEUEN TESTAMENT. Text in English, German. 1950. irreg., latest vol.269, 2010. price varies. **Document type:** *Monographic series, Academic/Scholarly.* **Description:** Examines philosophical discoveries in New Testament studies.
Indexed: IZBG.
Published by: Mohr Siebeck GmbH & Co. KG, Wilhelmstr 18, Tuebingen, 72074, Germany. TEL 49-7071-9230, FAX 49-7071-51104, info@mohr.de.

225 DEU ISSN 0340-9570
WISSENSCHAFTLICHE UNTERSUCHUNGEN ZUM NEUEN TESTAMENT. REIHE 2. Text in German. 1976. irreg., latest vol.302, 2011. price varies. **Document type:** *Monographic series, Academic/Scholarly.*
—CCC.
Published by: Mohr Siebeck GmbH & Co. KG, Wilhelmstr 18, Tuebingen, 72074, Germany. TEL 49-7071-9230, FAX 49-7071-51104, info@mohr.de.

200 USA
BV3750
➤ **WITNESS (ORLAND PARK).** Text in English. 1986. a. free (effective 2010). adv. bk.rev. cum.index: 1986-1994. back issues avail. **Document type:** *Journal, Academic/Scholarly.* **Description:** Scholarly forum and medium for the responsible sharing of ideas among those engaged in the teaching of evangelism, primarily at the seminary level, as well as those whose ministries involve them in serious research and writing in the field.
Formerly (until 2010): Academy for Evangelism in Theological Education. Journal (0894-9034)
Indexed: A21, R&TA, RI-1, RI-2.
Published by: Academy for Evangelism in Theological Education, c/o Al Tizon, Palmer Seminary, 6 E Lancaster Ave, Wynnewood, PA 19096. Circ: 400.

200.82 GBR ISSN 0962-2152
WOMAN ALIVE; the magazine for today's christian woman. Text in English. 1982. m. GBP 21 (effective 2009). **Document type:** *Magazine, Consumer.* **Description:** Covers Christian life-styles for women, includes articles on food, leisure, health, and Christian testimony.
Formerly (until 1991): Christian Woman (0269-0616)
Related titles: Online - full text ed.: free (effective 2009).
Published by: Christian Publishing and Outreach Ltd., Garcia Estate, Canterbury Rd, Worthing, West Sussex BN13 1BW, United Kingdom. TEL 44-1903-264556, FAX 44-1903-830066, sales@cpo.org.uk, http://www.cpo-online.org.uk/. Ed. Jackie Stead TEL 44-1903-604352. Adv. contact Paula Taylor TEL 44-1903-604342.

250 USA ISSN 0043-7379
BV676
WOMAN'S PULPIT. Text in English. 1922. q. USD 15 to members (effective 2000). bk.rev. illus. 8 p./no. 3 cols./p.; back issues avail. **Document type:** *Newsletter.*
Published by: International Association of Women Ministers, 579 Main St, Stroudsburg, PA 18360. FAX 717-421-7718, cjkz@enter.net, seater@hnet.net, cjk@epix.net, http://www.hcsinc.com/seater/iawml.html. Ed. Lavonne Althouse. Circ: 550.

WOMEN IN JOURNEY. *see* WOMEN'S INTERESTS

WOMEN TODAY MAGAZINE. *see* WOMEN'S INTERESTS

WOMEN'S FAITH & SPIRIT. *see* WOMEN'S INTERESTS

200 USA ISSN 1946-8717
WOMUUNWEB W & R. (Women & Religion) Text in English. 19??. q. free (effective 2009). back issues avail. **Document type:** *Newsletter, Trade.*
Former titles (until 2005): Womuunweb (1946-8709); (until 2000): Webworks
Media: Online - full content.
Published by: Unitarian Universalist Women & Religion, c/o Co-Convener Gretchen Ohmann, PO Box 1021, Benton Harbor, MI 49023. info@uuwr.org. Ed. Helen Popenoe.

200 028.5 NLD ISSN 0923-215X
WONDERWEL. Text in Dutch. 1988. 10/yr. EUR 15.50 domestic; EUR 17.50 in Belgium (effective 2010).
Published by: Gooi en Sticht, Postbus 5018, Kampen, 8260 GA, Netherlands. TEL 31-38-3392556, FAX 31-38-3311776, gens@kok.nl, http://www.kok.nl. Circ: 2,000.

200 NLD ISSN 1877-9093
WOODBROOKERS CAHIER. Text in Dutch. s-a. EUR 7.50 per vol. (effective 2011).
Former titles (until 2009): Barchemberichten (1569-6324); (until 2001): Woodbrookers Barchem. Huiselijkheden (0929-5534)
Published by: Vereniging Woodbrookers Barchem, Woodbrookersweg 1, Barchem, 7244 RB, Netherlands. TEL 31-573-441734, adm@woodbrookershuis.nl, http://www.woodbrookershuis.nl. Eds. Gerlof van Rheenen, Wouter Lookman.

200 NLD ISSN 1879-7016
HET WOORD DELEN. Text in Dutch. 5/yr. EUR 43 (effective 2010).
Published by: (Abdij van Berne, Werkgroep voor Liturgie), Uitgeverij Abdij van Berne, Postbus 60, Heeswijk, 5473 ZH, Netherlands. TEL 31-413-299299, FAX 31-413-299288, info@abdijvanberne.nl, http://www.uitgeverijberne.nl.

220 NLD ISSN 2211-2391
▼ **WOORDELIJK.** Text in Dutch. 2011. q. EUR 18.95 domestic; EUR 29.50 foreign; EUR 7 newsstand/cover (effective 2011). **Document type:** *Handbook/Manual/Guide, Consumer.*
Published by: Merweboek Uitgeverij, Postbus 217, Sliedrecht, 3360 AE, Netherlands. TEL 31-184-410224, FAX 1-184-411346, info@merweboek.nl, http://www.merweboek.nl. Ed. Henrieke Remmink.

WORD & DEED. *see* MEDICAL SCIENCES—Communicable Diseases

200 USA
WORD AND WORK. Text in English. 1908. m. USD 4.
Published by: Word, 2518 Portland Ave, Louisville, KY 40212-1040. Ed. Alex Wilson. Circ: 1,180.

200 GBR
WORD IN ACTION. Text in English. 1973. 3/yr. free (effective 2009). charts; illus. **Document type:** *Newspaper.*
Formerly: Bible Society News (0006-0755)
Published by: British and Foreign Bible Society, Stonehill Green, Westlea, Swindon, SN5 7DG, United Kingdom. TEL 44-1793-418100, contactus@biblesociety.org.uk. Circ: 150,000.

200 USA ISSN 0279-6007
WORD IN SEASON. Text in English. 1932. q. USD 7.20, CAD 10.45 to individuals (effective 2008). 96 p./no.; back issues avail. **Document type:** *Magazine, Consumer.* **Description:** Designed to be a daily devotional that enriches life with a contemporary message for today's Christian.
Related titles: Braille ed.; Online - full text ed.: price varies.
Published by: Augsburg Fortress Publishers, PO Box 1209, Minneapolis, MN 55440. TEL 800-328-4648, FAX 800-722-7766, info@augsburgfortress.org, http://www.augsburgfortress.org. Circ: 100,000.

200 079.94 IRL ISSN 1649-1297
THE WORD MAGAZINE. Text in English. 1953. m. EUR 25 domestic; EUR 35 foreign (effective 2007). adv. dance rev.; music rev.; play rev.; tel.rev.; video rev.; bk.rev. illus.; tr.lit. back issues avail. **Document type:** *Magazine, Consumer.* **Description:** Provides book and film reviews; articles on gardening, ecumenism, photography and lifestyles; Scripture readings and Gospel study; a children's page and crossword.
Published by: Divine Word Missionaries, Moyglare Rd, Maynooth, Co. Kildare, Ireland. TEL 353-1-5054467, FAX 353-1-5289184. Adv. contact Sarah MacDonald. Circ: 20,000.

200 USA
WORD OF FAITH. Text in English. 1968. m. free (effective 2009). back issues avail. **Document type:** *Magazine, Consumer.* **Description:** Features spiritual articles, testimonies that help to develop faith in life.
Related titles: Online - full text ed.
Published by: Kenneth Hagin Ministries, 1025 West Kenosha, Broken Arrow, OK 74012. TEL 918-258-1588 ext 1111.

200 USA
WORD OF LIFE QUARTERLY. Text in English. 1990. q.
Published by: Word of Life Fellowship, Rte 9, Schroon Lake, NY 12870. TEL 518-532-7111, FAX 518-532-7421. Ed. Mark Ward Sr. adv.: B&W page USD 1,895, color page USD 2,390. Circ: 40,000 (paid); 50,000 (controlled).

230 AUS ISSN 0813-7951
WORD OF SALVATION. Text in English. 1955. m.
Published by: Reformed Churches Publishing House, P.O. Box 161, Gosnells, W.A. 6110, Australia.

200 USA
WORD ONE. Text in English. 1973. 5/yr. free (effective 2011). **Document type:** *Newsletter, Trade.*
Published by: Claretian Publications, 205 W Monroe, Chicago, IL 60606. TEL 312-236-7782, FAX 312-236-8207, stjudeleague@claretians.org. Ed. Rev. Mark J Brummel.

200 USA
WORDS OF L I F E. Text in English. 1984. irreg. membership. **Document type:** *Newsletter.* **Description:** Focuses on homosexuality in the context of Christianity.
Published by: Living in Freedom Eternally, Inc., PO Box 353, New York, NY 10185. TEL 212-768-2366, FAX 212-768-2393, lifemin@bway.net. Ed., R&P Ronald Highley. Circ: 2,500 (controlled).

WORKING TOGETHER (SEATTLE); to prevent sexual and domestic violence. *see* CRIMINOLOGY AND LAW ENFORCEMENT

200 USA
THE WORKS: YOUR SOURCE FOR ABUNDANT LIVING. Text in English. q. USD 15 (effective 2001).
Published by: Crossroads Center, 711 W. Monroe St, Chicago, IL 60661. Ed. Mary Beth Sammons.

230 NLD ISSN 1874-6551
WORLD CHRISTIAN DATABASE. Text in English. 2007. irreg. EUR 1,670, USD 2,270 (effective 2010). **Document type:** *Academic/Scholarly.*
Media: Online - full text.
Published by: Brill, PO Box 9000, Leiden, 2300 PA, Netherlands. TEL 31-71-5353500, FAX 31-71-5317532, cs@brill.nl, http://www.brill.nl.

200 CHE ISSN 0084-1676
WORLD COUNCIL OF CHURCHES. GENERAL ASSEMBLY. ASSEMBLY - REPORTS. Text in English. 1948. irreg., latest vol.7, 1991. price varies. **Document type:** *Proceedings.*
Published by: (Publications Office), World Council of Churches, 150 route de Ferney, PO Box 2100, Geneva 2, 1211, Switzerland. TEL 41-22-791-6111, FAX 41-22-791-0361, TELEX 415730-OIK-CH. **Dist. in U.S. by:** World Council of Churches, Distribution Center, Rt 222 & Sharadin Rd, Box 346, Kutztown, PA 19530-0346.

200 CHE ISSN 0084-1684
WORLD COUNCIL OF CHURCHES. MINUTES AND REPORTS OF THE CENTRAL COMMITTEE MEETING. Text in English. 1948. irreg. (approx. a.), latest vol.48, 1997. price varies. **Document type:** *Proceedings, Corporate.*
Published by: (Publications Office), World Council of Churches, 150 route de Ferney, PO Box 2100, Geneva 2, 1211, Switzerland. TEL 41-22-791-6111, FAX 41-22-791-0361. **Dist. in U.S. by:** World Council of Churches, Distribution Center, Rt 222 & Sharadin Rd, Box 346, Kutztown, PA 19530-0346.

268 CHE
WORLD COUNCIL OF CHURCHES. OFFICE OF EDUCATION. EDUCATION NEWSLETTER. Text in English. 1972. 2/yr. donations. bk.rev.; film rev. illus. **Document type:** *Newsletter.*
Published by: (Programme Unit II), World Council of Churches, 150 route de Ferney, PO Box 2100, Geneva 2, 1211, Switzerland. TEL 41-22-791-6111, FAX 41-22-791-0361. Ed. C Payne. Circ: 4,000.

230 USA ISSN 1942-1001
WORLD NEWS & PROPHESY. Text in English. 1998. 10/yr. free (effective 2008). **Document type:** *Magazine, Consumer.* **Description:** Aims to increase awareness and understanding of current events as they relate to Biblical prophecy.
Published by: United Church of God, PO Box 541027, Cincinnati, OH 45254. TEL 513-576-9796, FAX 513-576-9795, info@ucg.org, http://www.ucg.org.

290 USA ISSN 0043-8804
BP300
WORLD ORDER; a Baha'i magazine. Text in English. N.S. 1966. q. USD 25 domestic; USD 30 foreign (effective 2009). bk.rev. cum.index: vols.1-12. reprints avail. **Document type:** *Magazine, Consumer.* **Description:** Devoted to consideration of the spiritual, moral, cultural and social challenges confronting world society at a time when, according to the Baha'i teaching, humanity must recognize its oneness and establish a global, just civilization.
Indexed: A21, A22, AmHI, H07, IAPV, MLA-IB, PCI, RI-1, RI-2, T02.
—Ingenta.
Published by: National Spiritual Assembly of the Baha'is of the United States, 1233 Central St, Evanston, IL 60201. TEL 847-733-3559, FAX 847-733-3578, http://www.bahai.us. Ed. Betty J Fisher. R&P Dale Spenner TEL 847-251-1854. Circ: 1,000. **Dist. by:** Baha'i Distribution Service, 415 Linden Ave, Wilmette, IL 60091. TEL 847-425-7950, FAX 847-425-7951, bds@usbnc.org.

207.2 USA ISSN 1063-7931
WORLD PULSE (WHEATON). Text in English. 1967. 24/yr. USD 29.95 domestic; USD 54.95 overseas (effective 2001). **Document type:** *Newsletter.* **Description:** Contains news and commentary about missions, politics and religion worldwide.
Former titles: Pulse (Wheaton) (0747-8631); (until 1984): Europe Pulse
Indexed: A22, INI.
—CCC.
Published by: Evangelism and Missions Information Service, Wheaton College, 500 College SAve, Wheaton, IL 60187. TEL 630-752-7158, FAX 630-752-7155. Ed. Deann Alford. Circ: 5,500.

WORLD UNION. *see* SOCIOLOGY

248 USA ISSN 0746-9241
BR1
WORLDWIDE CHALLENGE. Text in English. 1974. bi-m. USD 12.95; USD 17.45 foreign (effective 1999). illus.
Formerly (until Oct. 1974): World-Wide Impact
Published by: Campus Crusade for Christ, Inc., 100 Lake Hart Dr, Orlando, FL 32832. TEL 407-826-2390, 800-688-4992, FAX 407-826-2374. Ed. Judy Nelson. Pub. William R Bright. R&P Terri Oesterreich. Circ: 95,000; 95,000 (paid).

220 USA ISSN 0043-941X
BV175 CODEN: UWNAAX
➤ **WORSHIP.** Text in English. 1926. bi-m. USD 35 domestic; USD 55 foreign; USD 60 to libraries; USD 7.50 per issue (effective 2009). adv. bk.rev. illus. cum.index every 25 yrs. reprints avail. **Document type:** *Journal, Academic/Scholarly.* **Description:** Provides the best analysis, review, and in-depth comments on relevant, and controversial topics in liturgy and related Church issues.
Formerly (until 1951): Orate Fratres (0196-6898)
Related titles: Microfilm ed.: (from PQC); Online - full text ed.
Indexed: A21, A22, CERDIC, CLA, CPL, FR, MLA-IB, OTA, PCI, R&TA, RI-1, RI-2, RILM.
—BLDSC (9364.450000), IE, Ingenta, INIST.
Published by: (Saint John's Abbey), Liturgical Press, St John's Abbey, PO Box 7500, Collegeville, MN 56321. TEL 320-363-2213, 800-858-5450, FAX 320-363-3299, 800-445-5899, sales@litpress.org. Ed. Kevin Seasoltz TEL 320-363-3883. adv.: page USD 400; 4.375 x 7.5. Circ: 2,604.

200 USA ISSN 1559-6923
WORSHIP FACILITIES. Text in English. 2005. bi-m. free (effective 2007). **Document type:** *Magazine, Trade.* **Description:** Brings information on facilities design, renovation, financing, operation and maintenance.
Published by: (Worship Facilities Magazine), Production Media Inc., 1616 Evans Rd, Ste 104, Cary, NC 27513. TEL 919-677-4000, FAX 919-677-4001, http://www.pmipub.com. Ed. Brian Blackmore.

200 USA ISSN 1066-1247
WORSHIP LEADER MAGAZINE. Text in English. 1992. bi-m. USD 19.95 (effective 1999). adv. **Description:** Provides the tools, information, and resources church leaders need to enhance the worship experience. Non-denominational.
Indexed: CCR, ChrPI.
Published by: C C M Communications, 104 Woodmont Blvd, Ste 300, Nashville, TN 37205. TEL 615-386-3011, FAX 615-386-3380. Ed. Melissa Riddle. Pub. John W Styll. R&P Linda Pfnommer. Adv. contact David Berndt. B&W page USD 1,995, color page USD 2,395; trim 10.88 x 8.25. Circ: 50,000.

200 DEU ISSN 0342-6378
WORT UND ANTWORT; Zeitschrift fuer Fragen des Glaubens. Text in German. 1968. q. EUR 19.95; EUR 15.85 to students; EUR 6.25 newsstand/cover (effective 2006). adv. bk.rev. index. back issues avail. **Document type:** *Journal, Academic/Scholarly.*
Indexed: DIP, IBR, IBZ.
Published by: Matthias-Gruenewald-Verlag GmbH (Subsidiary of: Schwabenverlag AG), Senefelderstr 12, Ostfildern, 73760, Germany. TEL 49-711-44060, FAX 49-711-4406177, mail@gruenewaldverlag.de, http://www.gruenewaldverlag.de. Ed. Paulus Engelhardt. Adv. contact Nina Baab TEL 49-6131-928620. B&W page EUR 550; trim 130 x 207. Circ: 700 (paid and controlled).

R

220 NLD ISSN 1570-7008
WRITINGS FROM THE ANCIENT WORLD. Text in English. 1990. irreg., latest vol.26, 2007. price varies. **Document type:** *Monographic series, Academic/Scholarly.* **Description:** Presents translations of ancient Near Eastern texts dating from the beginning of the Sumerian civilization to the age of Alexander.
Indexed: IZBG.
Published by: (Society of Biblical Literature USA), Brill, PO Box 9000, Leiden, 2300 PA, Netherlands. TEL 31-71-5353500, FAX 31-71-5317532, cs@brill.nl.

220 NLD ISSN 1569-3600
➤ **WRITINGS FROM THE GRECO-ROMAN WORLD.** Text in English. 1972. irreg., latest vol.23, 2007. price varies. **Document type:** *Monographic series, Academic/Scholarly.* **Description:** Publishes translations of ancient texts that are important for scholars and students of religion.
Formerly (until 2001): Society of Biblical Literature. Texts and Translations (0145-3203)
Related titles: ◆ Supplement(s): Writings from the Greco-Roman World. Supplement Series. ISSN 1877-8534.
Indexed: IZBG.
—CCC.
Published by: (Society of Biblical Literature USA), Brill, PO Box 9000, Leiden, 2300 PA, Netherlands. TEL 31-71-5353500, FAX 31-71-5317532, cs@brill.nl.

220 DEU ISSN 0179-4566
WUERZBURGER STUDIEN ZUR FUNDAMENTALTHEOLOGIE. Text in German. 1986. irreg., latest vol.37, 2007. price varies. **Document type:** *Monographic series, Academic/Scholarly.*
Published by: Peter Lang GmbH (Subsidiary of: Peter Lang Publishing Group), Eschborner Landstr 42-50, Frankfurt Am Main, 60489, Germany. TEL 49-69-7807050, FAX 49-69-78070550, zentrale.frankfurt@peterlang.com, http://www.peterlang.com. Ed. Elmar Klinger.

267 028.5 NLD ISSN 1871-7888
XIST IN CHRIST. Text in Dutch. 1986. 10/yr. EUR 30.90; EUR 3.55 newsstand/cover (effective 2009). adv.
Formerly (until 2005): Kivive (1384-4172)
Published by: EB Media, Postbus 2101, Deventer, 7420 AC, Netherlands. TEL 31-88-3263333, FAX 31-88-3263339, mail@ebmedia.nl, http://www.ebmedia.nl/. Eds. Hanna Smallenbroek, Sjoerd Wielenga. adv.: color page EUR 635; trim 210 x 297. Circ: 6,000.

268 AUS ISSN 1832-097X
Y C W ACTION. (Young Christian Workers) Text in English. 1998. q. AUD 30 to non-members; AUD 20 to members (effective 2008). **Document type:** *Magazine, Consumer.* **Description:** Provides information and articles that highlight the everyday issues and actions in young workers lives.
Published by: Australian Young Christian Workers Movement, 40/A Mary St, Highgate, W.A. 6003, Australia. TEL 61-8-94227936, FAX 61-8-93282833, sara.kane@ycw.org.au, http://www.ycw.org.au. Ed. Sara Kane.

268 028.5 CAN ISSN 1719-959X
Y-GO. Text in English. 2003. q. free (effective 2006). **Document type:** *Magazine, Consumer.*
Published by: S I M International, 10 Huntingdale Blvd, Scarborough, ON M1W 2S5, Canada. TEL 416-497-2424, 800-294-6918, FAX 416-497-2444, info@sim.ca, http://www.sim.ca/index.php.

YEAR 'ROUND CHRISTMAS MAGAZINE. *see* ANTHROPOLOGY

200 USA ISSN 0195-9034
YEARBOOK OF AMERICAN AND CANADIAN CHURCHES. Text in English. 1916. a. **Document type:** *Yearbook, Consumer.* **Description:** Index for gauging trends in American and Canadian churches.
Former titles (until 1973): Yearbook of American Churches (0084-3644); (until 1932): The New Handbook of the Churches; (until 1931): The Handbook of the Churches; (until 1925): Year Book of the Churches Covering the Year ..; (until 1917): Federal Council. Year Book
Indexed: SRI.
Published by: Abingdon Press, 201 Eighth Ave S, PO Box 801, Nashville, TN 37202. TEL 800-251-3320, FAX 800-836-7802, orders@abingdonpress.com.

266 GBR ISSN 0951-726X
YES. Text in English. 1960. 3/yr. free domestic (effective 2009). bk.rev. illus. back issues avail. **Document type:** *Magazine, Consumer.* **Description:** Contains news, views, and feature articles on mission and church life in those countries in which CMS has a relationship with partner churches.
Incorporates: C M S Outlook
Related titles: Online - full text ed.: free (effective 2009).
—CCC.
Published by: Church Mission Society, Watlington Rd, Oxford, OX4 6BZ, United Kingdom. TEL 44-1865-787400, FAX 44-1865-776375, info@cms-uk.org. Ed. John Martin TEL 44-1865-787448.

200 GBR ISSN 0085-8374
YORK JOURNAL OF CONVOCATION. Text in English. 1856. irreg. GBP 5.50. **Document type:** *Proceedings.*
Published by: Convocation of York, c/o Synodal Secretary, Church House, West Walls, Carlishe CA3 8UE, United Kingdom. Ed. Canon D T I Jenkins. Circ: 400 (controlled).

268 USA ISSN 1550-8846
YOUNG ADULT TODAY. LEADER GUIDE. Variant title: Today leader. Text in English. 1986. q. USD 5.59 per issue (effective 2008). back issues avail. **Document type:** *Magazine, Consumer.* **Description:** Contains Bible commentary on the international uniform lesson series, teaching plans and other aids designed to challenge the teacher and students in the learning process.
Published by: Urban Ministries, Inc., Dept #4870, PO Box 87618, Chicago, IL 60680. TEL 708-868-7100, 800-860-8642, FAX 708-868-7105, customerservice@urbanministries.com, http://www.urbanministries.com.

268 USA ISSN 1550-8595
YOUNG ADULT TODAY. STUDENT MAGAZINE. Text in English. 1987. q. USD 3.49 per issue (effective 2008). back issues avail. **Document type:** *Magazine, Consumer.* **Description:** Contains Bible study guide lessons, including scripture passages, a lesson aim, focus, and outline, discussions on the lesson text, study questions, lesson applications, daily and weekly devotional readings, and student lessons.
Published by: Urban Ministries, Inc., Dept #4870, PO Box 87618, Chicago, IL 60680. TEL 708-868-7100, 800-860-8642, FAX 708-868-7105, customerservice@urbanministries.com.

268 USA ISSN 1540-9376
YOUNG TEEN STUDENT GUIDES. Text in English. 19??. q. USD 3.99 per issue (effective 2009). **Document type:** *Magazine, Consumer.*
Former titles (until 2002): Young Teen Study Guides (1093-1392); (until 1997): Y T (1080-9740); (until 1995): Teen Student Guide (1059-3349); (until 1992): Teen Student (0190-4590)
Published by: (General Council of the Assemblies of God), Gospel Publishing House, 1445 N Boonville Ave, Springfield, MO 65802. TEL 800-641-4310, FAX 417-862-5881, 800-328-0294, CustSrvReps@ag.org, http://www.gospelpublishing.com/.

YOUNG URBAN VIEWZ. *see* ETHNIC INTERESTS

207.2 USA ISSN 0044-1015
YOUR EDMUNDITE MISSIONS NEWS LETTER. Text in English. 1943. bi-m. USD 2. illus. **Document type:** *Newsletter.*
Published by: (Society of Saint Edmund), Southern Missions, Inc., 1428 Broad St, Selma, AL 36701. TEL 334-875-2359, FAX 205-875-8189. Ed. Roger J Lacharite. Circ: 54,500.

YOUTH AND CHRISTIAN EDUCATION LEADERSHIP. *see* EDUCATION

268 050 USA ISSN 1942-6968
YOUTH CONNEX. Text in English. 2008. bi-m. USD 18 (effective 2008). adv. **Document type:** *Magazine, Consumer.* **Description:** Addresses lifestyle topics including health, finance, career, education, spirituality, love and sex, community and relationships for Christian young adults.
Published by: Youth Connex Inc., PO Box 432, Burtonsville, MD 20866. TEL 866-238-0163. Ed. Joy Monkou. Pub. Nigel Williamson.

267.3 IND
YOUTH OF INDIA. Text in English. 18??. q. INR 100 (effective 2011). adv. **Document type:** *Magazine, Consumer.*
Former titles (until 1986): Yuvak (0044-1414); (until 1968): Association Men (0403-662X); (until 1949): Young Men of India, Burma and Ceylon; (until 1928): The Young Men of India; (until 1890): Indian Interpreter
Published by: National Council of YMCA's of India, Bharat Yuvak Bhawan, Jai Singh Rd, New Delhi, 110 001, India. TEL 91-11-23360769, FAX 91-11-23342859, office@ymcaindia.org.

220 USA ISSN 1540-6830
YOUTHWALK. Abbreviated title: Y W. Text in English. 1988. m. USD 29.74 domestic; USD 36.95 in Canada; USD 60.95 elsewhere; USD 3.95 newsstand/cover (effective 2011). **Document type:** *Magazine, Trade.* **Description:** Aims to provide religious guidance to teens, helping them to tackle the difficult issues they face. Special features inform, encourage and entertain through the scriptures.
Related titles: Supplement(s): Leader's Guide.
Published by: Walk Thru the Bible Ministries, Inc., 4201 N Peachtree Rd, Atlanta, GA 30341. TEL 800-361-6131, info@walkthru.org.

200 DEU ISSN 0943-8610
BL4
Z F R. (Zeitschrift fuer Religionswissenschaft) Text in German. 1993. 2/yr. EUR 47; EUR 26 newsstand/cover (effective 2009). back issues avail. **Document type:** *Journal, Academic/Scholarly.*
Indexed: DIP, IBR, IBZ, R&TA.
Published by: (Deutsche Vereinigung fuer Religionsgeschichte), Diagonal Verlag, Alte Kasseler Str 43, Marburg, 35039, Germany. TEL 49-6421-681936, FAX 49-6421-681944, post@diagonal-verlag.de, http://www.diagonal-verlag.de. Ed. Christoph Auffarth.

225 DEU ISSN 1435-2249
Z N T - ZEITSCHRIFT FUER NEUES TESTAMENT; das neue Testament in Universitaet, Kirche, Schule und Gesellschaft. Text in German. 1998. s-a. EUR 38 to institutions; EUR 44 combined subscription to institutions (print & online eds.); EUR 20 newsstand/cover (effective 2011). adv. **Document type:** *Journal, Academic/Scholarly.*
Related titles: Online - full text ed.
Indexed: DIP, IBR, IBZ, IZBG.
Published by: A. Francke Verlag GmbH, Dischinger Weg 5, Tuebingen, 72070, Germany. TEL 49-7071-97970, FAX 49-7071-979711, info@francke.de, http://www.francke.de. Ed. Stefan Alkier. Circ: 1,200 (paid and controlled).

266 NLD ISSN 1569-5956
Z Z G NIEUWS. Text in Dutch. 1834. q. free (effective 2008). bk.rev. illus.
Formerly (until 2000): Suriname Zending (0039-6141)
Published by: Zeister Zendingsgenootschap, Zusterplein 20, Zeist, 3700 AA, Netherlands. TEL 31-30-6927180, FAX 31-30-6917622, zzg@zzg.nl. Circ: 150,000.

201.6 AUS ISSN 0156-7500
ZADOK CENTRE READING GUIDES. Text in English. 1977. a. bk.rev. bibl. back issues avail. **Description:** Introduces five or six significant books in a particular field to help people evaluate the subject and its implications to Christian faith.
Published by: Zadok Institute for Christianity & Society, PO Box 2182, Fitzroy, VIC 3065, Australia. TEL 61-3-98900633, FAX 61-3-98900700, info@zadok.org.au, http://www.zadok.org.au.

201.6 AUS ISSN 1322-0705
ZADOK PAPERS. Text in English. 1977. q. AUD 4 per issue (effective 2009). back issues avail. **Document type:** *Monographic series, Trade.* **Description:** Extended evaluations of specific political, cultural or economic issues that deal with the subject area within the context of Christian values and beliefs.
Formed by the merger of: Zadok Centre. Series No. 1 (0156-7470); Zadok Centre. Series No. 2 (0156-7489)
Related titles: Online - full text ed.: AUD 2.50 per issue (effective 2009).
Published by: Zadok Institute for Christianity & Society, PO Box 2182, Fitzroy, VIC 3065, Australia. TEL 61-3-98900633, FAX 61-3-98900700, info@zadok.org.au. Ed. Gordon Preece. Circ: 1,000.

201.6 AUS ISSN 0810-9796
ZADOK PERSPECTIVES. Text in English. 1983. q. AUD 6 per issue (effective 2009). bk.rev. back issues avail. **Document type:** *Journal, Trade.* **Description:** Examines contemporary issues within the context of Christian belief.
Formerly (until 1983): Zadok Centre. News
Related titles: Online - full text ed.
Published by: Zadok Institute for Christianity & Society, PO Box 2182, Fitzroy, VIC 3065, Australia. TEL 61-3-98900633, FAX 61-3-98900700, info@zadok.org.au. Ed. Gordon Preece. Circ: 1,000.

230 DEU ISSN 0949-9571
BR129
➤ **ZEITSCHRIFT FUER ANTIKES CHRISTENTUM/JOURNAL OF ANCIENT CHRISTIANITY.** Text in English, German. 1997. 3/yr. EUR 192, USD 288 to institutions; EUR 221, USD 332 combined subscription to institutions (print & online eds.) (effective 2012). adv. reprint service avail. from SCH. **Document type:** *Journal, Academic/Scholarly.* **Description:** Aims to encourage dialogue between church history or historical scholarship on religion and classical scholarship on antiquity in all its subdisciplines.
Related titles: Online - full text ed.: ISSN 1612-961X. EUR 192, USD 288 to institutions (effective 2012).
Indexed: A01, A20, A21, A22, A26, AmHI, ArtHuCI, CurCont, DIP, E01, FR, I05, IBR, IBZ, R&TA, RI-1, SCOPUS, T02, W07.
—BLDSC (4929.005000), IE, Ingenta, INIST. **CCC.**
Published by: Walter de Gruyter GmbH & Co. KG, Genthiner Str 13, Berlin, 10785, Germany. TEL 49-30-260050, FAX 49-30-26005251, info@degruyter.com. Eds. Christoph Markschies, Mr. Hanns Christof Brennecke. Adv. contact Dietlind Makswitat TEL 49-30-260050. page EUR 200; trim 112 x 181. Circ: 400 (paid and controlled).

➤ **ZEITSCHRIFT FUER BAYERISCHE KIRCHENGESCHICHTE.** *see* RELIGIONS AND THEOLOGY—Protestant

200 NLD ISSN 0169-7536
➤ **ZEITSCHRIFT FUER DIALEKTISCHE THEOLOGIE.** Short title: Z D T h. Text in English, German. 1985. s-a. EUR 25 in Europe; USD 40 elsewhere; EUR 20 in Europe to students; USD 30 elsewhere to students (effective 2010). adv. bk.rev. bibl. back issues avail. **Document type:** *Journal, Academic/Scholarly.*
Indexed: DIP, IBR, IBZ, PCI.
Published by: Protestantse Theologische Universiteit, Postbus 5021, Kampen, 8260 GA, Netherlands. TEL 31-38-3371600, FAX 31-38-3371613, http://www.pthu.nl. Ed. Dr. Rinse Reeling Brouwer.

221 DEU ISSN 0044-2526
BS410
ZEITSCHRIFT FUER DIE ALTTESTAMENTLICHE WISSENSCHAFT. Text in Multiple languages. 1881. 4/yr. EUR 275, USD 413 to institutions; EUR 317, USD 476 combined subscription to institutions (print & online eds.) (effective 2012). adv. bk.rev. abstr. index. reprint service avail. from SCH. **Document type:** *Journal, Academic/Scholarly.* **Description:** Presents scholarly studies in the field of research on the Old Testament and early Judaism.
Former titles (until 1936): Zeitschrift fuer die Alttestamentliche Wissenschaft und die Kunde des Nachbiblischen Judentums (0934-2591); (until 1924): Zeitschrift fuer die Alttestamentliche Wissenschaft (0934-2796)
Related titles: Microfiche ed.: (from IDC); Microform ed.; Online - full text ed.: ISSN 1613-0103. EUR 275, USD 413 to institutions (effective 2012); ◆ Supplement(s): Zeitschrift fuer die Alttestamentliche Wissenschaft. Beihefte. ISSN 0934-2575.
Indexed: A01, A20, A21, A22, A26, ASCA, ArtHuCI, BibLing, CurCont, DIP, E01, FR, H14, I05, IBR, IBZ, IZBG, MLA-IB, OTA, P02, P10, P28, P48, P53, P54, PCI, PQC, R&TA, RASB, RI-1, RI-2, SCOPUS, T02, W07.
—BLDSC (9446.950000), IE, Infotrieve, Ingenta, INIST. **CCC.**
Published by: Walter de Gruyter GmbH & Co. KG, Genthiner Str 13, Berlin, 10785, Germany. TEL 49-30-260050, FAX 49-30-26005251, info@degruyter.com. Eds. Ernst-Joachim Waschke, Mr. Hans-Christoph Schmitt. Adv. contact Dietlind Makswitat TEL 49-30-260050. page EUR 500; trim 112 x 181. Circ: 1,200 (paid and controlled).

200 DEU ISSN 0934-2575
➤ **ZEITSCHRIFT FUER DIE ALTTESTAMENTLICHE WISSENSCHAFT. BEIHEFTE.** Text in English, German. 1896. irreg., latest vol.426, 2011. price varies. bibl. **Document type:** *Monographic series, Academic/Scholarly.*
Related titles: ◆ Supplement to: Zeitschrift fuer die Alttestamentliche Wissenschaft. ISSN 0044-2526.
Indexed: IZBG.
—CCC.
Published by: Walter de Gruyter GmbH & Co. KG, Genthiner Str 13, Berlin, 10785, Germany. TEL 49-30-260050, FAX 49-30-26005251, info@degruyter.com, http://www.degruyter.de. Eds. John Barton, Reinhard Kratz.

225 DEU ISSN 0044-2615
BS410
ZEITSCHRIFT FUER DIE NEUTESTAMENTLICHE WISSENSCHAFT UND DIE KUNDE DER AELTEREN KIRCHE. Text in German, English. 1900. 2/yr. EUR 161, USD 242 to institutions; EUR 186, USD 279 combined subscription to institutions (print & online eds.) (effective 2012). adv. bk.rev. bibl. index. cum.index: vols. 1-37, 1900-1938. reprint service avail. from SCH. **Document type:** *Journal, Academic/Scholarly.* **Description:** Provides a scholarly forum for the exegesis of the New Testament and knowledge of the early church.
Formerly (until 1921): Zeitschrift fuer die Neutestamentliche Wissenschaft und die Kunde des Urchristentums (0935-9257)
Related titles: Microform ed.; Online - full text ed.: ISSN 1613-009X. EUR 161, USD 242 to institutions (effective 2012); ◆ Supplement(s): Zeitschrift fuer die Neutestamentliche Wissenschaft und die Kunde der Aelteren Kirche. Beihefte. ISSN 0171-6441.
Indexed: A01, A20, A21, A22, A26, ASCA, ArtHuCI, BibLing, CERDIC, CurCont, DIP, E01, FR, H14, I05, IBR, IBZ, IZBG, P10, P28, P48, P53, P54, PCI, PQC, R&TA, RASB, RI-1, SCOPUS, T02, W07.
—IE, Infotrieve, INIST. **CCC.**
Published by: Walter de Gruyter GmbH & Co. KG, Genthiner Str 13, Berlin, 10785, Germany. TEL 49-30-260050, FAX 49-30-26005251, info@degruyter.com. Ed. Michael Wolter. Adv. contact Dietlind Makswitat TEL 49-30-260050. page EUR 500; trim 112 x 181. Circ: 1,050 (paid and controlled).

225 DEU ISSN 0171-6441
➤ **ZEITSCHRIFT FUER DIE NEUTESTAMENTLICHE WISSENSCHAFT UND DIE KUNDE DER AELTEREN KIRCHE. BEIHEFTE.** Text in German; Text occasionally in English. 1923. irreg., latest vol.186, 2011. price varies. back issues avail. **Document type:** *Monographic series, Academic/Scholarly.*
Related titles: ◆ Supplement to: Zeitschrift fuer die Neutestamentliche Wissenschaft und die Kunde der Aelteren Kirche. ISSN 0044-2615.
Indexed: IZBG.
Published by: Walter de Gruyter GmbH & Co. KG, Genthiner Str 13, Berlin, 10785, Germany. TEL 49-30-260050, FAX 49-30-26005251, info@degruyter.com, http://www.degruyter.de. Ed. Michael Wolter.

241 261 DEU ISSN 0044-2674
BJ1188.5
ZEITSCHRIFT FUER EVANGELISCHE ETHIK. Text in German. 1957. q. EUR 78 domestic; EUR 86 foreign; EUR 42 to students; EUR 24.95 newsstand/cover (effective 2011). adv. bk.rev. bibl. reprints avail. **Document type:** *Journal, Academic/Scholarly.*
Indexed: A20, A21, A22, ASCA, ArtHuCI, CERDIC, CurCont, DIP, FR, IBR, IBZ, RASB, RI-1, RI-2, SCOPUS, W07.
—IE, Infotrieve.
Published by: Guetersloher Verlagshaus (Subsidiary of: Verlagsgruppe Random House GmbH), Carl-Miele-Str 214, Guetersloh, 33311, Germany. TEL 49-5241-74050, FAX 49-5241-740548, info@gtvh.de, http://www.gtvh.de. Ed. Frank Surall. Circ: 950 (paid and controlled). **Subscr. to:** VVA Zeitschriftenservice, Postfach 7777, Guetersloh 33310, Germany. TEL 49-5241-801969, FAX 49-5241-809620.

200 DEU ISSN 0722-8856
ZEITSCHRIFT FUER GOTTESDIENST UND PREDIGT. Text in German. 1983. q. EUR 78; EUR 67.60 to students; EUR 20.85 newsstand/cover (effective 2011). bk.rev. **Document type:** *Journal, Academic/Scholarly.*
Indexed: DIP, IBR, IBZ.
Published by: Guetersloher Verlagshaus (Subsidiary of: Verlagsgruppe Random House GmbH), Carl-Miele-Str 214, Guetersloh, 33311, Germany. TEL 49-5241-74050, FAX 49-5241-740548, info@gtvh.de, http://www.gtvh.de. Ed. Werner Milstein. Circ: 3,200. **Subscr. to:** VVA Zeitschriftenservice, Postfach 7777, Guetersloh 33310, Germany. TEL 49-5241-801969, FAX 49-5241-809620.

200 DEU ISSN 1862-5886
BL4
ZEITSCHRIFT FUER JUNGE RELIGIONSWISSENSCHAFT. Text in Multiple languages. 2006. irreg. free (effective 2011). **Document type:** *Journal, Academic/Scholarly.*
Media: Online - full text.
Indexed: A01.

230.09 DEU ISSN 0044-2925
BR140
ZEITSCHRIFT FUER KIRCHENGESCHICHTE. Text in German. 1889. 3/yr. EUR 196.70; EUR 74 per issue (effective 2010). adv. bk.rev. abstr.; bibl. index. reprint service avail. from SCH. **Document type:** *Journal, Academic/Scholarly.*
Indexed: A20, A21, A22, ASCA, ArtHuCI, CERDIC, CurCont, DIP, FR, HistAb, IBR, IBZ, MLA-IB, P30, PCI, RI-1, RI-2, SCOPUS, W07.
—IE, Infotrieve, INIST. **CCC.**
Published by: W. Kohlhammer GmbH, Hessbruehlstr 69, Stuttgart, 70565, Germany. TEL 49-711-78630, FAX 49-711-78638204, kohlhammerkontakt@kohlhammer.de, http://www.kohlhammer.de. Ed. Roland Loeffler. Circ: 950.

207.2 DEU ISSN 0044-3123
BV2130
ZEITSCHRIFT FUER MISSIONSWISSENSCHAFT UND RELIGIONSWISSENSCHAFT. Text in English, French, German. 1911. 4/yr. EUR 42; EUR 12 per issue (effective 2010). adv. bk.rev. index. **Document type:** *Journal, Academic/Scholarly.*
Formerly (until 1950): Missionswissenschaft und Religionswissenschaft (0179-2970)
Indexed: A21, A22, BAS, CERDIC, CLA, DIP, FR, IBR, IBZ, MLA-IB, R&TA, RI-1, RI-2.
—IE, Infotrieve, INIST. **CCC.**
Published by: (Institut fuer Missionswissenschaftliche Forschungen), E O S Verlag, Erzabtei St. Ottilien, St.Ottilien, 86941, Germany. TEL 49-8193-71700, FAX 49-8193-71709, mail@eos-verlag.de.

200 DEU ISSN 0943-7592
ZEITSCHRIFT FUER NEUERE THEOLOGIEGESCHICHTE/JOURNAL FOR THE HISTORY OF MODERN THEOLOGY. Text in English, German. 1994. s-a. EUR 161, USD 242 to institutions; EUR 186, USD 279 combined subscription to institutions (print & online eds.) (effective 2012). adv. reprint service avail. from SCH. **Document type:** *Journal, Academic/Scholarly.* **Description:** Contains scholarly studies and articles on the history of theology since the Enlightenment.
Related titles: Online - full text ed.: ISSN 1612-9776. EUR 161, USD 242 to institutions (effective 2012).
Indexed: A21, A22, A26, DIP, E01, HistAb, I05, IBR, IBZ, P02, P28, P48, P53, P54, PQC, Philind, R&TA, RI-1, RI-2, T02.
—BLDSC (5001.010000), IE, Ingenta. **CCC.**
Published by: Walter de Gruyter GmbH & Co. KG, Genthiner Str 13, Berlin, 10785, Germany. TEL 49-30-260050, FAX 49-30-26005251, info@degruyter.com. Eds. Friedrich Wilhelm Graf, Dr. Richard E Crouter. Adv. contact Dietlind Makswitat TEL 49-30-260050. page EUR 150; trim 112 x 181. Circ: 400 (paid and controlled).

ZEITSCHRIFT FUER PAEDAGOGIK UND THEOLOGIE; der Evangelische Erzieher. *see* EDUCATION

200 NLD ISSN 0044-3441
BL4
➤ **ZEITSCHRIFT FUER RELIGIONS- UND GEISTESGESCHICHTE/JOURNAL OF RELIGIOUS AND INTELLECTUAL HISTORY.** Text in Dutch. 1948. q. EUR 267, USD 373 to institutions; EUR 291, USD 407 combined subscription to institutions (print & online eds.) (effective 2012). adv. bk.rev. bibl. cum.index: vols.1-39, 1948-1986. back issues avail.; reprint service avail. from PSC. **Document type:** *Journal, Academic/Scholarly.* **Description:** Publishes contributions relating to the history and comparison of religions, the history of German thought, and the history of ideas and ideologies.
Related titles: Online - full text ed.: ISSN 1570-0739. EUR 243, USD 339 to institutions (effective 2012) (from IngentaConnect).
Indexed: A20, A21, A22, ASCA, AmH&L, ArtHuCI, BAS, CA, CERDIC, CurCont, DIP, E01, FR, HistAb, I14, IBR, IBZ, IPB, IZBG, MLA-IB, P30, PCI, Philind, R&TA, RASB, RI-1, RI-2, SCOPUS, T02, W07.
—IE, Infotrieve, Ingenta, INIST. **CCC.**
Published by: Brill, PO Box 9000, Leiden, 2300 PA, Netherlands. TEL 31-71-5353500, FAX 31-71-5317532, cs@brill.nl. Ed. Joachim H Knoll. **Dist. by:** Turpin Distribution Services Ltd., Pegasus Dr, Stratton Business Park, Biggleswade, Bedfordshire SG18 8QB, United Kingdom. TEL 44-1767-604954, FAX 44-1767-601640, custserv@turpin-distribution.com, http://www.turpin-distribution.com/.

200 DEU ISSN 1430-7820
ZEITSCHRIFT FUER THEOLOGIE UND GEMEINDE. Text in German. 1996. a. EUR 12 (effective 2009). **Document type:** *Journal, Academic/Scholarly.*
Indexed: IBR, IBZ.
Published by: Gesellschaft fuer Freikirchliche Theologie und Publizistik e.V., Saarstr 14, Oldenburg, 26121, Germany. TEL 49-441-3407837, struebind@gftp.de.

ZHEXUE YANJIU/PHILOSOPHICAL RESEARCH. *see* PHILOSOPHY

200 HKG ISSN 1812-3651
ZHONGGUO SHENXUE YANJIUYUAN QIKAN/CHINA GRADUATE SCHOOL OF THEOLOGY JOURNAL. Text in Chinese, English. 1986. s-a. HKD 60 domestic; USD 10.50 in Asia; USD 15, CAD 19.50 elsewhere (effective 2006). **Document type:** *Journal, Academic/Scholarly.*
Related titles: Online - full text ed.: ISSN 1817-0900.
Indexed: A21, RI-1.
Published by: Zhongguo Shenxue Yanjiuyuan/China Graduate School of Theology, 12 Dorset Crescent, Kowloon Tong, Hong Kong. http://www.cgst.edu/.

ZHONGGUO ZHEXUESHI/HISTORY OF CHINESE PHILOSOPHY. *see* PHILOSOPHY

200 CHN ISSN 1006-7558
BL1790
ZHONGGUO ZONGJIAO/CHINA RELIGION. Text in Chinese. 1995. m. USD 62.40 (effective 2009). **Document type:** *Journal, Academic/Scholarly.*
Related titles: Online - full text ed.
—East View.
Published by: Zhongguo Zongjiao Shiwuju/State Bureau of Religious Affairs, 32, Jiaodaokoubei 3-dao, Beijing, 100007, China. TEL 86-10-64023355.

230 NLD ISSN 2210-7649
▼ **ZIJ EN ZEEUWS.** Text in Dutch. 2009. q. EUR 10; EUR 2.75 newsstand/cover (effective 2010). adv. **Document type:** *Magazine, Consumer.*
Address: Scheldestraat 60, Vlissingen, 4381 RV, Netherlands. TEL 31-118-431985, zijenzeeuws@live.nl, http://www.zijenzeeuws.nl. Eds. Corina Blok, Margriet Hackenberg. Adv. contact Henk Kats. page EUR 475; trim 210 x 297. Circ: 4,000.

220 ZAF ISSN 0028-3568
ZIONS FREUND. Text in English. 1969 (vol.9). q. ZAR 10.
Formerly: Neuer Zions Freund
Published by: Good News Missionary Society, PO Box 7848, Johannesburg, 2000, South Africa. TEL 011-729-9581. Ed. Sean O'Sullivan. Circ: 1,500.

230 DEU
ZISTERZIENSISCHE SPIRITUALITAET FUER DEN ALLTAG. Text in German. 2000. irreg., latest vol.8, 2010. price varies. **Document type:** *Monographic series, Academic/Scholarly.*
Published by: Verlag Schnell und Steiner GmbH, Leibnizstr 13, Regensburg, 93055, Germany. TEL 49-941-787850, FAX 49-941-7878516, post@schnell-und-steiner.de.

264 HRV ISSN 1331-2170
ZIVO VRELO. Text in Croatian. 1984. m. **Document type:** *Magazine, Consumer.*
Former titles (until 1990): Liturgijsko Pastoralni Listic Zivo Vrelo (1332-0505); (until 1989): Liturgijsko Pastoralni Listic (1331-2162)
Published by: Hrvatski Institut za Liturgijski Pastoral, Trg. sv. Franje 1, Zadar, 23000, Croatia.

277 HRV ISSN 0353-0434
ZNACI VREMENA; obitelski casopis za kriscansku renesansu. Text in Serbian. 1969. q. USD 4.
Related titles: Croatian ed.
Published by: Centar za Istrazivanje Biblije Dokumentaciju i Informacije, Klaiceva 40, Zagreb, 41000, Croatia. Eds. Tomislav Stefanovic, Zdenko Hlisc Bladt. Circ: 9,000.

200 POL ISSN 0044-488X
AP54
ZNAK. Text in Polish; Summaries in English, French. 1946. m. PLZ 78, USD 23; USD 75 in Europe; USD 90 in North America; USD 90 in Africa; USD 110 in South America; USD 110 in Asia; USD 135 in Australia. adv. bk.rev. index.
Indexed: BibLing, CERDIC, IBSS, MLA, MLA-IB, RASB.
Published by: Spoleczny Instytut Wydawniczy "Znak", Ul Kosciuszki 37, Krakow, 30105, Poland. TEL 48-12-8291410, FAX 48-12-4219814. Ed. Jaroslaw Gowin. Adv. contact Iwona Haberny. Circ: 3,000.

200 USA ISSN 2153-6481
▼ **ZOE LIFE MAGAZINE.** Text in English. 2009. bi-m. free (effective 2010). back issues avail. **Document type:** *Magazine, Consumer.* **Description:** Covers articles and information that will get a few steps closer to living the God-kind of life.
Media: Online - full text.
Published by: Soldier of Vision Entertainment, 244 Fifth Ave, Ste 2548, New York, NY 10001. TEL 212-726-1292, FAX 212-726-3292.

200 NLD ISSN 1383-2018
DE ZONDAG VIEREN. Text in Dutch. 1951. w. EUR 31 (effective 2009). **Document type:** *Newspaper, Consumer.*
Formerly (until 1994): Zondagsmis (0044-5002)
Published by: (Abdij van Berne, Werkgroep voor Liturgie), Grafische Bedrijven Berne B.V., Postbus 27, Heeswijk, 5473 ZG, Netherlands. TEL 33-413-291330, FAX 33-413-292270, http://www.uitgeverijberne.nl.

252 USA ISSN 0084-5558
ZONDERVAN PASTOR'S ANNUAL. Text in English. 1966. a. USD 22.99 per issue (effective 2012). reprints avail. **Document type:** *Journal, Trade.* **Description:** Contains planned and prepared sermons for every Sunday, Wednesday and special occasion of the year.
Published by: Zondervan Publishing House, 5300 Patterson Ave, SE, Grand Rapids, MI 49530.

200 CHN ISSN 1005-4162
BL9.C4
ZONGJIAO/RELIGION. Text in Chinese. bi-m. USD 55.80 (effective 2009). **Document type:** *Journal, Academic/Scholarly.* **Description:** Contains research on all religious denominations, their theories and histories.
Indexed: RASB.
Published by: Zhongguo Renmin Daxue Shubao Ziliao Zhongxin/Renmin University of China, Information Center for Social Sciences, Dongcheng-qu, 3, Zhangzizhong Lu, Beijing, 100007, China. TEL 86-10-64039458, FAX 86-10-64015080, center@zlzx.org, http://www.zlzx.org/. **Dist. by:** China International Book Trading Corp, 35 Chegongzhuang Xilu, Haidian District, PO Box 399, Beijing 100044, China. TEL 86-10-68412045, FAX 86-10-68412023, cibtc@mail.cibtc.com.cn, http://www.cibtc.com.cn.

200 CHN ISSN 1006-1312
BL9.C4
ZONGJIAOXUE YANJIU/STUDIES ON RELIGIONS. Text in Chinese. 1982. q. USD 53.20 (effective 2009). **Document type:** *Journal, Academic/Scholarly.*
Related titles: Online - full text ed.
Published by: Sichuan Daxue, Zongjiaoxue Yanjiusuo/Sichuan University, Religion Research Institute, Wekelou 2-Lou, Chengdu, Sichuan 610064, China. **Dist. by:** China International Book Trading Corp, 35 Chegongzhuang Xilu, Haidian District, PO Box 399, Beijing 100044, China. TEL 86-10-68412045, FAX 86-10-68412023, cibtc@mail.cibtc.com.cn, http://www.cibtc.com.cn.

215 USA ISSN 0591-2385
BL240.2
➤ **ZYGON**; journal of religion and science. Text in English. 1966. q. GBP 246 in United Kingdom to institutions; EUR 311 in Europe to institutions; USD 270 in the Americas to institutions; USD 481 elsewhere to institutions; GBP 284 combined subscription in United Kingdom to institutions (print & online eds.); EUR 358 combined subscription in Europe to institutions (print & online eds.); USD 311 combined subscription in the Americas to institutions (print & online eds.); USD 553 combined subscription elsewhere to institutions (print & online eds.) (effective 2012). adv. bk.rev. illus. index, cum.index: vols.1-20. back issues avail.; reprint service avail. from PSC. **Document type:** *Journal, Academic/Scholarly.* **Description:** Covers scholarly work that explores positive ways of relating contemporary scientific knowledge to the world's philosophical and religious heritage.
Related titles: Microfilm ed.: (from PQC); Online - full text ed.: ISSN 1467-9744. 1997. GBP 246 in United Kingdom to institutions; EUR 311 in Europe to institutions; USD 270 in the Americas to institutions; USD 481 elsewhere to institutions (effective 2012) (from IngentaConnect).
Indexed: A01, A02, A03, A08, A20, A21, A22, A25, A26, ASCA, AmHI, ArtHuCI, B04, B14, BRD, BRI, CA, CBRI, CERDIC, CurCont, DIP, E01, E08, F09, FR, FamI, G08, GSS&RPL, H07, H08, H09, H10, H14, HAb, HumInd, I05, IBR, IBZ, IPB, LID&ISL, OTA, P02, P10, P13, P28, P30, P43, P48, P53, P54, PCI, PQC, PerIslam, Philind, PsycholAb, R&TA, R05, RASB, RI-1, RI-2, RILM, S02, S03, S08, S09, S10, SCOPUS, SOPODA, SSCI, SociolAb, T02, W03, W07.
—BLDSC (9538.880000), IE, Infotrieve, Ingenta, INIST, Linda Hall. **CCC.**
Published by: (Institute on Religion in an Age of Science, Center for Advanced Study in Religion and Science), Wiley-Blackwell Publishing, Inc. (Subsidiary of: Wiley-Blackwell Publishing Ltd.), 111 River St, Hoboken, NJ 07030. TEL 201-748-6000, FAX 201-748-6088, info@wiley.com, http://www.wiley.com/WileyCDA/. Ed. Willem B Drees. Adv. contact Kristin McCarthy TEL 201-748-7683.

200 FRA ISSN 2106-7872
▼ **L'1VISIBLE.** Text in French. 2010. m. **Document type:** *Consumer.*
Related titles: Online - full text ed.: ISSN 2107-6634.
Published by: La Societe Prodeo, 20 Rue Jean-Baptiste Pigalle, Paris, 75009, France. TEL 33-1-55320500, FAX 33-1-55320505, http://www.l1visible.com/v1/index.php.

230 305.31 USA ISSN 1932-2690
3 V MAGAZINE; complete lifestyle for men. Text in English. bi-m. USD 12.95 (effective 2006). **Document type:** *Magazine, Consumer.* **Description:** Covers Christian spirituality in all aspects of a man's life, health & wealth.
Published by: 3 V Publishing Co., PO Box 143, McKeesport, PA 15134. TEL 412-896-3027, 877-279-5212.

4'S & 5'S FAMILY FUN. *see* CHILDREN AND YOUTH—For

230 USA ISSN 1048-4124
21ST CENTURY CHRISTIAN MAGAZINE. Text in English. 1938. m. USD 10.95.
Formerly (until 1990): 20th Century Christian (0162-6418)
Published by: 20th Century Christian Foundation, 2809 Granny White Pike, Nashville, TN 37204. TEL 615-383-3842. Ed. Mike Cope. Circ: 18,000.

230 USA ISSN 2162-089X
THE 7000 PROJECT JOURNAL. Text in English. 2004. m. free to members (effective 2011). **Document type:** *Journal, Trade.*
Published by: Be In Health, 4178 Crest Hwy, Thomaston, GA 30286. TEL 706-646-2074, http://beinhealth.com.

RELIGIONS AND THEOLOGY—Abstracting, Bibliographies, Statistics

016.2 USA
A T L A RELIGION DATABASE. Text in English. 200?. q. bk.rev. **Document type:** *Database, Trade.* **Description:** An online index of book reviews that cover all fields of religion.
Incorporates: Index to Book Reviews in Religion; Religion Index One : Periodicals; Religion Index Two: Multi-Author Works
Media: Online - full text.

R

Published by: American Theological Library Association, 300 S Wacker Dr, Ste 2100, Chicago, IL 60606. TEL 312-454-5100, 888-665-2852, FAX 312-454-5505, atla@atla.com.

016.282 USA ISSN 0737-3457
ABRIDGED CATHOLIC PERIODICAL AND LITERATURE INDEX. Variant title: Abridged Index. Text in English. 1983-1991; resumed 1994. q. bk.rev. abstr.; bibl. back issues avail. **Document type:** *Abstract/Index.*
Related titles: CD-ROM ed.; Supplement(s):.
Published by: Catholic Library Association, 100 North St, Ste 224, Pittsfield, MA 01201. TEL 413-443-2252, cla@cathla.org.

016.23 ESP ISSN 0211-4143
BR7
ACTUALIDAD BIBLIOGRAFICA DE FILOSOFIA Y TEOLOGIA; selecciones de libros. Text in Spanish. 1964. s-a. EUR 29 domestic; USD 43 foreign (effective 2009). adv. bk.rev. abstr.; bibl. index.
Formerly: Selecciones de Libros (0037-1181)
Indexed: CERDIC.
Published by: Instituto de Teologia Fundamental, Facultad de Teologia de Catalunya, Roger de Lluria, 13, Barcelona, 08010, Spain. TEL 34-93-3172338, FAX 34-93-3171094. Ed. Josep Boada. Circ: 600. **Subscr. to:** Selecciones de Teologia.

200.21 VAT ISSN 1010-6227
BX845
ANNUARIUM STATISTICUM ECCLESIAE/STATISTICAL YEARBOOK OF THE CHURCH/STATISTIQUE DE L'EGLISE. Text in English, French, Latin. 1969. a. charts; stat. **Document type:** *Journal, Academic/Scholarly.* **Description:** Statistics on the presence and Apostolic work of the Church in various countries and continents.
Formerly: Raccolta di Tavole Statistiche
Published by: (Vatican City. Vatican City. Secretariat of State/Citta del Vaticano. Segretaria di Stato, Vatican City. Ufficio Centrale di Statistica della Chiesa), Libreria Editrice Vaticana, 00120, Vatican City. TEL 379-6-69885003, FAX 379-6-69884716.

016.25571 VAT
ARCHIVUM BIBLIOGRAPHICUM CARMELI TERESIANI. Text in Latin. 1956. irreg. price varies. **Document type:** *Bibliography.*
Formerly: Archivum Bibliographicum Carmelitanum (0570-7242)
Published by: (Teresianum: Pontificia Facolta Teologica - Pontificio Istituto di Spiritualita ITA), Edizioni del Teresianum, Piazza San Pancrazio 5-A, Rome, 00152, Vatican City. TEL 39-06-58540248, FAX 39-06-58540300, http://www.teresianum.org. Ed. Fr. Manuel Diego Sanchez. Circ: 400.

016.28209 ITA ISSN 0066-6785
BR1.AL
ARCHIVUM HISTORIAE PONTIFICIAE. Text in English, French, German, Italian, Latin, Spanish; Summaries in Latin. 1963. a., latest vol.37, 1999. EUR 80 domestic; EUR 120 foreign (effective 2008). adv. bk.rev. bibl. back issues avail. **Document type:** *Monographic series, Academic/Scholarly.* **Description:** Provides a comprehensive bibliography of church history arranged chronologically and thematically.
Indexed: A22, CA, DIP, FR, HistAb, IBR, IBZ, MLA-IB, P30, PCI, T02. —IE.
Published by: (Pontificia Universita Gregoriana/Pontifical Gregorian University, Pontificia Universita Gregoriana, Facolta di Storia Ecclesiastica), Gregorian University Press/Editrice Pontificia Universita Gregoriana, Piazza della Pilotta 35, Rome, 00187, Italy. TEL 39-06-6781567, FAX 39-06-6780588, periodicals@biblicum.com, http://www.paxbook.com. Circ: 750.

016.2 USA
ATLA RELIGION. Text in English. q. **Document type:** *Database, Abstract/Index.*
Media: Online - full text.
Published by: American Theological Library Association, 300 S Wacker Dr, Ste 2100, Chicago, IL 60606. TEL 312-454-5100, 888-665-2852, FAX 312-454-5505, atla@atla.com.

200.021 AUS
AUSTRALIA. BUREAU OF STATISTICS. AUSTRALIAN STANDARD CLASSIFICATION OF RELIGIOUS GROUPS (ONLINE). Text in English. 1996. irreg., latest 2005. free (effective 2009). **Document type:** *Government.* **Description:** Describes how to code census and survey data in all ABS publications.
Formerly: Australia. Bureau of Statistics. Australian Standard Classification of Religious Groups (Print)
Media: Online - full text. **Related titles:** Diskette ed.
Published by: Australian Bureau of Statistics, Locked Bag 10, Belconnen, ACT 2616, Australia. TEL 61-2-92684909, 61-2-62527037, 300-135-070, FAX 61-2-62528103, client.services@abs.gov.au.

016.266 ITA ISSN 0394-9869
Z7838.M6
BIBLIOGRAFIA MISSIONARIA. Text in Italian. 1935. a., latest vol.63, 1999. USD 44 domestic; USD 58 in Europe; USD 60 elsewhere (effective 2009). bk.rev. **Document type:** *Bibliography.*
Formerly (until 1987): Bibliographia Missionaria
Published by: (Pontificia Universita Urbaniana VAT), Pontificia Biblioteca Missionaria, Via Urbano VIII, 16, Rome, RM 00165, Italy. TEL 39-06-69882351, FAX 39-06-69881871, http://www.urbaniana.edu/biblio/it/biblioteca/bibl_missionaria.htm. Ed. Willi Henkel. Circ: 1,000.

016.296 ARG
BIBLIOGRAFIA TEMATICA SOBRE JUDAISMO ARGENTINO. Text in English, Hebrew, Spanish, Yiddish. 1984. irreg., latest 1994. price varies. index. **Description:** Covers Jewish education in Argentina, anti-Semitism in Argentina, and the Jewish labor movement in Argentina; includes sociohistorical investigation.
Published by: (Centro de Documentacion e Informacion sobre Judaismo "Marc Turkow"), A.M.I.A., Ayacucho, 632 Piso 3, Buenos Aires, 1026, Argentina. TEL 54-114-3747877. Circ: 200.

016.2553 ITA ISSN 1723-3585
BIBLIOGRAPHIA FRANCISCANA. Text in Latin. 1931. a. price varies.
Related titles: ◆ Supplement to: Collectanea Franciscana. ISSN 0010-0749.
Published by: Frati Minori Cappuccini, Istituto Storico/Ordo Fratrum Minorum Capuccinorum, Circonvallazione Occidentale 6850, Rome, RM 00163, Italy. TEL 39-06-660521, FAX 39-06-66052532, http://www.istcap.org.

016.296 USA ISSN 0067-6853
BIBLIOGRAPHICA JUDAICA. Text in English. 1969. irreg. **Document type:** *Monographic series, Academic/Scholarly.*
Published by: Hebrew Union College - Jewish Institute of Religion (Cincinnati), 3101 Clifton Ave, Cincinnati, OH 45220. TEL 513-221-1875, FAX 513-221-0321, sjaffee@huc.edu, http://www.huc.edu. Ed. David J Gilner.

016.2 USA ISSN 0742-6836
BIBLIOGRAPHIES AND INDEXES IN RELIGIOUS STUDIES. Text in English. 1984. irreg., latest 2006. price varies. back issues avail. **Document type:** *Monographic series, Bibliography.* —BLDSC (1993.097500), IE, Ingenta.
Published by: Greenwood Publishing Group Inc. (Subsidiary of: A B C - C L I O), 88 Post Rd W, PO Box 5007, Westport, CT 06881. TEL 203-226-3571, 800-225-5800, FAX 877-231-6980, sales@greenwood.com, http://www.greenwood.com. Ed. Gary E Gorman.

016.282 VAT
BIBLIOTECA APOSTOLICA VATICANA. CATALOGHI E NORME DI CATALOGAZIONE. (In 9 subseries: A: Cataloghi ed Inventari di Manoscritti; B: Bibliografia del Manoscritti; C: Cataloghi di Mostre; D: Cataloghi di Stampati; E: Norme di Catalogazione; F: Cataloghi di Pubblicazioni; G: Storia delle Biblioteche Pontificie; H: Quaderni della Scuola di Biblioteconomia; I: Capellae Aposolicae Sixtinaeque Collectanea Acta Monumenta) Text in Italian. 1902. irreg., latest vol.59, 1996. price varies.
Published by: Biblioteca Apostolica Vaticana, 00120, Vatican City. TEL 396-6-69885051, FAX 396-6-69884795.

016.282 ITA
BIBLIOTHECA ASCETICO-MYSTICA. Text in Multiple languages. 1932. irreg., latest vol.7, 1995. price varies. **Document type:** *Bibliography.*
Published by: Frati Minori Cappuccini, Istituto Storico/Ordo Fratrum Minorum Capuccinorum, Circonvallazione Occidentale 6850, Rome, RM 00163, Italy. TEL 39-06-660521, FAX 39-06-66052532, http://www.istcap.org.

BULLETIN DE BIBLIOGRAPHIE BIBLIQUE. *see* RELIGIONS AND THEOLOGY

016.27112 BEL ISSN 0777-3331
BULLETIN D'HISTOIRE CISTERCIENNE/CISTERCIAN HISTORY ABSTRACTS. Text in English. 1987. biennial. back issues avail. **Document type:** *Bibliography.* **Description:** Provides a comprehensive overview of contemporary Cistercian studies, with abstract and complete references.
Related titles: ◆ Supplement to: Citeaux. ISSN 0009-7497.
Published by: Citeaux V.Z.W., Abdij OLVr van Nazareth, Abdijlaan 9, Brecht, 2960, Belgium. Ed., R&P Terryl N Kinder.

016.2629 GBR ISSN 0008-5650
KB49
CANON LAW ABSTRACTS; half-yearly review of periodical literature in canon law. Text in English. 1959. s-a. GBP 18, EUR 28, USD 36 to non-members; GBP 9, EUR 14 per issue to non-members; free to members (effective 2009). bk.rev. **Document type:** *Abstract/Index.*
Published by: Canon Law Society of Great Britain and Ireland, c/o David Hogan, St Bernadette's Presbytery, Gypsy Ln, Nunthorpe, Middlesbrough, TS7 0EB, United Kingdom. TEL 44-1642-316171, http://www.clsgbi.org. Ed. Rev. Paul Hayward.

016.282 USA ISSN 0008-8285
AI3
THE CATHOLIC PERIODICAL AND LITERATURE INDEX. Abbreviated title: C P L I. Text in English. 1930. q. (plus a. cumulation). adv. bk.rev. abstr.; bibl.; illus. back issues avail.; reprints avail. **Document type:** *Abstract/Index.*
Formerly (until 1968): Catholic Periodical Index (0363-6895); Incorporates (1888-1967): Guide to Catholic Literature (0145-191X)
Related titles: CD-ROM ed.: USD 995 (effective 2003); Microfilm ed.: (from PQC); Online - full content ed.: 2003.
Published by: Catholic Library Association, 100 North St, Ste 224, Pittsfield, MA 01201. TEL 413-443-2252, FAX 413-442-2252, cla@cathla.org. Adv. contact Anna LeMaire TEL 337-981-0908.

016.2804 FRA ISSN 1157-7452
Z7753
CENTRE PROTESTANT D'ETUDES ET DE DOCUMENTATION. LIBRESENS. Text in French. 1944. 10/yr. EUR 42 (effective 2008). adv. bk.rev. abstr.; bibl. index. **Document type:** *Bulletin.*
Former titles: Centre Protestant d'Etudes et de Documentation. Bulletin (0181-7671); Federation Protestante de France. Centre d'Etudes et de Documentation. Bulletin (0008-9842)
Indexed: CERDIC, OTA.
Published by: Centre Protestant d'Etudes et de Documentation, 47 Rue de Clichy, Paris, 75009, France. TEL 33-1-42800625, FAX 33-1-46331391, fpf-documentation@protestants.org. Ed. Gabrielle Cadier. Adv. contact Federica Cane. Circ: 1,350. **Co-sponsor:** Federation Protestante de France.

016.26 USA
CHRISTIAN PERIODICAL INDEX. Text in English. base vol. plus q. updates. USD 700 (effective 2005). **Document type:** *Database, Abstract/Index.*
Media: Online - full text. **Related titles:** CD-ROM ed.: USD 500 (effective 2005); ◆ Print ed.: Christian Periodical Index (Print).
Published by: Association of Christian Librarians Inc., PO Box 4, Cedarville, OH 45314.

016.26 USA
Z7753
CHRISTIAN PERIODICAL INDEX (PRINT). Abbreviated title: C P I. Text in English. 1957. s-a. bk.rev. illus. reprints avail. **Document type:** *Abstract/Index.* **Description:** Provides articles and reviews written from an evangelical perspective or of interest to the evangelical community.
Related titles: CD-ROM ed.: USD 500 (effective 2005); ◆ Online - full text ed.: Christian Periodical Index.
Indexed: RASB.
Published by: Association of Christian Librarians Inc., PO Box 4, Cedarville, OH 45314. TEL 937-766-2255, FAX 937-766-5499, info@acl.org. Ed. Douglas Butler.

016.25571 ITA ISSN 0394-7777
COLLECTANEA BIBLIOGRAPHICA CARMELITANA. Text in English, French, German, Italian, Latin, Spanish. 1958. irreg. price varies. adv. **Document type:** *Monographic series, Bibliography.* **Description:** Forum includes bibliographic studies relevant to Carmelite order.
Published by: (Order of Carmelites), Edizioni Carmelitane, Via Sforza Pallavicini 10, Rome, 00193, Italy. TEL 39-06-68100886, FAX 39-06-68100887, edizioni@ocarm.org, http://www.carmelites.info/edizioni/. Circ: 500.

016.23 DEU
DIETRICH'S INDEX PHILOSOPHICUS. Text in German, English, Italian. 1997. base vol. plus a. updates. EUR 569 to institutions (effective 2011). **Document type:** *Database, Abstract/Index.* **Description:** Contains over 950,000 articles from 5,500 humanities journals pertaining to the fields of philosophy, psychology, theology, and the history of religion.
Media: Online - full text.
Published by: De Gruyter Saur (Subsidiary of: Walter de Gruyter GmbH & Co. KG), Mies-van-der-Rohe-Str 1, Munich, 80807, Germany. TEL 49-89-769020, FAX 49-89-76902150, info@degruyter.com, http://www.saur.de.

016.22 ITA ISSN 1123-5608
Z7770
ELENCHUS OF BIBLICA. Variant title: Elenchus of Biblical Bibliography. Text in Italian. 1920. a., latest vol.13, 1997. **Document type:** *Bibliography.* **Description:** Bibliography covering all areas of investigation which involve the scientific study of the Bible.
Former titles (1933-1984): Elenchus Bibliographicus Biblicus (0392-7423); (1020-1932): Elenchus Bibliographicus (1123-5594)
Related titles: Online - full text ed.: ISSN 2038-6605; ◆ Supplement to: Biblica. ISSN 0006-0887.
Published by: Pontificio Istituto Biblico/Pontifical Biblical Institute, Via della Pilotta 25, Rome, 00187, Italy. TEL 39-06-695261, FAX 39-06-695266211, http://www.biblico.it. Ed. Robert Althann. Circ: 1,100.

200.21 USA ISSN 0363-7735
BV4025
FACT BOOK ON THEOLOGICAL EDUCATION. Text in English. 1969. biennial. USD 15 (effective 2010). adv. back issues avail.; reprints avail. **Document type:** *Journal, Academic/Scholarly.* **Description:** Provides statistical data useful for planning by theological institutions.
Related titles: Microfiche ed.: (from CIS); Online - full text ed.: free (effective 2010).
Indexed: SRI.
Published by: The Association of Theological Schools in the United States and Canada, 10 Summit Park Dr, Pittsburgh, PA 15275. TEL 412-788-6505, FAX 412-788-6510, ats@ats.edu.

255 ITA
FONTI E STUDI FRANCESCANI. Text in Italian. 1989. irreg., latest vol.9, 1998. price varies. **Document type:** *Monographic series, Academic/Scholarly.* **Description:** Contains specialized bibliographies in the field of Franciscan studies.
Published by: Centro Studi Antoniani, Piazza del Santo 11, Padua, PD 35123, Italy. TEL 39-049-8762177, FAX 39-049-8762187, asscsa@tin.it, http://www.centrostudiantoniani.it.

016.2 USA ISSN 1054-0946
Z7753
GUIDE TO SOCIAL SCIENCE AND RELIGION. Text in English. 1964. s-a. USD 118 in US & Canada; USD 128 elsewhere; USD 232 combined subscription in US & Canada print & online eds.; USD 242 combined subscription elsewhere print & online eds. (effective 2005). index. **Document type:** *Abstract/Index.*
Former titles (until 1988): Guide to Social Science and Religion in Periodical Literature (0017-5307); (until 1970): Guide to Religious and Semi-religious Periodicals (0533-9111)
Related titles: Online - full content ed.: USD 182 (effective 2005); Cumulative ed(s).
Published by: National Periodical Library, PO Box 3278, Clearwater, FL 33767. Ed., Pub. Albert M Wells. Circ: 450.

INDEX ISLAMICUS; a bibliography of publications on Islam and the Muslim world since 1906. *see* ETHNIC INTERESTS—Abstracting, Bibliographies, Statistics

016.296 ISR
Z6367
INDEX OF ARTICLES ON JEWISH STUDIES (ONLINE)/RESHIMAT MA'AMARIM BE-MADA'E HA-YAHADUT. Text in Multiple languages. 1969. base vol. plus irreg. updates. free (effective 2005). bk.rev. back issues avail. **Document type:** *Database, Abstract/Index.* **Description:** Bibliography of articles and book reviews dealing with all aspects of Jewish studies, and the land and state of Israel, in Hebrew and all European languages.
Formerly (until 2000): Index of Articles on Jewish Studies (Print) (0073-5817)
Media: Online - full text.
Published by: Jewish National and University Library, PO Box 39105, Jerusalem, 91390, Israel. TEL 972-2-6585974, FAX 972-2-6586315, jnl@ram1.huji.ac.il, http://jnul.huji.ac.il. Ed. Bitya Ben Shammai. Circ: 1,200.

016.296 USA ISSN 0019-4050
Z6367
INDEX TO JEWISH PERIODICALS. Text in English. 1963. a. USD 115 (effective 2005). adv. bk.rev. illus. 800 p./no.; back issues avail.; reprints avail. **Document type:** *Abstract/Index.* **Description:** Studies articles, book reviews, feature stories and other English-language writings on Jewish topics which appear in periodicals from the US, England, Israel, South Africa and Australia.
Related titles: CD-ROM ed.: USD 145 (effective 2005); Diskette ed.: USD 140 (effective 2003).
Address: PO Box 22780, Beachwood, OH 44122. TEL 216-921-5566, FAX 603-806-0575, index@jewishperiodicals.com. Ed. Lenore P Koppel. R&P, Adv. contact Harold H Koppel. Circ: 400.

016.22 NLD ISSN 0074-9745
Z7770
INTERNATIONAL REVIEW OF BIBLICAL STUDIES/INTERNATIONALE ZEITSCHRIFTENSCHAU FUER BIBELWISSENSCHAFT UND GRENZGEBIETE. Text in French, English, German. 1952. a. EUR 133 (effective 2009). adv. bk.rev. **Document type:** *Abstract/Index.*
Indexed: FR, OTA.

Published by: Brill, PO Box 9000, Leiden, 2300 PA, Netherlands. TEL 31-71-5353500, FAX 31-71-5317532, cs@brill.nl, http://www.brill.nl. Ed. Bernhard Lang. Circ: 1,000. **Dist. by:** Turpin Distribution Services Ltd., Pegasus Dr, Stratton Business Park, Biggleswade, Bedfordshire SG18 8QB, United Kingdom. TEL 44-1767-604954, FAX 44-1767-601640, custserv@turpin-distribution.com, http://www.turpin-distribution.com/.

016.2967 USA ISSN 1083-8341
Z6367
JEWISH BOOK WORLD. Text in English. 1982. q. USD 36 domestic; USD 45 in Canada; USD 60 elsewhere (effective 2009). adv. bk.rev. **Document type:** *Magazine, Consumer.* **Description:** Contains an annotated listing of new books of Jewish interest and full length reviews by prominent writers.
Indexed: IJP.
Published by: Jewish Book Council, 520 8th Avenue, 4th Fl, New York, NY 10018. TEL 212-201-2920, FAX 212-532-4952, jbc@jewishbooks.org. Ed. Carol E Kaufman.

JEWISH STUDIES SOURCE. *see* HISTORY—Abstracting, Bibliographies, Statistics

284.1021 ZMB
LUTHERAN CHURCH OF CENTRAL AFRICA. STATISTICAL REPORT. Text in English. 1970. a. USD 2.
Published by: Lutheran Church of Central Africa, PO Box CH 195, Lusaka, Zambia. TEL 260-1-281593, FAX 260-1-281523. Ed. Rev. Joel Spaude. Circ: 200.

016.2943 IND ISSN 0970-1435
M L B D NEWSLETTER. Text in English, Hindi. 1979. m. INR 2.50 per issue (effective 2011). bk.rev. abstr.; bibl.; illus. back issues avail. **Document type:** *Newsletter, Consumer.* **Description:** Focuses on Vedic and Buddhist works of literature and research.
Related titles: Online - full text ed.: free (effective 2011).
Indexed: RASB.
Published by: Motilal Banarsidass (Delhi), A-44, Naraina Industrial Area, Phase - I, New Delhi, 110 028, India. TEL 91-11-25795180, FAX 91-11-25797221, mlbd@mlbd.com. **Dist. in U.K. by:** M S Motilal Books Ltd.; **Dist. in U.S. by:** South Asia Books.

016.230 ZAF ISSN 0256-9507
BV2000
MISSIONALIA. Text in English. 1973. 3/yr. abstr. **Document type:** *Journal, Academic/Scholarly.* **Description:** Contains abstracts taken from a wide range of mission journals and periodicals from various parts of the world, and form a valuable tool for mission researchers.
Indexed: A21, A22, ISAP, R&TA, RI-1, SCOPUS.
—Ingenta. **CCC.**
Published by: Southern African Missiological Society, PO Box 35705, Menlo Park, 0102, South Africa. http://www.geocities.com/Athens/Parthenon/8409/sams.htm.

016.282 DEU ISSN 0171-550X
MITTEILUNGEN UND VERZEICHNISSE AUS DER BIBLIOTHEK DES BISCHOEFLICHEN PRIESTERSEMINARS ZU TRIER. Text in German. 1974. irreg., latest vol.25, 2008. price varies. **Document type:** *Monographic series, Academic/Scholarly.*
Published by: Paulinus Verlag GmbH, Maximineracht 11c, Trier, 54295, Germany. TEL 49-651-46080, FAX 49-651-4608221, verlag@paulinus.de.

016.297 GBR ISSN 0144-994X
BP1
NEW BOOKS QUARTERLY ON ISLAM & THE MUSLIM WORLD. Text in English. 1982. q. GBP 4. bk.rev.
Published by: Islamic Council of Europe, 16 Grosvenor Crescent, London, SW1X 7EP, United Kingdom.

016.225 USA
NEW TESTAMENT ABSTRACTS (ONLINE). Text in English. 1956. base vol. plus updates 3/yr. **Document type:** *Database, Abstract/Index.*
Media: Online - full text. **Related titles:** CD-ROM ed.: USD 100 to individuals; USD 250 to institutions (effective 2005); ◆ Print ed.: New Testament Abstracts (Print). ISSN 0028-6877.
Published by: (American Theological Library Association), Boston College, School of Theology and Ministry, 140 Commonwealth Ave, Chestnut Hill, MA 02467-3800. TEL 617-552-6501, 800-487-1167, FAX 617-552-0811, http://www.bc.edu/schools/stm/. Eds. Christopher R Matthews, Daniel J Harrington.

016.225 USA ISSN 0028-6877
BS410
NEW TESTAMENT ABSTRACTS (PRINT); a record of current literature. Text in English. 1956. 3/yr. USD 40 domestic; USD 50 foreign (effective 2010). adv. bk.rev. abstr.; illus. index, cum.index: vols. 1-15 (1956-1970). back issues avail.; reprints avail. **Document type:** *Abstract/Index.* **Description:** Provides a record of current literature on the study of the New Testament and its world.
Related titles: CD-ROM ed.: USD 100 to individuals; USD 250 to institutions (effective 2005); ◆ Online - full text ed.: New Testament Abstracts (Online).
Indexed: FR, RASB.
—BLDSC (6088.856000), INIST.
Published by: (American Theological Library Association), Boston College, School of Theology and Ministry, 140 Commonwealth Ave, Chestnut Hill, MA 02467-3800. TEL 617-552-6501, 800-487-1167, FAX 617-552-0811. Eds. Christopher R Matthews, Daniel J Harrington. adv.: page USD 175. Circ: 2,250. **Subscr. to:** Catholic Biblical Association of America, The Catholic University of America, Washington, DC 20064.

016.2 RUS
TA418.24
NOVAYA LITERATURA PO SOTSIAL'NYM I GUMANITARNYM NAUKAM. RELIGIOVEDENIE; bibliograficheskii ukazatel'. Text in Russian. 1959. m. USD 165 in United States (effective 2004). **Document type:** *Bibliography.* **Description:** Contains information about Russian and foreign books on the study of religions acquired by the INION library.
Formerly (until 1992): Novaya Sovetskaya i Inostrannaya Literatura po Obshchestvennym Naukam. Problemy Ateizma i Religii (0134-2932)
Indexed: RASB.
Published by: Rossiiskaya Akademiya Nauk, Institut Nauchnoi Informatsii po Obshchestvennym Naukam, Nakhimovskii pr-t 51/21, Moscow, 117997, Russian Federation. TEL 7-095-1288930, FAX 7-095-4202261, info@inion.ru, http://www.inion.ru. Ed. E I Serebryannaya. **Dist. by:** East View Information Services, 10601 Wayzata Blvd, Minneapolis, MN 55305. TEL 952-252-1201, 800-477-1005, FAX 952-252-1202, info@eastview.com, http://www.eastview.com.

NYCKELN TILL SVENSKA KYRKAN/KEY TO THE CHURCH OF SWEDEN; verksamhet och ekonomi. *see* RELIGIONS AND THEOLOGY

016.221 USA ISSN 0364-8591
BS410
OLD TESTAMENT ABSTRACTS. Text in English. 1978. 3/yr. USD 26; USD 9 per issue (effective 2009). adv. illus. Index. back issues avail.; reprints avail. **Document type:** *Catalog, Abstract/Index.* **Description:** Contains summaries and bibliographical data on articles and books on the Old Testament.
Related titles: CD-ROM ed.: USD 100 to individuals; USD 350 to institutions (effective 2005); Online - full text ed.
Indexed: CPL, P28, P53, P54, PQC, RASB.
Published by: (American Theological Library Association), Catholic Biblical Association of America, 433 Caldwell Hall, The Catholic University of America, Washington, DC 20064. TEL 202-319-5519, FAX 202-319-4799, cua-cathbib@cua.edu.

016.2 USA
PROQUEST RELIGION. Text in English. base vol. plus d. updates. **Document type:** *Database, Abstract/Index.*
Media: Online - full text.
Published by: ProQuest (Subsidiary of: Cambridge Information Group), 789 E Eisenhower Pky, PO Box 1346, Ann Arbor, MI 48106. TEL 734-761-4700, 800-521-0600, FAX 734-997-4040, 888-241-5612, info@proquest.com, http://www.proquest.com.

016.2897 USA
PROVIDENT BOOK FINDER. Text in English. 1970. 4/yr. free. bk.rev. back issues avail. **Description:** Each issue contains over 100 reviews of new books concentrating on peace, social concerns, theology, ethics, children's books and family life.
Published by: (Provident Bookstores), Mennonite Publishing House, 616 Walnut Ave, Scottdale, PA 15683. TEL 724-887-8500, FAX 724-887-3111. Ed., R&P Ron Meyer. Circ: 12,000.

016.2 016.1 USA
RELIGION AND PHILOSOPHY COLLECTION. Text in English. base vol. plus d. updates. **Document type:** *Database, Abstract/Index.*
Media: Online - full text.
Published by: Gale (Subsidiary of: Cengage Learning), 27500 Drake Rd, Farmington Hills, MI 48331. TEL 248-699-4253, 800-877-4253, FAX 248-699-8035, 877-363-4253, gale.customerservice@cengage.com, http://gale.cengage.com.

016.23 USA
BR1
➤ **RELIGIOUS & THEOLOGICAL ABSTRACTS.** Text in English. 1998. base vol. plus m. updates. USD 595 to institutions (effective 2009). abstr. index. back issues avail. **Document type:** *Database, Abstract/Index.* **Description:** Provides abstracts of articles from more than 400 scholarly periodicals on religion, including Christian, Jewish and other world religions, classified under Biblical, Theological, Historical or Practical headings.
Media: Online - full text.
—BLDSC (7356.480000).
Published by: (Religious & Theological Abstracts Inc.), Religious & Theological Abstracts, Inc., PO Box 215, Myerstown, PA 17067. TEL 717-866-6734, FAX 717-866-9280. Ed. William S Sailer. R&P Willaim S Sailer. Circ: 800.

016.2 USA ISSN 0319-485X
BL1
➤ **RELIGIOUS STUDIES REVIEW**; a quarterly review of publications in the field of religion and related disciplines. Text in English. 1975. q. GBP 149 combined subscription in United Kingdom to institutions (print & online eds.); EUR 189 combined subscription in Europe to institutions (print & online eds.); USD 233 combined subscription in the Americas to institutions (print & online eds.); USD 291 combined subscription elsewhere to institutions (print & online eds.) (effective 2012). bk.rev.; film rev.; video rev. bibl.; illus. index. 100 p./no. 2 cols./p.; back issues avail.; reprints avail. **Document type:** *Journal, Academic/Scholarly.* **Description:** Reviews and offers commentary on English-language books on religion, religious studies, and theology.
Related titles: Online - full text ed.: ISSN 1748-0922. GBP 127 in United Kingdom to institutions; EUR 159 in Europe to institutions; USD 198 in the Americas to institutions; USD 247 elsewhere to institutions (effective 2012) (from IngentaConnect).
Indexed: A01, A20, A21, A22, A26, AmHI, ArtHuCI, B04, BRD, BRI, BibLing, CA, CBRI, CERDIC, ChPerI, CurCont, DIP, E01, H07, H08, HAb, HumInd, I05, IBR, IBZ, IZBG, MEA&I, OTA, P30, PCI, R&TA, RI-1, RI-2, T02, W03, W07.
—BLDSC (7356.555000), IE, Infotrieve, Ingenta. **CCC.**
Published by: (Council of Societies for the Study of Religion), Wiley-Blackwell Publishing, Inc. (Subsidiary of: Wiley-Blackwell Publishing Ltd.), 111 River St, Hoboken, NJ 07030. TEL 201-748-6000, FAX 201-748-6088, info@wiley.com, http://www.wiley.com/WileyCDA/. Eds. David B Gray, Deepak Sarma.

230 GBR
RELIGIOUS TRENDS. Text in English. 1997. a. GBP 30 per issue (effective 2009). charts; illus.; maps; stat. cum.index. 176 p./no.; back issues avail. **Document type:** *Journal, Academic/Scholarly.* **Description:** Provides a statistical description of the UK population in religious terms for researchers, academics, church leaders, and librarians.
Published by: Christian Research, Trinity Business Centre, Stonehill Green, Westlea, Swindon, SN5 7DG, United Kingdom. TEL 44-1793-418388, FAX 44-1793-418118, admin@christian-research.org.uk, http://www.christian-research.org.uk/.

016.23 USA
RESEARCH IN MINISTRY (ONLINE); an index to Doctor of Ministry project reports and theses. Short title: R I M. Text in English. 1981. q. looseleaf. free (effective 2011). adv. abstr. **Document type:** *Database, Abstract/Index.*
Formerly (until 1998): Research in Ministry (Print)
Media: Online - full text.
Published by: American Theological Library Association, 300 S Wacker Dr, Ste 2100, Chicago, IL 60606. TEL 312-454-5100, 888-665-2852, FAX 312-454-5505, atla@atla.com.

016.23 USA ISSN 0036-6358
SCHOLARS' CHOICE; significant current theological literature from abroad. Text in English. 1960. s-a. bibl. **Document type:** *Journal, Academic/Scholarly.*
Published by: Union Theological Seminary, 3041 Broadway, 121st St, New York, NY 10027. TEL 212-662-7100, contactus@uts.columbia.edu, http://www.uts.columbia.edu. Ed. John B Trotti. **Co-publisher:** Presbyterian School of Christian Education.

016.2 NLD ISSN 0165-8794
Z7753
SCIENCE OF RELIGION; abstracts and index of recent articles. Text in English. 1976. s-a. EUR 192, USD 269 to institutions (effective 2012). reprint service avail. from PSC. **Document type:** *Abstract/Index.* **Description:** Aims to provide a systematic bibliography of articles which contribute in various ways to the academic study of religions.
Formerly: Science of Religion Bulletin
Indexed: CA, EI, IZBG.
—**CCC.**
Published by: Brill, PO Box 9000, Leiden, 2300 PA, Netherlands. TEL 31-71-5353500, FAX 31-71-5317532, cs@brill.nl. Ed. Katja Triplett. Circ: 350. **Dist. by:** Turpin Distribution Services Ltd., Pegasus Dr, Stratton Business Park, Biggleswade, Bedfordshire SG18 8QB, United Kingdom. TEL 44-1767-604954, FAX 44-1767-601640, custserv@turpin-distribution.com, http://www.turpin-distribution.com/.

016.221 GBR ISSN 0081-1440
SOCIETY FOR OLD TESTAMENT STUDY. BOOK LIST. Text in English. 1946. a., latest 2002. GBP 39.99 per issue to non-members; free to members (effective 2010). adv. bk.rev. index. back issues avail. **Document type:** *Journal, Academic/Scholarly.*
—**CCC.**
Published by: (Society for Old Testament Study), Continuum International Publishing Group, The Tower Bldg, 11 York Rd, London, SE1 7NX, United Kingdom. TEL 44-20-79220880, FAX 44-20-79287894, info@continuumbooks.com. Ed. George Rrooke. Circ: 1,200.

016.286132 USA ISSN 0081-3028
Z7845.B2
SOUTHERN BAPTIST PERIODICAL INDEX. Text in English. 1965. a., latest 2001. USD 95; USD 450 combined subscription print & online eds. (effective 2005). **Description:** Indexes theology, church music, Baptist history, missions, Christian life and education, child-rearing articles in about 50 periodical titles.
Related titles: CD-ROM ed.: Southern Baptist Periodical Index on CD-ROM. USD 450 per vol. to individuals; USD 550 per vol. to institutions (effective 2000); Online - full text ed.
Published by: Southwest Baptist University Library, 1600 University Ave., Bolivar, MO 65613. TEL 417-328-1614, 417-328-1625, FAX 417-328-1652. Ed. Eldonna DeWeese.

016.282 USA ISSN 1077-6648
SPIRIT OF BOOKS. Text in English. 1988. s-a. adv. **Document type:** *Catalog.* **Description:** Catalog of popular books of interest to Catholic bookstore customers.
Published by: Catholic Book Publishers Association, 8404 Jamesport Dr, Rockford, IL 61108. TEL 815-332-3245, FAX 815-332-3476, cpba3@aol.com, http://www.cbpa.org. Ed., Adv. contact Terry A Wessel. Circ: 250,000 (paid).

STUDIA POLONO-JUDAICA. SERIES BIBLIOGRAPHICA. *see* HISTORY—Abstracting, Bibliographies, Statistics

STUDIA POLONO-JUDAICA. SERIES LIBRORUM CONGRESSUS. *see* HISTORY—Abstracting, Bibliographies, Statistics

016.296 USA ISSN 0039-3568
Z7070
STUDIES IN BIBLIOGRAPHY AND BOOKLORE; devoted to research in the field of Jewish bibliography. Text in English, Hebrew, Multiple languages. 1953. irreg. price varies. bk.rev. bibl. cum.index: vols. 1-11. **Document type:** *Monographic series, Academic/Scholarly.*
Indexed: AmH&L, CA, ChLitAb, HistAb, IJP, L09, MEA&I, MLA-IB, OTA.
Published by: Hebrew Union College - Jewish Institute of Religion (Cincinnati), 3101 Clifton Ave, Cincinnati, OH 45220. TEL 513-221-1875, FAX 513-221-0321, sjaffee@huc.edu, http://www.huc.edu.

016.2 USA
TOPICS IN RELIGION: A BIBLIOGRAPHIC SERIES. Text in English. irreg. price varies. **Document type:** *Monographic series, Academic/Scholarly.*
Published by: Greenwood Publishing Group Inc. (Subsidiary of: A B C - C L I O), 88 Post Rd W, PO Box 5007, Westport, CT 06881. TEL 203-226-3571, 800-225-5800, FAX 877-231-6980, sales@greenwood.com, http://www.greenwood.com.

016.2876 USA
BX8382.2.A1
THE (YEAR) UNITED METHODIST DIRECTORY & INDEX RESOURCES. Text in English. 19??. a. USD 14 (print & CD-ROM eds.) (effective 2009). back issues avail. **Document type:** *Directory, Consumer.* **Description:** Includes a complete telephone and email directory of united methodist agencies, bishops, conference offices and jurisdictional offices.
Formerly (until 19??): United Methodist Directory & Index of Resources (0503-356X)
Related titles: CD-ROM ed.
Published by: United Methodist Publishing House, 201 8th Ave S, PO Box 801, Nashville, TN 37202. TEL 615-749-6000, 800-672-1789, FAX 615-749-6579, http://www.umph.org. Ed. Gwen Colvin.

016.230044 DEU ISSN 1436-2473
ZEITSCHRIFTENINHALTSDIENST THEOLOGIE; indices theologici. Text in German. s-a. index. back issues avail. **Document type:** *Abstract/Index.*
Media: CD-ROM. **Related titles:** Online - full text ed.
Published by: Universitaetsbibliothek Tuebingen, Theologische Abteilung, Postfach 2620, Tuebingen, 72016, Germany. TEL 49-7071-2972587, FAX 49-7071-293123. Ed. Hilger Weisweiler. Circ: 960. **Co-sponsor:** Deutsche Forschungsgemeinschaft.

RELIGIONS AND THEOLOGY—Buddhist

see also ASIAN STUDIES

294.30971 USA
AMERICAN BUDDHIST NEWS. Text in English. 1980. m. looseleaf. USD 25 (effective 2000). adv. bk.rev. back issues avail. **Document type:** *Newsletter.* **Description:** Covers Buddhism in the United States, Buddhism for beginners and advanced.
Former titles: American Buddhist; American Buddhist Newsletter (0747-900X); (until 1984): American Buddhist News
Published by: (American Buddhist Movement), Buddhist Press, 301 W 45th St, New York, NY 10036. TEL 212-489-1075. Ed., R&P Kevin O'Neil. Pub. Marian Valchar. Circ: 5,000.

294.3 USA ISSN 1932-393X
BQ2
THE BEST BUDDHIST WRITING (YEAR). Text in English. 2004. a., latest 2007. USD 16.95 per issue (effective 2008). **Document type:** *Journal, Consumer.*
Published by: Shambhala Publications, PO Box 308, Boston, MA 02117. TEL 617-424-0030, FAX 617-236 1563, custserv@shambhala.com, http://www.shambhala.com/index.cfm. Ed. Melvin McLeod.

294 USA ISSN 1533-8053
BQ2
BODHI. Text in English. 1997. q. USD 31 domestic; USD 35 in Canada; USD 52 elsewhere; USD 8 newsstand/cover domestic; USD 10 newsstand/cover in Canada (effective 2002). back issues avail. **Document type:** *Magazine, Consumer.* **Description:** Includes features and poetry from Buddhist masters of the Nyingma and Kangu lineages. Includes a schedule of teachings, Tsurluk Tibetan calendar, and a resource directory.
Published by: Nalandabodhi, 1111 East Madison, PMB 361, Seattle, WA 98122. TEL 425-814-8425. Eds. Amita Gupta, Carole Fleming, Cindy Shelton. Pubs. Dzogchen Ponlop Rinpoche, Martin Marvet.

294.3 LKA ISSN 0520-3325
BODHI LEAVES. Text in English. 1961. q. LKR 400, USD 30 (effective 2003). bk.rev. back issues avail. **Document type:** *Catalog, Abstract/Index.*
Related titles: E-mail ed.; Fax ed.; Online - full text ed.
Published by: Buddhist Publication Society, 54, Sangharaja Mawatha, P O Box 61, Kandy, Sri Lanka. TEL 94-8-223679, FAX 94-8-223679. Ed. Venerable Bhikkhu Bodhi.

294.3 NLD ISSN 1877-2498
BOEDDHISTISCHE WIJSHEDEN SCHEURKALENDER. Text in Dutch. 2008. a. EUR 8.99 (effective 2011).
Published by: Uitgeverij Verba, Birkstraat 143A, Soest, 3768 HE, Netherlands. TEL 31-33-4943909, FAX 31-33-4655174, info@uitgeverijdelantaarn.nl, http://www.ruitenbergboek.nl.

294.3 RUS
BUDDA; ezhemesyachnyi filosofsko-obrazovatel'nyi zhurnal. Text in Russian. 1996. m. USD 163 in the Americas (effective 2000).
Published by: Redaktsiya Budda, A-ya 14, Moscow, 117454, Russian Federation. TEL 7-095-1777418g. Ed. L L Kazimirovoi. **Dist. by:** East View Information Services, 10601 Wayzata Blvd, Minneapolis, MN 55305. TEL 952-252-1201, 800-477-1005, FAX 952-252-1202, info@eastview.com, http://www.eastview.com.

294.3927 USA
BUDDHA WORLD. Text in English. 1973. q. USD 12. back issues avail. **Description:** Zen Buddhist philosophy, theory, history, stories; events of the American Zen College.
Published by: American Zen College Press, 16815 Germantown Rd, Germantown, MD 20874. TEL 301-428-0665. Ed. Barbara Abrams. Circ: 1,000.

294.3 CAN ISSN 1499-9927
BUDDHADHARMA; the practitioner's quarterly. Text in English. 2002. q. CAD 26 domestic; USD 19.95 in United States; USD 36 elsewhere (effective 2008). adv. illus. **Description:** Brings in-depth reviews of the latest books on Buddhism, and articles about the people and issues that are of special interest to Buddhists. It reflects the growing sense of communication and common purpose among Buddhist sanghas in North America and internationally.
Address: 1660 Hollis St, Ste 701, Halifax, NS B3J 1V7, Canada. TEL 902-422-8404, FAX 902-423-2701, info@thebuddhadharma.com. Eds. Melvin McLeod, Tynette Deveaux. **Subscr. to:** 1345 Spruce St, Boulder, CO 80302-9687. TEL 877-786-1950.

294.3 AUS
BUDDHAZINE. Text in English. 1996. irreg. free (effective 2008). **Document type:** *Magazine, Consumer.* **Description:** Provides articles related to Buddhism.
Media: Online - full text.
Published by: BuddhaNet, 78 Bentley Rd, Tullera, NSW 2480, Australia. TEL 61-2-66282426, webmaster@buddhanet.net. Ed. Ven Pannyavaro.

294.3 USA ISSN 1933-3609
BQ2
BUDDHISM TODAY. Text in English. s-a. **Document type:** *Magazine, Consumer.*
Formerly (until 200?): Kagyu Life International
Published by: Diamond Way Buddhist Centers, 110 Merced Ave, San Francisco, CA 94127. TEL 415-661-6030, FAX 415-665-2241, dwbc@diamondway.org, http://www.diamondway.org.

294.367 USA
BUDDHISMS; a Princeton University Press series. Text in English. 1998. irreg., latest 2004. price varies. back issues avail. **Document type:** *Monographic series, Academic/Scholarly.* **Description:** Examines cultural, historical, moral, and ethical issues in Buddhism.
Published by: Princeton University Press, 41 William St, Princeton, NJ 08540. TEL 609-258-4900, 800-777-4726, FAX 609-258-6305, cpriday@pupress.co.uk. Ed. Stephen F Teiser. **Subscr. addr. in US:** California - Princeton Fulfillment Services, Inc., 1445 Lower Ferry Rd, Ewing, NJ 08618. TEL 609-883-1759, 800-777-4726, FAX 609-883-7413, 800-999-1958, orders@cpfsinc.com. **Dist. addr. in Canada:** University Press Group.; **Dist. addr. in UK:** John Wiley & Sons Ltd.

294.3 USA ISSN 0882-0945
BR128.B8
➤ **BUDDHIST - CHRISTIAN STUDIES.** Abbreviated title: B C S. Text in English. 1981. a. USD 25 per issue domestic to individuals; USD 37 per issue foreign to individuals; USD 40 per issue domestic to institutions; USD 52 per issue foreign to institutions; USD 16 per issue to students (effective 2009). adv. bk.rev. illus. back issues avail.; reprint service avail. from PSC. **Document type:** *Journal, Academic/Scholarly.* **Description:** Focuses on Buddhism and Christianity and their historical and contemporary interrelationship.
Related titles: Online - full text ed.: ISSN 1527-9472. 2000.
Indexed: A01, A03, A08, A21, A22, A26, AmHI, B04, B14, BRD, CA, E01, E08, G08, H07, H08, H14, HAb, HumInd, I05, P10, P28, P48, P53, P54, PCI, PQC, R&TA, R05, RASB, RI-1, RI-2, S09, T02, W03, W05.
—BLDSC (2357.252440), IE, Ingenta. **CCC.**
Published by: (Society for Buddhist-Christian Studies), University of Hawaii Press, Journals Department, 2840 Kolowalu St, Honolulu, HI 96822. TEL 808-956-8255, FAX 808-988-6052, uhpbooks@hawaii.edu. Ed. Mahinda Deegalle TEL 44-1225-875429. R&P Joel Bradshaw TEL 808-956-6790. Adv. contact Norman Kaneshiro TEL 808-956-8833. page USD 200; 4.75 x 7.75. Circ: 330.

294.34 LKA
BUDDHIST PUBLICATION SOCIETY NEWSLETTER. Text in English. 1985. 3/yr. LKR 400, USD 30 (effective 2003); includes Wheel and Bodhi Leaves. bk.rev. back issues avail. **Document type:** *Newsletter, Consumer.* **Description:** Provides instruction, news, and information of relevance to members of the society.
Related titles: E-mail ed.; Fax ed.; Online - full text ed.
Published by: Buddhist Publication Society, 54, Sangharaja Mawatha, P O Box 61, Kandy, Sri Lanka. TEL 94-8-223679, FAX 94-8-223679. Ed. Venerable Bhikkhu Bodhi. Circ: 4,000.

294.3 IND ISSN 0970-9754
BQ2
BUDDHIST STUDIES. Text in English, Hindi, Sanskrit. 1974. a. bk.rev. **Document type:** *Journal, Academic/Scholarly.*
Indexed: BAS.
—BLDSC (2357.253310).
Published by: University of Delhi, Department of Buddhist Studies, Rm No 307, Second Fl, Extension Bldg, Faculty of Arts, New Delhi, 110 007, India. TEL 7257725.

294.3 GBR ISSN 0265-2897
BQ2
➤ **BUDDHIST STUDIES REVIEW.** Abbreviated title: B S R. Text in English. 1984. s-a. USD 220 combined subscription in North America to institutions (print & online eds.); GBP 135 combined subscription elsewhere to institutions (print & online eds.) (effective 2012). adv. bk.rev. back issues avail.; reprints avail. **Document type:** *Journal, Academic/Scholarly.* **Description:** Contains articles on any aspect of Buddhism, covering the different cultural areas where Buddhism exists or has existed in Asia, historical and contemporary aspects, theoretical, practical and methodological issues, textual, linguistic, archaeological and art-historical studies.
Formed by the merger of (1976-1984): Pali Buddhist Review (0308-3756); (1977-1984): Linh-Son Publication d'Etudes Bouddhologiques (0294-619X); Which was formerly (1975-1977): Hoang Phap (0339-087X)
Related titles: Online - full text ed.: ISSN 1747-9681. USD 176 in North America to institutions; GBP 108 elsewhere to institutions (effective 2012).
Indexed: A21, DIP, IBR, IBZ, MLA-IB, RASB.
—IE. **CCC.**
Published by: (U K Association for Buddist Studies), Equinox Publishing Ltd., Unit S3, Kelham House, 3 Lancaster St, Sheffield, S6 3AF, United Kingdom. TEL 44-114-2725957, FAX 44-560-3459046, journals@equinoxpub.com, http://www.equinoxpub.com/. Ed. Peter Harvey. Adv. contact Val Hall.

294.3 IND
BUDDHIST TRADITION SERIES. Text in English, Sanskrit, Tibetan. 1985. irreg., latest vol.59, 2010. price varies. bibl. back issues avail. **Document type:** *Monographic series, Consumer.* **Description:** Publishes scholarly editions and translations of Buddhist texts in the Indian, Chinese and Tibetan traditions, and studies of cultural, historical and philosophical aspects of Buddhism.
Indexed: CIN, ChemAb, ChemTitl.
Published by: Motilal Banarsidass (Delhi), A-44, Naraina Industrial Area, Phase - I, New Delhi, 110 028, India. TEL 91-11-25795180, FAX 91-11-25797221, mlbd@mlbd.com, http://www.mlbd.com.

294.3 DEU
BUDDHISTISCHE MONATSBLAETTER. Text in German. 1955. q. bk.rev. bibl.; tr.lit. index. **Document type:** *Newsletter, Consumer.*
Published by: Buddhistische Gesellschaft Hamburg e.V., Beisserstr 23, Hamburg, 22337, Germany. TEL 49-40-6313696, FAX 49-40-6313690. Ed. Hans Gruber. Circ: 560 (controlled).

294.3 DNK ISSN 1395-0746
BUDDHISTISK FORUM. Text in Danish. 1993. s-a. DKK 150 membership (effective 2008). bk.rev. **Document type:** *Magazine, Consumer.* **Description:** Buddhist traditions and an attempt to open a dialog between Buddhism and the Western cultures.
Supersedes in part (1993-1994): Buddhistisk Forum. Medlemsblad (0909-1327)
Address: c/o Mugen Hilary Adler, Egely Kloster, Glappevej 12, Oestermarie, 3751, Denmark. TEL 45-50-179051, http://www.buddhistisk-forum.dk.

294.3 BRA ISSN 1808-0332
BUDISMO. Text in Portuguese. 2005. bi-m. BRL 12.90 newsstand/cover (effective 2007). **Document type:** *Magazine, Consumer.*
Published by: Digerati Comunicacao e Tecnologia Ltda., Rua Haddock Lobo 347, 12o andar, Sao Paulo, 01414-001, Brazil. TEL 55-11-32172600, FAX 55-11-32172617, http://www.digerati.com.br.

BUKKYO GEIJUTSU/ARS BUDDHICA. *see* ART

294.309 JPN ISSN 0288-6472
BQ6
BUKKYO SHIGAKU KENKYU/JOURNAL OF THE HISTORY OF BUDDHISM. Text in Japanese. 1949. s-a. JPY 25,000 per vol. (effective 2005). adv. bk.rev. bibl. Index. back issues avail. **Document type:** *Journal, Academic/Scholarly.*
Formerly: Bukkyo Shigaku (0022-5029)
Published by: Bukkyo Shigakukai/Society of the History of Buddhism, Ryukoku University, Okamura Research Lab., Shichijo Omiya, Shimogyo-ku, Kyoto, 600-8268, Japan. http://wwwsoc.nii.ac.jp/shb/. Circ: 500. **Dist. by:** Japan Publications Trading Co., Ltd., Book Export II Dept, PO Box 5030, Tokyo International, Tokyo 101-3191, Japan. TEL 81-3-32923753, FAX 81-3-32920410, infoserials@jptco.co.jp, http://www.jptco.co.jp.

294.3 FRA ISSN 1777-926X
LES CAHIERS BOUDDHIQUES. Text in French. 2005. irreg. **Document type:** *Journal.*
Published by: Universite Bouddhique Europeenne, 29 bd Edgar-Quinet, Paris, 75014, France. TEL 33-8-20205077, ube@club-internet.fr.

394.307 CAN ISSN 1710-825X
➤ **CANADIAN JOURNAL OF BUDDHIST STUDIES.** Text in English, French. 2005. a. **Document type:** *Journal, Academic/Scholarly.*
Related titles: Online - full text ed.: ISSN 1710-8268.
Published by: Nalanda College of Buddhist Studies, 47 Queen's Park Crescent East, Toronto, ON M5S 2C3, Canada. TEL 416-782-8227, 888-908-2544, FAX 416-978-7821.

294.3 CHN
CHAN/DEEP MEDITATION. Text in Chinese. 1989. bi-m. CNY 60 domestic; USD 25.20 foreign (effective 2005). **Document type:** *Journal, Academic/Scholarly.*
Related titles: Online - full text ed.
Published by: Hebei Sheng Fojiao Xiehui, 610, Yuhua Xilu, Shijiazhuang, Hebei 050081, China. TEL 86-311-83014060, FAX 86-311-83020851, namo@sjz.col.com.cn, http://www.hbfj.com.cn/. **Dist. by:** China International Book Trading Corp, 35 Chegongzhuang Xilu, Haidian District, PO Box 399, Beijing 100044, China. TEL 86-10-68412045, FAX 86-10-68412023, cibtc@mail.cibtc.com.cn, http://www.cibtc.com.cn.

294.3 USA ISSN 1932-2348
BQ4302
CHO TRIN/FA XUN; Dharma message. Text in English, Chinese. 2004. s-a. USD 10 (effective 2007). **Document type:** *Newsletter, Consumer.*
Published by: Tsechen Kunchab Ling, 12 Edmunds Lane, Walden, NY 12586. sakya@sakyatemple.org, http://www.sakyatemple.org/index.php.

294.30951 TWN
CHUNG-KUO FO CHIAO. Text in Chinese. m. charts; illus. **Description:** Chinese Buddhist magazine.
Address: Shih Pu Temple, 140 Nanchang St Sec 2, Taipei, Taiwan. TEL 02-321-4734.

294.3 GBR ISSN 1463-9947
BQ1
CONTEMPORARY BUDDHISM. Text in English. 2000 (Apr). s-a. GBP 199 combined subscription in United Kingdom to institutions (print & online eds.); EUR 264, USD 333 combined subscription to institutions (print & online eds.) (effective 2012). adv. reprint service avail. from PSC. **Document type:** *Journal, Academic/Scholarly.* **Description:** Publishes articles on the current state of buddhism from the view of the human sciences.
Related titles: Online - full text ed.: ISSN 1476-7953. GBP 179 in United Kingdom to institutions; EUR 238, USD 299 to institutions (effective 2012) (from IngentaConnect).
Indexed: A01, A02, A03, A08, A20, A21, A22, ArtHuCI, BrHumI, CA, CurCont, E01, IBR, IBZ, M02, P48, P53, P54, PQC, T02, W07.
—IE, Ingenta. **CCC.**
Published by: Routledge (Subsidiary of: Taylor & Francis Group), 4 Park Square, Milton Park, Abingdon, Oxon OX14 4RN, United Kingdom. subscriptions@tandf.co.uk, http://www.routledge.com. Eds. Dr. John Peacocke, Dr. Michael McGhee. Adv. contact Linda Hann TEL 44-1344-779945. **Subscr. to:** Taylor & Francis Ltd., Journals Customer Service, Sheepen Pl, Colchester, Essex CO3 3LP, United Kingdom. TEL 44-20-70175544, FAX 44-20-70175198, tf.enquiries@tfinforma.com.

294.3923 USA ISSN 0097-7209
BQ7662
CRYSTAL MIRROR; Tibetan Buddhism. Text in English. 1971. irreg., latest vol.12. price varies. illus. **Document type:** *Monographic series, Trade.*
Published by: (Tibetan Nyingma Meditation Center), Dharma Publishing, 2910 San Pablo Ave, Berkeley, CA 94702. TEL 510-548-5407, FAX 510-548-2230. Ed., R&P Leslie Bradburn.

294.3 TWN
DA-AI ZHIYOU/DA-AI MONTHLY. Text in Chinese. 2006. m. **Document type:** *Magazine, Consumer.*
Published by: Ciji Chuanbo Wenhua Zhiye Jijinghui/Tzu Chi Humanitarian Center, Zhongxiao East Rd., Section 3, 217 Alley, Lane 7, no.35, Taipei, Taiwan. TEL 886-2-28989000, FAX 886-2-28989977, kp_liu@tzuchi.org.tw, http://taipei.tzuchi.org.tw/.

294.3923 NLD ISSN 1876-2638
DE DALAI LAMA DAGKALENDER. Text in Dutch. 2006. a. EUR 14.95 (effective 2010).
Published by: B B N C Uitgevers bv, Schiehavenkade 206, Rotterdam, 3024 EZ, Netherlands. TEL 31-10-2540010, FAX 31-10-2540011, info@bbnc.nl, http://www.bbnc.nl.

294.3422 USA ISSN 0894-2056
DENSAL; karma triyana dharmachakra's newsletter. Text in English. 1979. q. USD 20 domestic; USD 40 foreign (effective 2005). bk.rev. tr.lit. back issues avail. **Document type:** *Newsletter, Consumer.* **Description:** Teaching and news of the Karma Kagyu Lineage of Tibetan Buddhism.
Published by: Karma Triyana Dharmachakra (K.T.D.), 352 Mead Mountain Rd, Woodstock, NY 12498. TEL 845-679-5906, FAX 845-679-4625. Ed. Naomi Schmidt. Circ: 1,200 (paid).

294.392 JPN ISSN 0387-5970
BQ8380
DHARMA WORLD. Text in English. 1974. 6/yr. USD 30. adv. bk.rev. 48 p./no.; back issues avail. **Document type:** *Magazine, Academic/Scholarly.* **Description:** For living Buddhism and interfaith dialogue.
Indexed: MLA-IB.
Published by: Kosei Publishing Co. Ltd., 7-1 Wada 2-chome, Suginami-ku, Tokyo, 1660012, Japan. TEL 81-3-5385-2319, FAX 81-3-5385-2331. Ed., R&P, Adv. contact Kazumasa Osaka. Pub. Teizo Kuriyama.

THE DHARMACHAKSU/DHARMA - VISION. *see* RELIGIONS AND THEOLOGY—Hindu

294.3 MNG
DHARMADUTA. Text in English. 1979. q. USD 8. illus. **Description:** Contains organization news, articles on history, culture, and comparative religion, all concerning Buddhism.
Formerly: Buddhists For Peace
Indexed: RASB.
Published by: Asian Buddhist Conference for Peace (ABCP), Ulan Bator, 51, Mongolia. TEL 976-1-50705, FAX 976-1-310014. Ed. B Wangchindorj. Circ: 3,000.

294.3 IND
DRELOMA. Text in English. 1978. 2/yr. free to members (effective 2011). adv. bk.rev. **Document type:** *Magazine, Trade.* **Description:** Contains articles about Dharma, as well as information about activities in the Drepung Loseling monastery.
Published by: Drepung Loseling Library Society, Lama Camp 2, Tibetan Col., Uttar Kannada, Karnataka 581 411, India. dllsociety@yahoo.com.in. Ed. Thubten Tendar.

294.3 JPN ISSN 0012-8708
BQ7300
➤ **EASTERN BUDDHIST.** Text in Japanese. N.S. 1965. s-a. JPY 3,000 domestic; USD 25 foreign (effective 2010). adv. bk.rev. illus. back issues avail.; reprints avail. **Document type:** *Journal, Academic/Scholarly.*
Related titles: Online - full text ed.
Indexed: A01, A03, A08, A20, A21, A22, A26, ASCA, AmHI, ArtHuCI, B04, BAS, BRD, CA, CurCont, E08, FR, G08, H07, H08, HAb, HumInd, I05, MLA, MLA-IB, PCI, PhilInd, R05, RI-1, RI-2, S09, SCOPUS, T02, W03, W07.
—BLDSC (3646.582000), IE, Infotrieve, Ingenta, INIST.
Published by: Eastern Buddhist Society, Otani University, Koyama, Kita-ku, Kyoto-shi, 603-8152, Japan. FAX 81-75-4314400, ebs@otani.ac.jp. Circ: 1,200.

294.30951 CHN ISSN 1004-2636
BQ3
FAYIN/VOICE DHARMA. Text in Chinese. 1981. m. USD 46.80 (effective 2009). **Document type:** *Journal, Academic/Scholarly.*
Related titles: Online - full text ed.
—East View, Ingenta.
Published by: Zhongguo Fojiao Xiehui/Buddhist Association of China, 25, Xisifunei Dajie, Beijing, 100034, China. TEL 86-10-66151260. **Dist. by:** China International Book Trading Corp, 35 Chegongzhuang Xilu, Haidian District, PO Box 399, Beijing 100044, China. TEL 86-10-68412045, FAX 86-10-68412023, cibtc@mail.cibtc.com.cn, http://www.cibtc.com.cn.

294.3 CHN ISSN 1004-2881
FOJIAO WENHUA/CULTURE OF BUDDHISM. Variant title: Buddhist Culture. Text in Chinese. 1989. bi-m. USD 48 (effective 2009). **Document type:** *Journal, Academic/Scholarly.*
Related titles: Online - full text ed.
—East View.
Published by: Zhongguo Fojiao Wenhua Yanjiusuo, 27, Beichang Jie, Xicheng-qu, Beijing, 100031, China. TEL 86-10-66038749. **Dist. by:** China International Book Trading Corp, 35 Chegongzhuang Xilu, Haidian District, PO Box 399, Beijing 100044, China. TEL 86-10-68412045, FAX 86-10-68412023, cibtc@mail.cibtc.com.cn, http://www.cibtc.com.cn.

294.3 GBR
FOREST SANGHA NEWSLETTER. Abbreviated title: F S N. Text in English. 1985. q. free (effective 2009). back issues avail. **Document type:** *Newsletter.* **Description:** Contains news, views, articles, forthcoming events, and contact addresses related to the Forest Sangha, a Buddhist monastic community.
Related titles: Online - full text ed.
Published by: Forest Sangha, Amaravati Buddhist Monastery, Great Gaddesden, St. Margaret's, Hemel Hempstead, Herts HP1 3BZ, United Kingdom. TEL 44-144-2842455, FAX 44-144-2843721, http://www.forestsangha.org.

294.3 GBR ISSN 1466-6596
FRIENDLY WAY. Text in English. 1966. q. free to members (effective 2009). bk.rev. **Document type:** *Magazine, Consumer.* **Description:** Contains information on Vipassana, or insight meditation, and Buddhism.
Related titles: E-mail ed.; Fax ed.
Published by: Buddhapadipa Temple, 14 Calonne Rd, Wimbledon Parkside, London, SW19 5HJ, United Kingdom. TEL 44-20-89461357, FAX 44-20-89445788, buddhapadipa@hotmail.com, http://www.buddhapadipa.org.

ICONOGRAPHY OF RELIGIONS. SECTION 12, EAST AND CENTRAL ASIA. *see* ART

294.3823 JPN ISSN 0287-1513
➤ **INSTITUTE FOR THE COMPREHENSIVE STUDY OF LOTUS SUTRA. JOURNAL/HOKKE BUNKA KENKYU.** Text in English, Japanese. 1975. a. not for sale; presentation copy avail. to institutions. bk.rev. illus. **Document type:** *Journal, Academic/Scholarly.*
Published by: Rissho University, Institute for the Comprehensive Study of Lotus Sutra/Rissho Daigaku Hokekyo Bunka Kenkyujo, 4-2-16 Osaki, Shinagawa-ku, Tokyo, 141-0032, Japan. TEL 81-3-5487-3253, FAX 81-3-5487-3255. Ed. Kokeu Sasaki. Circ: 500.

294.34436 USA ISSN 0161-1380
INTEGRAL YOGA. Text in English. 1970. q. USD 31 domestic; USD 32 in Canada & Mexico; USD 42 elsewhere; USD 6.25 per issue; free to qualified personnel (effective 2011). bk.rev. back issues avail. **Document type:** *Magazine, Consumer.* **Description:** Seeks who want to deepen their practice of Integral Yoga and their understanding of the many faith and wisdom traditions.
Published by: Integral Yoga Publications, Department W, 108 Yogaville Way, Buckingham, VA 23921. TEL 434-969-3121 ext 242, FAX 434-969-1303, letters@iymagazine.org.

294.365 CHE ISSN 0193-600X
BQ2
➤ **INTERNATIONAL ASSOCIATION OF BUDDHIST STUDIES. JOURNAL.** Text in English. 1977. s-a. free to members (effective 2010). adv. bk.rev. back issues avail. **Document type:** *Journal, Academic/Scholarly.*
Related titles: Microform ed.: (from PQC); Online - full text ed.
Indexed: A21, BAS, IBR, IBZ, RASB, RI-1, RI-2.
—BLDSC (4802.071000), Ingenta.
Published by: International Association of Buddhist Studies (I A B S), Dept of Oriental Languages and Cultures, University of Lausanne, BFSH2, Lausanne, 1015, Switzerland. FAX 41-79-3561766, iabs.treasurer@orient.unil.ch, http://www.iabsinfo.net.

294.3435 USA
INTERNATIONAL BUDDHIST MEDITATION CENTER. MONTHLY GUIDE. Text in English. 1970. 12/yr. looseleaf. donation. back issues avail. **Document type:** *Newsletter.* **Description:** Covers temple news, calendar of events, Buddhist issues and spiritual writings.
Formerly: International Buddhist Center. Monthly Guide
Published by: International Buddhist Meditation Center, 928 S New Hampshire Ave, Los Angeles, CA 90006. TEL 213-384-0850, FAX 213-386-6643. Pub. Rev. Raruna Dharna. Circ: 1,000.

294.35 USA ISSN 1076-9005
BQ2
➤ **JOURNAL OF BUDDHIST ETHICS.** Short title: J B E. Text in English. 1994. a. free (effective 2011). adv. bk.rev. back issues avail. **Document type:** *Journal, Academic/Scholarly.* **Description:** Promotes the study of Buddhist ethics. Publishes original research in vinaya, jurisprudence and legal, philosophical, medical and environmental ethics and related topics. Articles are published on an on-going basis.
Media: Online - full text.
Indexed: A21, A26, I05, P30, R&TA, RI-1, RI-2, S23.
Published by: Pennsylvania State University, Department of History &Religious Studies Program, 108 Weaver Bldg, University Park, PA 16802. TEL 814-865-1367, FAX 814-863-7840, dga11@psu.edu, http://history.psu.edu. Eds. Christopher Ives, Daniel Cozort.

➤ **THE JOURNAL OF BUDDHIST LITERATURE.** *see* LITERATURE

294.3 USA ISSN 1527-6457
➤ **JOURNAL OF GLOBAL BUDDHISM.** Short title: J G B. Text in English. 2000. irreg. free (effective 2011). bk.rev. **Document type:** *Journal, Academic/Scholarly.* **Description:** Established to promote the study of Buddhism's globalization and its transcontinental interrelatedness.
Media: Online - full text.
Indexed: A01, A21, A39, C27, C29, D03, D04, E13, P28, P48, P53, P54, PQC, R14, RI-1, S14, S15, S18.
—CCC. Eds. Charles Prebish, Martin Baumann.

294.3 JPN ISSN 0019-4344
BQ6
JOURNAL OF INDIAN AND BUDDHIST STUDIES/INDOGAKU BUNKKYOGAKU KENKYU. Text in Japanese. 1952. s-a. JPY 9,000, USD 14. bibl.; illus. index.
Indexed: FR, MLA-IB.
—Ingenta, INIST.
Published by: Japanese Association of Indian and Buddhist Studies/ Nihon Indogaku-Bukkyogakukai, c/o Dept of Indian Philosophy and Sanskrit Philology, Faculty of Letters University of, 7-3-1 Hongo, Bunkyo-ku, Tokyo, 113-0033, Japan. Circ: 3,000.

294.3928 USA
JOURNAL OF NICHIREN BUDDHISM. Text in English. 1979. q. membership. adv. bk.rev. **Document type:** *Bulletin.*
Published by: (Institute of Nichiren Buddhism), American Buddhist Press, 301 W 45th St, New York, NY 10036. TEL 212-489-1275, http://buddhismonline.us/html/tantrayana.htm. Ed. Kevin R O'Neil. R&P Kevin O'Neil. Adv. contact Marain Valchar. Circ: 500.

294.3 JPN ISSN 0452-3628
BQ6
KOMAZAWA DAIGAKU BUKKYO GAKUBU KENKYU KIYO/ KOMAZAWA UNIVERSITY. FACULTY OF BUDDHISM. JOURNAL. Text in Japanese. 1955. a. **Document type:** *Journal, Academic/ Scholarly.*
Supersedes in part (in 1960): Komazawa Daigaku Kenkyu Kiyo/Komazawa University. Journal (0452-361X)
Published by: Komazawa Daigaku, Bukkyo Gakubu/Komazawa University, Faculty of Buddhism, 1-23-1 Komazawa, Setagaya-ku, Tokyo, 154-8525, Japan. http://www.komazawa-u.ac.jp/gakubu/ bukkyo/index.html.

294.309519 KOR
KOREAN BUDDHISM. Text in English. irreg. **Document type:** *Newsletter.* **Description:** Book series.
Published by: Lotus Lantern International Buddhist Center, 148-5 Sokyok-dong, Chongno-gu, Seoul, 110-200, Korea, S. TEL 82-2-7355347, FAX 82-2-7207849, buddha@uriel.net, http:// www.buddhapia.com/mem/lotus/index.html. Ed. Won Myong Sunim.

294.3928 USA ISSN 1093-5169
BQ8400
LIVING BUDDHISM. Text in English. 1981. bi-m. USD 50 (effective 1998). **Document type:** *Magazine, Consumer.* **Description:** Publishes study material of the Soka Gakkai International and the Soka Gakkai International - USA, lay organizations that practice Nichiren Daishonin's Buddhism.
Formerly (until Jan. 1997): Seikyo Times
Published by: (Soka Gakkai International - U.S.A.), World Tribune Press, 606 Wilshire Blvd, Box 1427, Santa Monica, CA 90401. TEL 310-451-8811, FAX 310-260-8910, livingB1@aol.com. Ed. Jeff Farr. Pub. Guy McCloskey. Circ: 25,000.

294.3 KOR
LOTUS LANTERN INTERNATIONAL BUDDHIST CENTER. NEWSLETTER. Text in English. 1987. bi-m. USD 20. **Document type:** *Newsletter.*
Published by: Lotus Lantern International Buddhist Center, 148-5 Sokyok-dong, Chongno-gu, Seoul, 110-200, Korea, S. TEL 82-2-7355347, FAX 82-2-7207849, buddha@uriel.net, http:// www.buddhapia.com/mem/lotus/index.html. Ed. Won Myong Sunim.

M L B D NEWSLETTER. *see* RELIGIONS AND THEOLOGY—Abstracting, Bibliographies, Statistics

294.3 LKA
MAHINDA. Text in English. 1976. q. LKR 8, USD 2.
Published by: (Maha Mahinda International Dhammaduta Society), Buddhist English Speaking Society, 58 Sri Vipulasena Mawatha, Colombo, 10, Sri Lanka.

294.3923 USA ISSN 1075-4113
MANDALA; a Tibetan Buddhist journal. Text in English. 1987. bi-m. USD 19.95 domestic; USD 30 foreign; USD 4.95 per issue (effective 2007). adv. bk.rev. 84 p./no.; back issues avail. **Document type:** *Journal, Consumer.* **Description:** International news and information of interest to modern-day Tibetan Buddhist students.
Incorporates: Mandala Newsletter (1075-4121)
Related titles: Online - full text ed.
Indexed: ENW.
Address: 1632 SE 11th Ave, Portland, OR 97214-4702. TEL 866-808-3302. Ed., Pub. Nancy Patton. adv.: B&W page USD 415, color page USD 495; trim 10.63 x 8.13. Circ: 8,000.

MELANGES CHINOIS ET BOUDDHIQUES. NOUVELLE SERIE. *see* ASIAN STUDIES

294.3 USA
METTA. Text in English. 1972. m. looseleaf. free. bk.rev. **Document type:** *Newsletter.* **Description:** Gives information and personal insights on Buddhism, especially Jodo Shinshu. Includes information on events concerning Buddhism in Hawaii.
Published by: Honpa Hongwanji Mission of Hawaii, 1727 Pali Highway, Honolulu, HI 96813. TEL 808-522-9200, FAX 808-522-9209. Ed. Rev. Yoshiaki Fujitani. Circ: 1,775.

294.344 GBR ISSN 0026-3214
BL1400
THE MIDDLE WAY. Text in English. 1926. q. GBP 18 domestic to non-members; EUR 30 in Europe to non-members; GBP 27 elsewhere to non-members; free to members (effective 2009). bk.rev. illus. index. **Document type:** *Journal, Academic/Scholarly.* **Description:** Contains articles by noted Buddhist teachers and scholars on various aspects of Buddhist theory, practice, history, etc., as well as other material of ancillary interest.
Formerly (until 1943): Buddhism in England
Related titles: Online - full text ed.
Indexed: A21, A26, AmHI, B04, BRD, E08, G08, H07, H08, HAb, HumInd, I05, PCI, R05, RASB, RI-1, RI-2, S09, T02, W03, W05.
—BLDSC (5761.407000), IE, Ingenta.
Published by: Buddhist Society, 58 Eccleston Sq, London, SW1V 1PH, United Kingdom. TEL 44-20-78345858, FAX 44-20-79765238, info@thebuddhistsociety.org. Ed. Desmond Bidoulph.

294.3 JPN ISSN 0286-9837
BQ8950
MIKKYO BUNKA. Text in Japanese. 1947. q. **Document type:** *Journal, Academic/Scholarly.*
Published by: Koyasan Daigaku, Mikkyo Kenkyukai/Koyasan University, Esoteric Buddhist Society, 385 Koyasan, Koya-cho, Ito-gun, Wakayama, 648-0280, Japan. TEL 81-736-562390, FAX 81-736-562980.

294.3 USA
THE MINDFULNESS BELL; journal of the International Order of Interbeing. Text in English. 1990. 3/yr. USD 18 (effective 2000); USD 6 newsstand/cover. adv. back issues avail. **Document type:** *Journal, Academic/Scholarly.*
Related titles: Online - full text ed.
Published by: Community of Mindful Living, PO Box 38325, Charlotte, NC 28278. TEL 510-527-3751, FAX 510-525-7129. Ed., R&P, Adv. contact Leslie Rawls. Circ: 3,000 (paid).

MOKSHA JOURNAL; the journal of knowledge, enlightenment and freedom. *see* PHILOSOPHY

294.3927 USA ISSN 0896-8942
MOUNTAIN RECORD; the Zen practitioner's journal. Text in English. 1981. q. USD 15 domestic; USD 30 foreign (effective 2008). adv. bk.rev. **Document type:** *Magazine, Consumer.* **Description:** Covers both Eastern and Western religious traditions especially reflecting the impact of Zen Buddhism on social action, ecology, art, science and health.
Published by: Dharma Communications, Inc., PO Box 156, Mt. Tremper, NY 12457. TEL 914-688-7993, FAX 914-688-7911, http:// www.dharma.net/dchome.html. Circ: 5,000 (paid).

294.3 USA
NAMO BUDDHA NEWSLETTER. Text in English. 1992. 2/yr. USD 10. illus. **Document type:** *Newsletter.*
Published by: Namo Buddha Seminar, The Vajra Vidya Retreat Center Newsletter, Vajra Vidya, PO Box 1083, Crestone, CO 81131. http://www.vajravidyaretreatcenter.org/. Ed. Cornelia Hwang. Circ: 2,000 (controlled).

294.3 JPN ISSN 0547-2032
BQ684
NANTO BUKKYO/NANTO SOCIETY FOR BUDDHIST STUDIES. Text in Japanese. 1954. s-a. **Document type:** *Journal, Academic/Scholarly.*
Published by: Nanto Bukkyo Kenkyukai/Nanto Society for Buddhist Studies, 406-1 Zassi Town, Nara, 630-8587, Japan. TEL 81-742-202040, FAX 81-742-202041, http://www.todaiji.or.jp/nbk/index.html.

294.3 CAN ISSN 1913-0805
NEW CENTURY. Text in English. 2007. m. CAD 60 (effective 2007). **Document type:** *Magazine, Consumer.*
Published by: Soka Gakkai International Canada (S G I), 2050 Dufferin St, Toronto, ON M6E 3R6, Canada. TEL 416-654-3211.

294.3657 USA ISSN 0891-1177
BQ9460
ORDER OF BUDDHIST CONTEMPLATIVES. JOURNAL. Text in English. 1970. q. USD 20; USD 25 foreign (effective 1999). back issues avail. **Description:** Articles on the practical aspects of Buddhist meditation and training written by monks of the order and lay members of the congregation.
Former titles (until 1986): Shasta Abbey. Journal (0732-8508); Zen Mission Society. Journal
Published by: Order of Buddhist Contemplatives, 3724 Summit Dr, Mount Shasta, CA 96067-9102. TEL 530-926-4208, FAX 530-926-0428. Ed. Rev. Hogetsu Keith. R&P Shiko Rom. Circ: 560.

294.3 USA
QA431
➤ **PACIFIC WORLD.** Text in English. 1925. a. free (effective 2011). bk.rev. back issues avail. **Document type:** *Journal, Academic/ Scholarly.* **Description:** Devoted to the dissemination of historical, textual, critical and interpretive articles on Buddhism generally and Shinshu Buddhism particularly to both academic and lay readerships.
Former titles: Pacific World Journal; The Pacific World (0897-3644)
Related titles: Online - full text ed.

R

Indexed: BAS, CCMJ.
Published by: Institute of Buddhist Studies, 2140 Durant Ave, Ste 30, Berkeley, CA 94704. TEL 510-809-1444, FAX 510-809-1443, publications@shin-ibs.edu.

294.3 USA
PATHWAYS (WATSONVILLE). Text in English. 1979. 9/yr. USD 12 domestic; USD 15 in Canada; USD 20 elsewhere (effective 2000). adv. bk.rev. **Document type:** *Newsletter, Consumer.* **Description:** Includes information on current events and perspectives on the spiritual pathways, including teachings of the Baba Hari Dass and others.
Formerly: Gateways
Published by: Hanuman Fellowship, Mount Madonna Center, 445 Summit Rd, Watsonville, CA 95076-0759. TEL 408-847-0406, FAX 408-847-2683, programs@mountmadonna.org, http://www.mountmadonna.org/. Ed. Pratibha Sharan. R&P Pratibha Sharon. Circ: 600.

294.3 USA ISSN 2156-0099
BQ4570.W6
PRESENT. Text in English. 2008. s-a. free (effective 2010). **Document type:** *Newsletter, Consumer.* **Description:** The voice and activities of Theravada Buddhist women.
Media: Online - full text.
Published by: Alliance for Bhikkhunis, PO Box 2069, Santa Barbara, CA 93102-1058. allianceforbhikkhunis@gmail.com, http://www.bhikkhuni.net.

294.3927 USA ISSN 1084-1105
PRIMARY POINT. Text in English. 1983. 3/yr. USD 12 membership (effective 1999). adv. bk.rev. **Document type:** *Magazine, Consumer.* **Description:** Presents the practice of Zen Buddhism as taught by Zen Master Seung Sahn, with articles on contemporary issues in the Buddhist world.
Published by: Kwan Um School of Zen, 99 Pound Rd, Cumberland, RI 02864. TEL 401-658-1476, FAX 401-658-1188, kusz@kwanumzen.org. Ed., Adv. contact J W Harrington. R&P Dae Kwang. Circ: 4,000.

294.3 TWN
RENCHENG JIKAN. Text in Chinese. 1979. q. **Document type:** *Magazine, Consumer.*
Former titles (until 2007): Rencheng Huixun; (until 2005): Renchengfo Jizazhi
Address: 24-8, Dongchicun Dongxingxiang, Yuchih, 555, Taiwan. TEL 886-49-2896352, FAX 886-49-2898193, jen2896352@gmail.com.

294.3437 CAN
SHAMBHALA BANNER; news from the heart of the mandala. Text in English. m. CAD 30; USD 35 foreign. adv. **Document type:** *Newsletter.* **Description:** Covers education, social and economic issues, and other news from a Buddhist perspective.
Formerly: Nova Scotia Karma Ozong Banner
Published by: Karma Dzong, 1084 Tower Rd, Halifax, NS B3H 2Y5, Canada. TEL 902-420-1118, FAX 902-423-2750. Ed. Cynde Grieve. Pub. Karma Dzong. Adv. contact Molly Nudell. Circ: 500.

294.34 CAN ISSN 1190-7886
BQ2
SHAMBHALA SUN; buddhism culture meditation life. Text in English. 1978. bi-m. CAD 39 domestic; USD 28 in United States; USD 46 elsewhere (effective 2008). adv. bk.rev. illus. **Document type:** *Magazine, Consumer.* **Description:** Offers spiritual perspective on the arts, politics and social issues with particular emphasis on Buddhism.
Formerly (until Apr. 1992): Vajradhatu Sun (0882-0813)
Indexed: A21, C03, CBCARef, P48, PQC, RI-1, RI-2.
—CCC.
Address: 1660 Hollis St #603, Halifax, NS B3J 1V7, Canada. TEL 902-422-8404, FAX 902-423-2701, subscription@shambhalasun.com. Ed. Melvin McLeod. R&P Molly Deshong. Adv. contact Debra Ross. Circ: 35,000 (paid).

294.3 JPN ISSN 1349-0850
SHITENNOUJI KOKUSAI BUKKYOU DAIGAKU KIYOU/ INTERNATIONAL BUDDHIST UNIVERSITY BULLETIN. Text in Japanese. a. **Document type:** *Bulletin, Academic/Scholarly.*
Formed by the merger of: IBU Shitennouji Kokusai Bukkyou Daigaku Kiyou. Tanki Daigakubu; Which was formerly (until 1984): Shitennoji Kokusai Bukkyo Daigaku Tanki Daigakubu Kenkyu Kiyo/International Buddhist University. Junior College. Research Reports (0286-4193); (until 1981): Shitennoji Joshi Tanki Daigaku kenkyu Kiyo/Shitennoji Women's Junior College. Research Reports (0286-4169); (1981-1995): Shitennoji Kokusai Bukkyo Daigaku Bungakubu Kiyo/International Buddhist University. Faculty of Letters. Bulletin (0286-4185); Which was formerly (1969-1981): Shitennoji Joshi Daigaku Kiyo/Shitennoji Women's College. Review (0286-4177)
Indexed: RILM.
Published by: Shitennouji Kokusai Bukkyou Daigaku/International Buddhist University, 3-2-1Gakuenmae, Habikino, Osaka 583-8501, Japan. info@shitennoji.ac.jp, http://www.shitennoji.ac.jp/.

294.3923 USA ISSN 1059-3691
BQ7530
THE SNOW LION BUDDHIST NEWS & CATALOG. Text in English. 1985. q. USD 10 (effective 2007). adv. bk.rev. 56 p./no. 5 cols./p.; **Document type:** *Newsletter, Consumer.* **Description:** Contains up-to-date information on Tibetan Buddhist activities, Tibetan events, and the political situation in Tibet. Offers a large selection of books, audiotapes, videos, art, ritual items, and other cultural artifacts.
Related titles: Online - full text ed.
Published by: Snow Lion Publications, 605 W State St, Ithaca, NY 14850. TEL 607-273-8506, FAX 607-273-8508, info@snowlionpub.com. Ed. Jeff Cox. Circ: 30,000 (controlled and free).

294.3 CAN ISSN 1911-8155
SOKA. Variant title: Buddhist Humanism in Action. Text in English. 2007. m. **Document type:** *Magazine, Consumer.*
Published by: Soka Gakkai International Canada (S G I), 2050 Dufferin St, Toronto, ON M6E 3R6, Canada. TEL 416-654-3211.

294.3 JPN ISSN 0388-645X
TAISHO DAIGAKU SOGO BUKKYO KENKYUJO NENPO/INSTITUTE FOR COMPREHENSIVE STUDIES OF BUDDHISM. ANNUAL. Text in Japanese. 1979. a. **Document type:** *Journal, Academic/Scholarly.*
Indexed: RILM.
Published by: Taisho Daigaku, Sogo Bukkyo Kenkyujo/Taisho University, Institute for Comprehensive Studies of Buddhism, 3-20-1 Nishisugamo, Toshima-ku, Tokyo, 170-8470, Japan. http://www.tmx.tais.ac.jp/sobutsu/index2.html.

TIBET CONTACT-INFO. *see* HISTORY

TIBET.NU. *see* ETHNIC INTERESTS

294.3923 DEU ISSN 0938-3506
TIBET UND BUDDHISMUS; Vierteljahresheft des Tibetischen Zentrums e.V. Hamburg. Text in German. 1987. q. adv. bk.rev. back issues avail. **Document type:** *Academic/Scholarly.*
Formerly (until 1990): Zentrumsnachrichten
Published by: Tibetisches Zentrum e.V. Hamburg, Hermann-Balk-Str 106, Hamburg, 22147, Germany. TEL 49-40-6443585, FAX 49-40-6443515. Ed., R&P Birgit Stratmann. Adv. contact Lothar Wendler. Circ: 2,500.

294.3923 IND ISSN 0254-9808
TIBETAN BULLETIN. Text in English. 1969. bi-m. free (effective 2011). bk.rev.; music rev. **Document type:** *Bulletin, Trade.* **Description:** Covers events in Chinese occupied Tibet, activities within the Tibetan administration in exile, international human rights initiatives on behalf of Tibetans, as well as cultural and religious topics of general interest.
Related titles: Online - full text ed.: free.
Indexed: HRIR, RASB.
Published by: Central Tibetan Administration of His Holiness the Dalai Lama, Department of Information and International Relations, Central Tibetan Administration, Dharmsala, Himachal Pradesh 176 215, India. TEL 91-1892-222510, circulation@gov.tibet.net. Ed. Sherab Woeser.

294.34 USA ISSN 1055-484X
BQ2
TRICYCLE; the Buddhist review. Text in English. 1991. q. USD 24 domestic; USD 29 foreign; USD 34.95 combined subscription domestic; USD 39.95 combined subscription foreign (effective 2009). adv. bk.rev. illus. 128 p./no.; reprints avail. **Document type:** *Magazine, Consumer.* **Description:** Independent cultural review illuminated by a Buddhist point of view. Publishes interviews, art, fiction, profiles, reports on international news, and discussions of the applications of Buddhism in contemporary American society.
Related titles: Online - full text ed.
Indexed: A21, B04, BRD, BRI, CBRI, IAPV, R03, RGAb, RGPR, RI-1, RI-2, W03, W05.
Published by: The Tricycle Foundation, 92 Vandam St, 3rd Fl, New York, NY 10013. TEL 212-645-1143, FAX 212-645-1493. Ed., Pub. James Shaheen.

294.3 USA ISSN 1065-058X
BQ2
TURNING WHEEL; the journal of socially engaged Buddahism. Text in English. 1984. q. free to members (effective 2011). adv. film rev.; bk.rev. illus. 48 p./no. 2 cols./p.; back issues avail. **Document type:** *Magazine, Trade.* **Description:** Publishes articles, reviews, poems, interviews and graphics relating to Buddhist peace and social justice work in all traditions.
Formerly (until 1991): Buddhist Peace Fellowship Newsletter
Related titles: Online - full content ed.
Published by: Buddhist Peace Fellowship, PO Box 3470, Berkeley, CA 94703. TEL 510-655-6169, FAX 510-655-1369, membership@bpf.org. Ed. Everett Wilson TEL 510-655-6169. Circ: 10,000 (paid).

294.3 TWN
UNIVERSAL DOOR/P'U MEN; to promote humanistic Buddhism; to establish humanly pure land; of the public; international; of living. Text mainly in Chinese; Text occasionally in English. m. TWD 1,490, USD 65. adv.
Address: 117 Sec 3, San He Rd, Sanchung, Taipei, Taiwan. TEL 886-2-29813699, FAX 886-2-29889044. Ed. Man Kuang. Pub. Tzu Jung.

294.3 AUS ISSN 1036-4471
VESAK. Text in English. 1991. a. bk.rev. **Document type:** *Journal, Academic/Scholarly.* **Description:** Publishes articles on Buddhist mental culture relevant to contemporary society. Reports on mission's activities in Australia, New Zealand, Singapore and Malaysia.
Published by: Australian Buddhist Mission Inc., PO Box 16, Cherrybrook, NSW 2126, Australia. TEL 61-2-43751178, FAX 61-2-96513192, ykyau@sydney.net. Ed. Y K Yau. Circ: 2,000 (controlled).

294.3 DEU ISSN 1432-2382
VISION. Text in German. 1996. s-a. **Document type:** *Magazine, Consumer.*
—CCC.
Published by: Aro-Gemeinschaft Deutschland e.V., Postfach 101719, Moenchengladbach, 41017, Germany. TEL 49-2161-60627, FAX 49-2161-60636, info@aro-gemeinschaft.de, http://www.buddhismus-bb.de/aro.html.

294.34 MYS ISSN 0042-8094
VOICE OF BUDDHISM. Text mainly in English; Text occasionally in Chinese. 1963. s-a. MYR 5, USD 5. adv. bk.rev. illus. back issues avail. **Description:** Promotes the study and practice of Buddhism through articles and printed lectures. Also assists in the opening of schools and endowment funds.
Published by: Buddhist Missionary Society, Buddhist Temple, Brickfields, 123 Jalan Berhala, Kuala Lumpur, 50470, Malaysia. TEL 3-2741141. Ed. Tan Teik Beng. Circ: 6,500.

294.3 USA ISSN 1930-1049
THE VOICE OF CLEAR LIGHT. Text in English. 1992. m. **Document type:** *Newsletter, Consumer.*
Related titles: Online - full text ed.: ISSN 1930-1030. 2004.
Published by: Ligmincha Institute, 313 2nd St. SE., Ste #207, Charlottesville, VA 22902. TEL 434-977-6161, FAX 434-977-7020, Ligmincha@aol.com.

294.3 NLD ISSN 1574-2261
VORM & LEEGTE. Text in Dutch. 1968. q. EUR 28 domestic; EUR 32 in Belgium (effective 2009). adv.
Former titles (until 2004): Kwartaalblad Boeddhisme (1382-6956); (until 1995): Saddharma (0924-9818)
Published by: Uitgeverij Asoka, Postbus 61220, Rotterdam, 3002 HE, Netherlands. TEL 31-10-4113977, FAX 31-10-4113932, info@asoka.nl, http://www.asoka.nl. Adv. contact Anika van der Aa TEL 31-6-47175617. color page EUR 995; 186 x 242. Circ: 6,500.

294.3 THA
W F B REVIEW. Text in English. 1964. q. THB 180, USD 20 (effective 2001). adv. bk.rev. charts; illus. 50 p./no.; **Document type:** *Journal, Consumer.*
Former titles: World Fellowship of Buddhists. News Bulletin (0125-023X); World Fellowship of Buddhists. Review (0043-8464)
Indexed: BAS, RASB.
Published by: World Fellowship of Buddhists, Soi Medhinivet off Soi Sukhumvit 24, Sukhumvit Rd, 616 Benjasiri Park, Bangkok, 10110, Thailand. TEL 661-1284-89, FAX 661-0555, wfb_hq@asianet.co.th, http://www.wfb-hq.org. Ed. Pracha Chaowasilp. Circ: 1,000.

294.3 USA
WASHINGTON BUDDHIST. Text in English. 1969. q. USD 6. bk.rev.
Published by: Buddhist Vihara Society, 5017 16th St, N W, Washington, DC 20011. TEL 202-723-0773. Ed. Rev. M Dhamma. Circ: 1,000.

294.3 GBR ISSN 0144-9818
WESTERN BUDDHIST. Text in English. 1979. s-a. GBP 1.90. adv. bk.rev.
Indexed: RASB.
Published by: Scientific Buddhist Association, 30 Hollingbourne Gdns., Ealing, London, W13 8EN, United Kingdom. Ed. Paul Ingram. Circ: 550.

294.3 LKA ISSN 0049-7541
BL1400
WHEEL; a series of Buddhist publications. Text in English. 1958. q. LKR 400, USD 30 (effective 2003); includes Bodhi Leaves. bk.rev. back issues avail. **Document type:** *Monographic series, Academic/Scholarly.*
Related titles: E-mail ed.; Fax ed.; Online - full text ed.
Indexed: RASB.
Published by: Buddhist Publication Society, 54, Sangharaja Mawatha, P O Box 61, Kandy, Sri Lanka. TEL 94-8-223679, FAX 94-8-223679. Ed. Venerable Bhikkhu Bodhi. Circ: 4,000.

294.3 USA
WHEEL OF DHARMA. Text in English, Japanese. 1973. m. USD 8 (effective 2000). bk.rev. **Document type:** *Newspaper.* **Description:** Propagation of Buddhism and Jodo-Shinshu religion; organizational and layman education.
Published by: Buddhist Churches of America, 1710 Octavia St, San Francisco, CA 94109. TEL 415-776-5600, FAX 415-771-6293. Ed. Rev. Kodo Umezm. R&P Henry N Shibata. Circ: 13,600.

294.3923 USA ISSN 0043-5708
WIND BELL. Text in English. 1962. 2/yr. USD 6. bk.rev.
Media: Duplicated (not offset).
Published by: (Zen Center (San Francisco)), Wheelwright Press, 300 Page St, San Francisco, CA 94102. TEL 415-863-3136. Circ: 3,000.

294.3 THA ISSN 0084-1781
WORLD FELLOWSHIP OF BUDDHISTS. BOOK SERIES. Text in Thai. 1965. irreg. price varies.
Published by: World Fellowship of Buddhists, Soi Medhinivet off Soi Sukhumvit 24, Sukhumvit Rd, 616 Benjasiri Park, Bangkok, 10110, Thailand. TEL 661-1284-89, FAX 661-0555, wfb_hq@asianet.co.th, http://www.wfb-hq.org.

294.3928 USA ISSN 0049-8165
WORLD TRIBUNE. Text in English. 1964. w. USD 50 (effective 1998). bk.rev. illus. **Document type:** *Newspaper.* **Description:** Publishes news and study material about the Soka Gakkai International and Soka Gakkai International - USA, lay organizations that practice Nichiren Daishonon's Buddhism.
Published by: (Soka Gakkai International - U.S.A.), World Tribune Press, 606 Wilshire Blvd, Box 1427, Santa Monica, CA 90401. TEL 310-451-8811, FAX 310-260-8910. Ed. David McNeill. Pub. Fred M Zaitsu. Circ: 30,000.

294.3923 CHN
XIZANG FOJIAO/TIBETAN BUDDHISM. Text in Tibetan. s-a.
Published by: Zhongguo Fojiaohui, Xizang Fenhui/Chinese Society of Buddhism, Tibetan Chapter, 11, Niangre Lu, Lhasa, Xizang (Tibet) 850000, China. TEL 22282. Ed. Yixi Wangqiu.

294.3 SGP
YOUNG BUDDHIST. Text in Chinese, English. a. illus.
Published by: Singapore Buddhist Youth Organisations Joint Celebrations Committee, 83 Silat Rd, Singapore, Singapore.

294.3 USA
YUN LIN TEMPLE NEWS. Text in Chinese, English. s-a.?. **Document type:** *Newspaper.*
Published by: Tantric Buddhism Black Sect, Yun Lin Temple, 2959 Russell St, Berkeley, CA 94705.

294.3 CAN
ZANMAI. Text in English. 1986. 4/yr. USD 26 for 3 nos. adv. bk.rev. illus. **Description:** Contains transcripts of teisho and classes by the Sensei, essays, poetry, translations of classical texts.
Published by: (White Wind Zen Community), Great Matter Publications, P O Box 203, Sta A, Ottawa, ON K1N 8V2, Canada. TEL 613-232-7851, FAX 613-235-0472.

294.3927 DEU ISSN 0921-8335
ZEN. Text in German. 1988. a. bk.rev. illus. 48 p./no. 2 cols./p.; **Document type:** *Journal, Consumer.*
Related titles: Dutch ed.: ISSN 0921-5174. 1980.
Published by: Foerderverein Zengarten e.V., Huffertsheck 1, Lautzerath, 54619, Germany. TEL 49-6559-467, FAX 49-6559-1342, zenklausen@t-online.de, http://www.zenklausen.de. Eds. Adelheid Meutes Wilsing, Judith Bossert. Pub. Judith Bossert. Circ: 2,500.

294.3927 DEU
ZEN. Text in German. 1981. a. EUR 9 (effective 2008). adv. **Document type:** *Magazine, Consumer.*
Formerly (until 2000): Zen Extra
Published by: Zenklausen in der Eifel, Huffertsheck 1, Leidenborn, 54619, Germany. TEL 49-6551-467, info@zengarten-ev.de. Ed. Judith Bossert.

294.3927 USA
ZEN BOW; a publication of the Rochester Zen Center. Text in English. 1967. q. USD 16 domestic; USD 20 foreign (effective 2001). bk.rev. **Document type:** *Newsletter.* **Description:** Written by Rochester Zen Center members on Zen practice and current events at the center and its affiliates.
Formerly (until 1990): Zen Bow Newsletter; Supersedes (1967-1979): Zen Bow (0044-3956)
Media: Duplicated (not offset).

Indexed: NPI.
Published by: Rochester Zen Center, 7 Arnold Park, Rochester, NY 14607. TEL 716-473-9180, FAX 716-473-6846. Ed., R&P Richard von Sturmer. Circ: 900.

294.3927 USA ISSN 0513-9465
BQ9250
ZEN NOTES. Text in English. 1954. 4/yr. USD 10; USD 15 foreign (effective 2001). bk.rev. back issues avail.
Published by: First Zen Institute of America, 113 E 30th St, New York, NY 10016. TEL 212-686-2520. Ed. Peter Lamp. R&P Peter Haskel. Circ: 600.

ZEN RUBIES; an eclectic display of words and pictures. *see* LITERATURE

294.3 CAN
ZHEN FO BAO/TRUE BUDDHA NEWS. Text in Chinese, English. 1991. s-m. USD 30 (effective 2000). adv. **Document type:** *Newsletter.*
Published by: True Buddha Publication Society, 357 East Hasting St, Ste 200, Vancouver, BC V6A 1P3, Canada. TEL 604-685-5548, FAX 604-685-5598, lotuslight@mail.fronet.com, http://www.cosmo21.lotuslight.com. Ed., Pub. Lian Tzi. Adv. contact Ming Hui Lee. Circ: 210,000. **Subscr. to:** P O Box 88180, CPO, Vancouver, BC V6A 4A5, Canada.

294.3 TWN ISSN 1026-969X
BQ620
ZHONGHUA FOXUE YANJIU/CHUNG-HWA BUDDHIST STUDIES. Text in Chinese. 1997. a. **Document type:** *Journal, Academic/Scholarly.*
Published by: Zhonghua Foxue Yanjiusuo, 14-5 Sanjie Village, Jinshan 208, Taibei, 112, Taiwan.

RELIGIONS AND THEOLOGY—Eastern Orthodox

281.62 USA ISSN 1097-0924
BX7990.H48
A M A A NEWS. (Armenian Missionary Association of America) Text in Armenian, English. 1967. bi-m. per issue contribution. adv. bk.rev. illus. cum.index. **Document type:** *Newsletter.*
Formerly (until 1976): A M A A Newsletter; Incorporates: Armenian-American Outlook (0004-2307)
Published by: Armenian Missionary Association of America, Inc., 31 W Century Rd, Paramus, NJ 07652. TEL 201-265-2607, FAX 201-265-6015. Ed. Moses B Janbazian. Circ: 17,000.

281.9 USA ISSN 0885-9795
AGAIN; a call for the people of God to return to their roots in historic Orthodoxy once.. Text in English. 1978. q. USD 16 domestic; USD 17.50 foreign (effective Jun. 2001). 32 p./no.; back issues avail. **Document type:** *Magazine, Consumer.* **Description:** Contemporary journal of Eastern Orthodox thought, including history, theology, lives of saints, and contemporary issues.
Published by: (SS Peter and Paul Orthodox Church), Conciliar Press, 10090 A Hwy. 9, PO Box 76, Ben Lomond, CA 95005-0076. TEL 831-336-5118, FAX 831-336-8882, marketing@conciliarpress.com, http://www.conciliarpress.com. Ed., R&P Thomas Zell. Pub. Peter Gillgust. Circ: 5,000.

281.9 GRC
ANALECTA VLATADON. Text in Greek. irreg., latest vol.50. price varies.
Published by: Patriarchal Institute for Patristic Studies, 64 Heptapyrgiou, Thessaloniki, 546 34, Greece.

281.9 POL ISSN 1505-4454
ANTYFON; kwartalnik diecezji Przemysko-Nowosadeckiej. Text in Polish, Ukrainian. 1997. q. 48 p./no.
Published by: Osrodek Kultury Prawoslawnej Elpis, Ul Jana Brzechwy 2, Gorlice, 38300, Poland. TEL 48-18-3527210, ks1roman@poczta.onet.pl, orthodox@help.pl. Ed. Ks. Roman Dubec. Circ: 1,000.

281.9 CYP
APOSTOLOS VARNAVAS. Text in English, Greek. 1918. m. bk.rev.
Published by: Orthodox Church of Cyprus, Archbishopric of Nicosia, Nicosia, Cyprus. TEL 357-2-430696, FAX 357-2-432470. Ed. Andreas Mitsides. Circ: 1,500.

281.9 POL ISSN 1426-9201
ARCHE; kultura-tworczosc-krytyka. Text in Polish. 1988. q. 40 p./no.;
Formerly (until 1996): Wiadomosci Bractwa (1231-4897)
Published by: (Bractwo Mlodziezy Prawoslawnej w Polsce), Agencja Kanon, Ul Sloneczna 22, Warsaw, 00789, Poland. kanon@zigzag.pl. Ed. Jeremi Krolikowski. Circ: 2,000.

281.62 USA ISSN 1075-7066
THE ARMENIAN CHURCH. Text in English. 1980. bi-m. bk.rev. illus. back issues avail. **Document type:** *Magazine, Consumer.* **Description:** Provides a complete update of the events of the Church, words of the Primate and other clergy, and activities and accomplishments of Armenians in America.
Former titles (until 1987): Bema (0199-8765); Which Superseded in part (in 1980): The Armenian Church (0004-2315); (in 1980): Hayastaneayts' Ekeghets (0017-8667)
Indexed: CERDIC.
Published by: Diocese of the Armenian Church of America, 630 Second Ave, New York, NY 10016. TEL 212-686-0710, FAX 212-686-0245, tac@armeniandiocese.org.

281.9 GRC
ATHENISIN ETHNIKON KAI KAPODISTRAKION PANEPISTEMION. THEOLOGIKE SCHOLE. EPISTEMONIKE EPETERIS. Text in English, French, Greek. 1935. a.
Published by: Athenisin Ethnikon kai Kapodistrakion, Theologike Schole, Panepistimiou St, Athens, 143, Greece.

281.9 BLZ ISSN 0278-551X
AXIOS; the orthodox journal. Text in English. 1980. q. USD 15 (effective 1999). adv. bk.rev. **Document type:** *Newsletter.* **Description:** Presents challenges in ethics and theology.
Published by: Axios Newsletter Inc., PO Box 90, San Ignacio, Cayo, Belize. TEL 501-8-23284, FAX 501-8-23633. Ed. Daniel John Gorham. Adv. contact John Longsworth. Circ: 10,506.

281.9 USA ISSN 1947-5977
▼ **BIBLE IN THE CHRISTIAN ORTHODOX TRADITION.** Text in English. 2010. irreg. price varies. **Document type:** *Monographic series, Academic/Scholarly.* **Description:** Features books on biblical studies and orthodox Christianity.
Published by: Peter Lang Publishing, Inc. (Subsidiary of: Peter Lang Publishing Group), 29 Broadway, New York, NY 10006. TEL 212-647-7700, 800-770-5264, FAX 212-647-7707, customerservice@plang.com.

281.7 DEU
BIBLIA COPTICA. Text in German. 1995. irreg., latest 2009. price varies. **Document type:** *Monographic series, Academic/Scholarly.*
Published by: Harrassowitz Verlag, Kreuzberger Ring 7b-d, Wiesbaden, 65205, Germany. TEL 49-611-5300, FAX 49-611-530560, verlag@harrassowitz.de, http://www.harrassowitz.de. Ed. Karlheinz Schuessler.

281.7 EGY ISSN 1110-0001
BIBLIOTHEQUE D'ETUDES COPTES. Text in French. 1919. irreg., latest vol.18, 2005. price varies. back issues avail. **Document type:** *Monographic series.* **Description:** Scholarly studies of historical and linguistic topics relating to Coptic Egypt.
Published by: Institut Francais d'Archeologie Orientale du Caire, Kasr el-Aini, 37 Sharia Sheikh Aly Youssef, Mounira, PO Box 11562, Cairo, Egypt. FAX 20-2-3544635, ventes@ifao.egnet.net, http://www.ifao.egnet.net. Adv. contact Marie-Christine Michel TEL 20-2-7971622. **Dist. by:** Boustany's Publishing House, 29 Faggalah St, Cairo 11271, Egypt. TEL 20-2-5915315, FAX 20-2-4177915.

281.9 ROM ISSN 0257-4667
BX690
BISERICA ORTODOXA ROMANA. Text in Romanian. 1822. m.
Indexed: RASB.
Published by: Romanian Patriarchate, Aleea Dealul Mitropoliei 25, Bucharest, 040163, Romania. presa@patriarhia.ro. Ed. Rev. Dumitru Soare. Circ: 10,000.

230.19 SRB ISSN 0006-5714
BOGOSLOVLJE. Text in Serbo-Croatian. 1926. s-a. USD 15 per vol. foreign (effective 2008). bk.rev. **Document type:** *Journal, Academic/Scholarly.* **Description:** Presents articles by Orthodox and non-Orthodox theologians on various contemporary theological issues.
Published by: Univerzitet u Beogradu, Pravoslavni Bogoslovski Fakultet, 11b Mije Kovacevica, Belgrade, 11000. TEL 381-11-2762958, dekan@bfspc.bg.ac.yu, http://www.bfspc.bg.ac.yu. Ed. Maksim Vasiljevic. Circ: 1,200.

281.9 RUS ISSN 0320-0213
SD208.K32 CODEN: TPLKDU
BOGOSLOVSKIE TRUDY. Text in Russian. 1959. s-a. back issues avail.
Indexed: FR, RASB.
Published by: (Russkaya Pravoslavnaya Tserkov', Moskovskaya Patriarkhiya), Izdatel'stvo Moskovskoi Patriarkhii, Pogodinskaya 20, korp 2, Moscow, 119435, Russian Federation. TEL 7-095-2469848, pressmp@jmp.ru, http://212.188.13.168/izdat. Ed. Vladimir Silov'yev. Circ: 10,000.

281.9 POL ISSN 1233-6165
BRACTWO MLODZIEZY PRAWOSLAWNEJ DIECEZJI BIALOSTOCKO-GDANSKIEJ. LIST INFORMACYJNY. Text in Polish. 1987. bi-m. 32 p./no.
Published by: Bractwo Mlodziezy Prawoslawnej Diecezji Bialostocko-Gdanskiej, Ul Sw Mikolaja 3, Bialystok, 15420, Poland. TEL 48-85-7424527, FAX 48-85-7426528. Ed. Dariusz Grzybek. Circ: 700.

230.19 POL ISSN 0494-0997
CERKIEWNY WIESTNIK/TSERKOVNYI VESTNIK. Text in Belorussian, Polish, Russian, Ukrainian; Summaries in Polish. 1954. m. PLZ 16; PLZ 5 per issue (effective 2003). adv. illus. **Document type:** *Bulletin, Academic/Scholarly.* **Description:** Presents articles covering history and theology of the Orthodox Church.
Published by: Warszawska Metropolia Prawoslawna, Al Solidarnosci 52, Warsaw, 03402, Poland. TEL 48-22-6190886, FAX 48-22-6190886. Ed. Rev. Leonciusz Tofiluk. Adv. contact Fr Jerzy Doroszkiewicz. Circ: 1,500.

281.9 NLD ISSN 2210-7134
CHRISTENEN VOOR ISRAEL. NIEUWSBRIEF. Text in Dutch. 1978. irreg. (1-2/yr.). **Document type:** *Newsletter, Consumer.*
Published by: Stichting Christenen voor Israel, Postbus 1100, Nijkerk, 3860 BC, Netherlands. TEL 31-33-2458824, FAX 31-33-2463644, secretariaat@christenenvoorisrael.nl, http://christenenvoorisrael.nl.

281.9 USA ISSN 0734-0036
THE CHURCH MESSENGER (JOHNSTOWN)/CERKOVNYJ VISTNIK. Text in English. 1944. bi-w. USD 12 (effective 2000). adv. bk.rev.; film rev. illus. **Document type:** *Newspaper.*
Published by: American Carpatho-Russian Orthodox Greek Catholic Diocese, 312 Garfield St, Johnstown, PA 15906. TEL 814-539-9143, FAX 814-536-4699. Ed. Rev. Michael Rosco. Pub. Rev. John A. Barnik Jr. Circ: 6,200.

281.7 USA ISSN 1541-163X
BX130
COPTICA. Text in English. 2002. a. USD 15 newsstand/cover; free to members (effective 2002).
Published by: (St. Mark Foundation), St. Shenouda the Archimandrite Coptic Society, 1701 So. Wooster St., Los Angeles, CA 90035. TEL 310-558-1863, FAX 310-558-1863, http://www.stshenouda.com.

281.7 CAN ISSN 0229-1134
BX130
COPTOLOGIA; journal of Coptic thought and orthodox spirituality. Text in English. 1981. a. CAD 10, USD 8.50. bk.rev. **Document type:** *Journal, Academic/Scholarly.* **Description:** Research publication which is mainly concerned with the Egyptological sources and multiple meaning of the Coptic tradition.
Address: Don Mills Postal Sta, P O Box 235, Don Mills, ON M3C 2S2, Canada. TEL 416-391-1774. Ed. Fayek M Ishak. Circ: 450.

281.9 BEL ISSN 0070-0398
➤ **CORPUS SCRIPTORUM CHRISTIANORUM ORIENTALIUM: AETHIOPICA.** Text in Amharic. 1904. irreg. price varies. bk.rev. back issues avail. **Document type:** *Monographic series, Academic/Scholarly.*
Published by: (Universite Catholique de Louvain), Peeters Publishers, Bondgenotenlaan 153, Leuven, 3000, Belgium. TEL 32-16-235170, FAX 32-16-228500, http://www.peeters-leuven.be. **Co-sponsor:** Catholic University of America.

281.9 BEL ISSN 0070-0401
BR60.C5
➤ **CORPUS SCRIPTORUM CHRISTIANORUM ORIENTALIUM: ARABICA.** Text in Arabic. 1903. irreg. price varies. bk.rev. back issues avail. **Document type:** *Monographic series, Academic/Scholarly.*
Published by: (Universite Catholique de Louvain), Peeters Publishers, Bondgenotenlaan 153, Leuven, 3000, Belgium. TEL 32-16-235170, FAX 32-16-228500, http://www.peeters-leuven.be. **Co-sponsor:** Catholic University of America.

281.62 BEL ISSN 0070-041X
➤ **CORPUS SCRIPTORUM CHRISTIANORUM ORIENTALIUM: ARMENIACA.** Text in Armenian. 1953. irreg. price varies. bk.rev. back issues avail. **Document type:** *Monographic series, Academic/Scholarly.*
Published by: (Universite Catholique de Louvain), Peeters Publishers, Bondgenotenlaan 153, Leuven, 3000, Belgium. TEL 32-16-235170, FAX 32-16-228500, http://www.peeters-leuven.be. **Co-sponsor:** Catholic University of America.

281.9 BEL ISSN 0070-0428
➤ **CORPUS SCRIPTORUM CHRISTIANORUM ORIENTALIUM: COPTICA.** Text in Coptic. 1906. irreg. price varies. bk.rev. back issues avail. **Document type:** *Monographic series, Academic/Scholarly.*
Published by: (Universite Catholique de Louvain), Peeters Publishers, Bondgenotenlaan 153, Leuven, 3000, Belgium. TEL 32-16-235170, FAX 32-16-228500, http://www.peeters-leuven.be. **Co-sponsor:** Catholic University of America.

281.9 BEL ISSN 0070-0436
➤ **CORPUS SCRIPTORUM CHRISTIANORUM ORIENTALIUM: IBERICA.** Text in Georgian. 1950. irreg. price varies. bk.rev. back issues avail. **Document type:** *Monographic series, Academic/Scholarly.*
Published by: (Universite Catholique de Louvain), Peeters Publishers, Bondgenotenlaan 153, Leuven, 3000, Belgium. TEL 32-16-235170, FAX 32-16-228500, http://www.peeters-leuven.be. **Co-sponsor:** Catholic University of America.

281.9 BEL ISSN 0070-0444
BR60.C5
➤ **CORPUS SCRIPTORUM CHRISTIANORUM ORIENTALIUM: SUBSIDIA.** Text in English, French, German. 1950. irreg. price varies. bk.rev. **Document type:** *Monographic series, Academic/Scholarly.*
Published by: (Universite Catholique de Louvain), Peeters Publishers, Bondgenotenlaan 153, Leuven, 3000, Belgium. TEL 32-16-235170, FAX 32-16-228500, http://www.peeters-leuven.be. **Co-sponsor:** Catholic University of America.

281.9 BEL ISSN 0070-0452
➤ **CORPUS SCRIPTORUM CHRISTIANORUM ORIENTALIUM: SYRIACA.** Text in Syriac. 1903. irreg. price varies. bk.rev. back issues avail. **Document type:** *Monographic series, Academic/Scholarly.*
Published by: (Universite Catholique de Louvain), Peeters Publishers, Bondgenotenlaan 153, Leuven, 3000, Belgium. TEL 32-16-235170, FAX 32-16-228500, http://www.peeters-leuven.be. **Co-sponsor:** Catholic University of America.

281.9 USA ISSN 1059-9738
DESERT VOICE. Text in English. 1985. 5/yr. donation. adv. bk.rev. tr.lit. **Document type:** *Newspaper.*
Formerly: Orthodox Southwest (0897-7682)
Related titles: Online - full text ed.: ISSN 2150-9743.
Published by: (Monastery of St. Anthony the Great), St. Anthony the Great Orthodox Publications, PO Box 1432, Alamogordo, NM 88311-1432. Ed. Rev. Fr Bessarion Agioantonides. Circ: 4,000. **Subscr. to:** 3044 N 27th St, Phoenix, AZ 85016.

268.819 BGR
DUKHOVNA KULTURA. Text in Bulgarian. m. BGL 5,400 domestic; USD 44 foreign (effective 2002). **Document type:** *Journal, Consumer.*
Published by: Bulgarska Pravoslavna Tserkva, Svetii Sinod/Bulgarian Orthodox Church, the Holy Synod, Ul Oborishche 4, Sofia, 1090, Bulgaria. TEL 359-2-875611, FAX 359-2-870289, ort.church.bg@aster.net, http://bulch.tripod.com/boc/mainpage.htm. Ed. Angel Velichkov. **Dist. by:** Sofia Books, ul Silivria 16, Sofia 1404, Bulgaria. TEL 359-2-9586257, info@sofiabooks-bg.com, http://www.sofiabooks-bg.com.

230.071 RUS
DUKHOVNO-NRAVSTVENNOE VOSPITANIE. Text in Russian. 2001. bi-m. RUR 195 for 6 mos. domestic; USD 107 foreign (effective 2007). **Document type:** *Journal, Academic/Scholarly.* **Description:** Covers Orthodox education, ABCs of prayers, art of reading the Bible.
Published by: Izdatel'stvo Shkola Press, ul Rustaveli, dom 10, korpus 3, Moscow, 127254, Russian Federation. marketing@schoolpress.ru, http://www.schoolpress.ru. Circ: 3,000. **Dist. by:** East View Information Services, 10601 Wayzata Blvd, Minneapolis, MN 55305. TEL 952-252-1201, 800-477-1005, FAX 952-252-1202, info@eastview.com, http://www.eastview.com.

282 USA ISSN 0894-9786
EASTERN CATHOLIC LIFE. Text in English. 1965. bi-w. (Sun.). USD 12 (effective 2006). **Document type:** *Newspaper, Consumer.*
Related titles: Microform ed.
Published by: Eastern Catholic Life Press Association, 445 Lackawanna Ave, W, Paterson, NJ 07424. TEL 973-890-7794, FAX 973-890-7175, http://members.aol.com/byzruth/index.htm. Circ: 10,800. Wire service: CaNS.

281.9 HUN ISSN 0133-0047
EGYHAZI KRONIKA; keleti orthodox egyhazi folyoirat. Text in Hungarian. 1952. bi-m. HUF 300, USD 2 (effective 2000). back issues avail. **Document type:** *Newspaper.* **Description:** Contains ecclesiastic news and religious articles for Christian Orthodox people.
Published by: Magyar Orthodox Adminisztratura, Petofi ter 2, Budapest, 1052, Hungary. TEL 36-1-3184813. Ed. Dr. Feriz Berki. Circ: 500.

268.819 POL ISSN 1508-7719
BX200
ELPIS. Text in Polish. 1926. s-a. EUR 34 foreign (effective 2006). **Document type:** *Journal, Academic/Scholarly.*

R

Published by: Uniwersytet w Bialymstoku, Katedra Teologii Prawoslawnej, ul Sw Mikolaja 5, Bialystok, 15420, Poland. TEL 48-85-7443646, http://prawoslawie.uwb.edu.pl. **Dist. by:** Ars Polona, Obroncow 25, Warsaw 03933, Poland. TEL 48-22-5098609, FAX 48-22-5098610, arspolona@arspolona.com.pl, http://www.arspolona.com.pl.

281.9 DEU ISSN 1612-152X
ERFURTER STUDIEN ZUR KULTURGESCHICHTE DES ORTHODOXEN CHRISTENTUMS. Text in German. 2005. irreg., latest vol.4, 2008. price varies. **Document type:** *Monographic series, Academic/Scholarly.*
Published by: Peter Lang GmbH (Subsidiary of: Peter Lang Publishing Group), Eschborner Landstr 42-50, Frankfurt Am Main, 60489, Germany. TEL 49-69-7807050, FAX 49-69-78070550, zentrale.frankfurt@peterlang.com. Ed. Vasilios Makrides.

281.9 POL ISSN 1233-426X
FOS. Text in Polish. 1989. q. 16 p./no.
Published by: Bractwo Mlodziezy Prawoslawnej Diecezji Bialostocko-Gdanskiej, Ul Sw Mikolaja 3, Bialystok, 15420, Poland. TEL 48-85-7424527, FAX 48-85-7426528. Ed. Elzbieta Snarska. Circ: 1,000.

430 ARM
GANDZASAR THEOLOGICAL REVIEW. Text in Armenian. irreg.
Published by: Gandzasar Theological Center, Terian 91, Yerevan, Armenia. TEL 374-2-565933, 374-2-581232, FAX 374-2-565916.

281 USA
GREEK ORTHODOX ARCHDIOCESE OF NORTH AND SOUTH AMERICA. ANNUAL REPORT. Text in English. a.
Published by: Greek Orthodox Archdiocese, 8 E 79th St, New York, NY 10021.

230.19 USA ISSN 0017-3894
BX200
➤ **GREEK ORTHODOX THEOLOGICAL REVIEW.** Abbreviated title: G O T R. Text in English. 1954. q. USD 30 (effective 2009). bk.rev. illus. cum.index every 5 yrs. reprints avail. **Document type:** *Journal, Academic/Scholarly.* **Description:** Focuses on the theological issues faced by the Church today.
Related titles: CD-ROM ed.; Microform ed.: (from PQC); Online - full text ed.
Indexed: A01, A02, A03, A08, A21, A22, ABS&EES, AmHI, CA, CERDIC, DIP, H07, H14, IBR, IBZ, MLA-IB, OTA, P10, P28, P48, P53, P54, PCI, PQC, R&TA, RI-1, RI-2, RILM, T02.
—BLDSC (4214.905000).
Published by: (Holy Cross Greek Orthodox School of Theology, Hellenic College), Holy Cross Orthodox Press, 50 Goddard Ave, Brookline, MA 02445. TEL 617-850-1321, FAX 617-850-1457, press@hchc.edu. Ed. Thomas Fitzgerald.

281.9 GRC ISSN 1011-3010
BX610
➤ **GREGORIOS O PALAMAS.** Text in Greek. 1917. 5/yr. USD 50 (effective 2000). bk.rev. bibl. **Document type:** *Journal, Academic/Scholarly.*
Indexed: CERDIC, IZBG, MLA.
Published by: Metropolis Thessalonikes, PO Box 10335, Thessaloniki, Greece. FAX 30-31-230-722. Ed. Rev. Demetrios Vakaros. Circ: 1,000.

281.9 USA ISSN 1086-7600
THE HANDMAIDEN; a journal for women serving God within the orthodox faith. Text in English. 1996. q. USD 16.50 domestic; USD 17.50 foreign; USD 4.50 newsstand/cover (effective 2002). **Document type:** *Magazine, Consumer.* **Description:** Provides support, encouragement, spiritual teaching, and appropriate models for women committed to living the Orthodox Christian life.
Published by: Conciliar Press, 10090 A Hwy. 9, PO Box 76, Ben Lomond, CA 95005-0076. TEL 831-336-5118, FAX 831-336-8882, marketing@conciliarpress.com, http://www.conciliarpress.com.

281.9 CAN ISSN 0701-8290
HERALD (WINNIPEG)/VISNYK. Text in English, Ukrainian. 1924. s-m. CAD 25 domestic; CAD 30 in United States; CAD 45 elsewhere. **Document type:** *Newsletter.*
Indexed: MLA-IB.
Published by: Ecclesia Publishing Corp., 9 St John s Ave, Winnipeg, MB R2W 1G8, Canada. TEL 204-582-0996, FAX 204-582-5241. Ed. Rev. Ihor Kutash.

281.94971 GBR
HERALD OF THE SERBIAN ORTHODOX CHURCH IN WESTERN EUROPE. Text in English. 1951. 4/yr.
Published by: Religious Brotherhood of the Serbian Orthodox Church, 89 Lancaster Rd, London, W11 1QQ, United Kingdom. TEL 01-727-8367.

281.9478 USA ISSN 0437-6749
HOLAS CARKVY/VOICE OF THE CHURCH. Key Title: Golas Carkvy. Variant title: Church Messenger (Brooklyn). Text in Belorussian, English. 1955. s-a. USD 6. adv. bk.rev.; music rev. illus. back issues avail. **Document type:** *Newsletter.* **Description:** Deals with Byelorussian Christian-Orthodox theology, practices and traditions. Also contains information about cathedral activity in USA and in Belarus.
Published by: Byelorussian Autocephalous Orthodox Church, 401 Atlantic Ave, Brooklyn, NY 11217. TEL 718-875-0595, FAX 718-875-0595. Ed., Adv. contact Borys Daniluk. R&P Boris Daniluk. Circ: 500.

▼ **I P S E C JOURNAL.** *see* POLITICAL SCIENCE—International Relations

281.9 DEU
INSTITUT FUER ORTHODOXE THEOLOGIE. VEROEFFENTLICHUNGEN. Text in German. 1993. irreg., latest vol.9, 2006. price varies. **Document type:** *Monographic series, Academic/Scholarly.*
Published by: (Ludwig-Maximilians-Universitaet Muenchen, Institut fuer Orthodoxe Theologie), E O S Verlag, Erzabtei St. Ottilien, St.Ottilien, 86941, Germany. TEL 49-8193-71700, FAX 49-8193-71709, mail@eos-verlag.de.

INTERNATIONAL SOCIETY FOR ORTHODOX CHURCH MUSIC. PUBLICATIONS. *see* MUSIC

281.9 CAN ISSN 0021-1761
ISKRA. Text in English, Russian. 1943. 20/yr. CAD 60 domestic; CAD 70 foreign. adv. bk.rev. **Document type:** *Newsletter.* **Description:** Focuses on the history, culture, beliefs and present day activities of the Doukhobors.
Media: Duplicated (not offset). **Related titles:** Microfilm ed.: (from PQC).
Published by: Soyuz Dukhovnykh Obshchin Krista/Union of Spiritual Communities of Christ, P O Box 760, Grand Forks, BC V0H 1H0, Canada. TEL 250-442-8252, FAX 250-442-3433. Ed., R&P, Adv. contact Dmitri Popoff. Circ: 1,200.

JOURNAL OF COPTIC STUDIES. *see* HISTORY—History Of The Near East

JOURNAL OF EARLY CHRISTIAN STUDIES. *see* RELIGIONS AND THEOLOGY—Roman Catholic

281.9 GRC ISSN 1105-2139
KLERONOMIA. Text in English, French, German, Greek, Italian. 1969. 2/yr. USD 32. bk.rev. bibl. **Document type:** *Journal, Academic/Scholarly.*
Indexed: CERDIC, RI-1.
Published by: Patriarchal Institute for Patristic Studies, 64 Heptapyrgiou, Thessaloniki, 546 34, Greece. Ed. Panagiotis C Christou. Circ: 2,400.

281.5 GBR
KOINONIA. Text in English. 1940. 3/yr. free to members (effective 2009). bk.rev.; rec.rev. **Document type:** *Journal, Trade.* **Description:** Includes news items, theological and historical articles, correspondence and announcements of events.
Former titles (until 2003): E C N L; (until 1975): Eastern Churches News Letter (0012-8732); (until 1955): Eastern Churches Broadsheet; (until 1944): Stephen Graham's News Letter About the Orthodox Churches in War Time
Published by: Anglican & Eastern Churches Association, c/o Peter Doll, 39 The Motte, Abingdon, OX14 3NZ, United Kingdom. TEL 44-1235-520297, whtaylor@btconnect.com, http://www.aeca.org.uk/. Ed. Peter Doll.

281.9 USA ISSN 0279-8433
LIVING ORTHODOXY. Text in English. bi-m. USD 4.50 newsstand/cover (effective 2006).
Indexed: A21, RI-1.
Published by: Saint John of Kronstadt Press, 1180 Orthodox Way, Liberty, TN 37095-4366. TEL 615-536-5239, FAX 615-536-5945, info@sjkp.org, http://www.sjkp.org.

281.62 USA ISSN 0024-6476
LOOYS. Text in Armenian, English. 1953. m. (10/yr.). looseleaf. donation. bk.rev. **Document type:** *Newsletter.* **Description:** Covers parish activities; diocesan news on church in Armenia.
Published by: St. James Armenian Apostolic Church, 465 Mt Auburn St, Watertown, MA 02472. TEL 617-923-8860, FAX 617-926-5503, info@sthagop.com, http://www.sthagop.com. Ed. Rev. Arsen Barsamian. Circ: 2,500.

281.9 LBN ISSN 0025-4975
MASSIS. Text in Armenian. 1947. w. charts; illus.
Published by: Armenian Catholic Patriarchate, Rue de l'Hopital Grec Orthodoxe, Jeitawi 2400, Beirut, Lebanon. Ed. Fr Antranik Granian.

281.1 USA ISSN 0893-0872
MESSENGER (WORCESTER). Text in English. 192?. m. free. bk.rev. back issues avail. **Document type:** *Newsletter.*
Published by: Armenian Church of Our Saviour, 87 Salisbury St, Worcester, MA 01609. TEL 508-756-2931. Ed. Harold A Gregory. Circ: 750.

281.9 RUS
MOSKOVSKII TSERKOVNYI VESTNIK. Text in Russian. 1972. m. adv. **Document type:** *Newspaper.* **Description:** Covers activities of the Russian Orthodox Church and other local Orthodox churches, their relations with state agencies and society.
Related titles: Online - full content ed.: free.
Indexed: RASB.
Published by: (Russkaya Pravoslavnaya Tserkov', Moskovskaya Patriarkhiya), Izdatel'stvo Moskovskoi Patriarkhii, Pogodinskaya 20, korp 2, Moscow, 119435, Russian Federation. TEL 7-095-2469848, pressmp@jmp.ru, http://212.188.13.168/izdat. Ed. Vladimir Silov'yev. Circ: 100,000.

281.7 NLD ISSN 0929-2470
➤ **NAG HAMMADI AND MANICHAEAN STUDIES.** Text in Dutch. 1971. irreg., latest vol.65, 2008. price varies. back issues avail. **Document type:** *Monographic series, Academic/Scholarly.* **Description:** Scholarly discussions of Gnostic, Manichaean and early Christian religious topics based upon the papyrus Gospels found at Nag Hammadi, and Coptic and Manichaean texts from Dakhlah Oasis, Egypt. Includes translations, commentary on specific codices as well as analysis of textual and theological issues.
Formerly (until vol.36, 1994): Nag Hammadi Studies (0169-9350); Supersedes: Coptic Gnostic Library (0169-7749)
Indexed: IZBG.
—BLDSC (6013.235000).
Published by: Brill, PO Box 9000, Leiden, 2300 PA, Netherlands. TEL 31-71-5353500, FAX 31-71-5317532, cs@brill.nl, http://www.brill.nl. Eds. Johannes van Oort, Stephen Emmel. R&P Elizabeth Venekamp. **Dist. by:** Turpin Distribution Services Ltd., Pegasus Dr, Stratton Business Park, Biggleswade, Bedfordshire SG18 8QB, United Kingdom. TEL 44-1767-604954, FAX 44-1767-601640, custserv@turpin-distribution.com, http://www.turpin-distribution.com/.

266.19 NLD ISSN 2210-7266
NEMAGAZINE. Variant title: Near East Ministry Magazine. Text in Dutch. 1979. q. **Document type:** *Magazine, Consumer.*
Former titles (until 2010): N E M Nieuws (1387-0807); (until 1997): N E M Nieuwsbrief (0928-4192); (until 1992): Gebeds- en Nieuwsbrief (0928-4184)
Published by: Stichting Near East Ministry, Postbus 30, Voorthuizen, 3780 BA, Netherlands. TEL 31-342-471318, FAX 31-342-474896, info@nemnieuws.nl, http://www.nemnieuws.nl. Ed. Jededja Fijnenberg.

248.4819 NGA ISSN 1597-5282
NUGGETS. Text in English. 2001. w.
Published by: Living Word Ministries International Inc., PO Box 1453, Aba, Nigeria. TEL 234-82-223620, livingwordministries_ng@yahoo.com, http://www.lwmii.org.

281.9 USA ISSN 0029-7143
O L O G O S. Text in English. 1949. bi-m. USD 4.
Published by: (Orthodox Lore of the Gospel of Our Savior Mission), St. Photios National Shrine, 41 St. George St., St. Augustine, FL 32085. TEL 800-222-6727. Circ: 86,700.

281.9 USA
O S A MESSENGER. Text in English. 1925. bi-m. USD 3 to non-members (effective 2004); free to members. 8 p./no. 3 cols./p.; **Document type:** *Newsletter, Consumer.*
Former titles: U R O B A Messenger (0164-5978); Russian Messenger - Russkii Vestnik (0036-0287)
Published by: Orthodox Society of America, 29510 Lorain Rd, North Olmsted, OH 44070-3909. Ed., R&P George G Lichvarik. Circ: 3,000 (paid and free).

281.97 USA ISSN 0890-099X
BX496.A1
ORTHODOX AMERICA. Text in English. 1980. 8/yr. USD 10 domestic; USD 11 in Canada; USD 15 elsewhere (effective 2003). adv. bk.rev. 12 p./no.; back issues avail. **Document type:** *Newspaper, Consumer.* **Description:** Dedicated to traditional Eastern Orthodox Christianity containing articles on spiritual life, lives of saints, teachings of the Holy Fathers, contemporary issues and more.
Published by: (Russian Orthodox Church Outside of Russia), Nikodemos Orthodox Publication Society, PO Box 383, Richfield Springs, NY 13439-0383. TEL 315-858-1518. Ed., Pub. Mary Mansur. R&P, Adv. contact Katherine Mansur. Circ: 2,300.

281.9 USA ISSN 1074-0899
ORTHODOX CATHOLIC VOICE. Text in English. 1980. bi-m. USD 4 domestic; USD 5 foreign (effective 2003). adv. rec.rev.; bk.rev. 20 p./no. 2 cols./p.; back issues avail. **Document type:** *Newsletter.* **Description:** Focuses on religious topics with emphasis on the Eastern Orthodox Church and this diocese. News concerning faiths from around the world.
Published by: Orthodox Catholic Church of North and South America, PO Box 1213, Akron, OH 44309. TEL 330-753-1155. Ed., R&P Bishop Roman TEL 330-753-7717. Adv. contact R R Bernard. page USD 100; trim 11 x 8. Circ: 448.

281.947 USA ISSN 1524-7562
BX496.A1
ORTHODOX CHRISTIAN JOURNAL. Abbreviated title: O C J. Text in English. 1927. q. USD 12 domestic to non-members; USD 14 foreign to non-members; USD 3 per issue in North America to non-members includes South America; free to members (effective 2011). bk.rev. illus. index. back issues avail. **Document type:** *Journal, Academic/Scholarly.* **Description:** Features articles about the organization's activities and members, and about the Orthodox faith.
Formerly (until 1998): The Russian Orthodox Journal (0036-0317)
Related titles: Online - full text ed.: free (effective 2011).
Indexed: MLA-IB.
Published by: Fellowship of Orthodox Christians in America, 892 Scott St, Wilkes-Barre, PA 18705. TEL 570-825-3158, FAX 570-825-0136, orthodoxfellowship@yahoo.com. Ed. Nicholas D Ressetar.

281.9 USA ISSN 0048-2269
ORTHODOX CHURCH. Text in English. 1965. m. USD 15; USD 20 in Canada; USD 30 elsewhere (effective 1999). bk.rev. charts; illus. **Document type:** *Newspaper.* **Description:** Covers Orthodox and ecumenical church news. Includes feature articles and official announcements.
Indexed: CERDIC.
Published by: Orthodox Church in America, 7900 W 120 St, Palos Park, IL 60464. TEL 708-361-1684, FAX 708-923-1706. Ed. V Rev John Matusiak. Circ: 34,000.

281.97 USA ISSN 0145-7950
BX496.A5
ORTHODOX CHURCH IN AMERICA. YEARBOOK AND CHURCH DIRECTORY. Key Title: Yearbook and Church Directory of the Orthodox Church in America. Text in English. a. USD 15. charts; illus.; stat. **Document type:** *Directory.* **Description:** Complete listing of parishes and clergy, bishops, officers of church administration, institutions and publications in U.S. and Canada.
Supersedes: Russian Orthodox Greek-Catholic Church of America. Yearbook (0095-2257); Russian Orthodox Greek Catholic Church of America. Yearbook and Church Directory (0557-532X)
Published by: Orthodox Church in America (Syosset), Rte 25A, PO Box 675, Syosset, NY 11791. TEL 516-922-0550, FAX 516-922-0954. Ed. Gregory Havrilak. Circ: 3,000.

281.9 USA ISSN 0744-1495
ORTHODOX HERALD. Text in English. 1952. m. looseleaf. USD 8. bk.rev. 8 p./no. 3 cols./p.; **Document type:** *Newsletter.* **Description:** News about the Orthodox Christian faith and church, and the traditions and culture of people whose ancestors came from the former Austro-Hungarian empire and Russia.
Published by: Orthodox Herald, Inc, PO Box 9, Hunlock Creek, PA 18621. TEL 570-256-7232. Eds. Rev. Jorge Alberto Costa e Silva, Rev. W Basil Stroyen. Circ: 6,200 (paid).

281.9 USA ISSN 0030-5820
BX460
ORTHODOX LIFE. Text in English. 1950. bi-m. USD 12 (effective 2004).
Related titles: ◆ Russian ed.: Pravoslavnaya Zhyzn'. ISSN 0032-6992.
Indexed: A21, FamI, RI-1.
Published by: Holy Trinity Monastery, PO Box 36, Jordanville, NY 13361-0036.

281.9 GBR ISSN 0267-8470
ORTHODOX NEWS. Text in English. 1979. q. free (effective 2009). adv. bk.rev. **Document type:** *Newsletter, Trade.* **Description:** Features news relevant to the current affairs in the Orthodox Church.
Formerly (until 1984): Saint George Orthodox Information Service. News (0143-6201)
Published by: St. George Orthodox Information Service, The White House, Mettingham, Suffolk, Suffolk NR35 1TP, United Kingdom. TEL 44-1986-896708, StGeorgeOIS@aol.com.

281.9 USA ISSN 0731-2547
ORTHODOX OBSERVER. Text and summaries in English, Greek. 1971. m. USD 12; USD 55 foreign (effective 2008). adv. bk.rev. 32 p./no. 4 cols./p.; **Document type:** *Newspaper.*
Indexed: RASB.
Published by: (Greek Archdiocese of North and South America), Greek Orthodox Archdiocese, 8 E. 79th St., New York, NY 10021. TEL 212-570-3555, FAX 212-774-0239. Ed. Jim Golding. Adv. contact Lefteris H. Pissalidis. Circ: 130,000.

281.941 GBR ISSN 0950-8376
ORTHODOX OUTLOOK. Text in English. 1986. bi-m. GBP 28.44 domestic; EUR 42.50 in Europe; USD 54.57 in United States; CAD 67.80 in Canada; AUD 81.50 (effective 2010). bk.rev.; software rev.; video rev. 36 p./no. 3 cols./p.; back issues avail. **Document type:** *Magazine, Academic/Scholarly.* **Description:** News about the Orthodox Church in Britain and worldwide.
—BLDSC (6296.112095).
Published by: St. John Cassian Press, The Hermitage of the Mother of God, 1 Butterfly Cottages, Harkstead, Ipswich, IP9 1DB, United Kingdom. TEL 44-1473-788288. Ed. Fr. . Athanasius. Circ: 1,000.

281 USA ISSN 0030-5839
BX200
➤ **ORTHODOX WORD.** Text in English. 1965. bi-m. USD 19 domestic; USD 30 foreign (effective 2010). adv. bk.rev. illus. index. back issues avail.; reprints avail. **Document type:** *Journal, Academic/Scholarly.* **Description:** Covers traditional Christianity from Apostolic times. Features the lives of saints, especially of modern holy men and women, and offers spiritual guidance from ascetics and visionaries. Includes discussions of contemporary issues from an Orthodox perspective.
Related titles: Microfilm ed.: (from PQC).
Indexed: A21, A22, CERDIC, RASB, RI-1, RI-2.
Published by: St. Herman of Alaska Brotherhood, PO Box 70, Platina, CA 96076. stherman@stherman.com, http://www.stherman.com.

281.9 DEU ISSN 0933-8586
ORTHODOXES FORUM. Text in English, French, German, Greek. 1987. 2/yr. EUR 31.70 (effective 2010). adv. bk.rev. bibl.; illus. back issues avail. **Document type:** *Journal, Academic/Scholarly.*
Indexed: DIP, IBR, IBZ, PCI.
Published by: (Ludwig-Maximilians-Universitaet Muenchen, Kommunikation und Presse, Ludwig-Maximilians-Universitaet Muenchen, Institut fuer Orthodoxe Theologie), E O S Verlag, Erzabtei St. Ottilien, St.Ottilien, 86941, Germany. TEL 49-8193-71700, FAX 49-8193-71709, mail@eos-verlag.de. Circ: 600.

281.9 DEU ISSN 1433-5417
ORTHODOXIE AKTUELL; Informationen aus der Orthodoxen Kirche. Text in German. 1997. m. EUR 62 (effective 2011). **Document type:** *Magazine, Consumer.*
Published by: Gesellschaft Orthodoxe Medien e.V., Gruener Weg 40a, Bochum, 44791, Germany. TEL 49-234-501932, FAX 49-234-503576, info@kokid.de, http://www.kokid.de. Ed., R&P Nikolaus Thon.

281.9 DEU ISSN 1869-9057
▼ **ORTHODOXIE, ORIENT UND EUROPA.** Text in German. 2009. irreg., latest vol.3, 2010. price varies. **Document type:** *Monographic series, Academic/Scholarly.*
Published by: Ergon Verlag, Keesburgstr 11, Wuerzburg, 97074, Germany. TEL 49-931-280084, FAX 49-931-282872, service@ergon-verlag.de. Ed. Martin Tamcke.

281.9 SWE ISSN 0283-4545
ORTODOX TIDNING. Text in Danish, Norwegian, Swedish. 1961. m. adv. bk.rev. **Document type:** *Bulletin, Consumer.* **Description:** Contains theological and devotional material as well as information and news from the Orthodox churches worldwide.
Former titles (until 1985): Ortodox Orientering (0281-9465); (until 1981): Ortodox Tidning; (until 1975): Ortodox Kyrkotidning (0030-5952)
Published by: Ortodoxa Tidningsbokhandeln, Tulegatan 3, Stockholm, 11358, Sweden. TEL 46-8-6735788. Ed. Wolmar Holmstroem. Circ: 1,000.

281 DEU ISSN 0030-6487
BX100
OSTKIRCHLICHE STUDIEN. Text in English, French, German. 1952. q. EUR 50; EUR 25.60 newsstand/cover (effective 2010). adv. bk.rev. bibl. index. reprints avail. **Document type:** *Journal, Academic/Scholarly.* **Description:** Studies the history and theology of the Eastern Orthodox Churches.
Indexed: A21, BibInd, CERDIC, DIP, FR, HistAb, IBR, IBZ, PCI, R&TA, RI-1, RI-2, RILM.
—INIST.
Published by: (Ostkirchliches Institut Wuerzburg), Augustinus Verlag, Dominikanerplatz 8, Wuerzburg, 97070, Germany. TEL 49-931-660680, FAX 49-931-6606823, verlag@augustiner.de, http://www.augustiner.de/html/inhalt_set.htm?verlag. Circ: 500.

281.62 USA ISSN 1064-3087
BX124.U6
OUTREACH (NEW YORK). Text in English. 1978. 10/yr. free. adv. bk.rev. **Document type:** *Newspaper.*
Published by: Armenian Apostolic Church of America, 138 E 39th St, New York, NY 10016. TEL 212-689-7810, FAX 212-689-7168. Ed. Iris Papazian. Circ: 10,500 (controlled).

281.9 BEL
PATROLOGIA ORIENTALIS. Text in Multiple languages. 1903. irreg., latest vol.228, 2010. price varies. back issues avail. **Document type:** *Monographic series, Academic/Scholarly.*
Formerly: Patrologia Syriaca et Orientalis
Published by: Brepols Publishers, Begijnhof 67, Turnhout, 2300, Belgium. TEL 32-14-448020, FAX 32-14-428919, periodicals@brepols.net.

281.5 NLD ISSN 0032-2415
POKROF. Text in Dutch. 1954. 5/yr. EUR 17.50 (effective 2009). bk.rev. illus. index every 4 yrs. **Document type:** *Bulletin.*
Indexed: CERDIC.
Published by: Katholieke Vereniging voor Oecumene, Walpoort 10, 's-Hertogenbosch, 5211 DK, Netherlands. TEL 31-73-6136471, FAX 31-73-6126610, secretariaat@oecumene.nl. Ed. Dolf Langerhuizen.

281 GRC
POLYTECHNI OIKOGENEIA. Text in Greek. q. **Description:** Discusses activities of the Greek Orthodox church and activities for children.
Published by: Panhellenia Enosi Philon ton Polytechnon, 78D Akadimias St, Athens, 10678, Greece. TEL 30-1-3838-586, FAX 30-1-3839-509.

281.9 SRB ISSN 0555-0114
BX710
PRAVOSLAVLJE/ORTHODOXY; novine Srpske Patrijarsije. Text in Serbian. 1967. s-m. EUR 30, USD 35, CAD 40, AUD 45 (effective 2008). adv. bk.rev. **Document type:** *Magazine, Consumer.*
Published by: Srpska Patrijarsija, Kralja Petra 5, Belgrade, 11000. Ed. Miodrag Popovic. Circ: 7,500 (paid).

281.9 RUS
PRAVOSLAVNAYA BESEDA. Text in Russian. bi-m. USD 95 in United States.
Indexed: RASB.
Published by: Izdatel'stvo Khristianskaya Literatura, Ul Petrovka 28-2, Moscow, 103051, Russian Federation. TEL 7-095-2068727, FAX 7-095-2068727. Ed. V V Lebedev. **Dist. by:** East View Information Services, 10601 Wayzata Blvd, Minneapolis, MN 55305. TEL 952-252-1201, 800-477-1005, FAX 952-252-1202, info@eastview.com, http://www.eastview.com.

281.9 RUS
PRAVOSLAVNAYA MOSKVA. Text in Russian. 1993. s-m. USD 205 foreign (effective 2005). **Document type:** *Newspaper, Consumer.*
Published by: Tserkov' vo Imya Ikony Bozh'yei Materi Nechayannaya Radost'/Church in the Name of the Icon of Our Lady "Unexpected Joy", ul Sheremet'evskaya 33, Moscow, 127521, Russian Federation. info@orthodoxmoscow.ru. Ed. V Kharitonov Protoirei. **Dist. by:** East View Information Services, 10601 Wayzata Blvd, Minneapolis, MN 55305. TEL 952-252-1201, 800-477-1005, FAX 952-252-1202, info@eastview.com, http://www.eastview.com.

281.9 USA ISSN 0032-7018
BX460
PRAVOSLAVNAYA RUS'; tzerkovno-obshchestvennyi organ. Text in Russian. 1928. bi-w. USD 30 (effective 1999); including supplement. bk.rev. **Document type:** *Newspaper.*
Related titles: ◆ Supplement(s): Pravoslavnaya Zhyzn'. ISSN 0032-6992.
Indexed: CERDIC.
Published by: Holy Trinity Monastery, PO Box 36, Jordanville, NY 13361-0036. TEL 315-858-0940, FAX 315-858-0505. Ed. Archbishop Laurus. R&P Andrei Psarev. Circ: 2,000.

281.9 USA ISSN 0032-6992
BX460
PRAVOSLAVNAYA ZHYZN'/ORTHODOX LIFE. Text in Russian. 1950. m. USD 10.
Related titles: ◆ English ed.: Orthodox Life. ISSN 0030-5820; ◆ Supplement to: Pravoslavnaya Rus'. ISSN 0032-7018.
Indexed: ABS&EES, CERDIC, RASB, RI-1, RI-2.
Published by: Holy Trinity Monastery, PO Box 36, Jordanville, NY 13361-0036. TEL 315-858-0940, FAX 315-858-0505. Ed. Archbishop Laurus. R&P Andrei Psarev. Circ: 2,000.

281.9 ROM ISSN 1841-7663
ROMANIAN PATRIARCHATE NEWS BULLETIN. Text in English. 1971. 3/yr. free. **Document type:** *Newsletter, Consumer.*
Former titles (until 1996): Nouvelles de l'Eglise Orthodoxe Roumaine (1015-3349); (until 1987): Romanian Orthodox Church News (French Edition) (1015-3330)
Related titles: Online - full text ed.: ISSN 1841-7655.
Published by: Romanian Patriarchate, Aleea Dealul Mitropoliei 25, Bucharest, 040163, Romania. presa@patriarhia.ro. Ed. Vincentiu Ploiesteanu.

281.947 RUS ISSN 0132-862X
RUSSKAYA PRAVOSLAVNAYA TSERKOV'. MOSKOVSKAYA PATRIARKHIYA. ZHURNAL. Key Title: Zhurnal Moskovskoi Patriarkhii. Text in Russian. 1943. m. USD 170 foreign (effective 2005). adv. bk.rev. bibl.; illus. back issues avail. **Description:** Official chronicle of the Russian Orthodox Church. Covers the church life, theology and the church history.
Related titles: English ed.: Moscow Patriarchate. Journal. ISSN 0201-7318.
Indexed: CDSP, CERDIC, FR, RASB, RI-1, RI-2.
—East View.
Published by: (Russkaya Pravoslavnaya Tserkov', Moskovskaya Patriarkhiya), Izdatel'stvo Moskovskoi Patriarkhii, Pogodinskaya 20, korp 2, Moscow, 119435, Russian Federation. TEL 7-095-2469848, pressmp@jmp.ru, http://212.188.13.168/izdat. Ed. Vladimir Silov'yev. Circ: 10,000. **Dist. by:** East View Information Services, 10601 Wayzata Blvd, Minneapolis, MN 55305. TEL 952-252-1201, 800-477-1005, FAX 952-252-1202, info@eastview.com, http://www.eastview.com.

281.9 947 RUS
RUSSKII DOM. Text in Russian. 1998. m. USD 184 foreign (effective 2005). **Document type:** *Magazine, Consumer.* **Description:** Analyzes current political situation in Russia, appraises events in the spiritual, cultural and economic spheres of the country.
Published by: Redaktsiya Zhurnala Russkii Dom, a/ya 16, Moscow, 103031, Russian Federation. Ed. Aleksandr Krutov. **Dist. by:** East View Information Services, 10601 Wayzata Blvd, Minneapolis, MN 55305. TEL 952-252-1201, 800-477-1005, FAX 952-252-1202, info@eastview.com, http://www.eastview.com.

281.9 RUS
RUSSKII SOBOR. Text in Russian. irreg.
Indexed: RASB.
Published by: Russkii Natsional'nyi Sobor, Krasnoyarskaya 3, kom 2, Moscow, 107589, Russian Federation. TEL 7-095-9217174. **Dist. by:** East View Information Services, 10601 Wayzata Blvd, Minneapolis, MN 55305. TEL 952-252-1201, 800-477-1005, FAX 952-252-1202, info@eastview.com, http://www.eastview.com.

281.9 USA ISSN 0222-1543
BX598.A1
RUSSKOE VOZROZHDENIE/RUSSIAN RENAISSANCE; nezavisimyi russkii pravoslavnyi natsional'nyi al'manakh. Text in Russian. 1978. 3/yr. USD 10 per issue in US & Canada (effective 2005). adv. bk.rev. back issues avail. **Document type:** *Bulletin, Consumer.*
Indexed: ABS&EES, RASB.
Published by: St. Seraphim Foundation, PO Box 180262, Richmond Hill, NY 11418. TEL 201-768-3677, FAX 201-768-0866. Ed. Miliza K Holodny. R&P Tatyana Ilyinsky. Circ: 200.

281.62 USA
ST. MARY ARMENIAN CHURCH. BULLETIN. Text in Armenian, English. 196?. m. **Document type:** *Bulletin.*
Published by: St. Mary Armenian Church, PO Box 367, Yettem, CA 93670. Ed. Derstepanos Dingilian. Circ: 375.

268.819 USA ISSN 0897-7690
ST. PETER THE ALEUT ORTHODOX EDUCATIONAL SERIES. Text in English. 1983. bi-m. back issues avail. **Document type:** *Monographic series.*
Published by: (Monastery of St. Anthony the Great), St. Anthony the Great Orthodox Publications, PO Box 1432, Alamogordo, NM 88311-1432. Ed. Rev. Fr Bessarion Agioantonides. Circ: 50,000.

281.7 USA ISSN 1551-1324
BX130
SAINT SHENOUDA COPTIC QUARTERLY. Abbreviated title: S S C Q. Text in English. 1994 (Oct.). q. USD 10 domestic to non-members; USD 15 foreign to non-members; free to members (effective 2006). **Document type:** *Newsletter.*
Formerly (until Oct. 2004): St. Shenouda Coptic Newsletter
Published by: St. Shenouda the Archimandrite Coptic Society, 1701 So. Wooster St., Los Angeles, CA 90035. TEL 310-558-1863, FAX 310-558-1863.

230.19 USA ISSN 0036-3227
BX460
SAINT VLADIMIR'S THEOLOGICAL QUARTERLY. Abbreviated title: S V T Q. Text in English. 1953. q. USD 65 in US & Canada; USD 80 elsewhere (effective 2011). bk.rev. bibl.; illus. index. back issues avail.; reprints avail. **Document type:** *Journal, Academic/Scholarly.* **Description:** Publishes scholarly articles on Orthodox theology. Includes the history, liturgy, ecclesiology, scripture and pastoral theology of East and West, from an Orthodox perspective.
Formerly (until 1969): St. Vladimir's Seminary Quarterly (0360-6481)
Related titles: Microform ed.: N.S. (from PQC); Online - full text ed.
Indexed: A21, A22, ABS&EES, CERDIC, FR, MLA-IB, OTA, P30, R&TA, RASB, RI-1, RI-2, RILM.
—BLDSC (8070.208000), IE, Infotrieve, Ingenta, INIST. **CCC.**
Published by: St. Vladimir's Orthodox Theological Seminary, 575 Scarsdale Rd, Yonkers, NY 10707. TEL 914-961-8313, FAX 914-961-4507, svtq_subscriptions@svots.edu. Ed. Paul Meyendorff.

281.9 RUS ISSN 1817-7530
BR140
➤ **SCRINIUM.** Text in English, French, Russian, German. 2005. a. USD 134 per vol. (effective 2009). **Document type:** *Journal, Academic/Scholarly.* **Description:** Devoted to Church history. Its scope is the ancient and medieval Christian Church worldwide, especially Eastern/Oriental Christianity and Christian Origins.
Related titles: Online - full text ed.: ISSN 1817-7565; Supplement(s): Orientalia Judaica Christiana. 2008; Scripta Ecclesiastica. 2008.
Published by: Sankt-Peterburgskoe Obshchestvo Vizantino-Slavyanskih Issledovanii, PO Box 110, St. Petersburg, 194352, Russian Federation. byzantinorossica@gmail.com, http://byzantinorossica.org.ru. Ed. Basile Lourie. **Co-publisher:** Gorgias Press LLC.

281.9 GBR ISSN 0260-0382
THE SHEPHERD; an Orthodox Christian pastoral magazine. Text in English. 1980. m. GBP 15 domestic; GBP 21 foreign (effective 2009). adv. bk.rev. back issues avail. **Document type:** *Magazine, Trade.*
Indexed: RASB.
Published by: St. Edward Brotherhood, St Cyprian's Ave, Brookwood, Woking, Surrey GU24 0BL, United Kingdom. info@saintedwardbrotherhood.org. **Subscr. in Canada:** Mrs. Alexandra Adams; **Subscr. in the US:** Peter Nelson, PO Box 203, Fly Creek, NY 13337-0203.

281.9 UKR
SLOVO PROSVITY. Text in Ukrainian. m. USD 125 in United States.
Published by: Vseukrainske Tovaryvstvo Prosvita, Per Muzeinyi 8, Kiev, Ukraine. TEL 380-44-228-0130. **Dist. by:** East View Information Services, 10601 Wayzata Blvd, Minneapolis, MN 55305. TEL 952-252-1201, 800-477-1005, FAX 952-252-1202, info@eastview.com, http://www.eastview.com.

230.19 GBR ISSN 0144-8722
BX100
➤ **SOBORNOST.** Text in English. 1928. s-a. free to members (effective 2009). adv. bk.rev. illus. back issues avail.; reprints avail. **Document type:** *Journal, Academic/Scholarly.* **Description:** Contains articles dealing with Orthodox theology and church history, with particular reference to parallels in Western (Anglican and Roman) milieux. Reports on ecumenical concerns within this area.
Incorporates (1966-1978): Eastern Churches Review (0012-8740); Formerly (until 1935): Fellowship of St. Alban and St. Sergius. Journal
Related titles: Microform ed.: (from PQC).
Indexed: A20, A21, A22, ASCA, ArtHuCI, CERDIC, CPL, CurCont, DIP, FR, IBR, IBZ, PCI, R&TA, RI-1, RI-2, RILM, SCOPUS, W07.
—BLDSC (8318.020500), IE, Infotrieve, Ingenta, INIST. **CCC.**
Published by: Fellowship of St. Alban & St. Sergius, 1 Canterbury Rd, Oxford, OX2 6LU, United Kingdom. TEL 44-1865-552991, info@sobornost.org.

281.9 BGR ISSN 1310-0319
BX200
SOFIISKI UNIVERSITET SV. KLIMENT OHRIDSKI. BOGOSLOVSKI FAKULTET. GODISHNIK. Text in Bulgarian. 1905. a.
Former titles (until 1994): Dukhovna Akademiya Sv. Kliment Okhridski. Godishnik (0323-9578); (until 1951): Sofiiski Universitet. Bogoslovski Fakultet. Godishnik (1310-5469); Which superseded in part (in 1924): Sofiiski Universitet. Godishnik (1310-4942)
—Linda Hall.
Published by: (Sofiiski Universitet Sv. Kliment Ohridski, Bogoslovski Fakultet), Sofiiski Universitet Sv. Kliment Ohridski, Universitetsko Izdatelstvo/Sofia University St. Kliment Ohridski University Press, Akad G Bonchev 6, Sofia, 1113, Bulgaria. TEL 359-2-9792914.

281.9 USA ISSN 0038-1039
SOLIA - THE HERALD. Text in English, Romanian. 1936. bi-m. USD 15 domestic; USD 20 in Canada; USD 25 elsewhere (effective 2009). bk.rev. 24 p./no. 2 cols./p.; **Document type:** *Newspaper.*
Related titles: Online - full content ed.
Indexed: CERDIC.
Published by: Romanian Orthodox Episcopate of America, PO Box 185, Grass Lake, MI 49240-0185. TEL 517-522-4809, FAX 517-522-5907. Ed. Most Rev. Archbishop Nathaniel Popp. Circ: 6,000 (paid).

281.9 DEU
SOPHIA; Quellen oestlicher Theologie. Text in German. 1961. irreg., latest vol.35, 2008. price varies. **Document type:** *Monographic series, Academic/Scholarly.*
Published by: Paulinus Verlag GmbH, Maximineracht 11c, Trier, 54295, Germany. TEL 49-651-46080, FAX 49-651-4608221, verlag@paulinus.de, http://www.paulinus.de.

R

230.19 GBR ISSN 0950-2742
SOUROZH. Text in English. 1980. 4/yr. GBP 15, EUR 25 in Europe; USD 30, CAD 35, AUD 35 (effective 2005). bk.rev. Index. 56 p./no.; back issues avail. **Document type:** *Journal, Academic/Scholarly.*
Description: Covers Orthodox theology, current events, history, and ecumenical activities.
Indexed: A21, RI-1, RI-2.
—CCC.
Published by: Russian Orthodox Diocese of Sourozh, 94a Banbury Rd, Oxford, OX2 6JT, United Kingdom. TEL 44-1865-512701, FAX 44-1865-512882. Ed. Anthony Of Sourozh. R&P Basil Osborne. Circ: 600. **Subscr. to:** c/o E J Robertson, 13 Carver Rd, London SE24 9LS, United Kingdom. TEL 44-20-7733-9787.

281.9 USA ISSN 2159-7057
▼ **SPIRIT RISING.** Text in English. 2010. bi-m. USD 10.60 per issue (effective 2011). adv. **Document type:** *Magazine, Trade.*
Description: Aims to give practical and applicable information on living in and through the Word of God.
Related titles: Online - full text ed.: ISSN 2159-3744. free (effective 2011).
Published by: Pecan Tree Publishing, 2207 Jackson St, Ste 107, Hollywood, FL 33020. TEL 877-207-2442, FAX 877-842-3263, http://pecantreepress.com. Ed. LaWanda Scott.

230.19 ROM ISSN 1224-0869
BX320.2
➤ **STUDIA UNIVERSITATIS BABES-BOLYAI. THEOLOGIA ORTHODOXA.** Text in English, French, German, Romanian; Abstracts in English. 1992. s-a. exchange basis. bk.rev. abstr.; bibl.; illus. **Document type:** *Journal, Academic/Scholarly.*
Formerly: Studia Universitatis "Babes Bolyai". Theologia
Related titles: Online - full text ed.: ISSN 2065-9474.
Indexed: CA, T02.
Published by: Universitatea "Babes-Bolyai", Studia/Babes-Bolyai University, Studia, 51 Hasdeu Str, Cluj-Napoca, 400371, Romania. TEL 40-264-405352, FAX 40-264-591906, office@studia.ubbcluj.ro. Eds. Ioan Chirila, Valer Bel. **Dist by:** "Lucian Blaga" Central University Library, International Exchange Department, Clinicilor st no 2, Cluj-Napoca 400371, Romania. TEL 40-264-597092, FAX 40-264-597633, iancu@bcucluj.ro.

281.9 UKR
TAVRIDA PRAVOSLAVNAYA. Text in Ukrainian. m. USD 95 in United States.
Address: Ul Odesskaya 12, Simferopol, 333000, Ukraine. TEL 25-45-11.
Dist. by: East View Information Services, 10601 Wayzata Blvd, Minneapolis, MN 55305. TEL 952-252-1201, 800-477-1005, FAX 952-252-1202, info@eastview.com, http://www.eastview.com.

281.62 LBN ISSN 0040-0297
TCHAHERT/TORCH. Text in Armenian. 1966. s-a. USD 4. bk.rev. illus.
Published by: Armenian Evangelical Brotherhood Church, P O Box 4944, Beirut, Lebanon. Circ: 1,500.

281.9 GRC ISSN 0049-3635
THEOLOGIA. Text in English, French, German, Greek, Italian. 1923. q. USD 40. bk.rev. bibl.; illus. index. **Document type:** *Corporate.*
Indexed: BibLing, CERDIC, FR, IZBG, MLA-IB.
Published by: Holy Synod of the Church of Greece, 14 Ioannou Gennadiou St, Athens, 115 21, Greece. TEL 30-1-72-18-327. Ed. Evangelos Theodorou. Circ: 1,800.

281.75 ETH
TINSAE. Text in English. 1979. 3/yr. ETB 6.25, USD 3. charts; illus.
Description: Covers activities of the Ethiopian Orthodox Church including latest news involving prominent figures of the church.
Published by: Ethiopian Orthodox Mission, PO Box 3137, Addis Ababa, Ethiopia. Ed. Haddis Terrefe.

281.9 RUS
TOMSKIE PRAVOSLAVNYE VEDOMOSTI. Text in Russian. 1990. m. bk.rev. **Description:** Presents the history and life of the Eastern Orthodox church in Tomsk region.
Indexed: RASB.
Published by: Novosibirskaya Eparkhiya, Blagochinie Pravoslavnykh Khramov Tomskoi Oblasti, Ul Altaiskaya 47, Tomsk, 634029, Russian Federation. TEL 23-41-23. Circ: 10,000.

281.9 USA ISSN 1043-7878
BX738.H6
THE TRUE VINE. Text in English. 1989. q. USD 17 domestic; USD 23 foreign (effective 2006).
Indexed: A21, RI-1.
Published by: Holy Orthodox Church in North America, PO Box 129, Roslindale, MA 02131-0129.

281.9 RUS
TSERKOV' I SPASENIE. Text in Russian. 1991. w. **Document type:** *Newspaper.*
Published by: Pokrovskaya Tserkov', Ul Sovetskaya 187, Leninsk-Kuznetski, Kemerovskaya Oblast' 652500, Russian Federation. Ed. S Plaksin. Circ: 5,000.

281.9 BGR ISSN 0205-1362
TSURKOVEN VESTNIK. Text in Bulgarian. 26/yr. BGL 10,000 domestic; USD 88 foreign (effective 2002). **Document type:** *Newspaper.*
Published by: Bulgarska Pravoslavna Tserkva, Svetii Sinod/Bulgarian Orthodox Church, the Holy Synod, Ul Oborishche 4, Sofia, 1090, Bulgaria. TEL 359-2-875611, FAX 359-2-870289, ort.church.bg@aster.net, http://bulch.tripod.com/boc/mainpage.htm. Ed. Angel Velichkov. **Dist. by:** Sofia Books, ul Silivria 16, Sofia 1404, Bulgaria. TEL 359-2-9586257, info@sofiabooks-bg.com, http://www.sofiabooks-bg.com.

281.9 LBN ISSN 1814-7038
AT-TURATH AL-URTHUDUKSI/ORTHODOX LEGACY. Text in Arabic. 2004. m.
Published by: University of Balaband, Faculty of Science/Deir El-Balamand, El-Koura, Lebanon. TEL 961-6-930250, FAX 961-6-930278, info@balamand.edu.lb, http://www.balamand.edu.lb/english/index.asp.

281.9477 USA ISSN 0147-1015
BX738.U4
UKRAINIAN ORTHODOX WORD. Text in English. 1950. 10/yr. USD 30 domestic; USD 35 foreign (effective 2007). bk.rev.; film rev.; play rev. bibl.; stat. 32 p./no.; back issues avail. **Document type:** *Magazine, Consumer.* **Description:** Covers religious and ethnic topics of interest to the Ukrainian Orthodox community.
Related titles: Ukrainian ed.: Ukrains'ke Pravoslavne Slovo. ISSN 0195-0525.
Published by: Ukrainian Orthodox Church of the U.S.A., P.O. Box 495, South Bond Brook, NJ 08880. TEL 732-356-0090, FAX 732-356-5556, consistory@uocofusa.org. Ed. Rev. Hieromonk Daniel (Zelinsky). Circ: 8,000 (paid and controlled).

281.9 USA
VINEYARD/VRESHTA. Text in English, Albanian. 1970. bi-m. back issues avail.
Published by: Albanian Orthodox Archdiocese in America, 523 E Broadway, S, Boston, MA 02127-4415. TEL 617-268-7808. Ed. Nicholas Liolin. Circ: 2,800.

281.9 SRB ISSN 0353-1783
VINOGRAD GOSPODNJI; list za duhovnu kulturu. Text in Serbo-Croatian. 1978. 4/yr. free. back issues avail. **Description:** Examines the history of the Serbian Orthodox Church and its theology.
Published by: Uprava Parohije Uspenske, Uspenska br 2, Novi Sad, 21000. Ed. Dusan Petrovic.

281.9 AUS
VOICE OF ORTHODOXY. Text in English, Greek. 1980. m. AUD 20 (effective 2009). bk.rev. 16 p./no. 2 cols./p.; back issues avail. **Document type:** *Bulletin.* **Description:** Provides information about the Greek Orthodox Archdiocese of Australia.
Related titles: Online - full text ed.
Published by: Greek Orthodox Archdiocese of Australia, 242 Cleveland St, Redfern, NSW 2016, Australia. TEL 61-2-96985066, archmel@greekorthodox.org.au, http://www.greekorthodox.org.au. Circ: 3,500.

230.19 POL ISSN 0239-4499
WIADOMOSCI POLSKIEGO AUTOKEFALICZNEGO KOSCIOLA PRAWOSLAWNEGO. Text in Polish. 1971. m. PLZ 36; PLZ 3.50 per issue (effective 2003). adv. bk.rev. 20 p./no. 3 cols./p.; **Document type:** *Newspaper.* **Description:** Covers the news and activities of the Polish Autocephalous Orthodox Church.
Published by: Warszawska Metropolia Prawoslawna, Al Solidarnosci 52, Warsaw, 03402, Poland. TEL 48-22-6190886, FAX 48-22-6190886. Ed. Rev. Leonciusz Tofiluk. Adv. contact Fr Henryk Paprocki. Circ: 1,500.

RELIGIONS AND THEOLOGY—Hindu

see also ASIAN STUDIES

294.5 IND
THE ADVENT. Text in English. 1944. q. INR 50 domestic; USD 25 foreign (effective 2011). bk.rev. illus. back issues avail. **Document type:** *Magazine, Academic/Scholarly.* **Description:** Devotes to the exposition of Sri Aurobindo's vision of the future.
Indexed: BAS, CERDIC.
Published by: Sri Aurobindo Ashram Trust, SABDA, Pondicherry, Tamil Nadu 605 002, India. TEL 91-413-2233656, FAX 91-413-2223328, mail@sabda.in, http://www.sriaurobindoashram.org.

294.5 USA ISSN 0005-3643
F249.M8
➤ **BACK TO GODHEAD**; magazine of the Hare Krishna movement. Text in English. 1966. bi-m. USD 4.50 per issue (effective 2010). adv. bk.rev. illus.; tr.lit. index. back issues avail. **Document type:** *Magazine, Trade.* **Description:** Purports the Vedis scriptures and the belief by the cult of Vnisnauas that Lord Krishna is the supreme personality and encourages practicing bhakt.
Indexed: A21, RI-1, RI-2.
—Ingenta.
Published by: Bhaktivedanta Trust, PO Box 34074, Los Angeles, CA 90034. TEL 800-927-4152, FAX 310-837-1056, http://www.krsna.com/~btg. Circ: 20,000.

294.5 AUS
BHAVAN AUSTRALIA. Text in English. 2004. m. free to members (effective 2008). adv. back issues avail. **Document type:** *Magazine, Consumer.*
Formerly (until Jun.2005): Bhavan's News Australia (1449-3551)
Related titles: Online - full text ed.: free (effective 2008).
Published by: Bharatiya Vidya Bhavan Australia, GPO Box 4098, Sydney, NSW 2001, Australia. TEL 300-242-826, FAX 61-2-92679005, info@bhavanaustralia.org. Pub. Gambhir Watts.

294.5 CAN ISSN 1920-9339
▼ **CANADIAN HINDU LINK.** Text in English. 2009. q. free (effective 2010). back issues avail. **Document type:** *Journal, Consumer.*
Description: Aims to educate Hindu youths and young parents to help them understand and pass on their spiritual and cultural heritage to the new generation born or raised in Canada.
Related titles: Online - full text ed.
Published by: InderLekh Publications, 2546 Polland Dr, Mississauga, ON L5C 3H1, Canada. TEL 905-273-9563, FAX 905-273-9563. Ed. Ajit Adhopia.

CHAKRA; tidskrift foer indiske religioner. *see* RELIGIONS AND THEOLOGY

294.548 THA
THE DHARMACHAKSU/DHARMA - VISION. Text in Thai. 1894. m.
Description: Covers Buddhism and related subjects.
Published by: Foundation of Mahamakut Rajavidyalaya, Phra Sumeru Rd, Bangkok, 10200, Thailand. Ed. Wasin Indasara. Circ: 5,000.

294.5 IND ISSN 0971-1007
DIVINE LIFE. Text in English. 1938 (vol.32). m. bk.rev. illus. index. **Document type:** *Magazine, Consumer.*
Former titles (until 1990): Wisdom Light (0971-099X); (until 1986): Divine Life (0012-4206)
Indexed: RASB.
Published by: Divine Life Society, Rishikesh, Sivananda Nagar, Tehri Garhwal, Uttar Pradesh 249 192, India. TEL 91-135-2430040, FAX 91-135-2442046, generalsecretary@sivanandaonline.org, http://www.sivanandaonline.org. Ed. Swami Krishnananda.

GLOBAL VEDANTA; voice of the worldwide vedanta movement. *see* PHILOSOPHY

294.5 IND
HINDU REGENERATION. Text in English. 1971. q. adv. **Document type:** *Trade.*
Published by: (Hyderabad Branch), Bharat Sevasram Sangha, 211 Rash Behari Ave, Kolkata, West Bengal 700 019, India. TEL 91-33-24405178, FAX 91-33-24402326, http://www.bharatsevashramsangha.net/.

294.548 USA ISSN 0896-0801
BL1100
HINDUISM TODAY. Text in English. 1979. q. USD 35 in US & Canada; USD 45 in United Kingdom; USD 20 in India & Srilanka; USD 7.95 newsstand/cover (effective 2009). adv. bk.rev.; film rev.; video rev. back issues avail. **Document type:** *Magazine, Consumer.*
Description: Aims to foster Hindu solidarity as a unity in diversity among all sections and lineages.
Formerly (until Feb.1979): New Saivite World
Related titles: CD-ROM ed.; Online - full text ed.; Dutch ed.; Hindi ed.; ◆ Regional ed(s).: Hinduism Today (South Africa Edition). ISSN 1022-2154; Hinduism Today (Asian Edition); Hinduism Today (European Edition).
Indexed: A01, A21, APW, DYW, ENW, P48, PQC, RI-1, RI-2, T02.
Published by: Himalayan Academy Publications, 107 Kaholalele Rd, Kapaa, HI 96746. FAX 808-822-4351. Ed. Paramacharya Palaniswami. Pub. Bothinatha Veylanswami.

294.5 ZAF ISSN 1022-2154
HINDUISM TODAY (SOUTH AFRICA EDITION). Text in English. 1993 (vol.15). m. ZAR 42. adv. illus. **Document type:** *Newspaper.*
Related titles: ◆ Regional ed(s).: Hinduism Today. ISSN 0896-0801; Hinduism Today (European Edition); Hinduism Today (Asian Edition).
Published by: (Himalayan Academy), M B S Graphics, PO Box 13124, Laudium, Pretoria 0037, South Africa.

294.5 NLD ISSN 1875-4945
HINDULIFE MAGAZINE. Variant title: H L M. Text in Dutch. 2004. q. EUR 25 (effective 2011). **Document type:** *Magazine, Consumer.*
Published by: Stichting HinduLife, Kiotoweg 701, Rotterdam, 3047 BG, Netherlands. TEL 31-10-4621218, FAX 31-10-4621836.

ICONOGRAPHY OF RELIGIONS. SECTION 13, INDIAN RELIGIONS. *see* ART

294.5 CAN ISSN 1208-1167
INDIAN LIFE. Text in English. 1967. bi-m. USD 10. adv. bk.rev. **Document type:** *Newspaper.*
Former titles: Indian Life Magazine (0226-9317); (until 1979): Indian Christian
Related titles: Online - full text ed.
Indexed: A01, A02, A03, A08, A26, BNNA, C05, CPerI, G05, G06, G07, G08, I05, I07, S23, T02.
—CCC.
Published by: Intertribal Christian Communications, RPO Redwood Center, P O Box 3765, Sta B, Winnipeg, MB R2W 3R6, Canada. TEL 204-661-9333, 800-665-9275, FAX 204-661-3982. Ed., R&P Jim Uttley. Circ: 30,000.

294.5071 NLD ISSN 1022-4556
BL1100
➤ **INTERNATIONAL JOURNAL OF HINDU STUDIES.** Text in English. 1997. 3/yr. EUR 271, USD 338 combined subscription to institutions (print & online eds.) (effective 2012). adv. bk.rev. illus. index. reprint service avail. from PSC. **Document type:** *Journal, Academic/Scholarly.* **Description:** Considers Hinduism analytically and comparatively as a "form of life" as clarified by its contrasts and similarities to other historical and present day forms.
Related titles: Online - full text ed.: ISSN 1574-9282 (from IngentaConnect).
Indexed: A20, A21, A22, A26, AmHI, ArtHuCI, B04, BAS, BRD, CA, E01, H07, H08, H14, HAb, HumInd, P10, P28, P48, P53, P54, PQC, SCOPUS, T02, W03, W05, W07.
—IE, Ingenta. **CCC.**
Published by: (International Institute of India Studies CAN), Springer Netherlands (Subsidiary of: Springer Science+Business Media), Van Godewijckstraat 30, Dordrecht, 3311 GX, Netherlands. TEL 31-78-6576050, FAX 31-78-6576474, http://www.springer-sbm.de. Ed. Sushil Mittal.

294.5436 USA ISSN 0277-092X
B132.Y6
INTERNATIONAL YOGA GUIDE. Text in English. 1962. m. USD 24 (effective 2011). 24 p./no.; back issues avail.; reprints avail. **Document type:** *Guide, Trade.* **Description:** Contains timeless articles on yoga, Vedanta, philosophy, and the scientific explanation of mysticism. Provides enlightened examination of religious scriptures of the world, especially Hinduism.
Published by: Yoga Research Foundation, 6111 S W 74th Ave, Miami, FL 33143. TEL 305-666-2006, FAX 305-666-4443, info@yrf.org, http://www.yrf.org/.

294.5 IND
JATRA. Text in Marathi. 1963. a. INR 100 per issue (effective 2011). adv. **Document type:** *Magazine, Consumer.*
Published by: Menaka Prakashan Pvt. Ltd., 2117 Sadashiv Peth, Vijayanagar Colony, Pune, Maharashtra 411 030, India. TEL 91-20-24336960, sales@menakaprakashan.com, http://menakaprakashan.com. Ed., Pub. Anand Agashe.

294.507 USA
BR128.H5
JOURNAL OF HINDU - CHRISTIAN STUDIES. Text in English. 1988. a. USD 15 per issue to individuals; USD 30 per issue to institutions; free to members (effective 2011). bk.rev. 2 cols./p.; back issues avail. **Document type:** *Journal, Academic/Scholarly.* **Description:** Provides a world-wide forum for Hindu-Christian scholarly studies and dialogue.
Formerly (until 2004): Hindu - Christian Studies Bulletin (0844-4587)
Indexed: A21, R&TA, RI-1, RI-2.
Published by: Society for Hindu Christian Studies, c/o Bradley Malkovsky, 232 Malloy Hall, University of Notre Dame, Notre Dame, IN 46556. TEL 574-631-7128, info@hcstudies.org. Eds. Bradley J Malkovsky, Michael Amaladoss. **Editorial & subscr. addr. in India:** Anand Amaladass, Ed.

294.5 GBR ISSN 1756-4255
BL1100
➤ **THE JOURNAL OF HINDU STUDIES.** Text in English. 2008. 3/yr. GBP 64 in United Kingdom to institutions; EUR 96 in Europe to institutions; USD 128 in US & Canada to institutions; GBP 64 elsewhere to institutions; GBP 70 combined subscription in United Kingdom to institutions (print & online eds.); EUR 105 combined subscription in Europe to institutions (print & online eds.); USD 139 combined subscription in US & Canada to institutions (print & online eds.); GBP 70 combined subscription elsewhere to institutions (print & online eds.) (effective 2012). **Document type:** *Journal, Academic/Scholarly.* **Description:** Committed to a critical approach to Hindu Studies, focusing on annual themes that address overarching issues within the field.
Related titles: Online - full text ed.: ISSN 1756-4263. GBP 58 in United Kingdom to institutions; EUR 87 in Europe to institutions; USD 116 in US & Canada to institutions; GBP 58 elsewhere to institutions (effective 2012) (from IngentaConnect).
Indexed: A01, SCOPUS, T02.
—IE.
Published by: (The Oxford Centre for Hindu Studies), Oxford University Press, Great Clarendon St, Oxford, OX2 6DP, United Kingdom. TEL 44-1865-556767, FAX 44-1865-556646, jnl.orders@oup.co.uk, enquiry@oup.co.uk, http://www.oxfordjournals.org.

294.5 IND
KUMUDAM BAKTHI SPECIAL. Text in Tamil. bi-m. adv. back issues avail. **Document type:** *Magazine, Consumer.*
Related titles: Online - full text ed.; Telugu ed.: INR 250 domestic; USD 25 foreign (effective 2003).
Published by: Kumudam Publications Pvt. Ltd., 151 Purasawalkam High Rd, Chennai, Tamil Nadu 600 010, India. TEL 91-44-26422146, FAX 91-44-26425041, kumudam@vsnl.com.

294.5 USA ISSN 0276-0444
B130
MANANAM PUBLICATION SERIES. Text in English, Sanskrit. 1978. s-a. USD 20; USD 30 foreign (effective 1998). adv. bk.rev. charts; illus. back issues avail.
Published by: Chinmaya Mission, P O Box 129, Piercy, CA 95587. TEL 707-237-5321, FAX 707-247-3422, info-krishnalaya@chinmayamission.org. Circ: 1,300.

294.5 USA ISSN 1556-5262
BL1100
MARG; a path to your heritage. Text in English. 2005. bi-m. USD 20; USD 5 newsstand/cover (effective 2006). Index. back issues avail. **Document type:** *Magazine, Consumer.* **Description:** Covers Hindu dharma, philosophy, scriptures and culture.
Published by: The Marg Foundation, P O Box 2896, Montgomery Village, MD 20886-2896. TEL 301-963-4767, rameshwarpaul@hotmail.com. Ed., Pub. Rameshwar N Paul. Adv. contact Kshemendra N Paul TEL 703-689-0661. Circ: 4,000 (controlled).

294.5 CHE ISSN 1019-9969
MAYAPUR JOURNAL. Text in English. 1989. q. USD 15 (effective 2000). **Document type:** *Newsletter.*
Formerly (until 1992): Mayapur Newsletter (1015-552X)
Published by: Mayapur Association, PO Box 4742, Zug, 6304, Switzerland. TEL 41-1-2611220, FAX 41-1-2623114. Ed. Gaura-lila Dasa. R&P Gaura Lila Dasa. Circ: 1,000.

294.5435 USA ISSN 1075-9727
MEDITATOR'S NEWSLETTER. Text in English. 1994. m. looseleaf. USD 10 in United States; USD 12 in Canada (effective 2002). back issues avail. **Document type:** *Newsletter.* **Description:** Contains essays, poetry, and stories on issues of interest to meditators, contemplatives, and spiritual seekers. Compares traditional and current approaches to self-realization or enlightenment.
Related titles: E-mail ed.: 1998. free; Online - full text ed.: 1998. free.
Published by: Sacred Orchard Corporation, PO Box 298, Harriman, NY 10926-0298. TEL 845-782-3849, FAX 845-782-3849, mednews@sacredorchard.org, http://www.sacredorchard.org/. Eds., Pubs. Daryl Bailin TEL 845-782-3849, George Bailin. R&P Daryl Bailin TEL 845-782-3849. Circ: 100 (paid).

294.5 IND ISSN 0027-7770
NANAK PRAKASH PATRIKA. Text in English, Hindi, Panjabi. 1969. s-a. INR 50 per issue (effective 2011). bk.rev. back issues avail. **Document type:** *Journal, Academic/Scholarly.*
Published by: Punjabi University, Patiala, Punjab 147 002, India. TEL 91-175-3046533, http://www.punjabiuniversity.ac.in.

294.54 IND
NANDAN KANAN. Text in Bengali. 1975. m. **Document type:** *Journal, Trade.*
Published by: Adarsha Prakashani, c/o Society for the Formation of Character and Sequence, Ma-Mahajnan Mandir, P.O Inda, Kharagpur, 721 305, India. TEL 91-3222-225176. Circ: 10,000.

294.5 IND
NAVNEET HINDI. Text in Hindi. 1952. m. INR 220; INR 20 per issue (effective 2011). back issues avail. **Document type:** *Magazine, Consumer.* **Description:** Devoted to life, literature and culture of India in Hindi.
Related titles: Fax ed.
Address: Bharatiya Vidya Bhavan, Kulapati K.M. Munshi Marg, Mumbai, Maharashtra 400 007, India.

294.5 IND
NEELESHWARI. Text in Hindi. 198?. m. illus. **Document type:** *Magazine, Consumer.* **Description:** Contains spiritual, scriptural articles, stories, and interviews.
Formerly (until 1987): Shree Gurudev Ashram. Newsletter
Published by: (Shree Gurudev Ashram), Gurudev Siddha Peeth, PO. Ganeshpuri, Thane, Maharashtra 401 206, India. TEL 91-2522-302600, FAX 91-2522-261228, http://www.siddhayoga.org.in/Gurudev_Siddha_Peeth.html.

294.071 ZAF ISSN 1016-5320
➤ **NIDAN.** Text in English. 1989. a. ZAR 5 in Southern Africa; USD 5 overseas. abstr.; bibl. back issues avail. **Document type:** *Journal, Academic/Scholarly.* **Description:** Publishes original scholarly articles on topics of contemporary significance in the study of Hindu religion, philosophy and culture.
Indexed: A21, ISAP, PerIslam, RI-1, RI-2.
Published by: University of KwaZulu-Natal, King George V Avenue, Glenwood, Durban, KwaZulu-Natal 4041, South Africa. TEL 27-31-2602212, http://www.ukzn.ac.za. Ed. Anil Sooklal.

294.5 IND
OSHO TIMES INTERNATIONAL. Text in English, French, German, Hindi, Italian, Japanese, Polish, Portuguese, Spanish, Tamil. 1982. m. INR 330 (effective 2011). bk.rev. back issues avail.
Formerly (until 1988): Rajneesh Times International
Published by: Tao Publishing (Pvt.) Ltd., 17 Koregaon Park, Pune, Maharashtra 411 001, India. TEL 91-20-66019999, FAX 91-20-66019990.

294.5 IND ISSN 0032-6178
PRABUDDHA BHARATA/AWAKENED INDIA. Abbreviated title: P B. Text in English. 1896. m. INR 100 for India & Nepal; INR 1,100 for Sri Lanka and Bangladesh; GBP 18 in United Kingdom; EUR 25 in Europe; USD 30 elsewhere (effective 2011). adv. bk.rev. charts; illus. index. 60 p./no. 2 cols./p.; back issues avail. **Document type:** *Journal, Academic/Scholarly.* **Description:** Discusses Vedanta Philosophy or Universal religion and its application to daily life for followers of all religions and sects, irrespective of caste, creed or color.
Related titles: Online - full text ed.: free (effective 2011).
Indexed: BAS, MLA-IB.
—BLDSC (6579.250000).
Published by: (Ramakrishna Math & Mission Belur Math), Advaita Ashrama, 5 Dehi Entally Rd, Kolkata, West Bengal 700 014, India. TEL 91-33-22644000, FAX 91-33-22450050, mail@advaitaashrama.org.

294.5 IND ISSN 0973-2772
RAYS OF THE HARMONIST. Text in English. 1996. m. USD 212.50; USD 17.95 per issue (effective 2011). back issues avail. **Document type:** *Magazine, Consumer.*
Related titles: Online - full text ed.
Published by: Sri Gaudiya Vedanta Samiti, Opp Dist Hospital, Jawahar Hata, Mathura, U P 281 001, India. TEL 91-565-2502334, mathuramath@gmail.com.

294.5 IND
SAI SUDDHA. Text in English, Tamil, Telugu. 19??. m. illus. back issues avail. **Document type:** *Magazine, Consumer.*
Related titles: Online - full text ed.: free (effective 2011).
Published by: All India Sai Samaj, Alamelumangapuram, Mylapore, Chennai, Tamil Nadu 600 004, India. TEL 91-44-24640784, info@allindiasaisamaj.org, http://www.allindiasaisamaj.org.

294.5 IND
SAKTHI VIKATAN. Text in Tamil. 200?. s-m. INR 450 in state; INR 500 out of state; INR 2,450 elsewhere; INR 20 per issue in state; INR 22 per issue out of state (effective 2011). **Document type:** *Magazine, Consumer.*
Related titles: Online - full text ed.: INR 1,250, USD 29.07 includes all Vikatan publications (effective 2011).
Published by: Vasan Publications Pvt. Ltd., 757 Anna Salai, Chennai, Tamil Nadu 600 002, India. TEL 91-44-28524074, pubonline@vikatan.com, http://www.vikatan.com.

SATYA NILAYAM; Chennai journal of intercultural philosophy. *see* PHILOSOPHY

294.54 IND
SUDHI SAHITYA; a bilingual literary monthly. Text in Bengali, English. 1977. m. **Document type:** *Journal, Trade.*
Published by: Adarsha Prakashani, c/o Society for the Formation of Character and Sequence, Ma-Mahajnan Mandir, P.O Inda, Kharagpur, 721 305, India. TEL 91-3222-225176. Circ: 17,000.

294.5 USA
SWADHARMA (ONLINE); the voice of Dharma. Text in English. 2006. a. **Document type:** *Magazine, Consumer.* **Description:** Examines modern Hinduism though scholarly articles and personal reflections with the goal of creating better awareness of the tradition for both Hindus and non-Hindus.
Formerly (until 2008): Swadharma (Print) (1931-0471)
Published by: Harvard Dharma, Harvard University, University Hall, 1st Fl, Cambridge, MA 02138. harvarddharma@gmail.com, http://www.harvarddharma.org.

294.5 IND ISSN 0971-3964
TAPOVAN PRASAD; spirtual monthly of chinmaya mission worldwide. Text in English. 1963. m. INR 150 domestic; USD 25 foreign; INR 15 newsstand/cover (effective 2011). adv. bk.rev. **Document type:** *Magazine.* **Description:** Devoted to the propagation of Hindu philosophy, and Indian cultural and traditional values, particularly the teaching of Parama Poojya Swami Chinmayananda.
Published by: Chinmaya Mission, No 2, 13th Ave, Harrington Rd, Chennai, Tamilnadu 600 031, India. TEL 91-44-28363641.

VEDANTA. *see* PHILOSOPHY

294.5 FRA ISSN 1959-5387
VEDANTA. Text in French. 1957. q. EUR 12.20 (effective 2008). **Document type:** *Journal.*
Published by: Centre Vedantique Ramakrishna, 64 Bd Victor-Hugo, Gretz-Armainvilliers, 77220, France. TEL 33-1-64070311, FAX 33-1-64420357, centre.vedantique@wanadoo.fr.

THE VEDANTA KESARI; the lion of vedanta. *see* PHILOSOPHY

VIVEKANANDA VEDANTA SOCIETY OF CHICAGO. BULLETINS. *see* PHILOSOPHY

294.5 USA ISSN 2153-4632
▼ **YELLOW SUBMARINE.** Text in English. 2010 (Mar.). w. **Document type:** *Newsletter, Consumer.*
Media: E-mail.
Published by: Gita Nagari Press, 17305 N Village Main Blvd, Lewes, DE 19958-7220. TEL 302-703-2805, editor@gnpress.org, http://www.gnpress.org/.

RELIGIONS AND THEOLOGY—Islamic

297 USA ISSN 1062-5968
E184.E2
A I M. (Association of Indian Muslims) Text in English. 1987. q. USD 10 (effective 1999). adv. bk.rev. **Document type:** *Newsletter.*
Published by: Association of Indian Muslims of America, 11649 Masters Run, Elliot City, MD 21042. TEL 410-730-5456, FAX 410-922-0665. Ed., R&P, Adv. contact Kaleem Kawaja. Circ: 800.

297 USA ISSN 1536-2434
THE A M S S BULLETIN. (Association of Muslim Social Scientists) Text in English. 2000. q. 16 p./no. 3 cols./p.;
Formerly (until 2001): Association of Muslim Social Scientists Newsletter
Published by: Association of Muslim Social Scientists, P O Box 669, Herndon, VA 20172-0669. TEL 703-471-1133, FAX 703-471-3922, http://www.iiit.org. Ed. Layla Sein TEL 703-471-1133 ext 120.

A P S DIPLOMAT REDRAWING THE ISLAMIC MAP. *see* POLITICAL SCIENCE

297 ITA ISSN 0391-8130
ACCADEMIA NAZIONALE DEI LINCEI. FONDAZIONE LEONE CAETANI. Text in Multiple languages. 1905. irreg. **Document type:** *Monographic series, Academic/Scholarly.*
Formerly (until 1970): Accademia Nazionale dei Lincei. Fondazione Leone Caetani per gli Studi Mussulmani (0393-3709)
Indexed: P30.
Published by: (Accademia Nazionale dei Lincei), Bardi Editore, Via Piave 7, Rome, 00187, Italy. TEL 39-06-4817656, FAX 39-06-48912574, info@bardieditore.com, http://www.bardieditore.com.

297 IRN
➤ **AFAG AL-HIDARAH AL-ISLAMIYYAH.** Text in Arabic; Summaries in English. 1996. s-a. IRR 12,000 domestic; USD 25 foreign; IRR 3,500 newsstand/cover domestic; USD 12.50 newsstand/cover foreign (effective 2003). bk.rev. bibl.; charts; illus.; maps; stat. back issues avail. **Document type:** *Magazine, Academic/Scholarly.* **Description:** Covers Islamic philosophy and history.
Published by: Mu'assasah-i Mutala'at va Tahqiqat-i Farhangi/Cultural Studies and Research Institute, PO Box 14155-1871, Tehran, Iran. TEL 98-21-8036320, FAX 98-21-686317. Ed. Sadiq Ainawand. Circ: 1,000.

297 SLE ISSN 0044-653X
AFRICAN CRESCENT. Text in English. 1955. m. SLL 4. adv. bk.rev.
Published by: Ahmadiyya Muslim Mission, PO Box 353, Freetown, Sierra Leone. Ed. Maulana Khalil Mobashir. Circ: 1,000.

297.14 NGA ISSN 0065-468X
AHMADU BELLO UNIVERSITY. CENTRE OF ISLAMIC LEGAL STUDIES. JOURNAL. Text in English. 1966. irreg., latest vol.5, 1974. **Document type:** *Journal, Academic/Scholarly.*
Published by: Ahmadu Bello University, Centre of Islamic Legal Studies, PMB 1013, Samaru-Zaria, Kaduna, Nigeria.

297 SAU ISSN 1319-0725
AKHBAR AL-A'ALAM AL-ISLAMI. Text in Arabic; Summaries in English. 1966. w. USD 40. **Document type:** *Newspaper.*
Published by: Muslim World League/Rabitat al-Alam al-Islami, P O Box 538, Makkah, Saudi Arabia. TEL 966-2-5447905, FAX 966-2-5448196.

297.86 DNK ISSN 0108-7290
AKTIV ISLAM. Text in Danish. 1959. q. bk.rev. **Document type:** *Magazine, Consumer.* **Description:** Presents various different religious issues, with particular reference to the mission of the Ahmadiyya Movement in Islam.
Published by: Nusrat Djahan Moske/Nusrat Jahan Mosque, Eriksminde Alle 2, Hvidovre, 2650, Denmark. TEL 45-36-753502, FAX 56-36-750007. Ed. Ata-Ul-Qadir.

297 PAK ISSN 1995-7904
➤ **AL-ADWA.** Text in Arabic, English, Urdu. 1990. s-a. USD 15; USD 9 newsstand/cover (effective 2007). adv. **Document type:** *Journal, Academic/Scholarly.* **Description:** Devoted to publishing articles concerned with the religious and contemporary Muslim world.
Indexed: I14.
Published by: Sheikh Zayed Islamic Centre, University of the Punjab, Quaid-e-Azam Campus, Lahore, 54590, Pakistan. TEL 92-042-9231140, FAX 92-042-9231141, info@szic.pu.edu.pk. Ed. Abul Wafa. Circ: 500 (paid and controlled).

297 GBR ISSN 2044-0219
▼ **AL-HIDAYAH MAGAZINE.** Text in English. 2010. q. donations. adv. **Document type:** *Magazine, Trade.* **Description:** Serve as an intellectual and social medium addressing the diverse aspects of Muslim life and the challenges it brings.
Related titles: Online - full text ed.: ISSN 2044-0227. free (effective 2011).
Published by: Muslim Youth League UK, 37 Jessops Riverside, Brightside Ln, Sheffield, S9 2RX, United Kingdom. volunteer@hidayahmag.com. Eds. Jawed Iqbal, Samra Mursaleen, Tahseen Khalid.

297 IRN
AL-HUDA. Text in Arabic. m. USD 30 in Asia; USD 25 in Africa; USD 40 in Europe; USD 48 elsewhere (effective 2001). **Document type:** *Magazine, Consumer.*
Published by: Islamic Thought Foundation, P O Box 14155-3899, Tehran, Iran. TEL 98-21-88976635, FAX 98-21-8902725, i.t.f@iran-itf.com. Ed. Javad Jamil.

297.57 USA ISSN 1092-3772
BP1
AL-JUMUAH. Text in English. m. USD 30 domestic; USD 65 foreign (effective 2001). adv. **Document type:** *Magazine, Consumer.* **Description:** For people who are interested in understanding the beliefs and practices of Muslims.
Published by: Al-Muntada Al-Islami, Inc., PO Box 5387, Madison, WI 53705-5387. TEL 608-277-1855, FAX 608-277-0323. Ed., Pub. Hassen A Hassen Laidi. R&P Mounir Boughoula. Adv. contact Amin Farooqui. Circ: 15,000.

297 GBR ISSN 1319-5913
BP188.18.Y68
AL-MUSTAQBAL AL-ISLAMI (RIYAD)/ISLAMIC FUTURE. Text in Arabic. m. **Document type:** *Magazine, Consumer.*
Published by: World Assembly of Muslim Youth/Nadwat al-A'alamiyat li-l-Sabab al-Islami, 46 Goodge St, London, W1T 4LU, United Kingdom. TEL 44-20-7636-7010, FAX 44-20-7636-7080, wamy@wamy.co.uk, http://www.wamy.co.uk.

297 ZAF
AL-QALAM. Text in English. m. back issues avail. **Document type:** *Newspaper, Consumer.*
Related titles: Online - full content ed.
Published by: The Muslim Youth Movement of South Africa, PO Box 48112, Qualbert, 4078, South Africa. mymdbn@786.co.za, http://786.co.za/mym/.

297 IDN ISSN 0126-6357
AMANAH. Text in Indonesian. fortn.
Indexed: PerIslam.

R

Address: Jalan Garuda 69, Kemayoran, Jakarta, Indonesia. TEL 021-410254. Ed. Maskun Iskandar. Circ: 180,000.

297.93 USA ISSN 1062-1113
AMERICAN BAHA'I. Text in English, Persian, Modern, Spanish. 1970. 10/yr. free to members (effective 2005). **Document type:** *Newspaper.* **Description:** Current events in the Baha'i community.
Published by: National Spiritual Assembly of the Baha'is of the United States, 1233 Central St, Evanston, IL 60201. TEL 847-733-3559, FAX 847-733-3578, http://www.bahai.us. Ed. James Humphrey. R&P Dale Spenner TEL 847-251-1854. Circ: 97,000.

297.071 USA ISSN 0887-7653
BP1
➤ **AMERICAN JOURNAL OF ISLAMIC SOCIAL SCIENCES.** Abbreviated title: A J I S S. Text in English. 1984. q. USD 45 to individuals; USD 125 to institutions (effective 2009). bk.rev. charts; stat. cum.index: 1984-2002. back issues avail.; reprints avail. **Document type:** *Journal, Academic/Scholarly.* **Description:** Features scholarly research on all facets of Islam and the Muslim world: politics, history, economic philosophy, metaphysics, psychology, religious law, and Islamic thought, employing both empirical and theoretical analysis.
Formerly (until 1985): American Journal of Islamic Studies (0742-6763)
Related titles: Online - full text ed.
Indexed: A21, A22, AmH&L, CA, DIP, HistAb, I02, I13, IBR, IBZ, IBibSS, M10, P30, P42, PAIS, PCI, PSA, PerIslam, RI-1, RI-2, RILM, S02, S03, SCOPUS, SOPODA, SSA, SociolAb, T02.
—BLDSC (0826.830000), CIS, IE, Ingenta.
Published by: (Association of Muslim Social Scientists), International Institute of Islamic Thought, PO Box 669, Herndon, VA 20172. TEL 703-471-1133, FAX 703-471-3922, iiit@iiit.org, http://www.iiit.org. Eds. Zakyi Ibrahim, Ali A Mazrui.

297.092 USA ISSN 1545-3820
THE AMERICAN MUSLIM (ALEXANDRIA). Text in English. 2000 (Jan.). 4/yr. (4-5/yr.). USD 30 (effective 2003).
Published by: Muslim American Society, 3602 Forest Dr., Alexandria, VA 22302. TEL 703-998-6525, FAX 703-998-6526, mas@masnet.org, http://www.masnet.org. Ed. Dr. Souheil Ghannouchi.

297.0971 USA ISSN 1078-8808
BP67.A1
THE AMERICAN MUSLIM RESOURCE DIRECTORY. Text in English. 1992. a. USD 25. adv.
Indexed: PerIslam.
Published by: American Muslim Support Group, PO Box 5670, Bel Ridge, MO 63121. TEL 314-291-3711. Adv. contact Sheila Musaji.

297 TZA ISSN 0856-3861
AP9
AN-NUUR. Text in Swahili. 1991. w. TZS 19,200, USD 29. adv. back issues avail. **Document type:** *Newspaper.*
Published by: Islamic Propagation Centre, PO Box 55105, Dar Es Salaam, Tanzania. TEL 255-51-181365. Ed. Omar Junia Msangi. adv.: page TZS 250,000. Circ: 15,000.

297.09 EGY ISSN 0570-1716
BP1
ANNALES ISLAMOLOGIQUES. Text in Arabic, English, French. 1954. a., latest vol.34, 2000. EGP 212 domestic (effective 2001). back issues avail. **Document type:** *Journal, Academic/Scholarly.* **Description:** Research of history, archaeology and linguistics from the beginning of Islam to the 19th century.
Formerly (until 1963): Melanges Islamologiques (0254-2846)
Related titles: ◆ CD-ROM ed.: Bulletin Critique des Annales Islamologiques (CD-ROM Edition); ◆ Supplement(s): Annales Islamologiques. Supplement. ISSN 0254-282X.
Indexed: A21, BibLing, DIP, I14, IBR, IBZ, PCI, RI-1, RI-2.
—INIST.
Published by: Institut Francais d'Archeologie Orientale du Caire, Kasr el-Aini, 37 Sharia Sheikh Aly Youssef, Mounira, PO Box 11562, Cairo, Egypt. FAX 20-2-3544635, ventes@ifao.egnet.net, http://www.boustanys.com, http://www.ifao.egnet.net. Adv. contact Marie-Christine Michel TEL 20-2-7971622. Circ: 800. **Dist. by:** Boustany's Publishing House, 29 Faggalah St, Cairo 11271, Egypt. TEL 20-2-5915315, FAX 20-2-4177915.

297 ZAF
ANNUAL REVIEW OF ISLAM IN SOUTH AFRICA. Abbreviated title: A R I S A. Text in English. 1998. a. **Document type:** *Journal, Academic/Scholarly.*
Media: Online - full text.
Indexed: I14.
Published by: University of Cape Town, Department of Religious Studies, Private Bag 7701, Rondebosch, South Africa. Eds. Shaheed Mathee, Susana Molins Literas.

297 OMN
AL-AQIDAH. Text in Arabic. w. illus.
Published by: Aqidah, Ruwi, P O Box 4001, Muscat, Oman. TEL 701000, TELEX 3399. Ed. Said As Samhan Al Kathiri. Circ: 5,000.

ARAB LAW QUARTERLY. *see* LAW

ARABIC SCIENCES AND PHILOSOPHY; a historical journal. *see* HISTORY

297 327 GBR ISSN 1756-7335
ARCHES QUARTERLY. Text in English. 2006. q. back issues avail. **Document type:** *Journal, Academic/Scholarly.* **Description:** Provides analysis of the issues and developments in the arena of dialogue, civilizations, and a rapprochement between Islam and the West.
Formerly (until 2007): Arches (1755-4160)
Related titles: Online - full text ed.: ISSN 1756-7343. free (effective 2009).
Published by: The Cordoba Foundation Ltd., Westgate House, Level 7, Westgate Rd, Eailing, London, W5 1YY, United Kingdom. TEL 44-20-89913372, FAX 44-20-89913373, info@thecordobafoundation.com.

297 NLD ISSN 2210-2442
AS SIRAATA. Variant title: De Weg. Text in Dutch. 199?. q. EUR 12 (effective 2010). **Document type:** *Magazine, Consumer.*
Published by: Muslimvrouwenorganisatie Al Nisa, Postbus 9, Utrecht, 3500 AA, Netherlands. TEL 31-6-26232988, info@alnisa.nl, http://www.alnisa.nl.

297 NLD ISSN 0923-2044
ASFAR. Text in Dutch. 1977. irreg., latest vol.3, 1989. price varies. back issues avail. **Document type:** *Monographic series, Academic/Scholarly.*
Indexed: IZBG.
Published by: (Universiteit Leiden, Documentatiebureau Islam-Christendom), Brill, PO Box 9000, Leiden, 2300 PA, Netherlands. TEL 31-71-5353500, FAX 31-71-5317532, cs@brill.nl. R&P Elizabeth Venekamp. **Dist. by:** Turpin Distribution Services Ltd., Pegasus Dr, Stratton Business Park, Biggleswade, Bedfordshire SG18 8QB, United Kingdom. TEL 44-1767-604954, FAX 44-1767-601640, custserv@turpin-distribution.com, http://www.turpin-distribution.com/.

297 IRN ISSN 1019-0368
ASHINA. Text in Persian, Modern. 1991. m. USD 20 in the Middle East; USD 25 in Asia; USD 30 in North America; USD 15 in Africa.
Published by: Islamic Thought Foundation, P O Box 14155-3899, Tehran, Iran. TEL 98-21-844092, FAX 98-21-898295, i.t.f@iran-itf.com, http://www.iran-itf.com.

297.77 TUR ISSN 1303-295X
ATATURK UNIVERSITESI. ILAHIYAT FAKULTESI. DERGISI. Text in Turkish. 1982. a. **Document type:** *Journal, Academic/Scholarly.*
Formerly: Ataturk Universitesi Islami Ilimler Fakultesi Dergisi
Indexed: PerIslam.
Published by: Ataturk Universitesi, Ilahiyat Fakultesi/Ataturk University, Faculty of Theology, University Campus, Erzurum, 25240, Turkey. TEL 90-442-2312134, fkaraca@atauni.edu.tr, ata@atauni.edu.tr, http://www.atauni.edu.tr.

340.59 AUS ISSN 1838-2266
▼ ➤ **AUSTRALIAN JOURNAL OF ISLAMIC LAW, MANAGEMENT AND FINANCE.** Abbreviated title: A J I L M F. Text in English. 2010. q. free (effective 2011). back issues avail. **Document type:** *Journal, Academic/Scholarly.* **Description:** Addresses the advancement of contemporary research in the field of Islamic law, management and finance.
Related titles: Online - full text ed.
Published by: Centre for Islam and Social Sciences, PO Box 6131, Logan Central, QLD 4114, Australia. TEL 61-7-31333625, FAX 61-7-33038445, enquiries.ciss@gmail.com. Ed. Mohamad Sujimon.

297 FRA ISSN 0764-7573
DT193.5.B45
AWAL; cahier d'etudes berberes. Text in French. 1985. s-a. **Document type:** *Journal, Academic/Scholarly.*
Indexed: AnthLit, BibLing, FR, I14, PCI.
Published by: (Centre d'Etudes et de Recherches Amazigh), Editions de la Maison des Sciences de l'Homme, 54 Blvd Raspail, Paris, Cedex 6 75270, France. TEL 33-1-49542000, FAX 33-1-49542133, http://www.msh-paris.fr.

297.57 IRN ISSN 1023-7992
BP1
AYENEH-E PAZHOOHESH/MIRAT AL-TAHQIQ/MIRROR OF RESEARCH. Text in Persian, Modern; Summaries in Arabic, English. 1990. 6/yr. USD 30 in Europe; USD 33 in Asia; USD 37.50 in Australia (effective 2001). bk.rev. bibl. **Document type:** *Academic/Scholarly.* **Description:** Presents articles dealing with methodological issues and current research in Islamic culture, with extensive reviews of recent publications in the field, and news of research and translation projects underway.
Published by: Daftar-i Tablighat-i Islami-i Hawzah-i 'Ilmiyah-i Qum, P O Box 37185-3693, Qum, Iran. TEL 98-251-37729. Ed. Mohammed Ali Mahdavi Raad. Circ: 7,000.

297 USA ISSN 1530-7220
HQ1170
AZIZAH. Text in English. 2001. q. USD 30 domestic; USD 45 in Canada; USD 60 in Asia; USD 55 elsewhere (effective 2003). adv. **Document type:** *Magazine, Consumer.* **Description:** Covers issues faced by Muslim women in the United States and provides a positive image of Muslim women.
Related titles: Online - full text ed.
Indexed: ENW, GW.
Published by: Wow Publishing, Inc., PO Box 43410, Atlanta, GA 30336-0410. TEL 678-945-5800, FAX 678-945-1986, customerservice@azizahmagazine.com/, http://www.azizahmagazine.com/. adv.: page USD 500.

297.93 GBR ISSN 1354-8697
➤ **BAHA'I STUDIES REVIEW.** Abbreviated title: B S R. Text in English. 1991. a. GBP 210 per issue domestic to institutions; GBP 219 per issue in the European Union to institutions; USD 330 per issue in US & Canada to institutions; GBP 222 per issue elsewhere to institutions (effective 2011). adv. bk.rev. back issues avail. **Document type:** *Journal, Academic/Scholarly.* **Description:** Explores and discusses contemporary issues regarding the principles, history, and philosophy of the Baha'i faith.
Related titles: Online - full text ed.: ISSN 2040-1701. USD 265 per issue in US & Canada to institutions; GBP 177 per issue elsewhere to institutions (effective 2011).
Indexed: A21, AmHI, CA, H07, P48, P53, P54, PQC, RI-1, T02.
Published by: (Association for Baha'i Studies), Intellect Ltd., The Mill, Parnall Rd, Fishponds, Bristol, BS16 3JG, United Kingdom. TEL 44-117-9589910, FAX 44-117-9589911, info@intellectbooks.com. Eds. Ismael Velasco, Steve Cooney. Pub. Masoud Yazdani. **Subscr. to:** Turpin Distribution Services Ltd., Pegasus Dr, Stratton Business Park, Biggleswade, Bedfordshire SG18 8QB, United Kingdom. TEL 44-1767-604951, FAX 44-1767-601640, custserv@turpin-distribution.com, http://www.turpin-distribution.com/.

297.93 ISR ISSN 0045-1320
BAHA'I WORLD. Text mainly in English; Text occasionally in French, German, Persian, Modern. 1925. irreg., latest 2007. price varies.
Published by: Baha'i World Centre, P O Box 155, Haifa, 31001, Israel. FAX 04-358280, TELEX 46626-BAYT IL. Ed. Sherna Deamer. Circ: 15,000. **Dist. in U.S. by:** Baha'i Publishing Trust, 415 Linden Ave, Wilmette, IL 60091.

297.57 ZAF
AL-BALAAGH; dedicated to the expounding of Islam in its pristine purity. Text in English. 1976. 2/yr. ZAR 60; GBP 5 in United Kingdom; USD 10 elsewhere (effective 2008). 8 p./no.; **Document type:** *Newspaper.* **Description:** Offers a forum for the discussion of topics of interest to Muslims throughout the world.
Indexed: PerIslam.
Published by: Balaagh, PO Box 1925, Lensia, 1820, South Africa. http://www.al-balaagh.com.

297.4 NLD ISSN 1875-0664
BASIC TEXTS OF ISLAMIC MYSTICISM. Text in English. 2007. irreg., latest vol.2, 2008. price varies. **Document type:** *Monographic series, Academic/Scholarly.*
Indexed: IZBG.
Published by: Brill, PO Box 9000, Leiden, 2300 PA, Netherlands. TEL 31-71-5353500, FAX 31-71-5317532, cs@brill.nl. Ed. Bernd Radtke.

BEITRAEGE ZUR ISLAMISCHEN KUNST UND ARCHAEOLOGIE. *see* ART

297.77 DEU ISSN 1867-1578
▼ **BEITRAEGE ZUR ISLAMISCHEN RELIGIONSPAEDAGOGIK.** Text in German. 2009. irreg., latest vol.3, 2009. price varies. **Document type:** *Monographic series, Academic/Scholarly.*
Published by: Verlag Dr. Kovac, Leverkusenstr 13, Hamburg, 22761, Germany. TEL 49-40-3988800, FAX 49-40-39888055, info@verlagdrkovac.de. Ed. Bulent Ucar.

297.93 DEU
BELMONDA LETERO. Text in Esperanto. 1973. q. looseleaf. membership only. adv. bk.rev. **Document type:** *Newsletter, Consumer.* **Description:** News about the activities of Baha'i Esperantists around the world.
Published by: Bahaa Esperanto-Ligo, Eppsteiner Str 89, Hofheim-Langenhain, 65719, Germany. TEL 49-6192-992916, FAX 49-6192-992999, bahaaeligo@bahai.de, http://bahaaeligo.bahai.de. Circ: 500.

BERKELEY JOURNAL OF MIDDLE EASTERN AND ISLAMIC LAW. *see* LAW

297 DEU ISSN 0174-2477
BERLINER ISLAMSTUDIEN. Text in German. 1981. irreg., latest vol.16, 2001. price varies. **Document type:** *Monographic series, Academic/Scholarly.*
Published by: (Freien Universitaet Berlin, Institut fuer Islamwissenschaft), Franz Steiner Verlag GmbH, Birkenwaldstr 44, Stuttgart, 70191, Germany. TEL 49-711-25820, FAX 49-711-2582290, service@steiner-verlag.de, http://www.steiner-verlag.de.

297 IDN ISSN 0215-806X
DS611
BESTARI; edisi jurnal ilmiah. Text in Indonesian. 1991 (vol.4, no.6). bi-m.
Indexed: PerIslam.
Published by: Universitas Muhammadiyyah, Jalan Bandung 1, Malang, 51253, Indonesia.

297 NLD ISSN 1872-5481
BRILL CLASSICS IN ISLAM. Text in English. 2007. irreg., latest vol.6, 2011. price varies. **Document type:** *Monographic series, Academic/Scholarly.*
Indexed: IZBG.
Published by: Brill, PO Box 9000, Leiden, 2300 PA, Netherlands. TEL 31-71-5353500, FAX 31-71-5317532, cs@brill.nl.

BRILL'S ARAB AND ISLAMIC LAWS SERIES. *see* LAW

297 EGY
BP1
BULLETIN CRITIQUE DES ANNALES ISLAMOLOGIQUES (CD-ROM EDITION). Text in Arabic. 1984. a., latest vol.23, 2007. EGP 27 domestic; EUR 7.60 (effective 2001). bk.rev. back issues avail. **Document type:** *Academic/Scholarly.* **Description:** Annual review of books recently published in the field of Islamic and Arabic studies throughout the world.
Formerly (until vol.15 (1999)): Bulletin Critique des Annales Islamologiques (Print Edition) (0259-7373)
Media: CD-ROM. **Related titles:** ◆ Print ed.: Annales Islamologiques. ISSN 0570-1716.
Indexed: BibLing, DIP, IBR, IBZ, PCI.
Published by: Institut Francais d'Archeologie Orientale du Caire, Kasr el-Aini, 37 Sharia Sheikh Aly Youssef, Mounira, PO Box 11562, Cairo, Egypt. FAX 20-2-3544635, http://www.ifao.egnet.net. Eds. D Gimaret, M Cl Simeone Senelle. Circ: 800. **Dist. by:** Boustany's Publishing House, 29 Faggalah St, Cairo 11271, Egypt. TEL 20-2-5915315, FAX 20-2-4177915.

C I R S BRIEF. (Center for International and Regional Studies) *see* POLITICAL SCIENCE

297.071 AUS ISSN 1833-2447
C S C I ISLAMIC ISSUES BRIEFING PAPER SERIES. (Centre for the Study of Contemporary Islam) Text in English. 2005. 3/yr. **Document type:** *Monographic series, Academic/Scholarly.* **Description:** Provides an analysis of important contemporary issues relevant to Islam.
Published by: University of Melbourne, Centre for the Study of Contemporary Islam, Asia Institute, Sidney Myer Asia Centre, Melbourne, VIC 3010, Australia. TEL 61-3-83440155, FAX 61-3-93494974, csci-info@unimelb.edu.au, http://www.csci.unimelb.edu.au.

297.0971 CAN ISSN 0707-2945
CANADIAN MUSLIM. Text in Arabic, English. 1977. q. free. adv. bk.rev.
Published by: Ottawa Muslim Association, P O Box 2952, Sta D, Ottawa, ON S1P 5W9, Canada. TEL 613-725-0004. Ed. Saeed Bokhari. Circ: 2,000 (controlled).

297.283 GBR
CODEN: OSPBDN
THE CENTRE FOR ISLAMIC STUDIES AND THE CENTRE FOR THE STUDY OF INTERRELIGIOUS RELATIONS. NEWSLETTER. Text in English. 1979-1990; resumed 1996. 2/yr. free. adv. **Document type:** *Newsletter.*
Formerly (until 2007): Centre for the Study of Islam and Christian Muslim Relations. Newsletter (0143-8921)
Indexed: AMR.
—BLDSC (6107.145000).
Published by: University of Birmingham, The Centre for Islamic Studies and The Centre for the Study of Interreligious Relations, Elmfield House, Selly Oak Campus, Bristol Rd, Birmingham, B29 6LG, United Kingdom. TEL 44-121-4158373, FAX 44-121-4158376, theology@bham.ac.uk. Ed., R&P Dr. David Thomas. Adv. contact C A Bebawi.

297 USA ISSN 1935-2034
CHICAGO CRESCENT. Text in English. 2006. m. free (effective 2007). **Document type:** *Newsletter, Consumer.* **Description:** Features local, regional, and national politics, news and events relevant to Muslims and the Islamic community in the Chicago metropolitan area.
Related titles: Online - full text ed.
Published by: Council of Islamic Organizations of Greater Chicago, 231 S State St, Ste 300, Chicago, IL 60604. TEL 312-506-0070, 800-678-0753, FAX 312-506-0077. Ed. Faryal Ahmed.

297 FRA ISSN 1950-0653
COLLECTION ISLAM ET LAICITE. Text in French. 2006. irreg. back issues avail. **Document type:** *Monographic series, Academic/Scholarly.*
Published by: L' Harmattan, 5 Rue de l'Ecole Polytechnique, Paris, 75005, France. TEL 33-1-43257651, FAX 33-1-43258203, http://www.editions-harmattan.fr.

287.071 GBR ISSN 1740-7125
DS35.3
COMPARATIVE ISLAMIC STUDIES. Abbreviated title: C I S. Text in English. 2005. s-a. USD 220 combined subscription in North America to institutions (print & online eds.); GBP 135 combined subscription elsewhere to institutions (print & online eds.) (effective 2012). adv. bk.rev. back issues avail.; reprints avail. **Document type:** *Journal, Academic/Scholarly.* **Description:** Focuses on integrating Islamic studies into the general theoretical and methodological boundaries of liberal arts disciplines with an emphasis on those disciplines closely aligned with the contemporary study of religion.
Related titles: Online - full text ed.: ISSN 1743-1638. USD 176 in North America to institutions; GBP 108 elsewhere to institutions (effective 2012).
Indexed: A01, A02, A03, A08, CA, I02, T02.
—BLDSC (3363.782875), IE. **CCC.**
Published by: Equinox Publishing Ltd., Unit S3, Kelham House, 3 Lancaster St, Sheffield, S6 3AF, United Kingdom. TEL 44-114-2725957, FAX 44-560-3459046, journals@equinoxpub.com, http://www.equinoxpub.com/. Ed. Brannon M Wheeler. Adv. contact Val Hall.

297.2 USA ISSN 1051-0354
➤ **COMPARATIVE STUDIES ON MUSLIM SOCIETIES.** Text in English. 1987. irreg., latest vol.27, 1999. price varies. back issues avail. **Document type:** *Monographic series, Academic/Scholarly.* **Description:** Publishes papers on a wide variety of historical and theological topics of Islam.
—BLDSC (3363.834500). **CCC.**
Published by: University of California Press, Book Series, 2120 Berkeley Way, Berkeley, CA 94704. TEL 510-642-4247, FAX 510-643-7127, foundation@ucpress.edu. **Subscr. to:** California - Princeton Fulfillment Services, Inc., 1445 Lower Ferry Rd, Ewing, NJ 08618. TEL 800-777-4726, FAX 609-883-7413, 800-999-1958, orders@cpfsinc.com.

297 642 USA ISSN 1931-0072
BP184.9.D5
A COMPREHENSIVE LIST OF HALAL FOOD PRODUCTS IN U.S. AND CANADIAN SUPERMARKETS. Text in English. 1991. 3/yr. **Document type:** *Guide, Consumer.*
Published by: Muslim Consumer Group For Food Products, 10685 Rushmore Lane, Huntley, IL 60142. TEL 847-515-1008, 800-426-9550, FAX 847-515-1109, halalfoods@hotmail.com, http://www.muslimconsumergroup.com.

297 NLD ISSN 1872-0218
CONTEMPORARY ISLAM; dynamics of muslim life. Text in English. 2007. 3/yr. EUR 398, USD 481 combined subscription to institutions (print & online eds.) (effective 2012). bk.rev. reprint service avail. from PSC. **Document type:** *Journal, Academic/Scholarly.* **Description:** Focuses on the contemporary aspects of Islam and Muslim life, on presence of Muslims migrants in the West and western-born Muslims, and the relationship between Muslim identities and social life.
Related titles: Online - full text ed.: ISSN 1872-0226 (from IngentaConnect).
Indexed: A21, A22, A26, AmHI, BRD, CA, E01, E08, H07, H08, H12, HAb, HumInd, M08, P10, P28, P48, P53, P54, PAIS, PQC, S09, SCOPUS, SociolAb, T02, W03, W05.
—IE. **CCC.**
Published by: Springer Netherlands (Subsidiary of: Springer Science+Business Media), Van Godewijckstraat 30, Dordrecht, 3311 GX, Netherlands. TEL 31-78-6576050, FAX 31-78-6576474. Eds. Daniel Varisco, Gabriele Marranci.

297 QAT ISSN 2220-2757
▼ ➤ **CONTEMPORARY ISLAMIC STUDIES.** Text in English. 2010. free (effective 2011). **Document type:** *Journal, Academic/Scholarly.*
Media: Online - full text.
Published by: Bloomsbury Qatar Foundation Journals, Villa 3, Education City, PO Box 5825, Doha, Qatar. info@qscience.com. Ed. Hatem El-Karanshawy.

297 CAN ISSN 0705-3754
DS35.3
CRESCENT INTERNATIONAL. Text in English. 1972. s-m. GBP 24 in Europe to individuals; ZAR 100 in South Africa to individuals; USD 40 elsewhere to individuals; USD 60 to institutions (effective 2006). adv. bk.rev. back issues avail. **Document type:** *Magazine, Consumer.* **Description:** Covers the Islamic movement worldwide.
Related titles: Microfilm ed.
Indexed: PerIslam.
Address: PO Box 747, Gormley, ON L0H 1G0, Canada. TEL 905-887-8913, FAX 905-474-9293. Ed. Iqbal Siddiqui. Circ: 20,000. **Subscr. to:** 32 Warrington Ave, Slough SL1 3BQ, United Kingdom. TEL 44-1753-523719, FAX 44-1753-570231.

297 MUS
LE CROISSANT. Text in English, French. 1991 (vol.5). fortn.
Indexed: PerIslam.
Published by: Mauritian Islamic Mission, Rue Velore et Noor-e-Islam Mosque, Port Louis, Mauritius. Ed. Bashir Ahmade Oozeer.

297 GBR ISSN 1758-1222
CULTURES OF RESISTANCE. Text in English. 2008. s-a. back issues avail. **Document type:** *Magazine, Consumer.* **Description:** Aims to address the western hostile use of language intended to restrict debate related to mainstream Islamist movements and currents.
Related titles: Online - full text ed.: ISSN 1758-1230.
Published by: Conflicts Forum, London, United Kingdom. TEL 44-208-1449588, info@conflictsforum.com. Ed. Aisling Byrne.

297 320.5 USA ISSN 1940-834X
BP173.7
CURRENT TRENDS IN ISLAMIST IDEOLOGY. Text in English. 2005. s-a. back issues avail. **Document type:** *Journal, Academic/Scholarly.* **Description:** Examines religious and political developments in Islamic countries and the impact of Islamic ideologies around the world in relation to global politics and international relations.
Related titles: Online - full text ed.: ISSN 1940-8358. free (effective 2010).
Published by: Hudson Institute, 1015 15th St, NW, 6th Fl, Washington, DC 20005. TEL 202-974-2400, FAX 202-974-2410, info@hudson.org, http://www.hudson.org.

297.096 GBR ISSN 1352-7541
DAILY JANG LONDON. Text in English, Urdu. 1971. d. GBP 196. adv. bk.rev. back issues avail. **Document type:** *Newspaper.* **Description:** Provides news from U.K. and Indo-Pakistan subcontinent.
Published by: Jang Publications Ltd., 57 Lant St, London, SE1 1QN, United Kingdom. FAX 071-403-6740, TELEX 28208. Ed. Ashraf K Kazi. Circ: 19,427.

201.6 PHL ISSN 0115-866X
DS666.M8
DANSALAN QUARTERLY. Text in English. 1979. q. PHP 300 domestic; USD 15 foreign (effective 1999). bk.rev. **Document type:** *Journal, Academic/Scholarly.* **Description:** Focuses on Muslim Filipinos. Covers history, socio-economics, current issues on Muslim-Christian conflict, and political issues on Muslim Filipinos.
Indexed: AICP, BAS, IPP.
Published by: Dansalan College Foundation Inc., Gowing Memorial Research Center, PO Box 5430, Iligan City, Lanao Del Norte 9200, Philippines. TEL 63-63-520613. Ed. Manuel R Tawagon. Circ: 100.

297 SAU
AL-DA'WAH. Text in Arabic. w. **Document type:** *Consumer.* **Description:** Covers Islamic religious affairs.
Published by: Da'wah, P O Box 626, Riyadh, 11421, Saudi Arabia. TEL 966-2-4357249. Ed. Abdul Aziz Al Eissa.

297 LBY
AL-DA'WAH AL-ISLAMIYYAH. Text in Arabic, English, French. 1980. w.
Published by: World Islamic Call Society, P O Box 2682, Tripoli, Libya. TEL 218-21-4808461, TELEX 20407.

297.071 SAU ISSN 1319-2434
DA'WAT AL-HAQQ/CALL TO THE TRUTH. Text in Arabic. 1981. m. SAR 100, USD 27. **Description:** Publishes research on Islamic topics.
Published by: Muslim World League/Rabitat al-Alam al-Islami, P O Box 537-528, Makkah, Saudi Arabia. TEL 966-2-542-2733, FAX 966-2-544-2672, TELEX 440390. Circ: 1,000.

297.09 EGY ISSN 0342-1279
DT57
DEUTSCHES ARCHAEOLOGISCHES INSTITUT. ABTEILUNG KAIRO. MITTEILUNGEN. Text in German. 19??. a. EUR 84, USD 126 to institutions (effective 2012). **Document type:** *Monographic series, Academic/Scholarly.*
Indexed: A22, A30, A31, AIAP, B24, DIP, FR, IBR, IBZ, P30, SCOPUS, T02.
—BLDSC (5839.110000), IE, Ingenta, INIST. **CCC.**
Published by: Deutsches Archaeologisches Institut, Kairo/German Archaeological Institute - Cairo, 31, Abu el Feda, Zamalek, Cairo, 11211, Egypt. TEL 20-2-7351460, FAX 20-2-7370770, daik@soficom.com.eg, http://www.dainst.org/index_84_de.html.

AL-DIRASAT AL-ISLAMIYYAH. *see* LAW

DIRASAT. SHA'RIA AND LAW SCIENCES. *see* LAW

297.14 UAE
AL-DIYA'. Text in Arabic. 1978. q. **Description:** Covers topics related to the Qur'an, Hadith, and Sunna, as well as Islamic jurisprudence, literature, medicine, and interviews.
Published by: Da'irat al-Awqaf wal-Shu'un al-Islamiyyah/Department of Endowments and Islamic Affairs, P O Box 3135, Dubai, United Arab Emirates. TEL 695294. Ed. Isa Abdullah al-Mani' al-Hamadi. Circ: 10,000.

DOCUMENTA IRANICA ET ISLAMICA. *see* ASIAN STUDIES

297 NLD ISSN 1879-3657
▼ **E I REFERENCE GUIDES.** (Encyclopaedia of Islam) Text in English. 2009. irreg., latest vol.3, 2010. price varies. **Document type:** *Monographic series, Academic/Scholarly.*
Published by: Brill, PO Box 9000, Leiden, 2300 PA, Netherlands. TEL 31-71-5353500, FAX 31-71-5317532, cs@brill.nl.

297 IRN ISSN 1019-0775
ECHO OF ISLAM. Text in English. m. USD 35 in the Middle East; USD 40 in Europe; USD 45 in North America; USD 25 in Africa. **Document type:** *Magazine, Consumer.* **Description:** Contains current news of interest to the Muslim world. Covers political developments, Islamic uprisings, general news and views.
Indexed: PerIslam.
Published by: Islamic Thought Foundation, P O Box 14155-3899, Tehran, Iran. TEL 98-21-844092, FAX 98-21-898295, i.t.f@iran-itf.com. Ed. Morteza Shafi'y Shakib.

297 332 GBR
EDINBURGH GUIDES TO ISLAMIC FINANCE. Text in English. irreg. price varies. back issues avail. **Document type:** *Monographic series, Academic/Scholarly.*
Published by: Edinburgh University Press, 22 George Sq, Edinburgh, Scotland EH8 9LF, United Kingdom. TEL 44-131-6504218, FAX 44-131-6503286, journals@eup.ed.ac.uk.

700.48297 GBR
EDINBURGH STUDIES IN ISLAMIC ART. Text in English. irreg. price varies. back issues avail. **Document type:** *Monographic series, Academic/Scholarly.*
Published by: Edinburgh University Press, 22 George Sq, Edinburgh, Scotland EH8 9LF, United Kingdom. TEL 44-131-6504218, FAX 44-131-6503286, journals@eup.ed.ac.uk. Ed. Robert Hillenbrand.

ELAN; the guide to global muslim culture. *see* ETHNIC INTERESTS

297 USA ISSN 1557-5527
BP188.45
ELIXIR (NEW LEBANON). Text in English. 2005. s-a. **Document type:** *Magazine, Consumer.*
Published by: Sufi Order International, PO Box 480, New Lebanon, NY 12125. TEL 518-794-7834, secretariat@sufiorder.org, http://www.sufiorder.org.

297 230 ITA ISSN 1127-2252
ENCOUNTERS; documents for Muslim Christian understanding. Text in English. 1974. a. **Document type:** *Journal, Academic/Scholarly.* **Description:** Documents for Muslim-Christian understanding.
Published by: Pontificio Istituto di Studi Arabi e d'Islamistica (P I S A I), Viale di Trastevere 89, Rome, 00153, Italy. TEL 39-06-58392611, FAX 39-06-5882595, info@pisai.org, http://www.pisai.it.

297 GBR ISSN 1358-5770
BP172
➤ **ENCOUNTERS (LEICESTER);** journal of inter-cultural perspectives. Text in English. 1995. s-a. GBP 15 in Europe to institutions; GBP 20 elsewhere to institutions; GBP 5 per issue in Europe; GBP 7.50 per issue elsewhere (effective 2009). bk.rev. back issues avail. **Document type:** *Journal, Academic/Scholarly.* **Description:** Aims to provide a forum for a meticulous analysis and discussion of inter-religious dialogue, Islam and the West and Islamic resurgence.
Indexed: A21, AmHI, BrHumI, CA, H07, PCI, PerIslam, RI-1, S02, S03, SCOPUS, SOPODA, SociolAb, T02.
—IE, Ingenta.
Published by: Islamic Foundation, Markfield Conference Centre, Ratby Ln, Markfield, Leics LE67 9SY, United Kingdom. TEL 44-1530-244944, FAX 44-1530-244946, i.found@islamic-foundation.org.uk. Eds. Ataullah Siddiqui, Manazir Ahsan.

297 NLD ISSN 1875-9823
ENCYCLOPAEDIA ISLAMICA. Text in English. 2008. irreg., latest vol.3, 2011. price varies. **Document type:** *Monographic series, Academic/Scholarly.*
Related titles: Online - full text ed.: ISSN 1875-9831.
Published by: Brill, PO Box 9000, Leiden, 2300 PA, Netherlands. TEL 31-71-5353500, FAX 31-71-5317532, cs@brill.nl. Eds. Farhad Daftary, Wilferd Madelung.

297 NLD ISSN 1573-3912
ENCYCLOPAEDIA OF ISLAM ONLINE. Text in English. 2004. base vol. plus q. updates. EUR 2,420, USD 3,290 (effective 2010). **Document type:** *Database, Academic/Scholarly.*
Media: Online - full text. **Related titles:** French ed.: Encyclopedie de l'Islam en Ligne. ISSN 2210-5905. EUR 2,300, USD 3,130 (effective 2010).
Published by: Brill, PO Box 9000, Leiden, 2300 PA, Netherlands. TEL 31-71-5353500, FAX 31-71-5317532, cs@brill.nl, http://www.brill.nl.

297.07 NLD ISSN 1873-9830
DS37
ENCYCLOPAEDIA OF ISLAM THREE. Text in English. 2007. q. EUR 109, USD 153 per issue (effective 2011).
Related titles: Online - full text ed.: ISSN 1873-9849.
Indexed: IZBG.
Published by: Brill, PO Box 9000, Leiden, 2300 PA, Netherlands. TEL 31-71-5353500, FAX 31-71-5317532, cs@brill.nl. Eds. Denis Matringe, Everett Rowson, Gudrun Kraemer, John Nawas.

297 NLD ISSN 1875-3922
ENCYCLOPAEDIA OF THE QUR'AN ONLINE. Text in English. 200?. EUR 530, USD 720 (effective 2010). **Document type:** *Academic/Scholarly.*
Media: Online - full text.
Published by: Brill, PO Box 9000, Leiden, 2300 PA, Netherlands. TEL 31-71-5353500, FAX 31-71-5317532, cs@brill.nl.

ENCYCLOPAEDIA OF WOMEN AND ISLAMIC CULTURES. *see* WOMEN'S STUDIES

297 FRA ISSN 1769-5104
ESPRIT LIBRE MAGAZINE. Text in French. 2004. q. back issues avail. **Document type:** *Magazine, Consumer.*
Published by: Esprit Libre, 2 Rue Serge Gousseault, Beziers, 34500, France. TEL 33-6-10442508, libmag@voila.fr.

297 ITA ISSN 1722-943X
DS36.4
ETUDES ARABES. Text in Arabic, French. 1962. a. **Document type:** *Journal, Academic/Scholarly.*
Published by: Pontificio Istituto di Studi Arabi e d'Islamistica (P I S A I), Viale di Trastevere 89, Rome, 00153, Italy. TEL 39-06-58392611, FAX 39-06-5882595, info@pisai.org, http://www.pisai.it.

297 296 DEU ISSN 1863-9348
EX ORIENTE LUX; Rezeptionen und Exegesen als Traditionskritik. Text in German. 2003. irreg., latest vol.10, 2009. price varies. **Document type:** *Monographic series, Academic/Scholarly.*
Published by: Ergon Verlag, Keesburgstr 11, Wuerzburg, 97074, Germany. TEL 49-931-280084, FAX 49-931-282872, service@ergon-verlag.de, http://www.ergon-verlag.de.

297.14 PAK ISSN 0430-4055
BP1
FIKR-O-NAZAR. Text in Urdu. 1964. q. PKR 75, USD 20. adv. bk.rev. index. back issues avail. **Document type:** *Academic/Scholarly.* **Description:** Covers Islamic law, history, philosophy as well as other topics.
Published by: International Islamic University, Islamic Research Institute, Faisal Mosque Campus, P O Box 1243, Islamabad, 44000, Pakistan. TEL 92-51-850751, FAX 92-51-853360. Ed. Sahibzada Sajid Ur Rehman, Pub. Saeed Ahmad Shah.

297.87 USA ISSN 1090-7327
BP221.A1
THE FINAL CALL. Text in English. 1979. w. USD 45 domestic; USD 90 foreign (effective 2005). adv. **Document type:** *Newspaper, Consumer.* **Description:** Dedicated to the resurrection of the Black man and woman of America and the world.
Related titles: Online - full text ed.
Indexed: IIBP, PerIslam.
Published by: (Nation of Islam), Final Call Newspaper, 734 W 79th St, Chicago, IL 60620. TEL 773-602-1230, FAX 773-602-1013. Ed. James G Muhammad. Pub. Louis Farrakhan. **Subscr. to:** PO Box 79321, Atlanta, GA 30357-7321.

297 SAU
FIQH COUNCIL JOURNAL. Text in Arabic. 2/yr. USD 4 to individuals; USD 5 to institutions.
Published by: Muslim World League/Rabitat al-Alam al-Islami, P O Box 538, Makkah, Saudi Arabia. TEL 966-2-544-1622.

R

297 BGD
THE FORTNIGHTLY AHMADI. Text in Bengali. 1925. fortn. BDT 150; USD 100 foreign. adv. bk.rev. **Description:** Contains religious and moral articles.
Published by: Ahmadyya Art Press, 4 Bakshi Bazar Rd, Dhaka, 1211, Bangladesh. TEL 880-2-9662703, FAX 880-2-863414. Ed. Maqbul Ahmad Khan. Pub. M F K Molla. Adv. contact Abdul Awal Imran. Circ: 1,000 (paid).

297 DEU ISSN 0170-3285
FREIBURGER ISLAMSTUDIEN. Text in German. 1984. irreg., latest vol.23, 2005. price varies. **Document type:** *Monographic series, Academic/Scholarly.*
Published by: Franz Steiner Verlag GmbH, Birkenwaldstr 44, Stuttgart, 70191, Germany. TEL 49-711-25820, FAX 49-711-2582290, service@steiner-verlag.de, http://www.steiner-verlag.de.

297 USA ISSN 1556-8911
DS35.6
GLOBAL STUDIES: ISLAM AND THE MUSLIM WORLD. Text in English. 2005. biennial. **Document type:** *Magazine, Consumer.*
Published by: McGraw-Hill, Contemporary Learning Series (Subsidiary of: McGraw-Hill Companies, Inc.), 1221 Ave of the Americas, New York, NY 10020. TEL 212-904-2000, FAX 212-512-2000, customer.service@mcgraw-hill.com, http://www.mhhe.com/cls/.

297.5 DEU
GLOBALER LOKALER ISLAM. Text in German. 1998. irreg., latest vol.28, 2011. price varies. **Document type:** *Monographic series, Academic/Scholarly.*
Published by: Transcript, Muehlenstr 47, Bielefeld, 33607, Germany. TEL 49-521-63454, FAX 49-521-61040, live@transcript-verlag.de.

297 SAU
HAJJ. Text in Arabic, English. 1947. m. **Document type:** *Government.*
Published by: Ministry of Pilgrimage Affairs and Awqaf/Wizarat Shu'un al-Hajj wal-Awqaf, Sharia Omar bin al-Khattab, Riyadh, 11183, Saudi Arabia. TEL 966-1-4022200, TELEX 401603. Ed. Abdullah Bin Abdul Muttaleb Bogas.

297 PAK
HAMDARD FOUNDATION. REPORT. Text in English. 1980. biennial. free. **Document type:** *Corporate.*
Published by: Hamdard Foundation, Nazimabad No.3, Karachi, 74600, Pakistan. TEL 92-21-6616001, FAX 92-21-6611755. Circ: 2,000.

297 PAK ISSN 0250-7196
BP1
HAMDARD ISLAMICUS. Text in English. 1978. q. PKR 400, USD 60 (effective 2000). bk.rev. **Document type:** *Journal, Academic/Scholarly.*
Related titles: CD-ROM ed.
Indexed: A21, A22, AMR, BAS, CA, ExtraMED, HistAb, M10, MEA&I, MLA-IB, P30, PerIslam, RI-1, RI-2, T02.
—Ingenta.
Published by: Hamdard Foundation, Nazimabad No.3, Karachi, 74600, Pakistan. TEL 92-21-6616001, FAX 92-21-6611755. Ed. Sadia Rashid. Circ: 2,000.

297.57 NGA
AL-HAQQ; a periodic Islamic newspaper. Text in English. 1991 (vol.2, no.3). bi-m. **Document type:** *Newspaper.*
Indexed: PerIslam.
Published by: Hizbullah Movement of Nigeria, Marina, PO Box 5236, Lagos, Nigeria.

297.14 UAE
AL-HAQQ - SHARI'AH WA-QANUN. Text in Arabic. 1982. a. per issue exchange basis. **Document type:** *Academic/Scholarly.* **Description:** Focuses on Islamic jurisprudence and legal research, court rulings, and society activities.
Published by: Jam'iyat al-Huquqiyyin/Jurists' Association, PO Box 2233, Sharjah, United Arab Emirates. TEL 971-6-5354888, FAX 971-6-5542323, info@jurists-uae.com, http://jurists-uae.com. Ed. Dr. Mohamed A. Alroken. Circ: 1,000.

HARVARD MIDDLE EASTERN AND ISLAMIC REVIEW (ONLINE). *see* HISTORY—History Of The Near East

297 IND
BP1
➤ **HENRY MARTYN INSTITUTE. JOURNAL.** Abbreviated title: J H M I. Text in English. 1930-1986; resumed 1991. s-a. bk.rev. index. **Document type:** *Journal, Academic/Scholarly.* **Description:** Aims to promote inter-religious understanding with a special focus on the study of Islam. It also seeks to encourage reconciliation between people of different faiths within an overall framework of peace and justice.
Former titles (until 1998): Henry Martyn Institute of Islamic Studies. Bulletin (0970-6445); (until 1985): Christian Institute of Islamic Studies. Bulletin (0970-4698); (until 1978): Al-Basheer (0970-7107); (until 1972): Christian Institutes of Islamic Studies Bulletin (0009-5397); (until 1967): Henry Martyn Institute of Islamic Studies. Bulletin; (until 1960): Henry Martyn School of Islamic Studies. Bulletin; (until 19??): All-India Missionaries to Muslims League. News and Notes
Indexed: A21, AMR, I14, PerIslam, RI-1, RI-2.
Published by: Henry Martyn Institute, International Centre for Research, Interfaith Relations and Reconciliation, 6-3-128/1, Beside National Police Academy, Shivarampally, Hyderabad, 500 052, India. TEL 91-40-24014258, FAX 91-40-24014565, info@hmiindia.com.

297.14 BHR
AL-HIDAYAH. Text in Arabic. 1978. m.
Published by: Ministry of Justice and Islamic Affairs, Diplomatic Area, PO Box 450, Manama, Bahrain. TEL 531333. Ed. Abd al-Rahman bin Muhammad Rashid al-Khalifa.

297 IDN ISSN 0854-2414
AL-HIKMAH. Text in Indonesian. 1991 (vol.4). q.
Indexed: PerIslam.
Published by: Yayasan Mutthahhari, Jalan Kampus III 4, Bandung, 40283, Indonesia.

THE HISTORY OF CHRISTIAN-MUSLIM RELATIONS. *see* RELIGIONS AND THEOLOGY

297 HKG
HONG KONG MUSLIM HERALD. Text in English. 1992 (vol.14). m.
Indexed: PerIslam.
Address: PO Box 6488, G.P.O., Hong Kong, Hong Kong.

297 CMR
AL HOUDA; islamic cultural review. Text in French. q.
Published by: Houda, PO Box 1638, Yaounde, Cameroon. Ed. Ndam Njoya Adamou.

297.38 JOR
HUDA AL-ISLAM. Text in Arabic. 1956. m.
Published by: Ministry of Awqaf and Islamic Affairs, P O Box 659, Amman, Jordan. TEL 666141, TELEX 21559. Ed. Ahmad Muhammad Hulayyel.

297 USA
HUDAA. Text in English. m. USD 12 (effective 2001). back issues avail. **Document type:** *Magazine, Consumer.*
Published by: The Qur'an and Sunnah Society, PO Box 311071, Jamaica, NY 11431. TEL 718-262-0329, FAX 718-206-0804, info@qss.org.

297 NLD
I S I M DISSERTATIONS. Text in English. irreg. price varies. **Document type:** *Monographic series, Academic/Scholarly.*
Published by: (Universiteit van Amsterdam), International Institute for the Study of Islam in the Modern World, PO Box 11089, Leiden, 2301 EB, Netherlands. TEL 31-71-5277905, FAX 31-71-5277906, info@isim.nl, http://www.isim.nl.

297 NLD ISSN 1568-8313
I S I M PAPERS. Text in English. 2000. irreg. price varies. **Document type:** *Monographic series, Academic/Scholarly.*
Published by: (Universiteit van Amsterdam), International Institute for the Study of Islam in the Modern World, PO Box 11089, Leiden, 2301 EB, Netherlands. TEL 31-71-5277905, FAX 31-71-5277906, info@isim.nl, http://www.isim.nl.

ICONOGRAPHY OF RELIGIONS. SECTION 22, ISLAM. *see* ART

297.5 USA ISSN 1942-244X
ILLUME MAGAZINE. Text in English. 2006. bi-m. USD 24 domestic; USD 28 in Canada; USD 40 elsewhere (effective 2008). adv. **Document type:** *Magazine, Consumer.* **Description:** Aims to enlighten non-Muslims about Islam though scholarly articles, discourses, commentaries on current affairs, coverage of community events and articles on personal reflection.
Published by: Illume Media, 6167 Jarvis Ave #243, Newark, CA 94560. TEL 510-386-1171. Ed. Yahsmin Bobo. adv.: page USD 350.

297 ZAF ISSN 0258-932X
DS36.855
➤ **AL-ILM.** Text in English. 1981. a. bk.rev. **Document type:** *Journal, Academic/Scholarly.*
Indexed: ISAP, PerIslam.
Published by: University of KwaZulu-Natal, King George V Avenue, Glenwood, Durban, KwaZulu-Natal 4041, South Africa. TEL 27-31-2602212, http://www.ukzn.ac.za. Ed. S Salman Nadvi. Circ: 400.

➤ **INDEX ISLAMICUS**; a bibliography of publications on Islam and the Muslim world since 1906. *see* ETHNIC INTERESTS—Abstracting, Bibliographies, Statistics

297 NLD ISSN 1876-2123
▼ **INDEX ISLAMICUS. SUPPLEMENTS.** Text in English. 2010. a. **Document type:** *Monographic series, Academic/Scholarly.*
Related titles: ◆ Supplement to: Index Islamicus. ISSN 1360-0982.
Published by: Brill, PO Box 9000, Leiden, 2300 PA, Netherlands. TEL 31-71-5353500, FAX 31-71-5317532, cs@brill.nl, http://www.brill.nl.

297.57 USA
INDIAN MUSLIM RELIEF COMMITTEE. ANNUAL REPORT. Text in English. 1980. a. **Document type:** *Newsletter, Consumer.* **Description:** Documents plight of under-privileged minority communities with a special emphasis on Indian muslims.
Published by: Indian Muslim Relief Committee, 1000 San Antonio Rd, Palo Alto, CA 94303-4616. TEL 650-856-0440, FAX 650-856-0444, info@imrc.ws, http://www.imrc.ws. Ed. Manzoor Ghori.

297 AUS
INSIGHT (SYDNEY, 1986) (ONLINE). Text in English. 1986. irreg. **Document type:** *Journal, Trade.* **Description:** Covers a particular topic in each issue dealing with the clarification of concepts and development of ideas relevant to operational Islam in contemporary society.
Formerly (until Nov.1996): Insight (Print) (1321-4411)
Media: Online - full content.
Published by: Islamic Foundation for Education and Welfare, Bonnyrigg, PO Box 111, Sydney, NSW 2177, Australia. TEL 61-2-98238208, FAX 61-2-98233626.

297 001.3 MYS ISSN 0128-4878
BP1 CODEN: IDISE5
➤ **INTELLECTUAL DISCOURSE.** Text in English. 1993. s-a. MYR 30 domestic to individuals; USD 20 foreign to individuals; MYR 60 domestic to institutions; USD 35 foreign to institutions. bk.rev. **Document type:** *Journal, Academic/Scholarly.* **Description:** Covers the history, geography, political science, economics, anthropology, sociology, law, literature, religion, philosophy, international relations, environmental and developmental issues, as well as ethical questions related to Islam and the Muslim world.
Indexed: A01, CA, I14, L04, LISTA, SociolAb, T02.
Published by: (International Islamic University Malaysia, Kulliyah of Islamic Revealed Knowledge and Human Sciences), International Islamic University Malaysia, Research Centre, Jalan Gambak, Kuala Lumpur, 53100, Malaysia. TEL 60-3-20565010, FAX 60-3-20564862, rescentre@iiu.edu.my. Ed. Abdul Rashid Moten.

297.6 IND
INTERACTION. Text in English. s-a. **Document type:** *Newsletter, Consumer.* **Description:** Contains news, activities, and notes of the institute.
Indexed: BAS, Inspec.
Published by: Henry Martyn Institute, International Centre for Research, Interfaith Relations and Reconciliation, PO Box 153, Hyderabad, Andhra Pradesh 500 001, India. hmipublications@gmail.com.

297 PAK
IQRA. Text in Urdu. w. adv.
Indexed: PerIslam.
Published by: Independent Newspapers Corp. Pvt. Ltd., Printing House, I.I. Chundrigar Rd., P O Box 32, Karachi, (Sindh) 74200, Pakistan. FAX 92-21-2636066, subscription@akhbar-e-jehan.com. Ed., Pub. Mir Shakil-ur-Rahman. R&P Shahrukh Hasan TEL 92-21-2629523. Adv. contact Sarmad Ali.

AL-IQTISAD AL-ISLAMI/ISLAMIC ECONOMY. *see* BUSINESS AND ECONOMICS—Economic Situation And Conditions

297.57 320.082 GBR ISSN 1746-8728
DS251
IRAN BULLETIN - MIDDLE EAST FORUM; a political journal in defense of democracy and socialism. Variant title: Iran Bulletin - Middle East Left Forum. Text in English. 1986. q. GBP 10 domestic to individuals; EUR 18, USD 18 in Europe to individuals; EUR 20 elsewhere to individuals; USD 20 elsewhere to institutions; GBP 15 domestic to institutions; EUR 25, USD 25 in Europe to institutions; EUR 30, USD 30 elsewhere to institutions (effective 2009). bk.rev. back issues avail. **Document type:** *Journal, Academic/Scholarly.*
Former titles (until 2003): Iran Bulletin (0969-7462); (until 1993): International Rah e Kargar (0987-8343)
Indexed: LeftInd, M10, RASB.
Published by: BM Iran Bulletin, London, WC1N 3XX, United Kingdom. TEL 44-20-8961-0925. Eds. Ardeshir Mehrdad, Mehdi Kia, Yassamine Mather.

297.77 UAE
ISHRAQAT JEEL. Text in Arabic. 1984. a. **Description:** Covers topics relating to Islamic education for girls.
Published by: Madrasat al-Qadisiyyah al-I'dadiyyah al-Thanawiyyah lil-Banat, Jama'at al-Tarbiyah al-Islamiyyah, PO Box 5246, Abu Dhabi, United Arab Emirates. TEL 477606. Circ: 500.

297.57 UAE
AL-ISLAH/REFORM. Text in Arabic. 1978. bi-m. adv. **Document type:** *Academic/Scholarly.* **Description:** Presents an Islamic viewpoint on topics of interest to Muslims, including social, political, and cultural issues.
Published by: Jam'iyat al-Islah wal-Tawjih al-Ijtima'i/Society of Social Reform and Guidance, PO Box 4663, Dubai, United Arab Emirates. TEL 971-4-665962, FAX 971-4-662071. Ed. Ali Said Bin Essa. Adv. contact Mohammed Ali. color page AED 3,000. Circ: 15,000.

297 REU ISSN 0151-7163
BP1
AL ISLAM. Text in French. 1975. q.
Indexed: SPPI.
Published by: Centre Islamique de la Reunion, BP 437, Saint Pierre, Cedex 97459, Reunion. TEL 262-25-45-43, FAX 262-35-58-23. Ed. A Saeed Ingar. Circ: 1,200.

297 PAK
AL-ISLAM. Text in Urdu. 1973. w. PKR 400. adv. bk.rev.
Indexed: PerIslam.
Published by: Islam, c/o Jamiat Ahl-e-Hadith, 106 Ravi Rd., Lahore, Pakistan. FAX 042-54072, TELEX 46426 KARAM PK. Ed. Bashir Ansari. Circ: 4,000 (controlled).

297 DEU ISSN 0021-1818
DS36
DER ISLAM; Zeitschrift fuer Geschichte und Kultur des Islamischen Orients. Text in English, German, French. 1910. s-a. EUR 197, USD 296 to institutions; EUR 227, USD 341 combined subscription to institutions (print & online eds.) (effective 2012). adv. bk.rev. bibl.; illus. reprint service avail. from SCH. **Document type:** *Journal, Academic/Scholarly.*
Related titles: Online - full text ed.: ISSN 1613-0928. EUR 197, USD 296 to institutions (effective 2012); ◆ Supplement(s): Studien zur Geschichte und Kultur des Islamischen Orients. ISSN 1862-1295.
Indexed: A20, A21, A22, A26, ASCA, ArtHuCI, BAS, BibInd, BibLing, CurCont, DIP, E01, EI, ESPM, FR, I02, I05, I14, IBR, IBSS, IBZ, IPB, M08, M10, MLA, MLA-IB, NumL, P02, P10, P28, P48, P53, P54, PCI, PQC, RASB, RI-1, RI-2, RILM, SCOPUS, SSciA, W07.
—BLDSC (4583.013000), IE, Infotrieve, Ingenta, INIST. **CCC.**
Published by: Walter de Gruyter GmbH & Co. KG, Genthiner Str 13, Berlin, 10785, Germany. TEL 49-30-260050, FAX 49-30-26005251, info@degruyter.com. Ed. Lawrence Conrad. Adv. contact Dietlind Makswitat TEL 49-30-260050. Circ: 500 (paid and controlled).

297.283 GBR ISSN 0959-6410
BP172 CODEN: ICMREF
➤ **ISLAM AND CHRISTIAN - MUSLIM RELATIONS.** Abbreviated title: I C M R. Text in English. 1983. q. GBP 571 combined subscription in United Kingdom to institutions (print & online eds.); EUR 756, USD 947 combined subscription to institutions (print & online eds.) (effective 2012). adv. bk.rev. back issues avail.; reprint service avail. from PSC. **Document type:** *Journal, Academic/Scholarly.* **Description:** Deals with islam and christian-muslim relations worldwide, especially historical, regional or sociological themes.
Formerly (until 1990): Bulletin on Islam and Christian-Muslim Relations in Africa (0264-1356)
Related titles: Microfiche ed.; Online - full text ed.: ISSN 1469-9311. GBP 514 in United Kingdom to institutions; EUR 680, USD 853 to institutions (effective 2012) (from IngentaConnect).
Indexed: A01, A03, A08, A20, A21, A22, AmHI, ArtHuCI, BibInd, BibLing, BrHumI, CA, CCME, CurCont, DIP, E01, FR, H07, I02, I08, I13, I14, IBR, IBSS, IBZ, M10, MLA-IB, P10, P26, P28, P34, P42, P48, P53, P54, PAIS, PCI, PQC, PSA, PerIslam, R&TA, RI-1, RI-2, S02, S03, S11, SCOPUS, SOPODA, SociolAb, T02, W07.
—IE, Infotrieve, Ingenta, INIST. **CCC.**
Published by: (Centre for the Study of Islam and Christian-Muslim Relations), Routledge (Subsidiary of: Taylor & Francis Group), 4 Park Sq, Milton Park, Abingdon, Oxon OX14 4RN, United Kingdom. TEL 44-20-70176000, FAX 44-20-70176336, subscriptions@tandf.co.uk, http://www.routledge.com. Ed. David Thomas TEL 44-121-4158373. Adv. contact Linda Hann TEL 44-1344-779945. **Subscr. to:** Taylor & Francis Ltd., Journals Customer Service, Sheepen Pl, Colchester, Essex CO3 3LP, United Kingdom. TEL 44-20-70175544, FAX 44-20-70175198.

297.5 GBR ISSN 2041-871X
➤ **ISLAM AND CIVILISATIONAL RENEWAL**; a journal devoted to contemporary issues and policy research. Abbreviated title: I C R. Text in English. 2008. q. GBP 230, USD 380, EUR 270 combined subscription to institutions (print & online eds.); GBP 70, USD 115, EUR 80 combined subscription per issue to institutions (print & online eds.) (effective 2010). back issues avail. **Document type:** *Journal, Academic/Scholarly.* **Description:** Aims to promote advanced research on the contribution of Muslims to science and culture.
Formerly (until 2009): I A I S Journal of Civilisation Studies
Related titles: Online - full text ed.: ISSN 2041-8728. GBP 180, USD 300, EUR 210 to institutions; GBP 50, USD 85, EUR 60 per issue to institutions (effective 2010).
Published by: (International Institute of Advanced Islamic Studies Malaysia MYS), Pluto Journals, c/o Marston Book Services Ltd, PO Box 269, Abingdon, Oxfordshire OX14 4YN, United Kingdom. TEL 44-1235-465500, subscriptions@marston.co.uk. Ed. Mohammad Hashim Kamali.

297 IND ISSN 0973-2802
BP173.25
➤ **ISLAM AND MUSLIM SOCIETIES**; a social science journal. Text in English. 2005. s-a. **Document type:** *Journal, Academic/Scholarly.* **Description:** Provides a forum for scholars across the disciplines of sociology/ social anthropology, economics, history, political science, law, philosophy, and other related streams and provides open space for research and dialogue on Islam (except theological debates/ issues) and Muslim societies across the globe.
—BLDSC (4583.016500).
Published by: Serials Publications, 4830/24, Ansari Rd, Darya Ganj, New Delhi, 110 002, India. TEL 91-11-23245225, FAX 91-11-23272135, serialspublications.india@gmail.com, http://www.serialspublications.com/.

297 500 CAN ISSN 1703-7603
BP190.5.S3
➤ **ISLAM & SCIENCE.** Text in English. 2003. s-a. CAD 125 combined subscription domestic to institutions (print & online eds.); USD 120 combined subscription in United States to institutions (print & online eds.); USD 130 combined subscription elsewhere to institutions (print & online eds.) (effective 2012). bk.rev.; Website rev. index. back issues avail. **Document type:** *Journal, Academic/Scholarly.* **Description:** Explores, from Islamic perspectives, philosophical and religious implications of data that originate in the physical, biological and social sciences. Also publishes articles that enhance our understanding of the Islamic intellectual tradition with special emphasis on the Islamic scientific tradition.
Related titles: Online - full text ed.: ISSN 1703-762X.
Indexed: A01, CA, DIP, GSS&RPL, IBR, IBZ, M10, PQC, T02.
Published by: Center for Islam and Science, 349-52252 Range Rd 215, Sherwood Park, AB T8E 1B7, Canada. TEL 780-922-0927, FAX 780-922-0926. Ed. Dr. Muzaffar Iqbal.

297 IND ISSN 0021-1826
ISLAM AND THE MODERN AGE. Text in English. 1970. q. bk.rev. reprints avail. **Document type:** *Journal, Academic/Scholarly.*
Related titles: Urdu ed.: Islam Aur Asr-i-Jadeed.
Indexed: A22, AMR, BAS, I14, M10.
—BLDSC (4583.015000), IE, Infotrieve.
Published by: Zakir Husain Institute of Islamic Studies, Jamia Millia Islamia, Jamia Nagar, New Delhi, 110 025, India. TEL 91-11-26983578, 91-11-26910258, http://jmi.nic.in/OtherInstitutes/islamic.htm.

297 NLD ISSN 1876-3855
➤ **ISLAM ARASTIRMALARI.** Variant title: Journal of Islamic Research. Text in English, Arabic. 2008. s-a. **Document type:** *Journal, Academic/Scholarly.*
Published by: Islamitische Universiteit van Europa/Islamic University of Europe, Statenweg 300, Rotterdam, 3033 JA, Netherlands. TEL 31-10-4710026, FAX 31-10-4705855, rotterdam@iueurope.com, http://www.iueurope.com. Ed. Halit Unal.

297 TUR ISSN 1301-3289
BP1
ISLAM ARASTIRMALARI DERGISI/TURKISH JOURNAL OF ISLAMIC STUDIES. Text in Arabic, English, Turkish; Summaries in English. 1953. q. bk.rev. illus. **Document type:** *Journal, Academic/Scholarly.*
Formerly (until 1997): Islam Tetkikleri Enstitusu Dergisi
Related titles: Online - full text ed.
Indexed: I14, MLA-IB.
Published by: Turkiye Diyanet Vakfi, Islam Arastirmalari Merkezi, Icadiye Baglarbasi caddesi No 40, Uskudar, Istanbul, 34662, Turkey. TEL 90-216-4740850, FAX 90-216-4740874, isam@isam.org.tr. Ed. Bekir Kutukoglu. Circ: 1,000.

297 IRN ISSN 1019-0813
ISLAM CAGRISI. Text in Turkish. 1990 (no.69). m. USD 25 in the Middle East; USD 35 in Europe; USD 40 in North America.
Published by: Islamic Thought Foundation, P O Box 1415-3899, Teheran, Iran.

297 NLD ISSN 1570-3754
ISLAM IN AFRICA. Text in English. 2003. irreg., latest vol.9, 2008. price varies. **Document type:** *Monographic series, Academic/Scholarly.* **Description:** Presents issues of religious and intellectual traditions, social significance and organization, and other aspects of the Islamic presence in Africa.
Indexed: IZBG.
Published by: Brill, PO Box 9000, Leiden, 2300 PA, Netherlands. TEL 31-71-5353500, FAX 31-71-5317532, cs@brill.nl.

297 MAR ISSN 0851-1128
DS35.3
ISLAM TODAY/ISLAM AUJOURD'HUI. Text in Arabic, English, French. 1983. 2/yr. USD 6.
Indexed: PerIslam.
Address: B P 755, Rabat, Morocco. FAX 002127, TELEX 31845M. Ed. Abdulaziz Bin Othman Altwaijri. Circ: 15,000.

297.283 DEU ISSN 1616-8917
BP172
➤ **ISLAM UND CHRISTLICHER GLAUBE/ISLAM AND CHRISTIANITY.** Text and summaries in German, English. 2001. 2/yr. back issues avail. **Document type:** *Journal, Academic/Scholarly.*
Published by: (Institut fuer Islamfragen), Verlag fuer Theologie und Religionswissenschaft, Gogolstr 33, Nuernberg, 90475, Germany. TEL 49-911-831169, FAX 49-322-23760072, info@vtr-online.de, http://www.vtr-online.de. Pub. Thomas Mayer. Circ: 400 (paid and controlled).

297.14 DEU ISSN 1619-988X
ISLAM UND RECHT. Text in German. 2003. irreg., latest vol.7, 2010. price varies. **Document type:** *Monographic series, Academic/Scholarly.*
Published by: Peter Lang GmbH (Subsidiary of: Peter Lang Publishing Group), Eschborner Landstr 42-50, Frankfurt Am Main, 60489, Germany. TEL 49-69-7807050, FAX 49-69-78070550, zentrale.frankfurt@peterlang.com. Ed. Janbernd Oebbecke.

297 IRN
ISLAMI BAYRLAYK. Text in Azerbaijani. 1990. w.
Published by: Hawzah-i Hunari Sazman-i Tablighat-i Islami, 213 Summaiyah St., P O Box 1677-15815, Teheran, Iran.

297 USA
ISLAMIC AFFAIRS. Text mainly in English; Text occasionally in Arabic. 1969. w. USD 25. adv. bk.rev. charts; illus. **Document type:** *Newspaper.*
Formerly (until 1992): Action (New York) (0001-7388)
Published by: (National Council on Islamic Affairs), Islamic Affairs, PO Box 1028, Long Beach, NY 11561-0962. TEL 212-972-0460, FAX 212-682-1405. Ed. Dr. M T Mehdi. Adv. contact Ghazi Khankan. Circ: 15,000.

297 332.153 UAE ISSN 1319-1616
ISLAMIC ECONOMIC STUDIES. Text in English. a. price varies. reprints avail. **Document type:** *Monographic series, Academic/Scholarly.* **Description:** Features articles, reviews about Islamic economy. Includes references and citations.
Indexed: BAS, EconLit, JEL.
Published by: Islamic Research and Training Institute, Islamic Development Bank, P O Box 9201, Jeddah, 9201, United Arab Emirates. TEL 6361400, FAX 6378927, TELEX 601407-601137 ISDB SJ.

297.77 PAK ISSN 0578-8056
ISLAMIC EDUCATION. Text in English. 1968. bi-m. PKR 12, USD 2.50. adv. bk.rev. bibl.
Indexed: CPE.
Published by: All-Pakistan Islamic Education Congress, 7 Friends Colony, Multan Rd., Lahore, Pakistan. Ed. Muzaffar Hussain. Circ: 500.

297 GBR ISSN 1460-0676
ISLAMIC FOUNDATION NEWSLETTER. Text in English. 1992 (May). irreg. free (effective 2009). back issues avail. **Document type:** *Newsletter, Academic/Scholarly.* **Description:** Provides an insight into the Foundation's current activities and projects, a brief description of the Foundation's publications, new courses organized and other developments both inside the organization and outside in the community.
Related titles: Online - full text ed.
Published by: Islamic Foundation, Markfield Conference Centre, Ratby Ln, Markfield, Leics LE67 9SY, United Kingdom. TEL 44-1530-244944, FAX 44-1530-244946, i.found@islamic-foundation.org.uk.

297 USA
THE ISLAMIC HERALD; news from an Islamic perspective. Text in English. irreg. **Document type:** *Newspaper, Consumer.* **Description:** Covers various issue involving Islam with editorial articles and articles on current events.
Media: Online - full content.
Published by: The Islamic Herald herald@ais.org. Ed. Shabier Raffee.

297.09 NLD ISSN 0929-2403
➤ **ISLAMIC HISTORY AND CIVILIZATION.** Text in English, French, German. 1991. irreg., latest vol.73, 2008. price varies. back issues avail. **Document type:** *Monographic series, Academic/Scholarly.* **Description:** Publishes scholarly studies of topics relating to the history and culture of the Islamic world, including studies of institutions, historical figures, religious orders, architecture.
Formerly (until vol.4, 1994): Arab History and Civilization (0925-2908)
Indexed: IZBG.
—CCC.
Published by: Brill, PO Box 9000, Leiden, 2300 PA, Netherlands. TEL 31-71-5353500, FAX 31-71-5317532, cs@brill.nl, http://www.brill.nl. Eds. Sebastian Guenther, Wadad Kadi. R&P Elizabeth Venekamp. **Dist. in N. America by:** Brill, PO Box 605, Herndon, VA 20172-0605. TEL 703-661-1585, 800-337-9255, FAX 703-661-1501, cs@brillusa.com; **Dist. by:** Turpin Distribution Services Ltd., Pegasus Dr, Stratton Business Park, Biggleswade, Bedfordshire SG18 8QB, United Kingdom. TEL 44-1767-604954, FAX 44-1767-601640, custserv@turpin-distribution.com, http://www.turpin-distribution.com/.

297 USA ISSN 8756-2367
BP1 CODEN: ISHOFQ
ISLAMIC HORIZONS. Text in English. 1963. bi-m. USD 24 domestic to non-members; USD 29.95 in Canada to non-members; USD 60 elsewhere to non-members; USD 4 newsstand/cover; free to members (effective 2009). adv. software rev.; bk.rev. stat. 64 p./no.; back issues avail. **Document type:** *Magazine, Trade.* **Description:** Features significant articles on Muslim religion.
Incorporates (in 1995): I S N A Matters; Formerly (until 1976): M S A News
Related titles: Online - full text ed.: free (effective 2009).
Indexed: B04, BRD, ENW, P28, P48, P53, P54, PQC, PerIslam, R03, RGAb, RGPR, W03, W05.
—CIS, Ingenta.
Published by: Islamic Society of North America, PO Box 38, Plainfield, IN 46168. TEL 317-839-8157, FAX 317-839-1840. Ed., Adv. contact Omer Bin Abdallah TEL 703-742-8108. B&W page USD 1,450, color page USD 1,850; trim 8.125 x 10.875. Circ: 60,000.

297.14 NLD ISSN 0928-9380
K9
➤ **ISLAMIC LAW AND SOCIETY.** Text in English, French, German. 1994. 3/yr. EUR 353, USD 494 to institutions; EUR 385, USD 539 combined subscription to institutions (print & online eds.) (effective 2012). bk.rev. abstr.; bibl. index. back issues avail.; reprint service avail. from PSC,WSH. **Document type:** *Journal, Academic/Scholarly.* **Description:** Forum for comparative research in the field of Islamic law in Muslim and non-Muslim countries, covering both theory and practice, from its emergence up to the present. Discusses historical, juridical and social-scientific perspectives on Islamic law, including current legal issues and legislation.
Related titles: Online - full text ed.: ISSN 1568-5195. EUR 321, USD 449 to institutions (effective 2012) (from IngentaConnect).
Indexed: A01, A03, A08, A22, B07, CA, CCME, DIP, E01, FLP, I02, I14, IBR, IBSS, IBZ, IZBG, L03, M10, P42, PCI, PSA, S02, S03, SCOPUS, SociolAb, T02.
—IE, Infotrieve, Ingenta. **CCC.**
Published by: Brill, PO Box 9000, Leiden, 2300 PA, Netherlands. TEL 31-71-5353500, FAX 31-71-5317532, cs@brill.nl. Ed. David S Powers. **Dist. by:** Turpin Distribution Services Ltd., Pegasus Dr, Stratton Business Park, Biggleswade, Bedfordshire SG18 8QB, United Kingdom. TEL 44-1767-604954, FAX 44-1767-601640, custserv@turpin-distribution.com, http://www.turpin-distribution.com/.

➤ **ISLAMIC LEGAL STUDIES PROGRAM/BARNAMAJ DIRASAT AL-FIQH AL-ISLAMI.** *see* LAW—Civil Law

297 NLD ISSN 1877-9964
▼ **ISLAMIC MANUSCRIPTS AND BOOKS.** Text in English. 2010. irreg., latest vol.2, 2010. price varies. **Document type:** *Monographic series, Academic/Scholarly.*
Published by: Brill, PO Box 9000, Leiden, 2300 PA, Netherlands. TEL 31-71-5353500, FAX 31-71-5317532, cs@brill.nl. Ed. Arnoud Vrolijk.

297 USA ISSN 2159-9246
▼ **THE ISLAMIC MONTHLY**; politics, culture, society. Text in English. 2011. s-a. USD 9.99 per issue (effective 2011). adv. **Document type:** *Magazine, Consumer.* **Description:** Discusses issues and concerns related to Muslims in the modern world.
Related titles: Online - full text ed.: ISSN 2159-9254. free (effective 2011).
Published by: Amina Chaudary, Ed., PO Box 390032, Cambridge, MA 02139. amina@theislamicmonthly.com.

297 USA ISSN 1946-8946
➤ **ISLAMIC PERSPECTIVE**; quarterly journal for islamic culture, thought and civilization. Text in English. 2008. q. USD 19.99 per issue (effective 2009). back issues avail. **Document type:** *Journal, Academic/Scholarly.* **Description:** Aims to prepare the way for scientific and critical discussion about international cultural and reflective issues from islam or muslims point of view.
Published by: (Islamic Perspective Center for International Studies IRN), Xlibris Corporation, 1663 Liberty Dr, Ste 200, Bloomington, IN 47403. TEL 610-915-5214, 888-795-4274, FAX 610-915-0294, info@xlibris.com, http://www2.xlibris.com. Ed. Seyed Javad Miri.

297 NLD ISSN 0169-8729
➤ **ISLAMIC PHILOSOPHY, THEOLOGY AND SCIENCE**; texts and studies. Text in English, French, German. 1986. irreg., latest vol.78, 2008. price varies. back issues avail. **Document type:** *Monographic series, Academic/Scholarly.* **Description:** Publishes translations of medieval Islamic philosophical, theological scientific and medical texts, with commentary, as well as scholarly studies of aspects of Islamic philosophy, literature and ethics.
Indexed: CCMJ, IZBG, MSN, MathR.
—BLDSC (4583.025950).
Published by: Brill, PO Box 9000, Leiden, 2300 PA, Netherlands. TEL 31-71-5353500, FAX 31-71-5317532, cs@brill.nl, http://www.brill.nl. Ed. Hans Daiber. R&P Elizabeth Venekamp. **Dist. in N. America by:** Brill, PO Box 605, Herndon, VA 20172-0605. TEL 703-661-1585, 800-337-9255, FAX 703-661-1501, cs@brillusa.com; **Dist. by:** Turpin Distribution Services Ltd., Pegasus Dr, Stratton Business Park, Biggleswade, Bedfordshire SG18 8QB, United Kingdom. TEL 44-1767-604954, FAX 44-1767-601640, custserv@turpin-distribution.com, http://www.turpin-distribution.com/.

297 GBR ISSN 0021-1842
D198
THE ISLAMIC QUARTERLY; a review of Islamic culture. Text in English, Arabic. 1954. q. GBP 27.50 in Europe; GBP 32.50 elsewhere (effective 2009). bk.rev. back issues avail. **Document type:** *Journal, Academic/Scholarly.* **Description:** Contains articles relating to Islamic law, culture and arts.
Indexed: A21, A22, CA, FR, HistAb, I14, IBR, IBZ, M10, MLA-IB, P30, PCI, PerIslam, RI-1, RI-2, T02.
—BLDSC (4583.030000), IE, Infotrieve, Ingenta, INIST.
Published by: Islamic Cultural Centre, 146 Park Rd, London, NW8 7RG, United Kingdom. TEL 44-207-7252213, FAX 44-207-7240493, info@iccuk.org. Ed. Ahmad Al-Dubayan.

297 PAK ISSN 0578-8072
BP1
ISLAMIC STUDIES. Text in English. 1962. q. PKR 100, USD 30. adv. bk.rev. index. back issues avail.; reprints avail. **Document type:** *Journal, Academic/Scholarly.* **Description:** Covers Islamic law, history, political theory and philosophy as well as other topics.
Indexed: A21, A22, AMR, BAS, BibLing, DIP, FR, I02, I14, IBR, IBZ, M10, P10, P28, P30, P48, P53, P54, PAIS, PCI, PQC, PerIslam, RI-1, T02.
—IE, Infotrieve, Ingenta, INIST.
Published by: International Islamic University, Islamic Research Institute, Faisal Mosque Campus, P O Box 1243, Islamabad, 44000, Pakistan. TEL 92-51-926-1761, FAX 92-51-853360, http://www.iiu.edu.pk. Ed. Zafar Ishaq Ansari. Pub. Saeed Ahmad Shah. Circ: 3,000.

297.57 IND
THE ISLAMIC TIMES; the official organ of the Islamic Cultural Centre (India). Text in English. 1992. q. **Description:** Aims to enhance understanding among the various religions in India and elsewhere.
Published by: Islamic Cultural Centre (India), 317-321 Prospect Chambers Dr, Dr. D.N. Rd, Fort, Mumbai, Maharashtra 400 001, India. TEL 91-11-43535353.

297 IND
ISLAMIC VOICE. Text in English. 1976. m. INR 170 domestic; USD 16 foreign (effective 2011). bk.rev. **Document type:** *Newspaper, Consumer.*
Related titles: Online - full content ed.

R

Published by: Media House, Vivek Nagar Post Office, PO Box 4705, Bangalore, 560 047, India. TEL 91-80-25544483, FAX 91-80-25302770. Ed. Sadathullah Khan A W.

052 297.5 JOR ISSN 0969-7748
BP1

ISLAMICA MAGAZINE. Text in English. 1993. q. USD 29.95 in United States; USD 39.95 in Canada; GBP 15.95 in United Kingdom; EUR 44.95 in Europe; USD 49.95 elsewhere (effective 2008). adv. **Document type:** *Magazine, Consumer.* **Description:** Aims to broaden perspectives on traditional Islam and to provide a voice for Muslims to articulate their concerns and to establish cross-cultural relations between Muslim communities and their neighbours and co-religionists.
Indexed: ENW, P28, P48, P53, P54, PQC.
Address: 22 Queen Rania St, Sports City, Amman, 11191, Jordan. TEL 962-6-5153215, FAX 962-6-5153251, editor@islamicamagazine.com, info@islamicamagazine.com. Ed., Pub. Sohail Nakhooda. Adv. contact Alis Jusic. Circ: 10,000 (paid and controlled).

297.071 MYS ISSN 0126-5636
DS36.85

ISLAMIYYAT. Text in Arabic, English, Malay. 1977. s-a. MYR 20 per issue. abstr. **Document type:** *Journal, Academic/Scholarly.*
Indexed: PerIslam.
—Ingenta.
Published by: Perbit Universiti Kebangsaan Malaysia/National University of Malaysia Press, c/o Editor in Chief, Fakulti Pengajian Islam, Universiti Kebangsaan Malaysia, Bangi, Selangor D.E. 43600, Malaysia. TEL 60-3-89213515, FAX 60-3-89253902, penerbit@ukm.my, http://pkukmweb.ukm.my/~penerbit/. Ed. Ibrahim Abu Bakar.

297 SAU

➤ **JAMI'AT AL-IMAM MUHAMMAD IBN SA'UD AL-ISLAMIYYAH. IMADAT AL-BAHTH AL-ILMI. MAJALLAH/ISLAMIC UNIVERSITY OF IMAM MUHAMMAD IBN SAUD. DEANERY OF ACADEMIC RESEARCH. JOURNAL.** Text in Arabic, English. q. SAR 10 (effective 2003). **Document type:** *Journal, Academic/Scholarly.*
Formerly (until 1989): Jami'at al-Imam Muhammad Ibn Saud al Islamiyyah. Markaz al-Buhuth. Majallah
Published by: Jami'at al-Imam Muhammad Ibn Sa'ud al-Islamiyyah, Imadat al-Bahth al-Ilmi/Islamic University of Imam Muhammad Ibn Saud, Deanery of Academic Research, P O Box 18011, Riyadh, 11415, Saudi Arabia. TEL 966-1-2582247, FAX 966-1-2590261, http://www.imaum.com.sa. Ed. Dr. Turky Bin Sahw Al-Otaibi. Circ: 5,000.

➤ **JOURNAL OF ISLAMIC ECONOMICS, BANKING AND FINANCE.** *see* BUSINESS AND ECONOMICS—Banking And Finance

297.14 USA ISSN 1528-817X
K10

JOURNAL OF ISLAMIC LAW & CULTURE. Text in English. 1996. 3/yr. GBP 178 combined subscription in United Kingdom to institutions (print & online eds.); EUR 279, USD 347 combined subscription to institutions (print & online eds.) (effective 2012). back issues avail.; reprint service avail. from PSC,WSH. **Document type:** *Journal, Academic/Scholarly.* **Description:** Purpose of the Journal is to encourage scholarship and dialogue that fosters a deeper understanding of the law and public policy of Islamic religion and culture, particularly as it intersects with Western law and society, including the legal and social communities of the United States.
Formerly (until 2000): Journal of Islamic Law (1085-7141)
Related titles: Online - full text ed.: ISSN 1753-4534. GBP 160 in United Kingdom to institutions; EUR 251, USD 313 to institutions (effective 2012).
Indexed: A01, CA, FLP, P48, P53, P54, PQC, T02.
—CIS, IE, Ingenta. **CCC.**
Published by: (University of Arkansas, School of Law, Institute for Intercultural Relations), Routledge (Subsidiary of: Taylor & Francis Group), 325 Chestnut St, Ste 800, Philadelphia, PA 19106. TEL 800-354-1420, FAX 215-625-2940, journals@routledge.com, http://www.routledge.com. Ed. Aminah Beverly McCloud.

297 NLD ISSN 1878-4631
Z6611.I84

▼➤ **JOURNAL OF ISLAMIC MANUSCRIPTS.** Text in English. 2010. s-a. EUR 176, USD 246 to institutions; EUR 192, USD 269 combined subscription to institutions (print & online eds.) (effective 2012). **Document type:** *Journal, Academic/Scholarly.* **Description:** Explores the crucial importance of the handwritten book in the Muslim world. It is concerned with the written transmission of knowledge, the numerous varieties of Islamic book culture and the materials and techniques of bookmaking, namely codicology.
Related titles: Online - full text ed.: ISSN 1878-464X. EUR 160, USD 224 to institutions (effective 2012) (from IngentaConnect).
Indexed: A22, I02, L06, T02.
—**CCC.**
Published by: Brill, PO Box 9000, Leiden, 2300 PA, Netherlands. TEL 31-71-5353500, FAX 31-71-5317532. Ed. Jan Just Witkam.

➤ **JOURNAL OF ISLAMIC PHILOSOPHY.** *see* PHILOSOPHY

297 GBR ISSN 0955-2340
DS35.3

➤ **JOURNAL OF ISLAMIC STUDIES.** Text in English. 1990. 3/yr. GBP 221 in United Kingdom to institutions; EUR 333 in Europe to institutions; USD 377 in US & Canada to institutions; GBP 221 elsewhere to institutions; GBP 242 combined subscription in United Kingdom to institutions (print & online eds.); EUR 363 combined subscription in Europe to institutions (print & online eds.); USD 412 combined subscription in US & Canada to institutions (print & online eds.); GBP 242 combined subscription elsewhere to institutions (print & online eds.) (effective 2012). adv. bk.rev. back issues avail.; reprint service avail. from PSC. **Document type:** *Journal, Academic/Scholarly.* **Description:** Dedicated to the multi-disciplinary study of any aspect of Islam and the Islamic.
Related titles: Online - full text ed.: ISSN 1471-6917. GBP 202 in United Kingdom to institutions; EUR 303 in Europe to institutions; USD 343 in US & Canada to institutions; GBP 202 elsewhere to institutions (effective 2012) (from IngentaConnect).
Indexed: A01, A20, A21, A22, AmH&L, ArtHuCI, BibLing, BrHumI, CA, CurCont, E01, H14, HistAb, I02, I14, IBSS, M10, MLA-IB, P10, P28, P42, P47, P48, P53, P54, PCI, PQC, PSA, RI-1, RI-2, S02, S03, SociolAb, T02, W07.
—BLDSC (5008.550000), IE, Infotrieve, Ingenta. **CCC.**
Published by: (Oxford Centre for Islamic Studies), Oxford University Press, Great Clarendon St, Oxford, OX2 6DP, United Kingdom. TEL 44-1865-556767, FAX 44-1865-556646, enquiry@oup.co.uk, http://www.oxfordjournals.org. Ed. Farham Ahmad Nizami. Pub. Martin Green. Adv. contact Linda Hann TEL 44-1344-779945. **U.S. subscr. to:** Oxford University Press, 2001 Evans Rd, Cary, NC 27513. TEL 919-677-0977 ext 5777, 800-852-7323, FAX 919-677-1714, jnlorders@oup-usa.org, http://www.us.oup.com.

➤ **JOURNAL OF MIDDLE EASTERN AND ISLAMIC STUDIES IN ASIA.** *see* ASIAN STUDIES

➤ **JOURNAL OF MUSLIM MENTAL HEALTH.** *see* PSYCHOLOGY

297.5 GBR ISSN 1360-2004
BP52.5

➤ **JOURNAL OF MUSLIM MINORITY AFFAIRS.** Text and summaries in English. 1979. q. GBP 469 combined subscription in United Kingdom to institutions (print & online eds.); EUR 624, USD 778 combined subscription to institutions (print & online eds.) (effective 2012). adv. bk.rev. back issues avail.; reprint service avail. from PSC. **Document type:** *Journal, Academic/Scholarly.* **Description:** Devoted to the social, economic and political affairs of the muslim minority.
Formerly (until 1996): Institute of Muslim Minority Affairs. Journal (0266-6952)
Related titles: Online - full text ed.: ISSN 1469-9591. GBP 422 in United Kingdom to institutions; EUR 562, USD 700 to institutions (effective 2012) (from IngentaConnect).
Indexed: A01, A02, A03, A08, A21, A22, ASD, AmH&L, BAS, C12, CA, DIP, E01, H14, HRIR, HistAb, I02, I13, I14, IBR, IBSS, IBZ, ILD, LeftInd, M08, M10, MLA-IB, P02, P10, P28, P34, P42, P46, P47, P48, P53, P54, PAIS, PQC, PSA, PerIslam, RI-1, RI-2, RefugAb, S02, S03, S11, SCOPUS, SOPODA, SSA, SociolAb, T02.
—IE, Infotrieve, Ingenta. **CCC.**
Published by: (Institute of Muslim Minority Affairs), Routledge (Subsidiary of: Taylor & Francis Group), 4 Park Sq, Milton Park, Abingdon, Oxon OX14 4RN, United Kingdom. TEL 44-20-70176000, FAX 44-20-70176336, subscriptions@tandf.co.uk, http://www.routledge.com. Ed. Saleha S Mahmood. Adv. contact Linda Hann TEL 44-1344-779945. **Subscr. in N America to:** Taylor & Francis Inc., Customer Services Dept, 325 Chestnut St, 8th Fl, Philadelphia, PA 19106. TEL 215-625-8900, 800-354-1420, FAX 215-625-2940, customerservice@taylorandfrancis.com; **Subscr. to:** Taylor & Francis Ltd., Journals Customer Service, Sheepen Pl, Colchester, Essex CO3 3LP, United Kingdom. TEL 44-20-70175544, FAX 44-20-70175198.

297 IND ISSN 0971-3220

JOURNAL OF OBJECTIVE STUDIES. Text in English. 1989. s-a. INR 125 domestic to individuals; INR 150 SAARC to individuals; USD 30 elsewhere to individuals; INR 200 domestic to institutions; INR 250 SAARC to institutions; USD 40 elsewhere to institutions (effective 2011). bk.rev. back issues avail. **Document type:** *Journal, Academic/Scholarly.* **Description:** Encourages multifarious research activities and scholarly discussions on issues of vital social concern.
Indexed: I14, PerIslam.
—BLDSC (5024.900000).
Published by: Institute of Objective Studies, 162, Jogabai Main Rd, Jamia Nagar, PO Box 9725, New Delhi, 110025, India. TEL 91-11-26981187, FAX 91-11-26981104, ios1@vsnl.com. Eds. Ishtiyaque Danish, Z M Khan.

297.071 GBR ISSN 1465-3591
BP130

➤ **JOURNAL OF QUR'ANIC STUDIES.** Abbreviated title: J Q S. Text in English, Arabic. 1999. s-a. GBP 98 domestic to institutions; USD 194 in North America to institutions; GBP 108 elsewhere to institutions; GBP 122 combined subscription domestic to institutions (print & online eds.); USD 245 combined subscription in North America to institutions (print & online eds.); GBP 136 combined subscription elsewhere to institutions (print & online eds.) (effective 2012). bk.rev. back issues avail.; reprints avail. **Document type:** *Journal, Academic/Scholarly.* **Description:** Promotes the study of the Qur'an from a wide range of scholarly perspectives, reflecting the diversity of approaches characteristic of this field of scholarship.
Related titles: Online - full text ed.: ISSN 1755-1730. USD 158 in North America to institutions; GBP 88 elsewhere to institutions (effective 2012).
Indexed: A01, A03, A08, A21, CA, I02, I14, M10, MLA-IB, T02.
—**CCC.**
Published by: (University of London, Centre of Islamic Studies), Edinburgh University Press, 22 George Sq, Edinburgh, Scotland EH8 9LF, United Kingdom. TEL 44-131-6504218, FAX 44-131-6503286, journals@eup.ed.ac.uk. Adv. contact Ruth Allison TEL 44-131-6504220.

287 NLD ISSN 1877-6671

▼ **THE JOURNAL OF ROTTERDAM ISLAMIC AND SOCIAL STUDIES.** Variant title: J R I S S. Text in English. 2010. a. EUR 25 to individuals in Europe & North America; EUR 35 elsewhere to individuals; EUR 50 to institutions in Europe & North America; EUR 70 elsewhere to institutions (effective 2011). **Document type:** *Journal, Academic/Scholarly.*
Published by: (Islamitische Universiteit Rotterdam), IUR Press, Bergsingel 135, Rotterdam, 3037 GC, Netherlands. TEL 31-10-4854721, FAX 31-10-4843147, info@islamicuniversity.nl.

297 NLD ISSN 2210-5948

▼ **JOURNAL OF SUFI STUDIES.** Text in English. 2010. s-a. EUR 176, USD 246 to institutions; EUR 192, USD 269 combined subscription to institutions (print & online eds.) (effective 2012). **Document type:** *Journal, Academic/Scholarly.*
Related titles: Online - full text ed.: ISSN 2210-5956. EUR 160, USD 224 to institutions (effective 2012).
—**CCC.**
Published by: Brill, PO Box 9000, Leiden, 2300 PA, Netherlands. TEL 31-71-5353500, FAX 31-71-5317532, http://www.brill.nl.

297 MYS ISSN 1985-6830

➤ **JURNAL HADHARI.** Text in Arabic, English, Malay; Summaries in English. 2008. s-a. free. adv. bk.rev. abstr. back issues avail. **Document type:** *Journal, Academic/Scholarly.*
Published by: Jabatan Kemajuan Islam Malaysia/Department of Islamic Development Malaysia, Level 1, 4-9, Block D7, Federal Government Administration Centre, Putrajaya, 62519, Malaysia. TEL 60-3-88864842, FAX 60-3-88894951, http://www.islam.gov.my/portal/. **Co-publisher:** Universiti Kebangsaan Malaysia, Institut Islam Hadhari.

297 IRN ISSN 1025-5346
BP63.I68

KAUZAR. Text in Spanish. 1994. q. USD 35 in Asia; USD 40 in Europe; USD 40 in US, Canada & Australia; USD 25 in Africa (effective 2001). **Document type:** *Magazine, Consumer.*
Published by: Islamic Thought Foundation, P O Box 14155-3899, Tehran, Iran. TEL 98-21-88976635, FAX 98-21-8902725, i.t.f@iran-itf.com. Ed. Mohsen Rabbani.

KAYHAN ANDISHEH. *see* PHILOSOPHY

297 TUR ISSN 1309-2030

KELAM ARASTIRMALARI DERGISI. Text in Turkish. 2003. irreg. free (effective 2011). **Document type:** *Journal, Academic/Scholarly.*
Media: Online - full text.
Indexed: A01, T02. Ed. Ilyas Celebi.

KHERADNAMEH-E SADRA. *see* PHILOSOPHY

297.071 SAU

KING FAISAL CENTER FOR RESEARCH AND ISLAMIC STUDIES. NEWSLETTER. Text in Arabic. irreg. **Document type:** *Newsletter.*
Published by: King Faisal Center for Research and Islamic Studies, P O Box 51049, Riyadh, 11543, Saudi Arabia. TEL 4652255, FAX 4659993.

297.77 SAU

➤ **KING SAUD UNIVERSITY JOURNAL. EDUCATIONAL SCIENCES AND ISLAMIC STUDIES/JAMI'AT AL-MALIK SA'UD. MAJALLAH. AL-'ULUM AL-TARBAWIYYAH WAL-DIRASAT AL-ISLAMIYYAH.** (Other sections avail.: Administrative Sciences, Agricultural Sciences, Architecture and Planning, Arts, Computer and Information Sciences, Engineering Sciences, Science) Text in Arabic, English. 1989. m. charts; illus. back issues avail. **Document type:** *Journal, Academic/Scholarly.*
Formerly: King Saud University. Journal. Educational Sciences (1018-3620)
Published by: King Saud University, General Directorate for Academic Publishing and Press, PO Box 68953, Riyadh, 11537, Saudi Arabia. TEL 966-1-4672870, FAX 966-1-4672894, acksupress@ksu.edu.sa, http://printpress.ksu.edu.sa. Ed. Khalid A Ad-Dobaian. R&P Dr. Sulaiman Saleh Al-Ogle. Circ: 2,000.

297 DEU ISSN 1863-9801

KULTUR, RECHT UND POLITIK IN MUSLIMISCHEN GESELLSCHAFT. Text in German. 2001. irreg., latest vol.14, 2009. price varies. **Document type:** *Monographic series, Academic/Scholarly.*
Published by: Ergon Verlag, Keesburgstr 11, Wuerzburg, 97074, Germany. TEL 49-931-280084, FAX 49-931-282872, service@ergon-verlag.de, http://www.ergon-verlag.de.

297.77 GBR ISSN 0268-8352

LINK INTERNATIONAL: EDUCATIONAL NEWSLETTER. Text in English. 1986. bi-m. GBP 5 to individuals; GBP 7 to institutions. **Document type:** *Newsletter.*
Published by: Islamic Educational Publications, Muslim Community Studies, PO Box 139, Leicester, LE2 2YH, United Kingdom. TEL 01533-706714.

297.8 EGY

AL-LIWA' AL-ISLAMI/ISLAMIC BANNER/ISLAMIC STANDARD. Text in Arabic. 1982. w. **Document type:** *Newspaper, Consumer.* **Description:** Covers topics relating to Islamic fundamentalism.
Published by: Liwa' al-Islami, 11 Sharia Sharif Pasha, Cairo, Egypt. Ed. Muhammad Ali Sheta. Circ: 30,000.

297 IRN ISSN 0259-904X

LUQMAN. Text in French. 1985. 2/yr. IRR 7,000; GBP 13 in the Middle East; GBP 14 in Europe; GBP 15 elsewhere (effective 2001). back issues avail. **Document type:** *Academic/Scholarly.* **Description:** Deals primarily with Iranian studies, and Persian and comparative literatures.
Indexed: BibLing.
Published by: Markaz-i Nashr-i Danishgahi/Iran University Press, 85 Park Ave., P O Box 15875-4748, Tehran, Iran. TEL 98-21-8713232, FAX 98-21-8725954, pobox@iup-ir.com. Ed. Djavad Hadidi. Circ: 1,000.

297 305 USA ISSN 1943-8400
E184.M88

M S A LINK. (Muslim Students' Association) Text in English. 200?. s-a. **Document type:** *Magazine, Consumer.* **Description:** Focuses on the accomplishments of and issues facing Muslim students in the North America such as such as spirituality, activism and education.
Related titles: Online - full text ed.
Published by: M S A National, PO Box 1096, Falls Church, VA 22041. TEL 703-820-7900, FAX 703-820-7888, msalink@msanationa.org. Ed. Zalnab Khan.

297 PAK ISSN 0002-4015

AL-MA'ARIF. Text in Urdu. 1968. m. PKR 120. bk.rev. **Document type:** *Academic/Scholarly.* **Description:** Covers issues in Islamic philosophy, Islamic culture and Islamic history.
Formerly: Thaqafat
Published by: Institute of Islamic Culture, 2 Club Rd., Lahore 3, Pakistan. TEL 92-42-6363127. Ed. Rashid Ahmad Jullundhry. Circ: 500.

297.2 IRN ISSN 1015-2822
AP95.P3

MA'ARIF. Text in Persian, Modern. 1984. 3/yr. IRR 12,000; GBP 27 in the Middle East; GBP 28 in Europe; GBP 33 elsewhere (effective 2001). back issues avail. **Document type:** *Academic/Scholarly.* **Description:** Publishes articles and comparative studies relating to Islamic history, philosophy, theology and mysticism.
Indexed: BibLing.
Published by: Markaz-i Nashr-i Danishgahi/Iran University Press, 85 Park Ave., P O Box 15875-4748, Tehran, Iran. TEL 98-21-8713232, FAX 98-21-8725954, pobox@iup-ir.com. Ed. Nasrollah Pourjavady. Circ: 2,500.

297.2 PAK ISSN 2079-8563

➤ **MAARIF-E-RAZA.** Text in English. 2003. a. PKR 350, USD 20; free to qualified personnel (effective 2010). adv. bk.rev. a. index. back issues avail. **Document type:** *Journal, Academic/Scholarly.*

Related titles: Online - full text ed.: free (effective 2010); Urdu ed.: Ma'arif-i Raz'a. ISSN 2218-0834. 1980.
Published by: Imamahmadraza Research Institute, 25, Japan Mansion Raza (Regal) Chowk, Saddar, Karachi, 74400, Pakistan. TEL 92-21-32725150, Imamahmadraza@gmail.com. Eds. Dilawar Khan, Syed Wajahat Rasool. Pub. Majeedullah Qadiri. R&P Dilawar Khan.

297.14 EGY ISSN 1687-8310
MAGALLAT ITTIHAD AL-GAMI'AT AL-'ARABIYYAT LI-DIRASAT WA-BUHUTH AL-SHARI'AT AL-ISLAMIYYAT. Text in Arabic. 2008. a. **Document type:** *Journal, Academic/Scholarly.*
Published by: Al-Azhar University, Faculty of Shari'a and Law, El-Darrasa, Cairo, Egypt. TEL 202-395-2231. Ed. Dr. Abdel-Sameia Abdel-Wahhab Abou-El-Khair.

297 IRN ISSN 1019-0767
BP193.5
MAHJUBAH. Text in English. 1981. m. USD 35 in the Middle East; USD 40 in Europe; USD 45 in North America; USD 25 in Africa. **Document type:** *Magazine, Consumer.* **Description:** Islamic magazine for women.
Indexed: PerIslam.
Published by: Islamic Thought Foundation, P O Box 14155-3899, Tehran, Iran. TEL 98-21-844092, FAX 98-21-898295, i.t.f@iran-itf.com. Ed. Turan Jamshidian. R&P Mr. Beheshti. Circ: 30,000.

297 JOR ISSN 2079-5076
➤ **AL MAJALLA AL-URDUNNIYYA FI AL-DIRASAT AL-ISLAMIYAT/ JORDAN JOURNAL OF ISLAMIC STUDIES.** Text in Arabic, English, French; Summaries in Arabic, English. 2005. q. **Document type:** *Journal, Academic/Scholarly.* **Description:** Contains articles within the field of Islamic studies with the purpose of addressing contemporary challenges from a moderate Islamic perspective.
Published by: Al al-Bayt University, Deanship of Academic Research, PO Box 130111, Mafraq, 25113, Jordan. TEL 962-2-6297000 ext 2524, FAX 962-2-6297067, info@aabu.edu.jo. Ed., R&P Azmi Al-Sayyed Ahmad.

297 JOR
MAJALLAT AL-SHARIA. Text in Arabic. 1959. m. USD 20 to individuals; USD 40 to institutions. **Description:** General interest articles focusing on Islam, religious and health matters, issues in Jordanian society, as well as educational and entertainment topics.
Formerly: Theology - Sharia
Published by: League of Islamic Sciences, Yazid ben Abu Sufian St., P O Box 1829, Amman, Jordan. TEL 637203, FAX 819036. Ed. Hassan T Zibian.

MAJALLAT AL-SHARI'AH WAL-QANUN/JOURNAL OF SHARIA & LAW. *see* LAW

297.81 UAE
MANAAR AL-ISLAM. Text in Arabic. 1979. m. adv. bk.rev. **Document type:** *Magazine, Consumer.* **Description:** Discusses Islamic guidance, Quranic studies, Sunna, Islamic history and literature, family issues, and news of the Islamic world.
Published by: Ministry of Justice Islamic Affairs and Endowments, PO Box 2922, Abu Dhabi, United Arab Emirates. TEL 9712-6270049, FAX 9712-6265565, Alajleh@emirates.net.ae. Ed. Ali Mohammad Al Echlah. R&P, Adv. contact Ali Mohammad al-Echlah. Circ: 25,000 (paid).

297 USA
MANAR AL-HUDA. Text in Arabic. m. **Document type:** *Magazine, Consumer.*
Published by: Association of Islamic Charitable Projects, 4431 Walnut St, Philadelphia, PA 19104. TEL 215-387-8888, info@aicp.org, http://www.aicp.org/index.htm.

297 KEN
MAPENZI YA MUNGU. Text in Swahili. 1943. m. KES 25. adv. bk.rev.
Published by: East African Ahmadiyya Muslim Mission, PO Box 40554, Nairobi, Kenya. Ed. Jamil R Rafiq. Circ: 4,000.

297 GBR ISSN 0950-3110
DS36.85
➤ **AL-MASAQ**; Islam and the medieval mediterranean. Text in English, French. 1988. 3/yr. GBP 274 combined subscription in United Kingdom to institutions (print & online eds.); EUR 361, USD 453 combined subscription to institutions (print & online eds.) (effective 2012). adv. bk.rev. bibl. back issues avail.; reprint service avail. from PSC. **Document type:** *Journal, Academic/Scholarly.* **Description:** Devoted to the study of all aspects of the Arabo-Islamic medieval mediterranean studies.
Related titles: Microfilm ed.; Online - full text ed.: ISSN 1473-348X. GBP 246 in United Kingdom to institutions; EUR 324, USD 408 to institutions (effective 2012) (from IngentaConnect).
Indexed: A01, A03, A08, A22, BibLing, CA, E01, I02, I14, IBR, IBZ, M10, MLA-IB, P48, P53, P54, PQC, T02.
—IE, Infotrieve, Ingenta. **CCC.**
Published by: (The Society for the Medieval Mediterranean, University of Leeds), Routledge (Subsidiary of: Taylor & Francis Group), 4 Park Sq, Milton Park, Abingdon, Oxon OX14 4RN, United Kingdom. TEL 44-20-70176000, FAX 44-20-70176336, subscriptions@tandf.co.uk, http://www.routledge.com. Ed. Dr. Dionisius Agius. Adv. contact Linda Hann TEL 44-1344-779945. Circ: 200. **Subscr. to:** Taylor & Francis Ltd., Journals Customer Service, Sheepen Pl, Colchester, Essex CO3 3LP, United Kingdom. TEL 44-20-70175544, FAX 44-20-70175198. **Dist. in U.S. and Canada by:** Medieval Institute Press, Western Michigan University, Walwood Hall, 1903 W Michigan, Kalamazoo, MI 49008.

➤ **MEDIEN UND POLITISCHE KOMMUNIKATION - NAHER OSTEN UND ISLAMISCHE WELT.** *see* COMMUNICATIONS

➤ **MEDIEVAL ENCOUNTERS**; Jewish, Christian and Muslim culture in confluence and dialogue. *see* RELIGIONS AND THEOLOGY—Judaic

297 IRN
EL MENSAGE DE AZ-ZAQALAIN. Text in Spanish. q. USD 25 in Africa; USD 30 elsewhere (effective 2001). **Document type:** *Magazine, Academic/Scholarly.* **Description:** Contains articles and studies on Ahlul Beiyt's affairs.
Published by: Islamic Thought Foundation, P O Box 14155-3899, Tehran, Iran. TEL 98-21-88976635, FAX 98-21-8902725, i.t.f@iran-itf.com. Ed. Mohsen Rabbani.

297.57 USA ISSN 1071-5215
BP1
THE MESSAGE (JAMAICA). Text in English. 1989. m. USD 25; USD 2.50 newsstand/cover (effective 2005). adv. illus. **Document type:** *Magazine, Consumer.* **Description:** Provides an overview of the current issues that face American Muslims and the Muslim world at large. Includes international news, discussions of anti-Muslim bias in Western print and broadcast media, in-depth coverage of conditions in specific countries, advice and guidance on aspects of Islam.
Formerly (until 1993): Message International (1046-1019)
Indexed: PerIslam.
Published by: Islamic Circle of North America, 166-26 89th Ave, Jamaica, NY 11432. TEL 718-658-5163, FAX 718-658-5069, info@icna.org, http://www.icna.com. Ed. Mahbubur Rahman. Circ: 12,500 (controlled and free).

297 MUS
LE MESSAGE DE L'AHMADIYYAT. Text in French. 1965. m. USD 24. bk.rev. **Document type:** *Newspaper, Consumer.*
Formerly: Message
Published by: Ahmadiyya Muslim Association, PO Box 6, Rose Hill, Mauritius. TEL 230-464-1747, FAX 230-454-2223. Ed. Zafrullah Domun. Circ: 3,000.

297 IRN ISSN 1012-0734
LE MESSAGE DE L'ISLAM. Text in French. 1981. m. USD 35 in the Middle East; USD 40 in Europe; USD 45 in North America; USD 25 in Africa. **Document type:** *Magazine, Consumer.* **Description:** Contains articles and features on cultural, political, and religious issues of interest.
Indexed: MLA-IB.
Published by: Islamic Thought Foundation, P O Box 14155-3899, Tehran, Iran. TEL 98-21-844092, FAX 98-21-898295, i.t.f@iran-itf.com. Ed. Mahmood Reza Zainoddini. R&P Mr. Beheshti.

297 IRN
MESSAGE OF THAQALAYN; a quarterly journal of islamic studies. Text in English. q. USD 20 in Africa; USD 24 elsewhere (effective 2001). **Document type:** *Journal, Academic/Scholarly.* **Description:** Contains articles and studies on Ahlul Beiyt's affairs.
Published by: Islamic Thought Foundation, P O Box 14155-3899, Tehran, Iran. TEL 98-21-88976635, FAX 98-21-8902725, i.t.f@iran-itf.com. Ed. AliReza Foroughi.

297 GBR ISSN 2045-1040
▼ **MESSAGE OF THAQALAYN (UK EDITION)**; a quarterly journal of Islamic studies. Text in English. 2009. q. free to qualified personnel (effective 2010). back issues avail. **Document type:** *Journal, Academic/Scholarly.* **Description:** Presents the teachings of Islam in general and the School of the Ahlul Bayt (AS).
Related titles: Online - full text ed.: free (effective 2010).
Published by: Islamic Centre of England, 140 Maida Vale, London, W9 1QB, United Kingdom. TEL 44-20-76045500, FAX 44-20-76044898, icel@ic-el.com, http://www.ic-el.com. Eds. Fatima Khimji, Shahnaz Safieddin, Mohammad Ali Shomali.

297 SWE ISSN 1650-2949
BP1
MINARET; tidskrift foer svensk muslimsk kultur. Text in Swedish. 2001. q. SEK 240 domestic to individuals; SEK 275 in Scandinavia to individuals; SEK 300 elsewhere to individuals; SEK 340 to institutions; SEK 70 per issue (effective 2004). adv. **Document type:** *Magazine, Consumer.*
Related titles: Online - full text ed.
Published by: Svenska Islamiska Akademien, Aarstavaegan 29, Aarsta, 12052, Sweden. Ed. Muhamed Omar.

297 USA ISSN 0892-0559
DS35.3
THE MINARET (LOS ANGELES). Text in English. 1991 (vol.13). m. USD 25 (effective 2004). adv. bk.rev. **Document type:** *Magazine, Consumer.*
Indexed: PerIslam.
—Ingenta.
Published by: Islamic Center of Southern California, 434 S Vermont Ave, Los Angeles, CA 90020. TEL 213-384-4570, FAX 213-383-9674, http://www.islamctr.org. Ed. Aslam Abdullah. Adv. contact Faiqa Bashir. Circ: 8,000 (paid).

297 PAK
MINARET MONTHLY INTERNATIONAL. Text in English. 1964. m. USD 11 in Europe, Africa & Asia; USD 20 elsewhere; PKR 20 newsstand/cover domestic (effective 2000). adv. bk.rev. **Description:** Explores mission work in the country.
Formerly: Minaret (0026-4415)
Indexed: AMR, PerIslam.
Published by: World Federation of Islamic Missions, Islamic Centre, Abdul Aleem Siddiqi Rd., Block B N. Nazimabad, Karachi, 74700, Pakistan. TEL 92-21-6644156. Ed. Farid Uddin Ahmed. Circ: 1,200.

297 EGY
MINBAR AL-ISLAM/ISLAMIC PODIUM/PULPIT OF ISLAM. Text in Arabic, English, French, Spanish. 1942. m. USD 228 in North America (effective 2009). bibl.; illus.
Published by: (Egypt. Al-Majlis al-A'la lil-Shu'un al-Islamiyyah/Supreme Council for Islamic Affairs), Mu'assasat al-Ahram, Al-Ahram Building, Al-Galaa St., Cairo, Egypt. TEL 20-2-5747011, FAX 20-2-5792899. **Subscr. in N. America to:** Al-Ahram International, 405 Lexington Ave, 39th Fl, New York, NY 10174. TEL 212-972-6440, FAX 212-286-0285.

297.82 IRN
MISHKAT. Text in Persian, Modern. 1984. q. IRR 8,000 (effective 2003). back issues avail. **Document type:** *Academic/Scholarly.* **Description:** Publishes research on the Islamic sciences, culture and civilization and the teachings of Shiism.
Published by: Islamic Research Foundation, Astan Quds Razavi, P O Box 366-91735, Mashhad, Iran. TEL 98-511-2232501, FAX 98-511-2230005, islreafn@emamreza.net, http://www.islamic-rf.org. Ed. M. M. Rukni. Circ: 3,000. **Co-sponsor:** Astan Quds Razavi, Pub.

297 DEU ISSN 1436-8080
MITTEILUNGEN ZUR SOZIAL- UND KULTURGESCHICHTE DER ISLAMISCHEN WELT. Text in German. 1998. irreg., latest vol.28, 2009. price varies. **Document type:** *Monographic series, Academic/ Scholarly.*
Published by: Ergon Verlag, Keesburgstr 11, Wuerzburg, 97074, Germany. TEL 49-931-280084, FAX 49-931-282872, service@ergon-verlag.de, http://www.ergon-verlag.de.

297.4 USA
THE MOORISH SCIENCE MONITOR. Text in English. 1968. q. USD 3 per issue. adv. bk.rev. back issues avail. **Description:** Reports news of the Moorish Orthodox church, a syncretism of multi-media Sufism, heterodoxy, and ontological anarchism.
Published by: Ziggurat, 318 Brandon Rd., Rochester, NY 14622-2034. Ed. T Metzger.

297.2 DEU ISSN 0930-7338
BP1
MOSLEMISCHE REVUE. Text in German. 1924. q. EUR 45 domestic; EUR 55 foreign (effective 2010). adv. **Document type:** *Magazine, Consumer.* **Description:** Muslim theology, muslims and their life in Germany, dialogue between Christians and Moslem, news of the Islamic world.
Incorporates (1981-1989): Aktuelle Fragen (0724-2735)
Published by: Zentralinstitut Islam-Archiv-Deutschland, Am Kuhfuss 8, Soest, 59475, Germany. TEL 49-2921-60702, FAX 49-2921-65417, info@islamarchiv.de, http://www.islamarchiv.de. Ed. M Salim Abdullah. Circ: 900.

297.124 GBR ISSN 0266-2183
B753.I24
MUHYIDDIN IBN ARABI SOCIETY. JOURNAL. Text in English. 1982. s-a. free to members (effective 2009). bk.rev. back issues avail. **Document type:** *Journal, Academic/Scholarly.* **Description:** Contains translations and studies of works of Ibn Arabi.
—Ingenta.
Published by: Muhyiddin Ibn Arabi Society, PO Box 892, Oxford, OX2 7XL, United Kingdom. TEL 44-1865-511963, mias.uk@ibnarabisociety.org. Ed. Stephen Hirtenstein.

297 KEN ISSN 1995-6622
MUJTABA. Text in English. 2001. m. **Document type:** *Magazine, Consumer.*
Published by: Ahlul Bayt Islamic Sisters Network, PO Box 67486, Nairobi, Kenya. TEL 254-20-4449085, FAX 254-20-4448267, abisn@nbi.ispkenya.com.

297.74 ZAF ISSN 0027-4860
MUSLIM AFRICA. Text in English. 1969. m. USD 10. adv. **Description:** Highlights mission work in the country.
Indexed: PerIslam.
Published by: Islamic Missionary Society, PO Box 54125, Vrededorp, Transvaal 2141, South Africa. FAX 27-11-834-8241. Ed. M S Laher. Circ: 5,000.

297 ZAF ISSN 0027-4887
BP1
MUSLIM DIGEST; international magazine of Muslim affairs. Text in English. 1950. bi-m. USD 15. adv. illus.
Published by: Makki Publications, 100 Brickfield Rd, Durban, KwaZulu-Natal, South Africa.

MUSLIM GIRL; enlighten. celebrate. inspire. *see* CHILDREN AND YOUTH—For

297 USA ISSN 0883-816X
MUSLIM JOURNAL. Text in English. 1961. w. USD 49 (effective 2002). adv. **Document type:** *Newspaper.*
Former titles (until 1985): A M Journal (0744-7639); (until 1983): A M News (0744-7647); (until 1982): World Muslim News (0744-0014); (until 1981): Bilalian News (0161-8644); (until 1975): Muhammad Speaks (0027-3031)
Indexed: NewsAb, P23, P48, P53, PQC, PerIslam.
Published by: Muslim Journal Enterprises, Inc., 1141 175th St., Homewood, IL 60430-4604. muslimjrnl@aol.com. Ed. Ayesha K Mustafaa.

297 USA ISSN 1096-391X
BP1
THE MUSLIM MAGAZINE. Text in English. 1998. q. USD 400; USD 4 newsstand/cover (effective 2000). adv. back issues avail. **Document type:** *Magazine, Consumer.*
Related titles: E-mail ed.; Online - full text ed.
Published by: American Muslim Assistance, P. O. Box 1065, Fenton, MI 48430. TEL 810-714-2296, 888-278-6624, FAX 810-629-1770, staff@muslimmag.org. Ed. Mateen Siddiqui. Pub. Isaac Bojel. adv.: color page USD 950, B&W page USD 700. Circ: 40,000 (paid and controlled).

297 305.89 NLD ISSN 1570-7571
➤ **MUSLIM MINORITIES.** Text in English. 2003. irreg., latest vol.8, 2008. price varies. **Document type:** *Monographic series, Academic/ Scholarly.*
Indexed: IZBG.
Published by: Brill, PO Box 9000, Leiden, 2300 PA, Netherlands. TEL 31-71-5353500, FAX 31-71-5317532, cs@brill.nl, http://www.brill.nl.

297.0941 GBR ISSN 0956-5027
THE MUSLIM NEWS; news and views of Muslims in the United Kingdom. Text in English. 1989. m. GBP 12 domestic; GBP 17 foreign (effective 2009). adv. bk.rev. 8 p./no. 5 cols./p.; back issues avail. **Document type:** *Newspaper, Consumer.* **Description:** Provides objective news and views of Muslims in the United Kingdom.
Indexed: PerIslam.
Published by: Visitcrest Ltd., PO Box 380, Harrow, Mddx HA2 6LL, United Kingdom. TEL 44-20-88638586, FAX 44-20-88639370, editor@muslimnews.co.uk. Ed., Pub. Ahmed J Versi. Adv. contact Tahera Bhanji TEL 44-20-88638586. B&W page GBP 2,890, color page GBP 2,990; 266 x 380.

297 SAU
MUSLIM SOLIDARITY/MAJALLAT AL-TADAMUM AL-ISLAMI. Text in Arabic, English. m. free. bk.rev. bibl. **Document type:** *Government.*
Formerly: Majallat al-Hajj
Published by: Ministry of Pilgrimage Affairs and Awqaf/Wizarat Shu'un al-Hajj wal-Awqaf, Sharia Omar bin al-Khattab, Riyadh, 11183, Saudi Arabia. TEL 966-1-4022200. Ed. Abdullah Bin Abdul Muttaleb Bogas. Circ: 11,000.

297 USA
MUSLIM STAR. Text in English. 1953. m. USD 10. adv. bk.rev. illus.
Published by: Federation of Islamic Associations in the United States and Canada, 25341 Five Mile Rd, Redford, MI 48239. TEL 313-534-3295, FAX 313-534-1474. Ed. Nihad Hamed. Circ: 10,000 (paid).

R

297.57 USA ISSN 1085-3677
➤ **MUSLIM SUNRISE.** Text in English. 1921. q. USD 15; USD 4 newsstand/cover (effective 2010). adv. bk.rev. back issues avail.
Document type: *Journal, Academic/Scholarly.* **Description:** Provides a platform for public opinion on current problems confronting humanity and their solution. Features articles written by scholars discussing, as well as topics relating to other religions.
Related titles: Online - full text ed.
Published by: Ahmadiyya Muslim Community, 15000 Good Hope Rd, Silver Spring, DC 20905. TEL 301-879-0110, FAX 301-879-0115, info@alislam.org, http://www.alislam.org/. Ed. Falahud Din Shams.

297.283 USA ISSN 0027-4909
DS36
➤ **MUSLIM WORLD**; a journal devoted to the study of Islam and Christian-Muslim relations. Text in English. 1911. q. GBP 191 in United Kingdom to institutions; EUR 241 in Europe to institutions; USD 280 in the Americas to institutions; USD 373 elsewhere to institutions; GBP 220 combined subscription in United Kingdom to institutions (print & online eds.); EUR 278 combined subscription in Europe to institutions (print & online eds.); USD 323 combined subscription in the Americas to institutions (print & online eds.); USD 429 combined subscription elsewhere to institutions (print & online eds.) (effective 2012). adv. bk.rev. illus. index, cum.index: vols.1-25 (1911-1935), vols.26-50 (1936-1960). back issues avail.; reprint service avail. from PSC. **Document type:** *Journal, Academic/Scholarly.* **Description:** Covers research articles, book reviews, notices and surveys of periodicals.
Formerly (until 1948): The Moslem World (0362-4641)
Related titles: Microform ed.: (from PQC); Online - full text ed.: ISSN 1478-1913. GBP 191 in United Kingdom to institutions; EUR 241 in Europe to institutions; USD 280 in the Americas to institutions; USD 373 elsewhere to institutions (effective 2012) (from IngentaConnect).
Indexed: A01, A02, A03, A08, A11, A20, A21, A22, A25, A26, ABS&EES, AmHI, ArtHuCI, B04, BAS, BRD, C05, CA, CCME, CurCont, E01, E08, EI, FR, G08, H05, H07, H08, H09, H10, H14, HAb, HistAb, HumInd, I02, I05, I13, I14, IBR, IBZ, LeftInd, M06, M10, MASUSE, MEA&I, MLA, MLA-IB, P02, P10, P28, P30, P34, P42, P47, P48, P53, P54, PAIS, PCI, PQC, PSA, PerIslam, R&TA, R05, RASB, RI-1, RI-2, S02, S03, S05, S08, S09, SCOPUS, SociolAb, T02, U01, W03, W04, W05, W07, WBA, WMB.
—BLDSC (5991.150000), IE, Infotrieve, Ingenta, INIST. **CCC.**
Published by: (Duncan Black Macdonald Center), Wiley-Blackwell Publishing, Inc. (Subsidiary of: Wiley-Blackwell Publishing Ltd.), 111 River St, Hoboken, NJ 07030. TEL 201-748-6000, FAX 201-748-6088, info@wiley.com, http://www.wiley.com/WileyCDA/. Ed. Yahya M Michot.

297 GBR ISSN 0260-3063
DS35.3
MUSLIM WORLD BOOK REVIEW. Text in English. 1980. q. GBP 23 domestic to individuals; GBP 31 foreign to individuals; GBP 38 domestic to institutions; GBP 46 foreign to institutions; GBP 8 per issue domestic; GBP 11 per issue foreign (effective 2009). bk.rev. bibl. index. back issues avail. **Document type:** *Journal, Academic/Scholarly.* **Description:** Provides a critical analysis of the views expressed in the West and in the East on a variety of publications related to the Muslim world.
Indexed: A21, BibLing, DIP, I14, IBR, IBZ, M10, PerIslam, RASB, RI-1, RI-2.
—BLDSC (5991.160000), IE, Infotrieve.
Published by: Islamic Foundation, Markfield Conference Centre, Ratby Ln, Markfield, Leics LE67 9SY, United Kingdom. TEL 44-1530-244944, FAX 44-1530-244946, i.found@islamic-foundation.org.uk. Ed. Manazir Ahsan. **Co-sponsor:** International Institute of Islamic Thought, US.

MUSLIM WORLD JOURNAL OF HUMAN RIGHTS. *see* POLITICAL SCIENCE—Civil Rights

297 SAU
MUSLIM WORLD LEAGUE JOURNAL. Text in Arabic. 1973. m. USD 20 to individuals; USD 26 to institutions. index. **Description:** News and features of interest to Muslims throughout the world.
Related titles: English ed.
Indexed: PerIslam.
Published by: (Press and Publications Department), Muslim World League/Rabitat al-Alam al-Islami, P O Box 538, Makkah, Saudi Arabia. TEL 2-544-1622, FAX 2-544-1622, TELEX 440390. Ed. Hamid Hassan Al Radadi. Circ: 30,000.

297 CAN
MUSLIMEDIA. Text in English. fortn. **Document type:** *Newspaper, Consumer.* **Description:** Covers news and events in the Arab countries and Islamic related issues.
Media: Online - full content.
Published by: Crescent International, PO Box 747, Gormley, ON L0H 1G0, Canada. TEL 905-887-8913, FAX 905-474-9293. Ed. Iqbal Siddiqui. **Subscr. to:** 32 Warrington Ave, Slough SL1 3BQ, United Kingdom. TEL 44-1753-523719, FAX 44-1753-570231.

DIE MUSLIMISCHE. *see* ETHNIC INTERESTS

297.77 DEU ISSN 1439-6084
MUSLIMISCHE BILDUNGSGAENGE. Text in German. 1999. irreg. price varies. **Document type:** *Monographic series, Academic/Scholarly.*
Published by: Waxmann Verlag GmbH, Steinfurter Str 555, Muenster, 48159, Germany. TEL 49-251-265040, FAX 49-251-2650426, info@waxmann.com. Ed. Hasan Alacacioglu.

297.071 DEU ISSN 1869-9049
▼ **MUSLIMISCHE WELTEN**; empirische Studien zu Gesellschaft, Politik und Religion. Text in German. 2009. irreg., latest vol.2, 2010. price varies. **Document type:** *Monographic series, Academic/Scholarly.*
Published by: Ergon Verlag, Keesburgstr 11, Wuerzburg, 97074, Germany. TEL 49-931-280084, FAX 49-931-282872, service@ergon-verlag.de.

NEW BOOKS QUARTERLY ON ISLAM & THE MUSLIM WORLD. *see* RELIGIONS AND THEOLOGY—Abstracting, Bibliographies, Statistics

297 GBR
DS36.85
THE NEW EDINBURGH ISLAMIC SURVEYS. Text in English. 1962. irreg. price varies. back issues avail. **Document type:** *Monographic series, Academic/Scholarly.*
Formerly: Islamic Surveys (0075-093X)
—**CCC.**
Published by: Edinburgh University Press, 22 George Sq, Edinburgh, Scotland EH8 9LF, United Kingdom. TEL 44-131-6504218, FAX 44-131-6503286, journals@eup.ed.ac.uk. Ed. Carole Hillenbrand.

297.86 USA
BP1
NEW TREND; independent forum for the oppressed masses. Text in English. 1977. 9/m. free (effective 2005). adv. bk.rev.; film rev.
Document type: *Newsletter, Consumer.* **Description:** Islamic perspective on change and conflict in the world.
Media: Online - full text.
Indexed: PerIslam.
Published by: American Society for Education and Religion, Inc., PO Box 356, Kingsville, MD 21087-0356. TEL 443-859-5233, FAX 410-638-5965. Ed. Kaukab Siddique. adv.: page USD 300. Circ: 35,000 (paid and free).

297.5 AUS
NIDA'UL ISLAM. Text in Arabic. 1994 (Jan.). bi-m. **Description:** Contains Islamic perspectives of contemporary, social, political and economic events which affect the Ummah.
Related titles: Online - full content ed.; English ed.: The Call of Islam.
Published by: Islamic Youth Movement, PO Box 216, Lakemba, NSW 2195, Australia. TEL 61-2-97404460, FAX 61-2-97407921, nida@islam.org.au, http://www.islam.org.au/.

297.5 LBN
NOOR AL-ISLAM; thiqafiyyah islamiyyah - islamic cultural magazine. Text in Arabic, English. 1988. bi-m. USD 50 in the Middle East; USD 50 in Asia; USD 50 in Africa; USD 100 in United States; USD 100 in Europe (effective 2000). adv. bk.rev. illus. back issues avail. **Document type:** *Magazine, Academic/Scholarly.* **Description:** Discusses religious and cultural issues of interest to Muslims of all nations. Most issues include an article looking at the history and current status of Muslim communities within a particular country or ethnic group.
Indexed: PerIslam.
Published by: Imam Hussain Charitable - Cultural Foundation/ Muassasat al-Imam al-Husain al-Khairiyya al-Thiqafiyya, P O Box 25156, Beirut, Lebanon. TEL 961-1-823049, FAX 961-1-603379, TELEX 40512 KAMEC. Ed. Hussain Al Hakim. R&P, Adv. contact Jihad Abdallah. color page USD 350. Circ: 10,000.

297.071 DEU ISSN 1860-9775
NUR AL-HIKMA; Licht der Weisheit - interdisziplinaere Schriftenreihe zur Islamwissenschaft. Text in Arabic, German. 2005. irreg., latest vol.4, 2009. price varies. **Document type:** *Monographic series, Academic/Scholarly.*
Published by: Verlag Dr. Kovac, Leverkusenstr 13, Hamburg, 22761, Germany. TEL 49-40-3988800, FAX 49-40-39888055, info@verlagdrkovac.de.

297 USA
OUR ISLAM. Text in English. 1980. q. USD 12. adv. bk.rev. back issues avail.
Published by: (African Islamic Mission Inc.), A.I.M. Publications, PO Box 474143, Brooklyn, NY 11247-4143. FAX 212-789-0530. Ed. Alhaji Obaba Muhammad. Circ: 12,000.

297.071 GBR ISSN 2047-0312
▼ **PERSPECTIVES (YORK)**; teaching Islamic studies in higher education. Text in English. 2010. s-a. free to members (effective 2011). back issues avail. **Document type:** *Journal, Academic/Scholarly.* **Description:** Provides a forum for those involved in teaching Islamic studies and related subjects in higher education to share practice and resources.
Related titles: Online - full text ed.: ISSN 2047-0320. free (effective 2011).
Published by: Islamic Studies Network, c/o The Higher Education Academy, Innovation Way, York Science Park, Heslington, York, YO10 5BR, United Kingdom. TEL 44-1904-717500, islamicstudies@heacademy.ac.uk.

297.50 320.5 USA
➤ **PRINCETON STUDIES IN MUSLIM POLITICS.** Text in English. 1995. irreg., latest 2009. price varies. illus.; maps. back issues avail.
Document type: *Monographic series, Academic/Scholarly.*
Description: Examines political issues in Islamic nations throughout the ages.
Published by: Princeton University Press, 41 William St, Princeton, NJ 08540. TEL 609-258-4900, 800-777-4726, FAX 609-258-6305, cpriday@pupress.co.uk. Eds. Augustus Richard Norton, Dale F Eickelman. **Subscr. addr. in US:** California - Princeton Fulfillment Services, Inc., 1445 Lower Ferry Rd, Ewing, NJ 08618. TEL 609-883-1759, 800-777-4726, FAX 609-883-7413, 800-999-1958, orders@cpfsinc.com. **Dist. addr. in Canada:** University Press Group.; **Dist. addr. in UK:** John Wiley & Sons Ltd.

297 DEU ISSN 0942-6574
QUELLENSTUDIEN ZUR HADIT- UND RECHTSLITERATUR IN NORDAFRIKA. Text in German. 1992. irreg., latest 1997. price varies. **Document type:** *Monographic series, Academic/Scholarly.*
Published by: (Universitaet Bonn, Orientalisches Seminar), Harrassowitz Verlag, Kreuzberger Ring 7b-d, Wiesbaden, 65205, Germany. TEL 49-611-5300, FAX 49-611-530560, verlag@harrassowitz.de, http://www.harrassowitz.de. R&P Michael Langfeld. Adv. contact Robert Gietz.

297.122 PAK
QURANULHUDA. Text in English, Urdu. 1976. m. PKR 170, USD 40. adv. bk.rev. **Description:** Presents texts from the Qur'an with exhaustive commentary.
Indexed: PerIslam.
Published by: S.M.S.A. Hayat Ed. & Pub., Shahrah-e-Iraq, Qasr e Batool 28, P O Box 8677, Karachi, 74400, Pakistan. TEL 92-21-521292. Circ: 31,000.

197 AUS ISSN 1449-2555
REFLECTIONS (LAKEMBA). Text in English. 2003. irreg. **Document type:** *Magazine, Consumer.*
Related titles: Online - full content ed.
Published by: United Muslim Women Association Inc., 47 Wangee Rd, PO Box 264, Lakemba, NSW 2195, Australia. TEL 61-2-97506916, FAX 61-2-97507913, info@mwa.org.au, http://www.mwa.org.au. Eds. Feda Abdo, Samah Hadid.

297.21 DNK ISSN 1903-1106
REFLEKSION (MUSLIMERNES FAELLESRAAD). Text in Danish. 2006. q. DKK 250 (effective 2009). **Document type:** *Magazine, Consumer.*
Description: Scientific, spiritual and ideological aspects of Islam.
Formerly (until 2008): Refleksion (1901-3159)
Published by: Muslimernes Faellesraad, Noerrebrogade 37, Copenhagen N, 2200, Denmark. info@m-i-d.dk, http://www.m-i-d.dk.

RELIGION AND LAW REVIEW. *see* LAW

297 PAK ISSN 1605-0045
RENAISSANCE; a monthly Islamic journal. Text in English. 1991. m. PKR 200 in Pakistan; USD 20, GBP 10 foreign (effective 2001). adv.
Document type: *Journal, Academic/Scholarly.* **Description:** Aims to communicate the true message of Islam, to present the teachings of Islam in their pristine form and to apply its principles in current circumstances with a view to present positive solutions to the problems faced in the fields of law and politics, economics and sociology and indeed in all the other spheres of life.
Related titles: Online - full text ed.
Address: c/o Mr Azeem Ayub, 51-K Model Town, Lahore, Pakistan. Ed. Javed Ahmad Ghamidi. adv.: B&W page USD 15.

297.77 GBR ISSN 0034-6721
REVIEW OF RELIGIONS. Text in English. 1902. m. USD 30 (effective 2009). adv. bk.rev. index, cum.index. back issues avail.; reprints avail.
Document type: *Magazine, Trade.* **Description:** Aims to educate and inform its readers on religious, social, economic and political issues with particular emphasis on Islam.
Related titles: Microform ed.: (from PQC); Online - full text ed.
Indexed: A22, BAS, PerIslam.
Published by: Ahmadiyya Movement, 16 Gressenhall Rd, London, SW18 5QL, United Kingdom. TEL 44-20-88708517, FAX 44-20-88705234, info@ahmadiyya.org.uk, http://www.ahmadiyya.org.uk. Ed. Mansoor Ahmed Shah. Pub. Al Shirkatul Islamiyyah.

297 BIH ISSN 1512-6609
DS36
RIJASET ISLAMSKE ZAJEDNICE U BOSNI I HERCEGOVINI. GLASNIK/RIYASAT OF THE ISLAMIC COMMUNITY IN BOSNIA AND HERZEGOVINA. HERALD. Text in Bosnian; Summaries in Arabic, English. 1950. bi-m. **Document type:** *Journal, Academic/Scholarly.*
Former titles (until 1997): Rijaset Islamske Zajednice u Republici Bosni i Hercegovini. Glasnik (1512-6595); (until 1994): Rijaseta Islamske Zajednice u S F R J. Glasnik (0353-779X); (until 1990): Vrhovno Islamsko Starjesinstvo. Glasnik (0504-8273)
Indexed: PerIslam.
Published by: Rijaset Islamske Zajednice u Bosni i Hercegovini/Riyasat of the Islamic Community in Bosnia and Herzegovina, Zelenih beretki 17, Sarajevo, 71000, Bosnia Herzegovina. TEL 387-33-533000, FAX 387-33-441800, urednik@rijaset.ba, http://www.rijaset.ba. Ed. Mehmedalija Hadzic.

297.57 UAE
AL-RISALAH. Text in Arabic. 1987. m. per issue exchange basis.
Description: Covers topics of interest to Muslims.
Published by: Islamic Information Office, Publications Section, PO Box 1731, Sharjah, United Arab Emirates. TEL 372544. Circ: 1,000.

297 OMN
RISALAT AL-MASJID. Text in Arabic. m. illus. **Document type:** *Government.*
Published by: Diwan of Royal Court Affairs, Protocol Department, P O Box 6066, Muscat, Oman. TEL 704580. Ed. A Kareem.

297 IRN
RISALAT AL-TAQRIB. Text in Arabic. q. USD 15 in Africa; USD 20 elsewhere (effective 2001). **Document type:** *Journal, Academic/Scholarly.* **Description:** Presents studies and research on Islamic schools of thought and law.
Published by: Islamic Thought Foundation, P O Box 14155-3899, Tehran, Iran. TEL 98-21-88976635, FAX 98-21-8902725, i.t.f@iran-itf.com. Ed. Mohammad Ali Azarshab.

297 IRN
RISALATUTH THAQALAYN. Text in Arabic. q. USD 25 in Africa; USD 30 elsewhere (effective 2001). **Document type:** *Journal, Academic/Scholarly.* **Description:** Presents articles and studies on Ahlul Beiyt's affairs.
Published by: Islamic Thought Foundation, P O Box 14155-3899, Tehran, Iran. TEL 98-21-88976635, FAX 98-21-8902725, i.t.f@iran-itf.com. Ed. Foad Meghdadi.

297 FRA ISSN 1954-1562
RISSALA. Text in French. 2007. bi-m. back issues avail. **Document type:** *Magazine, Consumer.*
Published by: Federation Regionale de la Grande Mosquee de Paris (F R G M P), 22 Rue DeMarquette, Henin-Beaumont, 62110, France. TEL 33-6-22440546, kader.aoussedj@hotmail.fr, http://www.frgmp-nord.com.

297.071 JOR ISSN 1466-2361
BL1
ROYAL INSTITUTE FOR INTER-FAITH STUDIES. BULLETIN. Text in English. 1991. s-a. **Document type:** *Bulletin, Academic/Scholarly.*
Description: Provides a venue in the Arab world for the interdisciplinary study and rational discussion of religion and religious issues, with particular reference to Christianity in Arab and Islamic society.
Indexed: AmH&L, CA, HistAb, I14, MLA-IB, P30, P42, PSA, S02, S03, SCOPUS, SociolAb, T02.
Published by: Royal Institute for Inter-Faith Studies, PO Box 830562, Amman, 11183, Jordan. TEL 962-6-4618051, FAX 962-6-4618053, baker.hiyari@riifs.org, http://www.riifs.org.

297.09485 SWE ISSN 0283-684X
SALAAM. Text in Swedish. 1986. 6/yr. SEK 200 (effective 1998). bk.rev.
Document type: *Newspaper, Academic/Scholarly.* **Description:** Publishes articles and news items on Islam and the Muslim world, particularly Muslims in Sweden.
Published by: Islamiska Informationsfoereningen, Goetagatan 103 A, Fack 20163, Stockholm, 10460, Sweden. TEL 46-8-702-00-67, FAX 46-8-702-00-67. Ed. Helena Benaouda. R&P Mohamed Benaouda. Circ: 1,000.

297 TUR ISSN 1300-2511
SAMANYOLU; uc aylik egitim dergisi - quarterly magazine of the social sciences. Text and summaries in English, Turkish. 1990. q. TRY 40,000, USD 15 to individuals; USD 25 to institutions. adv. abstr.; bibl.; illus. **Document type:** *Journal, Academic/Scholarly.*
Description: Publishes articles in all disciplines of the social sciences, including historiography, education and sociology. Also addresses issues related to the role of religion in modern society.

ISSN 1019-0805
...amiyyat. Text in
...D 35 in Asia; USD 40
... in Africa. **Document**

...P O Box 14155-3899,
...98-21-898295, i.t.f@iran-

ISSN 1300-5057
...**FAKULTESI DERGISI.** Text in
...**ype:** *Journal, Academic/Scholarly.*
...d.

...esi, Ilahiyat Fakultesi, Meram Yeni Yol,
...Turkey. TEL 90-332-3238250, FAX
...selcuk.edu.tr.

JOR
SHARI'AH. Text in Arabic. 1959. fortn.
Published by: Shari'ah College, P O Box 585, Amman, Jordan. Circ: 5,000.

297.82 GBR
SHIA WORLD. Text in English. 1976. q. bk.rev. back issues avail. **Document type:** *Magazine, Consumer.*
Published by: World Federation of Khoja Shia Ithnaasheri Muslim Communities, Islamic Ctr, Wood Ln, PO Box 60, Stanmore, Mddx HA7 4LQ, United Kingdom. TEL 44-20-89549881, FAX 44-20-89549034, secretariat@world-federation.org, http://www.world-federation.org.

297.82 PAK
SHIAH. Text in Urdu. 1977 (vol.56). w. PKR 12.
Published by: Insaf Press, Railway Rd., Lahore, Pakistan.

SINGAPORE HALAL DIRECTORY. *see* AGRICULTURE

297 200.82 GBR ISSN 1756-1973
SISTERS. Text in English. 200?. q. GBP 19.99 domestic; GBP 24.99 foreign; GBP 17.99 to students; GBP 4.99 per issue domestic; GBP 3.99 per issue foreign (effective 2009). adv. back issues avail. **Document type:** *Magazine, Trade.* **Description:** Provides Muslim women inspiration for an Islamic life from deen and tarbiyah to food and fashion.
Related titles: Online - full text ed.: ISSN 1756-2333. GBP 7.99 (effective 2008).
Published by: Sisters Magazine, PO Box 2950, Mitcham, CR4 1UP, United Kingdom. TEL 44-208-1503117, info@sisters-magazine.com. Ed. Na'ima B Robert.

297 USA ISSN 1942-7948
SOCIOLOGY OF ISLAM & MUSLIM SOCIETIES. Text in English. 2008. 3/yr. back issues avail. **Document type:** *Newsletter, Consumer.* **Description:** Aims to study and understand the sociological aspects of Islam and Muslim societies.
Related titles: Online - full text ed.: ISSN 1942-7956. free (effective 2010).
Published by: Portland State University, Department of Sociology, PO Box 751, Portland, OR 97207. TEL 503-725-3926, FAX 503-725-3957, bhbj@pdx.edu, http://www.sociology.pdx.edu.

297 FRA ISSN 0585-5292
BP1
STUDIA ISLAMICA. Text in French. 1953. irreg. adv. reprints avail. **Document type:** *Journal, Academic/Scholarly.*
Related titles: Online - full text ed.
Indexed: A21, A22, BibLing, DIP, FR, HistAb, I14, IBR, IBZ, M10, MLA-IB, P30, PCI, PerIslam, PhilInd, RASB, RI-1, RI-2, SCOPUS.
—BLDSC (8482.950000), IE, Infotrieve, Ingenta, INIST. **CCC.**
Published by: Maisonneuve et Larose, 15 Rue Victor Cousin, Paris, 75005, France. TEL 33-1-44414930, FAX 33-1-43257741, maisonneuvelarose@yahoo.fr, http://www.maisonneuveetlarose.com/.

297 DEU ISSN 1862-1295
➤ **STUDIEN ZUR GESCHICHTE UND KULTUR DES ISLAMISCHEN ORIENTS.** Text in German. 1965. irreg., latest vol.27, 2011. price varies. **Document type:** *Monographic series, Academic/Scholarly.*
Formerly (until 2004): Studien zur Sprache, Geschichte und Kultur des Islamischen Orients (0585-6221)
Related titles: ◆ Supplement to: Der Islam. ISSN 0021-1818.
—CCC.
Published by: Walter de Gruyter GmbH & Co. KG, Genthiner Str 13, Berlin, 10785, Germany. TEL 49-30-260050, FAX 49-30-26005251, info@degruyter.com, http://www.degruyter.com. Ed. Lawrence Conrad.

297 USA ISSN 1523-9888
BP1
➤ **STUDIES IN CONTEMPORARY ISLAM.** Text in English. 1999. s-a. USD 15 to individuals; USD 30 to institutions (effective 2010). back issues avail. **Document type:** *Journal, Academic/Scholarly.* **Description:** Forum for scholarly dialogue and communication; it does not promote a particular point of view or ideology.
Published by: Youngstown State University, Center for Islamic Studies, 421 DeBartolo Hall, One University Plaza, Youngstown, OH 44555. TEL 330-941-1625, FAX 330-941-1600, mmir@ysu.edu.

297.14 NLD ISSN 1384-1130
➤ **STUDIES IN ISLAMIC LAW & SOCIETY.** Text in English. 1996. irreg., latest vol.30, 2007. price varies. back issues avail. **Document type:** *Monographic series, Academic/Scholarly.* **Description:** Publishes scholarly treatments of historical and contemporary issues in Islamic law and its interpretation.
Indexed: IZBG.
Published by: Brill, PO Box 9000, Leiden, 2300 PA, Netherlands. TEL 31-71-5353500, FAX 31-71-5317532, cs@brill.nl. R&P Elizabeth Venekamp. **Dist. in N. America by:** Brill, PO Box 605, Herndon, VA 20172-0605. TEL 703-661-1585, 800-337-9255, FAX 703-661-1501, cs@brillusa.com; **Dist. by:** Turpin Distribution Services Ltd., Pegasus Dr, Stratton Business Park, Biggleswade, Bedfordshire SG18 8QB, United Kingdom. TEL 44-1767-604954, FAX 44-1767-601640, custserv@turpin-distribution.com, http://www.turpin-distribution.com/.

297 USA
STUDIES IN LATE ANTIQUITY AND EARLY ISLAM. Abbreviated title: S L A E I. Text in English. 1992. irreg., latest vol.24, 2008. price varies. back issues avail. **Document type:** *Monographic series, Academic/Scholarly.* **Description:** Provides a basic resource for all those interested in late antiquity and Byzantium, early Islam and eastern Christianity, and Byzantine and Islamic archaeology and art history.
Published by: Darwin Press, Inc., PO Box 2202, Princeton, NJ 08543. TEL 609-737-1349, 866-772-9817, FAX 609-737-0929, books@darwinpress.com. Ed. Lawrence I Conrad.

297.4 GBR ISSN 0955-7385
BP189.7.K46
SUFI. Text in English. 1988. s-a. GBP 7 domestic to individuals; USD 12 in United States to individuals; USD 14 in Canada to individuals; EUR 7.50 in Europe to individuals; GBP 10 elsewhere to individuals; GBP 10.50, USD 15 to institutions (effective 2009). illus. **Document type:** *Journal, Trade.* **Description:** Designed for those seeking to understand the key messages of Sufism and devoted to the study of mysticism in all its aspects.
Indexed: M10.
Published by: Khaniqahi Nimatullahi Publications, The Editor, 41 Chepstow Place, London, W2 4TS, United Kingdom.

SUFISM; the science of the soul. *see* PSYCHOLOGY

297.57 IRN ISSN 1019-0791
AL-TAHIRAH. Text in Arabic. 1992 (no.30). m. USD 25 in the Middle East; USD 40 in Europe; USD 25 in Africa; USD 40 elsewhere. **Document type:** *Magazine, Consumer.* **Description:** Discusses the stats and activities of women in an Islamic context.
Published by: Islamic Thought Foundation, P O Box 14155-3899, Tehran, Iran. TEL 98-21-844092, FAX 98-21-898295, i.t.f@iran-itf.com.

297 PAK
TARJUMAN AL-HADITH. Text in Urdu. 1969. m. PKR 300. back issues avail.
Published by: Jamait E Ahl A Hadees Pakistan, 53 Lawrence Rd., Lahore, Pakistan. FAX 042-54072, TELEX 46424-KARAM-PK. Ed. Sajid Mir. Circ: 2,000.

297.57 IRN ISSN 0267-968X
BP1
➤ **AL-TAWHID**; a quarterly journal of Islamic thought and culture. Text in English. 1983. q. USD 35 in Asia; USD 25 in Africa; USD 40 elsewhere (effective 2003 - 2004). adv. bk.rev. back issues avail. **Document type:** *Magazine, Academic/Scholarly.* **Description:** Covers Quranic studies, hadith, Islamic law and jurisprudence, Islamic history and philosophy, mysticism, ethics, sociology, economics, political science and comparative religion.
Related titles: Online - full text ed.
Indexed: M10, PerIslam, R&TA, RASB.
Published by: Islamic Thought Foundation, P O Box 37165-111, Qum, Iran. Circ: 1,200.

297.93 DEU ISSN 1433-2078
TEMPORA. Text in German. 1960. a. bk.rev. bibl.; illus. cum.index. **Document type:** *Magazine, Consumer.*
Formerly (until 1997): Baha'i-Briefe (0005-3945)
Indexed: DIP, IBR, IBZ.
Published by: Nationale Geistige Rat der Baha'i in Deutschland e.V., Eppsteiner Str 89, Hofheim, 65719, Germany. TEL 49-6192-22921, FAX 49-6192-22936. Circ: 1,600 (controlled).

202.2 FRA ISSN 1761-211X
TERRES ET GENS D'ISLAM. Text in French. 2003. irreg. back issues avail. **Document type:** *Monographic series.*
Published by: Editions Karthala, 22-24 Boulevard Arago, Paris, 75013, France. TEL 33-1-43311559, FAX 33-1-45352705, karthala@orange.fr, http://www.karthala.com.

297 EGY ISSN 0257-4136
TEXTES ARABES ET ETUDES ISLAMIQUES. Text in Arabic, French. 1914. irreg., latest vol.42, 2008. price varies. back issues avail. **Document type:** *Monographic series.* **Description:** Presents critical editions of significant Arabic texts, bibliographies and studies in Islamic history, with an emphasis on Egypt.
Published by: Institut Francais d'Archeologie Orientale du Caire, Kasr el-Aini, 37 Sharia Sheikh Aly Youssef, Mounira, PO Box 11562, Cairo, Egypt. TEL 20-2-3571622, ventes@ifao.egnet.net. **Dist. by:** Boustany's Publishing House, 29 Faggalah St, Cairo 11271, Egypt. TEL 20-2-5915315, FAX 20-2-4177915.

297.18 NLD ISSN 1567-2808
TEXTS AND STUDIES ON THE QURAN. Text in English. 2004. irreg., latest vol.4, 2008. price varies. **Document type:** *Monographic series, Academic/Scholarly.*
Indexed: IZBG.
Published by: Brill, PO Box 9000, Leiden, 2300 PA, Netherlands. FAX 31-71-5317532, cs@brill.nl, http://www.brill.nl. Eds. Gerhard Boewering, Jane D McAuliffe.

297 NLD ISSN 1389-823X
THEMES IN ISLAMIC STUDIES. Text in English. 2000. irreg., latest vol.4, 2008. price varies. **Document type:** *Monographic series, Academic/Scholarly.*
Indexed: IZBG.
Published by: Brill, PO Box 9000, Leiden, 2300 PA, Netherlands. TEL 31-71-5353500, FAX 31-71-5317532, cs@brill.nl.

297 DNK ISSN 1901-9580
➤ **TIDSSKRIFT FOR ISLAMFORSKNING**; danske koranstudier. Text in Danish. 2006. s-a. bk.rev. back issues avail. **Document type:** *Journal, Academic/Scholarly.*
Media: Online - full content.
Published by: Forum for Islamforskning, c/o Garbi Schmidt, Forskningsinstituttet, Herluf Trolles Gade 11, Copenhagen K, 1052, Denmark. TEL 45-33-480896, info@islamforskning.dk. Ed. Brian Arly Jacobsen.

297 NGA ISSN 0331-5975
THE TRUTH; the Muslim weekly. Text in English. 1951. w. NGN 52, USD 5. adv. bk.rev. back issues avail. **Document type:** *Newspaper.*
Published by: Ahmadiyya Muslim Jamaat, 45 Idumagbo Ave, PO Box 418, Lagos, Nigeria. TEL 234-1-920105, FAX 234-1-668455, TELEX 26947 KESSAN NG. Ed. Alhaji M Habbebu. Circ: 5,000.

297 ZAF ISSN 0257-7062
BP1
➤ **TYDSKRIF VIR ISLAMKUNDE/JOURNAL FOR ISLAMIC STUDIES.** Text in Afrikaans, English. 1980. a. ZAR 100, USD 40 (effective 2000). **Document type:** *Journal, Academic/Scholarly.* **Description:** Publishes research into Islam in Africa and elsewhere.
Indexed: A21, PerIslam.
Published by: University of Cape Town, Centre of Contemporary Islam, Private Bag, Rondebosch, 7701, South Africa. cci@socsci.uct.ac.za. Ed. J A. Naude. Circ: 300.

297.5 PAK
➤ **ULOOM-E-ISLAMIYAH**; International. Text in Arabic, English, Sindhi, Urdu. 2005. s-a. PKR 250 (effective 2007). adv. **Document type:** *Journal, Academic/Scholarly.* **Description:** Contains articles on relations between Muslims and non-Muslims.
Published by: Maktabah Yadgar Shaikh-ul-Islam Pakistan Allama Shabbir Ahmed Usmani, 162, Sector 8/L, Orangi Town, Karachi, Pakistan. TEL 92-21-6659703, drsalahuddinsani@yahoo.com, http://www.auick.org. Ed., Pub. Salahuddin Sani. adv.: B&W page PKR 300, color page PKR 500. Circ: 500 (paid and controlled).

297 PAK ISSN 2073-5146
BP1
➤ **ULUM-E-ISLAMIA.** Text in English, Urdu; Summaries in English. 1975. s-a. free (effective 2009). Index. back issues avail.; reprints avail. **Document type:** *Journal, Academic/Scholarly.* **Description:** Covers research in all disciplines of Islamic studies: Quran, Hadith, Fiqh, Arabic, etc.
—CCC.
Published by: Islamia University of Bahawalpur, Faculty of Islamic Learning, Baghdad Campus, Bahawalpur, Pakistan. TEL 92-62-9255559, FAX 92-62-9255063, muloomi@hotmail.com, baghdadidgk@gmail.com. Ed. Shahid Hassan Rizvi. R&P Saleem Tariq Khan.

297.57 PAK
UNIVERSAL MESSAGE. Text in English. 1979. m. PKR 150, USD 25 (effective 1998). adv. bk.rev. bibl. back issues avail. **Document type:** *Journal, Academic/Scholarly.* **Description:** Teaches a better understanding of the religion, culture and history of Islam.
Indexed: PerIslam.
Published by: Islamic Research Academy, D-35, Block 5, Federal 'B' Area, Karachi, 75950, Pakistan. TEL 92-21-6349840, FAX 92-21-6361040. Ed. Shahid Hashmi. Circ: 1,000 (controlled).

297 LBN
UNIVERSITE SAINT-JOSEPH. FACULTE DES LETTRES ET DES SCIENCES HUMAINES. RECHERCHES. SERIE A: LANGUE ARABE ET PENSEE ISLAMIQUE. Text in French. 1956; N.S. 1971. irreg. price varies. **Document type:** *Monographic series, Academic/Scholarly.*
Indexed: BibLing.
Published by: (Universite Saint-Joseph, Faculte des Lettres et des Sciences Humaines), Dar el-Machreq S.A.R.L., rue Huvelin 2, P O Box 946, Beirut, Lebanon. machreq@cyberia.net.lb.

297 PAK ISSN 0042-8132
VOICE OF ISLAM. Text in English. 1968 (vol.16). m. PKR 10. adv. bk.rev.
Indexed: BAS, PerIslam.
Published by: Jamiyat-ul-Falah Karachi, P O Box 7141, Karachi 3, Pakistan. Ed. A A Alam. Circ: 5,000.

297 UGA
VOICE OF ISLAM. Text in English. m.
Indexed: PerIslam.
Published by: Ahmaddiya Muslim Association, PO Box 16085, Kampala, Uganda.

297 MUS
VOIX DE L'ISLAM. Text in English, French. 1951. m. MUR 5. back issues avail.
Indexed: PerIslam.
Published by: Abdool Azize Peeroo, Ed. & Pub., Parisot Rd., Mesnil, Phoenix, Mauritius.

297.9 NGA ISSN 0049-688X
WAR CRY. Text in English. 1921. q. NGN 15. bk.rev.
Published by: Salvation Army in Nigeria, Territorial Headquarters, PO Box 3025, Shomolu, Lagos, Nigeria. TEL 234-1-4975481, FAX 234-1-821497. Ed. Capt F O Oloruntoba. Circ: 4,500.

297.09033 NLD ISSN 0043-2539
DS36
➤ **DIE WELT DES ISLAMS/WORLD OF ISLAM**; internationale Zeitschrift fuer die Geschichte des Islams in der Neuzeit - international journal for the history of modern Islam. Text in English, French, German. 1913-1943; N.S. 1951. 4/yr. EUR 317, USD 443 to institutions; EUR 345, USD 483 combined subscription to institutions (print & online eds.) (effective 2012). bk.rev. index, cum.index: vols.1-35 (1951-1995). back issues avail.; reprint service avail. from PSC. **Document type:** *Journal, Academic/Scholarly.* **Description:** Focuses on the history and culture of the peoples of Islam from the end of the 18th century up to the present, with special attention given to literature.
Related titles: Microform ed.: (from SWZ); Online - full text ed.: ISSN 1570-0607. EUR 288, USD 403 to institutions (effective 2012) (from IngentaConnect).
Indexed: A01, A03, A08, A20, A21, A22, AmHI, ArtHuCI, BibInd, BibLing, CA, DIP, E01, H07, HistAb, I14, IBR, IBSS, IBZ, IZBG, M10, MLA-IB, P42, PCI, PSA, PerIslam, RASB, RI-1, RI-2, S02, S03, SCOPUS, SociolAb, T02, W07.
—BLDSC (9294.710000), IE, Infotrieve, Ingenta. **CCC.**
Published by: Brill, PO Box 9000, Leiden, 2300 PA, Netherlands. TEL 31-71-5353500, FAX 31-71-5317532, cs@brill.nl. Ed. Stefan Reichmuth. **Dist. by:** Turpin Distribution Services Ltd., Pegasus Dr, Stratton Business Park, Biggleswade, Bedfordshire SG18 8QB, United Kingdom. TEL 44-1767-604954, FAX 44-1767-601640, custserv@turpin-distribution.com, http://www.turpin-distribution.com/.

297 CHE ISSN 1661-6278
WELTEN DES ISLAMS/MONDES DE L'ISLAM/WORLDS OF ISLAM. Text in English, French, German. 2006. irreg., latest vol.2, 2007. price varies. **Document type:** *Monographic series, Academic/Scholarly.*
Published by: Peter Lang AG (Subsidiary of: Peter Lang Publishing Group), Hochfeldstr 32, Postfach 746, Bern 9, 3000, Switzerland. TEL 41-31-3061717, FAX 41-31-3061727, info@peterlang.com, http://www.peterlang.com.

297.7 AUT
▼ **WIENER ISLAMISCH-RELIGIONSPAEDAGOGISCHE STUDIEN.** Text in German. 2009. irreg. price varies. **Document type:** *Monographic series, Academic/Scholarly.*
Published by: Boehlau Verlag GmbH & Co.KG., Wiesingerstr 1, Vienna, W 1010, Austria. TEL 43-1-3302427, FAX 43-1-3302432, boehlau@boehlau.at. Ed. Ednan Aslan.

297 GBR
WORLD ASSEMBLY OF MUSLIM YOUTH. EUROPEAN NEWSLETTER. Text in English. 2001. irreg. **Document type:** *Newsletter, Consumer.* **Description:** Covers the activities of the Muslim Youth organizations in Europe.
Published by: World Assembly of Muslim Youth/Nadwat al-A'alamiyat li-l-Sabab al-Islami, 46 Goodge St, London, W1T 4LU, United Kingdom. TEL 44-20-7636-7010, FAX 44-20-7636-7080, wamy@wamy.co.uk, http://www.wamy.co.uk.

297.6 PAK ISSN 0084-2052
WORLD MUSLIM CONFERENCE. PROCEEDINGS. Text in English. biennial. **Document type:** *Proceedings.*
Related titles: ◆ Supplement to: Muslim World. ISSN 0464-0756.
Published by: World Muslim Congress/Motamar al-Alam al-Islami, Site 9-A Gulsha-e-Iqbal, Karachi, 75300, Pakistan. TEL 460712, FAX 466878, TELEX 24318-UMMAT-PK.

297 PAK ISSN 0084-2060
WORLD MUSLIM GAZETTEER. Text in English. 1964. quinquennial. USD 30.
Published by: World Muslim Congress/Motamar al-Alam al-Islami, Site 9-A Gulsha-e-Iqbal, Karachi, 75300, Pakistan. TEL 460712, FAX 466878. Ed. Inamullah Khan.

297.122 PAK ISSN 0044-0213
BP1
YAQEEN INTERNATIONAL. Text in Arabic, English. 1952. fortn. PKR 150; USD 20 in Europe; USD 20 in Japan; USD 30 in Australasia; USD 30 in the Americas. bk.rev. bibl. back issues avail. **Description:** Presents Islam as taught by the Quran and Sunnah.
Indexed: AMR, PerIslam.
Published by: Darut Tasnif, Iqbal Mansion, Off Shahrah-e-Liaquat, Near Naveed Clinic, Saddar, Karachi, 74400, Pakistan. TEL 92-21-5684325. Ed. Hafiz Muhammad Adil. Circ: 1,500. **Subscr. to:** Main Hub River Rd., Mujahidabad, Karachi 75760, Pakistan. TEL 92-21-2441182.

297 NLD ISSN 1877-1432
D1056.2.M87
▼ **YEARBOOK OF MUSLIMS IN EUROPE.** Text in English. 2009. a. price varies.
Published by: Brill, PO Box 9000, Leiden, 2300 PA, Netherlands. TEL 31-71-5353500, FAX 31-71-5317532, cs@brill.nl.

297 IRN ISSN 1024-9656
ZAMZAM; for young people. Text in English. 1995. m. USD 30 in Asia; USD 36 in Europe; USD 40 in US, Canada & Australia; USD 25 in Africa (effective 2001). **Document type:** *Magazine, Consumer.*
Related titles: Persian, Modern ed.: ISSN 1024-9664.
Published by: Islamic Thought Foundation, P O Box 14155-3899, Tehran, Iran. TEL 98-21-88976635, FAX 98-21-8902725, i.t.f@iran-itf.com. Ed. Maryam Tamhidi.

297 CHN ISSN 1004-3578
DS731.M87
ZHONGGUO MUSILIN/CHINA MUSLIM. Text in Chinese. 1957. bi-m. USD 21.60 (effective 2009). **Document type:** *Journal, Academic/Scholarly.*
Related titles: Online - full text ed.; Uigur ed.: Zhongguo Musilin (Weiwen). ISSN 1007-5836. CNY 18 domestic; USD 8.80 foreign (effective 2005).
—East View.
Published by: Zhongguo Musilin Jiaoxiehui/China Islamic Association, Xuanwu-qu, 103, Nanheng Xijie, Beijing, 100053, China. **Dist. by:** China International Book Trading Corp, 35 Chegongzhuang Xilu, Haidian District, PO Box 399, Beijing 100044, China. TEL 86-10-68412045, FAX 86-10-68412023, cibtc@mail.cibtc.com.cn, http://www.cibtc.com.cn.

RELIGIONS AND THEOLOGY—Judaic

see also ETHNIC INTERESTS

296 USA
A C H I M MAGAZINE. Text in English. 1967. q. USD 12 (effective 2000). adv. bk.rev. charts; illus.
Formerly: Brotherhood (0007-2435)
Published by: National Federation of Temple Brotherhoods, 633 3rd Ave, New York, NY 10017-6706. TEL 212-650-4100, FAX 800-765-6200, nftb@uahc.org, http://rj.org/nftb. Eds. Douglas Barden, Michael Geller. Circ: 40,000.

A D L ON THE FRONTLINE. *see* POLITICAL SCIENCE—Civil Rights

A J L NEWSLETTER. *see* LIBRARY AND INFORMATION SCIENCES

296.7 USA ISSN 1529-6423
BM75
A J S PERSPECTIVES; the newsletter of the association of jewish studies. Text in English. 1970-1998; N.S. 1999. s-a. membership. bk.rev. bibl. **Document type:** *Newsletter.*
Formerly (until 1999): Association for Jewish Studies Newsletter (0278-4033)
Related titles: Microfilm ed.
Indexed: IJP.
Published by: Association for Jewish Studies, MS011, Brandeis University, PO Box 549110, Waltham, MA 02254-9110. ajs@ajs.cjh.org. Eds. Bernard D Cooperman, Steven Fine. Circ: 1,700.

296.7 GBR ISSN 0364-...
BM1
➤ **A J S REVIEW.** Text in English. 1975. s-a. GBP 104, USD 180 to institutions; GBP 114, USD 193 combined subscription to institutions (print & online eds.) (effective 2012). adv. bk.rev. bibl. back issues avail.; reprints avail. **Document type:** *Journal, Academic/Scholarly.* **Description:** Publishes scholarly articles and book reviews covering the field of Jewish Studies, broadly defined, and representative of the Association for Jewish Studies.
Related titles: Online - full text ed.: ISSN 1475-4541. GBP 98, USD 168 to institutions (effective 2012).
Indexed: A20, A21, A22, ABS&EES, AmH&L, ArtHuCI, CA, DIP, E01, ENW, HistAb, I14, IBR, IBZ, JewAb, MLA-IB, P28, P30, P48, P53, P54, PQC, T02, W07.
—IE, Infotrieve, Ingenta. **CCC.**
Published by: (Association for Jewish Studies USA) Cambridge University Press, The Edinburgh Bldg, Shaftesbury Rd, Cambridge, CB2 8RU, United Kingdom. TEL 44-1223-312393, FAX 44-1223-315052, journals@cambridge.org, http://www.cambridge.org/uk. Eds. Elisheva Carlebach, Robert Goldenberg. adv.: B&W page USD 685, B&W page GBP 360; trim 115 x 190. Circ: 1,700. **Subscr. to:** Cambridge University Press, 32 Ave of the Americas, New York, NY 10013. TEL 212-337-5000, FAX 212-691-3239.

296.7 USA
DS150.R3
A M I T; building Israel. one child at a time. Text in English. 1926. q. membership. adv. bk.rev. illus. **Description:** Contains articles of interest to the Jewish community.
Former titles (until 1996): A M I T Magazine (1085-2891); (until 1995): A M I T Woman (0747-0258); (until 1984): American Mizrachi Woman (0161-3952); (until 1974): Mizrachi Woman (0026-7007)
Related titles: Online - full text ed.
Indexed: IJP.
Published by: Irgun Mitnadvot l'ma'an Yisrael v'Torata/Organization for Volunteers for Israel and Her Torah, 817 Broadway, New York, NY 10003. TEL 212-477-4720, 800-989-2648, FAX 212-353-2312, info@amitchildren.org. adv.: B&W page USD 1,200. Circ: 35,000.

A O J T NEWSLETTER. *see* EDUCATION

296 USA ISSN 1940-0144
DS101
A R I E L. Text mainly in Russian; Text occasionally in English. 200?. m. **Document type:** *Magazine, Consumer.*
Published by: American Russian Institute for Enrichment of Life, 6701 Old Pimlico Rd, Baltimore, MD 21209. TEL 410-764-5000, FAX 410-517-0770, info@arielonline.com.

296 SVK
ACTA JUDAICA SLOVACA. Text in Slovak. irreg. bibl.; illus. back issues avail. **Document type:** *Yearbook, Academic/Scholarly.*
Published by: Slovenske Narodne Muzeum, Muzeum Zidovskej Kultury, Vajanskeho nabr 2, Bratislava, 81436, Slovakia. TEL 421-2-52962973, FAX 421-2-52966653, nmc@snm.sk. Ed. Pavol Mestan.

AGADA; an illustrated Jewish literary magazine. *see* LITERATURE

AGENDA: JEWISH EDUCATION; a journal of public policy magazine. *see* EDUCATION—Teaching Methods And Curriculum

296.071 USA ISSN 1565-1525
BM538.S3
ALEPH: HISTORICAL STUDIES IN SCIENCE AND JUDAISM. Text in English. 2000. s-a. USD 94.50 combined subscription to institutions (print & online eds.) (effective 2012). adv. back issues avail.; reprint service avail. from PSC. **Document type:** *Journal, Academic/Scholarly.* **Description:** Explores the interface between Judaism and science in history.
Related titles: Online - full text ed.: ISSN 1553-3956. USD 62.50 to institutions (effective 2012).
Indexed: A01, A20, A22, A26, AmHI, ArtHuCI, B04, BRD, CA, E01, E08, G08, H05, H07, H08, HAb, HumInd, I05, I14, J01, MLA-IB, P02, P10, P28, P48, P53, P54, PQC, R05, S09, S11, SCOPUS, T02, W03, W05, W07.
—IE. **CCC.**
Published by: (Hebrew University of Jerusalem ISR), Indiana University Press, 601 N Morton St, Bloomington, IN 47404. TEL 812-855-8817, 800-842-6796, FAX 812-855-7931, journals@indiana.edu, http://iupress.indiana.edu. Ed. Gad Freudenthal. Circ: 150.

296.7 USA
DER ALGEMEINER JOURNAL. Text in English, Yiddish. 1972. w. USD 40; USD 250 foreign. adv. bk.rev.; film rev.; play rev. illus. **Document type:** *Newspaper.* **Description:** An independent publication serving the Jewish community in the U.S. and abroad.
Related titles: Diskette ed.
Published by: Algemeiner Journal, 508 Montgomery St., Brooklyn, NY 11225-3023. TEL 212-267-5561, FAX 212-267-5624. Ed., R&P Gershon Jacobson. Adv. contact Feige Braun. Circ: 212,000 (paid).

296 FRA ISSN 0002-6050
DS101
ALLIANCE ISRAELITE UNIVERSELLE EN FRANCE. CAHIERS; paix et droit. Text in French. 1947. irreg. (3-4/yr.). free to qualified personnel. bk.rev. bibl. **Document type:** *Journal, Consumer.*
Published by: Alliance Israelite Universelle en France, 45 Rue La Bruyere, Paris, 75009, France. TEL 33-1-53328853, FAX 33-1-48745133. Ed. Maguy Azria. Circ: 5,000.

296 USA ISSN 0741-465X
E184.J5
AMERICAN COUNCIL FOR JUDAISM. ISSUES. Text in English. 1958. q. free. bk.rev. **Document type:** *Bulletin.*
Formerly (until 1979): Brief (0006-9922)
Indexed: CLI.
Published by: American Council for Judaism, PO Box 9009, Alexandria, VA 22304. http://www.acjna.org. Ed., R&P Allan C Brownfeld. Pub. Alan V Stone. Circ: 8,000.

296 USA ISSN 0740-8528
JX1
AMERICAN COUNCIL FOR JUDAISM. SPECIAL INTEREST REPORT; a digest of news items and articles in the area of the council's interest. Text in English. 1968. m. free (effective 2005). back issues avail. **Document type:** *Bulletin.*
Published by: American Council for Judaism, PO Box 9009, Alexandria, VA 22304. TEL 703-836-2546. Ed., R&P Allan C Brownfeld. Pub. Alan V Stone. Circ: 8,000.

296.7
Add...
31...

296.7 USA
E184.J5
AMERICAN JEW... preservation a... Abbreviated title... personnel (effective ... **Document type:** Journ...
Formerly (until 1997): America... (0002-905X)
Media: Online - full text. **Related titles...**
Indexed: A20, A21, A22, ABS&EES, ASC..., IBR, IBZ, IJP, J01, JewAb, MEA&I, MLA..., RILM, T02.
—BLDSC (0820.921000), IE, Infotrieve, Ingenta.
Published by: American Jewish Archives, Jacob Rad..., 3101 Clifton Ave, Cincinnati, OH 45220. TEL 513-22..., 513-221-7812, aja@fuse.net.

296.7 USA ISSN 0...
DS101
AMERICAN JEWISH CONGRESS. CONGRESS MONTHLY; a journal ... opinion and Jewish affairs. Key Title: Congress Monthly. Text in English. 1933. bi-m. USD 20 domestic to non-members; USD 25 foreign to non-members; USD 4 newsstand/cover; free to members (effective 2009). bk.rev.; film rev.; play rev. **Document type:** *Magazine, Consumer.* **Description:** Covers all the issues of concern to the Jewish community-political, social, and cultural; Israel; U.S.; and international affairs.
Former titles (until 1985): American Jewish Congress Monthly (0739-1927); (until 1982): American Jewish Congress. Congress Monthly (0163-1365); (until 1975): American Jewish Congress. Congress Bi-Weekly (0010-5872)
Related titles: Online - full text ed.
Indexed: A22, ABS&EES, HRIR, IJP, IPARL, JewAb, MEA&I, P06, P30.
—Ingenta.
Published by: American Jewish Congress, 825 3rd Ave, Ste 18, New York, NY 10022. TEL 212-879-4500, FAX 212-758-1633, contact@ajcongress.org.

296.0971 USA ISSN 0164-0178
E184.J5
➤ **AMERICAN JEWISH HISTORY.** Abbreviated title: A J H. Text in English. 1893. q. USD 135 to institutions; USD 189 combined subscription to institutions (print & online eds.); USD 41 per issue to institutions (effective 2012). adv. bk.rev. bibl.; charts; illus. index. 124 p./no.; back issues avail.; reprint service avail. from PSC. **Document type:** *Journal, Academic/Scholarly.* **Description:** Focuses on every aspect of the American Jewish experience. Contains articles which shows the richness and complexity of Jewish life in America.
Former titles (until 1978): American Jewish Historical Quarterly (0002-9068); (until 1961): American Jewish Historical Society. Publications (0146-5511)
Related titles: Microfiche ed.; Microfilm ed.: (from PQC); Online - full text ed.: ISSN 1086-3141. USD 145 to institutions (effective 2012).
Indexed: A01, A02, A03, A08, A20, A21, A22, A25, A26, ABS&EES, ASCA, AmH&L, AmHI, ArtHuCI, B04, BRD, CA, CurCont, DIP, E01, E08, FR, G05, G06, G07, G08, H07, H08, H09, H10, HAb, HistAb, HumInd, I05, I07, IBR, IBZ, IJP, JewAb, M01, M02, M08, M10, MEA&I, MLA-IB, P02, P10, P30, P42, P48, P53, P54, PCI, PQC, PSA, R05, RASB, RI-1, RI-2, S02, S03, S08, S09, S23, SCOPUS, SociolAb, T02, W03, W05, W07, W09.
—BLDSC (0820.935000), IE, Infotrieve, Ingenta, INIST.
Published by: (American Jewish Historical Society), The Johns Hopkins University Press, 2715 N Charles St, Baltimore, MD 21218. TEL 410-516-6900, FAX 410-516-6968. Ed. Eric L Goldstein. Pub. William M Breichner. **Subscr. to:** PO Box 19966, Baltimore, MD 21211. TEL 410-516-6987, 800-548-1784, FAX 410-516-3866, jrnlcirc@press.jhu.edu.

296.7 USA ISSN 0002-9076
F265.J5
AMERICAN JEWISH TIMES OUTLOOK. Text in English. 1934. m. adv. **Document type:** *Bulletin.*
Published by: (Blumenthal Foundation), American Jewish Times, Inc., PO Box 33218, Charlotte, NC 28233-3218. TEL 704-372-3296, FAX 704-377-9237. Ed., R&P, Adv. contact Geri Zhiss. Circ: 9,000.

AMERICAN JEWISH WORLD; voice of Minnesota Jewry. *see* ETHNIC INTERESTS

296.025 USA ISSN 0065-8987
E184.J5 CODEN: AJYBEM
AMERICAN JEWISH YEAR BOOK. Text in English. 1899. a. USD 49.95 per issue (effective 2009). index. back issues avail. **Document type:** *Yearbook, Trade.* **Description:** Compendium of articles and directories relating to Jews worldwide.
Related titles: Microfiche ed.: (from CIS).
Indexed: ABS&EES, BibInd, FR, M10, P30, PCI, S02, S03, SOPODA, SRI, SociolAb, T02.
—INIST.
Published by: American Jewish Committee, PO Box 705, New York, NY 10150. TEL 212-751-4000, FAX 212-891-1450, PR@ajc.org.

296 USA ISSN 0003-102X
DS101
AMERICAN SEPHARDI. Text in English. 1966. s-a. USD 15. bk.rev. bibl.; illus. **Description:** Contains articles of interest to the Jewish community.
Indexed: MLA, MLA-IB.
Published by: Yeshiva University, Sephardic Studies Program, 500 W 185 St, New York, NY 10033. TEL 212-960-5277. Ed. H P Salomon. Circ: 7,000.

296.3 NLD ISSN 1385-2353
➤ **AMSTERDAM STUDIES IN JEWISH THOUGHT.** Text in English. 1996. irreg., latest vol.6, 1998. price varies. **Document type:** *Monographic series, Academic/Scholarly.* **Description:** Publishes monographic studies and collections of essays on Jewish philosophical and religious thought from antiquity to the present time.
Indexed: IZBG.

Published by: Brill, PO Box 9000, Leiden, 2300 PA, Netherlands. TEL 31-71-5353500, FAX 31-71-5317532, cs@brill.nl.

296.071 NLD ISSN 1871-6636
➤ **ANCIENT JUDAISM AND EARLY CHRISTIANITY.** Cover title: A J E C. Text in English. 1961. irreg., latest vol.77, 2011. price varies. back issues avail. **Document type:** *Monographic series, Academic/ Scholarly.* **Description:** Scholarly studies of early Jewish and Christian history, including studies of theology, law, textual and related issues.
Former titles (until 2004): Arbeiten zur Geschichte des Antiken Judentums und des Urchristentums (0169-734X); (until 1968): Arbeiten zur Geschichte des Spaetjudentums und Urchristentums (0066-5681)
Indexed: IZBG.
Published by: (Institutum Iudaicum, Tuebingen DEU), Brill, PO Box 9000, Leiden, 2300 PA, Netherlands. TEL 31-71-5353500, FAX 31-71-5317532, cs@brill.nl. R&P Elizabeth Venekamp. **Dist. by:** Turpin Distribution Services Ltd., Pegasus Dr, Stratton Business Park, Biggleswade, Bedfordshire SG18 8QB, United Kingdom. TEL 44-1767-604954, FAX 44-1767-601640, custserv@turpin-distribution.com, http://www.turpin-distribution.com/.

➤ **ANTISEMITISM AND XENOPHOBIA TODAY.** *see* POLITICAL SCIENCE—Civil Rights

➤ **ARBEITSINFORMATIONEN UEBER STUDIENPROJEKTE AUF DEM GEBIET DER GESCHICHTE DES DEUTSCHEN JUDENTUMS UND DES ANTISEMITISMUS.** *see* ETHNIC INTERESTS

296 FRA ISSN 0518-2840
DS101
L'ARCHE. Text in French. 1957. m. adv. **Document type:** *Magazine, Consumer.* **Description:** Looks at political and cultural aspects of judaism. Analyses current events.
Indexed: IBSS.
Published by: Fonds Social Juif Unifie, 39 rue de Broca, Paris, 75005, France. TEL 33-1-42171030, FAX 33-1-42171031, http://www.fsju.org. Ed. Meir Waintrater. Pub. David Saada. Adv. contact Myriam Ruszniewski. **Subscr. to:** D I P, 18-24 Quai de la Marne, Paris Cedex 19 75164, France. TEL 33-1-44848040, FAX 33-1-42005692, abo@dipinfo.fr, http://www.dipresse.com.

296 AUS ISSN 0814-8228
ARCHIVE OF AUSTRALIAN JUDAICA. CASUAL BULLETIN. Text in English. 1983. irreg. (1-2/yr.), latest 2008. bk.rev. abstr. back issues avail. **Document type:** *Bulletin.*
Related titles: Online - full text ed.: free (effective 2009).
Published by: University of Sydney, Archive of Australian Judaica, c/o Rare Books, Fisher Library, Sydney, NSW 2006, Australia. TEL 61-1-93514162, FAX 61-2-91140881, mdacy@library.usyd.edu.au. Ed. Marianne Dacy.

296 AUS ISSN 0816-3480
ARCHIVE OF AUSTRALIAN JUDAICA. MONOGRAPH. Text in English. 1985. irreg., latest 2009, 15th ed. AUD 15 per issue (effective 2009). 70 p./no.; back issues avail. **Document type:** *Monographic series, Consumer.*
Related titles: Online - full text ed.
Published by: University of Sydney, Archive of Australian Judaica, c/o Rare Books, Fisher Library, Sydney, NSW 2006, Australia. TEL 61-1-93514162, FAX 61-2-91140881, mdacy@library.usyd.edu.au. Ed. Marianne Dacy.

296 FRA ISSN 0003-9837
DS135.F8
ARCHIVES JUIVES; revue d'histoire des juifs de France. Text in French. 1965. s-a. bibl. index, cum.index (1965-1974; 1975-1979). back issues avail. **Document type:** *Journal, Academic/Scholarly.*
Related titles: Online - full text ed.
Indexed: FR, MLA-IB, NumL, PCI, SCOPUS.
—INIST.
Published by: (Commission Francaise des Archives Juives), Editions Les Belles Lettres, 95 Blvd Raspail, Paris, 75006, France. TEL 33-1-44398421, FAX 33-1-45449288, courrier@lesbelleslettres.com. Ed. Bernhard Blumenkranz. Circ: 650.

296 ITA ISSN 2035-6528
▼ **ARCHIVIO DI STUDI EBRAICI.** Text in Multiple languages. 2009. a. **Document type:** *Monographic series, Academic/Scholarly.*
Published by: Universita degli Studi di Napoli "L'Orientale", Dipartimento di Studi Asiatici, Piazza San Domenico Maggiore 12, Palazzo Corigliano, Naples, 80134, Italy. TEL 39-081-6909675, FAX 39-081-5527852, http://www.iuo.it.

296.7 USA ISSN 1053-5616
ARIZONA JEWISH POST. Text in English. 1946. fortn. adv. bk.rev. back issues avail. **Document type:** *Newspaper.* **Description:** Presents in-depth reporting of local, national, and international Jewish news.
Formerly: Arizona Post (0744-1509)
Related titles: Microfilm ed.: (from AJP).
Published by: Jewish Federation of Southern Arizona, 3822 E River Rd, Tucson, AZ 85718. TEL 520-577-9393, FAX 520-577-0734, cbaldwin@jfsa.org, http://jewishtucson.org/. Ed. Phyllis Bruan. Adv. contact Jerry Rosen. Circ: 10,500.

ARZA REPORT. *see* ETHNIC INTERESTS

296 DEU ISSN 1016-4987
DS135.G3
ASCHKENAS; Zeitschrift fuer Geschichte und Kultur der Juden. Text in German. 1991. 2/yr. EUR 119, USD 179 to institutions; EUR 138, USD 207 combined subscription to institutions (print & online eds.) (effective 2012). adv. bk.rev. reprint service avail. from SCH. **Document type:** *Journal, Academic/Scholarly.* **Description:** Explores and discusses the history and culture of the Ashkenazi Jews.
Related titles: Online - full text ed.: ISSN 1865-9438. EUR 119, USD 179 to institutions (effective 2012).
Indexed: A22, A26, CA, DIP, E01, HistAb, I05, IBR, IBZ, MLA-IB, P30, PCI, T02.
Published by: Walter de Gruyter GmbH & Co. KG, Genthiner Str 13, Berlin, 10785, Germany. TEL 49-30-260050, FAX 49-30-26005251, info@degruyter.com, http://www.degruyter.de. Eds. Hans Otto Horch, Markus Wenninger, Robert Juette. Circ: 320 (paid).

ASSIA. *see* MEDICAL SCIENCES

ASSOCIATION OF ADVANCED RABBINICAL AND TALMUDIC SCHOOLS. ACCREDITATION COMMISSION. HANDBOOK. *see* EDUCATION—Higher Education

296.7 USA
ATLANTA JEWISH LIFE. Text in English. 2001. q. **Document type:** *Magazine, Consumer.* **Description:** Captures the essence of life in Atlanta's Jewish community, including education, food, spirituality, home, philanthropy, shopping and more.
Published by: Leader Publishing Group, Inc., 3379 Peachtree Rd, NE, Ste 300, Atlanta, GA 30326. TEL 404-888-0555, 800-256-8271. Ed. Howard Lalli.

296.7 USA ISSN 0892-3345
ATLANTA JEWISH TIMES. Text in English. 1925. w. (Fri.). USD 49 in state; USD 65 out of state. adv. bk.rev. illus. **Document type:** *Newspaper.* **Description:** Contains articles of interest to the Jewish community.
Formerly: Southern Israelite (0038-4224)
Related titles: Microfiche ed.; Microfilm ed.: (from AJP).
Published by: Jewish Renaissance Media, 1117 Perimeter Center W., Ste. N-311, Atlanta, Fulton, GA 30338. TEL 404-564-4550. Ed. Bob Menaker. Pub. Stephen M. Levene. Adv. contact Shelley Lewis. Circ: 10,000. Wire service: JTA.

AUFBAU; Das juedische Monatsmagazin. *see* ETHNIC INTERESTS

296.071 AUS
AUSTRALIAN ASSOCIATION OF JEWISH STUDIES. NEWSLETTER (ONLINE). Variant title: A A J S. Newsletter. Text in English. 1989 (Oct.-Nov.). irreg., latest no.37, 2008. free to members (effective 2008). back issues avail. **Document type:** *Newsletter, Academic/ Scholarly.* **Description:** Contains information about annual conferences held by the association.
Formerly: Australian Association of Jewish Studies. Newsletter (Print) (1328-6889)
Media: Online - full text.
Published by: Australian Association of Jewish Studies, Holme Bldg, University of Sydney, PO Box 233, Sydney, NSW 2006, Australia. TEL 61-2-93514162, FAX 61-2-93512890, mdacy@library.usyd.edu.au, http://www.geocities.com/aajssite. Eds. Anna Rosenbaum, Marianne Dacy. Circ: 200 (controlled).

AUSTRALIAN JEWISH HISTORICAL SOCIETY. JOURNAL. *see* ETHNIC INTERESTS

296.09 AUS ISSN 0816-7141
DS135.A88
AUSTRALIAN JEWISH HISTORICAL SOCIETY. NEWSLETTER. Text in English. 1968. q. looseleaf. free to members (effective 2008). back issues avail. **Document type:** *Newsletter, Academic/Scholarly.*
Related titles: E-mail ed.
Published by: Australian Jewish Historical Society Inc., Level 2, Mandelbaum House, 385 Abercrombie St, Darlington, NSW 2008, Australia. ajhs@ozemail.com.au, http://www.ajhs.info. Ed. Julia Shapira.

AUSTRALIAN JEWISH NEWS (SYDNEY EDITION). *see* ETHNIC INTERESTS

296.071 AUS ISSN 1037-0838
DS135.A88
➤ **AUSTRALIAN JOURNAL OF JEWISH STUDIES.** Abbreviated title: A J J S. Text in English. 1987 (Aug.). a. free to members (effective 2008). bk.rev. 200 p./no.; back issues avail. **Document type:** *Journal, Academic/Scholarly.*
Formerly (until 1990): Menorah (0819-9957)
Indexed: A01, A11, A26, CA, CPerI, E08, I05, IJP, J01, MLA-IB, S09, T02.
—BLDSC (1809.115000), Ingenta.
Published by: Australian Association of Jewish Studies, Holme Bldg, University of Sydney, PO Box 233, Sydney, NSW 2006, Australia. TEL 61-2-93514162, FAX 61-2-93512890, mdacy@library.usyd.edu.au. Eds. Dvir Abramovich, Ziva Shavitsky. Circ: 100 (paid); 200 (controlled).

296.09 USA ISSN 0882-6501
DS101
AVOTAYNU; the international review of Jewish genealogy. Text in English. 1985. q. USD 38 in North America; USD 46 elsewhere (effective 2010). adv. bk.rev. illus. 68 p./no.; back issues avail.; reprints avail. **Document type:** *Journal, Academic/Scholarly.* **Description:** International review of Jewish genealogy. Correspondents in 16 countries regularly contribute articles of interest to persons tracing their Jewish family history.
Related titles: CD-ROM ed.
Indexed: IJP.
—Ingenta.
Published by: Avotaynu Inc., 155 N Washington Ave, Bergenfield, NJ 07621. TEL 201-387-7200, FAX 201-387-2855, info@avotaynu.com.

296 NLD ISSN 1879-7954
B. FOLKERTSMA STICHTING VOOR TALMUDICA. NIEUWSBRIEF. Text in Dutch. 199?. 3/yr.
Published by: B. Folkertsma Stichting voor Talmudica, Rapenburg 45, Amsterdam, 1011 TV, Netherlands. TEL 31-20-8455808, info@folkertsmastichting.nl.

296 DEU ISSN 0931-6418
DS101
BABYLON; Beitraege zur Juedischen Gegenwart. Text in German. 1986. s-a. back issues avail. **Document type:** *Academic/Scholarly.*
Indexed: DIP, IBR, IBZ, MLA-IB, PCI.
Published by: Verlag Neue Kritik KG, Kettenhofweg 53, Frankfurt Am Main, 60325, Germany. TEL 49-69-727576, FAX 49-69-726585.

296.7 USA ISSN 0005-450X
BALTIMORE JEWISH TIMES. Text in English. 1919. w. (Fri.). USD 46.15; USD 56.95 out of area (effective 2005). adv. play rev. illus. Supplement avail. **Document type:** *Newspaper, Consumer.*
Related titles: Microfilm ed.: (from AJP); Online - full text ed.
Indexed: DYW, ENW, P28, P48, P53, P54, PQC.
—CIS.
Address: 1040 Park Ave., Ste. 200, Baltimore, MD 21201-5634. TEL 410-752-3504, FAX 410-752-2375. Ed. Phil Jacobs. Pub. Andrew Buerger. R&P Melissa Whaley TEL 410-752-8129. Adv. contact Claudia Meyers. Circ: 20,000. Wire service: JTA.

296 ISR ISSN 0067-4109
BM1
BAR-ILAN: ANNUAL OF BAR-ILAN UNIVERSITY/UNIVERSITAT BAR-ILAN. SEFER HA-SHANA L'MADA'E HA-YAHADUT W'HA-RU'AH; studies in Judaica and the humanities. Text in Hebrew; Summaries in English. 1963. a., latest vol.31, 2006, May. USD 30 per issue (effective 2008). back issues avail. **Document type:** *Monographic series.*
Indexed: IHP, MLA-IB, OTA.
Published by: (Bar-Ilan University), Bar-Ilan University Press (Subsidiary of: Bar-Ilan University), Journals, Ramat-Gan, 52900, Israel. TEL 972-3-5318401, FAX 972-3-5353446, press@mail.biu.ac.il, http://www.biu.ac.il/Press. Ed. Zvi Arie Steinfeld.

220 ISR ISSN 0334-2255
BS1178.H4
➤ **BEER-SHEVA.** Text mainly in English; Text occasionally in Hebrew; Summaries in English. 1973. a., latest vol.14, 2000. price varies. illus. **Document type:** *Monographic series, Academic/Scholarly.* **Description:** Scholarly monographs on topics pertaining to Biblical archaeology and the ancient Near East.
Published by: (Ben-Gurion University of the Negev), Ben-Gurion University of the Negev Press, P O Box 653, Beersheva, Israel. FAX 972-7-6472913. Ed. Shmuel Ahituv. Circ: 1,000. **Dist. by:** Eisenbrauns Inc.; Bialik Institute, P O Box 92, Jerusalem 91000, Israel. TEL 972-2-6783554, FAX 972-2-6783706.

296 DEU ISSN 1613-575X
BEGEGNUNG (FRANKFURT AM MAIN); Juedische Studien. Text in German. 2004. irreg., latest vol.7, 2010. price varies. **Document type:** *Monographic series, Academic/Scholarly.*
Published by: Peter Lang GmbH (Subsidiary of: Peter Lang Publishing Group), Eschborner Landstr 42-50, Frankfurt Am Main, 60489, Germany. TEL 49-69-7807050, FAX 49-69-78070550, zentrale.frankfurt@peterlang.com. Ed. Dorothee Gelhard.

296 DEU ISSN 1612-4340
BEGEGNUNGEN; Zeitschrift fuer Kirche und Judentum. Text in German. 1903. q. EUR 15 (effective 2009). bk.rev. back issues avail. **Document type:** *Journal, Trade.*
Formerly (until 2001): Friede ueber Israel (0938-6408)
Published by: Evangelisch-Lutherischer Zentralverein fuer Begegnung von Christen und Juden e.V., Archivstr 3, Hannover, 30169, Germany. TEL 49-511-1241367, FAX 49-511-1241499, http://www.begegnung-christen-juden.de.

220 ISR ISSN 0005-979X
BS410
BEIT-MIQRA. Text in Hebrew. 1956. q. USD 70 (effective 2003). bk.rev. **Document type:** *Academic/Scholarly.* **Description:** Publishes Bible studies and research.
Indexed: A21, IHP, IZBG, MLA-IB, OTA, R&TA, RI-1.
Published by: World Jewish Bible Center, 12 Koresh St, P O Box 7024, Jerusalem, 94144, Israel. TEL 972-2-254851. Ed. David Hacohen. Circ: 1,400.

296 DEU ISSN 0722-0790
BEITRAEGE ZUR ERFORSCHUNG DES ALTEN TESTAMENTS UND DES ANTIKEN JUDENTUMS. Text in German. 1991. irreg., latest vol.56, 2010. price varies. **Document type:** *Monographic series, Academic/Scholarly.*
Indexed: IZBG.
Published by: Peter Lang GmbH (Subsidiary of: Peter Lang Publishing Group), Eschborner Landstr 42-50, Frankfurt Am Main, 60489, Germany. TEL 49-69-7807050, FAX 49-69-78070550, zentrale.frankfurt@peterlang.com. Eds. Matthias Augustin, Michael Mach. R&P Ruediger Brunsch.

296.5 ISR ISSN 0793-3894
BM1
BEKHOL DERAKHEKHA DA'EHU; journal of Torah and scholarship. Text in English, Hebrew. 1995. irreg., latest no.20, 2008. USD 20 per issue (effective 2011). **Document type:** *Journal, Academic/Scholarly.* **Description:** Includes articles in Hebrew and English relating to the interface between traditional Jewish scholarship and the sciences and humanities.
Indexed: IHP, P30.
Published by: (Bar-Ilan University), Bar-Ilan University Press (Subsidiary of: Bar-Ilan University), Journals, Ramat-Gan, 52900, Israel. TEL 972-3-5318401, FAX 972-3-5353446, press@mail.biu.ac.il, http://www.biu.ac.il/Press. Ed. Ely Merzbach.

BIBLIOGRAFIA TEMATICA SOBRE JUDAISMO ARGENTINO. *see* RELIGIONS AND THEOLOGY—Abstracting, Bibliographies, Statistics

BIBLIOGRAPHICA JUDAICA. *see* RELIGIONS AND THEOLOGY—Abstracting, Bibliographies, Statistics

BIBLIOTHEK DER ERINNERUNG. *see* HISTORY—History Of Europe

296.7 USA ISSN 1549-4799
HS2228.B4
B'NAI B'RITH MAGAZINE. Text in English. 1886. q. USD 12 domestic to non-members; USD 17 in Canada to non-members; USD 48 elsewhere to non-members; USD 36 elsewhere to members (effective 2010). adv. illus. index. back issues avail. **Document type:** *Magazine, Consumer.* **Description:** Explores the social, cultural, historical and political issues that affect the Jewish community in the United States and abroad.
Former titles (until 2003): The B'nai B'rith I J M (1544-0729); (until 2001): The B'nai B'rith International Jewish Monthly (0279-3415); (until 1981): The National Jewish Monthly (0027-9552); (until 1939): B'nai B'rith National Jewish Monthly (0731-5147); (until 1934): B'nai B'rith Magazine; (until 1924): B'nai B'rith News
Related titles: Online - full text ed.: free (effective 2010).
Indexed: A22, ABS&EES, IJP, L09, MEA&I, P30, PAIS.
Published by: B'nai B'rith International, 2020 K St, NW, 7th Fl, Washington, DC 20006. TEL 202-857-6600, 888-388-4224, foundation@bnaibrith.org.

296.7 USA ISSN 0006-5277
B'NAI B'RITH MESSENGER. Text in English. 1897. w. adv. bk.rev.; film rev.; play rev. illus. **Document type:** *Newspaper.*
Related titles: Microfilm ed.: (from AJP, PQC).
Published by: B'nai B'rith Messenger, Inc., PO Box 35915, Los Angeles, CA 90035-0915. TEL 310-659-2952. Ed. Rabbi Yale B Butler. Pub. Joe Bobker. R&P, Adv. contact Linda Cohen Carter TEL 213-933-0131. Circ: 67,000.

R

222.1 ISR ISSN 0333-6298
BM1
➤ **B'OR HA-TORAH**; science, the arts and modern life in the light of the Torah. Text in English. 1982. a., latest vol.17, 2007. ILS 25, USD 19 per issue (effective 2009). adv. bk.rev. abstr.; bibl.; charts; illus. index. 200 p./no. 2 cols./p.; back issues avail.; reprints avail. **Document type:** *Journal, Academic/Scholarly.* **Description:** Presents an international forum for students, academics, rabbis and artists on how the Torah permeates scientific and artistic creativity, social mores, and personal behavior. Contains poetry, critical articles, sources for study, and essays discussing contemporary situations and concerns and applications of Jewish law and ethics to these problems.
Related titles: English ed.
Indexed: A26, E08, I05, IHP, J01, T02.
Published by: Shamir, Association of Religious Professionals from the Former Soviet Union in Israel, 6 David Yellin St., P O Box 5749, Jerusalem, Israel. TEL 972-2-5385702, FAX 972-2-5385118, info@borhatorah.org, http://www.borhatorah.org. Ed. Herman Branover. R&P, Adv. contact Ilana Attia TEL 972-2-642-7521. page USD 500; 6.5 x 9.5. Circ: 5,000.

296.7 USA ISSN 8750-1961
BOSTON JEWISH TIMES. Text in English. 1945. fortn. USD 12. adv. bk.rev. illus. **Document type:** *Newspaper.*
Formerly: Jewish Times (Boston) (0021-6771)
Related titles: Microform ed.
Address: 15 School St, Boston, MA 02108. TEL 617-367-9100, FAX 617-367-9310. Ed. Robert Israel. Adv. contact Sarabeth Lukin. Circ: 11,500.

296 NLD ISSN 1571-5000
THE BRILL REFERENCE LIBRARY OF JUDAISM. Text in English. 2000. irreg., latest vol.27, 2007. price varies. **Document type:** *Monographic series, Academic/Scholarly.*
Formerly (until 2003): The Brill Reference Library of Ancient Judaism (1566-1237)
Indexed: IZBG.
—BLDSC (2284.110903).
Published by: Brill, PO Box 9000, Leiden, 2300 PA, Netherlands. TEL 31-71-5353500, FAX 31-71-5317532, cs@brill.nl. Eds. Alan J Avery-Peck, Dr. William Scott Green.

296 NLD ISSN 0926-2261
➤ **BRILL'S SERIES IN JEWISH STUDIES.** Text in Dutch. 1991. irreg., latest vol.45, 2011. price varies. back issues avail. **Document type:** *Monographic series, Academic/Scholarly.* **Description:** Scholarly monographs covering topics in Jewish history, language, society and culture up to the present era.
Indexed: IZBG.
—CCC.
Published by: Brill, PO Box 9000, Leiden, 2300 PA, Netherlands. TEL 31-71-5353500, FAX 31-71-5317532, cs@brill.nl. Ed. David S Katz. **Dist. by:** Turpin Distribution Services Ltd., Pegasus Dr, Stratton Business Park, Biggleswade, Bedfordshire SG18 8QB, United Kingdom. TEL 44-1767-604954, FAX 44-1767-601640, custserv@turpin-distribution.com, http://www.turpin-distribution.com/.

296.7 USA
BUFFALO JEWISH REVIEW. Text in English. 1918. w. (Fri.). USD 33 in state; USD 38 out of state (effective 2004). adv. **Document type:** *Newspaper, Consumer.*
Related titles: Microfilm ed.: (from AJP).
Address: 15 E Mohawk St, Buffalo, NY 14203. TEL 716-854-2192, FAX 716-854-2198. Ed. Rita Weiss. Pub. Arnold Weiss. Circ: 4,300 (paid). Wire service: JTA.

296.3 AUS ISSN 1832-6498
BULLETIN IN THE NOAHIDE LAWS. Text in English. 2005. irreg. AUD 5 per issue (effective 2009). back issues avail. **Document type:** *Bulletin.* **Description:** Covers the universal code of ethics set out in the Torah tradition for all humanity.
Published by: Institute for Judaism and Civilization, 88 Hotham St, East St Kilda, VIC 3183, Australia. admin@ijc.com.au.

296 GBR ISSN 0954-1179
DS135.M43
➤ **BULLETIN OF JUDAEO-GREEK STUDIES.** Text in English. 1987. s-a. GBP 20, USD 36 to institutions (effective 2009). adv. bk.rev. back issues avail. **Document type:** *Bulletin, Academic/Scholarly.* **Description:** Aims to serve as a means of communication for scholars in five continents researching in the area of Greek studies, which is attracting a rapidly-growing interest.
Indexed: PCI.
Address: University of Cambridge, Faculty of Divinity, West Rd, Cambridge, CB3 9BS, United Kingdom. FAX 44-1223-332582. Eds. Dr. James Aitken, Nicholas De Lange. Adv. contact Nicholas De Lange. Circ: 200.

296.3 USA ISSN 1058-8760
CODEN: APUPEI
C C A R JOURNAL; a reform Jewish quarterly. Text in English. 1953. q. USD 75; free to members (effective 2009). adv. bk.rev. illus. cum.index (25 yrs.). reprints avail. **Document type:** *Journal, Academic/Scholarly.* **Description:** Contains articles about contemporary topics that pertain to the leading members of the rabbinical, scholarly, and lay communities.
Former titles (until 1991): Journal of Reform Judaism (0149-712X); (until 1978): C C A R Journal (0007-7976)
Related titles: Microform ed.: free (effective 2009) (from PQC).
Indexed: A21, A22, IAJS, IBR, IBZ, IJP, JewAb, P30, R&TA, RI-1, RI-2, SCOPUS.
—BLDSC (3095.844000), IE, Ingenta.
Published by: (Central Conference of American Rabbis), C C A R Press, 355 Lexington Ave,, 18th Fl, New York, NY 10017. TEL 212-972-3636, FAX 212-692-0819, CCARpress@ccarnet.org. Ed. Susan E Laemmle.

296.4 USA ISSN 1945-2659
BM197.5
C J; voices of Conservative/Masorti Judaism. (Conservative Judaism) Text in English. 2007. s-a. adv. bk.rev. illus. 48 p./no. 3 cols./p.; back issues avail. **Document type:** *Magazine, Consumer.* **Description:** Serves as a communication vehicle for issues of interest or concern to Conservative Jews.
Formed by the merger of (1930-2007): Women's League Outlook (0043-7557); (19??-2007): United Synagogue Review (0041-8153); (1977-2007): Torchlight (1068-6134); Which was formerly (1941-1977): Torch (0049-416X)
Indexed: IJP, P30.
Published by: United Synagogue of Conservative Judaism, 820 Second Ave, New York, NY 10017. TEL 212-533-7800, FAX 212-353-9439, info@uscj.org. Ed. Scott Shindell. adv.: B&W page USD 3,100, color page USD 3,400; trim 8.25 x 10.5.

296 USA ISSN 0887-1639
C M J S CENTERPIECES. Text in English. 1985. a. free. bk.rev. charts; stat.
Published by: Cohen Center for Modern Jewish Studies, Brandeis University, Waltham, MA 02254. TEL 617-736-2063, FAX 617-736-2070. Ed. Sylvia Barack Fishman. Circ: 8,500.

296.7 FRA ISSN 1029-8878
DS101
CAHIERS DU JUDAISME. Text in French. 1965. 3/yr. EUR 39 domestic to individuals; EUR 46 foreign to individuals; EUR 32 domestic to students (effective 2008). adv. bk.rev. bibl. **Document type:** *Journal, Academic/Scholarly.* **Description:** Deals with Jewish history, philosophy, sociology and literature.
Formerly (until 1998): Alliance Israelite Universelle. Nouveaux Cahiers (0029-4705)
Indexed: FR, IBSS.
—INIST.
Published by: Alliance Israelite Universelle en France, 45 Rue La Bruyere, Paris, 75009, France. TEL 33-1-53328853, FAX 33-1-48745133. Ed. Anne Grynberg. Circ: 3,000.

296.7 USA
THE CALL. Text in English. 1933. bi-m. **Document type:** *Magazine, Consumer.*
Published by: (Yiddish Division), Workmen's Circle/Arbeter Ring, 45 E 33rd St, New York, NY 10016. TEL 212-889-6800, FAX 212-532-7518. Ed. Erica Sigmon.

CAMBRIDGE UNIVERSITY LIBRARY. GENIZAH SERIES. *see* BIBLIOGRAPHIES

296 CAN ISSN 0576-5528
F1035.J5
CANADIAN JEWISH ARCHIVES (NEW SERIES). Text in English. 1955; N.S. 1974. irreg., latest vol.49, 2007. CAD 16 per vol. (effective 2008). back issues avail. **Document type:** *Monographic series, Consumer.* **Description:** Contains documentation on all aspects of the Jewish presence in Quebec and Canada.
Published by: Canadian Jewish Congress, 100 Sparks St, Ste 650, Ottawa, ON K1p 5B7, Canada. TEL 613-233-8703, FAX 613-233-8748, canadianjewishcongress@cjc.ca, http://www.cjc.ca. Circ: 200.

296.7 CAN
CANADIAN JEWISH CONGRESS NEWSLETTER. Text in English. 2008 (Feb.). m. free. **Document type:** *Newsletter.*
Media: Online - full content.
Published by: Canadian Jewish Congress, 100 Sparks St, Ste 650, Ottawa, ON K1p 5B7, Canada. TEL 613-233-8703, FAX 613-233-8748, canadianjewishcongress@cjc.ca, http://www.cjc.ca. Ed. Jordan Kerbel.

296.7 CAN ISSN 0008-3941
CANADIAN JEWISH NEWS. Text in English, French. 1961. 50/yr. CAD 30.79 (effective 2003). adv. **Document type:** *Newspaper.* **Description:** Presents international, national and local news, including arts and business, of interest to the Canadian Jewish community.
Supersedes: Canadian Jewish Chronicle Review (0008-3925)
Related titles: Microfilm ed.: (from AJP, MMP); Online - full text ed.; ◆ Supplement(s): Viewpoints. ISSN 0042-5818.
Indexed: C03, CBCARef, CBPI, CPerI, G08, I05, P48, PQC, R05.
—CIS.
Address: 1500 Don Mills Rd, North York, ON M3B 3K4, Canada. TEL 416-391-1836, FAX 416-391-0829. Ed. Mordechai Ben Dat. Adv. contact Vera Gillman. Circ: 44,152.

296.071 AUT ISSN 1999-9283
CENTRUM FUER JUEDISCHE STUDIEN. SCHRIFTEN. Variant title: Schriften des Centrums fuer Juedische Studien. Text in German. 2002. irreg., latest vol.14, 2008. price varies. **Document type:** *Monographic series, Academic/Scholarly.*
Published by: (Karl-Franzens-Universitaet Graz, Centrum fuer Juedische Studien), StudienVerlag, Erlerstr 10, Innsbruck, 6020, Austria. TEL 43-512-395045, FAX 43-512-39504515, order@studienverlag.at, http://www.studienverlag.at.

296.7 USA ISSN 1537-0976
CHARLESTON JEWISH VOICE. Text in English. 19??. m. USD 12. adv. **Document type:** *Newspaper.* **Description:** Covers Jewish community efforts and news in and around Charleston, the U.S., Israel and the world.
Formerly (until 2001): Charleston Jewish Journal (1067-1587)
Published by: Charleston Jewish Federation, 1645 Wallenberg Blvd, Charleston, SC 29407. TEL 843-571-6565, FAX 803-556-6206. Ed., Adv. contact Ellen Katzman. Circ: 2,600.

296.7 USA
CHARLOTTE JEWISH NEWS. Text in English. 1978. 11/yr. free domestic to members area (effective 2005). **Document type:** *Newspaper, Consumer.*
Published by: Jewish Federation of Greater Charlotte, 5007 Providence Rd, Charlotte, NC 28226. TEL 704-944-6765, FAX 704-365-4507, http://www.jewishcharlotte.org. Ed. Amy Krakovitz Montoni. Adv. contact Rita Mond. Circ: 3,900 (free).

296.7 USA ISSN 1084-1881
CHICAGO JEWISH NEWS; Jewish Chicago's hometown newspaper. Text in English. 1994. w. USD 40; USD 35 to senior citizens (effective 2005). adv. **Document type:** *Newspaper.* **Description:** Open to and giving voice to all segments of the Chicago Jewish community.
Address: 5301 Dempster St., Ste. 100, Skokie, IL 60077-1800. TEL 847-966-0606, FAX 847-966-1656, info@chicagojewishnews.com. Ed., Pub. Joseph Aaron. Adv. contact Sara Belkov. B&W page USD 1,320, color page USD 1,920; 14 x 9.75. Circ: 13,000.

296.7 USA ISSN 1054-1365
F548.9.J5
CHICAGO JEWISH STAR. Text in English. 1991. bi-m. USD 25 (effective 2005). adv. film rev.; music rev.; play rev.; tel.rev.; video rev.; bk.rev. **Document type:** *Newspaper, Consumer.*
Related titles: Microfilm ed.; Online - full text ed.
Indexed: ENW.
Address: PO Box 268, Skokie, IL 60076-0268. chicago-jewish-star@mcimail.com. Ed., Adv. contact Douglas Wertheimer. R&P Gilla Margolese Wertheimer. Circ: 19,000 (controlled).

296.09 USA
➤ **CHICAGO STUDIES IN THE HISTORY OF JUDAISM.** Text in English. 1981. a. price varies. **Document type:** *Journal, Academic/Scholarly.*
Published by: University of Chicago, 5801 S Ellis Ave, Chicago, IL 60637. TEL 773-702-7899. Ed. William Scott Owen.

296 NLD ISSN 1876-3766
CHIDUSHIM. Text in Dutch. 1997. 3/yr. EUR 4.50 newsstand/cover (effective 2008).
Published by: Stichting Beit Ha'Chidush, Postbus 14613, Amsterdam, 1001 LC, Netherlands. TEL 31-79-3311981, info@beithachidush.nl. Ed. Pauline Kalkove.

CHOSEN WORDS. *see* ETHNIC INTERESTS

296.7 USA
THE CHRONICLE (SARASOTA). Text in English. 1971. fortn. **Document type:** *Newspaper.*
Published by: Sarasota - Manatee Jewish Federation, 580 S McIntosh Rd, Sarasota, FL 34232. TEL 813-371-4546, FAX 813-378-2947. Ed. Barry Millman.

CLEVELAND JEWISH NEWS. *see* ETHNIC INTERESTS

222.1 USA
COALITION: THE TORAH ACTION JOURNAL. Text in English, Yiddish. 1985. 5/yr. free. back issues avail. **Document type:** *Newspaper.* **Description:** Explores news and trends in the field of orthodox Jewish activism.
Published by: Agudath Israel of America, 42 Broadway, 14th Fl., New York, NY 10004-3889. TEL 212-797-9000. Ed. Rabbi A Shafran. Circ: 50,000.

296 BEL ISSN 0777-785X
COLLECTION DE LA REVUE DES ETUDES JUIVES. Text in French. 1980. irreg., latest 2010. price varies. back issues avail. **Document type:** *Monographic series, Academic/Scholarly.*
Related titles: ◆ Supplement to: Revue des Etudes Juives. ISSN 0484-8616.
—IE.
Published by: (Societe des Etudes Juives FRA), Peeters Publishers, Bondgenotenlaan 153, Leuven, 3000, Belgium. TEL 32-16-235170, FAX 32-16-228500, http://www.peeters-leuven.be.

COMMENTARIES ON EARLY JEWISH LITERATURE. *see* LITERATURE

296.7 USA ISSN 0010-2601
COMMENTARY; journal of significant thought and opinion on contemporary issues. Text in English. 1938. m. (except Jul./Aug. combined). USD 19.95 domestic; USD 38.95 in Canada; USD 44.95 elsewhere; USD 5.95 per issue (effective 2009). adv. bk.rev.; music rev. index. back issues avail.; reprints avail. **Document type:** *Magazine, Consumer.* **Description:** Focuses on contentious social and political issues.
Formerly (until 1945): Contemporary Jewish Record (0363-6909)
Related titles: Microform ed.; Online - full text ed.: ISSN 1943-4634. USD 12.95 (effective 2009).
Indexed: A01, A02, A03, A06, A08, A11, A20, A21, A22, A25, A26, ABCPolSci, ABS&EES, Acal, AmH&L, AmHI, B04, B05, BAS, BEL&L, BRD, C05, C12, CA, CBRI, CCME, CPerI, CWI, ChPerI, CurCont, DIP, E08, FamI, FutSurv, G05, G06, G07, G08, GEOBASE, GSS&RPL, H07, H08, H09, H10, HAb, HRIR, HistAb, HumInd, I05, I07, I13, IBR, IBRH, IBZ, IJP, IPARL, J01, JewAb, L05, L06, M01, M02, M06, MASUSE, MEA&I, MLA, MLA-IB, MRD, MagInd, P02, P05, P06, P10, P13, P27, P28, P30, P34, P42, P45, P48, P53, P54, PAIS, PCI, PMR, PQC, PRA, R03, R04, R05, R06, RASB, RGAb, RGPR, RI-1, RI-2, RILM, S02, S03, S05, S08, S09, S11, S23, SCOPUS, SSAI, SSAb, SSCI, SSI, T02, TOM, U01, W01, W02, W03, W05, W07.
—BLDSC (3333.600000), CIS, IE, Infotrieve, Ingenta. **CCC.**
Published by: American Jewish Committee, 165 E 56th St, New York, NY 10022. TEL 212-891-1400, FAX 212-751-4018, PR@ajc.org, http://www.ajc.org. Ed. John Podhoretz. Pub. Teri Schure. adv.: B&W page USD 3,430, color page USD 5,100; bleed 8.375 x 11.125. Circ: 27,000 (paid).

296.7 USA
COMMUNITY (LOUISVILLE). Text in English. 1975. bi-w. USD 20 domestic; USD 75 foreign (effective 2000). adv. bk.rev. **Document type:** *Newspaper.*
Published by: Jewish Community Federation of Louisville, 3630 Dutchmans Ln, Louisville, KY 40205. TEL 502-451-8840, FAX 502-458-0702, jfed@iglou.com, http://www.jewishlouisville.org. Ed. Shiela Wallace. Adv. contact Kay Hardy. Circ: 6,000 (controlled).

296.7 USA ISSN 1536-111X
DS101
COMMUNITY NEWS REPORTER. Variant title: J T A Community News Reporter. Text in English. m. USD 50 (effective 2001). **Document type:** *Newsletter.* **Description:** Focuses on honors, appointments and events within Jewish communities around the continent.
Media: Duplicated (not offset).
Published by: Jewish Telegraphic Agency, 330 Seventh Ave, 17th Fl, New York, NY 10001. newsdesk@JTA.org, http://www.jta.org. Ed. Lisa Hostein. Pub. Mark J Joffe.

296.7 USA ISSN 1047-9996
COMMUNITY REVIEW (HARRISBURG). Text in English. 1925. fortn. USD 25. adv. **Document type:** *Newspaper.*
Published by: United Jewish Community of Greater Harrisburg, 3301 N Front St, Harrisburg, PA 17110. TEL 717-236-9555, FAX 717-236-2552. Ed. Carol L Cohen. Adv. contact Linda Freedenberg. Circ: 2,200.

296 NLD ISSN 1877-4970
COMPENDIA RERUM IUDAICARUM AD NOVUM TESTAMENTUM. Text in English. 1976 (no.2). irreg., latest vol.12, 2009. price varies. **Document type:** *Monographic series, Academic/Scholarly.*
Published by: Brill, PO Box 9000, Leiden, 2300 PA, Netherlands. TEL 31-71-5353500, FAX 31-71-5317532, cs@brill.nl.

296.7 ARG
COMUNIDADES; periodico judio independiente. Text in Spanish. 1991 (vol.5). 17/yr. ARS 100,000. **Document type:** *Newspaper.*
Address: Sucursal Sarandi, Casilla de Correos 49, Buenos Aires, 1872, Argentina. TEL 54-114-2048801. Eds. Alberto Rotenberg, Natalio Steiner.

296.4 USA ISSN 0010-6542
BM197.5
➤ **CONSERVATIVE JUDAISM.** Text in English. 1945. q. USD 28 to individuals; USD 50 to institutions (includes libraries); USD 18 to students (effective 2009). bk.rev. cum.index: 1955-1963, 1963-1976. back issues avail. **Document type:** *Journal, Academic/Scholarly.* **Description:** Features articles which express a serious, critical inquiry of Jewish texts and traditions, legacy, and law.
Related titles: Online - full text ed.: ISSN 1947-4717.
Indexed: A21, A22, ABS&EES, E01, IJP, JewAb, MEA&I, MLA-IB, P30, PCI, R&TA, RI-1, RI-2, SCOPUS.
—BLDSC (3418.500000), IE, Infotrieve, Ingenta.
Published by: (Jewish Theological Seminary), Rabbinical Assembly, 3080 Broadway, New York, NY 10027. TEL 212-280-6000, FAX 212-749-9166, info@rabbinicalassembly.org. **Co-sponsor:** Jewish Theological Seminary.

➤ **CONTEMPORARY JEWRY**; a journal of social scientific inquiry. *see* ETHNIC INTERESTS

296.7 USA
CONTRAVERSIONS: JEWS AND OTHER DIFFERENCES. Text in English. 1979. irreg., latest 2003. price varies. back issues avail. **Document type:** *Monographic series, Academic/Scholarly.* **Description:** Takes a sharp, critical look at Jewish linguistic, literary, and sociocultural practices.
Published by: Stanford University Press (Subsidiary of: Stanford University), 1450 Page Mill Rd, Palo Alto, CA 94304. TEL 650-723-9434, FAX 650-725-3457, info@www.sup.org. Eds. Chana Kronfeld, Daniel Boyarin, Naomi Seidman. **In Europe:** Cambridge University Press, The Edinburgh Bldg, Shaftesbury Rd, Cambridge CB2 8RU, United Kingdom. TEL 44-1223-312393, FAX 44-1223-315052, information@cambridge.org, http://www.cambridge.org/uk; **In the Americas:** Cambridge University Press Distribution Center, 100 Brookhill Dr, West Nyack, NY 10994. TEL 845-353-7500, FAX 845-353-4141, http://www.cambridge.org.

COUNCIL OF JEWISH THEATRES NEWSLETTER. *see* THEATER

101 ISR ISSN 0334-2336
B154
DA'AT; Jewish philosophy and Kabbalah. Text in English, French, Hebrew; Summaries in English. 1978. irreg. (Jan.), latest no.62, 2008. price varies. bk.rev. bibl. cum.index: vols.1-20 in vol.20. back issues avail. **Document type:** *Journal, Academic/Scholarly.* **Description:** Devoted exclusively to all aspects of Jewish philisophy, Kabbalah and religious thought.
Indexed: IHP, JewAb.
Published by: (Bar-Ilan University, Department of Philosophy), Bar-Ilan University Press (Subsidiary of: Bar-Ilan University), Journals, Ramat-Gan, 52900, Israel. TEL 972-3-5318401, FAX 972-3-5353446, press@mail.biu.ac.il, http://www.biu.ac.il/Press. Eds. E Levinas, Moshe Hallamish. Circ: 600.

296 ISR
➤ **DAF L'TARBUT YEHUDIT.** Text in Hebrew. 1974. 8/yr. free (effective 2008). bk.rev. **Document type:** *Academic/Scholarly.* **Description:** Material collected from a variety of Jewish sources, devoting a different theme to each issue.
Media: Online - full text.
Published by: Ministry of Education, Department of Torah Culture (Subsidiary of: Ministry of Education), Jerusalem, 91911, Israel. TEL 972-2-5601345, FAX 972-2-5601370, http://cms.education.gov.il/EducationCMS/UNITS/Toranit. Ed. Dr. Arie Strikovsky. R&P Rabbi Aharon Angstreich. Circ: 7,500.

296.7 ARG
DAVKE; revista Israelita. Text in Spanish, Yiddish. 1949. q. bk.rev. bibl.
Address: Brandsen, 1634, Capital Federal, Buenos Aires 1287, Argentina. Ed. Salomon Suskovich.

296.68083025 USA ISSN 1543-4257
LC741
DAY SCHOOL DIRECTORY. Variant title: Directory of Day Schools in the United States and Canada. Text in English. 19??. a. **Document type:** *Directory, Academic/Scholarly.* **Description:** Lists addresses, phone, fax numbers and emails of elementary and secondary Hebrew day schools (Yeshivot) in the United States and Canada. Also includes administrative personnel, grades, language of instruction.
Formerly: Directory of Day Schools in the United States, Canada and Latin America
Published by: Torah Umesorah, National Society for Hebrew Day Schools, 1090 Coney Island Ave, Brooklyn, NY 11230. TEL 212-227-1000.

296.155 NLD ISSN 0929-0761
BM487.A6
➤ **DEAD SEA DISCOVERIES**; a journal of current research on the scrolls and related literature. Text in English. 1994. 3/yr. EUR 245, USD 344 to institutions; EUR 268, USD 375 combined subscription to institutions (print & online eds.) (effective 2012). bk.rev. abstr.; bibl. back issues avail.; reprint service avail. from PSC. **Document type:** *Journal, Academic/Scholarly.* **Description:** Publishes original research arising from the recent release of photographs of the previously unpublished Dead Sea Scrolls, and discusses the significance of the Qumran finds for the study of Palestinian Judaism and the history and ideas of early Christianity.
Related titles: Online - full text ed.: ISSN 1568-5179. EUR 223, USD 313 to institutions (effective 2012) (from IngentaConnect).
Indexed: A01, A03, A08, A21, A22, AmHI, BibInd, CA, DIP, E01, H07, IBR, IBZ, IJP, IZBG, J01, M10, OTA, PCI, R&TA, SCOPUS, T02.
—IE, Ingenta. **CCC.**
Published by: Brill, PO Box 9000, Leiden, 2300 PA, Netherlands. TEL 31-71-5353500, FAX 31-71-5317532, cs@brill.nl. Eds. Eibert J C Tigchelaar, Hindy Najman. **Dist. by:** Turpin Distribution Services Ltd., Pegasus Dr, Stratton Business Park, Biggleswade, Bedfordshire SG18 8QB, United Kingdom. TEL 44-1767-604954, FAX 44-1767-601640, custserv@turpin-distribution.com, http://www.turpin-distribution.com/.

296.7 USA
F335.J5
DEEP SOUTH JEWISH VOICE. Text in English. 1990. s-m. USD 18 (effective 2005). adv. bk.rev. **Document type:** *Newspaper, Consumer.* **Description:** Contains features and articles for the Alabama and Mississippi Jewish community.
Formerly (until 1999): Southern Shofar (1082-3484)
Indexed: ENW, J01.
Published by: Lawrence Brook, Ed. & Pub., PO Box 130052, Birmingham, AL 35213-0052. TEL 205-595-9255, FAX 205-595-9256. Ed., Pub. Lawrence Brook. Adv. contact Fred Benjamin. col. inch USD 10.70. Circ: 2,500 (paid and controlled). Wire service: JTA.

296 USA ISSN 0044-040X
DER YID; voice of American Orthodox Jewry. Text in Yiddish. 1951. w. (Thu.). USD 65 (effective 2006). adv. bk.rev. **Document type:** *Newspaper, Consumer.*
Related titles: Microfilm ed.: (from AJP).
Published by: (National Committee of Orthodox Jewish Communities), Der Yid Publishing, 84 Broadway, Brooklyn, NY 11211. TEL 718-302-0561, FAX 718-797-1985. Ed. Aron Friedman. Circ: 44,000.

296.7 USA ISSN 0011-9644
DETROIT JEWISH NEWS. Text in English. 1942. w. USD 56 in state; USD 75 out of state; USD 130 foreign. adv. bk.rev.; film rev.; play rev. illus. **Document type:** *Newspaper, Consumer.*
Incorporates (in 1951): Detroit Jewish Chronicle; Which was formerly (until 1947): Detroit Jewish Chronicle and the Legal Chronicle; (until 1932): Detroit Jewish Chronicle; (1916-1919): Jewish Chronicle
Related titles: Microfilm ed.: (from AJP).
Published by: Jewish Renaissance Media, 29200 Northwestern Hwy., Ste. 110, Southfield, Oakland, MI 48034. TEL 248-354-6060, FAX 248-304-8885. Ed. Robert Sklar. Pub. Arthur M. Horwitz. Adv. contact Meg Lyczak. Circ: 20,300. Wire service: JTA.

296.3 DEU
▼ **DEUTSCH-JUEDISCHE AUTOREN DES 19. JAHRHUNDERTS.** Text in German. 2010. irreg., latest vol.2, 2010. price varies. **Document type:** *Monographic series, Academic/Scholarly.*
Published by: Boehlau Verlag GmbH & Cie, Ursulaplatz 1, Cologne, 50668, Germany. TEL 49-221-913900, FAX 49-221-9139011, vertrieb@boehlau.de, http://www.boehlau.de.

DIMENSIONS (ONLINE); a journal of holocaust studies. *see* HISTORY

DOKUMENTE - TEXTE - MATERIALEN. *see* HISTORY—History Of Europe

DOWN SYNDROME AMONGST US. *see* MEDICAL SCIENCES—Psychiatry And Neurology

221 NLD ISSN 1569-3597
EARLY JUDAISM AND ITS LITERATURE. Text in English. 1991. irreg., latest vol.24, 2008. price varies. **Document type:** *Monographic series, Academic/Scholarly.* **Description:** Covers the history, culture and literature of early Judaism.
Indexed: IZBG.
Published by: (Society of Biblical Literature USA), Brill, PO Box 9000, Leiden, 2300 PA, Netherlands. TEL 31-71-5353500, FAX 31-71-5317532, cs@brill.nl.

EDITION MNEMOSYNE. *see* ETHNIC INTERESTS

296.071 DEU ISSN 1615-7443
➤ **EMIL-FRANK-INSTITUT. SCHRIFTEN.** Text in German. 1999. irreg., latest vol.13, 2011. price varies. **Document type:** *Monographic series, Academic/Scholarly.*
Published by: (Universitaet Trier, Emil-Frank-Institut), Paulinus Verlag GmbH, Maximineracht 11c, Trier, 54295, Germany. TEL 49-651-46080, FAX 49-651-4608221, verlag@paulinus.de, http://www.paulinus.de.

296 USA ISSN 1053-4113
BM1
EMUNAH. Text in English. 1988. 3/yr. **Document type:** *Magazine, Consumer.*
Related titles: Online - full text ed.
Indexed: IJP.
Published by: Emunah of America, 7 Penn Plaza, New York, NY 10001. TEL 212-564-9045, 800-368-6440. Ed. Faye Reichwald.

296.4 305.8924 USA
ERENSIA SEFARDI/HERENCIA SEFARDI/HERITAGE SEPHARADE/SEPHARDIC HERITAGE. Text in English. 1993. q. USD 30 to members. bk.rev. **Document type:** *Newsletter.* **Description:** Deals with the history and culture of the descendants of the Spanish and Portuguese Jews in the lands of exile and examines their daily lives from 1492 to the present.
Indexed: IJP.
Address: 46 Benson Pl, Fairfield, CT 06430. TEL 203-259-8530, FAX 203-256-8819. Ed. Albert de Vidas. Circ: 4,000.

296.0902 NLD ISSN 0169-815X
ETUDES SUR LE JUDAISME MEDIEVAL. Text in Dutch. 1968. irreg., latest vol.36, 2008. price varies. back issues avail. **Document type:** *Monographic series, Academic/Scholarly.* **Description:** Scholarly translation and discussion of texts and issues in medieval Judaism in Europe and the Middle East.
Indexed: IZBG.
Published by: Brill, PO Box 9000, Leiden, 2300 PA, Netherlands. TEL 31-71-5353500, FAX 31-71-5317532, cs@brill.nl, http://www.brill.nl. Ed. Paul Fenton. R&P Elizabeth Venekamp. **Dist. by:** Turpin Distribution Services Ltd., Pegasus Dr, Stratton Business Park, Biggleswade, Bedfordshire SG18 8QB, United Kingdom. TEL 44-1767-604954, FAX 44-1767-601640, custserv@turpin-distribution.com, http://www.turpin-distribution.com/.

296 305.8924 NLD
➤ **EUROPEAN JOURNAL OF JEWISH STUDIES.** Text in English. 1996. 3/yr. EUR 119, USD 167 to institutions; EUR 130, USD 182 combined subscription to institutions (print & online eds.) (effective 2012). reprint service avail. from PSC. **Document type:** *Journal, Academic/Scholarly.* **Description:** Publishes research articles, essays and shorter contributions on all aspects of Jewish studies.
Formerly (until 2006): E A J S Newsletter (1025-9996)
Related titles: Online - full text ed.: ISSN 1872-471X. EUR 108, USD 152 to institutions (effective 2012) (from IngentaConnect).
Indexed: A01, A20, A22, ArtHuCI, CA, E01, IZBG, J01, SCOPUS, T02, W07.
—IE. **CCC.**
Published by: (European Association for Jewish Studies GBR), Brill, PO Box 9000, Leiden, 2300 PA, Netherlands. TEL 31-71-5353500, FAX 31-71-5317532, cs@brill.nl. Ed. Giuseppe Veltri.

296.094 GBR ISSN 0014-3006
BM1
➤ **EUROPEAN JUDAISM**; a journal for the new Europe. Text in English. 1966. s-a. GBP 104 combined subscription domestic to institutions (print & online eds.); EUR 133 combined subscription in Europe to institutions (print & online eds.); USD 176 combined subscription elsewhere to institutions (print & online eds.) (effective 2011). adv. bk.rev. cum.index. back issues avail.; reprint service avail. from PSC. **Document type:** *Journal, Academic/Scholarly.* **Description:** Covers all aspects of contemporary European Jewish thought.
Related titles: Microfilm ed.: (from PQC); Online - full text ed.: ISSN 1752-2323. 2003. GBP 94 domestic to institutions; EUR 120 in Europe to institutions; USD 159 elsewhere to institutions (effective 2011) (from IngentaConnect).
Indexed: A01, A02, A03, A08, A26, B04, CA, DIP, E08, G08, I05, IBR, IBZ, IJP, J01, M10, MEA&I, MLA-IB, PCI, PhilInd, R05, S09, SSAI, SSAb, SSI, T02, W03, W05.
—Ingenta. **CCC.**
Published by: Berghahn Books Ltd, 3 Newtec Pl, Magdalen Rd, Oxford, OX4 1RE, United Kingdom. TEL 44-1865-250011, FAX 44-1865-250056, journals@berghahnbooks.com, http://www.berghahnbooks.com. Ed. Jonathan Magonet. **Dist. in Europe by:** Turpin Distribution Services Ltd., Pegasus Dr, Stratton Business Park, Biggleswade, Bedfordshire SG18 8QB, United Kingdom. TEL 44-1767-604951, FAX 44-1767-601640, berghahnjournalsuk@turpin-distribution.com, http://www.turpin-distribution.com/; **Dist. outside of Europe by:** Turpin Distribution Services Ltd., The Bleachery, 143 W St, New Milford, CT 06776. TEL 860-350-0041, FAX 860-350-0039, berghahnjournalsus@turpin-distribution.com. **Co-sponsors:** Michael Goulston Educational Foundation; Leo Baeck College.

➤ **EX ORIENTE LUX**; Rezeptionen und Exegesen als Traditionskritik. *see* RELIGIONS AND THEOLOGY—Islamic

296.7 USA ISSN 1051-340X
FORWARD (NEW YORK). Text in English. 1990. w. (Fri.). USD 49.95. **Document type:** *Newspaper.* **Description:** Publishes items of interest to the Jewish community.
Related titles: Microfilm ed.: (from IDC, PQC); Online - full text ed.
Indexed: ENW, LeftInd.
Published by: Forward Association, 45 E 33rd St, New York, NY 10016. TEL 212-889-8200, FAX 212-447-6406. Ed. J. J. Goldberg. Adv. contact Jerome Koenig. Circ: 40,000.

FRANCONIA JUDAICA. *see* HISTORY—History Of Europe

296.071 DEU ISSN 0721-3050
FRANKFURTER JUDAISTISCHE STUDIEN. Text in German. 1971. irreg., latest vol.10, 1998. price varies. **Document type:** *Monographic series, Academic/Scholarly.*
Published by: Peter Lang GmbH (Subsidiary of: Peter Lang Publishing Group), Eschborner Landstr 42-50, Frankfurt Am Main, 60489, Germany. TEL 49-69-7807050, FAX 49-69-78070550, zentrale.frankfurt@peterlang.com, http://www.peterlang.com.

296 AUT ISSN 0021-2334
DIE GEMEINDE. Text in German. 1958. m. adv. bk.rev. illus. back issues avail. **Document type:** *Newsletter, Consumer.*
Published by: Israelitische Kultusgemeinde Wien, Seitenstettengasse 4, Vienna, W 1010, Austria. TEL 43-1-53104105, FAX 43-1-53104108, office@ikg-wien.at, http://www.ikg-wien.at. Ed. Sonia Feiger. Adv. contact Manuela Schrank TEL 43-1-53104272. Circ: 6,000.

296 USA ISSN 0016-9145
GESHER. Text in English, Hebrew. a. USD 5.
Published by: (Yeshiva University, Student Organization of Yeshiva), Rabbi Isaac Elchanan Theological Seminary, 500 W 185th St, New York, NY 10033. TEL 212-960-5277.

296 USA
G'VANIM (LOS ANGELES). Text in English. 1972. bi-m. free. adv. bk.rev. back issues avail. **Document type:** *Newsletter.* **Description:** Provides information for gay, lesbian, bisexual and straight people at synagogue.
Formerly: G'vanim (Print)
Media: Online - full text. **Related titles:** Online - full text ed.
Published by: Beth Chayim Chadashim, 6090 West Pico Blvd, Los Angeles, CA 90035. TEL 323-931-7023, bcc@bcc-la.org. Ed. Larry Nathenson. Circ: 400.

296 USA ISSN 1944-3528
G'VANIM (RIVERDALE). Text in English. 2005. a. back issues avail. **Document type:** *Journal, Academic/Scholarly.* **Description:** Dedicated to promoting a pluralistic approach to Jewish thought through discussions of Bible, Rabbinic thought, halakhah, history and literature. Includes book reviews.
Formerly (until 2008): Academy for Jewish Religion. Journal (1944-3501)
Related titles: Online - full text ed.: ISSN 1944-3536.
Published by: Academy for Jewish Religion, 6301 Riverdale Ave, Riverdale, NY 10471. TEL 718-543-9360, FAX 718-543-1038. Ed. Bernard M Zlotowitz.

296 USA ISSN 1935-097X
BM1
HA-TANIN. Text in English. 1986. a. free (effective 2010). back issues avail. **Document type:** *Newsletter, Academic/Scholarly.* **Description:** Provides information on events and lectures sponsored by the Center, faculty and staff, gifts, Judaica library, graduates, courses, and special programs in Jewish studies.
Formerly (until 2006): Amudim
Related titles: Online - full text ed.
Published by: University of Florida, Center for Jewish Studies, 201 Walker Hall, PO Box 118020, Gainesville, FL 32611. TEL 352-392-9247, FAX 352-392-5378, center@jst.ufl.edu.

296 FRA ISSN 0292-7993
DS135.F8
HABONE; le batisseur. Text in French. 1977. q.
Published by: Consistoire Israelite de Marseille, 119 rue Breteuil, Marseille, 13006, France. TEL 33-4-91374964, FAX 33-4-91539872, http://www.consistoiremarseille.com/. Ed. Jacques Cohen. Circ: 5,000 (paid and controlled).

HADASSAH MAGAZINE. *see* ETHNIC INTERESTS

HALIKHOT SADEH/INSTITUTE FOR AGRICULTURAL RESEARCH ACCORDING TO THE TORAH. BULLETIN. *see* AGRICULTURE

R

HAMORE; revue trimestrielle des educateurs et enseignants juifs. *see* EDUCATION—Teaching Methods And Curriculum

HAVURAH. *see* RELIGIONS AND THEOLOGY—Other Denominations And Sects

HEBRAIC POLITICAL STUDIES. *see* POLITICAL SCIENCE

220 DEU ISSN 2192-2276

▼ ➤ **HEBREW BIBLE AND ANCIENT ISRAEL.** Text in English. 2012. q. EUR 49 to individuals; EUR 199 to institutions (effective 2012). **Document type:** *Journal, Academic/Scholarly.* **Description:** Focuses on Hebrew biblical texts in their ancient historical contexts.
Related titles: Online - full text ed.: ISSN 2192-2284. 2012.
Published by: Mohr Siebeck GmbH & Co. KG, Wilhelmstr 18, Tuebingen, 72074, Germany. TEL 49-7071-9230, FAX 49-7071-51104, info@mohr.de. Ed. Gary N Knoppers.

➤ **HEBREW STUDIES**; a journal devoted to Hebrew language and literature of all periods. *see* LITERATURE

296.68083 USA ISSN 0360-9049
BM11
➤ **HEBREW UNION COLLEGE. ANNUAL.** Text in English, French, German, Hebrew. 1919. a., latest 2007. cum.index: 1924-1982 in 1982 vol. 300 p./no.; back issues avail. **Document type:** *Journal, Academic/Scholarly.* **Description:** Provides an international forum for scholarly discussion in all areas of Judaic, biblical, and semitic studies.
Formerly (until 1924): Journal of Jewish Lore and Philosophy (0190-4361)
Related titles: Microfilm ed.: (from AJP); Online - full text ed.; ◆ Supplement(s): Hebrew Union College Annual Supplements. ISSN 0275-9993.
Indexed: A20, A21, A22, ASCA, AmH&L, ArtHuCI, BibLing, CA, CERDIC, FR, HistAb, IZBG, MLA-IB, OTA, P30, PCI, R&TA, RI-1, RI-2, SCOPUS, T02, W07.
—IE, INIST.
Published by: Hebrew Union College - Jewish Institute of Religion (Cincinnati), 3101 Clifton Ave, Cincinnati, OH 45220. TEL 513-221-1875, FAX 513-221-0321, sjaffee@huc.edu.

296.68083 USA ISSN 0275-9993
BM11
HEBREW UNION COLLEGE ANNUAL SUPPLEMENTS. Text in English. 1976. irreg. USD 18.75 per issue (effective 2010). **Document type:** *Monographic series, Academic/Scholarly.*
Related titles: ◆ Supplement to: Hebrew Union College. Annual. ISSN 0360-9049.
Indexed: OTA.
Published by: Hebrew Union College - Jewish Institute of Religion (Cincinnati), 3101 Clifton Ave, Cincinnati, OH 45220. TEL 513-221-1875, FAX 513-221-0321, sjaffee@huc.edu, http://www.huc.edu.

296.68 USA
HEBREW UNION COLLEGE - JEWISH INSTITUTE OF RELIGION. CHRONICLE. Text in English. 1972. s-a. free. bk.rev. bibl.; illus. **Document type:** *Newsletter.*
Formerly (until 1977): Hebrew Union College - Jewish Institute of Religion. Reporter
Published by: Hebrew Union College - Jewish Institute of Religion (New York), One W Fouth St, New York, NY 10012. TEL 212-824-2209. Ed. Jean Rosensaft. Circ: 13,000.

296.7 USA
HEBREW WATCHMAN. Text in English. w. (Thu.). USD 18; USD 0.50 newsstand/cover (effective 2004). **Document type:** *Newspaper, Consumer.*
Published by: Herman I. Goldberger, 4646 Poplar, Memphis, TN 38124-1183. TEL 901-763-2215. Ed., Pub. Herman I Goldberger. Circ: 3,000 (paid).

296.071 ITA ISSN 0393-6805
BS410
HENOCH. Text in English, French, German, Italian. 1979. s-a. EUR 46 domestic; EUR 56 foreign (effective 2009). back issues avail. **Document type:** *Journal, Academic/Scholarly.* **Description:** Contains historical and philological studies on Judaism.
Related titles: Supplement(s): Quaderni di Henoch. ISSN 1121-1067. 1989.
Indexed: A01, A21, A22, BibInd, BibLing, IBR, IBZ, IZBG, OTA, RI-1, T02.
—IE, Ingenta.
Published by: Editrice Morcelliana SpA, Via Gabriele Rosa 71, Brescia, BS 25121, Italy. TEL 39-030-46451, FAX 39-030-2400605, http://www.morcelliana.it.

296 USA ISSN 0732-0914
HERITAGE (WALTHAM). Text in English. 1968. s-a. USD 50 to members. **Document type:** *Newsletter.*
Former titles (until 1984): American Jewish Historical Society. Report; (until 1976): American Jewish Historical Society. News (0065-8944)
Related titles: Online - full content ed.
Indexed: MLA-IB.
Published by: American Jewish Historical Society, 15 W 16th St, New York, NY 10011. TEL 212-294-6160, info@ajhs.cjh.org. Ed. Michael Feldberg. Pub. Herbert Klein. Circ: 4,000.

296.7 USA ISSN 0199-0721
HERITAGE FLORIDA JEWISH NEWS. Text in English. 1976. w. (Fri.). USD 34.95; USD 0.75 newsstand/cover (effective 2005). adv. **Document type:** *Newspaper, Consumer.*
Address: PO Box 300742, Fern Park, FL 32730. TEL 407-834-8787, FAX 407-831-0507. Ed., Pub., R&P, Adv. contact Jeffrey Gaeser. Circ: 7,000 (paid).

296.7 USA
HIDDEN CHILD. Text in English. 1991. q. free to members (effective 2006). bk.rev. **Document type:** *Newsletter, Consumer.* **Description:** Examines issues of children who survived the Holocaust and their Jewish identity.
Related titles: Online - full text ed.
Published by: Hidden Child Foundation, 823 United Nations Plaza, New York, NY 10017. TEL 212-885-7900, FAX 212-867-0779. Circ: 5,200 (controlled). **Co-sponsor:** A D L.

HILLEL GATE. *see* ETHNIC INTERESTS

296.7 305.892 USA
HILLEL NOW; the newsletter for Jewish campus life. Text in English. s-a. **Document type:** *Newsletter.* **Description:** Provides information on campus campaign updates and events at the international, national, local and regional levels including grant and gift recognition.
Published by: Hillel: The Foundation for Jewish Campus Life, 800 8th St NW, Washington, DC 20001-3724. TEL 202-857-6560. Ed. Nurite Notarius Rosin.

296 ISR ISSN 0793-7474
HITKASHROUS. Text in Hebrew. 1994. w. free (effective 2008).
Published by: Chabad Youth Organization, PO Box 14, Kfar Chabad, 72915, Israel. TEL 972-3-9607588, FAX 03-9606169, chabad@inter.net.il, http://chabad.org.il. Ed. Menachem Brod.

HOLOCAUST STUDIES; a journal of culture and history. *see* HISTORY

HOLOCAUST STUDIES SERIES. *see* HISTORY

255.3 ISR ISSN 0333-7189
HOLY LAND REVIEW; illustrated quarterly of the Franciscan custody of the Holy Land. Text in English. 1975. q. USD 10 (effective 2008). adv. bk.rev. cum.index: 1975-1984. back issues avail. **Description:** Provides a Catholic voice on the troubled Middle East.
Published by: (Saint Saviour Franciscan Monastery), Franciscan Printing Press, PO Box 14064, Jerusalem, 91140, Israel. TEL 972-2-6266592, FAX 972-2-6272274, fpp@bezeqint.net, http://198.62.75.1/www1/ofm/fpp/FPPmain.html. Ed. James Heinsch. Circ: 5,000. **Subscr. in US to:** Holy Land Review, c/o Franciscan Monastery, 1400 Quincy St N E, Washington, DC 20017.

296.3 USA ISSN 0441-4195
BM1
HUMANISTIC JUDAISM. Text in English. 1967. q. USD 21 domestic; USD 31 in Canada & Mexico; USD 43 elsewhere; USD 30 domestic to libraries; USD 40 in Canada to libraries; USD 52 elsewhere to libraries (effective 2009). bk.rev. back issues avail. **Document type:** *Journal, Academic/Scholarly.* **Description:** Features an in depth examination of a topic of concern to Secular Humanistic Jews.
Indexed: IJP, JewAb.
Published by: Society for Humanistic Judaism, 28611 W 12 Mile Rd, Farmington Hills, MI 48334. TEL 248-478-7610, FAX 248-478-3159, info@shj.org.

296 NLD ISSN 1570-1581
I J S STUDIES IN JUDAICA. (Institute for Jewish Studies) Text in English. 2002. irreg., latest vol.6, 2008. price varies. **Document type:** *Monographic series, Academic/Scholarly.*
Indexed: IZBG.
Published by: Brill, PO Box 9000, Leiden, 2300 PA, Netherlands. TEL 31-71-5353500, FAX 31-71-5317532, cs@brill.nl. Ed. Mark Geller.

ICONOGRAPHY OF RELIGIONS. SECTION 23, JUDAISM. *see* ART

296.7 USA
ILLIANA NEWS. Text in English. 1976. 10/yr. free. adv. bk.rev. **Document type:** *Newsletter, Consumer.* **Description:** Contains articles on Israel, Jewish art, literature and lifestyle.
Published by: Jewish Federation, Inc. - Northwest Indiana, 2939 Jewett St., Highland, IN 46322. TEL 219-972-2250, FAX 219-972-4779. Ed. Nancy Webster.

IMAGES; a journal of Jewish art and visual culture. *see* ART

INDEX OF ARTICLES ON JEWISH STUDIES (ONLINE)/RESHIMAT MA'AMARIM BE-MADA'E HA-YAHADUT. *see* RELIGIONS AND THEOLOGY—Abstracting, Bibliographies, Statistics

INDEX TO JEWISH PERIODICALS. *see* RELIGIONS AND THEOLOGY—Abstracting, Bibliographies, Statistics

296.7 USA
INDIANA JEWISH POST AND OPINION. Text in English. 1933. w. USD 36; USD 2 per issue (effective 2011). adv. bk.rev. reprints avail. **Document type:** *Newspaper, Consumer.* **Description:** Contains articles of interest to the Jewish community.
Published by: Spokesman Co., Inc., 1111 East 54th St, Ste 119, Indianapolis, IN 46220. TEL 317-972-7800, FAX 317-972-7807, http://www.jewishpostopinion.com. Ed. Jennie Cohen. Pub. Gabriel Cohen. Adv. contact Barbara Lemaster. Circ: 129,301.

296.071 DEU ISSN 0344-4767
INFORMATION JUDENTUM. Text in German. 1978. irreg., latest vol.5, 2001. price varies. **Document type:** *Monographic series, Academic/Scholarly.*
Published by: Neukirchener Verlag, Andreas-Braem-Str 18-20, Neukirchen-Vluyn, 47506, Germany. TEL 49-2845-392222, FAX 49-2845-33689, info@nvg-medien.de, http://www.nvg-medien.de.

296.7 FRA ISSN 0020-0107
INFORMATION JUIVE. Text in French. 1948. m. EUR 33 domestic; EUR 41 foreign (effective 2009). adv. bk.rev. bibl. reprints avail. **Document type:** *Magazine.* **Description:** Studies the problems of Israel, aspects of Judaism in France and abroad, Jewish thought.
Incorporates (1950-1980): Journal de la Communaute (0021-8022)
Related titles: Microform ed.: (from PQC).
Published by: Consistoire Israelite de Paris, 17 rue Saint-Georges, Paris, 75009, France. TEL 33-1-48742987, FAX 33-1-48744197, http://www.consistoire.org. Ed. Victor Malka. Pub. Jacques Lazarus. Circ: 11,000.

296.18 USA
INTERCOM (NEW YORK, 1973). Text mainly in English; Text occasionally in Hebrew. 1973 (vol.14). s-a. USD 50 to members. bk.rev. **Description:** Addresses issues of science and Jewish law. Seeks to reconcile and resolve conflicts and challenges of science and Jewish law.
Published by: Association of Orthodox Jewish Scientists, 3 W 16th St, New York, NY 10011-6363. TEL 212-229-2340, FAX 212-229-2319. Ed. Rabbi Barry Freundel. Circ: 1,400.

296.7 USA ISSN 0047-0511
INTERMOUNTAIN JEWISH NEWS. Text in English. 1913. w. (Fri.). USD 55 (effective 2005). adv. bk.rev.; film rev. charts; illus. **Document type:** *Newspaper, Consumer.* **Description:** Contains international, national, regional and local news of interest to its Jewish readership.
Related titles: Microfilm ed.: (from AJP).
Address: 1275 Sherman St, Ste 214, Denver, CO 80203-2299. TEL 303-861-2234, FAX 303-832-6942. Ed., R&P Rabbi Hillel Goldberg. Pub., Adv. contact Miriam H Goldberg. B&W page USD 1,940.80. Circ: 9,520 (paid).

INTERNATIONAL ORGANIZATION FOR SEPTUAGINT AND COGNATE STUDIES. BULLETIN. *see* HUMANITIES: COMPREHENSIVE WORKS

ISRAEL AKTUEEL. *see* ETHNIC INTERESTS

ISSUES (SAN FRANCISCO); a messianic jewish perspective. *see* RELIGIONS AND THEOLOGY—Other Denominations And Sects

296.7 USA
E184.J5
J C C CIRCLE. Text in English. 1943. q. USD 25 (effective 1998). adv. bk.rev. **Document type:** *Newsletter, Consumer.* **Description:** Contains news and feature stories relevant to Jewish Community Center Movement, YM-YWHAs, camps and Jewish chaplains, Jewish organizations throughout North America.
Formerly (until 1997): Circle (1065-1551)
Related titles: Microfilm ed.: (from AJP).
Indexed: IJP.
Published by: Jewish Community Centers Association of North America, 15 E 26th St, New York, NY 10010-1579. TEL 212-532-4949, FAX 212-481-4174. Ed. Zimmy Zimberg. Adv. contact Estelle Heifetz. Circ: 32,000.

296.67 USA ISSN 1538-0777
BM729.W6
J O F A JOURNAL. (Jewish Orthodox Feminist Alliance) Text in English. 1998. q.
Published by: Jewish Orthodox Feminist Alliance, 15 E 26th St, Ste 915, New York, NY 10010. TEL 212-679-8500, jofa@rcn.com, http://www.jofa.org. Ed. Lisa Schlaff.

296.7 USA ISSN 0021-6763
J T A WEEKLY NEWS DIGEST. Text in English. 1935. w. USD 100 (effective 2001). **Document type:** *Newsletter.* **Description:** Summarizes international events of concern to and affecting Jews and Jewish communities.
Published by: Jewish Telegraphic Agency, 330 Seventh Ave, 17th Fl, New York, NY 10001. newsdesk@JTA.org, http://www.jta.org. Ed. Lisa Hostein. Pub. Mark T Joffe. Circ: 7,000.

296.7 USA
F899.S49
J T NEWS. Text in English. 1924. bi-w. USD 37.50 (effective 2004). adv. bk.rev. charts; illus. **Document type:** *Newspaper.*
Former titles: The Jewish Transcript (0021-678X); Transcript
Related titles: Microfilm ed.: (from AJP).
Published by: Jewish Federation of Greater Seattle, 2041 3rd Ave, Seattle, WA 98121-2418. Ed. Joel Magalnick. Pub. Karen Schachkes. Adv. contacts David Stahl, Lynn Feldhammer. Circ: 4,200. Wire service: JTA.

296.7 USA
J U F NEWS. (Jewish United Fund) Text in English. 1972. m. USD 10 donation. adv. bk.rev. **Document type:** *Newspaper, Consumer.* **Description:** Covers news of community service programs and events in the greater Chicago area.
Formerly: Chicago J U F News
Published by: Jewish United Fund - Jewish Federation of Metropolitan Chicago, One S Franklin St, Rm 701, Chicago, IL 60606. TEL 312-357-4848, FAX 312-855-2470. Ed. Aaron B Cohen. Pub. Michael B Kotzen. R&P Aaron Cohen. Adv. contact Janet Buzil. Circ: 55,000.

296.7 USA ISSN 0021-3799
J W V A BULLETIN. (Jewish War Veterans of the U.S.A.) Text in English. 1970 (vol.12). 3/yr. USD 1 (effective 1997). charts; illus. **Document type:** *Bulletin.* **Description:** Covers Jewish interests.
Published by: Jewish War Veterans Of The Usa, Inc.* National Ladies Auxiliary (Subsidiary of: Jewish War Veterans of the USA, Inc.), 1811 R St NW, Washington, DC 20009.

JABBOK. *see* RELIGIONS AND THEOLOGY

JAHRBUCH ZUR GESCHICHTE UND WIRKUNG DES HOLOCAUST. *see* HISTORY

296.7 USA ISSN 0447-7049
BM1
JEWISH ACTION. Text in English. 1950. q. USD 16 domestic; USD 20 in Canada; USD 60 elsewhere; free domestic to students (effective 2008). adv. bk.rev. illus. **Document type:** *Magazine, Consumer.*
Indexed: IJP, JewAb.
Published by: Union of Orthodox Jewish Congregations of America, 11 Broadway, New York, NY 10004. TEL 212-613-8146, FAX 212-613-0646, ja@ou.org. adv.: B&W page USD 2,535, color page USD 3,240; trim 8.375 x 10.875. Circ: 70,000.

296.7 USA ISSN 1077-2995
AN42.B6
JEWISH ADVOCATE. Text in English. 1902. w. (Fri.). USD 29.95 in New England; USD 40 in United States; USD 43 foreign. **Document type:** *Newspaper.*
Related titles: Microfilm ed.: (from AJP); Online - full text ed.
Indexed: DYW, ENW, I05.
Address: 15 School St, Boston, MA 02108. TEL 617-367-9100, FAX 617-367-9310. Eds. Richard Asinof, Richard Ferrer. Pub. Rabbi Y.A. Korff. Adv. contact Eleanor Grosser. Circ: 27,500 (paid). Wire service: JTA.

296.7 USA ISSN 0021-6305
DS101
JEWISH AFFAIRS. Text in English. 1970. bi-m. USD 7.50. adv. bk.rev. bibl.
Related titles: Microfilm ed.: (from AJP).
Indexed: RASB.
Published by: Communist Party, U S A, 235 W 23rd St, 7th Fl, New York, NY 10011. TEL 212-989-4994. Ed. Herbert Aptheker. Circ: 1,500.

220 ISR ISSN 0792-3910
BS410
➤ **JEWISH BIBLE QUARTERLY.** Text in English. 1972. q. USD 24 (effective 2005). adv. bk.rev. **Document type:** *Journal, Academic/Scholarly.* **Description:** Publishes original articles and translations from scholarly Hebrew journals on biblical themes. The only Jewish-sponsored, English language journal devoted exclusively to the Bible.
Former titles: Dor le-Dor (0334-2166); Bible Readers' Union Bulletin (0006-0771)
Related titles: Microfiche ed.; Online - full text ed.
Indexed: A01, A02, A03, A08, A21, A26, CA, FamI, G06, G07, G08, I05, IBSS, IJP, IZBG, J01, JewAb, OTA, R&TA, RI-1, RI-2, T02.

—BLDSC (4668.351280), IE, Ingenta.
Published by: Jewish Bible Association, PO Box 29002, Jerusalem, Israel. TEL 972-2-6216145. Ed. Dr. Shimon Bakon. R&P Dr. Joshua Backon TEL 972-2-6759145. Adv. contact Dr. Joshua Adler. Circ: 1,400 (paid).

➤ **JEWISH BOOK WORLD.** *see* RELIGIONS AND THEOLOGY—Abstracting, Bibliographies, Statistics

➤ **JEWISH BRAILLE REVIEW.** *see* HANDICAPPED—Visually Impaired

➤ **THE JEWISH CHRONICLE**; the world's leading Jewish newspaper. *see* ETHNIC INTERESTS

➤ **THE JEWISH CHRONICLE (PITTSBURGH).** *see* ETHNIC INTERESTS

296.7 USA ISSN 1068-1663
THE JEWISH CHRONICLE (WORCESTER). Text in English. 1926. bi-w. (Thu.). free; USD 20 subscr - mailed (effective 2008). **Document type:** *Newspaper, Consumer.*
Former titles (until 1992): The Jewish Chronicle-Leader (0747-0053); (until 1980): The Jewish Chronicle (0191-4952)
Published by: Mar-Len Publications, 131 Lincoln St, Worcester, MA 01605. TEL 508-752-2512, FAX 508-752-9057. Ed. Ellen Weingart. Pub. Sondra Shapiro. Adv. contact Reva Capellari TEL 508-752-2512 ext 125. Circ: 5,000 (free).

296 USA ISSN 8750-4197
JEWISH CHRONICLE (YONKERS); serving Southern Westchester. Text in English. 1968. 6/yr. USD 15 (effective 1998). adv. bk.rev.; film rev. back issues avail. **Document type:** *Newspaper.*
Published by: Jewish Council of Yonkers, 584 N Broadway, Yonkers, NY 10701. TEL 914-423-5009, FAX 914-423-5077. Ed., R&P Brian Stillman. Adv. contact Esther Marshall. Circ: 6,000.

296.7 USA ISSN 0021-6348
JEWISH CIVIC PRESS. Text in English. 1965. m. USD 15. adv. bk.rev.; film rev.; play rev. illus. **Document type:** *Newsletter.*
Related titles: Microfilm ed.: (from AJP).
Published by: Jewish Federation of Greater New Orleans, 924 Valmont St, New Orleans, LA 70115. TEL 504-895-8784, FAX 504-895-0433. Ed. Claire Tritt. R&P Abner L Tritt. Circ: 12,600 (controlled).

296.7 USA
JEWISH COMMUNITY NEWS. Text in English. 1941. bi-m. **Document type:** *Newsletter.*
Related titles: Microfilm ed.: (from AJP).
Published by: Jewish Federation of Southern Illinois, 6464 W Main, Ste 7A, Belleville, IL 62223. TEL 618-398-6100. Ed. Steven C Low.

296.7 USA ISSN 1042-2986
JEWISH COMMUNITY VOICE (CHERRY HILL). Text in English. 1941. fortn. USD 25 (effective 2008). adv. bk.rev. **Document type:** *Newspaper, Consumer.*
Formerly (until 1970): South Jersey Jewish Community Voice
Related titles: Microfilm ed.: 1941 (from AJP).
Published by: Jewish Federation of Southern New Jersey, 1301 Springdale Rd, Ste 250, Cherry Hill, NJ 08003-2769. TEL 856-751-9500, FAX 856-751-1697, http://www.jewishcommunityvoice.org/. Ed. Harriet Kessler. Adv. contact Sally Grossman. Circ: 11,200.

296.7 USA
JEWISH COMMUNITY VOICE (PORTLAND). Text in English. m. free. adv.
Published by: Jewish Federation, 57 Ashmont St, Portland, ME 04103. TEL 207-773-7254, FAX 207-772-2234. Ed. Rachel Michaud. Adv. contact Karen Lerman. B&W page USD 300; trim 15 x 10. Circ: 1,500.

JEWISH DENOMINATIONS IN AMERICA. *see* ETHNIC INTERESTS

296.7 USA ISSN 0021-6437
JEWISH EXPONENT. Text in English. 1887. w. (Thu.). USD 39.95. adv. bk.rev. illus. **Document type:** *Newspaper.* **Description:** Contains items of interest to the Jewish community.
Related titles: Microfilm ed.: (from AJP); Online - full text ed.
Indexed: ENW.
Published by: Jewish Federation of Greater Philadelphia, 2100 Arch St., Philadelphia, Philadelphia, PA 19103. TEL 215-832-0700, FAX 215-569-3389. Adv. contact Flora Klein. Circ: 80,000.

JEWISH GENEALOGICAL SOCIETY OF PHILADELPHIA. CHRONICLES. *see* GENEALOGY AND HERALDRY

296 USA
JEWISH GUARDIAN. Text in English. 1974. bi-m. USD 4.50. adv. bk.rev. illus.
Related titles: Microfilm ed.: (from AJP).
Published by: Neturei Karta of U.S.A. - Guardians of the Holy City, P O Box 2143, Brooklyn, New York, NY 11202. Ed. Mordecai Weberman. Circ: 10,000.

296.7 USA
JEWISH GUIDE TO BOSTON & NEW ENGLAND. Text in English. 1972. s-a. USD 11.95 (effective 1998). **Document type:** *Magazine, Consumer.*
Address: 15 School St, Boston, MA 02108. TEL 617-367-9100, FAX 617-367-9310. Ed. Rosie Rozenzweig.

JEWISH GUILD FOR THE BLIND. NEWSLETTER. *see* HANDICAPPED—Visually Impaired

296.7 USA ISSN 0021-6488
F395.J5
JEWISH HERALD-VOICE. Text in English. 1908. w. (plus 2 special issues). USD 35 (effective 1997). adv. bk.rev. illus. **Document type:** *Newspaper.*
Related titles: Microfilm ed.: (from AJP).
Address: 3403 Audley, Box 153, Houston, TX 77001. TEL 713-630-0391, FAX 713-630-0404. Ed. Jeanne F Samuels. Adv. contact Vicki Samuels. Circ: 6,600.

296.09 GBR ISSN 0962-9696
JEWISH HISTORICAL STUDIES. Text in English. 1893. biennial. GBP 30 per vol. to non-members; free to members (effective 2009). **Document type:** *Proceedings.*
Formerly (until 1982): Jewish Historical Society of England. Transactions & Miscellanies (0962-9688); Which was formed by the merger of (1925-1962): Jewish Historical Society of England. Miscellanies; (1894-1982): Jewish Historical Society of England. Transactions
Indexed: HistAb, PCI.
—BLDSC (4668.353770), IE, Ingenta.
Published by: Jewish Historical Society of England, 33 Seymour Pl, London, W1H 5AP, United Kingdom. TEL 44-20-77235852, FAX 44-20-77235852, info@jhse.org.

296.09 NLD ISSN 0334-701X
DS101 CODEN: JHEIAO
JEWISH HISTORY. Text in English, Hebrew. 1986. 4/yr. EUR 356, USD 367 combined subscription to institutions (print & online eds.) (effective 2012). adv. bk.rev. reprint service avail. from PSC. **Document type:** *Journal, Academic/Scholarly.* **Description:** Devoted exclusively to history and the Jews, is to broaden the limits of historical writing on the Jews.
Related titles: Online - full text ed.: ISSN 1572-8579 (from IngentaConnect).
Indexed: A01, A02, A03, A08, A20, A22, A26, AmH&L, ArtHuCI, BibLing, CA, E01, ENW, H05, HistAb, I02, I14, IHP, IJP, J01, JewAb, M08, M10, P10, P28, P48, P53, P54, PCI, PQC, R&TA, S02, S03, SCOPUS, T02, W07.
—BLDSC (4668.353800), IE, Infotrieve, Ingenta. **CCC.**
Published by: (Haifa University Press ISR), Springer Netherlands (Subsidiary of: Springer Science+Business Media), Van Godewijckstraat 30, Dordrecht, 3311 GX, Netherlands. TEL 31-78-6576050, FAX 31-78-6576474, http://www.springer.com. Ed. Kenneth Stow.

▼ **JEWISH ICONS.** *see* BIOGRAPHY

296.7 CAN ISSN 1910-9377
JEWISH INDEPENDENT. Text in English. 1930. w. CAD 46.50 domestic; USD 43 foreign (effective 2001). adv. bk.rev. illus. **Document type:** *Bulletin.*
Formerly (until 2005): Jewish Western Bulletin (0021-6879)
Related titles: Online - full text ed.: 2004.
Published by: Western Sky Communications Ltd., 291 East 2nd Ave., Ste 200, Vancouver, BC V5T 1B8, Canada. TEL 604-689-1520, FAX 604-689-1525, editor@jewishindependent.ca. Pub. Cynthia Ramsay. Circ: 2,402 (controlled).

296.7 USA
JEWISH JOURNAL. Text in English. 1976. s-w. (Tue. & Thu.). USD 150; free newsstand/cover (effective 2005). **Document type:** *Newspaper, Consumer.*
Related titles: Supplement(s): Directory of Jewish Life.
Published by: Forum Publishing Group (Subsidiary of: Tribune Company), 1701 Green Rd., Ste. B, Pompano Beach, FL 33064. TEL 954-698-6397, 800-275-8820, FAX 954-480-8426. Circ: 121,965 (paid and free). Wire service: JTA.

296.7 USA
JEWISH JOURNAL (VALLEY STREAM). Text in English. 1969. w.
Address: 11 Sunrise Plaza, Valley Stream, NY 11581. TEL 516-561-6900, FAX 516-561-6971. Ed. Harold Singer.

296.7 USA
JEWISH JOURNAL (YOUNGSTOWN). Text in English. 1987. s-m. USD 9 in city; USD 25 out of city (effective 2007). adv. bk.rev. **Document type:** *Newspaper.*
Published by: Youngstown Area Jewish Federation, 505 Gypsy Ln, Youngstown, OH 44504-1314. TEL 216-744-7902, FAX 216-744-7926. Ed., R&P Sherry Weinblatt. Adv. contact Phyllis Friedman. page USD 416; 12 x 9.75. Circ: 5,000. Wire service: JTA.

JEWISH JOURNAL - NORTH OF BOSTON. *see* PUBLISHING AND BOOK TRADE

296.7 USA ISSN 0888-0468
AP92
JEWISH JOURNAL OF GREATER LOS ANGELES. Text in English. 1986. w. USD 30 in state; USD 45 out of state; USD 120 elsewhere (effective 2000). adv. bk.rev. **Document type:** *Newspaper, Consumer.*
Formerly (until 1986): Los Angeles Jewish Community Bulletin (0194-4983)
Address: 3660 Wilshire Blvd, Ste 204, Los Angeles, CA 90010. TEL 213-368-1661, FAX 213-368-1684, ab871@lafn.org. Eds. Gene Lichtenstein, Rob Eshman. Pub. Stanley Hirsh. Circ: 58,000.

296.7 USA
JEWISH JOURNAL OF SAN ANTONIO. Text in English. 1973. m. (except July). free to qualified personnel. adv. bk.rev. back issues avail. **Document type:** *Newspaper, Consumer.* **Description:** Contains local, national, and international news and features of interest to the local Jewish community.
Related titles: Online - full text ed.: free.
Published by: Jewish Federation of San Antonio, 12500 NW Military Hwy No 200, San Antonio, TX 78231-1871. TEL 210-302-6960, http://www.jfsatx.org/. Ed. Barbara Richmond. Circ: 3,800.

JEWISH LAW ANNUAL. *see* LAW

JEWISH LAW IN CONTEXT. *see* LAW

JEWISH LAWYER. *see* LAW

296.7 USA
THE JEWISH LEADER. Text in English. 1974. bi-w. (Thu.). adv. **Document type:** *Newspaper, Consumer.*
Published by: Jewish Federation of Eastern Connecticut, 28 Channing St, Box 1468, New London, CT 06320. TEL 860-442-8062, FAX 860-443-4175. Ed. Mimi Perl. adv.: col. inch USD 9. Circ: 2,200 evening (paid).

296.7 USA ISSN 0021-6550
THE JEWISH LEDGER. Text in English. 1924. w. (Thu.). USD 30 (effective 2008). adv. bk.rev. illus. **Document type:** *Newspaper, Consumer.*
Related titles: Microfilm ed.: (from AJP).
Published by: Expositor Ledger Newspapers, 2535 Brighton Henrietta Town Line Rd, Rochester, NY 14623-2711. TEL 585-427-2468, FAX 585-427-8521. Ed., Adv. contact Barbara Morgenstern. R&P Jill Nabar. Circ: 8,000.

296.3642 ISR
➤ **JEWISH MEDICAL ETHICS AND HALACHA.** Text in English. 1988. s-a. (in 6 vols.). USD 30 (effective 2008). adv. **Document type:** *Journal, Academic/Scholarly.*
Formerly (until 2005): Jewish Medical Ethics (0793-2952)
Indexed: P30, SCOPUS.
Published by: Shaare Zedek Medical Center, Falk Schlesinger Institute for Medical Halachic Research, P O Box 3235, Jerusalem, 91031, Israel. TEL 972-2-6555266, FAX 972-2-6523295, medhal@szmc.org.il, http://www.szmc.org.il/machon. Ed. Rabbi Mordechai Dr Halperin. Circ: 500.

296.7 USA ISSN 1070-5848
JEWISH NEWS OF GREATER PHOENIX. Text in English. 1948. w. (Fri.). USD 48; USD 1.50 newsstand/cover (effective 2008). adv. 40 p./no. 5 cols./p.; **Document type:** *Newspaper, Consumer.* **Description:** Contains local, national, international news and features, as well as special sections. Also includes annual community directory.
Former titles: Greater Phoenix Jewish News (0747-444X); Phoenix Jewish News (0031-8353)
Related titles: Microform ed.; Online - full text ed.
Indexed: ENW.
Published by: Phoenix Jewish News, Inc., 1625 E Northern Ave, Ste 106, Phoenix, AZ 85020. TEL 602-870-9470, FAX 602-870-0426. R&P, Adv. contact Florence Eckstein. B&W page USD 2,731.25. Circ: 6,500 (paid). Wire service: JTA.

296.7 USA ISSN 1094-0243
JEWISH NEWS OF WESTERN MASSACHUSETTS. Text in English. 1945. bi-w. USD 25 in state; USD 33 out of state. adv. bk.rev. illus. **Document type:** *Newspaper.* **Description:** Contains articles of interest to the Jewish community.
Formerly (until 1992): Jewish Weekly News (0021-6860)
Related titles: Microfilm ed.: 1945 (from AJP).
Contact Owner: Jewish Advocate, 15 School St, Boston, MA 02108. TEL 617-367-9100, FAX 617-367-9310. Circ: 5,500. Wire service: JTA.

296.7 USA ISSN 1547-0733
THE JEWISH NEWS WEEKLY OF NORTHERN CALIFORNIA. Text in English. 1946. w. (Fri.). USD 42.50 (effective 2007). adv. bk.rev. **Document type:** *Newspaper, Consumer.*
Former titles (until 2003): Jewish Bulletin of Northern California (1067-8883); Northern California Jewish Bulletin (0745-0664); San Francisco Jewish Bulletin; Jewish Community Bulletin (0021-6364)
Related titles: Microfilm ed.: (from AJP, LIB); Online - full text ed.
Indexed: DYW, ENW.
—CIS.
Published by: San Francisco Jewish Community Publications, Inc., 225 Bush St, Ste 1480, San Francisco, CA 94104-4207. info@jweekly.com. Ed., Pub. Marc S Klein. Adv. contact Rhea Adler. Circ: 26,000.

296.7 USA
JEWISH OBSERVER (DEWITT). Text in English. 1978. bi-w. USD 30. adv. bk.rev.; film rev.; play rev. charts. back issues avail.
Published by: Syracuse Jewish Federation Inc., 5655 Thompson Rd, Syracuse, NY 13214-1234. TEL 315-445-2040, FAX 315-445-1559. Ed. Iris Petroff. R&P Marc Goldberg TEL 800-779-7896. Adv. contact Eileen Tobin. Circ: 4,650.

296.4 USA ISSN 0021-6615
BM1
JEWISH OBSERVER (NEW YORK). Text in English. 1963. m. (Sep.-June). USD 25 domestic; USD 40 foreign (effective 2009). adv. bk.rev. Index. back issues avail.; reprints avail. **Document type:** *Magazine, Consumer.* **Description:** Presents thought and opinion on Jewish affairs from an orthodox perspective.
Related titles: Microform ed.: (from PQC).
Indexed: A22, IJP.
Published by: Agudath Israel of America, 42 Broadway, 14th Fl., New York, NY 10004-3889. TEL 212-797-9000, FAX 646-254-1600. Ed. Rabbi Nisson Wolpin. Circ: 15,000.

296.7 CAN
JEWISH POST AND NEWS. Text in English. 1925. w. CAD 36.48, USD 70. adv. bk.rev. **Document type:** *Newspaper.*
Formed by the merger of (1925-1987): Jewish Post (0839-4687); (1925-1987): Western Jewish News (0839-4679)
Related titles: Microfilm ed.: (from AJP).
Address: 113 Hutchings St, Winnipeg, MB R2X 2V4, Canada. TEL 204-694-3332, FAX 204-694-3916. Ed. Matt Bellan. Pub. Bernie Bellan. Adv. contact Gail Frankel. Circ: 3,600.

296.7 USA ISSN 1073-9351
JEWISH POST OF NEW YORK. Text in English. 1974. m. USD 18 (effective 2000). adv. bk.rev. 80 p./no. 5 cols./p.; back issues avail. **Document type:** *Newspaper.* **Description:** Covers news of Jewish interest in New York area, Israel and worldwide.
Former titles (until 1991): Jewish Post and Renaissance of New York (0745-9238); (until 1983): Jewish Post of N Y
Published by: Link Marketing & Promotions, Inc, 262 West 38th St, Ste 904, New York, NY 10018. TEL 212-398-1313, FAX 212-398-3933. Ed. Gad Nahshon. R&P, Adv. contact Henry Levy. B&W page USD 3,000; trim 15 x 10. Circ: 42,000 (controlled and free).

296.7 USA ISSN 0021-6674
JEWISH PRESS (BROOKLYN). Text in English. 1949. w. USD 35 (effective 1998). adv. bk.rev.; film rev.; play rev.; software rev. bibl.; illus. 6 cols./p.; **Document type:** *Newspaper, Consumer.* **Description:** Concentrates on topics related to Israel and Jews worldwide.
Related titles: Microfilm ed.: (from AJP, PQC).
Indexed: RASB.
Published by: Jewish Press, Inc., c/o Irene Klass, Pub, 338 Third Ave, Brooklyn, NY 11215. TEL 718-330-1100, FAX 718-935-1215. Eds. Jason Maot, Sheila Abrams. Pub. Irene Klass. R&P Jerry Greenwald. Adv. contact Heshy Kornblit. Circ: 75,000 (paid).

296.7 USA ISSN 0021-6666
JEWISH PRESS (OMAHA). Text in English. 1921. w. USD 27 domestic; USD 32 foreign (effective 2001). adv. bk.rev. illus. **Document type:** *Newspaper.* **Description:** Contains local, national and international items of interest to the Jewish community.
Related titles: Microfilm ed.: (from AJP, PQC); Online - full text ed.
Indexed: ENW, P48, PQC.
Published by: Jewish Federation of Omaha, 333 S 132nd St, Omaha, NE 68154. TEL 402-334-6448, FAX 402-333-5422, jshpress@aol.com. Ed., R&P Carol Katzman TEL 402-334-6450. Adv. contact Larry Axelrod. Circ: 3,780.

296.7 USA ISSN 0895-4259
JEWISH PRESS OF PINELLAS COUNTY. Text in English. 1985. fortn. adv. **Document type:** *Newspaper.*

R

Published by: Jewish Press Group of Tampa Bay (FL), Inc., PO Box 6970, Clearwater, FL 33758-6970. TEL 727-535-4400, FAX 727-530-3039. Ed., R&P Karen Wolfson Dawkins. Pub., Adv. contact Jim Dawkins. Circ: 5,700.

296.7 USA
JEWISH PRESS OF TAMPA. Text in English. 1987. fortn. adv. **Document type:** *Newspaper.*
Published by: Jewish Press Group of Tampa Bay (FL), Inc., PO Box 6970, Clearwater, FL 33758-6970. TEL 727-871-2332, FAX 727-530-3039. Ed., R&P Karen W Dawkins. Pub., Adv. contact Jim Dawkins. Circ: 5,200.

JEWISH QUARTERLY. *see* ETHNIC INTERESTS

296.68 956 USA ISSN 0021-6682
DS101
THE JEWISH QUARTERLY REVIEW. Abbreviated title: J Q R. Text in English. 1888. q. USD 50 combined subscription to individuals (print & online eds.); USD 91 combined subscription to institutions (print & online eds.); USD 27 to students (effective 2011). bk.rev. bibl.; illus. index. back issues avail.; reprints avail. **Document type:** *Journal, Academic/Scholarly.* **Description:** Provides a forum for the study of religion, Judaica, Old and New Testaments, Semitic languages and ancient Near Eastern studies.
Related titles: Microfilm ed.: (from PMC, PQC); Online - full text ed.: ISSN 1553-0604. USD 42 to individuals; USD 82 to institutions (effective 2011).
Indexed: A01, A02, A03, A07, A08, A20, A21, A22, A26, A30, A31, AA, AICP, ASCA, AmHI, ArtInd, B04, BRD, BibLing, CA, E01, E08, ENW, FR, H07, H08, HAb, HumInd, I05, I14, IBR, IBZ, IJP, IZBG, J01, JewAb, L05, L06, M10, MEA&I, MLA, MLA-IB, OTA, P28, P30, P48, P53, P54, PCI, PQC, PhilInd, R&TA, RASB, RI-1, RI-2, S09, SociolAb, T02, W03, W05.
—IE, Ingenta, INIST. **CCC.**
Published by: University of Pennsylvania, Center for Advanced Judaic Studies, 420 Walnut St, Philadelphia, PA 19106. TEL 215-238-1290, FAX 215-238-1540, ruderman@sas.upenn.edu, http://www.cjs.upenn.edu/. Eds. David N Myers, Elliott Horowitz. **Dist. by:** Eisenbrauns Inc.

296.7 USA
JEWISH REPORTER. Text in English. 1976. bi-m. (Fri.). free (effective 2008). **Document type:** *Newspaper, Consumer.*
Related titles: Microfilm ed.: (from LIB).
Contact Owner: Jewish Federation of Las Vegas, 2317 Renaissance Dr., Las Vegas, NV 89119-7520. TEL 702-732-0556, 702-948-5129, FAX 702-732-3228, 702-967-1082. Circ: 20,000 (free).

296.7 USA ISSN 1547-7010
JEWISH REVIEW. Text in English. 1959. bi-m. (1st & 15th of mo.). free (effective 2008). adv. bk.rev.; music rev.; play rev.; tel.rev.; video rev. charts; illus.; maps. back issues avail. **Document type:** *Newspaper.* **Description:** Covers Jewish community efforts and events in and around Portland and worldwide.
Formerly (until 1986): Portland Jewish Review
Related titles: Microfilm ed.: (from AJP); Online - full text ed.
Published by: Jewish Federation of Portland, 6680 SW Capitol Hwy, Portland, OR 97204. TEL 503-245-6219, FAX 503-245-6603. Ed., R&P Paul Haist. Adv. contact Gail Halladay. Circ: 11,000 (free).

▼ **JEWISH REVIEW OF BOOKS.** *see* LITERATURE

THE JEWISH ROLE IN AMERICAN LIFE. *see* ETHNIC INTERESTS

296 USA ISSN 0898-7963
BM729.J4
JEWISH SCIENCE INTERPRETER; a message of health and happiness through the Jewish Faith. Text in English. 1922. 8/yr. USD 15 (effective 2001). adv. bk.rev.
Published by: (Society of Jewish Science), Jewish Science Publishing Co., 109 E 39th St, New York, NY 10016-0948. TEL 212-682-2626, FAX 212-682-9812. Ed. Pascal G Gondolfo. Circ: 1,000.

296.7 USA ISSN 0021-6704
DS101
➤ **JEWISH SOCIAL STUDIES**; history, culture and society. Text in English. 1939. 3/yr. USD 150.50 combined subscription to institutions (print & online eds.) (effective 2012). adv. bk.rev. cum.index every 25 yrs. back issues avail.; reprint service avail. from PSC. **Document type:** *Journal, Academic/Scholarly.* **Description:** Aims to enhance the understanding of Jewish life and the Jewish past through the study of history and the evolution of Jewish societies and cultures over time.
Related titles: Microform ed.; Online - full text ed.: ISSN 1527-2028. 1999. USD 99.50 to institutions (effective 2012).
Indexed: A01, A02, A03, A06, A08, A20, A21, A22, A26, ABS&EES, AbAn, AmH&L, AmHI, B04, BRD, CA, CBRI, DIP, E01, E08, ENW, FR, G06, G07, G08, H07, H08, H09, H10, HAb, HistAb, HumInd, I05, I07, I13, I14, IBR, IBSS, IBZ, IJP, J01, M01, M02, M10, MEA&I, MLA-IB, P06, P10, P28, P30, P34, P42, P43, P46, P48, P53, P54, PAIS, PCI, PQC, PSA, R&TA, R05, RI-1, RI-2, RILM, S02, S03, S05, S09, S23, SCOPUS, SOPODA, SSA, SociolAb, T02, W03, W04, W05.
—IE, Infotrieve, Ingenta, INIST. **CCC.**
Published by: Indiana University Press, 601 N Morton St, Bloomington, IN 47404. TEL 812-855-8817, 800-842-6796, FAX 812-855-7931, journals@indiana.edu, http://iupress.indiana.edu. Eds. Derek Penslar, Steven J Zipperstein. Circ: 400.

➤ **JEWISH STANDARD**; New Jersey's oldest English-Jewish newspaper. *see* JOURNALISM

296.7 CAN ISSN 0021-6739
AP92
JEWISH STANDARD. Text in English. 1929. fortn. CAD 20. adv. illus. **Description:** Covers activities of the Jewish community.
Published by: Julius Hayman Ltd., 1912A Avenue Rd, Ste E5, Toronto, ON M5M 4A1, Canada. TEL 416-537-2696, FAX 416-789-3872. Circ: 10,100.

THE JEWISH STATE. *see* ETHNIC INTERESTS

296 305.8924 USA ISSN 1040-4295
➤ **JEWISH STUDIES.** Text in English, Hebrew. 1986. irreg., latest vol.27, 2004. price varies. back issues avail. **Document type:** *Monographic series, Academic/Scholarly.*
Indexed: IJP.
Published by: Edwin Mellen Press, 415 Ridge St, PO Box 450, Lewiston, NY 14092. TEL 716-754-2266, FAX 716-754-4056, cservice@mellenpress.com.

296.071 305.8924 ISR ISSN 1565-7388
➤ **JEWISH STUDIES, AN INTERNET JOURNAL.** Abbreviated title: J S I J. Text in English, Hebrew; Summaries in English. 2002. irreg., latest vol.6. **Document type:** *Journal, Academic/Scholarly.* **Description:** Deals with all fields of Jewish studies.
Media: Online - full text.
Indexed: A21.
Published by: Bar-Ilan University, Faculty of Jewish Studies, Qiryat Ha-Universita, Ramat Gan, 52900, Israel. Ed. James L Kugel.

296 USA ISSN 1931-5511
DS101
JEWISH STUDIES AT PENN; the jewish studies annual newsletter. Text in English. 1987. a. free (effective 2010). **Document type:** *Newsletter, Academic/Scholarly.* **Description:** Highlights the events and programs in the Jewish community at University of Pennsylvania.
Related titles: Online - full text ed.: ISSN 1931-552X.
Published by: University of Pennsylvania, Jewish Studies Program, 711 Williams Hall, 255 S 36th St, Philadelphia, PA 19104. TEL 215-898-6654, FAX 215-573-6026, jsp-info@sas.upenn.edu.

296 USA ISSN 1935-6986
JEWISH STUDIES CLASSICS. Text mainly in English; Text occasionally in Hebrew, German. 2003. irreg., latest 2008. price varies. back issues avail. **Document type:** *Monographic series, Academic/Scholarly.* **Description:** Provides to academia standard works in Jewish Studies.
Published by: Gorgias Press LLC, 954 River Rd, Piscataway, NJ 08854. TEL 732-885-8900, FAX 732-885-8908, helpdesk@gorgiaspress.com, http://www.gorgiaspress.com/bookshop/default.aspx.

305.8924 USA
JEWISH STUDIES NEWSLETTER. Text in English. 1989. m. free. back issues avail. **Document type:** *Newsletter.* **Description:** Contains short articles and book reviews about Jewish studies.
Formerly: Jewish Studies Online
Media: Online - full text.
Published by: Michigan State University, 310 Auditorium Bldg, East Lansing, MI 48824. TEL 517-355-9300, FAX 517-355-8363, h-jucaic@h-net.msu.edu. Ed. Aviva Ben. **Co-sponsor:** Boston Hebrew College.

296 DEU ISSN 0944-5706
DS101
JEWISH STUDIES QUARTERLY. Text in German. 1993. q. EUR 59 to individuals; EUR 189 to institutions (effective 2012). adv. reprint service avail. from SCH. **Document type:** *Journal, Academic/Scholarly.*
Related titles: Online - full text ed.: ISSN 1868-6788 (from IngentaConnect).
Indexed: I14, IBR, IBZ, IJP, IZBG, JewAb, MLA-IB, OTA, PCI.
—BLDSC (4668.380330), IE, Ingenta.
Published by: Mohr Siebeck GmbH & Co. KG, Wilhelmstr 18, Tuebingen, 72074, Germany. TEL 49-7071-9230, FAX 49-7071-51104, info@mohr.de. Eds. Leora Batnitzky, Peter Schaefer. Adv. contact Tilman Gaebler. Circ: 450 (paid and controlled).

JEWISH STUDIES SOURCE. *see* HISTORY—Abstracting, Bibliographies, Statistics

JEWISH TELEGRAPH (GLASGOW EDITION). *see* ETHNIC INTERESTS

JEWISH TELEGRAPH (LEEDS EDITION). *see* ETHNIC INTERESTS

JEWISH TELEGRAPH (LIVERPOOL & MERSEYSIDE EDITION). *see* ETHNIC INTERESTS

JEWISH TELEGRAPH (MANCHESTER EDITION). *see* ETHNIC INTERESTS

296.4 ZAF
JEWISH TRADITION. Text in English. 1954. m. ZAR 60 (effective 2000). adv. bk.rev. charts; illus. **Document type:** *Journal, Academic/Scholarly.* **Description:** Official mouthpiece of South African Orthodox Jewry.
Formerly: Federation of Synagogues of South Africa. Federation Chronicle (0014-9314)
Published by: Union of Orthodox Synagogues of South Africa, PO Box 46518, Orange Grove, East London 2119, South Africa. TEL 27-11-485-4865, FAX 27-11-640-7528. Ed. R I Reznik. Circ: 15,000.

296.7 USA ISSN 0745-4708
JEWISH TRIBUNE. Text in English. 1971. w. (Fri.). USD 26 (effective 1999). adv. bk.rev. **Document type:** *Newspaper.*
Published by: Empire Publishing Corp., 115 Middle Neck Rd, Great Neck, NY 11021. TEL 516-829-4000, FAX 516-829-4776. Ed., Pub. Jerome Lippman. Adv. contact Harriet Feigenbaum. Circ: 10,235 (paid).

296.7 GBR ISSN 0021-6801
JEWISH VANGUARD. Text in English. 1948. q. GBP 1.20. adv. bk.rev.; film rev.; play rev.; rec.rev. illus.
Published by: Poale Zion - Labour Zionists, 48 College Rd, Wembley, Mddx HA9 8RJ, United Kingdom. TEL 44-181-904-8483, FAX 44-181-908-1936. Ed. Reginald Freeson. Circ: 5,000.

JEWISH VETERAN; the patriotic voice of American Jewry. *see* MILITARY

296 USA ISSN 2155-434X
JEWISH VOICE (BROOKLYN). Text in English. 2003. w. **Document type:** *Newspaper, Consumer.* **Description:** Jewish news for New York, New Jersey and Florida.
Published by: David Ben-Hooren, Ed. & Pub., 2154 E 4th St, Brooklyn, NY 11233. TEL 800-998-0885, FAX 718-617-0645, info@jewishvoiceny.com.

296.7 USA
JEWISH VOICE (DEAL PARK). Text in English. 1971. m. adv. bk.rev. **Document type:** *Newspaper.* **Description:** Discusses the local Jewish community.
Published by: Jewish Federation of Greater Monmouth County, 100 Grant Ave, Deal, NJ 07723. TEL 908-531-6200, FAX 908-531-9518. Ed. Suzanne G Michel.

296.7 USA ISSN 0021-6828
THE JEWISH VOICE (WILMINGTON). Text in English. 1931. fortn. USD 18. adv. bk.rev. **Document type:** *Newspaper.* **Description:** Covers the local Jewish community efforts, national events and world news.
Related titles: Microfiche ed.; Microfilm ed.: (from AJP).
Published by: Jewish Federation of Delaware, 100 W 10th St, Ste 301, Wilmington, DE 19801-1666. TEL 302-427-2100, FAX 302-427-2438. Ed. Jordan Sopinsky. R&P Dan Weintraub. Adv. contact Irv Epstein. Circ: 4,200.

296.7 USA ISSN 1539-2104
THE JEWISH VOICE & HERALD. Text in English. 1973. m. USD 11. adv. bk.rev. **Document type:** *Newspaper, Consumer.* **Description:** Covers Jewish community efforts and news in and around Rhode Island.
Formerly (until 2001): The Jewish Voice (Providence) (1065-7924)
Published by: Jewish Federation of Rhode Island, 130 Sessions St, Providence, RI 02906. TEL 401-421-4111, FAX 401-331-7961. Ed. Jane S Sprague. Pub. Steven A Rakitt. Adv. contact Seena Taylor. Circ: 7,500 (controlled).

296.7 USA ISSN 1527-3814
JEWISH VOICE & OPINION. Text in English. 1987. m. USD 15 (effective 1999). adv. bk.rev. **Document type:** *Newsletter.* **Description:** Carries articles and opinion pieces of interest to the observant Jewish community.
Address: 73 Dana Pl, Englewood, NJ 07631. TEL 201-569-2845, FAX 201-569-1739. Ed. Susan L Rosenbluth. Circ: 15,000.

296.4 USA ISSN 0745-5356
AP92
THE JEWISH WEEK. Variant title: New York Jewish Week. Text in English. 1970. w. USD 39 for New York City, Nassau, Suffolk and Westchester residents; USD 44 in US & Canada; USD 75 elsewhere (effective 2005). adv. bk.rev. charts; illus. **Document type:** *Newspaper, Consumer.* **Description:** Covers political, social, religious and cultural events concerning the Jewish people.
Formerly (until 1982): New York Jewish Week and American Examiner (0737-352X)
Related titles: Microfilm ed.: (from AJP); Online - full text ed.
Indexed: DYW, ENW.
Published by: The Jewish Week, Inc., 1501 Broadway, Ste 505, New York, NY 10036. TEL 212-921-7822, FAX 212-921-8420. Ed. Gary Rosenblatt. Pub. Rich Waloff. Adv. contact Gershon Fastow. Circ: 90,000 (paid). Wire service: AP.

JEWISH WOMAN. *see* WOMEN'S INTERESTS

296.7 USA ISSN 0199-4441
THE JEWISH WORLD. Text in English. 1965. w. (Thu.). USD 26 local; USD 30 elsewhere (effective 2005). adv. bk.rev.; play rev.; tel.rev. 24 p./no. 6 cols./p.; back issues avail. **Document type:** *Newspaper, Consumer.* **Description:** Covers local, regional, national, and international events of concern to Jews.
Published by: Jewish World, Inc., 1104 Central Ave, Albany, NY 12205-3428. TEL 518-459-8455, FAX 518-459-5289, albanywrld@aol.com, 685-9675@mcimail.com. Ed. Laurie Clevenson. Pub. Sam S Clevenson. Adv. contact Lisa Shaw. col. inch USD 13.99. Circ: 50,000. Wire service: JTA.

296.7 USA ISSN 1529-2487
DS101
JEWISH WORLD REVIEW. Text in English. 1997. 5/w. **Document type:** *Magazine, Consumer.* **Description:** Aimed at people of faith and those interested in learning more about contemporary Judaism from those who are deeply religious.
Media: Online - full text.
Address: TEL 718-972-9241. Ed., Pub. Binyamin Jolkovsky.

296.05 GBR ISSN 0075-3769
JEWISH YEAR BOOK. Text in English. 1896. a. GBP 35 per issue (effective 2009). bk.rev. back issues avail. **Document type:** *Yearbook, Trade.* **Description:** Designed to a guide to the structures and networks of the religious, social, educational, cultural and welfare organisations of the Jewish community across the British Isles.
Related titles: Microform ed.
—BLDSC (4668.381000).
Published by: Vallentine Mitchell Publishers, 29/45 High St, Edgware, Middlesex HA8 7UU, United Kingdom. TEL 44-20-89529526, FAX 44-20-89529242, info@vmbooks.com, http://www.vmbooksuk.com/. Ed. Stephen W Massil.

296.7 USA ISSN 2154-0209
F704.T929
JEWISHTULSA; the Jewish Tulsa review. Text in English. 1930. m. free to members; USD 15 (effective 2005). adv. bk.rev. **Document type:** *Newspaper, Consumer.*
Formerly (until 2010): Tulsa Jewish Review (1521-5482)
Related titles: Online - full text ed.
Published by: Jewish Federation of Tulsa, 2021 E 71st St, Tulsa, OK 74136-5408. TEL 918-495-1100, FAX 918-495-1220. Ed. Edward A Ulrich. Adv. contact Nancy Polishuk TEL 918-495-1100 ext. 3107. Circ: 1,400.

JEWS FOR JESUS NEWSLETTER. *see* RELIGIONS AND THEOLOGY—Other Denominations And Sects

JIDISCHE SCHTUDIES. *see* LINGUISTICS

296.7 DNK ISSN 0021-7131
JOEDISK ORIENTERING; dialog og debat. Text in Danish. 1966. 11/yr. adv. bk.rev. illus.; bibl. back issues avail. **Document type:** *Magazine, Consumer.* **Description:** Covers activities of the Danish Jewish community.
Formed by the merger of (1964-1966): Joedisk Debat (0449-0568); (1928-1966): Joedisk Samfund (0906-1363); Which was formerly (until 1941): Joedisk Familieblad (0907-5526)
Related titles: Online - full text ed.
Published by: Det Mosaiske Trossamfund. Det Joediske Samfund i Danmark/Jewish Denmark. The Jewish Community in Denmark, Ny Kongensgade 6, Copenhagen K, 1472, Denmark. TEL 45-33-128868, FAX 45-33-123357, mt@mosaiske.dk. Ed. Yigal Romm TEL 45-33-226158. Adv. contact Dorte Kjaer Burr TEL 45-23-477762. Circ: 3,000.

296 301 305.8924 ZAF ISSN 1013-8471
PJ3001
JOURNAL FOR SEMITICS/TYDSKRIF VIR SEMITISTIEK. Text in Multiple languages. 1989. s-a. ZAR 35 domestic; USD 28 foreign (effective 2003). **Document type:** *Journal, Academic/Scholarly.*
Indexed: ISAP, MLA-IB, OTA.
Published by: (Suider-Afrikaanse Veriniging vir Semitistiek/Southern African Society for Semitics), UniSA Press, PO Box 392, Pretoria, 0003, South Africa. TEL 27-12-4292953, FAX 27-12-4293449, unisa-press@unisa.ac.za, http://www.unisa.ac.za/press.

296.0935 NLD ISSN 0047-2212
BM176
➤ **JOURNAL FOR THE STUDY OF JUDAISM**; in the Persian, Hellenistic and Roman Period. Text in Dutch. 1970. 5/yr. EUR 377, USD 527 to institutions; EUR 411, USD 575 combined subscription to institutions (print & online eds.) (effective 2012). cum.index: vols.1-27, 1970-1996. Supplement avail.; back issues avail.; reprint service avail. from PSC. **Document type:** *Journal, Academic/Scholarly.* **Description:** International forum of scholarly discussions on the history, literature and religious ideas of Judaism in the Persian, Hellenistic and Roman period.
Related titles: Online - full text ed.: ISSN 1570-0631. EUR 343, USD 479 to institutions (effective 2012) (from IngentaConnect).
Indexed: A01, A02, A03, A08, A20, A21, A22, ArtHuCI, BibLing, CA, DIP, E01, FR, IBR, IBZ, IJP, IZBG, J01, JewAb, M10, MEA&I, OTA, PCI, R&TA, RASB, RI-1, RI-2, SCOPUS, T02, W07.
—IE, Infotrieve, Ingenta, INIST. **CCC.**
Published by: Brill, PO Box 9000, Leiden, 2300 PA, Netherlands. TEL 31-71-5353500, FAX 31-71-5317532, cs@brill.nl. Ed. Eibert J C Tigchelaar. **Dist. by:** Turpin Distribution Services Ltd., Pegasus Dr, Stratton Business Park, Biggleswade, Bedfordshire SG18 8QB, United Kingdom. TEL 44-1767-604954, FAX 44-1767-601640, custserv@turpin-distribution.com, http://www.turpin-distribution.com/.

296.071 NLD ISSN 1384-2161
➤ **JOURNAL FOR THE STUDY OF JUDAISM. SUPPLEMENT.** Text in English; Text occasionally in French, German. 1959. irreg., latest vol.131, 2008. price varies. back issues avail. **Document type:** *Monographic series, Academic/Scholarly.* **Description:** Scholarly studies on textual, historical, cultural, religious and social aspects of Judaism from the Persian period through late antiquity, including its influence on early Christianity.
Formerly (until vol.49, 1996): Studia Post Biblica (0169-9717)
Indexed: IZBG.
—BLDSC (8547.601400).
Published by: Brill, PO Box 9000, Leiden, 2300 PA, Netherlands. TEL 31-71-5353500, FAX 31-71-5317532, cs@brill.nl, http://www.brill.nl. Ed. Hindy Najman. R&P Elizabeth Venekamp. **Dist. by:** Turpin Distribution Services Ltd., Pegasus Dr, Stratton Business Park, Biggleswade, Bedfordshire SG18 8QB, United Kingdom. TEL 44-1767-604954, FAX 44-1767-601640, custserv@turpin-distribution.com, http://www.turpin-distribution.com/.

305.8924 296 956 USA ISSN 1935-0643
DS134
➤ **THE JOURNAL FOR THE STUDY OF SEPHARDIC AND MIZRAHI JEWRY.** Text in English. 2007. s-a. back issues avail. **Document type:** *Journal, Academic/Scholarly.* **Description:** Covers all aspects of the Sephardic and Mizrahi Jewish experience, including history, culture, philosophy, law, mysticism, art, languages, rituals, ethnicity, inter-religious dialogue, politics, religious customs, and life in Israel and the Diaspora.
Media: Online - full text.
Published by: Florida International University, College of Arts and Sciences, c/o Antonina Shachar, BBC, AC1-223, 3000 NE 151st St, Miami, FL 33181. TEL 305-919-5610, casdean@fiu.edu, http://cas.fiu.edu.

296.071 DEU ISSN 1869-3296
BM1
▼ **JOURNAL OF ANCIENT JUDAISM.** Text in English. 2010. 3/yr. EUR 89 to individuals; EUR 178 to institutions; EUR 34.90 newsstand/cover (effective 2011). **Document type:** *Journal, Academic/Scholarly.* **Description:** Addresses all issues of Jewish literature, culture, religion, and history from the Babylonian exile until the Talmudim.
Related titles: ◆ Supplement(s): Journal of Ancient Judaism. Supplements.
Published by: Vandenhoeck und Ruprecht, Theaterstr 13, Goettingen, 37073, Germany. TEL 49-551-508440, FAX 49-551-5084422, info@v-r.de.

296.071 DEU
▼ ➤ **JOURNAL OF ANCIENT JUDAISM. SUPPLEMENTS.** Text in English. 2010. irreg. price varies. **Document type:** *Monographic series, Academic/Scholarly.*
Related titles: ◆ Supplement to: Journal of Ancient Judaism. ISSN 1869-3296.
Published by: Vandenhoeck und Ruprecht, Theaterstr 13, Goettingen, 37073, Germany. TEL 49-551-508440, FAX 49-551-5084422, info@v-r.de.

227.87 CAN ISSN 1203-1542
BS1136
➤ **JOURNAL OF HEBREW SCRIPTURES.** Text in English. 1996. irreg. free (effective 2011). back issues avail. **Document type:** *Journal, Academic/Scholarly.* **Description:** Covers Hebrew scriptures and the Old Testament.
Media: Online - full text.
Indexed: A21, A39, C27, C29, D03, D04, E13, J01, R&TA, R14, RI-1, S14, S15, S18, T02.
—CCC.
Address: ehud.ben.zvi@ualberta.ca, http://www.arts.ualberta.ca/JHS/index.htm. Ed. Ehud Ben Zvi.

296.7 USA ISSN 0022-2089
HV1
➤ **JOURNAL OF JEWISH COMMUNAL SERVICE.** Text in English. 1899. q. USD 36 to individuals; USD 40 to institutions; USD 20 per issue; free to members (effective 2011). adv. bk.rev. charts. index, cum.index every 10 yrs. back issues avail.; reprints avail. **Document type:** *Journal, Academic/Scholarly.* **Description:** Contains articles which explores the issues and concerns the Jewish community has faced during these decades.
Former titles (until 1956): The Jewish Social Service Quarterly; (until 1924): Jewish Center Worker
Related titles: Microform ed.: (from PQC); Online - full text ed.
Indexed: A01, A03, A08, A22, ABS&EES, CA, IJP, J01, JewAb, MEA&I, P06, P30, P34, P43, PAIS, PsycholAb, S02, S03, SSA, SWR&A, SociolAb, T02.
—BLDSC (5009.500000), IE, Ingenta.
Published by: Jewish Communal Service Association, 3084 State Hwy 27, Ste 9, Kendall Park, NJ 08824-1657. info@jcsana.org. Ed. Gail Naron Chalew.

➤ **JOURNAL OF JEWISH EDUCATION.** *see* EDUCATION

➤ **JOURNAL OF JEWISH IDENTITIES.** *see* ETHNIC INTERESTS

➤ **JOURNAL OF JEWISH MUSIC AND LITURGY.** *see* MUSIC

296.4 GBR ISSN 0022-2097
BM1
➤ **JOURNAL OF JEWISH STUDIES.** Abbreviated title: J J S. Text in English; Text occasionally in French. 1948. s-a. GBP 100, USD 220 to institutions; GBP 120, USD 260 combined subscription to institutions (print & online eds.) (effective 2011). adv. bk.rev. bibl.; illus. index. back issues avail.; reprint service avail. from PSC. **Document type:** *Journal, Academic/Scholarly.* **Description:** Covers Jewish history, literature and culture throughout the ages.
Related titles: Microform ed.: (from PQC); Online - full content ed.
Indexed: A01, A02, A03, A08, A20, A21, A22, AMHA, ASCA, AmHI, ArtHuCI, BibLing, BrHumI, CA, CurCont, DIP, FR, FamI, H07, I14, IBR, IBSS, IBZ, IJP, JewAb, M01, M02, M10, MEA&I, MLA-IB, OTA, PCI, PhilInd, R&TA, RASB, RI-1, RI-2, SCOPUS, T02, W07.
—BLDSC (5009.600000), IE, Infotrieve, Ingenta, INIST. **CCC.**
Published by: Oxford Centre for Hebrew and Jewish Studies, Yarnton Manor, Yarnton, Oxford OX1 1PY, United Kingdom. TEL 44-1865-377946, FAX 44-1865-735034, enquiries@ochjs.ac.uk, http://www.ochjs.ac.uk. Eds. Geza Vermes, Dr. Sacha Stern. adv.: page GBP 240; 114 x 184. Circ: 1,000.

296.3 NLD ISSN 1053-699X
BM1 CODEN: JJTPE2
➤ **THE JOURNAL OF JEWISH THOUGHT AND PHILOSOPHY.** Text in English. 1991. 2/yr. EUR 284, USD 397 to institutions; EUR 309, USD 403 combined subscription to institutions (print & online eds.) (effective 2012). reprint service avail. from PSC. **Document type:** *Journal, Academic/Scholarly.* **Description:** Provides an international forum for Jewish thought, philosophy and intellectual history, with an emphasis on contemporary issues. Covers biblical studies, mysticism, literary criticism, political theory, sociology and anthropology.
Related titles: Online - full text ed.: ISSN 1477-285X. EUR 258, USD 361 to institutions (effective 2012) (from IngentaConnect); ◆ Supplement(s): Journal of Jewish Thought and Philosophy. Supplements. ISSN 1873-9008.
Indexed: A01, A20, A22, ASCA, ArtHuCI, CA, CurCont, E01, FR, IJP, IZBG, J01, JewAb, PhilInd, SCOPUS, SociolAb, T02, W07.
—BLDSC (5009.630000), IE, Infotrieve, Ingenta, INIST. **CCC.**
Published by: Brill, PO Box 9000, Leiden, 2300 PA, Netherlands. TEL 31-71-5353500, FAX 31-71-5317532, cs@brill.nl. Eds. Catherine Chalier, Eliott R Wolfson, Irene Kajon, Robert B Gibbs. **Dist. by:** Turpin Distribution Services Ltd., Pegasus Dr, Stratton Business Park, Biggleswade, Bedfordshire SG18 8QB, United Kingdom. TEL 44-1767-604954, FAX 44-1767-601640, custserv@turpin-distribution.com, http://www.turpin-distribution.com/.

296.1 NLD ISSN 1873-9008
JOURNAL OF JEWISH THOUGHT AND PHILOSOPHY. SUPPLEMENTS. Text in English. 2007. irreg., latest vol.8, 2008. price varies. **Document type:** *Monographic series.*
Related titles: ◆ Supplement to: The Journal of Jewish Thought and Philosophy. ISSN 1053-699X.
Indexed: IZBG.
Published by: Brill, PO Box 9000, Leiden, 2300 PA, Netherlands. TEL 31-71-5353500, FAX 31-71-5317532, cs@brill.nl. Eds. Christian Wiese, Eliott R Wolfson, Leora Batnitzky.

296 NLD ISSN 2210-5980
▼ **JOURNAL OF SEPHARDIC AND MIZRAHI STUDIES.** Text in English. 2210. s-a. EUR 93, USD 126 to institutions (print & online eds.) (effective 2011). **Document type:** *Journal, Academic/Scholarly.*
Related titles: Online - full text ed.: ISSN 2210-5999.
—CCC.
Published by: Brill, PO Box 9000, Leiden, 2300 PA, Netherlands. TEL 31-71-5353500, FAX 31-71-5317532, http://www.brill.nl.

296 305.8924 USA ISSN 1943-8214
DS133
▼ ➤ **JOURNAL OF SPANISH, PORTUGUESE, AND ITALIAN CRYPTO JEWS.** Abbreviated title: J O S P I C J. Text in English. 2009. a. USD 10 per issue to individuals; USD 20 per issue to institutions (effective 2011). adv. back issues avail. **Document type:** *Journal, Academic/Scholarly.* **Description:** Features research and developments in the study of Crypto Jews and their descendants in past and present manifestations.
Published by: Florida International University, School of International and Public Affairs, Modesto A. Maidique Campus, DM 445, Miami, FL 33199 . TEL 305-348-7266, international@fiu.edu, http://international.fiu.edu/. Eds. Dolores Sloan, Abraham D Lavender.

296 USA
JOURNAL OF TEXTUAL REASONING. Text in English. 2002. irreg. free (effective 2011). back issues avail. **Document type:** *Journal, Academic/Scholarly.*
Media: Online - full text.
Published by: Society of Textual Reasoning

296.3 USA ISSN 1094-5954
THE JOURNAL OF TEXTUAL REASONING. Text in English. 1991. irreg., latest 2007. bk.rev. back issues avail. **Document type:** *Journal, Academic/Scholarly.* **Description:** Includes information on the Bible, the Talmud, postmodern phiosophy, gender studies, Judaism, modern philosophy and culture, and hermeneutics.
Formerly (until 1996): Postmodern Jewish Bitnetwork
Related titles: Online - full text ed.: ISSN 1939-7518.
Published by: (Postmodern Jewish Philosophy Network), University of Virginia, Carruthers Hall, PO Box 400203, Charlottesville, VA 22904. TEL 434-924-4122, ureg@virginia.edu, http://www.virginia.edu.

JOURNAL ON JEWISH AGING. *see* GERONTOLOGY AND GERIATRICS

296 USA ISSN 2156-0390
JUDAIC STUDIES ACADEMIC PAPER SERIES. Text in English. 200?. irreg., latest 2008. free (effective 2010). back issues avail. **Document type:** *Monographic series.* **Description:** Covers research topics in the realm of Judaic studies including Jewish history, customs, tradition and religion.
Media: Online - full text.
Published by: Shelomo Alfassa Ed. & Pub. shelomo@alfassa.com.

296 ITA ISSN 1827-3262
JUDAICA. Text in Italian. 1999. irreg. **Document type:** *Monographic series, Academic/Scholarly.*
Published by: Alfredo Guida Editore, Via Port'Alba 20/23, Naples, 80134, Italy. TEL 39-081-446377, FAX 39-081-451883, libri@guida.it, http://www.guidaeditori.it.

296 CHE ISSN 0022-572X
DS101
JUDAICA; Beitraege zum Verstehen des Judentums. Text in French. 1945. q. CHF 57; CHF 69 in Europe; CHF 77 elsewhere. adv. bk.rev. **Document type:** *Academic/Scholarly.*
Indexed: A21, A22, CERDIC, DIP, FR, HistAb, I14, IBR, IBZ, OTA, PCI, RI-1, RI-2.
—IE, Infotrieve, INIST.
Published by: (Stiftung fuer Kirche und Judentum), Judaica Verlag, Austr 114, Basel, 4051, Switzerland. TEL 41-61-2719897, FAX 41-61-2719234. Ed. Nico Rubeli Guthauser. Adv. contact Urs Kessler. Circ: 1,020.

296.7 CZE ISSN 0022-5738
DS135.C95
➤ **JUDAICA BOHEMIAE.** Text in English, French, German, Russian. 1965. biennial. bk.rev. bibl.; stat. **Document type:** *Journal, Academic/Scholarly.* **Description:** Contains articles concerning the history of Jewish life and culture in Bohemia and Moravia.
Indexed: A20, ArtHuCI, CA, FR, HistAb, J01, PCI, RASB, SCOPUS, T02, W07.
—INIST.
Published by: Zidovske Museum v Praze/Jewish Museum in Prague, A Stare Skoly 1, 3, Prague, 11001, Czech Republic. TEL 420-2-21711576. Ed. Alexandr Putik. Circ: 500.

296 NLD ISSN 1384-9050
JUDAICA BULLETIN; mededelingenblad van de stichting Judaica Zwolle. Text in Dutch. 1987. q. EUR 7 (effective 2010). adv. bk.rev. back issues avail. **Document type:** *Bulletin, Academic/Scholarly.* **Description:** Includes articles concerning Judaism, the Hebrew language, and the Jewish religion.
Published by: Stichting Judaica Zwolle, Postbus 194, Zwolle, 8000 AD, Netherlands. info@judaica-zwolle.nl, http://www.judaica-zwolle.nl. Eds. S P van 't Riet, Dick Broeren.

JUDAICA LIBRARIANSHIP. *see* LIBRARY AND INFORMATION SCIENCES

296.7 USA ISSN 0022-5762
BM1
➤ **JUDAISM**; a quarterly journal of Jewish life and thought. Text in English. 1952. q. USD 20 domestic to individuals; USD 22 foreign to individuals; USD 35 to institutions; free to members (effective 2009). adv. bk.rev. illus. index, cum.index (20 yrs.). reprints avail. **Document type:** *Journal, Academic/Scholarly.* **Description:** Provides a forum for creative discussion and exposition of the religious, moral and philosophical concepts of Judaism, and their relevance to modern society.
Related titles: Microform ed.: (from PQC); Online - full text ed.
Indexed: A01, A02, A03, A08, A11, A20, A21, A22, A25, A26, ABS&EES, ASCA, AcaI, AmHI, ArtHuCI, B04, BRD, C05, CA, CERDIC, CPerI, CurCont, DIP, E08, FR, G08, GSS&RPL, H07, H08, H14, HAb, HumInd, I05, I07, IBR, IBZ, IJP, IZBG, J01, JewAb, L06, M01, M02, M10, MASUSE, MEA&I, MLA-IB, OTA, P02, P10, P13, P28, P30, P48, P53, P54, PCI, PQC, PhilInd, R&TA, R05, RI-1, RI-2, RILM, S08, S09, S23, SCOPUS, T02, U01, W03, W05, W07, WBA, WMB.
—BLDSC (5073.825000), IE, Infotrieve, Ingenta, INIST.
Published by: American Jewish Congress, 825 3rd Ave, Ste 18, New York, NY 10022. TEL 212-879-4500, FAX 212-758-1633, contact@ajcongress.org.

296 USA ISSN 1935-6978
JUDAISM IN CONTEXT. Text in English. 2005. irreg., latest 2008. price varies. back issues avail. **Document type:** *Monographic series, Academic/Scholarly.* **Description:** Focuses on cross-cultural interactions between Jews and their neighbors throughout history, primarily covering religion and society.
Published by: Gorgias Press LLC, 954 River Rd, Piscataway, NJ 08854. TEL 732-885-8900, FAX 732-885-8908, helpdesk@gorgiaspress.com, http://www.gorgiaspress.com/bookshop/default.aspx.

296.071 DEU ISSN 0175-9515
JUDAISTISCHE TEXTE UND STUDIEN. Text in German. 1972. irreg., latest vol.11, 1989. price varies. **Document type:** *Monographic series, Academic/Scholarly.*
Published by: Georg Olms Verlag, Hagentorwall 7, Hildesheim, 31134, Germany. TEL 49-5121-15010, FAX 49-5121-150150, info@olms.de.

296 DEU ISSN 0721-3131
JUDENTUM UND UMWELT; realms of judaism. Text in English, German. 1979. irreg., latest vol.79, 2008. price varies. **Document type:** *Monographic series, Academic/Scholarly.*
Published by: Peter Lang GmbH (Subsidiary of: Peter Lang Publishing Group), Eschborner Landstr 42-50, Frankfurt Am Main, 60489, Germany. TEL 49-69-7807050, FAX 49-69-78070550, zentrale.frankfurt@peterlang.com, http://www.peterlang.com.

JUEDISCHE ALLGEMEINE. *see* ETHNIC INTERESTS

JUEDISCHE BILDUNGSGESCHICHTE IN DEUTSCHLAND. *see* EDUCATION

296 DEU
JUEDISCHER ALMANACH. Text in German. 1992. a. **Document type:** *Academic/Scholarly.*
Published by: (Leo-Baeck-Institut), Juedischer Verlag, Lindenstr 29-35, Frankfurt Am Main, 60325, Germany. Ed. Jakob Hessing.

296.16 USA ISSN 1081-8561
BM526.K28
➤ **KABBALAH (CULVER CITY)**; journal for the study of Jewish mystical texts. Text in French, German, Hebrew, Italian, Spanish. 1996. a. USD 72 per vol. (effective 2011). adv. 1 cols./p.; back issues avail. **Document type:** *Journal, Academic/Scholarly.* **Description:** Provides a platform for articles and relatively short scholarly editions of Jewish mystical works, as well as studies, reviews and notes about related textual issues. Covers the whole spectrum of Jewish mystical literature, from antiquity to the present, including magic and Christian Kabbalah.
Indexed: A21, IHP, RI-1.

R

Published by: Cherub Press, 10736 Jefferson Blvd, Ste 518, Culver City, CA 90230. TEL 310-839-2329, FAX 310-839-2354, http://www.cherub-press.com. Ed. Daniel Abrams. **Dist. by:** AtlasBooks Distribution Service, 30 Amberwood Pky, Ashland, OH 44805. info@atlasbooks.com, http://www.atlasbooksdistribution.com.

296.16 ISR
KABBALAH TODAY. Text in English, Hebrew, Russian. 2006. m. free (effective 2008). **Document type:** *Newspaper, Consumer.* **Description:** Aims to share the ancient wisdom of Kabbalah in a contemporary style.
Published by: Bnei Baruch Kabbalah Education and Research Institute, PO Box 1552, Ramat Gan, 52115, Israel. TEL 972-3-9226723, FAX 972-3-9226741, english@kabbalah.info. Ed. Asaf Ohayon.

KANSAS CITY JEWISH CHRONICLE. *see* ETHNIC INTERESTS

KASHRUS FAXLETTER. *see* FOOD AND FOOD INDUSTRIES

KASHRUS MAGAZINE. *see* FOOD AND FOOD INDUSTRIES

296.7 USA
KENTUCKY JEWISH POST AND OPINION. Text in English. 1931. irreg. (2-3/yr.). adv. reprints avail. **Document type:** *Magazine, Consumer.* **Description:** Contains items of interest to the Jewish community.
Published by: Spokesman Co., Inc., 1111 East 54th St, Ste 119, Indianapolis, IN 46220. TEL 317-972-7800, FAX 317-972-7807, jpostopinion@gmail.com, http://www.jewishpostopinion.com.

296.7 USA ISSN 1068-6975
BM723
KEREM; creative explorations in Judaism. Text in English. 1993. irreg., latest vol.7. USD 8.50 per issue to individuals; USD 15 per issue to institutions (effective 2011). adv. 128 p./no.; **Document type:** *Journal, Academic/Scholarly.* **Description:** Aims to combine the best of modern thinking and a serious engagement with Jewish tradition.
Indexed: IJP.
Published by: Jewish Study Center Press, Inc., 3035 Porter St, N W, Washington, DC 20008. TEL 202-364-3006, FAX 202-364-3806. Eds. Gilah Langner, Sara R Horowitz.

296 USA
KEREM SHLOMO. Text in Hebrew. 1977. irreg. (10-12/yr.). USD 15. bibl. index. back issues avail.
Published by: Bobover Congregation, 1577 48th St, Brooklyn, NY 11219. TEL 718-438-2018. Ed. Shmerel Zitronenbaum. Circ: 2,500.

296.7 USA ISSN 0742-5031
KOL HA-T'NUAH/VOICE OF THE MOVEMENT. Text in English. 1975 (vol.32). m. USD 1.25. illus. **Description:** Covers Jewish interests.
Published by: National Young Judaea, 50 W 58th St, New York, NY 10019. TEL 212-247-9222, FAX 212-247-9240. Ed. David Dashefsky.

320.540 GBR ISSN 0260-6585
KOLEINU. Text in English; Text occasionally in Hebrew. 1980. q. membership (effective 2003). adv. bk.rev.; film rev. 24 p./no.; back issues avail. **Document type:** *Magazine, Consumer.*
Published by: Habonim-Dror Organisation, 523 Finchley Rd, London, NW3 7BD, United Kingdom. TEL 44-20-74359033, FAX 44-20-74314503, friends@habodror.org.uk, http://www.habodror.org.uk. Circ: 1,500 (controlled). **Co-sponsors:** World Zionist Organisation; United Jewish Israel Appeal.

KONSTANZER SCHRIFTEN ZUR SCHOAH UND JUDAICA. *see* ETHNIC INTERESTS

296.73 USA
KOSHER DIRECTORY. Text in English. a. adv. **Document type:** *Directory, Consumer.*
Published by: (Kashruth Division), Union of Orthodox Jewish Congregations of America, 11 Broadway, New York, NY 10004. TEL 212-613-8146, FAX 212-613-0646, ja@ou.org, http://www.ou.org/. Ed. Zahava Fulda. Circ: 20,000.

KOSHER SPIRIT. *see* HOME ECONOMICS

296 NLD ISSN 1877-1351
KRONIEK (UTRECHT). Text in Dutch. 1996. q. EUR 15 (effective 2011). **Document type:** *Bulletin, Consumer.*
Published by: Katholieke Raad voor Israel, Biltstraat 121, Postbus 13049, Utrecht, 3507 LA, Netherlands. TEL 31-30-2326931, FAX 31-30-2334601, info@kri-web.nl, http://www.kri-web.nl. Ed. Tineke de Lange.

296.7 USA ISSN 0023-513X
KULTUR UN LEBN. Text in Yiddish. 1967. q. USD 12 (effective 2000). illus. **Description:** Covers American and East European Jewish culture.
Formed by the merger of: Friend; Culture and Education
Published by: (Yiddish Division), Workmen's Circle/Arbeter Ring, 45 E 33rd St, New York, NY 10016. TEL 212-889-6800, FAX 212-532-7518. Ed. Joseph Mlotek. Circ: 40,000.

296.7 USA ISSN 0274-4961
F850.J5
LAS VEGAS ISRAELITE. Text in English. 1965. fortn. USD 24 (effective 2002). adv. bk.rev. illus. **Document type:** *Newspaper.* **Description:** Features fact-finding editorials of interest to the Jewish community of Las Vegas and the rest of the nation.
Related titles: Microfilm ed.: (from AJP, LIB).
Published by: Michael Tell, Ed. & Pub., PO Box 14096, Las Vegas, NV 89114. TEL 702-876-1255, FAX 702-364-1009. R&P, Adv. contact Michael Tell. Circ: 43,000. Wire service: JTA.

LATIN AMERICAN JEWISH STUDIES ASSOCIATION. NEWSLETTER. *see* HISTORY—History Of North And South America

296.1 USA ISSN 1050-0480
BM198
L'CHAIM; the weekly publication for every Jewish person. Text in English. 1988. w. cum.index. **Document type:** *Newsletter, Consumer.*
Related titles: E-mail ed.; Online - full text ed.
Published by: Lubavitch Youth Organization, 305 Kingston Ave, Brooklyn, NY 11213. TEL 718-953-1000, FAX 718-771-6553.

L'DOR V'DOR/FROM GENERATION TO GENERATION. *see* ETHNIC INTERESTS

LEIPZIGER BEITRAEGE ZUR JUEDISCHEN GESCHICHTE UND KULTUR. *see* ETHNIC INTERESTS

296 DEU
LEQACH. Text in German. irreg., latest vol.5. price varies. **Document type:** *Monographic series, Academic/Scholarly.*
Formerly (until 2001): Theologische Fakultaet Leipzig. Forschungsstelle Judentum. Mitteilungen und Beitraege
Indexed: IZBG, OTA.
Published by: Theologische Fakultaet Leipzig, Forschungsstelle Judentum, Otto-Schill-Str 2, Leipzig, 04109, Germany. TEL 49-341-9735410. Ed. Timotheus Arndt.

LIBRARY OF HOLOCAUST TESTIMONIES. *see* HISTORY

LIBRARY OF JEWISH LAW AND ETHICS. *see* LIBRARY AND INFORMATION SCIENCES

296.7 USA ISSN 0146-2334
BM729.W6
LILITH; the independent Jewish women's magazine. Text in English. 1976. q. USD 21 domestic; USD 27 in Canada; USD 29 elsewhere (effective 2004). adv. bk.rev. reprints avail. **Document type:** *Magazine, Consumer.* **Description:** Directed to Jewish women, featuring editorials, fiction, poetry, news.
Related titles: Microfilm ed.: (from PQC); Online - full text ed.
Indexed: ABS&EES, AltPI, DYW, ENW, FemPer, GW, IJP, JewAb, MEA&I, S02, S03, S21, W09, WSA, WSI.
—Ingenta.
Published by: Lilith Publications, Inc., 250 W 57th St, Ste 2432, New York, NY 10107-0172. TEL 212-757-0818, FAX 212-757-5705. Circ: 10,000.

296.1 USA
LIVING WITH MOSHIACH; a weekly digest about Moshiach for the visually impaired and the blind. Text in English. 1992. w. USD 18 (effective 2009). back issues avail. **Document type:** *Magazine, Consumer.* **Description:** Makes the prophecies about Moshiach (the Messiah) accessible to blind and visually impaired persons.
Media: Large Type (18 pt.). **Related titles:** Braille ed.; Online - full text ed.
Published by: Lubavitch Shluchim Conferences On The Moshiach Campaign, Committee For The Blind, c/o Enlightenment For The Blind, Inc, 602 N Orange Dr, Los Angeles, CA 90036. info@torah4blind.org.

LONG ISLAND JEWISH WORLD. *see* ETHNIC INTERESTS

296 ARG ISSN 0024-7693
LUZ; la revista judia independiente. Text in Spanish. 1931. fortn. ARS 30 for 6 mos. domestic; USD 120 for 6 mos. in the Americas; USD 140 for 6 mos. elsewhere. bk.rev. bibl.; illus.
Address: Paso, 684 Piso 2 O A, Buenos Aires, 1031, Argentina. Ed. David Elnecave Jr. Circ: 25,000.

296 CHE ISSN 1011-4009
DS135.S9
MAAJAN - DIE QUELLE. Text in German. 1986. q. adv. bk.rev. back issues avail. **Document type:** *Journal, Academic/Scholarly.* **Description:** Publishes articles concerning Jewish genealogy.
Published by: Schweizerische Vereinigung fuer Juedische Genealogie, Postfach 2774, Zuerich, 8021, Switzerland. TEL 41-1-4627883, FAX 41-1-4635288, reneloeb@tiscali.ch, http://www.eye.ch/swissgen/ver/jeinfo-d.htm. R&P, Adv. contact Rene Loeb. Circ: 500.

MAHUT; journal for Jewish literature & art. *see* ETHNIC INTERESTS

MAIMONIDEAN STUDIES. *see* LIBRARY AND INFORMATION SCIENCES

296.7 USA
MANHATTAN JEWISH SENTINEL. Text in English. w. (Fri.). free (effective 2006). **Document type:** *Newspaper, Consumer.*
Published by: Empire Publishing Corp., 115 Middle Neck Rd, Great Neck, NY 11021. TEL 516-829-4000, FAX 516-829-4776. Ed., Pub. Jerome Lippman. Adv. contact Harriet Feigenbaum. Circ: 40,000 evening (free).

296.7 USA ISSN 0892-1571
D804.3
➤ **MARTYRDOM AND RESISTANCE.** Text in English. 1973. bi-m. free to members (effective 2011). bk.rev. illus. back issues avail. **Document type:** *Journal, Academic/Scholarly.* **Description:** Contains articles of interest to the Jewish community.
Formerly: Martyrdom and Freedom
Related titles: Microfiche ed.; Online - full text ed.: free (effective 2011).
Published by: International Society for Yad Vashem, 500 Fifth Ave, 42nd Fl, New York, NY 10110. TEL 212-220-4304, FAX 212-220-4308, http://www.yadvashem.org. Eds. Yefim Krasnyanskiy, Eli Zborowski.

296.071 ISR ISSN 0334-1674
PJ4545
MASSOROT. Key Title: Mswrwt. Text in Hebrew. 1984 (Jan.). irreg., latest vol.15, 2010. USD 33 to non-members; USD 30 to members (effective 2010). **Document type:** *Monographic series, Academic/Scholarly.*
Published by: Magnes Press (Subsidiary of: Hebrew University of Jerusalem), Hebrew University, Jerusalem, The Sherman Building for Research Management, PO Box 39099, Jerusalem, 91390, Israel. TEL 972-2-658-6660, FAX 972-2-563-3370, info@magnespress.co.il, http://www.magnespress.co.il/website_en/index.asp?action=show_covers&covers_mode=home_page. Ed. Aharon Maman.

296.0902 NLD ISSN 1380-7854
CB351
➤ **MEDIEVAL ENCOUNTERS;** Jewish, Christian and Muslim culture in confluence and dialogue. Text in English. 1995. 3/yr. EUR 332, USD 465 to institutions; EUR 362, USD 507 combined subscription to institutions (print & online eds.) (effective 2012). adv. bk.rev. back issues avail.; reprint service avail. from PSC. **Document type:** *Journal, Academic/Scholarly.* **Description:** Promotes discussion and dialogue across cultural, linguistic and disciplinary boundaries about the interactions of Jewish, Christian and Muslim culture during the period from the 4th through the 15th century C.E.
Related titles: Online - full text ed.: ISSN 1570-0674. EUR 302, USD 423 to institutions (effective 2012) (from IngentaConnect).
Indexed: A01, A03, A08, A22, AmHI, CA, DIP, E01, H07, I14, IBR, IBZ, IZBG, J01, M10, MLA-IB, SCOPUS, T02.
—BLDSC (5534.265835), IE, Ingenta. **CCC.**
Published by: Brill, PO Box 9000, Leiden, 2300 PA, Netherlands. TEL 31-71-5353500, FAX 31-71-5317532, cs@brill.nl. Ed. Cynthia Robinson. **Dist. by:** Turpin Distribution Services Ltd., Pegasus Dr, Stratton Business Park, Biggleswade, Bedfordshire SG18 8QB, United Kingdom. TEL 44-1767-604954, FAX 44-1767-601640, custserv@turpin-distribution.com, http://www.turpin-distribution.com/.

➤ **MEGADIM.** *see* RELIGIONS AND THEOLOGY

296.3 ISR ISSN 0333-7081
BM1
MEHQ'RE YERUSHALAYIM B'MAHSHEVET YISRA'EL/JERUSALEM STUDIES IN JEWISH THOUGHT. Text in English. 1981. s-a. ILS 95, USD 30 (effective 1999). **Document type:** *Journal, Academic/Scholarly.* **Description:** Jewish thought throughout history; medieval and modern Jewish philosophy and mysticism.
Indexed: IHP.
Published by: Jewish National and University Library, Jewish National and University Library, PO Box 34165, Jerusalem, Israel. TEL 972-2-6585039, FAX 972-2-658-6315. Ed. Rachel Elior.

MENORAH. *see* ETHNIC INTERESTS

296 USA
MENORAH REVIEW. Text in English. 1984. q. free (effective 2011). bk.rev. **Document type:** *Journal, Academic/Scholarly.* **Description:** Covers Jewish interests.
Formerly: Menorah
Related titles: Online - full text ed.: (from PQC).
Published by: Virginia Commonwealth University, Judaic Studies Program, 312 N Shafer St, PO Box 842021, Richmond, VA 23284. TEL 804-827-0909, jspiro@vcu.edu, http://www.vcu.edu/judaicstudies/. Ed. Jack D Spiro TEL 804-828-1224.

296 URY
MENSAJE. Text in Spanish. 1978 (vol.4). bi-m.
Published by: Comite Central Israelita del Uruguay, Rio Negro, 1308, Montevideo, 11111, Uruguay. Ed. Jorge Sztarcevsky.

296.382 ISR ISSN 0333-9726
MESILOT; religious Zionism in action. Text in Hebrew. 1983. irreg. adv. bk.rev. **Document type:** *Bulletin, Consumer.*
Related titles: English ed.
Published by: Society for the Advancement of Religious Zionism, Mesilot, c/o Mr. S.R. Sacks, P O Box 7720, Jerusalem, Israel. TEL 972-2-258833, FAX 972-2-257418. R&P, Adv. contact Solly Sacks. Circ: 1,800.

MESSIANIC JEWISH LIFE. *see* RELIGIONS AND THEOLOGY—Other Denominations And Sects

MESSIANIC TESTIMONY. *see* RELIGIONS AND THEOLOGY—Other Denominations And Sects

HA-METIVTA. *see* LAW

296.7 USA
METRO JEWISH NEWS. Text in English. 1993. m. free. adv. **Document type:** *Newspaper, Consumer.*
Formerly: The Atlanta Maccabiah Press
Published by: Adler Publishing, Inc., 6168-C Glenridge Dr., N.E., Atlanta, GA 30328-4150. TEL 770-645-1940, FAX 770-645-1940. Ed., Pub. Andrew B Adler. adv.: B&W page USD 1,088. Circ: 12,000 (paid and free).

296.7 USA
METROWEST JEWISH REPORTER. Text in English. 1970. m. free. adv. bk.rev. **Document type:** *Newspaper.*
Published by: Combined Jewish Philanthropies of Greater Boston, 76 Salem End Rd, Framingham, MA 01702. TEL 508-879-5856, FAX 508-879-5856. Ed. Marcia T Rivin. Circ: 10,500.

296.0961 ISR
MI-MIZRAH UMI-MA'ARAV. Text mainly in Hebrew. 1974. irreg., latest vol.8, 2008. price varies. **Document type:** *Monographic series, Academic/Scholarly.* **Description:** Research in the history of the Jews in the Orient and North Africa.
Published by: (Bar-Ilan University), Bar-Ilan University Press (Subsidiary of: Bar-Ilan University), Journals, Ramat-Gan, 52900, Israel. TEL 972-3-5318401, FAX 972-3-5353446, press@mail.biu.ac.il, http://www.biu.ac.il/Press. Ed. Moshe Orfali.

MIDDEI CHODESH BECHODSHO. *see* EDUCATION—Teaching Methods And Curriculum

296.7 USA ISSN 0026-332X
DS149
MIDSTREAM; a monthly Jewish review. Text in English. 1955. bi-m. USD 18 domestic; USD 28 in Canada & Mexico; USD 38 elsewhere (effective 2009). bk.rev. back issues avail.; reprints avail. **Document type:** *Journal, Academic/Scholarly.* **Description:** Addresses the whole spectrum of contemporary Jewish life and culture, with special emphasis on the State of Israel and Zionism.
Related titles: Microform ed.: (from AJP, PQC); Online - full text ed.
Indexed: A22, A25, A26, ABS&EES, AES, AIPP, AmH&L, AmHI, CCME, CERDIC, E08, G06, G07, G08, GSS&RPL, HRIR, HistAb, I05, I07, IAJS, IBRH, IJP, JewAb, M10, MEA&I, MLA-IB, P06, P30, PAIS, RASB, S08, S09, S23, SCOPUS.
—Ingenta.
Published by: Theodor Herzl Foundation, 633 Third Ave, 21st Fl, New York, NY 10017. TEL 212-339-6020, FAX 212-318-6176, midstreamTHF@aol.com. Ed. Leo Haber.

MIKHTAV. *see* ETHNIC INTERESTS

296 810 USA ISSN 1544-144X
PN6067
MIMA'AMAKIM; creative expression on the Jewish religious experience. Text in English. 2000. a.
Address: 1326 Somerset Rd., Teaneck, NJ 07666. http://www.mimaamakim.org. Ed. Daniella Ross.

MINIMA JUDAICA. *see* HISTORY—History Of Europe

MISHKAN. *see* RELIGIONS AND THEOLOGY

MISHPAHA TOVA. *see* SOCIOLOGY

MNEMOSYNE. *see* ETHNIC INTERESTS

MODERN JUDAISM; a journal of Jewish ideas and experience. *see* ETHNIC INTERESTS

MOMENT; the magazine of Jewish culture, politics, and religion. *see* ETHNIC INTERESTS

MONITOR (WASHINGTON). *see* ETHNIC INTERESTS

296.7 USA ISSN 1940-5146
MOSHIACH TIMES. Text in English. 1981. bi-m. USD 15 domestic; USD 24 in Canada & Mexico; USD 36 elsewhere (effective 2010). back issues avail. **Document type:** *Magazine, Consumer.* **Description:** Contains stories, biographies, cartoon and humor, letters and games of contemporary and historical interest for Jewish children.
Indexed: IJP.

Published by: Tzivos HaShem, 792 Easter Pky, Brooklyn, NY 11213. TEL 718-467-0600, FAX 718-467-1300, http://www.kids.tzivoshashem.org. Ed. D S Pape TEL 718-907-8844.

296.7 ARG ISSN 0327-5930
MUNDO ISRAELITA; actualidad de la semana en Israel y en el mundo judio. Text in Spanish. 1923. w. USD 150. adv. bk.rev. illus. **Document type:** *Newspaper.*
Published by: Editorial Mundo Israelita, Pueyrredon 538, 2o Cpo., 1er piso, Dto. B, Buenos Aires, 1052, Argentina. TEL 54-114-9617999, FAX 54-114-9610763. Ed. Jose Kestelman.

296.074 ESP ISSN 0214-6975
DS135.S75
MUSEO SEFARDI. NOTICIAS. Text in Spanish. 1989. s-a. **Document type:** *Newsletter, Consumer.*
Published by: Museo Sefardi, Samuel Levi, S/N, Toledo, 45002, Spain.

MUSICA JUDAICA. *see* MUSIC

296 USA ISSN 0300-6689
LC701
N A T E NEWS. Text in English. 1955. 3/yr. free to members (effective 2005). adv. bk.rev. **Document type:** *Bulletin.*
Related titles: Online - full content ed.: free.
Published by: National Association of Temple Educators, 633 3rd Ave 7th Fl, New York, NY 10017-6778. TEL 212-452-6510, FAX 212-452-6512, nateoff@aol.com. Ed. Deborah Niederman. Circ: 1,200.

296.7 USA
N C J W JOURNAL. Text in English. 1940. s-a. USD 35 domestic; USD 60 foreign (effective 2007). adv. bk.rev. 32 p./no.; **Document type:** *Magazine, Consumer.* **Description:** Covers social issues, commentary, political news, women's empowerment news, advocacy news.
Former titles: Insight (New York, 1991); (until 1991): N C J W Journal (0161-2115); (until 1978): Council Woman (0148-2106)
Related titles: Online - full text ed.
Indexed: DYW, GW, P48, PQC.
Published by: National Council of Jewish Women, 53 W 23rd St, New York, NY 10010. TEL 212-645-4048, FAX 212-366-9135. Ed. Erica Brody. Circ: 96,000 (paid).

296.7 324.3 USA ISSN 0888-191X
DS150.L3
NA'AMAT WOMAN. Text in English. 1926. 4/yr. USD 5 to members; USD 10 to non-members (effective 2011). adv. bk.rev. illus. 32 p./no.; **Document type:** *Magazine, Consumer.* **Description:** Covers a wide spectrum of topics about Jewish life, culture and issues in the United States and Israel.
Formerly (until 1986): Pioneer Woman (0032-0021)
Related titles: Microfilm ed.: (from AJP); Online - full text ed.
Indexed: IJP, JewAb.
Published by: Na'amat U S A, International Movement of Zionist Women, 350 Fifth Ave, Ste 4700, New York, NY 10018. TEL 212-563-4962, FAX 212-563-5710, naamat@naamat.org. Ed., Pub. Judith A Sokoloff. Circ: 20,000.

NAHARAIM. *see* LITERATURE

NASHIM; a journal of Jewish women's studies and gender issues. *see* WOMEN'S STUDIES

NATIONAL COUNCIL OF JEWISH WOMEN. NEW YORK SECTION. BULLETIN. *see* SOCIAL SERVICES AND WELFARE

296.7 USA ISSN 1043-2795
NATIONAL JEWISH NEWS. Text in English. 1973. w. USD 45 (effective 1996 & 1997). adv. bk.rev.; film rev.; play rev. back issues avail. **Document type:** *Newspaper.*
Formerly (until 1986): Israel Today
Related titles: Microfilm ed.: (from AJP).
Address: 11071 Ventura Blvd, Studio City, CA 91604. TEL 818-786-4000, FAX 818-760-4648. Ed. Phil Blazer. R&P Miriam Fink. Circ: 106,000.

296.7 USA ISSN 0888-0379
THE NATIONAL JEWISH POST & OPINION. Text in English. 1931. w. USD 36; USD 2 per issue (effective 2011). adv. bk.rev. 5 cols./p.; back issues avail.; reprints avail. **Document type:** *Newspaper, Consumer.* **Description:** Contains items of interest to the Jewish community.
Formerly: Jewish Post and Opinion (0021-6658)
Related titles: Microfilm ed.: (from AJP, PQC).
—CIS.
Published by: Spokesman Co., Inc., 1111 East 54th St, Ste 119, Indianapolis, IN 46220. TEL 317-972-7800, FAX 317-972-7807. Ed. Jennie Cohen. Pub. Gabriel Cohen. Adv. contact Barbara Lemaster.

NETIVA; Wege deutsch-juedischer Geschichte. *see* HISTORY—History Of Europe

296.7 USA
NEW JERSEY JEWISH NEWS, JEWISH FEDERATION OF CENTRAL NJ EDITION. Text in English. 1981. w. **Document type:** *Newspaper.*
Formerly: Jewish Horizon
Related titles: ◆ Regional ed(s).: New Jersey Jewish News, United Jewish Communities of MetroWest NJ Edition; ◆ New Jersey Jewish News, Jewish Federation of Greater Middlesex County Edition; ◆ New Jersey Jewish News. ISSN 1532-9690; New Jersey Jewish News, United Jewish Federation of Princeton Mercer Bucks Edition.
Published by: United Jewish Communities of MetroWest, 901 State Route 10, Whippany, NJ 07981. TEL 973-887-3900, FAX 973-887-5999, Info@njjewishnews.com, http://www.njjewishnews.com.

296.7 USA
NEW JERSEY JEWISH NEWS, JEWISH FEDERATION OF GREATER MIDDLESEX COUNTY EDITION. Text in English. 1985. bi-m. USD 20 (effective 1988). adv. bk.rev. **Document type:** *Newspaper, Consumer.* **Description:** Covers the local Jewish community service efforts.
Formerly (until 2000): The Jewish Star (1527-1811)
Related titles: ◆ Regional ed(s).: New Jersey Jewish News, United Jewish Communities of MetroWest NJ Edition; ◆ New Jersey Jewish News, Jewish Federation of Central NJ Edition; ◆ New Jersey Jewish News. ISSN 1532-9690; New Jersey Jewish News, United Jewish Federation of Princeton Mercer Bucks Edition.
Published by: (Jewish Federation of Greater Middlesex County), United Jewish Communities of MetroWest, 901 State Route 10, Whippany, NJ 07981. Ed. Marlene A Heller. Adv. contact Ronnie Aaron. Circ: 17,000.

296.7 USA
NEW JERSEY JEWISH NEWS, UNITED JEWISH COMMUNITIES OF METROWEST NJ EDITION. Text in English. 1947. w. USD 25. **Document type:** *Newspaper.*
Formerly: MetroWest Jewish News
Related titles: ◆ Regional ed(s).: New Jersey Jewish News, Jewish Federation of Central NJ Edition; ◆ New Jersey Jewish News, Jewish Federation of Greater Middlesex County Edition; ◆ New Jersey Jewish News. ISSN 1532-9690; New Jersey Jewish News, United Jewish Federation of Princeton Mercer Bucks Edition.
Published by: United Jewish Federation of MetroWest, 901 Rte 10, Whippany, NJ 07981-1157. TEL 973-887-3900, FAX 973-887-4152, 973-887-4152. Ed. David Twersky. Circ: 26,000.

296.7 USA ISSN 1559-8098
THE NEW MEXICO JEWISH LINK. Text in English. 1971. m. free (effective 2007). adv. bk.rev. **Document type:** *Newspaper, Consumer.* **Description:** Covers statewide Jewish community news and carries national Jewish wire service articles.
Formerly (until 199?): The Link (Albuquerque)
Published by: Jewish Federation of Greater Albuquerque, 5520 Wyoming Blvd, N E, Albuquerque, NM 87109-3167. TEL 505-821-3214, 505-821-3214, FAX 505-821-3351, thelink@swcp.com, nmjlink@aol.com. Ed., R&P Tema Milstein. Adv. contact Susan Abonyi. Circ: 7,500.

▼ **NEW PERSPECTIVES ON MODERN JEWISH HISTORY.** *see* HISTORY

THE NEWSLETTER OF THE CAMPAIGN FOR JEWISH RENAISSANCE. *see* ETHNIC INTERESTS

290 610 DEU ISSN 1866-4040
NICOLAS-BENZIN-STIFTUNG. MITTEILUNGEN; Beitraege zur Kulturgeschichte des Judentums und der Geschichte der Medizin. Text in German. 2007. a. **Document type:** *Journal, Academic/Scholarly.*
Published by: Nicolas-Benzin-Stiftung, Ligusterweg 24, Frankfurt am Main, 60433, Germany. TEL 49-69-46939321, Wolf@Nicolas-Benzin-Stiftung.de, http://www.nicolas-benzin-stiftung.de.

296 SWE ISSN 0348-1646
NORDISK JUDAISTIK; scandinavian jewish studies. Text in Multiple languages. 1975. irreg., latest vol.24, 2010. **Document type:** *Monographic series, Academic/Scholarly.*
Published by: Saellskapet foer Judaistisk Forskning/Association for Jewish Studies, c/o Hanne Trautner-Kromann, Allhelgorna Kyrkogata 8, Lund, 22362, Sweden. TEL 46-8-2229041, hanne.trautner-kromann@teol.lu.se.

NORTHWEST JEWISH REPORTER. *see* ETHNIC INTERESTS

296.7 USA ISSN 8750-5290
OBSERVER (NASHVILLE). Text in English. 1934. fortn. USD 25 (effective 2000). adv. **Document type:** *Newspaper.* **Description:** Covers Jewish community efforts and events in and around Nashville.
Related titles: Microfilm ed.: (from AJP).
Published by: Jewish Federation of Nashville, 801 Percy Warner Blvd, Ste 102, Nashville, TN 37205. TEL 615-356-3242, FAX 615-352-0056, nashobserv@aol.com. Ed. Judith A Saks. Pub. Steven Edlstein. Adv. contact Carrie Mills. Circ: 3,300 (paid).

296.7 USA ISSN 0030-0942
OHIO JEWISH CHRONICLE. Text in English. 1922. w. USD 28 (effective 2000). adv. bk.rev. back issues avail. **Document type:** *Newspaper.* **Description:** Contains information for Jews.
Related titles: Microfilm ed.
Published by: O J C Publishing, 2862 Johnstown Rd, PO Box 30965, Columbus, OH 43230. TEL 614-337-2055, FAX 614-337-2059, ojc@iwaynet.net. Ed., R&P Roberta Keck. Pub. Stephen N Pinsky. Adv. contact Angela Miller. Circ: 3,000 (paid).

296 ISR ISSN 0793-6362
ORACHOT. Text in Hebrew. 1965. a. free. adv. **Document type:** *Bulletin, Consumer.*
Published by: Haifa Religious Council, 4 Shmuel Ben Adia St, P O Box 2405, Haifa, 31024, Israel. TEL 972-4-641186, FAX 972-4-667623. Ed. David Metzger. Circ: 3,000.

296.7 USA ISSN 1067-3784
BM730.A1
➤ **THE ORCHARD.** Text mainly in English; Section in Hebrew. 198?. s-a. free to qualified personnel (effective 2010). 20 p./no. 2 cols./p.; back issues avail. **Document type:** *Journal, Academic/Scholarly.* **Description:** Contains writings on Jewish studies and the modern state of Israel.
Related titles: Online - full text ed.: free (effective 2010).
Published by: Jewish Federations of North America, Wall St Station, PO Box 157, New York, NY 10268. TEL 212-284-6500, info@JewishFederations.org.

296.7 CAN ISSN 1196-1929
OTTAWA JEWISH BULLETIN. Text in English. 1974. 19/yr. CAD 25; CAD 32.10 foreign. adv. bk.rev. **Document type:** *Bulletin.* **Description:** Contains articles of interest to the Jewish community.
Formerly: Ottawa Jewish Bulletin and Review (0319-1303); Which was formed by the 1974 merger of: Ottawa Jewish Digest and Review (0319-1281); Ottawa Jewish Bulletin (0319-129X)
Published by: (Jewish Community Council of Ottawa), Ottawa Jewish Bulletin Publishing Co. Ltd., 1780 Kerr Ave, Ottawa, ON K2A 1R9, Canada. TEL 613-798-4696, FAX 613-798-4730. Ed. Myra Aronson. Adv. contact Kelly Green. Circ: 10,000.

220 NLD ISSN 0169-7226
BS1192
➤ **OUDTESTAMENTISCHE STUDIEN.** Text in English, German. 1942. irreg., latest vol.55, 2007. price varies. **Document type:** *Monographic series, Academic/Scholarly.* **Description:** Scholarly studies on linguistic, textual, historical and theological topics pertaining to the Old Testament.
Indexed: A22, BibLing, IZBG, OTA.
—IE, Infotrieve.
Published by: Brill, PO Box 9000, Leiden, 2300 PA, Netherlands. TEL 31-71-5353500, FAX 31-71-5317532, cs@brill.nl, http://www.brill.nl. Ed. B Becking. R&P Elizabeth Venekamp. **Dist. by:** Turpin Distribution Services Ltd., Pegasus Dr, Stratton Business Park, Biggleswade, Bedfordshire SG18 8QB, United Kingdom. TEL 44-1767-604954, FAX 44-1767-601640, custserv@turpin-distribution.com, http://www.turpin-distribution.com/.

➤ **OUTLOOK.** *see* LAW

800 296.7 USA ISSN 1093-1627
PJ5120
PAKN TREGER/BOOK PEDDLER. Text in English. 1981. s-a. USD 36 to members (effective 2011). adv. film rev.; music rev.; bk.rev. illus. 52 p./no.; back issues avail. **Document type:** *Magazine, Academic/Scholarly.* **Description:** Covers the tradition of the pakn tregers, who traveled from shtetl to shtetl in Eastern Europe bringing books and news of the outside world.
Formerly (until 1996): Book Peddler (0896-9523)
Related titles: Online - full text ed.
Indexed: IJP, JewAb, MLA-IB, RILM.
Published by: National Yiddish Book Center, 1021 West St, Amherst, MA 01002. TEL 413-256-4900, FAX 413-256-4700, yiddish@bikher.org.

PANU DERECH. *see* RELIGIONS AND THEOLOGY—Protestant

296.071 DEU ISSN 1614-6492
BM1
PARDES; Zeitschrift der Vereinigung fuer Juedische Studien. Text in German. 1997. s-a. EUR 8 per issue (effective 2009). **Document type:** *Journal, Academic/Scholarly.*
Formerly (until 2004): V J S - Nachrichten (1437-2843)
Related titles: Online - full text ed.: ISSN 1862-7684. 2005.
Published by: Universitaetsverlag Potsdam, Am Neuen Palais 10, Potsdam, 14469, Germany. TEL 49-331-9774458, FAX 49-331-9774625, ubpub@uni-potsdam.de, http://info.ub.uni-potsdam.de/verlag.htm.

296.071 GBR ISSN 1368-5449
PARKES-WIENER SERIES ON JEWISH STUDIES. Text in English. 1998. irreg. price varies. back issues avail. **Document type:** *Monographic series, Academic/Scholarly.* **Description:** Provides an outlet for innovative work on the interface between Judaism and ethnicity, popular culture, gender, class, space and memory.
Published by: Vallentine Mitchell Publishers, 29/45 High St, Edgware, Middlesex HA8 7UU, United Kingdom. TEL 44-20-89529526, FAX 44-20-89529242, info@vmbooks.com, http://www.vmbooksuk.com/. Eds. David Cesarani, Tony Kushner.

296.437 USA
PASSOVER DIRECTORY. Text in English. 1923. a.
Published by: Union of Orthodox Jewish Congregations of America, 11 Broadway, New York, NY 10004. TEL 212-613-8146, FAX 212-613-0646, ja@ou.org, http://www.ou.org/. Ed. Shelley Scharf.

PATTERNS OF PREJUDICE. *see* ETHNIC INTERESTS

296 ISR ISSN 0334-4088
DS101
➤ **PE'AMIM**; studies in Oriental Jewry. Text in Hebrew; Summaries in English. 1979. q. ILS 148, USD 65 (effective 2003). bk.rev. abstr.; charts; illus. Index. 160 p./no. 1 cols./p.; back issues avail. **Document type:** *Academic/Scholarly.* **Description:** Covers history, literature, and language of Sephardi and Oriental Jewry.
Indexed: IHP, MLA-IB, RILM.
Published by: Ben Zvi Institute for the Study of Jewish Communities in the East, P O Box 7660, Jerusalem, 91076, Israel. TEL 972-2-539-8844, FAX 972-2-561-2329, mahnonzvi@h2.hum.huji.ac.il, ybz.org.il. Ed. Avriel Bar-Levav. R&P Michael Glatzer TEL 972-2-5398848. Circ: 1,000.

296 USA ISSN 1542-9709
BM1
PERSPECTIVES (SKOKIE); journal of Jewish thought. Text in English. 2004 (Win). q. USD 18 (effective 2004).
Published by: Zionist Organization of Chicago, Institute for Public Affairs, 9131 N. Niles Cntr. Rd., Skokie, IL 60076. TEL 847-568-0244, FAX 847-568-1233, ZOC@ameritech.net, http://www.ZOCorg.org.

296 USA ISSN 1935-6897
PERSPECTIVES ON HEBREW SCRIPTURES AND ITS CONTEXTS. Text in English. 2006. irreg., latest 2009. price varies. back issues avail. **Document type:** *Monographic series, Academic/Scholarly.* **Description:** Presents articles about the Hebrew Bible, Biblical Hebrew and ancient Israelite society.
Formerly (until 2007): Perspectives on Hebrew Scriptures (1936-9867)
Published by: Gorgias Press LLC, 954 River Rd, Piscataway, NJ 08854. TEL 732-885-8900, FAX 732-885-8908, helpdesk@gorgiaspress.com, http://www.gorgiaspress.com/bookshop/default.aspx.

296.7 USA ISSN 1063-6269
DS135.C5
POINTS EAST (MENLO PARK). Text in English. 1985. 3/yr. looseleaf. free to members (effective 2010). bk.rev. back issues avail. **Document type:** *Journal, Academic/Scholarly.*
Indexed: J01.
Published by: Sino-Judaic Institute, 1823 East Prospect, Seattle, WA 98112. info@sino-judaic.org.

POLIN. *see* ETHNIC INTERESTS

296 USA ISSN 1550-1159
PRAEGER SERIES ON JEWISH AND ISRAELI STUDIES. Text in English. 2003. irreg., latest 2004. price varies. back issues avail. **Document type:** *Monographic series, Academic/Scholarly.*
Published by: Praeger Publishers (Subsidiary of: Greenwood Publishing Group Inc.), 88 Post Rd W, Westport, CT 06881. TEL 800-368-6868, tech.support@greenwood.com, http://www.greenwood.com. Ed. Leslie Stein.

296 USA ISSN 1091-1960
DS101
THE PRAGER PERSPECTIVE. Text in English. 1985. s-m. looseleaf. USD 48. bk.rev. bibl.; tr.lit. back issues avail. **Document type:** *Newsletter.*
Formerly (until 1996): Ultimate Issues (0888-3440)
Related titles: CD-ROM ed.: USD 24.95.
Indexed: IJP, JewAb.
Published by: Dennis Prager, Ed. & Pub., 10573 W Pico Blvd, 167, Los Angeles, CA 90064-2300. TEL 800-558-3958, FAX 310-558-4241. R&P Pat Havins TEL 800-225-8584. Circ: 6,000 (paid).

296 USA
PRAYER AND PRAISE. Text in English. 1949. m. free. **Document type:** *Newsletter.*
Published by: International Board of Jewish Missions, 1928 Hamill Rd, PO Box 1386, Hixson, TN 37343. TEL 423-876-8150, FAX 423-876-8156. Ed. Orman L Norwood. Circ: 1,500.

R

222.1106 DEU ISSN 1863-7442
PRI HA-PARDES. Text in German. 2007. irreg., latest vol.4, 2008. price varies. **Document type:** *Monographic series, Academic/Scholarly.*
Published by: Universitaetsverlag Potsdam, Am Neuen Palais 10, Potsdam, 14469, Germany. TEL 49-331-9774458, FAX 49-331-9774625, ubpub@uni-potsdam.de/, http://info.ub.uni-potsdam.de/verlag.htm.

PROOFTEXTS; a journal of Jewish literary history. *see* LITERATURE

296.155 POL ISSN 0867-8715
BM487.A62
THE QUMRAN CHRONICLE. Text in Multiple languages. 1990. 3/yr.
Indexed: OTA.
Published by: Enigma Press, ul Borsucza 3-58, Krakow, 30408, Poland. TEL 48-12-2674124, FAX 48-12-4226793.

296.4 USA
R C A RECORD. Text in English. 1953. q.
Formerly (until 1990): Rabbinical Council Record
Published by: Rabbinical Council of America, 305 Seventh Ave, 12th Fl, New York, NY 10001. TEL 212-807-9000, FAX 212-727-8452, http://www.rabbis.org.

296 ARG
RAICES; judaismo contemporaneo. Text in Spanish. 1991. q. USD 40. adv. **Document type:** *Consumer.*
Published by: (A.M.I.A. Comunidad Judia de Buenos Aires), Editorial Agedit S.A., Parana 866, Buenos Aires, 1017, Argentina. TEL 54-114-8125301, FAX 54-114-8039944. Eds. Alberto Iaccarino, Gustavo Borenstein. Adv. contact Alberto Iaccarino. B&W page USD 1,300, color page USD 4,300; 265 x 190. Circ: 10,000.

296.7 ESP ISSN 0212-6753
RAICES; revista judia de cultura. Text in Spanish. 1986. q. EUR 40 domestic; EUR 52 in Europe; EUR 56 elsewhere (effective 2010). bk.rev. **Document type:** *Journal, Academic/Scholarly.* **Description:** Provides opinion, analysis, and information on Jewish culture.
Related titles: Online - full text ed.
Indexed: MLA-IB.
Published by: Sefarad Editores, Apdo. de Correos 16.110, Madrid, 28080, Spain. Ed. Graciela Kohan. Pub. Jacobo Israel Garzon. Circ: 4,500. **Dist. by:** Asociacion de Revistas Culturales de Espana, C Covarruvias 9 2o. Derecha, Madrid 28010, Spain. TEL 34-91-3086066, FAX 34-91-3199267, info@arce.es, http://www.arce.es/.

016.296 ITA ISSN 0033-9792
DS101
RASSEGNA MENSILE DI ISRAEL. Text in English, French, Italian. 1924-1940; resumed 1947. 3/yr. bk.rev. charts; illus. index. **Document type:** *Magazine, Consumer.*
Indexed: FR, MLA-IB.
—INIST.
Published by: Unione delle Comunita Ebraiche Italiane (U C E I), Lungotevere Raffaello Sanzio 9, Rome, RM 00153, Italy. TEL 39-06-5803667, info@ucei.it, http://www.ucei.it. Ed. Giacomo Saban. Circ: 1,000.

296.7 USA ISSN 1072-3250
DS133
RECONSTRUCTIONISM TODAY. Text in English. 1994. 3/yr. USD 16 domestic; USD 20 foreign (effective 2003). bk.rev. index. 24 p./no.; back issues avail.; reprints avail. **Document type:** *Newsletter.*
Related titles: Microform ed.: (from PQC).
Indexed: HRIR, IJP, JewAb, MEA&I.
—CIS.
Published by: Jewish Reconstructionist Federation, 7804 Montgomery Ave 9, Elkins Park, PA 19027. TEL 215-782-8500, FAX 215-782-8805, press@jrf.org, http://www.jrf.org/. Ed. Lawrence Bush. Pub. Judy Wortman. R&P Pesha Leichter TEL 215-782-8500 ext 31. Circ: 15,000.

296.7 USA ISSN 0034-1495
DS133
➤ **RECONSTRUCTIONIST.** Text in English. 1935-1993; N.S. 1995. s-a. USD 45 for 2 yrs. to members; USD 50 for 2 yrs. to non-members (effective 2004). adv. bk.rev. 100 p./no.; **Document type:** *Journal, Academic/Scholarly.*
Incorporates (19??-19??): Federation of Reconstructionist Congregations and Havurot. Newsletter; Which was formerly (until 1980): Reconstructionist Federation of Congregations and Fellowships. Newsletter (0270-7357); (until 197?): Federation of Reconstructionist Congregations and Fellowships. Newsletter; (until 1974): Reconstructionist Federation Newsletter; (until 1973): Reconstructionist Newsletter (0486-1647)
Related titles: Microfilm ed.: N.S. (from PQC).
Indexed: A21, A22, IJP, JewAb, MLA-IB, P06, P30, PAIS, RI-1.
—CIS.
Published by: (Reconstructionist Rabbinical College), Reconstructionist Press, 101 Greenwood Ave, Ste 400, Jenkintown, PA 19046. TEL 215-885-5601, FAX 215-885-5603, press@jrf.org, http://jrf.org. Circ: 2,500.

296.4 USA ISSN 0482-0819
BM197
REFORM JUDAISM. Text in English. 1955. q. USD 12 domestic; USD 18 in Canada; USD 24 foreign; USD 3.50 per issue; free to members (effective 2009). adv. illus. back issues avail. **Document type:** *Magazine, Consumer.* **Description:** Links the institutions and affiliates of Reform Judaism with every Reform Jew. Covers developments within the movement while interpreting world events and Jewish tradition from a Reform perspective. Conveys the creativity, diversity, and dynamism of Reform Judaism.
Formerly (until 1972): Dimensions in American Judaism; Incorporates: Keeping Posted (0022-9636)
Related titles: Microfilm ed.: (from AJP).
Indexed: IJP, J01, JewAb, P30.
—Ingenta. **CCC.**
Published by: Union for Reform Judaism, 633 Third Ave, New York, NY 10017. TEL 212-650-4240, FAX 212-650-4249, SSchweitzer@urj.org, http://urj.org/index.cfm?. Adv. contact Keith Newman TEL 212-650-4244. B&W page USD 8,860, color page USD 11,230; trim 8 x 10.5. Circ: 300,000 (controlled).

296.7 USA
RENEWAL MAGAZINE. Text in English. 1984. 3/yr. adv. bk.rev. back issues avail. **Document type:** *Magazine, Consumer.* **Description:** Covers Jewish community efforts and events in southeastern Virginia.
Published by: United Jewish Federation of Tidewater, 5000 Corporate Woods Dr., Ste. 200, Virginia Bch, VA 23462-4429. TEL 757-671-1600, FAX 757-671-7613. Ed., R&P Reba Karp. Adv. contact Stewart Smokler. B&W page USD 725; trim 9.13 x 6.88. Circ: 6,000.

296.7 USA ISSN 1053-2676
THE REPORTER (NEW YORK, 1966). Text in English. 1967. q. USD 36 membership (effective 2005). adv. bk.rev.; film rev.; play rev. illus. **Document type:** *Magazine, Consumer.* **Description:** For the contemporary American Jewish woman. Features address issues concerning women, education, Jewish life and culture worldwide, Israel, politics, literature and the arts.
Formerly: Women's American O R T Reporter (0043-7514)
Related titles: Microfilm ed.: (from AJP).
Indexed: IJP, MLA-IB.
Published by: Women's America O R T, Inc., 250 Park Ave S., # 600, New York, NY 10003-1402. TEL 212-505-7700, FAX 212-674-3057. Ed. Aviva Patz. R&P Terese Loeb Kreuzer. adv.: B&W page USD 2,064, color page USD 2,458. Circ: 80,000.

296.7 USA
THE REPORTER (NEW YORK, 1971). Text in English. 1972. w. USD 25 domestic; USD 28 foreign (effective 2000). adv. bk.rev. **Document type:** *Newspaper.* **Description:** Presents local, national and international Jewish news.
Published by: Jewish Federation of Broome County, c/o Marc S Goldberg, Exec Ed, 500 Clubhouse Rd, Vestal, NY 13850. TEL 607-724-2360, FAX 607-724-2311, TReporter@aol.com. Ed., R&P Marc S Goldberg. Adv. contact Bonnie Rozen. Circ: 3,000 (paid).

296.7 USA
THE REPORTER (VESTAL). Text in English. 1971. w. (Fri.). USD 36 (effective 2009). adv. **Document type:** *Newspaper, Consumer.*
Published by: Jewish Federation of Broome County, Inc., 500 Clubhouse Rd., Vestal, NY 13850. TEL 607-724-2360, FAX 607-724-2311. Eds. Diana Sochor, Rabbi Rachel Esserman. Adv. contact Bonnie Rozen. col. inch USD 9.15. Circ: 3,000 (paid and free). Wire service: JTA.

296.68 USA ISSN 0098-468X
BM60
RESHIMAT HAVRE HISTADRUT HA-RABANIM DA-AMERIKA/ RABBINIC REGISTRY. Text in English, Hebrew. 19??. s-a. free to members.
Published by: Rabbinical Council of America, 305 Seventh Ave, 12th Fl, New York, NY 10001. TEL 212-807-9000, FAX 212-727-8452, office@rabbis.org, http://www.rabbis.org.

296.7 USA ISSN 1086-4490
BM700
RESHIMOT. Text in Hebrew. 1995. irreg. **Document type:** *Monographic series, Academic/Scholarly.*
—**CCC.**
Published by: Kehot Publication Society, 770 Eastern Pkwy, Brooklyn, NY 11213. TEL 718-778-0226, FAX 718-778-4148, yitzi@kehot.com, http://store.kehotonline.com.

296 USA ISSN 1936-6485
RESOURCE (SAN FRANCISCO); a guide to Jewish life in northern California. Text in English. 1990. a. **Document type:** *Directory, Consumer.* **Description:** Features information about providers of Jewish-oriented services and products, events and community centers in northern California.
Published by: San Francisco Jewish Community Publications, Inc., 225 Bush St, Ste 1480, San Francisco, CA 94104-4207. TEL 415-263-7200, FAX 415-263-7222, info@jweekly.com, http://www.jewishsf.com. Pub. Marc S Klein.

296.7 USA ISSN 1055-3703
D804.3
RESPONSE (LOS ANGELES). Text in English. 1978. q. USD 25 (effective 2005). **Document type:** *Newsletter.*
Related titles: Online - full text ed.: e-response. 2003.
Indexed: IJP.
Published by: Simon Wiesenthal Center, 1399 S Roxbury Dr, Los Angeles, CA 90035. TEL 310-553-9036, 800-900-9036, FAX 310-553-4521, information@wiesenthal.net, http://www.wiesenthal.com. Ed. Rabbi Abraham Cooper.

296.071 USA ISSN 1943-8257
▼ **REVIEW OF JEWISH THOUGHT AND INTELLECTUAL HISTORY.** Text in English. 2009 (Sep.). s-a. USD 120 (effective 2009). **Document type:** *Journal, Academic/Scholarly.* **Description:** Covers Jewish intellectual thought through the ages, including Rabbinic thought and mysticism, philosphy, Kabbalah and contemporary thought.
Published by: Academic Studies Press, 28 Montfern Ave, Brighton, MA 02135. TEL 617-782-6290, igor.nemirovsky@academicstudiespress.com. Eds. Dov Schwartz, Steven Harvey.

296 NLD ISSN 1568-4857
BM1 CODEN: LCAHAM
➤ **REVIEW OF RABBINIC JUDAISM.** Text in English. s-a. EUR 160, USD 223 to institutions; EUR 174, USD 244 combined subscription to institutions (print & online eds.) (effective 2012). bk.rev. back issues avail.; reprint service avail. from PSC. **Document type:** *Journal, Academic/Scholarly.* **Description:** Focuses on Rabbinic Judaism. Includes articles, essays on method and criticism, and related debate.
Formerly (until 2001): Annual of Rabbinic Judaism (1388-0365)
Related titles: Online - full text ed.: ISSN 1570-0704. EUR 145, USD 203 to institutions (effective 2012) (from IngentaConnect).
Indexed: A01, A02, A03, A08, A21, A22, C33, CA, E01, IZBG, J01, RI-1, T02.
—IE, Ingenta. **CCC.**
Published by: Brill, PO Box 9000, Leiden, 2300 PA, Netherlands. TEL 31-71-5353500, FAX 31-71-5317532, cs@brill.nl, http://www.brill.nl. Ed. Alan J Avery-Peck. **Dist. by:** Turpin Distribution Services Ltd., Pegasus Dr, Stratton Business Park, Biggleswade, Bedfordshire SG18 8QB, United Kingdom. TEL 44-1767-604954, FAX 44-1767-601640, custserv@turpin-distribution.com, http://www.turpin-distribution.com/.

296.7 ROM ISSN 0034-754X
REVISTA CULTULUI MOZAIC/REVIEW OF THE MOSAIC CREED. Text in English, Hebrew, Romanian. 1956. bi-m. USD 65. adv. bk.rev. illus. **Document type:** *Newspaper.*
Published by: Federatia Comunitatilor Evreiesti din Romania/Federation of Jewish Communities of Rumania, Str. Sf. Vineri 9-11, Bucharest, 70478, Romania. TEL 6132538, FAX 3120869, TELEX 10798. Ed. Haim Rimer. Circ: 9,000.

296.3 BEL ISSN 0484-8616
➤ **REVUE DES ETUDES JUIVES.** Text in French, English. 1880. s-a. EUR 100 combined subscription (print & online eds.) (effective 2011). adv. bk.rev. charts; illus. Index. reprint service avail. from PSC. **Document type:** *Journal, Academic/Scholarly.* **Description:** Scholarly discussion of religious, cultural, social and historical issues in Jewish studies.
Incorporated (1938-1961): Historia Judaica (1054-1330); (1881-1889): Actes et Conferences de la Societe des Etudes Juives (1149-8684); Which was formerly (until 1886): Annuaire de la Societe des Etudes Juives (1149-8641)
Related titles: Microfiche ed.: (from IDC); Online - full text ed.: ISSN 1783-175X; ◆ Supplement(s): Collection de la Revue des Etudes Juives. ISSN 0777-785X.
Indexed: A20, A21, A22, ASCA, AmH&L, ArtHuCI, BibLing, CA, CurCont, DIP, FR, HistAb, IBR, IBZ, MLA-IB, P30, PCI, RASB, RI-1, RI-2, SCOPUS, T02, W07.
—Infotrieve, INIST. **CCC.**
Published by: (Societe des Etudes Juives FRA), Peeters Publishers, Bondgenotenlaan 153, Leuven, 3000, Belgium. TEL 32-16-235170, FAX 32-16-228500, peeters@peeters-leuven.be, http://www.peeters-leuven.be. Ed. S C Mimouni. Circ: 1,800.

296 FRA ISSN 1280-9640
DS101
REVUE EUROPEENNE DES ETUDES HEBRAIQUES/EUROPEAN JOURNAL OF HEBREW STUDIES. Abbreviated title: R E E H. Text in Multiple languages. 1996. s-a. **Document type:** *Journal, Academic/Scholarly.*
Published by: Institut Europeen d'Etudes Hebraiques/European Association of Jewish Studies, Departement d'Etudes Juives et Hebraiques, Universite de Paris VIII, 2 Rue de la Liberte, Saint-Denis, 93526, France. TEL 33-1-49406839, FAX 33-1-48130263, reeh@univ-paris8.fr, http://www.eurojewishstudies.org.

RHODE ISLAND JEWISH HISTORICAL ASSOCIATION. NEWSLETTER. *see* HISTORY—History Of North And South America

296.09 USA ISSN 0556-8609
F90.J5
RHODE ISLAND JEWISH HISTORICAL NOTES. Text in English. 1954. a. free to members (effective 2010). bk.rev. bibl.; charts; illus.; stat. cum.index every 4 yrs. back issues avail. **Document type:** *Journal, Academic/Scholarly.* **Description:** Publishes articles on the history of Jewish people of Rhode Island.
Indexed: AmH&L, CA, T02.
Published by: Rhode Island Jewish Historical Association, 130 Sessions St, Providence, RI 02906. TEL 401-331-1360, FAX 401-331-1360, info@rijha.org, http://rijha.org/. Circ: 700.

296.3 USA
ROCKLAND COUNTY JEWISH HOLIDAY CONSUMER. Text in English. 1995. 5/yr. adv. **Description:** Covers Jewish Holidays, Israel, and universal Jewish themes. It also includes human interest, humor, inspirational, philosophical and informative articles, historical vignettes, practical Jewish customs and their meanings.
Published by: Jewish Holiday Consumer Newspapers, 8 Algonquin Circle, Monsey, NY 10952. TEL 845-371-3150, FAX 845-352-5117, jholiday@optonline.net, http://www.jewish-holiday.com. adv.: B&W page USD 1,150; trim 17 x 11. Circ: 19,800 (controlled).

930 296.071 DEU ISSN 1435-098X
ROMANIA JUDAICA; Studien zur juedischen Kultur in den romanischen Laendern. Text mainly in German. 1998. irreg., latest vol.8, 2008. price varies. **Document type:** *Monographic series, Academic/Scholarly.*
Published by: Max Niemeyer Verlag GmbH (Subsidiary of: Walter de Gruyter GmbH & Co. KG), Pfrondorfer Str 6, Tuebingen, 72074, Germany. TEL 49-7071-98940, FAX 49-7071-989450, info@niemeyer.de, http://www.niemeyer.de. Ed. Christoph Miething.

ROS CHODES. *see* ETHNIC INTERESTS

296.41 MYS ISSN 0036-2131
DS646.33
SABAH SOCIETY. JOURNAL. Text in English. 1961. irreg., latest vol.8, no.4, 1988. MYR 20 per issue. bk.rev.
Indexed: AnthLit, BAS, BibLing, EI, MLA-IB, Z01.
Published by: Sabah Society/Pertubuhan Sabah, PO Box 10547, Kota Kinabalu, Sabah 88806, Malaysia. Ed. Patricia Regis. Circ: 500.

THE SAGARIN REVIEW; the St. Louis Jewish literary journal. *see* LITERATURE

296.7 USA ISSN 0036-2964
F474.S29
ST. LOUIS JEWISH LIGHT; the newspaper of the Jewish community of Greater St. Louis. Text in English; Text occasionally in Hebrew, Yiddish. 1947. w. USD 36. adv. bk.rev. **Document type:** *Newspaper.*
Related titles: Microfilm ed.: (from AJP).
Published by: (Jewish Federation of St. Louis), St. Louis Jewish Light, Inc., 12 Millstone Campus Dr., St. Louis, MO 63146. TEL 314-432-3353, FAX 314-432-0515. Ed. Robert A Cohn. Circ: 14,000.

296.7 USA ISSN 0891-5814
SAN DIEGO JEWISH TIMES. Text in English. 1979. bi-w. USD 36 (effective 2008). adv. bk.rev.; music rev.; play rev. back issues avail. **Document type:** *Newspaper, Newspaper-distributed.*
Formerly (until 1986): Israel Today San Diego (0746-4207)
Address: 4731 Palm Ave, La Mesa, CA 91941-5221. TEL 619-463-5515. Ed. Carol Rosenberg. Circ: 16,000 (paid).

296.41 USA
SAVANNAH JEWISH NEWS. Text in English. 1949. m. USD 18. adv. **Document type:** *Newsletter.*
Formerly: Savannah Jewish Law
Related titles: Microfilm ed.: (from AJP).
Published by: Savannah Jewish Federation, 5111 Abercorn St, Box 23527, Savannah, GA 31403. TEL 912-355-8111. Ed. Midge Lasky Schildkraut. Adv. contact Midg Lasky Schildkraut. Circ: 1,500.

SCHRIFTENREIHE WISSENSCHAFTLICHER ABHANDLUNGEN DES LEO-BAECK-INSTITUTS. *see* HISTORY—History Of Europe

SCHWAEBISCHE FORSCHUNGSGEMEINSCHAFT. VEROEFFENTLICHUNGEN. REIHE 11: QUELLEN UND DARSTELLUNGEN ZUR JUEDISCHEN GESCHICHTE SCHWABENS. *see* HISTORY—History Of Europe

296 USA

SCRANTON FEDERATION REPORTER. Text in English. 1994. w. USD 20; USD 22 out of county (effective 2000). adv. bk.rev. **Document type:** *Newspaper.* **Description:** Presents local, national and internationall Jewish news.

Published by: Scranton-Lackawanna Jewish Federation, c/o Marc S Goldberg, Ed, 500 Clubhouse Rd, Vestal, NY 13850. TEL 607-724-2360, FAX 607-724-2311. Ed. Marc S Goldberg. R&P Marc S Golberg. Adv. contact Bonnie Rozen. Circ: 2,000 (paid).

296 USA ISSN 0278-2251
DS101

SEPHARDIC SCHOLAR. Text in English. 1973. a. USD 15. bk.rev.
Formerly (until 197?): American Society of Sephardic Studies Series
Indexed: MLA-IB.
Published by: (American Society of Sephardic Studies), Yeshiva University, Sephardic Studies Program, 500 W 185 St, New York, NY 10033. TEL 212-960-5277. Ed. D Attabe. Circ: 5,000.

296 ITA ISSN 0037-3265
DS101

SHALOM. Text in Italian. 1967. m. adv. bk.rev.; dance rev.; film rev.; music rev.; software rev.; tel.rev. illus.; stat.; tr.lit. 52 p./no. 4 cols./p.; back issues avail. **Document type:** *Magazine, Consumer.* **Description:** Covers Jewish communities in Italy.
Formerly: Voce della Comunita
Related titles: Fax ed.
Published by: Comunita Ebraica di Roma, Lungotevere Cenci, Rome, RM 00186, Italy. TEL 39-06-6876816, FAX 39-06-6832113. Ed. Giacomo Kahn. Circ: 10,000.

SHEMOT. *see* GENEALOGY AND HERALDRY

SHIRIM; a Jewish poetry journal. *see* LITERATURE—Poetry

296.7 USA ISSN 0049-0385
BM1

SH'MA; a journal of Jewish responsibility. Text in English. 1970. 10/yr. USD 29 domestic; USD 39 foreign (effective 2011). bk.rev. cum.index. back issues avail. **Document type:** *Journal, Academic/Scholarly.*
Related titles: Audio CD ed.; Microfilm ed.; Online - full text ed.: free (effective 2011).
Indexed: A22, IJP, JewAb, P30, SCOPUS.
Published by: Jewish Family & Life, Inc., PO Box 439, Congers, NY 10920. TEL 877-568-7462. Ed. Susan Berrin TEL 650-330-1545. Pub. Josh Rolnick.

296 USA ISSN 0882-8539
BM1

➤ **SHOFAR (ASHLAND);** an interdisciplinary journal of Jewish studies. Text in English. 1983. q. USD 100 domestic to institutions; USD 120 foreign to institutions (effective 2012). adv. back issues avail. **Document type:** *Journal, Academic/Scholarly.* **Description:** Provides scholarly articles, opinion pieces, readers' forums, pedagogical essays and book reviews in Jewish studies.
Related titles: Online - full text ed.: ISSN 1534-5165.
Indexed: A01, A03, A08, A22, A26, AmH&L, CA, E01, E08, ENW, G08, H07, H08, HAb, HistAb, HumInd, I02, I05, I14, J01, L05, L06, M08, M10, MLA-IB, OTA, P10, P28, P30, P48, P53, P54, PQC, R&TA, R05, RILM, S02, S03, S09, T02, W03, W04, W05.
—IE, Ingenta. **CCC.**
Published by: (Midwest Jewish Studies Association), Purdue University Press, Stewart Center 370, 504 W State St, West Lafayette, IN 47907. TEL 765-494-2038, FAX 765-496-2442, pupress@purdue.edu. Eds. Daniel Morris, Zev Garber.

296.7 USA

SHOFAR (CHATTANOOGA). Text in English. m. USD 25 (effective 1999). adv. bk.rev. **Description:** Discusses Jewish community efforts and events in and around Chattanooga, the US, Israel, and worldwide.
Indexed: IJP.
Published by: Jewish Community Federation of Greater Chattanooga, PO Box 8947, Chattanooga, TN 37414. TEL 423-493-0270, FAX 423-493-9997. Ed. Rachel Schulson. Circ: 1,100.

SHVUT; studies in Russian and East European Jewish history and culture. *see* ETHNIC INTERESTS

296 ISR ISSN 0793-7466

SICHAT HASHAVUA; the weekly sheet for every Jew. Text in Hebrew. 1987. w. adv. bk.rev. **Document type:** *Consumer.*
Published by: Chabad Youth Organization, PO Box 14, Kfar Chabad, 72915, Israel. TEL 03-9607588, FAX 03-9606169, chabad@inter.net.il, http://chabad.org.il. Ed. Menachem Brod.

296.0711 ISR ISSN 0334-6986
BM496.A1

SIDRA; a journal for the study of Rabbinic literature. Key Title: Sydr'. Text in Hebrew; Summaries in English. 1985. a., latest vol.23, 2008. USD 20 per issue (effective 2011). back issues avail. **Document type:** *Journal, Academic/Scholarly.* **Description:** Collection of research papers in various fields of Jewish oral law: the Mishna, the Babylonian and Jerusalem Talmuds, Midrashei Halakhah legends, translations and liturgical hymns, commentaries on the Geonim and the Rishonim.
Indexed: IHP.
Published by: (Bar-Ilan University, Talmud Department), Bar-Ilan University Press (Subsidiary of: Bar-Ilan University), Journals, Ramat-Gan, 52900, Israel. TEL 972-3-5318575, FAX 972-3-5353446, press@mail.biu.ac.il, http://www.biu.ac.il/Press. Ed. David Henshke.

SIMON-DUBNOW-INSTITUT FUER JUEDISCHE GESCHICHTE UND KULTUR E.V. AN DER UNIVERSITAET LEIPZIG. BULLETIN. *see* ETHNIC INTERESTS

SIMON-DUBNOW-INSTITUT. JAHRBUCH. *see* ETHNIC INTERESTS

SIMON-DUBNOW-INSTITUT. SCHRIFTEN. *see* ETHNIC INTERESTS

296 ISR ISSN 0334-4304

SINAI. Text in Hebrew. 1937. bi-m. USD 20 (effective 2003). bk.rev. back issues avail. **Document type:** *Journal, Academic/Scholarly.*
Indexed: IHP, MLA-IB.
Published by: Mosad HaRav Kook/Rabbi Kook Foundation, P O Box 642, Jerusalem, Israel. TEL 972-2-6526231, FAX 972-2-6526968. Ed. Rabbi Joseph Movshovitz. Circ: 1,500 (paid).

SINO-JUDAICA; occasional papers. *see* ETHNIC INTERESTS

SOLIDARITAET UND HILFE. *see* HISTORY—History Of Europe

296.7 USA

SOUTHEASTERN VIRGINIA JEWISH NEWS. Text in English. 1959. bi-w. adv. bk.rev. 20 p./no. 5 cols./p.; back issues avail. **Document type:** *Newspaper.* **Description:** Discusses local community-service projects and programs.
Formerly (until 1984): U J F Virginia News
Published by: United Jewish Federation of Tidewater, 5000 Corporate Woods Dr., Ste. 200, Virginia Bch, VA 23462-4429. TEL 757-671-1600, FAX 757-671-7613. R&P Reba Karp. Adv. contact Stewart Smokler. B&W page USD 845; trim 14 x 9.88. Circ: 5,900; 5,600 (paid).

296.0971 USA ISSN 1521-4206
F220.J5

➤ **SOUTHERN JEWISH HISTORY.** Text in English. 1998. a. USD 20 per issue to non-members; USD 15 per issue to members (effective 2010). bk.rev. illus. index. back issues avail. **Document type:** *Journal, Academic/Scholarly.* **Description:** Presents articles relating to the Jewish experience in the American South for an academic and an interested lay readership.
Indexed: AmH&L, CA, T02.
Published by: Southern Jewish Historical Society, PO Box 5024, Atlanta, GA 30302. info@jewishsouth.org. Ed. Mark K Bauman.

296.4 USA

STANFORD STUDIES IN JEWISH HISTORY AND CULTURE. Text in English. 1996. irreg., latest 2010. price varies. back issues avail. **Document type:** *Monographic series, Academic/Scholarly.* **Description:** Examines Jewish life in regard to gender, class and social conflict, and the nexus of class and religion and the state.
Published by: Stanford University Press (Subsidiary of: Stanford University), 1450 Page Mill Rd, Palo Alto, CA 94304. TEL 650-723-9434, FAX 650-725-3457, info@www.sup.org. Eds. Aron Rodrigue, Steven J Zipperstein. **In Europe:** Cambridge University Press, The Edinburgh Bldg, Shaftesbury Rd, Cambridge CB2 8RU, United Kingdom. TEL 44-1223-312393, FAX 44-1223-315052, information@cambridge.org, http://www.cambridge.org/uk; **In the Americas:** Cambridge University Press Distribution Center, 100 Brookhill Dr, West Nyack, NY 10994. TEL 845-353-7500, FAX 845-353-4141, http://www.cambridge.org.

296.7 USA

STARK JEWISH NEWS. Text in English. 1920. 10/yr. USD 12 (effective 2005). **Document type:** *Newspaper, Consumer.*
Related titles: Microfilm ed.: (from AJP).
Contact: Canton Jewish Community Federation, 2631 Harvard Ave, N W, Canton, OH 44709. TEL 330-452-6444, FAX 330-452-4487. Ed. Jamie Escola. Circ: 2,500 (paid).

296 ITA ISSN 1122-0716

STORIA DELL'EBRAISMO IN ITALIA; studi e testi. Text in Italian. 1980. irreg., latest vol.21, 2000. price varies. **Document type:** *Monographic series, Academic/Scholarly.*
Published by: Casa Editrice Leo S. Olschki, Viuzzo del Pozzetto 8, Florence, 50126, Italy. TEL 39-055-6530684, FAX 39-055-6530214, celso@olschki.it, http://www.olschki.it. Ed. P Joly Zorattini.

296 USA ISSN 1061-2858

STRAIGHTALK. Text in English. 1991. q. USD 18. adv. bk.rev. **Document type:** *Newsletter.*
Published by: Foundation for Jewish Studies, Inc., 1531 S Negley Ave, Pittsburgh, PA 15217. TEL 412-521-1959, FAX 412-521-2903. Ed., R&P Ronald A Brauner. Adv. contact Marcia F Goldman. Circ: 4,500 (paid).

STUDIA IN VETERIS TESTAMENTI PSEUDEPIGRAPHA. *see* RELIGIONS AND THEOLOGY

296.071 305.8924 NLD ISSN 1876-6153

STUDIA JUDAEOSLAVICA. Text in English. 2008. irreg., latest vol.1, 2008. price varies. **Document type:** *Monographic series.* **Description:** Covers all aspects of the history and culture of Jews in the Slavic world and the encounter between Jewish and Slavic cultures.
Indexed: IZBG.
Published by: Brill, PO Box 9000, Leiden, 2300 PA, Netherlands. TEL 31-71-5353500, FAX 31-71-5317532, cs@brill.nl. Ed. Alexander Kulik.

296 DEU ISSN 0585-5306

➤ **STUDIA JUDAICA;** Forschungen zur Wissenschaft des Judentums. Text in German. 1961. irreg., latest vol.62, 2011. price varies. back issues avail. **Document type:** *Monographic series, Academic/Scholarly.*
Published by: Walter de Gruyter GmbH & Co. KG, Genthiner Str 13, Berlin, 10785, Germany. TEL 49-30-260050, FAX 49-30-26005251, info@degruyter.com, http://www.degruyter.de. Ed. Guenter Stemberger.

296 ROM ISSN 1221-5163
DS135.R7

STUDIA JUDAICA. Text in English. 1991. a. per issue exchange basis. bk.rev. illus. **Document type:** *Journal, Academic/Scholarly.*
Published by: Universitatea "Babes-Bolyai", Moshe Carmilly Institute for Hebrew and Jewish History, Biblioteca Centrala Universitara, Str. Clinicilor 2, Cluj-Napoca, Romania. TEL 40-64-197092, FAX 40-64-197633. Ed. Ladislau Gyemant. Circ: 400.

STUDIA JUDAICA. *see* HISTORY—History Of Europe

STUDIA JUDAICA CRACOVIENSIA. *see* HISTORY—History Of Europe

296 USA ISSN 1052-4533
B689.Z7

THE STUDIA PHILONICA ANNUAL; studies in hellenistic judaism. (Notes: to be continued as occasional subseries of Brown Judaic Studies Series) Text in English. 1972-1980 (vol.6); resumed 1990. a. back issues avail. **Document type:** *Journal, Academic/Scholarly.* **Description:** Devoted to furthuring the study of Hellenistic Judaism, and in particular of the writings and thought of the great Hellenistic-Jewish.
Formerly (until 1989): Studia Philonica (0093-5808)
Indexed: A21, OTA, RI-1.
Published by: (Society of Biblical Literature), Brown University, Program in Judaic Studies, 163 George St, PO Box 1826, Providence, RI 02912. TEL 401-863-3912, FAX 401-863-3938, judaic@brown.edu, http://www.brown.edu/Departments/Judaic_Studies/.

STUDIA POLONO-JUDAICA. SERIES FONTIUM. *see* HISTORY—History Of Europe

296.071 BEL ISSN 1781-7838
DS135.N4

➤ **STUDIA ROSENTHALIANA;** journal of the history, culture and heritage of the Jews in the Netherlands. Text in Dutch, English, Hebrew; Summaries in English. 1967. a., latest 2009. EUR 70 combined subscription (print & online eds.) (effective 2011). bk.rev. illus. Index. back issues avail. **Document type:** *Journal, Academic/Scholarly.*
Related titles: Online - full text ed.: ISSN 1783-1792.
Indexed: ASCA, DIP, HistAb, IBR, IBZ.
—Infotrieve.
Published by: (Bibliotheca Rosenthaliana NLD), Peeters Publishers, Bondgenotenlaan 153, Leuven, 3000, Belgium. TEL 32-16-235170, FAX 32-16-228500, peeters@peeters-leuven.be, http://www.peeters-leuven.be. Ed. Emile G L Schrijver. Circ: 400.

➤ **STUDIES IN BIBLIOGRAPHY AND BOOKLORE;** devoted to research in the field of Jewish bibliography. *see* RELIGIONS AND THEOLOGY—Abstracting, Bibliographies, Statistics

➤ **STUDIES IN CONTEMPORARY JEWRY.** *see* ETHNIC INTERESTS

296.68 ISR ISSN 0333-9661
BM100

STUDIES IN JEWISH EDUCATION. Text in English. 1983. irreg., latest vol.13, 2008. price varies. back issues avail. **Document type:** *Monographic series, Academic/Scholarly.*
Indexed: CA, E03, ERI, IHP, J01, T02.
Published by: (Hebrew University of Jerusalem, Samuel Mendel Melton Centre for Jewish Education in Jerusalem), Magnes Press (Subsidiary of: Hebrew University of Jerusalem), Hebrew University, Jerusalem, The Sherman Building for Research Management, PO Box 39099, Jerusalem, 91390, Israel. TEL 972-2-5660341, FAX 972-2-5883688. Circ: 1,000.

305.8924 296.4 GBR

STUDIES IN JEWISH HISTORY. Text in English. 1987. irreg., latest 2004. price varies. illus. back issues avail. **Document type:** *Monographic series, Academic/Scholarly.* **Description:** Examines Jewish religion, culture, and thought throughout history.
Published by: Oxford University Press, Great Clarendon St, Oxford, OX2 6DP, United Kingdom. TEL 44-1865-556767, FAX 44-1865-556646, enquiry@oup.co.uk, http://www.oup-usa.org/catalogs/general/series/.

296 NLD ISSN 1874-9895

STUDIES IN JEWISH HISTORY AND CULTURE. Text in English. 2001. irreg., latest vol.20, 2008. price varies. **Document type:** *Monographic series, Academic/Scholarly.*
Formerly (until 2007): Studies in European Judaism (1568-5004)
Indexed: IZBG.
Published by: Brill, PO Box 9000, Leiden, 2300 PA, Netherlands. TEL 31-71-5353500, FAX 31-71-5317532, cs@brill.nl. Eds. Giuseppe Veltri, Hava Tirosh-Samuelson.

296 USA ISSN 1086-5403

STUDIES IN JUDAISM. Text in English. 2005. irreg., latest vol.4, 2009. price varies. **Document type:** *Monographic series, Academic/Scholarly.*
Published by: Peter Lang Publishing, Inc. (Subsidiary of: Peter Lang Publishing Group), 29 Broadway, New York, NY 10006. TEL 212-647-7706, 800-770-5264, FAX 212-647-7707, customerservice@plang.com. Ed. Yudit Kornberg Greenberg.

296.09049 NLD ISSN 0169-9660

➤ **STUDIES IN JUDAISM IN MODERN TIMES.** Text in Dutch. 1978. irreg., latest vol.10, 1992. price varies. back issues avail. **Document type:** *Monographic series, Academic/Scholarly.* **Description:** Scholarly discussions of religious, historical, literary and cultural issues relating to Judaism in Europe, North Africa and the Middle East in the early modern and modern period.
Indexed: IZBG.
Published by: Brill, PO Box 9000, Leiden, 2300 PA, Netherlands. TEL 31-71-5353500, FAX 31-71-5317532, cs@brill.nl, http://www.brill.nl. R&P Elizabeth Venekamp. **Dist. by:** Turpin Distribution Services Ltd., Pegasus Dr, Stratton Business Park, Biggleswade, Bedfordshire SG18 8QB, United Kingdom. TEL 44-1767-604954, FAX 44-1767-601640, custserv@turpin-distribution.com, http://www.turpin-distribution.com/.

220 NLD ISSN 1570-1336

STUDIES IN THE ARAMAIC INTERPRETATION OF SCRIPTURE. Text in English. 2002. irreg., latest vol.6, 2008. price varies. **Document type:** *Monographic series, Academic/Scholarly.*
Indexed: IZBG.
Published by: Brill, PO Box 9000, Leiden, 2300 PA, Netherlands. TEL 31-71-5353500, FAX 31-71-5317532, cs@brill.nl. Ed. Paul V M Flesher.

296.155 NLD ISSN 0169-9962

➤ **STUDIES ON THE TEXTS OF THE DESERT OF JUDAH.** Text in English, French, German. 1957. irreg., latest vol.81, 2008. price varies. back issues avail. **Document type:** *Monographic series, Academic/Scholarly.* **Description:** Scholarly translation and evaluation of Biblical texts from the papyrii and manuscripts of Wadi Qumran and the Dead Sea Scrolls, and related bibliographic, linguistic, cultural and historical aspects of ancient Judaism and early Christianity.
Indexed: IZBG.
Published by: Brill, PO Box 9000, Leiden, 2300 PA, Netherlands. TEL 31-71-5353500, FAX 31-71-5317532, cs@brill.nl, http://www.brill.nl. Ed. Florentino Garcia Martinez. R&P Elizabeth Venekamp. **Dist. by:** Turpin Distribution Services Ltd., Pegasus Dr, Stratton Business Park, Biggleswade, Bedfordshire SG18 8QB, United Kingdom. TEL 44-1767-604954, FAX 44-1767-601640, custserv@turpin-distribution.com, http://www.turpin-distribution.com/.

296.73 USA ISSN 1067-7518
BM1

SYNAGOGUE LIGHT - KOSHER LIFE. Text in English. 1933. q. adv. **Document type:** *Magazine, Consumer.* **Description:** Covers religious and current events, as well as cultural issues concerning the Jewish community and kosher life, including kosher food news, recipes, kosher restaurants, kosher travel, and kosher products available through mail-order catalogs. Covers documentary and educational CD-ROM's, software, and videos regarding Jewish subject matter and themes.
Formerly: Synagogue Light (0194-7109)

R

Published by: (Kosher Food Institute), Synagogue Light, Inc., 47 Beekman St, New York, NY 10038. TEL 212-227-7543. Ed. Rabbi Meyer Hager. Pub. Hal Gilbert. R&P Meyer Hager. Adv. contact Mark Warshow.

▼ **TABLET (NEW YORK, 2009)**; a new read on Jewish life. *see* ETHNIC INTERESTS

296 ISR ISSN 0334-3650
DS101
TARBIZ; a quarterly for Jewish studies. Text in Hebrew; Summaries in English. 1929. q. USD 48 to non-members; USD 43 to members (effective 2008). bk.rev. index. back issues avail. **Document type:** *Journal, Academic/Scholarly.*
Indexed: A01, A22, BibLing, CA, DIP, FR, IBR, IBZ, IHP, J01, MLA, MLA-IB, OTA, PCI, R&TA, RASB, T02.
—IE, Infotrieve, INIST.
Published by: (Hebrew University of Jerusalem), Magnes Press (Subsidiary of: Hebrew University of Jerusalem), Hebrew University, Jerusalem, The Sherman Building for Research Management, PO Box 39099, Jerusalem, 91390, Israel. TEL 972-2-658-6660, FAX 972-2-563-3370, info@magnespress.co.il, http://www.magnespress.co.il/website_en/index.asp?action=show_covers&covers_mode=home_page. Eds. Chava Turniansky, Israel Knohl. Circ: 700.

TAUBER INSTITUTE FOR THE STUDY OF EUROPEAN JEWRY SERIES. *see* HISTORY—History Of Europe

221 USA
➤ **TAUBMAN LECTURES IN JEWISH STUDIES.** Text in English. 1991 (no.2). irreg., latest vol.6, 2009. price varies. adv. back issues avail. **Document type:** *Monographic series, Academic/Scholarly.* **Description:** Explores Old Testament and later Hebrew poetry.
Related titles: Online - full text ed.
Published by: University of California Press, Book Series, 2120 Berkeley Way, Berkeley, CA 94704. TEL 510-642-4247, FAX 510-643-7127, foundation@ucpress.edu. **Subscr. to:** California - Princeton Fulfillment Services, Inc., 1445 Lower Ferry Rd, Ewing, NJ 08618. TEL 609-883-1759, 800-777-4726, FAX 800-999-1958, orders@cpfsinc.com.

296.18 ISR ISSN 0333-6883
BM520
TECHUMIN. Text in Hebrew. 1980. a. USD 18 (effective 1993). **Document type:** *Monographic series, Academic/Scholarly.* **Description:** Collection of monographs concerning modern society and Jewish law.
Related titles: CD-ROM ed.
Indexed: IHP.
Published by: Zomet Institute, Alon Shvut, Gush Etzion, 90433, Israel. TEL 972-2-9931442, FAX 972-2-9931889, zomet@netvision.net.il. Ed. Ezra Rosenfeld. Circ: 4,500.

296 ZAF ISSN 0040-2966
TEMPLE DAVID BULLETIN. Text in English. 1969. s-m. free. adv. bk.rev. **Document type:** *Bulletin.*
Formerly: Temple David Review
Published by: Durban Progressive Jewish Congregation, 369 Ridge Rd, Durban, KwaZulu-Natal, South Africa. FAX 27-31-292429. Circ: 535.

296.7 USA ISSN 0040-439X
TEXAS JEWISH POST; the Southwest's leading English - Jewish weekly newspaper. Text in English. 1947. w. (Thu.). USD 35 in state; USD 45 out of state (effective 2005). adv. bk.rev.; film rev.; play rev. illus. **Document type:** *Newspaper, Consumer.*
Related titles: Microfilm ed.: (from AJP).
Address: 3120 S. Freeway, Fort Worth, TX 76110. TEL 817-927-2831, FAX 817-429-0840. Ed., Pub. Rene Wisch. Circ: 8,000.

296 DEU ISSN 0721-8753
TEXTE UND STUDIEN ZUM ANTIKEN JUDENTUM. Text in English, French, German. 1981. irreg., latest vol.139, 2011. price varies. **Document type:** *Monographic series, Academic/Scholarly.*
Indexed: IZBG.
Published by: Mohr Siebeck GmbH & Co. KG, Wilhelmstr 18, Tuebingen, 72074, Germany. TEL 49-7071-9230, FAX 49-7071-51104, info@mohr.de, http://www.mohr.de.

296 DEU ISSN 0179-7891
TEXTS AND STUDIES IN MEDIEVAL AND EARLY MODERN JUDAISM. Text in English. 1986. irreg., latest vol.25, 2011. price varies. **Document type:** *Monographic series, Academic/Scholarly.*
Published by: Mohr Siebeck GmbH & Co. KG, Wilhelmstr 18, Tuebingen, 72074, Germany. TEL 49-7071-9230, FAX 49-7071-51104, info@mohr.de.

TIKKUN MAGAZINE; a bi-monthly Jewish critique of politics, culture and society. *see* LITERARY AND POLITICAL REVIEWS

TOLDOT. *see* ETHNIC INTERESTS

TOLDOT. *see* GENEALOGY AND HERALDRY

TOLEDO JEWISH NEWS; the monthly newspaper for the Jewish community of greater Toledo. *see* ETHNIC INTERESTS

222.1 USA ISSN 1050-4745
BM538.S3
TORAH U - MADDA JOURNAL. Text in English. 1989. a. membership.
Indexed: A21, IJP, JewAb, MLA-IB, P30, R&TA, RI-1, RI-2.
Published by: Yeshiva University, Torah U - Madda Project, 500 W 185th St, New York, NY 10033. TEL 212-960-5277.

296.4 NZL ISSN 1177-7982
TOROA-TE-NUKUROA. Text in English. 2007. irreg. **Document type:** *Journal, Trade.* **Description:** Helps to stemmed from the desire to name, locate and articulate the practices and thinking that underpins the Wananga.
Related titles: Online - full text ed.: ISSN 2230-2387.
Published by: Te Wananga O Aotearoa, 1 Dinsdale Rd, PO Box 1191, Rotorua, 3221, New Zealand. TEL 64-7-3492360, FAX 64-7-3492305, http://www.twoa.ac.nz.

296.4 USA ISSN 0041-0608
BM1 CODEN: TRADD2
TRADITION (NEW YORK). Text in English. 1958. q. USD 35 domestic to individuals; USD 40 in Canada to individuals; USD 45 elsewhere to individuals; USD 50 in Canada to institutions; USD 55 elsewhere to institutions; USD 70 combined subscription domestic to institutions (print & online eds.) (effective 2009). bk.rev. **Document type:** *Journal, Academic/Scholarly.*
Related titles: Online - full text ed.
Indexed: A20, A21, A22, ArtHuCI, CurCont, IBR, IBZ, IJP, JewAb, MEA&I, MLA-IB, OTA, P30, PCI, R&TA, RI-1, RI-2, RILM, SCOPUS, W07.
—BLDSC (8881.070300), IE, Ingenta.
Published by: Rabbinical Council of America, 305 Seventh Ave, 12th Fl, New York, NY 10001. TEL 212-807-9000, FAX 212-727-8452, office@rabbis.org. Ed. Rabbi Shalom Carmy.

296.071 AUT ISSN 1607-629X
DS135.E8
➤ **TRANSVERSAL**; Zeitschrift fuer Juedische Studien. Text in German. 2000. 2/yr. EUR 16; EUR 10.70 newsstand/cover (effective 2009). **Document type:** *Journal, Academic/Scholarly.*
Published by: (Karl-Franzens-Universitaet Graz, Centrum fuer Juedische Studien), StudienVerlag, Erlerstr 10, Innsbruck, 6020, Austria. TEL 43-512-395045, FAX 43-512-39504515, order@studienverlag.at, http://www.studienverlag.at.

296 DEU ISSN 0041-2716
DS101
TRIBUENE; Zeitschrift zum Verstaendnis des Judentums. Text in German. 1962. q. EUR 26; EUR 20 to students; EUR 8 newsstand/cover (effective 2007). adv. bk.rev. stat. **Document type:** *Magazine, Academic/Scholarly.*
Indexed: DIP, IBR, IBZ, PhilInd.
Published by: Tribuene Verlag, Habsburgerallee 72, Frankfurt Am Main, 60385, Germany. TEL 49-69-9433000, FAX 49-69-94330023. Ed., Adv. contact Elisabeth Reisch. B&W page EUR 1,250, color page EUR 2,150. Circ: 6,800 (paid and controlled).

TRUMAH; Zeitschrift der Hochschule fuer Juedische Studien Heidelberg. *see* ETHNIC INTERESTS

296 FRA ISSN 1149-6630
DS101
➤ **TSAFON**; revue d'etudes juives du Nord. Text in French. 1990. s-a. EUR 30; EUR 16 per issue (effective 2008). film rev.; bk.rev. 200 p./no.; **Document type:** *Journal, Academic/Scholarly.* **Description:** Covers literature, history and religion of the Jewish people and Israel.
Indexed: MLA-IB.
Published by: Association Jean Marie Delmaire, 62 rue Antoine LeFebvre, Villeneuve d'Ascq, 59650, France. TEL 33-3-20562540. Ed. D Delmaire. Circ: 150.

296.7 USA ISSN 1539-9591
TWIN CITIES JEWISH LIFE. Text in English. 2002 (Jun./Jul.). bi-m. free (effective 2009). **Document type:** *Newspaper.* **Description:** Aims to inform, educate, entertain and empower readers about issues of interest to the Twin Cities Jewish community.
Published by: Minneapolis Jewish Federation, 13100 Wayzata Blvd., Ste 200, Minnetonka, MN 55305. TEL 952-593-2600, FAX 952-593-2544. **Co-publisher:** United Jewish Fund and Council of St. Paul.

296 USA ISSN 1529-2819
TZEMACH NEWS SERVICE. Text in English. 1995. w. free. back issues avail. **Document type:** *Newsletter.* **Description:** Covers information regarding Israel and the Jewish people.
Formerly: F Y I - Israel in the News
Media: Online - full text.
Published by: Tzemach Institute for Biblical Studies, PO Box 181191, Casselberry, FL 32718. TEL 407-699-1011, FAX 407-699-6399. Ed., Pub., R&P Lee Underwood.

296.7 USA
U C S J MEMBERSHIP REPORT. Text in English. a. free. **Description:** Covers Jewish interests.
Formerly (until 1992): U C S J Quarterly Report (0897-0572)
Published by: Union of Councils for Jews in the Former Soviet Union, P O Box 11676, Cleveland Park, DC 20008. TEL 202-237-8262, FAX 202-237-2236, mnaftalin@ucsj.com, http://www.fsumonitor.com. Ed. David Waksberg.

296.7 USA
U C S J MONITOR. Text in English. bi-m. membership. **Document type:** *Newsletter.* **Description:** Contains news on Jewish issues concerning the transformation of the former Soviet Union to a democratic society.
Related titles: Online - full content ed.
Published by: Union of Councils for Jews in the Former Soviet Union, P O Box 11676, Cleveland Park, DC 20008. TEL 202-237-8262, FAX 202-237-2236, mnaftalin@ucsj.com, http://www.fsumonitor.com. Ed. David Waksberg.

296.65 USA ISSN 0363-3810
BM21
UNION OF AMERICAN HEBREW CONGREGATIONS. STATE OF OUR UNION. Text in English. biennial. **Document type:** *Monographic series.*
Published by: Union of American Hebrew Congregations, 633 Third Ave., 7th Fl, New York, NY 10017-6778. http://reformjudaismmag.org.

296.7 USA ISSN 0042-0506
AP91
UNSER TSAIT. Text in Yiddish. 1941. 6/yr. USD 20 domestic to individuals; USD 25 in Canada to individuals; USD 30 elsewhere to individuals; USD 30 in North America to institutions; USD 40 elsewhere to institutions (effective 2000). bk.rev.
Indexed: MLA, MLA-IB.
Published by: Jewish Labor Bund, Coordinating Committee, Atran Center, 25 E 21st St, 3rd Fl, New York, NY 10010. TEL 212-475-0059, FAX 212-473-5102. Ed., R&P Benjamin Nadel TEL 212-475-0055.

296.7 USA ISSN 1942-3292
VA JEWISH LIFE. Variant title: Virginia Jewish Life. Text in English. 2007. bi-m. USD 13 (effective 2008). adv. **Document type:** *Magazine, Consumer.* **Description:** Explores Jewish practice, history and holidays in Virginia, including art, food, book reviews, commentary, Jewish how-to's and education.
Published by: Friends of Lubavitch VA, Inc., 212 N Gaskins Rd, Richmond, VA 23238. TEL 804-740-2000, FAX 804-750-1341. Ed. Wendy Lusk. Adv. contact Rachel Teyssier. page USD 2,800.

220 NLD ISSN 0042-4935
BS410
➤ **VETUS TESTAMENTUM.** Text in English, French, German. 1951. 5/yr. EUR 391, USD 547 to institutions; EUR 426, USD 596 combined subscription to institutions (print & online eds.) (effective 2012). bk.rev. bibl. back issues avail.; reprint service avail. from PSC. **Document type:** *Journal, Academic/Scholarly.* **Description:** Covers the whole range of Old Testament study, including history, literature, religion and theology, language, and relevant contributions from archaeology and the study of the ancient Near East.
Related titles: Microform ed.; Online - full text ed.: ISSN 1568-5330. EUR 355, USD 497 to institutions (effective 2012) (from IngentaConnect); ◆ Supplement(s): Vetus Testamentum. Supplements. ISSN 0083-5889.
Indexed: A01, A03, A08, A20, A21, A22, ASCA, AmHI, ArtHuCI, BibLing, CA, CurCont, DIP, E01, FR, H07, IBR, IBZ, IZBG, MLA-IB, OTA, PCI, R&TA, RASB, RI-1, RI-2, SCOPUS, T02, W07.
—BLDSC (9231.470000), IE, Infotrieve, Ingenta, INIST. **CCC.**
Published by: (International Organization for the Study of the Old Testament), Brill, PO Box 9000, Leiden, 2300 PA, Netherlands. TEL 31-71-5353500, FAX 31-71-5317532, cs@brill.nl. Ed. A. van de Kooij. **Dist. by:** Turpin Distribution Services Ltd., Pegasus Dr, Stratton Business Park, Biggleswade, Bedfordshire SG18 8QB, United Kingdom. TEL 44-1767-604954, FAX 44-1767-601640, custserv@turpin-distribution.com, http://www.turpin-distribution.com/.

221 NLD ISSN 0083-5889
BS410 CODEN: GFFGEE
➤ **VETUS TESTAMENTUM. SUPPLEMENTS.** Text in Dutch. 1953. irreg., latest vol.123, 2008. price varies. back issues avail. **Document type:** *Monographic series, Academic/Scholarly.* **Description:** Publishes scholarly studies on topics relating to the Old Testament, the history and culture of the ancient Near East.
Related titles: ◆ Supplement to: Vetus Testamentum. ISSN 0042-4935.
Indexed: A22, IZBG, PCI.
—BLDSC (9231.475000), IE, Ingenta. **CCC.**
Published by: (International Organization for the Study of the Old Testament), Brill, PO Box 9000, Leiden, 2300 PA, Netherlands. TEL 31-71-5353500, FAX 31-71-5317532, cs@brill.nl, http://www.brill.nl. R&P Elizabeth Venekamp. **Dist. by:** Turpin Distribution Services Ltd., Pegasus Dr, Stratton Business Park, Biggleswade, Bedfordshire SG18 8QB, United Kingdom. TEL 44-1767-604954, FAX 44-1767-601640, custserv@turpin-distribution.com, http://www.turpin-distribution.com/.

296.7 USA
VOICE OF THE DUTCHESS JEWISH COMMUNITY. Text in English. 1990. m. free. adv. Website rev.; bk.rev. **Document type:** *Newspaper, Consumer.*
Published by: Jewish Federation of Dutchess County, 110 Grand Ave, Poughkeepsie, NY 12603. TEL 845-471-9811, FAX 843-471-0659, jfeddutchess@minsdpring.com. Ed. Sandy Gardner. Pub. Judith Huober TEL 845-229-9547. R&P Bonnie Meadow. Adv. contact Linda Lamorgese TEL 845-229-9547. Circ: 2,600 (controlled).

296 CAN ISSN 0703-153X
VOICE OF THE VAAD. Text in English, Hebrew, French. 1961. irreg. (3-4/yr.). free. adv. bk.rev. **Document type:** *Newsletter.*
Related titles: Online - full content ed.
Published by: Jewish Community Council of Montreal, 6825 Decarie Blvd, Montreal, PQ H3W 3E4, Canada. TEL 514-739-6363, FAX 514-739-7024, semanuel@mk.ca. Ed. Rabbi I L Hechtman.

296.7 USA ISSN 0746-7869
VORWAERTS/FORWARD. Text in Yiddish. 1897. w. (Fri.). USD 49.95 domestic; USD 79.95 in Canada; USD 84.95 elsewhere (effective 2005). **Document type:** *Newspaper, Consumer.*
Related titles: Microfilm ed.: (from IDC, PQC).
Published by: Forward Association, 45 E 33rd St, New York, NY 10016. TEL 212-889-8200, FAX 212-447-6406. Adv. contact Jerome Koenig. Circ: 10,000 (paid).

296 ISR ISSN 0042-9732
W I Z O REVIEW. Text in English. 1939. q. free. adv. bk.rev. illus. **Document type:** *Magazine, Academic/Scholarly.* **Description:** Contains news of the organizations policies and activities in Israel and around the world, as well as coverage of Israeli cultural and political issues.
Related titles: Spanish ed.: Revista W I Z O.
Published by: Women's International Zionist Organization, 38 David Hamelech Blvd, Tel Aviv, 64237, Israel. TEL 972-3-6923805, FAX 972-3-6923801, wreview@wizo.org. Ed., R&P Hillel Schenker. Circ: 20,000 (controlled).

▼ **WARSAW JEWISH AND GENOCIDE STUDIES.** *see* HISTORY—History Of Europe

296.7 USA ISSN 0746-9373
AP92
WASHINGTON JEWISH WEEK. Text in English. 1930. w. (Thu.). USD 42 domestic; USD 85 foreign (effective 2008). bk.rev. 48 p./no. 4 cols./p.; **Document type:** *Newspaper.*
Former titles (until 1983): Jewish Week (0272-7781); National Jewish Ledger
Related titles: Microfilm ed.: (from AJP); Online - full text ed.; Supplement(s): Bar-Bat Mitzvahs; Guide to Jewish Life; Weddings (Rockville).
Indexed: ENW, P28, P48, P53, P54, PQC.
Address: 11426 Rockville Pike, Ste 236, Rockville, MD 20852. TEL 301-230-2222, FAX 301-881-6362, publisher@washingtonjewishweek.com. Ed. Debra Rubin. Pub. Larry Fishbein. Adv. contact Eric Sodee. Circ: 13,000 (paid). Wire service: JTA.

296 BRA ISSN 2175-6163
▼ **WEBMOSAICA.** Text in Portuguese. 2009. s-a. free (effective 2011). **Document type:** *Journal, Academic/Scholarly.*
Media: Online - full text.
Published by: Instituto Cultural Judaico Marc Chagall, Rua General Joao Telles 329, 20 Andar, Porto Alegre, RS 90035-121, Brazil.

296.1 222.1 USA ISSN 0887-011X
BM198.54
WELLSPRINGS/MA'YANOT; a quarterly journal exploring the inner dimensions of Torah and Jewish life. Text in English. 1984. q. adv. bk.rev. tr.lit. back issues avail. **Document type:** *Magazine, Consumer.* **Description:** Explores issues of contemporary and social concern through a Hasidic perspective. Includes essays and dialogues on the arts and sciences.
Published by: Lubavitch Youth Organization, 305 Kingston Ave, Brooklyn, NY 11213. TEL 718-953-1000, FAX 718-771-6553. Ed. Baila Olidort.

296.09 USA ISSN 0749-5471
F591
WESTERN STATES JEWISH HISTORY. Text in English. 1968. q. free to members (effective 2011). bk.rev. charts; illus. index. 96 p./no.; back issues avail. **Document type:** *Journal, Academic/Scholarly.* **Description:** Studies Jewish history west of the Mississippi, including Alaska, Hawaii, the Pacific Rim, and western Mexico.
Formerly (until 1983): Western States Jewish Historical Quarterly (0043-4221)
Indexed: ABS&EES, AmH&L, CA, IJP, J01, P30, T02.
—Ingenta.
Published by: Western States Jewish History Association, 22711 Cass Ave, Woodland, CA 91364. TEL 818-225-9631, amrabbi@pacbell.net.

296.7 CAN
WINDSOR JEWISH FEDERATION. Text in English. 1942. q. **Document type:** *Newsletter.*
Address: 1641 Ouellette Ave, Windsor, ON N8X 1K9, Canada. TEL 519-973-1772, FAX 519-973-1774. Ed. Allen Juris.

296.7 USA ISSN 0043-6488
WISCONSIN JEWISH CHRONICLE. Text in English. 1921. w. USD 36 (effective 2000). adv. bk.rev.; film rev.; play rev. **Document type:** *Newspaper.*
Related titles: Microform ed.
Published by: Milwaukee Jewish Federation, Inc., 1360 N Prospect Ave, Milwaukee, WI 53202. TEL 414-390-5888, FAX 414-271-0487. Ed., R&P Vivian M Rothschild. Adv. contact Nadine Bonner. Circ: 5,300.

296.082 CAN ISSN 1209-9392
HQ1172
➤ **WOMEN IN JUDAISM**; a multidisciplinary journal. Text in English, French. 1997 (Apr.). s-a. free (effective 2011). adv. film rev.; video rev.; Website rev.; bk.rev. bibl. back issues avail. **Document type:** *Journal, Academic/Scholarly.* **Description:** Dedicated to gender-related issues in Judaism, featuring a variety of articles, essays and bibliographies that are thought-provoking and groundbreaking.
Media: Online - full text.
Indexed: A21, A26, A39, C03, C27, C29, CA, CBCARef, CPerI, CWI, D03, D04, E08, E13, ENW, FemPer, G08, G10, GW, I05, P10, P28, P48, P53, P54, PQC, R&TA, R14, RI-1, S09, S14, S15, S18, S23, T02.
—CIS. **CCC.**
Published by: Women in Judaism, Inc., 246-1054 Centre St, Thornhill, ON L4J 8E5, Canada. TEL 416-806-4013. Ed., Pub., R&P, Adv. contact Dina Ripsman Eylon. B&W page USD 100, color page USD 200.

296.382 ZAF
WOMEN'S ZIONIST ORGANIZATION OF SOUTH AFRICA. NEWS AND VIEWS. Text in English. 1949. a. membership. adv. bk.rev.; play rev. charts; illus.
Formerly: Women's Zionist Council of South Africa. News and Views (0043-7603)
Published by: Women's Zionist Organization of South Africa, PO Box 29203, Sandringham, 2131, South Africa. TEL 27-11-4851020, FAX 27-11-6401325. Ed. Sonia Benjamin. Circ: 12,500.

296 305.8924 ZAF ISSN 1991-119X
➤ **WORLD JOURNAL OF JEWISH STUDIES.** Text in English. 2006. q. USD 120 in Africa to individuals; USD 180 elsewhere to individuals; USD 350 in Africa to institutions; USD 450 elsewhere to institutions; USD 85 in Africa to students; USD 100 elsewhere to students (effective 2007). **Document type:** *Journal, Academic/Scholarly.*
Published by: (World Research Organization), Isis Press, PO Box 1919, Cape Town, 8000, South Africa. TEL 27-21-4471574, FAX 27-86-6219999, orders@unwro.org, http://www.unwro.org/isispress.html.

296.7 USA
WYOMING VALLEY JEWISH REPORTER. Text in English. 1995. bi-w. USD 20 domestic; USD 22 foreign (effective 2000). adv. bk.rev. **Document type:** *Newspaper.* **Description:** Reports on local news and events of interest to the Jewish community.
Published by: Jewish Federation of the Wyoming Valley, c/o Marc S Goldberg, Ed, 500 Clubhouse Rd, Vestal, NY 13850. TEL 607-724-2360, FAX 607-724-2311, TReporter@aol.com. Ed., R&P Marc S Goldberg. Adv. contact Bonnie Rozen. Circ: 2,000 (paid).

296 ISR ISSN 0084-3296
DS135.E83
➤ **YAD VASHEM STUDIES.** Text in English. 1957. a., latest vol.35. ILS 80 domestic each for vols. 27-34; USD 24 foreign each for vols. 27-34 (effective 2009). bk.rev. index, cum.index: vols.1-20 (1957-1990). 400 p./no.; back issues avail. **Document type:** *Journal, Academic/Scholarly.* **Description:** Committed to a multi-faceted and thorough examination of all aspects of the Holocaust.
Formerly (until 1976): Yad Vashem Studies on the European Jewish Catastrophe and Resistance (0792-3333)
Related titles: Hebrew ed.: ILS 80 (effective 2003).
Indexed: AmH&L, CA, HistAb, P30, PCI, T02.
—**CCC.**
Published by: Yad Vashem Martyrs' and Heroes' Remembrance Authority, P O Box 3477, Jerusalem, 91034, Israel. TEL 972-2-644-6400, FAX 972-2-644-3443, publishing@yadvashem.org.il, http://www.yadvashem.org.il. Ed., R&P David Silberklang TEL 972-2-644-3516. Circ: 750.

296.7 028.5 USA ISSN 1942-3365
YALDAH; a magazine for Jewish girls, by Jewish girls. Text in English. 2004. q. USD 26 domestic; USD 32 in Canada; USD 40 foreign (effective 2008). adv. **Document type:** *Magazine, Consumer.* **Description:** Promotes Jewish values and creativity for Jewish girls ages 8-14. Includes stories, articles, interviews, artwork, crafts, recipes, quizzes and puzzles.
Published by: Yaldah Magazine, PO Box 215, Sharon, MA 02067. TEL 416-890-8770. Ed. Leah Larson. adv.: page USD 600.

296 USA ISSN 0084-3369
YALE JUDAICA SERIES. Text in English. 1948. irreg., latest 2004. price varies. back issues avail. **Document type:** *Monographic series, Academic/Scholarly.*
—BLDSC (9370.100000).
Published by: Yale University Press, PO Box 209040, New Haven, CT 06520. TEL 203-432-0960, 800-405-1619, FAX 203-432-0948, customer.care@triliteral.org, http://yalepress.yale.edu/home.asp.

296.0711 USA
YESHIVA UNIVERSITY SEPHARDIC BULLETIN. Text in English. 1973. a. free. **Document type:** *Bulletin.*
Published by: Yeshiva University, Sephardic Studies Program, 500 W 185 St, New York, NY 10033. TEL 212-960-5277. Ed. Rabbi M Mitchell Serels. Circ: 24,000.

296.7 USA ISSN 0044-0418
BM198
DI YIDDISHE HEIM/JEWISH HOME. Text in English, Yiddish. 1958. q. USD 8. illus.
Published by: Kehot Publication Society, 770 Eastern Pkwy, Brooklyn, NY 11213. yitzi@kehot.com. Eds. Rachel Altein, Tema Gurary. Circ: 5,000.

296.7 USA ISSN 0513-5419
BM1
DOS YIDDISHE VORT. Text in Yiddish. 1953. 7/yr. USD 20 domestic; USD 25 foreign (effective 2000).
Published by: Agudath Israel of America, 42 Broadway, 14th Fl., New York, NY 10004-3889. TEL 212-297-9000, FAX 212-269-2843. Ed. Joseph Friedenson.

YIDISHE SHPRAKH/YIDDISH LANGUAGE. *see* LINGUISTICS

296 FRA ISSN 0338-9316
DS101
YOD; revue des etudes hebraiques et juives modernes et contemporaines. Text in French. 1975. a. **Document type:** *Journal, Academic/Scholarly.* **Description:** Studies the literature, history, and sociology of the Jewish people in Israel and the surrounding area in the 19th and 20th centuries.
Related titles: CD-ROM ed.
Indexed: FR, MLA-IB, P30.
Published by: Institut National des Langues et Civilisations Orientales (INALCO), 2 rue de Lille, Paris, Cedex 7 75343, France. TEL 33-1-70232600, FAX 33-1-70232699. Ed. Beatrice Philippe.

YOUR CHILD. *see* EDUCATION

296.7 USA ISSN 0098-3640
PJ5111
YUGNTRUF; Yiddish student quarterly. Text in Yiddish. 1964. 3/yr. USD 18 to individuals; USD 25 to institutions; USD 10 to students. adv. bk.rev. illus. **Document type:** *Bulletin.*
Indexed: MLA, MLA-IB.
Published by: Yugntruf - Youth for Yiddish, Inc., 200 W 72nd St, Ste 40, New York, NY 10023-2824. TEL 212-787-6675, FAX 212-799-1517. Ed. Elinor Robinson. Circ: 1,100.

296.7 CZE
ZIDOVSKE MUSEUM V PRAZE. ZPRAVODAJE. Text in Czech, English. q. free. Website rev. **Document type:** *Newsletter.*
Related titles: Online - full text ed.
Published by: Zidovske Museum v Praze/Jewish Museum in Prague, A Stare Skoly 1, 3, Prague, 11001, Czech Republic. TEL 420-2-21711576, salesjewishmuseum.cz.

296.09 ISR ISSN 0044-4758
DS101
➤ **ZION**; a quarterly for research in Jewish history. Text in Hebrew; Summaries in English. 1930. q. ILS 280 membership (effective 2008); USD 75 to individuals; USD 90 to institutions (effective 2003); for Zion and Historia. adv. bk.rev. bibl. reprints avail. **Document type:** *Journal, Academic/Scholarly.*
Formerly (until 1935): Ziyyon: Yedi'ot (0792-5271)
Indexed: A20, CA, FR, HistAb, IHP, IZBG, JewAb, OTA, P30, RASB, T02.
—INIST.
Published by: Historical Society of Israel, P O Box 4179, Jerusalem, 91041, Israel. TEL 972-2-5637171, 972-2-5650444, FAX 972-2-5662135, 972-2-6712388, shazar@netvision.net.il. Eds. Aharon Oppenheimer, Immanuel I Etkis, Jeremy Cohen. adv.: B&W page USD 250. Circ: 1,000.

296.382 GBR ISSN 0951-0575
THE ZIONIST REVIEW. Text in English. 1917. q. **Document type:** *Bulletin.*
Published by: Zionist Federation of Great Britain and Northern Ireland, Balfour House, 741 High Rd, London, N12 0BQ, United Kingdom. TEL 0181-343-9756, FAX 0181-446-0639. Ed. Joe Finklestone.

296 USA
ZRAIM. Text in English, Hebrew. 1972. q. USD 18. back issues avail.
Formerly: Akivon
Published by: Bnei Akiva, National Office, 7 Penn Plaza, Ste 205, New York, NY 10001-0041. TEL 212-889-5260, FAX 212-213-3053. Ed. Alex Bailey. Circ: 2,500.

296.7 053 USA ISSN 0044-5460
AP91
➤ **ZUKUNFT/TSUKUNFT.** Variant title: The Future. Text in Yiddish, English. 1892. s-a. bk.rev. reprints avail. **Document type:** *Journal, Academic/Scholarly.* **Description:** Covers literary themes.
Related titles: Microfilm ed.: (from AJP).
Indexed: MLA-IB.
Published by: Congress for Jewish Culture, 25 E 21st St, New York, NY 10010. TEL 212-505-8040, FAX 212-505-8044, kongres@earthlink.net, http://congressforjewishculture.org/.

RELIGIONS AND THEOLOGY—Other Denominations And Sects

289.9 KEN ISSN 1684-1476
BR1642.A35
➤ **A I C M A R BULLETIN.** (African Institute for Contemporary Mission and Research) Text in English. 2002. a. KES 500 domestic; USD 10 foreign (effective 2008). bk.rev. abstr.; bibl. back issues avail. **Document type:** *Journal, Academic/Scholarly.* **Description:** Aims to provide a forum for debate of contemporary issues from an evangelical and denominational viewpoint firmly grounded in biblical principles.
Indexed: A21.
Published by: African Institute for Contemporary Mission and Research (A I C M A R), PO Box 338, Butere, 50101, Kenya. TEL 254-56-620407, chadwicklibrary@aicmar.org. Ed. Fran Etemesi. Circ: 150.

289.1 USA ISSN 1058-3084
BX6181
A JOURNAL FROM THE RADICAL REFORMATION; a testimony to Biblical unitarianism. Text in English. 1991. s-a. USD 24 to individuals; USD 36 to institutions; USD 13 per issue domestic; USD 19 per issue foreign (effective 2010). adv. bk.rev. back issues avail. **Document type:** *Journal, Academic/Scholarly.*
Indexed: R&TA.
Published by: Church of God, General Conference, 2020 Avalon Pky, Ste 400, PO Box 2950, McDonough, GA 30253. TEL 678-833-1839, 800-347-4261, FAX 678-833-1853, info@abc-coggc.org. Eds. Anthony Buzzard, Kent Ross.

299.5 USA
BF1001
ABRASAX; magik and decadence. Text in English. 1988. a. USD 25 (effective 2000). adv. bk.rev. illus. **Document type:** *Yearbook, Consumer.* **Description:** Dedicated to persons interested in neo-paganism, occultism and others.
Former titles: Trident (Corpus Christi); (until 1995): Abrasax (1066-5455)
Published by: Abrasax Publications, PO Box 1219, Corpus Christi, TX 78403-1219. TEL 361-854-3821. Ed., Pub., Adv. contact James M Martin. Circ: 200.

289.9 ARG ISSN 0587-4300
ACTUALIDAD PASTORAL; revista mensual. Text in Spanish. 1968. q. ARS 80 domestic; USD 60 foreign (effective 2001). adv. bk.rev. charts; illus. index. back issues avail. **Document type:** *Newsletter, Academic/Scholarly.* **Description:** Covers Christianity around the world.
Address: C.C. 140, Abel Costa, 261, Moron, Buenos Aires 1708, Argentina. TEL 54-11-4489-5509, FAX 54-11-4489-5509, revistsap@actualidadpastoral.com. Ed. Carlos Vetrano. Pub. Raul Trotz. R&P, Adv. contact Elisa del Rosario Dondeni. page USD 1,000; 27 x 19. Circ: 2,000 (paid).

299.935 DNK ISSN 0109-1743
ADVANCE. Text in English, French, German, Italian. 1969. bi-m. membership. adv. bk.rev. illus. **Document type:** *Newsletter, Consumer.*
Published by: Church of Scientology, Advanced Organization Saint Hill Europe and Africa, Jernbanegade 6, Copenhagen V, 1608, Denmark. TEL 45-33-738888, FAX 45-33-738833. Circ: 70,000.

289.3 USA
AFFINITY. Text in English. 1977. m. free (effective 2007). **Document type:** *Newsletter, Consumer.* **Description:** Publication in support of gay and lesbian Mormons; focuses on education of authorities and lay members regarding homosexuality.
Published by: Affirmation: Gay & Lesbian Mormons, PO Box 46022, Los Angeles, CA 90046. TEL 661-367-2421, excom2005@affirmation.org. Circ: 750.

289.95 IND
AIM. Text in English. 1970. m. INR 100 (effective 2011). bk.rev. **Document type:** *Magazine, Consumer.* **Description:** Promotes partnership, the defense and confirmation of the Christian Gospel, as well as increasing Christian evangelicalism.
Supersedes: Evangelical Fellowship Quarterly
Published by: Evangelical Fellowship of India, Publication Trust, 805/92, Deepali Bldg, Nehru Pl, New Delhi, 110019, India. TEL 91-11-26431133, FAX 91-11-26285350, mail@efionline.org, http://www.efionline.org.

200 FRA ISSN 1778-6649
ALCHIMIE. Text in French. 2005. irreg. **Document type:** *Monographic series, Consumer.*
Published by: Editions de la Hutte, BP 8, Bonneuil-en-Valois, 60123, France. contact@editionsdelahutte.com, http://www.editionsdelahutte.com.

211.8 USA ISSN 0516-9623
BL2747.3
AMERICAN ATHEIST; a journal of atheist news and thought. Text in English. 1958. 10/yr. USD 40 domestic; USD 50 in Canada & Mexico; USD 70 elsewhere (effective 2008). adv. bk.rev. charts; illus.; stat.; tr.lit. index. back issues avail. **Document type:** *Magazine, Consumer.* **Description:** Provides an in-depth analysis of current state-church separation violations. Explores atheist history, science, pseudascience and the effects of religion.
Formerly: Poor Richard's Report (0032-4310)
Related titles: Online - full text ed.: ISSN 1935-8369. USD 35 (effective 2008).
Indexed: AltPI, G05, G06, G07, G08, I05, I07, IPARL, MLA-IB, P05, R05, RASB, S23.
Published by: American Atheist Press, Inc., PO Box 5733, Parsippany, NJ 07054-6733. TEL 908-276-7300, FAX 908-276-7402, info@atheists.org, http://www.americanatheist.org. Ed., R&P Frank Zindler TEL 614-299-1036. Circ: 50,000 (paid and free).

289.1 USA ISSN 1934-0818
THE AMERICAN UNITARIAN. Text in English. 2002. q. **Document type:** *Magazine, Consumer.*
Published by: American Unitarian Conference, 6806 Springfield Dr, Mason Neck, VA 22079. TEL 866-270-4116, info@americanunitarian.org, http://www.americanunitarian.org/index.html.

R

289.1 USA ISSN 2158-4613
THE APPLE TREE. Text in English. 19??. m. back issues avail. **Document type:** *Newsletter, Trade.* **Description:** Provides information about the First Unitarian Congregational Society.
Formerly (until 1975): First Congregational Church and Society. Bulletin (2158-4621)
Published by: First Unitarian Congregational Society, PO Box 89, Wilton, NH 03086. TEL 603-654-9518, admin@uuwilton.org.

240 MYS ISSN 0044-9180
ASIAN BEACON. Text in English. 1969. m. MYR 28 domestic; MYR 63, SGD 15 in Singapore; MYR 105, USD 28 elsewhere (effective 2008). adv. bk.rev.; film rev. illus. back issues avail. **Document type:** *Magazine, Consumer.*
Published by: Asian Beacon Fellowship, Jln Kelang Lama, PO Box 240, Kuala Lumpur, 58700, Malaysia. Circ: 4,500.

289.94 PHL ISSN 0118-8534
BR1644
ASIAN JOURNAL OF PENTECOSTAL STUDIES. Text in English. 1998. s-a. PHP 300 domestic; USD 15 in Asia; USD 20 elsewhere (effective 2003). adv. bk.rev. cum index: 1998-2003. 160 p./no. 1 cols./p.; back issues avail. **Document type:** *Journal, Consumer.* **Description:** Brings a forum for theological discussion in Asia and elsewhere.
Related titles: Online - full text ed.
Indexed: A01, A02, A03, A08, A21, CA, OTA, RI-1, T02.
Published by: Faculty of Asia Pacific Theological Seminary, PO Box 377, Baguio City, Benguet 2600, Philippines. TEL 63-74-4422779, FAX 63-74-4426378. Eds. William Menzies, Wonsuk Ma. Adv. contact Wonsuk Ma. page USD 50; 15 x 22. Circ: 510 (paid and controlled).

289.94 USA ISSN 0896-4394
BX8765.5.A1
ASSEMBLIES OF GOD HERITAGE. Text in English. 1981. a. USD 12.50 (effective 2000). adv. illus. 64 p./no.; **Document type:** *Magazine, Consumer.* **Description:** Focuses on the history of the Assemblies of God and other Pentecostal and Charismatic Christian believers. Covers doctrinal subjects, biographies, and denominational issues.
Related titles: Microfiche ed.
Indexed: A21, ChrPI, RI-1, RI-2.
Published by: (General Council of the Assemblies of God), Flower Pentecostal Heritage Center, 1445 N Boonville Ave, Springfield, MO 65802-1894. TEL 417-862-2781, 800-641-4310, FAX 417-862-6203, archives@ag.org, http://www.ifphc.org/. Ed., R&P Darrin Rodgers. Circ: 35,000 (paid).

299.936 DNK ISSN 0901-2982
AUDITOR; monthly journal of scientology. Text in Danish. 19??. m. **Document type:** *Magazine, Consumer.*
Published by: Church of Scientology, Advanced Organization Saint Hill Europe and Africa, Jernbanegade 6, Copenhagen V, 1608, Denmark. TEL 45-33-738888, FAX 45-33-738833.

299.936 USA ISSN 0004-7651
AUDITOR; the monthly scientology journal. Text in English. 1964. m. bk.rev. bibl.; illus. **Document type:** *Bulletin, Consumer.*
Published by: Church of Scientology International, American Saint Hill Organization, 6331 Hollywood Blvd, Ste 1200, Los Angeles, CA 90028. TEL 323-960-3500, FAX 323-960-3508, http://www.scientology.org/religion/groups/pg007.html.

289.9 AUS ISSN 1440-1991
➤ **AUSTRALASIAN PENTECOSTAL STUDIES.** Text in English. 1998. s-a. **Document type:** *Journal, Academic/Scholarly.* **Description:** Contains scholarly articles on variety of issues related to (but not limited to) Pentecostal and Charismatic spirituality specifically related to Australasia and beyond.
Formerly (until 2000): A P S Supplemental
Related titles: Online - full text ed.: free (effective 2009).
Published by: Southern Cross College of the Assemblies of God in Australia, 40 Hector St, Chester Hill, NSW 2162, Australia. TEL 61-2-96459000, FAX 61-2-96459099, info@scc.edu.au, http://scc.edu.au.

289.6 AUS ISSN 1326-0936
THE AUSTRALIAN FRIEND. Text in English. 19??. q. AUD 20 domestic to non-members; AUD 30 foreign to non-members; free to members (effective 2011). **Document type:** *Magazine, Consumer.* **Description:** Devoted to issues of interest to Australian quakers.
Former titles (until 1947): Friend of Australia and New Zealand; (until 1935): Australasian Friend; (until 1915): Australian Friend
Related titles: Online - full text ed.: free (effective 2011).
Published by: Religious Society of Friends (Quakers) in Australia, PO Box 556, Kenmore, QLD 4069, Australia. TEL 61-7-32012685, ymsecretary@quakers.org.au, http://www.quakers.org.au/.

289.92 USA ISSN 0005-237X
AP2
AWAKE! (Editions in 87 languages) Text in English. 1919. s-m. free (effective 2009). 32 p./no. 2 cols./p.; **Document type:** *Magazine, Consumer.* **Description:** Used by Jehovah's Witnesses as a teaching aid on current events and social issues.
Former titles (until 1946): Consolation; (until 1937): Golden Age
Published by: Watch Tower Bible and Tract Society of Pennsylvania, Inc., 25 Columbia Heights, Brooklyn, NY 11201. TEL 718-560-5600, FAX 718-560-5619.

289.5 USA
THE BANNER (ZANESVILLE); a newsletter for Christian Scientists. Text in English. 1987. q. (plus special editions). free. bk.rev. **Document type:** *Newsletter.* **Description:** Focuses on items of current interest and concern.
Indexed: GSS&RPL.
Published by: Andrew W. Hartsook, Ed. & Pub., 2040 Hazel Ave, Zanesville, OH 43701. Ed., Pub., R&P Andrew W Hartsook TEL 740-452-5692.

289.1 USA ISSN 2158-446X
THE BEACON. Text in English. 19??. m. free (effective 2010). back issues avail. **Document type:** *Newsletter, Trade.* **Description:** Explores and shares the story of members of the church with spiritual/political/cultural roots growing up in rural Kansas and invites others to explore the beginnings of their own stories.
Former titles (until 1999): Bismarck-Mandan Beacon (2158-4451); (until 19??): Unitarian Newsletter (2158-4443)
Published by: Bismarck-Mandan Unitarian Universalist Fellowship and Church, 818 East Divide Ave, Bismarck, ND 58501. TEL 701-223-6788, office@bismanuu.org.

289.1 USA ISSN 2158-5369
THE BEACON. Text in English. 19??. m. free to members (effective 2010). back issues avail. **Document type:** *Newsletter, Trade.* **Description:** Provides information about the First Unitarian Church.
Former titles (until 1973): The Baltimore Beacon (2158-5342); (until 1969): The Baltimore Unitarian Beacon (2158-5334)
Related titles: Online - full text ed.: free (effective 2010).
Published by: First Unitarian Church of Baltimore, 1 W Hamilton St, Baltimore, MD 21201. TEL 410-685-2330, FAX 410-685-4133, office@firstunitarian.net.

BEFRIENDING CREATION. *see* RELIGIONS AND THEOLOGY

289.3 810 USA ISSN 2153-8522
PS508.M67
▼ **THE BEST OF MORMONISM.** Text in English. 2009. a. USD 14.95 per issue (effective 2010). **Document type:** *Journal, Consumer.* **Description:** Features the best short fiction, poetry and essays by Mormon writers.
Published by: Curelom Books, 343 N 3rd W, Salt Lake City, UT 84103. TEL 801-355-5926.

294.6 IND ISSN 0378-1984
DS401
BHARATYA VIDYA. Text in English, Sanskrit. 1939. q. INR 100 domestic; USD 60 foreign; INR 30 per issue (effective 2011). back issues avail. **Document type:** *Journal, Trade.*
Indexed: CA, MLA, MLA-IB, P42, S02, S03, T02.
Published by: Bharatiya Vidya Bhavan, Kulapati K.M. Munshi Marg, Mumbai, Maharashtra 400 007, India. TEL 91-22-23631261, bhavan@bhavans.info. Eds. Jayantkrishna H Dave, S A Upadhyaya.

299.6 USA ISSN 1523-410X
BF1548
THE BLACK FLAME. Text in English. 1989. s-a. USD 8 per issue domestic for 2 nos.; USD 16 foreign for 2 nos. (effective 2007). adv. bk.rev. **Document type:** *Newsletter.* **Description:** Discusses Satanism and the occult world.
Published by: Hell's Kitchen Productions, Inc, PO Box 499, Radio City Sta, New York, NY 10101-0499. TEL 212-245-2329. Ed. Peter H Gilmore. Circ: 2,000.

289.7 CAN ISSN 0006-4327
BX8101
BLACKBOARD BULLETIN. Text in English. 1957. m. (10/yr.). USD 6. illus.
Published by: (Amish Church), Pathway Publishing Corporation, Rte. 4, Aylmer, ON N5H 2R3, Canada. Circ: 17,900.

292 USA
THE BLESSED BEE; a pagan family newsletter. Text in English. q. USD 13, USD 17 (effective 2001). adv. **Document type:** *Newsletter, Consumer.* **Description:** Filled with magic, features, stories and resources for Pagan families everywhere.
Published by: B B I Media, Inc., PO Box 641, Point Arena, CA 95468. TEL 707-882-2052, FAX 707-882-2793, bbimedia@mcn.org, http://www.bbimedia.com. Ed., R&P Anne Newkirk Niven.

289.7 CAN ISSN 0006-8209
DER BOTE; ein mennonitisches Familienblatt. Text and summaries in German. 1924. bi-w. CAD 40 domestic; USD 40 in United States; CAD 70 in Europe (effective 2004). adv. bk.rev. **Document type:** *Newspaper, Consumer.* **Description:** Contains news about Mennonite Church, reports from congregations, meditations, etc.
Related titles: Diskette ed.
Indexed: CERDIC.
Published by: Mennonite Church Canada, 600 Shaftesburg Blvd, Winnipeg, MB R3P 0M4, Canada. TEL 204-888-6781, FAX 204-831-5675, office@mennonitechurch.ca, http://www.mennonitechurch.ca. Ed. Isbrand Hiebert. R&P Jack Suderman. Adv. contact Lois Bergen. Circ: 3,570. **Co-sponsor:** Mennonite Church.

299.934 IND ISSN 0001-902X
BP500
BRAHMAVIDYA; the Adyar library bulletin. Variant title: Adyar Library Bulletin. Text in English, Sanskrit. 1937. a., latest vol.70, 2006. adv. bk.rev. cum.index: vols.1-51. back issues avail. **Document type:** *Journal, Academic/Scholarly.* **Description:** Studies on religions, philosophy and various aspects of Sanskrit and other Indian literature as well as editions of ancient texts and translations.
Related titles: Microfiche ed.: (from IDC).
Indexed: BibLing, DIP, IBR, IBZ, MLA, MLA-IB.
Published by: Adyar Library and Research Centre, Theosophical Society, The Theosophical Publishing House, Adyar, Chennai, Tamil Nadu 600 020, India. TEL 91-44-24913528, FAX 91-44-24901399, adyarlibrary@vsnl.net, http://ts-adyar.org/index.html. Circ: 500 (paid and controlled).

299.934 USA ISSN 0006-8918
HV1571
BRAILLE STAR THEOSOPHIST. Text in English. 1926. s-a. free. **Document type:** *Newsletter.*
Published by: Theosophical Book Association for the Blind, Inc., 54 Krotona Hill, Ojai, CA 93023. TBAB@compuserve.com. Circ: 2,500.

299 USA ISSN 1931-7514
BRANCHES. Text in English. 1988. bi-m. USD 20 (effective 2007). adv. **Document type:** *Magazine, Consumer.*
Published by: Branches Magazine, PO Box 30920, Indianapolis, IN 46230. TEL 317-255-5594. Circ: 20,000.

289.7 USA ISSN 0090-242X
HJ9013
THE BUDGET. Text in English. 1890. w. (Wed.). USD 42 domestic; USD 90 in Canada; USD 1 newsstand/cover (effective 2008). adv. 62 p./no. 6 cols./p.; **Document type:** *Newspaper, Consumer.* **Description:** Serves the Amish and Mennonite communities across the Americas.
Published by: Sugarcreek Budget Publishers, Inc., 134 N Factory St, Sugarcreek, OH 44681-0249. TEL 330-852-4634, FAX 330-852-4421. Pub. Keith Rathbun. Adv. contact Kathy Theiss. col. inch USD 10.95. Circ: 20,000 (paid).

289.97 GBR ISSN 0308-5252
C W I HERALD. Text in English. 1976. q. free (effective 2009). bk.rev. reprints avail. **Document type:** *Magazine, Trade.* **Description:** Provides information on what's happening in Israel and around the world.
Formed by the merger of (19??-1976): Herald; (1924-1976): Immanuel's Witness (0019-2759)
Related titles: Microform ed.: (from PQC).
Indexed: A22.
Published by: Christian Witness to Israel, 166 Main Rd, Sundridge, Sevenoaks, Kent TN14 6EL, United Kingdom. TEL 44-1959-565955, FAX 44-1959-565966, shalom@cwi.org.uk.

299.5 FRA ISSN 0766-1177
DS501
CAHIERS D'EXTREME - ASIE. Text in French. 1985. a.
Indexed: BAS, FR, PCI.
Published by: Ecole Francaise d'Extreme-Orient, 22 Avenue du President Wilson, Paris, 75116, France. TEL 33-1-53701837, FAX 33-1-53701838.

289.6 CAN ISSN 0382-7658
CANADIAN FRIEND; Quaker news and thought. Text in English. 1904. 5/yr. CAD 28 domestic; CAD 39 in United States; CAD 49 foreign (effective 2005). adv. bk.rev. 32 p./no.; back issues avail. **Document type:** *Magazine, Consumer.* **Description:** Articles on peace and social justice issues in accordance with the beliefs and activities of Quakers, particularly Canadian Quakers.
Indexed: PRA.
Published by: Canadian Yearly Meeting of the Religious Society of Friends (Quakers), 91A Fourth Ave, Ottawa, ON K1S 2L1, Canada. TEL 613-235-8553, 888-296-3222, FAX 613-235-1753, information@quaker.ca. Ed., R&P Anne-Marie Zilliacus. Adv. contact Anne Marie Zilliacus. page USD 100; trim 10.5 x 8. Circ: 1,100.

289.7 CAN ISSN 1480-042X
CANADIAN MENNONITE. Text in English. 1971. fortn. CAD 29.50 domestic; CAD 48 foreign (effective 2000). adv. bk.rev. index. **Description:** Canadian Mennonite news, features and comments.
Former titles (until 1997): Mennonite Reporter (0380-0121); (until 1971): Canadian Mennonite Reporter (0380-013X)
Related titles: CD-ROM ed.; Microfilm ed.: (from MML); Microform ed.: (from MML); Online - full text ed.
Indexed: C03, CBCARef, CBPI, P28, P48, P53, P54, PQC. —CIS.
Published by: Mennonite Publishing Service, 490 Dutton Drive, Unit C5, Waterloo, ON N2L 6H7, Canada. TEL 519-884-3810, FAX 519-884-3331. Ed., Pub. Ron Rempel. Circ: 18,000 (paid).

289.9 CAN ISSN 0820-554X
CANADIAN MESSENGER OF THE SACRED HEART. Text in English. 1891. m. CAD 14, USD 14; CAD 1.50 newsstand/cover (effective 2000). illus. back issues avail. **Document type:** *Newsletter, Consumer.*
Former titles (until 1983): Messanger of the Sacred Heart (0820-5531); (until 1982): Messenger (0706-6619); (until 1980): Messenger of the Sacred Heart (0708-3203); (until 1968): Messenger (0708-3211); (until 1962): Canadian Messenger of the Sacred Heart (0008-4425); (until 1899): Canadian Messenger (0708-322X)
Published by: Apostleship of Prayer, 661 Greenwood Ave, Toronto, ON M4J 4B3, Canada. TEL 416-466-1195. Ed. Rev. F J Power S J. Circ: 15,000.

289.6 CAN ISSN 1180-968X
CANADIAN QUAKER HISTORY JOURNAL. Text in English. 1972. s-a. CAD 15 to individuals; CAD 20 to institutions (effective 1999). bk.rev. bibl.; charts; illus.; stat. index, cum.index. **Document type:** *Journal, Academic/Scholarly.*
Formerly: Canadian Quaker Historic Newsletter (0319-3934)
Published by: Canadian Friends Historical Association, 60 Lowther Ave, Toronto, ON M5R 1C7, Canada. TEL 416-969-9675. Eds. Albert Schrauwers, Jane Zavitz Bond. R&P Albert Schrauwers. Circ: 150.

289.1 CAN ISSN 0527-9860
CANADIAN UNITARIAN. Text in English. 1957. q. free. bk.rev. **Document type:** *Newsletter.* **Description:** Provides information, opinion, profiles of members.
Published by: Canadian Unitarian Council, 55 Eglinton Ave E, Ste 705, Toronto, ON M4P 168, Canada. TEL 416-489-4121, FAX 416-489-9010. Ed. Nichola Martin Art Kilgour. Circ: 5,000.

260 JAM ISSN 0008-6436
CARIBBEAN CHALLENGE. Text in English. 1957. m. USD 14 (effective 1999). adv. **Document type:** *Magazine, Consumer.* **Description:** Provides a Christian magazine designed primarily to reach the "man in the street.".
Published by: Christian Literature Crusade, Inc., 55 Church St., P.O. Box 186, Kingston, Jamaica. TEL 876-92-27878, FAX 876-92-26969. Ed., Adv. contact John Keane. Circ: 18,000.

289.1 USA ISSN 2158-4532
CHALICE AND CHIMES. Text in English. 19??. m. (10/yr, Sep.-Jun.). free (effective 2010). back issues avail. **Document type:** *Newsletter, Trade.* **Description:** Celebrates diversity and supports spiritual growth and social responsibility in each child and adult.
Former titles (until 2000): Unitarian Universalist Society of Bangor. Newsletter (2158-4524); Unitarian Universalist Society of Bangor. New Chimes (2158-4516); (until 1995): First Universalist Church. Park Street Chimes (2158-4508); (until 1978): First Universalist Church. Bangor Universalist (2158-4494); (until 1976): First Universalist Church. Newsletter (2158-4486)
Published by: Unitarian Universalist Society of Bangor, 120 Park St, Bangor, ME 04401. TEL 207-947-7009, uubangor@gmail.com, www.uubangor.org.

289.1 USA ISSN 2157-572X
CHIMES. Text in English. 19??. w. back issues avail. **Document type:** *Newsletter, Consumer.*
Related titles: Online - full text ed.: free (effective 2010).
Published by: Westminster Unitarian Church, 119 Kenyon Ave, E Greenwich, RI 02818. TEL 401-822-3400, FAX 401-885-2710, westminsteruu@verizon.net. Ed. Renee Bucklin.

289.9 GBR
CHRISTIAN ENDEAVOUR PROGRAMME BOOK. Text in English. 1896. a. GBP 5 (effective 1999). adv. bk.rev. **Document type:** *Newsletter.* **Description:** Covers missions and missionary work in the UK.
Former titles: Christian Endeavour Topic Book; Christian Endeavour Year Book (0069-3863)
Published by: Christian Endeavour Union of Great Britain and Ireland, Wellesbourne House, Walton Rd, Wellesbourne, Warwick, CV35 9JB, United Kingdom. TEL 44-1789-470439, FAX 44-1789-470439. Ed., Adv. contact Goerge Campball. Circ: 1,000.

289.7 USA ISSN 0009-5419
CHRISTIAN LEADER. Text in English. 1937. m. USD 16 (effective 2000). adv. bk.rev. illus. index.
Indexed: A21, RI-1, RI-2.
Published by: U.S. Conference of Mennonite Brethren Churches, PO Box V, Hillsboro, KS 67063-0060. TEL 316-947-5543, chleader@southwind.net. Ed., Adv. contact Carmen Andres. Circ: 9,500.

260 GRC
CHRISTIAN LITERATURE. Text in Greek. irreg., latest vol.3. price varies.
Published by: Patriarchal Institute for Patristic Studies, 64 Heptapyrgiou, Thessaloniki, 546 34, Greece.

289.9 USA
CHRISTIAN NETWORKS JOURNAL. Text in English. 2001. q. USD 5 newsstand/cover domestic; USD 7 newsstand/cover in Canada (effective 2002).
Published by: Christian Networks Journala, 1000 W Wilshire, Ste.342, Oklahoma City, OK 73116. TEL 800-798-8915, http://www.cnj.org. Ed. Rev. Gordon McClellan.

289.9 GBR ISSN 0009-5559
CHRISTIAN ORDER. Text in English. 1960. m. GBP 25 domestic; USD 50 in United States; GBP 65 elsewhere (effective 2009). back issues avail. **Document type:** *Magazine, Consumer.* **Description:** Devoted to the defence and propagation of the One True Faith - Catholic, Apostolic and Roman - through incisive comment on current affairs in Church and State.
Related titles: Online - full text ed.
Indexed: CERDIC, CPL.
Address: PO Box 14754, London, SE19 2ZJ, United Kingdom. TEL 44-20-87711051, FAX 44-20-87711051. Ed. Rod Pead.

243 USA ISSN 1082-572X
BR1640.A1
CHRISTIAN RESEARCH JOURNAL. Text in English. 1975. bi-m. USD 39.50 in US & Canada; USD 79 elsewhere (effective 2010). adv. bk.rev. bibl. back issues avail. **Document type:** *Journal, Academic/ Scholarly.* **Description:** Specializes in in-depth, cutting-edge research of cults, the occult (including new age), religions, controversial new religious movements, and ethics from the perspective of evangelical Christianity.
Former titles (until 19??): Forward; Christian Research Institute. Newsletter (0045-6845)
Indexed: A21, CCR, RI-1, RI-2.
Published by: Christian Research Institute, PO Box 8500, Charlotte, NC 28271. TEL 888-700-0274, http://www.equip.org. **Subscr. in Canada to:** CRI Canada.

289.5 USA ISSN 0009-5613
BX6901
THE CHRISTIAN SCIENCE JOURNAL. Text in English. 1883. m. USD 68 domestic; USD 71.50 in Canada; USD 80 elsewhere (effective 2009). index. back issues avail. **Document type:** *Directory, Consumer.* **Description:** Provides instructive articles and verified reports of Christian healing that provides a working understanding of the divine principle and practice of Christian Science.
Related titles: Online - full text ed.
Indexed: CERDIC.
Published by: (First Church of Christ, Scientist), The Christian Science Publishing Society, PO Box 1291, Boston, MA 02117. TEL 888-424-2535, fischerm@csps.com. Ed. Marilyn Jones. **Subscr. to:** Subscriber Services, PO Box 37304, Boone, IA 50032-2304.

289.5 USA ISSN 1938-6176
CHRISTIAN SCIENCE QUARTERLY. BIBLE LESSONS (ENGLISH CITATION EDITION). Text in English. 1890. q. USD 20 (effective 2009). adv. **Document type:** *Magazine, Consumer.* **Description:** Contains the Bible Lesson citations (page and line references) to help the readers study each Lesson directly from the King James Version of the Bible and Science and Health.
Former titles (until 2007): Christian Science Quarterly Weekly Bible Lessons (1526-5838); (until 199?): Christian Science Quarterly. Bible Lessons (Citation Edition) (0145-7365); Which incorporated (198?-2000): Christian Science Quarterly. Bible Lessons (Study Edition) (1061-6713)
Media: Large Type (13 pt.). **Related titles:** French ed.: Livret Trimestriel de la Christian Science. Lecons Bibliques. ISSN 1520-4170; German ed.: Christian Science Vierteljahrsheft. Bibellektionen. ISSN 1520-4189; Italian ed.: Libretto Trimestrale della Christian Science. Lezioni Bibliche. ISSN 1520-6955; Portuguese ed.: Livrete Trimestral da Christian Science. Licoes Biblicas. ISSN 1520-698X; Spanish ed.: Cuaderno Trimestral de la Christian Science. Lecciones Biblicas. ISSN 1520-7013; Czech ed.: Ctvrtletnik Christian Science. Biblicke Lecke. ISSN 1520-3433; Danish ed.: Christian Science Kvartalshaefte. Bibelstudium; Dutch ed.: Christian Science Kwartaalboekje. Bijbellessen. ISSN 1520-345X; Greek ed.: Trimeniaio Periodiko tes Christian Science. Biblika Mathemata. ISSN 1520-4197; Japanese ed.: Christian Science Kotari. Seisho Kyokar. ISSN 1520-7048; Norwegian ed.: Christian Science Kvartalshefte. ISSN 1520-6963; Russian ed.: Ezhekvartal'nik Christian Science. Bibleiskie Uroki. ISSN 1520-703X; Swedish ed.: Christian Science Kvartalshaefte. Bibelstudium; Polish ed.: Kwartalnik Christian Science. Lekcje Biblijne. ISSN 1520-6971; Indonesian ed.: Buku Triwulanan Christian Science; ◆ Special ed. of: Christian Science Quarterly. Bible Lessons (Study Edition). ISSN 1938-6184.
Published by: (First Church of Christ, Scientist), The Christian Science Publishing Society, One Norway St, Boston, MA 02115. TEL 617-450-7034, 800-288-7090, fischerm@csps.com, http://www.csquarterly.com.

289.5 USA ISSN 1938-6184
CHRISTIAN SCIENCE QUARTERLY. BIBLE LESSONS (STUDY EDITION). Text in English. 1991. q. USD 98 domestic; USD 102.90 in Canada; USD 108 foreign (effective 2009). **Document type:** *Magazine, Consumer.*
Formerly (until 2007): Christian Science Quarterly. Bible Lessons (Full Text Edition) (1053-251X)
Related titles: Audio CD ed.: USD 150 domestic; USD 157.50 in Canada; USD 160 elsewhere (effective 2009); Audio cassette/tape ed.: USD 150 domestic; USD 157.50 in Canada; USD 160 elsewhere (effective 2009); Braille ed.; Diskette ed.: ISSN 1054-4550; Online - full text ed.: eBibleLesson. USD 9.95 per month (effective 2009); Large type ed. 16 pt.: Christian Science Quarterly. Bible Lessons (Full Text Large Type Edition). ISSN 1072-4486. 1994. USD 98 domestic; USD 102.90 in Canada; USD 108 elsewhere (effective 2009); ◆ Special ed(s).: Christian Science Quarterly. Bible Lessons (English Citation Edition). ISSN 1938-6176.
Published by: The Christian Science Publishing Society, One Norway St, Boston, MA 02115. TEL 617-450-7034, http://www.csquarterly.com.

289.5 USA ISSN 0009-563X
CHRISTIAN SCIENCE SENTINEL. Text in English. 1898. w. USD 79 domestic; USD 83 in Canada; USD 91 elsewhere (effective 2009). adv. index. 32 p./no. 2 cols./p.; back issues avail. **Document type:** *Magazine, Consumer.* **Description:** Examines events and trends from a spiritual perspective including articles and testimonies of healing.
Related titles: Audio cassette/tape ed.: ISSN 1065-1241. USD 96 (effective 1999); Online - full text ed.
Indexed: CERDIC.
—Ingenta.
Published by: (First Church of Christ, Scientist), The Christian Science Publishing Society, PO Box 955, Boston, MA 02117. TEL 617-450-7919, 888-882-9282. **Subscr. to:** Subscriber Services, PO Box 37304, Boone, IA 50032-2304.

289.9 PAK ISSN 0009-5699
CHRISTIAN VOICE; a weekly newspaper and review. Text in English. 1950. w. PKR 25. adv. bk.rev. bibl.; illus. **Document type:** *Newspaper.*
Published by: Archdiocese of Karachi, St. Patrick's High School, Sangster Rd., Saddar, Karachi, 0328, Pakistan. Ed. Fr Augustine P Varkey. Circ: 1,200.

289.9 POL ISSN 0209-0120
CHRZESCIJANIN. Text in Polish. 1929. bi-m. PLZ 24 domestic; USD 24 in US & Canada (effective 2000).
Published by: Kosciol Zielonoswiatkowy, Ul Sienna 68-70, Warsaw, 00825, Poland. TEL 48-22-6548296, FAX 48-22-6204073. Ed. Kazimierz Sosulski. Circ: 3,100.

289.9 USA ISSN 0009-630X
CHURCH ADVOCATE. Text in English. 1835. q. free. bk.rev. charts; illus. **Description:** Encourages an informed people to be the Church.
Formerly (until 1889): Gospel Publisher
Related titles: Microfilm ed.
Indexed: CERDIC.
Published by: Churches of God, General Conference, 700 E Melrose Ave, Findlay, OH 45040. TEL 419-424-1961, FAX 419-424-3433. Ed., R&P Mac Cordell.

289.3 USA
CHURCH NEWS (SALT LAKE CITY). Text in English. 1930. w. (Sat.). **Document type:** *Newspaper, Consumer.*
Published by: Deseret News Publishing Co., 30 E. 100 South, Salt Lake City, Salt Lake, UT 84111. Ed. Gerry Avant.

292 USA
CIRCLE MAGAZINE; celebrating nature, spirit & magic. Text in English. 1980. 4/yr. USD 25 domestic; USD 46 in Canada & Mexico; USD 48 elsewhere (effective 2010). adv. bk.rev. illus. back issues avail. **Document type:** *Magazine, Consumer.* **Description:** Provides news, views, notices, rituals, and other information pertaining to Wiccan ways, Paganism, Shamanism, Goddess Worship, Positive Magik, and related Pantheistic ways.
Formerly (until 1999): Circle Network News (1047-4196)
Published by: Circle Sanctuary, PO Box 9, Barneveld, WI 53507. TEL 608-924-2216, FAX 608-924-5961, circle@mhtc.net. Ed. Georgette Paxton. Adv. contact Theresa Jones.

289.7 USA ISSN 1083-818X
BX8128.W4
A COMMON PLACE. Text in English. 1995. q. free (effective 2011). back issues avail. **Document type:** *Magazine, Consumer.* **Description:** Introduces MCC's programs and partners and encourages readers to lives of service and peacemaking through stories of faith, struggle and blessing.
Related titles: Online - full text ed.: free (effective 2011).
Indexed: P30.
Published by: Mennonite Central Committee, 21 S 12th St, PO Box 500, Akron, PA 17501. TEL 717-859-1151, 888-563-4676, mailbox@mcc.org, http://www.mcc.org. Ed. Chery Zehr Walker.

289.1 USA ISSN 2159-564X
THE COMMUNICATOR. Text in English. 1962. m. **Document type:** *Newsletter, Trade.*
Published by: The Unitarian Society of Germantown, 6511 Lincoln Dr, Philadelphia, PA 19119. TEL 215-844-1157, FAX 215-844-1159, usguu@verizon.net, http://usguu.org.

289.1 USA
COMMUNICATOR (BOSTON). Text in English. 1976. 5/yr. price varies. back issues avail. **Document type:** *Newsletter.*
Formerly: U U W F Federation Newsletter
Published by: Unitarian Universalist Women's Federation, 25 Beacon St, Boston, MA 02108. TEL 617-742-2100. Ed. Ellen Spencer. Circ: 9,000.

289.1 USA ISSN 2151-4887
COMMUNITY COURIER. Variant title: Courier. Text in English. 19??. w. free to members (effective 2009). **Document type:** *Newsletter, Trade.*
Formerly (until 1971): Liberal
Published by: First Parish in Waltham, 50 Church St, Waltham, MA 02452. TEL 781-893-6240, sarahnwah@earthlink.net, http://www.walthamuu.org/. Ed. Judy Natale.

299 USA ISSN 2151-4089
BP600
COMPASSION. Text in English. 2000. a. **Document type:** *Magazine, Consumer.*
Formerly (until 200?): Falun Dafa Quarterly
Related titles: Online - full text ed.: ISSN 2151-4097. free (effective 2009).
Published by: Falun Dafa Information Center, PO Box 9175, Bardonia, NY 10954. TEL 888-842-4797, contact@faluninfo.net.

299.512 TWN
CONFUCIUS & MENCIUS SOCIETY OF THE REPUBLIC OF CHINA. JOURNAL. Text in Chinese. 1961. s-a. TWD 100, USD 4. bibl. cum.index.
Published by: Confucius-Mencius Society of the Republic of China, 45, Nan Hai Rd, Taipei, Taiwan. Ed. Tung Chin Yue.

289.9 USA
CONSCIOUS NEWSLETTER. Text in English. m. USD 35 donation. **Document type:** *Newsletter.*
Formerly: Christian Science Open Forum
Published by: Consciousness Network, 464 N 43rd St, Seattle, WA 98103. TEL 206-632-2018. Pub. Robert D Wells.

231.76 USA ISSN 0011-0671
BX7547.A1
COVENANT COMPANION. Text in English. 1926. m. USD 19.95 (effective 2000). adv. bk.rev.; film rev. index.
Indexed: CCR.
Published by: (Evangelical Covenant Church), Covenant Publications, 5101 N Francisco Ave, Chicago, IL 60625. TEL 773-784-3000, FAX 773-784-4366. Adv. contact Steve Luce. Circ: 22,000.

231.76 USA ISSN 0361-0934
BX7547.A1
THE COVENANT QUARTERLY. Text in English. 1941. q.
Indexed: A21, R&TA, RI-1.
—BLDSC (3485.882000), IE, Ingenta.
Published by: Covenant Publications, 5101 N Francisco Ave, Chicago, IL 60625. TEL 773-784-3000, communication@covchurch.org, http://www.covchurch.org.

289.9 GBR
COVENANT VIEWPOINT. Text in English. 1997. q. USD 17 in United Kingdom to non-members; GBP 10.50 overseas to non-members (effective 2000); with Covenant Voice. charts; illus. index.
Published by: Covenant Peoples Fellowship, 36 Shaftesbury Ave, Goring-by-Sea, Worthing, W Sussex BN12 4EQ, United Kingdom. TEL 44-1093-505919, FAX 44-1903-506746. R&P Rev. Kenneth Whittaker.

289 GBR
COVENANT VOICE. Text in English. 1945. q. GBP 8.50, USD 17 in United Kingdom to non-members; GBP 10.50 overseas to non-members (effective 2000); with Covenant Viewpoint. charts; illus. index. back issues avail.
Formerly (until June 1982): Brith (0007-0211)
Published by: Covenant Peoples Fellowship, 36 Shaftesbury Ave, Goring-by-Sea, Worthing, W Sussex BN12 4EQ, United Kingdom. TEL 44-1093-505919, FAX 44-1903-506746. Ed., R&P Rev. Kenneth Whittaker. Circ: 4,000.

230.0071 HRV ISSN 0352-4000
BR1 CODEN: UDK 215
CRKVA U SVIJETU. Text in Croatian; Abstracts in English, French, German. 1966. q. HRK 80; USD 25 foreign (effective 2001). bk.rev. 125 p./no. 1 cols./p.; **Document type:** *Academic/Scholarly.*
Indexed: RASB, RILM.
Address: Zrinsko Frankopanska 19, pp 329, Split, 21000, Croatia. TEL 385-21-386166, FAX 385-21-386188. Ed., R&P Nedjeljko A Ancic. Circ: 2,000.

266.02356 USA ISSN 0045-9119
CROSSROADS (INDIANAPOLIS). Text in English. 1972. q. USD 5, GBP 3 (effective 2004). adv. **Document type:** *Newsletter.* **Description:** Covers Christian Mission in the Middle East.
Published by: Middle East Christian Outreach, PO Box 531151, Indianapolis, IN 46253-1151. TEL 317-271-4026, FAX 317-271-4026. Ed. Peter D L Thomson. Circ: 5,000.

289.3 USA ISSN 0092-7147
BV4810
DAILY BREAD; a devotional guide for every day of the year. Text in English. 1969. a. USD 12 (effective 2008). **Document type:** *Magazine, Consumer.*
Published by: (Reorganized Church of Jesus Christ of Latter Day Saints), Herald Publishing House, 1001 W Walnut, Box 390, Independence, MO 64051. TEL 816-521-3015, 800-767-8181, FAX 816-521-3066, sales@heraldhouse.org, http://www.heraldhouse.org. Ed. Richard Brown. Circ: 10,000.

289.3 USA ISSN 0093-786X
BX8606
DESERET NEWS CHURCH ALMANAC. Text in English. 1974. a. USD 12.95 (effective 2007). 656 p./no.; **Document type:** *Magazine, Consumer.* **Description:** Covers reference information, history of the Church by country and state, leadership biographies, review of church news, historical chronology, and current church membership statistics.
Published by: Deseret News Publishing Co., PO Box 1257, Salt Lake City, UT 84110. TEL 801-237-2141, FAX 801-237-2524. Ed., R&P Gerry Avant. Pub. Jim M. Wall. Circ: 20,000.

289.3 USA ISSN 0012-2157
BX8601
➤ **DIALOGUE (SALT LAKE CITY);** a journal of mormon thought. Text in English. 1966. q. USD 37 domestic; USD 45 foreign; USD 100 to institutions (print or online ed.); USD 50 combined subscription domestic to individuals (print & online eds.); USD 58 combined subscription foreign to individuals (print & online eds.); USD 125 combined subscription to institutions (print & online eds.); USD 60 combined subscription (print & DVD eds.); USD 30 to students (effective 2009). adv. bk.rev. charts; illus. index, cum.index: 1966-1987. back issues avail.; reprints avail. **Document type:** *Journal, Academic/Scholarly.* **Description:** Contains articles, essays, poetry, fiction and art.
Related titles: CD-ROM ed.: New Mormon Studies; Microform ed.: (from PQC); Online - full text ed.: ISSN 1554-9399. USD 25 to individuals; USD 100 to institutions (effective 2009); Optical Disk - DVD ed.: ISSN 1554-9631. USD 42 (effective 2009).
Indexed: A01, A21, A22, AmH&L, CA, H14, HistAb, MLA-IB, P10, P28, P48, P53, P54, PQC, RI-1, RI-2, RILM, T02.
—IE, Ingenta. **CCC.**
Published by: Dialogue Foundation, PO Box 58423, Salt Lake City, UT 84158. dialoguebusiness@peoplepc.com. Ed. Kristine L Haglund. Adv. contact Lori Levinson. B&W page USD 250; 6 x 9. **Dist.by:** Signature Books.

R

289.7 CAN ISSN 0384-8515
BX8101
DIRECTION (WINNIPEG). Text in English. 1972. s-a. CAD 16 domestic; USD 15.50 foreign (effective 2001). bk.rev. back issues avail. **Document type:** *Journal, Academic/Scholarly.* **Description:** Aims to serve its constituency by addressing biblical, theological and church-related issues. Church and conference leaders, pastors, educators and informed church members are the intended audience.
Related titles: Online - full text ed.
Indexed: A21, OTA, RI-1.
—BLDSC (3590.248000), IE, Ingenta.
Published by: Kindred Productions, 169 Riverton Ave, Winnipeg, MB R2L 2E5, Canada. TEL 204-654-5765, FAX 204-654-1865, kindred@mbconf.ca. Ed. Douglas Miller. Pub. Marilyn Hudson. Circ: 350 (paid). **Co-sponsor:** Mennonite Brethrens of North America.

292.00250971 CAN ISSN 0848-3760
DIRECTORY TO CANADIAN PAGAN RESOURCES. Text in English. 1988. a. CAD 5, USD 5. **Document type:** *Directory.* **Description:** Covers all types of Pagan and occult resources available in Canada - witchcraft, Druid, womanspirit and feminist spirituality, Asatru and ceremonial magickal groups, bookstores, gatherings and newsletters and groups providing resources or services to these communities.
Published by: Obscure Pagan Press, c/o Sam Wagar, 32579 Oriole Crescent, Abbotsford, BC V2T 4C7, Canada. TEL 604-870-8715, swagar@home.com. Ed. Samuel Wagar.

286.13 USA ISSN 1539-1671
DISCIPLESWORLD. Text in English. 2002. m. USD 25 (effective 2005). adv. **Document type:** *Magazine, Consumer.* **Description:** Contains news, opinion, and mission for members of the Christian Church (Disciples of Christ).
Published by: Christian Church - Disciples of Christ, 130 East Washington St, Indianapolis, IN 46204-3645. TEL 317-635-3100, news@disciples.org, http://www.disciples.org. Adv. contact Fred Jones. B&W page USD 1,275; trim 8.375 x 10.875.

289 ITA
➤ **DOCUMENTA MISSIONALIA.** Text in English, French, Italian, Spanish. 1964. irreg., latest vol.26, 1999. price varies. **Document type:** *Monographic series, Academic/Scholarly.* **Description:** Publishes scholarly studies on missionary and cultural aspects of non-Christian peoples related to their religious, historical and ethnological contexts.
Published by: (Pontificia Universita Gregoriana, Facolta di Missiologia), Gregorian University Press/Editrice Pontificia Universita Gregoriana, Piazza della Pilotta 35, Rome, 00187, Italy. TEL 39-06-6781567, FAX 39-06-6780588, periodicals@biblicum.com, http://www.paxbook.com.

289.94 DNK ISSN 1604-6528
DOMINO. Text in Danish. 1932. 11/yr. adv. **Document type:** *Magazine, Consumer.*
Formerly (until 2005): Korsets Evangelium (0108-8114)
Related titles: Online - full text ed.
Published by: Frikirkenet, Lykkegaardsvej 100, Kolding, 6000, Denmark. TEL 4575-500200, lrh@apostolic.dk, http://www.frikirkenet.dk. Ed. Poul Kirk TEL 45-24-415125. Adv. contact Erik Damm. page DKK 9,000; 230 x 325.

289.7 NLD ISSN 0167-0441
BX8101
➤ **DOOPSGEZINDE BIJDRAGEN.** Text in Dutch. 1975. a. EUR 30 to individuals; EUR 35 to institutions (effective 2009). bk.rev. bibl.; illus. **Document type:** *Academic/Scholarly.* **Description:** Covers the history of Mennonitism and Anabaptism and related fields.
Related titles: Microfiche ed.: (from IDC).
Indexed: CERDIC.
Published by: Doopsgezinde Historische Kring, Singel 454, Amsterdam, 1017 AW, Netherlands. TEL 31-20-6230914, info@dhkonline.nl, http://www.dhklonline.nl. Ed. P Visser. Circ: 650.

299 DEU ISSN 0012-6063
BP595.A1
DIE DREI; Zeitschrift fuer Anthroposophie in Wissenschaft, Kunst und sozialem Leben. Text in German. 1921. m. EUR 49 domestic; EUR 54 foreign (effective 2008). adv. bk.rev. abstr.; illus. index. **Document type:** *Journal, Academic/Scholarly.*
Indexed: DIP, IBR, IBZ, RILM.
—CCC.
Published by: Anthroposophische Gesellschaft in Deutschland, Alt-Niederursel 45, Frankfurt am Main, 60439, Germany. TEL 49-69-95776121, FAX 49-69-582358, http://www.anthroposophie-de.com. adv.: page EUR 550; trim 130 x 200. Circ: 3,000 (paid and controlled).

299.16 USA ISSN 1540-4889
D70
➤ **E-KELTOI**; journal of interdisciplinary celtic studies. Text in English. 2003. irreg. free (effective 2011). **Document type:** *Journal, Academic/Scholarly.* **Description:** Aims to promote and disseminate research and communication related to Celtic cultures, past and present, in the academic arena as well as for the general public.
Media: Online - full text.
Indexed: A39, C27, C29, D03, D04, E13, R14, S14, S15, S18.
Published by: University of Wisconsin at Milwaukee, Center for Celtic Studies, Holton Hall 290, PO Box 413, Milwaukee, WI 53201. TEL 414-229-2608, FAX 414-229-6827, celtic@uwm.edu, http://www.uwm.edu/Dept/celtic. Ed. Bettina Arnold TEL 414-229-4583.

299 AUS ISSN 1449-8367
EARTHSONG JOURNAL. Text in English. 2004. s-a. AUD 30 domestic; AUD 35 foreign; AUD 12 newsstand/cover domestic; AUD 17 newsstand/cover foreign (effective 2009). back issues avail. **Document type:** *Magazine, Consumer.* **Description:** Aims to further development of eco-literacy and earth ethics.
Published by: Earthsong Project, PO Box 851, Parkville, VIC 3052, Australia. TEL 61-3-83590106, FAX 61-3-83590132, earthsong@pacific.net.au, http://www.earthsong.org.au/index.html. Ed. Anne Boyd.

284.2 266 NLD ISSN 0012-9119
ECHO; hervormd blad. Text in Dutch. 1952. 8/yr. EUR 10 (effective 2009). illus.
Published by: Hervormde Bond voor Inwendige Zending/Reformed Alliance for Home Mission, Johan van Oldenbarneveltlaan 10, Amersfoort, 3818 HB, Netherlands. TEL 31-33-4611949, FAX 31-33-4659204, secretariaat@izb.nl, http://www.izb.nl. Circ: 20,000.

299.6 NLD ISSN 0167-2665
ECHO UIT AFRIKA EN ANDERE WERELDDELEN. Text in Dutch. 1933. bi-m. charts; illus. **Document type:** *Bulletin, Consumer.*
Formerly: Echo uit Afrika (0012-9305)
Published by: Missiezusters van St. Petrus Claver/Missionary Sisters of St. Peter Claver, Bouillonstraat 4, Maastricht, 6211 LH, Netherlands. TEL 31-43-3212158, stpetrusclaver@filternet.nl, http://stpetrusclaver.filternet.nl/.

299 SWE ISSN 1401-7237
ELSA. Text in Swedish. 1988. q. SEK 100 membership (effective 2011). adv. **Document type:** *Magazine, Consumer.*
Formerly (until 1995): Kyrkor i Solidaritet Med Kvinnor (1102-755X)
Published by: Sveriges Ekumeniska Kvinnoraad/The Swedish Ecumenical Women's Council, c/o Ekumeniska Centret, PO Box 14038, Bromma, 16714, Sweden. TEL 46-8-4536800, sek@ekuc.se. Ed. Annika Damirjian.

289.94 NZL ISSN 1177-0546
EMPOWERED; magazine of the spirit empowered life. Text in English. q. **Document type:** *Magazine, Consumer.*
Formerly (until 2005): One Purpose Magazine
Published by: Assemblies of God in New Zealand Inc., PO Box 74138, Auckland, 1543, New Zealand. TEL 64-9-3584304, FAX 64-9-3584725, gensec@assembliesofgodnz.org.nz, http://www.agnz.org/.

299.514 USA ISSN 1073-7480
THE EMPTY VESSEL; a journal of Daoist philosophy and practice. Text in English. 1993. q. USD 20 domestic (effective 2008). adv. bk.rev.; video rev.; rec.rev. illus. 56 p./no.; back issues avail. **Document type:** *Magazine, Consumer.* **Description:** Dedicated to the exploration and dissemination of Daoist philosophy and practice.
Published by: The Abode of the Eternal Tao, 1991 Garfield St, Eugene, OR 97405. solala@abodetao.com. Ed. Solala Towler.

289.94 USA ISSN 1082-1791
ENRICHMENT; a journal for Pentecostal ministry. Text in English. 1965. q. USD 24 domestic; USD 54 foreign; USD 7 per issue (effective 2009). adv. bk.rev. bibl.; illus.; stat. back issues avail. **Document type:** *Journal, Trade.* **Description:** Features spiritual articles relevant to Pentecostal ministry.
Formerly (until 1996): Advance (0001-8589)
Related titles: Online - full text ed.
Indexed: CCR.
Published by: (General Council of the Assemblies of God), Gospel Publishing House, 1445 N Boonville Ave, Springfield, MO 65802. TEL 417-862-2781 ext 4095, 800-641-4310, FAX 417-862-5881, 800-328-0294, CustSrvReps@ag.org, http://www.gospelpublishing.com/. Adv. contact Steve Lopez TEL 417-862-2781 ext 4097. color page USD 2,358; bleed 8.125 x 11. Circ: 32,000.

289.3 USA ISSN 0884-1136
BX8601
ENSIGN. Text in English. 1971. m. USD 10; USD 1.50 per issue (effective 2009). charts; illus. back issues avail. **Document type:** *Magazine, Consumer.* **Description:** Contains the First Presidency Message and other words of latter-day prophets.
Formerly (until 1979): Ensign of the Church of Jesus Christ of Latter-day Saints (0013-8606); Which superseded (in 1970): Improvement Era; Which was formerly (until 1897): The Young Woman's Journal
Related titles: Audio cassette/tape ed.; Braille ed.; Online - full text ed.: free (effective 2009).
Published by: Church of Jesus Christ of Latter-day Saints, 50 E North Temple St, Salt Lake City, UT 84150. TEL 801-240-2950, 800-537-5971, FAX 801-240-5997. Eds. Spencer J Condie, Victor D Cave. **Subscr. to:** Distribution Services, P O Box 26368, Salt Lake City, UT 84126.

299 USA
ENSIGN TALKING BOOK. Text in English. 1976. m. USD 10 donation.
Media: Audio cassette/tape.
Published by: Church of Jesus Christ of Latter-day Saints, Internal Communications, 50 E North Temple, Salt Lake City, UT 84150. TEL 801-240-2477. Circ: 4,000.

261.705 GBR ISSN 1750-2217
➤ **EVANGELICAL REVIEW OF SOCIETY AND POLITICS.** Text in English. 2007. s-a. GBP 18 combined subscription to individuals (print & online eds.); GBP 25 combined subscription to institutions (print & online eds.) (effective 2009). adv. back issues avail. **Document type:** *Journal, Academic/Scholarly.* **Description:** Explores social and political issues from an interdisciplinary Evangelical perspective.
Related titles: Online - full text ed.: ISSN 1750-2225. GBP 10 to individuals; GBP 17 to institutions (effective 2009).
Indexed: P42, T02.
Published by: King's Evangelical Divinity School, Theology and Religious Studies, University of Wales, Lampeter, Ceredigion, SA48 7ED, United Kingdom. http://www.midbible.ac.uk/. Eds. Dr. Calvin Smith, Stephen Vantassel. adv.: page GBP 70; 14.8 x 21.

289.95 DEU ISSN 0930-8873
DER EVANGELISCHE BUCHBERATER. Text in German. 1947. q. EUR 25.40; EUR 5 newsstand/cover (effective 2009). bk.rev. index. back issues avail. **Document type:** *Magazine, Consumer.*
Indexed: IBR, IBZ.
Published by: Deutscher Verband Evangelischer Buechereien e.V., Buergerstr 2A, Goettingen, 37073, Germany. TEL 49-551-5007590, FAX 49-551-704415, dveb@dveb.info, http://www.ev-buchberater.de. Circ: 3,500.

289.9 USA ISSN 0738-8489
EVANGELIST (ALBANY). Text in English. 1926. w. USD 20 (effective 2001). adv. bk.rev.; film rev. 28 p./no.; back issues avail. **Document type:** *Newspaper.*
Related titles: Microfilm ed.
Published by: (Roman Catholic Diocese of Albany), Albany Catholic Press Association, Inc., 40 N Main Ave, Albany, NY 12203. TEL 518-453-6688, FAX 518-453-8448. Ed. James P Breig. Pub. Bishop Howard J Hubbard. Adv. contact Barbara R Oliver. Circ: 54,000.

269.2 USA ISSN 0014-3626
EVANGELIST (PASADENA). Text in English. 1960. q. USD 2 (effective 1999). bk.rev. illus.
Related titles: Arabic ed.; German ed.; Dutch ed.; Armenian ed.
Published by: Bible Land Mission, 2355 E Washington Blvd, Pasadena, CA 91104. TEL 818-798-7177, FAX 818-791-0036. Ed. Samuel Doctorian. R&P Paul Doctorian. Circ: 20,000.

289.95 USA
EVANGELIUMI HIRNOK/GOSPEL MESSENGER. Text in Hungarian. 1908. s-m. USD 20 (effective 2007). bk.rev. back issues avail. **Document type:** *Newsletter, Consumer.* **Description:** Writes largely in Hungarian with some English covering religious information.
Related titles: Online - full text ed.
Published by: Hungarian Baptist Convention of North America, 1370 Michigan Blvd., Lincoln Park, MI 48146. TEL 313-382-3735. Ed. Rev. A. Geza Herjeczki. Circ: 800 (paid and free).

289.3 USA ISSN 1550-3194
BX8627
➤ **THE F A R M S REVIEW.** (Foundation for Ancient Research and Mormon Studies) Text in English. 1989. a. USD 17.50 per issue (effective 2011). bk.rev. back issues avail. **Document type:** *Journal, Academic/Scholarly.* **Description:** Reviews books published in the past year on Mormon studies.
Former titles (until 2003): F A R M S Review of Books (1099-9450); (until 1996): Review of Books on the Book of Mormon (1050-7930)
Related titles: CD-ROM ed.; Online - full content ed.: USD 12.50 (effective 2003).
Indexed: A21, RI-1, RI-2.
Published by: Brigham Young University, The Neal A. Maxwell Institute for Religious Scholarship, The Neal A. Maxwell Institute for Religious Scholarship, Brigham Young University, Provo, UT 84602. TEL 801-422-9229, FAX 801-422-0040, maxwell_institute@byu.edu, http://mi.byu.edu.

295 USA ISSN 1068-2376
BL1500
F E Z A N A JOURNAL. Text mainly in English; Text occasionally in Persian, Modern. 1988. q. **Document type:** *Journal, Academic/Scholarly.* **Description:** Provides news and views, as well as educational and inspirational articles about the Zarathushti religion, culture and practices as they pertain to Zarathushtis in North America.
Published by: Federation of Zoroastrian Associations of North America, 8615 Meadowbrook Dr, Burr Ridge, IL 60527. TEL 630-468-2705, FAX 630-468-2705, admin@fezana.org.

289.6 USA
F L G C NEWSLETTER. Text in English. 1976. q. looseleaf. USD 10. bk.rev. **Document type:** *Newsletter.* **Description:** Carries articles of special interest to lesbian and gay Quakers, including current topics in same-sex marriage among Quakers.
Published by: Friends for Lesbian and Gay Concerns, 143 Campbell Ave, Ithaca, NY 14850. TEL 607-277-1024. Ed. Janis Kelly. Circ: 830.

289.1 USA ISSN 2158-4478
FAIRHOPE UNITARIAN FELLOWSHIP. NEWSLETTER. Text in English. 19??. m. free (effective 2010). back issues avail. **Document type:** *Newsletter, Trade.* **Description:** Contains members from different backgrounds, who represents a broad spectrum of conscientious, intellectual and spiritual perspectives.
Published by: Unitarian-Universalist Fellowship of Fairhope, 1150 Fairhope Ave, Fairhope, AL 36532. TEL 251-929-3207, fairhopeunitarian@att.net. Ed., Pub. Nancy Martin.

230 ZAF ISSN 0014-7044
FAITH FOR DAILY LIVING; a guide to confident Christian living. Text in English. 1960. bi-m. free.
Published by: Faith for Daily Living Foundation, PO Box 3737, Durban, KwaZulu-Natal, South Africa. Ed. Arnold J Walker. Circ: 120,000 (controlled).

299 USA ISSN 1931-5597
FAITHFULNESS IN THE FAMILY. Text in English. 2006. irreg. **Document type:** *Magazine, Consumer.*
Related titles: Spanish ed.: Fidelidad en la Familia. ISSN 1932-2682. 2002.
Published by: Faithfulness in the Family, Inc., PO Box 640, Oakhurst, CA 93644-0640. TEL 559-658-8598, edtuggy@faithfulnessinthefamily.org, http://www.faithfulnessinthefamily.org/index.html.

289.7 CAN ISSN 0014-7303
FAMILY LIFE. Text in English. 1968. m. (11/yr.). USD 9. bk.rev. illus. reprints avail.
Related titles: Microform ed.: (from PQC).
Indexed: A22.
Published by: (Amish Church), Pathway Publishing Corporation, Rte. 4, Aylmer, ON N5H 2R3, Canada. Circ: 23,300.

289.9 USA
FIERY SYNTHESIS. Text in English. 1965. 6/yr. donation. bk.rev. **Document type:** *Newsletter.*
Formerly: Blue Aquarius
Related titles: Online - full content ed.
Published by: Saraydarian Institute, PO Box 267, Sedona, AZ 86339. TEL 713-227-8887, FAX 713-227-5049, info@saraydarian.org. Ed. Joann Saraydarian. R&P Joann Saraydarian TEL 520-282-2655. Circ: 400.

299 GBR
FINDHORN FOUNDATION. GUEST PROGRAMME. Text in English. 1980. s-a. free. adv. 36 p./no.; **Document type:** *Catalog.* **Description:** Discusses courses, workshops, and programs and reflects on the Findhorn community spiritual philosophy.
Published by: Findhorn Foundation, The Park, Findhorn, Forres, IV36 0TZ, United Kingdom. TEL 44-1309-690311, FAX 44-1309-691301.

289.1 USA ISSN 2159-2721
THE FIRST UNITARIAN SOCIETY OF WESTCHESTER.NEWSLETTER. Text in English. 1947. m. **Document type:** *Newsletter, Trade.*
Former titles (until 19??): The Unitarian Church. Newsletter (2159-2713); (until 1970): The Unitarian Church. Newsletter (2159-2705); The Yonkers Unitarian (2159-2691)
Published by: The First Unitarian Society of Westchester, 25 Old Jackson Ave, Hastings-on-Hudson, NY 10706. TEL 914-478-2710, info@westchesteruu.org, http://www.westchesteruu.org/.

289 USA ISSN 0015-9182
BX7990
FOURSQUARE WORLD ADVANCE. Text in English. 1923. bi-m. free. bk.rev. illus.
Formerly: Foursquare Magazine
Published by: International Church of the Foursquare Gospel, 1910 Sunset Blvd, Ste 200, Box 26902, Los Angeles, CA 90026-0176. TEL 213-989-4234, FAX 213-989-4544. Ed. Ronald D Williams. R&P Ron Williams TEL 213-989-4220. Circ: 100,000.

289.3 USA ISSN 0009-4102
BX8605.1
FRIEND. Text in English. 1902. m. USD 8; USD 1.50 per issue (effective 2009). bk.rev. illus. index. back issues avail. **Document type:** *Magazine, Consumer.* **Description:** Contains stories and activities for children or parents with children - ages 3 to 11.
Formerly (until 19??): Children's Friend
Related titles: Braille ed.; Online - full text ed.: free (effective 2009).
Published by: Church of Jesus Christ of Latter-day Saints, 50 E North Temple St, Salt Lake City, UT 84150. TEL 801-240-2950, 800-537-5971, FAX 801-240-5997. Eds. Spencer J Condie, Victor D Cave. **Subscr. to:** Distribution Services, P O Box 26368, Salt Lake City, UT 84126.

289.6 GBR ISSN 0016-1268
FRIEND; a Quaker weekly journal. Text in English. 1843. w. GBP 72 domestic; GBP 94 foreign (effective 2009). adv. bk.rev. illus. index. back issues avail. **Document type:** *Newspaper, Consumer.* **Description:** Covers news, features, personal stories, arts, humour and friendship.
Related titles: Microform ed.: (from WMP); Online - full text ed.: GBP 45 (effective 2009).
Published by: Friend Publications Ltd., 173 Euston Rd, London, NW1 2BJ, United Kingdom. TEL 44-20-76631010, FAX 44-20-76631182. Adv. contact George Penaluna TEL 44-1535-630230. page GBP 595; 165 x 225. Circ: 4,500.

267 GBR ISSN 0071-9587
BX7676.A1
FRIENDS HISTORICAL SOCIETY. JOURNAL. Text in English. 1903. a. GBP 8, USD 16 to individuals; GBP 13, USD 26 to institutions. adv. bk.rev. **Document type:** *Journal, Academic/Scholarly.*
Indexed: AmH&L, CA, HistAb, P30, PCI, T02.
Published by: Friends Historical Society, c/o Friends House, Euston Rd, London, NW1 2BJ, United Kingdom. Ed. Howard F Gregg. Circ: 500.

289.6 USA ISSN 0016-1322
BX7601
FRIENDS JOURNAL; Quaker thought and life today. Text in English. 1955. m. USD 35 in North America; USD 43 elsewhere (effective 2005). adv. bk.rev. illus. index. reprints avail. **Document type:** *Magazine, Consumer.* **Description:** Includes articles on peace, social concerns, Quaker history, and spirituality. Contains poetry, news, humor, reports and classified advertisements on schools, publications, services and employment opportunities.
Formed by the merger (1827-1955): Friend (0362-8957); (1902-1955): Friends Intelligencer (0362-8965)
Related titles: Microform ed.: (from PQC); (from PQC).
Indexed: A22, GeoRef, MLA-IB, PRA.
Published by: Friends Publishing Corp., 1216 Arch St 2A, Philadelphia, PA 19107-2835. TEL 215-563-8629, FAX 215-568-1377, info@friendsjournal.org. Pub. Susan M Corson-Finnerty. R&P Kenneth Sutton. Adv. contact N Gulendran. page USD 525; trim 8.5 x 11. Circ: 8,500 (paid).

289.6 GBR ISSN 0016-1365
BX7748.I65
FRIENDS WORLD NEWS. Text in English. 1939. s-a. free to contributors. bk.rev. illus. back issues avail. **Document type:** *Newsletter.* **Description:** Presents articles from Quakers worldwide.
Indexed: CERDIC.
Published by: Friends World Committee for Consultation, 173 Euston Rd, London, NW1 2AX, United Kingdom. TEL 44-20-76631199, world@friendsworldoffice.org.

289.6 GBR ISSN 2044-5180
▼ **FUTURE LEADERS.** Text in English. 2010. a. GBP 5.95 per issue domestic; USD 11.99 per issue in United States (effective 2011). **Document type:** *Magazine, Consumer.* **Description:** Profiles some of Britain's brightest students of African and African Caribbean origin.
Published by: Powerful Media Ltd., Quay House, 2 Admirals Way, London, E14 9XG, United Kingdom. TEL 44-20-77887937, FAX 44-20-77883470, info@powerful-media.com. Ed. Adenike Adenitire.

289.9 USA
GEORGIAN ANNUAL. Text in English. 1989. a. USD 35. adv. bk.rev. illus. back issues avail.
Published by: Georgian Church, 1908 Verde St, Bakersfield, CA 93304. TEL 805-323-3309. Ed. Fauna.

289.9 USA
GEORGIAN MONTHLY. Text in English. 1976. 12/yr. USD 8. adv. bk.rev. illus. back issues avail.
Formerly: Georgian Newsletter
Published by: Georgian Church, 1908 Verde St, Bakersfield, CA 93304. TEL 805-323-3309. Ed. Fauna.

289.9 NLD ISSN 1876-2247
▼ **GLOBAL PENTECOSTAL AND CHARISMATIC STUDIES.** Text in English. 2009. irreg., latest vol.7, 2011. price varies. **Document type:** *Monographic series, Academic/Scholarly.* **Description:** Covers the Pentecostal and Charismatic movements with a historical, social scientific, and theological perspective.
Published by: Brill, PO Box 9000, Leiden, 2300 PA, Netherlands. TEL 31-71-5353500, FAX 31-71-5317532, cs@brill.nl. Eds. Andrew Davies, William Kay.

289.9 CAN ISSN 1481-2282
GOOD TIDINGS. Text in English. 1935. 10/yr. CAD 15, USD 20 (effective 2003). adv. bk.rev. illus. 20 p./no. 3 cols./p.; back issues avail. **Document type:** *Magazine, Consumer.* **Description:** Covers the Bible, church news, missions, and Christian service.
Published by: The Pentecostal Assemblies of Newfoundland and Labrador, Good Tidings Press, 57 Thorburn Rd, P O BOX 8895, Sta A, St. John's, NF A1B 3T2, Canada. TEL 709-753-6314, FAX 709-753-4945, paon@paon.nf.ca, http://www.paon.nf.ca. Ed. H Paul Foster. R&P Burton K Janes. Adv. contact Wanda Buckle. Circ: 7,500.

299 956 USA ISSN 1935-441X
GORGIAS MANDAEAN STUDIES. Text in English. 2007. irreg., latest vol.2, 2007. USD 349 per issue (effective 2010). **Document type:** *Monographic series, Academic/Scholarly.* **Description:** Addresses the religion, language, literature, and history of the Mandaean community of the Middle East.
Published by: Gorgias Press LLC, 954 River Rd, Piscataway, NJ 08854. TEL 732-885-8900, FAX 732-885-8908, helpdesk@gorgiaspress.com, http://www.gorgiaspress.com/bookshop/default.aspx.

299.514 USA
GREAT TAO. Text in English. 1986. q. USD 10 to members.
Published by: American Taoist and Buddhist Association, 81 Bowery St, New York, NY 10002.

289.9 GBR ISSN 0957-8935
THE GREATER WORLD NEWSLETTER. Text in English. 1928. q. free (effective 2009). bk.rev. back issues avail. **Document type:** *Newsletter, Academic/Scholarly.* **Description:** Disseminates spiritual teachings based on Christian Spiritualism.
Formerly (until 1989): Greater World (0046-6352)
Related titles: Online - full text ed.
Published by: Greater World Christian Spiritualist Association, Greater World Spiritual Centre, 3-5 Conway St, Fitzrovia, London, WIT 6BJ, United Kingdom. TEL 44-20-74367555, FAX 44-20-75803485, greaterworld@btconnect.com, http://www.greaterworld.co.uk/.

GREGORIOS O PALAMAS. *see* RELIGIONS AND THEOLOGY—Eastern Orthodox

289.9 AUS ISSN 1324-9428
GRID. Text in English. 1981. 3/yr. bk.rev. **Document type:** *Newsletter, Consumer.* **Description:** Covers Christian leadership and Third World development issues.
Published by: World Vision Australia, GPO Box 399C, Melbourne, VIC 3001, Australia. TEL 61-3-92872233, FAX 61-3-92872427, grid@wva.org.au, http://www.worldvision.com.au. Circ: 16,500.

243 CAN
HALLELUJAH! (VANCOUVER). Text in English. 1949. bi-m. bk.rev. illus. back issues avail. **Document type:** *Magazine, Consumer.* **Description:** Magazine of aggressive evangelical Christianity and social activism.
Formerly (until 1990): Truth on Fire (0821-6371)
Published by: Bible Holiness Movement, P O Box 223, Sta A, Vancouver, BC V6C 2M3, Canada. TEL 250-492-3376. Ed. Wesley H Wakefield. Circ: 10,000.

HALLESCHE FORSCHUNGEN. *see* HISTORY—History Of Europe

289.9 USA ISSN 1093-2372
HARE KRISHNA WORLD. Text in English. 1982. bi-m. adv. bk.rev. back issues avail. **Document type:** *Newspaper, Consumer.* **Description:** Offers news, events and services related to the Hare Krishna movement.
Formerly (until 1997): I S K C O N World Review (0748-2280)
Published by: International Society for Krishna Consciousness, PO Box 819, Alachua, FL 32616. TEL 386-462-2017, hkw@iskcon.net, http://hkw.iskcon.net. Ed. Mukunda Goswami. R&P Sarva Satya. Adv. contact Kunti Dasi. page USD 520; 10 x 15.5. Circ: 10,000 (paid).

299
HAVURAH. Text in English. 1983. q. **Description:** Deals with issues of interest to Jewish believers in Jesus.
Formerly (until 199?): Mishpochah Message (1068-4379)
Published by: Jews for Jesus, 60 Haight St, San Francisco, CA 94102. TEL 415-864-2600, FAX 415-552-8325, http://www.jewsforjesus.org. R&P Melissa Moskowitz.

289.9 USA
HEALING THOUGHTS. Text in English. 6/yr. USD 18; USD 25 foreign.
Published by: Plainfield Christian Science Church (Independent), 905 Prospect Ave, Box 5619, Plainfield, NJ 07060. TEL 908-756-4669.

289.1 USA
HEART TO HEART NEWSLETTER. Text in English. bi-m. back issues avail. **Description:** Contains news and articles about Church Universal and Triumphant, and the Royal Teton Ranch.
Formerly: Royal Teton Ranch News
Published by: The Summit Lighthouse, PO Box 5000, Corwin Springs, MT 59030-5000. TEL 406-484-9500, FAX 406-848-9555. Ed. Chris L Kelley.

248.4819 USA ISSN 2155-5826
▼ **HEARTS UP.** Text in English. 2009. m. free (effective 2010). back issues avail. **Document type:** *Consumer.* **Description:** Details on concepts and spiritual dynamics germane to discipleship beyond the elementary teachings of Christ and issues associated with real-life application and transformation during trials.
Media: Online - full text.
Published by: Keys To Understanding Life, 1551 N Walnut Ave, Ste 13-258, New Braunfels, TX 78130.

289.3 USA ISSN 1541-6143
HERALD (INDEPENDENCE); community of christ. Text in English. 1860. m. USD 26 in US & Canada; USD 35 elsewhere (effective 2002). adv. bk.rev. illus.; tr.lit. **Document type:** *Magazine, Trade.*
Formerly (until 2001): Saints' Herald (0036-3251)
Related titles: Microfilm ed.
Published by: (Reorganized Church of Jesus Christ of Latter Day Saints), Herald Publishing House, 1001 W Walnut, Box 390, Independence, MO 64051. TEL 816-521-3015, 800-767-8181, FAX 816-521-3066, http://www.cofchrist.org. Eds. James B. Hannah, Linda L Booth. Circ: 26,000.

289.5 USA ISSN 1520-7072
LE HERAUT DE LA CHRISTIAN SCIENCE. Text in French. m.
Formerly (unitl 1998): Le Heraut de la Science Chretienne (0145-7470)
Related titles: Swedish ed.: Kristen Vetenskaps Harold. ISSN 1934-3086; Spanish ed.: Heraldo de la Ciencia Cristiana. ISSN 1934-3000; Dutch ed.: De Christian Science Heraut. ISSN 1543-1495; German ed.: Der Christian Science Herold. ISSN 1520-7080. 1903; Italian ed.: Araldo della Christian Science. ISSN 1934-3051; Norwegian ed.: Kristen Vitenskaps Herold. ISSN 1934-3078; Danish ed.: Kristen Videnskabs Herold. ISSN 1934-3027; Greek ed.: Kerykas tes Christian Science. ISSN 1934-3035; Indonesian ed.: Bentara Ilmupengetahuan Kristen. ISSN 1934-3043; Japanese ed.: Kirisutokyo Kagaku Sakigake. ISSN 1934-306X; Portuguese ed.: Arauto da Ciencia Crista. ISSN 1934-2985.
Published by: The Christian Science Publishing Society, One Norway St, Boston, MA 02115. TEL 800-288-7090.

289.3 USA ISSN 0300-8851
HEROLD DER WAHRHEIT. Text in English, German. 1912. m. USD 8 (effective 2000). index. **Document type:** *Magazine, Consumer.*
Published by: Amish Publishing Association, c/o Schlabach Printing, Sec.-Treas., 2881 State Rte. 93, Sugercreek, OH 44681. TEL 330-852-4687, 888-406-2665, FAX 330-852-2689. Eds. Cephos Kauffman, Henry T Miller. Circ: 800 (paid).

299 USA ISSN 1540-4919
HONORBOUND. Text in English. 2001. q. USD 3 per issue (effective 2007). **Document type:** *Magazine, Consumer.*
Published by: General Council of the Assemblies of God, 1445 N Boonville Ave, Springfield, MO 65802-1894. TEL 417-862-2781, 877-840-4800, FAX 417-862-5881, info@ag.org, http://www.ag.org.

299 USA ISSN 1555-5674
HOPEGIVERS JOURNAL. Text in English. 2005. q. back issues avail. **Document type:** *Magazine, Consumer.*
Published by: Hopegivers International, PO Box 8808, Columbus, GA 31908. TEL 706-323-4673, 866-373-4673, http://www.hopegivers.org/Home.htm.

230 GBR
I C F QUARTERLY PAPERS. Text in English. 1963. q. GBP 15; GBP 23 foreign. bk.rev. **Document type:** *Newsletter.* **Description:** Contains articles helping industry, commerce and finance to operate within a framework of Christian principles and values to the ultimate benefit of all employees, management, shareholders, customers and the whole community.
Formerly: I C F Quarterly (0018-8913)
Published by: Industry Churches Forum, 86 Leadenhall St, London, EC3A 2BJ, United Kingdom. TEL 44-171-283-6120, FAX 44-171-549-9161. Ed. D Welbourn. Circ: 2,000.

291 USA ISSN 2154-820X
▼ **I C S A TODAY.** Text in English. 2010. 3/yr. **Document type:** *Magazine, Trade.* **Description:** Features news, announcements, profiles, essays and information on cults.
Related titles: Online - full text ed.: ISSN 2154-8218. 2010.
Published by: International Cultic Studies Association, PO Box 2265, Bonita Springs, FL 34133. TEL 239-514-3081, FAX 305-393-8193, mail@icsamail.com, http://www.icsahome.com.

ICONOGRAPHY OF RELIGIONS. SECTION 10, NORTH AMERICA. *see* ART

ICONOGRAPHY OF RELIGIONS. SECTION 11, ANCIENT AMERICA. *see* ART

ICONOGRAPHY OF RELIGIONS. SECTION 14, IRAN. *see* ART

ICONOGRAPHY OF RELIGIONS. SECTION 15, MESOPOTAMIA AND THE NEAR EAST. *see* ART

ICONOGRAPHY OF RELIGIONS. SECTION 16, EGYPT. *see* ART

ICONOGRAPHY OF RELIGIONS. SECTION 19, ANCIENT EUROPE. *see* ART

ICONOGRAPHY OF RELIGIONS. SECTION 7, AFRICA. *see* ART

ICONOGRAPHY OF RELIGIONS. SECTION 8, ARCTIC PEOPLES. *see* ART

ICONOGRAPHY OF RELIGIONS. SECTION 9, SOUTH AMERICA. *see* ART

293 USA ISSN 1937-397X
BL860
IDUNNA. Text in English. 1988. q. USD 25 (effective 2008). **Document type:** *Magazine, Consumer.* **Description:** Dedicated to the practice and promotion of pre-Christian heathen religion of German Northern Europe.
Published by: The Troth, PO Box 1369, Oldsmar, FL 34677. troth-contact@thetroth.org, http://www.thetroth.org. Pub. Mark Donegan.

299.935 DEU ISSN 1437-1898
BP605.N48
INFO3; Anthroposophie heute. Text in German. 1976. m. EUR 35 domestic; EUR 44 foreign (effective 2003). adv. film rev.; bk.rev. illus. back issues avail. **Document type:** *Magazine, Academic/Scholarly.*
Former titles (until 1998): Zeitschrift Info3 (0936-546X); (until 1983): Info3 (0721-5347).
Indexed: DIP, IBR, IBZ.
Published by: Info3 Verlag, Kirchgartenstr 1, Frankfurt Am Main, 60439, Germany. TEL 49-69-584647, FAX 49-69-584616, vertrieb@info3.de. Ed. Jens Heisterkamp. Pub. Ramon Bruell. Adv. contact Anke Okyere TEL 49-69-57000891. Circ: 16,000.

299.934 GBR ISSN 1465-4237
INSIGHT (LONDON, 1960). Text in English. 1929. q. free to members (effective 2009). bk.rev. illus. back issues avail. **Document type:** *Journal, Academic/Scholarly.* **Description:** Contains news, reviews and events in the field of spirituality and allied subjects under the metaphysical umbrella.
Former titles (until 1998): Theosophical Journal (0040-5876); (until 1960): Theosophical News & Notes
Published by: Theosophical Society in England, 50 Gloucester Pl, London, W1H 4EA, United Kingdom. TEL 44-20-75639817, info@theosoc.org.uk.

INSPIRED LIVING MAGAZINE. *see* LIFESTYLE

294.4 GBR ISSN 1748-1074
➤ **INTERNATIONAL JOURNAL OF JAINA STUDIES.** Text in English. 2005. q. free (effective 2009). **Document type:** *Journal, Academic/Scholarly.* **Description:** Dedicated to the promotion of scholarly exchange among academics, researchers, and students engaged in the study of the Jainism and Jain culture.
Media: Online - full text.
Published by: University of London, Centre of Jaina Studies, School of Oriental and African Studies, Thornhaugh St, London, WC1H 0XG, United Kingdom. TEL 44-20-76372388, FAX 44-20-74363844, jainstudies@soas.ac.uk, http://www.soas.ac.uk/jainastudies/. Ed. Peter Flugel.

289.3 GBR ISSN 1757-5532
➤ **INTERNATIONAL JOURNAL OF MORMON STUDIES.** Text in English. 2008. s-a. **Document type:** *Journal, Academic/Scholarly.*
Related titles: Online - full text ed.: free (effective 2011).
Indexed: A01, T02.
Address: 89 Victoria Park Rd, Tunstall, Stoke on Trent, Staffordshire ST6 6DX, United Kingdom. Ed. David M Morris.

289.9 USA ISSN 0886-6910
ISKCON REVIEW; academic perspectives on the Hare Krishna movement. Text in English. 1985. a. USD 6. bk.rev. back issues avail.
Published by: Institute for Vaishnava Studies, c/o Steven J Gelberg, 41 West Allens Ln, Philadelphia, PA 19119. TEL 215-242-6578. Circ: 1,200.

ISLAMIC DISCOURSE; a magazine of muslims in america. *see* SOCIAL SCIENCES: COMPREHENSIVE WORKS

R

289.9 USA ISSN 1092-4973
ISSACHARFILE; keeping church leaders in touch with the times. Text in English. 1917. m. USD 11.95 (effective 2001). bk.rev. bibl.; charts; illus. back issues avail. **Document type:** *Newsletter.*
Formerly: International Pentecostal Holiness Advocate (0145-6970)
Related titles: Microform ed.
Indexed: CERDIC.
Published by: (International Pentecostal Holiness Church), Lifesprings Resources, PO Box 12609, Oklahoma City, OK 73157. TEL 405-787-7110, FAX 405-789-3957. Ed. James D Leggett. Pub. Gregory K Hearn. R&P Shirley G Spencer. Circ: 2,500. **Subscr. to:** PO Box 9, Franklin, GA 30639. TEL 706-245-7272, FAX 706-245-5488, http://www.lifesprings.net.

299 USA ISSN 0741-0352
BR158
ISSUES (SAN FRANCISCO); a messianic jewish perspective. Text in English. 1978. bi-m. free (effective 2010). bk.rev. back issues avail. **Document type:** *Journal, Academic/Scholarly.*
Related titles: Online - full text ed.
Published by: (Jews for Jesus), A Messianic Jewish Perspective, 60 Haight St, San Francisco, CA 94102. TEL 415-864-2600, FAX 415-552-8325, jfj@jews-for-jesus.org. Eds. Matt Sieger, Susan Perlman. Circ: 40,000 (controlled).

294.4 IND ISSN 0021-4043
B162.5
JAIN JOURNAL. Text in English. 1966. q. INR 500 (effective 2011). bk.rev. bibl.; illus. index.
Indexed: DIP, IBR, IBZ.
—Ingenta.
Published by: Jain Bhawan, P-25 Kalakar St., Kolkata, West Bengal 700 007, India. TEL 91-33-22682655. **Subscr. to:** I N S I O Scientific Books & Periodicals, PO Box 7234, Indraprastha HPO, New Delhi 110 002, India.

294.4 GBR ISSN 1532-0472
BL1300
JAIN SPIRIT; advancing Jainism into the future. Text in English. 1999. q. GBP 16 membership (effective 2002). back issues avail. **Document type:** *Magazine, Consumer.* **Description:** Promotes one of the oldest vegetarian and environment-friendly cultures in the world. Janism is a culture which values and respects all living beings, irrespective of color or creed.
Published by: Jain Spirit Ltd, 14 Cowdray Office Centre, Cowdray Ave, Colchester, Essex CO1 1QB, United Kingdom. TEL 44-1206-500037, FAX 44-1206-500279, office@jainspirit.org.

299.56 JPN ISSN 0304-1042
BL2202
➤ **JAPANESE JOURNAL OF RELIGIOUS STUDIES.** Text in English. 1960. s-a. JPY 3,500 domestic to individuals; EUR 30 in Europe to individuals; USD 25 elsewhere to individuals; JPY 5,000 domestic to institutions; EUR 40 in Europe to institutions; USD 35 elsewhere to institutions (effective 2005). adv. bk.rev. illus.; stat. cum.index. reprints avail. **Document type:** *Journal, Academic/Scholarly.* **Description:** Presents academic studies of Japan's religions.
Formerly (until 1974): Contemporary Religions in Japan (0010-7557)
Related titles: Online - full text ed.: free (effective 2011).
Indexed: A20, A21, A22, ArtHuCI, BAS, CA, DIP, FR, IBR, IBZ, MLA-IB, P28, P48, P53, P54, PCI, PQC, R&TA, RASB, RI-1, RI-2, SCOPUS, T02, W07.
—BLDSC (4658.650000), IE, Infotrieve, Ingenta, INIST.
Published by: Nanzan Institute for Religion and Culture, 18 Yamazato-cho, Showa-ku, Nagoya, 466-8673, Japan. TEL 81-52-8323111, FAX 81-52-8336157, nirc@ic.nanzan-u.ac.jp, http://www.nanzan-u.ac.jp/SHUBUNKEN/index.htm. Ed. Paul I Swanson. Circ: 600.

➤ **JAPANESE RELIGIONS.** *see* RELIGIONS AND THEOLOGY

299 NLD ISSN 1570-078X
JERUSALEM STUDIES IN RELIGION AND CULTURE. Text in English. 2002. irreg., latest vol.9, 2008. price varies. **Document type:** *Monographic series, Academic/Scholarly.*
Indexed: IZBG.
Published by: Brill, PO Box 9000, Leiden, 2300 PA, Netherlands. TEL 31-71-5353500, FAX 31-71-5317532, cs@brill.nl. Eds. David Shulman, Guy Stroumsa.

299 USA ISSN 0740-5901
BR158
JEWS FOR JESUS NEWSLETTER. Text in English. 1973. m. free. bk.rev. illus. **Document type:** *Newsletter, Consumer.*
Related titles: Microfilm ed.
Published by: Jews for Jesus, 60 Haight St, San Francisco, CA 94102. TEL 415-864-2600, FAX 415-552-8325, jfj@jewsforjesus.org, http://www.jewsforjesus.org. Ed., R&P Ruth Rosen. Circ: 123,000 (controlled).

299 USA ISSN 1932-0442
JOTTINGS (GREENVILLE). Text in English. 2004. irreg. **Document type:** *Newsletter, Consumer.*
Published by: Mere Christianity Forum, Inc., PO Box 4261, Greenville, SC 29608. TEL 864-834-2228, http://www.mcfinc.org/home.

299 NLD ISSN 1569-2116
BL1060
➤ **JOURNAL OF ANCIENT NEAR EASTERN RELIGIONS.** Text in English. s-a. EUR 152, USD 212 to institutions; EUR 166, USD 232 combined subscription to institutions (print & online eds.) (effective 2012). back issues avail.; reprint service avail. from PSC. **Document type:** *Journal, Academic/Scholarly.* **Description:** Focuses on religions in the regions comprising Egypt, Mesopotamia, Syria-Palestine, and Anatolia from pre-historic times to the start of the common era. Also covers the cultural influence of these religions on neighboring areas, especially the western Mediterranean.
Related titles: Online - full text ed.: ISSN 1569-2124. EUR 138, USD 193 to institutions (effective 2012) (from IngentaConnect).
Indexed: A01, A02, A03, A08, A20, A21, A22, ArtHuCI, CA, E01, IZBG, M10, RI-1, SCOPUS, T02, W07.
—Ingenta. **CCC.**
Published by: Brill, PO Box 9000, Leiden, 2300 PA, Netherlands. TEL 31-71-5353500, FAX 31-71-5317532, cs@brill.nl. Ed. Chris Woods. **Dist. by:** Turpin Distribution Services Ltd., Pegasus Dr, Stratton Business Park, Biggleswade, Bedfordshire SG18 8QB, United Kingdom. TEL 44-1767-604954, FAX 44-1767-601640, custserv@turpin-distribution.com, http://www.turpin-distribution.com/.

299 USA ISSN 2150-2781
▼ **JOURNAL OF ATHEISM AND ALTERNATIVE WORSHIP.** Text in English. forthcoming 2011. q. **Document type:** *Journal, Academic/Scholarly.* **Description:** Publishes papers on the human tendency for worship, the consequences of this tendency, and the role of social intelligence and cultural norms in self-perception and emotional processes.
Media: Online - full content.
Published by: Kaiser Peer Publishing, PO Box 734, Churchville, NY 14428. TEL 585-393-1464, davidkaiser@spiritualneuroscience.org.

299.51 USA ISSN 0737-769X
BL1802
➤ **JOURNAL OF CHINESE RELIGIONS.** Text in English. 1975. a. USD 45 per issue to institutions; free to members (effective 2011). bk.rev. back issues avail. **Document type:** *Journal, Academic/Scholarly.*
Incorporates (1988-1997): Taoist Resources (1061-8805); Former titles (until 1982): Society for the Study of Chinese Religions. Bulletin (0271-3446); (until 1977): Society for the Study of Chinese Religions. Newsletter
Related titles: Online - full text ed.
Indexed: A21, BAS, RI-1.
—Ingenta.
Published by: Society for the Study of Chinese Religions, 2223 Fulton St, Rm 506, Ctr for Chinese Studies, UC-Berkeley, Berkeley, CA 94720. TEL 510-643-6328, FAX 510-643-7062, sscr@gsu.edu. Ed. Mark Csikszentmihalyi.

299.513 USA ISSN 1941-5516
BL1899
JOURNAL OF DAOIST STUDIES. Text in English. 2008 (Jun.). a. USD 22 per issue (effective 2011). **Document type:** *Journal, Academic/Scholarly.* **Description:** Contains three main parts: Academic Articles; Forum on Contemporary Practice; and News of the Field.
Related titles: Online - full text ed.: ISSN 1941-5524. USD 12 (effective 2011).
Indexed: A01, CA, T02.
Published by: Three Pines Press, PO Box 609, Dunedin, FL 34697. TEL 727-501-6915, FAX 815-301-2713, orders@threepinespress.com.

289.9 BEL ISSN 1783-1555
➤ **THE JOURNAL OF EASTERN CHRISTIAN STUDIES.** Text in Dutch, English, French, German; Summaries in English. 1948. s-a. EUR 60 combined subscription (print & online eds.) (effective 2011). adv. bk.rev. bibl.; illus. index, cum.index. 400 p./no.; **Document type:** *Journal, Academic/Scholarly.* **Description:** Review on Christianity in Eastern Europe and the Middle East.
Former titles (until 2001): Het Christelijk Oosten (0009-5141); (until 1964): Het Christelijk Oosten en Hereniging (1572-6614)
Related titles: Online - full text ed.: ISSN 1783-1520.
Indexed: A21, CERDIC, DIP, FR, IBR, IBZ, RASB.
—IE, INIST.
Published by: (Instituut voor Oosters Christendom NLD), Peeters Publishers, Bondgenotenlaan 153, Leuven, 3000, Belgium. TEL 32-16-235170, FAX 32-16-228500, peeters@peeters-leuven.be, http://www.peeters-leuven.be. Eds. B Groen, J Verheyden. Circ: 360.

293 USA ISSN 1555-6794
THE JOURNAL OF GERMANIC MYTHOLOGY AND FOLKLORE. Text in English. 2004. s-a. **Document type:** *Journal, Academic/Scholarly.* **Description:** Designed as forum to share new scholarship on topics relating to Germanic.
Related titles: Online - full text ed.: ISSN 1555-6808. free (effective 2010).
Published by: The Templin Foundation, Inc., 6533 W Howard Ave Ste 4, Milwaukee, WI 53200. http://templinfoundation.jgmf.org/.

JOURNAL OF HINDU - CHRISTIAN STUDIES. *see* RELIGIONS AND THEOLOGY—Hindu

289.7 CAN ISSN 0824-5053
BX8101
➤ **JOURNAL OF MENNONITE STUDIES.** Text in English, German. 1983. a. CAD 18 to individuals; CAD 25 to institutions (effective 2002). adv. bk.rev. back issues avail. **Document type:** *Journal, Academic/Scholarly.*
Indexed: A01, A21, AmH&L, C03, CA, CBCARef, HistAb, P48, PQC, RI-1, RILM, T02.
—CCC.
Published by: University of Winnipeg, 515 Portage Ave, Winnipeg, MB R3B 2E9, Canada. TEL 204-786-9391, FAX 204-774-4134, Roy.Loewen@uwinnipeg.ca. Ed. Royden Loewen. Circ: 600 (paid).

289.309 USA ISSN 0094-7342
BX8601
➤ **JOURNAL OF MORMON HISTORY.** Text in English. 1974. q. free to members (effective 2010). adv. bk.rev. back issues avail. **Document type:** *Journal, Academic/Scholarly.* **Description:** Publishes scholarly articles dealing with Mormon history.
Related titles: Online - full text ed.
Indexed: A21, AmH&L, CA, CERDIC, HistAb, P30, RI-1, RI-2, T02.
—Ingenta.
Published by: Mormon History Association, 10 West 100 South, Ste 610, Salt Lake City, UT 84101. Ed. Patricia Lyn Scott. Circ: 1,000.

299.6 NLD ISSN 0022-4200
BL2400 CODEN: JRAFF2
➤ **JOURNAL OF RELIGION IN AFRICA.** Text in English, French. 1967. q. EUR 284, USD 398 to institutions; EUR 310, USD 434 combined subscription to institutions (print & online eds.) (effective 2012). adv. bk.rev. bibl.; charts; illus. cum.index: vols.1-26 (1968-1996). back issues avail.; reprint service avail. from PSC. **Document type:** *Journal, Academic/Scholarly.* **Description:** Studies of the forms and history of religion on the African continent, with particular emphasis on sub-Saharan Africa and the relationships between Christianity and Islam in the region.
Incorporates (1971-1975): African Religious Research (0044-6602)
Related titles: Online - full text ed.: ISSN 1570-0666. EUR 258, USD 362 to institutions (effective 2012) (from IngentaConnect); ◆ Supplement(s): Studies of Religion in Africa. ISSN 0169-9814.
Indexed: A01, A02, A03, A08, A20, A21, A22, AICP, ASD, AmHI, ArtHuCI, CA, CCA, CERDIC, DIP, E01, FR, H07, HistAb, I14, IBR, IBSS, IBZ, IIBP, IZBG, M10, MLA-IB, P30, PCI, PerIslam, R&TA, RASB, RI-1, RI-2, RILM, S02, S03, SCOPUS, SOPODA, SociolAb, T02, W07.
—IE, Infotrieve, Ingenta, INIST. **CCC.**
Published by: Brill, PO Box 9000, Leiden, 2300 PA, Netherlands. TEL 31-71-5353500, FAX 31-71-5317532, cs@brill.nl. Eds. Adeline Masquelier, Brad Weiss. **Dist. by:** Turpin Distribution Services Ltd., Pegasus Dr, Stratton Business Park, Biggleswade, Bedfordshire SG18 8QB, United Kingdom. TEL 44-1767-604954, FAX 44-1767-601640, custserv@turpin-distribution.com, http://www.turpin-distribution.com/.

294.6 IND ISSN 0379-8194
BL2017
JOURNAL OF SIKH STUDIES. Text in English. 1974. s-a. INR 150 to individuals; INR 300 to institutions (effective 2011). bk.rev. **Document type:** *Journal, Academic/Scholarly.* **Description:** Aims to promote Sikh studies as a scientific discipline.
Indexed: IBR, IBZ.
Published by: Guru Nanak Dev University Press, c/o Ajaib Singh Brar, Amritsar, 143 005, India. TEL 91-183-2258802, vc@gndu.ac.in, http://www.gndu.ac.in/.

299.934 USA ISSN 2160-2433
▼ ➤ **JOURNAL OF SPIRITUALITY AND SPIRITUAL ADVANCEMENT.** Abbreviated title: J S S A. Text in English. 2011. s-a. free (effective 2011). **Document type:** *Journal, Academic/Scholarly.* **Description:** Contains professional articles, book reviews, and research papers in the fields of spirituality, spiritual advancement, and relevant subjects.
Media: Online - full text.
Published by: Panta Rhei Institute info@pantarheiinstitute.org.

289.3 USA ISSN 1948-7487
➤ **JOURNAL OF THE BOOK OF MORMON & RESTORATION SCRIPTURE.** Abbreviated title: J B M R S. Text in English. 1992. s-a. USD 25 (effective 2010). bk.rev. illus.; maps. back issues avail. **Document type:** *Journal, Academic/Scholarly.* **Description:** Aims to promote reader's understanding of the history, meaning, and significance of the scriptures revealed through the Prophet Joseph Smith.
Formerly (until 2008): Journal of Book of Mormon Studies (1065-9366)
Related titles: Online - full text ed.: free (effective 2009).
Indexed: A01.
Published by: Brigham Young University, The Neal A. Maxwell Institute for Religious Scholarship, The Neal A. Maxwell Institute for Religious Scholarship, Brigham Young University, Provo, UT 84602. TEL 801-422-9229, 800-327-6715, FAX 801-422-0040, maxwell_institute@byu.edu. Ed. Andrew H Hedges.

289.9 USA ISSN 1097-1769
BX9750.S45
JOURNAL OF UNIFICATION STUDIES. Abbreviated title: J U S. Text in English. 1997. a. **Document type:** *Journal, Academic/Scholarly.* **Description:** Addresses issues relating to the theological community and the professional ministry specific to Unification theology, themes and practice.
Related titles: Online - full text ed.: free (effective 2010).
Published by: Unification Theological Seminary, 30 Seminary Dr, Barrytown, NY 12507. TEL 845-752-3000, http://www.uts.edu.

289.109 USA ISSN 1550-0195
BX9803
➤ **JOURNAL OF UNITARIAN UNIVERSALIST HISTORY.** Text in English. 1925. a. USD 15 to non-members; free to members (effective 2011). bk.rev. back issues avail. **Document type:** *Journal, Academic/Scholarly.* **Description:** Presents scholarly articles on American, British, and Continental Unitarianism and Universalism.
Former titles (until 1997): Unitarian Universalist Historical Society. Proceedings (0731-4078); (until 1981): Unitarian Historical Society. Proceedings (0082-7819)
Related titles: Online - full text ed.: ISSN 1933-9208.
Indexed: A01, A21, AmH&L, CA, HistAb, MLA-IB, RI-1, T02.
Published by: Unitarian Universalist Historical Society, 27 Grove St, Scituate, MA 02066. membership@uuhs.org. Ed. Kathleen Parker.

294.6 USA ISSN 2155-6644
▼ **JOURNEY WITH THE GURUS.** Text in English. 2010 (Sep.). biennial. USD 28.95 per issue (effective 2011). **Document type:** *Magazine, Consumer.*
Published by: Sikh Education & Cultural Foundation, 30 Osborne Ave, Norwalk, CT 06855. TEL 203-853-2303, innid@aol.com.

289.1 USA ISSN 2158-4591
KALEIDOSCOPE. Text in English. 19??. bi-m. free (effective 2010). back issues avail. **Document type:** *Newsletter, Trade.* **Description:** Contains news about upcoming events and sermons, letters from the ministers of the Unitarian Society of Santa Barbara, and a variety of Unitarian Universalist related articles.
Formerly (until 1978): The Unitarian Society of Santa Barbara. Newsletter Calendar (2158-4605)
Published by: The Unitarian Society of Santa Barbara, 1535 Santa Barbara St, Santa Barbara, CA 93101. TEL 805-965-4583, FAX 805-965-6273, ussb@ussb.org. Ed. Jared Dawson.

KERNOS; revue internationale et pluridisciplinaire de religion grecque antique. *see* CLASSICAL STUDIES

289.9 USA
KOINONIA PARTNERS. NEWSLETTER. Text in English. 1944. q. free. **Document type:** *Newsletter.* **Description:** Discusses issues of community development, Christianity, and social justice relating to rural areas in the South.
Published by: Koinonia Partners, 1324 Georgia State Hwy 49 S, Americus, GA 31709.

299.51 CHN ISSN 1002-2627
B128.C8
KONGZI YANJIU/STUDIES ON CONFUCIUS. Text in Chinese. 1986. bi-m. USD 31.20 (effective 2009). **Document type:** *Journal, Academic/Scholarly.*
Related titles: Online - full text ed.
Indexed: MLA-IB.
—East View.
Published by: Zhongguo Kongzi Jijinhui/China Confucius Foundation, 2668, Dongweihuanlu Zhongduan, Jinan, Shandong 250100, China. TEL 81-531-8326129. **Dist. by:** China International Book Trading Corp, 35 Chegongzhuang Xilu, Haidian District, PO Box 399, Beijing 100044, China. TEL 86-10-68412045, FAX 86-10-68412023, cibtc@mail.cibtc.com.cn, http://www.cibtc.com.cn.

289.96 GBR
KOSMON UNITY. Text in English. 1946. s-a. GBP 5 for 2 yrs. (effective 1999). bk.rev.

Published by: (Confraternity of Faithists), Kosmon Press, BM-KCKP, London, WC1N 3XX, United Kingdom. Ed. Peter Andrews. Circ: 100. **Dist. in U.S. by:** Kosmon Service Center, PO Box 664, Salt Lake City, UT 84110.

289.9 USA ISSN 0882-4606
BP605.F34
KOSMON VOICE. Text in English. 1977. irreg. (5-6/yr.). USD 14 domestic; USD 20 foreign (effective 2000). bk.rev. **Document type:** *Newsletter, Consumer.* **Description:** Covers self-esteem, mind, and spiritual improvement, the Oahspe Bible, vegetarian diet, recipes, health, meditation, parenting, seeker discipline, letters, articles, meeting news, poetry, humor and science relating to the group's concerns.
Formerly: Kosmon News
Published by: Universal Faithists of Kosmon, PO Box 654, Mccook, NE 69001. TEL 308-345-6369, kosmon@nebi.com, http://oahsperesources.nebi.com/. Ed., R&P Erma J Lee. Circ: 100.

299 IND ISSN 0047-3693
B5134.K754
KRISHNAMURTI FOUNDATION. BULLETIN. Text in English. 1970. 3/yr. INR 75 domestic; USD 5 foreign (effective 2011). bk.rev. **Document type:** *Bulletin, Trade.*
Indexed: RASB.
Published by: Krishnamurti Foundation (India), Vasanta Vihar, 124 Greenways Rd, RA Puram, Chennai, 600 028, India. TEL 91-44-24937803, publications@kfionline.org.

289.6 SWE ISSN 0345-6005
BX7710
KVAEKARTIDSKRIFT. Text in Swedish. 1949. q. SEK 100; SEK 125 in Scandinavia; SEK 150 elsewhere (effective 1999). bk.rev. reprints avail. **Document type:** *Bulletin.* **Description:** Contains articles on religion, peace, justice and the integrity of creation.
Formerly (until 1974): Nordisk Kvaekartidskrift (0029-1404)
Published by: Vaennernas Samfund i Sverige/Society of Friends in Sweden (Quakers), Fack 9166, Stockholm, 10272, Sweden. TEL 46-33-12-2772, FAX 46-33-260652. Ed. Ingmar Hollsing. Circ: 500.

289.3 USA ISSN 1540-9678
L D S LIVING. (Latter Day Saints) Text in English. 2002 (Aug.). bi-m. USD 13.97; USD 3.95 newsstand/cover (effective 2002). **Document type:** *Magazine, Consumer.*
Published by: Legacy Publishing Corporation, 808 E. 1920 South, Ste. 1, Provo, UT 84606. TEL 801-373-2053, 800-585-3188, FAX 801-373-8859. Ed. Howard Collett.

289.1 USA ISSN 2158-4354
THE LAKES BEACON. Text in English. 19??. 9/yr. back issues avail. **Document type:** *Newsletter, Trade.* **Description:** Provides information about the First Unitarian Universalist Society.
Formerly (until 1980): The Lakes Beacon (2158-4346)
Related titles: Online - full text ed.: free (effective 2010).
Published by: Unitarian Universalist Society of Laconia, 172 Pleasant St, Laconia, NH 03246. TEL 603-524-6488, uusl@myfairpoint.net.

LATTERDAYBRIDE. *see* MATRIMONY

299.935 DEU ISSN 0174-6995
LAZARUS; Zeitschrift fuer Anthroposophie, Kunst und soziale Dreigliederung. Text in German. 1983. q. bk.rev. **Document type:** *Magazine, Consumer.*
Published by: Lazarus Verlag und Buchhandel GmbH, Fridtjof Nansen Str 7, Raisdorf, 24223, Germany. TEL 49-4307-6182, FAX 49-4307-839636. Ed., Pub., R&P Monika Neve.

792.8 AUS ISSN 0726-626X
LEAPING; magazine of Christian dance fellowship of Australia. Text in English. 1978. q. AUD 40 to members (effective 2008). adv. bk.rev. back issues avail. **Document type:** *Newsletter.*
Published by: Christian Dance Fellowship of Australia, 5/152 Culloden Rd, Marsfield, NSW, Australia. national@cdfa.org.au, http://www.cdfa.org.au/. Circ: 400.

289.9 DEU ISSN 1867-8661
LEITGEDANKEN ZUM GOTTESDIENST. Text in German. 1989. m. **Document type:** *Magazine, Consumer.*
Related titles: English ed.: Divine Service Guide. ISSN 1867-867X. 2008; French ed.: Pensees Directrices. ISSN 0995-5070. 19??; Spanish ed.: Pensamientos Guias para el Servicio Divino. ISSN 1869-1625. 1997; Italian ed.: Pensieri Guida. ISSN 1867-8688. 2007.
Published by: Verlag Friedrich Bischoff GmbH, Gutleutstr 298, Frankfurt Am Main, 60327, Germany. TEL 49-69-2696123, FAX 49-69-2696111, vertrieb@bischoff-verlag.de, http://www.bischoff-verlag.de.

289.7 CAN ISSN 0840-5972
LE LIEN DES FRERES MENNONITES. Text in French. 1981. m. (11/yr.). CAD 8 (effective 2000). bk.rev. illus.
Published by: Conference of Mennonite Brethren Churches of Canada, Board of Communications, 3 169 Riverton Ave, Winnipeg, MB R2L 2E5, Canada. TEL 204-669-6575, FAX 204-654-1865. Ed. Annie Brosseau. Circ: 700.

299.93 CAN
THE LIGHT WITHIN. Text in English. 1994. s-a. CAD 6 to non-members; free to members. adv. bk.rev. **Document type:** *Newsletter.* **Description:** Offers spiritual news.
Published by: Spiritualist Church of Canada, c/o Rev Kathyann Johnston, Ed, 674 Kennedy Rd, Toronto, ON M1K 2B5, Canada. TEL 416-439-1087. R&P, Adv. contact Rev. Kathyann Johnston.

269.2 AUS ISSN 0812-6240
THE LINK. Text in English. 1979. q. looseleaf. back issues avail. **Document type:** *Newsletter.* **Description:** Evangelical information from an international perspective.
Formerly: Missionary Society of Saint Paul. Link (0728-5493)
Published by: Missionary Society of St. Paul, 477 Royal Parade, Parkville, VIC 3050, Australia. TEL 61-3-93877433, FAX 61-3-93806625, parkville@paulistmissionaries.org, http://www.mssp.it.

289.94 USA ISSN 0190-3845
CODEN: EVEPEO
LIVE (SPRINGFIELD). Text in English. 1928. w. USD 3.49 per issue (effective 2009). **Document type:** *Magazine, Consumer.* **Description:** Includes fiction and nonfiction stories illustrating how God works in the lives of His people in practical ways.
Published by: Gospel Publishing House, 1445 N Boonville Ave, Springfield, MO 65802. TEL 800-641-4310, FAX 417-862-5881, 800-328-0294, CustSrvReps@ag.org, http://www.gospelpublishing.com/.

299.93 USA
THE LIVING LIGHT. Text in English. 1968. q. USD 5.
Former titles: The Living Light Philosophy; Serenity Sentinel
Published by: Living Light Publications, 2718 Decoy Dr, Sparks, NV 89436. TEL 775-626-4287, 800-626-4287, rlsalvation@sbcglobal.net, http://thelivinglightpublication.org/. Ed. Ronald C Cavender. Circ: 300.

289 NLD ISSN 1875-2578
LOPEND VUUR. Text in Dutch. 2001. q.
Formerly (until 2006): Nieuw Vuur (1570-4475); Which was formed by the merger of (1997-2000): C W N Nieuwsbrief (1387-3334); (1957-2000): Vuur (0920-1289)
Published by: Charismatische Werkgemeenschap Nederland, Dorpsstr 36, Streefkerk, 2959 AG, Netherlands. TEL 31-184-662048, FAX 31-184-662149, cwn.org@dbinet.nl. Eds. Joke Koelewijn, Maartje Fokkema.

289.7 360 USA
M C C ANNUAL REPORT. Text in English. 19??. a. free (effective 2011). **Document type:** *Journal, Trade.*
Published by: Mennonite Central Committee, 21 S 12th St, PO Box 500, Akron, PA 17501. TEL 717-859-1151, 888-563-4676, mailbox@mcc.org, http://www.mcc.org. Ed. Chery Zehr Walker.

M C C RESOURCE UPDATE. *see* SOCIAL SERVICES AND WELFARE

289.132 USA
M S U U NEWSLETTER: GLEANINGS. Text in English. 1974. q. membership only. adv. bk.rev. **Document type:** *Newsletter.* **Description:** Publishes information of interest to Unitarian Universalist women minister.
Formerly: M S U U Newsletter (0360-7046)
Published by: Ministerial Sisterhood Unitarian Universalist, c/o Universalist Unitarian Church, 740 E Main St, Santa Paula, CA 93060. TEL 805-525-8859. Ed. Rev. Shirley Ranck. R&P Rev. Marjorie N Leaming. Circ: 300 (controlled).

299.9 BEL
MANICHAEAN STUDIES. Text in English, French, German, Italian. 1991. irreg., latest vol.4, 2001. price varies. back issues avail. **Document type:** *Proceedings, Academic/Scholarly.* **Description:** Publishes original studies on religious and philosophical issues in Manichaean texts.
Published by: Brepols Publishers, Begijnhof 67, Turnhout, 2300, Belgium. FAX 32-14-428919, periodicals@brepols.net. Ed. Alois van Tongerloo.

289.1 USA ISSN 2151-4542
THE MEETING HOUSE NEWS. Text in English. 19??. m. free (effective 2009). back issues avail. **Document type:** *Newsletter, Consumer.* **Description:** Provides information about all the First Parish Church programs, including music, social action, religious education, pastoral care and more.
Former titles (until 1996): News from the Meeting House (2151-4534); (until 1986): From the Meeting House (2151-4550)
Related titles: Online - full text ed.
Published by: First Parish in Concord, 20 Lexington Rd, Concord, MA 01742. TEL 978-369-9602, fpcontact@firstparish.org. Ed. Kate Keleher.

289.7 USA ISSN 0025-9330
THE MENNONITE. Text in English. 1908. w. USD 34.95 in United States; USD 34 in Canada. adv. bk.rev. illus. index. **Description:** Devoted to informing and challenging the Christian fellowship as expressed in the Mennonite Church.
Formerly (until 1936): Gospel Herald (0017-2340)
Indexed: A21, A22, ChrPI, GSS&RPL, RI-1, RI-2.
Published by: Mennonite Church, 616 Walnut Ave., Scottsdale, PA 15683. TEL 724-887-8500, 800-790-2498, FAX 724-851-3111. Ed. J Lorne Peachey. Adv. contact Melanie Mueller. page USD 1,690; trim 22 x 8.5. Circ: 22,000. **Co-sponsor:** General Conference Mennonite Church.

289.7 CAN ISSN 0025-9349
MENNONITE BRETHREN HERALD. Text in English. 1962. bi-w. CAD 24 domestic; CAD 30 foreign (effective 2000). adv. bk.rev. illus. index. back issues avail. **Description:** Primarily for Mennonite Brethren in Canada. Information of events in church and world at large, and to meet the personal and corporate spiritual needs of the members, serves as vehicle of communication within the larger church body.
Published by: Conference of Mennonite Brethren Churches of Canada, Board of Communications, 3 169 Riverton Ave, Winnipeg, MB R2L 2E5, Canada. TEL 204-669-6575, FAX 204-654-1865, mr@mbconf.ca, mbherald@cdnmbconf.ca, http://www.mbherald.com. Ed. Jim Coggins. R&P, Adv. contact Susan Brandt. B&W page CAD 825; trim 11 x 8.25. Circ: 16,000.

289.7025 USA ISSN 1549-8913
BX8107
MENNONITE CHURCH U S A. DIRECTORY. (United States of America) Text in English. 1999. a. USD 19.99 per issue (effective 2011). **Document type:** *Directory, Trade.*
Formerly (until 2003): Mennonite Directory (1527-1722); Which was formed by the merger of (1951-1999): General Conference Mennonite Church. Handbook of Information; (1910-1999): Mennonite Yearbook and Directory (0275-1178); (199?-1999): Conference of Mennonites in Canada. Directory (1485-3485); Which superseded in part (in 199?): C M C Yearbook (1184-0420); Which was formerly (until 1989): Conference of Mennonites in Canada. Yearbook (0543-467X); (until 1966): Konferenz der Mennoniten in Kanada. Jahrbuch (0318-028X)
Published by: Herald Press, 1251 Virginia Ave, Harrisonburg, VA 22802. TEL 800-999-3534, FAX 877-271-0760, RussE@MennoMedia.org, http://www.heraldpress.com/.

289.7 CAN ISSN 0700-8066
MENNONITE HISTORIAN. Text in English. 1975. q. CAD 11 (effective 2006).
Published by: (Mennonite Heritage Centre), Canadian Conference of Mennonite Brethren Churches, Centre for Mennonite Brethren Studies, 600 Shaftesbury Blvd, Winnipeg, MB R3P 0M4, Canada. TEL 204-888-6781. Eds. Alf Redekipp, Conrad Stoesz. **Co-publisher:** Mennonite Heritage Centre.

289.7 USA ISSN 0025-9357
BX8101
MENNONITE HISTORICAL BULLETIN. Text in English. 1940. q. USD 25 (effective 2001). bk.rev. illus. cum.index every 10 yrs. **Document type:** *Bulletin.*
Related titles: Microfilm ed.: (from PQC).
Indexed: CERDIC, DIP, IBR, IBZ, PCI.
Published by: Historical Committee of the Mennonite Church, 1700 South Main St, Goshen, IN 46526. TEL 219-535-7477, FAX 219-535-7756. Ed., R&P John E Sharp. Circ: 400.

289.7 USA ISSN 1548-8500
BX8101
MENNONITE LIFE (ONLINE). Text in English. 1946. a. free (effective 2010). bk.rev. bibl.; charts; illus. cum.index every 5 yrs. back issues avail. **Document type:** *Magazine, Consumer.* **Description:** Contains articles related to Mennonite and Anabaptist history, faith, life and culture.
Formerly (in 2000): Mennonite Life (Print) (0025-9365)
Media: Online - full text.
Indexed: A21, A22, ABS&EES, AmH&L, HistAb, MLA-IB, R&TA, RI-1, RI-2, RILM.
Published by: Bethel College, 300 E 27th St, North Newton, KS 67117. TEL 316-283-2500, 800-522-1887, alumni@bethelks.edu.

289.7 USA ISSN 0025-9373
BX8101
➤ **MENNONITE QUARTERLY REVIEW.** Text in English; Text occasionally in Dutch, German, Multiple languages. 1926. q. USD 35 in US & Canada; USD 45 elsewhere; USD 10 per issue in US & Canada; USD 13 per issue elsewhere (effective 2009). bk.rev. bibl.; charts; illus. index, cum.index every 10 yrs. back issues avail.; reprints avail. **Document type:** *Journal, Academic/Scholarly.* **Description:** Contains articles on the Radical Reformation, Amish, Mennonites and Hutterites refereed by leading scholars in the pertinent field.
Supersedes (in 1927): Goshen College Record. Review Supplement
Related titles: E-mail ed.: USD 5 (effective 2009).
Indexed: A21, A22, A26, ABS&EES, AmH&L, CA, CERDIC, ChrPI, DIP, E08, FR, HistAb, I05, IBR, IBZ, MLA-IB, P30, PCI, PRA, R&TA, RI-1, RI-2, RILM, S09, T02.
—IE, Infotrieve, Ingenta, INIST.
Published by: (Mennonite Historical Society), Goshen College, 1700 S Main St, Goshen, IN 46526. TEL 574-535-7433, 800-348-7422, FAX 574-535-7438, info@goshen.edu. Ed. John D Roth. **Co-sponsor:** Associated Mennonite Biblical Seminary.

289.7 USA ISSN 0889-2156
MENNONITE WEEKLY REVIEW. Text in English. 1923. w. USD 42 domestic; USD 58 foreign (effective 2005). adv. bk.rev. illus. 14 p./no. 5 cols./p.; **Document type:** *Newspaper, Consumer.*
Published by: Mennonite Weekly Review, Inc., 129 W Sixth St, Box 568, Newton, KS 67114. Ed. Paul R Schrag. Pub. Robert M Schrag. Circ: 10,456 (paid). Wire service: RN.

289.7 DEU ISSN 0342-1171
BX8101
➤ **MENNONITISCHE GESCHICHTSBLAETTER.** Text in German. 1936. a. bk.rev. **Document type:** *Academic/Scholarly.* **Description:** Studies the history of the Mennonite Church and the Anabaptists.
Indexed: DIP, IBR, IBZ.
Published by: Mennonitischer Geschichtsverein, Am Hollerbrunnen 2A, Bolanden, 67295, Germany. mennoforsch@t-online.de. Eds. Christoph Wiebe, Hans Juergen Goertz. R&P Eckbert Driedger. Circ: 600. **Subscr. to:** Christel Schultz, Blumenweg 28, Dietzenbach 63128, Germany. TEL 49-6074-46146.

289.7 CAN ISSN 0025-9314
MENNONITISCHE RUNDSCHAU/MENNONITE REVIEW. Text in German. 1877. m. CAD 16 (effective 2000). adv. bk.rev. illus. index.
Published by: Conference of Mennonite Brethren Churches of Canada, Board of Communications, 3 169 Riverton Ave, Winnipeg, MB R2L 2E5, Canada. TEL 204-669-6575, FAX 204-654-1865, mr@mbconf.ca. Eds. Brigitte Penner, Marianne Dulder. Circ: 2,000.

299.934 DEU ISSN 0935-798X
DER MERKURSTAB; Zeitschrift fuer anthroposophische Medizin. Text in German. 1950. bi-m. EUR 70; EUR 25 to students (effective 2007). adv. bk.rev. **Document type:** *Journal, Academic/Scholarly.*
Indexed: AMED.
—GNLM. **CCC.**
Published by: Gesellschaft Anthroposophischer Aerzte in Deutschland e.V., Roggenstr 82, Filderstadt, 70794, Germany. TEL 49-711-7799711, FAX 49-711-7799712, ges.anth.aerzte@t-online.de, http://www.anthroposophischeaerzte.de. Adv. contact Petra Leber. page EUR 900; trim 175 x 248. Circ: 2,500 (paid and controlled).

289.4 USA
THE MESSENGER (JULIAN); official publication of the Swedenborgian Church. Text in English. 1852. m. USD 12 domestic; USD 15 foreign (effective 2000). bk.rev. charts; illus. index. **Document type:** *Newsletter.*
Formerly: New Church Messenger (0028-4424)
Indexed: MLA-IB.
Published by: Swedenborgian Church, Department of Communications, 11 Highland Ave, Newtonville, MA 02460-1852. TEL 617-969-4240, FAX 617-964-3258, manager@swedenborg.org. Ed., R&P Patte Wheat Le Van TEL 670-765-2915. Circ: 2,000.

296.4 USA
BV2619
MESSIANIC JEWISH LIFE. Text in English. 1928. q. USD 10; USD 2.75 newsstand/cover (effective 1999). adv. back issues avail. **Description:** Addresses Jewish culture, both Messianic and non-Messianic, exploring a wide range of topics, including "Ask the Rabbi," a forum that enables readers to submit questions to a well-known Messianic Rabbi.
Former titles (until May 1998): Messianic Jew; Hebrew Christian (0017-9477)
Media: Microfiche.
Indexed: CERDIC.
Published by: (International Messianic Jewish Alliance), Lederer Messianic Publications, 6204 Park Heights Ave, Baltimore, MD 21215. TEL 410-338-5505, FAX 410-764-1376. Ed. David Sedaca. Pub. Barry Rubin. Circ: 3,000 (controlled). **Subscr. to:** Messianic Jewish Life, I M J A, Box 6307, Virginia Beach, VA 23456. TEL 757-623-0424, FAX 757-627-4572.

296 GBR
MESSIANIC TESTIMONY. Text in English. 1973. q. free (effective 2009). bk.rev. **Document type:** *Newsletter, Trade.* **Description:** Information for supporters of the Messianic Testimony, a non-denominational and non-sectarian Christian mission bringing the Gospel of Jesus to Jewish people around the world.
Formerly (until 199?): The Messianic Witness; Which was formed by the 1973 merger of: Trusting and Toiling; Scattered Nation
Address: 15 Diddenham Ct, Lambwood Hill, Grazeley, Reading, Berkshire RG7 1JQ, United Kingdom. TEL 44-118-9885070, FAX 44-118-9885072, office@messianictestimony.com.

MIRROR (LANCASTER). *see* HISTORY—History Of North And South America

289.7 USA ISSN 0091-8296
BV2000
➤ **MISSIOLOGY**; an international review. Text in English. 1953. q. USD 30 combined subscription to individuals (print & online eds.); USD 40 combined subscription to institutions (print & online eds.); free to members (effective 2011). adv. bk.rev. index. 128 p./no.; reprints avail. **Document type:** *Journal, Academic/Scholarly.* **Description:** Multi-disciplinary journal for missionaries and professors of mission studies.
Supersedes (in 1973): Practical Anthropology (0032-633X)
Related titles: Microform ed.: (from PQC); Online - full text ed.: USD 20 to individuals; USD 30 to institutions (effective 2011).
Indexed: A21, A22, AICP, BAS, CERDIC, ChrPI, DIP, EI, FR, IBR, IBZ, MLA-IB, PCI, PerIslam, R&TA, RI-1, RI-2, RILM, SPPI.
—BLDSC (5828.912600), IE, Infotrieve, Ingenta.
Published by: American Society of Missiology, c/o W. Jay Moon, Sioux Falls Seminary, 2100 S Summit, Sioux Falls, SD 57105. TEL 605-336-6588, jmoon@sfseminary.edu. Ed. J Nelson Jennings TEL 314-434-4044 ext 4230. Adv. contact Jean Warren.

289.3 USA ISSN 2153-1226
▼ **MORMON ENTREPRENEUR.** Text in English. 2009. bi-m. free (effective 2010). back issues avail. **Document type:** *Magazine, Trade.*
Media: Online - full text.

299 USA
NARROW WAY. Text in English, Greek, Hebrew. 1970. bi-m. free to qualified personnel. **Document type:** *Newsletter.*
Published by: Assemblies of Yahweh, PO Box C, Bethel, PA 19507. TEL 717-933-4518. Ed. Jacob O Meyer. Circ: 1,200 (controlled).

299.5 BGD
NATIONAL COUNCIL OF CHURCHES, BANGLADESH. ANNUAL REPORT. Text in Bengali, English. a. stat.
Published by: National Council of Churches, Bangladesh, 395, New Eskaton Rd, Dhaka, 2, Bangladesh.

299.93 USA
NEW AGE TEACHINGS. Text in English. 1967. bi-m. per issue contribution. bk.rev. **Document type:** *Newsletter.*
Published by: Fare - Thee - Well Wholeness Center, PO Box 549, Huntington, MA 01050-0549. TEL 413-667-3600. Circ: 3,000.

289.4 USA ISSN 0275-0805
BX8701
➤ **NEW CHURCH LIFE**; a monthly magazine devoted to the teachings revealed through Emanuel Swedenborg. Text in English. 1891. m. bk.rev. **Document type:** *Magazine, Consumer.* **Description:** Contains sermons, religious articles and reviews, letters and church news.
Related titles: Online - full text ed.
Indexed: MLA-IB.
Published by: General Church of the New Jerusalem, PO Box 743, Bryn Athyn, PA 19009. TEL 267-502-4911, outreach@newchurch.org.

➤ **NEW DIRECTION**; Mormons & homosexuality. *see* HOMOSEXUALITY

289.3 USA ISSN 0164-5285
BX8605.1
NEW ERA (SALT LAKE CITY). Text in English. 1971. m. USD 8; USD 1.50 per issue (effective 2009). back issues avail. **Document type:** *Magazine, Consumer.* **Description:** Contains the words of the latter-day prophets and many testimonies and experiences of youth.
Related titles: Online - full text ed.: free (effective 2009).
Indexed: AIPP.
—Ingenta.
Published by: Church of Jesus Christ of Latter-day Saints, 50 E North Temple St, Salt Lake City, UT 84150. TEL 801-240-2950, 800-537-5971, FAX 801-240-5997, http://www.lds.org. Eds. Spencer J Condie, Victor D Cave. **Subscr. to:** Distribution Services, P O Box 26368, Salt Lake City, UT 84126.

289.1 USA ISSN 1933-8732
NEW MASSACHUSETTS UNIVERSALIST CONVENTION. NEWSLETTER. Text in English. 1998. s-a. **Document type:** *Newsletter, Consumer.*
Published by: The New Massachusetts Universalist Convention, 30 Briarwood Circle, N Easton, MA 02356-1706. info@nmuc.org, http://www.nmuc.org/index.htm.

292 NLD ISSN 1570-5994
THE NEW TESTAMENT IN THE GREEK FATHERS. Text in English. 1986. irreg., latest vol.9, 2008. price varies. **Document type:** *Monographic series.* **Description:** Provides a full presentation of the New Testament of a given Father or the selected works of a given Father.
Indexed: IZBG.
Published by: (Society of Biblical Literature USA), Brill, PO Box 9000, Leiden, 2300 PA, Netherlands. TEL 31-71-5353500, FAX 31-71-5317532, cs@brill.nl.

289.98 USA ISSN 0146-7832
NEW THOUGHT; a quarterly magazine dedicated to the spiritual enlightenment of the individual and of the world. Text in English. 1916. q. USD 15 (effective 2000). adv. bk.rev. illus.
Formerly (until 1950): New Thought Bulletin (0146-8170)
Published by: International New Thought Alliance, 5003 E Broadway Rd, Mesa, AZ 85206. TEL 980-830-2461. Ed. Blaine C Mays. Circ: 5,000.

289.1 USA ISSN 2156-4477
NEWS & VIEWS (OREGON CITY). Text in English. 19??. m. back issues avail. **Document type:** *Newsletter, Trade.* **Description:** Covers religious diversity, social justice, personal accountability, and spiritual growth for all ages in a historic welcoming community.
Related titles: Online - full text ed.: free (effective 2010).
Published by: Atkinson Memorial Church, 710 Sixth St, Oregon City, OR 97045. TEL 503-656-7296, FAX 815-366-7667, office@atkinsonchurch.org.

299 USA
NOT LIKE MOST. Text in English. 1995. irreg. USD 5 newsstand/cover domestic; USD 7 newsstand/cover foreign (effective 2001). **Document type:** *Magazine, Consumer.* **Description:** Covers news, music, interviews, and discussions on Satanism and the Church of Satan.
Published by: Purging Talon Publishing, PO Box 8131, Burlington, VT 05402. notlikemost@purgingtalon.com, http://purgingtalon.com/nlm/. Ed. Matt G Paradise.

290 USA ISSN 1092-6690
BL1
➤ **NOVA RELIGIO**; the journal of alternative and emergent religions. Abbreviated title: N R. Text in English. 1997. q. USD 215 combined subscription to institutions (print & online eds.) (effective 2012). adv. bk.rev. back issues avail.; reprint service avail. from PSC. **Document type:** *Journal, Academic/Scholarly.* **Description:** Presents scholarly interpretations and examinations of alternative religious movements.
Related titles: Online - full text ed.: ISSN 1541-8480. 2003 (Apr.). USD 171 to institutions (effective 2012).
Indexed: A20, A21, A22, ABS&EES, AmHI, ArtHuCI, BrHumI, CA, DIP, E01, H07, IBR, IBZ, MLA-IB, P10, P28, P42, P48, P53, P54, PQC, R&TA, RI-1, S02, S03, SociolAb, T02, W07.
—BLDSC (6179.355000), IE, Ingenta. **CCC.**
Published by: University of California Press, Journals Division, 2000 Ctr St, Ste 303, Berkeley, CA 94704. TEL 510-643-7154, 877-262-4226, FAX 510-642-9917, customerservice@ucpressjournals.com. Adv. contact Jennifer Rogers TEL 510-642-6188. Circ: 288. **Subscr. to:** 149 5th Ave, 8th Fl, New York, NY 10010. participation@jstor.org.

289.9 PRT ISSN 0029-5116
NOVAS DE ALEGRIA. Abbreviated title: N A. Text in Portuguese. 1943. m. adv. bk.rev. abstr.; illus.
Published by: Casa Publicadora da Convencao das Assembleias de Deus em Portugal, Avenida Almirante Gago Coutinho, 158, Lisbon, 1700, Portugal. TEL 351-21-8429190, FAX 351-21-840936, capu@capu.pt, http://www.capu.pt. Ed. Fernando Martinez da Silva. Circ: 10,000 (controlled).

292 USA ISSN 0892-5984
BF1001
OF A LIKE MIND. Text in English. 1983. q. USD 20 in United States; USD 25 in Canada; USD 30 elsewhere (effective 2000). adv. bk.rev. illus. reprints avail. **Document type:** *Newspaper.* **Description:** International, feminist perspective on Goddess religions, women's spirituality, paganism and earth connections.
Published by: Reformed Congregation of the Goddess - International, PO Box 6677, Madison, WI 53716. TEL 608-257-5858, rcgi@itis.com. Ed., R&P, Adv. contact Lynnie Levy. page USD 560; trim 11 x 8.5. Circ: 10,000.

289.4 CHE ISSN 0030-0101
OFFENE TORE; Beitraege zu einem neuen christlichen Zeitalter. Text in German. 1957. 6/yr. CHF 30, USD 15. bk.rev. **Document type:** *Bulletin.* **Description:** Covers new religious perspectives while providing contributions to a new Christian era.
Published by: Swedenborg Verlag, Postfach 1205, Zuerich, 8032, Switzerland. TEL 41-1-3835944, FAX 41-1-3822944. Ed. Dr. Friedemann Horn. Circ: 600.

299.93 USA
OMEGA NEW AGE DIRECTORY. Text in English. 1972. m. USD 10 in state; USD 15 domestic; USD 19 in Canada; USD 34 elsewhere (effective 2005). adv. bk.rev.; music rev.; video rev. back issues avail. **Document type:** *Magazine, Consumer.* **Description:** Contains national and local news of interest to the metaphysical community. Includes complete activity and group listings, coverage of holistic health issues and related items.
Published by: New Age Community Church, 6418 S 39th Ave, Phoenix, AZ 85041. TEL 602-237-3213, 800-888-66342, rodgers@aznewage.com. Ed., Adv. contact John Rodgers. B&W page USD 350, color page USD 425. Circ: 25,000.

299 CAN
ON THE MARCH!. Text in English. q. **Document type:** *Newsletter.* **Description:** Keeps friends and adherents informed of the news and prayer requests of the Movement.
Published by: Bible Holiness Movement, P O Box 223, Sta A, Vancouver, BC V6C 2M3, Canada. TEL 250-492-3376. Ed. Wesley H Wakefield.

289.1 USA ISSN 1549-5388
ONEVOICE (ANDERSON). Text in English. 2004. bi-m. **Document type:** *Magazine, Consumer.*
Related titles: Supplement(s): E-voice. ISSN 1549-537X. 2004.
Published by: Church of God Ministries, Inc., PO Box 2420, Anderson, IN 46018. TEL 765-642-0256, 800-848-2464, http://www.chog.org/Home/tabid/36/Default.aspx.

230 ITA ISSN 0030-5375
BX100
ORIENTALIA CHRISTIANA PERIODICA; commentarii de re orientali aetatis christianae sacra et profana. Text in English, French, German, Italian, Latin, Spanish. 1935. a. price varies. bk.rev. charts. index. back issues avail. **Document type:** *Monographic series, Academic/Scholarly.* **Description:** Covers articles in theology, patrology, liturgy, history, canon law, archaeology and similar aspects of the Christian East.
Indexed: A21, A22, ABS&EES, BibLing, CERDIC, DIP, FR, IBR, IBZ, MLA-IB, PCI, RASB, RI-1, RI-2, RILM, SCOPUS.
—IE, Infotrieve, INIST.
Published by: (Pontificio Istituto Orientale/Pontificum Institutum Studiorum Orientalium), Edizioni Orientalia Cristiana (Subsidiary of: Pontificio Istituto Orientale/Pontificum Institutum Studiorum Orientalium), Piazza Santa Maria Maggiore 7, Rome, 00185, Italy. TEL 39-06-447417104, FAX 39-06-4465576, http://www.pio.urbe.it. Circ: 1,000.

290 DEU ISSN 1869-0513
▼ **ORIENTALISCHE RELIGIONEN IN DER ANTIKE.** Text in German. 2009. irreg., latest vol.5, 2010. price varies. **Document type:** *Monographic series, Academic/Scholarly.*
Published by: Mohr Siebeck GmbH & Co. KG, Wilhelmstr 18, Tuebingen, 72074, Germany. TEL 49-7071-9230, FAX 49-7071-51104, info@mohr.de, http://www.mohr.de.

270.1 DEU ISSN 0946-3933
OUR FAMILY; magazine of the New Apostolic Church. Text in English. 1955. m. USD 86.40 (effective 2011). adv. **Document type:** *Magazine, Consumer.* **Description:** Denominational publication devoted to evangelism, to the promotion of faith and to the belief in God through the use of real life stories.
Related titles: ◆ German ed.: Unsere Familie. ISSN 0945-5027.
Published by: Verlag Friedrich Bischoff GmbH, Gutleutstr 298, Frankfurt Am Main, 60327, Germany. TEL 49-69-2696123, FAX 49-69-2696111, vertrieb@bischoff-verlag.de, http://www.bischoff-verlag.de. Circ: 82,000.

289.92 USA ISSN 1067-7259
BX8525
OUR KINGDOM MINISTRY. Text in English. 1956. m. looseleaf. **Document type:** *Newsletter, Consumer.* **Description:** Contains articles on biblical and religious subjects and how to teach religious texts. Aims to assist Jehovah's Witnesses to be better equipped for their ministry.
Related titles: French ed.; Spanish ed.; Korean ed.; Italian ed.
Published by: Watch Tower Bible and Tract Society of Pennsylvania, Inc., 25 Columbia Heights, Brooklyn, NY 11201. TEL 718-560-5600, FAX 718-560-5619, http://www.watchtower.org/. Circ: 1,325,500.

289.1 USA ISSN 2159-2756
OUR OUTLOOK. Text in English. 19??. m. **Document type:** *Newsletter, Trade.*
Formerly (until 1950): The Outlook
Published by: First Universalist Church of Rochester, 150 S Clinton Ave, Rochester, NY 14604. TEL 585-546-2826, office@uuroc.org, http://uuroc.org/.

289 USA ISSN 0744-6381
PACIFIC UNION RECORDER. Text in English. 1900. m. USD 11; USD 15 foreign (effective 1999). adv. charts; illus. back issues avail. **Description:** Informs, educates and inspires readers to action in all areas of ministry.
Related titles: Online - full text ed.
Published by: (Pacific Union Conference of Seventh Day Adventists), Pacific Press Publishing Association, 1350 N Kings Rd, Nampa, ID 83687. TEL 208-465-2509, FAX 208-465-2531. Ed. C. Elwyn Platner. R&P C Elwyn Platner. Adv. contact Jolynn Fisher. Circ: 60,000.

292 GBR ISSN 1357-5147
PAGAN DAWN. Text in English. 1968. q. GBP 12 domestic to non-members; GBP 15 foreign to non-members; free to members (effective 2009). adv. bk.rev. back issues avail. **Document type:** *Magazine, Consumer.* **Description:** Contains information on European paganism, witchcraft, wicca, druidry, heathenism and shamanism.
Formerly (until 1994): The Wiccan
Published by: Pagan Federation, The Secretary, BM Box 7097, London, WC1N 3XX, United Kingdom. TEL 44-7986-034387, Publications@paganfed.org. adv.: B&W page GBP 200, color page GBP 222.

292 CAN ISSN 0838-1550
PAGANS FOR PEACE. Text in English. 1983. bi-m. CAD 12, USD 10. adv. bk.rev. **Document type:** *Newsletter.*
Published by: (Pagans for Peace Network), Obscure Pagan Press, c/o Sam Wagar, 32579 Oriole Crescent, Abbotsford, BC V2T 4C7, Canada. TEL 604-870-8715, swagar@home.com. Ed. Samuel Wagar. Circ: 200 (paid).

294.6 IND ISSN 0970-7689
➤ **PANCHBATI SANDESH.** Text in English, Hindi, Panjabi. 1978. q. INR 300 (effective 2011). bk.rev. **Document type:** *Journal, Academic/Scholarly.* **Description:** Deals with the main tenets of Sikhism in particular and the traditional wisdom of all religions in general.
Published by: Punjabi University, 20 Pritam Rd, Dehra Dun, Uttar Pradesh 248 001, India. TEL 91-135-2653954, http://www.punjabiuniversity.ac.in/.

201.6 USA ISSN 0742-5368
PANTHEIST VISION. Text in English. 1980. q. USD 15 domestic; USD 25 foreign (effective 2000). bk.rev. back issues avail. **Document type:** *Newsletter.* **Description:** Espouses a way of life in opposition to anthropocentrism and in favor of reverence for the Earth, accepting nature as the ultimate context for human existence.
Published by: Universal Pantheist Society, PO Box 265, Big Pine, CA 93513. TEL 559-739-8527, pansociety@pantheist.net, http://www.pantheist.net. Ed. Harold W Wood Jr. R&P Harold Wood.

294.6 USA ISSN 1930-0107
THE PANTHIC WEEKLY. Text in English. 2005. w. **Document type:** *Newspaper, Consumer.*
Media: Online - full text.
Published by: Khalsa Press http://www.panthic.org.

289.1 USA ISSN 2156-3918
PARISH NOTES. Text in English. 19??. w. back issues avail. **Document type:** *Newsletter, Consumer.* **Description:** Features religious home free of creeds and guides all by love, reason, and conscience.
Former titles (until 2003): All Souls Bulletin (2156-390X); (until 2002): All Souls Unitarian Church. Newsletter (2156-3888); (until 2000): Parish Notes (2156-3845)
Related titles: Online - full text ed.: free (effective 2010).
Published by: All Souls Unitarian Church, 2952 S Peoria, Tulsa, OK 74114. TEL 918-743-2363, info@allsoulschurch.org.

295 IND ISSN 0971-3786
BL1500
PARSIANA. Text in English. 1964. s-m. INR 600 domestic; INR 3,250 foreign (effective 2011). adv. bk.rev. stat. back issues avail. **Document type:** *Magazine, Consumer.* **Description:** Covers activities of international Zoroastrian community.
Indexed: IndIndia, RASB.
Published by: Parsiana Publications Pvt. Ltd., K. K. (Navsari) Chambers, Ground Fl, (Opp. St. Cathedral School side entrance), 39B, Amrit Keshav Nayak Rd, Fort, Mumbai, 400 001, India. TEL 91-22-22078104, FAX 91-22-22075572. Ed. Jehangir R Patel. Adv. contact Jasmine D Driver.

270 GRC
PATRIARCHAL INSTITUTE FOR PATRISTIC STUDIES. THEOLOGICAL STUDIES. Text in Greek. irreg., latest vol.5. price varies.
Published by: Patriarchal Institute for Patristic Studies, 64 Heptapyrgiou, Thessaloniki, 546 34, Greece. Ed. Panagiotis C Christou.

289.7 USA
PEACE OFFICE NEWSLETTER. Text in English. 1970. q. donation. back issues avail. **Document type:** *Newsletter.* **Description:** Addresses and interprets international peace and justice issues from a peace church perspective.
Formerly (until 1988): Peace Section Newsletter
Related titles: Online - full text ed.: free (effective 2011).
Published by: Mennonite Central Committee, 21 S 12th St, PO Box 500, Akron, PA 17501. TEL 717-859-1151, 888-563-4676, mailbox@mcc.org, http://www.mcc.org. Ed. Lawrence Rupley.

289.7 974 USA ISSN 0148-4036
F160.M45
PENNSYLVANIA MENNONITE HERITAGE. Text in English. 1978. q. free to members (effective 2010). bk.rev. illus.; stat. cum.index: 1978-1982; 1983-1987; 1988-1992; 1993-1997. back issues avail. **Document type:** *Journal, Academic/Scholarly.* **Description:** Focuses on the historical background, religious thought and expression, culture, and genealogy of the Mennonite-related groups originating in Pennsylvania.
Supersedes (in 1978): Mennonite Research Journal (0025-9381)
Indexed: AmH&L, CA, GPAI, P30, RILM, T02.
—Ingenta.
Published by: Lancaster Mennonite Historical Society, 2215 Millstream Rd, Lancaster, PA 17602. TEL 717-393-9745, FAX 717-393-8751, lmhs@lmhs.org. Ed. Carolyn C Wenger.

289.94 CAN ISSN 0031-4927
BX8762
PENTECOSTAL TESTIMONY. Text in English. 1920. m. CAD 19.05 domestic; USD 24 foreign (effective 2004). adv. bk.rev. **Document type:** *Magazine, Consumer.*
Indexed: CERDIC.
Published by: Pentecostal Assemblies of Canada, 2450 Milltower Ct, Mississauga, ON L5N 5Z6, Canada. TEL 416-542-7400, FAX 416-542-7313. Ed. Rick P Hiebert. Adv. contact Bev Hynek. Circ: 23,000.

289.1 USA ISSN 2159-5747
THE PLOUGHSHARE. Text in English. 19??. m. back issues avail. **Document type:** *Newsletter, Consumer.*
Former titles (until 1972): The Flame (2159-5739); First Unitarian Church of Denver (2159-5720)
Related titles: Online - full text ed.: free (effective 2011).
Published by: First Unitarian Society of Denver, 1400 Lafayette St, Denver, CO 80218. TEL 303-831-7113, FAX 303-831-8458, office@fusden.org. Ed. Randle Loeb.

263.913 USA ISSN 0032-7700
PRESENT TRUTH AND HERALD OF CHRIST'S EPIPHANY. Text in English. 1918. bi-m. USD 5 (effective 2000).
Related titles: Danish ed.; French ed.; Polish ed.; Norwegian ed.; German ed.
Published by: Laymen's Home Missionary Movement, 1156 Saint Matthews Rd., Chester Sprgs, PA 19425-2700. TEL 610-827-7665. Ed. Bernard W Hedman. Circ: 1,100.

PROVIDENT BOOK FINDER. *see* RELIGIONS AND THEOLOGY—Abstracting, Bibliographies, Statistics

289.3 USA ISSN 0163-7274
PURPOSE. Text in English. 1968. m. USD 2.05 per issue (effective 2011). bk.rev. illus. back issues avail. **Document type:** *Magazine, Trade.*
Published by: Herald Press, 1251 Virginia Ave, Harrisonburg, VA 22802. TEL 800-999-3534, FAX 877-271-0760, RussE@MennoMedia.org, http://www.heraldpress.com/.

289.6 USA
QUAKER ACTION. Text in English. 1947. 3/yr. donations. illus. reprints avail. **Document type:** *Magazine, Trade.* **Description:** Program activities of the committee and editorial opinion, reviewed by a team of staff members.
Former titles (until 2004): Quaker Service Bulletin (0033-5096); (until 1970): Quaker Service; (until 1960): American Friends Service Committee. Bulletin (0033-510X); Which was formed by the merger of (1944-1947): Foreign Service Bulletin; (1940-1947): A F S E R C O News
Related titles: Online - full text ed.: free (effective 2011) (from PQC).
Indexed: HRIR.
Published by: American Friends Service Committee, Inc., 1501 Cherry St, Philadelphia, PA 19102. TEL 215-241-7000, FAX 215-241-7275, afscinfo@afsc.org.

289.6 CAN ISSN 0229-1916
QUAKER CONCERN. Text in English. 1967. 3/yr. bk.rev. illus. back issues avail. **Document type:** *Newsletter, Consumer.* **Description:** Contains updates on Canadian Friends Service Committee projects in peace and national concerns, international programs, aboriginal affairs.
Former titles (until 1976): Quaker Service Report (0703-9425); (until 1975): Canadian Friends Service Committee (0703-9417)
Published by: Canadian Friends Service Committee, 60 Lowther Ave, Toronto, ON M5R 1C7, Canada. TEL 416-920-5213, FAX 416-920-5214, cfsc-office@quaker.ca. Circ: 3,500.

289.6 USA ISSN 0033-5053
BX7635.A1
➤ **QUAKER HISTORY.** Text in English. 1902. s-a. free to members (effective 2009). bk.rev. bibl. cum.index every 5 yrs, vol.1-85. back issues avail.; reprints avail. **Document type:** *Journal, Academic/Scholarly.* **Description:** Contains articles on Quaker contributions to issues such as social justice, education and literature.
Former titles (until 1962): Friends' Historical Association. Bulletin (0361-1957); (until 1924): Friends' Historical Society of Philadelphia. Bulletin
Related titles: Microform ed.: (from PQC); Online - full text ed.: ISSN 1934-1504.
Indexed: A21, A22, AmH&L, BEL&L, BibInd, CA, CERDIC, E01, FR, HistAb, MLA-IB, P30, PCI, RI-1, RI-2, SCOPUS, T02.
—IE, Ingenta, INIST.
Published by: Friends Historical Association, Haverford College, 370 Lancaster Ave, Haverford, PA 19041. TEL 610-896-1161, FAX 610-896-1102, fha@haverford.edu, http://www.haverford.edu/library/fha/fha.html. Ed. Charles L Cherry TEL 610-519-6957.

289.6 USA ISSN 0033-5088
BX7601
QUAKER RELIGIOUS THOUGHT. Abbreviated title: Q R T. Text in English. 1959. irreg. (approx. 2/yr.). bk.rev. 50 p./no.; back issues avail. **Document type:** *Magazine, Consumer.* **Description:** Includes articles and reviews that explore the meaning and implications of Quaker faith.
Related titles: Microform ed.: USD 59.95 to individuals; USD 119.90 to institutions (from PQC).
Indexed: A21, A22, CERDIC, RI-1.
Published by: (Quaker Theological Discussion Group), Barclay Press, 211 N Meridian St, Ste 101, Newberg, OR 97132. TEL 503-538-9775, 800-962-4014, FAX 503-554-8597, info@barclaypress.com, http://www.barclaypress.com.

289.6 GBR ISSN 1363-013X
BX7601
➤ **QUAKER STUDIES.** Text in English. 1996. s-a. free to members (effective 2010). adv. back issues avail. **Document type:** *Journal, Academic/Scholarly.* **Description:** Covers all aspects of Quakerism, including the subject areas of aesthetics, anthropology, architecture, art, cultural studies, history, literature, peace studies, philosophy, research methodology, sociology, theology, and women's studies.
Related titles: Online - full text ed.
Indexed: A01, A03, A08, CA, P10, P28, P48, P53, P54, PQC, R&TA, SociolAb, T02.
Published by: Quaker Studies Research Association, c/o Centre for Postgraduate Quaker Studies, Woodbrooke Quaker Study Ctr, 1046 Bristol Rd, Birmingham, B29 6LJ, United Kingdom. TEL 44-121-4156782, FAX 44-121-4725173, B.P.Dandelion@bham.ac.uk, http://www.qsra.org/. Ed. Ben Pink Dandelion.

289.6 USA ISSN 1526-7482
BX7601
QUAKER THEOLOGY; a progressive journal and forum for discussion and study. Text in English. 1999 (Autumn). s-a.
Published by: Quest, PO Box 1344, Fayetteville, NC 28302-1344. quest@quaker.org. Ed. Chuck Fager.

289.6 GBR ISSN 2042-1680
BX7601
QUAKER VOICES. Text in English. 1905. bi-m. GBP 18 domestic; GBP 26 foreign (effective 2010). **Document type:** *Magazine, Trade.* **Description:** Contains articles, poems and graphics.
Former titles (until 2010): Quaker Monthly (0033-507X); (until 1964): Wayfarer (0144-915X); Which incorporated: Quaker World Service; (until 1922): Workers at Home and Abroad; (until 1913): The Quaker at Home & Abroad; (until 1911): The Friendly Messenger
Published by: Quaker Life of Britain Yearly Meeting of the Religious Society of Friends, Friends House, 173 - 177 Euston Rd, London, NW1 2BJ, United Kingdom. TEL 44-20-76631000, FAX 44-20-76631001, enquiries@quaker.org.uk. Ed. Trish Carn TEL 44-20-84465772.

289.6 USA ISSN 0737-8246
E184.F89
QUAKER YEOMEN. Text in English. 1974. q. USD 18. adv. bk.rev. bibl.; charts. index. back issues avail. **Document type:** *Newsletter.* **Description:** Newsletter of Quaker and related genealogy.
Indexed: GPAI.
Address: 1190 N.W. 183rd Ave., Beaverton, CO 97006. TEL 503-629-9047. Ed., Pub., R&P, Adv. contact Patti Smith Lamb. Circ: 300.

299.934 USA ISSN 1040-533X
BP500
THE QUEST (WHEATON). Text in English. 1912. bi-m. USD 20.94 domestic; USD 27.78 in Canada; USD 31.74 elsewhere (effective 2006). illus. **Document type:** *Magazine, Consumer.* **Description:** Covers philosophy, religion, science, and the arts from a Theosophical perspective.
Supersedes in part (1912-1998): American Theosophist (0003-1402)
Indexed: MLA-IB.
Published by: Theosophical Society in America, 1926 N Main St, Wheaton, IL 60187-3151. TEL 630-668-1571, FAX 630-668-4976, olcott@theosophical.org. Eds. Betty Bland, Donna Wimberley. R&P Donna Wimberley. Circ: 8,000.

289.95 USA ISSN 0273-7159
BV3750
RAILROAD EVANGELIST. Text in English. 1931. q. USD 6. **Description:** Interdenominational patriotic Christian magazine for the railroad and allied transportation industries.
Published by: (Railroad Evangelistic Association, Inc.), Bartel Printing Co., 310 Cedar St, Warsaw, IN 46580. TEL 317-844-3176. Ed. Esther Peterson. Circ: 2,500. **Subscr. to:** c/o Ann Grissom, 5272 Longstone Rd, Carmel, IN 46032.

289.94 028.5 USA
BV4450
RANGERS NOW. Text in English. 1971. a. free to members (effective 2009). **Document type:** *Magazine, Consumer.* **Description:** Features religious and inspirational subjects for boys.
Former titles (until 2008): High Adventure (0190-3802); (until 1986): Dispatch (0190-4264)
Published by: (Royal Rangers), Gospel Publishing House, 1445 N Boonville Ave, Springfield, MO 65802. TEL 800-641-4310, FAX 417-862-5881, 800-328-0294, CustSrvReps@ag.org, http://www.gospelpublishing.com/.

RECLAIMING QUARTERLY. *see* ENVIRONMENTAL STUDIES

289.7 CAN
REJOICE!. Text in English. 1965. q. CAD 17, USD 12 (effective 2002). adv. **Document type:** *Journal, Consumer.* **Description:** Designed for daily devotional reading. Purpose is to direct the reader to God.
Published by: Kindred Productions, 169 Riverton Ave, Winnipeg, MB R2L 2E5, Canada. TEL 204-654-5765, 800-545-7322, FAX 204-654-1865, kindred@mbconf.ca, http://www.kindredproductions.com. Ed., R&P Byron Rempel-Burkholder. Pub., Adv. contact Marilyn Hudson. Circ: 17,000. **Co-sponsors:** General Conference of Mennonite Brethren Churches; Mennonite Church; General Conference Mennonite Church.

290 DEU
RELIGION DER ROEMISCHEN PROVINZEN. Text in German. 2001. irreg., latest vol.4, 2008. price varies. **Document type:** *Monographic series, Academic/Scholarly.*
Published by: Mohr Siebeck GmbH & Co. KG, Wilhelmstr 18, Tuebingen, 72074, Germany. TEL 49-7071-9230, FAX 49-7071-51104, info@mohr.de.

299.5 GBR ISSN 1751-2689
BL1055
➤ **RELIGIONS OF SOUTH ASIA.** Abbreviated title: R O S A. Text in English. 2007 (Jun.). s-a. USD 220 combined subscription in North America to institutions (print & online eds.); GBP 135 combined subscription elsewhere to institutions (print & online eds.) (effective 2012). adv. bk.rev. back issues avail.; reprints avail. **Document type:** *Journal, Academic/Scholarly.* **Description:** Features papers by internationally respected scholars on some of the most vibrant and dynamic religious traditions of the world.
Related titles: Online - full text ed.: ISSN 1751-2697. USD 176 in North America to institutions; GBP 108 elsewhere to institutions (effective 2012).
Indexed: A21.
—IE. **CCC.**
Published by: Equinox Publishing Ltd., Unit S3, Kelham House, 3 Lancaster St, Sheffield, S6 3AF, United Kingdom. TEL 44-114-2725957, FAX 44-560-3459046, journals@equinoxpub.com, http://www.equinoxpub.com/. Eds. Anna S King, Dermot H Killingley. Adv. contact Val Hall.

289.9 AUS ISSN 1326-5857
RENEWAL JOURNAL. Text in English. 1993. s-a. back issues avail. **Document type:** *Journal, Academic/Scholarly.* **Description:** Comments on current developments in Christian renewal and revival.
Related titles: Online - full text ed.
Published by: Christian Heritage College School of Ministries, 322 Wecker Rd, PO Box 2111, Mansfield, QLD 4122, Australia. TEL 61-7-33438888, FAX 61-7-33439291, cmc@citipointe.com.au, http://www.citipointe.com.au/cmc/. Ed. Geoff Waugh.

289.3 USA ISSN 0191-0167
RESTORATION WITNESS; missionary magazine of the Reorganized Church of Jesus Christ of Latter-Day Saints. Text in English. 1963. bi-m. USD 12.75 to individuals; USD 11.50 groups; USD 15.25 foreign (effective 2000). adv. illus.; tr.lit. **Document type:** *Magazine, Trade.*
Published by: (Reorganized Church of Jesus Christ of Latter Day Saints), Herald Publishing House, 1001 W Walnut, Box 390, Independence, MO 64051. TEL 816-521-3015, FAX 816-521-3066. Circ: 4,000.

289.1 USA ISSN 1943-0310
RIGHTS NOW. Text in English. 3/yr. membership. back issues avail. **Document type:** *Newsletter.* **Description:** Discusses the human rights advocacy work of the organization, which supports programs for children in the U.S. and aids grassroots organizations overseas seeking social, political, cultural, and economic justice.
Formerly (until 2005): Unitarian Universalist Service. Service Committee News (1943-0302)
Related titles: Online - full text ed.
Published by: Unitarian Universalist Service Committee, 689 Massachusetts Ave, Cambridge, MA 02139. TEL 617-868-6600, 800-388-3920, FAX 617-868-7102, uusc@uusc.org. Ed. Meredith Barges. Circ: 25,000.

289.1 USA ISSN 2159-2748
THE ROCHESTER UNITARIAN. Text in English. 1951. s-m. back issues avail. **Document type:** *Newsletter, Consumer.*
Related titles: Online - full text ed.: free (effective 2011).
Published by: First Unitarian Church of Rochester, 220 Winton Rd S, Rochester, NY 14610. TEL 585-271-9070, FAX 585-244-5391, office@rochesterunitarian.org.

290 100 DEU ISSN 1611-5945
S A P E R E. (Scripta Antiquitatis Posterioris ad Ethicam Religionemque Pertinentia) Text in German. 2000. irreg., latest vol.18, 2011. price varies. **Document type:** *Monographic series, Academic/Scholarly.*
Published by: Mohr Siebeck GmbH & Co. KG, Wilhelmstr 18, Tuebingen, 72074, Germany. TEL 49-7071-9230, FAX 49-7071-51104, info@mohr.de.

299.7 USA ISSN 1930-5397
S U N Y SERIES IN NATIVE AMERICAN RELIGIONS. (State University of New York) Text in English. 1997. irreg., latest 2002. price varies. **Document type:** *Monographic series, Academic/Scholarly.*
Published by: State University of New York Press, 22 Corporate Woods Blvd, 3rd Fl, Albany, NY 12211. TEL 518-472-5000, 866-430-7869, FAX 518-472-5038, info@sunypress.edu.

289.9 USA
SABBATH SENTINEL; serving the Seventh-day Christian community. Text in English. 1945. bi-m. USD 15. adv. bk.rev. bibl.; illus. back issues avail.
Published by: Bible Sabbath Association, HC60 Box 8, Fairview, OK 73737. TEL 405-227-3200. Ed. Sydney Cleveland. Circ: 1,200.

299 USA
SACRED NAME BROADCASTER. Text in English. 1968. m. free. illus.
Published by: Assemblies of Yahweh, PO Box C, Bethel, PA 19507. TEL 717-933-4518. Ed. Jacob O Meyer. Circ: 17,000.

299 USA ISSN 1941-8167
BL1
SACRED TRIBES JOURNAL. Text in English. 2002. s-a. free (effective 2010). back issues avail. **Document type:** *Journal, Academic/Scholarly.* **Description:** Explores ways in which to bridge the gulf between the twin disciplines of cult apologetics and contextual missiology.
Media: Online - full text.
Address: 2065 Half Day Rd, Deerfield, IL 60073. TEL 800-345-8337. Ed. Michael T Cooper.

289.3 USA ISSN 0586-7282
SALT LAKE CITY MESSENGER. Text in English. 1964. irreg., latest vol.94, 1998. looseleaf. free. adv. **Document type:** *Newsletter.*
Published by: Utah Lighthouse Ministry, 1358 S W Temple St, Box 1884, Salt Lake City, UT 84110. TEL 801-485-8894, FAX 801-485-0312. Ed. Jerald Tanner. R&P Sandra Tanner. Circ: 20,000.

280.4 CAN ISSN 1718-5769
SALVATIONIST.CA. Text in English. 1886. m. CAD 29.80 domestic; CAD 36 in United States; CAD 41 elsewhere (effective 2006). **Document type:** *Magazine, Consumer.*
Formerly (until 2006): War Cry (0043-0218)

R

Published by: Salvation Army, Canada and Bermuda Territorial Headquarters, 2 Overlea Blvd, Toronto, ON M4H 1P4, Canada. TEL 416-425-2111, http://www.salvationarmy.ca.

299 USA ISSN 1935-0171
AP2
SALVO (CHICAGO). Text in English. 2006. q. USD 25.99 domestic; USD 32.99 in Canada; USD 37.99 elsewhere (effective 2008). **Document type:** *Magazine, Consumer.*
Published by: Fellowship of St. James, PO Box 410788, Chicago, IL 61641. TEL 773-481-1090, FAX 773-481-1095, fsj@fsj.org, http://www.fsj.org.

289.9 USA
SANCTUARY CIRCLES; events calendar newsletter. Text in English. 1980. 8/yr. USD 15 (effective 2000). **Document type:** *Newsletter.*
Published by: Circle Sanctuary, PO Box 9, Barneveld, WI 53507. TEL 608-924-2216, FAX 608-924-5961.

299.5 NLD ISSN 1566-1997
BL1790
SANJIAO WENXIAN. Text in French. 1997. irreg., latest vol.4, 2005. price varies. **Document type:** *Monographic series, Academic/Scholarly.*
Published by: (France. Centre National de la Recherche Scientifique FRA, Ecole Pratique des Hautes Etudes FRA, Research School of Asian, African and Amerindian Studies), CNWS Publications, Leiden University, PO Box 9515, Leiden, 2300 RA, Netherlands. TEL 31-71-5272987, FAX 31-71-5272939, cnwspublications@let.leidenuniv.nl.

322.1 IND
SANT SIPAHI. Text in Panjabi. 1945 (vol.27). m. USD 40 (effective 2011). back issues avail. **Document type:** *Magazine, Consumer.* **Description:** Covers Sikh politics and religion.
Address: 24 Shaheed Udham Singh Nagar, Jalandhar, Punjab 144 001, India.

299.6 MEX
SANTERIA CIENCIA Y RELIGION. Text in Spanish. 1993. bi-m.
Address: JARIPEO 115, Colinas del Sur, Mexico City, DF 01430, Mexico. TEL 525-6436366. Ed. Jose Rodriguez Brenas. Circ: 7,300.

299.936 USA ISSN 0036-8458
SCIENCE OF MIND MAGAZINE; a guide for spiritual living. Text in English. 1927. m. USD 19.95 domestic; USD 29.95 in Canada; USD 39.95 elsewhere (effective 2007). adv. bk.rev. illus. 112 p./no.; **Document type:** *Magazine, Consumer.*
Indexed: CERDIC.
Published by: United Church of Religious Science, 2600 W. Magnolia Blvd, Burbank, CA 91505. TEL 818-526-7757, FAX 818-556-2253. Ed. Amanda Pisani TEL 818-556-2215. Circ: 100,000.

289.3 USA
SCROLL. Text in English. 1888. w. (Tue.). USD 30 for 6 mos.; USD 60; free newsstand/cover (effective 2005). **Document type:** *Newspaper, Consumer.* **Description:** Consists of subjects of interest to the students of BYU-Idaho and reflect the values of sponsoring institution, the Church of Jesus Christ of Latter-Day Saints.
Published by: Brigham Young University - Idaho, 525 S Center, Rexburg, ID 83460. TEL 208-496-2900, FAX 208-496-2911. R&P Lee Warnick. Circ: 8,000 (paid and free).

299 ITA ISSN 1971-4394
LA SCUOLA DOMENICALE. Text in Italian. 1878. q. EUR 25 domestic; EUR 30 foreign (effective 2009). bk.rev. **Document type:** *Magazine, Consumer.*
Formerly (until 1895): Lezioni Internazionali per le Scuole Domenicali (1971-4408)
Published by: Federazione dell Chiese Evangeliche in Italia, Via Firenze 38, Rome, 00184, Italy. TEL 39-06-4825120, FAX 39-06-4828728, http://www.fedevangelica.it.

299.93 USA ISSN 0037-1564
B132.Y6
SELF-REALIZATION. Text in English. 1925. q. USD 6; USD 9 foreign (effective 1998). bk.rev. illus. index. back issues avail. **Description:** Features information on healing the body, mind and soul through the practical application of spiritual principles.
Published by: Self-Realization Fellowship, Inc., 3880 San Rafael Ave, Los Angeles, CA 90065. TEL 213-342-0336, 888-773-8680, FAX 213-342-9560. Ed. Christopher Bagley. Circ: 25,000.

294.6 GBR
THE SIKH COURIER INTERNATIONAL. Text in English. 1960 (Oct.). s-a. GBP 10, INR 300 membership (effective 2011). adv. bk.rev. back issues avail. **Document type:** *Magazine, Consumer.* **Description:** Contains scholarly and devotional articles on Sikh religion and philosophy. Profiles Sikh personalities.
Formerly: Sikh Courier (0037-511X)
Indexed: CERDIC, DIP, IBR, IBZ.
Published by: World Sikh Foundation, 33 Wargrave Rd, South Harrow, Midds HA2 8LL, United Kingdom. TEL 44-20-88649228, bablibharara@hotmail.com. Ed. Sukhbir Singh Kapoor TEL 44-20-88649228.

294.6 GBR ISSN 1744-8727
BL2017
➤ **SIKH FORMATIONS**; religion, culture, theory. Text in English. 2005. s-a. GBP 340 combined subscription in United Kingdom to institutions (print & online eds.); EUR 447, USD 562 combined subscription to institutions (print & online eds.) (effective 2012). adv. illus. back issues avail.; reprint service avail. from PSC. **Document type:** *Journal, Academic/Scholarly.* **Description:** Dedicated to anything related to Sikh culture, religion and history.
Related titles: Online - full text ed.: ISSN 1744-8735. GBP 306 in United Kingdom to institutions; EUR 402, USD 505 to institutions (effective 2012).
Indexed: A01, A21, A22, CA, E01, PQC, T02.
—IE, Ingenta. **CCC.**
Published by: Routledge (Subsidiary of: Taylor & Francis Group), 4 Park Sq, Milton Park, Abingdon, Oxon OX14 4RN, United Kingdom. TEL 44-20-70176000, FAX 44-20-70176336, subscriptions@tandf.co.uk, http://www.routledge.com. Adv. contact Linda Hann TEL 44-1344-779945. **Subscr. to:** Taylor & Francis Ltd., Journals Customer Service, Sheepen Pl, Colchester, Essex CO3 3LP, United Kingdom. TEL 44-20-70175544, FAX 44-20-70175198, tf.enquiries@tfinforma.com.

294.6 GBR ISSN 0266-9153
SIKH MESSENGER. Text in English. 1984. 4/yr. **Document type:** *Magazine, Consumer.*
Published by: Sikh Messenger Publications, Ste 405, Highland House, 165 The Broadway, Wimbledon, SW19 1NE, United Kingdom. TEL 44-208-5448037, FAX 44-208-5404148, sikhmessenger@aol.com, http://www.nsouk.co.uk/. Ed., R&P Mr. Indarjit Singh.

289.9 AUS
SLAVIC GOSPEL NEWS. Text in English. 1970. bi-m. Website rev. **Document type:** *Newsletter.* **Description:** Discusses and promotes Christianity in the former U.S.S.R. and other Slavic countries.
Published by: Slavic Gospel Association, PO Box 396, Noble Park, VIC 3174, Australia. TEL 61-3-95623434, FAX 61-3-95584020, email@sga.org.au, http://www.sga.org.au. Circ: 1,500.

289.1 USA ISSN 2152-4483
SMALL TALK (CONCORD). Text in English. 2003. m. back issues avail. **Document type:** *Newsletter, Academic/Scholarly.*
Published by: Unitarian Universalist Association, Northern New England District, 10 Ferry St, Ste #318, Concord, NH 03301. TEL 603-228-8704, FAX 603-226-3011, uua-me.nh.vt@comcast.net.

299.6 USA ISSN 1050-1940
SOCIETE. Text in English. 1986. 3/yr. USD 30 (effective 2000). back issues avail. **Description:** Covers voodoo and other neo-African religious belief systems, including magic and culture.
Published by: Technicians of the Sacred, 1317 N San Fernando Blvd, Ste 310, Burbank, CA 91504. Ed. Courtney Willis. Circ: 1,000.

289.6 USA ISSN 0024-0591
SPARK (NEW YORK). Text in English. 1970. 5/yr. membership only. bk.rev. bibl.; charts; illus.
Published by: New York Yearly Meeting of the Religious Society of Friends, 15 Rutherford Place, New York, NY 10003. nyym@compuserve.com, http://www.nyym.org. Ed. Helen Garay Toppins. Circ: 4,000.

289.9 DEU ISSN 1867-3538
SPIRIT (FRANKFURT AM MAIN). Text in German. 2002. bi-m. EUR 22.20 (effective 2011). **Document type:** *Magazine, Consumer.*
Published by: Verlag Friedrich Bischoff GmbH, Gutleutstr 298, Frankfurt Am Main, 60327, Germany. TEL 49-69-2696123, FAX 49-69-2696111, vertrieb@bischoff-verlag.de, http://www.bischoff-verlag.de.

289.1 USA ISSN 1934-0702
ST. LAWRENCE DISTRICT NEWS. Text in English. 19??. 3/yr. **Document type:** *Newsletter, Consumer.*
Formerly (until 2003): Lines (1934-0699)
Published by: Unitarian Universalist Association of Congregations, Saint Lawrence District, 695 Elmwood Ave, Buffalo, NY 14222-1697. TEL 716-882-0430, FAX 716-882-6337, http://www.uua.org/aboutus/professionalstaff/districtservices/43681.shtml.

289.1 USA ISSN 2159-5666
THE STEEL CHALICE. Text in English. 19??. m. back issues avail. **Document type:** *Newsletter, Consumer.* **Description:** Aims to build a diverse and transformative spiritual community, help people to live lives of wholeness, and promote justice, peace, and religious freedom.
Former titles (until 2000): First Unitarian Church (2159-5658); (until 1996): The Unitarian (2158-4885)
Related titles: Online - full text ed.: free (effective 2011).
Published by: First Unitarian Universalist Church of Youngstown, 1105 Elm St, Youngstown, OH 44505. TEL 330-746-3067, office@uuyo.org.

289.57 NLD ISSN 1572-8013
STICHTING GEESTELIJK-WETENSCHAPPELIJK GENOOTSCHAP "DE EEUW VAN CHRISTUS". DONATEURSBLAD. Text in Dutch. 2003. s-a.
Published by: (Stichting Geestelijk-Wetenschappelijk Genootschap "De Eeuw van Christus"), Stichting Jozef Rulof Belangen, Arnhemseweg 308, Apeldoorn, 7334 AB, Netherlands. TEL 31-55-5333335, FAX 31-55-5330034, info@jozefrulofbelangen.nl, http://www.jozefrulofbelangen.nl.

289 ITA ISSN 0080-3987
STUDIA MISSIONALIA. Text in Multiple languages. 1943. a., latest vol.50, 2001. price varies. index. back issues avail. **Document type:** *Monographic series, Academic/Scholarly.* **Description:** Includes subjects such as Islam, Buddhism, Hinduism, religious ethnology, revelation, worship and ritual, prayers, meditation, mystical experiences, morality and religion in Christianity and other religions.
Indexed: A21, CPL, DIP, FR, IBR, IBZ, PCI, R&TA, RI-1, RI-2, SCOPUS.
—BLDSC (8483.060000), INIST.
Published by: (Pontificia Universita Gregoriana, Facolta di Missiologia), Gregorian University Press/Editrice Pontificia Universita Gregoriana, Piazza della Pilotta 35, Rome, 00187, Italy. TEL 39-06-6781567, FAX 39-06-6780588, periodicals@biblicum.com, http://www.paxbook.com. Circ: 400.

290 DEU
STUDIA SAMARITANA. Text in German. 1969. irreg., latest vol.6, 2011. price varies. **Document type:** *Monographic series, Academic/Scholarly.*
Published by: Walter de Gruyter GmbH & Co. KG, Genthiner Str 13, Berlin, 10785, Germany. TEL 49-30-260050, FAX 49-30-26005251, info@degruyter.com, http://www.degruyter.de. Eds. Garry Knoppers, Magnar Kartveit, Stefan Schorch.

299 DEU ISSN 2190-3646
▼ **STUDIEN ZUR SPAETAEGYPTISCHEN RELIGION.** Text in German. 2010. irreg., latest vol.2, 2010. price varies. **Document type:** *Monographic series, Academic/Scholarly.*
Published by: Harrassowitz Verlag, Kreuzberger Ring 7b-d, Wiesbaden, 65205, Germany. TEL 49-611-5300, FAX 49-611-530560, verlag@harrassowitz.de, http://www.harrassowitz.de.

289.7 USA ISSN 0081-7538
STUDIES IN ANABAPTIST AND MENNONITE HISTORY. Text in English. 1929. irreg., latest vol.36, 1997. price varies.
Published by: (Mennonite Historical Society), Mennonite Publishing House, 616 Walnut Ave, Scottdale, PA 15683. TEL 724-887-8500, FAX 724-887-3111.

289.98 950 USA
➤ **STUDIES IN ASIAN THOUGHT AND RELIGION.** Text in English. 1983. irreg., latest vol.29, 2005. price varies. back issues avail. **Document type:** *Monographic series, Academic/Scholarly.*
Published by: Edwin Mellen Press, 415 Ridge St, PO Box 450, Lewiston, NY 14092. TEL 716-754-2266, FAX 716-754-4056, cservice@mellenpress.com.

243 USA ISSN 1052-0503
STUDIES IN EVANGELICALISM. Text in English. 1980. irreg., latest vol.17, 2000. price varies. **Document type:** *Monographic series, Academic/Scholarly.*
Published by: Scarecrow Press, Inc. (Subsidiary of: Rowman & Littlefield Publishers, Inc.), 4501 Forbes Blvd, Ste 200, Lanham, MD 20706. TEL 301-459-3366, 800-462-6420, FAX 301-429-5748, 800-338-4550, custserv@rowman.com, http://www.scarecrowpress.com. Eds. Donald W Dayton, Kenneth E Rowe. Pub. Mr. Edward Kurdyla TEL 301-459-3366 ext 5604.

299.5 DEU ISSN 0340-6792
STUDIES IN ORIENTAL RELIGIONS. Text in English, German. 1976. irreg., latest vol.59, 2010. price varies. **Document type:** *Monographic series, Academic/Scholarly.*
Published by: Harrassowitz Verlag, Kreuzberger Ring 7b-d, Wiesbaden, 65205, Germany. TEL 49-611-5300, FAX 49-611-530560, verlag@harrassowitz.de, http://www.harrassowitz.de.

289.3 USA ISSN 2151-7800
STUDIES IN THE BIBLE AND ANTIQUITY. Text in English. 1999 (Dec.). a. (until 2009 irreg.). USD 17.95 per issue (effective 2009). **Document type:** *Journal, Academic/Scholarly.* **Description:** Dedicated to Latter-Day Saint research on the Old Testament, New Testament and other texts topics in biblical and religious studies.
Formerly (until 2009): F A R M S Occasional Papers (1520-9652)
Indexed: A01.
Published by: Brigham Young University, The Neal A. Maxwell Institute for Religious Scholarship, The Neal A. Maxwell Institute for Religious Scholarship, Brigham Young University, Provo, UT 84602. TEL 801-422-9229, FAX 801-422-0040, maxwell_institute@byu.edu.

280.4 DEU ISSN 0170-9240
STUDIES IN THE INTERCULTURAL HISTORY OF CHRISTIANITY. Text in English, French, German. 1975. irreg., latest vol.152, 2010. price varies. **Document type:** *Monographic series, Academic/Scholarly.*
—BLDSC (8490.740000), IE, Ingenta.
Published by: Peter Lang GmbH (Subsidiary of: Peter Lang Publishing Group), Eschborner Landstr 42-50, Frankfurt Am Main, 60489, Germany. TEL 49-69-7807050, FAX 49-69-78070550, zentrale.frankfurt@peterlang.com, http://www.peterlang.com. Eds. Jan Jongeneel, Richard Friedli, Werner Ustorf.

299.6 NLD ISSN 0169-9814
➤ **STUDIES OF RELIGION IN AFRICA.** Text in Dutch. 1970. irreg., latest vol.35, 2008. price varies. bibl. back issues avail. **Document type:** *Monographic series, Academic/Scholarly.*
Related titles: ◆ Supplement to: Journal of Religion in Africa. ISSN 0022-4200.
Indexed: IZBG.
—BLDSC (8491.432000), IE, Ingenta.
Published by: Brill, PO Box 9000, Leiden, 2300 PA, Netherlands. TEL 31-71-5353500, FAX 31-71-5317532, cs@brill.nl, http://www.brill.nl. Ed. Paul Gifford. R&P Elizabeth Venekamp. **Dist. by:** Turpin Distribution Services Ltd., Pegasus Dr, Stratton Business Park, Biggleswade, Bedfordshire SG18 8QB, United Kingdom. TEL 44-1767-604954, FAX 44-1767-601640, custserv@turpin-distribution.com, http://www.turpin-distribution.com/.

289.93 GBR
SUDAN CHURCH REVIEW. Text in English. 1949. s-a. GBP 15 (effective 2009). bk.rev. back issues avail. **Document type:** *Newsletter.* **Description:** Provides news from church leaders and other workers in the Sudan. Includes news from supporting groups and organizations in UK.
Related titles: Online - full text ed.: free (effective 2009).
Published by: Sudan Church Association, Chairman, The Ven Michael Paget Wilkes, 1 Hill Top, Coventry, CV1 5AB, United Kingdom. TEL 44-2476-521337. Ed. Canon Cannon Timothy Biles TEL 44-1935-816247.

289.1 AUS
THE SUN. Text in English. 1950. bi-m. AUD 15 to non-members; free to members (effective 2009). back issues avail. **Document type:** *Newsletter, Trade.* **Description:** Official newsletter of Sydney Unitarian Church.
Former titles (until 2005): Unitarian Pioneer (0310-8384); (until 2004): Pioneer
Related titles: Online - full text ed.
Published by: Sydney Unitarian Church, PO Box 355, Darlinghurst, NSW 1300, Australia. TEL 61-2-93602038, info_syduni@yahoo.com.au. Ed. M R McPhee.

289.3 USA ISSN 0363-1370
AP2
SUNSTONE. Text in English. 1975. 6/yr. USD 36 domestic; USD 48 foreign; USD 26 domestic to students (effective 2005). adv. bk.rev. illus. index. **Document type:** *Magazine, Consumer.* **Description:** Examines the Mormon experience with scholarship, issues, and art.
Related titles: Online - full content ed.
Indexed: A21, CCR, RI-1, RI-2.
—Ingenta.
Published by: Sunstone Foundation, 343 N 300 W, Salt Lake City, UT 84103. TEL 801-355-5926, FAX 801-355-4043, info@sunstoneonline.com, http://www.sunstoneonline.com/. adv.: B&W page USD 700. Circ: 10,000 (paid).

292 SRB ISSN 1451-7191
SVETOSAVSKO ZVONCE. Text in Serbian. 1968. bi-m. CSD 50 domestic (effective 2007). **Document type:** *Magazine, Consumer.*
Published by: (Srpske Pravoslavne Crkve, Sveti Arhijerejski Sinod), Informativno Izdavacka Ustanova S P C, Kralja Petra br 5, Belgrade, 11000. TEL 381-11-3282588. Ed. Radmila Misev. Circ: 5,000.

290 USA ISSN 1932-3069
SYNAPSE (BOSTON). Text in English. 1983 (Mar.). 2/yr. free (effective 2007). adv. bk.rev. back issues avail.
Formerly: People Soup (0360-8247)
Published by: Unitarian Universalist Association, 25 Beacon St, Boston, MA 02108. TEL 617-742-2100, FAX 617-367-3237. Ed. Jennifer Harrison. Circ: 10,500 (controlled).

299 JPN ISSN 0040-3482
BL2222.T4
TENRIKYO. Text in English. 1962-1970; resumed 1976. m. JPY 1,520 domestic; JPY 1,680 in Asia; JPY 2,160 in Europe; JPY 2,160 in Africa; JPY 1,920 elsewhere (effective 2001). illus.; tr.lit. 4 p./no.; **Document type:** *Newsletter.* **Description:** Contains news related to the Tenrikyo church, and doctrinal articles.
Published by: Tenrikyo Overseas Department, Tenri, Nara, 632-8501, Japan. TEL 81-743-63-1511 ext 5364, FAX 81-743-62-5625. Ed. Hiroaki Yamazawa. R&P Yoshinori Onishi. Circ: 3,400.

THEOSOFIA; brotherhood, problems of society, religion and occult research. *see* PHILOSOPHY

299.934 USA ISSN 0951-497X
➤ **THEOSOPHICAL HISTORY**; a quarterly journal of research. Text in English. 1985-1989; resumed 1990. q. USD 22 in North America; USD 38 elsewhere; USD 8, GBP 4 per issue (effective 2010). bk.rev. bibl. index. back issues avail. **Document type:** *Journal, Academic/Scholarly.* **Description:** Publishes contributions related to the modern Theosophical Movement from the time of Helena Blavatsky, and to all groups deriving their teachings directly or indirectly from her or her immediate followers. Examines related movements or philosophies.
Related titles: Online - full text ed.: USD 2.50, GBP 1.50 (effective 2010).
Indexed: A21, RI-1, RI-2.
Address: c/o James A Santucci, Department of Comparative Religion, California State University, Box 6868, Fullerton, CA 92634. TEL 714-278-3727, jsantucci@fullerton.edu.

299.934 DEU ISSN 0177-8005
THEOSOPHIE HEUTE. Text in German. 1954. 3/yr. USD 10. back issues avail. **Document type:** *Academic/Scholarly.*
Published by: Theosophische Gesellschaft in Deutschland, c/o Hans Beetz, Argentinische Allee 159, Berlin, 14169, Germany. TEL 030-8131680. Circ: 1,200.

299.934 IND ISSN 0972-1851
BP500
THE THEOSOPHIST. Text in English. 1879. m. INR 100 (effective 2011). bk.rev. s-a. index. **Document type:** *Journal, Academic/Scholarly.* **Description:** Covers spiritual subjects, religion, science and philosophy.
Indexed: BAS, MLA-IB.
Published by: (Theosophical Society USA), Theosophical Publishing House, Adyar, Chennai, Tamil Nadu 600 020, India. TEL 91-44-24912474, intl.hq@ts-adyar.org.

299.934 AUS ISSN 1038-1139
THEOSOPHY IN AUSTRALIA. Text in English. 1926. q. AUD 12 domestic to non-members; AUD 20 foreign to non-members; free to members (effective 2010). bk.rev. index. 32 p./no. 2 cols./p.; **Document type:** *Magazine, Academic/Scholarly.* **Description:** Publishes articles on theosophy, comparative religion, philosophy and science, written mainly by members.
Incorporates (1934-1936): News and Notes; Formerly (until 1934): The Australian Theosophist
Published by: Theosophical Society in Australia, 4th Fl, 484 Kent St, Sydney, NSW 2000, Australia. TEL 61-2-92647056, FAX 61-2-92645857, tshq@austheos.org.au. Ed., R&P Dana Tatray.

260 ITA ISSN 0040-6686
TI SALUTO, FRATELLO!. Text in Italian. 1946. m. free. **Document type:** *Magazine, Consumer.* **Description:** Features letters of thanks from devoted Christians who have prayed for someone with an illness. Includes articles on religious community activities.
Published by: Diocesi di Treviso, Ufficio Pastorale della Salute, Via Longhin 7, Casa Toniolo, Treviso, TV 31100, Italy. http://www.webdiocesi.chiesacattolica.it/cci_new/PagineDiocesi/index.jsp?idPagina=23054.

284.2 266 NLD ISSN 0167-1057
TIJDING. Text in Dutch. q. free membership (effective 2009).
Published by: Hervormde Bond voor Inwendige Zending/Reformed Alliance for Home Mission, Johan van Oldenbarneveltlaan 10, Amersfoort, 3818 HB, Netherlands. TEL 31-33-4611949, FAX 31-33-4659204, secretariaat@izb.nl.

260 KEN
TODAY IN AFRICA. Text in English. 1967. bi-m. KES 170, USD 5. adv. bk.rev. back issues avail. **Document type:** *Magazine, Consumer.* **Description:** Aimed at singles 16 to 30 years old facing problems in decision making and family life. Discusses marriage and other relations, careers, religion, and health from a nondenominational Christian perspective.
Formerly: Today (0040-8387)
Indexed: CERDIC.
Published by: (Africa Inland Church), Kesho Publications, PO Box 60, Kijabe, Kenya. TEL 254-154-64211. Ed. Mwaura Njoroge. Adv. contact Joe Gacheru. B&W page KES 6,500. Circ: 13,000.

289.9 NGA ISSN 0189-0557
BR1463.N5
TODAY'S CHALLENGE. Text in English. 1951. bi-m. NGN 42, USD 15. adv. bk.rev. charts; illus.
Formerly: African Challenge (0001-9968)
Published by: (Evangelical Church of West Africa), E C W A Productions Ltd., PMB 2010, Jos, Benue, Nigeria. TEL 234-73-52230. Ed. Jacob Shaibu Tsado. Circ: 20,000.

289.94 USA ISSN 1540-9643
BX6198.A7
TODAY'S PENTECOSTAL EVANGEL. Text in English. 1913. w. USD 28.99 domestic; USD 52 foreign; USD 0.75 per issue (effective 2009). bk.rev. charts; illus. index. 32 p./no.; back issues avail. **Document type:** *Magazine, Consumer.* **Description:** Provides feature articles needed for a spiritual life.
Formerly (until 200?): Pentecostal Evangel (0031-4897)
Indexed: AIPP, GSS&RPL.
Published by: (General Council of the Assemblies of God), Gospel Publishing House, 1445 N Boonville Ave, Springfield, MO 65802. TEL 417-862-2781 ext 4109, 800-641-4310, FAX 417-862-0416, 800-328-0294, CustSrvReps@ag.org, http://www.gospelpublishing.com/. Ed. Ken Horn. Adv. contact Jodi Harmon. Circ: 200,000.

289.6 GBR ISSN 1745-0845
TOWARDS WHOLENESS. Text in English. 1972. 3/yr. free to members (effective 2009). bk.rev. **Document type:** *Newsletter, Consumer.* **Description:** Studies the practice of prayer and spiritual healing, alternative therapies, relaxation, and Quaker thought and practice.
Published by: Friends Fellowship of Healing, 78 Courtlands Ave, Lee, London, SE12 8JA, United Kingdom. clerk@quaker-healing.org.uk. Ed. Rosalind Smith.

284.2 266 NLD ISSN 0927-6254
TRANSMISSIE. Text in Dutch. 1991. q. free (effective 2009).
Formed by the merger of (1975-1991): Schakels (Amersfoort) (0927-6238); (19??-1991): Gereformeerde Zendingsbond in de Nederlandse Kerk, Hervormde Bond voor Zending op G.G. (0927-6246)
Published by: (Gereformeerde Zendingsbond in de Nederlandse Hervormde Kerk/Board of the Reformed Mission League in the Netherlands Reformed Church), Hervormde Bond voor Inwendige Zending/Reformed Alliance for Home Mission, Johan van Oldenbarneveltlaan 10, Amersfoort, 3818 HB, Netherlands. TEL 31-33-4611949, FAX 31-33-4659204, secretariaat@izb.nl.

299.6 USA
TRIDENT (WHITEHALL). Text in English. 1964. m. USD 49.95. adv. **Document type:** *Newsletter.* **Description:** Discusses issues concerning the modern philosophy of Satanism.
Published by: Embassy of S.A.T.A.N., PO Box 666, Whitehall, PA 18052. Ed. Ted Storm. Adv. contact Bernie Attorney.

TUATHA. *see* NEW AGE PUBLICATIONS

289.9 USA
U L C NEWS. Text in English. 1981 (vol.15). q. USD 10 domestic; USD 15 foreign (effective 2001). adv. bk.rev. illus. **Document type:** *Newsletter.* **Description:** Provides an overview of religion in today's growing society. Offers alternatives to established religions, doctrines and directions.
Formerly (until 1984): Universal Life
Related titles: Diskette ed.
Published by: Universal Life Church, 601 Third St, Modesto, CA 95351. TEL 209-527-8111, FAX 209-527-8116. Ed., R&P Kirby J Hensley. Adv. contact Matthew English. Circ: 100,000.

U P F TODAY. *see* POLITICAL SCIENCE—International Relations

289.1 USA ISSN 1930-7306
U U FELLOWSHIP FOCUS. (Unitarian Universalist) Text in English. 200?. m. **Document type:** *Newsletter, Consumer.*
Published by: Unitarian Universalist Fellowship of San Dieguito, PO Box 201, Solana Beach, CA 92075. http://www.uufsd.org/ourfellowship.html.

U U M N NOTES. *see* MUSIC

289.1 USA ISSN 1532-7450
U U WORLD. Text in English. 1970. 6/yr. USD 14 domestic; USD 20 foreign (effective 2007). adv. bk.rev. charts; illus. 3 cols./p.; **Document type:** *Journal, Consumer.* **Description:** Aims to help its readers build their faith and act on it more effectively in their personal lives, their congregations, their communities, and the world. It strives not only to be informative but also useful, provocative, and even prophetic.
Incorporates (1997-1004): U U & Me! (1093-2615); Former titles (until 2000): The World (Boston) (0892-2462); (until 1986): Unitarian Universalist World (0041-7122)
Related titles: Online - full text ed.
Indexed: A22, P28, P48, P53, P54, PQC.
—Ingenta.
Published by: Unitarian Universalist Association, 25 Beacon St, Boston, MA 02108. TEL 617-948-6518, http://www.uua.org. Ed., Pub. Tom Stites. Circ: 115,000.

289.1 USA ISSN 2159-2683
UNI-FIRE. Text in English. 19??. m. free (effective 2011). **Document type:** *Newsletter, Trade.* **Description:** Celebrates life, affirms the inherent worth and dignity of all people, seeks wisdom, and works for justice in the Yakima Valley.
Formerly (until 1992): Unitarian Universalist Church of Yakima. Newsletter (2159-2675)
Media: Online - full text.
Published by: Unitarian Universalist Church of Yakima, 225 N 2nd St, Yakima, WA 98901. TEL 509-453-8448, admin@uucyakima.org. Ed. Rob Sherwood.

299 USA
UNICORN (KIRKLAND). Text in English. 1977. 8/yr. USD 13 domestic; USD 17 foreign (effective 2001). bk.rev. illus. **Document type:** *Newsletter.* **Description:** Covers modern Neo-Pagan Revival literature.
Published by: Rowan Tree Church, PO Box 0691, Kirkland, WA 98083-0691. TEL 425-828-4124, FAX 425-803-2025. Ed. Rev. Paul Beyerl. Circ: 120 (paid).

289.1 USA ISSN 2157-5738
UNIGRAM. Text in English. 19??. bi-w. free to members (effective 2010). back issues avail. **Document type:** *Newsletter, Consumer.* **Description:** Designed to communicate to members and friends about First Universalist Church ministry, business and activities.
Related titles: Online - full text ed.: free (effective 2010).
Published by: First Universalist Church of Denver, 4101 E Hampden Ave, Denver, CO 80222. TEL 303-759-2770, FAX 303-759-2841, office@firstuniversalist.org. Ed. Kevin Lowry TEL 303-759-2770 ext 50.

289.1 GBR ISSN 0049-531X
THE UNITARIAN. Text in English. 1905. m. GBP 6 (effective 2009). adv. bk.rev. **Document type:** *Magazine, Consumer.*
Related titles: Microform ed.: (from PQC).
Published by: Manchester District Association, c/o Liz Shaw, Manager, UCM, Luther King House, Brighton Grove, Manchester, M14 5JP, United Kingdom. liz.shaw@lkh.co.uk. Ed. Frank Hytch TEL 44-121-449050.

289.133 GBR
UNITARIAN AND FREE CHRISTIAN CHURCHES. HANDBOOK AND DIRECTORY OF THE GENERAL ASSEMBLY. Text in English. 1890. a. (directory; quinquennial, handbook). GBP 5.
Formerly: Unitarian and Free Christian Churches. Yearbook of the General Assembly (0082-7797)
Published by: General Assembly of Unitarian Free Christian Churches, Essex Hall, 1-6 Essex St, Strand, London, WC2R 3HY, United Kingdom. Ed. Matthew Smith. Circ: 850.

289.132 GBR ISSN 0082-7800
BX9803
UNITARIAN HISTORICAL SOCIETY, LONDON. TRANSACTIONS. Text in English. 1917. a. free to members (effective 2009). adv. bk.rev. cum.index every 4 yrs. **Document type:** *Journal, Academic/Scholarly.* **Description:** Publishes articles, notes, original documents and reviews on the history of Unitarianism and its historical constituency of English Presbyterianism and general Baptists.
Related titles: Online - full text ed.
Indexed: PCI.
Published by: Unitarian Historical Society, c/o Dr. David Steers, 223 Upper Lisburn Rd, Belfast, BT10 0LL, United Kingdom. TEL 44-20-72402384, FAX 44-20-72403089, nspresb@hotmail.com. Ed., Adv. contact Alan Ruston TEL 44-1923-232110.

289.132 USA ISSN 0362-0492
BX9801
➤ **UNITARIAN UNIVERSALIST CHRISTIAN.** Text in English. 1945. a. USD 25 per issue to non-members; free to members (effective 2010). bk.rev. cum.index. back issues avail. **Document type:** *Journal, Academic/Scholarly.* **Description:** Contains theological and liturgical articles for liberal Protestant clergy and laity.
Former titles (until 1969): The Unitarian Christian (0364-3506); (until 1950): Our Faith (0364-3492)
Related titles: Microfiche ed.; Microfilm ed.
Indexed: A21, R&TA, RI-1, RI-2.
Published by: Unitarian Universalist Christian Fellowship, 349 Boston Post Rd, Weston, MA 02493. info@uuchristian.org.

289.1 USA ISSN 0082-7827
UNITARIAN UNIVERSALIST DIRECTORY. Text in English. 1961. a. USD 25 (effective 1999). adv. **Document type:** *Directory.*
Related titles: Online - full text ed.
Published by: (Publications Department), Unitarian Universalist Association, 25 Beacon St, Boston, MA 02108. TEL 617-742-2100, FAX 617-367-3237. Circ: 2,500.

289.97 USA ISSN 0162-3567
BX9890.U5
UNITY MAGAZINE. Text in English. 1889. bi-m. bk.rev. 48 p./no.; **Document type:** *Magazine, Consumer.* **Description:** Metaphysical journal with human interest stories, articles, photography, and poetry. Focuses on practical christianity and spirituality.
Related titles: Braille ed.
Published by: Unity School of Christianity, 1901 NW Blue Pkwy, Unity Village, MO 64065-0001. TEL 816-524-3550, FAX 816-251-3553, http://www.unityworldhq.org. Ed. Stephanie Stokes Oliver. R&P Kathy Robinson. Circ: 82,000.

289.6 GBR ISSN 0267-6648
BR127
UNIVERSALIST. Text in English. 1979. 3/yr. GBP 3 per issue to non-members; free to members (effective 2009). bk.rev. back issues avail. **Document type:** *Journal, Academic/Scholarly.* **Description:** Theology, religious experience and mysticism. Specializes in the universalist aspects of Quakerism, including interfaith and ecological issues.
Published by: Quaker Universalist Group, c/o Carol Wise, 24 Rose-Bank, Burley-in-Wharfedale, Ilkley, West Yorkshire LS29 7PQ, United Kingdom. anneviolin@hotmail.com. Ed. Hazel Nelson.

289.9 DEU ISSN 0945-5027
UNSERE FAMILIE; die Zeitschrift der Neuapostolischen Kirche. Text in German. 1933. fortn. EUR 63.60 (effective 2011). adv. **Document type:** *Magazine, Consumer.*
Related titles: Online - full text ed.; ◆ English ed.: Our Family. ISSN 0946-3933.
Published by: Verlag Friedrich Bischoff GmbH, Gutleutstr 298, Frankfurt Am Main, 60327, Germany. TEL 49-69-2696123, FAX 49-69-2696111, vertrieb@bischoff-verlag.de, http://www.bischoff-verlag.de. Circ: 82,000.

289.4 SWE ISSN 1100-4681
VAERLDARNAS MOETE; Nya Kyrkans tidning. Text in Swedish. 1876-1984; resumed 1989. q. SEK 100 (effective 1998). **Document type:** *Academic/Scholarly.*
Former titles (until 1984): Nya Kyrkans Tidning (0345-8695); (until 1891): Skandinavisk Nykyrk-Tidning
Published by: Nya Kyrkans Vaenner, Hornsgatan 62, 4 tr, Stockholm, 11821, Sweden. TEL 46-8-640-50-49, FAX 46-8-640-9-45. Ed. Olle Hjern. Circ: 1,100. **Subscr. to:** Groendalsvaegen 24, Stockholm 11766, Sweden. **Co-sponsor:** Herrens Nya Kyrka.

299 ESP ISSN 0210-0533
VIDA SOBRENATURAL. Text in Spanish. 1921. bi-m. EUR 20 domestic; EUR 30 foreign (effective 2009). bk.rev. abstr.; bibl. 100 p./no.; back issues avail. **Document type:** *Magazine, Consumer.*
Published by: Editorial San Esteban, Plaza Concilio de Trento s-n, Apartado 17, Salamanca, 37001, Spain. TEL 34-923-264781, FAX 34-923-265480, info@sanestebaneditorial.com, http://www.sanestebaneditorial.com/. Ed. Manuel Angel Martinez. Adv. contact Jose Ramon Enjamio.

289.7 USA ISSN 1492-7799
BX8101
VISION; a journal of church and theology. Text in English. 2000 (Fall). s-a. USD 12 domestic; CAD 18 in Canada; USD 14 elsewhere; USD 32 for 3 yrs. domestic; CAD 48 for 3 yrs. in Canada; USD 38 for 3 yrs. elsewhere (effective 2004). **Document type:** *Journal, Academic/Scholarly.*
Indexed: A21.
—CCC.
Published by: Institute of Mennonite Studies, 3003 Benham Ave, Elkhart, IN 46517-1999. TEL 574-296-6239, FAX 574-295-0092. Eds. Dan Epp-Tiessen TEL 204-487-3300, Mary H Schertz. R&P Barbara Nelson Gingerich. Adv. contact Dan Epp-Tiessen TEL 204-487-3300.

294.45697 IND ISSN 0042-8086
VOICE OF AHINSA. Text in English. 1951. m. bk.rev. illus. **Document type:** *Magazine, Trade.*
Published by: World Jain Mission/Virendra Prasad Jain, F-221, Beta II, Gautam Budh Nagar, Noida, Uttar Pradesh 207 247, India. TEL 91-120-4290000, FAX 91-120-4290000, jain.events@yahoo.com, http://jainworldmission.com.

299 CAN
VOICE OF CHOICE. Text in English. q. **Document type:** *Newsletter.*
Published by: (Religious Freedom Council of Christian Minorities), Bible Holiness Movement, P O Box 223, Sta A, Vancouver, BC V6C 2M3, Canada. TEL 250-492-3376. Ed. Wesley H Wakefield.

289.1 CAN ISSN 1705-4192
VOICES ACROSS BOUNDARIES. Text in English. 2003. 3/yr. CAD 30 for 2 yrs. to individuals; CAD 40 for 2 yrs. to institutions; CAD 6.50 newsstand/cover (effective 2006). **Document type:** *Magazine, Consumer.* **Description:** Provides a forum for social, cultural, ethical and spiritual questions.
Indexed: C03, CBCARef, PQC.
Published by: Across Boundaries Multifaith Institute, PO Box 437, Sta A, Toronto, ON M5W 1C2, Canada. TEL 416-850-3598, FAX 416-850-3599, admin@acrossboundaries.net.

299.7 USA
VOR TRU/OUR FAITH. Text in English. 1978. q. USD 18; USD 26 foreign. bk.rev. **Description:** Contains news of the Asatru faith (the ancient religion of the Northern European peoples) in North America. Includes articles, poems and letters.
Published by: World Tree Publications, PO Box 961, Payson, AZ 85547. Ed. Valgard Murray. Circ: 500.

289.5 USA
WARM LINE. Text in English. 10/yr. **Description:** Discusses ideas of interest to Christian Scientists in and out of the church.
Address: 9527 Bay Court, Carmel, CA 93923. TEL 408-625-0825.

289.7 USA
WASHINGTON MEMO (AKRON). Text in English. 1969. q. free (effective 2011). back issues avail. **Document type:** *Newsletter.* **Description:** Features in-depth analysis and theological reflection on the issues that shape and are shaped by public policy.
Formerly (until 1970): Memo From the Peace Section Washington Office
Related titles: Online - full text ed.: free (effective 2011).
Published by: Mennonite Central Committee, 21 S 12th St, PO Box 500, Akron, PA 17501. TEL 717-859-1151, 888-563-4676, mailbox@mcc.org, http://www.mcc.org.

289.92 USA ISSN 0043-1087
BX8525
WATCHTOWER; announcing Jehovah's kingdom. (Editions in 144 languages) Text in English. 1879. s-m. free (effective 2009). charts; illus.; maps. 32 p./no. 2 cols./p.; **Document type:** *Magazine, Consumer.* **Description:** Focuses on world events relevant to Bible prophecy.
Related titles: Braille ed.; Finnish Translation: Vartiotorni (Tavallinen). ISSN 0784-1418; Norwegian Translation: Vakttarnet (Ytre Enebakk). ISSN 0805-9268; Italian Translation: La Torre di Guardia. ISSN 0271-3004.
Published by: (Jehovah's Witnesses, Governing Body), Watchtower Bible & Tract Society of New York, 25 Columbia Hts, Brooklyn, NY 11201. TEL 718-625-5000, FAX 718-560-8850.

289.133 GBR
WAYMARK. Text in English. 1967. 10/yr. free to members (effective 2009). bk.rev. back issues avail. **Document type:** *Newsletter, Trade.*
Related titles: Online - full text ed.
Published by: St. Mark's Unitarian Church, St Mark's Church, 7 Castle Terr, Edinburgh, EH1 2DP, United Kingdom. enquire@edinburgh-unitarians.org.uk. Eds. Eric McFadd, Jane Aaronson.

289.1 DEU
WEGGEFAEHRTE. Text in German. 1963. s-a. **Document type:** *Magazine, Consumer.*
Published by: Bund Deutsch-Unitarischer Jugend e.V., Dorfstr 94, Nordholz, 27637, Germany. TEL 49-4741-901621, bduj@gmx.de. Circ: 100.

289.5 USA
WINDOW ON THE NEWS. Abbreviated title: W O T N. Text in English. 1998. fortn. **Document type:** *Newsletter.* **Description:** Reports on spiritual developments in the fields of science, theology, and medicine, from a Christian Science perspective.
Media: Online - full text.
Published by: (The First Church of Christ, Scientist), The Christian Science Publishing Society, One Norway St, Boston, MA 02115. TEL 617-450-7929, http://www.spirituality.com/.

WIR KINDER. *see* CHILDREN AND YOUTH—For

133 292 USA ISSN 2153-0467
▼ **WITCHES & PAGANS.** Text in English. 2009. q. USD 22 domestic; USD 30 in Canada; USD 33 elsewhere (effective 2010). adv. illus. back issues avail. **Document type:** *Magazine, Consumer.* **Description:** Dedicated to, featuring, and partially written by young or beginning Witches, Wiccans, Neo-Pagans, and other earth-based, ethnic, pre-Christian, shamanic, and magical practitioners.
Formed by the merger of (2002-2009): NewWitch (1546-2838); (1997-2009): PanGaia (1096-0996); Which was formerly (until 1997): The Green Man (1069-3211)
Published by: B B I Media, Inc., PO Box 687, Forest Grove, OR 97116. TEL 503-430-8817, 888-724-3966, bbimedia@mcn.org, http://www.bbimedia.com. Adv. contact Anne Newkirk Niven. B&W page USD 295; 7.5 x 9.5.

WORLD. *see* GENERAL INTEREST PERIODICALS—United States

289.9 USA ISSN 1058-4463
WORLDORAMA. Text in English. 1967. 10/yr. free. **Document type:** *Newsletter.*
Published by: Pentecostal Holiness Church, World Missions Ministries, PO Box 12609, Oklahoma City, OK 73157. TEL 405-787-7110, FAX 405-787-7729. Ed. M Donald Duncan. R&P Bruce E Martin. Circ: 45,000.

289.92 USA ISSN 0084-3849
(YEAR) YEARBOOK OF JEHOVAH'S WITNESSES. Variant title: Jehovah's Witnesses Yearbook. Text in English. 1927. a. free (effective 2011). charts; illus. Index. **Document type:** *Yearbook, Corporate.* **Description:** Reports on Jehovah's Witnesses missionary and relief activities worldwide.
Formerly (until 1934): The International Bible Students Association. Yearbook
Published by: Watch Tower Bible and Tract Society of Pennsylvania, Inc., 25 Columbia Heights, Brooklyn, NY 11201. TEL 718-560-5600, FAX 718-560-5619, http://www.watchtower.org/. **Co-sponsor:** International Bible Students Association.

292 USA
YGGDRASIL; Freya's folk. Text in English. 1984. q. USD 10; USD 13 foreign (effective 1999). adv. bk.rev.; film rev.; video rev.; music rev. back issues avail. **Document type:** *Newsletter.* **Description:** Focuses on pagan religion, mythology, culture, ethos, and runes.
Address: 537 Jones St, Ste 165, San Francisco, CA 94102-2007. Ed., R&P, Adv. contact Prudence Priest. page USD 20; trim 7.5 x 4.5. Circ: 300 (paid).

289.7 CAN
YOUNG COMPANION. Text in English. 1966. 11/yr. USD 6. bk.rev. bibl.; illus.
Formerly: Ambassador of Peace
Published by: (Amish Church), Pathway Publishing Corporation, Rte. 4, Aylmer, ON N5H 2R3, Canada. Eds. Christian Stoll, Joseph Stoll. Circ: 23,300.

299.514 CHN ISSN 1006-9593
BL1910
ZHONGGUO DAOJIAO/CHINESE TAOISM. Text in Chinese. 1987. bi-m. USD 18 (effective 2009). **Document type:** *Journal, Academic/Scholarly.*
Related titles: Online - full text ed.
—East View.
Published by: Zhongguo Daojiao Xiehui/Chinese Taoism Association, Baiyunguan Nei, Xibianmen Wai, Beijing, 100045, China. TEL 86-10-63448889. **Dist. by:** China International Book Trading Corp, 35 Chegongzhuang Xilu, Haidian District, PO Box 399, Beijing 100044, China. TEL 86-10-68412045, FAX 86-10-68412023, cibtc@mail.cibtc.com.cn, http://www.cibtc.com.cn.

RELIGIONS AND THEOLOGY—Protestant

A B H E NEWSLETTER. *see* EDUCATION—Higher Education

280.4 USA
A F A JOURNAL. Text in English. m. USD 20 (effective 2002). **Document type:** *Magazine, Consumer.* **Description:** Keeps Christian families informed about cultural trends, important issues, boycott information, and television programming.
Published by: American Family Association, PO Box 2440, Tupelo, MS 38803. TEL 662-844-5036, FAX 662-842-7798, afa@afa.net.

287.632 USA ISSN 1050-6039
A M E CHRISTIAN RECORDER. (African Methodist Episcopal) Key Title: Christian Recorder. Text in English. 1848. bi-w. (Mon.). USD 36 (effective 2010). **Document type:** *Newspaper, Trade.*
Former titles (until 1984): A M E Christian Recorder; (until 1961): The Christian Recorder; (until 1861): African Methodist Episcopal Church. Christian Recorder; (until 1852): African Methodist Episcopal Church. Christian Herald
Published by: African Methodist Episcopal Church, 500 Eighth Ave S, Nashville, TN 37203. TEL 615-254-0911, FAX 615-254-0912, cio@ame-church.com, http://www.ame-church.com. Ed. Dr. Calvin H Sydnor III. Pub. Dr. Johnny Barbour.

287.632 USA ISSN 0360-3725
BX8440
➤ **A M E CHURCH REVIEW.** (African Methodist Episcopal) Text in English. 1884. q. bk.rev. bibl.; charts; illus.; stat. back issues avail. **Document type:** *Journal, Academic/Scholarly.* **Description:** Provides a forum for the objective and analytical discussion of issues pertaining to religion, education, economics, politics, and international affairs.
Related titles: Microform ed.: (from PQC); Online - full text ed.
Indexed: A22, IIBP, RILM.
Published by: African Methodist Episcopal Church, 500 Eighth Ave S, Nashville, TN 37203. TEL 615-254-0911, FAX 615-254-0912, cio@ame-church.com, http://www.ame-church.com. Ed., Pub. Reverend Dennis C Dickerson.

284.1 DNK ISSN 0107-5055
BX8001
AALBORG STIFTSBOG. Text in Danish. 1959. a. illus. back issues avail. **Document type:** *Yearbook, Consumer.*
Formerly: Aalborg Stifts Julebog
Related titles: Online - full text ed.
Published by: Aalborg Stifts Landemode, Bispekontoret, Thulebakken 1, Aalborg, 9000, Denmark. TEL 45-98-188088, FAX 45-98-188068, kmaal@km.dk, http://www.aalborgstift.dk. Ed. Soeren Lodberg Hvas.

284.2 NLD ISSN 1875-3698
AANZET. Text in Dutch. 1981. 3/yr. EUR 10 (effective 2009).
Formerly (until 2005): Mivo + 16 (1568-895X)
Published by: Jeugdbond Gereformeerde Gemeenten, Postbus 79, Woerden, 3440 AB, Netherlands. TEL 31-348-489948, FAX 31-348-483466, info@jbgg.nl, http://www.jbgg.nl.

230 USA ISSN 1075-2250
BV4241
THE ABINGDON PREACHING ANNUAL. Text in English. 1987. a. **Document type:** *Handbook/Manual/Guide, Consumer.*
Former titles (until 1994): Abingdon Preacher's Annual (1047-5486); (until 1991): Minister's Annual
Published by: Abingdon Press, 201 Eighth Ave S, PO Box 801, Nashville, TN 37202. TEL 800-251-3320, FAX 800-836-7802, orders@abingdonpress.com.

ABUNDANT LIVING (SEARCY). *see* GERONTOLOGY AND GERIATRICS

286.132 USA ISSN 0162-1955
ACCENT (BIRMINGHAM). (Avail. in Leadership and Member editions) Text in English. 1970. m. (10/yr.). USD 16.95 for Leadership ed.; USD 15.95 membership (effective 2003). **Document type:** *Magazine, Consumer.* **Description:** Publication of interest to members and leaders of Southern Baptist Acteens organizations.
Published by: Woman's Missionary Union Auxiliary to the Southern Baptist Convention, 100 Missionary Ridge, PO Box 830010, Birmingham, AL 35283. TEL 205-991-8100, email@wmu.org, http://www.wmu.com/. Ed. Becky England. R&P Carol Causey. Circ: 40,000.

ACT AND INFORM. *see* PUBLIC ADMINISTRATION

286.132 USA
ACTEENS ACCESSORIES. Text in English. q. USD 20.99 (effective 2008). **Document type:** *Magazine, Consumer.*
Published by: Woman's Missionary Union Auxiliary to the Southern Baptist Convention, 100 Missionary Ridge, PO Box 830010, Birmingham, AL 35283. TEL 205-991-8100, 800-968-7301, FAX 205-995-4840, customer_service@wmu.org, http://www.wmu.com/. Ed. Becky England. R&P Carol Causey.

ADIAPHORA; Schriften zur Kunst und Kultur im Protestantismus. *see* ART

287.6 USA ISSN 0149-8347
ADULT BIBLE STUDIES. Text in English. 1967. q. USD 23.50 (effective 2009). back issues avail. **Document type:** *Magazine, Consumer.* **Description:** Bible-based, Christ-focused, United Methodist-approved curriculum for use in adult Sunday school classes, Wednesday evening Bible study, and small-group based studies.
Related titles: Audio cassette/tape ed.; Large type ed. 13 pt.: USD 26.50 (effective 2009); ◆ Special ed(s).: Adult Bible Studies Teacher. ISSN 1059-9118; USD 4.75 per issue (effective 2006).
Published by: (United Methodist Church), United Methodist Publishing House, 201 8th Ave S, PO Box 801, Nashville, TN 37202. TEL 615-749-6000, 800-672-1789, FAX 615-749-6579, customerservice@umph.com, http://www.umph.org.

268.87 USA
ADULT BIBLE STUDIES STUDENT. Text in English. q. USD 23.50; USD 5.25 per issue (effective 2009). back issues avail. **Document type:** *Magazine, Consumer.* **Description:** Designed for use in adult sunday school classes, wednesday evening bible study and small-group based studies.
Related titles: Audio cassette/tape ed.: USD 12 per issue (effective 2009); Large type ed. 13 pt.: USD 26.50; USD 5.95 per issue (effective 2009).
Published by: United Methodist Publishing House, 201 8th Ave S, PO Box 801, Nashville, TN 37202. TEL 615-749-6000, 800-672-1789, FAX 615-749-6579, customerservice@umph.com, http://www.umph.org. Pub. Neil M Alexander.

268.87 USA ISSN 1059-9118
ADULT BIBLE STUDIES TEACHER. Text in English. 19??. q. USD 36; USD 7.95 per issue (effective 2009). back issues avail. **Document type:** *Magazine, Consumer.* **Description:** Designed to help teachers prepare lessons for classes.
Former titles (until 1992): Adult Bible Studies. Teaching Helps (0742-0706); (until 1984): Adult Leader (0149-8355)
Related titles: Online - full text ed.; Large type ed. 13 pt.; ◆ Special ed. of: Adult Bible Studies. ISSN 0149-8347.
Published by: (United Methodist Church), United Methodist Publishing House, 201 8th Ave S, PO Box 801, Nashville, TN 37202. TEL 615-749-6000, 800-672-1789, FAX 615-749-6579, http://www.umph.org. Pub. Neil M Alexander.

280.4 USA ISSN 0746-6919
ADULT CHRISTIAN LIFE; adult Sunday school quarterly ages 25 & older. Variant title: Adult Quarterly. Text in English. 198?. q. USD 3.65 per issue (effective 2009). **Document type:** *Magazine, Consumer.* **Description:** Especially written for practical adult life experiences. These lessons provide clear biblical interpretations and stimulating discussions for everyday living.
Related titles: Online - full text ed.: ISSN 1947-2080. 2009. USD 3.95 per issue (effective 2009); Large type ed.: ISSN 1947-6604. 2009. USD 3.95 per issue (effective 2009).
Published by: R. H. Boyd Publishing Corporation, 6717 Centennial Blvd., Nashville, TN 37209-1017. TEL 877-474-2693, FAX 800-615-1815, customerservice@rhboyd.com, http://www.rhboydpublishing.com.

285 USA
ADULT QUARTERLY. Text in English. 1891. q. USD 9; USD 2.25 per issue (effective 2009). **Description:** Includes lesson topics, scripture portions, and daily Bible readings. Sunday school curriculum materials and sponsors retreats and activities for all ages.
Related titles: Online - full text ed.; Large type ed. 16 pt.: USD 13; USD 3.25 per issue (effective 2009).
Published by: Associate Reformed Presbyterian Center, Office of Christian Education, 1 Cleveland St, Greenville, SC 29601. TEL 864-232-8297, FAX 864-271-3729, mmalone@arpsynod.org, http://www.arpsynod.org. Ed. Rev. William B Evans. R&P Marge Malone TEL 864-232-8297 ext 233. Circ: 12,000 (paid).

280.4 USA
ADULT STUDY GUIDE. Text in English. q. USD 3.85 per issue (effective 1998). adv. illus.
Published by: Messenger Publishing House, 4901 Pennsylvania Ave, Joplin, MO 64804-0700. TEL 417-624-7050, FAX 417-624-7102. Ed. James B Gee. R&P Phil L Redding. Adv. contact Peggy Alleh. Circ: 15,000.

286.132 USA ISSN 0162-4148
ADVANCED BIBLE STUDY. COMMENTARY. Variant title: Bible Studies for Life: Advanced Bible Study Commentary. Text in English. 19??. q. price varies. back issues avail. **Document type:** *Magazine, Consumer.* **Description:** Designed for teachers and learners who desire extensive commentary and includes explanations for key words and concepts and bible background information.
Published by: LifeWay Christian Resources, 1 Lifeway Plz, Nashville, TN 37234. TEL 615-251-2000, 800-458-2772, FAX 615-251-5933, customerservice@lifeway.com, http://www.lifeway.com.

289.73 CHL ISSN 0718-4050
ADVENIMIENTO. Text in Spanish. 2004. s-a.
Published by: Universidad Adventista de Chile, Facultad de Teologia, Casilla 7-D, Chillan, Chile. TEL 56-42-433500, facultadtheologia@unach.cl, http://www.unach.cl/facultades/teologia/.

284.1 USA
ADVENT. Text in English. 1979. q. USD 20 (effective 2005). adv. **Document type:** *Newsletter, Consumer.* **Description:** Promotes gay and lesbian understanding in Lutheran churches.
Formerly: Adventus
Published by: Lutherans Concerned - San Francisco, 566 Vallejo St, Ste 25, San Francisco, CA 94133. TEL 415-956-2069, lcsf@lcna.org. Ed., R&P, Adv. contact Judy Streets TEL 510-525-8643. Circ: 700 (controlled).

286.3 NLD ISSN 0165-8603
ADVENT. Text in Dutch. 1899. 11/yr. free (effective 2009). illus.
Formerly: Adventbode (0001-8767)
Indexed: CERDIC.

Published by: Kerkgenootschap der Zevende-Dags Adventisten/ Seventh-Day Adventists, Amersfoortseweg 18, Huis ter Heide, 3712 BC, Netherlands. TEL 31-30-6939375, FAX 31-30-6915745, info@adventist.nl, http://www.adventist.nl. Ed. Dr. G Henk Koning.

286.7 USA ISSN 0741-4307
ADVENT CHRISTIAN WITNESS. Text in English. 1952. m. USD 12 in US & Canada; USD 14 elsewhere. bk.rev. illus. **Description:** Promotes the gospel of Jesus Christ and the teaching of the Advent Christian Church.
Formerly (until 1983): Advent Christian Witness to the World (0274-9289)
Published by: Advent Christian General Conference of America, PO Box 23152, Charlotte, NC 28227. TEL 704-545-6161, FAX 704-573-0712. Ed. Rev. Keith D Wheaton. Circ: 4,000 (paid).

286.7 DEU ISSN 0179-7999
ADVENTECHO; Gemeindezeitschrift der Siebenten - Tags - Adventisten. Text in German. 1895. 11/yr. EUR 43.20; EUR 3.10 newsstand/cover (effective 2009). adv. bk.rev. **Document type:** *Magazine, Consumer.*
Incorporates (1980-1990): AdventGemeinde (0232-6086); Formerly (until 1973): Der Adventbote (0179-8146)
Published by: Advent Verlag GmbH, Luener Rennbahn 14, Lueneburg, 21339, Germany. TEL 49-4131-983502, FAX 49-4131-9835500, info@advent-verlag.de. Ed., R&P Friedhelm Klingeberg. Circ: 6,000.

286.7 USA ISSN 0360-389X
BX6101
ADVENTIST HERITAGE; a journal of Adventist history. Text in English. 1974. q. bk.rev. illus. back issues avail. **Document type:** *Journal, Academic/Scholarly.* **Description:** Provides collection of items pertaining to the history of the Seventh-day Adventist Church and La Sierra University.
Related titles: Microfilm ed.: (from PQC).
Indexed: AmH&L, P30.
Published by: La Sierra University, 4500 Riverwalk Pky, Riverside, CA 92515. TEL 951-785-2000, 800-874-5587, FAX 951-785-2901, info@lasierra.edu. Ed. Arthur N Patrick. R&P Gary Chartier.

286.7 JPN
ADVENTIST LIFE. Text in Japanese. m. JPY 3,360; JPY 1,200 newsstand/cover (effective 2001).
Published by: Japan Union Conference of Seventh-Day Adventists, 846 Kami-Kawai-cho, Asahi-ku, Yokohama-shi, Kanagawa-ken 241-0802, Japan. TEL 81-45-921-1121, FAX 81-45-921-2319. Ed. Katsumi Higashide.

286.7 USA ISSN 0161-1119
BX6101
ADVENTIST REVIEW. Abbreviated title: A R. Text in English. 1849. w. (36/yr). USD 36.95 in North America; USD 65.45 elsewhere (effective 2009). bk.rev. index. back issues avail.; reprints avail. **Document type:** *Magazine, Consumer.* **Description:** Offers faith-building articles that nurture growing christians and proclaim the gospel of Jesus Christ.
Former titles (until 1978): Advent Review and Sabbath Herald (0095-2397); (until 1971): Review and Herald (0034-6381); (until 1961): Advent Review and Sabbath Herald; (until 1851): Second Advent Review and Sabbath Herald
Related titles: Online - full text ed.; Spanish ed.
Published by: (General Conference of Seventh-Day Adventists), Review and Herald Publishing Association, 12501 Old Columbia Pike, Silver Spring, MD 20904. TEL 301-680-6560, FAX 301-680-6638, info@rhpa.org, http://www.rhpa.org. Ed., Pub. Bill Knott. Circ: 30,000 (paid).

286.7 DEU ISSN 1435-2141
ADVENTISTICA; Forschungen zur Geschichte und Theologie der Siebenten-Tags-Adventisten. Text in German. 1985. irreg., latest vol.9, 2010. **Document type:** *Monographic series, Academic/ Scholarly.*
Formerly (until 2000): Archives of International Adventist History (0724-7575)
Published by: Peter Lang GmbH (Subsidiary of: Peter Lang Publishing Group), Eschborner Landstr 42-50, Frankfurt Am Main, 60489, Germany. TEL 49-69-7807050, FAX 49-69-78070550, zentrale.frankfurt@peterlang.com. Ed. Daniel Heinz.

ADVENTURE (NASHVILLE). *see* CHILDREN AND YOUTH—For

284.1 USA ISSN 0044-6467
BX8001
AFFIRM; our eternal Christ and his word for our changing and urgent needs. Text in English. 1971. bi-m. per issue contribution. bk.rev. **Description:** Dedicated to preserving theological heritage while looking at related developments in the Lutheran church.
Published by: Balance, Inc., PO Box 8390, Saint Louis, MO 63132-0390. TEL 414-444-4133. Ed. Rev. Thomas Baker. Circ: 104,000. **Subscr. to:** PO Box 8390, St. Louis, MO 63132-0390.

285 KEN ISSN 1026-2946
BR1642.A35
AFRICA JOURNAL OF EVANGELICAL THEOLOGY. Abbreviated title: A J E T. Text in English. 1982. s-a. KES 450 domestic; USD 24 elsewhere (effective 2009). bk.rev. 100 p./no.; back issues avail. **Document type:** *Journal, Academic/Scholarly.* **Description:** Provides African evangelical theologians with information about theology and ministry.
Formerly (until 1988): East Africa Journal of Evangelical Theology (1018-8975)
Related titles: Online - full text ed.
Indexed: A21, ChrPI, RI-1, RI-2.
—BLDSC (0732.160735).
Published by: Scott Theological College, PO Box 49, Machakos, Kenya. TEL 254-145-21423, http://www.atla.com/.

230.41 TZA ISSN 0856-0048
AFRICA THEOLOGICAL JOURNAL. Text in English. 1968. 3/yr. TZS 4,800 domestic; USD 15 in Africa; USD 25 in Europe; USD 27 elsewhere (effective 2000). adv. bk.rev.
Indexed: CERDIC, PLESA, R&TA, RI-1, RI-2.
—BLDSC (0732.189700).
Published by: All Africa Lutheran Churches Information and Coordination Centre, PO Box 314, Arusha, Tanzania. TELEX 42054 LUTHA TZ. Ed. Mutembe Gaetan. Circ: 1,500.

284.1 NAM ISSN 0400-714X
AY1201.S6
AFRIKANISCHER HEIMATKALENDER. Text in Afrikaans. 1929. a.

Published by: Der Evangelisch-Lutherischen Kirche in Namibia, PO Box 233, Windhoek, Namibia. TEL 264-61-236002, FAX 264-61-221470, delk@namibnet.com, http://www.elkin-delk.org.

280.4 KEN
AFROSCOPE. Text in English, French. 1972. q. donation. **Document type:** *Newsletter, Consumer.* **Description:** Covers Christian evangelicals in Africa and the world.
Related titles: French ed.
Published by: Association of Evangelicals in Africa, PO Box 49332, Nairobi, Kenya. TEL 254-2-714977, FAX 254-2-710254, info@aea.co.ke. Ed. Tokunboh Adeyomo. R&P Gilbert Okoronkwo. Circ: 2,500.

266.4 NOR ISSN 1502-5624
AGENDA 3:16. Text in Norwegian. 2001. m. NOK 450 (effective 2007). adv. **Document type:** *Magazine, Consumer.*
Formed by the merger of (1994-2000): Barn & Familie (0805-018X); (1883-2000): Santalen (0802-1708); (1848-2001): For Fattig og Rig (0804-9459); Which incorporates (1945-1983): Indremisjonslederen (0804-9610); Which was formerly (until 1976): Ungdomslederen (0804-9629)
Related titles: CD-ROM ed.: Agenda 3:16 (CD-ROM). ISSN 1890-0801.
Published by: Normisjon, PO Box 7153, St. Olavs Plass, Oslo, 0130, Norway. TEL 47-23-301000, FAX 47-23-301001, normisjon@normisjon.no, http://www.normisjon.no. Ed. Espen Utaker. Adv. contact Helge Soevde. page NOK 15,800; 240 x 297. Circ: 15,000.

280.4 FRA ISSN 1956-9157
AIMER ET SERVIR. Text in French. 1965. q. EUR 16; EUR 4 per issue (effective 2010). **Document type:** *Magazine, Consumer.*
Published by: Union Evangelique Medicale et Paramedicale, 21A Rue Haute, Bossendorf, 67270, France. TEL 33-3-88022881, uemp@wanadoo.fr. Ed. C Klopfenstein.

280.4 POL ISSN 1230-5030
AKCENTY. Text in Polish. 1991. s-a. PLZ 8; USD 12 in United States. back issues avail. **Document type:** *Bulletin.*
Published by: Kosciol Adwentystow Dnia Siodmego, Rada Okregu Warszawskiego, 1 Maja 39-208, Podkowa Lesna, K-warszawy, 05-807, Poland. TEL 48-22-7589214, FAX 48-22-278619, pistis@plearn.edu.pl. Ed. Arkadiusz Pietka.

267.6 NOR ISSN 0801-9975
AKT; tidsskrift for kirke, samfunn og kultur. Text in Norwegian. 1988. q. NOK 160 to individuals; NOK 250 to institutions; NOK 35 newsstand/ cover (effective 2001).
Published by: Norges Kristelige Studentforbund, Universitetsgata 20, Oslo, 0162, Norway. TEL 46-22-40-50-80, FAX 46-22-33-71-86. Ed. Oeyunn Syrstad Hoeydal.

286 USA ISSN 0738-7741
THE ALABAMA BAPTIST. Text in English. 1874. w. USD 19.95 to individuals; USD 12 for churches (effective 2009). 20 p./no.; **Document type:** *Newspaper, Consumer.*
Published by: (Alabama Baptist State Convention), The Alabama Baptist, Inc., 3310 Independence Dr, Birmingham, AL 35209. TEL 205-870-4720, 800-803-5201, FAX 205-870-8957, circulation@thealabamabaptist.org. Ed. Bobby S Terry. Adv. contact Sue Ann Miller. Circ: 100,000 (paid and free).

286 USA ISSN 0002-4147
THE ALABAMA BAPTIST HISTORIAN. Text in English. 1964. s-a. bk.rev. bibl. back issues avail. **Document type:** *Journal, Academic/Scholarly.*
Indexed: AmH&L, RILM.
Published by: Alabama Baptist Historical Society, PO Box 292286, Birmingham, AL 35229. TEL 205-726-2363, 800-325-9863, FAX 205-726-2363, llberg@samford.edu, http://www.abhconline.com.

353.538 USA
ALARMING CRY. Text in English. 1953. q. USD 15; USD 30 foreign (effective 2000). bk.rev. 22 p./no. 5 cols./p.; back issues avail. **Document type:** *Newspaper.* **Description:** Provides religious, political, and WWII update news for combat veterans of the South Pacific War; also covers UFOs.
Published by: Evangelistic Arm of All-American Bible Church, Inc., Biblical Enterprises, PO Box 48, Langley, WA 98260. TEL 360-579-3916. Ed. Rev. Robert P Le Roy. Circ: 3,000.

266.3 GBR ISSN 0140-1238
ALCUIN CLUB COLLECTIONS. Text in English. 1899. irreg. price varies. **Document type:** *Monographic series.*
—BLDSC (0786.805000).
Published by: (Alcuin Club), S P C K, 36 Causton St, London, SW1P 4ST, United Kingdom. TEL 44-20-75923900, FAX 44-20-75923939, spck@spck.org.uk, http://www.spck.org.uk.

283 AUS ISSN 1442-5572
ALIVE MAGAZINE; Australia's Christian magazine. Text in English. 1974. bi-m. AUD 32.50 in Australia & New Zealand; AUD 49.95 elsewhere; AUD 6.50 newsstand/cover (effective 2009). adv. bk.rev.; film rev.; music rev. index. 52 p./no.; back issues avail. **Document type:** *Magazine, Consumer.* **Description:** Satisfies family and lifestyle issues for a growing readership that is spiritually and socially conscious of its community's well-being worldwide. Includes world news, entertainment and the arts, healthy living, spiritual awareness, human rights, education and social issues.
Former titles (until 1999): On Being ALIVE (1440-0065); (until 1998): On Being (0312-3847)
Published by: Media Incorporated Pty Ltd., PO Box 163, North Sydney, NSW 2059, Australia. TEL 61-2-84373541, FAX 61-2-99861431, enquiries@mediaincorp.com. Pub. Matthew Danswan. Adv. contact Matthew Harvie TEL 61-2-90075373. page AUD 1,200; 210 x 297. Circ: 13,000.

287.6 USA ISSN 0891-8767
CODEN: BFPMAN
ALIVE NOW; devotional reading. Text in English. 1971. bi-m. USD 17.95 domestic; USD 23.95 foreign (effective 2008). bk.rev.; film rev. back issues avail. **Document type:** *Magazine, Consumer.* **Description:** Helps small groups and individuals find Christian meaning in their lives as they face challenges at home, at work, and in the community.
Related titles: Online - full text ed.
Published by: (United Methodist Church, General Board of Discipleship), The Upper Room Publications, 1908 Grand Ave, PO Box 340004, Nashville, TN 37203. TEL 615-340-7200, FAX 615-340-7275, urbooks@upperroom.org. Ed. Joann Evans Miller. Circ: 70,000 (paid).

287.96 GBR ISSN 0002-5623
ALL THE WORLD. Text in English. 1884. q. GBP 3 domestic; GBP 3.50 foreign (effective 2009). back issues avail. **Document type:** *Magazine, Trade.* **Description:** Features articles that cover the international work and mission of The Salvation Army.
Published by: Salvation Army, International Headquarters, 101 Queen Victoria St, London, EC4V 4EH, United Kingdom. TEL 44-20-73320101, FAX 44-20-72364681. Ed. Kevin Sims. **Subscr. to:** Salvationist Publishing and Supplies, Ltd., 66/78 Denington Rd, Denington Industrial Estate, Wellingborough, Northants NN8 2QH, United Kingdom. TEL 44-1933-445445, FAX 44-1933-445415, mail_order@sp-s.co.uk, http://www.sps-shop.com/.

280.4 SWE ISSN 1104-2060
ALLA LEDARE. Text in Swedish. 1944. q. SEK 120 (effective 1996).
Former titles (until 1992): Alla Tiders Ledare (0345-0279); (until vol.4, 1974): Kristne i Barn- och Ungdomsarbetet; (until 1966): Kristne
Published by: Pingstfoersamlingarnas Ungdomsarbete (PU), Fack 4025, Huddinge, 14104, Sweden. TEL 46-8-774-40-80, FAX 46-8-774-40-87.

285 NLD
ALLE VOLKEN. Text in Dutch. 1907. 4/yr. EUR 5 (effective 2009). bk.rev. illus. **Document type:** *Journal, Consumer.*
Formerly: Alle den Volcke (0002-5666)
Published by: Gereformeerde Zendingsbond in de Nederlandse Hervormde Kerk/Board of the Reformed Mission League in the Netherlands Reformed Church, Postbus 28, Driebergen, 3970 AA, Netherlands. TEL 31-343-512444, FAX 31-343-521392, info@gzb.org, http://www.gzb.org. Eds. Mathilde Schouwstra-van Hoorn, Wijgert Teeuwissen. Circ: 41,000.

266 USA ISSN 1040-6794
BX6700.A1
ALLIANCE LIFE; the magazine of the christian and missionary alliance. Text in English. 1882. m. USD 13; USD 17 in Canada; USD 18 elsewhere (effective 2001). adv. bk.rev. illus. index. back issues avail.; reprints avail. **Document type:** *Magazine, Consumer.* **Description:** Journal of Christian life and missions.
Formerly (until 1987): Alliance Witness (0745-3256)
Related titles: Microform ed.: (from PQC).
Indexed: ChrPI, GSS&RPL.
Published by: Christian and Missionary Alliance, PO Box 35000, Colorado Springs, CO 80935-3500. TEL 719-599-5999, FAX 719-593-8692, 70570.3457@compuserve.com. Ed. Stephen P Adams. Adv. contact Mike Saunier. Circ: 26,000.

284.8 AUT ISSN 0002-6514
BX4751
ALTKATHOLISCHE KIRCHENZEITUNG. Text in German. 1966. m. looseleaf. adv. bk.rev. illus. **Document type:** *Newspaper, Consumer.*
Formerly: Alt-Katholik
Published by: Altkatholische Kirche Oesterreichs, Wipplingerstr 6, Vienna, W 1010, Austria. TEL 43-1-5337133, FAX 43-1-533713315, info@altkatholiken.at, http://www.altkatholiken.at. Ed., Pub. Robert Freihsl. Adv. contact Sabine Kraft. Circ: 2,700.

284.2 NLD ISSN 0927-9938
AMBTELIJK CONTACT. Text in Dutch. 1962. m. EUR 12.50 (effective 2008).
Published by: Christelijke Gereformeerde Kerken in Nederland/Mission of the Christian Reformed Churches in the Netherlands, Ghandistr 2, Postbus 334, Veenendaal, 3900 AH, Netherlands. TEL 31-318-582350, lkb@cgk.nl, http://www.cgk.nl. Ed. D Quant.

280.4 USA
AMEN MINISTRIES WEBZINE. Text in English. w. free. **Document type:** *Newsletter.* **Description:** Covers a wide variety of topics of interest to the Christian life, including homeschooling, commentary on contemporary Christian issues, and teen views.
Media: Online - full text. Ed. Pat Veretto.

286.173025 USA
BX6207
AMERICAN BAPTIST PLANNING CALENDER: RESOURCE AND STAFF DIRECTORY. Text in English. 1971. a. USD 10.95 (effective 2000). **Document type:** *Directory.*
Formerly: American Baptist Churches in the U S A Directory (0091-9381); Supersedes: American Baptist Convention. Directory (0096-3380); American Baptist Convention. Yearbook
Published by: American Baptist Churches in the U S A, PO Box 851, Valley Forge, PA 19482-0851. TEL 800-222-3872, http://www.abc-usa.org. Ed. Richard W Schramm. Circ: 10,500.

286.173 USA ISSN 0745-3698
BX6201
➤ **AMERICAN BAPTIST QUARTERLY**; a Baptist journal of history, theology and ministry. Text in English. 1938. q. USD 40 domestic to members; USD 52 foreign to members (effective 2009). bk.rev. illus. Index. back issues avail.; reprints avail. **Document type:** *Journal, Academic/Scholarly.* **Description:** Features articles, research and documentation that focus on the current trends and issues in the life of American Baptists.
Formerly (until 1982): Foundations (0015-8992); Supersedes (in 1958): Chronicle (0360-5779)
Related titles: Microform ed.: (from PQC).
Indexed: A21, A22, AmH&L, CA, FR, HistAb, P30, R&TA, RI-1, RI-2, RILM, T02.
—BLDSC (0810.725000), IE, Ingenta, INIST.
Published by: American Baptist Historical Society, 3001 Mercer University Dr, Atlanta, GA 30341. TEL 678-547-6680.

266.6 USA
BX6201
AMERICAN BAPTISTS IN MISSION. Text in English. 1803. q. free. adv. bk.rev. charts; illus. **Document type:** *Magazine, Consumer.* **Description:** Seeks to share ministry news.
Former titles: American Baptist (0002-757X); (until 1970): Crusader; Mission
Published by: American Baptist Churches in the U S A, PO Box 851, Valley Forge, PA 19482-0851. TEL 800-222-3872, FAX 610-768-2275, http://www.abc-usa.org. Ed. Richard W Schramm. Circ: 37,500 (free).

284 BEL ISSN 1372-7281
ANALECTA BRUXELLENSIA. Text in Dutch, English, French, German; Summaries in English. 1996. a.
Indexed: OTA.

R

Published by: Universitaire Faculteit van Protestantse Godgeleerdheid/ Faculte Universitaire de Theologie Protestante, Bollandistenstraat, 40, Brussels, 1040, Belgium. TEL 32-2-7356746, FAX 32-2-7354731, protest@fac.ac.be, http://protestafac.ac.be/.

283 CAN ISSN 0517-7731
ANGLICAN. Text in English. 1958. m. CAD 20 (effective 2008). adv. bk.rev. **Document type:** *Newspaper, Consumer.*
Incorporates (in 1968): Toronto Diocesan Anglican Church Women. News and Views (0700-7582); Which was formerly (until 1968): A.C.W. News (0700-7604)
Related titles: Online - full content ed.
Indexed: CERDIC.
Published by: Anglican Church of Canada, Diocese of Toronto, 135 Adelaide St East, Toronto, ON M5C 1L8, Canada. TEL 416-363-6021, 800-668-8932, FAX 416-363-7678. Eds. Henrieta Paukov, Stuart Mann. Adv. contact Carol McCormick TEL 905-833-6200. Circ: 46,000.

283 USA ISSN 1059-6763
ANGLICAN ADVANCE. Text in English. 1875. q. USD 10 outside diocese; free in diocese (effective 2005). adv. bk.rev. illus. 16 p./no. 4 cols./p.; **Document type:** *Newspaper.* **Description:** Contains news of the Diocese, the Episcopal Church and the Anglican communion.
Formerly (until 1989): Advance (Chicago) (0001-8562)
Indexed: CERDIC.
Published by: Episcopal Diocese of Chicago, 65 E Huron St, Chicago, IL 60611. TEL 312-751-4200, FAX 312-787-4534, http://www.epischicago.org. Ed., R&P, Adv. contact David Skidmore TEL 312-751-4207. Pub. Bishop Jeffrey D. Lee. page USD 1,000, B&W 1/2 page USD 670. Circ: 17,000 (paid).

280.4 USA ISSN 1947-5640
▼ **ANGLICAN ANALECTS.** Text in English. forthcoming 2011. irreg. price varies. **Document type:** *Monographic series, Academic/Scholarly.* **Description:** A collection of Anglican texts originally from Grove Books.
Media: Online - full content.
Published by: Gorgias Press LLC, 954 River Rd, Piscataway, NJ 08854. TEL 732-885-8900, FAX 732-885-8908, sales@gorgiaspress.com, http://www.gorgiaspress.com/bookshop/default.aspx.

283.09 USA ISSN 0896-8039
BX5800
➤ **ANGLICAN AND EPISCOPAL HISTORY.** Text in English. 1932. q. USD 5 per issue domestic; USD 10 per issue foreign; free to members (effective 2009). adv. bk.rev.; Website rev. bibl.; charts; illus.; maps. index. 135 p./no. 1 cols./p.; back issues avail.; reprints avail. **Document type:** *Journal, Academic/Scholarly.* **Description:** Designed for the members of the Historical Society of the Episcopal Church.
Formerly (until 1987): Historical Magazine of the Protestant Episcopal Church (0018-2486)
Related titles: Microfilm ed.: (from PQC); Online - full text ed.
Indexed: A21, A22, AmH&L, BEL&L, CA, CERDIC, HistAb, MLA-IB, P02, P28, P30, P48, P53, P54, PCI, PQC, RI-1, RI-2, RILM, T02.
—BLDSC (0902.769200), IE, Ingenta.
Published by: Historical Society of the Episcopal Church, PO Box 1749, Harlingen, TX 78551. Ed. Edward Bond. Adv. contact Susan Johnson.

283.71 CAN ISSN 1193-9737
BX5605
ANGLICAN CHURCH DIRECTORY. Text in English. 1900. a. CAD 21.95 (effective 1999). adv. stat. **Document type:** *Directory.* **Description:** Includes addresses of all Canadian dioceses, parishes, clergy, colleges, chaplains, religious communities, missions together with General Synod officers and staff and statistics of the Anglican Church of Canada.
Formerly (until 1993): Anglican Year Book (0317-8765)
Published by: (Anglican Church of Canada), Anglican Book Centre Publishing, 600 Jarvis St, Toronto, ON M4Y 2J6, Canada. TEL 416-924-9192, FAX 416-924-2760. Ed., R&P Robert Maclennan. Adv. contact Beverly Nicholl. Circ: 1,000 (paid).

283 AUS ISSN 1833-7899
ANGLICAN CHURCH OF AUSTRALIA. DIOCESE OF GRAFTON. YEAR BOOK. Text in English. 1982. a. **Document type:** *Yearbook, Consumer.*
Published by: Anglican Church of Australia, Diocese of Grafton, P O Box 4, Grafton, VIC 2460, Australia. TEL 61-2-66424122, FAX 61-2-66431814.

283 CAN ISSN 0826-3205
ANGLICAN CHURCH OF CANADA. GENERAL SYNOD. JOURNAL. Text in English. 1894. triennial. **Document type:** *Proceedings.*
Former titles (until 1980): Anglican Church of Canada. General Synod. Journal of Proceedings (0380-2469); (until 1952): Church of England in Canada. General Synod. Journal of Proceedings (0381-1433)
Published by: Anglican Church of Canada, 600 Jarvis St, Toronto, ON M4Y 2J6, Canada. TEL 416-924-9192, FAX 416-921-0211. Circ: 450.

283 USA ISSN 0003-3278
BX5001
ANGLICAN DIGEST. Text in English. 1958. bi-m. USD 19; donation. adv. bk.rev. 64 p./no. 2 cols./p.; **Description:** Reflects the ministry of the faithful throughout the Anglican Communion.
Related titles: Audio cassette/tape ed.
Indexed: CERDIC.
Published by: (Society for Promoting and Encouraging Arts and Knowledge, Inc.), S P E A K, Inc., Hillspeak, Eureka Springs, AR 72632-9705. TEL 501-253-9701, FAX 501-253-1277. Ed. Rev. C Frederick Barbee. Adv. contact Tom Walker. Circ: 115,000.

283 AUS ISSN 1032-9234
ANGLICAN ENCOUNTER. Text in English. 1970. 11/yr. (Feb.-Dec.). adv. bk.rev. **Document type:** *Newspaper.* **Description:** Reports local, national, and international news and teachings of interest to members of the Anglican Church.
Published by: Anglican Diocese of Newcastle, PO Box 817, Newcatle West, NSW 2300, Australia. TEL 61-2-49263733, FAX 61-2-4926-1968, 61-2-4929-5418, info@angdon.com. Ed., R&P, Adv. contact Jillian Hodgins. Circ: 7,400.

283 AUS
THE ANGLICAN GAZETTE; magazine for the Anglican Church in Central Queensland. Text in English. 1890. m. AUD 16 (effective 2008). adv. bk.rev. **Document type:** *Magazine, Consumer.* **Description:** Provides information on bible and its interpretation.
Formerly: Church Gazette
Published by: Anglican Diocese of Rockhampton, PO Box 6158, C Q Mail Centre, QLD 4702, Australia. TEL 61-7-49273188, FAX 61-7-49224562. Ed. Raelyn James. Circ: 2,500.

283 AUS
THE ANGLICAN GUARDIAN (ONLINE). Text in English. 1906. m. (10/yr.). bk.rev.; film rev.; music rev. tr.lit. 12 p./no.; **Document type:** *Newspaper, Consumer.* **Description:** Provides information, education and resources relating to church growth, evangelism, ordination and formation.
Former titles (until 2007): Church Guardian (Print) (1449-0374); (until 2001): Adelaide Church Guardian (0001-8147)
Media: Online - full text.
Published by: Anglican Church of Australia, 26 King William Rd, North Adelaide, SA 5006, Australia. TEL 61-8-83059348, FAX 61-8-83059399. Circ: 3,000.

283.42 AUS ISSN 1443-5993
ANGLICAN HISTORICAL SOCIETY. JOURNAL. Text in English. 1956. s-a. AUD 20 to members (effective 2004). bk.rev.; play rev. illus.; maps. cum.index to 2000. 48 p./no.; back issues avail.; reprints avail. **Document type:** *Journal, Academic/Scholarly.* **Description:** Contains articles on clergy, people, churches, areas, denominations, and local and social history.
Formerly (until 2000): Church of England Historical Society (Diocese of Sydney). Journal (0009-6490)
Published by: Anglican Historical Society, Diocese of Sydney, GPO Box 2902, Sydney, NSW 2001, Australia. TEL 61-2-94895929. Ed. John C Hodge. Adv. contact H. M. Woolston. Circ: 150.

283.71 CAN ISSN 0847-978X
ANGLICAN JOURNAL/JOURNAL ANGLICAN. Text in English. 1875. m. (10/yr.). CAD 10 domestic; CAD 17 foreign (effective 2011). adv. bk.rev.; film rev. illus. **Document type:** *Newspaper, Consumer.* **Description:** The national newspaper of the Anglican Church of Canada.
Former titles (until 1989): Canadian Churchman (0008-3216); Anglican Journal - Journal Episcopal
Related titles: Microfilm ed.: (from MML, PQC); Microform ed.: (from MML); Online - full text ed.
Indexed: A26, C03, CBCARef, CBPI, CPerI, G08, I05, P28, P48, P53, P54, PQC, R05.
—CIS.
Published by: The Anglican Church of Canada, 80 Hayden St, Toronto, ON M4Y 3G2, Canada. TEL 416-924-9199, FAX 416-925-8811, http://www.anglican.ca. Ed. Kristin Jenkins. adv.: B&W page CAD 8,925, color page CAD 10,965. Circ: 160,000 (paid).

283 AUS
ANGLICAN MESSENGER; Western Australia's Anglican magazine. Text in English. 1947. m. AUD 30 (effective 2008). adv. bk.rev. **Document type:** *Magazine, Consumer.* **Description:** Covers local, national and international Anglican news.
Published by: Anglican Church in Western Australia, GPO Box W2067, Perth, W.A. 6846, Australia. TEL 61-8-93257455, FAX 61-8-92214118. Ed. Cheryl Herft TEL 61-8-93257455. Adv. contact Chris Davies. Circ: 6,000.

283 GBR ISSN 1474-4902
THE ANGLICAN PEACEMAKER. Text in English. 1961. q. GBP 7.50 domestic; GBP 10 foreign; GBP 2 per issue (effective 2009). adv. bk.rev. back issues avail. **Document type:** *Newsletter, Consumer.*
Former titles (until 2001): Challenge (0009-0999); Anglican Pacifist
Related titles: Online - full text ed.: free (effective 2009).
Indexed: Acal.
Published by: Anglican Pacifist Fellowship, c/o Secretary Dr Tony Kempster, 11 Weavers End, Hanslope, Milton Keynes, Cambs MK19 7PA, United Kingdom. TEL 44-1908-510642. Ed. Tony Kempster.

230.3 USA ISSN 0003-3286
BR1
➤ **ANGLICAN THEOLOGICAL REVIEW.** Abbreviated title: A T R. Text in English. 1918. q. USD 45 to individuals; USD 60 to institutions (effective 2010). adv. bk.rev. abstr.; illus. index, cum.index every 10 yrs. back issues avail.; reprints avail. **Document type:** *Journal, Academic/Scholarly.* **Description:** Aims to foster scholarly excellence and thoughtful conversation in and for the church.
Related titles: Microform ed.: (from PQC); Online - full text ed.
Indexed: A01, A02, A03, A08, A11, A21, A22, AmHI, CA, CERDIC, DIP, FR, H07, H14, IBR, IBZ, IZBG, M01, M02, MLA-IB, OTA, P10, P28, P30, P43, P48, P53, P54, PQC, PhilInd, R&TA, RI-1, RI-2, RILM, T02, U01, WBA, WMB.
—BLDSC (0902.770000), IE, Infotrieve, Ingenta, INIST.
Published by: Anglican Theological Review, Inc., 600 Haven St, Evanston, IL 60201. TEL 847-864-6024, FAX 847-328-9624. Ed. Ellen K Wondra. Adv. contact Jacqueline B Winter. page USD 150; 4.25 x 7.25.

266.3 GBR ISSN 0969-7373
BX5011
ANVIL; an Anglican Evangelical journal for theology and mission. Text in English. 1984. q. GBP 20 domestic; GBP 28.50 foreign; GBP 6 per issue (effective 2009). adv. bk.rev. back issues avail. **Document type:** *Journal, Academic/Scholarly.* **Description:** Aims to encourage clear and creative thinking and practice in theology and mission, through open, scholarly debate.
Indexed: A21, RI-1, RI-2.
—BLDSC (1565.470000), IE, Ingenta.
Published by: Anvil Trust, Wycliffe Hall, 54 Banbury Rd, Oxford, OX2 6PW, United Kingdom. subscription@anviljournal.co.uk. Ed. Andrew Goddard. Adv. contact Rob McDonald.

287 USA ISSN 0003-6552
BV4800
EL APOSENTO ALTO. Abbreviated title: E A A. (44 language editions available) Text in Spanish. 1938. bi-m. USD 11 in US & Canada; USD 17 elsewhere (effective 2008). illus. **Document type:** *Magazine, Consumer.* **Description:** Contains a meditation, a suggested Scripture reference, and a prayer focus for each day. Spanish edition of The Upper Room.
Related titles: Online - full content ed.: free; ◆ English ed.: The Upper Room. ISSN 0042-0735.
Published by: (United Methodist Church, General Board of Discipleship), The Upper Room Publications, 1908 Grand Ave, PO Box 340004, Nashville, TN 37203. TEL 615-340-7200, FAX 615-340-7275, urbooks@upperroom.org. Ed. Stephen D Bryant. Circ: 80,000 (paid).

283.73 USA
THE APOSTLE. Text in English. 1892. m. bk.rev. **Document type:** *Newspaper.* **Description:** Deals with Protestant news.
Former titles (until 1999): Alabama Apostle; (until 1998): Apostle (1041-3316); (until 1988): Alabama Churchman (8750-9679); (until 1985): Alabama Anglican (8756-2103)
Published by: Episcopal Diocese of Alabama, 521 N 20th St, Birmingham, AL 35203. TEL 205-715-2060. Ed., R&P Norma McKittrick. Circ: 13,500.

287 USA ISSN 0279-9804
APUNTES. Text in Spanish. 1981. q.
Indexed: A21, Chicano, RI-1.
Published by: Southern Methodist University, Perkins School of Theology Mexican American Program, PO Box 750133, Dallas, TX 75275-0133. TEL 214-768-2265, map@smu.edu, http://www.smu.edu/theology/MAP/.

280.4 DEU
ARBEITEN ZUR KIRCHENGESCHICHTE BAYERNS. Text in German. 1925. irreg., latest vol.89, 2010. price varies. **Document type:** *Monographic series, Academic/Scholarly.*
Formerly (until 2004): Einzelarbeiten aus der Kirchengeschichte Bayerns
Published by: Wissenschaftlicher Kommissionsverlag, Alter Festplatz 14, Stegaurach, 96135, Germany. TEL 49-951-6010962, FAX 49-951-6010961, verlag@wikommverlag.de. Ed. Dietrich Blaufuss.

280.4 DEU ISSN 0945-9472
ARBEITSHILFE ZUM WEITERGEBEN. Text in German. 1947. q. EUR 20.44 (effective 2009). bk.rev. back issues avail. **Document type:** *Newsletter, Trade.*
Formerly (until 1993): Zum Weitergeben (0936-7136)
Published by: Evangelische Frauen in Deutschland e.V., Berliner Allee 9-11, Hannover, 30175, Germany. TEL 49-511-897680, FAX 49-511-89768199, info@evangelischefrauen-deutschland.de, http://www.evangelischefrauen-deutschland.de.

280.4 DEU
ARCHIV ZUR WEIMARER AUSGABE DER WERKE MARTIN LUTHERS. Text in German. 1981. irreg., latest vol.10, 2010. price varies. **Document type:** *Monographic series, Academic/Scholarly.*
Published by: Boehlau Verlag GmbH & Cie, Ursulaplatz 1, Cologne, 50668, Germany. TEL 49-221-913900, FAX 49-221-9139011, vertrieb@boehlau.de, http://www.boehlau.de.

283.73 USA ISSN 0890-5258
ARKANSAS EPISCOPALIAN. Text in English. 1975 (vol.49). 9/yr. USD 3; donation. bk.rev. **Document type:** *Newspaper.*
Formerly (until 1985): Arkansas Churchman (0199-4611)
Published by: Episcopal Diocese of Arkansas, PO Box 164668, Little Rock, AR 72216-4668. TEL 501-372-2168. Ed. Julie Keller. Circ: 8,000 (controlled).

287.6 USA ISSN 1080-2819
ARKANSAS UNITED METHODIST. Text in English. 1881. bi-w. USD 12.50 (effective 2005). adv. **Document type:** *Newspaper, Consumer.* **Description:** Contains news, features and opinions relating to the United Methodist Church in Arkansas and its constituents. Includes national and international news and features on topics and events affecting the religious community.
Formerly (until 1983): Arkansas Methodist
Published by: (United Methodist Church), Arkansas Methodist, Inc., 715 Center St., Ste. 204, Little Rock, AR 72201-3547. TEL 501-324-8031, FAX 501-324-8018. Ed. Jane D Dennis. Adv. contact Laura Organ. Circ: 11,000.

230.044 USA
BX8001
THE ASBURY JOURNAL. Text in English. 1945. s-a. USD 20 to individuals; USD 40 to institutions (effective 2010). bk.rev. cum.index: 1946-66 in vol. 21. reprints avail. **Document type:** *Journal, Academic/Scholarly.* **Description:** Provides a scholarly forum for thorough discussion of issues relevant to Christian thought and faith, and to the nature and mission of the church. Addresses those concerns and ideas across the curriculum which interface with Christian thought, life and ministry.
Former titles (until vol.60, 2005): Asbury Theological Journal (1090-5642); (until vol.40, 1985): Asbury Seminarian (0004-4253)
Related titles: Microform ed.: (from PQC).
Indexed: A21, A22, CERDIC, ChrPI, OTA, P30, R&TA, RI-1, RI-2.
—IE, Infotrieve, Ingenta.
Published by: Asbury Theological Seminary, 204 N Lexington Ave, Wilmore, KY 40390. TEL 859-858-3581, 800-227-2879, http://www.asburyseminary.edu/index.shtml.

266.4 NOR ISSN 1504-5560
ASIAS MILLIONER; organ for evangelisk orientmisjon. Text in Norwegian. 1914. bi-m. free. back issues avail. **Document type:** *Magazine, Consumer.*
Former titles (until 2005): Med Evangeliet til Asiens Millioner (0808-0291); (until 1996): Orientmisjonaeren (0808-0283); (until 1951): Kinamisjonaeren (0808-0275)
Published by: Evangelisk Orientmisjon, Slemdalsveien 1, PO Box 5369, Majorstua, Oslo, 0304, Norway. TEL 47-22-609440, sven@eom.no. Ed. Allan Neset.

284.2 NLD ISSN 2211-8578
ASPECTEN VAN CHRISTELIJKE FILOSOFIE. Text in Dutch. 1981. q. **Document type:** *Bulletin, Consumer.*
Former titles (until 2009): Aspecten van Reformatorische Wijsbegeerte (0921-3031); (until 1987): Stichting voor Reformatorische Wijsbegeerte, Vereniging voor Calvinistische Wijsbegeerte. Informatie-Bulletin (0921-3074)
Published by: Stichting voor Reformatorische Wijsbegeerte/Association for Reformational Philosophy, Postbus 3206, Soest, 3760 DE, Netherlands. TEL 31-35-5880205, FAX 31-35-5880981, office.reform.philos@planet.nl, http://www.christelijkefilosofie.nl.

284.2 NLD ISSN 1874-8309
ASPECTS OF REFORMATIONAL PHILOSOPHY. Text in English. 2007. 3/yr. free (effective 2011). **Document type:** *Bulletin, Consumer.*
Media: Online - full text.
Published by: Stichting voor Reformatorische Wijsbegeerte/Association for Reformational Philosophy, Postbus 3206, Soest, 3760 DE, Netherlands. TEL 31-35-5880205, FAX 31-35-5880981, office.reform.philos@planet.nl.

285.7 USA ISSN 0362-0816
BX8999.A6
THE ASSOCIATE REFORMED PRESBYTERIAN. Text in English. 1976. m. USD 15 (effective 2000). adv. bk.rev. back issues avail.
Description: Devoted to the concerns of the Associate Reformed Presbyterian Church in relationship to its mission to the service of God.
Related titles: Microform ed.: (from PQC).
Indexed: A22.
Published by: Associate Reformed Presbyterian, Inc., General Synod of the Associate Reformed Presbyterian Church, One Cleveland St, Greenville, SC 29601-3696. TEL 864-232-8297, FAX 864-271-3729. Ed., R&P, Adv. contact Ben Johnston. Circ: 6,000 (paid).

ASSOCIATION OF CHRISTIANS IN HIGHER EDUCATION. FORUM. *see* EDUCATION—Higher Education

ATEMPAUSE; Die Bibellese-Zeitschrift fuer Frauen. *see* WOMEN'S INTERESTS

286.132 CAN ISSN 0004-6752
THE ATLANTIC BAPTIST. Text in English. 1827. m. CAD 21.95 domestic; CAD 29.95 foreign (effective 1999). adv. bk.rev. illus. index. back issues avail. **Document type:** *Magazine, Consumer.* **Description:** Covers general religion and family life, devotional and social action.
Published by: Board of Publication of the United Baptist Convention of the Atlantic Provinces, P O Box 909, Wolfville, NS B0P 1X0, Canada. TEL 902-678-7704, FAX 902-678-7704, abaptist@glinx.com. Ed., R&P, Adv. contact Gary Dunfield.

280.4 DEU ISSN 1430-9254
AUFATMEN; Gott begegnen - authentisch leben. Text in German. 1995. q. EUR 19.80; EUR 5.80 newsstand/cover (effective 2011). adv. back issues avail. **Document type:** *Magazine, Consumer.*
Published by: Bundes Verlag GmbH, Bodenborn 43, Witten, 58452, Germany. TEL 49-2302-930930, FAX 49-2302-93093689, info@bundes-verlag.de, http://www.bundes-verlag.de. Ed. Ulrich Eggers. Adv. contact Tim Mueller. Circ: 27,000 (paid).

266 CHE ISSN 0004-7880
BV2000
AUFTRAG. Text in German. 1967. 6/yr. CHF 24, USD 2 (effective 1999). illus. **Document type:** *Newsletter.* **Description:** Covers missionary activities in Third World countries. Includes announcements of events.
Published by: Kooperation Evangelischer Kirchen und Missionen, Missionstr 21, Basel, 4003, Switzerland. TEL 41-61-2688289, FAX 41-61-2688268. Ed. Armin Mettler. Circ: 25,000.

280.4 USA ISSN 0896-6990
AUGSBURG ADULT BIBLE STUDIES. LEADER GUIDE. Text in English. 1968. q. USD 6.25 per issue (effective 2009). 64 p./no.; back issues avail. **Document type:** *Magazine, Consumer.* **Description:** Contains extensive Bible backgrounds for each text, as well as a helpful process guide for each session.
Formerly (until 1987): A L C - L C A Augsburg Adult Bible Studies. Teacher's Guide
Published by: Augsburg Fortress Publishers, PO Box 1209, Minneapolis, MN 55440. TEL 800-328-4648, FAX 800-722-7766, info@augsburgfortress.org. Circ: 4,220.

280.4 USA ISSN 0896-6982
AUGSBURG ADULT BIBLE STUDIES. PARTICIPANT BOOK. Variant title: Augsburg Adult Bible Studies. Leader Guide. Text in English. 1968. q. USD 3.75 per issue (effective 2009). adv. back issues avail. **Document type:** *Magazine, Consumer.* **Description:** Provides timely topics based on selected books of the Bible.
Former titles (until 1987): A L C - L C A Augsburg Adult Bible Studies. Adult Quarterly; A L C - L C A Augsburg Adult Bible Studies
Published by: Augsburg Fortress Publishers, PO Box 1209, Minneapolis, MN 55440. TEL 800-328-4648, FAX 800-722-7766, info@augsburgfortress.org. Eds. Eileen Zahn, Mark Hinton. Circ: 33,000.

285 MTQ ISSN 0986-1491
AUJOURD'HUI DIMANCHE. Text in French. w.
Published by: Presbytere de Bellevue, Fort-de-France, Martinique. TEL 714897. Ed. Pere Gauthier. Circ: 12,000.

283 AUS ISSN 0812-0811
AUSTRALIAN LECTIONARY (YEAR). Text in English. 1978. a. AUD 9.95 (effective 2008). adv. **Document type:** *Journal, Consumer.*
—CCC.
Published by: (Anglican Church of Australia), Broughton Publishing, 32 Glenvale Cres, Mulgrave, VIC 3163, Australia. TEL 61-3-95607077. Circ: 12,000.

285.294 AUS ISSN 1445-7962
AUSTRALIAN PRESBYTERIAN. Text in English. 1966. m. (except Jan.). AUD 38.50 domestic; AUD 45 foreign (effective 2009). adv. bk.rev.; film rev.; music rev.; tel.rev. illus. back issues avail. **Document type:** *Magazine, Consumer.* **Description:** Provides information about the Presbyterian Church of Australia.
Former titles (until 1998): A P L Today; (until Aug.1991): Australian Presbyterian Living Today; (until 1991): Australian Presbyterian Life, Living Today; (until 1989): Australian Presbyterian Life (0005-0059); (until 1966): Presbyterian Life
Related titles: Online - full text ed.: AUD 27.50 (effective 2009).
Published by: Presbyterian Church of Australia, National Journal Committee, PO Box 375, Kilsyth, VIC 3137, Australia. TEL 61-3-97239684, FAX 61-3-97239685, austpres@bigpond.com, http://www.presbyterian.org.au/. Ed. Rev. Peter Hastie. R&P, Adv. contact Walter Bruining. page AUD 726; 180 x 240. Circ: 3,000.

280.4 USA
AWANA IDEAS. Text in English. 1962. q. bk.rev. **Document type:** *Magazine, Consumer.* **Description:** For leaders and supporters of Awana Clubs; contains mostly news about the Awana ministry, leadership aids and inspirational material.
Formerly (until 2001): Signal (Streamwood) (0893-0880)
Indexed: TelAb.
Published by: Awana Clubs International, 1 E Bode Rd, Streamwood, IL 60107. TEL 708-213-2000, FAX 708-213-9704. Ed. Beecher Bailey. R&P Sue Hickey. Circ: 100,000.

286.132 USA ISSN 0162-6833
AWARE. (Also avail.: q. Aware Picture Set; q. Aware Resource Kit) Text in English. 1970. q. USD 19.99 (effective 2006). **Document type:** *Magazine, Consumer.* **Description:** Publication of interest to leaders of Southern Baptist Girls in Action groups.
Published by: Woman's Missionary Union Auxiliary to the Southern Baptist Convention, 100 Missionary Ridge, PO Box 830010, Birmingham, AL 35283. TEL 205-991-8100, email@wmu.org, http://www.wmu.com/. Ed. Barbara Massey. R&P Carol Causey. Circ: 27,000 (paid).

280.4 USA ISSN 1540-9759
AWE; declaring the wondrous acts of god. Text in English. 2002. q. USD 19 domestic; USD 29 foreign (effective 2002).
Published by: Streams Publications, P. O. Box 550, North Sutton, NH 03260. TEL 603-927-4224, FAX 603-927-4883.

286 CAN ISSN 0833-4587
B C FELLOWSHIP BAPTIST. Text in English. 1927. m. CAD 7. bk.rev. **Document type:** *Newsletter.*
Formerly: B C Regular Baptist (0702-1003)
Published by: Fellowship of Evangelical Baptist Churches of British Columbia & Yukon, P O Box 800, Langley, BC V3A 8C9, Canada. TEL 604-888-3616, FAX 604-888-3601. Ed. Bruce Christiansen. Circ: 10,000.

286.025 CAN
B C O Q DIRECTORY. Text in English. a. CAD 20 (effective 1999). **Document type:** *Directory.*
Former titles: Baptist Directory; Baptist Yearbook
Published by: Baptist Convention of Ontario and Quebec, 195 The West Mall, Ste 414, Etobicoke, ON M9C 5K1, Canada. TEL 416-622-8600, FAX 416-622-2308. Ed. T Simmonds. Circ: 800.

280.4 USA ISSN 2162-0806
▼ **B F C ONEVOICE.** Text in English. 2011. q. USD 10 (effective 2011). **Document type:** *Magazine, Trade.*
Published by: Bible Fellowship Church, 3000 Fellowship Dr, Whitehal, PA 18052. TEL 888-724-5325 ext 706, http://www.bfc.org/.

266.6 GBR
B M S WORLD MISSION. ANNUAL REPORT AND FINANCIAL STATEMENTS (ONLINE). (Baptist Missionary Society) Text in English. 1792. a. free (effective 2009). **Description:** Reports the work of the Baptist Missionary Society for the year.
Former titles (until 2002): B M S World Mission. Annual Report and Financial Statements (Print); (until 2000): Baptist Missionary Society, Didcot. Annual Report (0067-4060); (until 1998): Baptist Missionary Society. Directory and Financial Report (0067-4079); (until 1985): Baptist Missionary Society. Annual Report
Media: Online - full text.
Published by: B M S World Mission, 129 Broadway, PO Box 49, Didcot, Oxfordshire OX11 8XA, United Kingdom. TEL 44-1235-517700, mail@bmsworldmission.org. Circ: 24,000.

284.2 USA ISSN 0005-5557
BANNER (GRAND RAPIDS). Text in English. 1866. s-m. USD 36.95 (effective 2001). adv. illus. index. reprints avail. **Description:** Contains news pertaining to the life of the church, as well as feature articles that address the Christian faith and life of the members and readers.
Formerly (until 1906): Banner of Truth (0731-6089)
Related titles: Microform ed.: (from PQC).
Indexed: A22, CERDIC, GSS&RPL.
Published by: (Christian Reformed Church), C R C Publications, 2850 Kalamazoo Ave S E, Grand Rapids, MI 49560. TEL 616-224-0796, FAX 616-224-0834. Ed. Rev. John Suk. R&P Joyce Kane TEL 616-224-0732. Adv. contact Rachel Katje. Circ: 29,500.

280.4 USA ISSN 1072-6357
THE BANNER OF SOVEREIGN GRACE TRUTH. Text in English. 1993. m. USD 15; USD 17.50 in Canada; USD 30 elsewhere (effective 2001). adv. bk.rev. back issues avail. **Description:** Official publication of the Heritage Netherlands Reformed Denomination.
Published by: Heritage Netherlands Reformed Denomination, 540 Crescent N E, Grand Rapids, MI 49503. TEL 616-977-0599. Ed. Joel R Beeke. Adv. contact Marv Vandentoorn. **Subscr. to:** Marvin VandenToorn, 2080 Brandon, Grand Rapids, MI 49504. TEL 616-453-1055.

284.2 GBR ISSN 0408-4748
THE BANNER OF TRUTH. Text in English. 1957. m. (11/yr.). GBP 15 domestic; USD 27.50 in United States; GBP 20 elsewhere; GBP 2 per issue domestic; GBP 3.50 per issue in United States (effective 2009). bk.rev. back issues avail. **Document type:** *Magazine, Academic/Scholarly.* **Description:** Aims to a serious approach to the Christian faith by means of devotional, historical and doctrinal studies, and seeks to show how that faith relates to modern issues and attitudes.
Related titles: Online - full text ed.: USD 15 in United States; GBP 12 in UK & elsewhere (effective 2009).
Indexed: ChrPI.
—CCC.
Published by: Banner of Truth Trust Publishers, The Grey House, 3 Murrayfield Rd, Edinburgh, EH12 6EL, United Kingdom. TEL 44-131-3377310, FAX 44-131-3467484, http://www.banneroftruth.co.uk. Ed. Rev Walter Chantry.

286 DNK ISSN 1901-4635
BAPTISK.DK. Text in Danish. 1886. 8/yr. back issues avail. **Document type:** *Magazine, Consumer.*
Former titles (until 2005): Baptist (0107-2528); (until 1969): Baptisternes Ugeblad (0107-2536); (until 1915): Evangelisten (0907-3779)
Related titles: Audio cassette/tape ed.; Online - full text ed.
Published by: Baptistkirken i Danmark, Laerdalsgade 7, Copenhagen S, 2300, Denmark. TEL 45-32-590708, FAX 45-32-590133, info@baptist.dk. Ed. Anne Marie Andersen TEL 45-32-340534.

286 RUS
BAPTIST. Text in Russian. q.
Related titles: Microfiche ed.: (from IDC).
Indexed: RASB.
Published by: Izdatel'stvo Protestant, Mukomol'nyi pr-d 1, korp 2, Moscow, 123290, Russian Federation. TEL 7-095-2597407. **Dist. by:** East View Information Services, 10601 Wayzata Blvd, Minneapolis, MN 55305. TEL 952-252-1201, 800-477-1005, FAX 952-252-1202, info@eastview.com, http://www.eastview.com.

286.193 NZL ISSN 1176-8711
BAPTIST. Text in English. 11/yr. adv. bk.rev.; music rev. **Document type:** *Magazine, Consumer.* **Description:** Provides news and features of interest to New Zealand Baptists and Christians generally.
Former titles (until 2002): The New Zealand Baptist (0027-7177); (until 1880): Baptist; The New Zealand Baptist incorporated: Baptist Assembly News
—CCC.
Published by: Baptist Union of New Zealand, PO Box 97543, South Auckland Mail Centre, Auckland, New Zealand. TEL 64-9-2787494, FAX 64-9-2787499, info@baptist.org.nz. Eds. Duncan Pardon, Fran Pardon. adv.: B&W page NZD 750, color page NZD 950; 260 x 370. Circ: 12,000 (controlled).

286.132 USA ISSN 0162-4180
BAPTIST ADULTS. Text in English. 19??. q. price varies. back issues avail. **Document type:** *Magazine, Consumer.* **Description:** Designed for all adults in discipleship training includes learning and training experiences in a relaxed atmosphere without detailed preparation and lengthy sessions.
Published by: LifeWay Christian Resources, 1 Lifeway Plz, Nashville, TN 37234. TEL 615-251-2000, 800-458-2772, FAX 615-251-5933, customerservice@lifeway.com, http://www.lifeway.com.

286 USA
BAPTIST AND REFLECTOR. Text in English. 1835. w. (Wed.). USD 11 domestic to individuals (effective 2004). **Document type:** *Newspaper.*
Published by: Tennessee Baptist Convention, 5001 Maryland Way, Brentwood, TN 37027. TEL 615-371-2003, 615-373-2255, FAX 615-371-2014. Ed. Lonnie Wilkey. Circ: 48,000 evening (paid and free).

286 USA ISSN 0745-5836
BAPTIST BIBLE TRIBUNE. Text in English. 1950. m. USD 12 (effective 1998). adv. bk.rev. back issues avail. **Document type:** *Newspaper.* **Description:** Publishes news articles concerning churches and missions of the Baptist Bible Fellowship International, an independent fellowship of fundamental Baptist churches of like faith and practice.
Related titles: Online - full text ed.
Published by: Baptist Bible Tribune, Inc., 720 E Kearney St, PO Box 309, Springfield, MO 65801. TEL 417-831-3996, FAX 417-831-1470. Ed., Pub. Mike Randall. R&P Keith Bassham. Adv. contact Tom Harper. color page USD 850. Circ: 28,000.

286 USA ISSN 0005-5689
BX6201
BAPTIST BULLETIN. Text in English. 1933. bi-m. USD 12 (effective 2010). adv. bk.rev. back issues avail. **Document type:** *Bulletin, Academic/Scholarly.* **Description:** Contains news, ministry ideas, and articles written from a Biblical and Baptist perspective.
Indexed: GSS&RPL.
—Ingenta.
Published by: General Association of Regular Baptist Churches, 1300 N Meacham Rd, Schaumburg, IL 60173. TEL 888-588-1600, http://www.garbc.org/. Adv. contact Jeanine Gower.

286 USA ISSN 8756-9612
THE BAPTIST CHALLENGE; voice of independent Baptists. Text in English. 1961. m. free. adv. bk.rev. illus.
Published by: Central Baptist Church, 15601 Taylor Loop Rd., Little Rock, AR 72223-4346. TEL 501-868-7703, 800-594-4876, FAX 501-868-7622. Circ: 7,500.

286 USA
BAPTIST COMMUNICATIONS ASSOCIATION. NEWSLETTER. Text in English. 1953. m. looseleaf. free to members (effective 2008). bk.rev. tr.lit. **Document type:** *Newsletter.*
Formerly: Baptist Public Relations Association Newsletter (Print)
Media: Online - full content.
Published by: Baptist Communications Association, c/o David Winfrey, 1880 Ivanhoe Court, Louisville, KY 40205. office@baptistcommunicators.org, webmaster@baptistcommunicators.org. Ed. Mary E Speidel. Circ: (controlled).

286 USA ISSN 0744-6985
BX6201
BAPTIST COURIER. Text in English. 1878. w. (Wed.). USD 11. **Document type:** *Newspaper, Consumer.* **Description:** Forum and news on religion.
Published by: Baptist Courier, Inc., 100 Manly St., Greenville, SC 29601-3025. Ed. Donald Kirkland. Adv. contact Debbie Groomes. Circ: 116,000.

286 USA
BAPTIST HERITAGE UPDATE. Text in English. 1985. 3/yr. looseleaf. free to members (effective 2009). 3 cols./p.; **Document type:** *Newsletter, Consumer.* **Description:** Provides a reports on the society's efforts to foster Baptist history.
Published by: Baptist History & Heritage Society, PO Box 728, Brentwood, TN 37024. TEL 800-966-2278, FAX 615-371-7939, http://www.baptisthistory.org. Circ: 1,000 (paid).

286 USA ISSN 0005-5719
BX6207 CODEN: TIVEDD
➤ **BAPTIST HISTORY AND HERITAGE.** Text in English. 1965. 3/yr. USD 30 domestic membership; USD 43 foreign membership; USD 20 domestic to students; USD 30 foreign to students; USD 25 domestic to senior citizens; USD 34 foreign to senior citizens (effective 2003); free to members (effective 2009). bk.rev. charts; illus. index. 120 p./no. 1 cols./p.; back issues avail. **Document type:** *Journal, Academic/Scholarly.* **Description:** Features significant articles on the Baptist history.
Related titles: Microfiche ed.; Microfilm ed.; Online - full text ed.
Indexed: A21, A22, A26, AmH&L, CA, CERDIC, ChrPI, DIP, E08, G08, H05, HistAb, I05, IBR, IBZ, P30, PCI, R&TA, R05, RI-1, RI-2, RILM, S09, SBPI, T02.
Published by: Baptist History & Heritage Society, PO Box 728, Brentwood, TN 37024. TEL 800-966-2278, FAX 615-371-7939. Ed. Pamela R Durso TEL 678-547-6095. Circ: 1,000 (paid).

286 USA
BAPTIST INFORMER. Text in English. 1878. m. USD 20 (effective 2005). **Document type:** *Newspaper, Consumer.*
Published by: General Baptist State Convention of North Carolina, Inc., 603 S Wilmington St, Raleigh, NC 27601. TEL 919-821-7466, FAX 919-836-0061. Ed., R&P Portia Brandon. Circ: 9,000 (controlled and free).

286 USA
BAPTIST LIFE. Text in English. 1849. m. free to members church; USD 12 to non-members (effective 2005). **Document type:** *Newspaper, Consumer.*
Related titles: Microfilm ed.

Published by: Baptist Convention of Maryland/Delaware, 10255 Old Columbia Rd, Columbia, MD 21046-1716. TEL 410-290-5290, FAX 410-290-6627. Ed. Bob Simpson. Circ: 21,000 (paid).

286.132 USA ISSN 0744-9518
BAPTIST MESSENGER. Text in English. 1912. w. USD 9 (effective 2000). adv. **Document type:** *Newspaper.* **Description:** Relates news of interest to Oklahoma Southern Baptists and global southern Baptists.
Published by: Baptist General Convention of Oklahoma, 3800 N May Ave, Oklahoma City, OK 73112-6506. TEL 405-942-3800, FAX 405-942-3075. Ed., R&P John Yeats. Adv. contact Jerry Pierce. Circ: 95,000 (paid). **Subscr. to:** PO Box 12130, Oklahoma City, OK 73157.

266.6025 USA ISSN 0091-2743
BX6209.B37
BAPTIST MISSIONARY ASSOCIATION OF AMERICA. DIRECTORY AND HANDBOOK. Key Title: Directory and Handbook - Baptist Missionary Association of America. Text in English. 1961. a. USD 7 (effective 1998). **Document type:** *Directory.*
Published by: (Baptist Missionary Association of America), Baptist News Service, PO Box 97, Jacksonville, TX 75766. TEL 903-586-2501, FAX 903-586-0378. Ed. James C Blaylock. Circ: 5,500 (controlled).

286 USA ISSN 0164-7423
BX6460.9.P77
BAPTIST PROGRESS (BROOKLYN). Text in English. 1966. q. **Document type:** *Magazine, Consumer.*
Published by: The Progressive National Baptist Convention, 601 50th St, NE, Washington, DC 20019. TEL 202-396-0558, 800-876-7600, FAX 202-398-4998, aabrams@pnbc.org, http://www.pnbc.org.

286 USA ISSN 0005-5751
BAPTIST PROGRESS (WAXAHACHIE). Text in English. 1912. w. USD 18 (effective 1998). adv. bk.rev. **Document type:** *Newspaper.*
Related titles: Microfilm ed.
Published by: Baptist Missionary Association of Texas, PO Box 2085, Waxahachie, TX 75165. http://www.bmaweb.net/baptistprogress. Ed. Lynn Stevens. Circ: 12,000 (controlled).

286 GBR ISSN 0005-576X
BX6276.A1
➤ **BAPTIST QUARTERLY.** Text in English. 1908. q. GBP 5 to non-members; free to members (effective 2009). adv. bk.rev. illus. index every 2 yrs.; cum.index: 1908-1921; 1922-1941; 1942-1964; 1965-1986; 1987-1996. back issues avail.; reprints avail. **Document type:** *Journal, Academic/Scholarly.* **Description:** For historians interested in Baptist matters.
Formerly (until 1922): Baptist Historical Society. Transactions
Related titles: CD-ROM ed.; Microfilm ed.: (from PQC).
Indexed: A21, A22, AmH&L, BAS, CA, CERDIC, DIP, FR, HistAb, IBR, IBZ, IZBG, P30, PCI, R&TA, RI-1, RI-2, RILM, T02.
—BLDSC (1863.150000), IE, Infotrieve, Ingenta, INIST.
Published by: Baptist Historical Society, Baptist House, 129 Broadway, PO Box 44, Didcot, Oxon OX11 8RT, United Kingdom. shepherd.peter@talk21.com. Ed. Ian M Randall.

286 USA ISSN 0005-5778
BAPTIST RECORD. Text in English. 1877. w. (Thu.). USD 9.35 (effective 2005). adv. bk.rev.; rec.rev. charts; illus. **Document type:** *Newspaper, Consumer.*
Related titles: Microform ed.
Indexed: CERDIC.
Published by: Mississippi Baptist Convention Board, PO Box 530, Jackson, MS 39205-0530. TEL 601-968-3800, FAX 601-292-3330. Ed., R&P William H Perkins Jr. Adv. contact Dana Richardson. Circ: 102,000.

286 USA
THE BAPTIST STANDARD. Text in English. 1888. bi-w. USD 20.50 (effective 2007). adv. bk.rev. 24 p./no. 5 cols./p.; **Document type:** *Magazine, Consumer.*
Published by: Baptist Standard Publishing Co., 2343 Lone Star Dr, Dallas, TX 75212. TEL 214-630-4571, FAX 214-638-8535. Ed. Marv Knox. Adv. contact Doug Hylton. Circ: 85,000 (controlled).

286 LBR
BAPTIST TIMES. Text in English. 1993. a. USD 10. **Document type:** *Newsletter.* **Description:** Reports on missionary news and contains words of inspiration.
Published by: Liberia Baptist Missionary and Educational Convention Inc., Ste. 217-128 ACDB Bldg., Careu and Warren Sts., P O Box 10 0390, Monrovia, Liberia. TEL 231-223269. Ed. Rev. Emil D E Sani Peal.

286 GBR ISSN 0005-5786
BAPTIST TIMES. Text in English. 1855. w. GBP 53 domestic; GBP 72 in Europe; GBP 88 elsewhere (effective 2009). adv. bk.rev.; music rev.; rec.rev. illus. back issues avail. **Document type:** *Newspaper, Consumer.* **Description:** Covers all aspects of the Baptist religion.
Former titles (until 1925): The Baptist Times and Freeman; (until 1899): Freeman : Organ of the Baptist Denomination
Related titles: Microfilm ed.: (from WMP); Online - full text ed.: GBP 30 (effective 2009).
Published by: Baptist Times Ltd., 129 The Broadway, PO Box 54, Didcot, Oxon OX11 8XB, United Kingdom. TEL 44-1235-517670, FAX 44-1235-517678. Ed. Mark Woods TEL 44-1235-517672. Adv. contact Tim Woods TEL 44-1865-407991.

286 USA ISSN 0888-9074
BAPTIST TRUMPET. Text in English. 1940. w. USD 15 (effective 2000). adv. **Document type:** *Newspaper.*
Published by: Baptist Missionary Association of Arkansas, PO Box 192208, Little Rock, AR 72219-2208. TEL 501-565-4601. Ed. David Tidwell. Adv. contact Diane Spriggs. Circ: 13,400.

286.025 GBR ISSN 0302-3184
BX6276.A1
BAPTIST UNION DIRECTORY. Text in English. 1861. a. GBP 15.50 per issue (effective 2009). adv. **Document type:** *Directory, Trade.* **Description:** Contains details of accredited ministers and churches in membership with the Baptist Union of Great Britain.
Former titles (until 1973): Baptist Handbook (0067-4052); (until 1961): Manual of the Baptist Denomination for .
Published by: Baptist Union of Great Britain, 129 Broadway, Po Box 44, Didcot, Oxfordshire OX11 8RT, United Kingdom. info@baptist.org.uk, http://www.baptist.org.uk.

286.171 CAN ISSN 0067-4087
BX6252.W47
BAPTIST UNION OF WESTERN CANADA. YEARBOOK. Text in English. 1907. a. CAD 20. **Document type:** *Corporate.*
Published by: Baptist Union of Western Canada, 302, 902-11 Ave S W, Calgary, AB T2R 0E7, Canada. TEL 403-228-9559, 800-820-2479, FAX 403-228-9048. Ed. Rev. Gerald Fisher. R&P Dana Cupples. Circ: 700 (controlled).

286 USA ISSN 0005-5808
BAPTIST WORLD. Text in English. 1954. q. donation. illus. reprints avail. **Description:** Informs Baptists about the work of the BWA and of what Baptists are doing worldwide.
Related titles: Microform ed.: (from PQC).
Indexed: A21, RASB, RI-1, RI-2.
Published by: Baptist World Alliance, Division of Communications, 405 N. Washington St., Falls Church, VA 22046-3410. TEL 703-790-8980. Ed., R&P Wendy Ryan. Circ: 11,000.

286 USA ISSN 0067-4095
BAPTIST WORLD ALLIANCE. CONGRESS REPORTS. Text in English. 1905. quinquennial. USD 10 (effective 1999). **Document type:** *Proceedings.*
Published by: Baptist World Alliance, Division of Communications, 405 N. Washington St., Falls Church, VA 22046-3410. TEL 703-790-8980, FAX 703-893-5160. Circ: 15,000.

286 NLD ISSN 1872-5678
BAPTISTEN.NL. Variant title: Baptisten Nederland. Text in Dutch. 1954. q. free (effective 2010). adv.
Formerly (until 2006): De Christen (0167-2355)
Related titles: CD-ROM ed.
Published by: Unie van Baptisten Gemeenten, Raadhuisplein 6-8, Barneveld, 3771 ER, Netherlands. TEL 31-342-712457, http://www.baptisten.nl. Ed. Erik van Duyl.

289.7 362.1 USA ISSN 2153-0556
BASIN AND TOWEL. Text in English. 1999. 3/yr. USD 6 to individuals; USD 12 to institutions (effective 2010). **Document type:** *Newsletter, Trade.* **Description:** Includes information and articles for members of the Association of Brethren Caregivers.
Formerly (until 2010): Caregiving (Elgin) (1523-441X)
Published by: Association of Brethren Caregivers, 1451 Dundee Ave, Elgin, IL 60120. TEL 800-323-8039, dkline@brethren.org, http://www.brethren.org.

284.2 USA ISSN 2154-6320
▼ **THE BAVINCK REVIEW.** Text in English. 2010 (Apr.). a. **Document type:** *Journal, Academic/Scholarly.* **Description:** Features research on the theology of Herman Bavinck and other Reformed theological scholarship.
Media: Online - full text.
Published by: Calvin Theological Seminary, 3233 Burton St SE, Grand Rapids, MI 49546. TEL 800-388-6034, FAX 616-957-6101, bltj@calvinseminary.edu. Ed. John Bolt.

284.1 DEU ISSN 1612-9938
BAYREUTH EVANGELISCH. Text in German. 1900. 6/yr. looseleaf. adv. bk.rev. abstr. **Document type:** *Bulletin, Consumer.*
Formerly (until 2003): Bayreuther Gemeindeblatt (0005-7282)
Published by: Evangelisch-Lutherische Dekanat Bayreuth, Kanzleistr 11, Bayreuth, 95447, Germany. TEL 49-921-596805, FAX 49-921-596888, christine.peetz.kga-bay@elkb.de. Ed. Gottfried Lindner. Circ: 4,000.

BEAUTIFUL GIRL; inside and out. *see* CHILDREN AND YOUTH—For

280.4 USA ISSN 2156-5031
THE BELL NOTE. Text in English. 19??. m. back issues avail. **Document type:** *Newsletter, Trade.*
Former titles (until 1982): First Universalist Church of East Liberty. News; (until 1973): First Universalist Church of East Liberty. Uni Uni-Press; (until 1972): First Universalist Church of East Liberty. Newsletter
Related titles: Online - full text ed.: free (effective 2010).
Published by: Universalist Unitarian Church of East Liberty, 2231 Jefferson Rd, Clarklake, MI 49234. TEL 517-529-4221, uucel_bellnote@yahoo.com. Eds. Kathy Haynes, Vicki Haynes.

261.8 DEU ISSN 0522-9014
BR45
➤ **BENSHEIMER HEFTE.** Text in German. 1951. irreg., latest vol.99, 2002. price varies. **Document type:** *Monographic series, Academic/Scholarly.*
Formerly (until 1961): Aus der Arbeit des Evangelischen Bundes (0421-8264)
Published by: Konfessionskundliches Institut des Evangelischen Bundes, Eifelstr. 35, Bensheim, 64625, Germany. TEL 49-6251-84330, FAX 49-6251-843328, ki-eb@t-online.de, http://www.ekd.de/ki/.

280.4 DEU
BERLIN - BRANDENBURGISCHES SONNTAGSBLATT DIE KIRCHE; evangelische Wochenzeitung. Text in German. 1995. w. (Sun.). EUR 100 (effective 2010). adv. **Document type:** *Newspaper, Consumer.*
Formed by the 1995 merger of: Kirche; Berlin - Brandenburgisches Sonntagsblatt (0941-2735); Which was formed by merger of (1945-1991): Berliner Sonntagsblatt (0341-454X); (1946-1991): Potsdamer Kirche (0232-5020)
Published by: Wichern Verlag GmbH, Georgenkirchstr 69-70, Berlin, 10249, Germany. TEL 49-30-28874811, FAX 49-30-28874820, info@wichern.de, http://www.wichern.de. Ed. Joachim Schmidt. Circ: 13,800.

230.044 DEU ISSN 0724-6137
BR4
BERLINER THEOLOGISCHE ZEITSCHRIFT. Text in German. 1949. s-a. EUR 24; EUR 12.50 per issue (effective 2010). **Document type:** *Magazine, Academic/Scholarly.* **Description:** Discusses theoretical and scientific problems of theology.
Formerly (until 1981): Theologia Viatorum (0342-4235)
Indexed: DIP, IBR, IBZ, IZBG, PCI.
Published by: (Humboldt-Universitaet zu Berlin, Theologische Fakultaet), Wichern Verlag GmbH, Georgenkirchstr 69-70, Berlin, 10249, Germany. TEL 49-30-28874811, FAX 49-30-28874820, info@wichern.de, http://www.wichern.de. Ed. Dr. Cilliers Breytenbach. Circ: 500.

285.734 DEU ISSN 0006-0615
BS410
BIBEL UND GEMEINDE. Text in German. 1900. q. bk.rev. **Document type:** *Journal, Academic/Scholarly.* **Description:** Theological journal of German evangelical fundamentalism.
Published by: Bibelbund e.V., Postfach 470268, Berlin, 12311, Germany. TEL 49-30-44039253, FAX 49-30-44039254, kontakt@bibelbund.de, http://www.bibelbund.christen.net. Ed. Karl Heinz Vanheiden. Circ: 3,500 (controlled).

280.4 DEU ISSN 1611-8367
BIBELLESEBUCH MITTENDRIN. Text in German. 1991. a. EUR 7 (effective 2009). **Document type:** *Magazine, Consumer.*
Formerly (until 2002): Bibellesebuch (0948-3004)
Published by: Bibellesebund e.V., Industriestr 2, Marienheide, 51709, Germany. TEL 49-2264-404340, FAX 49-2264-4043439, info@bibellesebund.de, http://www.bibellesebund.de.

230 USA ISSN 0899-7055
BIBLE DISCOVERY. Text in English. 19??. q. **Document type:** *Journal, Trade.*
—CCC.
Published by: Presbyterian Church - U.S.A., 100 Witherspoon St, Louisville, KY 40202. TEL 800-872-3283, 800-728-7228, http://www.pcusa.org/.

286.132 USA ISSN 1068-2775
BIBLE EXPRESS. Text in English. 1993. m. USD 24.95; USD 1.30 per issue (effective 2008). adv. back issues avail. **Document type:** *Magazine, Consumer.* **Description:** Contains separate devotional readings for boys and girls, reflective activities, timely articles and illustrations just for them.
Published by: LifeWay Christian Resources, 1 Lifeway Plz, Nashville, TN 37234. TEL 615-251-2000, 800-458-2772, FAX 615-251-5933, customerservice@lifeway.com.

220 GBR ISSN 0006-0763
BIBLE LANDS. Text in English. 1899. s-a. donation. bk.rev. illus. index. **Document type:** *Magazine, Trade.*
Published by: Jerusalem and the Middle East Church Association, 1 Hart House, The Hart, Farnham, Surrey GU9 7HJ, United Kingdom. TEL 44-1252-726994, FAX 44-1252-726994, http://www.jmeca.org.uk/. Ed. Canon Timothy Biles TEL 44-1935-816247.

268 USA ISSN 1557-4350
BIBLE STUDIES FOR LIFE: LEADER QUICKSOURCE. Text in English. 2006. q. USD 20.95 (effective 2006). back issues avail. **Document type:** *Magazine, Consumer.* **Description:** Features a discussion approach and contains one-page parable plans that allow the reader to use everyday household objects to teach as Jesus taught.
Formerly: Explore the Bible. Leader Quicksource (1552-7204)
Published by: LifeWay Christian Resources, 1 Lifeway Plz, Nashville, TN 37234. TEL 615-251-2000, 800-458-2772, FAX 615-251-5933, customerservice@lifeway.com, http://www.lifeway.com.

280.4 268 USA ISSN 1557-5020
BIBLE STUDIES FOR LIFE: LIFE/LIFEF X YOUNGER AND OLDER YOUTH LEADER GUIDE. Text in English. 2003 (Fall). q. USD 4.10 per issue (effective 2003).
Formerly (until 2006): Family Bible Study: Younger & Older Youth Leader Guide (1542-8583); Which was formed by the merger of (2000-2003): Family Bible Study: Younger Youth Leader Guide (1526-5889); (2000-2003): Family Bible Study Guide: Older Youth Leader Guide (1526-5552)
Published by: LifeWay Christian Resources, 1 Lifeway Plz, Nashville, TN 37234. TEL 615-251-2000, 800-458-2772, FAX 615-251-5933, customerservice@lifeway.com, http://www.lifeway.com.

280.4 268 USA ISSN 1557-492X
BIBLE STUDIES FOR LIFE: LIFE VENTURES LEADER GUIDE. Text in English. 2000 (Fall). q. price varies. back issues avail. **Document type:** *Magazine, Consumer.* **Description:** Challenges retired adults to discover new experiences in their service to the lord and to pass on to younger generations the legacy of their faith.
Formerly (until 2006): Family Bible Study: Life Ventures Leader Guide (1542-7374); (until 2003): Family Bible Study. Ventures & Pathways Leader Guide (1526-5684)
Published by: LifeWay Christian Resources, 1 Lifeway Plz, Nashville, TN 37234. TEL 615-251-2000, 800-458-2772, customerservice@lifeway.com, http://www.lifeway.com. Ed. Jerry Lemon.

268 USA ISSN 1557-4776
BIBLE STUDIES FOR LIFE: LIFE VENTURES LEARNER GUIDE. Text in English. 2000. q. price varies. back issues avail. **Document type:** *Magazine, Consumer.* **Description:** Aims to equip, encourage and minister to those in their retirement years, motivating them to share their valuable experiences with younger generations.
Former titles (until 2006): Family Bible Study. Life Ventures Learner Guide (1542-7366); (until 2003): Family Bible Study. Ventures Learner Guide (1526-5692)
Published by: LifeWay Christian Resources, 1 Lifeway Plz, Nashville, TN 37234. TEL 615-251-2000, 800-458-2772, FAX 615-251-5933, customerservice@lifeway.com, http://www.lifeway.com. Ed. Jerry Lemon.

280.4 USA ISSN 1945-0923
BS600.3
BIBLE STUDY; get into the word. Text in English. 2008. bi-m. USD 14.95 (effective 2010). adv. illus. **Document type:** *Magazine, Consumer.* **Description:** Suggests methods of Bible study and offering tips on Bible study tools. It includes advice and encouragement from pastors, teachers and scholars on Bible study.
Published by: Logos Bible Software, 1313 Commercial St, Bellingham, WA 98225-4307. TEL 360-527-1700, 800-875-6467, FAX 360-527-1707, customerservice@logos.com. Ed. Michael S Heiser.

268 USA ISSN 1557-4032
BIBLE TEACHING FOR KIDS: 3S-PREK MUSIC & MORE ENHANCED CD. (Kindergarten) Text in English. 2000. q. USD 11.95 per issue (effective 2008). back issues avail. **Document type:** *Magazine, Consumer.* **Description:** Contains everything you need to get three- and four-year-olds hopping, as well as relaxation tunes and instrumental tracks for those occasions when you want them to wind down.
Formerly (until 2006): Family Bible Study. Music for 3's-Pre-K (1544-175X)
Media: CD-ROM.

Published by: LifeWay Christian Resources, 1 Lifeway Plz, Nashville, TN 37234. TEL 615-251-2000, 800-458-2772, FAX 615-251-5933, customerservice@lifeway.com, http://www.lifeway.com.

268 USA ISSN 1557-4040
BIBLE TEACHING FOR KIDS: BABIES, 1S & 2S MUSIC & MORE ENHANCED CD. Variant title: Bible Teaching for Kids: Babies, 1s and 2s Music and More Enhanced CD. Text in English. 2000. q. USD 11.95 per issue (effective 2008). back issues avail. **Document type:** *Handbook/Manual/Guide, Consumer.* **Description:** Contains a collection of songs and music that can be used when teaching bible truths to tiny babies and active 2-year-olds.
Formerly (until 2006): Family Bible Study. Music for Babies, 1's & 2's (1544-2519)
Media: CD-ROM.
Published by: LifeWay Christian Resources, 1 Lifeway Plz, Nashville, TN 37234. TEL 615-251-2000, 800-458-2772, FAX 615-251-5933, customerservice@lifeway.com, http://www.lifeway.com.

268 USA ISSN 1557-4059
BIBLE TEACHING FOR KIDS: KINDERGARTEN MUSIC & MORE ENHANCED CD. Variant title: Music and More for Kindergarten Enhanced CD. Text in English. 2000. q. USD 11.95 per issue (effective 2008). back issues avail. **Document type:** *Handbook/Manual/Guide, Consumer.* **Description:** Features special unit songs designed for use with kindergarten curriculum, music for activities and instrumentals.
Formerly (until 2006): Family Bible Study. Music for Kindergarten (1544-0494)
Media: CD-ROM.
Published by: LifeWay Christian Resources, 1 Lifeway Plz, Nashville, TN 37234. TEL 615-251-2000, 800-458-2772, FAX 615-251-5933, customerservice@lifeway.com, http://www.lifeway.com.

286 USA ISSN 0740-7998
THE BIBLICAL EVANGELIST. Text in English. 1965-1980; resumed 1982. m. free (effective 2008). **Document type:** *Newsletter, Consumer.*
Formerly (until 1966): The Regular Baptist Evangelist
Related titles: Online - full text ed.
Published by: The Biblical Evangelist, 5717 Pine Drive, Raleigh, NC 27606-8947. TEL 919-852-0850. Ed. Robert L Sumner.

286.132 USA ISSN 0195-1351
BX6225
BIBLICAL ILLUSTRATOR. Text in English. 1974. q. USD 24.95; USD 34.35 combined subscription (print & CD-ROM eds.); USD 4.95 per issue (effective 2008). adv. back issues avail. **Document type:** *Magazine, Consumer.* **Description:** Includes Biblical backgrounds, geography, history, culture, archaeology, ancient religions and language studies.
Formerly (until 197?): Sunday School Lesson Illustrator (0162-4407)
Related titles: CD-ROM ed.
Indexed: OTA, SBPI.
Published by: LifeWay Christian Resources, 1 Lifeway Plz, Nashville, TN 37234. TEL 615-251-2000, 800-458-2772, FAX 615-251-5933, customerservice@lifeway.com. Ed. G B Howell.

285 USA ISSN 0006-0909
BIBLICAL MISSIONS. Text in English. 1935. irreg. (3-6/yr.). USD 6 (effective 2000). adv. bk.rev. illus. **Document type:** *Bulletin.*
Indexed: CERDIC.
Published by: The Independent Board for Presbyterian Foreign Missions, 246 W Walnut Ln, Philadelphia, PA 19144. TEL 215-438-0511, FAX 215-438-0560. Ed., R&P Rev. Edward Paauwe. Circ: 5,000.

286 USA ISSN 0279-8182
BIBLICAL RECORDER. Text in English. 1833. bi-w. (Fri.). USD 14 (effective 2006). adv. bk.rev. 4 cols./p.; **Document type:** *Newspaper.* **Description:** Covers news of churches, ministries, church staff, and denominational events.
Related titles: Magnetic Tape ed.
Published by: (Baptist State Convention of North Carolina), Biblical Recorder, Inc., 232 W. Millbrook Rd., Raleigh, Wake, NC 27609. TEL 919-847-2128, FAX 919-847-6939. Ed., Pub. Tony W. Cartledge. Adv. contact Jo Ellen Blaine. page USD 1,650. Circ: 65,000.

220.6 GBR ISSN 1365-6090
BIBLICAL STUDIES BULLETIN. Text in English. 1996. q. includes subscr. with Grove Biblical Series. back issues avail. **Document type:** *Newsletter, Academic/Scholarly.* **Description:** Contains news, reviews, surveys of useful commentaries, computer tidbits and off-beat humor relating to the field of biblical studies.
—CCC.
Published by: Grove Books Ltd., Ridley Hall Rd, Cambridge, CB3 9HU, United Kingdom. TEL 44-1223-464748, FAX 44-1223-464849, sales@grovebooks.co.uk. Ed. Richard Briggs.

280.4 SRB
BIBLIJSKE LEKCIJE. Text in Serbo-Croatian. q.
Published by: Unija Reformnog Pokreta Adventista Sedmog Dana, Moravska 8, Belgrade. Ed. Mladen Aradski.

280.4 SWE ISSN 0346-5438
BIBLIOTHECA HISTORICO-ECCLESIASTICA LUNDENSIS. Text in English, Swedish. 1972. irreg. price varies. **Document type:** *Monographic series, Academic/Scholarly.*
Published by: Lunds Universitet, Centrum foer Teologi och Religionsvetenskap/Lund University, Department of Theology and Religious Studies, Allhelgma Kyrkogata 8, Lund, 22362, Sweden.

230.044 USA ISSN 0006-1921
BR1 CODEN: BSTQAA
➤ **BIBLIOTHECA SACRA**; a theological quarterly. Text in English. 1864. q. USD 29 domestic to individuals; USD 39 foreign to individuals; USD 44 domestic to institutions; USD 49 foreign to institutions; USD 9 per issue domestic to individuals; USD 12 per issue foreign to individuals; USD 14 per issue domestic to institutions; USD 15 per issue foreign to institutions (effective 2011). bk.rev. abstr.; bibl. index. back issues avail.; reprints avail. **Document type:** *Journal, Academic/Scholarly.* **Description:** Provides biblical and theological instruction to biblical scholars, pastors, teachers and serious lay Bible students.
Incorporates (1863-1871): The Theological Eclectic; (1931-1939): Christian Faith and Life; Which was formed by the merger of (1913-1931): The Bible Champion; (1927-1931): The Essentialist; Which was formerly (until 1927): The Call to the Colors; Formed by the merger of (1858-1864): The Christian Review (2158-1738); (1858-1864): The Bibliotheca Sacra and Biblical Repository; Which was formerly (until 1858): The Bibliotheca Sacra and American Biblical Repository; Which was formed by the merger of (1844-1850): Bibliotheca Sacra and Theological Review; (1845-1850): The Biblical Repository and Classical Review (2156-9924); Which was formerly (until 1844): The American Biblical Repository (2155-5265)
Related titles: CD-ROM ed.: Theological Journal Library CD. USD 99.95 New & Updated CD (effective 2004); Microform ed.: (from PQC); Online - full text ed.
Indexed: A21, A22, CCR, CERDIC, ChrPI, GeoRef, H09, H10, IZBG, OTA, PCI, R&TA, R04, RI-1, RI-2, S05, SpeleolAb.
—BLDSC (2019.450000), IE, Ingenta.
Published by: Dallas Theological Seminary, 3909 Swiss Ave, Dallas, TX 75204. TEL 214-824-3094, FAX 214-841-3664.

280.4 ISL
BJARMI; kristilegt timarit. Text in Icelandic. 1906. 8/yr. ISK 2,450, USD 45. adv. back issues avail.
Published by: Kristilega Skolahreyfingin, PO Box 4060, Reykjavik, 124, Iceland. TEL 354-567-8899, FAX 354-567-8840. Ed. Gunnar J Gunnarsson. Circ: 1,000. **Co-sponsors:** Institutet foer Livsmedel och Bioteknik (S I K)/Swedish Institute for Food and Biotechnology; K F U M - K.

BLACK MINISTRIES. *see* ETHNIC INTERESTS

283 DEU ISSN 0341-9452
BLAETTER FUER PFAELZISCHE KIRCHENGESCHICHTE UND RELIGIOESE VOLKSKUNDE. Text in German. 1925. a. EUR 35 (effective 2010). bk.rev. index. back issues avail. **Document type:** *Yearbook, Academic/Scholarly.* **Description:** Contains information on Protestant church history in the southwestern portion of Germany.
Published by: (Verein fuer Pfaelzische Kirchengeschichte), Verlag Regionalkultur, Bahnhofstr 2, Ubstadt-Weiher, 76698, Germany. TEL 49-7251-367030, FAX 49-7251-3670329, kontakt@verlag-regionalkultur.de, http://www.verlag-regionalkultur.de.

280.4 DEU
BLICK IN DIE KIRCHE. Text in German. 1966. bi-m. EUR 12.50 (effective 2009). adv. bk.rev. **Document type:** *Magazine, Consumer.*
Published by: Evangelisches Medienzentrum Kurhessen-Waldeck, Heinrich-Wimmer-Str 4, Kassel, 34131, Germany. TEL 49-561-9307152, FAX 49-561-9307155, blick@ekkw.de, http://www.ekkw.de. Ed. Cornelia Barth. Adv. contact Petra Griessel. page EUR 800; trim 185 x 260. Circ: 20,000 (paid and controlled).

284.2 ZAF ISSN 0006-4947
BLOEMHEUWEL-NUUS. Text in Afrikaans. 1953. q. free. adv. bk.rev. bibl. **Document type:** *Academic/Scholarly.*
Published by: Nederduitse Gereformeerde Kerk Bloemfontein/Dutch Reformed Church, Bloemfontein, Bloemheuwel, 15 General Hertzog Straat, Bloemfontein, 9300, South Africa. Ed. Rev. H C J Flemming. Circ: 1,000.

284.1 USA ISSN 0279-9111
BX8001
BOND. Text in English. 1924. bi-m. USD 4 to non-members. illus. **Document type:** *Magazine, Consumer.* **Description:** Covers fraternal programs serving members, their families, churches and communities.
Published by: Lutheran Brotherhood, 625 Fourth Ave S, Minneapolis, MN 55415. TEL 612-340-7000. Ed. Gaelyn Beal. Circ: 711,000 (controlled).

284 200.82 NLD ISSN 0169-958X
BOND VAN CHRISTELIJKE GEREFORMEERDE VROUWENVERENIGINGEN. CONTACT. Text in Dutch. m.
Published by: (Bond van Christelijke Gereformeerde Vrouwenverenigingen), Confessioneel Gereformeerd Toerustingscentrum, Kooikersweg 360, 's-Hertogenbosch, 5224 AZ, Netherlands. TEL 31-73-6212166, info@cgb.nu. Ed. A S Rienstra.

BOOKS & CULTURE; a Christian review. *see* LITERATURE

BRAILLE EVANGELISM BULLETIN. *see* HANDICAPPED—Visually Impaired

280.4 DEU ISSN 0949-2577
BREMER KIRCHENZEITUNG; Das evangelische Magazin. Text in German. 1928. q. adv. 24 p./no. 3 cols./p.; **Document type:** *Magazine, Consumer.*
Published by: Bremische Evangelische Kirche, Franziuseck 2-4, Bremen, 28199, Germany. TEL 49-421-55970, FAX 49-421-5597265, webmaster@kirche-bremen.de. Circ: 16,233 (controlled).

280.4 DEU ISSN 0944-4734
BRENNPUNKT GEMEINDE. Text in German. 1952. bi-m. EUR 24.90; EUR 18.90 to students; EUR 4.20 newsstand/cover (effective 2008). bk.rev. **Document type:** *Magazine, Consumer.*
Formerly (until 1993): Das Missionarische Wort (0343-0006)
Published by: Arbeitsgemeinschaft Missionarische Dienste, Reichensteiner Weg 24, Berlin, 14195, Germany. TEL 49-30-83001313, FAX 49-30-83001333, amd@diakonie.de, http://www.a-m-d.de. Ed. Erhard Berneburg.

286.5 USA ISSN 0747-4288
BRETHREN EVANGELIST. Text in English. 1878. m. USD 15 to non-members; free to members (effective 2000). adv. index. back issues avail. **Document type:** *Newsletter.* **Description:** Contains inspirational articles and news of the Church and its ministries.
Published by: Brethren Church, 524 College Ave, Ashland, OH 44805. TEL 419-289-1708. Ed., R&P Richard C Winfield. Circ: 8,425.

286.5 USA ISSN 0006-9663
BX7801
BRETHREN LIFE AND THOUGHT; a quarterly journal published in the interest of the Church of the Brethren. Text in English. 1955. q. USD 30 to individuals; USD 45 to institutions (effective 2011). bk.rev. cum.index: vols.1-26, 27-42. back issues avail.; reprints avail. **Document type:** *Journal, Academic/Scholarly.*
Related titles: Microfilm ed.: (from PQC); Online - full text ed.
Indexed: A21, P30, R&TA, RI-1, RI-2, RILM.
—BLDSC (2279.732000).
Published by: (Brethren Journal Association), Bethany Theological Seminary, 615 National Rd W, Richmond, IN 47374. TEL 765-983-1800, 800-287-8822, contactus@bethanyseminary.edu.

283 GBR
BRITISH CHURCH NEWSPAPER. Abbreviated title: B C N. Text in English. 2002. m. GBP 15 domestic; GBP 27 foreign (effective 2009). adv. **Document type:** *Newspaper, Consumer.* **Description:** Contains news and commentary involving the Protestant religion in the Great Britain.
Published by: Timely Publications Ltd., 45 Rushy Way, Emerson's Green, Bristol, BS16 7ER, United Kingdom. TEL 44-117-9560190, FAX 44-117-9560190, editor.bcn@btinternet.com. Ed. Napler Malcom TEL 44-19-34712520. adv.: page GBP 140.

280.4 GBR
BUBBLES; for 5's and under. Text in English. 1984. q. GBP 1.99 per issue (effective 2010). back issues avail. **Document type:** *Magazine, Consumer.*
Former titles (until 2004): The S A L T Programme for 3 to 4 (0968-5367); (until 1993): Learning Together with Under 5's (0963-4878)
—CCC.
Published by: Scripture Union, 207-209 Queensway, Bletchley, Milton Keynes, Bucks MK2 2EB, United Kingdom. TEL 44-1908-856000, FAX 44-1908-856111, info@scriptureunion.org.uk.

284.1 NOR ISSN 0807-6375
BUDBAERETEN; organ for evanelisk-lutherske frikirke. Text in Norwegian. 1883. 23/yr. NOK 490 in Scandinavia; NOK 550 elsewhere (effective 2011). back issues avail. **Document type:** *Magazine, Consumer.*
Incorporates (1940-1976): Ungdomsbladet (0807-6383)
Related titles: CD-ROM ed.: ISSN 1504-6176. 1990.
Published by: (Evangelisk Luthersk Frikirke/Evangelical Lutheran Free Church of Norway), Norsk Luthersk Forlag, PO Box 23, Bekkelogshoegda, Oslo, 1109, Norway. TEL 47-22-748600, FAX 47-22-748601, post@frikirken.no, http://www.frikirken.no. Ed. Anne-Kristine Bjoergsvik Wiecek.

241.605 GBR ISSN 1751-5947
THE BULLETIN; news and reports from the Social Issues Team. Text in English. 1974. 3/yr. free (effective 2009). back issues avail. **Document type:** *Bulletin.* **Description:** Aims to keep evangelical churches and individual Christians informed of the implications of legislation and public policy on social issues in the UK.
Former titles (until 2006): Christian Citizenship Bulletin (Print) (1742-9900); (until 2002): Citizenship Bulletin (1476-4008); (until 1991): Christian Citizenship Bulletin
Related titles: Online - full text ed.: ISSN 1751-0953.
Published by: (Fellowship of Independent Evangelical Churches), Affinity (Partnership), Social Issues Team, PO Box 246, Bridgend, CF31 9FD, United Kingdom. TEL 44-1656-640130, admin@affinity.org.uk. Ed. Rod Badams TEL 44-1858-411554.

280.4 FRA ISSN 0760-8365
BX4800
BULLETIN D'INFORMATION PROTESTANT. Key Title: BIP. Text in French. 1961. 11/yr. EUR 27 (effective 2009). abstr. **Document type:** *Bulletin.*
Formerly: Service Protestant Francais de Presse et d'Information (0760-8616)
Media: Duplicated (not offset).
Published by: Federation Protestante de France, Service d'Information, 47 rue de Clichy, Paris, Cedex 9 75311, France. TEL 33-1-44534712, FAX 33-1-42814001, http://www.protestants.org/fpf. Ed. Myriam Delarbre. Circ: 1,200.

284.2 GBR ISSN 0045-3536
BX4800
BULWARK. Text in English. 1851. q. USD 7 foreign; USD 5 to libraries. bk.rev. **Document type:** *Newsletter.*
Published by: Scottish Reformation Society, The Magdalen Chapel, 41 Cowgate, Edinburgh, Midlothian, Scotland EH1 1JR, United Kingdom. TEL 41-131-220-1450. Ed. A Sinclair Horne. Circ: 4,200.

283 GBR ISSN 2044-1940
C; Connecting people and parishes. Variant title: C Magazine. Text in English. 2002. q. free to qualified personnel (effective 2010). back issues avail. **Document type:** *Magazine, Consumer.* **Description:** Contains a deanery stories and a gallery of photos from around the churches.
Published by: Diocese of Southwell & Nottingham, Communications Department, Dunham House, 8 Westgate, Southwell, Nottinghamshire NG25 0JL, United Kingdom. TEL 44-1636-814331, FAX 44-1636-815084, mail@southwell.anglican.org. Ed., Pub. Steve Legg.

268 USA
C E E PRESIDENTS REPORT. (Citizens for Excellence in Education) Text in English. 1983. m. free to members. bk.rev. bibl.; illus. **Description:** Information on issues of interest to Christian parents, teachers, pastors, and public school teachers.
Former titles: Education Newsline; Christians in Education (0742-3527)
Published by: National Association of Christian Educators, Citizens for Excellence in Education, PO Box 3200, Costa Mesa, CA 92628. TEL 714-546-2226, cee4kids@aol.com. Ed., R&P Kathi Hudson. Pub. Bob Simonds. Circ: 18,000.

285.834 USA
C J A NEWS. Text in English. q. USD 20 to members. **Description:** Covers justice and peace issues of interest to members of the United Church of Christ.
Published by: Christians for Justice Action, 233 North Country Rd, Mount Sinai, NY 11766. Eds. Donna Schaper, John Nelson. **Subscr. to:** Fred Tilinski, 1822 Peach St., St. Charles, MO 63303.

266 AUS ISSN 1444-0199
C M S CHECKPOINT. (Church Missionary Society) Text in English. 1925. q. AUD 20 to members. bk.rev. illus. back issues avail. **Document type:** *Newsletter, Consumer.* **Description:** Provides information on mission work in North Australia and overseas.
Former titles (until 1994): Checkpoint (0311-0737); (until 1971): The Open Door; (until 1937): Church Missionary Gleaner
Related titles: Online - full text ed.
Published by: Church Missionary Society - Australia Inc., Level 5, 51 Druitt St, Sydney, NSW 2000, Australia. TEL 61-2-92673711, FAX 61-2-92673703, nsw@cms.org.au.

280.4 305.089607305 USA ISSN 2150-0975
▼ **C R A N K.** (Christian Readers Answer in a Korrupt World) Text in English. 2010. q. **Document type:** *Magazine, Consumer.* **Description:** For urban Christians.
Related titles: Online - full text ed.: ISSN 2150-0983. 2009.

R

Published by: Thandiwe Clinton, Ed. & Pub., 67 Thorn Creek Way, Dallas, GA 30157. TEL 404-246-5181, teeplatinum@gmail.com.

283 GBR ISSN 0007-9073
C S C NEWSLETTER. Text in English. 1966. 3/yr. bk.rev. **Document type:** *Newsletter.* **Description:** For Anglican religious community.
Supersedes: Our Work
Indexed: CERDIC.
Published by: Community of the Sisters of the Church (UK Province), St Michael's Convent, 56 Ham Common, Richmond, Surrey TW10 7JH, United Kingdom. TEL 44-20-89408711, FAX 44-20-89485525, infoUK@sistersofthechurch.org. Ed. Sr. Judith . Circ: 2,200.

284 USA
C W U DIRECTORY - HANDBOOK. Text in English. a. free. **Document type:** *Directory.* **Description:** Posts dates for national and state CWU events; national meetings of supporting women's organizations and ecumenical partners; and information on CWU and church-related organizations.
Published by: Church Women United, 475 Riverside Dr, Rm 500, New York, NY 10115. TEL 212-870-2347, 800-298-5551, FAX 212-870-2338, cwu@churchwomen.org, http://www.churchwomen.org.

284.2 USA
CADET QUEST MAGAZINE. Text in English. 1958. 7/yr. USD 13.65 domestic; CAD 20.60 in Canada (effective 2007). adv. **Document type:** *Magazine, Consumer.* **Description:** For boys 9-14. Helps them see how God is at work in their lives and in the world around them.
Formerly (until 2003): Crusader Magazine
Published by: Calvinist Cadet Corps, 1333 Alger St, P O Box 7259, Grand Rapids, MI 49507. TEL 616-241-5616, FAX 616-241-5558, cadets@aol.com, http://www.calvinistcadets.org. Ed. G. Richard Broene. R&P G Richard Broene. Adv. contact Kathy Door. Circ: 13,000 (paid).

280.4 CHE
LES CAHIERS PROTESTANTS. Text in French. 1917. bi-m. CHF 48 (effective 2001). reprints avail. **Document type:** *Bulletin, Academic/ Scholarly.*
Published by: Evangile et Culture, 7 chemin des Cedres, Lausanne, 1004, Switzerland. TEL 41-21-6463723, FAX 41-21-6463723, evculture@bluewin.ch. Ed. Jean-Blaise Held.

283 CAN ISSN 0383-6509
CALEDONIA DIOCESAN TIMES. Text in English. 1960. m. CAD 10. bk.rev. illus. **Document type:** *Newsletter.*
Published by: Anglican Church of Canada, Diocese of Caledonia, P O Box 278, Prince Rupert, BC V8J 3P6, Canada. TEL 250-624-6013. Ed. Lisa Tyler. Circ: 2,500.

286.1794 USA ISSN 0008-1558
CALIFORNIA SOUTHERN BAPTIST. Text in English. 1941. m. USD 9.50 (effective 2008). adv. bk.rev. illus. index. 20 p./no. 4 cols./p.; **Document type:** *Newspaper.*
Published by: California Southern Baptist Convention, 678 E. Shaw Ave., Fresno, CA 93710-7704. TEL 559-229-9533, FAX 559-229-2824. Ed. Terry Barone. Circ: 11,000.

284.2 USA ISSN 1534-8318
BX9185
➤ **CALL TO WORSHIP**; liturgy, music, preeching and the arts. Text in English. 1963. q. USD 34.95 (effective 2011). bk.rev. index. back issues avail. **Document type:** *Journal, Academic/Scholarly.* **Description:** Seeks to develop an understanding of reformed piety, corporate worship, and the role of music in the life of the church.
Formerly (until 2001): Reformed Liturgy & Music (0362-0476)
Related titles: Microfiche ed.
Indexed: A21, A22, R&TA, RI-1, RI-2, RILM.
—Ingenta.
Published by: Presbyterian Church (U.S.A.), Office of Theology and Waship, 100 Witherspoon St, Louisville, KY 40202. TEL 800-728-7228, presbytel@pcusa.org, http://www.pcusa.org.

230.044 USA ISSN 0008-1795
BR1
➤ **CALVIN THEOLOGICAL JOURNAL.** Abbreviated title: C T J. Text in English. 1966. s-a. USD 26 (effective 2010). adv. bk.rev. abstr.; bibl. index. back issues avail. **Document type:** *Journal, Academic/ Scholarly.* **Description:** Covers all areas of theology (biblical, historical, systematic and pastoral) with specialization in Calvin studies. It aims at pastors and academics specializating in Calvin/ Reformation studies.
Related titles: Microfiche ed.; Online - full text ed.
Indexed: A21, A22, CERDIC, ChrPI, DIP, IBR, IBZ, IZBG, OTA, R&TA, RI-1, RI-2, RILM.
—BLDSC (3015.800000), IE, Ingenta.
Published by: Calvin Theological Seminary, 3233 Burton St SE, Grand Rapids, MI 49546. TEL 800-388-6034, FAX 616-957-6101. Ed. Arie C Leder.

287 BRA ISSN 1519-7018
BR7
➤ **CAMINHANDO.** Text in Portuguese. 1982. s-a. **Document type:** *Journal, Academic/Scholarly.*
Related titles: Online - full text ed.: ISSN 2176-3828. free (effective 2011).
Published by: Universidade Metodista de Sao Paulo, Faculdade de Teologia da Igreja Metodista, Rua do Sacramento 230, Rudge Ramos, Predio Alfa, Sala 222, Sao Bernardo do Campo, SP 09640-000, Brazil. TEL 55-11-43665958, FAX 55-11-43674899. Ed. Helmut Renders.

284.1 CAN ISSN 1487-9522
CANADA LUTHERAN (NATIONAL EDITION). Text in English. 1998. 9/yr. CAD 22.60 domestic to individuals; CAD 42 foreign to individuals (effective 2008). adv. back issues avail.
Formed by the merger of (1991-1998): Canada Lutheran (Manitoba/NW Ontario Edition (1201-6616); (1991-1998): Canada Lutheran (Alberta and the Territories Edition) (1201-6594); (1991-1998): Canada Lutheran (Saskatchewan Edition) (1201-6608); (1991-1998): Canada Lutheran (British Columbia Edition) (1201-6586); (1991-1998): Canada Lutheran (Eastern Edition) (1196-698X); Which superseded in part (in 1990): Canada Lutheran (National Edition) (0832-0179); Which was formed by the merger of (19??-1985): Shepherd (0383-8544); (1920-1985): Canada Lutheran (0008-2716); (1963-1985): Western Canada Lutheran (0382-0793); (1978-1985): Central Canada Lutheran (0708-7969); Which was formerly (until 1978): Central Canada Lutheran Circle 'N Dot (0705-8926); (until 1977): Circle 'N Dot (0319-468X); (until 1968): Central Canada Lutheran (0319-4671)
Published by: Evangelical Lutheran Church in Canada, 302-393 Portage Ave, Winnipeg, MB R3B 3H6, Canada. TEL 204-984-9177, tgallop@elcic.ca. Circ: 19,800 (paid).

286.171 CAN ISSN 0008-2988
CANADIAN BAPTIST. Text in English. 1854. m. (10/yr.). adv. bk.rev. index.
Related titles: Microfiche ed.: (from MML); Microform ed.: (from MML); Online - full text ed.
Indexed: C03, CBCARef, CBPI, CPerI, G08, PQC, RILM.
Published by: Baptist Convention of Ontario and Quebec, 195 The West Mall, Ste 414, Etobicoke, ON M9C 5K1, Canada. TEL 416-622-8600, FAX 416-622-0780. Ed. Carol Gouveia. Circ: 13,000.

283.71 282 CAN ISSN 0008-3208
➤ **CANADIAN CHURCH HISTORICAL SOCIETY JOURNAL.** Text in English. 1950. s-a. CAD 25 domestic; USD 25 foreign (effective 1999). bk.rev. cum.index. **Document type:** *Journal, Academic/ Scholarly.*
Related titles: Microfiche ed.: (from MML); Microfilm ed.: (from MML); Microform ed.: (from MML, PQC); Online - full text ed.
Indexed: A21, AmH&L, C03, CA, CBCARef, CERDIC, HistAb, P30, P48, PQC, RI-1, RI-2, T02.
Published by: Canadian Church Historical Society, c/o Quebec Diocesan Archives, Bishop s University, JIM 127, Lennoxville, PQ, Canada. TEL 819-822-9600, FAX 819-822-9661. Ed., R&P Richard Virr. Circ: 300.

283 941 GBR ISSN 0262-995X
BX5013.C3
CANTERBURY AND YORK SOCIETY. Text in English. 1905. irreg., latest vol.99, 2009. free to members (effective 2010). back issues avail. **Document type:** *Monographic series, Trade.*
Published by: (Canterbury and York Society), Boydell & Brewer Ltd., Whitwell House, St Audrys Park Rd, Melton, Woodbridge, IP12 1SY, United Kingdom. TEL 44-1394-610600, FAX 44-1394-610316, trading@boydell.co.uk, http://www.boydell.co.uk. Ed. Philippa Hoskin.

283 GBR ISSN 0950-6276
BX5195.C3
CANTERBURY CATHEDRAL CHRONICLE. Text in English. 1928. a. free to members (effective 2009). bk.rev. 52 p./no. 2 cols./p.; back issues avail. **Document type:** *Newsletter, Consumer.* **Description:** Contains articles about the cathedral and its environs, its life, its history, stained glass and paintings.
Published by: Friends of Canterbury Cathedral, Cathedral House, 8 The Precincts, Canterbury, Kent CT1 2EH, United Kingdom. TEL 44-1227-762862, FAX 44-1227-865222, enquiries@canterbury-cathedral.org, http://www.canterbury-cathedral.org.

CARING; the holistic ministries of the Salvation Army. *see* SOCIAL SERVICES AND WELFARE

284.1 USA ISSN 1559-8195
BV4012.2
CARING CONNECTIONS. Text in English. 2004. 3/yr. **Document type:** *Journal, Trade.*
Media: Online - full text.
Published by: Evangelical Lutheran Church in America, 8765 W Higgins Rd, Chicago, IL 60631. TEL 312-380-2949, FAX 312-380-2406, http://www.elca.org.

283.73 USA
CATHEDRAL. Text in English. 1986. q. free. **Document type:** *Newsletter.*
Formerly: Heights
Published by: Cathedral Church of St. John the Divine, 1047 Amsterdam Ave at 112th St, New York, NY 10025. TEL 212-316-7449, FAX 212-932-7348. Ed. Herbert J Katz. R&P Herbert Katz. Circ: 13,000 (controlled).

280.4 USA ISSN 0008-7874
NA4830
CATHEDRAL AGE; an international magazine devoted to activities relating to Washington National Cathedral. Text in English. 1925. q. USD 15 to non-members (effective 2007). bk.rev. illus. 36 p./no. 3 cols./p.; reprints avail. **Document type:** *Magazine, Consumer.*
Related titles: Microform ed.: (from PQC).
Indexed: A22.
—Ingenta.
Published by: Washington National Cathedral, Massachusetts & Wisconsin Aves, N W, Washington, DC 20016-5098. TEL 202-537-6200. Ed., R&P, Adv. contact Craig Stapert. Circ: 28,800.

280.4 USA ISSN 1093-4618
CEDARVILLE TORCH. Text in English. 1978. s-a. free (effective 2010). back issues avail. **Document type:** *Magazine, Trade.* **Description:** Features Bible-based articles that challenge and encourage evangelical Christians. Audience is adult Christians and alumni and friends of the university.
Published by: Cedarville University, 251 N Main St, Cedarville, OH 45314. TEL 937-766-7700, 800-233-2784. Ed. Bill Brown.

230 USA ISSN 0899-7063
CELEBRATE. Text in English. 19??. q. **Document type:** *Journal, Trade.*
—CCC.
Published by: Presbyterian Church - U.S.A., 100 Witherspoon St, Louisville, KY 40202. TEL 800-872-3283, 800-728-7228, http://www.pcusa.org/.

280.4 CHE ISSN 1015-1141
BR3
CENTRE PROTESTANT D'ETUDES DE GENEVE. BULLETIN. Text in French. 1948. bi-m. CHF 38 (effective 2000 & 2001). adv. **Document type:** *Bulletin.* **Description:** Covers theological and ethical inquiries conducted in the different centers in French-speaking Switzerland, particularly in Geneva.
Indexed: IZBG, OTA.
Published by: Centre Protestant d'Etudes de Geneve, Case Postale 3158, Geneva 3, 1211, Switzerland. TEL 41-22-8072737, FAX 41-22-8072738. Ed. Isabelle Graessle. Circ: 1,300.

CENTRE PROTESTANT D'ETUDES ET DE DOCUMENTATION. LIBRESENS. *see* RELIGIONS AND THEOLOGY—Abstracting, Bibliographies, Statistics

280.4 LKA ISSN 1391-7064
CEYLON CHURCHMAN. Text in English. 1867. bi-m. LKR 300, USD 11 (effective 2003). adv. bk.rev.; music rev. illus. 30 p./no. 2 cols./p.; back issues avail. **Document type:** *Magazine, Academic/Scholarly.*
Media: Large Type (11 pt.).
Published by: Dioceses of Colombo & Kurunagala, Diocesan Office, 368/3 Bauddhaloka Mawatha, Colombo, 7, Sri Lanka. TEL 00941-696208, FAX 00941-684811, diocol@eureka.lk. Eds. N Y Casie Chetty, Rev. Sydney Knight. Pub. Israel PaulRaj TEL 00941-328953. adv.: page LKR 2,500. Circ: 1,500.

266 USA ISSN 1084-2144
CHALLENGER (PETALUMA). Text in English. 1961. bi-m. free. back issues avail. **Document type:** *Magazine, Consumer.*
Published by: Chinese Christian Mission, 1269 N McDowell Blvd, Petaluma, CA 94975-0759. TEL 707-762-1314, FAX 707-762-1713, http://www.ccmusa.org. Ed. Carmen Tsui. R&P Maryann Yew. Circ: 11,200.

CHAMPION-VARIA. *see* HISTORY—History Of Europe

286.132 USA ISSN 1930-5893
BS410
CHANGNYON SONGGYONG YONGU/EXPLORE THE BIBLE: KOREAN BIBLE STUDIES. Text in Korean. 198?. q. USD 13.95 (effective 2007). **Description:** Contains Bible study material for Korean adults and youth in Sunday School.
Formerly (until 2000): Changnyon ul Wihan Songgyong Yongu (0747-9514)
Related titles: ◆ English ed.: Explore the Bible: Adult Study Guide Discovery. ISSN 1552-7212; ◆ Chinese ed.: Yan Jing Xi Lie. ISSN 1930-5907.
Published by: LifeWay Christian Resources, 1 Lifeway Plz, Nashville, TN 37234. TEL 615-251-2000, 800-458-2772, FAX 615-251-5933, customerservice@lifeway.com, http://www.lifeway.com.

283 362.41 GBR ISSN 0009-1529
CHANNELS OF BLESSING. Text in English. 1893. bi-m. GBP 0.53 per issue (effective 2009). **Document type:** *Bulletin.* **Description:** Contains digests articles from the Evangelical Christian Press; material includes news, overseas developments, commentary on current issues, personal experiences, Bible study, and devotional thought.
Media: Braille. **Related titles:** Diskette ed.; E-mail ed.
Published by: Royal National Institute of Blind People, 105 Judd St, London, WC1H 9NE, United Kingdom. TEL 44-20-73881266, FAX 44-20-73882034, magazines@rnib.org.uk, cservices@rnib.org.uk, http://www.rnib.org.uk/. **Co-sponsor:** Torch Trust for the Blind.

283.73 USA
CHAPLAIR. Text in English. 197?. irreg.
Published by: Assembly of Episcopal Hospitals and Chaplains, c/o James L Risk, Bishop Anderson House, 707 S Wood St, Chicago, IL 60612. TEL 312-563-4824, http://www.episcopalchaplain.org. Ed. James L Risk. Circ: 800.

280.4 DEU ISSN 0945-621X
CHARISMA. Text in German. 1974. q. EUR 15.50 domestic; EUR 21 in Europe; EUR 25 elsewhere (effective 2009). adv. bk.rev. back issues avail. **Document type:** *Magazine, Consumer.* **Description:** Provides information about the Charismatic Renewal movement worldwide, with special emphasis on the German speaking regions of Europe.
Incorporates (in 2007): Come (1611-9886); Which was formerly (1981-2002): Der Auftrag
Indexed: GSS&RPL.
Published by: Charisma-Verlag, Mendelssohnstr 2A, Duesseldorf, 40233, Germany. TEL 49-211-665451, FAX 49-211-665491, redaktion@charisma-verlag.de. Ed. Klaus Dieter Passon. Adv. contact Gerhard Bially. B&W page EUR 1,260, color page EUR 1,400; trim 210 x 297. Circ: 12,000.

CHARITY AND CHILDREN; the voice of child care in North Carolina. *see* CHILDREN AND YOUTH—About

283 GBR ISSN 0009-2126
CHEERING WORDS. Text in English. 1851. m. GBP 5.80 domestic; GBP 7.80 foreign (effective 2000 - 2001). bk.rev. illus. index. back issues avail. **Document type:** *Magazine, Consumer.*
Address: 22 Victoria Rd, Stamford, Lincs PE9 1HB, United Kingdom. TEL 44-1780-763780. Ed., Pub. David Oldham. Circ: 5,000 (paid and controlled).

280.4 GBR ISSN 0144-5707
CHICHESTER CATHEDRAL JOURNAL. Text in English. 1958. a. **Document type:** *Journal, Consumer.*
Published by: Friends of the Cathedral Church of Chichester, Visitors' Officer, The Royal Chantry, Cathedral Cloisters, Chichester, West Sussex PO19 1PX, United Kingdom. TEL 44-1243-782595, FAX 44-1243-536190, enquiries@chichester-cathedral.org.uk, http://www.fransnet.clara.net/chicath/.

283.42 GBR
CHICHESTER LEAFLET; monthly news from around the Chichester, Horsham, and Lewes and Hastings Archdeaconries. Variant title: Chichester Letter. Text in English. 1895. m. free. adv. bk.rev. back issues avail. **Document type:** *Newsletter, Consumer.*
Former titles (until 2008): Diocese of Chichester Letter; (until 2007): Chichester News (1750-8479); (until 2003): The Chichester Leaflet (1363-4410); Chichester News (0009-3785); Chichester Diocesan Leaflet
Related titles: Online - full text ed.: free (effective 2009).
Published by: Diocese of Chichester, Communications Department, Church House, 211 New Church Rd, Hove, BN3 4ED, United Kingdom. TEL 44-1273-421021, FAX 44-1273-421041, enquiry@diochi.org.uk. Adv. contact Lisa Williamson TEL 44-1273-425691.

283 GBR ISSN 1363-4550
CHICHESTER MAGAZINE. Text in English. 1988. q. adv. **Document type:** *Magazine, Consumer.* **Description:** Contains news, views, features, and pictures of around the diocese and the wider church.
Published by: Diocese of Chichester, Communications Department, Church House, 211 New Church Rd, Hove, BN3 4ED, United Kingdom. TEL 44-1273-421021, FAX 44-1273-421041, media@diochi.org.uk. Ed. Revd David Guest. Adv. contact Lisa Williamson TEL 44-1273-425691. page GBP 350.

266 USA ISSN 1045-6147
BR1280
CHINESE TODAY. Text in Chinese. 1961. m. free. back issues avail. **Document type:** *Magazine.*
Formerly: Chinese Christians Today
Published by: Chinese Christian Mission, 1269 N McDowell Blvd, Petaluma, CA 94975-0759. TEL 707-762-1314, FAX 707-762-1713, ccmlit@ix.netcom.com. Ed. Mandy Fung. R&P Anita Mo. Circ: 41,000.

200 CHE
CHRISCHONA PANORAMA. Text in German. 1913. 8/yr. CHF 20 (effective 2009). adv. **Document type:** *Magazine, Trade.*
Former titles (until 2006): Chrischona Magazin; (until 1990): Der Glaubensbote und Mitteilungen aus der Pilgermission St. Chrischona
Published by: Pilgermission St. Chrischona, Chrischonarain 200, Bettingen, 4126, Switzerland. TEL 41-61-6464557, FAX 41-61-6464277, medienstelle@chrischona.ch, http://www.chrischona.org. Ed. Michael Gross. Adv. contact Wolfgang Binninger. Circ: 12,500 (paid and controlled).

280.4 USA ISSN 0412-2968
CHRIST IN OUR HOME; light for today. Text in English. 1954. q. USD 7.20 domestic; USD 12.20 foreign (effective 2009). 96 p./no.; back issues avail. **Document type:** *Magazine, Consumer.* **Description:** Designed to be a lectionary-based devotional; it acknowledges all the festivals of the church, major and minor and celebrates people of great faith.
Related titles: Audio cassette/tape ed.: USD 11.50 (effective 2009); Large type ed. 20 pt.: USD 11 domestic; USD 16 foreign (effective 2009).
Published by: (Evangelical Lutheran Church in America), Augsburg Fortress Publishers, PO Box 1209, Minneapolis, MN 55440. TEL 800-328-4648, FAX 800-722-7766, info@augsburgfortress.org, http://www.augsburgfortress.org. Eds. Victor Eduardo Jortack, Virginia Bonde Zarth. Circ: 427,000.

280.4 DEU
CHRIST-ONLINE. Text in German. 6/yr. EUR 14.90 (effective 2009). **Document type:** *Magazine, Consumer.*
Published by: Christliche Verlagsgesellschaft mbH, Moltkestr 1, Dillenburg, 35683, Germany. TEL 49-2771-83020, FAX 49-2771-830230, info@cv-dillenburg.de, http://www.cv-dillenburg.de.

284 NLD ISSN 1877-6175
CHRISTELIJK WEEKBLAD. Variant title: C W. Text in Dutch. 1961. w. EUR 38 (effective 2011). adv. **Document type:** *Newspaper, Consumer.*
Formerly (until 2009): Centraal Weekblad (Landelijke Edition) (1381-7906)
Published by: FD-Periodieken bv, Postbus 412, Leeuwarden, 8901 BE, Netherlands. TEL 31-58-2987654, FAX 31-58-2987666, info@fdperiodieken.nl. Ed. Theo Klein. Pub. Marco van de Wetering.

283.42 GBR ISSN 0263-4023
CHRISTIAN AID NEWS. Text in English. 1969. q. free (effective 2009). bk.rev. back issues avail. **Document type:** *Magazine, Consumer.* **Description:** Provides news of projects benefiting the poor in developing countries with funds from the British charity, Christian Aid.
Related titles: Online - full text ed.
Published by: (Churches Together in Britain and Ireland), Christian Aid, 35 Lower Marsh, Waterloo, London, SE1 7RL, United Kingdom. info@christian-aid.org, http://www.christianaid.org.uk. Ed. Andrew Hogg TEL 44 -20-75232058.

286 USA ISSN 0746-0171
THE CHRISTIAN BAPTIST. Text in English. 1967. m. USD 12 (effective 2000). adv. bk.rev. **Document type:** *Newspaper.*
Related titles: Microform ed.: (from PQC).
Published by: Christian Baptist, PO Box 68, Atwood, TN 38220. TEL 901-662-7417. Ed. S T Tolley. Pub., R&P, Adv. contact S.T. Tolley. Circ: 3,500 (paid).

283 USA ISSN 0890-6793
BX5800
CHRISTIAN CHALLENGE. Text in English. 1962. 8/yr. USD 22 domestic; USD 25 in Canada; USD 30 elsewhere. adv. bk.rev. back issues avail. **Description:** News, opinions and spirituality of Anglican and Episcopal Christianity from a traditional viewpoint.
Related titles: Microfilm ed.
Indexed: A21, RI-1, RI-2.
Published by: Foundation for Christian Theology, 1215 Independence Ave, S E, Washington, DC 20003. TEL 202-547-5409, FAX 202-543-8704. Ed. Auburn Faber Traycik. Circ: 5,000.

284.2 CAN ISSN 1192-3415
CHRISTIAN COURIER. Text in English. 1945. bi-w. CAD 44 domestic; USD 40 foreign (effective 2007). adv. bk.rev.; film rev. illus. **Document type:** *Newspaper, Consumer.* **Description:** Serves as a discussion and information centre for North American Christians who wish to stay in touch with the activities of fellow Christians across the globe.
Former titles (until 1992): Calvinist Contact (0410-3882); (until 1951): Contact (0382-5949)
Published by: Reformed Faith Witness, 5 Joanna Dr, St Catharines, ON L2N 1V1, Canada. TEL 905-682-8311, 800-969-4838, FAX 905-682-8313. Ed. Harry der Nederlanden. Adv. contact Ineke Medcalf. Circ: 4,100 (paid).

286 USA ISSN 0362-0832
BX6201
CHRISTIAN INDEX (ATLANTA). Text in English. 1822. w. USD 12 (effective 2005). adv. bk.rev.; music rev. back issues avail. **Document type:** *Newspaper, Consumer.*
Related titles: Microfilm ed.
Published by: Georgia Baptist Convention, Executive Committee, 2930 Flowers Rd. S., Atlanta, GA 30341. TEL 770-936-5590. Ed. Dr. J. Gerald Harris. Circ: 63,000.

230.005 USA ISSN 1934-4295
CHRISTIAN INSIGHT. Text in English. 2006 (Nov.). m. adv. **Document type:** *Magazine, Consumer.*
Published by: Christian Insight Magazine, 3011 Oxfordshire Ln, Dallas, TX 75234-3615. TEL 800-975-6445, FAX 972-484-1700, info@christianinsightmag.com.

THE CHRISTIAN LIBRARIAN. *see* LIBRARY AND INFORMATION SCIENCES

CHRISTIAN LIBRARIAN. *see* LIBRARY AND INFORMATION SCIENCES

284.1 USA
CHRISTIAN MAGNIFIER. Text in English. 1955. m. USD 7; free to visually impaired (effective 2009). **Document type:** *Magazine, Consumer.* **Description:** Contains devotional and inspirational articles.
Media: Large Type (18 pt.). **Related titles:** Audio cassette/tape ed.: USD 7; free to visually impaired (effective 2009); ◆ Braille ed.: Tract Messenger. ISSN 0041-0357.
Published by: Lutheran Braille Evangelism Association, 1740 Eugene St, White Bear Lake, MN 55110-3312. TEL 651-426-0469, lbea@qwest.net. Ed. Rev. Dennis A Hawkinson.

285 GHA ISSN 0009-5478
CHRISTIAN MESSENGER. Text in English, Ga, Twi. 1883. m. USD 7.16 per issue. adv. bk.rev. bibl.; illus.; stat.
Related titles: Microfiche ed.: (from IDC); Microform ed.: (from PQC).
Indexed: CERDIC.
Published by: Presbyterian Book Depot, PO Box 3075, Accra, Ghana. TELEX 2525 PRESBY GH. Ed. G B K Owusu. Circ: 58,000.

284.1 USA ISSN 0009-5494
BX8001
CHRISTIAN MONTHLY. Text in English. 1944. m. USD 12 domestic; USD 14 in Canada; USD 25 elsewhere (effective 2000). adv. **Document type:** *Newsletter.*
Published by: (Apostolic Lutheran Church of America), Apostolic Lutheran Book Concern, PO Box 2126, Battle Ground, WA 98604-2126. TEL 360-687-4416. Ed. Linda Mattson. R&P, Adv. contact Neal Karlsen. Circ: 1,000 (paid).

284.1 USA ISSN 0009-5516
BR1
CHRISTIAN NEWS. Text in English. 1968. w. (except Aug.). USD 25 domestic; USD 30 foreign (effective 2000). bk.rev. stat. index. **Document type:** *Newspaper.*
Formerly (1962-1967): Lutheran News
Published by: Lutheran News, Inc., 3277 Boeuf Lutheran Rd, New Haven, MO 63068-2213. TEL 573-237-3110, FAX 573-237-3858. Ed. Rev. Herman J Otten. Circ: 6,000.

285 USA ISSN 0899-2584
BX8901
CHRISTIAN OBSERVER. Text in English. 1813. m. USD 27 domestic; USD 35 foreign (effective 2001). adv. bk.rev.; film rev.; play rev. abstr.; bibl.; charts; illus.; tr.lit. index. back issues avail. **Document type:** *Newspaper, Consumer.* **Description:** Encourages and edifies God's people and strengthens the Christian family.
Related titles: Microform ed.: (from PQC).
Published by: Christian Observer, Inc., 9400 Fairview Ave, Manassas, VA 20110-5802. TEL 703-335-2844. Ed. E P Elliott Jr. Pub. Francis M Elliott. R&P Edwin P Elliott. adv.: B&W page USD 200; 8.25 x 10.75. Circ: 1,400.

CHRISTIAN PERIODICAL INDEX. *see* RELIGIONS AND THEOLOGY—Abstracting, Bibliographies, Statistics

CHRISTIAN PERIODICAL INDEX (PRINT). *see* RELIGIONS AND THEOLOGY—Abstracting, Bibliographies, Statistics

CHRISTIAN RETAIL TRENDS REPORT. *see* BUSINESS AND ECONOMICS—Marketing And Purchasing

286.132 USA ISSN 0191-4294
BV4596.S5
CHRISTIAN SINGLE; the magazine for successful single living. Abbreviated title: C S. Text in English. 1979. m. USD 21.95; USD 3.95 per issue (effective 2008). adv. bk.rev. illus. back issues avail.; reprints avail. **Document type:** *Magazine, Consumer.* **Description:** Features high-quality, relevant information to single adults on various aspects of their lives.
Published by: LifeWay Christian Resources, 1 Lifeway Plz, Nashville, TN 37234. TEL 615-251-2000, 800-458-2772, FAX 615-251-5933, customerservice@lifeway.com. Eds. Larissa Arnault, Gena Rogers. Adv. contact Rhonda Edge Buescher. Circ: 36,500.

280.4 CAN ISSN 0835-412X
CHRISTIANWEEK; Canada's national Christian newspaper. Text in English. 1987. bi-w. CAD 34.95 domestic; CAD 59.95 foreign (effective 2000). adv. bk.rev.; film rev.; play rev. illus. 12 p./no. 5 cols./p.; back issues avail. **Document type:** *Newspaper.* **Description:** News and comments about Christian faith and life in Canada. Carries reporting and perspectives on a wide range of church, political and social issues. Targets leaders.
Related titles: Microfilm ed.
Indexed: CCR.
Published by: Fellowship for Print Witness Inc., P O Box 725, Winnipeg, MB R3C 2K3, Canada. TEL 204-982-2060, FAX 204-947-5632, editor@christianweek.org, http://www.christianweek.org. Ed. Doug Koop. Pub., R&P Bramwell Ryan. Adv. contact Julie Dykstra. Circ: 12,000.

280.4 USA ISSN 1945-4805
CHRISTMAS IN ZION. Text in English. 1984. a. USD 10 per issue (effective 2008). **Document type:** *Magazine, Consumer.*
Published by: Laestadian Lutheran Church, 279 N Medina St, Ste 150, Loretto, MN 55357. TEL 763-479-2422, http://laestadianlutheran.org. Ed. Paul Waaraniemi.

280.4 DEU ISSN 0942-0061
CHRISTSEIN HEUTE; Zeitschrift fuer Freie evangelische Gemeinden. Text in German. 1893. m. EUR 49.80; EUR 4.70 newsstand/cover (effective 2011). adv. bk.rev. back issues avail. **Document type:** *Magazine, Consumer.*
Formerly (until 1992): Der Gaertner (0342-3530)
Published by: Bundes Verlag GmbH, Bodenborn 43, Witten, 58452, Germany. TEL 49-2302-930930, FAX 49-2302-93093689, info@bundes-verlag.de, http://www.bundes-verlag.de. Ed. Arndt Schnepper. Adv. contact Juergen Bublitz. Circ: 5,500 (paid and controlled).

283 GBR ISSN 1755-6503
CHURCH ARMY. ANNUAL REPORT. Text in English. 1981. a. free. illus. **Document type:** *Corporate.* **Description:** Review of the year's work by the Church Army.
Former titles (until 1992): Church Army. Front Line Annual Report; Church Army. Front Line
Related titles: Online - full text ed.: ISSN 1755-6511.
Published by: Church Army, Marlowe House, 109 Station Rd, Sidcup, Kent DA15 7AD, United Kingdom. TEL 44-20-83099991, FAX 44-20-83093500, info@churcharmy.org.uk.

283.42 GBR ISSN 1751-3960
CHURCH ARMY. SHARE IT. Text in English. 1906. s-a. free (effective 2009). bk.rev. back issues avail. **Document type:** *Magazine, Trade.* **Description:** Contains reports on the activities of the Church Army.
Former titles (until 1992): Church Army. Frontline News; (until 1985): Church Army. Review; (until 19??): New Review; (until 1983): Church Army. Review (0009-6350)
Related titles: Online - full text ed.
Published by: Church Army, Marlowe House, 109 Station Rd, Sidcup, Kent DA15 7AD, United Kingdom. TEL 44-20-83099991, FAX 44-20-83093500, info@churcharmy.org.uk. Ed. Kofo Baptist TEL 44-20-83093515.

285 USA ISSN 0009-6393
BX9501
CHURCH HERALD. Text in English. 1826. 11/yr. USD 18 domestic; USD 23 foreign (effective 2005). adv. illus. reprints avail.
Related titles: Microfilm ed.
Indexed: A22, GSS&RPL.
Published by: (Reformed Church in America), Church Herald, Inc., 4500 60th St, Grand Rapids, MI 49512-9631. TEL 616-698-7071, FAX 616-698-6606. Ed. Christina Van Eyl. adv.: B&W page USD 2,410, color page USD 2,810. Circ: 110,000.

285 AUS ISSN 0156-224X
➤ **CHURCH HERITAGE.** Text in English. 1978. s-a. (one volume covers four numbers over two years). free to members (effective 2009). bk.rev. index. 76 p./no.; back issues avail. **Document type:** *Journal, Academic/Scholarly.* **Description:** Features articles and review of books with particular reference to congregational, methodist Presbyterian and Uniting traditions in Australia and the South Pacific.
Supersedes (in 1978): Australasian Methodist Historical Society. Journal and Proceedings (0084-6988); Church Records and Historical Society. Newsletter
Related titles: Online - full text ed.
Indexed: PCI, SPPI.
Published by: Uniting Church Records and Historical Society (NSW), PO Box 5081, Kingsdene, NSW 2118, Australia. Ed. Malcolm David Prentis.

283 GBR ISSN 0045-2831
CHURCH LADS' AND CHURCH GIRLS' BRIGADE. ANNUAL REPORT. Text in English. 1891. a. GBP 10 per issue UK only (effective 2000). bk.rev. **Document type:** *Corporate.*
Formerly: Brigade
Published by: Church Lads' and Church Girls' Brigade, 2 Barnsley Rd, Wath-upon-Dearne, Rotherham, S Yorks S63 6PY, United Kingdom. TEL 44-1709-876535, FAX 44-1709-878089, general-secretary@Church-Brigade.syol.com, http://www.clcgb.org.uk. Ed. J S Cresswell. R&P J.S. Cresswell. Circ: 1,200.

283.73 USA ISSN 8750-8613
CHURCH LIFE. Text in English. 1887. m. USD 1. adv. bk.rev. back issues avail.
Published by: Episcopal Diocese of Ohio, 2230 Euclid Ave, Cleveland, OH 44115. TEL 216-771-4815, FAX 216-623-0735. Ed. Dana C Speer. Circ: 23,000.

283.42 GBR ISSN 0009-6482
THE CHURCH OBSERVER. Text in English. 1948. 3/yr. GBP 1 per issue to non-members; free to members (effective 2009). adv. bk.rev. illus. back issues avail. **Document type:** *Magazine, Consumer.* **Description:** Covers Catholic faith and life within the Church of England.
Formed by the merger of (1870-1948): Church Union Gazette; (19??-1948): Platform
Related titles: Online - full text ed.: free (effective 2009).
Indexed: CERDIC.
Published by: Church Union, Faith House, 7 Tufton St, London, SW1P 3QN, United Kingdom. TEL 44-20-72226952, membership@churchunion.co.uk. Ed. Fr Ed Tomlinson. Adv. contact Mike Silver TEL 44-1634-401611. page GBP 150. **Co-sponsor:** Faith House Bookshop.

283.42 GBR ISSN 0307-7225
CHURCH OF ENGLAND. GENERAL SYNOD. REPORT OF PROCEEDINGS. Text in English. 19??. s-a. index. back issues avail. **Document type:** *Proceedings, Trade.* **Description:** Provides a verbatim report of the sessions of the general synod of the Church of England.
Formerly (until 1970): Church of England. National Assembly. Report of proceedings
Published by: Church of England, General Synod, Church House, Great Smith St, Westminster, London, SW1P 3NZ, United Kingdom. TEL 44-20-78981000. **Subscr. to:** Church House Publishing.

283.42 GBR ISSN 0964-816X
CHURCH OF ENGLAND NEWSPAPER. Abbreviated title: C E N. Text in English. 1828. w. GBP 60 domestic; GBP 80 in Europe; GBP 100 elsewhere (effective 2009). adv. bk.rev.; film rev.; rec.rev. illus. back issues avail. **Document type:** *Newspaper, Consumer.* **Description:** Provides news of the Church of England, of the Anglican Communion worldwide and on Christian charities and missionary organizations. Covers theological developments and how Christian faith applies to everyday life and problems.
Incorporates (1886-1991): Christian Week; Which was formerly (until 1987): British Weekly and Christian Record; Which was formed by the merger of: British Weekly and Christian World (0007-1951); Christian Record
Related titles: Online - full text ed.: GBP 20 (effective 2009).
Published by: Religious Intelligence Ltd., 14 Great College St, Westminster, London, SW1P 3RX, United Kingdom. TEL 44-20-78781001, FAX 44-20-78781031. Ed. Colin Blakely TEL 44-20-78781002. Adv. contact Chris Turner TEL 44-20-78781004. color page GBP 1,025, B&W page GBP 925; 265 x 365.

283.42 GBR ISSN 0069-3987
BX5015
CHURCH OF ENGLAND YEARBOOK. Text in English. 1883. a. GBP 39 per issue (effective 2010). **Document type:** *Yearbook, Trade.* **Description:** Contains list holders of office in the English dioceses with details of associated organizations.
Formerly (until 1963): Church of England. Official Yearbook
Published by: Church House Publishing, Church House, Great Smith St, London, SW1P 3AZ, United Kingdom. TEL 44-20-78981451, FAX 44-20-78981449.

R

280.4 USA ISSN 0745-6778
CHURCH OF GOD EVANGEL. Text in English. 1910. m. USD 15 domestic; USD 24 foreign (effective 2009). bk.rev. 40 p./no.; **Document type:** *Magazine, Consumer.*
Related titles: Microform ed.
Indexed: GSS&RPL.
Published by: Church of God Publishing House, 1080 Montgomery Ave, Cleveland, TN 37320-2250. http://www.churchofgod.cc/. Circ: 49,000.

266 USA ISSN 0009-6504
CHURCH OF GOD MISSIONS. Text in English. 1951. bi-m. USD 10; USD 13 foreign. adv. bk.rev. illus.
Published by: Church of God, Missionary Board, PO Box 2337, Anderson, IN 46018. TEL 765-648-2142, FAX 765-642-4279. Ed. J David Reames. R&P J. David Reames. Circ: 6,000.

280.4 GBR ISSN 0009-6512
THE CHURCH OF IRELAND GAZETTE. Text in English. 1856. w. GBP 45 domestic; GBP 85 in Ireland; GBP 70 elsewhere (effective 2009). adv. bk.rev. back issues avail. **Document type:** *Newspaper, Consumer.* **Description:** Aims to communicate events from throughout the Church of Ireland.
Formerly (until 1900): The Irish Ecclesiastical Gazette
Related titles: Audio CD ed.
Published by: Church of Ireland Press, 3 Wallace Ave, Lisburn, BT27 4AA, United Kingdom. TEL 44-28-92675743, FAX 44-28-92667580, press@ireland.anglican.org, http://www.ireland.anglican.org. Ed. Canon Ian Ellis.

285.233 GBR ISSN 0069-3995
BX9076
CHURCH OF SCOTLAND. YEARBOOK. Text in English. 1885. a. adv. index. **Document type:** *Yearbook.* **Description:** Designed to be a guide to the Church of Scotland for ministers and office bearers.
—CCC.
Published by: (Church of Scotland), St. Andrew Press, 121 George St, Edinburgh, EH2 4YN, United Kingdom. TEL 44-131-2255722, info@crossreach.org.uk.

283 GBR ISSN 0009-658X
CHURCH TIMES. Text in English. 1863. w. adv. bk.rev. illus. index. 5 cols./p.; reprints avail. **Document type:** *Newspaper.* **Description:** Features news of the Anglican Church.
Incorporates: Anvil
Related titles: Microfilm ed.: (from PQC).
Indexed: A21, RI-1, RI-2.
Published by: G.J. Palmer & Sons Ltd., 13-17 Long Ln, London, EC1A 9PN, United Kingdom. TEL 44-20-77761060. Adv. contact Stephen Dutton. **Subscr. to:** 16 Blyburgate, Beccles, Suffolk NR34 9TB, United Kingdom.

283 USA
CHURCHART PRO. Text in English. 1993. m. looseleaf. USD 149.95 (effective 1999). illus. back issues avail. **Document type:** *Newsletter.* **Description:** Provides layout and design ideas for church publications.
Former titles: ChurchArt Pro on Disk (1083-8848); (until 1995): ChurchArt Plus on Disk (1072-1975)
Related titles: CD-ROM ed.; Diskette ed.; Online - full text ed.
Published by: Communication Resources Inc., PO Box 36269, Canton, OH 44735-6269. TEL 800-992-2144. Ed. Stan Purdum.

230.3 GBR ISSN 0009-661X
BX5011
➤ **CHURCHMAN**; a journal of Anglican theology. Text in English. 1879. q. GBP 24 in Europe; GBP 29 elsewhere; GBP 19 to students; GBP 6 per issue; free to members (effective 2009). adv. bk.rev. index. 96 p./no.; back issues avail. **Document type:** *Journal, Academic/Scholarly.* **Description:** Features articles that deal with current issues, historical themes, and the Evangelical doctrine.
Related titles: Microfilm ed.
Indexed: A21, CERDIC, ChrPI, FamI, MLA-IB, OTA, RI-1, RI-2, RILM.
—BLDSC (3189.930000). **CCC.**
Published by: Church Society, Dean Wace House, 16 Rosslyn Rd, Watford, Herts WD18 0NY, United Kingdom. TEL 44-1923-235111, FAX 44-1923-800362, enquiries@churchsociety.org, http://www.churchsociety.org. Ed. Gerald Bray. Adv. contact David Phillips. page BRL 50.

284 USA ISSN 0009-6598
BV4415
CHURCHWOMAN. Text in English. 1934. q. USD 10 (effective 1998). bk.rev. illus. **Description:** Addresses the concerns of today's women of faith: children, peacemaking, the discovery of gifts, health and wholeness, inclusive language, partnerships of empowerment, worship, land, homelessness, criminal justice, and poverty of women and children.
Published by: Church Women United, 475 Riverside Dr, Rm 500, New York, NY 10115. TEL 212-870-2347, 800-298-5551, FAX 212-870-2338, cwu@churchwomen.org. Circ: 7,000.

287.6 USA ISSN 0146-9924
BX8382.2.A1
CIRCUIT RIDER (NASHVILLE). Text in English. 1976. q. USD 25; free to qualified personnel (effective 2008). adv. 32 p./no.; back issues avail. **Document type:** *Magazine, Consumer.* **Description:** Addresses the spiritual, intellectual, and practical needs of pastors serving local churches.
Related titles: Online - full text ed.
—CCC.
Published by: United Methodist Publishing House, 201 8th Ave S, PO Box 801, Nashville, TN 37202. TEL 615-749-6000, 800-672-1789, FAX 615-749-6579. Pub. Neil M Alexander. Adv. contact Melissa King TEL 615-749-6615. Circ: 42,000 (controlled).

280.4 SVK ISSN 0139-9217
CIRKEVNE LISTY. Text in Slovak. 1887. m. **Document type:** *Magazine, Consumer.*
Published by: Tranoscius a.s., Tranovskeho 1, Liptovsky Mikulas, 031 80, Slovakia. TEL 421-44-5523070, FAX 421-44-5523070, sefredaktor@tranoscius.sk.

287 GBR ISSN 0950-8732
CIRPLAN. Text in English. 1955. 2/yr. GBP 1.50 domestic; GBP 3 overseas (effective 2005). bk.rev. 30 p./no.; back issues avail. **Document type:** *Bulletin.* **Description:** Provides current and historical information on Methodist circuit regulations, preaching appointments, and preaching plans.
Media: Duplicated (not offset).
Published by: Society of Cirplanologists, Cadeby, 34 Fernhill Crescent, Bacup, Lancs OL13 8JU, United Kingdom. TEL 44-1706-873042. Ed., R&P Ken F Bowden. Circ: 120.

280.4 GBR ISSN 1362-914X
CLOSER TO GOD; reading the Bible in the power of the Holy Spirit. Text in English. 1999. q. GBP 14 domestic; GBP 18 in Europe (effective 2010); GBP 20 elsewhere (effective 2009); GBP 3.50 per issue (effective 2010). back issues avail. **Document type:** *Magazine, Consumer.* **Description:** Offers a complete devotional experience for those seeking a deeper, richer meeting with God through his word and spirit.
Incorporates (in 1999): Alive to God (0963-2743)
Related titles: Online - full text ed.
—CCC.
Published by: Scripture Union, 207-209 Queensway, Bletchley, Milton Keynes, Bucks MK2 2EB, United Kingdom. TEL 44-1908-856000, FAX 44-1908-856111, info@scriptureunion.org.uk. Ed. Phil Andrews. **Subscr. to:** Mail Order, PO Box 5148, Milton Keynes MLO, Bucks MK2 2YZ, United Kingdom. TEL 44-1908-856006, FAX 44-1908-856020, mailorder@scriptureunion.org.uk.

285.8 GBR
Y COFIADUR. Text in English. 1923. a. **Description:** Covers the history of Welsh congregational churches and institutions.
Published by: Undeb Yr Annibynwyr Cymraeg, c/o Ty John Penry, Abertawe/Swansea, SA14AL, United Kingdom.

200 600 USA ISSN 2151-3147
BV652.95
COLLIDE MAGAZINE; where the media and the church converge. Text in English. 2007. bi-m. USD 16 (effective 2009). bk.rev.; film rev.; music rev.; software rev.; tel.rev.; video rev. back issues avail. **Document type:** *Magazine, Consumer.* **Description:** Covers media and technology for creative church leaders.
Related titles: Online - full text ed.: USD 8 (effective 2009).
Published by: R T Creative Group, 9330 LBJ Fwy, Ste 800, Dallas, TX 75243. TEL 866-283-4276, http://www.rtcreativegroup.com/. Ed. Scott McClellan. Pub. Rob Thomas. Adv. contact Kami Stroope.

283.73 USA ISSN 0883-6728
COLORADO EPISCOPALIAN. Text in English. 1939. bi-m. free (effective 2005). adv. bk.rev. **Document type:** *Newspaper, Consumer.* **Description:** Provides news about the Episcopal Church for members in Colorado.
Related titles: Online - full text ed.
Published by: Diocese of Colorado, 1300 Washington St, Denver, CO 80203-2008. TEL 303-837-1173, FAX 303-837-1311, ceneus@colorododocese.org. Ed., Adv. contact Beckett Stokes. Circ: 19,000 (controlled).

266.6132 USA ISSN 0010-3179
BV2520.A1
COMMISSION; International Missions magazine. Text in English. 1849. m. USD 8.75; USD 17.25 foreign (effective 1999). adv. illus. index. **Description:** Reports on international Christian missions work. Content includes features on Southern Baptist missionaries and volunteers and their work.
Indexed: PerIslam, SBPI.
Published by: Southern Baptist Convention, International Mission Board, 3806 Monument Ave, Box 6767, Richmond, VA 23230-0767. TEL 804-219-1327, 800-866-3621, FAX 804-219-1410. Ed. Mary Jane Welch. Pub. Dan Allen. Adv. contact Tammy Dunkum. Circ: 90,000.

266.4 USA ISSN 2153-2958
▼ **COMMISSIONSTORIES**; experience, explore, engage. Text in English. 2009. q. back issues avail. **Document type:** *Magazine, Consumer.* **Description:** Focuses on today's issues facing international missions.
Published by: I M B Connecting, 3806 Monument Ave, PO Box 6767, Richmond, VA 23230. TEL 800-999-3113, http://www.imb.org. Ed. Bill Bangham.

286.732 GBR
COMMUNICATOR (WATFORD). Text in English. 1987. q. **Document type:** *Newsletter.* **Description:** Reports on church activities and events with devotional and inspirational articles as well as theological discussion articles.
Published by: South England Conference of Seventh-Day Adventists, Communication Department, Seventh-day Adventist Church, 25 St Johns Rd, Watford, Herts WD1 1PZ, United Kingdom. TEL 44-1923-232728, FAX 44-1923-250582, sstanciu@secadventist.org.uk, http://www.secadventist.org/. Ed. Dr. Richard de Lisser.

230.044 CZE ISSN 0010-3713
BR1.A1
➤ **COMMUNIO VIATORUM**; a theological journal. Text in English, German. 1958. 3/yr. EUR 48.20 foreign (effective 2009). bk.rev. index. 100 p./no.; **Document type:** *Journal, Academic/Scholarly.* **Description:** Includes articles on theology, philosophy and history.
Indexed: A20, A21, ArtHuCI, FR, IZBG, MLA-IB, OTA, PhilInd, R&TA, RI-1, RI-2, RILM, W07.
Published by: Univerzita Karlova v Praze, Evangelicka Teologicka Fakulta/Charles University in Prague, Protestant Theological Faculty, Cerna 9, p schr 529, Prague 1, 11555, Czech Republic. TEL 420-22-1988214, FAX 420-22-1988215. Circ: 1,000. **Dist. by:** Kubon & Sagner Buchexport - Import GmbH, Hessstr 39-41, Munich 80798, Germany. TEL 49-89-542180, FAX 49-89-54218218, postmaster@kubon-sagner.de, http://www.kubon-sagner.de.

285 USA
COMMUNIQUE (COLUMBUS, 1974). Text in English. 1974. m. (except Aug.). USD 5 (effective 2000). adv. bk.rev. back issues avail. **Document type:** *Newspaper.*
Published by: Presbyterian Church (U.S.A.), Synod of the Covenant, 6172 Busch Blvd, Ste 3000, Columbus, OH 43229. TEL 614-436-3310, FAX 614-846-5582. Ed., R&P, Adv. contact Doris Campbell. Circ: 18,000.

378.073 USA
COMPASS POINTS (NEW YORK). Text in English. 1993. s-a. free. back issues avail. **Document type:** *Newsletter.*
Published by: Colleges and Universities of the Anglican Communion, c/o the Assn of Episcopal Colleges, 815 Second Ave, Ste 315, New York, NY 10017-4594. TEL 212-716-6148, FAX 212-986-5039. R&P Hal Clark. Circ: 10,000.

COMPASSION MAGAZINE (COLORADO SPRINGS). *see* PSYCHOLOGY

284.1 USA ISSN 0741-9872
CONCORD (CHICAGO). Text in English. 1976. q. USD 20 (effective 2002). bk.rev. back issues avail. **Document type:** *Newsletter.* **Description:** Serves as the official publication of Lutherans Concerned/North America. The organization affirms God's love to people of alll sexual orientations, promoting justice by creating an "inclusive Lutheran church and helping Christians reconcile their spirituality and sexuality in an uplifting way.".
Related titles: Online - full text ed.
Indexed: CA, T02.
—CIS.
Published by: Lutherans Concerned North America, 2466 Sharondale, Atlanta, GA 30305. Ed. Peggy Yingst. R&P Bob Gibeling TEL 404-266-9615. Circ: 1,200.

284.1 USA ISSN 0010-5260
BX8001
CONCORDIA HISTORICAL INSTITUTE QUARTERLY; a journal for the history of Lutheranism in America. Text in English. 1928. q. USD 28 to non-members; free to members (effective 2010). bk.rev. charts; illus.; tr.lit. cum.index every 4 yrs. back issues avail.; reprints avail. **Document type:** *Journal, Academic/Scholarly.* **Description:** Features articles and book reviews on the history of Lutheranism in America.
Related titles: Microfilm ed.
Indexed: A21, A22, AmH&L, CA, GPAI, HistAb, MLA-IB, P30, R&TA, RI-1, RI-2, T02.
—Ingenta.
Published by: (Lutheran Church - Missouri Synod), Concordia Historical Institute, 804 Seminary Pl, St Louis, MO 63105. TEL 314-505-7900, FAX 314-505-7901, mhuggins@chi.lcms.org. Ed. Carol Geisler.

284.1 USA ISSN 2152-3312
CONCORDIA NEWS. Text in English. 2006. m. free to members (effective 2010). back issues avail. **Document type:** *Newsletter, Consumer.*
Related titles: Online - full text ed.: ISSN 2152-3320; Large type ed.: ISSN 2152-3339.
Published by: (Concordia Cemetery Association), Concordia Lutheran Church, 6637 80th Ave, N, Glyndon, MN 56547. TEL 218-233-0459. Eds. Karolynn Teigen-Decker, Sylvia Teigen.

284.1 DEU ISSN 1432-4431
BX8001
CONFESSIO AUGUSTANA; Das lutherische Magazin fuer Religion, Gesellschaft und Kultur. Abbreviated title: C A. Text in German. 1996. q. EUR 18.80; EUR 4.70 newsstand/cover (effective 2010). adv. **Document type:** *Journal, Academic/Scholarly.*
Published by: (Gesellschaft fuer Innere und Aeussere Mission im Sinne der Lutherischen Kirche e.V.), Freimund Verlag, Missionsstr 3, Neuendettelsau, 91564, Germany. TEL 49-9874-689330, FAX 49-9874-6893399, kontakt@freimund-verlag.de, http://www.freimund-buchhandlung.de/verlag/.

284 NLD ISSN 1388-1043
CONFESSIONEEL. Variant title: H W Confessioneel. Text in Dutch. bi-w. EUR 49.55 domestic; EUR 78.80 foreign; EUR 25.50 to students (effective 2010). adv.
Former titles (until 1998): Hervormd Weekblad (0165-4985); (until 1930): Gereformeerde Kerk
Published by: Koninklijke BDU Uitgeverij BV, Postbus 67, Barneveld, 3770 AB, Netherlands. TEL 31-342-494911, FAX 31-342-413141, tijdschriften@bdu.nl, http://www.bduuitgevers.nl. Ed. D van Duijvenbode. adv.: B&W page EUR 654; trim 210 x 297.

285.8 USA
CONGREGATIONAL BIBLE REVIVAL NEWS. Text in English. 1974. q. adv. **Document type:** *Newspaper.*
Published by: Congregational Bible Churches International, PO Box 47311, Wichita, KS 67201-7311. TEL 316-262-3706, FAX 316-263-5162. Ed. Dr. M L Webber. Adv. contact Rev. Brent Turnipseed. B&W page USD 75. Circ: 5,000 (controlled).

CONGREGATIONAL LIBRARY. BULLETIN. *see* LIBRARY AND INFORMATION SCIENCES

285 GBR ISSN 0266-7088
CONGREGATIONAL YEAR BOOK. Text in English. 1973. a. GBP 20 per issue (effective 2009). stat. index. back issues avail. **Document type:** *Yearbook, Consumer.* **Description:** Contains all the information of churches, ministers, areas and much more.
Published by: Congregational Federation, 6 Castle Gate, Nottingham, NG1 7AS, United Kingdom. TEL 44-115-9111460, FAX 44-115-9111462, admin@congregational.org.uk.

285.8 USA ISSN 0010-5856
BX7101
CONGREGATIONALIST. Text in English. 1816. irreg. free (effective 2001). adv. bk.rev. illus.
Published by: National Association of Congregational Christian Churches, 8473 S Howell Ave, Oak Creek, WI 53154. TEL 414-764-1620. Ed. Mary K Woolsey. Circ: 6,500.

285.8 USA
CONGREGATIONS: THE ALBAN JOURNAL; resources for people who care about congregations. Text in English. 1975. bi-m. USD 50 membership (effective 2000). bk.rev. illus. index, cum.index. **Document type:** *Newsletter.*
Formerly (until 1992): Action Information
Indexed: CCR.
Published by: Alban Institute, Inc., 7315 Wisconsin Ave, Ste 1250 W, Bethesda, MD 20814-3211. TEL 301-718-4407. Ed., R&P Lisa Kinney. Circ: 8,100.

284.1 USA ISSN 1941-5249
CONNECTIONS (FERGUS FALLS); for evangelical Lutheran Christians. Text in English. 2008. 6/yr. USD 20 (effective 2008). adv. **Document type:** *Magazine, Consumer.* **Description:** For Evangelical Lutheran Christians filled with meaty articles as well as lighter spiritual fare, and sponsoring monthly contests.
Published by: Bible Alive Ministries, PO Box 372, Fergus Falls, MN 56538. TEL 218-731-0662, http://bible-aliveministries.com. Ed. Kent Groethe. adv.: page USD 400.

283.73 USA ISSN 2155-7551
▼ **CONNECTIONS (SAGINAW).** Text in English. 2010. q. **Document type:** *Magazine, Consumer.* **Description:** News and information for the Episcopal Diocese of Eastern Michigan.

Published by: Episcopal Diocese of Eastern Michigan, 924 N Niagara St, Saginaw, MI 48602. TEL 989-752-6020, FAX 989-752-6120, http://www.eastmich.org/index.html.

283.42 GBR ISSN 1359-1762
CONTACT (ALDERSHOT). Text in English. 1920. 3/yr. GBP 2 per issue to non-members; free to members (effective 2009). bk.rev. back issues avail. **Document type:** *Magazine, Trade.* **Description:** Contains inspirational articles, profiles, and announcements of conferences and affiliations pertaining to the activities of Christian officers in the British armed forces.
Formerly (until 1981): Practical Christianity (0032-6364)
Related titles: Online - full text ed.: free (effective 2009).
Indexed: CERDIC.
Published by: The Armed Forces' Christian Union, Havelock House, Barrack Rd, Aldershot, Hants GU11 3NP, United Kingdom. TEL 44-1252-311221, office@afcu.org.uk. Eds. Rachel Farmer, Simon Farmer.

280.4 AUS ISSN 1030-7052
CONTACT (BOX HILL). Text in English. 1986. q. free (effective 2008). adv. back issues avail. **Document type:** *Magazine, Consumer.* **Description:** Provides information and news items about the work and the staff of the Christian Radio Missionary Fellowship.
Formerly (until 1994): Closer Contact (1036-4013)
Related titles: E-mail ed.: free (effective 2008); Online - full text ed.
Published by: Christian Radio Missionary Fellowship, 5 Court St, PO Box 39, Box Hill, VIC 3128, Australia. TEL 61-3-98902338, FAX 61-3-98996063, crmf-aust@maf.org.au.

287.1 GBR
CONTACT (SHEFFIELD). Text in English. 1849. m. GBP 8. adv. **Document type:** *Newsletter.*
Formerly: Christian Words
Published by: Wesleyan Reform Union, Wesleyan Reform Church House, 123 Queen St, Sheffield, S Yorks S1 2DU, United Kingdom. TEL 44-114-272-1938, FAX 44-114-272-1965. Ed. Rev. A J Williams. Circ: 1,500.

286 USA ISSN 1945-9696
CONVERGE POINT. Text in English. 1911. bi-m. adv. bk.rev. charts; illus. back issues avail. **Document type:** *Magazine, Consumer.* **Description:** Reports on the events and people of the Baptist General Conference, its churches and constituent organizations. Includes advice and teachings about Christian living.
Former titles (until 2008): B G C World (1546-3257); (until 2003): Standard (0038-9382); Which incorporated (1944-1961): The Mission Post; Which was formerly (until 1944): Missionsposten; (1906-1922): Finska Missions-Posten
Related titles: Online - full text ed.
Published by: Converge Worldwide, 2002 S Arlington Heights Rd, Arlington, IL 60005. TEL 847-228-0200, FAX 847-228-5376, http://www.scene3.org/. Ed. Bob Putman.

285.834 USA
CORLETTER. Text in English. 1986. q. USD 10 (effective 1999). adv. bk.rev. **Document type:** *Newsletter.*
Published by: National Council of the Churches of Christ, Ecumenical Networks, 475 Riverside Dr, Rm 880, New York, NY 10115-0050. TEL 212-870-2155, FAX 212-870-2817. Ed., Pub., R&P, Adv. contact Barbara George. Circ: 3,575.

287 GBR ISSN 0574-1009
CORNISH METHODIST HISTORICAL ASSOCIATION JOURNAL. Text in English. 1960. a. GBP 3 domestic; GBP 5 foreign (effective 2001). bk.rev. **Document type:** *Newsletter, Academic/Scholarly.*
Address: c/o Barrie S. May, Pelmear Villa, Carharrack, Redruth, Cornwall TR16 5RB, United Kingdom. TEL 44-1209-820381. Ed. C A Appleby. Circ: 300 (controlled).

266 GBR
COUNCIL FOR WORLD MISSION. ANNUAL REPORT. Text in English. 1993. a. bk.rev. **Document type:** *Corporate.* **Description:** Includes the annual report of the Council's activities, including environmental studies, religion and theology, and ethnic interests.
Former titles: Bicentenary Brochure; (until 1995): Beyond Ourselves; Which superseded: C W M Report (0069-8857)
Published by: Council for World Mission, Ipalo House, 32-34 Great Peter St, London, SW1P 2DB, United Kingdom. TEL 44-20-72224214, FAX 44-20-72331747, council@cwmission.org, http://www.cwmission.org. Ed. Nick Sireau. Circ: 5,000.

285.8 USA ISSN 0746-3030
THE COURIER (ST. LOUIS). Text in English. 10/yr.
Formerly (until 198?): The United Courier (0194-9829)
Published by: United Church of Christ, Missouri Mid-South Conference, 411 E Lockwood Ave, St. Louis, MO 63119. TEL 314-962-8740, 877-877-5884, FAX 314-918-2610, http://www.mmsucc.org. Ed. Sandy Roland.

287.6 USA
COVENANT DISCIPLESHIP CONNECTION. Text in English. 1985. m. free (effective 2009). bk.rev. back issues avail. **Document type:** *Newsletter, Consumer.* **Description:** Designed to educate, encourage and empower covenant discipleship group members and class leaders in their daily Christian living, by reviewing resources, exploring issues and sharing information.
Formerly (until 2009): Covenant Discipleship Quarterly (1052-3790)
Media: E-mail.
Published by: (United Methodist Church), General Board of Discipleship (Subsidiary of: United Methodist Church), PO Box 340003, Nashville, TN 37203-0003. TEL 877-899-2780. Ed. Steven Manskar. Circ: 900.

284 NLD ISSN 0167-2304
CREDO. Text in Dutch. 1974. m.
Published by: (Confessioneel Gereformeerd Beraad), Confessioneel Gereformeerd Toerustingscentrum, Kooikersweg 360, 's-Hertogenbosch, 5224 AZ, Netherlands. TEL 31-73-6212166, info@cgb.nu.

301.6 NOR ISSN 0804-7529
CREDO; det kristne studentermagasinet. Text in Norwegian. 1933. 8/yr. NOK 298 (effective 2001). adv. bk.rev.; film rev.; music rev. **Document type:** *Magazine.* **Description:** Concerned with the relationship between Church and society, Christianity and science, and new religiousness, especially for young people.
Address: St. Olavs Plass, Postboks 6707, Oslo, 0130, Norway. TEL 47-22-20-89-35, FAX 47-22-20-61-43. Ed. Kaare Rune Hauge. Adv. contact Solveig Schanke Eikum. color page NOK 5,800; 200 x 200. Circ: 2,000 (paid and controlled); 800.

280.4 ITA ISSN 0394-0284
IL CRISTIANO; mensile di edificazione e d'informazione. Text in Italian. 1888. m. EUR 15 domestic; EUR 25 foreign (effective 2008). **Document type:** *Magazine, Consumer.*
Published by: Associazione Stampe Pubblicazioni Evangeliche (A S P E), Via Campo della Fiera 16, Anghiari, AR 52031, Italy. Ed. Paolo Moretti. Circ: 4,200.

280.4 USA ISSN 0892-5712
BR1
CRISWELL THEOLOGICAL REVIEW. Abbreviated title: C T R. Text in English. 1986. s-a. USD 25 to individuals; USD 30 to libraries; USD 15 per issue (effective 2010). back issues avail. **Document type:** *Journal, Academic/Scholarly.*
Indexed: A21, ChrPI, OTA, RI-1.
Published by: The Criswell College, 4010 Gaston Ave, Dallas, TX 75246. TEL 214-821-5433, 800-899-0012, FAX 214-370-0497, http://www.criswell.edu. Ed. Alan Streett.

283 GBR ISSN 0955-0747
CROCKFORD'S CLERICAL DIRECTORY. Text in English. 1858. biennial. GBP 56 per issue (effective 2010). **Document type:** *Directory, Trade.* **Description:** Contains the biographies of over 26,000 Anglican clergy as well as comprehensive supplementary information including diocesan maps, indexes of English, Welsh and Irish benefices and churches.
Formerly (until 1860): The Clerical Directory
Related titles: Online - full text ed.: GBP 29.36 per issue (effective 2010).
—BLDSC (3487.680000). **CCC.**
Published by: Church House Publishing, Church House, Great Smith St, London, SW1P 3AZ, United Kingdom. TEL 44-20-78981012, FAX 44-20-78981769, http://www.chpublishing.co.uk.

286 FRA ISSN 1950-8492
CROIRE ET VIVRE; une aventure a partager. Text in French. 1946. m. (10/yr). EUR 16 (effective 2009). bk.rev. **Document type:** *Magazine, Consumer.*
Formerly (until 2006): Croire et Servir (0755-7205)
Published by: (Federation des Eglises Evangeliques Baptistes), Croire Publications, 48 Rue de Lille, Paris, 75007, France. http://www.publicroire.com. Ed. Andre Thobois. Circ: 20,000.

285.834 AUS ISSN 1037-826X
CROSSLIGHT. Text in English. 19??. m. free (effective 2009). adv. bk.rev.; music rev. illus. 16 p./no.; back issues avail. **Document type:** *Newspaper.* **Description:** Features stories, comments and letters that reflect the depth and diversity of the uniting church.
Former titles (until 1992): Church and Nation (0314-6200); (until 1977): New Spectator (0300-3736); (until 1971): Spectator
Published by: Uniting Church in Australia Synod of Victoria, Level 1, 130 Little Collins St, Melbourne, VIC 3000, Australia. TEL 61-3-92515200, FAX 61-3-96504490. Ed. Kim Cain. Circ: 25,000.

283.72 CAN ISSN 1489-0631
CROSSTALK. Text in English. 1978. 10/yr. CAD 12; USD 20 foreign (effective 2000). adv. bk.rev. **Document type:** *Newspaper.* **Description:** News and views of the Anglican Diocese of Ottawa.
Former titles (1998): Crosstalk and Anglican Journal (1196-7374); (until 1990): Crosstalk and Anglican Journal Episcopal (0845-4795); (until 1989): Crosstalk (0706-8069)
Published by: Anglican Church of Canada, Diocese of Ottawa, 71 Bronson Ave, Ottawa, ON K1R 6G6, Canada. TEL 613-232-1451, FAX 613-232-1451, ottawa_crosstalk@ecunet.org. Ed., R&P Susan Becker Davidson. Pub. Rev. Peter Coffin. Adv. contact Robert Browning. Circ: 14,063 (paid).

THE CRUSADER. *see* COLLEGE AND ALUMNI

CRUSADER (ALPHARETTA). *see* CHILDREN AND YOUTH

283 CAN ISSN 0382-4314
CRUSADER (TORONTO). Text in English. 1928. 3/yr. free. illus. back issues avail. **Description:** Provides personal articles describing the vaious elements in the postings of church army personnel.
Formerly (until 1972): Anglican Crusader (0382-4306)
Published by: Church Army in Canada, 50 Gervais Dr 301, Toronto, ON M3C 123, Canada. TEL 416-385-9686, FAX 416-385-9689. Ed. Bruce Smith. Circ: 8,000 (controlled).

285 USA ISSN 0011-2968
CUMBERLAND FLAG. Text in English. 1915. m. USD 8.
Published by: General Assembly Second Cumberland Presbyterian Church, 226 Church St, Huntsville, AL 35801. TEL 205-536-7481.

285 USA ISSN 0011-2976
THE CUMBERLAND PRESBYTERIAN. Text in English. 1829. 11/yr. USD 24 (effective 2000 - 2001). adv. bk.rev. illus. **Description:** A denominational news and features magazine.
Published by: Cumberland Presbyterian Church, PO Box 155, Lincoln, IL 62656-0155. TEL 217-732-2813. Ed. Patricia P Richards. adv.: B&W page USD 400; trim 11 x 8.5. Circ: 4,660.

230.41 USA ISSN 0098-2113
BX8061.M7
CURRENTS IN THEOLOGY AND MISSION. Text in English. 1974. bi-m. adv. bk.rev. back issues avail.; reprints avail. **Document type:** *Journal, Academic/Scholarly.* **Description:** Contains theological and practical articles for ministers.
Incorporates (1974-1986): Preaching Helps (0098-2156)
Related titles: Microform ed.: (from PQC); Online - full text ed.
Indexed: A21, A22, A26, CERDIC, DIP, E08, G08, I05, IBR, IBZ, IZBG, OTA, P30, R&TA, R05, RI-1, RI-2, RILM, S09.
—BLDSC (3505.203000), IE, Infotrieve, Ingenta.
Published by: Lutheran School of Theology at Chicago, 1100 E 55th St, Chicago, IL 60615. TEL 773-256-0700. Ed. Kurt K Hendel TEL 773-256-0776. Circ: 3,000.

280.4 AUT ISSN 0011-4057
CURSILLO; Evangelium Heute. Text in German. 1964. m. bk.rev. bibl. **Document type:** *Magazine, Consumer.*
Formerly: Karat
Published by: Arbeitsgemeinschaft der Diozesansekretariate der Cursillo-Bewegung, Bennogasse 21, Vienna, W 1080, Austria. TEL 43-1-4055318, FAX 43-1-4081015, cursillo@ins.at. Ed. Josef G Cascales.

280.4 GBR ISSN 0143-0076
Y CYLCHGRAWN EFENGYLAIDD. Text in English. 1948. q. adv. bk.rev. illus. back issues avail. **Document type:** *Journal, Trade.* **Description:** Contains articles on a wide range of subjects relating to the historic evangelical faith of the Christian Church and news of the contemporary religious scene.
Published by: Evangelical Movement of Wales, Bryntirion, Bridgend, CF31 4DX, United Kingdom. TEL 44-1656-655886, FAX 44-1656-665919, office@emw.org.uk.

280.4 USA
D R C MISSISSIPPI NEWSLETTER. Text in English. 1972. irreg. free. **Document type:** *Newsletter.*
Published by: Delta Resources Committee, Inc., 300 N Edison St, Box 584, Greenville, MS 38702. TEL 601-335-3121, FAX 601-335-3123. Ed. Roger A Smith. Circ: 1,500 (controlled).

284.2 ZAF
D R C NEWS. (Dutch Reformed Church) Text in English. 1958. s-a. free. bk.rev. **Document type:** *Newsletter.*
Former titles: D R C Africa News (0250-0353); (until 1976): D R C Newsletter (0011-5118)
Published by: (Ecumenical Department), Nederduitse Gereformeerde Kerk in Suid-Afrika/Dutch Reformed Church in South Africa, PO Box 4445, Pretoria, 0001, South Africa. TEL 27-12-3228900, FAX 27-12-3223803, http://www.ngkerk.org.za. Circ: 2,000.

280.4 DEU
D Z M AKTUELL. (Deutsche Zeltmission) Text in German. 1902. m. bk.rev. bibl.; illus. back issues avail. **Document type:** *Magazine, Trade.*
Former titles (until 2005): Zeltgruss-News; (until 2002): Zeltgruss; (until 2000): Zeltgruss der Deutschen Zeltmission; (until 1909): Gruss aus der Zeltmission
Published by: Deutsche Zeltmission e.V., Patmosweg 10, Siegen-Geisweid, 57078, Germany. TEL 49-271-8800100, FAX 49-271-8800150, web@dzm.de, http://www.deutsche-zeltmission.de.

287.6 USA ISSN 0742-065X
DAILY BIBLE STUDY. Text in English. 1984. q. USD 23; USD 6.25 per issue (effective 2009). back issues avail. **Document type:** *Magazine, Consumer.* **Description:** Helps individuals to develop the discipline of studying the Bible every day.
Media: Large Type (14 pt.). **Related titles:** Online - full text ed.
—**CCC.**
Published by: (United Methodist Church), United Methodist Publishing House, 201 8th Ave S, PO Box 801, Nashville, TN 37202. TEL 615-749-6000, 800-672-1789, FAX 615-749-6579, http://www.umph.org. Ed. Wayne G Reece. Pub. Neil M Alexander.

283 USA ISSN 0011-538X
DAILY BLESSING. Text in English. 1959. s-a. USD 7 (effective 1999).
Published by: Oral Roberts Evangelistic Association Inc., 7777 South Lewis Ave, Box 2187, Tulsa, OK 74171-0001. TEL 918-495-7307. Ed. Oral Roberts.

283 GBR ISSN 0963-4797
DAILY BREAD (LONDON); practical help from the Bible. Text in English. 1937. q. GBP 14 domestic; GBP 18 in Europe; GBP 20 elsewhere; GBP 3.50 per issue (effective 2010). back issues avail. **Document type:** *Magazine, Consumer.* **Description:** Explores bible study geared to the individual.
Related titles: Braille ed.; Online - full text ed.: GBP 2.50 per issue (effective 2010).
—**CCC.**
Published by: Scripture Union, 207-209 Queensway, Bletchley, Milton Keynes, Bucks MK2 2EB, United Kingdom. TEL 44-1908-856000, FAX 44-1908-856111. Ed. Andrew Clark. **Subscr. to:** Mail Order, PO Box 5148, Milton Keynes MLO, Bucks MK2 2YZ, United Kingdom. TEL 44-1908-856006, FAX 44-1908-856020, mailorder@scriptureunion.org.uk.

R

283 GBR
DAILY BREAD (PETERBOROUGH). Text in English. 19??. m. GBP 0.70 per issue (effective 2009). **Document type:** *Bulletin, Consumer.* **Description:** Provides a daily commentary on portions of the scripture for visually impaired persons.
Media: Braille. **Related titles:** Diskette ed.; E-mail ed.
Published by: Royal National Institute of Blind People, 105 Judd St, London, WC1H 9NE, United Kingdom. TEL 44-20-73881266, FAX 44-20-73882034, helpline@rnib.org.uk, http://www.rnib.org.uk/.

DAILY DEVOTIONS FOR THE DEAF. *see* HANDICAPPED—Hearing Impaired

284.6 GBR
DAILY WATCHWORDS. Text in English. 1722. a. **Document type:** *Bulletin, Trade.*
Published by: Moravian Union Inc., Book Room, 5 Muswell Hill, London, N103TJ, United Kingdom. TEL 44-20-88833409, FAX 44-20-88150105, office@moravian.org.uk. Ed. Rev Paul Gubi TEL 44-1225-442730. Circ: 5,000.

280.4 USA ISSN 0011-5525
DAILY WORD. Text in English. 1924. m. USD 12.95 domestic (effective 2009). **Document type:** *Magazine, Consumer.* **Description:** Covers daily devotional readings, with articles and poetry on spiritual inspiration, human relations, and everyday living.
Formerly: Unity Daily Word (0041-8188)
Related titles: Audio cassette/tape ed.: free to visually impaired (effective 2009); Braille ed.: free to visually impaired (effective 2009); Large type ed. 18 pt.: USD 10.95 domestic; USD 17.95 in Canada; USD 34.95 elsewhere (effective 2009); ♦ Spanish ed.: La Palabra Diaria. ISSN 0475-4816.
Indexed: A22.
Published by: Unity School of Christianity, 1901 NW Blue Pkwy, Unity Village, MO 64065-0001. TEL 816-524-3550, FAX 816-251-3553, unity@unityworldhq.org, http://www.unityworldhq.org. Ed. Colleen Zuck. Pub. Lynne Brown. Circ: 1,200,000.

280.4 DEU ISSN 1611-1729
BV2440
DARUM; Zeitschrift fuer Mission und Oekumene. Text in German. 1983. bi-m. EUR 15; EUR 3 newsstand/cover (effective 2009). bk.rev. 32 p./no.; back issues avail. **Document type:** *Newsletter, Consumer.* **Description:** Information about mission and ecumenical matters concerning churches in Africa and Asia.

Published by: Evangelisches Missionswerk in Suedwestdeutschland e.V./Association of Churches and Missions in South Western Germany, Vogelsangstr 62, Stuttgart, 70197, Germany. TEL 49-711-636780, FAX 49-711-6367855, info@ems-online.org.

280.4 DEU ISSN 1611-1737
BV2440
DARUM-JOURNAL; Suedwestdeutsches Magazin aus Mission und Oekumene. Text in German. bi-m. free (effective 2009). 16 p./no.; **Document type:** *Magazine, Consumer.*
Published by: Evangelisches Missionswerk in Suedwestdeutschland e.V./Association of Churches and Missions in South Western Germany, Vogelsangstr 62, Stuttgart, 70197, Germany. TEL 49-711-636780, FAX 49-711-6367855, info@ems-online.org. Ed., R&P Birte Peterson TEL 49-711-6367867.

284.1 USA ISSN 1550-4166
DAVEY AND GOLIATH'S DEVOTIONS; for families on the go. Text in English. 1939. q. USD 8.75 to individuals (effective 2009). back issues avail. **Document type:** *Magazine, Consumer.*
Formerly (until 2004): Home Altar (1042-5888)
Published by: Augsburg Fortress Publishers, PO Box 1209, Minneapolis, MN 55440. TEL 800-328-4648, FAX 800-722-7766, info@augsburgfortress.org, http://www.augsburgfortress.org. Ed. Davey . Circ: 50,000.

286 USA ISSN 0045-9771
THE DEACON. Text in English. 1970. q. USD 14.95; USD 3.10 per issue (effective 2008). adv. cum.index every 3 yrs. back issues avail. **Document type:** *Magazine, Consumer.* **Description:** Enables deacons to learn more about their ministry role in their church and community.
Indexed: SBPI.
Published by: LifeWay Christian Resources, 1 Lifeway Plz, Nashville, TN 37234. TEL 615-251-2000, 800-458-2772, FAX 615-251-5933, customerservice@lifeway.com.

DEAF MISSIONS ENEWS. *see* HANDICAPPED—Hearing Impaired

280.4 USA ISSN 0011-7307
BV3750
DECISION. Text in English. 1960. m. USD 15 in North America; USD 32 elsewhere (effective 2010). illus. index, cum.index. back issues avail. **Document type:** *Magazine, Consumer.* **Description:** Encourages, teaches and strengthens Christians; and reports on the crusade ministry of Billy Graham and associate evangelists.
Related titles: Audio cassette/tape ed.: free; Braille ed.: free; Online - full text ed.
Indexed: A22, CCR, ChrPI, GSS&RPL.
Published by: Billy Graham Evangelistic Association, PO Box 668886, Charlotte, NC 28266. TEL 704-401-2432, 877-247-2426. Ed. Bob Paulson. **Subscr. in Australia to:** Decision, G.P.O., PO Box 4807, Sydney, NSW 2001, Australia; **Subscr. in Canada to:** Decision, Stn M, PO Box 2276, Calgary, AB T2P 5M8, Canada; **Subscr. in New Zealand to:** Decision, PO Box 870, Auckland, New Zealand; **Subscr. in the UK to:** Decision, PO Box 2032, Woodford Green IG9 5AP, United Kingdom; **Subscr. in the US and elsewhere to:** Decison, PO Box 668886, Charlotte, NC 28266-8886. **Co-publisher:** Christian Services for the Blind International, Inc.

283 GBR ISSN 1467-5706
DERBY DIOCESAN DIRECTORY AND CLERGY LIST. Text in English. 1927. a. looseleaf. adv. **Document type:** *Directory.* **Description:** Contains a list of clergy readers, church wardens, secretaries, treasurers, and other church people in 270 parishes for the Derby Diocese.
Formerly (until 1998): Derby Diocesan Year Book and Clergy List (0305-0874)
Published by: Diocese of Derby, Derby Diocesan Communications Committee, Derby Church House, Full St, Derby, DE1 3DR, United Kingdom. TEL 44-1332-388650, http://www.derby.anglican.org/.

286 USA ISSN 1094-8473
DETROIT BAPTIST SEMINARY JOURNAL. Abbreviated title: D B S J. Text in English. 1996. a. USD 11 for 2 yrs. domestic; USD 14 for 2 yrs. foreign (effective 2010). back issues avail. **Document type:** *Journal, Academic/Scholarly.* **Description:** Publishes articles on systematic theology, Old and New Testament studies, historical theology, and pastoral theology.
Indexed: A21, ChrPI, OTA, R&TA, RI-1.
Published by: Detroit Baptist Theological Seminary, 4801 Allen Rd, Allen Park, MI 48101. TEL 313-381-0111, 800-866-0111, FAX 313-381-0798, info@dbts.edu.

284.1 USA ISSN 1521-1444
DETROIT LUTHERAN. Text in English. 1941. m. USD 12 (effective 2008). adv. bk.rev. **Document type:** *Newspaper.*
Former titles (until 1998): T L C Lutheran News (1088-2073); (until 1996): Tri-Country Lutheran (0744-9437); (until 1982): Detroit and Suburban Lutheran (0011-9660)
Published by: Lutheran Center Association of Southeastern Michigan, 16259 Nine Mile Rd., Eastpointe, MI 48021. TEL 586-774-2831, 800-572-6711, FAX 586-774-5269. Ed., Adv. contact Betty J Mueller. B&W page USD 325. Circ: 8,500.

200 ISR
DEUTSCHE EVANGELISCHE INSTITUT FUER ALTERTUMSWISSENSCHAFT DES HEILIGEN LANDES. JAHRBUCH. Text in German. 1989. a. **Document type:** *Yearbook, Academic/Scholarly.* **Description:** Aims to strengthen ties between research in the Holy Land and all aspects of Protestant theology.
Indexed: IZBG.
Published by: Deutsche Evangelische Institut fuer Altertumswissenschaft des Heiligen Landes, PO Box 18463, Jerusalem, 91184, Israel. TEL 972-2-6284792, FAX 972-2-6287388, dei_ger@netvision.net.il, http://www.dei-jerusalem.de.

DEUTSCHER HUGENOTTEN-GESELLSCHAFT. GESCHICHTSBLAETTER. *see* HISTORY—History Of Europe

280.4 DEU ISSN 0939-9771
BX8001
DEUTSCHES PFARRERBLATT. Text in German. 1897. m. EUR 47 domestic; EUR 54 foreign; EUR 5 newsstand/cover (effective 2009). adv. **Document type:** *Journal, Trade.*
Published by: (Verband der Vereine Evangelischer Pfarrerinnen und Pfarrer in Deutscgland e.V.), Evangelischer Presseverlag Pfalz GmbH, Beethovenstr 4, Speyer, 67346, Germany. TEL 49-6232-24926, FAX 49-6232-132344, redaktion@evpfalz.de, http://www.evpfalz.de. Ed. Peter Haigis. adv.: B&W page EUR 1,450. Circ: 19,000 (controlled).

DEVELOPING PRIMARY R E. (Religious Education) *see* EDUCATION—Teaching Methods And Curriculum

DEVELOPING SECONDARY R E. (Religious Education) *see* EDUCATION—Teaching Methods And Curriculum

280.4 USA
DEVOTIONS; a daily guide for December, January, February. Text in English. 1957. q. USD 3.99 (effective 2009). back issues avail. **Document type:** *Magazine, Consumer.* **Description:** Contains scripture, meditation and song that correlates to each week's lesson in the quarter.
Related titles: Large type ed. 18 pt.: USD 4.99 (effective 2009).
Published by: Standard Publishing, 8805 Governor's Hill Dr, Ste 400, Cincinnati, OH 45249. TEL 513-931-4050, 800-543-1353, FAX 877-867-5751, customerservice@standardpub.com, http://www.standardpub.com. Ed. Garry Allen. Circ: 167,500.

287 028.5 USA ISSN 1088-0054
DEVO'ZINE; just for teens. Text in English. 1996. bi-m. USD 21.95 (effective 2008). bk.rev.; film rev.; music rev. illus. **Document type:** *Magazine, Consumer.* **Description:** Written by youth (and youth workers) themselves, it links teens with their peers and helps strengthen their faith. Includes scripture, meditations, prayers, feature articles, reflection questions, extreme color graphics, etc.
Related titles: Online - full text ed.
Published by: (United Methodist Church, General Board of Discipleship), The Upper Room Publications, 1908 Grand Ave, PO Box 340004, Nashville, TN 37203. TEL 615-340-7200, FAX 615-340-7275, urbooks@upperroom.org. Ed. Sandy Miller. Circ: 85,000 (paid).

284 NLD ISSN 1572-7459
DIACOON. Text in Dutch. 1982. bi-m. EUR 10 (effective 2008).
Formerly (until 2003): A D M A Info (0924-6398)
Published by: Christelijke Gereformeerde Kerken in Nederland, Deputaten Diaconaat, Postbus 334, Veenendaal, 3900 AH, Netherlands. TEL 31-318-582367, diac.bur@cgk.nl.

280.4 AUT
DIAKONIE; Zeitschrift fuer Freunde und Mitarbeiter des Evangelischen Diakoniewerkes Gallneukirchen. Text in German. 1875. bi-m. adv. bk.rev. **Document type:** *Newsletter, Consumer.*
Formerly: Gallneukirchner Bote (0016-4143)
Published by: Evangelisches Diakoniewerk Gallneukirchen, Martin Boos Strasse 4, Gallneukirchen, O 4210, Austria. TEL 43-7235-63251, FAX 43-7235-63251201, a.kloesch@diakoniewerk.at, http://diakoniewerk.at/. Eds. Andrea Kloesch, Gerhard Gaebler. R&P Andrea Kloesch. Circ: 7,200.

230.044 DEU ISSN 0174-5506
DIAKRISIS. Text in German. 1979. q. EUR 10 (effective 2008). bk.rev. cum.index: 1980-1984. back issues avail. **Document type:** *Journal, Academic/Scholarly.*
Published by: Theologischer Konvent Bekennender Gemeinschaften, Schulstr 1, Gomaringen, 72810, Germany. TEL 49-7072-920343, FAX 49-7072-920344, Institut-Diakrisis@t-online.de. Ed. Peter Beyerhaus. Circ: 2,500 (controlled).

DIALOGUE. *see* GENERAL INTEREST PERIODICALS—Africa

283.713 CAN ISSN 1184-6283
DIALOGUE (KINGSTON). Text in English. 1960. m. (10/yr.). CAD 10 (effective 2000). adv. bk.rev. **Document type:** *Newspaper.* **Description:** Provides news, opinion, features concerning interests of the Anglican parishes in the Diocese of Ontario in eastern Ontario.
Formerly (until 1991): Ontario Churchman (0030-2848)
Published by: Synod of the Diocese of Ontario, Dialogue Board of Directors, 90 Johnson St, Kingston, ON K7L 1X7, Canada. TEL 613-544-4774, FAX 613-547-3745. Ed., R&P Francie Healy TEL 613-548-4617. Adv. contact Jane Miller. Circ: 6,086.

283 GUY
DIOCESAN MAGAZINE. Text in English. bi-m. **Description:** Anglican interests.
Published by: Diocese of Guyana, Barrack St 49, Kingston, Georgetown, Guyana. Ed. Blanche E Duke.

283 CAN ISSN 0382-9391
DIOCESAN TIMES. Text in English. 1946. m. (except July-Aug.). CAD 5. adv. **Document type:** *Newspaper.*
Published by: (Anglican Diocese of Nova Scotia), Diocesan Times Publishing Co., 5732 College St, Halifax, NS B3H 1X3, Canada. TEL 902-832-0960. Ed., R&P Robert Martin. Circ: 17,500.

283 USA ISSN 2160-4525
DIOLOG. Text in English. 19??. q. USD 25 to non-members; free to members (effective 2011). **Document type:** *Magazine, Trade.* **Description:** Report news and feature stories on the people, the ministries and the congregations in the Diocese of Texas.
Former titles (until 2011): The Texas Episcopalian (1074-441X); (until 1990): The Texas Episcopal Churchman (0746-9314); Texas Churchman
Published by: The Episcopal Diocese of Texas, 1225 Texas Ave, Houston, TX 77002. TEL 713-520-6444, 800-318-4452, FAX 713-520-5723, adoyle@epicenter.org.

289.94 GBR ISSN 0957-9397
DIRECTION. Text in English. 1919. m. GBP 24 domestic; GBP 31.95 in Europe; GBP 41.95 elsewhere; GBP 1.70 newsstand/cover (effective 2009). adv. bk.rev.; music rev.; video rev. back issues avail.; reprints avail. **Document type:** *Magazine, Consumer.* **Description:** Addresses current issues affecting the Christian Church in a lively manner for all ages.
Formerly (until 1989): Elim Evangel (0013-6182)
Indexed: OTA.
Published by: Elim Pentecostal Church, Elim International Ctr, De Walden Rd, West Malvern, Worcestershire WR14 4DF, United Kingdom. TEL 44-845-3026750, FAX 44-845-3026752, info@elimhq.net. Ed. John Glass. Circ: 9,000. **Subscr. to:** New Life Publishing Co., PO Box 777, Nottingham NG11 6ZZ, United Kingdom. TEL 44-115-8240777.

DIRECTORY OF MINISTRIES IN HIGHER EDUCATION. *see* EDUCATION—Higher Education

280.4 USA ISSN 0273-5865
BV4485
DISCIPLESHIP JOURNAL. Abbreviated title: D J. Text in English. 1981. bi-m. USD 3.96 per issue (effective 2009). adv. index. **Document type:** *Journal, Consumer.* **Description:** Provides articles that help believers to develop a deeper relationship with Jesus Christ and guides in understanding the Bible and applying it to daily life and ministry.
Indexed: CCR, ChrPI.
Published by: NavPress Publishing Group, PO Box 35002, Colorado Springs, CO 80935. TEL 719-548-9222, 800-366-7788, FAX 800-343-3902, customerservice@navpress.com.

286 USA ISSN 0732-9881
BX7301
DISCIPLIANA. Text in English. 1941. s-a. USD 25 to libraries; free to members (effective 2010). bk.rev. bibl. 32 p./no.; back issues avail. **Document type:** *Journal, Academic/Scholarly.* **Description:** Provides a brand new historical essay in each issue, as well as other articles and information of interest to our readers.
Former titles (until 1960): The Harbinger and Discipliana; (until 1953): Discipliana
Related titles: Microfilm ed.
Indexed: A21, RI-1, RI-2.
Published by: Disciples of Christ Historical Society, 1101 Nineteenth Ave S, Nashville, TN 37212. TEL 615-327-1444, 866-834-7563, FAX 615-327-1445, mail@discipleshistory.org.

286.132 USA ISSN 1930-1782
DISCIPULADO CRISTIANO. Variant title: Discipulado: Herramienta de Crecimiento Espiritual Para Todo Cristiano. Text in Portuguese. 1963. q. price varies. back issues avail. **Document type:** *Magazine, Consumer.* **Description:** Features a series of important bible studies to be taken either in small groups or individually.
Formerly (until 1995): La Fe Bautista (0162-4504)
Published by: LifeWay Christian Resources, 1 Lifeway Plz, Nashville, TN 37234. TEL 615-251-2000, 800-458-2772, FAX 615-251-5933, customerservice@lifeway.com, http://www.lifeway.com.

286.132 USA ISSN 0162-198X
DISCOVERY (BIRMINGHAM). Text in English. 1970. m. USD 14.99 (effective 2006). **Document type:** *Magazine, Consumer.* **Description:** For girls, grades 1-4, who are members of Southern Baptist Girls in Action organization.
Published by: Woman's Missionary Union Auxiliary to the Southern Baptist Convention, 100 Missionary Ridge, PO Box 830010, Birmingham, AL 35283. TEL 205-991-8100, email@wmu.org, http://www.wmu.com/. Ed. Barbara Massey. R&P Carol Causey. Circ: 90,000 (paid).

230 USA ISSN 1934-3132
DIVINE FAVOR GOSPEL MAGAZINE. Text in English. 2006. q. USD 19 (effective 2007). **Document type:** *Magazine, Consumer.* **Description:** Features information about church, worship and the Southern Baptist community in Alabama.
Published by: Billionaire Record Label & Publishing Firm, PO Box 110682, Birmingham, AL 35211. TEL 205-401-0192. Pub. Derlesia Sims.

DOCTRINA ET PIETAS; Zwischen Reformation und Aufklaerung. *see* HISTORY—History Of Europe

284.2 NLD ISSN 0165-4349
BR900
➤ **DOCUMENTATIEBLAD NADERE REFORMATIE.** Text in Dutch. 1977. 2/yr. EUR 21 (effective 2008). adv. bk.rev. bibl.; illus. back issues avail. **Document type:** *Academic/Scholarly.* **Description:** Publishes information on the history of Dutch Reformed pietism and further reformation.
Incorporates (1993-2003): Nieuwsbrief S S N R (1382-757X)
Published by: (Stichting Studie der Nadere Reformatie), Boekencentrum Uitgevers, Goudstraat 50, Postbus 29, Zoetermeer, 2700 AA, Netherlands. TEL 31-79-3615481, FAX 31-79-3615489, info@boekencentrum.nl, http://www.boekencentrum.nl. Ed. Dr. A Goudriaan. Circ: 500.

284.2 NLD ISSN 0923-7771
DOCUMENTATIEBLAD VOOR DE NEDERLANDSE KERKGESCHIEDENIS NA 1800. Text in Dutch. 1977. 2/yr. EUR 24 domestic; EUR 29.50 in Belgium; EUR 13 newsstand/cover (effective 2009). back issues avail. **Document type:** *Academic/Scholarly.*
Formerly (until 1989): Documentatieblad voor de Nederlandse Kerkgeschiedenis van de Negentiende Eeuw (0166-0144)
Published by: (Vrije Universiteit Amsterdam, Historisch Documentatiecentrum voor het Nederlands Protestantisme), Kok Tijdschriften, Postbus 5018, Kampen, 8260 GA, Netherlands. TEL 31-38-3392555, http://www.kok.nl.

286 NLD ISSN 1872-2229
DOOPSGEZIND NL. Text in Dutch. 1946. bi-w. EUR 57 (effective 2008). adv.
Formerly (until 2006): Algemeen Doopsgezind Weekblad (0167-1715)
Published by: Algemene Doopsgezinde Societeit Nederland, Singel 454, Amsterdam, 1017 AW, Netherlands. TEL 31-20-6230914, FAX 31-20-6278919, ads@doopsgezind.nl, http://www.doopsgezind.nl.

280.4 GBR
THE DOOR. Text in English. 1989. 10/yr. free to qualified personnel (effective 2009). bk.rev. **Document type:** *Newspaper, Trade.* **Description:** Designed for the churches and schools in the diocese of Oxford.
Formerly (until 1989): Oxford Diocesan Magazine
Published by: (Oxford Diocesan Board of Finance), Oxford Diocesan Publications Ltd., Diocesan Church House, North Hinksey, Oxford, Oxon OX2 0NB, United Kingdom. TEL 44-1865-208200, FAX 44-1865-790470. Ed. Jo Duckles TEL 44-1865-208227.

283 USA
DOOR OF HOPE MAGAZINE. Text in English. 1972. m. USD 25. adv. bk.rev.; film rev.; play rev. bibl.; tr.lit. **Document type:** *Newsletter.*
Former titles: Door of Hope International; Door of Hope
Published by: Door of Hope International, PO Box 10460, Glendale, CA 91209. TEL 818-249-6025, FAX 818-249-6026. Ed. Paul Haralan Popov. Adv. contact Ivette Moradian. Circ: 5,000.

266.82 NLD ISSN 1380-474X
DOORGEVEN. Text in Dutch. 1906. 5/yr. free (effective 2008). adv. bk.rev. illus.; stat. **Description:** Covers missionary activities Third world countries.

Incorporates (in 1995): Ga (0921-0962); Formed by the 1994 merger of: Zendingsblad (0042-1650); (1979-1993): Werkwoord (1380-4758)
Published by: Christelijke Gereformeerde Kerken in Nederland/Mission of the Christian Reformed Churches in the Netherlands, Ghandistr 2, Postbus 334, Veenendaal, 3900 AH, Netherlands. TEL 31-318-582350, FAX 31-318-582351, lkb@cgk.nl, http://www.cgk.nl. Ed. Rita Blankenstijn. Circ: 33,500.

DORDT CROSSINGS. *see* EDUCATION

268 GBR ISSN 0012-5695
DOUAI MAGAZINE. Text in English. 1894. a. free (effective 2009). adv. bk.rev. illus. back issues avail. **Document type:** *Magazine, Consumer.*
Related titles: Online - full text ed.
Published by: Douai Abbey, Upper Woolhampton, Reading, Berks RG7 5TQ, United Kingdom. TEL 44-118-9715300, FAX 44-118-9715305, info@douaiabbey.org.uk. Ed. Gervase Holdaway.

284.1 DEU ISSN 0012-608X
DREIKOENIGSBOTE. Text in German. 1951. 3/yr. free (effective 2009). bibl. **Document type:** *Bulletin, Consumer.*
Published by: Evangelisch-Lutherische Dreikoenigsgemeinde, Tucholskystr 40, Frankfurt Am Main, 60598, Germany. TEL 49-69-681771, FAX 49-69-68600772, dreikoenigsgemeinde@t-online.de, http://www.dreikoenigsgemeinde.de.

284.1 028.5 SWE ISSN 1654-9457
DROPPEN. Text in Swedish. 1952. 36/yr. SEK 240 (effective 2008). 8 p./no. 2 cols./p.; **Document type:** *Bulletin, Consumer.* **Description:** Magazine for young children.
Former titles (until 2207): Evangelisk-Lutherska Barntidning Droppen (1404-2185); (until 1997): Luthersk Barntidning (0345-7389)
Related titles: Online - full text ed.
Published by: Missionssaellskapet Bibeltrogna Vaenner, Smala Graend 5, Stockholm, 11139, Sweden. TEL 46-8-55923104, FAX 46-8-225922. Ed. Johanna Nyholm.

280.4 SVK ISSN 0862-8319
DUHA. Text in Slovak. 1990. m. EUR 10 (effective 2011). adv. **Document type:** *Magazine, Consumer.*
Published by: Tranoscius a.s., Tranovskeho 1, Liptovsky Mikulas, 031 80, Slovakia. TEL 421-44-5523070, FAX 421-44-5523070, sefredaktor@tranoscius.sk.

280.4 DEU
DURCHBLICK UND DIENST. Text in German. 1969. bi-m. EUR 11.70 (effective 2002). back issues avail. **Document type:** *Newsletter, Consumer.*
Published by: Liebenzeller Gemeinschaftsverband, Postfach 1205, Bad Liebenzell, 75375, Germany. TEL 49-7052-920886, FAX 49-7052-5347, lgv-redaktion@t-online.de, http://www.lgv-online.de. Ed. Rev. Friedhelm Geiss. Circ: 5,200.

284.2 USA
DUTCH CHURCH TRANSCRIPTS. Text in English. 1985. s-a. looseleaf. USD 15. back issues avail. **Description:** Transcriptions of Dutch Reformed Church records in the United States.
Formerly: Dutch American Genealogist
Published by: Reformed Church Archives, 21 Seminary Place, New Brunswick, NJ 08901. TEL 908-296-1779. Ed. Russell L Gasero. Circ: 125.

286.132 USA ISSN 1078-2788
E C; nurturing godly families for 60 yeasrs. (Essential Connection) Text in English. 1995. m. USD 24.95; USD 2.95 per issue (effective 2008). adv. back issues avail. **Document type:** *Magazine, Consumer.* **Description:** Features in-depth articles on living for Christ in the midst of the student culture, as well as daily devotions and scripture readings.
Published by: LifeWay Christian Resources, 1 Lifeway Plz, Nashville, TN 37234. TEL 615-251-2000, 800-458-2772, FAX 615-251-5933, customerservice@lifeway.com. Ed. Mandy Crow. Adv. contact Rhonda Edge Buescher. color page USD 4,257; trim 7 x 9.5. Circ: 60,900.

266.4 SWE ISSN 0282-0668
E F S MISSIONSTIDNING BUDBAERAREN. Variant title: Budbaeraren. Text in Swedish. 1958. w. SEK 465 (effective 2006). adv. back issues avail. **Document type:** *Newsletter, Consumer.*
Formerly (until 1981): E F S-Budbaeraren (0345-2638)
Related titles: Online - full text ed.
Published by: Evangeliska Fosterlandsstiftelsen, Sysslomansgatan 4, Uppsala, 75170, Sweden. TEL 46-18-169800, FAX 46-18-169801, efs@efs.svenskakyrkan.se. Ed. Per Erik Lund TEL 46-18-169823. Adv. contact Gunnel Karlsson TEL 46-18-169828.

266 DEU
E M S - JAHRESBERICHT. (Evangelisches Missionswerk in Suedwestdeutschland) Text in German. 1974. a. free (effective 2009). 46 p./no.; **Document type:** *Journal, Trade.*
Former titles (until 2004): Evangelisches Missionswerk in Suedwestdeutschland. Jahresbericht; (until 2003): E M S - Impulse; (until 2002): E M S - Jahrbuch; (until 1984): Empfangen, Weitergeben
Published by: Evangelisches Missionswerk in Suedwestdeutschland e.V./Association of Churches and Missions in South Western Germany, Vogelsangstr 62, Stuttgart, 70197, Germany. TEL 49-711-636780, FAX 49-711-6367855, info@ems-online.org. Ed. Bernhard Dinkelaker. Circ: 8,000 (controlled).

E P D MEDIEN. (Evangelischer Pressedienst) *see* COMMUNICATIONS

654.19 215 DEU ISSN 1612-2216
E P D SOZIAL. (Evangelischer Pressedienst) Text in German. 2001. w. EUR 237.60 (effective 2007). adv. **Document type:** *Magazine, Trade.*
Published by: Gemeinschaftswerk der Evangelischen Publizistik e.V., Emil-von-Behring-Str 3, Frankfurt Am Main, 60439, Germany. TEL 49-69-580980, FAX 49-69-58098272, info@gep.de, http://www.gep.de. adv.: B&W page EUR 580. Circ: 727 (controlled).

280.4 DEU
E P D WOCHENSPIEGEL. AUSGABE OST. (Evangelischer Pressedienst) Text in German. 1995. w. EUR 10.70 per month (effective 2009). **Document type:** *Newspaper, Consumer.*
Formerly (until 1995): E P D - Landesdienst Ost
Published by: Evangelischer Pressedienst, Landesdienst Ost, Ziegelstr 30, Berlin, 10117, Germany. TEL 49-30-28303911, FAX 49-30-28303913, berlin@epd.de, http://www.epd.de/ost/ost_index.html. Ed. Hans Juergen Roeder.

283.73 USA
E P F NEWSLETTER. Text in English. 1939. q. USD 30 to members (effective 1999). bk.rev. **Document type:** *Newsletter.*
Published by: Episcopal Peace Fellowship, 637 S. Dearborn St., Chicago, IL 60605-1839. TEL 202-783-3380. Circ: 2,500.

286.132 USA ISSN 1540-5567
EARLY YEARS (WINCHESTER). Text in English. 1969. q. USD 9.75 (effective 2007). **Document type:** *Magazine, Consumer.* **Description:** Consists of leaflets with Bible stories, pictures, and songs for parents and Sunday school teachers of preschoolers ages 4-6.
Former titles (until 1999): Kindergarten Connection (1522-0036); (until 1999): Growing (Nashville) (0162-4512)
Related titles: Spanish ed.: ISSN 1540-5575.
Published by: LifeWay Christian Resources, 1 Lifeway Plz, Nashville, TN 37234. TEL 615-251-2000, 800-458-2772, FAX 615-251-5933, customerservice@lifeway.com, http://www.lifeway.com.

284.2 NLD ISSN 1878-4348
DE EARN. Text in Frisian. 1998. 5/yr. EUR 12.50 (effective 2011).
Published by: Frysk Oekumenysk Wurkferban Earnewald, Waldyk 9, Aldwald, 9294 LG, Netherlands. TEL 31-6-20600409. Eds. Dr. Rienk Klooster, Tine van Minnen.

266 USA ISSN 0012-8406
BV3400
EAST ASIA'S MILLIONS. Text in English. 1892. a. free. adv. bk.rev. illus. index. **Description:** Covers mission work in East Asia.
Former titles: East Asia Millions; China's Millions
Related titles: Microform ed.: (from PQC); Online - full text ed.
Indexed: A22.
Published by: O M F International, 10 W Dry Creek Cir, Littleton, CO 80120-4413. TEL 303-730-4160, 800-422-5330, FAX 303-730-4165. Ed. E David Dougherty. R&P, Adv. contact Patrice Nelson. Circ: 15,000 (controlled).

284.1 CAN ISSN 0831-4446
THE EASTERN SYNOD LUTHERAN. Text in English. 1920. 10/yr. CAD 10 (effective 2000). adv. bk.rev. **Document type:** *Newspaper.* **Description:** Contains denominational news and information.
Supersedes in part: Canada Lutheran (0008-2716)
Published by: Evangelical Lutheran Church in Canada, Eastern Synod, 74 Weber W, Kitchener, ON N2H 3Z3, Canada. FAX 519-743-4291. Ed., R&P Jane Wahl TEL 519-743-1461. Adv. contact W Phil Heinze. Circ: 23,000.

280.4 GBR ISSN 0956-618X
K5
ECCLESIASTICAL LAW JOURNAL. Text in English. 1987. 3/yr. GBP 119, USD 223 combined subscription to institutions (print & online eds.) (effective 2012). bk.rev. back issues avail.; reprint service avail. from PSC. **Document type:** *Journal, Academic/Scholarly.* **Description:** Discusses issues in Church law and reviews pertinent cases.
Related titles: Online - full text ed.: ISSN 1751-8539.
Indexed: A01, A12, A20, A22, ABIn, ArtHuCI, B04, CLA, CurCont, E01, ELJI, I01, ILP, L03, LJI, P28, P48, P51, P53, P54, PCI, PQC, T02, W07.
—Ingenta. **CCC.**
Published by: (Ecclesiastical Law Society), Cambridge University Press, The Edinburgh Bldg, Shaftesbury Rd, Cambridge, CB2 8RU, United Kingdom. TEL 44-1223-312393, FAX 44-1223-315052, journals@cambridge.org, http://www.cambridge.org/uk. Ed. Mark Hill. Adv. contact Rebecca Roberts TEL 44-1223-325083. Circ: 600.

280.4 FRA ISSN 0397-0736
ECHANGES; journal de l'eglise reformee..Provence, Cote d'Azur, Corse. Text in French. 1955. m. adv. bk.rev.; film rev. illus. **Description:** News about the Protestant religion and theology. Provides chronicles of the parishes of Provence-Cote d'Azur.
Formerly: Eglise Reformee Vous Parle
Indexed: MLA-IB, PdeR.
Published by: Association Echanges, 34 bd. des Platanes, Marseille, 13009, France. TEL 91-26-17-49. Ed. Eric Trocme. Circ: 4,000.

283 GBR
ECHOES (BATH). Text in English. 1872. m. GBP 18 domestic; GBP 22 foreign (effective 2009); subscr. includes Daily Prayer Guide. bk.rev. illus.; maps; stat. 52 p./no.; back issues avail. **Document type:** *Newsletter, Consumer.* **Description:** Stimulates interest in various aspects of missionary work of the Christian Brethren, worldwide.
Media: Large Type. **Related titles:** Online - full text ed.; Print ed.
Published by: Echoes of Service, 124 Wells Rd, Bath, BA2 3AH, United Kingdom. TEL 44-1225-310893, FAX 44-1225-480134, echoes@echoes.org.uk.

220 DEU ISSN 0944-9124
ECHT; das Magazin Ihrer evangelischen Kirche. Text in German. 1993. q. adv. **Document type:** *Magazine, Consumer.*
Published by: Medienhaus - Zentrum fuer Evangelische Publizistik und Medienarbeit in Hessen und Nassau, Rechneigrabenstr 10, Frankfurt Am Main, 60311, Germany. TEL 49-69-92107210, FAX 49-69-92107201, medienhaus@ekhn.de, http://www.ev-medienhaus.de. Ed. J Rainer Didszuweit. Adv. contact Erika Richter. B&W page EUR 12,000, color page EUR 15,000; trim 220 x 300. Circ: 1,099,462 (controlled).

280.4 DEU
ECHT.; Im Glauben wachsen. Text in German. q. EUR 19.90; EUR 5.50 newsstand/cover (effective 2009). adv. **Document type:** *Magazine, Consumer.*
Published by: Born-Verlag, Leuschnerstr 74, Kassel, 34134, Germany. TEL 49-561-4095107, FAX 49-561-4095112, info.born@ec-jugend.de, http://www.born-buch.de. Ed. Thorsten Riewesell.

280.4 USA
ECU - LINK. Text in English. 1986. irreg. (3-4/yr.). USD 6 (effective 2000). **Document type:** *Newsletter.* **Description:** An ecumenical newsletter to help create community among the Council's member communions.
Published by: National Council of Churches, Department of Communication, 475 Riverside Dr, Rm 850, New York, NY 10115. TEL 212-870-2227, FAX 212-870-2030. Ed. Sarah Vilankulu. Circ: 5,000 (paid and controlled).

THE EDGE. *see* CHILDREN AND YOUTH—For

280.4 AUS ISSN 0726-4143
EDITOR'S CLIP SHEETS. Text in English. 1980. m. looseleaf. AUD 75; AUD 95 combined subscription (print & online eds.) (effective 2009). adv. **Document type:** *Newsletter, Trade.* **Description:** Features articles on devotion, short stories, puzzles and Bible illustrations.
Related titles: Online - full text ed.
Published by: Mediacom Associates Inc., PO Box 610, Unley, SA 5061, Australia. TEL 61-8-83711399, 800-811-311, FAX 61-8-82978719, admin@mediacom.org.au. Circ: 1,500.

266.4 SWE ISSN 1651-2820
EFS.NU; en tidning om EFS missionsarbete. (Evangeliska Fosterlandsstiftelsen) Text in Swedish. 2001. 5/yr. free. back issues avail. **Document type:** *Magazine, Consumer.*
Related titles: Online - full text ed.
Published by: Evangeliska Fosterlandsstiftelsen, Sysslomansgatan 4, Uppsala, 75170, Sweden. TEL 46-18-169800, FAX 46-18-169801, efs@efs.svenskakyrkan.se. Eds. Lotta Ring, Martin Nilsson.

266 DEU ISSN 0949-216X
EINEWELT; Magazin aus Mission und Oekumene. Text in German. 1915. bi-m. EUR 15; EUR 3 newsstand/cover (effective 2006). adv. bk.rev. illus. index. 32 p./no.; back issues avail. **Document type:** *Magazine, Consumer.*
Former titles: Weltmission (0723-6204); Wort in der Welt (0341-082X); Allgemeine Missionsnachrichten (0002-5909)
Published by: (Evangelisches Missionswerk), Missionshilfe Verlag, Normannenweg 17-21, Hamburg, 20537, Germany. TEL 49-40-25456143, FAX 49-40-2542987, demh@emw-d.de. Ed., Pub. Martin Keiper. R&P Margrit Gerlach. Adv. contact Elke Rahn. page EUR 1,995. Circ: 35,910 (paid and controlled).

230 DEU
EINS; gemeinsam glauben, miteinander handeln. Text in German. 1993. 4/yr. adv. **Document type:** *Magazine, Consumer.*
Formerly (until 2004): Evangelische Allianz Intern
Published by: (Deutsche Evangelische Allianz e.V.), Bundes Verlag GmbH, Bodenborn 43, Witten, 58452, Germany. TEL 49-2302-930930, FAX 49-2302-93093689, info@bundes-verlag.de, http://www.bundes-verlag.de. Ed. Joerg Podworny. Adv. contact Juergen Bublitz. Circ: 23,000 (controlled).

286 USA ISSN 2159-8088
▼ ➤ **ELEUTHERIA.** Text in English. 2010. s-a. free (effective 2011). **Document type:** *Journal, Academic/Scholarly.*
Media: Online - full text.
Published by: Liberty Baptist Theological Seminary and Graduate School, 1971 University Blvd, CN 2500, Lynchburg, VA 24502. TEL 434-592-4140, FAX 434-522-0415, LBTS@liberty.edu, http://www.liberty.edu.

280.4 USA ISSN 2151-4569
THE EMERSONIAN. Text in English. 19??. m. back issues avail. **Document type:** *Newsletter, Consumer.*
Formerly (until 1975): Emerson Window
Related titles: Online - full text ed.: free (effective 2009).
Published by: Emerson Unitarian Universalist Church, 1900 Bering Dr, Houston, TX 77057. TEL 713-782-8250, FAX 713-782-8261.

280.4 USA ISSN 1546-6973
BS410
EMMAUS JOURNAL. Text in English. 1990. s-a. USD 7 domestic; CAD 10 in Canada; USD 10 elsewhere (effective 2010). bk.rev. Index. 130 p./no.; back issues avail. **Document type:** *Journal, Academic/Scholarly.* **Description:** Dedicated to the exposition of the Bible, biblical doctrine, and practical issues of the Christian life and church, as well as historical and doctrinal issues that affect the Brethren movement.
Related titles: CD-ROM ed.: Theological Journal Library CD. USD 99.95 New & Updated CD (effective 2004).
Indexed: ChrPI, R&TA.
Published by: Emmaus Bible College, 2570 Asbury Rd, Dubuque, IA 52001. TEL 319-588-8000, FAX 563-588-1216, info@emmaus.edu.

283 GBR ISSN 1350-5130
ENCOUNTER WITH GOD (UK EDITION); Bible studies for thought and action. Text in English. 1923. q. GBP 15.80 domestic; GBP 20 in Europe; GBP 23 elsewhere (effective 2010). back issues avail. **Document type:** *Magazine, Consumer.*
Formerly (until 1994): Daily Notes (0963-4819)
Related titles: Online - full text ed.: GBP 3 per issue (effective 2010).
—**CCC.**
Published by: Scripture Union, 207-209 Queensway, Bletchley, Milton Keynes, Bucks MK2 2EB, United Kingdom. TEL 44-1908-856000, FAX 44-1908-856111, info@scriptureunion.org.uk. Ed. Andrew Clark.

266.6 GBR ISSN 1756-2481
ENGAGE (DIDCOT). Text in English. 1918. bi-m. GBP 9.90 (effective 2000). back issues avail. **Document type:** *Bulletin.*
Former titles (until 2008): World Mission (1472-2488); (until 2001): Missionary Herald (0264-1372); (until 1918): Baptist Missionary Society. Herald
Published by: B M S World Mission, 129 Broadway, PO Box 49, Didcot, Oxfordshire OX11 8XA, United Kingdom. TEL 44-1235-517700, mail@bmsworldmission.org, http://www.bmsworldmission.org. Ed. Jan Kendall. Circ: 18,000.

280.4 322.1 GBR
ENGLISH CHURCHMAN & ST. JAMES'S CHRONICLE. Text in English. 1843. fortn. GBP 16 domestic; GBP 30 in Europe; GBP 28 foreign (effective 2009). adv. bk.rev. 4 cols./p.; back issues avail. **Document type:** *Newspaper, Consumer.* **Description:** Discusses a variety of ethical and philosophical issues from a Christian perspective.
Former titles (until 1963): English Churchman & Saint James's Chronicle; English Churchman (0013-8223)
—BLDSC (3773.311000).
Published by: English Churchman Trust Ltd., 64 Ripley Rd, Worthing, W Sussex BN11 5NH, United Kingdom. TEL 44-1908-505555, FAX 44-1908-600019, admin@englishchurchman.com.

280.4 DEU ISSN 0013-9092
ENTSCHEIDUNG (HOLZGERLINGEN). Text in German. 1963. bi-m. EUR 15; EUR 3 newsstand/cover (effective 2003). adv. bk.rev. bibl. **Document type:** *Magazine, Consumer.*
Published by: (Billy Graham Evangelistic Association Deutschland e.V.), Haenssler Verlag GmbH, Max-Eyth-Str 41, Holzgerlingen, 71088, Germany. TEL 49-7031-74140, FAX 49-7031-7414119, info@haenssler.de, http://www.haenssler.de. Ed. Irmhild Baerend. Circ: 50,000.

R

280.4 DEU ISSN 0343-6519
ENTWURF; religionspaedagogische Mitteilungen. Text in German. 1970. 4/yr. EUR 58; EUR 13.50 newsstand/cover (effective 2011). adv. Website rev.; bk.rev. cum.index. back issues avail. **Document type:** *Magazine, Trade.* **Description:** Provides teaching aids, materials, and discussions for religious education teachers.
Indexed: DIP, IBR, IBZ.
Published by: (Fachgemeinschaft Evangelischer Religionslehrer in Wuerttemberg), Erhard Friedrich Verlag GmbH, Im Brande 17, Seelze, 30926, Germany. TEL 49-511-400040, FAX 49-511-40004170, info@friedrich-verlag.de, http://www.friedrich-verlag.de. Circ: 5,000 (paid and controlled).

283.73 USA
EPISCOPAL CLERICAL DIRECTORY. Text in English. 1925. biennial. USD 39.95. **Document type:** *Directory.*
Published by: Church Hymnal Corporation, 445 Fifth Ave, New York, NY 10016-0109. TEL 212-592-1800, 800-242-1918. Ed. Johnny Ross. Circ: 5,300.

283.73 USA
EPISCOPAL DIOCESE OF MICHIGAN. Text in English. 1952. m. USD 6. adv.
Address: 4800 Woodward Ave, Detroit, MI 48201-1310. TEL 313-832-4400. Ed. Jeanie Wylie. Circ: 10,000.

283.73 USA ISSN 1545-6676
THE EPISCOPAL EVANGELICAL JOURNAL. Text in English. 1994 (Jul.). s-a. USD 10 to non-members; free to members (effective 2003).
Published by: Evangelical Fellowship of the Anglican Communion, 1283 Earlford Dr., Pittsburgh, PA 15227-1520. http://www.episcopalian.org/efac/index.htm. Ed. Philip Wainwright.

283.73 USA ISSN 2155-7071
▼ **EPISCOPAL KENTUCKY QUARTERLY.** Text in English. 2010. q. **Document type:** *Magazine, Academic/Scholarly.*
Published by: Episcopal Diocese of Kentucky, 425 S Second St, Ste 200, Louisville, KY 40202. TEL 502-584-7148, lmoore@epicopalchurch.org, http://www.episcopalky.org/.

283.747 USA ISSN 1543-2092
THE EPISCOPAL NEW YORKER. Text in English. 19??. bi-m. USD 15 (effective 1998). adv. illus. **Document type:** *Newspaper.* **Description:** Strives to communicate the news of the Diocese, its parishes and the world Anglican community in a way that is relevant to the lives of the readers.
Published by: Episcopal Diocese of New York, 1047 Amsterdam Ave, New York, NY 10025. TEL 212-316-7400, FAX 212-316-7405, info@diocesny.org. Ed., Adv. contact Debra Wagner. Circ: 32,951.

285 USA ISSN 2153-3482
EPISCOPAL NEWS MONTHLY. Text in English. 1828. m. adv. bk.rev. illus. back issues avail. **Document type:** *Bulletin, Trade.* **Description:** Focuses on reporting and analysis of local, regional, national and international news.
Former titles (until 2010): Episcopal Life (1050-0057); (until 1990): The Episcopalian (0013-9629); (until 1960): Forth; (until 1940): The Spirit of Missions; (until 1836): Protestant Episcopal Church in the United States of America. Domestic and Foreign Missionary Society. Missionary Record; (until 1833): Protestant Episcopal Church in the United States of America. Domestic and Foreign Missionary Society. Periodical Paper; (until 1831): Protestant Episcopal Church in the United States of America. Domestic and Foreign Missionary Society. Missionary Paper; (until 1830): Protestant Episcopal Church in the United States of America. Domestic and Foreign Missionary Society. Quarterly Papers
Published by: Episcopal Church, 815 2nd Ave, New York, NY 10017. TEL 212-716-6000, 800-334-7626, news@episcopalchurch.org, http://www.episcopalchurch.org. Ed. Mary Frances Schjonberg TEL 212-716-6314. Adv. contact Thomas Cahill.

280.4 USA
THE EPISCOPAL TIMES. Text in English. 8/yr. free (effective 2005). **Document type:** *Newspaper, Consumer.*
Published by: Episcopal Diocese of Massachusetts, 138 Tremont St., Boston, MA 02111-1319. TEL 617-482-4826, FAX 617-451-6446. Ed. Tracy J. Sukraw. Circ: 40,000 (free).

287 GBR ISSN 0308-0382
BR1
EPWORTH REVIEW. Text in English. 1973. q. GBP 20 (effective 2010). adv. abstr. back issues avail. **Document type:** *Journal, Academic/Scholarly.* **Description:** Contains theological, biblical and discussion articles written by leading names in the academic world and the ministry.
Indexed: A21, R&TA, RI-1, RI-2, RILM.
—BLDSC (3794.470000), IE, Ingenta.
Published by: Methodist Publishing House, 17 Tresham Rd, Orton Southgate, Peterborough, PE2 6SG, United Kingdom. TEL 44-1733-235962, FAX 44-1733-390325, resources@methodistchurch.org.uk, http://www.mph.org.uk.

285 USA
EQUIP FOR MINISTRY. Text in English. bi-m. adv. **Description:** Contains a variety of resource materials for local Presbyterian leaders.
Published by: Christian Education & Publications of the Presbyterian Church of America, 1852 Century Place, Atlanta, GA 30345. TEL 404-320-3388, FAX 404-329-1280. Ed. Charles Dunahoo. Adv. contact William Savage.

280.4 DEU ISSN 0171-6204
ERNEUERUNG IN KIRCHE UND GESELLSCHAFT. Text in German. 1977. q. adv. bk.rev. **Document type:** *Bulletin, Consumer.*
Formerly (until 1977): Charismatische Erneuerung der Kirche (0938-099X)
Address: Westerhudestr 38, Salzkotten, 33154, Germany. TEL 49-5258-4889, redaktion@zeitschrift-erneuerung.de. Ed. Richard Martin Schleyer.

280.4 DEU ISSN 0179-1583
ERWECKLICHE STIMME. Text in German. 1960. m. adv. bk.rev. illus. **Document type:** *Newsletter.*
Published by: Geistliches Ruestzentrum Krelingen, Krelingen 37, Walsrode, 29664, Germany. TEL 49-5167-970-0, FAX 49-5167-970160. Ed. Wilfried Reuter. Circ: 22,000.

280.4 FRA
ESQUISSE D'UNE PHILOSOPHIE DE LA RELIGION. Text in French. 1956. irreg., latest 2010.
Formerly: Esprit et Liberte (0071-1330)
Indexed: CLA.
Published by: Librairie Fischbacher, 33 rue de Seine, Paris, 75006, France. TEL 33-1-43268487, FAX 33-1-43264887, http://www.librairiefischbacher.fr.

286.132 USA ISSN 1555-3108
ESTUDIOS BIBLICOS LIFEWAY PARA ADULTOS. MANUAL PARA EL LIDER. Variant title: Manual para el Lider. Text in Spanish. 1982. q. price varies. back issues avail. **Document type:** *Magazine, Consumer.* **Description:** Contains bible exposition, teaching plans with options, ministry helps and more that helps to reach and teach adults of all ages.
Former titles (until 200?): El Interprete Maestros (0740-0063); (until 1983): Maestros de Adultos (0744-3005)
Published by: LifeWay Christian Resources, 1 Lifeway Plz, Nashville, TN 37234. TEL 615-251-2000, 800-458-2772, FAX 615-251-5933, customerservice@lifeway.com, http://www.lifeway.com. Ed. Oscar Fernedez.

284.1 BRA ISSN 0101-3130
BR7
➤ **ESTUDOS TEOLOGICOS.** Text in Portuguese; Summaries in Portuguese, Spanish, English. 1946. q. BRL 15 domestic; USD 16 in Latin America; USD 18 in United States (effective 2001). bk.rev. back issues avail. **Document type:** *Journal, Academic/Scholarly.*
Indexed: A21, IBR, IBZ, OTA, RI-1.
Published by: Escola Superior de Teologia, Caixa Postal 14, Sao Leopoldo, RS 93001-970, Brazil. TEL 55-51-5901455, FAX 55-51-5901603, est@est.com.br, http://www.est.com.br. Ed. Osmar L. Witt.

230.044 FRA ISSN 0014-2239
BR3
ETUDES THEOLOGIQUES ET RELIGIEUSES. Text in French. 1926. q. EUR 34 domestic; EUR 38 foreign (effective 2010). adv. bk.rev. bibl. index. 150 p./no.; reprints avail. **Document type:** *Journal, Academic/Scholarly.* **Description:** Contains articles on the principal disciplines of theology: Bible, history of Christianity, history of religion, doctrine, religious psychology, practical theology.
Related titles: Microfilm ed.: (from PQC).
Indexed: A20, A21, A22, ASCA, ArtHuCI, CERDIC, CurCont, DIP, FR, IBR, IBZ, IZBG, OTA, PCI, R&TA, RI-1, RI-2, SCOPUS, W07.
—BLDSC (3822.310000), IE, Ingenta, INIST.
Published by: Institut Protestant de Theologie, 13 rue Louis Perrier, Montpellier, 34000, France. TEL 33-4-67064576, FAX 33-4-67064591, contact@revue-etr.org, http://www.revue-etr.org. Ed., Pub., R&P Hubert Bost. Adv. contact Jean Berlin. Circ: 2,350.

230.044 GBR ISSN 0960-2720
BL1.A1
EUROPEAN JOURNAL OF THEOLOGY; a new journal for a new Europe. Text in English. 1992. s-a. USD 58.20 to individuals (print or online ed.); USD 87.30 to institutions (print or online ed.); USD 69.80 combined subscription to individuals (print & online eds.); USD 104.80 combined subscription to institutions (print & online eds.) (effective 2010). bk.rev. reprint service avail. from IRC. **Document type:** *Journal, Academic/Scholarly.* **Description:** Seeks to reflect the variety of European evangelical theology.
Related titles: Online - full text ed.
Indexed: A01, A02, A03, A08, A21, CA, OTA, R&TA, RI-1, RI-2, T02.
—BLDSC (3829.746500), IE, Ingenta.
Published by: The Paternoster Press, c/o Aplhagraphics, 6 Angel Row, Nottingham, NG1 6HL, United Kingdom. TEL 44-115-8523614, FAX 44-115-8523601, periodicals@alphagraphics.co.uk, http://www.paternosterperiodicals.com.

289.94 GBR ISSN 1812-4461
➤ **EUROPEAN PENTECOSTAL THEOLOGICAL ASSOCIATION. JOURNAL.** Variant title: Journal of the European Pentecostal Theological Association. Text in English. 1981. a. free to members (effective 2009). **Document type:** *Journal, Academic/Scholarly.* **Description:** Aims to stimulate theological discussion and encourage an interchange of ideas and information.
Formerly (until 1996): E P T A Bulletin (0774-6210)
Indexed: A01, A21, CA, R&TA, RI-1, T02.
Published by: European Pentecostal Theological Association, c/o Anne Dyer, Secretary, Mattersey Hall, Mattersey, Nottinghamshire DN10 5HD, United Kingdom. TEL 44-1777-817663, library@matterseyhall.co.uk, http://www.epta.nu.

287 USA ISSN 0162-1890
EVANGEL. Text in English. w. USD 7.40 (effective 2000). back issues avail. **Document type:** *Magazine, Trade.*
Indexed: GSS&RPL.
Published by: (Free Methodist Church of North America), Free Methodist Publishing House, PO Box 535002, Indianapolis, IN 46253-5002. TEL 317-244-3660, FAX 317-244-1247. Ed., R&P Julie Innes. Pub. John Van Valin. Circ: 25,000.

286 CAN ISSN 0014-3324
EVANGELICAL BAPTIST. Text in English. 1953. 5/yr. CAD 12 (effective 2001). adv. bk.rev. illus.
Published by: Fellowship of Evangelical Baptist Churches in Canada, 679 Southgate Dr, Guelph, ON N1G 4S2, Canada. TEL 519-821-4830, FAX 519-821-9829. Ed. Rev. Terry Cuthbert. R&P, Adv. contact Ginette Cotnoir TEL 450-621-3248. Circ: 6,000.

286.171 CAN ISSN 0317-266X
EVANGELICAL BAPTIST CHURCHES IN CANADA. FELLOWSHIP YEARBOOK. Key Title: Fellowship Yearbook. Text in English. 1959. a. illus.
Formerly: Missions Digest and Year Book (0544-439X)
Published by: Fellowship of Evangelical Baptist Churches in Canada, 679 Southgate Dr, Guelph, ON N1G 4S2, Canada. TEL 519-821-4830, FAX 519-821-9829. Ed. Rev. Terry Cuthbert. R&P Jean Brubacher.

285.734 USA ISSN 0014-3332
BX7548.A1
EVANGELICAL BEACON. Text in English. 1931. 7/yr. USD 12. adv. bk.rev. illus. **Description:** Information, inspiration and evangelism for members.
Published by: Evangelical Free Church of America, 901 E 78th St, Minneapolis, MN 55420. TEL 612-854-1300. Ed. Carol Madison. Adv. contact Jan Delay. Circ: 33,000.

280 USA ISSN 1534-7478
BV4200
EVANGELICAL HOMILETICS SOCIETY. JOURNAL. Text in English. 2001 (Dec.). irreg.
Published by: Evangelical Homiletics Society, 130 Essex St., South Hamilton, MA 01982. http://www.evangelicalhomiletics.com. Ed. Scott M. Gibson.

284.1 USA ISSN 1058-3696
BX8048.3
EVANGELICAL LUTHERAN CHURCH IN AMERICA (YEAR). Abbreviated title: E L C A. Short title: E L C A Yearbook. Text in English. 1961. a. USD 25.99 per issue (effective 2009). adv. 775 p./no.; **Document type:** *Yearbook.* **Description:** Provides a roster of listings of congregations, ordained ministers, associates in ministry and agencies, and more.
Formerly (until 1988): American Lutheran Church. Yearbook (1050-477X)
Published by: (Evangelical Lutheran Church in America), Augsburg Fortress Publishers, PO Box 1209, Minneapolis, MN 55440. TEL 800-328-4648, FAX 800-722-7766, info@augsburgfortress.org. Circ: 15,000.

280.4 GBR ISSN 1743-4092
THE EVANGELICAL MAGAZINE. Text in English. 1955. bi-m. bk.rev. bibl.; illus. back issues avail. **Document type:** *Magazine, Consumer.* **Description:** Contains articles on a wide range of subjects relating to the historic evangelical faith of the Christian Church and news of the contemporary religious scene.
Formerly (until 2003): Evangelical Magazine of Wales (0421-8094)
Published by: Evangelical Movement of Wales, Bryntirion, Bridgend, CF31 4DX, United Kingdom. TEL 44-1656-655886.

283 GBR ISSN 0014-3367
BR1
EVANGELICAL QUARTERLY; an international review of Bible and theology. Text in English. 1929. q. USD 63.30 to individuals (print or online ed.); USD 95 to institutions (print or online ed.); USD 76 combined subscription to individuals (print & online eds.); USD 114 combined subscription to institutions (print & online eds.) (effective 2010). adv. bk.rev. illus. index. reprints avail. **Document type:** *Journal, Academic/Scholarly.* **Description:** Articles on a variety of biblical and theological topics.
Related titles: Microfilm ed.: (from PQC); Online - full text ed.
Indexed: A01, A02, A03, A08, A21, A22, CA, CERDIC, ChrPI, DIP, IBR, IBZ, MLA-IB, OTA, PCI, R&TA, RI-1, RI-2, T02.
—BLDSC (3830.700000), IE, Ingenta. **CCC.**
Published by: The Paternoster Press, c/o Aplhagraphics, 6 Angel Row, Nottingham, NG1 6HL, United Kingdom. TEL 44-115-8523614, FAX 44-115-8523601, periodicals@alphagraphics.co.uk, http://www.paternosterperiodicals.com. **Dist. in U.S. & Canada by:** The Paternoster Press, P O Box 11127, Birmingham, AL 35201-1127.

285 USA ISSN 0890-703X
BR1640.A1
EVANGELICAL STUDIES BULLETIN. Text in English. 1984. q. USD 7.50 (effective 2005). bk.rev.
Indexed: A21, RI-1.
Published by: Institute for the Study of American Evangelicals, Wheaton College, Wheaton, IL 61087. isae@wheaton.edu.

285.734 USA ISSN 0360-8808
BR21
➤ **EVANGELICAL THEOLOGICAL SOCIETY. JOURNAL.** Abbreviated title: J E T S. Text in English. 1958. q. free to members (effective 2010). adv. bk.rev. illus. Index. 192 p./no.; back issues avail.; reprints avail. **Document type:** *Journal, Academic/Scholarly.* **Description:** Contains articles on Old and New Testament and theological issues.
Formerly (until 1969): E T S Bulletin (0361-5138)
Related titles: CD-ROM ed.: Theological Journal Library CD. USD 99.95 New & Updated CD (effective 2004); Microform ed.: (from PQC); Online - full text ed.
Indexed: A21, A22, CERDIC, ChrPI, IZBG, OTA, P10, P28, P30, P48, P53, P54, PQC, PhilInd, R&TA, RI-1, RI-2, RILM.
—BLDSC (4741.650000), IE, Infotrieve, Ingenta.
Published by: Evangelical Theological Society, 2825 Lexington Rd, PO Box 927, Louisville, KY 40280. TEL 502-897-4387, FAX 502-897-4386. Ed. Andreas Kostenberger. Adv. contact J Michael Thigpen. page USD 750. Circ: 5,000.

280.4 CZE ISSN 1211-6793
BX4854.C9
EVANGELICKY CASOPIS CESKY BRATR. Text in Czech. 1924. 18/yr. CZK 290 (effective 2008). bk.rev. 16 p./no. 2 cols./p.; back issues avail.; reprints avail. **Document type:** *Journal.* **Description:** Provides articles on theological, ethical and educational subjects; includes information on the work of local congregations and church workers.
Formerly (until 1991): Cesky Bratr (0009-0778)
Related titles: Diskette ed.
Published by: Ceskobratrska Cirkev Evangelicka, Synodi Rada, Jungmannova 9, Prague, 11121, Czech Republic. TEL 420-2-24999236. Ed. Jan Mamula. Circ: 4,600.

284.1 HUN ISSN 0133-1302
BX8001
EVANGELIKUS ELET. Text in Hungarian. 1933. w. HUF 1,820, USD 42 (effective 1997). **Document type:** *Newspaper.*
Published by: (Evangelical - Lutheran Church), Evangelikus Sajtoosztaly, Ulloai ut 24, Budapest, 1085, Hungary. TEL 36-1-1171108, FAX 36-1-1175478. Ed. Mihaly Toth Szollos. Circ: 12,000.

284.1 DEU
EVANGELISCH-LUTHERISCHE DEKANAT WUERZBURG. MONATSGRUSS. Text in German. 1959. m. **Document type:** *Magazine, Consumer.*
Former titles (until 1987): Gemeinde der Evangelisch-Lutherischen Dekanats Wuerzburg. Monatsgruss; (until 1972): Evangelisch-Lutherischer Dekanatsbezirk. Gemeinde der Evangelisch-Lutherischen Dekanats Wuerzburg. Monatsgruss
Published by: Evangelisch-Lutherische Dekanat Wuerzburg, Friedrich-Ebert-Ring 27c, Wuerzburg, 97072, Germany. TEL 49-931-7962574, FAX 49-931-7962575, kga@ekwue.de, http://www.ekwue.de. Ed. Reinhard Finke. Circ: 15,000 (controlled).

284.1 DEU ISSN 0423-8346
EVANGELISCH-LUTHERISCHE LANDESKIRCHE SACHSENS. AMTSBLATT. Text in German. 1949. 2/m. bk.rev.; play rev. abstr. index. **Document type:** *Bulletin, Consumer.*

Published by: (Evangelisch-Lutherisches Landeskirchenamt Sachsens), Saechsisches Druck- und Verlagshaus AG, Tharandter Str 23-27, Dresden, 01159, Germany. TEL 49-351-4203-0, FAX 49-351-4203260, service@sdv.de, http://www.sdv.de. Ed. Brigitte Pinsker. Adv. contact Hannelore Leuthold. Circ: 2,100.

266.41 DEU
EVANGELISCH-LUTHERISCHES MISSIONSWERK IN NIEDERSACHSEN. JAHRBUCH (YEAR). Text in German. 1954. a. bk.rev. back issues avail. **Document type:** *Bulletin.* **Description:** Deals with articles about the work of the missionaries of the Missionswerk, and about the countries in which they work.
Formerly (until 1979): Hermannsburger Mission im Jahre (Year)
Published by: (Evangelisch-Lutherisch Missionswerk in Niedersachsen), Missionshandlung Hermannsburg, Postfach 1109, Hermannsburg, 29314, Germany. TEL 49-5052-690, FAX 49-5052-69222, zentrale-de@elm-mission.net, http://www.elm-mission.net. Circ: 2,000.

280.4 DEU ISSN 0342-2763
EVANGELISCHE KINDERKIRCHE; Zeitschrift fuer Mitarbeiterinnen und Mitarbeiter im Kindergottesdienst. Text in German. 1924. q. EUR 14.20 (effective 2011). bk.rev. **Document type:** *Magazine, Consumer.*
Published by: (Wuerttembergische Evangelische Landesverband fuer Kindergottesdienst e.V.), Verlag Junge Gemeinde, Postfach 100355, Leinfelden-Echterdingen, 70747, Germany. TEL 49-711-990780, FAX 49-711-9907825, vertrieb@junge-gemeinde.de, http://www.junge-gemeinde.de. Ed. Gottfried Mohr. Circ: 50,000 (paid).

285.734 DEU ISSN 0014-343X
BX7560
EVANGELISCHE KIRCHE IN DEUTSCHLAND. AMTSBLATT. Text in German. 1946. m. EUR 24; EUR 2.20 newsstand/cover (effective 2006). index. back issues avail. **Document type:** *Bulletin.*
Published by: Kirchenamt der Evangelische Kirche in Deutschland, Herrenhaeuser Str 12, Hannover, 30419, Germany. TEL 49-511-27960, FAX 49-511-2796707, info@ekd.de. Circ: 1,150.

280.4 DEU
EVANGELISCHE KIRCHE IN MITTELDEUTSCHLAND. AMTSBLATT. Text in German. 1869. m. **Document type:** *Bulletin, Consumer.* **Description:** Events and information on evangelical churches in western part of Germany.
Former titles (until 2009): Foederation Evangelischer Kirchen in Mitteldeutschland. Amtsblatt; (until 2005): Evangelische Kirche der Kirchenprovinz Sachsen. Amtsblatt (0232-6310); (until 1956): Kirchenprovinz Sachsen zu Magdeburg. Kirchliches Amtsblatt; (until 1927): Amtliche Mitteilungen des Evangelischen Konsistoriums der Provinz Sachsen; (until 1918): Amtliche Mitteilungen des Koeniglichen Konsistoriums der Provinz Sachsen
Published by: Evangelische Kirche in Mitteldeutschland, Dr.-M.-Mitzenheim-Str 2a, Eisenach, 99817, Germany. TEL 49-3691-678404, FAX 49-3691-678449, presse.eisenach@ekmd.de, http://www.ekmd.desum/.

285.734 DEU ISSN 0014-3529
EVANGELISCHE LANDESKIRCHE IN WUERTTEMBERG. AMTSBLATT. Text in German. 1855. m. EUR 25; EUR 2 newsstand/cover (effective 2009). index. **Document type:** *Bulletin, Consumer.* **Description:** Focuses on church matters including changes in constitution, by-laws, regulations, obligations for pastors and congregations.
Published by: Evangelische Landeskirche in Wuerttemberg, Evangelischer Oberkirchenrat, Gaensheidestr 4, Stuttgart, 70184, Germany. TEL 49-711-21490, FAX 49-711-21499236, komm.emh@elk-wue.de. Circ: 3,600.

284.1 DEU
EVANGELISCHE LUTHERISCHE KIRCHE IN BAYERN. PFARRER- UND PFARRERINNENVEREIN. KORRESPONDENZBLATT. Text in German. 1876. 11/yr. EUR 4.60 per quarter (effective 2009). adv. bk.rev. index. 16 p./no. 3 cols./p.; back issues avail. **Document type:** *Newsletter, Consumer.*
Published by: Evangelische Lutherische Kirche in Bayern, Pfarrer- und Pfarrerinnenverein, Kirchplatz 3, Markt Einersheim, 97348, Germany. TEL 49-9326-99980, FAX 49-9326-99982, info@pfarrerverein.de. Ed. Martin Ost.

284.1 DEU ISSN 0014-326X
EVANGELISCHE-LUTHERISCHE KIRCHE IN THUERINGEN. AMTSBLATT. Text in German. 1948. s-m. bk.rev. **Document type:** *Bulletin.*
Published by: (Evangelischen Kirche in Mitteldeutschland), Wartburg Verlag GmbH, Lisztstr 2a, Weimar, 99423, Germany. TEL 49-3643-246144, FAX 49-3643-246118, buch@wartburgverlag.de, http://www.guh-cms.de/wv/catalog/index.php.

280.4 DEU ISSN 1612-7811
EVANGELISCHE ORIENTIERUNG; Zeitschrift des Evangelischen Bundes. Text in German. 1954. q. EUR 20 membership (effective 2009). back issues avail. **Document type:** *Magazine, Consumer.*
Formerly (until 2000): Evangelischer Bund (0933-7857)
Indexed: DIP, IBR, IBZ.
Published by: Evangelischer Bund, Konfessionskundliches Institut, Postfach 1255, Bensheim, 64602, Germany. TEL 49-6251-843311, FAX 49-6251-843328, webmaster@ki-eb.de. Ed. Walter Fleischmann-Bisten.

280.4 DEU ISSN 1862-8249
EVANGELISCHE SONNTAGS-ZEITUNG. Text in German. 1946. w. (Sun.). EUR 1.20 newsstand/cover (effective 2006). adv. bk.rev. **Document type:** *Newspaper, Consumer.*
Former titles (until 2004): Evangelische Kirchenzeitung (0942-1513); (until 1989): Weg und Wahrheit (0170-6136)
—CCC.
Published by: Medienhaus - Zentrum fuer Evangelische Publizistik und Medienarbeit in Hessen und Nassau, Rechneigrabenstr 10, Frankfurt Am Main, 60311, Germany. TEL 49-69-92107210, FAX 49-69-92107201, medienhaus@ekhn.de, http://www.ev-medienhaus.de. Ed. Wolfgang Weissgerber. adv.: B&W page EUR 2,004, color page EUR 3,674. Circ: 16,934 (controlled).

284.1 DEU
EVANGELISCHE ZEITUNG FUER NIEDERSACHSEN. Text in German. 1946. w. EUR 59.40 (effective 2006). adv. bk.rev. **Document type:** *Newspaper, Consumer.*
Former titles: Niedersaechsische Evangelische Zeitung fuer die Evangelische-Lutherische Landeskirche Braunschweig, Hannover und Oldenburg (0720-1974); (until 1980): Niedersaechsische Evangelische Zeitung (0171-8606); (until 1975): Botschaft (0006-8268)
Published by: Lutherisches Verlagshaus GmbH, Knochenhauerstr 38-40, Hannover, 30159, Germany. TEL 49-511-1241720, FAX 49-511-3681098, info@lvh.de, http://www.lvh.de. Ed. Michael Eberstein. Adv. contact Christine Smolin. B&W page EUR 2,400, color page EUR 4,200. Circ: 26,921 (controlled).

285.734 AUT ISSN 0036-6943
EVANGELISCHER BUND IN OESTERREICH. SCHRIFTENREIHE. Text in German. 1956. q. **Document type:** *Monographic series.*
Incorporates: Martin Luther
Published by: Evangelischer Bund in Oesterreich, Ungargasse 9-10, Vienna, W 1030, Austria. TEL 43-1-7125461, FAX 43-1-7125475. Ed. Paul Weiland. Circ: 8,000.

284.1 DEU
EVANGELISCHER KIRCHENBOTE; Sonntagsblatt fuer die Pfalz. Text in German. 1852. w. EUR 8.40 per quarter (effective 2009). adv. **Document type:** *Newspaper, Consumer.*
Formerly (until 1887): Evangelischer Kirchenbote fuer die Pfalz
Published by: Evangelischer Presseverlag Pfalz GmbH, Beethovenstr 4, Speyer, 67346, Germany. TEL 49-6232-24926, FAX 49-6232-132344, redaktion@evpfalz.de, http://www.evpfalz.de. Ed. Hartmut Metzger.

280.4 AUT
EVANGELISCHER KIRCHENBOTE LINZ. Text in German. 1952. 5/yr. adv. bk.rev. **Document type:** *Newsletter, Consumer.*
Published by: Evangelischer Pfarrgemeinde Linz, Johan Konrad Vogel Str 2a, Linz, O 4020, Austria. TEL 43-732-773260, FAX 43-732-7732685, evang.kirchenbote@liwest.at, http://www.linz-evang.at. Circ: 6,400.

285.734 DEU ISSN 0014-360X
EVANGELISCHES GEMEINDEBLATT FUER WUERTTEMBERG. Text in German. 1905. w. (Sun.). EUR 58.80; EUR 33 to students (effective 2009). adv. bk.rev. illus. **Document type:** *Newspaper, Consumer.*
Published by: (Evangelische Gesellschaft Stuttgart e.V.), Evangelische Gemeindepresse GmbH, Augustenstr 124, Stuttgart, 70197, Germany. TEL 49-711-6010074, FAX 49-711-6010070, verlag@evanggemeindeblatt.de. Ed. Petra Ziegler. Adv. contact Wolfgang Schmoll TEL 49-711-6010066. B&W page EUR 4,200; trim 200 x 280. Circ: 79,040 (controlled).

284 DNK ISSN 1901-533X
EVANGELISK ALLIANCE. NYHEDSBREV. Text in Danish. 1907. s-a. illus. back issues avail. **Document type:** *Newsletter, Consumer.*
Formerly (until 2004): Alliancebladet (0900-4726)
Related titles: Online - full text ed.
Published by: Evangelisk Alliance, Peter Bangs Vej 1 D, Frederiksberg, 2000, Denmark. TEL 45-38-384915, FAX 45-38-384917, info@evengeliskalliance.dk.

280.4 FRA ISSN 1146-4771
EVANGILE ET LIBERTE. Text in French. 1885. m. adv. bk.rev. bibl. **Document type:** *Newsletter, Consumer.*
Published by: Association Evangile et Liberte, c/o Pasteur Christian Mazel, Les Genets, Residence St. Michel, Apt-en-luberon, 84400, France. TEL 33-4-90745637, FAX 33-4-90745637. Ed. Christian E Mazel. R&P Christian Mazel. Adv. contact Mr. Burgelin.

280.4 SRB ISSN 0014-3642
EVANJELICKY HLASNIK. Text in Serbo-Croatian. 1965. m. bk.rev.
Published by: Slovenska Evanjelicka a.v. Cirkev v Srbsku, Vuka Karadzica 2, Novi Sad, 21000. Ed. Rev. Ondrej Petkovsky. Circ: 4,200.

280.4 SVK ISSN 0139-8768
EVANJELICKY POSOL SPOD TATIER. Text in Slovak. 1910. w. EUR 23.40 (effective 2011). adv. **Document type:** *Newspaper, Consumer.*
Published by: Tranoscius a.s., Tranovskeho 1, Liptovsky Mikulas, 031 80, Slovakia. TEL 421-44-5523070, FAX 421-44-5523070, sefredaktor@tranoscius.sk.

283 GBR
EXETER DIOCESAN DIRECTORY. Text in English. 1946. a. adv. back issues avail. **Document type:** *Directory.* **Description:** Provides parish information covered in the diocese of Exeter.
Published by: Diocese of Exeter, The Old Deanery, The Cloisters, Exeter, EX1 1HS, United Kingdom. TEL 44-1392-272686.

268.86132 USA ISSN 1092-7174
EXPLORE THE BIBLE: ADULT COMMENTARY. Variant title: Explore the Bible: Commentary. Text in English. 1979. q. price varies. back issues avail. **Document type:** *Magazine, Consumer.* **Description:** Features in-depth bible exposition with suggestions for further study.
Formerly (until 199?): Bible Book Study Commentary (0164-4440)
Published by: LifeWay Christian Resources, 1 Lifeway Plz, Nashville, TN 37234. TEL 615-251-2000, 800-458-2772, FAX 615-251-5933, customerservice@lifeway.com, http://www.lifeway.com.

286.132 USA ISSN 1930-5877
EXPLORE THE BIBLE: ADULT LEADER GUIDE - LEADER. Variant title: Explore the Bible: Leader Guide. Text in English. 1978. q. USD 9.55 (effective 2009). back issues avail. **Document type:** *Magazine, Consumer.* **Description:** Contains in-depth bible expositions and life applications.
Former titles (until 200?): Explore the Bible. Adult Teacher (1092-7190); (until 1996): Bible Book Study for Adult Teachers (0162-4202)
Published by: LifeWay Christian Resources, 1 Lifeway Plz, Nashville, TN 37234. TEL 615-251-2000, 800-458-2772, FAX 615-251-5933, customerservice@lifeway.com, http://www.lifeway.com.

286.132 USA ISSN 1556-3731
EXPLORE THE BIBLE: ADULT LEARNER GUIDE (LARGE PRINT EDITION). Variant title: Explore the Bible: Learner Guide Large Print. Text in English. q. USD 9.75; USD 1.90 per issue (effective 2009). back issues avail. **Document type:** *Magazine, Consumer.* **Description:** Provides a systematic and comprehensive study of both the new and old testaments.
Former titles (until 200?): Explore the Bible: Adult Large Print (1092-7166); (until 1996): Bible Book Study for Adults. Large Print Edition
Media: Large Type (18 pt.). **Related titles:** Audio CD ed.: USD 57.55 (effective 2009).
Published by: LifeWay Christian Resources, 1 Lifeway Plz, Nashville, TN 37234. TEL 615-251-2000, FAX 615-251-5933, customerservice@lifeway.com, http://www.lifeway.com. Ed. Janice Meier TEL 615-251-2660.

268.86132 USA ISSN 1552-7212
EXPLORE THE BIBLE: ADULT STUDY GUIDE DISCOVERY. Variant title: Explore the Bible: Discovery Study Guide. Text in English. q. price varies. back issues avail. **Document type:** *Magazine, Consumer.* **Description:** Serves as an interactive Bible study resource.
Former titles (until 2005): Explore the Bible: Adult Study Guide (1091-7292); (until 1996): Bible Book Study Guide (0731-8391)
Related titles: ◆ Korean ed.: Changnyon Songgyong Yongu. ISSN 1930-5893; ◆ Chinese ed.: Yan Jing Xi Lie. ISSN 1930-5907.
Published by: LifeWay Christian Resources, 1 Lifeway Plz, Nashville, TN 37234. TEL 615-251-2000, 800-458-2772, FAX 615-251-5933, customerservice@lifeway.com, http://www.lifeway.com.

286.132 305.908162 USA ISSN 1930-1790
EXPLORING THE BIBLE: BIBLE STUDIES FOR THE DEAF. Variant title: Explore the Bible: Deaf. Text in English. 19??. q. price varies. back issues avail. **Document type:** *Magazine, Consumer.* **Description:** Designed to be a special learner resource, which is written by hearing-impaired writers using text with simplified language to facilitate signing American sign language.
Incorporates: Adult Bible Lessons for the Deaf; Former titles (until Fall 2001): Sunday School Lessons Special Ministries (0748-5360); (until 1984): Sunday School Lessons Simplified (0162-4873)
Published by: LifeWay Christian Resources, 1 Lifeway Plz, Nashville, TN 37234. TEL 615-251-2000, 800-458-2772, FAX 615-251-5933, customerservice@lifeway.com, http://www.lifeway.com.

286 ARG ISSN 0327-2222
EXPOSITOR BAUTISTA. Text in Spanish. 1908. m. ARS 25, USD 50 (effective 1997). adv. charts; illus. **Document type:** *Newspaper.*
Published by: Convencion Evangelica Bautista Argentina, Virrey Liniers 42, Piso 4, Buenos Aires, 1174, Argentina. TEL 54-114-8642711. Ed., R&P Raul Guzman. Pub. Miguel A Manceri. Adv. contact Isabel Sadosky.

284.1 USA ISSN 1074-1712
FAITH AND FELLOWSHIP. Text in English. 1933. m. USD 14.50. bk.rev.
Published by: (Church of the Lutheran Brethren), Faith and Fellowship Press, PO Box 655, Fergus Falls, MN 56538-0655. TEL 218-736-7357, FAX 218-736-2200. Ed. Rev. David Rinden. Circ: 7,000 (paid).

280.4 CAN ISSN 0832-1191
FAITH TODAY; seeking to inform, equip and inspire Christians across Canada. Text in English. 1983. bi-m. CAD 19.26 domestic; CAD 25.26 in United States; CAD 31.26 elsewhere (effective 2004 - 2005). adv. bk.rev. **Document type:** *Magazine, Consumer.* **Description:** Informs Canadian Christians on issues facing church and society and on events and trends within the church community.
Formerly (until 1986): Faith Alive
Indexed: CCR, ChrPI.
Published by: Evangelical Fellowship of Canada, Station M.I.P., P O Box 3745, Markham, ON L3R 0Y4, Canada. TEL 905-479-5885, FAX 905-479-4742, http://www.efc-canada.com. Eds. Bill Fledderus, Karen Stiller. Pub. Bruce Clemenger. Adv. contact Brian Shephard TEL 705-792-5025. Circ: 18,000.

280.4 AUT
FAMILIENPERSPEKTIVEN; das Internetmagazin fuer Familien, Spiritualitaet und Lebensgestaltung. Text in German. m. adv. **Document type:** *Consumer.* **Description:** Provides guidance and advice on living a more spiritual and Christian family life.
Media: Online - full text.
Address: redaktion@familienperspektiven.at, http://www.familienperspektiven.at. Ed., Adv. contact Karl Ebinger.

285 USA
▼ ➤ **FAMILY AND COMMUNITY MINISTRIES (ONLINE).** Text in English. 2010. q. **Document type:** *Journal, Academic/Scholarly.*
Media: Online - full text. **Related titles:** Microfilm ed.
Published by: Baylor University, School of Social Work, 1 Bear Pl, Ste 97320, Waco, TX 76798. TEL 254-710-2326, FAX 254-710-6455, CFCM@baylor.edu, http://www.baylor.edu/social_work/index.php. Ed. Jon Singletary.

268 USA ISSN 1559-2162
FAMILY BIBLE STUDY: BIBLE TEACHING FOR KINDERGARTEN; Leader Guide. Text in English. 1969. q.
Former titles (until 2006): Bible Teaching for Kindergarten. Leader Guide (1522-0044); Preschool Bible Teacher. C. (0732-9458); (until 19??): Guide C for Preschool Teachers (0162-4490)
Published by: LifeWay Christian Resources, 1 Lifeway Plz, Nashville, TN 37234. TEL 615-251-2000, 800-458-2772, FAX 615-251-5933, customerservice@lifeway.com, http://www.lifeway.com.

280.4 FRA
FEDERATION PROTESTANTE DE FRANCE. ANNUAIRE (ONLINE). Key Title: Annuaire de la France Protestante. Text in French. 1952. a. **Document type:** *Directory.*
Former titles (until 200?): Federation Protestante de France. Annuaire (Print) (0240-5164); (until 1979): France Protestante (0071-9064)
Media: Online - full text.
Published by: Federation Protestante de France, Service d'Information, 47 rue de Clichy, Paris, Cedex 9 75311, France. TEL 33-1-44534700, FAX 33-1-42814001, http://www.protestants.org/fpf.

200 CHE ISSN 1424-5434
FERMENT. Text in German. 1894. bi-m. CHF 52; CHF 9 newsstand/cover (effective 2010). adv. **Document type:** *Magazine, Consumer.*
Formerly (until 1959): Rosenkranz (1424-5590)
Published by: Schweizer Pallottiner, Friedbergstr 16, Gossau, 9201, Switzerland. TEL 41-71-3885340, FAX 41-71-3885348, provinzialat@pallottiner.ch, http://www.pallottiner.ch. Ed. Andreas Baumeister.

283 372.41 GBR
FESTIVAL OF NINE LESSONS AND CAROLS (YEAR). Text in English. 19??. a. GBP 2.75 combined subscription per issue (print & CD-ROM eds.) (effective 2009). **Document type:** *Magazine, Consumer.* **Description:** Designed to enable blind and visually impaired persons to participate in the traditional King's College Christmas Eve carol service.
Media: Braille. **Related titles:** Audio cassette/tape ed.; CD-ROM ed.

R

Published by: Royal National Institute of Blind People, 105 Judd St, London, WC1H 9NE, United Kingdom. TEL 44-20-73881266, FAX 44-20-73882034, helpline@rnib.org.uk, http://www.rnib.org.uk/.

280.4 NLD ISSN 2210-9986
▼ **FESTUS.** Text in Dutch. 2010. s-a. EUR 25 domestic; EUR 35 foreign; EUR 15 newsstand/cover (effective 2010).
Published by: (Protestantse Kerk in Nederland, Bezinningscentrum, Stichting Kerk en Wereld), Boekencentrum Uitgevers, Goudstraat 50, Postbus 29, Zoetermeer, 2700 AA, Netherlands. TEL 31-79-3615481, FAX 31-79-3615489, info@boekencentrum.nl, http://www.boekencentrum.nl.

285 BRA ISSN 1517-5863
BX9042.B66
➤ **FIDES REFORMATA.** Abstracts in English; Text in Portuguese. 1996. s-a. BRL 40 for 2 yrs. (effective 2004). abstr. **Document type:** *Journal, Academic/Scholarly.*
Formerly (until 2002): Fides Reformata et Semper Reformanda Est
Indexed: A01, A21, C01, CA, F03, F04, FR, R&TA, RI-1, T02.
—INIST.
Published by: (Centro Presbiteriano de Pos-Graduacao Andrew Jumper), Universidade Presbiteriana Mackenzie (Subsidiary of: Instituto Presbiteriano Mackenzie), Rua da Consolacao 896, Pr.2, Sao Paulo-SP, SP 01302-907, Brazil. FAX 55-11-32142582, 55-11-32368302, biblio.per@mackenzie.br, http://www.mackenzie.com.br. Eds. Tarcizio de Carvalho, Valdeci Santos.

280.4 GBR
FIRST!. Text in English. 1886. bi-m. GBP 5.64 domestic; GBP 7.56 in Europe; GBP 7.98 elsewhere (effective 2009). adv. cum.index. back issues avail. **Document type:** *Magazine, Consumer.*
Former titles (until 2005): Life Indeed; (until 1966): Bright Words for Pilgrims to the Heavenly City
Published by: Faith Mission, Govan House, 548 Gilmerton Rd, Edinburgh, EH17 7JD, United Kingdom. TEL 44-131-6645814, FAX 44-131-6642260, hq@faithmission.org. Ed. Lin Pearson.

280.4 USA ISSN 2159-5704
FIRST PARISH POST. Text in English. 19??. w. **Document type:** *Newsletter, Trade.*
Formerly (until 1995): The First Parish in Weston (2159-5690)
Published by: First Parish Church in Weston, 349 Boston Post Rd, Weston, MA 02493. TEL 781-893-7798, FAX 781-647-9684, http://www.firstparishweston.org/.

286.132 USA
FIRST STEPS IN MISSIONS. Text in English. 1994. a. USD 13.99 per issue (effective 2008). **Document type:** *Magazine, Consumer.*
Description: Features creative ideas just for preschoolers, including songs, clip art, bulletin board ideas and reproducible patterns.
Published by: Woman's Missionary Union Auxiliary to the Southern Baptist Convention, 100 Missionary Ridge, PO Box 830010, Birmingham, AL 35283. TEL 205-991-8100, 800-968-7301, FAX 205-995-4840, customer_service@wmu.org, http://www.wmu.com/. Ed. Rhonda Reeves. R&P Carol Causey.

266 GBR ISSN 0015-4822
FLYING ANGEL NEWS. Text in English. 1958. 3/yr. GBP 2, USD 4 (effective 2009). illus. back issues avail. **Document type:** *Newspaper, Trade.*
Related titles: Online - full text ed.: free (effective 2009).
Published by: Mission to Seafarers, Saint Michael Paternoster Royal, College Hill, London, EC4R 2RL, United Kingdom. TEL 44-20-72485202, FAX 44-20-72484761, pr@missiontoseafarers.org. Ed. Richard Rhydderch.

286 GBR ISSN 0143-7925
FOCUS (GRANTHAM). Text in English. 1979. q. GBP 2.95 domestic; GBP 5 foreign. adv. illus. **Document type:** *Bulletin.*
—CCC.
Published by: Stanborough Press Ltd., Alma Park, Grantham, Lincs NG31 9SL, United Kingdom. TEL 44-1476-591700, FAX 44-1476-77144. Ed. D N Marshall. Pub. P Hammond. R&P, Adv. contact Edward Johnson. Circ: 25,000.

266 USA
FOCUS ON MISSIONS. Text in English. 1970. 3/yr. free to members (effective 2005). bk.rev. back issues avail. **Document type:** *Newsletter, Trade.* **Description:** Covers news on missions worldwide.
Published by: Fellowship of Missions, 11650 Northland Dr, Rockford, MI 49341. Ed. Rev. Leigh Adams. Circ: 3,000 (free).

FONDATION DE L'ARMEE DU SALUT. LE MAGAZINE. see SOCIAL SERVICES AND WELFARE

284.1 SWE ISSN 1652-8581
FORSKNING FOER KYRKAN. Text in Swedish. 2005. irreg. **Document type:** *Monographic series.*
Published by: Svenska Kyrkan/Church of Sweden, Kyrkans Hus, Sysslomansgatan 4, Uppsala, 75170, Sweden. TEL 46-18-169600, FAX 46-18-169707, info@svenskakyrkan.se, http://www.svenskakyrkan.se.

280.4 DEU ISSN 0724-9780
FORUM LOCCUM. Text in German. 1982. 4/yr. adv. bibl.; illus. cum.index: 1982-1984. 24 p./no. 3 cols./p.; back issues avail. **Document type:** *Newsletter, Consumer.* **Description:** Protestant publication discussing religion, Church, human ethics, humanities and social science. Includes activities of the Protestant Academies.
Published by: Evangelische Akademie Loccum, Muenchehaeger Str 6, Rehburg-Loccum, 31547, Germany. TEL 49-5766-81105, FAX 49-5766-81900, reinhard.behnisch@evlka.de. Ed., Adv. contact Reinhard Behnisch TEL 49-5766-81105.

283.73 USA
FORWARD (ERIE); a witness to the Good News of Jesus Christ in the Episcopal Church Diocese of Northwestern Pennsylvania. Text in English. 1948. m. (10/yr.). **Document type:** *Newsletter.*
Formerly: Forward in Erie (0015-8623)
Published by: Episcopal Diocese of Northwestern Pennsylvania, 145 W Sixth St, Erie, PA 16501. TEL 814-456-4203. Ed. Rev. Dr William S Pugliese. Circ: 3,800.

280.4 USA ISSN 1058-6784
FORWARD DAY BY DAY; a manual of daily Bible reading and devotions. Text in English, Spanish. 1935. q. USD 18 for 2 yrs. domestic; USD 21 for 2 yrs. in Canada; USD 24 for 2 yrs. elsewhere (effective 2009). 96 p./no.; **Document type:** *Magazine, Consumer.*
Related titles: Audio cassette/tape ed.: free to elderly and disabled (effective 2009); Braille ed.: free to visually impaired (effective 2009); E-mail ed.: USD 6 (effective 2009); Large type ed. 18 pt.: USD 15 domestic; USD 18 in Canada; USD 21 elsewhere (effective 2009); Spanish ed.: Dia a Dia. USD 18 for 2 yrs. domestic; USD 21 for 2 yrs. in Canada; USD 24 for 2 yrs. elsewhere (effective 2009).
Published by: Forward Movement Publications, 300 W 4th St, Ste 200, Cincinnati, OH 45202-2666. TEL 800-543-1813, orders@forwarddaybyday.com. Ed. Richard Schmidt. Circ: 400,000.

284.1 USA
FORWARD IN CHRIST- NORTHWESTERN LUTHERAN. Text in English. 1914. m. USD 10 domestic; USD 25 foreign (effective 2000). bk.rev. index. **Description:** Contains news and informative and inspirational articles.
Former titles: Forward - Northwestern Lutheran (1526-2529); Northwestern Lutheran (0029-3512)
Indexed: CCR, CERDIC.
Published by: Wisconsin Evangelical Lutheran Synod, 2929 N Mayfair Rd, Milwaukee, WI 53222-4398. TEL 414-256-3230, FAX 414-256-3899. Ed. Rev. Gary P Baumler. R&P Nicole Moline. Circ: 60,000.

285 USA ISSN 1554-4958
FOURTH QUARTERLY. Text in English. 2004 (Fall). q.
Published by: Fourth Presbyterian Church of Bethesda, 5500 River Rd, Bethesda, MD 20816. 301-320-3600, http://www.4thpres.org. Ed. Jules Grisham.

280.4 FRA
BX4843.A2
FRANCE PROTESTANTE ET LES EGLISES DE LANGUE FRANCAISE. Text in French. 1922 (40th ed.). a., latest 2010. price varies. **Document type:** *Monographic series.*
Formerly: Annuaire Protestant: la France Protestante et les Eglises de Langue Francaise (0066-362X)
Published by: Librairie Fischbacher, 33 rue de Seine, Paris, 75006, France. TEL 33-1-43268487, FAX 33-1-43264887, http://www.librairiefischbacher.fr.

285.234 GBR ISSN 2042-2970
BX9084.A1
FREE CHURCH OF SCOTLAND. THE RECORD. Text in English, Gaelic. 1843. m. (11/yr.). GBP 25; GBP 1.50 newsstand/cover (effective 2010). adv. bk.rev. back issues avail.; reprints avail. **Document type:** *Magazine, Consumer.* **Description:** Contains theological and devotional material. Includes comment on current affairs, church notices, and articles of ecclesiastical interest.
Formerly (until 2009): Free Church of Scotland. Monthly Record (0016-0334); Which superseded in part (in 1901): Free Church of Scotland Monthly
Related titles: Online - full text ed.: free to qualified personnel (effective 2010).
Published by: Free Church of Scotland, Youth and Publications Committee, 15 N Bank St, The Mound, Edinburgh, EH1 2LS, United Kingdom. TEL 44-131-2265286, FAX 44-131-2200597, offices@freechurchofscotland.org.uk. Ed. David Robertson.

287 USA ISSN 1081-8898
FREE METHODIST WORLD MISSION PEOPLE. Text in English. 1897. q. free. **Document type:** *Magazine, Trade.* **Description:** Provides news and features about cross-cultural communication and world evangelization in the Free Methodist denomination.
Formerly (until 1995): Missionary Tidings (1043-0725)
Published by: Free Methodist World Missions, 770 N High School Rd, Indianapolis, IN 46214. TEL 317-244-3660, FAX 317-241-1248. Ed., R&P Paula J. Innes. Pub. Dr. Arthur Brown. Circ: 16,000 (paid).
Subscr. to: PO Box 535002, Indianapolis, IN 46253-5002.

280.4 DEU ISSN 0342-3549
FREUND DER KINDER. Text in German. 6/yr. **Document type:** *Magazine, Consumer.*
Published by: Christliche Verlagsgesellschaft mbH, Moltkestr 1, Dillenburg, 35683, Germany. TEL 49-2771-83020, FAX 49-2771-830230, info@cv-dillenburg.de, http://www.cv-dillenburg.de. Ed. Hartmut Jaeger.

280.4 DEU ISSN 1610-1588
FRIEDEN FUER SIE. Text in German. 1860. m. EUR 6; EUR 0.50 newsstand/cover (effective 2009). back issues avail. **Document type:** *Magazine, Consumer.*
Formerly (until 2002): Friedensbote
Published by: Oncken Verlag GmbH, Muendener Str 13, Kassel, 34123, Germany. TEL 49-561-520050, FAX 49-561-5200550, zeitschriften@oncken.de, http://www.oncken.de. Ed. Hinrich Schmidt. Circ: 28,000.

280.4 GBR ISSN 0016-1292
FRIENDLY COMPANION. Text in English. 1857. m. GBP 11.50 domestic (effective 2009). adv. back issues avail. **Document type:** *Bulletin, Consumer.* **Description:** Focuses on scriptural teaching and everyday experiences for children and teens.
Formerly (until 1875): The Friendly Companion and Illustrated Instructor
Published by: Gospel Standard Publications, 12B Roundwood Ln, Harpenden, Herts AL5 3BZ, United Kingdom. TEL 44-1582-765448, publications@gospelstandard.org, http://www.gospelstandard.org/.

280.4 USA ISSN 2156-504X
THE FRONT STEPS. Text in English. 19??. bi-m. free to members (effective 2010). back issues avail. **Document type:** *Newsletter, Consumer.*
Related titles: Online - full text ed.: free (effective 2010).
Published by: First Unitarian Church of Portland, 1034 SW 13th Ave, Portland, OR 97205. TEL 503-228-6389, FAX 503-228-2676, office@firstunitarianportland.org. Ed. Craig Towers TEL 503-228-6389 ext 13.

266.2 NLD ISSN 1574-7824
FRONTTAAL. Text in Dutch. 1972. 3/yr.
Former titles (until 2004): Zending Zonder Grenzen (0929-208X); (until 1992): Vervolgd Christendom (0167-1774)
Published by: Stichting Zending over Grenzen, Postbus 1222, Almere, 1300 BE, Netherlands. TEL 31-36-5363615, info@zendingovergrenzen.nl.

285.734 DEU ISSN 0016-2434
FUER ARBEIT UND BESINNUNG. Variant title: A und B fuer Arbeit und Besinnung. Text in German. 1947. 2/m. EUR 50.24 (effective 2011). adv. bk.rev. index. **Document type:** *Magazine, Trade.*
Published by: (Evangelischer Oberkirchenrat), Evangelische Gemeindepresse GmbH, Augustenstr 124, Stuttgart, 70197, Germany. TEL 49-711-6010040, FAX 49-711-6010076, kontakt@elk-wue.de, http://www.elk-wue.de.

287 DEU ISSN 0016-2442
FUER HEUTE. Text in German. 1968. w. EUR 14 (effective 2005). **Document type:** *Magazine, Consumer.*
Formed by the 1968 merger of: Gute Botschaft; Friedensglocke
Published by: (Evangelisch-methodistische Kirche), Medienwerk der Evangelisch-Methodistischen Kirche, Ludolfusstr 2-4, Frankfurt am Main, 60487, Germany. TEL 49-69-24252120, FAX 49-69-24252128, medienwerk@emk.de, http://www.emk.de. Circ: 13,000.

280.4 USA ISSN 0896-5749
FUNDAMENTAL NEWS SERVICE. Text in English. 1960. bi-m. USD 10 donation. bk.rev. **Document type:** *Newsletter, Consumer.*
Published by: American Council of Christian Churches, PO Box 5455, Bethlehem, PA 18015-0455. TEL 610-865-3009, FAX 610-865-3033. Ed. Ralph Colas. Circ: 15,000.

286 USA ISSN 0016-2744
FUNDAMENTALIST. Text in English. 1927. bi-m. bk.rev. **Document type:** *Newsletter, Consumer.* **Description:** Promotional news from the World Baptist Fellowship.
Indexed: CERDIC.
Published by: (World Baptist Fellowship), Knifty Ideas Printing, PO Box 13459, Arlington, TX 76094-0459. TEL 817-274-7161, FAX 817-861-1992. Ed. Dr. Wendell Hiers. Circ: 8,000.

284.1 DNK ISSN 0107-8399
FYENS STIFTSBOG. Text in Danish. 1969. a. illus. **Document type:** *Yearbook, Consumer.*
Related titles: Diskette ed.
Indexed: MLA-IB, NAA.
Published by: Fyens Stift, Klingenborg 2, Odense, 5100, Denmark. TEL 45-66-123024, FAX 45-66-123524, kmfyn@km.dk, http://www.fyensstift.dk.

286.132 USA ISSN 1083-3277
G A WORLD. (Girls in Action) Text in English. 1995. m. USD 14.99 (effective 2007). **Document type:** *Magazine, Consumer.*
Description: For girls, grades 5 and 6, who are members of the Southern Baptist Girls in Action organization.
Published by: Woman's Missionary Union Auxiliary to the Southern Baptist Convention, 100 Missionary Ridge, PO Box 830010, Birmingham, AL 35283. TEL 205-991-8100, email@wmu.org, http://www.wmu.com/. Ed. Barbara Massey. R&P Carol Causey. Circ: 55,000 (paid).

284.1 DEU ISSN 1437-1146
GEHET HIN! - MISSIONSBLATT; Zeitschrift der Lutherische Kirchenmission (Bleckmarer Mission). Text in German. 1899. bi-m. free (effective 2011). bk.rev. illus. back issues avail. **Document type:** *Newsletter, Consumer.* **Description:** Discusses missionary and evangelistic work worldwide.
Formerly: Missionsblatt (0948-1567)
Published by: Lutherische Kirchenmission e.V., Teichkamp 4, Bergen, 29303, Germany. TEL 49-5051-986911, FAX 49-5051-986945, lkm@selk.de, http://www.mission-bleckmar.de. Ed. Markus Nietzke. Circ: 5,700 (controlled).

280.4 DEU ISSN 0016-6073
BX6201
DIE GEMEINDE (KASSEL). Text in German. 1946. fortn. EUR 67.20; EUR 2.80 newsstand/cover (effective 2009). adv. bk.rev. abstr.; illus. index. **Document type:** *Magazine, Consumer.*
—CCC.
Published by: (Bund Evangelisch-Freikirchlicher Gemeinden), Oncken Verlag GmbH, Muendener Str 13, Kassel, 34123, Germany. TEL 49-561-520050, FAX 49-561-5200550, zeitschriften@oncken.de, http://www.oncken.de. Ed. Frank Fornagon. adv.: B&W page EUR 1,100, color page EUR 1,940. Circ: 9,500 (paid and controlled).

215 DEU ISSN 0936-0107
GEMEINDEBRIEF. Text in German. 1971. bi-m. adv. **Document type:** *Journal, Trade.*
Published by: Gemeinschaftswerk der Evangelischen Publizistik e.V., Emil-von-Behring-Str 3, Frankfurt Am Main, 60439, Germany. TEL 49-69-580980, FAX 49-69-58098272, info@gep.de, http://www.gep.de. adv.: B&W page EUR 980. Circ: 7,358 (controlled).

284.2 NLD ISSN 1567-5610
GEREFORMEERD KERKBLAD. Text in Dutch. 2000. bi-w. EUR 49.55 domestic; EUR 78.80 foreign; EUR 25.20 to students (effective 2010). adv. **Document type:** *Newsletter, Consumer.*
Formed by the merger of (2000-2000): Gereformeerd Kerkblad West- en Zuid-Nederland (1567-5602); Which was formerly (1996-2000): Gereformeerd Kerkblad voor Holland, Zeeland, Noord-Brabant en Limburg (1384-8666); (1964-1996): Gereformeerd Kerkblad voor Zuid-Holland, Zeeland, Noord-Brabant en Limburg (0167-3416); (1979-2000): Gereformeerd Kerkblad Midden-Nederland (1389-9325); (1979-2000): Gereformeerd Kerkblad Enschede (1389-9538); Both of which superseded in part (in 1999): Gereformeerd Kerkblad (1384-3850)
Published by: Koninklijke BDU Uitgeverij BV, Postbus 67, Barneveld, 3770 AB, Netherlands. TEL 31-342-494911, FAX 31-342-413141, tijdschriften@bdu.nl, http://www.bduuitgevers.nl. Ed. H J Messelink. Adv. contact Hendrik Jan Joosten TEL 31-342-494267. B&W page EUR 534; trim 210 x 297. Circ: 5,000.

284.2 ZAF ISSN 0378-407X
GEREFORMEERDE VROUEBLAD. Text in Afrikaans. 1947. m. ZAR 60 (effective 1999).
Published by: (Gereformeerde Kerke in Suid-Afrika/Reformed Churches in South Africa), Deputate Kerklike Tydskrifte GKSA, PO Box 20008, Noordbrug, Potchefstroom 2522, South Africa. Ed. M Venter. Circ: 6,400.

280.4 CHE ISSN 0016-9021
GESCHAEFTSMANN UND CHRIST. Text in German. 1960. m. (10/yr.). CHF 32 (effective 2001). bk.rev. illus. 42 p./no.; **Document type:** *Magazine, Trade.* **Description:** Devoted to Christianity's role in the business world, and the problem of applying Christian principles to the business community. Includes list of events.
Published by: Internationale Vereinigung Christlicher Geschaeftsleute, Gruppe Zurich, PO Box 29, Zuerich, 8034, Switzerland. http://www.ivcg.org. Circ: 15,000.

280.4 CHE
▼ **GESCHICHTE DES GOTTESDIENSTES IN DEN EVANGELISCH-REFORMIERTEN KIRCHEN DER DEUTSCHSCHWEIZ.** Text in German. 2010 (Jun.). irreg. price varies. **Document type:** *Monographic series, Academic/Scholarly.*
Published by: Theologischer Verlag Zurich, Badenerstr 73, Zurich, 8026, Switzerland. TEL 41-44-2993355, FAX 41-44-2993358, tvz@ref.ch.

280.4 282 DEU
GESCHICHTE DES KIRCHLICHEN LEBENS. Text in German. 1991. irreg., latest vol.8, 2008. price varies. **Document type:** *Monographic series, Academic/Scholarly.*
Published by: Verlag Herder GmbH, Hermann-Herder-Str 4, Freiburg Im Breisgau, 79104, Germany. TEL 49-761-27170, FAX 49-761-2717520, kundenservice@herder.de, http://www.herder.de.

284.2 DEU ISSN 0072-4238
➤ **GESELLSCHAFT FUER NIEDERSAECHSISCHE KIRCHENGESCHICHTE. JAHRBUCH.** Text in German. 1896. a. EUR 15 membership (effective 2005). bk.rev. **Document type:** *Journal, Academic/Scholarly.*
Indexed: B24, DIP, IBR, IBZ.
Published by: Gesellschaft fuer Niedersaechsische Kirchengeschichte, Goethestr 27, Hannover, 30169, Germany. TEL 49-511-1241755, FAX 49-511-1241770, Hans.Otte@evlka.de, http://www.kirchengeschichte-niedersachsen.de. Circ: 250.

283 AUS
GIPPSLAND ANGLICAN. Text in English. 1904. m. adv. bk.rev.; film rev. back issues avail. **Document type:** *Newspaper, Consumer.* **Description:** Regional Anglican newspaper for Anglicans in the Diocese of Gippsland.
Former titles (until 1980): Gippsland Anglican Church News; (until 1968): Church of England in the Diocese of Gippsland. Church News
Published by: Anglican Diocese of Gippsland, Church News Board, 453 Raymond St, Sale, VIC 3850, Australia. TEL 61-3-51442044, FAX 61-3-51447183, registrar@gippsanglican.org.au. Ed., R&P Rev. Donald Crewe TEL 61-3-56331021. Adv. contact Merle Sheean. Circ: 4,500.

280.4 DNK ISSN 1603-6816
GIV DET STOERSTE TIL DE MINDSTE; evangeliet til boernene. Text in Danish. 1984-1992; resumed 1995. q. free (effective 2004). illus. **Document type:** *Magazine, Consumer.*
Formerly (until 2003): Soendagskolekontakt (0109-2375)
Published by: Danmarks Folkekirkelige Soendagsskoler, Korskaervej 25, Fredericia, 7000, Denmark. TEL 45-75-926100, FAX 45-75-926146, kontakt@soendagsskoler.dk, http://www.soendagsskoler.dk. Ed. Mikael Arendt Laursen.

266.5 CAN ISSN 0017-0720
GLAD TIDINGS. Text in English. 1925. bi-m. CAD 11 (effective 2002). bk.rev. illus. index. 48 p./no.; back issues avail. **Description:** Covers mission work in the world.
Media: Large Type. **Related titles:** Audio cassette/tape ed.; Microfiche ed.
Published by: Women's Missionary Society, 50 Wynford Dr, Toronto, ON M3C 1J7, Canada. TEL 416-441-1111, FAX 416-441-2825, jstevenson@presbyterian.ca. Ed. L June Stevenson. R&P L. June Stevenson. Circ: 5,000 (paid).

THE GLASS (NORTHWOOD); towards a Christian understanding of literature. *see* LITERATURE

284.1 DEU ISSN 0323-8202
BX9798.U5
GLAUBE UND HEIMAT; evangelische Wochenzeitung fuer Thueringen. Text in German. 1946. w. EUR 39 domestic; EUR 49.90 foreign (effective 2010). adv. bk.rev. **Document type:** *Newspaper, Consumer.*
Published by: (Evangelischer Presseverband in Mitteldeutschland e.V. USA), Wartburg Verlag GmbH, Lisztstr 2a, Weimar, 99423, Germany. TEL 49-3643-246144, FAX 49-3643-246118, buch@wartburgverlag.de, http://www.guh-cms.de/wv/catalog/index.php. Ed. Martin Hanusch. adv.: B&W page EUR 2,436, color page EUR 3,410.40. Circ: 11,591 (controlled).

280.4 USA
GLOBAL MINISTRIES NEWS. Text in English. 1805. 2/yr. **Document type:** *Newsletter.* **Description:** Contains news and views of mission activities.
Former titles (until 2001): Whole Earth Newsletter; Missionary Herald; Goodnews
Published by: Global Ministries, 130 E Washington St, Indianapolis, IN 46204 . TEL 317-635-3100, FAX 317-635-4363, dom@disciples.org. Eds. Marianne Collar, Sandra J Rooney. R&P Sandra J Rooney. Circ: 11,000.

GLORY SONGS. *see* MUSIC

283 GBR ISSN 0256-4726
GO. Text in English. 1872. q. free. bk.rev. 16 p./no.; **Document type:** *Magazine, Consumer.* **Description:** Contains challenging and thought-provoking articles relating to cross-cultural mission and is designed to encourage people to play their part in bringing Christ's love to the peoples of Asia, the Arab World and the UK.
Published by: Interserve England and Wales, 5/6 Walker Ave, Wolverton Mill, Milton Keynes, MK12 5TW, United Kingdom. TEL 44-1908-552700, FAX 44-1908-552779, info@interserve.org.uk, http://www.interserve.org. Circ: 20,000.

266 DEU
GO FUER GOTT. Text in German. 1909. bi-m. illus. back issues avail. **Document type:** *Magazine, Consumer.*
Formerly: Missionsglocke der Liebenzeller Mission
Published by: Liebenzell Mission, Liobastr 17, Bad Liebenzell, 75378, Germany. TEL 49-7052-170, FAX 49-7052-17100, info@liebenzell.org, http://www.liebenzell.org. Ed., R&P Doris Eberhardh TEL 49-7052-17297. Circ: 11,000.

285 GBR ISSN 0017-1700
Y GOLEUAD/LIGHT. Text in English. 1871. w. adv. bk.rev. **Document type:** *Newspaper.*
—BLDSC (4201.223050).
Published by: Presbyterian Church of Wales, Tabernacle Chapel, 81 Merthyr Rd, Whitchurch, Cardiff, Wales CF14 1DD, United Kingdom. TEL 44-29-20627465, FAX 44-29-20616188, swyddfa.office@ebcpcw.org.uk, http://www.ebcpcw.org.uk/. Ed. R Maldwyn Thomas. R&P, Adv. contact June Jones. Circ: 5,000.

283 GBR ISSN 0262-2874
GOOD NEWS (BIRMINGHAM). Text in English. 1837. s-a. GBP 1 per issue (effective 2009). adv. bk.rev. illus. back issues avail. **Document type:** *Magazine, Trade.* **Description:** Covers articles on priesthood.
Formerly (until 1981): Home Mission News
Related titles: Online - full text ed.: free (effective 2009).
Published by: Additional Curates Society for England and Wales, Gordon Browning House, 8 Spitfire Rd, Birmingham, Warks B24 9PB, United Kingdom. TEL 44-121-3825533, FAX 44-121-3826999, info@additionalcurates.co.uk.

287.6 USA ISSN 0436-1563
BX8201
GOOD NEWS (WILMORE). Text in English. 1967. bi-m. USD 14.95. adv. bk.rev. back issues avail. **Description:** Covers United Methodist related current issues, testimonies and inspirational pieces.
Published by: Forum for Scriptural Christianity, Inc., 308 E Main St, Box 150, Wilmore, KY 40390. TEL 606-858-4661, FAX 606-858-4972. Ed. James V Heidinger II. Circ: 20,000.

280.4 USA ISSN 2152-484X
GOOD PREACHER. Text in English. 1989. bi-m. USD 79.99 (effective 2010). **Document type:** *Magazine, Trade.* **Description:** Provides scripture, lessons, sermons and sermon reviews for ministers.
Formerly (until 2009): Lectionary Homiletics (1043-2310)
Published by: Preaching Conference, PO Box 843, Amelia, VA 23002. TEL 804-937-1695, dhowell39@verizon.net.

280.4 GBR
GOSPEL MAGAZINE. Text in English. 1766. bi-m. GBP 5.50 (effective 2009). bk.rev. 36 p./no.; back issues avail. **Document type:** *Magazine, Consumer.* **Description:** Covers a variety of religious, ethical, and moral issues from a Christian perspective.
Incorporates: Protestant Beacon; British Protestant
Published by: Gospel Magazine Trust, 15 Bridge St, Knighton, Powys LD7 1BT, United Kingdom. Ed. Edward Malcolm.

280.4 GBR ISSN 0017-2367
GOSPEL STANDARD. Text in English. 1835. m. GBP 16.50 domestic (effective 2009). adv. bk.rev. back issues avail. **Document type:** *Magazine, Academic/Scholarly.* **Description:** Presents information relating to the Gospel Standard Societies; includes free grace sermons and articles concerning the doctrines of grace and experience of the Truth.
Formerly (until 1852): Gospel Standard or Feeble Christian's Support
Indexed: CERDIC.
Published by: Gospel Standard Publications, 12B Roundwood Ln, Harpenden, Herts AL5 3BZ, United Kingdom. TEL 44-1582-765448, publications@gospelstandard.org, http://www.gospelstandard.org/. Ed. Benjamin Ashworth Ramsbottom.

286 GBR ISSN 0046-6239
GRACE. Text in English. 1833. m. GBP 19.50 domestic; GBP 22.50 in Europe; GBP 26.50 elsewhere; GBP 1.85 newsstand/cover (effective 2009). adv. bk.rev. back issues avail. **Document type:** *Magazine, Consumer.* **Description:** A Reformed Baptist magazine for all Christians with articles and news.
Published by: Grace Magazine Trust, 4 Beechwood Rd, Caterham, CR3 6NA, United Kingdom. TEL 44-1883-344327.

286 GBR
GRACE BAPTIST MISSION HERALD. Text in English. 1899. q. free (effective 2009). back issues avail. **Document type:** *Magazine, Consumer.*
Formerly (until 1983): Strict Baptist Mission Herald
Related titles: Online - full text ed.
Published by: Grace Baptist Mission, 12 Abbey Close, Abingdon, Oxon OX14 3JD, United Kingdom. TEL 44-1235-520147, FAX 44-1235-559796.

280.4 USA ISSN 2160-2425
▼ **GRACE NEWS.** Text in English. 2010. q. free (effective 2011). **Document type:** *Newsletter, Trade.*
Related titles: Online - full text ed.
Published by: Grace of God Ministries International, 3950, 48th St, Bladensburg, MD 20710. TEL 301-277-1733, FAX 301-277-2992, http://www.graceofgodministries.com.

GREAT BRITAIN. ROYAL ARMY CHAPLAINS' DEPARTMENT. JOURNAL. *see* MILITARY

283 GBR ISSN 1365-490X
GROVE BIBLICAL SERIES. Text in English. 1996. q. GBP 10; GBP 3.50 per issue (print or online ed.) (effective 2009); subscr. includes Biblical Studies Bulletin. back issues avail. **Document type:** *Monographic series, Trade.* **Description:** Aims to make the best in current thinking about the Bible and its application accessible to those teaching and preaching in the local church.
Related titles: Online - full text ed.
—CCC.
Published by: Grove Books Ltd., Ridley Hall Rd, Cambridge, CB3 9HU, United Kingdom. TEL 44-1223-464748, FAX 44-1223-464849, sales@grovebooks.co.uk.

283 GBR ISSN 1367-0840
GROVE EVANGELISM SERIES. Variant title: Church Army Evangelism Series. Text in English. 1988. q. GBP 10; GBP 3.50 per issue (print or online ed.) (effective 2009). back issues avail. **Document type:** *Monographic series, Trade.* **Description:** Provides concise explorations of key areas in evangelism.
Formerly (until 1996): Grove Booklets on Evangelism (0953-4946)
Related titles: Online - full text ed.
—CCC.
Published by: Grove Books Ltd., Ridley Hall Rd, Cambridge, CB3 9HU, United Kingdom. TEL 44-1223-464748, FAX 44-1223-464849, sales@grovebooks.co.uk.

283 GBR ISSN 1470-8531
GROVE RENEWAL SERIES. Text in English. 2000. q. GBP 10; GBP 3.50 per issue (print or online ed.) (effective 2009). back issues avail. **Document type:** *Monographic series, Trade.* **Description:** Explores key issues raised by the charismatic renewal movement in the church.
Related titles: Online - full text ed.
—CCC.
Published by: Grove Books Ltd., Ridley Hall Rd, Cambridge, CB3 9HU, United Kingdom. TEL 44-1223-464748, FAX 44-1223-464849, sales@grovebooks.co.uk.

283 GBR ISSN 0144-1728
GROVE WORSHIP SERIES. Text in English. 1972. q. GBP 10; GBP 3.50 per issue (print or online ed.) (effective 2009). back issues avail. **Document type:** *Monographic series, Trade.* **Description:** Provides clear and concise explorations of aspects of worship in the local church, and also aims to comment on all recent Anglican liturgical revision.
Supersedes in part (in 1980): Grove Booklet on Ministry and Worship (0305-3067)
Related titles: Online - full text ed.
—CCC.
Published by: Grove Books Ltd., Ridley Hall Rd, Cambridge, CB3 9HU, United Kingdom. TEL 44-1223-464748, FAX 44-1223-464849, sales@grovebooks.co.uk.

283 GBR ISSN 1748-3492
GROVE YOUTH SERIES. Text in English. 2005. q. GBP 10; GBP 3.50 per issue (print or online ed.) (effective 2009). back issues avail. **Document type:** *Monographic series, Trade.* **Description:** Provides clear and concise explorations of Christian youth ministry.
Related titles: Online - full text ed.
—CCC.
Published by: Grove Books Ltd., Ridley Hall Rd, Cambridge, CB3 9HU, United Kingdom. TEL 44-1223-464748, FAX 44-1223-464849, sales@grovebooks.co.uk.

230.0071 USA ISSN 1543-3668
BV1610
GROWTH; the journal of the Association for Christians in Student Development. Text in English. 2001 (Spr.). a.
Published by: Association for Christians in Student Development, c/o Skip Trudeau, Taylor University, 236 West Reade Ave., Upland, IN 46989-1001. amuia@acsdhome.org, http://www.acsdhome.org/. Eds. Skip Trudeau, Tim Herrmann.

280.4 DNK ISSN 0107-4164
PT8130.Z5
➤ **GRUNDTVIG STUDIER.** Variant title: Grundtvigstudier. Text in Danish, English. 1948. a. DKK 240 membership (effective 2009). bk.rev. abstr.; bibl. 250 p./no.; back issues avail. **Document type:** *Monographic series, Academic/Scholarly.*
Indexed: A21, BibInd, MLA, MLA-IB, RI-1, RI-2, RILM.
—CCC.
Published by: Grundtvig-Selskabet af 8. September 1947, c/o Kirkeligt Samfund, Vartorv, Farvergade 27, Copenhagen K, 1463, Denmark. TEL 45-33-732800. **Subscr. to:** Forlaget Vartov, Farvergade 27, Copenhagen K 1463, Denmark.

286.73 USA ISSN 0017-5226
GUIDE (HAGERSTOWN); true stories pointing to Jesus. Text in English. 1953. w. USD 54.95 (effective 2009). adv. illus. index. reprints avail. **Document type:** *Magazine, Consumer.* **Description:** Features true stories that show how following Jesus makes a positive difference in kids' lives.
Related titles: Microfilm ed.: (from PQC).
Published by: (General Conference of Seventh-Day Adventists), Review and Herald Publishing Association, 55 W Oak Ridge Dr, Hagerstown, MD 21740. TEL 301-393-4037, info@rhpa.org, http://www.rhpa.org. Ed. Randy Fishell. Adv. contact Genia Blumenberg TEL 301-393-3170. color page USD 630; trim 5.187 x 8.25. Circ: 27,000.

283 USA
GUIDE FOR BIBLICAL STUDIES. Text in English. 1885. q. USD 4 per issue (effective 2010). adv. back issues avail. **Document type:** *Handbook/Manual/Guide, Trade.* **Description:** Based on international Sunday school lessons for Christian teaching.
Published by: Church of the Brethren, General Board, 1451 Dundee Ave, Elgin, IL 60120. TEL 847-742-5100, 800-323-8039, FAX 847-742-6103, cobweb@brethren.org, http://www.brethren.org. Circ: 15,000.

280.4 DEU ISSN 0017-5730
GUSTAV-ADOLF-BLATT. Text in German. 1955. q. EUR 7.16; EUR 1.95 per issue (effective 2010). adv. bk.rev. **Document type:** *Magazine, Consumer.* **Description:** Provides general information about minority Protestant churches.
Published by: (Gustav-Adolf-Werk e.V. Diasporawerk der Evangelischen Kirche in Deutschland), Verlag des Gustav-Adolf-Werks e.V., Pistorisstr 6, Leipzig, 04229, Germany. TEL 49-341-490620, FAX 49-341-4770505, info@gustav-adolf-werk.de, http://www.gustav-adolf-werk.de. Ed. Maaja Pauska. adv.: page EUR 1,000; trim 210 x 297. Circ: 14,000.

GUTER START. *see* CHILDREN AND YOUTH—For

284.1 248.14895 DNK ISSN 0108-7541
BX8034.H33
HADERSLEV STIFTSBOG. Text in Danish. 1946. a. back issues avail. **Document type:** *Yearbook, Consumer.*
Formerly (until 1966): Haderslav Stifts Aarbog
Published by: Haderslev Stift, Ribe Landevej 37, Haderslev, 6100, Denmark. TEL 45-74-522025, FAX 45-74-533606, kmhad@km.dk, http://www.haderslevstift.dk.

HANDBELLS; for directors and ringers. *see* MUSIC

284 NLD ISSN 1877-234X
HANDELINGEN VAN DE GENERALE SYNODE EN VAN DE KLEINE SYNODE VAN DE PROTESTANTSE KERK IN NEDERLAND. Text in Dutch. 2005. a. EUR 27.50 (effective 2011).
Published by: (Protestantse Kerk in Nederland, Generale Synode), Boekencentrum Uitgevers, Goudstraat 50, Postbus 29, Zoetermeer, 2700 AA, Netherlands. TEL 31-79-3615481, FAX 31-79-3615489, info@boekencentrum.nl, http://www.boekencentrum.nl.

268.841 USA
HAPPY TIMES. Text in English. 1964. m. USD 9.96 (effective 2009). **Document type:** *Magazine, Consumer.* **Description:** Contains Christian stories, poems, colorful activity pages and special projects for active 3- to 5-year-olds and their parents.
Related titles: Microfilm ed.
Published by: (Lutheran Church - Missouri Synod, Board for Parish Services), Concordia Publishing House, 3558 S Jefferson, St Louis, MO 63118. TEL 314-268-1000, 800-325-3040, FAX 800-490-9889, order@cph.org. Ed. Earl H Gaulke. Pub. Rev. Paul T McCain. Circ: 49,000.

280.4 DEU ISSN 1863-7752
DAS HAUSKREISMAGAZIN; Glauben gemeinsam Leben. Text in German. 1977. q. EUR 16; EUR 5.90 newsstand/cover (effective 2011). adv. back issues avail. **Document type:** *Magazine, Consumer.*

R

Former titles (until 2006): Treffpunkt Bibel (1431-2050); (until 1996): Gemeindebibelschule (0344-2233)
Published by: Bundes Verlag GmbH, Bodenborn 43, Witten, 58452, Germany. TEL 49-2302-930930, FAX 49-2302-93093689, info@bundes-verlag.de, http://www.bundes-verlag.de. Ed. Christof Klenk. Adv. contact Tim Mueller. Circ: 14,000 (paid and controlled).

280.4 USA ISSN 2150-4768
▼ **HAVING CHURCH FOR WOMEN.** Text in English. 2009. bi-m. USD 29 (effective 2009). **Document type:** *Magazine, Consumer.* **Description:** Offers tips, letters of hope, stories of love, insight into the soul and life giving truth for Christian women.
Published by: Having Church Ministries, LLC, PO Box 5422, Suffolk, VA 23435. TEL 757-513-5467, info@havingchurchministries.com, http://havingchurchministries.com/.

283.73 USA ISSN 0274-7154
HAWAIIAN CHURCH CHRONICLE. Text in English. 1910. 10/yr. free to members (effective 2008). bk.rev. **Document type:** *Newspaper, Consumer.*
Published by: Episcopal Church in Hawaii, 229 Queen Emma Sq, Honolulu, HI 96813-2304. TEL 808-536-7776, FAX 808-538-7194, stmoore@episcopalhawaii.org, http://www.episcopalhawaii.org. Pub. Rt. Rev. Robert Fitzpatrick. Circ: 7,600.

286 USA
HEARTBEAT (ANTIOCH). Text in English. 1961. 6/yr. free. **Document type:** *Monographic series.* **Description:** News, profiles, and personal experiences pertaining to the foreign missionary work of Free Will Baptists.
Published by: Free Will Baptist Foreign Missions, PO Box 5002, Antioch, TN 37011-5002. TEL 615-731-6812, FAX 615-731-5345, charity@nafwb.org. Ed., R&P Don Robirds. Circ: 20,000 (controlled).

280.4 CHE
HEILSARMEE ZEITUNG. Text in German. 1884. 24/yr. CHF 35 (effective 2000). **Document type:** *Newspaper, Consumer.*
Formerly: Kriegsruf
Related titles: French ed.: Journal de l'Amee du Salut.
Address: Laupenstr 5, Postfach 6575, Bern, 3001, Switzerland. TEL 41-31-3880591, FAX 41-31-3880595, redaktion@swi.salvationarmy.org. Ed. Hedy Brenner. Circ: 12,900.

286.3 USA
HELPING HAND IN BIBLE STUDY. Text in English. 1884. q. USD 9 (effective 1999). back issues avail. **Document type:** *Magazine, Consumer.* **Description:** Bible study lessons, based on international Bible lessons for Christian teaching for Seventh Day Baptists.
Published by: (Seventh Day Baptist Board of Christian Education), American Sabbath Tract and Communication Council, 3120 Kennedy Rd, Box 1678, Janesville, WI 53547-1678. TEL 608-752-5055. Ed. Ernest K Bee Jr. R&P Ernest Bee Jr. Circ: 2,400.

285 CUB ISSN 0864-0270
HERALDO CRISTIANO. Text in Spanish. bi-m.
Published by: Iglesia Presbiteriana, Apdo. 154, Matanzas, Cuba. TEL 61-1558. Ed. Jacobo Guiribitey.

283.73 CUB
HERALDO EPISCOPAL. Text in Spanish. 1938. q. USD 6. bk.rev. **Description:** Channels communication between the Anglican and Christian Cuban communities and the world church.
Published by: Iglesia Episcopal Cubana, Centro Diocesano, Calle 13, no.874 e-4 y 6, Vedado, La Habana, Cuba. TEL 7-32-1120. Ed. Rev. Juan Quevedo. Circ: 2,000.

280.4 NLD ISSN 1879-4564
▼ **HERSTELD HERVORMDE KERK. LEDENINFORMATIEBLAD.** Text in Dutch. 2009. q. adv.
Published by: Hersteld Hervormde Kerk, De Vendelier, Vendelier 51-D, Veenendaal, 3905 PC, Netherlands. TEL 31-318-505541, bureau@hersteldhervormdekerk.nl. Eds. B Noteboom, J Kwakkel, L W Ruijgrok.

284 NLD ISSN 1572-7998
HERVORMD KERKBLAD. Text in Dutch. 1982. 23/yr. EUR 18 (effective 2009).
Formerly (until 2004): Het Gekrookte Riet (1382-1067)
Published by: Hersteld Hervormde Kerk, De Vendelier, Vendelier 51-D, Veenendaal, 3905 PC, Netherlands. TEL 31-318-505541, bureau@hersteldhervormdekerk.nl, http://www.hersteldhervormdekerk.nl. Ed. T de Jong.

280.4 ZAF ISSN 0259-949X
BX9624.A1
DIE HERVORMER. Text in Afrikaans. 1909. s-m. ZAR 25.30 (effective 1999). adv. bk.rev. **Document type:** *Newspaper.*
Indexed: ISAP.
Published by: Nederduitsch Hervormde Kerk van Afrika, PO Box 5777, Pretoria, 0001, South Africa. TEL 27-12-3228885, FAX 27-12-3227906. Ed. W A Dreyer. Circ: 12,500.

280.4 DEU ISSN 0941-5475
HESSISCHES PFARRBLATT. Text in German. 1971. bi-m. index. back issues avail. **Document type:** *Newsletter, Consumer.* **Description:** Covers church problems and matters of the pastoral profession.
Published by: Pfarrerinnen- und Pfarrerverein in der Evang. Kirche in Hessen und Nassau e.V., Melsunger Str 8A, Frankfurt Am Main, 60389, Germany. TEL 49-69-471820, FAX 49-69-479487, PfarrvereinFFM@aol.com, http://www.dike.de/Pfarrerinnen-Pfarrerverein/index.html. Ed. Martin Zentgraf. Circ: 2,700.

283 ZAF ISSN 0018-1684
BX5700.6.A1
HIGHWAY. Text in Afrikaans, English. 1940. m. ZAR 20, USD 12. adv. bk.rev. **Document type:** *Newspaper.*
Published by: Anglican Diocese of Kimberley and Kuruman, PO Box 45, Kimberley, 8300, South Africa. TEL 27-531-32433, FAX 27-531-812730. Ed. Canon Oswald Swartz. Circ: 2,300.

287.6 974 USA ISSN 0439-2191
BX8235
HISTORIAN'S DIGEST. Text in English. 1959. q. looseleaf. free to members (effective 2009). back issues avail. **Document type:** *Newsletter, Academic/Scholarly.* **Description:** Provides information about the United Methodist Church.
Related titles: Online - full text ed.: free (effective 2009).
Published by: (Historical Society of The United Methodist Church), United Methodist Church, General Commission on Archives & History, 36 Madison Avenue, PO Box 127, Madison, NJ 07940. TEL 973-408-3189, FAX 973-408-3909, gcah@gcah.org, http://www.gcah.org. Ed. Joy Donovan TEL 304-594-3914.

280.4 USA ISSN 0360-9030
E172
HISTORICAL FOOTNOTES (ST. LOUIS). Text in English. 1955. q. free to members (effective 2010). bk.rev. bibl. back issues avail. **Document type:** *Newsletter, Trade.*
Formerly (until 1962): Concordia Historical Institute. Message from Headquarters
Related titles: Online - full text ed.: free (effective 2010).
Published by: Concordia Historical Institute, 804 Seminary Pl, St Louis, MO 63105. TEL 314-505-7900, FAX 314-505-7901, mhuggins@chi.lcms.org. Ed. Marvin A Huggins.

285 GBR
HISTORICAL SOCIETY OF THE PRESBYTERIAN CHURCH OF WALES. JOURNAL. Text in English, Welsh. 1916. a. bk.rev.
Published by: Historical Society of the Presbyterian Church of Wales, The Manse, Caradog Rd, Aberystwyth, Dyfed, United Kingdom. Ed. Rev. Gomer M Roberts. Circ: 600.

286 USA ISSN 0018-3229
HOGAR CRISTIANO. Text in Spanish. 1957. q. USD 10 (effective 1999). adv. illus.
Published by: Casa Bautista de Publicaciones, PO Box 4255, El Paso, TX 79914. TEL 915-566-9656. Ed. Exequiel San Martin. R&P Norberto Herrera. Adv. contact Jorge A Rousselin. Circ: 20,000.

286.132 USA ISSN 0018-4071
BV4485
HOMELIFE; a Christian family magazine. Text in English. 1947. m. USD 21.95; USD 3.95 per issue (effective 2008). adv. 66 p./no.; back issues avail. **Document type:** *Magazine, Consumer.* **Description:** Provides tools that equip families to experience dynamic, healthy and Christ-centered living.
Indexed: SBPI.
Published by: LifeWay Christian Resources, 1 Lifeway Plz, Nashville, TN 37234. TEL 615-251-2000, FAX 615-251-5933, customerservice@lifeway.com. Eds. Beckman Ivey, Rene A Holt, Ivey Harrington Beckman. Adv. contact Rhonda Edge Buescher. color page USD 11,288; trim 8.125 x 10.875. Circ: 306,000.

284.1 USA ISSN 2152-6923
➤ **HOMILETIC (ONLINE).** Abbreviated title: H M L T C. Text in English. 1976. s-a. free (effective 2011). back issues avail. **Document type:** *Journal, Academic/Scholarly.* **Description:** Explores disciplines related to religious communication, biblical interpretation, theology, worship, art and media, human sciences and culture, and communication theory.
Media: Online - full text.
Published by: (Academy of Homiletics), Religious Speech Communication Association, Vanderbilt Divinity School, 210 21st Ave, Nashville, TN 37240. TEL 615-343-1229. Eds. Dale Andrews, John S McClure.

283 USA ISSN 1040-6255
HOMILETICS; the art of writing and preaching sermons. Text in English. 1989. q. USD 59.95 (effective 1999). **Document type:** *Journal, Trade.* **Description:** Provides sermon resources for Protestant pastors.
Related titles: Diskette ed.
Indexed: CCR.
Published by: Communication Resources Inc., PO Box 36269, Canton, OH 44735-6269. TEL 800-992-2144. Ed. Timothy Merrill.

280.4 305.31 USA ISSN 1540-0816
HONORBOUND MAGAZINE FOR MEN. Text in English. 2002. q.
Published by: Gospel Publishing House, 1445 N Boonville Ave, Springfield, MO 65802. TEL 800-641-4310, FAX 417-862-5881, 800-328-0294, CustSrvReps@ag.org, http://www.gospelpublishing.com/.

280.4 USA ISSN 1041-5270
HORIZONS UNLIMITED. Text in English. 1987-1996 (Jul.); resumed 1998 (Nov.). s-a. free. **Document type:** *Magazine, Consumer.* **Description:** Biblically based teachings by Clinton and Sarah Utterbach, fellowship's pastors and a variety of guest writers. Focus is on the result of practical application of biblical principles in the lives of individuals featured.
Published by: Redeeming Love Christian Center, 145 W Rt 59, Box 577, Nanuet, NY 10954-9963. TEL 914-623-9300, FAX 914-623-0521, http://www.redeemingcc.org. Ed., R&P Deborah D Walker. Circ: 44,000.

280.4 DEU ISSN 1436-3437
HUGENOTTEN. Text in German. 1929. q. EUR 36 membership; EUR 6 newsstand/cover (effective 2009). bk.rev. abstr.; bibl.; illus. **Document type:** *Journal, Academic/Scholarly.*
Formerly (until 1998): Der Deutsche Hugenott (0012-0294)
—CCC.
Published by: Deutscher Hugenotten-Gesellschaft e.V., Hafenplatz 9a, Bad Karlshafen, 34385, Germany. TEL 49-5672-1433, FAX 49-5672-925072, info@hugenotten.de. Ed. Andreas Flick. Circ: 1,500.

283.71 CAN ISSN 0018-7917
HURON CHURCH NEWS. Text in English. 1950. 10/yr. CAD 15; CAD 23 foreign (effective 1998). adv. bk.rev. illus. **Document type:** *Newspaper.*
Published by: Anglican Church of Canada, Diocese of Huron, 255 Queens Ave, Ste 903, London, ON N6A 5R8, Canada. TEL 519-434-6893, FAX 519-673-4151. Ed. David Parson. Pub. Percy O'Driscoll. Adv. contact Bonnie Rollins. Circ: 26,000.

280.4 DNK ISSN 1901-5976
ML3142
➤ **HYMNOLOGI**; nordisk tidsskrift. Text in Danish, Norwegian, Swedish; Summaries in English, German. 1972. q. DKK 275 membership (effective 2009). bk.rev. illus. back issues avail. **Document type:** *Journal, Academic/Scholarly.* **Description:** Discusses hymnology and new hymns from Denmark, Norway, Sweden and Finland.
Formerly (until 2006): Hymnologiske Meddelelser (0106-4940)
Indexed: MLA, MLA-IB, RILM.
Published by: Salmehistorisk Selskab, c/o Institut for Kirkehistorie, Koebmagergade 44-46, Copenhagen K, 1150, Denmark. TEL 45-35-323623, FAX 45-35-323638, pbc@teol.ku.dk. Ed. Ove Paulsen TEL 45-98-318470. Circ: 700. **Co-publisher:** Teologisk Paedagogisk Center.

280.4 AUT
I C O - INFORMATION CHRISTLICHER ORIENT. Text in German. 2001. m. EUR 10 (effective 2001). **Document type:** *Magazine, Consumer.* **Description:** Contains information on events, history, monuments and places pertaining to Christian churches in the Middle East.
Published by: Initiative Christlicher Orient, Bethlehemstr 20, Linz, 4020, Austria. TEL 43-732-773578, FAX 43-732-773578, ico@utanet.at, http://www.8ung.at/auslaender/ico.

280.4 DEU ISSN 0721-8796
IDEA-SPEKTRUM; Nachrichten und Meinungen aus der evangelischen Welt. Text in German. 1979. 48/yr. EUR 6.40 per month to individuals; EUR 8.50 per month to institutions; EUR 4.48 per month to students (effective 2009). adv. bk.rev. 35 p./no.; back issues avail. **Document type:** *Magazine, Consumer.*
Related titles: CD-ROM ed.; English ed.; Supplement(s): Idea-Spezial.
Published by: Evangelische Nachrichtenagentur Idea e.V., Postfach 1820, Wetzlar, 35528, Germany. TEL 49-6441-9150, FAX 49-6441-915118, idea@idea.de, http://www.idea.de. adv.: B&W page EUR 1,760, color page EUR 2,543; trim 194 x 272. Circ: 30,051 (paid).

280.4 CHE
IDEASPEKTRUM SCHWEIZ. Text in German. 1975. w. CHF 128 (effective 2001). adv. bk.rev. illus.; tr.lit. **Document type:** *Magazine, Consumer.*
Former titles (until 1999): Idea Magazin; Idea Schweiz; (until 1986): Schweizerische Arbeitsgemeinschaft fuer Evangelisation
Published by: (Informationsdienst der Schweizerischen Evangelischen Allianz), Idea Schweiz, Postfach, Zurich, 8023, Switzerland. TEL 41-1-4474411, FAX 41-1-4474410, redaktion@ideaschweiz.ch, http://www.ideaschweiz.ch. Ed. Fritz Herrli. Circ: 4,500. **Subscr. to:** bv-media, Schaffhauserstr 18, Zurich 8023, Switzerland. TEL 41-1-3504350, FAX 41-1-3504351, info@bv-media.ch.

284.1 BRA ISSN 0103-779X
➤ **IGREJA LUTERANA**; revista semestral de teologia. Text in Portuguese. 1941. s-a. BRL 15, USD 18 (effective 2003). adv. bk.rev. bibl. back issues avail. **Document type:** *Academic/Scholarly.* **Description:** For pastors and theologians of Brazil and abroad.
Indexed: OTA.
Published by: Seminario Concordia, Caixa Postal 202, S. Leopoldo, RS 93001-970, Brazil. TEL 55-51-592-9035. Ed., Pub. Acir Raymann. Circ: 600.

280.4 TZA ISSN 0856-1931
IJA WEBONERE. Text in Swahili, Niger-Congo. 1968 (vol.14). bi-m. looseleaf. TZS 300, USD 30. adv. stat.
Published by: Evangelical Lutheran Church in Tanzania, North Western Diocese, PO Box 277, Bukoba, Tanzania. TELEX 58387-ELCT-TZ. Ed. Rev. J Kalugendo.

286.1773 USA ISSN 0019-1868
ILLINOIS BAPTIST. Text in English. 1905. w. USD 7.50. bk.rev. charts; illus.; stat. **Document type:** *Newspaper.*
Related titles: Microform ed.
Published by: Illinois Baptist State Association, PO Box 19247, Springfield, IL 62794. TEL 217-786-2600. Ed. Ferrell Foster. Circ: 10,800.

284.2 ZAF ISSN 0378-4088
IMBONGI YENKOSI. Text in Zulu. 1952. m. (11/yr.).
Published by: Reformed Churches in South Africa/Gereformeerde Kerke in Suid-Afrika, c/o South African Council of Churches, PO Box 62098, Marshalltown, 2107, South Africa. TEL 27-11-4921380, FAX 27-11-4921448, info@sacc.org.za, http://www.sacc.org.za. Ed. Rev. W L Kurpershoek. Circ: 2,150.

286.6 USA ISSN 0194-0422
IMPACT (CLAREMONT). Text in English. 1978. a. USD 5 (effective 2006).
Indexed: A21, RI-1.
Published by: Disciples Seminary Foundation, 300 W Foothill Blvd, Claremont, CA 91711-2709. TEL 909-624-0712, FAX 909-626-4100, info@dsf.edu. Eds. Mary Anne Parrott, Rod Parrott.

266.6 USA ISSN 0019-2821
BV2360
IMPACT (LITTLETON). Text in English. 1943. 4/yr. free. bk.rev.; film rev. charts; illus.; stat.; tr.lit. **Description:** Discusses mission work in the world.
Formerly: Conservative Baptist Impact
Published by: C B International, 1501 W Mineral Ave, Littleton, CO 80120. TEL 800-487-4224. Ed. James P Long. Circ: 40,375.

284.2 ZAF ISSN 1018-6441
➤ **IN DIE SKRIFLIG.** Text in Afrikaans, Dutch, English; Summaries in English, Afrikaans. 1966. q. ZAR 110 domestic; USD 35 foreign (effective 2003). adv. video rev.; bk.rev. abstr.; bibl. Index. back issues avail. **Document type:** *Journal, Academic/Scholarly.* **Description:** Publishes theological research articles in the Reformational tradition.
Related titles: Online - full text ed.
Indexed: A21, ISAP, IZBG, OTA, R&TA, RI-1, RI-2.
—BLDSC (4372.460400).
Published by: (Potchefstroom University for Christian Higher Education/ Potchefstroomse Universiteit vir Christelike Hoer Onderwys, Gereformeerde Teologiese Vereniging), Buro vir Wetenskaplike Tydskrifte/Bureau for Scholarly Journals, Private Bag X6001, Potchefstroom, 2520, South Africa. TEL 27-18-299-4081, FAX 27-18-299-4084, http://www.puk.ac.za. Ed. P P Kruger. R&P Susan Lourens TEL 27-18-299-4081. Circ: 327 (paid).

286.5 USA ISSN 1940-2937
IN PART. Text in English. 1887. q. USD 15 to non-members; free to members (effective 2006). bk.rev. back issues avail. **Document type:** *Magazine, Consumer.* **Description:** Promotes the doctrine, teaching and ministry of the Brethren in Christ Church.
Former titles (until 2007): Seek (Grantham) (1555-4619); (until 2005): Visitor (Grantham); (until 1999): Evangelical Visitor (0745-0486)
Related titles: Online - full content ed.: ISSN 1940-2945.
Published by: (Board for Media Ministries of the Brethren in Christ Church), Evangel Publishing House, PO Box A, Grantham, PA 17027. TEL 717-697-2634, FAX 717-697-7714, rross@messiah.edu, http://www.bic-church.org. Ed., R&P Ron Ross. Circ: 5,000 (paid).

284.1 USA
IN PARTNERSHIP. Text in English. 1978. q. free. adv. **Document type:** *Newsletter.* **Description:** Presents news and notes on the Christian Social Mission from Lutheran Social Services in New York.
Former titles: On the Edge (New York); Which superseded: Focus (Brooklyn); Which was formerly: Our70's
Indexed: SpeleolAb.
Published by: Lutheran Social Services of Metropolitan New York, Inc., 27 Park Pl, New York, NY 10007-2502. FAX 212-366-4886. Ed. Teena Isaacs Dorn. R&P, Adv. contact Teena Dorn TEL 212-366-6330. Circ: 16,000.

280.4 DEU
IN SPIRIT; Zeitschrift fuer geisterfuelltes Christsein. Text in German. 1948. 5/yr. EUR 2.30 newsstand/cover (effective 2005). adv. **Document type:** *Magazine, Consumer.*
Formerly: Stimme der Wahrheit (1433-528X)
Published by: Gemeinde Gottes e.V., Schurwald Str 10, Urbach, 73660, Germany. TEL 49-7181-9875-0, FAX 49-7181-9875-20. Ed., R&P Heinrich Scherz TEL 49-7183-6786. Pub. Paul Schmidgall. Adv. contact Marc Brenner. Circ: 3,500 (paid).

280.4 GBR ISSN 2042-1796
▼ **IN TOUCH WITH HEAVEN.** Text in English. 2009. q. GBP 9.99 per issue (effective 2011). **Document type:** *Handbook/Manual/Guide, Consumer.* **Description:** Helps people to recharge spiritual batteries and move forward with the Lord.
Published by: Divine Encounter Publication, 685-689 Old Kent Rd, London, SE15 1JS, United Kingdom. TEL 44-20-76399852, info@divineencounterministry.org.

286 USA ISSN 8756-1816
THE INDEPENDENT BAPTIST VOICE. Text in English. 1982. w. USD 25 in county; USD 27 elsewhere; USD 0.75 newsstand/cover (effective 2005). adv. **Document type:** *Newspaper, Consumer.* **Description:** Carries news of Baptist churches throughout New York State.
Published by: Newspaper Publishers, Llc., 1035 Conklin Rd, Conklin, NY 13748. TEL 607-775-0472, FAX 607-775-5863. Pub. Donald Einstein. adv.: col. inch USD 2.60. Circ: 1,110 (paid).

284.154 IND
INDIAN LUTHERAN NEWSLETTER. Text in English. 1967. bi-m. free to members (effective 2011). bk.rev. **Document type:** *Newsletter, Trade.*
Former titles (until 1991): Indian Lutheran; (until 1980): Gospel Witness (0017-2391)
Related titles: Online - full text ed.
Published by: United Evangelical Lutheran Churches in India, Martin Luther Bhavan, 95, Purasavakkam High Rd, Chennai, Tamil Nadu 600 010, India. TEL 91-44-26430008, FAX 91-44-26611364, augustinejkumar@uelci.org, http://www.uelci.org/.

284.1 DNK ISSN 0902-9532
BV2650
INDRE MISSIONS TIDENDE. Variant title: I M T. Text in Danish. 1854. w. DKK 698; DKK 460 to students (effective 2009). adv. back issues avail. **Document type:** *Consumer.*
Published by: Kirkelig Forening for den Indre Mission/The Church Association for the Inner Mission in Denmark, Korskaersvej 25, Fredericia, 7000, Denmark. TEL 45-75-926100, FAX 45-75-926146, post@indremission.dk, http://www2.indremission.dk. Eds. Holger Skovengaard TEL 45-82-271220, Peter Nord Hansen TEL 45-82-271201. Adv. contact Inge Mortensen TEL 45-82-271224. Circ: 9,000.

280.4 FRA ISSN 2106-5896
INFOS C P. (Conseillers Presbyteraux) Text in French. 2006. 11/yr. **Document type:** *Bulletin, Consumer.*
Published by: Union des Eglises Protestantes d'Alsace et de Lorraine, BP 80022, Strasbourg, 67081, France. TEL 33-3-88259000, FAX 33-3-88259099, contact@uepal.fr.

283.73 USA ISSN 2150-5780
THE INLAND EPISCOPALIAN. Text in English. 19??. m. free to members (effective 2009). **Document type:** *Newspaper.* **Description:** Contains news, features and other information about the life and ministry of the church in the Diocese and beyond.
Formerly (until 1995): Columbia Churchman
Published by: The Episcopal Diocese of Spokane, 245 E 13th Ave, Spokane, WA 99202. TEL 509-624-3191, 800-359-2587, FAX 509-747-0049, campcross@spokanediocese.org.

201.6 GBR
INSAKA. Text in English. 1993. q. free to members. **Document type:** *Newsletter.* **Description:** Serves as a forum for news and views affecting the equal participation of women and men in mission and in the life of the church.
Formerly (until no.2, 1993): Community of Women and Men in Mission. Newsletter
Published by: (Community of Women and Men), Council for World Mission, Ipalo House, 32-34 Great Peter St, London, SW1P 2DB, United Kingdom. TEL 44-20-72224214, FAX 44-20-72331747, council@cwmission.org, http://www.cwmission.org.

284.1 SWE
INSIDAN - KRISTEN UNGDOMSTIDNING. Text in Swedish. 8/yr. SEK 150 (effective 1998). adv. **Document type:** *Bulletin.* **Description:** Evangelical Lutheran publication for teen-agers.
Formerly (until 1997): Ungdomsbladet
Published by: Kristna Ungdomsfoerbundet i Sydsverige, c/o Missionssaellskapet Bibeltrogna Vaenner, Fack 6160, Stockholm, 10233, Sweden. TEL 46-8-33-2-5-23, FAX 46-8-34-58-18. Ed. Per Bergstroem. Adv. contact Cecilia Andersson. Circ: 900.

280.4 GBR ISSN 1474-1628
INSIDE OUT. Text in English. 1997. bi-m. free to qualified personnel (effective 2009). **Document type:** *Magazine, Consumer.* **Description:** Covers events and concerns affecting the council and its member churches.
Formerly: News Share
Published by: (Communication Unit), Council for World Mission, Ipalo House, 32-34 Great Peter St, London, SW1P 2DB, United Kingdom. TEL 44-20-72272505, FAX 44-20-72331747, council@cwmission.org, http://www.cwmission.org.

286.1415 GBR
➤ **INSIGHT.** Variant title: A B C Insight. Text in English. 1877. bi-m. GBP 19, EUR 20 (effective 2010). adv. music rev.; Website rev.; bk.rev. 24 p./no.; **Document type:** *Magazine, Academic/Scholarly.* **Description:** Aims to inform readers about the life in churches of the Association of Baptist churches in Ireland; impart instruction in the Christian faith, stimulate thought in relation to Biblical interpretation and stimulate the application of Biblical truth to personal and social life.
Former titles (until 2007): Irish Baptist Life; (until 2000): Irish Baptist; (until 1930): Irish Baptist Magazine
Published by: Association of Baptist Churches in Ireland, 19 Hillsborough Rd, Moira, Co. Down BT67 0HG, United Kingdom. abc@thebaptistcentre.org, http://www.baptistsinireland.org/. Ed., R&P, Adv. contact Miss Agnes Borland. page GBP 170; trim 180 x 255. Circ: 2,400.

286.732 USA ISSN 0020-1944
INSIGHT (HAGERSTOWN). Text in English. 1970. w. USD 54.95 includes Cornerstone Quarterly (effective 2009). adv. bk.rev.; music rev. illus. reprints avail. **Document type:** *Magazine, Consumer.* **Description:** Designed to help seventh-day adventist teenagers grow in a friendship with god; solve life's problems; choose positive christian values and principles to live by; and provide an Internet forum for discussion and interaction with other SDA teens.
Supersedes: Youth's Instructor
Published by: (General Conference of Seventh-Day Adventists), Review and Herald Publishing Association, 55 W Oak Ridge Dr, Hagerstown, MD 21740. TEL 301-393-4038, info@rhpa.org, http://www.rhpa.org. Ed. Dwain Neilson Esmond. Adv. contact Genia Blumenberg TEL 301-393-3170. B&W page USD 864, color page USD 1,440; trim 7 x 9. Circ: 11,000.

285.1 USA ISSN 1056-0548
INSIGHTS (AUSTIN). Text in English. s-a. free (effective 2005).
Supersedes in part (in 1990): Austin Presbyterian Theological Seminary. Bulletin (0191-8613)
Indexed: A21, A22, RI-1.
Published by: Austin Presbyterian Theological Seminary, 100 E 27th St, Austin, TX 78705. TEL 512-472-6736.

283.73 GBR ISSN 1748-5371
INSPIRES. Text in English. 1981. m. (10/yr). GBP 10 domestic; GBP 12 foreign; GBP 0.80 per issue (effective 2010). adv. bk.rev. **Document type:** *Magazine, Consumer.* **Description:** Covers a wide and varied range of topics of local and global interest or concern, highlighting what's going on across the province, and featuring comment, opinion and reflection from various contributors.
Former titles (until 2005): The Scottish Episcopalian (0969-4161); (until 1992): Newscan (0263-2497); Which superseded in part (in 1981): Outlook (0306-2295); Which was formerly (until 1971): Scan Advance (0305-1021)
Published by: Scottish Episcopal Church, 21 Grosvenor Crescent, Edinburgh, EH12 5EE, United Kingdom. TEL 44-131-2256357, FAX 44-131-3467247, office@scotland.anglican.org.

285 USA ISSN 1543-1975
THE INSTITUTE FOR REFORMED THEOLOGY. BULLETIN. Text in English. 1999 (Fall). irreg.
Published by: The Institute for Reformed Theology, 3401 Brook Rd., Richmond, VA 23227. TEL 804-278-4381, FAX 804-278-4393, info@reformedtheology.org, http://www.reformedtheology.com. Ed. Robert Johnson.

280.4 USA ISSN 1550-9346
INTEEN. STUDENT. Text in English. 1971. q. USD 3.49 per issue (effective 2008). illus. back issues avail. **Document type:** *Magazine, Consumer.* **Description:** Presents a christian perspective on social, economic, and ethical issues African-American teenagers face.
Published by: Urban Ministries, Inc., Dept #4870, PO Box 87618, Chicago, IL 60680. TEL 708-868-7100, 800-860-8642, FAX 708-868-7105, customerservice@urbanministries.com. Circ: 62,000.

230.071 USA ISSN 1547-0474
BV1460
INTEGRITE; a faith & learning journal. Text in English. 2002 (Fall). a. USD 10 to individuals; USD 20 to institutions (effective 2004). **Document type:** *Journal, Academic/Scholarly.*
Related titles: Online - full text ed.: ISSN 1547-0873.
Indexed: MLA-IB.
Published by: Missouri Baptist University, Faith and Learning Committee, 1 College Park Dr., St. Louis, MO 63141. TEL 314-392-2311, FAX 314-392-2390. Ed. John J. Han.

283.73 USA
INTERCHANGE (CINCINNATI). Text in English. 1971. 6/yr. USD 10 to non-members (effective 2000). adv. bk.rev. illus.; stat. back issues avail. **Document type:** *Newspaper.*
Related titles: Online - full content ed.
Published by: Episcopal Diocese of Southern Ohio, 412 Sycamore St, Cincinnati, OH 45202-4179. TEL 513-421-0311, FAX 513-421-0315. Ed., R&P Rev. John E Lawrence. Circ: 13,500.

286 CAN ISSN 0383-6061
INTERCOM (GUELPH). Text in English, French. 1968. q. adv.
Published by: Fellowship of Evangelical Baptist Churches in Canada, 679 Southgate Dr, Guelph, ON N1G 4S2, Canada. TEL 519-821-4830, FAX 519-821-9829. Ed. Rev. Terry Cuthbert. R&P Ginette Cotnoir TEL 450-621-3248.

266 USA ISSN 0272-6122
BV2350
INTERNATIONAL BULLETIN OF MISSIONARY RESEARCH. Text in English. 1950. q. USD 23 (effective 2010). adv. bk.rev. bibl.; stat. cum.index: 1977-1980, 1981-1984, 1985-1988, 1989-1992, 1993-1996, 1997-2000. 48 p./no. 2 cols./p.; back issues avail.; reprints avail. **Document type:** *Journal, Academic/Scholarly.* **Description:** Features articles and book reviews written by leading specialists on Christian mission from around the world-scholars from varied academic disciplines and theological perspectives.
Formed by the merger of: Gospel in Context (0193-8320); (1977-1980): Occasional Bulletin of Missionary Research (0364-2178); Which was formerly (until 1977): Missionary Research Library. Occasional Bulletin (0026-606X)
Related titles: Microform ed.: N.S. (from PQC); Online - full text ed.: N.S. free (effective 2010).
Indexed: A01, A02, A03, A08, A21, A22, A26, AmHI, B04, B14, BRD, BRI, CA, CBRI, CCR, CERDIC, ChPerI, ChrPI, DIP, E08, G06, G07, G08, GSS&RPL, H07, H08, H14, HAb, HumInd, I05, IBR, IBZ, M01, M02, P02, P10, P28, P48, P53, P54, PCI, PQC, PerIslam, R&TA, R05, RI-1, RI-2, S09, T02, W03, W05.
—BLDSC (4538.080000), IE, Infotrieve, Ingenta.
Published by: Overseas Ministries Study Center, 490 Prospect St, New Haven, CT 06511. TEL 203-624-6672, FAX 203-865-2857, info@omsc.org, http://www.omsc.org. Ed. Jonathan J Bonk. Adv. contact Charles A Roth.

286 CHE ISSN 0946-1507
INTERNATIONAL THEOLOGICAL STUDIES. Text in English. 1994. irreg., latest vol.4, 2002. price varies. **Document type:** *Monographic series, Academic/Scholarly.*
Published by: Peter Lang AG (Subsidiary of: Peter Lang Publishing Group), Hochfeldstr 32, Postfach 746, Bern 9, 3000, Switzerland. TEL 41-31-3061717, FAX 41-31-3061727, info@peterlang.com. Ed. Thorwald Lorenzen.

287.6 USA ISSN 0020-9678
BV1460
INTERPRETER (NASHVILLE); program ideas for United Methodists. Text in English. 1957. 8/yr. USD 8 domestic (effective 2001). adv. bk.rev.; music rev.; software rev.; video rev.; Website rev. charts; illus.; tr.lit. 44 p./no.; back issues avail. **Document type:** *Magazine, Trade.* **Description:** Targeting United Methodist leaders, emphasizes church implementation of program ideas.
Formed by the 1969 merger of: Spotlight and Methodist Story; Methodist Story
Related titles: Microfilm ed.: (from PQC); Online - full text ed.
Indexed: A22, MPI.
Published by: United Methodist Communications, PO Box 320, Nashville, TN 37202. TEL 615-742-5107, FAX 615-742-5460. Ed. M Garlinda Burton. Pub. Arvin R Luchs. R&P Tanya Simmons. Adv. contact J May TEL 847-823-4545. B&W page USD 3,250, color page USD 4,000; trim 9.38 x 7. Circ: 239,000; 20,097 (paid). **Dist by:** Banta Publishing, PO Box 305127, Nashville, TN 37230-5127. TEL 615-386-6136.

283 GBR
INTO VIEW. Text in English. q. bk.rev. **Document type:** *Newsletter.*
Published by: British Youth for Christ, Youth For Christ, PO Box 5254, Halesowen, W Mids B63 3DG, United Kingdom. TEL 44-121-550-8055, FAX 44-121-550-9979, yfc@yfc.co.uk. Ed. Lynne Norman. Circ: 8,000 (controlled).

ISLAM UND CHRISTLICHER GLAUBE/ISLAM AND CHRISTIANITY.
see RELIGIONS AND THEOLOGY—Islamic

280.4 DEU
J S - DAS MAGAZIN FUER LEUTE BEIM BUND. (Junge Soldaten) Text in German. 1986. m. EUR 4 newsstand/cover (effective 2006). adv. **Document type:** *Magazine, Consumer.*
Published by: Gemeinschaftswerk der Evangelischen Publizistik e.V., Emil-von-Behring-Str 3, Frankfurt Am Main, 60439, Germany. TEL 49-69-580980, FAX 49-69-58098272, info@gep.de, http://www.gep.de. Ed. Barbara Kamprad. adv.: page EUR 2,500. Circ: 25,810 (paid and controlled).

284.2 NLD
JAARBOEK VAN DE CHRISTELIJKE GEREFORMEERDE KERKEN IN NEDERLAND. Text in Dutch. 1909. a. EUR 9.95 (effective 2008). adv. stat. **Description:** Lists addresses of churches, ministers, church officials, church organizations, Reformed societies, and Reformed churches abroad. Also includes names of church deputees and periodicals.
Published by: (Christelijke Gereformeerde Kerken in Nederland/Mission of the Christian Reformed Churches in the Netherlands), Buijten en Schipperheijn B.V., Postbus 22708, Amsterdam, 1100 DE, Netherlands. TEL 31-20-5241010, FAX 31-20-5241011, http://www.buijten.nl, info@buijten.nl.

280.4 AUT ISSN 1013-6991
BX4841
JAHRBUCH FUER DIE GESCHICHTE DES PROTESTANTISMUS IN OESTERREICH. Text in German. 1880. a. bk.rev. **Document type:** *Bulletin, Consumer.*
Formerly (until 1980): Gesellschaft fuer die Geschichte des Protestantismus in Oesterreich. Jahrbuch (1013-6983)
Indexed: DIP, FR, IBR, IBZ, RILM.
—INIST.
Published by: Gesellschaft fuer die Geschichte des Protestantismus in Oesterreich, Rooseveltplatz 10-8, Vienna, W 1090, Austria. TEL 43-222-4791523. Ed. Gustav Reingrabner. Circ: 30.

284 DEU ISSN 0933-3835
BR1640.A1
JAHRBUCH FUER EVANGELIKALE THEOLOGIE. Text in German. 1987. a. EUR 14.90 (effective 2004).
Indexed: DIP, IBR, IBZ, IZBG, OTA.
Published by: (Arbeitskreis fuer Evangelikale Theologie), R. Brockhaus Verlag, Postfach 2220, Haan, 42766, Germany. TEL 49-2104-968600, FAX 49-2104-967880, info@brockhaus-verlag.de, http://www.brockhaus-verlag.de.

284.1 264.23 DEU ISSN 0075-2681
ML3168
➤ **JAHRBUCH FUER LITURGIK UND HYMNOLOGIE.** Text in German. 1955. a., latest vol.48, 2009. EUR 46.90 (effective 2010). bk.rev. **Document type:** *Journal, Academic/Scholarly.*
Indexed: A21, CERDIC, DIP, FR, IBR, IBZ, PCI, RI-1, RILM.
—BLDSC (4631.640000), INIST.
Published by: (International Fellowship of Research in Hymnology), Vandenhoeck und Ruprecht, Theaterstr 13, Goettingen, 37073, Germany. TEL 49-551-508440, FAX 49-551-5084422, info@v-r.de. Circ: 1,000.

283 JAM ISSN 0047-1720
JAMAICA CHURCHMAN. Text in English. 1970. m. USD 1.10, GBP 0.75. adv. illus.
Published by: Anglican Diocese of Jamaica, Anglican Church Office, Kingston, 5, Jamaica. Ed. Barbara Gloudon. Circ: 6,000.

266 JPN ISSN 0021-440X
JAPAN HARVEST. Text in English. 1951. q. JPY 2,500, USD 20; USD 25 foreign (effective 1999). adv. bk.rev. charts; illus. **Document type:** *Journal, Consumer.* **Description:** Discusses mission work in the country.

R

Published by: Japan Evangelical Missionary Association, 2-1 Kanda-Surugadai, Chiyoda-ku, Tokyo, 101-0062, Japan. TEL 81-3-3295-1949, FAX 81-3-3295-1949. Ed. Gerald B D May. R&P, Adv. contact Mizuko Matsushita TEL 81-33-295-1354. Circ: 1,200.

284.2 POL ISSN 0446-7035
BX9480.P7
JEDNOTA; miesiecznik religijno-spoleczny poswiecony polskiemu ewangelicyzmowi i ekumenii. Text in Polish. 1926. m. PLZ 24, USD 60. index. back issues avail. **Description:** For members of the Evangelical-Reformed Church and those interested in Evangelicism.
Published by: Konsystorz Kosciola Ewangelicko-Reformowanego, Al Solidarnosci 76 a, Warsaw, 00145, Poland. TEL 48-22-312383, FAX 48-22-310827. Circ: 1,000.

280.4 USA ISSN 1057-266X
BV4200
JOURNAL FOR PREACHERS. Text in English. 1977. q. USD 16 domestic; USD 19 in Canada; USD 22 elsewhere (effective 2006). **Document type:** *Journal, Academic/Scholarly.* **Description:** Covers cultural issues, theological ideas, liturgical seasons, and social concerns.
Related titles: Online - full text ed.
Indexed: A21, RI-1, RILM.
Address: PO Box 520, Decatur, GA 30031-0520.

280.4 USA ISSN 1949-8233
JOURNAL FOR STAR WISDOM. Text in English. 1991. a. USD 20 per issue (effective 2010). **Document type:** *Journal, Consumer.* **Description:** Features a guide to the connections between stellar configurations during the life of Christ and those of today.
Formerly (until 2010): Christian Star Calendar
Published by: SteinerBooks, Incorporated, 610 Main St, Great Barrington, MA 01230. TEL 413-528-8233, FAX 413-528-8826, service@steinerbooks.org.

286.7 USA ISSN 0021-8480
LC586.A3
THE JOURNAL OF ADVENTIST EDUCATION. Text in English, Portuguese, French. 1939. 5/yr. USD 18.25 domestic; USD 21.25 foreign (effective 2010). adv. bk.rev. charts; illus. index. back issues avail. **Document type:** *Journal, Academic/Scholarly.* **Description:** Features informational and practical articles on a variety of topics relating to Christian education.
Formerly (until 1967): Journal of True Education
Published by: General Conference of Seventh-Day Adventists, 12501 Old Columbia Pike, Silver Spring, MD 20904. TEL 301-680-6000, FAX 301-680-6090, http://www.adventist.org. Ed. Beverly J Robinson-Rumble.

283 GBR ISSN 1740-3553
BX5001
JOURNAL OF ANGLICAN STUDIES. Text in English. 2003 (Jun.). s-a. GBP 106, USD 203 to institutions; GBP 110, USD 209 combined subscription to institutions (print & online eds.) (effective 2012). adv. back issues avail.; reprint service avail. from PSC. **Document type:** *Journal, Academic/Scholarly.* **Description:** Covers history, theology, worship, ethics, scripture, canon law, aesthetics, education, any aspect that has a place in the tradition of Anglican faith and practice.
Related titles: Online - full text ed.: ISSN 1745-5278. GBP 104, USD 198 to institutions (effective 2012).
Indexed: A01, A02, A03, A08, CA, T02.
—IE. **CCC.**
Published by: (General Synod Office AUS), Cambridge University Press, The Edinburgh Bldg, Shaftesbury Rd, Cambridge, CB2 8RU, United Kingdom. TEL 44-1223-312393, FAX 44-1223-315052, journals@cambridge.org, http://www.cambridge.org/uk. Ed. Bruce Kaye. Adv. contact Rebecca Roberts TEL 44-1223-325083.

239 USA
JOURNAL OF CHRISTIAN APOLOGETICS. Text in English. s-a. USD 16. **Document type:** *Journal, Academic/Scholarly.* **Description:** Covers issues of philosophy, theology, biblical studies, ethics, science, and cult studies as these subjects relate to apologetics.
Related titles: CD-ROM ed.: Theological Journal Library CD. USD 99.95 New & Updated CD (effective 2004).
Published by: Michigan Theological Seminary, 41550 E. Ann Arbor Trail, Plymouth, MI 48170. TEL 888-687-2737, FAX 734-207-9582.

268.8373 USA
JOURNAL OF CHRISTIAN EDUCATION. Text in English. 1936. q. USD 25 (effective 2009). adv. bk.rev.; film rev.; rec.rev. charts; illus. **Document type:** *Journal, Consumer.* **Description:** Features new creative and productive ideas designed to expand and strengthen the educational ministry of the Church.
Former titles: Journal of Christian Education of the African Methodist Episcopal Church; (until 1982): Journal of Religious Education of the African Methodist Episcopal Church (0276-0770); (until 1980): Journal of Religious Education (0022-4219); (until 1974): Journal of Religious Education of the African Methodist Episcopal Church
Published by: African Methodist Episcopal Church, Christian Education Department, 500 Eighth Ave S, Nashville, TN 37203. TEL 800-525-7282, FAX 615-726-1866, cedoffice@ameced.com. Ed. Daryl B Ingram. **Subscr. to:** P O Box 331947, Nashville, TN 37203.

THE JOURNAL OF CHRISTIAN HEALING. *see* PSYCHOLOGY

280.4 USA ISSN 2152-6397
▼➤ **JOURNAL OF FAMILY MINISTRY.** Text in English. 2010 (Oct.). s-a. USD 30 domestic; USD 50 foreign (effective 2011). **Document type:** *Journal, Trade.* **Description:** Features news and information for family-centered churches and ministries.
Published by: Southern Baptist Theological Seminary, Center for Christian Family Ministry, 2825 Lexington Rd, Louisville, KY 40280. TEL 502-897-4347, tjones@sbts.edu. Ed. Dr. Timothy P Jones.

280.4 ARG ISSN 1668-2610
JOURNAL OF LATIN AMERICAN HERMENEUTICS. Text in English; Text occasionally in French, German. 2004. s-a. free (effective 2007). **Document type:** *Journal, Academic/Scholarly.*
Media: Online - full text.
Indexed: A01, CA, T02.
Published by: Instituto Universitario I S E D E T, Camacua 282, Buenos Aires, 1406, Argentina. TEL 54-11-46325030, FAX 54-11-46332825, info@isedet.edu.ar.

284 USA ISSN 1538-5264
BJ1251
JOURNAL OF LUTHERAN ETHICS. Text in English. 2001. m. free (effective 2009). bk.rev. back issues avail. **Document type:** *Journal, Academic/Scholarly.* **Description:** Dedicated to promoting awareness of, study of, and conversation about Christian ethics in the Lutheran tradition.
Media: Online - full text.
Published by: Evangelical Lutheran Church in America, Division for Church in Society, ELCA Churchwide Organization, 8765 W Higgins Rd, Chicago, IL 60631 . TEL 773-380-2700, 800-638-3522, FAX 773-380-1465, info@elca.org. Ed. Rev. Kaari Reierson TEL 773-380-2894.

289.94 NLD ISSN 0966-7369
BR1644
JOURNAL OF PENTECOSTAL THEOLOGY. Text in English. 1992. s-a. EUR 209, USD 293 to institutions; EUR 228, USD 319 combined subscription to institutions (print & online eds.) (effective 2012). adv. reprint service avail. from PSC. **Document type:** *Journal, Academic/Scholarly.* **Description:** Covers the areas of biblical studies, modern theology, ethics and practical theology.
Related titles: Online - full text ed.: ISSN 1745-5251. EUR 190, USD 266 to institutions (effective 2012) (from IngentaConnect).
Indexed: A01, A03, A08, A21, A22, CA, ChrPI, DIP, E01, IBR, IBZ, IZBG, R&TA, RI-1, RI-2, T02.
—IE. **CCC.**
Published by: (Church of God Theological Seminary USA), Brill, PO Box 9000, Leiden, 2300 PA, Netherlands. TEL 31-71-5353500, FAX 31-71-5317532, cs@brill.nl. Ed. John Christopher Thomas.

285 USA ISSN 1521-9216
BX8935
➤ **JOURNAL OF PRESBYTERIAN HISTORY.** Text in English. 1901. s-a. free to members (effective 2009). bk.rev. abstr.; illus.; bibl. annual. 72 p./no.; back issues avail.; reprints avail. **Document type:** *Journal, Academic/Scholarly.* **Description:** Intended to inform, nurture, and promote among its readers an understanding and appreciation of religious history in its cultural setting, specifically Presbyterian and reformed history.
Former titles (until 1997): American Presbyterians (0886-5159); (until 1985): Journal of Presbyterian History (0022-3883); (until 1962): Presbyterian Historical Society. Journal (0147-3735); (until 1943): Presbyterian Historical Society. Department of History. Journal (0149-2330); (until 1930): Presbyterian Historical Society. Journal
Related titles: Microfilm ed.; Online - full text ed.
Indexed: A20, A21, A22, ASCA, AmH&L, ArtHuCI, BAS, BEL&L, CA, CurCont, DIP, FR, HistAb, IBR, IBZ, PCI, R&TA, RI-1, RI-2, RILM, SCOPUS, T02, W07.
—INIST.
Published by: Presbyterian Historical Society (Subsidiary of: Presbyterian Church - U.S.A.), 425 Lombard St, Philadelphia, PA 19147. TEL 215-627-1852, FAX 215-627-0509, refdesk@history.pcusa.org.

285.235 GBR ISSN 0967-3938
BR770
➤ **JOURNAL OF WELSH RELIGIOUS HISTORY.** Text mainly in English; Text occasionally in Welsh. 1993; N.S. 2001. a., latest vol.2, 2002. GBP 14 domestic; GBP 16 foreign (effective 2003). bk.rev. bibl.; charts; illus.; maps. 128 p./no. 1 cols./p.; back issues avail. **Document type:** *Journal, Academic/Scholarly.*
Formed by the merger of (1946-1993): Historical Society of the Church in Wales. Journal; (1984-1993): Journal of Welsh Ecclesiastical History (0266-5603)
Indexed: BrArAb, HistAb.
Published by: Centre for the Advanced study of Religion in Wales, c/o Dr. G. Tudur, Dept. of Theology, University of Wales Bangor, Bangor, LL57 2DG, United Kingdom. TEL 44-1248-382079, FAX 44-1248-383759. Eds. D D Morgan, Geraint Tudur, Robert Pope. Pub. Geraint Tudur. Circ: 300 (paid).

259.2 USA ISSN 1541-0412
THE JOURNAL OF YOUTH MINISTRY; the academic journal of youth ministry educators. Text in English. 2002. s-a. USD 25 domestic to individuals; USD 30 to institutions; USD 30 foreign (effective 2002).
Related titles: Online - full text ed.
Indexed: A01, A02, A03, A08, A21, CA, ChrPI, T02.
Published by: Gordon College, Dept. of Youth Ministries, Frost Hall, 255 Grapevine Rd., Wenham, MA 01984. TEL 978-927-2300, http://www.gordon.edu/youthmin/. Ed. Mark Cannister.

280.4 AUS ISSN 0817-4466
BX9890.U34
JOURNEY. Text in English. 1987. 11/yr. (except Jan.). free to members (effective 2009). adv. bk.rev.; film rev. charts; illus. 12 p./no.; back issues avail. **Document type:** *Newspaper.*
Former titles (until 1986): Life and Times (0314-6235); (until 1977): The Methodist Times; (until 1950): Queensland Methodist Times; (until 1927): The Methodist Leader; Which was formed by the merger of (1889-18??): The Queensland Christian Witness and Methodist Journal; (189?-1897): The Christian Ensign
Related titles: Microfilm ed.
Published by: Uniting Church in Australia Queensland Synod, 60 Bayliss St, Auchenflower, PO Box 674, Brisbane, QLD 4001, Australia. TEL 61-7-33779910, FAX 61-7-33779796, http://www.ucaqld.com.au. Ed. Bruce Mullan TEL 61-7-33779801. Adv. contact Mardi Lumsden TEL 61-7-33779795. Circ: 15,500.

286.132 USA ISSN 1073-4473
JOURNEY: A WOMAN'S GUIDE TO INTIMACY WITH GOD. Text in English. 1994. m. USD 24.95; USD 3.50 per issue (effective 2008). adv. back issues avail. **Document type:** *Magazine, Consumer.* **Description:** Offers guidance for a growing, personal relationship with god and also deals with issues and real-life situations.
Published by: LifeWay Christian Resources, 1 Lifeway Plz, Nashville, TN 37234. TEL 615-251-2000, 800-458-2772, FAX 615-251-5933, customerservice@lifeway.com. Circ: 217,000.

JOYCE; Was Frauen inspiriert. *see* WOMEN'S INTERESTS

280.4082 USA ISSN 0164-4882
THE JOYFUL WOMAN; a fresh perspective on biblical living. Text in English. 1978. bi-m. USD 19.95 domestic; USD 26.95 foreign (effective 2001). adv. bk.rev. illus. back issues avail. **Document type:** *Magazine, Consumer.* **Description:** Covers every facet of a Christian woman's life.
Published by: Joyful Christian Ministries, PO Box 90028, Chattanooga, TN 37412. TEL 423-892-6753, FAX 423-892-4902. Ed. Carol Parks. R&P, Adv. contact Reba Bowman. B&W page USD 716, color page USD 820. Circ: 6,000.

280.4 USA ISSN 0893-1607
JUBILEE; the monthly newsletter of Prison Fellowship. Text in English. 1977. m. free. **Document type:** *Newsletter.*
Published by: Prison Fellowship, 2204, Ashburn, VA 20146-9104. TEL 703-478-0100, FAX 703-478-0452. Ed. Becky Beane. Circ: 180,000.

285.834 AUT ISSN 0022-6289
JUNGE GEMEINDE; das Magazin fuer evangelische Kinder- und Jugendarbeit. Text in German. 1948. q. adv. bk.rev.; film rev. abstr. 24 p./no.; back issues avail. **Document type:** *Magazine, Consumer.* **Description:** Contains information of interest to those involved in evangelical work with Austrian youth. Includes readers' letters, reports and announcements of events.
Published by: Evangelische Jugend Oesterreich, Liechtensteinstr 20, Vienna, W 1090, Austria. TEL 43-1-3179266, FAX 43-1-317926716, office@ejoe.at, http://start.at/ejoe. Ed. Thomas Dasek. Adv. contact Joachim Hoffleit. Circ: 3,800.

JUNGSCHAR; Christliche Zeitschrift fuer Kids. *see* CHILDREN AND YOUTH—For

285 CUB ISSN 0864-0254
JUPRECU. Text in Spanish. 3/yr.
Published by: Iglesia Presbiteriana, Apdo. 154, Matanzas, Cuba. TEL 809 61-1558. Ed. Francisco Marrero.

280.4 USA ISSN 1069-3459
JUST BETWEEN US. Text in English. 1992. q. USD 14.95 (effective 2001). adv. bk.rev. 32 p./no.; back issues avail. **Description:** Published for ministry wives and women in church and missions leadership to provide encouragement, support and inspiration from a biblical perspective.
Related titles: E-mail ed.; Fax ed.; Online - full text ed.
Indexed: CCR, ChrPI.
Published by: Telling the Truth Media Ministries, 777 S Barker Rd, Brookfield, WI 53045. TEL 262-786-6478, 800-260-3342, FAX 262-796-5752, http://www.tellingthetruth.org. Ed. Jill Briscoe. R&P Suzan Braun. Adv. contact Tempy McCombe TEL 262-780-1817. Circ: 7,500 (paid).

287.6 USA ISSN 1073-8479
KALEIDOSCOPE (COLUMBIA); a magazine about today's Christians. Text in English. 1993. bi-m. USD 18. adv. bk.rev. **Document type:** *Magazine, Consumer.* **Description:** Written for and about active Christians striving to make a positive difference in today's world.
Published by: Balto-Washington Conference, United Methodists, 9720 Patuxent Woods Dr, Ste 100, Columbia, MD 21046-1526. TEL 800-492-2525. Ed. James E Skillington. Adv. contact Trisk Twentey. B&W page USD 2,675, color page USD 3,025; trim 10.88 x 8.25. Circ: 110,000.

280.4 AUS
KEEPING IN TOUCH. Text in English. 3/yr. **Document type:** *Newsletter.*
Media: Online - full text.
Published by: The Full Gospel Churches of Australia, 184 Williams Rd, Caboolture, QLD 4510, Australia. TEL 61-7-54952124, FAX 61-7-54958500, office@fullgospelaustralia.org.au.

280.4 NLD ISSN 1568-8712
KERKBEHEER. Text in Dutch. 2001. 11/yr. EUR 25 to non-members; EUR 22 to members (effective 2010). adv. **Document type:** *Bulletin, Trade.* **Description:** Covers financial accounting and administration for churches.
Formed by the merger of (1952-2001): Administratie en Beheer (0165-4527); (1959-2001): Kerkvoogdij (0167-255X); Which was formerly (1927-1959): Vereeniging van Kerkvoogdijen in de Nederlandsche Hervormde Ker. Maandblad (0929-2152); (1920-1927): Orgaan van de Vereeniging van Kerkvoogdijen in de Nederlandsche Hervormde Kerk (0929-2144)
Published by: (Landelijk Verband van Commissies van Beheer van de Gereformeerde Kerken in Nederland), Vereniging voor Kerkrentmeesterlijk Beheer, Postbus 176, Dordrecht, 3300 AD, Netherlands. TEL 31-78-6393666, FAX 31-78-6315949, info@kerkrentmeester.nl, http://www.kerkrentmeester.nl. Ed. R M Belder TEL 31-78-6393661. adv.: B&W page EUR 464; 17.6 x 26. Circ: 8,000.

284.2 ZAF ISSN 0023-0596
KERKBLAD. Text in Afrikaans. 1873. fortn. ZAR 107 (effective 1999). adv. bk.rev.
Published by: (Gereformeerde Kerke in Suid-Afrika/Reformed Churches in South Africa), Deputate Kerklike Tydskrifte GKSA, PO Box 20008, Noordbrug, Potchefstroom 2522, South Africa. Ed. M Venter. Circ: 9,300.

284.2 ZAF
DIE KERKBODE; amptelike blad van die Nederduitse Gereformeerde Kerk. Text in Afrikaans. 1849. s-m. (20/yr.). USD 2 (effective 2001). adv. bk.rev. back issues avail. **Document type:** *Newspaper.*
Indexed: ISAP.
Published by: Nederduitse Gereformeerde Kerk in Suid-Afrika/Dutch Reformed Church in South Africa, PO Box 4445, Pretoria, 0001, South Africa. TEL 27-12-3228900, FAX 27-12-3223803, http://www.ngkerk.org.za. Ed. G S J Moller. adv.: B&W page ZAR 7,469, color page ZAR 9,816; 260 x 380. Circ: 44,350.

284.1 NLD ISSN 1380-460X
KERKINFORMATIE. Text in Dutch. 1994. m. (11/yr.). EUR 17.50 domestic; EUR 24 foreign (effective 2010). adv. **Document type:** *Magazine, Consumer.*
Published by: Protestantse Kerk in Nederland, Protestants Landelijk Dienstencentrum, Postbus 8504, Utrecht, 3503 RM, Netherlands. TEL 31-30-8801880, FAX 31-30-8801300, servicedesk@pkn.nl, http://www.pkn.nl. adv.: color page EUR 2,250; trim 210 x 297. Circ: 14,500.

287.9 AUS
KID ZONE. Text in English. 1890. w. illus. **Document type:** *Newspaper.*
Formerly: Young Soldier (0300-3264)
Published by: (Salvation Army GBR), Salvation Army, Australia Eastern Territory Territorial Headquarters, 140 Elizabeth St, PO Box A435, Sydney South, NSW 1232, Australia. TEL 61-2-92641711, http://www.salvos.org.au. Circ: 15,000.

287.96 GBR ISSN 1363-5662
KIDS ALIVE. Text in English. 1881. w. GBP 25 (effective 2010). bk.rev.; rec.rev. illus. **Document type:** *Magazine, Consumer.* **Description:** Contains quizzes, puzzles, craft activities, recipes, posters, competitions and cartoon Bible stories.
Formerly (until 1996): Young Soldier (0044-0906)
Published by: Salvation Army, London NE DHQ, Maldon Road, Hatfield Peverel, Chelmsford, Essex CM3 2HL, United Kingdom. TEL 44-1245-383000, londonnortheast@salvationarmy.org.uk, http://www1.salvationarmy.org.uk/uki/www_uki.nsf.

263.1 USA
KIDS' MINISTRY IDEAS. Abbreviated title: K M I. Text in English. 1971. q. USD 27.45 (effective 2009). adv. **Document type:** *Magazine, Consumer.* **Description:** Designed to bringing teacher/leader growth and continued training to those in the forefront of children's ministry.
Formerly (until 1998): Kids' Stuff
Published by: (General Conference of Seventh-Day Adventists), Review and Herald Publishing Association, 55 W Oak Ridge Dr, Hagerstown, MD 21740. TEL 301-393-3178, info@rhpa.org, http://www.rhpa.org. Ed. Candy DeVore. Adv. contact Genia Blumenberg TEL 301-393-3170. B&W page USD 468, color page USD 702; trim 8.125 x 10.625. Circ: 3,500.

286.732 ZAF
KINDERGARTEN. Text in English. 1994. q. illus.
Published by: South African Union Conference of Seventh-Day Adventists, PO Box 468, Bloemfontein, 9300, South Africa.

286.732 ZAF
KINDERTUIN. Text in Afrikaans. q. illus.
Formerly (until 1994): Primkin-maatjie Kindertuin
Published by: South African Union Conference of Seventh-Day Adventists, PO Box 468, Bloemfontein, 9300, South Africa.

280.4 USA ISSN 2153-4055
▼ **THE KINGDOM BELIEVER'S JOURNAL.** Text in English. 2010 (Apr.). q. USD 10; USD 3 newsstand/cover (effective 2011). **Document type:** *Journal, Consumer.* **Description:** Features Bible verses and instruction on living God's kingdom principle.
Related titles: Online - full text ed.: ISSN 2153-4616. 2010 (Apr.).
Published by: Barrye Harmon Ministries, PO Box 701055, Tulsa, OK 74170. TEL 918-574-2314, pastor@barryeharmon.com.

284 DEU ISSN 0949-8672
DIE KIRCHE; evangelische Wochenzeitung in Mitteldeutschland. Text in German. 1979. w. EUR 42 domestic; EUR 52 foreign; EUR 21 to students; EUR 0.85 newsstand/cover (effective 2009). adv. **Document type:** *Newspaper, Consumer.*
Formerly (until 1995): Die Kirche. Ausgabe fuer die Kirchenprovinz Sachsen (0232-5098)
Published by: Wartburg Verlag GmbH, Lisztstr 2a, Weimar, 99423, Germany. TEL 49-3643-246144, FAX 49-3643-246118, buch@wartburgverlag.de, http://www.guh-cms.de/wv/catalog/index.php. Ed. Martin Hanusch. Adv. contact Stefanie Rost. Circ: 4,192 (paid and controlled).

280.4 DEU ISSN 0173-4636
BV638
KIRCHE IM LAENDLICHEN RAUM. Text in German. 1950. q. EUR 15 (effective 2009). bk.rev. back issues avail. **Document type:** *Bulletin, Consumer.*
Former titles (until 1979): Kirche im Dorf (0450-3007); (until 1953): Deutscher Dorfkirchenfreund (0173-4601)
Published by: Evangelische Landjugendakademie, Dieperzbergweg 13-17, Altenkirchen, 57610, Germany. TEL 49-2681-95160, FAX 49-2681-70206, info@lja.de. Ed. Werner Jung.

285.734 DEU ISSN 0075-6210
BX8020.A2
KIRCHLICHES JAHRBUCH FUER DIE EVANGELISCHE KIRCHE IN DEUTSCHLAND. Text in German. a. EUR 36.95 (effective 2010). **Document type:** *Yearbook, Academic/Scholarly.*
Indexed: DIP, IBR, IBZ.
Published by: Guetersloher Verlagshaus (Subsidiary of: Verlagsgruppe Random House GmbH), Carl-Miele-Str 214, Guetersloh, 33311, Germany. TEL 49-5241-74050, FAX 49-5241-740548, info@gtvh.de, http://www.gtvh.de.

284.1 CAN
KIRKEBLADET/CHURCH NEWSLETTER. Text in Danish, English. 1935. m. adv. illus. **Document type:** *Newsletter.* **Description:** Publishes news, information on heritage of the church and community, as well as news from Denmark.
Published by: The Danish Lutheran Church of Vancouver, 6010 Kincaid St, Burnaby, BC V5G 4N3, Canada. TEL 604-298-6112, FAX 604-525-9840, glud@msn.com. Ed. Kai Glud. Circ: 1,550.

284.1489 266 DNK ISSN 0905-071X
KIRKELIG FORENING FOR DEN INDRE MISSION I DANMARK. AARBOG. Text in Danish. 1906. a. adv. illus. **Description:** Contains reports of Den Kirkelige Forening for den Indre Mission i Danmark.
Formerly (until 1988): Det Nye Aar (0108-8297)
Published by: Kirkelig Forening for den Indre Mission/The Church Association for the Inner Mission in Denmark, Korskaersvej 25, Fredericia, 7000, Denmark. TEL 45-75-926100, FAX 45-75-926146, post@indremission.dk, http://www2.indremission.dk.

284.1 ISL ISSN 1021-8351
KIRKJURITID. Text in Icelandic. 1935. q.
Indexed: RILM.
Published by: Prestafelag Islands, Kirkjutorg 4, Reykjavik, Iceland. TEL 354-562-1525.

KLARTEXT. *see* CHILDREN AND YOUTH—For

268 ZAF ISSN 0023-270X
➤ **KOERS**; bulletin vir Christelike wetenskap - bulletin for Christian scholarship. Text in Afrikaans, English; Summaries in English, Afrikaans. 1934. 4/yr. ZAR 80 domestic; USD 35 foreign (effective 2003). bk.rev.; video rev. abstr.; bibl. index. back issues avail. **Document type:** *Journal, Academic/Scholarly.*
Indexed: ISAP, OTA.
Published by: (Potchefstroom University for Christian Higher Education/ Potchefstroomse Universiteit vir Christelike Hoer Onderwys), Buro vir Wetenskaplike Tydskrifte/Bureau for Scholarly Journals, Private Bag X6001, Potchefstroom, 2520, South Africa. TEL 27-18-299-4081, FAX 27-18-299-4084, bwtscl@puknet.puk.ac.za, http://www.puk.ac.za. Ed. Annette L Combrink. R&P Susan Lourens TEL 27-18-299-4081. Circ: 300. **Co-sponsor:** Die Koersvereniging.

230.044 USA ISSN 1047-1057
BR1
➤ **KOINONIA**; the Princeton Theological Seminary graduate forum. Text in English; Text occasionally in French, German, Greek, Hebrew. 1989. a. bk.rev. bibl. back issues avail. **Document type:** *Journal, Academic/Scholarly.* **Description:** Promotes interdisciplinary discussion of new and emerging areas and issues in the study of religion and theology.
Indexed: A21, RI-1, RI-2.
Published by: Princeton Theological Seminary, 64 Mercer St, PO Box 821, Princeton, NJ 08542. TEL 609-921-8300, http://www3.ptsem.edu.

280.4 DEU ISSN 1611-325X
KOMM!; Magazin fuer junge Christ. Text in German. 1997. bi-m. EUR 14.90 (effective 2009). **Document type:** *Magazine, Consumer.*
Published by: Christliche Verlagsgesellschaft mbH, Moltkestr 1, Dillenburg, 35683, Germany. TEL 49-2771-83020, FAX 49-2771-830230, info@cv-dillenburg.de, http://www.cv-dillenburg.de.

280.4 CZE ISSN 0139-505X
KOSTNICKE JISKRY. Variant title: Evangelicky Tydenik. Text in Czech. 1919. w. CZK 481 (effective 2010). adv. **Document type:** *Magazine, Consumer.*
Published by: Kostnicka Jednota, Jecna 19, Prague 2, 120 00, Czech Republic. TEL 420-224-919607. Ed. Ladislav Meckovsky.

284.1 DEU
KREIS DER FREUNDE UND FOERDERER DER LUTHERISCHEN THEOLOGISCHEN HOCHSCHULE IN OBERURSEL. MITTEILUNGEN. Text in German. 1960. 2/yr. **Document type:** *Newsletter.*
Published by: Kreis der Freunde und Foerderer der Lutherischen Theologischen Hochschule in Oberursel e.V., Altkoenigstr 150, Oberursel, 61440, Germany. Ed. Wilhelm Rothfuchs.

286.96 DEU
DER KRIEGSRUF; Zeitschrift der Heilsarmee. Text in German. 1890. w. EUR 33 domestic; EUR 50 foreign (effective 2005). bk.rev.; rec.rev. 12 p./no.; back issues avail. **Document type:** *Corporate.* **Description:** Official organ of the Salvation Army in Germany.
Related titles: E-mail ed.; Fax ed.; Online - full text ed.
Published by: Heilsarmee Verlag, Salierring 23-27, Cologne, 50677, Germany. TEL 49-221-208190, FAX 49-221-2081943. Circ: 15,000.

285 MWI
KUUNIKA. 1909. m. bk.rev.
Published by: (Christian Literature Fund), Presbyterian Church of Central Africa, Nkhoma Synod, P.O. Nkhoma, Lilongwe, Malawi. Ed. Rev. M C Nkhalambayausi. Circ: 6,000.

284.1 SWE ISSN 0345-6757
BX8001
KYRKA OCH FOLK. Text in Swedish. 1924. w. SEK 320 domestic; SEK 350 in Nordic countries; SEK 420 elsewhere (effective 2001). adv. 12 p./no. 3 cols./p.; **Document type:** *Newspaper.* **Description:** Covers the interests of the members of the Church of Sweden.
Published by: Kyrkliga Foerbundet foer Evangelisk-Luthersk Tro, Traringen 52 1/2, Goeteborg, 41679, Sweden. TEL 46-31-7074293, FAX 46-31-7074295. Ed. Josef Axelsson. R&P Per Anders Grunnan TEL 46-31-7074294. Adv. contact Jan Sandstrom.

284.1 SWE ISSN 0283-7846
KYRKFACK. Text in Swedish. 1954. 4/yr. SEK 120 (effective 2001). **Document type:** *Newsletter.*
Former titles (until 1986): Svenska Kyrkans Personalfoerbund - Meddelande; (until 1979): Svenska Praestfoerbundet - Meddelande; (until 1967): Meddelanden fraan Svenska Praestfoerbundet
Published by: Kyrkans Akademikerforbund, PO Box 19609, Stockholm, 10432, Sweden. TEL 46-8-441-85-60, FAX 46-8-441-85-77. Ed. Bror Holm.

284.1 SWE ISSN 0345-682X
KYRKLIG SAMLING KRING BIBELN OCH BEKAENNELSEN; informationsblad som utges av Kyrklig Samlings stoedfoerening. Variant title: Kring Bibeln och Bekaennelsen. Text in Swedish. 1960. irreg. (4-6/yr.). SEK 25 (effective 1993).
Published by: Kyrklig Samling, I Nordanstig, Kaerrdalsv 42, Goeteborg, 41729, Sweden.

284.2 ZAF
L I G. Text in Afrikaans. 1937. w. adv. bk.rev. illus.
Formerly: Die Voorligter (0042-8728)
Related titles: Online - full text ed.: Lig. ISSN 1605-9018. 2000.
Indexed: CERDIC, ISAP.
Published by: Nederduitse Gereformeerde Kerk in Suid-Afrika/Dutch Reformed Church in South Africa, Privaatsak X18, Wellington, 7654, South Africa. TEL 27-21-864-8200, FAX 27-21-864-8242, http://www.ngkerk.org.za. Circ: 132,000.

261.8328 USA
L I R S BULLETIN. Text in English. 1964. 2/yr. free to qualified personnel. **Document type:** *Bulletin.* **Description:** Articles about immigration ranging from news of previous immigrants to why the church is involved in helping refugees. Updates on LIRS activities in resettlement and advocacy, and on developments in US immigration policy.
Formerly: L I R S Information Bulletin
Published by: Lutheran Immigration and Refugee Service, 700 Light St, Baltimore, MD 21230-3850. TEL 212-532-6350, FAX 212-683-1329. Ed. Benjamin Bankson. Circ: 6,000.

284.1 CHE ISSN 0174-1756
BX8001
L W F DOCUMENTATION/LUTHERISCHE RUNDSCHAU. Text in English. 1954. irreg., latest vol.50, 2005. price varies. bk.rev. index. **Document type:** *Monographic series, Academic/Scholarly.*
Supersedes in part (in 1978): Lutheran World (0024-760X)
Related titles: Online - full text ed.
Indexed: A21, CERDIC, CWI, DIP, FR, IBR, IBZ, RI-1, RI-2. —BLDSC (5309.530000), Ingenta, INIST.
Published by: Lutheran World Federation, 150 Route de Ferney, Geneva 20, 1211, Switzerland. TEL 41-22-7916111, FAX 41-22-7916630, info@lutheranworld.org, http://www.lutheranworld.org. Circ: 4,595.

284.1 CHE ISSN 1025-2290
L W F STUDIES. Text in English. 1993. irreg. **Document type:** *Monographic series, Academic/Scholarly.*
Related titles: Online - full text ed.
Indexed: CWI.
Published by: Lutheran World Federation, 150 Route de Ferney, Geneva 20, 1211, Switzerland. TEL 41-22-7916111, FAX 41-22-7916630, info@lutheranworld.org, http://www.lutheranworld.org.

280.4 USA ISSN 0893-5262
LAD. Text in English. 1987. m. USD 1.29 per issue (effective 2011). illus. back issues avail. **Document type:** *Magazine, Consumer.* **Description:** Provides students in grades 1-3 with devotional readings and humor. Discusses ministry activities.
Indexed: AgrLib.
Published by: North American Mission Board, 4200 N Point Pky, Alpharetta, GA 30022. TEL 770-410-6000, 800-634-2462, FAX 770-410-6082, http://www.namb.net/.

280.4 USA ISSN 1096-5890
LATIN AMERICA EVANGELIST. Text in English. 1921. q. GBP 121, USD 10 (effective 2000). **Document type:** *Magazine, Consumer.* **Description:** Focuses on Latin America and the Christian Church there.
Indexed: CCR.
Published by: Latin America Mission, PO Box 52 7900, Miami, FL 33152. TEL 305-884-8400, FAX 305-885-8649, evangelist@lam.org, http://www.lam.org. Ed. Susan J. Griswold Loobie. Pub. David R Befus. R&P Susan J Griswold Loobie. Circ: 17,000.

263.1 USA ISSN 1942-4221
LEAD; leadership - education - advent - discipleship. Text in English. 198?. q. USD 34.95 (effective 2009). adv. **Document type:** *Magazine, Consumer.* **Description:** Provides program ideas, training and encouragement for people who are leading out in Sabbath schools in the Seventh-day Adventist church.
Former titles (until 2008): Sabbath School Leadership (1092-082X); (until 1997): Celebration (0887-1094)
Related titles: Spanish ed.
Published by: (General Conference of Seventh-Day Adventists), Review and Herald Publishing Association, 55 W Oak Ridge Dr, Hagerstown, MD 21740. TEL 301-393-4095, info@rhpa.org, http://www.rhpa.org. Ed. Faith Johnson Crumbly. Adv. contact Genia Blumenberg TEL 301-393-3170. B&W page USD 813; trim 8.125 x 10.625. Circ: 8,200.

280.4 DEU ISSN 0343-4591
LEBENDIGE SEELSORGE; Zeitschrift fuer alle Fragen der Seelsorge. Text in German. 1949. bi-m. EUR 32.20; EUR 24 to students; EUR 6.40 newsstand/cover (effective 2010). bk.rev. **Document type:** *Magazine, Consumer.*
Related titles: ◆ Supplement(s): Lebendige Katechese. ISSN 0171-4171.
Indexed: DIP, E-psyche, IBR, IBZ.
Published by: Echter Verlag GmbH, Dominikanerplatz 8, Wuerzburg, 97070, Germany. TEL 49-931-660680, FAX 49-931-6606823, info@echter-verlag.de, http://www.echter.de. Ed. Erich Garhammer. Circ: 4,000.

280.4 DEU ISSN 1865-2972
LEBENSLAUF; Wach glauben - mutig handeln - dankbar geniessen. Text in German. 1970. bi-m. EUR 22.80; EUR 4.60 newsstand/cover (effective 2011). adv. **Document type:** *Magazine, Consumer.*
Former titles (until 2007): 55plus (1612-8133); (until 2003): Senior (0342-7544)
Published by: Bundes Verlag GmbH, Bodenborn 43, Witten, 58452, Germany. TEL 49-2302-930930, FAX 49-2302-93093689, info@bundes-verlag.de, http://www.bundes-verlag.de. Ed. Ulrich Eggers. Adv. contact Juergen Bublitz. Circ: 13,000 (paid and controlled).

268 USA ISSN 0889-4051
LECCIONES CRISTIANAS. LIBRO DEL MAESTRO. Text in Spanish. 1986. q. **Document type:** *Journal, Trade.* —CCC.
Published by: Cokesbury, 201 8th Ave, S, PO Box 801, Nashville, TN 37202. TEL 615-749-6000, 800-672-1789, FAX 615-749-6578, cokes_serv@cokesbury.com, http://www.cokesbury.com.

284.1 DEU ISSN 0931-6191
LERNORT GEMEINDE; Zeitschrift fuer Theologische Praxis. Text in German. 1984. 4/yr. EUR 25; EUR 7.50 newsstand/cover (effective 2006). adv. **Document type:** *Magazine, Consumer.*
Published by: Lutherisches Verlagshaus GmbH, Knochenhauerstr 38-40, Hannover, 30159, Germany. TEL 49-511-1241720, FAX 49-511-3681098, info@lvh.de, http://www.lvh.de. adv.: B&W page EUR 500. Circ: 1,200 (paid and controlled).

280.4 DEU ISSN 0173-4199
DIE LESEPREDIGT. Text in German. 1967. a. EUR 49.95 (effective 2010). **Document type:** *Bulletin, Consumer.*
Published by: Guetersloher Verlagshaus (Subsidiary of: Verlagsgruppe Random House GmbH), Carl-Miele-Str 214, Guetersloh, 33311, Germany. TEL 49-5241-74050, FAX 49-5241-740548, info@gtvh.de, http://www.gtvh.de.

280.4 CAN ISSN 0829-0954
LIBERATION. Text in English. 1972. q. free. illus. **Document type:** *Newsletter, Consumer.*
Formerly (until 1984): Encounter (0315-0097)
Indexed: GSS&RPL.
Published by: Wilderness Ministries, c/o Ken Campbell, PO Box 130, Tumbler Ridge, BC V0C 2W0, Canada. TEL 250-242-3525, kencampbell@kencampbell.ca, http://www.kencampbell.ca. Ed. Ken Cambell. Circ: 35,000.

LIBRARIANS' CHRISTIAN FELLOWSHIP NEWSLETTER (ONLINE). *see* LIBRARY AND INFORMATION SCIENCES

230 USA ISSN 1048-4698
LIBRARY OF EARLY CHRISTIANITY. Text in English. 1986. irreg. **Document type:** *Monographic series, Academic/Scholarly.*
Published by: Westminster John Knox Press, Rm 2047, 100 Witherspoon St, Louisville, KY 40202. TEL 502-569-5052, FAX 502-569-8308, publicity@wjkbooks.com, http://www.ppcbooks.com.

280.4 DEU ISSN 0047-4584
BX8001
LICHT UND LEBEN. Text in German. 1889. m. adv. bk.rev. **Document type:** *Bulletin.* **Description:** Aims to disseminate knowledge about the Bible and Christianity. Discusses missionary activities.
Published by: (Evangelische Gesellschaft fuer Deutschland e.V.), Schriftenmission, Kaiserstr 78, Wuppertal, 42329, Germany. TEL 49-202-27850-0, FAX 49-202-2785040. Ed. Volker Heckl. Adv. contact Herbert Becker. Circ: 6,000.

R

283 DEU
LICHTSTRAHLEN; taegliche Bibellese. Text in German. 1897. a. EUR 4.50 (effective 2009). **Document type:** *Magazine, Consumer.*
Published by: (Deutscher E C - Verband), Born-Verlag, Leuschnerstr 74, Kassel, 34134, Germany. TEL 49-561-4095107, FAX 49-561-4095112, info.born@ec-jugend.de, http://www.born-buch.de. Circ: 50,000.

285.233 GBR ISSN 0024-306X
BX9075.A1
LIFE & WORK. Text in English. 1879. m. GBP 22 domestic (effective 2009). bk.rev. illus. back issues avail. **Document type:** *Magazine, Consumer.* **Description:** Contains wide range of articles, news and views relating to the life of the church and its people in Scotland.
Related titles: Online - full text ed.; Gaelic ed.
Indexed: CERDIC.
Published by: Church of Scotland, 121 George St, Edinburgh, EH2 4YN, United Kingdom. TEL 44-131-2255722, FAX 44-131-2402207. Ed. Lynne McNeil.

286.6 NZL ISSN 2230-2646
▼ **LIFE INTEGRATING FAITH TOGETHER.** Abbreviated title: L I F T. Text in English. 2010. q. NZD 12 domestic; NZD 15 in Australia; NZD 20 elsewhere (effective 2011). adv. back issues avail. **Document type:** *Magazine, Consumer.*
Published by: Windsor Park Baptist Church, Mairangi Bay, PO Box 65275, Auckland, 0754, New Zealand. http://www.windsorpark.org.nz/. Ed. Julie Belding. Adv. contact Debbie McCann TEL 64-9-4770002.

286.132 USA ISSN 1557-4865
LIFE WORDS: K J V LEADER GUIDE. (King James Version) Variant title: Life Words: King James Version Leader Guide. Text in English. 1956. q. USD 9.55 (effective 2009). back issues avail. **Document type:** *Magazine, Consumer.* **Description:** Focuses on the development of godly values, growth in biblical knowledge, and understanding of a life of Christlike excellence.
Former titles (until 2006): Family Bible Series. Adult Learner Guide K J V (1526-5269); (until 2000): Family Bible Series: Adult Teacher (1079-5243); (until 1996): Adult Teacher (0400-5880)
Related titles: Online - full text ed.: free.
Published by: LifeWay Christian Resources, 1 Lifeway Plz, Nashville, TN 37234. TEL 615-251-2000, 800-458-2772, FAX 615-251-5933, customerservice@lifeway.com, http://www.lifeway.com.

286.132 USA ISSN 1557-4873
LIFE WORDS: K J V LEADER GUIDE (LARGE PRINT EDITION). (King James Version) Variant title: Bible Studies for Life: Lifewords K J V Learner Guide Large Print. Life Words K J V Learner Guide. Text in English. q. USD 9.75 (effective 2009). back issues avail. **Document type:** *Magazine, Consumer.* **Description:** Helps teachers effectively guide adults of all ages in purposeful bible study.
Former titles (until 2006): Family Bible Series. Adult Learner Guide K J V (Large Print Edition) (1526-5277); (until 2000): Family Bible Series. Senior Adults; Sunday School Senior Adults (0585-9328)
Media: Large Type (14 pt.). **Related titles:** Audio CD ed.: USD 57.55 (effective 2009); Online - full text ed.: free.
Published by: LifeWay Christian Resources, 1 Lifeway Plz, Nashville, TN 37234. TEL 615-251-2000, 800-458-2772, FAX 615-251-5933, customerservice@lifeway.com, http://www.lifeway.com. Ed. Michael Livingston.

284.1 USA ISSN 1098-5859
LIFEDATE. Text in English. 1986. q. free. stat. back issues avail. **Document type:** *Newsletter.* **Description:** Features news and commentary from a Biblical Law/Gospel perspective on life issues such as abortion,chastity, euthanasia and end of life.
Related titles: Online - full text ed.
Published by: Lutherans For Life, 1229 South G Ave, Bldg B, Bldg B, Ste 100, Nevada, IA 50201-2778. TEL 515-382-2077, 888-364-5433, FAX 515-382-3020, info@lutheransforlife.org, http://www.lutheransforlife.org. Ed., R&P Lowell J Highby. Pub. Rev. Dr. James I Lamb. Circ: 18,000.

280.4 028.5 USA ISSN 2155-2770
▼ **LIFEWAY KIDS WORSHIP BULLETINS.** Text in English. forthcoming 2010 (Oct.). q. USD 12.95 per issue (effective 2011). **Document type:** *Bulletin, Consumer.* **Description:** Offers age-appropriate activities that help reinforce what kids learn in Sunday School.
Media: CD-ROM.
Published by: LifeWay Christian Resources, 1 Lifeway Plz, Nashville, TN 37234. TEL 615-251-2000, FAX 615-251-5933, customerservice@lifeway.com, http://www.lifeway.com.

284.2 ZAF
LIGDRAER. Text in English. 1940. m. ZAR 46.63; ZAR 117.03 foreign (effective 1998). adv. bk.rev. bibl.; illus.; stat. index. **Document type:** *Newspaper.* **Description:** Provides articles relevant to Christian daily life, news about the church at an international, national and congregational level.
Former titles: Ligdraer - Ligstraal; Ligdraer (0024-3272); Which incorporates: Ligstraal
Published by: Uniting Reformed Church in Southern Africa, Private Bag X1, Belhar, 7507, South Africa. TEL 27-21-9522151, FAX 27-21-9528638. Ed. Dr. P J A Fourie. Adv. contact S A Petersen. Circ: 21,000.

266 USA
LIGHT AMONG THE LEAST REACHED. Text in English. 1962. q. free. bk.rev. **Document type:** *Newsletter.* **Description:** Provides information and reports on ministries which establish churches in many lands, primarily among Asian-people groups.
Formerly: Eastern Challenge (0898-9346)
Published by: Christar, PO Box 14866, Reading, PA 19612-4866. TEL 610-375-0300, 800-755-7955, FAX 610-375-6862, info@christar.org, http://www.christar.org. Ed., R&P Byron Barnshaw Jr. Circ: 22,000 (controlled).

287 USA ISSN 0024-3299
LIGHT AND LIFE. Text in English. 1896. bi-m. USD 16 (effective 2005). adv. **Description:** Interactive magazine for Christians.
Indexed: GSS&RPL.
Published by: (Free Methodist Church of North America), Free Methodist Publishing House, PO Box 535002, Indianapolis, IN 46253-5002. TEL 317-244-3660, FAX 317-244-1247. Circ: 19,000.

280.4 GBR ISSN 0140-8267
LIGHT FOR OUR PATH. Text in English. 1956. a. GBP 8.50 per issue (effective 2010). **Document type:** *Yearbook, Consumer.* **Description:** Covers a variety of themes, showing how the old and new testaments read together can reveal the depth, richness and relevance of the bible for today's world.
—CCC.
Published by: (International Bible Reading Association), Christian Education Publishing, 1020 Bristol Rd, Selby Oak, Birmingham, B29 6LB, United Kingdom. TEL 44-121-4724242, FAX 44-121-4727575, enquiries@christianeducation.org.uk, http://www.christianeducation.org.uk. Ed. Kate Hughes.

280.4 GBR
LIGHT FOR THE LAST DAYS. Text in English. 1987. q. GBP 5 domestic; GBP 7 foreign (effective 2009). back issues avail. **Document type:** *Magazine, Trade.* **Description:** Contains articles on current national and international events and their significance to the fulfilment of Biblical prophecies.
Related titles: Online - full text ed.
Address: Box BM - 4226, London, WC1N 3XX, United Kingdom. Circ: 6,000.

LIGHTNING BUG; christian magazine for children. *see* CHILDREN AND YOUTH—For

LIKEREKE NTLAFATSONG. *see* GENERAL INTEREST PERIODICALS—Lesotho

287 GBR ISSN 0265-2226
LINCOLNSHIRE METHODIST HISTORY SOCIETY. JOURNAL. Text in English. 1963. 2/yr. free to members (effective 2009). bk.rev. **Document type:** *Journal, Academic/Scholarly.* **Description:** Covers all aspects of the history of Methodism in historic Lincolnshire.
Supersedes in part (in 1977): Epworth Witness and Lincolnshire Methodist History Society. Journal
Published by: Lincolnshire Methodist History Society, c/o J.S. English, Ed, 1 Dorton Ave, Gainsborough, Lincs DN21 1UB, United Kingdom.

286 CAN ISSN 0380-4100
LINK & VISITOR; a Baptist magazine for women. Text in English. 1878. 6/yr. CAD 14 domestic; CAD 16 foreign (effective 2000). adv. bk.rev. index. back issues avail. **Document type:** *Magazine, Consumer.* **Description:** "Encourages and equips Canadian Christian women to be effective disciples of Jesus.".
Formerly (until 1927): Canadian Missionary Link (0710-9288)
Published by: Baptist Women's Missionary Society of Ontario & Quebec, 414-195 The West Mall, Etobicoke, ON M9C 5K1, Canada. TEL 416-622-8600. Ed., R&P, Adv. contact Esther Barnes. Pub. Nancy Webb. Circ: 4,500 (paid).

287.6 USA
LINKS (NASHVILLE). Text in English. 1997. q. free. bk.rev. illus. back issues avail. **Document type:** *Newsletter.* **Description:** Examines various national issues from a Methodist perspective.
Published by: (Board of Discipleship), United Methodist Church, 201 Eighth Ave S, Nashville, TN 37202. TEL 615-749-6512, FAX 615-749-6512.

LITSOAKOTLENG EDUCATIONAL CALENDAR. *see* GENERAL INTEREST PERIODICALS—Lesotho

LITSOAKOTLENG MAGAZINE; Bukana e hlophisitsoeng ka har'a naha molemong oa Basotho. *see* GENERAL INTEREST PERIODICALS—Lesotho

284.1 USA ISSN 1935-1593
THE LITTLE LUTHERAN. Text in English. 2007. 10/yr. USD 24.95 (effective 2008). **Document type:** *Magazine, Consumer.* **Description:** Contains art, stories, prayers, songs and activities for children.
Related titles: Online - full text ed.
Published by: Augsburg Fortress Publishers, PO Box 1209, Minneapolis, MN 55440. TEL 800-328-4648, FAX 800-722-7766, info@augsburgfortress.org, http://www.augsburgfortress.org. Ed. Elizabeth Hunter.

280.4 USA ISSN 1098-5840
LIVING (NEVADA); a family life companion. Text in English. 1988. q. USD 15 domestic; USD 20 in Canada and Australia (effective 2001). illus. back issues avail. **Document type:** *Magazine, Consumer.* **Description:** Offers Biblical, pro-life alternatives through personal stories and feature articles.
Published by: Lutherans For Life, 1229 South G Ave, Bldg B, Bldg B, Ste 100, Nevada, IA 50201-2778. TEL 515-382-2077, 888-364-5433, FAX 515-382-3020, info@lutheransforlife.org, http://www.lutheransforlife.org. Ed., Pub. Rev. Dr. James I Lamb. R&P Linda D Bartlett TEL 515-648-3785. Circ: 700.

283.73 USA ISSN 0024-5240
BX5800
LIVING CHURCH; an independent weekly record of the news of the Church and the views of Episcopalians. Text in English. 1941. w. USD 42.50; USD 2 newsstand/cover (effective 2005). adv. bk.rev. illus. **Document type:** *Magazine, Consumer.*
Formerly (until 1942): The Living Church and the Layman's Magazine (0161-8482); Which was formed by the merger of (1940-1941): The Layman's Magazine of the Living Church (0161-8474); (1878-1941): The Living Church (0161-8466)
Indexed: MLA-IB.
Published by: Living Church Foundation, Inc., 816 E Juneau Ave, Milwaukee, WI 53203. TEL 414-276-5420, 877-822-8228, FAX 414-276-7483. Adv. contacts Lila Thurber, Tom Parker. Circ: 9,000 (paid).

280.4 USA ISSN 1069-0182
LIVING LIFE; monthly Christian quiet time guide. Text in English. 1992. m. USD 60 (effective 2009). **Document type:** *Magazine, Consumer.* **Description:** Provides daily meditation, reflection and devotional Bible study.
Related titles: Korean ed.: Saengmyeong Ui Salm. ISSN 1227-4666. 1992; Spanish ed.: Vida Viva. ISSN 2150-5888. 2009 (Dec.); Regional ed(s).: Tiempo con Dios es Vida Viva (Latin America Edition). ISSN 2150-2501.
Published by: Duranno International Ministry, 616 S Westmoreland Ave, Los Angeles, CA 90005. TEL 213-382-5400, usduranno@duranno.com, http://www.duranno.com/english/introduce.asp.

280.4 USA ISSN 2154-8072
▼ **LIVING THE 31 PROVERBS LIFE.** Text in English. 2010 (Apr.). w. free. **Document type:** *Newsletter, Consumer.* **Description:** For women devoted to living the Proverbs 31 life.
Media: E-mail.
Published by: Patricia Samuels Ministries, PO Box 16, Cedar Hill, TX 75106. TEL 214-331-0954, info@patriciasamuels.org, http://www.patriciasamuels.org.

286.132 USA ISSN 0162-4261
LIVING WITH TEENAGERS; a christian parenting magazine. Abbreviated title: L W T. Text in English. 1978. m. USD 21.95; USD 3.95 per issue (effective 2008). back issues avail. **Document type:** *Magazine, Consumer.* **Description:** Offers practical answers to real-life questions from a christian perspective.
Published by: LifeWay Christian Resources, 1 Lifeway Plz, Nashville, TN 37234. TEL 615-251-2000, 800-458-2772, FAX 615-251-5933, customerservice@lifeway.com. Ed. Bop Bunn. Adv. contact Rhonda Edge Buescher. Circ: 38,000.

280.4 GBR
LLANDAFF DIOCESAN DIRECTORY. Text in English. a. GBP 3. bibl. index. **Document type:** *Directory.*
Published by: Llandaff Diocesan Board of Finance/Esgobaeth Llandaf Bwrdd Cyllid, Heol Fair, Llandaff, Cardiff, S Glam CF5 2EE, United Kingdom. TEL 01222-578899, FAX 01222-576198. Ed. M J Beasant. Circ: 1,000.

284.1 USA ISSN 1064-0398
BX8001
LOGIA. Text in English. 1990. q. USD 25 domestic; USD 31 in Canada & Mexico; USD 36 elsewhere (effective 2005). **Description:** Publishes articles on exegetical, historical, systematic, and liturgical theology that promote the orthodox theology of the Evangelical Lutheran Church.
Formerly (until 1992): Lutheran Confessional Review (1060-0930)
Indexed: A21, R&TA, RI-1, RILM.
Published by: Luther Academy, 314 Pearl St., Mankato, MN 56001.

280.4 USA ISSN 1555-2993
BX7312.A1
THE LOOKOUT (CINCINNATI). Text in English. 1894. w. USD 26.99 (effective 2008). back issues avail. **Document type:** *Magazine, Consumer.* **Description:** Designed to provide christian adults with true-to-the-bible teaching and current information that will help them to mature as individual believers, develop godly homes and live in the world as faithful witnesses of christ.
Published by: Standard Publishing, 8805 Governor's Hill Dr, Ste 400, Cincinnati, OH 45249. TEL 513-931-4050, 800-543-1353, FAX 877-867-5751, customerservice@standardpub.com, http://www.standardpub.com. Pub., R&P Mark A Taylor. Circ: 90,000.

286 USA ISSN 0024-6743
LOUISIANA BAPTIST BUILDER. Text in English. 1953. m. USD 7 (effective 2008). adv. bk.rev. illus. **Document type:** *Newspaper, Consumer.* **Description:** Contains news from the churches of Louisiana, BMA of America, and departmental news.
Address: Bobby Kelley, Ed, 979 Patrick Church Rd, Bernice, LA 71222. TEL 225-454-8138, buck_hughes@yahoo.com. Ed. Leroy Mayfield. Circ: 1,364.

280.4 CAN ISSN 1718-2263
LUMIERE SUR MON SENTIER/LIGHT ON MY PATH. Text in French. 2006. bi-m. **Document type:** *Journal, Consumer.*
Published by: Eglise Chretienne Reformee de Beauce/Christian Reformed Church of Beauce, CP 402, Beauce, Beauce, PQ G5Y 5C8, Canada. http://www.ecrb.org.

284.1 DEU ISSN 0340-6210
BR323.5
LUTHER. Text in German. 1919. 3/yr. EUR 27; EUR 14.90 newsstand/cover (effective 2011). adv. bk.rev. index. **Document type:** *Journal, Academic/Scholarly.*
Indexed: A21, CERDIC, DIP, FR, IBR, IBZ, MLA-IB, PCI, RI-1, RI-2, RILM.
—INIST. **CCC.**
Published by: (Luther-Gesellschaft), Vandenhoeck und Ruprecht, Theaterstr 13, Goettingen, 37073, Germany. TEL 49-551-508440, FAX 49-551-5084422, info@v-r.de. Ed. Hellmut Zschoch. Circ: 1,400 (paid and controlled).

284.1 AUT
DIE LUTHER-KIRCHE. Text in German. 1948. q. **Document type:** *Bulletin, Consumer.*
Published by: Evangelische Gemeinde A.B. Wien-Waehring, Martinstr 25, Vienna, W 1180, Austria. pfarramt@lutherkirche.at, http://www.lutherkirche.at. Ed. Uwe Kuehneweg. Circ: 4,000.

284.1 USA ISSN 0024-743X
BX8001
THE LUTHERAN; news magazine of the Evangelical Lutheran church in America. Text in English. 1860. m. USD 15.95 combined subscription to individuals (print & online eds.) (effective 2008). adv. bk.rev.; film rev. 60 p./no.; back issues avail. **Document type:** *Magazine, Consumer.* **Description:** Contains news and activities of the Evangelical Lutheran Church in America, news of the world of religion, ethical reflections on issues in society, and personal Christian experience.
Incorporates (in 1987): Lutheran Standard (0024-7545)
Related titles: Microform ed.: (from PQC); Online - full text ed.: USD 11.95 (effective 2008).
Indexed: A22, CERDIC, GSS&RPL, P28, P48, P53, P54, PQC.
—Ingenta.
Published by: (Evangelical Lutheran Church in America), Augsburg Fortress Publishers, PO Box 1209, Minneapolis, MN 55440. TEL 800-328-4648, FAX 800-722-7766, info@augsburgfortress.org, http://www.augsburgfortress.org. Ed. Daniel J Lehmann. Adv. contact Joel Stombres. page USD 10,000; bleed 8.375 x 10.75. Circ: 326,000.

284.1 USA
THE LUTHERAN ANNUAL. Text in English. 1910. a. USD 17.99 per issue (effective 2009). adv. 700 p./no.; **Document type:** *Directory, Consumer.* **Description:** Designed to serve as a reference tool for and about churches, schools, pastors, church professionals, and church agencies.

Published by: (Lutheran Church - Missouri Synod), Concordia Publishing House, 3558 S Jefferson, St Louis, MO 63118. TEL 314-268-1000, 800-325-3040, FAX 800-490-9889, order@cph.org. Ed. Fred Baue. Pub. Rev. Paul T McCain. adv.: page USD 1,500; 7 x 10. Circ: 16,000.

284.1 AUS ISSN 0726-4305
BX8009
LUTHERAN CHURCH OF AUSTRALIA. YEARBOOK. Text in English. 1887. a. **Document type:** *Directory.*
Former titles (until 1969): Lutheran Yearbook; Which was formed by the merger of (1944-1966): The Lutheran Almanac; Which was formerly (until 1944): Christian Book Almanac; (until 1926): Aurricht's Almanac for Church and Home; (until 1925): G. Auricht's Book Almanac for Australia; (until 1918) : Christlicher Volks-Kalender fuer Australien ; (1919-1966): The Australian Lutheran Alamanac for the (Year); Which was formerly (until 1918): Luther Almanac for the 400th Anniversary of the Beginning of the Great Reformation
—CCC.
Published by: (Lutheran Church of Australia), Openbook Publishers, GPO Box 1368, Adelaide, SA 5001, Australia. TEL 61-8-82234552, FAX 61-8-82235103.

LUTHERAN CHURCH OF CENTRAL AFRICA. STATISTICAL REPORT. *see* RELIGIONS AND THEOLOGY—Abstracting, Bibliographies, Statistics

284.171025 CAN ISSN 0316-800X
BX8063.C2
LUTHERAN CHURCHES IN CANADA. DIRECTORY. Text in English. 1954. a. CAD 10 (effective 2000). adv. **Document type:** *Directory.*
Published by: Lutheran Council in Canada, 302 393 Portage Ave, Winnipeg, MB R3B 3H6, Canada. TEL 204-984-9150, FAX 204-984-9185. Ed. L C Gilbertson. R&P L.C. Gilbertson. Adv. contact Toni Walker. Circ: 1,600.

284.1 USA ISSN 0458-497X
BR1
➤ **LUTHERAN DIGEST.** Text in English. 1953. q. USD 16 (effective 2009). adv. 64 p./no.; **Document type:** *Magazine, Consumer.*
Related titles: Audio cassette/tape ed.: free (effective 2011); Braille ed.: 1990. free (effective 2011); ◆ Large type ed. 22 pt.: Lutheran Digest (Large Print Edition).
Published by: Lutheran Digest, Inc., PO Box 4250, Hopkins, MN 55343. TEL 952-933-2820, FAX 952-933-5708. Ed. David L Tank. Pub. Randy Schwanz. Circ: 101,000 (paid and controlled).

➤ **LUTHERAN DIGEST (LARGE PRINT EDITION).** *see* HANDICAPPED—Visually Impaired

268.841 USA ISSN 0024-7448
LC573
LUTHERAN EDUCATION. Text in English. 1865. 5/yr. adv. bk.rev. illus. index. **Document type:** *Magazine, Consumer.*
Related titles: Microfilm ed.: (from PQC); Online - full text ed.
Indexed: A22, B04, BRD, CA, CERDIC, E02, E03, E06, ERI, EdA, EdI, T02, W03, W05.
Published by: Concordia University, 7400 Augusta St, River Forest, IL 60305-1499. TEL 708-209-3073, FAX 708-209-3176, http://cuchicago.edu/. Ed., R&P, Adv. contact Jonathan Barz. Circ: 4,200.

284.1 USA ISSN 0024-7456
BX8001
LUTHERAN FORUM; an independent journal. Text in English. 1967. q. USD 26.95 includes Forum letter (effective 2010). adv. bk.rev. illus.; stat. 50 p./no.; Supplement avail.; back issues avail.; reprints avail. **Document type:** *Magazine, Academic/Scholarly.*
Supersedes: American Lutheran Magazine
Related titles: Microform ed.: (from PQC).
Indexed: A21, A22, CERDIC, R&TA, RI-1, RI-2, RILM.
Published by: American Lutheran Publicity Bureau, PO Box 327, Delhi, NY 13753. http://www.alpb.org. Ed. Sarah Hinlicky Wilson.

284.1 USA ISSN 0046-4732
LUTHERAN FORUM. FORUM LETTER. Text in English. 1972. m. included with subscr. to Lutheran Forum. 8 p./no.; back issues avail.; reprints avail. **Document type:** *Newsletter, Consumer.* **Description:** Provides readers with information and viewpoints from all sides of Lutheranism.
Related titles: Microfilm ed.: (from PQC).
Indexed: A21, CERDIC, RI-1.
Published by: American Lutheran Publicity Bureau, PO Box 327, Delhi, NY 13753. dkralpb@aol.com. Ed. Richard O Johnson. Circ: 3,100.

284.1 USA ISSN 0090-3817
BX8011.A1
LUTHERAN HISTORICAL CONFERENCE. ESSAYS AND REPORTS. Text in English. 1964. biennial. USD 20 to members (effective 2000). **Document type:** *Proceedings.* **Description:** Contains papers presented at biennial meetings that are of interest to professional Lutheran historians, librarians, and archivists.
Indexed: A21, R&TA, RI-1, RI-2.
Published by: Lutheran Historical Conference, c/o Concordia Historical Institute, 801 DeMun Ave, St. Louis, MO 63105. TEL 314-505-7900. Ed. Marvin A Huggins. Circ: 350.

284.1 USA ISSN 0460-0274
BX8001
LUTHERAN HISTORICAL CONFERENCE. NEWSLETTER. Text in English. 1963. q. looseleaf. free to members (effective 2010). bk.rev. bibl. back issues avail. **Document type:** *Newsletter, Trade.* **Description:** Contains items of interest to archivists, librarians and historians, plus technical notes and bibliographical resources. Conference is intended to foster effective cooperation among persons and institutions concerned with research, documentation, and preservation of the resources revealing experiences of Lutheranism in North America.
Related titles: Online - full text ed.: free (effective 2010).
Indexed: RI-1.
Published by: Lutheran Historical Conference, ELCA Archives, 321 Bonnie Lane, Elk Grove Village, IL 60007. TEL 847-690-9410, FAX 847-690-9502, ewittman@elca.org, http://luthhist.org/. Ed. Joel Thoreson. Circ: 225 (paid).

284.1 USA ISSN 1070-5252
BX8042.P4
LUTHERAN HISTORICAL SOCIETY OF EASTERN PENNSYLVANIA. PERIODICAL. Text in English. 1950. s-a. USD 7.50 to members (effective 2000). bk.rev. back issues avail. **Document type:** *Proceedings.*
Formerly: Lutheran Historical Society of Eastern Pennsylvania
Published by: Lutheran Historical Society of Eastern Pennsylvania, Lutheran Theological Seminary, 7301 Germantown Ave, Philadelphia, PA 19119. Ed. Mahlon H Hellerich. Circ: 550.

284.1 USA ISSN 0360-6945
BX8001
LUTHERAN JOURNAL. Text in English. 1937. q. USD 15 (effective 1998). adv. bk.rev. illus. **Document type:** *Journal, Consumer.*
Former titles (1943-1947): Northwest Lutheran Journal; Lutheran Home Journal
Indexed: AIPP.
Published by: Macalester Park Publishing Co., Inc., 7317 Cahill Rd., Edina, MN 55439. TEL 612-941-6830, FAX 612-941-3010. Ed. Rev. Armin U Deye. Pub. Michael Beard. R&P Stephani Karges. Adv. contact Karen Beard. Circ: 125,000 (controlled).

284.1 USA ISSN 0024-7464
BX8001
LUTHERAN LAYMAN. Text in English. 1929. bi-m. donation. bk.rev. illus. 16 p./no.; back issues avail. **Document type:** *Magazine, Trade.* **Description:** Contains religious news for the International Lutheran Laymen's League and all Lutheran laity.
Published by: International Lutheran Laymen's League, Lutheran Hour Ministries, 660 Mason Ridge Center, St. Louis, MO 63141-8557. TEL 314-317-4100, 800-944-3450, FAX 314-317-4295, lh_min@lhm.org, http://www.lhm.org. Ed. Gerald Perschbacher. Circ: 125,000 (controlled).

LUTHERAN MESSENGER FOR THE BLIND. *see* HANDICAPPED—Visually Impaired

284.1 USA ISSN 0885-9922
BX8001
LUTHERAN PARTNERS. Text in English. 1985. bi-m. USD 13 in North America; USD 19.50 elsewhere (effective 2009). adv. bk.rev. back issues avail. **Document type:** *Magazine, Consumer.* **Description:** Covers information about voices of real people doing real ministry in the real world.
Former titles (until 1985): LCA Partners; (until 1979): Partners
Published by: Augsburg Fortress Publishers, PO Box 1209, Minneapolis, MN 55440. TEL 800-328-4648, FAX 800-722-7766, info@augsburgfortress.org, http://www.augsburgfortress.org. Ed. William A Decker TEL 773-380-2884. Adv. contact Jeannette May TEL 847-823-4545. color page USD 1,550; trim 8.375 x 10.875. Circ: 20,000. **Co-sponsor:** Evangelical Lutheran Church in America (ELCA), Division for Ministry.

284.1 USA
BX8001
LUTHERAN QUARTERLY. Abbreviated title: L Q. Text in English. 1949-1977; N.S. 1987. q. USD 30 domestic; USD 38 foreign (effective 2009). bk.rev. index. 128 p./no.; back issues avail. **Document type:** *Journal, Consumer.* **Description:** Aims to provide a forum for the discussion of Christian faith and life on the basis of the Lutheran confession; for the application of the principles of the Lutheran Church to the changing problems of religion and society; for the fostering of world Lutheranism; and for the promotion of understanding between Lutherans and other Christians.
Formerly (until 1978): Lutheran Quarterly (0024-7499); Which was formed by the merger of (1928-1949): Lutheran Church Quarterly; (1922-1949): Augustana Quarterly
Indexed: A20, A21, AmH&L, CA, CERDIC, HistAb, MLA-IB, P30, R&TA, RI-1, RI-2, RILM, T02.
—IE, Ingenta.
Published by: Lutheran Quarterly, Inc., PO Box 465, Hanover, PA 17331. Ed. Paul Rorem.

284.1 USA ISSN 0024-7510
BX8001
LUTHERAN SENTINEL. Text in English. 1917. m. USD 8. bk.rev. **Document type:** *Newsletter.* **Description:** Contains articles on religious topics, the Church Year, and Synod news.
Published by: Evangelical Lutheran Synod, 1451 Pearl Place, Escondido, CA 92027. TEL 619-745-0583, FAX 619-743-4440. Ed., R&P Theodore G Gullixson. Circ: 6,500. **Dist. by:** Stoyles Graphic Services, 19 8th St, S E, Mason City, IA 50401.

284.1 USA ISSN 0024-7537
BX8061
LUTHERAN SPOKESMAN. Text in English. 1958. m. USD 13 (effective 2008). bk.rev. **Description:** Testamentary commentary on issues relevant to the Church of the Lutheran Confession, with official notices and news pertaining to its activities.
Related titles: Online - full text ed.: 1958.
Published by: Church of the Lutheran Confession (Minneapolis), 2750 Oxford St. N, Roseville, MN 55113. TEL 361-241-5147, pgflei@prairie.lakes.com, http://www.primenet.com/~mpkelly/clc/spokesman.html. Ed., R&P Rev. Paul Fleischer. Pub. Benno Sydow. Circ: 2,500.

284.1 AUS ISSN 0024-7553
LUTHERAN THEOLOGICAL JOURNAL. Text in English. 1930. 3/yr. AUD 33 domestic; AUD 40 foreign (effective 2009). bk.rev. back issues avail. **Document type:** *Journal, Academic/Scholarly.*
Formerly (until 1967): Australasian Theological Review
Related titles: Online - full text ed.
Indexed: A21, A22, AEI, CERDIC, OTA, P28, P30, P48, P53, P54, PQC, RI-1, RI-2, RILM.
—Ingenta. **CCC.**
Published by: (Lutheran Church of Australia, Australian Lutheran College), Openbook Publishers, GPO Box 1368, Adelaide, SA 5001, Australia. TEL 61-8-81240070, FAX 61-8-82234552.

230.41 USA ISSN 0362-0581
BV4070
LUTHERAN THEOLOGICAL SEMINARY BULLETIN. Text in English. 1921. q. free. bk.rev. **Description:** Discusses theological and ecclesiastical issues, primarily to its immediate constituency, but also to a broader readership of interested persons.
Formerly: Gettysburg Seminary Bulletin (0016-9366)
Related titles: Microform ed.: (from PQC); Online - full text ed.
Indexed: A21, P28, P48, P53, P54, PQC, RI-1, RI-2.
Published by: Lutheran Theological Seminary, 61 N W Confederate Ave, Gettysburg, PA 17325. TEL 717-334-6286, FAX 717-334-3469. Ed. Susan Karen Hedahl. Circ: 3,500.

284.1 USA ISSN 0024-757X
BX8001
THE LUTHERAN WITNESS; a magazine for the lay people of the Lutheran Church - Missouri Synod. Text in English. 1882. m. USD 22 (effective 2009). adv. bk.rev. illus. 32 p./no.; **Document type:** *Magazine, Consumer.* **Description:** Features synodical news, reports from Lutherans around the world, features, columns, Q and A's and a Bible study.
Related titles: Audio cassette/tape ed.: free (effective 2011); Braille ed.: free (effective 2011); ◆ Large type ed. 22 pt.: Lutheran Witness (Large Print Edition).
Indexed: A22, CCR, GSS&RPL.
Published by: (Lutheran Church - Missouri Synod), Concordia Publishing House, 3558 S Jefferson, St Louis, MO 63118. TEL 314-268-1000, 800-325-3040, FAX 800-490-9889, service@cph.org. Pub. Rev. Paul T McCain. adv.: page USD 7,013; 7.125 x 9.625. Circ: 200,000 (paid).

284.1 USA
LUTHERAN WITNESS (LARGE PRINT EDITION). Text in English. m. free (effective 2011). **Document type:** *Magazine, Consumer.*
Media: Large Type (22 pt.). **Related titles:** Audio cassette/tape ed.: free (effective 2011); Braille ed.: free (effective 2011); ◆ Print ed.: The Lutheran Witness. ISSN 0024-757X.
Published by: (Lutheran Church - Missouri Synod), Lutheran Library for the Blind, 7550 Watson Rd, St Louis, MO 63119. TEL 314-918-0415, 888-215-2455, blind.mission@blindmission.org.

284.1082 USA ISSN 0896-209X
BX8001
LUTHERAN WOMAN TODAY. Text in English. 1908. 10/yr. USD 12 (effective 2008). adv. index. 64 p./no.; back issues avail. **Document type:** *Magazine, Consumer.* **Description:** Offers a mix of articles, theological reflections, devotions, and stories of comfort and challenge that lift up the mission of Women of the ELCA.
Formed by the 1987 merger of: Lutheran Woman (0024-7596); Scope (0036-8997)
Related titles: Audio cassette/tape ed.: USD 11.50 (effective 2002); Braille ed.
Indexed: AIPP.
Published by: Women of the Evangelical Lutheran Church in America (ELCA), 8765 W Higgins Rd, Chicago, IL 60631-4189. TEL 773-380-2700, 800-638-3522, FAX 773-380-2419, http://www.elca.org. Ed. Deb Bogaert. adv.: color page USD 4,500; trim 8.125 x 10.5. Circ: 95,806 (paid and controlled).

284.1 USA
LUTHERAN WOMAN'S QUARTERLY. Text in English. 1942. q. USD 5.50 (effective 2009). bk.rev. back issues avail. **Document type:** *Magazine, Consumer.* **Description:** Publishes short stories of interest to women, along with articles on mission projects.
Former titles: L W M L Quarterly; Lutheran Woman's Quarterly
Related titles: Audio cassette/tape ed.: free (donation); Braille ed.: free (donation); Large type ed. 22 pt.: free (donation).
Published by: Lutheran Church - Missouri Synod, Lutheran Women's Missionary League, PO Box 411993, St. Louis, MO 63141-9998. TEL 314-268-1531, 800-252-5965, FAX 314-268-1532, lwml@lwml.org. Ed., R&P Nancy Graf Peters. Circ: 200,000. **Subscr. to:** Lutheran Library for the Blind, 1333 S Kirkwood Rd, St Louis, MO 63122. TEL 888-215-2455, FAX 314-965-0959, blind.library@lcms.org.

284.1 DEU ISSN 0949-880X
LUTHERISCHE BEITRAEGE. Text in German. 1996. q. EUR 24, USD 30; EUR 12, USD 15 to students (effective 2006). adv. bk.rev. **Document type:** *Bulletin.* **Description:** Articles of confessional Lutheran doctrine.
Address: Greifswaldstr 2b, Braunschweig, 38124, Germany. TEL 49-531-2504962, FAX 49-531-2505401. Ed., R&P, Adv. contact Johannes Junker. Circ: 400 (paid).

230.41 DEU ISSN 0170-3846
BX8009
LUTHERISCHE THEOLOGIE UND KIRCHE. Text in German. 1977. q. EUR 18.90 (effective 2009). adv. bk.rev. 50 p./no.; back issues avail. **Document type:** *Journal, Academic/Scholarly.* **Description:** Studies Lutheran theology.
Indexed: DIP, IBR, IBZ.
Published by: (Lutherische Theologische Hochschule in Oberursel), Edition Ruprecht, Postfach 1716, Goettingen, 37007, Germany. TEL 49-551-4883751, FAX 49-551-4883753, info@edition-ruprecht.de. Circ: 800.

284.1 DEU ISSN 0342-0914
BR327.A1
➤ **LUTHERJAHRBUCH.** Text in German. 1919. a., latest vol.75, 2008. EUR 39.90 per issue (effective 2010). **Document type:** *Journal, Academic/Scholarly.*
Indexed: A21, DIP, FR, HistAb, IBR, IBZ, MLA-IB, PCI, RI-1, RI-2.
—INIST.
Published by: (Luther-Gesellschaft), Vandenhoeck und Ruprecht, Theaterstr 13, Goettingen, 37073, Germany. TEL 49-551-508440, FAX 49-551-5084422, info@v-r.de. Ed. Helmar Junghans.

284.1 AUT ISSN 0024-7626
DIE LUTHERKIRCHE; Pfarrblatt. Text in German. 1948. q. free (effective 2010). **Document type:** *Bulletin, Consumer.*
Published by: Evangelische Gemeinde A.B. Wien-Waehring, Martinstr 25, Vienna, W 1180, Austria. TEL 43-1-4064534, FAX 43-1-406453422, pfarramt@lutherkirche.at, http://www.lutherkirche.at. Ed. Uwe Kuehneweg.

266 DEU
M B K - MISSION AKTUELL. Text in German. 1927. q. looseleaf. 4 p./no.; back issues avail. **Document type:** *Newsletter, Consumer.* **Description:** Reports on social and missionary work in Japan and Hong Kong.
Formerly (until 1992): M B K - Mission. Nachrichten
Published by: M B K - Mission e.V., Postfach 560, Bad Salzuflen, 32067, Germany. TEL 49-5222-180523, FAX 49-5222-180556, mbk.mission@t-online.de. Ed. Doris Oehlenschlaeger. Circ: 2,600.

R

287 GBR ISSN 2043-9105
M E T CONNEXION. Text in English. 19??. q. free to members (effective 2010). **Document type:** *Magazine, Trade.* **Description:** Provides a source of material to keep abreast of evangelical thinking and what God is doing through the witness of Christian people across the world.
Formerly (until 2008): Headline (1367-1626)
Published by: Methodist Evangelicals Together, 7, Gledhow Park Rd, Leeds, LS7 4JX, United Kingdom.

284 NLD ISSN 1385-0326
MAANDBRIEF VOOR LEERHUIS EN LITURGIE. Text in Dutch. 1996. m. EUR 25 domestic; EUR 32.50 in Europe; EUR 40 elsewhere (effective 2010).
Published by: Stichting Leerhuis en Liturgie, Postbus 17268, Amsterdam, 1001 JG, Netherlands. TEL 31-20-6256940, leerhuis@leerhuisenliturgie.nl. Ed. Kees Kok.

286 ZAF ISSN 1019-5092
BX6153.4.A356
MARANATHA. Text in Afrikaans, English. 1940. bi-m. donation. adv. **Document type:** *Newsletter.* **Description:** Communicates news of church activities and provides devotional inspiration.
Supersedes (in 1992): South African Union Lantern (0038-2795); Suid-Afrikaanse Unie-Lantern (0377-0796)
Published by: South African Union Conference of Seventh-Day Adventists, PO Box 468, Bloemfontein, 9300, South Africa. TEL 27-51-447-8271, FAX 27-51-448-8059, 74532.1700@compuserve.com. Ed., R&P P B Peters. Circ: 13,008 (controlled).

280.4 USA
MARANATHA CHRISTIAN JOURNAL. Text in English. 1996. d. free. **Description:** Reports newsworthy events and activities affecting today's Christians.
Media: Online - full text.
Published by: Matrix Development, 12240 Perris Blvd, Ste 112, Moreno Valley, CA 92557. TEL 909-247-0958, FAX 909-242-5538. Ed. George Lawson.

280.4 USA
MARS HILL AUDIO JOURNAL. Text in English. bi-m. USD 48 (effective 2005). **Document type:** *Magazine, Consumer.* **Description:** Its purpose id to assist Christians who desire to move from thoughtless consumption of modern culture to a vantage point of thoughtful engagement.
Media: Audio CD. **Related titles:** Audio cassette/tape ed.: USD 36 (effective 2004).
Published by: Mars Hill Audio, PO Box 7826, Charlottesville, VA 22906-7826. TEL 434-990-9000, FAX 434-990-9090, tapes@marshillaudio.org, http://www.marshillaudio.org.

280.4 USA ISSN 1066-3959
BS410
MASTER'S SEMINARY JOURNAL. Text in English. 1990. s-a. USD 14 domestic to individuals; USD 18 foreign to individuals; USD 20 domestic to institutions; USD 24 foreign to institutions (effective 2005). back issues avail. **Description:** Contains scholarly articles dealing with the Biblical text, theology.
Related titles: CD-ROM ed.: Theological Journal Library CD. USD 99.95 New & Updated CD (effective 2004).
Indexed: A21, ChrPI, GSS&RPL, OTA, R&TA, RI-1.
Published by: Master's Seminary, 13248 Roscoe Blvd., Sun Valley, CA 91352-3798. TEL 818-909-5619, 800-225-5867, webmaster@tms.edu.

286.132 USA ISSN 0162-427X
MATURE LIVING. Text in English. 1977. m. USD 21.95; USD 3.95 per issue (effective 2008). adv. back issues avail. **Document type:** *Magazine, Consumer.* **Description:** Focuses on the interests and needs of adults over the age of 55, such as finances, grandparenting and nostalgia.
Published by: LifeWay Christian Resources, 1 Lifeway Plz, Nashville, TN 37234. TEL 615-251-2000, 800-458-2772, FAX 615-251-5933, customerservice@lifeway.com. Eds. Rene A Holt, David T Seay. Adv. contact Rhonda Edge Buescher. color page USD 11,618; trim 8.125 x 10.875. Circ: 317,000.

287.6 USA ISSN 0025-6021
BV4580.A1
MATURE YEARS. Text in English. 1954. q. USD 25; USD 6.45 per issue (effective 2009). illus. 112 p./no. 2 cols./p.; back issues avail. **Document type:** *Magazine, Consumer.* **Description:** Contains articles of interest to elderly persons, written from a religious perspective.
Supersedes: Mature Years
Media: Large Type (14 pt.). **Related titles:** Online - full text ed.
Indexed: A22, MPI.
—CCC.
Published by: (United Methodist Church), United Methodist Publishing House, 201 8th Ave S, PO Box 801, Nashville, TN 37202. TEL 615-749-6000, 800-672-1789, FAX 615-749-6579, http://www.umph.org. Ed. Wayne G Reece. Pub. Neil M Alexander. Circ: 55,000 (paid).

MEDIA UPDATE (ONLINE). *see* MUSIC

283 AUS ISSN 1324-5724
MELBOURNE ANGLICAN. Text in English. 1966. m. AUD 29.95 domestic; AUD 49.95 foreign (effective 2009). adv. bk.rev.; film rev.; play rev.; music rev.; tel.rev. illus. 20 p./no.; back issues avail. **Document type:** *Newspaper, Consumer.* **Description:** Brings current issues in the Church into debate and scrutiny.
Formerly (until 1994): See (0037-0754)
Published by: Anglican Media Melbourne, The Anglican Centre, 209 Flinders Ln, Melbourne, VIC 3000, Australia. TEL 61-3-96534221, FAX 61-3-96505237, media@melbourne.anglican.com.au. Ed. Roland Ashby TEL 61-3-9653-4215. Adv. contact Bryce Amner TEL 61-3-96534219. Circ: 13,359.

285 USA ISSN 1550-7351
MEMPHIS THEOLOGICAL SEMINARY. JOURNAL. Text in English. 1953. a. free to qualified personnel (effective 2011). back issues avail. **Document type:** *Journal, Academic/Scholarly.*
Formerly (until 1991): The Cumberland Seminarian (0590-3386)
Related titles: Online - full text ed.
Indexed: A21, FamI, RI-1.
Published by: Memphis Theological Seminary, 168 E Pkwy S, Memphis, TN 38104. TEL 901-458-8232.

286 GBR ISSN 2041-5354
MEN MATTERS. Text in English. 1918. q. GBP 4 (effective 2000). adv. bk.rev. back issues avail. **Document type:** *Magazine, Consumer.*
Incorporates (in 2008): World Outlook; (until 1945): Layman
—BLDSC (9356.958000).
Published by: Baptist Men's Movement, 5 Elizabeth Dr, PO BOX 44, Wantage, Oxon OX12 9YA, United Kingdom. TEL 44-1235-768660, secretary@baptistmen.org.uk. Circ: 1,100 (controlled).

287 MEX ISSN 0026-0185
MESIAS; boletin semanal de la iglesia Metodista. Text in Spanish. 1971 (vol.8). w.
Published by: Iglesia Metodista el Mesias, Balderas 47, Mexico, DF, Mexico.

286 USA ISSN 0271-5732
BV2520.A2
MESSAGE (NEW CUMBERLAND). Text in English. 1927. q. free. 24 p./no.; **Document type:** *Magazine, Consumer.*
Formerly: Message (Association of Baptists for Evangelism in the Orient)
Published by: Association of Baptists for World Evangelism, PO Box 8585, Harrisburg, PA 17105. info@abwe.org, http://www.abwe.org/. Ed. Angela Shuff. Circ: 130,000.

284.2 FRA ISSN 1632-6768
MESSAGER (STRASBOURG). Text in French, German. 1945. w. adv. bk.rev. illus.
Formerly (until 2001): Messager Evangelique (0026-0274)
Published by: Eglise de la Confession d'Ausburg, 4 Rue Gustave Dore, Strasbourg, 67000, France. TEL 33-3-88233340. Ed. Fritz Westphal. Circ: 20,000. **Co-sponsor:** Eglise Reforme d'Alsace et de Lorraine.

286.7 ITA ISSN 0392-6346
IL MESSAGGERO AVVENTISTA. Text in Italian. 1926. m. EUR 22 (effective 2009). **Document type:** *Magazine, Consumer.*
Formerly (until 1929): Rivista Avventista (0394-3550)
Related titles: Online - full text ed.
Published by: (Unione Italiana delle Chiese Cristiane Avventiste), Edizioni A D V, Via Chiantigiana, 30, Falciani, Impruneta, FI 50023, Italy. TEL 39-055-2326291, FAX 39-055-2326241, info@edizioniadv.it, http://www.edizioniadv.it. Ed. Franco Evangelisti. Circ: 1,600.

286 SGP ISSN 0026-0371
MESSENGER. Text in English. 1968 (vol.18). bi-m. SGD 3.50. illus.
Published by: Southeast Asia Union Mission of Seventh-Day Adventists, 251 Upper Serangoon Rd, Singapore, 347688, Singapore. Ed. Loralyn Horning. Circ: 2,000 (controlled).

286 USA
MESSENGER (DUNN). Text in English. 1960. m. USD 6.50 (effective 2000). bk.rev.
Published by: Pentecostal Free Will Baptist Church, Inc., PO Box 1568, Dunn, NC 28335. TEL 910-892-4161, FAX 910-892-6876. Ed. George Thomas. R&P Pam Kennedy. Circ: 3,010.

286.5 USA ISSN 0026-0355
BX7801
MESSENGER (ELGIN). Text in English. 1851. m. USD 12.50. adv. bk.rev.; film rev. index.
Published by: Church of the Brethren, General Services Commission, 1451 Dundee Ave, Elgin, IL 60120-1694. TEL 847-742-5100, FAX 847-742-6103. Ed. Kermon Thomasson. Pub. Dale E Minnich. Adv. contact Nevin Dulabaum. Circ: 23,000.

286.7 GBR ISSN 0309-3654
MESSENGER (GRANTHAM). Text in English. 1895. fortn. GBP 13; GBP 27 foreign. adv. bk.rev. **Document type:** *Bulletin.*
Formerly: British Advent Messenger (0045-2874)
Indexed: RASB.
—CCC.
Published by: Stanborough Press Ltd., Alma Park, Grantham, Lincs NG31 9SL, United Kingdom. TEL 44-1476-591700, FAX 44-1476-77144. Ed. D N Marshall. Pub. P Hammond. R&P, Adv. contact Edward Johnson. Circ: 10,000.

286 USA
THE MESSENGER (OMAHA). Text in English. 1911. 6/yr. USD 1. bk.rev. illus. **Document type:** *Newsletter.*
Formerly: Nebraska Baptist Messenger
Published by: American Baptist Churches of Nebraska, 6404 Maple St, Omaha, NE 68104. TEL 402-556-4730, FAX 402-556-1910. Ed. Rovert C Molby. Circ: 3,875.

286.5 USA
MESSENGER OF TRUTH. Text in Ukrainian. 1927. bi-m. USD 12. bk.rev. illus.
Published by: All-Ukrainian Evangelical Baptist Convention, 6751 Riverside Dr, Berwyn, IL 60402-2227. TEL 312-788-0999. Ed. O R Harbuziuk. Circ: 5,000.

287 GBR
METHODIST CONFERENCE. MINUTES AND YEARBOOK. Text in English. 1932. a. GBP 29 per issue (effective 2010). 508 p./no.; **Document type:** *Directory, Academic/Scholarly.* **Description:** Covers information about Methodist conference.
Published by: Methodist Publishing House, 17 Tresham Rd, Orton Southgate, Peterborough, PE2 6SG, United Kingdom. TEL 44-1733-235962, FAX 44-1733-390325, resources@methodistchurch.org.uk, http://www.mph.org.uk.

287 GBR
METHODIST DIARY. Text in English. 1850. a. GBP 6.50 per issue (effective 2010). 100 p./no.; back issues avail. **Document type:** *Bulletin, Consumer.* **Description:** Provides information for preachers.
Published by: Methodist Publishing House, 17 Tresham Rd, Orton Southgate, Peterborough, PE2 6SG, United Kingdom. TEL 44-1733-235962, FAX 44-1733-390325, resources@methodistchurch.org.uk, http://www.mph.org.uk.

287 USA ISSN 0026-1238
BX8235
➤ **METHODIST HISTORY.** Text in English. 1948. q. USD 20 domestic; USD 25 in Canada; USD 30 elsewhere; USD 10 domestic to students; USD 14 in Canada to students; USD 18 elsewhere to students (effective 2009). bk.rev. charts; illus. cum index: 1962-July 1982, October 1982-1997. back issues avail.; reprints avail. **Document type:** *Journal, Academic/Scholarly.* **Description:** Covers articles, book reviews, pictures and illustrations, news and other information about the history of the Wesleyan and Methodist heritage.
Supersedes in part (in 1962): World Parish (0510-9272)
Related titles: Microfilm ed.: (from PQC).
Indexed: A21, A22, AmH&L, BAS, CA, CERDIC, FR, HistAb, MLA-IB, MPI, P30, R&TA, RI-1, RI-2, RILM, T02.
—BLDSC (5746.350000), IE, Infotrieve, Ingenta, INIST.
Published by: (Historical Society of The United Methodist Church), United Methodist Church, General Commission on Archives & History, 36 Madison Avenue, PO Box 127, Madison, NJ 07940. TEL 973-408-3189, FAX 973-408-3909, gcah@gcah.org. Ed. Robert J Williams.

287 GBR ISSN 0026-1262
METHODIST RECORDER. Text in English. 1861. w. GBP 58.50; GBP 1.10 per issue (effective 2009). adv. bk.rev.; play rev.; rec.rev. charts; illus. back issues avail. **Document type:** *Newspaper, Consumer.* **Description:** Features about the life and history of the Methodist Church.
Related titles: Microfilm ed.: (from PQC, WMP).
Published by: Methodist Newspaper Co. Ltd., 122 Golden Ln, London, EC1Y 0TL, United Kingdom. TEL 44-20-72518414, FAX 44-20-72518600. **Dist. by:** Comag.

287 USA ISSN 1946-5254
▼ ➤ **METHODIST REVIEW**; a journal of Wesleyan and Methodist studies. Text in English. 2009. a. free (effective 2011). **Document type:** *Journal, Academic/Scholarly.* **Description:** Research on Wesleyan and Methodist studies, including biblical, theological, ethical, philosophical, practical, historical, and social-scientific topics and methodologies.
Media: Online - full text.
Indexed: T02.
Published by: (Emory University, Candler School of Theology), The Methodist Review, Inc., 1001 9th Ave, Nashville, TN 37203-4729. TEL 615-340-7000, rex.matthews@emory.edu.

287 SWE ISSN 0543-6206
METODISTKYRKANS I SVERIGE AARSBOK; utgiven enligt konferensens beslut. Text in Swedish. 1908. a. SEK 100 (effective 1999). stat. **Document type:** *Bulletin.* **Description:** Reports on the work of the Methodist Church in Sweden.
Formerly (until 1939): Metodist-Episkopal-Kyrkans i Sverige Aarsbok
Published by: Metodistkyrkan i Sverige/United Methodist Church in Sweden, Fack 45130, Stockholm, 10430, Sweden. FAX 46-31-55-79. Ed. Rev. Alf Englund. Circ: 400.

287.6 USA ISSN 0026-2072
MICHIGAN CHRISTIAN ADVOCATE. Text in English. 1873. m. USD 20 (effective 2005). adv. bk.rev. illus. 16 p./no.; back issues avail. **Document type:** *Newspaper, Consumer.*
Published by: (United Methodist Church, West Michigan and Detroit Annual Conferences), Michigan Christian Advocate Publishing Co., 316 Springbrook Ave, Adrian, MI 49221. TEL 517-265-2075, FAX 517-263-7422. Circ: 7,500 (paid).

284.1 USA
MICHIGAN LUTHERAN. Text in English. 1922. m. USD 6. adv. bk.rev.; film rev. **Document type:** *Newspaper.* **Description:** Presents the work of the Michigan District and its congregations to the membership of the church in the area, for information, motivation, and inspiration.
Published by: Lutheran Church - Missouri Synod, Michigan District, 3773 Geddes Road, Ann Arbor, MI 48105. TEL 313-665-3791, FAX 313-665-0255. Ed. Walt Rummel. Adv. contact Alice Pearson. Circ: 76,000 (controlled).

286 USA ISSN 1543-6977
BX6201
MIDWESTERN JOURNAL OF THEOLOGY. Text in English. 2003 (Spr.). s-a. USD 20 (effective 2003).
Published by: Midwestern Baptist Theological Seminary, 5001 N. Oak Trafficway, Kansas City, MO 64118. TEL 816-414-3700, http://www.mbts.edu.

284.1 CAN ISSN 1193-1825
MIERA DRAUDZES VESTIS. Text in Latvian. 1953. bi-m. CAD 15. adv. bk.rev. **Document type:** *Bulletin.* **Description:** News of events in the church, and articles and news of interest to the Latvian community.
Formerly (until 1991): Draudzes Vestis (0701-0214)
Published by: Peace Latvian Lutheran Church, 83 Main St, Ottawa, ON K1S 1B5, Canada. TEL 613-230-4085. Ed. Rev. Maris Ludviks. Circ: 170.

280.4 USA
MIRACLES NOW. Text in English. 1997. bi-m.
Published by: Oral Roberts Evangelistic Association Inc., 7777 South Lewis Ave, Box 2187, Tulsa, OK 74171-0001. TEL 918-495-7307.

266.4 NOR ISSN 0800-5346
MISJONSTIDENDE; aktuelt om misjon og kirke. Text in Norwegian. 1845. m. NOK 340 (effective 2007). back issues avail. **Document type:** *Magazine, Consumer.*
Formerly (until 1984): Norsk Misjonstidende (0800-5842); Which icorporated (1924-1931): Lys over Sudan (1500-2365); (1884-1924): Missionslaesning for Kvindeforeninger (1500-5917); (1916-1924): Kamp og Seier (1500-3280); Which was formerly (1900-1916): Kamp og Seier paa Missionsmarken (1500-3272)
Related titles: Audio cassette/tape ed.: Misjonstidende (CD-ROM). ISSN 1890-1026. 2003; Online - full text ed.: ISSN 1890-0593.
Published by: Det Norske Misjonsselskab, PO Box 226, Sentrum, Stavanger, 4001, Norway. TEL 47-51-516100, FAX 47-51-516161, infosenter@nms.no, http://ww.nms.no.

284.1 USA ISSN 1068-3151
BV2540.A1
MISSIO APOSTOLICA. Text in English. 1993. s-a. bk.rev. **Document type:** *Magazine, Consumer.*
Indexed: A21, RI-1.
Published by: Lutheran Society for Missiology, 801 De Mun Ave, St. Louis, MO 63105. info@lsfmissiology.org, http://lsfmissiology.org/.

286.6 USA ISSN 1947-2781
▼ **MISSIO DEI**; a journal of mission theology and praxis. Text in English. 2010 (Aug.). s-a. USD 6.99 (effective 2011). **Document type:** *Journal, Academic/Scholarly.* **Description:** Provides a forum for exploring the tradition, practice and missions of the Churches of Christ and the wider Stone-Campbell Restoration Movement.
Media: Online - full text.
Published by: The Missio Dei Foundation, 11409 Morning Glory Tr, Austin, TX 78750. TEL 931-563-0347, gemckinzie@gmail.com.

283 NZL
MISSION ACTION. Text in English. 1981. 3/yr. free. charts; illus. back issues avail. **Document type:** *Newsletter.* **Description:** Reports news from partner organizations and topics of current missiological concern.
Former titles (until 1999): World Mission News; Mission There and Here (0111-4824)
Related titles: Online - full text ed.
Published by: Anglican Missions Board of the Church in Aotearoa New Zealand & Polynesia, 32 Mulgrave St, PO Box 12012, Wellington, 6038, New Zealand. TEL 64-4-4735172, FAX 64-4-4995553, 64-4-4995553, info@angmissions.org.nz. Circ: 18,000.

280.4 USA
BV2050
MISSION HANDBOOK. U.S. AND CANADIAN PROTESTANT MINISTRIES OVERSEAS. Text in English. 1951. irreg. (every 3-5 yrs.), latest 19th ed., 2004-2006. price varies. Index. **Document type:** *Directory, Trade.* **Description:** Presents detailed data on Canadian and U.S. Christian missionary agencies, cross-indexed by ministry, state, province, countries of services, and church tradition. Includes interpretive essays.
Former titles: Mission Handbook. U.S. and Canadian Protestant Ministries Overseas; (until 2003): Mission Handbook. U.S. and Canadian Christian Ministries Overseas; (until 1996): Mission Handbook. USA / Canada Christian Ministries Overseas; Mission Handbook: U S A - Canada Protestant Ministries Overseas (1050-771X); (until 1986): Mission Handbook: North American Protestant Ministries Overseas (0093-8130); North American Protestant Ministries Overseas (0078-1339)
Published by: Evangelism and Missions Information Service, Wheaton College, Billy Graham Center, 500 College Ave., Wheaton, IL 60187. TEL 630-752-7158, FAX 630-752-7155, emis@wheaton.edu, http://bgc.gospelcom.net/emis/. Circ: 1,500.

266 DEU ISSN 1430-9092
MISSION WELTWEIT. Text in German. 1986. bi-m. **Document type:** *Bulletin.*
Formerly (until 1996): Voelker Rufen (0933-6117)
Published by: Liebenzell Mission, Liobastr 17, Bad Liebenzell, 75378, Germany. TEL 49-7052-170, FAX 49-7052-17100, info@liebenzell.org, http://www.liebenzell.org. Circ: 20,500.

266 USA
MISSIONARY HERALD. Text in English. m. USD 2 domestic (effective 2000). back issues avail. **Document type:** *Newsletter.* **Description:** Contains missionary reports and religious articles to inform readers of missionary activities on various foreign mission fields.
Related titles: Microform ed.: (from PQC).
Published by: Evangelistic Faith Missions, PO Box 609, Bedford, IN 47421. TEL 812-275-7531, FAX 812-275-7532. Ed., R&P J Stevan Manley.

266.6 USA
MISSIONARY REPORTER. Text in English. 1946. q. looseleaf. membership. **Document type:** *Newsletter.* **Description:** Covers the minutes of the board meetings. Includes reports of workers on various missionary projects.
Published by: Seventh Day Baptist Missionary Society, 119 Main St, Westerly, RI 02891. TEL 401-596-4326, FAX 401-348-9494. Ed. Brenda Palmer. R&P G Kirk Looper. Circ: 250.

266.6 USA
MISSIONS; update. Text in English. 1975. m. looseleaf. free. **Document type:** *Newsletter.* **Description:** National and international coverage of the society's activities.
Published by: (Seventh Day Baptist Missionary Society), American Sabbath Tract and Communication Council, Seventh Day Baptist Center, Box 1678, Janesville, WI 53547. TEL 608-752-5055, FAX 608-752-7711. Ed. Kirk Looper. Circ: 200. **Subscr. to:** Seventh Day Baptist Missionary Society, 119 Main St, Westerly, RI 02891. TEL 401-596-4326.

286.132 USA
MISSIONS LEADER. Text in English. 1970. q. USD 17.99 (effective 2008). **Document type:** *Magazine, Consumer.* **Description:** Provides a planning tool for all the missions leaders in the church including WMU directors and leaders, pastors and other church staff.
Former titles (until 199?): Dimension (Churchwide Edition); (until 199?): Dimension (Birmingham) (0162-6825)
Related titles: Online - full text ed.
Published by: Woman's Missionary Union Auxiliary to the Southern Baptist Convention, 100 Missionary Ridge, PO Box 830010, Birmingham, AL 35283. TEL 205-991-8100, 800-968-7301, FAX 205-995-4840, customer_service@wmu.org, http://www.wmu.com/. Ed. Nell Branum. R&P Carol Causey. Circ: 20,000 (paid).

286.132 USA
MISSIONS LEADER - ASSOCIATIONAL EDITION. Text in English. q. USD 19.99 (effective 2008). **Document type:** *Magazine, Consumer.* **Description:** Provides information for associational WMU leaders, directors of missions and on mission council members.
Formerly: Dimension (Associational Edition); Supersedes in part (in 199?): Dimension (Birmingham) (0162-6825)
Published by: Woman's Missionary Union Auxiliary to the Southern Baptist Convention, 100 Missionary Ridge, PO Box 830010, Birmingham, AL 35283. TEL 205-991-8100, 800-968-7301, FAX 205-995-4840, customer_service@wmu.org, http://www.wmu.com/.

266.6132 USA ISSN 1083-3293
MISSIONS MOSAIC. Text in English. 1995. m. USD 20.99 (effective 2009). adv. bk.rev. illus. reprints avail. **Document type:** *Magazine, Consumer.* **Description:** Features women's issues, bible study, pray, how to minister and witness and spiritual development.
Incorporates (in Sep.1996): Prayer Patterns; Formed by the merger of (1970-1995): Contempo (0162-1971); Royal Service (0035-9084); Which was formerly: Our Mission Fields
Related titles: Online - full text ed.
Published by: Woman's Missionary Union Auxiliary to the Southern Baptist Convention, 100 Missionary Ridge, PO Box 830010, Birmingham, AL 35283. TEL 205-991-8100, 800-968-7301, FAX 205-995-4840, customer_service@wmu.org, http://www.wmu.com/. Ed. Joanne Parker. R&P Carol Causey. adv.: color page USD 2,500; trim 8 x 10.5. Circ: 235,000 (paid).

266 GBR
MISSIONS TO SEAFARERS. ANNUAL REPORT & ACCOUNTS. Text in English. 1856. a. free (effective 2009). index. **Document type:** *Report, Trade.*
Former titles (until 200?): Missions to Seafarers. Annual Report; Missions to Seamen Annual Report; Missions to Seamen Handbook (0076-9401)
Related titles: Online - full text ed.
Published by: Mission to Seafarers, Saint Michael Paternoster Royal, College Hill, London, EC4R 2RL, United Kingdom. TEL 44-20-72485202, FAX 44-20-72484761, pr@missiontoseafarers.org. Ed. Gillian Ennis.

283.73 USA ISSN 1942-8154
THE MISSISSIPPI EPISCOPALIAN. Text in English. 19??. m. (except Jun. and Aug.). **Document type:** *Newsletter, Consumer.* **Description:** Includes stories of local or diocesan-wide interest, church and pastor updates and memorial information for Episcopal church members in Mississippi.
Published by: Episcopal Diocese of Mississippi, 118 N Congress St, Jackson,, MS 39201. TEL 601-948-5954. Ed. Rev. Scott Lenoir.

287.6 USA
MISSISSIPPI UNITED METHODIST ADVOCATE. Text in English. 1947. fortn. USD 9.50. adv. bk.rev. **Document type:** *Newspaper.*
Formerly: Mississippi Methodist Advocate (0026-6329)
Published by: United Methodist Church, Mississippi Conference, PO Box 1093, Jackson, MS 39215. TEL 601-354-0515. Ed. Rev. J R Woodrick. Circ: 15,000 (controlled).

280.4 DEU
MITEINANDER UNTERWEGS; Frauen im Bund Evangelisch-Freikirchlicher Gemeinden. Text in German. bi-m. EUR 6.90; EUR 1.15 newsstand/cover (effective 2007). **Document type:** *Magazine, Consumer.*
Published by: Oncken Verlag GmbH, Muendener Str 13, Kassel, 34123, Germany. TEL 49-561-520050, FAX 49-561-5200550, zeitschriften@oncken.de, http://www.oncken.de.

284.1 DEU ISSN 1436-9397
MITTEILEN; Hermannsburger Missionsblatt. Text in German. 1853. bi-m. free (effective 2009). bk.rev. illus.; maps. 48 p./no. 3 cols./p.; back issues avail. **Document type:** *Bulletin, Consumer.*
Formerly (until 1993): Hermannsburger Missionsblatt
Published by: Evangelisch-Lutherisches Missionswerk in Niedersachsen, Georg Haccius Str 9, Hermannsburg, 29320, Germany. TEL 49-5052-690, FAX 49-5052-69222, zentrale-de@elm-mission.net.

280.4 DEU
MITTENDRIN (DILLENBURG). Text in German. 1996. 4/yr. EUR 9.20 (effective 2009). **Document type:** *Magazine, Consumer.*
Published by: Christliche Verlagsgesellschaft mbH, Moltkestr 1, Dillenburg, 35683, Germany. TEL 49-2771-83020, FAX 49-2771-830230, info@cv-dillenburg.de, http://www.cv-dillenburg.de.

285 USA ISSN 1076-7169
BX9401
MODERN REFORMATION. Text in English. 1986. bi-m. USD 22 domestic; USD 25 in Canada; USD 40 in Europe; USD 45 elsewhere (effective 2004). **Document type:** *Magazine, Consumer.*
Indexed: ChrPI.
—Ingenta. **CCC.**
Address: 1725 Bear Valley Pkwy, Escondido, CA 92027. TEL 800-890-7556.

280.4 305.4 USA ISSN 2154-2546
▼ **THE MODEST WOMAN.** Text in English. 2010. bi-m. USD 4 per issue (effective 2010). **Document type:** *Magazine, Consumer.* **Description:** For Christian women of virtue, integrity, and class.
Media: Online - full text.
Published by: Sensational Christian Creations, 5613 Old Boyce Rd, Boyce, LA 71409. TEL 318-787-2606, shanetria@shanetria.com.

284.2 ZAF ISSN 0378-410X
MOLAETSA-MOLAETSA. Text in Sotho, Southern, Tswana. 1957. 8/yr.
Formerly: Rugama
Published by: Reformed Churches in South Africa/Gereformeerde Kerke in Suid-Afrika, c/o South African Council of Churches, PO Box 62098, Marshalltown, 2107, South Africa. Ed. H A Louw. Circ: 2,500.

280.4 DEU ISSN 0540-6226
BX8022.R5
MONATSHEFTE FUER EVANGELISCHE KIRCHENGESCHICHTE DES RHEINLANDES. Text in German. 1952. m. EUR 30 (effective 2011). **Document type:** *Journal, Academic/Scholarly.*
Indexed: DIP, IBR, IBZ.
Published by: (Rheinland Kultur GmbH), Dr. Rudolf Habelt GmbH, Am Buchenhang 1, Bonn, 53115, Germany. TEL 49-228-9238322, FAX 49-228-923836, info@habelt.de, http://www.habelt.de.

284.6 USA ISSN 1041-0961
BX8551
MORAVIAN (BETHLEHEM, 1856). Text in English. 1856. m. (combined Jan.-Feb., July-Aug.). USD 10 to non-members; USD 13 to members. adv. bk.rev. charts; illus.; maps; stat. index. **Document type:** *Newsletter.*
Former titles: North American Moravian (0027-1012); Moravian and Wachovia Moravian
Related titles: Microfilm ed.
Published by: Moravian Church in America - North and South, Board of Communications, Box 1245, Bethlehem, PA 18016. TEL 610-867-0594, FAX 610-866-9223. Ed., Pub. Hermann I Weinlick. Adv. contact Nena M Asguith. Circ: 24,000.

284.6 GBR
MORAVIAN MESSENGER. Text in English. 19??. m. free to members (effective 2009). adv. bk.rev. illus. back issues avail. **Document type:** *Magazine, Trade.* **Description:** Covers details about the Moravian Church in the British Province.
Formerly: Moravian Message
Related titles: Online - full text ed.
Published by: Moravian Union Inc., Book Room, 5 Muswell Hill, London, N103TJ, United Kingdom. TEL 44-20-88833409, office@moravian.org.uk. Ed. Judith Ashton.

286.132 USA ISSN 0162-4288
MORE (NASHVILLE). Text in English. 19??. m. USD 24.95; USD 1.40 per issue (effective 2008). adv. back issues avail. **Document type:** *Magazine, Consumer.* **Description:** Features meaningful, 10-minute devotions that are simple enough for use by children developing the habit of daily bible reading.
Published by: LifeWay Christian Resources, 1 Lifeway Plz, Nashville, TN 37234. TEL 615-251-2000, 800-458-2772, FAX 615-251-5933, customerservice@lifeway.com.

MORE LIGHT UPDATE. *see* HOMOSEXUALITY

284.2 ZAF ISSN 0378-4126
MURUMIWA. Text in Tsonga. 1950. bi-m.
Related titles: Ed.
Published by: Reformed Churches in South Africa/Gereformeerde Kerke in Suid-Afrika, c/o South African Council of Churches, PO Box 62098, Marshalltown, 2107, South Africa. TEL 27-11-4921380, FAX 27-11-4921448, info@sacc.org.za, http://www.sacc.org.za.

MUSIC TIME. *see* MUSIC

280.4083 USA ISSN 0027-5387
MY DEVOTIONS. Text in English. 1958. q. USD 9 (effective 2009). illus. **Document type:** *Magazine, Consumer.* **Description:** Guides the children to the word through stories and situations to which they can relate.
Related titles: Braille ed.: free (effective 2011); ◆ Large type ed. 22 pt.: My Devotions (Large Print Edition).
Published by: Concordia Publishing House, 3558 S Jefferson, St Louis, MO 63118. TEL 314-268-1000, 800-325-3040, FAX 800-490-9889, order@cph.org. Pub. Rev. Paul T McCain. Circ: 70,000.

284.1 USA
MY DEVOTIONS (LARGE PRINT EDITION). Text in English. m. free (effective 2011). **Document type:** *Magazine, Consumer.* **Description:** Publishes devotional pieces for children ages 8-13.
Media: Large Type (22 pt.). **Related titles:** Braille ed.: free (effective 2011); ◆ Print ed.: My Devotions. ISSN 0027-5387.
Published by: (Lutheran Church - Missouri Synod), Lutheran Library for the Blind, 7550 Watson Rd, St Louis, MO 63119. TEL 314-918-0415, 888-215-2455, blind.mission@blindmission.org.

280.4 POL ISSN 1428-3697
MYSL PROTESTANCKA; kwartalnik spoleczno-kulturalny. Text in Polish. 1997. q.
Published by: Fundacja Kultury Chrzescijanskiej, ul Warszawska 18, Katowice, 40006, Poland. redakcja@protestantyzm.media.pl, http://www.protestantyzm.media.pl. Ed. Jan Szturc.

284.1 DEU
N M - NORDELBISCHE MISSION; Breklumer Sonntagsblatt fuers Haus. Text in German. 1974. bi-m. bk.rev. **Document type:** *Newsletter.* **Description:** Lutheran publication covering missionary work and development aid in all parts of the world, especially developing countries in the Southern Hemisphere. Includes letters from readers.
Published by: Nordelbisches Zentrum fuer Weltmission und Kirchlichen Weltdienst, Agathe-Lasch-Weg 16, Hamburg, 22605, Germany. TEL 49-40-881810, FAX 49-40-88181210, info@nmz-mission.de. Circ: 8,000.

284 NLD ISSN 1873-8818
NAAST/. Text in Dutch. 1976. m. **Document type:** *Magazine, Consumer.*
Formerly (until 2007): Tot aan de Einden der Aarde (1381-902X)
Published by: Gereformeerde Kerken in Nederland, Postbus 770, Amersfoort, 3800 AT, Netherlands. info@gkv.nl, http://www.gkv.nl. Ed. Tjerk S de Vries. Circ: 48,500.

220 GBR ISSN 0077-3557
NATIONAL BIBLE SOCIETY OF SCOTLAND. ANNUAL REPORT. Text in English. 1860. a. free. **Document type:** *Corporate.*
Related titles: ◆ Supplement to: Word at Work.
Published by: Scottish Bible Society, 7 Hampton Terr, Edinburgh, EH12 5XU, United Kingdom. info@scottishbiblesociety.org. Ed. Pauline Hurst. R&P Colin Hay. Circ: 1,000.

284.2 ZAF ISSN 0024-8665
NEDERDUITSE GEREFORMEERDE KERK VAN NATAL GEMEENTE VRYHEID. MAANDBRIEF. Text in English. 1965. m. looseleaf. free. adv.
Published by: Nederduitse Gereformeerde Kerk van Natal Gemeentevryheid, Smalstraat 82, Vryheid, KwaZulu-Natal, South Africa. Ed. E Oberholster. Circ: 600 (controlled).

284.2 ZAF ISSN 0378-9888
BR9.A34
➤ **NEDERDUITSE GEREFORMEERDE TEOLOGIESE TYDSKRIF.** Text in English. 1959. q. ZAR 72 in South Africa & Namibia; ZAR 82 elsewhere (effective 2000). bk.rev. bibl. index. **Document type:** *Journal, Academic/Scholarly.*
Related titles: Online - full text ed.
Indexed: CERDIC, ISAP, IZBG, OTA.
—BLDSC (6069.150000).
Published by: Nederduitse Gereformeerde Kerk in Suid-Afrika/Dutch Reformed Church in South Africa, PO Box 4445, Pretoria, 0001, South Africa. TEL 27-12-3228900, FAX 27-12-3223803, http://www.ngkerk.org.za. Circ: 1,800 (controlled).

285 USA ISSN 0745-418X
NETWORK NEWS (BLUFFTON). Text in English. 19??. q. USD 40; USD 50 membership (effective 2002).
Related titles: Online - full text ed.
Indexed: A01, A02, A03, A08, B07, C06, C07, C12, CA, M01, M02, MicrocompInd, P34, T02, V02, W09.
Published by: Witherspoon Society, 1419 Claredon Dr, Wayzata, MN 55391. TEL 952-473-2711. Ed. Doug King.

280.4 USA ISSN 2156-0358
▼ **NEUE.** Text in English. 2010. q. USD 12 (effective 2010). **Document type:** *Magazine, Consumer.* **Description:** Connects, inspires and gives voice to innovators and leaders shaping the future of the Church.
Published by: Relevant Media Group, Inc., 600 Rinehart Rd, Lake Mary, FL 32771. TEL 407-333-7152, FAX 407-333-7153, info@relevantmediagroup.com, http://www.relevantmediagroup.com.

285 USA ISSN 0199-3518
NEW HORIZONS (WILLOW GROVE). Text in English. 1935. 11/yr. USD 15 domestic; USD 20 foreign (effective 2005). adv. bk.rev. illus.
Formerly (until 1980): Presbyterian Guardian (0032-7522)
Indexed: CERDIC.

R

Published by: Orthodox Presbyterian Church, Committee on Christian Education, P O Box P, Willow Grove, PA 19090-0920. TEL 215-830-0900, FAX 215-830-0350. Ed., R&P Thomas E Tyson. Circ: 11,300.

285 USA
THE NEW SOUTHERN PRESBYTERIAN REVIEW. Variant title: Christ Theological Seminary. Text in English. 200?. q. **Document type:** *Journal, Academic/Scholarly.* **Description:** Covers free debate and discussion. Works to renew every idea, activity, relationship, and institution of human existance, beginning with the heart, according to the Creation Mandate of Genesis.
Indexed: R&TA.
Published by: Chalcedon Presbyterian Church, 302 Pilgrim Mill Rd, Cumming, GA 30040. TEL 770-205-9390, FAX 770-205-9363, http://www.chalcedon.org.

287 AUS ISSN 0726-2612
NEW TIMES. Text in English. 19??. m. (except Jan.). adv. bk.rev. illus. back issues avail. **Document type:** *Newspaper, Consumer.*
Former titles (until 1982): Central Times (0038-2949); (until 1971): South Australian Methodist; (until 1941): Australian Christian Commonwealth
Related titles: Online - full text ed.
Indexed: CERDIC, MLA-IB.
Published by: (Uniting Church in Australia, Synod of South Australia), New Times Inc., GPO Box 2145, Adelaide, SA 5001, Australia. TEL 61-8-82025112. Ed. Jill Freear TEL 61-8-83264230. Adv. contact Russell Baker TEL 61-8-83616822. B&W page AUD 1,620. Circ: 12,000.

NEW WORLD OUTLOOK; United Methodist missions. *see* RELIGIONS AND THEOLOGY

283 CAN ISSN 0549-0898
NEWFOUNDLAND CHURCHMAN. Text in English. 1888. m. CAD 5, USD 7.50. adv. bk.rev.
Published by: Anglican Church of Newfoundland, 19 Kingsbridge Rd, St. John's, NF A1C 3K4, Canada. TEL 709-576-6697. Ed. Hollis Hiscock. Circ: 33,000.

285.8 USA ISSN 0362-1510
BX7101
NEWS FROM THE CONGREGATIONAL CHRISTIAN HISTORICAL SOCIETY. Text in English. 1969. s-a. membership. **Document type:** *Newsletter.* **Description:** News and announcements pertaining to the members and activities of this Boston-based church historical society.
Published by: Congregational Christian Historical Society, Inc., 14 Beacon St., Boston, MA 02108. TEL 617-523-0470, FAX 617-523-0491. Ed. Harold F Worthley. Circ: 1,100 (paid).

287.6 USA ISSN 1073-4910
NEWSCOPE; the national weekly for United Methodist leaders. Text in English. 1973. w. looseleaf. USD 28 domestic; USD 38 foreign (effective 2009). back issues avail. **Document type:** *Newsletter, Trade.* **Description:** Provides up-to-the-minute reports on united methodist church news and other happenings of interest to united methodists.
Related titles: E-mail ed.: USD 16 (effective 2009); Online - full text ed.: USD 15.
Published by: United Methodist Publishing House, 201 8th Ave S, PO Box 801, Nashville, TN 37202. TEL 615-749-6000, 800-672-1789, FAX 615-749-6579, customerservice@umph.com. Ed. John F Kutsko TEL 615-749-6385. Pub. Neil M Alexander. R&P R Lewis TEL 615-749-6422. Circ: 8,000.

280.4 AUS
NEWSFLASHES. Text in English. 19??. q. back issues avail. **Document type:** *Newsletter.*
Related titles: Online - full text ed.: free (effective 2009).
Published by: Pocket Testament League of Australia (P T L), PO Box 253, Kingsgrove, NSW 1480, Australia. TEL 61-2-95022982, FAX 61-2-91507374, tptl@ay.com.au. Ed. Ronnie Goh.

283 USA ISSN 0885-6966
THE NEWSLETTER NEWSLETTER. Text in English. 1979. m. looseleaf. USD 44.95 (effective 2005). back issues avail. **Document type:** *Newsletter, Trade.* **Description:** Contains editorial, production, design and distribution advice for church newsletter editors.
Related titles: Online - full text ed.
Published by: Communication Resources Inc., PO Box 36269, Canton, OH 44735-6269. TEL 800-992-2144. Ed. Stan Purdum.

283 CAN ISSN 0703-5888
NIAGARA ANGLICAN. Text in English. 1954. 10/yr. CAD 15 (effective 2011). adv. bk.rev. **Document type:** *Newspaper, Consumer.*
Address: 252 James St N, Hamilton, ON L8R 2L3, Canada. TEL 905-527-1316, FAX 905-527-1281, editor@niagara.anglican.ca. Eds. Christopher Grabiec, Larry Perks. R&P Larry Perks. Adv. contact Roddie Gould Perks. Circ: 18,500.

280.4 NLD ISSN 0167-3602
NIEUW LEVEN. Text in Dutch. 1962. m. EUR 10 (effective 2010). **Document type:** *Newspaper, Consumer.* **Description:** Inspirational and evangelical publication.
Published by: Stichting Johan Maasbach Wereldzending, Apeldoornselaan 2, The Hague, 2573 LM, Netherlands. TEL 31-70-3635929, FAX 31-70-3107111, info@maasbach.com, http://www.maasbach.com. Ed. Maasbach David.

266 DEU
NORDDEUTSCHE MISSION. MITTEILUNGEN. Text in German. 1949. bi-m. free. **Document type:** *Newsletter, Consumer.*
Published by: Norddeutsche Mission, Berckstr 27, Bremen, 28359, Germany. TEL 49-421-4677038, FAX 49-421-4677907, info@norddeutschemission.de, http://www.norddeutschemission.de. Ed. Antje Wodtke.

280.4 DEU
DIE NORDELBISCHE; Wochenzeitung fuer Gemeinde und Gesellschaft. Text in German. 1924. w. EUR 67.20; EUR 1.50 newsstand/cover (effective 2009). adv. **Document type:** *Newspaper, Consumer.*
Former titles (until 2003): Nordelbische Kirchenzeitung; (until 1978): Nordelbische Kirchenzeitung - Kirche in Schleswig Holstein; (until 1976): Die Kirche der Heimat; (until 1949): Am Sehrohr der Zeit
Published by: Evangelischer Presseverband Nord e.V., Gartenstr 20, Kiel, 24103, Germany. TEL 49-431-55779241, FAX 49-431-55779297, gemeinde@nordelbische.de. Ed. Carsten Splitt. Circ: 12,500 (paid and controlled).

280.4 DEU ISSN 0938-3697
BX8001
NORDELBISCHE STIMMEN; Monatszeitschrift fuer haupt- und ehrenamtliche Mitarbeiter in Hamburg und Schleswig-Holstein. Text in German. 1977. m. adv. bk.rev. index. back issues avail. **Document type:** *Bulletin, Consumer.*
Published by: Evangelischer Presseverband Nord e.V., Gartenstr 20, Kiel, 24103, Germany. TEL 49-431-55779241, FAX 49-431-55779297, gemeinde@nordelbische.de, http://www.nordelbische.de. Circ: 3,000.

266.2 SWE ISSN 0345-8571
NORDISK OESTMISSION. Text in Swedish. 1964. q. SEK 50 (effective 2011). **Document type:** *Magazine, Consumer.* **Description:** Contains information about Lutheran mission in East Europe, Ukraine, Latvia, etc.
Related titles: Online - full text ed.
Address: c/o Martin Wihlborg, Torsgatan 36, Moelndal, 43138, Sweden. TEL 46-31-162480. Ed. Bengt Westholm.

285 USA
NOR'EASTER LEADERSHIP NEWS. Text in English. 1985. bi-m. USD 10 (effective 2000). back issues avail. **Document type:** *Newsletter.* **Description:** Covers Presbyterians in the Northeast US.
Formerly: Nor'easter (Syracuse) (1060-2755)
Published by: Presbyterian Church (U.S.A.), Synod of the Northeast, 65811 Hevitage Landing Dr, East Syracuse, NY 13057. TEL 315-446-5990, FAX 315-446-5708. Ed., R&P Lida Dawson Price. Circ: 20,000 (controlled).

266 USA
NORTH AMERICAN MISSIONS. Text in English. 1950. 3/yr. free. bk.rev. **Document type:** *Newsletter.*
Formerly: Round Table (Sarasota)
Published by: Association of North American Missions, 160 Tolbert Farm Rd, Beckley, WV 25801-8824. TEL 304-256-0596, FAX 304-256-0988. Ed. Dr. Roy Anderson. Circ: 5,000 (controlled).

287.6 USA ISSN 1933-0626
NORTH CAROLINA CONFERENCE CHRISTIAN ADVOCATE. Text in English. 1855. m. USD 15 (effective 2007). adv. bk.rev. **Document type:** *Newspaper, Consumer.*
Formerly (until 2005): North Carolina Christian Advocate (0029-2435)
Published by: (United Methodist Church, North Carolina Conference and Western North Carolina Conference), N C Conference Communications, 1307 Glenwood Ave, PO Box 10955, Raleigh, NC 27605. TEL 919-832-9560, 800-849-4433, http://nccumc.org. Ed. Bill Norton. Circ: 11,000.

283.73 USA
THE NORTHEAST (PORTLAND). Text in English. m. free subscr - mailed domestic to members; domestic voluntary donations. **Document type:** *Newspaper, Consumer.*
Published by: Episcopal Diocese of Maine, 143 State St, Portland, ME 04357. TEL 207-772-1953, FAX 207-773-0095. Ed. Heidi Shott. Circ: 10,000 (controlled).

280.4 ITA ISSN 1973-980X
NOTIZIE DA RIESI/NOUVELLES DE RIESI. Text in Multiple languages. 1961. bi-m. **Document type:** *Magazine, Consumer.*
Published by: Servizio Cristiano Istituto Valdese, Via Monte degli Ulivi 6, Riesi, CL 93016, Italy. TEL 39-0934-922906.

280.4 ITA
NOTIZIE EVANGELICHE. Short title: N E V. Text in Italian. 1980. w. bk.rev. **Document type:** *Bulletin, Consumer.* **Description:** Contains news about Protestant and evangelical churches, and the ecumenical movement in Italy and abroad.
Related titles: Diskette ed.; Online - full text ed.
Published by: Federation of Protestant Churches in Italy, Via Firenze, 38, Rome, RM 00184, Italy. TEL 39-06-4825120, FAX 39-06-4828728, nev@fcei.it, http://www.fcei.it.

286.132 USA ISSN 0469-1733
NUESTRA TAREA. Text in Spanish. 1955. q. USD 20.99 (effective 2008). **Document type:** *Magazine, Consumer.* **Description:** Provides missions information, ideas and inspiration to become more involved in the great commission for the Hispanic woman.
Related titles: Online - full text ed.
Published by: Woman's Missionary Union Auxiliary to the Southern Baptist Convention, 100 Missionary Ridge, PO Box 830010, Birmingham, AL 35283. TEL 205-991-8100, 800-968-7301, FAX 205-995-4840, customer_service@wmu.org, http://www.wmu.com/. Eds. Elizabeth Rivera, Steve Murdock. R&P Carol Causey. Circ: 3,500 (paid).

280.4 DOM ISSN 0029-5752
NUESTRO AMIGO. Text in Spanish. 1931. m. free.
Published by: Iglesia Evangelica Dominicana, Apartado 727, Santo Domingo, Dominican Republic. Ed. Herman Gonzalez Roca. Circ: 2,500.

280.4 780 USA ISSN 1947-590X
▼ **[NXTLVL] MAGAZINE**; Christ. life. music. Text in English. 2009. d. free per issue (effective 2009). **Document type:** *Magazine, Consumer.* **Description:** An urban pop culture publication with a spiritual perspective on life and culture.
Media: Online - full content.
Published by: Ogadi Fields, Ed. & Pub., 22822 Spellbrook Bend Ln, Richmond, TX 77407. TEL 301-318-8499, ofields@nxtlvlmag.com.

286.7 FIN ISSN 0355-3280
NYKYAIKA; suomen adventti kirkon viikkolehti. Text in Finnish. 1897. w. EUR 77 domestic; EUR 89.40 In Nordic countries; EUR 112.80 elsewhere; EUR 5 per issue (effective 2005). back issues avail. **Document type:** *Newspaper, Consumer.* **Description:** Publishes a weekly journal for the Seventh-Day Adventist congregation and a monthly evangelistic journal for the general public.
Related titles: Audio cassette/tape ed.: ISSN 1455-8866. 1995; Braille ed.: ISSN 0355-3299. 1974.
Published by: (Suomen Adventtikirkko/Seventh-Day Adventist Church in Finland), Kirjatoimi, PO Box 94, Tampere, 33101, Finland. TEL 358-3-3611200, FAX 358-3-3600454, kirjatoimi@kirjatoima.fi. Ed., R&P Klaus Kalliokoski. Adv. contact Anne Said.

280.4 USA
OBADIAH MAGAZINE. Text in English. 2001. q. USD 15 domestic; USD 18 in Canada; USD 20 elsewhere (effective 2000). adv. **Document type:** *Magazine, Consumer.* **Description:** Provides content for ecumenical Christians who live to love and serve the Lord.
Published by: Obadiah Press, 1826 Crossover Rd, PMB 108, Fayetteville, AR 72703. TEL 715-536-3167, obadiahpress@aol.com, http://www.obadiahpress.com. Ed. Tina Miller. adv.: B&W page USD 490; trim 8.25 x 10.75. Circ: 10,000 (paid and controlled).

286 NGA ISSN 1115-232X
OGBOMOSO JOURNAL OF THEOLOGY. Text in English. 1986. a. **Document type:** *Journal, Academic/Scholarly.*
Indexed: A21, R&TA, RI-1.
Published by: Nigerian Baptist Theological Seminary, PO Box 30, Ogbomoso, Western State, Nigeria.

286 USA ISSN 1554-3323
ONE MAGAZINE (ANTIOCH). Text in English. 2005. bi-m. **Document type:** *Magazine, Consumer.*
Published by: National Association of Free Will Baptists, 5233 Mt. View Rd, Antioch, TN 37013-2306. TEL 615-731-6812 615.731.6812, 877-767-7659, FAX 615-731-0771, http://nafwb.net/tp42/Default.asp?ID=767. Ed. Keith Burden.

284.2 NLD ISSN 0030-3356
OPBOUW. Text in Dutch. 1957. fortn. EUR 41.75 domestic; EUR 78 in Europe; EUR 103.50 elsewhere; EUR 20.50 to students (effective 2009). adv. bk.rev. illus. **Document type:** *Magazine, Consumer.*
Related titles: E-mail ed.
Published by: Gereformeerde Persvereniging Opbouw, c/o N Schenk, Droogoven 7, Wijk bij Duurstede, 3961 EW, Netherlands. TEL 31-343-575027, adm.opbouw@opbouwonline.nl. Eds. Matthias Huijgen, Sander Klos. adv.: page EUR 430; 180 x 266. Circ: 2,500.

284.2 NLD
OPEN DEUR. Text in Dutch. 1936. m. EUR 27 domestic; EUR 43.10 foreign; EUR 3.35 newsstand/cover (effective 2008). bk.rev. illus.
Formerly: Open Deur. Goede Tijding (0165-229X); Which was formed by the merger of (1970-1977): Open Deur (0030-3402); (1922-1977): Goede Tijding (0922-3606)
Published by: Boekencentrum Uitgevers, Goudstraat 50, Postbus 29, Zoetermeer, 2700 AA, Netherlands. TEL 31-79-3615481, FAX 31-79-3615489, info@boekencentrum.nl, http://www.boekencentrum.nl. Ed. Esther van der Panne. **Co-sponsors:** Dutch Reformed Church; Geref. Foundation; Roman Catholic Church; Lutheran Church.

280.4 USA ISSN 0888-8833
OPEN HANDS; resources for ministries affirming the diversity of human sexuality. Text in English. 1985. q. USD 20 domestic; USD 25 foreign (effective 2005). adv. bk.rev. bibl. back issues avail. **Document type:** *Magazine, Consumer.*
Formerly (until 1986): Manna for the Journey
Published by: Reconciling Congregation Program Inc., 3801 N Keeler, Chicago, IL 60641. TEL 773-736-5526, FAX 773-736-5475. Ed. Chris Glaser. Pub., Adv. contact Mark Bowman. Circ: 3,000. **Co-sponsor:** More Light, Open and Affirming, Reconciled in Christ, Welcoming & Affirming programs.

286.132 USA ISSN 0162-4296
BV4800
OPEN WINDOWS. Text in English. 19??. q. USD 10.95 (effective 2009). adv. back issues avail. **Document type:** *Magazine, Consumer.* **Description:** Provides believers with a plan for a meaningful 10-minute or longer devotional time.
Related titles: CD-ROM ed.: ISSN 1556-5351. 2005. USD 58.35 (effective 2009); ◆ Large type ed. 14 pt.: Open Windows. Large Print Edition.
Published by: LifeWay Christian Resources, 1 Lifeway Plz, Nashville, TN 37234. TEL 615-251-2000, 800-458-2772, FAX 615-251-5933, customerservice@lifeway.com. Ed. Woody Parker.

OPEN WINDOWS. LARGE PRINT EDITION. *see* HANDICAPPED—Visually Impaired

266.4 DNK ISSN 1903-6051
BV2355.D3
▼ **ORD TIL HANDLING.** Text in Danish. 2009. 6/yr. free. adv. bk.rev. abstr.; illus. back issues avail. **Document type:** *Newsletter, Consumer.*
Formed by the merger of (2000-2008): Danmission (1399-8277); Which was formed by the merger of (1834-2000): Dansk missionsblad (0011-6378); (1996-2000): Mission i Asien (1397-498X); Which was formerly (1896-1996): Santalposten (0106-391X); (2007-2008): Netvaerk (1902-5769); Which was formerly (2000-2005): Netvaerk i Danmission (1600-1079); (until 2000): D M S- Kredsen (0907-1946); (until 1992): D M S Nyt (0900-6524); (1966-1975): D M S Kredsen (0907-1954)
Related titles: Online - full text ed.
Published by: Danmission, Strandagervej 24, Hellerup, 2900, Denmark. TEL 45-39-629911, FAX 45-39-620206, danmission@danmission.dk. Ed. Tove Lind Iversen.

284.2 USA ISSN 1525-3503
ORDAINED SERVANT. Text in English. 19??. q. **Document type:** *Journal, Consumer.*
Related titles: Online - full text ed.: ISSN 1931-7115. 1992.
Published by: Orthodox Presbyterian Church, 607 N Easton Rd., Bldg. E, Box P, Willow Grove, PA 19090-0920. TEL 215-830-0900, FAX 215-830-0350, http://opc.org.

283.73 USA ISSN 1068-8811
OREGON EPISCOPAL CHURCH NEWS. Text in English. 1861. 9/yr. adv. bk.rev. illus.; stat. **Description:** News related to Episopal Church members in Western Oregon.
Former titles: Oregon Episcopal Churchman; Oregon Churchman (0030-4646)
Published by: Episcopal Diocese of Oregon, 11800 S W Military Ln, Portland, OR 97219-8436. TEL 503-636-5613, FAX 503-636-5616. Ed. Arlene Christianson Pickard. Circ: 11,000.

280.4 DEU
ORIENTIERUNG. Text in German. 1965. q. EUR 10.40; EUR 2.90 newsstand/cover (effective 2009). **Document type:** *Magazine, Consumer.*
Formerly (until 1974): Der Bibelleser
Published by: Bibellesebund e.V., Industriestr 2, Marienheide, 51709, Germany. TEL 49-2264-404340, FAX 49-2264-4043439, info@bibellesebund.de.

280.4 DEU
ORIENTIERUNG PLUS; Arbeitshilfe fuer Bibelgespraechskreise. Text in German. q. EUR 14.80; EUR 4 newsstand/cover (effective 2009). **Document type:** *Magazine, Consumer.*

Published by: Bibellesebund e.V., Industriestr 2, Marienheide, 51709, Germany. TEL 49-2264-404340, FAX 49-2264-4043439, info@bibellesebund.de.

284.2 USA ISSN 0889-0501
F574.G7
➤ **ORIGINS (GRAND RAPIDS).** Text in English. 1983. s-a. free to members (effective 2011). bk.rev. bibl.; charts; illus.; maps. http://www.calvin-edu/hh/origindx.htm. 48 p./no. 2 cols./p.; back issues avail. **Document type:** *Journal, Academic/Scholarly.* **Description:** Covers Dutch-American history, society, economics, religion, and genealogy.
Published by: Calvin College Archives, 1855 Knollcrest Cir SE, Grand Rapids, MI 49546. TEL 616-526-6313, crcarchives@calvin.edu. Circ: 2,400 (paid).

280.4 DEU
OUR VOICES; EMS women's network. Text in English, German, Indonesian. 1992. a. donation. 34 p./no.; **Document type:** *Magazine, Consumer.*
Published by: Evangelisches Missionswerk in Suedwestdeutschland e.V./Association of Churches and Missions in South Western Germany, Vogelsangstr 62, Stuttgart, 70197, Germany. TEL 49-711-636780, FAX 49-711-6367855, info@ems-online.org, http://www.ems-online.org. Ed. Gabriele Mayer. Circ: 1,000 (paid and controlled).

266 USA ISSN 1537-2758
OUTREACH. Text in English. 1901. 3/yr. USD 10; free to members (effective 2009). back issues avail. **Document type:** *Magazine, Trade.* **Description:** Provides information on mission work in 18 countries.
Former titles (until 2001): O M S Outreach (0274-9459); (until 1973): The Missionary Standard (0738-4521)
Published by: O M S International, 941 Fry Rd, PO Box A, Greenwood, IN 46142. TEL 317-881-6751, FAX 317-888-5275, info@omsinternational.org. Ed., R&P Susan Griswold Loobie. Circ: 48,000.

283 GBR
P I O S A. Text in English. 1982. a. GBP 1 per issue (effective 2009). back issues avail. **Document type:** *Bulletin.*
Published by: Province of the Indian Ocean Support Association, St Martin's Rectory, Horn St., Folkestone, Kent CT20 3JJ, United Kingdom. TEL 44-1303 238509. Ed. P C A Harbridge. Pub. H C Jones. Circ: 800.

286 NZL ISSN 1177-0228
PACIFIC JOURNAL OF BAPTIST RESEARCH. Text in English. 1996. s-a. **Document type:** *Journal, Academic/Scholarly.* **Description:** Seeks to promote understanding of the Baptist story worldwide.
Formerly (until 2005): New Zealand Journal of Baptist Research (1173-9312)
Indexed: R&TA.
Published by: New Zealand Baptist Historical Society, PO Box 12149, Auckland, New Zealand. martin@carey.ac.nz.

280.4 CHL ISSN 0718-4417
LA PALABRA VIVIENTE. Text in Spanish. 2006. 3/yr.
Published by: Crearte Producciones, Casilla 234-11, Santiago, Chile. lapalabraviviente@gmail.com, http://www.lapalabraviviente.cl/default.htm.

PANORAMA (PITTSBURGH, 1960). *see* COLLEGE AND ALUMNI

299 DEU ISSN 0944-2626
PANU DERECH. Text in German. 1989. irreg., latest vol.16, 1998. **Document type:** *Monographic series, Academic/Scholarly.* **Description:** Publishes articles and papers on Christian-Jewish relations and dialogue in Germany and throughout the world.
Published by: Gesellschaft fuer Christlich-Juedische Zusammenarbeit in Lippe e.V., Hornsche Str. 38, Detmold, 32756, Germany. TEL 49-5231-29758, FAX 49-5231-29758, gfcjz.lippe@t-online.de, http://www.gfcjz-lippe.home.pages.de.

287 NLD ISSN 0924-7688
PARAKLEET. Text in Dutch. 1981. q. EUR 18 (effective 2010). adv. bk.rev. back issues avail. **Document type:** *Bulletin, Academic/Scholarly.* **Description:** Contains information on systematic theology, exegesis, pastoral, and church history.
Published by: Verenigde Pinkster- en Evangeliegemeenten, Rotholm 20, kr. 3.01, Urk, 8321 DK, Netherlands. TEL 31-527-687005, FAX 31-527-686987, info@vpe.nl, http://www.vpe.nl.

286.132 USA ISSN 1074-326X
PARENTLIFE; a Christian parenting magazine. Variant title: Parent Life. Text in English. 1994. m. USD 22.95; USD 3.95 per issue (effective 2008). adv. illus. back issues avail.; reprints avail. **Document type:** *Magazine, Consumer.* **Description:** Offers help, information and advice in various areas such as health, education, discipline, safety and spiritual development.
Formed by the merger of (197?-1994): Living with Children (0456-3271); (19??-1994): Living with Preschoolers (0162-4350)
Related titles: Special ed(s).: BabyLife.
Published by: LifeWay Christian Resources, 1 Lifeway Plz, Nashville, TN 37234. TEL 615-251-2000, 800-458-2772, FAX 615-251-5933, customerservice@lifeway.com. Eds. Kathryn Collins, William Summey. Adv. contact Rhonda Edge Buescher. Circ: 77,000.

280.4 200 USA ISSN 2156-4345
THE PARISH POST. Text in English. 1958. m. **Document type:** *Newsletter, Consumer.* **Description:** Contains details on current events and committee work as well as a message the Pastor.
Related titles: Online - full text ed.: free (effective 2010).
Published by: The First Parish Church United, 48 Main St, Westford, MA 01886. TEL 978-692-8350, fpcuwestford@verizon.net, http://www.firstparishwestford.com/.

283 GBR ISSN 0031-2436
PARSON AND PARISH. Text in English. 1938. s-a. free to members (effective 2009). adv. bk.rev. back issues avail. **Document type:** *Magazine, Trade.* **Description:** Covers current church affairs, articles of general theological and pastoral interest, and correspondence.
Related titles: Online - full text ed.
Published by: English Clergy Association, The Old School, Norton Hawkfield, Near Pensford, Bristol, BS39 4HB, United Kingdom. TEL 44-1275-830017, FAX 44-1275-830017, benoporto-eca@yahoo.co.uk. Ed. Rev. Jonathan Redvers Harris TEL 44-1983-565953.

287 GBR ISSN 0079-0117
PARTNERS IN LEARNING; worship and learning resources for all ages. Text in English. 1968. a. adv. **Document type:** *Journal, Academic/Scholarly.*
—CCC.
Published by: Methodist Church, 25 Marylebone Rd, London, NW1 5JR, United Kingdom.

283 300 CRI ISSN 1016-9857
PASOS. Text in Spanish. 1985. bi-m. USD 12 in Latin America; USD 18 elsewhere.
Indexed: OTA.
Published by: (Departamento Ecumenico de Investigaciones), Editorial D E I, Apdo. 390, Sabanilla, San Jose 2070, Costa Rica. TEL 506-2530229, FAX 506-2531541, TELEX 3472 ADEI CR, publicaciones@dei-cr.org.

283.73 USA ISSN 1931-8219
PATHWAYS (ATLANTA). Text in English. 1963. q. **Document type:** *Journal, Consumer.*
Former titles (until 2006): Connecting (1930-5761); (until 2005): DioLog (1073-6549); (until 1991): Diocese (0417-5077); (until 1963): Diocesan Record
Published by: Episcopal Diocese of Atlanta, 2744 Peachtree Rd, Atlanta, GA 30305. TEL 404-601-5320, 800-537-6743, FAX 404-601-5330, http://www.episcopalatlanta.org/index.html.

PEDALPOINT. *see* MUSIC

287 MYS
PELITA METHODIST. Text in English. 1977. m. MYR 10; MYR 20 overseas. adv. bk.rev. **Document type:** *Newsletter.*
Former titles: Methodist Message (0026-1254); Malaysia Methodist
Published by: Methodist Church in Malaysia/Gereja Methodist Malaysia, Methodist Headquarters, 69 Jalan 5-31, Petaling Jaya, Selangor, Malaysia. Ed. Rev. Ng Ee Lin. Circ: 2,000.

284.1 NLD ISSN 1871-1626
PENTAGRAM (BULGAARSE EDITION). Text in Bulgarian. 2004. q.
Published by: (Lectorium Rosicrucianum), Uitgeverij Rozecruis Pers, Bakenessergracht 5, Haarlem, 2011 JS, Netherlands. TEL 31-23-5323852, FAX 31-23-5329453, info@rozekruispers.com, http://www.rozekruispers.com.

289.94 USA ISSN 0031-4919
BX8773.15.A1
PENTECOSTAL MESSENGER. Text in English. 1919. m. USD 12 (effective 2005). adv. **Document type:** *Magazine, Consumer.*
Indexed: CERDIC.
Published by: (Pentecostal Church of God of America), Messenger Publishing House, 4901 Pennsylvania Ave, Joplin, MO 64804-0700. TEL 417-624-7050, FAX 417-624-7102, http://www.pcg.org/publishinghouse/. Eds. John Mallinak, Phil L Redding. adv.: B&W page USD 453. Circ: 8,000 (paid and free).

280.4 AUT ISSN 0031-5141
PERCHTOLDSDORFER PFARRBOTE. Text in German. 1950. m. per issue contribution. **Document type:** *Journal, Trade.*
Published by: Pfarramt Perchtoldsdorf, Wenzel Frey Gasse 2, Perchtoldsdorf, N 2380, Austria. TEL 43-1-8692547, FAX 43-1-869254715, evang.perchtoldsdorf@aon.at, http://www.evang-perchtoldsdorf.at. Circ: 4,700.

284. USA ISSN 0888-5281
PERSPECTIVES (GRAND RAPIDS); a journal of reformed thought. Text in English. 1986. 10/yr. USD 30 domestic; CAD 35 in Canada (effective 2010). adv. bk.rev. biennial index. back issues avail. **Document type:** *Journal, Academic/Scholarly.* **Description:** Expresses the Reformed faith theologically and engages issues that Reformed Christians meet in personal, ecclesiastical and societal life.
Incorporates (1951-1990): Reformed Journal (0486-252X)
Related titles: Microform ed.: (from PQC).
Indexed: A21, A22, CERDIC, ChrPI, MLA-IB, P30, R&TA, RI-1, RI-2, RILM.
—Ingenta. **CCC.**
Published by: Reformed Church Press, 4500 60th St, SE, Grand Rapids, MI 49512. TEL 616-698-7071, FAX 616-698-6606, subscriptions@rca.org, http://www.rca.org/. Eds. James Bratt, Scott Hoezee, Steve Mathonnet-VanderWell.

286 USA ISSN 0093-531X
BX6201
➤ **PERSPECTIVES IN RELIGIOUS STUDIES.** Text in English. 1974. q. USD 18 domestic to individuals; USD 25 domestic to institutions; USD 40 foreign; free to members (effective 2011). bk.rev. abstr.; bibl.; charts; illus.; stat. cum.index: 1974-1983. back issues avail. **Document type:** *Journal, Academic/Scholarly.*
Related titles: Microfilm ed.: (from PQC); Online - full text ed.
Indexed: A21, A22, BRM, CERDIC, FamI, IZBG, OTA, R&TA, RI-1, RI-2. —BLDSC (6428.163500), IE, Ingenta.
Published by: National Association of Baptist Professors of Religion, c/o Steven R. Harmon, 110 N Main St, Noel Hall, PO Box 7327, Boiling Springs, NC 28017. sharmon@gardner-webb.edu, http://www.nabpr.org/. Ed. Mikeal C Parsons.

280.4 DEU ISSN 1616-9182
PERSPEKTIVE; Christliche Monatszeitschrift fuer Jung und Alt. Text in German. 2001. m. EUR 29.40; EUR 2.60 newsstand/cover (effective 2009). **Document type:** *Magazine, Consumer.*
Formed by the merger of (1968-2001): Die Wegweisung (0342-6351); (1939-2001): Die Botschaft (1616-9190)
Published by: Christliche Verlagsgesellschaft mbH, Moltkestr 1, Dillenburg, 35683, Germany. TEL 49-2771-83020, FAX 49-2771-830230, info@cv-dillenburg.de, http://www.cv-dillenburg.de.

287.6 POL ISSN 0209-3898
PIELGRZYM POLSKI. Text in Polish. 1926. m. USD 13 domestic; USD 17 foreign (effective 2000). adv. back issues avail. **Document type:** *Newsletter.* **Description:** Presents religions and socio-cultural issues from the United Methodist Church perspective.
Published by: Wydawnictwo Kosciola Ewangelicko-Metodystycznego, Ul Mokotowska 12, Warsaw, 00561, Poland. TEL 48-22-6285328, FAX 48-22-6285328, umc@elc.com.pl, http://www.kem.com.pl. Ed., Adv. contact Rev. Zbigniew Kaminski. Circ: 1,000.

280.4 DEU ISSN 0172-6943
BR1650.A1
PIETISMUS UND NEUZEIT; Jahrbuch zur Geschichte des neueren Protestantismus. Text in German. 1974. a., latest vol.35, 2009. price varies. index. back issues avail. **Document type:** *Journal, Academic/Scholarly.*
Indexed: A21, DIP, IBR, IBZ, RI-1, RI-2.
Published by: Vandenhoeck und Ruprecht, Theaterstr 13, Goettingen, 37073, Germany. TEL 49-551-508440, FAX 49-551-5084422, info@v-r.de.

283 AUS ISSN 1035-1035
THE PIONEER. Text in English. 1932-1990; N.S. 1991. 3/yr. donation. bk.rev. back issues avail. **Document type:** *Newsletter, Consumer.* **Description:** Provides information on evangelism of church army work and challenge to evangelism.
Published by: Church Army in Australia, PO Box 12, Hazelbrook, NSW 2779, Australia. TEL 61-2-47591360, FAX 61-2-47591359, office@churcharmy.com.au, http://www.churcharmy.com.au.

266 AUS
PIONEERS DOWN UNDER. Text in English. 1989. q. back issues avail. **Description:** Work of mission staff in partnership with nationals all over the world. Informs supporters and those not involved in the work.Mobilizes teams to glorify God among the unreached by initiating church planting movements in partnership with local churches. PDU seeks to inform and inspire its readers regarding PIONEERS work around the globe.
Formerly (until 1998): Light and Life
Published by: Pioneers of Australia Inc., PO Box 200, Blackburn, VIC 3130, Australia. TEL 800-787-889, info@pioneers.org.au, http://www.pioneers.org.au. Circ: 5,000.

266.04 NLD ISSN 0032-0056
PIONIER. Text in Dutch. 1939. 9/yr. free (effective 2008). bk.rev. illus.; charts; bibl. 16 p./no. 2 cols./p.; back issues avail. **Document type:** *Newsletter, Consumer.* **Description:** Missionary magazine in Dutch language.
Published by: (Stichting Alliance Zendings - Centrum Parousia), C A M A - Zending, Amersfoortseweg 44, Maarn, 3951 LC, Netherlands. TEL 31-343-443392, FAX 31-343-441404, zending@cama.nl, http://www.camazending.nl.

280.4 CHE
PLATTFORM. Text in German. 1995. q. free. bk.rev.; film rev.; music rev. back issues avail. **Document type:** *Newsletter.*
Published by: Junge Kirche - Zwinglibund, Brauerstr 60, Zuerich, 8004, Switzerland. TEL 01-2410707. Ed. Bruno Sommer.

280.4 USA ISSN 2154-2856
▼ **PLOWPOINT.** Text in English. forthcoming 2010 (May). q. USD 4.95 per issue (effective 2010). **Description:** News and information from the Plowpoint Ministry.
Related titles: Online - full text ed.: ISSN 2154-2864. forthcoming 2010 (May).
Published by: Plowpoint Press, PO Box 979, Graham, NC 27253. TEL 336-226-0282, kelly@plowpoint.org, http://www.plowpoint.org.

283.73 NLD ISSN 0272-0965
BR1644
PNEUMA. Text in English. 1979. 3/yr. EUR 224, USD 315 to institutions; EUR 245, USD 343 combined subscription to institutions (print & online eds.) (effective 2012). bk.rev. back issues avail.; reprint service avail. from PSC. **Document type:** *Journal, Academic/Scholarly.* **Description:** A medium for the international discussion of scholarly issues related to Pentecostal and Charismatic studies.
Related titles: Online - full text ed.: ISSN 1570-0747. EUR 204, USD 286 to institutions (effective 2012) (from IngentaConnect).
Indexed: A01, A02, A03, A08, A21, A22, CA, E01, IZBG, RI-1, RI-2, T02. —BLDSC (6541.106000), IE, Ingenta. **CCC.**
Published by: (Society for Pentecostal Studies USA), Brill, PO Box 9000, Leiden, 2300 PA, Netherlands. TEL 31-71-5353500, FAX 31-71-5317532, cs@brill.nl. Ed. Frank D Macchia. Circ: 600. **Dist. by:** Turpin Distribution Services Ltd., Pegasus Dr, Stratton Business Park, Biggleswade, Bedfordshire SG18 8QB, United Kingdom. TEL 44-1767-604954, FAX 44-1767-601640, custserv@turpin-distribution.com, http://www.turpin-distribution.com/.

287.6 028.5 USA ISSN 0278-565X
POCKETS. Text in English. 1981. m. (except Jan.). USD 21.95 domestic; CAD 27.95 foreign (effective 2008). illus. 48 p./no.; back issues avail. **Document type:** *Magazine, Consumer.* **Description:** Includes stories, scriptures, prayers, and games for children ages 6-12.
Related titles: Online - full text ed.
Published by: (United Methodist Church, General Board of Discipleship), The Upper Room Publications, 1908 Grand Ave, PO Box 340004, Nashville, TN 37203. TEL 615-340-7200, FAX 615-340-7267, customerassistance@upperroom.org. Ed. Lynn W Gilliam. Circ: 90,000 (paid).

287 DEU ISSN 1432-7589
PODIUM. Text in German. 1963. m. EUR 27.60 (effective 2002). **Document type:** *Magazine, Consumer.*
Formerly: E M K Aktuell (0342-1937)
Published by: (Evangelisch - Methodistische Kirche), Medienwerk der Evangelisch-Methodistischen Kirche, Ludolfusstr 2-4, Frankfurt am Main, 60487, Germany. TEL 49-711-8300051, FAX 49-711-8300082, medienwerk@emk.de, http://www.emk.de. Ed. Karl-Heinz Hecke. Circ: 2,800.

POKOLENIE. *see* CHILDREN AND YOUTH—About

284.1 USA ISSN 0032-4884
PORTALS OF PRAYER; daily devotions for adults. Text in English. 1937. q. USD 9 (effective 2009); (Spanish, Braille, & Audio Cassette Editions avail. from Lutheran Library For the Blind, 888-215-2455 blind.library@lcms.org). adv. 1 cols./p.; back issues avail. **Document type:** *Magazine, Consumer.* **Description:** Features a Bible reading, meditation and prayer in an easy-to-read format.
Related titles: Audio cassette/tape ed.: free (effective 2009); Braille ed.: free (effective 2009); Large type ed. 20 pt.: USD 11 (effective 2009); Spanish ed.: Portales de Oracion. ISSN 1942-1060.
Published by: Concordia Publishing House, 3558 S Jefferson, St Louis, MO 63118. TEL 314-268-1000, 800-325-3040, FAX 800-490-9889, order@cph.org. Ed. Rev. Eric Forss. Pub. Rev. Paul T McCain. adv.: page USD 4,140; 3.75 x 5. Circ: 750,000 (paid).

R

287 PRT ISSN 1646-5482
PORTUGAL EVANGELICO. Text in Portuguese. 1920. 3/yr. EUR 4.50 domestic; EUR 9 foreign (effective 2010). bk.rev. illus. **Document type:** *Magazine, Consumer.*
Published by: Igreja Metodista Portuguesa, Praca Coronel Pacheco 23, Oporto, 4050-453, Portugal. TEL 351-22-2007410, FAX 351-22-2086961.

284.1 FRA ISSN 0032-5228
POSITIONS LUTHERIENNES. Text in French. 1953. q. EUR 35 domestic to individuals; EUR 42 domestic to institutions; EUR 47 foreign (effective 2008). bk.rev. bibl. **Document type:** *Journal.*
Indexed: CERDIC, FR, IZBG.
—INIST.
Published by: Association Positions Lutheriennes, 16 rue Chauchat, Paris, 75009, France. TEL 33-1-47708030. Ed. J N Peres. Circ: 550.

280.4 FRA ISSN 0751-5987
POUR LA VERITE. Text in French. 1936. 10/yr. bk.rev.
Published by: Union des Eglises Evangeliques Libres de France, 23 rue Benard, Paris, 75014, France. TEL 33-1-46573809. Ed. Mireille Boissonnat. Circ: 1,000. **Subscr. to:** Violette Ronchetti, 13 sentier des Piottes, Noisy-le-Grand 93160, France. FAX 33-1-48460066.

230.044 DNK ISSN 0106-6218
PRAESTEFORENINGENS BLAD. Text in Danish. 1897. w. free membership; DKK 836 to students (effective 2009). adv. bk.rev. **Document type:** *Magazine, Trade.*
Formerly (until 1911): Maanedsblad for den Danske Folkekirke
Published by: Den Danske Praesteforening, Linnetgade 25, Copenhagen K, 1361, Denmark. TEL 45-35-260555, ddp@praesteforening.dk. Ed. Jakob Broennum TEL 45-20-218087. adv.: page DKK 3,154; 124 x 196. Circ: 4,000 (controlled).

268 DEU ISSN 1860-6946
BV1460
PRAXIS GEMEINDEPAEDAGOGIK. Text in German. 1948. q. EUR 36 domestic; EUR 44 foreign; EUR 12 newsstand/cover (effective 2009). adv. bk.rev. 64 p./no.; back issues avail. **Document type:** *Journal, Academic/Scholarly.* **Description:** Contains discussions, curricula, teaching instructions and news.
Former titles (until 2005): Christenlehre - Religionsunterricht - Praxis (1860-692X); (until 1998): Die Christenlehre (0009-5192)
Indexed: DIP, IBR, IBZ.
Published by: Evangelische Verlagsanstalt GmbH, Blumenstr 76, Leipzig, 04155, Germany. TEL 49-341-7114115, FAX 49-341-7114150, info@eva-leipzig.de, http://www.eva-leipzig.de. Ed. Martin Steinhaeuser. Adv. contact Christine Herrmann TEL 49-341-7114122. page EUR 680; trim 175 x 255. Circ: 1,500 (paid).

280.4 USA ISSN 1094-2572
PRAY!. Text in English. 1997. bi-m. back issues avail. **Document type:** *Magazine, Consumer.* **Description:** Features articles that provide Biblical encouragement, inspiration, and practical help for prayer life.
Indexed: CCR, ChrPI.
Published by: NavPress Publishing Group, PO Box 35002, Colorado Springs, CO 80935. TEL 719-548-9222, 800-366-7788, FAX 800-343-3902, customerservice@navpress.com.

230 USA ISSN 1531-8265
PREACHING GREAT TEXTS. Text in English. 2001. q. USD 49.95 in United States; USD 55.95 in Canada; USD 68.95 elsewhere (effective 2002).
Address: 13540 E. Boundary Rd., Bldg. 2, Ste. 105, Midlothian, VA 23112-3943. TEL 800-866-8631, FAX 804-744-0253, webmaster@preachtext.com.

280.4 NLD ISSN 0923-0343
PREDIKANT EN SAMENLEVING. Text in Dutch. 1923. 6/yr. EUR 30 to institutions (effective 2008). adv. bk.rev. back issues avail. **Document type:** *Bulletin.* **Description:** News and information for Dutch predikants.
Related titles: Online - full text ed.
Published by: Bond van Nederlandse Predikanten, Cornelis Houtmanstraat 2, Utrecht, 3572 LV, Netherlands. TEL 31-30-2716133, FAX 31-30-2733429, bnp@predikanten.nl, http://www.predikanten.nl. Ed. F T Bos. adv.: B&W page EUR 775, color page EUR 925; trim 210 x 297. Circ: 3,700.

284 NLD ISSN 1388-8943
PREEKSCHRIFT. Text in Dutch. 1998. a. EUR 13.50 (effective 2008).
Published by: (Confessioneel Gereformeerd Beraad), Confessioneel Gereformeerd Toerustingscentrum, Kooikersweg 360, 's-Hertogenbosch, 5224 AZ, Netherlands. TEL 31-73-6212166, info@cgb.nu.

285 AUS ISSN 0729-3542
PRESBYTERIAN BANNER. Text in English. 1985. m. (except Jan.). AUD 25 domestic; AUD 40 foreign (effective 2009). adv. bk.rev. back issues avail. **Document type:** *Magazine, Trade.* **Description:** Serves as a forum for edification of the Biblical Reformed faith.
Related titles: Online - full text ed.
Published by: Presbyterian Church of Eastern Australia, 33 Tallowood St, South Grafton, NSW 2460, Australia. rowlandw@optushome.com.au, http://www.pcea.org.au. Ed. Rev. Ray Murray. Circ: 400.

285 USA
PRESBYTERIAN CHURCH (U.S.A.). MINUTES OF THE GENERAL ASSEMBLY. Text in English. 19??. a. back issues avail. **Document type:** *Proceedings, Trade.*
Formerly (until 1983): United Presbyterian Church in the United States of America. Minutes of the General Assembly (0082-8548)
Related titles: Online - full text ed.: free (effective 2010).
Published by: Presbyterian Church - U.S.A., 100 Witherspoon St, Louisville, KY 40202. TEL 502-569-5637, 800-728-7228, FAX 502-569-8632, presbytel@pcusa.org, http://www.pcusa.org/.

285 CAN ISSN 0079-4996
PRESBYTERIAN CHURCH IN CANADA. GENERAL ASSEMBLY. ACTS AND PROCEEDINGS. Text in English. a. CAD 14 (effective 2000). **Document type:** *Proceedings.*
Published by: Presbyterian Church in Canada, 50 Wynford Dr, North York, ON M3C 1J7, Canada. TEL 416-441-1111.

285 GBR ISSN 0032-7530
THE PRESBYTERIAN HERALD. Text in English. 1943. 10/yr. GBP 15 domestic; GBP 25 in Europe; GBP 22 elsewhere (effective 2009). adv. bk.rev. **Document type:** *Magazine, Trade.* **Description:** Features articles on Christian ideas, along with news and views from home and abroad.
Incorporates (in 1947): Irish Presbyterian; Witness (Belfast); Presbyterian Church in Ireland. Missionary Herald
Indexed: CERDIC.
Published by: Presbyterian Church in Ireland, Church House, Fisherwick Pl, Belfast, N Ireland BT1 6DW, United Kingdom. TEL 44-28-90322284, FAX 44-28-90417307, info@presbyterianireland.org. adv.: page GBP 450; trim 210 x 284. Circ: 16,000.

285 CMR
PRESBYTERIAN MESSENGER. Text in English. 1979. q. XOF 12,000 (effective 2002). **Document type:** *Newsletter.*
Formerly (until 2001): Presbyterian Newsletter
Published by: Presbyterian Communication Department, BP 19, Buea, Cameroon. TEL 237-32-22-77, FAX 237-32-23-13, TELEX 5613, achowahumenei@yahoo.com. Ed. Rev. Achowah Umenei. Circ: 2,500.

285 USA ISSN 0032-7565
BX8901
THE PRESBYTERIAN OUTLOOK. Text in English. 1819. w. (43/yr.). USD 44.95; USD 4 per issue (effective 2009). adv. bk.rev. illus. 24 p./no. 3 cols./p.; reprints avail. **Document type:** *Newspaper.* **Description:** Includes news, letters, articles, columns, editorials, Sunday school lessons, and ministerial changes.
Related titles: Microform ed.: (from PQC).
Indexed: A22.
Published by: Presbyterian Outlook Foundation, 2112 W. Laburnum Ave, Ste. 109, Richmond, Richmond, VA 23227. TEL 804-359-8442, FAX 804-353-6369. Adv. contact George Whipple. col. inch USD 64. Circ: 8,500 (paid).

285 CAN ISSN 0032-7573
PRESBYTERIAN RECORD. Text in English. 1876. m. CAD 18 domestic; CAD 25 foreign (effective 2005). adv. bk.rev.; film rev. index.
Related titles: Microfiche ed.: (from MML); Microfilm ed.; Microform ed.: (from MML); Online - full text ed.
Indexed: A26, C03, CBCARef, CBPI, CPerI, G06, G07, G08, I05, P48, PQC, R05.
Published by: Presbyterian Church in Canada, 50 Wynford Dr, North York, ON M3C 1J7, Canada. TEL 416-441-1111, FAX 416-441-2825. Ed. John Congram. adv.: B&W page CAD 2,230, color page CAD 2,850. Circ: 51,000.

285 USA
THE PRESBYTERIAN SUN. Text in English. 1954. bi-m. free (effective 2005). adv. reprints avail. **Document type:** *Newspaper, Consumer.*
Former titles: The Presbyterian (0893-4134); (until 1973): Texas Presbyterian (0040-4616)
Related titles: Microfilm ed.: (from PQC).
Indexed: OTA.
Published by: Synod of the Sun, 1925 E Belt Line Rd., Ste 220, Carrollton, TX 75006-5826. TEL 214-390-1894, 877-748-6777, FAX 214-390-0755, synodsun@synodsun.org, http://www.synodsun.org. Ed., R&P Rev. Shane Whisler. Adv. contact Beth Hernandez. color page USD 3,000. Circ: 95,000 (controlled).

285 USA ISSN 1083-2181
BV2570.A1
PRESBYTERIANS TODAY. Text in English. 1924. 10/yr. USD 19.95 (effective 2010). adv. bk.rev.; music rev.; play rev.; software rev.; tel.rev.; video rev. charts; illus. Index. 44 p./no. 3 cols./p.; back issues avail. **Document type:** *Magazine, Consumer.* **Description:** Covers interpretation of the work of the church and other religious news, discussions of contemporary issues, information for both individuals and congregations.
Former titles (until 1995): Presbyterian Survey (0032-759X); (until 1924): The Missionary Survey; Which was formed by the merger of (1908-1911): Home Mission Herald; (1868-1911): The Missionary (0362-9007)
Related titles: Microform ed.: (from PQC).
Indexed: A22, CCR.
Published by: Presbyterian Church - U.S.A., 100 Witherspoon St, Louisville, KY 40202. TEL 502-569-5637, 800-728-7228, FAX 502-569-8632, presbytel@pcusa.org, http://www.pcusa.org/. Ed. Eva Stimson TEL 502-569-5637 ext 5635. Pub. Jeffrey Lawrence TEL 502-569-5637 ext 5093. Adv. contact Katie Cannon. **Subscr. to:** PO Box 52, Congers, NY 10920. TEL 800-558-1669.

285 USA ISSN 0193-6212
BX8990.A1
PRESBYTERION; covenant seminary review. Text in English. 1975. s-a. USD 8.50 (effective 2010). bk.rev. **Document type:** *Journal, Academic/Scholarly.* **Description:** Covers all theological disciplines in a scholarly, yet readable manner.
Related titles: Microform ed.
Indexed: A21, CERDIC, ChrPI, OTA, R&TA, RI-1, RI-2.
—BLDSC (6609.673000).
Published by: Covenant Theological Seminary, 12330 Conway Rd, St Louis, MO 63141. TEL 314-434-4044, info@covenantseminary.edu, http://www.covenantseminary.edu/.

280.4 USA
PROCLAIM!. Text in English. 1988. bi-m. back issues avail. **Document type:** *Newsletter.* **Description:** Focuses primarily on Evangelistic ministry of LPEA worldwide.
Formerly: L P E A HeartBeat
Published by: Luis Palau Evangelistic Association, PO Box 1173, Portland, OR 97207. TEL 503-614-1500, FAX 503-614-1599, lpea@palau.org, http://www.gospelcom.net/lpea. Ed. Kimberly Claassen. Circ: 15,000.

285 USA ISSN 1041-2689
PROCLAIM (PETALUMA). Text in Chinese. 1988. bi-m. free. back issues avail. **Document type:** *Magazine.*
Published by: Chinese Christian Mission, 1269 N McDowell Blvd, Petaluma, CA 94975-0759. TEL 707-762-1314, FAX 707-762-1713, ccmlit@ix.netcom.com. Ed. Mandy Fung. R&P Anita Mo. Circ: 13,300.

287.6 USA ISSN 1934-7316
BX8201
THE PROGRESSIVE CHRISTIAN. Text in English. 1823. bi-m. USD 29.59 (effective 2007). adv. bk.rev. back issues avail. **Document type:** *Newspaper, Consumer.*
Former titles (until 2006): Zion's Herald (0098-9282); Which incorporated (19??-1994): Maine United Methodist (0745-0273); (until 1974): Methodist Churchman; (until 1970): Zion's Herald (0044-4790)
Related titles: Microform ed.: (from PQC); Online - full text ed.
Indexed: B04, BRD, R03, RGAb, RGPR, W03, W05.
Published by: United Methodist Church, 566 Commonwealth Ave, Boston, MA 02215-2510. TEL 617-266-3900. Ed. Ann Whiting. Circ: 5,000.

283 USA ISSN 1543-3595
LC383
PROLOGUE (NEW YORK); a journal of colleges & universities of the Anglican communion. Text in English. 1999. a.
Published by: Colleges and Universities of the Anglican Communion, c/o the Assn of Episcopal Colleges, 815 Second Ave, Ste 315, New York, NY 10017-4594. TEL 212-716-6148, FAX 212-986-5039, office@cuac.org. Ed. Allan K. Beavis.

280.4 RUS
PROTESTANT. Text in Russian. 1982. q.
Formerly: Samizdat Review
Indexed: RASB.
Address: Mukomol'nyi pr-d 1, korp 2, Moscow, 123290, Russian Federation. TEL 7-095-2599397, FAX 7-095-2926511.

280.4 GBR ISSN 1357-5155
PROTESTANT TRUTH. Text in English. 1846. bi-m. adv. bk.rev. illus. **Document type:** *Magazine, Trade.*
Formerly (until 1995): The Churchman's Magazine (0009-6636); Incorporates: Wickliffe Preachers Messenger
Related titles: Microform ed.: (from PQC).
Published by: Protestant Truth Society Inc., 184 Fleet St, London, EC4A 2HJ, United Kingdom. TEL 44-207-4054960, info@protestant-truth.org. Ed. Samuel McKay.

280.4 ITA ISSN 0033-1767
BR5
PROTESTANTESIMO. Text in Italian. 1946. q. bk.rev. bibl. cum.index: 1946-1988. **Document type:** *Journal, Academic/Scholarly.*
Indexed: A21, CERDIC, DIP, FR, IBR, IBZ, IZBG, OTA, RI-1, RI-2, RILM.
—INIST.
Published by: (Facolta Valdese di Teologia), Claudiana Editrice, Via San Pio V, 15, Torino, 10125, Italy. TEL 39-011-6689804, FAX 39-011-657542, info@claudiana.it, http://www.claudiana.it.

158 280.4 USA ISSN 2153-0343
▼ **THE PROVIDENT.** Variant title: The Provident E-Zine. Text in English. 2011 (Jan.). m. free. **Document type:** *Newsletter, Consumer.* **Description:** Provides tips and tools for inspiring Christ-centered transformation in your own life and in the lives of those you influence.
Media: E-mail.
Published by: Providential Coaching, 419 The Parkway, Greer, SC 29650. TEL 864-469-9453, info@providentialcoaching.com, http://www.providentialcoaching.com.

285.2 CAN ISSN 1910-958X
PROVISIONARIES; the planned giving magazine. Text in English. 2005. irreg. **Document type:** *Magazine, Consumer.*
Published by: Presbyterian Church in Canada, The Life and Mission Agency. Resource Production and Communication (Subsidiary of: Presbyterian Church in Canada), 50 Wynford Dr., Toronto, ON M3C 1J7, Canada. TEL 416-441-1111, 800-619-7301, FAX 416-441-2825, pccweb@presbycan.ca, http://www.presbyterian.ca/rpc/index.html.

280.4 DEU
PUR. Text in German. 1971. q. EUR 9.80; EUR 2.75 newsstand/cover (effective 2009). **Document type:** *Magazine, Consumer.*
Formerly (until 1998): Geradeaus
Published by: Bibellesebund e.V., Industriestr 2, Marienheide, 51709, Germany. TEL 49-2264-404340, FAX 49-2264-4043439, info@bibellesebund.de.

230 285.9 USA ISSN 1946-8652
BX9323
▼ **PURITAN REFORMED JOURNAL.** Abbreviated title: P R J. Text in English. 2009. s-a. USD 20 domestic; USD 30 in Canada; USD 35 elsewhere (effective 2009). back issues avail. **Document type:** *Journal, Academic/Scholarly.*
Published by: Puritan Reformed Theological Seminary, 2965 Leonard St NE, Grand Rapids, MI 49525. TEL 616-977-0599, info@puritanseminary.org. Ed. Joel R Beeke TEL 616-977-0599 ext 123.

266.2 362 USA
▼ **PURPOSE DRIVEN CONNECTION (ONLINE).** Text in English. 2009. q. **Document type:** *Magazine, Consumer.*
Formerly (until 2009): Purpose Driven Connection (Print)
Media: Online - full text.
Published by: Purpose Driven Connection Ed. Rick Warren.

286.132 USA ISSN 1075-0126
QUARTZ HILL JOURNAL OF THEOLOGY. Text in English. 1994. q. bk.rev. illus. biennial cum.index. back issues avail. **Document type:** *Journal, Academic/Scholarly.* **Description:** Publishes contemporary studies of the Bible, theology and Biblical languages from a Southern Baptist perspective.
Related titles: Online - full text ed.
Published by: (Quartz Hill Community Church), Quartz Hill School of Theology, 43543 51st St W, Quartz Hill, CA 93536. TEL 661-722-0891, FAX 661-943-3484, info@theology.edu.

284.1 DEU ISSN 0341-9495
QUATEMBER; Vierteljahreshefte fuer Erneuerung und Einheit der Kirche. Text in German. 1936. q. EUR 28; EUR 7.50 newsstand/cover (effective 2006). **Document type:** *Magazine, Consumer.*
Indexed: DIP, IBR, IBZ, RILM.
—CCC.
Published by: Lutherisches Verlagshaus GmbH, Knochenhauerstr 38-40, Hannover, 30159, Germany. TEL 49-511-1241720, FAX 49-511-3681098, info@lvh.de, http://www.lvh.de. Ed. Frank Lilie. Circ: 1,100.

284.2 ZAF ISSN 0033-6637
QUO VADIS (POTCHEFSTROOM). Text in Afrikaans. 1950. 10/yr. ZAR 3.50 (effective 1999).
Published by: (Gereformeerde Kerke in Suid-Afrika/Reformed Churches in South Africa), Deputate Kerklike Tydskrifte GKSA, PO Box 20008, Noordbrug, Potchefstroom 2522, South Africa. Ed. M Venter. Circ: 4,800.

285 USA ISSN 1534-259X
BX9401
R E C FOCUS. Text in English. 1981. q. USD 15 to First World institutions (effective 2000); donations elsewhere. **Document type:** *Journal, Academic/Scholarly.*

Incorporates: R E C Theological Forum; Former titles (until Dec. 2000): R E S Mission Bulletin (1081-6267); R E S World Diaconal Bulletin
Published by: Reformed Ecumenical Council, 2050 Breton Rd, S E, Ste 102, Grand Rapids, MI 49546-5547. TEL 616-949-2910, rvhrec@aol.com. Ed. Richard L van Houten. Circ: 1,300.

285 USA
R E C NEWS EXCHANGE. Text in English. 1964. m. USD 10 to first world institutions (effective 2001); donations elsewhere. **Document type:** *Newsletter.*
Formerly: R E S News Exchange (0033-6904)
Published by: Reformed Ecumenical Council, 2050 Breton Rd, S E, Ste 102, Grand Rapids, MI 49546-5547. TEL 616-949-2910, rvhrec@aol.com. Ed. Richard L van Houten. Circ: 2,000.

280.4 GBR
RAINBOW (LONDON). Text in English. 1841. q. free (effective 2009). **Document type:** *Magazine, Consumer.* **Description:** Designed for children and contains information on the worldwide church.
Former titles (until 1993): Junkanoo; (until 1991): Window (0306-9028); (until 1974): At Home and Abroad (0044-9830)
Related titles: Microfiche ed.: (from IDC).
Published by: Methodist Church, 25 Marylebone Rd, London, NW1 5JR, United Kingdom. Ed. Penny Fuller.

284 GBR ISSN 2045-1954
RE. Variant title: Re Magazine. Text in English. 1985. m. GBP 22.95 domestic; GBP 31.95 in Europe; GBP 41.95 elsewhere (effective 2010). adv. **Document type:** *Magazine, Consumer.* **Description:** Provides news, articles and interviews to encourage and build-up everyone in Assemblies of God.
Former titles (until 2010): Joy (1355-6703); (until 1994): Redemption (0966-8098)
Published by: Assemblies of God Inc., PO Box 7634, Nottingham, NG11 6ZY, United Kingdom. TEL 44-115-9217272, FAX 44-115-9217273, info@aog.org.uk, http://www.aog.org.uk. Ed. Peter Wreford. Circ: 5,500.

285 USA
REACH (GRAND RAPIDS). Text in English. bi-m. back issues avail. **Document type:** *Newsletter.* **Description:** Deals with church growth issues for pastors and church leaders in the Christian Reformed Church of North America.
Published by: (Christian Reformed Church of North America), Christian Reformed Home Missions, 2850 Kalamazoo Ave, S E, Grand Rapids, MI 49560. TEL 616-246-0822, FAX 616-246-0834. Ed. Donald J McCrory. Circ: 12,500.

285 GBR
REACHOUT. Text in English. 1880. bi-m. GBP 7, EUR 9 domestic; GBP 10, EUR 19 foreign; GBP 1.20, EUR 1.50 newsstand/cover (effective 2009). adv. bk.rev. illus. back issues avail. **Document type:** *Magazine, Academic/Scholarly.* **Description:** Provides articles on Christian living, mission, church growth, conferences and more.
Former titles (until 2006): Christian Irishman; (until 1883): Key of Truth
Related titles: Online - full text ed.: free (effective 2009).
Published by: Irish Mission of the Presbyterian Church in Ireland, Church House, Belfast, Co Antrim BT1 6DW, United Kingdom. TEL 44-28-90322284, FAX 44-28-90417301, info@presbyterianireland.org, http://www.presbyterianireland.org. Ed. Robin Fairbairn.

283.42 GBR ISSN 0300-3469
THE READER (LONDON). Text in English. 1904. q. GBP 5 domestic; GBP 1.75 newsstand/cover (effective 2009). adv. bk.rev. back issues avail. **Document type:** *Magazine, Consumer.* **Description:** Focuses on religion, the ministry, and the lay ministry in the Anglican Church.
Former titles (until 1946): The Lay Reader; (until 1906): The Reader and Layworker
—CCC.
Published by: Church of England, Central Readers' Council, Church House, Great Smith St, London, SW1P 3AZ, United Kingdom. TEL 44-20-78981000, http://www.cofe.anglican.org. Ed. Heather Fenton. Adv. contact Janice Cruse.

READY. *see* MILITARY

230 USA ISSN 1542-0922
REASON & REVELATION. Text in English. 1981. m. USD 8 domestic; USD 13 foreign (effective 2002).
Published by: Apologetics Press, Inc., 230 Landmark Dr., Montgomery, AL 36117-2752. TEL 334-272-8558, FAX 334-270-2002, mail@apologeticspress.org. Ed. Bert Thompson.

286.7 AUS ISSN 0819-5633
RECORD. Text in English. 1987. w. back issues avail. **Document type:** *Magazine, Trade.*
Former titles (until 1987): South Pacific Record and Adventist World Survey (0818-7258); (until 1986): Australasian Record and Advent World Survey (0818-724X); (until 1953): Australasian Record
Related titles: Online - full text ed.: free (effective 2009).
Published by: Seventh-Day Adventist Church, South Pacific Division, 148 Fox Valley Rd, Locked Bag 2014, Wahroonga, NSW 2076, Australia. Ed. Nathan Brown.

284.2 GBR ISSN 0306-7262
BX9890.U25
REFORM. Text in English. 1972. m. (11/yr.). GBP 19.80; GBP 1.80 per issue (effective 2009). adv. bk.rev.; film rev. illus. back issues avail. **Document type:** *Magazine, Consumer.* **Description:** Covers Christian Biblical information.
Formed by the merger of (1951-1973): Congregational Monthly (0010-583X); Which was formerly (until 1951): Congregational Church Monthly; (1967-1973): Outlook (0030-7203); Which was formerly (until 1967): The Messenger; (until 1965): Presbyterian Messenger
Related titles: Online - full text ed.: free (effective 2009).
Indexed: A01.
—CCC.
Published by: The United Reformed Church in the United Kingdom, West St, Bourne, Lincolnshire PE10 9PH, United Kingdom. TEL 44-20-79168630, urc@urc.org.uk. Ed. Kay Parris.

252 940 USA ISSN 1937-3708
REFORMATION TEXTS WITH TRANSLATION (1350-1650). THEOLOGY AND PIETY. Text mainly in English; Text occasionally in Latin, German. 2002. irreg. price varies. **Document type:** *Monographic series, Academic/Scholarly.*
Published by: Marquette University Press, PO Box 3141, Milwaukee, WI 53201. TEL 414-288-1564, FAX 414-288-7813, maureen.kondrick@marquette.edu, http://www.mu.edu/mupress. Ed. Ian Christopher Levy.

284.2 GBR ISSN 0034-3048
REFORMATION TODAY. Text in English. 19??. bi-m. GBP 13 in Europe; USD 25 in US, Canada & New Zealand; USD 20 in Australia; USD 15 in Brazil; ZAR 75 in South Africa; SGD 35 in Singapore & Malaysia (effective 2009). bk.rev. charts. 32 p./no. 1 cols./p.; back issues avail. **Document type:** *Magazine, Trade.* **Description:** Presents Bible study material, biographies, and news of Reformed churches worldwide.
Formerly (until 1970): Christians Pathway
Indexed: CERDIC.
Address: 75 Woodhill Rd, Leeds, LS16 7BZ, United Kingdom. Ed. Erroll Hulse.

284.2 DEU ISSN 0171-3469
REFORMATIONSGESCHICHTLICHE STUDIEN UND TEXTE. Text in German. 1906. irreg., latest vol.155, 2010. price varies. **Document type:** *Monographic series, Academic/Scholarly.*
Related titles: Microfiche ed.: (from BHP).
Published by: Aschendorff Verlag GmbH & Co. KG, Soester Str 13, Muenster, 48135, Germany. TEL 49-251-6900, FAX 49-251-6904570, buchverlag@aschendorff.de, http://www.aschendorff-buchverlag.de. Ed. Klaus Ganzer. R&P Dirk F Passmann. Adv. contact Petra Landsknecht.

284.2 HUN
REFORMATUS EGYHAZ. Text in Hungarian. 1949. m. USD 35.50.
Published by: Hungarian Reformed Church, Abonyi utca 21, Budapest, 1146, Hungary. TEL 122-7870. Ed. Ferenc Dusicza. Circ: 1,600.

284.2 HUN ISSN 0482-086X
BX9440
REFORMATUSOK LAPJA. Text in Hungarian. 1957. w. USD 37.
Published by: Reformed Church, PO Box 424, Budapest, 1395, Hungary. TEL 117-6809. Ed. Attila P Komlos. Circ: 40,000.

280.4 FRA ISSN 0223-5749
REFORME; chaque semaine un regard protestant sur l'actualite. Text in French. 1945. w. EUR 108; EUR 66 to students (effective 2009). adv. bk.rev. illus. 12 p./no.; **Document type:** *Newspaper.*
Related titles: Online - full text ed.: EUR 60 (effective 2009).
Indexed: RASB.
Address: 53-55 avenue du Maine, Paris, 75014, France. TEL 33-01-43203267, FAX 33-01-43214286, reforme@club-internet.fr, http://www.reforme.net. Ed., R&P Remy Hebding. Pub. Jean Luc Mouton. Adv. contact Daphne Faure. Circ: 10,000.

284.2 USA
REFORMED REVIEW (ONLINE). Text in English. 1947. 3/yr. free (effective 2011). bk.rev. bibl. cum.index. reprints avail. **Document type:** *Journal, Academic/Scholarly.*
Former titles (until 2004): Reformed Review (Print) (0034-3064); (until 1955): The Western Seminary Bulletin (0361-5480)
Media: Online - full text. **Related titles:** Microform ed.: (from PQC).
Indexed: A21, CERDIC, MLA-IB, R&TA, RI-1, RI-2.
—IE, Ingenta.
Published by: Western Theological Seminary, 101 E 13th St, Holland, MI 49423. TEL 800-392-8554. Ed. Christopher Dorn.

284.2 CHE ISSN 0034-3056
BX8901
REFORMED WORLD. Text in English. 1931. q. CHF 18, USD 13.50, GBP 8; CHF 34, USD 25.50, GBP 15 for 2 yrs.; CHF 49, USD 36.50, GBP 21.50 for 3 yrs. (effective 2005). bk.rev. index. back issues avail.; reprints avail. **Document type:** *Journal, Academic/Scholarly.*
Former titles (until 1971): Reformed and Presbyterian World (1607-6710); (until 1955): The Presbyterian World (1607-6702)
Related titles: Microfilm ed.: (from PQC).
Indexed: A21, A22, CERDIC, DIP, IBR, IBZ, R&TA, RI-1, RI-2.
Published by: World Alliance of Reformed Churches, 150 route de Ferney, PO Box 2100, Geneva 2, 1211, Switzerland. TEL 41-22-7916240, FAX 41-22-7916505, 41-22-7916235, http://www.warc.ch. Eds., R&Ps Rev. Odair Pedroso Mateus TEL 41-22-7916239, Paraic Reamonn. Adv. contact Rev. Odair Pedroso Mateus TEL 41-22-7916239. Circ: 3,000 (paid and controlled).

284.2 USA ISSN 0890-8583
REFORMED WORSHIP; resources in liturgy and music. Text in English. 1986. q. USD 25.95 domestic; CAD 36.95 in Canada; USD 33.95 elsewhere (effective 2005). bk.rev. back issues avail. **Document type:** *Magazine, Consumer.* **Description:** Provides worship leaders and committees with practical assistance in planning, structuring, and conducting congregational worship in the Reformed tradition.
Indexed: A21, CCR, RI-1, RI-2, RILM.
Address: 2850 Kalamazoo Ave SE, Grand Rapids, MI 49546. TEL 800-777-7270, FAX 616-224-0803. Ed. Emily Brink. Circ: 4,000 (paid).

284.2 DEU
REFORMIERT. Text in German. 1961. q. free membership (effective 2009). **Document type:** *Magazine, Consumer.*
Published by: Evangelisch-Reformierte Kirchen in Bayern und Nordwestdeutschland, Saarstr 6, Leer, 26789, Germany. TEL 49-491-91980, FAX 49-491-9198240, info@reformiert.de.

280.4 DEU ISSN 1866-6639
RELIGIONSUNTERRICHT AN BERUFSBILDENDEN SCHULEN. Text in German. 1969. q. EUR 20; EUR 7 newsstand/cover (effective 2011). illus. **Document type:** *Journal, Academic/Scholarly.*
Former titles (until 2003): R A B S (0342-5525); (until 1977): Religionspaedagogik an Berufsbildenden Schulen (0341-0021)
Indexed: DIP, IBR, IBZ.
Published by: Papenbusch Verlag, Unnaer Str 50, Menden, 58706, Germany. TEL 49-2373-1790980, FAX 49-2373-1744010, info@papenbusch.de, http://www.papenbusch.de. Circ: 2,100 (paid and controlled).

283.132 USA ISSN 0738-7318
RELIGIOUS HERALD. Text in English. 1828. 40/yr. USD 13 (effective Jan. 2000). adv. 12 p./no. 4 cols./p.; back issues avail. **Document type:** *Newspaper.* **Description:** News for the Virginia Baptist community.
Address: PO Box 8377, Richmond, VA 23226-0377. TEL 804-672-1973, FAX 804-672-8323. Ed. Dr. Michael J. Clingenpeel. Adv. contact Barbara Francis. Circ: 23,000.

285 USA
RENEWS (LOUISVILLE). Text in English. q. **Document type:** *Newsletter.* **Description:** Provides resources for the Presbyterian Church (U.S.A.).
Formerly (until 1989): Open Letter (0194-7125)
Published by: Presbyterians for Renewal, 8134 New La Grange Rd, Ste 227, Louisville, KY 40222-0069.

322.1 USA ISSN 0364-6661
BX6201
REPORT FROM THE CAPITAL. Text in English. 1946. 24/yr. USD 10. bk.rev. back issues avail. **Document type:** *Newsletter.* **Description:** Provides news, views and articles about religious liberty and church-state separation.
Indexed: SBPI.
Published by: Baptist Joint Committee on Public Affairs, 200 Maryland Ave, N E, Washington, DC 20002. TEL 202-544-4226, FAX 202-544-2094. Ed. Larry Chesser. Circ: 10,000.

284.1 USA ISSN 0360-7119
REPORTER (ST. LOUIS). Text in English. 1954. m. USD 15 (effective 2002). adv. **Document type:** *Newspaper.*
Formerly (until 1975): Advance (St. Louis) (0001-8570)
Related titles: Microform ed.: (from PQC).
Published by: Lutheran Church - Missouri Synod, 1333 S Kirkwood Rd, St. Louis, MO 63122. infocenter@lcms.org. Ed. David Mahsman. Adv. contact Bruce Kueck. Circ: 62,000.

287.6 USA ISSN 0034-5725
RESPONSE (NEW YORK, 1969). Text in English. 1969. m. (11/yr., combined Jul.-Aug.). USD 12 (effective 1999). illus. index.
Supersedes (1940-1969): Methodist Woman
Indexed: MEA&I.
Published by: (Women's Division), United Methodist Church, General Board of Global Ministries, 475 Riverside Dr, Rm 1476, New York, NY 10115. TEL 212-870-3755. Ed. Alma Graham. Circ: 60,000.

RETHINKING MISSION (ONLINE). *see* RELIGIONS AND THEOLOGY

280.4 NLD ISSN 0169-9539
REVEIL; onafhankelijk christelijk maandblad. Text in Dutch. 1964. m. (10/yr.). EUR 27; EUR 2.75 newsstand/cover (effective 2010). adv. bk.rev. 32 p./no. 3 cols./p.; back issues avail. **Document type:** *Magazine, Consumer.* **Description:** Deals with church, raising children, work, politics, sports and Christian views on several subjects of daily life.
Published by: Stichting Reveil, PO Box 241, Wierden, 7640 AE, Netherlands. TEL 31-546-577475, FAX 31-546-577477. adv.: page EUR 245; 180 x 260. Circ: 2,700 (paid).

286 USA ISSN 0034-6373
BX6201
REVIEW AND EXPOSITOR; a quarterly baptist theological journal. Abbreviated title: R & E. Text in English. 1904. q. USD 35 domestic to individuals; USD 50 foreign to individuals; USD 60 domestic to libraries; USD 75 foreign to libraries (effective 2010). adv. bk.rev. illus. index. back issues avail.; reprints avail. **Document type:** *Journal, Academic/Scholarly.* **Description:** Features articles dedicated to free and open inquiry of issues related to the Church's mission in the contemporary world.
Formerly (until 1906): The Baptist Review and Expositor (0190-5856)
Related titles: Microform ed.: (from PQC); Online - full text ed.
Indexed: A21, A22, CERDIC, MLA-IB, OTA, R&TA, RI-1, RI-2, RILM, SBPI.
—BLDSC (7786.940000), IE, Ingenta. **CCC.**
Published by: Review & Expositor, Inc., PO Box 6681, Louisville, KY 40206. TEL 502-327-8347, FAX 502-327-8347, Office@rande.org.

280.4 NIC
REVISTA DE HISTORIA DEL PROTESTANTISMO NICARAGUENSE. Text in Spanish. 1990. a. NIC 50, USD 12. **Document type:** *Academic/Scholarly.*
Published by: Centro Inter-Eclesial de Estudios Teologicos y Sociales, Instituto de Historia Protestante y Filosofia, Plaza El SOL, 1 c al sur 50 vrs. arriba,, Apdo. RP-082, Managua, Nicaragua. TEL 506-2-673033, FAX 506-2-671010. Ed. Noel Gonzalez Garcia.

280.4 USA
REVITALIZATION (WILMORE). Text in English. q. **Document type:** *Magazine, Consumer.*
Published by: Center for the Study of World Christian Revitalization Movements, 204 N Lexington Ave, Wilmore, KY 40390. revitalization@asburyseminary.edu.

287 ITA
RIFORMA; l'eco delle valli valdesi. Text in Italian. w. EUR 70 domestic (effective 2009). **Document type:** *Newspaper, Consumer.*
Formerly: Luce (Turin)
Related titles: Online - full text ed.
Published by: Edizioni Protestanti, Via San Pio V, 15, Turin, TO 10125, Italy. TEL 39-011-655278, FAX 39-011-657542. Circ: 5,000.

284.8 USA ISSN 1046-5030
ROLA BOZA/GOD'S FIELD. Text in English, Polish. 1923. bi-w. (Sat.). USD 10. **Document type:** *Newspaper.*
Published by: (Polish National Catholic Church), Rola Boza Publishing Co., 529 E Locust St, Scranton, PA 18505. TEL 717-343-6017. Circ: 7,200 (paid).

280.4 NLD ISSN 1570-470X
RONDUIT INSITE. Text in Dutch. 1984. 6/yr. EUR 12 (effective 2009). adv. **Document type:** *Magazine, Consumer.*
Former titles (until 2001): Ronduit Magazine (1382-7693); (until 1993): EO-Ronduit-Club-Magazine (0168-9584)
Published by: Evangelische Omroep, Postbus 21000, Hilversum, 1202 BA, Netherlands. TEL 31-35-6474747, FAX 31-35-6474727, eo@eo.nl, http://www.eo.nl. Eds. Jirska Alberts, Frank van der Velde. adv.: color page EUR 1,823; trim 210 x 275. Circ: 58,000.

266.4 NOR ISSN 0803-4729
ROPET FRA OEST. Text in Norwegian. 1971. bi-m. free. **Document type:** *Magazine, Consumer.*
Related titles: CD-ROM ed.: ISSN 1890-1719. 1997; Online - full text ed.
Published by: Norsk Misjon i Oest/Norwegian Mission in the East, Trondheimsveien 137, PO Box 6603, Rodeloekka, Oslo, 0502, Norway. TEL 47-23-408800, FAX 47-23-408801, post@nmio.no, http://www.nmio.no. Circ: 18,000.

R

280.4 USA ISSN 2155-1448
▼ **ROSALIN'S MINISTRY III.** Text in English. forthcoming 2010 (Apr.). w. **Document type:** *Consumer.* **Description:** Weekly recordings of Rosalin Pugh's ministry.
Media: CD-ROM.
Published by: Rosalin Pugh, Ed. & Pub., PO Box 6333, Vallejo, CA 94591. TEL 510-812-7464, bsharrp@aol.com.

280.4 USA ISSN 2153-4977
▼ **RULERS' WORLD NEWS.** Text in English. forthcoming 2011. m. **Document type:** *Newspaper, Consumer.* **Description:** Addresses the condition of Christianity and the effect of the plurastic world on the church.
Related titles: Online - full text ed.: ISSN 2153-5019. forthcoming 2011.
Published by: John S. Famodimu, Ed. & Pub., 9119 Bedell Ln, Brooklyn, NY 11236. TEL 914-338-3107, jfamodimu@yahoo.com.

RUMINATE; faith in literature and art. *see* LITERATURE

286.132 USA ISSN 1081-8189
S B C LIFE. (Southern Baptist Convention) Text in English. 1927. 10/yr. USD 14.95 to individuals; USD 5 bulk subscription (effective 2005). adv. bk.rev. illus. index. back issues avail. **Document type:** *Journal, Academic/Scholarly.*
Formerly (until Sept. 1993): Baptist Program (0005-5743)
Indexed: CCR, SBPI.
Published by: Southern Baptist Convention, Executive Committee, 901 Commerce St, Nashville, TN 37203-3630. TEL 615-244-2355, FAX 615-782-8684, jrevell@sbc.net. Ed. A William Merrell. R&P John Revell. Adv. contact Linda Baker. Circ: 70,000.

266 USA ISSN 0279-6716
S O W. (Save Our World) Text in English. 1962. q. free. charts; illus.; stat. **Description:** Provides news and feature articles on international missions, to promote interest in missionary work among the constituency of the Church of God.
Published by: (Church of God World Missions), Pathway Press, PO Box 2250, Cleveland, TN 37320-2250. TEL 615-476-3361, FAX 615-478-7521. Ed. Robert McCall. Circ: 87,000.

285.29305 NZL ISSN 1175-5202
S P A N Z. (Spanning Presbyterians in Aotearoa New Zealand.) Text in English. 2001 (May). q. NZD 18 domestic; free domestic to Presbyterian and Uniting parishes. (effective 2009). adv. **Document type:** *Magazine, Consumer.* **Description:** Covers topical issues of interest to Presbyterian and Uniting churchgoers, as well as telling the stories of churches engaging successfully with their communities.
Supersedes in part (1987-2001): Crosslink (0113-2024); Which was formed by the merger of (1979-1986): Focus; Which was formerly: New Citizen; (1966-1973): The New Zealand Methodist; (1984-1986): Outreach; Which was formerly: Presbyterian News and Views; (until 1967): News and Views of Presbyterian Overseas Missions; (1899-1986): Outlook (0048-2463); Which was formerly (1894-1898): Christian Outlook
Related titles: Online - full text ed.
Published by: Presbyterian Church of Aotearoa New Zealand, PO Box 9049, Aotearoa, Wellington, New Zealand. TEL 64-4-8016000, FAX 64-4-8016001, info@presbyterian.org.nz.

286.3 USA ISSN 0036-214X
BX6390
SABBATH RECORDER. Text in English. 1844. m. free. bk.rev. illus. **Document type:** *Magazine, Consumer.* **Description:** Contains inspirational and informational news for and about Seventh Day Baptists.
Related titles: Microfilm ed.
Published by: American Sabbath Tract and Communication Council, Seventh Day Baptist Center, Box 1678, Janesville, WI 53547. TEL 608-752-5055, FAX 608-752-7711. Ed., R&P Kevin Butler. Circ: 1,800.

286.732 USA ISSN 0098-9517
BX6101
SABBATH WATCHMAN. Text in English. 1926. bi-m. USD 12; USD 15 foreign (effective 2001). bk.rev. illus. 24 p./no. 3 cols./p.; **Document type:** *Newsletter, Newspaper-distributed.*
Published by: Religious Liberty Publishing Association, 2877 E Florence Ave, Huntington Park, CA 90255. TEL 310-862-5252, FAX 310-862-7166, brankocholich@aol.com. Ed. Evelyn Holmstroem. R&P Branko Cholich. Circ: 650. **Co-sponsor:** Seventh-Day Adventist Church Reform Movement, American Union.

280.4 CHE
SAEMANN; evangelisch-reformierte Monatszeitung. Text in German. 1884. m. CHF 12.50 domestic; CHF 19.20 foreign (effective 2000). bk.rev. bibl.; illus. **Document type:** *Bulletin, Consumer.* **Description:** Provides content and information for local Protestant denominations.
Published by: Verein Saemann, Postfach 7822, Bern, 3001, Switzerland. TEL 41-31-3981820, FAX 41-31-3981823, saemann@swissonline.ch. Ed. Samuel Geiser. Circ: 270,000 (paid).
Dist. by: Laenggass Druck AG, Postfach, Bern 3001, Switzerland. TEL 41-31-3077575, FAX 41-31-3077580.

286 SWE ISSN 1103-6206
SAENDAREN; mitt i vardagen mitt i waerlden. Text in Swedish. 1992. bi-w. SEK 459 (effective 2004). adv. bk.rev.; play rev. **Document type:** *Magazine, Consumer.*
Formed by the merger of (1868-1992): Veckoposten (0346-4091); (1882-1992): Svensk Veckotidning (0039-6826); Incorporates (1975-1985): Missionstidningen Familjevennen (0347-089X); Incorporates (1904-1981): Vinterny
Related titles: Audio cassette/tape ed.
Published by: (Svenska Baptistsamfundet/Co-sponsor: Svenska Missionsfoerbundet, Svenska Missionsfoerbundet), Svensk Frikyrkopress AB, Tegnargatan 8, PO Box 6302, Stockholm, 11381, Sweden. TEL 46-8-6740700, FAX 46-8-6122423. Ed. Magnus Stenberg TEL 46-8-6740707. Circ: 16,000 (paid and controlled).

284 GRC ISSN 0036-357X
SALPISMA. Text in Greek. 1945. 3/m. USD 20. bk.rev. cum.index every 4 yrs. **Description:** Contains articles in Biblical theology and contemporary issues from a Biblical perspective; includes Christian literature such as poetry and novels.
Indexed: CERDIC.
Published by: Free Evangelical Churches of Greece, 3 Alkiviadou, Athens, 104 39, Greece. TEL 30-1-8210159. Ed. Sotis Alexandris. Circ: 1,500.

287.96 GBR ISSN 0080-567X
SALVATION ARMY YEAR BOOK. Text in English. 1906. a. GBP 6.49 per issue (effective 2009). index. **Document type:** *Directory, Trade.* **Description:** Contains annual reports and information regarding the International Salvation Army.
Published by: (Salvation Army), Salvationist Publishing and Supplies, Ltd., 66/78 Denington Rd, Denington Industrial Estate, Wellingborough, Northants NN8 2QH, United Kingdom. TEL 44-1933-445445, FAX 44-1933-445415, mail_order@sp-s.co.uk, http://www.sps-shop.com/.

287.9 GBR
SALVATIONIST. Text in English. 1907. w. GBP 0.60 per issue to members (effective 2010). back issues avail. **Document type:** *Newspaper.* **Description:** Designed for the members and friends of The Salvation Army.
Formerly (until 1986): The Musician of the Salvation Army
Related titles: Online - full text ed.
Published by: Salvation Army, 101 Queen Victoria St., London, EC4P 4EP, United Kingdom. londonnortheast@salvationarmy.org.uk, http://www1.salvationarmy.org.uk/uki/www_uki.nsf. Eds. Christine Clement TEL 44-20-73674890, Christine Clement TEL 44-20-73674890.

266.4 NOR ISSN 0809-5779
SAMENES VENN. Text in Norwegian. 1926. 22/yr. NOK 240 (effective 2005). **Document type:** *Newsletter, Consumer.*
Formed by the merger of (1910-1926): Lappernes Ven (0809-5795); (1916-1926): Norsk Finnemisjons Blad (0809-5760)
Published by: Norges Samemisjon, Kongens Gate 14 B, Trondheim, 7011, Norway. TEL 47-73-876250, FAX 47-73-876260, hovedkontoret@samemisjonen.no, http://www.samemisjonen.no. Ed. Rigmor Hoelmo.

264 DNK ISSN 0107-6736
SAMFUNDET DANSK KIRKESANG. AARSKRIFT. Text in Danish. 1940. a. DKK 100 membership (effective 2009). back issues avail. **Document type:** *Yearbook, Consumer.*
Indexed: RILM.
Published by: Samfundet Dansk Kirkesang, c/o Michael Hemmingsen, Sindshvilevej 1, Frederiksberg, 2000, Denmark. TEL 45-22-440297, hemmingsenmichael@hotmail.com, http://www.kirkesang.dk.

287 SWE ISSN 1403-2457
SANDEBUDET. Text in Swedish. 1869. bi-m. **Document type:** *Bulletin.*
Formerly (until 1996): Svenska Sandebudet (0346-2390); Which incorporated (1967-1996): Metodistkyrkans Kvinnor (0345-7923); Which was formerly: Tidskrift foer Metodistkyrkans Kvinnor; Incorporates (1953-1983): Metod (0345-7915)
Published by: Metodistkyrkan i Sverige/United Methodist Church in Sweden, Fack 45130, Stockholm, 10430, Sweden.

283 GBR
THE SARUM LINK. Text in English. 1987. m. GBP 5 (effective Apr. 2003). adv. Website rev.; music rev.; play rev.; video rev.; bk.rev. charts; illus.; stat.; tr.lit. 16 p./no.; back issues avail. **Document type:** *Newspaper, Consumer.* **Description:** Contains news and commentary relating to people and events in the Anglican Diocese of Salisbury for members of local churches and community.
Published by: Church of England, Cross Publications, The Old Bakehouse, 1242A Evesham Rd, Astwood Bank, Worcester, B96 6AA, United Kingdom. cross.publications@virgin.net. Ed., R&P Nicky Davies TEL 44-1722-339447. Adv. contact Sue Medcalfe TEL 44-1527-892945. Circ: 37,500. **Subscr. to:** Church House, Crane St, Salisbury, Wilts SP1 2QB, United Kingdom.

283 KEN
SAUTI NYIKANI. Text in Swahili. 1964. bi-m. free. **Document type:** *Newspaper.*
Published by: Evangel Publishing House, Private Bag 28963, Nairobi, Kenya. TEL 254-2-8020334, FAX 254-2-860840. Circ: 10,000.

283 TZA
SAUTI YA JIMBO. Text in Swahili. q. **Description:** Provides Anglican diocesan, provincial, and world news.
Published by: Church of the Province of Tanzania, PO Box 899, Dodoma, Tanzania.

287.96 KEN
SAUTI YA VITA. Text in English, Swahili. 1928. m. KES 6. **Document type:** *Newsletter.* **Description:** Includes testimonies, information about officers, as well as articles about work for youth, the women's organisation, health education, the AIDs programme, and general news about Salvation Army's work in Kenya and internationally.
Published by: Salvation Army, PO Box 40575, Nairobi, Kenya. TEL 254-2-227541, FAX 254-2-335538, Kenya_CS@EAF.salvationarmy.org. Ed. Julius Omukonyi. Pub. Hezekiel Anzeze. Circ: 20,540.

248 USA
SAY AMEN; magazine for living in Christian authority. Text in English. 1995. q. USD 11; USD 3 newsstand/cover (effective 1999 & 2000). adv. bk.rev.; film rev.; music rev.; software rev.; tel.rev.; video rev. charts; illus.; stat. back issues avail. **Document type:** *Magazine, Consumer.* **Description:** Aims to create an understanding of living a Christ-based life, encouraging readers to take authoritative action over their lives, homes and communities. Includes an annual women's and an annual men's edition as well as regular features such as "4youth Only," Relationships, Testimony, and advice on health, prosperity and knowledge.
Published by: Word Communications, Inc., 5645 Hunters Chase Dr, Lithonia, GA 30038. TEL 770-808-4595, FAX 770-808-0046. Ed. Vikki R Conwell. Pub. Faye J Shannon. Adv. contact Byron E Whatley. B&W page USD 3,400, color page USD 4,000; 10.5 x 8.5. Circ: 50,000. **Subscr. to:** PO Box 360658, Decatur, GA 30036-0658.

283 DEU ISSN 0947-5435
BR1110
SCHNELLER-MAGAZIN; Magazin ueber christliches Leben im Nahen Osten. Text in German. 1885. q. free to members (effective 2009). back issues avail. **Document type:** *Magazine, Consumer.* **Description:** Information on orphanages in Jordan and Lebanon and other Middle East issues.
Former titles (until 1991): Schneller Bote (0344-8525); (until 1969): Bote aus Zion (0174-8491)
Published by: Evangelischer Verein fuer die Schneller-Schulen e.V., Vogelsangstr 62, Stuttgart, 70197, Germany. TEL 49-711-636780, FAX 49-711-6367855, evs@ems-online.org. Ed. Wiltrud Roesch-Metzler. Circ: 14,600 (controlled).

230.017 DEU ISSN 1614-0540
SCHULE IN EVANGELISCHER TRAEGERSCHAFT. Text in German. 2001. irreg., latest vol.14, 2011. price varies. **Document type:** *Monographic series, Academic/Scholarly.*
Published by: Waxmann Verlag GmbH, Steinfurter Str 555, Muenster, 48159, Germany. TEL 49-251-265040, FAX 49-251-2650426, info@waxmann.com. Eds. Christel R Kaiser, Juergen Frank, Volker Elsenbast.

342.4940852 CHE ISSN 1420-9497
K23
SCHWEIZERISCHE JAHRBUCH FUER KIRCHENRECHT/ANNUAIRE SUISSE DE DROIT ECCLESIAL. Text in French, German. 1997. a. CHF 90 (effective 2010). **Document type:** *Journal, Academic/Scholarly.*
Published by: (Schweizerisches Vereinigung fuer Evangelisches Kirchenrecht), Peter Lang AG (Subsidiary of: Peter Lang Publishing Group), Hochfeldstr 32, Postfach 746, Bern 9, 3000, Switzerland. TEL 41-31-3061717, FAX 41-31-3061727, info@peterlang.com, http://www.peterlang.com. Ed. Dieter Kraus. Circ: 250 (paid).

342.4940852 CHE ISSN 1422-3163
SCHWEIZERISCHES JAHRBUCH FUER KIRCHENRECHT. BEIHEFT. Text in German. 1997. irreg., latest vol.6, 2009. price varies. **Document type:** *Monographic series, Academic/Scholarly.*
Published by: Peter Lang AG (Subsidiary of: Peter Lang Publishing Group), Hochfeldstr 32, Postfach 746, Bern 9, 3000, Switzerland. TEL 41-31-3061717, FAX 41-31-3061727, info@peterlang.com, http://www.peterlang.com. Ed. Dieter Kraus.

280.4 USA ISSN 0036-8032
BX9749
SCHWENKFELDIAN. Text in English. 1903. 3/yr. USD 4 to non-members. bk.rev. illus. **Document type:** *Newsletter.*
Published by: (Schwenkfelder Church), Board of Publication of the Schwenkfelder General Conference, 105 Seminary St, Pennsburg, PA 18073-1898. TEL 215-679-3103. Ed. Andrew C Anders. Circ: 2,000.

230.044 GBR ISSN 0265-4539
BR1
SCOTTISH BULLETIN OF EVANGELICAL THEOLOGY; a journal for those interested in serious theology. Abbreviated title: S B E T. Text in English. 1983. s-a. GBP 14 domestic; GBP 16 foreign (effective 2009). adv. bk.rev. 128 p./no.; back issues avail.; reprint service avail. from IRC. **Document type:** *Journal, Academic/Scholarly.* **Description:** Concentrates on Scottish and Reformed theology.
Supersedes in part (in 1983): Scottish Evangelical Theology Society Bulletin (0262-1053); Which was formerly (until 1981): Scottish Tynedale Bulletin
Indexed: A21, IZBG, R&TA, RI-1, RI-2, RILM.
—BLDSC (8206.542000), IE, Ingenta.
Published by: (Scottish Evangelical Theology Society), Rutherford House, 1 Hill St, Edinburgh, EH2 3JP, United Kingdom. TEL 44-131-2201735, info@rutherfordhouse.org.uk, http://www.rutherfordhouse.org.uk/ie.html. **Co-sponsor:** Scottish Evangelical Theology Society.

283.73 GBR ISSN 0260-0617
BX5225
SCOTTISH EPISCOPAL CHURCH YEARBOOK. Text in English. 1879. a. GBP 8 per issue (effective 2010). index. **Document type:** *Bulletin.*
Formerly (until 1979): Episcopal Church in Scotland. Year Book and Directory
Published by: Scottish Episcopal Church, 21 Grosvenor Crescent, Edinburgh, EH12 5EE, United Kingdom. TEL 44-131-2256357, FAX 44-131-3467247, office@scotland.anglican.org, http://www.scotland.anglican.org/.

280.4 GBR ISSN 2045-4570
▼ **SCOTTISH REFORMATION SOCIETY. HISTORICAL JOURNAL.** Text in English. 2010. a. **Document type:** *Journal, Academic/Scholarly.* **Description:** Aims to publish scholarly articles, written from an evangelical perspective, on subjects connected with Scottish church history.
Published by: Scottish Reformation Society, The Magdalen Chapel, 41 Cowgate, Edinburgh, Midlothian, Scotland EH1 1JR, United Kingdom. TEL 44-131-2201450, info@scottishreformationsociety.org.uk. Eds. A Sinclair Horne, Douglas Somerset.

280.4 ZAF ISSN 0254-1807
➤ **SCRIPTURA**; international journal of bible, religion and theology in southern Africa. Text mainly in English; Text occasionally in Afrikaans, French, German, Xhosa, Zulu. 1980. q. ZAR 90 domestic to individuals; USD 60 foreign to individuals; ZAR 120 domestic to institutions; USD 120 foreign to institutions (effective 2004). bk.rev. illus. **Document type:** *Academic/Scholarly.* **Description:** Publishes contibutions to the fields of Bible, religion and theology. Special attention is given to topics and issues emerging from or relevant to southern Africa.
Related titles: Online - full text ed.
Indexed: A21, A22, DIP, IBR, IBZ, ISAP, IZBG, OTA, R&TA, RI-1, RI-2. —BLDSC (8213.237300), IE, Ingenta.
Published by: Universiteit Stellenbosch, Department of Religion/Stellenbosch University, Private Bag X1, Matieland, 7602, South Africa. TEL 27-21-8089111, FAX 27-21-8082031. Ed. Johann Kinghorn.

280.4 AUS
SCRIPTURE UNION NEWS. Text in English. 19??. q. bk.rev. back issues avail. **Document type:** *Newsletter.* **Description:** Provides information about the Scripture union in spreading the God's message to people.
Former titles (until 1996): S U News (0725-6140); (until 1981): Relations
Related titles: Online - full text ed.: free (effective 2009).
Published by: Scripture Union (A.C.T.), 4 Campion St, Deakin, ACT 2600, Australia. TEL 61-2-62513677, FAX 61-2-62512953, suact@su.org.au, http://www.su.org.au/aut.

283.42 IRL ISSN 0332-0618
BX5410
SEARCH; Church of Ireland journal. Text in English. 1978. 3/yr. EUR 15 (effective 2005). bk.rev. **Document type:** *Journal, Academic/Scholarly.* **Description:** For teachers in primary and secondary schools, people of responsibility in parishes, as well as the clergy.
Formed by the merger of (1970-1976): New Divinity (0791-1556); (1973-1976): Resources (0791-1564)

—BLDSC (8213.809000).
Published by: Religious Education Resource Centre, Holy Trinity Church, Rathmines, Dublin, 6, Ireland. Circ: 600.

286 USA ISSN 0739-2281
SEARCHING TOGETHER. Text in English. 1972. q. GBP 6 in United Kingdom; AUD 6 in Australia; USD 10 elsewhere (effective 2011). bk.rev. back issues avail.; reprints avail. **Document type:** *Magazine, Trade.* **Description:** Explores church issues and biblical teachings. Includes new publications information.
Formerly (until 1981): Baptist Reformation Review (0276-7945)
Related titles: Microform ed.: (from PQC).
Indexed: A21, A22, CERDIC, R&TA, RI-1, RI-2.
Published by: Word of Life Church, PO Box 548, Saint Croix Falls, WI 54024. TEL 715-338-2796, contact@wolc.com, http://www.wolc.com.

286 USA ISSN 0037-0606
BV4800
THE SECRET PLACE. Text in English. 1938. q. USD 11.20 for 2 yrs. (effective 2009). **Document type:** *Magazine, Consumer.* **Description:** A devotional guide to be used with the Bible at home.
Related titles: Braille ed.: USD 16 (effective 2007); Large type ed. 14 pt.: USD 16.20 for 2 yrs. (effective 2009).
Published by: (American Baptist Churches in the U S A), Judson Press, PO Box 851, Valley Forge, PA 19482-0851. Ed. Kathleen Hayes. Circ: 112,000.

284.1 USA ISSN 0897-5663
BX8001
SEEDS FOR THE PARISH. Text in English. 1972. 6/yr. free to qualified personnel. bk.rev. **Description:** Reports on new resources and services available to clergy and lay congregational leaders.
Supersedes (in 1988): Congregation (0361-8862)
Related titles: Diskette ed.
Published by: Evangelical Lutheran Church in America, 8765 W Higgins Rd, Chicago, IL 60631. TEL 312-380-2949, FAX 312-380-2406. Ed. Elizabeth Hunter. Circ: 190,000 (controlled).

286 PRT ISSN 0037-1874
SEMEADOR BAPTISTA. Text in Portuguese. 1926. m. bk.rev. illus. **Document type:** *Newspaper.*
Published by: Convencao Baptista Portuguesa/Portuguese Baptist Convention, R Goncalves Crespo, 33-3oF, Lisbon, 1100-000, Portugal. TEL 351-21-4362718. Ed. Pedro Guedes. Circ: 1,250.

284.1 USA ISSN 1526-0674
SEMINARY RIDGE REVIEW. Text in English. 1998. s-a. **Document type:** *Magazine, Consumer.* **Description:** Faculty publication intended as a theological round table for alumni, rostered church leaders and scholars. It offers perspectives highlighting the unique history and theology of the Lutheran Theological Seminary at Gettysburg, eastern Lutheranism and the issues that emerge in the cross-currents of theological and cultural debates.
Formerly: Lutheran Theological Seminary Bulletin
Related titles: Online - full text ed.
Indexed: A21, R&TA, RI-1.
Published by: Lutheran Theological Seminary at Gettysburg (Subsidiary of: Lutheran Theological Seminary), 61 Seminary Ridge, Gettysburg, PA 17325. TEL 717-334-6286, info@ltsg.edu. Eds. Dr. Brooks Schramm, Dr. Maria E Erling, Dr. Susan Karen Hedahl.

SENIOR MUSICIAN. *see* MUSIC

280.4 CAN ISSN 0848-1741
SERVANT MAGAZINE. Text in English. 1989. 4/yr. donation. bk.rev. **Document type:** *Bulletin.* **Description:** Features world news section related to the Church, moral issues, articles devoted to important figures, education and encouragement for today's Christian.
Indexed: CCR.
Published by: Prairie Bible Institute, Three Hills, AB T0M 2A0, Canada. TEL 403-443-5511, FAX 403-443-5540. Ed. Phil R Callaway. Circ: 25,000.

280.4 CMR
SERVITEUR. Text in French. m.
Address: PO Box 1405, Yaounde, Cameroon. Ed. Daniel Ako'o. Circ: 3,000.

283 USA ISSN 1059-9576
BR1
SEWANEE THEOLOGICAL REVIEW. Text in English. 1957. q. USD 24 to individuals; USD 28 to libraries (effective 2011). bk.rev. index, cum.index: 1956-1967, 1967-1977. back issues avail.; reprints avail. **Document type:** *Journal, Academic/Scholarly.* **Description:** Engages readers in Anglican theological reflection.
Formerly (until 1991): St. Luke's Journal of Theology (0036-309X)
Related titles: Microfilm ed.: (from PQC); Online - full text ed.
Indexed: A21, A22, CERDIC, MLA-IB, OTA, P28, P30, P48, P53, P54, PQC, R&TA, RI-1, RI-2, RILM.
—BLDSC (8254.252000), IE, Ingenta.
Published by: University of the South, School of Theology, 735 University Ave, Sewanee, TN 37383. TEL 931-598-1000, http://theology.sewanee.edu/.

251 GBR ISSN 1471-5015
SHARING GOD'S WORD. Text in English. 1987. a. **Document type:** *Magazine, Consumer.*
Formerly (until 2000): Preachers' Handbook (0269-2767)
—CCC.
Published by: International Bible Reading Association, 1020 Bristol Rd, Selly Oak, Birmingham, B29 6LB, United Kingdom. TEL 44-121-4724242, FAX 44-121-4727575, enquiries@christianeducation.org.uk, http://www.christianeducation.org.uk.

283 AUS ISSN 1837-5022
THE SHEPHERD. Text in English. 1955. s-a. back issues avail. **Document type:** *Magazine, Trade.*
Supersedes in part (in 1960): Canberra North Anglican
Related titles: Online - full text ed.: free (effective 2010).
Published by: Parish of All Saints, PO Box 328, Dickson, ACT 2602, Australia. TEL 61-2-62487420, FAX 61-2-62486500, admin@allsaintsainslie.org.au.

THE SHEPHERD'S VOICE. *see* CHILDREN AND YOUTH—For

284.2 USA
SHINE BRIGHTLY. Text in English. 1970. 9/yr. USD 13.25 (effective 2006). bk.rev. **Document type:** *Magazine, Consumer.* **Description:** Christian publication for girls 9-14.
Formerly: Touch
Published by: (GEMS - Calvinettes), GEMS Girls' Clubs, PO Box 7259, Grand Rapids, MI 49510-7244. TEL 616-241-5616, FAX 616-241-5558, servicecenter@gemsgc.org. Ed. Sara Lynne Hilton.

286.372 TZA
SIKILIZA. Text in Swahili. q. USD 1.60 per issue (effective 1993).
Published by: Seventh Day Adventist, PO Box 635, Mzumbe-Morgoro, Tanzania. TEL 255-56-3338, FAX 255-56-4374. Ed. G H Mbwana. Circ: 10,000.

286 USA
THE SILENT REMINDER. Text in English. 1968. bi-w. free (effective 2000). **Document type:** *Newsletter.* **Description:** Reports news and events of the Deaf Ministry of the First Baptist Church Silent Friends Chapel.
Published by: Silent Friends Chapel, First Baptist Church, 1707 San Jacinto, Dallas, TX 75201. TEL 201-969-2440, FAX 214-969-7830. Ed., R&P Rev. Dale Withrow. Circ: 450.

SILVER WINGS - MAYFLOWER PULPIT; poems. *see* LITERATURE—Poetry

280.4 USA ISSN 2153-0149
▼ **SIN NO MORE.** Text in English. 2010. m. free (effective 2010). **Document type:** *Newsletter, Consumer.* **Description:** Newsletter of the Gospel's Grace.
Media: Online - full text.
Published by: Anthony Love and Associates, 2314 Station House Ln, Odenton, MD 21113. TEL 202-271-9121, brotherlove@gospelsgrace.org.

287.96 GBR
SING TO THE LORD. Text in English. 1886. 3/yr. **Document type:** *Bulletin.*
Formerly (until 1994): Musical Salvationist (0027-464X)
Published by: Salvation Army, Territorial Headquarters, 101 Queen Victoria St, London, EC4P 4EP, United Kingdom. TEL 44-171-387-3768, FAX 44-171-236-3491. Ed. Richard Phillips. R&P Tina Shepherd. Circ: 23,000.

SINGLES SCENE - SPIRIT & LIFE. *see* SINGLES' INTERESTS AND LIFESTYLES

SIRJONZORG. *see* HANDICAPPED—Visually Impaired

280.4 USA ISSN 0700-5202
SLAVNA NADEJE/GLORIOUS HOPE. Text in English, Czech, Slovak. 1974. bi-m. free (2001). 24 p./no. 3 cols./p.; back issues avail. **Document type:** *Newsletter.*
Published by: Czechoslovak Baptist Convention of the United States and Canada, Rt 4 Box 58D, Philippi, WV 26416. TEL 304-457-4287, FAX 304-457-3043, sommer@ab.edu, http://www.ab.edu/czslbaptconv. Ed. Natasha Legierski. Circ: 1,300.

284.2 ZAF ISSN 0037-685X
SLINGERVEL. Text in Afrikaans. 1959. m. ZAR 46 (effective 1999). bk.rev.
Published by: (Gereformeerde Kerke in Suid-Afrika/Reformed Churches in South Africa), Deputate Kerklike Tydskrifte GKSA, PO Box 20008, Noordbrug, Potchefstroom 2522, South Africa. Ed. M Venter. Circ: 7,850.

201.6 USA ISSN 0731-0234
SOCIAL QUESTIONS BULLETIN. Text in English. 1911. bi-m. USD 12 to individuals; USD 15 to institutions (effective 2001). bk.rev. back issues avail.; reprints avail. **Document type:** *Newsletter.*
Related titles: Microform ed.: (from PQC).
Indexed: CERDIC.
Published by: Methodist Federation for Social Action, 212 East Capitol St, NE, Washington, DC 20003. TEL 202-546-8806, FAX 202-546-6811, http://www.olg.com/mfsa. Ed. Rev. Kathryn J Johnson. Circ: 2,500.

284.2 FRA ISSN 0035-3884
BX9401
SOCIETE CALVINISTE DE FRANCE. REVUE REFORMEE. Text in French. 1950. q. bk.rev. index, cum.index every 10 yrs.
Indexed: FR, OTA, PCI.
—INIST. **CCC.**
Published by: Faculte de Theologie Reformee, 33 av. Jules Ferry, Aix En Provence, 13100, France. TEL 33-42-26-1355, FAX 33-42-93-2263. Ed. Paul Wells. Circ: 1,300.

280.4 FRA ISSN 0037-9050
BX9450
SOCIETE DE L'HISTOIRE DU PROTESTANTISME FRANCAIS. BULLETIN. Text in French. 1852. q. EUR 50 domestic to individuals; EUR 62 foreign to individuals; EUR 14 per issue (effective 2010). bk.rev. bibl.; charts; illus.; stat. index, cum.index. back issues avail.; reprints avail. **Document type:** *Journal, Academic/Scholarly.*
Former titles (until 1903): Societe de l'Histoire du Protestantisme Francais. Bulletin Historique et Litteraire (1141-0558); (until 1866): Societe de l'Histoire du Protestantisme Francais. Bulletin (1141-054X)
Indexed: A21, A22, AmH&L, B24, CA, CERDIC, DIP, FR, HistAb, IBR, IBZ, MLA-IB, PCI, RI-1, RI-2, T02.
—IE, Infotrieve, INIST.
Published by: Societe de l'Histoire du Protestantisme Francais, 54 rue des Saints Peres, Paris, 75007, France. Ed. Andre Encreve. Circ: 2,200. **Subscr to:** Librairie Droz S.A., Case Postale 389, Geneva 12 1211, Switzerland. TEL 41-22-3466666, FAX 41-22-3472391.

289.94 USA ISSN 2153-2737
SOCIETY FOR PENTECOSTAL STUDIES. NEWSLETTER (ONLINE). Text in English. 1970. s-a. free (effective 2010). bk.rev. bibl. back issues avail. **Document type:** *Newsletter, Trade.*
Formerly (until 2009): Society for Pentecostal Studies. Newsletter (Print)
Published by: Society for Pentecostal Studies, PO Box 3802, Cleveland, TN 37320. Eds. Darrin J Rodgers, Mark E Roberts TEL 918-495-6899.

284.1 DEU ISSN 0232-5527
DER SONNTAG (LEIPZIG); Wochenzeitung fuer die Evangelisch-Lutherische Landeskirche Sachsens. Text in German. 1946. w. EUR 42 domestic; EUR 54 foreign (effective 2009). adv. bk.rev. back issues avail. **Document type:** *Newspaper, Consumer.*
Published by: (Evangelisch-Lutherisches Landeskirchenamt Sachsens), Evangelische Verlagsanstalt GmbH, Blumenstr 76, Leipzig, 04155, Germany. TEL 49-341-7114115, FAX 49-341-7114150, info@eva-leipzig.de, http://www.eva-leipzig.de. Ed. Christine Reuther. Adv. contact Christine Herrmann TEL 49-341-7114122. B&W page EUR 2,436, color page EUR 4,263; trim 282 x 400. Circ: 12,429 (paid and controlled).

285 DEU ISSN 0722-2831
SONNTAGSBLATT; evangelische Wochenzeitung fuer Bayern. Text in German. 1892. w. EUR 64.90 (effective 2009). adv. bk.rev. charts; illus. **Document type:** *Newsletter, Consumer.*
Former titles (until 1981): Sonntagsblatt fuer die Evangelisch-Lutherische Kirche in Bayern. Gemeindeblatt fuer Muenchen und Oberbayern (0721-1015); (until 1981): Muenchner Gemeindeblatt (0721-1007); (until 1971): Evangelisches Gemeindeblatt fuer Muenchen (0014-3588)
Published by: Evangelischer Presseverband fuer Bayern e.V., Birkerstr 22, Munich, 80636, Germany. TEL 49-89-121720, FAX 49-89-12172138, info@epv.de, http://www.epv.de. Ed. Helmut Frank. Pub. Roland Gertz. adv.: page EUR 969. Circ: 11,716.

284.1 DEU ISSN 1868-5331
SONNTAGSBLATT (AUSGABE OBERFRANKEN); evangelische Wochenzeitung fuer Bayern. Text in German. 1998. w. EUR 64.90 (effective 2009). adv. bk.rev. illus.; stat. **Document type:** *Newspaper, Consumer.*
Supersedes in part (in 2008): Sonntagsblatt (Ausgabe Oberfranken und Unterfranken) (1615-8504); Which was formed by the merger of (1981-1998): Sonntagsblatt (Ausgabe Unterfranken) (1615-8490); (1968-1998): Sonntagsblatt (Ausgabe Oberfranken) (0722-3145); Which was formerly (until 1981): Sonntagsblatt fuer die Evangelisch-Lutherische Kirche in Bayern. Ausgabe Oberfranken (0014-3391); Which was formed by the merger of (1949-1968): Evangelisches Gemeindeblatt fuer Hof und Umgebung (0722-0685); (1913-1968): Sonntagsblatt fuer den Evangelisch-Lutherischen Kirchenbezirk Bamberg (0722-0677); Which was formerly (until 1957): Bamberger Evangelisches Gemeindeblatt (0722-0669)
Published by: (Evangelisch-Lutherischer Landeskirchenrat), Evangelischer Presseverband fuer Bayern e.V., Birkerstr 22, Munich, 80636, Germany. TEL 49-89-121720, FAX 49-89-12172138, info@epv.de, http://www.epv.de.

284.2 DEU
SONNTAGSBLATT (LEER); fuer evangelish-reformierte Gemeinden. Text in German. 1891. 2/m. EUR 24 (effective 2009). **Document type:** *Newspaper, Consumer.*
Published by: Evangelisch-Reformierte Kirchen in Bayern und Nordwestdeutschland, Saarstr 6, Leer, 26789, Germany. TEL 49-491-91980, FAX 49-491-9198240, info@reformiert.de. Ed. Susanne Eggert.

280.4 DEU
SONNTAGSGRUSS UND BESINNUNG. Text in German. 1989. w. **Document type:** *Newspaper, Consumer.*
Formerly (until 1995): Sonntagsgruss und Kraft fuer den Tag (0940-5216); Which was formed by the merger of (1973-1989): Sonntagsgruss (0940-5208); (1948-1989): Kraft fuer den Tag (0940-5194)
Published by: Aussaat Verlag, Andreas Braem Str 18-20, Neukirchen-Vluyn, 47506, Germany. TEL 49-2845-392225, FAX 49-2845-33689, info@nvg-medien.de, http://www.nvg-medien.de. Eds. Klaus Guenther, Manfred Juelicher. R&P Klaus Guenther.

283.73 USA ISSN 0194-8040
SOUNDINGS (MINNEAPOLIS). Text in English. 1976. 6/yr. USD 10 (effective 2000). adv. bk.rev. **Document type:** *Newspaper, Consumer.* **Description:** Provides news and current issues of concern to Episcopalians in Minnesota.
Published by: Episcopal Diocese of Minnesota, 1730 Clifton Pl, Ste 201, Minneapolis, MN 55403. TEL 612-871-5311, FAX 612-871-0552. Ed., R&P, Adv. contact Susan Barksdale. B&W page USD 720; trim 11 x 17. Circ: 16,000.

286.168 ZAF
SOUTH AFRICAN BAPTIST HANDBOOK. Text in English. 1885. a. ZAR 47, USD 15 (effective 1999). back issues avail. **Document type:** *Directory.*
Published by: Baptist Union of Southern Africa, Private Bag X45, Wilropark, 1731, South Africa. TEL 27-11-7685980, FAX 27-11-7685983. Circ: 1,200.

287.6 USA ISSN 1078-8166
BX8201
SOUTH CAROLINA UNITED METHODIST ADVOCATE. Text in English. 1837. m. USD 12 (effective 2000). adv. bk.rev. illus. **Document type:** *Newspaper.*
Former titles: South Carolina Methodist Advocate (0038-3147); Southern Christian Advocate
Published by: (United Methodist Church, South Carolina Conference), Southern Christian Advocate, 4908 Colonial Dr, Columbia, SC 29203. TEL 803-786-9483, FAX 803-735-8168. Ed. Karl F Davie Burgdorf. R&P Karl F. Davie Burgdorf TEL 803-786-9486. Adv. contact Allison Trussell. Circ: 10,000.

286.132 USA ISSN 0081-3001
SOUTHERN BAPTIST CONVENTION. ANNUAL. Text in English. 1845. a. USD 10 (effective 2000). cum.index 1845-1953; 1954-1965.
Related titles: Microfilm ed.
Published by: Southern Baptist Convention, Executive Committee, 901 Commerce St, Nashville, TN 37203-3630. jrevell@sbc.net. Circ: 35,000.

286.132 USA ISSN 0038-3848
SOUTHERN BAPTIST EDUCATOR. Text in English. 1947 (vol.12). 4/yr. bk.rev. bibl.; stat. index. **Document type:** *Magazine, Consumer.*
Related titles: Online - full text ed.
Published by: Association of Southern Baptist Colleges & Schools, 8120 Sawyer Brown Rd., Ste. 108, Nashville, TN 37221-1410. TEL 615-673-1896, FAX 615-242-2153, tim_fields@baptistschools.org. Ed., R&P Tim Fields. Circ: 10,500.

R

286 USA ISSN 1520-7307
BX6462.7
THE SOUTHERN BAPTIST JOURNAL OF THEOLOGY. Text in English. 1997. q. USD 25 domestic to individuals; USD 50 foreign to individuals; USD 40 domestic to institutions; USD 65 foreign to institutions (effective 2010). **Document type:** *Journal, Academic/Scholarly.* **Description:** Features insightful articles by the faculty of southern seminary as well as leading evangelical scholars from around the world.
Indexed: A21, RI-1.
Published by: Southern Baptist Theological Seminary, 2825 Lexington Rd, Louisville, KY 40280. TEL 800-626-5525, campustechnology@sbts.edu.

SOUTHERN BAPTIST PERIODICAL INDEX. *see* RELIGIONS AND THEOLOGY—Abstracting, Bibliographies, Statistics

283 AUS ISSN 1445-0089
SOUTHERN CROSS. Text in English. 1961. m. free local Anglican churches; AUD 44 (effective 2009). adv. bk.rev.; film rev. back issues avail. **Document type:** *Newspaper, Consumer.* **Description:** Studies applied theology, information and debate on current issues.
Former titles (until 1999): Southern Cross Newspaper (1444-9978); (until 1995): Southern Cross Sydney (0313-5861)
Published by: Anglican Media Council, Parramatta, PO Box W185, Westfield, NSW 22150, Australia. TEL 61-2-88608860, newspaper@anglicanmedia.com.au. Circ: 23,000.

286.132 USA ISSN 1078-2613
THE SOUTHERN SEMINARY MAGAZINE. Text in English. 1932. q. free (effective 2010). **Document type:** *Magazine, Consumer.*
Formerly (until 19??): The Tie (0040-7232)
Indexed: SBPI.
Published by: Southern Baptist Theological Seminary, 2825 Lexington Rd, Louisville, KY 40280. TEL 800-626-5525, campustechnology@sbts.edu.

286.132 USA ISSN 0038-4917
SOUTHWESTERN NEWS. Text in English. 1941. q. free (effective 2010). reprints avail. **Document type:** *Newsletter, Trade.* **Description:** Provides information about students.
Indexed: CCR, SBPI.
Published by: Southwestern Baptist Theological Seminary, Box 22000, Fort Worth, TX 76122. TEL 817-923-1921, registrar@swbts.edu.

286.732 USA
SOUTHWESTERN UNION RECORD. Text in English. 1902. m. USD 10 (effective 2000). adv. **Description:** Focuses on inspirational material and news and promotion of Seventh-Day Adventists' churches and institutions in Arkansas, Louisiana, Oklahoma, Texas, and New Mexico.
Published by: Southwestern Union Conference of Seventh Day Adventists, PO Box 4000, Burleson, TX 76028. TEL 817-295-0476, FAX 817-447-2443. Ed., R&P Jean Thomas. Adv. contact Carla Baker. Circ: 24,500.

SPARK (MARKET HARBOROUGH). *see* HANDICAPPED—Visually Impaired

286.3 USA ISSN 0890-0264
BX6101
SPECTRUM (ROSEVILLE). Text in English. 1969. q. USD 39.95 domestic; USD 59.95 foreign (effective 2011). adv. bk.rev.; film rev. bibl.; charts; illus. cum.index every 5 yrs. 80 p./no.; back issues avail. **Document type:** *Magazine, Trade.* **Description:** Journal of opinion and scholarship for Seventh-day Adventist and other Christian readers.
Related titles: Online - full text ed.
Indexed: PhilInd.
Published by: Association of Adventist Forums, PO Box 619047, Roseville, CA 95661. TEL 916-774-1080, FAX 916-791-4938. Adv. contact Carlyn Ferrari TEL 916-774-1080.

286 USA ISSN 1061-6160
CODEN: NOINEK
SPECTRUM (WHEATON). Text in English. 1992. bi-m. bk.rev. **Document type:** *Newsletter.* **Description:** Informative, inspirational, and educational, concerning national, home missions, and international missions.
Published by: (Conservative Baptist Association of America), C B America, 3686 Stagecoach Rd., Unit E, Longmont, CO 80504-5660. TEL 720-283-3030, 888-627-1995, FAX 720-283-3333. Ed. Rev. Ed Mitchell. R&P Sylvia Allen. Circ: 3,100.

285.8 USA ISSN 2156-4329
THE SPIRE. Text in English. 19??. m. (except Jul. and Aug.). back issues avail. **Document type:** *Newsletter, Consumer.*
Former titles (until 1982): First Church of Christ. Newsletter; (until 197?): First Church of Christ. Parish News Letter (2156-3926)
Related titles: Online - full text ed.: free (effective 2010).
Published by: First Church of Christ, 250 Main St, Wethersfield, CT 06109. TEL 860-529-1575, FAX 860-721-7861, fcw@firstchurch.org. Ed. Dave Gilbert TEL 860-529-1575 ext 225.

280.4 USA ISSN 1098-1039
SPIRIT (JOPLIN). Text in English. 1998. m. USD 850 (effective 2001). adv. **Description:** Provides devotional and inspirational life experiences using short essays or testimonies.
Indexed: CPL.
Published by: Messenger Publishing House, 4901 Pennsylvania Ave, Joplin, MO 64804-0700. TEL 417-624-7050, FAX 417-624-7102, http://www.pcg.org/publishinghouse/. Eds. Aaron M Wilson, James B Gee. Circ: 12,000 (paid).

283.73 USA
THE SPRINGFIELD CURRENT. Text in English. 1890. m. bk.rev. 20 p./no.; back issues avail. **Document type:** *Newspaper.* **Description:** Contains items of interest to Episcopalians in the Springfield, Illinois, area.
Supersedes in part: Illinois Churchman
Related titles: Online - full content ed.
Published by: Episcopal Dioceses of Quincy and Springfield (Illinois), 821 S Second St, Springfield, IL 62704. Ed. Paul C Baker. Circ: 7,200 (controlled).

286.132 USA ISSN 1085-7966
STAND FIRM; God's challenge for today's man. Text in English. 1996. m. USD 24.95; USD 3.50 per issue (effective 2008). adv. back issues avail. **Document type:** *Magazine, Consumer.* **Description:** Contains daily devotions, feature articles, interviews, reviews and practical ways to apply biblical truths.
Published by: LifeWay Christian Resources, 1 Lifeway Plz, Nashville, TN 37234. TEL 615-251-2000, 800-458-2772, FAX 615-251-5933, customerservice@lifeway.com. Eds. Tammy Drolsum, Tim Walker, Woody Parker. Circ: 79,000.

286 USA ISSN 0038-9447
STANDARD BEARER (SACRAMENTO). Text in English. 1973 (vol.11). q. USD 9. adv. illus.
Indexed: RehabLit.
Published by: (Seventh-Day Adventist Reform Movement), Northwestern Publishing Association, PO Box 245360, Sacramento, CA 95824-5360. TEL 209-245-3131. Ed. Alfon Sas Balbachas. Circ: 2,000.

280.4 GBR
STAR IN THE EAST. Text in English. 1883. 3/yr. free (effective 2009). bk.rev. back issues avail. **Document type:** *Magazine, Trade.* **Description:** Features articles concerned with the care of needy children in the lands of the Bible.
Related titles: Online - full text ed.: free (effective 2009).
Indexed: NumL.
Published by: BibleLands, PO Box 50, High Wycombe, Bucks HP15 7QU, United Kingdom. TEL 44-1494-897950, FAX 44-1494-897951, info@biblelands.org.uk. Ed. Caroline Rance.

287.632 USA ISSN 0038-9870
STAR OF ZION. Text in English. 1876. bi-m. USD 38 (effective 2005). adv. bk.rev. illus. reprints avail. **Document type:** *Newspaper, Consumer.*
Related titles: Microfilm ed.: (from PQC).
Published by: African Methodist Episcopal Zion Church, PO Box 26770, Charlotte, NC 28221-6770. TEL 704-599-4630, FAX 704-688-2556. Ed., Pub. Mike Lisby. Circ: 11,000.

286 NLD ISSN 1574-6305
STARTKRANT. Text in Dutch. 1997. a.
Published by: (Confessioneel Gereformeerd Toerustingscentrum, Confessionele Vereniging in de Nederlandse Hervormde Kerk, Protestantse Kerk in Nederland, Evangelisch Werkverband), FD-Periodieken bv, Postbus 690, Leeuwarden, 8901 BL, Netherlands. TEL 31-58-2987653, FAX 31-58-2987666. Ed. Thea Westerbeek. Circ: 100,000.

STATE OF THE FAMILY. *see* SOCIOLOGY

285.233 GBR
STEDFAST. Text in English. 1930. bi-m. GBP 1.25 newsstand/cover (effective 2009). adv. back issues avail. **Document type:** *Journal, Consumer.* **Description:** Provides information about the United Free Church of Scotland.
Related titles: Online - full text ed.: free (effective 2009).
Published by: United Free Church of Scotland, 11 Newton Pl, Glasgow, Lanarkshire G3 7PR, United Kingdom. TEL 44-141-3323435, FAX 44-141-3331973, gensec@ufcos.org.uk, http://www.ufcos.org.uk. Ed. John Fulton.

286.6 USA ISSN 1097-6566
BX7075.A1
STONE-CAMPBELL JOURNAL. Text in English. 1998. s-a. USD 18 domestic to individuals; USD 27 foreign to individuals; USD 22 domestic to institutions; USD 27 foreign to institutions (effective 2004). adv. back issues avail. **Document type:** *Journal, Academic/Scholarly.* **Description:** Provides a forum for biblical interpretation, history, philosophy, theology, and cultural criticism to those who follow the perspectives of the Stone-Campbell Movement.
Indexed: A21, ChrPI, OTA, R&TA, RI-1.
Published by: College Press Publishing Company, PO Box 1132, Joplin, MO 64802-1132. TEL 800-289-3300, books@collegepress.com, http://www.collegepress.com. Ed. William R. Baker TEL 513-244-8688. Adv. contact Carol DeWelt.

287 USA
THE STORY (DELAWARE). Text in English. 1989. s-a. free. back issues avail. **Document type:** *Magazine, Consumer.* **Description:** Contains news for students, staff, faculty, alumni, and friends of the school.
Published by: Methodist Theological School in Ohio, 3081 Columbus Pike, PO Box 8004, Delaware, OH 43015-0931. TEL 740-363-1146, FAX 740-362-3135, library@mtso.edu, http://www.mtso.edu. R&P Linda Ogden TEL 740-362-3121.

284.1 USA
STRENGTH FOR THE DAY; God's words of hope and healing. Text in English. 1962. m. USD 16.20 (effective 2009); (Braille & Large Print Editions avail. from Lutheran Library For the Blind, 888-215-2455, blind.library@lcms.org). 16 p./no.; back issues avail. **Document type:** *Magazine, Consumer.* **Description:** Guides the readers to deal with many issues and emotions of daily life-stress, illness, fatigue, loss and anxiety.
Related titles: Braille ed.: free (effective 2009); Large type ed. 22 pt.: free (effective 2009).
Published by: Concordia Publishing House, 3558 S Jefferson, St Louis, MO 63118. TEL 314-268-1000, 800-325-3040, FAX 800-490-9889, order@cph.org. Ed. Rev. Matthew Harrison. Pub. Rev. Paul T McCain. Circ: 10,000 (paid).

287.9 NLD ISSN 0167-1006
STRIJDKREET. Text in Dutch. 1887. fortn. bk.rev. 16 p./no.; back issues avail. **Document type:** *Newsletter, Consumer.*
Related titles: Audio cassette/tape ed.
Published by: Salvation Army, Spoordreef 10, Almere, 1315 GN, Netherlands. TEL 31-36-5398111, FAX 31-36-5331458, ldhnl@legerdesheils.nl.

284.2 ZAF
STROOIDAK. Text in Afrikaans. 1949. q. looseleaf. free.
Formerly: Paarlse Padwyser (0030-8455)
Published by: Nederduitse Gereformeerde Gemeente die Paarl/Dutch Reformed Church, Paarl, Hoofstraat 144, Paarl, Cape Province, South Africa. Ed. J C P B Nieuwoudt. Circ: 1,000.

230.044 ITA ISSN 1125-7326
➤ **STUDI DI TEOLOGIA.** Text in Italian. N.S. 1988. s-a. adv. bk.rev. bibl. index. 110 p./no.; back issues avail. **Document type:** *Journal, Academic/Scholarly.* **Description:** Contains biblical and theological studies.
Indexed: DIP, IBR, IBZ.
Published by: Istituto di Formazione Evangelica e Documentazione (I F E D), Via P M Vermigli 13, Padua, PD 35100, Italy. TEL 39-049-619623, http://www.ifeditalia.org. Ed. Leonardo De Chirico. R&P Luisa Luisetto. Adv. contact Giuliana Luisetto. Circ: 1,000 (paid).

299.2 NLD ISSN 0081-6914
STUDIA SEMITICA NEERLANDICA. Text in English. 1956. irreg., latest vol.53, 2009. price varies. **Document type:** *Monographic series, Academic/Scholarly.*
Indexed: IZBG.
Published by: Brill, PO Box 9000, Leiden, 2300 PA, Netherlands. TEL 31-71-5353500, FAX 31-71-5317532, cs@brill.nl. Ed. K A D Smelik.

280.4 ROM ISSN 1582-5418
BR9.H8
➤ **STUDIA UNIVERSITATIS BABES-BOLYAI. THEOLOGIA REFORMATA TRANSYLVANICA.** Text in English, French, German, Hungarian. 1992. s-a. exchange basis. bk.rev. abstr.; bibl.; illus. **Document type:** *Journal, Academic/Scholarly.*
Related titles: Online - full text ed.: ISSN 2065-9482.
Indexed: CA, T02.
Published by: Universitatea "Babes-Bolyai", Studia/Babes-Bolyai University, Studia, 51 Hasdeu Str, Cluj-Napoca, 400371, Romania. TEL 40-264-405352, FAX 40-264-591906, office@studia.ubbcluj.ro. Ed. Janos Molnar. **Dist by:** "Lucian Blaga" Central University Library, International Exchange Department, Clinicilor st no 2, Cluj-Napoca 400371, Romania. TEL 40-264-597092, FAX 40-264-597633, iancu@bcucluj.ro.

280.4 AUT
STUDIEN UND TEXTE ZUR KIRCHENGESCHICHTE UND GESCHICHTE. Text in German. 1975. irreg., latest vol.41, 1987. price varies. back issues avail. **Document type:** *Monographic series, Academic/Scholarly.*
Indexed: RI-2.
Published by: Boehlau Verlag GmbH & Co.KG., Wiesingerstr 1, Vienna, W 1010, Austria. TEL 43-1-3302427-0, FAX 43-1-3302432. Ed. Peter Barton. Circ: 800.

280.4 DEU ISSN 0935-5898
STUDIEN ZUR THEOLOGIE UND PRAXIS DER SEELSORGE. Text in German. 1989. irreg., latest vol.80, 2010. price varies. **Document type:** *Monographic series, Academic/Scholarly.*
Published by: Echter Verlag GmbH, Dominikanerplatz 8, Wuerzburg, 97070, Germany. TEL 49-931-660680, FAX 49-931-6606823, info@echter-verlag.de, http://www.echter.de.

STUDIES IN MODERN BRITISH RELIGIOUS HISTORY. *see* HISTORY—History Of Europe

285.9 USA ISSN 1048-8553
BX9354.2
STUDIES IN PURITAN AMERICAN SPIRITUALITY. Text in English. 1990. a. USD 99.95 per vol. domestic; GBP 64.95 per vol. in United Kingdom (effective 2010). back issues avail. **Document type:** *Monographic series, Academic/Scholarly.* **Description:** Addresses spiritual concerns that existed in Puritan America.
Indexed: AmH&L, CA, MLA-IB.
Published by: Edwin Mellen Press, 415 Ridge St, PO Box 450, Lewiston, NY 14092. TEL 716-754-2266, FAX 716-754-4056, cservice@mellenpress.com. Ed. Michael Schuldiner.

284.2 NLD ISSN 1571-4799
➤ **STUDIES IN REFORMED THEOLOGY.** Text in English. 1996. irreg., latest vol.17, 2008. price varies. **Document type:** *Monographic series.* **Description:** Covers current issues in the field of systematic, historical and Biblical theology.
Indexed: IZBG.
Published by: Brill, PO Box 9000, Leiden, 2300 PA, Netherlands. TEL 31-71-5353500, FAX 31-71-5317532, cs@brill.nl. Ed. Eddy Van der Borght.

285.7 USA ISSN 1067-4268
BX9422.2
STUDIES IN REFORMED THEOLOGY AND HISTORY. Text in English. 1993 (Win.). irreg., latest vol.10. price varies. **Document type:** *Monographic series, Academic/Scholarly.*
Published by: Princeton Theological Seminary, 64 Mercer St, PO Box 821, Princeton, NJ 08542. TEL 609-921-8300, http://www3.ptsem.edu.

285 CUB ISSN 0864-0262
SU VOZ. Text in Spanish. a.
Published by: Iglesia Presbiteriana, Apdo. 154, Matanzas, Cuba. TEL 809 61-1558. Ed. Francisco Marrero.

280.4 FIN ISSN 1797-0326
SUOMEN EVANKELIS-LUTERILAINEN KIRKKO. KIRKKOHALLITUKSEN YLEISKIRJE (ONLINE). Text in Finnish. 1949. irreg. back issues avail. **Document type:** *Consumer.*
Former titles (until 2007): Suomen Evankelis-Luterilainen Kirkko. Kirkkohallituksen Yleiskirje (Print) (0781-9501); (until 1985): Kirkkohallituksen Ohjeita ja Tiedotuksia (Print) (0356-3901)
Media: Online - full content. **Related titles:** Swedish ed.: Evangelisk-Lutherska Kyrkan i Finland. Cirkulaer (Online). ISSN 1797-0334. 1949.
Published by: Suomen Evankelis-Luterilainen Kirkko/Evangelical Lutheran Church of Finland, PO Box 185, Helsinki, 00161, Finland. TEL 358-9-18021, FAX 358-9-1802350, kirkkohallitus@evl.fi.

280.4 DNK ISSN 1904-223X
SUPERFROE. Text in Danish. 2003. 10/yr. DKK 115 (effective 2008). **Document type:** *Magazine, Consumer.*
Former titles (until 2010): Konrad (1902-4193); (until 2007): Boerne- og Juniorbladet Konrad (1603-1156); Which was formed by the merger of (1981-2003): Nemli' (0901-649X); (1949-2003): Boernebladet (0105-7081); Which incorporated (1982-1989): Alle Boerns Jul (0109-050X); Which was formerly (1976-1982): Boernebladets Jul (0105-709X)
Related titles: Online - full text ed.: ISSN 1904-2361. 2010.
Published by: Danmarks Folkekirkelige Soendagsskoler, Korskaervej 25, Fredericia, 7000, Denmark. TEL 45-75-926100, FAX 45-75-926146, kontakt@soendagsskoler.dk. Ed. Bente Graugaard Nielsen.

266 SWE ISSN 0346-217X
SVENSK MISSIONSTIDSKRIFT/SWEDISH MISSIOLOGICAL THEMES. Variant title: S M T. Text in Swedish, English, French. 1913. q. SEK 150 in Scandinavia to individuals; SEK 200 elsewhere to individuals; SEK 300 in Scandinavia to institutions; SEK 400 elsewhere to institutions (effective 2007). adv. bk.rev. cum index: 1997-2004. back issues avail. **Document type:** *Journal, Academic/Scholarly.* **Description:** Publishes articles on missiological research from the Nordic countries as well as internationally. Publishes extended reviews on doctoral dissertations in missiology from the Nordic countries.
Indexed: A21, BAS, R&TA, RI-1, RI-2.
Published by: Svenska Institutet foer Missionsforskning/Swedish Institute of Missionary Research, PO Box 1526, Uppsala, 75145, Sweden. TEL 46-18-130065, info@teol.uu.se, http://www.teol.uu.se/homepage/SIM/index.htm. Ed. Magnus Lundberg.

286 USA ISSN 1931-6038
SYMSONIA BAPTIST. NEWSLETTER. Text in English. 2006. m. **Document type:** *Newsletter, Consumer.*
Published by: Symsonia Baptist Church, P.O. Box 343, Symsonia, KY 42082. TEL 270-851-3527, http://25425.lifewaylink.com/templates/lif01bl/default.asp?id=25425.

283 USA ISSN 1088-4335
SYNTHESIS C E. (Christian Education) Text in English. 1990. w. (mailed m.). USD 120 (effective 2011). **Document type:** *Handbook/Manual/Guide, Trade.* **Description:** Bible study aids, including readings, interpretations and questions.
Related titles: E-mail ed.: USD 110 (effective 2011).
Published by: Sedgwick Publishing Company, PO Box 328, Boyds, MD 20841. TEL 301-528-0011, FAX 301-599-7679, support@pnmsi.com. Ed. H King Oehmig. Pub. Tod Sedgwick.

T C MAGAZINE. (Teenage Christian) *see* CHILDREN AND YOUTH—For

T E A R TIMES. (The Evangelical Alliance Relief) *see* SOCIAL SERVICES AND WELFARE

T E C. (Teens Erleben Christus) *see* CHILDREN AND YOUTH—For

268 USA ISSN 1064-881X
TABLETALK. Text in English. 1977. m. USD 20 domestic; USD 30 foreign; USD 3 newsstand/cover (effective 2007). bk.rev. 80 p./no.; back issues avail. **Document type:** *Magazine, Consumer.* **Description:** Publishes articles by leading Christian writers, and daily Bible studies for those interested in Christian education.
Indexed: CCR.
Published by: Ligonier Ministries Inc., 400 Technology Park, Lake Mary, FL 32746. TEL 407-333-4244, FAX 407-333-4233. Ed. Burk Parsons. Circ: 55,000 (paid).

280.4 TWN
TAIWAN MISSION QUARTERLY. Text in English. 1991 (Jul.). q. (Jan., Apr., Jul. & Oct.). TWD 300, USD 10 in Asia; TWD 600, USD 20 elsewhere (effective 2001). back issues avail. **Document type:** *Journal, Consumer.* **Description:** Provides community information, resources, religious articles and columns for Protestant missionaries in Taiwan.
Published by: Taiwan Missionary Fellowship, PO Box 22, Taichung, 400, Taiwan. TEL 886-4-236-1901, FAX 886-4-358-6261, tmq@mail.com, http://www.members.aol.com/taimission/.

286 AUS ISSN 0815-6964
TASMANIAN BAPTIST ADVANCE. Text in English. 1958. q. AUD 10 (effective 2010). adv. bk.rev. bibl. back issues avail. **Document type:** *Newsletter.* **Description:** Covers church news, church history and general denominational interest.
Formerly (until 1983): Advance (0815-6956)
Published by: Baptist Union of Tasmania, 8 Hobart Rd, PO Box 275, Kings Meadows, TAS 7249, Australia. TEL 61-3-63434463, FAX 61-3-63436779, info@tasbaptists.org.au, http://www.tasbaptists.org.au. adv.: B&W page AUD 160. Circ: 1,500.

284.1 USA
TE DEUM; alumni newsletter. Text in English. 1978. s-a. free. illus. back issues avail. **Document type:** *Newsletter.* **Description:** Features articles about the Trinity Lutheran Seminary, its curriculum, faculty and alumni.
Published by: Trinity Lutheran Seminary, Office of Communications, 2199 E Main St, Columbus, OH 43209. TEL 614-235-4136, FAX 614-238-0263, advancement@trinity.capital.edu, http://www.trinitylutheranseminary.edu. Ed. Jan Ray. Circ: 10,000.

230.41 USA
TE DEUM TODAY. Text in English. s-a. **Document type:** *Newsletter.* **Description:** Provides news, schedules and information about speakers and events at the seminary.
Published by: Trinity Lutheran Seminary, Office of Communications, 2199 E Main St, Columbus, OH 43209. TEL 614-235-4136, FAX 614-238-0263, advancement@trinity.capital.edu, http://www.trinitylutheranseminary.edu. Ed. Jan Ray.

280.4 USA ISSN 1554-7779
TEACH KIDS!. Text in English. 1942. bi-m. USD 24 domestic; USD 30 foreign (effective 2007). adv. bk.rev. index. **Document type:** *Magazine, Consumer.* **Description:** Gives Sunday school teachers and other Christian education workers instruction and tools to teach 5- to 12-year-olds the Bible.
Former titles (until Sep.-Oct. 2005): Evangelizing Today's Child (0891-3846); (until 1974): Child Evangelism
Related titles: Online - full text ed.: ISSN 1554-8236.
Indexed: ChrPI.
Published by: Child Evangelism Fellowship Inc., 17482 Ste Hwy M, PO Box 348, Warrenton, MO 63383. TEL 636-456-4321, FAX 636-456-9935, custserv@cefinc.org, http://www.cefinc.org/etcmag/. Ed. Elsie Lippy. R&P Billie Parman. Adv. contact Tim Noe. color page USD 899. Circ: 10,000 (paid).

280.4 USA ISSN 1941-6172
TEACH KIDS! ESSENTIALS. Text in English. 2008. m. USD 36 (effective 2008). **Document type:** *Magazine, Consumer.* **Description:** Contains insights and ideas presented in a succinct, easy-to-read format.
Published by: Child Evangelism Fellowship Inc., 17482 Ste Hwy M, PO Box 348, Warrenton, MO 63383. TEL 636-456-4321, FAX 636-456-9935, custserv@cefinc.org, http://www.cefonline.com/.

268.841 USA ISSN 0894-7821
TEACHER'S INTERACTION; a magazine for Sunday school teachers. Text in English. 1960. q. USD 16 (effective 2009). bk.rev. illus. index. **Document type:** *Magazine, Consumer.* **Description:** Features articles, activities, classroom ideas and music that expand the teacher's knowledge base.
Formerly (until 1987): Interaction (0020-5117)
Related titles: Microform ed.: (from PQC).
Indexed: A22.
Published by: (Board for Parish Services), Concordia Publishing House, 3558 S Jefferson, St Louis, MO 63118. TEL 314-268-1000, 800-325-3040, FAX 800-490-9889, order@cph.org. Ed. Tom Nummela. Pub. Rev. Paul T McCain. Circ: 17,000.

280.4 DEU ISSN 1660-4156
TEENSMAG; Trends, Glaube, Action, Tiefgang. Text in German. 1985. bi-m. EUR 19.20; EUR 3.80 newsstand/cover (effective 2011). adv. back issues avail. **Document type:** *Magazine, Consumer.*
Formerly (until 1995): Teens (1660-4776)
Published by: Bundes Verlag GmbH, Bodenborn 43, Witten, 58452, Germany. TEL 49-2302-930930, FAX 49-2302-93093689, info@bundes-verlag.de, http://www.bundes-verlag.de. Ed. Annette Penno. Adv. contact Gabriel Furchert. Circ: 28,000 (paid and controlled).

280.4 DNK ISSN 1902-9179
TENDO. Text in Danish. 1891. 4/yr. DKK 180 (effective 2008). **Document type:** *Magazine, Consumer.*
Formerly (until 2008): Raadgiveren (0105-7073)
Published by: Danmarks Folkekirkelige Soendagsskoler, Korskaervej 25, Fredericia, 7000, Denmark. TEL 45-75-926100, FAX 45-75-926146, kontakt@soendagsskoler.dk, http://www.soendagsskoler.dk. Ed. Mikael Arendt Laursen.

280.4 CZE ISSN 1211-1872
BR9.C95
➤ **TEOLOGICKA REFLEXE**; casopis pro teologii. Text in Czech. 1995. s-a. CZK 130 domestic; EUR 28.90 foreign (effective 2009). **Document type:** *Journal, Academic/Scholarly.*
Indexed: A21, RI-1.
Published by: Univerzita Karlova v Praze, Evangelicka Teologicka Fakulta/Charles University in Prague, Protestant Theological Faculty, Cerna 9, p schr 529, Prague 1, 11555, Czech Republic. TEL 420-22-1988214, FAX 420-22-1988215. Ed. Jindrich Halama. **Dist. by:** Kubon & Sagner Buchexport - Import GmbH, Hessstr 39-41, Munich 80798, Germany. TEL 49-89-542180, FAX 49-89-54218218, postmaster@kubon-sagner.de, http://www.kubon-sagner.de.

230.044 NLD ISSN 0040-5612
THEOLOGIA REFORMATA. Text in Dutch. 1958. q. EUR 40; EUR 30 to students; EUR 11.50 newsstand/cover (effective 2008). adv. bk.rev. index.
Indexed: CERDIC.
—BLDSC (8814.510500), IE.
Published by: (Gereformeerde Bond in de Hervormde Kerk), Bureau Gereformeerde Bond, Kleine Fluitersweg 253, Apeldoorn, 7316 MX, Netherlands. TEL 31-55-5766660, FAX 31-55-5767707. Ed. Dr. J de Gier TEL 31-318-617091.

283 GBR ISSN 0308-6089
THEOLOGICAL RENEWAL. Text in German. 1975. q. **Document type:** *Journal, Trade.*
—CCC.
Published by: Grove Books Ltd., Ridley Hall Rd, Cambridge, CB3 9HU, United Kingdom. TEL 44-1223-464748, FAX 44-1223-464849, sales@grovebooks.co.uk, http://www.grovebooks.co.uk.

283 362.41 GBR ISSN 0049-3651
THEOLOGICAL TIMES. Text in English. 1950. q. GBP 1.16 per issue (effective 2009). **Document type:** *Magazine, Consumer.* **Description:** Features articles from theological periodicals covering many aspects of churchmanship.
Media: Braille. **Related titles:** Audio cassette/tape ed.; Diskette ed.; E-mail ed.
Published by: Royal National Institute of Blind People, 105 Judd St, London, WC1H 9NE, United Kingdom. TEL 44-20-73881266, FAX 44-20-73882034, helpline@rnib.org.uk, http://www.rnib.org.uk.

220 DEU ISSN 0939-5121
➤ **THEOLOGIE FUER DIE PRAXIS.** Text in German. 1978. 2/yr. EUR 12.90 (effective 2009). bk.rev. back issues avail. **Document type:** *Journal, Academic/Scholarly.*
Published by: Edition Ruprecht, Postfach 1716, Goettingen, 37007, Germany. TEL 49-551-4883751, FAX 49-551-4883753, info@edition-ruprecht.de. Eds. Christof Voigt, Holger Eschmann, Joerg Barthel. Pub., R&P Reinhilde Ruprecht. **Dist. by:** Brockhaus Commission, Kreidlerstr 9, Kornwestheim 70806, Germany. TEL 49-7154-13270, FAX 49-7154-132713, info@brocom.de, http://www.brocom.de.

230.044 USA ISSN 1529-899X
THEOLOGY NEWS AND NOTES. Text in English. 1954. s-a. free to qualified personnel (effective 2011). back issues avail. **Document type:** *Journal, Academic/Scholarly.* **Description:** Offers articles of theological reflection.
Related titles: Online - full text ed.
Indexed: A21, CCR, RI-1.
Published by: Fuller Theological Seminary, 135 N Oakland Ave, Pasadena, CA 91182. TEL 626-584-5200, 800-235-2222, alum-alumni@dept.fuller.edu.

285 USA
THESE DAYS. Text in English. 1970. bi-m.
Published by: Presbyterian Publishing Corporation, 100 Witherspoon St., Louisville, KY 40202-1396. Ed. Kay Snodgrass. Circ: 200,000.

287.6 USA ISSN 1092-7085
BX8248.M3
THIRD CENTURY METHODISM. Text in English. 1962. irreg. (3-4/yr.). looseleaf. USD 10 (effective 2001). bk.rev. bibl.; illus.; maps; stat. back issues avail. **Document type:** *Newsletter.*
Published by: United Methodist Historical Society, Lovely Lane Museum, 2200 St Paul St, Baltimore, MD 21218. TEL 401-889-4458, FAX 410-889-1501. Ed. Rev. Edwin Schell. Circ: 545 (paid).

280 USA ISSN 2152-8837
▼ **THRIVING FAMILY.** Text in English. 2009. bi-m. USD 9.99 (effective 2010). back issues avail. **Document type:** *Magazine, Consumer.* **Description:** Provides readers with articles and advice that will help to strengthen their marriage, develop new parenting skills and build a strong family.
Related titles: Online - full text ed.
Published by: Focus on the Family, 8605 Explorer Dr, Colorado Springs, CO 80920. TEL 719-531-3400, 800-232-6459, FAX 719-531-3424, http://www.focusonthefamily.com. Ed. Susan Mathis. Pub. Robert E Dubberley.

283 CHN ISSN 1006-1274
BR1280
TIAN FENG/HEAVENLY WIND. Text in Chinese. 1945. m. USD 28.80 (effective 2009). **Document type:** *Bulletin.*
—East View.
Published by: Zhongguo Jidujiao Xiehui/China Christian Council, 3rd Fl, 169 Yuanmingyuan Rd, Shanghai, 200002, China. TEL 86-21-6321-0487, FAX 86-21-6323-2605, tfceshen@online.sh.cn. Ed. Cheng En Shen. Circ: 120,000. **Co-sponsor:** National Committee of Protestant Three-self Patriotic Movement.

286.7 NOR ISSN 0804-8916
TIDENS TALE. Text in Norwegian. 1901. bi-m. NOK 128 (effective 2007). back issues avail. **Document type:** *Magazine, Consumer.*
Formerly (until 1928): Evangeliets Sendebud (0804-8924)
Related titles: Online - full text ed.
Published by: (Syvendedags-Adventistsamfunnet i Norge), Norsk Bokforlag A-S, Vik Senter, Roeyse, 3530, Norway. TEL 47-32-461550, FAX 47-32-461551, salg@noskbokforlag.no, http://www.norskbokforlag.no. Ed. Widar Ursett.

230.044 NOR ISSN 0040-7194
BX8001
TIDSSKRIFT FOR TEOLOGI OG KIRKE; Norwegian periodical for church and theology. Text in Norwegian; Summaries in English. 1930. q. NOK 488 to individuals; NOK 765 to institutions; NOK 280 to students (effective 2010). bk.rev. bibl. index. back issues avail. **Document type:** *Journal, Academic/Scholarly.* **Description:** Focuses on research in theology and the Church.
Related titles: Online - full text ed.: ISSN 1504-2952. NOK 865 (effective 2010).
Indexed: DIP, FR, IBR, IBZ, IZBG, OTA.
—BLDSC (8828.180000), INIST.
Published by: Universitetsforlaget AS/Scandinavian University Press (Subsidiary of: Aschehoug & Co.), Sehesteds Gate 3, P O Box 508, Sentrum, Oslo, 0105, Norway. TEL 47-24-147500, FAX 47-24-147501, post@universitetsforlaget.no, http://www.universitetsforlaget.no. Ed. Peder Gravem. Circ: 500.

280.4 AUS ISSN 1030-0295
TODAY (LAWSON); family magazine. Text in English. 1966. m. (except Jan.). illus. **Document type:** *Bulletin.* **Description:** Includes stories, testimonies, bible teaching and photos.
Incorporates (1979-1992): Today's Young Life (1030-0309); (1962-1992): Letterstick (0727-5854)
Published by: Mission Publications of Australia, 19 Cascade St, PO Box 21, Lawson, NSW 2785, Australia. TEL 61-2-47591003, FAX 61-2-47591001.

260 USA ISSN 1538-6775
TODAY'S CHRISTIAN MAN. Text in English. 2001 (Nov./Dec.). bi-m. USD 19.95 (effective 2002). adv.
Published by: Hagstrom Publishing, Inc., P.O. Box 12683, Dallas, TX 75225-0683. TEL 214-739-9400, 866-739-1427 (toll free), FAX 214-739-9401, info@todayschristianman.com. Ed., Pub. Bradford S. Hagstrom.

284.1 USA ISSN 1084-4775
TODAY'S LIGHT. Text in English. 1996. bi-m. USD 24 (effective 2009); (Braille & Large Print Editions avail. from Lutheran Library For the Blind. Tel. 888-215-2455; E-mail: blind.library@lcms.org). charts; illus.; maps. 84 p./no.; back issues avail. **Document type:** *Magazine, Consumer.* **Description:** Guides the readers through the entire Bible.
Related titles: Braille ed.: free (effective 2009); Large type ed. 22 pt.: free (effective 2009).
Published by: Concordia Publishing House, 3558 S Jefferson, St Louis, MO 63118. TEL 314-268-1000, 800-325-3040, FAX 800-490-9889, order@cph.org. Ed. Rodney Rathman. Pub. Rev. Paul T McCain. Circ: 12,000 (paid).

283.73 280.4 USA ISSN 1098-7975
TODAY'S READINGS. Text in English. 1993. q. USD 41.60 (effective 2003). **Document type:** *Magazine, Consumer.* **Description:** Provides Sunday readings for the Episcopal Church.
Formerly (until 1998): Lectionary Insert
Published by: Forward Movement Publications, 300 W 4th St, Ste 200, Cincinnati, OH 45202-2666. http://www.forwardmovement.org. Ed. E S Gleason.

280.4 GBR ISSN 1361-1429
TOGETHER WITH CHILDREN. Text in English. 1956. 9/yr. GBP 17 in United Kingdom; GBP 22 elsewhere (effective 2001). adv. bk.rev. illus. **Document type:** *Magazine, Consumer.* **Description:** For those concerned with children's Christian education.
Former titles: Together (0307-5982); Church Teacher (0009-6571)
Indexed: CCR, CERDIC.
—CCC.
Published by: National Society, Church House, Great Smith St, London, SW1P 3NZ, United Kingdom. TEL 44-20-7898-1518, FAX 44-20-7898-1493, http://www.natsoc.org.uk. Ed. Jayne Hall. R&P John Kanes TEL 44-20-7898-1357. Adv. contact Sheridan James TEL 44-20-7898-1524. Circ: 3,000.

285.293 NZL ISSN 1175-6020
TOUCHSTONE. Text in English. 1899. 11/yr. adv. back issues avail. **Document type:** *Newsletter, Consumer.* **Description:** Seeks to explore Faith issues for today and report on the life and work of Methodist Churches and co-operative ventures.
Supersedes in part (1987-2001): Crosslink (0113-2024); Which was formerly (until 1987): Outlook (0048-2463); Which was formed by the merger of (18??-1899): Focus; (18??-1899): Outreach; (until 1899): Christian Outlook; Outlook incorporated: Four Square
Related titles: Online - full text ed.: ISSN 1179-6677. free (effective 2010).

R

Published by: Methodist Church of New Zealand, PO Box 931, Christchurch, 8140, New Zealand. TEL 64-3-3666049, FAX 64-3-3649439. Ed. Paul Titus TEL 64-3-3816912. Adv. contact Pieter van den Berg TEL 64-3-3107781.

TRACT MESSENGER. *see* HANDICAPPED—Visually Impaired

280.4 AUS
TRANSFORM (EAGLE FARM). Text in English. 1953. 4/yr. back issues avail. **Document type:** *Newsletter, Consumer.* **Description:** Provides details of union activities.
Former titles (until 2007): S U News; State of the Union
Published by: Scripture Union of Queensland, 800 Kingsford Smith Dr, PO Box 1167, Eagle Farm, QLD 4009, Australia. TEL 61-7-36322222, FAX 61-7-36322299, info@suqld.org.au, http://www.suqld.org.au.

TRANSMISSION. *see* RELIGIONS AND THEOLOGY

284.2 949.2 NLD ISSN 0928-1282
TRANSPARANT. Text in Dutch. 1990. q. EUR 27.50; EUR 13.75 to students (effective 2008). adv.
Incorporates (1993-1996): Transparant. Onderwijskatern (0929-0133)
Published by: (Vereniging van Christen-Historici), Boekencentrum Uitgevers, Goudstraat 50, Postbus 29, Zoetermeer, 2700 AA, Netherlands. TEL 31-79-3615481, FAX 31-79-3615489, info@boekencentrum.nl, http://www.boekencentrum.nl. Ed. A A van der Schans.

280.4 CAN ISSN 0229-4362
TRANSPORTEUR; au service du personnel dans le transport et les industries connexes. Text in French. 1983. bi-m. free.
Formerly: Bonne Nouvelle pour le Transporteur
Published by: Christian Transportation Inc., 2222 S Sheridan Way, Unit 5, Bldg 2, Mississauga, ON L5J 2M4, Canada. TEL 416-822-2700. Ed. Louis G Voyer. Circ: 6,300.

255.42 GBR
TRINITARIAN BIBLE SOCIETY. QUARTERLY RECORD (ONLINE). Text in English. 19??. q. free (effective 2009). back issues avail. **Document type:** *Magazine, Trade.* **Description:** Reports on Scripture publication and distribution; includes articles on Bible translation and textual questions.
Media: Online - full text.
Published by: Trinitarian Bible Society, Tyndale House, Dorset Rd, London, SW19 3NN, United Kingdom. TEL 44-20-85437857, FAX 44-20-85436370.

283.73 USA ISSN 1937-5328
BR1
TRINITY JOURNAL FOR THEOLOGY & MINISTRY. Text in English. 2007 (Sep.). s-a. ((Spr./Fall)). USD 30 (effective 2010). **Document type:** *Journal, Academic/Scholarly.* **Description:** Provides information about theology & ministry.
Published by: Trinity Episcopal School for Ministry, 311 11th St, Ambridge, PA 15003. TEL 724-266-3838, 800-874-8754, FAX 724-266-4617, info@tsm.edu.

THE TRINITY REVIEW. *see* PHILOSOPHY

TRINITY SEMINARY REVIEW. *see* EDUCATION—Higher Education

240 USA ISSN 1943-6645
TRUTH POINTS. Text in English. 2008. w. **Document type:** *Newsletter, Consumer.*
Media: E-mail.
Published by: Called to Destiny, PO Box 2769, Alvin, TX 77512. TEL 800-604-7037, info@calledtodestiny.org, http://www.calledtodestiny.org. Ed. Gail Wiggins.

280.4 USA
TRUTH VS. TRADITION. Text in English. bi-m. free. **Document type:** *Newsletter.* **Description:** Deals with many traditions that have come to be accepted as Bible truth by the world today.
Media: Online - full text. Ed. Larry Wolfe.

280.4 DEU ISSN 0930-732X
TUTZINGER BLAETTER. Text in German. 1975. q. **Document type:** *Newsletter, Consumer.*
Published by: Evangelische Akademie Tutzing, Schlossstr 2-4, Tutzing, 82327, Germany. TEL 49-8158-2510, FAX 49-8158-251137, http://www.ev-akademie-tutzing.de, info@ev-akademie-tutzing.de. Ed. Axel Schwanebeck. Circ: 10,000.

286.1 ZAF ISSN 1013-1116
TYDSKRIF VIR CHRISTELIKE WETENSKAP. Text in Afrikaans. 1965. s-a. **Document type:** *Journal.*
Indexed: ISAP, OTA.
Published by: Die Vereniging vir Christelike Hoeer Onderwys/ Association for Christian Higher Education, Posbus 1824, Bloemfontein, 9300, South Africa. TEL 27-51-4484464, FAX 27-51-4484669, vcho@mjvn.co.za, http://www.vcho.co.za.

285.235 GBR
TYST. Text in Welsh. 1867. w. GBP 35; GBP 32.25 foreign (effective 1999). adv. bk.rev. **Document type:** *Newspaper.*
Published by: Union of Welsh Independents, 11 St Helens Rd, Swansea, SA1 4AL, United Kingdom. TEL 44-1792-467040, FAX 44-1792-650647. R&P, Adv. contact Gareth Rees. Circ: 1,200.

284.1 USA
U L S TODAY. Text mainly in English; Text occasionally in Slovak. 1894. bi-m. free. adv. bk.rev. **Document type:** *Newsletter.*
Formerly (until Jan. 1996): United Lutheran (0041-7300)
Published by: United Lutheran Society, Box 947, Ligonier, PA 15658-0947. TEL 724-238-9505, FAX 724-238-9506. Ed., R&P Matthew M Blistan Jr. Circ: 5,000.

287.6 USA
U M CONNECTION. (United Methodist) Text in English. s-m. USD 15 (effective 2000). adv.
Published by: Balto-Washington Conference, United Methodists, 9720 Patuxent Woods Dr, Ste 100, Columbia, MD 21046-1526. TEL 800-492-2525. Ed. Dean Snyder. Adv. contact Sharon Porter TEL 800-492-2525 ext 420. B&W page USD 648, color page USD 964.

U S P G PRAYER DIARY. *see* RELIGIONS AND THEOLOGY

280.4 DEU
UEBER LAND; evangelische Perspektiven zu Land und Oekologie. Text in German. 1971. 2/yr. bk.rev. back issues avail. **Document type:** *Bulletin, Trade.*
Former titles: Evangelischer Informationsdienst fuer Jugend- und Erwachsenenbildung auf dem Lande; Evangelischer Informationsdienst fuer Jugend- und Erwachsenbildung
Published by: Evangelische Landjugendakademie, Dieperzbergweg 13-17, Altenkirchen, 57610, Germany. TEL 49-2681-95160, FAX 49-2681-70206, info@lja.de.

284.1 TZA
UHURU NA AMANI. Text in Swahili. fortn. **Description:** Evangelical-Lutheran publication.
Address: PO Box 3033, Arusha, Tanzania. TEL 255-3221, TELEX 42054. Ed. Elias G B Goroi. Circ: 15,000.

284.2 NLD
UIT DE LEVENSBRON. Text in Dutch. 10/yr. EUR 38.50; EUR 30 to students (effective 2008).
Published by: Stichting Uit de Levensbron, Vlieland 198, Utrecht, 3524 AD, Netherlands. TEL 31-30-2892440, udl@kooier.nl.

284.2 ZAF ISSN 0378-4134
UMTHOMBO WAMANDLA. Text in Xhosa. 1972. bi-m.
Published by: Reformed Churches in South Africa/Gereformeerde Kerke in Suid-Afrika, c/o South African Council of Churches, PO Box 62098, Marshalltown, 2107, South Africa. TEL 27-11-4921380, FAX 27-11-4921448, info@sacc.org.za, http://www.sacc.org.za. Ed. W D Graham. Circ: 860.

230.0071 USA ISSN 0362-1545
➤ **UNION SEMINARY QUARTERLY REVIEW.** Abbreviated title: U S Q R. Text in English. 1945. q. adv. bk.rev. bibl.; illus. index. back issues avail.; reprints avail. **Document type:** *Journal, Academic/Scholarly.* **Description:** Contains features articles and book reviews by established and emergent biblical scholars, historians, ethicists, theologians, and other academic, church and social commentators.
Formed by the merger of (1939-1945): Union Review (0362-9031); (1925-1945): Union Theological Seminary. Alumni Bulletin
Related titles: Microfilm ed.: (from PQC).
Indexed: A21, A22, CERDIC, OTA, P30, PCI, PhilInd, R&TA, RI-1, RI-2. —Ingenta. **CCC.**
Published by: Union Theological Seminary, 3041 Broadway, 121st St, New York, NY 10027. TEL 212-662-7100, contactus@uts.columbia.edu, http://www.uts.columbia.edu. Circ: 1,500. **Co-publisher:** Presbyterian School of Christian Education.

➤ **UNITARIAN UNIVERSALIST CHRISTIAN.** *see* RELIGIONS AND THEOLOGY—Other Denominations And Sects

284.6 DEU ISSN 0344-9254
BX8551
UNITAS FRATRUM; Zeitschrift fuer Geschichte und Gegenwartsfragen der Bruedergemeine. Text in German. 1977. s-a. EUR 25; EUR 12.50 to students (effective 2009). bk.rev. abstr.; bibl. back issues avail. **Document type:** *Journal, Academic/Scholarly.* **Description:** Contains scholarly and historical articles on the Moravian Church and its members.
Indexed: A21, AmH&L, CA, DIP, HistAb, IBR, IBZ, MLA-IB, RI-1, RI-2, T02.
—CCC.
Published by: Verein fuer Geschichte und Gegenwartsfragen der Bruedergemeine, Zittauer Str 24, Herrnhut, 02745, Germany. TEL 49-35873-48731, FAX 49-35873-48799, http://www.ebu.de. Ed. Paul Peucker. Circ: 500.

286 CAN ISSN 0082-7843
BX6251
UNITED BAPTIST CONVENTION OF THE ATLANTIC PROVINCES. YEARBOOK. Text in English. 1963. a. price varies. index. **Document type:** *Corporate.*
Published by: United Baptist Convention of the Atlantic Provinces, 1655 Manawagonish Rd, Saint John, NB E2M 3Y2, Canada. TEL 506-635-1922, FAX 506-635-0366. Ed., R&P Harry G Gardner. Circ: 2,200.

285.834 USA ISSN 0882-7214
UNITED CHURCH NEWS. Text in English. 1985. m. (except Jan. & Aug.). free. adv. illus. back issues avail. **Document type:** *Newspaper.* **Description:** News and features of the people, churches and agencies of the United Church of Christ.
Incorporates: Keeping You Posted (0361-8668)
Published by: United Church of Christ, Office of Communication, 700 Prospect Ave, Cleveland, OH 44115-1100. TEL 216-736-2218, FAX 216-736-2223, ucnews@ecunet.org. Ed., Pub., R&P, Adv. contact Rev. Robert Chase TEL 216-736-2173. Circ: 80,000.

285.834 CAN ISSN 0041-7238
BX9881.A1
THE UNITED CHURCH OBSERVER. Text in English. 1925. m. CAD 12 domestic; CAD 25 foreign; CAD 2 newsstand/cover (effective 2000). adv. bk.rev.; film rev.
Related titles: Microfilm ed.: (from PQC).
Indexed: A22, C03, CBCARef, CBPI, CPerI, G08, I05, P48, PQC, PRA, R05, RILM.
Published by: (United Church of Canada), Observer Publication Inc., 478 Huron St, Toronto, ON M5R 2R3, Canada. TEL 416-960-8500, FAX 416-960-8477, general@ucobserver.org, http://www.ucobserver.org. Ed. Muriel Duncan. Circ: 120,000 (paid).

287.92 CAN ISSN 0848-4449
BX9881
UNITED CHURCH OF CANADA. YEAR BOOK AND DIRECTORY. Text in English. 1925. a. CAD 20 (effective 1998). **Document type:** *Directory.*
Formerly: United Church of Canada. Year Book (0082-7886)
Published by: United Church of Canada, 3250 Bloor St W, Ste 300, Etobicoke, ON M8X 2Y4, Canada. TEL 416-231-5931, 800-268-3781, FAX 416-231-3103. Circ: 4,000.

285.834 USA ISSN 0360-9782
BX7245.5
UNITED CHURCH OF CHRIST. PENSION BOARDS (ANNUAL REPORT). Key Title: Pension Boards. Text in English. 1967. a. free. **Document type:** *Corporate.*
Published by: United Church of Christ, Pension Board, 475 Riverside Dr, 10th Fl, New York, NY 10115-1126. TEL 212-870-2790, FAX 212-870-2877. Ed. Edmund Tortora. Circ: 22,681.

285.233 GBR ISSN 0082-7908
BX9089
UNITED FREE CHURCH OF SCOTLAND. HANDBOOK. Text in English. 1930. a. GBP 3 (effective 2000). **Document type:** *Bulletin.*
Published by: United Free Church of Scotland, 11 Newton Pl, Glasgow, Lanarkshire G3 7PR, United Kingdom. TEL 44-141-3323435, FAX 44-141-3331973, gensec@ufcos.org.uk, http://www.ufcos.org.uk. Ed. John Fulton. Circ: 600.

287.6 USA ISSN 0503-3551
BX8382.2.A1
UNITED METHODIST CHURCH. GENERAL MINUTES OF THE ANNUAL CONFERENCES. Key Title: General Minutes of the Annual Conferences of the United Methodist Church. Text in English. 1968. a. USD 28 paperbound ed.; USD 40 cloth ed. (effective 1999). illus. **Document type:** *Proceedings.* **Description:** Directory of the churches and personnel of the United Methodist Church. Includes local church statistical data.
Related titles: Microfiche ed.: (from IDC).
Published by: United Methodist Church, General Council on Finance and Administration, 1200 Davis St, Evanston, IL 60201-4193. TEL 847-869-3345, FAX 847-869-3359, bbabbitt@gcfa.org. Ed., R&P Beth Babbitt. Pub. Sandra Kelley Lackore. Circ: 1,500.

287.6 USA ISSN 1081-079X
UNITED METHODIST LIFE. Text in English. 1957. 10/yr. USD 6; free to all Iowa local officers. adv. illus. **Document type:** *Newspaper.*
Former titles (until 1995): Hawkeye (Des Moines) (0887-0829); Hawkeye United Methodist (0017-8632); Hawkeye Methodist
Published by: United Methodist Church, Iowa Conference, 500 E Court Ave, Suite C, Des Moines, IA 50309-2019. TEL 515-283-1991, FAX 515-283-0863. Ed. Brenda R P Henning. Pub. George Wylie. R&P, Adv. contact Eryn O'Hare. Circ: 14,000.

287.6 USA ISSN 0737-5581
UNITED METHODIST REPORTER. Text in English, Spanish. 1847. w. USD 26. adv. bk.rev. charts; illus. **Document type:** *Newspaper.*
Incorporates (in 1996): United Methodist Review; Former titles (until 1972): Texas Methodist - United Methodist Reporter; Texas Methodist (0040-4489)
Related titles: Microfilm ed.
Published by: United Methodist Communications Council, PO Box 660275, Dallas, TX 75266. TEL 214-630-6495, FAX 214-630-0079. Ed. John A Lovelace. Circ: 450,000.

285.232 GBR
UNITED REFORMED CHURCH (GREAT BRITAIN). UNITED REFORMED CHURCH YEAR BOOK. Text in English. 1973. a. GBP 15 per issue (effective 2009). adv. **Document type:** *Yearbook.* **Description:** Covers yearly information about the United Reformed Church in the United Kingdom.
Former titles (until 2001): United Reformed Church in the United Kingdom. The United Reformed Church Year Book; (until 1982): United Reformed Church in England and Wales. United Reformed Church Year Book (0069-8849)
Related titles: CD-ROM ed.: GBP 6 per issue (effective 2009).
—CCC.
Published by: The United Reformed Church in the United Kingdom, 86 Tavistock Pl, London, WC1H 9RT, United Kingdom. TEL 44-20-79162020, FAX 44-20-79162021, urc@urc.org.uk.

283.42 GBR
UNITED REFORMED CHURCH. DIARY. Text in English. 19??. a. GBP 5.95 per issue (effective 2010). **Document type:** *Bulletin.* **Description:** Features include, 7-day per page, church related dates, forward planner for 2011, holiday dates, URC useful addresses, maps and telephone & address page.
Published by: The United Reformed Church in the United Kingdom, 86 Tavistock Pl, London, WC1H 9RT, United Kingdom. TEL 44-20-79162020, FAX 44-20-79162021, urc@urc.org.uk, http://www.urc.org.uk.

285.232 GBR ISSN 0049-5433
BX9890.U25
UNITED REFORMED CHURCH HISTORY SOCIETY. JOURNAL. Text in English. 1973. s-a. GBP 18.50 domestic; GBP 20 foreign (effective 2010). bk.rev. Index. back issues avail. **Document type:** *Journal, Academic/Scholarly.* **Description:** Covers the history of the constituent, 16th-20th centuries.
Formed by the 1973 merger of: Congregational Historical Society. Transactions; Presbyterian Historical Society. Journal (0079-5011)
Related titles: Microform ed.: (from PQC).
Indexed: AmH&L, CA, CERDIC, FR, HistAb, P30, PCI, T02.
—BLDSC (4910.640000), INIST.
Published by: United Reformed Church History Society, Westminster College, Madingley Rd, Cambridge, CB3 0AA, United Kingdom. TEL 44-1223-741300, mt212@hermes.cam.ac.uk, http://www.urc.org.uk/what_we_do/groups/history/history_society.

283.42 GBR
UNITED REFORMED CHURCH, YORKSHIRE PROVINCE, PROVINCIAL HANDBOOK. Text in English. 1973. a. GBP 2. adv. **Document type:** *Directory.* **Description:** Names and addresses of churches' officers and committees.
Published by: United Reformed Church (Yorkshire Province), 43 Hunslet Ln, Leeds, LS10 1JW, United Kingdom. TEL 44-1132-451267, FAX 44-1132-341145. Ed. Colin Mundy. Circ: 450.

280.4 AUS ISSN 1323-6377
UNITING CHURCH STUDIES. Text in English. 1995. s-a. back issues avail. **Document type:** *Journal, Consumer.*
Indexed: A21, RI-1.
Published by: United Theological College, 16 Masons Dr, N Parramatta, NSW 2151, Australia. TEL 61-2-88388927, FAX 61-2-96836617, utc@nsw.uca.org.au, http://www.utc.uca.org.au.

UNSERE GEMEINDE. *see* HANDICAPPED—Hearing Impaired

280.4 DEU
UNSERE KIRCHE - DER WEG - SONNTAGSGRUSS. Text in German. 1935. w. EUR 4.95 per month (effective 2009). adv. **Document type:** *Newsletter, Consumer.*
Published by: Evangelische Medien Agentur, Cansteinstr 1, Bielefeld, 33647, Germany. TEL 49-521-94400, FAX 49-521-9440181, zentrale@presseverband-bielefeld.de, http://www.medienhaus-bielefeld.de. Circ: 58,074 (paid and controlled).

287 DEU ISSN 1436-607X
UNTERWEGS (STUTTGART); Zeitschrift der Evangelisch-methodistischen Kirche. Text in German. 1968. w. EUR 50 (effective 2002). adv. bk.rev. bibl.; illus.; stat. **Document type:** *Magazine, Consumer.*

Formerly (until 1998): Wort und Weg (0043-9444); Which was formed by the 1968 merger of: Evangelischer Botschaft; Evangelist
Published by: (Evangelisch-methodistische Kirche), Medienwerk der Evangelisch-Methodistischen Kirche, Ludolfusstr 2-4, Frankfurt am Main, 60487, Germany. TEL 49-69-24252120, FAX 49-69-24252128, medienwerk@emk.de, http://www.emk.de. Ed. Karl-Heinz Hecke. adv.: page EUR 1,120; trim 184 x 254. Circ: 7,500 (controlled).

287.6 USA ISSN 0042-0735
BV4800
THE UPPER ROOM; daily devotional guide. Text in English. 1935. bi-m. USD 11 domestic; CAD 14.25 in Canada (effective 2009). back issues avail. **Document type:** *Magazine, Consumer.* **Description:** Contains meditation, prayer, suggested scripture reading, and a prayer focus for each day.
Related titles: Audio cassette/tape ed.: USD 35 (effective 2009); Braille ed.: free; Online - full content ed.: free; Large type ed. 18 pt.: USD 12 domestic; CAD 15.50 in Canada (effective 2009); ◆ Spanish ed.: El Aposento Alto. ISSN 0003-6552.
Published by: (United Methodist Church, General Board of Discipleship), The Upper Room Publications, 1908 Grand Ave, PO Box 340004, Nashville, TN 37203. TEL 615-340-7200, FAX 615-340-7275, urbooks@upperroom.org. Ed. Stephen D Bryant. Circ: 2,000,000 (paid).

266.4 SWE ISSN 0042-1553
UTE OCH HEMMA; svenska kyrkan i utlandet. Text in Swedish. 1928. q. SEK 100 (effective 2006). adv. bk.rev. illus. indes. **Document type:** *Magazine, Consumer.* **Description:** The Swedish Church's work abroad.
Published by: Naemnden foer Svenska Kyrkan i Utlandet, Sysslomansgatan 4, Uppsala, 75170, Sweden. TEL 46-18-169500, FAX 46-18-169567, skut@svenskakyrkan.se. Eds. Lena Sjoestroem, Marja Anne Casparsson.

280.4 DEU ISSN 1431-2549
V E D D FORUM. Text in German. 1913. bi-m. membership. **Document type:** *Newsletter, Consumer.*
Former titles (until 1992): Diakon (0343-3692); (until 1977): Mannliche Diakonie (0343-3633)
Published by: Verband Evangelischer Diakonen- und Diakoninnen-Gemeinschaften in Deutschland e.V., Kurt-Schumacher-Str 2, Kassel, 34117, Germany. TEL 49-561-7399421, FAX 49-561-7399422, vedd@vedd.de, http://www.vedd.de.

284.1 DEU ISSN 1617-0741
V E L K D - INFORMATIONEN. Text in German. 1969. q. bk.rev. **Document type:** *Newsletter, Consumer.*
Published by: Vereinigte Evangelisch - Lutherische Kirche Deutschlands, Lutherisches Kirchenamt, Postfach 510409, Hannover, 30634, Germany. TEL 49-511-6261226, FAX 49-511-6261511, http://www.velkd.de. Ed. Udo Hahn. Circ: 4,500.

284.1 USA ISSN 0042-2568
BT734
VANGUARD (MILWAUKEE, 1954). Text in English. 1954. bi-m. membership. bk.rev. illus. reprints avail. **Document type:** *Newspaper.* **Description:** Focuses on issues of justice.
Related titles: Microform ed.: (from PQC); Online - full content ed.
Published by: Lutheran Human Relations Association, 1821 N. 16th St., Milwaukee, WI 53205-1626. TEL 414-536-0585, FAX 414-536-0690. Ed., R&P Joyce Caldwell. Circ: 7,000.

266.6 USA ISSN 0042-3459
VENTANA; missionary magazine for women. Text in Spanish. 1931. q. USD 10 (effective 1999). adv. illus.
Published by: Casa Bautista de Publicaciones, PO Box 4255, El Paso, TX 79914. TEL 915-566-9656. Ed. Alicia Zorzoli. R&P Norberto Herrera. Adv. contact Jorge A Rousselin. Circ: 20,000.

280.4 FRA ISSN 2108-2308
VERS DIMANCHE +. Text in French. 1966. m. **Document type:** *Consumer.*
Formerly (until 2010): Christ Source de Vie (0181-1959)
Published by: Association Christ Source de Vie, 9 Rue Montplaisir, Toulouse, 31400, France. http://www.ndweb.org/versdimanche.

284.14895 DNK ISSN 1399-2317
VIBORG STIFTS BOG. Variant title: Viborg Stifsbog. Text in Danish. 1942. a. DKK 125 per issue (effective 2010). illus. **Document type:** *Yearbook, Consumer.* **Description:** Articles on Danish ecclesial matters.
Formerly (until 1998): Viborg Stifts Aarbog (0107-8925)
Published by: Viborg Stift, Domkirkestraede 1, Viborg, 8800, Denmark. TEL 45-86-620911, FAX 45-86-623709, kmvib@km.dk, http://www.viborgstift.dk. Ed. Thomas Frank.

286 AUS ISSN 0726-4097
VICTORIAN BAPTIST WITNESS; the voice of victorian baptists. Text in English. 1931. m. AUD 36 domestic to individuals; AUD 12 foreign to individuals; AUD 10 for churches (effective 2008). adv. bk.rev. back issues avail. **Document type:** *Magazine, Consumer.* **Description:** Includes news and features of interest to Baptist Church members.
Formerly: Propagandist
Published by: Baptist Union of Victoria, PO Box 377, Hawthorn, VIC 3122, Australia. TEL 61-3-98806100, FAX 61-3-98806123, info@buv.com.au. Ed. Matthew J Bevis TEL 61-3-98806155. adv.: page AUD 1,510, color page AUD 2,160; 240 x 315. Circ: 6,200.

280.4 USA ISSN 0745-9173
VICTORY (SAN DIEGO). Text in English. 1964. bi-m.
Formerly (until 1983): Deeper Life
Related titles: Spanish ed.: ISSN 8750-2534.
Published by: Morris Cerullo World Evangelism, PO Box 85277, San Diego, CA 92186. TEL 858-277-2200, FAX 858-277-5111. Ed. Bill Jones. Circ: 130,000.

286.7 USA ISSN 1941-2568
VIDA ADVENTISTA EN LA DIVISION INTERAMERICANA. Text in Spanish. 2008. q. **Document type:** *Magazine, Consumer.*
Published by: Inter American Division Publishing Association, 2905 NW 87th Ave, Doral, FL 33171. TEL 305-599-0037, FAX 305-592-8999, mail@iadpa.org, http://iadpa.org.

280.4 CHL ISSN 0718-5340
VIDA Y PAZ. Text in Spanish. 2007. bi-m.
Media: Online - full text.
Published by: Centro Evangelistico Internacional, Ministerio Rodolfo Mejia, Guillermo Gallardo 221, Puerto Mont, Chile. vidaypaz@genesiscreacionweb.net, http://www.ministeriorodolfomejia.com/.

280.4 CHE
LA VIE PROTESTANTE BERNE - JURA. Text in French. 1992. m. bk.rev. 3 cols./p.; **Document type:** *Bulletin, Consumer.* **Description:** Presents articles on Protestantism and religion in general.
Related titles: Diskette ed.; Fax ed.
Published by: Fondation Visage Protestant, Acherweg 70-D, Case Postale 130, Tramelan, 2720, Switzerland. TEL 41-32-487-5679, FAX 41-32-344-2928. **Dist. by:** Ediprim, Case Postale 1144, Bieme 2501, Switzerland. TEL 41-32-344-2929, FAX 41-32-344-2928.

280.4 384.54 NLD ISSN 1872-194X
VIER. Text in Dutch. 2005. q. EUR 13 (effective 2009). **Document type:** *Magazine, Consumer.*
Published by: Nederlandse Christelijke Radio Vereniging, Postbus 25000, Hilversum, 1202 HB, Netherlands. TEL 31-35-6719911, FAX 31-35-6719285, http://www.ncrv.nl.

286.1755 USA ISSN 0083-6311
BX6248.V8
THE VIRGINIA BAPTIST REGISTER. Text in English. 1962. a. USD 10 per issue (effective 2011). bk.rev. cum.index every 5 yrs. **Document type:** *Journal, Academic/Scholarly.* **Description:** Covers early Virginia Baptist history.
Related titles: Microfilm ed.
Indexed: AmH&L.
Published by: Virginia Baptist Historical Society, PO Box 34, University Of Richmond, VA 23173. TEL 804-289-8434, FAX 804-289-8953.

283.73 USA ISSN 1535-3621
VIRGINIA EPISCOPALIAN. Text in English. 1922. m. (except Aug.). USD 5 (effective 2005). adv. bk.rev. **Document type:** *Newspaper, Consumer.*
Formerly (until 1986): Virginia Churchman
Published by: Episcopal Diocese of Virginia, 110 W Franklin, Richmond, VA 23220. TEL 800-346-2373, FAX 804-644-6928. Circ: 28,000.

287.6 USA ISSN 0891-5598
VIRGINIA UNITED METHODIST ADVOCATE. Text in English. 1832. m. USD 12 (effective 1999). adv. bk.rev.
Former titles (until 1984): Virginia Advocate (0042-6458); Virginia Methodist Advocate
Published by: (United Methodist Church, Virginia Conference), Virginia United Methodist Communications, Inc., 4016 W Broad St, Richmond, VA 23230-3916. TEL 804-359-9451, FAX 804-359-5904. Ed. Alvin J Horton. Circ: 16,000.

201.7 NLD ISSN 0921-7711
VISIE. Text in Dutch. 1970. w. EUR 59.75 domestic; EUR 61.25 foreign (effective 2009). adv. bk.rev. **Document type:** *Magazine, Consumer.*
Incorporates (1976-1984): Alpha (0166-4182)
Published by: Evangelische Omroep, Postbus 21000, Hilversum, 1202 BA, Netherlands. TEL 31-35-6474747, FAX 31-35-6474727, eo@eo.nl. Eds. Mirjam Hollebrandse, Arie Kok. adv.: color page EUR 3,176; trim 210 x 296. Circ: 151,695.

266.6 AUS
VISION. Text in English. 1950. q. AUD 15 (effective 2008); Subscr. includes Prayer Guide. bk.rev. index. back issues avail. **Document type:** *Magazine, Consumer.* **Description:** Publishes articles about activities of the organization worldwide, issues related to mission.
Related titles: Online - full text ed.: free.
Published by: Global Interaction, PO Box 273, Hawthorn, VIC 3122, Australia. TEL 61-3-98194944, FAX 61-3-98191004, info@globalinteraction.org.au. Ed. Rosalind Gooden. Circ: 7,000.

280.4 USA
VISIONS OF GLORY MAGAZINE. Text in English. 1994. m. free. **Document type:** *Magazine, Consumer.* **Description:** Focuses on the glory of God and fullness of Christ.
Media: Online - full text.
Published by: Bethel Christian Center of Vandergrift, Inc, PO Box 178, Vandergrift, PA 15690-0178. TEL 724-568-1566, FAX 724-567-1530. Ed., R&P Stephen J Myers Jr.

286 USA ISSN 1547-9285
VITAL WOMAN MAGAZINE. Text in English. 1956. 3/yr. USD 12 (effective 2003). adv. bk.rev. **Document type:** *Bulletin.*
Former titles (until 2002): On the Way with American Baptist Women; (until 1995): American Baptist Woman (0191-0183)
Published by: American Baptist Women's Ministries, PO Box 851, Valley Forge, PA 19482-0851. TEL 610-768-2283, FAX 610-768-2275, info@abwministries.org, http://www.abwministries.org. Ed. Sandra Hasenauer. Circ: 7,000.

286 305.4 USA ISSN 1945-2381
VOCARE. Text in English. 1983. 3/yr. **Document type:** *Journal, Trade.*
Formerly (until 2005): Folio (0741-1537)
Published by: Baptist Women in Ministry, c/o McAfee School of Theology, 3001 Mercer University Ave, Atlanta, GA 30341. http://www.bwim.info.

287.6 USA ISSN 1079-3461
THE VOICE (BIRMINGHAM); the official publication of the United Methodist Church in North Alabama. Text in English. 1881. m. USD 17.50 (effective 2005). adv. bk.rev. **Document type:** *Newspaper, Consumer.* **Description:** Contains latest news and announcements from the North Alabama Conference, columns from Conference leaders, and articles to enhance the ministry of your local church.
Formerly: United Methodist Christian Advocate (8750-7668)
Published by: North Alabama Conference of the United Methodist Church, Office of Communication, 898 Arkadelphia Rd, Birmingham, AL 35204-3498. TEL 205-226-7972, 888-448-6423, FAX 205-226-7975. Ed., Pub., R&P, Adv. contact Danette Clifton TEL 205-226-7973. Circ: 160,000 (paid).

283.73 USA ISSN 0277-2272
THE VOICE (NEWARK); serving the Episcopal Church in northern New Jersey. Text in English. 1878. 9/yr. per issue contribution. adv. bk.rev. charts; illus.; stat. cum.index. 12 p./no. 3 cols./p.; back issues avail. **Document type:** *Newspaper, Consumer.* **Description:** Covers news of interest to the Episcopal Churches in northern New Jersey.
Formerly: Newark Churchman (0028-8853)
Published by: Episcopal Diocese of Newark, Episcopal House, 31 Mulberry St, Newark, NJ 07102. TEL 973-430-9914, FAX 973-622-3503. Ed., R&P, Adv. contact Johanna Young. Circ: 15,300.

201.7 USA ISSN 1529-9414
VOICE OF PROPHECY NEWS. Text in English. 1942. 3/yr. free to qualified personnel. 32 p./no. 3 cols./p.; back issues avail. **Document type:** *Magazine, Consumer.* **Description:** Reports on the North American activities of the oldest, continuously aired religious radio broadcast since 1929.
Related titles: Online - full content ed.
Published by: Voice of Prophecy, Inc., 101 W Cochran St, Simi Valley, CA 93065. TEL 805-955-7657, FAX 805-955-7703, gospel@vop.com, http://www.vop.com. Ed., R&P Eldyn Karr. Circ: 45,000.

284.1 USA ISSN 1945-4791
THE VOICE OF ZION. Text in English. 1974. m. USD 46 (effective 2008). **Document type:** *Newsletter, Consumer.*
Related titles: CD-ROM ed.
Published by: Laestadian Lutheran Church, 279 N Medina St, Ste 150, Loretto, MN 55357. TEL 763-479-2422, http://laestadianlutheran.org. Ed. Paul Waaraniemi.

280.4 DEU
VOLLTREFFER; Pfiffige Zeitschrift fuer Jungen und Maedchen. Text in German. m. EUR 9.20 (effective 2009). **Document type:** *Magazine, Consumer.*
Published by: Christliche Verlagsgesellschaft mbH, Moltkestr 1, Dillenburg, 35683, Germany. TEL 49-2771-83020, FAX 49-2771-830230, info@cv-dillenburg.de, http://www.cv-dillenburg.de.

284.2 AUS ISSN 0728-0912
VOX REFORMATA; Australasian journal for Christian scholarship. Text in English. 1962. a., latest 2007, 72th ed. bk.rev. index. back issues avail. **Document type:** *Journal, Academic/Scholarly.* **Description:** Devoted to specific topics of theological, biblical and ecclesiastical interest.
Related titles: Microfiche ed.
Indexed: A22, CERDIC, OTA.
Published by: Reformed Theological College, 125 Pigdons Rd, Waurn Ponds, Geelong, VIC 3216, Australia. TEL 61-3-52442955, FAX 61-3-52436055, admin@rtc.vic.edu.au.

284 NLD ISSN 1876-0627
VRIJZINNIG. Text in Dutch. 2008. q. EUR 15 (effective 2010).
Published by: (V-Link, Vrijzinnige Jeugd- en Jongerenorganisatie), Vereniging van Vrijzinnige Protestanten, Joseph Haydnlaan 2a, Utrecht, 3533 AE, Netherlands. TEL 31-30-8801497, info@vrijzinnig.nl, http://www.vrijzinnig.nl.

280.4 USA ISSN 2150-3745
▼ **W I S E.** (Walking in Spiritual Excellence) Text in English. 2009. q. USD 12.97 domestic; USD 19.96 in Canada; USD 32.97 elsewhere; USD 4 newsstand/cover (effective 2010). adv. back issues avail. **Document type:** *Magazine, Consumer.* **Description:** Features practical wisdom which helps individuals to live a Godly life.
Related titles: Online - full text ed.: ISSN 2150-3753.
Published by: Kingdom Life Publishers, PO Box 681614, Charlotte, NC 28216. TEL 704-827-0876, 866-996-8181, kingdomlifepublishers@wisdomenterprise.net, http://wisdomenterprise.net/wisdompublishing.aspx. Ed. Rhonda Mouton.

287.9 ZAF ISSN 0043-0250
WAR CRY. Text in English. 1884. m. ZAR 40; ZAR 65 foreign (effective 1999). bk.rev. illus. **Document type:** *Newspaper.*
Published by: Salvation Army, PO Box 1018, Johannesburg, 2000, South Africa. TEL 27-11-4033614, FAX 27-11-4035368. Ed. Maj Jenny Harms. Pub. Israel L Gaither. Circ: 8,800.

287.9 GBR ISSN 0043-0226
WAR CRY. Text in English. 1879. w. GBP 26 domestic; GBP 41 foreign (effective 2010). adv. bk.rev. illus. **Document type:** *Bulletin.* **Description:** Features a variety of articles on Christianity.
Related titles: Online - full text ed.
Indexed: ABS&EES.
Published by: Salvation Army, 101 Newington Causeway, London, SE1 6BN, United Kingdom. TEL 44-20-73674900, FAX 44-20-73674710, londonnortheast@salvationarmy.org.uk, http://www1.salvationarmy.org.uk/uki/www_uki.nsf. Eds. Nigel Bovey, Christine Clement TEL 44-20-73674890. **Dist. by:** Salvationist Publishing and Supplies, Ltd., 66/78 Denington Rd, Denington Industrial Estate, Wellingborough, Northants NN8 2QH, United Kingdom.

287.96 USA ISSN 0043-0234
BX9701
THE WAR CRY. Text in English. 1881. fortn. USD 7.50 domestic (effective 1999); USD 8 in Canada; USD 9 elsewhere (effective 2001). bk.rev. **Document type:** *Magazine, Consumer.*
Indexed: ABS&EES, GSS&RPL.
Published by: Salvation Army (Alexandria), 615 Slaters Ln, Alexandria, VA 22313. TEL 703-684-5500, FAX 703-684-5539, http://publications.salvationarmyusa.org. Ed. Col Marlene Chase. R&P Cynthia Hall. Circ: 300,000.

287.96 NZL ISSN 0043-0242
WAR CRY. Text in English. 1883. 48/yr. NZD 68.70 domestic (effective 2009); NZD 0.60 newsstand/cover (effective 1999). bk.rev. back issues avail. **Document type:** *Magazine, Consumer.* **Description:** Covers Salvation Army and religious news and devotional material.
Related titles: Microfilm ed.
—CCC.
Published by: Salvation Army, Marion Sq, PO Box 6015, Wellington, 6141, New Zealand. TEL 64-4-3845649, FAX 64-4-8026259, http://www.salvationarmy.org.nz/. Circ: 9,000 (paid).

285 USA
WASHINGTON REPORT TO PRESBYTERIANS. Text in English. 1979. bi-m. USD 20 (effective 1999). **Document type:** *Newsletter.* **Description:** Advocates the public policy positions of the General Assembly of the Presbyterian Church (U.S.A.).
Published by: Presbyterian Church (U.S.A.), Washington Office, 110 Maryland Ave, N E, Washington, DC 20002. TEL 202-543-1126, FAX 202-543-7755. Ed. Catherine A Sunshine. Circ: 1,000.

283.73 USA
WASHINGTON WINDOW. Text in English. 1933. m. USD 5 to non-members; USD 3 to members (effective 2005). adv. bk.rev. charts; illus.; stat. **Document type:** *Newspaper, Consumer.*
Formerly (until 2006): Washington Diocese (0043-0544)
Related titles: Microfilm ed.
Indexed: CERDIC.

R

Published by: Episcopal Diocese of Washington, Episcopal Church House, Mount Saint Alban, N W, Washington, DC 20016-5094. TEL 202-537-6560, 800-642-4427, FAX 202-364-6605. Ed. Deborah Kennedy. Circ: 21,500.

280.4 GBR ISSN 1351-4768
WATCHING AND WAITING. Text in English. 1919. q. GBP 3.75 (effective 2009). bk.rev. back issues avail. **Document type:** *Bulletin.* **Description:** Features spiritual articles on Christianity.
Published by: Sovereign Grace Advent Testimony, c/o Secretary, Stephen A Toms, 1 Donald Way, Chelmsford, Essex CM2 9JB, United Kingdom. satoms@hotmail.co.uk.

287 USA ISSN 0890-6491
BV4485
WEAVINGS; a journal of the Christian spiritual life. Text in English. 1986. bi-m. USD 29.35 domestic; USD 35.95 foreign (effective 2009). bk.rev. illus. back issues avail.; reprints avail. **Document type:** *Magazine, Consumer.* **Description:** Explores contemporary issues, organized around a single theme, through articles, meditations, poetry, and fiction.
Related titles: E-mail ed.; Online - full text ed.
Indexed: A21, ChrPI, RI-1, RI-2.
Published by: (United Methodist Church, General Board of Discipleship), The Upper Room Publications, 1908 Grand Ave, PO Box 340004, Nashville, TN 37203. TEL 615-340-7200, FAX 615-340-7275, urbooks@upperroom.org. Ed. John S Mogabgab. Circ: 40,000 (paid).

280.4 DEU
WEISSES KREUZ; Zeitschrift fuer Lebensfragen. Text in German. 1970. 4/yr. EUR 6 (effective 2011). adv. **Document type:** *Magazine, Consumer.*
Formerly (until 2000): Sexualethik und Seelsorge
Published by: Bundes Verlag GmbH, Bodenborn 43, Witten, 58452, Germany. TEL 49-2302-930930, FAX 49-2302-93093689, info@bundes-verlag.de, http://www.bundes-verlag.de. Adv. contact Juergen Bublitz. Circ: 10,000 (controlled).

284.2 NLD ISSN 0167-1227
DE WEKKER. Text in Dutch. 1891. w. EUR 43 domestic; EUR 60 foreign; EUR 21.50 to students (effective 2008). adv.
Published by: Christelijke Gereformeerde Kerken in Nederland/Mission of the Christian Reformed Churches in the Netherlands, Ghandistr 2, Postbus 334, Veenendaal, 3900 AH, Netherlands. TEL 31-318-582350, lkb@cgk.nl, http://www.cgk.nl. Eds. Dr. H K Sok, Dr. G van Roekel.

266 DEU ISSN 1866-3109
WELTWEIT VERBUNDEN. Text in German. 1837. q. free (effective 2009). **Document type:** *Magazine, Consumer.* **Description:** Reports on mission work throughout the world.
Former titles (until 2008): Daheim und Draussen (0177-1817); (until 1984): Herrnhuter Arbeit Daheim und Draussen (0177-1825); (until 1957): Nachrichten aus der Herrnhuter Arbeit Daheim und Draussen; (until 1949): Nachrichten aus der Mission der Herrnhuter Bruedergemeine; (until 1940): Missionsblatt der Bruedergemeine
Published by: Herrnhuter Missionshilfe e.V., Badwasen 6, Bad Boll, 73087, Germany. TEL 49-7164-942185, FAX 49-7164-942199, info@herrnhuter-missionshilfe.de, http://www.herrnhuter-missionshilfe.de. Ed., R&P Andreas Tasche. Circ: 34,000 (controlled).

280.4 DEU ISSN 0938-0868
WERKSTATT FUER LITURGIE UND PREDIGT. Text in German. 1991. 11/yr. EUR 114 (effective 2011). **Document type:** *Journal, Academic/Scholarly.*
Published by: Bergmoser und Hoeller Verlag GmbH, Karl-Friedrich-Str 76, Aachen, 52072, Germany. TEL 49-241-93888123, FAX 49-241-93888134, kontakt@buhv.de.

280.4 DEU ISSN 1618-8497
WERKSTATT SPEZIAL. Text in German. 2008. base vol. plus bi-m. updates. EUR 29.90 base vol(s).; EUR 90 updates (effective 2011). **Document type:** *Trade.*
Published by: Bergmoser und Hoeller Verlag GmbH, Karl-Friedrich-Str 76, Aachen, 52072, Germany. TEL 49-241-93888123, FAX 49-241-93888134, kontakt@buhv.de.

287.1 GBR ISSN 0043-2873
BX8203.W51
WESLEY HISTORICAL SOCIETY. PROCEEDINGS. Text in English. 1897. 3/yr. GBP 6.25 to non-members; GBP 4.25 to members (effective 2009). bk.rev. bibl.; charts; illus.; maps. index, cum.index: vols.1-30 (1897-1958); vols.31-50 (1957-1996). 1 cols./p.; back issues avail. **Document type:** *Proceedings, Academic/Scholarly.* **Description:** Features history of methodism in the British isles.
Indexed: A21, AmH&L, CERDIC, FR, HistAb, P30, PCI, RI-1, RI-2. —BLDSC (6832.400000), IE, Infotrieve, Ingenta, INIST.
Published by: Wesley Historical Society, 26 Roe Cross Green, Mottram, Hyde, Ches SK14 6LP, United Kingdom. president@wesleyhistoricalsociety.org.uk. Ed. E Alan Rose TEL 44-1457-763485.

287.6 USA ISSN 0190-6097
BX8201
WESLEYAN CHRISTIAN ADVOCATE. Text in English. 1836. w. USD 14. adv. bk.rev.
Published by: (United Methodist Church, North and South Georgia Conferences), Jacob's Religious List, 104 Ansel Dr, Clinton, SC 20325-2808. TEL 404-659-0002, FAX 404-659-1727. Ed. G Ross Freeman. Circ: 30,980.

287.1 USA
BX9995.W4
WESLEYAN LIFE. Text in English. 1842. q. adv. bk.rev. **Document type:** *Journal, Consumer.* **Description:** Provides doctrinal, devotional, inspirational and practical articles.
Formerly: Wesleyan Advocate (0043-289X); Which was formed by the 1968 merger of: Pilgrim Holiness Advocate; (1884 -1968): Wesleyan Methodist (0190-6100)
Related titles: Microfiche ed.: (from IDC); Microfilm ed.
Indexed: CCR, ChrPI, GSS&RPL.
Published by: (Wesleyan Church), Wesley Publishing House, PO Box 50434, Indianapolis, IN 46250. FAX 317-774-7913, communications@wesleyan.org. Ed. Norman G. Wilson. Pub. Don Cady. Adv. contact Julie Alexander. B&W page USD 500, color page USD 750. Circ: 50,000 (controlled).

287.1 USA ISSN 0092-4245
BR1
WESLEYAN THEOLOGICAL JOURNAL. Text in English. 1966. s-a. adv. bk.rev. reprints avail. **Document type:** *Journal, Consumer.*
Related titles: Microform ed.: 1966 (from PQC).
Indexed: A21, A22, CERDIC, ChrPI, P30, R&TA, RI-1, RI-2, RILM. —BLDSC (9298.673700), IE, Infotrieve, Ingenta.
Published by: Wesleyan Theological Society, 185, Pasadena, CA 91102-0185. http://www.wesley.nnu.edu/wts. Ed. Paul Bassett. Circ: 1,200.

286 USA ISSN 0043-4132
WESTERN RECORDER. Text in English. 1826. w. (Wed.). USD 11.66 to individuals; USD 9.25 churches (effective 2007). adv. **Document type:** *Newspaper.*
Related titles: Microform ed.: (from PQC).
Published by: (Kentucky Baptist Convention), Western Recorder, Inc., PO Box 43969, Louisville, KY 40253. TEL 502-244-6470, FAX 502-244-6474. Ed. Trennis Henderson. R&P, Adv. contact Mauri Smith. Circ: 40,000 (paid).

285 USA ISSN 1056-0556
WINDOWS. Text in English. 3/yr.
Supersedes in part (in 1989): Austin Presbyterian Theological Seminary. Bulletin (0191-8613)
Indexed: A22.
Published by: Austin Presbyterian Theological Seminary, 100 E 27th St, Austin, TX 78705. TEL 512-472-6736, http://www.austinseminary.edu/. Ed. Randall Whittington.

284.1 USA ISSN 0362-5648
BX8001
WISCONSIN LUTHERAN QUARTERLY. Text in English. 1904. q. USD 22 domestic; USD 23.10 in Canada; USD 39.60 elsewhere; USD 5.50 per issue domestic; USD 5.83 per issue in Canada (effective 2011). bk.rev. **Document type:** *Journal, Academic/Scholarly.* **Description:** Serves the theological and professional growth of those whom the seminary is training for the public ministry and of those already active in this ministry.
Former titles (until 1960): Quartalschrift (0363-6615); (until 1947): Theologische Quartalschrift (0363-7255)
Indexed: A21, R&TA, RI-1.
Published by: Northwestern Publishing House, 1250 N 113th St, Milwaukee, WI 53226. TEL 414-615-5733, 800-662-6022, FAX 414-475-7684.

322.1 USA ISSN 0197-8896
BX5800
THE WITNESS. Text in English. 1917. m. USD 35 domestic; USD 45 foreign (effective 2000). bk.rev. illus. **Document type:** *Journal, Consumer.* **Description:** Concentrates on peace, social and economic justice, the mission of the Church and the Gospel message. Each issue focuses on a theme providing a variety of viewpoints.
Related titles: Microfiche ed.; Microfilm ed.
Indexed: A21, A22, AltPI, CERDIC, RI-1, RI-2.
Published by: Episcopal Church Publishing Co., 7012 Michigan Ave., Detroit, MI 48210-2872. TEL 313-841-1967, FAX 313-841-1956. Eds. Jeanie Wylie Kellerman, Julie A Wortman. R&P Marianne Arbogast. Adv. contact Wes Todd. Circ: 6,000.

280.4 USA ISSN 1078-9650
WOMEN OF SPIRIT; sharing faith, hope and love. Text in English. 1995. bi-m. USD 22 (effective 2009). adv. **Document type:** *Magazine, Consumer.* **Description:** Designed to stimulate spiritual vitality, to nurture emotional growth, to foster balanced, healthy living and to encourage a dynamic christian witness in the home and community.
Related titles: French ed.: La femme desprit. ISSN 1946-5602; Spanish ed.: Mujeres de Espiritu. ISSN 1938-047X.
Published by: Review and Herald Publishing Association, 55 W Oak Ridge Dr, Hagerstown, MD 21740. TEL 301-393-4082, info@rhpa.org, http://www.rhpa.org. Ed. Lori Peckham. Adv. contact Genia Blumenberg TEL 301-393-3170. B&W page USD 900, color page USD 1,400; trim 8.125 x 10.625. Circ: 42,500.

268 ZAF ISSN 0257-8921
BX9595.S6
WOORD & DAAD/WORD & ACTION; kwartaalblad van die Reformatoriese beweging van Suider-Afrika. Text in Afrikaans, English. 1961. q. illus. 28 p./no.; back issues avail. **Document type:** *Magazine, Consumer.* **Description:** Comments on topical issues from a Reformational Christian perspective.
Related titles: Online - full text ed.
Indexed: ISAP.
Published by: (Potchefstroom University for Christian Higher Education, Institute for Reformational Studies/Potchefstroomse Universiteit vir Christelike Hoer Onderwys, Instituut vir Reformatoriese Studie), Woord en Daad/Word and Action, Posbus 20011, Noordbrug, 2522, South Africa. TEL 27-18-299-4082, FAX 27-18-299-1562. Ed. W du Plessis. R&P, Adv. contact Eunice Strydom. Circ: 502.

284 NLD ISSN 0165-2443
BX9470
WOORD EN DIENST. Text in Dutch. 1952. 24/yr. EUR 57.50 domestic; EUR 95 overseas; EUR 44.25 to students; EUR 3.85 newsstand/cover (effective 2008). adv. bk.rev. illus.
Published by: Boekencentrum Uitgevers, Goudstraat 50, Postbus 29, Zoetermeer, 2700 AA, Netherlands. TEL 31-79-3615481, FAX 31-79-3615489, info@boekencentrum.nl, http://www.boekencentrum.nl. Ed. Kees Posthumus. adv.: B&W page EUR 725, color page EUR 850; trim 210 x 297. Circ: 5,000.

286 USA ISSN 0049-7959
WORD AND WAY. Text in English. 1895. bi-w. USD 17.50 to individuals (effective 2009). adv. bk.rev. illus. back issues avail. **Document type:** *Newspaper, Trade.* **Description:** Features news of Missouri Baptist and Southern Baptist churches.
Former titles (until 1947): Word and Way and Central Baptist; (until 1913): Word and Way; Which incorporated (in 1896): Central Baptist
Published by: Missouri Baptist Convention, 3236 Emerald Ln, Ste 400, Jefferson City, MO 65109. TEL 573-635-5939, FAX 573-635-1774, newsletter@wordandway.org. Ed. Bill Webb TEL 573-635-5939 ext 206. Adv. contact Ken Satterfield TEL 573-635-5939 ext 208.

230.044 USA ISSN 0275-5270
BR1
WORD & WORLD; theology for Christian ministry. Text in English. 1981. q. USD 28 domestic to individuals; USD 33 foreign to individuals; USD 35 to institutions; USD 8 per issue (effective 2010). adv. bk.rev. Index. back issues avail. **Document type:** *Journal, Academic/Scholarly.* **Description:** Journal for pastors and scholars who seek to relate the work of theology to the ministry of the Christian church.
Related titles: Microfilm ed.: (from PQC); Supplement(s): Word & World. Supplement. ISSN 1550-0071. 1992.
Indexed: A21, A22, FamI, OTA, P30, R&TA, RI-1, RI-2, RILM. —BLDSC (9347.841200), IE, Infotrieve, Ingenta.
Published by: Luther Seminary, 2481 Como Ave, St. Paul, MN 55108. TEL 651-641-3482, FAX 651-641-3354, ww@luthersem.edu, http://www.luthersem.edu/. Ed. Frederick J Gaiser TEL 651-641-3210. Circ: 3,000.

220 GBR
WORD AT WORK. Text in English. s-a. free. **Document type:** *Magazine, Trade.*
Related titles: Online - full text ed.: free; ◆ Supplement(s): National Bible Society of Scotland. Annual Report. ISSN 0077-3557.
Published by: Scottish Bible Society, 7 Hampton Terr, Edinburgh, EH12 5XU, United Kingdom. TEL 44-131-3379701, FAX 44-131-3370641, info@scottishbiblesociety.org, http://www.scottishbiblesociety.org/. Circ: 50,000.

280.4 USA
WORD FOR TODAY. Text in English. d. **Document type:** *Bulletin.* **Description:** Soul food for discipleship growth.
Media: Online - full text.
Address: PO Box 8000, Costa Mesa, CA 92628. TEL 800-272-9673.

280.4 GBR ISSN 1476-3893
WORDS FOR TODAY. Text in English. 1973. a. GBP 8.50 per issue (effective 2010). **Document type:** *Yearbook, Consumer.* **Description:** Contains daily religious notes. Writers are drawn from around the globe and from many different traditions. It includes Jewish as well as Christian biblical scholars and presents a lively and often radical approach to the text.
Formerly (until 2000): Notes on Bible Readings (0140-8275) —CCC.
Published by: Christian Education Publishing, 1020 Bristol Rd, Selby Oak, Birmingham, B29 6LB, United Kingdom. TEL 44-121-4724242, FAX 44-121-4727575, enquiries@christianeducation.org.uk, http://www.christianeducation.org.uk. Ed. Nicola Slee.

284 CHE
WORLD ALLIANCE OF REFORMED CHURCHES. UPDATE. Text in English, French, German, Spanish. 1962. q. CHF 15, USD 10, GBP 6.50 (effective 2003). 16 p./no. 3 cols./p.; back issues avail. **Document type:** *Bulletin, Consumer.*
Formerly (until 1991): Reformed and Presbyterian Press Service
Published by: World Alliance of Reformed Churches, 150 route de Ferney, PO Box 2100, Geneva 2, 1211, Switzerland. TEL 41-22-7916240, FAX 41-22-7916505, 41-22-7916235, sjr@warc.ch, http://www.warc.ch. Ed., R&P Paraic Reamonn.

287 USA
WORLD METHODIST HISTORICAL SOCIETY. HISTORICAL BULLETIN. Text in English. 1961. q. free to members (effective 2011). bk.rev. illus. back issues avail. **Document type:** *Bulletin, Trade.*
Formerly (until 19??): World Methodist Historical Society. News Bulletin
Related titles: Online - full text ed.: free (effective 2011).
Published by: World Methodist Historical Society, PO Box 127, Madison, NJ 07940. http://www.gcah.org/site/pp.aspx?c=ghKJI0PHIoE&b=3761527.

261 USA
WORLD VISION MAGAZINE. Text in English. 1972. q. free (effective 2009). illus.; charts; maps; stat. 32 p./no. 3 cols./p.; back issues avail. **Document type:** *Magazine, Consumer.* **Description:** Affirms people responding to God's call to care for the poor by providing information, inspiration and opportunities for action linking them with children and families in nearly 90 countries where world vision ministers.
Former titles (until 2003): World Vision Today; (until 1997): World Vision; Which was formed by the merger of (1957-1972): World Vision Magazine (0043-9215); (196?-1972): World Vision Heartline
Related titles: Online - full text ed.
Indexed: ChrPI.
Published by: World Vision, Inc., Dept W, PO Box 9716, Federal Way, WA 98063. TEL 253-815-1000, info@worldvision.org. Ed. Milana McLead.

280.4 USA
WORLDWIDE NEWS. Text in English. 1917. 4/yr. free. **Document type:** *Newsletter.* **Description:** Provides information on The Pocket Testament League outreach, particularly Scripture distribution and evangelism worldwide.
Published by: The Pocket Testament League, PO Box 800, Lititz, PA 17543-7026. TEL 717-626-1919, FAX 717-626-5553. Ed., R&P Mary Barr. Circ: 15,000.

286 USA ISSN 1935-4959
WORSHIP KIDSTYLE (CHILDREN'S EDITION). Variant title: Worship KidStyle: Children All-In-One Pack. Text in English. 2007 (Fall). q. price varies. back issues avail. **Document type:** *Magazine, Consumer.* **Description:** Contains cool arts and crafts that bring focus on the creator, as well as life application videos that tell stories for kids in grades 1-6.
Related titles: Audio CD ed.: ISSN 1935-4967.
Published by: LifeWay Christian Resources, 1 Lifeway Plz, Nashville, TN 37234. TEL 615-251-2000, FAX 615-251-5933, customerservice@lifeway.com.

286 USA ISSN 1935-4975
WORSHIP KIDSTYLE (PRESCHOOL EDITION). Variant title: Worship KidStyle: Preschool All-In-One Pack. Text in English. 2007 (Fall). q. price varies. back issues avail. **Document type:** *Magazine, Consumer.* **Description:** Contains cool arts and crafts that bring focus on the creator, as well as life application videos that tell stories for kids in kindergarten.
Related titles: Audio CD ed.: ISSN 1935-4983.
Published by: LifeWay Christian Resources, 1 Lifeway Plz, Nashville, TN 37234. TEL 615-251-2000, 800-458-2772, FAX 615-251-5933, customerservice@lifeway.com, http://www.lifeway.com.

280.4 DEU
WORT FUER DIE WOCHE. Text in German. 56/yr. **Document type:** *Bulletin, Consumer.*
Published by: Aussaat Verlag, Andreas Braem Str 18-20, Neukirchen-Vluyn, 47506, Germany. TEL 49-2845-392225, FAX 49-2845-33689, info@nvg-medien.de, http://www.nvg-medien.de.

280.4 DEU ISSN 0930-3995
DAS WORT FUER HEUTE. Text in German. 1984. bi-m. looseleaf. free (effective 2009). illus. **Document type:** *Magazine, Consumer.*
Formed by the merger of (1969-1984): Wittener Andachtskalender (0930-3987); (1949-1984): Taegliches Brot (0492-1267); (1958-1984): Kasseler Abreisskalender (0930-3979)
Published by: Christliche Verlagsgesellschaft mbH, Moltkestr 1, Dillenburg, 35683, Germany. TEL 49-2771-83020, FAX 49-2771-830230, info@cv-dillenburg.de, http://www.cv-dillenburg.de. Ed. Hartmut Jaeger. Circ: 28,800.

280.4 DEU ISSN 0342-3085
WORT UND DIENST. Text in German. 1930. a. **Document type:** *Journal, Academic/Scholarly.*
Formerly (until 1948): Theologische Schule Bethel. Jahrbuch (0931-6302)
Indexed: IBR, IBZ, IZBG, OTA.
Published by: Kirchliche Hochschule Bethel, Remterweg 45, Bielefeld, 33617, Germany. TEL 49-521-1443948, FAX 49-521-1444700, rektorat.kihobethel@uni-bielefeld.de, http://www.bethel.de/kiho/.

280.4 DEU
WOW!; Schuelerkalender. Text in German. 1898. a. EUR 4.95 (effective 2009). **Document type:** *Magazine, Consumer.*
Formerly: Okay
Published by: (Deutscher E C - Verband), Born-Verlag, Leuschnerstr 74, Kassel, 34134, Germany. TEL 49-561-4095107, FAX 49-561-4095112, info.born@ec-jugend.de, http://www.born-buch.de. Circ: 16,000.

280.4 USA ISSN 2151-4127
▼ **XTRAORDINARY**; the Christian living magazine. Text in English. forthcoming 2011. bi-m. **Document type:** *Magazine, Consumer.* **Description:** Informs the public about spiritual matters and issues affecting everyday life, including career, finance, personal and health issues.
Published by: Abiola Dada-Lajumoke, Ed. & Pub., PO Box 165175, Irving, TX 75016. TEL 817-724-9436, publisher@christianlivingmagazine.com.

280.4 305.89607305 USA ISSN 2155-1405
▼ **Y S G 2 MAGAZINE.** (Young, Successful and Godly Too!) Text in English. 2010. q. USD 30 (effective 2010). **Document type:** *Magazine, Consumer.* **Description:** For young, successful African-American Christians.
Related titles: Online - full text ed.: ISSN 2155-1413. forthcoming 2010 (July).
Address: 10945 State Bridge Rd, 401-301, Alpharetta, GA 30022. TEL 678-266-0172, rp@ysg2.com.

286.132 USA ISSN 1930-5907
YAN JING XI LIE. Text in Chinese. 1988. q. price varies. back issues avail. **Document type:** *Magazine, Consumer.* **Description:** Designed to be a bible-book study and includes a teaching plan.
Formerly (until 200?): Cheng Nian Qing Nian Yan Jing Ke Cheng (0897-0742)
Related titles: ◆ English ed.: Explore the Bible: Adult Study Guide Discovery. ISSN 1552-7212; ◆ Korean ed.: Changnyon Songgyong Yongu. ISSN 1930-5893.
Published by: LifeWay Christian Resources, 1 LifeWay Plz, Nashville, TN 37234. TEL 615-251-2000, 800-458-2772, FAX 615-251-5933, customerservice@lifeway.com, http://www.lifeway.com.

THE (YEAR) UNITED METHODIST DIRECTORY & INDEX RESOURCES. *see* RELIGIONS AND THEOLOGY—Abstracting, Bibliographies, Statistics

280.4 USA ISSN 0044-0388
YEVANHELSKYJ RANOK/EVANGELICAL MORNING. (Includes an English section: Ukrainian Christian Herald, Protestant monthly) Text in English. 1905. q. USD 5. adv. bk.rev. illus. reprints avail.
Published by: Ukrainian Evangelical Alliance of North America, 5610 Trowbridge Dr., Dunwoody, GA 30338. TEL 404-394-7795. Ed. Rev. W Borowsky. Circ: 500.

YOUNG MUSICIANS. *see* MUSIC

287.96 USA ISSN 0746-861X
YOUNG SALVATIONIST. Text in English. 1985. m. USD 4. music rev. **Document type:** *Magazine, Consumer.* **Description:** Youth paper to provide guidance for Christian living and to teach the history, goals and principles of The Salvation Army.
Formerly: Young Soldier (0744-5032)
Published by: Salvation Army (Alexandria), 615 Slaters Ln, Alexandria, VA 22313. TEL 703-684-5500, FAX 703-684-5539, http://publications.salvationarmyusa.org. Ed. Tim Clark. R&P Cynthia Hall. Circ: 48,000.

283 GBR ISSN 0966-2855
YOUTHWORK; ideas, resources & guidance for youth ministry. Text in English. 1992. m. GBP 29 domestic; GBP 40.30 in Europe; GBP 43 elsewhere; GBP 3 newsstand/cover (effective 2009). adv. bk.rev. back issues avail. **Document type:** *Magazine, Consumer.* **Description:** Provides resources, ideas, and how-to features on church-based youth work.
Related titles: Online - full text ed.: free (effective 2009).
Published by: C C P Ltd, PO Box 17911, London, SW1P 4YX, United Kingdom. TEL 44-20-73161472, FAX 44-20-73161453. Ed. Martin Saunders. Adv. contact Candy O'Donovan TEL 44-20-73161456. B&W page GBP 390; trim 186 x 270. Circ: 9,000 (paid).

280.4 USA
BV4447
YOUTHWORKER JOURNAL. Abbreviated title: Y W J. Text in English. 1984. bi-m. USD 39.95 domestic; USD 46.95 foreign (effective 2009). adv. back issues avail. **Document type:** *Magazine, Consumer.* **Description:** Contains youth ministry resources with youth ministry game ideas, fundraiser tools, insightful interviews with today's top youth workers, independent reviews.
Formerly (until 2004): Youthworker (0747-3486)
Indexed: CCR, ChrPI.
Published by: Salem Publishing, 104 Woodmont Blvd, Ste 300, Nashville, TN 37205. TEL 615-312-4250, 800-527-5226, FAX 615-385-4112, customerservice@salempublishing.com, http://www.salempublishing.com. Adv. contact Dede Donatelli-Tarrant TEL 805-987-5072.

283 DEU ISSN 1434-548X
Z - DIE ZEITUNG FUER EVANGELISCHE JUGENDARBEIT. Text in German. 1958. q. back issues avail. **Document type:** *Magazine, Consumer.*
Former titles (until 1997): Nachrichten, Informationen, Aktuelles (1433-2736); (until 199?): Evangelische Jugend in Bayern. Nachrichten (0937-1729)
Published by: Amt fuer Evangelische Jugendarbeit, Hummelsteiner Weg 100, Nuernberg, 90459, Germany. TEL 49-911-4304284, FAX 49-911-4304205, afj@ejb.de. Ed. Christina Frey-Scholz. Circ: 3,500 (controlled).

280.4 DEU
ZEICHEN. Text in German. 1973. q. bk.rev. back issues avail. **Document type:** *Magazine, Consumer.*
Published by: Aktion Suehnezeichen Friedensdienste e.V., Auguststr 80, Berlin, 10117, Germany. TEL 49-30-28395184, FAX 49-30-28395135, asf@asf-ev.de. Ed., R&P Johannes Zerger. Circ: 12,000.

280.4 270 DEU ISSN 0342-4316
ZEITSCHRIFT FUER BAYERISCHE KIRCHENGESCHICHTE. Text in German. 1926. a. EUR 30 per issue (effective 2011). adv. bk.rev. back issues avail. **Document type:** *Journal, Academic/Scholarly.* **Description:** Consists of articles concerning church history in Bavaria.
Indexed: B24, DIP, FR, IBR, IBZ, RILM.
—INIST.
Published by: (Verein fuer Bayerische Kirchengeschichte), Wissenschaftlicher Kommissionsverlag, Alter Festplatz 14, Stegaurach, 96135, Germany. TEL 49-951-6010962, FAX 49-951-6010961, verlag@wikommverlag.de. Ed. Dietrich Blaufuss. Pub. Helmut Baier. Circ: 800.

262.9804 DEU ISSN 0044-2690
K30
ZEITSCHRIFT FUER EVANGELISCHES KIRCHENRECHT. Text in German. 1951. q. EUR 124 to individuals; EUR 169 to institutions (effective 2012). adv. bk.rev. index. reprint service avail. from SCH. **Document type:** *Journal, Academic/Scholarly.* **Description:** Examines the problems of Protestant ecclesiastical law and the relation between church and state in Germany.
Related titles: Online - full text ed.: ISSN 1868-7369 (from IngentaConnect).
Indexed: A22, CERDIC, DIP, FLP, IBR, IBZ, PCI.
—IE, Infotrieve. **CCC.**
Published by: Mohr Siebeck GmbH & Co. KG, Wilhelmstr 18, Tuebingen, 72074, Germany. TEL 49-7071-9230, FAX 49-7071-51104, info@mohr.de. R&P Jill Sopper. Adv. contact Tilman Gaebler. Circ: 600 (paid and controlled).

230.044 DEU ISSN 0044-3549
BR4
ZEITSCHRIFT FUER THEOLOGIE UND KIRCHE. Text in German. 1891. q. EUR 74 to individuals; EUR 169 to institutions; EUR 32 to students (effective 2012). adv. index. reprint service avail. from SCH. **Document type:** *Journal, Academic/Scholarly.* **Description:** Studies all areas of theological research and the teachings of the church.
Related titles: Online - full text ed.: ISSN 1868-7377 (from IngentaConnect); ◆ Supplement(s): Zeitschrift fuer Theologie und Kirche. Beiheft. ISSN 0513-9147.
Indexed: A20, A21, A22, ASCA, ArtHuCI, CERDIC, CurCont, DIP, FR, IBR, IBZ, MLA-IB, OTA, PCI, R&TA, RASB, RI-1, RI-2, SCOPUS, W07.
—IE, Ingenta, INIST. **CCC.**
Published by: Mohr Siebeck GmbH & Co. KG, Wilhelmstr 18, Tuebingen, 72074, Germany. TEL 49-7071-9230, FAX 49-7071-51104, info@mohr.de. Ed. Eberhard Juengel. R&P Jill Sopper. Adv. contact Tilman Gaebler. Circ: 2,200 (paid and controlled).

230.044 DEU ISSN 0513-9147
ZEITSCHRIFT FUER THEOLOGIE UND KIRCHE. BEIHEFT. Text in German. 1959. irreg., latest vol.10, 1998. price varies. **Document type:** *Monographic series, Academic/Scholarly.*
Related titles: ◆ Supplement to: Zeitschrift fuer Theologie und Kirche. ISSN 0044-3549.
Indexed: FR, OTA.
—Infotrieve, INIST.
Published by: Mohr Siebeck GmbH & Co. KG, Wilhelmstr 18, Tuebingen, 72074, Germany. TEL 49-7071-9230, FAX 49-7071-51104, info@mohr.de, http://www.mohr.de.

ZEITSCHRIFTENINHALTSDIENST THEOLOGIE; indices theologici. *see* RELIGIONS AND THEOLOGY—Abstracting, Bibliographies, Statistics

284.1 DEU ISSN 1616-4164
ZEITZEICHEN; evangelische Kommentare zu Religion und Gesellschaft. Text in German. 2000. m. EUR 58.20; EUR 29.10 to students (effective 2007). adv. **Document type:** *Magazine, Consumer.* **Description:** Contains articles and features on all aspects of religion and society from a Protestant perspective.
Formed by the merger of (1968-2000): Evangelische Kommentare (0300-4236); (1878-2000): Reformierte Kirchenzeitung (0724-5939); (1998-2000): Zeichen der Zeit - Lutherische Monatshefte (1436-0810); Which was formed by the merger of (1947-1998): Zeichen der Zeit (0044-2038); (1962-1998): Lutherische Monatshefte (0024-7618)
Indexed: DIP, IBR, IBZ, RILM.
—BLDSC (9497.583500).
Published by: Kreuz Verlag GmbH & Co. KG, Postfach 800669, Stuttgart, 70506, Germany. TEL 49-711-788030, FAX 49-711-7880310, service@kreuzverlag.de, http://www.kreuzverlag.de. Ed. Helmut Kremers. Adv. contact Martin Dubberke. B&W page EUR 1,130, color page EUR 1,680. Circ: 13,800 (paid and controlled).

294 CHE ISSN 0514-8693
ZUERCHER BEITRAEGE ZUR REFORMATIONSGESCHICHTE. Text in German. 1970. irreg., latest vol.21, 2003. price varies. **Document type:** *Monographic series, Academic/Scholarly.*
Published by: Peter Lang AG (Subsidiary of: Peter Lang Publishing Group), Hochfeldstr 32, Postfach 746, Bern 9, 3000, Switzerland. TEL 41-31-3061717, FAX 41-31-3061727, info@peterlang.com, http://www.peterlang.com.

280.4 DEU ISSN 0722-3234
ZUVERSICHT UND STAERKE. Text in German. 1982. bi-m. EUR 4.50 newsstand/cover (effective 2003). back issues avail. **Document type:** *Journal, Academic/Scholarly.*
Published by: (Ludwig-Hofacker-Vereinigung), Haenssler Verlag GmbH, Max-Eyth-Str 41, Holzgerlingen, 71088, Germany. TEL 49-7031-74140, FAX 49-7031-7414119, info@haenssler.de, http://www.haenssler.de. Circ: 3,000.

264 941.74 CHE ISSN 0254-4407
ZWINGLIANA. Text in English, French, German. 1897. a. CHF 50, EUR 30 (effective 2010). **Document type:** *Journal, Academic/Scholarly.* **Description:** Presents the history of the Reformation and Protestantism in Switzerland, with emphasis on the life and work of Ulrich Zwingli.
Indexed: A21, CA, DIP, FR, HistAb, IBR, IBZ, MLA-IB, P30, R&TA, RI-1, T02.
—INIST.
Published by: (Universitaet Zuerich, Institut fuer Schweizerische Reformationsgeschichte), Theologischer Verlag Zurich, Badenerstr 73, Zurich, 8026, Switzerland. TEL 41-44-2993355, FAX 41-44-2993358, tvz@ref.ch. Eds. Alfred Schindler, Emidio Campi.

266 GBR
4 CORNERS. Text in English. 1931. 3/yr. bk.rev. **Document type:** *Newsletter.* **Description:** Contains articles, biographical sketches, and profiles of the missionary ministry of U F M Worldwide.
Formerly (until 1999): Light and Life
Related titles: Online - full text ed.: free (effective 2009).
Published by: U F M Worldwide, c/o Peter Milsom, Director, 145 Faringdon Rd, Swindon, Wiltshire, United Kingdom. TEL 44-1793-610515, info@ufm.org.uk. Ed. Rev. Richard Myerscough.

24TRETTON; pedagogik i svenska kyrkan. *see* EDUCATION

280.4 USA
365 DEVOTIONS. Text in English. 1957. a. USD 14.99 base vol(s). per issue (effective 2009). back issues avail. **Document type:** *Magazine, Consumer.*
Published by: Standard Publishing, 8805 Governor's Hill Dr, Ste 400, Cincinnati, OH 45249. TEL 513-931-4050, 800-543-1353, FAX 877-867-5751, customerservice@standardpub.com, http://www.standardpub.com. Ed. Garry Allen.

RELIGIONS AND THEOLOGY—Roman Catholic

282 PER ISSN 1609-9885
A C I DIGITAL. (Agencia Catolica de Informaciones en America Latina Digital) Text in Spanish. 1997. d.
Media: Online - full text.
Published by: Agencia Catolica de Informaciones en America Latina, Apdo Postal 040062, Lima, 4, Peru. aciprensa@aciprensa.com, http://www.aciprensa.com/.

282 CZE ISSN 1214-5769
A D SPECIAL; magazine pro mlade. Text in Czech. 1990. q. CZK 25 per issue (effective 2009). adv. **Document type:** *Magazine, Consumer.* **Description:** Youth magazine written from Christian point of view.
Supersedes in part (in 2004): A D Magazin (1212-9615); Which was formerly (until 1999): Anno Domini (0862-6952)
Published by: Portal, Klapkova 2, Prague 8, 18200, Czech Republic. TEL 420-2-83028111, FAX 420-2-83028112, naklad@portal.cz, http://www.portal.cz. Ed. Josef Beranek. R&P Jindrich Sirovatka. Circ: 7,500 (paid).

282 KEN ISSN 0250-4650
BX1675.A1
A F E R; African ecclesiastical review. Text in English. 1959. q. KES 800 domestic; USD 58 in Africa; USD 87 in Asia & Europe; USD 97 in the Americas (effective 2003). bk.rev. index. 96 p./no.; back issues avail. **Document type:** *Journal, Academic/Scholarly.* **Description:** Aims at making Christ's message relevant through reflection, discussion, informed views, documentation and pastoral ministry experience.
Formerly (until 1975): African Ecclesiastical Review (0001-1134)
Related titles: Online - full text ed.
Indexed: A21, CLA, CPL, DIP, IBR, IBZ, MLA-IB, PLESA, RI-1, RI-2.
—BLDSC (0731.235000).
Published by: (Amecea Pastoral Institute), AMECEA Gaba Publications, PO Box 4002, Eldoret, Kenya. TEL 254-321-61218, FAX 254-321-62570, gabapubs@net2000ke.com. Ed. Sr. Justin Nabushawo. Circ: 2,500.

255 FRA ISSN 1779-4811
A I M. BULLETIN. (Alliance Inter-Monasteres) Text in French. 1965. irreg. EUR 25 in Europe; CAD 40 in Canada (effective 2008). bk.rev. illus. **Document type:** *Bulletin.*
Former titles (until 2005): Bulletin de l'A I M pour l'Aide et le Dialogue (1143-0567); (until 1985): Aide Inter-Monasteres. Bulletin (0758-8240); (until 1968): Bulletin de Liaison des Monasteres d' Afrique (0758-8232)
Related titles: English ed.; German ed.; Italian ed.
—**CCC.**
Published by: Alliance Inter-Monasteres, 7 rue d'Issy, Vanves, 92170, France. TEL 33-1-46646005, aim.vanves@wanadoo.fr. Ed. Dom Marie-Bernard de Soos. Circ: 1,800. **Dist. in the US by:** Alliance for International Monasticism, c/o St Scholastica Priory, 355 E. 9th St, Erie, PA 16503.

A I M: LITURGY RESOURCES. *see* MUSIC

ABRIDGED CATHOLIC PERIODICAL AND LITERATURE INDEX. *see* RELIGIONS AND THEOLOGY—Abstracting, Bibliographies, Statistics

271.3 USA ISSN 0065-0633
ACADEMY OF AMERICAN FRANCISCAN HISTORY. DOCUMENTARY SERIES. Text in English. 1951. irreg., latest vol.11, 1979. price varies. **Document type:** *Monographic series, Academic/Scholarly.*
Published by: Academy of American Franciscan History, 1712 Euclid Ave, Berkeley, CA 94709. TEL 510-548-1755.

271.3 USA ISSN 0065-0641
ACADEMY OF AMERICAN FRANCISCAN HISTORY. MONOGRAPH SERIES. Text in English. 1953. irreg., latest vol.14, 1997. price varies. back issues avail. **Document type:** *Monographic series, Trade.*
Published by: Academy of American Franciscan History, 1712 Euclid Ave, Berkeley, CA 94709. TEL 510-548-1755, acadafh@aol.com, http://www.aafh.org.

R

282 USA ISSN 0888-0247
ACADIANA CATHOLIC. Text in English. 1954. m. USD 12. adv. bk.rev. Supplement avail. **Document type:** *Newspaper.*
Published by: Diocese of Lafayette, 1408 Carmel Ave, Lafayette, LA 70501. TEL 337-261-5513, 337-261-5652. Ed. Thomas Sommers. Pub. Michael Jarrell. adv.: page USD 960. Circ: 28,000. Wire service: CaNS.

262.13 VAT ISSN 0001-5199
KBU26
ACTA APOSTOLICAE SEDIS. COMMENTARIUM OFFICIALE. Text in Latin, Multiple languages. 1909. m. index. back issues avail.; reprints avail. **Document type:** *Journal, Academic/Scholarly.* **Description:** Contains official commentary of the Holy See with information on Papal activites.
Related titles: Microfiche ed.: (from IDC).
Indexed: A22, CERDIC, CPL, PCI.
—IE, Infotrieve.
Published by: (Vatican City. Vatican City. Secretariat of State/Citta del Vaticano. Segretaria di Stato), Libreria Editrice Vaticana, 00120, Vatican City. TEL 379-6-69885003, FAX 379-6-69884716. Circ: 6,000.

282 POL ISSN 0137-3064
BR9.P6
ACTA MEDIAEVALIA. Text in Latin, Polish; Summaries in French. 1973. irreg., latest vol.14. price varies. **Document type:** *Monographic series, Academic/Scholarly.*
Indexed: RASB.
Published by: (Katolicki Uniwersytet Lubelski, Miedzywydzialowy Zaklad Historii Kultury w Sredniowieczu), Wydawnictwo Towarzystwa Naukowego Katolickiego Uniwersytetu Lubelskiego, ul Gliniana 21, Lublin, 20616, Poland. TEL 48-81-5250193, tnkul@kul.lublin.pl, http://www.kul.lublin.pl/tn/wydawnfr.html.

262.13 ITA ISSN 0065-1443
BX1528.A2
ACTA NUNTIATURAE GALLICAE. Text in French. 1961. irreg., latest vol.16, 1984. price varies. **Document type:** *Monographic series, Academic/Scholarly.* **Description:** Consists of critical editions of the correspondence of Papal Nuncios to the French court during the sixteenth century.
Published by: (Pontificia Universita Gregoriana, Facolta di Storia Ecclesiastica), Gregorian University Press/Editrice Pontificia Universita Gregoriana, Piazza della Pilotta 35, Rome, 00187, Italy. TEL 39-06-6781567, FAX 39-06-6780588, periodicals@biblicum.com, http://www.paxbook.com. Circ: 1,000.
Co-sponsor: Ecole Francaise de Rome.

282 ITA ISSN 0001-6411
ACTA ORDINIS FRATRUM MINORUM. Text in Multiple languages. 1882. 3/yr. index, cum.index. reprints avail. **Document type:** *Journal, Academic/Scholarly.*
—BLDSC (0582.505000).
Published by: Frati Minori, Curia Generale/Ordo Fratrum Minorum, Via di Santa Maria Mediatrice 25, Rome, 00165, Italy.

282 VAT
ACTA ROMANORUM PONTIFICUM. Text in Italian. 1977. irreg., latest 1985, no.7-8. price varies.
Published by: Biblioteca Apostolica Vaticana, 00120, Vatican City. TEL 396-6-69885051, FAX 396-6-69884795.

262.3 CAN ISSN 0823-552X
ACTUALITE DIOCESAINE. Text in English. 1970. m. CAD 12. adv. bk.rev. **Document type:** *Newspaper.*
Formerly (until 1983): Rythme de Notre Eglise (0383-0152)
Published by: Eglise Catholique, Diocese de Saint-Jean-Longueuil, c/o Micheline Le Royer, 740 bd Ste Foy, C P 40, Longueuil, PQ J4K 4X8, Canada. TEL 514-679-1100, FAX 514-679-1102. Circ: 8,000.

266.2 ITA ISSN 1826-0756
AD GENTES. Text in Italian. 1997. s-a. EUR 20 domestic; EUR 25 in Europe; EUR 40 elsewhere (effective 2009). **Document type:** *Magazine, Consumer.*
Published by: Editrice Missionaria Italiana (E M I), Via di Corticella 179/4, Bologna, 40128, Italy. TEL 39-051-326027, FAX 39-051-327552, ordini@emi.it, http://www.emi.it.

266.2 ITA
AFRICA (TREVIGLIO). Text in Italian. 1922. bi-m. EUR 25 domestic; EUR 35 foreign (effective 2009). **Document type:** *Magazine, Consumer.*
Published by: (Missionari d'Africa Padri Bianchi), Editrice Missionaria Italiana (E M I), Via di Corticella 179/4, Bologna, 40128, Italy. TEL 39-051-326027, FAX 39-051-327552, ordini@emi.it, http://www.emi.it.

305.896 121 282 USA ISSN 1946-8989
AFRICAN AMERICAN HISTORY MONTH. Variant title: Daily Devotions. Text in English. 200?. a. USD 2.10 per issue (effective 2009). back issues avail. **Document type:** *Journal, Trade.* **Description:** Contains an inspirational meditation based on a scripture passage and on African American history, and a prayer based on the theme.
Published by: Abingdon Press, 201 Eighth Ave S, PO Box 801, Nashville, TN 37202. TEL 800-251-3320, FAX 800-836-7802, orders@abingdonpress.com.

282.68 KEN ISSN 1013-171X
BR1359
➤ **AFRICAN CHRISTIAN STUDIES.** Text in English. 1985. q. KES 575; USD 52 in Africa; USD 86 in Europe & Middle East; USD 105 elsewhere (effective 2001). 1 cols./p.; back issues avail. **Document type:** *Monographic series, Academic/Scholarly.* **Description:** African Theology.
Indexed: PLESA.
—BLDSC (0732.380000).
Published by: (Catholic University of Eastern Africa, Catholic University of Eastern Africa, Faculty of Theology), C U E A Publications, Karen, PO Box 24205, Nairobi, Kenya. TEL 254-2-891601, FAX 254-2-891261, admin@cuea.edu. Ed. Rev. Patrick Ryan. Circ: 350.

220 NGA ISSN 0795-7602
AFRICAN JOURNAL OF BIBLICAL STUDIES. Text in English. 1986. s-a. NGN 400 domestic; USD 40 foreign (effective 2003). adv. bk.rev. **Document type:** *Journal, Academic/Scholarly.* **Description:** Dedicated to publishing articles that reflect African biblical studies.
Indexed: BibLing, OTA.
Published by: Nigerian Association for Biblical Studies, c/o Department of Religious Studies, University of Ibadan, Ibadan, Oyo, Nigeria. TEL 234-8033290864, adamod@juno.com. Ed., R&P, Adv. contact David Tuesday Adamo. Circ: 500.

266.2 IRL
AFRICAN MISSIONARY. Text in English. 1914. 3/yr. free (effective 2005). bk.rev. back issues avail. **Document type:** *Magazine, Consumer.*
Former titles: S M A - The African Missonary; African Missionary (0044-6580)
Published by: Society of African Missions, Blackrock Rd, Cork, Ireland. TEL 353-21-4292871, FAX 353-21-4293873. Ed. Fr. Thomas J Curran. Circ: 40,000.

282 DEU ISSN 0002-3000
AKADEMISCHE MONATSBLAETTER. Text in German. 1887. 10/yr. EUR 4.50 newsstand/cover (effective 2006). adv. bk.rev. index. **Document type:** *Bulletin, Academic/Scholarly.*
Published by: Kartellverband Katholischer Deutscher Studentenvereine, Postfach 101680, Marl, 45746, Germany. TEL 49-2365-5729010, FAX 49-2365-5729051, sekretariat@kartellverband.de, http://www.kartellverband.de. adv.: B&W page EUR 1,800. Circ: 14,900 (controlled).

282.7123 CAN ISSN 0316-473X
ALBERTA CATHOLIC DIRECTORY. Text in English. 1920. a. CAD 17 (effective 1998). adv. **Document type:** *Directory.* **Description:** Lists all priests, parishes, religious orders and other Catholic organizations.
Published by: Western Catholic Reporter, 8421 101 Ave, Edmonton, AB T6A 0L1, Canada. TEL 403-465-8030, FAX 403-465-8031. Ed. Glen Argan. Adv. contact Linda Keer. Circ: 1,200 (paid).

282 IRL
ALIVE!. Text in English. m. adv. **Document type:** *Magazine, Consumer.*
Address: St. Mary's Priory, Tallaght, Dublin, 24, Ireland. TEL 353-1-4048187, FAX 353-1-4596784. Circ: 250,000 (controlled).

246.96 USA
ALIVE AND WELL SAINT PATRICK'S CATHEDRAL. Text in English. 1976 (vol.56). m. USD 6. adv. bk.rev. illus.
Former titles: Alive and Well and Living in New York City Saint Patrick's Cathedral; St. Patrick's Cathedral Bulletin
Published by: (St. Patrick's Parish House), Cathedral Publications (New York), 14 E 51st St, New York, NY 10022. TEL 212-753-2261. Ed. Michael Hoffman. Circ: 5,000.

ALLGEMEINER CAECILIEN-VERBAND. SCHRIFTENREIHE. *see* MUSIC

230.2 ITA ISSN 1126-8476
ALOISIANA. Text in Italian. 1960. irreg., latest vol.30, 2001. price varies. **Document type:** *Monographic series, Academic/Scholarly.*
Indexed: FR.
—INIST.
Published by: (Pontificia Facolta Teologica dell'Italia Meridionale), Gregorian University Press/Editrice Pontificia Universita Gregoriana, Piazza della Pilotta 35, Rome, 00187, Italy. TEL 39-06-6781567, FAX 39-06-6780588, periodicals@biblicum.com, http://www.paxbook.com.

282 100 ITA ISSN 1126-8557
BX800.A1
➤ **ALPHA OMEGA**; rivista di filosofia e teologia dell'Ateneo Pontificio Regina Apostolorum. Text and summaries in Multiple languages. 1998. 3/yr. EUR 31 domestic (effective 2008). bk.rev. back issues avail. **Document type:** *Journal, Academic/Scholarly.* **Description:** A periodical of philosophical and theological studies published under the auspices of the Faculties of Philosophy and Theology of the Pontifical Athenaeum Regina Apostolorum.
Indexed: CPL, DIP, FR, IBR, IBZ, PhilInd.
—INIST.
Published by: Ateneo Pontificio Regina Apostolorum/Pontifical Athenaeum Regina Apostolorum, Dipartimento Pubblicazioni, Via degli Aldobrandeschi 190, Rome, 00163, Italy. TEL 39-06-66527800, FAX 39-06-66527840, publications@upra.org. Circ: 600.

271.1 DEU ISSN 0949-8869
ALT UND JUNG METTEN. Text in German. 1926. s-a. bk.rev. **Document type:** *Magazine, Consumer.* **Description:** Information on subjects concerning the Metten Abbey and the Benedictine Order.
Published by: Abtei Verlag Metten, Abteistr 3, Metten, 94526, Germany. TEL 49-991-9108120, FAX 49-991-9108178, http://www.kloster-metten.de. Ed. Stephan Haering. Circ: 3,000.

282.7285 NIC ISSN 0254-1688
AMANECER; reflexion Cristiana en la nueva Nicaragua. Text in Spanish. 1981. 10/yr. USD 25. bk.rev.
Indexed: C01, LeftInd, M10.
Published by: Centro Ecumenico Antonio Valdivieso, De la Casa Ricardo Morales, 6 C. al Sur No. 1208, Apdo 3205, Managua, Nicaragua. Ed. Jose Arguello. Circ: 2,500.

230.2 USA ISSN 0002-7049
BX801
AMERICA; the national catholic weekly. Text in English. 1909. w. USD 48 domestic; USD 70 in Canada; USD 80 elsewhere (effective 2009). adv. bk.rev.; film rev.; play rev. illus. s-a. index. 32 p./no.; back issues avail.; reprints avail. **Document type:** *Magazine, Consumer.* **Description:** Contains timely and thought-provoking articles written by prestigious writers and theologians.
Supersedes in part (in 1909): The Messenger; Which was formerly (1866-1902): The Messenger of the Sacred Heart of Jesus
Related titles: CD-ROM ed.; Microform ed.: ISSN 0364-989X (from PQC); Online - full text ed.: ISSN 1943-3697. USD 24 (effective 2009).
Indexed: A01, A02, A03, A08, A22, A25, A26, A33, ABS&EES, AcaI, AmHI, B04, B05, B14, BAS, BRD, BRI, C04, C05, C12, CBRI, CERDIC, CPL, CPerI, ChPerI, Chicano, E03, E07, E08, ERI, F01, F02, G05, G06, G07, G08, GSS&RPL, H07, H14, HRIR, I05, I07, L09, M01, M02, M05, M06, MASUSE, MEA&I, MLA-IB, MRD, MagInd, OTA, P02, P04, P05, P10, P13, P28, P30, P34, P47, P48, P53, P54, PCI, PMR, PQC, PRA, R03, R04, R05, R06, RASB, RGAb, RGPR, RILM, S02, S03, S08, S09, S23, SCOPUS, T02, TOM, W03, W05.
—BLDSC (0809.660000), IE, Infotrieve, Ingenta. **CCC.**
Published by: America Press Inc., 106 W 56th St, New York, NY 10019. TEL 212-581-4640, FAX 212-399-3596, america@americapress.org, http://www.americapress.org. Ed. Drew Christiansen. Pub. Jan Attridge. Circ: 44,872 (paid).

282.8 PER
AMERICA LATINA. BOLETIN. Text in Spanish. 1978 (Feb., no.15). irreg. illus.
Published by: Movimiento Internacional de Estudiantes Catolicos, Centro de Documentacion, Apdo. 3564, Lima, 100, Peru.

282 USA ISSN 1084-1008
AMERICAN ACADEMY OF MINISTRY. JOURNAL. Text in English. 1993. q. **Document type:** *Journal, Academic/Scholarly.*
Indexed: R&TA.
Published by: The American Academy of Ministry, 133 Holiday Court., Ste 111, Franklin, TN 37067. TEL 800-288-9673, FAX 615-599-8985, mail@ministry.org.

271.1 USA ISSN 0002-7650
BX3001
➤ **THE AMERICAN BENEDICTINE REVIEW.** Text in English. 1950. q. USD 30 domestic; USD 35 in Canada; USD 45 elsewhere; USD 7.50 per issue (effective 2011). bk.rev. index. back issues avail. **Document type:** *Journal, Academic/Scholarly.* **Description:** Publishes research on the history and spirituality of the monastic movement, including its current issues.
Related titles: Microform ed.: (from PQC).
Indexed: A01, A22, ABS&EES, AmH&L, CA, CPL, FR, HistAb, MLA, MLA-IB, OTA, P30, PCI, PhilInd, R&TA, RI-1, RILM, T02.
—BLDSC (0810.785000), IE, Infotrieve, Ingenta, INIST.
Published by: American Benedictine Review, Inc., Assumption Abbey, Box A, Richardton, ND 58652. TEL 701-974-3315, FAX 701-974-3317, abredit@assumptionabbey.com. Ed. Terrence Kardong.

230.2 973 USA
AMERICAN CATHOLIC IDENTITIES; a documentary history series. Text in English. 1999. irreg. price varies. back issues avail. **Document type:** *Monographic series, Academic/Scholarly.* **Description:** Provides commentary on primary documents in the history of the United States Catholic Church.
Published by: (Maryknoll Fathers and Brothers), Orbis Books (Subsidiary of: Maryknoll Fathers and Brothers), Dept WEB, PO Box 302, Maryknoll, NY 10545. TEL 800-258-5838, FAX 914-941-7005, orbisbooks@maryknoll.org, http://www.orbisbooks.com. Ed. Christopher J Kauffman.

AMERICAN CATHOLIC PHILOSOPHICAL ASSOCIATION. PROCEEDINGS. *see* PHILOSOPHY

282.74811 973 USA ISSN 2161-8542
➤ **AMERICAN CATHOLIC STUDIES.** Text in English. 1886. q. USD 40 domestic; USD 60 foreign (effective 2011). adv. bk.rev. index, cum.index. back issues avail. **Document type:** *Journal, Academic/Scholarly.*
Formerly (until 2000): American Catholic Society of Philadelphia. Records (0002-7790); Which incorporated (1887-1912): The American Catholic Historical Researches (2155-5273); Which was formerly (until 1887): Catholic Historical Researches (2157-4634); (until 1885): Historical Researches in Western Pennsylvania, Principally Catholic; American Catholic Historical Researches incorporated (in 1900): Griffin's Journal
Related titles: Online - full text ed.: ISSN 2161-8534 (from BHP).
Indexed: A22, AmH&L, CA, CPL, HistAb, MLA-IB.
—Ingenta.
Published by: American Catholic Historical Society of Philadelphia, Villanova University, 800 Lancaster Ave, St. Mary's Hall, Villanova, PA 19085. TEL 610-519-5470, FAX 610-519-7304. Eds. Dr. Margaret McGuinness, Dr. Rodger Van Allen.

282 USA ISSN 1081-4019
BX801
AMERICAN CATHOLIC STUDIES NEWSLETTER. Text in English. 1975. s-a. USD 12 for 2 yrs.; USD 15 for 3 yrs. (effective 2003). bk.rev. bibl. **Document type:** *Newsletter.* **Description:** Directed to scholars, graduate students, librarians and archivists with a research interest in the history of the US Catholic church in any of its aspects.
Indexed: CPL.
Published by: University of Notre Dame, 538 Grace Hall, Notre Dame, IN 46556. TEL 574-631-5441, FAX 574-631-8471, cushwa.1@nd.edu. R&P Paula Brach. Circ: 2,000.

255 USA
AMERICAN MONASTIC NEWSLETTER. Text in English. 1947. 3/yr. free to members (effective 2010). bk.rev.; software rev.; video rev.; rec.rev. 2 cols./p.; back issues avail.; reprints avail. **Document type:** *Newsletter, Trade.* **Description:** Includes news, commentaries, reviews of interest to members of monastic communities and others associated with monastic studies.
Published by: American Benedictine Academy, Saint Benedict's House, 415 S Crow St, Pierre, SD 57501. TEL 605-224-0969, bennii@dakota2k.net. Ed. Judith Sutera.

282 USA ISSN 0279-6201
AMERYKA/AMERICA - UKRAINIAN CATHOLIC WEEKLY; Ukrainskyi katolyts'kyi chasopys. Text in English, Ukrainian. 1912. w. **Document type:** *Newspaper, Consumer.*
Indexed: MLA-IB.
Published by: Providence Association of Ukrainian Catholics, 817 N Franklin St, Philadelphia, PA 19123. TEL 215-627-2445, 877-857-2284, info@provassn.com.

AMICI. *see* LIBRARY AND INFORMATION SCIENCES

282 ISR
AMICI DI TERRA SANTA. Text in Italian. 1972. q.
Published by: (Convento Saint Salvatore, Associazione Amici di Terra Santa), Franciscan Printing Press, PO Box 14064, Jerusalem, 91140, Israel. TEL 972-2-6286594, FAX 972-2-6284717, fpp@bezeqint.net, http://198.62.75.5/opt/xampp/custodia/tsancta/00fpp.php. **Subscr. to:** Centro di Propaganda e Stampa di Terra Santa, Via Giovanni Gherardini, 7, Milan, MI 20145, Italy. TEL 39-2-311327.

282 DOM
AMIGO DEL HOGAR. Text in Spanish. 1983 (no.442). m. USD 12.
Address: Apdo Postal 1104, Santo Domingo, Dominican Republic. Ed. Juan Rodriquez. Circ: 23,000.

282 USA
AMIGOS DE JESUS. Text in English, Spanish. 1998. w. USD 99 domestic; USD 109 foreign (effective 2011). **Document type:** *Journal, Trade.* **Description:** Designed specifically for Hispanic children living and growing up in the United States.

Published by: Claretian Publications, 205 W Monroe, Chicago, IL 60606. TEL 312-236-7782, FAX 312-236-8207, stjudeleague@claretians.org. Ed. Carmen Aguinaco.

282 FRA ISSN 1252-1469
AMITIES; les communautes francophones dans le monde. Text in French. N.S. 1915. q. EUR 15 (effective 2002). adv. bk.rev. bibl.; stat. index. back issues avail. **Document type:** *Magazine, Consumer.* **Description:** General news on topics interesting Roman Catholics in France and abroad (history, sociology, ethics, etc) seen from a French cultural point of view.
Formerly (until 1994): Amities Catholiques Francaises (0998-2671)
Indexed: FR.
Published by: Amities Catholiques Francaises dans le Monde, 58 Av. de Breteuil, Paris, 75007, France. TEL 33-1-72366881, FAX 33-1-73729651, agfe@cef.fr. Ed. Dominique de la Motte. Adv. contact Claire Richard. Circ: 1,100.

255.3 ITA
ANACLETA TOR. (Terzo Ordine Regolare) Text in English, Italian, Spanish; Summaries in English, Italian. 1913. q. bk.rev. abstr.; bibl. back issues avail. **Document type:** *Journal, Academic/Scholarly.* **Description:** Covers the spirituality and history of Franciscanism, with a focus on the Third Order Regular.
Published by: (Terzo Ordine Regolare di San Francesco d'Assisi), Editrice Franciscanum, Via Tor dei Conti 31a, Rome, 00184, Italy. TEL 39-075-812268, FAX 39-075-816340, linotemperini@tiscali.it, http://www.franciscanum.it. Circ: 700 (paid).

255.4 ITA ISSN 0392-2855
BX2901
ANALECTA AUGUSTINIANA. Text in Latin, Multiple languages. 1905. a. 400 p./no.; back issues avail. **Document type:** *Journal, Academic/Scholarly.* **Description:** Historical studies.
Indexed: A21, BAS, DIP, IBR, IBZ, MLA-IB, PCI, RI-1, RI-2.
Published by: Istituto Patristico Augustinianum/Institutum Patristicum Augustinianum, Via Paolo VI 25, Rome, 00193, Italy. http://www.patristicum.org. Circ: 1,000.

282 ITA ISSN 0066-135X
ANALECTA BIBLICA. Text in Multiple languages. 1952. irreg., latest vol.147, 2001. price varies. **Document type:** *Monographic series, Academic/Scholarly.* **Description:** Most issues are doctoral dissertations, some are critical editions of texts.
Published by: Pontificio Istituto Biblico/Pontifical Biblical Institute, Via della Pilotta 25, Rome, 00187, Italy. TEL 39-06-695261, FAX 39-06-695266211, http://www.biblico.it. Ed. Pietro Bovati.

282 BEL ISSN 0003-2468
BX4655
➤ **ANALECTA BOLLANDIANA**; revue critique d'hagiographie - journal of critical hagiography. Text in English, French, German, Italian, Latin, Spanish; Summaries in English. 1882. s-a. EUR 85 (effective 2003). bk.rev. index, cum.index every 20 yrs. (vols.1-100). 240 p./no.; back issues avail. **Document type:** *Journal, Academic/Scholarly.* **Description:** Studies the lives of saints from early Christianity to the Renaissance.
Indexed: A21, A22, BibInd, CERDIC, DIP, FR, IBR, IBZ, MLA, MLA-IB, PCI, RASB, RI-1, RI-2, SCOPUS.
—IE, Infotrieve, INIST.
Published by: Societe des Bollandistes, Bd St Michel 24, Brussels, 1040, Belgium. TEL 32-2-739-3338, FAX 32-2-739-3332, info@bollandistes.be, http://www.bollandistes.be.

282 POL ISSN 0209-0864
BX1751.2
➤ **ANALECTA CRACOVIENSIA.** Text in Polish; Summaries in Latin, French, German. 1969. a. **Document type:** *Journal, Academic/Scholarly.*
Indexed: A21, FR, IZBG, RI-1.
—INIST.
Published by: (Papieska Akademia Teologiczna w Krakowie/Pontifical Academy of Theology in Krakow), Wydawnictwo Naukowe Papieskiej Akademii Teologicznej w Krakowie, ul Franciszkanska 1, pok 037, Krakow, 31004, Poland. wydawnictwo@pat.krakow.pl. Ed. Josef Makselon.

255.3 ITA
ANALECTA FRANCISCANA. Text in Latin. 1885. irreg., latest vol.12, 1983. price varies. **Document type:** *Monographic series, Academic/Scholarly.*
Published by: Collegio San Bonaventura/Collegium S Bonaventurae ad Claras Aquas, Via Vecchia per Marino 28-30, Grottaferrata, 00046, Italy. http://www.fratiquaracchi.it.

282 ITA ISSN 0066-1376
➤ **ANALECTA GREGORIANA.** Text in English, French, German, Italian, Latin, Spanish. 1930. irreg., latest vol.282, 2001. price varies. **Document type:** *Monographic series, Academic/Scholarly.* **Description:** Contains research studies on sacred scripture, theology, patristics, church law, philosophy, church history, ecumenism, non-Christian religions and more.
Published by: (Pontificia Universita Gregoriana/Pontifical Gregorian University), Gregorian University Press/Editrice Pontificia Universita Gregoriana, Piazza della Pilotta 35, Rome, 00187, Italy. TEL 39-06-6781567, FAX 39-06-6780588, periodicals@biblicum.com, http://www.paxbook.com. Ed. Angel Anton.

282 ITA ISSN 1971-369X
BX3800.A1
ANALECTA MERCEDARIA. Text in Multiple languages. 1982. a. **Document type:** *Monographic series, Academic/Scholarly.*
Published by: Institutum Historicum Ordinis de Mercede, Via Monte Carmelo 3, Rome, 00166, Italy. http://www.ordinedellamercede.org.

255.71 ITA ISSN 0394-7726
ANALECTA ORDINIS CARMELITARUM. Text in Italian. 1909. s-a. EUR 19 (effective 2009). adv. **Document type:** *Bulletin, Consumer.* **Description:** Official documents of the Carmelite Order; also news and brief historical articles.
Indexed: DIP, IBR, IBZ.
Published by: (Institutum Carmelitanum), Edizioni Carmelitane, Via Sforza Pallavicini 10, Rome, 00193, Italy. TEL 39-06-68100886, FAX 39-06-68100887, edizioni@ocarm.org, http://www.carmelites.info/edizioni/. Ed. Emanuele Boaga. Circ: 500.

262.3 BEL ISSN 0066-1414
ANALECTA VATICANO-BELGICA. DEUXIEME SERIE. SECTION A: NONCIATURE DE FLANDRE. Text in French. 1924. irreg., latest vol.75, 1993. price varies. **Document type:** *Monographic series.* **Description:** Correspondence from and to nuncios in the Southern Low Countries during the 16th, 17th and 18th centuries.
Published by: (Institut Historique Belge de Rome), Brepols Publishers, Begijnhof 67, Turnhout, 2300, Belgium. TEL 32-14-448020, FAX 32-14-428919, periodicals@brepols.net, http://www.brepols.net. Circ: (controlled).

262.3 BEL ISSN 0066-1422
ANALECTA VATICANO-BELGICA. DEUXIEME SERIE. SECTION B: NONCIATURE DE COLOGNE. Text in French. 1956. irreg., latest vol.8, 1995. price varies. **Document type:** *Monographic series.* **Description:** Correspondence from and to nuncios in the Southern Low Countries during the 16th, 17th and 18th centuries.
Published by: (Institut Historique Belge de Rome), Brepols Publishers, Begijnhof 67, Turnhout, 2300, Belgium. FAX 32-14-428919, periodicals@brepols.net. Circ: (controlled).

262.3 BEL ISSN 0066-1430
ANALECTA VATICANO-BELGICA. DEUXIEME SERIE. SECTION C: NONCIATURE DE BRUXELLES. Text in French. 1956. irreg., latest vol.12, 1996. price varies. **Document type:** *Monographic series.* **Description:** Correspondence from and to nuncios in 19th century Belgium.
Published by: (Institut Historique Belge de Rome), Brepols Publishers, Begijnhof 67, Turnhout, 2300, Belgium. FAX 32-14-428919, periodicals@brepols.net. Circ: (controlled).

262.13 BEL ISSN 0066-1449
ANALECTA VATICANO-BELGICA. PREMIERE SERIE: DOCUMENTS RELATIFS AUX ANCIENS DIOCESES DE CAMBRAI, LIEGE, THEROUANNE ET TOURNAI. Text in French. 1906. irreg., latest vol.32, 1987. price varies. **Document type:** *Monographic series.* **Description:** Letters from and supplications to the Popes concerning the Southern Low Countries during the 14th and 15th centuries.
Published by: (Institut Historique Belge de Rome), Brepols Publishers, Begijnhof 67, Turnhout, 2300, Belgium. FAX 32-14-428919, periodicals@brepols.net. Circ: (controlled).

282 USA
THE ANCHOR; Fall River diocesan newspaper for Southeast Massachusetts, Cape Cod & the Islands. Text in English. 1957. w. USD 14 domestic; USD 25 foreign (effective 2005). adv. film rev. illus. back issues avail. **Document type:** *Newspaper, Consumer.*
Related titles: Microfilm ed.
Published by: (Roman Catholic Diocese of Fall River), Anchor Publishing Co., 887 Highland Ave, PO Box 7, Fall River, MA 02722. TEL 508-675-7151, FAX 508-675-7048. Ed. Mr. David BF Jolivet. Pub. Rev. Sean O'Malley. R&P, Adv. contact Rosemary Dussault. Circ: 31,000 (paid). Wire service: CaNS.

282 VAT ISSN 1123-5772
BX800.A1
➤ **ANGELICUM**; periodicum trimestre pontificae studiorum universitatis a Santo Thoma Aquinate in Urbe. Text in English, French, German, Italian, Spanish. 1924. q. bk.rev. abstr. 250 p./no.; back issues avail. **Document type:** *Journal, Academic/Scholarly.* **Description:** Scholarly articles on a variety of topics related to the Catholic faith.
Formerly (until 1925): Unio Thomistica (1123-5780)
Indexed: CERDIC, CLA, DIP, FR, IBR, IBZ, IPB, IZBG, MLA, MLA-IB, OTA.
—BLDSC (0900.930000), IE, Infotrieve, Ingenta, INIST.
Published by: Pontificia Universita San Tommaso d'Aquino - Angelicum, Largo Angelicum 1, Vatican City, 00184, Vatican City. TEL 39-06-67021, FAX 39-06-6790407, http://www.angelicum.org. Ed. Boguslaw Kochaniewicz. R&P, Adv. contact Stefano Serafini.

282 USA ISSN 1073-5003
THE ANGELUS; a journal of Roman Catholic tradition. Text in English. 1978. m. USD 35 domestic; USD 55 foreign; USD 45 combined subscription domestic (print & online eds.); USD 65 combined subscription foreign (print & online eds.) (effective 2010). back issues avail. **Document type:** *Journal, Academic/Scholarly.* **Description:** A review of ideas according to Thomistic philosophy; current trends examined by the light of the principles of the Catholic faith and reason. Reviews major events in the Church from a traditional standpoint.
Related titles: Online - full text ed.
Published by: Angelus Press, Inc., 2915 Forest Ave, Kansas City, MO 64109. TEL 800-966-7337, FAX 816-753-3557, http://www.angeluspress.org/. Circ: 3,000.

255.53 GRC
ANICHTI ORIZONTES - ANGHELIAFOROS. Text in Greek. 1900. m. USD 25 (effective 2000). adv. bk.rev. bibl.
Former titles (until 1977): Anichti Orizontes (1105-3216); (until 1975): Angheliaforos (1105-3496)
Published by: Mone Pateron Iesouitons/Jesuit Fathers, 27 Smyrnis St, Athens, 104 39, Greece. TEL 30-1-8835-911. Ed. Fr Michael Roussos. Circ: 3,500.

282 ITA ISSN 2038-2561
ANNALES FRANCISCANI. Text in Italian. 2006. s-a. **Document type:** *Magazine, Consumer.*
Published by: Casa Mariana Editrice, Casa Mariana, Maria SS deel Buon Consiglio, Frigento, AV, Italy. http://www.casamarianaeditrice.info.

282 ITA ISSN 0394-8226
BR5
ANNALES THEOLOGICI. Text in Multiple languages. 1987. s-a. EUR 70 combined subscription domestic to institutions (print & online eds.); EUR 110 combined subscription foreign to institutions (print & online eds.) (effective 2009). **Document type:** *Journal, Academic/Scholarly.*
Related titles: Online - full text ed.: ISSN 1972-4934. 2007.
Indexed: FR, OTA, R&TA.
—INIST.
Published by: (Pontificia Universita della Santa Croce), Fabrizio Serra Editore (Subsidiary of: Accademia Editoriale), c/o Accademia Editoriale, Via Santa Bibbiana 28, Pisa, 56127, Italy. TEL 39-050-542332, FAX 39-050-574888, accademiaeditoriale@accademiaeditoriale.it, http://www.libraweb.net.

282.09 ITA ISSN 1120-4001
ANNALI DI STORIA DELL'ESEGESI. Text in Italian. 1984. s-a. EUR 47.50 domestic; EUR 62.70 in the European Union; EUR 67.80 elsewhere (effective 2008). **Document type:** *Monographic series, Academic/Scholarly.*
Indexed: IZBG, OTA, PCI, SCOPUS.
Published by: Centro Editoriale Dehoniano, Via Scipione dal Ferro 4, Bologna, BO 40138, Italy. TEL 39-051-4290451, FAX 39-051-4290491, ced-amm@dehoniane.it, http://www.dehoniane.it.

282 BEL
➤ **ANNUA NUNTIA LOVANIENSIA.** Text in English, French, German, Dutch. 1960. a., latest vol.39, 1997. price varies. back issues avail. **Document type:** *Monographic series, Academic/Scholarly.*
Published by: (Universite Catholique de Louvain, Faculte de Theologie et de Droit Canonique), Leuven University Press, Blijde Inkomststraat 5, Leuven, 3000, Belgium. TEL 32-16-325345, FAX 32-16-325352, university.press@upers.kuleuven.ac.be, http://www.kuleuven.ac.be/upers.

262.3 FRA ISSN 0153-3533
ANNUAIRE DU DIOCESE DE LYON. Text in French. 1826. a. EUR 29.50 (effective 2008). **Description:** Discusses departments, parishes, communities, and various groups of the Diocese.
Formerly (until 1972): Ordo et Annuaire de l'Archdiocese de Lyon
Published by: Association Diocesaine de Lyon, 6 Av. Adolphe Max, Lyon, Cedex 5 69321, France. TEL 33-4-78384658, contact@e-diocese-lyon.com, http://don-lyon.nuxit.net.

282 ITA ISSN 0066-4464
ANNUARIO CATTOLICO D'ITALIA. Text in Italian. 1956. biennial. EUR 110 (effective 2009). index. **Document type:** *Directory.* **Description:** Yearbook about the Catholic Church, Cadres and institutions in Italy.
Published by: Editoriale Italiana, Via Vigliena 10, Rome, 00192, Italy. TEL 39-06-3230177, FAX 39-06-3211359, info@editoriale.it, http://www.editoriale.it.

282 USA ISSN 1060-0345
BX3601
THE ANTHONIAN. Text in English. 1927. q. USD 10 (effective 2000). **Document type:** *Magazine, Consumer.* **Description:** Promotes devotion to St. Anthony of Padua and presents the works of the Franciscans of Holy Name Province along the eastern U.S. and abroad.
Published by: St. Anthony's Guild, 127 W 31 St, New York, NY 10001-3403. TEL 212-594-6224, FAX 212-594-2769. Ed., R&P Fr Cassian Miles TEL 212-594-6224. Circ: 90,000 (paid).

282 USA ISSN 1543-9925
BX1970.A1
ANTIPHON; a journal for liturgical renewal. Text in English. 1996. 3/yr. USD 15 (effective 2003).
Indexed: CPL.
Published by: Society for Catholic Liturgy, PO Box 594, Mundelein, IL 60060. TEL 847-837-4542, FAX 847-837-4545, http://www.liturgysociety.org. Ed. M. Frances Mannion.

282 ITA ISSN 0003-6064
BX804
ANTONIANUM. Text in English, French, German, Italian, Latin, Spanish. 1925. q. bk.rev. abstr.; bibl. index, cum.index. reprints avail. **Document type:** *Journal, Academic/Scholarly.* **Description:** Publishes inedited works on the Sacred Scripture, theology (dogmatic, moral, and pastoral), the history of the church, of theology, of spirituality, canon law, philosophy, human sciences and especially medieval and Franciscan studies.
Indexed: A21, A22, CA, CERDIC, DIP, FR, HistAb, IBR, IBZ, IPB, IZBG, MLA, MLA-IB, OTA, PCI, PhilInd, R&TA, RI-1, S02, S03, SociolAb, T02.
—IE, Infotrieve, INIST.
Published by: Pontificio Ateneo Antonianum, Via Merulana 124, Rome, 00185, Italy. TEL 39-06-70373502, FAX 39-06-70373604, segreteriapaa@ofm.org.

282 DEU
ANTONIUS. Text in German. 1894. 11/yr. EUR 8 (effective 2009). **Document type:** *Magazine, Trade.*
Formerly (until 1959): Antonius von Padua
Published by: Bayerische Franziskanerprovinz, Sankt-Anna-Str 19, Munich, 80538, Germany. TEL 49-89-211260, FAX 49-89-21126111, prov.muenchen@franziskaner.de.

271 DEU ISSN 0721-1937
ANZEIGER FUER DIE SEELSORGE; Zeitschrift fuer Pastoral und Gemeindepraxis. Text in German. 1891. 11/yr. EUR 33; EUR 4 newsstand/cover (effective 2010). adv. back issues avail. **Document type:** *Magazine, Consumer.*
Published by: Verlag Herder GmbH, Hermann-Herder-Str 4, Freiburg Im Breisgau, 79104, Germany. TEL 49-761-27170, FAX 49-761-2717520, kundenservice@herder.de, http://www.herder.de. Ed. Klaus Vellguth. Adv. contact Friederike Ward TEL 49-761-2717407. Circ: 11,746 (paid and controlled).

282 VAT ISSN 0392-2359
K1
APOLLINARIS. Text in Italian. 1928. 2/yr. USD 90.
Indexed: CERDIC, CLA, DIP, DoGi, FR, IBR, IBZ, MLA, MLA-IB, PCI.
—INIST.
Published by: (Pontificio Istituto Utriusque Iuris), Pontificia Universita Lateranense/Pontificia Universitas Lateranensis, Piazza S. Giovanni in Laterano 4, Vatican City, 00120, Vatican City. Ed. Domingo Andres Giuterrez.

282 CAN ISSN 1491-7181
APOSTOLAT INTERNATIONAL. Text in French. 1929. bi-m. CAD 8, USD 8. **Document type:** *Newsletter.* **Description:** Religious topics on the Roman Catholic home and missions abroad.
Formerly (until 1999): Apostolat (0706-9928)
Published by: Missionary Oblates of Mary Immaculate, 8844 Notre Dame Est, Montreal, PQ H1L 3M4, Canada. TEL 514-351-9310, FAX 514-351-1314. Ed. Rev. Guy Gaudreau. Circ: 21,000.

282 LKA
➤ **AQUINAS JOURNAL.** Text in English. 1984. a. LKR 75 domestic; USD 10 foreign (effective 1999). bk.rev. **Document type:** *Journal, Academic/Scholarly.* **Description:** Discusses ethical, moral, religious, and cultural issues in various fields.

R

Published by: Aquinas College of Higher Studies, 990 Marandana Rd., Colombo, 8, Sri Lanka. TEL 94-1-694709, FAX 94-1-678463. Ed. Rev. Don Gerald Chrispin Leo. Circ: 500; 350 (paid).

282 IND
ARASARADI JOURNAL OF THEOLOGICAL REFLECTION. Text in English. 1986. s-a. **Document type:** *Journal, Academic/Scholarly.*
Indexed: A21, R&TA, RI-1.
Published by: Tamilnadu Theological Seminary, Arasaradi, Madurai, 625 010, India. TEL 91-452-2602351, tts@md2.vsnl.net.in.

282.77178 USA
ARCHDIOCESE OF CINCINNATI ALMANAC DIRECTORY AND BUYER'S GUIDE. Text in English. 1959. a. USD 15. adv. stat. **Document type:** *Directory.*
Published by: (Archdiocese of Cincinnati), Catholic Telegraph, 100 E 8th St, Cincinnati, OH 45202. TEL 513-421-3131. Ed. James Stackpoole. Circ: 3,000.

262.3 ESP
ARCHIDIOCESIS DE MADRID-ALCALA. BOLETIN OFICIAL. Text in Spanish. 1878. s-m. USD 13. adv. bibl. index. back issues avail.
Published by: Arzobispado de Madrid, Bailen, 8, Madrid, 28013, Spain. TEL 34-91-4546400, infomadrid@planalfa.es. Ed. J Gonzalez Prado. Circ: 1,500.

282 DEU ISSN 0003-9160
ARCHIV FUER KATHOLISCHES KIRCHENRECHT. Text in German, Latin. 1857. s-a. EUR 128 (effective 2010). adv. bibl. index. **Document type:** *Journal, Academic/Scholarly.*
Indexed: A22, CERDIC, CLA, DIP, FR, IBR, IBZ.
—IE, INIST.
Published by: Verlag Ferdinand Schoeningh GmbH, Postfach 2540, Paderborn, 33055, Germany. TEL 49-5251-1275, FAX 49-5251-127860, info@schoeningh.de, http://www.schoeningh.de. Circ: 550.

282.45 ITA ISSN 0390-8240
HN39.I8
ARCHIVIO PER LA STORIA DEL MOVIMENTO SOCIALE CATTOLICO IN ITALIA. BOLLETTINO. Text in Italian. 1966. 3/yr. EUR 60 domestic to institutions; EUR 95 foreign to institutions (effective 2009). **Document type:** *Journal, Academic/Scholarly.* **Description:** Covers history of the Social-Catholic movement in Italy.
Related titles: Online - full text ed.: ISSN 1827-7977. 2003.
Indexed: CA, DIP, HistAb, IBR, IBZ, P30, RASB, T02.
Published by: (Universita Cattolica del Sacro Cuore), Vita e Pensiero (Subsidiary of: Universita Cattolica del Sacro Cuore), Largo Gemelli 1, Milan, 20123, Italy. TEL 39-02-72342335, FAX 39-02-72342260, redazione.vp@mi.unicatt.it, http://www.vitaepensiero.it. Ed. Alberto Cova. Circ: 650.

255.71 ITA ISSN 0394-7734
ARCHIVIUM HISTORICUM CARMELITANUM. Text in English, French, German, Italian, Latin, Spanish. 1961. irreg. price varies. adv. **Document type:** *Monographic series, Academic/Scholarly.* **Description:** Covers Carmelite history; an order in the Catholic religion.
Published by: (Order of Carmelites), Edizioni Carmelitane, Via Sforza Pallavicini 10, Rome, 00193, Italy. TEL 39-06-68100886, FAX 39-06-68100887, edizioni@ocarm.org, http://www.carmelites.info/edizioni/. Circ: 500.

255.4 ESP ISSN 0211-2035
ARCHIVO AGUSTINIANO. Text in English, French, Italian, Spanish. 1914-1935; resumed 1950-1965; resumed 1976. a. USD 45 foreign; EUR 44 in Europe. bk.rev. cum.index: 1914-1927; 1928-1959. back issues avail. **Document type:** *Journal, Academic/Scholarly.*
Formerly (until 1927): Archivo Historico Hispano-Agustiniano (0211-2019)
Indexed: FR.
—INIST.
Published by: (Provincia Agustiniana del Santisimo Nombre de Jesus de Filipinas), Editorial Estudio Agustiniano, Paseo Filipinos, 7, Valladolid, 47007, Spain. TEL 34-983-306800, FAX 34-983-397896, edestagus@adenet.es. Eds. Carlos Alonso, J Balmori. Adv. contact J Balmori. Circ: 300.

255.2 ESP ISSN 0211-5255
BX3544.A1
ARCHIVO DOMINICANO. Text in Spanish. 1980. a. EUR 40 (effective 2009). bk.rev. charts; illus. 360 p./no.; back issues avail. **Document type:** *Yearbook, Academic/Scholarly.*
Published by: (Instituto Historico Dominicano de San Esteban), Editorial San Esteban, Plaza Concilio de Trento s-n, Apartado 17, Salamanca, 37001, Spain. TEL 34-923-264781, FAX 34-923-265480, info@sanestebaneditorial.com, http://www.sanestebaneditorial.com/. Ed. Jose Barrado Barquilla.

262.3 GTM
ARCHIVO HISTORICO ARQUIDIOCESANO "FRANCISCO DE PAULA GARCIA PELAEZ". BOLETIN. Text in Spanish. 199?. s-a.
Published by: Archivo Historico Arquidiocesano "Francisco de Paula Garcia Pelaez", Palacio Arzobispal, 7a Avda. 6-21, ZONA, 1, Guatemala City, 01001, Guatemala. Ed. Ramiro Ordonez Jonama.

282 ESP ISSN 0210-1629
BX880
ARCHIVO TEOLOGICO GRANADINO. Text in Spanish. 1938. a. **Document type:** *Journal, Academic/Scholarly.* **Description:** Covers theological studies of the period 1500-1800.
Indexed: BibLing, FR, OTA, P09, PCI.
—INIST.
Published by: Facultad de Teologia de Granada, Campus Universitario de Cantuja s/n, Granada, 18080, Spain. TEL 34-958-185252, FAX 34-958-162559, info@eol-granada.com, http://www.teol.granada.com/. Circ: 400.

ARCHIVUM BIBLIOGRAPHICUM CARMELI TERESIANI. *see* RELIGIONS AND THEOLOGY—Abstracting, Bibliographies, Statistics

271.3 ITA ISSN 0004-0665
BX3601
ARCHIVUM FRANCISCANUM HISTORICUM. Abbreviated title: AFH. Text in English, French, German, Italian, Latin, Spanish. 1908. s-a. price varies. bk.rev. bibl.; charts; illus. cum.index: 1908-1957. reprints avail. **Document type:** *Monographic series, Academic/Scholarly.* **Description:** Contains studies, articles, and notes on Franciscan history, 13th-19th centuries.
Indexed: AmH&L, B24, BAS, BibInd, CERDIC, DIP, FR, HistAb, IBR, IBZ, IPB, MLA, MLA-IB, P30, PCI, T02.
—INIST.
Published by: (Commissione Storica), Collegio San Bonaventura/Collegium S Bonaventurae ad Claras Aquas, Via Vecchia per Marino 28-30, Grottaferrata, 00046, Italy. http://www.fratiquaracchi.it. Circ: 600.

ARCHIVUM HISTORIAE PONTIFICIAE. *see* RELIGIONS AND THEOLOGY—Abstracting, Bibliographies, Statistics

255.53 ITA ISSN 0037-8887
BX3701
➤ **ARCHIVUM HISTORICUM SOCIETATIS IESU.** Text and summaries in English, French, German, Italian, Latin, Portuguese, Spanish. 1932. s-a. bk.rev. bibl. cum.index: 1932-1951, 1952-1961, 1962-1981. reprints avail. **Document type:** *Journal, Academic/Scholarly.* **Description:** Contains research articles on history of Jesuits worldwide.
Related titles: Online - full text ed.
Indexed: AmH&L, B24, BAS, BibInd, CA, CPL, DIP, FR, HistAb, IBR, IBZ, MLA-IB, PCI, SPPI, T02.
—INIST.
Published by: Institutum Historicum Societatis Iesu/Jesuit Historical Institute, Via dei Penitenzieri 20, Rome, 00193, Italy.

282 POL ISSN 0518-3766
BR950
➤ **ARCHIWA, BIBLIOTEKI I MUZEA KOSCIELNE/ARCHIVA, BIBLIOTHECAE ET MUSEA ECCLESIASTICA.** Text in Polish; Summaries in German; Text occasionally in English. 1959. s-a. price varies. bk.rev. index. **Document type:** *Journal, Academic/Scholarly.*
Indexed: DIP, FR, IBR, IBZ, IIPA, RASB.
—INIST.
Published by: (Katolicki Uniwersytet Lubelski, Osrodek Archiwow Bibliotek i Muzeow Koscielnych), Katolicki Uniwersytet Lubelski, Al Raclawickie 14, Lublin, 20-950, Poland. TEL 48-81-5338022, FAX 48-81-5338022. Ed. Stanislaw Tylus. Circ: 800.

282.767 USA ISSN 1057-8439
ARKANSAS CATHOLIC. Text in English. 1911. w. USD 18 (effective 1999). adv. 16 p./no. 4 cols./p.; **Document type:** *Newspaper.*
Address: 2500 N Tyler, Box 7417, Little Rock, AR 72217-7417. TEL 501-664-0340, FAX 501-664-9075. Ed., R&P Malea Hargett. Pub. Peter J Sartain. Adv. contact Tara Little. Circ: 7,000. Wire service: CaNS.

282.755295 USA ISSN 0361-3712
ARLINGTON CATHOLIC HERALD. Text in English. 1976. w. (Thu.). USD 15. adv. bk.rev. illus. **Document type:** *Newspaper.* **Description:** Local, national, international news and features of Catholic interest.
Related titles: Microfilm ed.
Published by: Arlington Catholic Herald, Inc., 200 N Glebe Rd, Ste 600, Arlington, VA 22203. TEL 703-841-2590, FAX 703-524-2782. Ed. Michael Flach. Pub. Most Rev. Paul S. Loverde. Circ: 56,000. Wire service: CaNS.

282 NLD ISSN 1872-4906
ARNULFUS POST. Text in Dutch. 1995. 5/yr.
Published by: (Arnulfus Stichting), Katholiek Nieuwsblad, Postbus 1270, 's-Hertogenbosch, 5200 BH, Netherlands. TEL 31-73-6123480, FAX 31-73-6890065. Circ: 13,000.

220 MLT
L-ART IMQADDSA; rivista biblika. Text in Maltese. 1955; N.S. 1980. bi-m. bk.rev. illus.; maps. back issues avail. **Document type:** *Consumer.* **Description:** Covers topics related to the Christian religion, Biblical studies, religious art and history, archaeological discoveries, and related news of interest.
Published by: (Kummissarjat ta' l-Art Imqaddsa tal-Provincja Frangiskana Maltija), Edizzjoni Tau, 291 Triq San Pawl, Valetta, VLT 07, Malta. TEL 356-242254, FAX 356-221560. Ed. Rev. P Marcello Ghirlando. Circ: 2,140.

262.3 CHL
ARZOBISPADO DE SANTIAGO. VICARIA DE LA SOLIDARIDAD. ESTUDIOS. Text in Spanish. 1978. irreg.
Published by: Arzobispado de Santiago, Vicaria de la Solidaridad, Casilla 30D, Plaza De Armas, 444, Santiago, Chile.

262.3 ESP
ARZOBISPADO DE SEVILLA. BOLETIN OFICIAL ECLESIASTICO. Text in Spanish. 1854. m. adv. bk.rev. **Document type:** *Bulletin, Consumer.*
Published by: Arzobispado de Sevilla, Oficina Diocesana de Informacion, Apartado Postal 6, Sevilla, 41080, Spain. arzobispado@archisevilla.org, 34-95-4505515, http://www.diocesisdesevilla.org/.

266.2 ITA ISSN 1125-3576
ASIA NEWS. Text in Italian. 1987. m. (10/yr.). **Document type:** *Magazine, Consumer.* **Description:** Covers the Roman Catholic Church, non-Christian religions, missionary work, human rights, refugees, and the environment in Asia.
Related titles: Online - full text ed.; ◆ Supplement to: Mondo e Missione. ISSN 0026-6094.
Published by: Pontificio Istituto Missioni Estere, Via F D Guerrazzi, Rome, 00152, Italy. TEL 39-06-5839151, FAX 39-06-5894228, http://www.pime.org/. Circ: 2,200.

282 ESP ISSN 2171-4347
ASIDONENSE. Text in Spanish. 2006. a. **Document type:** *Magazine, Consumer.*
Published by: Instituto Superior de Ciencias Religiosas Asidonense, Plaza de Arroyo, 50, Jerez de Frontera, Cadiz, 11403, Spain. TEL 34-956-338800, http://www.diocesisdejerez.org/ISCRA/default.htm.

230.2 ITA ISSN 0004-4970
ASPRENAS; rivista di teologia. Text in Italian. 1953. q. adv. bk.rev. charts; illus. **Document type:** *Journal, Academic/Scholarly.* **Description:** Contains studies and research on all aspects of theological science; Bible, patristics, systematic and practical theology, ecumenism, with particular attention to their cultural contexts and their relationship to the humanities.
Indexed: CERDIC, MLA-IB, OTA.
Published by: Pontificia Facolta Teologica dell'Italia Meridionale, Viale Colli Aminei 2, Naples, 80131, Italy. TEL 39-081-7410000, FAX 39-081-7437580, http://www.pftim.it. Circ: 1,000.

ASSOCIATION OF JESUIT COLLEGES AND UNIVERSITIES AND JESUIT SECONDARY EDUCATION ASSOCIATION DIRECTORY. *see* EDUCATION—Higher Education

282 USA ISSN 2162-2299
AT HOME WITH OUR FAITH; nurturing the spirituality of your family. Text in English. 1976. 9/yr. USD 12 domestic; USD 22 foreign (effective 2011). reprints avail. **Document type:** *Newsletter, Consumer.* **Description:** Offers parents fresh new insights on important parenting topics.
Formerly (until 199?): Bringing Religion Home
Published by: Claretian Publications, 205 W Monroe, Chicago, IL 60606. TEL 312-236-7782, FAX 312-236-8207, http://www.claretians.org.

282 HUN ISSN 1219-9915
➤ **ATHANASIANA.** Text in Hungarian; Summaries in English, French, German, Italian. 1995. s-a. HUF 800, USD 10 (effective 2010). bk.rev. back issues avail. **Document type:** *Journal, Academic/Scholarly.* **Description:** Covers Byzantine theology, liturgy, and church history.
Related titles: Online - full text ed.: ISSN 1588-0184.
Published by: Szent Atanaz Gorogkatolikus Hittudomanyi Foiskola/St. Athanasius Greek Catholic Theological College, Bethlen G. u. 13-19, Nyiregyhaza, 4400, Hungary. TEL 36-42-597600, FAX 36-42-597600. Ed., Pub. Istvan Ivancso. R&P Janos Soltesz.

282 USA
AUGUSTINIAN HISTORICAL INSTITUTE. SERIES. Text in English. 1990. irreg., latest vol.4, 2003. price varies. **Document type:** *Monographic series, Academic/Scholarly.*
Published by: (Augustinian Historical Institute), Peter Lang Publishing, Inc. (Subsidiary of: Peter Lang Publishing Group), 29 Broadway, New York, NY 10006. TEL 212-647-7700, 800-770-5264, FAX 212-647-7707, customerservice@plang.com.

AUGUSTINIAN STUDIES. *see* PHILOSOPHY

255.4 BEL ISSN 0004-8003
BR65.A9
AUGUSTINIANA; revue pour l'etude de Saint Augustin et de l'Ordre des Augustins. Text in English, French, German, Latin. 1951. q. EUR 38 (effective 2003). bk.rev. bibl. index. **Document type:** *Journal, Academic/Scholarly.*
Indexed: A21, A22, BibInd, CERDIC, DIP, FR, IBR, IBZ, MLA, MLA-IB, PCI, RI-1, RI-2.
—IE, Infotrieve, INIST.
Published by: Augustijns Historisch Instituut/Institut Historique Augustinien, Pakenstraat 65, Heverlee-Leuven, 3001, Belgium. TEL 32-16-404440, FAX 32-16-405733, klooster.heverlee@augustijnen.be. Ed. T van Bavel.

255.4 ITA ISSN 0004-8011
B1
AUGUSTINIANUM. Text in Italian. 1961. s-a. bk.rev. index. 280 p./no.; back issues avail. **Document type:** *Journal, Academic/Scholarly.* **Description:** Patristic studies.
Indexed: A21, A22, DIP, FR, IBR, IBZ, MLA, MLA-IB, OTA, PCI, RI-1, RI-2.
—BLDSC (1791.700000), IE, Infotrieve, Ingenta, INIST.
Published by: Istituto Patristico Augustinianum/Institutum Patristicum Augustinianum, Via Paolo VI 25, Rome, 00193, Italy. TEL 39-06-68006238, FAX 39-06-68006298, http://www.patristicum.org. Ed. Vittorino Grossi. Circ: 1,000.

271.4 ESP ISSN 0004-802X
AUGUSTINUS; revista trimestral publicada por los Padres Agustinos Recoletos. Text in Spanish. 1956. q. adv. bk.rev. bibl. index. back issues avail. **Document type:** *Journal, Academic/Scholarly.* **Description:** Studies on the life, doctrine, thought, spirituality and influence of St. Augustine.
Indexed: A22, CERDIC, DIP, FR, IBR, IBZ, IPB, MLA, MLA-IB, P09, PCI, PhilInd.
—IE, Infotrieve, INIST.
Published by: Orden de Agustinos Recoletos, General Davila, 5 Bajo D, Madrid, 28003, Spain. TEL 34-91-5342070, FAX 34-91-5544801, oar.sezeq.ad@teleline.es.

282.9 AUS ISSN 0727-3215
➤ **AUSTRALASIAN CATHOLIC RECORD.** Text in English. 1895. q. AUD 50 (effective 2004). adv. bk.rev. bibl. index. back issues avail. **Document type:** *Journal, Academic/Scholarly.* **Description:** Seeks to be a form for the discussion of contemporary issues facing the church, particularly in Australasia. It has a special interest in Australian church history. Each issues is devoted to a theme, but there is always space for articles of broad interest reflecting local scholarship.
Related titles: Online - full text ed.
Indexed: A01, AusPAIS, CLA, CPL, MLA-IB, P28, P30, P48, P53, P54, PCI, PQC, T02.
—BLDSC (1793.630000), IE, Ingenta.
Address: 99 Albert Rd, Strathfield, NSW 2135, Australia. TEL 61-2-97529500, FAX 61-2-97466022. Ed., Pub. Rev. Gerard Kelly. adv.: B&W page AUD 150; trim 19 x 13. Circ: 1,800.

282 AUS ISSN 0084-7259
BX1685.A1
AUSTRALIAN CATHOLIC HISTORICAL SOCIETY. JOURNAL. Text in English. 1954. a. free to members (effective 2011). bk.rev. back issues avail. **Document type:** *Journal, Academic/Scholarly.* **Description:** Provides articles and book reviews on Australian catholic history as well as a brief record of catholic society activities.
Related titles: Online - full text ed.: ISSN 1838-6571.
Indexed: A26, AusPAIS, E08, G08, I05, PCI, S09.
Published by: Australian Catholic Historical Society, PO Box A621, Sydney S, NSW 1235, Australia. dgleeson@nd.edu.au.

282 AUS ISSN 1448-6326
➤ **AUSTRALIAN EJOURNAL OF THEOLOGY.** Text in English. 2003. s-a. free (effective 2011). back issues avail. **Document type:** *Journal, Academic/Scholarly.* **Description:** Focuses on scholarly exchange within the Australian and international theological community on different disciplines, including humanities, philosophy, arts, sciences, ethical and legal studies, sociology and history.
Media: Online - full text.
Indexed: A39, C27, C29, D03, D04, E13, R14, S14, S15, S18.
Published by: Australian Catholic University, School of Theology, Brisbane Campus, 1100 Nudgee Rd, Banyo, QLD 4014, Australia. http://www.acu.edu.au/acu_national/Schools/theology/. Ed. Gerard Hall TEL 61-7-36237254.

282 BRA ISSN 1980-7872
AVE MARIA. Variant title: Revista Ave Maria. Text in Portuguese. 1898. s-m. adv. bk.rev. illus. **Document type:** *Magazine, Consumer.*
Related titles: Online - full text ed.
Published by: Editora Ave Maria, Rua Martim Francisco 636, Sta cecilia, Sao Paulo, SP 01226-000, Brazil. Circ: 50,000 (controlled).

271.71 USA
AYLESFORD CARMELITE NEWSLETTER. Text in English. 1984. q. USD 2 (effective 1998). bk.rev. back issues avail. **Document type:** *Newsletter.* **Description:** Deals with Carmelite spirituality and recent trends in the involvement of the laity in Carmel.
Published by: Lay Carmelite Office, 8501 Bailey Road, Darien, IL 60561. TEL 630-969-5050, FAX 630-969-5536. Ed. Rev. Peter Byrth. Pub. Rev. Leo McCarthy. Circ: 12,000 (controlled).

282 CAN ISSN 0007-0483
B C CATHOLIC. Variant title: British Columbia Catholic. Text in English. 1931. w. CAD 32 domestic; CAD 50 in United States; CAD 65 foreign (effective 2000). adv. bk.rev.; film rev.; play rev. illus. **Document type:** *Newspaper.*
Published by: Vancouver Archdiocese, 150 Robson St, Vancouver, BC V6B 2A7, Canada. TEL 604-683-0281, FAX 604-683-8117. Ed. Paul Schratz. Circ: 20,000.

268.432 DEU ISSN 0948-0188
B D K J JOURNAL. Text in German. 1952. m. EUR 12; EUR 2 newsstand/cover (effective 2009). adv. bk.rev. stat. back issues avail. **Document type:** *Magazine, Trade.*
Formerly (until 1992): Bund der Deutschen Katholischen Jugend. Informationsdienst (0007-5833)
Published by: Bund der Deutschen Katholischen Jugend, Carl-Mosterts-Platz 1, Duesseldorf, 40477, Germany. TEL 49-211-46930, FAX 49-211-4693120, info@bdkj.de. adv.: B&W page EUR 502. Circ: 2,000 (controlled). **Co-sponsor:** Jugendhaus Duesseldorf e.V.

282 DEU ISSN 1865-4576
B K U - JOURNAL; Nachrichten - Berichte - Kommentare. (Bund Katholischer Unternehmer) Text in German. 1949. q. EUR 4 newsstand/cover (effective 2009). **Document type:** *Magazine, Consumer.*
Formerly (until 1999): B K U Rundbrief (0934-8514)
Published by: Bund Katholischer Unternehmer e.V., Georgstr 18, Cologne, 50676, Germany. TEL 49-221-272370, FAX 49-221-2723727, service@bku.de. Ed. Peter Unterberg.

282 ITA ISSN 0005-3783
BADIA GRECA DI GROTTAFERRATA. BOLLETTINO. Text in English, French, Italian, Spanish. 1910. a. EUR 45 domestic; EUR 50 foreign (effective 2008). bk.rev. illus. cum.index every 10 yrs. back issues avail. **Document type:** *Bulletin, Consumer.* **Description:** Features Medieval Bizantine culture and history.
Formerly (until1921): Roma e l'Oriente (1120-9186)
Indexed: CERDIC, FR.
Published by: (Monastero Esarchico di Grottaferrata), Badia Greca di Grottaferrata, Corso del Popolo, 128, Grottaferrata, RM 00046, Italy. TEL 39-06-9459309, FAX 39-06-9458311. Circ: 500.

282 DEU ISSN 1436-0802
BAYERISCHES SONNTAGSBLATT; Wochenzeitschrift fuer die katholische Familie. Text in German. 1879. w. (Sun.). looseleaf. EUR 88.40; EUR 1.70 newsstand/cover (effective 2009). adv. bk.rev.; film rev. abstr.; illus. **Document type:** *Newspaper, Consumer.*
Formerly (until 1994): Bayerisches Sonntagsblatt fuer die Katholische Familie (0005-7177)
Published by: Bayerisches Sonntagsblatt Verlags GmbH, Lange Str 335, Hamm, 59067, Germany. TEL 49-2381-9404030, FAX 49-2381-9404070. Ed., R&P Heribert Boeller. Adv. contact Rudolf Thiemann. B&W page EUR 1,260, color page EUR 2,016. Circ: 14,066 (paid and controlled).

282.763 USA ISSN 0274-8126
THE BAYOU CATHOLIC. Text in English. 1980. w. (Thu.). USD 15 (effective 2000). adv. illus. 24 p./no. 5 cols./p.; back issues avail. **Document type:** *Newspaper.* **Description:** Geared toward Roman Catholics living in Southern Louisiana. Covers church and church related community news and some sports.
Published by: (Diocese of Houma-Thibodaux), H T Publishing Co., 2779 Hwy, 311, Schriever, LA 70395. TEL 504-850-3132, FAX 504-850-3215, editor@cajux.net. Ed., Pub., R&P Louis G Aguirre. Adv. contact Peggy Adams. B&W page USD 776.10, color page USD 1,058; trim 13 x 9.81. Circ: 37,000 (paid). Wire service: CaNS.

282.477 CAN ISSN 0382-6384
BEACON; Ukrainian rite bi-monthly. Text in English. 1966. bi-m. CAD 18 (effective 2001). adv. bk.rev. **Document type:** *Magazine, Academic/Scholarly.* **Description:** Covers news and theological articles, as well as human-interest articles in the life of the Ukrainian community.
Related titles: ◆ Ukrainian ed.: Svitlo. ISSN 0039-7164.
Published by: (Order of Saint Basil-the-Great in Canada), Basilian Press, 265 Bering Ave, Toronto, ON M6J 3G9, Canada. TEL 416-234-1212. Ed., Pub., R&P Rev. Ignatius Holowaychuk. Adv. contact Bro Stephen Krysak. Circ: 1,300.

255.1 DEU ISSN 0936-3858
BEITRAEGE ZUR GESCHICHTE DES ALTEN MOENCHTUMS UND DES BENEDIKTINERTUMS. Text in German. 1912. irreg., latest vol.46, 1999. price varies. **Document type:** *Monographic series, Academic/Scholarly.*
Formerly (until 1984): Beitraege zur Geschichte des Alten Moenchtums und des Benediktinerordens (0342-1341)
Published by: Aschendorff Verlag GmbH & Co. KG, Soester Str 13, Muenster, 48135, Germany. TEL 49-251-6900, FAX 49-251-6904570, buchverlag@aschendorff.de, http://www.aschendorff-buchverlag.de.

BEITRAEGE ZUR NEUEREN ORDENS- UND FROEMMIGKEITSGESCHICHTE. *see* HISTORY—History Of Europe

230.2 DEU ISSN 0067-5172
BEITRAEGE ZUR OEKUMENISCHEN THEOLOGIE. Text in German. 1967. irreg., latest vol.27, 1997. price varies. **Document type:** *Monographic series, Academic/Scholarly.* **Description:** Scholarly publication about the ecumenical movement in the Catholic Church and the beliefs of contemporary theologians. Each issue covers a distinctive topic.
Indexed: IBR, IBZ.
Published by: Verlag Ferdinand Schoeningh GmbH, Postfach 2540, Paderborn, 33055, Germany. TEL 49-5251-1275, FAX 49-5251-127860, info@schoeningh.de, http://www.schoeningh.de. Eds. Johannes Gamberoni, Winifred Schulz. Circ: 500.

282 PRT ISSN 1645-1309
BEM AVENTURADOS FRANCISCO E JACINTA MARTO. Text in Portuguese. 2001. q. **Document type:** *Bulletin, Consumer.*
Related titles: Online - full text ed.; Polish ed.: Boldog Marto Ferenc es Jacinta. ISSN 1645-1368. 2005; French ed.: Les Bienheureux Francois et Jacinte Marto. ISSN 1645-1325. 2005; English ed.: Blessed Francisco and Jacinta Marto. ISSN 1645-1341. 2005; Italian ed.: I Beati Francesco e Giacinta Marto. ISSN 1645-1333. 2005; Spanish ed.: Beatos Francisco y Jacinta Marto. ISSN 1645-1317. 2005.
Published by: Secretariado dos Pastorinhos, Rua de sao Pedro 9, Fatima, 2496-908, Portugal. TEL 351-249-539780, FAX 351-249-539789.

255.1 NLD ISSN 0005-8734
BENEDICTIJNS TIJDSCHRIFT; voor Evangelische bezinning. Text in Dutch. 1937. q. EUR 11 (effective 2010). adv. bk.rev. bibl. back issues avail. **Document type:** *Journal, Trade.*
Formerly (until 1969): Benedictijns Tijdschrift voor Bezinning op Kerkelijk en Kloosterlijk Leven
Indexed: CERDIC.
Published by: Sint-Adelbertabdij, Abdijlaan 26, Egmond-Binnen, 1935 BH, Netherlands. TEL 31-72-5061415, gastenpater.adelbertabdij@xs4all.nl, http://www.abdijvanegmond.nl.

255.100941 GBR ISSN 1751-4673
BENEDICTINE CULTURE; a journal of practical theology produced by the Benedictine Study and Arts Centre at Ealing Abbey. Text in English. 2006 (Sep.). irreg. GBP 2.50 per vol. domestic; GBP 3 per vol. foreign (effective 2009). bk.rev.; music rev. **Document type:** *Journal, Academic/Scholarly.*
Published by: Benedictine Study & Arts Centre, 74 Castlebar Rd, Ealing, London, W5 2DD, United Kingdom. TEL 44-20-88622156, FAX 44-20-88622133, centre@bsac.ac.uk, http://www.bsac.ac.uk/site/index.html. Ed. James Leachman.

255.1 GBR ISSN 0522-8883
BX3050.E9
THE BENEDICTINE YEARBOOK (YEAR). Variant title: Benedictine and Cistercian Monastic Yearbook. Text in English. 1863. a. GBP 3.50, EUR 3.78 (effective 2009). **Document type:** *Yearbook.* **Description:** Official guide to the abbeys, priories, parishes and schools of the monks and nuns following the Rule of St Benedict in Great Britain, Ireland and their overseas foundations.
Supersedes: Benedictine Almanac
—BLDSC (1891.380000).
Published by: Ampleforth Abbey Trading, Ampleforth Abbey, Ampleforth, York YO62 4EN, United Kingdom. TEL 44-1439-766778, FAX 44-1439-766778, feedback@ampleforth.org.uk, http://www.ampleforth.org.uk/. Circ: 5,000.

255.1 USA ISSN 0005-8726
BX3001
BENEDICTINES. Text in English. 1946. s-a. USD 15 domestic; USD 18 in Canada & Mexico; USD 20 elsewhere (effective 2011). bk.rev. illus. cum.index: vols.1-9, 10-20, 21-30. 2 cols./p.; back issues avail.; reprints avail. **Document type:** *Journal, Academic/Scholarly.* **Description:** Explores issues of interest to monastic women and men. Contains articles on scripture, spirituality, community life, ministry, prayer and liturgy.
Formerly (until 1966): The Benedictine Review (0148-947X)
Related titles: Online - full text ed.: free (effective 2011) (from PQC).
Indexed: A01, A22, CERDIC, CPL, FR, MLA-IB.
Published by: (Mount St. Scholastica Convent), Mount St. Scholastica, Inc., 801 S 8th St, Atchison, KS 66002. TEL 913-360-6200, FAX 913-360-6190, patterson@mountosb.org. Ed. Barbara Ann Mayer TEL 913-342-0938.

282 DEU
BERCKERS TASCHENKALENDER. Text in German. 1955. a. EUR 5.60 (effective 2009). **Document type:** *Bulletin, Consumer.*
Former titles (until 1994): Berckers Katholischer Taschenkalender; (until 1984): Berckers Taschenkalender; (until 1976): Berckers Katholischer Taschenkalender
Published by: Butzon und Bercker GmbH, Hoogeweg 71, Kevelaer, 47623, Germany. TEL 49-2832-9290, FAX 49-2832-929211, service@bube.de, http://www.butzonbercker.de. Circ: 8,000.

282 NLD ISSN 0167-3904
BERNE. Text in Dutch. 1948. bi-m. EUR 17.20 domestic; EUR 22 foreign (effective 2010). **Document type:** *Magazine, Consumer.*
Published by: Uitgeverij Abdij van Berne, Postbus 60, Heeswijk, 5473 ZH, Netherlands. TEL 31-413-299299, FAX 31-413-299288, info@abdijvanberne.nl, http://www.uitgeverijberne.nl.

282 ITA
LA BIBBIA NELLA STORIA. Text in Italian. 1984. irreg. **Document type:** *Monographic series, Academic/Scholarly.*
Published by: Centro Editoriale Dehoniano, Via Scipione dal Ferro 4, Bologna, BO 40138, Italy. TEL 39-051-4290451, FAX 39-051-4290491, ced-amm@dehoniane.it.

220 DEU ISSN 0006-0593
BIBEL HEUTE. Text in German. 1965. q. EUR 22; EUR 12 to students (effective 2010). adv. bk.rev. illus. index, cum.index. 24 p./no.; **Document type:** *Journal, Academic/Scholarly.*
Indexed: CERDIC, DIP, IBR, IBZ.
Published by: Katholisches Bibelwerk e.V., Silberburgstr 121, Stuttgart, 70176, Germany. TEL 49-711-6192050, FAX 49-711-6192077, bibelinfo@bibelwerk.de, http://www.bibelwerk.de. Circ: 25,000.

220 DEU ISSN 0006-0623
BS410
BIBEL UND KIRCHE. Text in German. 1946. q. EUR 22; EUR 12 to students (effective 2010). adv. bk.rev. abstr. index. 48 p./no.; **Document type:** *Journal, Academic/Scholarly.*
Indexed: CERDIC, DIP, IBR, IBZ, IZBG, OTA.
—BLDSC (1947.810000).
Published by: Katholisches Bibelwerk e.V., Silberburgstr 121, Stuttgart, 70176, Germany. TEL 49-711-6192050, FAX 49-711-6192077, bibelinfo@bibelwerk.de, http://www.bibelwerk.de. Ed. Franz-Josef Ortkemper.

282 DEU
BIBELLESE PLAN. Text in German. a. EUR 1.50 (effective 2001). 16 p./no.; **Document type:** *Bulletin, Consumer.*
Formerly: Leseplan Jahreslosung
Published by: Katholisches Bibelwerk e.V., Silberburgstr 121, Stuttgart, 70176, Germany. TEL 49-711-6192050, FAX 49-711-6192077, bibelinfo@bibelwerk.de. Ed. Wolfgang Baur.

220 BRA
BIBLIA - GENTE. Text in Portuguese. 1978. w. BRL 100. illus.
Published by: (Pia Sociedade de Sao Paulo), Edicoes Paulinas, Via Raposo Tavares Km 18.5, Centro, Caixa Postal 8107, Sao Paulo, SP 01065-970, Brazil. Ed. A C D'Elboux. Circ: 120,000.

220 ESP ISSN 2171-2026
BS300
▼ **BIBLIAS HISPANICAS.** Text in Spanish. 2009. a. **Document type:** *Monographic series, Academic/Scholarly.*
Published by: Fundacion San Millan de la Cogolla, Plaza del Convento, s-n, San Millan de la Cogolla, La Rioja, 26226, Spain. TEL 34-94-1373389, FAX 34-94-1373390.

220 ITA ISSN 0006-0887
BIBLICA. Text in English, French, German, Italian, Latin, Spanish. 1920. q. bk.rev. index, cum.index: vols.1-25, vols.26-50. back issues avail. **Document type:** *Journal, Academic/Scholarly.* **Description:** Explores the scientific study of scripture.
Related titles: Online - full text ed.: free (effective 2011); ◆ Supplement(s): Elenchus of Biblica. ISSN 1123-5608.
Indexed: A20, A21, A22, ASCA, ArtHuCI, BibLing, CERDIC, CurCont, DIP, FR, IBR, IBZ, IZBG, MLA-IB, OTA, PCI, PerIslam, R&TA, RI-1, RI-2, SCOPUS, W07.
—IE, Infotrieve, INIST.
Published by: Pontificio Istituto Biblico/Pontifical Biblical Institute, Via della Pilotta 25, Rome, 00187, Italy. TEL 39-06-695261, FAX 39-06-695266211, http://www.biblico.it. Ed. Horacio Simian-Yofre. Circ: 1,800.

220 ITA
BIBLICA ET ORIENTALIA. Text in Italian, English, French, German. 1928. irreg., latest vol.45, 1997. price varies. **Document type:** *Monographic series, Academic/Scholarly.* **Description:** Covers aspects of the Bible which are directly related to the ancient Near Eastern background out of which the Bible came.
Published by: Pontificio Istituto Biblico/Pontifical Biblical Institute, Via della Pilotta 25, Rome, 00187, Italy. TEL 39-06-695261, FAX 39-06-695266211, http://www.biblico.it. Ed. Agustinus Gianto.

BIBLIOGRAFIA MISSIONARIA. *see* RELIGIONS AND THEOLOGY—Abstracting, Bibliographies, Statistics

BIBLIOGRAPHIA FRANCISCANA. *see* RELIGIONS AND THEOLOGY—Abstracting, Bibliographies, Statistics

BIBLIOTECA APOSTOLICA VATICANA. CATALOGHI E NORME DI CATALOGAZIONE. *see* RELIGIONS AND THEOLOGY—Abstracting, Bibliographies, Statistics

282 VAT
BIBLIOTECA APOSTOLICA VATICANA. EDIZIONI ILLUSTRATE. (In 3 subseries: A: Illustrazioni di Codici; B: Illustrazioni di Documenti; C: Illustrazioni di Monumenti) Text in Italian. 1902. irreg. price varies.
Published by: Biblioteca Apostolica Vaticana, 00120, Vatican City. TEL 396-6-69885051, FAX 396-6-69884795.

282 VAT
BIBLIOTECA APOSTOLICA VATICANA. STUDI E TESTI. Text in Italian. 1900. irreg., latest vol.388, 1998. price varies.
Indexed: CCMJ, RASB.
Published by: Biblioteca Apostolica Vaticana, 00120, Vatican City. TEL 396-6-69885051, FAX 396-6-69884795.

BIBLIOTHECA ASCETICO-MYSTICA. *see* RELIGIONS AND THEOLOGY—Abstracting, Bibliographies, Statistics

255.3 ITA
BIBLIOTHECA FRANCISCANA ASCETICA MEDII AEVI. Text in Latin. 1904. irreg., latest vol.13, 1997. price varies. **Document type:** *Monographic series, Academic/Scholarly.*
Published by: Collegio San Bonaventura/Collegium S Bonaventurae ad Claras Aquas, Via Vecchia per Marino 28-30, Grottaferrata, 00046, Italy. http://www.fratiquaracchi.it.

271.53 ITA ISSN 2037-8254
BIBLIOTHECA INSTITUTI HISTORICI SOCIETATIS IESU. Text in Italian. 1941. irreg., latest vol.50, 1997. adv. back issues avail. **Document type:** *Monographic series, Academic/Scholarly.* **Description:** Contains research monographs on history of the Jesuits worldwide.
Published by: Institutum Historicum Societatis Iesu/Jesuit Historical Institute, Via dei Penitenzieri 20, Rome, 00193, Italy.

282 ITA ISSN 1971-3703
BIBLIOTHECA MERCEDARIA. Text in Multiple languages. 1986. irreg. **Document type:** *Monographic series, Academic/Scholarly.*
Formerly (until 2006): Biblioteca Mercedaria (1971-3835)
Published by: Institutum Historicum Ordinis de Mercede, Via Monte Carmelo 3, Rome, 00166, Italy. http://www.ordinedellamercede.org.

282 ITA ISSN 0067-8163
BIBLIOTHECA SERAPHICO-CAPUCCINA. SECTIO HISTORICA. Text in Italian. 1932. irreg., latest vol.60, 1999. price varies. index. **Document type:** *Monographic series, Academic/Scholarly.*
Published by: Frati Minori Cappuccini, Istituto Storico/Ordo Fratrum Minorum Capuccinorum, Circonvallazione Occidentale 6850, Rome, RM 00163, Italy. TEL 39-06-660521, FAX 39-06-66052532, http://www.istcap.org.

BIBLIOTHEKE; Zeitschrift fuer katholische Buecherei- und Medienarbeit. *see* LIBRARY AND INFORMATION SCIENCES

262.3 BEL ISSN 0067-8279
BIBLIOTHEQUE DE LA REVUE D'HISTOIRE ECCLESIASTIQUE. Text in Dutch, English, French, Italian. 1928. irreg. **Document type:** *Monographic series, Academic/Scholarly.*
Published by: Universite Catholique de Louvain, Bureau de la Revue d'Histoire Ecclesiastique, Bibliotheque, College Erasme, Louvain-la-Neuve, 1348, Belgium. Ed. Roger Aubert. Circ: 500.

262.9 DEU
BISCHOEFLICHES ORDINARIAT AUGSBURG. RECHTSSAMMLUNG. Text in German. 1990. a. **Document type:** *Bulletin.*

R

Published by: (Bischoefliches Ordinariat Augsburg), Verlag Bischoefliches Ordinariat Augsburg, Postfach 110349, Augsburg, 86028, Germany. TEL 49-821-3166291, FAX 49-821-3166189.

266.2 AUS
BLAZE. Text in English. 1990. q. free (effective 2009). back issues avail. **Document type:** *Magazine, Trade.* **Description:** Aims to present subjects with a clear proclamation of bible truth and Christian teaching.
Related titles: Online - full text ed.: free (effective 2009).
Published by: Flame Ministries International, Subiaco E, PO Box 8133, Perth, W.A. 6008, Australia. TEL 61-8-93823668, FAX 61-8-83824080, fmi@flameministries.org.

282 SVN ISSN 0006-5722
BR9.S5
BOGOSLOVNI VESTNIK. Text in Slovenian; Text occasionally in English, German. 1921-1944; resumed 1965. q. USD 53 (effective 2005). bk.rev.
Related titles: Online - full text ed.: ISSN 1581-2987. 1999.
Indexed: FR, MLA-IB.
—BLDSC (2118.180100), INIST.
Published by: Univerza v Ljubljani, Teoloska Fakultet, Poljanska 4, p p 2007, Ljubljana, 1000, Slovenia. TEL 386-1-4345810. Ed. Anton Mlinar. Circ: 700.

282 HRV ISSN 0352-3101
BOGOSLOVSKA SMOTRA. Text in Serbo-Croatian. 1910. q. **Document type:** *Journal, Academic/Scholarly.*
Indexed: A26, RILM.
Published by: Sveuciliste u Zagrebu, Katolicki Bogoslovni Fakultet, Katehetski Institut, Vlaska 38, pp 432, Zagreb, HR-10001, Croatia. TEL 385-1-4890402, FAX 385-1-4814704. Ed. Tomislav Z Tensek.

282.599 PHL ISSN 0116-1830
BOLETIN ECLESIASTICO DE FILIPINAS; official organ of the Catholic hierarchy of the Philippines. Text in English. 1923. bi-m. PHP 370, USD 40; PHP 65, USD 8 newsstand/cover (effective 1999). adv. bk.rev. bibl. index. **Description:** Contains pastoral and encyclical letters, documents from the Catholic Bishops' Conference of the Philippines, homiletics, canon law cases, and continued priestly formation articles.
Indexed: BAS, CLA.
Published by: University of Santo Tomas, Ecclesiastical Faculties, Ecclesiastical Publications Office, Espana St, Manila, 1008, Philippines. TEL 731-3522, FAX 731-3522, publishing@ust.edu.ph. Ed. Vincente Cajilig. Circ: 1,200.

282 BOL
BOLIVIA: GUIA ECLESIASTICA. Text in Spanish. 1977. irreg., latest vol.3. USD 15. illus. **Document type:** *Directory.*
Formerly: Guia de la Iglesia
Published by: Conferencia Episcopal Boliviana, Secretariado General, Casilla 7857, La Paz, Bolivia. TEL 377878, FAX 02-392326.

282 ITA ISSN 0404-9462
BOLLETTINO DI S. NICOLA. Text mainly in Italian. 1906. m. bk.rev. bibl. index. back issues avail. **Document type:** *Magazine, Consumer.*
Published by: Padri Domenicani della Basilica di S. Nicola di Bari, Basilica di S. Nicola, Bari, BA 70122, Italy.

282 ITA ISSN 0391-5867
IL BOLLETTINO SALESIANO; rivista fondata da San Giovanni Bosco. Text in Italian. 1877. m. free. bk.rev. bibl.; illus. back issues avail. **Document type:** *Magazine, Consumer.*
Related titles: Online - full text ed.
Published by: Fondazione Don Bosco nel Mondo, Via della Pisana 1111, Rome, RM 00163, Italy. TEL 39-06-656121, FAX 39-06-65612643, donbosconelmondo@sdb.org, http://www.fdbnm.org. Circ: 350,000.

282.09 ITA ISSN 0394-1841
BOLLETTINO STORICO DELLA BASILICATA. Text in Italian. 1985. a. EUR 15.49 (effective 2004). bk.rev. **Document type:** *Journal, Academic/Scholarly.*
Indexed: B24.
Published by: Edizioni Osanna Srl, Via Appia 3a, Venosa, PZ 85029, Italy. TEL 39-0972-35952, FAX 39-0972-35723, osanna@osannaedizioni.it, http://www.osannaedizioni.it.

241.66 USA
BONDINGS. Text in English. 1978. q. USD 10 domestic; USD 15 foreign (effective 2003). adv. bk.rev. back issues avail. **Document type:** *Newspaper, Consumer.* **Description:** Addresses issues relating to homosexuality and the Catholic Church.
Published by: New Ways Ministry, 4012 29th St., Mt. Rainier, MD 20712. TEL 301-277-5674, FAX 301-864-6948. Ed., R&P, Adv. contact John Gallagher. Circ: 1,500 (paid); 3,200 (controlled).

282 DEU ISSN 0006-7113
BONIFATIUSBLATT. Text in German. 1849. q. EUR 2.50 (effective 2009). illus.; stat. **Document type:** *Newsletter, Consumer.* **Description:** Reports on Catholic minorities, so-called "Diaspora-Church", in Germany and Scandinavian countries.
Related titles: Talking Book ed.
Published by: Bonifatiuswerk der Deutschen Katholiken e.V., Kamp 22, Paderborn, 33098, Germany. TEL 49-5251-29960, FAX 49-5251-299688, info@bonifatiuswerk.de, http://www.bonifatiuswerk.de. Ed. Christoph Schommer. Circ: 280,000 (controlled).

282 DEU ISSN 0935-8897
BONIFATIUSBOTE. Text in German. 1884. w. (Sun.). EUR 6.55 per month (effective 2010). adv. **Document type:** *Newspaper, Consumer.*
Published by: (Bischoefliches Generalvikariat Fulda), Gesellschaft fuer kirchliche Publizistik Mainz GmbH, Erich-Dombrowski-Str 2, Mainz, 55127, Germany. TEL 49-6131-484150, FAX 49-6131-484158, hkaus@vrm.de. Ed. Johannes Becher. Adv. contact Sylvia Ehrengard. B&W page EUR 3,206; trim 325 x 458. Circ: 8,702 (paid and controlled).

255.3 CAN ISSN 0225-0233
BONNE NOUVELLE. Text in French. 1911. 10/yr. CAD 8. adv. bk.rev. bibl.; charts; illus.; stat. back issues avail.
Indexed: CERDIC.
Published by: Secular Franciscan Order, 5730 bd Pie 9, Montreal, PQ H1X 2B9, Canada. TEL 514-727-8483. Circ: 4,000.

230.2 DEU
BONNER BEITRAEGE ZUR KIRCHENGESCHICHTE. Text in German. 1972. irreg., latest vol.28, 2011. price varies. **Document type:** *Monographic series, Academic/Scholarly.*
Published by: Boehlau Verlag GmbH & Cie, Ursulaplatz 1, Cologne, 50668, Germany. TEL 49-221-913900, FAX 49-221-9139011, vertrieb@boehlau.de, http://www.boehlau.de.

282 USA ISSN 1930-255X
THE BOSTON CATHOLIC TELEVISION MONTHLY. Text in English. 2005. m. **Document type:** *Magazine, Consumer.*
Published by: Boston Catholic Television, 34 Chestnut St, Watertown, MA 02472-2339. http://www.catholictv.org.

282 NLD ISSN 0006-8349
BOUWEN AAN DE NIEUWE AARDE. Text in Dutch. 1953. bi-m. EUR 15 domestic; EUR 17.50 foreign (effective 2010). bk.rev. 40 p./no. 2 cols./p.; **Description:** Promotes renewal of the Christian church by the power of the Holy Spirit.
Published by: Stichting Bouwen aan de Nieuwe Aarde, Prins Karelstraat 100, Helmond, 5701 VM, Netherlands. TEL 31-492-554644, info@kcv-net.nl, http://kcv.nl.dnnmax.com. Ed. K Slijkerman.

282 SVN ISSN 1318-9328
BOZJE OKOLJE. Text in Slovenian; Summaries in English. 1977. bi-m. EUR 21 (effective 2007). **Document type:** *Magazine, Consumer.*
Published by: Druzina, Krekov trg 1, p.p. 95, Ljubljana, 1001, Slovenia. TEL 386-1-3602845, FAX 386-1-3602800. Ed. Marjan Pogacnik. Circ: 2,500.

268 NLD ISSN 0920-9476
DE BRANDENDE LAMP; Informatiebulletin van de titus brandsma stichting. Text in Dutch. 1980. q. EUR 10 (effective 2010). illus. **Document type:** *Newsletter, Consumer.* **Description:** Discusses issues of the Catholic Church.
Published by: Titus Brandsma Stichting (Tibrasti), Haagweg 141, Rijswijk (ZH), 22 SAG, Netherlands. TEL 31-70-3954938, janla.r@kpnplanet.nl, http://www.we-believe-in-god.com. Ed. J A A Leechburch Auwers.

282 SVN ISSN 1408-0192
BRAT FRANCISEK; slovenska revija s Franciskovim duhom. Text in Slovenian. 1948. bi-m. EUR 8.35 (effective 2007). bk.rev. 48 p./no.; back issues avail. **Document type:** *Magazine, Consumer.* **Description:** Focuses on Franciscan spirituality, the secular Franciscan order and ecology.
Formerly (until 1993): Srecanja (0038-8777)
Indexed: MLA-IB.
Published by: Zalozba Brat Francisek, Presernov trg 4, Ljubljana, Slovenia. TEL 386-1-2429312, FAX 386-1-2429313, zbf@rkc.si, http://franciskani.rkc.si/zbf/zalozba.html. Ed. Mihael S Vovk. Circ: 2,000.

282 RUS
BRATSKII VESTNIK. Text in Russian. 1993. bi-m. USD 145 in the Americas (effective 2000).
Indexed: RASB.
Published by: Federatsiya Soyuzov Evangel'skikh Khristian-Baptistov, Malyi Vuzovskii per., 3, Moscow, 109028, Russian Federation. TEL 7-095-9179626. **Dist. by:** East View Information Services, 10601 Wayzata Blvd, Minneapolis, MN 55305. TEL 952-252-1201, 800-477-1005, FAX 952-252-1202, info@eastview.com, http://www.eastview.com.

282 CAN ISSN 0821-168X
THE BREAD OF LIFE. Text in English. 1977. bi-m. CAD 30 (effective 2000). adv. bk.rev. **Document type:** *Newsletter, Consumer.* **Description:** Designed to encourage spiritual growth in areas of renewal in the Catholic Church today.
Published by: C.C.S.O. Bread of Life Renewal Centre, P O Box 395, Hamilton, ON L8N 3H8, Canada. TEL 905-529-4496, FAX 905-529-5373. Ed., R&P Rev. Peter B Coughlin. Adv. contact Christine Labrosse. Circ: 3,500.

282 GBR
BRIDGE (KINGSTON-UPON-THAMES). Text in English. 1959. q. free (effective 2009). back issues avail. **Document type:** *Magazine, Trade.* **Description:** Provides international news of the work of the organization and its personnel, including publicity, information, communication with friends and supporters. Summarizes the Catholic Church's teaching on various subjects.
Published by: Sons of Divine Providence, 13 Lower Teddington Rd, Hampton Wick, Kingston upon Thames, Surrey KT1 4EU, United Kingdom. TEL 44-20-89775130, FAX 44-20-89770105, info@sonsofdivine.org. Ed., R&P Malcolm Dyer.

255.3 ITA
BULLARIUM FRANCISCANUM. Text in Latin. 1939. irreg., latest vol.30, 1990. price varies. **Document type:** *Monographic series, Academic/Scholarly.*
Published by: Collegio San Bonaventura/Collegium S Bonaventurae ad Claras Aquas, Via Vecchia per Marino 28-30, Grottaferrata, 00046, Italy. http://www.fratiquaracchi.it.

262 FRA ISSN 0007-4322
BX802
BULLETIN DE LITTERATURE ECCLESIASTIQUE. Text in French. 1899. q. EUR 58 domestic; EUR 65 foreign (effective 2009). bk.rev. bibl. index. back issues avail. **Document type:** *Journal, Academic/Scholarly.*
Former titles (until 1899): Institut Catholique de Toulouse. Bulletin Theologique, Scientifique et Litteraire (0988-2340); (until 1889): Institut Catholique de Toulouse. Bulletin (0988-2332)
Indexed: CERDIC, DIP, FR, IBR, IBZ, IPB, MLA, MLA-IB, OTA, RILM.
—INIST.
Published by: Institut Catholique de Toulouse, 31 rue de la Fonderie, BP 7012, Toulouse, Cedex 7 31068, France. TEL 33-5-61368100, FAX 33-5-61368108. Ed. Pierre Deberge. Circ: 700.

200.92 FRA ISSN 0337-7148
BULLETIN DE SAINT-SULPICE. Text in French, English, Spanish. 1953. a. USD 20 foreign (effective 2000). **Document type:** *Bulletin.* **Description:** Studies on the development of Catholic clergy.
Formerly (until 1970): Compagnie de Saint Sulpice. Bulletin du Comite des Etudes
Published by: Compagnie des Pretres de Saint-Sulpice, 6 rue du Regard, Paris, 75006, France.

BULLETIN D'HISTOIRE CISTERCIENNE/CISTERCIAN HISTORY ABSTRACTS. *see* RELIGIONS AND THEOLOGY—Abstracting, Bibliographies, Statistics

282 GBR
C A F O D MAGAZINE. Text in English. 1993. 3/yr. free. bk.rev.
Published by: Catholic Fund for Overseas Development, Stockwell Rd, Romero Close, London, SW9 9TY, United Kingdom. TEL 44-207-7337900, FAX 44-207-2749630. Ed. Christina Holt. Circ: 20,000.

266.2 GBR
C A F O D REPORT. Text in English. 1966. s-a. free. **Document type:** *Magazine, Consumer.*
Formerly (until 1992): C A F O D Journal
Published by: Catholic Fund for Overseas Development, Stockwell Rd, Romero Close, London, SW9 9TY, United Kingdom. TEL 44-207-7337900, FAX 44-207-2749630, TELEX 893347 CAFOD G. Ed. Christina Holt. Circ: 16,000 (free).

282.73 USA ISSN 1092-9770
BX905
C A R A CATHOLIC MINISTRY FORMATION DIRECTORY; US Catholic institutions for the training of candidates for the priesthood, the diaconate, and lay ministry. Text in English. 1965. biennial. USD 47 (effective 2000). back issues avail. **Document type:** *Directory.*
Formerly (until 1997): C A R A Seminary Directory
Published by: Center for Applied Research in the Apostolate, 2300 Wisconsin Ave, NW, Suite 400, Washington, DC 20007. TEL 202-687-8080, FAX 202-687-8083, cara@georgetown.edu, http://cara.georgetown.edu/. Ed. Bryan T Froehle. Circ: 500 (paid).

282 USA
C C I C A ANNUAL. Text in English. 1982. a. USD 12 (effective 1999). back issues avail. **Document type:** *Proceedings.*
Published by: Catholic Commission on Intellectual and Cultural Affairs, c/o University of Notre Dame, 1135 Flanner Hall, Notre Dame, IN 46556-5611. TEL 219-631-8471, FAX 219-631-8471. Ed. R Scott Appleby. Circ: 350.

C H A C INFO/INFO A C C S. *see* HEALTH FACILITIES AND ADMINISTRATION

C P F I NEWSLETTER. *see* PHARMACY AND PHARMACOLOGY

282 COD ISSN 0008-0047
BL2400
CAHIERS DES RELIGIONS AFRICAINES. Text in English, French. 1967. s-a. USD 35. adv. bk.rev. bibl.; illus. **Document type:** *Journal, Academic/Scholarly.*
Indexed: A21, AICP, ASD, CCA, CERDIC, FR, MLA-IB, P30, RI-1, RI-2, RILM.
Published by: Faculte Catholique de Kinshasa, BP 1534, Kinshasa-Limite, Congo, Dem. Republic. TEL 78476. Ed. Vincent Mulago. Circ: 1,000. **Co-sponsor:** Centre d'Etudes de Religions Africaines.

282 CMR
CAMEROON PANORAMA. Text in English. 1962. m.
Address: BP 46, Buea, Cameroon. TEL 32-22-40. Ed. Sr Mercy Horgan. Circ: 4,000.

282 NLD ISSN 0008-221X
CAMILLUSBODE. Text in Dutch. 1950. s-a. free (effective 2010). **Document type:** *Bulletin.*
Formerly: St. Camillusbode
Published by: Provincialaat van de Camillianen, Heinsbergerweg 174, Roermond, 6045 CK, Netherlands. TEL 31-475-321985, FAX 31-475-324784. Circ: 2,000.

282 ITA ISSN 1971-1867
CAMPANIA SERAFICA. Text in Italian. 1927. m. **Document type:** *Magazine, Consumer.*
Published by: Telediffusione Cattolica - Editori Cappuccini Napoli (T D C - E C N), Via Macedonia 13, Naples, 80137, Italy. TEL 39-081-7519403, FAX 39-081-7519374, www.ofmcappuccininapoli.it.

262.9 CAN ISSN 0703-1963
CANADIAN CANON LAW SOCIETY. NEWSLETTER. Text and summaries in English, French. 1975. s-a. membership. back issues avail.
Published by: Canadian Canon Law Society, 223 Main St, Ottawa, ON K1S 1C4, Canada. TEL 613-751-4024, FAX 613-751-4036. Ed. Michael Tremblay. Circ: 400.

282.71 CAN ISSN 1182-9214
BX1419
CANADIAN CATHOLIC HISTORICAL ASSOCIATION. BULLETIN. Text in English. 1986. biennial.
Indexed: C05, CA, T02.
Published by: Canadian Catholic Historical Association, c/o Secretary General, 1155 Yonge St, Toronto, ON M4T 1W2, Canada. TEL 416-968-3683, FAX 416-921-1673. Ed. Terry Fay.

CANADIAN CHURCH HISTORICAL SOCIETY JOURNAL. *see* RELIGIONS AND THEOLOGY—Protestant

264 CAN
CANADIAN CONFERENCE OF CATHOLIC BISHOPS. NATIONAL BULLETIN ON LITURGY. Key Title: National Bulletin on Liturgy. Text in English. 1965. 4/yr. CAD 17 domestic; USD 20 in United States; USD 27 elsewhere. bk.rev. cum.index: 1965-77, 1978-85. back issues avail.; reprints avail. **Document type:** *Bulletin.* **Description:** For parishes, schools, communities as they prepare, celebrate, and improve their life of worship and prayer. Primarily pastoral in scope.
Formerly: Canadian Catholic Conference. National Bulletin on Liturgy (0084-8425)
Related titles: Microfilm ed.: (from PQC).
Indexed: A22, CPL, RILM.
—CCC.
Published by: Canadian Conference of Catholic Bishops, Publications Service/Conference des Eveques Catholiques du Canada, 90 Parent Ave, Ottawa, ON K1N 7B1, Canada. TEL 613-241-9461, FAX 613-241-5090. Ed. J Frank Henderson. R&P Johanne Gnassi. Circ: 3,500.

CANON LAW ABSTRACTS; half-yearly review of periodical literature in canon law. *see* RELIGIONS AND THEOLOGY—Abstracting, Bibliographies, Statistics

282 DEU ISSN 0722-4567
CANONISTICA. Text in German. 1979. irreg., latest vol.7, 1982. price varies. **Document type:** *Monographic series, Academic/Scholarly.*
Published by: Paulinus Verlag GmbH, Maximineracht 11c, Trier, 54295, Germany. TEL 49-651-46080, FAX 49-651-4608221, verlag@paulinus.de, http://www.paulinus.de.

268.434 CAN ISSN 0835-2003
CARAVAN; a resource for those engaged in animating adult faith formation. Text in English. 1987. q. CAD 16 domestic; USD 18 in United States; USD 24 elsewhere. bk.rev. charts; illus.; stat. **Document type:** *Bulletin.* **Description:** News about workshops, research, upcoming conferences.
Published by: Canadian Conference of Catholic Bishops, Publications Service/Conference des Eveques Catholiques du Canada, 90 Parent Ave, Ottawa, ON K1N 7B1, Canada. TEL 613-241-9461, FAX 613-241-5090. Ed. Joanne Chafe. Circ: 1,000.

282.092 PHL
CARDINAL BEA STUDIES. Short title: C B S. Text in English. 1970. irreg., latest vol.7, 1977.
Published by: Cardinal Bea Institute for Ecumenical Studies, PO Box 4082, Manila, Philippines. Ed. Pedro S de Achutegui. Circ: 750.

282 LTU ISSN 0236-2716
BX2347
CARITAS. Text in Lithuanian. 1989. m. USD 15. bk.rev.
Published by: Lithuanian Caritas Federation, Vilniaus 29, Kaunas, 3000, Lithuania. TEL 370-7-209683, FAX 370-7-205549. Ed. Albina Pribushauskaite. Circ: 13,000.

CARITAS UPDATE; the Catholic agency for justice, peace and development. *see* SOCIAL SERVICES AND WELFARE

255.71 ITA ISSN 0394-7742
BX3201
CARMEL IN THE WORLD. Text in English. 1961. 3/yr. EUR 10 (effective 2009). adv. **Document type:** *Magazine, Consumer.* **Description:** Features readings on Carmelite spirituality, especially for laity.
Published by: (Order of Carmelites), Edizioni Carmelitane, Via Sforza Pallavicini 10, Rome, 00193, Italy. TEL 39-06-68100886, FAX 39-06-68100887, edizioni@ocarm.org, http://www.carmelites.info/edizioni/. Circ: 800.

255.71 ITA ISSN 0394-7750
CARMEL IN THE WORLD PAPERBACKS. Text in English, Italian, Spanish. 1982. irreg. price varies. adv. **Document type:** *Monographic series, Academic/Scholarly.* **Description:** Forum includes Carmelite spirituality biography and popular treatment.
Published by: (Institutum Carmelitanum), Edizioni Carmelitane, Via Sforza Pallavicini 10, Rome, 00193, Italy. TEL 39-06-68100886, FAX 39-06-68100887, edizioni@ocarm.org, http://www.carmelites.info/edizioni/. Circ: 1,000.

255.71 USA ISSN 0887-123X
BX3201
CARMELITE DIGEST. Text in English. q. USD 15; USD 19 foreign.
Published by: Discalced Carmelites, PO Box 3180, San Jose, CA 95156. TEL 408-286-8505, FAX 408-287-8748. Ed. David Centner. adv.: B&W page USD 300; trim 8.5 x 5.5. Circ: 2,500 (paid).

255.71 USA
CARMELITE REVIEW. Text in English. 1962. q. USD 10 (effective 1999). back issues avail. **Document type:** *Newspaper.* **Description:** Keeps English speaking Carmelite priests and brothers up to date on information on their lives and ministry.
Published by: Canadian - American Carmelite Province, Society of Mt. Carmel in Illinois, 6725 Reed Rd, Houston, TX 77087-6830. TEL 713-644-5741, FAX 708-969-3376. Ed., R&P Rev. William Harry. Pub. Rev. Leo McCarthy. Circ: 725.

255.71 ITA ISSN 0008-6673
BX3201
CARMELUS; commentarii ab Instituto Carmelitano editi. Text in English, French, German, Italian, Latin, Spanish. 1954. 2/yr. EUR 31 domestic; EUR 37 foreign (effective 2009). adv. bk.rev. bibl. index. back issues avail. **Document type:** *Journal, Academic/Scholarly.* **Description:** Contains original articles on theology, with emphasis on spirituality and mariology and history.
Indexed: A22, BibInd, DIP, FR, IBR, IBZ, MLA-IB.
—IE, Ingenta, INIST.
Published by: (Order of Carmelites), Edizioni Carmelitane, Via Sforza Pallavicini 10, Rome, 00193, Italy. TEL 39-06-68100886, FAX 39-06-68100887, edizioni@ocarm.org, http://www.carmelites.info/edizioni/. Circ: 600.

282 FRA ISSN 2105-7338
CARREFOURS D'ALSACE. Text in French. 1987. m.
Related titles: German ed.: ISSN 2105-7346.
Published by: Alsace Media, 16 Rue Brulee, Strasbourg, France. TEL 33-3-88212424, FAX 33-3-88212436, http://www.diocese-alsace.fr.

282 USA
CASA CRY. Text in English. 1972. m. free. back issues avail.; reprints avail. **Document type:** *Newsletter.* **Description:** Update on work of Casa Maria Catholic Worker community.
Published by: Casa Maria Catholic Worker, 5206, Milwaukee, WI 53205-0206. TEL 414-344-5745. Ed. Don Timmerman. Circ: 2,220.

CATALYST (BOTSFORD). *see* SOCIAL SERVICES AND WELFARE

282 ITA ISSN 0391-5433
CATECHESI. Text in Italian. 1932. 6/yr. EUR 25 domestic; EUR 35 foreign (effective 2009). **Document type:** *Magazine, Consumer.*
Indexed: CERDIC.
Published by: (C E C Don Bosco), Editrice Elledici, Corso Francia 214, Cascine Vica - Rivoli, TO 10098, Italy. TEL 39-011-9552111, FAX 39-011-9574048, mail@elledici.org, http://www.elledici.org.

282 USA ISSN 1547-7908
BX1968
CATECHETICAL LEADER. Abbreviated title: C L. Text in English. bi-m. USD 24 to non-members; free to members (effective 2005). **Document type:** *Magazine, Consumer.*
Published by: National Conference for Catechetical Leadership, 3021 4th St N E, Washington, DC 20017. TEL 202-636-3826, FAX 202-832-2712, http:www.nccl.org. Ed. Joyce A Crider.

238 USA ISSN 0008-7726
BX1968
CATECHIST. Text in English. 1967. 7/yr. USD 24.95 domestic; USD 28.95 foreign (effective 2005). bk.rev.; film rev. illus. **Document type:** *Magazine, Consumer.* **Description:** Articles, announcements, and services pertaining to Catholic education.
Related titles: Online - full text ed.
Indexed: A22, CERDIC, CPL, E03, ERI, MRD, P02, P18, P28, P48, P53, P54, P55, PQC, T02.
—CCC.
Published by: Peter Li Education Group, 2621 Dryden Rd, Ste 300, Dayton, OH 45439. TEL 937-293-1415, 800-523-4625, FAX 937-293-1310, http://www.peterli.com. Eds. Kass Dotterweich, Mary Noschang. Adv. contacts Bret Thomas, Rosemarie Brown. Circ: 52,000.

282 ITA ISSN 1825-1757
CATECHISTI PARROCCHIALI. Text in Italian. 1964. m. **Document type:** *Magazine, Consumer.*
Published by: Paoline Editoriale, Via Po 75, Rome, 00145, Italy. fsp@paoline.it, http://www.paoline.it.

282 USA ISSN 1040-659X
CATECHUMENATE; a journal of Christian initiation. Text in English. 1978. bi-m. USD 20 domestic; USD 25 foreign (effective 2009). bk.rev. index. back issues avail. **Document type:** *Journal, Academic/Scholarly.* **Description:** Contains essential information for catechists of children and adults, parish staff, and parents.
Formerly (until 1987): Chicago Catechumenate
Indexed: CPL.
Published by: Liturgy Training Publications, 3949 South Racine Ave, Chicago, IL 60609. TEL 773-579-4900, 800-933-1800, orders@ltp.org.

282 GBR ISSN 0008-7769
CATENA. Text in English. 1917. m. GBP 1.50 newsstand/cover; free (effective 2009). back issues avail. **Document type:** *Journal, Academic/Scholarly.* **Description:** Designed for the members of the Catena Association members.
Related titles: Online - full text ed.
—CCC.
Published by: Catenian Association, c o Jai Milward, 1 Copthall House, 2nd Fl, Station Sq, Coventry, West Midlands CV1 2FY, United Kingdom. TEL 44-24-76224533, FAX 44-24-76224544, membership.catena@btconnect.com. Ed. Gil Whale TEL 44-1543-256041.

282 GBR
THE CATHOLIC. Text in English. 1896. a. USD 20. adv. bk.rev. bibl. **Description:** Contains reports for members of the society detailing publishing work carried out and financial position.
Formerly (until Jul. 1989): The Catholic (0411-275X)
Published by: Incorporated Catholic Truth Society, 40-46 Harleyford Rd, London, SE11 5AY, United Kingdom. TEL 44-20-7640-0042, FAX 44-20-7640-0046. Ed. Christopher Ralls. Circ: 25,000 (controlled).

282 USA ISSN 0745-399X
CATHOLIC ACCENT. Text in English. 1961. w. (Thu.). USD 14 in state to individuals; USD 16 out of state to individuals; USD 35 foreign. adv. **Document type:** *Newspaper.*
Related titles: Microform ed.; Online - full text ed.
Published by: Greensburg Catholic Accent and Communications, Inc., 723 E Pittsburgh St, Greensburg, PA 15601. TEL 724-834-4010, FAX 724-836-5650. Ed. Angela A Burrows. Adv. contact Rose Marie Govi. Circ: 54,000. Wire service: CaNS.

282 USA ISSN 0008-7904
CATHOLIC ADVANCE. Text in English. 1901. w. USD 20 in state; USD 24 out of state. adv. bk.rev. **Document type:** *Newspaper.*
Formerly: Advance
Related titles: Microform ed.
Published by: Catholic Diocese of Wichita, 424 N Broadway, Wichita, KS 67202. TEL 316-263-6262, 316-269-3965. Ed. Christopher M Riggs. Adv. contact Karin Eckberg. Circ: 37,500. Wire service: CaNS.

282.74932 USA ISSN 1084-3213
BX1418.N5
CATHOLIC ADVOCATE. Text in English. 1951. bi-w. (Wed.). USD 15; USD 0.50 per issue (effective 2008). adv. bk.rev.; film rev. **Document type:** *Newspaper, Consumer.*
Formerly: Newark Catholic Advocate
Published by: Catholic Archdiocese of Newark, 171 Clifton Ave, PO Box 9500, Newark, NJ 07104-9500. TEL 973-497-4200, FAX 973-497-4192. Pub. Michael Gabriele. Adv. contact Marge P. McCue. B&W page USD 3,300; 14 x 19.5. Circ: 125,000 (controlled and free). Wire service: CNS.

282 USA ISSN 0045-5970
BX2348.A1
CATHOLIC AGITATOR. Text in English. 1971. 8/yr. USD 1. adv. bk.rev.
Published by: (Ammon Hennacy House of Hospitality), Los Angeles Catholic Worker, 632 N Brittania St, Los Angeles, CA 90033. TEL 213-267-8789. Ed. Jeff Dietrich. Circ: 6,000.

282 USA
CATHOLIC AID NEWS. Text in English. 1895. m. membership. **Document type:** *Newspaper.* **Description:** News articles and announcements pertaining to the members and activities of this association.
Published by: Catholic Aid Association, 3499 N. Lexington Ave., St. Paul, MN 55126-8098. TEL 651-490-0170, FAX 651-490-0746. Ed. Colleen Kingsbury. Circ: 40,000.

282 NGA ISSN 1115-8832
THE CATHOLIC AMBASSADOR. Text in English. 1980. q. NGN 300, USD 20; NGN 50 newsstand/cover (effective 2002). adv. bk.rev. back issues avail. **Document type:** *Magazine, Consumer.* **Description:** Helps the faithful take an interest in the Universal Church. Contains news of activities and coverage of issues both in Nigeria and the world.
Formerly: Ambassador Newsletter
Related titles: Diskette ed.
Published by: (Missionary Society of St. Paul - Nigeria), Ambassador Publications, PMB 2011, Iperu Remo, Osun State, Nigeria. TEL 234-37-620022, FAX 234-37-620699. Ed. Augustine Etemma Inwang. Adv. contact Iffrok Edem Inyang. B&W page NGN 5,000. Circ: 20,000 (paid).

282 USA ISSN 1044-1581
THE CATHOLIC ANSWER. Abbreviated title: T C A. Text in English. 1987. bi-m. USD 21.95 combined subscription (print & online eds.) (effective 2009). adv. back issues avail. **Document type:** *Magazine, Consumer.* **Description:** Supplies Catholics with answers on what the church teaches, how to live their faith, and what their Catholic heritage is.
Related titles: Online - full text ed.
Indexed: A01.
Published by: Our Sunday Visitor, Inc., 200 Noll Plz, Huntington, IN 46750. TEL 260-356-8400, 800-348-2440, FAX 260-356-8472, osvbooks@osv.com. Ed. Paul Thigpen.

282.41 GBR ISSN 0261-4316
BX801 CODEN: MACRDS
CATHOLIC ARCHIVES. Text in English. 1981. a., latest no.23, 2003, May. free to members (effective 2009). back issues avail. **Document type:** *Journal, Academic/Scholarly.* **Description:** Provides guide to the history and use of the archives of the Roman Catholic Church in the UK and Ireland.
Indexed: CERDIC.
Published by: Catholic Archives Society, c o Judith Smeaton, 33 Middlethorpe Dr, York, YO24 1NA, United Kingdom. TEL 44-1904-704525.

282 GBR
CATHOLIC ARCHIVES SOCIETY. BULLETIN. Text in English. 1980. a. free to members (effective 2009). back issues avail. **Document type:** *Bulletin, Trade.* **Description:** Contains notes on seminars, local meetings and the society's annual conference.
Former titles (until 1999): C A S Bulletin (1353-0232); (until 1993): C A S Newsletter (0262-6896)
Published by: Catholic Archives Society, c o Judith Smeaton, 33 Middlethorpe Dr, York, YO24 1NA, United Kingdom. TEL 44-1904-704525, archive@ampleforth.org.uk.

220 USA ISSN 0008-7912
BS410
➤ **CATHOLIC BIBLICAL QUARTERLY.** Text in English. 1939. q. adv. bk.rev. illus. index, cum.index. back issues avail.; reprints avail. **Document type:** *Journal, Academic/Scholarly.* **Description:** Contains articles and notices of a scholarly nature on the scripture.
Related titles: Microfilm ed.; Online - full text ed.
Indexed: A01, A02, A03, A08, A11, A20, A21, A22, A25, A26, ASCA, AmHI, ArtHuCI, B04, BRD, BibLing, CA, CERDIC, CPL, CurCont, DIP, E08, FR, G08, H07, H08, H09, H10, H14, HAb, HumInd, I05, IBR, IBZ, IZBG, M01, M02, MEA&I, MLA-IB, OTA, P02, P10, P13, P28, P48, P53, P54, PCI, PQC, R&TA, R05, RI-1, RI-2, S08, S09, SCOPUS, T02, W03, W05, W07, WBA, WMB.
—BLDSC (3093.010000), IE, Infotrieve, Ingenta, INIST.
Published by: Catholic Biblical Association of America, 433 Caldwell Hall, The Catholic University of America, Washington, DC 20064. TEL 202-319-5519, FAX 202-319-4799, cua-cathbib@cua.edu.

➤ **CATHOLIC BOOK PUBLISHERS ASSOCIATION DIRECTORY.** *see* PUBLISHING AND BOOK TRADE

363 USA ISSN 1520-0272
CATHOLIC CAMPAIGN FOR AMERICA. CAMPAIGN UPDATE. Text in English. 1996. irreg.
Published by: Catholic Campaign for America, 2444 Solomons Island Rd, Ste 201, Annapolis, MD 21401. TEL 410-571-6300, 866-275-8784, FAX 410-571-6365, inquiries@cpjustice.org, http://www.cpjustice.org/.

CATHOLIC CEMETERY. *see* FUNERALS

282 USA ISSN 0008-7971
CATHOLIC CHRONICLE. Text in English. 1934. m. USD 21 domestic; USD 42 foreign; USD 1.50 newsstand/cover (effective 2008). adv. bk.rev.; music rev.; play rev.; software rev.; tel.rev.; video rev. charts; illus.; maps; stat. 44 p./no. 6 cols./p.; back issues avail. **Document type:** *Newspaper.* **Description:** Features national, international, and local news of interest to Catholic readers in 19 northwest Ohio counties.
Published by: (Catholic Diocese of Toledo), Catholic Chronicle, Inc., 4913 Harroun Rd, Box 1866, Toledo, OH 43603-1866. TEL 419-885-6397, FAX 419-885-6398. Ed., R&P Patricia Lynn Morrison TEL 888-805-6397. Pub. Rev. James R. Hoffman. Circ: 100,000 (paid). Wire service: CaNS.

282 LCA
CATHOLIC CHRONICLE. Text in English. 1957. m. XEC 1. adv.
Formerly: Castries Catholic Chronicle
Published by: Archdiocese of Castries, c/o Benedictine Nuns, Box 778, Castries, St. Lucia. TEL 758-20790. Ed. Patrick A B Anthony. Circ: 2,500.

282 USA ISSN 0746-0511
THE CATHOLIC COMMENTATOR. Text in English. 1962. bi-w. (Wed.). USD 12. adv. **Document type:** *Newspaper.* **Description:** Covers local and world news, and diocesan communications.
Published by: Roman Catholic Diocese of Baton Rouge, 1800 S Acadian Thruway, Baton Rouge, LA 70808. TEL 225-387-0983, FAX 225-336-8710. Ed. Laura G Deavers. Pub. Rev. John Carville. Adv. contact Wanda Koch. Circ: 53,000. Wire service: CaNS. **Subscr. to:** PO Box 14746, Baton Rouge, LA 70898.

282 GBR ISSN 2042-907X
▼ **CATHOLIC COMPANION.** Text in English. 2010. m. GBP 12; GBP 1 per issue (effective 2011). **Document type:** *Magazine, Trade.*
Published by: Universe Media Group Ltd., 4th Fl, Landmark House, Station Rd, Cheadle Hulme, Cheshire SK8 7JH, United Kingdom. TEL 44-161-4881758, http://www.totalcatholic.com/tc.

282 FRA
CATHOLIC COUNTER-REFORMATION IN THE XXTH CENTURY. Text in English. 1970. m. bk.rev.
Related titles: Dutch ed.; French ed.: La Contre-Reforme Catholique au XXe Siecle. FRF 80 in France; CAD 30 in North America; FRF 120 elsewhere (effective 2000).
Published by: Contre Reforme Catholique, Maison Saint-Joseph, St Parres les Vaudes, 10260, France. Ed. Frere Gerard Cousin. Circ: 4,500. **Subscr. to:** Centre de Renaissance Catholique des Laurentides, Maison Sainte-Therese, 255 chemin de la Reserve, RR2, Shawinigan, PQ G9N 6T6, Canada.

282 USA ISSN 1054-2728
CATHOLIC COURIER. Text in English. 1889. m. (1st Wed.). USD 20; USD 3 newsstand/cover (effective 2008). bk.rev.; film rev.; video rev. charts; illus.; maps. 40 p./no. 4 cols./p.; back issues avail. **Document type:** *Newspaper, Consumer.* **Description:** Newspaper of the 12-county Rochester, NY diocese. Includes local, national and international church news, feature articles, columns, commentary and reviews.
Formerly: Courier-Journal
Related titles: Microfilm ed.
Published by: (Roman Catholic Diocese of Rochester, N.Y.), Rochester Catholic Press Association, Inc., 1136 Buffalo Rd, Rochester, NY 14624. TEL 585-529-9530. Ed. Karen M. Franz. Pub. Most Rev. (Bishop) Matthew H. Clark. Circ: 113,858 (paid). Wire service: CaNS.

282 USA ISSN 0008-7998
BX801
CATHOLIC DIGEST. Text in English. 1936. 11/yr. USD 19.95 domestic; USD 39.95 foreign (effective 2009). adv. bk.rev. illus. 125 p./no.; back issues avail.; reprints avail. **Document type:** *Magazine, Consumer.* **Description:** Provides articles essential for a life guided by faith.
Former titles (1937): The Catholic Digest of Catholic Books and Magazines; (until 1936): Catholic Book and Magazine Digest
Indexed: A22, CCR, CERDIC, CPL, M02.
Published by: Bayard Inc. (Subsidiary of: Bayard Presse), PO Box 6015, New London, CT 06320. TEL 860-437-3012, 800-321-0411, FAX 860-437-3013, cservice@bayard-us.com, http://www.bayard-inc.com. Ed. Dan Connors. Adv. contact Paul P Bourque TEL 860-437-3012 ext 155. color page USD 15,687; trim 5.29 x 7.375. **Subscr. to:** PO Box 51547, Boulder, CO 80321. TEL 800-678-2836.

282.025 USA
CATHOLIC DIRECTORY (SAN DIEGO). Text in English. 1936. a. USD 23 (effective 2000). adv. **Document type:** *Directory.*
Published by: Roman Catholic Diocese of San Diego, PO Box 81869, San Diego, CA 92138. TEL 858-490-8266, FAX 858-490-8355. Ed. Cyril Jones Kellett. Pub. Robert Brom. Adv. contact Ann Burke. Circ: 2,000.

282.411 GBR ISSN 0306-5677
BX1497.A3
CATHOLIC DIRECTORY FOR SCOTLAND. Text in English. 1828. a. **Document type:** *Directory.* **Description:** Includes details of the hierarchy of the Catholic Church in Scotland, details of the Dioceses, an alphabetical list of the clergy with addresses, specialised ministries, ordinations, obituaries, Catholic societies and institutions, Diocesan statistics, listed church buildings and a chronicle of the past years' events.
Formerly: Catholic Directory for the Clergy and Laity in Scotland (0069-1232)
—BLDSC (3093.019000).
Published by: Burns Publications Ltd., c/o Michael Burns, 20 William Wood Park, Netherlee, Glasgow, G44 3TD, United Kingdom. TEL 44-141-5718856.

282.025 GBR ISSN 0143-7615
BX1491.A1
CATHOLIC DIRECTORY OF ENGLAND AND WALES. Text in English. 1838. a. GBP 29.50 per issue (effective 2010). adv. back issues avail. **Document type:** *Directory, Consumer.* **Description:** Lists contact details for all clergy, catholic schools and catholic orders & associations.
Former titles (until 1973): Catholic Directory (0069-1224); (until 1944): Catholic Directory, Ecclesiastical Register and Almanac; (until 1856): Catholic Directory and Ecclesiastical Register; (until 1850): Catholic Directory, Almanack and Ecclesiastical Register; (until 1844): Catholic Directory and Annual Register
—CCC.
Published by: Gabriel Communications Ltd., 4th Fl, Landmark House, Station Rd, Cheadle Hulme, Cheshire SK8 7JH, United Kingdom. TEL 44-161-4881700, digitaldownloads@totalcatholic.com. Ed. Joseph Kelly TEL 44-161-4881700.

282.68 ZAF ISSN 0379-4652
CATHOLIC DIRECTORY OF SOUTHERN AFRICA. Text in English. 1906. biennial. ZAR 30. adv. stat. index. **Document type:** *Directory.* **Description:** Guide to all Catholic organizations and institutions comprising the ecclesiastical territories of South Africa, Botswana, and Swaziland.
Published by: Southern African Catholic Bishops' Conference, Office for Social Communications, PO Box 941, Pretoria, 0001, South Africa. TEL 27-12-3236458, FAX 27-12-3266218. Eds. Fr Emil Blaser, Johnson Mkhabela. Adv. contact Fr. Emil Blaser. Circ: 2,500.

262.3097526 USA
CATHOLIC DIRECTORY OF THE ARCHDIOCESE OF BALTIMORE. Text in English. 1921. a. USD 25 (effective 1998). adv. **Document type:** *Directory.*
Formerly: Archdiocese of Baltimore. Directory
Published by: (Archdiocese of Baltimore, Inc.), Cathedral Foundation, Inc., 880 Park Ave, PO Box 777, Baltimore, MD 21201. TEL 443-524-3150, FAX 443-524-3155, dmedinger@catholicreview.org, http://www.catholicreview.org. Adv. contact Chic Davis. Circ: 1,900.

262.3 USA
CATHOLIC DIRECTORY OF THE DIOCESE OF ALBANY. Text in English. 1957. a. USD 11 (effective 2001). adv. **Document type:** *Directory.* **Description:** Lists churches, staff, agencies, organizations, and institutions of Albany Roman Catholic Diocese, covering 14 counties in upstate New York.
Published by: Albany Catholic Press Association, Inc., 40 N Main Ave, Albany, NY 12203. TEL 518-453-6688, FAX 518-453-8448. Ed. James P Breig. Pub. Bishop Howard J Hubbard. Adv. contact Barbara R Oliver.

282 USA
CATHOLIC EAST TEXAS. Text in English. 1987. s-m. USD 15 (effective 2004). **Document type:** *Newspaper, Consumer.*
Published by: (Catholic Diocese of Tyler), Catholic East Texas, 1015 ESE Loop 323, Tyler, TX 75701-9663. TEL 903-534-1077, FAX 903-534-1370, djones@dioceseoftyler.org, http://www.dioceseoftyler.org. Ed. Jim D'Avignon. Pub. Bishop Alvaro Corrada. Circ: 13,000 (paid).

CATHOLIC EDUCATION. *see* EDUCATION

CATHOLIC EDUCATION CIRCULAR. *see* EDUCATION

282 AUS ISSN 1833-4202
CATHOLIC EDUCATION OFFICE. ANNUAL REPORT. Variant title: C E O M Annual Report. Text in English. 2005. a. free (effective 2008). back issues avail. **Document type:** *Report, Trade.* **Description:** Presents key activities and achievements associated with the six priority areas identified in the CEOM strategic plan, namely, leadership, religious education, governance, access and equity, planned provision and excellence and innovation.
Related titles: Online - full text ed.: free (effective 2008).
Published by: Catholic Education Office Melbourne, James Goold House, 228 Victoria Parade, PO Box 3, East Melbourne, VIC 8002, Australia. TEL 61-3-92670228, FAX 61-3-94159325, director@ceo.melb.catholic.edu.au, http://www.ceo.melb.catholic.edu.au.

282 USA
CATHOLIC EXPLORER. Text in English. 1960. w. USD 20. adv. bk.rev. **Document type:** *Newspaper.*
Former titles (until October, 1998): New Catholic Explorer (1044-8322); (until Aug. 1988): Joliet Catholic Explorer
Published by: Roman Catholic Diocese of Joliet, St Charles Borromeo Pastoral Center, 402 S Independence Blvd, Romeoville, IL 60446-2264. TEL 815-838-6475, FAX 815-834-4068. Ed. Mary Breslin. Pub., R&P Rev. Joseph L. Imesch. Adv. contact Don Birsa. B&W page USD 651. Circ: 28,000 (paid).

262.3 USA ISSN 0162-7031
CATHOLIC EXPONENT. Text in English. 1944. bi-w. USD 20 (effective 2006). adv. Supplement avail. **Document type:** *Newspaper.* **Description:** Official newspaper for six-county diocese of Youngstown in northeast Ohio. Looks at world, national, and diocesan events from a Catholic perspective.
Published by: Catholic Exponent, Inc., 144 W. Wood St, Youngstown, OH 44503. TEL 330-744-5251, FAX 330-744-5252. Pub. Bishop Thomas J Tobin. Circ: 40,500. Wire service: CaNS.

201.6 USA
CATHOLIC FAMILY PERSPECTIVES. Text in English. 1996. m. **Document type:** *Newsletter.*
Formerly: Catholic Family Perspectives Weekly
Media: Online - full text.
Address: 195 Lark St, Rochester, NY 14613. TEL 716-254-1811. Ed., Pub., R&P John F Wagner Jr.

282 USA ISSN 0008-8056
CATHOLIC FREE PRESS. Text in English. 1951. w. (Fri.). USD 19 domestic; USD 45 foreign. adv. bk.rev. illus. Supplement avail. **Document type:** *Newspaper.*
Related titles: Microfilm ed.
Published by: (Roman Catholic Bishop of Worcester), Catholic Free Press, 47 Elm St, Worcester, MA 01609. Eds. Gerard E Goggins, Margaret Russell. Pub. Rev. Daniel P. Reilly. R&P Gerard E Goggins. Adv. contact Robert Ballantine. Circ: 20,000 (paid). Wire service: CaNS.

282 USA ISSN 8756-4068
RA975
CATHOLIC HEALTH WORLD. Text in English. 1985. s-m. (22/yr.). USD 35 domestic; USD 40 foreign (effective 2003). adv. 8 p./no. 4 cols./p.; back issues avail. **Document type:** *Newspaper.* **Description:** Contains national and regional news, features, human interest items, articles on people and health care legislation, and reports of events.
Related titles: Online - full text ed.
—CCC.
Published by: Catholic Health Association of the United States, 4455 Woodson Rd., St. Louis, MO 63134. TEL 314-427-2500, FAX 314-427-0029, http://www.chausa.org. Ed. Monica Bayer Heaton. Pub. Rev. Michael D Place. Adv. contact Donna Troy TEL 314-253-3450. Circ: 11,500.

282 GBR ISSN 0008-8072
THE CATHOLIC HERALD. Text in English. 1894. w. GBP 62 domestic; GBP 85 in Europe includes Ireland; GBP 100 elsewhere; GBP 1.20 per issue (effective 2009). adv. bk.rev.; music rev. index. back issues avail. **Document type:** *Newspaper, Consumer.* **Description:** Contains news, features, arts, and letters to the editor.
Incorporates (18??-1894): London Catholic Herald; (18??-1894): South Coast Catholic Herald
Related titles: Microfilm ed.: (from WMP); Online - full text ed.: GBP 38 (effective 2009).
—CCC.
Published by: Catholic Herald Ltd., Herald House, 15 Lambs Passage, Bunhill Row, London, EC1Y 8TQ, United Kingdom. TEL 44-20-74483602, subscriptions@catholicherald.co.uk. Eds. Luke Coppen, Damian Thompson. Adv. contact James Quantrill TEL 44-20-74483610. page GBP 2,700; 340 x 540.

282 USA ISSN 1094-589X
CATHOLIC HERALD (MILWAUKEE). Text in English. 1869. w. USD 45 non-parish members; USD 38 parish members (effective 2004). adv. **Document type:** *Newspaper, Consumer.*
Published by: Milwaukee Catholic Press Apostolate, Inc., 3501 S Lake Dr, Box 07913, Milwaukee, WI 53235-0913. TEL 414-769-3500, 877-769-7699, FAX 414-769-3468. Pub. Timothy Dolan. Adv. contact Timothy Walter. Circ: 23,000.

282.09 USA ISSN 0008-8080
BX1404
➤ **THE CATHOLIC HISTORICAL REVIEW.** Text in English. 1915. q. USD 60 to institutions (print or online ed.); USD 84 combined subscription to institutions (print & online eds.) (effective 2009). adv. bk.rev. bibl. cum.index: vols.1-20, 21-50. 178 p./no.; back issues avail.; reprint service avail. from PSC. **Document type:** *Journal, Academic/Scholarly.* **Description:** Publishes articles, review articles, book reviews, and lists of books received in all areas of church history.
Related titles: Microfilm ed.: (from PMC, PQC); Online - full text ed.: ISSN 1534-0708.
Indexed: A01, A02, A03, A07, A08, A20, A21, A22, A25, A26, A30, A31, AA, ABS&EES, ASCA, AmH&L, AmHI, ArtHuCI, ArtInd, B04, B14, BEL&L, BRD, BRI, CA, CBRI, CPL, CurCont, DIP, E01, E08, FR, G08, H07, H08, H09, H10, H14, HAb, HistAb, HumInd, I05, I07, IBR, IBZ, M01, M02, MASUSE, MEA&I, MLA-IB, OTA, P02, P10, P13, P28, P30, P48, P53, P54, PCI, PQC, R&TA, R05, RASB, RI-1, RI-2, S08, S09, SCOPUS, T02, W03, W04, W05, W07, W09.
—BLDSC (3093.070000), IE, Infotrieve, Ingenta, INIST. **CCC.**
Published by: Catholic University of America Press, 620 Michigan Ave, NE, 240 Leahy Hall, Washington, DC 20064. FAX 202-319-4985, cua-press@cua.edu, http://cuapress.cua.edu. Eds. Robert Trisco, David J McGonagle. **Co-sponsor:** American Catholic Historical Association.

282 USA ISSN 1531-3980
BX801
CATHOLIC HORIZONS. Text in English. 2001. q. USD 35 domestic to individuals; USD 47 foreign to individuals; USD 50 domestic to institutions; USD 67 foreign to institutions (effective 2002).
Published by: Catholic Horizons Publishing, P. O. Box 2122, Carbondale, IL 62902-2122. FAX 618-529-7396. Ed. Angela Elrod-Sadler.

282 USA ISSN 1075-2943
BX802
CATHOLIC INTERNATIONAL. Text in English. 1990. q. USD 69.95 domestic; USD 109.95 foreign (effective 2004). **Description:** Provides readers with contemporary church issues, national and international news and developments, and papal messages.
Indexed: CPL.
—CCC.
Published by: Cathedral Foundation, Inc., 880 Park Ave, PO Box 777, Baltimore, MD 21201. TEL 443-524-3150, 888-768-9555, FAX 443-524-3155.

THE CATHOLIC JOURNALIST. *see* JOURNALISM

282 USA
CATHOLIC KEY. Text in English. 1969. w. USD 18; USD 30 foreign (effective 1999). adv. bk.rev. back issues avail. **Document type:** *Newspaper.*
Published by: Diocese of Kansas City, St. Joseph, 300 E 36th St, Box 419037, Kansas City, MO 64141-6037. TEL 816-756-1850, FAX 816-753-6205. Ed., R&P Albert de Zutter. Pub. Raymond J. Boland. Adv. contact Betsy Peters. Circ: 20,500.

282 AUS ISSN 0008-8145
THE CATHOLIC LEADER. Text in English. 1928. w. AUD 72 (effective 2008). adv. bk.rev.; film rev.; play rev. illus.
Related titles: Online - full text ed.
Published by: The Catholic Leader, GPO Box 282, Brisbane, QLD 4001, Australia. TEL 61-7-3336-9355, FAX 61-7-3236-4897, editor@catholicleader.com.au, http://www.catholicleader.com.au. Ed. G C Coleman. Circ: 20,000.

282 GBR ISSN 1356-2959
CATHOLIC LIFE. Text in English. 1995. m. GBP 36 (effective 2010). back issues avail. **Document type:** *Magazine, Consumer.* **Description:** Aims to explore both contemporary and historical aspects of catholic faith.
Published by: Gabriel Communications Ltd., 4th Fl, Landmark House, Station Rd, Cheadle Hulme, Cheshire SK8 7JH, United Kingdom. TEL 44-161-4881700, digitaldownloads@totalcatholic.com. Eds. Lynda Walker TEL 44-161-4881756, Joseph Kelly TEL 44-161-4881700. Circ: 11,000.

282 USA
CATHOLIC LIFE. Text in English. 1997. m. USD 24. adv. bk.rev. **Document type:** *Magazine, Consumer.*
Published by: Catholic Treasures Inc., 135 W Foothill Blvd, Ste A, Monrovia, CA 91017-1734. TEL 626-359-4893, 800-257-4893, FAX 626-359-6933. Ed. Charles Coulombe. Adv. contact Brian Feeney.

282 USA ISSN 0164-9418
BX801
THE CATHOLIC LIGHT. Text in English. 1899. bi-w. USD 10; USD 12 foreign (effective 2004). adv. 14 p./no. 6 cols./p.; **Document type:** *Newspaper.*
Published by: Catholic Light, 300 Wyoming Ave, Scranton, PA 18503. TEL 717-346-8915, FAX 717-346-8917. Ed., R&P William R Genello TEL 570-207-2229. Circ: 49,300. Wire service: CaNS.

261.561 GBR ISSN 0008-8226
CATHOLIC MEDICAL QUARTERLY. Text in English. 1923. q. free to members (effective 2009). adv. bk.rev. bibl. index. back issues avail. **Document type:** *Directory, Consumer.* **Description:** Consists of information about bio-ethics, the Guild's activities and letters.
Indexed: P30, PCI.
Published by: Catholic Medical Association, 60 Grove End Rd, Brampton House, London, NW8 9NH, United Kingdom. TEL 44-20-72664246, FAX 44-20-72664813, enquiries@catholicdoctors.org.uk.

282 USA ISSN 0008-8234
CATHOLIC MESSENGER. Text in English. 1882. w. USD 27 domestic; USD 130 foreign (effective 2009). adv. bk.rev. 10 p./no. 6 cols./p.; **Document type:** *Newspaper, Consumer.*
Related titles: Microform ed.
Published by: Roman Catholic Diocese of Davenport, PO Box 460, Davenport, IA 52805-0460. cathmess@sau.edu. Eds. Barb Arland-Fye, Rev. Francis C Henricksen. Pub. Bishop Martin Amos. adv.: col. inch USD 7.10. Circ: 19,200 (paid). Wire service: CaNS.

282.778 USA ISSN 1083-6977
CATHOLIC MISSOURIAN. Text in English. 1957. w. (Fri.). USD 13 (effective 2006). adv. bk.rev. illus. 16 p./no.; **Document type:** *Newspaper.*
Published by: Diocese of Jefferson City, 2207 W Main St, Jefferson City, Cole, MO 65109. Ed. Jay Nies. Pub. Bishop John R. Gaydos. Adv. contact Kelly Martin. col. inch USD 8.03. Circ: 21,000. Wire service: CaNS.

282 USA ISSN 1087-2604
THE CATHOLIC MOMENT. Text in English. 1945. w. USD 25 (effective 2008). adv. bk.rev. 16 p./no. 5 cols./p.; **Document type:** *Newspaper.* **Description:** Addresses general social, religious, educational, health, and familial issues through a Catholic perspective.
Former titles (until Dec. 1994): Sunday Visitor; Lafayette Sunday Visitor
Related titles: Microfilm ed.
Published by: Diocese of Lafayette-in-Indiana, Local Church of Northcentral Indiana, PO Box 1603, Lafayette, IN 47902-1603. TEL 765-742-2050, FAX 765-742-7513. Ed. Kevin Cullen. R&P Thomas A Russell. Adv. contact Carolyn McKinney. col. inch USD 13; trim 11.5 x 14.5. Circ: 29,000. Wire service: CaNS.

282 CAN ISSN 0701-0788
CATHOLIC NEW TIMES. Text in English. 1976. s-m. (20/yr.). CAD 24, USD 33 (effective 1999). adv. bk.rev.
Related titles: Microfiche ed.; Microfilm ed.: (from MML); Microform ed.: (from MML).
Indexed: A01, A26, C03, CBCARef, CBPI, CPerI, G05, G06, G07, G08, I05, P48, PQC, R05.
—CIS.
Published by: New Catholic Times Inc., 80 Sackville St, Toronto, ON M5A 3E5, Canada. TEL 416-361-0761, FAX 416-361-0796. Ed., R&P Joyce Murray CSJ. Adv. contact Stephanie Lamb. Circ: 9,000.

282 USA ISSN 1527-4756
BX801
THE CATHOLIC NEW WORLD. Text in English. 1892. bi-w. (Sun.). USD 25 (effective 2001). adv. bk.rev.; film rev.; music rev.; play rev.; tel.rev.; video rev. **Document type:** *Newspaper.*
Former titles: New World (1043-3538); Chicago Catholic (0149-970X); New World (0028-7016)

Related titles: Microform ed.
Indexed: CERDIC.
Published by: (Catholic Archdiocese of Chicago), New World Publications, 721 N. LaSalle St, Chicago, IL 60610. TEL 312-243-1300, FAX 312-243-1526. Ed., R&P Thomas H Sheridan. Pub. Cardinal Francis E George. Adv. contact Dawn Vidmar. Circ: 75,000. Wire service: CaNS.

282 USA ISSN 0278-1174
CATHOLIC NEW YORK. Text in English. 1981. m. USD 12 domestic; USD 1 newsstand/cover (effective 2005). adv. bk.rev. 44 p./no. 6 cols./p.; **Document type:** *Newspaper.*
Related titles: Microfiche ed.
Published by: (Roman Catholic Archdiocese of New York), Ecclesiastical Communications Corp., 1011 First Ave, New York, NY 10022. TEL 212-688-2399, FAX 212-688-2642. Ed., R&P John Woods. Adv. contact Arthur L McKenna TEL 212-688-2399. Circ: 135,906.

282 TTO
CATHOLIC NEWS. Text in English. 1892. w. TTD 2, USD 0.32 per issue (effective 2001). adv. bk.rev. back issues avail. **Document type:** *Newspaper.* **Description:** Contains news of the Church, locally and worldwide, social commentary, and spiritual reading.
Published by: (Roman Catholic Archdiocese), Printing Services Ltd., 31 Independence Sq, Port-of-Spain, Trinidad, Trinidad & Tobago. TEL 868-623-6093, FAX 868-623-9468. Ed. Michel de Verteuil. Circ: 14,000 (paid).

282 USA ISSN 1080-0956
THE CATHOLIC NORTHWEST PROGRESS. Text in English. 1897. w. (Thu.). USD 20 (effective 2010). adv. **Document type:** *Newspaper, Consumer.*
Former titles (until 1994): The Progress (0739-6023); (until 19??): Catholic Northwest Progress
Related titles: Online - full text ed.: free (effective 2010).
Published by: Archdiocese of Seattle, 910 Marion St, Seattle, WA 98104. TEL 206-382-4850, FAX 206-382-3487. Ed. Steve Kent. Adv. contact Keri Hake. Circ: 18,365.

282 USA
CATHOLIC OBSERVER. Text in English. 1954. bi-w. (Fri.). USD 15 (effective 2004). **Document type:** *Newspaper, Consumer.* **Description:** Contains national and international news of the Catholic Church as well as local information. Includes columns by local writers, the bishop's column, arts and book reviews, religious education features, a children's page, letters to the editor and syndicated columns by Catholic writers.
Published by: (Diocese of Springfield, Massachusetts), Catholic Communications Corporation, 65 Elliott St, Springfield, MA 01105. TEL 413-737-4744, m.dupont@diospringfield.org. Ed. Rebecca Drake. Adv. contact Ron Pitruzello. Circ: 12,000 (paid). Wire service: CaNS.

282 USA ISSN 0008-8277
CATHOLIC PEACE FELLOWSHIP BULLETIN. Text in English. 1965. 2/yr. donation. bk.rev. illus. **Description:** Reports on events and views in the peace and disarmament movement.
Published by: Catholic Peace Fellowship, 339 Lafayette St, New York, NY 10012. TEL 212-673-8990. Ed. Bill Ofenloch. Circ: 4,000.

282 USA ISSN 1083-1223
CATHOLIC PEACE VOICE. Text in English. 1975. 4/yr. USD 35 to members. bk.rev. 20 p./no.; **Document type:** *Newspaper.* **Description:** Covers the world of Christianity and peace.
Formerly: Pax Christi U S A (0897-9545)
Related titles: Microfilm ed.; Online - full text ed.
Published by: Pax Christi U S A, National Catholic Peace Movement, c/o National Office, 532 W Eighth St, Erie, PA 16502-1343. TEL 814-453-4955, FAX 814-452-4784, http://www.nonviolence.org/pcusa. Ed. Dave Robinson. Circ: 20,000.

THE CATHOLIC PERIODICAL AND LITERATURE INDEX. *see* RELIGIONS AND THEOLOGY—Abstracting, Bibliographies, Statistics

THE CATHOLIC PHARMACIST. *see* PHARMACY AND PHARMACOLOGY

282 GBR ISSN 0008-8293
CATHOLIC PICTORIAL. Text in English. 1962. w. GBP 0.60 newsstand/cover (effective 2001). adv. bk.rev.; music rev.; tel.rev. illus. 24 p./no.; back issues avail. **Document type:** *Newspaper, Consumer.*
Published by: Catholic Pictorial Ltd., Pier Head, Media House, Mann Island, Liverpool, L3 1DQ, United Kingdom. TEL 44-151-236-2191, FAX 44-151-236-2216. Ed. David Mahon. Adv. contact Fiona Barnet. Circ: 50,000.

282 USA
THE CATHOLIC POST. Text in English. 1944. w. (Fri.). USD 20 in state; USD 21 out of state; USD 40 elsewhere (effective 2004). **Document type:** *Newspaper, Consumer.*
Published by: Catholic Diocese of Peoria, 409 N E Monroe, Peoria, IL 61603. TEL 309-673-3603. Ed. Tom Dermody. Adv. contact Sonia Nelson. Circ: 26,000 (paid).

282 USA ISSN 1536-2388
CATHOLIC QUOTE; instant inspiration. Text in English. 1974 (vol.37). m. USD 5. index. back issues avail.
Published by: Rev. Jerome Pokorny, Ed. & Pub., Valparaiso, NE 68065. Circ: 7,000.

282 CAN ISSN 0383-1620
CATHOLIC REGISTER. Text in English. 1893. w. (47/yr.). CAD 31.95; USD 55.95 in United States (effective 2001). adv. bk.rev.; film rev.; Website rev. abstr. back issues avail. **Document type:** *Newspaper.* **Description:** Contains news and views from a Catholic perspective.
Formerly: Canadian Register (0008-4913)
Published by: Canadian Register Ltd., 1155 Yonge St, Ste 401, Toronto, ON M4T 1W2, Canada. TEL 416-934-3410, FAX 416-934-3409. Ed., Pub., R&P Joseph Sinasac. Adv. contact Steven Tyson. Circ: 20,000 (paid).

282 USA
CATHOLIC REGISTER. Text in English. 1931. bi-w. (Mon.). USD 12 (effective 2005). **Document type:** *Newspaper, Consumer.*
Published by: Diocese of Altoona-Johnstown, PO Box 413, Hollidaysburg, PA 16648. TEL 814-695-7563, FAX 814-695-7517, srmary@dioceseaj.org. Ed. Rev. Timothy P Stein. Pub. Rev. Joseph V Adamec. Adv. contact Bruce Tomaselli. Circ: 37,000 (controlled). Wire service: CaNS.

282 USA ISSN 0008-8315
CATHOLIC REVIEW (BALTIMORE). Text in English. 1913. w. (Thu.). USD 45 (effective 2009). adv. bk.rev. **Document type:** *Newspaper, Consumer.*
Related titles: Online - full content ed.: free.
Published by: Cathedral Foundation, Inc., 880 Park Ave, PO Box 777, Baltimore, MD 21201. dmedinger@catholicreview.org. Pub. Cardinal William H. Keeler. Adv. contact Chic Davis. Circ: 69,300. Wire service: CaNS.

282 USA ISSN 1089-6570
HN51
CATHOLIC RURAL LIFE. Text in English. 1922. s-a. USD 25 to individuals; USD 100 to institutions (effective 2000). bk.rev. illus.
Former titles (until 1996): Earth Matters (1041-9276); (until 1988): Catholic Rural Life (0008-8331)
Published by: National Catholic Rural Life Conference, 4625 Beaver Ave, Des Moines, IA 50310. TEL 515-270-2634, FAX 515-270-9447, ncrlc@aol.com, http://www.ncrlc.com. Circ: 3,000.

282.025 USA ISSN 1525-5298
CATHOLIC SAN FRANCISCO; Marin, San Francisco and San Mateo Counties. Text in English. w. adv. stat. **Document type:** *Newspaper.*
Formerly: Catholic Directory (San Francisco)
Related titles: Online - full text ed.: free (effective 2010).
Published by: Archdiocese of San Francisco, 1 Peter Yorke Way, San Francisco, CA 94109-6602. TEL 415-614-5632, FAX 415-614-5641, healym@sfarchdiocese.org. Pub. Rev. Geroge H Niederauer. Circ: 100,000 (controlled).

282 USA ISSN 0162-2102
CATHOLIC SENTINEL (ARCHDIOCESE OF PORTLAND, OREGON). Text in English. 19??. w. (Wed.). **Document type:** *Newspaper.*
Published by: Oregon Catholic Press, 5536 NE Hassalo St, PO Box 18030, Portland, OR 97218. TEL 503-281-1191, 800-548-8749, liturgy@ocp.org, http://www.ocp.org. Wire service: CaNS.

282 USA ISSN 1091-0905
BT738
THE CATHOLIC SOCIAL SCIENCE REVIEW. Text in English. 1996. a. USD 20 (effective 2009). bk.rev. **Document type:** *Journal, Academic/Scholarly.* **Description:** Publishes articles, book reviews, and essays in the social sciences or humanities.
Related titles: Online - full text ed.: ISSN 1944-6292. free (effective 2011).
Indexed: A01, CA, CPL, R&TA, T02.
Published by: (Society of Catholic Social Scientists), Catholic Social Science Press, c/o Dr Stephen Krason, Franciscan University of Steubenville, 1235 University Blvd, Steubenville, OH 43952. TEL 740-283-6245 ext 2366, FAX 740-283-6401, scss@franciscan.edu, http://www.catholicsocialscientists.org/SCSS_Home.htm. Ed. Mark Lowery. Pub. Stephen M Krason. **Dist. by:** Franciscan University Press, 1235 University Blvd, Steubenville, OH 43952. TEL 740-283-6357, 888-333-0381, FAX 740-284-5454, upress@franciscan.edu, http://press.franciscan.edu/.

282.764 USA ISSN 1098-5468
BX1415.T4
➤ **CATHOLIC SOUTHWEST.** Text in English. 1990. a. USD 25 per issue to libraries; USD 6 per issue to non-members; free to members (effective 2010). bk.rev. illus. back issues avail. **Document type:** *Journal, Academic/Scholarly.* **Description:** Devoted to publish research and writing on the Catholic experience in Texas and the Southwest, particularly as expressed through art, architecture, music, literature, and related spheres of cultural study within a historical context.
Formerly (until 1996): Journal of Texas Catholic History and Culture (1048-2431)
Related titles: Diskette ed.
Indexed: AmH&L, CA, HistAb, T02.
Published by: (Texas Catholic Conference), Texas Catholic Historical Society, 1625 Rutherford Ln, Bldg D, Austin, TX 78754. http://www.onr.com/user/cat/TCHS.htm. Ed. Roy Barkley. **Subscr. to:** Texas Catholic Conference.

268 USA ISSN 0896-2715
CATHOLIC SPIRIT (AUSTIN). Text in English, Spanish. 1983. m. USD 12 (effective 2005). adv. bk.rev. **Document type:** *Newspaper, Consumer.* **Description:** Provides news and religious education to families in the diocese.
Published by: Diocese of Austin, PO Box 13327, Austin, TX 78711. TEL 512-476-4888, FAX 512-469-9537. Ed., R&P Helen Osman. Adv. contact Peggy Schott. Circ: 33,000 (paid).

282 USA
CATHOLIC SPIRIT (DAYTON). Text in English. 1911. w. USD 26.95. **Document type:** *Newspaper.*
Formerly: Catholic Bulletin
Published by: Catholic Bulletin, 244, Dayton, MN 55102. TEL 612-291-4444. Ed. Mike Krokos. Pub. Harry J Flynn. R&P Robert Zyskowski. Adv. contact Janet Smith. Circ: 87,000.

282 USA
THE CATHOLIC SPIRIT (ST. PAUL, MN). Text in English. 1911. w. (Thu.). USD 21.95 (effective 2004). 24 p./no. 4 cols./p.; **Document type:** *Newspaper.*
Formerly: Catholic Bulletin
Published by: St. Paul Catholic Bulletin, 244 Dayton Ave, St. Paul, MN 55102. TEL 651-291-4444, FAX 651-291-4460. Ed. Mike Krokos. Pub. Harry J Flynn. Adv. contact Janet Smith. Circ: 87,500 (paid). Wire service: CaNS.

282 USA ISSN 1088-6176
CATHOLIC SPIRIT (WHEELING). Text in English. 1934. 10/yr. USD 15 (effective 1998). adv. bk.rev.; film rev. **Document type:** *Newspaper.*
Published by: Catholic Diocese of Wheeling-Charleston, PO Box 951, Wheeling, WV 26003-0119. TEL 304-233-0880, FAX 304-233-0890. Adv. contact Janice Danison. Circ: 4,600.

282 USA ISSN 0411-2741
BX801
THE CATHOLIC STANDARD. Text in English. 1951. w. USD 31. adv. bk.rev. illus. **Document type:** *Newspaper.*
Indexed: P30.
Published by: Archdiocese of Washington, 145 Taylor St, NE, PO Box 4464, Washington, DC 20017. TEL 301-853-4599, FAX 301-853-3349. Ed. Mark Zimmermann. Pub. Theodore Cardinal McCarric, Adv. contact Steve Stedman. Circ: 50,000. Wire service: CNS.

282 GBR ISSN 0008-8366
CATHOLIC STANDARD. Text in English. 1938. w. GBP 40. adv. bk.rev. illus. **Document type:** *Newspaper.* **Description:** Irish edition of Catholic Herald.
Indexed: CERDIC, HRIR.
Published by: Catholic Herald Ltd., Herald House, 15 Lambs Passage, Bunhill Row, London, EC1Y 8TQ, United Kingdom. TEL 44-171-588-3101, FAX 44-171-256-9728. Ed. William Oddie. Adv. contact James Hughes. Circ: 5,000.

282 GUY
CATHOLIC STANDARD. Text in English. 1905. w.
Address: Oronoque St 293, Queenstown, PO Box 10720, Georgetown, Guyana. TEL 2-61540. Ed. Fr Andrew Morrison. Circ: 10,000.

282 USA ISSN 1074-021X
THE CATHOLIC STANDARD & TIMES. Text in English. 1985. w. (Thu.). **Document type:** *Newspaper, Consumer.*
Formed by the merger of (1866-1895): Catholic Standard; (1892-1895): Catholic Times
Contact Owner: Archdiocese of Philadelphia, 222 N 17th St, Philadelphia, PA 19103. TEL 215-587-3660. Wire service: CaNS.

282 USA
CATHOLIC STAR HERALD. Text in English. 1951. w. (Fri.). USD 27 (effective 2005). adv. **Document type:** *Newspaper, Consumer.*
Formerly: Camden Catholic Star Herald
Published by: Diocese of Camden, 15 N Seventh St, Camden, NJ 08102. TEL 856-756-7900, FAX 856-756-7938, galante@camdendiocese.org. Pub. Rev. Joseph A Galante. Adv. contact Dennis Ezekiel. Circ: 40,000 (paid). Wire service: CaNS.

282 USA ISSN 1533-0230
CATHOLIC SUN (PHOENIX); serving the church of phoenix. Text in English. 1985. 21/yr. USD 20 in state; USD 25 out of state (effective 2009). adv. bk.rev. **Document type:** *Newspaper.*
Related titles: Microfiche ed.
Published by: Roman Catholic Diocese of Phoenix, 400 E Monroe St, Phoenix, AZ 85004. TEL 602-354-2139, FAX 602-354-2429. Ed. Rob DeFrancesco. Pub. Bishop Thomas J. Olmsted. Adv. contact Jennifer Ellis. Circ: 104,505 (paid). Wire service: CaNS. **Subscr. to:** PO Box 13549, Phoenix, AZ 85002.

262.3 USA ISSN 0744-267X
Discard
CATHOLIC SUN (SYRACUSE). Text in English. 1893. w. USD 20; USD 25 foreign. adv. bk.rev. back issues avail. **Document type:** *Newspaper.* **Description:** Publication for the Roman Catholic diocese of Syracuse.
Related titles: Microfilm ed.
Published by: Syracuse Catholic Press, Inc., 421 S Warren St, Syracuse, NY 13202-2603. TEL 315-422-8153, 800-333-0571, FAX 315-422-7549. Ed., R&P Anne Checkosky. Pub. Bishop James Moynihan. Adv. contact Dan Cetola. Circ: 35,700 (paid).

CATHOLIC TEACHERS GAZETTE. *see* EDUCATION

282 USA ISSN 1073-6689
THE CATHOLIC TELEGRAPH. Text in English. 1831. w. (Fri.). USD 24 (effective 2002). adv. bk.rev.; film rev. **Document type:** *Newspaper, Consumer.*
Related titles: Microform ed.: (from PQC).
Published by: (Archdiocese of Cincinnati), Catholic Telegraph, 100 E 8th St, Cincinnati, OH 45202. Eds. Lenore Christopher, Tricia Hempel. Pub. Rev. Daniel Pilarczyk. Adv. contact Tim Mayer. Circ: 32,000. Wire service: CaNS.

282.025 USA ISSN 0147-5959
BX1417.N4
CATHOLIC TELEPHONE GUIDE. Text in English. a. USD 32 (effective 2000 - 2001). adv. 352 p./no. 3 cols./p.; **Document type:** *Directory.*
Published by: Catholic News Publishing Co., Inc. (Subsidiary of: School Guide Publications), 210 North Ave, New Rochelle, NY 10801. TEL 914-632-1220, 800-433-7771, FAX 914-632-3412. Ed. Nancy Lappin. Pub., Adv. contact Myles Ridder TEL 914-632-1220. B&W page USD 2,260; 10 x 7. Circ: 10,000 (paid).

230.2 USA ISSN 0069-1267
CATHOLIC THEOLOGICAL SOCIETY OF AMERICA. PROCEEDINGS. Text in English. 1946. a. USD 25 (effective 2004). index, cum.index. reprints avail. **Document type:** *Proceedings.*
Related titles: Microform ed.: (from PQC).
Indexed: CERDIC, CPL.
Published by: Catholic Theological Society of America, c/o Dr. Dolores Christie, John Carroll University, 20700 N Park Blvd, University Hights, OH 44118. dlchristie@aol.com, http://www.jcu.edu/ctsa. Ed. Michael Downey. R&P Dolores Christine. Circ: 1,600.

282 USA ISSN 1051-693X
CATHOLIC THOUGHT FROM LUBLIN. Text in English. 1990. irreg., latest vol.11, 2002. price varies. **Document type:** *Monographic series, Academic/Scholarly.*
Published by: Peter Lang Publishing, Inc. (Subsidiary of: Peter Lang Publishing Group), 29 Broadway, New York, NY 10006. TEL 212-647-7700, 212-647-7706, 800-770-5264, FAX 212-647-7707, customerservice@plang.com. Ed. Andrew Woznicki.

282 USA
CATHOLIC TIMES. Text in English. 1937. 26/yr. USD 25 domestic (effective 2009). adv. bk.rev. **Document type:** *Newspaper.*
Formerly (until 2006): Times Review (0746-0759)
Published by: Diocese of La Crosse, 3710 East Ave S, La Crosse, WI 54601. TEL 608-788-7700, FAX 608-788-8413. Ed. Stan Gould. Pub. Bishop Jerome E. Listecki. Circ: 30,000 (paid). Wire service: CaNS.

282 GBR ISSN 1351-7945
CATHOLIC TIMES. Text in English. 1993. w. GBP 52 (effective 2010). back issues avail. **Document type:** *Newspaper, Consumer.*
—CCC.
Published by: Gabriel Communications Ltd., 4th Fl, Landmark House, Station Rd, Cheadle Hulme, Cheshire SK8 7JH, United Kingdom. TEL 44-161-4881700, digitaldownloads@totalcatholic.com. Eds. Kevin Flaherty TEL 44-161-4881753, Joseph Kelly TEL 44-161-4881700.

262.3 USA ISSN 0745-6050
CATHOLIC TIMES (COLUMBUS). Text in English. 1951. w. (49/yr.). USD 25 (effective 2005). adv. bk.rev.; film rev. back issues avail. **Document type:** *Newspaper, Consumer.* **Description:** Newspaper of the Diocese of Columbus.
Related titles: Magnetic Tape ed.; Microfilm ed.

R

Published by: Catholic Times, Inc., 197 E. Gay St, Columbus, OH 43216. Ed., R&P Mark Moretti. Pub. Bishop James A Griffin. Circ: 26,000. Wire service: CaNS.

282 USA
CATHOLIC TIMES (SAGINAW). Text in English. 1991. w. (Fri.). USD 25.95; USD 0.75 per issue (effective 2005). back issues avail. **Document type:** *Newspaper, Consumer.*
Published by: G.L.S. Diocesan Reports, Inc., 1520 Court St, Box 1405, Saginaw, MI 48605. TEL 989-793-7661, FAX 989-793-7663. Ed. Anne Seebaldt. Adv. contact Lisa Briggs. Circ: 5,918 (paid). Wire service: CaNS.

282 USA
CATHOLIC TIMES (SPRINGFIELD). Text in English. 1896. w. (Thu.). USD 15 (effective 2008). **Document type:** *Newspaper, Consumer.*
Published by: Diocese of Springfield, PO Box 3187, Springfield, IL 62708-3187. TEL 217-698-8500, FAX 217-698-0619, ksass@dio.org, http://www.dio.org. Ed. Kathie Sass. Adv. contact Paula Ruot. Circ: 46,000 (paid). Wire service: CaNS.

282 USA ISSN 1081-4353
CATHOLIC TRANSCRIPT. Text in English. 1898. m. USD 12. adv. bk.rev. 32 p./no. 5 cols./p.; **Document type:** *Newspaper.*
Related titles: Microfilm ed.: 1898.
Published by: Archdiocese of Hartford, 467 Bloomfield Ave, Bloomfield, CT 06002. TEL 800-726-2391. Pub. Archbishop Henry J Mansell. R&P Carole Cronsell. Adv. contact Jeff Guerrette. col. inch USD 28. Circ: 86,000 (paid).

282 USA ISSN 0162-7023
CATHOLIC UNIVERSE BULLETIN. Text in English. 1874. 25/yr. (alternate Fri.). USD 25 (effective 2009). adv. bk.rev.; film rev. index. back issues avail. **Document type:** *Newspaper.* **Description:** Contains world news and religious happenings, a recipe column, and church and social news.
Published by: Catholic Universe Bulletin Pub. Co., Inc., 1404 E 9th St, 6th flr, Cleveland, OH 44114-2556. TEL 216-696-6525, FAX 216-696-6519. Eds. Dennis Sadowski, Nancy Erickson. Pub. Bishop Richard G Lennon. Adv. contact David Sarosy. Circ: 31,200 (paid). Wire service: AP, CaNS.

262.9 USA ISSN 1530-6119
K3
➤ **CATHOLIC UNIVERSITY LAW REVIEW.** Text in English. 1950. q. USD 40 domestic; USD 45 foreign; free to members (effective 2009). adv. bk.rev. index. back issues avail.; reprint service avail. from WSH. **Document type:** *Journal, Academic/Scholarly.* **Description:** Publishes on a quarterly basis, articles submitted by legal scholars and practitioners, as well as significant student work.
Former titles (until 1995): Catholic University Law Review (0008-8390); (until 1975): Law Review
Related titles: Microfiche ed.: (from WSH); Microfilm ed.: (from PMC, WSH); Microform ed.: (from WSH); Online - full text ed.
Indexed: A20, A22, A26, ABRCLP, ASCA, B04, CA, CLI, CPL, CurCont, Faml, G08, I01, I03, I05, ILP, LRI, LegCont, P30, R05, SCOPUS, SSCI, T02, W07.
—BLDSC (3093.249000), CIS, IE, Infotrieve, Ingenta.
Published by: Catholic University of America, Columbus School of Law, 3600 John McCormack Rd, N E, Ste 248, Washington, DC 20064. TEL 202-319-5140, http://law.cua.edu.

282 USA
CATHOLIC UPDATE. Abbreviated title: C U. Text in English. 1973. m. USD 14 domestic; USD 21.20 in Canada; USD 23.60 elsewhere; USD 0.55 per issue (effective 2011). adv. back issues avail. **Document type:** *Newsletter, Trade.* **Description:** Covers Roman Catholic concerns and practices.
Related titles: Online - full text ed.
Indexed: CPL, P28.
Published by: (Franciscan Friars of St. John the Baptist Province), St. Anthony Messenger Press, 28 W Liberty St, Cincinnati, OH 45202. TEL 513-241-5615, 800-488-0488, FAX 513-241-0399, stanthony@americancatholic.org, http://www.americancatholic.org.

282 USA ISSN 0008-8404
CATHOLIC VIRGINIAN. Text in English. 1946. w. USD 10. adv. bk.rev.; film rev. charts; illus. **Document type:** *Newspaper.*
Published by: Diocese of Richmond, c/o Most Rev Walter F Sullivan, Bishop of Richmond, 800 Cathedral Pl, Box 26843, Richmond, VA 23261. TEL 804-359-5654. Ed. Charles E Mahon. Circ: 38,827.

282 GHA ISSN 0008-8412
CATHOLIC VOICE. Text in English. 1926. m. USD 72. illus.
Indexed: CERDIC.
Published by: (Archdiocese of Cape Coast), Catholic Mission Press, PO Box 60, Cape Coast, Ghana. Ed. Rev. Gabriel D Mensah. Circ: 6,000.

282 USA ISSN 0279-0645
BX801
CATHOLIC VOICE (OAKLAND). Text in English. 1963. bi-w. USD 8; USD 18 outside Diocese. adv. bk.rev. **Document type:** *Newspaper.*
Related titles: Microfilm ed.: (from LIB).
Published by: Diocese of Oakland, 3014 Lake Shore Ave, Oakland, CA 94610. TEL 510-893-5339, FAX 510-893-4734, cathvoice@aol.com. Ed., R&P Monica Clark. Pub. Most Rev. John S. Cummins. Adv. contact Tim Holden. Circ: 85,000. Wire service: CaNS.

282 USA ISSN 0744-9585
CATHOLIC VOICE (OMAHA). Text in English. 1903. 21/yr. (Fri.). USD 23 (effective 2005). adv. bk.rev. back issues avail. **Document type:** *Newspaper.*
Related titles: Microfiche ed.
Published by: (Catholic Archbishop of Omaha, Nebraska), Catholic Voice Publishing Co., 6060 N W Radial Highway, Box 4010, Omaha, NE 68104. TEL 402-558-6611, FAX 402-558-6614. Ed. Charles Wieser. R&P Stephen M Kent. Adv. contact Randy A. Grosse. col. inch USD 29.25. Circ: 69,023. Wire service: CaNS.

282 USA ISSN 1045-7496
CATHOLIC WEEK. Text in English. 1934. w. USD 14 inside diocese; USD 19 outside diocese; USD 22 in state; USD 30 foreign. adv. bk.rev. **Document type:** *Newspaper.* **Description:** Local, national, and international news with a Catholic perspective.
Address: PO Box 349, Mobile, AL 36601. TEL 334-432-3529, FAX 334-434-1547. Ed., R&P Larry G Wahl. Pub. Rev. Oscar H. Lipscomb. Adv. contact Mary Ann Stevens. Circ: 16,353.

282 AUS ISSN 0008-8420
CATHOLIC WEEKLY. Abbreviated title: C W. Text in English. 1942. w. AUD 80 (effective 2008). adv. bk.rev. illus. back issues avail. **Document type:** *Newspaper, Consumer.* **Description:** Acts as a catholic family newspaper offering international, national and local news.
Formed by the merger of (1895-1942): The Catholic Press; (1850-1942): The Freeman's Journal; Which was formerly (until 1850): The Australasian Chronicle
Related titles: Online - full text ed.: ISSN 1833-0460.
Published by: Catholic Press Newspaper Co Pty Ltd., Polding Centre, Level 8, 133 Liverpool St, Sydney, NSW 2000, Australia. TEL 61-2-93905400, FAX 61-2-93905401, cwaccountant@catholicweekly.com.au. Adv. contact Trevor Kenneally. page AUD 2,070; trim 290 x 400.

282 USA ISSN 0008-8439
CATHOLIC WEEKLY. Text in English. 1942. w. USD 25.95 domestic; USD 34.50 foreign (effective 2005). adv. bk.rev.; film rev. 8 p./no.; back issues avail. **Document type:** *Newspaper, Consumer.* **Description:** Coverage of current local, national and world news from a Catholic perspective.
Published by: G.L.S. Diocesan Reports, Inc., 1520 Court St., Saginaw, MI 48602. TEL 989-793-7661, FAX 989-793-7663, glsdiorepo@aol.com. Ed. Steve Sirianni. Adv. contact Jean Milburn. Circ: 11,613 (paid). Wire service: CaNS.

282 USA ISSN 0008-8447
CATHOLIC WITNESS. Text in English. 1966. bi-w. (Fri.). USD 9 to non-members (effective 2005). bk.rev. illus. **Document type:** *Newspaper, Consumer.* **Description:** Regional, national and international news of religious events.
Related titles: Microfilm ed.
Published by: (Roman Catholic Diocese of Harrisburg), Harrisburg Catholic Publishing Associates, 4800 Union Deposit Rd, Box 2555, Harrisburg, PA 17105. TEL 717-657-4804, FAX 717-657-7673. Ed. Rev. T R Haney. R&P Rev. T.R. Haney. Circ: 73,000. Wire service: CNS.

CATHOLIC WOMAN. *see* WOMEN'S INTERESTS

331.11 USA ISSN 0008-8463
BX801
CATHOLIC WORKER. Text in English. 1933. d. USD 0.25 domestic; USD 0.30 foreign; USD 0.01 per issue (effective 2005). bk.rev. **Document type:** *Newspaper.*
Related titles: Microform ed.: (from PQC).
Indexed: CPL, PRA.
Published by: New York Catholic Worker, 36 E First St, New York, NY 10003. TEL 212-777-9617. Ed. Frank Donovan. Circ: 89,000.

282 USA ISSN 0008-8471
CATHOLIC WORKMAN. Text in English. 1970 (vol.63). m. USD 5 to non-members. stat. **Document type:** *Newspaper, Consumer.* **Description:** Covers religious articles, news and activity calendar.
Address: PO Box 47, New Prague, MN 56071. TEL 612-758-2229, FAX 612-758-6221. Ed. Jill Pampach. Circ: 8,500 (controlled).

282 USA ISSN 1058-8159
BX801
THE CATHOLIC WORLD REPORT. Abbreviated title: C W R. Text in English. 1991. m. USD 39.95 domestic; USD 53.75 in Canada; USD 50.95 elsewhere (effective 2009). **Document type:** *Magazine, Consumer.* **Description:** Features significant articles from an orthodox Catholic perspective.
Related titles: Spanish ed.
Published by: Ignatius Press, PO Box 1339, Ft. Collins, CO 80522. TEL 800-353-2324, info@ignatius.com, http://www.ignatius.com. Ed. George Neumayr. Pub. Rev. Joseph Fessio. **Subscr. to:** PO Box 46, Bathgate, ND 58216. TEL 800-651-1531.

282 DEU ISSN 0008-8501
BR4
CATHOLICA; Vierteljahresschrift fuer oekumenische Theologie. Text in German. 1932. 4/yr. EUR 49.90; EUR 39.90 to students; EUR 15.40 newsstand/cover (effective 2011). adv. bk.rev. bibl. index. reprints avail. **Document type:** *Journal, Academic/Scholarly.*
Related titles: Online - full text ed.
Indexed: A01, A21, CPL, DIP, FR, IBR, IBZ, PCI, RASB, RI-1, RI-2, SCOPUS, T02.
—INIST. **CCC.**
Published by: (Johann Adam Moehler-Institut Paderborn), Aschendorff Verlag GmbH & Co. KG, Soester Str 13, Muenster, 48135, Germany. TEL 49-251-6900, FAX 49-251-6904570, buchverlag@aschendorff.de, http://www.aschendorff-buchverlag.de. Circ: 550 (paid and controlled).

282 FRA
CATHOLICISME HIER, AUJOURD'HUI, DEMAIN. Text in French. 1935. irreg., latest vol.70, 1997. back issues avail. **Document type:** *Monographic series, Academic/Scholarly.*
Published by: Letouzey et Ane Editeurs, 87 bd. Raspail, Paris, 75006, France. TEL 33-1-45488014, FAX 33-1-45490343. R&P Florence Letouzey.

CATHOLICS IN COALITION FOR JUSTICE AND PEACE NATIONAL NEWSLETTER. *see* POLITICAL SCIENCE—International Relations

282.44 FRA ISSN 1771-0405
CATHOLIQUES EN FRANCE. Text in French. 2005. m. EUR 49 domestic; EUR 66 foreign (effective 2007). back issues avail. **Document type:** *Magazine, Consumer.*
Formerly (until 2005): S N O P (0760-8373)
Published by: Conference des Eveques de France, 106 Rue du Bac, Paris, Cedex 07 75341, France. revue@cef.fr.

282 FRA ISSN 2106-7732
CATHOLIQUES EN VENDEE. Text in French. 1876. 23/yr. EUR 33 domestic; EUR 53 foreign; EUR 1.60 per issue (effective 2010). **Document type:** *Magazine, Consumer.*
Former titles (until 2010): Eglise de Lucon (1620-901X); (until 1999): La Semaine Catholique du Diocese de Lucon (1279-3361)
Related titles: Supplement(s): Catholiques en Vendee. Hors-Serie Vocations Vendee. ISSN 2108-8284. 1968.
Published by: Service de Communication du Diocese de Lucon, BP 219, Lucon, 85402, France. http://catholique-vendee.cef.fr.

282 ESP ISSN 1886-4945
BR7
CAURIENSIA; revista anual de ciencias eclesiasticas. Text in Multiple languages; Summaries in Spanish, English. 2006. a. EUR 24 domestic; EUR 30 in Europe; EUR 35 elsewhere (effective 2010). bk.rev. bibl. back issues avail. **Document type:** *Journal, Academic/ Scholarly.*
Related titles: Online - full text ed.
Indexed: CA, F04, T02.
—INIST.
Published by: Instituto Teologico San Pedro de Alcantara, Avenida de la Universidad 3, Caceres, 10004, Spain. TEL 34-927-245400, FAX 34-927-245440. Ed. Manuel Lazaro Pulido. R&P Ramon de la Trinidad Pinero Marino.

282 CAN ISSN 0843-2538
CELEBRATE. Text in English. 1940. bi-m. CAD 25.95 domestic; USD 24.95 in United States; USD 29.95 elsewhere (effective 2000). **Document type:** *Journal, Academic/Scholarly.* **Description:** Aimed at catechists, religion teachers, homilists and liturgy planners.
Formerly: Homiletic Service (0381-7466)
Published by: Novalis, St Paul University, 223 Main St, Ottawa, ON K1S 1C4, Canada. TEL 613-751-4040, 800-387-7164, FAX 613-782-3004. Ed. Bernadette Gasslein.

264.36 USA ISSN 1098-9994
CELEBREMOS!/LET US CELEBRATE!. Text in English, Spanish. 1998. q. USD 25 (effective 2011). **Document type:** *Magazine, Trade.* **Description:** Bilingual missal contains all prayers, readings, Orders of Mass, and commentaries in both languages on facing pages.
Published by: World Library Publications, Inc. (Subsidiary of: J.S. Paluch Co., Inc.), 3708 River Rd, Ste 400, Franklin Park, IL 60131. TEL 847-233-2752, 800-621-5197, FAX 847-233-2762, 888-957-3291, wlpcs@jspaluch.com. Ed. Mr. Peter Kolar.

282 FRA ISSN 0240-4656
CELEBRER. Text in French. irreg. price varies. Supplement avail.
Published by: (Centre National de Pastorale Liturgique), Editions du Cerf, 29 Boulevard La Tour Maubourg, Paris, 75340 Cedex 07, France. http://www.editionsducerf.fr.

CELEBRIAMO; rivista bimestrale di musica vocale per la liturgia. *see* MUSIC

282 ITA ISSN 0393-9901
IL CENACOLO. Text in Italian. 1923. m. index.
Formerly (until 1930): L'Eco del Seminario Beato Pietro Giuliano Eymard (0393-991X)
Published by: Padri Sacramentini, Via Longari 7, Ponteranica, BG 24010, Italy. TEL 39-035-571355, FAX 39-035-574294, ordini@sacramentini.it, http://www.sacramentini.it.

282 USA
EL CENTINELA. Text in Spanish. 1995. m. USD 15; free to qualified personnel (effective 2011). back issues avail. **Document type:** *Newspaper, Consumer.*
Contact Owner: Oregon Catholic Press, 5536 NE Hassalo St, PO Box 18030, Portland, OR 97218. TEL 503-281-1191, 800-548-8749, liturgy@ocp.org, http://www.ocp.org.

THE CENTRE FOR ISLAMIC STUDIES AND THE CENTRE FOR THE STUDY OF INTERRELIGIOUS RELATIONS. NEWSLETTER. *see* RELIGIONS AND THEOLOGY—Islamic

282 CAN ISSN 1718-7567
CENTRE ROSALIE-CADRON-JETTE. BULLETIN. Text in French. 1997. q. **Document type:** *Newsletter, Consumer.*
Formerly (until 2005): Rosalie, Lumiere et Tendresse sur nos Pas (1912-2543)
Related titles: English ed.: Rosalie-Cadron-Jette Centre Newsletter. ISSN 1718-7575. 1997.
Published by: Centre Rosalie-Cadron-Jette/Rosalie-Cadron-Jette Centre, 12435, Ave. de la Misericorde, Montreal, PQ H4J 2G3, Canada. TEL 514-332-0550, FAX 514-331-1262, rosalie.cadron@sympatico.ca, http://www.smisericorde.org/Fcrcj.htm.

255.1 ITA
CENTRO STORICO BENEDETTINO ITALIANO. BOLLETTINO INFORMATIVO. Text in Italian. irreg., latest vol.12, 1998. **Document type:** *Bulletin, Consumer.* **Description:** Offers essays on the Italian monastic tradition and details happenings within the Benedictine center.
Published by: Centro Storico Benedettino Italiano, Badia S. Maria del Monte, Cesena, FC 47023, Italy. TEL 39-0547-302161, http://www.abbaziadelmonte.it.

255 ITA
CENTRO STUDI ANTONIANI. COLLANA. Text in Italian. 1977. irreg., latest vol.29, 1997. price varies. **Document type:** *Monographic series, Academic/Scholarly.* **Description:** Contains scholarly articles about Franciscan studies.
Published by: Centro Studi Antoniani, Piazza del Santo 11, Padua, PD 35123, Italy. TEL 39-049-8762177, FAX 39-049-8762187, asscsa@tin.it, http://www.centrostudiantoniani.it.

255 ITA
CENTRO STUDI ANTONIANI. VARIA. Text in Italian. irreg., latest vol.27, 1998. price varies. **Document type:** *Monographic series, Academic/ Scholarly.*
Published by: Centro Studi Antoniani, Piazza del Santo 11, Padua, PD 35123, Italy. TEL 39-049-8762177, FAX 39-049-8762187, asscsa@tin.it, http://www.centrostudiantoniani.it.

262.13 USA
CENTRUM JANA PAWLA II BIULETYN. Text in Polish. 1979. 5/yr. USD 5. bk.rev. back issues avail. **Document type:** *Newsletter.* **Description:** Biographical information, memoirs, publications and activities.
Related titles: ◆ English ed.: Pope John Paul II Center Newsletter.
Indexed: RASB.
Published by: Pope John Paul II Center, Orchard Lake Schools, Orchard, Lake, MI 48324. TEL 313-683-0408. Ed. Rev. Roman Nir. Circ: 328.

282 SVN ISSN 0009-0387
CERKEV V SEDANJEM SVETU. Text in Slovenian. 1967. bi-m. EUR 24 (effective 2007). bk.rev. bibl. **Document type:** *Magazine, Consumer.*
Published by: Druzina, Krekov trg 1, p.p. 95, Ljubljana, 1001, Slovenia. TEL 386-1-3602845, FAX 386-1-3602800. Ed. Peter Kvaternik. Circ: 2,500.

282 GBR ISSN 0009-1014
CHALLENGE (SANDBACH); the magazine of St. Mary's Church, Sandbach. Text in English. 1964. m. GBP 2.40. adv. bk.rev. charts; illus. **Document type:** *Newsletter.*
Published by: St. Mary's Parochial Church Council, 55 Cookesmere Ln, Sandbach, Ches CW11 1BQ, United Kingdom. TEL 44-1270-763033, FAX 44-1270-764719. Ed. Nora Williams. Circ: 450.

282 USA
CHAP-LETT. Text in English. 3/yr. USD 15.
Published by: American Catholic Correctional Chaplains, PO Box 888, Ashland, KY 41101. TEL 606-928-6414. Ed. Rev. John P Noe. Circ: 350.

242 FRA ISSN 1775-6502
CHEMIN DE CROIX. Text in French. 2005. irreg. **Document type:** *Monographic series, Academic/Scholarly.*
Published by: Abbaye Notre Dame du Sacre Coeur de Chambarand, Monastere de Chambarand, Roybon, 38940, France.

282 FRA ISSN 1244-8869
CHEMINS DE DIALOGUE. Text in French. 1993. s-a. **Document type:** *Monographic series, Consumer.*
Published by: Institut Catholique de la Mediterranee (I C M), Le Mistral - 11 Impasse Flammarion, Marseille, 13001, France. TEL 33-4-91503550, FAX 33-4-91503555, icm@cathomed.cef.fr, http://cathomed.cef.fr.

230.0071 USA ISSN 0009-3718
BX801
CHICAGO STUDIES. Text in English. 1962. 3/yr. USD 17.50 (effective 2009). bk.rev. Index. back issues avail.; reprints avail. **Document type:** *Journal, Trade.* **Description:** Covers the concerns of the church and its ministry.
Related titles: Microform ed.: (from PQC).
Indexed: A22, CERDIC, CLA, CPL, OTA, P30, R&TA.
—BLDSC (3172.730000), IE.
Published by: Liturgy Training Publications, 3949 South Racine Ave, Chicago, IL 60609. TEL 773-579-4900, 800-933-1800, orders@ltp.org.

282 USA
CHIPS FROM THE FORESTERS TREE. Text in English. 1981. bi-m. back issues avail. **Document type:** *Newsletter.* **Description:** Features membership news with inspirational and religious contents.
Published by: Catholic Association of Foresters, 347 Commonwealth Ave, Boston, MA 02115. TEL 617-536-8221, 800-282-2263, FAX 617-536-2819. Ed. J A McVeigh. Circ: 5,500 (controlled).

200 DEU ISSN 1436-0489
CHORINER FORSCHUNGEN. Text in German. 1998. irreg., latest vol.2, 1998. price varies. **Document type:** *Monographic series, Academic/Scholarly.*
Published by: Trafo Verlag, Finkenstr 8, Berlin, 12621, Germany. TEL 49-30-61299418, FAX 49-30-61299421, info@trafoberlin.de, http://www.trafoberlin.de.

282 FRA ISSN 0252-2578
CHRETIENS DE L'EST. Text in French. 1974. q. **Document type:** *Magazine, Trade.*
—CCC.
Published by: Aide a l'Eglise en Detresse, 29, rue du Louvre, Mareil-Marly, 78750, France. TEL 33-1-39173010, FAX 33-1-39173019, sgd@aed-france.org, http://www.aed-france.org.

282 FRA ISSN 2108-9094
▼ **CHRETIENS MAGAZINE.** Text in French. 2010. 10/yr. EUR 33 domestic; EUR 39 foreign (effective 2010). **Document type:** *Magazine, Consumer.*
Published by: Rassemblement a Son Image, 1169 Av du Rouergue, Rodez, 12000, France. TEL 33-5-65780195.

282 DEU ISSN 0170-5148
CHRIST IN DER GEGENWART; katholische Wochenzeitschrift. Text in German. 1948. w. looseleaf. EUR 41.60 for 6 mos.; EUR 28.60 for 6 mos. to students; EUR 2.20 newsstand/cover (effective 2010). adv. index. back issues avail. **Document type:** *Newsletter, Consumer.*
Published by: Verlag Herder GmbH, Hermann-Herder-Str 4, Freiburg Im Breisgau, 79104, Germany. TEL 49-761-27170, FAX 49-761-2717520, kundenservice@herder.de, http://www.herder.de. Adv. contact Friederike Ward TEL 49-761-2717407.

282 DEU ISSN 0930-5718
BX4751
CHRISTEN HEUTE; Zeitung der Alt-Katholiken fuer Christen heute. Text in German. 1873; N.S. 1956. m. EUR 20 domestic; EUR 26.50 foreign (effective 2006). bk.rev. back issues avail. **Document type:** *Bulletin.*
Formerly (until 1984): Alt-Katholische Kirchenzeitung (0002-6522)
Published by: Katholisches Bistum der Alt-Katholiken in Deutschland, Gregor-Mendel-Str 28, Bonn, 53115, Germany. TEL 49-228-232285, FAX 49-228-238314, ordinariat@alt-katholisch.de, http://www.alt-katholisch.de. Ed., R&P Matthias Ring. **Subscr. to:** Christen Heute, Osterdeich 1, Nordstrand 25845, Germany. FAX 49-4842-1511, versand@christen-heute.de.

282 USA ISSN 1050-4125
CHRISTIAN STUDIES. Text in English. 1980. s-a. free (effective 2011). back issues avail. **Document type:** *Journal, Academic/Scholarly.*
Formerly (until 1989): Institute for Christian Studies. Faculty Bulletin
Related titles: Online - full text ed.
Indexed: A01, A03, A08, A21, CA, RI-1, T02.
Published by: Austin Graduate School of Theology, 7640 Guadalupe St, Austin, TX 78752. TEL 512-476-2772, FAX 512-476-3919, info@austingrad.edu.

268 POL ISSN 1508-5813
CHRISTIANITAS; religia, kultura, spoleczenstwo. Text in Polish. 1999. q. **Document type:** *Magazine, Consumer.*
Published by: Klub Ksiazki Katolickiej, P.O. Box 101, Brwinow, 05840, Poland. TEL 48-61-8652995, FAX 48-61-8652995. Ed. Pawel Milcarek.

255.71 AUT ISSN 0009-5796
CHRISTLICHE INNERLICHKEIT; Schrift fuer Gebet und gelebtes Christentum. Text in German. 1965. bi-m. EUR 15 (effective 2010). bk.rev. **Document type:** *Journal, Consumer.*
Address: Silbergasse 35, Vienna, O 1190, Austria. TEL 43-1-320334010, FAX 43-1-3281364, ci@karmel.at, http://www.karmel.at/ci/. Ed. P Antonio Sagardoy. Circ: 5,000.

282 USA ISSN 8755-6901
CHRISTOPHER NEWS NOTES. Text in English. 1945. 10/yr. free (effective 2009). back issues avail. **Document type:** *Newsletter, Consumer.* **Description:** Features articles for inspiration and ideas.
Related titles: Online - full text ed.
Published by: Christophers, Inc., 5 Hanover Sq, 11th Fl, New York, NY 10004. TEL 212-759-4050, 888-298-4050, FAX 212-838-5073, mail@christophers.org. Ed. Stephanie Raha. Circ: 600,000.

268 DEU ISSN 0009-5818
CHRISTOPHORUS (FRANKENTHAL). Text in German. 1955. q. adv. bk.rev. charts. 40 p./no. 2 cols./p.; **Document type:** *Journal, Academic/Scholarly.*
Published by: Christophorus, Anselm-Feuerbach-Str 24, Frankenthal, 67227, Germany. TEL 49-6233-34013, FAX 49-6233-34015, G.H.Fehrenbach@t-online.de. Ed. Paul Niewalda. Circ: 900 (controlled).

230.2 USA ISSN 0883-5667
BV4000
CHURCH. Text in English. 1985. q. USD 33 domestic to individuals; USD 39 foreign to individuals; USD 39 domestic to institutions; USD 45 foreign to institutions (effective 2005). adv. bk.rev. back issues avail. **Document type:** *Magazine, Trade.* **Description:** For Catholic pastoral ministers. Publishes articles on theology, moral issues, scripture, liturgy, parish and staff administration, religious education, spirituality, and practical examples of successful parish programs.
Indexed: CPL.
Published by: National Pastoral Life Center, 18 Bleecker St, New York, NY 10012-2404. TEL 212-431-7825, FAX 212-274-9786, nplc@nplc.org, http://www.nplc.org. Ed. Karen Sue Smith. R&P, Adv. contact Mary Good. Circ: 8,600 (paid).

CIAO AMICI; il messaggero dei bambini. *see* CHILDREN AND YOUTH—For

282 ESP ISSN 0210-0398
BX805
CIENCIA TOMISTA. Text in Spanish. 1910. 3/yr. EUR 50 (effective 2009). bk.rev. abstr.; bibl. 210 p./no.; back issues avail. **Document type:** *Journal, Academic/Scholarly.*
Indexed: CERDIC, CPL, DIP, FR, IBR, IBZ, IPB, MLA, MLA-IB, OTA.
—INIST.
Published by: (Facultad Teologica de San Esteban), Editorial San Esteban, Plaza Concilio de Trento s-n, Apartado 17, Salamanca, 37001, Spain. TEL 34-923-264781, FAX 34-923-265480, info@sanestebaneditorial.com, http://www.sanestebaneditorial.com/. Ed. Alberto Escallada Tijero. Circ: 700.

271.12 BEL ISSN 0009-7497
BX3401
➤ **CITEAUX**; commentarii cistercienses. Text in Dutch, English, French, German, Italian, Portuguese, Spanish; Summaries in French, German, English. 1950. s-a. USD 48 foreign (effective 1999). bk.rev. bibl.; illus. index, cum.index: 1950-1974. back issues avail. **Document type:** *Journal, Academic/Scholarly.* **Description:** Publishes articles concerning all aspects and periods of Cistercian history, art, archeology, law, economy, liturgy and spirituality.
Formerly (until 1958): Citeaux in de Nederlanden (0774-4927)
Related titles: Microfiche ed.; ◆ Supplement(s): Bulletin d'Histoire Cistercienne. ISSN 0777-3331.
Indexed: FR, MLA, MLA-IB, PCI.
—IE, INIST.
Published by: Citeaux V.Z.W., Abdij OLVr van Nazareth, Abdijlaan 9, Brecht, 2960, Belgium. 104124.3655@compuserve.com. Ed., Pub., R&P Terryl N Kinder. Circ: 500 (paid).

271.12 BEL
CITEAUX. COLLECTION STUDIA ET DOCUMENTA. Text in French. irreg., latest 1998. price varies. back issues avail. **Document type:** *Academic/Scholarly.* **Description:** Contains scholarly editions of texts and documents pertaining to the Cistercian order.
Published by: Citeaux V.Z.W., Abdij OLVr van Nazareth, Abdijlaan 9, Brecht, 2960, Belgium. Ed., R&P Terryl N Kinder.

271.12 BEL
CITEAUX. COLLECTION TEXTES ET DOCUMENTS. Text in French. 1988. irreg., latest 1995. price varies. back issues avail. **Document type:** *Monographic series, Academic/Scholarly.* **Description:** Contains scholarly examinations of texts and issues in Cistercian history and life.
Published by: Citeaux V.Z.W., Abdij OLVr van Nazareth, Abdijlaan 9, Brecht, 2960, Belgium. Ed., R&P Terryl N Kinder.

255.4 ESP ISSN 0009-7756
AP60
LA CIUDAD DE DIOS; revista Agustiniana. Text in Spanish. 1881. q. EUR 60 in the European Union; EUR 90 elsewhere (effective 2009). bk.rev. bibl. index. 250 p./no.; back issues avail. **Document type:** *Journal, Academic/Scholarly.* **Description:** Contains manuscripts on religion, philosophy and history.
Formerly (until 1936): Religion y Cultura (0211-8971); Which was formed by the merger of (1887-1927): La Ciudad de Dios (0211-8963); (1903-1927): Espana y America (0211-898X)
Related titles: Fax ed.; Microfilm ed.: (from PQC).
Indexed: CERDIC, CPL, FR, IBR, IBZ, IPB, IZBG, MLA, MLA-IB.
—INIST.
Published by: Ediciones Escurialenses, Real Monasterio del Escorial, San Lorenzo del Escorial, Madrid, 28200, Spain. TEL 34-91-8869109, FAX 34-91-8965011, edes@edes.es, http://www.edes.es. Circ: 550.

282 ITA ISSN 0009-8167
AP37
CIVILTA CATTOLICA. Text in Italian. 1850. s-m. EUR 70 domestic; EUR 100 in the European Union; USD 150 in United States (effective 2008). adv. bk.rev.; film rev.; play rev. bibl. index, cum.index: 1940-1960, 1960-1970, 1970-1980, 1980-1990. **Document type:** *Magazine, Consumer.* **Description:** Covers the important problems faced by society and the Church and offers articles on theological, philosophical, moral, social, political and literary subjects.
Related titles: Fax ed.; Online - full text ed.
Indexed: A21, A22, CERDIC, CPL, FR, I13, IBR, IBZ, MLA-IB, P30, PCI, RASB, RI-1, RI-2.
—IE, Infotrieve, INIST.
Published by: Compagnia di Gesu, Via di Porta Pinciana, 1, Rome, RM 00187, Italy. TEL 39-06-69792039, FAX 39-06-69792022. Circ: 20,000.

230.2 ITA ISSN 0578-4182
CLARETIANUM; commentaria theologica. Text in Multiple languages. 1961. a. price varies. bk.rev. bibl. **Document type:** *Magazine, Consumer.*
Formerly (until 1993): Theologica
Indexed: CERDIC, CLA, OTA.
Published by: Claretianum. Istituto di Teologia della Vita Consacrata, Largo Lorenzo Mossa 4, Rome, RM 00165, Italy. TEL 39-06-660681, FAX 39-06-66068303, istvitcons@libero.it, http://www.claretianum.org. Ed. Bruno Proietti. Circ: 300.

282 MAC
CLARIM. Text in Portuguese. 1948. w. MOP 450 (effective 2000). adv. 24 p./no. 6 cols./p.; **Document type:** *Newspaper.* **Description:** Covers religion, education, social assistance, and government.
Published by: Diocese of Macau, Rua Central, 26 A, Macau. TEL 573860, FAX 307867. Ed., R&P, Adv. contact Albino Bento Pais. Circ: 1,100.

282 USA
CLARION HERALD. Text in English. 1963. bi-w. (Wed.). USD 15 in state; USD 17 out of state (effective 2006). adv. **Document type:** *Newspaper, Consumer.*
Related titles: Microfilm ed.
Published by: Archdiocese of New Orleans, 1000 Howard Ave, Ste 400, New Orleans, LA 70113. TEL 504-524-4777, FAX 504-596-3020. Pub. Rev. Rev. Alfred C Hughes. Adv. contact Maureen O'Connor Austin. col. inch USD 31.50. Circ: 75,000 (paid). Wire service: CaNS.

282.09 ESP
COLECCION HISTORIA DE LA IGLESIA. Text in Spanish. 1971. irreg., latest vol.32, 1999. price varies. back issues avail. **Document type:** *Monographic series, Academic/Scholarly.*
Published by: (Universidad de Navarra, Facultad de Teologia), Universidad de Navarra, Servicio de Publicaciones, Campus Universitario, Pamplona, 31009, Spain. TEL 34-948-256850, FAX 34-948-256854, http://www.unav.es/publicaciones/.

230.2 ESP
COLECCION TEOLOGICA. Text in Spanish. 1971. irreg., latest 2010. price varies. back issues avail. **Document type:** *Monographic series, Academic/Scholarly.*
Published by: (Universidad de Navarra, Facultad de Teologia), Universidad de Navarra, Servicio de Publicaciones, Campus Universitario, Pamplona, 31009, Spain. TEL 34-948-256850, FAX 34-948-256854, http://www.unav.es/publicaciones/.

255.71 ITA ISSN 0394-7769
COLLATIONES MARIALES INSTITUTI CARMELITANI. Text in English, French, German, Italian, Latin, Spanish. 1960. irreg. price varies. adv. **Document type:** *Monographic series, Academic/Scholarly.*
Published by: (Order of Carmelites), Edizioni Carmelitane, Via Sforza Pallavicini 10, Rome, 00193, Italy. TEL 39-06-68100886, FAX 39-06-68100887, edizioni@ocarm.org, http://www.carmelites.info/edizioni/. Circ: 500.

COLLECTANEA BIBLIOGRAPHICA CARMELITANA. *see* RELIGIONS AND THEOLOGY—Abstracting, Bibliographies, Statistics

271.12 BEL ISSN 0378-4916
COLLECTANEA CISTERCIENSIA; revue trimestrielle de spiritualite monastique. Text in French. 1934. q. EUR 30 in Europe; EUR 32.50 elsewhere (effective 2003). bk.rev. bibl. cum.index: 1959-1970, 1971-1980, 1981-1990. 120 p./no.; back issues avail. **Document type:** *Magazine, Academic/Scholarly.* **Description:** Publishes studies on the various monastic traditions, both oriental and occidental, information pertaining to the dialogue between Christian and non-Christian monasticism, and reports on events in the monastic world, including congresses, meetings, and relevant publications.
Formerly (until 1965): Collectanea Ordinis Cisterciensium Reformatorum
Related titles: Microform ed.: (from PQC).
Indexed: CERDIC, CPL, DIP, FR, IBR, IBZ, MLA-IB, PCI, RILM.
—BLDSC (3299.400000), IE, Infotrieve, INIST.
Published by: Abbaye Notre Dame de Soleilmont, Administration "Cisterciensia", Fleurus, 6220, Belgium. TEL 32-7-1380209, FAX 32-7-1385662, coll.cist@skynet.be. Ed. Bernard-Joseph Samain. **U.K. subscr. to:** Mt. St. Bernard Abbey, Coalville, Leics LE67 5UL, United Kingdom; **U.S. subscr. to:** Mississippi Abbey, 8400 Abbey Hill, Dubuque, IA 52003-9576.

271.3 ITA ISSN 0010-0749
BX3601
COLLECTANEA FRANCISCANA. Text in English, French, German, Italian, Latin, Portuguese, Spanish. 1931. q. bk.rev. bibl. index, cum.index: 1931-1970. **Document type:** *Journal, Academic/Scholarly.*
Related titles: ◆ Supplement(s): Bibliographia Franciscana. ISSN 1723-3585.
Indexed: A22, B24, BibInd, CERDIC, DIP, FR, IBR, IBZ, IPB, MLA-IB.
—IE, INIST.
Published by: Frati Minori Cappuccini, Istituto Storico/Ordo Fratrum Minorum Capuccinorum, Circonvallazione Occidentale 6850, Rome, RM 00163, Italy. TEL 39-06-660521, FAX 39-06-66052532.

230.0071 POL ISSN 0137-6985
COLLECTANEA THEOLOGICA. Text in Polish. 1931. q. EUR 74 foreign (effective 2006). **Document type:** *Journal, Academic/Scholarly.*
Indexed: FR, IBR, IBZ, IZBG, OTA.
—INIST.
Published by: Wydawnictwo Uniwersytetu Kardynala Stefana Wyszynskiego, Ul Dewajtis 5, Warsaw, 01815, Poland. wydawnictwo@uksw.edu.pl, http://www.uksw.edu.pl/wydawn/wydawnictwo.htm. **Dist. by:** Ars Polona, Obroncow 25, Warsaw 03933, Poland. TEL 48-22-5098609, FAX 48-22-5098610, arspolona@arspolona.com.pl, http://www.arspolona.com.pl.

230.2 ITA ISSN 1970-2817
COLLECTIO OLIVIANA. Text in Multiple languages. 1999. irreg. price varies. **Document type:** *Monographic series, Academic/Scholarly.*
Published by: Collegio San Bonaventura/Collegium S Bonaventurae ad Claras Aquas, Via Vecchia per Marino 28-30, Grottaferrata, 00046, Italy. http://www.fratiquaracchi.it.

230.2 USA ISSN 1074-9403
➤ **COLLEGE THEOLOGY SOCIETY. ANNUAL PUBLICATION.** Text in English. 19??. a. free to members (effective 2010). **Document type:** *Monographic series, Academic/Scholarly.*
Formerly (until 19??): College Theology Society. Annual Publications (0276-2064)

R

—BLDSC (1093.300000).
Published by: College Theology Society, c/o Bradford Hinze, Fordham University, Theology, 441 E Fordham Rd, Bronx, NY 10458. TEL 718-817-3364, http://www.collegetheology.org.

282 USA
THE COLORADO CATHOLIC HERALD. Text in English. 1984. bi-m. (1st & 3rd Fri.). USD 15 in state; USD 20 out of state (effective 2006). **Document type:** *Newspaper.*
Formerly (until 2006): The Catholic Herald
Published by: Diocese of Colorado Springs, 228 N. Colorado Ave, Colorado Springs, CO 80903. TEL 719-636-2345, FAX 719-636-1216. Pub. Michael J Bishop Sheridan. Adv. contact Mary Theresa Thomas. Circ: 30,000 (controlled and free). Wire service: CaNS.

266.2 USA ISSN 0095-4438
BV3410
COLUMBAN MISSION. Text in English. 1918. 8/yr. USD 10 (effective 2000). adv. bk.rev. **Description:** Describes the mission apostolate of Columban-sponsored missionaries & elicits support for that work.
Formerly: Columban Fathers Mission
Published by: (St. Columban's Foreign Mission Society), Columban Fathers, St Columbans, NE 68056. FAX 402-291-4984, editor@columban.org. Ed., R&P Rev. John Burger. Pub. Rev. Brendan O'Sullivan. Adv. contact William Zuerlein. Circ: 100,000 (controlled).

282 USA ISSN 0010-1869
COLUMBIA (NEW HAVEN). Text in English. 1921. m. USD 6 domestic to non-members; USD 8 foreign to non-members; free to members (effective 2009). bk.rev. illus. Index. reprints avail. **Document type:** *Magazine, Consumer.* **Description:** Provides features and columns demonstrating how groups and families can cooperate to improve society, written predominantly by members of a Catholic fraternal organization.
Related titles: Online - full text ed.: free (effective 2009).
Indexed: CPL.
Published by: Knights of Columbus, 1 Columbus Plz, New Haven, CT 06510. TEL 203-752-4000, 800-380-995, FAX 203-752-4109, info@kofc.org, http://www.kofc.org. **Subscr. to:** PO Box 1670, New Haven, CT 06507.

266.2 USA ISSN 0279-3652
COMBONI MISSIONS. Text in English. 1948. q. USD 6. illus. **Description:** Informs readers about Third World situations and about the congregation's mission work.
Former titles: Verona Missions (0164-4211); Verona Fathers Missions (0042-4234)
Published by: Comboni Missionaries of the Heart of Jesus, 8108 Beechmont Ave, Cincinnati, OH 45255. TEL 513-474-4997, FAX 513-474-0382. Ed. Jose Marques. Circ: 25,000 (controlled).

COMMONWEAL; a review of religion, politics & culture. *see* LITERARY AND POLITICAL REVIEWS

282 DEU ISSN 0010-3497
COMMUNICATIO SOCIALIS; internationale Zeitschrift fuer Kommunikation in Religion, Kirche und Gesellschaft. Text in German; Summaries in English, French, Spanish. 1968-1988; resumed. q. EUR 40.50; EUR 32 to students; EUR 11.90 newsstand/cover (effective 2007). adv. bk.rev.; film rev. **Document type:** *Journal, Academic/Scholarly.* **Description:** Catholic publication dealing with mass media and religion, the Catholic press, and communication in theology. Includes list of book and magazine references.
Indexed: CA, CERDIC, CommAb, DIP, IBR, IBZ, S02, S03, SCOPUS, SOPODA, SPPI, SociolAb, T02.
—CCC.
Published by: Matthias-Gruenewald-Verlag GmbH (Subsidiary of: Schwabenverlag AG), Senefelderstr 12, Ostfildern, 73760, Germany. TEL 49-711-44060, FAX 49-711-4406177, mail@gruenewaldverlag.de, http://www.gruenewaldverlag.de. Ed. Dr. Franz Josef Eilers. Adv. contact Nina Baab TEL 49-6131-928620. B&W page EUR 350; trim 110 x 200. Circ: 420 (paid).

262.9 VAT ISSN 0393-0327
BX1935
COMMUNICATIONES. Key Title: Communicationes - Pontificia Codici Iuris Canonici Recognoscendo. Text in Italian. 1969. s-a. EUR 24 domestic; EUR 31 foreign (effective 2002). back issues avail. **Document type:** *Academic/Scholarly.* **Description:** Organ of the Pontifical Commission for the right interpretation of the Code of Canon Law.
Indexed: CERDIC, CLA, CPL, PCI.
Published by: (Pontificia Commissio Codici Iuris Canonici Recognoscendo), Libreria Editrice Vaticana, 00120, Vatican City. TEL 379-6-69885003, FAX 379-6-69884716.

230.0071 GBR ISSN 0094-2065
BX801
➤ **COMMUNIO;** international Catholic review. Text in English. 1972. q. USD 142, GBP 82 to institutions (effective 2011). adv. index, cum.index. back issues avail.; reprint service avail. from PSC. **Document type:** *Journal, Academic/Scholarly.* **Description:** Journal of theological and cultural reflection from a Catholic perspective by noted theologians, philosophers, and other scholars.
Related titles: Microform ed.: (from PQC); Online - full text ed.: GBP 62, USD 109 to institutions (effective 2006).
Indexed: A21, A22, CPL, DIP, IBR, IBZ, MLA-IB, OTA, P30, PCI, R&TA, RI-1, RI-2.
—BLDSC (3363.543600), IE, Infotrieve, Ingenta. **CCC.**
Published by: Sage Publications Ltd. (Subsidiary of: Sage Publications, Inc.), 1 Oliver's Yard, 55 City Rd, London, EC1Y 1SP, United Kingdom. TEL 44-20-73248500, FAX 44-20-73248600, info@sagepub.co.uk, http://www.uk.sagepub.com/home.nav. Ed. David L Schindler. **Subscr. outside UK & Europe to:** Communio, Inc., PO Box 4557, Washington, DC 20017. TEL 202-526-0251, FAX 202-526-1934, sales@communio-icr.com.

264.36 ESP ISSN 0010-3705
BR7
COMMUNIO; commentarii internationales de ecclesia et theologia. Text in Spanish. 1968. s-a. adv. bk.rev. cum.index. 250 p./no.; **Document type:** *Journal, Academic/Scholarly.*
Indexed: A21, CERDIC, OTA, RI-1, RILM.
Published by: Estudio General Dominicano, Provincia Betica (Espana), Apartado 820, Sevilla, 41080, Spain. FAX 34-54-904367. Ed. Antonio Larios Ramos. Adv. contact Modesto Sanchez. Circ: 500.

282 DEU ISSN 1439-6165
BX803
COMMUNIO. Text in German. 1972. bi-m. EUR 35.50 (effective 2009). adv. bk.rev. **Document type:** *Magazine, Consumer.*
Formerly (until 1995): Internationale Katholische Zeitschrift (0341-8693)
Indexed: A21, CERDIC, DIP, FR, IBR, IBZ, IZBG, LID&ISL, MLA-IB, OTA, RASB, RI-1, RI-2.
Published by: Communio Verlagsgesellschaft mbH (Subsidiary of: Schwabenverlag AG), Senefelderstr 12, Ostfildern, 73760, Germany. TEL 49-711-4406140, FAX 49-711-4406138. Ed. Jan-Heiner Tueck. Adv. contact Sabrina Reusch. B&W page EUR 550; trim 165 x 240. Circ: 1,800 (paid).

282 FRA ISSN 0338-781X
COMMUNIO. Text in French. 1975. bi-m. EUR 59 domestic; EUR 59 in Belgium; EUR 59 in Switzerland; EUR 61 elsewhere (effective 2008). **Document type:** *Journal, Academic/Scholarly.*
Indexed: FR, MLA-IB, RILM.
—INIST. **CCC.**
Published by: Association Communio, 5 Passage Saint-Paul, Paris, 75004, France. TEL 33-1-42782843, FAX 33-1-42782840.

282 CHL ISSN 0717-4799
COMMUNIO; revista catolica internacional de lengua hispana para America Latina. Text in Spanish. 1999. s-a. back issues avail. **Document type:** *Journal, Academic/Scholarly.*
Published by: Universidad Gabriela Mistral, Ave Ricardo Lyon 1177, Santiago de Chile, Chile. TEL 56-2-4144545, ugmistral@ugm.cl, http://www.ugm.cl/main/.

255.53 USA ISSN 0886-1293
COMPANY; a magazine of the American Jesuits. Text in English. 1983. q. free (effective 2005). bk.rev. **Document type:** *Magazine, Consumer.*
Related titles: Online - full text ed.
Address: P O Box 60790, Chicago, IL 60660. TEL 773-761-9432, FAX 773-761-9443. Ed., R&P Martin McHugh. Pub. Daniel Flaherty. Circ: 110,000 (controlled).

230.2 AUS ISSN 1036-9686
➤ **COMPASS;** a review of topical theology. Text in English. 1967. q. AUD 30 (effective 2009). bk.rev. 48 p./no.; back issues avail. **Document type:** *Journal, Academic/Scholarly.* **Description:** Features analysis of topical theology.
Former titles (until 1990): Compass Theology Review (0819-4602); (until 1973): Compass (0311-1210)
Related titles: Online - full text ed.
Indexed: A01, P28, P48, P53, P54, PQC, T02.
—CIS, Ingenta.
Published by: (Missionaries of the Sacred Heart), Compass, PO Box 229, Kensington, NSW 1465, Australia. TEL 61-2-95163542, FAX 61-2-95163536, http://www.chevaliercentre.org/. Ed., R&P Barry Brundell TEL 61-2-95163542.

282 ESP ISSN 2171-5793
COMUNIDADE. Text in Spanish. 1994. bi-m. **Document type:** *Bulletin, Consumer.*
Related titles: ◆ Supplement to: Obispado de Orense. Boletin Oficial. ISSN 2171-5807.
Published by: Obispado de Orense, Rua Progeso No. 26, Orense, 32080, Spain. TEL 34-988-366141, FAX 34-988-366142, orcuria@obispadodeourense.com, http://www.obispadodeourense.com.

282 ESP ISSN 0212-6729
CONFER; revista de vida religiosa. Text in Spanish. 1961. q. USD 56 (effective 2001). **Document type:** *Magazine, Consumer.* **Description:** Covers all aspects of a life devoted to the church. Directed to male and female members of religious communities.
Published by: Conferencia Espanola de Religiosos y Religiosas, Avda Alfonso XIII, 97, Madrid, 28016, Spain. TEL 34-91-5193635, FAX 34-91-5195557. Ed., R&P Isidro Hernandez. Adv. contact Luis Ortiz. Circ: 4,500.

282 ESP ISSN 0214-0683
CONFERENCIA EPISCOPAL ESPANOLA. BOLETIN OFICIAL. Text in Spanish. 1984. q. back issues avail. **Document type:** *Bulletin, Consumer.*
Published by: Conferencia Episcopal Espanola, C/ Anastro 1, Madrid, 28033, Spain. TEL 34-91-3439600 34-91-343 96 00, conferenciaepiscopal@planalfa.es, http://www.conferenciaepiscopal.es.

282 ITA
CONFERENZA ITALIANA SUPERIORI MAGGIORI. ARCHIVIO DI NOTIZIE. Text in Italian. 1960. bi-m. free. **Document type:** *Newsletter, Consumer.*
Published by: Conferenza Italiana Superiori Maggiori, Via degli Scipioni 256 B, Rome, 00192, Italy. TEL 39-06-3216455, FAX 39-06-3222950, http://www.cism-italia.org.

270.092 USA ISSN 1550-0500
CONNECT! (NEW BERLIN); uniting word & world. Text in English. 1972. bi-m. looseleaf. USD 69.95; USD 15 per issue (effective 2011). adv. **Document type:** *Journal, Trade.* **Description:** Includes homily resource for ministers and priests.
Former titles (until 1994): Nova (1047-2398); Nova et Vetera
Related titles: CD-ROM ed.: USD 59.95 (effective 2011); Online - full text ed.: USD 39.95; USD 10 per issue (effective 2011).
Indexed: OTA.
Published by: Liturgical Publications Inc., 2875 South James Dr, New Berlin, WI 53151. TEL 800-950-9952, CustomerService@LPiResourceCenter.comCustomerService@LPiResourceCenter.com, http://www.4lpi.com.

282 USA ISSN 0740-6835
CONSCIENCE; a news journal of prochoice Catholic opinion. Text in English. 1980. q. USD 15 domestic; USD 25 foreign; free to libraries (effective 2011). adv. bk.rev. Index. 48 p./no. 3 cols./p.; back issues avail. **Document type:** *Magazine, Trade.* **Description:** Explores sexual and reproductive ethics, the people and agendas of the religious right, as well as the role of the church in the civil state.
Related titles: Online - full text ed.
Indexed: A26, AmHI, B14, BRI, CBRI, CWI, G05, G06, G07, G08, GW, H07, I05, IAPV, P30, P48, PAIS, PQC, R05, S21, SCOPUS, T02, W09.
Published by: Catholics for Choice, 1436 U St, NW, Ste 301, Washington, DC 20009. TEL 202-986-6093, FAX 202-332-7995, cfc@catholicsforchoice.org. Ed. David Nolan.

282 USA ISSN 0884-7010
CONSECRATED LIFE. Text in English. 1975. s-a. USD 15 domestic; USD 20 foreign (effective 2007). back issues avail. **Document type:** *Magazine, Consumer.* **Description:** Contains news and notices of religious activities, and statements of the Holy Father pertinent to religious life and decisions.
Indexed: CPL.
Published by: Institute on Religious Life, PO Box 7500, Libertyville, IL 60048. TEL 877-267-1195, FAX 877-267-2044. Circ: 2,000.

282 AUS ISSN 0810-7025
CONTACT (SCORESBY). Text in English. 1959. q. AUD 10 for 10 issues (effective 2010). illus. 36 p./no.; back issues avail. **Document type:** *Magazine, Consumer.* **Description:** Contains teaching articles on the faith and feature articles on many interesting aspects of Australian Church history.
Related titles: Online - full text ed.: free (effective 2009).
Published by: Confraternity of Christ the Priest, PO Box 1272, Doncaster, VIC 3109, Australia. TEL 61-3-98420144, FAX 61-3-98420155, contact@christthepriest.com. Ed. Thomas Casanova.

282 USA ISSN 2154-9958
CONTEMPORARY CATHOLIC. Text in English. 2007. m. free (effective 2010). **Document type:** *Newsletter, Consumer.* **Description:** Provides news for modern Catholics.
Media: Online - full content.
Published by: The Contemporary Catholics, 1539 Shire Cir, Iverness, IL 60067. TEL 708-710-3460, fatherjim@contemporarycatholics.org.

282 ITA ISSN 2038-1204
CONVENTO FRANCESCANO DI DINGO. BIBLIOTECA. QUADERNI. Key Title: Quaderni della Biblioteca del Convento Francescano di Dongo. Text in Italian. 1990. 3/yr. **Document type:** *Journal, Academic/Scholarly.*
Published by: Edizioni Biblioteca Francescana, Piazza Sant' Angelo 2, Milan, 20121, Italy. info@bibliotecafrancescana.it, http://www.bibliotecafrancescana.it.

282 ITA ISSN 1828-7743
BR5
CONVIVIUM ASSISIENSE. Text in Italian. 1993. s-a. **Document type:** *Magazine, Consumer.*
Indexed: OTA.
Published by: Cittadella Editrice, Via Ancaiani 3, Assisi, PG 06081, Italy. TEL 39-075-813595, FAX 39-075-813719, http://www.cittadellaeditrice.com.

255.3 USA ISSN 0010-8685
CORD; a franciscan spiritual review. Text in English. 1951. q. USD 30 domestic; USD 35 foreign (effective 2010). adv. bk.rev. bibl.; illus. back issues avail. **Document type:** *Journal, Academic/Scholarly.* **Description:** Provides articles of historical interest, as well as articles dealing with contemporary applications.
Indexed: CERDIC, MLA-IB.
Published by: Franciscan Institute (Subsidiary of: St. Bonaventure University), c/o St. Bonaventure University, 3261 W State Rd, St. Bonaventure, NY 14778. TEL 716-375-2000, FAX 716-375-2139, franinst@sbu.edu, http://franciscaninstitute.sbu.edu. Ed. Daria R Mitchell TEL 716-375-2160. Pub. Michael F Cusato TEL 716-375-2143.

282 ESP ISSN 0210-1858
CORINTIOS XIII; revista de teologia y pastoral de la caridad. Variant title: Corintios Trece. Text in Spanish. 1977. q. EUR 28.38 (effective 2008). back issues avail. **Document type:** *Monographic series, Consumer.*
Published by: Caritas Espanola, San Bernardo, 99 bis 7a, Madrid, 28015, Spain. TEL 34-91-4441000, FAX 34-91-5934882, publicaciones@caritas-espa.org, http://www.caritas.es.

282 DEU ISSN 0070-0320
BR302
CORPUS CATHOLICORUM. Text in German. 1919. irreg., latest vol.48, 2007. price varies. **Document type:** *Monographic series, Academic/Scholarly.*
Published by: Aschendorff Verlag GmbH & Co. KG, Soester Str 13, Muenster, 48135, Germany. TEL 49-251-6900, FAX 49-251-6904570, buchverlag@aschendorff.de, http://www.aschendorff-buchverlag.de.

282 BEL ISSN 0589-7963
CORPUS CHRISTIANORUM. CONTINUATIO MEDIAEVALIS. Text in Latin. 1966. irreg. (5-10/yr.), latest vol.167, 1997. back issues avail. **Document type:** *Monographic series, Academic/Scholarly.* **Description:** Publishes critical editions of medieval texts from the eight to the fifteenth century.
Related titles: CD-ROM ed.
Published by: Brepols Publishers, Begijnhof 67, Turnhout, 2300, Belgium. FAX 32-14-428919, periodicals@brepols.net.

225 BEL ISSN 2031-4876
CORPUS CHRISTIANORUM. SERIES APOCRYPHORUM. Text in Multiple languages. 1983. irreg., latest vol.12, 1999. back issues avail. **Document type:** *Monographic series, Academic/Scholarly.* **Description:** Publishes critical editions of New Testament apocrypha.
Published by: (Association pour l'Etude de la Litterature Apocryphe Chretienne), Brepols Publishers, Begijnhof 67, Turnhout, 2300, Belgium. FAX 32-14-428919, periodicals@brepols.net.

282 BEL ISSN 1780-4582
CORPUS CHRISTIANORUM. SERIES LATINA. Text in Latin. 1952. irreg. (3-4/yr.). back issues avail. **Document type:** *Monographic series.*
Related titles: CD-ROM ed.
Published by: Brepols Publishers, Begijnhof 67, Turnhout, 2300, Belgium. FAX 32-14-428919, periodicals@brepols.net.

282 DEU ISSN 0589-7998
CORPUS CONSUETUDINUM MONASTICARUM. Text in Latin. 1963. irreg., latest vol.14, 1999. price varies. **Document type:** *Monographic series, Academic/Scholarly.*
Published by: Verlag Franz Schmitt, Kaiserstr 99-101, Siegburg, 53721, Germany. TEL 49-2241-62925, FAX 49-2241-53891, verlagschmitt@aol.com, http://www.verlagfranzschmitt.de.

282 FRA ISSN 2107-0482
LE CORPUS DES MESSES ANONYMES DU X VE SIECLE. Text in Latin. 2008. **Document type:** *Database.*
Media: Online - full text.

Published by: Universite de Tours (Francois-Rabelais), Centre d'Etudes Superieures de la Renaissance de Tours. Programme Ricercar, 59, Rue Nericault-Destouches, BP 11328, Tours Cedex, 37013, France. TEL 33-2-47367784, FAX 33-2-47367762, ricercar@univ-tours.fr, http://ricercar.cesr.univ-tours.fr/index.htm.

282 ITA
COSCIENZA. Text in Italian. 1946. 6/yr. bk.rev. illus. index. **Document type:** *Journal, Academic/Scholarly.*
Indexed: CERDIC.
Published by: Movimento Ecclesiale di Impegno Culturale, Via della Conciliazione 1, Rome, 00193, Italy. TEL 39-06-6861867, FAX 39-06-6875577, http://www.meic.net.

253.5 USA ISSN 0160-7960
CODEN: COVADQ
➤ **COUNSELING AND VALUES.** Abbreviated title: C V J. Text in English. 1956. s-a. GBP 71 in United Kingdom to institutions; EUR 82 in Europe to institutions; USD 100 elsewhere to institutions; GBP 82 combined subscription in United Kingdom to institutions (print & online eds.); EUR 95 combined subscription in Europe to institutions (print & online eds.); USD 115 combined subscription elsewhere to institutions (print & online eds.) (effective 2012). adv. bk.rev. abstr.; bibl.; illus. 80 p./no.; back issues avail.; reprint service avail. from PSC. **Document type:** *Journal, Academic/Scholarly.* **Description:** Focuses on the role of values, ethics, spirituality, and religion in counseling and psychology.
Former titles (until 1971): National Catholic Guidance Conference Journal (0027-8912); (until 1964): Catholic Counselor
Related titles: Microform ed.: (from PQC); Online - full text ed.: ISSN 2161-007X. GBP 71 in United Kingdom to institutions; EUR 82 in Europe to institutions; USD 100 elsewhere to institutions (effective 2012).
Indexed: A01, A02, A03, A08, A21, A22, A26, B04, BRD, C12, CA, CPL, CWI, E-psyche, E02, E03, E06, E07, E08, ERI, ERIC, EdA, EdI, FamI, G08, HEA, I05, M01, M02, P03, P04, P18, P25, P30, P43, P48, P53, P54, P55, PQC, PsycInfo, PsycholAb, R05, RI-1, RI-2, S02, S03, S09, SCOPUS, SWR&A, T02, W03, W05.
—BLDSC (3481.320000), CIS, IE, Infotrieve, Ingenta. **CCC.**
Published by: (Association for Spiritual, Ethical and Religious Values in Counseling), American Counseling Association, 5999 Stevenson Ave, Alexandria, VA 22304. TEL 800-347-6647, FAX 703-823-0252, 800-473-2329. Ed. Richard E Watts TEL 936-294-4658. Adv. contact Kathy Maguire TEL 703-823-9800 ext 207. Circ: 2,300.

282 USA
COURIER (WINONA). Text in English. 1910. m. USD 5 (effective 2005). adv. 16 p./no. 5 cols./p.; **Document type:** *Newspaper, Consumer.*
Formerly: Winona Courier
Published by: Diocese of Winona, 55 W. Sanborn St., PO Box 949, Winona, MN 55987. TEL 507-454-4643, FAX 507-454-8106. Ed. Rose A Hammes. Adv. contact Shelley Duffy. Circ: 40,000 (paid and controlled). Wire service: AP, NYT.

282 ITA ISSN 1123-3281
CREDEREOGGI; dossiers di orientamento e aggiornamento teologico. Text in Italian. 1980. bi-m. EUR 30 domestic; EUR 40 foreign (effective 2009). back issues avail. **Document type:** *Magazine, Consumer.*
Published by: Messaggero di Sant' Antonio Editrice, Via Orto Botanico 11, Padua, PD 35123, Italy. TEL 39-049-8225777, FAX 39-049-8225650, info@santantonio.org, http://www.edizionimessaggero.it. Circ: 3,000.

282 NOR ISSN 1503-7959
CREDIMUS; katolsk blad for unge voksne. Text in Norwegian. 2004. q. NOK 150 (effective 2006). back issues avail. **Document type:** *Magazine, Consumer.*
Related titles: Online - full text ed.
Published by: Norges Unge Katolikker, Akersveien 16A, Oslo, 0177, Norway. TEL 47-23-219540, FAX 47-23-219543, nuk@nuk.no. Eds. Marta Bivand, Kristine Dingstad. Circ: 1,200.

270.1 ITA ISSN 0011-1465
CRISTO AL MONDO/CHRIST AU MONDE/CHRIST TO THE WORLD; international review of Apostolic experiences. Text in English. 1955. 5/yr. EUR 18 in Europe; EUR 25 elsewhere (effective 2008). bk.rev.
Related titles: French ed.
Indexed: CERDIC, CPL, P30.
Published by: Christ to the World, Via di Propaganda 1 c, Rome, 00187, Italy. http://www.christ-to-the-world.com.

282 USA ISSN 0574-4350
THE CRITERION. Text in English. 1960. w. (Fri.). USD 0.75 per issue; USD 22 (effective 2005). **Document type:** *Newspaper, Consumer.*
Published by: Archdiocese of Indianapolis, 1400 N Meridian St, Indianapolis, IN 46202. TEL 317-236-1400, FAX 317-236-1593, info@archindy.org. Ed. Greg Otolski. Pub. Rev. Daniel M Buechlein. Circ: 74,000 (paid). Wire service: CaNS.

261.57 USA ISSN 0011-149X
Z1219
CRITIC (CHICAGO); a Catholic review of culture and the arts. Text in English. 1942-1981; resumed 1985. q. USD 17. illus. reprints avail.
Related titles: Microform ed.: (from PQC).
Indexed: A22, BRI, CBRI, CPL, MLA-IB, PCI.
Published by: Thomas More Association, 205 W Monroe St, 6th Fl, Chicago, IL 60606. TEL 312-609-8880, FAX 312-609-8891. Circ: 2,500.

282 FRA ISSN 0242-6056
LA CROIX. Text in French. 1883. d. (304 issues). EUR 300 domestic; EUR 390 in the European Union; EUR 485 elsewhere (effective 2005). **Document type:** *Newspaper, Consumer.* **Description:** Covers bioethics, education, the environment, religious news from a Catholic perspective.
Related titles: Microfilm ed.: (from PQC).
Indexed: MLA-IB, RASB.
—CIS. **CCC.**
Published by: Bayard Presse, 3-5 rue Bayard, Paris, 75393 Cedex 08, France. TEL 33-1-44356060, FAX 33-1-44356161, redactions@bayard-presse.com, http://www.bayardpresse.com. Ed. Bruno Frappat. Circ: 89,558.

282 BEN
CROIX DE BENIN. Text in French. 1946. fortn.
Address: BP 105, Cotonou, Benin. TEL 32-11-19. Ed. Barthelemy Cakpo Assogba.

282 PHL
CROSS; national Catholic magazine. Text in English. 1945. bi-m. PHP 6, USD 1. adv. bk.rev.
Former titles (until 1988): Crossline; (until 1986): Cross
Published by: Knights of Columbus in the Philippines, P.O. Box 510, Manila, Philippines. Ed. Ben S De Castro. Circ: 51,000.

382 ESP ISSN 2171-5505
▼ **CUADERNOS RUAJ.** Text in Spanish. 2010. bi-m. **Document type:** *Magazine, Consumer.*
Published by: Semillas Servicios Editoriales, Apdo de Correos No. 7001, Sevilla, 41005, Spain. TEL 34-954-579572.

282 BRA
CULTURA E FE. Text in Portuguese. 1978. q. USD 20. bk.rev.
Description: Review of culture from a Roman Catholic point of view.
Published by: Instituto de Desenvolvimento Cultural, Rua Vicente da Fontoura 1578, Santana, Porto Alegre, 90640-002, Brazil. idc@idc.org.br, http://www.idc.org.br.

322.1 USA ISSN 1080-9058
HN51
CULTURE WARS MAGAZINE. Text in English. 1995. m. (11/yr.). USD 30 domestic; USD 35 in Canada; USD 40 elsewhere; USD 4 per issue (effective 2005). adv. bk.rev. index. back issues avail. **Document type:** *Magazine, Consumer.* **Description:** Based on the premise that the Founding Fathers understood that there is no social order or progress without moral citizens. Focuses on events and issues concerning faith and morals, family, and culture from a Roman Catholic and Christian perspective.
Incorporates (1981-Dec. 1996): Fidelity Magazine
Published by: Ultramontane Associates, Inc., 206 Marquette Ave, South Bend, IN 46617. TEL 574-289-9786, FAX 574-289-1461, http://www.culturewars.com. Ed. E Michael Jones. Pub. E. Michael Jones. R&P, Adv. contact Ruth Jones. B&W page USD 400; trim 9.5 x 7.25. Circ: 7,000.

CURRICULUM HANDBOOK FOR PARENTS. GRADE 1 (CATHOLIC SCHOOL VERSION). *see* EDUCATION—Teaching Methods And Curriculum

CURRICULUM HANDBOOK FOR PARENTS. GRADE 2 (CATHOLIC SCHOOL VERSION). *see* EDUCATION—Teaching Methods And Curriculum

CURRICULUM HANDBOOK FOR PARENTS. GRADE 3 (CATHOLIC SCHOOL VERSION). *see* EDUCATION—Teaching Methods And Curriculum

CURRICULUM HANDBOOK FOR PARENTS. GRADE 4 (CATHOLIC SCHOOL VERSION). *see* EDUCATION—Teaching Methods And Curriculum

CURRICULUM HANDBOOK FOR PARENTS. GRADE 5 (CATHOLIC SCHOOL VERSION). *see* EDUCATION—Teaching Methods And Curriculum

CURRICULUM HANDBOOK FOR PARENTS. GRADE 6 (CATHOLIC SCHOOL VERSION). *see* EDUCATION—Teaching Methods And Curriculum

CURRICULUM HANDBOOK FOR PARENTS. GRADE 7 (CATHOLIC SCHOOL VERSION). *see* EDUCATION—Teaching Methods And Curriculum

CURRICULUM HANDBOOK FOR PARENTS. GRADE 8 (CATHOLIC SCHOOL VERSION). *see* EDUCATION—Teaching Methods And Curriculum

CURRICULUM HANDBOOK FOR PARENTS. GRADE 9 (CATHOLIC SCHOOL VERSION). *see* EDUCATION—Teaching Methods And Curriculum

CURRICULUM HANDBOOK FOR PARENTS. SENIOR HIGH SCHOOL (CATHOLIC SCHOOL VERSION). *see* EDUCATION—Teaching Methods And Curriculum

CURRICULUM MATTERS. *see* EDUCATION

282 DEU ISSN 0590-4501
CUSANUS-GESELLSCHAFT. KLEINE SCHRIFTEN. Text in German. 1963. irreg., latest vol.19, 2011. price varies. **Document type:** *Monographic series, Academic/Scholarly.*
Published by: (Cusanus-Gesellschaft), Paulinus Verlag GmbH, Maximineracht 11c, Trier, 54295, Germany. TEL 49-651-46080, FAX 49-651-4608221, verlag@paulinus.de, http://www.paulinus.de.

282 DEU ISSN 0590-451X
B765.N54
CUSANUS-GESELLSCHAFT. MITTEILUNGEN UND FORSCHUNGSBEITRAEGE. Text in German. 1961. irreg., latest vol.32, 2010. price varies. **Document type:** *Monographic series, Academic/Scholarly.*
Indexed: A22, DIP, FR, IBR, IBZ, MLA-IB, P30.
—INIST.
Published by: (Cusanus-Gesellschaft), Paulinus Verlag GmbH, Maximineracht 11c, Trier, 54295, Germany. TEL 49-651-46080, FAX 49-651-4608221, verlag@paulinus.de, http://www.paulinus.de.

282 100 DEU ISSN 1869-9502
CUSANUS-JAHRBUCH. Text in German. 2001. a. **Document type:** *Journal, Academic/Scholarly.*
Formerly (until 2009): Litterae Cusanae (1617-5611)
Published by: (Cusanus-Gesellschaft), Paulinus Verlag GmbH, Maximineracht 11c, Trier, 54295, Germany. TEL 49-651-46080, FAX 49-651-4608221, verlag@paulinus.de, http://www.paulinus.de.

282 POL ISSN 1230-7297
CZAS SERCA; dwumiesiecznik religijno-spoleczny. Text in Polish. 1991. bi-m. PLZ 16. bk.rev. **Document type:** *Newspaper.* **Description:** Aims to inform and educate.
Published by: (Zgromadzenie Ksiezy Najswietszego Serca Jezusowego), Wydawnictwo Ksiezy Sercanow, Ul Saska 2, Krakow, 30715, Poland. TEL 48-12-6562042, FAX 48-12-6562042. Ed. Fr Grzegorz Piatek. R&P Fr Gabriel Pisarek. Circ: 9,000.

282 POL ISSN 0137-4087
CZESTOCHOWSKIE STUDIA TEOLOGICZNE/CZESTOCHOWA THEOLOGICAL STUDIES. Text in Polish. 1973. irreg.
Indexed: IZBG.
Published by: Czestochowskie Wydawnictwo Archidiecezjalne Regina Poloniae, Al Najsw Maryi Panny 54, Czestochowa, 42200, Poland. TEL 48-34-629850, FAX 48-34-651182.

261.8344 DNK ISSN 0109-1476
D K K F - NYT. (Danmarks Katolske Kvindeforening) Text in Danish. 1981. q. illus. **Document type:** *Newsletter, Consumer.*
Published by: Danmarks Katolske Kvindeforening, c/o Benedicte Knudsen, Urlev Kirkevej 7, Hedensted, 7511, Denmark. TEL 45-75-687511, http://www.dkkf.dk. Ed. Vivian Tiedemann TEL 45-33-259340.

282 ITA
DALLO SCOGLIO DI SANTA RITA. Text in Italian. 1940. m. bk.rev. **Document type:** *Magazine, Consumer.*
Related titles: Online - full text ed.
Published by: Santuario di Santa Rita, Roccaporena di Cascia, PE 06043, Italy.

255.3 USA
DANICA; hrvatski tjednik. Text in Croatian; Summaries in Croatian, English. 1921. w. USD 30. adv. bk.rev.
Published by: (Croatian Center Association), Croatian Franciscan Press, 4851 Drexel Blvd, Chicago, IL 60615. TEL 312-268-2819. Ed. Fr Castimir Majic. Circ: 5,000.

DAPPLED THINGS. *see* LITERATURE

282 USA ISSN 0011-6637
DARBININKAS. Text in Lithuanian. 1915. w. USD 30. adv. bk.rev. **Document type:** *Newspaper.*
Indexed: RASB.
Published by: Franciscan Fathers, 341 Highland Blvd, Brooklyn, NY 11207. TEL 718-827-1352, FAX 718-827-2964. Ed. Rev. Dr Cornelius Bucmys. Adv. contact Albina Zumbakis.

282 DEU ISSN 0933-0771
DIACONIA CHRISTI. Text in German. 1966. s-a. EUR 40 membership (effective 2010). adv. bk.rev. bibl. back issues avail. **Document type:** *Newsletter, Consumer.*
Formerly (until 1987): Diaconia XP (0343-3218)
Published by: Internationales Diakonatszentrum, Postfach 9, Rottenburg, 72101, Germany. TEL 49-7472-169737, FAX 49-7472-169607, idz@bo.drs.de. Circ: 1,000 (paid and controlled).

282 ITA ISSN 0391-545X
DIAGROUP. Text in Italian. 1980. bi-m. **Document type:** *Magazine, Consumer.* **Description:** Aimed at highschool students, this publication is unique in Europe in that each issue consists of 12 slides and a manual for the teacher/instructor.
Published by: Editrice Elledici, Corso Francia 214, Cascine Vica - Rivoli, TO 10098, Italy. TEL 39-011-9552111, FAX 39-011-9574048, mail@elledici.org, http://www.elledici.org.

282 DEU ISSN 0341-9592
BX1913
DIAKONIA; internationale Zeitschrift fuer praktische Theologie. Text in German. 1966. bi-m. EUR 84 to institutions; EUR 69 to individuals; EUR 14.80 newsstand/cover (effective 2010). adv. bk.rev. bibl.; stat. index. **Document type:** *Journal, Academic/Scholarly.* **Description:** Reflections and reports of church and parish life, practical theology and the influence of social changes on parishes and theology.
Indexed: A01, CPL, DIP, IBR, IBZ, P30.
—IE.
Published by: Verlag Herder GmbH, Hermann-Herder-Str 4, Freiburg Im Breisgau, 79104, Germany. TEL 49-761-27170, FAX 49-761-2717520, kundenservice@herder.de, http://www.herder.de. Ed. Veronika Prueller Jagenteufel. Adv. contact Friederike Ward TEL 49-761-2717407.

282 NIC
DIAKONIA; servicio de la fe y promocion de la justicia. Text in Spanish. 1977. q. USD 25. back issues avail. **Description:** Religious publication that aids those involved in religion. Looks at problematic aspects that Christianity and other religions face in Latin America. Includes articles, research and other writings of spirituality.
Indexed: CERDIC.
Published by: Centro Ignaciano de Centro America, Apartado C-31, Managua, 13, Nicaragua. Circ: 600.

282 USA
THE DIALOG. Text in English. 1964. w. (Thu.). free to parish members; USD 0.50 newsstand/cover; USD 20 (effective 2007). **Document type:** *Newspaper.*
Formerly: Wilmington Dialog
Published by: Diocese of Wilmington, 1925 Delaware Ave, Wilmington, DE 19806. TEL 302-573-3109, FAX 302-573-6948. Ed. Jim Grant. Pub. Bishop Michael Saltarelli. Adv. contact Sue Uniatowski. Circ: 50,000 (paid and free). Wire service: CaNS.

282 FRA ISSN 1951-5367
DIALOGUE ET VERITE. Text in French. 2006. s-a. **Document type:** *Monographic series, Consumer.*
Published by: Institut Catholique de la Mediterranee (I C M), Le Mistral - 11 Impasse Flammarion, Marseille, 13001, France. TEL 33-4-91503550, FAX 33-4-91503555, icm@cathomed.cef.fr, http://cathomed.cef.fr.

282 DEU
DIASPORA - M I V A; Verkehrshilfe des Bonifatiuswerkes. (Motorisierende Innerdeutsche Verkehrs-Arbeitsgemeinschaft) Text in German. 1949. s-a. free (effective 2009). back issues avail. **Document type:** *Newsletter, Trade.*
Published by: Bonifatiuswerk der Deutschen Katholiken e.V., Kamp 22, Paderborn, 33098, Germany. TEL 49-5251-29960, FAX 49-5251-299688, info@bonifatiuswerk.de, http://www.bonifatiuswerk.de. Ed. Christoph Schommer. Circ: 45,000.

DICTIONAIRE DES RACINES SEMITIQUES. *see* ASIAN STUDIES

282 PRT ISSN 0253-1674
BR7
DIDASKALIA. Text in Multiple languages; Summaries in English, French. 1971. s-a. USD 60 (effective 2003). bk.rev. **Document type:** *Academic/Scholarly.*
Indexed: CERDIC, FR, OTA.
—INIST.
Published by: Universidade Catolica Portuguesa, Faculdade de Teologia, Palma de Cima, Lisbon, 1600, Portugal. TEL 351-1-7214155, FAX 351-1-7270256, didaskalia@ft.ucp.pt. Ed. Jose Jacinto Ferreira de Farias. Circ: 500.

R

282.08664 USA ISSN 0147-1139
DIGNITY - U S A. Text in English. 1969. q. USD 45. bk.rev. tr.lit.
Document type: *Newsletter.* **Description:** Contains news, theological reflection, opinion and other material of interest to Dignity members, gay and lesbian Catholics, and progressive Catholics in general.
Indexed: L01, L02.
Address: 1500 Massachusetts Ave N W, Ste 11, Washington, DC 20005. TEL 202-861-0017, FAX 202-429-9808, http://www.dignityusa.org. Ed., R&P David Floss. Circ: 2,500 (paid); 500 (controlled).

250 BEL ISSN 0012-2866
DIMANCHE. Text in French. 1935. w. adv. bk.rev. illus. **Document type:** *Newspaper.* **Description:** Parish newspaper distributed by local parishes.
Address: Pl de Vannes 20, Mons, 7000, Belgium. TEL 32-65-352885, FAX 32-65-346370. Ed. Fr Charles Delhez. Adv. contact Cyril Becovart. Circ: 375,000 (paid and controlled).

262.3 USA ISSN 1072-7922
DIOCESAN DIALOGUE; a newsletter for television Mass producers. Text in English. 1986. a. USD 5 (effective 2007). adv. back issues avail.; reprints avail. **Document type:** *Newsletter, Consumer.* **Description:** Includes news about the work of offices of communication in various Roman Catholic dioceses in the US, especially those that produce religious services on television.
Published by: American Catholic Press, 16565 S State St, South Holland, IL 60473. TEL 708-331-5485, FAX 708-331-5484. Ed. Rev. Michael Gilligon. Circ: 850 (paid and controlled).

262.3025 GBR
DIOCESAN DIRECTORY (CARLISLE). Text in English. 1879. a. looseleaf. GBP 3, USD 6. **Document type:** *Directory.*
Published by: Carlisle Diocesan Board of Finance, Church House, West Walls, Carlisle, Lancs CA3 8UE, United Kingdom. TEL 01228-22573, FAX 01228-48469. Circ: 600 (paid).

282 ITA ISSN 2038-5323
DIOCESI DI IMOLA. BOLLETTINO. Text in Italian. 1975. 3/yr. **Document type:** *Bulletin, Consumer.*
Former titles (until 2008): Bollettino della Chiesa Particolare (2038-5331); (until 2003): Diocesi di Imola. Bollettino (2038-534X)
Published by: (Diocesi di Imola), Editrice Il Nuovo Diario Messaggero, Via Emilia 77-79, Imola, 40026, Italy. TEL 39-0542-22178, FAX 39-0542-29804, diario@nuovodiario.com, http://www.nuovodiario.com.

262.3 AUT
DIOEZESE GURK. JAHRBUCH/KRSKE SKOFIJE. ZBORNIK. Text in German, Slovenian. 1978. a. EUR 8 (effective 2005). adv. bk.rev. back issues avail. **Document type:** *Bulletin, Consumer.*
Published by: Katholische Kirche in Kaernten, Dioezese Gurk, Mariannengasse 2, Klagenfurt, K 9020, Austria. TEL 43-463-57770, FAX 43-463-577701079, info@kath-kirche-kaernten.at, http://www.kath-kirche-kaernten.at. Circ: 7,000.

262.3 AUT
DIOEZESE LINZ. JAHRBUCH. Text in German. a. adv. bk.rev. back issues avail. **Document type:** *Yearbook, Consumer.*
Published by: Katholische Kirche in Oberoesterreich, Dioezese Linz, Herrenstr 19, Linz, O 4020, Austria. TEL 43-732-76101130, FAX 43-732-76101137, post@dioezese-linz.at, http://www.dioezese-linz.at. Ed. Wolfgang Katzboeck. Circ: 30,000.

282 DEU ISSN 1433-1314
DIRECT. Text in German. 1971. q. adv. bk.rev.; film rev.; play rev. back issues avail. **Document type:** *Newsletter, Consumer.* **Description:** Periodical for members of KSJ, a secondary school student's youth group.
Related titles: Online - full text ed.
Published by: Katholische Studierende Jugend, Gabelsbergerstr 19, Cologne, 50674, Germany. TEL 49-221-9420180, FAX 49-221-94201822, zeitschriften@ksj.de, http://ksj.de. Ed. Clemens Dittges. Adv. contact Olaf Roettig. Circ: 4,000.

282.025 PER
DIRECTORIO ECLESIASTICO. Text in Spanish. 1993. irreg. PEN 38 domestic; USD 11.02 foreign (effective 2000).
Published by: Conferencia Episcopal Peruana, Jr Estados Unidos 838, Jesus Maria, Lima, 11, Peru. TEL 51-1-463-1010, FAX 51-1-463-6125, sgc@iglesiacatolica.org.pe, http://www.ekeko.rcp.net.pe/IAL/cep.

282 DEU
DIRECTORIUM FUER DAS BISTUM TRIER. LITURGISCHER KALENDER. Text in German. 1937. a. **Document type:** *Bulletin, Consumer.*
Published by: Paulinus Verlag GmbH, Maximineracht 11c, Trier, 54295, Germany. TEL 49-651-46080, FAX 49-651-4608221, verlag@paulinus.de, http://www.paulinus.de. Circ: 450.

262.3 USA
DIRECTORY OF CATHOLIC DIOCESE OF SPOKANE. Text in English. a. adv. **Document type:** *Directory.*
Published by: Catholic Diocese of Spokane, PO Box 1453, Spokane, WA 99210-1453. TEL 509-358-7340, FAX 509-358-7302. Ed. Deacon Eric Meisfjord. Pub. Bishop William S Skylstad. Adv. contact Nancy Loberg.

262.3 DEU
DIREKTORIUM SPIRENSE - OFFIZIUM UND MESSFEIER. Text in German. 1824. a. **Document type:** *Directory, Trade.*
Published by: Bischoefliches Ordinariat Speyer, Kleine Pfaffengasse 16, Speyer, 67346, Germany. TEL 49-6232-1020, FAX 49-6232-102300, pressestelle@bistum-speyer.de, http://www.bistum-speyer.de. Circ: 2,700.

282 ITA ISSN 1828-8146
DISSERTATIO. SERIES MEDIOLANENSIS. Text in Italian. 1992. irreg. price varies. **Document type:** *Monographic series, Academic/Scholarly.* **Description:** Publishes the theses of students who graduate in Theology from universities in Northern Italy.
Published by: Libreria Editrice Glossa, Piazza Paolo VI 6, Milan, 20121, Italy. TEL 39-02-877609, FAX 39-02-72003162, http://www.glossaeditrice.it.

282 ITA ISSN 1828-812X
DISSERTATIO. SERIES ROMANA. Text in Italian. 1991. irreg. price varies. **Document type:** *Monographic series, Academic/Scholarly.* **Description:** Publishes the theses of students who graduate in Theology from universities in Southern Italy.
Published by: Libreria Editrice Glossa, Piazza Paolo VI 6, Milan, 20121, Italy. TEL 39-02-877609, FAX 39-02-72003162, http://www.glossaeditrice.it.

230.2 DEU
DISSERTATIONEN. KANONISTISCHE REIHE. Text in German. 1988. irreg., latest vol.21, 2006. price varies. **Document type:** *Monographic series, Academic/Scholarly.*
Published by: E O S Verlag, Erzabtei St. Ottilien, St.Ottilien, 86941, Germany. TEL 49-8193-71700, FAX 49-8193-71709, mail@eos-verlag.de.

230.2 DEU
DISSERTATIONEN. PHILOSOPHISCHE REIHE. Text in German. 1983. irreg., latest vol.25, 2010. price varies. **Document type:** *Monographic series, Academic/Scholarly.*
Published by: E O S Verlag, Erzabtei St. Ottilien, St.Ottilien, 86941, Germany. TEL 49-8193-71700, FAX 49-8193-71709, mail@eos-verlag.de.

230.2 DEU
DISSERTATIONEN. THEOLOGISCHE REIHE. Text in German. 1987. irreg., latest vol.90, 2009. price varies. **Document type:** *Monographic series, Academic/Scholarly.*
Published by: E O S Verlag, Erzabtei St. Ottilien, St.Ottilien, 86941, Germany. TEL 49-8193-71700, FAX 49-8193-71709, mail@eos-verlag.de.

282 ESP ISSN 2171-5769
DIVERSARUM RERUM. Text in Spanish. 2006. a. **Document type:** *Bulletin, Consumer.*
Related titles: ◆ Supplement to: Obispado de Orense. Boletin Oficial. ISSN 2171-5807.
Published by: Obispado de Orense, Rua Progeso No. 26, Orense, 32080, Spain. TEL 34-988-366141, FAX 34-988-366142, orcuria@obispadodeourense.com, http://www.obispadodeourense.com.

282 VAT ISSN 0012-4222
BR1.A1
DIVINITAS. Text in Italian. 1957. 3/yr. adv. bk.rev. cum.index every 10 yrs.
Indexed: DIP, FR, IBR, IBZ, MLA-IB, R&TA.
—BLDSC (3604.276000), INIST.
Published by: Mons. Brunero Gherardini, Canonico della Basilica di San Pietro, Vatican City, 00120, Vatican City. Ed. Msgr. Brunero Gherardini.

230.2 IRL ISSN 0012-446X
BX2350.2
➤ **DOCTRINE AND LIFE.** Text in English. 1951. 10/yr. EUR 35.94 domestic; GBP 27 in Great Britain & Northern Ireland; EUR 38.44 in Europe; USD 44 elsewhere (effective 2004). adv. bk.rev. index. back issues avail.; reprints avail. **Document type:** *Journal, Academic/Scholarly.* **Description:** Maintains a dialogue between the inheritance of Christian faith and the concerns of today's world - political, artistic and economic.
Related titles: Microfilm ed.: (from PQC).
Indexed: CERDIC, CPL, MLA-IB, OTA.
—BLDSC (3608.030000), IE, Ingenta. **CCC.**
Published by: Dominican Publications, 42 Parnell Sq, Dublin, Dublin 1, Ireland. TEL 353-1-8721611, 353-1-8731355, FAX 353-1-8731760, sales@dominicanpublications.com. Ed. Rev. Bernard Treacy. Circ: 5,000.

282 FRA ISSN 0012-4613
BX802
LA DOCUMENTATION CATHOLIQUE. Text in French. 1919. bi-m. EUR 79 domestic; EUR 89 foreign (effective 2009). adv. index. **Document type:** *Magazine, Consumer.* **Description:** Presents church texts in their entirety as a source of inspiration for study, reflexion and meditation.
Related titles: Online - full text ed.; English ed.: Catholic International. ISSN 1155-3197.
Indexed: A21, A22, CERDIC, CPL, FR, RASB, RI-1, RI-2, S02, S03.
—IE, Infotrieve.
Published by: Bayard Presse, 3-5 rue Bayard, Paris, 75393 Cedex 08, France. TEL 33-1-44356060, FAX 33-1-44356161, redactions@bayard-presse.com, http://www.bayardpresse.com. Ed. Vincent Cabanac. Circ: 18,000.

282 VAT ISSN 1022-8659
BX1795.H4
DOLENTIUM HOMINUM. Text in Multiple languages. 1986. 3/yr. **Document type:** *Magazine, Consumer.*
Indexed: P30, SCOPUS.
Published by: Pontifical Council for Pastoral Care, Voa della Conciliazione 3, Vatican City, 00120, Vatican City. TEL 39-06-69883138, FAX 39-06-69883139, opersanit@hlthwork.va, http://www.healthpastoral.org.

282 DEU
DER DOM. Text in German. w. EUR 5.80 per month (effective 2009). adv. **Document type:** *Newspaper, Consumer.*
Formerly (until 1946): Leo
Published by: Bonifatius GmbH, Karl-Schurz-Str 26, Paderborn, 33100, Germany. TEL 49-5251-153245, FAX 49-5251-153133, mail@bonifatius.de, http://www.bonifatius.de. Ed. Christian Schlichter. Adv. contact Karl Wegener. B&W page EUR 2,228.80, color page EUR 2,979.20; trim 204 x 280. Circ: 61,643 (controlled).

255.3 ITA ISSN 0012-5288
LA DOMENICA. Text in Italian. 1921. w. (61 issues). EUR 13 (effective 2008). **Document type:** *Magazine, Consumer.*
Published by: Edizioni San Paolo, Piazza Soncino 5, Cinisello Balsamo, MI 20092, Italy. TEL 39-02-660751, FAX 39-02-66075211, sanpaoloedizioni@stpauls.it, http://www.edizionisanpaolo.it.

282 BRA
DOMINGO. Text in Portuguese. 1932. w. USD 100. Supplement avail.
Published by: (Pia Sociedade de Sao Paulo), Edicoes Paulinas, Via Raposo Tavares Km 18.5, Centro, Caixa Postal 8107, Sao Paulo, SP 01065-970, Brazil. Ed. Virgilio Ciaccio. Circ: 253,000.

255.3 NLD ISSN 0012-5504
DOORTOCHT; schakel tussen mensen met een Franciscaanse visie. Text in Dutch. 1963. 6/yr. EUR 12 (effective 2009). bk.rev. illus.
Incorporates (1962-1989): Schakel ('s-Hertogenbosch) (0167-2908)
Published by: Orde van Franciscaanse Seculieren, c/o Mariette Fleur, Sec., Graaf Adolfstr 20, Leerdam, 4141 JK, Netherlands. TEL 31-345-841880, info@ofsnederland.nl.

282 ITA ISSN 0393-3547
DOSSIER CATECHISTA. Text in Italian. 1984. 8/yr. EUR 9 domestic; EUR 17 foreign (effective 2009). **Document type:** *Magazine, Consumer.*
Published by: Editrice Elledici, Corso Francia 214, Cascine Vica - Rivoli, TO 10098, Italy. TEL 39-011-9552111, FAX 39-011-9574048, mail@elledici.org, http://www.elledici.org.

282 FRA ISSN 1285-719X
LES DOSSIERS DE L'ACTUALITE. Text in French. 1977. m. (10/yr.). EUR 32 domestic; EUR 45 in Europe; EUR 45 DOM-TOM; EUR 50 elsewhere (effective 2009 & 2010). **Document type:** *Magazine, Consumer.* **Description:** Aims to help secondary school pupils and university students to gain a better understanding of current affairs and to provide them with tools to analyze the world around them.
Formerly (until 1997): Les Pages de l'Evenement (0152-0741)
Published by: Bayard Presse, 3-5 rue Bayard, Paris, 75393 Cedex 08, France. TEL 33-1-44356060, FAX 33-1-44356161, redactions@bayard-presse.com, http://www.bayardpresse.com. Ed. Jean-Luc Macia. Circ: 12,000.

282 GBR ISSN 0012-5806
BX801
DOWNSIDE REVIEW; a quarterly of Catholic thought. Text in English. 1880. q. adv. bk.rev. index. back issues avail.; reprint service avail. from PSC. **Document type:** *Journal, Consumer.* **Description:** Provides a forum for the scholarly discussion and debate on a wide range of topics, including monastic history, theology, philosophy, Scripture studies and spirituality.
Related titles: Microfiche ed.
Indexed: A21, A22, CERDIC, CPL, DIP, FR, IBR, IBZ, IPB, MLA, MLA-IB, OTA, PCI, Phillnd, R&TA, RI-1, RI-2, RILM.
—BLDSC (3620.100000), IE, Infotrieve, Ingenta, INIST.
Published by: Downside Abbey, Stratton-on-the-Fosse, Radstock, Bath, BA3 4RH, United Kingdom. TEL 44-1761-235161, FAX 44-1761-235124, monks@downside.co.uk, http://www.downsideabbey.co.uk/. Ed. Desmond O'Keeffe.

282 USA
DRAUGAS. Text in Lithuanian. 1909. d. (Tue.-Sat.). USD 0.50 newsstand/cover; USD 0.75 newsstand/cover Sat.; USD 100 (effective 2005). adv. **Document type:** *Newspaper, Consumer.*
Indexed: RASB.
Published by: Lithuanian Catholic Press Society, 4545 W. 63rd St., Chicago, IL 60629-5589. TEL 773-585-9500, FAX 773-585-8284. Ed. Danute Bindokas. Adv. contact Danja Mackevicius. Circ: 7,000 (paid and controlled).

282 SVN ISSN 0416-3885
BX806.S5
DRUZINA/FAMILY; verski tednik - Catholic weekly. Text in Slovenian. 1952. w. EUR 65 (effective 2007). back issues avail. **Document type:** *Magazine, Consumer.*
Address: Krekov trg 1, p.p. 95, Ljubljana, 1001, Slovenia. TEL 386-1-3602845, FAX 386-1-3602800. Ed. Franci Petric. Circ: 100,000.

255 USA ISSN 0419-8379
THE DUNWOODIE REVIEW. Text in English. 1961. irreg. USD 25 to individuals; USD 35 to institutions (effective 2003).
Published by: St. Joseph's Seminary, 201 Seminary Ave., Yonkers, NY 10704. TEL 914-968-6200. Ed. Nicholas Callaghan.

282 BEL ISSN 2032-5215
▼ **E T - STUDIES.** Text in Multiple languages. 2009. s-a. EUR 45 combined subscription (print & online eds.) (effective 2011). **Document type:** *Journal, Academic/Scholarly.*
Formerly (until 2008): Europaeische Gesellschaft fuer Katholische Theologie. Bulletin (0939-3897)
Related titles: Online - full text ed.: ISSN 2033-4273.
Published by: (Europaeische Gesellschaft fuer Katholische Theologie/ Association Europeenne de Theologie Catholique NLD), Peeters Publishers, Bondgenotenlaan 153, Leuven, 3000, Belgium. TEL 32-16-235170, FAX 32-16-228500, peeters@peeters-leuven.be, http://www.peeters-leuven.be.

253 PHL ISSN 0116-0257
EAST ASIAN PASTORAL REVIEW; a quarterly with focus on Asia for all church ministers and theology in context, interested laity and theological students. Text in English. 1979. q. bk.rev. bibl. 105 p./no.; back issues avail. **Document type:** *Journal, Academic/Scholarly.*
Formed by the merger of: Teaching All Nations (0040-0564); Good Tidings (0436-1571); Amen
Indexed: BAS, CPL, IPP.
Published by: East Asian Pastoral Institute, U.P. Campus, PO Box 221, Quezon City, 1101, Philippines. TEL 63-2-4265901, FAX 63-2-4266143, eapisec@pusit.admu.edu.ph. Ed. Rev. Jose Mario C Francisco, S J. Circ: 2,000.

282 USA
EAST TENNESSEE CATHOLIC. Text in English. 1991. s-m. (Sun.). USD 15 (effective 2005). 12 p./no. 6 cols./p.; **Document type:** *Newspaper, Consumer.*
Published by: Roman Catholic Diocese of Knoxville, 805 Northshore Dr., Knoxville, TN 37919-6206. TEL 865-584-3307, FAX 865-584-8124. Ed. Mary Weaver. Pub. Joseph E. Kurtz. Circ: 18,300 (controlled).

EASTERN CATHOLIC LIFE. *see* RELIGIONS AND THEOLOGY—Eastern Orthodox

282.766 USA
EASTERN OKLAHOMA CATHOLIC. Text in English. 1974. bi-w. USD 24 (effective 2005). **Document type:** *Newspaper, Consumer.*
Published by: Diocese of Tulsa, PO Box 690240, Tulsa, OK 74169-0240. TEL 918-294-1904, FAX 918-294-0920, jim.sellars@dioceseoftulsa.org, http://www.dioceseoftulsa.org. Ed., Adv. contact Jim Sellars. Pub. Bishop Edward J Slattery. Circ: 20,000 evening (paid). Wire service: CaNS.

282 FRA ISSN 0766-6101
EAUX - VIVES. Text in French. 1941. m. adv. illus.
Address: 21 bd. Voltaire, Paris, 75011, France.

282 100 800 ITA
➤ **ECCLESIA**; revista de cultura catolica. Text in Spanish. 1987. q. EUR 40 domestic (effective 2008). bk.rev. Index. back issues avail. **Document type:** *Journal, Academic/Scholarly.*
Indexed: CPL.
Published by: Ateneo Pontificio Regina Apostolorum/Pontificial Athenaeum Regina Apostolorum, Dipartimento Pubblicazioni, Via degli Aldobrandeschi 190, Rome, 00163, Italy. TEL 39-06-66527800, FAX 39-06-66527840, publications@upra.org. Circ: 1,000.

282 ESP ISSN 0012-9038
BX2348.A1
ECCLESIA. Text in Spanish. 1941. w. adv. bk.rev.; film rev. bibl.; charts; illus. index. back issues avail. **Document type:** *Magazine, Consumer.*
Description: Covers religious information and documentation.
Indexed: CERDIC, MLA-IB.
Published by: Conferencia Episcopal Espanola, C/ Anastro 1, Madrid, 28033, Spain. TEL 34-91-3439600 34-91-343 96 00, conferenciaepiscopal@planalfa.es, http://www.conferenciaepiscopal.es. Ed. Jose Antonio Carro Celada. Circ: 25,000.

282 ITA ISSN 2036-9239
ECCLESIA MATER. Text in Italian. 1963. 3/yr. EUR 20 domestic; EUR 22 foreign (effective 2011). bk.rev. illus. Supplement avail. **Document type:** *Magazine, Consumer.*
Incorporates: Mater Ecclesiae (0025-522X)
Related titles: Supplement(s): Quaderni di Ecclesia Mater.
Published by: Istituto Suore Figlie della Chiesa, Viale Vaticano, 62, Rome, RM 00165, Italy. TEL 39-06-39740818, FAX 39-06-39750889.

282 ITA ISSN 1010-3872
BV169
ECCLESIA ORANS. Text in Italian. 1984. 3/yr. EUR 40 domestic; EUR 50 foreign (effective 2009). **Document type:** *Journal, Academic/Scholarly.*
Indexed: CPL, RILM.
Published by: Pontificio Istituto Liturgico, Piazza Cavalieri di Malta 5, Rome, 00153, Italy. TEL 39-06-5791320, FAX 39-06-5791366, publicazioni@santanselmo.org.

266.2 ITA
ECCO TUA MADRE. Text in Italian. 6/yr. EUR 10 domestic; EUR 20 foreign (effective 2009). **Document type:** *Magazine, Consumer.*
Description: Catholic newsletter featuring articles on events in the church, prayers and interviews with missionaries.
Published by: Santuario Madonna della Milicia, Piazza Matrice 18, Altavilla Milicia, PA 90010, Italy. TEL 39-091-951304, FAX 39-091-951634, http://www.madonnamilicia.it.

261.8328 DEU ISSN 0252-2527
ECHO DER LIEBE. Text in German. 1959. 8/yr. free to benefactors. back issues avail. **Document type:** *Newsletter, Consumer.* **Description:** News about the persecuted Church and refugees in Eastern Europe and the Third World.
Related titles: Online - full text ed.; ◆ English ed.: Mirror. ISSN 0252-2535; French ed.: Aide a l'Eglise en Detresse. Bulletin. ISSN 0252-2519; Italian ed.: L' Eco dell'Amore. ISSN 0252-2551; Portuguese ed.: Ajuda a Igreja Que Sofre. Boletim. ISSN 0873-3317; Dutch ed.: Echo der Liefde. ISSN 0252-2543; Spanish ed.: Ayuda a la Iglesia Necesitada. Boletin. ISSN 0252-256X.
Published by: Kirche in Not - Ostpriesterhilfe e.V., Bischof-Kindermann-Str 23, Koenigstein im Taunus, 61462, Germany. TEL 49-6174-2910, FAX 49-6174-3423, info@acn-intl.org, http://www.acn-intl.org. Ed. Juergen Liminski. Circ: 1,000,000 (controlled).

282 SYC
L'ECHO DES ILES. Text in Creoles and Pidgins, English, French. fortn.
Description: Roman Catholic publication.
Published by: Echo des Iles, PO Box 138, Victoria, Mahe, Seychelles. Ed. P Symphorien. Circ: 2,800.

255.9 USA
ECHO Z AFRYKI I INNYCH KONTYNENTOW. Text in Polish. 1892. m. USD 8 domestic; USD 12 in Canada (effective 2000). **Description:** Aims to make mission world known and loved by faithful.
Published by: Missionary Sisters of St. Peter Claver, St. Mary's Mission House, 265 Century Ave., St. Paul, MN 55125. TEL 651-738-9704, FAX 651-738-9704. Ed. Sr M Krystyna Kucza. Circ: 8,000.

282 CRI
ECO CATOLICO. Text in Spanish. 1931. w.
Address: Avda. 10, Calles 5 y 7, Apdo. 1064, San Jose, Costa Rica. TEL 22-5903. Ed. Armando Alfaro. Circ: 20,000.

282 ITA
L'ECO DI GIBILMANNA. Text in Italian. 1919. bi-m. free. bk.rev.
Document type: *Magazine, Consumer.*
Published by: Frati Minori Cappuccini, Provincia di Messina/Ordo Fratrum Minorum Capuccinorum, Santuario Maria SS. di Gibilmanna, Cefalu, PA 90010, Italy.

282 ITA
L'ECO DI SAN GABRIELE. Text in Italian. 1913. m. EUR 20 domestic; EUR 25 foreign (effective 2009). **Document type:** *Magazine, Consumer.*
Published by: Editoriale Eco, Via Santuario, 187, San Gabriele Dell'addolorata, TE 64048, Italy. Circ: 130,000.

282 FRA ISSN 0992-6887
EGLISE A LYON. Text in French. m. EUR 35 in Europe; EUR 45 in Africa; EUR 48 in North America; EUR 50 elsewhere (effective 2008). Supplement avail.; back issues avail. **Document type:** *Magazine.*
Description: Review of the diocese.
Former titles (until 1983): Eglise a Lyon et a Saint Etienne (0996-3251); (until 1972): Eglise de Lyon (0996-374X)
Published by: Association Diocesaine de Lyon, 6 Av. Adolphe Max, Lyon, Cedex 5 69321, France. TEL 33-4-78384658, contact@e-diocese-lyon.com, http://don-lyon.nuxit.net.

282 FRA ISSN 2104-9424
EGLISE A MARSEILLE. Text in French. 188?. m. **Document type:** *Consumer.*
Former titles (until 2010): L' Eglise Aujourd'hui a Marseille (1639-4321); (until 1969): Bulletin Religieux de Marseille (1639-4313)
Published by: Association Diocesaine Marseille, 14, Place Colonel Edon, Marseille Cedex 07, 13284, France. TEL 33-4-91529427, http://marseille.catholique.fr.

282.691 MDG
EGLISE CATHOLIQUE A MADAGASCAR. Cover title: Annuaire de l'Eglise Catholique a Madagascar. Text in French, Malagasy. a.
Published by: Imprimerie Catholique, 127 Arabe Lenine Vladimir, Antananarivo, Madagascar.

282 CAN ISSN 1719-8658
EGLISE CATHOLIQUE. DIOCESE DE GASPE. ANNUAIRE. Text in French. 1973. biennial. **Document type:** *Journal, Trade.*
Former titles (until 2001): Eglise Catholique. Diocese de Gaspe. Annuaire Diocesain (0843-2783); (until 1985): Notre Eglise Diocesaine (0843-2775)
Published by: Eglise Catholique. Diocese de Gaspe, 172, Jacques-Cartier, Gaspe, PQ G4X 1M9, Canada. TEL 418-368-2274, FAX 418-368-3772, http://www.gaspesie.net/diocesegaspe/main.htm.

282 FRA ISSN 1620-9001
L'EGLISE DANS LE MONDE. Text in French. 1981. q. **Document type:** *Magazine, Consumer.*
Formerly (until 2000): Eglise en Detresse (0991-2231)
—CCC.
Published by: Aide a l'Eglise en Detresse, 29, rue du Louvre, Mareil-Marly, 78750, France. TEL 33-1-39173010, FAX 33-1-39173019, sgd@aed-france.org, http://www.aed-france.org.

282.449 FRA ISSN 1775-013X
EGLISE DANS LES HAUTES-ALPES; mensuel de l'eglise catholique du diocese de Gap. Text in French. 1987. m. EUR 30; EUR 3 per issue (effective 2006). **Document type:** *Newsletter, Consumer.*
Formerly (until 2005): Eglise de Gap (1279-337X)
Published by: Bayard Service Edition Mediterranee, Centre la Baume, 1770 Chemin de la Blaque, Aix-en-Provence, 13090, France.

282 FRA ISSN 0013-2330
EGLISE EN ALSACE. Text in French. 1967. m. adv. bk.rev.
Indexed: CERDIC.
Published by: Archeveche de Strasbourg, Seminaires Diocesains, 16 rue Brulee, Strasbourg, Cedex 67081, France. TEL 33-3-88212424, FAX 33-3-88212436.

282 FRA ISSN 1777-3245
EGLISE EN SARTHE. Text in French. 2005. m. EUR 32 (effective 2009).
Document type: *Magazine.*
Formerly (until 2005): Eglise du Mans (0296-8673)
Published by: Eglise Catholique, Diocese du Mans, 4 place du Cardinal Grente, Le Mans Cedex 2, 72016, France. TEL 33-2-43288209.

EICHSTAETTER MATERIALIEN. *see* EDUCATION—Teaching Methods And Curriculum

282 DEU ISSN 1617-3996
AS182.M892
EICHSTAETTER UNIVERSITAETSREDEN. Text in German. 1978. irreg., latest vol.118, 2010. price varies. **Document type:** *Monographic series, Academic/Scholarly.*
Formerly (until 1999): Eichstaetter Hochschulreden (0344-2896)
Indexed: GeoRef, SpeleolAb.
Published by: (Katholische Universitaet Eichstaett-Ingolstadt), Medienhaus Kastner AG, Schlosshof 2-6, Wolnzach, 85283, Germany. TEL 49-8442-92530, FAX 49-8442-2289, verlag@kastner.de, http://www.kastner.de.

282 DEU ISSN 1862-3700
EINFACH LEBEN; ein Brief von Anselm Gruen. Text in German. 2006. 11/yr. EUR 41.60; EUR 3.95 newsstand/cover (effective 2010).
Document type: *Journal, Academic/Scholarly.*
Published by: Verlag Herder GmbH, Hermann-Herder-Str 4, Freiburg Im Breisgau, 79104, Germany. TEL 49-761-27170, FAX 49-761-2717520, kundenservice@herder.de, http://www.herder.de. Ed. Rudolf Walter.

264.02036 USA ISSN 0013-6719
BX801
EMMANUEL; magazine of Eucharist spirituality. Text in English. 1895. m. (except Jan.-Feb. & Jul.-Aug.). USD 19.95 domestic; USD 24.95 foreign (effective 2000). adv. bk.rev. bibl. index.
Indexed: CPL, OTA.
Published by: Congregation of Blessed Sacrament, 5384 Wilson Mills Rd, Cleveland, OH 44143. TEL 440-449-2103, FAX 440-449-3862. Ed. Rev. Anthony Schueller. Adv. contact Judy Strah. Circ: 4,000 (paid).

282 CAN ISSN 0317-851X
EN EGLISE. Text in French. 1974. m. CAD 15. bk.rev. illus. **Document type:** *Newsletter.* **Description:** Contains information about Catholic members and diocese life.
Published by: Eglise Catholique, Diocese de Chicoutimi, Office des Communications Sociales, 602 Racine Est, Chicoutimi, PQ G7H 6J6, Canada. TEL 418-543-0783. Ed. M l'abbe Jacques Bouchard. Circ: 1,450.

282 NLD ISSN 1872-6518
EN TOCH. Text in Dutch. 1979. q. EUR 10 (effective 2009).
Address: Jurastr 20, Heerlen, 6412 EW, Netherlands. TEL 31-45-5725016.

282 DEU ISSN 1612-9407
ENGAGIERT; die christliche frau. Text in German. 2003. 11/yr. EUR 20 (effective 2006). bk.rev. back issues avail. **Document type:** *Bulletin.*
Formed by the merger of (1901-2002): Christliche Frau (0009-5788); (1998-2002): Engagiert (1437-0913)
Published by: Katholischer Deutscher Frauenbund e.V., Schraudolphstr 1, Munich, 80799, Germany. TEL 49-89-28623740, FAX 49-89-28623733. Ed. Gabriele Kloeckner TEL 49-2831-94472. Circ: 28,000.

255.1 GBR
ENGLISH BENEDICTINE CONGREGATION. ORDO. Abbreviated title: E B C. Text in English. 1885. a. GBP 2.40 per issue (effective 2009).
Document type: *Directory, Trade.* **Description:** Directory of the Divine Office and Mass for use in the Abbeys and churches of this congregation.
Related titles: Online - full text ed.
Published by: Ampleforth Abbey, Ampleforth, York, YO62 4EN, United Kingdom. TEL 44-1439-766000, FAX 44-1439-766724, enquiries@benedictines.org.uk, http://www.ampleforth.org.uk/.

266.2 ESP ISSN 0425-1466
BT595
EPHEMERIDES MARIOLOGICAE; international revue of mariology. Text in Spanish. 1951. q. USD 35 domestic; USD 57 foreign (effective 2008). adv. bk.rev. index. back issues avail. **Document type:** *Monographic series, Consumer.*
Indexed: CERDIC, MLA-IB.
Published by: (Ephemerides Mariologicae), Claretian Fathers/Misioneros Claretianos, Buen Suceso, 22, Madrid, 28008, Spain. TEL 34-91-5401262, FAX 34-91-5400066, pcl@planalfa.es, http://vidareligiosa.com/. Ed. Ernesto Barea-Amorena. Adv. contact Lola Hiniesto. Circ: 550.

230.2 BEL ISSN 0013-9513
BR1.A1
➤ **EPHEMERIDES THEOLOGICAE LOVANIENSES**; revue de theologie et de droit canon de Louvain - Leuvens tijdschrift voor theologie en kerkelijk recht - Louvain journal of theological and canonical studies. Text in English, French, German. 1924. q. EUR 100 combined subscription (print & online eds.) (effective 2011). bibl. index. back issues avail. **Document type:** *Journal, Academic/Scholarly.*
Description: Publishes articles reflecting the full scope of theological research, with an international calendar of meetings and congresses.
Related titles: CD-ROM ed.; Online - full text ed.: ISSN 1783-1423; ◆ Supplement(s): Bibliotheca Ephemeridum Theologicarum Lovaniensium.
Indexed: A20, A21, A22, ArtHuCI, BibLing, CERDIC, CLA, CPL, CurCont, DIP, FR, IBR, IBZ, IPB, IZBG, MLA-IB, OTA, PCI, PhilInd, R&TA, RI-1, RI-2, SCOPUS, W07.
—BLDSC (3793.500000), IE, Infotrieve, Ingenta, INIST. **CCC.**
Published by: (Universite Catholique de Louvain), Peeters Publishers, Bondgenotenlaan 153, Leuven, 3000, Belgium. TEL 32-16-235170, FAX 32-16-228500, peeters@peeters-leuven.be, http://www.peeters-leuven.be. Ed. G Van Belle.

282 470 NLD
ERASMI OPERA OMNIA. Text in Dutch. irreg., latest vol.9, 2005. price varies. **Document type:** *Monographic series, Academic/Scholarly.*
Published by: Elsevier BV (Subsidiary of: Elsevier Science & Technology), Radarweg 29, PO Box 211, Amsterdam, 1000 AE, Netherlands. TEL 31-20-4853911, FAX 31-20-4852457, JournalsCustomerServiceEMEA@elsevier.com, http://www.elsevier.com.

255.1 DEU ISSN 0013-9963
BX3001
➤ **ERBE UND AUFTRAG**; Monastische Welt. Text in German. 1928. q. EUR 32; EUR 9 newsstand/cover (effective 2009). adv. bk.rev. abstr.; bibl.; illus. index. 80 p./no.; reprints avail. **Document type:** *Journal, Academic/Scholarly.*
Former titles (until 1958): Benediktinische Monatsschrift (0930-4924); (until 1949): Benediktinische Monatschrift zur Pflege Religiosen und Geistigen Lebens (0930-5947)
Indexed: DIP, FR, IBR, IBZ, IZBG, MLA-IB, OTA, RILM.
Published by: Beuroner Kunstverlag, Abteistr 2, Beuron, 88631, Germany. TEL 49-7466-17228, FAX 49-7466-17209, webmaster@beuroner-kunstverlag.de, http://www.beuroner-kunstverlag.de. Ed., R&P Albert Schmidt. Adv. contact Joachim Schlude TEL 49-7466-17227. page EUR 450; trim 125 x 185. Circ: 1,200 (paid).

282 DEU ISSN 1618-0216
ERZBISTUM BAMBERG. AMTSBLATT. Text in German, Latin. 1878. m. bk.rev. stat. index. **Document type:** *Bulletin, Trade.*
Formerly (until 2001): Amtsblatt fuer die Erzdioezese Bamberg (0003-2328)
Published by: Erzbischoefliches Ordinariat Bamberg, Domplatz 2, Bamberg, 96049, Germany. TEL 49-951-5020, FAX 49-951-502271, eckert@erzbistum-bamberg.de, http://www.erzbistum-bamberg.de. Circ: 900.

271.4 ESP ISSN 0425-340X
ESTUDIO AGUSTINIANO. Text in English, French, Italian, Spanish. 1966. 3/yr. EUR 49 in Europe; USD 50 foreign. bk.rev. index. back issues avail. **Document type:** *Journal, Academic/Scholarly.* **Description:** Publishes articles of philosophy and theology from the institute's professors and other investigators.
Formerly (until 1967): Archivo Teologico Agustiniano (0211-2043)
Indexed: BAS, CERDIC, CLA, FR, OTA.
—INIST.
Published by: (Estudio Teologico Agustiniano), Editorial Estudio Agustiniano, Paseo Filipinos, 7, Valladolid, 47007, Spain. TEL 34-983-306800, FAX 34-983-397896, edestagus@adenet.es. Eds. J Balmori, Pio de Luis. Adv. contact J Balmori. Circ: 400.

282 ESP ISSN 0210-7074
ESTUDIOS JOSEFINOS. Text in Spanish. 1947. s-a. EUR 22 domestic; EUR 30 in Europe; USD 40 rest of world (effective 2008). bk.rev. back issues avail. **Document type:** *Magazine, Consumer.*
Published by: Centro Josefino Espanol, C San Benito, 3, Valladolid, 47003, Spain. TEL 34-983-330169, FAX 34-983-380956, centrojosefino@ocd.castilla.org, http://www.centrojosefino.com/. Circ: 600.

261.561 USA ISSN 1071-3778
ETHICS AND MEDICS. Text in English. 1976. m. USD 28 domestic to individuals; USD 38 foreign to individuals; USD 55 to institutions; free to members (effective 2010). cum.index: 1976-1996. back issues avail. **Document type:** *Magazine, Consumer.* **Description:** Provides analysis and commentary on matters of current interest in health care, medicine, and law in order to help priests and religious, health professionals, students, and lay catholics understand and appreciate the moral teaching of the Church regarding life and health.
Related titles: Online - full text ed.: ISSN 1938-1638.
Indexed: A01, CPL, H05, P30, SCOPUS, T02.
—CCC.
Published by: National Catholic Bioethics Center, 6399 Drexel Rd, Philadelphia, PA 19151. TEL 215-877-2660, FAX 215-877-2688, info@ncbcenter.org.

282 POL ISSN 0860-8024
DK4120
ETHOS. Text in Polish. 1988. q. EUR 43 foreign (effective 2006).
Document type: *Journal, Academic/Scholarly.*
Published by: Katolicki Uniwersytet Lubelski, Instytut Jana Pawla II, Al Raclawickie 14, Lublin, 20950, Poland. TEL 48-81-4453218, FAX 48-81-4453217, http://www.kul.lublin.pl/m_wydzialowe/i_JPII. Ed. Ks. Tadeusz Styczen. Circ: 2,000. **Dist. by:** Ars Polona, Obroncow 25, Warsaw 03933, Poland. TEL 48-22-5098609, FAX 48-22-5098610, arspolona@arspolona.com.pl, http://www.arspolona.com.pl.

230.2 FRA ISSN 0014-1941
ETUDES; revue de culture contemporaine. Text in French. 1856. m. EUR 92 domestic; EUR 92 in Belgium; EUR 115.58 in Switzerland; EUR 105.79 in Canada; EUR 110 elsewhere (effective 2009). adv. bk.rev. abstr.; bibl. index, cum.index: 1961-1978, 1979-1990. **Document type:** *Academic/Scholarly.*
Related titles: Online - full text ed.
Indexed: A22, BAS, CERDIC, CPL, DIP, FR, I13, IBR, IBSS, IBZ, ILD, MLA, MLA-IB, NAA, P30, PAIS, PCI, PdeR, RILM.

R

—BLDSC (3816.555000), IE, Infotrieve, Ingenta, INIST.
Published by: Assas Editions, 14 rue d'Assas, Paris, 75006, France. TEL 33-1-44394848, FAX 33-1-40490192, redaction.etudes@ser-sa.com. Ed. Pierre de Charentenay. Circ: 15,000.

282 CAN ISSN 1193-199X
BX940S6
ETUDES D'HISTOIRE RELIGIEUSE. Text in French. 1934. a. CAD 30 membership individuals; CAD 40 membership institutions; CAD 15 membership students (effective 2004).
Former titles (until 1990): Societe Canadienne d'Histoire de l'Eglise Catholique. Sessions d'Etude (0318-6172); (until 1966): Societe Canadienne d'Histoire de l'Eglise Catholique. Rapport (0318-6164)
Indexed: A01, AmH&L, CA, CPL, FR, T02.
—INIST.
Published by: (Societe Canadienne d'Histoire de l'Eglise Catholique, Section Francaise), Universite Saint-Paul, Centre de Recherche en Histoire Religieuse du Canada, 223, rue Main, Ottawa, ON K1S 1C4, Canada. TEL 613-236-1393, FAX 613-782-3001, crh-rc-rhc@ustpaul.uottawa.ca, http://web.ustpaul.uottawa.ca/fr/recherche/centrehistoire.htm.

268 DEU ISSN 1866-0851
EULENFISCH; Limburger Magazin fuer Religion und Bildung. Text in German. 1976. q. EUR 3.50 per issue to non-members (effective 2009). **Document type:** *Magazine, Trade.*
Former titles (until 2008): Informationen fuer Religionslehrerinnen und Religionslehrer (0937-8162); (until 1989): Informationen fuer Religionslehrer (0178-8493)
Related titles: Online - full text ed.: ISSN 1617-9234. 2001.
—CCC.
Published by: Bischoefliches Ordinariat Limburg, Rossmarkt 4, Limburg, 65549, Germany. TEL 49-6431-2950, FAX 49-6431-295476, ordinariat@bistumlimburg.de, http://www.bistumlimburg.de.

282 VAT ISSN 0394-9850
BX804
EUNTES DOCETE; Commentaria Urbaniana. Text in Italian. 1948. q. bk.rev. bibl. back issues avail. **Document type:** *Journal, Academic/Scholarly.*
Indexed: CERDIC, FR.
—INIST.
Published by: (Pontificia Universita Urbaniana), Urbaniana University Press, Via Urbano VIII, 16, 00120, Vatican City. TEL 39-06-69882132, FAX 39-06-69882182, uupamm@pcn.net.

262.9 BEL ISSN 1370-5954
BR735
EUROPEAN JOURNAL FOR CHURCH AND STATE RESEARCH/ REVUE EUROPEENNE DES RELATIONS EGLISES - ETAT. Text in English. 1991. a., latest vol.10, 2003. EUR 65 combined subscription (print & online eds.) (effective 2011). adv. bk.rev. back issues avail. **Document type:** *Journal, Academic/Scholarly.* **Description:** Aims to follow up on the changes in the relationship between church and state by presenting a report for each country of the European Union.
Related titles: Online - full text ed.: ISSN 1783-1458.
Indexed: A21, FR, IBSS, RI-1, SCOPUS.
—INIST.
Published by: (Universite Catholique de Louvain, Faculte de Theologie et de Droit Canonique), Peeters Publishers, Bondgenotenlaan 153, Leuven, 3000, Belgium. TEL 32-16-235170, FAX 32-16-228500, peeters@peeters-leuven.be, http://www.peeters-leuven.be. Ed. Rik Torfs.

230.2 ESP ISSN 0214-6827
BR7
EXCERPTA E DISSERTATIONIBUS IN SACRA THEOLOGICA. Text in Spanish. 1975. irreg., latest vol.13, 1987. EUR 30 in the European Union; USD 43 elsewhere (effective 2009). **Document type:** *Monographic series, Academic/Scholarly.*
Related titles: Online - full text ed.
Indexed: A01, CA, F03, F04, T02.
Published by: (Universidad de Navarra, Facultad de Teologia), Universidad de Navarra, Servicio de Publicaciones, Campus Universitario, Pamplona, 31009, Spain. http://www.unav.es/publicaciones/.

230.2 DEU
EXTEMPORALIA; Fragen der Theologie und Seelsorge. Text in German. 1985. irreg., latest vol.22, 2009. price varies. **Document type:** *Monographic series, Academic/Scholarly.*
Published by: E O S Verlag, Erzabtei St. Ottilien, St.Ottilien, 86941, Germany. TEL 49-8193-71700, FAX 49-8193-71709, mail@eos-verlag.de.

266.2 USA ISSN 0884-7533
BX801
EXTENSION; Magazine of Catholic Missionary Work in America. Text in English. 1906. m. free. illus.; maps. 24 p./no. 3 cols./p.; back issues avail. **Document type:** *Magazine, Trade.* **Description:** Discusses mission work in the US.
Indexed: CERDIC, CPL.
Published by: Catholic Church Extension Society of the United States, 150 S Wacker Dr, 20th Fl, Chicago, IL 60606-4200. TEL 312-236-7240, FAX 312-236-5276. Ed., R&P Bradley Collins TEL 312-795-6068. Pub. Richard Ritter. Circ: 95,000 (controlled).

282 NLD ISSN 0167-3211
F M (UTRECHT). (Franciscaans Maandblad) Text in Dutch. 1971. m. EUR 28; EUR 2.80 newsstand/cover (effective 2009).
Published by: Franciscaanse Beweging in Nederland, Van der Does de Willeboissingel 11, Den Bosch, 5211 CA, Netherlands. TEL 31-73-6131340.

266.2 AUS
F M I NEWSLETTER. Text in English. 19??. m. **Document type:** *Newsletter.* **Description:** Aims to evangelise the unbeliever that they may know Jesus Christ as Lord and Savior, the Baptism of the Holy Spirit, the Baptism of Fire and the fullness of life within the Church.
Related titles: Online - full text ed.
Published by: Flame Ministries International, Subiaco E, PO Box 8133, Perth, W.A. 6008, Australia. TEL 61-8-93823668, FAX 61-8-83824080, fmi@flameministries.org, http://www.flameministries.org/.

FACE UP. *see* CHILDREN AND YOUTH—For

282 USA
FAIRFIELD COUNTY CATHOLIC. Text in English. 1984. m. USD 15 to non-members; free to members (effective 2006). adv. **Document type:** *Newspaper, Consumer.*
Contact Owner: Roman Catholic Diocese of Bridgeport, 238 Jewett Ave, Bridgeport, CT 06606-2892. TEL 203-372-4301, FAX 203-374-2044. adv.: page USD 33. Circ: 90,000 (controlled).

282 GBR ISSN 1356-126X
FAITH. Text in English. 1968. bi-m. GBP 25 domestic; GBP 29 in Europe; USD 49.99 in United States; GBP 28 elsewhere; GBP 17 to students; GBP 5 per issue (effective 2009). adv. bk.rev. 40 p./no. 2 cols./p.; back issues avail. **Document type:** *Journal, Academic/Scholarly.*
Formerly (until 1970): Kephas
Published by: Faith - Magazine (Subsidiary of: Faith Keyway Trust), 16a off Coniston Way, Reigate, RH2 0LN, United Kingdom. TEL 44-1737-770016, FAX 44-1737-770016. Ed. Hugh MacKenzie TEL 44-20-84516720. Adv. contact Scott Deeley. page GBP 300; 190 x 270.

282 USA
FAITH (ERIE). Text in English. 2005. bi-m. USD 15 (effective 2006). adv. **Document type:** *Magazine, Consumer.*
Related titles: Online - full text ed.
Published by: Catholic Diocese of Erie, 429 E Grandview Blvd, Erie, PA 16504. TEL 814-824-1160, FAX 814-824-1170, http://www.eriercd.org/. Ed. Anne Marie Welsh TEL 814-824-1167. Adv. contact Carolyn A Risinger TEL 814-824-1168. color page USD 2,892; trim 8.75 x 11. Circ: 68,014 (paid).

230.2 305.8 USA
FAITH & CULTURES SERIES. Text in English. 19??. irreg. price varies. back issues avail. **Document type:** *Monographic series, Academic/Scholarly.* **Description:** Provides questions that arise as Christian faith attempts to respond to its new global reality.
Published by: Orbis Books (Subsidiary of: Maryknoll Fathers and Brothers), Dept WEB, PO Box 302, Maryknoll, NY 10545. TEL 800-258-5838, FAX 914-941-7005, orbisbooks@maryknoll.org.

268 249 USA
FAITH & FAMILY; the magazine of catholic living. Text in English. 1966. q. USD 11.95 (effective 2005). 95 p./no.; **Document type:** *Magazine, Consumer.*
Former titles (until Dec. 2000): Catholic Faith & Family (1099-923X); (until 199?): Catholic Twin Circle (0273-6136); (until 19??): Twin Circle (0041-4654)
Indexed: MLA-IB.
Published by: Circle Media, 432 Washington Ave, North Haven, CT 06473-1309. cmsp@circlemedia.com, http://www.circlemedia.com. Ed. April Thomas Hooper. Circ: 32,000.

282 USA ISSN 1935-0384
FAITH GRAND RAPIDS. Text in English. 200?. m. USD 15 domestic; USD 25 foreign (effective 2007). **Document type:** *Magazine, Consumer.*
Published by: Catholic Diocese of Grand Rapids, 660 Burton St SE, Grand Rapids, MI 49507. TEL 616-243-0491, FAX 616-243-4910, http://www.faithgrandrapids.org/.

230.2 282 USA
FAITH MEETS FAITH SERIES. Text in English. 19??. irreg. price varies. back issues avail. **Document type:** *Monographic series, Academic/Scholarly.* **Description:** Promotes dialogue by providing an open forum for exchanges among followers of different religious paths.
Published by: Orbis Books (Subsidiary of: Maryknoll Fathers and Brothers), Dept WEB, PO Box 302, Maryknoll, NY 10545. TEL 800-258-5838, FAX 914-941-7005, orbisbooks@maryknoll.org.

282 USA
FAITHLIFE. Text in English. 1874. bi-w. USD 10 (effective 2011). adv. **Document type:** *Bulletin, Consumer.*
Formerly (until 2006): Lake Shore Visitor
Related titles: Online - full text ed.
Published by: Roman Catholic Diocese of Erie, 429 E Grandview Blvd, Erie, Erie, PA 16504-2603. TEL 814-824-1161, FAX 814-824-1170, news@eriercd.org. Ed. Anne-Marie Welsh. Pub. Bishop Donald W Trautman. Adv. contact Brenda Williams. Circ: 62,000 (paid). Wire service: CaNS.

282 ITA ISSN 0393-3555
FAMIGLIA DOMANI. Text in Italian. q. EUR 20.50 domestic; EUR 28 foreign (effective 2009). **Document type:** *Magazine, Consumer.*
Published by: Editrice Elledici, Corso Francia 214, Cascine Vica - Rivoli, TO 10098, Italy. TEL 39-011-9552111, FAX 39-011-9574048, mail@elledici.org, http://www.elledici.org.

282 PRT
FAMILIA CRISTA. Text in Portuguese. 1954. m. EUR 17.50 domestic; EUR 32 in Europe; EUR 44 elsewhere (effective 2005). **Document type:** *Newsletter.* **Description:** Covers family problems, and the pastoral and Catholic ways.
Published by: Sociedade Sao Paulo, Rua D. Pedro de Cristo 10-12, Lisbon, 1749-092, Portugal. TEL 351-21-8437620, FAX 351-21-8437629. Circ: 27,500.

282 MEX
FAMILIA CRISTIANA. Text in Spanish. 1953. m. MXN 60; USD 80 foreign. adv. **Document type:** *Magazine, Consumer.*
Published by: Ediciones Paulinas, S.A., Apdo. 69-766, 04460 Coyoacan, Mexico City, DF, Mexico. TEL 525-5491454, FAX 525-6709392. Ed., R&P Gregorio E Hidalgo. Adv. contact Ezequiel Tovar. Circ: 55,000.

282 USA
THE FAMILY DIGEST (MINNEAPOLIS). Text in English. 1945. bi-m. adv. **Document type:** *Magazine, Trade.* **Description:** Publishes general-interest articles dedicated to the joy and fulfillment of Catholic family and parish life. Distributed through Catholic parishes. Article topics include family life, parish life, spiritual life, Catholic church traditions, saint's lives, prayer, how-to and seasonal.
Formerly: Parish Family Digest
Published by: Family Digest, PO Box 26126, Minneapolis, MN 55426. TEL 612-929-6765. Ed. Corine B Erlandson. Pub., Adv. contact Clancy Mylan. R&P Corine Erlandson. Circ: 150,000.

248.4 USA
THE FAMILY FRIEND. Text in English. 1905. q. membership. bk.rev. back issues avail. **Description:** Official publication for society members. Publishes articles that relate to member recognition and benevolent activities.; society business and programs; as well as those regarding religious, seasonal, educational, and family topics.
Published by: Catholic Family Life Insurance, PO Box 11563, Milwaukee, WI 53211. TEL 414-961-0500, FAX 414-961-0103. Ed. Kari Lueneberg. Circ: 36,500.

266.2 AUS
THE FAR EAST; mission magazine of the Columban fathers. Text in English. 1920. 10/yr. AUD 10 domestic; AUD 15 in New Zealand (effective 2009). back issues avail. **Document type:** *Magazine, Consumer.* **Description:** Features articles and photographs by Columban missionaries from those countries where the missionaries work.
Published by: St. Columban's Mission Society, PO Box 752, Niddrie D.C., VIC 3042, Australia. TEL 61-3-93759475, FAX 61-3-93796040, info@columban.org.au. Ed. Fr. Gary Walker.

282 USA ISSN 0014-8814
FATHERS OF THE CHURCH. Text in English. 1947. irreg., latest 2005. price varies. back issues avail. **Document type:** *Monographic series, Academic/Scholarly.*
—CCC.
Published by: Catholic University of America Press, 620 Michigan Ave, NE, 240 Leahy Hall, Washington, DC 20064. TEL 800-537-5487, FAX 202-319-4985, cua-press@cua.edu, http://cuapress.cua.edu.

282 USA ISSN 0014-8830
FATIMA FINDINGS; the smallest newspaper on earth for the greatest cause in heaven. Text in English. 1946. m. USD 10; USD 10.50 foreign (effective 1999). back issues avail. **Document type:** *Newspaper.* **Description:** Spreads knowledge of and devotion to Our Blessed Lady of Fatima and her message.
Published by: Reparation Society of the Immaculate Heart of Mary, Inc., Fatima House, 7920 Beverly Ave, Baltimore, MD 21234. TEL 410-665-1199. Ed., R&P Rev. Casimir M Peterson. Circ: 1,000 (controlled).

282 PRT ISSN 1647-2438
FATIMA LUZ E PAZ (PORTUGUESE EDITION). Text in Portuguese. 2004. q. **Document type:** *Magazine, Consumer.*
Published by: Santuario de Nossa Senhora de Fatima, Apartado 31, Fatima, 2496-908, Portugal. TEL 351-249-539600, FAX 351-249-539605, http://www.santuario-fatima.pt.

053.1 DEU ISSN 0343-7205
FEIERABEND; Christliches Monatsblatt fuer aeltere Menschen. Text in German. 1950. m. EUR 3.55; EUR 0.35 newsstand/cover (effective 2010). **Document type:** *Newsletter, Consumer.*
Published by: Echter Verlag GmbH, Dominikanerplatz 8, Wuerzburg, 97070, Germany. TEL 49-931-660680, FAX 49-931-6606823, info@echter-verlag.de, http://www.echter.de.

282 USA ISSN 1534-200X
FELLOWSHIP OF CATHOLIC SCHOLARS QUARTERLY. Text in English. 197?. q. USD 40 (effective 2005).
Formerly (until 1996): Fellowship of Catholic Scholars Newsletter (1084-3035)
Published by: Fellowship of Catholic Scholars, c/o Dr Bernard Dobranski, Ave Maria School of Law, 3475 Plymouth Rd, Ann Arbor, MI 48105. TEL 734-827-8043.

282 ESP ISSN 2171-4673
FERVOROSA HERMANDAD D LA SANTA CRUZ, SANTA CARIDAD Y NUESTRA SENORA DEL ROSARIO. BOLETIN. Text in Spanish. 1991. s-a. **Document type:** *Bulletin, Consumer.*
Published by: Fervorosa Hermandad de la Santa Cruz, Santa Caridad y Nuestra Senora del Rosario, Calle Carlos Mauricio Morales, 20, La Palma, 21700, Spain.

220 CAN ISSN 0225-2112
FEUILLET BIBLIQUE. Text in French. 1958. w. (except Jul. & Aug.). CAD 22 (effective 2000). bk.rev. bibl. index. **Document type:** *Bulletin.*
Formerly: Parole-Dimanche
Published by: Archeveche de Montreal, Centre Biblique, 2000 rue Sherbrooke Ouest, Montreal, PQ H3H 1G4, Canada. TEL 514-925-4300, FAX 514-931-3432. Ed. Rev. Yves Guillemette. Circ: 5,000.

282 ITA ISSN 1125-9418
LA FIACCOLA. Text in Italian. 1916. m. bk.rev. back issues avail. **Document type:** *Magazine, Consumer.*
Related titles: Microfilm ed.: (from PQC).
Published by: Associazione Amici del Seminario Arcivescovile di Milano, Via San Carlo 2, Seveso, MI 20030, Italy. FAX 39-02-72023494. Ed. Don Fabio Viscardi. Circ: 18,000.

282 USA ISSN 1041-7710
FIDELIS ET VERUS/FAITHFUL AND TRUE. Text in English. 1985. q. USD 10. adv. bk.rev. 10 p./no. 2 cols./p.; back issues avail. **Document type:** *Newspaper.* **Description:** Exposes infiltration of church by Masons and Communists. Teaches traditional Catholic doctrine and practices.
Published by: Children of Mary, PO Box 350333, Ft. Lauderdale, FL 33335-0333. TEL 800-910-8187, FAX 800-910-8187, jwalsh2@juno.com. Ed., R&P, Adv. contact John Walsh. B&W page USD 100. Circ: 2,000 (paid).

282 ITA ISSN 2036-9093
FIDES CATHOLICA. Text in Italian. 2006. s-a. **Document type:** *Magazine, Consumer.*
Published by: Casa Mariana Editrice, Casa Mariana, Maria SS deel Buon Consiglio, Frigento, AV, Italy. http://www.casamarianaeditrice.info.

FILM-DIENST; das Film-Magazin. *see* MOTION PICTURES

282 028.5 FRA ISSN 1777-1692
FILOTEO. Text in French. 1988. bi-m. EUR 54.80 domestic; EUR 62.30 in the European Union; EUR 62.30 DOM-TOM; EUR 64.80 elsewhere (effective 2009 & 2010). **Document type:** *Magazine, Consumer.* **Description:** Provides youngsters with an introduction to Christian life.
Formerly (until 2005): Grain de Soleil (0993-0787)
Published by: Bayard Presse, 3-5 rue Bayard, Paris, 75393 Cedex 08, France. TEL 33-1-44356060, FAX 33-1-44356161, redactions@bayard-presse.com, http://www.bayardpresse.com. Ed. Delphine Sauliere. Circ: 39,700.

282 USA ISSN 0275-6145
E184.S64
FIRST CATHOLIC SLOVAK UNION OF AMERICA. MINUTES OF ANNUAL MEETING. Key Title: Minutes of the Annual Meeting of the First Catholic Slovak Union of the United States of America and Canada. Text in English. a.

Published by: First Catholic Slovak Union, PO Box 318013, Cleveland, OH 44131-8013.

282 DEU
FIT DURCH TIP. Text in German. 1969. 5/yr. adv. **Document type:** *Bulletin.*
Published by: Kolpingwerk Dioezesanverband Muenster, Gerlever Weg 1, Coesfeld, 48653, Germany. TEL 49-221-207010, FAX 49-221-2070138, info@kolping.de, http://www.kolping.de. Circ: 1,000.

282.759 USA ISSN 0746-4584
FLORIDA CATHOLIC (MIAMI EDITION). Text in English. 1939. w. USD 24 in state; USD 30 out of state; USD 95 foreign (effective 2009). adv. bk.rev.; film rev. **Document type:** *Newspaper, Consumer.*
Incorporates (1939-1990): The Voice (Miami) (8750-538X); (1982-1984): Southern Catholic (0745-1121)
Related titles: ◆ Regional ed(s).: Gathered; Florida Catholic (Orlando Edition); Florida Catholic (Venice Edition); Florida Catholic (Palm Beach Edition); Florida Catholic (Pensacola - Tallahassee Edition).
Published by: (Archdiocese of Miami), The Florida Catholic, Inc., 50 E. Robinson St., Orlando, FL 32801. TEL 407-373-0075, 888-275-9953. Circ: 144,000. Wire service: CaNS.

282.44862 FRA ISSN 0015-5365
FOI ET VIE DE L'EGLISE AU DIOCESE DE TOULOUSE; semaine catholique de Toulouse. Text in French. 1860. m. (10/yr). EUR 40 (effective 2008). adv. bk.rev. bibl. index.
Published by: Diocese de Toulouse, Service de la Communication, 28 Rue de l'Aude, Toulouse, 31500, France. TEL 33-5-61806997. Circ: 1,800.

282.415 IRL
THE FOLD. Text in English. m. adv. **Document type:** *Magazine, Consumer.*
Former titles: The New Fold (0790-6838); (until 1982): The Fold (0790-682X)
Published by: Diocese of Cork and Ross, Redemption Rd., Cork, Ireland. TEL 353-21-4301717, FAX 353-21-4301557. adv.: page EUR 330; 7.25 x 10.7. Circ: 7,000 (controlled).

282 HUN ISSN 1585-1370
➤ **FOLIA ATHANASIANA.** Text in Hungarian; Summaries in English, French, German, Italian. 1999. a. HUF 1,400, USD 20 per issue (effective 2010). bk.rev. back issues avail. **Document type:** *Monographic series, Academic/Scholarly.*
Published by: Szent Atanaz Gorogkatolikus Hittudomanyi Foiskola/St. Athanasius Greek Catholic Theological College, Bethlen G. u. 13-19, Nyiregyhaza, 4400, Hungary. TEL 36-42-597600, FAX 36-42-597600. Ed., Pub. Istvan Ivancso. R&P Janos Soltesz.

282 POL ISSN 0867-8294
BX1564.A1
➤ **FOLIA HISTORICA CRACOVIENSIA.** Text in Polish, English. 1989. s-a. **Document type:** *Journal, Academic/Scholarly.*
Published by: (Papieska Akademia Teologiczna w Krakowie, Wydzial Historii Kosciola), Wydawnictwo Naukowe Papieskiej Akademii Teologicznej w Krakowie, ul Franciszkanska 1, pok 037, Krakow, 31004, Poland. wydawnictwo@pat.krakow.pl. Ed. Jacek Urban.

➤ **FONTI E STUDI FRANCESCANI.** *see* RELIGIONS AND THEOLOGY—Abstracting, Bibliographies, Statistics

262.9 AUT ISSN 0429-1581
FORSCHUNGEN ZUR KIRCHLICHEN RECHTSGESCHICHTE UND ZUM KIRCHENRECHT. Text in German. 1957. irreg., latest vol.28, 2004. price varies. **Document type:** *Monographic series, Academic/Scholarly.*
Published by: Boehlau Verlag GmbH & Co.KG., Wiesingerstr 1, Vienna, W 1010, Austria. TEL 43-1-3302427, FAX 43-1-3302432, boehlau@boehlau.at, http://www.boehlau.at.

FORUM; contactblad voor inrichtende machten, pedagogische begeleiders en directies van het Katholieke Onderwijs. *see* EDUCATION

262.9 POL ISSN 1643-8388
KB51
FORUM IURIDICUM. Text in Polish. 2002. a. USD 23 foreign (effective 2006). **Document type:** *Journal, Academic/Scholarly.*
Published by: (Papieski Wydzial Teologiczny w Warszawie, Sekcja Bobolanum, Katedra Prawa Kanonicznego i Wyznaniowego), Wydawnictwo Rhetos, ul Rakowiecka 61, Warsaw, 02532, Poland. wydawnictwo@rhetos.pl, http://www.rhetos.pl. Ed. Witold Adamczewski.

282 DEU ISSN 0178-1626
BX1751.2.A1
FORUM KATHOLISCHE THEOLOGIE; Vierteljahresschrift fuer das Gesamtgebiet der katholischen Theologie. Text in German. 1985. q. **Document type:** *Journal, Academic/Scholarly.*
Indexed: DIP, FR, IBR, IBZ, PCI.
—INIST.
Published by: Schneider Druck GmbH, Erlbacherstr 102, Rothenburg ob der Tauber, 91541, Germany. TEL 49-9861-4000, FAX 49-9861-40016, info@rotabene.de, http://www.rotabene.de.

266.2 DEU ISSN 1862-9008
FORUM WELTKIRCHE. Text in German. 1873. 6/yr. EUR 30; EUR 24 to students; EUR 6 newsstand/cover (effective 2010). adv. bk.rev. abstr.; bibl.; charts; illus. index. **Document type:** *Newsletter, Consumer.*
Former titles (until 2006): K M - Forum Weltkirche (1439-1694); (until 1999): K M - Die Katholischen Missionen; Katholischen Missionen (0022-9407)
Published by: (Internationales Katholisches Missionswerk (MISSIO)), Verlag Herder GmbH, Hermann-Herder-Str 4, Freiburg Im Breisgau, 79104, Germany. TEL 49-761-27170, FAX 49-761-2717520, kundenservice@herder.de, http://www.herder.de. Adv. contact Friederike Ward TEL 49-761-2717407.

271.3 DEU ISSN 0173-5543
FRAENKISCHER HAUSKALENDER UND CARITASKALENDER. Text in German. 1949. a. **Document type:** *Bulletin, Consumer.*
Formerly (until 1968): Fraenkischer Hauskalender (0173-5527)
Published by: Echter Verlag GmbH, Dominikanerplatz 8, Wuerzburg, 97070, Germany. TEL 49-931-660680, FAX 49-931-6606823, info@echter-verlag.de, http://www.echter.de. Circ: 14,000.

282.77 FRA ISSN 0766-4125
FRANCE CATHOLIQUE. Text in French. 1972. w. EUR 110 domestic; EUR 122 foreign (effective 2009). adv. bk.rev. **Document type:** *Newspaper.*
Formerly (until 1985): France Catholique - Ecclesia (0244-528X); Which was formed by the merger of (1949-1972): Ecclesia (0766-7337); (1972-1972): Ecclesia, Reponses Chretiennes (0766-7353); (1968-1972): Reponses Chretiennes aux Problemes d'Aujourd'hui (0766-7345); (1932-1972): La France Catholique (0766-4117); Which was formerly (until 1932): L' Action Catholique de France (0766-737X); (1925-1930): Correspondance Hebdomadaire de la F N C (0766-7361)
Related titles: ◆ Supplement(s): T L Catho. ISSN 1763-8321.
Indexed: RASB.
Published by: Societe de Presse France Catholique, 60 rue de Fontenay, Le Plessis-Robinson, 92350, France. TEL 33-1-42605281. Ed. Paul Guinard. Circ: 20,000.

268 ITA ISSN 1828-4671
FRANCESCO IL VOLTO SECOLARE. Text in Italian. 2003. m. **Document type:** *Magazine, Consumer.*
Published by: Ordine Francescano Secolare d'Italia, Centro Tau, Via della Cannella 8, Capodacqua di Assisi, Italy. TEL 39-075-8064531, FAX 39-075-8065792, segreteria.assisi@ofs.it, http://www.ofs.it.

255.3 NLD ISSN 0015-9794
FRANCISCAANS LEVEN; tijdschrift tot verdieping en vernieuwing van de Franciskaanse beweging in Nederland en Vlaanderen. Text in Dutch. 1917. bi-m. EUR 22; EUR 5 newsstand/cover (effective 2009). bk.rev. bibl. index, cum.index. **Document type:** *Magazine, Academic/Scholarly.*
Published by: Franciscaanse Beweging in Nederland, Van der Does de Willeboissingel 11, Den Bosch, 5211 CA, Netherlands. TEL 31-73-6131340, http://www.franciscaansebeweging.nl.

282 NLD
FRANCISCAANS LEVEN SPECIAL. Text in Dutch. s-a. EUR 10; EUR 5 newsstand/cover (effective 2009).
Published by: Franciscaanse Beweging in Nederland, Van der Does de Willeboissingel 11, Den Bosch, 5211 CA, Netherlands. TEL 31-73-6131340, http://www.franciscaansebeweging.nl.

255.3 GBR ISSN 0532-579X
BX 5184
FRANCISCAN. Text in English. 1959. 3/yr. GBP 7 domestic; GBP 8 in Europe; GBP 9 elsewhere (effective 2010). bk.rev. 16 p./no.; back issues avail. **Document type:** *Newsletter, Consumer.* **Description:** Includes articles on Franciscan themes, as well as news of the Society.
Formerly (until 1962): The Franciscan News
Related titles: Audio cassette/tape ed.; Online - full content ed.
Indexed: A21, RI-1, RI-2.
—BLDSC (4032.783650).
Published by: Society of St. Francis, St. Francis House, 113 Gillott Rd, Birmingham, B16 0ET, United Kingdom. TEL 44-121-4548302, FAX 44-121-4559784, franciscan@franciscans.org.uk. Circ: 3,500. **Subscr. to:** The Subscriptions Secretary, The Friary, Hilfield, Dorchester, Dorset DT2 7BE, United Kingdom. franciscansubscriptions@franciscans.org.uk.

271.3 USA ISSN 0080-5459
BX3601
FRANCISCAN STUDIES. Text in English. 1924. a. USD 60 per issue domestic; USD 70 per issue foreign (effective 2010). back issues avail.; reprints avail. **Document type:** *Journal, Academic/Scholarly.* **Description:** Contains articles in the languages of western world on Franciscan history, sources, philosophy, and theology.
Related titles: Microform ed.: (from PQC); Online - full text ed.: ISSN 1945-9718.
Indexed: A01, A22, CA, CERDIC, CPL, DIP, E01, FR, IBR, IBZ, IPB, MLA, MLA-IB, PCI, PhilInd, RASB, RI-2, RILM, T02.
—BLDSC (4032.785000).
Published by: Franciscan Institute (Subsidiary of: St. Bonaventure University), c/o St. Bonaventure University, 3261 W State Rd, St. Bonaventure, NY 14778. TEL 716-375-2000, FAX 716-375-2139, franinst@sbu.edu, http://franciscaninstitute.sbu.edu. Ed. Dr. Jean-Francois Godet-Calogeras TEL 716-375-2149. Pub. Michael F Cusato TEL 716-375-2143.

FRANCISCANUM; revista de las ciencias del espiritu. *see* PHILOSOPHY

282 DEU
FRANZISKANER MISSION. Text in German. 1894. 4/yr. **Document type:** *Magazine, Trade.*
Former titles (until 1968): Antoniusbote; (until 1906): Der Sendbote des Heiligen Antonius von Padua
Address: Franziskanerstr 1, Dortmund, 44143, Germany. TEL 49-231-1763375, FAX 49-231-17633770, info@franziskanermission.de, http://www.franziskanermission.de.

282 ITA
FRATI MINORI CAPPUCCINI. ISTITUTO STORICO. VARIA. Text in Italian. 1973. irreg., latest vol.20, 1997. price varies. **Document type:** *Monographic series, Academic/Scholarly.*
Published by: Frati Minori Cappuccini, Istituto Storico/Ordo Fratrum Minorum Capuccinorum, Circonvallazione Occidentale 6850, Rome, RM 00163, Italy. TEL 39-06-660521, FAX 39-06-66052532, http://www.istcap.org.

244 DEU ISSN 0342-0213
FREIBURGER DIOEZESAN-ARCHIV. Text in German. 1865. irreg., latest vol.129. price varies. **Document type:** *Monographic series, Academic/Scholarly.*
Indexed: DIP, IBR, IBZ, RILM.
Published by: Verlag Herder GmbH, Hermann-Herder-Str 4, Freiburg Im Breisgau, 79104, Germany. TEL 49-761-27170, FAX 49-761-2717520, kundenservice@herder.de, http://www.herder.de.

230.2 CHE ISSN 0016-0725
BR45
FREIBURGER ZEITSCHRIFT FUER PHILOSOPHIE UND THEOLOGIE. Text in French, German. 1914. 2/yr. CHF 65, EUR 43 (effective 2011). bk.rev. bibl. index. reprints avail. **Document type:** *Journal, Academic/Scholarly.*
Indexed: A21, A22, BibInd, CERDIC, DIP, FR, IBR, IBZ, IPB, MLA, MLA-IB, PCI, PhilInd, RASB, RI-1, RI-2.
—IE, Infotrieve, INIST.
Published by: (Institut fuer Oekumenische Studien), Editions Saint-Paul Fribourg, Perolles 42, Fribourg, 1700, Switzerland. TEL 41-26-4264331, FAX 41-26-4264330, info@paulusedition.ch, http://www.paulusedition.ch. Circ: 600.

282 USA ISSN 1089-7496
FRONTLINE REPORT. Text in English. bi-m. bk.rev. **Document type:** *Newsletter.* **Description:** Offers a newsletter to inform readers of the SMA Missionary activities in Africa and in the United States.
Published by: Society of African Missions, Inc., 23 Bliss Ave, Tenafly, NJ 07670. TEL 201-567-0450, 800-318-1209, FAX 201-541-1280. Ed. Linda Telesco. Pub., R&P Ulick Bourke. Circ: 90,000.

FUNKKORRESPONDENZ. *see* COMMUNICATIONS—Radio

282 IRL ISSN 0016-3120
BX801
THE FURROW; a journal for the contemporary church. Text in English. 1950. m. EUR 38 in Ireland; GBP 29 in United Kingdom; EUR 44 elsewhere; EUR 26 to students; EUR 2.30 newsstand/cover (effective 2005). bk.rev. s-a. index. 64 p./no. 1 cols./p.; back issues avail.; reprints avail. **Document type:** *Journal, Academic/Scholarly.* **Description:** Provides a forum for discussing the challenges facing the Church today and of the resources available to meet them.
Related titles: Microform ed.: (from PQC).
Indexed: CERDIC, CLA, CPL, OTA, P30, PhilInd, RILM.
—BLDSC (4059.400000). **CCC.**
Published by: Furrow Trust, St. Patrick's College, Maynooth, Co. Kildare, Ireland. TEL 353-1-7083741, FAX 353-1-7083908, furrow.office@may.ie. Ed. Ronan Drury. Circ: 8,000.

G BABY. *see* CHILDREN AND YOUTH—For

266.2 USA ISSN 1945-3140
THE GABRIEL; a journal of independent sacramental spirituality. Text in English. 2008. q. USD 24.95; USD 6.95 per issue (effective 2009). back issues avail. **Document type:** *Journal, Trade.* **Description:** Highlights the best of the old and independent Catholic Churches in North America has to offer.
Related titles: Online - full text ed.: ISSN 1945-3159. free (effective 2009).
Published by: The Old Catholic Publishing Group, 227 Tennessee Ave NE, Washington, DC 20002. TEL 888-650-1817, http://www.ocpublishing.org. Ed. Matthew Velic. Pub. Michael V Seneco.

GANLEY'S CATHOLIC SCHOOLS IN AMERICA. *see* EDUCATION—Guides To Schools And Colleges

282 USA
GATHERED. Text in English. bi-m. **Document type:** *Magazine, Consumer.*
Formerly (until Oct.2008): Florida Catholic (St. Petersburg Edition)
Related titles: ◆ Regional ed(s).: Florida Catholic (Miami Edition). ISSN 0746-4584; Florida Catholic (Venice Edition); Florida Catholic (Pensacola - Tallahassee Edition); Florida Catholic (Palm Beach Edition); Florida Catholic (Orlando Edition).
Published by: (Diocese of St. Petersburg), The Florida Catholic, Inc., 50 E. Robinson St., Orlando, FL 32801. TEL 407-373-0075, 888-275-9953.

282 GBR ISSN 1358-832X
GAZETA NIEDZIELNA. Text in Polish. 1949. w. USD 130 (effective 2005). adv. bk.rev.; film rev.; play rev.; dance rev.; music rev. 6 cols./p.; back issues avail. **Document type:** *Newspaper, Consumer.*
Published by: Veritas Foundation Publication Centre, 63 Jeddo Rd, London, W12 9EE, United Kingdom. TEL 44-20-8749-4957, FAX 44-20-8749-4965. Ed., R&P Z E Walaszewski. Adv. contact D Mytko. Circ: 3,000.

282 DEU
GEIST UND AUFTRAG; Zeitschrift der Missionarischen Heilig-Geist-Gemeinschaft. Text in German. 1921. q. bk.rev. **Document type:** *Magazine, Consumer.*
Published by: Missionarische Heilig-Geist-Gemeinschaft Steyl e.V./Charitable Cooperation of the Missionary Holy Spirit Association Steyl e.V., Postfach 2308, Nettetal, 41310, Germany. TEL 49-77-3764235, FAX 49-77-3740224. Ed., R&P Sr. Gabriele Hoelzer. Circ: 35,000.

282 DEU ISSN 1615-3669
GEIST UND WORT. Text in German. 2000. irreg., latest vol.15, 2009. price varies. **Document type:** *Monographic series, Academic/Scholarly.*
Published by: Verlag Dr. Kovac, Leverkusenstr 13, Hamburg, 22761, Germany. TEL 49-40-3988800, FAX 49-40-39888055, info@verlagdrkovac.de. Ed. Erwin Moede.

282 DEU ISSN 1618-8322
GEMEINDE CREATIV; zeitschrift fuer engagierte katholiken. Text in German. 1957. 6/yr. EUR 12.50 (effective 2006). adv. bk.rev. 32 p./no.; **Document type:** *Newsletter, Consumer.*
Formerly (until 2002): Die Lebendige Zelle (0931-8887)
Published by: Landeskomitee der Katholiken in Bayern, Schaefflerstr 9, Munich, 80333, Germany. TEL 49-89-21372800, FAX 49-89-21372802, info@landeskomitee.de, http://www.landeskomitee.de. Ed. Gabriele Riffert. Adv. contact Ursula Pech. Circ: 5,400.

282 266.2 200.82 FRA ISSN 1638-7929
GENERATIONS FEMME. Text in French. 2003. irreg. EUR 30 for 6 issues (effective 2008). back issues avail. **Document type:** *Magazine, Consumer.*
Formed by the merger of (1996-200?): En Equipe A C G F au Service de l'Evangile (1279-7464); Which was formerly (until 1996): En Equipe au Service de l'Evangile (0395-1766); (1992-2002): Horizon Femme (1163-7978); Which was formerly (until 1992): Le Gue (0395-1480); (until 1976): Militantes A C G F (0395-1472)
Published by: Action Catholique des Femmes, 98 rue de l'Universite, Paris, 75007, France. TEL 33-1-40626500, FAX 33-1-40626518, http://www.actioncatholiquedesfemmes.org.

282 USA
THE GEORGIA BULLETIN. Text in English. 1962. w. (Thu.). USD 18 (effective 2005). **Document type:** *Newspaper, Consumer.*
Published by: Catholic Archdiocese of Atlanta, 680 W Peachtree St, N W, Atlanta, GA 30308-1984. TEL 404-897-5500, FAX 404-877-5505, gkeiser@georgiabulletin.org, http://www.archatl.com. Ed. Gretchen R Keiser. Pub. Rev. Wilton D Gregory. Adv. contact Tom Aisthorpe. Circ: 72,000 (paid). Wire service: CaNS.

282 NLD ISSN 1878-8718
GERARDUS. Text in Dutch. 1920. m. EUR 10 (effective 2009). 16 p./no.; **Document type:** *Magazine, Consumer.*
Former titles (until 2009): Gerardus Klok (1571-697X); (until 2000): Sint Gerardus Klok (0167-2673)

R

Published by: Redemptoristenklooster, Wittemer Allee 32, Wittem, 6286 AB, Netherlands. TEL 31-43-4501741, FAX 31-43-4503055, info@gerardus.nl, http://www.redemptoristen.nl.

GESCHICHTE DES KIRCHLICHEN LEBENS. *see* RELIGIONS AND THEOLOGY—Protestant

DE GIDS OP MAATSCHAPPELIJK GEBIED; blad met mening. *see* LABOR UNIONS

IL GIORNALINO; settimanale dei ragazzi. *see* CHILDREN AND YOUTH—For

282 HRV ISSN 0436-0311
GLAS KONCILA. Text in Croatian. 1962. w. HRK 260 domestic; EUR 71.50 in Europe (effective 2002). adv. **Document type:** *Newspaper, Consumer.*
Related titles: Online - full text ed.: ISSN 1333-9087.
Address: Kaptol 8, p.p. 216, Zagreb, 10001, Croatia. TEL 385-1-4814828, FAX 385-1-4814832. Ed. Ivan Miklenic.

266.2 USA ISSN 0746-3022
GLENMARY CHALLENGE. Text in English. 1937. q. donation. charts; illus.; stat. back issues avail. **Document type:** *Magazine, Consumer.* **Description:** Focuses on problems and promise of rural United States and how Glenmary Home Missioners serve the spiritual and material needs of rural America.
Formerly: Glenmary's Challenge (0017-1182)
Published by: Glenmary Home Missioners, PO Box 465618, Cincinnati, OH 45246-5618. TEL 513-874-8900, FAX 513-874-1690, challenge@glenmary.org. Ed. Karen Hurley. Pub. Rev. Jerry Dorn. R&P Jean Bach. Circ: 110,000 (controlled).

282 USA
THE GLOBE (SIOUX CITY). Text in English. 1953. w. (Thu.). USD 20 diocese; USD 22 outside diocese (effective 2005). **Document type:** *Newspaper, Consumer.*
Formerly: Sioux City Globe
Published by: Catholic Diocese of Sioux City, 1825 Jackson St, Sioux City, IA 51105. TEL 712-255-2550, FAX 712-255-4901. Ed. Renee Webb. Circ: 29,000 (paid). Wire service: CaNS.

282 LKA
GNANARTHAPRADEEPAYA. Text in Singhalese. 1866. w.
Published by: Colombo Catholic Press, Borella, 2 Gnanarthapradeepaya Mawatha, Colombo, 8, Sri Lanka. TEL 1-695984. Ed. Rev. Fr Bertram Dabrera. Circ: 26,000.

282 USA ISSN 0199-3429
GOD'S WORD TODAY. Text in English. 1979. m. USD 17.95; USD 1.95 newsstand/cover. bk.rev. charts; illus.; maps. back issues avail. **Document type:** *Magazine, Consumer.*
Published by: University of St. Thomas, Fulfillment House, PO Box 56915, Boulder, CO 80322-6915. TEL 808-246-7390. Ed. George A Martin. Pub. L Thomas Kelly. Circ: 50,000 (paid).

282 FRA ISSN 1144-8814
GOLIAS. Text in French. 1985. bi-m. EUR 38 domestic; EUR 50 foreign (effective 2009). back issues avail. **Document type:** *Magazine, Consumer.*
Indexed: IBSS.
Published by: Golias France, B.P. 3045, Villeurbanne, Cedex 69605, France. TEL 33-4-78038747, FAX 33-4-78844203, redaction.golias@orange.fr, http://golias-editions.fr.

282 FRA ISSN 1962-3070
GOLIAS HEBDO. Text in French. 2007. w. (52/yr). EUR 39 domestic; EUR 50 foreign (effective 2009). **Document type:** *Magazine, Consumer.* **Description:** Covers world news items that involve the Catholic church.
Published by: Golias France, B.P. 3045, Villeurbanne, Cedex 69605, France. TEL 33-4-78038747, FAX 33-4-78844203, redaction.golias@orange.fr, http://golias-editions.fr.

282 DEU ISSN 0946-8943
GOTTES VOLK. Text in German. 1986. 8/yr. EUR 91.80; EUR 12 newsstand/cover (effective 2005). **Document type:** *Journal, Trade.*
Related titles: Supplement(s): Gottes Volk Sonderband. ISSN 1437-4021. 199?.
Published by: Katholisches Bibelwerk e.V., Silberburgstr 121, Stuttgart, 70176, Germany. TEL 49-711-6192050, FAX 49-711-6192077, bibelinfo@bibelwerk.de, http://www.bibelwerk.de.

282 DEU ISSN 0343-8732
GOTTESDIENST; Information und Handreichung der Liturgischen Institute Deutschlands, Oesterreichs und der Schweiz. Text in German. 1967. s-m. EUR 47.50; EUR 35 to students; EUR 2.50 newsstand/cover (effective 2010). adv. bk.rev. back issues avail. **Document type:** *Newsletter, Consumer.*
Published by: Verlag Herder GmbH, Hermann-Herder-Str 4, Freiburg Im Breisgau, 79104, Germany. TEL 49-761-27170, FAX 49-761-2717520, kundenservice@herder.de, http://www.herder.de. Adv. contact Friederike Ward TEL 49-761-2717407. Circ: 12,500.

282 DEU ISSN 0945-4667
GOTTESDIENSTE VORBEREITEN. Text in German. 1996. bi-m. EUR 59.70 (effective 2011). **Document type:** *Journal, Trade.*
Published by: Bergmoser und Hoeller Verlag GmbH, Karl-Friedrich-Str 76, Aachen, 52072, Germany. TEL 49-241-93888123, FAX 49-241-93888134, kontakt@buhv.de.

282.68 ZAF ISSN 1012-5930
➤ **GRACE AND TRUTH**; a journal of catholic reflection for Southern Africa. Text in English. 1980. 3/yr. ZAR 90 domestic; GBP 26, USD 43 in Africa; GBP 31, USD 47 in Europe; USD 52 elsewhere (effective 2001). bk.rev. index. 64 p./no.; back issues avail. **Document type:** *Journal, Academic/Scholarly.* **Description:** Concerned with the development of the Catholic church and society in Southern Africa.
Indexed: ISAP.
Published by: St. Joseph's Theological Institute, Private Bag 6004, Hilton, KwaZulu-Natal 3245, South Africa. TEL 27-331-433293, FAX 27-331-431232, stjoseph@nu.ac.za. Ed., R&P Christopher Chatteris TEL 27-333306274. Circ: 500.

282 USA ISSN 8755-9323
GREEN BAY CATHOLIC COMPASS. Text in English. 1978. w. (45/yr.). USD 25; USD 27 foreign. adv. **Document type:** *Newspaper.* **Description:** Provides local and world news, features, opinion columns, and youth pages for Catholics in the Green Bay Diocese.
Related titles: Microfiche ed.
Published by: (Catholic Diocese of Green Bay), Green Bay Register, Inc., 1825 Riverside Dr, Box 23825, Green Bay, WI 54305-3825. TEL 414-437-7531, FAX 414-437-0694. Ed. Tony Staley. Pub. Bishop Robert J Banks. R&P Tony Kuick. Adv. contact John Klozotsky Jr. Circ: 14,500 (paid).

282 ITA ISSN 0017-4114
BX800.A1
➤ **GREGORIANUM.** Text in English, French, German, Italian, Latin, Spanish. 1920. q. bk.rev. bibl. index, cum.index: vols.1-31 (1920-1950). **Document type:** *Monographic series, Academic/Scholarly.* **Description:** A scientific review of theology and philosophy with occasional discussions of problems in Church history, canon law, and the social sciences.
Related titles: Microfiche ed.: (from IDC).
Indexed: A21, A22, CERDIC, CLA, CPL, DIP, FR, IBR, IBZ, IPB, IZBG, MLA-IB, OTA, PCI, Philind, RI-1, RI-2, SCOPUS.
—BLDSC (4215.300000), IE, Infotrieve, Ingenta, INIST.
Published by: (Pontificia Universita Gregoriana/Pontifical Gregorian University), Gregorian University Press/Editrice Pontificia Universita Gregoriana, Piazza della Pilotta 35, Rome, 00187, Italy. TEL 39-06-6781567, FAX 39-06-6780588, periodicals@biblicum.com, http://www.paxbook.com. Circ: 1,200.

266.2 DEU
GRENZENLOS; eine Welt in Schule und Gemeinde. Text in German. 1950. s-a. bk.rev. **Document type:** *Academic/Scholarly.*
Former titles (until 2005): Schule und Mission; (until 1959): Heilige Kindheit
Published by: Kindermissionswerk, Stephanstr 35, Aachen, 52064, Germany. TEL 49-241-44610, FAX 49-241-446140, kontakt@kindermissionswerk.de, http://www.kindermissionswerk.de, http://www.sternsinger.de. Circ: 7,800.

271.3 USA ISSN 1936-4903
BX3601
GREYFRIARS REVIEW. Text in English. 1987. q. USD 42 (effective 2010). back issues avail. **Document type:** *Journal, Academic/Scholarly.* **Description:** Contains resource for Franciscan theology, spirituality, and history in English translation.
Indexed: CPL.
Published by: Franciscan Institute (Subsidiary of: St. Bonaventure University), c/o St. Bonaventure University, 3261 W State Rd, St. Bonaventure, NY 14778. TEL 716-375-2000, FAX 716-375-2139, franinst@sbu.edu, http://franciscaninstitute.sbu.edu. Ed. Michael Blastic.

282 DEU
GUCKLOCH. Text in German. 1973. q. free. back issues avail. **Document type:** *Corporate.*
Published by: Katholische Junge Gemeinde, Dioezesanverband Muenster, Rosenstr 16, Muenster, 48143, Germany. TEL 0251-495500. Ed. Uta Forbrig.

GUIA DE CENTROS EDUCATIVOS CATOLICOS. *see* EDUCATION—Guides To Schools And Colleges

282 USA
GUIDE TO RELIGIOUS MINISTRIES FOR CATHOLIC MEN AND WOMEN. (Published in 3 regional editions) Text in English. 1979. a. USD 10 (effective 2000). adv. tr.lit.
Former titles: Religious Community Profiles; Guide to Religious Ministries for Catholic Men and Women; Guide to Religious Careers for Catholic Men and Women
Published by: Catholic News Publishing Co., Inc. (Subsidiary of: School Guide Publications), 210 North Ave, New Rochelle, NY 10801. TEL 914-632-1220, 800-433-7771, FAX 914-632-3412. Ed. Mari Castrovilla. Pub. Myles Ridder TEL 914-632-1220. adv.: B&W page USD 1,210; trim 7 x 4.5. Circ: 45,000.

282 ESP
GUIONES LITURGICOS. Text in Spanish. s-a. EUR 16 per issue (effective 2008). **Document type:** *Bulletin, Consumer.*
Published by: Caritas Espanola, San Bernardo, 99 bis 7a, Madrid, 28015, Spain. TEL 34-91-4441000, FAX 34-91-5934882, publicaciones@caritas-espa.org, http://www.caritas.es.

282 USA
GULF PINE CATHOLIC. Text in English. 1983. bi-w. (Fri.). USD 12.50 (effective 2008). **Document type:** *Newspaper, Consumer.*
Published by: Catholic Diocese of Biloxi, 1790 Popps Ferry Rd, Biloxi, MS 39532. TEL 228-702-2126, FAX 228-702-2128. Ed., Adv. contact Shirley Henderson. Pub. Bishop Thomas J Rodi. Circ: 17,000 (paid). Wire service: CaNS.

223 ITA ISSN 1124-1225
BX4655.2
➤ **HAGIOGRAPHICA**; rivista di agiografia e biografia. Text in English, French, German, Italian. 1994. a., latest vol.6, 1999. back issues avail. **Document type:** *Journal, Academic/Scholarly.* **Description:** Publishes articles relating to topics in hagiography and biography, with particular emphasis on medieval European history.
Published by: (Societa Internazionale per lo Studio del Medioevo Latina), S I S M E L Edizioni del Galluzzo, Casella Postale 90, Tavarnuzze, FI 50023, Italy. TEL 39-055-2374537, FAX 39-055-2373454, http://www.sismel.it.

➤ **HAKIMANI**; Jesuit journal of social justice in Eastern Africa. *see* SOCIOLOGY

282 USA ISSN 1942-9371
HARVEST (PORTLAND). Text in English. 200?. bi-m. USD 12 (effective 2008). adv. **Document type:** *Magazine, Consumer.*
Published by: Roman Catholic Bishop of Portland, 510 Ocean Av, PO Box 11559, Portland, ME 04104. TEL 207-773-6471, FAX 207-773-0182, http://www.portlanddiocese.net/info.php?info_id=205. Ed. Lois Czerniak.

282.969 USA ISSN 1045-3636
HAWAII CATHOLIC HERALD. Text in English. 1936. fortn. USD 15. adv. bk.rev.
Published by: Roman Catholic Bishop of Honolulu, 1184 Bishop St, Honolulu, HI 96813. TEL 808-533-1791, FAX 808-521-8428. Ed. Patrick Downes. Circ: 8,000.

282 POL ISSN 0017-9914
HEJNAL MARIACKI; miesiecznik o tematyce religijno-kulturalno-spolecznej. Text in Polish. 1956. m. USD 6. adv. illus.
Published by: Chrzescijanskie Stowarzyszenie Dobroczynne, ul Boleslawska 23, Klucze, 32310, Poland. TEL 48-32-6471441, chsd@chsd.org.pl, http://www.chsd.org.pl. Circ: 5,000.

282 DEU
HELIAND KORRESPONDENZ. Text in German. 1969. q. bk.rev. **Document type:** *Bulletin.*
Published by: Kreis Katholischer Frauen im Heliandbund, Gabelsbergerstr 19, Cologne, 50674, Germany. TEL 49-6234-7544, FAX 49-6234-7544. Circ: 1,700. **Subscr. to:** Lilienstr 61, Mutterstadt 67112, Germany.

282 TWN
HENGYI: CHENGSHU JIAOYOU DE ZAZHI/COSTANTINIAN: MAGAZINE FOR MATURE CATHOLICS. Text in Chinese. 1951. bi-m. **Document type:** *Magazine, Consumer.*
Published by: Tianzhu Jiaozhu Tuhui/Congregatio Discipulorum Domini, 108, Zhongzheng Lu, Hsinchuang, Taipei 242, Taiwan. TEL 886-2-22769146, FAX 886-2-22769146, maiantai@ms1.hinet.net. Eds. Shuhua Zhang, Jiaxiang Liu. Circ: 1,000.

282 USA ISSN 0746-4185
EL HERALDO CATOLICO/CATHOLIC HERALD; Spanish language newspaper. Text in Spanish, English. 1979. m. free at Spanish language masses (effective 2009). adv. bk.rev. 16 p./no. 5 cols./p.; **Document type:** *Newspaper, Consumer.*
Related titles: Microfilm ed.: (from LIB).
Published by: Roman Catholic Diocese of Sacramento, 2110 Broadway, Sacramento, CA 95818-2541. TEL 916-733-0200, FAX 916-733-0195. Ed. Julie Sly. Pub. Jaime K Soto. Adv. contact Cathy Joyce. Circ: 35,000. Wire service: CaNS.

282 DEU ISSN 0018-0645
BX803
HERDER - KORRESPONDENZ; Monatshefte fuer Gesellschaft und Religion. Text in German. 1946. m. EUR 72 for 6 mos.; EUR 54 for 6 mos. to students; EUR 12 newsstand/cover (effective 2010). adv. bk.rev. index. **Document type:** *Newsletter, Consumer.*
Indexed: A01, A22, AIAP, CPL, DIP, IBR, IBZ, MLA-IB, RASB, RILM.
—IE, Infotrieve.
Published by: Verlag Herder GmbH, Hermann-Herder-Str 4, Freiburg Im Breisgau, 79104, Germany. TEL 49-761-27170, FAX 49-761-2717520, kundenservice@herder.de, http://www.herder.de. Ed. Ulrich Ruh. Adv. contact Bettina Schillinger-Wegmann. Circ: 7,500 (paid and controlled).

THE HIBERNIAN. *see* HISTORY—History Of Europe

291.72 268 FRA ISSN 1957-5246
BV2100
HISTOIRE & MISSIONS CHRETIENNES. Text in French. 2007. q. EUR 70 domestic; EUR 80 in Europe; EUR 80 DOM-TOM; EUR 80 in Africa; EUR 95 elsewhere (effective 2009). **Document type:** *Journal, Consumer.*
Published by: Editions Karthala, 22-24 Boulevard Arago, Paris, 75013, France. TEL 33-1-43311559, FAX 33-1-45352705, karthala@orange.fr, http://www.karthala.com.

282.71 CAN ISSN 1193-1981
➤ **HISTORICAL STUDIES.** Text in English, French. 1933. a., latest vol.67, 2001. CAD 35 domestic; CAD 40 in United States; CAD 45 in Europe; CAD 20 to students (effective 2002). bk.rev. abstr. 340 p./no. 1 cols./p.; back issues avail. **Document type:** *Journal, Academic/Scholarly.* **Description:** Features papers that were read at both the annual conferences.
Former titles (until 1990): Canadian Catholic Historical Studies (0827-1704); (until 1984): Canadian Catholic Historical Association. Study Sessions (0318-6156); (until 1966): Canadian Catholic Historical Association. Report (0318-6148)
Related titles: CD-ROM ed.; Online - full text ed.
Indexed: A26, AmH&L, C03, CA, CBCARef, CPL, CPerI, E08, G08, HistAb, I05, P30, P48, PQC, S09, T02.
—**CCC.**
Published by: Canadian Catholic Historical Association, c/o Secretary General, 1155 Yonge St, Toronto, ON M4T 1W2, Canada. TEL 416-934-3400, ext 501, 416-934-0606, FAX 416-934-3444, terry.fay@utoronto.ca, http://www.umanitob.ca/colleges/st_pauls/ccha. Eds. Mark G McGowan, Richard A Lebrun. Circ: 350 (paid).

262.13 BEL
➤ **HISTORY OF VATICAN II.** Text in English. 1996. irreg., latest 2006. price varies. bk.rev. 600 p./no.; back issues avail. **Document type:** *Monographic series, Academic/Scholarly.*
Published by: Peeters Publishers, Bondgenotenlaan 153, Leuven, 3000, Belgium. TEL 32-16-235170, FAX 32-16-228500, http://www.peeters-leuven.be.

282 USA ISSN 1068-0330
HLAS NARODA/VOICE OF THE NATION. Text in Czech, English, Slovak. w. USD 30. back issues avail. **Document type:** *Newspaper.*
Published by: Czech-American Heritage Center, 159, Berwyn, IL 60402-0159. TEL 312-656-1050. Ed. Vojtech Vit.

282 USA
HOLY CROSS. NEWSLETTER. Text in English. 1965 (vol.4). 3/yr. per issue contribution. **Document type:** *Newspaper.*
Formerly (until 1978): Holy Cross News (0018-3725)
Published by: Order of the Holy Cross, Holy Cross Monastery, Box 99, West Park, NY 12493. TEL 914-384-6660. Circ: 24,000.

HOLY LAND REVIEW; illustrated quarterly of the Franciscan custody of the Holy Land. *see* RELIGIONS AND THEOLOGY—Judaic

HOMELIFE; the Philippines' family magazine. *see* GENERAL INTEREST PERIODICALS—Philippines

253 USA ISSN 0018-4268
BX801
HOMILETIC AND PASTORAL REVIEW. Text in English. 1900. m. (bi-m. Aug.-Sep.). USD 26 domestic; USD 35.82 in Canada; USD 34 elsewhere; USD 4 per issue (effective 2009). adv. bk.rev. index. reprints avail. **Document type:** *Magazine, Trade.* **Description:** Contains articles by great Catholic writers on doctrine, spiritual guidance, morality and authentic pastoral practice as well as provides deep insights into pressing pastoral issues of the Church's life and mission.
Former titles (until 1920): Homiletic Monthly and Pastoral Review; (until 1918): Homiletic Monthly; (until 1917): Homiletic Monthly and Catechist
Related titles: Microform ed.: (from PQC).
Indexed: A21, A22, CERDIC, CLA, CPL, L09, MLA-IB, OTA, P30, RI-1, RI-2.
—IE.

Published by: Ignatius Press, 2515 McAllister St, San Francisco, CA 94118. http://www.ignatius.com. Ed. Kenneth Baker. Adv. contact Evelyn C Campbell. **Subscr. to:** PO Box 46, Bathgate, ND 58216. TEL 800-651-1531.

255 POL ISSN 0208-757X
HOMO DEI. Text in Polish. 1932. q. EUR 45 foreign (effective 2006). **Document type:** *Journal.*
Published by: Warszawska Prowincja Redemptorystow, ul Zamojskiego 56, Krakow, 30532, Poland. TEL 48-12-2598120, FAX 48-12-2598121. **Dist. by:** Ars Polona, Obroncow 25, Warsaw 03933, Poland. TEL 48-22-5098609, FAX 48-22-5098610, arspolona@arspolona.com.pl, http://www.arspolona.com.pl.

282.5125 HKG ISSN 0073-3210
HONG KONG CATHOLIC CHURCH DIRECTORY/HSIANG-KANG T'IEN CHU CHIAO SHOU TS'E. Text in Chinese, English. 1954. a. USD 11.54 (effective 2001). adv. 628 p./no.; **Document type:** *Directory.* **Description:** Includes personnel of Curiae, churches, diocesan organizations, pious associations, Catholic schools, social services and religious congregations.
Published by: Catholic Truth Society, 11 Fl, Catholic Diocese Centre, 16 Caine Rd, Hong Kong, Hong Kong. TEL 852-2810-9381, FAX 852-2521-8700. Ed., R&P Louis Lee. Pub., Adv. contact Rev. Edward Khong TEL 852-2522-1009. Circ: 1,900. **Dist. by:** Catholic Centre, 16/F, Grand Bldg, 15-18 Connaught Rd, Central, Hong Kong. TEL 852-2525-7063, FAX 852-2521-7969, bookshop@catholiccentre.org.hk.

230.2 USA ISSN 0360-9669
BR1
➤ **HORIZONS (VILLANOVA).** Text in English. 1974. s-a. free to members (effective 2010). bk.rev. illus. reprints avail. **Document type:** *Journal, Academic/Scholarly.* **Description:** Explores developments in Catholic theology, the total Christian tradition, human religious experience, and the concerns of creative teaching in the college and university environment.
Formerly (until 19??): 21st Century Genetics Cooperative
Related titles: Microfilm ed.: (from PQC); Online - full text ed.
Indexed: A20, A21, A22, ArtHuCI, CA, CPL, CurCont, FamI, OTA, RI-1, RI-2, SCOPUS, T02, W07.
—BLDSC (4326.794400), IE, Infotrieve, Ingenta.
Published by: (Council of Societies for the Study of Religion), College Theology Society, c/o The Editor, St. Mary's Hall, 800 Lancaster Ave, Villanova University, Villanova, PA 19085. TEL 610-519-6917. Ed. Anthony J Godzieba.

255.3 USA ISSN 0018-6910
HRVATSKI KATOLICKI GLASNIK; mjesecnik za duhovnu izgradnju iseljenih Hrvata. Text in English. 1942. m. USD 5. adv. bk.rev. illus.
Indexed: CERDIC.
Published by: (Croatian Franciscan Fathers), Croatian Franciscan Press, 4851 Drexel Blvd, Chicago, IL 60615. TEL 312-268-2819. Ed. Fr Harvoslav Ban O F M. Circ: 3,000.

255.53 USA ISSN 0197-3096
BV4012
➤ **HUMAN DEVELOPMENT (CHICAGO).** Text in English. 1980. q. USD 36 combined subscription domestic (print & online eds.); USD 40 combined subscription foreign (print & online eds.) (effective 2009). bk.rev. back issues avail. **Document type:** *Magazine, Academic/Scholarly.* **Description:** Designed for people involved in religious leadership, education, spiritual direction, pastoral care and religious information.
Related titles: Online - full text ed.: USD 20 (effective 2009).
Indexed: A01, A02, A03, A08, A22, C28, CA, CPL, E03, ERI, G10, P04, RASB, S02, S03, T02.
—BLDSC (4336.052000), IE, Infotrieve.
Published by: Regis University, 3333 Regis Blvd, Denver, CO 80221. TEL 303-458-4143, 800-388-2366, FAX 303-964-5530. Eds. Robert Hamma, Rev. William A Barry.

266.2 USA ISSN 0899-420X
HUMAN LIFE INTERNATIONAL. SPECIAL REPORT. Text in English. 1981. m. looseleaf. stat. cum.index: 1981-1996. back issues avail. **Document type:** *Newsletter, Trade.* **Description:** Accounts of Rev. Welch's and Rev. Habiger's pro-life missionary travels.
Formerly: Human Life International. Letter Dr. Report
Published by: Human Life International, 4 Family Life, Front Royal, VA 22630. TEL 540-635-7884, FAX 540-622-2838. R&P, Adv. contact James Price. Circ: 30,000.

282 FRA ISSN 2116-9306
I C E S. ANNALES. (Institut Catholique d'Etudes Superieures) Text in French. 2007. a. **Document type:** *Journal, Academic/Scholarly.*
Formerly (until 2011): Vendee. Annales (1960-7032)
Published by: Institut Catholique d'Etudes Superieures, BP 691, La Roche-sur-Yon, 85000, France. http://www.ices.fr.

282.091734 VAT
I C R A - AGRIMISSIO INFORMATION. (International Catholic Rural Association) Text in English. 1964. q. Free. adv. bk.rev. cum.index. back issues avail. **Document type:** *Bulletin.* **Description:** Facilitates contact, exchange and joint endeavor among all Catholic rural and agricultural organizations throughout the world; stimulate mutual help on an international level between these organizations; help to find Christian-inspired solutions to social, religious and moral aspects of rural problems.
Formerly: Information Bulletin for Catholic Rural Organizations
Published by: International Catholic Rural Association - Agrimissio, Palazzo San Calisto, Vatican City, 00120, Vatican City. TEL 39-6-69887123, FAX 39-6-69887223, info@icra-agrimissio.org, http://www.icra-agrimissio.org. Ed. Msgr. Biagio Notarangelo. Circ: 1,800.

ICONOGRAPHIA FRANCISCANA. *see* ART

282.796 USA ISSN 1080-4463
IDAHO CATHOLIC REGISTER. Text in English. 1958. s-m. USD 16 domestic; USD 35 foreign (effective 2005). adv. bk.rev. **Document type:** *Newspaper.*
Formerly: Idaho Register (0891-5792)
Published by: Catholic Diocese of Idaho, 303 Federal Way, Boise, ID 83705. TEL 208-342-1311, FAX 208-342-0224. Pub. Michael Driscoll. adv.: page USD 746. Circ: 16,000 (paid). Wire service: CaNS.

282 DEU
IDEENREICH. Text in German. 1990. q. **Document type:** *Magazine, Consumer.*
Published by: Katholische Studierende Jugend, Gabelsbergerstr 19, Cologne, 50674, Germany. TEL 49-221-9420180, FAX 49-221-94201822, bundesamt@ksj.de.

282 DEU ISSN 1616-1033
IDEENWERKSTATT GOTTESDIENST. Text in German. 2000. 6/yr. EUR 19.90 newsstand/cover (effective 2010). **Document type:** *Journal, Academic/Scholarly.*
Published by: Verlag Herder GmbH, Hermann-Herder-Str 4, Freiburg Im Breisgau, 79104, Germany. TEL 49-761-27170, FAX 49-761-2717520, kundenservice@herder.de, http://www.herder.de.

282 HUN ISSN 0864-8557
BX2355
IGEN. Text in Hungarian. 1989. m.
Indexed: RILM.
Published by: Igen Katolikus Kulturalis Egyesulet, Ferenciek tere 7-8 III lph II em 10, Budapest, 1053, Hungary. TEL 36-1-3175369, igen@igen.hu.

282.4686 ESP
IGLESIA DE SEVILLA. Text in Spanish. s-a. back issues avail. **Document type:** *Bulletin, Consumer.*
Published by: Arzobispado de Sevilla, Oficina Diocesana de Informacion, Apartado Postal 6, Sevilla, 41080, Spain. arzobispado@archisevilla.org, 34-95-4505515, http://www.diocesisdesevilla.org/. Ed. Angel G Gomez Guillen. Circ: 16,000.

282 ITA ISSN 1828-2377
BX3701
IGNAZIANA; rivista di ricerca teologica. Text in Multiple languages. 2006. s-a. free (effective 2011). **Document type:** *Journal, Academic/Scholarly.*
Media: Online - full text.
Indexed: A01, T02.
Published by: Centro di Spiritualita Ignaziana (Naples), Viale S Ignazio di Loyola 51, Cangiani, Naples, 80131, Italy. TEL 39-081-3724811, FAX 39-081-5464413. Ed. Giuseppe Piva.

282 DEU ISSN 0939-4656
IM DIENST DER KIRCHE; die groesste Fachzeitschrift fuer alle Kirchenangestellten. Text in German. 1919. q. bk.rev.; music rev. bibl. **Document type:** *Journal, Consumer.*
Published by: Zentralverband Katholischer Kirchenangestellter e.V., Breite Str 101, Cologne, 50667, Germany. TEL 49-221-2570420, FAX 49-221-2570319, mail@zkd-online.de, http://www.zkd-online.de/.

282 FRA ISSN 0750-3407
IMAGES DU MOIS. Text in French. 1962. m. **Document type:** *Magazine, Consumer.*
Published by: Vie Catholique Illustree, 163 bd. Malesherbes, Paris, Cedex 17 75017, France. TEL 33-1-48884500, FAX 33-1-48884533. Ed. Francois Leroux. Circ: 50,000.

282 ITA ISSN 2037-4585
IMMACULATA MEDIATRIX. Text in Italian. 2001. 3/yr. **Document type:** *Magazine, Consumer.*
Published by: Casa Mariana Editrice, Casa Mariana, Maria SS deel Buon Consiglio, Frigento, AV, Italy. http://www.casamarianaeditrice.info.

282 NLD ISSN 1877-2412
IMPRESSIE. Text in Dutch. 1990. irreg. (1-2/yr.). free (effective 2011). **Document type:** *Newsletter, Academic/Scholarly.*
Formerly (until 2008): Erasmusplein (0924-8668)
Published by: Katholiek Documentatie Centrum, Postbus 9100, Nijmegen, 6500 HA, Netherlands. TEL 31-24-3612457, FAX 31-24-3612403, info@kdc.ru.nl. Eds. Anne-Lies van Diessen, Lodewijk Winkeler.

282 DEU ISSN 0946-3178
IMPRIMATUR. Text in German. 1968. 7/yr. EUR 32 (effective 2008). **Document type:** *Journal, Academic/Scholarly.*
Indexed: P30.
Published by: Arbeitskreis Imprimatur, Walter Gieseking Str 12, Saarbruecken, 66123, Germany. TEL 49-681-9102506, FAX 49-681-9102509. Ed. Erhard Bertel.

282 ITA ISSN 0992-7484
IN CAMMINO. Text in Italian. 1988. 7/yr. EUR 18.30 domestic; EUR 27.80 in the European Union; EUR 32 elsewhere (effective 2008). **Document type:** *Magazine, Consumer.*
Published by: Centro Editoriale Dehoniano, Via Scipione dal Ferro 4, Bologna, BO 40138, Italy. TEL 39-051-4290451, FAX 39-051-4290491, ced-amm@dehoniane.it, http://www.dehoniane.it.

282 NLD ISSN 0019-3151
IN DE RECHTE STRAAT. Text in Dutch. 1958. q. EUR 5.75 domestic; EUR 7.50 in Europe; EUR 11 foreign (effective 2010). bk.rev. illus. **Description:** Discusses dialogue and witness with the Catholic Church and helps ex-priests who left their church for reasons of conscience.
Related titles: Spanish ed.: En la Calle Recta. ISSN 0165-5264.
Indexed: CERDIC.
Published by: Stichting In de Rechte Straat, Prins Hendrikweg 4, Bennekom, 6721 AD, Netherlands. TEL 31-318-431298, FAX 31-318-431395, secr@irs.nu.

IN HIS HANDS. *see* HANDICAPPED—Visually Impaired

282 USA ISSN 2150-9824
BX1754
THE INCARNATE WORD. Abbreviated title: T I W. Text in English. 2006. s-a. USD 53 for 2 yrs.; USD 15 per issue (effective 2009). back issues avail. **Document type:** *Journal, Trade.* **Description:** Aimed at prolonging the Mystery of the Incarnation of the Word in all mankind, in the entire man, and in every manifestation of man.
Related titles: Online - full text ed.: free (effective 2009).
Published by: Religious Family of the Institute of the Incarnate Word in the USA, 113 E 117th St, New York, NY 10035. TEL 212-534-5257, FAX 212-534-5258.

282 ITA
➤ **INCULTURATION.** Text in Italian, English, French. 1982. irreg., latest vol.21, 2001. price varies. **Document type:** *Monographic series, Academic/Scholarly.* **Description:** Working papers on living faith and cultures.
Published by: (Pontificia Universita Gregoriana/Pontifical Gregorian University, Centre "Culture e Religioni"), Gregorian University Press/Editrice Pontificia Universita Gregoriana, Piazza della Pilotta 35, Rome, 00187, Italy. TEL 39-06-6781567, FAX 39-06-6780588, periodicals@biblicum.com, http://www.paxbook.com.

282 NGA ISSN 0331-7110
THE INDEPENDENT. Text in English. 1960. w. **Description:** Independent Roman Catholic-based publication.
Published by: Independent, Bodija Rd., PMB 5109, Ibadan, Oyo, Nigeria. Ed. F B Cronin Coltsman. Circ: 13,000.

282 VAT
INDEX ACTORUM ROMANORUM PONTIFICUM. Text in Italian. 1975. irreg., latest vol.7, 1993. price varies.
Published by: Biblioteca Apostolica Vaticana, 00120, Vatican City. TEL 396-6-69885051, FAX 396-6-69884795.

282 USA ISSN 0020-1510
INLAND REGISTER. Text in English. 1942. 17/yr. USD 15 domestic; USD 20 foreign (effective 2009). adv. bk.rev. **Document type:** *Newspaper.*
Published by: Catholic Diocese of Spokane, PO Box 1453, Spokane, WA 99210-1453. TEL 509-358-7300. Ed. Deacon Eric Meisfjord. Pub. Bishop William S Skylstad. Adv. contact Nancy Loberg. Circ: 11,000. Wire service: CaNS.

282 GBR ISSN 0020-157X
BX2597
➤ **THE INNES REVIEW.** Text in English. 1950. s-a. GBP 75 domestic to institutions; USD 146 in North America to institutions; GBP 80 elsewhere to institutions; GBP 94 domestic to institutions (print & online eds.); USD 183 in North America to institutions (print & online eds.); GBP 100 elsewhere to institutions (print & online eds.) (effective 2012). adv. illus. cum.index: 1950-1959. back issues avail.; reprints avail. **Document type:** *Journal, Academic/Scholarly.* **Description:** Designed for the study of the part played by the Catholic Church in the history of the Scottish nation.
Related titles: Online - full text ed.: ISSN 1745-5219. USD 125 in North America to institutions; GBP 68 elsewhere to institutions (effective 2012).
Indexed: A01, A03, A08, A22, BrArAb, CA, E01, HistAb, MLA-IB, NumL, PCI, T02.
—BLDSC (4515.460000), IE, Ingenta. **CCC.**
Published by: (Scottish Catholic Historical Association), Edinburgh University Press, 22 George Sq, Edinburgh, Scotland EH8 9LF, United Kingdom. TEL 44-131-6504218, FAX 44-131-6503286, journals@eup.ed.ac.uk. Ed. Dr. Eila Williamson. Adv. contact Ruth Allison TEL 44-131-6504220.

268 375 ITA ISSN 1121-1555
INSEGNARE RELIGIONE. Text in Italian. 1988. 5/yr. EUR 21 domestic; EUR 31.50 foreign (effective 2009). **Document type:** *Magazine, Consumer.* **Description:** For teachers of religion at all levels.
Published by: Editrice Elledici, Corso Francia 214, Cascine Vica - Rivoli, TO 10098, Italy. TEL 39-011-9552111, FAX 39-011-9574048, mail@elledici.org, http://www.elledici.org.

262.13 USA ISSN 1068-8579
BX801
INSIDE THE VATICAN; Catholic news magazine. Text in English. 1993. 10/yr. USD 49.95 domestic; USD 74.95 foreign (effective 2010). adv. Supplement avail. **Document type:** *Magazine, Consumer.* **Description:** Covers news and activities of the Vatican. Special features include Vatican News, Vatican Watch, Churches of Rome, and Photo Essays.
Related titles: ◆ German ed.: Vatican-Magazin. ISSN 1865-1577; Polish ed.: Na Watykanie. ISSN 1233-7625. 1995.
Indexed: CPL.
Published by: Urbi et Orbi Communications, PO Box 57, New Hope, KY 40052-0057. TEL 270-325-5499, 800-789-9494, FAX 270-325-3091, service@insidethevatican.com. Ed. Robert Moynihan. R&P Dennis Musk TEL 270-325-3061. Adv. contact Joyce Rogers TEL 270-325-3061. Circ: 20,000 (paid); 15,000 (controlled).

282 PHL ISSN 0119-2787
INSPIRE; a magazine for today's Catholic. Text in English. 1999. m. PHP 260, USD 37 (effective 2000). back issues avail. **Document type:** *Magazine, Consumer.* **Description:** Covers teachings, testimonies, and other features to help Catholics live out their faith in the modern world.
Published by: Seedtime Publishing, Inc., 51 10th St, Rolling Hills Village, New Manila, Quezon City, 1112, Philippines. TEL 63-2-7222621, FAX 63-2-7218723, inspiremag@email.com. Ed. Rissa Singson. Pub. Didi Maranon. Adv. contact Raul Lanting. Circ: 4,000 (paid and controlled).

282 DEU ISSN 1867-5794
INSTITUT-PAPST-BENEDIKT XVI. MITTEILUNGEN. Text in German. 2008. a. EUR 24.95 (effective 2011). **Document type:** *Journal, Academic/Scholarly.*
Published by: (Institut-Papst-Benedikt XVI), Verlag Schnell und Steiner GmbH, Leibnizstr 13, Regensburg, 93055, Germany. TEL 49-941-787850, FAX 49-941-7878516, post@schnell-und-steiner.de, http://www.schnell-und-steiner.de.

282 ESP ISSN 1135-8513
INSTITUTO IGNACIO DE LOYOLA. ANUARIO. Text in Spanish. 1995. a. **Document type:** *Journal, Academic/Scholarly.*
Published by: (Universidad de Deusto, Instituto Ignacio de Loyola), Universidad de Deusto, Departamento de Publicaciones, Apdo 1/E, Bilbao, 48080, Spain. TEL 34-94-4139162, FAX 34-94-4456817, publicaciones@deusto.es.

282 AUS ISSN 1832-4282
INTER NOS; confraternity news. Text in English. 2000. s-a. free (effective 2008). back issues avail. **Document type:** *Newsletter.*
Related titles: Online - full content ed.
Published by: Australian Confraternity of Catholic Clergy, PO Box 246, Jamison, ACT 2614, Australia. http://www.australianccc.org. Ed. Paul-Anthony McGavin TEL 61-2-62516547.

282 IRL
INTERCOM. Text in English. m. adv. **Document type:** *Magazine, Consumer.*
Address: Veritas House, 7-8 Lower Abbey St., Dublin, 1, Ireland. TEL 353-1-8788177, FAX 353-1-8786507. adv.: B&W page EUR 476, color page EUR 762; 185 x 270. Circ: 7,500 (controlled).

282 BEL ISSN 0770-4720
INTERFACE; lettre d'information trimestrielle. Text in Dutch. 1981. q. adv. bk.rev. back issues avail. **Document type:** *Newsletter.*

R

Published by: (Centre Informatique et Bible), Informatique & Bible a.s.b.l., Rue de l'Abbaye, 11, Denee, 5537, Belgium. TEL 32-82-699647, FAX 32-82-223269, cib@cibmaredsous.be, http://www.cibmaredsous.be. Ed. R F Poswick. Circ: 3,000.

282 USA ISSN 0273-6187
INTERMOUNTAIN CATHOLIC. Text in English, Spanish. 1899. w. (Fri.; bi-w Jul. & Aug.). USD 20; USD 30 foreign (effective 1998). adv. bk.rev.; film rev.; play rev. index. 16 p./no. 6 cols./p.; back issues avail. **Document type:** *Newspaper.*
Published by: Catholic Diocese of Salt Lake City, 27 C St, Salt Lake City, UT 84103. TEL 801-328-8641, FAX 801-328-9680. Ed., R&P Barbara S Lee. Pub. Bishop George H. Niederauer. Adv. contact Lon W Schiffbaoer. Circ: 13,700. Wire service: CaNS. **Subscr. to:** PO Box 2489, Salt Lake City, UT 84110.

282 VAT ISSN 0074-5782
INTERNATIONAL EUCHARIST CONGRESS. PROCEEDINGS. Text in Italian. irreg., latest 1993, 45th, Seville, Spain. **Document type:** *Proceedings.*
Published by: Pontificio Comitato per i Congressi Eucaristici Internazionali, Palazzo S. Calisto, 00120, Vatican City. Ed. H E Cardinal Edouard Gagnon.

230.071 GBR ISSN 1942-2539
▼ **INTERNATIONAL STUDIES IN CATHOLIC EDUCATION.** Text in English. 2009 (Mar.). s-a. GBP 173 combined subscription in United Kingdom to institutions (print & online eds.); EUR 275, USD 343 combined subscription to institutions (print & online eds.) (effective 2012). **Document type:** *Journal, Academic/Scholarly.* **Description:** Aims to provide an international forum for articles of a theological, philosophical, historical and social scientific nature, as well as empirical research perspectives on Catholic education.
Related titles: Online - full text ed.: ISSN 1942-2547. 2009. GBP 155 in United Kingdom to institutions; EUR 248, USD 309 to institutions (effective 2012).
Indexed: CA, E03, T02.
—IE. **CCC.**
Published by: Taylor & Francis Ltd. (Subsidiary of: Taylor & Francis Group), 4 Park Sq, Milton Park, Abingdon, Oxfordshire OX14 4RN, United Kingdom. TEL 44-1235-828600, FAX 44-1235-829000, info@tandf.co.uk. Ed. Gerald Grace.

230.017 ITA
➤ **INTERRELIGIOUS AND INTERCULTURAL INVESTIGATION.** Text in Italian, English, French. 1999. irreg., latest vol.5, 2001. price varies. **Document type:** *Monographic series, Academic/Scholarly.*
Published by: (Gregorian Research Centre on Cultures and Religions), Gregorian University Press/Editrice Pontificia Universita Gregoriana, Piazza della Pilotta 35, Rome, 00187, Italy. TEL 39-06-6781567, FAX 39-06-6780588, periodicals@biblicum.com, http://www.paxbook.com.

230.2 USA
INTRODUCING.. Variant title: Introducing Series. Text in English. 1999. irreg. price varies. back issues avail. **Document type:** *Monographic series, Academic/Scholarly.* **Description:** Provides a introduction to distinct genres of theology.
Published by: Orbis Books (Subsidiary of: Maryknoll Fathers and Brothers), Dept WEB, PO Box 302, Maryknoll, NY 10545. TEL 800-258-5838, FAX 914-941-7005, orbisbooks@maryknoll.org.

282 IRL ISSN 1393-6832
IRISH CATHOLIC. Text in English. 1888. w. EUR 72.80 domestic; EUR 109.20 in United Kingdom; EUR 114.20 elsewhere (effective 2005). adv. bk.rev. illus. **Document type:** *Newspaper, Consumer.*
Former titles (until 1896): The Irish Catholic and Nation (1393-6824); (until 1891): Irish Catholic (1393-6816)
Published by: Irish Catholic Ltd., 55 Lower Gardiner St., Dublin, 1, Ireland. TEL 353-1-8555619, ger@irishcatholic.ie, info@irishcatholic.ie. Ed. Bridget Anne Ryan. Adv. contact Gerhard Crowley. Circ: 39,000.

282.025 IRL ISSN 0075-0735
BX1503.A3
IRISH CATHOLIC DIRECTORY. Text in English. 1838. a. EUR 42.50 (effective 2005). adv. index. **Document type:** *Directory, Consumer.*
—BLDSC (4571.125000).
Published by: (Roman Catholic Church in All Ireland), Veritas Book Co. Ltd., Veritas House, 7-8 Lower Abbey St., Dublin, Ireland. TEL 353-1-8788177, FAX 353-1-8786507, publications@veritas.ie, http://www.veritas.ie.

282 USA ISSN 1937-8106
THE IRISH IN AMERICA. Text in English. 1999. irreg., latest 2001. price varies. back issues avail. **Document type:** *Monographic series, Academic/Scholarly.* **Description:** Examines the history and culture of the Irish in the United States.
Published by: (Cushwa Center for the Study of American Catholicism), University of Notre Dame Press, 310 Flanner Hall, Notre Dame, IN 46556. TEL 574-631-6346, FAX 574-631-8148, undpress.1@nd.edu. **Dist. overseas by:** Eurospan Group, c/o Turpin Distribution Pegasus Dr, Stratton Business Park, Biggleswade, Bedfordshire SG18 8TQ, United Kingdom. TEL 44-1767-604972, FAX 44-1767-601640, eurospan@turpin-distribution.com, http://www.eurospangroup.com; **Dist. by:** c/o Chicago Distribution Ctr, 11030 S Langley Ave, Chicago, IL 60628. TEL 773-702-7000, 800-621-2736, FAX 773-702-7212, 800-621-8476.

282 ESP ISSN 1131-7027
ISIDORIANUM; revista semestral de estudios eclesiasticos superiores. Text in Spanish; Abstracts in English. 1967. s-a. bk.rev. back issues avail. **Document type:** *Journal, Academic/Scholarly.*
Indexed: OTA.
Published by: Centro de Estudios Teologicos de Sevilla, Cardenal Buenos Monreal s-n, Apdo. 1180 AP, Seville, 41012, Spain. TEL 34-5-4231323, FAX 34-5-4231122, cetsevilla@terra.es, http://www.cetsevilla.com/. Ed. Luis Fernando Alvarez Gonzalez. Circ: 800.

282 MDG
ISIKA MIANAKAVY. Text in Malagasy. 1958. m.
Address: Ambatonena, Fianarantsoa, 301, Madagascar. Ed. J Ranaivomanana. Circ: 21,000.

282 ITA
ISTITUTO DI SCIENZE RELIGIOSE IN TRENTO. PUBBLICAZIONI. SERIES MAIOR. Text in Italian. 1981. irreg. **Document type:** *Monographic series, Academic/Scholarly.*
Published by: Centro per le Scienze Religiose, Via Santa croce 77, Trento, 38122, Italy. TEL 39-0461-210231, info-scienzereligiose@fbk.eu, http://isr.fbk.eu/it/.

230.0071 ITA
➤ **ISTITUTO DI SCIENZE RELIGIOSE. SAGGI. NUOVA SERIE.** Text in Italian. 1993. irreg., latest vol.2, 1999. price varies. **Document type:** *Monographic series, Academic/Scholarly.* **Description:** Publishes research and manuals of the professors of the Institute of Religious Studies and of their scholarly collaborators, with a focus on interdisciplinary studies.
Published by: (Pontificia Universita Gregoriana, Istituto di Scienze Religiose), Gregorian University Press/Editrice Pontificia Universita Gregoriana, Piazza della Pilotta 35, Rome, 00187, Italy. TEL 39-06-6781567, FAX 39-06-6780588, periodicals@biblicum.com, http://www.paxbook.com.

235.2 BRA ISSN 1517-7807
ITAICI REVISTA DE ESPIRITUALIDADE INACIANA. Text in Portuguese. 1989. 4/yr. BRL 30 domestic; USD 40 foreign (effective 2001). **Description:** Deals with Ignation spirituality and the spiritual exercises of St. Ignacious of Loyola.
Published by: Centro de Espiritualidade Inaciana de Itaici, Vila Kostka, Caixa Postal 09, Indaiatuba, SP 13330-000, Brazil. TEL 55-19-38948555, FAX 55-19-38948866, revistaitaici@apoiocom.com.br. Ed., Pub. Luis Gonzalez Quevedo. Adv. contact Debora Beatriz Scarton. Circ: 1,200.

255.1 945 ITA
ITALIA BENEDETTINA; studi e documenti di storia monastica. Text in Italian. 1979. irreg., latest vol.15, 1995. price varies. **Document type:** *Monographic series, Academic/Scholarly.* **Description:** Provides information regarding the Italian monastic history.
Published by: Centro Storico Benedettino Italiano, Badia S. Maria del Monte, Cesena, FC 47023, Italy. TEL 39-0547-302161, http://www.abbaziadelmonte.it.

ITALIA MISSIONARIA. *see* CHILDREN AND YOUTH—For

255.3 PRT ISSN 0021-3209
ITINERARIUM; revista quadrimestral de cultura. Text in Portuguese. 1955. 3/yr. bk.rev. bibl. index, cum.index: 1955-1970. back issues avail. **Document type:** *Consumer.*
Indexed: CERDIC, DIP, IBR, IBZ, MLA-IB, OTA.
—BLDSC (4588.660000).
Published by: (Portuguese Franciscans), Editorial Franciscana, Largo da Luz, 11, Lisbon, 1600-498, Portugal. TEL 351-21-7142700, FAX 351-21-7145019, http://www.editorialfranciscana.org/. Ed. Jose Antonio da Silva Soares. Circ: 350.

268.432 USA
IT'S OUR WORLD; mission news from the Holy Childhood Association. (In 3 editions Prek-1; 2-5, 6-8 as of 2003.) Text in English. 1974 (vol.74). 3/yr. illus. **Document type:** *Newspaper, Consumer.* **Description:** Seeks to help Catholic children cultivate an awareness and appreciation of children of other cultures.
Formerly: Annals of the Holy Childhood (0003-4940)
Published by: (Pontifical Association of the Holy Childhood), Holy Childhood Association, 366 Fifth Ave, New York, NY 10001. TEL 212-563-8700, FAX 212-563-8725, pmsusa@propfaith.org, http://www.missionsla.org/missionprograms/hca/hca_home.html. Eds. Sr. Joanne Madden, Mary Connors. Circ: 200,000 (controlled).

262.9 ITA ISSN 1120-6462
K9
IUS ECCLESIAE; rivista internazionale di diritto canonico. Text in Italian. 1989. 3/yr. EUR 135 combined subscription domestic to institutions (print & online eds.); EUR 180 combined subscription foreign to institutions (print & online eds.) (effective 2009). **Document type:** *Journal, Academic/Scholarly.* **Description:** Examines canonic law, guidelines and universal rights.
Related titles: Online - full text ed.: ISSN 1972-5671. 2007.
Indexed: CLA, DIP, DoGi, IBR, IBZ, PCI.
Published by: (Pontificia Universita della Santa Croce), Fabrizio Serra Editore (Subsidiary of: Accademia Editoriale), c/o Accademia Editoriale, Via Santa Bibbiana 28, Pisa, 56127, Italy. TEL 39-050-542332, FAX 39-050-574888, accademiaeditoriale@accademiaeditoriale.it, http://www.libraweb.net.

255.53 ZMB ISSN 1990-4479
BX3747.Z33
J C T R BULLETIN. Text in English. 1988. q. ZMK 30,000 domestic; USD 25 foreign (effective 2006). **Description:** Promotes the study and action on issues linking Christian faith and social justice in Zambia and Malawi.
Related titles: Online - full text ed.: ISSN 1990-4487.
Published by: Jesuit Centre for Theological Reflection, PO Box 37774, Lusaka, 10101, Zambia. TEL 260-1-290410, FAX 260-1-290759.

282 DEU
J G AKTUELL. Text in German. q. free. **Document type:** *Bulletin.*
Published by: Josefs-Gesellschaft e.V., Alarichstr 40, Cologne, 50679, Germany. TEL 49-221-88998-0. Ed. Alfred Hovestaedt.

382 NLD ISSN 0924-042X
JAARBOEK VOOR LITURGIE - ONDERZOEK. Text in Dutch. 1985. a. EUR 25 (effective 2010). back issues avail. **Document type:** *Journal, Academic/Scholarly.*
Published by: Rijksuniversiteit Groningen, Instituut voor Christelijk Cultureel Erfgoed/Institute for Christian Cultural Heritage, Oude Boteringestraat 38, Groningen, 9712 GK, Netherlands. TEL 31-50-3634587, FAX 31-50-3636200, lit.inst@rug.nl, http://www.rug.nl/ggw/onderzoek/onderzoeksinstituten/icce/index. Ed. Paul Post. **Co-sponsor:** Universiteit van Tilburg, Liturgisch Instituut/Tilburg University, Liturgical Institute.

282 USA ISSN 1946-3804
JACOB'S WELL. Text in English. 1982. q. free to members (effective 2009). adv. **Document type:** *Newsletter.* **Description:** Contains information about education resources pertinent to divorce recovery, remarriage and blended families.
Published by: North American Conference of Separated and Divorced Catholics, PO Box 10, Hancock, MI 49930. TEL 906-482-0494, FAX 906-482-7470, office@nacsdc.org, http://www.nacsdc.org.

282 USA ISSN 1545-892X
JACOB'S WELL PROFESSIONAL NEWSLETTER. Text in English. q. USD 60 membership (effective 2005). adv. **Document type:** *Newsletter.*
Published by: North American Conference of Separated and Divorced Catholics, PO Box 360, Richland, OR 97870. TEL 541-893-6089, FAX 541-893-6089. Ed. Irene Varley. R&P, Adv. contact Krista Dennis.

282 AUT
JAHRBUCH DER ERZDIOEZESE WIEN. Text in German. 1950. a. adv. illus. **Document type:** *Bulletin, Consumer.*
Formerly: Jahrbuch fuer die Kirche von Wien
Published by: Pastoralamt der Erzdioezese Wien, Stephansplatz 6-6, Vienna, W 1010, Austria. TEL 43-1-515523363, FAX 43-1-515523366, pastoralamt@edw.or.at, http://www.pastoralamt.at. Ed. Franz Ferstl. Adv. contact Walburga Barta.

262.3 DEU ISSN 1863-8139
JAHRBUCH FUER GESCHICHTE UND KUNST IM BISTUM HILDESHEIM. Text in German. 1927. a. bk.rev. back issues avail. **Document type:** *Journal, Academic/Scholarly.*
Formerly (until 2005): Diozese Hildesheim in Vergangenheit und Gegenwart (0341-9975)
Indexed: B24, DIP, IBR, IBZ.
Published by: (Verein fuer Geschichte und Kunst in Bistum Hildesheim e.V.), Verlag Schnell und Steiner GmbH, Leibnizstr 13, Regensburg, 93055, Germany. TEL 49-941-787850, FAX 49-941-7878516, post@schnell-und-steiner.de, http://www.schnell-und-steiner.de. Circ: 1,100.

282 DEU ISSN 0075-2754
JAHRBUCH FUER SALESIANISCHE STUDIEN. Text in German. 1963. a. price varies. adv. bk.rev. back issues avail. **Document type:** *Academic/Scholarly.*
Indexed: DIP, IBR, IBZ.
Published by: (Arbeitsgemeinschaft fuer Salesianische Studien), Franz Sales Verlag, Rosental 1, Eichstaett, 85072, Germany. TEL 49-8421-5379, FAX 49-8421-80805, info@franz-sales-verlag.de, http://www.franz-sales-verlag.de. Ed. Gottfried Prinz. Pub. Herbert Winklehner. Adv. contact Peter Keller.

282 DEU ISSN 0934-8611
JAKOBUS-STUDIEN. Text in German. 1988. irreg., latest vol.18, 2009. price varies. **Document type:** *Monographic series, Academic/Scholarly.*
Published by: Gunter Narr Verlag, Postfach 2567, Tuebingen, 72015, Germany. TEL 49-7071-97970, FAX 49-7071-75288, info@narr.de, http://www.narr.de. Eds. Klaus Herbers, Robert Ploetz.

282 USA
JEDNOTA/UNION. Text in English, Slovak. 1891. w. USD 25; USD 30 foreign (effective 2006). illus. 4 cols./p.; **Document type:** *Newspaper, Consumer.*
Published by: First Catholic Slovak Union, 6611 Rockside Rd, Independence, OH 44131-2398. TEL 216-642-9406. Ed. Anthony X. Sutherland. Circ: 16,000.

230.2 IND ISSN 0970-1117
➤ **JEEVADHARA**; an international theological journal. Text in Malayalam. 1971. m. INR 60 domestic; USD 24 foreign (effective 2011). bk.rev. index. **Document type:** *Journal, Academic/Scholarly.* **Description:** Covers Anthropology, Sacred Scriptures, Systematic Theology, Ecclesiology, Ecumenism and Spirituality.
Related titles: English ed.: ISSN 0970-1125. INR 100 domestic; USD 24 foreign (effective 2003).
Indexed: OTA.
Published by: Jeevadhara Theological Society, Malloossery P O, Kottayam, Kerala 686 041, India. TEL 91-481-2392530, ktm_jeeva123@sancharnet.in.

271.53 USA ISSN 1524-1815
JESUIT BULLETIN. Text in English. 1922. 3/yr. free. adv. back issues avail. **Document type:** *Monographic series.* **Description:** Provides information about the people, spirituality, and works of the Missouri Province Jesuits. For friends, colleagues and benefactors.
Published by: Society of Jesus, Jesuits of the Missouri Province, 4511 W. Pine Blvd., St. Louis, MO 63108. TEL 314-977-7363, FAX 314-977-7362, office4511@jesuits-mis.org. Ed., R&P Rev. David L Fleming TEL 314-977-7363. Circ: 28,000.

JESUIT SOCIAL SERVICES NEWS. *see* SOCIAL SERVICES AND WELFARE

255 DEU
JESUITICA; Quellen und Studien zu Geschichte, Kunst und Literatur der Gesellschaft Jesu im deutschsprachigen Raum. Text in German. 1997. irreg., latest vol.15, 2010. price varies. **Document type:** *Monographic series, Academic/Scholarly.*
Published by: Verlag Schnell und Steiner GmbH, Leibnizstr 13, Regensburg, 93055, Germany. TEL 49-941-787850, FAX 49-941-7878516, post@schnell-und-steiner.de.

282 NLD ISSN 1879-8950
JESUITICA NEERLANDICA. Text in Dutch. 2002. irreg., latest vol.2, 2006. **Document type:** *Monographic series, Academic/Scholarly.*
Published by: Nederlands Instituut voor Jezuieten Studies/Netherlands Institute for Jesuit Studies, Singel 448, Amsterdam, 1017 AV, Netherlands. TEL 31-20-3446650, http://www.nijsnijs.nl.

255.53 GBR
JESUITS AND FRIENDS. Text in English. 1985. 3/yr. back issues avail. **Document type:** *Magazine, Trade.* **Description:** Designed for the British province Jesuits and their associates.
Formed by the 1985 merger of: Jesuit Missions; To Our Friends
Related titles: Online - full text ed.: free (effective 2009).
Published by: (British Province of the Society of Jesus), Jesuit Missions, 11 Edge Hill, London, SW19 4LR, United Kingdom. TEL 44-208-9460466, FAX 44-208-9462292, director@jesuitmissions.org.uk, http://www.jesuitmissions.org.uk/. Ed. Ged Clason.

282 ITA
JESUS CARITAS. Text in Italian. 1961. q. USD 41.22 (effective 2008). adv. bk.rev. **Document type:** *Magazine, Consumer.*
Published by: Comunita Jesus Caritas, Abbazia di Sassovivo, Foligno, PG 06034, Italy. Circ: 2,500.

282 CAN ISSN 0383-2635
JESUS MARIE NOTRE TEMPS. Text in French. 1971. m. CAD 12 domestic; USD 15 in United States; EUR 18 in Europe; EUR 28 elsewhere (effective 2004). **Document type:** *Newspaper, Consumer.*
Incorporates (1977-1999): Annoncer Jesus-Christ (0705-1018); Formerly (until 1973): Marie et Notre Temps (0383-2627)
Published by: Jesus Marie et Notre Temps, 5055 Rue Saint-Dominique, Montreal, PQ H2T 1V1, Canada. TEL 514-271-7731.

282 BEL
JEUNES EN MOUVEMENT. Text in French. 1976. q. EUR 8.68 (effective 2005). adv. bk.rev. **Document type:** *Bulletin.* **Description:** Covers current topics of interest to young persons between the ages of 16 and 30.
Published by: Conseil de la Jeunesse Catholique, 43, Rue de la Charite, Bruxelles, 1210, Belgium. TEL 32-2-230-3283, FAX 32-2-230-6811, cjc@cjc.be. Ed. Georges Gilkinet. R&P Donatienne Coppetiers. Adv. contact VincentPhilippe Gengler.

255.53 BEL ISSN 1871-1944
JEZUIETEN. Text in Dutch. 1968. q.
Incorporates (1968-2004): Nederlandse Jezuieten (0167-2967)
Published by: (Nederlandse Provincie van de Societeit van Jezus NLD, Vlaamse Provincie van de Societeit van Jezus), Paters Jezuieten, Koninginnelaan 141, Brussel, 1030, Belgium. TEL 32-2-2050150, FAX 32-2-2050151, jesuits.flanders@jesuits.net.

230.2 USA ISSN 1071-8257
THE JOSEPHINUM JOURNAL OF THEOLOGY. Text in English. 1982. s-a. USD 10 domestic; USD 15 foreign (effective 2005). adv. bk.rev. back issues avail. **Document type:** *Journal, Academic/Scholarly.* **Description:** Provides a forum for pastoral and theological essays.
Indexed: A21, CPL, FamI, MLA-IB, OTA, RI-1.
Published by: (Pontifical College Josephinum, School of Theology), Pontifical College Josephinum, 7625 N High St, Columbus, OH 43235-1498. TEL 614-885-5585, FAX 614-885-2307. Ed. James Keating. Adv. contact Elizabeth V Palmer. B&W page USD 100.

282 USA
JOSEPHINUM MAGAZINE. Text in English. 1976. 2/yr. free. **Document type:** *Newsletter.* **Description:** For alumni of the Josephinum.
Formerly: Josephinum Newsletter (0021-759X); Supersedes: Josephinum Review
Published by: Pontifical College Josephinum, 7625 N High St, Columbus, OH 43235-1498. TEL 614-885-5585, FAX 614-885-2307, http://www.pcj.edu. Ed., R&P Lisa Komp. Circ: 3,500.

282 FRA ISSN 0021-7794
LE JOURNAL DE LA PAIX. Text in French. 1951. q. EUR 30 (effective 2008). adv. bk.rev.; film rev. abstr.; bibl.; charts; illus. **Document type:** *Magazine, Consumer.*
Indexed: IBSS.
Published by: Pax Christi France, 5 Rue Morere, Paris, 75014, France. TEL 33-1-44490636, pax.christi-france@wanadoo.fr. Circ: 21,030.

JOURNAL OF CATHOLIC HIGHER EDUCATION. *see* EDUCATION—Higher Education

JOURNAL OF CATHOLIC LEGAL STUDIES. *see* LAW

JOURNAL OF CATHOLIC SCHOOL STUDIES. *see* EDUCATION

282 USA ISSN 1548-0712
BX1753
➤ **JOURNAL OF CATHOLIC SOCIAL THOUGHT.** Text in English. 2004 (Win.). s-a. USD 40 domestic; USD 60 foreign (effective 2010). adv. back issues avail. **Document type:** *Journal, Academic/Scholarly.*
Related titles: Online - full text ed.: ISSN 2153-9979. USD 64 to individuals; USD 120 to institutions (effective 2010).
Indexed: CPL, SociolAb.
Published by: (Villanova University, Office for Mission Effectiveness), Philosophy Documentation Center, PO Box 7147, Charlottesville, VA 22906. TEL 434-220-3300, FAX 434-220-3301, order@pdcnet.org, http://www.pdcnet.org. Adv. contact Greg Swope.

230 USA ISSN 1067-6341
BR66
➤ **JOURNAL OF EARLY CHRISTIAN STUDIES.** Abbreviated title: J E C S. Text in English. 1981. q. USD 160 to institutions; USD 224 combined subscription to institutions (print & online eds.); USD 48 per issue to institutions (effective 2012). adv. bk.rev. illus. 160 p./no.; back issues avail.; reprint service avail. from PSC. **Document type:** *Journal, Academic/Scholarly.* **Description:** Publishes original scholarly studies on the early history and theology of the Christian church from C.E. 100-700.
Formerly (until 1993): The Second Century (0276-7899); Incorporates (1972-1993): Patristics (0360-652X)
Related titles: Online - full text ed.: ISSN 1086-3184. N.S. USD 168 to institutions (effective 2012).
Indexed: A01, A03, A08, A20, A21, A22, ASCA, AmHI, ArtHuCI, BRD, CA, CurCont, DIP, E01, FamI, H07, H08, H14, HAb, HumInd, IBR, IBZ, IZBG, L&LBA, M10, MLA-IB, P10, P28, P48, P53, P54, PCI, PQC, Perlslam, R&TA, RI-1, RI-2, S02, S03, SCOPUS, T02, W03, W07.
—BLDSC (4970.703000), IE, Infotrieve, Ingenta. **CCC.**
Published by: (North American Patristics Society), The Johns Hopkins University Press, 2715 N Charles St, Baltimore, MD 21218. TEL 410-516-6900, FAX 410-516-6968. Ed. David Brakke TEL 812-855-3531. Pub. William M Breichner. **Subscr. to:** PO Box 19966, Baltimore, MD 21211. TEL 410-516-6987, 800-548-1784, FAX 410-516-3866, jrnlcirc@press.jhu.edu.

▼➤ **JOURNAL OF JESUIT BUSINESS EDUCATION.** *see* BUSINESS AND ECONOMICS

282 BEL ISSN 2034-3515
▼ **THE JOURNAL OF MEDIEVAL MONASTIC STUDIES.** Text in Multiple languages. 2012. a. EUR 75 combined subscription (print & online eds.) (effective 2012). **Document type:** *Journal, Academic/Scholarly.*
Related titles: Online - full text ed.: ISSN 2034-3523.
Published by: Brepols Publishers, Begijnhof 67, Turnhout, 2300, Belgium. TEL 32-14-448020, FAX 32-14-428919, periodicals@brepols.net, http://www.brepols.net.

268 AUS ISSN 1442-018X
➤ **JOURNAL OF RELIGIOUS EDUCATION.** Text in English. 1952. q. AUD 40 domestic; AUD 45 foreign (effective 2004). bk.rev. cum.index: 1952-2003. back issues avail. **Document type:** *Journal, Academic/Scholarly.* **Description:** Disseminates writings and research in religious education and catechesis — and in related areas such as spirituality, theology, moral and faith development, cultural contexts, ministry and schooling. It includes a variety of feature sections — on contemporary educational issues, book reviews, conferences, resources and practical hints for teachers.
Former titles (until 1999): Word in Life: Journal of Religious Education (0155-6894); (until 1977): Our Apostolate
Related titles: CD-ROM ed.
Indexed: AEI, CERDIC, E03.
Published by: Australian Catholic University, 223 Antill St, Watson, ACT 2602, Australia. TEL 61-6-62091148, FAX 61-6-62091178. Ed., R&P Louise Welbourne. Circ: 800 (controlled).

282 USA
JOYFULL NOISE. Text in English. 2001. bi-m. USD 24; USD 5 newsstand/cover (effective 2002). adv. **Document type:** *Magazine, Consumer.*
Published by: Kalos Communications, Inc., Box 160, Sartell, MN 56377. TEL 320-203-0260, http://www.joyfullnoise.com. Ed. Paul Dunham. Pub. Paula Dunham.

282 USA
JUNIOR MESSENGER. Text in English. m.
Published by: Roman Catholic Diocese of Belleville, Chancery Office, 222 S Third St, Belleville, IL 62220. TEL 618-235-9601, FAX 618-235-7416. Ed. Julie Wier. Circ: 5,000.

262.9 USA ISSN 0022-6858
K10
➤ **JURIST**; studies in church order and ministry. Text in English. 1941. s-a. USD 50 (effective 2011). adv. bk.rev. index, cum.index. reprint service avail. from PSC. **Document type:** *Journal, Academic/Scholarly.* **Description:** Devoted to the study and promotion of canon law.
Related titles: Microfilm ed.: (from PQC); Online - full text ed.
Indexed: A01, A22, A26, ABRCLP, B04, CERDIC, CLA, CLI, CPL, DIP, FLP, FR, FamI, G08, I01, I03, I05, IBR, IBZ, ILP, LRI, P30, PCI, S02, S03, T02.
—IE, Ingenta, INIST. **CCC.**
Published by: Catholic University of America, Department of Canon Law, 345 Caldwell Hall, Washington, DC 20064. TEL 202-319-5492, FAX 202-319-4187, cua-canonlaw@cua.edu.

261 POL ISSN 1429-3803
K10
JUS MATRIMONIALE. Text in Polish. 1996. a. **Document type:** *Journal, Academic/Scholarly.*
Published by: Wydawnictwo Uniwersytetu Kardynala Stefana Wyszynskiego, Ul Dewajtis 5, Warsaw, 01815, Poland. wydawnictwo@uksw.edu.pl, http://www.uksw.edu.pl/wydawn/wydawnictwo.htm.

282 GBR ISSN 2041-9201
▼ **JUSTICE**; social issues: a Catholic perspective. Text in English. 2009. bi-m. GBP 3.50 per issue domestic; CAD 6.75 per issue in Canada; USD 6 per issue in United States; PHP 260 per issue in Philippines (effective 2011). adv. **Document type:** *Magazine, Consumer.* **Description:** Contains articles from a wide range of contributors reflecting all aspects of the Catholic Church rich history of social teaching - including the environment, migration, the world of work, the economy, poverty and conflict.
Related titles: Online - full text ed.: free (effective 2011).
Published by: Universe Media Group Ltd., 4th Fl, Landmark House, Station Rd, Cheadle Hulme, Cheshire SK8 7JH, United Kingdom. TEL 44-161-4881758. Ed. Lee Siggs. Adv. contact Carol Malpass TEL 44-1785-660543.

282 DEU ISSN 1434-4386
K A B IMPULS. Text in German. 1891. m. (11/yr.). bk.rev. **Document type:** *Newsletter.*
Formerly (until 1997): Katholische Arbeitnehmer-Zeitung (0945-1897); Which was formed by the 1989 merger of: Katholische Arbeitnehmer-Zeitung (Ausgabe West) (0945-1935); Which was formerly (until 1985): Gemeinsame Zeitung Katholische Arbeitnehmer-Bewegung (Ausgabe West) (0175-5161); Katholische Arbeitnehmer-Zeitung (Ausgabe Sued) (0945-2044); Which was formerly (until 1985): Gemeinsame Zeitung Katholische Arbeitnehmer-Bewegung (Ausgabe Sued) (0175-5153)
Published by: (Katholische Arbeitnehmer-Bewegung Deutschlands), Ketteler Verlag GmbH, Schlosshof 1, Waldmuenchen, 93449, Germany. TEL 49-9972-941451, FAX 49-9972-941455, kontakt@ketteler-verlag.de, http://www.ketteler-verlag.de/. Circ: 170,000.

282 DEU ISSN 1439-6025
K A + DAS ZEICHEN. Text in German. 1999. m. adv. **Document type:** *Magazine, Trade.*
Formed by the merger of (1893-1999): Das Zeichen (0342-6416); (1926-1999): Katholisches Apostolat (1439-5347)
Published by: Herz-Jesu-Provinz der Pallottiner, Vinzenz-Pallotti-Str 14, Friedberg, 86316, Germany. TEL 49-821-600520, FAX 49-821-60052252, info@pallottiner.org, http://www.pallottiner.org. Circ: 60,000 (controlled).

282 949.2 NLD ISSN 1574-2296
K D C CURSOR. Text in Dutch. 1984. irreg., latest vol.12, 2006.
Published by: Katholiek Documentatie Centrum, Postbus 9100, Nijmegen, 6500 HA, Netherlands. TEL 31-24-3612457, FAX 31-24-3612403, info@kdc.ru.nl.

282 300 NLD ISSN 0923-5310
K D C SCRIPTA. Text in Dutch. 1988. irreg., latest vol.9, 1997. EUR 4.50 per vol. (effective 2010). **Document type:** *Monographic series.*
Published by: Katholiek Documentatie Centrum, Postbus 9100, Nijmegen, 6500 HA, Netherlands. TEL 31-24-3612457, FAX 31-24-3612403, info@kdc.ru.nl.

230.2 DEU
K F H MAINZ. SCHRIFTENREIHE. (Katholische Fachhochschule) Variant title: Schriftenreihe der KFH Mainz. Text in German. 2006. irreg., latest vol.4, 2009. price varies. **Document type:** *Monographic series, Academic/Scholarly.*
Published by: (Katholische Fachhochschule Mainz), E O S Verlag, Erzabtei St. Ottilien, St.Ottilien, 86941, Germany. TEL 49-8193-71700, FAX 49-8193-71709, mail@eos-verlag.de.

K R O MAGAZINE. (Katholieke Radio Omroep) *see* COMMUNICATIONS—Television And Cable

282 200.82 NLD ISSN 1574-7131
K V O.NU. Text in Dutch. 2004. q.
Published by: Katholieke Vrouwenorganisatie, Spoorlaan 350, Postbus 91, Tilburg, 5000 MA, Netherlands. TEL 31-13-5324050, secretariaat@kvo.nu, http://www.kvo.nu. Ed. A op den Buijs.

282 AUT
KAERNTNER KIRCHENZEITUNG. Text in German. 1945. w. EUR 32 (effective 2005). bk.rev. **Document type:** *Newspaper, Consumer.* **Description:** News and comments from and about the local and international Catholic worlds.
Published by: Katholische Kirche in Kaernten, Dioezese Gurk, Tarviser Str 30, Klagenfurt, 9020, Austria. TEL 43-463-58772551, FAX 43-463-58772559, info@kath-kirche-kaernten.at. Ed. Ingeborg Jakl. Circ: 13,000 (controlled).

255 AUT
KAISER KARL GEBETSLIGA FUER DEN VOELKERFRIEDEN. JOURNAL. Text in German. 1953. a. **Document type:** *Bulletin, Consumer.* **Description:** Contains biographical and historical articles on the Austro-Hungarian Emperor Karl and efforts to promote him to sainthood.
Formerly: Stille Schar (0081-5594)
Published by: (Kaiser Karl Gebetsliga fuer den Voelkerfrieden), Gebetsliga Praesidium, Diefenbachgasse 45-47-3-1-7, Vienna, W 1150, Austria. gebetsliga@stvincent.edu, http://facweb.stvincent.edu/academics/finearts/gebetsliga/index.html. Ed., Pub., R&P Johannes Parsch. Circ: 5,000.

282 POL ISSN 0860-410X
KALENDARZ SLOWA BOZEGO. Text in Polish. 1979. a. PLZ 4, USD 1.50 per issue. adv. back issues avail.
Published by: (Ksieza Werbisci), Wydawnictwo Ksiezy Werbistow Verbinum, Ostrobramska 98, Warsaw, 04118, Poland. TEL 48-22-6107870, FAX 48-22-6107775. Ed. Marek Grzech. Circ: 200,000.

282 HRV ISSN 0353-2828
BX806.S4
KANA. Text in Croatian. 1970. m. **Document type:** *Magazine, Consumer.*
Published by: Krscanska Sadasnjost, Marulicev Trg. 14, p.p. 434, Zagreb, 10000, Croatia. TEL 385-1-4828222, FAX 385-1-4828227.

282 LTU ISSN 0235-8050
KATALIKU PASAULIS. Text in Lithuanian. 1989. m. USD 45.
Published by: (Lithuanian Catholic Church), Publishing House of the Episcopalian Conference, Pranciskonu 3-6, Vilnius, 2000, Lithuania. TEL 0122-222263, FAX 0122-222122. Ed. Ausvydas Belickas. Circ: 13,000.

282 DEU ISSN 0342-5517
KATECHETISCHE BLAETTER; Zeitschrift fuer Religionsunterricht, Gemeindekatechese, Kirchliche Jugendarbeit. Text in German. 1875. bi-m. EUR 46.20; EUR 9 newsstand/cover (effective 2011). adv. bk.rev.; film rev.; play rev. illus. index. back issues avail. **Document type:** *Journal, Academic/Scholarly.*
Formerly (until 1977): Katechetische Blaetter, Kirchliche Jugendarbeit (0341-0013)
Indexed: DIP, IBR, IBZ, RILM.
—**CCC.**
Published by: (Deutscher Katecheten-Verein e.V.), Koesel-Verlag GmbH und Co. (Subsidiary of: Verlagsgruppe Random House GmbH), Flueggenstr 2, Munich, 80639, Germany. TEL 49-89-178010, FAX 49-89-17801111, leserservice@koesel.de. Ed. Helga Kohler-Spiegel. Circ: 5,000 (paid and controlled). **Co-sponsor:** Arbeitsstelle fuer Jugendseelsorge der Deutschen Bischofskonferenz.

282 SWE ISSN 0282-0234
KATEKETNYTT; tidskriften foer kateketer. Text in Swedish. 1966. 3/yr. SEK 75 in Sweden to non-Catechists; SEK 25 per issue in Sweden; free in Sweden to Catechists (effective 2005). bk.rev. **Document type:** *Magazine, Trade.*
Formerly (until 1979): Katolskt Pedagogiskt Forum
Published by: Katolska Pedagogiska Naemnden, Goetgatan 64, PO Box 4198, Stockholm, 10264, Sweden. TEL 46-8-4626630, FAX 46-8-4629435, kpn@katolskakyrkan.se, http://www.kpn.se.

282 CAN ISSN 0315-8020
KATERI; Lily of the Mohawks. Text in French. 1949. q. CAD 5 (effective 2000). **Document type:** *Newsletter.* **Description:** News about Kateri Tekawitha's life and virtues, and about native peoples of America.
Related titles: English ed.
Published by: Cause for the Canonization of Blessed Kateri Tekakwitha, P O Box 70, Kahnawake, PQ J0L 1B0, Canada. TEL 450-638-1546, FAX 450-632-6031. Ed., R&P Rev. Jacques Bruyere. Pub. Rev. Jacques Bruyere S J. Circ: 9,000 (paid and controlled).

KATHOLIEK DOCUMENTATIE CENTRUM. BRONNEN EN STUDIES. *see* LIBRARY AND INFORMATION SCIENCES

282 NLD ISSN 0168-244X
HET KATHOLIEK NIEUWSBLAD. Text in Dutch. 1983. w. EUR 108; EUR 69 to students (effective 2009). adv. illus. back issues avail. **Document type:** *Newspaper, Consumer.* **Description:** Reports news and events and discusses issues of interest to the Roman Catholic community in the Netherlands and Belgium.
Related titles: Online - full text ed.: ISSN 1876-1178.
Published by: Katholiek Nieuwsblad, Postbus 1270, 's-Hertogenbosch, 5200 BH, Netherlands. TEL 31-73-6123480, FAX 31-73-6890065, 31-73-6128530. Ed. Ed Arons.

282 NLD ISSN 1387-3482
KATHOLIEKE DOCUMENTATIE CENTRUM. MEMOREEKS. Text in Dutch. 1975. irreg., latest vol.27, 2009. price varies. **Document type:** *Monographic series.*
Published by: (Katholiek Documentatie Centrum), Uitgeverij Valkhof Pers, Postbus 1391, Nijmegen, 6501 BJ, Netherlands. TEL 31-24-3607250, FAX 31-24-3603269, info@valkhofpers.nl, http://www.valkhofpers.nl.

282 DEU ISSN 0343-4605
KATHOLISCHE BILDUNG. Text in German. 1974. m. (11/yr.). **Document type:** *Bulletin.*
Indexed: DIP, IBR, IBZ.
—**CCC.**
Published by: Verein Katholischer Deutscher Lehrerinnen, Hedwig-Dransfeld-Platz 4, Essen, 45143, Germany. TEL 49-201-623029, FAX 49-201-621587, info@vkdl.de, http://www.vkdl.de.

282 AUT ISSN 0022-9377
KATHOLISCHE FRAUENBEWEGUNG OESTERREICHS. FUEHRUNGSBLATT. Text in German. 1951. q. bk.rev. **Document type:** *Newsletter, Consumer.*
Published by: Katholisches Frauenwerk in Oesterreich, Spiegelgasse 3-2, Vienna, W 1010, Austria. TEL 43-1-515523697, FAX 43-1-515523764, office@kfb.at, http://www.kfb.at. Eds. Susanne Degenhart, Veronika Handschuh. Circ: 2,500.

282 DEU
DER KATHOLISCHE MESNER. Text in German. 1950. bi-m. EUR 7 (effective 2006). adv. **Document type:** *Magazine, Trade.*

Published by: Sankt Ulrich Verlag GmbH, Hafnerberg 2, Augsburg, 86152, Germany. TEL 49-821-502420, FAX 49-821-5024241, verlag@suv.de, http://www.suv.de. adv.: B&W page EUR 235. Circ: 3,295 (controlled).

282 DEU ISSN 0945-859X
KATHOLISCHE SONNTAGSZEITUNG FUER DAS BISTUM AUGSBURG. Text in German. 1946. w. EUR 25.50 per quarter (effective 2011). adv. bk.rev. 40 p./no. 4 cols./p.; back issues avail. **Document type:** *Newspaper, Consumer.*
Formerly (until 1993): Kirchenzeitung fuer die Diozeese Augsburg
Published by: Sankt Ulrich Verlag GmbH, Postfach 111920, Augsburg, 86044, Germany. TEL 49-821-50242, FAX 49-821-5024241, info@uv-media.de. adv.: B&W page EUR 1,885, color page EUR 3,045. Circ: 37,712 (paid and controlled).

282 DEU
KATHOLISCHE SONNTAGSZEITUNG FUER DAS BISTUM REGENSBURG. Text in German. 1926. w. (Sun.). EUR 20.70 per quarter (effective 2011). adv. **Document type:** *Newspaper, Consumer.*
Formerly (until 2003): Regensburger Bistumsblatt (0034-3250)
Published by: (Bischoeflicher Stuhl Regensburg), Sankt Ulrich Verlag GmbH, Postfach 111920, Augsburg, 86044, Germany. TEL 49-821-50242, FAX 49-821-5024241, info@uv-media.de. Circ: 100,000.

282 DEU
KATHOLISCHE SONNTAGSZEITUNG FUER DAS ERZBISTUM BERLIN. Text in German. 1990. w. EUR 21.15 per quarter (effective 2011). **Document type:** *Newspaper, Consumer.*
Formerly (until 2003): Katholische Kirchenzeitung fuer das Bistum Berlin (0944-0666); Which was formed by the merger of (1954-1990): St.-Hedwigsblatt (0487-2088); (1945-1990): Petrusblatt (0342-9091)
Published by: Sankt Ulrich Verlag GmbH, Postfach 111920, Augsburg, 86044, Germany. TEL 49-821-50242, FAX 49-821-5024241, info@uv-media.de.

282 DEU
KATHOLISCHE SONNTAGSZEITUNG FUER DEUTSCHLAND. Text in German. 1885. w. EUR 18.45 per quarter (effective 2011). adv. **Document type:** *Newspaper, Consumer.*
Published by: Sankt Ulrich Verlag GmbH, Postfach 111920, Augsburg, 86044, Germany. TEL 49-821-50242, FAX 49-821-5024241, info@uv-media.de. adv.: B&W page EUR 2,000, color page EUR 3,280. Circ: 85,739 (paid).

KATHOLISCHE UNIVERSITAET EICHSTAETT. VORLESUNGSVERZEICHNIS. *see* EDUCATION—Guides To Schools And Colleges

282 DEU
KATHOLISCHEN MILITAERBISCHOF FUER DIE DEUTSCHE BUNDESWEHR. VERORDNUNGSBLATT. Text in German, Latin. 1965. 8/yr. **Document type:** *Bulletin.*
Published by: Katholisches Militaerbischofsamt, Postfach 190199, Bonn, 53037, Germany. TEL 0228-9121-0, FAX 0228-9121-105. Circ: 350.

KATHOLISCHER BERUFSVERBAND FUER PFLEGEBERUFE. MITTEILUNGSBLATT. *see* MEDICAL SCIENCES

282 DEU ISSN 0170-7302
KATHOLISCHES LEBEN UND KIRCHENREFORM IM ZEITALTER DER GLAUBENSSPALTUNG. Text in German. 1927. irreg., latest vol.69, 2009. price varies. **Document type:** *Monographic series, Academic/Scholarly.*
Formerly (until 1966): Katholisches Leben und Kaempfen im Zeitalter der Glaubensspaltung (0170-7310)
Published by: Aschendorff Verlag GmbH & Co. KG, Soester Str 13, Muenster, 48135, Germany. TEL 49-251-6900, FAX 49-251-6904570, buchverlag@aschendorff.de, http://www.aschendorff-buchverlag.de. Eds. Heribea Surolinsky, Klaus Ganzer. R&P Dirk F Passmann. Adv. contact Petra Landsknecht.

282 DEU ISSN 0179-7395
KATHOLISCHES SONNTAGSBLATT. Text in German. 1850. w. EUR 67.20 (effective 2007); EUR 1.45 newsstand/cover (effective 2006). adv. **Document type:** *Newspaper, Consumer.*
Published by: Schwabenverlag AG, Senefelderstr 12, Ostfildern, 73760, Germany. TEL 49-711-4406140, FAX 49-711-4406138, info@schwabenverlag.de. Ed. Reiner Schlotthauer. Adv. contact Wolfgang Schmoll. B&W page EUR 2,856; trim 230 x 305. Circ: 56,275 (paid and controlled).

230.2 POL
KATOLICKI UNIWERSYTET LUBELSKI. WYDZIAL TEOLOGICZNO-KANONICZNY. ROZPRAWY. Text in Polish; Summaries in English, French. 1947. irreg. price varies. index.
Published by: Katolicki Uniwersytet Lubelski, Towarzystwo Naukowe, ul Gliniana 21, Lublin, 20616, Poland. Circ: 3,150.

230.0071 POL ISSN 0044-4405
AS262.L84
KATOLICKI UNIWERSYTET LUBELSKI. ZESZYTY NAUKOWE. Text in Polish; Summaries in English, French. 1958. q. (in 4 vols.). price varies. bk.rev. illus. index. **Document type:** *Academic/Scholarly.*
Indexed: DIP, FR, IBR, IBZ, IZBG, RASB.
—Linda Hall.
Published by: Katolicki Uniwersytet Lubelski, Towarzystwo Naukowe, ul Gliniana 21, Lublin, 20616, Poland. Circ: 1,125.

282 CZE ISSN 0862-5557
KATOLICKY TYDENIK. Text in Czech. 1949. w. CZK 572; CZK 11 newsstand/cover (effective 2010). adv. **Document type:** *Newspaper, Consumer.*
Formerly (until 1990): Katolicke Noviny (0231-7516)
Published by: Katolicky Tydenik, s.r.o., Londynska 44, Prague 2, 120 00, Czech Republic. TEL 420-224-250395, FAX 420-224-257041. Ed. Antonin Randa. Adv. contact Hana Culikova.

282 DNK ISSN 0902-297X
KATOLSK ORIENTERING. Text in Danish. 1969. bi-w. adv. bk.rev. **Document type:** *Newsletter, Consumer.*
Formerly (until 1975): Katolsk Forum (0902-2988)
Related titles: Online - full text ed.
Published by: Den Katolske Kirke i Danmark/The Catholic Church of Denmark, Gl. Kongevej 15, Copenhagen V, 1610, Denmark. TEL 45-33-556040, FAX 45-33-556041, http://www.katolsk.dk. Eds. Lisbeth Ruetz, Niels Messerschmidt. Adv. contact Lisbeth Roenne. Circ: 8,700.

282 DEU ISSN 0138-2543
KATOLSKI POSOL. Text in Sorbian, Lower. 1863. w. **Document type:** *Journal, Academic/Scholarly.*
Published by: (Towarstwo Cyrila a Metoda), Domowina Verlag GmbH, Tuchmacherstr 27, Bautzen, 02625, Germany. TEL 49-3591-5770, FAX 49-3591-577207, domowinaverlag@t-online.de, http://www.domowinaverlag.de.

282.485 SWE ISSN 1402-3385
KATOLSKT MAGASIN. Text in Swedish. 1926. 14/yr. SEK 240 domestic; SEK 330 other Scandinavian countries; SEK 370 in Europe; SEK 450 elsewhere. **Document type:** *Newspaper.* **Description:** Acts as a forum for the Swedish Catholic church and Catholics in Swedish society. Focuses on the state of the Church in Sweden and worldwide, faith, ethics and culture.
Former titles (until 1997): Katolskt Kyrkotidning (0345-6110); (until 1960): Hemmet och Helgedomen; (until 1959): Katolska Foersamlingsbladet Hemmet och Helgedomen; (until 1940): Hemmet och Helgedomen
Published by: Stiftelsen Katolsk Kyrkotidning, PO Box 4032, Stockholm, 10261, Sweden. TEL 46-8-7148066, FAX 46-8-6438061, redaktionen@katolsktmagasin.press.se. Ed. Gustaf von Essen. Circ: 2,500 (paid).

230.2 JPN ISSN 0387-3005
KATORIKKU KENKYU. Text in Japanese; Summaries in English. 1961. a. JPY 1,240 (effective 2003). bk.rev. back issues avail. **Document type:** *Academic/Scholarly.* **Description:** Contains articles in all fields of Christian theology and philosophy, past and present, written by scholars born or living in Japan.
Formerly (until 1971): Katorikku Shingaku (0387-2998)
Indexed: IZBG, OTA.
Published by: Sophia University, Theological Society/Jochi Daigaku, Nerima-ku, 4-32-11 Kamishiyakujii, Tokyo, 177-0044, Japan. TEL 81-3-5991-0343, FAX 81-3-5991-6928. Ed. Tadahiko Iwashima. Circ: 1,020 (controlled).

282 ZAF ISSN 0022-9687
KEHILWENYANE; dikgang tsa bodumedi le morafe. Text and summaries in English. 1958. m. ZAR 1 per issue. bk.rev. abstr.; illus.; stat.
Indexed: CERDIC.
Published by: (Roman Catholic Diocese of Kimberley), Kehilwenyane Publications, PO Box 309, Kimberley, 8300, South Africa. Ed. Kgalalelo G Makadu. Circ: 5,600.

282 BEL
KERK EN LEVEN. Text in Dutch. 1944. w. free (effective 2005). adv. bk.rev. back issues avail. **Document type:** *Newspaper.* **Description:** Covers all aspects of contemporary Catholic life, including education, social and community issues, and problems of Third World development, and related topics.
Published by: N.V. Halewijn, Halewijnlaan 92, Antwerp, 2050, Belgium. TEL 32-3-210-0940, FAX 32-3-210-0936, redaktie.kerklev@kerknet.be, http://www.kerknet.be/kerkenleven. Ed. Mark Van de Voorde. Pub., R&P Johan Cornille. Adv. contact Arnold Scheerder. Circ: 680,000.

230.071 POL ISSN 1643-2444
➤ **KERYKS**; miedzynarodowy przeglad katechetyczno-pedagogiczno-religijny. Text in Polish, German. 2002. s-a. **Document type:** *Journal, Academic/Scholarly.*
Published by: (Katolicki Uniwersytet Lubelski, Towarzystwo Naukowe, Katolicki Uniwersytet Lubelski, Wydzial Teologii, Instytut Pastoralno-Katechetyczny), Wydawnictwo Towarzystwa Naukowego Katolickiego Uniwersytetu Lubelskiego, ul Gliniana 21, Lublin, 20616, Poland. TEL 48-81-5250193, tnkul@kul.lublin.pl. Ed. Cyprian Rogowski.

262.13 GBR
KEYS OF PETER. Text in English. 1969. bi-m. GBP 6 (effective 2000). bk.rev. **Document type:** *Bulletin.* **Description:** Catholic publication covering religious and world affairs in relation to the Christian social order and Papal teaching.
Published by: Petrine Publications, 157 Vicarage Rd, London, E10 5DU, United Kingdom. TEL 44-181-539-3876. Ed. Ronald King.

268 NLD ISSN 1381-2327
KINDSCHAP GODS; de genadegave kind gods to mogen zijn. Text in Dutch. 1994. q. **Document type:** *Newsletter, Consumer.* **Description:** Contains devotional readings.
Published by: Goddelijke Genade (Unio Divinae Gratiae), Postbus 30163, Landgraaf, 6370 KD, Netherlands. Ed. L F M Terranea.

282 TZA ISSN 0856-2563
KIONGOZI/LEADER; gazeti la wananchi. Text in Swahili. 1950. fortn. TZS 200 for 6 mos. bk.rev. **Document type:** *Newspaper.*
Incorporates: Ecclesia (0012-9046)
Published by: Catholic Publishers Ltd., PO Box 9400, Dar Es Salaam, Tanzania. TEL 255-51-29505. Ed. Chrysostom C Rweyemamu. Circ: 20,000.

282 DEU ISSN 0946-5804
KIRCHE HEUTE. Text in German. 1948. 11/yr. EUR 29 domestic; EUR 34 foreign; EUR 20 to students (effective 2007). adv. bk.rev. back issues avail. **Document type:** *Magazine, Consumer.*
Formerly (until 1994): Offerten-Zeitung fuer die Katholische Geistlichkeit und Engagierte Glaeubige (0946-5812)
Published by: Kirche Heute Verlags GmbH, Postfach 1406, Altoetting, 84498, Germany. TEL 49-8671-880430, FAX 49-8671-880431. Ed. Daniel Langhans. Adv. contact Maria Kugler. color page EUR 1,540, B&W page EUR 1,195. Circ: 10,872 (controlled).

282 DEU
KIRCHE UND LEBEN. Text in German. 1946. w. EUR 21.90 per quarter; EUR 1.50 newsstand/cover (effective 2008). adv. **Document type:** *Newspaper, Consumer.*
Published by: B M V Bistumszeitung Muenster, Auf dem Graben 2, Recklinghausen, 45657, Germany. TEL 49-2361-5828833, FAX 49-2361-5828856, info@bmv-verlag.de, http://www.bmv-verlag.de. Circ: 127,593 (paid and controlled).

282 DEU
KIRCHE UND SCHULE. Text in German. 1972. q. **Document type:** *Newsletter, Consumer.*
Published by: Bischoefliches Generalvikariat Muenster, Domplatz 27, Muenster, 48135, Germany. TEL 49-251-4956301, FAX 49-251-4956075, medien@bistum-muenster.de. Ed. Stephan Chmielus. Circ: 5,000 (controlled).

282 DEU ISSN 1431-5637
KIRCHENBOTE; Wochenzeitung fuer das Bistum Osnabrueck. Text in German. 1926. w. EUR 1.15 newsstand/cover (effective 2006). adv. **Document type:** *Newspaper, Consumer.*
Former titles (until 1988): Kirchenbote des Bistums Osnabrueck (0175-9167); (until 1936): Kirchenbote fuer Stadt und Bistum Osnabrueck (0175-9175)
Published by: Kirchenbote des Bistums Osnabrueck, Kleine Domsfreiheit 23a, Osnabrueck, 49074, Germany. TEL 49-541-318500, FAX 49-541-318530, vertrieb@kirchenbote.de. Ed. Bernhard Remmers. Pub. Theo Moench-Tegeder. Adv. contact Stefan Grasser. B&W page EUR 4,032, color page EUR 5,376. Circ: 31,046 (paid and controlled).

KIRCHENMUSIKALISCHE MITTEILUNGEN DER DIOEZESE ROTTENBURG-STUTTGART. *see* MUSIC

KIRCHENMUSIKALISCHES JAHRBUCH. *see* MUSIC

282 DEU ISSN 0936-9627
KIRCHENZEITUNG FUER DAS BISTUM AACHEN. Text in German. 1933. w. EUR 5.95 per month (effective 2009). adv. bk.rev.; music rev.; tel.rev.; video rev. back issues avail. **Document type:** *Newspaper, Consumer.*
Published by: (Bistum Aachen), Einhard Verlag GmbH, Tempelhofer Str 21, Aachen, 52068, Germany. TEL 49-241-16850, FAX 49-241-1685253, info@einhardverlag.de, http://www.einhardverlag.de. Ed. Berthold Fischer. Adv. contact Holger Twardy. page EUR 1,900.80; trim 205 x 288. Circ: 43,138 (controlled).

282 DEU
KIRCHENZEITUNG FUER DAS BISTUM EICHSTAETT. Text in German. 1934. w. EUR 64.80; EUR 1 newsstand/cover (effective 2007). **Document type:** *Newspaper, Consumer.*
Address: Sollnau 2, Eichstaett, 85072, Germany. TEL 49-8421-97810, FAX 49-8421-978120. Circ: 28,328 (controlled).

282 DEU
KIRCHENZEITUNG FUER DAS ERZBISTUM KOELN. Text in German. 1946. w. EUR 70.20; EUR 1.40 newsstand/cover (effective 2006). adv. **Document type:** *Newspaper, Consumer.*
Published by: J.P. Bachem Verlag GmbH, Ursulaplatz 1, Cologne, 50668, Germany. TEL 49-221-16190, FAX 49-221-1619205, info@bachem-verlag.de, http://www.bachem-verlag.de. Ed. Erich Laeufer. R&P Lambert Bachem. Adv. contact Klaus Boscanin. page EUR 3,404.80. Circ: 1,314,643 (paid and controlled).

282 DEU
KIRCHENZEITUNG HILDESHEIM; Die Woche im Bistum Hildesheim. Text in German. w. EUR 71.40; EUR 1.45 newsstand/cover (effective 2009). adv. **Document type:** *Newspaper, Consumer.*
Published by: Bernward Mediengesellschaft mbH, Domhof 24, Hildesheim, 31134, Germany. TEL 49-5121-307800, FAX 49-5121-307801, info@bernward-medien.de, http://www.bernward-medien.de. Ed. Matthias Bode. adv.: B&W page EUR 3,091.20, color page EUR 5,140.80. Circ: 18,317 (paid and controlled).

268.432 UGA
KIZITO; a children's magazine. Text in Luganda. 1957. 3/yr. UGX 500 per issue. **Document type:** *Academic/Scholarly.* **Description:** Promotes Catholic principles while educating children from all walks of life.
Indexed: L09.
Published by: Kampala Archdiocese, c/o Sr. Olivia Nakiganda, Ed., PO Box 14, Kampala, Kisubi, Uganda. Ed. M O Nakiganda.

282 DEU ISSN 0948-6216
KLERUSBLATT. Text in German. 1925. m. adv. **Document type:** *Newsletter, Consumer.*
Indexed: RILM.
Published by: Klerusverband e.V., Stephansplatz 3, Munich, 80337, Germany. TEL 49-89-265464, FAX 49-89-266671, klerusverband@t-online.de. adv.: B&W page EUR 647.

255 NLD ISSN 2210-7126
DE KLUIS. Text in Dutch. 1957. q. EUR 15 (effective 2010). **Document type:** *Newsletter, Consumer.*
Formerly (until 2010): Abdijleven (0167-2207)
Published by: Stichting Vrienden van de Achelse Kluis, c/o J Roothans, Dommelstraat 34, Valkenswaard, 5551 TA, Netherlands. TEL 31-40-2014036.

KOLEDARCEK. *see* CHILDREN AND YOUTH—For

282 USA
KOLPING BANNER. Text in English. 1929. m. USD 10. **Document type:** *Newsletter.* **Description:** Serves as a religious, fraternal, and social service magazine.
Published by: Cath. Kolping Society of America, PO Box 4097, Clifton, NJ 07015-4907. TEL 973-478-8635. Ed., R&P Ed J Farkas. Circ: 2,000.

KOLPING OESTERREICH. *see* CHILDREN AND YOUTH—For

282 DEU
KONRADSBLATT. Text in German. 1916. w. (Sun.). EUR 69 (effective 2008); EUR 1.30 newsstand/cover (effective 2007). adv. **Document type:** *Magazine, Consumer.* **Description:** Discusses current religious issues.
Published by: (Erbistum Freiburg), Badenia Verlag und Druckerei GmbH, Rudolf-Freytag-Str 6, Karlsruhe, 76189, Germany. TEL 49-721-95450, FAX 49-721-9545125, verlag@badeniaverlag.de, http://www.badeniaverlag.de. Ed. Klaus Nientiedt. Adv. contact Siegfried Fernschild. B&W page EUR 2,968, color page EUR 5,880; trim 225 x 295. Circ: 61,834 (paid and controlled).

282 AUT ISSN 0023-3676
KONTAKT DREI UND ZWANZIG. Text in German. 1954. bi-m. bk.rev. **Document type:** *Newsletter, Consumer.*
Formerly: Liesinger Pfarrblatt
Published by: Pfarre Atzgersdorf, Kirchenplatz 1, Vienna, W 1230, Austria. TEL 43-1-8659348, FAX 43-1-86593484, pfarre.atzgersdorf@gmx.at, http://www.pfarre-atzgersdorf.at. Circ: 2,100.

282 DEU
KRANKENBRIEF. Text in German. 1947. m. **Document type:** *Magazine, Consumer.*
Published by: Paulinus Verlag GmbH, Maximineracht 11c, Trier, 54295, Germany. TEL 49-651-46080, FAX 49-651-4608221, verlag@paulinus.de.

282 HKG
KUNG KAO PO/CATHOLIC CHINESE WEEKLY. Text in Chinese. 1928. w. HKD 400 domestic; HKD 430 in China; HKD 550 elsewhere; HKD 5 newsstand/cover (effective 2001). adv. bk.rev.
Address: 16 Caine Rd, 11th Fl, Hong Kong, Hong Kong. TEL 852-2522-0487, FAX 852-2521-3095, kkp@catholic.org.hk. Ed. Leung Peter. R&P Fr. Louis Ha. Adv. contact Mary Leung. Circ: 30,000 (paid).

LABOR LIFE. *see* BUSINESS AND ECONOMICS—Labor And Industrial Relations

282 MDG
LAKROAN'I MADAGASIKARA. Text in French, Malagasy. 1927. w.
Address: Maison Jean XXIII, Mahamasina Sud, Antananarivo, 101, Madagascar. TEL 26141. Ed. Louis Rasolo. Circ: 16,000.

282 DEU
LAND AKTIV. Text in German. 1949. bi-m. EUR 8.70 (effective 2007). adv. bk.rev. **Document type:** *Newspaper, Consumer.*
Former titles (until 2001): Land Aktuell (0340-7837); (until 1970): Dorf Aktuell (0012-5547)
Published by: Katholische Landvolkbewegung Deutschland e.V., Drachenfelsstr 23, Bad Honnef-Rhoendorf, 53604, Germany. TEL 49-2224-71031, FAX 49-2224-78971, bundesstelle@landvolk.de, http://landvolk.de/bund/. Ed., Adv. contact Katharina Knierim. B&W page EUR 820, color page EUR 1,520; trim 184 x 239. Circ: 11,000.

230.2 PHL ISSN 0116-4856
BR1
LANDAS; journal of Loyola School of Theology. Text in English. 1987. s-a. PHP 150, USD 18 (effective 2001). bk.rev. 140 p./no.; **Description:** Features articles on scripture, theology, ethics and spirituality written from the perspective of authors, most of them Filipinos, working and teaching in the Philippines.
Indexed: OTA.
Published by: (Loyola Institute for Studies on Development of Man and Society), Loyola School of Theology, Ateneo de Manila University, PO Box 4082, Manila, Philippines. TEL 632-99-15-61, FAX 632-921-7311, lambino@hotmail.com, water0828@yahoo.com. Ed. Miguel S J Lambino. Circ: 500.

282 VAT ISSN 1010-7215
BX800.A1
LATERANUM. Text in Italian. 1976. 3/yr. USD 78. bk.rev.
Indexed: A22, CERDIC, OTA, PCI.
—IE.
Published by: Pontificia Universita Lateranense/Pontificia Universitas Lateranensis, Piazza S. Giovanni in Laterano 4, Vatican City, 00120, Vatican City. Ed. Marcello Bordoni.

264 870 USA
LATIN LITURGY ASSOCIATION NEWSLETTER. Text in English. 1976. q. USD 15 (effective 2000). adv. bk.rev. back issues avail. **Document type:** *Newsletter.* **Description:** Promotes the use of Latin in the rites of the Roman Catholic Church.
Published by: Latin Liturgy Association, c/o Mr. Scott Calta, Secretary - LLA, PO Box 1308, Dallas, GA 30132-0022. Ed., R&P James Pauer TEL 718-979-6685. Circ: 1,000.

282 USA ISSN 1064-556X
BX1970.A1
LATIN MASS; a journal of Catholic culture. Text in English. 1992. q. USD 28.95 (effective 2004). adv. **Document type:** *Magazine, Consumer.*
Published by: Keep the Faith, Inc., 70 Lake St., Ramsey, NJ 07446-2030. info@keepthefaith.org, http://www.keepthefaith.org. Ed. Fr. James McLucas. R&P Liz Altham TEL 203-288-2500. Adv. contact Steve Terenzio. Circ: 11,000.

268 USA ISSN 1541-602X
LAY WITNESS. Text in English. 197?. bi-m. free to members (effective 2009). adv. bk.rev.; film rev. charts; illus.; stat. 58 p./no.; back issues avail. **Document type:** *Magazine, Consumer.* **Description:** Covers current events in the church, the holy father's intentions for the month, and provides formation through biblical and catechetical articles with real-life applications for everyday Catholics.
Formerly (until 1979): Catholics United for the Faith. Newsletter
Published by: Catholic United for the Faith, 827 N Fourth St, Steubenville, OH 43952. TEL 740-283-2484, 800-693-2484, FAX 740-283-4011.

282.996 NGA ISSN 0331-5193
THE LEADER. Text in English. 1956. fortn. NGN 600; NGN 1,700 foreign. **Document type:** *Newspaper.* **Description:** Informs and educates Nigerian Catholics on issues facing the country and the Church, so they can form their opinions and contribute meaningfully to these issues that affect their lives and faith.
Published by: Archdiocese of Owerri, PMB 1017, Owerri, Nigeria. TEL 234-230932. Ed. Kevin C Akagha. Circ: 27,000 (paid).

282 USA ISSN 1072-7930
LEAFLET MISSAL. Text in English. 1929. bi-m. USD 30 (effective 2007). illus. 136 p./no. 2 cols./p.; back issues avail. **Document type:** *Journal, Consumer.* **Description:** Provides Bible readings, prayer texts and hymns.
Published by: American Catholic Press, 16565 S State St, South Holland, IL 60473. TEL 708-331-5485, FAX 708-331-5484, acp@acpress.org, http://www.acpress.org. Ed. Rev. Michael Gilligon. Circ: 125,000 (paid).

282 370 AUS ISSN 1326-8198
LEARNING MATTERS. Text in English. 2005. s-a. USD 22 domestic (effective 2007).
Formed by the merger of (1982-2005): Crosslinks (0727-6435); (1982-2005): Curriculum Exchange (0727-6826); (1983-2005): Diversity (0812-0102)
Related titles: Online - full text ed.
Published by: Catholic Education Office Melbourne, James Goold House, 228 Victoria Parade, PO Box 3, East Melbourne, VIC 8002, Australia. TEL 61-3-92670228, FAX 61-3-94159325, director@ceo.melb.catholic.edu.au, http://www.ceo.melb.catholic.edu.au.

282 USA ISSN 0194-9799
THE LEAVEN (KANSAS CITY). Text in English. 1939. w. USD 12. adv. bk.rev.; film rev. **Document type:** *Newspaper.* **Description:** Covers local news, national and international news on issues of concern and interest to Catholics.
Formerly: Eastern Kansas Register (0012-883X)
Published by: Catholic Archdiocese of Kansas City, 12615 Parallel Pkwy, Kansas City, KS 66109. TEL 913-721-1575. Ed. Rev. Mark Goldasich. Adv. contact Wilma Plake. Circ: 45,500.

282 DEU ISSN 0171-4171
LEBENDIGE KATECHESE. Text in German. 1981. s-a. adv. bk.rev. back issues avail. **Document type:** *Bulletin.*
Related titles: ◆ Supplement to: Lebendige Seelsorge. ISSN 0343-4591.
Indexed: DIP, IBR, IBZ.
—BLDSC (5179.622800).
Published by: Seelsorge Verlag Echter, Postfach 5560, Wuerzburg, 97005, Germany. TEL 49-931-6671-0, FAX 49-931-6671151. Ed. Lothar Roos. Adv. contact Thomas Haeussner.

282 DEU ISSN 0023-9941
LEBENDIGES ZEUGNIS. Text in German. 1885. q. EUR 12 (effective 2009). bk.rev. **Document type:** *Newsletter, Consumer.* **Description:** Examines topics in the fields of religion, philosophy and ethics.
Formerly (until 1946): Akademische Bonifatius-Korrespondenz (0174-8033)
Indexed: CERDIC, DIP, IBR, IBZ.
Published by: Bonifatiuswerk der Deutschen Katholiken e.V., Kamp 22, Paderborn, 33098, Germany. TEL 49-5251-29960, FAX 49-5251-299688, info@bonifatiuswerk.de, http://www.bonifatiuswerk.de. Circ: 4,600 (paid).

282.4585 MLT
LEHEN IS-SEWWA. Text in Maltese. 1928. w. (Sat.). adv. 5 cols./p.; back issues avail. **Document type:** *Newspaper.* **Description:** Publishes news and commentary on events and issues of interest to Maltese Catholics.
Published by: Malta Catholic Action, Catholic Institute, Floriana, VLT 16, Malta. TEL 353-225847. Ed. Paul Sailba. Adv. contact Virgil Bugeja.

280 ESP ISSN 2171-4444
▼ **LEPE COFRADE.** Text in Spanish. 2010. a. **Document type:** *Magazine, Consumer.*
Published by: Consejo General de Hermandades y Cofradias de la Ciudad de Huelva, Apdo de Correos 588, Huelva, 21080, Spain. TEL 34-959-221142, http://www.consejohermandadeshuelva.com.

282.6885 LSO
LESOTHO CATHOLIC DIRECTORY. Text in English. 1977. irreg., latest 1988. USD 10. stat. **Document type:** *Directory.* **Description:** Lists statistics, personnel, addresses and services of the Catholic Church in Lesotho.
Published by: (Lesotho Catholic Bishops Conference), Mazenod Printing Works Pty. Ltd., PO Box 39, Mazenod, 160, Lesotho. FAX 266-310131, TELEX 4271 LO. Ed. F Mairot. Circ: 500.

282 220 USA ISSN 1555-4147
BS410
LETTER & SPIRIT. Text in English. 2005. a. USD 11.95 per issue (effective 2007). **Document type:** *Journal, Consumer.*
Published by: Emmaus Road Publishing, 827 N. Fourth St, Steubenville, OH 43952. TEL 800-398-5470, FAX 740-283-4011, questions@emmausroad.org, http://www.emmausroad.org/index.aspx?SID=8&Tab=Home. Ed. Scott Hahn.

282 ITA ISSN 1827-3246
LETTERA AGLI AMICI. Text in Italian. 1984. s-a. **Document type:** *Newsletter, Consumer.*
Formerly (until 2002): Qiqajon di Bose (1827-3238)
Published by: Monastero di Bose, Edizioni Qiqajon, Cascina Bose 6, Magnano, BI 13887, Italy. TEL 39-015-679185, FAX 39-015-679294, segreteria@monasterodibose.it, http://www.monasterodibose.it.

255 FRA ISSN 0750-3695
LETTRE DE TAIZE. Text in French. 1970. bi-m. EUR 4.50 domestic; EUR 6 foreign (effective 2009). **Document type:** *Newsletter.*
Related titles: Dutch ed.: Brief uit Taize. ISSN 1260-4763; English ed.: Letter from Taize. ISSN 1258-9993; Spanish ed.: Carta de Taize. ISSN 1258-9977; Italian ed.: Lettera da Taize. ISSN 1260-4755; German ed.: Brief aus Taize. ISSN 1258-9985.
Published by: Communaute de Taize, Taize, 71250, France. editions@taize.fr. Circ: 20,000.

282 FRA ISSN 1963-2029
LA LETTRE DES EDITIONS DE GOLIAS; l'aventure chretienne autrement. Text in French. 198?. bi-m. **Document type:** *Newsletter, Consumer.*
Formerly (until 2008): La Lettre de Golias (1247-3669)
Published by: Golias France, B.P. 3045, Villeurbanne, Cedex 69605, France. TEL 33-4-78038747, FAX 33-4-78844203, redaction.golias@orange.fr, http://golias-editions.fr. Ed. Christian Terras.

282 LUX
LETZEBURGER SONNDESBLAD. Text in German. 1867. irreg.
Published by: Editions Saint Paul, 4, rue Hogenberg, Luxembourg, L-2988, Luxembourg. TEL 352-49-93-281, FAX 352-49-93-384. Ed. Andre Heiderscheid.

282 ITA ISSN 0024-1997
LA LIBERTA. Text in Italian. 1952. w. **Document type:** *Newspaper, Consumer.*
Related titles: Online - full text ed.
Indexed: MLA.
Published by: Editoriale Liberta SpA, Via Benedettine 68, Piacenza, RE 29100, Italy.

282 DEU ISSN 0171-5895
LIBORIUSBLATT. Text in German. 1898. w. EUR 1.50 newsstand/cover (effective 2011). adv. **Document type:** *Newspaper, Consumer.*
Published by: Verlag Liboriusblatt GmbH & Co. KG, Lange Str 335, Hamm, 59067, Germany. TEL 49-2381-940400, FAX 49-2381-9404070, verlag@liborius.de. Ed. Heribert Boeller. adv.: B&W page EUR 3,701.25, color page EUR 5,922.

282 AUT
LICHTENTALER PFARRNACHRICHTEN. Text in German. 1978. 4/yr. free. adv.
Published by: Pfarre Lichtental, Marktgasse 40, Vienna, W 1090, Austria. Circ: 5,000.

282 SYR
LE LIEN; revue du patriarcat Grec-Melkite Catholique. Text in Arabic. 1936. bi-m. SYP 23,000 domestic (effective 2000); USD 50 foreign. adv. bk.rev. illus. back issues avail. **Description:** Covers news of the Patriarchate, ecumenism, liturgy, and other religious topics.
Published by: Patriarcat Grec-Melkite Catholique, P O Box 22249, Damascus, Syria. TEL 963-11-5433129, FAX 963-11-5431266. Ed. Patriarch Maximos V Hakim. Pub. Fr Groeges Jabaly. R&P, Adv. contact Lucienne Vandenplas TEL 963-11-4413111. Circ: 2,500.

282 FRA ISSN 1766-9634
LE LIEN. Text in French. 1966. q.
Former titles (until 2004): Le Lien entre les Parents de Pretres, Religieux et Religieuses (1273-8611); (until 1996): Lien entre les Meres et Peres de Pretres, Religieux et Religieuses (0180-5428); (until 1977): Lien entre les Meres et Peres de Pretres (0024-2926)
Published by: Association Nationale des Parents de Pretres, Religieux et Religieuses, 58 Av. de Breteuil, Paris, 75007, France. courriel@apprr.cef.fr.

282 USA ISSN 0024-3450
BX4020.A1
LIGUORIAN. Text in English. 1913. 10/yr. USD 20 domestic; USD 27 foreign (effective 2009). adv. bk.rev. illus. **Document type:** *Magazine, Consumer.* **Description:** Provides practical advice and information for adult Catholics in a rapidly changing world.
Related titles: Audio cassette/tape ed.; Microfiche ed.: (from PQC); Online - full text ed.; Supplement(s): Season of Wonder; Journey to Glory.
Indexed: A22, CERDIC, CPL, P28, P30, P48, P53, P54, PQC, S02, S03.
—CCC.
Published by: (Redemptorist Pastoral), Liguori Publications, One Liguori Dr, Liguori, MO 63057. TEL 636-464-2500, 800-325-9521, liguori@liguori.org, http://www.liguori.org.

282 USA
LILY OF THE MOHAWKS. Text in English. 1936. q. USD 5 to members (effective 2000). bk.rev. back issues avail. **Document type:** *Newsletter.*
Published by: Tekakwitha League, Auriesville, NY 12016. TEL 518-853-3153. Ed. Marie McClumpha. Circ: 3,500.

282 610.73 USA ISSN 1681-9594
LINK INTERNATIONAL. Text in English. 1987. q.
Formerly (until 2001): Christian Nurse International (1010-7355)
Indexed: C06, C07, C08, CINAHL, P30, SCOPUS.
—CCC.
Published by: Nurses' Christian Fellowship International, P O Box 7895, Madison, WI 53707-7895. TEL 608-274-4823 ext 402, ncf@intervarsity.org, http://www.intervarsity.org.

282 DEU ISSN 1438-4396
LINZER PHILOSOPHISCH-THEOLOGISCHE BEITRAEGE. Text in German. 2000. irreg., latest vol.19, 2009. price varies. **Document type:** *Monographic series, Academic/Scholarly.*
Published by: (Katholisch-Theologische Privatuniversitaet Linz AUT), Peter Lang GmbH (Subsidiary of: Peter Lang Publishing Group), Eschborner Landstr 42-50, Frankfurt Am Main, 60489, Germany. TEL 49-69-7807050, FAX 49-69-78070550, zentrale.frankfurt@peterlang.com.

264 USA ISSN 1059-7786
BX1970.A1
LITURGICAL MINISTRY. Text in English. 1992. q. USD 35 domestic; USD 49 foreign; USD 54 to libraries; USD 11 per issue (effective 2009). back issues avail. **Document type:** *Journal, Academic/Scholarly.* **Description:** Designed for diocesan and parish liturgy committee members, liturgists and musicians, teachers, clergy, and liturgical scholars alike.
Related titles: Online - full text ed.
Indexed: A21, CPL, R&TA, RI-1, RI-2, RILM.
Published by: Liturgical Press, St John's Abbey, PO Box 7500, Collegeville, MN 56321. TEL 320-363-2213, 800-858-5450, FAX 320-363-3299, 800-445-5899, sales@litpress.org.

264 CAN
LITURGIE, FOI ET CULTURE. Text in French. 1965. q. CAD 20 domestic; USD 22 in Canada; USD 30 elsewhere. bk.rev. illus. **Document type:** *Bulletin.*
Former titles: Conference des Eveques Catholiques du Canada. Bulletin National de Liturgie; Conference Catholique Canadienne. Bulletin National de Liturgie (0384-5087)
Published by: Canadian Conference of Catholic Bishops, Publications Service/Conference des Eveques Catholiques du Canada, 90 Parent Ave, Ottawa, ON K1N 7B1, Canada. TEL 613-241-9461, FAX 613-241-5090. Ed. M l'Abbe Paul Boily. Circ: 1,400.

282 AUS ISSN 1039-0464
LITURGY NEWS. Text in English. 1971. q. AUD 24 domestic; AUD 32 foreign (effective 2008). bk.rev.; music rev. illus. 16 p./no.; back issues avail. **Document type:** *Magazine, Consumer.* **Description:** Provides latest liturgical news. The content provides a balance between practical help and background articles.
Published by: Archdiocese of Brisbane, Liturgical Commission, GPO Box 282, Brisbane, QLD 4001, Australia. TEL 61-7-33369444, FAX 61-7-32211705. Eds. Mr. Barry Copley TEL 61-7-33922798, Dr. Tom W Elich TEL 61-7-33369443. Circ: 2,500 (paid).

282 USA ISSN 1055-5463
LIVING FAITH; daily Catholic devotions. Text in English. 1985. q. USD 10 domestic; USD 12 in Canada (effective 2009). **Document type:** *Magazine, Consumer.* **Description:** Provides daily reflection based on a Scripture passage from the daily Mass. Includes readings for daily Mass listed at the bottom of each devotion.
Formerly: Living Words (0884-1330)
Related titles: Large type ed. 14 pt.: USD 12 domestic; USD 16 in Canada (effective 2009).
Published by: Creative Communications for the Parish, 1564 Fencorp Dr, Fenton, MO 63026. TEL 636-305-9777, FAX 636-305-9333. Ed. James E Adams. Pub. Larry Neeb. R&P Mark Neilsen. Circ: 650,000 (paid).

282 USA ISSN 1947-2862
ML3086
▼ **LIVING LITURGY FOR CANTORS.** Text in English. 2009. a. USD 9.95 per issue (effective 2009). **Document type:** *Handbook/Manual/Guide, Trade.* **Description:** A resource to help cantors prepare themselves to sing the responsorial psalm.
Published by: Liturgical Press, St John's Abbey, PO Box 7500, Collegeville, MN 56321. TEL 320-363-2213, FAX 320-363-3299, sales@litpress.org.

282 USA ISSN 1949-1166
BX2015.A4
▼ **LIVING LITURGY SUNDAY MISSAL**; celebrating the eucharist. Text in English. 2010. a. USD 9.95 per issue (effective 2010). **Document type:** *Trade.* **Description:** Liturgical content includes gospel reflections, readings and congregational responses.
Published by: Liturgical Press, St John's Abbey, PO Box 7500, Collegeville, MN 56321. TEL 800-858-5450, FAX 800-445-5899, sales@litpress.org.

282 USA
LIVING THE WORD; Scripture reflections and commentaries for Sundays and Holy Days. Text in English. 1986. a. USD 9.95 per issue (effective 2011). 240 p./no.; **Document type:** *Magazine, Consumer.* **Description:** Contains the year's Lectionary readings, along with commentary and discussion questions for Sundays and holy days.
Formerly: Living the Word, Not Only on Sunday (1079-4670)
Published by: World Library Publications, Inc. (Subsidiary of: J.S. Paluch Co., Inc.), 3708 River Rd, Ste 400, Franklin Park, IL 60131. TEL 847-233-2752, 800-621-5197, FAX 847-233-2762, 888-957-3291, wlpcs@jspaluch.com. Circ: 40,000.

282 PHL
LIVING WATER. Text in English. 1994. bi-m. PHP 95 domestic; USD 16 foreign (effective 2001). adv. 65 p./no.; back issues avail. **Document type:** *Magazine, Consumer.* **Description:** Features reflections based on Scripture to help Christians live out their faith.
Published by: Springs Foundation, Inc., ECR 51 10th St, Rolling Hills Village, New Manila, Quezon City, 1112, Philippines. TEL 632-7226749, FAX 632-7218723, springs@elimrevival.com, http://www.elimrevival.com. Ed. Mich Dumlao. Pub. Rissa Singson. R&P Marcelino Catan. Adv. contact Beth De Los Reyes. page USD 200; 6 x 3.25. Circ: 10,000.

282 CAN ISSN 1481-9244
LIVING WITH CHRIST COMPLETE - AMERICAN EDITION. Text in English. 1999. m. (plus 2 special issues). USD 18.95 in United States; USD 40 elsewhere (effective 2000).
Published by: Novalis, St Paul University, 223 Main St, Ottawa, ON K1S 1C4, Canada. TEL 613-236-1393, FAX 613-782-3004, http://www.novalis.ca. Ed. Louise Pambrun. **Subscr. to:** 49 Front St E, 2nd Fl, Toronto, ON M5E 1B3, Canada. TEL 800-387-7164, FAX 800-204-4140.

LIVING WITH CHRIST - COMPLETE EDITION. *see* MUSIC

282 CAN
LIVING WITH CHRIST - LARGE PRINT EDITION. Text in English. 1992. m. CAD 27.50 domestic; USD 27.50 in United States; USD 50 elsewhere (effective 2000); includes 2 special issues.
Published by: Novalis, St Paul University, 223 Main St, Ottawa, ON K1S 1C4, Canada. TEL 613-236-1393, FAX 613-782-3004, http://www.novalis.ca. Ed. Louise Pambrun. **Subscr. to:** 49 Front St E, 2nd Fl, Toronto, ON M5E 1B3, Canada. TEL 800-387-7164, FAX 800-204-4140.

LIVING WITH CHRIST - SUNDAY EDITION. *see* MUSIC

271.9 ESP
LLUVIA DE ROSAS. Text in Spanish. 1923. bi-m. USD 25. **Description:** Presents the life and doctrine of Saint Teresa del Nino Jesus. Includes articles on Carmelite spirituality and missions, and on life in and the activities of the Sanctuary.
Related titles: Microfilm ed.
Published by: Santuario de Santa Teresita, Apartado 1112, Lerida, 25080, Spain. TEL 973-268038, FAX 973-275886, ocdcat2@redestb.es. Ed. Angel Maria Brinas Gonzalo. Circ: 20,000.

282 CAN ISSN 0024-5895
BX4711.74
➤ **LOGOS**; a journal of eastern christian studies. Variant title: Lohos. (Supplement: Homiletychnyi Dodatok) Text in English, Ukrainian, French. 1950-1983; N.S. 1993. 2/yr. CAD 37.45 domestic; USD 30 in United States; USD 35 elsewhere (effective 2006). bk.rev. bibl. index. **Document type:** *Journal, Academic/Scholarly.* **Description:** Contains articles devoted to Eastern Christian studies, emphasizing both Orthodox and Catholic Eastern Churches.
Indexed: A21, ABS&EES, FR, MLA-IB, RI-1.
—INIST.
Published by: Saint Paul University, Metropolitan Andrey Sheptytsky Institute of Eastern Christian Studies (Subsidiary of: Saint Paul University/Universite Saint-Paul), 223 Main St, Ottawa, ON K1S 1C4, Canada. TEL 613-236-1393, FAX 613-782-3026, sheptytsky@ustpaul.ca, http://web.ustpaul.uottawa.ca/Sheptytsky/index.htm. Ed. Andriy Chirovsky.

282 100 800 306 USA ISSN 1091-6687
BX1795.C85
➤ **LOGOS (ST. PAUL)**; a journal of Catholic thought and culture. Text in English. 1997. q. 1 cols./p.; back issues avail. **Document type:** *Journal, Academic/Scholarly.* **Description:** Explores interdisciplinary issues of Christianity as shaped by Catholic theology and practice.
Related titles: Online - full text ed.: ISSN 1533-791X.
Indexed: A01, A02, A03, A08, A20, A22, AmHI, ArtHuCI, CA, CPL, CurCont, E01, H07, MLA-IB, R&TA, SCOPUS, T02, W07.
—IE. **CCC.**
Published by: University of St. Thomas (St. Paul), Center for Catholic Studies, 2115 Summit Ave, Mail #55-S, St. Paul, MN 55105. TEL 651-962-5705, 800-328-6819, FAX 651-962-5710. Ed. Michael C Jordan.

282 USA ISSN 1948-4747
HD101
▼ **THE LONERGAN REVIEW.** Text in English. 2009. a. USD 20 per issue (effective 2009). **Document type:** *Journal, Academic/Scholarly.*
Related titles: Online - full text ed.: ISSN 1948-4755. 2009.
Published by: Seton Hall University, Bernard J. Lonergan Institute, 400 South Orange Ave, Walsh 431, South Orange, NJ 07079. TEL 973-275-2431, lonerganinstitute@shu.edu, http://www.shu.edu/catholic-mission/lonergan/.

282.74721 USA ISSN 0024-6255
LONG ISLAND CATHOLIC. Text in English. 1962. w. (Wed.). USD 20 domestic; USD 27 foreign (effective 2005). adv. bibl.; charts; illus.; tr.lit. **Document type:** *Newspaper, Consumer.*
Address: 200 W. Centennial Ave., Ste. 201, Box 9000, Roosevelt, NY 11575. TEL 516-594-1000, FAX 516-594-1092. Ed. Liz O'Connor. adv.: page USD 3,315; 10 x 11.2. Circ: 118,388. Wire service: CaNS.

282 DEU
LOURDES-ROSEN. Text in German. 1880. q. membership. **Document type:** *Newsletter, Consumer.*
Published by: Deutscher Lourdes Verein Koeln e.V., Schwalbengasse 10, Cologne, 50667, Germany. TEL 49-221-9922210, FAX 49-221-99222129, info@lourdes-verein.de, http://www.deutscher-lourdes-verein.de. Circ: 25,000 (controlled).

282 BEL ISSN 0024-6964
BX801
➤ **LOUVAIN STUDIES.** Text in English. 1966. q. EUR 40 combined subscription (print & online eds.) (effective 2011). bk.rev. index. back issues avail. **Document type:** *Journal, Academic/Scholarly.* **Description:** Aims to promote international dialogue and reflection on contemporary theological, ethical and pastoral issues. Edited by the Faculty of Theology of the Katholieke Universiteit Leuven, Belgium.
Related titles: Microform ed.: (from PQC); Online - full text ed.: ISSN 1783-161X.
Indexed: A21, A22, CERDIC, CLA, CPL, IPB, IZBG, OTA, P30, R&TA, RI-1, RI-2.
—BLDSC (5296.360000), IE, Infotrieve, Ingenta. **CCC.**
Published by: (Universite Catholique de Louvain, Faculte de Theologie et de Droit Canonique), Peeters Publishers, Bondgenotenlaan 153, Leuven, 3000, Belgium. TEL 32-16-235170, FAX 32-16-228500, peeters@peeters-leuven.be, http://www.peeters-leuven.be. Circ: 1,500.

282 ITA
LUISA LA SANTA; il periodico del divin volere. Text in Italian. 19??. m. **Document type:** *Magazine, Consumer.* **Description:** Religious forum covering various religious topics, also includes calendar of events.
Published by: Pia Associazione Luisa Piccarreta, Via Luisa Piccarreta 25-27, Corato, BA 70033, Italy. http://www.luisalasanta.com/it/. Ed. Suor Assunta Marigliano.

371.07 BEL ISSN 0024-7324
BX800.A1
LUMEN VITAE; revue internationale de catechese et de pastorale. Text in French. 1946. q. EUR 45 domestic; EUR 55 in Europe; EUR 63 elsewhere (effective 2012). adv. bk.rev. bibl. index. 120 p./no.; back issues avail. **Document type:** *Journal, Academic/Scholarly.*
Related titles: Microform ed.: (from PQC).
Indexed: A22, B04, BRD, CERDIC, CPL, DIP, E02, EdA, EdI, FR, IBR, IBZ, MLA-IB, R&TA, W03.
—IE, Infotrieve. **CCC.**
Published by: (International Centre for Religious Education), Lumen Vitae Press, Rue Washington 186, Brussels, B-1050, Belgium. TEL 32-2-3490370, FAX 32-2-3490385. Ed., R&P Henri Derroitte. Adv. contact Gabriella Tihon Gyorffy. Circ: 1,800.

M I E C SERVICO DE DOCUMENTACION. *see* EDUCATION—Higher Education

282 ITA
LA MADONNA DEL DIVINO AMORE; bollettino mensile del santuario. Text in Italian. 1932. m. free. bk.rev. illus. **Document type:** *Bulletin, Consumer.* **Description:** Deals with religious events for young people and community affairs sponsored by local church organizations.
Published by: Associazione Fuoco del Divino Amore, Vicolo del Divino Amore 12, Rome, 00186, Italy. TEL 39-06-71353303, FAX 39-06-71353304. Circ: 100,000.

282 ITA
MADRE DI DIO; mensile mariano fondato da don Giacomo Alberione. Text in Italian. 1932. m. (11/yr.). EUR 13.50 (effective 2008). adv. bk.rev. back issues avail. **Document type:** *Magazine, Consumer.* **Description:** Religious publication covering religious news with special emphasis on the Virgin Mary.
Related titles: E-mail ed.; Fax ed.; Online - full text ed.
Published by: Edizioni San Paolo, Piazza Soncino 5, Cinisello Balsamo, MI 20092, Italy. TEL 39-02-660751, FAX 39-02-66075211, sanpaoloedizioni@stpauls.it, http://www.edizionisanpaolo.it. Circ: 9,500.

282 ESP ISSN 1132-3388
MADRE Y MAESTRA. Text in Spanish. 1860. m. (except July-Aug. combined). adv. bk.rev. illus. **Document type:** *Magazine, Consumer.* **Description:** Covers religion, theology, mission work, socialogy and world and church news.
Formerly (until 1957): Nuestra Senora del Sagrado Corazon. Anales (1132-337X)
Published by: Misioneros del Sagrado Corazon de Jesus, Avda Pio XII, 31, Madrid, Madrid 28016, Spain. TEL 34-1-3599600, FAX 34-1-3501889.

268 ITA ISSN 0024-9696
IL MAESTRO. Text in Italian. 1944. m. adv. bk.rev. illus.; stat. **Document type:** *Magazine, Trade.* **Description:** Presents articles from educators and others related to the field on the issues of school systems, the quality of education and the politics of schooling throughout Italy.
Indexed: IBR, IBZ.
Published by: Associazione Italiana Maestri Cattolici, Clivio di Monte del Gallo 50, Rome, RM 00165, Italy. TEL 39-06-634651, FAX 39-06-39375903, a.i.m.c@flashnet.it, http://www.aimc.it. Circ: 60,000.

282 NLD ISSN 1874-0480
MAGAZINE VAN HET BISDOM BREDA. Text in Dutch. 2007. q. EUR 7.50; EUR 2.50 newsstand/cover (effective 2009). adv.
Published by: Bisdom van Breda, Postbus 90189, Breda, 4800 RN, Netherlands. TEL 31-76-5223444, FAX 31-76-5216244, secretariaat@bisdombreda.nl, http://bisdom.essence-information.nl. adv.: B&W page EUR 1,162; trim 185 x 267. Circ: 5,000.

282 CAN ISSN 0025-0007
MAGNIFICAT. Text in French. 1965. 10/yr. CAD 10 domestic; CAD 14 in United States; CAD 20 elsewhere (effective 2004). illus. **Document type:** *Magazine, Consumer.* **Description:** Spirituality and religious informations, biographies of the Saints, news stories.
Related titles: English ed.: ISSN 0381-0852.
Indexed: MLA-IB.
Published by: Apostles of Infinite Love, Monastery of the Apostles, PO Box 4478, Mont-TremblantJ8E 1A1, PQ J8E 1A1, Canada. apotres@magnificat.ca, http://www.magnificat.qc.ca. Circ: 2,000 (paid).

282 AUS
MAJELLAN; champion of the family. Text in English. 1949 (Jan.). q. AUD 16 for 2 yrs.; AUD 2, NZD 2.50 newsstand/cover (effective 2009). 48 p./no.; back issues avail. **Document type:** *Magazine, Consumer.* **Description:** Contains articles relating to marriage and family life.
Published by: Redemptorist Congregation, PO Box 43, Brighton, VIC 3186, Australia. TEL 61-3-95922777, FAX 61-3-95931337.

282 CHE ISSN 0025-2972
MARIA; marianischer digest. Text in German. 1950. 6/yr. CHF 19.50 (effective 2000). adv. bk.rev. illus. **Document type:** *Magazine, Consumer.*
Address: Postfach 6407, Bern, 3001, Switzerland. TEL 41-31-221380. Ed. Josef Gruebel. Circ: 19,500.

282 CHE ISSN 1420-8644
MARIA HEUTE. Text in German. 1969. m. CHF 32 (effective 2001). 24 p./no. 4 cols./p.; **Document type:** *Newspaper, Consumer.*
Formerly: Mater Nostra
Related titles: French ed.: Stella Maris. ISSN 1420-8598. CHF 34 (effective 2001).
Published by: Parvis Verlag, Hauteville, 1648, Switzerland. TEL 41-26-9159393, FAX 41-26-9159399. Ed. Jean-Marie Castella. Pub. Andre Castella. R&P Jean Marie Castella. Circ: 9,000 (paid).

282 AUT ISSN 0025-2999
MARIAHILFER PFARRBOTE. Text in German. 1924. q. per issue contribution. bk.rev. abstr.; charts; illus.; stat. index.
Published by: Pfarramt Mariahilf, Barnabitengasse 14, Vienna, W 1060, Austria. Ed. Waldemar Posch. Circ: 3,000.

255.9 USA
MARIAN HELPER. Text in English. 1947. q. free to members (effective 2005); USD 2.25 newsstand/cover (effective 2009). bk.rev. back issues avail. **Document type:** *Magazine, Trade.* **Description:** Emphasizes the work of the Marians, including the divine Marian message and devotion.
Formerly (until 2001): The Association of Marian Helpers Bulletin
Related titles: Online - full text ed.: free (effective 2009).
Indexed: APW.
Published by: Association of Marian Helpers, Eden Hill, Stockbridge, MA 01263. TEL 413-298-3691, 800-462-7426, FAX 413-298-3583, EADM@marian.org. Ed. Dan Valenti. Pub. Bro. Andrew Maczynski, MIC.

282 USA ISSN 0464-9680
BT596
MARIAN STUDIES. Text in English. 1950. a. USD 20 domestic to institutions; USD 25 foreign to institutions (effective 2010). bibl. cum.index. 200 p./no.; back issues avail. **Document type:** *Journal, Academic/Scholarly.* **Description:** Contains proceedings of society's annual convention.
Indexed: A22, CPL, FR.
—BLDSC (5373.555000), INIST.
Published by: Mariological Society of America, Marian Library, University of Dayton, Dayton, OH 45469. TEL 937-229-4294, FAX 937-229-4258, cecilia.mushenheim@notes.udayton.edu.

271.9 ITA
MARIANUM. Text in Multiple languages. 1939. s-a. adv. bk.rev. **Document type:** *Journal, Academic/Scholarly.* **Description:** Offers to the Church a serious theological reflection on Mary the Mother of God.
Indexed: CPL, MLA.
Published by: Pontificia Facolta Teologica Marianum, Viale Trenta Aprile 6, Rome, 00153, Italy. TEL 39-06-58391601, FAX 39-06-5880292, marianum@marianum.it, http://www.marianum.it.

282 NLD ISSN 1878-8734
MARIENBURG. Text in Dutch. 1984. q. EUR 20 (effective 2011). **Document type:** *Magazine, Consumer.*
Former titles (until 2009): M V-nu (1572-7564); (until 2003): Vereniging Marienburg. Nieuwsbrief (0169-8648); (until 1985): Marienburg-Groep. Nieuwsbrief (0926-096X)
Published by: Secretariaat Marienburgvereniging, Postbus 675, Amersfoort, 3800 AR, Netherlands. TEL 31-33-4690070, secretariaat@marienburgvereniging.nl, http://www.marienburgvereniging.nl. Ed. Lambert van Gelder.

282 DEU ISSN 1862-7013
MARIOLOGISCHES JAHRBUCH. Text in German. 1997. a. free (effective 2011). **Document type:** *Journal, Academic/Scholarly.*
Media: Online - full text.
Published by: Internationaler Mariologischer Arbeitskreis Kevelaer (I M A K), Maasstrasse 2, Kevelaer, 47623, Germany. TEL 49-2832-799900, FAX 49-2832-978202, mail@imak-kevelaer.de, http://www.imak-kevelaer.de.

241 301 USA ISSN 1530-5430
BV4012.2
MARRIAGE & FAMILY: A CHRISTIAN JOURNAL. Text in English. 1997. q. USD 24.95 domestic; USD 31.19 foreign (effective 2005). bk.rev. Index. back issues avail. **Document type:** *Journal, Consumer.*
Indexed: ChrPI, FamI, P03, PsycholAb, R&TA.
Published by: American Association of Christian Counselors, PO Box 739, Forest, VA 24551. TEL 800-526-8673, FAX 434-525-9480, http://www.aacc.net. Ed. Gary J Oliver. R&P Tim Clinton. Circ: 12,589.

255.53 CAN
MARTYRS' SHRINE MESSAGE. Text in English. 1937. s-a. CAD 10. back issues avail. **Description:** Promotes devotion to the North American Jesuit Martyrs and pilgrimages to their Canadian national shrine.
Published by: Jesuit Fathers of Upper Canada, 69 Marmaduke St, Toronto, ON M6R 1T3, Canada. TEL 416-763-4664, FAX 416-921-1864, 74163.2472@compuserve.com. Circ: 15,000.

266.2 USA ISSN 0025-4142
BV2300
MARYKNOLL MAGAZINE. Text in English. 1907. 10/yr. USD 15 (effective 2009). illus. index. 60 p./no.; back issues avail. **Document type:** *Magazine, Consumer.* **Description:** Covers mission work in underdeveloped countries.
Former titles (until 1939): Field Afar (0271-7204)
Related titles: Microform ed.: (from PQC); ◆ Spanish ed.: Revista Maryknoll. ISSN 0274-9092; ◆ Supplement(s): Maryknoll Study Guide.
Indexed: CERDIC, CPL.
—Ingenta.

Published by: Maryknoll Fathers and Brothers, PO Box 304, Maryknoll, NY 10545. mkweb@maryknoll.org, https://www.maryknollsociety.org/i.

266.2 371.33 USA
MARYKNOLL STUDY GUIDE. Text in English. 1999. m. free. illus. back issues avail. **Document type:** *Magazine, Consumer.* **Description:** Offers teachers information on teaching about cultural, religious, spiritual, and social justice issues facing peoples around the world.
Media: Online - full content. **Related titles:** ◆ Supplement to: Maryknoll Magazine. ISSN 0025-4142.
Published by: Maryknoll Missioners, PO Box 307, Maryknoll, NY 10545-0307. TEL 914-762-6364, 800-818-5276, FAX 914-762-7031, mmaf@mmkl-mmaf.org, http://www.maryknoll.org/MARYKNOLL/MMAF/welcom_mf.htm.

282 DEU ISSN 0934-8522
MATERIALDIENST DES KONFESSIONSKUNDLICHEN INSTITUTS. Text in German. 1950. bi-m. EUR 18; EUR 9 to students; EUR 3 newsstand/cover (effective 2009). bk.rev. **Document type:** *Journal, Academic/Scholarly.* **Description:** Ecumenical issues as they relate to the Roman Catholic Church.
Formerly (until 1970): Evangelischer Bund. Konfessionskundliches Institut. Materialdienst (0580-5554)
Indexed: DIP, FR, IBR, IBZ.
—INIST.
Published by: Evangelischer Bund, Konfessionskundliches Institut, Postfach 1255, Bensheim, 64602, Germany. TEL 49-6251-843311, FAX 49-6251-843328, webmaster@ki-eb.de.

268 POL ISSN 1426-2673
MATERIALY HOMILETYCZNE. Text in Polish. 1974. bi-m. PLZ 133 domestic; EUR 103 foreign (effective 2006). adv. **Document type:** *Journal, Academic/Scholarly.* **Description:** Aims to help priests with sermons and catecheses.
Published by: Wydawnictwo Sw. Stanislawa BM Archidiecezji Krakowskiej, ul Straszewskiego 2, Krakow, 31101, Poland. TEL 48-12-4295217, FAX 48-12-4214970, wydawnictwo@stanislawbm.pl. **Dist. by:** Ars Polona, Obroncow 25, Warsaw 03933, Poland. TEL 48-22-5098609, FAX 48-22-5098610, arspolona@arspolona.com.pl, http://www.arspolona.com.pl.

282 POL ISSN 0076-5244
MATERIALY ZRODLOWE DO DZIEJOW KOSCIOLA W POLSCE. Text in Polish. 1965. irreg. price varies.
Published by: Katolicki Uniwersytet Lubelski, Towarzystwo Naukowe, ul Gliniana 21, Lublin, 20616, Poland. Ed. Jerzy Kloczowski. Circ: 1,000. **Dist. by:** Ars Polona, Obroncow 25, Warsaw 03933, Poland. **Co-sponsor:** Instytut Geografii Historycznej Kosciola w Polsce przy K.U.L.

282 SVN
MAVRICA/RAINBOW. Text in Slovenian. m. EUR 24.62 (effective 2007). **Document type:** *Magazine, Consumer.*
Published by: Druzina, Krekov trg 1, p.p. 95, Ljubljana, 1001, Slovenia. TEL 386-1-3602845, FAX 386-1-3602800. Ed. Melita Kosir. Circ: 50,000.

282 NLD
➤ **MEANDER (KAMPEN).** Text in Dutch. 1993. irreg., latest vol.11, 2008. price varies. back issues avail. **Document type:** *Monographic series, Academic/Scholarly.* **Description:** Features studies on all contemporary aspects of the Catholic liturgy: historical, theological, and pastoral.
Supersedes (in 1993): Liturgie in Perspectief
Published by: (Universiteit van Tilburg, Liturgisch Instituut/Tilburg University, Liturgical Institute), Uitgeverij Abdij van Berne, Postbus 60, Heeswijk, 5473 ZH, Netherlands. TEL 31-413-299299, FAX 31-413-299288, info@abdijvanberne.nl, http://www.uitgeverijberne.nl.

282.8 COL ISSN 0121-4977
BX1751.2
MEDELLIN; teologia y pastoral para America Latina. Text in Spanish. 1975. q. COP 35,000; COP 50 in Latin America; COP 60 in Africa; COP 70 in Europe. bk.rev.; film rev. back issues avail. **Document type:** *Monographic series.*
Indexed: CPL, OTA.
Published by: Consejo Episcopal Latinoamericano, Instituto Teologico Pastoral, Transversal 67 No. 173-71, Apartado Aereo 253353, Bogota, DE, Colombia. TEL 57-1-6776521, FAX 57-1-6714004, TELEX 41388 CELA CO. Ed. P Tony Mifsud S J. R&P P Tony Mifsud. Circ: 2,000.

266.2 USA
MEDICAL MISSION NEWS. Text in English. 1931. q. free. **Description:** Distribution of medicines to 6,000 mission units in 60 countries, placement of healthcare professionals and para-professionals in clinical facilities the world over, and indigenous training.
Incorporates (1962-1992): Professional Placement Newsnotes
Published by: Catholic Medical Mission Board, Inc., 10 W 17th St, New York, NY 10011. TEL 212-242-7757, FAX 212-807-9161. Ed. Shirley Stephenson. Circ: 55,000.

230.2 NLD ISSN 1572-6991
THE MEDIEVAL FRANCISCANS. Text in English. 2004. a. price varies. **Document type:** *Yearbook, Academic/Scholarly.*
Indexed: IZBG.
Published by: Brill, PO Box 9000, Leiden, 2300 PA, Netherlands. TEL 31-71-5353500, FAX 31-71-5317532, cs@brill.nl, http://www.brill.nl. Ed. Steven J McMichael.

230.2 FRA ISSN 0025-8911
BR3
➤ **MELANGES DE SCIENCE RELIGIEUSE.** Text in French; Abstracts in English, French. 1944. q. adv. bk.rev. cum.index: vols.1-27, 1944-1970. back issues avail.; reprints avail. **Document type:** *Journal, Academic/Scholarly.* **Description:** Covers theology, philosophy, the histories of religions, institutions, law, anthropology, sociology, pedagogy, literature and art.
Indexed: A21, CERDIC, CPL, DIP, FR, IBR, IBZ, IPB, IZBG, MLA, MLA-IB, OTA, PCI, R&TA, RASB, RI-1, RI-2.
—INIST.
Published by: Institut Catholique de Lille, 60 bd. Vauban, BP 109, Lille, Cedex 59016, France. TEL 33-3-20134089, FAX 33-3-20134090, martine.golon@fupl.asso.fr. Ed. Philippe Henne. R&P, Adv. contact Martine Golon. Circ: 500 (controlled).

230.2 CHL ISSN 0716-0062
MENSAJE. Text in Spanish. 1951. m. (10/yr.). CLP 24,000 domestic; USD 85 in the Americas; USD 110 elsewhere (effective 2003). adv. bk.rev.; film rev.; play rev. bibl.; illus.; stat. cum.index. **Document type:** *Magazine, Consumer.* **Description:** Church review that deals with theological, social, cultural, economic and political issues of Chile and South America.
Related titles: Online - full text ed.
Indexed: C01, H21, HRIR, I04, I05, P08, RILM.
Published by: (Compania de Jesus, Provincia Chilena), Residencia San Roberto Bellarmino, Casilla 10445, Almirante Barroso, 24, Santiago, Chile. TEL 56-2-6960653, FAX 56-2-6717030. Ed. Antonio Delfau S. Pub. Ernesto Espindola. R&P Antonio Delfau S. Adv. contact Paola Barrera TEL 56-2-6980617. B&W page CLP 210,000, color page CLP 380,000; 152 x 211. Circ: 6,000.

282.772 USA
THE MESSAGE (EVANSVILLE). Text in English. 1970. w. (Fri.). USD 23 (effective 2005). adv. **Document type:** *Newspaper, Consumer.*
Published by: (Diocese of Evansville), Catholic Press of Evansville, 4200 N Kentucky Ave, Box 4169, Evansville, IN 47724-0169. TEL 812-424-5536, FAX 812-424-0972. Ed. Paul R Leingang. Pub. Rev. Gerald A Gettelfinger. adv.: col. inch USD 8. Circ: 7,000 (paid). Wire service: CaNS.

282 FRA ISSN 0026-0290
MESSAGES DU SECOURS CATHOLIQUE. Text in French. 1945. 11/yr. free to members. adv. bk.rev. charts; illus.; stat. **Document type:** *Newspaper, Consumer.*
Published by: Secours Catholique, 106 Rue du Bac, Paris, 75007, France. TEL 33-1-45497300, info@secours-catholique.org. Circ: 700,000.

282 ITA ISSN 1972-8239
MESSAGGERO CAPPUCCINO. Abbreviated title: M C. Text in Italian. 1957. bi-m. EUR 24 domestic; EUR 40 foreign (effective 2009). bk.rev. back issues avail.
Published by: Missioni Cappuccini Emilia-Romagna, Via Villa Clelia 16, Imola, BO 40026, Italy.

MESSAGGERO DEI RAGAZZI. see CHILDREN AND YOUTH—For

282 ITA ISSN 0026-0312
MESSAGGERO DI SANT' ANTONIO. Text in Italian. 1898. m. EUR 18 domestic (effective 2008). adv. bk.rev.; film rev. back issues avail. **Document type:** *Magazine, Consumer.*
Formerly (until 19??): Il Messaggero di Sant' Antonio di Padova (2035-441X)
Related titles: English ed.: Messenger of Saint Anthony. EUR 16 (effective 2002); French ed.: Le Messeger de Saint Antoine. EUR 26 (effective 2002); German ed.: Sendbote des Hl. Antonius. EUR 23 (effective 2002); Spanish ed.: Mensajero de San Antonio. EUR 20 (effective 2002); Portuguese ed.; Romanian ed.; Polish ed.: Postaniec Sw. Antoniego.
Published by: (Frati Minori Conventuali della Provincia Padovana/Ordo Fratrum Minorum Conventualium), Messaggero di Sant' Antonio Editrice, Via Orto Botanico 11, Padua, PD 35123, Italy. TEL 39-049-8225777, FAX 39-049-8225650, info@santantonio.org, http://www.edizionimessaggero.it. Circ: 1,000,000.

282 ITA
MESSAGGI CARISMATICI CATTOLICI. Text in Italian. 1999. m. **Document type:** *Newspaper, Consumer.* **Description:** Devoted to the messages and revelations received by charismatic Christian individuals.
Published by: Edizioni Segno SRL, Via E. Fermi 80, Tavagnacco (UD), 33010, Italy. TEL 39-04-32575179, FAX 39-04-32575589, info@edizionisegno.it, http://www.edizionisegno.it.

282 ITA ISSN 0036-116X
IL MESSAGGIO DELLA SANTA CASA; mensuale del Santuario di Loreto. Text in Italian. 1881. m. EUR 18 domestic; EUR 20 foreign (effective 2009). bk.rev. illus. **Document type:** *Magazine, Consumer.*
Related titles: English ed.: Shrine of the Holy House. Loreto. GBP 6 in United Kingdom; USD 10 in United States.
Published by: Congregazione Universale della Santa Casa, Loreto (Ancona), 60025, Italy. TEL 39-071-970104, FAX 39-071-976837, santuarioloreto@tin.it. Circ: 36,000.

282 USA ISSN 0279-3911
THE MESSENGER (BELLEVILLE). Text in English. 1907. w. (36/yr.). USD 19 (effective 1997). adv. bk.rev.; film rev. **Document type:** *Newspaper.*
Related titles: Microfilm ed.
Published by: Roman Catholic Diocese of Belleville, Chancery Office, 222 S Third St, Belleville, IL 62220. TEL 618-235-9601, FAX 618-235-7416. Ed. Raphael H Middeke. Circ: 15,000. **Subscr. to:** 2620 Lebanon Ave, Belleville, IL 62221.

230.07 USA
MESSENGER (COVINGTON); serving the Diocese of Covington. Text in English. 193?. w. (44/yr.). USD 19; USD 40 foreign. adv. bk.rev. 16 p./no. 4 cols./p.; **Document type:** *Newspaper.* **Description:** Discusses news topics and religious, philosophical, and moral issues of concern to the community.
Published by: Roman Catholic Diocese of Covington, PO Box 15550, Covington, KY 41015. TEL 859-392-1500. Ed. Tim Fitsgerald. Pub. Bishop Robert W Foys. Adv. contact Bob Schuck. Circ: 28,000 (paid).

282 HRV ISSN 1331-8837
MI. Text in Croatian. 1977. m. **Document type:** *Newspaper, Consumer.*
Published by: Hrvatski Katolicki Zbor Mi, Ilica 29, Zagreb, 10000, Croatia. TEL 385-1-428844, FAX 385-1-424338. Ed. Vladimir Loncarevic.

282 CAN ISSN 0317-8498
MICHAEL; for the triumph of the Immaculate. Text in English. 1955. bi-m. CAD 10 (effective 1999). **Document type:** *Newspaper.* **Description:** Promotes the application of the teachings of the Roman Catholic Church in every aspect of social life, especially in economics with the social credit philosophy of Scottish engineer, Clifford Hugh Douglas.
Published by: Louis Even Institute, 1101 Principale St, Rougemont, PQ J0L 1M0, Canada. TEL 514-469-2209, FAX 514-469-2601. Ed. Gilberte Cote Mercier. Circ: 35,000.

282.774 USA
MICHIGAN CATHOLIC. Text in English. 1872. w. (Fri.). USD 24 (effective 2008). **Document type:** *Newspaper, Consumer.*
Published by: (Archdiocese of Detroit), Michigan Catholic, 305 Michigan Ave, Detroit, MI 48226. TEL 313-224-8000, FAX 313-224-8009, infodesk@aod.org, http://www.aodonline.org. Circ: 30,000 (paid). Wire service: CaNS.

282.09 GBR
➤ **MIDLAND CATHOLIC HISTORY.** Text in English. 1963. a. GBP 5 (effective 2002). bibl. **Document type:** *Journal, Academic/Scholarly.*
Formerly: Worcestershire Recusant
Published by: Midland Catholic History Society, c/o Vincent Burke, 16 Brandhall Ct, Wolverhampton Rd, Warley, W Mids B68 8DE, United Kingdom. Eds. Michael Greenslade, Michael Hodgetts. Circ: 150.

255.9 ITA ISSN 1123-9441
MILES IMMACULATAE; rivista di cultura mariana e di formazione kolbiana. Summaries in English, French; Text in Italian. 1965. s-a. bk.rev. abstr.; bibl. index. back issues avail. **Document type:** *Magazine, Consumer.* **Description:** Contains theological studies on Mariology and Kolbian spirituality.
Related titles: E-mail ed.; Fax ed.
Published by: Centro Internazionale Milizia dell'Immacolata, Via di San Teodoro 42, Rome, 00186, Italy. TEL 39-06-679382, FAX 39-06-69941017, MIinternational@ofmconv.org, http://www.mi-international.org. Circ: 2,000.

230.2 IRL ISSN 0332-1428
BR1
➤ **MILLTOWN STUDIES.** Text in English. 1977. s-a. EUR 20 in Ireland & UK; EUR 25 in the European Union; USD 30 elsewhere (effective 2011). bk.rev. illus. **Document type:** *Journal, Academic/Scholarly.* **Description:** Studies various aspects of Catholicism in the areas of theology, philosophy, ministry, and spirituality.
Indexed: DIP, IBR, IBZ, IPB, OTA.
—BLDSC (5774.350000).
Published by: Milltown Institute of Theology & Philosophy, Milltown Park, Dublin, 6, Ireland. TEL 353-1-2698388, FAX 353-1-2692528, info@milltown-institute.ie. Ed. Joe Egan. Circ: 200.

282 DEU
MINI (EICHSTAETT); Taschenkalender fuer Ministrantinnen, Ministranten und junge Christen. Text in German. 1949. a. EUR 4.60 per issue (effective 2005). bk.rev. back issues avail. **Document type:** *Bulletin, Consumer.*
Published by: Franz Sales Verlag, Rosental 1, Eichstaett, 85072, Germany. TEL 49-8421-9348931, FAX 49-8421-9348935, info@franz-sales-verlag.de, http://www.franz-sales-verlag.de. Pub. Herbert Winklehner. Circ: 50,000.

282 DEU ISSN 0947-9449
MINIBOERSE. Text in German. 1960. q. EUR 16.35 (effective 2010). adv. bk.rev. back issues avail. **Document type:** *Newsletter, Consumer.* **Description:** Articles and information for those responsible for altar servants and youth choir members.
Formerly (until 1995): Im Heiligen Dienst (0938-3190)
Published by: Verlag Haus Altenberg, Postfach 320520, Duesseldorf, 40420, Germany. TEL 49-211-4693160, FAX 49-211-469372, verkauf-verlag@jugendhaus-duesseldorf.de, http://www.jugendhaus-duesseldorf.de. Circ: 3,000.

282 028.5 SVN ISSN 0353-0485
MINISTRANT. Text in Slovenian. 1981. 5/school-academic yr. **Document type:** *Magazine, Consumer.* **Description:** Provides information about the Church in Slovenia, ministry groups, education and liturgy.
Published by: Salve d.o.o., Rakovniska 6, Ljubljana, 1001, Slovenia. TEL 386-1-4277310, FAX 386-1-4273040, info@salve.si, http://www.salve.si. Eds. Branko Balazic, Marko Suhoversnik. Circ: 6,500.

255.71 ESP ISSN 0214-3879
MIRIAM; revista mariana universal. Text in Spanish. 1949. bi-m. bk.rev. bibl.; illus. index. **Document type:** *Magazine, Consumer.*
Published by: Padres Carmelitas Descalzos, Triana, 9, Madrid, 28016, Spain. Circ: 5,500.

255 CHE
MIRJAM; Monatszeitschrift der weltoffenen Frau. Text in German. 1934. m. CHF 36. adv. bk.rev.; film rev.; play rev. illus. index.
Formerly: Ancilla (0003-2867)
Published by: (Arbeitsstelle Bildungsdienst), Verlag U. Cavelti AG, Gossau Sg, 9202, Switzerland. TEL 01-2521011, FAX 01-2611354. Ed. Annelies Schuepp. Circ: 16,000.

282.08691 DEU ISSN 0252-2535
MIRROR; aid to the Church in Need. Text in English. 1959. 8/yr. free to benefactors. illus. back issues avail. **Document type:** *Newsletter, Consumer.* **Description:** News about the church and persecuted refugees in Eastern Europe and the Third World.
Related titles: Online - full text ed.; ◆ German ed.: Echo der Liebe. ISSN 0252-2527; French ed.: Aide a l'Eglise en Detresse. Bulletin. ISSN 0252-2519; Italian ed.: L' Eco dell'Amore. ISSN 0252-2551; Portuguese ed.: Ajuda a Igreja Que Sofre. Boletim. ISSN 0873-3317; Dutch ed.: Echo der Liefde. ISSN 0252-2543; Spanish ed.: Ayuda a la Iglesia Necesitada. Boletin. ISSN 0252-256X.
Published by: Kirche in Not - Ostpriesterhilfe e.V., Bischof-Kindermann-Str 23, Koenigstein im Taunus, 61462, Germany. TEL 49-6174-2910, FAX 49-6174-3423, info@acn-intl.org, http://www.acn-intl.org. Eds. Claude Piel, Juergen Liminski.

282 USA
THE MIRROR (SPRINGFIELD). Text in English. 1965. w. (Fri., Sep.-May; bi-w.: June-Aug.). USD 14 (effective 2008). **Document type:** *Newspaper, Consumer.*
Published by: Diocese of Springfield - Cape Girardeau, 601 S Jefferson Ave, Springfield, MO 65806. TEL 417-866-0841, FAX 417-866-1140. Ed. Leslie Eidson. Pub. James Vann Johnston Jr. Adv. contact Angie Toben. Circ: 17,400 (controlled and free). Wire service: CaNS.

282 ESP ISSN 0213-0742
BX1977.S7
MISCEL.LANIA LITURGICA CATALANA. Text in Multiple languages. 1978. irreg. EUR 10 (effective 2009). **Document type:** *Journal, Academic/Scholarly.*
Related titles: Online - full text ed.: ISSN 2013-4010. 1978.
Published by: Institut d'Estudis Catalans, Carrer del Carme 47, Barcelona, 08001, Spain. TEL 34-932-701620, FAX 34-932-701180, informacio@iecat.net, http://www2.iecat.net.

R

271.3 ITA ISSN 0026-587X
MISCELLANEA FRANCESCANA; rivista trimestrale di scienze teologiche e di studi francescani. Text in English, French, Italian, Latin. 1886. q. USD 45. bk.rev. illus. index. **Document type:** *Journal, Academic/Scholarly.*
Formerly (until 1935): Miscellanea Francescana di Storia, di Lettere, di Arti (1124-6812)
Indexed: A01, B24, CA, FR, IPB, MLA, MLA-IB, T02.
—INIST.
Published by: Pontificia Facolta Teologica S. Bonaventura, Via del Serafico 1, Rome, 00142, Italy. TEL 39-06-5192007, FAX 39-06-5192067, seraphicum1@ofmconv.org, http://www.bon.ofmconv.org.

262.13 ITA ISSN 0080-3979
MISCELLANEA HISTORIAE PONTIFICIAE. Text in English, French, German, Italian, Spanish. 1939. irreg., latest vol.64, 1997. price varies. **Document type:** *Monographic series, Academic/Scholarly.* **Description:** Contains research studies on themes of the history of the Papacy.
Published by: (Pontificia Universita Gregoriana/Pontifical Gregorian University, Pontificia Universita Gregoriana, Facolta di Storia Ecclesiastica), Gregorian University Press/Editrice Pontificia Universita Gregoriana, Piazza della Pilotta 35, Rome, 00187, Italy. TEL 39-06-6781567, FAX 39-06-6780588, periodicals@biblicum.com, http://www.paxbook.com.

282 AUS ISSN 1443-8364
MISLI/THOUGHTS; religious and cultural monthly in Slovenian language. Text in Slovenian. 1952. m. bk.rev. back issues avail. **Document type:** *Newspaper.* **Description:** Provides information on Slovenian cultural and religious life in Australia.
Published by: Franciscan Fathers, Slovenian Mission, Baraga House, 19 A Beckett St, Kew, VIC 3101, Australia.

266.2 PRT ISSN 1647-9203
MISSAOMP. (Obras Missionarias Pontificias) Text in Portuguese. 1950. q. **Document type:** *Report, Academic/Scholarly.*
Formerly (until 2002): Obras Missionarias Pontificias. Anais (0874-7989)
Published by: Obras Missionarias Pontificias, Rua Ilha do Principe 19, Lisbon, 1170-182, Portugal. TEL 351-21-8148428, FAX 351-21-8139611, missio.omp@netcabp.pt, http://www.opf.pt.

266.2 DEU ISSN 0945-3407
MISSIO AKTUELL. Text in German. 1969. bi-m. EUR 10 membership (effective 2008). bk.rev. **Document type:** *Magazine, Consumer.*
Former titles (until 1991): Mission Aktuell (0945-3385); Which was formed by the merger of (1933-1969): Weltmission (Aachen) (0945-3369); (1962-1969): C R - Illustrierte (0945-3342); Which was formerly (1960-1962): C R - Presse-Bild (0945-3334); (19??-1960): Christi Reich in der Weltmission (0945-330X); (1964-1969): Weltmission (Muenchen) (0945-3350); Which was formerly (1948-1964): Weltmission der Katholischen Kirche (0945-3970)
—CCC.
Published by: Missio Internationales Katholisches Missionswerk e.V., Goethestr 43, Aachen, 52064, Germany. TEL 49-241-750700, FAX 49-241-7507237, info@missio-aachen.de. Ed. Franz Jussen. Circ: 500,000.

266.2 CAN ISSN 1920-9126
MISSIO DEI; a new kind of journal. Text in English. 2008. m. free (effective 2010). back issues avail. **Document type:** *Journal, Academic/Scholarly.* **Description:** Emphasizes for the whole spectrum of Christian leaders in the Greater Toronto Area and beyond.
Media: Online - full text.
Published by: Tyndale University College & Seminary, 25 Ballyconnor Ct, Toronto, ON M2M 4B3, Canada. TEL 416-226-6380, FAX 416-226-6746, info@tyndale.ca. Ed. Ian W Scott.

266.2 GBR ISSN 0962-8142
MISSION OUTLOOK. Text in English. 1950. q. GBP 10 domestic; GBP 14 foreign (effective 2009). **Document type:** *Bulletin.* **Description:** Aims to keep a diverse readership up to date with today's thoughts, developments and challenges regarding the Mission of the Church on a world scale.
Formerly (until 1990): Outlook (0030-7211)
Published by: Pontifical Mission Societies, 23 Eccleston Sq, London, SW1V 1NU, United Kingdom. TEL 44-20-78219755, FAX 44-20-76308466, director@missio.org.uk. Ed. John Dale.

266.2 GBR ISSN 0967-8379
MISSION TODAY. Text in English. 1937. q. free to members (effective 2009). bk.rev. back issues avail. **Document type:** *Magazine, Consumer.* **Description:** Contains articles by lay people, religious sisters and priests about the missions, prayer, the Bible and topical issues from a Catholic perspective.
Former titles (until 1991): Missions, Missionaries and Young Churches; (until 1989): Missions and Missionaries
Related titles: Online - full text ed.: free (effective 2009).
Published by: Association for the Propagation of the Faith, 23 Eccleston Sq, London, SW1V 1NU, United Kingdom. TEL 44-20-78219755, FAX 44-20-76308466, apf@missio.org.uk, http://www.pontificalmissionsocieties.co.uk/apf/index.php. Ed. John Dale. Circ: 203,000.

266.2 USA ISSN 1542-6130
MISSION UPDATE. Text in English. 1971. q. USD 40 membership (effective 2005). bk.rev. 8 p./no.; **Document type:** *Newsletter, Trade.* **Description:** Mission Animation & Education.
Formerly: Mission Intercom
Related titles: Online - full content ed.
Published by: United States Catholic Mission Association, 3029 Fourth St, N E, Washington, DC 20017. TEL 202-832-3112, FAX 202-832-3688, uscma@uscatholicmission.org. Ed. Kevin F Day. Circ: 1,500.

266.2 ITA
MISSIONARI DEL P I M E. Text in Italian. 1914. m. (11/yr.). adv. bk.rev. **Document type:** *Newsletter, Consumer.*
Formerly (until 1959): Propaganda Missionaria
Published by: Pontificio Istituto Missioni Estere, Via F D Guerrazzi, Rome, 00152, Italy. TEL 39-2-438220, FAX 39-2-4695193. Ed. Gian Paolo Gualzetti. Circ: 50,000.

266.2 AUS ISSN 1444-4178
MISSIONARIES OF THE SACRED HEART. ANNALS AUSTRALASIA; journal of Catholic culture. Text in English. 1889. bi-m. adv. bk.rev.; film rev.; video rev. bibl.; illus.; stat. 44 p./no.; back issues avail. **Document type:** *Journal, Academic/Scholarly.*
Former titles (until 1999): Missionaries of the Sacred Heart. Annals Australia (0812-9355); (until 1981): Missionaries of the Sacred Heart. Annals (0812-9363); (until 1967): The Annals of Our Lady of the Sacred Heart (0812-9371); (until 1925): The Australian Annals of Our Lady of the Sacred Heart
Indexed: Gdlns.
Published by: (Missionaries of the Sacred Heart), Chevalier Press, 1 Roma Ave, PO Box 13, Kensington, NSW 2031, Australia. TEL 61-2-96627894, FAX 61-2-96621910. Ed., R&P, Adv. contact Paul Stenhouse. Circ: 14,000.

282 ITA ISSN 2035-4436
IL MISSIONARIO FRANCESCANO. Text in Italian. 1933. m. EUR 12 (effective 2010). **Document type:** *Magazine, Consumer.*
Published by: Centro Nazionale Missionario Francescano, Santuario Santa Maria delle Grazie, Piazza Santa Maria 1, Zagarolo, RM 00039, Italy.

266.2 USA ISSN 0026-6086
BV1230
MISSIONHURST. Text in English. 1948. 6/yr. free to qualified personnel. illus. **Document type:** *Proceedings, Consumer.*
Published by: (Congregation of the Immaculate Heart of Mary), Missionhurst, Inc., 4651 N 25th St, Arlington, VA 22207-3500. TEL 703-528-3800, FAX 703-522-7864. Ed. Fr. Bill Wyndaele. Circ: 80,000 (controlled).

266.2 FRA ISSN 1957-3928
MISSIONNAIRES SERVITEURS DES PAUVRES DU TIERS-MONDE. Text in French. 2007. 3/yr.
Published by: Aide aux Serviteurs des Pauvres du Tiers-Monde, Abbaye Notre-Dame, Fontgombault, 36220, France. TEL 33-2-54371256, serviteursfr@hotmail.com, http://www.sptm.hu/fr_index.html.

255.3 CAN ISSN 0700-4192
MISSIONS DES FRANCISCAINS. Text in French. 1923. q. USD 10.
Published by: Syndics Apostoliques des Freres Mineurs (Franciscains), 2000 Rene Levesque Ouest, Montreal, PQ H3H 1R6, Canada. TEL 514-932-6094, FAX 514-932-4134. Ed. George L Morin. Circ: 6,000.

266.2 DEU ISSN 0179-0102
MISSIONSBLAETTER. Text in German. 1888. q. free (effective 2009). bk.rev. back issues avail. **Document type:** *Bulletin, Consumer.*
Indexed: IBR, IBZ.
Published by: Erzabtei St. Ottilien, St Ottilien, 86941, Germany. TEL 49-8193-710, FAX 49-8193-71332, presse@erzabtei.de, http://www.erzabtei.de. Ed. Martin Wild. Circ: 15,000.

266.2 DEU
MISSIONSKALENDER - JAHRBUCH ST. OTTILIEN. Text in German. 1888. a. back issues avail. **Document type:** *Bulletin, Consumer.*
Formerly: Missionskalender
Published by: Erzabtei St. Ottilien, St Ottilien, 86941, Germany. TEL 49-8193-710, FAX 49-8193-71332, presse@erzabtei.de, http://www.erzabtei.de. Ed., R&P Cyrill Schaefer.

282 DEU ISSN 1618-9264
MISSIONSZENTRALE DER FRANZISKANER. BERICHTE, DOKUMENTE, KOMMENTARE. Text in German. 1979. q. **Document type:** *Journal, Trade.*
Published by: Missionszentrale der Franziskaner, Albertus-Magnus-Str 39, Bonn, 53177, Germany. TEL 49-228-953540, FAX 49-228-9535440, info@missionszentrale.de. Ed. Norbert Arntz. Circ: 26,000 (controlled).

266.2 POL ISSN 0209-1348
MISYJNE DROGI. Text in Polish. 1983. bi-m. PLZ 20. back issues avail. **Description:** Presents missionary activities around the world.
Published by: Misjonarze Oblaci Maryi Niepokalanej, Ul Ostatnia 14, Poznan, 60102, Poland. TEL 48-61-306517, FAX 48-61-305513. Ed. Fr Alfons Kupka. Circ: 30,000 (paid).

282 SVN ISSN 1408-0672
MLADINSKA KNJIZNICA. Text in Slovenian. 1972. irreg., latest vol.30, 2010. price varies. **Document type:** *Monographic series, Academic/Scholarly.*
Published by: Salve d.o.o., Rakovniska 6, Ljubljana, 1001, Slovenia. TEL 386-1-4277310, FAX 386-1-4273040, info@salve.si, http://www.salve.si.

230.2 USA
MODERN SPIRITUAL MASTERS. Text in English. 1999. irreg. price varies. back issues avail. **Document type:** *Monographic series, Academic/Scholarly.* **Description:** Contains writing and vision of the spiritual masters of the twentieth century.
Published by: Orbis Books (Subsidiary of: Maryknoll Fathers and Brothers), Dept WEB, PO Box 302, Maryknoll, NY 10545. TEL 800-258-5838, FAX 914-941-7005, orbisbooks@maryknoll.org. Ed. Robert N Ellsberg.

282 LSO
MOELETSI OA BASOTHO/COUNSELLOR OF BASOTHO. 1933. w. adv. 10 p./no. 5 cols./p.; **Document type:** *Newspaper.* **Description:** Roman Catholic oriented publication.
Published by: Mazenod Institute, PO Box 18, Mazenod, Lesotho. TEL 266-350465, 266-350224, FAX 266-350010, TELEX 4271, mzprws@lesoff.co.za. Ed. Fr. F. S. Shopane. Adv. contact Mrs. Celina Rasephei. B&W page LSL 1,100. Circ: 7,000.

282 SVN ISSN 1318-5462
MOHORJEV KOLEDAR. Text in Slovenian. 1961. a. EUR 16 (effective 2010). **Document type:** *Magazine, Consumer.*
Published by: Mohorjeva Druzba, Presernova c 23, pp 150, Celje, 3001, Slovenia. TEL 386-3-4264800, FAX 386-3-4264810, info@mohorjeva-druzba-ce.si, http://www.mohorjeva.org.

282 USA
EL MOMENTO CATOLICO. Text in Spanish, English. 19??. irreg. price varies based on number of issues. **Document type:** *Monographic series, Trade.* **Description:** Discusses a topic of faith and society and challenges the reader with questions and reflection about the role of Catholicism in the Hispanic community.
Published by: Claretian Publications, 205 W Monroe, Chicago, IL 60606. TEL 312-236-7782, FAX 312-236-8207, stjudeleague@claretians.org.

MOMENTUM (WASHINGTON). *see* EDUCATION

MONASTIC ORDERS. *see* HISTORY—History Of Europe

255.1 945 ITA
MONASTICON ITALIAE; repertorio topo-bibliografio dei monasteri italiani. Text in Italian. irreg., latest vol.3, 1986. price varies. **Document type:** *Monographic series, Academic/Scholarly.* **Description:** Dedicated to the Benedictine monasteries according to their geographical order. Provides an historical explanation for each monastery, with an indication of the manuscript and printed sources.
Published by: Centro Storico Benedettino Italiano, Badia S. Maria del Monte, Cesena, FC 47023, Italy. TEL 39-0547-302161, http://www.abbaziadelmonte.it.

282 FRA ISSN 1763-3346
LE MONDE DES RELIGIONS. Text in French. 1953. bi-m. EUR 29 (effective 2010). adv. bk.rev.; film rev. bibl.; illus. index. **Document type:** *Journal, Academic/Scholarly.* **Description:** Examines the religious aspects of world events.
Former titles (until 2003): Actualite des Religions (1265-6240); Actualite Religieuse; Actualites Religieuse dans le Monde (0757-3529); (until 1983): Informations Catholiques Internationales (0020-0441); (until 1955): Actualite Religieuse dans le Monde (0400-4620)
Indexed: FR, IBSS, PAIS, PdeR, RASB.
—CCC.
Published by: Malesherbes Publications, 8 Rue Jean-Antoine de Baif, Paris, Cedex 13 75012, France. TEL 33-1-48885105, FAX 33-1-42270419. Circ: 30,000.

220 ITA ISSN 1120-7353
IL MONDO DELLA BIBBIA. Text in Italian. 1990. 5/yr. EUR 33 domestic; EUR 43 foreign (effective 2009). **Document type:** *Magazine, Consumer.*
Published by: Editrice Elledici, Corso Francia 214, Cascine Vica - Rivoli, TO 10098, Italy. TEL 39-011-9552111, FAX 39-011-9574048, mail@elledici.org, http://www.elledici.org.

266.2 ITA ISSN 0026-6094
BV2130
MONDO E MISSIONE. Text in Italian. 1872. m. (10/yr.). EUR 32 domestic; EUR 45 foreign (effective 2009). bk.rev. illus. index. **Document type:** *Magazine, Consumer.* **Description:** Covers missionary work in third world countries.
Formerly: Missioni Cattoliche
Related titles: Online - full text ed.; ◆ Supplement(s): Asia News. ISSN 1125-3576.
Indexed: CERDIC.
Published by: Pontificio Istituto Missioni Estere, Via F D Guerrazzi, Rome, 00152, Italy. TEL 39-2-438220, FAX 39-2-4695193. Ed. P Giancarlo Politi. Circ: 30,000.

262.3 ITA
MONITORE DIOCESANO; organo ufficiale della curia vescovile. Text in Italian. 1917. 3/yr. **Document type:** *Bulletin, Consumer.*
Published by: Diocesi di Caltanisetta/Curia Vescovile, Via Cairoli 8, Caltanisetta, 93100, Italy. curia@diocesicaltanisetta.it, http://www.diocesicaltanisetta.it.

282.786 USA ISSN 0883-7899
MONTANA CATHOLIC. Text in English. 1932. 16/yr. USD 18 domestic; USD 27 foreign. adv. bk.rev. back issues avail. **Document type:** *Newspaper.* **Description:** News and feature of the Catholic Church in Western Montana.
Formerly (until 1985): Westmont Word (8750-4715)
Published by: Roman Catholic Diocese of Helena, 515 N Ewing, Box 1729, Helena, MT 59624. TEL 406-442-5820, FAX 406-442-5191. Eds. Cathy Tilzey, Eric M Schiedermayer. Pub. Msgr. Kevin S O'Neill. R&P Eric M Schiedermayer. Circ: 8,800. Wire service: CaNS.

282 ITA ISSN 0077-1449
MONUMENTA HISTORICA ORDINIS MINORUM CAPUCCINORUM. Text in Italian, Latin. 1937. irreg., latest vol.26, 1999. price varies. index.
Published by: Frati Minori Cappuccini, Istituto Storico/Ordo Fratrum Minorum Capuccinorum, Circonvallazione Occidentale 6850, Rome, RM 00163, Italy. TEL 39-06-660521, FAX 39-06-66052532, http://www.istcap.org.

271.53 ITA
MONUMENTA HISTORICA SOCIETATIS IESU. Text in Italian. irreg., latest vol.150, 1997. adv. back issues avail. **Document type:** *Monographic series, Academic/Scholarly.* **Description:** Editions of documents regarding early history of Jesuits and of Jesuit missions worldwide.
Related titles: Microfiche ed.: (from IDC).
Published by: Institutum Historicum Societatis Iesu/Jesuit Historical Institute, Via dei Penitenzieri 20, Rome, 00193, Italy. Ed., Adv. contact Thomas McCoog.

282 VAT ISSN 0077-1457
MONUMENTA IURIS CANONICI. SERIES A, CORPUS GLOSSATORIUM. Text in Multiple languages. 1969. irreg. price varies.
Related titles: ◆ Series: Monumenta Iuris Canonici. Series C, Subsidia. ISSN 0544-991X; ◆ Monumenta Iuris Canonici. Series B, Corpus Collectionum. ISSN 1012-5876.
Published by: Biblioteca Apostolica Vaticana, 00120, Vatican City. TEL 396-6-69885051, FAX 396-6-69884795.

282 VAT ISSN 1012-5876
MONUMENTA IURIS CANONICI. SERIES B, CORPUS COLLECTIONUM. Text in Multiple languages. 1973. irreg. price varies.
Related titles: ◆ Series: Monumenta Iuris Canonici. Series C, Subsidia. ISSN 0544-991X; ◆ Monumenta Iuris Canonici. Series A, Corpus Glossatorium. ISSN 0077-1457.
Published by: Biblioteca Apostolica Vaticana, 00120, Vatican City. TEL 396-6-69885051, FAX 396-6-69884795.

282 VAT ISSN 0544-991X
MONUMENTA IURIS CANONICI. SERIES C, SUBSIDIA. Text in Multiple languages. 1965. irreg. price varies.
Related titles: ◆ Series: Monumenta Iuris Canonici. Series B, Corpus Collectionum. ISSN 1012-5876; ◆ Monumenta Iuris Canonici. Series A, Corpus Glossatorium. ISSN 0077-1457.
Published by: Biblioteca Apostolica Vaticana, 00120, Vatican City. TEL 396-6-69885051, FAX 396-6-69884795.

282 ESP ISSN 0210-0851
MORALIA; revista de ciencias morales. Text in Spanish. 1963. q. EUR 32 domestic; EUR 65 in Europe; EUR 55 elsewhere (effective 2010). adv. bk.rev. back issues avail. **Document type:** *Academic/Scholarly.*

Formerly (until vol.16, 1978): Pentecostes (0479-9828)
Related titles: Online - full text ed.: ISSN 2174-0704. 200?.
Indexed: A01, CA, CERDIC, CPL, FR, IBR, IBZ, OTA, T02.
—INIST.
Published by: Instituto Superior de Ciencias Morales, Felix Boix, 13, Madrid, 28036, Spain. TEL 34-913-453600, FAX 34-913458679, moralia@iscm.edu. Ed., R&P, Adv. contact Rev. Alberto De Mingo. Circ: 1,000.

271.71 GBR ISSN 0307-5958
MOUNT CARMEL; a quarterly review of the spiritual life. Text in English. 1953. q. GBP 10 domestic; GBP 14, USD 28 foreign; GBP 2.50 per issue (effective 2009). bk.rev. **Document type:** *Bulletin, Consumer.* **Description:** Promotes personal growth in the christian experience and practice of prayer.
—BLDSC (5978.735000).
Published by: Discalced Carmelite, Carmelite Priory, Boars Hill, Oxford, OX1 5HB, United Kingdom. TEL 44-1865-735133, FAX 44-1865-739832, priory@carmelite.org.uk. Ed. James McCaffrey.

282 PRT ISSN 1647-7596
MOVIMENTO DO SANTUARIO DE FATIMA. BOLETIM. Text in Portuguese. 1986. a. **Document type:** *Bulletin, Consumer.*
Formerly (until 1994): Movimento dos Cruzados de Fatima. Boletim (0872-0509)
Published by: Movimento do Santuario de Fatima, Ap 31, Santuario de Fatima, Fatima, 2496-908, Portugal. http://www.santuario-fatima.pt.

230.2 DEU
MUENCHENER KIRCHENHISTORISCHE STUDIEN. Text in German. irreg., latest vol.11, 2006. EUR 60 per vol. (effective 2010). **Document type:** *Monographic series, Academic/Scholarly.*
Published by: W. Kohlhammer GmbH, Hessbruehlstr 69, Stuttgart, 70565, Germany. TEL 49-711-78630, FAX 49-711-78638204, kohlhammerkontakt@kohlhammer.de, http://www.kohlhammer.de.

230.2 DEU ISSN 0580-1370
MUENCHENER THEOLOGISCHE STUDIEN. HISTORISCHE ABTEILUNG. Text in German. 1951. irreg., latest vol.40, 2004. price varies. **Document type:** *Monographic series, Academic/Scholarly.*
Published by: E O S Verlag, Erzabtei St. Ottilien, St.Ottilien, 86941, Germany. TEL 49-8193-71700, FAX 49-8193-71709, mail@eos-verlag.de.

230.2 DEU ISSN 0580-1397
MUENCHENER THEOLOGISCHE STUDIEN. KANONISTISCHE ABTEILUNG. Text in German. 1951. irreg., latest vol.64, 2009. price varies. **Document type:** *Monographic series, Academic/Scholarly.*
Published by: E O S Verlag, Erzabtei St. Ottilien, St.Ottilien, 86941, Germany. TEL 49-8193-71700, FAX 49-8193-71709, mail@eos-verlag.de, http://www.eos-verlag.de.

230.2 DEU ISSN 0580-1389
MUENCHENER THEOLOGISCHE STUDIEN. SYSTEMATISCHE ABTEILUNG. Text in German. 1950. irreg., latest vol.69, 2007. price varies. **Document type:** *Monographic series, Academic/Scholarly.*
Published by: E O S Verlag, Erzabtei St. Ottilien, St.Ottilien, 86941, Germany. TEL 49-8193-71700, FAX 49-8193-71709, mail@eos-verlag.de.

230.2 DEU ISSN 0580-1400
BR4
MUENCHENER THEOLOGISCHE ZEITSCHRIFT. Text in German. 1950. q. EUR 31; EUR 8.80 newsstand/cover (effective 2010). bk.rev. back issues avail. **Document type:** *Journal, Academic/Scholarly.*
Indexed: A21, DIP, IBR, IBZ, IPB, IZBG, MLA-IB, OTA, PCI, RI-1, RI-2.
Published by: (Ludwig-Maximilians-Universitaet Muenchen, Kommunikation und Presse), E O S Verlag, Erzabtei St. Ottilien, St.Ottilien, 86941, Germany. TEL 49-8193-71700, FAX 49-8193-71709, mail@eos-verlag.de. Circ: 350 (controlled).

282 DEU
MUENCHNER KIRCHENZEITUNG. Text in German. 1901. w. EUR 5.35 per month; EUR 1.40 newsstand/cover (effective 2007). adv. **Document type:** *Newspaper, Consumer.*
Address: Herzog-Wilhelm-Str 5, Munich, 80331, Germany. TEL 49-89-23225200, FAX 49-89-23225240. Ed. Johannes Schiessl. Pub. Erich Jooss. Adv. contact Michael Brandl. B&W page EUR 2,400, color page EUR 3,525. Circ: 39,681 (paid and controlled).

282 ITA ISSN 2038-7989
MUSEUM COMBONIANUM. Text in Multiple languages. 1948. irreg. **Document type:** *Monographic series, Academic/Scholarly.*
Published by: Missionari Comboniani, Vicolo Pozzo 1, Verona, 37129, Italy. http://www.comboni.org.

MUSICA SACRA. *see* MUSIC

282 USA
MY DAILY VISITOR. Text in English. 1955. bi-m. USD 13.95 (effective 2009). **Document type:** *Magazine, Consumer.* **Description:** Provides spiritual support for those caring for family members with health and age issues.
Published by: Our Sunday Visitor, Inc., 200 Noll Plz, Huntington, IN 46750. TEL 260-356-8400, 800-348-2440, FAX 260-356-8472, osvbooks@osv.com. Eds. . Monica, Bill Dodds.

N A F I M NEWSLETTER. *see* EDUCATION—Special Education And Rehabilitation

N C E A NOTES. *see* EDUCATION

282.93 NZL ISSN 1174-0086
N Z CATHOLIC. (New Zealand) Text in English. 1934. fortn. NZD 70 domestic; NZD 110 in Australia & South Pacific; NZD 120 elsewhere (effective 2009). adv. bk.rev.; film rev.; play rev. bibl. **Document type:** *Newspaper, Consumer.* **Description:** Covers Catholic national and international news, features, scripture, family life, ecumenical news, and Church history.
Formerly (until 1996): New Zealandia (0114-5207); Which supersedes (in 1989): Zealandia (0044-202X)
—CCC.
Published by: Roman Catholic Bishop of Auckland, Ponsonby, PO Box 147-000, Auckland, 1034, New Zealand. TEL 64-9-3603067, FAX 64-9-3603065. Ed. Gavin Abraham. Pub. Patrick Dunn. Circ: 7,200 (paid).

NARTHEX; tijdschrift voor levensbeschouwing en educatie. *see* EDUCATION

282 USA ISSN 0164-470X
NASA NADA/OUR HOPE. Text in English, Croatian. 1921. m. USD 20 (effective 2005). bk.rev. **Document type:** *Magazine, Consumer.*
Published by: Croatian Catholic Union of USA & Canada, 1 East Old Ridge Rd, Hobart, IN 46342. TEL 219-942-1191, FAX 219-942-8808. Ed. Melchior Masina. Circ: 3,500.

282 SVN
NASE OBCESTVO; glasilo zupnije Svete Trojice v Ljubljani. Text in Slovenian. 1980. m. free.
Published by: Zupnijski Urad Sveta Trojica, Slovenska cesta 21, pp 1618, Ljubljana, 1001, Slovenia. TEL 386-1-2524864. Circ: 500.

282 POL ISSN 0137-3218
BX1564
➤ **NASZA PRZESZLOSC**; studia z dziejow kosciola i kultury katolickiej w Polsce. Text in Polish; Summaries in German, English. 1946. 2/yr. EUR 21 foreign (effective 2005). bk.rev. cum.index: 1946-1988. 550 p./no. 1 cols./p.; back issues avail. **Document type:** *Journal, Academic/Scholarly.* **Description:** Covers the history of the catholic church in Poland.
Indexed: CERDIC, HistAb, P30, RASB.
Published by: Instytut Wydawniczy "Nasza Przeszlosc", ul Strzelnica 6, Krakow, 30125, Poland. TEL 48-12-4251859. Ed. Jan Dukala. Circ: 1,000. **Dist. by:** Ars Polona, Obroncow 25, Warsaw 03933, Poland. TEL 48-22-5098609, FAX 48-22-5098610, arspolona@arspolona.com.pl, http://www.arspolona.com.pl.

➤ **THE NATIONAL CATHOLIC BIOETHICS QUARTERLY.** *see* PHILOSOPHY

282 USA ISSN 0027-8920
NATIONAL CATHOLIC REGISTER; America's leading news from a Catholic perspective. Text in English. 1928. w. (Sun.). USD 59.95 (effective 2005). adv. bk.rev.; film rev. illus. **Document type:** *Newspaper, Consumer.* **Description:** Contains facts, reports, in-depth stories and commentary on items and events of interest to Catholics.
Formerly: Denver Register
Related titles: Online - full text ed.
Indexed: CPL.
Published by: Circle Media, 432 Washington Ave, North Haven, CT 06473-1309. Ed., Pub. Fr. Owen Kearns. Adv. contact Eileen Schreck. Circ: 35,000. Wire service: CaNS.

282 USA ISSN 0027-8939
NATIONAL CATHOLIC REPORTER; the independent weekly. Text in English. 1964. 26/yr. USD 43.95 combined subscription domestic (print & online eds.); USD 78.95 combined subscription foreign (print & online eds.) (effective 2009). adv. bk.rev. illus. back issues avail.; reprints avail. **Document type:** *Magazine, Consumer.* **Description:** Independent progressive views on religious, social and moral issues.
Related titles: Microform ed.: (from PQC); Online - full text ed.: USD 34.95 worldwide (effective 2004).
Indexed: A01, A03, A08, A22, A26, CERDIC, CLFP, CPL, Chicano, E08, G05, G06, G07, G08, H14, HlthInd, I05, I07, L01, L02, M06, MagInd, P02, P05, P10, P13, P28, P30, P34, P48, P53, P54, PQC, PRA, R05, RASB, S02, S03, S09, S23, T02.
Published by: National Catholic Reporter Publishing Co., 115 E Armour Blvd, Kansas City, MO 64111-1203. TEL 816-531-0538, FAX 816-968-2280, ncrsub@ncronline.org. Ed., Pub. Joe Feuerherd. Adv. contact Vicki Breashears. page USD 2,388; trim 10.43 x 14.5. Circ: 50,000 (paid). Wire service: CaNS.

261.834 USA ISSN 1061-9615
NETWORK CONNECTION; national Catholic social justice lobby. Text in English. 1971. bi-m. USD 40. charts; illus. index. back issues avail.
Formerly: Network (Washington, 1971) (0199-5723)
Published by: Network, 25 E Street NW, Ste 200, Washington, DC 20001-1522. TEL 202-347-9797, FAX 202-347-9864, network@igc.apc.org. Ed. Beth Baker. Pub. Kathy Thornton. Circ: 10,000.

282 DEU ISSN 0930-1143
NEUE GESPRAECHE; Handreichungen fuer Familien und Gruppen. Text in German. bi-m. EUR 7.70 (effective 2001). **Document type:** *Bulletin, Consumer.*
Published by: (Arbeitsgemeinschaft fuer Katholische Familienbildung e.V.), Patmos Verlag GmbH, Am Wehrhahn 100, Duesseldorf, 40211, Germany. TEL 49-211-16795-0, FAX 49-211-1679575, service@patmos.de, http://www.patmos.de.

282 DEU ISSN 1868-3258
NEUE MITTE; Zeitschrift der Katholiken in Wirtschaft und Verwaltung. Text in German. 1972. q. EUR 9.20; EUR 2.30 newsstand/cover (effective 2010). adv. bk.rev. **Document type:** *Magazine, Consumer.*
Formerly (until 2001): K K V - Forum Neue Mitte (0943-7584); Which incorporated (1949-1971): Kreuzschiff (0450-9307)
Published by: K K V - Bundesverband der Katholiken in Wirtschaft und Verwaltung e.V., Bismarckstr 61, Essen, 45128, Germany. TEL 49-201-879230, FAX 49-201-8792333, info@kkv-bund.de. Circ: 9,000 (paid and controlled).

262.3 AUT
NEUES ARCHIV FUER DIE GESCHICHTE DER DIOEZESE LINZ. Text in German. 1981. irreg. price varies. bk.rev. Supplement avail.; back issues avail. **Document type:** *Monographic series, Academic/Scholarly.*
Published by: Dioezesanarchiv Linz, Harrachstrasse 7, Linz, 4020, Austria. TEL 43-732-7712058608, FAX 43-732-7712058100, archiv@dioezese-linz.at, http://www.dioezese-linz.at/dioezesanarchiv. Eds. Johannes Ebner, Monika Wuerthinger.

282 DEU ISSN 0720-2024
BX1538.M3
NEUES JAHRBUCH FUER DAS BISTUM MAINZ. Text in German. 1946. a. EUR 16.80 (effective 2009). **Document type:** *Journal, Academic/Scholarly.*
Formerly (until 1977): Jahrbuch fuer das Bistum Mainz (0720-2113)
Indexed: RILM.
Published by: Bistum Mainz, Infoladen, Bischofsplatz 2, Mainz, 55116, Germany. TEL 49-6131-253844, FAX 49-6131-253845, Infoladen@Bistum-Mainz.de, http://www.bdkj-mainz.de/bm/dcms/sites/bistum/bistum/ordinariat/dezernate/dezernat_Z/publikationen/index.html.

271.2 GBR ISSN 0028-4289
BX801
➤ **NEW BLACKFRIARS**; a review: edited by the Dominicans of the English Province. Text in English. 1920; N.S. 1964. bi-m. GBP 175 in United Kingdom to institutions; EUR 221 in Europe to institutions; USD 251 in the Americas to institutions; USD 342 elsewhere to institutions; GBP 202 combined subscription in United Kingdom to institutions (print & online eds.); EUR 255 combined subscription in Europe to institutions (print & online eds.); USD 289 combined subscription in the Americas to institutions (print & online eds.); USD 394 combined subscription elsewhere to institutions (print & online eds.) (effective 2012). adv. bk.rev. index. back issues avail.; reprint service avail. from PSC. **Document type:** *Journal, Academic/Scholarly.* **Description:** Surveys theology, philosophy, sociology and the arts from the standpoint of Christian principles and their application to the modern world.
Formed by the merger of (1920-1964): Blackfriars (1754-2014); (1946-1964): Life of the Spirit (0269-3593)
Related titles: Microfilm ed.: N.S. (from PQC); Online - full text ed.: ISSN 1741-2005. GBP 175 in United Kingdom to institutions; EUR 221 in Europe to institutions; USD 251 in the Americas to institutions; USD 342 elsewhere to institutions (effective 2012) (from IngentaConnect).
Indexed: A01, A21, A22, A26, CA, CERDIC, CPL, DIP, E01, IBR, IBZ, MEA&I, MLA-IB, OTA, P30, PCI, RASB, RI-1, RI-2, T02.
—BLDSC (6082.270000), IE, Ingenta. **CCC.**
Published by: (English Dominicans), Wiley-Blackwell Publishing Ltd. (Subsidiary of: John Wiley & Sons, Inc.), 9600 Garsington Rd, Oxford, OX4 2DQ, United Kingdom. TEL 44-1865-776868, FAX 44-1865-714591, customer@wiley.co.uk, http://www.wiley.com/WileyCDA/. Ed. Fergus Kerr.

282 USA ISSN 1053-6558
THE NEW CATHOLIC MISCELLANY. Text in English. 1822. w. (Thu.). USD 19. adv. **Document type:** *Newspaper.*
Published by: Roman Catholic Diocese of Charleston, 119 Broad St, Box 818, Charleston, SC 29402. TEL 803-724-8375, FAX 803-724-8368. Ed. Deirdre Mays. Pub. Bishop David B Thompson. Adv. contact Nancy Schwerin. Circ: 23,450. Wire service: CaNS.

282 USA
NEW CATHOLIC REVIEW; contemporary Catholic Christianity. Text in English. 1982. m. USD 36. back issues avail.
Published by: Dayspring Press, Inc., 18600 W 58 Ave, Golden, CO 80403-1070. Ed. John C Brainerd.

282 USA ISSN 1067-6406
NEW EARTH. Text in English. 1938. 11/yr. adv. 16 p./no. 4 cols./p.; back issues avail. **Document type:** *Newspaper.*
Formerly (until May 1980): Catholic Action News (0008-7890)
Related titles: Online - full text ed.
Published by: Catholic Diocese of Fargo, Communications Office, 5201 Bishops Blvd, Ste A, Fargo, ND 58104. TEL 701-356-7958, tanya.watterud@fargodiocese.org. Ed. Tanya Watterud. Pub. Fr. Samuel J Aquila. Circ: 31,000.

282 CAN ISSN 0838-0341
NEW FREEMAN. Text in English. 1900. w. CAD 20; CAD 30 foreign (effective 1999). adv. bk.rev. **Document type:** *Newspaper.*
Related titles: Microfilm ed.
Published by: New Freeman Ltd., One Bayard Dr, Saint John, NB E2L 3L5, Canada. TEL 506-653-6806, FAX 506-653-6812. Ed., Adv. contact Bill Donovan. Pub. Faber MacDonald. Circ: 6,950.

NEW HIBERNIA REVIEW/IRIS EIREANNACH NUA. *see* ANTHROPOLOGY

282 USA ISSN 0149-4244
BR1
NEW OXFORD REVIEW. Abbreviated title: N O R. Text in English. 1940. m. (11/yr.). USD 19 domestic; USD 29 foreign; USD 39 combined subscription foreign (print & online eds.) (effective 2009). bk.rev. illus. 48 p./no.; back issues avail.; reprints avail. **Document type:** *Magazine, Consumer.* **Description:** Features articles on orthodoxy, evangelism, social justice, peace, and traditional family values.
Former titles (until 1977): American Church News (0002-791X); (until 1959): A C U News
Related titles: Microform ed.: (from PQC); Online - full text ed.: USD 25 (effective 2009).
Indexed: A01, A21, A22, CCR, CPL, GSS&RPL, MLA-IB, P28, P34, P48, P53, P54, PQC, RI-1, RI-2, T02.
—BLDSC (6084.872000), IE, Ingenta.
Published by: New Oxford Review, Inc., 1069 Kains Ave, Berkeley, CA 94706. TEL 510-526-5374, FAX 510-526-3492. Ed., Adv. contact Pieter Vree TEL 510-526-5374.

230.2 USA ISSN 0896-4297
NEW THEOLOGY REVIEW. Abbreviated title: N T R. Text in English. 1988. q. USD 35 domestic to individuals; USD 47 foreign to individuals; USD 52 to libraries; USD 10.50 per issue (effective 2009). adv. Index. **Document type:** *Journal, Academic/Scholarly.* **Description:** Provides a wide range of articles reflecting the importance of theology in modern times.
Indexed: A01, CPL, OTA, P30, R&TA.
Published by: Liturgical Press, St John's Abbey, PO Box 7500, Collegeville, MN 56321. TEL 320-363-2213, 800-858-5450, FAX 320-363-3299, 800-445-5899, sales@litpress.org. adv.: page USD 350; 4.5 x 7.5. Circ: 1,058.

230.071 USA ISSN 1941-9562
NEW WINESKINS; a journal of the Jesuit School of Theology at Berkeley. Text in English. 2006. s-a. **Description:** Includes theological reflections, homilies and exegesis from individuals affiliated with the Jesuit School of Theology at Berkeley.
Related titles: Online - full text ed.: ISSN 1941-9570.
Published by: Jesuit School of Theology at Berkeley, 1735 Le Roy Ave, Berkeley, CA 94709. TEL 510-549-5000, 800-824-0122, FAX 510-841-8536. Ed. Bobbi Dykema Katsanis.

282 GBR ISSN 0951-5399
THE NEWMAN. Text in English. 1950; N.S. 1972. a. back issues avail. **Document type:** *Newsletter.* **Description:** Contains articles of a scholarly nature as well as newsletter items of specific interest to members.
Former titles (until 1987): Newman Newsletter (0143-6600); (until 1976): Newman (0048-0207)
—BLDSC (6102.282000).

R

Published by: Newman Association, 20-22 Bedford Row, London, WC1R 4JS, United Kingdom. secretary@newman.org.uk. Ed. Martin Ward. Circ: 3,000.

282 USA ISSN 1547-9080
BX4705.N5

➤ **NEWMAN STUDIES JOURNAL.** Abbreviated title: N S J. Text in English. 2004 (Spr.). s-a. USD 30 to individuals; USD 58 to institutions; USD 75 combined subscription to individuals (print & online eds.); USD 209 combined subscription to institutions (print & online eds.); USD 15 per issue to individuals; USD 29 per issue to institutions (effective 2010). adv. back issues avail. **Document type:** *Journal, Academic/Scholarly.* **Description:** Provides Newman-related articles in diverse fields, including philosophy, theology, spirituality, history, literature, and education.
Related titles: Online - full text ed.: ISSN 2153-6945. USD 48 to individuals; USD 174 to institutions (effective 2010).
Published by: National Institute for Newman Studies, 211 N Dithridge St, Pittsburgh, PA 15213. TEL 412-681-4375, FAX 412-681-4376, newmanstudies@comcast.net. Eds. Gerard H McCarren, John T Ford. **Subscr. to:** Philosophy Documentation Center, PO Box 7147, Charlottesville, VA 22906. TEL 434-220-3300, FAX 434-220-3301, order@pdcnet.org, http://www.pdcnet.org.

282 VNM
NGUOI CONG GIAO VIET-NAM/VIETNAMESE CATHOLIC. Text in Vietnamese. 1984. fortn.
Published by: Committee for Solidarity of Patriotic Vietnamese Catholics, 59 Trang Thi, Hanoi, Viet Nam. TEL 56242. Ed. Pham Van Kham.

262.52 VAT ISSN 0390-2935
NICOLAUS; rivista di teologia ecumenico-patristica. Text in Italian. 1973. s-a. **Document type:** *Journal, Academic/Scholarly.*
Indexed: CERDIC.
—BLDSC (6110.105000).
Published by: Pontificia Universita San Tommaso d'Aquino - Angelicum, Largo Angelicum 1, Vatican City, 00184, Vatican City. TEL 39-06-67021, FAX 39-06-6790407, http://www.angelicum.org.

282 USA
NORTH CAROLINA CATHOLIC. Text in English. 1946. s-m. (Sun.). USD 16 (effective 2005). **Document type:** *Newspaper, Consumer.*
Related titles: Microfilm ed.
Contact Owner: Roman Catholic Diocese of Raleigh, 715 Nazareth St, Raleigh, NC 27606-2187. TEL 919-821-9730, FAX 919-821-9705. Circ: 58,000 Sunday (paid). Wire service: CaNS.

282 USA
NORTH COUNTRY CATHOLIC. Text in English. 1946. w. (Wed.). USD 23 within diocese area; USD 25 out of area; USD 45 in Canada (effective 2006). adv. **Document type:** *Newspaper, Consumer.*
Published by: Diocese of Ogdensburg, 308 Isabella St, Ogdensburg, NY 13669. TEL 315-393-2920, FAX 315-394-0670, http://www.dioogdensburg.org. Ed. Mary Lou Kilian. Pub. Bishop Robert J. Cunningham. Adv. contact Scott Wilson. col. inch USD 8.75. Circ: 8,000 (paid and free). Wire service: CaNS.

282.764 USA ISSN 0899-7020
NORTH TEXAS CATHOLIC. Text in English. 1985. w. USD 18 (effective 1998). adv. bk.rev. charts; illus. back issues avail. **Document type:** *Newspaper.* **Description:** Contains local, state, national, and international news relating to the church and the people of the church. Also Catholic view of the ways church teaching has a bearing on the major issues of the day. Audience is mainstream Catholics in the churches of the Diocese of Ft. Worth.
Published by: Catholic Diocese of Ft. Worth, 800 W Loop 820 South, Ft Worth, TX 76108. TEL 817-560-3300, FAX 817-244-8839. Ed., R&P Jeff Hensley. Pub. Bishop Joseph P Delaney. Adv. contact Marta Lindley. Circ: 24,000 (paid).

282 USA
NORTHERN CROSS. Text in English. 1970. m. free to members in diocese (effective 2006). **Document type:** *Newspaper, Consumer.*
Formerly (until 2005): Catholic Outlook
Published by: Diocese of Duluth, 2830 E Fourth St, Duluth, MN 55812. TEL 218-724-9111, FAX 218-724-1056. Pub. Bishop Dennis M. Schnurr. Circ: 20,000 (controlled).

282.772 USA ISSN 1074-2778
NORTHWEST INDIANA CATHOLIC. Text in English. 1987. w. USD 25 to qualified personnel (effective 2009). adv. bk.rev. 18 p./no. 6 cols./p.; **Document type:** *Newspaper, Consumer.*
Related titles: Online - full text ed.
Published by: Catholic Diocese of Gary, 9292 Broadway, Merrillville, IN 46410-7088. TEL 219-769-9292, FAX 219-738-9034. Ed., Adv. contact Steve Euvino. Pub. Dale J Melczek. B&W page USD 840, color page USD 965; trim 17 x 11. Circ: 20,457 (paid). Wire service: CaNS.

253 ITA ISSN 0029-3903
NOTE DI PASTORALE GIOVANILE. Text in Italian. 1967. 9/yr. EUR 36.50 domestic; EUR 54 foreign (effective 2009). bk.rev. index. **Document type:** *Magazine, Consumer.*
Indexed: CERDIC.
Published by: (C E C Don Bosco), Editrice Elledici, Corso Francia 214, Cascine Vica - Rivoli, TO 10098, Italy. TEL 39-011-9552111, FAX 39-011-9574048, mail@elledici.org, http://www.elledici.org. Circ: 6,000.

282 POL
NOTIFICATIONES E CURIA METROPOLITANA CRACOVIENSI. Text in Polish. 1863. q. **Document type:** *Newsletter.* **Description:** Provides information for Catholic priests and Catholic institutions on Papal and Episcopal documents, theology, ethics, church law.
Published by: Kuria Metropolitalna Krakow, Wydzial Koordynacji Duszpasterstwa, Ul Franciszkanska 3, Krakow, 31004, Poland. TEL 48-12-211406, FAX 48-12-211533. Ed. Fr Szymon Fedorowicz. Circ: 1,200.

282 VAT ISSN 0029-4306
NOTITIAE. Text in English, French, Latin. 1965. m. EUR 26 domestic; EUR 37 foreign (effective 2002). illus. index. back issues avail. **Document type:** *Journal, Academic/Scholarly.* **Description:** Contains news of the Congregation for Divine Worship and information on liturgical matters.
Indexed: CERDIC, CLA, CPL.
Published by: Libreria Editrice Vaticana, 00120, Vatican City. TEL 379-6-69885003, FAX 379-6-69884716.

282 FRA ISSN 2106-9565
NOTRE EGLISE. Text in French. 1906. m. **Document type:** *Bulletin, Consumer.*
Former titles (until 2010): Bulletin Diocesain (0991-7241); (until 1939): Bulletin Religieux du Diocese de Bayonne (0991-7225)
Published by: Eglise Catholique, Diocese de Bayonne, 16 Place Mgr Vansteenberghe, Bayonne, 64100, France. TEL 33-5-59591688, FAX 33-5-59598881, dir.bulletin.diocesain@eveche-bayonne.org, http://www.diocese-bayonne.org.

282.6668 CIV
LA NOUVELLE; magazine d'information de l'Eglise Catholique en Cote d'Ivoire. Text in French. 1989-1994; resumed 1997. bi-m. XOF 5,000. back issues avail.
Published by: Eglise Catholique en Cote d'Ivoire, 01 BP 1287, Abidjan, 01, Ivory Coast. TEL 21-69-79. Ed. Pierre Trichet. Circ: 3,500.

282 PRT ISSN 1646-5016
NOVA ET VETERA. Text in Portuguese. 2006. m. **Document type:** *Newspaper, Consumer.*
Published by: Milita Sanctae Mariae, Rua de Guadalupe 73, Braga, 4710-298, Portugal. TEL 351-253-611609, http://milicia.com.sapo.pt.

282 CHE ISSN 0029-5027
AP24
NOVA ET VETERA (FRENCH EDITION). Text in French. 1926. q. CHF 50. bk.rev. index. reprints avail. **Document type:** *Bulletin.*
Related titles: ◆ English ed.: Nova et Vetera (English Edition). ISSN 1542-7315.
Indexed: CERDIC, DIP, FR, IBR, IBZ, IPB, OTA.
—INIST.
Published by: Editions Saint-Augustin, Saint-Maurice, 1890, Switzerland. Ed. Georges Cottier.

282 ITA ISSN 0078-253X
NOVARIEN. Text in Italian. 1967. a. free to members (effective 2008). bk.rev. **Document type:** *Magazine, Consumer.*
Indexed: FR, MLA-IB.
Published by: Associazione di Storia Ecclesiastica Novarese, Via Pietro Micca 24, Novara, 28100, Italy. Circ: 1,000.

262.9 BEL
➤ **NOVUM COMMENTARIUM LOVANIENSE IN CODICEM IURIS CANONICI.** Text in Dutch. 1992. irreg., latest 2005. price varies. bk.rev. back issues avail. **Document type:** *Monographic series, Academic/Scholarly.* **Description:** Discusses Roman Catholic Canon Law.
Published by: (Universite Catholique de Louvain, Faculte de Theologie et de Droit Canonique), Peeters Publishers, Bondgenotenlaan 153, Leuven, 3000, Belgium. TEL 32-16-235170, FAX 32-16-228500, http://www.peeters-leuven.be. Ed. R Toefs.

282 USA
NUESTRA PARROQUIA. Text in English, Spanish. 1991. m. USD 48 domestic; USD 58 foreign (effective 2011). **Document type:** *Bulletin, Trade.* **Description:** Includes homily guides with practical advice for running a multicultural parish.
Published by: Claretian Publications, 205 W Monroe, Chicago, IL 60606. TEL 312-236-7782, FAX 312-236-8207, stjudeleague@claretians.org.

282 ARG ISSN 0029-585X
NUEVA POMPEYA. Text in Spanish. 1924. m. ARS 20,000. index.
Published by: (Santuario de la Virgen del Rosario), Orden de los Frailes Menores Capuchinos, Esquiu 974, C.C. 14-Suc.37, Buenos Aires, Argentina. Ed. R P Andres Guirao. Circ: 18,000.

NUNTIATURBERICHTE AUS DEUTSCHLAND NEBST ERGAENZENDEN AKTENSTUECKEN. *see* HISTORY

282 ITA
NUOVA UMANITA. Text in Italian. 1979. bi-m. EUR 25 domestic; EUR 31 in Europe; EUR 36 elsewhere (effective 2010). **Document type:** *Magazine, Consumer.* **Description:** Features articles on justice, solidarity and other topics in the humanities.
Published by: Citta Nuova Editrice, Via Pieve Torina 55, Rome, 00156, Italy. TEL 39-06-3216212, FAX 39-06-3207185, comm.editrice@cittanuova.it, http://www.cittanuova.it.

O I E C BULLETIN. *see* EDUCATION

282 ESP ISSN 2171-5807
OBISPADO DE ORENSE. BOLETIN OFICIAL. Key Title: Boletin Oficial del Obispado de Orense. Text in Spanish. 1851. m. **Document type:** *Bulletin, Consumer.*
Related titles: ◆ Supplement(s): Diversarum Rerum. ISSN 2171-5769; ◆ Comunidade. ISSN 2171-5793.
Published by: Obispado de Orense, Rua Progeso No. 26, Orense, 32080, Spain. TEL 34-988-366141, FAX 34-988-366142, orcuria@obispadodeourense.com, http://www.obispadodeourense.com.

282 FRA ISSN 1778-2155
OBJECTIONS. Text in French. 2005. 10/yr. EUR 20 to individuals (effective 2008).
Published by: Association pour la Diffusion de la Culture Chretienne, 22 rue Fremicourt, Paris, 75015, France. TEL 33-1-40264178. Ed. Guillaume de Tanouarn.

261.58 USA
OBLATES. Text in English. 1943. bi-m. membership. back issues avail. **Document type:** *Newspaper.* **Description:** Articles and poetry espousing positive Christian direction for primarily middle-age to older Catholic adults.
Published by: Missionary Association of Mary Immaculate, 9480 N De Mazenod Dr, Belleville, IL 62223-1160. TEL 618-398-4848. Ed. Christine Portell. Circ: 500,000 (controlled).

282 HRV ISSN 0351-3947
BX806.S4
OBNOVLJENI ZIVOT/LIFE RENEWED; casopis za religioznu kulturu. Text in Croatian; Summaries in English. 1919-1945; resumed 1971. q. HRK 120 domestic; EUR 25 in Europe; USD 45 elsewhere (effective 2002). adv. bk.rev. abstr.; bibl.; stat. index. back issues avail. **Document type:** *Journal.*
Related titles: E-mail ed.; Online - full text ed.
Indexed: FR, R&TA.
—INIST.
Published by: Filozofsko-Teoloski Institut Druzbe Isusove/Institute of Philosophy and Theology, S.J., Jordanovac 110, Zagreb, 10001, Croatia. TEL 385-1-2354050, FAX 385-1-2354049. Ed. Ivan Sestak. Adv. contact Josip Jelenic TEL 385-1-2354064. Circ: 1,500.

282 USA ISSN 0745-9491
CODEN: PHSMA2
THE OBSERVER (MONTEREY). Text in English. 1967. m. USD 45 (effective 2005). adv. bk.rev. 24 p./no. 5 cols./p.; **Document type:** *Newspaper, Consumer.*
Indexed: B02, B15, B17, B18, G04, G08, PROMT.
Published by: Diocese of Monterey, PO Box 2079, Monterey, CA 93942. TEL 831-373-2919, FAX 831-373-1175, http://www.dioceseofmonterey.org. Ed., R&P Kevin Drabinski. Pub. Most Rev. Sylvester Ryan. Circ: 16,500.

282 USA ISSN 0029-7739
THE OBSERVER (ROCKFORD). Text in English. 1935. w. (Fri.). USD 26 (effective 2005). adv. bk.rev.; film rev. **Document type:** *Newspaper, Consumer.*
Related titles: Microfilm ed.
Indexed: HECAB.
Published by: Catholic Diocese of Rockford, 555 Coleman Center Dr, PO Box 7044, Rockford, IL 61125. TEL 815-399-4300, FAX 815-399-5266. Eds. Owen Phelps Jr., Penny Weigert. Pub. Thomas G Doran. Adv. contact Ron Bergman. Circ: 32,500 (paid). Wire service: CaNS.

262.3 MWI ISSN 0300-4651
AN275.L5
ODINI/WELCOME. Text in English. 1950. fortn. MWK 137.50, USD 9; MWK 160, USD 11 foreign. adv. bk.rev. illus. **Document type:** *Newspaper.*
Formerly (until 1984): African
Published by: (Diocese of Lilongwe), Likuni Press and Publishing House, PO Box 133, Lilongwe, Malawi. TEL 265-721388, FAX 265-721141. Ed. Paul I Akomenji. Circ: 12,000 (controlled).

282 AUT
OESTERREICHISCHE AKADEMIE DER WISSENSCHAFTEN. KOMMISSION ZUR HERAUSGABE DES CORPUS DER LATEINISCHEN KIRCHENVAETER. VEROEFFENTLICHUNGEN. Text in German. irreg. 416 p./no.; back issues avail. **Document type:** *Monographic series, Academic/Scholarly.*
Published by: (Oesterreichische Akademie der Wissenschaften, Kommission zur Herausgabe des Corpus der Lateinischen Kirchenvaeter), Verlag der Oesterreichischen Akademie der Wissenschaften, Postgasse 7/4, Vienna, W 1011, Austria. TEL 43-1-515813402, FAX 43-1-515813400, verlag@oeaw.ac.at, http://www.verlag.oeaw.ac.at. Ed. Marie Therese Wieser.

282.025 USA ISSN 0078-3854
BX845
OFFICIAL CATHOLIC DIRECTORY. Abbreviated title: O C D. Text in English. 1817. a. adv. Supplement avail. **Document type:** *Directory, Trade.* **Description:** Lists 60,000 church leaders - from clergy to laity - in every Catholic institution in the United States, including all Catholic possessions, and a description of the governing body of Rome.
Incorporates (19??-2001): The official Catholic Directory. Education Guide (1544-5968); Former titles (until 1913): Official Catholic Directory and Clergy List; (until 1906): Catholic Directory, Almanac and Clergy List-Quarterly; (until 1900): Hoffmanns Catholic Directory, Almanac and Clergy List Quarterly
Related titles: Online - full text ed.
Indexed: SRI.
—CCC.
Published by: National Register Publishing (Subsidiary of: Marquis Who's Who LLC.), 300 Connell Dr, Ste 2000, Berkeley Heights, NJ 07922. TEL 800-473-7020, FAX 908-673-1189, NRPsales@marquiswhoswho.com, http://www.nationalregisterpub.com. Adv. contact Anne Collins TEL 212-689-2500 ext 2503.

OLIVER LEONARD KAPSNER, O.S.B. CATALOGING BULLETIN. *see* LIBRARY AND INFORMATION SCIENCES

282 SUR
OMHOOG. Text in French. 1953. w. USD 30; USD 50 foreign. adv. bk.rev. **Document type:** *Newsletter.*
Published by: Roman Catholic Church of Suriname, Communication Commission, Gravenstraat 21, PO Box 1802, Paramaribo, Suriname. TEL 597-472521, FAX 597-473904. Ed. Rev. Sebastian Mulder. R&P Nico Waagmeester TEL 597-424312.

282 USA ISSN 1552-2016
BX1617
ONE (NEW YORK). Text in English. 1974. bi-m. USD 12 (effective 2005). illus. **Document type:** *Journal, Trade.* **Description:** Informs members of ecumenical and interfaith endeavors, projects and programs developed by the church in the Near East, and cultural and spiritual items.
Former titles (until 2004): C N E W A World (1535-6671); (until 2001): Catholic Near East; (until 1987): Catholic Near East Magazine (0164-0674)
Indexed: Perlslam.
Published by: Catholic Near East Welfare Association, 1011 First Ave, New York, NY 10022-4195. TEL 212-826-1480, FAX 212-826-8979, cnewa@cnewa.org, http://www.cnewa.org. Ed. Michael J L La Civita. R&P Michael La Civita TEL 212-826-1480 ext. 600. Circ: 100,000 (controlled).

282 GBR ISSN 0030-252X
BX1781
ONE IN CHRIST; a Roman Catholic ecumenical review. Text in English. 1965. q. GBP 26 domestic; GBP 29 in Europe; GBP 32 elsewhere (effective 2003). adv. bk.rev. bibl. index. reprints avail. **Document type:** *Journal, Academic/Scholarly.* **Description:** Offers documentation and comment on current ecumenical initiatives, with items on the theology, history and spirituality of ecumenism.
Incorporates: Ecumenical Notes
Related titles: Microfilm ed.: (from PQC).
Indexed: A01, A21, CA, CERDIC, CPL, FR, OTA, RI-1, RI-2, T02.
—BLDSC (6260.230000).
Published by: Vita et Pax-Foundation for Unity, Monastery of Christ our Saviour, Turvey, Beds MK43 8DH, United Kingdom. TEL 44-1234-881432, FAX 44-1234-881538. Ed., R&P Gregory van der Kleij. Circ: 800.

282 USA
ONE VOICE (BIRMINGHAM). Text in English. 1971. w. (Fri.). USD 17 (effective 2005). **Document type:** *Newspaper, Consumer.*
Formerly: Birmingham One Voice
Published by: Birmingham Catholic Press, Inc., 2121 Third Ave, N, Birmingham, AL 35206. TEL 205-838-8305, FAX 205-838-8319, http://www.bhmdiocese.org. Circ: 19,500 (paid). Wire service: CaNS.

282 NLD ISSN 1574-3934
OP WEG NAAR KERSTMIS. Text in Dutch. 2000. a. EUR 4.20 (effective 2008).
Published by: (Abdij van Berne, Werkgroep voor Liturgie), Uitgeverij Abdij van Berne, Postbus 60, Heeswijk, 5473 ZH, Netherlands. TEL 31-413-299299, FAX 31-413-299288, info@abdijvanberne.nl, http://www.uitgeverijberne.nl.

OPUS DEI AWARENESS NETWORK. *see* RELIGIONS AND THEOLOGY

L'ORA DI RELIGIONE. *see* EDUCATION

282 ITA ISSN 0030-4174
ORA ET LABORA; quaderni di interesse monastico. Text in Italian. 1947. q. bk.rev. bibl. back issues avail. **Document type:** *Magazine, Consumer.* **Description:** Examines the origins of the monastic life.
Indexed: CERDIC.
Published by: Monastero S. Benedetto, Monache Benedettine dell'Adorazione, Via Felice Bellotti 10, Milan, 20129, Italy. http://spazio.csi2000.it/benedettine-milano/?q=node/15.

282 CAN ISSN 0701-4090
ORATOIRE. Text in French. 1912. bi-m. CAD 8. illus. **Document type:** *Journal, Academic/Scholarly.*
Related titles: ◆ English ed.: The Oratory. ISSN 0384-1871.
Published by: Oratoire Saint-Joseph du Mont-Royal, 3800 Chemin Queen Mary, Montreal, PQ H3V 1H6, Canada. TEL 514-733-8211, FAX 514-733-9735, http://www.saint-joseph.org. Circ: 55,000.

282 CAN ISSN 1206-050X
ORATOIRE SAINT JOSEPH. CAHIERS. Text in English, French. 1953. irreg. CAD 20. bk.rev. bibl.; illus. index, cum.index: 1953-1972; 1973-1992. **Document type:** *Monographic series, Academic/Scholarly.*
Formerly (until 1996): Cahiers de Josephologie (0007-9774)
Indexed: A21, CPL, FR, OTA, RI-1, RI-2.
—INIST.
Published by: Oratoire Saint-Joseph du Mont-Royal, 3800 Chemin Queen Mary, Montreal, PQ H3V 1H6, Canada. TEL 514-733-8211, FAX 514-733-9735. Ed. Pierre Robert. Circ: 600.

282 CAN ISSN 0384-1871
THE ORATORY. Text in English. 1927. bi-m. CAD 10, USD 8. **Document type:** *Newsletter, Consumer.*
Related titles: ◆ French ed.: Oratoire. ISSN 0701-4090.
Published by: St. Joseph's Oratory, 3800 Queen Mary Rd, Montreal, PQ H3V 1H6, Canada. TEL 514-733-8211, FAX 514-733-9735, revue@ost.qc.ca, http://www.saint.joseph.org. Ed., R&P Gilles Leblanc. Circ: 8,500.

282 ITA ISSN 0039-3045
BX4055.A1
ORDINE DEI SERVI DI MARIA. STUDI STORICI. Text and summaries in English, French, German, Italian, Portuguese, Spanish. 1933. s-a. adv. bk.rev. bibl.; charts; illus.; pat.; stat. index. **Document type:** *Journal, Academic/Scholarly.*
Indexed: FR.
—INIST.
Published by: Ordine dei Servi di Maria, Istituto Storico, Viale Trenta Aprile 6, Rome, 00153, Italy. TEL 39-06-5814441, http://www.servidimaria.org/it/index.htm. Circ: 300. **Co-sponsor:** Centro Edizioni Marianum.

282 CAN ISSN 1912-0680
ORDO. Text in English. 1968. a. CAD 13.95 per issue (effective 2007). **Document type:** *Journal, Consumer.*
Former titles (until 2005): Guidelines for Pastoral Liturgy (0317-7203); (until 1973): Liturgical Calendar (0317-7211)
Published by: Canadian Conference of Catholic Bishops, Publications Service/Conference des Eveques Catholiques du Canada, 90 Parent Ave, Ottawa, ON K1N 7B1, Canada. TEL 613-241-9461, FAX 613-241-5090, http://www.cccb-publi-cecc.com.

264 POL ISSN 1234-1762
OREMUS. Text in Polish. 1995. m. USD 23 foreign. index. **Description:** Provides liturgical texts for daily mass, including short meditations; mass readings, common prayer and features on liturgy.
Published by: Wydawnictwo Ksiezy Marianow, Ul Sw Bonifacego 9, Warsaw, 02914, Poland. TEL 48-22-6519970, FAX 48-22-6519055. Ed. Dariusz Mazewski. Circ: 8,000.

266.2 CAN ISSN 0472-0490
ORIENT. Text in English. 1953. bi-m. CAD 6 (effective 2000). adv. illus.
Indexed: M10, MLA-IB, PRA.
Published by: Missions des Peres de Sainte-Croix, 4901 rue Piedmont, Montreal, PQ H3V 1E3, Canada. TEL 514-731-6231, FAX 514-731-7820. Ed., R&P Marcel Descheneaux. Adv. contact Marc Gagnon. Circ: 9,000.

282 SLV
ORIENTACION. Text in Spanish. 1953. w.
Address: 1a Calle Poniente 3412, San Salvador, El Salvador. TEL 24-5166, FAX 26-4979. Ed. Fr Jesus Delgado. Circ: 8,000.

220 DEU ISSN 0946-5065
ORIENTALIA BIBLICA ET CHRISTIANA. Text in German. 1991. irreg., latest vol.17, 2009. price varies. **Document type:** *Monographic series, Academic/Scholarly.*
Published by: Harrassowitz Verlag, Kreuzberger Ring 7b-d, Wiesbaden, 65205, Germany. TEL 49-611-5300, FAX 49-611-530560, verlag@harrassowitz.de, http://www.harrassowitz.de.

ORIENTALIA CHRISTIANA ANALECTA. *see* ASIAN STUDIES

253 ITA ISSN 0472-0784
ORIENTAMENTI PASTORALI. Text in Italian. 1953. m. EUR 36.30 domestic; EUR 56.50 in Europe; EUR 62.40 elsewhere (effective 2008). **Document type:** *Magazine, Consumer.*
Indexed: CERDIC.
Published by: (Centro di Orientamento Pastorale), Centro Editoriale Dehoniano, Via Scipione dal Ferro 4, Bologna, BO 40138, Italy. TEL 39-051-4290451, FAX 39-051-4290491, ced-amm@dehoniane.it, http://www.dehoniane.it. Circ: 4,500.

282 CHE ISSN 0030-5502
BX803
ORIENTIERUNG; katholische Blaetter fuer weltanschauliche Information. Text in German. 1937. s-m. looseleaf. CHF 65 domestic; EUR 50 in Germany & Austria; EUR 61 elsewhere; CHF 50 to students (effective 2006). adv. bk.rev. abstr.; bibl.; stat. index, cum.index. 12 p./no.; **Document type:** *Magazine, Consumer.*
Indexed: CERDIC, MLA-IB, OTA.
Published by: Institut fuer Weltanschauliche Fragen, Scheideggstr 45, Zuerich, 8002, Switzerland. TEL 41-44-2049050, FAX 41-44-2049051. Ed. Nikolaus Klein. Circ: 6,690 (paid).

282.73 USA
BX801
ORIGINS, C N S DOCUMENTARY SERVICE. Key Title: Origins (Washington). Text in English. 1971. 47/yr. USD 114 to individuals; USD 144 combined subscription to individuals print & online eds. (effective 2011); Institutional subscription price varies. Please contact publisher.
Formerly: Origins, N C Documentary Service (0093-609X)
Related titles: Online - full text ed.: USD 99 to individuals (effective 2011); Institutional subscription varies. Please contact publisher.
Indexed: A22, CERDIC, CLA, CPL, P30, S02, S03, SCOPUS.
—BLDSC (6291.263900), IE, Ingenta.
Published by: Catholic News Service, 3211 Fourth St, NE, Washington, DC 20017. TEL 202-541-3250, FAX 202-541-3255, cns@catholicnews.com, http://www.catholicnews.com. Circ: 9,000.

255 ITA ISSN 1973-0500
ORIZZONTI MONASTICI. Text in Italian. 1991. irreg. price varies. **Document type:** *Monographic series, Academic/Scholarly.*
Published by: Abbazia San Benedetto, Seregno, MI 20038, Italy. TEL 39-362-231772. Ed. Valerio Cattana.

282 VAT ISSN 0391-688X
L'OSSERVATORE ROMANO (DAILY); unicuique suum - non praevalebunt. Text in Italian. 1861. d. EUR 198 domestic; EUR 325 in the European Union; EUR 396 in Europe outside European Union; EUR 761 Africa, Asia, Latin America; EUR 927 elsewhere (effective 2004). adv. **Document type:** *Newspaper, Consumer.*
Related titles: Microfilm ed.: (from PQC); Online - full text ed.: ISSN 1563-6259; ◆ Alternate Frequency ed(s).: L' Osservatore Romano (Italian Edition. Weekly). ISSN 1563-6232. w.
Indexed: CPL, RASB.
Published by: Osservatore Romano, .00120, Vatican City. TEL 39-06-69883461, FAX 39-06-69883675, http://www.vatican.va/news_services/or/home_ita.artl. Ed. Mario Agnes. Circ: 41,000.

282 VAT ISSN 1563-6178
L'OSSERVATORE ROMANO (ENGLISH EDITION. WEEKLY). Text in English. 1967. w. EUR 58 domestic; EUR 120 in the European Union; EUR 130 in Europe outside the European Union; EUR 110 Africa, Asia, Latin America; EUR 162 elsewhere (effective 2004). **Document type:** *Newspaper, Consumer.*
Related titles: Online - full text ed.: ISSN 1563-6186. 199?; ◆ Italian ed.: L' Osservatore Romano (Italian Edition. Weekly). ISSN 1563-6232; ◆ Spanish ed.: L' Osservatore Romano (Spanish Edition. Weekly). ISSN 1563-6216; ◆ Polish ed.: L' Osservatore Romano (Polish Edition. Monthly). ISSN 1563-6267; ◆ German ed.: L' Osservatore Romano (German Edition. Weekly). ISSN 0179-7387; ◆ French ed.: L' Osservatore Romano (French Edition. Weekly). ISSN 1017-3862; ◆ Portuguese ed.: L' Osservatore Romano (Portuguese Edition. Weekly). ISSN 1563-6194.
Published by: Osservatore Romano, .00120, Vatican City. TEL 39-06-69883461, FAX 39-06-69883675, http://www.vatican.va/news_services/or/home_ita.artl.

282 VAT ISSN 1017-3862
L'OSSERVATORE ROMANO (FRENCH EDITION. WEEKLY). Text in French. 1949. w. EUR 58 domestic; EUR 120 in the European Union; EUR 130 in Europe outside the European Union; EUR 110 Africa, Asia, Latin America; EUR 162 elsewhere (effective 2004). **Document type:** *Newspaper, Consumer.*
Related titles: Online - full text ed.: ISSN 1563-616X; ◆ Italian ed.: L' Osservatore Romano (Italian Edition. Weekly). ISSN 1563-6232; ◆ English ed.: L' Osservatore Romano (English Edition. Weekly). ISSN 1563-6178; ◆ Polish ed.: L' Osservatore Romano (Polish Edition. Monthly). ISSN 1563-6267; ◆ Portuguese ed.: L' Osservatore Romano (Portuguese Edition. Weekly). ISSN 1563-6194; ◆ German ed.: L' Osservatore Romano (German Edition. Weekly). ISSN 0179-7387; ◆ Spanish ed.: L' Osservatore Romano (Spanish Edition. Weekly). ISSN 1563-6216.
Published by: Osservatore Romano, .00120, Vatican City. TEL 39-06-69883461, FAX 39-06-69883675, http://www.vatican.va/news_services/or/home_ita.artl.

282 VAT ISSN 0179-7387
L'OSSERVATORE ROMANO (GERMAN EDITION. WEEKLY). Text in German. 1971. w. **Document type:** *Newspaper, Consumer.*
Related titles: CD-ROM ed.: ISSN 1616-2749; ◆ Italian ed.: L' Osservatore Romano (Italian Edition. Weekly). ISSN 1563-6232; ◆ English ed.: L' Osservatore Romano (English Edition. Weekly). ISSN 1563-6178; ◆ Polish ed.: L' Osservatore Romano (Polish Edition. Monthly). ISSN 1563-6267; ◆ Portuguese ed.: L' Osservatore Romano (Portuguese Edition. Weekly). ISSN 1563-6194; ◆ French ed.: L' Osservatore Romano (French Edition. Weekly). ISSN 1017-3862; ◆ Spanish ed.: L' Osservatore Romano (Spanish Edition. Weekly). ISSN 1563-6216.
Published by: Osservatore Romano, .00120, Vatican City. TEL 39-06-69883461, FAX 39-06-69883675, http://www.vatican.va/news_services/or/home_ita.artl.

282 VAT ISSN 1563-6232
L'OSSERVATORE ROMANO (ITALIAN EDITION. WEEKLY). Text and summaries in Italian. 1950. w. EUR 58 domestic; EUR 120 in the European Union; EUR 130 in Europe outside the European Union; EUR 110 Africa, Asia, Latin America; EUR 162 elsewhere (effective 2004). **Document type:** *Newspaper, Consumer.*
Related titles: Online - full text ed.: ISSN 1563-6240. 199?; ◆ German ed.: L' Osservatore Romano (German Edition. Weekly). ISSN 0179-7387; ◆ French ed.: L' Osservatore Romano (French Edition. Weekly). ISSN 1017-3862; ◆ Polish ed.: L' Osservatore Romano (Polish Edition. Monthly). ISSN 1563-6267; ◆ Portuguese ed.: L' Osservatore Romano (Portuguese Edition. Weekly). ISSN 1563-6194; ◆ Spanish ed.: L' Osservatore Romano (Spanish Edition. Weekly). ISSN 1563-6216; ◆ English ed.: L' Osservatore Romano (English Edition. Weekly). ISSN 1563-6178; ◆ Alternate Frequency ed(s).: L' Osservatore Romano (Daily). ISSN 0391-688X. d.
Published by: Osservatore Romano, .00120, Vatican City. TEL 39-06-69883461, FAX 39-06-69883675, http://www.vatican.va/news_services/or/home_ita.artl.

282 VAT ISSN 1563-6267
L'OSSERVATORE ROMANO (POLISH EDITION. MONTHLY). Text in Polish. 1980. m. EUR 20 domestic; EUR 54 in the European Union; EUR 58 in Europe outside the European Union; EUR 66 Africa, Asia, Latin America; EUR 88 elsewhere (effective 2004).
Related titles: ◆ Italian ed.: L' Osservatore Romano (Italian Edition. Weekly). ISSN 1563-6232; ◆ German ed.: L' Osservatore Romano (German Edition. Weekly). ISSN 0179-7387; ◆ Spanish ed.: L' Osservatore Romano (Spanish Edition. Weekly). ISSN 1563-6216; ◆ English ed.: L' Osservatore Romano (English Edition. Weekly). ISSN 1563-6178; ◆ French ed.: L' Osservatore Romano (French Edition. Weekly). ISSN 1017-3862; ◆ Portuguese ed.: L' Osservatore Romano (Portuguese Edition. Weekly). ISSN 1563-6194.
Published by: Osservatore Romano, .00120, Vatican City. TEL 39-06-69883461, FAX 39-06-69883675, http://www.vatican.va/news_services/or/home_ita.artl.

282 VAT ISSN 1563-6194
L'OSSERVATORE ROMANO (PORTUGUESE EDITION. WEEKLY). Text in Portuguese. 1970. w. EUR 58 domestic; EUR 120 in the European Union; EUR 130 in Europe outside the European Union; EUR 110 Africa, Asia, Latin America; EUR 162 elsewhere (effective 2004). **Document type:** *Newspaper, Consumer.*
Related titles: Online - full text ed.: ISSN 1563-6208. 199?; ◆ Italian ed.: L' Osservatore Romano (Italian Edition. Weekly). ISSN 1563-6232; ◆ English ed.: L' Osservatore Romano (English Edition. Weekly). ISSN 1563-6178; ◆ Polish ed.: L' Osservatore Romano (Polish Edition. Monthly). ISSN 1563-6267; ◆ German ed.: L' Osservatore Romano (German Edition. Weekly). ISSN 0179-7387; ◆ French ed.: L' Osservatore Romano (French Edition. Weekly). ISSN 1017-3862; ◆ Spanish ed.: L' Osservatore Romano (Spanish Edition. Weekly). ISSN 1563-6216.
Published by: Osservatore Romano, .00120, Vatican City. TEL 39-06-69883461, FAX 39-06-69883675, http://www.vatican.va/news_services/or/home_ita.artl.

282 VAT ISSN 1563-6216
L'OSSERVATORE ROMANO (SPANISH EDITION. WEEKLY). Text in Spanish. 1969. w. EUR 58 domestic; EUR 120 in the European Union; EUR 130 in Europe outside the European Union; EUR 110 Africa, Asia, Latin America; EUR 162 elsewhere (effective 2004). **Document type:** *Newspaper, Consumer.*
Related titles: Online - full text ed.: ISSN 1563-6224. 199?; ◆ Italian ed.: L' Osservatore Romano (Italian Edition. Weekly). ISSN 1563-6232; ◆ English ed.: L' Osservatore Romano (English Edition. Weekly). ISSN 1563-6178; ◆ Polish ed.: L' Osservatore Romano (Polish Edition. Monthly). ISSN 1563-6267; ◆ German ed.: L' Osservatore Romano (German Edition. Weekly). ISSN 0179-7387; ◆ French ed.: L' Osservatore Romano (French Edition. Weekly). ISSN 1017-3862; ◆ Portuguese ed.: L' Osservatore Romano (Portuguese Edition. Weekly). ISSN 1563-6194.
Published by: Osservatore Romano, .00120, Vatican City. TEL 39-06-69883461, FAX 39-06-69883675, http://www.vatican.va/news_services/or/home_ita.artl.

282 DEU ISSN 1439-2089
BX1490.4.A1
OST - WEST EUROPAEISCHE PERSPEKTIVEN. Text in German. 1961. q. EUR 19.80; EUR 6.50 newsstand/cover (effective 2008). adv. **Document type:** *Journal, Academic/Scholarly.* **Description:** Provides background information and a forum for discussions involving problems in Middle and Eastern Europe.
Former titles (until 2000): Katholischer Arbeitskreis fuer Zeitgeschichtliche Fragen. Ost-West Informationsdienst (0939-3137); Katholischer Arbeitskreis fuer Zeitgeschichtliche Fragen. Informationsdienst (0176-5493)
Indexed: DIP, IBR, IBZ.
Published by: (Renovabis), Matthias-Gruenewald-Verlag GmbH (Subsidiary of: Schwabenverlag AG), Senefelderstr 12, Ostfildern, 73760, Germany. TEL 49-711-44060, FAX 49-711-4406177, mail@gruenewaldverlag.de, http://www.gruenewaldverlag.de. Eds. Dietger Demuth, Stefan Vesper. adv.: B&W page EUR 550; trim 118 x 182. Circ: 1,200 (paid and controlled).

320.2 DEU
OTTILIANER REIHE. Text in German. 2001. irreg., latest vol.12, 2010. price varies. **Document type:** *Monographic series, Academic/Scholarly.*
Published by: E O S Verlag, Erzabtei St. Ottilien, St.Ottilien, 86941, Germany. TEL 49-8193-71700, FAX 49-8193-71709, mail@eos-verlag.de.

282.71 CAN ISSN 0030-6843
OUR FAMILY; Canada's Catholic family monthly magazine. Text in English. 1949. m. CAD 17.98, USD 24.98. adv. illus.
Published by: Missionary Oblates of St. Mary's Province of Canada, P O Box 249, Battleford, SK S0M 0E0, Canada. TEL 306-937-7771, FAX 306-937-7644. Ed. Marie Louise Ternier Gommers. R&P N Gregoire. Circ: 8,000.

282 AUS ISSN 1833-0126
OUR LADY'S ROSARY MAKERS OF AUSTRALIA. ANNUAL REPORT. Text in English. 1998. a., latest 2007. free (effective 2009). **Document type:** *Corporate.*
Published by: Our Lady's Rosary Makers of Australia Inc, PO Box 216, Coonamble, NSW 2829, Australia. TEL 61-2-68221474, FAX 61-2-68221070, olrmaust@ozemail.com.au, http://www.ourladysrosarymakers.org.au/.

R

262.3 USA ISSN 0030-6924
OUR NORTHLAND DIOCESE. Text in English. 1946. s-m. USD 12.30 in parish; USD 14 out of parish (effective 2006). adv. bk.rev. **Document type:** *Newspaper, Consumer.* **Description:** Publishes inspirational news for the Diocese of Crookston.
Published by: Northland Diocese Association, PO Box 610, Crookston, MN 56716-0610. TEL 218-281-4533, FAX 218-281-3328. Ed., Adv. contact Carol J Evenson. Circ: 14,000. Wire service: CaNS.

282 USA ISSN 0030-6967
BX801
OUR SUNDAY VISITOR. Abbreviated title: O S V. Text in English. 1912. w. (Sun.). USD 38.95 combined subscription (print & online eds.) (effective 2009). bk.rev.; film rev.; play rev. illus. 20 p./no. 5 cols./p.; back issues avail. **Document type:** *Magazine, Consumer.* **Description:** Features important national and international religious events reported from a Catholic perspective including critical news, information, and spiritual guidance.
Related titles: Online - full text ed.
Indexed: CPL, S02, S03.
Published by: Our Sunday Visitor, Inc., 200 Noll Plz, Huntington, IN 46750. TEL 260-356-8400, 800-348-2440, FAX 260-356-8472, osvbooks@osv.com.

282 USA
AY81.R6
OUR SUNDAY VISITOR'S CATHOLIC ALMANAC. Text in English. 1904. a. USD 28.95 per issue (effective 2009). index. **Document type:** *Directory.* **Description:** Provides Catholic teaching and informative articles for researchers, homilists, writers, media professionals, students, and teachers.
Former titles (until 1996): Catholic Almanac (0069-1208); (until 1969): National Catholic Almanac; (until 1940): Franciscan Almanac; (until 1936): Franciscan Almanac Edition; (until 1931): Saint Anthony's Almanac
Related titles: Microfiche ed.: (from CIS).
Indexed: SRI.
Published by: Our Sunday Visitor, Inc., 200 Noll Plz, Huntington, IN 46750. TEL 260-356-8400, 800-348-2440, FAX 260-356-8472, osvbooks@osv.com, http://www.osv.com.

282 NLD ISSN 1568-2862
OVEREEN. Text in Dutch. 1986. s-a. EUR 16 (effective 2010).
Formerly (until 2001): Oosterse Christenen Dichtbij (1380-9059)
Published by: Katholieke Vereniging voor Oecumene, Walpoort 10, 's-Hertogenbosch, 5211 DK, Netherlands. TEL 31-73-6136471, FAX 31-73-6126610, secretariaat@oecumene.nl.

282 USA ISSN 0030-7564
OVERVIEW (CHICAGO); a continuing survey of issues affecting Catholics. Text in English. 1968. m. (11/yr.). USD 15.95. **Description:** Issues pertaining to the Catholic faith.
Published by: Thomas More Association, 205 W Monroe St, 6th Fl, Chicago, IL 60606. TEL 312-609-8880. Ed. Sara Miller. Circ: 4,000.

282 100 VAT
➤ **P A T H.** Text mainly in Italian; Text occasionally in English, French, German, Spanish. 2002. s-a. EUR 20 domestic; EUR 25 foreign; EUR 12 newsstand/cover (effective 2004 - 2005). bk.rev. back issues avail. **Document type:** *Journal, Academic/Scholarly.* **Description:** Contains arfticles theological and philosophical in nature which address questions of faith, religion and culture.
Published by: Libreria Editrice Vaticana, 00120, Vatican City. TEL 379-6-69885003, FAX 379-6-69884716. **Co-sponsor:** Pontificia Academia Theologica.

255.1 GBR ISSN 0266-6014
P A X; quarterly of the Benedictines of Prinknash. (Prinknash Abbey) Text in English. 1904. 2/yr. donation. bk.rev. back issues avail. **Document type:** *Magazine, Consumer.*
Indexed: MLA-IB.
—BLDSC (6413.041000).
Published by: Prinknash Abbey, c/o The Editor, PAX Newsletter, Prinknash Abbey, Cranham, Glos GL4 8EX, United Kingdom. Ed. Fr. Mark Hargreaves TEL 44-1452-813592. Circ: 400 (controlled).

266.2 USA ISSN 1066-5943
P I M E WORLD. Text in English. 1954. 10/yr. USD 5. reprints avail. **Document type:** *Newsletter.*
Formerly (until 1991): Catholic Life (0008-8218)
Related titles: Microfilm ed.: (from PQC).
Indexed: CERDIC.
Published by: Pontifical Institute for Foreign Missionaries, 17330 Quincy St, Detroit, MI 48221-2765. TEL 313-342-4066, FAX 313-342-6816. Ed. Paul W Witte. Pub. Rev. Bruno Piccolo. Circ: 26,200.

282 DEU ISSN 0340-7993
PAEPSTE UND PAPSTTUM. Text in English, German, Italian. 1971. irreg., latest vol.38, 2010. price varies. **Document type:** *Monographic series, Academic/Scholarly.*
Published by: Anton Hiersemann Verlag, Haldenstr 30, Stuttgart, 70376, Germany. TEL 49-711-5499710, FAX 49-711-54997121, info@hiersemann.de, http://www.hiersemann.de.

262.13 ESP ISSN 1132-0591
LA PALABRA. Text in Spanish. 1965. m. adv. **Document type:** *Magazine, Consumer.* **Description:** Contains reports, comments, dossiers, essays, interviews, and teachings of the Pope.
Published by: Ediciones Palabra S.A., Paseo Castellana, 210, Madrid, 28046, Spain. TEL 34-91-3507739, FAX 34-91-3590230, epalsa@edicionespalabra.es, http://www.edicionespalabra.es/. Ed. Belen Martin G. Cabiedes. Pub. Jose Miguel Perosanz. R&P Belen Martin G Cabiedes. Adv. contact Arturo Hernansanz. Circ: 20,000.

282 USA ISSN 0896-1727
LA PALABRA ENTRE NOSOTROS. Text in Spanish. 1984. bi-m. USD 18; USD 23 foreign (effective 1998). bk.rev. back issues avail.
Related titles: ◆ English ed.: The Word Among Us. ISSN 0742-4639; Polish ed.; Portuguese ed.; Japanese ed.
Published by: Word Among Us, 319 W Town Pl, Ste 319, St. Augustine, FL 32092. TEL 301-874-1700, 800-775-9673, FAX 301-874-2190, wordamongus@wau.org. Ed. Leo Zanchettin. Pub. Jeffrey C Smith. R&P Pat Sullivan. Circ: 35,000 (paid).

230.2 DEU
PALLOTTINISCHE STUDIEN ZU KIRCHE UND WELT. Text in German. 1997. irreg., latest vol.10, 2009. price varies. **Document type:** *Monographic series, Academic/Scholarly.*
Published by: E O S Verlag, Erzabtei St. Ottilien, St.Ottilien, 86941, Germany. TEL 49-8193-71700, FAX 49-8193-71709, mail@eos-verlag.de.

282 USA ISSN 0274-9009
PAN Z WAMI. Text in English. 6/yr. **Document type:** *Newsletter.*
Published by: Polish American Liturgical Center, PO Box 538, Keego Harbor, MI 48320-0538. TEL 810-683-0409.

230.2 POL
PAPIESKI FAKULTET TEOLOGICZNY WE WROCLAWIU. ROZPRAWY NAUKOWE. Text in Polish. irreg., latest vol.13. **Document type:** *Monographic series, Academic/Scholarly.*
Published by: Papieski Fakultet Teologiczny we Wroclawiu, Pl Katedralny 14, Wroclaw, 50329, Poland. TEL 48-71-229970, FAX 48-71-229970.

280.4 USA ISSN 0279-7828
PARISH COMMUNICATION. Text in English. 1981. q. USD 23 domestic; USD 30 foreign (effective 2005). bk.rev. abstr.; stat. back issues avail. **Document type:** *Newsletter, Trade.* **Description:** Presents seasonal graphics, quotes from saints and modern leaders, weekly essays, puzzles, calendars, and sketches to be used in parish bulletins and newsletters.
Related titles: Diskette ed.
Published by: Fred B. Estabrook Company, Inc., PO Box 428, New Hampton, NH 03256-0428. Circ: 1,100 (controlled and free).

264 USA ISSN 0164-6443
PARISH LITURGY. Text in English. 1978. q. USD 26 (effective 2005). bk.rev.; music rev. illus. 40 p./no. 2 cols./p.; back issues avail. **Document type:** *Magazine, Trade.* **Description:** Serves the personnel of Roman Catholic parishes, with special emphasis on preparation of the Sunday Eucharist celebration.
Published by: American Catholic Press, 16565 S State St, South Holland, IL 60473. TEL 708-331-5485, FAX 708-331-5484, http://www.americancatholicpress.org. Ed. Rev. Michael Gilligon. Circ: 1,200 (paid).

250 USA ISSN 0271-728X
BX801
PARISH VISITOR. Text in English. 1924. q. USD 2 (effective 2001). **Description:** Publishes articles about the life and work of the parish visitors. Includes articles of a general religious nature.
Published by: Parish Visitors of Mary Immaculate, PO Box 658, Monroe, NY 10950. TEL 914-783-2251. Ed. George A Morton. R&P George Morton. Circ: 13,500.

282 ZAF ISSN 0031-2088
PARISHIONER. Text in English. 1902. 10/yr. per issue contribution. adv. bk.rev. **Document type:** *Newsletter.*
Published by: Cathedral of St. Mary the Virgin, PO Box 2029, Johannesburg, 2000, South Africa. TEL 27-11-333-2537, FAX 27-11-29-0051. Ed. Lynda Wyngaard. Circ: 1,500.

282 ITA
PAROLA SPIRITO E VITA. Text in Italian. 1979. s-a. EUR 29 domestic; EUR 38.90 in the European Union; EUR 41.20 elsewhere (effective 2008). back issues avail. **Document type:** *Magazine, Consumer.*
Indexed: IZBG.
Published by: Centro Editoriale Dehoniano, Via Scipione dal Ferro 4, Bologna, BO 40138, Italy. TEL 39-051-4290451, FAX 39-051-4290491, ced-amm@dehoniane.it, http://www.dehoniane.it. Circ: 3,000.

282 ITA ISSN 0031-2398
PAROLE DI VITA; bimestrale dell'Associazione Biblica Italiana. Text in Italian. 1955. bi-m. EUR 25 domestic; EUR 30 foreign (effective 2009). bk.rev. index. **Document type:** *Magazine, Consumer.*
Indexed: OTA.
Published by: Messaggero di Sant' Antonio Editrice, Via Orto Botanico 11, Padua, PD 35123, Italy. TEL 39-049-8225777, FAX 39-049-8225650, info@santantonio.org, http://www.edizionimessaggero.it. Circ: 3,000.

282.85 PER
PASTORAL ANDINA. Text in Spanish. 1974. bi-m. USD 30 domestic; USD 40 foreign. **Document type:** *Newspaper.* **Description:** Current news on the Catholic Church and pastoral activities in the southern Andes of Peru.
Indexed: AICP.
Published by: Instituto de Pastoral Andina, Apdo Postal 1018, Cuzco, Peru. TEL 51-84-238068, FAX 51-84-225205. Circ: 3,500.

PASTORAL LITURGY. *see* MUSIC

282 USA ISSN 1079-4751
PASTORAL PATTERNS. Text in English. 1973. q. USD 14.95 per issue domestic; USD 24.95 per issue foreign (effective 2011). **Document type:** *Magazine, Trade.* **Description:** Provides a worship liturgy resource presenting optional texts and suggestions for use in Roman Catholic services.
Related titles: Online - full text ed.: USD 9 (effective 2011); ◆ Spanish ed.: Palabras Pastorales. ISSN 1541-8138.
Published by: World Library Publications, Inc. (Subsidiary of: J.S. Paluch Co., Inc.), 3708 River Rd, Ste 400, Franklin Park, IL 60131. TEL 847-233-2752, 800-621-5197, FAX 847-233-2762, 888-957-3291, wlpcs@jspaluch.com. Ed. Mary Brewick. Circ: 32,500 (paid).

200.92 GBR
BX801
THE PASTORAL REVIEW. Text in English. 1930. bi-m. GBP 34.40 domestic; GBP 43.75 foreign; GBP 6.57 per issue domestic; GBP 6.96 per issue in Europe; AUD 19.76 per issue in Australia; USD 14.33 per issue in United States; CAD 18.44 per issue in Canada; GBP 7.75 per issue elsewhere (effective 2009). adv. bk.rev. index. back issues avail.; reprints avail. **Document type:** *Journal, Academic/Scholarly.* **Description:** Aims to reach all those actively involved in all aspects of pastoral responsibilities within the Church.
Former titles (until 2004): Priests and People (0952-6390); (until 1987): The Clergy Review (0009-8736)
Indexed: CERDIC, CLA, CPL, OTA, P30.
—CCC.
Published by: (Catholic Church), Tablet Publishing Co. Ltd., 1 King St Cloisters, Clifton Walk, London, W6 0QZ, United Kingdom. TEL 44-20-87488484, FAX 44-20-87481550, tablet@subscription.co.uk. Ed. Rev. Michael Hayes. Adv. contact Margaret Beaman TEL 44-1903-885623. color page GBP 350, B&W page GBP 290; trim 149 x 216.

282 DEU
PASTORALBLATT. Text in German. 1948. m. EUR 33.55; EUR 2.80 newsstand/cover (effective 2005). adv. **Document type:** *Newsletter.*
Published by: J.P. Bachem Verlag GmbH, Ursulaplatz 1, Cologne, 50668, Germany. TEL 49-221-16190, FAX 49-221-1619205, info@bachem-verlag.de, http://www.bachem-verlag.de. R&P Lambert Bachem.

268 DEU ISSN 0555-9308
PASTORALTHEOLOGISCHE INFORMATIONEN. Text in German. 1968. 2/yr. EUR 30; EUR 18 per issue (effective 2006). **Document type:** *Journal, Academic/Scholarly.*
Indexed: A21, RI-1.
Published by: Konferenz der Deutschsprachigen Pastoraltheologen e.V., Postfach 1429, Schwerte, 58209, Germany. konferenz@pastoraltheologie.de. Ed. Reinhard Feiter.

255 POL ISSN 1505-9634
PASTORES. Text in Polish. 1998. q. EUR 33 foreign (effective 2005).
Published by: Wydawnictwo Diecezji Pelplinskiej Bernardinum, ul Bpa Dominika 11, Pelplin, 83130, Poland. TEL 48-58-5361757, sekretarzpastores@bernardinum.csc.pl, http://www.bernardinum.com.pl. Ed. Miroslaw Cholewa. **Dist. by:** Ars Polona, Obroncow 25, Warsaw 03933, Poland. TEL 48-22-5098609, FAX 48-22-5098610, arspolona@arspolona.com.pl, http://www.arspolona.com.pl.

282 USA ISSN 2159-1806
▼ **PASTORES DABO VOBIS.** Text in English. 2010. bi-m. free (effective 2011). **Document type:** *Newsletter, Trade.*
Media: Online - full text.
Published by: The National Black Catholic Seminarians Association, c/o Christopher S Rhodes, Theological College, 401 Michigan Ave, NE, Washington, DC 20017. nbcseminarians@gmail.com, http://www.nbccongress.org/seminarians/. Ed. Desmond Drummer.

282 PRT ISSN 1645-0817
PATRIARCADO DE LISBOA. ANUARIO. Text in Portuguese. 2000. a. **Document type:** *Magazine, Consumer.*
Published by: Patriarcado de Lisboa, Mosterio de Sao Vicente de Fora, Campo de Santa Clara, Lisbon, 1100-472, Portugal. info@patriarcado-lisboa.pt, http://www.patriarcado-lisboa.pt.

230.2 DEU
PATRISTISCHES ZENTRUM KOINONIA-ORIENS. SCHRIFTENREIHE. Text in German. 1979. irreg., latest vol.54, 2008. price varies. **Document type:** *Monographic series, Academic/Scholarly.*
Published by: (Patristisches Zentrum Koinonia-Oriens e.V.), E O S Verlag, Erzabtei St. Ottilien, St.Ottilien, 86941, Germany. TEL 49-8193-71700, FAX 49-8193-71709, mail@eos-verlag.de.

282 DEU ISSN 1436-9214
PAULINUS; Wochenzeitung im Bistum Trier. Text in German. 1875. w. EUR 68.20 (effective 2011). adv. **Document type:** *Newspaper, Consumer.* **Description:** Provides news and items of interest to members of the Catholic diocese of Trier.
Incorporates (1970-1997): Trierer Forum (1436-9206)
Published by: Paulinus Verlag GmbH, Maximineracht 11c, Trier, 54295, Germany. TEL 49-651-46080, FAX 49-651-4608221, verlag@paulinus.de, http://www.paulinus.de. Ed. Bruno Sonnen.

230.2 SWE ISSN 1403-7467
PAULUS; tidskrift foer konservativ och katolsk kultur. Text in Swedish. 1999. bi-m. SEK 1,020 (effective 2000). bk.rev. illus.; tr.lit. **Document type:** *Consumer.*
Media: Online - full text.
Published by: Bo Cavefors Ed. & Pub., Fack 4552, Malmo, 20320, Sweden. TEL 46-40-97-58-79. R&P Bo Cavefors TEL 46-40-95879. Circ: 100.

282 CHE
PAULUS-AKADEMIE ZUERICH. SCHRIFTEN. Text in German. 2003. irreg., latest vol.6, 2009. price varies. **Document type:** *Monographic series, Academic/Scholarly.*
Published by: (Paulus-Akademie Zuerich), Theologischer Verlag Zurich, Badenerstr 73, Zurich, 8026, Switzerland. TEL 41-44-2993355, FAX 41-44-2993358, tvz@ref.ch, http://www.tvz-verlag.ch.

230.0732 CAN ISSN 0031-3335
PAX REGIS. Text in English. 1942. s-a. USD 3. illus. **Description:** Articles and news for alumni of the Seminary of Christ the King, and for those interested in Roman Catholic seminary education.
Published by: Westminster Abbey Ltd., Dewdney Trunk Rd, Mission, BC V2V 4J2, Canada. TEL 604-826-8975. Ed. Alban Riley. Circ: 1,500.

282 PRT
PAZ E ALEGRIA. Text in Portuguese. 1907. m. bk.rev.
Supersedes: Alma (0002-6239)
Published by: Familia Franciscana Portuguesa, Rua Serpa Pinto, 7, Lisbon, 1200, Portugal. jufra@mail.pt. Circ: 3,000.

282 028.5 SVN ISSN 1580-4275
PEDAGOSKA ZBIRKA. Text in Slovenian. 1996. irreg., latest vol.4, 2004. price varies. **Document type:** *Monographic series, Academic/Scholarly.*
Published by: Salve d.o.o., Rakovniska 6, Ljubljana, 1001, Slovenia. TEL 386-1-4277310, FAX 386-1-4273040, info@salve.si, http://www.salve.si.

282 NLD ISSN 2211-6281
PEERKE DONDERS. Text in Dutch. 1961. q. **Document type:** *Magazine, Consumer.*
Formerly (until 2011): Petrus Donders (1382-0389)
Published by: Stichting Vrienden Petrus Donders, De Schans 95, Tilburg, 5011 EN, Netherlands. TEL 31-13-4550663, info@norbertijnentilburg.nl. Eds. Ronald Peeters, Paul Spapens.

282 FRA ISSN 1166-7095
PENTECOTE. Text in French. 194?. m. EUR 26.60 domestic; EUR 34 in Europe; EUR 36.50 elsewhere (effective 2009). **Document type:** *Magazine, Consumer.*
Formerly (until 1974): Viens et Vois (1166-7109)
Published by: Editions Viens et Vois, 22 Rue Paul Bert, Decines, 69150, France. TEL 33-4-78497171, FAX 33-4-72057139, info@viensetvois.fr.

282 IDN ISSN 0553-6448
PERABA. Text in Indonesian, Javanese. w.
Formerly (until 1968): Praba
Address: Bintaran Kidul 5, Yogyakarta, Indonesia. Ed. W Kartosoeharsono.

282 ITA ISSN 1974-5249
PERCORSI AGOSTINIANI. Text in Italian. 2008. s-a. EUR 15 domestic; EUR 20 foreign (effective 2010). **Document type:** *Magazine, Consumer.*
Published by: Provincia Agostiniana d'Italia, Convento Santa Rita, Via Colle delle Rose 30, Riano, RM 00060, Italy. TEL 39-06-9036121, FAX 39-06-9036213.

262.9 ITA
PERIODICA DE RE CANONICA. Text in English, French, German, Italian, Latin, Spanish. 1903. q. index. **Document type:** *Monographic series, Academic/Scholarly.* **Description:** Offers research, articles and timely essays on the most recent Church legislation regarding collegiality, marriage, consecrated life, and secularization.
Former titles (1927-1991): Periodica de Re Morali Canonica Liturgica (0031-529X); (1919-1927): Periodica de Re Canonica et Morali Utilia Praesertim Religiosis et Missionariis; (1911-1919): De Religiosis et Missionariis Supplementa et Monumenta Periodica
Indexed: CLA, CPL, DIP, DoGi, FR, IBR, IBZ.
—IE.
Published by: (Pontificia Universita Gregoriana/Pontifical Gregorian University), Gregorian University Press/Editrice Pontificia Universita Gregoriana, Piazza della Pilotta 35, Rome, 00187, Italy. TEL 39-06-6781567, FAX 39-06-6780588, periodicals@biblicum.com, http://www.paxbook.com. Circ: 1,000.

200 BRA ISSN 0031-5486
PERMANENCIA. Variant title: Revista Permanencia. Text in Portuguese. 1968. m. **Document type:** *Magazine, Consumer.*
Published by: Editora Permanencia, Rua Cosme Velho 1204, Rio de Janeiro, RJ 22211-091, Brazil. Ed. Julio Fleichman.

PETITE ETOILE. *see* CHILDREN AND YOUTH—For

282 CHE
PFARRBLATT. Text in French, German. 1910. w. CHF 32 (effective 1999). back issues avail. **Document type:** *Newspaper.*
Published by: Pfarrblatt-Gemeinschaft Bern, Lenghausgasse 24, Bern 7, 3000, Switzerland. TEL 41-31-3275050, FAX 41-31-3275055. Ed. Angelika Boesch. adv.: B&W page CHF 980. Circ: 47,500 (paid).

▼ **PFLEGE LEBEN**; Pflege - Werte - Zukunft. *see* SOCIAL SERVICES AND WELFARE

282.599 CAN
PHILIPPINES. Text in English, French. 1963. q. CAD 1.
Published by: Centre cor Jesu (Philippines), 328 rue Chapel, Ottawa, ON K1N 7Z3, Canada. Ed. Gerard Lefebvre. Circ: 1,500.

282 POL ISSN 0860-9985
PIELGRZYM. Text in Polish. 1869-1939; resumed 1989. fortn. PLZ 28; PLZ 1 newsstand/cover. adv. bk.rev.; tel.rev. illus. back issues avail. **Description:** Covers religious subjects, social problems, family life, church activies in the local area, sacral art and architecture.
Published by: Wydawnictwo Diecezjalne, Ul Biskupa Dominika 11, Pelplin, 83130, Poland. TEL 48-69-361775, TELEX 0512736. Circ: 15,000.

PIK PAK BOOM KIDDIE MAGZINE. *see* CHILDREN AND YOUTH—For

282 DEU
DER PILGER. Text in German. 1848. w. EUR 1.32 newsstand/cover (effective 2007). adv. **Document type:** *Magazine, Consumer.*
Published by: Pilger-Druckerei GmbH, Brunckstr 17, Speyer, 67346, Germany. TEL 49-6232-318360, FAX 49-6232-318379, redaktion@pilger-druckerei.de. Ed. Norbert Roenn. Adv. contact Susanne Rottmann. B&W page EUR 1,425, color page EUR 2,550. Circ: 27,087 (paid and controlled).

282 USA
THE PILOT. Text in English. 1829. w. (Fri.). USD 35; USD 1 newsstand/cover (effective 2008). **Document type:** *Newspaper, Consumer.*
Published by: Archdiocese of Boston, 66 Brooks Dr, Braintree, MA 02184-3839. TEL 617-746-5889, FAX 617-779-4562. Ed. Antonio Enrique. Pub. Cardinal Sean O'Malley. Adv. contact Larry Ricardo. Circ: 34,000 (paid). Wire service: CaNS.

282 USA ISSN 0032-0323
PITTSBURGH CATHOLIC. Text in English. 1844. w. USD 19 (effective 2010). adv. bk.rev.; film rev.; play rev. illus. **Document type:** *Newspaper, Consumer.*
Related titles: Online - full text ed.
Published by: (Catholic Diocese of Pittsburgh), Pittsburgh Catholic Publishing Associates, 135 First Ave., Ste. 200, Pittsburgh, PA 15222. TEL 412-471-1252, FAX 412-471-4228. Ed. William Cone. Pub. Most. Rev. D.W. Wuerl. Adv. contact Cynthia Scott. Circ: 110,866.

230.2 FRA
POINT THEOLOGIQUE. Text in French. irreg. **Document type:** *Monographic series.*
Indexed: RI-2.
Published by: Editions Beauchesne, 7 cite Cardinal Lemoine, Paris, 75005, France. TEL 33-1-53100818, FAX 33-1-53108519, contact@editions-beauchesne.com, http://www.editions-beauchesne.com. Ed. Charles Kannengiesser.

282 POL ISSN 1428-5673
➤ **POLONIA SACRA.** Text in Polish. 1918. a. **Document type:** *Journal, Academic/Scholarly.*
Former titles (until 1948): Nova Polonia Sacra (1428-9911); (until 1924): Polonia Sacra (1428-9903)
Published by: (Papieska Akademia Teologiczna w Krakowie/Pontifical Academy of Theology in Krakow), Wydawnictwo Naukowe Papieskiej Akademii Teologicznej w Krakowie, ul Franciszkanska 1, pok 037, Krakow, 31004, Poland. wydawnictwo@pat.krakow.pl.

➤ **POMME D'API SOLEIL**; pour parler des grandes questions avec les 4 a 8 ans. *see* CHILDREN AND YOUTH—For

920 262.13 USA
POPE JOHN PAUL II CENTER NEWSLETTER. Text in English. 1979. 5/yr. USD 5. **Document type:** *Newsletter.* **Description:** Includes biographical information, memoirs, publications and activities.
Related titles: ◆ Polish ed.: Centrum Jana Pawla II Biuletyn.
Published by: Pope John Paul II Center, Orchard Lake Schools, Orchard, Lake, MI 48324. TEL 313-683-0408. Ed. Alfred H Jantz.

282 PRT ISSN 1647-1237
O POVO DO LIMA. Text in Portuguese. 1975. bi-w. **Document type:** *Newspaper, Consumer.*
Published by: Milita Sanctae Mariae, Rua de Guadalupe 73, Braga, 4710-298, Portugal. TEL 351-253-611609, http://milicia.com.sapo.pt.

255.1 CAN ISSN 0032-664X
PRAIRIE MESSENGER. Text in English. 1923. 46/yr. CAD 26, USD 66.50 (effective 1999). adv. bk.rev.; film rev. illus.
—CCC.
Published by: Order of St. Benedict, Inc., Muenster, SK S0K 2Y0, Canada. TEL 306-682-1772, FAX 306-682-5285. Ed., R&P Andrew Britz. Adv. contact Corie Hetzel. Circ: 7,300.

282 DEU ISSN 1610-1847
PRAXIS GOTTESDIENST. Text in German. 2002. m. EUR 22.80; EUR 2.40 newsstand/cover (effective 2010). **Document type:** *Journal, Academic/Scholarly.*
Published by: Verlag Herder GmbH, Hermann-Herder-Str 4, Freiburg Im Breisgau, 79104, Germany. TEL 49-761-27170, FAX 49-761-2717520, kundenservice@herder.de, http://www.herder.de.

282 DEU ISSN 0172-7478
PRAXIS IN DER GEMEINDE; Materialien und Erfahrungen. Text in German. 1979. q. EUR 19.40; EUR 5.40 newsstand/cover (effective 2008). adv. bk.rev. cum.index. back issues avail. **Document type:** *Journal, Academic/Scholarly.*
Published by: Matthias-Gruenewald-Verlag GmbH (Subsidiary of: Schwabenverlag AG), Senefelderstr 12, Ostfildern, 73760, Germany. TEL 49-711-44060, FAX 49-711-4406177, mail@gruenewaldverlag.de. Ed. Anneliese Hueck. Adv. contact Nina Baab TEL 49-6131-928620. B&W page EUR 750; trim 120 x 200. Circ: 1,100 (paid and controlled).

282 DEU ISSN 0032-7212
DER PREDIGER UND KATECHET; Praktische katholische Zeitschrift fuer die Verkuendigung des Glaubens. Text in German. 1850. 6/yr. EUR 37.80; EUR 8.90 newsstand/cover (effective 2008). adv. index. **Document type:** *Journal, Consumer.*
Related titles: Online - full text ed.: EUR 49.90 (effective 2008).
—CCC.
Published by: Schwabenverlag AG, Senefelderstr 12, Ostfildern, 73760, Germany. TEL 49-711-4406140, FAX 49-711-4406138, info@schwabenverlag.de, http://www.schwabenverlag.de. adv.: B&W page EUR 850. Circ: 6,200 (paid and controlled).

282 USA ISSN 8750-9326
EL PREGONERO. Text in Spanish. 1977. w. (Thu.). free (effective 2005). 32 p./no. 6 cols./p.; **Document type:** *Newspaper.*
Related titles: Online - full text ed.
Indexed: ENW, P23, P48, P53, PQC.
Published by: (Centro Catolico Hispano), Carroll Publishing Company, 1058 Thomas Jefferson St, N W, Washington, DC 20007. rafael@elpreg.org. Ed. Rafael Roncal. Adv. contact Francisco Vega. Circ: 50,000 (free). Wire service: CNS, CaNS. **Co-sponsor:** Archdiocese of Washington.

253 CAN ISSN 0383-8307
PRETRE ET PASTEUR; revue des agents de pastorale. Text in English. 1898. m. (except Jul./Aug. combined). CAD 30.49; CAD 50 foreign. bk.rev. index. back issues avail. **Document type:** *Newspaper.* **Description:** Provides priests and other ministers with up-to-date pastoral and liturgical theology.
Former titles (until 1970): Revue Eucharistique du Clerge (0383-8293); (until 1936): Annales des Pretres - Adorateurs et de la Ligue Sacerdotale de la Communion (0703-3567); Association des Pretres - Adorateurs et la Ligue Sacerdotale de la Communion. Annales (0841-5404); Association des Pretres - Adorateurs. Annales (0841-5390)
Published by: Blessed Sacrament Fathers, 4450 St Hubert, Montreal, PQ H2J 2W9, Canada. TEL 514-525-6210, FAX 514-521-8752. Ed. Jean-Yves Garneau. R&P Jean Yves Garneau TEL 514-524-8760. Circ: 2,700 (paid).

262.3 FRA ISSN 0032-7956
PRETRES DIOCESAINS. Text in French. 1863. 10/yr. EUR 50 domestic; EUR 70 foreign; EUR 5 per issue (effective 2010). bk.rev. abstr.; bibl. index. 48 p./no.; **Document type:** *Magazine.* **Description:** Intended for those involved in the clergy. Addresses problems in the Catholic church as well as spiritual issues. Features Biblical studies and a bibliographic section.
Former titles (until 1948): L' Union Apostolique (1271-5700); (until 1920): Etudes Ecclesiastiques sur les Devoirs du Sacerdoce (1271-5697); (until 1868): Pretres du Sacre-Coeur. Annales (1271-5689)
Published by: Union Apostolique du Clerge, 179 rue de Tolbiac, Paris, 75013, France. TEL 33-1-45893253, FAX 33-1-45899330, http://www.uac.fr/pages/indexpag.html.

282 CAN ISSN 1203-8946
PRIERES MISSIONNAIRES. Text in French. 1994. m. CAD 10 (effective 2003). illus. 81 p./no. 1 cols./p.; back issues avail. **Document type:** *Newsletter.* **Description:** Prayers and short celebrations in a missionary spirit.
Published by: Missionnaires de la Consolata, 2505 Boul Gouin O, Montreal, PQ H3M 1B5, Canada. TEL 514-334-1910, FAX 514-332-1940, http://www.consolata.qc.ca. Ed. Jean Pare. Circ: 250 (paid); 50 (controlled).

282 USA ISSN 0032-8200
BX803
THE PRIEST. Text in English. 1925. m. USD 40.95 combined subscription (print & online eds.) (effective 2009). adv. bk.rev. tr.lit. 52 p./no. 3 cols./p.; reprints avail. **Document type:** *Magazine, Consumer.* **Description:** Parish product showcase for Roman Catholic priests and deacons, with homily aids and commentary.
Supersedes (in 1945): Acolyte
Related titles: Microform ed.: (from PQC); Online - full text ed.
Indexed: A01, A22, CERDIC, CPL, P28, P30, P53, P54, PQC.
Published by: Our Sunday Visitor, Inc., 200 Noll Plz, Huntington, IN 46750. TEL 260-356-8400, 800-348-2440, FAX 260-356-8472, osvbooks@osv.com. Ed. Msgr. Owen Campion.

282 AUS ISSN 0818-9005
THE PRIEST. Text in English. 1986. s-a. **Document type:** *Journal, Trade.*
Published by: Australian Confraternity of Catholic Clergy, PO Box 246, Jamison, ACT 2614, Australia. acccsecretariat@gmail.com, http://www.australianccc.org. Ed. Paul-Anthony McGavin TEL 61-2-62516547.

282 DEU ISSN 0172-0929
PRIESTERJAHRHEFT. Text in German. 1926. a. free (effective 2009). **Document type:** *Newsletter, Trade.* **Description:** Sermon material for Catholic priests in Germany for the "Diaspora-Sonntag".
Published by: Bonifatiuswerk der Deutschen Katholiken e.V., Kamp 22, Paderborn, 33098, Germany. TEL 49-5251-29960, FAX 49-5251-299688, info@bonifatiuswerk.de, http://www.bonifatiuswerk.de. Ed. Clemens Kathke. Circ: 20,000 (controlled).

282 FRA ISSN 0982-4944
PRIONS EN EGLISE. Text in French. 1987. m. EUR 34 domestic; EUR 39 in the European Union; EUR 39 DOM-TOM; EUR 45 elsewhere (effective 2009). **Document type:** *Magazine, Consumer.* **Description:** This monthly magazine of daily prayer offers commentaries for Sunday Mass, suggestions for liturgical activities and other aids to prayer.
Published by: Bayard Presse, 3-5 rue Bayard, Paris, 75393 Cedex 08, France. TEL 33-1-44356060, FAX 33-1-44356161, redactions@bayard-presse.com, http://www.bayardpresse.com. Ed. Pere Benoit Gschwind. Circ: 470,000.

282 CAN ISSN 0383-8285
PRIONS EN EGLISE - EDITION COMPLETE. Text in French. 1965. m. CAD 17.95 domestic; USD 15.95 in United States; USD 39.95 elsewhere (effective 2000).
Related titles: ◆ English ed.: Living with Christ - Complete Edition. ISSN 0703-6752.
Published by: Novalis, St Paul University, 223 Main St, Ottawa, ON K1S 1C4, Canada. TEL 613-236-1393, FAX 613-782-3004, http://www.novalis.ca. Ed. Pierre Dufresne. **Subscr. to:** 49 Front St E, 2nd Fl, Toronto, ON M5E 1B3, Canada. TEL 800-387-7164, FAX 800-204-4140.

282 CAN ISSN 0383-8277
PRIONS EN EGLISE - EDITION DOMINICALE. Text in French. 1936. w. (plus 2 special issues).
Related titles: ◆ English ed.: Living with Christ - Sunday Edition. ISSN 0703-6760.
Published by: Novalis, St Paul University, 223 Main St, Ottawa, ON K1S 1C4, Canada. TEL 613-236-1393, FAX 613-782-3004. Ed. Pierre Dufresne. Pub. Michael O'Hearn. **Subscr. to:** C.P. 990, Ville Mont-royal, PQ H3P 3M8, Canada.

282 FRA
PRIONS EN EGLISE - GRAND CARACTERES. Text in English. 1988. m. (plus one special issue). EUR 40 domestic; EUR 45 DOM-TOM; EUR 45 in the European Union; EUR 46 elsewhere (effective 2009).
Published by: Bayard Presse, 3-5 rue Bayard, Paris, 75393 Cedex 08, France. TEL 33-1-44356060, FAX 33-1-44356161, redactions@bayard-presse.com, http://www.bayardpresse.com. Ed. Pere Benoit Gschwind.

282 FRA ISSN 1769-4981
PRIONS EN EGLISE JUNIOR (2004). Text in French. 1992. bi-m. EUR 29 domestic; EUR 36.50 DOM-TOM; EUR 36.50 in the European Union; EUR 39 elsewhere (effective 2009 & 2010). **Document type:** *Magazine, Consumer.* **Description:** Helps children 8 to 12 years old to understand the Gospel.
Supersedes (in 2004): Les Lectures de la Messe (1266-670X); Which was formerly (until 199?): Prions en Eglise Junior (1168-0024)
Published by: Bayard Presse, 3-5 rue Bayard, Paris, 75393 Cedex 08, France. TEL 33-1-44356060, FAX 33-1-44356161, redactions@bayard-presse.com, http://www.bayardpresse.com. Ed. Delphine Sauliere.

282 USA
PRO ECCLESIA MAGAZINE. Text in English. 1965; N.S. 1990. q. USD 20 (effective 1999). adv. bk.rev. illus. **Description:** Examines attacks against the Catholic church and provides answers based on Catholic teachings.
Formerly (until 1990): Pro Ecclesia; Incorporates: Common Good; Talks of Pope John Paul II; Which was formerly: Talks of Pope Paul VI
Indexed: RI-1, RI-2.
Published by: Pro Ecclesia Foundation, 350 Fifth Ave, Rm 3304, New York, NY 10118-0110. TEL 212-673-7447. Ed., R&P Timothy A Mitchell. Circ: 5,000 (paid).

282 POL ISSN 1232-6437
PRO PATRIA; magazyn katolicko-spoleczny. Text in Polish. 1992. bi-m. PLZ 20. adv. illus. back issues avail. **Description:** Provides cultural, socio-political information on the Chelm Region from the Catholic perspective.
Published by: Towarzystwo Kulturalno-Oswiatowe Pro Patria, Ul Ks Piotra Skargi 7-8, Chelm, 22100, Poland. TEL 651096. Ed. Andrzej Miskur. Adv. contact Andrzej Miskur.

282 BEL ISSN 0778-6735
➤ **PROBLEMES D'HISTOIRE DES RELIGIONS.** Text in French. 1971-1989; N.S. 1990. a. price varies. back issues avail. **Document type:** *Monographic series, Academic/Scholarly.*
Formerly (until 1990): Problemes d'Histoire du Christianisme (0778-6751)
Indexed: CERDIC, DIP, IBR, IBZ, RI-2.
Published by: (Universite Libre de Bruxelles, Institut d'Etude des Religions et de la Laicite), Editions de l'Universite de Bruxelles (Subsidiary of: Universite Libre de Bruxelles), Av Paul Heger 26, CP 163, Brussels, 1000, Belgium. TEL 32-2-650-3799, FAX 32-2-650-3794. Ed. Alain Dierkens TEL 32-2-650-3809.

262.3 ITA
PROCULUS. Text in Italian. 1917. q. adv. **Document type:** *Magazine, Consumer.* **Description:** Covers theology, history, archeology and life in the diocese.
Former titles (until 1987): Diocesi di Pozzuoli. Bollettino Ecclesiastico (1972-8174); (until 1934): La Voce della Verita (1972-8166)
Published by: Diocesi di Pozzuoli/Curia Vescovile, Via Campi Flegrei 12, Pozzuoli, NA 80078, Italy. TEL 39-081-5261204, info@diocesipozzuoli.org, http://www.diocesipozzuoli.org.

282 POL ISSN 0137-8384
PRZEWODNIK KATOLICKI. Text in Polish. 1895. w. PLZ 46.80 domestic; USD 17.24 in United States; PLZ 0.90 newsstand/cover. adv.
Published by: Drukarnia i Ksiegarnia Sw. Wojciecha, Pl Wolnosci 1, Poznan, 60967, Poland. TEL 48-61-529186, FAX 48-61-523746. Ed. Marek Jedraszewski. adv.: page PLZ 1,756.80. Circ: 40,000 (controlled).

282 NOR ISSN 1503-8998
Q KATOLSK UNGDOM; blad for unge katolikker. Text in Norwegian. 1946. q. back issues avail. **Document type:** *Magazine, Consumer.*
Former titles (until 2003): Katolsk Ungdom (1500-2934); (until 1957): Ignis (1500-3434)
Related titles: Online - full text ed.

R

Published by: Norges Unge Katolikker, Akersveien 16A, Oslo, 0177, Norway. TEL 47-23-219540, FAX 47-23-219543, nuk@nuk.no. Ed. Martin Bjoernland. Circ: 2,000.

262.9 ITA ISSN 1124-1179
K17

QUADERNI DI DIRITTO ECCLESIALE. Text in Italian. 1988. q. **Document type:** *Magazine, Consumer.*
Indexed: CLA.
Published by: Editrice Ancora, Via G Battista Niccolini 8, Milan, 20154, Italy. TEL 39-02-3456081, FAX 39-02-34560866, editrice@ancora-libri.it, http://www.ancora-libri.it.

282 POL ISSN 1234-2289
QUAESTIONES SELECTAE. Text in Polish. 1994. 2/yr. **Document type:** *Journal, Academic/Scholarly.*
Indexed: IZBG.
Published by: Wyzsze Seminarium Duchowne Zakonu Braci Mniejszych, al Jan Kasprowicza 26, Wroclaw 8, 51161, Poland. TEL 48-71-3273401, FAX 48-71-3273431, rektor@franciszkanie.com, http://www.franciszkanie.com.

282 AUT ISSN 1817-0358
QUART. Text in German. 19??. q. **Document type:** *Magazine, Consumer.*
Formerly (until 2001): Actio Catholica (0400-4256)
Published by: Katholische Aktion Oesterreich, Forum Kunst-Wissenschaft-Medien, Otto-Mauer-Zentrum, Waehringerstr 2-4, Vienna, 1090, Austria. TEL 43-1-317616531, forum-kwm@kaoe.at, http://www.kaoe.at.

255.2 DEU ISSN 0942-4059
QUELLEN UND FORSCHUNGEN ZUR GESCHICHTE DES DOMINIKANERORDENS. Text in German. 1992. irreg., latest vol.16, 2008. price varies. **Document type:** *Monographic series, Academic/Scholarly.*
Published by: Akademie Verlag GmbH (Subsidiary of: Oldenbourg Wissenschaftsverlag GmbH), Markgrafenstr 12-14, Berlin, 10969, Germany. TEL 49-30-4220060, FAX 49-30-42200657, info@akademie-verlag.de, http://www.akademie-verlag.de.

262.13 USA ISSN 1044-0518
BX1793
QUOTE..UNQUOTE; a public information service. Text in English. 1980. m. looseleaf. free (effective 2005). Website rev. 12 p./no.; back issues avail. **Document type:** *Bulletin.* **Description:** Comments from notable persons and publications about papal and Vatican affairs and activities within the context of traditional Catholicism.
Published by: (Catholic Traditionalist Movement, Inc.), C T M Publications, Inc., 210 Maple Ave, Westbury, NY 11590-3117. TEL 516-333-6470, FAX 516-333-7535, http://www.latinmass-ctm.org. Ed., R&P Gommar A De Pauw TEL 516-333-6470.

282 CAN ISSN 0035-3795
BX2350A1R6
R N D. (Revue Notre-Dame) Text in French. 1903. m. CAD 15; CAD 28 foreign (effective 1999). adv. illus. **Description:** Studies social and religious formation.
Indexed: PdeR.
Published by: Missionnaires du Sacre-Coeur, 2215 rue Marie Victorin, Sillery, Quebec, PQ G1T 1J6, Canada. TEL 418-681-3581, FAX 418-681-1139. Ed. Paul Desaulniers. Pub. Paul Eugene Chabot. Adv. contact Thomas Maurais. Circ: 130,000.

282 IND ISSN 0048-668X
RALLY. Text in English. 1973 (vol.50). m. bk.rev. **Document type:** *Magazine, Trade.*
Published by: All India Catholic University Federation, 52 Sterling Rd, Chennai, Tamil Nadu 600 034, India. TEL 91-44-28272283, FAX 91-44-28229573, aicuf@aicuf.net. Circ: 1,500.

282 GBR ISSN 0033-9245
RANSOMER. Text in English. 1893. 3/yr. USD 15 (effective 2001). adv. bk.rev. **Document type:** *Newsletter.*
Published by: Guild of Our Lady of Ransom, 31 Southdown Rd, London, SW20 8QJ, United Kingdom. TEL 44-20-8947-2598, FAX 44-20-8944-6208. Ed. Msgr. Anthony George Stark. Circ: 1,750 (controlled).

282 CAN ISSN 0381-7482
RASSEMBLER. Text in English. 1940. 6/yr. CAD 24.69 domestic; USD 24.95 in United States; USD 29.95 elsewhere (effective 2000).
Published by: Novalis, St Paul University, 223 Main St, Ottawa, ON K1S 1C4, Canada. TEL 613-236-1393, FAX 613-782-3004, http://www.novalis.ca. Ed. Lise Lachance. **Subscr. to:** 49 Front St E, 2nd Fl, Toronto, ON M5E 1B3, Canada. TEL 800-387-7164, FAX 800-204-4140.

230.2 DEU
▼ **RATZINGER-STUDIEN.** Text in German. 2009. irreg., latest vol.2, 2010. price varies. **Document type:** *Monographic series, Academic/Scholarly.*
Published by: Verlag Friedrich Pustet, Gutenbergstr 8, Regensburg, 93051, Germany. TEL 49-941-920220, FAX 49-941-92022330, verlag@pustet.de, http://www.pustetverlag.de.

282 GBR
REAL LIFE. Text in English. 1947. q. GBP 12 (effective 2009). bk.rev.; film rev.; play rev. **Document type:** *Bulletin.* **Description:** Provides information about Young Christian Workers.
Formerly: New Life (London, 1947) (0028-6079)
Related titles: Online - full text ed.: free (effective 2009).
Published by: Young Christian Workers, St Joseph's, off St Joseph's Grove, Watford Way, Hendon, London, NW4 4TY, United Kingdom. TEL 44-20-82036290, FAX 44-20-82036291, info@ycwimpact.com, http://www.ycwimpact.com.

282 IRL ISSN 0034-0960
REALITY. Text in English. 1936. m. (11/yr.). EUR 1.25 newsstand/cover (effective 2005). adv. bk.rev. illus. **Document type:** *Bulletin.*
Formerly (until 1966): The Redemptorist Record (0791-153X)
Indexed: CERDIC.
Published by: Redemptorist Publications, 75 Orwell Rd., Rathgar, Dublin, Dublin 6, Ireland. TEL 353-1-4922488, FAX 353-1-4922654, info@redemptoristpublications.com, http://www.redemptoristpublications.com. Ed. Gerard Moloney. Adv. contact Gary Hanlon. color page EUR 700. Circ: 12,000.

282 FRA ISSN 0034-1258
BL3 CODEN: ANKHEW
➤ **RECHERCHES DE SCIENCE RELIGIEUSE.** Text in French; Summaries in English. 1910. q. EUR 68 domestic; EUR 77 foreign (effective 2009). bk.rev. index, cum.index: 1910-1960. reprints avail. **Document type:** *Journal, Academic/Scholarly.*
Indexed: A21, A22, Biblnd, C33, CERDIC, DIP, FR, IBR, IBZ, IPB, IZBG, MLA, MLA-IB, OTA, PCI, RI-1, RI-2, SCOPUS.
—BLDSC (7309.160000), IE, Infotrieve, Ingenta, INIST. **CCC.**
Published by: Association Recherches de Science Religieuse, 14 rue d'Assas, Paris, 75006, France. TEL 33-1-44394847, FAX 33-1-44394841, r.s.r@wanadoo.fr. Ed. Pierre Gibert. Circ: 1,400 (paid).

282.94 AUS ISSN 1038-0493
THE RECORD (DARLINGHURST). Text in English. 1900. q. AUD 10. bk.rev. illus. index. **Document type:** *Magazine, Consumer.* **Description:** Provides pictures and articles relating to society work of helping the needy in Australia or overseas.
Formerly: Saint Vincent de Paul Record (0036-3219)
Published by: Saint Vincent de Paul Society, 243, Deakin West, ACT 2600, Australia. TEL 61-2-62021200, julies@svdpnatcl.org.au. Ed. John McNamara. Circ: 19,000.

262.3 USA ISSN 0746-8474
THE RECORD (LOUISVILLE). Text in English. 1879. w. (Thu.). USD 16 subscr - mailed; USD 0.50 newsstand/cover (effective 2005). adv. **Document type:** *Newspaper, Consumer.*
Published by: Archdiocese of Louisville, 1200 South Shelby St, Louisville, KY 40203-2600. TEL 502-636-0296, FAX 502-585-2466, comm@archlou.org, http://www.archlou.org. Adv. contact Rick Goetz. col. inch USD 28. Circ: 69,000 (paid).

282.94 AUS ISSN 1327-3531
THE RECORD (WEST PERTH). Text in English. 1874. w. bk.rev. **Document type:** *Newspaper, Consumer.* **Description:** Publishes Catholic news for Western Australian Catholics.
Former titles (until 1922): W A Record; (until 1888): West Australian Catholic Record
Published by: Record (West Perth), 587 Newcastle St, West Perth, W.A. 6005, Australia. TEL 61-8-92277080, FAX 61-8-92277087, cathrec@iinet.net.au.

940 282 GBR ISSN 0034-1932
BX1491.A1
RECUSANT HISTORY. Text in English. 1951. s-a. GBP 15, USD 30; GBP 20, USD 40 foreign. adv. index, cum.index every 2 yrs. back issues avail.
Formerly (until 1957): Biographical Studies, 1534-1829 (0268-4195)
Indexed: A22, AmHI, B24, BrArAb, BrHumI, CERDIC, FR, H07, HistAb, IBR, IBZ, MLA-IB, NumL, PCI, RILM, SCOPUS, T02.
—BLDSC (7331.155000), IE, Infotrieve, Ingenta, INIST.
Published by: Catholic Record Society, c/o Secretary L. Gooch, 12 Melbourne Pl, Wolsingham, Bishop Auckland, Durham DL13 3EH, United Kingdom. Circ: 800.

282 ITA ISSN 0034-3498
IL REGNO. Text in Italian. 1956. fortn. EUR 52 domestic; EUR 87.40 in the European Union; EUR 99.40 elsewhere (effective 2008). adv. bk.rev. bibl. index, cum.index. **Document type:** *Magazine, Consumer.* **Description:** It alternates every 15 days the publication of a section called Attualita (featuring problems and discussions about recent Church events and original interviews) with a section called Documenti (new documents issued by the Roman Catholic Church.).
Published by: Centro Editoriale Dehoniano, Via Scipione dal Ferro 4, Bologna, BO 40138, Italy. TEL 39-051-4290451, FAX 39-051-4290491, ced-amm@dehoniane.it, http://www.dehoniane.it. Circ: 12,000.

282 DEU ISSN 0341-3322
REGNUM; Schoenstatt - International Reflexion und Dialog. Text in German. 1965. q. EUR 19.60 (effective 2005). bk.rev. back issues avail. **Document type:** *Academic/Scholarly.*
Indexed: DIP, IBR, IBZ.
Published by: Patris Verlag, Postfach 1162, Vallendar, 56171, Germany. TEL 49-261-604090, FAX 49-261-671192, info@patris-verlag.de. Circ: 1,700.

266.2 USA ISSN 0048-7155
REIGN OF THE SACRED HEART. Text in English. 1934. q. illus.
Published by: Priests of the Sacred Heart, 6889 S Lovers Ln, Hales Corners, WI 53130. TEL 414-425-3383, FAX 414-425-5719. Ed. Fr. Frank. R&P John Cain. Circ: 490,000 (controlled).

282 ITA ISSN 0391-853X
RELIGIONE E SOCIETA (ROME); storia della chiesa e dei movimenti cattolici. Text in Italian. 1977. irreg., latest vol.31. price varies. **Document type:** *Monographic series, Academic/Scholarly.*
Published by: Edizioni Studium, Via Cassiodoro 14, Rome, 00193, Italy. TEL 39-06-6865846, FAX 39-06-6875456, info@edizionistudium.it, http://www.edizionistudium.it.

268 DEU ISSN 0173-0339
➤ **RELIGIONSPAEDAGOGISCHE BEITRAEGE.** Short title: R p B. Text in German. 1978. s-a. EUR 20.50; EUR 11.50 newsstand/cover (effective 2008). bk.rev. index. back issues avail. **Document type:** *Journal, Academic/Scholarly.* **Description:** Catholic publication concerned with the teaching of religion. Contains articles on the church, Bible, Catholic doctrine, and social issues.
Indexed: DIP, IBR, IBZ.
Published by: Arbeitsgemeinschaft Katholische Religionspaedagogik und Katechetik, c/o Prof Herbert A Zwergel, Universitaet Kassel, Standort Hollaendischer Platz, Diagonale 9, Zimmer 0407, Kassel, 34109, Germany. TEL 49-561-8043493, FAX 49-561-8043541, zwergel@uni-kassel.de. Ed. Werner Simon. Circ: 400.

230.0071 DEU ISSN 0341-8960
RELIGIONSUNTERRICHT AN HOEHEREN SCHULEN. Text in German. 1958. bi-m. EUR 28.90 domestic; EUR 33.90 foreign (effective 2001). adv. bk.rev. index. **Document type:** *Journal, Academic/Scholarly.* **Description:** Discusses topics in Catholic education; includes reports of current events and issues, as well as new publications.
Indexed: CERDIC, DIP, IBR, IBZ.
—**CCC.**
Published by: (Bundesverband der Katholischen Religionslehrer an Gymnasien e.V.), Patmos Verlag GmbH, Am Wehrhahn 100, Duesseldorf, 40211, Germany. TEL 49-211-16795-0, FAX 49-211-1679575, service@patmos.de, http://www.patmos.de. Ed. Theo Ahrens. Circ: 2,000.

282 USA ISSN 0279-0459
BX2385
RELIGIOUS LIFE. Text in English. 1976. bi-m. USD 20 domestic; USD 25 foreign (effective 2007). adv. bk.rev. 32 p./no.; back issues avail. **Document type:** *Newsletter, Consumer.* **Description:** Serves the Catholic religious communities and laity by fostering a more effective understanding of the Church's teaching on religious life.
Published by: Institute on Religious Life, PO Box 7500, Libertyville, IL 60048. TEL 877-267-1195, FAX 877-267-2044. Ed., R&P Michael Wick. Circ: 3,800 (paid and controlled).

282 IRL ISSN 0332-4346
➤ **RELIGIOUS LIFE REVIEW.** Text in English. 1961. bi-m. EUR 21.56 domestic; GBP 16.20 in Great Britain & Northern Ireland; EUR 23.06 in Europe; USD 26.40 elsewhere (effective 2004). **Document type:** *Journal, Academic/Scholarly.* **Description:** Provides a forum concentrating on problems of religious life or on questions which, though of interest to other Christians, might usefully be discussed in a more limited context.
Formerly (until 1980): Doctrine and Life. Supplement (0419-5078)
Published by: Dominican Publications, 42 Parnell Sq, Dublin, Dublin 1, Ireland. TEL 353-1-8731355, 353-1-8721611, FAX 353-1-8731760, sales@dominicanpublications.com. Ed. Austin Flannery.

282 USA
REMNANT OF ISRAEL. Text in English. 1976. q. free; free. back issues avail. **Document type:** *Newsletter.*
Published by: Remnant of Israel Publications, New Hope, KY 40052. TEL 502-325-3081. Ed. Mark Drogin. Circ: 15,000.

282 DEU ISSN 0340-8280
BX803
RENOVATIO; Zeitschrift fuer das interdisziplinaere Gespraech. Text in German. 1945. 4/yr. EUR 12.78; EUR 7.67 to students; EUR 4.10 newsstand/cover (effective 2002). adv. bk.rev. reprints avail. **Document type:** *Magazine, Academic/Scholarly.*
Formerly: Katholische Gedanke (0022-9385)
Indexed: CERDIC, DIP, IBR, IBZ.
Published by: Katholischer Akademikerverband Deutschlands e.V., Linder Weg 44, Marl, 45746, Germany. TEL 49-2365-5729090, FAX 49-2365-5729091, geschaeftsstelle@kavd.de, http://www.kavd.de. adv.: page EUR 330. Circ: 6,500.

REPORT ON THE IMPLEMENTATION OF THE CHARTER FOR THE PROTECTION OF CHILDREN AND YOUNG PEOPLE. *see* CHILDREN AND YOUTH—About

282 CAN ISSN 0034-6284
REVEIL MISSIONNAIRE. Text in French. 1966. bi-m. CAD 7 (effective 2003). adv. illus. 16 p./no. 2 cols./p.; back issues avail. **Document type:** *Newsletter.*
Published by: Missionnaires de la Consolata, 2505 Boul Gouin O, Montreal, PQ H3M 1B5, Canada. TEL 514-334-1910, FAX 514-332-1940, joseph@netrover.com, http://www.consolata.qc.ca. Ed. Jean Pare. Pub. Ghislaine Crete. Circ: 20,000.

289.9 USA ISSN 0034-639X
BX2400
➤ **REVIEW FOR RELIGIOUS**; a journal of Catholic spirituality. Text in English. 1942. q. USD 30 domestic; USD 36 foreign; USD 10 per issue (effective 2011). bk.rev. index. 112 p./no.; back issues avail. **Document type:** *Journal, Academic/Scholarly.* **Description:** Publishes articles on prayer and ministry, pastoral approaches to living and working with others, and concise book reviews and thoughtful poetry.
Related titles: Audio cassette/tape ed.; Microform ed.: (from PQC); Online - full text ed.
Indexed: A22, BRI, CBRI, CERDIC, CLA, CPL, MLA-IB, OTA, P30.
—**CCC.**
Published by: Jesuits of the Missouri Province, 3601 Lindell Blvd, Saint Louis, MO 63108. TEL 314-633-4610, FAX 314-633-4611. Ed. David L Fleming S J.

255.4 ESP ISSN 0211-612X
BX805
REVISTA AGUSTINIANA. Text in Spanish. 1960. 3/yr. EUR 18 (effective 2009). back issues avail. **Document type:** *Magazine, Consumer.*
Formerly (until 1980): Revista Agustiniana de Espiritualidad (0484-6370)
Indexed: A21, FR, IPB, IZBG, MLA-IB, PhilInd, RI-1, RILM.
—INIST.
Published by: Ediciones y Distribuciones Isla, Paso de la Alameda, 39, Madrid, 28440, Spain. TEL 34-91-8549590, FAX 34-91-8549612, editorial@agustinianas.es, http://www.agustinianas.com/. Ed. Rafael Lazcano Gonzalez.

282 CHL ISSN 0716-033X
LA REVISTA CATOLICA. Text in Spanish. 1843. q. CLP 16,000 domestic; USD 40 in Latin America; USD 50 elsewhere (effective 2002). adv. bk.rev. 88 p./no.; **Document type:** *Magazine, Academic/Scholarly.* **Description:** Presents theological topics, news of the Catholic world, information on Catholic literature.
Indexed: C01.
Published by: Seminario Pontificio Mayor de Santiago Chile, Casilla 3-D, Walker Martinez, 2020, La Florida, Santiago, Chile. TEL 56-2-2853119, FAX 56-2-285679, semin@cmet.net. Ed. Rodrigo Fernandois Polanco. Pub. Armando Carrasco Jara. Circ: 1,200.

280 CRI ISSN 1018-5763
REVISTA DE INTERPRETACION BIBLICA LATINOAMERICANA. Abbreviated title: R I B L A. Text in Spanish. 1988. 3/yr. **Document type:** *Magazine, Trade.*
Indexed: A21, OTA, RI-1.
Published by: Departamento Ecumenico de Investigaciones, Apdo. 390-2070, Sabanilla de Montes de Oca, San Jose, Costa Rica.

272.2 ESP ISSN 1131-5571
BX1735
REVISTA DE LA INQUISICION. Text in Spanish. 1991. a., latest vol.8, 1999. back issues avail. **Document type:** *Journal, Academic/Scholarly.* **Description:** Focuses on Roman Catholic religion with special emphasis on the inquisition period in Spain.
Related titles: Online - full text ed.: ISSN 1988-2785.
Indexed: CA, FR, HistAb, MLA-IB, T02.
—INIST.

Published by: (Universidad Complutense de Madrid, Instituto de Historia de la Inquisicion), Universidad Complutense de Madrid, Servicio de Publicaciones, C/ Obispo Trejo 2, Ciudad Universitaria, Madrid, 28040, Spain. TEL 34-91-3941127, FAX 34-91-3941126, servicio.publicaciones@rect.ucm.es, http://www.ucm.es/publicaciones.

262.9 ESP ISSN 0034-9372
K19 CODEN: REDCE4
REVISTA ESPANOLA DE DERECHO CANONICO. Text in French, Italian, Latin, Spanish; Summaries in English, Latin, Spanish. 1946. 2/yr. bk.rev. bibl. index, cum.index every 20 yrs. **Document type:** *Journal, Academic/Scholarly.*
Incorporates (in 1984): Colectanea de Jurisprudencia Canonica (0210-0711)
Indexed: CERDIC, CLA, DIP, FR, IBR, IBZ, P09, PCI, R&TA.
—INIST.
Published by: Universidad Pontificia de Salamanca, Servicio de Publicaciones, Calle Compania 5, Salamanca, 37002, Spain. TEL 34-923-277100. Ed. Yolanda Benito de Tapia. Circ: 1,000.

282 USA ISSN 0274-9092
BV2300.C35
REVISTA MARYKNOLL. Text in Spanish, English. 1980. 10/yr. USD 15 Donation (effective 2009). adv. illus. back issues avail. **Document type:** *Magazine, Consumer.* **Description:** Dedicated and directed toward Hispanics, their concerns and religiosity at home and abroad.
Related titles: ◆ English ed.: Maryknoll Magazine. ISSN 0025-4142.
Published by: Maryknoll Fathers and Brothers, PO Box 308, Maryknoll, NY 10545. TEL 914-941-7590, 888-627-9566, FAX 914-944-3613, mkweb@maryknoll.org, https://www.maryknollsociety.org/i.

282.85 PER
REVISTA PERUANA DE HISTORIA ECLESIASTICA. Text in Spanish. a. bk.rev. **Document type:** *Monographic series, Academic/Scholarly.* **Description:** Specializes in the history of the Catholic Church in Peru.
Published by: Academia Peruana de Historia Eclesiastica, Calle Hatun-Rumiyoc, 414, Apdo Postal 148, Cuzco, Peru. TEL 51-84-225211, FAX 51-84-222781. Ed. Severo Aparicio Quispe.

230.2 PER ISSN 1026-0021
BX1751.2
➤ **REVISTA TEOLOGICA LIMENSE.** Text in Spanish; Summaries in English, Spanish. 1966. 3/yr. USD 20 domestic; USD 40 in Latin America; USD 50 elsewhere (effective 2005). bk.rev. **Document type:** *Journal, Academic/Scholarly.* **Description:** Covers theology, education, philosophy, and history.
Indexed: OTA.
Published by: Facultad de Teologia Pontificia y Civil de Lima, C Carlos Bondy, no 700, Pueblo Libre, Apdo Postal 21 0135, Lima, Peru. TEL 51-14-4610013, FAX 51-14-4610245, cinte@ftpcl.edu.pe, http://ftpcl.edu.pe. Ed. Alfredo Garcia Quesada. Circ: 700.

230.2 COD ISSN 1016-2461
BR3
REVUE AFRICAINE DE THEOLOGIE. Text in English, French; Summaries in French. 1977. s-a. USD 70. back issues avail. **Document type:** *Journal, Academic/Scholarly.*
Indexed: CERDIC, PLESA.
Published by: Faculte Catholique de Kinshasa, BP 1534, Kinshasa-Limite, Congo, Dem. Republic.

255.1 BEL ISSN 0035-0893
BX3001
REVUE BENEDICTINE; de critique, d'histoire et de litterature religieuses. Text in English, French, German, Italian. 1884. 2/yr. bk.rev. abstr. index. back issues avail. **Document type:** *Journal, Academic/Scholarly.* **Description:** Studies occidental ecclesiastical history, with emphasis on biblical, patristic and monastic texts.
Formerly (until 1889): Messager des Fideles (1370-0103)
Related titles: Microfiche ed.: (from IDC).
Indexed: A22, DIP, FR, IBR, IBZ, MLA, MLA-IB, OTA, PCI, SCOPUS.
—IE, Infotrieve, INIST.
Published by: Abbaye de Maredsous, Denee, 5537, Belgium. TEL 32-82-698211, FAX 32-82-698321. Ed. Pierre-Maurice Bogaert. Circ: 1,000.

255.77 FRA ISSN 1163-3697
REVUE DES EQUIPES SAINT VINCENT. Text in French. 3/yr. bk.rev.
Former titles (until 1992): Equipes Saint Vincent (0763-5184); (until 1973): Echos des Charites de St. Vincent de Paul (0070-8305)
Published by: Federation Francaise des Equipes Saint-Vincent, 67 rue de Sevres, Paris, 75006, France. TEL 33-1-45441756, FAX 33-1-42229194, federation@equipes-saint-vincent.com, http://www.equipes-saint-vincent.com. Ed. Mauricette Borloo. Circ: 4,000.

230.2 FRA ISSN 0035-2217
BX802
REVUE DES SCIENCES RELIGIEUSES. Text in French. 1911. q. adv. bk.rev. abstr.; bibl. index. **Document type:** *Journal, Academic/Scholarly.* **Description:** Aims to present all fields of theology through concise and scientific articles.
Formerly (until 1914): Ancienne Litterature et d'Archeologie Chretienne. Bulletin (0996-2719)
Related titles: Microform ed.: (from SWZ).
Indexed: A21, A22, CERDIC, DIP, FR, IBR, IBZ, IPB, MLA-IB, OTA, PCI, R&TA, RI-1, RI-2.
—BLDSC (7948.500000), IE, Infotrieve, Ingenta, INIST.
Published by: Universite de Strasbourg II (Marc Bloch/Sciences Humaines), Faculte de Theologie Catholique, Palais Universitaire, Strasbourg, 67084, France. TEL 33-3-88259729, FAX 33-3-88379209, theo-catho@unistra.fr. Ed., R&P, Adv. contact Marie-Anne Vannier. Pub. Marie Anne Vannier. Circ: 1,100.

282 FRA ISSN 1148-6503
REVUE DU ROSAIRE. Text in French. 1927. 10/yr. EUR 24.80 domestic; EUR 27.90 DOM-TOM; EUR 31.70 elsewhere (effective 2009). **Document type:** *Journal, Consumer.*
Address: Couvent des Dominicains, 9 Rue Saint-Francois-de-Paule, Nice, 06300, France. TEL 33-4-93526555, FAX 33-4-92174101.

282.09 BEL ISSN 0035-3620
REVUE MABILLON. Text in French, Latin; Summaries in English, French. 1905; N.S. 1990. a., latest vol.16, 2005. EUR 74 (effective 2012). adv. abstr.; bibl.; charts; illus. index. back issues avail. **Document type:** *Journal, Academic/Scholarly.* **Description:** Studies the history of religious life and spirituality in the Middle Ages and modern times. Publishes previously unpublished texts and iconography.
Indexed: B24, DIP, FR, IBR, IBZ, MLA-IB, RASB.
—BLDSC (7926.770000), INIST.
Published by: (Institut de Recherche et d'Histoire des Textes FRA), Brepols Publishers, Begijnhof 67, Turnhout, 2300, Belgium. TEL 32-14-448030, FAX 32-14-428919, periodicals@brepols.net, http://www.brepols.net. Ed. Jean Becquet.

230.2 BEL ISSN 0080-2654
BL3
REVUE THEOLOGIQUE DE LOUVAIN. Text in French. 1970. 4/yr. EUR 45 combined subscription (print & online eds.) (effective 2011). bk.rev. cum.index: vols.1-10, 1970-1979; vols.11-20, 1980-1989 vols. 21-30, 1990-1999. 150 p./no.; back issues avail. **Document type:** *Journal, Academic/Scholarly.*
Related titles: Online - full text ed.: ISSN 1783-8401; ◆ Supplement(s): Revue Theologique de Louvain. Cahiers. ISSN 0771-601X.
Indexed: A20, A21, A22, ASCA, ArtHuCI, CPL, CurCont, FR, IBR, IBZ, IPB, IZBG, OTA, PCI, RI-1, RI-2, SCOPUS, W07.
—BLDSC (7956.080000), IE, Ingenta, INIST.
Published by: (Universite Catholique de Louvain, Faculte de Theologie et de Droit Canonique), Peeters Publishers, Bondgenotenlaan 153, Leuven, 3000, Belgium. TEL 32-16-235170, FAX 32-16-228500, peeters@peeters-leuven.be, http://www.peeters-leuven.be. Ed. A Haquin. Circ: 1,000.

230.2 BEL ISSN 0771-601X
➤ **REVUE THEOLOGIQUE DE LOUVAIN. CAHIERS.** Key Title: Cahiers de la Revue Theologique de Louvain. Text in French. 1980. irreg., latest 2009. price varies. back issues avail. **Document type:** *Monographic series, Academic/Scholarly.* **Description:** Examines theological issues in Catholicism.
Related titles: ◆ Supplement to: Revue Theologique de Louvain. ISSN 0080-2654.
Indexed: CERDIC, CLA, OTA.
Published by: (Universite Catholique de Louvain, Faculte de Theologie et de Droit Canonique), Peeters Publishers, Bondgenotenlaan 153, Leuven, 3000, Belgium. TEL 32-16-235170, FAX 32-16-228500, http://www.peeters-leuven.be.

282 USA ISSN 1938-8675
RHODE ISLAND CATHOLIC; faith, family & life since 1875. Text in English. 1875. w. (Thu.). USD 25 domestic (effective 2007). adv. **Document type:** *Newspaper.*
Formerly (until 2007): Providence Visitor (8750-5452)
Published by: Providence Visitor, 184 Broad St, Providence, RI 02903. TEL 401-272-1010, FAX 401-421-8418. Ed., R&P, Adv. contact Michael K Brown. col. inch USD 16.25. Circ: 40,000. Wire service: CaNS.

282 ITA ISSN 0393-3830
BX4045.A1
RICERCHE STORICHE SALESIANE; rivista semestrale di storia religiosa e civile. Text in Italian. 1982. s-a. EUR 28 domestic; EUR 35 foreign (effective 2008). bk.rev. **Document type:** *Journal, Academic/Scholarly.* **Description:** Features study and research on the history of St. John Bosco and the Salesians, as well as religious history and civilization.
Indexed: DIP, IBR, IBZ.
Published by: (Istituto Storico Salesiano), Universita Pontificia Salesiana, Editrice L A S, Piazza dell'Ateneo Salesiano 1, Rome, 00139, Italy. TEL 39-06-87290626, FAX 39-06-87240629, las@ups.urbe.it, http://las.ups.urbe.it.

220 ITA ISSN 0394-980X
BS410
RICERCHE STORICO BIBLICHE. Text in Italian. 1989. s-a. EUR 45.40 domestic; EUR 56.60 in the European Union; EUR 58.90 elsewhere (effective 2008). **Document type:** *Journal, Academic/Scholarly.*
Indexed: A21, DIP, IBR, IBZ, IZBG, OTA, PCI, RI-1, RI-2.
Published by: Centro Editoriale Dehoniano, Via Scipione dal Ferro 4, Bologna, BO 40138, Italy. TEL 39-051-4290451, FAX 39-051-4290491, ced-amm@dehoniane.it, http://www.dehoniane.it.

230.2 ITA ISSN 0042-7586
BX804
LA RIVISTA DEL CLERO ITALIANO. Text in Italian. 1920. m. EUR 40 domestic to institutions; EUR 65 foreign to institutions (effective 2009). adv. bk.rev. bibl. index. **Document type:** *Journal, Academic/Scholarly.* **Description:** Looks at many different issues in theology and various religious cultures.
Related titles: Online - full text ed.
Indexed: CERDIC, DIP, IBR, IBZ, RASB.
Published by: (Universita Cattolica del Sacro Cuore), Vita e Pensiero (Subsidiary of: Universita Cattolica del Sacro Cuore), Largo Gemelli 1, Milan, 20123, Italy. TEL 39-02-72342335, FAX 39-02-72342260, redazione.vp@mi.unicatt.it, http://www.vitaepensiero.it. Ed. Bruno Maggioni. Circ: 4,300.

282 ITA ISSN 0394-0594
RIVISTA DI ASCETICA E MISTICA. Text in Italian. 1929. q. EUR 26 (effective 2008). bk.rev. back issues avail. **Document type:** *Journal, Academic/Scholarly.*
Former titles (since 1978): Nuova Rivista di Ascetica e Mistica (0394-0586); (until 1976): Rassegna di Ascetica e Mistica. S. Caterina da Siena (0394-0578); Which was formed by the merger of (1950-1970): S. Caterina da Siena (1120-0308); (1956-1970): Rivista di Ascetica e Mistica (0485-232X); Which was formerly: Vita Cristiana (1120-0316)
Published by: Convento di S. Marco, Via Camillo Cavour, 56, Florence, FI 50129, Italy. TEL 055-287628. Ed. F Sbaffoni.

230.2 ITA
RIVISTA DI TEOLOGIA DELL'EVANGELIZZAZIONE. Text in Italian. s-a. EUR 26.90 domestic; EUR 38 in Europe; EUR 42 elsewhere (effective 2010). **Document type:** *Journal, Academic/Scholarly.*
Published by: Centro Editoriale Dehoniano, Via Scipione dal Ferro 4, Bologna, BO 40138, Italy. TEL 39-051-4290451, FAX 39-051-4290491, ced-amm@dehoniane.it, http://www.dehoniane.it.

230.2 ITA ISSN 0391-0946
BJ1188.5
RIVISTA DI TEOLOGIA MORALE. Text in Italian. 1969. q. EUR 37.50 domestic; EUR 47.90 in the European Union; EUR 50.20 elsewhere (effective 2008). **Document type:** *Journal, Academic/Scholarly.*
Indexed: A21, DIP, FR, IBR, IBZ, R&TA, RI-1.
—INIST.
Published by: Centro Editoriale Dehoniano, Via Scipione dal Ferro 4, Bologna, BO 40138, Italy. TEL 39-051-4290451, FAX 39-051-4290491, ced-amm@dehoniane.it, http://www.dehoniane.it. Circ: 2,500.

282 ITA ISSN 1974-4749
RIVISTA ECUMENICA. Text in Italian. 2008. bi-m. **Document type:** *Journal, Consumer.*
Published by: Editrice Domenicana Italiana, Via G Marotta 12, Naples, 80133, Italy. http://www.edi.na.it.

282 ITA ISSN 0035-6956
RIVISTA LITURGICA. Text in Italian. 1914-1994; resumed 1997. bi-m. EUR 40 domestic; EUR 60 in Europe; EUR 65 elsewhere (effective 2009). bk.rev. cum.index: 1914-1974. **Document type:** *Magazine, Consumer.*
Indexed: CERDIC.
Published by: (Universita Pontificia Salesiana VAT), Messaggero di Sant' Antonio Editrice, Via Orto Botanico 11, Padua, PD 35123, Italy. TEL 39-049-8225777, FAX 39-049-8225650, info@santantonio.org, http://www.edizionimessaggero.it. Circ: 2,000.

262.3 ITA
RIVISTA PASTORALE. Text in Italian. 1910. bi-m. adv. illus. **Document type:** *Magazine, Consumer.* **Description:** Covers regional conferences and other news concerning the diocese.
Formerly: Bollettino Ecclesiastico (0006-6788)
Published by: Arcidiocesi di Reggio Calabria - Bova, Curia Metropolitana, Via Tommaso Campanella 63, Reggio Calabria, 89127, Italy. TEL 39-0965-385511, FAX 39-0965-330963, curia@reggiocalabria.chiesacattolica.it, http://www.webdiocesi.chiesacattolica.it/cci_new/vis_diocesi.jsp?idDiocesi=165.

282 ITA ISSN 1971-1859
BX3139.N36
RIVISTA STORICA DEI CAPPUCCINI DI NAPOLI. Text in Italian. 1972. a. EUR 26 in Europe; EUR 32 elsewhere (effective 2008). adv. bk.rev. index. **Document type:** *Journal, Academic/Scholarly.*
Formerly (until 2005): Studi e Ricerche Francescane (1824-9442)
Indexed: CERDIC.
Published by: Telediffusione Cattolica - Editori Cappuccini Napoli (T D C - E C N), Via Macedonia 13, Naples, 80137, Italy. TEL 39-081-7519403, FAX 39-081-7519374. Ed. Ferdinando Mastroianni.

282 CHE ISSN 1420-6730
RIVISTA TEOLOGICA DI LUGANO/LUGANO THEOLOGICAL REVIEW/REVUE THEOLOGIQUE DE LUGANO. Text in French, German, Italian. 1996. q. CHF 69 in Europe (effective 2004). bk.rev.
Indexed: OTA.
Published by: Facolta di Teologia di Lugano, Via Buffi 13, Lugano, 6904, Switzerland. TEL 41-91-9138555, FAX 41-91-9138556, info@teologialugano.ch. Ed. Dr. A. Tombolini.

268 ITA ISSN 0391-108X
ROCCA. Text in Italian. 1940. fortn. adv. bk.rev. **Document type:** *Magazine, Consumer.*
Published by: Cittadella Editrice, Via Ancaiani 3, Assisi, PG 06081, Italy. TEL 39-075-813595, FAX 39-075-813719, http://www.cittadellaeditrice.com. Circ: 130,000.

282 POL ISSN 1233-1457
ROCZNIKI TEOLOGICZNE/ANNALS OF THEOLOGY. Text in Polish, English. 1949. a. **Document type:** *Journal, Academic/Scholarly.*
Formerly (until 1991): Roczniki Teologiczno-Kanoniczne (0035-7723)
Indexed: BibInd, FR, IBR, IBZ, IZBG, OTA.
—INIST.
Published by: Katolicki Uniwersytet Lubelski, Towarzystwo Naukowe, ul Gliniana 21, Lublin, 20616, Poland. TEL 48-81-5250193, FAX 48-81-5243177, tnkul@kul.lublin.pl, http://www.kul.lublin.pl/tn.

282 DEU ISSN 0035-7812
ROEMISCHE QUARTALSCHRIFT FUER CHRISTLICHE ALTERTUMSKUNDE UND KIRCHENGESCHICHTE. Text in German. 1905. s-a. EUR 178; EUR 90 newsstand/cover (effective 2010). adv. bk.rev. charts; illus. reprint service avail. from SCH. **Document type:** *Journal, Academic/Scholarly.*
Indexed: A22, AIAP, B24, DIP, FR, IBR, IBZ, MLA-IB, NumL, PCI, SCOPUS.
—IE, Infotrieve, INIST. **CCC.**
Published by: Verlag Herder GmbH, Hermann-Herder-Str 4, Freiburg Im Breisgau, 79104, Germany. TEL 49-761-27170, FAX 49-761-2717520, kundenservice@herder.de, http://www.herder.de.

282 USA
➤ **ROMAN CATHOLIC STUDIES.** Text in English. 1987. irreg., latest vol.27, 2010. price varies. back issues avail. **Document type:** *Monographic series, Academic/Scholarly.*
Published by: Edwin Mellen Press, 415 Ridge St, PO Box 450, Lewiston, NY 14092. TEL 716-754-2266, FAX 716-754-4056, cservice@mellenpress.com.

282 PRT ISSN 0035-8274
ROSARIO DE MARIA; publicacao mensal de espiritualidade rosario mariana. Text in Portuguese. 1944. m. bk.rev. illus. index.
Published by: Dominican Convent Friars-Fatima, Secretariado Nacional do Rosario, Fatima, 2495, Portugal. Ed. L Cerdeira. Circ: 7,000.

282 ITA ISSN 1824-1204
IL ROSARIO DI PADRE PIO. Text in Italian. 2004. s-a. **Document type:** *Magazine, Consumer.*
Published by: Edizioni Piemme SpA, Via Galeotto del Carretto 10, Casale Monferrato, AL 15033, Italy. TEL 39-0142-3361, FAX 39-0142-74223, http://piemme3.bluestudio.it.

282 ITA ISSN 0035-8282
IL ROSARIO E LA NUOVA POMPEI. Text in Italian. 1884. m. bk.rev. **Document type:** *Magazine, Consumer.* **Description:** Covers the many religious, charitable and social activities and initiatives of the Sanctuary of Our Lady of the Rosary of Pompei.
Related titles: English ed.
Published by: Pontificio Santuario di Pompei, Piazza B Longo 1, Pompei, NA 80045, Italy. TEL 39-081-8577321, FAX 39-081-8503357, rnp@santuario.it. Ed. Nicola Nicoletti.

282 ITA ISSN 1825-0718
ROSETUM. Text in Italian. m. **Document type:** *Magazine, Consumer.*
Former titles (until 1991): Nuovo Fra Ginepro (1825-070X); (until 1970): Fra Ginepro (1825-0696)

R

Published by: Centro Francescano Culturale Artistico Rosetum, Via Pisanello 1, Milan, Italy. TEL 39-02-40092015, FAX 39-02-40092195, info@rosetum.it, http://www.rosetum.it.

282 USA ISSN 0745-3299
AY76
ROZE MARYI. Text in Polish. 1944. q. USD 6. bk.rev.
Published by: Association of Marian Helpers, Eden Hill, Stockbridge, MA 01263. TEL 413-298-3691. Ed. Bro. Andrew Maczynski, MIC. Circ: 9,500.

220 POL ISSN 0209-0872
BS410
➤ **RUCH BIBLIJNY I LITURGICZNY.** Text in Polish; Summaries in English, Italian, French, German. 1948. q. PLZ 32 domestic; EUR 30 in Europe (effective 2006). bk.rev. **Document type:** *Journal, Academic/Scholarly.* **Description:** Covers bible studies and Roman Catholic liturgy.
Indexed: IZBG, OTA.
Published by: Polskie Towarzystwo Teologiczne/Polish Theological Society, ul Kanonicza 3, Krakow, 31002, Poland. TEL 48-12-4225690, zarzad@ptt.net.pl. Ed. Rev. Jerzy Chmiel. Circ: 800.

282 DEU
RUHRWORT; Wochenzeitung im Bistum Essen. Text in German. 1958. w. EUR 6.85 per month (effective 2009). adv. **Document type:** *Newspaper, Consumer.*
Published by: Essener Kirchenzeitung Verlagsgesellschaft mbH, Alfredistr 31, Essen, 45127, Germany. TEL 49-201-810900, FAX 49-201-8109010. Ed. Ulrich Engelberg. adv.: B&W page EUR 3,461.50; trim 312 x 430. Circ: 27,113 (paid and controlled).

268 AUT ISSN 0013-2489
RUNDBRIEF EHEMALIGER SCHUELER UND FREUNDE DER SCHULBRUEDER. Text in German. 1948. s-a. adv. bk.rev. abstr.; bibl.; charts; illus.; stat. **Document type:** *Newsletter, Consumer.*
Published by: Provinzialat der Brueder der Christlichen Schulen, Anton Boeck Gasse 20, Vienna, W 1210, Austria. TEL 43-1-29125501, FAX 43-1-2912595. Circ: 3,000.

282 USA
RURAL LANDSCAPES; a newsletter of faith, community and resources. Text in English. 1981. 6/yr. USD 25 to individuals; USD 100 to institutions (effective 2000). **Document type:** *Newsletter.*
Formerly (until 1993): Common Ground (Des Moines) (0746-5114)
Published by: National Catholic Rural Life Conference, 4625 Beaver Ave, Des Moines, IA 50310. TEL 515-270-2634, FAX 515-270-9447. Circ: 3,000.

266.2 CAN ISSN 1924-3553
S A M S UPDATE. (South American Missionary Society in Canada) Text in English. 198?. 3/yr. free (effective 2010). back issues avail. **Document type:** *Newsletter, Trade.* **Description:** Aims to encourage interest in mission and in South and Central America amongst Canadian Anglicans.
Former titles (until 2010): S A M S News (0839-1513); (until 1987): S A M S Canada News (0833-8469)
Related titles: Online - full text ed.: free (effective 2010).
Published by: S A M S Canada, PO Box 21082, Barrie, ON L4M 6J1, Canada. TEL 705-728-7151, FAX 705-728-6716, office@samscanada.ca.

268 USA
S C R C SPIRIT. Text in English. 1973. bi-m. looseleaf. free to members. adv. **Document type:** *Newsletter, Consumer.* **Description:** Provides teaching articles and lists events for the Catholic charismatic renewal.
Former titles (until 1994): S C R C Vision (1041-4045); S C R C Newsletter
Published by: Southern California Renewal Communities, 9795 Cabrini Dr, Ste 105, Burbank, CA 91504-1739. TEL 818-771-1361, FAX 818-771-1379, spirit@fea.net, http://www.scrc.org. Ed. Fr Bill Delaney S J. R&P, Adv. contact Sandy Berardino. Circ: 13,500.

282 ITA ISSN 1824-9892
SACERDOS (ITALIAN EDITION). Text in Italian. 1994. bi-m. **Document type:** *Magazine, Consumer.*
Related titles: English ed.: Sacerdos (English Edition). ISSN 1824-9868; Portuguese ed.: Sacerdos (Portuguese Edition). ISSN 1824-9876; Spanish ed.: Sacerdos (Spanish Edition). ISSN 1824-985X.
Published by: Edizioni A R T (Adveniat Regnum Tuum), Via G Sottile 18, Novara, 28100, Italy. TEL 39-0321-612799, http://www.edizioniart.it.

234.13 IRL ISSN 1649-4458
SACRED HEART MESSENGER. Text in English. 1888. m. EUR 18 domestic; GBP 13.50 in United Kingdom; EUR 25 foreign (effective 2005). charts; illus.; pat.; tr.mk. **Document type:** *Bulletin.* **Description:** Publication of the Apostleship of prayer- practical spirituality, family appeal, modern and balanced.
Formerly (until 1973): Irish Messenger of the Sacred Heart (0021-1303)
Published by: (Jesuit Fathers), Messenger Publications, 37 Lower Leeson St., Dublin, 2, Ireland. TEL 353-1-6767491, FAX 353-1-6611606, sj-shm@clubi.ie. Ed. Patrick Carberry. Circ: 120,000.

282 USA
SACRED HISTORY MAGAZINE. Text in English. 2005. bi-m. USD 24.95 (effective 2007). adv. illus. **Document type:** *Magazine, Consumer.*
Address: 1800 Thibodo Rd, Ste 230, Vista, CA 92081. TEL 760-597-9314, 888-937-6484, FAX 760-597-9318, info@sacredhistorymagazine.com. Ed. James Rietveld. Pub. James Griffith.

282 POL ISSN 1232-1575
BX1564.A1
SAECULUM CHRISTIANUM. Text in Polish. 1994. s-a. **Document type:** *Journal, Academic/Scholarly.*
Published by: (Uniwersytet Kardynala Stefana Wyszynskiego, Wydzial Nauk Historycznych i Spolecznych), Wydawnictwo Uniwersytetu Kardynala Stefana Wyszynskiego, Ul Dewajtis 5, Warsaw, 01815, Poland. wydawnictwo@uksw.edu.pl, http://www.uksw.edu.pl/wydawn/wydawnictwo.htm.

282 CAN ISSN 1922-3838
SAINT ANNE. THE ANNALS. Text in English. 1878. bi-m. USD 21 in US & Canada; GBP 11 in Ireland; CAD 25 elsewhere (effective 2010). adv. bk.rev. back issues avail. **Document type:** *Magazine, Consumer.*
Former titles (until 2009): Sainte Anne de Beaupre. The Annals (0318-434X); (until 1974): Good St. Anne de Beaupre. Annuals (0318-4331); (until 19??): St. Anne de Beaupre. Annuals (1484-2092)
Related titles: French ed.: Sainte Anne de Beaupre. ISSN 0318-4366.
Published by: Redemptorist Fathers, Ste-Anne de Beaupre Province Quebec, 10018 Ave Royale, Sainte Anne De Beaupre, PQ G0A 3C0, Canada. TEL 418-827-3781, 800-363-3585, FAX 418-827-8771, secretariat@ssadb.qc.ca.

282 USA
ST. ANSGAR'S BULLETIN. Text in English. 1910. a. USD 15 domestic membership; USD 25 foreign membership (effective 2005). illus.; stat. **Document type:** *Bulletin.*
Published by: St. Ansgar's Scandinavian Catholic League, c/o Patricia Sullivan, Sec., 3 East 28th St, 8th Fl, New York, NY 10016. aobrien@fordham.edu. Pub. Astrid M O'Brien. Circ: 1,400 (paid).

282 USA ISSN 0036-276X
BX801
SAINT ANTHONY MESSENGER. Text in English. 1893. m. USD 32 domestic; USD 52 foreign (effective 2009). adv. bk.rev.; film rev.; Website rev. index. 64 p./no.; reprints avail. **Document type:** *Magazine, Consumer.* **Description:** Features inspiring articles for the modern Catholic whose beliefs are steeped in a rich, abiding tradition.
Related titles: Microform ed.: (from PQC); Online - full text ed.: free (effective 2009).
Indexed: A22, CERDIC, CPL, P28, P30, P48, P53, P54, PQC.
Published by: (Franciscan Friars of St. John the Baptist Province), Franciscan Communication, 28 W Liberty St, Cincinnati, OH 45202. TEL 513-241-5615, 800-488-0488. Ed. Pat McCloskey. Adv. contact Peggie Jones. B&W page USD 4,157, color page USD 5,671; trim 7.875 x 10.5.

262.3 USA ISSN 0036-3022
AP2
ST. LOUIS REVIEW. Text in English. 1941. w. (Fri.). USD 20 (effective 2005). adv. bk.rev.; film rev. illus. **Document type:** *Newspaper, Consumer.*
Formerly: St. Louis Register
Related titles: Microfilm ed.
Published by: Catholic Archdiocese of St. Louis, 462 N Taylor Ave, St Louis, MO 63108. TEL 314-531-9700, FAX 314-531-2269, slreview@swbell.net. Pub. Archbishop Raymond Bur. Adv. contact Tom Courtaway. Circ: 90,000 (paid). Wire service: CaNS.

282 GBR ISSN 0036-3111
ST. MARTIN'S REVIEW; the journal with the international outlook. Text in English. 1893. m. GBP 8; GBP 10 foreign. adv. bk.rev.; play rev. illus. **Document type:** *Bulletin.*
Published by: St.-Martin-in-the-Fields Church, 5 St Martins Pl, London, WC2, United Kingdom. TEL 44-171-930-1862. Ed. Rev. Schuennemann. Circ: 1,500.

253 ESP ISSN 1138-1094
SAL TERRAE; revista de teologia pastoral. Text in Spanish. 1912. m. (11/yr.). EUR 45 domestic; EUR 56 in Europe; USD 67 elsewhere (effective 2009). **Document type:** *Magazine, Consumer.*
Formerly (until 1964): Sal Terrae. Parte Teorica (1138-1078); Which superseded in part (in 1954): Sal Terrae (0211-4569)
Related titles: Online - full text ed.: EUR 39 (effective 2009).
Indexed: CERDIC, CLA.
—CCC.
Published by: Editorial Sal Terrae, Poligono de Raos, Parcela 14-I, Maliano, Cantabria, 34600, Spain. TEL 34-942-369198, salterrae@salterrae.es. Ed. Enrique Sanz Gimenez-Rico.

371.07 USA ISSN 0036-3480
BV2300.S24
SALESIAN. Text in English. 1950. s-a. free (effective 2009). illus. back issues avail. **Document type:** *Magazine, Consumer.* **Description:** Contains informational, educational, and narrative material about the world-wide Salesian Missions, which ministers specifically to poor and abandoned youth.
Related titles: Online - full text ed.: free (effective 2009); Spanish ed.
Published by: Salesian Missions, 2 Lefevre Ln, New Rochelle, NY 10801. TEL 914-633-8344, FAX 914-633-7404, info@salesianmissions.org. Ed. Brother Emile Dube.

282 IRL ISSN 0790-1216
SALESIAN BULLETIN. Text in English. 1939. q. EUR 10 (effective 2005). bk.rev. 24 p./no.; back issues avail. **Document type:** *Bulletin.*
Published by: Salesians of Don Bosco Media, Salesian College, Celbridge, Co Kildare, Ireland. TEL 353-1-6275060, FAX 353-1-6303601, sdbmedia@eircom.net. Ed. Fr. Pat Egan. Circ: 15,000. **Subscr. to:** Salesian Missions, PO Box 50, Pallaskenry, Co. Limerick, Ireland.

282 ITA ISSN 0036-3502
BX800.A1
SALESIANUM. Text in English, French, German, Italian, Latin, Spanish. 1939. q. EUR 40 domestic; EUR 50 foreign (effective 2008). bk.rev. **Document type:** *Journal, Academic/Scholarly.* **Description:** Features sections that deal with theology, philosophy, canon law, and religious research.
Indexed: CERDIC, CLA, DIP, FR, IBR, IBZ, IPB, IZBG, MLA, MLA-IB, R&TA.
—INIST.
Published by: (Universita Pontificia Salesiana VAT), Universita Pontificia Salesiana, Editrice L A S, Piazza dell'Ateneo Salesiano 1, Rome, 00139, Italy. TEL 39-06-87290626, FAX 39-06-87240629, las@ups.urbe.it, http://las.ups.urbe.it. Circ: 1,000.

282 SVN ISSN 0353-0477
SALEZIJANSKI VESTNIK/SALESIAN BULLETIN; glasilo za salezijansko druzino. Text in Slovenian. 1904. 6/yr. free. **Document type:** *Bulletin.* **Description:** Contains information on the Church in Slovenia, Salesian society, missions, education, and Mariology.
Published by: (Salezijanski Inspektorat), Salve d.o.o., Rakovniska 6, Ljubljana, 1001, Slovenia. TEL 386-1-4277310, FAX 386-1-4273040, info@salve.si, http://www.salve.si. Ed. Janez Potocnik. Circ: 12,500.

282 ESP ISSN 0036-3537
BX805
SALMANTICENSIS. Text in Spanish. 1954. 3/yr. looseleaf. EUR 43 domestic; EUR 52 in Europe; EUR 60 elsewhere (effective 2008). bk.rev. bibl. index. **Document type:** *Journal, Academic/Scholarly.*
Indexed: A21, CERDIC, DIP, FR, IBR, IBZ, IPB, IZBG, MLA-IB, OTA, RI-1, RI-2.
—INIST.
Published by: Universidad Pontificia de Salamanca, Servicio de Publicaciones, Calle Compania 5, Salamanca, 37002, Spain. TEL 34-923-277100.

282 POL ISSN 1426-0662
SALWATOR. Text in Polish. 1934-1943; resumed 1947-1952; resumed 1996. bi-m. adv. bk.rev. **Description:** Aims to attract candidates to priesthood and religious life.
Published by: (Prowincjalat Salwatorianow), Wydawnictwo Salwatorianskie, Ul Sw Jacka 16, Krakow, 30364, Poland. TEL 58-12-665327, FAX 48-12-668824. Ed. Fr Bogdan Giemza Sds. Circ: 3,500. **Subscr. to:** B Glowackiego 3, Trzebinia 32540, Poland.

255.77 ITA
LA SAN VINCENZO IN ITALIA. Text in Italian. 1856. bi-m. EUR 10 (effective 2009). bk.rev. **Document type:** *Magazine, Consumer.*
Formerly: Samaritano (0036-3723)
Published by: Societa di San Vincenzo de Paoli, Consiglio Nazionale Italiano, Via della Pigna 13a, Rome, 00186, Italy. TEL 39-06-6796989, FAX 39-06-6789309. Ed. Antonio Strambi. Circ: 4,000.

230.2 ITA ISSN 1824-2367
SANCTORUM. Text in Italian. 2004. s-a.
Related titles: Online - full text ed.: ISSN 2036-5829.
Published by: (Associazione Italiana per lo Studio della Santita, dei Culti e dell'Agiografia (A I S S C A)), Viella Libreria Editrice, Via delle Alpi 32, Rome, 00198, Italy. TEL 39-06-8417758, FAX 39-06-85353960, info@viella.it, http://www.viella.it. Ed. Sofia Boesch Gajano.

282 AUS ISSN 1449-9606
SANDPIPER (BENDIGO). Text in English. 2004. m. **Document type:** *Newspaper, Consumer.* **Description:** Provides information about the Diocese of Sandhurst.
Published by: Diocese of Sandhurst, Diocesan Chancery, PO Box 201, Bendigo, VIC 3552, Australia. TEL 61-3-54412544, FAX 61-3-54418278, chancery@sand.catholic.org.au, http://www.sand.catholic.org.au. Ed. Damian Griffin.

282 USA
SANGRE DE CRISTO NEWSNOTES. Text in English. 1973. s-a. USD 10. bk.rev. back issues avail. **Document type:** *Newsletter.* **Description:** Deals with the Roman Catholic and Christian education, Marian apparitions, and Christian uniy in the renewed church of Jesus Christ.
Address: 210 S Second St, Box 89, Westcliffe, CO 81252. TEL 719-783-2840. Ed. Fr Dan E Jones. Circ: 450 (paid and controlled).

282 ITA ISSN 1970-4755
SANTI E BEATI. EROI DELLA FEDE. Text in Italian. 2006. w. **Document type:** *Magazine, Consumer.*
Published by: R C S Libri (Subsidiary of: R C S Mediagroup), Via Mecenate 91, Milan, 20138, Italy. TEL 39-02-5095-2248, FAX 39-02-5095-2975, http://rcslibri.corriere.it/libri/index.htm.

282 ITA ISSN 2035-2905
SANTI PROTETTORI. Text in Italian. 2008. m. **Document type:** *Magazine, Consumer.*
Published by: Sprea Editori Srl, Via Torino 51, Cernusco sul Naviglio, MI 20063, Italy. TEL 39-02-92432222, FAX 39-02-92432236, editori@sprea.it, http://www.sprea.it.

261.57 ITA ISSN 0391-7819
BX4684
IL SANTO; rivista francescana di storia dottrina arte. Text in English, French, Italian. 1961. 3/yr. EUR 45 domestic; EUR 55 foreign (effective 2009). bk.rev. abstr. index. back issues avail. **Document type:** *Journal, Academic/Scholarly.* **Description:** Covers the history of Franciscanism, with particular attention given to St. Anthony.
Indexed: AIAP, B24, DIP, IBR, IBZ, RILM.
Published by: Centro Studi Antoniani, Piazza del Santo 11, Padua, PD 35123, Italy. TEL 39-049-8762177, FAX 39-049-8762187, asscsa@tin.it, http://www.centrostudiantoniani.it. Ed. Luciano Bertazzo.

266.2 ITA ISSN 0036-4622
IL SANTUARIO DELLA MADONNA DELLE ROCCHE. Text in Italian. 1920. bi-m. free. bibl.; charts; illus.; stat. index. **Document type:** *Bulletin, Consumer.*
Published by: Passionisti, Molare, AL 15074, Italy.

282 ITA ISSN 1120-7825
LA SAPIENZA DELLA CROCE; rivista di cultura e spiritualita della passione. Text in Italian. 1986. q. **Document type:** *Magazine, Consumer.*
Related titles: Online - full text ed.
Published by: C I P I, Piazza dei Santi Giovanni E Paolo 13, Rome, 00184, Italy. TEL 39-06-77271474, FAX 39-06-7008012, cipi@pcn.net.

SCHOOLBESTUUR. *see* EDUCATION

268 GBR ISSN 0261-5703
SCHOOLS OF PRAYER. Text in English. 1980. 3/yr. GBP 9 domestic; GBP 10 in Europe; GBP 14 elsewhere. bk.rev. illus. **Description:** For those involved with celebrating the liturgy with young people. Contains ideas for prayer and worship in school, parish and home. Includes practical suggestions, background articles, and examples of liturgies from other communities.
Published by: Roman Catholic Diocese of Northampton, Religious Education Service, c/o Business Manager, Thevenet Centre, Thornton College, Milton Keynes, MK17 OHJ, United Kingdom. TEL 44-1280-814004, FAX 44-1280-814004. Eds. A Tomalak, K McGinnell. Circ: 400 (paid).

220 NLD ISSN 0167-3114
SCHRIFT; populair bijbeltijdschrift. Text in Dutch. 1953. bi-m. EUR 35.50 domestic; EUR 40 in Belgium; EUR 45 in Europe; EUR 50 elsewhere; EUR 6.50 newsstand/cover (effective 2009). bk.rev. **Description:** Catholic publication devoted to Biblical studies.
Formerly (until 1969): Boek der Boeken (0006-5544)
Indexed: CERDIC, IZBG.
Published by: Gooi en Sticht, Postbus 5018, Kampen, 8260 GA, Netherlands. TEL 31-38-3392556, FAX 31-38-3311776, gens@kok.nl, http://www.kok.nl. Ed. Ellen van Wolde.

282 DEU
SCHRIFTEN DES ARCHIVS DES ERZBISTUMS MUENCHEN UND FREISING. Text in German. 2001. irreg., latest vol.14, 2010. price varies. **Document type:** *Monographic series, Academic/Scholarly.*
Published by: Verlag Schnell und Steiner GmbH, Leibnizstr 13, Regensburg, 93055, Germany. TEL 49-941-787850, FAX 49-941-7878516, post@schnell-und-steiner.de.

DER SCHUETZENBRUDER; Zeitschrift fuer die Schuetzenfamilie. *see* CLUBS

SCHWAEBISCHE FORSCHUNGSGEMEINSCHAFT. VEROEFFENTLICHUNGEN. REIHE 2: URKUNDEN UND REGESTEN. B: DIE REGESTEN DER BISCHOEFE UND DES DOMKAPITELS VON AUGSBURG. see HISTORY—History Of Europe

282 CHE ISSN 1420-5041
BX803
SCHWEIZERISCHE KIRCHENZEITUNG. Text in German. 1832. w. CHF 123; CHF 3 newsstand/cover (effective 1999). adv. bk.rev. back issues avail. **Document type:** *Newspaper.*
Related titles: Online - full text ed.
Published by: Multicolor Print AG, Maihofstr 76, Luzern, 6006, Switzerland. TEL 41-429-5386, FAX 41-429-5367. Ed. Rolf Weibel. adv.: B&W page CHF 990; trim 261 x 189. Circ: 3,000 (paid).

260 CHE ISSN 1420-1380
SCHWEIZERISCHES KATHOLISCHES SONNTAGSBLATT. Text in German. 1886. w. **Document type:** *Newspaper, Consumer.*
Published by: Schmid - Fehr AG, Hauptstr 22-22a, Goldach, 9403, Switzerland. TEL 41-71-8440303, FAX 41-71-8440345, info@schmid-fehr.ch, http://www.schmid-fehr.ch.

220 GBR ISSN 0036-9780
BS410
SCRIPTURE BULLETIN. Text in English. 1946. s-a. GBP 10 domestic; GBP 12 foreign; free to members (effective 2009). bk.rev. **Document type:** *Bulletin, Academic/Scholarly.* **Description:** Aims to keep readers informed of current trends in biblical scholarship.
Formerly (until 1969): Scripture
Related titles: Diskette ed.
Indexed: A01, A22, CPL, IZBG, OTA, PCI, T02.
—BLDSC (8213.240000).
Published by: Catholic Biblical Association of Great Britain, Department of Theology and Religious Studies, Liverpool Hope University, Hope Park, Taggart Ave, Liverpool, L16 9JD, United Kingdom. millsm@hope.ac.uk. Ed. Ian Boxall.

207.8 USA
SCRIPTURE FROM SCRATCH. Text in English. 1994. irreg. USD 0.55 per issue (effective 2011). adv. back issues avail. **Document type:** *Newsletter, Trade.* **Description:** Discusses Scripture-based topics for Catholics.
Published by: St. Anthony Messenger Press, 28 W Liberty St, Cincinnati, OH 45202. TEL 513-241-5615, 800-488-0488, FAX 513-241-0399, stanthony@americancatholic.org, http://www.americancatholic.org.

207.8 IRL ISSN 0332-1150
BS534.5
SCRIPTURE IN CHURCH. Text in English. 1970. q. EUR 40.73 domestic; GBP 29.20 in Great Britain & Northern Ireland; EUR 40.13 in Europe; USD 50.72 elsewhere (effective 2004). back issues avail. **Document type:** *Journal, Consumer.* **Description:** Intended as an aid to understanding the Scripture readings at Mass.
Indexed: OTA.
—CCC.
Published by: Dominican Publications, 42 Parnell Sq, Dublin, Dublin 1, Ireland. TEL 353-1-8721611, 353-1-8731355, FAX 353-1-8731760, sales@dominicanpublications.com. Ed. Martin MacNamara. Circ: 6,200.

371.0712 268 ITA ISSN 0036-9810
BR5
SCUOLA CATTOLICA. Text in Italian. 1873. q. bk.rev. index. **Document type:** *Magazine, Consumer.*
Indexed: CERDIC, IZBG, MLA-IB, OTA.
Published by: Editrice Ancora, Via G Battista Niccolini 8, Milan, 20154, Italy. TEL 39-02-3456081, FAX 39-02-34560866, editrice@ancora-libri.it, http://www.ancora-libri.it. Circ: 1,100.

282 USA
SEASONAL MISSALETTE; worship resource. Text in English. 19??. q. USD 25 (effective 2011). **Document type:** *Magazine, Trade.* **Description:** Contains all of the appointed Scriptures, acclamations, and prayers from the Lectionary and Sacramentary, as well as scriptural commentary.
Media: Large Type.
Published by: World Library Publications, Inc. (Subsidiary of: J.S. Paluch Co., Inc.), 3708 River Rd, Ste 400, Franklin Park, IL 60131. TEL 847-233-2752, 800-621-5197, FAX 847-233-2762, 888-957-3291, wlpcs@jspaluch.com.

282 USA ISSN 2154-8757
BS543
▼ **SEAT OF WISDOM.** Text in English. 2010 (May). s-a. free (effective 2011). **Document type:** *Journal, Academic/Scholarly.*
Media: Online - full text.
Published by: Seminary of the Immaculate Conception, 440 W Neck Rd, Huntington, NY 11743. TEL 631-423-0483, FAX 631-423-2346, mhoonhout@icseminary.edu, http://www.icseminary.edu. Ed. Dr. Michael A Hoonhout.

282 ITA ISSN 1592-9973
IL SEGNO DEL SOPRANNATURALE. Text in Italian. 1988. m. bk.rev. 36 p./no.; back issues avail. **Document type:** *Magazine, Consumer.* **Description:** Includes detailed reports on the signs of the times such as miracles, healings, apparitions and charisms.
Published by: Edizioni Segno SRL, Via E. Fermi 80, Tavagnacco (UD), 33010, Italy. TEL 39-04-32575179, FAX 39-04-32575589, info@edizionisegno.it, http://www.edizionisegno.it.

282.68 COG ISSN 0488-2024
SEMAINE AFRICAINE. Text in French. 1952. w.
Indexed: RASB.
Address: BP 2080, Brazzaville, Congo, Republic. Ed. Bernard Mackiza. Circ: 8,000.

230.0732 VAT ISSN 0582-6314
SEMINARIUM; a review for seminaries, ecclesiastical vocations, universities. Text in Multiple languages. 1950; N.S. 1961. q. EUR 31 domestic; EUR 34 foreign (effective 2002). bk.rev. bibl. index. back issues avail. **Document type:** *Academic/Scholarly.* **Description:** Commentaries for seminaries, ecclesiastical vocations and universities, edited by the Congregation for Catholic Education.
Indexed: CERDIC, CPL, MLA-IB.
Published by: (Pontifical Society for Priestly Vocations), Libreria Editrice Vaticana, 00120, Vatican City. TEL 379-6-69885003, FAX 379-6-69884716. Circ: 2,500.

282 PRY
SENDERO. Text in Spanish. 2/w.
Address: ALBERDI, 874, Asuncion, Paraguay. TEL 21-95941. Ed. Ilde Silvero. Circ: 15,000.

282 ITA
SETTIMANA. Text in Italian. w. EUR 50.50 domestic; EUR 86.80 in the European Union; EUR 94 elsewhere (effective 2008). **Document type:** *Magazine, Consumer.*
Published by: Centro Editoriale Dehoniano, Via Scipione dal Ferro 4, Bologna, BO 40138, Italy. TEL 39-051-4290451, FAX 39-051-4290491, ced-amm@dehoniane.it, http://www.dehoniane.it.

282 USA ISSN 0192-7418
SHARE. Text in English. 1970. 3/yr. USD 4. adv. **Description:** Contains news of the organization and covers topics of national current and moral interest.
Published by: Catholic Daughters of America, 10 W 71st St, New York, NY 10023-4298. TEL 212-877-3041, FAX 301-816-8840. Ed. Peggy Eastman. Circ: 140,000.

263.041 USA
SHRINE BULLETIN. Text in English. 1978. 3/yr. USD 1 (effective 1999). **Document type:** *Bulletin.* **Description:** Calendar of monthly and daily events and pilgrimage information for the Shrine of the Immaculate Heart of Mary.
Published by: Blue Army of Our Lady of Fatima, U S A, Inc., 674 Mountain View Rd, Box 976, Washington, NJ 07882. TEL 908-689-1701, FAX 908-689-6279.

300 VEN ISSN 0254-1645
SIC. Text in Spanish. 1938. 10/yr. adv. bk.rev.; film rev. abstr.; bibl.; charts; illus.; stat. index.
Published by: Fundacion Centro Gumilla, Edificio Centro Valores Local 2 Esq. Luneta, Apdo 4838, Caracas, DF 1010-A, Venezuela. TEL 582-564-7557, FAX 582-5618205. Ed. Arturo Sosa S J. Circ: 6,500.

SIEGBURGER STUDIEN. see HISTORY—History Of Europe

SIGNES D'AUJOURD'HUI; la revue de l'animation liturgique. see MUSIC

SIGNES MUSIQUES; la revue du chant liturgique. see MUSIC

282 SWE ISSN 0347-0423
BX806.S8
SIGNUM; katolsk orientering om kyrka, kultur och samhaelle. Text in Swedish. 1975. 9/yr. SEK 310 domestic; SEK 360 in Scandinavia; SEK 410 in Europe; SEK 460 elsewhere; SEK 40 per issue (effective 2007). adv. bk.rev.; music rev. cum index: 1975-1994. back issues avail. **Document type:** *Magazine, Consumer.* **Description:** Provides a Catholic orientation of the Church, culture and society. Publishes articles on social issues, religion, humanities, arts and sciences.
Formed by the merger of (1920-1975): Credo (0011-1120); (1963-1975): K I T. Katolsk Informationstjenst (0345-6102)
Related titles: Online - full text ed.
Indexed: BAS, MLA-IB.
Published by: Newmaninstitutet. Katolsk Institut foer Teologi, Filosofi och Kultur/Newman Institute for Catholic Studies, Traedgaardsgatan 14, Uppsala, 75309, Sweden. adm@newman.se, http://www.newmaninstitut.nu. Eds. Franz-Josef Holin TEL 46-18-695686, Ulf Jonsson. Circ: 2,300.

SINGENDE KIRCHE; Zeitschrift fuer katholische Kirchenmusik. see MUSIC

228 NLD ISSN 1878-4941
SINT-JANSCENTRUM. Text in Dutch. 2002. a.
Published by: (Sint-Janscentrum), R.K. Instelling Sonnius, Papenhuist 4, 's-Hertogenbosch, 5211 LC, Netherlands. TEL 31-73-6123055, FAX 31-73-6145315, info@sonnius.nl.

266.2 USA
SISTER MIRIAM TERESA LEAGUE OF PRAYER BULLETIN. Text in English. 1946. q. USD 5. **Document type:** *Bulletin.* **Description:** Publicizes the life and mission of Sr. Miriam Teresa, a candidate for canonization.
Published by: Sisters of Charity, PO Box 476, Convent Station, NJ 07961-0476. TEL 201-605-3300. Ed. Marian Jose Smith. R&P Sr Marian Jose Smith. Circ: 3,000.

282 POL ISSN 0137-3447
SLASKIE STUDIA HISTORYCZNO-TEOLOGICZNE. Text in Multiple languages. 1968. irreg. **Document type:** *Academic/Scholarly.*
Indexed: IZBG.
Published by: Uniwersytet Slaski w Katowicach, Wydzial Teologiczny, ul Jordana 18, Katowice, 40043, Poland. TEL 48-32-3569056, FAX 48-32-3569055, sekretariat@wtl.us.edu.pl, http://www.wtl.us.edu.pl.

282.4373 USA ISSN 0897-8107
SLOVAK CATHOLIC FALCON. Text in English. 1911. w. (Wed.). USD 25 (effective 2005). bk.rev. illus. **Document type:** *Newspaper, Consumer.*
Formerly: Katolicky Sokol (0745-1571)
Published by: Slovak Catholic Sokol, 205 Madison St, Passaic, NJ 07055. TEL 973-777-2605, FAX 973-779-8245. Ed. Daniel F Tanzone. Circ: 10,000.

282 POL ISSN 1230-8668
SLOWO; dziennik katolicki. Text in Polish. 1947. 5/w. adv. illus. **Document type:** *Newspaper.*
Formerly (until 1993): Slowo Powszechne (0137-9283)
Indexed: RASB.
Published by: Inco-veritas sp. z o.o., Ul Mokotowska 43, Warsaw, 00551, Poland. TEL 48-22-6286011, FAX 48-22-6283387. Ed. Adam Wieczorek. Circ: 60,000. **Co-publisher:** Wydawnictwo Civitas Christiana.

282 USA ISSN 0892-5100
SLOWO I LITURGIA. Text in Polish. 1970. q. looseleaf. USD 25.
Published by: Polish American Liturgical Center, PO Box 538, Keego Harbor, MI 48320-0538. TEL 810-683-0409. Ed. Msgr. Jan Jagodzinski. Circ: 130.

220 POL ISSN 0867-7573
SLOWO WSROD NAS. Text in Polish. 1990. m. PLZ 20; USD 22 foreign. bk.rev. index. **Description:** Provides daily biblical meditation and articles for general audience.
Published by: Wydawnictwo Ksiezy Marianow, Ul Sw Bonifacego 9, Warsaw, 02914, Poland. TEL 48-22-6519970, FAX 48-22-6519055. Ed. Dariusz Mazewski. Circ: 20,000.

201.6 USA ISSN 0037-7767
HN37.C3
SOCIAL JUSTICE REVIEW; pioneer American journal of Catholic social action. Text in English. 1908. bi-m. USD 20 domestic; USD 30 foreign (effective 2011). bk.rev. back issues avail. **Document type:** *Journal, Academic/Scholarly.* **Description:** To defend human dignity.
Formerly (until 1940): Central-Blatt and Social Justice
Related titles: Microfilm ed.
Indexed: A22, CERDIC, CPL, MLA-IB, P30, RASB, S02, S03.
—Ingenta.
Published by: Catholic Central Union of America, 3835 Westminster Pl, St. Louis, MO 63108. TEL 314-371-1653, FAX 314-371-0889.

SOCIAL WORK PRACTICE MONOGRAPH SERIES. see SOCIAL SERVICES AND WELFARE

282 CAN ISSN 1484-7450
SOCIETE CANADIENNE D'HISTOIRE DE L'EGLISE CATHOLIQUE. BULLETIN. Text in French. s-a. **Document type:** *Bulletin.*
Formerly (until 1997): Societe Canadienne d'Histoire de l'Eglise Catholique. Bulletin de Liaison (1183-6490)
Related titles: Online - full content ed.
Published by: Societe Canadienne d'Histoire de l'Eglise Catholique, Secretariat du Centre interuniversitaire d'Etudes Quebecoises, Universite du Quebec a Trois-Rivieres, 3351, Boulevard des Forges, Trois-Rivieres, PQ G9A 5H7, Canada. TEL 819-376-5011 ext 3668, FAX 819-376-5179, http://www.cieq.uqtr.ca/schec/accueil.html.

282 ECU
SOLIDARIDAD. Text in Spanish. 1982. m.
Published by: Confederation of Catholic Office Staff and Students, Calle ORIENTE, 725, Quito, Pichincha, Ecuador. TEL 2-216-541. Circ: 15,000.

282 CAN ISSN 1910-4588
SOLIDARITY RESOURCE BOOK. THIRSTING FOR JUSTICE. Text in English. 2004. irreg. **Document type:** *Handbook/Manual/Guide, Consumer.*
Published by: Canadian Catholic Organization for Development and Peace, 10 St Mary St, Ste 420, Toronto, ON M4Y 1P9, Canada. TEL 416-922-1592, 800-494-1401, FAX 416-922-0957, ccodp@devp.org, http://www.devp.org.

282 170 AUS ISSN 1839-0366
▼ ➤ **SOLIDARITY: THE JOURNAL OF CATHOLIC SOCIAL THOUGHT AND SECULAR ETHICS.** Text in English. 2011. s-a. free. bk.rev. back issues avail. **Document type:** *Journal, Academic/Scholarly.* **Description:** Provides a forum for the discussion of social ethics, social justice and Catholic social thought.
Media: Online - full text. **Related titles:** Print ed.
Published by: University of Notre Dame Australia, Centre for Faith Ethics and Society, c/o Matt Beard, 104 Broadway, PO Box 944, Broadway, NSW 2007, Australia. TEL 61-2-82044189, http://www.nd.edu.au/university/University%20Research/CentreFaithEthics&Society.shtml. Pub. Sandra Lynch. **Co-sponsor:** Catholic Archdiocese of Sydney, Justice and Peace Office.

282 DEU ISSN 1617-6421
DER SONNTAG (LIMBURG). Text in German. 2000. w. EUR 6.55 per month (effective 2010). adv. **Document type:** *Newspaper, Consumer.*
Formed by the merger of (1947-2000): Der Sonntag. Ausgabe A (0720-9630); (1947-2000): Der Sonntag. Ausgabe AW (0720-9649); (1947-2000): Der Sonntag. Ausgabe AWF (0720-9665); All of which superseded in part: Der Sonntag (0172-0279)
Published by: Gesellschaft fuer kirchliche Publizistik Mainz GmbH, Erich-Dombrowski-Str 2, Mainz, 55127, Germany. TEL 49-6131-484150, FAX 49-6131-484158, hkaus@vrm.de. Ed. Bernhard Perrefort.

282 USA
SOONER CATHOLIC. Text in English. 1974. bi-w. (Sun.). free to members (donations accepted); USD 20 to non-members (effective 2005). **Document type:** *Newspaper, Consumer.*
Related titles: Microfilm ed.
Published by: Archdiocese of Oklahoma City, PO Box 32180, Oklahoma City, OK 73123. TEL 405-721-5651, FAX 405-721-5210. Ed. Ray Dyer. Pub. Archbishop E.J. Beltran. Circ: 30,000 (controlled and free). Wire service: CaNS.

282 USA ISSN 0194-7958
BX4711.31
SOPHIA; the journal of the eparchy of newton for melkite Greek Catholics in the United States. Text in English. 1971. q. USD 15 (effective 2010). illus. **Document type:** *Journal, Academic/Scholarly.*
Related titles: Online - full text ed.: free (effective 2010).
Indexed: CPL.
Published by: Melkite Diocese of Newton, 3 VFW Pky, West Roxbury, MA 02131. TEL 617-323-9922, FAX 617-323-0188. Ed. Rev. Robert Rabbat. Pub. Cyril Bustros.

282 USA ISSN 0038-1756
SOUL (WASHINGTON, NEW JERSEY); national Catholic magazine. Variant title: The Message of Fatima Today. Text in English. 1950. q. USD 9.95 domestic; USD 12.95 in Canada; USD 13.95 elsewhere (effective 2007). charts; illus. 44 p./no.; **Document type:** *Magazine, Consumer.* **Description:** National Roman Catholic magazine articulating the Catholic faith through the medium of the Fatima message.
Published by: Blue Army of Our Lady of Fatima, U S A, Inc., 674 Mountain View Rd, Box 976, Washington, NJ 07882. TEL 908-213-2223, FAX 908-213-2263, service@bluearmy.com, httyp://www.wafusa.org. Ed. Michael LaCorte TEL 908-689-1700 ext 16. Circ: 55,000.

282 USA ISSN 0038-187X
BX1752
SOUNDS OF TRUTH AND TRADITION. Text in English. 1965. irreg. free to qualified personnel. bk.rev. **Document type:** *Monographic series.*
Indexed: CERDIC.
Published by: (Catholic Traditionalist Movement, Inc.), C T M Publications, Inc., 210 Maple Ave, Westbury, NY 11590-3117. TEL 516-333-6470, FAX 516-333-7535. Ed., R&P Gommar A De Pauw TEL 516-333-6470.

282.764 USA
SOUTH PLAINS CATHOLIC. Text in English. 1984. s-m. USD 9. adv. **Document type:** *Newspaper.* **Description:** Provides information, communication, and inspiration for the Catholic community on the Texas South Plains.

R

Published by: Diocese of Lubbock, PO Box 98700, Lubbock, TX 79499-8700. TEL 806-792-3643, FAX 806-792-3943. Ed. Deacon Leroy Behnke. R&P Pat Behnke. Adv. contact Mark Roberti. Circ: 9,400 (paid).

282 USA ISSN 0745-9343
SOUTH TEXAS CATHOLIC. Text in English, Spanish. 19??. w. USD 15 (effective 2005). adv. bk.rev. **Document type:** *Newspaper, Consumer.*
Address: PO Box 2620, Corpus Christi, TX 78403-2620. TEL 361-882-6191, FAX 361-883-2556. Ed., R&P Paula Goldapp. Pub. Bishop Edmond Carmody. adv.: col. inch USD 15. Circ: 42,500 (paid and controlled). Wire service: CaNS.

282.09 GBR ISSN 0269-8390
BX1491.A1
SOUTH WESTERN CATHOLIC HISTORY. Text in English. 1983. a. GBP 3 (effective 2001). bk.rev. **Document type:** *Journal, Academic/Scholarly.* **Description:** Covers architectural, theological and biographical studies of the English Roman Catholic community (1558-1950).
Address: c/o Dominic Aidan Bellenger, Ed, Downside Abbey, Stratton-on-the-Fosse, Bath, Avon BA3 4RJ, United Kingdom. TEL 44-1761-232219, FAX 44-1761-233575. Ed., R&P Dom Aidan Bellenger. Circ: 250.

282 USA ISSN 2159-7529
THE SOUTHEAST ALASKA CATHOLIC. Text in English. 1970. bi-w. (except June, July & Aug. (pub. monthly)). free to qualified personnel (effective 2011). illus. **Document type:** *Newspaper, Consumer.*
Formerly (until 2011): The Inside Passage
Published by: Diocese of Juneau, 415 Sixth St, Ste 300, Juneau, AK 99801. TEL 907-586-2227 ext 25, FAX 907-463-3237, juneaudiocese@gci.net. Ed. Karla Donaghey TEL 907-586-2227 ext 32.

282 ZAF ISSN 0038-4011
SOUTHERN CROSS. Text in English. 1920. w. (Wed.). ZAR 260 domestic; ZAR 3.50 newsstand/cover; ZAR 380 in Africa; ZAR 566 elsewhere (effective 2002). adv. bk.rev.; Website rev. illus. back issues avail. **Document type:** *Newspaper.* **Description:** Publishes local and international Catholic church or church-related news and opinion.
Indexed: CERDIC.
Published by: (Southern African Catholic Bishops' Conference), Catholic Newspaper and Publishing Co. Ltd., PO Box 2372, Cape Town, 8000, South Africa. TEL 27-21-4655007, FAX 27-21-4653850. Ed., R&P Gunther Simmermacher TEL 27-21-4655007. Adv. contact Pamela Davids. B&W page ZAR 1,265. Circ: 10,530 (paid).

282 USA ISSN 0745-0257
SOUTHERN CROSS (SAN DIEGO). Text in English. 1912. m. USD 15 (effective 2008). adv. bk.rev.; film rev.; play rev. illus.; tr.lit. 32 p./no. 4 cols./p.; back issues avail. **Document type:** *Newspaper.*
Published by: Roman Catholic Diocese of San Diego, PO Box 81869, San Diego, CA 92138. Ed. Fr. Charles Fuld. Adv. contact Donna K Moore. col. inch USD 30. Circ: 32,000. Wire service: CaNS.

282 USA
SOUTHERN CROSS (SAVANNAH). Text in English. 1920. w. (Thu.). USD 20 (effective 2004). **Document type:** *Newspaper, Consumer.*
Contact Owner: Catholic Diocese of Savannah, 601 E Liberty St, Savananah, GA 31401. TEL 912-201-4100, communications@diosav.org. Circ: 12,000 (paid). Wire service: CaNS.

282.781 USA ISSN 0038-4690
SOUTHWEST KANSAS REGISTER; the newspaper of the Diocese of Doge City. Text in English. 1966. fortn. USD 27 (effective 2006). adv. bk.rev. illus. **Document type:** *Newspaper.*
Published by: Catholic Diocese of Dodge City, 910 Central, P O Box 137, Dodge City, KS 67801. TEL 620-227-1519, FAX 620-227-1570. Ed. David Myers. Pub. Bishop Ronald M. Gilmore. Adv. contact Timothy F. Wenzl. Circ: 6,295. Wire service: CaNS.

282 DEU ISSN 0584-5882
SOZIALES SEMINAR INFORMATIONEN; politisch-soziale Bildung in katholischer Traegerschaft. Text in German. 1952. s-a. free (effective 2008). **Document type:** *Journal, Academic/Scholarly.*
Published by: Akademie Franz-Hitze-Haus, Kardinal-von-Galen-Ring 50, Muenster, 48149, Germany. TEL 49-251-98180, FAX 49-251-9818480, info@franz-hitze-haus.de, http://www.franz-hitze-haus.de. Circ: 6,000 (controlled).

271.4 AUT
SPECIMINA EINES LEXICON AUGUSTINIANUM. Text in German. 1987. a. EUR 20 (effective 2003). **Document type:** *Journal, Academic/Scholarly.* **Description:** Contains a series of terms and words focussing and attracting essential and significant Augustinian thoughts in lexicographic processing.
Published by: Verlag der Oesterreichischen Akademie der Wissenschaften, Postfach 471, Vienna, W 1011, Austria. TEL 43-1-515813402, FAX 43-1-515813400, verlag@oeaw.ac.at, http://verlag.oeaw.ac.at. Eds. Peter Schilling, Werner Hensellek.

282 ITA
SPICILEGIUM BONAVENTURIANUM. Text in Latin. 1963. irreg., latest vol.29, 1997. price varies. **Document type:** *Monographic series, Academic/Scholarly.*
Published by: Collegio San Bonaventura/Collegium S Bonaventurae ad Claras Aquas, Via Vecchia per Marino 28-30, Grottaferrata, 00046, Italy. http://www.fratiquaracchi.it.

271.3 USA ISSN 1088-9191
BX3601
SPIRIT AND LIFE. Text in English. 1992. irreg., latest vol.14, 2010. price varies. back issues avail. **Document type:** *Monographic series, Academic/Scholarly.* **Description:** Provides results of a conference held at the Franciscan Institute.
Published by: Franciscan Institute (Subsidiary of: St. Bonaventure University), c/o St. Bonaventure University, 3261 W State Rd, St. Bonaventure, NY 14778. TEL 716-375-2000, FAX 716-375-2139, franinst@sbu.edu, http://franciscaninstitute.sbu.edu.

282 USA ISSN 0038-7592
SPIRIT & LIFE. Text in English. 1905. 6/yr. USD 15 domestic; USD 18 foreign (effective 2001). bk.rev. illus. 24 p./no.; back issues avail.; reprints avail. **Description:** For readers who want short, pithy reading material which will inspire them and give them impetus to live out their Christ-life on a day-to-day basis. Aims to engender spirit and life in the Church from the stance of its Benedictine publishers.
Related titles: Microform ed.: (from PQC).
Indexed: A22, CERDIC.
Published by: (Benedictine Sisters of Perpetual Adoration), Benedictine Publications Center, 800 N Country Club Rd, Tucson, AZ 85716-4507. TEL 520-325-6401, FAX 520-321-4358, http://www.benedictinesisters.org. Ed., R&P Sr Lenora Black Osb. Circ: 10,000.

SPIRIT OF BOOKS. *see* RELIGIONS AND THEOLOGY—Abstracting, Bibliographies, Statistics

282 GBR ISSN 1748-5088
SPIRIT OF THE SEASON. Abbreviated title: S O S. Text in English. 2000. bi-m. free (effective 2009). back issues avail. **Document type:** *Journal, Consumer.* **Description:** Provides reflection and information in the area of worship.
Related titles: Online - full text ed.: ISSN 1748-5096.
Published by: Liturgy Office (England & Wales), 39 Eccleston Sq, London, SW1V 1PL, United Kingdom. TEL 44-20-79014850, FAX 44-20-79014821, Liturgy.Office@cbcew.org.uk.

255 USA ISSN 1933-1762
BX3682.A1
SPIRITAN HORIZONS. Text in English. 2006. a., latest 2008. back issues avail. **Document type:** *Journal, Academic/Scholarly.* **Description:** Seeks to further research into the history, spirituality, and tradition of the Congregation of the Holy Spirit and to promote creative fidelity to the Spiritan charism in the contemporary world.
Related titles: Online - full text ed.: ISSN 1935-0759.
Published by: Duquesne University, Center for Spiritan Studies, 600 Forbes Ave, Pittsburgh, PA 15282.

266.2 IRL ISSN 1393-273X
SPIRITUALITY. Text in English. 1995. bi-m. EUR 30.35 domestic; EUR 29.92 in Great Britain and Northern Ireland; EUR 34.25 in Europe; EUR 46.92 elsewhere (effective 2005). bk.rev. illus. back issues avail. **Document type:** *Journal, Consumer.* **Description:** Informs readers of Biblical and liturgical teachings and wisdom, along with those of noteworthy theologians and mystics.
Indexed: CPL, MLA-IB.
—CCC.
Published by: Dominican Publications, 42 Parnell Sq, Dublin, Dublin 1, Ireland. TEL 353-1-8721611, 353-1-8731355, FAX 353-1-8731760, sales@dominicanpublications.com. Ed. Rev. Thomas Jordan. **Subscr. in N. America:** Orbis Books, Dept WEB, PO Box 302, Maryknoll, NY 10545. TEL 914-941-7636 ext 2477, 914-941-7636, FAX 914-941-7005, orbisbooks@maryknoll.org. **Co-publisher:** Orbis Books.

282 DEU
SPUREN - ESSAYS ZU KULTUR UND GLAUBE. Text in German. 2008. irreg., latest vol.4, 2010. price varies. **Document type:** *Monographic series, Academic/Scholarly.*
Published by: E O S Verlag, Erzabtei St. Ottilien, St.Ottilien, 86941, Germany. TEL 49-8193-71700, FAX 49-8193-71709, mail@eos-verlag.de, http://www.eos-verlag.de.

282 USA
ST. CLOUD VISITOR. Text in English. 1938. w. (Thu.). USD 18 (effective 2005). **Document type:** *Newspaper, Consumer.*
Published by: Diocese of St. Cloud, PO Box 1068, St. Cloud, MN 56302. TEL 320-251-2340. Ed. Pat Morrison. Pub. John Kinney. Adv. contact Rose K Fuchs. Circ: 43,000 (paid). Wire service: CaNS.

282 NOR ISSN 0802-6726
ST. OLAV; katolsk kirkeblad. Text in Norwegian. 1889. bi-m. **Document type:** *Magazine, Consumer.*
Incorporates (1959-2009): Broen (0804-9297); (1950-1978): Klippen (1891-6929); (1950-1968): Stella Maris
Related titles: CD-ROM ed.: ISSN 0809-7097.
Published by: Norsk Katolsk Bisperaad, Akersveien 5, Oslo, 0177, Norway. TEL 47-23-219500, FAX 47-22-219501, nkb@katolsk.no. Ed. Heidi Haugros Oeyma. Circ: 43,700 (controlled and free).

282 NLD ISSN 0038-8904
STAD GODS. Text in Dutch. 1932. bi-m. bk.rev. illus.
Published by: Zusters Augustinessen van Sint Monica, Klooster De Stad Gods, Soestdijkerstraatweg 151, Hilversum, 1213 VZ, Netherlands. TEL 31-35-6837528, http://www.zustersaugustinessen.nl. Circ: 50,000.

282 GHA ISSN 0038-9374
STANDARD; national Catholic weekly. Text in English. 1938. w. GHC 7.
Media: Duplicated (not offset).
Indexed: MLA-IB.
Published by: (Ghana Catholic Hierarchy), Catholic Mission Press, PO Box 60, Cape Coast, Ghana. Ed. Rev. Martin T Peters. Circ: 11,000.

282 ITA
LA STELLA DEL MARE. Text in Italian. 1908. m. EUR 12 (effective 2009). **Document type:** *Newsletter, Consumer.*
Formerly: Santuario di N.S.D. Grazie e di S. Maria Goretti (0036-4630)
Published by: Passionisti Scala Santa, Santuario di Nettuno, Nettuno, RM 00048, Italy. TEL 39-06-9854011.

282.48 DEU
DIE STERNSINGER; diaspora. Text in German. 1949. q. EUR 1.50 (effective 2009). back issues avail. **Document type:** *Magazine, Consumer.* **Description:** Contains articles and features for children promoting religious themes and education.
Published by: Bonifatiuswerk der Deutschen Katholiken e.V., Kamp 22, Paderborn, 33098, Germany. TEL 49-5251-29960, FAX 49-5251-299688, info@bonifatiuswerk.de. Ed. Christoph Schommer. Circ: 280,000 (controlled).

282 USA ISSN 0744-771X
STEUBENVILLE REGISTER. Text in English. 1945. fortn. USD 15 in state; USD 17 domestic; USD 24 foreign (effective 2000). adv. **Document type:** *Newspaper.*
Related titles: Microfiche ed.
Published by: Diocese of Steubenville (Ohio), 422 Washington St, Box 160, Steubenville, OH 43952. TEL 740-282-3631, FAX 740-282-3238. Ed., R&P Pat DeFrancis. Pub. Gilbert I Sheldon. Adv. contact Janice Ward. page USD 54,027. Circ: 17,900.

282 DEU ISSN 0039-1492
AP30
STIMMEN DER ZEIT. Text in German. 1871. m. EUR 55.20 for 6 mos.; EUR 40.80 for 6 mos. to students; EUR 11 newsstand/cover (effective 2010). bk.rev. reprints avail. **Document type:** *Newsletter, Consumer.*
Indexed: A22, CERDIC, CPL, DIP, FR, HistAb, IBR, IBZ, MLA, MLA-IB, OTA, P30, PRA, PhilInd, RASB, RILM.
—IE, Infotrieve, INIST. **CCC.**
Published by: Verlag Herder GmbH, Hermann-Herder-Str 4, Freiburg Im Breisgau, 79104, Germany. TEL 49-761-27170, FAX 49-761-2717520, kundenservice@herder.de, http://www.herder.de. Ed. Andreas Batlogg. Adv. contact Friederike Ward TEL 49-761-2717407. Circ: 5,000.

220 RUS ISSN 1562-1421
BR9.R9
STRANITSY. BOGOSLOVIE, KUL'TURA, OBRAZOVANIE/PAGES: THEOLOGY, CULTURE, EDUCATION. Text in Russian. 1996. q. USD 76 foreign to institutions (effective 2003). back issues avail. **Document type:** *Academic/Scholarly.* **Description:** Covers a broad range of theological and philosophical issues, biblical studies, liturgics, ecology, church history, and art history.
—East View.
Published by: Bibleisko-Bogoslovskii Institut Svyatogo Apostola Andreya/St. Andrew's Biblical Theological College, ul Ierusalimskaya, d.3, Moscow, 109316, Russian Federation. standrews@standrews.ru, http://www.standrews.ru. Ed. A Bodrov. R&P A Pospelov. **Dist. by:** East View Information Services, 10601 Wayzata Blvd, Minneapolis, MN 55305. TEL 952-252-1201, 800-477-1005, FAX 952-252-1202, info@eastview.com, http://www.eastview.com.

282 ITA ISSN 0039-2901
BX804 CODEN: BSIBAC
STUDI CATTOLICI; mensile di studi ed attualita. Text in Italian. 1957. m. EUR 50 domestic; EUR 80 foreign (effective 2008). bk.rev. bibl.; charts; illus. index. **Document type:** *Magazine, Consumer.*
Indexed: CERDIC, MLA-IB.
Published by: Edizioni A R E S, Via Antonio Stradivari 7, Milan, 20131, Italy. TEL 39-02-29514202, FAX 39-02-520163, info@ares.mi.it, http://www.ares.mi.it. Ed. Cesare Cavalleri.

282 ITA ISSN 2036-8437
STUDIA ANSELMIANA. Text in Multiple languages. 1933. irreg. **Document type:** *Monographic series, Academic/Scholarly.*
Published by: Pontificio Ateneo S. Anselmo, Piazza dei Cavalieri di Malta 5, Rome, 00153, Italy. TEL 39-06-5791320, FAX 39-06-5791366, http://www.santanselmo.org.

282 ITA ISSN 2036-8461
STUDIA ANSELMIANA. ANALECTA LITURGICA. Text in Multiple languages. 1976. irreg. **Document type:** *Monographic series, Academic/Scholarly.*
Published by: Pontificio Ateneo S. Anselmo, Piazza dei Cavalieri di Malta 5, Rome, 00153, Italy. TEL 39-06-5791320, FAX 39-06-5791366, http://www.santanselmo.org.

282 ITA ISSN 2036-847X
STUDIA ANSELMIANA. ANALECTA MONASTICA. Text in Multiple languages. 1948. irreg. **Document type:** *Monographic series, Academic/Scholarly.*
Published by: Pontificio Ateneo S. Anselmo, Piazza dei Cavalieri di Malta 5, Rome, 00153, Italy. TEL 39-06-5791320, FAX 39-06-5791366, http://www.santanselmo.org.

282 ITA ISSN 2036-8453
STUDIA ANSELMIANA. SACRAMENTUM. Text in Italian. 1973. irreg. **Document type:** *Monographic series, Academic/Scholarly.*
Published by: Pontificio Ateneo S. Anselmo, Piazza dei Cavalieri di Malta 5, Rome, 00153, Italy. TEL 39-06-5791320, FAX 39-06-5791366, http://www.santanselmo.org.

282 POL ISSN 1642-5650
STUDIA BOBOLANUM. Text in Polish, English; Abstracts in English. 2001. q. PLZ 72 domestic; USD 35 foreign (effective 2006).
Indexed: IZBG.
Published by: (Papieski Wydzial Teologiczny w Warszawie, Sekcja Bobolanum), Wydawnictwo Rhetos, ul Rakowiecka 61, Warsaw, 02532, Poland. wydawnictwo@rhetos.pl, http://www.rhetos.pl.

262.9 CAN ISSN 0039-310X
➤ **STUDIA CANONICA/CANON LAW**; a Canadian canon law review. Text in English, French, Latin. 1967. s-a. CAD 50 domestic; CAD 65, USD 45 foreign (effective 2004). adv. bk.rev. 288 p./no.; reprints avail. **Document type:** *Journal, Academic/Scholarly.*
Related titles: CD-ROM ed.; Microfiche ed.: (from MML); Microform ed.: (from MML); Online - full text ed.
Indexed: A20, A21, A22, ArtHuCI, C03, CBCARef, CERDIC, CLA, CLI, CPL, DIP, FR, IBR, IBZ, ICLPL, P48, PCI, PQC, RI-1, RI-2, W07.
—CIS, INIST. **CCC.**
Published by: Saint Paul University, Faculty of Canon Law (Subsidiary of: Saint Paul University/Universite Saint-Paul), 223 Main St, Ottawa, ON K1S 1C4, Canada. TEL 613-751-4017, FAX 613-751-4036, http://www.ustpaul.ca. Ed. Roch Page. R&P, Adv. contact Patrick Cogan. Circ: 1,300 (paid).

271.4 ITA
STUDIA EPHEMERIDIS AUGUSTINIANUM. Text in Italian. 1967. irreg., latest vol.74, 2001. price varies. back issues avail. **Document type:** *Monographic series, Academic/Scholarly.* **Description:** Patristic studies.
Published by: Istituto Patristico Augustinianum/Institutum Patristicum Augustinianum, Via Paolo VI 25, Rome, 00193, Italy. TEL 39-06-68006238, FAX 39-06-68006298, http://www.patristicum.org.

230.2 900 ITA ISSN 1970-4879
BX819.3.O68
STUDIA ET DOCUMENTA. Text in Multiple languages. 2007. a. **Document type:** *Journal, Academic/Scholarly.*
Published by: (Istituto Storico San Josemaria Escriva), Edusc, Piazza Sant'Apollinare 49, Rome, 00186, Italy. TEL 39-06-681641, FAX 39-06-68164400, setd@edusc.it.

255.3 POL ISSN 0860-0775
STUDIA FRANCISZKANSKIE. Text in Polish. 1984. a. USD 15 per vol. (effective 2006).
Indexed: IZBG.
Published by: Klasztor OO. Franciszkanow, ul Franciszkanska 2, Poznan, 61768, Poland. TEL 48-61-8523637, poznan@franciszkanie.gdansk.pl, http://www.ofmconv.opoka.org.pl/poznan. Ed. Salezy Tomczak.

255 ESP ISSN 0039-3258
BX2400
STUDIA MONASTICA; commentarium ad rem monasticam historice investigandam. Text in Catalan, English, French, German, Italian, Latin, Portuguese, Spanish. 1959. s-a. adv. bk.rev. abstr.; bibl.; charts; illus. index. **Document type:** *Journal, Academic/Scholarly.*
Indexed: A20, ASCA, ArtHuCI, BibInd, CERDIC, CurCont, FR, MLA, MLA-IB, P09, PCI, SCOPUS, W07.
—BLDSC (8483.063000), INIST. **CCC.**
Published by: Publicacions de l' Abadia de Montserrat, Ausias Marc 92-98, Barcelona, 08013, Spain. TEL 34-932-450303, FAX 34-932-473594, http://www.pamsa.com. Ed. Manuel Nin. Circ: 800.

261 306.85 POL ISSN 1429-2416
BX1751.2
STUDIA NAD RODZINA. Text in Polish. 1997. s-a. **Document type:** *Journal, Academic/Scholarly.*
Published by: (Uniwersytet Kardynala Stefana Wyszynskiego, Wydzial Teologiczny, Instytut Studiow nad Rodzina), Wydawnictwo Uniwersytetu Kardynala Stefana Wyszynskiego, Ul Dewajtis 5, Warsaw, 01815, Poland. wydawnictwo@uksw.edu.pl, http://www.uksw.edu.pl/wydawn/wydawnictwo.htm.

230.2 CHE ISSN 1662-6540
STUDIA OECUMENICA FRIBURGENSIA. Variant title: Cahiers Oecumeniques. Text in German. 1968. irreg., latest vol.50, 2009. price varies. **Document type:** *Monographic series, Academic/Scholarly.*
Formerly (until 2006): Freiburger Zeitschrift fuer Philosophie und Theologie. Oekumenische Beihefte (1422-4380)
Published by: Academic Press Fribourg, Perolles 42, Fribourg, 1705, Switzerland. TEL 41-26-4264311, FAX 41-26-4264300, info@paulusedition.ch, http://www.paulusedition.ch/academic_press/.

282 POL ISSN 0585-5470
BR9.P6
STUDIA PHILOSOPHIAE CHRISTIANAE. Text in Polish. 1965. s-a. **Document type:** *Journal, Academic/Scholarly.*
Indexed: FR, PhilInd.
—INIST.
Published by: (Uniwersytet Kardynala Stefana Wyszynskiego, Wydzial Filozofii Chrzescijanskiej), Wydawnictwo Uniwersytetu Kardynala Stefana Wyszynskiego, Ul Dewajtis 5, Warsaw, 01815, Poland. wydawnictwo@uksw.edu.pl, http://www.uksw.edu.pl/wydawn/wydawnictwo.htm.

282 POL
STUDIA PLOCKIE. Text in Polish. a. PLZ 29 per vol. (effective 2006). **Document type:** *Journal, Academic/Scholarly.*
Indexed: IZBG.
Published by: Diecezja Plocka, ul Tumska 3, Plock, 09402, Poland. TEL 48-24-2622640, http://www.diecezja.plock.opoka.org.pl.

282 POL ISSN 0239-801X
STUDIA TEOLOGICZNE. Text in Polish, English. 1983. irreg. price varies. **Document type:** *Monographic series, Academic/Scholarly.*
Indexed: IZBG.
Published by: Kuria Arcybiskupia, ul Ostrow Tumski 2, Poznan, 61109, Poland. TEL 48-61-8524282, FAX 48-61-8519748, kuria@archpoznan.org.pl, http://www.archpoznan.org.pl.

230.2 POL ISSN 0585-5594
BR9.P6
STUDIA THEOLOGICA VARSAVIENSIA. Text in Polish. 1963. s-a. **Document type:** *Journal, Academic/Scholarly.*
Indexed: IBR, IBZ, IZBG, OTA.
—INIST.
Published by: (Uniwersytet Kardynala Stefana Wyszynskiego, Wydzial Teologiczny), Wydawnictwo Uniwersytetu Kardynala Stefana Wyszynskiego, Ul Dewajtis 5, Warsaw, 01815, Poland. wydawnictwo@uksw.edu.pl, http://www.uksw.edu.pl/wydawn/wydawnictwo.htm.

230.2 ROM ISSN 1224-8754
BX1751.2
➤ **STUDIA UNIVERSITATIS BABES-BOLYAI. THEOLOGIA CATHOLICA.** Text in English, French, German, Italian, Romanian; Abstracts in English. 1996. q. exchange basis. **Document type:** *Journal, Academic/Scholarly.*
Related titles: Online - full text ed.: ISSN 2065-9458.
Indexed: CA, T02.
Published by: Universitatea "Babes-Bolyai", Studia/Babes-Bolyai University, Studia, 51 Hasdeu Str, Cluj-Napoca, 400371, Romania. TEL 40-264-405352, FAX 40-264-591906, office@studia.ubbcluj.ro. Eds. Dan Ruscu, Simona Stefana Zetea. **Dist by:** "Lucian Blaga" Central University Library, International Exchange Department, Clinicilor st no 2, Cluj-Napoca 400371, Romania. TEL 40-264-597092, FAX 40-264-597633, iancu@bcucluj.ro.

282 ROM ISSN 1582-2524
BX800.A1
➤ **STUDIA UNIVERSITATIS BABES-BOLYAI. THEOLOGIA CATHOLICA LATINA.** Text in English, French, German, Hungarian, Italian. 2000. s-a. bk.rev. abstr.; bibl.; illus. **Document type:** *Journal, Academic/Scholarly.*
Related titles: Online - full text ed.: ISSN 2065-944X.
Indexed: CA, T02.
Published by: Universitatea "Babes-Bolyai", Studia/Babes-Bolyai University, Studia, 51 Hasdeu Str, Cluj-Napoca, 400371, Romania. TEL 40-264-405352, FAX 40-264-591906, office@studia.ubbcluj.ro, http://www.studia.ubbcluj.ro. Eds. Janos Vik, Jozsef Marton. **Dist by:** "Lucian Blaga" Central University Library, International Exchange Department, Clinicilor st no 2, Cluj-Napoca 400371, Romania. TEL 40-264-597092, FAX 40-264-597633, iancu@bcucluj.ro.

282 ROM ISSN 1454-8933
BX806.R6
➤ **STUDIA UNIVERSITATIS BABES-BOLYAI. THEOLOGIA GRAECO-CATHOLICA VARADIENSIS.** Text and summaries in English, French, German, Italian, Romanian; Abstracts in English. 1999. s-a. exchange basis. bk.rev. abstr.; bibl.; illus. **Document type:** *Journal, Academic/Scholarly.*
Related titles: Online - full text ed.: ISSN 2065-9466.
Indexed: CA, T02.
—INIST.
Published by: Universitatea "Babes-Bolyai", Studia/Babes-Bolyai University, Studia, 51 Hasdeu Str, Cluj-Napoca, 400371, Romania. TEL 40-264-405352, FAX 40-264-591906, office@studia.ubbcluj.ro. Eds. Ovidiu Pop, Virgil Bercea. **Dist by** "Lucian Blaga" Central University Library, International Exchange Department, Clinicilor st no 2, Cluj-Napoca 400371, Romania. TEL 40-264-597092, FAX 40-264-597633, iancu@bcucluj.ro.

255.1 DEU ISSN 0303-4224
BX3001
STUDIEN UND MITTEILUNGEN ZUR GESCHICHTE DES BENEDIKTINERORDENS UND SEINER ZWEIGE. Text in German. 1880. a. EUR 56.50 (effective 2010). bk.rev. illus. cum.index. **Document type:** *Journal, Academic/Scholarly.*
Indexed: A22, B24, DIP, FR, IBR, IBZ, MLA-IB, RILM.
—IE, Infotrieve, INIST.
Published by: (Bayerische Benediktinerakademie), E O S Verlag, Erzabtei St. Ottilien, St.Ottilien, 86941, Germany. TEL 49-8193-71700, FAX 49-8193-71709, mail@eos-verlag.de.

271.1 DEU ISSN 0722-253X
STUDIEN UND MITTEILUNGEN ZUR GESCHICHTE DES BENEDIKTINERORDENS UND SEINER ZWEIGE. ERGAENZUNGSBAND. Text in German. 1926. irreg., latest vol.46, 2009. price varies. **Document type:** *Monographic series, Academic/Scholarly.*
Indexed: FR.
—INIST.
Published by: E O S Verlag, Erzabtei St. Ottilien, St.Ottilien, 86941, Germany. TEL 49-8193-71700, FAX 49-8193-71709, mail@eos-verlag.de.

282 DEU ISSN 1439-362X
STUDIEN UND QUELLEN ZUR GESCHICHTE DER KREUZZUEGE UND DES PAPSTTUMS. Text in German. 2000. irreg. price varies. **Document type:** *Monographic series, Academic/Scholarly.*
Published by: Peter Lang GmbH (Subsidiary of: Peter Lang Publishing Group), Eschborner Landstr 42-50, Frankfurt Am Main, 60489, Germany. TEL 49-69-7807050, FAX 49-69-78070550, zentrale.frankfurt@peterlang.com, http://www.peterlang.com.

282 943 DEU
▼ **STUDIEN ZUM FRAUENSTIFT GANDERSHEIM UND SEINEN EIGENKLOESTERN.** Text in German. 2009. irreg., latest vol.3, 2010. price varies. **Document type:** *Monographic series, Academic/Scholarly.*
Published by: Verlag Schnell und Steiner GmbH, Leibnizstr 13, Regensburg, 93055, Germany. TEL 49-941-787850, FAX 49-941-7878516, post@schnell-und-steiner.de.

230.2 DEU ISSN 0081-7295
STUDIEN ZUR GESCHICHTE DER KATHOLISCHEN MORALTHEOLOGIE. Text in German. 1955 (vol.3). irreg., latest vol.37, 2001. price varies. **Document type:** *Monographic series, Academic/Scholarly.*
Published by: Verlag Friedrich Pustet, Gutenbergstr 8, Regensburg, 93051, Germany. TEL 49-941-920220, FAX 49-941-92022330, verlag@pustet.de, http://www.pustetverlag.de. Ed. Johannes Gruendel. Circ: 500.

230 DEU
STUDIEN ZUR GESCHICHTE, KUNST UND KULTUR DER ZISTERZIENSER. Text in German. 1996. irreg., latest vol.30, 2010. price varies. **Document type:** *Monographic series, Academic/Scholarly.*
Published by: Lukas Verlag fuer Kunst- und Geistesgeschichte, Kollwitzstr 57, Berlin, 10405, Germany. TEL 49-30-44049220, FAX 49-30-4428177, lukas.verlag@t-online.de.

268 DEU ISSN 1611-0277
STUDIEN ZUR KIRCHENGESCHICHTE. Text in German. 2002. irreg., latest vol.10, 2009. price varies. **Document type:** *Monographic series, Academic/Scholarly.*
Published by: Verlag Dr. Kovac, Leverkusenstr 13, Hamburg, 22761, Germany. TEL 49-40-3988800, FAX 49-40-39888055, info@verlagdrkovac.de.

STUDIEN ZUR KOELNER KIRCHENGESCHICHTE. *see* HISTORY—History Of Europe

282 DEU
STUDIEN ZUR MONASTISCHEN KULTUR. Text in German. 2008. irreg., latest vol.3, 2009. price varies. **Document type:** *Monographic series, Academic/Scholarly.*
Published by: E O S Verlag, Erzabtei St. Ottilien, St.Ottilien, 86941, Germany. TEL 49-8193-71700, FAX 49-8193-71709, mail@eos-verlag.de, http://www.eos-verlag.de.

253 DEU ISSN 0341-6909
STUDIEN ZUR PASTORALLITURGIE. Text in German. 1976. irreg., latest vol.24, 2010. price varies. **Document type:** *Monographic series, Academic/Scholarly.*
Published by: Verlag Friedrich Pustet, Gutenbergstr 8, Regensburg, 93051, Germany. TEL 49-941-920220, FAX 49-941-92022330, verlag@pustet.de, http://www.pustetverlag.de.

230.2 DEU
STUDIEN ZUR THEOLOGIE UND GESCHICHTE. Text in German. 1989. irreg., latest vol.15, 2001. price varies. **Document type:** *Monographic series, Academic/Scholarly.*
Published by: E O S Verlag, Erzabtei St. Ottilien, St.Ottilien, 86941, Germany. TEL 49-8193-71700, FAX 49-8193-71709, mail@eos-verlag.de, http://www.eos-verlag.de.

282 NLD ISSN 0169-9512
➤ **STUDIES IN GREEK AND ROMAN RELIGION.** Text in Dutch. 1980. irreg., latest vol.7, 1991. price varies. back issues avail. **Document type:** *Monographic series, Academic/Scholarly.* **Description:** International studies in Hellenic and Roman theology.
Indexed: IZBG.
Published by: Brill, PO Box 9000, Leiden, 2300 PA, Netherlands. TEL 31-71-5353500, FAX 31-71-5317532, cs@brill.nl, http://www.brill.nl. R&P Elizabeth Venekamp. **Dist. by:** Turpin Distribution Services Ltd., Pegasus Dr, Stratton Business Park, Biggleswade, Bedfordshire SG18 8QB, United Kingdom. TEL 44-1767-604954, FAX 44-1767-601640, custserv@turpin-distribution.com, http://www.turpin-distribution.com/.

255.53 ITA
SUBSIDIA AD HISTORIAM S.I. (Societatis Iesu) Text in Italian. 2001. irreg. **Document type:** *Magazine, Academic/Scholarly.*
Published by: Institutum Historicum Societatis Iesu/Jesuit Historical Institute, Via dei Penitenzieri 20, Rome, 00193, Italy.

223 BEL ISSN 0777-8112
➤ **SUBSIDIA HAGIOGRAPHICA.** Text in English, French, German, Italian, Latin. 1886. irreg., latest vol.84, 2003. price varies. back issues avail. **Document type:** *Monographic series, Academic/Scholarly.* **Description:** Takes a critical look at the lives of saints.
Published by: Societe des Bollandistes, Bd St Michel 24, Brussels, 1040, Belgium. TEL 32-2-739-3338, FAX 32-2-739-3332, info@bollandistes.be, http://www.bollandistes.be.

255.3 ITA ISSN 0562-4649
SUBSIDIA SCIENTIFICA FRANCISCALIA. Text in French, German, Italian, Latin. 1962. irreg., latest vol.9, 1999. price varies. index. **Document type:** *Monographic series, Academic/Scholarly.*
Published by: Frati Minori Cappuccini, Istituto Storico/Ordo Fratrum Minorum Capuccinorum, Circonvallazione Occidentale 6850, Rome, RM 00163, Italy. TEL 39-06-660521, FAX 39-06-66052532, http://www.istcap.org. Circ: 500.

282 ITA ISSN 2037-822X
SUDI AGOSTINIANI. Text in Italian. 1999. irreg. **Document type:** *Monographic series, Academic/Scholarly.*
Published by: Citta Nuova Editrice, Via Pieve Torina 55, Rome, 00156, Italy. TEL 39-06-3216212, FAX 39-06-3207185, comm.editrice@cittanuova.it, http://www.cittanuova.it.

230.002 100 GRC ISSN 1105-3208
SUGHRONA BEMATA. Text in Greek. 1970. q.
Formerly (until 1977): Problemata Theologias (1105-347X)
Published by: Mone Pateron Iesouitons/Jesuit Fathers, 27 Smyrnis St, Athens, 104 39, Greece. TEL 30-1-8835-911. Ed. Theodoros Kontidis.

268 AUS ISSN 0312-7044
THE SUMMIT. Text in English. 1974. q. AUD 44 domestic; AUD 66 foreign; AUD 14.50 per issue (effective 2008). music rev.; bk.rev. 48 p./no.; back issues avail. **Document type:** *Journal, Consumer.* **Description:** Aims to act as a resource for catechesis from the lectionary. Also provides commentary for local implementation of the R.C.I.A.
Published by: Catholic Archdiocese of Melbourne, Office for Worship, 383 Albert St, PO Box 146, East Melbourne, VIC 3002, Australia. TEL 61-3-99265677, FAX 61-3-99265617, info@melbourne.catholic.org.au. Ed. Paul Talor TEL 61-3-94123324.

282 HKG
SUNDAY EXAMINER. Text in English. 1946. w. HKD 330 domestic; HKD 340 in China; HKD 440 elsewhere. adv. bk.rev. **Document type:** *Newspaper.*
Address: 11-F, Catholic Diocese Centre, 16 Caine Rd, Hong Kong, Hong Kong. TEL 852-2522-0487, FAX 852-2521-3095. Ed. John J Casey. Circ: 3,000.

230.2 CAN ISSN 1715-6149
SUNDAY MISSAL FOR YOUNG CATHOLICS. Text in English. 2006. a. CAD 6 per issue (effective 2006). 288 p./no.; **Document type:** *Journal, Consumer.*
Published by: Novalis, 4475 Frontenac St, Montreal, PQ H2H 2S2, Canada. TEL 514-278-3020, 800-387-7164, FAX 514-278-0072, http://www.novalis.ca.

282 USA
SUPERIOR CATHOLIC HERALD. Text in English. 1953. w. (Thu.). USD 18 to members; USD 33 to non-members (effective 2006). **Document type:** *Newspaper, Consumer.*
Formerly: Catholic Herald Citizen
Address: PO Box 969, Superior, WI 54880. TEL 715-392-8268, FAX 715-392-8656. Pub. Bishop Raphael Fliss. Circ: 20,000 (controlled and free). Wire service: CaNS.

255.4 ITA
SUSSIDI PATRISTICI. Text in Italian. 1981. irreg., latest vol.12, 2001. price varies. back issues avail. **Document type:** *Monographic series, Academic/Scholarly.*
Published by: Istituto Patristico Augustinianum/Institutum Patristicum Augustinianum, Via Paolo VI 25, Rome, 00193, Italy. TEL 39-06-68006238, FAX 39-06-68006298, http://www.patristicum.org.

282 SVK ISSN 1336-0205
SVATE PISMO PRE KAZDEHO. Text in Slovak. 2001. m. **Document type:** *Magazine, Consumer.*
Published by: Vydavatel'stvo Don Bosco, Mileticova 7, Bratislava, 821 08, Slovakia. TEL 421-2-55572226, FAX 421-2-55574992, donbosco@donbosco.sk, http://www.donbosco.sk.

282 CAN ISSN 0039-7164
SVITLO/LIGHT. Text in Ukrainian. 1939. m. USD 25 (effective 2001). adv. **Document type:** *Journal, Academic/Scholarly.*
Related titles: ◆ English ed.: Beacon. ISSN 0382-6384.
Published by: Basilian Press, 265 Bering Ave, Toronto, ON M6J 3G9, Canada. TEL 416-234-1212, FAX 416-234-1213. Ed., Pub., R&P Rev. Basil Cymbalisty. Adv. contact Bro Stephen Krysak. Circ: 2,000.

282 BIH ISSN 1512-6986
BX1612.B54
SVJETLO RIJECI/LIGHT OF THE WORD; vjerski list/religious newspaper. Text in Croatian. 1983. m. looseleaf. USD 66 foreign (effective 2007). **Document type:** *Newspaper.*
Published by: Franjevacka Provincija Bosna Srebrena, Svjetlo Rijeci, Zagrebacka 18, Sarajevo, 71000, Bosnia Herzegovina. svjetlo@svjetlorijeci.com. Ed. Mirko Filipovic TEL 387-33-726205. Circ: 10,000.

SZKOLY POBOZNE; mlodziezowy kwartalnik katolicki. *see* EDUCATION

R

282 USA ISSN 0039-8845
BX801
THE TABLET (NEW YORK). Text in English. 1908. w. USD 26 domestic; USD 41 foreign (effective 2005). adv. bk.rev. illus. back issues avail. **Document type:** *Newspaper, Consumer.* **Description:** Promotes the churches teachings and public image, including discussions and opinion on religious and secular issues.
Formerly: Brooklyn Tablet
Related titles: Microfilm ed.: (from PQC); Microform ed.
Indexed: CPL, MLA-IB, P30.
—CCC.
Published by: (Roman Catholic Diocese of Brooklyn), The Tablet (New York), 310 Prospect Park W., Brooklyn, NY 11215. TEL 718-965-7333, FAX 718-965-7337. Ed. Edward Wilkinson. Pub. Thomas V. Daily. adv.: page USD 2,650. Circ: 80,000 (paid).

282 DEU ISSN 0492-1283
TAG DES HERRN; katholisches Kirchenblatt. Text in German. 1951. w. EUR 4.25 per month (effective 2007). adv. bk.rev. **Document type:** *Newspaper, Consumer.* **Description:** Covers news of the Catholic Church, including events, issues and questions.
Related titles: Online - full text ed.
Published by: (Berliner Bischofskonferenz), St. Benno Buch- und Zeitschriftenverlagsgesellschaft mbH, Stammerstr 11, Leipzig, 04159, Germany. TEL 49-341-467770, FAX 49-341-4677740, service@st-benno.de, http://www.st-benno.de. Ed. Matthias Holluba. adv.: page EUR 3,360. Circ: 25,878 (controlled).

282 POL ISSN 0239-4472
TARNOWSKIE STUDIA TEOLOGICZNE. Text in Polish, English. 1977. s-a. **Document type:** *Journal, Academic/Scholarly.*
Indexed: IZBG.
Published by: (Papieska Akademia Teologiczna w Krakowie, Wydzial Teologiczny w Tarnowie), Wydawnictwo Diecezji Tarnowskiej Biblos, Pl Katedralny 6, Tarnow, 33100, Poland. TEL 48-14-6212777, biblos@wsd.tarnow.pl, http://www.biblos.pl.

282 AUS
THE TASMANIAN CATHOLIC. Text in English. 1995. bi-m. adv. **Document type:** *Newspaper, Consumer.*
Formerly (until 2005): The Standard (Hobart)
Published by: Archdiocese of Hobart, P.O. Box 62, Hobart, TAS 7001, Australia. TEL 61-3-62086230, FAX 61-3-62086292. Ed. Pip Barnard. Pub. Archbishop Adrian Doyle. adv.: B&W page AUD 760, color page AUD 890; 205 x 292. Circ: 16,000.

282 DEU ISSN 1618-0550
TAUWETTER; eine franziskanische Zeitschrift. Text in German. 1986. 4/yr. **Document type:** *Magazine, Consumer.*
Published by: Missionszentrale der Franziskaner, Albertus-Magnus-Str 39, Bonn, 53177, Germany.

282 HUN ISSN 1215-282X
BX880
TAVLATOK. Text in Hungarian. 1991. q. USD 36 foreign (effective 2006). **Document type:** *Journal.*
Indexed: RILM.
Published by: Jezus Tarsasaga Magyar Rendtartomanya, Sodras u 13, Budapest, 1026, Hungary. TEL 36-1-2008054, FAX 36-1-2750269.

282 COD ISSN 1013-7769
BR3
TELEMA. Text in French. 1975. q. USD 50. adv. bk.rev. **Description:** Contains articles on pastroal and spirituality with emphasis on African thought.
Indexed: CCA, CERDIC, IBR, IBZ, OTA.
Published by: Jesuit Fathers of the Central Africa Province, BP 3724, Kinshasa-Gombe, Congo, Dem. Republic. Ed. Simon Decloux. Circ: 1,200.

282 REU
TEMOIGNAGE CHRETIEN DE LA REUNION. Text in French. w.
Indexed: RASB.
Address: 21 bis rue de l'Est, Saint-Denis, Cedex 97465, Reunion. Ed. Rene Payet. Circ: 2,000.

282 USA ISSN 1041-1569
TENNESSEE REGISTER; a voice of Tennessee Catholic life. Text in English. 1937. bi-w. USD 23 (effective 2005). adv. **Document type:** *Newspaper, Consumer.* **Description:** News of social or religious significance to Catholics in Middle Tennessee.
Related titles: Microfilm ed.; Online - full content ed.
Published by: Diocese of Nashville, 2400 21st Ave., S., Nashville, TN 37212-8411. TEL 615-783-0770, 800-273-0256, FAX 615-783-0285. Ed. Rick Musacchio. Pub. Rev. David Choby. Adv. contact Byron Warner. Circ: 15,000. Wire service: CaNS.

230.2 BRA ISSN 0103-314X
BX805
TEOCOMUNICACAO. Text in Portuguese. 1971. q. BRL 38 (effective 2007). bk.rev. **Document type:** *Journal, Academic/Scholarly.*
Related titles: Online - full text ed.: free (effective 2011).
Indexed: C01, CA, OTA, T02.
Published by: (Pontificia Universidade Catolica do Rio Grande do Sul, Instituto de Teologia, Pontificia Universidade Catolica do Rio Grande do Sul), Editora da P U C R S, Avenida Ipiranga 6681, Predio 33, Porto Alegre, RS 90619-900, Brazil. http://www.pucrs.br/edipucrs/.

230.2 HUN ISSN 0133-1779
TEOLOGIA; hittudomanyi folyoirat. Text in Hungarian. 1967. 4/yr. HUF 290, USD 30. adv. bk.rev. **Document type:** *Academic/Scholarly.*
Indexed: CERDIC, OTA.
Published by: (Pazmany Peter Katolikus Egyetem Hittudomanyi Kara), Teologia Kiadohivatala, Papnovelde utca 7, Budapest, 1053, Hungary. TEL 36-1-4473701, FAX 36-1-1173471. Ed. Laszlo Vanyo. Adv. contact Andrea Gyorffy. Circ: 1,000.

230.2 CHL ISSN 0049-3449
BR7
TEOLOGIA Y VIDA. Text in Spanish. 1960. q. CLP 25,000 domestic; USD 95 foreign (effective 2011). adv. bk.rev. abstr.; bibl. cum.index: 1960-1979. back issues avail. **Document type:** *Academic/Scholarly.*
Related titles: Online - full text ed.: ISSN 0717-6295. 2000. free (effective 2011) (from SciELO).
Indexed: A20, ArtHuCI, CLA, CPL, DIP, FR, IBR, IBZ, OTA, SCOPUS, W07.
—INIST.
Published by: Pontificia Universidad Catolica de Chile, Facultad de Teologia, Jaime Guzman Errazuriz 3300, Casilla 316, Santiago, 22, Chile. ccoz@puc.cl. Ed. Cecilia Coz Canas. Pub., Adv. contact Waldo Romo Perez TEL 56-2-6865074. Circ: 700.

282 SVN ISSN 1408-3655
TEOLOSKA KNJIZNICA. Text in Slovenian. 1988. irreg., latest vol.20, 2003. price varies. **Document type:** *Monographic series, Academic/Scholarly.*
Published by: Salve d.o.o., Rakovniska 6, Ljubljana, 1001, Slovenia. TEL 386-1-4277310, FAX 386-1-4273040, info@salve.si, http://www.salve.si.

282 SVN ISSN 1408-3000
TEOLOSKI PRIROCNIKI. Text in Slovenian. 1973. irreg. **Document type:** *Monographic series, Academic/Scholarly.*
Published by: Mohorjeva Druzba, Presernova c 23, pp 150, Celje, 3001, Slovenia. TEL 386-3-4264800, FAX 386-3-4264810, info@mohorjeva-druzba-ce.si, http://www.mohorjeva.org.

271.97 VAT ISSN 0392-4556
BX800.A1
TERESIANUM. Text in Multiple languages. 1947. s-a. EUR 31 (effective 2004). **Document type:** *Academic/Scholarly.*
Formerly (until 1982): Ephemerides Carmeliticae
Indexed: CERDIC, FR, MLA-IB, OTA, PCI.
—INIST.
Published by: (Teresianum: Pontificia Facolta Teologica - Pontificio Istituto di Spiritualita ITA), Edizioni del Teresianum, Piazza San Pancrazio 5-A, Rome, 00152, Vatican City. TEL 39-06-58540248, FAX 39-06-58540300, http://www.teresianum.org. Ed. R P Virgilio Pasquetto. Circ: 800.

282 ITA
TESI GREGORIANA. (In 9 series: Teologia, Diritto Canonico, Filosofia, Storia Ecclesiastica, Missiologia, Scienze Sociali, Spiritualita, Psicologia, Scienze Religiose) Text in Multiple languages. 1995. irreg. price varies. **Document type:** *Monographic series, Academic/Scholarly.* **Description:** Publishes doctoral theses that earned summa cum laude or magna cum laude at Universita Gregoriana.
Published by: (Pontificia Universita Gregoriana/Pontifical Gregorian University), Gregorian University Press/Editrice Pontificia Universita Gregoriana, Piazza della Pilotta 35, Rome, 00187, Italy. TEL 39-06-6781567, FAX 39-06-6780588, periodicals@biblicum.com, http://www.paxbook.com.

282.764 USA ISSN 0899-6296
TEXAS CATHOLIC. Text in English. 1952. bi-w. USD 15 (effective 2005). adv. bk.rev. **Document type:** *Newspaper, Consumer.* **Description:** Interprets secular and religious events from the Catholic viewpoint for Catholics in Dallas, Texas.
Related titles: Microfilm ed.
Address: PO Box 190347, Dallas, TX 75219. TEL 214-528-8792, FAX 214-528-3411. Adv. contact Tony Ramirez. col. inch USD 28. Circ: 50,000 (paid). Wire service: AP, CaNS.

282.764 USA
TEXAS CATHOLIC HERALD. Text in English. 1964. bi-w. (2nd & 4th Fri. of mo.). USD 10 in state; USD 15 out of state (effective 2005). adv. **Document type:** *Newspaper, Consumer.*
Related titles: Microfilm ed.
Published by: Catholic Diocese of Galveston-Houston, 1700 San Jacinto, Houston, TX 77002. TEL 713-659-5461, FAX 713-659-3444. Pub. Joseph A Fiorenza. adv.: B&W page USD 1,900; trim 10.5 x 13.5. Circ: 78,000 (controlled and free). Wire service: CaNS.

255.71 ITA ISSN 0394-7793
TEXTUS ET STUDIA HISTORICA CARMELITANA. Text in English, French, German, Italian, Latin, Spanish. 1954. irreg. price varies. adv. **Document type:** *Monographic series, Academic/Scholarly.* **Description:** Forum covers a Carmelite history; critical editions.
Published by: (Order of Carmelites), Edizioni Carmelitane, Via Sforza Pallavicini 10, Rome, 00193, Italy. TEL 39-06-68100886, FAX 39-06-68100887, 39-06-68307200, http://www.carmelites.info/edizioni/. Circ: 500.

230 COL ISSN 0120-3649
THEOLOGICA XAVERIANA. Text in Spanish. 1951. s-a. COP 60,000 domestic; USD 60 foreign (effective 2010). adv. bk.rev. index. back issues avail. **Document type:** *Journal, Academic/Scholarly.*
Formerly (until 1975): Ecclesiastica Xaveriana (0012-9054)
Related titles: Online - full text ed.: ISSN 2011-219X.
Indexed: A01, CA, CLA, F03, F04, FR, I04, I05, IBR, IBZ, T02.
—INIST.
Published by: Pontificia Universidad Javeriana, Facultad de Teologia, Carrera 10 No. 65-48, Apartado Aereo 54953, Bogota, DE, Colombia. TEL 57-1-2124846, FAX 57-1-2123360. Ed. Jose Alfredo Noratto Gutirrez. Circ: 300.

230.2 DEU ISSN 0049-366X
BR4
THEOLOGIE UND GLAUBE. Text in German. 1943. q. EUR 39.80; EUR 12.30 per issue (effective 2011). adv. bk.rev. **Document type:** *Journal, Academic/Scholarly.* **Description:** Covers a variety of theological issues: Church history, ethics, Bible, and liturgy.
Supersedes in part (in 1947): Theologie und Seelsorge (1864-4589); Which was formed by the merger of (1883-1943): Pastor Bonus (1864-4740); (1909-1943): Theologie und Glaube (1864-4767); (1930-1943): Ostdeutsches Pastoralblatt
Indexed: CERDIC, CLA, DIP, FR, IBR, IBZ, MLA-IB, OTA, PCI, RI-1.
—INIST. **CCC.**
Published by: (Theologische Fakultaet Paderborn), Aschendorff Verlag GmbH & Co. KG, Soester Str 13, Muenster, 48135, Germany. TEL 49-251-6900, FAX 49-251-6904570, buchverlag@aschendorff.de, http://www.aschendorff-buchverlag.de. Eds. Dieter Hattrup, Hans F Fuhs.

230.2 DEU ISSN 1863-1215
THEOLOGIE UND HOCHSCHULE. Text in German. 2006. irreg., latest vol.3, 2006. price varies. **Document type:** *Monographic series, Academic/Scholarly.*
Published by: Verlagshaus Monsenstein und Vannerdat OHG, Am Hawerkamp 31, Muenster, 48155, Germany. TEL 49-251-232990, FAX 49-251-3999447, service@mv-verlag.de, http://www.mv-verlag.de. Ed. Eric Steinhauer.

282 100 DEU ISSN 0040-5655
BX803
THEOLOGIE UND PHILOSOPHIE. Text in German. 1926. q. EUR 192; EUR 49.80 newsstand/cover (effective 2010). adv. bk.rev. bibl. index. reprints avail. **Document type:** *Journal, Academic/Scholarly.*
Formerly (until 1966): Scholastik (0932-4038)
Indexed: A21, A22, BibInd, BibLing, CERDIC, CLA, DIP, FR, IBR, IBZ, IPB, MLA-IB, PCI, PhilInd, RASB, RI-1, RI-2.
—IE, Infotrieve, INIST.
Published by: Verlag Herder GmbH, Hermann-Herder-Str 4, Freiburg Im Breisgau, 79104, Germany. TEL 49-761-27170, FAX 49-761-2717520, kundenservice@herder.de, http://www.herder.de.

230.2 DEU ISSN 0342-1430
BR4
THEOLOGISCHE QUARTALSCHRIFT. Text in German. 1819. q. EUR 37.80 (effective 2004). index. reprints avail. **Document type:** *Journal, Academic/Scholarly.*
Formerly (until 1968): Tubinger Theologische Quartalschrift (0937-0838)
Indexed: A21, A22, BibLing, DIP, FR, IBR, IBZ, IPB, IZBG, OTA, R&TA, RI-1, RI-2.
—IE, Infotrieve, INIST. **CCC.**
Published by: Ludwig Auer GmbH, Heilig-Kreuz-Str 16, Donauwoerth, 86609, Germany. TEL 49-906-73130, FAX 49-906-73184, org@auer-medien.de, http://www.auer-medien.de. Ed. Hans Reinhard Seeliger.

230.2 DEU ISSN 0040-568X
BR4
THEOLOGISCHE REVUE. Text in German. 1902. 6/yr. EUR 109; EUR 19.90 newsstand/cover (effective 2011). adv. bk.rev. bibl. index. reprints avail. **Document type:** *Journal, Academic/Scholarly.*
Indexed: A22, BibInd, BibLing, CERDIC, DIP, FR, IBR, IBZ, IPB, PCI.
—IE, Infotrieve, INIST. **CCC.**
Published by: (Westfaelische Wilhelms-Universitaet Muenster, Katholisch-Theologische Fakultaet), Aschendorff Verlag GmbH & Co. KG, Soester Str 13, Muenster, 48135, Germany. TEL 49-251-6900, FAX 49-251-6904570, buchverlag@aschendorff.de, http://www.aschendorff-buchverlag.de. Ed. Thomas Bremer. Circ: 900 (paid and controlled).

271.9 FRA ISSN 1168-5638
THERESE DE LISIEUX. Text in French. 1925. m. EUR 30 domestic; EUR 40 foreign (effective 2008). bk.rev. **Document type:** *Magazine.*
Formerly: Sainte Therese de Lisieux. Annales (0994-6373)
Published by: Association Ste. Therese, 33 Rue du Carmel, Lisieux, Cedex 14102, France. TEL 33-2-31485500, FAX 33-2-31485525. Ed., R&P Raymond Zambelli. Circ: 35,000.

282 USA ISSN 1049-4561
THIS ROCK. Text in English. 1990. 10/yr. USD 39.95 domestic; USD 59.95 in Canada & Mexico; USD 76.50 elsewhere (effective 2007). **Document type:** *Magazine, Consumer.* **Description:** Explains and defends the tenets of the Catholic faith and presents practical ways to spread God's truth.
Published by: Catholic Answers, 2020 Gillespie Way, El Cajon, CA 92020. TEL 619-387-7200, 888-291-8000, FAX 619-387-0042, orders@catholic.com. Pub. Karl Keating.

230.2 USA ISSN 0040-6325
BX801
➤ **THOMIST**; a speculative quarterly review. Text in English. 1939. q. USD 30 domestic; USD 45 foreign; USD 35 combined subscription domestic (print & online eds.); USD 50 combined subscription foreign (print & online eds.) (effective 2010). bk.rev. bibl. index, cum.index: vol.1-50, 1939-1986; vol.51-55, 1987-1991; vol.56-60, 1992-1996; vol.61-65, 1997-2001. 176 p./no.; reprint service avail. from PSC. **Document type:** *Journal, Academic/Scholarly.* **Description:** Publishes scholarly articles and book reviews in theology and philosophy.
Related titles: Microfilm ed.: (from PQC); Online - full text ed.: USD 20 (effective 2010).
Indexed: A20, A21, A22, ASCA, ArtHuCI, CERDIC, CPL, CurCont, DIP, FR, IBR, IBZ, IPB, MLA-IB, P30, PCI, PhilInd, R&TA, RASB, RI-1, RI-2, SCOPUS, W07.
—BLDSC (8820.234000), IE, Infotrieve, Ingenta, INIST.
Published by: (Dominican Fathers, Province of St. Joseph), Thomist Press, 487 Michigan Ave, NE, Washington, DC 20017. TEL 202-495-3866, FAX 202-636-4460. Ed. Joseph Torchia.

282 330 USA
THRIVENT. Text in English. 1904. q. free to members (effective 2009). **Document type:** *Magazine, Consumer.* **Description:** Covers information ranging from families to finance.
Former titles (until Aug.2002): Correspondent Bond (1539-0128); (until Jun.2002): Correspondent (0740-6452)
Published by: Thrivent Financial for Lutherans, 625 Fourth Ave S, Minneapolis, MN 55415. TEL 920-734-5721, 800-847-4836, FAX 800-225-2264. Ed. Donna Mulder.

282.79494 USA ISSN 0040-6791
THE TIDINGS. Text in English. 1895. w. (Fri.). USD 23 (effective 2006). **Document type:** *Newspaper, Consumer.*
Formerly: The Los Angeles Tidings
Related titles: Microfilm ed.: (from LIB); Microform ed.
Indexed: MLA-IB.
Published by: Roman Catholic Archdiocese of Los Angeles, 3424 Wilshire Blvd, Los Angeles, CA 90010. TEL 213-637-7360, FAX 213-637-6360, info@la-archdiocese.org, http://www.la-archdiocese.org. Ed. Mike Nelson. Pub. Msgr. Msgr. Lloyd Torgerson. Circ: 92,000 (controlled and free). Wire service: CaNS.

282 ESP ISSN 2173-4321
TIEMPO DE PASION. Text in Spanish. 199?. a. **Document type:** *Magazine, Consumer.*
Published by: Ayuntamiento de Cantillana, Nuesro Padre Jess s-n, Cantillana, 41320, Spain. TEL 34-955751700, http://www.cantillana.es/.

230.2 NLD ISSN 0168-9959
➤ **TIJDSCHRIFT VOOR THEOLOGIE.** Text in Dutch; Summaries in English. 1838. q. EUR 49.95 in Europe to individuals; EUR 55 elsewhere to individuals; EUR 97.50 domestic to institutions; EUR 115 foreign to institutions; EUR 35 to students (effective 2011). bk.rev. index. back issues avail. **Document type:** *Journal, Academic/Scholarly.*

Former titles (until 1961): Studia Catholica (0166-3771); (until 1924): Katholiek (0167-0778); Which incorporated (1905-1906): Geschiedkundige Bladen (1878-5131); (until 1842): Godsdienstig Geschied- en Letterkundig Tijdschrift voor Roomsch-Katholyken (0167-1294)
Indexed: A22, CERDIC, DIP, IBR, IBZ, IPB, IZBG, MLA-IB, OTA, PCI, R&TA.
—IE, Infotrieve.
Address: Postbus 9103, Nijmegen, 6500 HD, Netherlands. TEL 31-24-3611503. Ed. Dr. Stephan van Erp.

282 USA ISSN 2158-8562
TODAY'S CATHOLIC. Text in English. 1943. m. USD 15 in state; USD 20 out of state (effective 2011). bk.rev. back issues avail. **Document type:** *Newspaper, Trade.*
Former titles (until 2010): Chronicle of Catholic Life (1041-1984); (until 1988): Catholic Crosswinds (0888-1464)
Published by: Diocese of Pueblo, 101 N Greenwood St, Pueblo, CO 81003. TEL 719-544-9861, http://www.dioceseofpueblo.org/. Wire service: CaNS.

282 USA ISSN 0891-1533
TODAY'S CATHOLIC (FORT WAYNE). Text in English. 1926. w. (Sun.). USD 20 (effective 1999). adv. bk.rev.; film rev. charts; illus.; stat. back issues avail. **Document type:** *Newspaper.* **Description:** Roman Catholic diocesan newspaper.
Related titles: Talking Book ed.
Published by: Bishop John M. D'Arcy, Pub., PO Box 11169, Fort Wayne, IN 46856. TEL 219-456-2824, FAX 219-744-1473. Ed. William Cone. Adv. contact Dee Dee Dahm. Circ: 19,000. Wire service: CaNS.

282 USA ISSN 0745-3612
TODAY'S CATHOLIC (SAN ANTONIO). Text in English, Spanish. 1892. fortn. USD 12 domestic; USD 65 foreign (effective 2005). adv. bk.rev. **Document type:** *Newsletter.* **Description:** Covers family-oriented Catholic news.
Address: PO Box 28410, San Antonio, TX 78228. TEL 210-734-2620, FAX 210-734-2939. Ed. Jordan McMorrough. Pub. Archbishop Jose H Gomez. Adv. contact Judy Cevera. Circ: 24,000 (paid).

TODAY'S CATHOLIC TEACHER. *see* EDUCATION

282 USA ISSN 0199-8803
TODAY'S MISSAL; masses for sunday and holy days with daily mass propers. Text in English. q. USD 12.25 5 to 24 subscriptions; USD 12.95 newsstand/cover domestic; USD 15.95 newsstand/cover in Canada (effective 2007). **Document type:** *Magazine, Consumer.*
Published by: O C P Publications, 5536 NE Hassalo, Portland, OR 97213. TEL 800-548-8749, FAX 800-462-7329, http://www.ocp.org. Ed. Eric Schumock. Pub. John J Limp.

250 USA ISSN 2154-5243
TODAY'S PARISH; ideas and inspiration for pastors, parish ministers, and leaders. Text in English. 1969. bi-m. USD 24.95 (effective 2010). adv. bk.rev. abstr.; illus. back issues avail. **Document type:** *Magazine, Trade.* **Description:** Covers practical ideas for fostering lively communities of active parishioners.
Former titles (until 2010): Today's Parish Minister (1936-7465); (until 2006): Today's Parish (0040-8549)
Indexed: CERDIC, CPL.
—CCC.
Published by: Bayard Inc. (Subsidiary of: Bayard Presse), 1 Montauk Ave, Ste 200, New London, CT 06320. TEL 800-321-0411, cservice@bayard-us.com, http://www.bayard-inc.com. Ed. Nick Wagner. Adv. contact Rosanne Coffey. B&W page GBP 785, color page GBP 1,115; bleed 8.5 x 11.25.

TOSCANAOGGI. *see* LIFESTYLE

322.1 USA ISSN 0897-327X
BR1
TOUCHSTONE (CHICAGO); a journal of mere christianity. Text in English. 1986. m. USD 34.95 domestic; USD 41.95 in Canada; USD 46.95 elsewhere (effective 2007). adv. bk.rev. back issues avail. **Document type:** *Magazine, Consumer.* **Description:** Contains information and news pertaining to priests, spirituality, and articles on various ministries.
Indexed: A01, A03, A21, AIAP, AmHI, CA, H07, P34, RI-1, RI-2, T02.
Published by: Fellowship of St. James, PO Box 410788, Chicago, IL 61641. TEL 773-481-1090, FAX 773-481-1095, fsj@fsj.org, http://www.fsj.org. Ed. David Mills. adv.: B&W page USD 800, color page USD 1,600; bleed 8.25 x 10.875. Circ: 10,000.

282 USA ISSN 2152-8748
▼ **THE TRADITIONALIST.** Text in English. 2009. q. USD 36.75 foreign; USD 29.75 combined subscription domestic (print & E-Mail eds.); USD 7.50 per issue (effective 2010). adv. **Document type:** *Magazine, Consumer.* **Description:** Features writing and reports from all parts of the world by noted Catholics and talented young writers.
Related titles: E-mail ed.; Online - full text ed.: ISSN 2152-8764.
Published by: Roger A. McCaffrey, Ed. & Pub., PO Box 993, Ridgefield, CT 06877. Ed., Pub. Roger A McCaffrey.

230.2 USA
TRADITIONS OF CHRISTIAN SPIRITUALITY SERIES. Text in English. 1998. irreg. price varies. back issues avail. **Document type:** *Monographic series, Academic/Scholarly.* **Description:** Provides historical and thematic treatments of their subjects.
Published by: Orbis Books (Subsidiary of: Maryknoll Fathers and Brothers), Dept WEB, PO Box 302, Maryknoll, NY 10545. TEL 800-258-5838, FAX 914-941-7005, orbisbooks@maryknoll.org.

230.2 ITA
TRADIZIONE CATTOLICA. Text in Italian. N.S. 1986. q. bk.rev. **Document type:** *Magazine, Consumer.* **Description:** Covers traditional theology, doctrines, and spirituality of the church.
Published by: Fraternita Sacerdotale San Pio X, Distretto Italia, Via Mavoncello 25, Spadarolo, RN 47037, Italy.

282.09 NLD ISSN 0778-8304
BX1549.A1
➤ **TRAJECTA**; tijdschrift voor de geshiedenis van het katholiek leven in de Nederlanden. Text in Dutch; Summaries in English. 1959. 4/yr. EUR 32; EUR 16 to students; EUR 10 newsstand/cover (effective 2008). adv. bk.rev. abstr.; bibl.; illus. index, cum.index 1959-1991. reprints avail. **Document type:** *Academic/Scholarly.* **Description:** Scholarly treatment of the history of Catholic life in the Low Countries.
Formerly (until 1992): Archief voor de Geschiedenis van de Katholieke Kerk in Nederland (0003-8326); Which was formed by the merger of (1875-1957): Archief voor de Gescheidenis van het Aartsbisdom Utrecht (0921-996X); (1873-1958): Haarlemsche Bijdragen (0927-7870); Which was formerly (until 1934): Bijdragen voor de Geschiedenis van het Bisdom van Haarlem (0927-7862)
Indexed: A21, A22, CA, FR, HistAb, IBR, IBZ, P30, PCI, RI-1, T02.
—IE, Infotrieve, INIST.
Published by: Katholiek Documentatie Centrum, Postbus 9100, Nijmegen, 6500 HA, Netherlands. TEL 31-24-3612457, FAX 31-24-3612403, info@kdc.ru.nl, http://www.ru.nl/kdc.

282 FRA ISSN 1241-8986
TRAJETS; Cahiers Universitaires Catholiques. Text in French. 1911. q. bk.rev.; music rev. bibl. index. **Document type:** *Magazine, Consumer.* **Description:** Keeps readers abreast of current cultural and religious issues at home and abroad.
Former titles (until 1992): Cahiers Universitaires Catholiques (0223-5935); (until 1948): Cahiers de la Paroisse Universitaires (1141-0299); (until 1946): Bulletin Joseph Lotte (1141-0280); (until 1929): Bulletin des Professeurs Catholiques de l'Universite (1141-0272)
Indexed: FR, IBSS.
Published by: Association Joseph Lotte, 170 bd. du Montparnasse, Paris, 75014, France. TEL 33-1-43352850, FAX 33-1-43216934. Ed. Marie Helene Depardon. Pub. Maurice Montabrut. Circ: 1,600.

371.0712 282 001.3 300 FRA ISSN 1286-9449
BR3
TRANSVERSALITES; revue de l'Institut Catholique de Paris. Text in French. 1949. q. **Document type:** *Academic/Scholarly.* **Description:** Quarterly journal with contributions on subjects taught in the Institut Catholique de Paris.
Former titles (until 1996): Institut Catholique de Paris. Revue (0294-4308); (until 1982): Institut Catholique de Paris. Nouvelles (0294-4294)
Indexed: A21, FR, IBSS, MLA-IB.
—BLDSC (9026.700650), INIST.
Published by: Institut Catholique de Paris, 21 rue d'Assas, Paris, Cedex 6 75270, France. TEL 33-1-44395296, FAX 33-1-45445277, recherche@icp.fr. Ed. Michel Quesnel.

282 DEU
TRIERER CUSANUS LECTURE. Text in German. 1994. irreg., latest vol.16, 2010. price varies. **Document type:** *Monographic series, Academic/Scholarly.*
Published by: Cusanus-Gesellschaft, Gestade 18, Bernkastel-Kues, 54470, Germany. TEL 49-6531-54118, FAX 49-6531-54107, cusanus@bernkastel-kues.de, http://www.nikolaus-von-kues.de.

282 ESP
TRINIDAD Y LIBERACION. Text in Spanish. m. EUR 12 (effective 2010). **Document type:** *Magazine, Consumer.*
Formerly: Hoja Trinitaria
Published by: Secretariado Trinitario Ediciones, Avda Filiberto Villalobos, 80, Salamanca, 37007, Spain. TEL 34-92-3235602, http://www.secretariadotrinitario.org/.

TRUE GIRL. *see* CHILDREN AND YOUTH—For

382 ESP ISSN 0211-7207
DP402.T25
TURIASO. Text in Spanish. 1980. a. back issues avail.
Related titles: Online - full text ed.
Indexed: GeoRef, RILM.
Published by: Centro de Estudios Turiasonenses, Bajos del Palacio Episcolar, C. Rua Alta de Beques, s-n, Tarazona, Zaragoza 50500, Spain. TEL 34-976-642861, FAX 34-976-643462, info@ceturiasonenses.org.

282 USA ISSN 1063-4525
THE U P CATHOLIC. (Upper Peninsula) Text in English. 1971. s-m. USD 20. adv. bk.rev. **Document type:** *Newspaper.* **Description:** Covers local, national and international news both religious and secular.
Formerly: Upper Peninsula Catholic (0747-1440)
Published by: Diocese of Marquette, PO Box 548, Marquette, MI 49855-0548. TEL 906-226-8821, FAX 906-226-6941. Ed. Joseph Zyble. Pub. Bishop James Garland. R&P Joseph K Zyble. Adv. contact Sandra L Paull Numikoski. page USD 432. Circ: 5,000.

282.73 USA ISSN 0041-7548
BX801
U S CATHOLIC. Text in English. 1968. m. USD 29 domestic; USD 39 foreign (effective 2011). adv. bk.rev. illus. reprints avail. **Document type:** *Magazine, Consumer.* **Description:** Provides informative features, interviews and essays on Catholic life, contemporary Catholic thought, social justice concerns, faith and work, scripture, prayer, current events, and popular culture.
Formerly (until 1972): U S Catholic and Jubilee (0096-3356); Which was formed by the merger of (1953-1968): Jubilee (0449-3486); (1963-1968): U S Catholic; Which was formerly (until 1963): St. Jude
Related titles: Microform ed.: (from PQC); Online - full text ed.
Indexed: A01, A02, A03, A08, A22, A26, B04, BRD, CERDIC, CPL, G05, G06, G07, G08, GSS&RPL, H14, I05, I07, L09, M01, M02, M06, MASUSE, MagInd, P02, P10, P28, P30, P34, P48, P53, P54, PMR, PQC, R03, R04, R05, RGAb, RGPR, RILM, S23, T02, W03, W05.
—Ingenta.
Published by: Claretian Publications, 205 W Monroe, Chicago, IL 60606. TEL 312-236-7782, FAX 312-236-8207.

282 USA ISSN 0735-8318
BX1404
U S CATHOLIC HISTORIAN. Text in English. 1980. q. USD 45 in US & Canada to individuals; USD 50 elsewhere to individuals; USD 60 in US & Canada to institutions; USD 65 elsewhere to institutions (effective 2009). adv. illus. back issues avail.; reprint service avail. from PSC. **Document type:** *Journal, Academic/Scholarly.*
Related titles: Online - full text ed.: ISSN 1947-8224.
Indexed: A22, AmH&L, CPL, E01, MLA-IB, T02.
—CCC.
Published by: (U.S. Catholic Historical Society), Catholic University of America Press, 620 Michigan Ave, NE, 240 Leahy Hall, Washington, DC 20064. FAX 202-319-4985, cua-press@cua.edu, http://cuapress.cua.edu. Ed. Christopher Kauffman. adv.: page USD 150, 1/2 page USD 100. Circ: 1,279 (paid). **Subscr. to:** Kable Fulfillment Services, Inc., PO Box 573, Mt. Morris, IL 61054. TEL 815-734-5981, FAX 815-734-5204.

282.021 USA
U S CATHOLIC MISSION HANDBOOK. Text in English. 1950. biennial. free membership (effective 2003). charts; stat. **Document type:** *Directory.* **Description:** Missionary statistics in the US and abroad.
Former titles (until 1994): Report on U S Catholic Overseas Mission; Mission Handbook; United States Catholic Mission Council. Handbook; United States Catholic Missionary Personnel Overseas (0082-9560)
Related titles: Online - full content ed.
Indexed: SRI.
Published by: United States Catholic Mission Association, 3029 Fourth St, N E, Washington, DC 20017. TEL 202-832-3112, FAX 202-832-3688, http://www.uscatholicmission.org. Circ: 1,500.

282 ITA
L'ULIVO. Text in Italian. q.
Published by: Congregazione Benedettina di Monte Oliveto, c/o Abbazia Monte Oliveto Maggiore, Chiusure, SI 53020, Italy. http://www.monteolivetomaggiore.it. Ed. D Diego Donatelli.

282 USA ISSN 0041-6258
ULTREYA. Text in English. 1959. bi-m. USD 12; USD 16 foreign (effective 1999). bk.rev. illus.
Published by: U S Cusillo Movement, National Secretariat, 4500 W Davis, PO Box 210226, Dallas, TX 75211. TEL 214-339-6321, FAX 214-339-6322. Ed. Thomas E Sarg. Circ: 4,000.

282 USA ISSN 1527-635X
UNIDOS EN CRISTO/UNITED IN CHRIST. Text in English, Spanish. 1999. 3/yr. back issues avail. **Document type:** *Magazine, Consumer.*
Related titles: Special ed(s).: Unidos en Cristo (Daily Mass Proper Edition). ISSN 1939-2524.
Published by: Oregon Catholic Press, 5536 NE Hassalo St, PO Box 18030, Portland, OR 97218. TEL 503-281-1191, 800-548-8749, liturgy@ocp.org.

282 USA
L'UNION. Text in English, French. 1902. q. membership. bk.rev.
Published by: Union Saint-Jean-Baptiste, 68 Cumberland St, Plaza Center, P O Box F, Woonsocket, RI 02895-0989. TEL 401-769-0520, 800-225-USJB, FAX 401-766-3014. Ed. Joseph E Gadbois. Pub. Louise R Champigny. Circ: 16,000 (free). **Co-sponsor:** Catholic Family Life Insurance.

230.2 ITA
UNITA E CARISMI. Text in Italian. 1991. bi-m. **Document type:** *Magazine, Consumer.*
Published by: Movimento dei Focolari, Via di Frascati 306, Rocca di Papa, RM 00040, Italy. TEL 39-06-947989, FAX 39-06-94749320, sif@focolare.org.

282 GBR ISSN 0041-8226
THE UNIVERSE. Text in English. 1860. w. GBP 57 (effective 2010). adv. bk.rev. illus. back issues avail. **Document type:** *Newspaper, Consumer.*
Former titles (until 1967): Universe and Catholic Times; (until 1962): The Universe; (until 1912): The Universe and Catholic Weekly; (until 1909): The Universe
—CCC.
Published by: Gabriel Communications Ltd., 4th Fl, Landmark House, Station Rd, Cheadle Hulme, Cheshire SK8 7JH, United Kingdom. TEL 44-161-4881700, digitaldownloads@totalcatholic.com. Ed. Joseph Kelly TEL 44-161-4881700.

230.2 CHL ISSN 0069-3596
BX805
UNIVERSIDAD CATOLICA DE CHILE. FACULTAD DE TEOLOGIA. ANALES. Text in Spanish. 1940. a. cum.index: 1940-1969. **Document type:** *Monographic series.*
Indexed: CPL, FR.
—INIST.
Published by: Pontificia Universidad Catolica de Chile, Facultad de Teologia, Jaime Guzman Errazuriz 3300, Casilla 316, Santiago, 22, Chile. Eds. Antonio Rehbein Pesce, Cecilia Coz Canas. Circ: 500.

230.2 ESP
UNIVERSIDAD PONTIFICIA COMILLAS DE MADRID. PUBLICACIONES. SERIE 1: ESTUDIOS. Text in Spanish. 1975. irreg., latest vol.32, 1984. **Document type:** *Monographic series, Academic/Scholarly.*
Related titles: Series: Universidad Pontificia Comillas de Madrid. Publicaciones. Serie 1: Estudios: Teologia. ISSN 0211-2752; Universidad Pontificia Comillas de Madrid. Publicaciones. Serie 1: Estudios: Canon. ISSN 0211-2760; Universidad Pontificia Comillas de Madrid. Publicaciones. Serie 1: Estudios: Filosofia. ISSN 0211-2779.
Published by: Universidad Pontificia Comillas de Madrid, Comision de Publicaciones, C Alberto Aguilera, 23, Madrid, 28015, Spain.

230.2 BEL
UNIVERSITE CATHOLIQUE DE LOUVAIN. FACULTE DE THEOLOGIE ET DE DROIT CANONIQUE. COLLECTION DES DISSERTATIONS PRESENTEES POUR L'OBTENTION DU GRADE DE MAITRE A LA FACULTE DE THEOLOGIE OU A LA FACULTE DE DROIT CANONIQUE. Text in French. 1841. irreg., latest vol.8, 1998, series quarto. **Document type:** *Monographic series, Academic/Scholarly.*
Formerly: Universite Catholique de Louvain. Facultes de Theologie et de Droit Canonique. Dissertationes ad Gradum Magistri in Facultate Theologica Vel in Facultate Iuris Canonici Consequendum Conscriptae
Published by: Universite Catholique de Louvain, Faculte de Theologie et de Droit Canonique, College Albert Deschamps, Grand' Place 45, Louvain-la-Neuve, 1348, Belgium. R&P Monique Gheysens TEL 32-10-47-4592.

230.2 BEL ISSN 0076-1230
UNIVERSITE CATHOLIQUE DE LOUVAIN. FACULTE DE THEOLOGIE ET DE DROIT CANONIQUE. TRAVAUX DE DOCTORAT. NOUVELLE SERIE. Text in French, Spanish, English. 1969. irreg., latest vol.19, 2000. **Document type:** *Monographic series, Academic/Scholarly.*
Formerly: Universite Catholique de Louvain. Faculte de Theologie et de Droit Canonique. Travaux de Doctorat en Theologie et en Droit Canaonique. Nouvelle Serie
Published by: Universite Catholique de Louvain, Faculte de Theologie et de Droit Canonique, College Albert Deschamps, Grand' Place 45, Louvain-la-Neuve, 1348, Belgium. R&P Monique Gheysens TEL 32-10-47-4592. Circ: 100.

R

261.58 USA ISSN 1069-8051
UPSOUTH; "your writing can change the world!". Text in English. 1993. q. USD 12 domestic; USD 3 newsstand/cover (effective 2005). bk.rev.; film rev. back issues avail. **Document type:** *Newsletter.* **Description:** Contains articles, essays, and poems on the hobbies, spiritual issues, and religious experiences of Catholic southern writers and seeks to foster a dialogue among the members of this audience. Also shows a strong interest in the culture of the U.S. South, as well as spiritual and religious poetry.
Published by: Upsouth Ventures, 323 Bellevue Ave, Bowling Green, KY 42101. TEL 270-535-2346, galen@ky.net. Ed., Pub., R&P Galen Smith Sr. Circ: 100 (paid).

255.71 ITA ISSN 0394-7807
VACARE DEO. Text in English, French, German, Italian, Latin, Spanish. 1956. irreg. price varies. adv. **Document type:** *Monographic series, Academic/Scholarly.* **Description:** Forum includes Carmelite spirituality; critical editions.
Published by: (Order of Carmelites), Edizioni Carmelitane, Via Sforza Pallavicini 10, Rome, 00193, Italy. TEL 39-06-68100886, FAX 39-06-68100887, edizioni@ocarm.org, http://www.carmelites.info/edizioni/. Circ: 500.

230.2 DEU ISSN 1865-1577
VATICAN-MAGAZIN. Text in German. 2006. m. EUR 50 domestic; EUR 60 foreign; EUR 44.50 to students (effective 2009). adv. **Document type:** *Magazine, Consumer.*
Formerly (until 2007): Inside the Vatican (German Edition) (1932-4723)
Related titles: ◆ English ed.: Inside the Vatican. ISSN 1068-8579; Polish ed.: Na Watykanie. ISSN 1233-7625. 1995.
Published by: Fe-Medienverlags GmbH, Hauptstr 22, Kisslegg, 88353, Germany. TEL 49-7563-92005. adv.: color page EUR 1,199; trim 210 x 275. Circ: 5,000 (paid).

262.13 USA ISSN 0889-0595
VATICAN VOICES AND NOTABLE PAPAL QUOTES. Text in English. 1979. w. looseleaf. USD 20. index.
Published by: Truth, Inc., 7346 W. Greenfield Ave., W. Allis, WI 53214. TEL 414-258-2665. Ed. Rev. Cletus Healy S J. Circ: 100.

266.2 ITA
VENGA IL TUO REGNO. Text in Italian. 1945. m. (10/yr.). bk.rev. **Document type:** *Magazine, Consumer.* **Description:** Missionary magazine for families containing mainly correspondence from missionaries working in Asia, Africa, South America, and Oceania.
Published by: Pontificio Istituto Missioni Estere, Via F D Guerrazzi, Rome, 00152, Italy. TEL 39-06-5839151, FAX 39-06-5894228, http://www.pime.org/. Circ: 10,000.

VEREIN FUER AUGSBURGER BISTUMSGESCHICHTE. JAHRBUCH. *see* HISTORY—History Of Europe

282 HRV ISSN 0352-5708
VERITAS; glasnik sv Antuna Padovanskoga. Text in Croatian. 1962. m. HRK 110 domestic; USD 33 foreign (effective 2000). adv. back issues avail. **Document type:** *Newsletter, Academic/Scholarly.*
Published by: Hrvatska Provincija sv Jeronima Franjevaca Konventualaca, Sveti Duh 31, Zagreb, 10000, Croatia. TEL 385-1-3777127, FAX 385-1-3777252. Ed., Pub. Ilija Miskic. R&P, Adv. contact Marko Puskaric TEL 385-1-3771888. Circ: 6,500 (paid); 500 (controlled).

282 USA ISSN 0042-4145
VERMONT CATHOLIC TRIBUNE. Text in English. 1957. bi-w. USD 12. adv. bk.rev.; film rev. illus. **Document type:** *Newspaper.*
Related titles: Microfilm ed.
Published by: Vermont Catholic Press Association, 351 North Ave, Burlington, VT 05401-2999. TEL 802-658-6110, FAX 802-658-0436. Ed., R&P Pat Gore. Pub. Bishop Kenneth Angell. Adv. contact Ginny Couture. Circ: 22,000. Wire service: CaNS.

262.3 ITA ISSN 0042-4242
VERONA FEDELE; settimanale cattolico d'informazione. Text in Italian. 1946. w. adv. bk.rev. **Document type:** *Newspaper.*
Related titles: Online - full text ed.
Published by: Editrice Verona Fedele s.r.l., Via Pieta' Vecchia, 4, Verona, VR 37121, Italy.

268 CAN ISSN 0042-434X
VERS DEMAIN. Text in French. 1939. 7/yr. CAD 10, USD 14. charts; illus. **Document type:** *Newspaper.* **Description:** Promotes the application of the teachings of the Roman Catholic Church in every aspect of social life, especially in economics with the social credit philosophy of Scottish engineer Clifford Hugh Douglas.
Published by: (Institut Louis Even Pelerins de Saint Michel, Pilgrims of Saint Michael USA), Louis Even Institute, 1101 Principale St, Rougemont, PQ J0L 1M0, Canada. TEL 514-469-2209, FAX 514-469-2601. Ed. Gilberte Cote Mercier. Circ: 35,000.

282 PRT ISSN 0873-1233
BX2350.A1
VIA SPIRITUS; revista de historia da spiritualidade e do sentimento religioso. Text in Portuguese. 1994. a. **Document type:** *Journal, Academic/Scholarly.*
Related titles: Online - full text ed.: free (effective 2011).
Published by: Universidade do Porto, Faculdade de Letras, Praca Gomes Teixeira, Oporto, 4099-002, Portugal. TEL 351-220-408000, FAX 351-220-408186, up@up.pt, http://www.up.pt.

268 AUS ISSN 1833-525X
VICTORIAN CATHOLIC SCHOOLS PARENT BODY. Text in English. 2006. q. **Document type:** *Bulletin, Consumer.*
Published by: Catholic Education Office Melbourne, James Goold House, 228 Victoria Parade, PO Box 3, East Melbourne, VIC 8002, Australia. TEL 61-3-92670228, FAX 61-3-94159325, director@ceo.melb.catholic.edu.au.

282 ESP ISSN 0505-4605
VIDA NUEVA. Text in Spanish. 1944. w. adv. bk.rev. **Document type:** *Newspaper, Consumer.*
Formerly (until 1957): Pax (0211-6375)
Indexed: FR.
Published by: PPC Editorial, Agastia 80, Madrid, 28043, Spain. TEL 34-91-744-4550, FAX 34-91-7444891. Ed. Rosario Marin Malave.

282 ESP ISSN 0211-9749
VIDA RELIGIOSA. Text in Spanish. 1944. s-m. (except July-Aug.). adv. bk.rev. bibl.; charts; stat.; tr.lit. index. back issues avail. **Document type:** *Magazine, Consumer.*
Indexed: CERDIC, CLA.
Published by: Misioneros Hijos del Inmaculado Corazon de Maria (Claretianos), Buen Suceso, 22, Madrid, 28008, Spain. TEL 34-91-5401261, FAX 34-91-5400066, pcl@infonegocio.com, http://www.infonegocio.com/claret. Circ: 10,000 (controlled).

230.2 IND ISSN 0970-1079
VIDYAJYOTI JOURNAL OF THEOLOGICAL REFLECTION. Text in English. 1938. m. bk.rev. bibl. index. back issues avail. **Document type:** *Journal, Trade.* **Description:** Concerned with the life and thought of the church in India, inter-religious dialogue, theology and social concerns.
Former titles (until 1986): Vidyajyoti (0970-1222); (until 1975): Clergy Monthly
Indexed: CLA, OTA, R&TA.
—BLDSC (9234.501000).
Published by: Vidyajyoti Educational and Welfare Society (VIEWS), 4 A Raj Nivas Marg, New Delhi, 110 054, India.

282 FRA ISSN 0042-5362
VIE CATHOLIQUE DU BERRY. Text in French. 1865. bi-w. EUR 32 (effective 2008). adv. bk.rev. **Document type:** *Bulletin.*
Incorporates: Vocation (1144-2549); Formerly: Semaine Religieuse du Diocese de Bourges (1141-1562)
Published by: Association Diocesaine de Bourges, Archeveche de Bourges, 4 avenue du 95e de Ligne, BP 95, Bourges, Cedex 18020, France. TEL 33-2-48231290, FAX 33-2-48249418. Ed. Jean Soulcie. Pub. Carmel de Bourges. Circ: 400,000.

282 CAN ISSN 0380-8254
VIE LITURGIQUE. Text in English. 1968. 8/yr. CAD 43.86 domestic; USD 41.95 in United States; USD 62.95 elsewhere (effective 2000).
Published by: Novalis, St Paul University, 223 Main St, Ottawa, ON K1S 1C4, Canada. TEL 613-236-1393, FAX 613-782-3004, http://www.novalis.ca. Ed. Claude Auger. **Subscr. to:** 49 Front St E, 2nd Fl, Toronto, ON M5E 1B3, Canada. TEL 800-387-7164, FAX 800-204-4140.

282 CAN ISSN 0318-9392
VIE OBLATE/OBLATE LIFE. Text in English, French. 1942. 3/yr. CAD 20 (effective 2000). bk.rev. cum.index: 1942-1961, 1962-1990. back issues avail. **Document type:** *Newsletter.* **Description:** Deals with Oblate community life, pastoral methods, constitutions and rules, spirituality and history of the institute.
Formerly: Etudes Oblates (0318-9384)
Address: 175 rue Main, Ottawa, ON K1S 1C3, Canada. TEL 613-237-0580, FAX 613-232-4064. Ed. Romuald Boucher. Circ: 500.

271.9 FRA ISSN 0994-639X
VIE THERESIENNE. Text in French. 1961. q. EUR 30 domestic; EUR 40 foreign (effective 2008). bk.rev. **Document type:** *Bulletin.*
Published by: Association Ste. Therese, 33 Rue du Carmel, Lisieux, Cedex 14102, France. TEL 33-2-31485500, FAX 33-2-31485525, http://therese-de-lisieux.cef.fr/. Ed., R&P Raymond Zambelli. Circ: 2,500.

282 HUN ISSN 0042-6024
BX806.H8
VIGILIA. Text in Hungarian; Summaries in English, French, German. 1935. m. HUF 480, USD 35. bk.rev.
Indexed: CERDIC, RASB, RILM.
Address: Kossuth Lajos utca 1, PO Box 111, Budapest, 1364, Hungary. TEL 117-7246, FAX 117-4895. Ed. Laszlo Lukacs. Circ: 10,000. **Subscr. to:** Kultura, PO Box 149, Budapest 1389, Hungary.

253 USA ISSN 1527-2370
VISION (MILWAUKEE). Text in English. 1968. 10/yr. USD 44 (effective 2000). bk.rev. **Document type:** *Newsletter.* **Description:** Provides a forum for discussion and communication among Catholic chaplains who work primarily in health care and prisons and other interested readers on issues of Catholic religion.
Formerly (until 1991): Camillian
Indexed: CERDIC.
Published by: National Association of Catholic Chaplains, 3501 S Lake Dr, Box 07473, Milwaukee, WI 53207-0473. TEL 414-483-4898, FAX 414-483-6712. Ed. Rev. Joseph J Driscoll. R&P, Adv. contact Susan Cubar. Circ: 3,600 (paid).

282 PRI ISSN 1526-8616
EL VISITANTE DE PUERTO RICO. Text in Spanish. 1975. w. USD 46 in area (effective 2006). adv. bk.rev. 28 p./no.; back issues avail. **Document type:** *Newspaper, Consumer.* **Description:** Follows Roman Catholic church philosophy and applies it to social, moral, cultural and political issues.
Related titles: Microfilm ed.
Published by: El Visitante, PO Box 41305, Minillas Sta, San Juan, 00940-1305, Puerto Rico. adv.: B&W page USD 800, color page USD 1,340. Circ: 59,000 (controlled).

282 USA
VISITOR (ST. CLOUD). Text in English. 1938. w. USD 17 (effective 2000). adv. bk.rev. **Document type:** *Newspaper.*
Published by: Diocese of St. Cloud, 305 N. Seventh Ave., St. Cloud, MN 56303. TEL 320-251-3022, FAX 320-251-0424. Ed., R&P Joe Towalski. Adv. contact Rose Kruger Fuchs. **Subscr. to:** PO Box 1068, St. Cloud, MN 56302.

282 ITA ISSN 0042-7233
VITA CATTOLICA. Text in Italian. 1916. w. EUR 42 (effective 2009). adv. illus. **Document type:** *Magazine, Consumer.*
Indexed: MLA-IB.
Published by: (Diocesi di Cremona), Nuova Editrice Cremonese S.r.l., Via Stenico 3, Cremona, CR 26100, Italy. TEL 39-0372-20666, FAX 39-0372-35721.

282 ITA ISSN 0042-7276
VITA GIUSEPPINA. Text in Italian. 1895. m. adv. bk.rev. illus. index, cum.index. back issues avail. **Document type:** *Magazine, Consumer.*
Indexed: MLA-IB.
Published by: Congregazione di S. Giuseppe (Giuseppini del Murialdo), Via Belvedere Montello 77, Rome, 00166, Italy. TEL 39-06-6242851, FAX 39-06-6240846. Circ: 16,000.

282 ITA ISSN 0042-7284
LA VITA IN CRISTO E NELLA CHIESA; mensile per l'animazione liturgica. Text in Italian. 1951. m. EUR 21 domestic (effective 2009). adv. bk.rev. illus. index. **Document type:** *Magazine, Consumer.* **Description:** Religious forum devoted to Christians. Includes articles on the church, liturgical art, ecumenism, prayer and observance of religious holidays in modern day context.
Published by: Provincia Italiana Pie Discepole del Divin Maestro, Via Gabriele Rossetti 17, Rome, 00152, Italy. TEL 39-06-5839321, FAX 39-06-583932271, http://www.pddm.org. Circ: 17,000.

282 ITA ISSN 1825-2923
VITA NUOVA. Text in Italian. 1919. w. illus. back issues avail. **Document type:** *Magazine, Consumer.*
Indexed: E-psyche.
Published by: Opera Diocesana San Bernardo degli Uberti, Piazza Duomo 1, Parma, 43100, Italy. TEL 39-0521-380511, FAX 39-0521-380528, http://www.diocesi.parma.it.

230.2 DEU
VITA REGULARIS ABHANDLUNGEN. Text in German. 1996. irreg., latest vol.42, 2009. price varies. **Document type:** *Monographic series, Academic/Scholarly.*
Supersedes in part (in 2003): Vita Regularis
Published by: Lit Verlag, Grevener Str/Fresnostr 2, Muenster, 48159, Germany. TEL 49-251-6203222, FAX 49-251-231972, lit@lit-verlag.de.

230.2 DEU
VITA REGULARIS EDITIONEN. Text in German. 1996. irreg., latest vol.3, 2005. price varies. **Document type:** *Monographic series, Academic/Scholarly.*
Supersedes in part (in 2003): Vita Regularis
Published by: Lit Verlag, Grevener Str/Fresnostr 2, Muenster, 48159, Germany. TEL 49-251-235091, FAX 49-251-231972, lit@lit-verlag.de.

282 ITA ISSN 1123-5470
BR5
VIVENS HOMO. Text in Italian. 1990. s-a. EUR 39.70 domestic; EUR 51.30 in the European Union; EUR 55.30 elsewhere (effective 2008). **Document type:** *Magazine, Consumer.*
Indexed: FR, MLA-IB, OTA, R&TA.
—INIST.
Published by: Centro Editoriale Dehoniano, Via Scipione dal Ferro 4, Bologna, BO 40138, Italy. TEL 39-051-4290451, FAX 39-051-4290491, ced-amm@dehoniane.it, http://www.dehoniane.it.

282.71 CAN ISSN 1492-9295
VIVRE EN EGLISE. Text in French. 1882. s-m. CAD 30 (effective 2001). adv. bibl. index. back issues avail.
Former titles (until Sep.2000): Eglise de Montreal (0381-0380); (until 1968): Votre Eglise (0381-0372); (until 1967): Eglise de Montreal (0381-0364); (until 1965): Semaine Religieuse de Montreal (0381-0356)
Published by: Eglise de Montreal, 2000 rue Sherbrooke Ouest, Montreal, PQ H3H 1G4, Canada. TEL 514-925-4300 ext 250, FAX 514-925-4336, revue@archevech-mtl.qc.ca. Ed. Huguette Bergeron-Fortin. Adv. contact Josee Roy. Circ: 2,500.

282.08691 CAN ISSN 0823-2687
VIVRE ENSEMBLE; bulletin de liaison en pastorale interculturelle. Text in English. 4/yr. CAD 10. adv. **Description:** Aims to welcome immigrants entering Quebec to the church.
Published by: Centre Justice et Foi, Secteur des Communautes Culturelles, 25 rue Jarry Ouest, Montreal, PQ H2P 1S6, Canada. Adv. contact Therese Benguerel.

282 USA ISSN 1075-6663
VOCATIONS AND PRAYERS. Text in English. 1990. q. USD 15 in North America; USD 22 elsewhere (effective 2005). **Document type:** *Magazine, Consumer.* **Description:** Provides ideas on how to improve vocation ministry and promotes prayer for priestly and Catholic vocations.
Published by: Rogationist of the Heart of Jesus, 6635 Tobias Ave, Van Nuys, CA 91405. TEL 818-782-1765, FAX 818-782-1794.

262.3 ITA
VOCE DEI BERICI; settimanale di informazione dell Diocesi di Vicenza. Text in Italian. 1949. w. EUR 40 (effective 2009). **Document type:** *Newspaper, Consumer.*
Address: Borgo Santa Lucia 51, Vicenza, VI 36100, Italy. TEL 39-0444-301711, FAX 39-0444-302750, lavocedeiberici@lavocedeiberici.it.

282 ITA
LA VOCE DI FERRARA - COMACCHIO. Text in Italian. 1954. w. adv. bk.rev. **Document type:** *Magazine, Consumer.*
Formerly: La Voce di Ferrara (0042-7853); Which was formed by the merger of: La Voce; La Croce
Published by: Arcidiocesi di Ferrara-Comacchio/Cura Vescovile, Comacchio, FE 44022, Italy. Circ: 4,000.

282 DEU ISSN 0724-2778
BX803
UNA VOCE KORRESPONDENZ. Text in German, Latin. 1970. bi-m. bk.rev. index. back issues avail. **Document type:** *Bulletin, Consumer.*
Indexed: DIP, IBR, IBZ.
Published by: Una Voce Korrespondenz Schriftleitung, Geldorpstr 73, Cologne, 50733, Germany. una.voce@t-online.de, http://www.unavoce.de. Ed. Rudolf Kaschewsky. Circ: 2,500.

282 ITA
VOCE SERAFICA DELLA SARDEGNA. Text in Italian, Sardinian; Section in French; Summaries in Italian. 1921. m. adv. bk.rev. index. **Document type:** *Magazine, Consumer.* **Description:** Covers the Catholic religion and Capuchin information from Sardinia and Corsica.
Related titles: Microfiche ed.
Published by: Frati Minori Cappuccini, Provincia di Sardegna/Ordo Fratrum Minorum Capuccinorum, Via Sant Ignazio Da Laconi, 94, Cagliari, CA 09123, Italy. http://www.vol.it/vocenet/index.html. Circ: 23,000 (paid); 3,000 (controlled).

282 JOR
VOICE OF THE HOLY LAND/SAWT EL-'ARD EL-MUKADDAS. Text in Arabic. 1968. m. JOD 10,000. adv. bk.rev.
Published by: Catholic Bureau of Press and Publication, P O Box 5634, Amman, Jordan. TEL 694095, FAX 692502. Ed. Raouf Najjar. Circ: 10,000.

262.3 USA ISSN 8750-5975
VOICE OF THE SOUTHWEST; serving the Catholic Diocese of Gallup. Text in English. 1970. m. USD 10 domestic (effective 2000). adv. bk.rev. **Document type:** *Newspaper.*
Published by: Diocese of Gallup, PO Box 1338, Gallup, NM 87305. TEL 505-863-4406, FAX 505-325-8860. Ed., R&P Rev. Timothy Farrell. Pub. Rev. Donald E Pelotte. Adv. contact Ella M Roanhorse. page USD 200; 14.5 x 10. Circ: 2,800 (paid).

282 POL ISSN 0860-9411
➤ **VOX PATRUM.** Text in Polish. 1981. s-a. **Document type:** *Journal, Academic/Scholarly.*
Indexed: IZBG.
Published by: (Katolicki Uniwersytet Lubelski, Miedzywydzialowy Zaklad Badan nad Antykiem Chrzescijanskim), Katolicki Uniwersytet Lubelski, Al Raclawickie 14, Lublin, 20-950, Poland. TEL 48-81-5338022, FAX 48-81-5338022. Ed. Stanislaw Longosz.

271.53 HRV ISSN 0352-9215
VRELA I PRINOSI. Text in Croatian. 1932. a. **Document type:** *Journal, Academic/Scholarly.*
Indexed: RILM.
Published by: Filozofsko-Teoloski Institut Druzbe Isusove/Institute of Philosophy and Theology, S.J., Jordanovac 110, Zagreb, 10001, Croatia. http://www.ftidi.hr.

371.0712 282 FRA ISSN 1291-4088
➤ **VUES D'ENSEMBLE.** Text in French. 1966. q. **Document type:** *Journal, Academic/Scholarly.*
Former titles (until 1998): Ensemble (1162-0978); (until 1990): Ensemble d'Ecoles Superieures et de Facultes Catholiques (0336-3678); (until 1974): Ensemble Universitaire de Facultes Libres. Ecoles et Instituts (0336-366X); (until 1970): Facultes Catholiques de Lille. Bulletin Trimestriel (0181-4559)
Published by: Institut Catholique de Lille, 60 bd. Vauban, BP 109, Lille, Cedex 59016, France. TEL 33-3-20134089, FAX 33-3-20134090. Circ: 15,000.

282 USA ISSN 1068-168X
WANDERER. Text in English. 1867. w. (Thu.). USD 65 domestic; USD 75 foreign; USD 80 combined subscription (print & online eds.) (effective 2009). bk.rev. back issues avail. **Document type:** *Newspaper, Consumer.* **Description:** Provides news and commentary from an orthodox Catholic perspective including vital issues affecting the Catholic Church to the political events that threaten the Catholic faith.
Related titles: Microfilm ed.: (from PQC); Online - full text ed.: USD 50; USD 2.50 per issue (effective 2009).
Published by: Wanderer Printing Co., 201 Ohio St, St. Paul, MN 55107. TEL 651-224-5733, FAX 651-224-9666. Ed. A J Matt Jr.

282 USA ISSN 0043-1583
BX806.R8
THE WAY (PHILADELPHIA)/SHLIAKH; Ukrainian Catholic bi-weekly. Text in English, Ukrainian. 1939. bi-w. (Sun.). USD 20. bk.rev. illus. **Document type:** *Newspaper.*
Published by: (Ukrainian Catholic Archdiocese of Philadelphia), Apostolate, Inc., 827 N Franklin St, Philadelphia, PA 19123-2004. TEL 215-922-5231. Eds. Iwan Skoczylas, Rev. Robert Hitchens. Circ: 6,500. Wire service: CaNS.

255.3 USA ISSN 0273-8295
BX801
WAY OF ST. FRANCIS. Text in English. 1948. 6/yr. USD 12 domestic; USD 14 foreign (effective 2000). adv. bk.rev. illus. **Document type:** *Newsletter.* **Description:** Franciscan life and spirituality.
Formerly: Way-Catholic Viewpoints (0043-1591)
Indexed: CERDIC.
Published by: Franciscan Friars of California, Inc., 1500 34th Ave, Oakland, CA 94601-3092. TEL 916-443-5717, FAX 916-443-2019. Ed., R&P Camille Francevich TEL 707-763-9189. Pub. Finian McGinn. Circ: 3,100 (paid).

282 USA
WEEKDAY HOMILY HELPS. Text in English. 1981. 5/w. looseleaf. USD 60 domestic; USD 72 in Canada; USD 82 elsewhere (effective 2011). adv. back issues avail. **Document type:** *Newsletter, Trade.* **Description:** Aid to Catholic clergy on preaching.
Related titles: E-mail ed.: USD 60 (effective 2011).
Published by: St. Anthony Messenger Press, 28 W Liberty St, Cincinnati, OH 45202. TEL 513-241-5615, 800-488-0488, FAX 513-241-0399, stanthony@americancatholic.org, http://www.americancatholic.org.

282 DEU ISSN 1439-4499
WEGE MIT FRANZISKUS. Text in German. 1999. 4/yr. **Document type:** *Magazine, Trade.*
Published by: Provinzialat der Thueringischen Franziskanerprovinz, Am Frauenberg 1, Fulda, 36039, Germany. TEL 49-661-109536, FAX 49-661-109539, prov.fulda@franziskaner.de, http://www.franziskaner.de.

282 DEU ISSN 0373-5885
WELT DES KINDES; Die Fachzeitschrift fuer Kindertageseinrichtungen. Text in German. 1915. bi-m. EUR 29; EUR 24 to students; EUR 6 newsstand/cover (effective 2011). adv. **Document type:** *Journal, Academic/Scholarly.*
Indexed: DIP, IBR, IBZ.
—INIST. **CCC.**
Published by: (Verband Katholischer Tageseinrichtungen fuer Kinder Bundesverband e.V.), Koesel-Verlag GmbH und Co. (Subsidiary of: Verlagsgruppe Random House GmbH), Flueggenstr 2, Munich, 80639, Germany. TEL 49-89-178010, FAX 49-89-17801111, leserservice@koesel.de, http://www.koesel.de. Circ: 11,000 (controlled).

282.782 USA
WEST NEBRASKA REGISTER. Text in English. 1930. w. USD 13.
Published by: Diocese of Grand Island, 311 W 17th St, 804 W Division, Grand Island, NE 68802. TEL 308-382-4660. Ed. Francis Curran. adv.: B&W page USD 200. Circ: 16,842.

282 USA
WEST RIVER CATHOLIC. Text in English. 1973. m. USD 25 in state; USD 60 out of state (effective 2009). adv. **Document type:** *Newspaper, Consumer.*
Published by: Diocese of Rapid City, 606 Cathedral Dr., Rapid City, Pennington, SD 57701. TEL 605-343-3541, FAX 605-348-7985, lhallstrom@diocr.org, http://www.rapidcitydocese.org. Ed. Laurie Hallstrom. Adv. contact Leon Lunders. B&W page USD 400. Circ: 12,000 evening (paid and free). Wire service: CaNS.

282 USA ISSN 0273-7345
WEST TEXAS ANGELUS. Text in English, Spanish. 1964. m. USD 10 (effective 1998). adv. bk.rev. **Document type:** *Newspaper.*
Formerly: Texas Concho Register (0040-425X)
Published by: Catholic Diocese of San Angelo, 804 Ford St, San Angelo, TX 76905. TEL 325-651-7500, FAX 325-651-6688. Ed. Peter N. Micale. Pub. Most Rev. Michael D. Pfeifer. Circ: 20,000. **Subscr. to:** PO Box 1829, San Angelo, TX 76902-1829.

282 USA ISSN 0745-516X
BX801
WEST TEXAS CATHOLIC. Text in English. 1936. w. USD 15 for 20 issues (effective 2008). adv.
Formerly: West Texas Register (0043-3187)
Published by: Roman Catholic Diocese of Amarillo, c/o Bishop John W Yanta, Box 5644, Amarillo, TX 79117-5644. TEL 806-383-2137, FAX 806-383-2243. Ed., R&P, Adv. contact Cathy Lexa. Pub. John W Yanta. Circ: 8,600.

282 CAN ISSN 0512-5235
WESTERN CATHOLIC REPORTER. Text in English. 1965. w. CAD 25, USD 50 (effective 1999). adv. **Document type:** *Newspaper.*
Published by: Great Western Press Ltd., 8421 101 Ave, Edmonton, AB T6A 0L1, Canada. TEL 780-465-8030, FAX 780-465-8031. Ed. Glen Argan. Adv. contact Linda Keer. B&W page USD 1,073. Circ: 38,000.

282 USA
WESTERN KENTUCKY CATHOLIC. Text in English. 1985. 10/yr. USD 10 (effective 2008). 48 p./no. 4 cols./p.; **Document type:** *Newspaper, Consumer.*
Published by: Roman Catholic Diocese of Owensboro, 600 Locust St., Owensboro, KY 42301-2130. TEL 270-683-1545, FAX 270-683-6883. Ed. Mel Howard. Pub. Rev. John J. McRaith. Circ: 19,400 (paid). Wire service: CaNS.

282 USA ISSN 1079-1205
WESTERN NEW YORK CATHOLIC. Text in English. 1873. m. USD 16 (effective 2005). **Document type:** *Newspaper, Consumer.* **Description:** Focuses on sharing local faith and service activities and their connection to the national and global mission of the Church.
Related titles: E-mail ed.
Published by: Diocese of Buffalo, 795 Main St, Buffalo, NY 14203-1215. TEL 716-847-8700, FAX 716-847-8722, dob@buffalodiocese.org. Ed. Kevin Keenan. Pub. Bishop Edward Kmiec. Adv. contact Kelly Scozzaro. Circ: 70,000 (paid).

262.13 POL ISSN 1230-6541
WIADOMOSCI ARCHIDIECEZJI LUBELSKIEJ; dicta et facta memoranda. Text in Polish. 1918. q. PLZ 20 (effective 2002). bk.rev. index. **Description:** Publishes official documents concerning the Pope, the Episcopate and the Archbishop.
Formerly (until 1992): Wiadomosci Diecezjalne Lubelskie
Published by: Kuria Metropolitalna w Lublinie, Ul Prymasa S Wyszynskiego 2, Lublin, 20950, Poland. TEL 48-81-5321058, FAX 48-81-5321225, TELEX 643599 KDL PL, z.wojtowicz@kuria.lublin.pl. Ed. Rev. Zbigniew Wojtowicz. Circ: 700.

282 POL ISSN 1230-7165
WIADOMOSCI DIECEZJALNE SIEDLECKIE. Text in Polish. 1918. m. **Document type:** *Bulletin.*
Formerly (until 1992): Wiadomosci Diecezjalne Podlaskie (0239-2763)
Related titles: Diskette ed.
Published by: Kuria Diecezjalna Siedlecka, Ul Pilsudskiego 62, Siedlce, 08100, Poland. TEL 23126, FAX 448744.

262.3 POL ISSN 1230-302X
WIADOMOSCI DIECEZJI LOWICKIEJ. Text in Polish. 1992. bi-m. PLZ 15. bk.rev. bibl.; maps; stat. **Document type:** *Bulletin.* **Description:** Presents documents and news from the Lowicz Diocese, theological disertations, church history.
Published by: Kuria Diecezji Lowickiej, Rynek Kosciuszki 26, Lowicz, 99400, Poland. TEL 48-46-374349, FAX 48-46-376340. Ed. Fr Stanislaw Banach. Circ: 600.

282 POL ISSN 0511-9405
WIEZ. Text in Polish. 1958. m. USD 6 per issue in Europe; USD 6.50 per issue in North America (effective 2006). **Document type:** *Journal, Academic/Scholarly.*
Indexed: IZBG, MLA-IB.
Published by: Wydawnictwo Wiez, ul Trebacka 3, Warsaw, 00074, Poland. TEL 48-22-8272917, FAX 48-22-8267983. Ed. Zbigniew Nosowski.

261.58 USA ISSN 1522-2314
WINDHOVER; a journal of Christian literature. Text in English. 1997. s-a. USD 10 (effective 2000). adv. bk.rev.; film rev.; play rev. back issues avail. **Description:** Publishes fiction, poetry, and drama that reflects a Christian perspective in literature.
Published by: University of Mary Hardin-Baylor, PO Box 8008, Belton, TX 76513. TEL 254-295-4564, dwnixon@umhb.edu. Ed. Donna Walker-Nixon. Adv. contact Donna Walker Nixon. page USD 80; 9 x 6. Circ: 500.

282 USA
WINONA COURIER. Text in English. 1910. m. USD 5. **Document type:** *Newspaper.*
Published by: Diocese of Winona, 55 W. Sanborn St., PO Box 949, Winona, MN 55987. TEL 507-454-4643. Ed. Ivan J Kubista. Circ: 39,200.

282.775 USA
WISCONSIN PASTORAL HANDBOOK. Text in English. 1962. a. USD 37 (effective 2000). adv. **Document type:** *Directory.* **Description:** Directory for all five Catholic dioceses in Wisconsin.
Formerly: Official Wisconsin Pastoral Handbook
Published by: Milwaukee Catholic Press Apostolate, Inc., 3501 S Lake Dr, Box 07913, Milwaukee, WI 53235-0913. TEL 414-769-3472. R&P Ethel Gintoft TEL 414-769-3478. Adv. contact Timothy Walter. Circ: 2,300 (controlled).

282 AUT ISSN 1012-3067
WISSENSCHAFT UND GLAUBE. Text in German. 1988. q. **Document type:** *Journal, Academic/Scholarly.*
Indexed: P30.
Published by: Wiener Katholische Akademie, Ebendorfer Str 8/2/10, Vienna, W 1010, Austria. TEL 43-1-4023917, http://stephanscom.at/edw/akademie.html.

230.2 DEU ISSN 0043-678X
BR4
WISSENSCHAFT UND WEISHEIT; Franziskanische Studien zu Theologie, Philosophie und Geschichte. Text in German. 1934. 2/yr. EUR 39; EUR 24 newsstand/cover (effective 2011). adv. bk.rev. index. **Document type:** *Journal, Academic/Scholarly.*
Incorporates (1914-1993): Franziskanische Studien (0016-0067)
Indexed: A22, DIP, FR, IBR, IBZ, IPB, OTA, PhilInd, RILM.
—Infotrieve, INIST.

Published by: (Koelnische Franziskanerordensprovinz), Aschendorff Verlag GmbH & Co. KG, Soester Str 13, Muenster, 48135, Germany. TEL 49-251-6900, FAX 49-251-6904570, buchverlag@aschendorff.de, http://www.aschendorff-buchverlag.de. Circ: 500.

282 USA ISSN 0745-0427
THE WITNESS (DIOCESAN) NEWSPAPER. Text in English. 1923. w. (Sun.). USD 18 in diocese; USD 20 outside diocese (effective 2005). adv. bk.rev. back issues avail. **Document type:** *Newspaper, Consumer.* **Description:** Provides national, international, and local news. Includes announcements, op-ed, entertainment, television reviews, and obituaries.
Published by: (Archdiocese of Dubuque), Witness Publishing Company, 1229 Mt Loretta Ave, P O Box 917, Dubuque, IA 52004-0917. TEL 563-588-0556, FAX 563-588-0557. Ed. Sister Carol Hoverman. Pub. Archbishop Jerome Hanus. Adv. contact Judith Bandy. col. inch USD 7. Circ: 20,321. Wire service: CaNS.

220 USA ISSN 0742-4639
THE WORD AMONG US; a catholic devotional magazine based on the daily mass readings. Text in English. 1981. m. (11/yr.). USD 24.95 combined subscription domestic (print & online eds.); USD 21.95 to senior citizens (print & online eds.); USD 3.50 newsstand/cover domestic; USD 4 newsstand/cover in Canada (effective 2008). bk.rev. back issues avail. **Document type:** *Magazine, Consumer.* **Description:** Catholic Bible study and practical guide to Christian living.
Related titles: Online - full text ed.; ◆ Spanish ed.: La Palabra entre Nosotros. ISSN 0896-1727; Polish ed.; Portuguese ed.; Japanese ed.
Indexed: P28, P48, P53, P54, PQC.
Published by: Word Among Us, 319 W Town Pl, Ste 319, St. Augustine, FL 32092. TEL 301-874-1700, 800-775-9673, FAX 301-874-2190, wordamongus@wau.org. Ed. Leo Zanchettin. Pub. Jeff Difato. Circ: 200,000. **Subscr. to:** Spring Arbor Distributors Inc., 10885 Textile Rd, Belleville, MI 48111. TEL 313-481-0900, 800-395-2681.

282 CAN ISSN 1480-0675
WORDS OF LIFE. Text in English. 1998. m. CAD 14.95 domestic; USD 14.95 in United States; USD 39.95 elsewhere (effective 2000).
Published by: Novalis, St Paul University, 223 Main St, Ottawa, ON K1S 1C4, Canada. TEL 613-236-1393, FAX 613-782-3004, http://www.novalis.ca. Ed. Caryl Green. **Subscr. to:** 49 Front St E, 2nd Fl, Toronto, ON M5E 1B3, Canada. TEL 800-387-7164, FAX 800-204-4140.

282 ZMB
WORKERS' CHALLENGE; from the workers to the workers. Text in English. 1982. bi-m. ZMK 2 per issue.
Published by: Workers' Pastoral Centre, PO Box 270035, Kitwe, Zambia. Eds. Clement Katongo, Fr Elias Afwenye. Circ: 18,000.

230.2 POL ISSN 1231-1731
WROCLAWSKI PRZEGLAD TEOLOGICZNY. Text in Polish; Contents page in English. 1993. s-a. PLZ 20; USD 20 in United States. bk.rev. back issues avail. **Document type:** *Academic/Scholarly.* **Description:** For theologians and theology students, clergy and laymen.
Indexed: IZBG.
Published by: Papieski Fakultet Teologiczny we Wroclawiu, Pl Katedralny 14, Wroclaw, 50329, Poland. TEL 48-71-229970, FAX 48-71-229970. Ed. Rev. Prof Ignacy Dec. Circ: 750.

282 DEU
WUERZBURGER KATHOLISCHES SONNTAGSBLATT. Text in German. 1850. w. EUR 118.80 (effective 2010). adv. **Document type:** *Newspaper, Consumer.*
Address: Kardinal-Doepfner-Platz 5, Wuerzburg, 97070, Germany. TEL 49-931-38611200, FAX 49-931-38611299, info@sobla.de. Ed., Pub. Wolfgang Bullin. Adv. contact Ernst Reusch. Circ: 49,635 (paid and controlled).

282.787 USA ISSN 0746-5580
WYOMING CATHOLIC REGISTER. Text in English. 1952. 4/yr. USD 15 (effective 2008). bk.rev. illus.; tr.lit. **Document type:** *Newspaper, Consumer.*
Address: 2121 Capitol Ave, Cheyenne, WY 82001. TEL 307-638-1530, FAX 307-367-7936. Eds. Scott Farris, Timothy J Stransky. Pub. Bishop Joseph Hart. Adv. contact Scott Farris. Circ: 20,000. Wire service: CaNS. **Subscr. to:** PO Box 1468, Cheyenne, WY 82003-1468.

266.2 USA
XAVERIAN MISSIONS NEWSLETTER. Text in English. 1951. 3/yr. looseleaf. USD 5 (effective 2005). **Document type:** *Newsletter, Consumer.* **Description:** Carries reports on Xaverian foreign missions and on related subjects involving the work of the Xaverian missionaries. Includes correspondence from missionaries, appeals for vocations, and news of activities on the home front.
Published by: Xaverian Missionaries, 101 Summer St, PO Box 5857, Holliston, MA 01746-5857. TEL 508-429-2144, askforinfo@xaviermissionaries.org. Circ: 25,000.

282 USA
XAVIER CATHOLIC REVIEW. Text in English. 1943. bi-m. free to blind and visually impaired (effective 2009). **Document type:** *Magazine, Consumer.* **Description:** Includes articles from Catholic periodicals.
Formerly: Catholic Review (New York) (0008-8323)
Media: Large Type (24 pt.). **Related titles:** Audio cassette/tape ed.; Braille ed.
Published by: Xavier Society for the Blind, 154 E 23rd St, New York, NY 10010. TEL 212-473-7800, 800-637-9193, FAX 212-473-7801. Ed. Rev. Thomas Danny. Circ: 3,200.

299.6 266.2 GBR ISSN 2046-7583
YOUNG AFRICA. Text in English. 1927. bi-m. free (effective 2011). bk.rev. back issues avail. **Document type:** *Magazine, Consumer.* **Description:** Presents the missionary work of the Catholic Church in Africa and matters concerning Africa.
Former titles (until 200?): White Fathers - White Sisters (0262-1061); (until 1969): White Fathers
Published by: Missionaries of Africa in Britain, 129 Lichfield Rd, Sutton Coldfield, W Mids B74 2SA, United Kingdom. TEL 44-20-89597421, suttonlink@dial.pipex.com, http://www.thewhitefathers.org.uk.

THE YOUNGSTER; the magazine for the young minister of the word. *see* CHILDREN AND YOUTH—For

R

282 POL ISSN 1425-7777
ZAMOJSKI INFORMATOR DIECEZJALNY. Text in Latin, Polish. 1992. q. PLZ 15. bk.rev. index. **Document type:** *Bulletin.* **Description:** Covers Catholic theology, canon law, church documents.
Published by: Diecezja Zamojsko - Lubaczowska, Kuria Diecezjalna, Ul Hetmana J Zamoyskiego 1, Zamosc, 22400, Poland. TEL 48-84-6279521, FAX 48-846279521, kuria@zamosc.opoka.org.pl, http://www.zamosc.opoka.org.pl. Ed. Franciszek Greniuk.

282 SVN ISSN 1580-4445
ZBIRKA FRANCISEK MED NAMI. Text in Slovenian. 1998. irreg., latest vol.10, 2010. price varies. **Document type:** *Monographic series, Academic/Scholarly.*
Published by: Mohorjeva Druzba, Presernova c 23, pp 150, Celje, 3001, Slovenia. TEL 386-3-4264800, FAX 386-3-4264810, info@mohorjeva-druzba-ce.si, http://www.mohorjeva.org.

266.2 USA ISSN 0514-2482
ZEAL. Text in English. 1952. 3/yr. free.
Published by: (St. Elizabeth Mission Society), Franciscan Sisters of Allegany, St. Elizabeth Mothehouse, 115 E Main St, Allegany, NY 14706. TEL 716-373-0200. Ed. Sr Marie Dolores Gionta. Circ: 10,000.

282 DEU ISSN 0044-2895
BX803
ZEITSCHRIFT FUER KATHOLISCHE THEOLOGIE. Text in German. 1877. q. EUR 75; EUR 20 newsstand/cover (effective 2010). adv. bk.rev. bibl. index, cum.index. reprints avail. **Document type:** *Journal, Academic/Scholarly.*
Indexed: A21, A22, CERDIC, CLA, DIP, FR, IBR, IBZ, IPB, IZBG, LID&ISL, MLA-IB, OTA, PCI, RASB, RI-1, RI-2.
—IE, INIST.
Published by: (Universitaet Innsbruck AUT, Universitaet Berlin, Theologische Fakultaet), Echter Verlag GmbH, Dominikanerplatz 8, Wuerzburg, 97070, Germany. TEL 49-931-660680, FAX 49-931-6606823, info@echter-verlag.de, http://www.echter.de.

282 DEU
ZENTRALKOMITEE DER DEUTSCHEN KATHOLIKEN. MITTEILUNGEN (E-MAIL). Text in German. 1969. m. free. **Document type:** *Newsletter.*
Formerly (until 200?): Zentralkomitee der Deutschen Katholiken. Mitteilungen (Print)
Media: E-mail.
Published by: Zentralkomitee der deutschen Katholiken, Hochkreuzallee 246, Bonn, 53175, Germany. TEL 49-228-382970, FAX 49-228-3829744, info@zdk.de, http://www.zdk.de. Ed. Stefan Vesper. Circ: 2,000.

282 CHN
ZHONGGUO TIANZHUJIAO/CATHOLIC CHURCH IN CHINA. Text in Chinese. 1980. bi-m. CNY 19.20 domestic; USD 9 foreign (effective 2005). **Document type:** *Journal, Academic/Scholarly.*
Published by: Zhongguo Tianzhujiao Aiguohui, Xicheng-qu, 14, Liuyin Jie, Beijing, 100009, China. TEL 86-10-66184321, FAX 86-10-66185740.

282 DEU ISSN 0179-6658
ZUR DEBATTE. Text in German. 1970. bi-m. EUR 19 (effective 2006). **Description:** Extracts of lectures given at conferences at the academy.
Indexed: MLA-IB.
Published by: Katholische Akademie in Bayern, Mandlstr 23, Munich, 80802, Germany. TEL 49-89-381020, FAX 49-89-38102103, info@kath-akademie-bayern.de, http://www.katholische-akademie-bayern.de.

282 USA ISSN 0897-2435
BX801
30 DAYS IN THE CHURCH AND IN THE WORLD. Text in English. 1988. m. (11/yr.). USD 45. adv. index. back issues avail. **Description:** International Catholic news.
Related titles: Arabic ed.; French ed.; Spanish ed.; Italian ed.; Portuguese ed.; German ed.
Published by: Italcoser Corporation, One Penn Plaza, Ste 3515, New York, NY 10119-3595. Ed. Giulio Andreotti. Circ: 10,000. **Subscr. to:** 35 02 48th Ave, Long Island City, NY 11101-2421.

282 ITA ISSN 0390-4539
30 GIORNI; nella chiesa e nel mondo. Text in Italian. 1983. m. (11/yr.). EUR 45 domestic; EUR 60 in Europe; EUR 25 Africa and Brazil; EUR 70 elsewhere (effective 2008). adv. back issues avail. **Document type:** *Magazine, Consumer.* **Description:** International Catholic news.
Published by: 30Giorni, Via Francesco Antolisei 25, Rome, RM 00173, Italy. TEL 39-06-724031, FAX 39-06-7231576. Ed. Giulio Andreotti.

RESPIRATORY DISEASES

see MEDICAL SCIENCES—Respiratory Diseases

RHEUMATOLOGY

see MEDICAL SCIENCES—Rheumatology

ROADS AND TRAFFIC

see TRANSPORTATION—Roads And Traffic

ROBOTICS

see COMPUTERS—Artificial Intelligence ; COMPUTERS—Robotics

ROMAN CATHOLICISM

see RELIGIONS AND THEOLOGY—Roman Catholic

RUBBER

see also ENGINEERING—Chemical Engineering ; PLASTICS

ANNUAL BOOK OF A S T M STANDARDS. VOLUME 09.01. RUBBER, NATURAL AND SYNTHETIC - GENERAL TEST METHODS; CARBON BLACK. (American Society for Testing and Materials) *see* ENGINEERING—Engineering Mechanics And Materials

ANNUAL BOOK OF A S T M STANDARDS. VOLUME 09.02. RUBBER PRODUCTS, INDUSTRIAL - SPECIFICATIONS AND RELATED TEST METHODS; GASKETS; TIRES. (American Society for Testing and Materials) *see* ENGINEERING—Engineering Mechanics And Materials

678 DEU
ASBEST-HANDBUCH. Text in German. 2 base vols. plus a. updates. EUR 68 base vol(s).; EUR 29.65 per issue (effective 2009). **Document type:** *Monographic series, Trade.*
Published by: Erich Schmidt Verlag GmbH & Co. (Berlin), Genthiner Str 30 G, Berlin, 10785, Germany. TEL 49-30-2500850, FAX 49-30-250085305, esv@esvmedien.de, http://www.erich-schmidt-verlag.de.

678 668 FRA
ASSOCIATION FRANCAISE DES INGENIEURS ET CADRES DU CAOUTCHOUC ET DES PLASTIQUES. ANNUAIRE. Text in French. 1956. biennial. membership. adv. bk.rev.
Formerly: Association Francaise des Ingenieurs du Caoutchouc et des Plastiques. Annuaire (0066-9229)
Published by: Association Francaise des Ingenieurs et Cadres du Caoutchouc et des Plastiques, 60 rue Auber, Vitry-Seine, 94408, France. FAX 45-21-03-50, TELEX 202963.

AUSTRALIAN TYRE DEALER. *see* TRANSPORTATION—Automobiles

678.2029 GBR
B R P P A RUBBER AND POLYURETHANE DIRECTORY. Text in English. 1968. a. free (effective 2009). Website rev. **Document type:** *Directory, Trade.* **Description:** Contains over 1000 products, services, materials and equipment offered by the rubber and polyurethane industry and details of association members, including their full addresses, and fax and telephone numbers.
Former titles (until 2006): B M R A Rubber and Polyurethane Directory (0955-8772); (until 1984): British Rubber Industry Directory (0266-397X)
Related titles: E-mail ed.; Fax ed.
Published by: British Rubber and Polyurethane Products Association, 6 Bath Pl, Rivington St, London, EC2A 3JE, United Kingdom. TEL 44-845-3016852, FAX 44-845-3016853, info@brppa.co.uk.

BRITISH PLASTICS AND RUBBER MAGAZINE. *see* PLASTICS

678.2 IND
BUSINESS GUIDE TO RUBBER INDUSTRY. Text in English. 19??. a. INR 450 per issue (effective 2011). **Document type:** *Directory, Trade.* **Description:** Helps in locating the right type of materials and services required for the rubber industry. Information on the various sub-sectors supporting the rubber products manufacturing industry becomes very relevant and this guide helps to serve this objective.
Published by: Rubber Board, Ministry of Commerce and Industry, PO Box 1122, Kottayam, 686 002, India. TEL 91-481-2301231, FAX 91-481-2571380, info@rubberboard.org.in, http://www.rubberboard.org.in.

BUSINESS RATIO REPORT. THE RUBBER AND TYRE INDUSTRY. *see* BUSINESS AND ECONOMICS—Production Of Goods And Services

BUSINESS TIMES. *see* BUSINESS AND ECONOMICS

678.2 ARG
TS1870 CODEN: CAUCDV
CAUCHOTECNIA. Text in Spanish. 1994. 4/yr. USD 43 in Latin America and Argentina; USD 50 elsewhere and Argentina (effective 2000). adv. bk.rev. charts; illus.; stat. **Document type:** *Trade.* **Description:** Issues cover a topic in technology of the rubber industry.
Supersedes (1958-1994): Revista Caucho (0528-3280)
Published by: Federacion Argentina de la Industria del Caucho, Avda. Leandro N. Alem, 1067 Piso 16, Buenos Aires, 1001, Argentina. TEL 54-114-3132009, FAX 54-114-3129892. Ed. Antonio C Castro. Adv. contact A Cortez Ruiz. Circ: 500.

CHINA PLASTIC AND RUBBER JOURNAL/ZHONGGUO CUOLIAO XIANGJIAO; a plastic and rubber journal for P.R. China. *see* PLASTICS

678.2 IND
DIRECTORY OF WORLD IMPORTERS OF RUBBER PRODUCTS. Text in English. 19??. a. INR 300 per issue (effective 2011). **Document type:** *Directory, Trade.* **Description:** Helps to bring foreign buyers of rubber and rubber products closer to Indian exporters. The 2nd edition of this directory contains more than 2700 entries giving names, addresses and product description of major importers in the field of rubber and rubber based products.
Related titles: CD-ROM ed.: INR 400 per issue (effective 2011).
Published by: Rubber Board, Ministry of Commerce and Industry, PO Box 1122, Kottayam, 686 002, India. TEL 91-481-2301231, FAX 91-481-2571380, info@rubberboard.org.in, http://www.rubberboard.org.in.

678.2 JPN ISSN 1349-7308
TA401
E-JOURNAL OF SOFT MATERIALS. Text in English. 2005. a. **Document type:** *Journal, Academic/Scholarly.*
Media: Online - full content.
Published by: Nihon Gomu Kyoukai/Society of Rubber Industry of Japan, 1-5-26 Motoakasaka, Minato-ku, Tokyo, 107-0051, Japan. TEL 81-3-34012957, FAX 81-3-34014143, srij@srij.or.jp, http://www.srij.or.jp/.

678.2 668.4 KOR ISSN 2092-9676
ELASTOMERS AND COMPOSITES. Text in English. 1966. q. **Description:** Covers all aspects of elastomeric polymers and plastics, and their composites with reinforcing fillers including organic and inorganic fillers and fibers. Topics include: Synthesis and molecular design of elastomeric polymers, compounding technology, rheology and processing technology, mold design and molding technology, nancomposites with organic and inorganic fillers, physical properties, chemical properties, aging properties, numerical analysis of properties, chemical analysis, lifetime production, surface and adhesive properties between polymers and fillers and fibers, and other key technologies.
Former titles (until 2008): Elraseu To'meo/Elastomer (1226-8526); (until 1998): Go'mu Haghoeji/Korean Institute of Rubber Industry. Journal (0253-3138)
—BLDSC (3670.156000), IE.
Published by: Han-guk Gomu Hakoe/Rubber Society of Korea, Rm. 803 & 804 Woojung Town, 1488-7 gwanyang-2dong, Dongan-gu, Anyang-si, Gyeonggi-do 431-846, Korea, S. TEL 82-31-4227224, FAX 82-31-4227223, cnah@chonbuk.ac.kr, http://www.elastomer.or.kr. Ed. Changwoon Nah.

EURO TELEX. MECANIQUE. *see* PLASTICS

678 GBR ISSN 0266-4151
TS1870 CODEN: ERJODH
EUROPEAN RUBBER JOURNAL. Abbreviated title: E R J. Text in English. 1884. bi-m. GBP 93; GBP 124 combined subscription (print & online eds.) (effective 2010). illus. back issues avail.; reprints avail. **Document type:** *Magazine, Trade.* **Description:** Covers commercial and technical developments pertinent to the rubber processing and manufacturing industries.
Former titles (until 1982): European Rubber Journal and Urethanes Today (0260-5317); (until 1980): European Rubber Journal (0305-2222); (until 1973): Rubber Journal (0035-9505); (until 1964): Rubber and Plastics Weekly; (until 1961): Rubber Journal and International Plastics; (until 1957): Rubber Journal; (until 1955): India Rubber Journal (0367-9985); (until 1911): India-Rubber and Gutta-Percha and Electrical Trades Journal
Related titles: E-mail ed.: GBP 100 email & online eds. (effective 2007); Microform ed.: (from PQC); Online - full text ed.: GBP 103 (effective 2010); Supplement(s): Rubbicana European Rubber Directory & Buyers Guide; Global Tire Report.
Indexed: A09, A10, A22, B01, B02, B03, B06, B07, B09, B11, B15, B17, B18, CA, CBNB, G04, G06, G07, G08, I05, KES, RefZh, SCOPUS, T01, T02, TTI, V03, V04.
—BLDSC (3829.960000), CASDDS, CIS, IE, Infotrieve, Ingenta, INIST, Linda Hall. **CCC.**
Published by: Crain Communications, Ltd., 3rd Fl, 21 St Thomas St, London, SE1 9RY, United Kingdom. TEL 44-20-74571400, FAX 44-20-74571440, http://www.crain.co.uk. Ed. David Shaw. Pub., Adv. contact Paul Mitchell TEL 44-20-74571431. **Subscr. to:** The Coach House, Turners Dr, Thatcham, Berkshire RG1 4QB, United Kingdom. TEL 44-1635-879382, FAX 44-1635-868594.

338.476 ARG ISSN 0533-4500
GUIA DE LA INDUSTRIA DEL CAUCHO. Text in Spanish. 1961. biennial. ARS 50, USD 50; or exchange basis. adv. **Document type:** *Directory.*
Published by: Federacion Argentina de la Industria del Caucho, Avda. Leandro N. Alem, 1067 Piso 16, Buenos Aires, 1001, Argentina. TEL 54-114-3132009, FAX 54-114-3129892. Ed. Antonio C Castro. Adv. contact A Cortez Ruiz. Circ: 3,000.

GUIDE PLASTIQUES ET CAOUTCHOUC. *see* BUSINESS AND ECONOMICS—Trade And Industrial Directories

678 DEU ISSN 0176-1625
TS1870 CODEN: GFKUED
GUMMI, FASERN, KUNSTSTOFFE; Fachmagazin fuer die Polymerindustrie. Text in German. 1948. m. EUR 280; EUR 25 newsstand/cover (effective 2011). adv. bk.rev. bibl.; charts; illus.; pat.; stat. index. **Document type:** *Magazine, Trade.*
Former titles (until 1984): Gummi, Asbest, Kunstoffe (0017-5595); (until 1961): Gummi und Asbest (0367-5424)
Indexed: A22, ASCA, AcoustA, CIN, CPEI, ChemAb, ChemTitl, DokArb, Englnd, IBR, IBZ, IPackAb, PST, R18, RefZh, SCOPUS, TM.
—BLDSC (4230.950000), CASDDS, IE, Infotrieve, Ingenta, INIST, Linda Hall. **CCC.**
Published by: Dr. Gupta Verlag, Postfach 104125, Ratingen, 40852, Germany. TEL 49-2102-93450, FAX 49-2102-934520, info@gupta-verlag.de, http://www.gupta-verlag.de. Ed., Pub. Heinz Gupta. Adv. contact Cynthia Freyer.

678 DEU ISSN 0017-5609
GUMMIBEREIFUNG; Fachzeitschrift fuer Vulkanisation, Runderneuerung, Reifenhandel und Zubehoer. Variant title: Auto Raeder Reifen - Gummibereifung. Text in German. 1924. m. EUR 120 domestic; EUR 142.80 foreign; EUR 9.50 newsstand/cover (effective 2008). adv. bk.rev. bibl.; charts; illus.; mkt.; pat. index. **Document type:** *Magazine, Trade.* **Description:** For the tire trade industry. Information on tire technology, retreading, marketing, and recycling.
Indexed: CISA, ChemAb, R18, RefZh.
—INIST.
Published by: B V A Bielefelder Verlag GmbH & Co. KG, Niederwall 53, Bielefeld, 33602, Germany. TEL 49-521-595514, FAX 49-521-595518, kontakt@bva-bielefeld.de, http://www.bva-bielefeld.de. Ed. Karlheinz Mutz. adv.: B&W page EUR 2,480, color page EUR 3,950; trim 185 x 286. Circ: 7,797 (paid and controlled).

678 CHE ISSN 0073-0076
HANDBUCH DER INTERNATIONALEN KAUTSCHUKINDUSTRIE/ INTERNATIONAL RUBBER DIRECTORY/MANUEL INTERNATIONAL DE CAOUTCHOUC. Text in English, French, German. 1955. every 10 yrs. CHF 600. **Document type:** *Directory.*
Published by: Verlag fuer Internationale Wirtschaftsliteratur GmbH, Postfach 28, Zuerich, 8047, Switzerland. FAX 41-1-4010545. Ed. Walter Hirt.

678.2 MEX
HULEQUIPO. Text in Spanish. 1978. m. adv.
Address: Queretaro No. 229-402, Mexico City, DF 06700, Mexico. Ed. Carlos Villagran Arevalo. Circ: 5,000.

INDIAN RUBBER STATISTICS. *see* RUBBER—Abstracting, Bibliographies, Statistics

678 ITA
TS1870 CODEN: INGOAF
L'INDUSTRIA DELLA GOMMA - ELASTICA. Text in Italian. 1957. m. (10/yr.). EUR 90 domestic; EUR 100 in Europe; EUR 130 elsewhere (effective 2009). adv. bk.rev. abstr.; charts; illus.; mkt.; pat.; stat.; tr.lit. index. **Document type:** *Magazine, Trade.* **Description:** Technical and economic news for the rubber industry.
Formerly: Industria della Gomma (0019-7556)
Indexed: CIN, ChemAb, ChemTitl, R18.
—CASDDS, INIST.
Published by: (Associazione Nazionale fra le Industrie della Gomma Cavi Elettrici ed Affini/Italian Rubber and Manufacturers Association), Gesto Editore Srl, Via Mercato 28, Milan, MI 20121, Italy. TEL 39-02-8051511, FAX 39-02-89013553, gesto@gestoeditore.it, http://www.modainitaly.it.

678 ITA
L'INDUSTRIA ITALIANA DELLA GOMMA. GUIDA/GUIDE TO THE ITALIAN RUBBER INDUSTRY. Text in English, French, German. 1962. a. price varies. **Document type:** *Directory, Trade.* **Description:** Directory of Italian rubber manufacturers and their suppliers.
Formerly: Annuario dell'Industria Italiana della Gomma (0066-4499)
Published by: Gesto Editore Srl, Via Mercato 28, Milan, MI 20121, Italy. TEL 39-02-8051511, FAX 39-02-89013553, gesto@gestoeditore.it, http://www.modainitaly.it.

INSTITUTO DE CIENCIA Y TECNOLOGIA DE POLIMEROS. MEMORIA. *see* PLASTICS

678 USA ISSN 1070-6488
CODEN: PGISF2
INTERNATIONAL INSTITUTE OF SYNTHETIC RUBBER PRODUCERS. PROCEEDINGS ANNUAL GENERAL MEETING. Text in English. 1969. a. USD 250 (effective 2005). **Document type:** *Proceedings, Trade.* **Description:** Contains scientific papers on industrial hygiene, polymer development, raw material and product situations.
Formerly (until 1992): International Institute of Synthetic Rubber Producers. Annual Meeting Proceedings (0146-3977)
Related titles: CD-ROM ed.: ISSN 1932-958X. 200?.
Indexed: CIN, ChemAb, ChemTitl.
—CASDDS.
Published by: International Institute of Synthetic Rubber Producers, 2077 S Gessner Rd Ste 133, Houston, TX 77063-1123. TEL 713-783-7511, FAX 713-783-7253, TELEX 791062. Circ: 350.

J E C COMPOSITES. *see* PLASTICS

JOURNAL OF ADHESION SCIENCE AND TECHNOLOGY; the international journal of theoretical and basic aspects of adhesion science and its applications in all areas of technology. *see* PLASTICS

678 MYS ISSN 1511-1768
SB290 CODEN: JRREFG
JOURNAL OF RUBBER RESEARCH. Text in English. 1928. q. USD 50 (effective 2004). bibl.; charts. index, cum.index. **Document type:** *Journal, Academic/Scholarly.* **Description:** Publishes results and reviews on all aspects of rubber, including genetics, breeding and selection; tissue culture and vegetative propagation: anatomy and physiology; exploitation: tapping systems and stimulation; agronomic practices and management; nutrition and fertilizer usage; soils: classification, chemistry, microbiology, use and management; diseases and pests; mechanization; biochemistry and biotechnology; chemistry and physics of rubber; technology of dry rubber and latex; rubber processing and presentation, product manufacture, end uses and rubber industrialization; tires; nr and sr blends; and, effluent treatment and utilization.
Former titles (until 1997): Journal of Natural Rubber Research (0127-7065); (until 1986): Rubber Research Institute of Malaysia. Journal (0035-953X); (until 1973): Kuala Lumpur. Rubber Research Institute of Malaya. Journal
Indexed: A22, A34, A35, A36, A37, AgBio, BA, BAS, C25, C30, CABA, CIN, ChemAb, ChemTitl, D01, E12, F08, F11, F12, GH, H16, I11, MSCI, MaizeAb, N02, N03, OR, P32, P37, P40, PGrRegA, PHN&I, R12, R13, R18, RA&MP, S12, S13, S16, SCI, SCOPUS, TAR, VS, W07, W10, W11.
—BLDSC (5052.125020), CASDDS, IE, Infotrieve, Ingenta, Linda Hall.
Published by: Malaysian Rubber Board, 148, Jalan Ampang, PO Box 10508, Kuala Lumpur, 50716, Malaysia. TEL 603-9206 2000, FAX 603-2163 3139, general@lgm.gov.my. Eds. Kanesan Solomalai, Wan Abdul Rahaman Wan Yaacob. Circ: 700.

678 DEU ISSN 0948-3276
CODEN: KKGKB5
➤ **K G K. KAUTSCHUK, GUMMI, KUNSTSTOFFE**; international technical journal for polymer materials. Text in English, German. 1947. 10/yr. EUR 269 domestic; EUR 278 foreign; EUR 31 per issue (effective 2010). adv. bk.rev. abstr.; bibl.; charts; illus.; pat. index. **Document type:** *Journal, Trade.* **Description:** Covers high polymeric materials, auxiliary materials and additives, as well as machines and testing equipment for the caoutchouc and rubber industries.
Formerly (until 1993): Kautschuk und Gummi Kunststoffe (0022-9520)
Related titles: Microfilm ed.: (from PMC); Online - full text ed.
Indexed: A22, C33, CBNB, CPEI, ChemAb, ChemTitl, CurCont, EngInd, MSCI, R18, RefZh, SCI, SCOPUS, TM, W07.
—BLDSC (5088.050000), CASDDS, IE, Infotrieve, Ingenta, INIST, Linda Hall. **CCC.**
Published by: (Verband der Deutschen Kautschukgesellschaften), Huethig GmbH & Co. KG, Postfach 102869, Heidelberg, 69018, Germany. TEL 49-6221-4890, FAX 49-6221-489279, aboservice@huethig.de, http://www.huethig.de. Ed. Martina Bechstedt. Adv. contact Ludger Aulich. Circ: 1,982 (controlled).

➤ **KAMI INSATSU PURASUCHIKKU GOMU SEIHIN TOUKEI GEPPOU/MONTHLY REPORT OF PAPER, PRINTING, PLASTICS PRODUCTS AND RUBBER PRODUCTS STATISTICS.** *see* PAPER AND PULP

678 540 RUS ISSN 0022-9466
CODEN: KCRZAE
➤ **KAUCHUK I REZINA.** Text in Russian; Summaries in English. 1927. bi-m. USD 83 foreign (effective 2005). adv. bk.rev. bibl.; illus. index. 52 p./no. 2 cols./p.; back issues avail. **Document type:** *Journal, Academic/Scholarly.* **Description:** Covers elastomers: science, processing, application; tires, rubber goods of various types; rubbers, hermetics, and adhesives. Also includes composition of rubber compounds, instruments, tests, physics, mechanics and physical chemistry. Aimed at researchers, engineers, and post-graduate students.
Related titles: E-mail ed.; Fax ed.
Indexed: CIN, ChemAb, ChemTitl, R18, RefZh, SCOPUS.
—BLDSC (0088.500000), CASDDS, East View, INIST, Linda Hall. **CCC.**
Address: M Trubetskaya 28, Moscow, 119992, Russian Federation. TEL 7-095-2429607, FAX 7-095-2421245, kir@niiemi.ru. Ed., Pub. Sergei V Reznichenko. R&P, Adv. contact Maya Bukhina TEL 7-095-2429687. B&W page USD 250, color page USD 350; trim 230 x 170. Circ: 600 (paid). **Dist. by:** M K - Periodica, ul Gilyarovskogo 39, Moscow 129110, Russian Federation. TEL 7-095-2845008, FAX 7-095-2813798, info@periodicals.ru, http://www.mkniga.ru.

678.2 GBR
KEY NOTE MARKET REPORT: RUBBER MANUFACTURING & PROCESSING. Variant title: Rubber Manufacturing & Processing. Text in English. 199?. irreg., latest 1999, Mar. GBP 235 per issue (effective 2008). **Document type:** *Report, Trade.* **Description:** Provides an overview of a specific UK market segment and includes executive summary, market definition, market size, industry background, competitor analysis, current issues, forecasts, company profiles, and more.
Formerly: Key Note Report: Rubber Manufacturers and Processors
Related titles: CD-ROM ed.; Online - full text ed.
Published by: Key Note Ltd. (Subsidiary of: Bonnier Business Information), Field House, 72 Oldfield Rd, Hampton, Mddx TW12 2HQ, United Kingdom. TEL 44-20-84818750, FAX 44-20-87830049, info@keynote.co.uk, http://www.keynote.co.uk. Ed. Phillippa Smith.

KEY NOTE MARKET REPORT: THE TYRE INDUSTRY. *see* BUSINESS AND ECONOMICS—Production Of Goods And Services

KOVACH TIRE REPORT. *see* TRANSPORTATION—Automobiles

678 630 MYS ISSN 0032-096X
SB290 CODEN: RRMPA5
MALAYSIAN RUBBER BOARD. PLANTERS BULLETIN. Text in English. 1952. q. MYR 12, USD 24 (effective 2000). bk.rev. charts; illus.; mkt.; pat.; tr.mk. index, cum.index every 4 and 8 yrs. **Document type:** *Bulletin.*
Indexed: ChemAb, R18.
Published by: Malaysian Rubber Board, 148, Jalan Ampang, PO Box 10508, Kuala Lumpur, 50716, Malaysia. TEL 603-9206 2000, FAX 603-2163 3139, general@lgm.gov.my, http://www.lgm.gov.my/. Ed. Wan Abdul Rahaman Wan Yaacob. Circ: 6,000.

633.895 MYS ISSN 0127-9785
MALAYSIAN RUBBER BOARD. RUBBER GROWERS' CONFERENCE - PROCEEDINGS. Text in English. biennial. USD 150. charts; illus. **Document type:** *Proceedings.*
Formerly: Rubber Research Institute of Malaysia. Planters Conference Proceedings (0126-5849)
Indexed: ChemAb.
Published by: Rubber Research Institute of Malaysia, Public Relations, Publications and Library Unit/Sains Institut Penyelidikan Getah Malaysia, PO Box 10150, Kuala Lumpur, 50908, Malaysia. TEL 60-3-456-7033, FAX 60-3-457-3512, TELEX MA 30369. Circ: 1,000.

678.2 MYS ISSN 0126-8309
HD9161.M32
MALAYSIAN RUBBER PRODUCERS' COUNCIL. ANNUAL REPORT/ MAJLIS PENGELUAR-PENGELUAR GETAH MALAYSIA. LAPURAN TAHUNAN. Text in English, Malay. 1951. a. MYR 12. stat. **Document type:** *Corporate.*
Formerly: Rubber Producers' Council of Malaysia. Annual Report
Published by: Malaysian Rubber Producers' Council/Majlis Pengeluar-Pengeluar Getah Malaysia, PO Box 12688, Kuala Lumpur, 50786, Malaysia. TEL 2482677. Circ: 600.

633.895 MYS
MALAYSIAN RUBBER PRODUCERS' COUNCIL. MONTHLY BULLETIN. Text in English. 1957. m. MYR 166. charts; stat. **Document type:** *Bulletin.*
Former titles (until 1973): Malaysian Rubber Producers' Council. Monthly Statistical Bulletin (0303-1640); (until 1966): Rubber Producers' Council of Malaysia. Monthly Statistical Bulletin (0126-5865)
Published by: Malaysian Rubber Producers' Council/Majlis Pengeluar-Pengeluar Getah Malaysia, PO Box 12688, Kuala Lumpur, 50786, Malaysia.

678.32 USA ISSN 0026-8496
HD9061.U54
MODERN TIRE DEALER; covering tire sales and car service. Abbreviated title: M T D. Text in English. 1919. m. USD 65 domestic; USD 99 in Canada; USD 198 elsewhere (effective 2008); includes Facts Issue. adv. bk.rev. illus.; tr.lit. back issues avail.; reprints avail. **Document type:** *Magazine, Trade.* **Description:** Provides up to date information and trends in the tire industry and includes marketing analysis, business trends, merchandising and sales methods.
Related titles: Online - full text ed.
Indexed: A15, A22, ABIn, B02, B15, B17, B18, BusI, G04, G06, G07, G08, I05, P16, P48, P51, P52, P53, P54, PQC, R18, T&II.
—IE, Infotrieve.
Published by: Bobit Business Media, 3520 Challenger St, Torrance, CA 90503. TEL 310-533-2400, FAX 310-533-2500, order@bobit.com, http://www.bobit.com. Eds. Bob Ulrich, Mike Manges. Pub. Greg Smith. adv.: B&W page USD 10,240, color page USD 13,230; trim 7.875 x 10.75. Circ: 32,002 (controlled).

MUANYAG ES GUMI/PLASTICS AND RUBBER. *see* PLASTICS

678.2 IND
NATURAL RUBBER & RUBBER PRODUCTS EXPORTERS IN INDIA. DIRECTORY. Text in English. 19??. a. INR 250 per issue (effective 2011). **Document type:** *Directory, Trade.* **Description:** Provides the list of firms exporting natural rubber, details of exporters of rubber products in India, product-wise details of exporters are given on the basis of exporter code number. For each organization, name and their contact addresses including e-mail and web address, name of the contact person, products manufactured, export destinations and category of exporter are given.
Published by: Rubber Board, Ministry of Commerce and Industry, PO Box 1122, Kottayam, 686 002, India. TEL 91-481-2301231, FAX 91-481-2571380, info@rubberboard.org.in, http://www.rubberboard.org.in.

678.2 IND
SB291.H4 CODEN: IJNREZ
➤ **NATURAL RUBBER RESEARCH.** Text in English. 1988. s-a. INR 400, USD 50 (effective 2011). bibl.; charts; abstr.; illus. 80 p./no. 2 cols./p.; back issues avail. **Document type:** *Journal, Trade.* **Description:** Features biological and technological aspects of natural rubber, including propagation techniques and planting methods, morphology and anatomy, growth and productivity and many other disciplines.
Formerly (until 2004): Indian Journal of Natural Rubber Research (0970-2431)
Related titles: Online - full text ed.
Indexed: A34, A35, ATA, AgBio, AgrForAb, Agrind, B23, B25, BIOSIS Prev, BP, C25, C30, CABA, CIN, ChemAb, ChemTitl, D01, E12, F08, F11, F12, FCA, G11, H16, I11, ISA, MycolAb, N02, N04, N05, O01, OR, P32, P40, PGegResA, PGrRegA, PHN&I, R07, R11, R12, R13, RA&MP, S13, S16, S17, VS, W10, W11.
—BLDSC (6040.810000), CASDDS.
Published by: Rubber Board, Ministry of Commerce and Industry, PO Box 1122, Kottayam, 686 002, India. TEL 91-481-2301231, FAX 91-481-2571380, info@rubberboard.org.in, http://www.rubberboard.org.in. Eds. C Kuruvilla Jacob, James Jacob.

678.32 ESP ISSN 1132-1474
NEUMATICOS Y ACCESORIOS; revista para el comercio, montaje, y reparacion de neumaticos. Text in English, Spanish. 1991. m. EUR 82 domestic; EUR 100 in Europe; EUR 150 elsewhere (effective 2009). adv. back issues avail. **Document type:** *Magazine, Trade.* **Description:** For tire repairers and dealers.
Published by: Reed Business Information SA (Subsidiary of: Reed Business Information International), C Albarracin 34, Madrid, 28037, Spain. TEL 34-91-3755800, FAX 34-91-4562499, rbi@rbi.es. Ed. Nuria Alvarez TEL 34-91-3755800. Circ: 3,500 (controlled).

678 JPN ISSN 0029-022X
HD9161.J3 CODEN: NGOKAF
NIHON GOMU KYOKAISHI/SOCIETY OF RUBBER INDUSTRY OF JAPAN. JOURNAL. Text in Japanese; Summaries in English, Japanese. 1928. m. subscr. incld. with membership. adv. bk.rev.; Website rev. abstr.; bibl.; charts; pat. cum.index. **Document type:** *Journal, Academic/Scholarly.*
Formerly (until 1931): Gomu/Rubber Society, Japan. Journal (0367-4924)
Indexed: A22, A28, APA, BrCerAb, C&ISA, CA/WCA, CIA, CerAb, CivEngAb, CorrAb, E&CAJ, E11, EEA, EMA, ESPM, EnvEAb, H15, INIS AtomInd, M&TEA, M09, MBF, METADEX, R18, SolStAb, T04, WAA.
—BLDSC (4897.000000), CASDDS, IE, Ingenta, INIST, Linda Hall. **CCC.**
Published by: Nihon Gomu Kyoukai/Society of Rubber Industry of Japan, 1-5-26 Motoakasaka, Minato-ku, Tokyo, 107-0051, Japan. TEL 81-3-34012957, FAX 81-3-34014143, srij@srij.or.jp, http://www.srij.or.jp/. Circ: 4,000.

NOTICIERO DEL PLASTICO. *see* PLASTICS

678 GBR ISSN 1356-2584
HD9662.E42
OUTLOOK FOR ELASTOMERS (YEAR). Text in English. 1994. a. SGD 1,500 per issue (effective 2010). stat. back issues avail. **Document type:** *Report, Trade.* **Description:** Reviews the world rubber economy, summarizes data of the rubber economy in each member nation and forecasts the production and consumption of rubber for the coming year.
Published by: (International Rubber Study Group, Secretariat), International Rubber Study Group, Heron House, 109/115 Wembley Hill Rd, Wembley, Mddx HA9 8DA, United Kingdom. TEL 44-20-89005400, FAX 44-20-89032848, irsg@rubberstudy.com.

PANORAMA PLASTICO; la revista mexicana del plastico. *see* PLASTICS

PLASTICS AND RUBBER ASIA. *see* PLASTICS

PLASTICS & RUBBER WEEKLY. *see* PLASTICS

PLASTICS NEWS. *see* PLASTICS

PLASTICS NEWS CHINA E-WEEKLY. *see* PLASTICS

PLASTICS, RUBBER AND COMPOSITES; macromolecular engineering. *see* PLASTICS

PLASTIKA I GUMA. *see* PLASTICS

PNEU MAG. *see* TRANSPORTATION—Automobiles

PNEU REVUE. *see* TRANSPORTATION—Automobiles

678 FRA ISSN 0296-9386
LE PNEUMATIQUE; industrie - distribution - rechapage. Text in French. 1929. 5/yr. EUR 82 domestic; EUR 94 in Europe; EUR 112 elsewhere (effective 2009). adv. 80 p./no.; **Document type:** *Magazine, Corporate.*
Incorporated (1974-1983): Le Pneu (0771-0372)
Published by: (Les Professionnels du Pneu), Editions V B, 7 Rue Jean Mermoz, Versailles, 78000, France. TEL 33-1-39208805, FAX 33-1-39208806, vblcda@lcda.fr. Ed. Eric Bigourdan. Adv. contact Helene Hernandez. Circ: 7,000.

678.32 ITA
PNEURAMA. Text in Italian. 1970. bi-m. free. adv. **Document type:** *Magazine, Trade.*
Published by: Edit Prom s.r.l., Via A G Ragazzi 9, Anzola dell'Emilia, BO 40011, Italy. TEL 39-051-733000, FAX 39-051-731886. Circ: 15,000 (controlled).

POLIMERI; casopis za plastiku i gumu. *see* PLASTICS

POLYMER CURING TECHNOLOGIES. *see* PLASTICS

678.4 668.4 JPN ISSN 0032-4779
POLYMER FRIENDS FOR RUBBER, PLASTICS AND FIBER/PORIMA NO TOMO. Text in Japanese. 1964. m. JPY 2,400, USD 6.66. adv. charts; illus. index.
Published by: Taiseisha Ltd., Publishing Division, 1-5 Kyobashi, Chuo-ku, Tokyo, 104-0031, Japan. Ed. Sadanori Itonori. Circ: 3,000.

POLYMERS AND POLYMER COMPOSITES. *see* PLASTICS

▼ **POLYMERS FROM RENEWABLE RESOURCES.** *see* PLASTICS

678.2 USA
POLYTOPICS. Text in English. q. **Document type:** *Newsletter.*
Published by: Polyurethane Manufacturers Association, Bldg C, Ste 20, 800 Roosevelt Rd, Glen Ellyn, IL 60137. TEL 630-858-2670, FAX 630-790-3095. Ed. Jenny Hofmeister.

PROGRESS IN RUBBER, PLASTICS AND RECYCLING TECHNOLOGY. *see* ENGINEERING—Chemical Engineering

678 LKA ISSN 1391-0051
R R I S L BULLETIN. Text in English. a. LKR 25; LKR 160 foreign.
Document type: *Bulletin.*
Supersedes: R R I C Bulletin
Indexed: A35, A36, A37, AgBio, AgrForAb, C30, CABA, E12, F08, F11, F12, GH, H16, I11, N02, N03, O01, OR, P32, P40, PGrRegA, PHN&I, R07, R12, R13, RA&MP, S13, S16, S17, SLSI, T05, TAR, W10, W11.
—Linda Hall.
Published by: Rubber Research Institute of Sri Lanka, Dartonfield, Agalawatta, Sri Lanka. TEL 34-47426, FAX 34-47427.

RADNEWS. *see* PLASTICS

338.476 ESP ISSN 0212-2138
REVISTA DEL CAUCHO. Text in Spanish. 1950. bi-m. EUR 56 domestic; EUR 116 foreign (effective 2009). back issues avail. **Document type:** *Magazine, Consumer.*
Formerly (until 1979): Caucho (0210-0991)
Related titles: Online - full text ed.
Indexed: IECT.
—IE.
Published by: Consorcio Nacional de Industriales del Caucho, C Sino, 18 Bajo, Madrid, 28007, Spain. TEL 34-91-4458412, FAX 34-91-4478111, info@consorciocaucho.es. Ed. Jose Ignacio Izquierdo Marlasca. Circ: 1,500.

678.2 IND
RUBBER. Text in Malayalam. 19??. a. INR 50 per issue (effective 2011). **Document type:** *Magazine, Trade.* **Description:** Presents articles, features and notes for providing guidance to rubber growers in modern scientific methods of rubber cultivation and processing.
Published by: Rubber Board, Ministry of Commerce and Industry, PO Box 1122, Kottayam, 686 002, India. TEL 91-481-2301231, FAX 91-481-2571380, info@rubberboard.org.in, http://www.rubberboard.org.in.

678 USA ISSN 0300-6123
RUBBER & PLASTICS NEWS; the rubber industry's international newspaper. Abbreviated title: R P N. Text in English. 1971. bi-w. USD 99 domestic; USD 138 in Canada; USD 140 elsewhere (effective 2009). adv. bk.rev. charts; illus.; stat.; abstr. cum.index. back issues avail.; reprints avail. **Document type:** *Newspaper, Trade.*
Description: Contains commentary, editorials, news items, and technical notes on legislative, technological, financial and corporate issues that affect the rubber industry worldwide.
Related titles: Microfiche ed.: (from PQC); Online - full text ed.: USD 99 (effective 2009); ◆ Supplement(s): Rubber Directory and Buyers Guide (Year). ISSN 1557-1718.
Indexed: A09, A10, A22, B01, B03, B06, B07, B09, B11, CBNB, CWI, I05, P34, PROMT, R18, T02, V03, V04.
—BLDSC (8040.030000), CIS, INIST. **CCC.**
Published by: Crain Communications, Inc., 1725 Merrimen Rd, Ste 300, Akron, OH 44313. TEL 330-836-9180, FAX 330-836-2831, info@crain.com, http://www.crain.com. Ed. Edward Noga. Pub. David E Zielasko. adv.: color page USD 2,323; trim 8.25 x 10.875. Circ: 16,254 (paid).

678.2 IND
RUBBER ASIA; the complete magazine on rubber. Text in English. 1985. bi-m. INR 800 domestic; USD 100 foreign; INR 150 per issue domestic; USD 20 per issue foreign (effective 2011). adv. back issues avail. **Document type:** *Magazine, Trade.* **Description:** Covers all sectors of the rubber industry including technology, production and marketing.
Related titles: Online - full text ed.
Indexed: R18.
Published by: Dhanam Publications Pvt. Ltd., Dhanam House, 29/609, Cheruparambath Rd, Kadavanthra, Cochin, Kerala 682 020, India. TEL 91-484-2315840, FAX 91-484-2317872, danam@satyam.net.in.

678 IND ISSN 0970-4124
SB290 CODEN: BRUBAV
RUBBER BOARD BULLETIN. Text in English. 1951. q. INR 20 per vol. domestic (effective 2011). **Document type:** *Bulletin, Government.* **Description:** Contains articles of interest to planters and research contributions of Rubber Research Institute of India.
Indexed: ATA, ChemAb, ISA.
Published by: Rubber Board, Ministry of Commerce and Industry, c/o Editori-in-Chief, Kottayam, Kerala 686 009, India. TEL 91-481-2578316, FAX 91-481-2578317, info@rubberboard.org.in. Ed. P N Nair.

678 USA ISSN 0035-9475
TS1870 CODEN: RCTEA4
➤ **RUBBER CHEMISTRY AND TECHNOLOGY.** Text in English. 1928. q. USD 480 to individuals; USD 580 to institutions; USD 380 to members; USD 880 combined subscription to individuals (print & online eds.); USD 1,380 combined subscription to institutions (print & online eds.); USD 380 combined subscription to members (print & online eds.) (effective 2011). adv. bk.rev. abstr.; charts; illus. index. **Document type:** *Journal, Academic/Scholarly.* **Description:** Provides papers on fundamental research, technical development, and chemical engineering relating to rubber and its allied substances.
Related titles: Microform ed.: (from PQC); Online - full text ed.: ISSN 1943-4804. USD 450 to individuals; USD 950 to institutions; free to members (effective 2011).
Indexed: A05, A15, A22, A23, A24, ABIn, AS&TA, AS&TI, ASCA, B04, B13, C&ISA, C10, C33, CA, CCI, CPEI, ChemAb, ChemTitl, CurCR, CurCont, E&CAJ, EngInd, FR, HRIS, ISMEC, ISR, Inspec, MSCI, P26, P48, P51, P52, P54, P56, PQC, R16, R18, RefZh, SCI, SCOPUS, SolStAb, T02, W07.
—BLDSC (8041.000000), CASDDS, IE, Infotrieve, Ingenta, INIST, Linda Hall. **CCC.**
Published by: American Chemical Society, Rubber Division, PO Box 499, Akron, OH 44309. TEL 330-972-7814, crobinson@rubber.org.

678 GBR ISSN 0035-9483
TS1870 CODEN: RUDVAX
RUBBER DEVELOPMENTS. Text in English. 1947. s-a. free. adv. bk.rev. bibl.; charts; illus. index. **Document type:** *Journal, Trade.*
Description: A review of developments in natural rubber research, technology and use.
Incorporates (1970-1990): N R Technology (0307-9007)
Indexed: ABIPC, CBNB, CEABA, CIN, Cadscan, ChemAb, ChemTitl, IPackAb, LeadAb, P06, R18, SCOPUS, WSCA, Zincscan.
—CASDDS, Ingenta, Linda Hall. **CCC.**
Published by: Tun Abdul Razak Research Center, Brickendonbury, Brickendon, Hertford, Herts SG13 8NL, United Kingdom. TEL 44-1992-584966, FAX 44-1992-554837. Ed. G M Reader. Adv. contact B Livesay. Circ: 10,000.

338.476 USA ISSN 1557-1718
HD9161.U5
RUBBER DIRECTORY AND BUYERS GUIDE (YEAR); a directory of rubber product manufacturers and rubber industry suppliers in North America. Text in English. 1978. a. USD 89 per issue (effective 2009). adv. **Document type:** *Directory, Trade.*
Formerly (until 1999): Rubbicana: Rubber Directory and Buyers Guide (Year) (1076-710X)
Related titles: Online - full text ed.; ◆ Supplement to: Rubber & Plastics News. ISSN 0300-6123.
—**CCC.**
Published by: (Rubber and Plastic News), Crain Communications, Inc., 1725 Merrimen Rd, Ste 300, Akron, OH 44313. TEL 330-836-9180, FAX 330-836-2831, info@crain.com, http://www.crain.com. Ed. Edward Noga. Pub. David E Zielasko. **Subscr. to:** 1155 Gratiot Ave, Detroit, MI 48207. TEL 313-446-0480, 800-678-9595.

678.2 DEU ISSN 1863-7116
RUBBER, FIBRES, PLASTICS INTERNATIONAL. Abbreviated title: R F P. Text in German. 2006. bi-m. EUR 120; EUR 25 newsstand/cover (effective 2011). adv. **Document type:** *Magazine, Trade.*
Published by: Dr. Gupta Verlag, Postfach 104125, Ratingen, 40852, Germany. TEL 49-2102-93450, FAX 49-2102-934520, info@gupta-verlag.de, http://www.gupta-verlag.de.

678.2 IND
RUBBER GROWERS COMPANION. Text in English. 1962. a. **Document type:** *Handbook/Manual/Guide, Trade.* **Description:** Details of various aspects of rubber cultivation and processing, information on the activities and development schemes of the Rubber Board and statistics pertaining to the rubber industry are incorporated in the publication.
Published by: Rubber Board, Ministry of Commerce and Industry, PO Box 1122, Kottayam, 686 002, India. TEL 91-481-2301231, FAX 91-481-2571380, info@rubberboard.org.in, http://www.rubberboard.org.in.

678 IND ISSN 0035-9491
TS1885.I5 CODEN: RUIDA4
RUBBER INDIA. Text in English. 1949. m. bk.rev. **Document type:** *Newsletter, Trade.* **Description:** Devoted to the dissemination of information within the rubber industry.
Indexed: B03, ChemAb, ChemTitl, R18.
—BLDSC (8043.800000), IE, Ingenta. **CCC.**
Published by: (All India Rubber Industries Association), Scientific Publishers, 5-A, New Pali Rd, PO Box 91, Jodhpur, Rajasthan 342 001, India. TEL 91-291-2433323, FAX 91-291-2624154, info@scientificpub.com, http://www.scientificpub.com.

678 GBR ISSN 1681-4894
RUBBER INDUSTRY REPORT. Text in English. 19??. q. SGD 2,500; SGD 1,000 per issue (effective 2009). **Document type:** *Report, Trade.* **Description:** Provides an economic analysis of natural and synthetic rubber markets and factors influencing the demand, supply and price; special articles on topics relating to the rubber industry and news of IRSG activities.
Formerly (until 2001): International Rubber Digest (0020-8655)
Indexed: IIS, R18.
Published by: International Rubber Study Group, Heron House, 109/115 Wembley Hill Rd, Wembley, Mddx HA9 8DA, United Kingdom. TEL 44-20-89005400, FAX 44-20-89032848, irsg@rubberstudy.com.

678 USA ISSN 0361-0640
TS1877
RUBBER RED BOOK; directory of the rubber industry. Text in English. 1936. a. USD 112 domestic; USD 134 foreign (effective 2002). **Document type:** *Directory, Trade.*
Formerly: Elastomerics Rubber Red Book
Related titles: CD-ROM ed.: USD 995 (effective 2002).
—**CCC.**
Published by: Lippincott & Peto, Inc., 1867 W Market St, PO Box 5451, Akron, OH 44313. TEL 216-864-2122. Ed. Don R Smith. Pub. Job H Lippincot. Circ: 4,400.

678.2 IND ISSN 0970-2490
RUBBER RESEARCH INSTITUTE OF INDIA. ANNUAL REPORT. Text in English. 1987. a. free (effective 2011). **Document type:** *Report, Trade.* **Description:** Presents major research accomplishments of the Rubber Research Institute of India.
Published by: Rubber Board, Ministry of Commerce and Industry, PO Box 1122, Kottayam, 686 002, India. TEL 91-481-2301231, FAX 91-481-2571380, info@rubberboard.org.in, http://www.rubberboard.org.in.

678.2 IND
RUBBER RESEARCH INSTITUTE OF INDIA. CONFERENCE PROCEEDINGS. Text in English. 1974. irreg., latest no.18, 2005. back issues avail. **Document type:** *Proceedings, Trade.*
Published by: Rubber Board, Ministry of Commerce and Industry, PO Box 1122, Kottayam, 686 002, India. TEL 91-481-2301231, FAX 91-481-2571380, info@rubberboard.org.in, http://www.rubberboard.org.in.

633.895 MYS ISSN 0126-8279
SB290
RUBBER RESEARCH INSTITUTE OF MALAYSIA. ANNUAL REPORT. Text in English. 1951. a. MYR 25, USD 30. charts; illus.; stat. **Document type:** *Corporate.*
Formerly (until 1973): Kuala Lumpur. Rubber Research Institute of Malaya. Annual Report (0370-7032)
—Linda Hall.
Published by: Rubber Research Institute of Malaysia, Public Relations, Publications and Library Unit/Sains Institut Penyelidikan Getah Malaysia, PO Box 10150, Kuala Lumpur, 50908, Malaysia. TEL 60-3-456-7022, FAX 60-3-457-3512, TELEX MA 30369. Circ: 1,700.

633.895 MYS ISSN 0126-9410
RUBBER RESEARCH INSTITUTE OF MALAYSIA. TECHNOLOGY BULLETIN. Text in English. irreg. USD 25 (effective 2000). **Document type:** *Bulletin, Academic/Scholarly.*
Formerly (unitl 1980): R R I M Technology Centre Bulletin
Published by: Rubber Research Institute of Malaysia, Public Relations, Publications and Library Unit/Sains Institut Penyelidikan Getah Malaysia, PO Box 10150, Kuala Lumpur, 50908, Malaysia. TEL 60-3-456-7033, FAX 60-3-457-3512, TELEX MA 30369, dg@lgm.gov.my, http://www.lgm.gov.my. Circ: 1,500.

678 LKA ISSN 1013-2198
TS1870
RUBBER RESEARCH INSTITUTE OF SRI LANKA. ANNUAL REVIEW. Text in English. a. LKR 50; LKR 320 foreign.
Supersedes: Rubber Research Institute of Ceylon. Annual Review
—Linda Hall.
Published by: Rubber Research Institute of Sri Lanka, Dartonfield, Agalawatta, Sri Lanka. TEL 34-47426, FAX 34-47427.

678 668.4 LKA ISSN 0379-1130
TS1870 CODEN: JRRLDZ
RUBBER RESEARCH INSTITUTE OF SRI LANKA. JOURNAL. Text in English. 1976 (vol.53). a. LKR 50; LKR 320 foreign. adv. bk.rev. charts; illus. **Document type:** *Journal, Academic/Scholarly.*
Formerly (until 1976): Rubber Research Institute of Sri Lanka. Quarterly Journal (0035-9521)
Indexed: ATA, ChemAb, SLSI.
—CASDDS, Linda Hall.
Published by: Rubber Research Institute of Sri Lanka, Dartonfield, Agalawatta, Sri Lanka. TEL 34-47426, FAX 34-47427. Ed. Dr. L M K Tillekerathe. Circ: 1,000.

678.2 668.4 ZAF ISSN 0258-9737
RUBBER SOUTHERN AFRICA. Text in English. 1985. bi-m. ZAR 74.10 domestic; ZAR 80 in Africa; ZAR 104 elsewhere. **Document type:** *Journal, Trade.* **Description:** Contains information on rubber compounding, moulding, tire manufacturing, repair and marketing.
Indexed: ISAP.
—INIST, Linda Hall.
Published by: George Warman Publications (Pty.) Ltd., Rondebosch, PO Box 705, Cape Town, 7701, South Africa. info@gwarmanpublications.co.za, http://www.gwarmanpublications.co.za. Ed. Martin Wells. Circ: 1,113.

678 USA ISSN 0035-9572
TS1870 CODEN: RUBWAQ
RUBBER WORLD. Text in English. 1889. 16/yr. USD 34 domestic; USD 39 in Canada; USD 149 elsewhere (effective 2010). adv. bk.rev. bibl.; charts; illus.; mkt.; stat.; tr.lit. index. back issues avail.; reprints avail. **Document type:** *Magazine, Trade.*
Former titles (until 1954): India Rubber World (0096-5790); (until 1899): India Rubber World and Electrical Trades Review
Related titles: CD-ROM ed.; Microform ed.: (from PMC, PQC); Online - full text ed.: free (effective 2010).
Indexed: A09, A10, A22, A23, A24, B01, B02, B06, B07, B08, B09, B13, B15, B17, B18, BusI, C&ISA, C12, CIN, CPEI, ChemAb, ChemTitl, E&CAJ, EngInd, G04, G06, G07, G08, I05, KES, M01, M02, P06, R18, RefZh, S22, SCOPUS, SRI, SolStAb, T&II, T02, V02, V03, V04.
—BLDSC (8047.000000), CASDDS, IE, Infotrieve, Ingenta, INIST, Linda Hall. **CCC.**
Published by: Lippincott & Peto, Inc., 1867 W Market St, PO Box 5451, Akron, OH 44313. TEL 330-864-2122, FAX 330-864-5298. Ed. Don R Smith. Pub. Job H Lippincot.

678 USA
RUBBER WORLD BLUE BOOK OF MATERIALS, COMPOUNDING INGREDIENTS AND MACHINERY FOR RUBBER. Text in English. 1916. a. USD 111; USD 139 foreign. adv. **Document type:** *Directory.*
Published by: Lippincott & Peto, Inc., 1867 W Market St, PO Box 5451, Akron, OH 44313. TEL 216-864-2122. Ed. Don R Smith. Adv. contact Dennis Kennelly.

678 USA
RUBBER WORLD PRODUCT NEWS. Text in English. q. Included in subscription to Rubber World Magazine. **Description:** Covers new products in the rubber industry.
Published by: Lippincott & Peto, Inc., 1867 W Market St, PO Box 5451, Akron, OH 44313. TEL 216-864-2122. Pub. Job H Lippincot.

SVET POLIMERA/WORLD OF POLYMERS. *see* PLASTICS

678 USA ISSN 1070-6461
SYNTHETIC RUBBER MANUAL. Text in English. triennial. USD 250 (effective 2005). **Description:** Lists over 2000 individual polymers and elastomers with technical and quality criteria.
Published by: International Institute of Synthetic Rubber Producers, 2077 S Gessner Rd Ste 133, Houston, TX 77063-1123. TEL 713-783-7511, FAX 713-783-7253, info@iisrp.com, http://www.iisrp.com. Eds. Leon Loh, James L McGraw.

678.32 USA
TIRE AND RIM ASSOCIATION YEAR BOOK. Text in English. 1927. a. USD 55 (effective 2001). **Document type:** *Yearbook, Trade.*
Description: Includes standards for tire, rim and valve interchangeability.
Formerly: Tire and Rim Association. Standards Year Book (0082-4496)
Related titles: CD-ROM ed.: USD 200 to individuals; USD 400 to institutions (effective 2001).
Published by: Tire and Rim Association, Inc., Crown Pointe, 175 Montrose Ave. W., No. 150, Copley, OH 44321. TEL 216-666-8121. Ed. J F Pacuit. Circ: 4,500.

TIRE BUSINESS. *see* TRANSPORTATION—Automobiles

678.32 USA
TIRE RETAILING TODAY. Text in English. 1997. bi-m. USD 13 (effective 2005). **Document type:** *Magazine, Trade.*
Published by: Tire Association of North America, 11921 Freedom Dr., Ste. 550, Reston, VA 20190. TEL 703-736-8082, FAX 703-904-4339. Ed. Bob Griendling. Circ: 4,000 (paid).

678.32 USA ISSN 1046-7157
TIRE RETREADING - REPAIR JOURNAL; a technical digest for tire retreaders. Text in English. 1956. m. USD 50 in US & Canada; USD 60 elsewhere (effective 2000). adv. index. back issues avail.
Document type: *Journal, Trade.* **Description:** Discusses matters of interest to tire retread production employees, retread and repair material sales personnel, equipment sales people, and other professionals in the tire and transportation industries.
Formed by the merger of (1982-1989): Tire Repair Journal (0731-7298); Retreader's Journal (0482-430X)

Published by: (International Tire and Rubber Association), Tire Industry Publication Service, Inc., PO Box 37203, Louisville, KY 40233-7203. TEL 502-968-8900, 800-426-8835, FAX 502-964-7859. Ed. Marvin Bozarth. Adv. contact Bunny McDermott. B&W page USD 550. Circ: 2,650 (controlled).

TIRE REVIEW; the authority on tire dealer profitability. *see* TRANSPORTATION—Automobiles

678.32 USA ISSN 0090-8657
TL270 CODEN: TSTCAU
➤ **TIRE SCIENCE AND TECHNOLOGY.** Text in English. 1973. q. USD 125 to non-members; USD 75 to members (effective 2010). bibl.; charts; illus. index. back issues avail. **Document type:** *Journal, Academic/Scholarly.* **Description:** Contains scientific articles on tire technology.
Related titles: Online - full text ed.: ISSN 1945-5852. USD 175 to non-members; free to members (effective 2010).
Indexed: A22, ApMecR, CPEI, EngInd, GeoRef, Inspec, R18, SCOPUS, TM.
—BLDSC (8858.403000), IE, Infotrieve, Ingenta, INIST, Linda Hall. **CCC.**
Published by: Tire Society Inc., PO Box 1502, Akron, OH 44309. TEL 330-972-7814, FAX 330-972-5269, office@tiresociety.org, http://www.tiresociety.org/. Ed. Michael Kaliske.

678.32 GBR ISSN 1462-4729
TIRE TECHNOLOGY INTERNATIONAL. Text in English. 1998. q. free (effective 2009). adv. back issues avail. **Document type:** *Magazine, Trade.* **Description:** Covers all aspects of tire design, tire materials and tire manufacturing technology.
Related titles: Online - full text ed.; Supplement(s): Tire Technology International (Annual Edition). ISSN 0969-7217. 1993.
Indexed: HRIS, R18.
—BLDSC (8858.403250). **CCC.**
Published by: U K & International Press (Subsidiary of: AutoIntermediates Ltd.), Abinger House, Church St, Dorking, Surrey RH4 1DF, United Kingdom. TEL 44-1306-743744, FAX 44-1306-887546, info@ukintpress.com, http://www.ukipme.com. Ed. Adam Gavine. Adv. contact Colin Scott.

678.2 629.286 AUS
THE TYRE AND RIM ASSOCIATION OF AUSTRALIA STANDARDS MANUAL. Text in English. 1958. a. price varies. 260 p./no.; **Document type:** *Yearbook, Trade.*
Published by: Tyre and Rim Association of Australia, Ste 1, 795 Glenferrie Rd, Hawthorn, VIC 3122, Australia. TEL 61-3-98180759, FAX 61-3-9818-0750, info@tyreandrim.org.au.

678.32 GBR ISSN 0041-4859
TYRES AND ACCESSORIES. Text in English. 1946. m. GBP 60 combined subscription domestic (print & online eds.); GBP 70 combined subscription in Europe (print & online eds.); GBP 90 combined subscription elsewhere (print & online eds.) (effective 2009). adv. bk.rev. illus. back issues avail. **Document type:** *Magazine, Trade.*
Related titles: Online - full text ed.
Indexed: ChemAb, R18, RefZh.
—IE, Infotrieve.
Published by: Tyre Industry Publications Ltd., 6a Salem St, Stoke-on-Trent, Staffordshire ST1 5PR, United Kingdom. TEL 44-1782-214224, FAX 44-1782-286589, info@tyrepress.com. Circ: 7,000.

678 668.4 FRA ISSN 1635-0502
UNION DES SYNDICATS DES PME DU CAOUTCHOUC ET DE LA PLASTURGIE. Text in French. 1949. irreg. adv. charts; illus.; mkt. **Description:** Periodical of economic research on plastics.
Former titles (until 2001): Union des Industries et de la Distribution des Plastiques et du Caoutchouc. Informations Mensuelles (1240-974X); (until 1992): Informations du Caoutchouc et des Plastiques (0247-3518); (until 1974): Informations du Caoutchouc (0020-0468)
Address: 37-39 rue de Pommard, Paris, 75012, France. TEL 33-1-55782898, FAX 33-1-55782899, http://www.ucaplast.fr/. Circ: 2,000.

URETHANES TECHNOLOGY INTERNATIONAL. *see* PLASTICS

▼ **URETHANES TECHNOLOGY INTERNATIONAL NORTH AMERICA.** *see* PLASTICS

678.2 USA ISSN 0083-5218
TS1890
VANDERBILT RUBBER HANDBOOK. Text in English. 1926. irreg. USD 100 (effective 1999). index. **Document type:** *Handbook/Manual/Guide, Trade.* **Description:** Contains technical information for those directly connected with the compounding and processing of rubber and synthetic elastomers in their dry form.
Related titles: CD-ROM ed.: CD-ROM Blue Book (Year).
Published by: R.T. Vanderbilt Co., Inc., 30 Winfield St, Norwalk, CT 06855. TEL 203-853-1400, FAX 203-853-1452. Ed., R&P Robert F Ohm. **CD-ROM subscr. to:** Rubber World Magazine, 1867 W Market St, PO Box 5451, Akron, OH 44313. TEL 330-864-2122, FAX 330-864-5298.

678.2 CHN ISSN 1000-890X
HD9161.C5 CODEN: XIGOED
XIANGJIAO GONGYE/CHINA RUBBER INDUSTRY. Text in Chinese; Contents page in Chinese, English. 1953. m. USD 74.40 (effective 2009). **Document type:** *Journal, Academic/Scholarly.*
Related titles: Online - full text ed.
Indexed: CIN, ChemAb, ChemTitl, R18.
—BLDSC (3180.234280), CASDDS, East View, IE, Ingenta.
Published by: Beijing Xiangjiao Gongye Yanjiu Shejiyuan/Beijing Research and Design Institute of Rubber Industry, Fushi Lu Jia #19, Beijing, 100039, China. TEL 86-10-51338152, FAX 86-10-68156717, http://www.china-rp.com.cn/.

XIANGSU JISHU YU ZHUANGBEI/CHINA RUBBER / PLASTICS TECHNOLOGY & EQUIPMENT. *see* PLASTICS

RUBBER—Abstracting, Bibliographies, Statistics

678.2 CAN ISSN 1481-9724
CANADA. STATISTICS CANADA. RUBBER AND PLASTIC PRODUCTS INDUSTRIES (ONLINE)/CANADA. STATISTIQUE CANADA. INDUSTRIES DES PRODUITS EN CAOUTCHOUC ET EN MATIERE PLASTIQUE. Text in English, French. 1985. a. CAD 40 domestic; USD 40 foreign (effective 1999). **Document type:** *Government.*
Formerly (until 1997): Canada. Statistics Canada. Rubber and Plastic Products Industries (Print) (0835-0027); Which was formed by the merger of (1919-1985): Canada. Statistics Canada. Rubber Products Industries (0300-0214); Which was formerly (until 1970): Canada. Statistics Canada. Rubber Industries (0700-0111); (until 1960): Canada. Dominion Bureau of Statistics. Rubber Products Industry (0700-012X); (1981-1985): Canada. Statistics Canada. Plastics Industries (0319-9053); Which was formed by the merger of (1950-1981): Canada. Statistics Canada. Plastics Fabricating Industry (0384-4196); Which was formerly (until 1970): Canada. Statistics Canada. Plastics Fabricator, n.e.ss (0575-9323); Which superseded in part (in 1960): Canada. Statistics Canada. Miscellaneous Industries (0410-5508); (19??-1981): Canada. Statistics Canada. Manufacturers of Plastics and Synthetic Resins (0527-5571); Which was formerly (until 1960): Canada. Statistics Canada. Primary Plastics Industries (0527-6055)
Media: Online - full content.
—CCC.
Published by: Statistics Canada, Operations and Integration Division (Subsidiary of: Statistics Canada/Statistique Canada), Circulation Management, 120 Parkdale Ave, Ottawa, ON K1A 0T6, Canada. TEL 613-951-7277, 800-267-6677, FAX 613-951-1584.

678 IND ISSN 0073-6651
INDIAN RUBBER STATISTICS. Text in English. 1958. a. INR 250 per issue (effective 2011). **Document type:** *Directory, Trade.* **Description:** Covers statistics relating to area, production, import, consumption, price etc of rubber, manufacturers and dealers of rubber products, taxation, labour and various other topics. A guide for industrialists and researchers.
Published by: Rubber Board, Ministry of Commerce and Industry, PO Box 1122, Kottayam, 686 002, India. TEL 91-481-2301231, FAX 91-481-2571380, info@rubberboard.org.in, http://www.rubberboard.org.in.

338.1738952 MYS ISSN 0127-6778
MALAYSIA. DEPARTMENT OF STATISTICS. MONTHLY RUBBER STATISTICS, MALAYSIA/MALAYSIA. JABATAN PERANGKAAN. PERANGKAAN GETAH BULANAN, MALAYSIA. Key Title: Perangkaan Bulanan Getah Bagi Malaysia. Text in English, Malay. 1968. m. MYR 5 per issue (effective 1999). **Document type:** *Government.*
Published by: Malaysia. Department of Statistics/Jabatan Perangkaan, Jalan Cenderasari, Kuala Lumpur, 50514, Malaysia. TEL 60-3-294-4264, FAX 60-3-291-4535.

633.895 310 MYS ISSN 0127-8509
MALAYSIA. DEPARTMENT OF STATISTICS. RUBBER STATISTICS HANDBOOK, MALAYSIA/MALAYSIA. JABATAN PERANGKAAN. BUKU MAKLUMAT PERANGKAAN GETAH, MALAYSIA. Text in English. 1988. irreg., latest 1996. MYR 28. **Document type:** *Government.*
Published by: Malaysia. Department of Statistics/Jabatan Perangkaan, Jalan Cenderasari, Kuala Lumpur, 50514, Malaysia. TEL 60-3-294-4264, FAX 60-3-291-4535, jpmeto@po.jaring.my, jpukp@po.jaring.my.

678 668.4 016 GBR
TS1870
R A P R A ABSTRACTS. (Rubber and Plastics Research Association) Text in English. 1923. m. price varies. adv. bk.rev. stat. index. back issues avail. **Document type:** *Abstract/Index.* **Description:** Provides a comprehensive up-to-date survey of current information from all around the globe, relevant to the rubber, plastics, composites and associated industries. Material is selected from more than 500 journals, conference proceedings, books, trade and technical literature, US and EP patents, standards and government publications.
Related titles: ◆ CD-ROM ed.: Rapra Abstracts - CD-ROM; ◆ Online - full text ed.: Rapra Abstracts Database.
—CCC.
Published by: iSmithers, Shawbury, Shrewsbury, Shrops SY4 4NR, United Kingdom. TEL 44-1939-250383, FAX 44-1939-251118, info@ismithers.net, http://www.ismithers.net.

R A P R A REVIEW REPORTS; expert overviews covering the science and technology of rubbers and plastics. (Rubber and Plastics Research Association) *see* PLASTICS—Abstracting, Bibliographies, Statistics

678 668.4 GBR
RAPRA ABSTRACTS - CD-ROM. Text in English. 1991. m. price varies. **Document type:** *Abstract/Index.*
Formerly (until 1993): Plastics and Rubbers Materials Disk (0961-9305); Incorporates: Polymer Patent Abstracts (1357-0706)
Media: CD-ROM. **Related titles:** ◆ Online - full text ed.: Rapra Abstracts Database; ◆ Print ed.: R A P R A Abstracts.
—CCC.
Published by: iSmithers, Shawbury, Shrewsbury, Shrops SY4 4NR, United Kingdom. TEL 44-1939-250383, FAX 44-1939-251118, info@ismithers.net, http://www.ismithers.net.

678 668.4 016 GBR
RAPRA ABSTRACTS DATABASE. Text in English. base vol. plus updates. **Document type:** *Database, Abstract/Index.*
Media: Online - full text. **Related titles:** ◆ CD-ROM ed.: Rapra Abstracts - CD-ROM; ◆ Print ed.: R A P R A Abstracts.
Published by: iSmithers, Shawbury, Shrewsbury, Shrops SY4 4NR, United Kingdom. TEL 44-1939-250383, info@ismithers.net, info@rapra.net, http://www.rapra.net.

678 GBR
RAPRA ABSTRACTS. RUBBER MATERIALS. Text in English. bi-m. price varies. **Document type:** *Abstract/Index.*
Media: CD-ROM.
Published by: iSmithers, Shawbury, Shrewsbury, Shrops SY4 4NR, United Kingdom. TEL 44-1939-250383, FAX 44-1939-251118, info@ismithers.net, http://www.ismithers.net.

338.476 310 USA
RUBBER MANUFACTURERS ASSOCIATION. STATISTICAL REPORT. MONTHLY TIRE REPORT. Text in English. 1974. m. USD 2,800 (effective 2011). charts; stat. **Document type:** *Report, Trade.* **Description:** Shows import-export activity of passenger car, light and heavy truck, and bus tires. Includes statistics on tire shipments.
Related titles: Online - full text ed.
Indexed: SRI.
Published by: Rubber Manufacturers Association, 1400 K St, NW, Ste 900, Washington, DC 20005. TEL 202-682-4800.

678 GBR ISSN 0035-9548
HD9161.A1
RUBBER STATISTICAL BULLETIN. Text in English. 1935. q. SGD 2,500; SGD 1,000 per issue (effective 2009). 48 p./no.; back issues avail. **Document type:** *Bulletin, Trade.* **Description:** Provides statistics on the production, consumption, import and export of natural and synthetic rubbers for many countries for the current and preceding year.
Formerly (until 1946): International Rubber Regulatory Commission. Statistical Bulletin
Related titles: Microfiche ed.: (from CIS).
Indexed: IIS, P06, R18, RASB.
Published by: International Rubber Study Group, Heron House, 109/115 Wembley Hill Rd, Wembley, Mddx HA9 8DA, United Kingdom. TEL 44-20-89005400, FAX 44-20-89032848, irsg@rubberstudy.com.

678.2021 IND
RUBBER STATISTICAL NEWS. Text in English. 1975 (July). m. INR 50 (effective 2011). **Document type:** *Report, Trade.* **Description:** Contains relevant and up-to-date statistics on rubber.
Related titles: Online - full text ed.: free (effective 2011).
Published by: Rubber Board, Ministry of Commerce and Industry, PO Box 1122, Kottayam, 686 002, India. TEL 91-481-2301231, FAX 91-481-2571380, info@rubberboard.org.in, http://www.rubberboard.org.in.

678 GBR
WORLD RUBBER STATISTICS HANDBOOK. Text in English. 1974. quadrennial. SGD 3,000 per vol. (effective 2009). 73 p./no.; **Document type:** *Handbook/Manual/Guide, Trade.* **Description:** Covers all aspects of the world elastomer rubber economy and associated products. Provides statistics on natural and synthetic rubber production and statistics on the production and use of cars.
Related titles: Diskette ed.: GBP 175 (effective 1999); Microfiche ed.: (from CIS).
Indexed: IIS.
Published by: International Rubber Study Group, Heron House, 109/115 Wembley Hill Rd, Wembley, Mddx HA9 8DA, United Kingdom. TEL 44-20-89005400, FAX 44-20-89032848, irsg@rubberstudy.com.

338.476 USA
WORLDWIDE RUBBER STATISTICS. Text in English. 1975. a. USD 205 in North America; USD 215 elsewhere (effective 1999). **Description:** Covers synthetic and natural rubber industry. Lists producers, tabulates plant production, provides forecasts and gives statistical histories.
Published by: International Institute of Synthetic Rubber Producers, 2077 S Gessner Rd Ste 133, Houston, TX 77063-1123. TEL 713-783-7511, FAX 713-783-7253. Ed. B Theismann.

R

SCHOOL ORGANIZATION AND ADMINISTRATION

see EDUCATION—School Organization And Administration

SCIENCE FICTION, FANTASY, HORROR

see LITERATURE—Science Fiction, Fantasy, Horror

SCIENCES: COMPREHENSIVE WORKS

500 USA ISSN 1041-8857
Q181.A1
A A A S REPORT: RESEARCH AND DEVELOPMENT. Text in English. 1976. a. USD 19.95 per issue to non-members; USD 15.96 per issue to members (effective 2009). back issues avail. **Document type:** *Report, Trade.* **Description:** Details information on the President's proposed federal research and development budget.
Former titles (until 1984): American Association for the Advancement of Science. Report. Research & Development.; (until 1979): American Association for the Advancement of Science. Research and Development in the Federal Budget (0147-6289); (until 1977): American Association for the Advancement of Science. Report. Research & Development.
Related titles: Online - full text ed.
Indexed: B02, B15, B17, B18, G04, G05, G06, G07, G08, I05, SRI.
Published by: American Association for the Advancement of Science, 1200 New York Ave, NW, Washington, DC 20005. TEL 202-326-6400, FAX 202-371-9849, development@aaas.org.

A B C. *see* CHILDREN AND YOUTH—For

500 BRA ISSN 1414-7149
A D A P E C. ARQUIVOS. (Associacao Paranaense para o Desenvolvimento do Ensino da Ciencia. Arquivos) Key Title: Arquivos da Apadec. Text in Portuguese. 1997. s-a. BRL 18 to members; BRL 22 to non-members (effective 2006). **Document type:** *Journal, Academic/Scholarly.*
Indexed: C01.
Published by: Associacao Paranaense para o Desenvolvimiento do Ensino da Ciencia, Ave Colombo 5790 Bloco 104, Saa 1, Maringa, Parana, 8720-900, Brazil. sec-cic@uem.br, http://www.apadec.hpg.ig.com.br/.

A F P SCIENCES; bulletin information scientifique, technique, medicale. *see* MEDICAL SCIENCES

500 070 FRA
A F P SCIENCES SUR CD-ROM. Text in French. s-a. USD 1,600 (effective 1996). **Description:** Contains the complete text of documents prepared by AFP's Scientific Department from dispatches of AFP offices around the world.
Media: CD-ROM. **Related titles:** ◆ Print ed.: A F P Sciences.
Published by: Agence France-Presse, 11-15 Place de la Bourse, Paris, 75002, France. TEL 33-1-40414646, contact@afp.com, http://www.afp.com.

500 JPN ISSN 1346-602X
HC465.H53
A I S T TODAY (ENGLISH EDITION). (Advanced Industrial Science and Technology) Text in English. 2001. q.
Related titles: ◆ Japanese ed.: Sansouken Today. ISSN 1880-0041.
Indexed: A28, APA, BrCerAb, C&ISA, CA/WCA, CIA, CPEI, CerAb, CivEngAb, CorrAb, E&CAJ, E11, EEA, EMA, ESPM, EngInd, EnvEAb, GeoRef, H15, M&TEA, M09, MBF, METADEX, SCOPUS, SolStAb, T04, WAA.
—BLDSC (0785.456300), Linda Hall.
Published by: National Institute of Advanced Industrial Science and Technology/Sangyou Gijutsu Sougou Kenkyuujo, 1-1-1 Umezono, Tsukuba Central 2, Tsukuba, Ibaraki 305-8563, Japan. TEL 81-29-8626217, FAX 81-29-8626212.

▼ **A L T E X. ETHIK.** (Alternatives to Animal Experimentation) *see* ANIMAL WELFARE

500 IND ISSN 0975-9573
▼ **A N U JOURNAL OF NATURAL SCIENCE.** Text in English. 2009. s-a. **Document type:** *Journal, Academic/Scholarly.*
Published by: Acharya Nagarjuna University, Nagarjuna Nagar, Guntur, Andhra Pradesh 522 510, India. TEL 91-863-2293007, FAX 91-863-2293378, http://www.nagarjunauniversity.ac.in.

A N U REPORTER. *see* COLLEGE AND ALUMNI

500 AUT
A P A - JOURNAL. FORSCHUNG. Text in German. w. EUR 380 combined subscription for print & online eds. (effective 2003). **Document type:** *Journal, Trade.*
Related titles: Online - full text ed.
Published by: Austria Presse Agentur, Gunoldstr 14, Vienna, W 1190, Austria. TEL 43-1-360600, FAX 43-1-360603099, kundenservice@apa.at, http://www.apa.at.

500 FIN ISSN 1456-5080
A PROPOS; Suomen akatemien lehti. Variant title: Apropos. Text in Finnish. 1976. q. free (effective 2005). **Document type:** *Journal, Academic/Scholarly.*
Former titles (until 1999): Suomen Akatemia. Tiedottaa (0357-2781); (until 1979): Suomen Akatemia. Tiedotuslehti (0358-951X)
Related titles: Online - full text ed.
Published by: Suomen Akatemia/The Academy of Finland, Vilhonvuorenkatu 6, PO Box 99, Helsinki, 00501, Finland. TEL 358-9-774881, FAX 358-9-77488299, keskus@aka.fi. Ed. Riitta Tirronen TEL 358-9-77488369.

500 600 IDN ISSN 0217-5460
HC441.A1 CODEN: AJSDFX
A S E A N JOURNAL ON SCIENCE AND TECHNOLOGY FOR DEVELOPMENT. Text in English. 1984. s-a.
Indexed: INIS AtomInd.
—BLDSC (1739.956700), IE, Ingenta.
Published by: Association of South East Asian Nations, ASEAN Secretariat, Jalan Sisingamangaraja 70 A, Jakarta, 12110, Indonesia. TEL 62-21-7262991, FAX 62-21-7398234, public@aseansec.org, http://www.aseansec.org.

507.4 USA ISSN 1528-820X
Q105.A1
A S T C DIMENSIONS. Text in English. 1974. bi-m. USD 55 domestic to non-members; USD 65 foreign to non-members; USD 40 domestic to members; USD 50 foreign to members (effective 2011). adv. bk.rev. charts; illus. back issues avail. **Document type:** *Journal, Academic/Scholarly.* **Description:** Reports on new interactive exhibitions at member institutions, issues related to informal science education and to science museums and related institutions.
Formerly (until 1999): A S T C Newsletter (0895-7371)
Related titles: Audio cassette/tape ed.; Diskette ed.
Published by: Association of Science-Technology Centers, 1025 Vermont Ave, NW, Ste 500, Washington, DC 20050. TEL 202-783-7200, FAX 202-783-7207, info@astc.org.

A S T I S BIBLIOGRAPHY. *see* SCIENCES: COMPREHENSIVE WORKS—Abstracting, Bibliographies, Statistics

A W I S MAGAZINE. *see* WOMEN'S INTERESTS

500 DEU
AACHENER BEITRAEGE ZUR WISSENSCHAFTS- UND TECHNIKGESCHICHTE DES 20. JAHRHUNDERTS. Text in German. irreg., latest vol.6, 2008. price varies. **Document type:** *Monographic series, Academic/Scholarly.*
Published by: G N T Verlag, Schlossstr. 1, Diepholz, 49356, Germany. TEL 49-5441-927129, FAX 49-5441-927127, service@gnt-verlag.de.

500 CHE ISSN 0379-2722
AARGAUISCHE NATURFORSCHENDE GESELLSCHAFT. MITTEILUNGEN. Text in German. 1863. irreg., latest vol.36, 2005. price varies. **Document type:** *Monographic series, Academic/Scholarly.*
Indexed: Z01.
Published by: Aargauische Naturforschende Gesellschaft, Im Wygarte 3, Anglikon, 5611, Switzerland. http://www.ang.ch.

ABHANDLUNGEN ZUR GESCHICHTE DER MEDIZIN UND DER NATURWISSENSCHAFTEN. *see* MEDICAL SCIENCES

500 ITA ISSN 1125-4203
ACADEMIA. Text in Italian, English, German. 1995. q. free (effective 2008). **Document type:** *Magazine, Consumer.* **Description:** Publishes reports, interviews on current topics, reports from throughout Europe and informative photos and illustrations.
Published by: Accademia Europea Bolzano (E U R A C)/European Academy Bolzano, Viale Druso 1, Bolzano, Italy. TEL 39-0471-055055, FAX 39-0471-055059. Circ: 8,500.

500 USA ISSN 1553-992X
▼ **ACADEMIA ARENA.** Text in English. 2009. bi-m. **Document type:** *Magazine, Trade.*
Related titles: Online - full text ed.: ISSN 2158-771X.
Published by: Marsland Press, PO Box 21126, Lansing, MI 48909. TEL 347-321-7172, FAX 718-404-5362, sciencepub@gmail.com, http://www.sciencepub.net.

500 BRA ISSN 0001-3765
Q33 CODEN: AABCAD
➤ **ACADEMIA BRASILEIRA DE CIENCIAS. ANAIS/ANNALS OF THE BRAZILIAN ACADEMY OF SCIENCES.** Text in English. 1917. q. BRL 85 domestic to individuals; USD 85 foreign to individuals; BRL 100 domestic to institutions; USD 100 foreign to institutions (effective 2005). bk.rev. bibl.; charts; illus. index. 160 p./no.; back issues avail.; reprints avail. **Document type:** *Journal, Academic/Scholarly.* **Description:** Contains papers and reviews on such subject areas as mathematics, physics, chemistry, biology, earth sciences, and engineering.
Former titles (until 1928): Academia Brasileira de Sciencias. Revista (0100-2252); (until 1922): Revista de Sciencias (0100-2368); (until 1919): Sociedade Brasileira de Sciencias. Revista (0100-2317)
Related titles: Online - full text ed.: ISSN 1678-2690. 2000. free (effective 2011).
Indexed: A20, A22, A34, A35, A36, A37, A38, AgBio, AgrForAb, AnBeAb, B21, B23, B25, BIOSIS Prev, BP, C01, C25, C30, CABA, CCMJ, CIN, ChemAb, ChemTitl, CurCont, E12, E17, EMBASE, ESPM, EntAb, ExcerpMed, F08, F11, F12, FCA, G11, GH, GeoRef, H16, H17, I11, IBR, IBZ, INIS AtomInd, IndMed, IndVet, Inspec, MEDLINE, MSN, MaizeAb, MathR, MycolAb, N02, N03, N05, O01, OR, P30, P32, P33, P37, P39, P40, PGegResA, PGrRegA, PHN&I, PN&I, R07, R08, R10, R11, R12, R13, RA&MP, RASB, RM&VM, Reac, S12, S13, S16, S17, SCI, SCOPUS, SoyAb, SpeleolAb, T05, TAR, VITIS, VS, W07, W08, W10, W11, Z01, Z02.
—BLDSC (0860.000000), AskIEEE, CASDDS, IE, Infotrieve, Ingenta, INIST, Linda Hall. **CCC.**
Published by: Academia Brasileira de Ciencias, Rua Anfilofio de Carvalho, 29-3A, Centro, Rio de Janeiro, RJ 20030-060, Brazil. TEL 55-21-2220-4794, FAX 55-21-2532-5807, http://www.scielo.br/aabc, http://www.abc.org.br. Ed. Lucia Mendoca Previato. Adv. contact Isa Maioli. Circ: 800.

500 ESP ISSN 1130-4723
ACADEMIA CANARIA DE CIENCIAS. REVISTA. Text in Spanish. 1990. a.
Indexed: CCMJ, IECT, MSN, MathR, Z01, Z02.
Published by: Academia Canaria de Ciencias, Santiago Cuadrado, 2, Santa Cruz De Tenerife, Canary Islands 38006, Spain. http://webpages.ull.es/users/acanacie/Academia.htm.

500 COL ISSN 0370-3908
Q33 CODEN: RCCFAO
ACADEMIA COLOMBIANA DE CIENCIAS EXACTAS, FISICAS Y NATURALES. REVISTA. Text in Multiple languages. 1936. q. **Description:** Publishes articles in the fields of biology, botany, biochemistry, earth sciences, ecology, physics, mathematics, zoology, and the history and philosophy of science.
Related titles: Online - full text ed.
Indexed: A26, C01, CA, CCMJ, F04, GeoRef, I04, I05, MSN, MathR, T02, Z01, Z02.
—INIST.
Published by: Academia Colombiana de Ciencias Exactas, Fisicas y Naturales, Apartado 44763, Bogota, DC 1, Colombia. TEL 57-268-3290, FAX 57-244-3186.

500 DOM ISSN 1023-9065
Q29
ACADEMIA DE CIENCIAS DE LA REPUBLICA DOMINICANA. ANUARIO. Text in English, French, Spanish; Summaries in Spanish. 1975. a. USD 55 (effective 1995).
Published by: (Academia de Ciencias de la Republica Dominicana), Editora Taller, Apdo. 2190, Isabel la Catolica 260, Santo Domingo, Dominican Republic. TEL 809-682-9369, FAX 809-689-7259.

500 ESP ISSN 1132-6360
CODEN: MACZEJ
ACADEMIA DE CIENCIAS EXACTAS, FISICAS, QUIMICAS Y NATURALES DE ZARAGOZA. MONOGRAFIAS. Text in Spanish. 1988. irreg. **Document type:** *Monographic series, Academic/Scholarly.*
Indexed: CCMJ, GeoRef, IECT, Inspec, SpeleolAb, Z02.
Published by: Academia de Ciencias Exactas Fisico-Quimicas y Naturales, Facultad de Ciencias, C Pedro Cerbuna, 12, Zaragoza, 50009, Spain. TEL 34-976-761128, FAX 34-976-761125, acz@posta.unizar.es, http://www.unizar.es/acz/.

500 ESP ISSN 0370-3207
Q65 CODEN: RACZA2
ACADEMIA DE CIENCIAS EXACTAS, FISICO-QUIMICAS Y NATURALES. REVISTA. Text in English, French, German, Spanish. 1916. irreg. price varies. **Document type:** *Journal, Academic/Scholarly.*
Indexed: CCMJ, CIN, CIS, ChemAb, ChemTitl, GeoRef, IBR, IBZ, IECT, Inspec, MSN, MathR, RefZh, SpeleolAb, Z02.
—BLDSC (7801.000000), AskIEEE, CASDDS, INIST, Linda Hall. **CCC.**
Published by: Academia de Ciencias Exactas Fisico-Quimicas y Naturales, Facultad de Ciencias, C Pedro Cerbuna, 12, Zaragoza, 50009, Spain. TEL 34-976-761128, FAX 34-976-761125, acz@posta.unizar.es. Ed. J Casas.

500 510 VEN ISSN 0366-1652
Q33 CODEN: BOCVAE
➤ **ACADEMIA DE CIENCIAS FISICAS MATEMATICAS Y NATURALES. BOLETIN.** Text in Spanish. 1934. 2/yr. free. bibl.; charts; illus. back issues avail. **Document type:** *Journal, Academic/Scholarly.*
Indexed: C01, ChemAb, GeoRef, MathR, SpeleolAb, Z01, Z02.
—Linda Hall.
Published by: Academia de Ciencias Fisicas Matematicas y Naturales, Palacio de las Academias, Apdo 1421, Caracas, DF 1010-A, Venezuela. TEL 58-212-4834133, FAX 58-212-4846611, acfiman@cantv.net, http://www.academiasnacionales.gov.ve. Ed. Eugenio de Bellard-Pietri. Circ: 500.

500 ARG ISSN 0325-2051
Q33 CODEN: BANCAG
ACADEMIA NACIONAL DE CIENCIAS. BOLETIN. Text in Spanish. 1874. m.
Indexed: B25, BIOSIS Prev, C01, CCMJ, GeoRef, IBR, IBZ, Inspec, MSN, MathR, MycolAb, P30, Z02.
—Linda Hall.
Published by: Academia Nacional de Ciencias, Velez Sarfield 229, Casilla de Correo 36, Cordoba, 5000, Argentina.

500 ARG ISSN 0365-1185
Q33 CODEN: ACFBAA
ACADEMIA NACIONAL DE CIENCIAS EXACTAS, FISICAS Y NATURALES DE BUENOS AIRES. ANALES. Text in Spanish. 1928. irreg. **Document type:** *Monographic series, Academic/Scholarly.*
Indexed: CABA, E12, GeoRef, I11, INIS AtomInd, N02, R07, S13, S16, W11, Z01.
—INIST, Linda Hall.
Published by: Academia Nacional de Ciencias Exactas, Fisicas y Naturales, Av Alvear 1711, 4 piso, Buenos Aires, 1014, Argentina. TEL 54-1-4811-2998, FAX 54-1-4811-6951, acad@ancefn.org.ar.

500 ARG ISSN 0327-5426
ACADEMIA NACIONAL DE CIENCIAS EXACTAS, FISICAS Y NATURALES DE BUENOS AIRES. MONOGRAFIAS. Text in Spanish. 1982. irreg. **Document type:** *Monographic series, Academic/Scholarly.*
Indexed: GeoRef, Z01.
Published by: Academia Nacional de Ciencias Exactas, Fisicas y Naturales, Av Alvear 1711, 4 piso, Buenos Aires, 1014, Argentina. TEL 54-1-4811-2998, FAX 54-1-4811-6951, acad@ancefn.org.ar.

500 ARG
ACADEMIA NACIONAL DE CIENCIAS EXACTAS, FISICAS Y NATURALES DE BUENOS AIRES. NOTICIAS. Text in Spanish. 1998. irreg. **Document type:** *Monographic series, Academic/Scholarly.*
Published by: Academia Nacional de Ciencias Exactas, Fisicas y Naturales, Av Alvear 1711, 4 piso, Buenos Aires, 1014, Argentina. TEL 54-1-4811-2998, FAX 54-1-4811-6951, acad@ancefn.org.ar.

500 ARG ISSN 0325-3406
Q33 CODEN: ANCMC5
ACADEMIA NACIONAL DE CIENCIAS. MISCELANEA. Text in Spanish. 1920. irreg.
Indexed: C01, GeoRef, IBR, IBZ, Z01.
—Linda Hall.
Published by: Academia Nacional de Ciencias, Velez Sarfield 229, Casilla de Correo 36, Cordoba, 5000, Argentina.

500 BEL
CODEN: MKAWAW
ACADEMIAE ANALECTA. KLASSE VAN DE NATUURWETENSCHAPPEN. Text in Dutch, English; Summaries in English. 1938. irreg., latest vol.60, no.1, 1998. price varies. back issues avail. **Document type:** *Monographic series, Academic/Scholarly.*
Former titles: Koninklijke Academie voor Wetenschappen, Letteren en Schone Kunsten van Belgie. Mededelingen. Klasse der Wetenschappen (0770-1098); (until 1972): Koninklijke Vlaamse Academie voor Wetenschappen, Letteren en Schone Kunsten van Belgie. Mededelingen. Klasse der Wetenschappen (0369-285X)
Indexed: GeoRef, Inspec, P30, SpeleolAb.
—AskIEEE, CASDDS, INIST, Linda Hall.
Published by: Koninklijke Vlaamse Academie van Belgie voor Wetenschappen en Kunsten/The Royal Flemish Academy of Belgium for Science and the Arts, Hertogsstraat 1, Brussels, 1000, Belgium. TEL 32-2-5502323, FAX 32-2-5502325, info@kvab.be, http://www.kvab.be. Ed. G Verbeke. Circ: 600. **Dist. by:** Brepols Publishers, Begijnhof 67, Turnhout 2300, Belgium. TEL 32-14-402500, FAX 32-14-428919.

500 600 BGR ISSN 1311-4360
Q1.A3
ACADEMIC OPEN INTERNET JOURNAL. Text in English. 2000. bi-m. adv. **Document type:** *Journal, Academic/Scholarly.* **Description:** Publishes papers from scientists from around the world.
Media: Online - full text.
Indexed: Inspec.
Published by: Bourgas University, Technical College, Aleksandrovska 101 Str, Bourgas, 8000, Bulgaria. TEL 359-56-26182, FAX 359-56-26182, info@acadjournal.com. Eds. Andrey Nenov, Sotir Sotirov.

▼ **ACADEMIC RESEARCH INTERNATIONAL.** *see* HUMANITIES: COMPREHENSIVE WORKS

ACADEMICA. *see* HUMANITIES: COMPREHENSIVE WORKS

500 FRA ISSN 0065-0552
Q46
ACADEMIE DES SCIENCES. ANNUAIRE. Text in French. 1917. a. **Document type:** *Academic/Scholarly.* **Description:** Informs readers of the present state of l'Academie des Sciences, list of prizes and grants available at the university, member addresses.
Indexed: RASB.
—Linda Hall.
Published by: Academie des Sciences, 23 Quai Conti, Paris, 75006, France. TEL 33-1-44414385, FAX 33-1-44414354.

ACADEMIE DES SCIENCES. COMPTES RENDUS. BIOLOGIES. *see* BIOLOGY

500 FRA ISSN 1631-0713
QE1 CODEN: CRSPEA
➤ **ACADEMIE DES SCIENCES. COMPTES RENDUS. GEOSCIENCE.** Text and summaries in English, French. 1836. 12/yr. EUR 595 in Europe to institutions; EUR 419.10 in France to institutions; JPY 58,400 in Japan to institutions; USD 673 elsewhere to institutions (effective 2012). charts; illus. Index. **Document type:** *Journal, Academic/Scholarly.* **Description:** Covers the fields of climate and environment, geosciences of the surface, oceanography, stratigraphy, tectonics, geodynamics, and the history of science.
Formerly (until 2001): Academie des Sciences. Comptes Rendus. Serie 2a. Sciences de la Terre et des Planetes (1251-8050); Which superseded in part (in 1994): Academie des Sciences. Comptes Rendus. Serie 2. Mecanique, Physique, Chimie, Sciences de la Terre, Sciences de l'Univers (0764-4450); Which was formerly (until 1984): Academie des Sciences. Comptes Rendus des Sciences. Serie 2: Mecanique - Physique, Chimie, Sciences de l'Univers, Sciences de la Terre (0750-7623); (until 1981): Academie des Sciences. Comptes Rendus des Seances. Serie 2: Mecanique, Physique, Chimie, Sciences de la Terre, Sciences de l'Univers (0249-6305); Which was formed by the 1981 merger of: Academie des Sciences. Comptes Rendus Hebdomadaires des Seances. Serie B: Sciences Physiques (0335-5993); Academie des Sciences. Comptes Rendus Hebdomadaires des Seances. Serie C: Sciences Chimiques (0567-6541)
Related titles: Microform ed.: (from PMC); Online - full text ed.: ISSN 1778-7025 (from IngentaConnect, ScienceDirect); Abridged ed.
Indexed: A&AAb, A01, A03, A08, A20, A22, A26, A33, A36, A37, ASCA, ASFA, AgrForAb, ApMecR, B21, BA, C25, C30, CA, CABA, CIN, ChemAb, ChemTitl, CurCont, E12, ESPM, F08, F12, FCA, FR, G11, GEOBASE, GH, GeoRef, GeotechAb, I05, I11, INIS AtomInd, ISR, IndMed, Inspec, M&GPA, MaizeAb, MathR, OR, P33, P37, P39, PetrolAb, PhysBer, R08, R11, R12, RefZh, S12, S13, S16, SCI, SCOPUS, SpeleolAb, T02, T05, TAR, TriticAb, VITIS, VS, W07, W11, Z01.
—BLDSC (3384.692000), AskIEEE, CASDDS, IE, Ingenta, INIST, Linda Hall, PADDS. **CCC.**
Published by: (Academie des Sciences), Elsevier Masson (Subsidiary of: Elsevier Health Sciences), 62 Rue Camille Desmoulins, Issy les Moulineaux, Cedex 92442, France. TEL 33-1-71165500, FAX 33-1-71165600, infos@elsevier-masson.fr. Eds. J. Touret, M. Herbillon. Circ: 3,200.

500 800 FRA ISSN 1146-7282
AS162
ACADEMIE DES SCIENCES ET LETTRES DE MONTPELLIER. BULLETIN MENSUEL. Text in French. 1909. m. **Document type:** *Bulletin, Academic/Scholarly.*
Indexed: FR.
—INIST, Linda Hall.
Published by: Academie des Sciences et Lettres de Montpellier, 60 rue des Etats Generaux, Montpellier, 34965, France. TEL 33-4-67134394.

500 FRA ISSN 1631-0462
ACADEMIE DES SCIENCES. LETTRE. Text in French. 1966. 3/yr. back issues avail. **Document type:** *Journal, Academic/Scholarly.*
Supersedes in part (in 2001): Academie des sciences et du CADAS. Lettre (1250-5331); Which was formerly (until 1993): Nouvelles de l'Academie (0246-1226); Which superseded in part (in 1984): Comptes Rendus des Seances de l'Academie des Sciences. Vie Academique (0249-6321); Which was formerly (until 1979): Comptes Rendus Hebdomadaires des Seances de l'Academie des Sciences. Vie Academique (0151-0525)
Related titles: Online - full text ed.: ISSN 2102-5398. free.
Indexed: CIS.
—Linda Hall.
Published by: Academie des Sciences, 23 Quai Conti, Paris, 75006, France. TEL 33-1-44414385, FAX 33-1-44414354, http://www.academie-sciences.fr.

500 FRA ISSN 1635-8597
Q46
➤ **ACADEMIE LORRAINE DE SCIENCES. BULLETIN.** Text in French. 1889. q. adv. bk.rev. **Document type:** *Journal, Academic/Scholarly.*
Former titles (until 2001): Academie et Societe Lorraines de Sciences. Bulletin (0567-6576); (until 1963): Societe Lorraine des Sciences. Bulletin (0366-340X); (until 1961): Societe des Sciences de Nancy. Bulletin Mensuel (1155-1119); (until 1936): Societe des Sciences de Nancy. Bulletin (1155-1100); (until 1920): Societe des Sciences de Nancy. Bulletin de Seances (1155-1097); Which incorporated (1873-1899): Societe des Sciences de Nancy. Bulletin (0366-3604)
Related titles: Microfilm ed.; Online - full text ed.
Indexed: B25, BIOSIS Prev, ChemAb, FR, GeoRef, IBR, IBZ, MycolAb, P30, RefZh, SpeleolAb, VITIS, Z01.
—INIST, Linda Hall.
Published by: Academie Lorraine des Sciences, Communaute Urbaine du Grand Nancy, 22-24 Viaduc Kennedy, C.O.36, Nancy, 54035, France. TEL 33-06-11539022. Adv. contact JM Keller. Circ: 600.

500 001.3 MDG ISSN 1021-0474
DT469.M21 CODEN: BUMTAW
ACADEMIE MALGACHE. BULLETIN D'INFORMATION ET DE LIAISON. Text in French. 1902. 2/yr. **Document type:** *Bulletin.*
Formerly (until 1988): Academie Malgache. Bulletin (0366-4473)
Indexed: GeoRef, PLESA, SpeleolAb.
Published by: Academie Malgache, Tsimbazaza, BP 6217, Antananarivo, Madagascar.

500 MDG ISSN 0374-9002
DT469.M21 CODEN: MEACAW
ACADEMIE MALGACHE. MEMOIRES. Text in French. 1926. irreg. **Document type:** *Monographic series.*
Indexed: GeoRef, SpeleolAb.
Published by: Academie Malgache, Tsimbazaza, BP 6217, Antananarivo, Madagascar.

ACADEMIE ROYALE DES SCIENCES, DES LETTRES ET DES BEAUX-ARTS DE BELGIQUE. ANNUAIRE. *see* HUMANITIES: COMPREHENSIVE WORKS

500 BEL ISSN 0001-4141
AS242 CODEN: BCSAAF
ACADEMIE ROYALE DES SCIENCES, DES LETTRES ET DES BEAUX-ARTS DE BELGIQUE. CLASSE DES SCIENCES. BULLETIN. Text in French. 1832. s-a. EUR 45 per issue (effective 2003). charts; illus.; stat.; abstr. index. 250 p./no.; **Document type:** *Bulletin, Academic/Scholarly.*
Supersedes in part (in 1899): Academie Royale des Sciences, des Lettres et des Beaux-Arts de Belgique. Bulletins (0770-7509); Which was formerly (until 1846): Academie Royale des Sciences et Belles-Lettres de Bruxelles. Bulletins (0770-7355)
Indexed: CCMJ, ChemAb, GeoRef, H09, H10, IBR, IBZ, Inspec, MSN, MathR, P30, PCI, S05, SpeleolAb, Z02.
—AskIEEE, CASDDS, INIST, Linda Hall.
Published by: Academie Royale des Sciences, des Lettres et des Beaux-Arts de Belgique/Koninklijke Vlaamse Academie van Belgie voor Wetenschappen en Kunsten, Palais des Academies, Rue Ducale 1, Brussels, 1000, Belgium. TEL 32-2-5502211, FAX 32-2-25502205, arb@cfwb.be, http://www.arb.cfwb.be. Ed. Leo Houziaux. Adv. contact Beatrice Denuit TEL 32-2-5502221. Circ: 600 (controlled).

500 BEL ISSN 0365-0936
QA483 CODEN: ABSCA3
ACADEMIE ROYALE DES SCIENCES, DES LETTRES ET DES BEAUX-ARTS DE BELGIQUE. CLASSE DES SCIENCES. MEMOIRES. Text in French. 1904. irreg. price varies. 200 p./no.; **Document type:** *Monographic series.*
Indexed: CCMJ, GeoRef, Inspec, MSN, MathR, SpeleolAb, Z02.
—AskIEEE, CASDDS, INIST, Linda Hall.
Published by: Academie Royale des Sciences, des Lettres et des Beaux-Arts de Belgique/Koninklijke Vlaamse Academie van Belgie voor Wetenschappen en Kunsten, Palais des Academies, Rue Ducale 1, Brussels, 1000, Belgium. TEL 32-2-5502211, FAX 32-2-25502205, http://www.arb.cfwb.be. Ed. Leo Houziaux. Adv. contact Beatrice Denuit TEL 32-2-5502221. Circ: 500 (controlled).

500 940 BEL ISSN 0001-4176
JV2802 CODEN: AOBSAN
ACADEMIE ROYALE DES SCIENCES D'OUTRE-MER. BULLETIN DES SEANCES/KONINKLIJKE ACADEMIE VOOR OVERZEESE WETENSCHAPPEN. MEDEDELINGEN DER ZITTINGEN. Text in Dutch, French. 1929; N.S. 1955. q. bk.rev. illus.; charts. index, cum.index every 10 yrs. Supplement avail.; back issues avail. **Document type:** *Proceedings, Academic/Scholarly.*
Former titles (until 1959): Academie Royale des Sciences Coloniales. Bulletin des Seances (0365-6578); (until 1954): Institut Royal Colonial Belge. Bulletin des Seances (0367-6935)
Indexed: A34, AICP, ASD, AgrForAb, BA, BP, BibLing, CABA, CCA, ChemAb, E12, F08, F12, FR, GH, GeoRef, H16, HistAb, I11, N02, N03, O01, P30, R12, RASB, RILM, RefZh, S13, S16, SpeleolAb, T05, VS, W11, Z01.
—BLDSC (2895.015000), CASDDS, INIST, Linda Hall.
Published by: Academie Royale des Sciences d'Outre-Mer/Koninklijke Academie voor Overzeese Wetenschappen, Defacqzstraat 1/3, Brussels, 1000, Belgium. TEL 32-2-538-0211, FAX 32-2-539-2353, kaowarsom@skynet.be, http://users.skynet.be/kaowarsom. Ed. Y Verhasselt.

500 610 BEL ISSN 0379-1920
ACADEMIE ROYALE DES SCIENCES D'OUTRE-MER. CLASSE DES SCIENCES NATURELLES ET MEDICALES. COLLECTION IN 4. Text in French. 1960. q.
Formerly (until 1963): Academie Royale des Sciences d'Outre-Mer. Classe des Sciences Naturelles et Medicales. Collection in 4. Memoires (0777-155X)
Indexed: GeoRef, Z01.
Published by: Academie Royale des Sciences d'Outre-Mer/Koninklijke Academie voor Overzeese Wetenschappen, Defacqzstraat 1/3, Brussels, 1000, Belgium.

500 BEL ISSN 0770-1896
ACADEMIE ROYALE DES SCIENCES D'OUTRE-MER. CLASSE DES SCIENCES NATURELLES ET MEDICALES. COLLECTION IN 8/KONINKLIJKE ACADEMIE VOOR OVERZEESE WETENSCHAPPEN. KLASSE VOOR NATUUR- EN GENEESKUNDIGE WETENSCHAPPEN. VERZAMELING IN 8. Text in Dutch, English, French. 1931; N.S. 1955. irreg., latest vol.24, no.4, 1999. price varies. back issues avail. **Document type:** *Monographic series, Academic/Scholarly.*
Former titles (until 1964): Academie Royale des Sciences d'Outre-Mer. Classe des Sciences Naturelles et Medicales. Memoires - Collection in 8 (0567-6606); (until 1960): Academie Royale des Sciences Coloniales. Classe des Sciences Naturelles et Medicales. Memoires - Collection in 8 (0770-6766); (until 1954): Institut Royal Colonial Belge. Section des Sciences Naturelles et Medicales. Memoires - Collection in 8 (0367-6994)
Indexed: SpeleolAb.
—INIST, Linda Hall.
Published by: Academie Royale des Sciences d'Outre-Mer/Koninklijke Academie voor Overzeese Wetenschappen, Defacqzstraat 1/3, Brussels, 1000, Belgium. TEL 32-2-5384772, FAX 32-2-5392353. Ed. Y Verhasselt.

500 940 BEL ISSN 0373-7063
CODEN: AOTMAR
ACADEMIE ROYALE DES SCIENCES D'OUTRE-MER. CLASSE DES SCIENCES TECHNIQUES. COLLECTION IN 4. Text in French. 1960. q.
Formerly (until 1963): Academie Royale des Sciences d'Outre-Mer. Classe des Sciences Techniques. Collection in 4. Memoires (0770-6618)
Indexed: GeoRef.
—INIST, Linda Hall.
Published by: Academie Royale des Sciences d'Outre-Mer/Koninklijke Academie voor Overzeese Wetenschappen, Defacqzstraat 1/3, Brussels, 1000, Belgium.

500 BEL ISSN 0777-1525
ACADEMIE ROYALE DES SCIENCES D'OUTRE-MER. CLASSE DES SCIENCES TECHNIQUES. COLLECTION IN 8/KONINKLIJKE ACADEMIE VOOR OVERZEESE WETENSCHAPPEN. KLASSE VOOR TECHNISCHE WETENSCHAPPEN. VERZAMELING IN 8. Text in Dutch, English, French. 1930; N.S. 1955. irreg., latest vol.19, no.2, 1997. price varies. back issues avail. **Document type:** *Monographic series, Academic/Scholarly.*
Former titles (until 1964): Academie Royale des Sciences d'Outre-Mer, Classe des Sciences techniques. Memoires in 8 (0777-1517); (until 1960): Academie Royales des Sciences Coloniales. Classe des Sciences Techniques. Memoires in 8 (0777-1509); (until 1955): Institut Royal Colonial Belge. Section des Sciences Techniques. Memoires - Collection in 8 (0777-1487)
Indexed: SpeleolAb.
Published by: Academie Royale des Sciences d'Outre-Mer/Koninklijke Academie voor Overzeese Wetenschappen, Defacqzstraat 1/3, Brussels, 1000, Belgium. TEL 32-2-5380211, FAX 32-2-5392353. Ed. Y Verhasselt.

500 570 SRB ISSN 0352-5740
QH7 CODEN: BASNA6
ACADEMIE SERBE DES SCIENCES ET DES ARTS. CLASSE DES SCIENCES MATHEMATIQUES ET NATURELLES. BULLETIN SCIENCES NATURELLES. Text in French. 1952. s-a. price varies. **Document type:** *Journal, Academic/Scholarly.*
Supersedes in part: Academie Serbe des Sciences et des Arts. Classe des Sciences Mathematiques et Naturelles. Bulletin. Nouvelle Serie (0001-4184)
Related titles: ◆ Serbo-Croatian ed.: Srpska Akademija Nauka i Umetnosti. Odeljenje Prirodno-Matematickih Nauka. Glas. ISSN 0374-7956.
Indexed: B25, BIOSIS Prev, CIN, ChemAb, ChemTitl, GeoRef, IBR, IBZ, MinerAb, MycolAb, RefZh, Z01.
—CASDDS, INIST, Linda Hall.
Published by: Srpska Akademija Nauka i Umetnosti/Serbian Academy of Arts and Sciences, Knez Mihailova 35, Belgrade, 11000. TEL 381-11-2027154, FAX 381-11-2027178, izdavacka@sanu.ac.rs, http://www.sanu.ac.rs. Ed. Vladimir Pantic. Circ: 1,000.

500 USA ISSN 1939-2966
Q11 CODEN: TNYAAE
➤ **ACADEMY EBRIEFINGS.** Text in English. 1881. irreg., latest 2010. free (effective 2010). adv. back issues avail.; reprints avail. **Document type:** *Monographic series, Academic/Scholarly.* **Description:** Designed to provide scientists the information in unique multimedia presentations that contains meeting summaries.
Formerly (until 2003): New York Academy of Sciences. Transactions (Print) (0028-7113)
Media: Online - full text. **Related titles:** Microform ed.: (from PQC).
Indexed: CADCAM, ChemAb, GeoRef, MathR, P06, P30, SpeleolAb.
—CASDDS, GNLM, INIST. **CCC.**
Published by: New York Academy of Sciences, 7 World Trade Ctr, 250 Greenwich St, 40th Fl, New York, NY 10007. TEL 212-298-8600, info@nyas.org. Adv. contact Alexis Clements TEL 212-298-8636.

500 USA ISSN 0096-7750
QH1
ACADEMY OF NATURAL SCIENCES OF PHILADELPHIA. MONOGRAPHS. Text in English. 1935. irreg., latest vol.22, 1982. price varies. bibl.; charts; illus.; stat. back issues avail. **Document type:** *Monographic series, Academic/Scholarly.* **Description:** Features larger systematic reviews of special taxonomic groups.
Indexed: GeoRef, SpeleolAb.
—Linda Hall. **CCC.**
Published by: Academy of Natural Sciences of Philadelphia, 1900 Benjamin Franklin Pky, Philadelphia, PA 19103. TEL 215-299-1000, scipubseditor@ansp.org.

500 USA ISSN 0097-3157
QH1 CODEN: PANPA5
➤ **ACADEMY OF NATURAL SCIENCES OF PHILADELPHIA. PROCEEDINGS.** Text in English. 1841. irreg. (2-3/yr). USD 45 per issue (effective 2010). bibl.; charts; illus.; stat. back issues avail.; reprints avail. **Document type:** *Proceedings, Academic/Scholarly.*
Related titles: Online - full text ed.: ISSN 1938-5293.
Indexed: A20, A22, A29, ASCA, ASFA, Agr, B&BAb, B19, B20, B21, B23, B25, BIOSIS Prev, BiolDig, CABA, CurCont, E01, E12, ESPM, F08, F12, GenetAb, GeoRef, H09, H10, H16, I10, IBR, IBZ, ISR, MycolAb, OR, P32, P40, PGegResA, R07, S05, S13, S16, SCI, SCOPUS, SWRA, SpeleolAb, VirolAbstr, W07, WildRev, Z01.
—BLDSC (6618.000000), IE, Infotrieve, Ingenta, INIST, Linda Hall. **CCC.**
Published by: Academy of Natural Sciences of Philadelphia, 1900 Benjamin Franklin Pky, Philadelphia, PA 19103. TEL 215-299-1000, scipubseditor@ansp.org.

500 USA ISSN 0097-3254
CODEN: AYSPAX
ACADEMY OF NATURAL SCIENCES OF PHILADELPHIA. SPECIAL PUBLICATIONS. Text in English. 1922. irreg., latest vol.21. price varies. bibl.; charts; illus.; stat. back issues avail. **Document type:** *Monographic series, Academic/Scholarly.*
Indexed: GeoRef, IBR, IBZ, SpeleolAb.
—Linda Hall. **CCC.**
Published by: Academy of Natural Sciences of Philadelphia, 1900 Benjamin Franklin Pky, Philadelphia, PA 19103. TEL 215-299-1000, scipubseditor@ansp.org.

S

500 ITA ISSN 0515-2143
Q54
ACCADEMIA DELLE SCIENZE DELL'ISTITUTO DI BOLOGNA. ATTI. CLASSI DI SCIENZE FISICHE. MEMORIE. Text in Italian. 1907. irreg. **Document type:** *Journal, Academic/Scholarly.*
Formerly (until 1912): Reale Accademia delle Scienze dell'Istituto di Bologna. Atti. Classi di Scienze Fisiche. Memorie (0376-0847)
Indexed: Inspec, P30.
—INIST.
Published by: Universita degli Studi di Bologna, Accademia delle Scienze dell'Istituto di Bologna, Via Zamboni 31, Bologna, 40126, Italy. TEL 39-051-222596, FAX 39-051-265249, http://www.unibo.it/Portale/Divulgazione+scientifica/Accademia/default.htm.

500 ITA ISSN 0365-0057
ACCADEMIA DELLE SCIENZE DELL'ISTITUTO DI BOLOGNA. ATTI. CLASSI DI SCIENZE FISICHE. RENDICONTI. Text in Italian. 1954. s-a. **Document type:** *Journal, Academic/Scholarly.*
Indexed: GeoRef, IBR, IBZ, Inspec, Z02.
—INIST, Linda Hall.
Published by: Universita degli Studi di Bologna, Accademia delle Scienze dell'Istituto di Bologna, Via Zamboni 31, Bologna, 40126, Italy. TEL 39-051-222596, FAX 39-051-265249, http://www.unibo.it/Portale/Divulgazione+scientifica/Accademia/default.htm.

500.2 510 ITA ISSN 0001-4419
Q54 CODEN: AATFAA
ACCADEMIA DELLE SCIENZE DI TORINO. ATTI. CLASSE DI SCIENZE FISICHE, MATEMATICHE E NATURALI. Text in Italian. 1866. bi-m. price varies. charts; illus. cum.index: vols. 50-100. **Document type:** *Journal, Academic/Scholarly.*
Formerly (until 1946): Reale Accademia delle Scienze di Torino. Atti. Part 1. Classe di Scienze Fisiche, Matematiche e Naturali; Which superseded in part (in 1927): Reale Accademia delle Scienze di Torino. (1122-1364)
Related titles: Supplement(s): Accademia delle Scienze di Torino. Atti. Classe di Scienze Fisiche, Matematiche e Naturali. Supplementi. ISSN 1971-5781.
Indexed: ApMecR, CCMJ, ChemAb, IBR, IBZ, Inspec, MSN, MathR, Z01, Z02.
—CASDDS, INIST, Linda Hall.
Published by: Accademia delle Scienze di Torino, Via Maria Vittoria 3, Turin, 10123, Italy. TEL 39-011-5620047, FAX 39-011-532619, info@accademia.csi.it, http://www.accademiadellescienze.it. Circ: 600.

500 ITA ISSN 1120-1630
ACCADEMIA DELLE SCIENZE DI TORINO. MEMORIE. CLASSE DI SCIENZE FISICHE, MATEMATICHE E NATURALI. Text in Italian, English. 1759. a., latest vol.25, 2001. charts; illus. back issues avail. **Document type:** *Journal, Academic/Scholarly.*
Former titles (until 1951): Reale Accademia delle Scienze di Torino. Memorie. Part 1. Classe di Scienze Fisiche, Matematiche e Naturali (1120-1614); Which superseded in part (in 1915): Reale Accademia delle Scienze di Torino. Memorie (1120-1592); Which was formerly (until 1818): Academie Royale des Sciences de Turin (1120-1576); Which was formed by the 1813 merger of: Academie Imperiale des Sciences Litterature et Beaux-Arts de Turin. Memoires. Sciences Physiques et Mathematiques (1120-1568); Academie Imperiale des Sciences Litterature et Beaux-Arts de Turin. Memoires. Litterature et Beaux-Arts (1120-1584); both of which superseded (in 1803): Academie des Sciences de Turin. Memoires (1120-1533); (1786-1793): Academie Royale des Sciences de Turin. Memoires (1120-1525); (1761-1773): Societe de Turin. Melanges de Philosophie et de Mathematiques (1120-1517); (until 1761): Societatis Privatae Taurinensis. Miscellanea Philosophico Mathematica (1120-1509)
Indexed: CCMJ, MSN, MathR.
—INIST.
Published by: Accademia delle Scienze di Torino, Via Maria Vittoria 3, Turin, 10123, Italy. TEL 39-011-5620047, FAX 39-011-532619, info@accademia.csi.it, http://www.accademiadellescienze.it. Circ: 600.

500 ITA ISSN 1125-0402
ACCADEMIA DELLE SCIENZE DI TORINO. QUADERNI. Text in Multiple languages. 1995. irreg. **Document type:** *Monographic series, Academic/Scholarly.*
Indexed: CCMJ, MSN, MathR.
Published by: Accademia delle Scienze di Torino, Via Maria Vittoria 3, Turin, 10123, Italy. TEL 39-011-5620047, FAX 39-011-532619, info@accademia.csi.it, http://www.accademiadellescienze.it.

500 ITA ISSN 0370-3568
Q54.N2 CODEN: RASFAM
ACCADEMIA DELLE SCIENZE FISICHE E MATEMATICHE. RENDICONTO. Text in Italian. 1862. a. EUR 25 domestic; EUR 31.50 in the European Union; EUR 38.50 elsewhere (effective 2008). bibl.; illus.; stat. back issues avail. **Document type:** *Proceedings, Academic/Scholarly.*
Former titles (until 1861): Reale Accademia delle Scienze di Napoli. Rendiconto (0393-6945); (until 1857): Societa Reale Borbonica. Accademia delle Scienze. Rendiconto (0393-6937); (1842-1850): Societa Reale Borbonica di Napoli. Sezione Accademia delle Scienze. Rendiconto delle Adunanze e de' Lavori (0393-6929)
Indexed: CCMJ, GeoRef, MSN, MathR, Z02.
—INIST, Linda Hall.
Published by: (Accademia delle Scienze di Napoli), Liguori Editore, Via Posillipo 394, Naples, 80123, Italy. TEL 39-081-7206111, FAX 39-081-7206244, liguori@liguori.it, http://www.liguori.it. Pub. Guido Liguori. Circ: 600.

500 ITA ISSN 1122-651X
Q54
ACCADEMIA LIGURE DI SCIENZE E LETTERE. ATTI. Text in English, French, Italian. 1890. a. **Document type:** *Journal, Academic/Scholarly.*
Former titles (until 1946): Reale Accademia Ligure di Scienze e Lettere. Atti (0365-0278); (until 1941): Accademia Ligure di Scienze e Lettere. Atti (1941) (0392-2219); (until 1940): Societa di Scienze e Lettere di Genova. Atti (1122-6501); (until 1935): Societa Linguistica di Scienze e Lettere. Atti (1122-6498); (until 1921): Societa Linguistica di Scienze Naturali e Geografiche. Atti (1122-648X)
Indexed: CCMJ, ChemAb, GeoRef, IBR, IBZ, Inspec, MLA-IB, MSN, MathR, SpeleolAb, Z02.
—INIST, Linda Hall.
Published by: Accademia Ligure di Scienze e Lettere, Palazzo Ducale, Piazza Giacomo Matteotti, 5, Genoa, GE 16123, Italy. TEL 39-010-565570, FAX 39-010-566080. Circ: 800.

500 ITA ISSN 0365-0359
QC1 CODEN: AAPFAO
➤ **ACCADEMIA PELORITANA DEI PERICOLANTI. CLASSE DI SCIENZE FISICHE MATEMATICHE E NATURALI. ATTI.** Text in Multiple languages. 1878. irreg. **Document type:** *Journal, Academic/Scholarly.*
Supersedes in part (in 1944): Accademia Peloritana dei Pericolanti. Classe di Scienze Fisiche, Matematiche e Biologiche (0365-5520); Which was formerly (until 1935): Reale Accademia Peloritana. Atti (0365-592X)
Related titles: Online - full text ed.: ISSN 1825-1242. 2004. free (effective 2011).
Indexed: A01, CA, Inspec, T02, Z02.
—Linda Hall.
Published by: Accademia Peloritana dei Pericolanti, Piazza Pugliatti 1, Messina, 98122, Italy. TEL 39-090-6764874, FAX 39-090-6764875.

500 ITA ISSN 0365-0294
CODEN: AAMBAV
ACCADEMIA PELORITANA DEI PERICOLANTI. CLASSE DI SCIENZE MEDICO - BIOLOGICHE. ATTI. Text in Multiple languages. 1878. a. **Document type:** *Journal, Academic/Scholarly.*
Supersedes in part (in 1942): Accademia Peloritana dei Pericolanti. Classe di Scienze Fisiche, Matematiche e Biologiche. Atti (0365-5520); Which was formerly (until 1935): Reale Accademia Peloritana. Atti (0365-592X)
—Linda Hall.
Published by: Accademia Peloritana dei Pericolanti, Piazza Pugliatti 1, Messina, 98122, Italy. TEL 39-090-6764874, FAX 39-090-6764875.

623 510 530 ITA ISSN 1124-0350
ACCADEMIA ROVERETANA DEGLI AGIATI. ATTI. FASC. B: CLASSE DI SCIENZE MATEMATICHE, FISICHE E NATURALI. Text in Italian. a. **Document type:** *Journal, Academic/Scholarly.*
Indexed: Z01.
Published by: Accademia Roveretana degli Agiati, di Scienze, Lettere ed Arti, Piazza Rosmini 5, Rovereto, TN I-38068, Italy. TEL 39-0464-436663, FAX 39-0464-487672, info@agiati.org, http://www.agiati.org.

500 ITA ISSN 0392-0836
DG402
ACCADEMIA TOSCANA DI SCIENZE E LETTERE LA COLOMBARIA. ATTI E MEMORIE. Text in Italian. N.S. 1947. a., latest vol.66, 2001. price varies. **Document type:** *Monographic series, Academic/Scholarly.*
Indexed: B24, BibLing, DIP, IBR, IBZ, MLA-IB, P30.
Published by: (Accademia Toscana di Scienze e Lettere La Colombaria), Casa Editrice Leo S. Olschki, Viuzzo del Pozzetto 8, Florence, 50126, Italy. TEL 39-055-6530684, FAX 39-055-6530214, celso@olschki.it, http://www.olschki.it.

500 060 ITA ISSN 0065-0781
ACCADEMIA TOSCANA DI SCIENZE E LETTERE LA COLOMBARIA. STUDI. Text in Italian. 1953. irreg., latest vol.196, 2001. price varies. **Document type:** *Monographic series, Academic/Scholarly.*
Indexed: AIAP, DIP, IBR, IBZ, RASB.
Published by: (Accademia Toscana di Scienze e Lettere La Colombaria), Casa Editrice Leo S. Olschki, Viuzzo del Pozzetto 8, Florence, 50126, Italy. TEL 39-055-6530684, FAX 39-055-6530214, celso@olschki.it, http://www.olschki.it. Circ: 1,000.

507.1 CAN ISSN 1193-7114
ACCELERATOR. Text in English. 1964. irreg. (2-3/yr.). CAD 20 foreign (effective 2000). adv. bk.rev. illus.; stat. **Document type:** *Newsletter.*
Former titles (until 1988): Accelerator Newsletter (0712-1377); (until 1980): Saskatchewan Science Teachers' Society. Newsletter (0712-1369); (until 1976): Saskatchewan Science Teachers' Society (0316-2893)
Media: Duplicated (not offset).
Indexed: C03, CEI, P11, P52, P56, PQC.
—CCC.
Published by: (Saskatchewan Science Teachers' Society), Saskatchewan Teachers' Federation, 2317 Arlington Ave., Saskatoon, SK S7J 2H8, Canada. stf@stf.sk.ca. Circ: 300.

500 USA ISSN 0898-9621
Q180.55.E9 CODEN: ARQAEZ
➤ **ACCOUNTABILITY IN RESEARCH**; policies and quality assurance. Text in English. 1989. bi-m. GBP 965 combined subscription in United Kingdom to institutions (print & online eds.); EUR 1,033, USD 1,289 combined subscription to institutions (print & online eds.) (effective 2012). adv. bk.rev. reprint service avail. from PSC. **Document type:** *Journal, Academic/Scholarly.* **Description:** Covers historical perspectives, data auditing, research policies, ethical issues, legal issues and standards for data analysis.
Related titles: Microfiche ed.; Microfilm ed.; Online - full text ed.: ISSN 1545-5815. GBP 868 in United Kingdom to institutions; EUR 930, USD 1,160 to institutions (effective 2012) (from IngentaConnect).
Indexed: A20, A22, B01, B06, B07, B09, CA, E01, EMBASE, ESPM, ExcerpMed, MEDLINE, P30, P48, P50, P52, P56, PQC, RiskAb, SCI, SCOPUS, SWR&A, T02, W07.
—IE, Infotrieve, Ingenta. **CCC.**
Published by: Taylor & Francis Inc. (Subsidiary of: Taylor & Francis Group), 325 Chestnut St, Ste 800, Philadelphia, PA 19106. TEL 215-625-2940, 800-354-1420, orders@taylorandfrancis.com, http://www.taylorandfrancis.com. Ed. Dr. Adil E Shamoo. Adv. contact Linda Hann TEL 44-1344-779945.

➤ **ACTA ACADEMIAE ABOENSIS, SERIES B: MATHEMATICA ET PHYSICA.** *see* MATHEMATICS

500 BRA ISSN 0044-5967
QH111 CODEN: AAMZAZ
➤ **ACTA AMAZONICA.** Text in English, Portuguese, Spanish. 1971. irreg. (1-3/yr.). BRL 75 domestic to individuals; USD 50 foreign to individuals; BRL 100 domestic to institutions; USD 100 foreign to institutions (effective 2005). bk.rev. back issues avail. **Document type:** *Journal, Academic/Scholarly.* **Description:** Publication in pure and applied sciences including botany, agronomy, aquatic biology, tropical pathology, forest research, zoology and wood technology.
Related titles: Online - full text ed.: free (effective 2011).
Indexed: A22, A34, A35, A36, A37, A38, ASFA, AgBio, AgrForAb, ApicAb, B21, B23, B25, BA, BIOSIS Prev, BP, C01, C25, C30, CABA, CIN, ChemAb, ChemTitl, ChemoAb, D01, E12, E17, ESPM, EntAb, F08, F11, F12, FCA, FR, G11, GH, GeoRef, H16, H17, HPNRM, I11, IBR, IBZ, INIS AtomInd, IndVet, LT, MaizeAb, MycolAb, N02, N03, N04, O01, OR, P32, P33, P37, P39, P40, PGegResA, PGrRegA, PHN&I, PN&I, R07, R08, R11, R12, R13, RA&MP, RM&VM, RRTA, S13, S16, S17, SCOPUS, SSciA, SWRA, SoyAb, SpeleolAb, T05, TAR, VS, W10, W11, WildRev, Z01.
—BLDSC (0593.100000), CASDDS, IE, Ingenta, INIST.
Published by: Instituto Nacional de Pesquisas da Amazonia, Av Andre Araujo, N 2936 Petropolis, PO Box 478, Manaus, AM 69083-000, Brazil. TEL 55-92-6433220, FAX 55-92-6433223, acta@inpa.gov.br. Ed. Ozorio Jose de Menezes Fonseca. Circ: 1,500.

500 VEN ISSN 0001-5504
Q22 CODEN: ACVEAU
➤ **ACTA CIENTIFICA VENEZOLANA.** Text in Spanish; Summaries in English, Spanish. 1950. 4/yr. VEB 200 domestic to institutions; USD 180 foreign to institutions (effective 2009). adv. bk.rev. abstr.; bibl.; charts; illus.; stat. index, cum.index. 70 p./no.; back issues avail. **Document type:** *Journal, Academic/Scholarly.* **Description:** Research papers and essays discussing general scientific problems, not exclusively based on original experimental results.
Related titles: Online - full text ed.; Supplement(s): Acta Cientifica Venezolana. Suplemento. ISSN 0375-8370.
Indexed: A22, ASCA, ASFA, B21, B25, BIOBASE, BIOSIS Prev, C01, CCMJ, CIN, CTO, ChemAb, ChemTitl, DBA, DIP, DentInd, EMBASE, ESPM, ExcerpMed, GeoRef, IABS, IBR, IBZ, INIS AtomInd, IndMed, MEDLINE, MSN, MathR, MycolAb, P30, SCOPUS, SpeleolAb, Z01, Z02.
—CASDDS, IE, Infotrieve, Ingenta, INIST.
Published by: Asociacion Venezolana para el Avance de la Ciencia, Av. Neveri, Colinas de Bello Monte, Apdo. 47286, Caracas, Venezuela. TEL 58-2-7521002, FAX 58-2-7511420. Ed., R&P, Adv. contact Juscelino Tovar Rodriguez. Circ: 500.

720 551 BRA ISSN 0102-1249
QE235 CODEN: AGLEDC
ACTA GEOLOGICA LEOPOLDENSIA. Text in Spanish, English, Portuguese. 1976. 2/yr. **Document type:** *Journal, Academic/Scholarly.*
Related titles: ◆ Series of: Estudos Tecnologicos. ISSN 0101-5303.
Indexed: GeoRef, SpeleolAb.
Published by: Universidade do Vale do Rio dos Sinos (UNISINOS), Av Unisinos 950, Sao Leopoldo, RS 93022-000, Brazil. TEL 55-51-5908131, FAX 55-51-5908132, http://www.unisinos.br.

500.9 610 DEU ISSN 0001-5857
Q1 CODEN: ACHLAG
ACTA HISTORICA LEOPOLDINA. Text in German. 1963. irreg., latest vol.56, 2010. price varies. bibl.; charts; illus. **Document type:** *Monographic series, Academic/Scholarly.*
Indexed: CCMJ, DIP, EMBASE, ExcerpMed, FR, IBR, IBZ, MEDLINE, MSN, MathR, P30, SCOPUS, Z02.
—INIST, Linda Hall.
Published by: (Deutsche Akademie der Naturforscher Leopoldina, Archiv fuer Geschichte der Naturforschung und Medizin), Wissenschaftliche Verlagsgesellschaft mbH, Postfach 101061, Stuttgart, 70009, Germany. TEL 49-711-25820, FAX 49-711-2582290, service@wissenschaftliche-verlagsgesellschaft.de, http://www.wissenschaftliche-verlagsgesellschaft.de. Circ: 1,200.

509 610.9 DNK ISSN 0065-1311
CODEN: AHSMA7
ACTA HISTORICA SCIENTIARUM NATURALIUM ET MEDICINALIUM. Text in English, German. 1942. irreg., latest vol.45, 2010. price varies. back issues avail. **Document type:** *Monographic series, Academic/Scholarly.*
Indexed: EMBASE, ExcerpMed, GeoRef, IndMed, MEDLINE, P30, SpeleolAb.
—GNLM, Infotrieve, Linda Hall. **CCC.**
Published by: (Denmark. Koebenhavns Universitetsbibliotek, Natur- og Sundhedsvidenskabelige Fakultetsbibliotek/Copenhagen University Library, Faculty Library of Natural- and Health Sciences), Museum Tusculanum Press, c/o University of Copenhagen, Njalsgade 126, Copenhagen S, 2300, Denmark. TEL 45-35-329109, FAX 45-35-329113, info@mtp.dk, http://www.mtp.dk. **Dist. by:** Editions Picard, Editions Picard, Paris 75006, France. TEL 33-1-43269778, FAX 33-1-43264264.

505 DNK ISSN 0105-6824
AS281
ACTA JUTLANDICA. NATURVIDENSKABELIG SERIE. Variant title: Natural Science Series. Naturvidenskabelig Serie. Text in Multiple languages. 1939. irreg. price varies. back issues avail. **Document type:** *Monographic series, Academic/Scholarly.*
Related titles: ◆ Series of: Acta Jutlandica. ISSN 0065-1354.
Published by: (Det Laerde Selskab i Aarhus), Aarhus Universitetsforlag/Aarhus University Press, Langelandsgade 177, Aarhus N, 8200, Denmark. TEL 45-89-425370, FAX 45-89-425380, unipress@au.dk.

500 616.99 PHL ISSN 0065-1370
CODEN: ACTMEF
ACTA MANILANA, SERIES A: NATURAL AND APPLIED SCIENCES. Text and summaries in English. 1965. a. PHP 80, USD 15 (effective 1999). back issues avail. **Document type:** *Academic/Scholarly.* **Description:** Papers dealing with all aspects of the natural sciences.
Indexed: B25, BAS, BIOSIS Prev, INIS AtomInd, IPP, Inspec, MycolAb.
—AskIEEE, IE, Ingenta, Linda Hall.
Published by: (University Of Santo Tomas, Research Center for the Natural Sciences), University of Santo Tomas Publishing House (U S T P H), Beato Angelico Bldg, Espana, Manila, Philippines. TEL 63-2-7313522 ext 8252/8278, FAX 63-2-7313522, http://www.ust.edu.ph. Circ: 500.

500 600 MEX ISSN 0567-7785
T4 CODEN: AMXCB4
ACTA MEXICANA DE CIENCIA Y TECNOLOGIA. Text in English, Spanish. 1967. irreg., latest vol.14, 1980. bibl.; charts; illus. index.
Indexed: C01, CIN, ChemAb, ChemTitl, Inspec, MathR, Z02.
—AskIEEE, CASDDS, INIST, Linda Hall.
Published by: Instituto Politecnico Nacional, Comision de Operacion y Fomento de Actividades Academicas, Unidad Profesional Zacatenco, Col Lindavista, Mexico City, DF 07738, Mexico. Circ: 1,000.

500 BRA ISSN 2177-3610
▼ **ACTA MONOGRAFICA.** Text in Portuguese. 2010. irreg. free (effective 2011). **Document type:** *Journal, Academic/Scholarly.*
Media: Online - full text.
Address: editor@actamonografica.org, http://www.actamonografica.org. Ed. Valdi Lopes Tutunji.

ACTA REGIAE SOCIETATIS SCIENTIARUM ET LITTERARUM GOTHOBURGENSIS. INTERDISCIPLINARIA. *see* HUMANITIES: COMPREHENSIVE WORKS

500 708.371 CZE ISSN 1801-5972
➤ **ACTA RERUM NATURALIUM.** Text in Czech. 2005. a. **Document type:** *Journal, Academic/Scholarly.* **Description:** Publishes original articles, points of view and reviews on all aspects of natural sciences.
Related titles: Online - full text ed.: ISSN 1803-1587.
Published by: Muzeum Vysociny Jihlava, Masarykovo nam 55, Jihlava, 58601, Czech Republic. TEL 420-56-7573893, muzeum@muzeum.ji.cz. Ed. Dr. Karel Maly.

500 USA ISSN 1947-7929
QC1
▼ ➤ **ACTA SCIENTIAE.** Text in English. 2009. irreg. back issues avail. **Document type:** *Journal, Academic/Scholarly.* **Description:** Publishes papers devoted to analysis of fundamental aspects of science.
Related titles: Online - full text ed.: ISSN 1947-7937. USD 49.95 (effective 2009).
Published by: New York Sofia Institute, 149 W 12th St, New York, NY 10011. TEL 212-463-7435, learnsmart101@newyorksofiainstitute.org, http://www.newyorksofiainstitute.org. Ed. Vesselin C Noninski.

500 610 MEX ISSN 0188-6266
AS63.A1 CODEN: ACUNFO
➤ **ACTA UNIVERSITARIA.** Text in Spanish; Summaries in English, Spanish. 1990. 3/yr. USD 45 foreign (effective 2011). bk.rev. abstr.; bibl.; charts; illus. **Document type:** *Journal, Academic/Scholarly.* **Description:** Publishes research and commentary on social, agricultural, and engineering sciences.
Related titles: Online - full text ed.: 2001. free (effective 2011).
Indexed: C01.
—BLDSC (0669.060000).
Published by: Universidad de Guanajuato, Direccion de Investigacion y Posgrado, Lascurain de Retana 5, Col Centro, Guanajuato, GTO 36000, Mexico. TEL 52-473-7320006, FAX 52-473-7329312. Ed., R&P Esperanza Vargas-Pacheco. Circ: 1,500.

➤ **ACTA UNIVERSITATIS GOTHOBURGENSIS.** *see* HUMANITIES: COMPREHENSIVE WORKS

500 FIN ISSN 0355-3191
Q1 CODEN: AUOADB
➤ **ACTA UNIVERSITATIS OULUENSIS. SERIES A. SCIENTIAE RERUM NATURALIUM.** Text in Multiple languages. 1971. irreg. back issues avail. **Document type:** *Monographic series, Academic/Scholarly.*
Related titles: Online - full text ed.: ISSN 1796-220X.
Indexed: CCMJ, GeoRef, INIS AtomInd, MSN, MathR, Z02.
—IE, Ingenta, Linda Hall.
Published by: Oulun Yliopisto, Julkaisupalvelut/University of Oulu. Publications Committee, Pentti Kaiteran Katu 1, PO Box 8000, Oulu, 90014, Finland. TEL 358-8-5531011, FAX 358-8-5534112, university.of.oulu@oulu.fi, http://www.oulu.fi. Eds. Mikko Siponen TEL 358-8-5531984, Olli Vuolteenaho TEL 358-8-5375302.

500 FIN ISSN 1455-1616
AS145.A1
ACTA UNIVERSITATIS TAMPERENSIS. Text in Finnish, English. 1965. irreg. **Document type:** *Monographic series, Academic/Scholarly.*
Former titles (until 1996): Acta Universitatis Tamperensis. Series A (0496-7909); (until 1966): Acta Academiae Socialis. Ser. A (0496-7887)
Indexed: CIS, MSN.
Published by: Tampereen Yliopisto/University of Tampere, Kalevantie 4, Tampere, Finland. TEL 358-3-355111, FAX 358-3-2134473, kirjaamo@uta.fi, http://www.uta.fi.

500 610 SWE ISSN 0346-5462
➤ **ACTA UNIVERSITATIS UPSALIENSIS.** Text in Multiple languages. 1861. irreg. price varies. bibl.; charts; illus. index. back issues avail. **Document type:** *Monographic series, Academic/Scholarly.*
Formerly (until 1960): Uppsala Universitets Aarsskrift (0372-4654)
Related titles: ◆ Series: Digital Comprehensive Summaries of Uppsala Dissertations from the Faculty of Social Sciences. ISSN 1652-9030; ◆ Uppsala Studies in History of Ideas. ISSN 1653-5197; ◆ Figura. Nova Series. ISSN 0071-481X; ◆ Statsvetenskapliga Foereningen i Uppsala. Skrifter. ISSN 0346-7538; ◆ Studia Historica Upsaliensia. ISSN 0081-6531; ◆ Studia Musicologica Upsaliensia. Nova Series. ISSN 0081-6744; ◆ Studia Philologiae Scandinavicae Upsaliensia. ISSN 0081-6809; ◆ Uppsala Studies in Education. ISSN 0347-1314; ◆ Studia Uralica Upsaliensia. ISSN 1101-7430; ◆ Symbolae Botanicae Upsalienses. ISSN 0082-0644; ◆ Studia Anglistica Upsaliensia. ISSN 0562-2719; ◆ Studia Ethnologica Upsaliensia. ISSN 0346-900X; ◆ Uppsala Studies in Cultural Anthropology. ISSN 0348-5099; ◆ Uppsala Studies in Economic History. ISSN 0346-6493; ◆ Historia Litterarum. ISSN 0440-9078; ◆ Studia Romanica Upsaliensia. ISSN 0562-3022; ◆ Studia Germanistica Upsaliensia. ISSN 0585-5160; ◆ Acta Bibliothecae R. Universitatis Upsaliensis. ISSN 0346-7465; ◆ Acta Instituti Upsaliensis Jurisprudentiae Comparativae. ISSN 0502-7497; ◆ Aesthetica Upsaliensia. ISSN 0349-6708; ◆ Boreas (Uppsala). ISSN 0346-6442; ◆ Comprehensive Summaries of Uppsala Dissertations from the Faculty of Arts. ISSN 1102-2043; ◆ Comprehensive Summaries of Uppsala Dissertations from the Faculty of Medicine. ISSN 0282-7476; ◆ Comprehensive Summaries of Uppsala Dissertations from the Faculty of Pharmacy. ISSN 0282-7484; ◆ Historia Religionum. ISSN 0439-2132; ◆ Nomina Germanica. ISSN 0349-3075; ◆ Studia Biblica Upsaliensia. ISSN 1101-878X; ◆ Studia Byzantina Upsaliensia. ISSN 0283-1244; ◆ Studia Celtica Upsaliensia. ISSN 1104-5515; ◆ Studia Graeca Upsaliensia. ISSN 0562-2743; ◆ Studia Historico-Ecclesiastica Upsaliensia. ISSN 0562-2751; ◆ Studia Indoeuropaea Upsaliensia. ISSN 0346-6469; ◆ Studia Psychologica Clinica Upsaliensia. ISSN 1100-3278; ◆ Studia Psychologica Upsaliensia. ISSN 0586-8858; ◆ Studia Philosophica Upsaliensia. ISSN 0585-5497; ◆ Studia Oeconomiae Negotiorum. ISSN 0586-884X; ◆ Studia Sociologica Upsaliensia. ISSN 0585-5551; ◆ Studia Statistica Upsaliensia. ISSN 1104-1560; ◆ Studier i Ide- och Laerdomshistoria. ISSN 0348-212X; ◆ Studies in Bioethics and Research Ethics. ISSN 1402-3148; ◆ Uppsala Studies in Social Ethics. ISSN 0346-6507; ◆ Uppsala Studies in Faith and Ideologies. ISSN 1102-7878; ◆ Uppsala Studies on Eastern Europe. ISSN 1104-6481; ◆ Uppsala Women's Studies. A, Women in Religion. ISSN 0283-944X; ◆ Studia Multiethnica Upsaliensia. ISSN 0282-6623; ◆ Uppsala North American Studies Series. ISSN 1104-0807; ◆ Psychologia et Sociologia Religionum. ISSN 0283-149X; ◆ Studia Iranica Upsaliensia. ISSN 1100-326X; ◆ Studia Latina Upsaliensia. ISSN 0562-2859; ◆ Studia Semitica Upsaliensia. ISSN 0585-5535; ◆ Studia Slavica Upsaliensia. ISSN 0562-3030; ◆ Nova Acta Regiae Societatis Scientiarum Upsaliensis. A, Astronomy and Mathematical Sciences. ISSN 0346-6523; ◆ Nova Acta Regiae Societatis Scientiarum Upsaliensis. C, Botany, General Geology, Physical Geography, Palaeontology and Zoology. ISSN 0374-5929; ◆ Skrifter Roerande Uppsala Universitet. B, Inbjudningar. ISSN 0566-3091; ◆ Uppsala Dissertations from the Faculty of Medicine. ISSN 0282-8928; ◆ Uppsala Dissertations from the Faculty of Science and Technology. ISSN 1104-2516; ◆ Skrifter Roerande Uppsala Universitet. C, Organisation och Historia. ISSN 0502-7454; ◆ Uppsala Women's Studies. B, Women in the Humanities. ISSN 0283-4995; ◆ Uppsala Studies in Media and Communication. ISSN 1651-4777; ◆ Studia Turcica Upsaliensia. ISSN 0346-6477; ◆ Comprehensive Summaries of Uppsala Dissertations from the Faculty of Science and Technology. ISSN 1104-232X; ◆ Ars Suetica. ISSN 0066-7919.
Indexed: BibLing, GeoRef, INIS AtomInd, MLA, PCI, RASB, SpeleolAb.
Published by: (Kungliga Vetenskaps-Societeten i Uppsala/Royal Society of Sciences at Uppsala), Uppsala Universitet, Acta Universitatis Upsaliensis/University Publications from Uppsala, PO Box 256, Uppsala, 75105, Sweden. TEL 46-18-4716804, FAX 46-18-4716804, acta@ub.uu.se, http://www.ub.uu.se/upu/auu/index.html. Ed. Bengt Landgren. **Dist. by:** Almqvist & Wiksell International, PO Box 614, Soedertaelje 15127, Sweden. TEL 46-8-5509497, FAX 46-8-55016710.

500 ARG ISSN 1666-7573
Q1
ACTAS DE LA ACADEMIA LUVENTICUS/LUVENTICUS ACADEMY. TRANSACTIONS. Text in Spanish. 2001. irreg. **Document type:** *Academic/Scholarly.*
Related titles: Online - full content ed.: ISSN 1666-7581; Online - full text ed.
Indexed: A26, I04, I05.
Published by: Academia de Ciencias Luventicus/Luventicus Academy of Sciences, Pasaje Monroe 2766, Rosario, 2000, Argentina. TEL 54-341-4487316, contact@luventicus.org, http://luventicus.org/. Eds. A Luetich, J J Luetich.

ACTION (OTTAWA)/ACTION - BULLETIN DU COMITE NATIONAL CANADIEN; newsletter of the Canadian National Committee. *see* ENVIRONMENTAL STUDIES

500 DEU ISSN 0940-2241
ADADEMIE GEMEINNUTZIGER WISSENSCHAFTEN ZU ERFURT. MATHEMATISCH-NATURWISSENSCHAFTLICHEN KLASSE. SITZUNGSBERICHTE. Text in German. 1991. irreg., latest vol.11, 2001. price varies. **Document type:** *Monographic series, Academic/Scholarly.*
Indexed: MSN, Z02.
Published by: Akademie Gemeinnuetziger Wissenschaften zu Erfurt e.V., Gotthardtstr 24, Erfurt, 99051, Germany. TEL 49-3641-937792, FAX 49-3641-937796, sekretariat@akademie-erfurt.de, http://www.akademie-erfurt.de.

▼ **ADVANCE JOURNAL OF FOOD SCIENCE AND TECHNOLOGY.** *see* NUTRITION AND DIETETICS

500 INT ISSN 2219-7478
▼ **THE ADVANCED SCIENCE JOURNAL.** Text in English. 2010. m. free. adv. cum.index:2010-2011. back issues avail. **Document type:** *Journal, Academic/Scholarly.* **Description:** Publishes multi-disciplinary research articles in natural science, social science and applied science. Audience include scientific researchers in the public and private sectors, government agencies, educators and the general public worldwide.
Media: Online - full text. **Related titles:** CD-ROM ed.; Print ed.: ISSN 2219-746X.
Published by: The Advanced Science Journal, 2964 Columbia St., Ste.32268, Torrance, CA 90503. uk.mail@advancedscience.org, us.mail@advancedscience.org, ua.mail@advancedscience.org. Ed., Pub., R&P, Adv. contact Roman Davydov.

500 USA ISSN 1936-6612
Q179.9
➤ **ADVANCED SCIENCE LETTERS.** Abbreviated title: A S L. Text in English. 2008 (Jun.). q. USD 1,180; USD 2,080 combined subscription (print & online eds.) (effective 2010). adv. back issues avail. **Document type:** *Journal, Academic/Scholarly.* **Description:** Covers research activities in all areas of Physical Sciences, Engineering, Biological Sciences/Health Sciences, Mathematical Sciences, Engineering, Computer and Information Sciences, Geosciences etc.
Related titles: Online - full text ed.: ISSN 1936-7317. USD 1,880 (effective 2010) (from IngentaConnect).
Indexed: B&BAb, B19, B20, B21, CurCont, ESPM, NSA, SCI, SCOPUS, W07.
Published by: American Scientific Publishers, 26650 The Old Rd, Ste 208, Valencia, CA 91381. TEL 661-799-7200, FAX 661-254-1207, order@aspbs.com. Ed. Hari Singh Nalwa. **Subscr. to:** 25650 N Lewis Way, Stevenson Ranch, CA 91381.

▼ ➤ **ADVANCES IN ADAPTIVE DATA ANALYSIS.** *see* ENGINEERING

500 IND ISSN 0976-8610
▼ **ADVANCES IN APPLIED SCIENCE RESEARCH.** Text in English. 2010 (Aug.). s-a. free (effective 2011). back issues avail. **Document type:** *Journal, Academic/Scholarly.* **Description:** Covers all types of review and research articles related to applied biological and chemical sciences.
Media: Online - full text.
Indexed: A01.
Published by: Pelagia Research Library, 20, Kumbha Nagar, Udaipur, India. TEL 91-982-8173650, info@pelagiaresearchlibrary.com. Ed. H P Singh. Pub., R&P C S Sharma.

500 BGR ISSN 1312-6164
Q180.B8
ADVANCES IN BULGARIAN SCIENCE. Text and summaries in English. 2005. q. BGL 56 domestic; USD 38 foreign (effective 2006). abstr.; bibl.; charts; illus.; stat. **Document type:** *Journal, Academic/Scholarly.* **Description:** Covers the advances of contemporary Bulgarian science in specific research fields of human knowledge.
Related titles: Online - full text ed.
Indexed: A01, CA, RefZh, T02.
Published by: National Centre for Information and Documentation (N A C I D), 52A G M Dimitrov Blvd, Sofia, 1125, Bulgaria. TEL 359-2-8173824, FAX 359-2-9713120. Circ: 300.

500 600 SGP ISSN 0219-5259
QA402
➤ **ADVANCES IN COMPLEX SYSTEMS.** Abbreviated title: A C S. Text in English. 2001 (vol.4). bi-m. SGD 1,162, USD 722, EUR 604 combined subscription to institutions (print & online eds.) (effective 2012). adv. back issues avail. **Document type:** *Journal, Academic/Scholarly.* **Description:** Aims to provide a medium of communication for multidisciplinary approaches, either empirical or theoretical, to the study of complex systems.
Related titles: Online - full text ed.: ISSN 1793-6802. SGD 1,056, USD 656, EUR 549 to institutions (effective 2012).
Indexed: A01, A02, A03, A08, A20, A22, BioEngAb, CA, CCMJ, CMCI, CurCont, E01, ESPM, HPNRM, MSN, MathR, S01, SCI, SCOPUS, SSciA, T02, W07, Z02.
—BLDSC (0704.103520), IE, Ingenta. **CCC.**
Published by: World Scientific Publishing Co. Pte. Ltd., 5 Toh Tuck Link, Singapore, 596224, Singapore. TEL 65-6466-5775, FAX 65-6467-7667, wspc@wspc.com.sg, http://www.worldscientific.com. Ed. Frank Schweitzer. **Dist. in the US by:** World Scientific Publishing Co., Inc., 27 Warren St, Ste 401-402, Hackensack, NJ 07601. TEL 201-487-9655, 800-227-7562, FAX 201-487-9656, 888-977-2665, wspc@wspc.com; **Dist. by:** World Scientific Publishing Ltd., 57 Shelton St, London WC2H 9HE, United Kingdom. TEL 44-207-8360888, FAX 44-207-8362020, sales@wspc.co.uk.

363.7 NLD ISSN 1574-0919
ADVANCES IN GLOBAL CHANGE RESEARCH. Text in English. 1999. irreg., latest vol.37, 2009. price varies. **Document type:** *Monographic series, Academic/Scholarly.* **Description:** Addressees key issues facing the global environment.
Indexed: GeoRef.
Published by: Springer Netherlands (Subsidiary of: Springer Science+Business Media), Van Godewijckstraat 30, Dordrecht, 3311 GX, Netherlands. TEL 31-78-6576050, FAX 31-78-6576474. Ed. Martin Beniston.

500 600 VEN
ADVANCES IN MATERIALS SCIENCE & TECHNOLOGY. Text in English; Summaries in Multiple languages. 1996. irreg. adv. bk.rev. bibl. back issues avail.; reprints avail. **Document type:** *Journal, Academic/Scholarly.* **Description:** All basic and applied aspects of the physics and chemistry of new materials, ceramics, alloys, calcogenide compounds, semiconductors, porous media, thin film, semimetals, electrochemistry.
Published by: Centro de Investigacion y Reproduccion de Especies Silvestres, Apartado Postal 397, Merida, 5101, Venezuela. cires@ciens.ula.ve, http://www.ciens.ula.ve/~cires. Ed., Pub. Hector Fernando Aguilar. Adv. contact Lieselotte Hoeger de Aguilar. Circ: 3,000.

500 JOR ISSN 1995-0772
➤ **ADVANCES IN NATURAL AND APPLIED SCIENCES.** Text in English. 2007. 3/yr. **Document type:** *Journal, Academic/Scholarly.* **Description:** Publishes research results in the areas of natural and applied sciences.
Related titles: Online - full text ed.: ISSN 1998-1090. free (effective 2011).
Indexed: A01, A26, CA, E08, I05, SCOPUS, T02.
Published by: American - Eurasian Network for Scientific Information, A E N S I Publications, c/o Dr. Abdel Rahman Mohammad Said Al-Tawaha, Al Hussein Bin Talal University, Biological Department, PO Box 20, Ma'an, Jordan. TEL 962-2-7305196. Ed., R&P, Adv. contact Abdel Rahman Al-Tawaha.

500 CAN ISSN 1715-7862
Q1
➤ **ADVANCES IN NATURAL SCIENCE.** Text in English. 2008. s-a. **Document type:** *Journal, Academic/Scholarly.*
Related titles: Online - full text ed.: ISSN 1715-7870. free (effective 2011).
Indexed: A01, A26, CA, CPerI, E08, I05, P15, P48, P52, P56, PQC, S09, T02.
Published by: Canadian Research & Development Center of Sciences and Cultures, 3-265 Melrose, Montreal, PQ H4H 1T2, Canada. http://www.cscanada.org. Ed. Jenny Ding.

500 VNM
ADVANCES IN NATURAL SCIENCES. Text in English. q. **Document type:** *Journal, Academic/Scholarly.*
Formerly: National Centre for Science and Technology of Vietnam. Proceedings
Indexed: PQC.
Published by: National Centre for Science and Technology of Vietnam, Hoang Quoc Viet Road, Cau Giay, Hanoi, Viet Nam. **Dist. by:** XunhaSaba, 32, Hai Ba Trung Str., Hoan Kiem Dist, HaNoi, Viet Nam. TEL 84-4-8262989, FAX 84-4-8252860, xunhasaba@hn.vnn.vn, http://www.xunhasaba.com.vn/.

500 620 GBR
▼ ➤ **ADVANCES IN NATURAL SCIENCES: NANOSCIENCE AND NANOTECHNOLOGY.** Text in English. 2010. q. back issues avail. **Document type:** *Journal, Academic/Scholarly.* **Description:** Covers all aspects of nanoscience and nanotechnology.
Related titles: Online - full text ed.: ISSN 2043-6262. free (effective 2011).
Published by: (National Centre for Science and Technology of Vietnam VNM), Institute of Physics Publishing Ltd., Dirac House, Temple Back, Bristol, BS1 6BE, United Kingdom. TEL 44-117-9297481, FAX 44-117-9301178, http://publishing.iop.org/.

S

500 DEU ISSN 1992-0628
➤ **ADVANCES IN SCIENCE AND RESEARCH.** Text in English. 2007. irreg. **Document type:** *Journal, Academic/Scholarly.* **Description:** Presents collections of communications in all fields of science and research.
Related titles: Online - full text ed.: ISSN 1992-0636. free (effective 2011).
Indexed: A01, P52, T02.
Published by: Copernicus GmbH, Bahnhofsallee 1e, Goettingen, 37081, Germany. TEL 49-551-9003390, FAX 49-551-90033970, info@copernicus.org, http://www.copernicus.org.

500 CHE ISSN 1662-0356
ADVANCES IN SCIENCE AND TECHNOLOGY. Text in English. 2006. irreg. EUR 590 to institutions (effective 2007). **Document type:** *Monographic series, Academic/Scholarly.*
Media: Online - full content. **Related titles:** CD-ROM ed.: ISSN 1661-819X.
Published by: Trans Tech Publications Ltd., Laubisrutistr 24, Stafa-Zurich, 8712, Switzerland. TEL 41-1-9221022, FAX 41-44-9221033, info@ttp.net, http://www.ttp.net. Ed. P Vincenzini.

500 NLD ISSN 1386-9817
ADVIESRAAD VOOR HET WETENSCHAPS- EN TECHNOLOGIEBELEID. NIEUWSBRIEF. Text in Dutch. 1997. 3/yr. free (effective 2008).
Published by: Adviesraad voor het Wetenschaps- en Technologiebeleid, Javastraat 42, Den Haag, 2585 AP, Netherlands. TEL 31-70-3639922, FAX 31-70-3608992, http://www.awt.nl/nl/index.html.

AEON; a journal of interdisciplinary science. *see* SOCIAL SCIENCES: COMPREHENSIVE WORKS

500 600 USA ISSN 0277-6499
TL789.8.U5
AERONAUTICS AND SPACE REPORT OF THE PRESIDENT. ACTIVITIES. Text in English. 1958. a. back issues avail.; reprints avail. **Document type:** *Report, Government.*
Former titles (until 1971): Aeronautics and Space Report of the President (0566-7186); (until 1969): U.S. Aeronautics and Space Activities (0500-2818)
Indexed: GeoRef.
Published by: U.S. National Aeronautics and Space Administration, Scientific and Technical Information Office, 300 E St S.W., Washington, DC 20546. TEL 202-358-0171, FAX 202-358-3469, histinfo@hq.nasa.gov. Ed. Giny Cheong.

509 USA ISSN 1549-4470
AESTIMATIO; critical reviews in the history of science. Text in English. 2004. a. **Document type:** *Journal, Academic/Scholarly.*
Related titles: CD-ROM ed.: ISSN 1549-4489; Online - full text ed.: ISSN 1549-4497. free (effective 2011).
Indexed: A01, T02.
Published by: Institute for Research in Classical Philosophy and Science (I R C P S), 3 Nelson Ridge Rd, Princeton, NJ 08540-7423. iscps@IRCPS.org, http://www.ircps.org/index.htm. Ed. Alan C Bowen.

500 600 KEN ISSN 1607-9949
AFRICAN JOURNAL OF SCIENCE AND TECHNOLOGY/JOURNAL AFRICAIN DE SCIENCE ET TECHNOLOGIE. Text in English, French. 2000. s-a. USD 80 (effective 2005). bibl.; charts; illus.; maps. back issues avail. **Document type:** *Journal, Academic/Scholarly.*
Formed by the merger of (1986-1999): African Journal of Science and Technology. Series A. Technology (1010-5263); (1986-1999): African Journal of Science and Technology. Series B. Basic Sciences (1010-5271); (1990-1999): African Journal of Science and Technology. Series C. General
Related titles: Online - full text ed.: free (effective 2011).
Indexed: A34, A37, A38, B23, C25, C30, CABA, E12, F08, F12, FCA, G11, GH, H16, I11, LT, MaizeAb, N02, N04, P32, P33, PHN&I, R07, R08, R11, S12, S13, S16, T05, W10.
Published by: Reseau Africain d'Instituts Scientifiques et Techniques/ African Network of Scientific and Technical Institutions, ANSTI-RAIST Secretariat UNESCO ROSTA, PO Box 30592, Nairobi, Kenya. TEL 254-2-622620, FAX 254-2-622538, J.Massaquoi@unesco.org, nairobi@unesco.org. Ed. Dr. Norbert Opiyo-Akech.

AGAINST ALL REASON; propaganda, politics, power. *see* PSYCHOLOGY

500 NOR ISSN 0808-9655
AGDER NATURMUSEUM. AARBOK. Text in Norwegian. 1965. a., latest vol.173, 2001. NOK 100 (effective 2003). adv. **Document type:** *Yearbook, Academic/Scholarly.*
Formerly (until 1994): Kristiansand Museum. Aarbok (0333-3124)
Published by: Agder Naturmuseum, Gimlemoen 1887, Kristiansand, 4686, Norway. TEL 47-38-092388, FAX 47-38-092378, ekspedisjonen.naturmuset@kristiansand.kommune.no. Ed. Roar Solheim. Adv. contact Ingrid Heimdal. Circ: 500.

500 600 PHL
AGHAM MINDANAW. Text in English. 2003. irreg. **Document type:** *Journal, Academic/Scholarly.*
Published by: Ateneo de Davao University, Research and Publication Office, Emilio Jacinto St, Davao City, 8016, Philippines. Ed. Lourdes Simbol.

700 JPN ISSN 0388-7367
AS552.K343
AICHI KYOIKU DAIGAKU KENKYU HOKOKU. GEIJUTSU, HOKEN TAIIKU, KASEI, GIJUTSU KAGAKU. Text in Japanese. 1975. a. per issue exchange basis.
Published by: Aichi University of Education/Aichi Kyoiku Daigaku, 1 Hirosawa-Igaya-cho, Kariya-shi, Aichi-ken 448-0000, Japan. Circ: 600.

510 500 JPN ISSN 0365-3722
Q4 CODEN: AKDSA5
AICHI KYOIKU DAIGAKU KENKYU HOKOKU. SHIZEN KAGAKU/ AICHI UNIVERSITY OF EDUCATION. NATURAL SCIENCE BULLETIN. Text and summaries in English, Japanese. 1952. a. **Document type:** *Bulletin.*
Formerly (until 1967): Aichi Gakugei Daigaku Kenkyu Hokoku. Shizen Kagaku (0515-779X)
Indexed: INIS AtomInd.
Published by: Aichi University of Education/Aichi Kyoiku Daigaku, 1 Hirosawa-Igaya-cho, Kariya-shi, Aichi-ken 448-0000, Japan.

500 EGY ISSN 1110-7634
AIN SHAMS UNIVERSITY. FACULTY OF EDUCATION. JOURNAL. SCIENTIFIC SECTION/MAGALLAT KULLIYAT AL-TARBIYYAT AL-QISM AL-'ILMI. Text in English. 198?. irreg., latest 2006. **Document type:** *Journal, Academic/Scholarly.*
Formed by the merger of (1977-198?): Ain Shams University. Faculty of Education. Journal. Section A: Mathematics & Physics (1110-1296); (19??-198?): Ain Shams University. Faculty of Education. Journal. Section B: Chemistry & Biology (1687-7403)
Published by: Ain Shams University, Faculty of Education, Heliopolis, Cairo, Egypt. TEL 20-2-4506842. Ed. Yusri Afifi Afifi.

500 TJK ISSN 1026-9541
AS581 CODEN: DANTAL
AKADEMIAI ILMHOI CUMHURII TOCIKISTON. DOKLADHOI. Text in Russian. 1951. a. illus. index. **Document type:** *Journal, Academic/ Scholarly.*
Formerly (until 1992): Akademiya Nauk Tadzhikskoi S.S.R. Doklady (0002-3469)
Indexed: CIN, CTFA, ChemAb, ChemTitl, GeoRef, Inspec, MathR, RASB, SpeleolAb, Z02.
—CASDDS, INIST. **CCC.**
Published by: Akademiai Ilmhoi Cumhurii Tocikiston/Academy of Sciences of the Republic of Tajikistan, 33 Rudaki Ave, Dushanbe, 734025, Tajikistan. TEL 992-372-215083, FAX 992-372-214911, ulmas@tajik.net. Circ: 700.

001.3 500 DEU ISSN 0084-6104
AS182 CODEN: AWLJAY
AKADEMIE DER WISSENSCHAFTEN UND DER LITERATUR, MAINZ. JAHRBUCH. Text in German. 1950. a. price varies. **Document type:** *Monographic series, Academic/Scholarly.*
Indexed: BibLing, GeoRef, IBR, IBZ, MLA-IB, RASB, SpeleolAb.
—Linda Hall.
Published by: Akademie der Wissenschaften und der Literatur Mainz, Geschwister-Scholl-Str 2, Mainz, 55131, Germany. TEL 49-6131-5770, FAX 49-6131-577206, generalsekretariat@adwmainz.de, http://www.adwmainz.de.

510 500 DEU ISSN 0002-2993
Q49 CODEN: AWLMA9
AKADEMIE DER WISSENSCHAFTEN UND DER LITERATUR, MAINZ. MATHEMATISCH - NATURWISSENSCHAFTLICHE KLASSE. ABHANDLUNGEN. Text in English, French, German. 1950. irreg., latest 2008. EUR 72 per vol. (effective 2009). abstr.; charts; illus. index. **Document type:** *Monographic series, Academic/Scholarly.*
Indexed: ASFA, B21, CCMJ, ChemAb, ESPM, GeoRef, SpeleolAb.
—CASDDS, INIST, Linda Hall.
Published by: (Akademie der Wissenschaften und der Literatur Mainz, Mathematisch - Naturwissenschaftliche Klasse), Franz Steiner Verlag GmbH, Birkenwaldstr 44, Stuttgart, 70191, Germany. TEL 49-711-25820, FAX 49-711-2582290, service@steiner-verlag.de, http://www.steiner-verlag.de.

500 DEU ISSN 0373-9767
➤ **AKADEMIE DER WISSENSCHAFTEN ZU GOETTINGEN. JAHRBUCH.** Text in German. 1939. a. EUR 68, USD 102 to institutions; EUR 78, USD 117 combined subscription to institutions (print & online eds.) (effective 2012). **Document type:** *Journal, Academic/Scholarly.*
Related titles: Online - full text ed.: ISSN 1868-9191. EUR 68, USD 102 to institutions (effective 2012).
Indexed: A01, BibLing, FR, IBR, IBZ, SpeleolAb, T02.
Published by: (Akademie der Wissenschaften zu Goettingen), Walter de Gruyter GmbH & Co. KG, Genthiner Str 13, Berlin, 10785, Germany. TEL 49-30-260050, FAX 49-30-26005251, info@degruyter.com.

500 CZE ISSN 1210-9525
AS142.P7
AKADEMIE VED CESKE REPUBLIKY. AKADEMICKY BULLETIN. Text in Czech. 1955. m. free. **Document type:** *Bulletin, Academic/ Scholarly.* **Description:** Features articles about the latest scientific findings, exchanges of opinion at the Academy and the scientific community at home and abroad, reports or photo reports from important events.
Formerly (until 1993): Ceskoslovenska Akademie Ved. Bulletin (0322-8010)
Published by: (Akademie Ved Ceske Republiky), Nakladatelstvi Akademia, Vodickova 40, Prague 1, 110 00, Czech Republic. TEL 420-2-24942584, FAX 420-2-24941982, http://www.academia.cz.

AKADEMIYA NAUK ARMENII. IZVESTIYA. SERIYA TEKHNICHESKIKH NAUK/HAYASTANI HANRAPETUTIAN GITUTSUNNERI AZGAIN ACADEMIAY TEKHNIKAKAN GITUTSUNNERY HANDES. *see* TECHNOLOGY: COMPREHENSIVE WORKS

500 UKR ISSN 1027-3239
AS262 CODEN: VNUKAC
AKADEMIYA NAUK UKRAINY. VISNYK. Text in Ukrainian. 1928. bi-m. USD 145. **Document type:** *Academic/Scholarly.*
Formerly (until 199?): Akademiya Nauk Ukrainskoi S.S.R. Visnyk (0372-6436)
Related titles: Microfiche ed.: (from IDC).
Indexed: ASFA, B21, Djerelo, ESPM, RASB.
—CASDDS, East View, INIST, Linda Hall.
Published by: Natsional'na Akademiya Nauk Ukrainy, Prezydium/ National Academy of Sciences of Ukraine, Presidium, Ul Tereshchenkovskaya 3, Kiev, Ukraine. TEL 380-44-224-7118. Ed. B E Paton. **Dist. by:** East View Information Services, 10601 Wayzata Blvd, Minneapolis, MN 55305. TEL 952-252-1201, 800-477-1005, FAX 952-252-1202, info@eastview.com, http://www.eastview.com; M K - Periodica, ul Gilyarovskogo 39, Moscow 129110, Russian Federation. TEL 7-095-2845008, FAX 7-095-2813798, info@periodicals.ru, http://www.mkniga.ru.

500 UZB ISSN 1019-8954
CODEN: DANUAO
AKADEMIYA NAUK UZBEKISTANA. DOKLADY. MATEMATIKA, TEKHNICHESKIE NAUKI, ESTESTVOZNANIE. Text in Uzbek. 1944. m.
Formerly (until 1992): Akademiya Nauk Uzbekskoi S.S.R. Doklady (0134-4307)
Indexed: CCMJ, CIN, CIS, ChemAb, ChemTitl, GeoRef, INIS AtomInd, RASB, RefZh, SpeleolAb, Z01, Z02.
—CASDDS, East View, INIST, Linda Hall. **CCC.**
Published by: (O'zbekiston Respublikasi Fanlar Akademiyasi/Academy of Sciences of Uzbekistan), Izdatel'stvo Fan, Ya Gulyamov ul 70, k 105, Tashkent, 700047, Uzbekistan.

500 RUS ISSN 1727-2769
AKADEMIYA NAUK VYSSHEI SHKOLY ROSSII. DOKLADY. Text in Russian. 1999. s-a. RUR 220 per issue domestic; USD 80 foreign (effective 2005). **Document type:** *Journal, Academic/Scholarly.*
Formerly (until 2003): Akademiya Nauk Vysshei Shkoly. Sibirskoe Otdelenie. Doklady (1681-0031)
Indexed: RefZh.
—East View.
Published by: (Akademiya Nauk Vysshei Shkoly Rossii, Novosibirskoe Otdelenie/Russian Higher Education Academy of Sciences, Siberian Branch), Izdatel'stvo Sibirskogo Otdeleniya Rossiiskoi Akademii Nauk/Publishing House of the Russian Academy of Sciences, Siberian Branch, Morskoi pr 2, a/ya 187, Novosibirsk, 630090, Russian Federation. TEL 7-3832-300570, FAX 7-3832-333755, psb@ad-sbras.nsc.ru. Ed. A S Vostrikov. **Dist. by:** East View Information Services, 10601 Wayzata Blvd, Minneapolis, MN 55305. TEL 952-252-1201, 800-477-1005, FAX 952-252-1202, info@eastview.com, http://www.eastview.com.

500 JPN
AKITA EIYOU TANKI DAIGAKU. RONSO/AKITA KEIZAIHOKA UNIVERSITY. COLLECTED PAPERS. Text in Japanese. 1957. s-a. **Document type:** *Journal, Academic/Scholarly.*
Former titles (until 2005): Akita Keizai Hoka Daigaku. Tanki Daigakubu. Ronso/Akita Keizai Hoka University. Junior College. Collected Papers (1345-742X); (until 1997): Akita Tanki Daigaku. Ronso/Akita Junior College. Collected Papers (0910-8807); Which superseded in part (in 1984): Akita Keizai Hoka Daigaku. Ronso/Akita University of Economics and Law. Collected Papers (0289-2200); Which was formerly (until 1983): Akita Keizai Daigaku. Ronso/Akita Junior College. Collected Papers (0387-4737)
Indexed: RILM.
Published by: Akita Eiyou Tanki Daigaku, 46-1, Morisawa, Shimokitadezakura, Akita, 010-8515, Japan. http://www.akeihou-u.ac.jp/.

AKITA-KENRITSU HAKUBUTSUKAN KENKYU HOKOKU/AKITA PREFECTURAL MUSEUM. ANNUAL REPORT. *see* MUSEUMS AND ART GALLERIES

500 JPN ISSN 0285-0257
AKITA SHIZENSHI KENKYU. Text in Japanese. 1973. a.
Published by: Akita Natural History Association/Akita Shizenshi Gakkai, c/o Mr Jun Takado, 6-36 Yabase-Tagoro 2-chome, Akita-shi, 010-0972, Japan.

500 RUS ISSN 1680-2721
AKTUAL'NYE PROBLEMY SOVREMENNOI NAUKI; informatsionno-analiticheskii zhurnal. Text in Russian. 2001. bi-m. USD 149 in United States (effective 2004). **Document type:** *Journal, Academic/ Scholarly.* **Description:** Publishes scientific research articles by Russian and CIS scholars in various areas of science.
Indexed: RefZh.
Published by: Izdatel'stvo Kompaniya Sputnik+, Ryazanskii pr-kt, dom 8a, Moscow, 109428, Russian Federation. TEL 7-095-7304774, http://www.sputnikplus.ru. **Dist. by:** East View Information Services, 10601 Wayzata Blvd, Minneapolis, MN 55305. TEL 952-252-1201, 800-477-1005, FAX 952-252-1202, info@eastview.com, http://www.eastview.com.

500 DNK ISSN 1399-2309
AKTUEL NATURVIDENSKAB. Text in Danish. 1999. bi-m. DKK 276 (effective 2009). adv. back issues avail. **Document type:** *Magazine, Consumer.*
Incorporates (1917-2008): Naturens Verden (0028-0895)
Related titles: Online - full text ed.: ISSN 1602-3544. 200?.
Published by: Aarhus Universitet, Det Naturvidenskabelige Fakultet/ Aarhus University, Faculty of Science, Ny Munkegade 120, Bygning 1520, Aarhus C, 8000, Denmark. TEL 45-89-423588, FAX 45-89-423596, mail@science.au.dk, http://www.nat.au.dk. Eds. Joergen Dahlgaard TEL 45-89-425555, Erik Meinecke Schmidt. Adv. contact Joergen Dahlgaard TEL 45-89-425555. page DKK 7,000; 180 x 250.

500 USA ISSN 0002-4112
Q11 CODEN: JAASAJ
ALABAMA ACADEMY OF SCIENCE. JOURNAL. Text in English. 1926. q. free to members (effective 2011). adv. bk.rev. abstr.; illus. reprints avail. **Document type:** *Proceedings, Academic/Scholarly.*
Related titles: Microform ed.: (from PQC); Online - full text ed.: ISSN 2162-2922.
Indexed: A01, A22, A26, ASFA, Agr, AmH&L, B21, CA, ChemAb, E08, ESPM, G01, G08, GeoRef, I05, P30, RASB, S06, S09, SASA, SWRA, SpeleolAb, T02, W08, WildRev, Z01.
—CASDDS, Ingenta, Linda Hall.
Published by: (Alabama Academy of Science), Auburn University Press, 101 Cary Hall, Auburn University, Zoology, Auburn, AL 36849. Ed. Safaa Al-Hamdani TEL 205-782-5801.

500 USA ISSN 0196-1039
ALABAMA MUSEUM OF NATURAL HISTORY. BULLETIN. Text in English. 1975. irreg.
Indexed: Z01.
Published by: University of Alabama Museums, Alabama Museum of Natural History Moundeville Archaeological Park, Box 870340, Tuscaloosa, AL 35487-0340. TEL 205-348-9742.

507.1 ESP ISSN 1133-9837
ALAMBIQUE; didactica de las ciencias experimentales. Text in Spanish. 1994. q. EUR 58.50 domestic; EUR 61.50 foreign (effective 2009). bk.rev. index. **Document type:** *Monographic series, Academic/ Scholarly.*
Published by: Editoral Grao, C Hurtado, 29, Barcelona, 08022, Spain. TEL 34-93-4080464, FAX 34-93-3524337, web@grao.com, http://www.grao.com. Circ: 2,500 (paid).

ALAMEDA. *see* EDUCATION

500 USA ISSN 1545-4967
SB482.A6
ALASKA PARK SCIENCE. Text in English. 2002 (Win.). s-a.
Published by: U.S. Department of the Interior, National Park Service, Alaska Support Office, 2525 Gambell St. Ste. 107, Anchorage, AK 99503-2892. TEL 907-257-2437. Ed. Monica Shah.

ALBERTA GEOLOGICAL SURVEY. REPORTS. *see* TECHNOLOGY: COMPREHENSIVE WORKS

ALBERTA RESEARCH COUNCIL. ANNUAL REPORT. *see* TECHNOLOGY: COMPREHENSIVE WORKS

ALEPH: HISTORICAL STUDIES IN SCIENCE AND JUDAISM. *see* RELIGIONS AND THEOLOGY—Judaic

505 MEX
ALEPHZERO; revista de ciencia y divulgacion. Text in Spanish. 1995. bi-m. back issues avail.
Published by: Universidad de las Americas, Puebla, Santa Catarina Martir, Cholula, Puebla, 72820, Mexico. TEL 52-22-293166, http://www.udlap.mx. Ed. Miguel Angel Mendez Rojas.

500 EGY ISSN 1110-0176
CODEN: ALSEEF
➤ **ALEXANDRIA SCIENCE EXCHANGE.** Text in English; Summaries in Arabic, English. 1981. q. USD 15 to individuals; USD 40 to institutions (effective 2004). abstr. **Document type:** *Journal, Academic/Scholarly.* **Description:** Publishes original research in various disciplines of science.
Indexed: CIN, ChemAb, ChemTitl, FS&TA.
—BLDSC (0786.945000), CASDDS, IE, Ingenta.
Published by: A.M. Balba Group for Soil and Water Research, College of Agriculture, University of Alexandria, El-Shatby, Alexandria, 21545, Egypt. TEL 20-3-5975405, FAX 20-3-5954684. Ed. Abdel-Munaem M Balba.

500 FRA ISSN 1144-5645
➤ **ALLIAGE**; culture, science, technique. Text in French. 1989. q. EUR 52 domestic; EUR 61 foreign; EUR 13 newsstand/cover (effective 2003). adv. film rev.; music rev.; play rev.; bk.rev. bibl.; illus. 120 p./no.; back issues avail. **Document type:** *Journal, Academic/Scholarly.* **Description:** Alliage is a magazine which confronts sciences, technologies and culture.
Related titles: Online - full text ed.
Published by: Association Nicoise d'Animation et d'Information Scientifique (A N I S), 78 route de Saint-Pierre-de-Feric, Nice, 06000, France. Ed., R&P, Adv. contact Roselyne Chaumont TEL 33-4-93868793. Pub. Jean Marc Levy Leblond. Circ: 1,500; 1,000 (paid).

500 SWE ISSN 1652-3318
ALLT OM VETENSKAP. Text in Swedish. 2004. 11/yr. SEK 539 domestic; SEK 1,079 in Europe; SEK 1,139 elsewhere (effective 2011). adv. back issues avail. **Document type:** *Magazine, Consumer.*
Published by: Allt om Vetenskap AB, Industrigatan 2 A, Stockholm, 11285, Sweden. TEL 46-8-7585260, http://www.alltomvetenskap.se. Ed. Lasse Zernell. Pub. Michael Journath. Adv. contact Lena Sjoedell.

500 BEL ISSN 1792-2593
▼ **ALMAGEST**; international journal for the history of scientific ideas. Text in Multiple languages. 2010. s-a. EUR 72 combined subscription (print & online eds.) (effective 2012). **Document type:** *Journal, Academic/Scholarly.*
Related titles: Online - full text ed.
—Linda Hall.
Published by: Brepols Publishers, Begijnhof 67, Turnhout, 2300, Belgium. TEL 32-14-448020, FAX 32-14-428919, periodicals@brepols.net, http://www.brepols.net.

500 ITA ISSN 2037-4801
▼ **ALMANACCO DELLA SCIENZA.** Text in Italian. 2009. fortn. **Document type:** *Magazine, Consumer.*
Media: Online - full text.
Published by: Consiglio Nazionale delle Ricerche (C N R)/Italian National Research Council, Piazzale Aldo Moro 7, Rome, 00185, Italy. TEL 39-06-49931, FAX 39-06-4461954, http://www.cnr.it. Ed. Rita Bugliosi.

500 NZL ISSN 0111-1957
ALPHA. Text in English. 1980. irreg., latest vol.132, 2008. NZD 5 per issue (effective 2008). **Document type:** *Monographic series, Academic/Scholarly.* **Description:** Educational leaflets depicting science and technology with a New Zealand context.
Related titles: Online - full text ed.: ISSN 1178-1351. free (effective 2008).
Indexed: GeoRef, SpeleolAb.
—CCC.
Published by: (Royal Society of New Zealand), R S N Z Publishing, PO Box 598, Wellington, 6001, New Zealand. TEL 64-4-4727421, FAX 64-4-4731841, http://www.rsnz.org. Circ: 2,000.

AMBIO; a journal of the human environment. *see* ENVIRONMENTAL STUDIES

AMERICAN ACADEMY OF ARTS AND SCIENCES. BULLETIN. *see* HUMANITIES: COMPREHENSIVE WORKS

AMERICAN HERITAGE OF INVENTION & TECHNOLOGY. *see* TECHNOLOGY: COMPREHENSIVE WORKS

500 001.3 300 USA ISSN 2162-139X
▼ ➤ **AMERICAN INTERNATIONAL JOURNAL OF CONTEMPORARY RESEARCH.** Text in English. 2011. bi-m. free. bk.rev. abstr.; bibl. back issues avail.; reprints avail. **Document type:** *Journal, Academic/Scholarly.* **Description:** Publishes original papers, review papers, conceptual framework, analytical and simulation models, case studies, empirical research, technical notes, and book reviews. Topic areas include: Business and economics; humanities and social science; and science and technology.
Related titles: Online - full text ed.
Published by: Centre for Promoting Ideas, 432 Claremont Ave, New York, NY 10027. TEL 540-831-5888, info.cpi.usa@hotmail.com, http://www.cpinet.info. Ed. Andrew Lessard. Pub., R&P Mamin Ullah.

500 620 BGD ISSN 1608-3679
Q1
AMERICAN INTERNATIONAL UNIVERSITY-BANGLADESH JOURNAL OF SCIENCE AND ENGINEERING. Text in English. 2002. a. **Document type:** *Journal, Academic/Scholarly.* **Description:** Covers a wide area in the field of science and engineering, insight into the scientific and engineering practices and theoretical underpinnings.
Indexed: Inspec.
Published by: American International University-Bangladesh, House #77/C, Road #4, Banani, Dhaka, 1213, Bangladesh. TEL 880-2-8815386, FAX 880-2-8813233, aiub@citechno.net, http://www.aiub.edu. Ed. Carmen Z Lamagna.

500 001.3 300 USA ISSN 2154-4646
▼ **AMERICAN JOURNAL OF ACADEMIC RESEARCH.** Text in English. 2010 (Oct.). q. free (effective 2011). **Document type:** *Journal, Academic/Scholarly.* **Description:** Features scholarly research by undergraduates on a wide variety of topics.
Media: Online - full text.
Published by: Bio Tech System, PO Box 31932, Edmond, OK 73003. editorial@btsjournals.com.

500 USA ISSN 1546-9239
T1
➤ **AMERICAN JOURNAL OF APPLIED SCIENCES.** Text in English. 2004. m. USD 4,800 (effective 2009). **Document type:** *Journal, Academic/Scholarly.* **Description:** Publishes original articles, reviews and short communications of a high scientific and ethical standard in applied science.
Related titles: Online - full text ed.: ISSN 1554-3641. free (effective 2011).
Indexed: A26, A34, A35, A36, A37, A38, A39, AgBio, AgrForAb, B23, BA, BP, C10, C25, C27, C29, C30, CA, CABA, D01, D03, D04, E08, E12, E13, F08, F11, F12, FCA, G01, G08, G11, GH, H16, H17, I05, I11, IndVet, Inspec, LT, MaizeAb, N02, N03, N04, O01, OR, P32, P33, P40, PGegResA, PHN&I, R07, R08, R11, R12, R13, R14, RA&MP, RM&VM, RRTA, S06, S09, S12, S13, S14, S15, S16, S17, S18, SCOPUS, SoyAb, T02, T05, TAR, TriticAb, VS, W10, W11.
—BLDSC (0821.050000), IE, Ingenta.
Published by: Science Publications, 244, 5th Ave, Ste 207, New York, NY 10001. TEL 845-510-3028, FAX 866-250-7082, support@scipub.org, http://www.thescipub.com.

500 USA ISSN 2153-649X
▼ ➤ **AMERICAN JOURNAL OF SCIENTIFIC AND INDUSTRIAL RESEARCH.** Text in English. 2010 (June). q. USD 1,200 (effective 2011). **Document type:** *Journal, Academic/Scholarly.*
Media: Online - full text. **Related titles:** CD-ROM ed.: ISSN 2153-6503. forthcoming 2010 (June).
Published by: Science Hub, PO Box 3423, Milford, CT 06460. TEL 203-500-7280, customer@scihub.org, http://www.scihub.org/.

500 USA ISSN 1536-4585
➤ **AMERICAN JOURNAL OF UNDERGRADUATE RESEARCH.** Abbreviated title: A J U R. Text in English. 2002 (Jun.). q. adv. back issues avail. **Document type:** *Journal, Academic/Scholarly.* **Description:** Covers research in the pure and applied sciences, mathematics, engineering, technology, and related areas in education.
Published by: University of Northern Iowa, Physics Bldg., Rm 205, Cedar Falls, IA 50614. FAX 319-273-7136, hrs-mail@uni.edu, http://www.uni.edu. Ed., Adv. contact Cliff Chancey TEL 319-273-2425. **Subscr. to:** Physics 215, Cedar Fall, IA 50614.

➤ **AMERICAN MEN AND WOMEN OF SCIENCE**; a biographical directory of today's leaders in physical, biological and related sciences. *see* BIOGRAPHY

500.9 USA ISSN 0003-0031
QH1 CODEN: AMNAAF
➤ **AMERICAN MIDLAND NATURALIST.** Text in English. 1909. q. USD 55 to individuals; USD 95 in the Americas to institutions; USD 100 elsewhere to institutions; USD 35 to students (effective 2009). bibl.; charts; illus. index, cum.index: vols.1-60, 61-100. back issues avail.; reprints avail. **Document type:** *Journal, Academic/Scholarly.* **Description:** Covers the spectrum of laboratory and field studies in biology, ecology, life histories, evolution and physiology.
Formerly (until Apr.1909): The Midland Naturalist (0271-6844)
Related titles: Microfiche ed.: (from IDC); Microform ed.: (from PQC); Online - full text ed.: ISSN 1938-4238.
Indexed: A01, A03, A08, A20, A22, A25, A26, A34, A35, A37, A38, ASCA, ASFA, AgBio, Agr, AgrForAb, AnBeAb, B&AI, B04, B10, B21, B23, B25, BA, BIOBASE, BIOSIS Prev, BRD, C12, C25, C30, CA, CABA, ChemAb, CurCont, D01, E01, E04, E05, E08, E12, E17, ESPM, EntAb, F08, F11, F12, FCA, G03, G08, G11, GEOBASE, GH, GSA, GSI, GardL, GenetAb, GeoRef, H09, H16, H17, HPNRM, I05, I11, IABS, IBR, IBZ, INIS AtomInd, ISR, IndVet, KWIWR, LT, M01, M02, MaizeAb, MycolAb, N04, O01, OR, P02, P10, P11, P15, P26, P32, P33, P37, P40, P48, P52, P53, P54, P56, PGegResA, PGrRegA, PN&I, PQC, PlantSci, R07, R08, R11, R13, RA&MP, RRTA, S04, S08, S09, S10, S13, S16, S17, SCI, SCOPUS, SSciA, SWRA, SoyAb, SpeleolAb, T02, TAR, TriticAb, VS, W03, W05, W07, W08, W10, WildRev, Z01.
—BLDSC (0843.000000), CASDDS, IE, Infotrieve, Ingenta, INIST, Linda Hall.
Published by: University of Notre Dame, Department of Biological Sciences, Rm 285 GLSC, PO Box 369, Notre Dame, IN 46556. TEL 574-631-7481, FAX 574-631-7413, biology.biosadm.1@nd.edu. Ed. William E Evans.

➤ **AMERICAN MUSEUM OF NATURAL HISTORY. ANNUAL REPORT.** *see* MUSEUMS AND ART GALLERIES

➤ **AMERICAN MUSEUM OF NATURAL HISTORY. BIENNIAL REPORT.** *see* MUSEUMS AND ART GALLERIES

500 USA ISSN 0003-0996
LJ85 CODEN: AMSCAC
AMERICAN SCIENTIST. Text in English. 1913. bi-m. USD 28 domestic; USD 36 in Canada; USD 44 elsewhere; USD 6.95 per issue domestic; USD 8.95 per issue foreign (effective 2010). adv. bk.rev. bibl.; illus. index, cum.index: vols.34-61 (1946-1973). back issues avail.; reprints avail. **Document type:** *Journal, Academic/Scholarly.* **Description:** Contains reviews of important scientific work in all fields, from molecular biology to computer engineering.
Formerly (until 1942): Sigma XI Quarterly (0096-977X)
Related titles: Microform ed.: (from PMC, PQC); Online - full text ed.: ISSN 1545-2786.
Indexed: A01, A02, A03, A05, A08, A20, A22, A23, A24, A25, A26, A33, AS&TA, AS&TI, ASCA, ASFA, AbAn, AcaI, Agr, AnBeAb, B04, B05, B13, B14, B20, B21, BIOSIS Prev, BRD, BRI, BibAg, BiolDig, BrArAb, C10, CA, CADCAM, CBRI, CDA, CIS, Cadscan, ChemAb, CompR, CurCont, CurPA, E04, E05, E08, E11, E17, ESPM, EnerRev, EntAb, EnvAb, EnvInd, FutSurv, G01, G03, G05, G06, G07, G08, GEOBASE, GSA, GSI, GardL, GeoRef, HPNRM, HRIS, I05, I07, IBR, IBZ, ISR, IndMed, Inspec, KWIWR, LeadAb, M&GPA, M02, M06, MASUSE, MEA&I, MLA-IB, MathR, MycolAb, NRN, NSA, NumL, P02, P05, P10, P11, P13, P15, P26, P30, P34, P48, P52, P53, P54, P56, PMR, PQC, PollutAb, PsycholAb, RASB, RILM, RefSour, S01, S02, S03, S04, S06, S08, S09, S10, S23, SCI, SCOPUS, SPPI, SSciA, SWRA, SociolAb, SpeleolAb, T02, T04, W03, W05, W07, W08, WildRev, Zincscan.
—BLDSC (0857.000000), AskIEEE, CASDDS, GNLM, IE, Infotrieve, Ingenta, INIST, Linda Hall. **CCC.**
Published by: Sigma XI, Scientific Research Society, 3106 East NC Highway 54, PO Box 13975, Research Triangle Park, NC 27709. TEL 919-549-4691, 800-243-6534, FAX 919-549-0090, info@sigmaxi.org, http://www.sigmaxi.org/. Ed. David Schoonmaker. Pub. Jerome F Baker.

AMERICAN SOCIETY FOR INFORMATION SCIENCE AND TECHNOLOGY. BULLETIN (ONLINE). *see* LIBRARY AND INFORMATION SCIENCES

500 IRN ISSN 1015-0951
CODEN: AMIREB
AMIRKABIR; journal of science & technology. Key Title: Amir Kabir. Text in Persian, Modern. 1985. s-a.
Indexed: CIN, CPEI, ChemAb, ChemTitl, EngInd, INIS AtomInd, SCOPUS.
—CASDDS.
Published by: Amirkabir University, Office of Vice Chancellor in Research Affairs, Hafez Ave., Tehran 15, Iran. TEL 98-21-6406591, FAX 98-21-6419728. Ed. M Sohrabi.

500 600 TUR ISSN 1302-3160
Q4
➤ **ANADOLU UNIVERSITESI BILIM VE TEKNOLOJI DERGISI/ ANADOLU UNIVERSITY JOURNAL OF SCIENCES AND TECHNOLOGY.** Abstracts in English, Turkish; Text in Turkish. s-a. **Document type:** *Journal, Academic/Scholarly.* **Description:** Publishes original papers in the fields of pure sciences, engineering sciences, and health sciences.
Related titles: Online - full text ed.: ISSN 2146-0205. free (effective 2011).
Indexed: A01, CA, T02, Z01.
Published by: Anadolu Universitesi, Fen Bilimleri Enstitusu/Anadolu University, Graduate School of Sciences, Eskisehir, 26470, Turkey. FAX 90-222-3354122. Ed. Ridvan Say.

509 POL ISSN 1230-1159
H8
ANALECTA; studia i materialy z dziejow nauki. Text in Polish; Summaries in English. 1992. s-a. EUR 35 foreign (effective 2006). illus. **Document type:** *Journal, Academic/Scholarly.*
Formed by the merger of (1986-1992): Studia i Materialy z Dziejow Nauki Polskiej. Seria 1. Historia Nauk Spolecznych (0860-1011); (1984-1992): Studia i Materialy z Dziejow Nauki Polskiej. Seria 2. Historia Nauk Scislych, Przyrodniczych i Technicznych (0860-102X); Which was formed by the merger of (1958-1984): Studia i Materialy z Dziejow Nauki Polskiej. Seria D, Historia Techniki i Nauk Technicznych (0081-6604); (1957-1984): Studia i Materialy z Dziejow Nauki Polskiej. Seria C, Historia Nauk Matematycznych, Fizyko-Chemicznych i Geologiczno-Geograficznych (0081-6590); (1957-1984): Studia i Materialy z Dziejow Nauki Polskiej. Seria B, Historia Nauk Biologicznych i Medycznych (0081-6582)
Indexed: AgrLib, FR, P30, RASB.
Published by: Polska Akademia Nauk, Instytut Historii Nauki, Palac Staszica, ul Nowy Swiat 72, pok 9, Warsaw, 00330, Poland. TEL 48-22-8268754, FAX 48-22-8266137, ihn@ihnpan.waw.pl, http://www.ihnpan.waw.pl. Ed. Halina Lichocka. Circ: 320. **Dist. by:** Ars Polona, Obroncow 25, Warsaw 03933, Poland. TEL 48-22-5098609, FAX 48-22-5098610, arspolona@arspolona.com.pl, http://www.arspolona.com.pl.

500 ROM ISSN 1220-4161
ANALELE BANATULUI. STIINTELE NATURII. Text in Romanian. 1983. a.
Published by: Muzeul Banatului Timisoara, Piata Huniade, nr 1, Timisoara, 300002, Romania. TEL 40-256-491339, FAX 40-256-201321, http://www.infotim.ro/mbt.

500 ROM ISSN 0378-8989
QH301 CODEN: AUBBDH
ANALELE UNIVERSITATII BUCURESTI. BIOLOGIE. Text in English, French, Romanian. 1969. a. **Document type:** *Journal, Academic/Scholarly.*
Supersedes in part (1974-1976): Analele Universitatii Bucuresti. Stiintele Naturii (0254-8887); Which was formed by the merger of (1969-1973): Analele Universitatii Bucuresti. Chimie (0068-3140); (1969-1973): Analele Universitatii Bucuresti. Biologie Animala (0068-3124); (1969-1973): Analele Universitatii Bucuresti. Biologie Vegetala (0068-3132); (1969-1973): Analele Universitatii Bucuresti. Geografie (0068-3191); (1969-1973): Analele Universitatii Bucuresti. Geologie (0068-3183); (1969-1973): Analele Universitatii Bucuresti. Fizica (0068-3108); (1969-1973): Analele Universitatii Bucuresti. Matematica - Mecanica (0068-3272)
Indexed: B25, BIOSIS Prev, MycolAb, SpeleolAb, Z01.
—BLDSC (0869.410000), INIST, Linda Hall.
Published by: Universitatea din Bucuresti, Bd. Gh. Gheorghiu-Dej 64, Bucharest, Romania.

500 630 PER ISSN 0003-2484
Q4 CODEN: ANCNA6
ANALES CIENTIFICOS. Text in Spanish; Summaries in English. 1963. q. PEN 10, USD 6. adv. index. **Document type:** *Academic/Scholarly.*
Indexed: ChemAb.
—CASDDS, INIST.
Published by: Universidad Nacional Agraria "La Molina", Av La Universidad s-n, Lima, Peru. secgeneral@lamolina.edu.pe, http://www.lamolina.edu.pe. Ed. Antonio Bacigalupo. Circ: 1,000.

ANALOG SCIENCE FICTION & FACT. *see* LITERATURE—Science Fiction, Fantasy, Horror

508 GRC
ANDRIAKA MELETEMATA. Text in Greek. 1994. irreg. USD 15 (effective 2003).
Published by: Kaireios Library, Andros, 845 00, Greece. TEL 30-22820-22262, FAX 30-22820-24504, 30-282-24504, kaireios@otenet.gr. Ed. Demetrios I Polemis.

S

500 CHN ISSN 1000-2162
ANHUI DAXUE XUEBAO (ZIRAN KEXUE BAN)/ANHUI UNIVERSITY. JOURNAL (NATURAL SCIENCE EDITION). Text in Chinese. 1960. bi-m. USD 18 (effective 2009). adv. **Document type:** *Journal, Academic/Scholarly.* **Description:** Contains scientific papers on mathematics, physics, chemistry, biology and engineering.
Related titles: Online - full text ed.: (from WanFang Data Corp.).
Indexed: CCMJ, INIS AtomInd, RefZh, Z02.
—BLDSC (0902.916793), East View.
Published by: Anhui Daxue Xuebao Bianjibu, 3, Feixi Lu, Longhe Xiao-qu, Xingzheng Bei Lou 322, Hefei, Anhui 230039, China. TEL 86-551-5107145, FAX 86-551-5107157, http://xuebao.ahu.edu.cn/. Ed. Zuxiu Zheng. Adv. contact Haiyan Lu. Circ: 2,000. **Dist. overseas by:** China International Book Trading Corp, 35 Chegongzhuang Xilu, Haidian District, PO Box 399, Beijing 100044, China. TEL 86-10-68412045, FAX 86-10-68412023, cibtc@mail.cibtc.com.cn, http://www.cibtc.com.cn.

ANHUI DIANZI XINXI ZHIYE JISHU XUEYUAN XUEBAO/ANHUI VOCATIONAL COLLEGE OF ELECTRONICS & INFORMATION TECHNOLOGY. JOURNAL. *see* SOCIAL SCIENCES: COMPREHENSIVE WORKS

500 CHN ISSN 2095-0977
➤ **ANHUI GONGCHENG DAXUE XUEBAO/ANHUI POLYTECHNIC UNIVERSITY. JOURNAL.** Text in Chinese; Abstracts in Chinese, English. 1983. q. CNY 40, USD 40; CNY 10 per issue (effective 2011 & 2012).
Former titles (until 2010): Anhui Gongcheng Keji Xueyuan Xuebao (Ziran Kexue Ban)/Anhui University of Technology and Science. Journal (Natural Science) (1672-2477); (until 2003): Anhui Jidian Xueyuan Xuebao/Anhui Institute of Mechanical and Electrical Engineering. Journal (1007-5240)
Related titles: Online - full text ed.
Indexed: RefZh.
Published by: Anhui Gongcheng Daxue/Anhui Polytechnic University, Beijing Middle Rd., Wuhu, Anhui 241000, China. TEL 86-553-2871234, FAX 86-553-2871234. Ed. Hong Gan. Circ: 700. **Dist. by:** China International Book Trading Corp, 35 Chegongzhuang Xilu, Haidian District, PO Box 399, Beijing 100044, China. TEL 86-10-68412045, FAX 86-10-68412023, cibtc@mail.cibtc.com.cn, http://www.cibtc.com.cn.

500 CHN ISSN 1006-4540
ANHUI JIANZHU GONGYE XUEYUAN XUEBAO (ZIRAN KEXUE BAN)/ANHUI INSTITUTE OF ARCHITECTURE INDUSTRY. JOURNAL. Text in Chinese. 1993. bi-m. CNY 10 newsstand/cover (effective 2006). **Document type:** *Journal, Academic/Scholarly.*
Related titles: Online - full text ed.
Published by: Anhui Jianzhu Gongye Xueyuan, 856, Liujinzhai Nan Lu, Hefei, 230022, China. TEL 86-551-3513091, FAX 86-551-3517457.

500 600 CHN ISSN 1007-7855
ANHUI KEJI/ANHUI SCIENCE & TECHNOLOGY. Text in Chinese. m.
Formerly (until 1996): Zhongwai Jishu Qingbao/Technical Information from China and Foreign Countries
Published by: (Anhui Sheng Keji Qingbao Yanjiusuo/Anhui Provincial Institute of Science and Technology Information), Anhui Keji Zazhishe, 287, Chaohu Lu, Hefei, 230001, China. TEL 86-551-2611252, FAX 86-551-2678453.

500 CHN ISSN 1673-8772
ANHUI KEJI XUEYUAN XUEBAO/ANHUI SCIENCE AND TECHNOLOGY UNIVERSITY. JOURNAL. Text in Chinese. 1984. bi-m. **Document type:** *Journal, Academic/Scholarly.*
Former titles (until 2006): Anhui Jishu Shifan Xueyuan Xuebao/Anhui Technical Teachers College. Journal (1672-3589); (until 1999): Anhui Nongye Jishu Shifan Xueyuan Xuebao/Anhui Agrotechnical Teachers College. Journal (1007-3302)
Related titles: Online - full text ed.
Published by: Anhui Keji Xueyuan/Anhui Science and Technology University, 9, Donghua Lu, Fengyangxian, Chuzhou, 233100, China. TEL 86-550-6732247, FAX 86-550-6732036.

500 CHN ISSN 1672-1098
ANHUI LIGONG DAXUE XUEBAO (ZIREN KEXUE BAN)/ANHUI UNIVERSITY OF SCIENCE AND TECHNOLOGY. JOURNAL (NATURAL SCIENCES). Text in Chinese. 1981. q. CNY 20; CNY 5 newsstand/cover (effective 2005). **Document type:** *Journal, Academic/Scholarly.*
Former titles (until 2003): Huainan Gongye Xueyuan Xuebao (Ziran Kexue Ban)/Huainan Institute of Technology. Journal (Natural Sciences) (1671-0932); (until 1998): Huainan Kuangye Xueyuan Xuebao (Ziran Kexue Ban) (1001-7038)
Related titles: Online - full text ed.
Indexed: A32, ESPM, PollutAb, RefZh, SWRA.
—BLDSC (0902.916798).
Published by: Anhui Ligong Daxue/Anhui University of Science and Technology, Journal Editorial Board, Huainan, Anhui 232001, China. TEL 86-554-6668044, http://www.aust.edu.cn.

500 CHN ISSN 1672-352X
ANHUI NONGYE DAXUE XUEBAO/ANHUI AGRICULTURAL UNIVERSITY. JOURNAL. Text in Chinese. 1957. q. USD 12 (effective 2009). **Document type:** *Journal, Academic/Scholarly.*
Related titles: Online - full text ed.
Indexed: A29, A34, A35, A36, A37, A38, AEBA, ASFA, AgBio, AgrForAb, B&BAb, B19, B21, B23, BA, BP, C25, C30, CABA, D01, E12, ESPM, F08, F11, F12, FCA, G11, GH, GenetAb, H16, H17, I10, I11, IndVet, LT, MaizeAb, N02, N03, N04, N05, O01, OR, P32, P33, P37, P38, P39, P40, PGegResA, PGrRegA, PHN&I, PN&I, R07, R08, R11, R12, R13, RA&MP, RM&VM, RRTA, S12, S13, S16, S17, SoyAb, T05, TAR, TriticAb, VS, VirolAbstr, W10, W11, Z01.
—BLDSC (0902.916850), Ingenta.
Published by: Anhui Nongye Daxue, 130, Changjiang Xi Lu, Hefei, 230036, China. TEL 86-551-2810205, FAX 86-551-2810103.

500 CHN
CODEN: ASXZEG
ANHUI SHIFAN DAXUE XUEBAO (ZIRAN KEXUE BAN)/ANHUI NORMAL UNIVERSITY. JOURNAL. Text in Chinese. 1957. bi-m. adv. **Document type:** *Journal, Academic/Scholarly.*
Former titles (until 1998): Anhui Shida Xuebao (1001-2443); (until 1974): Anhui Shifan Daxue Xuebao (Ziran Kexue Ban); Which superseded in part (in 1959): Anhui Shifan Xueyuan Xuebao
Related titles: ◆ CD-ROM ed.: Chinese Academic Journals Full-Text Database. Education & Social Sciences; Online - full text ed.
Indexed: A28, APA, ASFA, B21, BrCerAb, C&ISA, CA/WCA, CIA, CIS, CerAb, CivEngAb, CorrAb, E&CAJ, E11, EEA, EMA, ESPM, EnvEAb, H15, M&TEA, M09, MBF, METADEX, PEI, RefZh, SSciA, SWRA, SolStAb, T04, WAA, Z02.
—BLDSC (0902.917500), Linda Hall.
Published by: Anhui Shifan Daxue/Anhui Normal University, 1, Beijing Dong Lu, Wuhu, 241000, China. TEL 86-553-3869664, FAX 86-553-3869521. adv.: page CNY 3,500, page USD 50. **Dist. by:** China International Book Trading Corp, 35 Chegongzhuang Xilu, Haidian District, PO Box 399, Beijing 100044, China. TEL 86-10-68412045, FAX 86-10-68412023, cibtc@mail.cibtc.com.cn, http://www.cibtc.com.cn.

ANHUI YEJIN KEJI ZHIYE XUEYUAN XUEBAO/ANHUI VOCATIONAL COLLEGE OF METALLURGY AND TECHNOLOGY. JOURNAL. *see* SOCIAL SCIENCES: COMPREHENSIVE WORKS

590 USA
ANIMAL NATURAL HISTORY SERIES. Text in English. 1996. irreg., latest vol.9, 2005. price varies. back issues avail. **Document type:** *Monographic series, Academic/Scholarly.* **Description:** Covers information about the bird roadrunner.
Published by: University of Oklahoma Press, 2800 Venture Dr, Norman, OK 73069. TEL 405-325-2000, 800-627-7377, FAX 405-364-5798, 800-735-0476, kbenson@ou.edu.

500 SWE ISSN 0504-0736
ANNALES ACADEMIAE REGIAE SCIENTIARUM UPSALIENSIS. Variant title: Kungliga Vetenskapssamhaellet i Uppsala. Aarsbok. Text in Swedish. 1957. a. **Document type:** *Academic/Scholarly.*
Indexed: B25, BIOSIS Prev, MycolAb.
—INIST.
Published by: Kungliga Vetenskapssamhaellet i Uppsala/Royal Society of Sciences at Uppsala, Aasgraend 7, Uppsala, 75310, Sweden. TEL 46-18-103211, sten.lunell@kvac.uu.se.

ANNALES DU MUSEUM DU HAVRE. *see* MUSEUMS AND ART GALLERIES

500 001 USA ISSN 1079-5146
Q167
➤ **THE ANNALS OF IMPROBABLE RESEARCH**; resarch that makes people LAUGH and then THINK. Abbreviated title: A I R. Text in English. 1995. bi-m. USD 37 domestic; USD 46 in Canada & Mexico; USD 59 elsewhere; USD 6.50 newsstand/cover domestic; USD 9.50 newsstand/cover in Canada (effective 2010). illus. back issues avail.; reprints avail. **Document type:** *Journal, Academic/Scholarly.* **Description:** Contains humorous articles about science and scientists.
Related titles: Online - full text ed.: ISSN 1935-6862. free (effective 2010); ◆ Supplement(s): The Mini-Annals of Improbable Research. ISSN 1076-500X.
—IE, Ingenta.
Published by: Annals of Improbable Research, PO Box 380853, Cambridge, MA 02238. TEL 617-491-4437, FAX 617-661-0927, info@improbable.com, http://www.improbable.com. Ed. Marc Abrahams.

509 GBR ISSN 0003-3790
Q1 CODEN: ANNSA8
➤ **ANNALS OF SCIENCE**; a review of the history of science since the thirteenth century. Text in English. 1936. q. GBP 951, EUR 1,254, USD 1,575 combined subscription to institutions (print & online eds.) (effective 2009). adv. bk.rev. bibl.; illus. index. back issues avail.; reprint service avail. from PSC. **Document type:** *Journal, Academic/Scholarly.* **Description:** Directed to all who are interested in the evolution of science and its impact on the development of related arts and industries.
Related titles: Microfiche ed.: (from PQC); Online - full text ed.: ISSN 1464-505X. GBP 903, EUR 1,191, USD 1,496 to institutions (effective 2009) (from IngentaConnect).
Indexed: A01, A02, A03, A08, A20, A22, A28, APA, ASCA, AmH&L, AmHI, ArtHuCI, B04, B07, BRD, BrCerAb, BrGeoL, BrHumI, C&ISA, CA, CA/WCA, CCMJ, CIA, CIS, CLOSS, CPEI, Cadscan, CerAb, ChemAb, CivEngAb, CorrAb, CurCont, DIP, E&CAJ, E01, E11, EEA, EMA, EMBASE, ERIC, ESPM, EngInd, EnvEAb, ExcerpMed, FR, G03, GSA, GSI, GeoRef, H07, H15, HistAb, IBR, IBZ, ISR, Inspec, LeadAb, M&TEA, M09, MBF, MEDLINE, METADEX, MLA-IB, MSN, MathR, P11, P26, P30, P52, P54, P56, PCI, PQC, RASB, RILM, SCI, SCOPUS, SSCI, SolStAb, SpeleolAb, T02, T04, W03, W07, WAA, Z02, Zincscan.
—AskIEEE, CASDDS, IE, Infotrieve, Ingenta, INIST, Linda Hall. **CCC.**
Published by: Taylor & Francis Ltd. (Subsidiary of: Taylor & Francis Group), 4 Park Sq, Milton Park, Abingdon, Oxfordshire OX14 4RN, United Kingdom. TEL 44-20-70176000, FAX 44-20-70176336, subscriptions@tandf.co.uk, http://www.taylorandfrancis.com. Ed. Trevor H Levere. Adv. contact Linda Hann. **Subscr. addr. in N. America:** Taylor & Francis Inc., Customer Services Dept, 325 Chestnut St, 8th Fl, Philadelphia, PA 19106. TEL 215-625-8900, 800-354-1420, FAX 215-625-2940, customerservice@taylorandfrancis.com; **Subscr. to:** Journals Customer Service, Sheepen Pl, Colchester, Essex CO3 3LP, United Kingdom. TEL 44-20-70175544, FAX 44-20-70175198, tf.enquiries@tfinforma.com.

508.074 ZAF ISSN 1562-5273
QH195.S6 CODEN: ACPVAI
➤ **ANNALS OF THE EASTERN CAPE MUSEUMS.** Text in English. 1961. irreg., latest vol.3, 2002. price varies. back issues avail. **Document type:** *Monographic series, Academic/Scholarly.*
Formed by the 2000 merger of: Annals of the Cape Provincial Museums: Natural History (0570-1880); Annals of the Cape Provincial Museums: Human Sciences (0256-6699)
Indexed: A29, AICP, B20, B21, B25, BIOSIS Prev, ESPM, EntAb, GeoRef, I10, ISAP, MycolAb, OceAb, SpeleolAb, VirolAbstr, WildRev, Z01.
Published by: Albany Museum, Somerset St, Grahamstown, East Cape 6139, South Africa. TEL 27-46-622312, FAX 27-46-622398, amfg@giraffe.ru.ac.za. Ed. F C de Moor. **Co-sponsors:** East London Museum; Port Elizabeth Museum; Kaffrarian Museum, King William's Town.

500 ESP ISSN 1136-470X
ANO CERO. Text in Spanish. 1990. m. adv. **Document type:** *Magazine, Consumer.*
Published by: Editorial America Iberica, C. Miguel Yuste 33bis, Madrid, 28037, Spain. TEL 34-91-3277950, FAX 34-91-3044746, editorial@eai.es, http://www.eai.es/. Ed. Enrique de Vicente. adv.: page EUR 3,650; trim 210 x 285.

500 CHN ISSN 1007-4260
ANQING SHIFAN XUEYUAN XUEBAO (ZIRAN KEXUE BAN)/ANQING TEACHERS COLLEGE. JOURNAL (NATURAL SCIENCE EDITION). Text in Chinese. 1995. q. back issues avail. **Document type:** *Journal, Academic/Scholarly.*
Related titles: Online - full text ed.
Published by: Anqing Shifan Xueyuan, 128, Hunan Lu, Anqing, 246011, China. TEL 86-556-5500129, FAX 86-556-5500148, http://www.aqtc.edu.cn/.

500 DEU ISSN 0942-0398
Q124.95
ANTIKE NATURWISSENSCHAFT UND IHRE REZEPTION. Text in German. 1990. irreg., latest vol.19, 2009. EUR 18 per vol. (effective 2010). **Document type:** *Monographic series, Academic/Scholarly.*
Indexed: IBR, IBZ.
Published by: Wissenschaftlicher Verlag Trier, Bergstr 27, Trier, 54295, Germany. TEL 49-651-41503, FAX 49-651-41504, wvt@wvttrier.de. Ed. Georg Woehrle.

500 JPN ISSN 1346-1311
AOMORI AKENOHOSHI TANKI DAIGAKU KENKYU KIYO/AOMORI AKENOHOSHI JUNIOR COLLEGE RESEARCH BULLETIN. Text in Japanese. 1968. a. **Document type:** *Journal, Academic/Scholarly.*
Formerly (until 1999): Aomori Akenohoshi Tanki Daigaku Kiyo (0289-8977)
Indexed: RILM.
Published by: Aomori Akenohoshi Tanki Daigaku/Aomori Akenohoshi Junior College, 2-6-32 Namiuchi, Aomori, 030-0961, Japan. http://www.aomori-akenohoshi.ac.jp/.

500 NOR ISSN 0803-6926
APOLLON; forskningsmagasin fra universitetet i Oslo. Text in Norwegian. 1962. q. free (effective 2004). back issues avail. **Document type:** *Journal, Academic/Scholarly.* **Description:** Science and research magazine from the University of Oslo.
Former titles (until 1992): Akademisk Kvartal (0802-9784); (until 1989): Nytt fra Universitetet i Oslo (0800-708X)
Related titles: Online - full text ed.: ISSN 0806-3702. 1994; English ed.: ISSN 0809-9189. 1996-2004; resumed 2008.
Published by: Universitetet i Oslo/University of Oslo, PO Box 1072, Blindern, Oslo, 0317, Norway. http://www.uio.no. Ed. Harald Aas.

500 USA ISSN 0882-4347
APPLIED ORGONOMETRY; notes from the workshop of applied orgonometry. Text in English. 1986. 3/yr. looseleaf. USD 25.
Published by: R R P Publishers, PO Box 8, Easton, PA 18044-0008. TEL 215-252-1199. Ed. Jacob Meyerowitz.

016.5 016.6 USA
APPLIED SCIENCE & TECHNOLOGY INDEX. Text in English. 1983. (updated weekly on OCLC)), base vol. plus d. updates. USD 2,845 (effective 2011). **Document type:** *Database, Abstract/Index.*
Media: Online - full text. **Related titles:** CD-ROM ed.: ISSN 1063-8695. USD 1,495; Magnetic Tape ed.; ◆ Print ed.: Applied Science & Technology Index (Print). ISSN 0003-6986.
Published by: H.W. Wilson, 950 University Ave, Bronx, NY 10452. TEL 718-588-8400, 800-367-6770, FAX 718-590-1617, 800-590-1617, custserv@hwwilson.com.

500 CHE ISSN 2076-3417
▼ ➤ **APPLIED SCIENCES.** Text in English. forthcoming 2011. q. free (effective 2011). **Document type:** *Journal, Academic/Scholarly.*
Media: Online - full text.
Published by: M D P I AG, Postfach, Basel, 4005, Switzerland. TEL 41-61-6837734, FAX 41-61-3028918, http://www.mdpi.org/. Ed. Ophelia Han.

500 510 SAU ISSN 1015-4442
Q82 CODEN: AGSREJ
➤ **ARAB GULF JOURNAL OF SCIENTIFIC RESEARCH.** Text in Arabic, English. 1983. 3/yr. SAR 100 domestic to individuals; USD 25 foreign to individuals; SAR 200 domestic to institutions; USD 50 foreign to institutions (effective 1999). back issues avail. **Document type:** *Journal, Academic/Scholarly.*
Formed by the 1989 merger of: Arab Gulf Journal of Scientific Research. Section A: Mathematical and Physical Sciences (0259-8930); Arab Gulf Journal of Scientific Research. Section B: Agricultural and Biological Sciences (0259-8949); Which superseded: Arab Gulf Journal of Scientific Research (0256-4548)
Indexed: A34, A35, A36, A37, A38, ASCA, ASFA, AgBio, AgrForAb, B21, B23, BA, BIOBASE, BioDAb, C25, C30, CABA, CCMJ, CIN, CRFR, CTFA, ChemAb, ChemTitl, E04, E05, E12, ESPM, EntAb, F08, F12, FCA, FLUIDEX, G11, GEOBASE, GH, GeoRef, H16, H17, I11, IABS, INIS AtomInd, IndVet, Inspec, MSN, MaizeAb, MathR, N02, N03, N04, N05, O01, OR, OceAb, P32, P33, P37, P39, P40, PHN&I, PlantSci, PollutAb, R07, R08, R12, R13, RA&MP, RM&VM, S&MA, S12, S13, S16, S17, SCI, SCOPUS, SSciA, SWRA, SpeleolAb, T05, TAR, TriticAb, VS, W07, W10, W11, Z01, Z02.
—BLDSC (1583.226630), AskIEEE, CASDDS, IE, Ingenta, INIST, Linda Hall.
Published by: Arab Bureau of Education for the Gulf States, P O Box 94693, Riyadh, 11614, Saudi Arabia. TEL 966-1-4774644, FAX 966-1-4783165, TELEX 401441 TARBIA SJ. Ed. Daham Alani. Circ: 2,000.

➤ **ARAB LEAGUE EDUCATIONAL, SCIENTIFIC, AND CULTURAL ORGANIZATION. INFORMATION NEWSLETTER.** *see* EDUCATION

➤ **ARABIAN JOURNAL FOR SCIENCE AND ENGINEERING.** *see* ENGINEERING

➤ **ARABIC SCIENCES AND PHILOSOPHY**; a historical journal. *see* HISTORY

500 ESP ISSN 1132-2292
ARANZADIANA; aranzadiko berriak. Text in Spanish. 1953. a. free to members. **Document type:** *Bulletin, Academic/Scholarly.* **Description:** Reviews the association's activities.
Indexed: GeoRef, Z01.
Published by: Sociedad de Ciencias Aranzadi/Zientzi Elkartea, Calle del Alto de Zorroaga 11, Donostia, San Sebastian 20014, Spain. TEL 34-943-466142, FAX 34-943-455811, idazkatitza@aranzadi-zientziak.org, http://www.aranzadi-zientziak.org.

ARAUCARIA C&T. (Araucaria Ciencia e Tecnologia) *see* TECHNOLOGY: COMPREHENSIVE WORKS

500 NLD ISSN 0166-459X
ARCHIEF. Text in Dutch. 1769. irreg. price varies.
Former titles (until 1856): Zeeuwsch Genootschap der Wetenschappen. Nieuwe Werken (2210-3627); (until 1839): Zeeuwsch Genootschap der Wetenschappen. Nieuwe Verhandelingen (2210-3651); (until 1807): Verhandelingen Uitgegeven door het Zeeuwsch Genootschap der Wetenschappen te Vissingen (2210-366X)
Published by: Koninklijk Zeeuwsch Genootschap der Wetenschappen, Kousteensedijk 7, Middelburg, 4331 JE, Netherlands. TEL 31-118-654347, FAX 31-118-654439, info@zeeuwsgenootschap.nl.

ARCHIMEDES; natural science magazine for the whole family. *see* CHILDREN AND YOUTH—For

500 NLD ISSN 1385-0180
T14.7
ARCHIMEDES (NEW SERIES); new studies in the history and philosophy of science and technology. Text in English. 1964-19??; resumed 1996. irreg., latest vol.24, 2009. price varies. bk.rev. illus. **Document type:** *Monographic series, Academic/Scholarly.* **Description:** Aims to further the integration of the histories of science and technology, to investigate the technical, social and practical histories of specific developments in science and technology, and to bring the histories of science and technology into closer contact with the philosophy of science.
Formerly: Archimedes (0003-8377)
Indexed: MSN.
—BLDSC (1597.515000), IE.
Published by: Springer Netherlands (Subsidiary of: Springer Science+Business Media), Van Godewijckstraat 30, Dordrecht, 3311 GX, Netherlands. TEL 31-78-6576050, FAX 31-78-6576474. Ed. Jed Z Buchwald.

508 DEU ISSN 0518-3189
ARCHIV DER FREUNDE DER NATURGESCHICHTE IN MECKLENBURG. Text in German. 1954. a. EUR 8 (effective 2002).
Indexed: ASFA, B21, ESPM, GeoRef, IBR, IBZ, Z01.
—Linda Hall.
Published by: (Universitaet Rostock, Fachbereich Biologie), Universitaet Rostock, Presse- und Informationsstelle, Universitaetsplatz 1, Rostock, 18051, Germany. TEL 49-381-498-1013, FAX 49-381-498-1032, pressestelle@uni-rostock.de, http://www.uni-rostock.de.

509 DEU ISSN 0003-9519
Q125 CODEN: AHESAN
➤ **ARCHIVE FOR HISTORY OF EXACT SCIENCES.** Text in English; Text occasionally in French, German, Italian, Latin, Spanish. 1960. bi-m. EUR 1,098, USD 1,358 combined subscription to institutions (print & online eds.) (effective 2012). adv. bibl.; charts. index. reprint service avail. from PSC. **Document type:** *Journal, Academic/Scholarly.* **Description:** Focuses on mathematics and natural philosophy. Includes examination of the physical sciences.
Related titles: Microform ed.: (from PQC); Online - full text ed.: ISSN 1432-0657 (from IngentaConnect).
Indexed: A01, A03, A08, A20, A22, A26, ASCA, ArtHuCI, BrArAb, CA, CCMJ, CIS, CMCI, CurCont, E01, FR, HistAb, IBR, IBZ, ISR, MSN, MathR, P30, RASB, S01, SCI, SCOPUS, T02, W04, W07, Z02.
—BLDSC (1634.430000), IE, Infotrieve, Ingenta, INIST, Linda Hall. **CCC.**
Published by: Springer (Subsidiary of: Springer Science+Business Media), Tiergartenstr 17, Heidelberg, 69121, Germany. TEL 49-6221-4870, FAX 49-6221-345229. Eds. J Z Buchwald, J J Gray. **Subscr. in the Americas to:** Springer New York LLC, Journal Fulfillment, PO Box 2485, Secaucus, NJ 07096. TEL 800-777-4643, 201-348-4033, FAX 201-348-4505, journals-ny@springer.com, http://www.springer.com; **Subscr. to:** Springer Distribution Center, Kundenservice Zeitschriften, Haberstr 7, Heidelberg 69126, Germany. TEL 49-6221-3454303, FAX 49-6221-3454229, subscriptions@springer.com.

509 CHE ISSN 1661-464X
Q67 CODEN: ASGVAH
➤ **ARCHIVES DES SCIENCES.** Text in English, French, German, Italian. 1981. 3/yr. adv. illus. back issues avail. **Document type:** *Proceedings, Academic/Scholarly.*
Formerly (until 2004): Archives des Sciences et Compte Rendu des Seances de la Societe de Physique et d'Histoire Naturelle de Geneve (0252-9289); Which was formed by the merger of (1884-1981): Compte Rendu des Seances de la Societe de Physique et d'Histoire Naturelle de Geneve (0583-8401); (1948-1981): Archives des Sciences (0003-9705); Which was formerly (1846-1947): Archives des Sciences Physiques et Naturelles (0365-7116); (1841-1846): Archives de l'Electricite (0259-6598)
Related titles: Microfiche ed.: (from BHP); Microfilm ed.: (from PMC).
Indexed: A20, A22, ApMecR, B21, B25, BIOSIS Prev, CPEI, CTA, ChemAb, ChemoAb, CurCont, Englnd, GeoRef, IBR, IBZ, ISR, Inspec, MathR, MycolAb, NSA, P30, RASB, SCI, SCOPUS, SpeleolAb, VITIS, W07, Z01.
—BLDSC (1642.000000), AskIEEE, CASDDS, IE, Infotrieve, Ingenta, INIST, Linda Hall.
Published by: Societe de Physique et d'Histoire Naturelle de Geneve, Museum d'Histoire Naturelle, Case Postale 6434, Geneva 6, 1211, Switzerland. TEL 41-22-4186321, FAX 41-22-4186301. Ed. Robert Degli Agosti TEL 41-22-7057404.

500.9 BEL ISSN 0003-9810
Q1 CODEN: AIHSAB
➤ **ARCHIVES INTERNATIONALES D'HISTOIRE DES SCIENCES.** Text in English, French, German, Italian, Spanish, Russian. 1919; N.S. 1972. 2/yr. EUR 83 (effective 2012). adv. bk.rev. bibl.; charts; illus. index. back issues avail. **Document type:** *Journal, Academic/ Scholarly.*
Formerly (until 1947): Archeion (Rome) (0392-7865); (until 1928): Archivio di Storia della Scienza (0393-9316)
Indexed: A22, AmH&L, CA, CCMJ, ChemAb, DIP, EMBASE, ExcerpMed, FR, GeoRef, HistAb, IBR, IBZ, IPB, MEDLINE, MLA-IB, MSN, MathR, P30, PCI, Perlslam, RASB, SCOPUS, SpeleolAb, T02, Z02.
—IE, INIST, Linda Hall.
Published by: (Istituto della Enciclopedia Italiana ITA), Brepols Publishers, Begijnhof 67, Turnhout, 2300, Belgium. TEL 32-14-448020, FAX 32-14-428919, periodicals@brepols.net. Ed. Eberhard Knobloch. Circ: 1,200.

500 IND ISSN 0975-508X
▼ ➤ **ARCHIVES OF APPLIED SCIENCE RESEARCH.** Text in English. 2009. q. free (effective 2011). Index. back issues avail. **Document type:** *Journal, Academic/Scholarly.* **Description:** Publishes full length research papers, reviews, short communications, book review and notes dealing with entire aspects of applied sciences like agricultural & soil, animal & veterinary, biological, forensic, marine, petroleum & gas, pharmaceutical, polymer, medical, biomedical materials, chemical physics, computational chemistry, food & food industry, marine technology, medical technology, medicine research, nanotechnology, synthetic drugs, textile industry & fabrics etc.
Media: Online - full text.
Indexed: A01, A34, A35, A36, A37, A38, AgBio, AgrForAb, B21, B23, C25, C30, CABA, D01, E12, F08, F11, F12, FCA, G11, GH, H16, H17, I11, MaizeAb, N02, N03, N04, O01, P32, P33, P39, P40, R07, R08, R11, R12, R13, S12, S13, S16, SoyAb, T02, T05, TAR, W10, W11.
Published by: Scholars Research Library, 20, Kumbha Nagar, Sector4, Udaipur, Rajasthan, India. TEL 91-982-8173650, editor@scholarsresearchlibrary.com, http://www.scholarsresearchlibrary.com/.

508.09 GBR ISSN 0260-9541
Z7403
➤ **ARCHIVES OF NATURAL HISTORY.** Abbreviated title: A N H. Text in English. 1936. s-a. GBP 115 domestic to institutions; USD 231 in North America to institutions; GBP 128 elsewhere to institutions; GBP 144 combined subscription domestic to institutions (print & online eds.); USD 289 combined subscription in North America to institutions (print & online eds.); GBP 160 combined subscription elsewhere to institutions (print & online eds.) (effective 2012). adv. bk.rev. bibl.; illus. index. back issues avail.; reprints avail. **Document type:** *Journal, Academic/Scholarly.* **Description:** Features papers on the history and bibliography of natural history in its broadest sense, and in all periods and all cultures.
Formerly (until 1981): Society for the Bibliography of Natural History. Journal (0037-9778)
Related titles: Online - full text ed.: ISSN 1755-6260. USD 190 in North America to institutions; GBP 103 elsewhere to institutions (effective 2012).
Indexed: A22, BrGeoL, CA, DIP, GeoRef, HistAb, IBR, IBZ, MLA-IB, P30, SCOPUS, SPPI, SpeleolAb, T02, W08, WildRev, Z01.
—BLDSC (1637.947000), IE, Infotrieve, Ingenta, INIST, Linda Hall. **CCC.**
Published by: (Society for the History of Natural History), Edinburgh University Press, 22 George Sq, Edinburgh, Scotland EH8 9LF, United Kingdom. TEL 44-131-6504218, FAX 44-131-6503286, journals@eup.ed.ac.uk. Ed. Dr. E Charles Nelson. Adv. contact Ruth Allison TEL 44-131-6504220.

500 ITA ISSN 1122-0929
ARCHIVIO DELLA CORRISPONDENZA DEGLI SCIENZIATI ITALIANI. Text in Italian. 1985. irreg., latest vol.14, 1999. price varies. **Document type:** *Monographic series, Academic/Scholarly.*
Indexed: CCMJ.
Published by: (Istituto e Museo di Storia della Scienza), Casa Editrice Leo S. Olschki, Viuzzo del Pozzetto 8, Florence, 50126, Italy. TEL 39-055-6530684, FAX 39-055-6530214, celso@olschki.it, http://www.olschki.it.

ARCHIWUM ENERGETYKI. *see* ENGINEERING

919 551 CAN ISSN 0004-0843
G600 CODEN: ATICAB
➤ **ARCTIC.** Text and summaries in English, French, Russian. 1947. q. USD 25 per issue to non-members; free to members (effective 2011). bk.rev. abstr.; bibl.; charts; illus.; maps. index. back issues avail.; reprints avail. **Document type:** *Journal, Academic/Scholarly.* **Description:** Contains articles in area of scholarship dealing with the polar and subpolar regions of the world.
Related titles: Microfilm ed.; Microform ed.: (from PQC); Online - full text ed.: ISSN 1923-1245.
Indexed: A01, A02, A03, A08, A20, A22, A26, A33, A34, A36, A37, A38, ABS&EES, ASCA, ASFA, ASTIS, AbAn, AgrForAb, AmH&L, ArcBib, B21, B23, B25, BIOBASE, BIOSIS Prev, BNNA, C03, C25, C30, CA, CABA, CBCARef, CBPI, CPerI, ChemAb, CurCont, E&PHSE, E04, E05, E08, E12, E17, ESPM, EnvAb, EnvInd, F08, F12, FCA, FR, G08, G11, GEOBASE, GH, GP&P, GeoRef, H17, HPNRM, HistAb, I05, I11, IABS, IBR, IBZ, ISR, IndVet, KWIWR, LT, M&GPA, MLA-IB, MycolAb, N02, N03, OceAb, OffTech, P32, P33, P37, P40, P48, P52, P56, PGegResA, PQC, PetrolAb, PollutAb, R07, R08, R12, RASB, RRTA, RefZh, S06, S09, S13, S16, S17, SCI, SCOPUS, SSciA, SWRA, SpeleolAb, T02, TAR, TriticAb, VS, W07, W08, W10, W11, WildRev, Z01.
—BLDSC (1663.000000), CASDDS, CIS, IE, Infotrieve, Ingenta, INIST, Linda Hall, PADDS. **CCC.**
Published by: (Social Sciences and Humanities Research Council of Canada), Arctic Institute of North America, University of Calgary, 2500 University Dr N W, Calgary, AB T2N 1N4, Canada. TEL 403-220-7515, FAX 403-282-4609, arctic@ucalgary.ca. Ed. Karen McCullough TEL 403-220-4049. **Subscr. to:** University Microfilms International, 300 N. Zeeb Rd, PO Box 1346, Ann Arbor, MI 48106. TEL 734-761-4700, http://www.proquest.com.

577 USA ISSN 1523-0430
G575 CODEN: AAARFO
➤ **ARCTIC, ANTARCTIC, AND ALPINE RESEARCH**; an interdisciplinary journal. Text in English. 1969. q. USD 225 domestic to institutions; USD 275 foreign to institutions; USD 270 combined subscription domestic to institutions (print & online eds.); USD 290 combined subscription foreign to institutions (print & online eds.); USD 65 per issue domestic to institutions; USD 75 per issue foreign to institutions (effective 2011). bk.rev. bibl.; charts; illus.; stat.; maps. index. back issues avail.; reprints avail. **Document type:** *Journal, Academic/ Scholarly.* **Description:** Presents original research pertaining to cold environments, both past and present.
Formerly (until 1999): Arctic and Alpine Research (0004-0851)
Related titles: Microform ed.: (from PQC); Online - full text ed.: ISSN 1938-4246.
Indexed: A20, A22, A29, A33, A34, ASCA, AbAn, Agr, B20, B21, B23, B25, BIOBASE, BIOSIS Prev, C25, C30, CA, CABA, ChemAb, CurCont, E01, E04, E05, E12, E17, ESPM, EnvAb, EnvInd, F08, F11, F12, G11, GEOBASE, GH, GeoRef, H16, HPNRM, I10, I11, IABS, ISR, IndVet, KWIWR, LT, M&GPA, MycolAb, N04, N05, O01, OR, P32, P33, P37, P40, PGegResA, PollutAb, R07, R08, R12, R13, RRTA, RefZh, S13, S16, S17, SCI, SCOPUS, SSciA, SWRA, SoyAb, SpeleolAb, T02, TAR, TriticAb, VS, VirolAbstr, W07, W08, W10, W11, WildRev, Z01.
—BLDSC (1663.068000), CASDDS, IE, Infotrieve, Ingenta, INIST, Linda Hall. **CCC.**
Published by: University of Colorado, Institute of Arctic and Alpine Research, 1560 30th St, 450 UCB, Boulder, CO 80309. TEL 303-492-6387, FAX 303-492-3287, instaar@colorado.edu. Eds. Anne E Jennings, Bill Bowman.

508.311 910 USA ISSN 1045-4764
G615
➤ **ARCTIC RESEARCH OF THE UNITED STATES.** Text in English. 1987. s-a. back issues avail. **Document type:** *Journal, Academic/ Scholarly.*
Related titles: Online - full text ed.
Indexed: A22, A26, E08, ESPM, G08, GeoRef, I05, M&GPA, S06, S09, SSciA, SpeleolAb, WildRev.
—BLDSC (1663.163000), Linda Hall.
Published by: U.S. Department of Commerce, National Science Foundation, 4201 Wilson Blvd, Ste 245, Arlington, VA 22230. TEL 703-292-5111, 800-877-8339, info@nsf.gov.

509.798 USA
ARCTIC SCIENCE CONFERENCE. PROCEEDINGS. Text in English. 1950. a. USD 17. **Document type:** *Proceedings.*
Former titles: Alaska Science Conference. Proceedings (0084-6120); (until 1969): Science in Alaska (0191-2151)
Indexed: GeoRef, SpeleolAb, WildRev.
Published by: American Association for the Advancement of Science, Arctic Division, PO Box 80271, Fairbanks, AK 99708. TEL 907-474-7487. Circ: 600.

500 USA ISSN 0193-8509
Q11.A72 CODEN: JNASDB
ARIZONA-NEVADA ACADEMY OF SCIENCE. JOURNAL. Text in English. 1959. s-a. free to members (effective 2010). adv. bk.rev. charts; illus. back issues avail. **Document type:** *Journal, Academic/ Scholarly.*
Formerly (until 1978): Arizona Academy of Science. Journal (0004-1378)
Related titles: Online - full text ed.: ISSN 1533-6085; ◆ Supplement(s): Arizona-Nevada Academy of Science. Journal. Proceedings.
Indexed: Agr, B25, BIOSIS Prev, ChemAb, EIA, EnvAb, GeoRef, MycolAb, SASA, SpeleolAb, Z01.
—CASDDS, Ingenta, Linda Hall. **CCC.**
Published by: Arizona-Nevada Academy of Science, Biomedical Sciences, Midwestern University, 19555 N 59th Ave, Glendale, AZ 85308. TEL 623-572-3666, FAX 623-572-3673, pchave@midwestern.edu. Adv. contact Robert Reavis.

500 USA
Q11.A72
ARIZONA-NEVADA ACADEMY OF SCIENCE. JOURNAL. PROCEEDINGS. Text in English. 19??. a. free to qualified personnel (effective 2010). back issues avail. **Document type:** *Proceedings, Academic/Scholarly.* **Description:** Covers meeting schedule, plus abstracts for the talks and posters.
Former titles (until 2001): Arizona-Nevada Academy of Science. Journal. Proceedings Supplement (0895-4860); (until 1978): Arizona Academy of Science. Journal. Proceedings Supplement
Related titles: Online - full text ed.; ◆ Supplement to: Arizona-Nevada Academy of Science. Journal. ISSN 0193-8509.
Indexed: GeoRef.
—Linda Hall.
Published by: Arizona-Nevada Academy of Science, Biomedical Sciences, Midwestern University, 19555 N 59th Ave, Glendale, AZ 85308. TEL 623-572-3666, FAX 623-572-3673, pchave@midwestern.edu, http://www.arizonanevadaacademyofscience.org. Ed. Florence Slater TEL 623-845-3619.

500 061.67 USA
AS36 CODEN: AKASAO
➤ **ARKANSAS ACADEMY OF SCIENCE. JOURNAL.** Text in English. 1941. a. free to members (effective 2011). back issues avail. **Document type:** *Journal, Academic/Scholarly.*
Formerly (until 1997): Arkansas Academy of Science. Proceedings (0097-4374)
Related titles: Online - full text ed.
Indexed: AbAn, BibAg, CIN, ChemAb, ChemTitl, GeoRef, SASA, SpeleolAb, WildRev, Z01.
—CASDDS.
Published by: Arkansas Academy of Science, Div of Math & Sciences, Univ of Arkansas at Monticello, Monticello, AR 71656. Ed. Mostafa Hemmati TEL 479-968-0340.

500 FIN ISSN 1235-0583
ARKTISEN KESKUS. TIEDOTTEITA/ARCTIC CENTRE. REPORTS. Text in Multiple languages. 1991. irreg., latest vol.43, 2004. price varies. back issues avail. **Document type:** *Monographic series, Academic/Scholarly.*
Indexed: A33, GeoRef.
Published by: Lapin Yliopisto, Arktinen Keskus/University of Lapland. Arctic Centre, University of Lapland, PO Box 122, Rovaniemi, 96100, Finland. TEL 358-16-3412758, FAX 358-16-3412777, Http://www.arcticcentre.org.

500 PRT ISSN 0870-6581
QH132.A9
ARQUIPELAGO. CIENCIAS DA NATUREZA. Variant title: Arquipelago. Serie Ciencias da Natureza. Text in English, Portuguese. 1980. a. **Description:** Publishes scientific articles, brief notes, and reviews on the natural environment of the archipelago of the Azores and the surrounding region.
Related titles: ◆ Supplement(s): Arquipelago. Ciencias Biologicas e Maritimas. ISSN 0873-4704.
Indexed: GeoRef, IBR, IBZ, MLA-IB.
Published by: Universidade dos Acores/University of the Azores, Camous de Ponta Delgada, Ponta Delgada, 9501-801, Portugal. Ed. Helen Rost Martins.

S

ARTNODES; revista d'art, ciencia i tecnologia. *see* ART

500 600 USA
ARTS AND SCIENCES NEWSLETTER. Text in English. 1984. s-a. membership. **Document type:** *Newsletter.*
Published by: Vermont Academy of Arts and Sciences, 2 Buxton Ave, Middletown Springs, VT 05757. TEL 802-235-2302. Ed. Frances B Krouse. Circ: 500.

500 ESP ISSN 1132-9319
ARXIUS DE LES SECCIONS DE CIENCIES. Text in Catalan. 1990. irreg. back issues avail. **Document type:** *Journal, Academic/Scholarly.*
Indexed: Z01.
Published by: Institut d'Estudis Catalans, Carrer del Carme 47, Barcelona, 08001, Spain. TEL 34-932-701620, FAX 34-932-701180, informacio@iecat.net, http://www2.iecat.net.

500 001.3 JPN ISSN 1341-3589
ASAHI DAIGAKU IPPAN KYOIKU KIYO/ASAHI UNIVERSITY JOURNAL OF LIBERAL ARTS AND SCIENCE. Text in Japanese. 1975. a.
Former titles (until 1992): Asahi Daigaku Kyoyobu Kenkyu Hokoku/Asahi University. School of Liberal Arts. Journal (0912-0947); (until 1984): Gifu Shika Daigaku Shingakubu Kenkyu Hokoku/Gifu College of Dentistry. Predental Faculty. Journal (0386-5665)
—BLDSC (5010.307000).
Published by: Asahi Daigaku/Asahi University, 1851 Hozumi, Motosu-gun, Gifu 501-0296, Japan. http://www.asahi-u.ac.jp/.

ASIA - PACIFIC FORUM ON SCIENCE LEARNING AND TEACHING. *see* EDUCATION

ASIA PACIFIC JOURNAL OF LIFE SCIENCES. *see* ASIAN STUDIES

ASIAN GEOGRAPHIC. *see* CONSERVATION

500 PAK ISSN 1992-1454
➤ **ASIAN JOURNAL OF SCIENTIFIC RESEARCH.** Text in English. 2006. 4/yr. **Document type:** *Journal, Academic/Scholarly.*
Description: Addresses both applied and theoretical issues. The scope of the journal encompasses research articles, original research reports, reviews and short communications in the fields of applied and theoretical sciences, biology, chemistry, physics, zoology, medical studies, environmental sciences, mathematics, statistics, geology, engineering, computer science, social sciences, natural sciences, technological sciences, linguistics, medicine, industrial, and all other applied and theoretical sciences.
Related titles: Online - full text ed.: free (effective 2011).
Indexed: A01, A29, A34, A37, A38, AgrForAb, AnBeAb, B20, B21, BA, C25, C30, CABA, D01, E12, E17, ESPM, EntAb, F08, F11, F12, FCA, G11, GH, H16, H17, I11, IndVet, M&GPA, MaizeAb, N02, N03, N04, O01, OR, OceAb, P32, P33, P37, P39, P40, R07, R11, R12, R13, RA&MP, S13, S16, SCOPUS, SWRA, SoyAb, T02, T05, TAR, VS, ViroIAbstr, W11.
Published by: A N S I Network, 308 Lasani Town, Sargodha Rd, Faisalabad, 38090, Pakistan. TEL 92-41-8787087, FAX 92-41-8815544, sarwarm@ansimail.org, http://ansinet.com.

500 PAK ISSN 2221-4291
▼ **ASIAN TRANSACTIONS ON BASIC & APPLIED SCIENCES.** Text in English. 2011. 6/yr. back issues avail. **Document type:** *Journal, Academic/Scholarly.*
Media: Online - full text. **Related titles:** Online - full text ed.: free.
Published by: A T Publisher, Fazl-e-Haq Rd, Blue Area, Islamabad, 44000, Pakistan. editor@asian-transactions.org, http://www.asian-transactions.org/index.htm.

500 600 PAK ISSN 2221-4283
▼ **ASIAN TRANSACTIONS ON SCIENCE & TECHNOLOGY.** Text in English. 2011. 6/yr. back issues avail. **Document type:** *Journal, Academic/Scholarly.*
Media: Online - full text. **Related titles:** Online - full text ed.: free.
Published by: A T Publisher, Fazl-e-Haq Rd, Blue Area, Islamabad, 44000, Pakistan. editor@asian-transactions.org, http://www.asian-transactions.org/index.htm.

500 BGD ISSN 1016-6947
Q80.B3
ASIATIC SOCIETY OF BANGLADESH. JOURNAL: SCIENCE; man and nature of Asia. Text in English. 1956. s-a. BDT 400, USD 40 per issue. **Document type:** *Journal, Academic/Scholarly.*
Supersedes in part (in 1975): Asiatic Society of Bangladesh. Journal (0377-0540); Which was formerly (until 1972): Asiatic Society of Pakistan. Journal (0571-317X)
—BLDSC (4701.610000).
Published by: Asiatic Society of Bangladesh, Ramna, 5 Old Secretariat Rd Nimtali, Dhaka, 1000, Bangladesh. TEL 88-2-9560500, FAX 88-2-9667586. Ed. S M Humayun Kabir. Pub. Sajahan Miah. Circ: 1,000.

500 RUS ISSN 1608-9014
ASPIRANT I SOISKATEL. Text in Russian. 2000. bi-m. USD 93 in United States (effective 2004). **Document type:** *Journal, Academic/Scholarly.* **Description:** Publishes scientific research articles written by students and applicants for graduate degrees in various sciences.
Indexed: RefZh.
Published by: Izdatel'stvo Kompaniya Sputnik+, Ryazanskii pr-kt, dom 8a, Moscow, 109428, Russian Federation. TEL 7-095-7304774, sputnikplus2000@mail.ru, http://www.sputnikplus.ru. **Dist. by:** East View Information Services, 10601 Wayzata Blvd, Minneapolis, MN 55305. TEL 952-252-1201, 800-477-1005, FAX 952-252-1202, info@eastview.com, http://www.eastview.com.

500 IND ISSN 0587-1921
Q73 CODEN: JASYBQ
➤ **ASSAM SCIENCE SOCIETY. JOURNAL.** Abbreviated title: JASS. Text and summaries in English. 1955. s-a. **Document type:** *Journal, Academic/Scholarly.* **Description:** Intended for researchers of all branches of science.
Indexed: CIS, Inspec, MathR, P30, Z02.
Published by: Assam Science Society, Jawaharnagar, Khanapara, Guwahati, 781022, India. TEL 91-361-2363258, secretary@assamsciencesociety.com, www.assamsciencesociety.com.

500 600 ZAF ISSN 0373-4250
T1 CODEN: ATSAAL
ASSOCIATED SCIENTIFIC AND TECHNICAL SOCIETIES OF SOUTH AFRICA. ANNUAL PROCEEDINGS. Text in English. 1921. a. free. back issues avail. **Document type:** *Proceedings.*
Indexed: IMMAb, Inspec.
—AskIEEE.
Published by: Associated Scientific and Technical Societies of South Africa, PO Box 93480, Yeoville, 2143, South Africa. TEL 27-11-4871512, FAX 27-11-6481876. Circ: (controlled).

500 CAN ISSN 0066-8842
Q21 CODEN: AACFAR
ASSOCIATION CANADIENNE - FRANCAISE POUR L'AVANCEMENT DES SCIENCES. ANNALES. Text in English. 1935. a. CAD 12.
Description: Summaries of all the communications presented at the association's congress.
Indexed: ArcBib, GeoRef, SpeleolAb.
—CASDDS.
Published by: Association Francophone pour le Savoir, 425 rue de la Gauchetiere E, Montreal, PQ H2L 2M7, Canada. TEL 514-849-0045, FAX 514-849-5558. Circ: 4,000.

500 CAN
ASSOCIATION CANADIENNE - FRANCAISE POUR L'AVANCEMENT DES SCIENCES. CAHIERS SCIENTIFIQUES. Text in English. irreg. price varies. **Document type:** *Monographic series, Academic/Scholarly.*
Formerly: Cahiers de l'A C F A S
Published by: Association Francophone pour le Savoir, 425 rue de la Gauchetiere E, Montreal, PQ H2L 2M7, Canada. TEL 514-849-0045, FAX 514-849-5558.

500.9 FRA ISSN 1167-9786
ASSOCIATION DES NATURALISTES DES YVELINES. BULLETIN. Text in French. N.S. 1974 (4th). q. EUR 18 domestic; EUR 30 foreign (effective 2008). illus. **Document type:** *Bulletin.*
Former titles (until 1992): Societe Versaillaise des Sciences Naturelles. Bulletin (0336-8300)
Indexed: GeoRef, SpeleolAb.
—INIST.
Published by: Association des Naturalistes des Yvelines, La Villa de Chevreloup, 34 route de Versailles, Rocquencourt, 78150, France. TEL 33-1-39555606. Circ: 500.

500.9 MLI
ASSOCIATION DES NATURALISTES DU MALI. BULLETIN. Text in French. a. **Document type:** *Bulletin.*
Published by: Association des Naturalistes du Mali, BP 1746, Bamako, Mali.

500 CAN ISSN 1498-5845
QC21
ASSOCIATION FRANCOPHONE POUR LE SAVOIR. DECOUVRIR. Text in French. 1959. 5/yr. CAD 48 to individuals; CAD 95 to institutions; CAD 27 to students (effective 2001). adv. bk.rev. back issues avail. **Document type:** *Magazine, Academic/Scholarly.* **Description:** A multi-disciplinary magazine addressed to members of the scientific community in the university, college, public, parapublic and private sectors.
Former titles (until 2000): Association Canadienne - Francaise pour l'Avancement des Sciences. Interface (0826-4864); (until 1984): Association Canadienne - Francaise pour l'Avancement des Sciences. Bulletin (0066-8850)
Indexed: PdeR.
—INIST. **CCC.**
Published by: Association Francophone pour le Savoir, 425 rue de la Gauchetiere E, Montreal, PQ H2L 2M7, Canada. TEL 514-849-0045, FAX 514-849-5558, acfas@acfas.ca, http://www.acfas.ca. R&P Danielle Ovellet. Adv. contact Chantal St. Denis. B&W page CAD 1,075, color page CAD 1,950; trim 11 x 8.5. Circ: 8,500.

ASSOCIATION NATIONALE DE LA RECHERCHE TECHNIQUE. LETTRE EUROPEENNE. *see* TECHNOLOGY: COMPREHENSIVE WORKS

500 BHR ISSN 1815-3852
➤ **ASSOCIATION OF ARAB UNIVERSITIES FOR BASIC AND APPLIED SCIENCES. JOURNAL/MAJALLAT ITTIHAD AL-JAMI'AT AL-'ARABIYYAT LI-L-'ULUM AL-'ASASIYYAT WA-AL-TATBIQITTAT.** Text in English; Summaries in Arabic, English. 2005. s-a. USD 15 (effective 2007). Index. back issues avail. **Document type:** *Journal, Academic/Scholarly.*
Related titles: Online - full text ed.: (from ScienceDirect).
Indexed: C10, CA, T02.
—**CCC.**
Published by: University of Bahrain, College of Science, PO Box 32038, Isa, Bahrain. TEL 973-17437555, FAX 973-17449662, alnaserw@sci.uob.bh, http://www.uob.edu.bh. Ed. H A Al-Maskati. Pub., R&P W E Alnaser. Circ: 500 (paid and controlled).

➤ **ASSOCIATION OF COLLEGE AND RESEARCH LIBRARIES. SCIENCE AND TECHNOLOGY SECTION SIGNAL.** *see* LIBRARY AND INFORMATION SCIENCES

500 300 COL ISSN 0124-213X
➤ **EL ASTROLABIO.** Text in Spanish, English. 1999. s-a. free to qualified personnel (effective 2009). abstr.; bibl. back issues avail. **Document type:** *Journal, Academic/Scholarly.*
Related titles: CD-ROM ed.
Published by: Gimnasio Campestre, Calle 165 Numero 8A, Bogota, Colombia. TEL 57-1-6684400, FAX 57-1-5261710. Eds. Juan Antonio Casas Pardo, Luz Helena Aljure.

500 EGY ISSN 1110-0184
ASWAN SCIENCE AND TECHNOLOGY BULLETIN/NASRAT ASWAN LIL-A!LUM WA AL-TIKNULUGYYAA. Text in English. 1979. s-a. **Document type:** *Bulletin, Academic/Scholarly.*
Published by: South Valley University, Faculty of Science, c/o Dr. Muhammad Abd-Allah, Aswan, Egypt. TEL 20-97-480450.

500 001.3 ITA ISSN 1724-2371
ATENEO DI SCIENZE, LETTERE ED ARTI DI BERGAMO. ALBUM. Text in Italian. 2001. irreg. **Document type:** *Journal, Academic/Scholarly.*
Published by: Ateneo di Scienze, Lettere ed Arti di Bergamo, Via Torquato Tasso 4, Bergamo, 24124, Italy. http://www.ateneobergamo.it.

500 001.3 ITA ISSN 1724-2363
ATENEO DI SCIENZE, LETTERE ED ARTI DI BERGAMO. QUADERNI. Text in Italian. 1999. irreg. **Document type:** *Monographic series, Academic/Scholarly.*
Published by: Ateneo di Scienze, Lettere ed Arti di Bergamo, Via Torquato Tasso 4, Bergamo, 24124, Italy. http://www.ateneobergamo.it.

500 700 ITA ISSN 0004-6558
ATENEO VENETO; rivista di scienze, lettere ed arti. Text in Italian. 1812. s-a. bk.rev. bibl.; charts; illus. index, cum.index. **Document type:** *Journal, Academic/Scholarly.* **Description:** Covers Venetian history and culture, humanities in general.
Former titles (until 1924): Ateneo Veneto. Atti (1722-3571); (until 1920): L'Ateneo Veneto (1722-3555); (until 1881): Ateneo Veneto. Atti (1722-3563); (until 1860): Esercitazioni Scientifiche e Letterarie (1722-3547); (until 1817): Ateneo Veneto. Sessioni Pubbliche (1722-3539)
Indexed: B24, IBR, IBZ, MLA, MLA-IB, P30, RILM.
Address: Campo S. Fantin 1897, Venice, VE, Italy. TEL 39-041-5224459. Circ: 1,000.

500 CAN
ATLANTIC SCIENCE. Text in English. 1975. 3/yr. free. **Description:** News about members of the council and research conducted by scientists in the Atlantic provinces.
Formerly: A P I C S News
Published by: Atlantic Provinces Council on the Sciences, Memorial University of Newfoundland, P O Box 4200, St. John's, NF A1C 5S7, Canada. TEL 709-737-8918, FAX 709-737-4569. Ed. Joan Atkinson. Circ: 3,000.

500 USA ISSN 1541-5031
ATLANTIS RISING. Text in English. 1994. bi-m. USD 24.95 domestic; USD 45.05 in Canada; USD 51.95 in Mexico; USD 55.55 in Europe; USD 59.45 in Asia; USD 59.45 in Africa (effective 2002). adv.
Description: Covers unexplained phenomena, mysteries and alternative science.
Address: PO Box 441, Livingston, MT 59047. TEL 406-222-0875, FAX 406-222-3078. Ed., Pub. Doug Kenyon.

▼ **ATLAS JOURNAL OF SCIENCE EDUCATION.** *see* EDUCATION

500 USA ISSN 0077-5630
QE565 CODEN: ATOBA4
ATOLL RESEARCH BULLETIN. Text in English. 1951. irreg., latest vol.581, 2010. price varies. back issues avail.; reprints avail. **Document type:** *Bulletin, Academic/Scholarly.*
Related titles: Microfilm ed.: 1951 (from BHP); Online - full text ed.: ISSN 1943-9660.
Indexed: A34, AICP, ASFA, Agr, AgrForAb, B21, B25, BIOSIS Prev, CABA, E12, E17, ESPM, F08, F12, GEOBASE, GH, GeoRef, H16, I11, MycolAb, OceAb, P30, P33, P39, S13, S16, SCOPUS, SPPI, SpeleolAb, T05, TAR, Z01.
—BLDSC (1768.000000), INIST, Linda Hall. **CCC.**
Published by: Smithsonian Institution Press, SI Bldg, Rm 153, MRC 010, PO Box 37012, Washington, DC 20013. TEL 202-633-3017, FAX 202-633-6877, schol.press@si.edu, http://www.si.edu. Ed. Ian G Macintyre.

AULA; revista de ensenanza e investigacion educativa. *see* EDUCATION

500 AUS ISSN 1442-679X
Q1 CODEN: SRCHAA
AUSTRALASIAN SCIENCE. Text in English. 1997. m. AUD 68 domestic to individuals; AUD 85 foreign to individuals; AUD 209 domestic to institutions; AUD 245 foreign to institutions; AUD 99 domestic to secondary schools; AUD 125 foreign to secondary schools; AUD 7.95 per issue (effective 2008). adv. bk.rev. illus. 48 p./no.; back issues avail. **Document type:** *Journal, Academic/Scholarly.* **Description:** Provides a forum for news, discussion and debate of recent scientific and technological developments in the Asia Pacific region.
Formerly (until 2000): Australasian Science Incorporating Search (1440-3919); Which was formed by the merger of (1938-1997): Search (0004-9549); Which was formerly (until 1970): Australian Journal of Science (0365-3668); (1980-1997): Australasian Science (1322-2384); Which was formerly (until 1993): Australasian Science Magazine (1036-0875); (until 1990): Australian Science Magazine (0729-6924); (until 1981): Science Mag (0159-9062)
Related titles: Online - full text ed.
Indexed: A11, A20, A22, A33, AEI, AESIS, ARI, ASCA, ASFA, B21, CA, E04, E05, ERO, ESPM, GeoRef, INIS AtomInd, Inspec, M01, M02, P10, P11, P18, P19, P26, P30, P48, P52, P53, P54, P55, P56, PCI, PQC, RASB, S11, SCOPUS, SpeleolAb, T02, U01, WBA, WMB, WildRev.
—BLDSC (1796.334600), CASDDS, IE, Ingenta, INIST, Linda Hall. **CCC.**
Published by: Control Publications Pty. Ltd., PO Box 2155, Wattletree, VIC 3145, Australia. TEL 61-3-95000015, FAX 61-3-95000255, advertise@control.com.au. Ed., Pub. Guy Nolch. R&P Barnaby Griggs. Adv. contact Joanna Dettl TEL 61-7-35116246. color page AUD 1,190; trim 210 x 297.

500 AUS ISSN 1833-9891
AUSTRALIA IN ANTARCTICA. Text in English. 2006. a.
Media: Online - full text.
Published by: Australian Government. Antarctic Division, Channel Highway, Kingston, TAS 7050, Australia. TEL 61-3-6232-3209, FAX 61-3-6232-3288.

500 AUS ISSN 1448-2037
AUSTRALIAN ACADEMY OF SCIENCE. ANNUAL REPORT. Text in English. 2001. a. free (effective 2008). back issues avail. **Document type:** *Report, Academic/Scholarly.* **Description:** Provides information on activities conducted, the upcoming challenges and plan of action by the Australian Academy of Science for every calendar year.
Formerly: Annual Report of the Council
Related titles: Online - full text ed.: free (effective 2008).
Published by: Australian Academy of Science, GPO Box 783, Canberra, ACT 2601, Australia. TEL 61-2-62019400, FAX 61-2-62019494, eb@science.org.au.

500 AUS
AUSTRALIAN ACADEMY OF SCIENCE. NATIONAL COMMITTEE FOR THE HISTORY AND PHILOSOPHY OF SCIENCE. ANNUAL LECTURE. Text in English. a.
Published by: Australian Academy of Science, National Committee for the History and Philosophy of Science, G.P.O. Box 783, Canberra, ACT 2601, Australia. TEL 61-2-62475777, FAX 61-2-62574620, eb@science.org.au, http://www.science.org.au/academy.

500 AUS ISSN 1031-9204
AUSTRALIAN ACADEMY OF SCIENCE. NEWSLETTER. Text in English. 1980. q. free (effective 2008). back issues avail. **Document type:** *Newsletter, Academic/Scholarly.* **Description:** Provides details of conferences conducted by Australian Academy of Science.
Formerly (until 1981): Australian Academy of Science. Science Report (0159-5458)

Related titles: Online - full text ed.: free (effective 2008).
Published by: Australian Academy of Science, GPO Box 783, Canberra, ACT 2601, Australia. TEL 61-2-62019400, FAX 61-2-62019494, eb@science.org.au. Ed. Neville Fletcher.

500 PAK ISSN 1991-8178
SB107
➤ **AUSTRALIAN JOURNAL OF BASIC AND APPLIED SCIENCES.** Abbreviated title: A J B A S. Text in English. 2006. q. USD 80 combined subscription print & CD-ROM eds. (effective 2007). **Document type:** *Journal, Academic/Scholarly.*
Related titles: CD-ROM ed.; Online - full text ed.: free (effective 2011).
Indexed: A01, A34, A35, A36, A37, A38, AgBio, AgrForAb, B23, BA, BP, C25, C30, CA, CABA, D01, E12, F08, F11, F12, FCA, G11, GH, H16, H17, I11, IndVet, LT, MaizeAb, N02, N03, N04, N05, O01, OR, P32, P33, P37, P38, P39, P40, PGegResA, PGrRegA, PHN&I, PN&I, R07, R08, R11, R12, R13, RA&MP, RM&VM, RRTA, S12, S13, S16, S17, SCOPUS, SoyAb, T02, T05, TAR, TriticAb, VS, W10, W11, Z01.
Published by: INSInet Publications, International Network for Scientific Information, P-112, St # 10, Haseeb Shaheed Colony, Hilal Road, Faisalabad, Punjab, Pakistan. TEL 92-333-6616624, editor@insinet.net, composer_editor@yahoo.com, http://www.insinet.net.

500 AUS ISSN 1448-9791
CODEN: TOLSEE
➤ **AUSTRALIAN LIFE SCIENTIST**; first for life science research. Abbreviated title: A L S. Text in English. 2003. bi-m. free to qualified personnel (effective 2008). adv. **Document type:** *Journal, Academic/Scholarly.* **Description:** Takes a multidisciplinary approach to provide Australia's life science professionals with reports on the latest developments in biological and medical science, laboratory techniques and biotechnology.
Incorporates (1989-2003): Today's Life Science (1033-6893)
Indexed: A01, A11, A22, CA, SCOPUS, T02.
—BLDSC (1813.848000), GNLM, IE, Ingenta. **CCC.**
Published by: I D G Communications Pty. Ltd., PO Box 295, St Leonards, NSW 1590, Australia. TEL 61-2-94395133, FAX 61-2-94395512, don_kennedy@idg.com.au, http://www.idg.com.au. Ed. Kate McDonald TEL 61-2-99022765. Adv. contact Ric Hudson TEL 61-2-99022732. Circ: 8,000.

➤ **AUSTRALIAN MUSEUM. RECORDS.** *see* BIOLOGY—Zoology

➤ **AUSTRALIAN MUSEUM, SYDNEY. RECORDS SUPPLEMENT.** *see* BIOLOGY—Zoology

➤ **AUSTRALIAN MUSEUM. TECHNICAL REPORTS (ONLINE).** *see* BIOLOGY—Zoology

500 AUT
AUSTRIA. BUNDESMINISTERIUM FUER WISSENSCHAFT UND VERKEHR. FORSCHUNGSBERICHT. Text in German. 1968. triennial. free. stat. **Document type:** *Government.* **Description:** Report to the Austrian Parliament on the current situation of scientific research.
Former titles: Austria. Bundesministerium fuer Wissenschaft, Verkehr und Kunst. Forschungsbericht; Austria. Bundesministerium fuer Wissenschaft, Forschung und Kunst. Forschungsbericht; Austria. Bundesministerium fuer Wissenschaft und Forschung. Bericht der Bundesregierung an den Nationalrat (0300-2772)
Published by: Bundesministerium fuer Wissenschaft und Verkehr, Bankgasse 1, Vienna, W 1014, Austria. TEL 43-1-531205150, FAX 43-1-531205155, TELEX 111157. Ed. Reinhard Schurawitzki. R&P Wolfgang Fingernagel.

500 600 ITA ISSN 1828-9274
CC1
AUTOMATA. Text in Multiple languages. 2006. irreg. price varies. **Document type:** *Monographic series, Academic/Scholarly.*
Published by: L' Erma di Bretschneider, Via Cassiodoro 19, Rome, 00193, Italy. TEL 39-06-6874127, FAX 39-06-6874129, lerma@lerma.it, http://www.lerma.it.

500 FRA ISSN 2106-640X
▼ **AUX FRONTIERES DE LA SCIENCE.** Text in French. 2010. q. EUR 8 newsstand/cover (effective 2011). **Document type:** *Magazine, Consumer.*
Published by: Export Press, 91 Rue de Turenne, Paris, 75003, France. TEL 33-1-40291451, FAX 33-1-42720743, dir@exportpress.com, http://www.exportpress.com.

500 MEX
AVACIENT. Text in Spanish. 1996. q. **Document type:** *Journal, Academic/Scholarly.*
Published by: Instituto Tecnologico de Chetumal, Ave Insurgentes 330 Esq Andres Quintana Roo, Chetumal, Quintana Roo, 77013, Mexico. TEL 52-983-8322330, FAX 52-983-8321019. Ed. Abel Zapata Dittrich.

500 MEX ISSN 0185-1411
AVANCE Y PERSPECTIVA. Text in Spanish. 1980. bi-m. USD 150 (effective 2002).
Indexed: C01, RefZh.
Published by: Instituto Politecnico Nacional, Centro de Investigacion y Estudios Avanzados (C I N V E S T A V), Ave Instituto Politecnico Nacional 2508, Col San Pedro Zacatenco, Mexico City, 07360, Mexico. TEL 52-57477000, FAX 52-57473800, http://www.cinvestav.mx.

500 600 ECU ISSN 1390-3012
AVANCES DE LA CIENCIA Y LA TECNOLOGIA. Text in Spanish. 2005. bi-m. **Document type:** *Bulletin, Academic/Scholarly.*
Related titles: Online - full text ed.
Published by: Secretaria Nacional de Ciencia y Tecnologia, Fundacion para la Ciencia y la Tecnologia, Ave Patria 850 y 10 de Agosto, Edif. Banco de Prestamos Piso 9, Mariscal, Pichincha, Quito, 17, Ecuador. TEL 593-2-2505142, FAX 593-2-2509054, root@fundacyt.org.ec, http://www.fundacyt.ec/. Ed. Maria del Carmen Cevallos.

500 620 CHL ISSN 0718-8706
▼ **AVANCES EN CIENCIAS E INGENIERIA.** Abbreviated title: A C I. Text in Spanish. 2010. q. free (effective 2011). **Document type:** *Journal, Academic/Scholarly.*
Media: Online - full text.
Published by: Universidad Mayor, Business School, Avda Americo Vespucio Sur 357, Santiago, Chile. Ed. Carlos J Rojas.

500 CUB ISSN 1029-3450
➤ **AVANZADA CIENTIFICA.** Text in Spanish; Abstracts in English, Spanish. 1998. q. free (effective 2011). back issues avail. **Document type:** *Journal, Academic/Scholarly.* **Description:** Covers environment, medicine, science, take of decisions, information of management, knowledge management, educational sciences, energy, etc. Audience include scientists, students, and investigators.
Media: Online - full text.
Published by: Ministerio de Ciencia, Tecnologia y Medio Ambiente, Centro de Informacion Cientifica y Tecnologica, c/ Jovellanos No. 4 e/ Medio y Rio, Matanzas, Matanzas CP 40100, Cuba. TEL 53-45-242483, silvio@cigetmtz.atenas.inf.cu. Pub., R&P Silvio Curiel Lorenzo.

600 IND ISSN 0970-6607
AWISHKARA. Text in Hindi. 1971. m. INR 150 domestic; USD 60 foreign (effective 2011). bk.rev. abstr.; charts; illus. **Document type:** *Magazine, Trade.*
Indexed: ISA.
Published by: National Research Development Corporation, Kailash Colony Ext, 20-22 Zamroodpur Community Centre, New Delhi, 110 048, India. TEL 91-80-23341255, FAX 91-80-23347555, nrdc@bgl.vsnl.net.in. Ed. R K Anthwal TEL 91-80-29240401 ext 344.

500 700 NLD ISSN 1387-6783
AZIMUTH. Text in English. 1998. irreg., latest vol.2, 2000. price varies. **Document type:** *Monographic series, Academic/Scholarly.* **Description:** Aims to reach the individual scientist interested in gaining a wider perspective and a deeper insight into the communications between specialists.
Related titles: Online - full text ed.
Indexed: SCOPUS.
—BLDSC (1841.530500). **CCC.**
Published by: Elsevier BV (Subsidiary of: Elsevier Science & Technology), Radarweg 29, PO Box 211, Amsterdam, 1000 AE, Netherlands. TEL 31-20-4853911, FAX 31-20-4852457, JournalsCustomerServiceEMEA@elsevier.com.

500 CAN ISSN 1912-3280
S900
B C NATURE. Text in English. 1964. q. CAD 15 (effective 1999). adv. bk.rev. **Document type:** *Newsletter.*
Former titles (until 2006): B.C. Naturalist (0228-8842); (until 1980): Federation of British Columbia Naturalists. Newsletter (0046-3566); (until 1969): British Columbia Nature Council. Newsletter (0380-3155)
Indexed: WildRev.
Published by: Federation of British Columbia Naturalists, 307 1367 W Broadway Ave, Vancouver, BC V6H 4A9, Canada. TEL 604-737-3057, FAX 604-738-7175, fbcnclublink@telus.net, http://www.naturalists.bc.ca. Circ: 6,500.

500 GBR ISSN 1753-6561
R106
➤ **B M C PROCEEDINGS.** Text in English. 2007. irreg. free (effective 2011). adv. back issues avail.; reprints avail. **Document type:** *Proceedings, Academic/Scholarly.* **Description:** Contains full articles and meeting abstracts from various conferences.
Media: Online - full text.
Indexed: A01, CA, P30, T02.
Published by: BioMed Central Ltd. (Subsidiary of: Springer Science+Business Media), 236 Gray's Inn Rd, London, WC1X 8HB, United Kingdom. TEL 44-20-31922000, FAX 44-20-31922010, info@biomedcentral.com. Ed. Dr. Melissa Norton. Adv. contact Natasha Bailey TEL 44-20-31922231.

509 GBR
B S H S GUIDE TO INSTITUTIONS. Text in English. 1992. a. free (effective 2010). back issues avail. **Document type:** *Directory, Trade.*
Formerly: Guide to History of Science Courses in Britain
Media: Online - full text.
Published by: British Society for the History of Science, PO Box 3401, Norwich, NR7 7JF, United Kingdom. TEL 44-1603-516236, FAX 44-1603-208563, membership@bshs.org.uk.

500 GBR ISSN 0963-0902
B S H S MONOGRAPHS. Text in English. 1979. irreg., latest vol.13, 2007. price varies. **Document type:** *Monographic series, Academic/Scholarly.*
Indexed: Z01.
—BLDSC (2354.170000).
Published by: British Society for the History of Science, PO Box 3401, Norwich, NR7 7JF, United Kingdom. TEL 44-1603-516236, FAX 44-1603-208563, membership@bshs.org.uk. Ed. Joe Cain.

500 FRA ISSN 1770-1368
QC1U6 CODEN: BTUPAJ
LE B U P PHYSIQUE CHIMIE. (Bulletin Union des Professeurs) Text in French. 1907. m. **Document type:** *Bulletin, Trade.*
Formerly (until 2003): Union des Physiciens. Bulletin (0366-3876)
Indexed: INIS AtomInd, RefZh.
—INIST.
Published by: Union des Professeurs de Physique et de Chimie, 44 Bd Saint-Michel, Paris, 75270 Cedex 06, France. TEL 33-1-43256153, FAX 33-1-43250748, http://www.udppc.asso.fr.

500 DEU ISSN 2190-0574
B U W OUTPUT. Text in German. 1993. s-a. **Document type:** *Journal, Academic/Scholarly.*
Formerly (until 2009): Output (0944-0046)
Published by: Bergische Universitaet Wuppertal, Gausstr 20, Wuppertal, 42097, Germany. TEL 49-202-4390, FAX 49-202-4392899, presse@uni-wuppertal.de, http://www.uni-wuppertal.de. Ed. Michael Kroemer. Circ: 2,000 (controlled).

LE BAC EN TETE. PHYSIQUE-CHIMIE. *see* EDUCATION

LE BAC EN TETE. SCIENCES DE LA VIE ET DE LA TERRE. *see* EDUCATION

500 BHS ISSN 1022-2189
Q29
➤ **BAHAMAS JOURNAL OF SCIENCE.** Text in English. 1993. s-a. BSD 40 domestic; USD 40 foreign (effective 2001). adv. bk.rev. illus. 64 p./no.; back issues avail. **Document type:** *Journal, Academic/Scholarly.*
Indexed: ASFA, B21, ESPM, EntAb, ViroIAbstr.
Published by: Media Publishing Ltd (Subsidiary of: Media Enterprises Ltd.), PO Box N 9240, Nassau, Bahamas. TEL 242-325-8210, FAX 242-325-8065, info@bahamasmedia.com. Ed., R&P, Adv. contact Neil E Sealey. Circ: 350 (paid).

500 SDN
AL-BAHITH AS-SAGEER/YOUNG RESEARCHER. Text in Arabic. 1975. s-a.
Published by: National Centre for Research, Documentation and Information Centre, P O Box 2404, Khartoum, Sudan. TEL 249-11-770776, FAX 249-11-770701.

001.3 CHN ISSN 1002-9567
AP95.C4
BAIKE ZHISHI/ENCYCLOPEDIC KNOWLEDGE. Text in Chinese. 1979. m. USD 55.20 (effective 2009). adv. **Document type:** *Magazine, Academic/Scholarly.* **Description:** Popular science periodical.
Related titles: Online - full text ed.
—East View.
Published by: Zhongguo Dabaike Quanshu Chubanshe, 17 Fuchengmen Beidajie, Beijing, 100037, China.

500 IND ISSN 0447-9483
Q1 CODEN: JSRBA9
BANARAS HINDU UNIVERSITY. JOURNAL OF SCIENTIFIC RESEARCH. Text in English. 1950. s-a. **Document type:** *Journal, Academic/Scholarly.*
Indexed: Inspec.
Published by: Banaras Hindu University, Varanasi, Uttar Pradesh 221 005, India. **Subscr. to:** I N S I O Scientific Books & Periodicals.

500 BGD ISSN 0378-8121
Q80.B3 CODEN: JBACDF
➤ **BANGLADESH ACADEMY OF SCIENCES. JOURNAL.** Text in English. 1977. 2/yr. bk.rev. 150 p./no.; back issues avail. **Document type:** *Journal, Academic/Scholarly.*
Related titles: Online - full text ed.: free (effective 2011).
Indexed: A22, CIN, ChemAb, ChemTitl, INIS AtomInd, Inspec.
—BLDSC (4707.662000), AskIEEE, CASDDS, IE, Ingenta, Linda Hall.
Published by: Bangladesh Academy of Sciences, c/o Department of Chemistry, Dhaka University, Dhaka, 1000, Bangladesh. TEL 880-2-9110425, FAX 880-2-8615583, dumail@du.bangla.net, hshabbir@bdmail.net, bas@bdmail.net. Ed. K M Sultanul Aziz.

500 BGD ISSN 0304-9809
Q1 CODEN: BJSIBL
BANGLADESH JOURNAL OF SCIENTIFIC AND INDUSTRIAL RESEARCH. Text in English. 1964. q. BDT 100; USD 24 foreign. **Document type:** *Journal, Academic/Scholarly.* **Description:** Reports the findings of scientific and industrial research conducted in Bangladesh, India, Pakistan and Africa.
Formerly (until Jan. 1973): Scientific Researches (0036-8830)
Indexed: A34, A35, A37, A38, AgBio, AgrForAb, B23, BA, BP, C25, C30, CABA, CIN, ChemAb, ChemTitl, D01, E12, F08, F11, F12, FCA, FS&TA, GH, H16, H17, I11, IndVet, Inspec, MaizeAb, N02, N03, N04, O01, OR, P32, P33, P37, P38, P39, P40, PGegResA, PGrRegA, PHN&I, R07, R08, R11, R12, R13, RA&MP, RM&VM, S12, S13, S16, S17, SoyAb, T05, TAR, TriticAb, VS, W10, W11, WildRev, Z01.
—AskIEEE, CASDDS, Ingenta, INIST, Linda Hall.
Published by: Bangladesh Council of Scientific and Industrial Research (BCSIR), Mirpur Rd Dhanmondi, Dhaka, 1205, Bangladesh. TEL 880-2-500078, FAX 880-2-863022. Ed. M Nizamuddin.

BANGLADESH JOURNAL OF SOIL SCIENCE. *see* AGRICULTURE—Crop Production And Soil

500 BGD
BANGLADESH SCIENCE CONFERENCE. PROCEEDINGS. Text in Bengali. a. **Document type:** *Proceedings.*
Published by: (Bangladesh Association for the Advancement of Science), University of Dhaka, Ramna, Dhaka, 1000, Bangladesh.

BANWA. *see* HUMANITIES: COMPREHENSIVE WORKS

500 300 CHN ISSN 1674-2494
BAODING XUEYUAN XUEBAO/BAODING UNIVERSITY. JOURNAL. Text in Chinese. 1999. bi-m. back issues avail. **Document type:** *Journal, Academic/Scholarly.*
Formerly (until 2008): Baoding Shi-Zhuan Xuebao/Baoding Teachers College. Journal (1008-4584); Which was formed by the 1999 merger of: Baoding Shi-Zhuan Xuebao (Zhexue Shehui Kexue Ban); Baoding Shi-Zhuan Xuebao (Ziran Kexue Ban)
Related titles: Online - full text ed.
Published by: Baoding Xueyuan, 3027, Qi-yi Dong Lu, Baoding, 071000, China. TEL 86-312-5972218, FAX 86-312-5972218, http://www.bdu.edu.cn/.

500 CHN ISSN 1007-1261
➤ **BAOJI WENLI XUEYUAN XUEBAO (ZIRAN KEXUE)/BAOJI UNIVERSITY OF ARTS AND SCIENCES. JOURNAL (NATURAL SCIENCES EDITION).** Text in Chinese; Abstracts in Chinese, English. 1979-1980 (May); resumed 1982. q. adv. abstr. Index. back issues avail. **Document type:** *Journal, Academic/Scholarly.*
Former titles (until 1993): Baoji Shifan Xueyuan Xuebao (Ziran Kexue Ban)/Baoji College of Arts and Science. Journal (Natural Science Edition); (until 1990): Baoji Shiyuan Xuebao (Ziran Kexue Ban); (until 1985): Jiaoxue yu Keyan (Ziran Kexue); Which superseded in part (in 1984): Jiaoxue yu Keyan (Zonghe Ban); Which was formerly (until 1982): Baoji Shiyuan Xuebao
Related titles: Online - full text ed.
Indexed: CCMJ, MSN, MathR, RefZh, Z02.
Published by: Baoji Wenli Xueyuan/Baoji College of Arts and Sciences, 44, Baoguang Lu, Baoji, Shaanxi 721007, China. TEL 86-917-3361019. Ed. Zhu-Ping Deng. Pub. Bin Cao. **Dist. by:** China International Book Trading Corp, 35 Chegongzhuang Xilu, Haidian District, PO Box 399, Beijing 100044, China. TEL 86-10-68412045, FAX 86-10-68412023, cibtc@mail.cibtc.com.cn, http://www.cibtc.com.cn.

500 RUS
BASHKIRSKII UNIVERSITET. VESTNIK. Text in Russian. 1996. 3/yr.
Related titles: Online - full text ed.
Published by: Bashkirskii Gosudarstvennyi Universitet/Bashkir State University, ul. Frunze, 32, Ufa, 450077, Russian Federation. TEL 7-3472-226370, FAX 7-3472-331677, rector@bsu.bashedu.ru, http://www.bashedu.ru/firstbgu_e.htm.

S

500 DEU ISSN 0084-6090
AS182 CODEN: BAWJAE
BAYERISCHE AKADEMIE DER WISSENSCHAFTEN. JAHRBUCH. Text in German. 1912. a. EUR 28 per vol. (effective 2010). index. back issues avail. **Document type:** *Yearbook, Academic/Scholarly.*
Indexed: BibLing, DIP, GeoRef, IBR, IBZ, MLA-IB, RASB, SpeleolAb.
—Linda Hall.
Published by: (Bayerische Akademie der Wissenschaften/Bavarian Academy of Sciences and Humanities), Verlag C.H. Beck oHG, Wilhelmstr 9, Munich, 80801, Germany. TEL 49-89-381890, FAX 49-89-38189398, bestellung@beck.de, http://www.beck.de.

500.9 DEU ISSN 0005-6995
AS182 CODEN: ABWMAJ
➤ **BAYERISCHE AKADEMIE DER WISSENSCHAFTEN. MATHEMATISCH-NATURWISSENSCHAFTLICHE KLASSE. ABHANDLUNGEN.** Text in German. 1829. irreg., latest vol.176, 2008. price varies. **Document type:** *Monographic series, Academic/Scholarly.*
Former titles (until 1926): Bayerische Akademie der Wissenschaften. Mathematisch-Physikalische Klasse. Abhandlungen (0176-7038); (until 1919): Koeniglich Bayerischen Akademie der Wissenschaften. Mathematisch-Physikalische Klasse. Abhandlungen (0176-7100)
Related titles: ◆ Series: Nova Kepleriana. Neue Folge. ISSN 0078-2246.
Indexed: ApMecR, CCMJ, ChemAb, GeoRef, MSN, MathR, SpeleolAb, Z01.
—INIST, Linda Hall. **CCC.**
Published by: Bayerische Akademie der Wissenschaften/Bavarian Academy of Sciences and Humanities, Alfons-Goppel-Str 11, Munich, 80539, Germany. TEL 49-89-230311141, FAX 49-89-230311281, webmaster@badw.de.

500 510 DEU ISSN 0340-7586
CODEN: AMNSB2
➤ **BAYERISCHE AKADEMIE DER WISSENSCHAFTEN. MATHEMATISCH-NATURWISSENSCHAFTLICHE KLASSE. SITZUNGSBERICHTE.** Text in German. 1871. irreg., latest 2004. price varies. **Document type:** *Monographic series, Academic/Scholarly.*
Formerly (until 1955): Bayerische Akademie der Wissenschaften zu Muenchen. Mathematisch-Naturwissenschaftliche Klasse. Sitzungsberichte (0376-1037)
Indexed: CCMJ, GeoRef, IBR, IBZ, MSN, MathR, SpeleolAb, Z02.
—INIST, Linda Hall.
Published by: Bayerische Akademie der Wissenschaften/Bavarian Academy of Sciences and Humanities, Alfons-Goppel-Str 11, Munich, 80539, Germany. TEL 49-89-230311141, FAX 49-89-230311281, webmaster@badw.de.

➤ **BAYERISCHE AKADEMIE DER WISSENSCHAFTEN. PHILOSOPHISCH-HISTORISCHE KLASSE. ABHANDLUNGEN, N.F.** *see* HUMANITIES: COMPREHENSIVE WORKS

➤ **BAYERISCHE AKADEMIE DER WISSENSCHAFTEN. PHILOSOPHISCH-HISTORISCHE KLASSE. SITZUNGSBERICHTE.** *see* HUMANITIES: COMPREHENSIVE WORKS

500 NGA ISSN 2006-6996
▼ **BAYERO JOURNAL OF PURE AND APPLIED SCIENCES.** Text in English. 2009. s-a. **Document type:** *Journal, Academic/Scholarly.*
Related titles: Online - full text ed.: free (effective 2011).
Indexed: A34, A35, A36, A37, A38, AgrForAb, B23, C25, C30, CABA, E12, F08, FCA, GH, H16, MaizeAb, N02, N03, N04, P32, P33, R07, R08, S13, T05, W10, W11.
Published by: Bayero University, Faculty of Science, PMB 3011, Kano, Nigeria. Ed. M D Mukhtar.

500 CHN ISSN 1001-5477
BEIFANG GONGYE DAXUE XUEBAO/NORTH CHINA UNIVERSITY OF TECHNOLOGY. JOURNAL. Text in Chinese. 1989. q. CNY 5 newsstand/cover (effective 2006). **Document type:** *Journal, Academic/Scholarly.*
Related titles: Online - full text ed.
Published by: Beifang Gongye Daxue/North China University of Technology, 5, Shijingshan Jinyuanzhuang, Beijing, 100041, China. TEL 86-10-88803374.

500 CHN ISSN 1009-4822
BEIHUA DAXUE XUEBAO (ZIRAN KEXUE BAN)/BEIHUA UNIVERSITY. JOURNAL (NATURAL SCIENCE EDITION). Text in Chinese. 2000. bi-m. USD 37.20 (effective 2009). **Document type:** *Journal, Academic/Scholarly.*
Incorporates (1985-1999): Jilin Linxueyuan Xuebao/ Jilin Forestry Institute. Journal (1004-6992); (1980-1999): Jilin Yixueyuan Xuebao/Jilin Medical College. Journal (1007-3914)
Related titles: Online - full content ed.; Online - full text ed.
—BLDSC (4707.882000), East View.
Published by: Beihua Daxue/Beihua University, 15, Jilin Dajie, Jilin, 132033, China. TEL 81-432-4602730. **Dist. by:** China International Book Trading Corp, 35 Chegongzhuang Xilu, Haidian District, PO Box 399, Beijing 100044, China. TEL 86-10-68412045, FAX 86-10-68412023, cibtc@mail.cibtc.com.cn, http://www.cibtc.com.cn.

500 300 CHN ISSN 1673-7938
BEIHUA HANGTIAN GONGYE XUEYUAN XUEBAO/NORTH CHINA INSTITUTE OF ASTRONAUTIC ENGINEERING. JOURNAL. Text in Chinese. 1986. bi-m. **Document type:** *Journal, Academic/Scholarly.*
Formerly (until 2006): Huabei Hangtian Gongye Xueyuan Xuebao (1009-2145)
Related titles: Online - full text ed.
Published by: Huabei Hangtian Gongye Xueyuan, 130 Xinxiang, Langfang, 065000, China. TEL 86-316-2083330, FAX 86-316-2083230.

500 CHN ISSN 0479-8023
CODEN: PCTHAP
BEIJING DAXUE XUEBAO (ZIRAN KEXUE BAN)/ACTA SCIENTIARUM NATURALIUM UNIVERSITATIS PEKINENSIS/BEIJING UNIVERSITY. JOURNAL (NATURAL SCIENCE EDITION). Text in Chinese. 1955-1966; resumed 1977. bi-m. USD 66.60 (effective 2009). **Document type:** *Academic/Scholarly.* **Description:** Publishes research papers and dissertations on various fields of natural sciences.
Related titles: Online - full content ed.; Online - full text ed.
Indexed: A22, CCMJ, CIS, EngInd, GeoRef, INIS AtomInd, Inspec, MSN, MathR, RefZh, SCOPUS, SpeleolAb, Z01, Z02.
—BLDSC (0663.190000), AskIEEE, CASDDS, East View, IE, Ingenta, INIST, Linda Hall.
Published by: (Beijing University), Beijing University Press, Haidian-qu, Beijing, 100871, China. TEL 86-1-2501216. Ed. Gao Congshou. Circ: 5,500. **Dist. by:** China International Book Trading Corp, 35 Chegongzhuang Xilu, Haidian District, PO Box 399, Beijing 100044, China. TEL 86-10-68412045, FAX 86-10-68412023, cibtc@mail.cibtc.com.cn, http://www.cibtc.com.cn.

500 CHN
BEIJING DIANLI GAODENG ZHUANKE XUEXIAO XUEBAO (ZIRAN KEXUE BAN)/BEIJING ELECTRIC POWER COLLEGE. JOURNAL (NATURAL SCIENCE EDITION). Text in Chinese. 1992. m. **Document type:** *Journal, Academic/Scholarly.*
Supersedes in part: Beijing Dianli Gaodeng Zhuanke Xuexiao Xuebao (1009-0118)
Related titles: Online - full text ed.
Published by: Beijing Dianli Gaodeng Zhuanke Xuexiao, 42, Fucheng Lu, Beijing, 100036, China. TEL 86-10-86931100.

BEIJING DIANZI KEJI XUEYUAN XUEBAO/BEIJING ELECTRONIC SCIENCE AND TECHNOLOGY INSTITUTE. JOURNAL. *see* SOCIAL SCIENCES: COMPREHENSIVE WORKS

500 CHN ISSN 1001-0564
BEIJING FUZHUANG XUEYUAN XUEBAO (ZIRAN KEXUE BAN)/BEIJING INSTITUTE OF CLOTHING TECHNOLOGY. JOURNAL. Text in Chinese. 1981. q. CNY 5 newsstand/cover (effective 2006). **Document type:** *Journal, Academic/Scholarly.*
Formerly (until 1988): Beijing Huaxian Gongxueyuan Xuebao/Beijing Institute of Chemical Fibre Technology. Journal (1000-1468)
Related titles: Online - full text ed.
Indexed: A28, APA, BrCerAb, C&ISA, CA/WCA, CIA, CerAb, CivEngAb, CorrAb, E&CAJ, E11, EEA, EMA, ESPM, EnvEAb, H15, M&TEA, M09, MBF, METADEX, SCOPUS, SolStAb, T04, WAA, WTA.
—BLDSC (1878.331140), Linda Hall.
Published by: Beijing Fuzhuang Xueyuan/Beijing Institute of Clothing Technology, Heping Jie Beikou Yinghua Lu Jia, 2, Beijing, 100029, China. TEL 86-10-64288370, FAX 86-10-64210962.

500 CHN ISSN 0254-0037
T4 CODEN: BGDXD6
BEIJING GONGYE DAXUE XUEBAO/BEIJING UNIVERSITY OF TECHNOLOGY. JOURNAL. Text in Chinese. 1974. q. USD 62.40 (effective 2009). **Document type:** *Journal, Academic/Scholarly.*
Related titles: Online - full text ed.
Indexed: A28, APA, BrCerAb, C&ISA, CA/WCA, CCMJ, CIA, CPEI, CerAb, CivEngAb, CorrAb, E&CAJ, E11, EEA, EMA, ESPM, EngInd, EnvEAb, H15, Inspec, M&TEA, M09, MBF, METADEX, MSN, MathR, RefZh, SCOPUS, SolStAb, T04, WAA, Z02.
—BLDSC (4707.892000), East View, Linda Hall.
Published by: Beijing Gongye Daxue/Beijing University Of Technology, 100, Pingyueyuan, Zhixinyuan 317-shi, Beijing, 100022, China. http://www.bjpu.edu.cn/. **Dist. by:** China International Book Trading Corp, 35 Chegongzhuang Xilu, Haidian District, PO Box 399, Beijing 100044, China. TEL 86-10-68412045, FAX 86-10-68412023, cibtc@mail.cibtc.com.cn, http://www.cibtc.com.cn.

500 CHN ISSN 1671-4628
TP1 CODEN: BHXKE7
BEIJING HUAGONG DAXUE XUEBAO (ZIRAN KEXUE BAN)/BEIJING UNIVERSITY OF CHEMICAL TECHNOLOGY. JOURNAL (NATURAL SCIENCE EDITION). Text in Chinese. 1974. bi-m. CNY 10 newsstand/cover (effective 2006). 96 p./no.; **Document type:** *Journal, Academic/Scholarly.*
Former titles (until 2002): Beijing Huagong Daxue Xuebao (1007-2640); (until 1995): Beijing Huagong Xueyuan Xuebao (Ziran Kexue Ban)/Beijing Institute of Chemical Technology. Journal (Natural Science) (1000-5668)
Related titles: ◆ CD-ROM ed.: Chinese Academic Journals Full-Text Database. Science & Engineering, Series B. ISSN 1007-8029; Online - full text ed.
Indexed: A28, APA, BrCerAb, C&ISA, CA/WCA, CIA, CerAb, CivEngAb, CorrAb, E&CAJ, E11, EEA, EMA, ESPM, EngInd, EnvEAb, H15, M&TEA, M09, MBF, METADEX, PollutAb, SCOPUS, SWRA, SolStAb, T04, WAA.
—BLDSC (4707.892760), CASDDS, IE, Ingenta, Linda Hall.
Published by: Beijing Huagong Daxue/Beijing University of Chemical Technology, Dianjiaolou 122, 127, 15, Beisanhuan Dong Lu, Beijing, 100029, China. TEL 86-10-64434926 ext 801, FAX 86-10-64434926 ext 803.

600 CHN ISSN 1004-0579
CODEN: JBITE5
BEIJING INSTITUTE OF TECHNOLOGY. JOURNAL. Text in English; Summaries in English, Chinese. 1992. q. USD 20.80 (effective 2009). **Document type:** *Journal, Academic/Scholarly.* **Description:** Publishes research in various mathematical, engineering, and scientific disciplines.
Related titles: Online - full text ed.; ◆ Chinese ed.: Beijing Ligong Daxue Xuebao. ISSN 1001-0645.
Indexed: A28, APA, BrCerAb, C&ISA, CA/WCA, CCMJ, CIA, CPEI, CerAb, CivEngAb, CorrAb, E&CAJ, E11, EEA, EMA, ESPM, EngInd, EnvEAb, H15, Inspec, M&TEA, M09, MBF, METADEX, MSN, MathR, RefZh, SCOPUS, SolStAb, T04, TM, WAA, Z02.
—BLDSC (4707.889600), AskIEEE, CASDDS, East View, IE, Ingenta, Linda Hall.
Published by: Beijing Ligong Daxue/Beijing Institute of Technology, 5, Zhongguancun Nan Dajie, Haidian-qu, Beijing, 100081, China. http://www.bit.edu.cn/. Ed. Peiran Yan. **Dist. outside China by:** China International Book Trading Corp, 35 Chegongzhuang Xilu, Haidian District, PO Box 399, Beijing 100044, China. TEL 86-10-68412045, FAX 86-10-68412023, cibtc@mail.cibtc.com.cn, http://www.cibtc.com.cn.

500 CHN ISSN 1673-0291
TA1001
BEIJING JIAOTONG DAXUE XUEBAO (ZIRAN KEXUE BAN)/BEIJING JIAOTONG UNIVERSITY. JOURNAL (NATURAL SCIENCE EDITION). Text in Chinese. 1975. bi-m. USD 24.60 (effective 2009). **Document type:** *Journal, Academic/Scholarly.*
Formerly (until 2004): Beijing Jiaotong Daxue Xuebao/North Communications University. Journal (1000-1506)
Related titles: Online - full text ed.
Indexed: A28, APA, B21, BrCerAb, C&ISA, CA/WCA, CIA, CerAb, CivEngAb, CorrAb, E&CAJ, E11, EEA, EMA, ESPM, EngInd, EnvEAb, H&SSA, H15, M&TEA, M09, MBF, METADEX, RefZh, SCOPUS, SolStAb, T04, WAA, Z02.
—BLDSC (1878.331235), East View, Linda Hall.
Published by: Beijing Jiaotong Daxue, Xizhimen Wai, 3, Shangyuancun, Beijing, 100044, China. Ed. Hu Shuliang.

500 CHN ISSN 1673-6923
BEIJING JIAOYU XUEYUAN XUEBAO (ZIRAN KEXUE BAN). Text in Chinese. 2006. q. CNY 20 (effective 2010). **Document type:** *Journal, Academic/Scholarly.*
Supersedes in part (in 2006): Beijing Jiaoyu Xueyuan Xuebao/Beijing Institute of Education. Journal (1008-228X); Which incorporated (1999-2000): Beijing Shi Chengren Jiaoyu Xueyuan Xuebao/Journal of Beijing Adult Educational College (1008-2212); Beijing Jiaoyu Xueyuan Xuebao was formerly (1987-1989): Beijing Jiaoyu Xueyuan Xuekan
Related titles: Online - full text ed.
Published by: Beijing Jiaoyu Xueyuan/Beijing Institute of Education, 2, Dewai Shenfeng Jie, Zhonghe Lou Rm.602, Beijing, 100011, China. TEL 86-10-82089136.

500 600 CHN
BEIJING KEJIE BAO/BEIJING SCIENCE TECHNOLOGY REPORT. Text in English. w. **Document type:** *Newspaper, Academic/Scholarly.*
Related titles: Online - full content ed.
Published by: Beijing Qingnian Bao Wangji Chuanbo Jizhu Youxian Gongsi, Beijing Qingnian Bao Dasha, Chaoyang-qu, 23, Baijia Zhuan Dongli, Beijing, 100026, China. webmaster@ynet.com, http://www.ynet.com/.

500 CHN ISSN 1005-0310
BEIJING LIANHE DAXUE XUEBAO (ZIRAN KEXUE BAN). Text in Chinese. 1987. q. **Document type:** *Journal, Academic/Scholarly.*
Supersedes in part (in 2003): Beijing Lianhe Daxue Xuebao
Related titles: Online - full text ed.
Published by: Beijing Lianhe Daxue/Beijin Union University, 97, Sihuan Dong Lu, Beijing, 100101, China. TEL 86-10-64900023, FAX 86-10-64900023.

500 CHN ISSN 1001-0645
T4 CODEN: BLXUEV
BEIJING LIGONG DAXUE XUEBAO. Text in Chinese; Summaries in Chinese, English. 1956. bi-m. USD 62.40 (effective 2009). **Document type:** *Journal, Academic/Scholarly.* **Description:** Publishes research papers in various engineering and scientific disciplines.
Related titles: Online - full text ed.; ◆ English ed.: Beijing Institute of Technology. Journal. ISSN 1004-0579.
Indexed: A28, APA, ApMecR, BrCerAb, C&ISA, CA, CA/WCA, CCMJ, CIA, CIN, CPEI, CerAb, ChemAb, ChemTitl, CivEngAb, CorrAb, E&CAJ, E11, EEA, EMA, ESPM, EngInd, EnvEAb, H15, ISMEC, Inspec, M&GPA, M&TEA, M09, MBF, METADEX, MSN, MathR, P42, RefZh, S02, S03, SCOPUS, SolStAb, T02, T04, WAA, Z02.
—BLDSC (4707.889500), CASDDS, East View, Linda Hall.
Published by: Beijing Ligong Daxue/Beijing Institute of Technology, 5, Zhongguancun Nan Dajie, Haidian-qu, Beijing, 100081, China. http://www.bit.edu.cn/. Ed. Fengxiang Mei.

500 CHN ISSN 1000-1522
SD221 CODEN: BLDXE8
BEIJING LINYE DAXUE XUEBAO/BEIJING FORESTRY UNIVERSITY. JOURNAL. Text in Chinese. 1979. bi-m. USD 133.20 (effective 2009). adv. bk.rev. **Document type:** *Journal, Academic/Scholarly.*
Related titles: Online - full text ed.; ◆ English ed.: Forestry Studies in China. ISSN 1008-1321.
Indexed: A22, A28, A34, A35, A36, A37, APA, AgBio, AgrForAb, B21, B23, BA, BP, BrCerAb, C&ISA, C25, C30, CA/WCA, CABA, CIA, CerAb, CivEngAb, CorrAb, D01, E&CAJ, E11, E12, E17, EEA, EMA, ESPM, EngInd, EnvEAb, F08, F11, F12, FCA, G11, GH, H15, H16, I10, I11, LT, M&GPA, M&TEA, M09, MBF, METADEX, MaizeAb, N02, N04, N05, O01, OR, P32, P33, P40, PGegResA, PGrRegA, PHN&I, R07, R08, R11, R12, R13, RA&MP, RM&VM, RRTA, RefZh, S12, S13, S16, S17, SSciA, SolStAb, SoyAb, T04, T05, TAR, TriticAb, VS, W10, W11, WAA, Z01.
—BLDSC (4707.887000), CASDDS, East View, IE, Ingenta.
Published by: (Xuebao Bianjibu), Beijing Linye Daxue/Beijing Forestry University, 35, Qinghua Dong Lu, Beijing, 100083, China. TEL 86-10-62337673, FAX 86-10-62337605.

500 CHN ISSN 0476-0301
QH7 CODEN: BSDKDH
BEIJING SHIFAN DAXUE XUEBAO (ZIRAN KEXUE BAN)/BEIJING NORMAL UNIVERSITY. JOURNAL (NATURAL SCIENCE EDITION). Text in Chinese. 1956. bi-m. USD 79.80 (effective 2009). **Document type:** *Journal, Academic/Scholarly.*
Related titles: Online - full text ed.
Indexed: A22, CCMJ, CIN, ChemAb, ChemTitl, INIS AtomInd, Inspec, MSN, MathR, RefZh, Z01, Z02.
—BLDSC (4707.890900), CASDDS, East View, IE, Ingenta, Linda Hall.
Published by: Beijing Shifan Daxue/Beijing Normal University, Keji Lou A-qu, Rm. 216, Beijing, 100875, China. **Dist. outside of China by:** China International Book Trading Corp, 35 Chegongzhuang Xilu, Haidian District, PO Box 399, Beijing 100044, China. TEL 86-10-68412045, FAX 86-10-68412023, cibtc@mail.cibtc.com.cn, http://www.cibtc.com.cn/.

500 DEU ISSN 0232-1556
BEITRAEGE ZUR ALEXANDER-VON-HUMBOLDT-FORSCHUNG. Text in German. 1968. irreg., latest vol.28, 2007. price varies. **Document type:** *Monographic series, Academic/Scholarly.* **Description:** Studies various aspects of Humboldt's life.
Indexed: Z02.
Published by: Akademie Verlag GmbH (Subsidiary of: Oldenbourg Wissenschaftsverlag GmbH), Markgrafenstr 12-14, Berlin, 10969, Germany. TEL 49-30-4220060, FAX 49-30-42200657, info@akademie-verlag.de, http://www.akademie-verlag.de.

500 940 DEU
BEITRAEGE ZUR D D R - WISSENSCHAFTSGESCHICHTE. REIHE A: DOKUMENTE. (Deutsche Demokratische Republik) Text in German. 2003. irreg. price varies. **Document type:** *Monographic series, Academic/Scholarly.*
Published by: Akademische Verlagsanstalt AVA, Oststr 41, Leipzig, 04317, Germany. TEL 49-341-9900440, FAX 49-341-9900440, info@univerlag-leipzig.de.

500 940 DEU
BEITRAEGE ZUR D D R - WISSENSCHAFTSGESCHICHTE. REIHE B: ARBEITSMATERIALIEN UND TEXTE. (Deutsche Demokratische Republik) Text in German. 2002. irreg., latest vol.2, 2005. price varies. **Document type:** *Monographic series, Academic/Scholarly.*
Published by: Akademische Verlagsanstalt AVA, Oststr 41, Leipzig, 04317, Germany. TEL 49-341-9900440, FAX 49-341-9900440, info@univerlag-leipzig.de.

500 DEU
BEITRAEGE ZUR D D R - WISSENSCHAFTSGESCHICHTE. REIHE C: STUDIEN. (Deutsche Demokratische Republik) Text in German. 2008. irreg. price varies. **Document type:** *Monographic series, Academic/Scholarly.*
Published by: Akademische Verlagsanstalt AVA, Oststr 41, Leipzig, 04317, Germany. TEL 49-341-9900440, FAX 49-341-9900440, info@univerlag-leipzig.de, http://www.univerlag-leipzig.de.

500 DEU ISSN 1861-1478
BEITRAEGE ZUR GESCHICHTE DER DEUTSCHEN FORSCHUNGSGEMEINSCHAFT. Text in German. 2006. irreg., latest vol.5, 2010. price varies. **Document type:** *Monographic series, Academic/Scholarly.*
Published by: Franz Steiner Verlag GmbH, Birkenwaldstr 44, Stuttgart, 70191, Germany. TEL 49-711-25820, FAX 49-711-2582290, service@steiner-verlag.de, http://www.steiner-verlag.de.

500 DEU ISSN 0522-6570
BEITRAEGE ZUR GESCHICHTE DER WISSENSCHAFT UND DER TECHNIK. Text in German. 1961. irreg., latest vol.21, 1990. price varies. illus. **Document type:** *Monographic series, Academic/ Scholarly.*
Published by: (Deutsche Gesellschaft fuer Geschichte der Medizin, Naturwissenschaft und Technik e.V.), Franz Steiner Verlag GmbH, Birkenwaldstr 44, Stuttgart, 70191, Germany. TEL 49-711-25820, FAX 49-711-2582290, service@steiner-verlag.de, http://www.steiner-verlag.de.

500 BEL
BELGIUM. FONDS VOOR WETENSCHAPPELIJK ONDERZOEK - VLAANDEREN. JAARVERSLAG (ONLINE EDITION). Text in Dutch; Summaries in English. 1928. a. **Document type:** *Yearbook, Government.* **Description:** Report of activities of the Fund for Scientific Research - Flanders (Belgium) and its associated funds.
Former titles: Belgium. Fonds voor Wetenschappelijk Onderzoek - Vlaanderen. Jaarverslag (Print Edition) (0067-5407); (until 1996): Belgium. Nationaal Fonds voor Wetenschappelijk Onderzoek. Jaarverslag; Which superseded (in 1989): Belgium Fonds National de la Recherche Scientifique. Rapport Annuel
Media: Online - full text.
Published by: Fonds voor Wetenschappelijk Onderzoek - Vlaanderen, Egmontstraat 5, Brussels, 1000, Belgium. TEL 32-2-5129110, FAX 32-2-5125890, http://www.fwo.be. Ed. Jose Traest.

507 BEL
BELGIUM. FONDS VOOR WETENSCHAPPELIJK ONDERZOEK - VLAANDEREN. LIJST DER KREDIETGENIETERS. Text in Dutch; Summaries in English. 1928. a. back issues avail. **Document type:** *Government.* **Description:** Lists scientific projects supported by the Fund for Scientific Research - Flanders and its associated funds.
Formerly (until 1996): Belgium. Nationaal Fonds voor Wetenschappelijk Onderzoek. Lijst der Kredietgenieters; Which superseded (in 1989): Belgium. Fonds National de la Recherche Scientifique. Liste des Beneficiaires d'une Subvention
Published by: Fonds voor Wetenschappelijk Onderzoek - Vlaanderen, Egmontstraat 5, Brussels, 1000, Belgium. TEL 32-2-5129110, FAX 32-2-5125890, http://www.fwo.be. Ed. Jose Traest. Circ: 1,500.

500 CHE ISSN 1662-3118
▼ **BEOBACHTER NATUR.** Text in German. 2009. 10/yr. CHF 58 domestic; CHF 75 in Europe; CHF 89 elsewhere (effective 2011). adv. **Document type:** *Magazine, Consumer.*
Published by: Axel Springer Schweiz AG (Subsidiary of: Axel Springer Verlag AG), Foerrlibuckstr 70, Zuerich, 8005, Switzerland. TEL 41-43-4445111, FAX 41-43-4445091, info@axelspringer.ch, http://www.axelspringer.ch. Circ: 76,000 (paid).

500.9 DEU ISSN 0067-5806
BERICHTE DES VEREINS NATUR UND HEIMAT UND DES NATURHISTORISCHEN MUSEUMS ZU LUEBECK. Text in German. 1959. irreg. (every 2-3 yrs.). **Document type:** *Monographic series.*
Indexed: Z01.
—Linda Hall.
Published by: Museum fuer Natur und Umwelt, Muehlendamm 1-3, Luebeck, 23552, Germany. TEL 49-451-1224122, FAX 49-451-1224199, naturmuseum@luebeck.de. Circ: 800.

500 DEU ISSN 0170-6233
Q124.6 CODEN: BEWID8
BERICHTE ZUR WISSENSCHAFTSGESCHICHTE; Organ der Gesellschaft fuer Wissenschaftsgeschichte. Text in German; Summaries in English. 1978. q. GBP 147 in United Kingdom to institutions; EUR 280 in Europe to institutions; USD 288 elsewhere to institutions; GBP 170 combined subscription in United Kingdom to institutions (print & online eds.); EUR 323 combined subscription in Europe to institutions (print & online eds.); USD 331 combined subscription elsewhere to institutions (print & online eds.) (effective 2012). bk.rev. illus. reprint service avail. from PSC. **Document type:** *Journal, Academic/Scholarly.*
Related titles: Online - full text ed.: ISSN 1522-2365. GBP 147 in United Kingdom to institutions; EUR 280 in Europe to institutions; USD 288 elsewhere to institutions (effective 2012).
Indexed: A20, A22, ArtHuCI, BibLing, CA, CCMJ, DIP, EMBASE, ExcerpMed, FR, HistAb, IBR, IBZ, MEDLINE, MSN, MathR, P30, PCI, RASB, SCI, SCOPUS, SSCI, T02, W07, Z02.
—BLDSC (1938.400000), IE, Ingenta, INIST, Linda Hall. **CCC.**
Published by: Wiley - V C H Verlag GmbH & Co. KGaA (Subsidiary of: John Wiley & Sons, Inc.), Postfach 101161, Weinheim, 69451, Germany. TEL 49-6201-606400, FAX 49-6201-606184, subservice@wiley-vch.de, http://www.wiley-vch.de. Ed. Cornelius Borck. Circ: 750. **Subscr. in the Americas to:** John Wiley & Sons, Inc., 111 River St, Hoboken, NJ 07030. TEL 201-748-6645, subinfo@wiley.com; **Subscr. outside Germany, Austria & Switzerland to:** John Wiley & Sons Ltd., The Atrium, Southern Gate, Chichester, West Sussex PO19 8SQ, United Kingdom. TEL 44-1243-779777, FAX 44-1243-775878.

500 IDN ISSN 0125-9156
Q4
BERITA ILMU PENGETAHUAN DAN TEKNOLOGI. Cover title: Berita I P T E K. Text in English, Indonesian. 1957. q. USD 15. bk.rev. bibl. **Document type:** *Journal, Academic/Scholarly.*
Formerly: Berita L.I.P.I. (0005-9137)
Media: Microform.
Indexed: BAS, GeoRef, SpeleolAb.
Published by: Indonesian Institute of Sciences/Lembaga Ilmu Pengetahuan Indonesia, Jalan Jenderal Gatot Subroto 10, PO Box 250 JKT, Jakarta, 10002, Indonesia. TEL 62-21-525-1542. Ed. Djoko Pitono. **Subscr. to:** Yayasan Memajukan Jasa Informasi, Gedung PDII-LIPI Lt. V. Jl. Jend. Gatot Subroto 10, PO Box 4509, Jakarta 12710, Indonesia.

500 DEU
▼ **BERLIN STUDIES IN KNOWLEDGE RESEARCH.** Text in English. 2011. irreg., latest vol.3, 2012. price varies. **Document type:** *Monographic series, Academic/Scholarly.*
Published by: Walter de Gruyter GmbH & Co. KG, Genthiner Str 13, Berlin, 10785, Germany. TEL 49-30-260050, FAX 49-30-26005251, info@degruyter.com, http://www.degruyter.de. Eds. Guenter Abel, James Conant.

500 DEU ISSN 0930-7583
BERLINER AUSGABEN. Text in German. 1991. irreg. price varies. **Document type:** *Monographic series, Academic/Scholarly.*
Published by: Frommann-Holzboog Verlag e.K., Koenig-Karl-Str 27, Stuttgart, 70372, Germany. TEL 49-711-9559690, FAX 49-711-9559691, info@frommann-holzboog.de, http://www.frommann-holzboog.de.

500 DEU ISSN 0171-3302
AS181
BERLINER WISSENSCHAFTLICHE GESELLSCHAFT. JAHRBUCH. Text in German. 1978. a. EUR 34 (effective 2009). **Document type:** *Journal, Academic/Scholarly.*
Indexed: MLA-IB.
Published by: Berliner Wissenschaftliche Gesellschaft e.V., Robert-Koch-Platz 7, Berlin, 10115, Germany. TEL 49-30-2832267, FAX 49-30-2832267, mail@bwg-berlin.de, http://www.bwg-berlin.de. Circ: 500.

507 DEU ISSN 0344-578X
LC1047.G3
BERUFSBILDUNGSBERICHT. Variant title: Grundlagen und Perspektiven fuer Bildung und Wissenschaft. Berufsbildungsbericht. Text in German. 1977. a. **Document type:** *Trade.*
Published by: Bundesministerium fuer Bildung und Forschung, Hannoversche Str 28-30, Berlin, 10115, Germany. TEL 49-30-18570, FAX 49-30-18575503, information@bmbf.bund.de.

500 600 JPN ISSN 0285-1008
BESSATSU SAIENSU. Text in Japanese. 8/yr. price varies. **Description:** Covers current topics in science with photographs and easy-to-understand explanations.
Published by: Nikkei Science Inc. (Subsidiary of: Nihon Keizai Shimbun, Inc.), 2-2-1 Uchisaiwai-cho, Chiyoda-ku, Tokyo, 100-0011, Japan. TEL 03-5255-2125, FAX 03-3293-2759, TELEX J22308-NIHONKEIZAI. Eds. K Ohtake, S Katayose. Circ: 28,751.

500 800 USA ISSN 1530-1508
Q1
THE BEST AMERICAN SCIENCE AND NATURE WRITING (YEAR). Text in English. 2000. irreg. USD 14.95 per issue (effective 2010). adv. 352 p./no.; back issues avail.; reprints avail.
Published by: Houghton Mifflin Harcourt Publishing Company, 215 Park Ave S, New York, NY 10003. TEL 212-420-5846, FAX 212-420-5850, trade_publicity@hmco.com. Ed. Tim Folger.

THE BEST STUDY SERIES FOR G E D. SCIENCE. (General Education Development) *see* EDUCATION

500 IND ISSN 0971-7706
BHARATIYA VAIGYANIK EVAM AUDYOGIK ANUSANDHAN PATRIKA. Abbreviated title: B V A A P. Text in Hindi. 1993. s-a. INR 400, USD 60; INR 200, USD 30 per issue (effective 2011). back issues avail. **Document type:** *Journal, Academic/Scholarly.*
Related titles: Online - full text ed.: ISSN 0975-2412. free (effective 2011).
Published by: National Institute of Science Communication and Information Resources (N I S C A I R), Dr. K.S. Krishnan Marg, New Delhi, 110 012, India. TEL 91-11-25841647, FAX 91-11-25847062, sales@niscair.res.in. Ed. Pradeep Sharma.

500 378 DEU ISSN 1863-8775
BI.RESEARCH; Forschungsmagazin der Universitaet Bielefeld. Text in German, English. 1990. s-a. adv. abstr.; illus. 80 p./no. 2 cols./p.; **Document type:** *Magazine, Academic/Scholarly.*
Formerly (until 2006): Forschung an der Universitaet Bielefeld (0937-2873)
Related titles: Online - full text ed.
Published by: Universitaet Bielefeld, Referat fuer Kommunikation, Postfach 100131, Bielefeld, 33501, Germany. TEL 49-521-1064146, FAX 49-521-1062964, pressestelle@uni-bielefeld.de. Eds. Hans-Martin Kruckis, Sabine Schulze. Adv. contact Marlies Laege-Knuth. Circ: 3,800 (controlled).

BIANJI XUEBAO/ACTA EDITOLOGICA. *see* PUBLISHING AND BOOK TRADE

500 ITA ISSN 0394-5065
BIBLIOTECA DI STORIA DELLA SCIENZA. Text in Italian. 1947. irreg., latest vol.43, 2000. price varies. **Document type:** *Monographic series, Academic/Scholarly.* **Description:** Examines the history of science.
Formerly (until 1987): Rivista di Storia delle Scienze Mediche e Naturali. Biblioteca (0080-326X)
Indexed: FR, MLA-IB, P30.
Published by: Casa Editrice Leo S. Olschki, Viuzzo del Pozzetto 8, Florence, 50126, Italy. TEL 39-055-6530684, FAX 39-055-6530214, celso@olschki.it, http://www.olschki.it.

500 ITA ISSN 2038-3533
▼ **BIBLIOTECA GALILEIANA.** Text in Multiple languages. 2010. irreg. **Document type:** *Monographic series, Academic/Scholarly.*
Published by: Casa Editrice Leo S. Olschki, Viuzzo del Pozzetto 8, Florence, 50126, Italy. TEL 39-055-6530684, FAX 39-055-6530214, celso@olschki.it, http://www.olschki.it.

500 COL ISSN 0120-484X
BIBLIOTECA JOSE JERONIMO TRIANA (SERIAL). Text in English, Spanish. 1983. irreg. per issue exchange basis. **Document type:** *Monographic series, Academic/Scholarly.*
Indexed: Z01.
Published by: Universidad Nacional de Colombia, Instituto de Ciencias, PO Box 7495, Bogota, CUND, Colombia. TEL 57-1-3165305, FAX 57-1-3165365, dicn@ciencias.ciencias.unal.edu.co, http://www.icn.unal.edu.co. Ed. Gloria Galeano. Pub. Gary Stiles. R&P Jaime Uribe M. Circ: 1,000.

500 CAN ISSN 1920-9932
BIG SCIENCE. Text in English. 2002. m. free to members (effective 2010). back issues avail. **Document type:** *Newsletter, Academic/Scholarly.* **Description:** Aims to teaching science in an interactive environment.
Formerly (until 2007): Big Little Science Centre. Newsletter (1920-9924)
Related titles: Online - full text ed.: ISSN 1920-9940. free to members (effective 2010).
Published by: Big Little Science Centre, Station Main, PO Box 882, Kamloops, BC V2C 5M8, Canada. TEL 250-554-2572, gord@blscs.org. Ed. Gordon R Gore TEL 250-579-5722.

500.9 DEU ISSN 0006-2375
Q3 CODEN: BIWIAX
BILD DER WISSENSCHAFT; das Magazin fuer Wissenschaft und Technik. Text in German. 1964. m. EUR 77.40 domestic; EUR 86.40 foreign; EUR 7.30 newsstand/cover (effective 2011). adv. bk.rev. bibl.; charts; illus. index. **Document type:** *Journal, Academic/Scholarly.*
Incorporates (1992-2000): Illustrierte Wissenschaft (0942-7090); (1969-1973): X (0720-6313)
Indexed: A22, CEABA, ChemAb, DIP, GeoRef, IBR, IBZ, KWIWR, MLA-IB, NumL, P30, RASB, RILM, SpeleolAb, TM.
—BLDSC (2058.950000), CASDDS, IE, Infotrieve, Ingenta, Linda Hall. **CCC.**
Published by: Konradin Verlag Robert Kohlhammer GmbH, Ernst Mey Str 8, Leinfelden-Echterdingen, 70771, Germany. TEL 49-711-75940, FAX 49-711-7594390, info@konradin.de, http://www.konradin.de. Ed. Wolfgang Hess. Adv. contact Julia Raudenbusch. Circ: 91,127 (paid and controlled).

BILDUNG+ SCIENCE. *see* CHILDREN AND YOUTH—About

BIOGRAPHY TODAY SCIENTISTS & INVENTORS SERIES; profiles of people of interest to young readers. *see* BIOGRAPHY

500 USA ISSN 1934-8630
R857.M3
➤ **BIOINTERPHASES.** Text in English. 2006. q. adv. back issues avail. **Document type:** *Journal, Academic/Scholarly.* **Description:** Provides an interdisciplinary platform for scientific exchange among the biology, chemistry, physics, and materials sciences communities.
Related titles: Online - full text ed.: ISSN 1559-4106. 2007. free (effective 2011).
Indexed: C10, Inspec, MEDLINE, P30, T02.
—BLDSC (2072.357000). **CCC.**
Published by: (American Vacuum Society), American Institute of Physics, 1 Physics Ellipse, College Park, MD 20740. TEL 301-209-3100, FAX 301-209-0843, aipinfo@aip.org, http://www.aip.org. Ed. Michael Grunze TEL 49-6221-548461. **Subscr. to:** PO Box 503284, St Louis, MO 63150. TEL 516-576-2270, 800-344-6902, FAX 516-349-9704, subs@aip.org.

➤ **BIOLOGICAL RHYTHM RESEARCH.** *see* BIOLOGY

➤ **BIOLOGIE, CHEMIE, ZEMEPIS.** *see* EDUCATION

➤ **BIOSCIENCE RESEARCH.** *see* BIOLOGY

500 USA ISSN 0893-1348
CODEN: OPBMAU
BISHOP MUSEUM OCCASIONAL PAPERS. Text in English. 1898. irreg., latest vol.108, 2010. price varies. back issues avail.; reprints avail. **Document type:** *Monographic series, Academic/Scholarly.* **Description:** Contains original contributions in anthropology, history, and the natural sciences of Hawaii and the Pacific.
Formerly (until 1984): Bernice P. Bishop Museum. Occasional Papers (0067-6160)
Related titles: Online - full text ed.: free (effective 2010).
Indexed: AICP, ASFA, B21, B25, BIOSIS Prev, EntAb, FR, GeoRef, MycolAb, SpeleolAb, Z01.
—Ingenta, INIST, Linda Hall.
Published by: (Bernice Pauahi Bishop Museum), Bishop Museum Press, 1525 Bernice St, Honolulu, HI 96817. TEL 808-847-3511, FAX 808-841-8968, press@bishopmuseum.org, http://www.bishopmuseum.org.

500 USA ISSN 1085-455X
QH70.U6 CODEN: BMUREE
BISHOP MUSEUM TECHNICAL REPORT. Text in English. 1992. irreg., latest vol.51, 2010. back issues avail. **Document type:** *Monographic series, Trade.*
Related titles: Online - full text ed.: free (effective 2010).
Indexed: Z01.
Published by: Bishop Museum Press, 1525 Bernice St, Honolulu, HI 96817. TEL 808-847-3511, FAX 808-841-8968, press@bishopmuseum.org, http://www.bishopmuseum.org.

500 COL ISSN 0120-4211
BISTUA; revista de la Facultad de Ciencias Basicas. Text in Spanish. 1986. s-a. USD 20 (effective 2010). back issues avail. **Document type:** *Journal, Academic/Scholarly.*
Related titles: Online - full text ed.: free (effective 2011).
Indexed: A32, AnBeAb, B21, E17, ESPM, EntAb, F04, SWRA.
Published by: Universidad de Pamplona, Facultad de Ciencias Basicas, Km. 1 Via Bucaramanga, Bucaramanga, Santander, Colombia. informacion@unipamplona.edu.co, http://www.unipamplona.edu.co/. Ed. Alfonso Quijano.

508 NLD ISSN 2210-416X
BLAD. Text in Dutch. 200?. q. EUR 26.50 membership (effective 2010).
Published by: (IVN Vereniging voor Natuur- en Milieueducatie, Afdeling Noord-Kennemerland), Koninklijke Nederlandse Natuurhistorische Vereniging, Afdeling Regio Alkmaar, Halsstraat 10, Alkmaar, 1816 CN, Netherlands. TEL 31-72-5113975. **Co-publisher:** IVN Vereniging voor Natuur- en Milieueducatie, Afdeling Noord-Kennemerland.

378.4 DEU ISSN 0942-928X
BLICK IN DIE WISSENSCHAFT; Forschungsmagazin der Universitaet Regensburg. Text in German. 1992. a. EUR 7.50 per issue (effective 2011). adv. **Document type:** *Journal, Academic/Scholarly.*
Related titles: Online - full text ed.

S

Published by: (Universitaet Regensburg), Verlag Schnell und Steiner GmbH, Leibnizstr 13, Regensburg, 93055, Germany. TEL 49-941-787850, FAX 49-941-7878516, post@schnell-und-steiner.de. Adv. contact Silvia Dechant. color page EUR 3,229, B&W page EUR 2,170; trim 186 x 260. Circ: 5,000 (paid and controlled).

508 971 CAN ISSN 0006-5099
CODEN: BLJYA3

➤ **BLUE JAY.** Text in English. 1942. 4/yr. CAD 25 domestic; CAD 30 foreign (effective 2005). adv. bk.rev. charts; illus.; maps. 64 p./no. 2 cols./p.; back issues avail. **Document type:** *Journal, Academic/Scholarly.* **Description:** General interest scientific information dealing with the natural history of Saskatchewan.
Indexed: A22, B25, BIOSIS Prev, MycolAb, WLR, WildRev, Z01.
—BLDSC (2114.150000), Ingenta. **CCC.**
Published by: Nature Saskatchewan, 1860 Lorne St, Rm 206, Regina, SK S4P 2L7, Canada. TEL 306-780-9273, FAX 306-780-9263, pdumont@naturesask.com, http://www.nature.sask.com. adv.: B&W 1/4 page CAD 125. Circ: 2,000.

500 330 ITA ISSN 2039-1471

▼ **BOCCONI & SPRINGER SERIES.** Text in English. 2010. q.
Description: Covers a wide variety of topics in the fields of mathematics, statistics, finance, economics and financial economics.
Related titles: Online - full text ed.: ISSN 2039-148X.
Published by: (Universita Bocconi), Springer Italia Srl (Subsidiary of: Springer Science+Business Media), Via Decembrio 28, Milan, 20137, Italy. TEL 39-02-54259722, FAX 39-02-55193360, springer@springer.it.

500 DEU ISSN 0523-8226

BOETHIUS; Texte und Abhandlungen zur Geschichte der Mathematik und der Naturwissenschaften. Text in German. 1962. irreg., latest vol.64, 2010. price varies. illus. **Document type:** *Monographic series, Academic/Scholarly.*
Indexed: CCMJ.
—Linda Hall.
Published by: Franz Steiner Verlag GmbH, Birkenwaldstr 44, Stuttgart, 70191, Germany. TEL 49-711-25820, FAX 49-711-2582290, franz.steiner.verlag@t-online.de, http://www.steiner-verlag.de.

500 CHN ISSN 1673-0569
CODEN: BDXZBL

BOHAI DAXUE XUEBAO (ZIRAN KEXUE BAN)/BOHAI UNIVERSITY. JOURNAL (NATURAL SCIENCE EDITION). Text in Chinese. 1980. q. CNY 20, USD 20 (effective 2008 & 2009). **Document type:** *Journal, Academic/Scholarly.* **Description:** Covers Sci-tech service, chemistry and chemical engineering, physics, engineering, mathematics, and information science.
Formerly (until 2004): Jinzhou Shifan Xueyuan Xuebao (Zike Ban) (1007-533X)
Related titles: Online - full text ed.
Indexed: RefZh, Z02.
—BLDSC (2118.260000), IE, Ingenta.
Published by: Bohai Daxue/Bohai University, No.19, High-Tech Industrial Park, Keji Road, Jinzhou, Liaoning 121013, China. TEL 86-416-5189063, FAX 86-416-5189063, http://www.bhu.edu.cn/. Ed. Chuanfu Jiang. Circ: 1,000. **Dist. by:** China International Book Trading Corp, 35 Chegongzhuang Xilu, Haidian District, PO Box 399, Beijing 100044, China. TEL 86-10-68412045, FAX 86-10-68412023, cibtc@mail.cibtc.com.cn, http://www.cibtc.com.cn.

500 300 BRA ISSN 0103-1589

BOLETIM CULTURAL. Text in Portuguese; Summaries in English, Portuguese. 1987. a., latest vol.29, 2001. BRL 20 per issue domestic; USD 10 per issue foreign (effective 2003). bk.rev. abstr.; bibl.; charts; illus.; maps. 75 p./no.; back issues avail. **Document type:** *Bulletin, Consumer.* **Description:** Contains original works of technical and didactic character from different areas of knowledge. Directed to the academic community in general.
Indexed: MLA-IB.
Published by: Universidade do Sagrado Coracao, Rua Irma Arminda, 10-50, Bauru, SP 17011-160, Brazil. TEL 55-14-2357111, FAX 55-14-2357219, edusc@edusc.com.br, http://www.usc.br. Ed. Mari lene Cabello Di Flora. Pub. Lina Ana Santarosa. R&P Luis Eugenio Vescio TEL 55-14-2357111. Adv. contact Luzia Bianchi TEL 55-14-2357111. Circ: 500.

500 CUB

BOLETIN DE EVENTOS CIENTIFICO-TECNICOS. Text in Spanish. w.
Published by: Academia de Ciencias de Cuba, Instituto de Documentacion e Informacion Cientifico-Tecnica (I D I C T), Capitolio Nacional, Prado y San Jose, Habana, 2, Cuba.

500 ECU ISSN 0366-1830
Q4 CODEN: BOICAL

BOLETIN DE INFORMACIONES CIENTIFICAS NACIONALES. Text in Spanish. 1947. irreg., latest vol.126, 1997. bibl. **Document type:** *Academic/Scholarly.*
Indexed: C01, MLA-IB.
Published by: Casa de la Cultura Ecuatoriana, Avenida 6 de Diciembre 332, Quito, Ecuador. Ed. Celin Astudillo Espinosa. Circ: 1,000.

500 PER ISSN 0253-0015
F3401 CODEN: BLIMEY

BOLETIN DE LIMA; revista cientifica y cultural. Text in Spanish; Summaries in English, German, Spanish. 1979. bi-m. USD 100 domestic; USD 120 foreign. adv. bk.rev. **Document type:** *Journal, Academic/Scholarly.* **Description:** Presents research relating to Peru in the fields of biology, ecology, geography, history, archaeology, folklore, medicine, oceanography, and natural sciences.
Indexed: AICP, IBR, IBZ, MLA-IB, RASB.
—BLDSC (2207.480000). **CCC.**
Published by: Editorial Los Pinos E.I.R.L., Casilla 18-1027, Lima, 18, Peru. TEL 51-14-460031, FAX 51-14-460031. Ed., R&P Fernando Villiger. Circ: 1,500 (paid).

500 CUB ISSN 1028-0855

BOLETIN DE NOVEDADES CIENTIFICO-TECNICAS. Text in Spanish. 1997. m.
Media: Online - full text.
Published by: Instituto de Informacion Cientifica y Tecnologica, Prado entre Dragones y San Jose, Apdo 2035, Havana, 10200, Cuba. TEL 537-635500, FAX 537-338237, comercial@idict.cu.

500.9 IND ISSN 0006-6982
QH1 CODEN: JBOMAA

➤ **BOMBAY NATURAL HISTORY SOCIETY. JOURNAL.** Text in English. 1886. 3/yr. free to members (effective 2011). bk.rev. charts; illus. back issues avail. **Document type:** *Journal, Academic/Scholarly.*
Description: Contains up-to-date information on Ecology, Natural History and Biology for researchers.
Related titles: Online - full text ed.: (from IDC).
Indexed: A22, A29, A34, A35, A38, ASFA, AgBio, AgrForAb, B20, B21, B23, B25, BAS, BIOSIS Prev, C25, C30, CABA, E12, ESPM, F08, F11, F12, FCA, G11, GeoRef, H16, I10, I11, KWIWR, LT, MycolAb, N02, N04, O01, P32, P33, P39, P40, PGegResA, R07, R08, R13, RA&MP, S13, S16, SCOPUS, SpeleolAb, TAR, VITIS, VirolAbstr, W08, W10, W11, WildRev, Z01.
—BLDSC (4709.900000), IE, Ingenta, INIST, Linda Hall.
Published by: Bombay Natural History Society, Hornbill House, Shaheed Bhagat Singh Rd, Mumbai, Maharashtra 400 001, India. TEL 91-22-22821811, FAX 91-22-22837615, info@bnhs.org.

➤ **B'OR HA-TORAH**; science, the arts and modern life in the light of the Torah. *see* RELIGIONS AND THEOLOGY—Judaic

501 NLD ISSN 0068-0346
Q174 CODEN: BPSCDD

➤ **BOSTON STUDIES IN THE PHILOSOPHY OF SCIENCE**; Boston colloquium for the philosophy of science. Text in English. 1963. irreg., latest vol.280, 2009. price varies. **Document type:** *Proceedings, Academic/Scholarly.* **Description:** Looks into and reflects on interactions between epistemological and historical dimensions.
Indexed: A22, CCMJ, FR, MathR, PhilInd, RASB.
—BLDSC (2251.830000), IE, Ingenta, INIST. **CCC.**
Published by: Springer Netherlands (Subsidiary of: Springer Science+Business Media), Van Godewijckstraat 30, Dordrecht, 3311 GX, Netherlands. TEL 31-78-6576050, FAX 31-78-6576474, http://www.springer.com. Eds. Juergen Renn, Kostas Gavroglu, Robert S Cohen.

500 DEU ISSN 0068-0737
CODEN: ABWGAZ

BRAUNSCHWEIGISCHE WISSENSCHAFTLICHE GESELLSCHAFT. ABHANDLUNGEN. Text in German. 1949. a. EUR 25 per vol. (effective 2010). **Document type:** *Monographic series, Academic/Scholarly.*
Indexed: CCMJ, GeoRef, IBR, IBZ, Inspec, MSN, MathR, RefZh, SpeleolAb, Z02.
—INIST, Linda Hall.
Published by: (Braunschweigische Wissenschaftliche Gesellschaft), Verlag Erich Goltze GmbH und Co. KG, Hans-Boeckler-Str 7, Postfach 1944, Goettingen, 37009, Germany. TEL 49-551-506760, FAX 49-551-5067622, info@goltze.de, http://www.goltze.de. Ed. Claus-Artur Scheier.

500 BRA

BRAZIL. CONSELHO NACIONAL DE DESENVOLVIMENTO CIENTIFICO E TECNOLOGICO. PROGRAMA DO TROPICA SEMI-ARIDO (PUBLICACION). Text in Portuguese. irreg. charts; stat.
Published by: Conselho Nacional de Desenvolvimento Cientifico e Tecnologico, Programa do Tropico Semi-Arido, Av. W-3 Norte Q-507-B, Brasilia, DF 11-1142, Brazil. Ed. Domingos Carvalho da Silva.

500 BRA

BRAZIL. CONSELHO NACIONAL DE DESENVOLVIMENTO CIENTIFICO E TECNOLOGICO. RELATORIO DE ATIVIDADES. Text in Portuguese. 1975. irreg.
Published by: Conselho Nacional de Desenvolvimento Cientifico e Tecnologico, SEPN 507 Norte Bloco B, Brasilia, DF 70740901, Brazil. FAX 061-274-1950.

500 IND ISSN 0974-2433

BREAKTHROUGH. Text in English. 1992. q. INR 10 (effective 2011). **Document type:** *Journal, Academic/Scholarly.*
Published by: Breakthrough Science Society, c/o G S Padmakumar, 43/20, Chenganath, Ayyappankavu, Cochin, Kerala 682 018, India. TEL 91-484-2091162, http://www.bsskerala.org.

500 CRI ISSN 0304-3711
QH7 CODEN: BRNSBE

BRENESIA; revista de biodiversidad y conservacion - journal of biodiversity and conservation. Text in Multiple languages; Summaries in Spanish; Abstracts in English, Spanish. 1972. 2/yr. CRC 1,500 domestic; USD 25 foreign (effective 2010); or exchange basis. illus. **Document type:** *Journal, Academic/Scholarly.*
Supersedes: Revista Historia Natural de Costa Rica
Indexed: A34, A35, ASFA, AgBio, AgrForAb, ApicAb, B21, B23, B25, BIOSIS Prev, C01, C25, C30, CABA, E12, ESPM, F08, F11, F12, G11, GH, GeoRef, H16, H17, IBR, IBZ, IndVet, LT, MycolAb, O01, P32, P33, P37, P40, PGegResA, R07, R08, RM&VM, RRTA, S13, S16, S17, SpeleolAb, T05, TAR, VS, W10, WildRev, Z01.
—INIST, Linda Hall.
Published by: Museo Nacional de Costa Rica, Apdo 749, San Jose, 1000, Costa Rica. http://www.museocostarica.go.cr. Ed. Joaquin Sanchez Gonzalez.

509 610.9 NLD ISSN 1876-6595

➤ **BRILL'S SERIES IN THE HISTORY OF THE ENVIRONMENT.** Variant title: B S H E. Text in English. 2008. irreg., latest vol.2, 2010. price varies. **Document type:** *Monographic series, Academic/Scholarly.*
Description: Includes historical and archaeological studies and the history of ideas and medicine.
Published by: Brill, PO Box 9000, Leiden, 2300 PA, Netherlands. TEL 31-71-5353500, FAX 31-71-5317532, cs@brill.nl. Ed. Aleks Pluskowski.

➤ **BRILL'S STUDIES IN INTELLECTUAL HISTORY.** *see* HUMANITIES: COMPREHENSIVE WORKS

➤ **BRILL'S TEXTS AND SOURCES IN INTELLECTUAL HISTORY.** *see* HUMANITIES: COMPREHENSIVE WORKS

509 GBR ISSN 0141-3325
QH84.2

BRITISH ANTARCTIC SURVEY. ANNUAL REPORT. Text in English. 1969. a. **Document type:** *Corporate.* **Description:** Includes reports from the nine BAS science programs, developments in infrastructure and technology, international collaborations, influence in global affairs, environmental protection, science in society, recruitment and career development.
Indexed: GeoRef, SpeleolAb.
—BLDSC (7383.680000), Linda Hall.
Published by: British Antarctic Survey, High Cross, Madingley Rd, Cambridge, CBE OET, United Kingdom. TEL 44-1223-221400, FAX 44-1223-362616, information@bas.ac.uk. Circ: 700.

509 GBR ISSN 0007-0874
Q125 CODEN: BJHSAT

➤ **BRITISH JOURNAL FOR THE HISTORY OF SCIENCE.** Abbreviated title: B J H S. Text in English. 1949. q. GBP 167, USD 312 to institutions; GBP 170, USD 321 combined subscription to institutions (print & online eds.) (effective 2012). adv. bk.rev. charts; illus. index. back issues avail.; reprint service avail. from PSC. **Document type:** *Journal, Academic/Scholarly.* **Description:** Covers all aspects of the history of science.
Formerly (until 1962): British Society for the History of Science. Bulletin (0950-5636)
Related titles: Microform ed.: (from PQC); Online - full text ed.: ISSN 1474-001X. GBP 155, USD 293 to institutions (effective 2012).
Indexed: A01, A02, A03, A08, A20, A22, A26, ASCA, AmH&L, AmHI, ArtHuCI, B04, BRD, BrGeoL, CA, CCMJ, CIS, CLOSS, ChemAb, CurCont, DIP, E01, E08, EMBASE, ESPM, EnvEAb, ExcerpMed, FR, G03, G08, GSA, GSI, GeoRef, H07, H08, H09, H10, HAb, HistAb, HumInd, I05, IBR, IBSS, IBZ, ISR, Inspec, L09, MEA&I, MEDLINE, MSN, MathR, P02, P10, P11, P26, P30, P48, P52, P53, P54, P56, PCI, PQC, PhilInd, RASB, S05, S09, S10, SCOPUS, SSCI, SpeleolAb, T02, W03, W07, Z01, Z02.
—BLDSC (2309.400000), AskIEEE, IE, Infotrieve, Ingenta, INIST, Linda Hall. **CCC.**
Published by: (British Society for the History of Science), Cambridge University Press, The Edinburgh Bldg, Shaftesbury Rd, Cambridge, CB2 8RU, United Kingdom. TEL 44-1223-312393, FAX 44-1223-315052, journals@cambridge.org, http://www.cambridge.org/uk. Ed. Simon Schaffer. R&P Linda Nicol TEL 44-1223-325702. Adv. contact Rebecca Roberts TEL 44-1223-325083. page GBP 515, page USD 975. Circ: 1,500. **Subscr. to:** Cambridge University Press, 32 Ave of the Americas, New York, NY 10013. TEL 212-337-5000, FAX 212-691-3239, journals_subscriptions@cup.org.

501 GBR ISSN 0007-0882
Q175 CODEN: BJPIA5

➤ **THE BRITISH JOURNAL FOR THE PHILOSOPHY OF SCIENCE.** Text in English. 1950. q. GBP 141 in United Kingdom to institutions; EUR 211 in Europe to institutions; USD 274 in US & Canada to institutions; GBP 141 elsewhere to institutions; GBP 154 combined subscription in United Kingdom to institutions (print & online eds.); EUR 230 combined subscription in Europe to institutions (print & online eds.); USD 299 combined subscription in US & Canada to institutions (print & online eds.); GBP 154 combined subscription elsewhere to institutions (print & online eds.) (effective 2012). adv. bk.rev. bibl.; illus. index. 196 p./no.; back issues avail.; reprint service avail. from PSC. **Document type:** *Journal, Academic/Scholarly.* **Description:** Addresses the study of the logic, the method, and the philosophy of science, including the social sciences.
Related titles: Microfiche ed.; Online - full text ed.: ISSN 1464-3537. GBP 123 in United Kingdom to institutions; EUR 184 in Europe to institutions; USD 239 in US & Canada to institutions; GBP 123 elsewhere to institutions (effective 2012) (from IngentaConnect).
Indexed: A01, A02, A03, A08, A20, A22, A26, ASCA, AmHI, ArtHuCI, B04, BRD, CA, CCMJ, CIS, CMCI, CPM, CurCont, DIP, E01, E08, FR, G08, H07, H08, H09, H10, H14, HAb, HumInd, I05, IBR, IBRH, IBZ, IPB, ISR, Inpharma, Inspec, L&LBA, MLA-IB, MSN, MathR, P02, P10, P11, P26, P30, P48, P52, P53, P54, P56, PCI, PQC, PhilInd, PsycholAb, RASB, S09, S10, SCI, SCOPUS, SSCI, T02, W03, W07, Z02.
—BLDSC (2316.000000), AskIEEE, IE, Infotrieve, Ingenta, INIST, Linda Hall. **CCC.**
Published by: (British Society for the Philosophy of Science), Oxford University Press, Great Clarendon St, Oxford, OX2 6DP, United Kingdom. TEL 44-1865-556767, FAX 44-1865-556646, enquiry@oup.co.uk, http://www.oxfordjournals.org. Eds. Alexander Bird TEL 44-117-9287826, James Ladyman TEL 44-117-9287609. Adv. contact Linda Hann TEL 44-1344-779945.

509 GBR

BRITISH SOCIETY FOR THE HISTORY OF SCIENCE. LIST OF THESES. Text in English. 1970. a. free (effective 2010). back issues avail. **Document type:** *Academic/Scholarly.*
Media: Online - full text.
Published by: British Society for the History of Science, PO Box 3401, Norwich, NR7 7JF, United Kingdom. TEL 44-1603-516236, FAX 44-1603-208563, membership@bshs.org.uk.

BRUNIANA & CAMPANELLIANA. *see* PHILOSOPHY

500 USA

BUFFALO SOCIETY OF NATURAL SCIENCES. OCCASIONAL PAPERS. Text in English. 1976. irreg., latest vol.4, 1990. price varies.
Published by: Buffalo Society of Natural Sciences, 1020 Humboldt Pkwy, Buffalo, NY 14211. TEL 716-896-5200, FAX 716-897-6723.

500 ALB

BULETINI I SHKENCAVE TEKNIKE/BULLETIN DES SCIENCES TECHNIQUES. Text in Albanian; Summaries in French. q. USD 7.20.
Published by: Enver Hoxha Universitet, Tirana, Albania.

500 370 BGR ISSN 1313-1958

➤ **BULGARIAN JOURNAL OF SCIENCE AND EDUCATION POLICY.** Abbreviated title: B J S E P. Text in Bulgarian, English. 2007. s-a. free. bk.rev. illus. cum.index. back issues avail.; reprints avail. **Document type:** *Journal, Academic/Scholarly.* **Description:** Covers all aspects of science and education theory, policy, practice (Especially in science education) and management, including biographical portraits of prominent scholars and educators of any nation.
Related titles: Online - full text ed.: ISSN 1313-9118. free (effective 2011).
Indexed: E03, T02.
Published by: Sofiiski Universitet Sv. Kliment Ohridski, Universitetsko Izdatelstvo/Sofia University St. Kliment Ohridski University Press, 1 James Bourchier Blvd., Sofia, 1164, Bulgaria. TEL 359-2-8629049, FAX 359-2-9625438, unipress@press.uni-sofia.bg, http://www.uni-sofia.bg/index.php/bul/universitet_t/drugi_strukturni_zvena/samostoyatelni_zvena/universitetsko_izdatelstvo. Ed. B V Toshev. Pub. D. Tomov.

500 BGR ISSN 0007-3989
AS343
BULGARSKA AKADEMIIA NA NAUKITE. SPISANIE. Text in Bulgarian; Summaries in English. 1956. bi-m. BGL 7.80; USD 120 foreign (effective 2002). illus. reprint service avail. from IRC. **Document type:** *Journal.* **Description:** Reflects the scientific events in the Bulgarian Academy of Sciences, its programs and research communities; national and international scientific events; scientific problems, discussions, announcements.
Indexed: A28, APA, BSLBiol, BSLEcon, BSLMath, BrCerAb, C&ISA, CA/WCA, CIA, CerAb, CivEngAb, CorrAb, E&CAJ, E11, EEA, EMA, ESPM, EnvEAb, H15, M&TEA, M09, MBF, METADEX, P30, RASB, RefZh, SolStAb, T04, WAA.
—INIST, Linda Hall. **CCC.**
Published by: (Bulgarska Akademiya na Naukite/Bulgarian Academy of Sciences), Sofiiski Universitet Sv. Kliment Ohridski, Universitetsko Izdatelstvo/Sofia University St. Kliment Ohridski University Press, Akad G Bonchev 6, Sofia, 1113, Bulgaria. Ed. G Brankov. Circ: 800. **Dist. by:** Hemus, 6 Rouski Blvd., Sofia 1000, Bulgaria; **Dist. by:** Sofia Books, ul Silivria 16, Sofia 1404, Bulgaria. TEL 359-2-9586257, info@sofiabooks-bg.com, http://www.sofiabooks-bg.com.

500 BGR ISSN 1310-1331
Q69 CODEN: DBANEH
BULGARSKA AKADEMIYA NA NAUKITE. DOKLADI/ACADEMIE BULGARE DES SCIENCES. COMPTES RENDUS/BULGARIAN ACADEMY OF SCIENCES. PROCEEDINGS. Text in English, French, German, Russian. 1948. m. BGL 2.70 per issue. illus. index. reprint service avail. from IRC. **Document type:** *Journal, Academic/Scholarly.*
Formerly (until 1991): Bolgarskaya Akademiya Nauk. Doklady (0366-8681)
Indexed: A28, ABSML, AESIS, APA, B25, BIOSIS Prev, BSLBiol, BSLGeo, BSLMath, BrCerAb, C&ISA, CA/WCA, CCMJ, CIA, CerAb, ChemAb, CivEngAb, CorrAb, E&CAJ, E11, EEA, EMA, GeoRef, H15, IBR, IBZ, INIS AtomInd, IndMed, Inspec, M&TEA, M09, MBF, METADEX, MSN, MathR, MinerAb, MycolAb, P30, RefZh, SCI, SCOPUS, SolStAb, SpeleolAb, T04, W07, WAA, Z01.
—AskIEEE, CASDDS, IE, Infotrieve, INIST. **CCC.**
Published by: (Bulgarska Akademiya na Naukite/Bulgarian Academy of Sciences), Akademichno Izdatelstvo Prof. Marin Drinov/Prof. Marin Drinov Academic Publishing House, Akad G Bonchev 6, Sofia, 1113, Bulgaria. TEL 359-2-720922, FAX 359-2-8704054, http://m-drinov.bas.bg. **Dist. by:** Hemus, 6 Rouski Blvd., Sofia 1000, Bulgaria.

BULLETIN HISTORIQUE ET SCIENTIFIQUE DE L'AUVERGNE. *see* HISTORY—History Of Europe

500 300 USA ISSN 0270-4676
Q175.4 CODEN: BSTSDJ
➤ **BULLETIN OF SCIENCE, TECHNOLOGY & SOCIETY.** Text in English. 1981. bi-m. adv. bk.rev. illus. Index. back issues avail.; reprint service avail. from PSC. **Document type:** *Journal, Academic/Scholarly.* **Description:** Contains articles designed to provide a means of communication within as wide a spectrum of the science and technology community as possible.
Related titles: Microform ed.: (from MIM, PQC); Online - full text ed.: ISSN 1552-4183. USD 835, GBP 492 to institutions (effective 2011).
Indexed: A01, A02, A03, A08, A20, A22, A34, A35, A36, A37, ASCA, AgBio, B07, B21, BA, C25, CA, CABA, CMM, CommAb, D01, E-psyche, E01, E03, E12, ERI, ERIC, ESPM, EnerRev, F08, F12, FCA, FR, GH, GeoRef, H&SSA, H04, H16, I11, MaizeAb, N02, OR, P04, P30, P32, P34, P37, P38, P40, P42, PAIS, PGegResA, PSA, PhilInd, R07, R12, RASB, S02, S03, S12, S13, S16, SCOPUS, SOPODA, SSA, SSciA, SociolAb, SoyAb, T02, TAR, V02, VS, W10, W11.
—BLDSC (2887.760000), IE, Infotrieve, Ingenta, INIST, Linda Hall. **CCC.**
Published by: Sage Publications, Inc., 2455 Teller Rd, Thousand Oaks, CA 91320. TEL 805-499-9774, 800-818-7243, FAX 805-499-0871, 800-583-2665, info@sagepub.com. Ed. Bill Vanderburg. Circ: 350 (paid).

543 KOR ISSN 1225-0163
QD71
BUNSEOG GWAHAG/ANALYTICAL SCIENCE AND TECHNOLOGY. Text in Korean. 1988. q. **Document type:** *Journal, Academic/Scholarly.*
Indexed: INIS AtomInd.
—IE, Ingenta.
Published by: Han'gug Bunseog Gwahaghoe/Korean Society of Analytical Science, Kyung Hee University, Department of Chemistry, 17 Haengdang-dong, Sungdong-gu, Seoul, 133-791, Korea, S. TEL 82-2-22204252, FAX 82-2-22204253, koanal@naver.com, http://www.koanal.or.kr/.

500 USA
BUSINESS - SCIENCE - TECHNOLOGY DEVELOPMENTS AND NEWS. Text in English. 1964. m. s-a. index.
Formerly: U S - R and D (0436-2225)
Published by: Government Data Publications, Inc., 2300 M St, NW, Washington, DC 20037. TEL 800-275-4688, FAX 718-998-5960, gdp@govdata.com, http://www.govdata.com.

500 USA
BYTES OF SCIENCE; an Internet magazine. Text in English. 1999. irreg. bk.rev. **Description:** Presents articles as tutorials and introductory pieces on various areas of science.
Media: Online - full text.
Published by: George Mason University, School of Information Technology and Engineering, Department of Electric and Computer Engineering, 4400 University Dr., Fairfax, VA 22030-4444.

C A P S T JOURNAL. (Chinese Association of Professionals in Science and Technology) *see* ETHNIC INTERESTS

500 ZAF
C A S M E NEWSLETTER. Text in English. 1993. q. **Document type:** *Newsletter.*
Published by: Centre for the Advancement of Science and Mathematics Education, PO Box 17112, Congella, 4013, South Africa. http://www.und.ac.za/und/casme/index.html.

507.1 GBR ISSN 0264-3138
C A S T M E JOURNAL. Text in English. 1960. 3/yr. free to members (effective 2009). adv. bk.rev. illus. reprints avail. **Document type:** *Journal, Academic/Scholarly.* **Description:** Original research articles on science, technology and mathematics, and social implications thereof.
Former titles (until 1982): C A S M E Journal (0261-5916); (until 1980): Science Teacher (0036-8547)
Indexed: CPE, Inspec.
—BLDSC (3064.300000), IE.
Published by: Commonwealth Association of Science Technology & Math Educators, c/o Dr Bridget Egan, University of Winchester, Faculty of Education, Winchester, SO22 4NR, United Kingdom. Bridget.Egan@winchester.ac.uk. Ed. Dr. Brudget A Egan. Circ: 10,000.

500 FRA ISSN 1626-0198
C E A ANNUAL REPORT (YEAR). (Commissariat a l'Energie Atomique) (Includes Financial Statements (Year)) Text in English, French. 1998. a. free.
Media: Online - full text.
Published by: Commissariat a l'Energie Atomique, Direction de la Communication, Batiment Le Ponant D, 25 Rue Leblanc, Paris, 75015, France. TEL 33-1-40561000.

C E N D O T E C DOSSIER. (Centro Franco-Brasileiro de Documentacao Tecnica e Cientifica Dossier) *see* TECHNOLOGY: COMPREHENSIVE WORKS

500 600 ARG ISSN 1668-8910
C E T. REVISTA DE CIENCIAS EXACTAS E INGENIERIA. (Ciencias Exactas y Tecnologia) Text in Spanish. 1992. s-a. back issues avail. **Document type:** *Journal, Academic/Scholarly.*
Related titles: Online - full text ed.: ISSN 1668-9178. 1992.
Published by: Universidad Nacional de Tucuman, Facultad de Ciencias Exactas y Tecnologia, Avda. Independencia 1800, San Miguel de Tucuman, Tucuman, Argentina. TEL 54-381-4363004, revista@herrera.unt.edu.ar, http://www.herrera.unt.edu.ar/facet/. Ed. Juan Manuel Yalour.

C I R A S NEWS. (Center for Industrial Research and Service) *see* TECHNOLOGY: COMPREHENSIVE WORKS

500 CAN ISSN 1190-9382
C I S T I OCCASIONAL PAPER. Text in English, French. 1995. irreg., latest 2008. price varies. **Document type:** *Monographic series, Academic/Scholarly.*
Indexed: ASFA, B21, ESPM.
Published by: (Canada Institute for Scientific and Technical Information), National Research Council Canada (N R C)/Conseil National de Recherches Canada (C N R C), NRC Communications & Corporate Relations, 1200 Montreal Rd, Bldg M-58, Ottawa, ON K1A 0R6, Canada. TEL 613-993-9101, FAX 613-952-9907, info@nrc-cnrc.gc.ca, http://www.nrc-cnrc.gc.ca.

500 001.3 300 600 CHN
C N K I WEB. (China National Knowledge Infrastructure) Text in Chinese, English. 1996 (Dec.). base vol. plus d. updates. USD 3,000 per series (effective 2003). adv. Index. back issues avail. **Document type:** *Database, Academic/Scholarly.* **Description:** Provides a comprehensive database with a collection of 6600 academic journals, containing 10 million bibliographies, 4 million Abstracts and 3 million full-text literatures.
Formerly: China Journal Net
Media: Online - full content. **Related titles:** ◆ CD-ROM ed.: Chinese Academic Journals Full-Text Database. Medicine & Hygiene; ◆ Chinese Academic Journals Full-Text Database. Science & Engineering, Series A. ISSN 1007-8010; ◆ Chinese Academic Journals Full-Text Database. Science & Engineering, Series B. ISSN 1007-8029; ◆ Chinese Academic Journals Full-Text Database. Science & Engineering, Series C. ISSN 1007-8037; ◆ Chinese Academic Journals Full-Text Database. Education & Social Sciences; ◆ Chinese Academic Journals Full-Text Database. Literature, History & Philosophy. ISSN 1007-8061; ◆ Chinese Academic Journals Full-Text Database. Economics, Politics & Laws. ISSN 1007-807X; ◆ Chinese Academic Journals Full-Text Database. Electronic Technology & Information Science. ISSN 1008-6293; ◆ Chinese Academic Journals Full-Text Database. Agriculture.
Published by: Tsinghua Tongfang Optical Disc Co., Ltd., Room 1300, Huaye Building, Tsing Hua University, PO BOX 84-48, Beijing, 100084, China. TEL 86-1-62791819, FAX 86-1-62791944, Beijing@cnki.net, http://www.cnki.net. R&P Zhang Li. adv.: page USD 200. **Co-sponsor:** Tsinghua University, School of Law.

500 ITA ISSN 1593-9715
C N R REPORT. (Consiglio Nazionale delle Ricerche) Text in Italian. 1998. a. **Document type:** *Magazine, Consumer.*
Related titles: Online - full text ed.
Published by: Consiglio Nazionale delle Ricerche (C N R)/Italian National Research Council, Piazzale Aldo Moro 7, Rome, 00185, Italy. TEL 39-06-49931, FAX 39-06-4461954.

500 001.3 FRA ISSN 0994-7647
C N R S. JOURNAL. Variant title: Le Journal du C N R S. Text in French. 1988. m. (10/yr). **Document type:** *Magazine, Academic/Scholarly.*
Related titles: Online - full text ed.: free.
—INIST.
Published by: Centre National de la Recherche Scientifique, Campus Gerard-Megie, 3 Rue Michel-Ange, Paris, 75794, France. TEL 33-1-44964000, FAX 33-1-44965390.

C N R S PLUS. (Centre Nationale de la Recherche Scientifique) *see* BIBLIOGRAPHIES

500 FRA ISSN 0538-6918
Q10
C O D A T A NEWSLETTER. (Committee on Data for Science and Technology) Text in English. 1968. q. free. adv. bk.rev. bibl. **Document type:** *Newsletter, Trade.*
Indexed: AESIS.
—INIST, Linda Hall.
Published by: (Committee on Data for Science and Technology (C O D A T A)), International Council for Science/Conseil International pour la Science, 5 Rue Auguste Vacquerie, Paris, 75116, France. Ed. Edgar F Westrum Jr. Circ: 6,500.

▼ **C P S. WORKING PAPERS.** (Centre for Philosophy and Science Studies) *see* PHILOSOPHY

507 NZL ISSN 1177-7923
C R E S T NEWZ. (Creativity in Science and Technology) Text in English. 200?. 3/yr. free. back issues avail. **Document type:** *Newsletter.*
Media: Online - full text.
Published by: Crest NZ, c/o Royal Society of New Zealand, PO Box 598, Wellington, 1640, New Zealand. TEL 64-4-4705789, FAX 64-4-4731841, crest@royalsociety.org.nz.

500 CAN ISSN 1912-192X
C R T I SUMMER SYMPOSIUM. PROCEEDINGS OF THE (YEAR)/ SYMPOSIUM D'ETE DE L'I R T C. PROGRAMME. (Chemical, Biological, Radiological, and Nuclear (C B R N) Research and Technology Initiative) Text in English. 2003. a. **Document type:** *Proceedings, Trade.*
Related titles: Online - full text ed.
Published by: Defence Research and Development Canada/Recherche et Developpement pour la Defense Canada, Knowledge and Information Management, Ottawa, ON K1A 0K2, Canada. TEL 613-995-2971, FAX 613-996-0392, candidinfo@drdc-rddc.gc.ca, http://www.drdc-rddc.gc.ca/home_e.asp.

500 ESP ISSN 1577-1687
C S I C BASES DE DATOS. (Consejo Superior de Investigaciones Cientificas) Text in Spanish. 1994. 4/yr. **Document type:** *Directory, Bibliography.*
Media: Optical Disk - DVD. **Related titles:** Online - full text ed.
Published by: Consejo Superior de Investigaciones Cientificas (C S I C), Joaquin Costa 22, Madrid, 28002, Spain. TEL 34-91-5635482, FAX 34-91-5642644, sdi@cindoc.csic.es, http://www.csic.es.

500 600 ZAF
C S I R ANNUAL REPORT - TECHNOLOGY IMPACT. (Council for Scientific and Industrial Research) Text in English. 1945. a. free. **Document type:** *Corporate.* **Description:** Features the year's scientific and technological research, development and implementation successes, executive overviews and financial financial statements.
Incorporates: C S I R Technology Impact; Incorporates: W N N R Tegnologie Inslag; Formerly: C S I R Annual Report (0370-8454)
—BLDSC (1158.330000), INIST.
Published by: Council for Scientific and Industrial Research (C S I R), PO Box 395, Pretoria, 0001, South Africa. TEL 27-12-8412911, FAX 27-12-3491153, http://www.csir.co.za. Circ: 10,000.

500 GHA
C S I R HANDBOOK. Text in English. 1970. irreg. back issues avail.
Published by: Council for Scientific and Industrial Research, PO Box M32, Accra, Ghana. http://www.csir.org.gh.

C S S E. (Cultural Studies of Science Education) *see* EDUCATION—Teaching Methods And Curriculum

THE C T N S BULLETIN. *see* RELIGIONS AND THEOLOGY

600 ARG ISSN 1668-0030
Q175.52.L37
➤ **C T S. CIENCIA, TECNOLOGIA Y SOCIEDAD.** Text in Spanish, Portuguese; Summaries in English, Spanish. 2003. 4/yr. USD 60 domestic to individuals; EUR 25 foreign to individuals; USD 60 domestic to institutions; EUR 40 foreign to institutions. back issues avail. **Document type:** *Journal, Academic/Scholarly.* **Description:** Adresses the relationships between science, technology and society.
Related titles: Online - full text ed.: C T S. Revista Iberoamericana de Ciencia, Tecnologia y Sociedad. ISSN 1850-0013. 2003. free (effective 2011) (from SciELO).
Indexed: A26, F04, I04, I05, IBSS.
Published by: Centro de Estudios sobre Ciencia, Desarrollo y Educacion Superior, Mansilla 2698 Piso 2, Buenos Aires, Argentina. TEL 54-11-49638778, FAX 54-11-49638811, secretaria@revistacts.net, http://www.centroredes.org.ar. Eds. Mario Albornoz, Miguel Angel Quintanilla. R&P, Adv. contact Claudio Alfaraz. Circ: 600 (paid).

500.9 ARG
CABLE SEMANAL. Text in Spanish. 1996 (no. 1999). w. back issues avail. **Document type:** *Academic/Scholarly.*
Related titles: E-mail ed.; Online - full text ed.
Published by: Universidad de Buenos Aires, Facultad de Ciencias Exactas y Naturales, Cuidad Universitaria, Nunez - Pabellon 2, Buenos Aires, 1428, Argentina. TEL 54-11-4573300, info@fcen.uba.ar, http://fcen.uba.ar/.

500 BRA ISSN 0104-1096
S494.5.I5
CADERNOS DE CIENCIA E TECNOLOGIA. Text in Portuguese, English. 1984. q.
Formerly (until 1991): Cadernos de Difusao de Tecnologia (0102-1869)
Related titles: Online - full text ed.
Indexed: A34, A35, A37, A38, AgBio, Agr, C25, CA, CABA, D01, E12, F08, F12, FCA, G11, H16, I11, N02, N04, P32, P33, P40, PGegResA, PN&I, R07, R11, R12, R13, RA&MP, RM&VM, S02, S03, S13, S16, SociolAb, SoyAb, T02, VS, W11.
Published by: Empresa Brasileira de Pesquisa Agropecuaria, Parque Estacao Biologica - PqEB s-n, Brasilia, 70770-901, Brazil. TEL 55-61-4484433, FAX 55-61-3471041.

509 101 BRA ISSN 0101-3424
Q124.6
CADERNOS DE HISTORIA E FILOSOFIA DA CIENCIA. Text in Portuguese. 1980. irreg.
Indexed: C01, MSN, MathR, PhilInd, Z02.
Published by: Universidade Estadual de Campinas, Centro de Logica Epistemologia e Historia da Ciencia/State University of Campinas, Center for Logic, Epistemology and History of Science, Cidade Universitaria, Caixa Postal 6133, Campinas, SP 13083-970, Brazil. logica@cle.unicamp.br.

500 FRA ISSN 1157-4887
LES CAHIERS DE SCIENCE & VIE. Text in French. 1991. bi-m. EUR 32 (effective 2008). back issues avail. **Document type:** *Magazine, Consumer.* **Description:** Focuses on the history of science.
Published by: Mondadori France, 1 Rue du Colonel Pierre-Avia, Paris, Cedex 15 75754, France. TEL 33-1-46484848, contact@mondadori.fr, http://www.mondadori.fr. Circ: 50,000 (paid).

500 CHE ISSN 1420-4223
LES CAHIERS DE SCIENCES NATURELLES. Text in French. 1996. irreg. **Document type:** *Monographic series, Academic/Scholarly.*
Indexed: BIOSIS Prev, MycolAb, Z01.
Published by: La Murithienne, Societe Valaisanne des Sciences Naturelles, Secretariat, Musee Cantonale d'Histoire Naturelle, Av de la Gare 42, CP 2251, Sion, 1950, Switzerland. TEL 41-27-6064732, FAX 41-27-6064734, lamurithienne@vs.ch, http://www.murithienne.unibe.ch.

S

508 FRA ISSN 0008-0039
QH3 CODEN: CNBNAN
CAHIERS DES NATURALISTES. Text in French. 1946. q. bk.rev. bibl.; charts; illus. index. back issues avail. **Document type:** *Bulletin, Academic/Scholarly.* **Description:** This bulletin covers all sectors of natural sciences.
Indexed: B25, BIOSIS Prev, ChemAb, GeoRef, MycolAb, RefZh, SpeleolAb, Z01.
—INIST.
Published by: Les Naturalistes Parisiens, 45 rue de Buffon, Paris, 75005, France. FAX 33-01-40793699, http://www.chez.com/naturalistes. Ed. Claude Dupuis. Circ: 500.

509 FRA ISSN 0753-6712
CAHIERS D'HISTOIRE ET DE PHILOSOPHIE DES SCIENCES. Text in French. 1977; N.S. 1982. q. **Document type:** *Journal, Academic/Scholarly.*
Indexed: CCMJ, FR, MSN, MathR, Z02.
—INIST.
Published by: (Societe Francaise d'Histoire des Sciences et des Techniques), Centre National de la Recherche Scientifique, Campus Gerard-Megie, 3 Rue Michel-Ange, Paris, 75794, France. TEL 33-1-44964000, FAX 33-1-44965390, cnrseditions@cnrseditions.fr, http://www.cnrs.fr.

500 370.116 NLD ISSN 2211-0798
LES CAHIERS DU RESEAU FRANCO-NEDERLANDAIS/FRANS-NEDERLANDSE NETWERK. CAHIERS. Text in Dutch, French. 2006. a.
Published by: (Reseau Franco-Neerlandais FRA), Frans-Nederlandse Academie, Kromme Nieuwegracht 46, Utrecht, 3512 HJ, Netherlands. TEL 31-30-2537012, secretariaatFNA@uu.nl, http://frnl.nl. Circ: 3,000. **Co-publisher:** Reseau Franco-Neerlandais.

500 FRA ISSN 1243-1923
CAHIERS POUR L'HISTOIRE DE LA RECHERCHE. Variant title: Cahiers pour l'Histoire du C N R S, 1939 - 1989. Text in French. 1988. irreg. price varies. **Document type:** *Monographic series, Academic/Scholarly.*
Formerly (until 1991): Cahiers pour l'Histoire du C N R S (1144-5785)
—INIST.
Published by: Centre National de la Recherche Scientifique, Campus Gerard-Megie, 3 Rue Michel-Ange, Paris, 75794, France. TEL 33-1-44964000, FAX 33-1-44965390, http://www.cnrseditions.fr.

500 FRA ISSN 0008-0462
LES CAHIERS RATIONALISTES. Text in French. 1931. 10/yr. EUR 8 per issue (effective 2010). bk.rev. index. **Document type:** *Bulletin.*
Indexed: RASB, RILM.
Published by: Union Rationaliste, 14 rue de l'Ecole Polytechnique, Paris, 75005, France. TEL 33-1-46330350, http://www.union-rationaliste.org. Ed. Alain Policar.

500 EGY ISSN 2090-1631
CAIRO UNIVERSITY. FACULTY OF SCIENCE. BULLETIN. A: PHYSICAL SCIENCES/NASHRAT KULLIYYAT AL-'ULUM. JAMI'AT AL-QAHIRAT. A: AL-'ULUM AL-TABI'IYYAT. Text in English. 1934. a. **Document type:** *Bulletin, Academic/Scholarly.*
Supersedes in part (in 2006): Cairo University. Faculty of Science. Bulletin (1110-0966)
—INIST.
Published by: (Cairo University, Faculty of Science), Cairo University, Faculty of Science. Library, University Compound, Library of the Faculty of Science, Giza, Egypt. TEL 20-2-567-6638, FAX 20-2-572-8843. Ed. Dr. Nazhmi Abdel-Lattif Kassab.

500 AUS ISSN 1443-4482
CAL-LABORATE. Text in English. 1997. s-a. back issues avail. **Document type:** *Journal, Consumer.* **Description:** Focuses on eLearning, collaborative teaching developments and laboratory teaching.
Related titles: Online - full text ed.: ISSN 1443-4490. 1997. free (effective 2008).
Indexed: AEI, ERO.
Published by: UniServe Science, Carslaw Bldg F07, University of Sydney, Sydney, NSW 2006, Australia. TEL 61-2-93512960, FAX 61-2-93512175, uniserve@mail.usyd.edu.au. Ed. Roger Lewis.

500 COL ISSN 0366-5232
QH7 CODEN: CALDAK
CALDASIA. Text in English, French, Portuguese, Spanish. 1942. 3/yr. COP 35,000 domestic; USD 45 foreign (effective 2010). bibl.; illus. **Document type:** *Journal, Academic/Scholarly.*
Related titles: Online - full text ed.: free (effective 2011).
Indexed: A26, A34, AgrForAb, B25, BIOSIS Prev, C25, C30, CABA, E12, F08, F11, F12, G11, GH, GeoRef, H16, H17, I04, I05, I11, IBR, IBZ, IndVet, MycolAb, O01, P32, P33, P39, P40, PGegResA, R07, R08, R12, R13, RA&MP, S13, S16, SCI, SCOPUS, SpeleolAb, T05, TAR, VITIS, VS, W07, W10, W11, WildRev, Z01.
—INIST.
Published by: Universidad Nacional de Colombia, Instituto de Ciencias, PO Box 7495, Bogota, CUND, Colombia. TEL 57-1-3165305, FAX 57-1-3165365, dicn@ciencias.ciencias.unal.edu.co, http://www.icn.unal.edu.co. Ed. Orlando J Rangel. R&P Jaime Uribe M. Circ: 1,000.

306 USA
LB1585.3
CALIFORNIA JOURNAL OF SCIENCE EDUCATION (ONLINE). Text in English. 1969. s-a. free to members (effective 2011). back issues avail. **Document type:** *Journal, Academic/Scholarly.* **Description:** Focuses on critical issues in science education.
Former titles (until 2008): California Journal of Science Education (Print) (1531-2488); (until 2000): C S T A Journal (1531-6556); (until 199?): California Science Teacher's Journal
Media: Online - full text.
Indexed: CA, E03, ERI, GeoRef, T02.
Published by: California Science Teachers Association, 3800 Watt Ave, Ste 100, Sacramento, CA 95821. TEL 916-979-7004, FAX 916-979-7023, admin@cascience.org.

509 USA
➤ **CALIFORNIA STUDIES IN THE HISTORY OF SCIENCE.** Text in English. 1989. irreg., latest vol.11, 1997. price varies. back issues avail. **Document type:** *Monographic series, Academic/Scholarly.* **Description:** Publishes research on various phases of the history of science.
Published by: University of California Press, Book Series, 2120 Berkeley Way, Berkeley, CA 94704. TEL 510-642-4247, FAX 510-643-7127, foundation@ucpress.edu. **Subscr. to:** California - Princeton Fulfillment Services, Inc., 1445 Lower Ferry Rd, Ewing, NJ 08618. TEL 609-883-1759, 800-777-4726, FAX 800-999-1958, orders@cpfsinc.com.

500 CMR
➤ **CAMEROON ACADEMY OF SCIENCES. JOURNAL.** Text in English, French. 2000. 3/yr. XAF 20,000 domestic; USD 30 in Africa; USD 40 in Europe & Asia; USD 60 in the Americas (effective 2007). back issues avail. **Document type:** *Journal, Academic/Scholarly.* **Description:** Devoted to all aspects of fundamental and applied research. Publishes topical reviews on science and technology in development, arts, humanities and culture.
Related titles: Online - full text ed.
Indexed: O01, PGegResA, PHN&I, S16, Z01.
Published by: Cameroon Academy of Science, Box 63, S W Provice, Cameroon. titanji@aol.com. Ed. Vincent P Titanji.

➤ **CAMINHOS DO COHECIMENTO.** *see* HUMANITIES: COMPREHENSIVE WORKS

500 DEU ISSN 0945-0041
CAMPUS. Text in German. 1977. q. free. adv. **Document type:** *Newspaper.* **Description:** Contains general information on scientific research at Essen University.
Former titles (until 1993): Essener Universitaetsberichte (0935-3658); (until 1987): Hochschuljournal Essen
Published by: Universitaet - Gesamthochschule Essen, Universitaetsstr 2, Essen, 45141, Germany. TEL 49-201-18320, FAX 49-201-1833008. Circ: 8,400.

500 026 CAN ISSN 0714-3648
Q224.3.C2
CANADA INSTITUTE FOR SCIENTIFIC AND TECHNICAL INFORMATION. ANNUAL REPORT/INSTITUT CANADIEN DE L'INFORMATION SCIENTIFIQUE ET TECHNIQUE. RAPPORT ANNUEL. Text in English. a. free. **Document type:** *Corporate.*
Former titles: Canada Institute for Scientific and Technical Information. Report (0703-0320); National Science Library of Canada. Annual Report (0077-5576)
Related titles: Online - full text ed.
Indexed: ASFA, B21, ESPM.
—Linda Hall. **CCC.**
Published by: (Canada Institute for Scientific and Technical Information), National Research Council Canada (N R C)/Conseil National de Recherches Canada (C N R C), NRC Communications & Corporate Relations, 1200 Montreal Rd, Bldg M-58, Ottawa, ON K1A 0R6, Canada. TEL 613-993-9101, FAX 613-952-9907, info@nrc-cnrc.gc.ca, http://www.nrc-cnrc.gc.ca. Circ: 4,000.

500.9 CAN ISSN 0008-3550
QH1 CODEN: CAFNAK
➤ **THE CANADIAN FIELD-NATURALIST.** Text in English, French. 1879. q. CAD 40 to individuals; CAD 50 to institutions (effective 2011). bk.rev. bibl.; charts; illus.; maps. cum.index: vol.index in issue 4 of each vol. back issues avail. **Document type:** *Journal, Academic/Scholarly.*
Former titles (until 1919): Ottawa Naturalist (0316-4411); (until 1887): Ottawa Field-Naturalists' Club. Transactions (0316-442X)
Indexed: A20, A22, A34, A35, A36, A38, ASCA, ASFA, AgBio, AgrForAb, AnBeAb, B21, B23, B25, BIOBASE, BIOSIS Prev, C25, C30, CA, CABA, CRFR, CurCont, E04, E05, E12, E17, ESPM, EnvAb, EnvInd, F08, F11, F12, G11, GEOBASE, GH, GardL, GeoRef, H16, H17, I11, IABS, ISR, IndVet, KWIWR, LT, MycolAb, N04, O01, OceAb, P32, P33, P37, P40, PGegResA, PGrRegA, PN&I, PlantSci, R07, R08, RefZh, S13, S16, S17, SCI, SCOPUS, SSciA, SWRA, SpeleolAb, T02, VS, W07, W08, W10, W11, WildRev, Z01.
—BLDSC (3023.000000), IE, Infotrieve, Ingenta, INIST, Linda Hall. **CCC.**
Published by: Ottawa Field-Naturalists' Club, Westgate, P O Box 35069, Ottawa, ON K1Z 1A2, Canada. TEL 613-722-3050, subscriptions@canadianfieldnaturalist.ca. Ed. Carolyn Callaghan. Circ: 2,000.

500 CAN ISSN 1925-7430
▼ ➤ **CANADIAN JOURNAL OF APPLIED SCIENCES.** Text in English. 2011. q. free. **Document type:** *Journal, Academic/Scholarly.* **Description:** Publishes as original research papers, reviewed articles, case reports, peer reviews, and short communications on the analytical characterization, discovery, methodologies and production of scientific moiety and their utilization with respective therapeutic outcomes.
Media: Online - full text.
Published by: Intellectual Consortium of Drug Discovery & Technology Development Incorporation, 34-115 V N., Saskatoon, SK S7L3E4, Canada. TEL 306-261-9809, http://icdtd.wordpress.com/. Ed. M. Shoaib Akhtar. R&P Taha Nazir.

500 CAN ISSN 1715-9997
Q1
➤ **CANADIAN JOURNAL OF PURE AND APPLIED SCIENCES.** Text in English. 2007. s-a. **Document type:** *Journal, Academic/Scholarly.* **Description:** Aims at promoting research worldwide in Agricultural Sciences, Biological Sciences, Chemical Sciences, Computer and Mathematical Sciences, Engineering, Environmental Sciences, Medicine and Physics.
Related titles: Online - full text ed.: ISSN 1920-3853. free (effective 2011).
Indexed: A34, A35, A37, AgBio, AgrForAb, BA, BP, C25, C30, CABA, D01, E12, F08, F11, F12, FCA, G11, GH, H16, H17, I11, IndVet, LT, MaizeAb, N02, N03, N04, OR, P32, P33, P37, P39, P40, PGegResA, PGrRegA, PHN&I, R07, R08, R13, RA&MP, RM&VM, S12, S13, S16, S17, SoyAb, T05, TriticAb, VS, W10.
Published by: S E N R A Academic Publishers, 7845 15th St., Burnaby, BC V3N 3A3, Canada. TEL 778-389-9141.

500 510 600 USA ISSN 1492-6156
Q181.A1
➤ **CANADIAN JOURNAL OF SCIENCE, MATHEMATICS AND TECHNOLOGY EDUCATION/REVUE CANADIENNE DE L'ENSEIGNEMENT DES SCIENCES, DES MATHEMATIQUES ET DES TECHNOLOGIES.** Text in English, French. 2000. q. GBP 185 combined subscription in United Kingdom to institutions (print & online eds.); EUR 241, USD 307 combined subscription to institutions (print & online eds.) (effective 2012). adv. back issues avail.; reprint service avail. from PSC. **Document type:** *Journal, Academic/Scholarly.* **Description:** Provides an international forum for the publication of original articles written in a variety of styles, including research investigations using experimental, qualitative, ethnographic, historical, philosophical or case study approaches.
Related titles: Online - full text ed.: ISSN 1942-4051. GBP 166 in United Kingdom to institutions; EUR 217, USD 276 to institutions (effective 2012).
Indexed: A01, A02, A03, A08, C03, CA, CEI, E03, ERI, P11, P48, P49, P52, P56, PQC, S01, T02.
—BLDSC (3035.560000), IE, Ingenta. **CCC.**
Published by: Routledge (Subsidiary of: Taylor & Francis Group), 325 Chestnut St, Ste 800, Philadelphia, PA 19106. TEL 800-354-1420, FAX 215-625-2940, journals@routledge.com, http://www.routledge.com.

500.9 CAN ISSN 0317-6401
CODEN: CPLPDS
CANADIAN PLAINS PROCEEDINGS. Text in English. 197?. irreg., latest vol.29, 1997. price varies. **Document type:** *Monographic series, Academic/Scholarly.*
Indexed: Agr, GeoRef, SpeleolAb.
—BLDSC (3043.870000), CASDDS.
Published by: Canadian Plains Research Center, University of Regina, 3737 Wascana Pky, Regina, SK S4S 0A2, Canada. TEL 306-585-5056, FAX 306-585-4699.

500.9 920 CAN ISSN 1205-3341
CANADIAN PLAINS REFERENCE WORKS. Text in English. 1988. irreg. price varies. **Document type:** *Monographic series, Academic/Scholarly.*
Formerly: Canadian Plains Biographies (1192-8999)
Published by: Canadian Plains Research Center, University of Regina, 3737 Wascana Pky, Regina, SK S4S 0A2, Canada. TEL 306-585-5056, FAX 306-585-4699.

500.9 CAN ISSN 0384-8930
CANADIAN PLAINS REPORTS. Text in English. 1977. irreg., latest vol.10, 1996. price varies. **Document type:** *Monographic series, Academic/Scholarly.*
Published by: Canadian Plains Research Center, University of Regina, 3737 Wascana Pky, Regina, SK S4S 0A2, Canada. TEL 306-585-5056, FAX 306-585-4699.

500.9 CAN ISSN 0317-6290
CANADIAN PLAINS STUDIES. Text in English. 1973. irreg., latest vol.34, 1996. price varies. **Document type:** *Monographic series, Academic/Scholarly.*
Published by: Canadian Plains Research Center, University of Regina, 3737 Wascana Pky, Regina, SK S4S 0A2, Canada. TEL 306-585-5056, FAX 306-585-4699.

507 CAN ISSN 1913-1925
➤ **CANADIAN YOUNG SCIENTIST JOURNAL**; a forum for the next generation of Canadian thinkers. Text in English. 2008. 3/yr. CAD 112 to individuals; CAD 365 to institutions (effective 2008). adv. bibl.; charts; illus. back issues avail. **Document type:** *Journal, Academic/Scholarly.* **Description:** Seeks to spark new interest in scientific research and science careers amoung young people.
Indexed: E03.
Address: 5863 Leslie St, 126, Toronto, ON M2H 1J8, Canada. TEL 416-727-5106, FAX 416-395-3294. Ed., Pub., R&P, Adv. contact Alexandre Noukhovitch. B&W page CAD 600, color page CAD 1,300. Circ: 2,000 (paid and controlled).

➤ **CANGZHOU SHIFAN ZHUANKE XUEXIAO XUEBAO/CANGZHOU TEACHERS' COLLEGE. JOURNAL.** *see* SOCIAL SCIENCES: COMPREHENSIVE WORKS

500 USA
AS32 CODEN: CIWYAO
CARNEGIE INSTITUTION. YEARBOOK. Text in English. 1902. a. free (effective 2010). bibl.; illus. back issues avail. **Document type:** *Yearbook, Trade.* **Description:** Features scientific research by the institution's astronomers, earth scientists, and biologists.
Formerly (until 199?): Director of the Geophysical Laboratory. Annual Report (0576-792X); Which superseded in part (in 1907): Carnegie Institution of Washington. Year Book (0069-066X)
Related titles: Online - full text ed.
Indexed: AESIS, ChemAb, GeoRef, Inspec, MLA-IB, MinerAb, P30, SpeleolAb.
—INIST, Linda Hall.
Published by: Carnegie Institution of Washington, 1530 P St, NW, Washington, DC 20005. TEL 202-387-6400, FAX 202-387-8092, http://www.carnegieinstitution.org. Ed. Tina McDowell TEL 202-939-1120.

508 USA ISSN 0097-4463
AS36 CODEN: CIMUAU
➤ **CARNEGIE MUSEUM OF NATURAL HISTORY. ANNALS.** Key Title: Annals of Carnegie Museum. Text in English. 1901. q. USD 90 domestic to institutions; USD 125 foreign to institutions (effective 2010). charts; illus. index. back issues avail. **Document type:** *Journal, Academic/Scholarly.* **Description:** Contributions in organismal biology, earth sciences and anthropology.
Related titles: Online - full text ed.: ISSN 1943-6300.
Indexed: A22, A34, ASCA, B21, B23, B25, BIOSIS Prev, CABA, CurCont, E12, EntAb, F08, F12, GEOBASE, GH, GeoRef, IBR, IBZ, ISR, MycolAb, OR, P32, P33, PGegResA, R07, R08, RefZh, S13, S16, SCI, SCOPUS, SpeleolAb, VS, W07, WildRev, Z01.
—BLDSC (1022.000000), IE, Ingenta, INIST, Linda Hall. **CCC.**
Published by: Carnegie Museum of Natural History, Office of Scientific Publications, 4400 Forbes Ave, Pittsburgh, PA 15213. TEL 412-622-3287, FAX 412-665-2751, scipubs@clpgh.org, http://www.clpgh.org/cmnh/scipub.

508 USA ISSN 0145-9058
CODEN: BCMHD9
CARNEGIE MUSEUM OF NATURAL HISTORY. BULLETIN. Text in English. 1976. irreg., latest vol.40, 2009. price varies. bibl.; charts; illus. index. back issues avail. **Document type:** *Bulletin, Academic/Scholarly.* **Description:** Contains monographs in organismal biology, earth sciences and anthropology.
Indexed: B21, EntAb, GeoRef, SpeleolAb, WildRev, Z01.
—Linda Hall. **CCC.**
Published by: Carnegie Museum of Natural History, Office of Scientific Publications, 4400 Forbes Ave, Pittsburgh, PA 15213. TEL 412-622-3287, FAX 412-665-2751, scipubs@clpgh.org, http://www.clpgh.org/cmnh/scipub.

500.9 USA ISSN 0145-9031
CODEN: SPCHDX
CARNEGIE MUSEUM OF NATURAL HISTORY. SPECIAL PUBLICATIONS. Text in English. 1975. irreg., latest vol.21, 2002. price varies. back issues avail. **Document type:** *Monographic series, Academic/Scholarly.* **Description:** Contains variety of monographs in natural history.
Indexed: B25, BIOSIS Prev, GeoRef, MycolAb, SpeleolAb, Z01.
—BLDSC (8373.850000).
Published by: Carnegie Museum of Natural History, Office of Scientific Publications, 4400 Forbes Ave, Pittsburgh, PA 15213. TEL 412-622-3287, FAX 412-665-2751, scipubs@clpgh.org, http://www.clpgh.org/cmnh/scipub.

500 USA
CARNEGIESCIENCE. Text in English. 19??. 3/yr. free to members (effective 2010). 20 p./no.; back issues avail. **Document type:** *Newsletter, Trade.* **Description:** Features current activities of the institution's astronomers, biologists, and earth scientists.
Former titles (until 2005): Spectra; (until 19??): C I W Newsletter
Related titles: Online - full content ed.: free (effective 2010).
Published by: Carnegie Institution of Washington, 1530 P St, NW, Washington, DC 20005. TEL 202-387-6400, FAX 202-387-8092. Ed. Tina McDowell TEL 202-939-1120.

CATALOGO DE TESES E DISSERTACOES. *see* EDUCATION—Higher Education

500 300 NIC
CATEDRA; revista de ciencia, cultura y educacion. Text in Spanish. 1991. q. **Document type:** *Academic/Scholarly.*
Published by: Universidad Nacional Autonoma de Nicaragua, Facultad de Ciencias de la Educacion, Recinto Universitario Ruben Dario, Managua, Nicaragua.

CELLULAR AND MOLECULAR LIFE SCIENCES. *see* BIOLOGY

509 USA ISSN 0008-8994
Q1 CODEN: CENTA4
➤ **CENTAURUS;** an international journal of the history of science and its cultural aspects. Text in English, French, German. 1957. q. GBP 391 in United Kingdom to institutions; EUR 496 in Europe to institutions; USD 659 in the Americas to institutions; USD 765 elsewhere to institutions; GBP 450 combined subscription in United Kingdom to institutions (print & online eds.); EUR 571 combined subscription in Europe to institutions (print & online eds.); USD 758 combined subscription in the Americas to institutions (print & online eds.); USD 880 combined subscription elsewhere to institutions (print & online eds.) (effective 2012). adv. bk.rev. bibl.; illus. cum.index: vols.1-30, 1950-1984 in vol.32. back issues avail.; reprint service avail. from PSC. **Document type:** *Journal, Academic/Scholarly.*
Related titles: Online - full text ed.: ISSN 1600-0498. GBP 391 in United Kingdom to institutions; EUR 496 in Europe to institutions; USD 659 in the Americas to institutions; USD 765 elsewhere to institutions (effective 2012) (from IngentaConnect).
Indexed: A01, A03, A08, A20, A22, A26, ASCA, AmH&L, AmHI, CA, CCMJ, CIS, ChemAb, DIP, E01, EMBASE, ExcerpMed, FR, GeoRef, H07, HistAb, I14, IBR, IBZ, IndMed, MEA&I, MEDLINE, MLA-IB, MSN, MathR, P30, PCI, RASB, RILM, S01, SCOPUS, SpeleolAb, T02, Z02.
—BLDSC (3104.000000), IE, Infotrieve, Ingenta, INIST, Linda Hall. **CCC.**
Published by: Wiley-Blackwell Publishing, Inc. (Subsidiary of: Wiley-Blackwell Publishing Ltd.), Commerce Pl, 350 Main St, Malden, MA 02148. TEL 781-388-8200, FAX 781-388-8210, info@wiley.com, http://www.wiley.com/WileyCDA/. Ed. Ida Stamhuis.

➤ **CENTRALE VIDENSKABSETISKE KOMITE. AARSBERETNING/ CENTRAL SCIENTIFIC - ETHICAL COMMITTEE OF DENMARK. REPORT.** *see* PHILOSOPHY

500 FRA ISSN 1627-3516
CENTRE DE COSERVATION ET D'ETUDE DES COLLECTIONS. CAHIERS SCIENTIFIQUES. Text in French; Abstracts in English. 2000. s-a. **Document type:** *Journal, Academic/Scholarly.*
Indexed: FR, GeoRef, Z01.
—INIST.
Published by: Museum d'Histoire Naturelle de Lyon, 28 Bd des Belges, Lyon, 69006, France. TEL 33-4-72690500, FAX 33-4-78946225, museum@rhone.fr.

508 ESP ISSN 0213-3598
CODEN: BENNED
CENTRE D'ESTUDIS DE LA NATURA DEL BARCELONES-NORD. BUTLLETI. Text in Catalan. 1985. s-a. EUR 25 Sat.; EUR 40. back issues avail. **Document type:** *Bulletin, Academic/Scholarly.*
Indexed: GeoRef, Z01.
Published by: Centre d'Estudis de la Natura del Barcelones-Nord, Apartat de Correus, 3, Santa Coloma de Gramenet, Barcelona, 08921, Spain.

500 FRA ISSN 0366-7634
CODEN: COINAV
CENTRE NATIONAL DE LA RECHERCHE SCIENTIFIQUE. COLLOQUES INTERNATIONAUX. Text in French. 1949. irreg., latest 2002. price varies.
Indexed: GeoRef, P30.
—CCC.
Published by: Centre National de la Recherche Scientifique, Campus Gerard-Megie, 3 Rue Michel-Ange, Paris, 75794, France. TEL 33-1-44964000, FAX 33-1-44965390, cnrseditions@cnrseditions.fr, http://www.cnrseditions.fr.

500 FRA ISSN 1777-9251
CENTRE NATIONAL DE LA RECHERCHE SCIENTIFIQUE. CRISTAL. Key Title: Cristal du C N R S. Text in French. 1981. a. **Description:** Reports on the winners of innovative and original scientific accomplishments.
Supersedes in part (in 2005): Les Medailles du C N R S (1632-0948)
Published by: Centre National de la Recherche Scientifique, Campus Gerard-Megie, 3 Rue Michel-Ange, Paris, 75794, France. TEL 33-1-44964000, FAX 33-1-44965390, http://www.cnrs.fr.

500 FRA ISSN 1777-0378
CENTRE NATIONAL DE LA RECHERCHE SCIENTIFIQUE. LES MEDAILLES D'OR. Key Title: Les Medailles d'Or. Text in French. 1981. a. free.
Supersedes in part (in 2004): Les Medailles du C N R S (1632-0948)
Published by: Centre National de la Recherche Scientifique, Campus Gerard-Megie, 3 Rue Michel-Ange, Paris, 75794, France. TEL 33-1-44964000, FAX 33-1-44965390.

500 CUB ISSN 1562-3297
CENTRO DE INFORMACION Y GESTION TECNOLOGICA. AVANCES. Text in Spanish. 1999. q. back issues avail. **Document type:** *Journal, Academic/Scholarly.*
Indexed: CA, F04, T02.
Published by: Ministerio de Ciencia, Tecnologia y Medio Ambiente, Centro de Informacion y Gestion Tecnologica, Colon No 106 Esq Maceo y Virtudes, Pinar del Rio, 20100, Cuba. TEL 53-82-752232, FAX 53-82-752294, cicitma@vega.inf.cu, http://www.citma.pinar.cu/. Ed. Juan Jose Blanco Barreda.

CENTRO JOURNAL. *see* HUMANITIES: COMPREHENSIVE WORKS

500 ITA ISSN 0394-0705
CODEN: CCLADS
CENTRO LINCEO INTERDISCIPLINARE BENIAMINO SEGRE. CONTRIBUTI. Text in Italian. 1974. irreg. **Document type:** *Monographic series, Academic/Scholarly.*
Formerly (until 1987): Centro Linceo Interdisciplinare di Scienze Matematiche e Loro Applicazioni. Contributi (0391-8041)
Indexed: Z01.
—CASDDS.
Published by: (Accademia Nazionale dei Lincei, Centro Linceo Interdisciplinare Beniamino Segre), Bardi Editore, Via Piave 7, Rome, 00187, Italy. TEL 39-06-4817656, FAX 39-06-48912574, info@bardieditore.com, http://www.bardieditore.com.

CENTRO UNIVERSITARIO DE ESTUDIOS GENERALES. REVISTA. *see* SOCIAL SCIENCES: COMPREHENSIVE WORKS

CENTRULUI PENTRU DIALOG INTRE STIINTE SI TEOLOGIE. BULETINUL/CENTER FOR DIALOGUE BETWEEN SCIENCES AND THEOLOGY. BULLETIN. *see* RELIGIONS AND THEOLOGY

630 CHN ISSN 1671-7449
CESHI JISHU XUEBAO/JOURNAL OF TEST AND MEASUREMENT TECHNOLOGY. Text in Chinese. 1986. bi-m. USD 31.20 (effective 2009). back issues avail. **Document type:** *Journal, Academic/Scholarly.*
Formerly (until 2002): Huabei Gongxueyuan. Ceshi Jishu Xuebao (1008-6374)
Related titles: Online - full text ed.
Indexed: RefZh, SCOPUS.
—BLDSC (5069.037000), IE, Ingenta.
Published by: Zhongbei Daxue Chubanbu/Press of North University of China, Xueyuan Lu, Taiyuan, 030051, China. TEL 86-351-3925798, FAX 86-351-3922085, http://xuebao.nuc.edu.cn/. **Dist. by:** China International Book Trading Corp, 35 Chegongzhuang Xilu, Haidian District, PO Box 399, Beijing 100044, China. TEL 86-10-68412045, FAX 86-10-68412023, cibtc@mail.cibtc.com.cn, http://www.cibtc.com.cn.

500 600 LKA
CEYLON INSTITUTE OF SCIENTIFIC & INDUSTRIAL RESEARCH. ANNUAL REPORT. Text in English. 1956. a. USD 25. **Document type:** *Corporate.*
Published by: Ceylon Institute of Scientific & Industrial Research, 363 Bauddhaloka Mawatha, P O Box 787, Colombo, 7, Sri Lanka. Ed. Nirmala M Pieris. R&P P M Jayatissa. Circ: 300.

500 600 LKA
CEYLON INSTITUTE OF SCIENTIFIC & INDUSTRIAL RESEARCH. NEWS BULLETIN. Text in English. 1992. q. **Document type:** *Newsletter.*
Published by: Ceylon Institute of Scientific & Industrial Research, 363 Bauddhaloka Mawatha, P O Box 787, Colombo, 7, Sri Lanka. Ed. Dilmani Warnasuriye. R&P P M Jayatissa. Circ: 500.

500 LKA ISSN 1391-1465
CEYLON JOURNAL OF SCIENCE. PHYSICAL SCIENCES. Text in English. a. LKR 150, USD 16 (effective 2000 - 2001). **Document type:** *Journal, Academic/Scholarly.* **Description:** Interdisciplinary journal in physical sciences devoted to papers on original scientific research of high quality in chemistry, computer science, geology, mathematics, meteorology, physics, statistics, science education and related disciplines.
Published by: University of Peradeniya, P.O. Box 35, Peradeniya, Sri Lanka. librarian@pdn.ac.lk, http://www.pdn.ac.lk. Ed. M A K L Dissanayake.

500 USA
CHAIN REACTION; stories of science and learning from Arizona state university. Text in English. 1998. s-a. free (effective 2007). illus. back issues avail. **Document type:** *Magazine, Consumer.* **Description:** Stories of science and learning on specific themes targeted at middle school students and their teachers.
Related titles: Online - full text ed.; ◆ Supplement to: Kievskie Vedomosti.
Published by: Arizona State University, A S U Research Publications, Admin. Bldg. Rm 165, PO Box 873803, Tempe, AZ 85287-3803. TEL 480-965-1266, FAX 480-965-9684, cstorad@asu.edu. Ed. Conrad J Storad. Circ: 150,000 (controlled).

500 CHE ISSN 2078-1547
▼ ➤ **CHALLENGES.** Text in English. 2010. q. free (effective 2011). **Document type:** *Journal, Academic/Scholarly.* **Description:** Provides an advanced forum for presenting research proposals and discussing open problems.
Media: Online - full text.
Published by: M D P I AG, Postfach, Basel, 4005, Switzerland. TEL 41-61-6837734, FAX 41-61-3028918, http://www.mdpi.org/. Ed. Andreas Manz TEL 49-681-9382210.

500 CHN ISSN 1009-8984
CHANGCHUN GONGCHENG XUEYUAN XUEBAO (ZIRAN KEXUE BAN)/CHANGCHUN INSTITUTE OF TECHNOLOGY. JOURNAL (NATURAL SCIENCE EDITION). Text in Chinese. 2000. q. **Document type:** *Journal, Academic/Scholarly.*
Formed by the merger of (1991-2000): Changchun Jianzhu Gaodeng Zhuanke Xuexiao Xuebao/Changchun Architectural College. Journal (1008-7478); (1999-2000): Changchun Shuili Dianli Gaodeng Zhuanke Xuexiao Xuebao/Changchun Institute of Hydraulic and Electric Engineering. Journal (1009-198X)
Published by: Changchun Gongcheng Xueyuan, 395, Shangping Da Lu, Changchun, 130012, China. FAX 86-431-85711240, 86-431-85940805.

500 CHN ISSN 1672-9870
CHANGCHUN LIGONG DAXUE XUEBAO (ZIRAN KEXUE BAN)/ CHANGCHUN UNIVERSITY OF SCIENCE AND TECHNOLOGY. JOURNAL (NATURAL SCIENCE EDITION). Text in Chinese. 1978. q. CNY 60; CNY 15 newsstand/cover (effective 2010). **Document type:** *Journal, Academic/Scholarly.*
Formerly (until 2002): Changchun Guangxue Jingmi Jixie Xueyuan Xuebao/Changchun Institute of Optics and Fine Mechanics. Journal (1004-485X)
Related titles: Online - full text ed.
Published by: Changchun Ligong Daxue, 7186, Weixing Lu, Changchun, 130022, China. TEL 86-431-85582724.

500 CHN ISSN 1673-1409
CHANGJIANG DAXUE XUEBAO (ZIRAN KEXUE BAN)/YANGTZE UNIVERSITY. JOURNAL (NATURAL SCIENCE EDITION). Text in Chinese. 2004. q. **Document type:** *Journal, Academic/Scholarly.*
Related titles: Online - full text ed.; ◆ Special ed(s).: Changjiang Daxue Xuebao (Ziran Kexue Ban, Yixue Juan); ◆ Changjiang Daxue Xuebao (Ziran Kexue Ban, Ligong Juan); ◆ Changjiang Daxue Xuebao (Ziran Kexue Ban, Nongxue Juan).
Published by: Changjiang Daxue/Yangtze University, 1, Nanhuan Lu, Jingzhou, 434023, China. http://qks.yangtzeu.edu.cn/main/.

CHANGSHA DAXUE XUEBAO/CHANGSHA UNIVERSITY. JOURNAL. *see* SOCIAL SCIENCES: COMPREHENSIVE WORKS

500 CHN ISSN 1672-9331
CHANGSHA LIGONG DAXUE XUEBAO (ZIRAN KEXUE BAN)/ CHANGSHA UNIVERSITY OF SCIENCE AND TECHNOLOGY. JOURNAL (NATURAL SCIENCE). Text in Chinese. 1988. q. **Document type:** *Journal, Academic/Scholarly.*
Related titles: Online - full text ed.
Indexed: RefZh, Z02.
Published by: Changsha Ligong Daxue/Changsha University of Science and Technology, 45, Chiling Lu, Tushuguan B, 3/F, Changsha, 410076, China. TEL 86-731-85258192.

CHANGZHI XUEYUAN XUEBAO/CHANGZHI UNIVERSITY. JOURNAL. *see* SOCIAL SCIENCES: COMPREHENSIVE WORKS

300 CHN ISSN 1671-0436
CHANGZHOU GONGXUEYUAN XUEBAO/CHANGZHOU INSTITUTE OF TECHNOLOGY. JOURNAL. Text in Chinese. 1987. bi-m. **Document type:** *Journal, Academic/Scholarly.*
Formerly (until 2000): Changzhou Gongye Jishu Xueyuan Xuebao
Related titles: Online - full text ed.
Published by: Changzhou Gongxueyuan/Changzhou Institute of Technology, 299, Tongjiang Nan Lu, Changzhou, 213002, China. TEL 86-519-85217535, FAX 86-519-85217535.

CHANYE YU KEJI LUNTAN/INDUSTRIAL AND SCIENCE TRIBUNE. *see* BUSINESS AND ECONOMICS

001.9 CAN ISSN 0706-5337
CHAOS. Text in English. 1978. 8/yr. CAD 16.
Indexed: CMCI.
—Infotrieve.
Published by: Res Bureaux, P O Box 1598, Kingston, ON K7L 5C8, Canada. TEL 613-542-7277.

500 001.3 RUS ISSN 1994-2796
➤ **CHELYABINSKII GOSUDARSTVENNYI UNIVERSITET. VESTNIK.** Text in Russian. 1991. q. RUR 1,247 for 6 mos. domestic (effective 2010). **Document type:** *Journal, Academic/Scholarly.* **Description:** Presents scientific research results in the following areas: philosophy, sociology and cultural studies, philology and art history, history, economics, law and physics.
Related titles: Online - full text ed.
Indexed: RefZh, Z02.
Published by: Chelyabinskii Gosudarstvennyi Universitet, ul Brat'yev Kashirinyh 129, Chelyabinsk, 454021, Russian Federation. TEL 7-351-7997134, sahan@csu.ru, http://www.csu.ru. Ed. A Yu Shatin. Circ: 1,000.

500 RUS ISSN 1727-7434
CHELYABINSKII NAUCHNYI TSENTR. IZVESTIYA/CHELYABINSK SCIENTIFIC CENTER. PROCEEDINGS. Text in English, Russian. 1997. q. free (effective 2003). **Description:** Publishes research results in the fields of mathematics, computer science, natural science, and environmental issues.
Media: Online - full content.
Indexed: CCMJ, MSN, MathR, Z01.
Published by: Rossiiskaya Akademiya Nauk, Ural'skoe Otdelenie, Chelyabinskii Nauchnyi Tsentr/Russian Academy of Sciences, Ural Branch, Chelyabinsk Scientific Center, 68 Kommuny Str, Chelyabinsk, 454000, Russian Federation. TEL 7-351-2336920, FAX 7-351-2335672. Ed. German P Vyatkin.

500 NLD ISSN 1872-1400
CHEMICAL, PHYSICAL AND BIOLOGICAL ASPECTS OF CONFINED SYSTEMS. Text in English. 2006. irreg., latest vol.1, 2006. price varies. **Document type:** *Monographic series, Academic/Scholarly.*
Published by: Elsevier BV (Subsidiary of: Elsevier Science & Technology), Radarweg 29, PO Box 211, Amsterdam, 1000 AE, Netherlands. TEL 31-20-4853911, FAX 31-20-4852457, JournalsCustomerServiceEMEA@elsevier.com, http://www.elsevier.com. Ed. Abderrazzak Douhal.

S

500 CHN ISSN 1004-5422
CHENGDU DAXUE XUEBAO (ZIRAN KEXUE BAN)/CHENGDU UNIVERSITY. JOURNAL (NATURAL SCIENCE EDITION). Text in Chinese. 1982. q. CNY 8 newsstand/cover (effective 2006). **Document type:** *Journal, Academic/Scholarly.* **Description:** Publishes scientific research results and technology news in the natural sciences, including food processing and industrial management.
Related titles: Online - full text ed.
Indexed: MSN.
Published by: Chengdu Daxue/Chengdu University, Waidongshiling Zhen, Chengdu, 610106, China. TEL 86-28-84616197.

500 MNG ISSN 1673-260X
CHIFENG XUEYUAN XUEBAO (ZIRAN KEXUE BAN)/CHIFENG UNIVERSITY. JOURNAL (NATURAL SCIENCE). Text in Chinese. m. **Document type:** *Journal, Academic/Scholarly.*
Formerly (until 2004): Chifeng Jiaoyu Xueyuan Xuebao/Chifeng Education College. Journal (1008-9152)
Related titles: Online - full text ed.
Published by: Chifeng Xueyuan, 1, Jichang Lu, Hongshan-qu, Chifeng, 024000, Mongolia. TEL 86-476-2205717, http://www.cfxy.cn/.

500 IRN ISSN 1022-7806
DS318.72
CHIKIDAH-I TAZAHHA-YI TAHQIQ DAR DANISHGAHHA VA MARAKIZ-I TAHQIQATI IRAN/CURRENT RESEARCH IN IRANIAN UNIVERSITIES AND RESEARCH CENTERS. Text in Persian, Modern. 1993. q. USD 75 (effective 2003). 550 p./no.; back issues avail. **Document type:** *Academic/Scholarly.* **Description:** Reports on the research projects carried out in Iran.
Published by: Iranian Information & Documentation Center (IRANDOC), 1188 Enqelab Ave., P O Box 13185-1371, Tehran, Iran. TEL 98-21-6494955, FAX 98-21-6462254, journal@irandoc.ac.ir, http://www.irandoc.ac.ir. Ed. Hussein Gharibi.

500 CHN
CHINA ASSOCIATION FOR SCIENCE AND TECHNOLOGY. PROCEEDINGS. Text in English. irreg. **Document type:** *Proceedings, Academic/Scholarly.*
Published by: (China Association for Science and Technology), Kexue Chubanshe/Science Press, 16 Donghuang Cheng Genbei Jie, Beijing, 100717, China. TEL 86-10-64000246, FAX 86-10-64030255, http://www.sciencep.com/.

500 CHN ISSN 1007-8010
CHINESE ACADEMIC JOURNALS FULL-TEXT DATABASE. SCIENCE & ENGINEERING, SERIES A. Text in Chinese, English. base vol. plus m. updates. USD 4,160 to institutions (effective 2003). **Document type:** *Database, Academic/Scholarly.* **Description:** Contains several science & engineering journals published in China, covering mathematics, mechanics, physics, astronomy, biology, climatology, geography, geology, & oceanography.
Media: CD-ROM. **Related titles:** ◆ Online - full content ed.: C N K I Web; Online - full text ed.; ◆ Print ed.: Dongwuxue Yanjiu. ISSN 0254-5853; ◆ Bopuxue Zazhi. ISSN 1000-4556; ◆ Redai Qixiang Xuebao. ISSN 1004-4965; ◆ Guangxi Zhiwu. ISSN 1000-3142; ◆ Gaoxiao Dizhi Xuebao. ISSN 1006-7493; ◆ Cehui Kexue. ISSN 1009-2307; ◆ Dizhi Zaihai yu Huanjing Baohu. ISSN 1006-4362; ◆ Dadi Celiang yu Diqiu Donglixue. ISSN 1671-5942; ◆ Yanshi Lixue yu Gongcheng Xuebao. ISSN 1000-6915; ◆ Nanjing Shehui Kexue. ISSN 1001-8263; ◆ Haiyang Tongbao. ISSN 1001-6392; ◆ Guangxue Xuebao. ISSN 0253-2239; ◆ Advances in Atmospheric Sciences. ISSN 0256-1530.
Published by: Tsinghua Tongfang Optical Disc Co., Ltd., Room 1300, Huaye Building, Tsing Hua University, PO BOX 84-48, Beijing, 100084, China. TEL 86-1-62791819, FAX 86-1-62791944, Beijing@cnki.net, http://www.cnki.net. **Co-sponsor:** Tsinghua University, School of Law.

500 CHN ISSN 1007-8029
CHINESE ACADEMIC JOURNALS FULL-TEXT DATABASE. SCIENCE & ENGINEERING, SERIES B. Text in Chinese, English. 1994. m. USD 4,160 to institutions (effective 2003). **Document type:** *Database, Academic/Scholarly.* **Description:** Includes 782,688 full-text articles from 667 academic journals, covering topics such as chemistry, chemical industry, mineralogy, metallurgy, metallography, petroleum, natural gas, coal, light industry, material, environment.
Media: CD-ROM. **Related titles:** ◆ Online - full content ed.: C N K I Web; Online - full text ed.; ◆ Print ed.: Huadong Ligong Daxue Xuebao. ISSN 1006-3080; ◆ Shiyou Huagong Gaodeng Xuexiao Xuebao. ISSN 1006-396X; ◆ Shiyou Huagong. ISSN 1000-8144; ◆ Jinshu Rechuli. ISSN 0254-6051; ◆ Shuyou Shiyan Dizhi. ISSN 1001-6112; ◆ Beijing Huagong Daxue Xuebao (Ziran Kexue Ban). ISSN 1671-4628.
Published by: Tsinghua Tongfang Optical Disc Co., Ltd., Room 1300, Huaye Building, Tsing Hua University, PO BOX 84-48, Beijing, 100084, China. TEL 86-1-62791819, FAX 86-1-62791944, Beijing@cnki.net, http://www.cnki.net. **Co-sponsor:** Tsinghua University, School of Law.

500 CHN ISSN 1007-8037
CHINESE ACADEMIC JOURNALS FULL-TEXT DATABASE. SCIENCE & ENGINEERING, SERIES C. Text in Chinese, English. 1994. m. USD 4,160 to institutions (effective 2003). **Document type:** *Abstract/Index.* **Description:** Includes 635,931 full-text articles from 786 academic journals and covers disciplines such as machinery, instrumentation, metrology, electrical engineering, motive power, architecture, communication and transportation, weapon, aviation, space technology, atomic energy, engineering college journal.
Media: CD-ROM. **Related titles:** ◆ Online - full content ed.: C N K I Web; Online - full text ed.; ◆ Print ed.: Zhizao Jishu yu Jichuang. ISSN 1005-2402; ◆ Dongli Gongcheng. ISSN 1000-6761.
Published by: Tsinghua Tongfang Optical Disc Co., Ltd., Room 1300, Huaye Building, Tsing Hua University, PO BOX 84-48, Beijing, 100084, China. TEL 86-1-62791819, FAX 86-1-62791944, Beijing@cnki.net, http://www.cnki.net. **Co-sponsor:** Tsinghua University, School of Law.

500 CHN ISSN 1003-3572
Q4
CHINESE ACADEMY OF SCIENCES. BULLETIN. Text in English. q. USD 44.40 (effective 2009). 112 p./no.; **Document type:** *Journal, Academic/Scholarly.* **Description:** Publishes research results, science and technology development trends. Some of the articles are original, not translations.
Related titles: ◆ Chinese ed.: Zhongguo Kexueyuan Yuankan. ISSN 1000-3045.
—East View.
Published by: Zhongguo Kexueyuan/Chinese Academy of Sciences, PO Box 8712, Beijing, 100080, China. TEL 86-10-62627791. **Dist. by:** Haiyang Chubanshe, International Department, 8 Dahuisi Rd, Haidian District, Beijing 100081, China. TEL 86-10-62179976, FAX 86-10-62173569, oceanpress@china.com, http://www.oceanpress.cn/; China International Book Trading Corp, 35 Chegongzhuang Xilu, Haidian District, PO Box 399, Beijing 100044, China. TEL 86-10-68412045, FAX 86-10-68412023, cibtc@mail.cibtc.com.cn, http://www.cibtc.com.cn.

500 CHN ISSN 1001-6538
Q4 CODEN: CSBUEF
➤ **CHINESE SCIENCE BULLETIN.** Text in English. 1950. s-m. EUR 1,610, USD 2,005 combined subscription to institutions (print & online eds.) (effective 2012). adv. index. 88 p./no.; back issues avail. **Document type:** *Journal, Academic/Scholarly.* **Description:** Publishes up-to-date scientific achievements in all fields of natural sciences in China, and presents concise reports on the latest research in basic and applied sciences with a column "letters" covering briefly the most recent research news.
Formerly (until 1988): Kexue Tongbao (Foreign Language Edition) (0250-7862)
Related titles: Online - full text ed.: ISSN 1861-9541; ◆ Chinese ed.: Kexue Tongbao. ISSN 0023-074X.
Indexed: A01, A02, A03, A08, A20, A22, A26, A29, AIDS&CR, ASCA, ASFA, B07, B20, B21, B25, BIOSIS Prev, C13, CA, CCMJ, CIN, CIS, ChemAb, ChemTitl, CurCont, E01, E11, ESPM, GeoRef, ISR, Inspec, M&GPA, MOS, MSN, MathR, MycolAb, NPU, NucAcAb, P30, PollutAb, S01, SCI, SCOPUS, SWRA, SpeleolAb, T02, T04, ViroIAbstr, W07, W08, Z01, Z02.
—BLDSC (3181.086000), AskIEEE, CASDDS, East View, IE, Ingenta, INIST, Linda Hall. **CCC.**
Published by: (Chinese Academy of Sciences/Zhongguo Kexueyuan), Zhongguo Kexue Zazhishe/Science in China Press, 16 Donghuangchenggen North Street, Beijing, 100717, China. TEL 86-10-64019820, FAX 86-10-64016350, sale@scichina.com, http://www.scichina.com/. Ed. Jianbai Xia. Circ: 5,000. **Dist. outside of China by:** Springer, Haber Str 7, Heidelberg 69126, Germany. TEL 49-6221-3454303, FAX 49-6221-3454229, subscriptions@springer.com. **Co-publisher:** Springer.

507.11 BGD ISSN 1561-1167
Q80.B3 CODEN: CUSCDP
THE CHITTAGONG UNIVERSITY JOURNAL OF SCIENCE. Text in English. 1977. every 2 yrs.?. BDT 100 domestic; USD 15 foreign (effective 1999).
Formerly (until 1998): Chittagong University Studies. Part II: Science (0253-5459)
Indexed: CCMJ, CIN, CIS, ChemAb, ChemTitl, Inspec, MSN, ST&MA.
—AskIEEE, CASDDS, IE, Ingenta.
Published by: University of Chittagong, Chittagong, Bangladesh. Ed. Hamida Banu.

500 CHN
AS451 CODEN: CPAOD4
CHONGQING DAXUE XUEBAO (ZIRAN KEXUE BAN)/CHONGQING UNIVERSITY. JOURNAL (NATURAL SCIENCE EDITION). Text in Chinese. 1960. m. **Document type:** *Journal, Academic/Scholarly.*
Formerly: Chongqing Daxue Xuebao (1000-582X)
Related titles: Online - full text ed.
Indexed: A&ATA, A28, APA, BrCerAb, C&ISA, CA/WCA, CIA, CIN, CPEI, CerAb, ChemAb, ChemTitl, CivEngAb, CorrAb, CybAb, E&CAJ, E11, EEA, EMA, ESPM, EnvEAb, H15, M&TEA, M09, MBF, METADEX, RASB, SCOPUS, SolStAb, T04, WAA.
—CASDDS, East View, Linda Hall.
Published by: Chongqing Daxue/Chongqing University, 174, Shapingba Zheng Jie, Chongqing, Sichuan 400044, China. TEL 86-23-65102302, FAX 86-23-65112294. **Dist. by:** China International Book Trading Corp, 35 Chegongzhuang Xilu, Haidian District, PO Box 399, Beijing 100044, China. TEL 86-10-68412045, FAX 86-10-68412023, cibtc@mail.cibtc.com.cn, http://www.cibtc.com.cn.

500 CHN ISSN 1672-058X
CHONGQING GONGSHANG DAXUE XUEBAO (ZIRAN KEXUE BAN)/CHONGQING TECHNOLOGY AND BUSINESS UNIVERSITY. JOURNAL (NATURAL SCIENCES EDITION). Text in Chinese. 1983. bi-m. CNY 6 newsstand/cover (effective 2006). **Document type:** *Journal, Academic/Scholarly.*
Formerly (until 2002): Yuzhou Daxue Xuebao (Ziran kexue Ban)/Yuzhou University. Journal (Natural Science) (1006-3293)
Related titles: Online - full text ed.
Published by: Chongqing Gongshang Daxue, 58, Xuefu Dadao, Chongqing5, 400067, China. TEL 86-23-62769495.

500 CHN ISSN 1671-0924
CHONGQING GONGXUEYUAN XUEBAO (ZIRAN KEXUE BAN)/CHONGQING INSTITUTE OF TECHNOLOGY. JOURNAL (NATURAL SCIENCE EDITION). Text in Chinese. 1987. m. CNY 120, USD 15 (effective 2007). **Document type:** *Journal, Academic/Scholarly.*
Related titles: Online - full text ed.
Published by: Chongqing Gongxueyuan/Chongqing Institute of Technology, 4, Xingsheng Rd, Yangjiaping, Jiulongpe Division, Chongqing, 400050, China. TEL 86-23-68820073, FAX 86-23-68667984 86-23-68667984. Ed. Quan-li Liu.

CHONGQING JIAOYU XUEYUAN XUEBAO/CHONGQING COLLEGE OF EDUCATION. JOURNAL. *see* SOCIAL SCIENCES: COMPREHENSIVE WORKS

500 600 CHN
CHONGQING KEJI/CHONGQING SCIENCE AND TECHNOLOGY. Text in Chinese. m.
Published by: Chongqing Shi Kexue Jishu Weiyuanhui/Chongqing Science and Technology Commission, 236, Renmin Lu, Chongqing, Sichuan 630015, China. TEL 352263. Ed. Zhou Yongxin.

500 CHN ISSN 1673-1980
CHONGQING KEJI XUEYUAN XUEBAO (ZIRAN KEXUE BAN)/CHONGQING UNIVERSITY OF SCIENCE AND TECHNOLOGY. JOURNAL (NATURAL SCIENCE EDITION). Text in Chinese. 1999. bi-m. **Document type:** *Journal, Academic/Scholarly.*
Formerly (until 2003): Chongqing Shiyou Gaodeng Zhuanke Xuexiao Xuebao/Chongqing Petroleum College. Journal (1008-9845)
Related titles: Online - full text ed.
Published by: Chongqing Keji Xueyuan/Chongqing University of Science and Technology, 419, Xingzheng Lou, Chongqing, 401331, China. TEL 86-23-65023856, http://www.cqust.cn/default.htm.

500 CHN ISSN 1672-6693
CHONGQING SHIFAN DAXUE XUEBAO (ZIRAN KEXUE BAN)/CHONGQING NORMAL UNIVERSITY. JOURNAL (NATURAL SCIENCE EDITION). Text in Chinese; Abstracts and contents page in Chinese, English. 1984. q. USD 14.40 (effective 2009). **Document type:** *Magazine, Academic/Scholarly.*
Formerly: Chongqing Shifan Xueyuan Xuebao (Ziran Kexue Ban)/Chongqing Teachers College. Journal (Natural Science Edition) (1001-8905)
Related titles: Online - full text ed.: free (effective 2011).
Indexed: A34, A35, AgBio, C25, CABA, CCMJ, E12, F08, F12, G11, GH, I11, LT, MSN, MathR, P32, P33, P39, R07, R08, R12, R13, S13, S16, TAR, W11, Z01.
—BLDSC (4729.336500), IE.
Published by: Chongqing Shifan Daxue/Chongqing Normal University, 12, Tianchen Road, Shapingba District, Chongqing, 400047, China. TEL 86-23-65362431, FAX 86-23-65362431. Ed. Xiang Huang. **Dist. by:** China International Book Trading Corp, 35 Chegongzhuang Xilu, Haidian District, PO Box 399, Beijing 100044, China. TEL 86-10-68412045, FAX 86-10-68412023, cibtc@mail.cibtc.com.cn, http://www.cibtc.com.cn.

CHONGQING UNIVERSITY. JOURNAL. *see* SOCIAL SCIENCES: COMPREHENSIVE WORKS

500 CHN ISSN 1673-8012
CHONGQING WENLI XUEYUAN XUEBAO (ZIRAN KEXUE BAN)/CHONGQING UNIVERSITY OF ARTS AND SCIENCES. JOURNAL. Text in Chinese. 1988. q. CNY 6.50 newsstand/cover (effective 2006). **Document type:** *Journal, Academic/Scholarly.*
Former titles (until 2002): Yuxi Xueyuan Xuebao (Ziran Kexue Ban)/Western Chongqing University. Journal (Nature Science Edition) (1671-7538); (until 2001): Yuzhou Jiaoyu Xueyuan Xuebao/Yuzhou College of Education. Journal (1008-648X)
Published by: Chongqing Wenli Xueyuan, Yongchuan, Chongqing, 402168, China. TEL 86-23-49682273.

500 CHN
CHONGQING YOUDIAN DAXUE XUEBAO (ZIRAN KEXUE BAN)/CHONGQING INSTITUTE OF POSTS AND TELECOMMUNICATIONS. JOURNAL (NATURAL SCIENCE EDITION). Text in Chinese; Abstracts in English. 1988. bi-m. **Document type:** *Journal, Academic/Scholarly.*
Former titles: Chongqing Youdian Xueyuan Xuebao (Ziran Kexue Ban) (1673-825X); Chongqing Youdian Xueyuan Xuebao (Zike Ban) (1004-5694)
Related titles: Online - full text ed.
Indexed: A28, APA, BrCerAb, C&ISA, CA/WCA, CIA, CerAb, CivEngAb, CorrAb, E&CAJ, E11, EEA, EMA, ESPM, EnvEAb, H15, Inspec, M&TEA, M09, MBF, METADEX, SolStAb, T04, WAA.
—BLDSC (3181.559501), Linda Hall.
Published by: Congqing Youdian Daxue/Chongqing University of Posts and Telecommunications, Nanan-qu, Huangjiaoping, Chongqing, 400065, China. TEL 86-23-62461032, FAX 86-23-62471771, http://www.cqupt.edu.cn/. Ed. Yinguo Li. **Dist. by:** China International Book Trading Corp, 35 Chegongzhuang Xilu, Haidian District, PO Box 399, Beijing 100044, China. TEL 86-10-68412045, FAX 86-10-68412023, cibtc@mail.cibtc.com.cn, http://www.cibtc.com.cn.

550 330 DEU ISSN 0578-0160
LF2861.C5
CHRISTIANA ALBERTINA. Text in German. 1965. s-a. adv. back issues avail. **Document type:** *Journal, Academic/Scholarly.*
Formerly (until 1966): Christian-Albrechts-Universitaet zu Kiel. Mitteilungsblatt (0450-2353)
Indexed: GeoRef, P30, SpeleolAb.
Published by: Christian Albrechts Universitaet zu Kiel, Rektorat, Christian-Albrechts-Platz 4, Kiel, 24118, Germany. TEL 49-431-88000, FAX 49-431-8802072, mail@uni-kiel.de, http://www.uni-kiel.de.

500 COD ISSN 0009-6040
CHRONIQUE DE L'I R S A C. Text in English, French. 1966. 3/yr. USD 2. abstr.; illus.
Published by: Institut pour la Recherche Scientifique en Afrique Centrale, Lwiro- Bukavu, Congo, Dem. Republic.

500 CHN ISSN 1671-0037
CHUANGXIN KEJI/SCIENCE NEW GROUND. Text in Chinese. 1988. m. CNY 72 domestic; USD 18 in Hong Kong, Macau & Taiwan; USD 36 elsewhere (effective 2007). **Document type:** *Journal, Academic/Scholarly.*
Related titles: Online - full text ed.
Address: 3, Zheng Liu Jie, Zhengzhou, 450003, China. TEL 86-371-65998844, FAX 86-371-65941765. **Dist. by:** China International Book Trading Corp, 35 Chegongzhuang Xilu, Haidian District, PO Box 399, Beijing 100044, China. TEL 86-10-68412045, FAX 86-10-68412023, cibtc@mail.cibtc.com.cn, http://www.cibtc.com.cn.

500 600 CHN ISSN 1674-5256
CHUANGYI SHIJIE/CREATIVITY. Text in Chinese. 1978. m. USD 80.40 (effective 2009).
Former titles (until 2009): Shijie Faming/World Invention (1003-1049); (until 1980): Guowai Faming
—East View.
Published by: Zhongguo Zhishi Chanquan Baoshe, Haidian-qu, Jimen, 6, Xitucheng Lu, Beijing, 100088, China. TEL 86-10-82803936.

500 620 JPN ISSN 1341-7304
CHUO DAIGAKU RIKOGAKU KENKYUJO NENPO/CHUO UNIVERSITY. INSTITUTE OF SCIENCE AND ENGINEERING. ANNUAL REPORT. Text in Japanese. 1994. a. **Document type:** *Academic/Scholarly.*
Related titles: Online - full text ed.
Published by: Chuo Daigaku, Rikogaku Kenkyujo/Chuo University, Institute of Science and Engineering, 1-13-27 Kasuga, Bunkyo-ku, Tokyo, 112-8551, Japan. TEL 81-3-38171600, FAX 81-3-38171677, http://www.chuo-u.ac.jp/chuo-u/ins_science/index_j.html.

500 620 JPN ISSN 1343-0068
CODEN: CDRRFG
CHUO DAIGAKU RIKOGAKU KENKYUJO RONBUNSHU/JOURNAL OF THE INSTITUTE OF SCIENCE AND ENGINEERING, CHUO UNIVERSITY. Text in Japanese. 1995. irreg. **Document type:** *Journal, Academic/Scholarly.*

Related titles: Online - full text ed.
Indexed: Z02.
—BLDSC (4786.900000).
Published by: Chuo Daigaku, Rikogaku Kenkyujo/Chuo University, Institute of Science and Engineering, 1-13-27 Kasuga, Bunkyo-ku, Tokyo, 112-8551, Japan. TEL 81-3-38171600, FAX 81-3-38171677, http://www.chuo-u.ac.jp/chuo-u/ins_science/index_j.html.

CHUZHONGSHENG TIANDI/WORLD FOR THE JUNIOR STUDENTS. *see* CHILDREN AND YOUTH—For

500 300 MEX ISSN 1405-6550
Q4 CODEN: CIENA3
CIENCIA. Text in Spanish; Summaries in English, Spanish. 1940. q. USD 78 to individuals; USD 158 to institutions. adv. bk.rev. index. back issues avail. **Document type:** *Academic/Scholarly.*
Former titles: Ciencia. Academia Mexicana de Ciencias (0185-075X); (until 1980): Ciencia. Patronato de Ciencia (0185-0806)
Indexed: ASFA, B21, B25, BIOSIS Prev, C01, CIN, ChemAb, ChemTitl, ESPM, IBR, IBZ, Inspec, MycolAb, P30, RASB, Z01.
—AskIEEE, INIST, Linda Hall.
Published by: Academia de la Investigacion Cientifica A.C., Ave. San Jeronimo 260, Jardines del Pedregal de San Angel, Mexico City, DF 04500, Mexico. TEL 52-5-5506278, FAX 52-5-5501143. Ed. Fernando del Rio. Circ: 3,000.

500 600 MEX ISSN 2007-1175
CIENCIA; revista de difusion cientifica y tecnologica universitaria autonoma de nuevo leon. Key Title: Ciencia UANL. Text in Spanish. 1998. q. **Document type:** *Journal, Academic/Scholarly.*
Published by: Universidad Autonoma de Nuevo Leon, Secretaria de Investigacion y Postgrado, Ave Universitaria s-n Torre de Rectoria 7o. Piso, Ciudad Universitaria, San Nicolas de los Garza, Nuevo Leon 66451, Mexico. TEL 52-81-83294022, FAX 52-81-83763076, http://www.uanl.mx/.

500 PRT ISSN 1647-5232
CIENCIA. Text in Portuguese. 1991. irreg. **Document type:** *Magazine, Consumer.*
Published by: Relogio d'Agua Editores Lda., Rua Sylvio Rebelo 15, Lisbon, 1000-282, Portugal. TEL 351-218-474450, FAX 351-218-470775, relogiodagua@relogiodagua.pt, http://www.relogiodagua.pt.

500 ECU ISSN 1390-1117
CIENCIA. Text in Spanish.
Indexed: INIS AtomInd.
Published by: Escuela Politecnica del Ejercito, Campus Politecnico, Av El Progreso s/n, Sangolqui, Ecuador. TEL 593-2-2334950, FAX 593-2-2334952, http://www.espe.edu.ec/.

500 CUB
CIENCIA. Text in Spanish. s-a. USD 15 in the Americas; USD 16 in Europe.
Published by: (Academia de Ciencias de Cuba, Instituto de Documentacion e Informacion Cientifico-Tecnica (I D I C T)), Ediciones Cubanas, Obispo 527, Havana, Cuba.

500 DOM
CIENCIA. Text in Spanish. 1972. q. DOP 8, USD 11. bibl.; charts; illus.
Published by: Universidad Autonoma de Santo Domingo, Direccion de Investigaciones Cientificas, Apdo. 1355, Santo Domingo, Dominican Republic. Ed. Jose del Castillo.

500 CHL ISSN 0717-8948
CIENCIA ABIERTA. Text in Spanish, English. 1984. q. back issues avail. **Document type:** *Journal, Academic/Scholarly.*
Media: Online - full text.
Published by: Universidad de Chile, Facultad de Ciencias Fisicas y Matematicas, Campus Universitario, Santiago, Chile. rrppfcfm@ce.uchile.cl, http://ingenieria.uchile.cl/.

500 600 CHL ISSN 0717-3849
CIENCIA AL DIA INTERNACIONAL. Text in Spanish. 1998. s-a. back issues avail. **Document type:** *Journal, Academic/Scholarly.*
Media: Online - full text.
Published by: Ciencia al Dia golowasch@stg.rutgers.edu. Ed. Jorge Golowasch.

500 ESP ISSN 1988-7884
CIENCIA COGNITIVA; revista electronica de divulgacion. Text in Spanish. 2007. m. free (effective 2011). **Document type:** *Journal, Academic/Scholarly.*
Media: Online - full text.
Address: divulgacion@cienciacognitiva.org. Ed. Julio Santiago De Torres.

500 600 ARG ISSN 0327-5566
H53.A55
➤ **CIENCIA, DOCENCIA Y TECNOLOGIA.** Text in Spanish; Abstracts in English, Portuguese, Spanish. 1990. s-a. USD 55 (effective 2011). **Document type:** *Journal, Academic/Scholarly.* **Description:** Focuses on the geographical scope of the Argentine Republic and Latin American countries.
Related titles: Online - full text ed.: ISSN 1851-1716. 2007. free (effective 2011) (from SciELO).
Indexed: C01, CA, L&LBA, S02, S03, SSA, SociolAb, T02.
—IE.
Published by: Editorial de la Universidad Nacional de Entre Rios, Casa de la UNER, Cordoba 475, Parana, 3100, Argentina. TEL 54-343-4321118, FAX 54-343-4321123, eduner@uner.edu.ar. Ed. Silvia M Storani. Adv. contact Paola Carolina Campo. Circ: 350 (controlled).

500 BRA ISSN 0009-6725
Q4 CODEN: CCUPAD
➤ **CIENCIA E CULTURA.** Text in English, Portuguese; Summaries in English, Portuguese. 1949. bi-m. adv. bk.rev. bibl.; charts; illus. cum.index: 1948-1996. reprints avail. **Document type:** *Journal, Academic/Scholarly.* **Description:** Includes reviews, reports, research articles, news and comments.
Related titles: Online - full text ed.: free (effective 2011).
Indexed: A22, A29, ASFA, B21, B25, BIOSIS Prev, BioDAb, C01, C25, C30, CABA, CIN, ChemAb, ChemTitl, E12, ESPM, F08, F11, F12, G11, GeoRef, I11, IBR, IBZ, LT, MLA-IB, MycolAb, P30, R12, RRTA, S13, S16, SCOPUS, SWRA, SpeleolAb, TAR, ToxAb, W11.
—CASDDS, Infotrieve, Ingenta, INIST, Linda Hall.
Published by: Sociedad Brasileira para o Progresso da Ciencia (S B P C), Rua Maria Antonia 294, 4o Andara, Sao Paulo, 01222-010, Brazil. TEL 55-11-32592766, FAX 55-11-3106-1002, socios@sbpcnet.org.br, http://www.sbpcnet.org.br. Ed. Carlos Vogt. Circ: 1,500.

500 620 BRA ISSN 0103-944X
CIENCIA & ENGENHARIA. Text in Portuguese. 1992. s-a. **Document type:** *Journal, Academic/Scholarly.*
Indexed: CPEI, Englnd, SCOPUS.
Published by: Universidade Federal de Uberlandia, Av Engenheiro Diniz 1178, Uberlandia, MG 38400-902, Brazil. TEL 55-34-2394811, FAX 55-34-2350099, http://www.ufu.br.

500 370 BRA ISSN 1414-5111
CIENCIA & ENSINO. Text in Portuguese. 1996. s-a. **Document type:** *Journal, Academic/Scholarly.*
Related titles: Online - full text ed.: ISSN 1980-8631. free (effective 2011).
Published by: Universidade Estadual de Campinas, Faculdade de Educacao, Ave Bertrand Russell 801, Cidade Universitaria "Zeferino Vaz", Campinas, SP 13083-861, Brazil. TEL 55-19-37885571, FAX 55-19-37885633, http://www.unicamp.br. Ed. Henrique Cesar da Silva.

500 ARG ISSN 0009-6733
Q4 CODEN: CIBAAH
CIENCIA E INVESTIGACION. Text in Spanish. 1945. m. USD 15. adv. bk.rev. bibl.; charts; illus. index.
Indexed: ChemAb, P30.
—CASDDS, INIST, Linda Hall.
Published by: Asociacion Argentina para el Progreso de las Ciencias, Ave. Alvear No. 1711 Piso 4, Buenos Aires, 1014, Argentina. TEL 54-11-47713043, FAX 54-11-48116951. Ed. Horacio H Camacho. Circ: 2,000.

508 BRA ISSN 0100-8307
Q4 CODEN: CNATD5
CIENCIA E NATURA. Text in Portuguese. 1979. s-a. back issues avail. **Document type:** *Journal, Academic/Scholarly.*
Indexed: Z01.
Published by: Universidade Federal de Santa Maria, Centro de Ciencias Naturais e Exatas, Camus da UFSM Sala 1110 Predio 13, Santa Maria, RS 97105-900, Brazil. TEL 55-55-2208735, mligia@smaill.ufsm.br. Ed. Gervasio Annes Degrazia.

500 GTM ISSN 1607-5684
CIENCIA EN ACCION. Text in Spanish. 1996. s-a. back issues avail. **Document type:** *Academic/Scholarly.*
Related titles: Online - full text ed.: ISSN 1607-5692. 1996.
Published by: Universidad del Valle de Guatemala, Instituto de Investigaciones, 18 Ave 11-95, Zona 15, Vista Hermosa, Guatemala, 01901, Guatemala. Ed. Charles MacVean.

500 BRA ISSN 0101-8515
Q4 CODEN: CIHOEP
➤ **CIENCIA HOJE.** Text in Portuguese. 1982. m. adv. bk.rev. back issues avail. **Document type:** *Magazine, Consumer.* **Description:** Written by scientists and journalists for the general public on all fields of scientific knowledge.
Related titles: Online - full text ed.
Indexed: A22.
—BLDSC (3196.330000), IE, Ingenta.
Published by: Sociedad Brasileira para o Progresso da Ciencia (S B P C), Rua Maria Antonia 294, 4o Andara, Sao Paulo, 01222-010, Brazil. TEL 55-11-32592766, socios@sbpcnet.org.br, http://www.sbpcnet.org.br. Circ: 30,000.

500 ARG ISSN 0327-1218
Q4
CIENCIA HOY. Text in Spanish. 1988. bi-m. ARS 45 (effective 2006). back issues avail. **Document type:** *Journal, Academic/Scholarly.*
Related titles: Online - full text ed.: ISSN 1666-5171. 1998.
Published by: Asociacion Civil Ciencia Hoy, Ave Corrientes, 2835, Cuerpo A 50-A, Buenos Aires, 1193, Argentina. TEL 54-11-49611824, FAX 54-11-49621330, rvcihoy@criba.edu.ar. Ed. Patricio Garrahan.

500 CUB
CIENCIA, INNOVACION Y DESARROLLO. Short title: Cinde. Text in Spanish. q. USD 30.
Published by: Ministerio de la Ciencia la Tecnologia y el Medio Ambiente, Instituto de Documentacion e Information Cientifica y Tecnologica, Apartado Postal 2213, Havana, 10200, Cuba. TEL 62-6501, FAX 62-6501. Ed. Andres Castillo Bernal.

500 600 MEX
CIENCIA PARA TODOS. Text in Spanish. 1974. m. MXN 130, USD 14. adv. bk.rev.
Formerly: Ciencia Popular
Published by: Publicaciones Herrerias, S.A., Morelos 16, planta baja, Mexico City, DF 06040, Mexico. Ed. Jose Pichel. Circ: 15,000.

500 600 MEX ISSN 2007-1310
▼ **CIENCIA TECNOLOGIA E INNOVACION PARA EL DESARROLLO DE MEXICO.** Text in Spanish. 2009. w. back issues avail. **Document type:** *Journal, Academic/Scholarly.*
Media: Online - full text.
Address: Guasinai Esq. Aquiles Serdan, Col. Guayura, La Paz, Baja California 23090, Mexico. TEL 52-612-1240245. Ed. Patricia Alzaga Mayagoitia.

500 300 BOL ISSN 2077-3323
CIENCIA Y CULTURA. Text in Spanish. 1997. s-a. back issues avail. **Document type:** *Journal, Academic/Scholarly.*
Related titles: Online - full text ed.
Published by: Universidad Catolica Boliviana, Avenida 14 de Septiembre 4807, Esquina Calle 2, Obrajes, La Paz, Bolivia. TEL 591-2-2782222, FAX 591-2-2786749, http://www.ucb.edu.bo. Ed. Carlos Rosso Orosco.

500 790.1 ESP
CIENCIA Y DEPORTE. Text in Spanish. 6/yr. back issues avail. **Document type:** *Magazine, Consumer.*
Related titles: Online - full text ed.: Cienciaydeporte.net. ISSN 1698-8388. 2004.
Address: Comercio, 4, bajo C 1a escalera, Madrid, 28007, Spain. TEL 1-433-45-23. Ed. Antonio Ramon Garica Torres.

500 600 MEX ISSN 0185-0008
Q4 CODEN: CIDED8
CIENCIA Y DESARROLLO. Text in Spanish. 1975. bi-m. MXN 120; USD 42 in North America; USD 50 in Europe; USD 60 elsewhere (effective 1999). adv. bk.rev. bibl. index. **Document type:** *Academic/Scholarly.* **Description:** Covers diverse themes such as medicine, anthropology, architecture, biology, astronomy, physics and chemistry.
Related titles: Online - full text ed.
Indexed: ASFA, B21, C01, ChemAb, ESPM, P30, RASB.
—CASDDS, IE, Infotrieve, Linda Hall.
Published by: Consejo Nacional de Ciencia y Tecnologia, Ave Insurgentes Sur 1582, Col Credito Constructor, Mexico, D.F., 03940, Mexico. TEL 52-5-3277400 ext. 7737, FAX 52-5-5702730. Ed. Alfredo Gomez. Adv. contact Jose Luis Miranda Salgado. Circ: 8,000.

500 MEX ISSN 0187-8786
Q23
LA CIENCIA Y EL HOMBRE. Text in Spanish. 1988. 3/yr. USD 21 (effective 2001). **Document type:** *Academic/Scholarly.*
Indexed: C01.
—Linda Hall.
Published by: Universidad Veracruzana, Direccion Editorial, Apdo. Postal 97, Xalapa, Ver. 91001, Mexico. TEL 52-28-174435, FAX 52-28-185980. Pub. Rafael Bulle-Goyri.

500.1 ECU ISSN 0009-6768
Q33 CODEN: CINQAN
CIENCIA Y NATURALEZA. Text and summaries in English, Spanish. 1957. s-a. per issue exchange basis. bibl.; charts; illus. index.
Indexed: C01, ChemAb, GeoRef, SpeleolAb.
—INIST, Linda Hall.
Published by: Universidad Central del Ecuador, Instituto de Ciencias Naturales, Casilla 633, Quito, Pichincha, Ecuador. Ed. Francisco Latorre. Circ: 2,500.

500 DOM ISSN 0378-7680
HC157.D6
CIENCIA Y SOCIEDAD. Text in Spanish; Summaries in English. 1975. q. adv. bk.rev. bibl.; charts. **Document type:** *Journal, Academic/Scholarly.*
Related titles: Online - full text ed.: free (effective 2011).
Indexed: C01, CA, F04, IBR, IBZ, MLA-IB, P30, PAIS, T02.
Published by: Instituto Tecnologico de Santo Domingo, Apdo Postal 342-9, Santo Domingo, Dominican Republic. Ed. Antonio Fernandez.

500 CRI ISSN 0378-052X
CODEN: CITEDK
CIENCIA Y TECNOLOGIA. Text in Spanish. 1976. s-a. adv. **Document type:** *Journal, Academic/Scholarly.*
Related titles: Online - full text ed.
Indexed: A26, C01, CCMJ, GeoRef, I04, I05, IBR, IBZ, MSN, MathR, RASB, SpeleolAb, Z02.
—CASDDS.
Published by: Universidad de Costa Rica, Editorial, Sede Rodrigo Facio Brenes, Montes de Oca, San Jose, Costa Rica. TEL 506-207-4000, FAX 506-224-8214, direccion@editorial.ucr.ac.cr, http://editorial.ucr.ac.cr. Ed. Rodrigo Carboni.

500 600 ESP ISSN 1579-4091
CIENCIA Y TECNOLOGIA EN (YEAR). Text in Spanish. 2000. a., latest 2005. **Document type:** *Directory, Trade.*
Related titles: Online - full text ed.: ISSN 1579-4105.
Published by: Asociacion Espanola de Periodismo Cientifico (A E P C), Calle Isla Cristina 72, San Roman de los Montes, Toledo 45646, Spain. http://www.agendadelacomunicacion.com/aepc/.

500 ESP
Q65 CODEN: CINSAT
CIENCIAS. Text in Spanish. 1934. q. adv.
—CASDDS.
Published by: Asociacion Espanola para el Progreso de las Ciencias, Valverde, 22, Madrid, 28004, Spain. Circ: 1,500.

500 MEX ISSN 0187-6376
Q23 CODEN: ESABFA
➤ **CIENCIAS.** Text in Spanish. 1982. q. **Document type:** *Journal, Academic/Scholarly.* **Description:** Dedicated to making the general population more knowledgeable about science and encouraging young researchers to participate in an open dialogue.
Related titles: Online - full text ed.: free (effective 2011).
Indexed: C01.
—IE.
Published by: Universidad Nacional Autonoma de Mexico, Facultad de Ciencias, Cub. 319, 320 and 321, Circuito Exterior, Ciudad Universitaria, Mexico City, DF 04510, Mexico. TEL 52-5-6224935, FAX 52-5-6160326, revista@astroscu.unam.mx, revista@servidor.unam.mx, http://www.fciencias.unam.mx/revista/ciencias/ciencis.html. Ed. Patricia Magana.

➤ **CIENCIAS TECNICAS FISICAS Y MATEMATICAS.** *see* TECHNOLOGY: COMPREHENSIVE WORKS

500 370 ESP ISSN 1699-6712
LB1585
CIENCIES; revista del professorat de ciencies de primaria i secundaria. Text in Catalan. 2005. irreg. free (effective 2011). **Document type:** *Journal, Academic/Scholarly.*
Media: Online - full text.
Published by: Universitat Autonoma de Barcelona, Servei de Publicacions, Edifici A, Bellaterra, Cardanyola del Valles, Barcelona, 08193, Spain. TEL 34-93-5811022, FAX 34-93-5813239, sp@uab.es, http://www.uab.es/publicacions/.

500 ARG ISSN 1852-866X
▼ **CIENTIFICAMENTE, EXACTAS Y NATURALES.** Text in Spanish. 2009. q. **Document type:** *Journal, Academic/Scholarly.*
Published by: Universidad Nacional de Catamarca, Facultad de Ciencias Exactas y Naturales, Ave Belgrado, P., San Fernando del Valle, Catamarca, 47000, Argentina. TEL 54-3833-420900, http://www.exactas.unca.edu.ar. Ed. Josefina Vera Araoz.

508 001.3 NAM ISSN 1012-4926
Q85.8 CODEN: CIMBEB
CIMBEBASIA. Text in English; Summaries in French, German. 1962. irreg. (approx a.). price varies. charts; illus. back issues avail. **Document type:** *Monographic series, Academic/Scholarly.*
Formed by the merger of (1962-1988): Cimbebasia. Series A, Natural History (0590-6342); (1962-1988): Cimbebasia. Series B, Cultural History (0253-2522); Both of which superseded in part (in 1967): Cimbebasia (0578-2732)
Indexed: AICP, B25, BIOSIS Prev, GeoRef, IBR, IBZ, ISAP, MycolAb, SpeleolAb, Z01.
—Ingenta, INIST.
Published by: National Museum of Namibia, PO Box 77203, Windhoek, Namibia. TEL 061-2934360. Ed. John Kinahan. Circ: 400.

508 NAM ISSN 0578-2724
CIMBEBASIA. MEMOIR. Text mainly in English; Summaries in French, German. 1967. irreg., latest vol.6, 1985. price varies. index. back issues avail. **Document type:** *Monographic series.*
Indexed: B25, BIOSIS Prev, MycolAb, Z01.
—INIST.
Published by: National Museum of Namibia, PO Box 77203, Windhoek, Namibia. TEL 061-2934360. Ed. John Kinahan. Circ: 400.

500 600 JPN
CLASS N K TECHNICAL BULLETIN. Text in English. 1983. a. free. **Document type:** *Bulletin, Academic/Scholarly.*
Formerly (until 1993): Nippon Kaiji Kyokai. Technical Bulletin
Indexed: BMT, HRIS.
Published by: Nippon Kaiji Kyokai, 4-7 Kioi-cho, Chiyoda-ku, Tokyo, 102-8567, Japan. TEL 81-43-2945451, FAX 81-43-2947204, isd@classnk.or.jp. Ed. Minoru Okami. Circ: 2,500 (controlled).

500 FRA ISSN 0298-6248
QC791.9 CODEN: CEACES
CLEFS C E A. (Commissariat a l'Energie Atomique) Text in French. 1986. s-a. free. **Document type:** *Journal, Trade.*
Related titles: Online - full text ed.: ISSN 1625-9718.
Indexed: A22, CIN, ChemAb, ChemTitl, INIS AtomInd, Inspec.
—BLDSC (3278.558000), CASDDS, IE, Ingenta, INIST, Linda Hall.
Published by: Commissariat a l'Energie Atomique, Direction de la Communication, Batiment Le Ponant D, 25 Rue Leblanc, Paris, 75015, France. TEL 33-1-64502059, http://www.cea.fr.

500 CUB ISSN 1607-2863
COCUYO. Text in Spanish. 1995. s-a.
Indexed: Z01.
Published by: Museo Nacional de Historia Natural, Calle Obispo 61, Plaza de Armas, Habana, Cuba. TEL 53-863-9361, FAX 53-862-0353, http://www.cuba.cu/ciencia/citma/ama/museo.

500 COL ISSN 0120-5986
COLCIENCIAS. CARTA. Text in Spanish. 1970. m.
Published by: Colciencias, Transversal 9A No. 133-28, PO Box 051580, Bogota, CUND, Colombia. TEL 57-1-216-9800, FAX 57-1-625-1788, TELEX 44305. Ed. Julia Patricia Aguirre Guzman.

500 ESP
➤ **COLECCION CIENCIAS, HUMANIDADES E INGENIERIA.** Abbreviated title: Coleccion C H I. Text in Spanish. 1975. irreg. (approx. 4/yr.). price varies. **Document type:** *Monographic series, Academic/Scholarly.*
Published by: Colegio de Ingenieros de Caminos Canales y Puertos, Almagro 42, Madrid, 28010, Spain. TEL 34-91-3081988, FAX 34-91-3083931, docu@ciccp.es, http://www.ciccp.es. Ed. Marisa Marco.

➤ **COLLANA SAPERI.** *see* HUMANITIES: COMPREHENSIVE WORKS

500 ITA ISSN 2036-1181
COLLANA SCIENTIFICA. ATTI DI CONVEGNI E MISCELLANEE. Text in Italian. 2004. irreg. **Document type:** *Proceedings, Academic/Scholarly.*
Published by: (Universita degli Studi di Salerno), Rubbettino Editore, Viale Rosario Rubbettino 10, Soveria Mannelli, CZ 88049, Italy. TEL 39-0968-662034, FAX 39-0968-662055, segreteria@rubbettino.it, http://www.rubbettino.it.

500 NZL ISSN 0112-2479
COLLECTED PAPERS FROM THE JOURNAL OF THE ROYAL SOCIETY OF NEW ZEALAND. Text in English. 1984. irreg. price varies. **Document type:** *Journal, Academic/Scholarly.*
Indexed: MLA-IB.
Published by: (Royal Society of New Zealand), R S N Z Publishing, PO Box 598, Wellington, 6001, New Zealand. TEL 64-4-4727421, FAX 64-4-4731841, sales@rsnz.org, http://www.rsnz.org. Ed. Carolyn M King.

500 ITA
COLLECTIO MONOGRAPHICA MINOR; collana a cura dell'Instituto Comeliana di Lugano. Text in Italian. 1976. irreg., latest vol.4, 1978. price varies. **Document type:** *Monographic series, Academic/Scholarly.*
Published by: (Istituto Comeliana di Lugano), Fabrizio Serra Editore (Subsidiary of: Accademia Editoriale), c/o Accademia Editoriale, Via Santa Bibbiana 28, Pisa, 56127, Italy. TEL 39-050-542332, FAX 39-050-574888, accademiaeditoriale@accademiaeditoriale.it, http://www.libraweb.net.

500 FRA ISSN 1257-9130
COLLECTION CURSUS. SCIENCES. Variant title: Cursus. Sciences. Text in French. 1993. irreg. price varies. **Document type:** *Monographic series, Academic/Scholarly.*
Published by: Armand Colin, 21 Rue du Montparnasse, Paris, 75283 Cedex 06, France. TEL 33-1-44395447, FAX 33-1-44394343, infos@armand-colin.fr, http://www.armand-colin.com.

COLLECTION FORUM. *see* MUSEUMS AND ART GALLERIES

COLLECTION NORDICANA. *see* ANTHROPOLOGY

500 FRA ISSN 1281-6213
COLLECTION PATRIMOINES NATURELLES. Text in French. 1990. irreg. price varies. **Document type:** *Monographic series, Academic/Scholarly.*
—INIST.
Published by: Museum National d'Histoire Naturelle, 57 Rue Cuvier, CP 39, Paris, 05 75231, France. TEL 33-1-40793777, http://www.mnhn.fr. Ed. Jacques Trouvilliez.

500 USA
QH1
COLLECTIONS & EVENTS. Text in English. 1920. bi-m. USD 5 domestic; USD 6 in Canada; free to members (effective 2005). illus. **Document type:** *Magazine, Consumer.* **Description:** Membership newsletter devoted to activities and collections of the Buffalo Museum of Science, the Society of Natural History, and Tifft Nature Preserve.
Former titles: Collections (Buffalo) (0160-0664); (until vol.56, 1976): Science on the March (0036-8474); (until 1958): Hobbies (0899-8736)
Indexed: GeoRef, RASB, SpeleolAb.
—Linda Hall.
Published by: Buffalo Society of Natural Sciences, 1020 Humboldt Pkwy, Buffalo, NY 14211. TEL 716-896-5200, FAX 716-897-6723. Ed. Renata Toney. Circ: 10,000 (controlled).

500 DEU ISSN 0949-8788
AS182.M2332
COLLOQUIA ACADEMICA. GEISTESWISSENSCHAFTEN. Text in German. 1996. a. price varies. **Document type:** *Monographic series, Academic/Scholarly.*
Published by: (Akademie der Wissenschaften und der Literatur), Franz Steiner Verlag GmbH, Birkenwaldstr 44, Stuttgart, 70191, Germany. TEL 49-711-25820, FAX 49-711-2582290, service@steiner-verlag.de, http://www.steiner-verlag.de.

500 DEU ISSN 0949-8133
Q49
COLLOQUIA ACADEMICA. NATURWISSENSCHAFTEN. Text in German. 1996. a. price varies. **Document type:** *Monographic series, Academic/Scholarly.*
—Linda Hall.
Published by: (Akademie der Wissenschaften und der Literatur), Franz Steiner Verlag GmbH, Birkenwaldstr 44, Stuttgart, 70191, Germany. TEL 49-711-25820, FAX 49-711-2582290, service@steiner-verlag.de, http://www.steiner-verlag.de.

500 BRA ISSN 1413-7313
COLLOQUIUM. Text in Portuguese. 1996. s-a.
Indexed: SociolAb.
Published by: (Universidade do Oeste Paulista), Oeste Noticias Grafica e Editora Ltda., Rua Kametaro Morishita 95, Presidente Prudente, SP 19050-700, Brazil. TEL 55-18-229-0300, FAX 55-18-229-0366, comercial@oestenoticias.com.br, sac@oestenoticias.com.br, http://www.oestenoticias.com.br/assinante.htm.

500 COL ISSN 0120-5595
➤ **COLOMBIA: CIENCIA Y TECNOLOGIA.** Text in Spanish. 1983. q. COP 8,000, USD 20. adv. bk.rev. charts; illus.; stat. **Document type:** *Academic/Scholarly.* **Description:** Presents studies in science and technology.
Formerly (since 1986): Ciencia y Tecnologia
Indexed: C01.
Published by: Colciencias, Transversal 9A No. 133-28, PO Box 051580, Bogota, CUND, Colombia. TEL 57-1-216-9800, FAX 57-1-625-1788, TELEX 44305. Ed. Julia Patricia Aguirre Guzman. Circ: 3,500.

500 USA ISSN 0096-2279
AS36 CODEN: JCOQAT
COLORADO-WYOMING ACADEMY OF SCIENCES. JOURNAL. Text in English. 1929. a., latest 2007. abstr. **Document type:** *Journal, Academic/Scholarly.*
Related titles: Online - full text ed.
Indexed: A26, E08, G08, GeoRef, I05, S06, S09, SASA, SpeleolAb, WildRev.
—Linda Hall.
Published by: Colorado-Wyoming Academy of Science, c/o David Gilliam, School of Behavioral Sciences, 501 20th St, University of Northern Colorado, PO Box 94, Greeley, CO 80639.

THE COLUMBIA SCIENCE AND TECHNOLOGY LAW REVIEW. *see* LAW

500 200 USA ISSN 1559-1409
COLUMBIA SERIES IN SCIENCE AND RELIGION. Text in English. 2000. irreg., latest 2009. price varies. back issues avail. **Document type:** *Monographic series, Academic/Scholarly.*
Published by: Columbia University Press, 61 W 62nd St, New York, NY 10023. TEL 212-459-0600, FAX 212-459-3678, orderentry@perseusbooks.com. Ed. Jennifer Crewe.

500 USA ISSN 1932-765X
➤ **COLUMBIA UNDERGRADUATE SCIENCE JOURNAL.** Abbreviated title: C U S J. Text in English. 2006. a. back issues avail. **Document type:** *Journal, Academic/Scholarly.* **Description:** Publishes manuscripts of the highest scholarship resulting from significant scientific research or outstanding scientific analysis.
Related titles: Online - full text ed.: ISSN 1932-7641. free (effective 2011).
Indexed: A01, CA, T02.
Published by: Columbia University Libraries, c/o CUL LDPD, 207A Butler Library, MC 1114, New York, NY 10027. journalism@libraries.cul.columbia.edu, http://www.columbia.edu/cu/lweb/. Eds. Asya Izraelit, Kimmy Szeto.

➤ **COMMUNICATIONS IN NONLINEAR SCIENCE AND NUMERICAL SIMULATION.** *see* MATHEMATICS

➤ **COMPENSATION OF LIFE SCIENTISTS IN THE UNITED STATES OF AMERICA.** *see* BUSINESS AND ECONOMICS—Labor And Industrial Relations

500 USA
COMPLEMENTARY SCIENCE. Text in English. 2003. irreg., latest 2008. price varies. **Document type:** *Monographic series, Academic/Scholarly.*
Published by: Academic Press (Subsidiary of: Elsevier Science & Technology), 525 B St, Ste 1900, San Diego, CA 92101-4495. TEL 619-231-6616, FAX 619-699-6422, JournalCustomerService-usa@elsevier.com, http://www.elsevierdirect.com/imprint.jsp?iid=5.

500 SGP ISSN 1793-4540
COMPLEX SYSTEMS AND INTERDISCIPLINARY SCIENCE. Text in English. 2007. irreg., latest vol.3, 2007. price varies. back issues avail. **Document type:** *Monographic series, Academic/Scholarly.* **Description:** Focuses on fundamental principles in the understanding, function and design of complex systems, with emphasis on generic aspects which recur across subjects and application domains.
Indexed: CCMJ, MSN, MathR.
—BLDSC (3364.584300), IE.
Published by: World Scientific Publishing Co. Pte. Ltd., 5 Toh Tuck Link, Singapore, 596224, Singapore. TEL 65-6466-5775, FAX 65-6467-7667, wspc@wspc.com.sg, http://www.worldscientific.com. Eds. Felix Reed-Tsochas, Neil Johnson. **Dist. by:** World Scientific Publishing Ltd., 57 Shelton St, London WC2H 9HE, United Kingdom. TEL 44-207-8360888, FAX 44-207-8362020, sales@wspc.co.uk; World Scientific Publishing Co., Inc., 27 Warren St, Ste 401-402, Hackensack, NJ 07601. TEL 201-487-9655, 800-227-7562, FAX 201-487-9656, 888-977-2665, wspc@wspc.com.

500 USA
COMPLEXITY DIGEST. Text in English. 1999. w. back issues avail. **Media:** Online - full text. **Related titles:** E-mail ed. Eds. Dean LeBaron, Gottfried Mayer.

500 510 NLD ISSN 1871-3033
COMPUTATIONAL METHODS IN APPLIED SCIENCES. Text in English. 2004. irreg., latest vol.16, 2008. price varies. **Document type:** *Monographic series, Academic/Scholarly.* **Description:** Covers the fields of mathematical and computational methods and modelling and their applications to major areas such as fluid dynamics, structural mechanics, semiconductor modelling, electromagnetics and CAD/CAM.
Indexed: P30.
Published by: Springer Netherlands (Subsidiary of: Springer Science+Business Media), Van Godewijckstraat 30, Dordrecht, 3311 GX, Netherlands. TEL 31-78-6576050, FAX 31-78-6576474. Ed. Eugenio Onate. Pub. Nathalie Jacobs.

COMPUTATIONAL, NUMERICAL AND MATHEMATICAL METHODS IN SCIENCES AND ENGINEERING. *see* ENGINEERING

509 609 ESP ISSN 1576-4826
CONECTA/CONECTA: BULLETIN OF NEWS IN THE HISTORY OF SCIENCE AND TECHNOLOGY; Boletin de Noticias sobre Historia de la Ciencia, la Medicina y la Tecnologia. Text in English, Spanish. 1995. fortn. **Document type:** *Bulletin, Academic/Scholarly.* **Description:** Aims to disseminate news and information to teachers, researchers, and other interested people on the history of science and technology.
Media: Online - full text.
Address: c/o Enrique Perdiguero, Miguel Hernandez University, Apartado de Correos 18, San Juan (Alicante), 03550, Spain. TEL 34-65919514, FAX 34-65919551. Ed., Pub., R&P Enrique Perdiguero.

CONFIGURATIONS; a journal of literature, science and technology. *see* LITERATURE

500 600 SWE ISSN 0074-9540
CONGRES INTERNATIONAL D'HISTOIRE DES SCIENCES. ACTES. Text in Swedish. 1947. quadrennial. **Document type:** *Proceedings.*
Published by: International Union of the History & Philosophy of Science, c/o Tore Frangsmyr, Office of History of Science, Uppsala University, Fack 256, Uppsala, 75105, Sweden.

500 FRA CODEN: CSSSAM
CONGRES NATIONAL DES SOCIETES HISTORIQUES ET SCIENTIFIQUES. ACTES. SECTION DES SCIENCES. Text in French. 1961. a. price varies. **Document type:** *Proceedings.*
Former titles: Congres National des Societes Savantes. Actes. Section des Sciences (0996-357X); (until 1985): Congres National des Societes Savantes. Comptes Renduus. Section des Sciences (0300-8010)
Indexed: GeoRef, SpeleolAb.
—CASDDS, Linda Hall. **CCC.**
Published by: Comite des Travaux Historiques et Scientifiques, 1 rue Descartes, Paris, Cedex 5 75231, France. TEL 33-1-46-34-47-57. Ed. Martine Francois.

▼ **CONGRESO DE INVESTIGACION. PROCEEDINGS.** *see* HUMANITIES: COMPREHENSIVE WORKS

CONGRESSIONAL REPORT: SCIENCE, ENERGY & ENVIRONMENT. *see* PUBLIC ADMINISTRATION

CONNECT (BRATTLEBORO); teachers' innovations in K - 8 science, math and technology. *see* EDUCATION—Teaching Methods And Curriculum

CONNECTED. *see* CHILDREN AND YOUTH—For

001.3 500 USA ISSN 0069-8970
Q11
CONNECTICUT ACADEMY OF ARTS AND SCIENCES. MEMOIRS. Text in English. 1810. irreg., latest vol.27, 2003. price varies. illus. back issues avail. **Document type:** *Monographic series, Trade.*
Related titles: Microform ed.: (from PQC).
Indexed: GeoRef, SpeleolAb.
—Linda Hall.
Published by: Connecticut Academy of Arts and Sciences, PO Box 208211, New Haven, CT 06520. TEL 203-432-3113, FAX 203-432-5712, caas@yale.edu.

CONNECTICUT ACADEMY OF ARTS AND SCIENCES. TRANSACTIONS. *see* HUMANITIES: COMPREHENSIVE WORKS

CONNECTICUT GEOLOGIC AND NATURAL HISTORY BULLETINS. *see* EARTH SCIENCES—Geology

500 600 MEX ISSN 0188-3240
CONOZCA MAS. Text in Spanish. 1990. m. MXN 279 domestic (effective 2010). **Document type:** *Magazine, Consumer.* **Description:** Covers a broad spectrum of current scientific and technological topics.
Published by: Editorial Televisa, Vasco de Quiroga 2000, Edificio E, Colonia Santa Fe, Mexico City, DF 01210, Mexico. TEL 52-55-52612761, FAX 52-55-52612704, info@editorialtelevisa.com, http://www.esmas.com/editorialtelevisa/.

CONTACT (RICHMOND); newsletter of the science teachers' association of victoria. *see* EDUCATION—Teaching Methods And Curriculum

CONTEMPORARY TRENDS AND ISSUES IN SCIENCE EDUCATION. *see* LIBRARY AND INFORMATION SCIENCES

500 NGA
➤ **CONTINENTAL JOURNAL OF APPLIED SCIENCES.** Text in English. 2007. a. NGN 2,500 domestic to individuals; USD 120 foreign to individuals; NGN 500 domestic to institutions; USD 200 foreign to institutions (effective 2010). Index. back issues avail.; reprints avail. **Document type:** *Journal, Academic/Scholarly.* **Description:** Contains original articles focusing on theories, methods and applications in applied science, engineering and technology.
Related titles: Online - full text ed.
Published by: Wilolud Journals, 2 Church Ave, Oke Eri qrt, Oba Ile, Ondo State 340001, Nigeria. TEL 234-803-4458674, managingeditor.olawale71@gmail.com. Ed. E.I. Adeyeye.

500 BRA ISSN 1516-7240
QH117
CONTRIBUICOES AVULSAS SOBRE A HISTORIA NATURAL DO BRASIL. SERIE HISTORIA DA HISTORIA NATURAL. Text in Portuguese. 1999. irreg.
Indexed: Z01.
Published by: Universidade Federal Rural do Rio de Janeiro, Instituto de Biologia, BR-465, Km 7, Seropedica, Rio de Janeiro, 23851-970, Brazil. http://www.ufrrj.br/institutos/ib/inicio.htm.

550 USA ISSN 0459-8113
Q11 CODEN: LAMSAX
➤ **CONTRIBUTIONS IN SCIENCE.** Text in English; Abstracts occasionally in Spanish. 1957. irreg., latest vol.517, 2008. back issues avail. **Document type:** *Monographic series, Academic/Scholarly.* **Description:** Covers topics in science.
Incorporates (1972-1978): Science Bulletin (0076-0935); Which was formerly (until 1972): Natural History Museum of Los Angeles County. Science Bulletin (0149-4155); (until 197?): Los Angeles County Museum of Natural History. Science Bulletin; (until 1966): Los Angeles County Museum. Science Bulletin
Related titles: Online - full text ed.: free (effective 2010).
Indexed: B25, BIOSIS Prev, GeoRef, MycolAb, RefZh, SpeleolAb, WildRev, Z01.
—Ingenta, INIST, Linda Hall.
Published by: Natural History Museum of Los Angeles County, 900 Exposition Blvd, Los Angeles, CA 90007. TEL 213-763-3426, FAX 213-763-3583, members@nhm.org.

500 CHE ISSN 1660-9972
CONTRIBUTIONS TO NATURAL HISTORY. Text in English. 2003. irreg. **Document type:** *Monographic series, Academic/Scholarly.*
Indexed: GeoRef, Z01.
Published by: Naturhistorisches Museum, Bernastr 15, Bern, 3005, Switzerland. TEL 41-31-3507111, FAX 41-31-3507499, contact@nmbe.ch, http://www.nmbe.unibe.ch/.

500 ESP ISSN 1575-6343
Q1
➤ **CONTRIBUTIONS TO SCIENCE.** Text in English; Summaries in English, Catalan. 1998. s-a. EUR 18.70 (effective 2009). Index. back issues avail. **Document type:** *Journal, Academic/Scholarly.*
Related titles: Online - full text ed.: ISSN 2013-410X. 1999.
—BLDSC (3461.225000), IE.
Published by: Institut d'Estudis Catalans, Carrer del Carme 47, Barcelona, 08001, Spain. TEL 34-932-701620, FAX 34-932-701180, informacio@iecat.net, http://www2.iecat.net. Ed. Salvador Reguant. Pub. Salvador Alegret.

500 DEU ISSN 0340-6857
CONTUBERNIUM. Text in German. 1971. irreg., latest vol.75, 2011. price varies. **Document type:** *Monographic series, Academic/Scholarly.*
Published by: Franz Steiner Verlag GmbH, Birkenwaldstr 44, Stuttgart, 70191, Germany. TEL 49-711-25820, FAX 49-711-2582290, service@steiner-verlag.de, http://www.steiner-verlag.de.

500 AUS
CODEN: CRSHEK
CORESEARCH. Text in English. irreg.
Indexed: INIS AtomInd.
Published by: C S I R O, Internal Communication, P O Box 225, Dickson, ACT 2602, Australia. TEL 61-2-62766639, FAX 61-2-62766273, publishing@csiro.au, http://www.publish.csiro.au/.

600 CHL ISSN 0717-3024
CORREO DE LA INNOVACION. Text in Spanish. 1996. q.
Published by: Ministerio de Economia, Programa de Innovacion Technologica, Ave Bernando O'Higgins 1316, Ofic 31, Santiago, Chile. TEL 56-2-696-1689, FAX 56-2-695-8698, sepit@pit.minecon.cl, http://www.innovacion.cl/.

COSINUS. *see* CHILDREN AND YOUTH—For

500 AUS ISSN 1832-522X
➤ **COSMOS**; the science of everything. Text in English. 2005. bi-m. AUD 49 in Australia & New Zealand; AUD 65 elsewhere; AUD 9.95 newsstand/cover (effective 2009). adv. back issues avail. **Document type:** *Magazine, Academic/Scholarly.* **Description:** Treats science as culture, covering it from many angles: art, design, travel, interviews, humor, history and opinion.
Related titles: Online - full text ed.
Published by: Luna Media Pty Ltd, PO Box 302, Sydney, NSW 2012, Australia. TEL 61-2-93108500, FAX 61-2-96984899, enquiries@lunamedia.com.au, http://www.lunamedia.com.au. Ed. Wilson da Silva TEL 61-2-93108502. Pub., Adv. contact Kylie Ahern TEL 61-2-93108501. Circ: 20,000.

500.9 GBR ISSN 0011-023X
COUNTRY-SIDE; a wildlife magazine. Text in English. 1905. a. free to members (effective 2009). bk.rev. illus.; stat. back issues avail. **Document type:** *Magazine, Consumer.* **Description:** Features on meetings, rambles, conferences and the like which should be of interest to the naturalist.
Incorporates (1980-1982): British Naturalist (0144-9761); Formerly (until 1920): Country-Side Leaflet
Indexed: F&GI, G05, G06, G07, G08, KWIWR.
Published by: British Naturalists' Association, c/o General Secretary, PO Box 5682, Corby, Northamptonshire NN17 2ZW, United Kingdom. TEL 44-1536-262977, info@bna-naturalists.org. **Subscr. to:** Mrs. Y. Griffiths.

508 FRA ISSN 0011-0477
LE COURRIER DE LA NATURE; revue nationale de protection de la nature. Text in French. 1967. bi-m. EUR 35 (effective 2009). adv. bk.rev. bibl.; illus. index. back issues avail.
Formerly (until 1977): Courrier de la Nature, l'Homme et l'Oiseau (1162-4671)
Indexed: RefZh.
—BLDSC (3482.969000), IE, Ingenta, INIST.
Published by: Societe Nationale de Protection de la Nature, 9 rue Cels, Paris, 75014, France. TEL 33-1-43201539, FAX 33-1-43201571, snpn@wanadoo.fr. Ed. M Gallois. Circ: 20,000.

500 DZA ISSN 1112-3338
COURRIER DU SAVOIR SCIENTIFIQUE ET TECHNIQUE/BARID AL-MA'RIFAT AL-'ILMIYYAT WA AL-TIQNIYYAT. Text in Arabic, French. 2001. s-a.
Published by: Universite Mohamed Khider de Biskra, Direction de la Publication, BP 145, Biskra, 07000, Algeria.

500 USA ISSN 0070-1416
Q11
CRANBROOK INSTITUTE OF SCIENCE, BLOOMFIELD HILLS, MICHIGAN. BULLETIN. Text in English. 1931. irreg., latest vol.62, 1996. price varies. adv. bk.rev. reprints avail. **Document type:** *Bulletin.* **Description:** Disseminates scientific information concerning Michigan and the Great Lakes region. Aimed at practicing scientists, serious students and the interested public.
Published by: Cranbrook Institute of Science, PO Box 801, Bloomfield Hills, MI 48303-0801. TEL 313-645-3203, FAX 313-645-3050. Ed., R&P Marion M Sisneros.

CREATION; ex nihilo. *see* RELIGIONS AND THEOLOGY

CREATION MATTERS. *see* RELIGIONS AND THEOLOGY

231.765 USA ISSN 0092-9166
BS651
➤ **CREATION RESEARCH SOCIETY QUARTERLY.** Abbreviated title: C R S Q. Text in English. 1964. q. USD 38 domestic to non-members; USD 56 in Canada & Mexico to non-members; USD 73 elsewhere to non-members; free to members (effective 2010); subscr. includes Creation Matters. bk.rev. index. back issues avail.; reprints avail. **Document type:** *Journal, Academic/Scholarly.* **Description:** Presents original research and reviews pertinent to the study of origins science, creation and evolution.
Related titles: Microfilm ed.: (from PQC); Online - full text ed.: free to members (effective 2010).
Indexed: A22, ChrPI, Z01.
Published by: Creation Research Society, PO Box 8263, St. Joseph, MO 64508. TEL 928-636-1153, contact@creationresearch.org. Ed. Kevin L Anderson.

500 CHL ISSN 0716-0313
CRECES. Text in Spanish. 1979. m. USD 70. adv. bk.rev.
Indexed: IBR, IBZ.
Address: Bustos, 2030, Providencia, Santiago, Chile. TEL 2-496692, TELEX 341011. Ed. Fernando Monckeberg. Circ: 12,000.

500 MNE ISSN 0350-5464
QH7 CODEN: GOPUEX
CRNOGORSKA AKADEMIJA NAUKA I UMJETNOSTI. ODJELJENJE PRIRODNIH NAUKA. GLASNIK. Text in Serbian. 1974. a. EUR 5 per issue (effective 2007). **Document type:** *Journal, Academic/Scholarly.*
Indexed: GeoRef, RefZh, Z01.
—Linda Hall.
Published by: Crnogorska Akademija Nauka i Umjetnosti, Odjeljenje Prirodnih Nauka, Rista Stijovica 5, Podgorica, 81000. TEL 381-81-655456, FAX 381-81-655451, canu@cg.yu, http://www.canu.cg.yu.

500 FRA ISSN 1250-6028
CROISEE DES SCIENCES. Variant title: Collection Croisee des Sciences. Text in French. 1994. irreg. price varies. **Document type:** *Monographic series, Academic/Scholarly.*
Published by: Centre National de la Recherche Scientifique, Campus Gerard-Megie, 3 Rue Michel-Ange, Paris, 75794, France. TEL 33-1-44964000, FAX 33-1-44965390, http://www.cnrseditions.fr.

CRONOS. *see* MEDICAL SCIENCES

500 300 USA ISSN 1075-5608
CROSS-THINKING FOR DISCOVERY AND CREATIVITY. Text in English. 1992. q. looseleaf. USD 12. back issues avail.
Published by: Cross-Thinking, PO Box 449, Reese, MI 48757. TEL 517-662-4169. Eds. Deborah Italvorson, Kermit Kranz.

500 GBR ISSN 0309-6149
CROYDON NATURAL HISTORY & SCIENTIFIC SOCIETY. BULLETIN. Text in English. 1967. 3/yr. bk.rev. bibl. **Document type:** *Bulletin, Trade.* **Description:** Contains the notice of the Annual general meeting of the society, the Directors' report and the Accountants' report as well as various articles, usually of local interest, and general society information.
Published by: Croydon Natural History & Scientific Society Ltd., 96a Brighton Rd, South Croydon, Surrey CR2 6AD, United Kingdom. Ed. J Greig.

507 CAN ISSN 0381-8047
CODEN: CRUCDE
CRUCIBLE. Text in English. 196?. 5/yr. free to members. adv. bk.rev. illus. **Document type:** *Magazine, Trade.* **Description:** Covers innovative approaches to science education for high school teachers.
Indexed: C03, CEI, P11, P48, P52, P56, PQC.
—CASDDS.
Published by: S T A O / A P S O, Box 771, Dresden, ON N0P 1M0, Canada. TEL 800-461-2264, FAX 800-754-1654, paul_weese@stao.org, http://www.stao.org/index.html. Circ: 2,600.

500 600 ARG ISSN 1852-0626
CUADERNOS DE CIENCIA Y TECNICA. Text in Spanish. 2003. s-a. **Document type:** *Journal, Academic/Scholarly.*
Published by: Universidad Nacional de la Pampa, Coronel Gil No. 353, Santa Rosa, Argentina. TEL 54-2954-451600, info@unlpam.edu.ar, http://www.unlpam.edu.ar/.

500 600 MEX ISSN 2007-0411
CULTURA CIENTIFICA Y TECNOLOGICA. Text in Spanish. 2004. irreg. **Document type:** *Journal, Academic/Scholarly.*
Related titles: Online - full text ed.: free (effective 2011).
Indexed: F04, T02.
Published by: Universidad Autonoma de Ciudad Juarez, Henri Dunant 4016, Zona Pronaf, Ciudad Juarez, Chihuahua 32310, Mexico. TEL 52-656-6882100. Ed. Victoriano Garza Almanza.

CULTURAL STUDIES OF SCIENCE EDUCATION. *see* EDUCATION—Teaching Methods And Curriculum

▼ **CULTURE FRAME.** *see* HUMANITIES: COMPREHENSIVE WORKS

500 USA ISSN 1947-9794
▼➤ **CURRENT ADVANCES IN SCIENCE & TECHNOLOGY.** Abbreviated title: C A S T. Text in English, Chinese. 2009 (Dec.). m. free (effective 2010). **Document type:** *Journal, Academic/Scholarly.* **Description:** Includes original research, reviews and commentary from all disciplines within science and technology.
Media: Online - full content.
Published by: The C A S T Journal, 2252 Spring Pointe Dr, Baton Rouge, LA 70810. TEL 225-578-9670, qilongxu@gmail.com.

➤ **CURRENT SCIENCE.** *see* CHILDREN AND YOUTH—For

500 IND ISSN 0011-3891
Q1 CODEN: CUSCAM
➤ **CURRENT SCIENCE**; a fortnightly journal of research. Text in English. 1932. fortn. INR 1,000 domestic to individuals; USD 100 foreign to individuals; INR 3,000 domestic to institutions; USD 300 foreign to institutions; INR 100, USD 15 per issue; free to members (effective 2011). adv. bk.rev. illus. index. 120 p./no. 2 cols./p.; back issues avail.; reprints avail. **Document type:** *Journal, Academic/Scholarly.* **Description:** Contains original research and review articles that involve science and scientific activities.
Related titles: Microfilm ed.: (from PQC); Online - full text ed.: 1997. free (effective 2011).
Indexed: A01, A20, A22, A28, A29, A34, A35, A36, A37, A38, APA, ASFA, AgBio, AgrForAb, ApicAb, B20, B21, B23, B25, BA, BIOSIS Prev, BP, BrCerAb, C&ISA, C25, C30, CA, CA/WCA, CABA, CCMJ, CIA, CLL, CTA, CTFA, CerAb, ChemAb, ChemoAb, CivEngAb, CorrAb, CurCR, CurCont, D01, DBA, E&CAJ, E11, E12, E17, EEA, EMA, ESPM, EntAb, EnvEAb, F08, F11, F12, FCA, FR, FS&TA, FaBeAb, G02, G11, GH, GenetAb, GeoRef, H&SSA, H15, H16, H17, I10, I11, INIS AtomInd, ISR, IndVet, Inspec, LT, M&GPA, M&TEA, M09, MBF, METADEX, MSN, MaizeAb, MathR, MycolAb, N02, N03, N04, N05, NSA, NucAcAb, NumL, O01, OR, P30, P32, P33, P34, P37, P38, P39, P40, PGegResA, PGrRegA, PHN&I, PN&I, PollutAb, R07, R08, R11, R12, R13, R16, RA&MP, RM&VM, RRTA, S&MA, S12, S13, S16, S17, SCI, SCOPUS, SSciA, SWRA, SolStAb, SoyAb, SpeleolAb, T02, T04, T05, TAR, TOSA, ToxAb, TriticAb, VITIS, VS, VirolAbstr, W07, W08, W10, W11, WAA, Z01.
—BLDSC (3504.000000), AskIEEE, CASDDS, GNLM, IE, Infotrieve, Ingenta, INIST, Linda Hall.
Published by: (Current Science Association), Indian Academy of Sciences, C.V. Raman Ave, Sadashivanagar, PO Box 8005, Bangalore, Karnataka 560 080, India. TEL 91-80-22661200, FAX 91-80-23616094, office@ias.ernet.in. Ed. P Balaram.

505 USA ISSN 1946-5203
CURRENTS (LOS ALAMOS). Text in English. 2000. m. free (effective 2009). back issues avail. **Document type:** *Magazine, Trade.* **Description:** Focuses on the people behind the Los Alamos National Laboratory's science and other initiatives.
Formerly (until 2008): Los Alamos News Letter
Media: Online - full content.
Published by: Los Alamos National Laboratory, Bikini Atoll Rd, SM 30, PO Box 1663, Los Alamos, NM 87545. TEL 505-664-5265. Ed. Paris-Chitanvis Jacqueline TEL 505-665-7779.

500 NOR ISSN 1890-081X
D K N V S 'S MEDDELELSER. (Det Kongelige Norske Videnskabers Selskab) Text in Norwegian. 2005. irreg. **Document type:** *Monographic series, Consumer.*
Related titles: Online - full text ed.
Published by: Det Kongelige Norske Videnskabers Selskab/The Royal Norwegian Society of Sciences and Letters, Erling Skakkes Gate 47 C, Trondheim, 7491, Norway. TEL 47-73-592157, FAX 47-73-595895, postmaster@dknvs.no, http://www.dknvs.no.

DAEDALUS. *see* HUMANITIES: COMPREHENSIVE WORKS

DAEDALUS (STOCKHOLM); tekniska museets aarsbok. *see* MUSEUMS AND ART GALLERIES

500 JPN ISSN 0912-2346
AS552.D3
DAITO BUNKA DAIGAKU KIYO. SHIZEN KAGAKU/DAITO BUNKA UNIVERSITY. BULLETIN. NATURAL SCIENCES. Text and summaries in English, Japanese. a.
Published by: Daito Bunka University/Daito Bunka Daigaku, 9-1, Takashimadaira, 1-chome, Itabashi-ku, Tokyo, 175, Japan.

507.11 USA
DAKOTA SCIENTIST. Text in English. 1921. m. free. **Document type:** *Newspaper.* **Description:** News of issues and trends in technology and applied science education and ccollege activities.
Published by: North Dakota State College of Science, Information Publications, Wahpeton, ND 58076-0002. TEL 701-671-2248, FAX 701-671-2145. Ed. Blayne F Helgeson. Circ: 4,000.

500 CHN ISSN 1672-2345
➤ **DALI XUEYUAN XUEBAO/DALI UNIVERSITY. JOURNAL.** Text in Chinese; Abstracts in Chinese, English. 1980. m. CNY 120, USD 120; CNY 10, USD 10 per issue (effective 2009). **Document type:** *Journal, Academic/Scholarly.*
Formerly (until 2002): Dali Shi-Zhuan Xuebao (1008-9748); Which supersedes in part (in 1985): Xiaguan Shi-Zhuan Xuebao; Which was formerly (until 1981): Xiaguan Shi-Zhuan
Related titles: Online - full text ed.
Published by: Dali Xueyuan/Dali University, 2, Gucheng Hongsheng Lu, Dali, 671003, China. TEL 86-872-2219939, FAX 86-872-2219938, xbzk@dali.edu.cn, eoj@dali.edu.cn, http://www.dali.edu.cn/. Ed. Jinfu Qian. Circ: 1,500.

500 CHN ISSN 1674-1404
HD9720.1 CODEN: DGDXAP
➤ **DALIAN GONGYE DAXUE XUEBAO/DALIAN DALIAN POLYTECHNIC UNIVERSITY. JOURNAL.** Text in Chinese; Abstracts in Chinese, English. 1981. bi-m. CNY 10 per issue (effective 2010). **Document type:** *Journal, Academic/Scholarly.* **Description:** Covers the latest developments of theoretical and applied researches in the fields of Science and Engineering.
Formerly (until 2007): Dalian Qinggongye Xueyuan Xuebao/Dalian Institute of Light Industry. Journal (1005-4014)
Related titles: Online - full text ed.
Indexed: A28, A32, A35, A37, APA, AgBio, B&BAb, B19, B21, BrCerAb, C&ISA, C25, CA/WCA, CABA, CIA, CerAb, CivEngAb, CorrAb, E&CAJ, E11, E12, EEA, EMA, ESPM, EnvEAb, F08, F11, F12, FCA, GH, H15, H16, I10, I11, LT, M&TEA, M09, MBF, METADEX, MaizeAb, N02, N03, O01, P32, P40, R13, RA&MP, RRTA, S12, S13, S16, SWRA, SolStAb, SoyAb, T04, T05, WAA.
—BLDSC (4732.664500), IE, Ingenta, Linda Hall.
Published by: Dalian Gongye Daxue/Dalian Polytechnic University, 1, Qinggongyuan, Ganjingzi District, Dalian, 116034, China. TEL 86-411-86324490, FAX 86-411-86323650. Ed. Gui-wei Liu. Circ: 1,500.

500 CHN ISSN 1006-7736
HE561
DALIAN HAISHI DAXUE XUEBAO/DALIAN MARITIME UNIVERSITY. JOURNAL. Text in Chinese. 1957. q. back issues avail. **Document type:** *Journal, Academic/Scholarly.*
Formerly: Dalian Haiyun Xueyuan Xuebao/Dalian Marine College. Journal (1000-1689)
Related titles: Online - full text ed.
Indexed: A28, APA, B21, BrCerAb, C&ISA, CA/WCA, CIA, CerAb, CivEngAb, CorrAb, E&CAJ, E11, EEA, EMA, ESPM, EnvEAb, H&SSA, H15, M&TEA, M09, MBF, METADEX, RefZh, SCOPUS, SolStAb, T04, WAA.
—Linda Hall.

Published by: Dalian Haishi Daxue Qikanshe, 7, Gangwan St., Rm.401, Times Bldg., Dalian, 116001, China. TEL 86-411-84727810, FAX 86-411-84729692.

500 CHN ISSN 1673-9590
Q295 CODEN: DTXBEI
DALIAN JIAOTONG DAXUE XUEBAO/DALIAN INSTITUTE OF RAILWAY TECHNOLOGY. JOURNAL. Text in Chinese; Abstracts in Chinese, English. 1980. bi-m. CNY 90, USD 90; CNY 15 newsstand/cover (effective 2009). **Document type:** *Journal, Academic/Scholarly.*
Formerly (until 2007): Dalian Tiedao Xueyuan Xuebao/Dalian Institute of Railway Technology. Journal (1000-1670)
Related titles: Online - full text ed.
—BLDSC (3517.773000).
Published by: Dalian Jiaotong Daxue, 794, Huanghe Lu, Dalian, 116028, China. TEL 86-411-84109976, FAX 86-411-84109369. Ed. Jiping Ge.

500 CHN ISSN 1000-8608
T4 CODEN: DLXUEJ
DALIAN LIGONG DAXUE XUEBAO/DALIAN UNIVERSITY OF TECHNOLOGY. JOURNAL. Text in Chinese; Abstracts in Chinese, English. 1950. bi-m. CNY 15 newsstand/cover (effective 2009). **Document type:** *Journal, Academic/Scholarly.* **Description:** Covers the latest developments of theoretical and applied researches in the fields of engineering, electronics, computer science, applied mathematics and physics.
Related titles: Online - full text ed.
Indexed: A22, A28, APA, ASFA, ApMecR, BrCerAb, C&ISA, CA/WCA, CCMJ, CIA, CPEI, CerAb, CivEngAb, CorrAb, E&CAJ, E11, EEA, EMA, ESPM, EngInd, EnvEAb, H15, Inspec, M&TEA, M09, MBF, METADEX, MSN, MathR, OceAb, RefZh, SCOPUS, SolStAb, T04, WAA, Z02.
—BLDSC (4732.666000), AskIEEE, CASDDS, East View, IE, Ingenta, INIST, Linda Hall.
Published by: Dalian Ligong Daxue/Dalian University of Technology, 320 Xinxiang, Dalian, 116023, China. TEL 86-411-84708608, FAX 86-411-84701466. Ed. Geng-Dong Cheng. Circ: 1,500. **Dist. overseas by:** China International Book Trading Corp, 35 Chegongzhuang Xilu, Haidian District, PO Box 399, Beijing 100044, China. TEL 86-10-68412045, FAX 86-10-68412023, cibtc@mail.cibtc.com.cn, http://www.cibtc.com.cn.

500 CHN ISSN 1009-315X
AS452.D34
DALIAN MINZU XUEYUAN XUEBAO/DALIAN NATIONALITIES UNIVERSITY. JOURNAL. Text in Chinese; Abstracts in Chinese, English. 1999. bi-m. CNY 48 domestic; USD 40 foreign; USD 8 newsstand/cover (effective 2007). **Document type:** *Journal, Academic/Scholarly.*
Related titles: Online - full text ed.
Indexed: A28, A34, A35, A36, A37, APA, AgBio, B23, BrCerAb, C&ISA, C25, C30, CA/WCA, CABA, CIA, CerAb, CivEngAb, CorrAb, D01, E&CAJ, E11, E12, EEA, EMA, ESPM, EnvEAb, F08, F12, G11, GH, H15, H16, IndVet, L&LBA, LT, M&TEA, M09, MBF, METADEX, MaizeAb, N02, N03, N04, O01, OR, P32, P40, PAIS, PGrRegA, PHN&I, PSA, R12, S13, S16, SociolAb, SolStAb, T04, TAR, VS, W10, W11, WAA, Z02.
Published by: Dalian Minzu Xueyuan/Dalian Nationalities University, Dalian Development Zone, 18, Liaohe Xi Lu, Dalian, 116600, China. TEL 86-411-87656296, FAX 86-411-87656295. Ed. Yu-qing Zhao.

500 SYR
➤ **DAMASCUS UNIVERSITY JOURNAL FOR THE BASIC SCIENCES.** Text in Arabic, English, French; Summaries in English, French. 1996. **Document type:** *Journal, Academic/Scholarly.*
Published by: University of Damascus, c/o Y. Koudsi, Ed., P O Box 31753, Damascus, Syria. Ed. Dr. Yahia Koudsi.

500 DNK ISSN 1901-7138
DANISH COUNCILS FOR INDEPENDENT RESEARCH. ANNUAL REPORT. Text in English. 2006. a. **Document type:** *Corporate.*
Related titles: Online - full text ed.: ISSN 1901-7146; ◆ Danish ed.: Det Frie Forskningsraad. Aarsrapport. ISSN 1604-6765.
Published by: (Det Frie Forskningsraad/Danish Councils on Independent Research), Forsknings- og Innovationsstyrelsen/Danish Agency for Science, Technology and Innovation, Bredgade 40, Copenhagen K, 1260, Denmark. TEL 45-35-446200, FAX 45-35-446201, fi@fi.dk, http://www.fi.dk.

500 IRN ISSN 1607-9884
DANISHGAH-I AL-ZAHRA. 'ULUM-I PAYAH/AL-ZAHRA UNIVERSITY. JOURNAL OF SCIENCE. Text in Arabic. 1989. s-a.
Indexed: INIS AtomInd.
Published by: Danishgah-i Al-Zahra/Al-Zahra University, PO Box 1993891167, Vanak, Tehran, Iran. TEL 98-21-80440519, FAX 98-21-8035187, http://www.alzahra.ac.ir/.

DANYAG; journal of studies in the humanities, education and the sciences, basic and applied. *see* HUMANITIES: COMPREHENSIVE WORKS

DAQING SHIFAN XUEYUAN XUEBAO/DAQING NORMAL UNIVERSITY. JOURNAL. *see* SOCIAL SCIENCES: COMPREHENSIVE WORKS

500 SAU ISSN 1319-0148
AL DARAT. Text in Arabic. 1975. q. **Document type:** *Magazine, Academic/Scholarly.*
Indexed: P30.
Published by: King Abdulaziz Foundation for Research and Archives, PO Box 2945, Riyadh, 11461, Saudi Arabia. TEL 966-4011999, FAX 966-4013597, info@darah.org.sa, http://www.darah.org.sa.

500 ITA ISSN 1824-2448
DARWIN. Text in Italian. 2004. bi-m. EUR 25 (effective 2008). **Document type:** *Magazine, Consumer.*
Published by: Arnoldo Mondadori Editore SpA, Via Mondadori 1, Segrate, 20090, Italy. TEL 39-02-66814363, FAX 39-030-3198412, http://www.mondadori.com.

500 CHN ISSN 1002-6908
DAZHONG KEXUE/POPULAR SCIENCE. Text in Chinese. 1980. m. CNY 60 (effective 2009). **Document type:** *Magazine, Consumer.*
Published by: Guizhou Sheng Kexue Jishu Xiehui/Guizhou Association for Science and Technology, 48, Ruijin Nan Lu, Guiyang, 550002, China. TEL 86-851-5833752, gzkx2008@126.com, http://www.gzast.org/index111.asp.

500 CHN ISSN 0255-7800
QH7
DAZIRAN/NATURE. Text in Chinese. q. USD 37.20 (effective 2009).
Indexed: GeoRef, ISR, SpeleolAb.
—East View, Linda Hall.
Published by: (Beijing Ziran Bowuguan/Beijing Natural History Museum), Daziran Zazhishe, 126 Tianqiao Nandajie, Beijing, 100050, China. TEL 754431. Ed. Jin Jianming.

500 CHN ISSN 1000-4041
CODEN: TATAF5
➤ **DAZIRAN TANSUO/EXPLORATION OF NATURE.** Text in Chinese. 1983. m. USD 49.20 (effective 2009). bk.rev. **Document type:** *Journal, Academic/Scholarly.* **Description:** Covers new theories of natural science, interdisciplinary programs, scientific studies, and history of science and technology.
Related titles: Online - full text ed.
—CASDDS, East View.
Published by: Sichuan Kexue Jishu Chubanshe, Yi-Huan Lu Nan 1-Duan, no.1, Hongxi Huayuan Hongyun Lou C3-1406, Chengdu, Sichuan 610021, China. Circ: 4,000 (paid).

500 ESP ISSN 1577-1261
F1401
DEBATE Y PERSPECTIVAS. Text in Multiple languages. 2000. a. **Document type:** *Magazine, Consumer.*
Published by: Fundacion Mapfre, Paseo de Recoletos, 23, Madrid, 28004, Spain. TEL 34-91-5812353, FAX 34-91-5816070, fundacion.informacion@mafre.com, http://www.fundacionmapfre.com.

505 FRA ISSN 1621-0085
DECOUVERTE. Text in French. 1972. m. (10/yr.). EUR 25 domestic; EUR 31 foreign (effective 2009). adv. bk.rev. illus. back issues avail.
Formerly (until 1999): Palais de la Decouverte. Revue (0339-7521)
Indexed: FR, GeoRef, INIS AtomInd, P30, SpeleolAb.
—BLDSC (3540.280000), INIST, Linda Hall.
Published by: Palais de la Decouverte, Av. Franklin D. Roosevelt, Paris, 75008, France. TEL 33-1-56432023. Ed., Pub. Michel Demazure. R&P, Adv. contact Martine Pene. Circ: 5,000 (paid).

500 001.3 ITA ISSN 1974-1960
DEDALUS; laboratorio di scienza, filosofia, cultura. Text in Italian. 2006. q. **Document type:** *Journal, Academic/Scholarly.*
Published by: Associazione Culturale AlboVersorio, Via Torino 11B, Senago, MI 20030, Italy. TEL 39-340-9247340, http://www.alboversorio.it. Eds. Laura Querci, Massimiliano Cappuccio.

DEFENCE SCIENCE JOURNAL. *see* MILITARY

500 FRA ISSN 1163-619X
LES DEFIS DU C E A; mensuel d'informations generales et scientifiques. (Commissariat a l'Energie Atomique) Text in French. 1991. m. free.
Indexed: INIS AtomInd.
Published by: Commissariat a l'Energie Atomique, Direction de la Communication, Batiment Le Ponant D, 25 Rue Leblanc, Paris, 75015, France. http://www.cea.fr. Ed. Brigitte Morin Blanch. Pub. Jean Louis Chambon.

500 600 CZE ISSN 0300-4414
CODEN: DVTDAE
➤ **DEJINY VED A TECHNIKY/HISTORY OF SCIENCES AND TECHNOLOGY.** Text in Czech; Summaries in English, French, German. 1968. q. EUR 109, USD 130 foreign (effective 2009). bk.rev. index. **Document type:** *Journal, Academic/Scholarly.* **Description:** History of natural sciences, medicine and technology, including the history of scientific institutions, conditions of scientific work, and social status of scientists.
Indexed: CA, FR, HistAb, MathR, P30, RASB, SCOPUS, T02, Z02.
—Linda Hall.
Published by: Spolecnost pro Dejiny Ved a Techniky/Society for the History of Science and Technology, Gabcikova 2362/10, Prague 8, 18200, Czech Republic. TEL 420-2-86010118, barvikova@mua.cas.cz. Ed. Pavel Drabek. Circ: 1,000. **Subscr. to:** Myris Trade Ltd., V Stihlach 1311, PO Box 2, Prague 4 14201, Czech Republic. TEL 420-2-34035200, FAX 420-2-34035207, myris@myris.cz, http://www.myris.cz.

500 600 CHL ISSN 0717-7887
DELEGATION REGIONALE DE COOPERATION DANS LE CONE SUD ET LE BRESIL. BULLETIN ELETRONIQUE. Text in French. 2002. m. **Document type:** *Bulletin, Trade.*
Media: Online - full text.
Published by: Comision Nacional de Investigacion Cientifica y Tecnologica, Canada 308, Piso 2, Providencia, Santiago de Chile, Chile. TEL 56-2-3654463, FAX 56-2-6551395, http://www.conicy.cl.

500 EGY ISSN 1012-5965
Q1 CODEN: DJSCES
DELTA JOURNAL OF SCIENCE. Text in English. 1977. a. **Document type:** *Journal, Academic/Scholarly.*
—BLDSC (3548.292500).
Published by: Tanta University, Faculty of Science, Tanta University Press, Tanta, Egypt. TEL 20-40-3344352 ext 112. Ed. Dr. Muhammad Ezzat Abdel-Munssef.

500 USA ISSN 0190-1850
QH70.U62
DENVER MUSEUM OF NATURAL HISTORY. ANNUAL REPORT. Text in English. a. **Document type:** *Corporate.*
Indexed: GeoRef, SpeleolAb.
Published by: Denver Museum of Nature & Science, 2001 Colorado Blvd, Denver, CO 80205. TEL 303-370-8334, FAX 303-331-6492. Ed. Michelle Kubiic. R&P Michelle Kubic.

500 USA ISSN 1948-9293
QH45.5
▼ **DENVER MUSEUM OF NATURE & SCIENCE ANNALS.** Text in English. 2009. irreg. (2-4/yr.). price varies. **Document type:** *Journal, Academic/Scholarly.* **Description:** Research on anthropology, geology, paleontology, botany, zoology, space and planetary sciences, and health sciences.
Related titles: Online - full text ed.: ISSN 1948-9307. free (effective 2009).
Indexed: Z01.
Published by: Denver Museum of Nature & Science, 2001 Colorado Blvd, Denver, CO 80205. TEL 303-322-7009, 800-925-2250, kris.haglund@dmns.org.

500 GBR ISSN 1478-0585
DESIGN AND NATURE. Text in English. 2002. irreg., latest vol.9, 2008. price varies. back issues avail. **Document type:** *Monographic series, Academic/Scholarly.* **Description:** Provides in depth coverage of such topics as mathematics in nature, evolution, natural selection, vision and acoustic systems, robotics, shape in nature, biomimetics, and creativity.
Indexed: EngInd, SCOPUS, SSciA.
Published by: W I T Press, Ashurst Lodge, Ashurst, Southampton, Hants SO40 7AA, United Kingdom. TEL 44-238-0293223, FAX 44-238-0292853, marketing@witpress.com.

500 DEU ISSN 0070-3974
DEUTSCHE FORSCHUNGSGEMEINSCHAFT. DENKSCHRIFTEN ZUR LAGE DER DEUTSCHEN WISSENSCHAFT. Text in German. 1957. irreg., latest 2008. price varies. bk.rev. **Document type:** *Monographic series, Academic/Scholarly.*
Related titles: Online - full text ed.
Published by: (Deutsche Forschungsgemeinschaft), Wiley - V C H Verlag GmbH & Co. KGaA (Subsidiary of: John Wiley & Sons, Inc.), Postfach 101161, Weinheim, 69451, Germany. TEL 49-6201-606400, FAX 49-6201-606184, subservice@wiley-vch.de, http://www.wiley-vch.de.

500 DEU ISSN 0070-3982
DEUTSCHE FORSCHUNGSGEMEINSCHAFT. FORSCHUNGSBERICHTE. Text in German. 1957. irreg., latest 2004. price varies. **Document type:** *Monographic series, Academic/Scholarly.*
Indexed: GeoRef, SpeleolAb.
Published by: (Deutsche Forschungsgemeinschaft), Wiley - V C H Verlag GmbH & Co. KGaA (Subsidiary of: John Wiley & Sons, Inc.), Postfach 101161, Weinheim, 69451, Germany. TEL 49-6201-606400, FAX 49-6201-606184, subservice@wiley-vch.de, http://www.wiley-vch.de. Ed. Gerd Mauer.

500 DEU
AS182.D39
DEUTSCHE FORSCHUNGSGEMEINSCHAFT. JAHRESBERICHT. AUFGABEN UND ERGEBNISSE. Text in German. 1921. a. **Document type:** *Bulletin, Trade.*
Former titles (until 2000): Deutsche Forschungsgemeinschaft. Jahresbericht. Band 1: Aufgaben und Ergebnisse (0942-7813); (until 1991): Deutsche Forschungsgemeinschaft. Taetigkeitsbericht (0934-9030); (until 1980): Deutsche Forschungsgemeinschaft. Jahresbericht. Band 1: Taetigkeitsbericht (0340-1359); Which superseded in part (in 1970): Bericht der Deutschen Forschungsgemeinschaft ueber Ihre Taetigkeit (0418-8411); Which was formerly (until 1952): Bericht der Notgemeinschaft der Deutschen Wissenschaft ueber Ihre Taetigkeit (0340-1308)
Indexed: GeoRef, RASB, SpeleolAb.
—BLDSC (4633.915200), INIST.
Published by: Deutsche Forschungsgemeinschaft, Kennedyallee 40, Bonn, 53175, Germany. TEL 49-228-8851, FAX 49-228-8852777, postmaster@dfg.de.

500 DEU ISSN 0934-9049
DEUTSCHE FORSCHUNGSGEMEINSCHAFT. JAHRESBERICHT. PROGRAMME UND PROJEKTE. Text in German. 1921. a. **Document type:** *Bulletin, Trade.*
Formerly (until 1981): Deutsche Forschungsgemeinschaft. Jahresbericht. Band 2: Programme und Projekte (0340-1251); Which superseded in part (in 1970): Bericht der Deutschen Forschungsgemeinschaft ueber Ihre Taetigkeit (0418-8411); Which was formerly (until 1952): Bericht der Notgemeinschaft der Deutschen Wissenschaft ueber Ihre Taetigkeit (0340-1308)
Indexed: SpeleolAb.
—GNLM, INIST.
Published by: Deutsche Forschungsgemeinschaft, Kennedyallee 40, Bonn, 53175, Germany. TEL 49-228-8851, FAX 49-228-8852777, postmaster@dfg.de.

500 DEU ISSN 0418-842X
F1203
DEUTSCHE FORSCHUNGSGEMEINSCHAFT. MEXIKO-PROJEKT; eine deutsch-mexikanische interdisziplinaere Regionalforschung im Becken von Puebla-Tlaxcala. Text in German, Spanish. 1968. irreg., latest vol.21, 1991. price varies. **Document type:** *Monographic series, Academic/Scholarly.*
Indexed: GeoRef, SpeleolAb.
Published by: (Deutsche Forschungsgemeinschaft), Franz Steiner Verlag GmbH, Birkenwaldstr 44, Stuttgart, 70191, Germany. TEL 49-711-25820, FAX 49-711-2582290, service@steiner-verlag.de, http://www.steiner-verlag.de. Ed. Wilhelm Lauer. R&P Sabine Koerner.

500 BGD ISSN 1022-2502
AS472.D3 CODEN: DJOSEM
THE DHAKA UNIVERSITY JOURNAL OF SCIENCE. Text in English. 1970 (vol.18). irreg.?. bibl.; charts. **Document type:** *Journal, Academic/Scholarly.*
Former titles (until 1997): Dhaka University Studies. Part B: Science (0259-7365); Dacca University Studies. Part B: Science (0253-5467)
Related titles: CD-ROM ed.
Indexed: BAS, ExtraMED, P30.
—CASDDS.
Published by: (Department of Physics), University of Dhaka, Ramna, Dhaka, 1000, Bangladesh.

500 CHN ISSN 1673-9140
DIANLI KEXUE YU JISHU XUEBAO/JOURNAL OF ELECTRIC POWER SCIENCE AND TECHNOLOGY. Variant title: Electric Science and Technology. Text in English; Abstracts and contents page in Chinese, English. 1986. q. CNY 10 per issue (effective 2011). **Document type:** *Journal, Academic/Scholarly.*
Former titles (until 2004): Changsha Dianli Xueyuan Xuebao (Ziran Kexue Ban)/Changsha University of Electric Power. Journal (Natural Science Edition) (1006-7140); (until 1994): Changsha Shui-Dian Shi-Yuan Xuebao. Ziran Kexue Ban/Changsha Normal University of Water Resources and Electric Power. Journal. Natural Science Edition (1004-8898)
Related titles: Online - full text ed.
Indexed: A22, A32, CCMJ, ESPM, Inspec, MSN, MathR, PollutAb, SCOPUS, SSciA, SWRA, Z02.
—BLDSC (4725.124580), East View, IE, Ingenta.

Published by: Changsha Ligong Daxue/Changsha University of Science and Technology, 45, Chiling Lu, Tushuguan B, 4/F, Changsha, 410076, China. TEL 86-731-2617279, http://www.cscu.edu.cn/. Ed. Xiangjun Zeng. **Dist. by:** China International Book Trading Corp, 35 Chegongzhuang Xilu, Haidian District, PO Box 399, Beijing 100044, China. TEL 86-10-68412045, FAX 86-10-68412023, cibtc@mail.cibtc.com.cn, http://www.cibtc.com.cn.

500 CHN ISSN 1003-8930
DIANLI XITONG JIQI ZIDONG HUAXUE BAO/C S U - E P S A. PROCEEDINGS. Text in Chinese. 1989. bi-m. USD 37.20 (effective 2009). **Document type:** *Journal, Academic/Scholarly.*
Related titles: Online - full text ed.
Indexed: A28, APA, BrCerAb, C&ISA, CA/WCA, CIA, CerAb, CivEngAb, CorrAb, E&CAJ, E11, EEA, EMA, ESPM, EnvEAb, H15, Inspec, M&TEA, M09, MBF, METADEX, RefZh, SolStAb, T04, WAA.
Published by: Tianjin Daxue, Zidong Huaxue Yuan, Nankai-qu, Tianjin, 300072, China. TEL 86-22-27401056, FAX 86-22-27400866.

DIDATTICA DELLE SCIENZE E INFORMATICA NELLA SCUOLA. *see* EDUCATION—Teaching Methods And Curriculum

501 149 SRB ISSN 0350-1272
DIJALEKTIKA/DIALECTICS; casopis za metodolosko filozofske probleme matematickih, prirodnih i tehnickih nauka. Text in Serbo-Croatian. 1966. q. YUN 40.
Indexed: RASB.
Published by: Univerzitet u Beogradu, Studentski trg 1, Belgrade, Serbia 11000. Eds. Andrija Stojkovic, Milorad Bertolino.

509 USA ISSN 1099-5757
DIO; the international journal of scientific history. Text in English. 1991. 3/yr. **Document type:** *Journal, Academic/Scholarly.*
Formerly (until 1993): Dio and the Journal for Hysterical Astronomy (1041-5440)
Related titles: Online - full text ed.: free (effective 2011).
Indexed: A01, GardL, T02.
—Linda Hall.
Published by: Dio, Inc., Box 19935, Baltimore, MD 21211-0935. TEL 410-889-1414, FAX 410-889-4749. Ed. Dennis Duke. Pub. Dennis Rawlins.

500 JOR ISSN 1560-456X
Q1
➤ **DIRASAT: PURE SCIENCES.** Text in English, Arabic. 1974. s-a. JOD 9 domestic to individuals; JOD 11 domestic to institutions; USD 30 foreign (effective 2010). index, cum.index. back issues avail. **Document type:** *Journal, Academic/Scholarly.* **Description:** Publishes scholarly research in all pure sciences subjects.
Supersedes in part (in 1996): Dirasat: Pure Science and Engineering (1026-3756)
Indexed: B25, BIOSIS Prev, CCMJ, GeoRef, MSN, MathR, MycolAb, Z01.
Published by: University of Jordan, Deanship of Academic Research, Amman, 11942, Jordan. FAX 962-6-5300815, dirasata@ju.edu.jo. Eds. Mohammad H Al-Surakhi, Neveen Al-Zagha, Fuad A Kittaneh TEL 962-6-5355000 ext 25100. Circ: 1,000 (controlled).

500 ZWE
DIRECTORY OF ORGANIZATIONS CONCERNED WITH SCIENTIFIC RESEARCH AND TECHNICAL SERVICES IN ZIMBABWE. Text in English. 1959. triennial. USD 20. **Document type:** *Directory.*
Formerly: Directory of Organizations Concerned with Scientific Research and Technical Services in Rhodesia
Published by: Scientific Liaison Office, Causeway, PO Box CY 294, Harare, Zimbabwe. TEL 263-4-700573, FAX 263-4-728799.

500 NGA ISSN 0070-6280
DIRECTORY OF SCIENTIFIC RESEARCH IN NIGERIA. Text in English. 1968. a. **Document type:** *Directory.*
Published by: Science Association of Nigeria, University of Ibadan, PO Box 4039, Ibadan, Oyo, Nigeria.

502.9 PAK
DIRECTORY OF THE SCIENTISTS, TECHNOLOGISTS, AND ENGINEERS OF THE P C S I R. Text in English. 1972. irreg. **Document type:** *Directory.*
Published by: Pakistan Journal of Scientific and Industrial Research, Scientific Information Centre, PCSIR Laboratories Campus, Shahrah-e-Dr. Salimuzzaman Siddiqui, Karachi, 75280, Pakistan. TEL 92-21-34651739, FAX 92-21-34651738. Circ: (controlled).

500 600 USA ISSN 0274-7529
CODEN: JMOEDW
DISCOVER; science, technology and the future. Text in English. 1980. m. USD 19.95 domestic (effective 2009). adv. bk.rev. illus. back issues avail.; reprints avail. **Document type:** *Magazine, Consumer.* **Description:** Provides extensive coverage of science and technology in nontechnical language.
Related titles: Microform ed.: (from PQC); Online - full text ed.; ◆ Esperanto ed.: Discover en Espanol. ISSN 1095-8924.
Indexed: A01, A02, A03, A08, A11, A20, A21, A22, A25, A26, AIA, ARG, Acal, Agr, B04, B07, BIOSIS Prev, BRD, BiolDig, C04, C05, C12, CADCAM, CPerI, E08, EnvAb, EnvInd, G01, G03, G05, G06, G07, G08, G09, GSA, GSI, GdIns, GeoRef, H05, HlthInd, I05, I06, I07, ISR, M01, M02, M04, M06, MASUSE, MagInd, MycolAb, P02, P10, P11, P13, P15, P26, P30, P34, P48, P52, P53, P54, P56, PMR, PQC, R03, R06, RGAb, RGPR, RGYP, RI-1, RehabLit, RoboAb, S04, S06, S08, S09, S10, S23, SCOPUS, SpeleolAb, T02, TOM, U01, V02, W03, W05, WBA, WMB, WildRev.
—BLDSC (3595.870000), CASDDS, IE, Infotrieve, Ingenta, Linda Hall. **CCC.**
Published by: Discover Magazine, 90 Fifth Av, 11th Fl, New York, NY 10011. adv.: B&W page USD 37,035, color page USD 50,045. Circ: 1,088,269.

570 CAN ISSN 0319-8480
QH1
➤ **DISCOVERY.** Text in English. N.S. 1972. biennial. CAD 15; CAD 7.50 per issue (effective 2003). adv. bk.rev. charts; maps. Index. 64 p./no. 2 cols./p.; back issues avail. **Document type:** *Journal, Academic/Scholarly.* **Description:** Covers natural history topics, particularly ornithology, botany and conservation, but also entomology, mycology, mamalogy and marine biology in British Columbia.
Related titles: Microfiche ed.: (from MML); Microform ed.: N.S. (from MML).
Indexed: BiolDig, C03, CBPI, CEI, CPerI, P11, P48, PQC, WildRev.
Published by: Vancouver Natural History Society, P O Box 3021, Vancouver, BC V6B 3X5, Canada. TEL 604-737-3074, FAX 604-876-3313. Ed., R&P, Adv. contact Marian Coope TEL 604-224-6192. Pub. Benwell Atkins. page CAD 150. Circ: 1,000 (controlled).

500 KEN ISSN 1015-079X
Q85.2 CODEN: DIINE4
➤ **DISCOVERY AND INNOVATION.** Text in English. 1989. q. KES 1,500 domestic to individuals; USD 80 in Africa to individuals; USD 150 elsewhere to individuals; KES 3,000 domestic to institutions; USD 140 in Africa to institutions; USD 250 elsewhere to institutions (effective 2007). adv. illus. index. reprints avail. **Document type:** *Journal, Academic/Scholarly.* **Description:** Takes a multidisciplinary approach to covering progress in scientific research, technological innovation, and issues that affect these two areas.
Related titles: Online - full text ed.
Indexed: A22, A34, A35, A36, A37, A38, ASCA, ASD, ASFA, AbAn, AgBio, AgrForAb, B21, B25, BA, BIOSIS Prev, BP, C25, C30, CABA, CIN, ChemAb, ChemTitl, CurCont, E12, ESPM, F08, F11, F12, FCA, G11, GH, H16, H17, I11, IIBP, IndVet, MaizeAb, MycolAb, N02, N03, N04, O01, OR, P30, P32, P33, P37, P38, P39, P40, PAIS, PGegResA, PGrRegA, PHN&I, PLESA, PN&I, R07, R08, R11, R12, R13, RA&MP, RM&VM, S12, S13, S16, S17, SCI, SCOPUS, SoyAb, T05, TAR, TriticAb, VS, W07, W11, Z01.
—BLDSC (3596.330000), CASDDS, IE, Infotrieve, Ingenta.
Published by: (Third World Academy of Sciences, African Academy of Sciences), Academy Science Publishers, PO Box 14798, Nairobi, Kenya. TEL 254-2-8844015, FAX 254-2-884406, asp@africaonline.co.ke, http://www.aasciences.org. Ed. S Akatch. adv.: B&W page KES 20,000,500, color page USD 1,500.

508 USA ISSN 1026-0226
QA402.3 CODEN: DDNSFA
➤ **DISCRETE DYNAMICS IN NATURE AND SOCIETY**; an international multidisciplinary research and review journal. Text in English. 1997. irreg. USD 195 (effective 2011). **Document type:** *Journal, Academic/Scholarly.* **Description:** Aims to foster links between basic and applied research relating to discrete dynamics of complex systems encountered in the natural and social sciences.
Related titles: Online - full text ed.: ISSN 1607-887X. free (effective 2011) (from IngentaConnect).
Indexed: A01, A02, A03, A08, A22, A26, A28, A39, APA, BrCerAb, C&ISA, C10, C27, C29, CA, CA/WCA, CCMJ, CIA, CIS, CMCI, CerAb, CivEngAb, CorrAb, CurCont, D03, D04, E&CAJ, E01, E11, E13, EEA, EMA, ESPM, EnvEAb, H15, I05, Inspec, M&TEA, M09, MBF, METADEX, MSN, MathR, P49, P52, R14, S14, S15, S18, SCI, SCOPUS, SolStAb, T02, T04, W07, WAA, Z02.
—BLDSC (3597.026000), IE, Infotrieve, Ingenta. **CCC.**
Published by: Hindawi Publishing Corporation, 410 Park Ave, 15th Fl, PMB 287, New York, NY 10022. FAX 866-446-3294, info@hindawi.com. Ed. Vladimir Gontar.

500 BRA ISSN 1808-1002
DISCUTINDO CIENCIA. Text in Portuguese. 2005. bi-m. BRL 47.40 (effective 2006). **Document type:** *Journal, Academic/Scholarly.*
Published by: Editora Escala Ltda., Av Prof Ida Kolb, 551, Casa Verde, Sao Paulo, 02518-000, Brazil. TEL 55-11-38552100, FAX 55-11-38579643, escala@escala.com.br, http://www.escala.com.br.

500 CHE ISSN 1424-2818
▼ **DIVERSITY.** Text in English. 2009. irreg. free (effective 2011). **Document type:** *Journal, Academic/Scholarly.*
Media: Online - full text.
Indexed: A01, A34, A35, AgBio, C25, ESPM, F08, H16, P32, SSciA, T02, Z01.
Published by: M D P I AG, Postfach, Basel, 4005, Switzerland. TEL 41-61-6837734, FAX 41-61-3028918, http://www.mdpi.org/. Ed. Michael Wink.

500 VEN
DIVULGA. Text in Spanish. q.
Published by: Universidad Nacional Experimental del Tachira, Comision de Cultura, Ave. Universidad-Paramillo, Apdo 436, San Cristobal, Tachira 5001, Venezuela. Ed. Gilberto A Labrador.

500 ESP ISSN 1988-8023
DIVULGACION CIENTIFICA, INNOVACION E INVESTIGACION HISPANICA. Text in Spanish. 2008. s-w.
Media: Online - full text.
Published by: Divulgacion Cientifica revista@latierrachica.com.

500 FRA ISSN 1957-3367
DOCSCIENCES. Text in French. 2007. 3/yr. EUR 7 newsstand/cover (effective 2007). **Document type:** *Journal.*
Published by: Academie de Versailles, Centre Regional de Documentation Pedagogique, 584 Rue de Fourny, B P 326, Buc, Cedex 78533, France. TEL 33-1-39457878, FAX 33-1-39457845, http://www.crdp2.ac-versailles.fr.

500 SWE ISSN 0347-5719
DOCUMENTA. Text in Swedish. 1972. irreg. (1-5/yr.). bibl.; illus. back issues avail. **Document type:** *Monographic series, Academic/Scholarly.*
Published by: Kungliga Vetenskapsakademien/Royal Swedish Academy of Sciences, PO Box 50005, Stockholm, 10405, Sweden. TEL 46-8-6739500, FAX 46-8-155670.

500 FRA ISSN 0046-0478
DOCUMENTATION PAR L'IMAGE; revue d'historie, geographie and sciences. Text in French. 1933. 5/yr. EUR 47.50 (effective 2009). adv. illus. **Document type:** *Magazine, Trade.*
—CCC.
Published by: Editions Nathan, 25 Av. Pierre de Coubertin, Paris, Cedex 13 75211, France. FAX 33-1-45872662, http://www.nathan.fr. Ed. Anick Lestage. R&P Corinne Dupuis. Adv. contact Luc Leherlcy.

DOCUMENTS HISTORIQUES DES SCIENCES. *see* HISTORY—History Of Europe

DOGAR'S GENERAL KNOWLEDGE DIGEST. *see* POLITICAL SCIENCE

DONGBEI DAXUE XUEBAO (ZIRAN KEXUE BAN)/NORTHEASTERN UNIVERSITY. JOURNAL (NATURAL SCIENCES). *see* TECHNOLOGY: COMPREHENSIVE WORKS

500 CHN ISSN 1000-1832
QH7 CODEN: DSZKEE
DONGBEI SHI-DAXUEBAO (ZIRAN KEXUE BAN)/NORTHEAST NORMAL UNIVERSITY. JOURNAL (NATURAL SCIENCE EDITION). Text in Chinese. 1951. q. USD 26.80 (effective 2009). abstr.; charts. 128 p./no.; **Document type:** *Journal, Academic/Scholarly.*
Formerly (until 1979): Jilin Shi-Da Xuebao (Zhexue Shehui Kexue Ban) (1001-7798)
Related titles: Online - full text ed.
Indexed: B25, BIOSIS Prev, CCMJ, MSN, MathR, MycolAb, RefZh, Z01, Z02.
—BLDSC (4834.152000), CASDDS, East View.
Published by: Dongbei Shifan Daxue/Northeast Normal University, 5268 Renmin Dajie, Changchun, 130024, China. TEL 86-431-5268024, http://www.nenu.edu.cn. Circ: 1,000.

500 CHN ISSN 1671-0444
TS1300
DONGHUA DAXUE XUEBAO (ZIRAN BAN)/DONGHUA UNIVERISTY. JOURNAL (NATURAL SCIENCE EDITION). Text in English. 1956. bi-m. USD 24.60 (effective 2009). **Document type:** *Journal, Academic/Scholarly.*
Related titles: Online - full content ed.; Online - full text ed.
Indexed: A28, APA, BrCerAb, C&ISA, CA/WCA, CIA, CerAb, CivEngAb, CorrAb, E&CAJ, E11, EEA, EMA, ESPM, EnvEAb, H15, M&TEA, M09, MBF, METADEX, SolStAb, T04, WAA.
—East View.
Published by: Donghua Daxue/Donghua University, 1882, Yanan Xilu, Shanghai, 200051, China. TEL 86-21-62373643, http://www.dhu.edu.cn/.

500 620 CHN ISSN 1001-0505
T4 CODEN: DDXUEV
➤ **DONGNAN DAXUE XUEBAO (ZIRAN KEXUE BAN)/SOUTHEAST UNIVERSITY. JOURNAL (NATURAL SCIENCE EDITION).** Text in Chinese; Abstracts in Chinese, English. 1955. bi-m. USD 21.60 (effective 2009). **Document type:** *Journal, Academic/Scholarly.* **Description:** Covers various branches of science and engineering.
Formerly (until 1989): Nanjing Gongxueyuan Xuebao (0254-4180)
Related titles: Online - full text ed.
Indexed: A28, APA, BrCerAb, C&ISA, CA/WCA, CCMJ, CIA, CPEI, CerAb, CivEngAb, CorrAb, E&CAJ, E11, EEA, EMA, ESPM, EngInd, EnvEAb, GeoRef, H15, Inspec, M&TEA, M09, MBF, METADEX, MSN, MathR, RefZh, SCOPUS, SolStAb, SpeleolAb, T04, WAA, Z02.
—CASDDS, East View, Linda Hall.
Published by: Dongnan Daxue/Southeast University, 2, Sipailou, Nanjing, Jiangsu 210096, China. TEL 86-25-83794323, FAX 86-25-57712719. Ed. Shan-feng Mao. **Dist. by:** China International Book Trading Corp, 35 Chegongzhuang Xilu, Haidian District, PO Box 399, Beijing 100044, China. TEL 86-10-68412045, FAX 86-10-68412023, cibtc@mail.cibtc.com.cn, http://www.cibtc.com.cn.

500.9 ITA ISSN 0417-9927
QL1 CODEN: DRNAAF
DORIANA. Text and summaries in English, French, German, Italian, Spanish. 1949. irreg., latest vol.308, 1998. per issue exchange basis only. back issues avail. **Document type:** *Monographic series, Academic/Scholarly.* **Description:** Discusses natural history of the area.
Related titles: ◆ Supplement to: Museo Civico di Storia Naturale "Giacomo Doria", Genoa. Annali. ISSN 0365-4389.
Indexed: A29, B21, B25, BIOSIS Prev, CABA, E12, EntAb, GeoRef, MycolAb, P33, R07, R08, SpeleolAb, Z01.
—INIST.
Published by: Museo Civico di Storia Naturale "Giacomo Doria", Via Brigata Liguria 9, Genoa, 16121, Italy. http://www.museodoria.it.

500.9 913 GBR ISSN 0070-7112
DA670.D69
DORSET NATURAL HISTORY AND ARCHAEOLOGICAL SOCIETY. PROCEEDINGS. Variant title: D N H & A S Proceedings. Text in English. 1877. a. free to members (effective 2009). charts; illus.; maps. Index. back issues avail.; reprints avail. **Document type:** *Proceedings.* **Description:** Covers all aspects of natural history, geology, archaeology, local history, biography in Dorset.
Formerly (until 1929): Dorset Natural History and Antiquarian Field Club. Proceedings
Indexed: AIAP, B24, BrArAb, BrGeoL, GeoRef, NumL, RILM, SpeleolAb, Z01.
—BLDSC (6691.000000). **CCC.**
Published by: Dorset County Museum, High W St, Dorchester, Dorset DT1 1XA, United Kingdom. TEL 44-1305-262735, FAX 44-1305-257180, enquiries@dorsetcountymuseum.org.

500 FRA ISSN 1772-3809
LES DOSSIERS DE LA RECHERCHE. Text in French. 2004. q. back issues avail. **Document type:** *Magazine, Consumer.*
Formerly (until 2004): La Recherche. Hors Serie (1622-7530)
Published by: Sophia Publications, 74 Av. du Maine, Paris, 75014, France. TEL 33-1-44101010, FAX 33-1-44101394.

500 USA
DREXEL FACULTY PUBLICATION. Text in English. 1978. a. free. **Document type:** *Bibliography.*
Supersedes (1971-1978): Drexel Research Conference. Summary Report (0085-0071)
Published by: (Office of Sponsored Projects), Drexel University, 32nd & Chestnut Sts, Philadelphia, PA 19104. TEL 215-895-2499, FAX 215-895-1619. Ed. Dr. Kenneth N Geller. Circ: 200.

500 FRA ISSN 2106-8224
▼ **DROSOPHILE.** Text in French. 2010. q. **Document type:** *Journal, Academic/Scholarly.*
Published by: Universite de Trou-les-Pommes, 200 Rue de la Mairie, Brienne, 71290, France. http://www.drosophile.net.

500 COL ISSN 0121-3199
DUGANDIA. Text in Spanish. 1989. s-a. **Document type:** *Journal, Academic/Scholarly.*
Published by: Universidad del Atlantico, Departamento de Fisica, Oficina 201C, Km 7 Antigua Via a Puerto Colombia, Barranquilla, Colombia. fisica2002@uniatlantico.edu.co, http://www.uniatlantico.edu.co.

509 NLD ISSN 1570-2154
DUTCH CLASSICS ON HISTORY OF SCIENCE. Text in Multiple languages. 1961. irreg. price varies. **Document type:** *Monographic series, Academic/Scholarly.*

S

Published by: Hes & De Graaf Publishers BV, Postbus 540, Houten, 3990 GH, Netherlands. TEL 31-30-6380071, FAX 31-30-6380099, info@hesdegraaf.com, http://www.hesdegraaf.com.

DYNAMICAL SYSTEMS (ONLINE). *see* COMPUTERS

DYNAMICAL SYSTEMS (PRINT). *see* COMPUTERS

507 607 DNK ISSN 1604-7877
DYNAMO. Text in Danish. 2005. q. free. back issues avail. **Document type:** *Magazine, Consumer.* **Description:** Articles featuring the ongoing technical/scientific research at DTU.
Related titles: Online - full text ed.: ISSN 1604-7885.
Published by: Danmarks Tekniske Universitet/Technical University of Denmark, Anker Engelundsvej 1, Bygning 101 A, Lyngby, 2800, Denmark. TEL 45-45-252525, FAX 45-45-881799, dtu@dtu.dk. Eds. Tine Kortenbach, Dan Jensen TEL 45-45-251020.

600 MNG
DZALUU DZOHION BUTEEGCH/YOUNG INVENTOR. Text in Mongol. 1981. q. USD 1. adv. bk.rev.
Published by: Editorial Office for Mongolian Youth, P.O. Box 1053, Ulan Bator, 210613, Mongolia. TEL 29651. Ed. S Batmonh. Circ: 21,000.

500 600 MEX ISSN 1665-5745
QH7
E-GNOSIS. Text in Spanish. 2003. a. back issues avail. **Document type:** *Monographic series, Academic/Scholarly.*
Media: Online - full text.
Published by: Universidad de Guadalajara, Apartado Postal 1-2130, Guadalajara, JALISCO 44600, Mexico. TEL 52-33-36164399, FAX 52-322- 2232982, http://www.udg.mx/.

500 PHL ISSN 2094-1749
▼ **E - INTERNATIONAL SCIENTIFIC RESEARCH JOURNAL.** Text in English. 2009. q. free (effective 2011). **Document type:** *Journal, Academic/Scholarly.*
Media: Online - full text.
Published by: BCTA Inc. http://www.peerc.com. Ed. A Anand.

500 600 GRC ISSN 1790-5613
Q9
E-JOURNAL OF SCIENCE & TECHNOLOGY. Text in Greek, English. 2005. a. free (effective 2011). **Document type:** *Journal, Academic/Scholarly.*
Media: Online - full text.
Indexed: A34, A35, A36, AgBio, BA, C10, C30, CA, CABA, D01, E12, GH, H16, I11, LT, N02, N03, N04, OR, P32, P33, P40, PGegResA, PGrRegA, PHN&I, R12, RM&VM, RRTA, S12, S13, S16, T02, T05, TAR, W11.

500 600 BEL ISSN 1784-0732
E-NEWSLETTER FOR SCIENCE AND TECHNOLOGY. Text in English. 2006. irreg. **Document type:** *Newsletter, Academic/Scholarly.* **Description:** Provides a platform for reporting any recent scientific or technological findings.
Published by: European Academy of Sciences, Bd d'Avroy 280, Liege, 4000, Belgium. TEL 32-4-2536716, FAX 32-2-2532870, http://www.eurasc.org.

500 COL ISSN 2011-1827
E-REVISTA. Text in Spanish. 2007. s-a. **Document type:** *Journal, Academic/Scholarly.*
Published by: Universidad Catolica de Manizales, Carrera 23 No. 606-3, Manizales, Caldas, Colombia. TEL 57-6-8782900, FAX 57-6-8782950, http://www.ucm.edu.co/.

500 FRA ISSN 0293-082X
E S F COMMUNICATIONS. (European Science Foundation) Text in English. 1981. irreg.
Related titles: Online - full text ed.
Published by: European Science Foundation, 1 Quai Lezay Marnesia, Strasbourg, 67080 Cedex, France. TEL 33-3-88767100, FAX 33-3-88370532, esf@esf.org, http://www.esf.org.

500 GBR ISSN 1465-9581
E S P NOW!. Text in English. 1999. irreg. **Document type:** *Monographic series, Academic/Scholarly.*
—CCC.
Published by: G T I Specialist Publishers, The Barns, Preston Crowmarsh, Wallingford, Oxon OX10 6SL, United Kingdom. TEL 44-1491-826262, FAX 44-1491-833146, http://www.groupgti.com.

E S R. (Electronic - Science - Radio) *see* COMMUNICATIONS—Radio

500 CHE ISSN 1423-6958
E T H - BIBLIOTHEK. A: WISSENSCHAFTSGESCHICHTE. Text in German. 2000. irreg., latest vol.2, 2001. price varies. back issues avail. **Document type:** *Monographic series, Academic/Scholarly.*
Supersedes in part (1948-1999): E T H - Bibliothek. Schriftenreihe (1421-6302)
Indexed: CCMJ, MSN, MathR.
Published by: Eidgenoessische Technische Hochschule, Bibliothek, Raemistr 101, Zurich, 8092, Switzerland. TEL 41-1-6322183, FAX 41-1-6321087, info@library.ethz.ch, http://www.ethbib.ethz.ch. R&P Rudolf Mumenthaler. Circ: 250 (paid and controlled).

E X S. (Experientia Supplementum) *see* BIOLOGY

EARLY SCIENCE AND MEDICINE; a journal for the study of science, technology and medicine in the pre-modern period. *see* MEDICAL SCIENCES

500 ETH ISSN 1992-0407
➤ **EAST AFRICA JOURNAL OF SCIENCES.** Text in English. 2007. s-a. **Document type:** *Journal, Academic/Scholarly.* **Description:** Covers the fields of agriculture, forestry, natural resources, education, natural and social sciences, and human and animal health sciences.
Published by: Alemaya University, Research and Extension Office, PO Box 138, Dire Dawa, Ethiopia. TEL 251-25-6610713, FAX 251-25-6610712. Ed. Dr. Tadele Tefera.

500 600 USA ISSN 1875-2160
Q127.E26
EAST ASIAN SCIENCE, TECHNOLOGY AND SOCIETY; an international journal. Abbreviated title: E A S T S. Text in English. 2007. q. USD 50 to individuals; USD 294 to institutions; USD 324 combined subscription to institutions (print & online eds.); USD 74 per issue to institutions (effective 2012). adv. reprint service avail. from PSC. **Document type:** *Journal, Academic/Scholarly.* **Description:** Contains research and commentary on how society and culture, and the dynamics of science, technology and medicine, are mutually shaped and co-produced.
Related titles: Online - full text ed.: ISSN 1875-2152. USD 260 to institutions (effective 2012) (from IngentaConnect).
Indexed: A22, A26, E01, E08, P52, P56, PQC, S09, SCOPUS.
—IE. **CCC.**
Published by: Duke University Press, 905 W Main St, Ste 18 B, Durham, NC 27701. TEL 919-688-5134, 888-651-0122, FAX 919-688-2615, 888-651-0124, subscriptions@dukeupress.edu, http://www.dukeupress.edu. Ed. Daiwie Fu.

EASYSCIENCE. *see* CHILDREN AND YOUTH—For

500 FRA ISSN 0183-7478
ECOLE PRATIQUE DES HAUTES ETUDES, SECTION DES SCIENCES RELIGIEUSES. ANNUAIRE. Text in French. 1892. a., latest 2009. **Document type:** *Academic/Scholarly.*
Formed by the merger of (1973-1975): Ecole Pratique des Hautes Etudes, 5e Section, Sciences Religieuses. Vie de la Section. Annuaire (0183-7451); (1973-1975): Ecole Pratique des Hautes Etudes, 5e Section, Sciences Religieuses. Comptes Rendus des Conferences. Annuaire (0183-746X); Both of which superseded in part (in 1973): Annuaire .. - Ecole Pratique des Hautes Etudes, Section des Sciences Religieuses (0183-7443); Which was formerly (until 1915): Ecole Pratique des Hautes Etudes, Section des Sciences Religieuses. Rapport Sommaire sur les Conferences (Year). et le Programme des Conferences (Year) (1267-9240); Which superseded in part (in 1892): Ecole Pratique des Hautes Etudes. Rapport (1254-0617)
Related titles: Online - full text ed.: ISSN 1969-6329. 2009.
Published by: Ecole Pratique des Hautes Etudes, Section des Sciences Religieuses (Subsidiary of: Ecole Pratique des Hautes Etudes), 46, Rue de Lille, Paris, 75007, France. TEL 33-1-53636120, FAX 33-1-53636194, http://www.ephe.sorbonne.fr.

EDUCATION IN SCIENCE. *see* EDUCATION

EDUCYT. *see* EDUCATION—Higher Education

500.9 EST ISSN 0131-5862
QH7
EESTI LOODUS/ESTONIAN NATURE. Text in Estonian; Summaries in English. 1958. m. EUR 25.56 (effective 2011). bk.rev. abstr.; charts; illus.; maps. **Document type:** *Magazine, Consumer.* **Description:** Covers Estonian environment, its research and protection.
Indexed: INIS AtomInd.
Published by: (Eesti Teaduste Akadeemia/Estonian Academy of Sciences), Loodusajakiri, Endla 3, Tallinn, 10122, Estonia. TEL 372-6-104105, FAX 372-6-104109, loodusajakiri@loodusajakiri.ee. Ed. Toomas Kukk. Circ: 5,000.

EGERTON JOURNAL. *see* HUMANITIES: COMPREHENSIVE WORKS

EGITANIA SCIENCIA. *see* HUMANITIES: COMPREHENSIVE WORKS

500 EGY ISSN 2090-231X
Q1
EGYPTIAN JOURNAL OF PURE AND APPLIED SCIENCES. Text in English. 1990. s-w. **Document type:** *Journal, Academic/Scholarly.*
Formerly (until 2010): Ain Shams Science Bulletin (1110-0397)
Indexed: SpeleolAb.
Published by: Ain Shams University, University Hospital, Abbassia, Cairo, Egypt. TEL 20-2-4821096, FAX 20-2-4821031. Ed. Dr. Muhammad M Abdel-Fattah Muhammad.

500 JPN ISSN 0919-5203
Q4
EHIME DAIGAKU RIGAKUBU KIYO/EHIME UNIVERSITY. FACULTY OF SCIENCE. MEMOIRS. Text in Japanese. 1992. s-a.?. **Document type:** *Academic/Scholarly.*
Indexed: GeoRef, SpeleolAb.
Published by: Ehime Daigaku, Rigakubu, 2-5 Bunkyo-cho, Matsuyama-shi, Ehime-ken 790-0826, Japan. TEL 81-899-24-7111, FAX 81-899-23-2545. Ed. Toshiyuki Suzuki.

500 DEU ISSN 1615-5971
EINBLICKE IN DIE WISSENSCHAFT. Text in German. 1992. irreg., latest 2002. price varies. **Document type:** *Monographic series, Academic/Scholarly.*
Published by: Vieweg und Teubner Verlag (Subsidiary of: Springer Fachmedien Wiesbaden GmbH), Abraham-Lincoln-Str 46, Wiesbaden, 65189, Germany. TEL 49-611-78780, FAX 49-611-7878400, info@viewegteubner.de, http://www.viewegteubner.de.

500 ESP ISSN 0214-9001
EKAIA. Text in Basque. 1989. s-a. EUR 10 (effective 2009). back issues avail. **Document type:** *Journal, Academic/Scholarly.* **Description:** Educational journal of science and technology which addresses the problems and solutions of utilizing the Basque language in terms of science and technology.
Related titles: Online - full text ed.
Published by: (Universidad del Pais Vasco, Facultad de Ciencias), Universidad del Pais Vasco, Servicio Editorial, Apartado 1397, Bilbao, 48080, Spain. TEL 34-94-6015126, FAX 34-94-4801314, luxedito@lg.ehu.es.

500 USA ISSN 1067-7399
ELECTRIC SPACE CRAFT; a journal of interactive research. Text in English. 1991. q. back issues avail. **Document type:** *Journal, Academic/Scholarly.* **Description:** Contains individual exploratory research, publishing articles by amateurs and professionals from the fields of engineering, physics, education and science.
—BLDSC (3672.620000), IE, Ingenta.
Published by: Electric Spacecraft, Inc., 322 Sunlight Dr, Leicester, NC 28748. TEL 828-683-0313, FAX 828-683-3511, contact@electricspacecraft.comaft.com.

500 ARM ISSN 1728-791X
ELECTRONIC JOURNAL OF NATURAL SCIENCES. Text in English. 2003. s-a. **Document type:** *Journal, Academic/Scholarly.*
Media: Online - full text.
Indexed: A01, A03, A08, CA, T02, Z01.
Published by: National Academy of Sciences of the Republic of Armenia, 24, Marshall Baghramian Ave, Yerevan, 375019, Armenia. TEL 374-10-527031, FAX 374-10-569281, academy@sci.am, http://www.sci.am.

500 POL ISSN 1505-0297
➤ **ELECTRONIC JOURNAL OF POLISH AGRICULTURAL UNIVERSITIES.** Text in English. 1998. s-a. free (effective 2011). **Document type:** *Journal, Academic/Scholarly.* **Description:** Publishes original scientific papers on agronomy, animal husbandry, agricultural engineering, biotechnology, civil engineering, economics, environmental development, fisheries, food science and technology, forestry, geodesy and cartography, horticulture, wood technology, and veterinary medicine.
Media: Online - full content.
Indexed: A38, AgrAg, B23, CA, F12, FS&TA, G11, H17, I11, O01, P37, P38, P40, PGegResA, PGrRegA, PHN&I, PN&I, R11, R13, S12, S13, S16, T02, Z01.
Published by: (Uniwersytet Przyrodniczy w Poznaniu/Poznan University of Life Sciences), Wydawnictwo Uniwersytetu Przyrodniczego we Wroclawiu, ul Sopocka 23, Wroclaw, 50344, Poland. wyd@up.wroc.pl, http://wydawnictwo.ar.wroc.pl. Ed. Sobota Jerzy.

➤ **ELECTRONIC JOURNAL OF SCIENCE AND MATHEMATICS EDUCATION.** *see* EDUCATION—Computer Applications

➤ **ELECTRONIC JOURNAL OF SCIENCE EDUCATION.** *see* EDUCATION

500 SVK ISSN 0323-2778
ELEKTRON. Text in Slovak. 1973. m. USD 0.50. adv. bk.rev..
Related titles: Online - full text ed.
Published by: (Socialisticky Svaz Mladeze C.S.S.R.), Smena Publishing House, Prazska 11, Bratislava, 81284, Slovakia. TEL 406-06. Ed. Eduard Drobny. Circ: 55,000.

500 HUN ISSN 0013-6077
ELET ES TUDOMANY. Text in Hungarian. 1946. w.
Related titles: Online - full content ed.: ISSN 1418-1665.
Indexed: HBB.
Published by: (Tudomanyos Ismeretterjeszto Tarsulat), Magyar Hivatalos Kozlonykiado/Hungarian Official Journal Publisher, Somogyi Bela u. 6, Budapest, 1085, Hungary. http://www.mhk.hu. Circ: 30,000.

500 600 ESP ISSN 0213-3687
ELHUYAR: ZIENTZIA ETA TEKNIKA. Text in Basque. 1985. m. adv. **Document type:** *Bulletin, Consumer.*
Published by: Elhuyar Kultur Elkartea, Asteasuain Poligonoa, 14, Pabilioia, Txikierdi Auzoa, Usurbil, (Gipuzkoa) 20170, Spain. TEL 34-43-363040, FAX 34-43-363144, adliakaria@elhuyar.com, http://www.elhuyar.com. Ed. Eustakio Arrojeia. R&P Inaki Irazabalbeitia. Adv. contact Bernardo Kortabarria.

500 EGY
EL-ELM/SCIENCES MONTHLY MAGAZINE. Text in Arabic. 1976. m. adv. illus.
Published by: Dar al-Tahrir, 24 Sharia Zakaria Ahmed, Cairo, Egypt. TEL 02-741611, FAX 02-749949, http://www.eltahrir.net. Circ: 25,000.

500 FRA ISSN 0396-4957
ENCYCLOPEDIE D'UTOVIE; revue mensuelle de science populaire. Text in French. 1976. m. price varies. **Document type:** *Journal, Consumer.*
Published by: Editions d' Utovie, 402 Rte des Pyrenees, Bats, 40320, France. TEL 33-5-58791793, FAX 33-5-58791959, utovie@wanadoo.fr, http://www.utovie.com. Ed. Jean Marc Carite.

500 GBR ISSN 0160-9327
Q1 CODEN: ENDEAS
➤ **ENDEAVOUR**; a quarterly magazine reviewing the history and philosophy of science in the service of mankind. Text in English. 1942; N.S. 1977. q. EUR 623 in Europe to institutions; JPY 86,400 in Japan to institutions; USD 694 elsewhere to institutions (effective 2012). adv. bk.rev. charts; illus. index, cum.index: 1942-1961 (in 2 vols.). back issues avail.; reprints avail. **Document type:** *Journal, Academic/Scholarly.* **Description:** Contains articles discussing current advances in science and technology, as well as examinations of issues in the history and philosophy of science of enduring interest to practicing scientists, engineers and general readers.
Related titles: Microfiche ed.: N.S. (from MIM); Microfilm ed.: N.S. (from PQC); Online - full text ed.: ISSN 1873-1929. 199? (from IngentaConnect, ScienceDirect).
Indexed: A&ATA, A01, A02, A03, A08, A20, A22, A25, A26, A34, A35, A36, A38, AgBio, ApMecR, B04, B05, B21, B25, BIOBASE, BIOSIS Prev, BP, BRD, BioDAb, BrTechI, C&ISA, CA, CABA, CBTA, CCMJ, CIN, CISA, Cadscan, ChemAb, ChemTitl, CurCont, D01, E&CAJ, E08, E11, E12, EMBASE, EngInd, ExcerpMed, F&EA, FR, G03, G08, GH, GSA, GSI, GeoRef, H16, HRIS, I05, IABS, IMMAb, ISMEC, ISR, IndMed, Inspec, LT, LeadAb, M&GPA, MEDLINE, MLA-IB, MSN, MathR, MycolAb, N02, N03, N05, P02, P10, P11, P30, P32, P33, P37, P39, P40, P48, P52, P53, P54, P56, PQC, PsycholAb, RA&MP, S08, S09, S10, S13, S16, SCI, SCOPUS, SolStAb, SpeleolAb, T02, T04, T05, TriticAb, VS, W03, W07, W10, W11, WildRev, Zincscan.
—BLDSC (3740.000000), AskIEEE, CASDDS, IE, Infotrieve, Ingenta, INIST, Linda Hall. **CCC.**
Published by: Elsevier Ltd., Trends Journals (Subsidiary of: Elsevier Science & Technology), 84 Theobald's Rd, London, WC1X 8RR, United Kingdom. TEL 44-20-76114000, FAX 44-20-76114485, JournalsCustomerServiceEMEA@elsevier.com. Ed. E Henry Nicholls.

➤ **ENERGY EDUCATION SCIENCE & TECHNOLOGY, PART A: ENERGY SCIENCE AND RESEARCH.** *see* ENERGY

➤ **ENGINEERING & SCIENCE.** *see* ENGINEERING

500 BRA ISSN 1415-6938
ENSAIOS E CIENCIA. Text in Portuguese. 1997. q. **Document type:** *Journal, Academic/Scholarly.*
Indexed: C01, Z01.
Published by: Universidade para o Desenvolvimento do Estado e da Regiao do Pantanal, Rua Ceara, 333, Miguel Couto Campo Grande, Mato Grosso do Sul, 79003-010, Brazil. TEL 55-67-3488073, FAX 55-67-3488021, editora@uniderp.br, http://www.uniderp.br/. Ed. Maria Ines Affonseca Jardim. Circ: 600.

500.9 JPN ISSN 0386-5037
ENSHU NO SHIZEN/NATURE OF ENSHU. Text in Japanese. 1978. a. JPY 1,000. **Description:** Contains original papers, reviews, and commentary.
Published by: Enshu Shizen Kenkyukai/Society for the Study of Nature, Enshu, c/o Mr Hideo Toda, 895-3 Kanasashi, Inasa-gun, Inasa-cho, Shizuoka-ken 431-2213, Japan.

ENVIRONMENT, SCIENCE AND SOCIETY. *see* ENVIRONMENTAL STUDIES

500 BEL
EOS. Text in Dutch. 11/yr. EUR 39; EUR 4.95 newsstand/cover (effective 2009). **Document type:** *Magazine, Consumer.*
Published by: Uitgeverij Cascade, Katwilgweg 2 bus 5, Antwerpen, 2050, Belgium. TEL 32-36-802561, FAX 32-36-802564. Ed. Raf Scheers. Circ: 27,337.

500 FRA ISSN 1953-5783
EOS. Text in French. 2006. bi-m. EUR 4.95 newsstand/cover (effective 2011). **Document type:** *Magazine, Consumer.*
Published by: Export Press, 91 Rue de Turenne, Paris, 75003, France. TEL 33-1-40291451, FAX 33-1-42720743, dir@exportpress.com, http://www.exportpress.com.

500 BEL
EOS SCIENCES. Text in French. 10/yr. EUR 45; EUR 4.95 newsstand/cover (effective 2009). **Document type:** *Magazine, Consumer.*
Published by: Uitgeverij Cascade, Katwilgweg 2 bus 5, Antwerpen, 2050, Belgium. TEL 32-36-802561, FAX 32-36-802564. Ed. Raf Scheers. Circ: 20,000.

500 600 NLD ISSN 0165-0904
CODEN: episda
EPISTEME; a series in the foundational methodological, philosophical, psychological, sociological and political aspects of the sciences, pure and applied. Text in English. 1975. irreg., latest vol.24, 2000. price varies. **Document type:** *Monographic series, Academic/Scholarly.*
Related titles: Online - full text ed.
Indexed: ASD, CCMJ, MathR.
—BLDSC (3793.845000), CASDDS, Ingenta.
Published by: Springer Netherlands (Subsidiary of: Springer Science+Business Media), Van Godewijckstraat 30, Dordrecht, 3311 GX, Netherlands. TEL 31-78-6576050, FAX 31-78-6576474. Ed. Mario Bunge.

500 100 ITA ISSN 1824-8462
AS221
EPISTEME (ONLINE); an international journal of science, history and philosophy. Text in English, Italian. 2000. irreg. back issues avail. **Document type:** *Journal, Academic/Scholarly.* **Description:** Emphasizes unconventional points of view in discussions of science, history and philosophy.
Formerly (until 2004): Episteme (Print) (1593-3482)
Media: Online - full text.
Published by: Morlacchi Editore, Piazza Morlacchi 7-9, Perugia, 06123, Italy. TEL 39-075-5716036, FAX 39-075-5725297, editore@morlacchilibr.com, http://www.morlacchilibri.com.

EPISTEMOLOGIA; rivista italiana di filosofia della scienza. *see* PHILOSOPHY

500 610 GBR ISSN 1754-1417
EPOSTERS.NET; the online journal of scientific posters. Text in English. 2005. irreg. free (effective 2009). back issues avail. **Document type:** *Journal, Trade.* **Description:** Features scientific or medical poster.
Media: Online - full text.
Published by: Technology Networks Ltd., Wood View, Bull Lane Industrial Estate, Sudbury, CO10 0FD, United Kingdom. TEL 44-1787-319234, FAX 44-1787-319235, Promotion@TechnologyNetworks.net.

500 POL ISSN 0137-4990
➤ **ERGONOMIA.** Text in Polish; Summaries in English. 1978. q. EUR 66 foreign (effective 2006). bk.rev. **Document type:** *Journal, Academic/Scholarly.*
Indexed: ErgAb.
Published by: Polska Akademia Nauk, Komitet Ergonomii/Polish Academy of Sciences, Committee of Ergonomics, ul Grzegorzecka 20, Krakow, 31531, Poland. TEL 48-12-4219351, mmpokors@cyf-kr.edu.pl. Ed. Andrzej Jozefik. R&P Anrzej Jozefik. **Dist. by:** Ars Polona, Obroncow 25, Warsaw 03933, Poland. TEL 48-22-5098609, FAX 48-22-5098610, arspolona@arspolona.com.pl, http://www.arspolona.com.pl.

500 DEU ISSN 0340-8833
ERNST-MACH-INSTITUT, FREIBURG. BERICHT. Text in German. 1966. irreg. **Document type:** *Monographic series, Academic/Scholarly.*
Formerly (until 196?): Ernst-Mach-Institut, Freiburg. Wissenschaftlicher Bericht (0071-1217)
Published by: Fraunhofer-Institut fuer Kurzzeitdynamik - Ernst-Mach-Institut, Eckerstr 4, Freiburg Im Breisgau, 79104, Germany. TEL 49-761-27140, FAX 49-761-2714316, birgit.bindnagel@emi.fraunhofer.de, http://www.emi.fraunhofer.de.

500 600 VEN ISSN 0798-1015
ESPACIOS. Text in Spanish. 1980. 3/yr. **Document type:** *Journal, Academic/Scholarly.*
Related titles: Online - full text ed.: free (effective 2011).
Indexed: SCOPUS.
Published by: Talleres de Impresos Omar, Av Suapure, Quinta Sicoris, Colinas de Bello Monte, Caracas, 1010-A, Venezuela.

500 600 BRA ISSN 1678-1643
ESPIRAL; revista electronica. Text in Portuguese. 1999. q. back issues avail. **Document type:** *Journal, Academic/Scholarly.*
Media: Online - full content.
Published by: Universidade de Sao Paulo, Nucleo Jose Reis de Divulgacao Cientifica, Ave Prof. Luio Martins Rodrigues, 442, Bloco 9, Sala 10, Cidade Universitaria, Sao Paulo, 05508-900, Brazil. TEL 55-11-30914021, FAX 55-11-30914329, revista.espiral@yahoo.com.br. Ed. Crodowaldo Pavan.

500 FRA ISSN 1961-3679
L'ESSENTIEL DE LA SCIENCE. Text in French. 2008. q. EUR 32 for 2 yrs. (effective 2010). **Document type:** *Magazine, Consumer.*
Published by: Lafont Presse, 53 Rue du Chemin Vert, Boulogne-Billancourt, 92100, France. TEL 33-1-46102121, FAX 33-1-45792211, http://www.lafontpresse.fr.

500 600 BRA ISSN 1809-046X
ESTACAO CIENTIFICA. Text in Portuguese. 2005. 3/yr. back issues avail. **Document type:** *Journal, Academic/Scholarly.*
Media: Online - full text.
Published by: Faculdade Estacio de Sa de Juiz de Fora, Campus Rio Branco, Ave Presidente Joao Goulart 600, Cruzeiro do Sul, Juiz de Fora, MG, Brazil. TEL 55-32-32493600, estacaocientifica@estacio.br. Ed. Daniela Borges Lima de Souza.

500 RUS ISSN 1684-2626
T4
ESTESTVENNYE I TEKHNICHESKIE NAUKI. Text in Russian. 2002. bi-m. USD 135 in United States (effective 2004). **Document type:** *Journal, Academic/Scholarly.* **Description:** Publishes scientific research articles written by students and applicants for graduate degrees in Natural and Technical Sciences.
Indexed: RefZh.
—East View.
Published by: Izdatel'stvo Kompaniya Sputnik+, Ryazanskii pr-kt, dom 8a, Moscow, 109428, Russian Federation. TEL 7-095-7304774, sputnikplus2000@mail.ru, http://www.sputnikplus.ru. **Dist. by:** East View Information Services, 10601 Wayzata Blvd, Minneapolis, MN 55305. TEL 952-252-1201, 800-477-1005, FAX 952-252-1202, info@eastview.com, http://www.eastview.com.

500 ESP ISSN 1133-5777
ESTRATOS. Text in Spanish. 1986. 4/yr. adv. bk.rev. back issues avail. **Document type:** *Magazine, Consumer.*
Indexed: GeoRef, IECT, INIS AtomInd, SpeleolAb.
Published by: Empresa Nacional de Residuos Radioactivos, Emilio Vargas, 7, Madrid, 28043, Spain. TEL 34-91-5668160, FAX 34-91-5668169, registro@enresa.es, http://www.enresa.es/. Ed. Jorge Fernandez. Circ: 6,000.

ESTUDIOS SOBRE PATRIMONIO, CULTURA Y CIENCIAS MEDIEVALES. *see* HUMANITIES: COMPREHENSIVE WORKS

720 620 551 BRA ISSN 0101-5303
CODEN: ESTTEM
ESTUDOS TECNOLOGICOS. Text in Portuguese; Summaries in English. 1976. 5/yr. USD 24 (effective 1999). bibl.; charts; illus. **Document type:** *Journal, Academic/Scholarly.*
Related titles: ◆ Series: Matematica Fisica. ISSN 0102-3896; ◆ Acta Geologica Leopoldensia. ISSN 0102-1249.
Indexed: ASFA, B21, C01, ESPM, GeoRef, OTA, SpeleolAb.
Published by: Universidade do Vale do Rio dos Sinos (UNISINOS), Av Unisinos 950, Sao Leopoldo, RS 93022-000, Brazil. TEL 55-51-5908131, FAX 55-51-5908132, http://www.unisinos.br.

200 AUT ISSN 1021-8122
ETHICA - WISSENSCHAFT UND VERANTWORTUNG. Text in German; Abstracts in English. 1993. q. EUR 36.50 (effective 2003). bk.rev. 112 p./no.; back issues avail. **Document type:** *Journal, Academic/Scholarly.*
Formerly (until 1993): Impulse aus Wissenschaft und Forschung
Indexed: DIP, IBR, IBZ.
Published by: Resch Verlag, Maximilianstr 8, Innsbruck, 6010, Austria. TEL 43-512-574772, FAX 43-512-586463, igw@uibk.ac.at, http://www.uibk.ac.at/c/cb/index-en.html. Ed. Andreas Resch. Circ: 500.

500 170 USA ISSN 2151-805X
R724
▼ **ETHICS IN BIOLOGY, ENGINEERING AND MEDICINE.** Text in English. 2010 (Mar.). q. USD 650 to institutions (effective 2011). **Document type:** *Journal, Academic/Scholarly.* **Description:** Features scholarly research on ethical issues that surround biomedical research and the development of new biomaterials, implants, devices and treatments.
Related titles: Online - full text ed.: ISSN 2151-8068. 2010 (Mar.).
Indexed: ESPM.
Published by: Begell House Inc., 50 Cross Hwy, Redding, CT 06896. TEL 203-938-1300, FAX 203-938-1304, orders@begellhouse.com.

179.1 DEU ISSN 1866-8526
ETHICS OF SCIENCE AND TECHNOLOGY ASSESSMENT. Text in English, German. 1998. irreg., latest vol.37, 2010. price varies. **Document type:** *Monographic series, Academic/Scholarly.* **Description:** Serves to publish the results of the Europaeische Akademie's work concerning the scientific study of the consequences of scientific and technological advances for individual and social life and for the natural environment.
Formerly (until 2007): Wissenschaftsethik und Technikfolgenbeurteilung (1860-4803)
Related titles: Online - full text ed.: ISSN 1860-4811.
—BLDSC (9340.257000).
Published by: Springer (Subsidiary of: Springer Science+Business Media), Tiergartenstr 17, Heidelberg, 69121, Germany. TEL 49-6221-4870, FAX 49-6221-345229, subscriptions@springer.com. Ed. Carl Friedrich Gethmann.

ETHIK IN DEN WISSENSCHAFTEN. *see* PHILOSOPHY

500 ARG ISSN 0326-9442
BJ57
ETICA & CIENCIA. Text in English, Spanish. 1987. 2/yr. USD 4 per issue (effective 1998). back issues avail. **Document type:** *Journal, Academic/Scholarly.* **Description:** Includes articles on scientific ethics and moral questions of scientists.
Published by: Zagier & Urruty Publicaciones, P.O. Box 94, Sucursal 19, Buenos Aires, 1419, Argentina. TEL 54-114-5721050, FAX 54-114-5725766. Ed. Patricia Morales. Circ: 1,500.

500 IRN ISSN 1022-7822
ETTELA' RESANI/JOURNAL OF INFORMATION SCIENCES. Text in Persian, Modern; Abstracts in English. 1993. q. USD 53 (effective 2005). 110 p./no.; back issues avail. **Document type:** *Bulletin.* **Description:** Contains technical items and information.
Indexed: CA, L04, LISTA, T02.
Published by: Iranian Information & Documentation Center (IRANDOC), 1188 Enqelab Ave., P O Box 13185-1371, Tehran, Iran. TEL 98-21-6494955, FAX 98-21-6462254, journal@irandoc.ac.ir, http://www.irandoc.ac.ir. Ed. Hussein Gharibi.

500 IRN
ETTELA'AT-E ELMI. Text in Persian, Modern. 1987. m. GBP 40 in Iran; GBP 40 in Pakistan; GBP 46 in Japan; GBP 46 in Europe; GBP 62 in North America; GBP 62 in Australia (effective 1999). adv. **Document type:** *Consumer.* **Description:** Covers developments and advances in all fields of science and technology, including relevant medical and health related issues.
Published by: Ettela'at Publications, Mirdamad Blvd., Naft-e Jonubi St., Ettala'at Bldg., Tehran, 1549951199, Iran. TEL 98-21-29993666, FAX 98-21-3111223. Ed. Mrs. Sayyedeh Tahereh Ghassemi. Circ: 50,000.

▼ **DIE ETTLINGER KINDER-SOMMERAKADEMIE.** *see* CHILDREN AND YOUTH—For

ETUDES MARNAISES. *see* HUMANITIES: COMPREHENSIVE WORKS

EURASIA; journal of mathematics, science & technology education. *see* EDUCATION—Teaching Methods And Curriculum

EUREKA; a periodical for the instruction of science and technology. *see* EDUCATION

EUROPAEISCHE STUDIEN ZUR IDEEN- UND WISSENSCHAFTSGESCHICHTE/EUROPEAN STUDIES IN THE HISTORY OF SCIENCE AND IDEAS. *see* SOCIAL SCIENCES: COMPREHENSIVE WORKS

508 ESP ISSN 2171-6722
EUROPARC. ANUARIO. Key Title: Anuario EUROPARC. Text in Spanish. 2002. a. **Document type:** *Yearbook, Academic/Scholarly.*
Published by: Federacion de Parques Naturales y Nacionales de Europa, Facultad de Ciencias, Modulo 08, 5a. Planta, Desp. 504, Madrid, 28049, Spain. TEL 34-91-3967676, FAX 34-91-47973558, fundacion.gbernaldez@uam.es, http://www.uam.es/otros/fungobe/.

500 BEL ISSN 1784-0686
THE EUROPEAN ACADEMY OF SCIENCES. ANNALS. Text in English. 2003. a.
Related titles: Online - full text ed.: ISSN 1784-357X.
Published by: European Academy of Sciences, Bd d'Avroy 280, Liege, 4000, Belgium. TEL 32-4-2536716, FAX 32-2-2532870.

300 100 NLD ISSN 1879-4912
▼ **EUROPEAN JOURNAL FOR PHILOSOPHY OF SCIENCE.** Text in English. 2011. 3/yr. EUR 315, USD 387 combined subscription to institutions (print & online eds.) (effective 2012). **Document type:** *Journal, Academic/Scholarly.*
Related titles: Online - full text ed.: ISSN 1879-4920. 2011.
Indexed: SCOPUS.
—IE. **CCC.**
Published by: Springer Netherlands (Subsidiary of: Springer Science+Business Media), Van Godewijckstraat 30, Dordrecht, 3311 GX, Netherlands. TEL 31-78-6576050, FAX 31-78-6576474. Ed. Carl Hoefer.

500 TUR
➤ **THE EUROPEAN JOURNAL OF INVASIVE SCIENCES.** Text in English. s-a. free (effective 2011). **Document type:** *Journal, Academic/Scholarly.*
Media: Online - full text.
Published by: Suleyman Demirel Universitesi, Dogu Kampusu Guzel Sanatlar Fakultesi Binasi, Cunur, Isparta, Turkey. TEL 90-246-2113559, FAX 90-246-2113551, http://w3.sdu.edu.tr/.

500 GBR ISSN 1450-216X
➤ **EUROPEAN JOURNAL OF SCIENTIFIC RESEARCH.** Text in English. 2005. m. free (effective 2011). **Document type:** *Journal, Academic/Scholarly.* **Description:** Covers research articles, original research reports, reviews, short communication and scientific commentaries in the fields of applied and theoretical sciences, biology, chemistry, physics, zoology, environmental sciences, mathematics, statistics, geology, engineering, computer science, social sciences, natural and technological sciences, linguistics, medicine, industrial, and all other applied and theoretical sciences.
Media: Online - full text.
Indexed: A01, CA, P34, T02.
Published by: (European Association for Comparative Economic Studies ITA), EuroJournals, 115 Ashby Rd., Leicestershire, LE153AB, United Kingdom. editor@eurojournals.com. Ed. Adrian M Steinberg.

500 GBR ISSN 0957-0748
HD6497.E85 CODEN: DELSE6
EUROPEAN PROFESSIONAL & LEARNED SOCIETIES. DIRECTORY. Text in English. 1989. irreg., latest vol.6, 2004. GBP 147.50 per issue (effective 2009). **Document type:** *Directory, Trade.* **Description:** Contains lists of 6,000 European national professional and learned societies outside Ireland and the UK.
Supersedes in part (in 1989): Directory of European Associations. Part 2: National Learned, Scientific and Technical Societies (0309-5339)
Related titles: Online - full text ed.
—BLDSC (3593.528500). **CCC.**
Published by: C.B.D. Research Ltd., Chancery House, 15 Wickham Rd, Beckenham, Kent BR3 5JS, United Kingdom. TEL 44-20-86507745, FAX 44-20-86500768, cbd@cbdresearch.com. Circ: 4,000. **Dist. in the U.S. by:** Gale Research Co.

500 BEL
EUROPEAN R T D INSIGHT; news on EU research policy and programmes. Text in English. m. free (effective 2001). **Description:** Provides the latest news on European Union (EU) policy, research, education, training and culture, new publications and on-line resources.
Media: Online - full text.
Published by: U K R O, Rue de la Loi 83, BP10, Brussels, B-1040, Belgium. TEL 32-2-2301535, FAX 32-2-2304803, ukro@bbsrc.ac.uk, http://www.ukro.ac.uk. **Co-sponsor:** British Council.

500 GBR ISSN 1062-7987
AS9 CODEN: EURREK
➤ **EUROPEAN REVIEW.** Abbreviated title: E R. Text in English. 1993. q. GBP 191, USD 329 to institutions; GBP 202, USD 356 combined subscription to institutions (print & online eds.) (effective 2012). adv. back issues avail.; reprints avail. **Document type:** *Journal, Academic/Scholarly.* **Description:** Promotes intra-European studies relating to society, education, and research from an interdisciplinary approach, including the humanities, law, economics, social sciences, cognitive science, mathematics, medicine, natural sciences, and technological sciences.
Related titles: Microform ed.: (from PQC); Online - full text ed.: ISSN 1474-0575. GBP 179, USD 315 to institutions (effective 2012).
Indexed: A01, A03, A08, A22, ASSIA, B21, BrHumI, CA, E01, E03, FR, GEOBASE, I13, IBSS, MLA-IB, NSA, P10, P11, P21, P26, P30, P34, P42, P48, P52, P54, P56, PQC, PRA, PSA, RILM, S02, S03, SCOPUS, SSA, SociolAb, T02.
—BLDSC (3829.935100), IE, Infotrieve, Ingenta. **CCC.**
Published by: (Academia Europaea), Cambridge University Press, The Edinburgh Bldg, Shaftesbury Rd, Cambridge, CB2 8RU, United Kingdom. TEL 44-1223-312393, FAX 44-1223-315052, journals@cambridge.org, http://www.cambridge.org/uk. Ed. Theo d'Haen. Adv. contact Rebecca Roberts TEL 44-1223-325083. **Subscr. to:** Cambridge University Press, 32 Ave of the Americas, New York, NY 10013. TEL 212-337-5000, FAX 212-691-3239, journals_subscriptions@cup.org.

S

500 USA ISSN 1937-3198
EUROPEAN SCIENCE AND TECHNOLOGY REVIEW. Text in English. 2007 (Jul.). m. USD 120 (effective 2010). back issues avail. **Document type:** *Newsletter, Academic/Scholarly.*
Media: Online - full text.
Indexed: P11, P41, P48, P52, P56, PQC.
Published by: Transatlantic Euro-American Multimedia LLC, PO Box 6793, Portsmouth, VA 23703. service@teamultimedia.com.

EUROPEAN SCIENCE EDITING. *see* PUBLISHING AND BOOK TRADE

500 FRA
EUROPEAN SCIENCE FOUNDATION. ANNUAL REPORT/EUROPEAN SCIENCE FOUNDATION. RAPPORT ANNUEL. Text in English, French. 1981. a.
Related titles: Online - full text ed.
Published by: European Science Foundation, 1 Quai Lezay Marnesia, Strasbourg, 67080 Cedex, France. TEL 33-3-88767100, FAX 33-3-88370532, esf@esf.org, http://www.esf.org.

500 FRA
EUROPEAN SCIENCE FOUNDATION. SCIENTIFIC PAPERS AND POSITION PAPERS. Text in English. irreg.
Published by: European Science Foundation, 1 Quai Lezay Marnesia, Strasbourg, 67080 Cedex, France. TEL 33-3-88767100, FAX 33-3-88370532, esf@esf.org, http://www.esf.org.

500 FRA ISSN 1560-7623
EUROPEAN SCIENCE POLICY BRIEFING. Text in English. irreg.
Related titles: Online - full text ed.
Published by: European Science Foundation, 1 Quai Lezay Marnesia, Strasbourg, 67080 Cedex, France. TEL 33-3-88767100, FAX 33-3-88370532, esf@esf.org, http://www.esf.org.

500 FRA ISSN 2108-7237
EVALUATION DE LA RECHERCHE EN S H S. (Sciences Humaines et Sociales) Text in French, English. 2008. irreg.
Media: Online - full text.
Address: http://evaluation.hypotheses.org.

EVANGELIUM UND WISSENSCHAFT; Beitraege zum interdisziplinaeren Gespraech. *see* RELIGIONS AND THEOLOGY

600 500 IND ISSN 0531-495X
EVERYMAN'S SCIENCE. Text in English. 1966. bi-m. INR 50 to individuals; INR 200 to institutions (effective 2011). adv. back issues avail. **Document type:** *Academic/Scholarly.* **Description:** Contains popular science articles.
Related titles: Online - full text ed.: free (effective 2011).
Indexed: RefZh.
Published by: Indian Science Congress Association, c/o Dr. Vijay Laxmi Saxena, General Secretary, 14 Dr Biresh Guha St, Kolkata, West Bengal 700 017, India. TEL 91-33-2474530, FAX 91-33-2402551, iscacal@vsnl.net. Ed. S S Katiyar.

EVOLUTIONARY PSYCHOLOGY; an international journal of evolutionary approaches to psychology and behavior. *see* PSYCHOLOGY

500 DEU ISSN 1868-6478
▼ ➤ **EVOLVING SYSTEMS.** Text in English. 2010. 4/yr. EUR 326, USD 437 combined subscription to institutions (print & online eds.) (effective 2012). **Document type:** *Journal, Academic/Scholarly.*
Related titles: Online - full text ed.: ISSN 1868-6486. 2010.
Indexed: SCOPUS.
—CCC.
Published by: Springer (Subsidiary of: Springer Science+Business Media), Tiergartenstr 17, Heidelberg, 69121, Germany. TEL 49-6221-4870, FAX 49-6221-345229, subscriptions@springer.com.

500 USA
EXCITEMENT AND FASCINATION OF SCIENCE; reflections by eminent scientists. Text in English. 1965. irreg., latest vol.4, 1995. adv. back issues avail. **Document type:** *Monographic series, Academic/Scholarly.* **Description:** Presents autobiographical essays by prominent scientists.
Published by: Annual Reviews, PO Box 10139, Palo Alto, CA 94303. TEL 650-493-4400, FAX 650-424-0910, 800-523-8635, service@annualreviews.org, http://www.annualreviews.org.

508 GBR ISSN 1367-7047
EXMOOR NATURALIST. Text in English. 1975. irreg. free to members. **Document type:** *Magazine, Consumer.*
Indexed: Z01.
Published by: Exmoor Natural History Society, The Secretary, 12 King George Rd, Minehead, Somerset TA24 5JD, United Kingdom. TEL 44-1643-707624, carol.enhs@virgin.net.

500 NLD ISSN 1871-7306
Q4
EXPLORE. Text in Dutch. 1985. 6/yr. EUR 39.95 (effective 2009). adv. bk.rev. index. **Document type:** *Journal, Academic/Scholarly.* **Description:** Publishes articles on topics relating to the physical and biological sciences, new technologies, anthropology and the natural world.
Former titles (until 2005): Mens en Wetenschap (0921-559X); (until 1987): Aarde en Kosmos - D J O (0921-769X); Which was formed by the merger of (1974-1985): D J O - De Jonge Onderzoeker (0166-4697); (1974-1985): Aarde en Kosmos (0166-4786); And which incorporates (1970-1985): Spiegel der Natuur (0165-8409); (1975-1985): Technovisie (0165-5329); Which was formerly (1971-1975): M T S - er (0921-7681)
—IE, Infotrieve.
Published by: Beta Publishers, Postbus 2696, Amersfoort, 3800 GE, Netherlands. TEL 31-33-4535060, FAX 31-33-4535065, info@betapublishers.nl, http://www.betapublishers.nl. Eds. Feri Roseboom, Gijs van Hengstum. Pub. Dr. Roeland Dobbelaer. Adv. contact Bart van der Wal TEL 31-38-4606384. color page EUR 4,750; 178 x 253. Circ: 15,000.

708.11 508 AUS ISSN 1833-752X
QH1
EXPLORE. Text in English. 2006. q. **Document type:** *Magazine, Consumer.*
Formed by the merger of (1988-2006): Muse (1445-310X); (1996-2006): Nature Australia (1324-2598); Which was formerly (until 1995): A N H (1324-2059); (until 1992): Australian Natural History (0004-9840); (1921-1961): Australian Museum Magazine (0155-3496)
—Ingenta, INIST, Linda Hall.
Published by: Australian Museum, 6 College St, Sydney, NSW 2010, Australia. TEL 61-2-93206200, FAX 61-2-93206073, http://www.austmus.gov.au.

500 USA ISSN 1091-8361
➤ **EXPLORE! (PRESCOTT)**; for the integrative health professional & health conscious consumer. Text in English. 199?. bi-m. **Document type:** *Journal, Academic/Scholarly.*
Related titles: Online - full text ed.: USD 29.95 to members (effective 2011).
—BLDSC (3842.209150), IE, Ingenta.
Published by: Explore Publications, Inc., PO Box 11510, Prescott, AZ 86304. TEL 800-320-6036, explorerpub@sos.net.

500 USA ISSN 1550-8307
R733
EXPLORE: THE JOURNAL OF SCIENCE & HEALING. Text in English. 2005 (Jan.). bi-m. USD 214 in United States to institutions; USD 284 elsewhere to institutions (effective 2012). adv. back issues avail.; reprints avail. **Document type:** *Journal, Academic/Scholarly.* **Description:** Addresses the scientific principles behind, and applications of, healing practices from a variety of sources, including conventional, alternative, and cross-cultural medicine.
Related titles: Online - full text ed.: ISSN 1878-7541 (from ScienceDirect).
Indexed: A20, A26, C06, C07, CA, CurCont, EMBASE, ExcerpMed, I05, MEDLINE, P30, R10, Reac, SCI, SCOPUS, T02, W07.
—BLDSC (3842.209125), IE, Ingenta. **CCC.**
Published by: Elsevier Inc. (Subsidiary of: Elsevier Science & Technology), 1600 John F Kennedy Blvd, Philadelphia, PA 19103. TEL 215-239-3900, FAX 215-238-7883, JournalCustomerService-usa@elsevier.com, http://www.elsevier.com. Eds. Ben Kligler, Dean Radin. Circ: 700.

508 USA ISSN 0014-5009
QH1 CODEN: EXPOAI
EXPLORER (CLEVELAND). Text in English. 1938. q. bk.rev. charts; illus. Index. back issues avail. **Document type:** *Magazine, Consumer.* **Description:** Addresses natural history, environmental, conservation and general science topics for members of natural history museums, science centers, and schools.
Indexed: BiolDig, GeoRef, SpeleolAb.
—Ingenta.
Published by: Cleveland Museum of Natural History, One Wade Oval Dr, University Circle, Cleveland, OH 44106. TEL 216-231-4600. Ed. Megan Harding. Circ: 10,300.

500 CAN ISSN 1499-4569
EYE ON SCIENCE; a student journal in science and technology. Text in English. 2001. q. **Document type:** *Journal, Academic/Scholarly.*
Indexed: C03, CEI, P11, P48, P52, P56, PQC.
Published by: Ontario Institute for Studies in Education, 252 Bloor St West, 11th Fl, Toronto, ON M5S 1V6, Canada. TEL 416-483-7345.

500 USA ISSN 0092-9824
Q11
F A S PUBLIC INTEREST REPORT. Text in English. 1946. bi-m. USD 25 to individuals; USD 50 to institutions (effective 1999). back issues avail. **Document type:** *Newsletter.*
Formerly: F A S Newsletter
Related titles: Online - full text ed.
Indexed: HRIR, P30, RASB.
Published by: Federation of American Scientists, 1725 DeSales St, NW, 6th Fl, Washington, DC 20036. TEL 202-546-3300, FAX 202-675-1010. Ed. Jeremy Stone. Circ: 4,000.

500 NOR
F F I PUBLICATION. (Forsvarets Forskningsinstitutt) Text and summaries in English. 1953. irreg. **Document type:** *Monographic series, Academic/Scholarly.*
Former titles (until 1996): N D R E Publication (0800-4412); (until 1980): Norway. Forsvarets Forskningsinstitutt. N D R E Report (0085-4301)
—INIST.
Published by: Forsvarets Forskningsinstitutt/Norwegian Defence Research Establishment, PO Box 25, Kjeller, 2027, Norway. TEL 47-63-807000, FAX 47-63-807115, ffi@ffi.no, http://www.ffi.no. Circ: (controlled).

605 GBR ISSN 1475-1704
Q1
F S T JOURNAL. (Foundation for Science and Technology) Text in English. 1985. q. GBP 55 to non-members; free to members (effective 2009). back issues avail. **Document type:** *Journal, Academic/Scholarly.*
Formerly (until 2001): Technology, Innovation and Society (0951-2918)
Related titles: Online - full text ed.
—CCC.
Published by: The Foundation for Science and Technology, 10 Carlton House Terrace, London, SW1Y 5AH, United Kingdom. TEL 44-20-73212220, FAX 44-20-73212221, office@foundation.org.uk.

500 370 BRA ISSN 1678-1244
F U C A M P. CADERNOS. (Fundacao Carmelitana Mario Palmerio) Text in Portuguese. 2002. a. **Document type:** *Journal, Academic/Scholarly.*
Related titles: Online - full text ed.
Published by: Fundacao Carmelitana Mario Palmerio (F U C A M P), Av Brasil Oeste s/n, Jardim Zenith, Monte Carmelo, MG 38500-000, Brazil. TEL 55-34-38425272. Ed. Joao Francisco Natal Greco.

FACHPROSAFORSCHUNG - GRENZUEBERSCHREITUNGEN. *see* LITERATURE

500 PRT ISSN 1645-3360
FACULDADE DE CIENCIAS DO PORTO. DEPARTAMENTO DE GEOLOGIA. PUBLICACOES. Text in Portuguese. 1935-1993; resumed 2001. irreg. **Document type:** *Report, Consumer.*
Formerly (until 1993): Faculdade de Ciencias do Porto. Museu e Laboratorio Mineralogico e Geologico. Publicacoes (0370-0631)
Published by: Universidade do Porto, Faculdade de Ciencias, Rua do Campo Alegre s/n, Oporto, 4169-007, Portugal. TEL 351-220-402000, http://sigarra.up.pt/fcup/.

500 300 CHN ISSN 1006-8341
FANGZHI GAOXIAO JICHU KEXUE XUEBAO/BASIC SCIENCES JOURNAL OF TEXTILE UNIVERSITIES. Text in Chinese; Abstracts in Chinese, English. 1987. q. **Document type:** *Journal, Academic/Scholarly.*
Formerly (until 1995): Fangzhi Jichu Kexue Xuebao/Journal of Textile Basic Science (1002-123X)
Related titles: Online - full text ed.
Indexed: A28, APA, BrCerAb, C&ISA, CA/WCA, CCMJ, CIA, CerAb, CivEngAb, CorrAb, E&CAJ, E11, EEA, EMA, ESPM, EnvEAb, H15, M&TEA, M09, MBF, METADEX, MSN, MathR, SCOPUS, SolStAb, T04, WAA, WTA, Z02.
Published by: Xi'an Gongcheng Daxue/Xi'an Polytechnic University, 19, Jinhua Nan Lu, 179 Xinxiang, Xi'an, 710048, China. TEL 86-29-82330074, FAX 86-29-83235130, http://www.xpu.edu.cn.

FARQUHAR STUDENT JOURNAL. *see* HUMANITIES: COMPREHENSIVE WORKS

500 SWE ISSN 0014-8903
CODEN: FUOFAA
➤ **FAUNA OCH FLORA**; Svensk faunistik och floristik. Text in Swedish; Summaries in English. 1906. q. SEK 200 domestic; SEK 250 in Scandinavia; SEK 300 elsewhere (effective 2004). adv. bk.rev. charts; illus. **Document type:** *Academic/Scholarly.* **Description:** Articles on biology, zoology, botany, ecology, geology, astronomy, fossils, natural history and nature in general.
Indexed: GeoRef, SpeleolAb, Z01.
Published by: (Stiftelsen foer Svensk Faunistik och Floristik), Sveriges Lantbruksuniversitet, ArtDatabanken/Swedish University of Agricultural Sciences. Swedish Species Information Center, Baeckloesavaegen 8, PO Box 7007, Uppsala, 75007, Sweden. TEL 46-18-672577, FAX 46-18-673480, artdatabanken@artdata.slu.se. Eds. Ragmar Hall TEL 46-18-671977, Tomas Carlberg TEL 46-18-672579. adv.: B&W page SEK 4,000. Circ: 7,000.

500 CAN ISSN 0824-0310
Q180.C2
FEDERAL SCIENTIFIC ACTIVITIES. Text in English, French. 1978. a.
Former titles (until 1983): Canada. Ministry of State for Science and Technology. Federal Science Activities (0706-2206); Canada. Ministry of State for Science and Technology. Federal Science Programs (0701-7391)
Related titles: Online - full text ed.: ISSN 1480-8684.
Indexed: A01, A03, A08, C04, C05, CA, T02.
Published by: Statistics Canada/Statistique Canada, Publications Sales and Services, Ottawa, ON K1A 0T6, Canada. http://www.statcan.gc.ca.

FEDERAL SCIENTISTS AND ENGINEERS. *see* BUSINESS AND ECONOMICS—Personnel Management

500 CHN ISSN 1006-6144
FENXI KEXUE XUEBAO/JOURNAL OF ANALYTICAL SCIENCE. Text in Chinese. 1985. bi-m. CNY 5 domestic (effective 2000). **Document type:** *Journal, Academic/Scholarly.*
Formerly (until 1993): Henliang Fenxi
Related titles: Online - full text ed.
Indexed: A22, A28, A40, APA, BrCerAb, C&ISA, CA/WCA, CIA, CerAb, CivEngAb, CorrAb, E&CAJ, E11, EEA, EMA, ESPM, EnvEAb, H15, M&TEA, M09, MBF, METADEX, SolStAb, T04, WAA.
—BLDSC (4928.600000), IE, Ingenta, Linda Hall.
Published by: (Nanjing Daxue, Beijing Daxue), Wuhan Daxue Huaxue yu Fezi Kexue Xueyuan/Wuhan University, College of Chemistry and Molecular Sciences, Wuchang, Luojiashan, Whuhan, 430072, China. TEL 86-27-68752248, http://www.chem.whu.edu.cn/.

506 LUX ISSN 1682-5519
FERRANTIA. Text in Multiple languages. 1981. irreg. **Document type:** *Journal, Academic/Scholarly.*
Former titles (until 2001): Musee National d'Histoire Naturelle de Luxembourg. Travaux Scientifiques (1017-3366); (until 1987): Musee d'Histoire Naturelle. Travaux Scientifiques (0251-2424)
Related titles: Online - full text ed.: ISSN 1812-0539.
Indexed: Z01.
—INIST, Linda Hall.
Published by: Musee National d'Histoire Naturelle, 25 rue Munster, Luxembourg, 2160, Luxembourg. TEL 352-462233, http://www.mnhn.lu.

FEUILLETS DU NATURALISTE. *see* CHILDREN AND YOUTH—For

FIBEROPTIC PRODUCT NEWS TECHNOLOGY REFERENCE MANUAL. *see* COMMUNICATIONS—Telephone And Telegraph

500 100 ITA ISSN 1970-7274
FILOSOFIA E SCIENZA NELL'ETA MODERNA. SER.1. STUDI. Text in Italian. 1971. irreg. **Document type:** *Monographic series, Academic/Scholarly.*
Former titles (until 2002): Filosofia e Scienza nel Cinquecento e nel Seicento. Ser 1, Studi (1973-0004); (until 1981): Centro di Studi del Pensiero Filosofico del Cinquecento e del Seicento in Relazione ai Problemi della Scienza. Pubblicazioni. Ser.1, Studi (1973-0012)
Published by: (Consiglio Nazionale delle Ricerche (C N R), Istituto per la Storia del Pensiero Filosofico e Scientifico Moderno), Franco Angeli Edizioni, Viale Monza 106, Milan, 20127, Italy. TEL 39-02-2837141, FAX 39-02-26144793, redazioni@francoangeli.it, http://www.francoangeli.it.

500 100 ITA ISSN 1973-0063
FILOSOFIA E SCIENZA NELL'ETA MODERNA. SER 3. TESTI INEDITI O RARI. Text in Italian. 1976. irreg. price varies. **Document type:** *Monographic series, Academic/Scholarly.*
Former titles (until 2002): Filosofia e Scienza nel Cinquecento e nel Seicento. Ser. 3. Testi (1973-0055); (until 1982): Centro di Studi del Pensiero Filosofico del Cinquecento e del Seicento in Relazione ai Problemi della Scienza. Ser. 3. Testi (1973-0047)
Published by: (Consiglio Nazionale delle Ricerche (C N R), Istituto per la Storia del Pensiero Filosofico e Scientifico Moderno), Franco Angeli Edizioni, Viale Monza 106, Milan, 20127, Italy. TEL 39-02-2837141, FAX 39-02-26144793, redazioni@francoangeli.it, http://www.francoangeli.it.

FILOSOFSKIE NAUKI (MOSCOW). *see* PHILOSOPHY

500.021 600.021 FIN ISSN 0785-885X
Q127.F5
FINLAND. TILASTOKESKUS. SCIENCE AND TECHNOLOGY IN FINLAND. Text in English. 1990. irreg., latest 2005. EUR 60 (effective 2008). **Document type:** *Government.*
Related titles: ◆ Finnish ed.: Finland. Tilastokeskus. Tiede ja Teknologia. ISSN 0785-0719; ◆ Series of: Finland. Tilastokeskus. Suomen Virallinen Tilasto. ISSN 1795-5165.
Published by: Tilastokeskus/Statistics Finland, Tyopajakatu 13, Statistics Finland, Helsinki, 00022, Finland. TEL 358-9-17341, FAX 358-9-17342279, http://www.stat.fi.

500.021 600.021 FIN ISSN 0785-0719
FINLAND. TILASTOKESKUS. TIEDE JA TEKNOLOGIA. Text in Finnish. 1990. irreg., latest 2005. EUR 60 (effective 2008). **Document type:** *Government.*
Related titles: ◆ English ed.: Finland. Tilastokeskus. Science and Technology in Finland. ISSN 0785-885X; ◆ Series of: Finland. Tilastokeskus. Suomen Virallinen Tilasto. ISSN 1795-5165.
Published by: Tilastokeskus/Statistics Finland, Tyopajakatu 13, Statistics Finland, Helsinki, 00022, Finland. TEL 358-9-17341, FAX 358-9-17342279, http://www.stat.fi.

500.021 600.021 FIN ISSN 1795-536X
FINLAND. TILASTOKESKUS. TIEDE, TEKNOLOGIA JA TIETOYHTEISKUNTA/FINLAND. STATISTICS FINLAND. SCIENCE, TECHNOLOGY, AND INFORMATION SOCIETY/ FINLAND. STATISTIKCENTRALEN. VETENSKAP, TEKNOLOGI OCH INFORMATIONSSAMHAELLE. Text in English, Finnish, Swedish. 1968. irreg. EUR 37 (effective 2008). **Document type:** *Government.*
Former titles (until 2005): Finland. Tilastokeskus. Tiede, Teknologia ja Tutkimus (1457-1218); (until 1998): Finland. Tilastokeskus. Tiede ja Teknologia (1236-5858); Which superseded in part (in 1993): Finland. Tilastokeskus. Koulutus ja Tutkimus (0784-8242); Which was formerly (until 1988): Finland. Tilastokeskus. K O Koulutus ja Tutkimus (0355-2268)
Related titles: Online - full text ed.; ◆ Series: Finland. Tilastokeskus. Tutkimus- ja Kehittamisrahoitus Valtion Talousarviossa. ISSN 1459-9066; ◆ Finland. Tilastokeskus. Tutkimus- ja Kehittamistoiminta Suomessa. ISSN 1457-4101.
Published by: Tilastokeskus/Statistics Finland, Tyopajakatu 13, Statistics Finland, Helsinki, 00022, Finland. TEL 358-9-17341, FAX 358-9-17342279.

500 TUR ISSN 1308-9072
➤ **FIRAT UNIVERSITESI MUHENDISLIK BILIMLERI DERGISI/FIRAT UNIVERSITY JOURNAL OF SCIENCE AND ENGINEERING.** Text in Turkish, English. 1986. s-a. **Document type:** *Journal, Academic/ Scholarly.* **Description:** Contains article related to basic and applied science studies.
Formerly: Firat Universitesi Fen ve Muhendislik Bilimleri Dergisi (1300-2708); Which superseded in part (in 1989): Firat University. Science and Technology Journal (1012-0181)
Related titles: Online - full text ed.: free (effective 2010).
Indexed: Z01.
Published by: Firat Universitesi, Rektorlugu, Elazig, 23119, Turkey. posta@firat.edu.tr, http://www.firat.edu.tr.

500 ITA ISSN 1014-2800
FLORA, FAUNA Y AREAS SILVESTRES. Text in English, Spanish. 1986. q. **Document type:** *Newsletter, Trade.*
Indexed: C01.
Published by: Food and Agriculture Organization of the United Nations (F A O), Viale delle Terme di Caracalla, Rome, RM 00153, Italy. TEL 39-06-5705-1, FAX 39-06-5705-3360, publications-sales@fao.org, http://www.fao.org.

578.012 ESP ISSN 1138-5952
FLORA MONTIBERICA. Text in Spanish. 1995. 3/yr.
Related titles: Online - full text ed.: ISSN 1988-799X. 2004.
Address: Jardin Botanico - UV, C Quart, 82, Valencia, 46008, Spain. http://www.floramontiberica.org/entrada.htm. Ed. Gonzalo Mateo Sanz.

578.012 DNK ISSN 0015-3818
QH7 CODEN: FLFAAN
➤ **FLORA OG FAUNA.** Text in Danish; Summaries in English. 1893. q. DKK 190 membership; DKK 215 to institutional members; DKK 230 foreign (effective 2009). bk.rev. illus. index. **Document type:** *Journal, Academic/Scholarly.* **Description:** Original papers on taxonomy, distribution, biology, ecology and conservation of Danish plants and animals.
Indexed: ASFA, B21, B25, BIOSIS Prev, ESPM, MycolAb, SCOPUS, SWRA, VirolAbstr, Z01.
—INIST.
Published by: Naturhistorisk Forening for Jylland, c/o Henrik Sell, Naturhistorisk Museum, Universitetsparken, Aarhus C, 8000, Denmark. TEL 45-86-129777, FAX 45-86-130882, sell@nathist.dk. Ed. Jon Feilberg TEL 45-57-600125.

508 USA
FLORIDA MUSEUM OF NATURAL HISTORY. SPECIAL PUBLICATION. Text in English. 19??. irreg. back issues avail. **Document type:** *Trade.*
Indexed: Z01.
Published by: Florida Museum of Natural History, PO Box 117800, Gainesville, FL 32611. TEL 352-273-1940, FAX 352-846-0287, members@flmnh.ufl.edu, http://www.flmnh.ufl.edu.

500 USA ISSN 0098-4590
Q11 CODEN: FLSCAQ
➤ **FLORIDA SCIENTIST.** Text in English. 1936. q. free to members (effective 2010). adv. bk.rev. charts; illus.; stat. index. 75 p./no. 1 cols./p.; back issues avail.; reprints avail. **Document type:** *Journal, Academic/Scholarly.* **Description:** Scientific and educational material in many categories of science for professionals, nonprofessionals, students and laypersons.
Former titles (until 1973): Florida Academy of Sciences. Quarterly Journal (0015-3850); (until 1945): Florida Academy of Sciences. Proceedings (0097-0581)
Related titles: Microform ed.: (from PQC).
Indexed: A22, ANAG, ASFA, Agr, AnBeAb, B21, B25, BIOSIS Prev, BiolDig, CIN, ChemAb, ChemTitl, E11, E17, EIP, ESPM, EntAb, GeoRef, MycolAb, OceAb, P11, P48, P52, P56, PQC, PollutAb, RefZh, SASA, SSciA, SWRA, SpeleolAb, T04, W08, WildRev, Z01.
—BLDSC (3956.130000), CASDDS, IE, Ingenta, INIST, Linda Hall.
Published by: Florida Academy of Sciences, Inc., 777 E Princeton St, Orlando, FL 32803. TEL 407-514-2079, FAX 407-514-2081, floridaacademyofsciences@osc.org. Ed. Thomas J Manning TEL 229-333-7178.

500 USA ISSN 1043-4275
FLORIDA STATE UNIVERSITY RESEARCH IN REVIEW. Text in English. 1969. q. free. bk.rev. charts; illus.
Formerly (until 1989): Florida State University Bulletin: Research in Review (0885-2073)
Indexed: IFP, PAIS.
—Ingenta.
Published by: Florida State University, Office of Graduate Studies and Research, 109 HMB R 23, Tallahassee, FL 32306. TEL 904-644-8634. Ed. Frank H Stephenson. Circ: 9,500.

500 NLD ISSN 1386-6184
TA349 CODEN: FTCOF9
➤ **FLOW, TURBULENCE AND COMBUSTION.** Text in English. 1966. 8/yr. EUR 1,675, USD 1,770 combined subscription to institutions (print & online eds.) (effective 2012). adv. reprint service avail. from PSC. **Document type:** *Journal, Academic/Scholarly.* **Description:** Publishes original theoretical and experimental contributions and research reports relating to fluid dynamics and heat and mass transfer, with an emphasis on applied research.
Formerly (until 1998): Applied Scientific Research (0003-6994); Which was formed by the 1966 merger of: Applied Scientific Research. Section A. Mechanics, Heat (0365-7132); Applied Scientific Research. Section B. Electrophysics, Acoustics, Optics, Mathematical Methods (0365-7140)
Related titles: Microform ed.: (from PQC); Online - full text ed.: ISSN 1573-1987 (from IngentaConnect).
Indexed: A20, A22, A26, A28, APA, APIAb, ASCA, ASFA, ApMecR, BibLing, BrCerAb, C&ISA, C10, CA, CA/WCA, CEA, CEABA, CIA, CPEI, CerAb, ChemAb, CivEngAb, CorrAb, CurCont, E&CAJ, E01, E11, EEA, EMA, ESPM, EngInd, EnvEAb, GeoRef, H15, I05, IBR, IBZ, ISMEC, ISR, Inspec, M&TEA, M09, MBF, METADEX, MathR, PetrolAb, RefZh, SCI, SCOPUS, SolStAb, SpeleolAb, T02, T04, TCEA, W07, WAA, Z02.
—BLDSC (3958.438000), AskIEEE, CASDDS, IE, Infotrieve, Ingenta, INIST, Linda Hall. **CCC.**
Published by: Springer Netherlands (Subsidiary of: Springer Science+Business Media), Van Godewijckstraat 30, Dordrecht, 3311 GX, Netherlands. TEL 31-78-6576050, FAX 31-78-6576474, http://www.springer.com. Ed. K Hanjalic.

500 FRA ISSN 1154-2721
T57.85
FLUX; cahiers scientifiques internationaux reseaux et territoires. Text in English, French; Summaries in English, French. 1989. 4/yr. EUR 80 domestic to institutions; EUR 90 in Europe to institutions; EUR 105 elsewhere to institutions (effective 2009). **Document type:** *Journal, Academic/Scholarly.*
Formerly (until 1989): Groupement de Recherche "Reseaux". Cahier (1162-9630)
Related titles: Microfiche ed.
Indexed: FR, GEOBASE, IBSS, RefZh, SCOPUS.
—INIST.
Published by: (France. Centre National de la Recherche Scientifique), Association Metropolis, 7 Route de Bercheres, Les Duveaux, 28410, France. TEL 33-2-37822826, FAX 33-2-37822827. Eds. Marianne Ollivier-Trigalo, Olivier Coutard.

500 GRC ISSN 1108-6661
FOCUS. Text in Greek. 2000. m. adv. **Document type:** *Magazine, Consumer.* **Description:** Contains articles and features on the scientific mysteries of the Earth and universe, including evolution, animal behavior, exotic lands and new technologies.
Related titles: Online - full text ed.
Published by: Liberis Publications S.A./Ekdoseon Lymperi A.E., Ioannou Metaxa 80, Karelas, Koropi 19400, Greece. TEL 30-210-6688000, FAX 30-210-6688300, info@liberis.gr, http://www.liberis.gr. Ed. Christos Tsanakas. Adv. contact Sofia Salemi. Circ: 27,490 (paid).

500 ITA ISSN 1824-954X
FOCUS DOMANDE & RISPOSTE. Text in Italian. 2004. m. adv. **Document type:** *Magazine, Consumer.*
Published by: Gruner + Jahr (G + J) Mondadori SpA (Subsidiary of: Arnoldo Mondadori Editore SpA), Corso Monforte 54, Milan, 20122, Italy. TEL 39-02-76210206, FAX 39-02-76013439, info@gujm.it. Circ: 240,000 (paid).

500 600 JAM ISSN 1010-9552
FOCUS ON SCIENCE AND TECHNOLOGY. Text in English. 2/yr. **Document type:** *Magazine, Consumer.*
Published by: Scientific Research Council, PO Box 350, Kingston, 6, Jamaica. TEL 876-927-1771, FAX 876-927-1840, infosrc@cwjamaica.com, http://www.src-jamaica.org.

500 708.39 HUN ISSN 0134-1243
QH7 CODEN: FHNME7
FOLIA HISTORICO-NATURALIA MUSEI MATRAENSIS. Text in Hungarian, German. 1972. a. **Document type:** *Journal, Academic/ Scholarly.*
Indexed: Z01.
Published by: Matra Muzeum, Kossuth utca 40, Gyongyos, 3200, Hungary. TEL 36-37-311447, FAX 36-37-311884, matramuz@enternet.hu, http://www.matramuzeum.hu.

FOND ZA NAUCNA ISTRAZIVANJA. BILTEN. *see* HUMANITIES: COMPREHENSIVE WORKS

500 FRA ISSN 0980-157X
GN1
FONDATION FYSSEN. ANNALES. Text in French. 1985. a. **Document type:** *Monographic series, Academic/Scholarly.*
Indexed: AICP, FR.
—INIST.
Published by: Fondation Fyssen, 194 Rue de Rivoli, Paris, 75001, France. TEL 33-1-42975316, FAX 33-1-42601795, http://www.fondation-fyssen.org.

FONDAZIONE GIORGIO RONCHI. ATTI. *see* PHYSICS—Optics

500 FRA ISSN 0295-6977
FONDEMENTS DES SCIENCES. Text in French. 1983. irreg. price varies. **Document type:** *Monographic series, Academic/Scholarly.*
Published by: (Universite de Strasbourg I (Louis Pasteur)), Centre National de la Recherche Scientifique, Campus Gerard-Megie, 3 Rue Michel-Ange, Paris, 75794, France. TEL 33-1-44964000, FAX 33-1-44965390, http://www.cnrseditions.fr.

500 001.3 ITA ISSN 1724-2355
FONTI. Variant title: Ateneo di Scienze, Lettere ed Arti di Bergamo. Fonti. Text in Italian. 2002. irreg. **Document type:** *Monographic series, Academic/Scholarly.*
Published by: Ateneo di Scienze, Lettere ed Arti di Bergamo, Via Torquato Tasso 4, Bergamo, 24124, Italy. http:// www.ateneobergamo.it.

571.3 JPN ISSN 0911-6036
➤ **FORMA.** Text in English. 1989. 4/yr. free domestic to members; USD 80 foreign to members; USD 150 to non-members (effective 2002). 100 p./no.; back issues avail. **Document type:** *Journal, Academic/ Scholarly.* **Description:** Covers a variety of scientific research motivated by an interest in forms.
Indexed: CCMJ, MSN, MathR, Z02.
—IE, Ingenta. **CCC.**
Published by: (Society for Science on Form Japan/Katachi no Kagakkai), K T K Scientific Publishers, 2003 Sansei Jiyugaoka Haimu, 5-27-19 Okusawa, Setagaya-ku, Tokyo, 158-0083, Japan. TEL 81-3-3718-7500, FAX 81-3-3718-4406, forma@terrapub.co.jp, http:// www.terrapub.co.jp. Ed., R&P Ryuji Takaki TEL 81-42-388-7224. Circ: 500.

500 DEU ISSN 1868-9035
FORSCHEN; Wissenschaftsmagazin. Text in German. 1995. s-a. adv. **Document type:** *Magazine, Trade.*
Formerly (until 2009): Thema Forschung (1434-7768)
Indexed: GeoRef.
Published by: (Technische Universitaet Darmstadt), V M M Wirtschaftsverlag GmbH & Co. KG, Kleine Grottenau 1, Augsburg, 86150, Germany. TEL 49-821-44050, FAX 49-821-4405409, info@vmm-wirtschaftsverlag.de, http://www.vmm-wirtschaftsverlag.de. Circ: 6,000 (controlled).

500 DEU ISSN 0172-1518
Q180.G4
FORSCHUNG. Text in German. 1958. q. GBP 47 in United Kingdom to institutions; EUR 65 in Europe to institutions; USD 92 elsewhere to institutions; GBP 55 combined subscription in United Kingdom to institutions (print & online eds.); EUR 75 combined subscription in Europe to institutions (print & online eds.); USD 107 combined subscription elsewhere to institutions (print & online eds.) (effective 2012). adv. bk.rev. back issues avail.; reprint service avail. from PSC. **Document type:** *Journal, Academic/Scholarly.*
Formerly (until 1979): Deutsche Forschungsgemeinschaft. Mitteilungen (0417-1780)
Related titles: Online - full text ed.: ISSN 1522-2357. GBP 47 in United Kingdom to institutions; EUR 65 in Europe to institutions; USD 92 elsewhere to institutions (effective 2012); ◆ English Translation: German Research. ISSN 0172-1526.
Indexed: A22, DIP, GeoRef, IBR, IBZ, RASB, RefZh, SOPODA, SociolAb, SpeleolAb, T02.
—GNLM, IE, Ingenta. **CCC.**
Published by: (Deutsche Forschungsgemeinschaft), Wiley - V C H Verlag GmbH & Co. KGaA (Subsidiary of: John Wiley & Sons, Inc.), Postfach 101161, Weinheim, 69451, Germany. TEL 49-6201-606400, FAX 49-6201-606184, subservice@wiley-vch.de, http://www.wiley-vch.de. Ed. Marco Finetti. Circ: 15,000.

500 DEU ISSN 0176-263X
FORSCHUNG AKTUELL; Wissenschaft fuer die Praxis. Text in German. 1984. 2/yr. free. index. back issues avail. **Document type:** *Journal, Academic/Scholarly.*
Indexed: GeoRef, SpeleolAb.
Published by: Technische Universitaet Berlin, Presse- und Informationsreferat, Str des 17 Juni 135, Berlin, 10623, Germany. TEL 49-30-31423922, FAX 49-30-314-23909, pressestelle@tu-berlin.de, http://www.tu-berlin.de/presse/. Ed. Kristina Zerges. Circ: 7,000.

500 DEU ISSN 0175-0992
FORSCHUNG FRANKFURT. Text in German. 1983. q. EUR 14; EUR 10 to students; EUR 2.50 newsstand/cover (effective 2006). adv. back issues avail. **Document type:** *Academic/Scholarly.*
Indexed: DIP, IBR, IBZ, VITIS.
Published by: Johann Wolfgang Goethe Universitaet Frankfurt am Main, Senckenberganlage 31, Frankfurt Am Main, 60054, Germany. TEL 49-69-7980, FAX 49-69-79828383, http://www.uni-frankfurt.de. Ed. Ulrike Jaspers TEL 49-69-79823266. Circ: 5,000.

500 DEU ISSN 0942-1386
FORSCHUNGS-JOURNAL; Universitaet Muenster. Variant title: Westfaelische Wilhelms-Universitaet. Journal. Text in German. 1992. 2/yr. EUR 5 per issue (effective 2006). **Document type:** *Journal, Academic/Scholarly.*
Published by: (Westfaelische Wilhelms-Universitaet Muenster), Waxmann Verlag GmbH, Steinfurter Str 555, Muenster, 48159, Germany. TEL 49-251-265040, FAX 49-251-2650426, info@waxmann.com, http://www.waxmann.com.

500 DEU ISSN 1437-496X
FORSCHUNGSINSTITUT GASTEIN-TAUERNREGION. BERICHTE. Text in German, English. 1996. irreg., latest vol.5, 2004. price varies. **Document type:** *Monographic series, Academic/Scholarly.*
Published by: Peter Lang GmbH (Subsidiary of: Peter Lang Publishing Group), Eschborner Landstr 42-50, Frankfurt Am Main, 60489, Germany. TEL 49-69-7807050, FAX 49-69-78070550, zentrale.frankfurt@peterlang.com, http://www.peterlang.com. Ed. Hans Adam.

500 DEU ISSN 1437-322X
FORSCHUNGSZENTRUM ROSSENDORF. WISSENSCHAFTLICH-TECHNISCHE BERICHTE. Text in German. irreg., latest vol.345, 2002. **Document type:** *Monographic series, Academic/Scholarly.*
Indexed: GeoRef.
—BLDSC (9332.848500).
Published by: Forschungszentrum Rossendorf e.V., Postfach 510119, Dresden, 01314, Germany. TEL 49-351-2600, FAX 49-351-2690461, contact@fz-rossendorf.de, http://www.fz-rossendorf.de.

500 600 SWE ISSN 1654-8876
➤ **FORSKNING.** Text in Swedish. 1985. 5/yr. SEK 270 to individuals; SEK 360 to institutions; SEK 200 to students; SEK 55 newsstand/cover (effective 2004). adv. 76 p./no.; **Document type:** *Magazine, Academic/Scholarly.* **Description:** Forum for Swedish technology and science research.
Former titles (until 2008): Teknik och Vetenskap (1402-5701); (until 1997): Teknik och Naturvetenskap (1402-4314); (until 1990): Teknik och Vetenskap (0282-9274)
Published by: Forskningsfoerlaget AB, Soedra Larmgatan 14, Goeteborg, 41116, Sweden. TEL 46-31-7010736, FAX 46-31-7010704, lars@forskning.com. Ed., Pub. Lars Alvegaard. Adv. contact Lars Alfredsson TEL 46-31-836932. B&W page SEK 14,300, color page SEK 18,150; trim 186 x 270. Circ: 17,000 (paid and controlled).

S

500 NOR ISSN 0804-7545
FORSKNING. Variant title: Bladet Forskning. Text in Norwegian. 1993. 4/yr. free (effective 2003). **Document type:** *Journal, Academic/ Scholarly.*
Incorporates (1988-1995): Kultur og Samfunn (0804-6506); Which was formerly (until 1993): Nytt fra Norges Forskningsraad (0804-8843); (until 1992): N O R A S Nytt (0802-1597); (1993-1995): Industri og Energi (0804-6492); (1993-1995): Bioproduksjon og Foredling (0804-6484); Which was formed by the merger of (1984-1993): N F F R-Nytt (0804-8940); (1987-1993): N L V F-Kontakt (0804-8851)
Related titles: Online - full text ed.: ISSN 1504-4882.
Published by: Norges Forskningsraad/The Research Council of Norway, P O Box 2700, St Hanshaugen, Oslo, 0131, Norway. TEL 47-22-037000, FAX 47-22-037001, post@forskningsradet.no. Ed. Mona Gravningen Rygh TEL 47-22-037082.

500 SWE ISSN 0015-7937
CODEN: FSFMA6
FORSKNING & FRAMSTEG. Text in Swedish. 1966. 10/yr. SEK 649 (effective 2011). adv. bk.rev. charts; illus. cum index:1977-1986. 62 p./no. 3 cols./p.; back issues avail. **Document type:** *Magazine, Consumer.* **Description:** A general interest popular science magazine.
Related titles: Online - full text ed.
Indexed: GeoRef, MLA-IB, NAA, RASB, SpeleolAb.
—CASDDS.
Published by: Stiftelsen Forskning och Framsteg, P O Box 1191, Stockholm, 11191, Sweden. TEL 46-8-55519800, FAX 46-8-55519899. Ed. Patrik Hadenius TEL 46-8-55110955. Circ: 41,000.

FORTEAN TIMES. *see* PARAPSYCHOLOGY AND OCCULTISM

333.72 929.6 598 GBR ISSN 0309-7560
DA880.F8
➤ **FORTH NATURALIST AND HISTORIAN SERIES.** Abbreviated title: F N H. Text in English. 1976. a., latest vol.27, 2004. GBP 8 per vol. (effective 2009). bk.rev. cum.index every 5 yrs. 1 cols./p.; back issues avail. **Document type:** *Journal, Academic/Scholarly.* **Description:** Promotes research in the natural history, environment and heritage of central Scotland.
Indexed: ASFA, B21, ESPM, Z01.
—BLDSC (4017.700000).
Published by: Forth Naturalist and Historian Editorial Board, c/o Mike Thomas, Chairman, SBES, Stirling University, Stirling, FK9 4LA, United Kingdom. TEL 44-1786-467839, m.f.thomas@stir.ac.uk. Ed. Neville Dix.

500 DEU ISSN 1613-1622
FORUM (MANNHEIM). Text in German. 1998. 4/yr. adv. **Document type:** *Journal, Academic/Scholarly.*
Formed by the merger of (1984-1998): Mannheimer Berichte (0934-9472); (1968-1998): Gesellschaft der Freunde der Universitaet Mannheim. Mitteilungen (0937-3306)
Indexed: FR, IBR, IBZ.
Published by: Universitaet Mannheim, Abteilung fuer Kommunikation und Fundraising, Schloss, Mannheim, 68131, Germany. TEL 49-621-1811016. Ed. Achim Fischer. Circ: 7,000 (controlled).

500 200 DEU ISSN 1438-0773
FORUM T T N. (Technik Theologie Naturwissenschaften) Text in German. 1999. irreg., latest vol.19, 2008. price varies. **Document type:** *Monographic series, Academic/Scholarly.*
Published by: (Ludwig-Maximilians-Universitaet Muenchen, Institut Technik-Theologie-Naturwissenschaften), Herbert Utz Verlag GmbH, Adalbertstr 57, Munich, 80799, Germany. TEL 49-89-27779100, FAX 49-89-27779101, utz@utzverlag.com.

500 DEU ISSN 0178-6563
AS181
FORUM WISSENSCHAFT; das kritische Wissenschaftsmagazine. Text in German. 1984. q. EUR 26 domestic; EUR 30 foreign; EUR 7 newsstand/cover (effective 2009). adv. bk.rev. bibl.; illus. **Document type:** *Journal, Academic/Scholarly.* **Description:** Deals with science and research policy, and the social responsibility of scientists.
Formerly (until 1984): Bund Demokratischer Wissenschaftler. Forum (0178-6555)
Related titles: Diskette ed.; Online - full text ed.
Indexed: GeoRef, IBR, IBZ, SpeleolAb.
Published by: Bund Demokratischer Wissenschaftlerinnen und Wissenschaftler e.V., Gisselberger Str 7, Marburg, 35037, Germany. TEL 49-6421-21395, FAX 49-6421-24654, verlag@bdwi.de. adv.: B&W page EUR 329; trim 186 x 262. Circ: 1,900 (paid and controlled).

500 CHN ISSN 1008-0171
FOSHAN KEXUE JISHU XUEYUAN XUEBAO (ZIRAN KEXUE BAN)/FOSHAN UNIVERSITY. JOURNAL (NATURAL SCIENCE EDITION). Text in Chinese. 1983. bi-m. CNY 5 newsstand/cover (effective 2007). **Document type:** *Journal, Academic/Scholarly.*
Supersedes in part (in 1998): Foshan Daxue Xuebao/Foshan University. Journal (1004-2520); Which was formerly: Foshan Daxue Foshan Shi-Zhuan Xuebao/Foshan University and Foshan Normal College. Journal (1001-8190)
Related titles: Online - full text ed.
Indexed: Z02.
—BLDSC (4754.952750).
Published by: Foshan Kexue Jishu Xueyuan/Foshan University, 18, Jiangwan Yi Lu, Foshan, Guangdong 528000, China.

500 NZL ISSN 1177-3464
FOUNDATION FOR RESEARCH, SCIENCE AND TECHNOLOGY. ANNUAL REPORT. Text in English. 1990. a.
Formerly (until 1999): Foundation for Research, Science and Technology. Report (1170-9588)
Related titles: Online - full text ed.: ISSN 1177-7338.
Published by: Foundation for Research, Science and Technology, Level 11, AT&T Tower, 15-17 Murphy St, PO Box 12240, Thorndon, Wellington, 6144, New Zealand. TEL 64-4-9177800, FAX 64-4-9177850.

500 600 NZL ISSN 1177-7281
FOUNDATION FOR RESEARCH, SCIENCE AND TECHNOLOGY. STATEMENT OF INVESTMENT OUTCOMES. Text in English. 200?. a.
Related titles: Online - full text ed.: ISSN 1177-7346.
Published by: Foundation for Research, Science and Technology, Level 11, AT&T Tower, 15-17 Murphy St, PO Box 12240, Thorndon, Wellington, 6144, New Zealand. TEL 64-4-9177800, FAX 64-4-9177850.

500 USA
FOUNDATIONS FOR ORGANIZATIONAL SCIENCE SERIES. Text in English. 1995. irreg., latest 2007. price varies. back issues avail. **Document type:** *Monographic series, Academic/Scholarly.*
Published by: Sage Publications, Inc., Books (Subsidiary of: Sage Publications, Inc.), 2455 Teller Rd, Thousand Oaks, CA 91320. TEL 800-818-7243, FAX 800-583-2665, books.claim@sagepub.com. **Subscr. outside N. America to:** Sage Publications Ltd.; **Subscr. to:** Sage Publications India Pvt. Ltd.

500 001 NLD ISSN 1233-1821
Q175 CODEN: FOSCFI
➤ **FOUNDATIONS OF SCIENCE.** Text in English. 1995. q. EUR 535, USD 558 combined subscription to institutions (print & online eds.) (effective 2012). adv. reprint service avail. from PSC. **Document type:** *Journal, Academic/Scholarly.* **Description:** Provides foundational issues of science without unnecessary technicalities yet faithful to the scientific content; focuses on methodological and philosophical topics of foundational significance concerning the structure and the growth of science.
Related titles: Online - full text ed.: ISSN 1572-8471 (from IngentaConnect).
Indexed: A01, A03, A08, A20, A22, A26, ArtHuCI, BibLing, CA, CCMJ, E01, FR, G08, I05, IPB, MSN, MathR, PhilInd, SCI, SCOPUS, T02, W07, Z02.
—BLDSC (4025.423000), IE, Infotrieve, Ingenta, INIST, Linda Hall. **CCC.**
Published by: (Association for Foundations of Science, Language and Cognition), Springer Netherlands (Subsidiary of: Springer Science+Business Media), Van Godewijckstraat 30, Dordrecht, 3311 GX, Netherlands. TEL 31-78-6576050, FAX 31-78-6576474, http://www.springer.com. Ed. Diederik Aerts.

➤ **FRAG DOCH MAL DIE MAUS**; Dein Wissensmagazin mit der Maus. *see* CHILDREN AND YOUTH—For

➤ **FRANCIS BACON RESEARCH TRUST. JOURNAL**; studies in ancient wisdom. *see* PHILOSOPHY

500 DNK ISSN 1604-6765
DET FRIE FORSKNINGSRAAD. AARSRAPPORT. Text in Danish. 2005. a.
Related titles: Online - full text ed.: ISSN 1604-8997; ◆ English ed.: Danish Councils for Independent Research. Annual Report. ISSN 1901-7138.
Published by: (Det Frie Forskningsraad/Danish Councils on Independent Research), Forsknings- og Innovationsstyrelsen/Danish Agency for Science, Technology and Innovation, Bredgade 40, Copenhagen K, 1260, Denmark. TEL 45-35-446200, FAX 45-35-446201, fi@fi.dk, http://www.fi.dk.

500 SGP ISSN 1793-5733
FRONTIERS OF RESEARCH WITH THE CHINESE ACADEMY OF SCIENCES. Text in English. 2008. irreg., latest vol.2, 2008. price varies. back issues avail. **Document type:** *Monographic series, Academic/Scholarly.*
Indexed: CCMJ, MSN, MathR.
Published by: World Scientific Publishing Co. Pte. Ltd., 5 Toh Tuck Link, Singapore, 596224, Singapore. TEL 65-6466-5775, FAX 65-6467-7667, wspc@wspc.com.sg, http://www.worldscientific.com. **Dist. by:** World Scientific Publishing Ltd., 57 Shelton St, London WC2H 9HE, United Kingdom. TEL 44-207-8360888, FAX 44-207-8362020, sales@wspc.co.uk; World Scientific Publishing Co., Inc., 27 Warren St, Ste 401-402, Hackensack, NJ 07601. TEL 201-487-9655, 800-227-7562, FAX 201-487-9656, 888-977-2665, wspc@wspc.com.

500 JPN ISSN 0915-8502
FRONTIERS SCIENCE SERIES. Text in English. 1991. irreg., latest no.37. **Document type:** *Monographic series, Academic/Scholarly.*
Indexed: GeoRef.
—BLDSC (4042.061000), IE, Ingenta.
Published by: Universal Academy Press, Inc., BR-Hongo-5 Bldg, 6-16-2, Hongo, Bunkyo-ku, Tokyo, 113-0033, Japan. TEL 81-3-38137232, FAX 81-3-38135932, general@uap.co.jp.

500 TWN ISSN 1016-1538
FU JEN STUDIES. NATURAL SCIENCES. Text in English. 1968. a. **Document type:** *Journal, Academic/Scholarly.*
Former titles (until 197?): Jen Studies. Natural Sciences & Foreign Languages (1018-7251); (until 1969): Fu Jen studies (0532-7725)
Published by: Fu Jen Catholic University, College of Science and Engineering/Furen Daxue, Ligong Xueyuan, 510 Chung Cheng Rd, Hsinchung, Taipei, 242, Taiwan. TEL 886-2-29031111 ext 2411, FAX 886-2-29014749, http://www.se.fju.edu.tw/.

500 CHN ISSN 0427-7104
Q4 CODEN: FHPTAY
FUDAN XUEBAO (ZIRAN KEXUE BAN)/FUDAN UNIVERSITY. JOURNAL (NATURAL SCIENCE EDITION). Text in Chinese. 1935. bi-m. **Document type:** *Journal, Academic/Scholarly.*
Formerly: Fudan Daxue Xuebao (Ziran Kexue Ban)
Related titles: Online - full text ed.
Indexed: B25, BIOSIS Prev, C31, CCMJ, CIN, ChemAb, ChemTitl, INIS AtomInd, Inspec, MSN, MathR, MycolAb, RefZh, Z01, Z02.
—BLDSC (4755.440000), CASDDS, Linda Hall.
Published by: Fudan Daxue/Fudan University, 220 Handan Lu, Shanghai, 200433, China. TEL 86-21-65642666, FAX 86-21-65642666. Ed. Fu Jia Yang. **Dist. outside China by:** China International Book Trading Corp, 35 Chegongzhuang Xilu, Haidian District, PO Box 399, Beijing 100044, China. TEL 86-10-68412045, FAX 86-10-68412023, cibtc@mail.cibtc.com.cn, http://www.cibtc.com.cn.

FUJIAN SHI-DA FUQING FENXIAO XUEBAO/FUJIAN NORMAL UNIVERSITY. FUQING BRANCH. JOURNAL. *see* SOCIAL SCIENCES: COMPREHENSIVE WORKS

500 CHN ISSN 1000-5277
Q4 CODEN: FSDKES
FUJIAN SHIFAN DAXUE XUEBAO (ZIRAN KEXUE BAN)/FUJIAN TEACHERS UNIVERSITY. JOURNAL (NATURAL SCIENCE EDITION). Text in Chinese. 1956. q. USD 18 (effective 2009). **Document type:** *Journal, Academic/Scholarly.*
Formerly (until 1984): Fujian Normal University. Journal (Natural Science Edition)
Related titles: Online - full text ed.
Indexed: A22, ASFA, B21, CCMJ, CIN, ChemAb, ChemTitl, ESPM, MSN, MathR, Z02.
—BLDSC (4755.512250), CASDDS, East View, IE, Ingenta.
Published by: Fujian Shifan Daxue/Fujian Normal University, 8, Shangsan Lu, Cangshan-qu, Fuzhou, Fujian 350007, China. TEL 86-591-83464002, http://www.fjtu.edu.cn. **Dist. by:** China International Book Trading Corp, 35 Chegongzhuang Xilu, Haidian District, PO Box 399, Beijing 100044, China. TEL 86-10-68412045, FAX 86-10-68412023, cibtc@mail.cibtc.com.cn, http://www.cibtc.com.cn.

500 JPN ISSN 0071-9781
FUKUI DAIGAKU KYOIKUGAKUBU KIYO. DAI 2-BU. SHIZEN KAGAKU/FUKUI UNIVERSITY. FACULTY OF EDUCATION. MEMOIRS. SERIES 2: NATURAL SCIENCE. Text and summaries in English, Japanese. 1961. a. free. **Document type:** *Academic/ Scholarly.* **Description:** Contains original papers.
Published by: Fukui University, Faculty of Education/Fukui Daigaku Kyoikugakubu, 9-1 Bunkyo 3-chome, Fukui-shi, 910-0017, Japan. Ed. Terutsugu Ando.

510 JPN ISSN 0532-811X
Q4 CODEN: FKDRAN
FUKUOKA KYOIKU DAIGAKU KIYO. DAI-3-BUNSATSU. SUGAKU, RIKA, GIJUTSUKA HEN/FUKUOKA UNIVERSITY OF EDUCATION. BULLETIN. PART 3: MATHEMATICS, NATURAL SCIENCES AND TECHNOLOGY. Text in English, Japanese; Summaries in English. 1951. a. **Document type:** *Bulletin, Academic/Scholarly.*
Former titles (until 1966): Fukuoka Gakugei Daigaku, Dai-3-Bu, Rika-Hen/Fukuoka Gakugei University. Bulletin. Part 3: Natural Sciences (0429-842X); (until 1955): Fukuoka Gakugei Daigaku Kiyo. Dai 2-bu, Rika Keito/Fukuoka Gakugei University. Bulletin. Part 2, Natural Sciences (0286-4371); Which superseded in part (in 1953): Fukuoka Gakugei Daigaku Kiyo (0286-4363)
Indexed: CCMJ, CIN, ChemAb, ChemTitl, MSN, MathR, RefZh, Z02.
—BLDSC (2523.115000), CASDDS, INIST, Linda Hall.
Published by: Fukuoka Kyoiku Daigaku/Fukuoka University of Education, 1-1 Akamabunkyomachi, Munakata, Fukuoka 811-4192, Japan. http://www.fukuoka-edu.ac.jp/.

500 SGP ISSN 1793-6047
TA401
FUNCTIONAL MATERIALS LETTERS. Abbreviated title: F M L. Text in English. 2008. q. SGD 444, USD 286, EUR 224 combined subscription to institutions (print & online eds.) (effective 2012). adv. back issues avail. **Document type:** *Journal, Academic/Scholarly.* **Description:** Covers novel and cutting-edge interdisciplinary scientific research on functional materials, providing a forum for communication amongst materials scientists and engineers, chemists, and physicists in the dynamic field associated with functional materials.
Related titles: Online - full text ed.: ISSN 1793-7213. SGD 404, USD 260, EUR 204 to institutions (effective 2012).
Indexed: A22, CurCont, E01, MSCI, SCI, SCOPUS, W07.
—IE.
Published by: World Scientific Publishing Co. Pte. Ltd., 5 Toh Tuck Link, Singapore, 596224, Singapore. TEL 65-6466-5775, FAX 65-6467-7667, wspc@wspc.com.sg, http://www.worldscientific.com. Ed. Li Lu. **Dist. by:** World Scientific Publishing Ltd., 57 Shelton St, London WC2H 9HE, United Kingdom. TEL 44-207-8360888, FAX 44-207-8362020, sales@wspc.co.uk; World Scientific Publishing Co., Inc., 27 Warren St, Ste 401-402, Hackensack, NJ 07601. TEL 201-487-9655, 800-227-7562, FAX 201-487-9656, 888-977-2665, wspc@wspc.com.

060 ARG
FUNDACION BARILOCHE. MEMORIA ANUAL. Text in Spanish. a.
Published by: Fundacion Bariloche, Casilla de Correos 138, San Carlos de Bariloche, Rio Negro 8400, Argentina. TEL 54-2944-422050.

FUNDACION LA CAIXA. PANORAMA. *see* MUSEUMS AND ART GALLERIES

FUSION; Forschung und Technik fuer das 21. Jahrhundert. *see* ENERGY

FUTURE SEX. *see* SINGLES' INTERESTS AND LIFESTYLES

500 USA ISSN 0016-3317
CB158 CODEN: FUTUAC
THE FUTURIST; a journal of forecasts, trends, and ideas about the future. Text in English. 1967. bi-m. free to members (effective 2010). adv. bk.rev. charts; illus. cum.index: 1967-1975, 1976-1980, 1981-1983, 1984-1988, 1987-1991. back issues avail.; reprints avail. **Document type:** *Magazine, Consumer.* **Description:** Focuses on trends and developments that are likely to have a major impact on the way we will live in the years ahead.
Related titles: Microform ed.: (from PQC); Online - full text ed.
Indexed: A01, A02, A03, A08, A11, A12, A13, A17, A20, A21, A22, A25, A26, A33, ABIn, AIA, ASCA, AcaI, AgeL, B01, B02, B04, B06, B07, B08, B09, B14, B15, B17, B18, BPIA, BRD, BRI, BiolDig, BusI, C05, C12, C28, CA, CBRI, CCR, CPerI, Chicano, CompB, CurCont, DIP, E02, E03, E07, E08, EIA, EIP, ERI, EdA, EdI, Emerald, EnerRev, EnvAb, EnvInd, FutSurv, G01, G04, G05, G06, G07, G08, H09, I05, I07, IBR, IBZ, ILD, Inspec, M01, M02, M05, M06, MASUSE, MEA&I, MagInd, ORMS, P02, P04, P10, P11, P13, P18, P19, P26, P27, P30, P34, P41, P47, P48, P51, P52, P53, P54, P55, P56, PMR, PQC, PRA, PersLit, QC&AS, R03, R04, R05, R06, RASB, RGAb, RGPR, RI-1, RI-2, S02, S03, S05, S06, S08, S09, S11, S23, SCOPUS, SOPODA, SSAI, SSAb, SSCI, SSI, SWR&A, SociolAb, T&II, T02, Telegen, U01, W01, W02, W03, W05, W07, W09.
—BLDSC (4060.700000), IE, Infotrieve, Ingenta. **CCC.**
Published by: World Future Society, 7910 Woodmont Ave, Ste 450, Bethesda, MD 20814. info@wfs.org. Ed. Edward S Cornish. Adv. contact Jeff Cornish.

500 200 ITA ISSN 1971-6885
UN FUTURO PER L'UOMO. Text in Italian. 1974. 2/yr. adv. bk.rev. back issues avail. **Document type:** *Journal, Academic/Scholarly.*
Formerly (until 2000): Il Futuro dell'Uomo (0390-217X)
Published by: Il Segno dei Gabrielli Editori, Via Cengia 67, loc.Nogarine, San Pietro in Cariano, VE 37020, Italy. TEL 39-045-7725543, FAX 39-045-6858595, http://www.gabriellieditore.it.

FUTUROLOGY. *see* TECHNOLOGY: COMPREHENSIVE WORKS

500 CHN ISSN 1672-3813
FUZA XITONG YU FUZAXING KEXUE/COMPLEX SYSTEMS AND COMPLEXITY SCIENCE. Text in Chinese. 2004. q. **Document type:** *Journal, Academic/Scholarly.*

Related titles: Online - full text ed.
Indexed: A28, APA, BrCerAb, C&ISA, CA/WCA, CIA, CerAb, CivEngAb, CorrAb, E&CAJ, E11, EEA, EMA, ESPM, EnvEAb, H15, M&TEA, M09, MBF, METADEX, SolStAb, T04, WAA.
Published by: Fuza Xitong yu Fuzaxing Kexue Zazhishe, Qingdao Daxue, 308, Ningxia Lu, Qingdao, 266071, China. TEL 86-532-85953597.

500 CHN ISSN 1000-2243
CODEN: FDXKEN
FUZHOU DAXUE XUEBAO (ZIRAN KEXUE BAN)/FUZHOU UNIVERSITY. JOURNAL (NATURAL SCIENCE EDITION). Text in Chinese. 1961. bi-m. USD 24.60 (effective 2009). **Document type:** *Journal, Academic/Scholarly.* **Description:** Covers mathematics, computer science, physics, electrical engineering, civil engineering, chemistry and other fields of science.
Related titles: Online - full text ed.
Indexed: A28, APA, BrCerAb, C&ISA, CA/WCA, CCMJ, CIA, CIN, CerAb, ChemAb, ChemTitl, CivEngAb, CorrAb, E&CAJ, E11, EEA, EMA, ESPM, EnvEAb, H15, M&TEA, M09, MBF, METADEX, MSN, MathR, RefZh, SolStAb, T04, WAA, Z02.
—BLDSC (4755.520000), CASDDS, Linda Hall.
Published by: Fuzhou Daxue/Fuzhou University, 523, Gongye Lu, Fuzhou, Fujian 350002, China. TEL 86-591-87893102, http://www.fzu.edu.cn.

500 NLD ISSN 1875-4546
FYSISCH-MATHEMATISCHE FACULTEITSVERENIGING. PERIODIEK. Text in Dutch. 1996. 5/yr. EUR 15 (effective 2011). adv. **Document type:** *Magazine, Consumer.*
Related titles: Online - full text ed.: ISSN 1875-4538.
Published by: Fysisch-Mathematische Faculteitsvereniging, Nijenborgh 4, Groningen, 9747 AG, Netherlands. TEL 31-50-3634948, FAX 31-50-3634155, bestuur@fmf.nl, www.fmf.nl. Circ: 1,200.

500 600 GBR ISSN 1366-7831
G I S T GLOBAL INFORMATION ON SCIENCE AND TECHNOLOGY. Text in English. 1997. m.
Published by: Pera Business Connection, Melton Mowbray, Leicester LE13 0PB, United Kingdom. FAX 44-01664-501555.

500 DEU ISSN 0344-9629
G K S S. (Gesellschaft fuer Kernenergieverwertung in Schiffbau und Schiffahrt) Text in German. 1971. irreg. **Document type:** *Monographic series, Academic/Scholarly.*
Indexed: GeoRef, RefZh.
—BLDSC (4179.968000), IE, Ingenta.
Published by: G K S S Forschungszentrum Geesthacht GmbH, Max-Planck-Str. 1, Geesthacht, 21502, Germany. TEL 49-4152-870, FAX 49-4152-871802, contact@gkss.de, http://www.gkss.de.

500 DEU ISSN 1430-7278
G K S S FORSCHUNGSZENTRUM. JAHRESBERICHT. (Gesellschaft fuer Kernenergieverwertung in Schiffbau und Schiffahrt) Text in German. 1971. a. **Document type:** *Journal, Academic/Scholarly.*
Former titles (until 1994): G K S S Jahresbericht (0174-4933); (until 1976): Gesellschaft fuer Kernenergieverwertung in Schiffbau und Schiffahrt. Jahresbericht (0174-4941)
Indexed: GeoRef.
Published by: G K S S Forschungszentrum Geesthacht GmbH, Max-Planck-Str. 1, Geesthacht, 21502, Germany. TEL 49-4152-870, FAX 49-4152-871802, contact@gkss.de, http://www.gkss.de.

500 DEU
G-O.DE WISSEN ONLINE. (Geoscience Online) Text in German. d. adv. **Document type:** *Academic/Scholarly.* **Description:** Presents articles and research on natural sciences in an informative and entertaining manner.
Media: Online - full content.
Published by: M M C D GmbH, Schadowstr 70, Duesseldorf, 40212, Germany. TEL 49-211-162268, FAX 49-211-162257, info@mmcd.de, http://www.mmcd.de. Ed. Dieter Lohmann. **Co-publisher:** Springer.

500 TUR ISSN 1303-9709
➤ **G U FEN BILIMLERI DERGISI/G U JOURNAL OF SCIENCE.** (Gazi Universitesi) Text in English, Turkish. 1994. q. **Document type:** *Journal, Academic/Scholarly.*
Formerly (until 2003): Gazi Universitesi Fen Gilimler Enstitusu Dergisi (1300-1833)
Related titles: Online - full text ed.
Indexed: A01, A28, APA, BrCerAb, C&ISA, CA, CA/WCA, CIA, CPEI, CerAb, CivEngAb, CorrAb, E&CAJ, E11, EEA, EMA, ESPM, EnvEAb, H15, INIS AtomInd, M&TEA, M09, MBF, METADEX, SCOPUS, SWRA, SolStAb, T02, T04, WAA, Z01.
Published by: Gazi Universitesi, Fen Bilimleri Enstitusu, Eti Mahallesi, Ali Suavi Sokak, No. 15, 5 kat Maltepe, Ankara, Turkey. TEL 90-312-2323226. Ed. Yilmaz Yildirir.

➤ **GAIA**; oekologische Perspektiven in Natur-, Geistes- und Wirtschaftswissenschaften. *see* HUMANITIES: COMPREHENSIVE WORKS

500 JPN ISSN 0387-2440
Q4
GAKUJUTSU GEPPO/JAPANESE SCIENTIFIC MONTHLY. Text in Japanese; Summaries in English. 1948. m. JPY 800. abstr.
Description: Contains reviews, commentary, and news.
Indexed: INIS AtomInd, JPI.
—Ingenta.
Published by: Japan Society for the Promotion of Science, 3-1 Koji-Machi 5-chome, Chiyoda-ku, Tokyo, 102-0083, Japan.

500 JPN
Q77
GAKUJUTSU NO DOKO/TRENDS IN THE SCIENCES; S C J forum. Text in Japanese. 1960. m. JPY 720 newsstand/cover (effective 2001). 100 p./no.; **Document type:** *Journal, Academic/Scholarly.*
Formerly (until 1996): Nihon Gakujutsu Kaigi Geppo/Science Council of Japan. Monthly Report (0029-019X)
Published by: Nihon Gakujutsu Kyoryoku Zaidan/Japan Science Support Foundation (Subsidiary of: Nihon Gakujutsu Kaigi/Science Council of Japan), 3-24-20 Nishiazabu, Minatoku, Tokyo, 106-0031, Japan. TEL 81-3-5410-0242, FAX 81-3-5410-1822. Circ: 3,000.

577 ECU ISSN 1390-2830
QH123 CODEN: NOGAB2
➤ **GALAPAGOS RESEARCH.** Text in English. 1963. s-a. USD 25 to individuals; USD 50 to institutions (effective 2011). adv. bk.rev. **Document type:** *Journal, Academic/Scholarly.* **Description:** Covers science and conservation in Galapagos, the Galapagos National Park Service, and the Charles Darwin Research Station.
Formerly (until 2003): Noticias de Galapagos (0550-1067)
Indexed: B25, BIOSIS Prev, CTO, WildRev, Z01.
Published by: Charles Darwin Foundation, Puerto Ayora, Santa Cruz Island, Galapagos, Ecuador. TEL 593-5-2526146, FAX 593-5-2526146, cdrs@fcdarwin.org.ec, http://www.darwinfoundation.org/english/pages/index.php. Ed. Alan Tye.

500 ITA ISSN 1971-6052
GALILAEANA; journal of Galilean studies. Text and summaries in Italian; Text occasionally in English, French. 2004. a. EUR 86 combined subscription per vol. foreign to institutions (print & online eds.) (effective 2012). **Document type:** *Journal, Academic/Scholarly.*
Related titles: Online - full content ed.: ISSN 1825-3903. 2004.
Published by: Casa Editrice Leo S. Olschki, Viuzzo del Pozzetto 8, Florence, 50126, Italy. TEL 39-055-6530684, FAX 39-055-6530214, celso@olschki.it. Eds. Massimo Bucciantini, Michele Camerota.

500 ISR ISSN 0793-0453
GALILEO (TEL AVIV). Text in Hebrew. 1993. m. ILS 384 (effective 2008). **Document type:** *Magazine, Consumer.*
Related titles: Online - full text ed.: ILS 192 (effective 2008).
Published by: S B C Group, 8 Shefa Tal St., Tel Aviv, 67013, Israel. TEL 972-3-565-2100, FAX 972-3-562-6476, sherut@sbc.co.il, http://www.sbc.co.il/Index.asp.

500 028.5 ISR ISSN 1565-4583
GALILEO TSA'IR/YOUNG GALILEO. Text in Hebrew. 2004. m. ILS 315 (effective 2008). **Document type:** *Magazine, Consumer.* **Description:** A magazine of science for curious children of age seven and above including nature, history, philosophy, biology, and physics.
Related titles: Online - full text ed.: ILS 120 (effective 2008).
Published by: S B C Group, 8 Shefa Tal St., Tel Aviv, 67013, Israel. TEL 972-3-565-2100, FAX 972-3-562-6476, sherut@sbc.co.il, http://www.sbc.co.il/Index.asp.

500 CHN ISSN 1004-0366
GANSU KEXUE XUEBAO/JOURNAL OF GANSU SCIENCE. Text in Chinese. 1989. q. CNY 32 domestic; USD 8 in Hong Kong, Macau & Taiwan; USD 14 elsewhere (effective 2007). **Document type:** *Journal, Academic/Scholarly.*
Related titles: Online - full text ed.
Published by: Gansu-sheng Kexueyuan, 177 Dingxi Nan Lu, Lanzhou, 730000, China. TEL 86-931-8613844, FAX 86-931-8616127. **Dist. by:** China International Book Trading Corp, 35 Chegongzhuang Xilu, Haidian District, PO Box 399, Beijing 100044, China. TEL 86-10-68412045, FAX 86-10-68412023, cibtc@mail.cibtc.com.cn, http://www.cibtc.com.cn.

500 CHN ISSN 1672-691X
GANSU LIANHE DAXUE XUEBAO (ZIRAN KEXUE BAN)/GANSU LIANHE UNIVERSITY. JOURNAL (NATURAL SCIENCES). Text in Chinese. 1985. bi-m. USD 21.60 (effective 2009). **Document type:** *Journal, Academic/Scholarly.*
Formerly: Gansu Jiaoyu Xueyuan Xuebao (Ziran Kexue Ban)/Gansu Education College. Journal (Natural Science Edition) (1007-9912)
Related titles: Online - full text ed.
—East View.
Published by: Gansu Lianhe Daxue/Gansu Lianhe University, 400, Yantan Bei Mian Tan, Lanzhou, Gansu 730000, China. Ed. Chang Xing Xie.

500 CHN ISSN 1007-9831
GAO-SHI LI-KE XUEKAN/TEACHERS' COLLEGE AND UNIVERSITY. JOURNAL OF SCIENCE. Text in Chinese. 1979. q. CNY 5 newsstand/cover (effective 2006). **Document type:** *Journal, Academic/Scholarly.*
Formerly: Qiqihaer Shifan Xueyuan Xuebao (Ziran Kexue Ban) (1000-9884)
Related titles: Online - full text ed.
Published by: Qiqihaer Daxue/Qiqihaer University, 30, Wenhua Dajie, Qiqihaer, 161006, China. TEL 86-452-2738212.

500 CHN ISSN 1006-7353
GAODENG HANSHOU XUEBAO (ZIRAN KEXUE BAN)/JOURNAL OF HIGHER CORRESPONDENCE EDUCATION (NATURAL SCIENCE EDITION). Text in Chinese. 1987. bi-m. USD 5.50 (effective 2006). **Document type:** *Journal, Academic/Scholarly.*
Related titles: Online - full text ed.
Published by: Huazhong Shifan Daxue, Chengren Jiaoyu Xueyuan, Wuhan, 430079, China. TEL 86-27-67867240, FAX 86-27-67861802.

508 AUS
GEELONG NATURALIST. Text in English. 19??. m. AUD 26 domestic; AUD 45 foreign; free to members (effective 2009). **Document type:** *Magazine, Trade.* **Description:** Features all the natural history happenings in and around Geelong.
Formerly: G F N C Monthly News
Published by: Geelong Field Naturalists Club Inc., Box 1047, Geelong, VIC 3220, Australia. gfnc@vicnet.net.au.

500 DEU ISSN 1435-571X
Q4
GEGENWORTE; Hefte fuer den Disput ueber Wissen. Text in German. 1998. s-a. EUR 22.80; EUR 14 newsstand/cover (effective 2011). adv. **Document type:** *Journal, Academic/Scholarly.* **Description:** Provides a forum for discussion and debate involving all scientific disciplines.
Indexed: DIP, IBR, IBZ, PhilInd.
Published by: (Berlin-Brandenburgische Akademie der Wissenschaften), Akademie Verlag GmbH (Subsidiary of: Oldenbourg Wissenschaftsverlag GmbH), Markgrafenstr 12-14, Berlin, 10969, Germany. TEL 49-30-4220060, FAX 49-30-42200657, info@akademie-verlag.de, http://www.akademie-verlag.de. Ed. Wolfert von Rahden. Adv. contact Christina Gericke. Circ: 1,500 (paid and controlled).

500 GBR ISSN 0016-6588
GENERAL SYSTEMS BULLETIN. Text in English. 1956. a. free to members (effective 2009). back issues avail. **Document type:** *Bulletin, Academic/Scholarly.*
Related titles: Online - full text ed.: ISSN 1996-5370. 200?. free (effective 2009).
Published by: International Society for the Systems Sciences, 47 Southfield Rd, Pocklington, York YO42 2XE, United Kingdom. TEL 44-1759-302718, FAX 44-1759-302718, isssoffice@dsl.pipex.com. Ed. Jennifer Wilby.

500 600 JPN ISSN 1345-3610
RA565.A1
GENRYU. Text in Japanese. 1999. irreg. **Document type:** *Journal, Academic/Scholarly.*
Related titles: Online - full content ed.; Online - full text ed.
Published by: Japan Science and Technology Corp., Kawaguchi Center Bldg, 1-8, Honcho 4-chome, Kawaguchi City, Saitama 332-0012, Japan. TEL 81-48-226-5630, 81-48-226-5601, FAX 81-48-226-5751, http://www.jst.go.jp/.

GEO. *see* GEOGRAPHY

500 DEU ISSN 1614-6913
GEO KOMPAKT. Text in German. 2004. q. EUR 31; EUR 8.50 newsstand/cover (effective 2010). adv. **Document type:** *Magazine, Consumer.*
Published by: Gruner + Jahr AG & Co, Am Baumwall 11, Hamburg, 20459, Germany. TEL 49-40-37030, FAX 49-40-37035601, info@gujmedia.de, http://www.guj.de. Adv. contact Sabine Plath. color page EUR 10,100. Circ: 100,000 (paid and controlled).

500 POL ISSN 1733-8387
➤ **GEOCHRONOMETRIA**; journal on methods and applications of absolute chronology. Text in English. 1986. q. EUR 237, USD 292 combined subscription to institutions (print & online eds.) (effective 2012). **Document type:** *Journal, Academic/Scholarly.* **Description:** Aims to integrate the scientists developing different methods of absolute chronology and using them in different fields of earth and other natural sciences and archaeology.
Related titles: Online - full text ed.: ISSN 1897-1695. 2001.
Indexed: A01, A20, B22, CA, CurCont, GeoRef, SCI, SCOPUS, T02, W07.
—BLDSC (4117.130000), IE.
Published by: Politechnika Slaska, Instytut Fizyki/Silesian University of Technology, Krzywoustego 2, Gliwice, 44100, Poland. TEL 48-32-2372216, FAX 48-32-2371778, rjp10@polsl.pl, http://fizyka.polsl.pl. Ed. Anna Pazdur. **Co-publisher:** Springer.

500 USA ISSN 0147-9369
Q11 CODEN: GJSCDQ
➤ **GEORGIA JOURNAL OF SCIENCE.** Text in English. 1943. q. free to members (effective 2010). adv. abstr.; bibl.; charts; illus.; stat. cum.index: 1943-1967. back issues avail. **Document type:** *Journal, Academic/Scholarly.*
Formerly (until 1977): Georgia Academy of Science. Bulletin (0016-8114)
Related titles: Microform ed.: (from PQC); Online - full text ed.: free (effective 2010).
Indexed: A01, A22, A26, CA, E08, G08, GeoRef, I05, P10, P11, P26, P30, P48, P52, P53, P54, P56, PQC, S06, S09, S10, SASA, SpeleolAb, T02, W08, WildRev, Z01.
—CASDDS, Ingenta, Linda Hall.
Published by: Georgia Academy of Science, c/o Mitch Lockhart, Biology Department, Valdosta State University, 1500 N Patterson St, BC 2035, Valdosta, GA 31698. TEL 229-333-5767, FAX 229-245-6585, jmlockha@valdosta.edu, http://www.gaacademy.org. Ed. John V Aliff TEL 678-630-7530.

500 GEO ISSN 0132-1447
AS262 CODEN: BGASFC
GEORGIAN ACADEMY OF SCIENCES. BULLETIN/SAKARTVELOS METSNIEREBATA AKADEMIA. MOAMBE. Text in English; Summaries in Georgian. 1940. bi-m. USD 730 foreign (effective 2007). bibl. index. **Document type:** *Journal, Academic/Scholarly.*
Former titles: Akademiya Nauk Gruzii. Soobshcheniya; (until 1991): Akademiya Nauk Gruzinskoi S.S.R. Soobshcheniya
Indexed: CCMJ, CIN, CIS, ChemTitl, MSN, MathR, NumL, P30, RASB, RefZh, ST&MA, SpeleolAb, Z01, Z02.
—INIST. **CCC.**
Published by: Sakartvelos Metsnierebata Akademia/Georgian Academy of Sciences, Rustaveli pr 52, Tbilisi, 380008, Georgia. TEL 995-32-995480, FAX 995-32-998823. Ed. Tamaz Gamkrelidze. Circ: 1,400. **Dist. by:** East View Information Services, 10601 Wayzata Blvd, Minneapolis, MN 55305. TEL 952-252-1201, 800-477-1005, FAX 952-252-1202, info@eastview.com, http://www.eastview.com.

GEORGIAN INTERNATIONAL JOURNAL OF SCIENCE, TECHNOLOGY AND MEDICINE. *see* MEDICAL SCIENCES

500 909.07 ITA ISSN 2038-3657
▼ **GERBERTUS.** Text in Multiple languages. 2010. a. **Document type:** *Journal, Academic/Scholarly.*
Related titles: CD-ROM ed.: ISSN 2038-3630; Online - full text ed.: ISSN 2038-355X.
Published by: International Center for Relativistic Astrophysics, Dipartimento di Fisica, Universita degli Studi di Roma "La Sapienza", Piazzale Aldo Moro 5, Rome, 00185, Italy. TEL 39-06-4991142554, FAX 39-06-4454992. Ed. Costantino Sigismondi.

500 DEU ISSN 0172-1526
GERMAN RESEARCH. Text in English. 1983. 3/yr. GBP 40 in United Kingdom to institutions; EUR 70 in Europe to institutions; USD 75 elsewhere to institutions; GBP 46 combined subscription in United Kingdom to institutions (print & online eds.); EUR 82 combined subscription in Europe to institutions (print & online eds.); USD 87 combined subscription elsewhere to institutions (print & online eds.) (effective 2012). adv. reprint service avail. from PSC. **Document type:** *Journal, Academic/Scholarly.* **Description:** Covers the arts and humanities as well as the many fields of natural science.
Related titles: Online - full text ed.: ISSN 1522-2322. GBP 40 in United Kingdom to institutions; EUR 70 in Europe to institutions; USD 75 elsewhere to institutions (effective 2012); ◆ Translation of: Forschung. ISSN 0172-1518.
Indexed: GeoRef, MLA-IB, RILM, SpeleolAb.
—IE, Ingenta. **CCC.**

S

Published by: (Deutsche Forschungsgemeinschaft), Wiley - V C H Verlag GmbH & Co. KGaA (Subsidiary of: John Wiley & Sons, Inc.), Postfach 101161, Weinheim, 69451, Germany. TEL 49-6201-606400, FAX 49-6201-606184, subservice@wiley-vch.de, adsales@wiley-vch.de, http://www.wiley-vch.de. Ed. Marco Finetti. Circ: 8,000. **Subscr. in the Americas to:** John Wiley & Sons, Inc., 111 River St, Hoboken, NJ 07030. TEL 201-748-6645, subinfo@wiley.com; **Subscr. outside Germany, Austria & Switzerland to:** John Wiley & Sons Ltd., The Atrium, Southern Gate, Chichester, West Sussex PO19 8SQ, United Kingdom. TEL 44-1243-779777, FAX 44-1243-775878.

GESELLSCHAFT FUER UNIVERSITAETS- UND WISSENSCHAFTSGESCHICHTE. VEROEFFENTLICHUNGEN. *see* EDUCATION—Higher Education

500.9 DEU ISSN 0037-5942
GESELLSCHAFT NATURFORSCHENDER FREUNDE ZU BERLIN. SITZUNGSBERICHTE. NEUE FOLGE. Text in German. 1961. a. EUR 50 per vol. (effective 2011). **Document type:** *Monographic series, Academic/Scholarly.*
Indexed: GeoRef, SpeleolAb, Z01.
—Linda Hall. **CCC.**
Published by: (Gesellschaft Naturforschender Freunde zu Berlin), Verlag Goecke und Evers, Sportplatzweg 5, Keltern-Weiler, 75210, Germany. TEL 49-7236-7174, FAX 49-7236-7325, books@goeckeevers.de, http://www.goeckeevers.de.

GESNERUS; Swiss journal of the history of medicine and sciences. *see* MEDICAL SCIENCES

GESNERUS. SUPPLEMENT. *see* MEDICAL SCIENCES

500 GHA ISSN 0855-6768
➤ **GHANA JOURNAL OF DEVELOPMENT STUDIES.** Text in English. s-a. GHC 30,000 domestic; USD 25 foreign (effective 2007). **Document type:** *Journal, Academic/Scholarly.* **Description:** Publishes works on development policy, programming and projects, whether analytical, evaluative, basic, applicative and/or descriptive.
Related titles: Online - full text ed.
Indexed: AgrForAb, CABA, E12, F08, F12, GH, IBSS, IIBP, LT, R12, RRTA, S13, S16, T05, TAR, W11.
Published by: University for Development Studies, Faculty of Integrated Development Studies, Center for Research and Graduate Studies, PO Box 24, Navrongo, Ghana. Ed. Agnes A Apusigah.

500 GHA ISSN 0016-9544
Q1 CODEN: GHJSAC
➤ **GHANA JOURNAL OF SCIENCE.** Text in English. 1961. s-a. GHC 8,000 domestic; USD 15, GBP 10 foreign (effective 2004). adv. bk.rev. charts; illus.; maps. back issues avail. **Document type:** *Journal, Academic/Scholarly.* **Description:** Publishes papers of a scientific and technical nature from Ghana and elsewhere.
Related titles: Microfilm ed.: (from PQC).
Indexed: ChemAb, GeoRef, SpeleolAb.
—CASDDS, Ingenta, INIST, Linda Hall.
Published by: National Science and Technology Press, PO Box 32, Accra, Ghana. TEL 233-21-778808, FAX 223-21-777655, http://www.csir.org.gh. Ed. A K Ahafia. R&P F J K Adotevi. Adv. contact F.J.K. Adotevi. Circ: 500.

600 500 GHA ISSN 0855-3823
Q1
➤ **GHANA SCIENCE ASSOCIATION. JOURNAL.** Text in English. 1998. 3/yr. GHC 75,000 domestic to individuals; USD 75 foreign to individuals; GHC 200,000 domestic to institutions; USD 200 foreign to institutions (effective 2007). back issues avail. **Document type:** *Journal, Academic/Scholarly.* **Description:** Publishes scholarly articles in all disciplines of science and technology.
Related titles: Online - full text ed.
Indexed: A34, A38, AgrForAb, BA, C25, C30, CABA, E12, F08, F11, F12, FCA, G11, GH, H16, I11, INIS AtomInd, IndVet, LT, N02, N03, OR, P32, P40, PGegResA, PHN&I, R07, R11, R12, R13, RA&MP, RRTA, S12, S13, S16, S17, T05, TAR, VS, W10, W11.
Published by: Ghana Science Association, Box LG 7, Accra, Legon, Ghana. gsa@ug.edu.gh. Ed. Menyeh Aboagye.

508 GIB ISSN 1352-8726
CODEN: NGOSE9
GIBRALTAR NATURE NEWS. Key Title: Gibraltar Ornithological & Natural History Society. Newsletter. Text in English. 1979. 2/yr. free (effective 2003). 12 p./no. 3 cols./p.; **Document type:** *Newspaper.*
Indexed: WildRev.
Published by: Gibraltar Ornithological & Natural History Society, Gibraltar Natural History Field Centre, Jew's Gate, Upper Rock Nature Reserve, P O Box 843, Gibraltar, Gibraltar. TEL 350-72639, FAX 350-74022, publish@gonhs.org, http://www.gonhs.org. Ed. John E Cortes.

500 JPN ISSN 0533-9529
Q4 CODEN: GDGKAD
GIFU DAIGAKU KYOIKUGAKUBU KENKYU HOKOKU. SHIZEN KAGAKU/GIFU UNIVERSITY. FACULTY OF EDUCATION. SCIENCE REPORT. NATURAL SCIENCE. Text in Japanese, English; Summaries in English. 1953. a. **Document type:** *Report, Academic/Scholarly.*
Indexed: CCMJ, ChemAb, JPI, MSN, MathR, Z01, Z02.
Published by: Gifu Daigaku, Kyoikugakubu, Chiryo Kyoikugaku Kenkyushitsu/Gifu University, Faculty of Education, 1-1 Yanagi-To, Gifu, 501-1112, Japan.

507.4 JPN ISSN 0388-550X
GIFU-KEN HAKUBUTSUKAN CHOSA KENKYU HOKOKU/GIFU PREFECTURAL MUSEUM. BULLETIN. Text and summaries in Japanese, English. 1980. a. free. **Document type:** *Bulletin.* **Description:** Contains research reports from the museum.
Published by: Gifu Prefectural Museum/Gifu-ken Hakubutsukan, Hyakunen Koen, Oyana, Seki-shi, Gifu-ken 501-3941, Japan. TEL 0575-28-3111, FAX 0575-28-3110.

GLASGOW NATURALIST. *see* BIOLOGY

500 600 USA ISSN 0886-6236
QH344 CODEN: GBCYEP
➤ **GLOBAL BIOGEOCHEMICAL CYCLES**; an international journal of global change. Text in English. 1987. q. USD 750 domestic to institutions; USD 782 foreign to institutions (effective 2009). charts; illus. back issues avail.; reprints avail. **Document type:** *Journal, Academic/Scholarly.* **Description:** Features scholarly papers in the broad areas of global change involving the geosphere and biosphere.
Related titles: Microfiche ed.: USD 465; Online - full text ed.: ISSN 1944-9224. USD 90 to individuals; USD 420 to institutions (effective 2009).
Indexed: A22, A33, A34, A37, A38, ASCA, ASFA, Agr, AgrForAb, B21, BA, C25, C30, C33, CABA, CIN, ChemAb, ChemTitl, CurCont, E04, E05, E12, E17, ESPM, F08, F11, F12, FCA, FLUIDEX, G11, GEOBASE, GH, GeoRef, H16, I11, INIS AtomInd, ISR, M&GPA, MaizeAb, N02, OR, OceAb, P10, P11, P26, P30, P32, P40, P48, P52, P53, P54, P56, PGegResA, PGrRegA, PQC, PollutAb, R07, R11, S12, S13, S16, SCI, SCOPUS, SPINweb, SSciA, SWRA, SpeleolAb, T02, TAR, TriticAb, W07.
—BLDSC (4195.352000), CASDDS, IE, Infotrieve, Ingenta, INIST, Linda Hall. **CCC.**
Published by: American Geophysical Union, 2000 Florida Ave, NW, Washington, DC 20009. TEL 202-462-6900, 800-966-2481, FAX 202-328-0566, service@agu.org. Ed. Meinrat O Andreae.

➤ **GLOBAL ENVIRONMENTAL POLITICS.** *see* ENVIRONMENTAL STUDIES

500 NGA ISSN 1118-0579
➤ **GLOBAL JOURNAL OF PURE AND APPLIED SCIENCES.** Text in English. 1995. q. NGN 3,000 domestic; USD 160 foreign (effective 2007). bk.rev. 100 p./no. 2 cols./p.; back issues avail.; reprints avail. **Document type:** *Journal, Academic/Scholarly.* **Description:** Covers multi-disciplinary research in biological sciences, agricultural sciences, chemical sciences, mathematical and computer sciences, physics, engineering, environmental sciences and medicine.
Related titles: Online - full text ed.
Indexed: A34, A36, A37, A38, AgrForAb, B23, BA, BP, C25, C30, CABA, CIS, D01, E12, ESPM, F08, F11, F12, FCA, G11, GH, H16, H17, I11, INIS AtomInd, IndVet, MaizeAb, N02, N03, N04, O01, OR, P32, P33, P37, P38, P39, P40, PGegResA, PGrRegA, PHN&I, PN&I, R07, R08, R11, R12, R13, RA&MP, RM&VM, S12, S13, S16, S17, SoyAb, T05, TAR, TriticAb, VS, W10, W11, Z01.
—IE, Ingenta.
Published by: Global Journal Series, c/o Prof Barth N Ekwueme, University of Calabar, Unical Post Office, PO Box 3651, Calabar, Cross River State, Nigeria. bachudo@yahoo.com. Ed. Barth N Ekwueme.

500 600 MYS ISSN 1985-9406
▼ **GLOBAL JOURNAL OF TECHNOLOGY AND OPTIMIZATION.** Text in English. 2010. a. free (effective 2011). **Document type:** *Journal, Academic/Scholarly.* **Description:** Publishes specialized reviews in biotechnology, power optimization, controllers and real-time computing. Contains papers on the development and use of industrial and systems engineering tools and techniques including operations research, statistics, information systems, work measurement, and human factors applications.
Media: Online - full text.
Indexed: A01, P10, P48, P51, P52, P53, P54, PQC, T02.
Published by: Power Control Optimization pcoglobal@gmail.com. Ed. Nader Barsoum.

500 NGA ISSN 0795-6770
➤ **GLOBAL SCIENCE JOURNAL**; an international journal of science. Text and summaries in English. 1988. m. USD 15 (effective 2003). adv. **Document type:** *Academic/Scholarly.*
Published by: Global Science Union, Ugbowo, PO Box 10123, Benin City, Nigeria. Ed. O S A Aromose.

500 001.3 GBR ISSN 1474-7731
JZ1308
➤ **GLOBALIZATIONS.** Text in English. 2004. q. GBP 458 combined subscription in United Kingdom to institutions (print & online eds.); EUR 606, USD 762 combined subscription to institutions (print & online eds.) (effective 2012). adv. back issues avail.; reprint service avail. from PSC. **Document type:** *Journal, Academic/Scholarly.* **Description:** Dedicated to opening the widest possible space for discussion of alternatives to a narrow economic understanding of globalization.
Related titles: Online - full text ed.: ISSN 1474-774X. GBP 412 in United Kingdom to institutions; EUR 545, USD 686 to institutions (effective 2012) (from IngentaConnect).
Indexed: A01, A03, A08, A22, CA, CurCont, E01, E04, E05, IBSS, LeftInd, P34, P42, PAIS, PSA, S02, S03, SSCI, SociolAb, T02, W07.
—IE, Ingenta. **CCC.**
Published by: Routledge (Subsidiary of: Taylor & Francis Group), 4 Park Square, Milton Park, Abingdon, Oxon OX14 4RN, United Kingdom. subscriptions@tandf.co.uk, http://www.routledge.com. Ed. Barry Gills TEL 44-191-2227742. Adv. contact Linda Hann TEL 44-1344-779945. **Subscr. to:** Taylor & Francis Ltd., Journals Customer Service, Sheepen Pl, Colchester, Essex CO3 3LP, United Kingdom. TEL 44-20-70175544, FAX 44-20-70175198, tf.enquiries@tfinforma.com.

500 300 DEU ISSN 0944-0321
➤ **GLOBULUS.** Text in German. 1993. a. EUR 10.50 (effective 2002). back issues avail. **Document type:** *Journal, Academic/Scholarly.*
Published by: (Natur- und kulturwissenschaftliche Gesellschaft), Polygon Verlag, Kilian-Leib-Str. 137, Eichstaett, 85072, Germany. TEL 49-8421-907730, FAX 49-8421-907735, kontakt@polygon-verlag.de, http://www.polygon-verlag.de. Ed., R&P Karl Roettel. Circ: 500 (paid).

500 JPN ISSN 0385-7433
GOCHO/OKOCHI MEMORIAL FOUNDATION. JOURNAL. Text in Japanese. irreg. JPY 600. **Description:** Contains reviews, commentary, and news of the foundation.
Published by: Okochi Kinenkai/Okochi Memorial Foundation, 17-1 Toranomon 1-chome, Minato-ku, Tokyo, 105-0001, Japan.

GOENC FOCUS MAGAZINE. *see* EDUCATION—Teaching Methods And Curriculum

GOETEBORGS NATURHISTORISKA MUSEUM. AARSTRYCK. *see* MUSEUMS AND ART GALLERIES

500 SWE ISSN 0348-6788
GOTHENBURG STUDIES IN THE HISTORY OF SCIENCE AND IDEAS. Text in Swedish. 1979. irreg., latest vol.16, 2001. price varies; also exchange basis. **Document type:** *Monographic series, Academic/Scholarly.*
Related titles: ◆ Series of: Acta Universitatis Gothoburgensis. ISSN 0346-7740.
Published by: Acta Universitatis Gothoburgensis, Renstroemsgatan 4, P O Box 222, Goeteborg, 40530, Sweden. TEL 46-31-773-17-33, FAX 46-31-163-797. Ed. Sven Eric Liedman.

GR K G - GRUNDLAGENSTUDIEN AUS KYBERNETIK UND GEISTESWISSENSCHAFT; Humankybernetik. *see* COMPUTERS—Cybernetics

500 ITA ISSN 1827-3556
LA GRANDE BIBLIOTECA DELLA SCIENZA. Text in Italian. 2006. w. **Document type:** *Magazine, Consumer.*
Published by: R C S Libri (Subsidiary of: R C S Mediagroup), Via Mecenate 91, Milan, 20138, Italy. TEL 39-02-5095-2248, FAX 39-02-5095-2975, http://rcslibri.corriere.it/libri/index.htm.

GREAT BRITAIN. LABORATORY OF THE GOVERNMENT CHEMIST. REPORT AND ACCOUNTS. *see* BUSINESS AND ECONOMICS—Accounting

508.78 USA ISSN 1052-5165
QH104.5.G73 CODEN: GPLREB
➤ **GREAT PLAINS RESEARCH.** Text in English. 1991. s-a. USD 25 domestic to individuals; USD 34 in Canada to individuals; USD 38 elsewhere to individuals; USD 50 domestic to institutions; USD 60 in Canada to institutions; USD 75 elsewhere to institutions; USD 8 per issue (effective 2010). adv. bk.rev. abstr.; bibl.; charts; illus. 192 p./no.; back issues avail. **Document type:** *Journal, Academic/Scholarly.* **Description:** Contains reviews of books and reports on symposia and conferences that included sessions on topics pertaining to the Great Plains.
Indexed: ASFA, AmH&L, B21, B25, BIOBASE, BIOSIS Prev, CA, E17, ESPM, GEOBASE, IABS, M&GPA, MycolAb, P10, P11, P42, P52, P56, PQC, PSA, S02, S03, SCOPUS, SOPODA, SSA, SWRA, SociolAb, SpeleolAb, T02, W08, WildRev.
—BLDSC (4214.564500), IE, Ingenta.
Published by: University of Nebraska at Lincoln, Center for Great Plains Studies, 1155 Q St, PO Box 880214, Lincoln, NE 68588. TEL 402-472-3082, FAX 402-472-0463, cgps@unl.edu. Ed. Dr. Robert F Diffendal Jr. Circ: 500.

508 ITA ISSN 1593-5205
GREDLERIANA. Text in Multiple languages. 2001. a. EUR 20 (effective 2009). 352 p./no.; **Document type:** *Journal, Academic/Scholarly.*
Indexed: B21, B25, BIOSIS Prev, EntAb, MycolAb, RefZh, Z01.
—BLDSC (4214.817500).
Published by: Museo di Scienze Naturali dell'Alto Adige, Via Bottai 1, Bolzano, 39100, Italy. TEL 39-0471-412960, FAX 39-0471-412979, info@museonatura.it, http://www.naturmuseum.it.

500 USA ISSN 1559-5374
GREENWOOD GUIDES TO GREAT IDEAS IN SCIENCE. Variant title: Guides to Great Ideas in Science. Text in English. 2006. irreg. price varies. back issues avail. **Document type:** *Monographic series, Academic/Scholarly.* **Description:** Narrates the development of a particular scientific concept from ancient times to the present day.
Related titles: Online - full text ed.
Published by: Greenwood Publishing Group Inc. (Subsidiary of: A B C - C L I O), 88 Post Rd W, PO Box 5007, Westport, CT 06881. TEL 203-226-3571, 800-225-5800, FAX 877-231-6980, sales@greenwood.com. Ed. Brian Baigrie.

500 100 200 DEU ISSN 0933-5366
GRENZFRAGEN. Text in German. 1972. irreg., latest vol.34, 2009. price varies. **Document type:** *Monographic series, Academic/Scholarly.*
Supersedes (1957-1970): Naturwissenschaft und Theologie (0547-9762)
Published by: (Goerres-Gesellschaft), Verlag Karl Alber, Hermann-Herder-Str 4, Freiburg, 79104, Germany. TEL 49-761-2717436, FAX 49-761-2717212, info@verlag-alber.de. Ed. Ludger Honnefelder.

500 AUT ISSN 1021-8130
GRENZGEBIETE DER WISSENSCHAFT. Text in German; Abstracts in English. 1951. q. EUR 34 (effective 2003). bk.rev. 96 p./no.; back issues avail. **Document type:** *Journal, Academic/Scholarly.*
Formerly (until 1967): Verborgene Welt
Indexed: DIP, IBR, IBZ, P30, RILM.
Published by: Resch Verlag, Maximilianstr 8, Innsbruck, 6010, Austria. TEL 43-512-574772, FAX 43-512-586463, igw@uibk.ac.at, http://www.uibk.ac.at/c/cb/index-en.html. Ed. Andreas Resch. Circ: 500.

GRUNDLAGENPROBLEME UNSERER ZEIT. *see* SOCIAL SCIENCES: COMPREHENSIVE WORKS

GUANGDONG JISHU SHIFAN XUEYUAN XUEBAO/GUANGDONG POLYTECHNIC NORMAL UNIVERSITY. JOURNAL. *see* SOCIAL SCIENCES: COMPREHENSIVE WORKS

GUANGDONG QINGGONG ZHIYE JISHU XUEYUAN XUEBAO/ GUANGDONG INDUSTRY TECHNICAL COLLEGE. JOURNAL. *see* SOCIAL SCIENCES: COMPREHENSIVE WORKS

300 CHN ISSN 1009-2633
GUANGXI DAXUE WUZHOU FENXIAO XUEBAO/GUANGXI UNIVERSITY. WUZHOU BRANCH. JOURNAL. Text in Chinese. 1991. q. CNY 10 newsstand/cover (effective 2006). **Document type:** *Journal, Academic/Scholarly.*
Related titles: Online - full text ed.
Published by: Guangxi Daxue, Wuzhou Fenxiao, 82, Fumin San-Lu, Wuzhou, 543002, China. TEL 86-774-5839976.

500 CHN ISSN 1001-7445
CODEN: GDXZEB
➤ **GUANGXI DAXUE XUEBAO (ZIRAN KEXUE BAN)/GUANGXI UNIVERSITY. JOURNAL (NATURAL SCIENCE EDITION).** Text in Chinese; Abstracts in Chinese, English. 1976. bi-m. CNY 60, USD 60; CNY 10 per issue (effective 2010 & 2011). **Document type:** *Journal, Academic/Scholarly.* **Description:** Covers civil and architectural engineering, chemistry and chemical engineering, mechanical engineering, and computer science.
Related titles: Online - full text ed.
Indexed: CCMJ, ESPM, MSN, MathR, RefZh, SWRA, Z02.
—BLDSC (4757.656750), East View, IE, Ingenta.
Published by: Guangxi Daxue/Guangxi University, No.100, Uversity Rd., Nanning, Guangxi 530004, China. TEL 86-771-3235713, FAX 86-771-2313009. Ed. Bao-shan Chen. Circ: 1,000.

500 CHN ISSN 1005-9164
GUANGXI KEXUE/GUANGXI SCIENCES. Text in Chinese. 1994. q. **Document type:** *Journal, Academic/Scholarly.*
Related titles: Online - full text ed.
—BLDSC (4223.859223).
Published by: Guangxi Kexueyuan/Guangxi Academy of Science, No.32, Xinghu Road, Nanning 530022, Guangxi 530022, China. TEL 86-771-2503922, FAX 86-771-2503923, gxas@gxas.cn. Ed. Zheng-you Zhang.

500 CHN ISSN 1002-7378
GUANGXI KEXUEYUAN XUEBAO/GUANGXI ACADEMY OF SCIENCE. JOURNAL. Text in Chinese. 1982. q. CNY 2.50 newsstand/cover domestic (effective 2003). **Document type:** *Journal, Academic/Scholarly.*
Related titles: Online - full text ed.
—BLDSC (4996.539000).
Published by: Guangxi Kexueyuan/Guangxi Academy of Science, No.32, Xinghu Road, Nanning 530022, Guangxi 530022, China. TEL 86-771-2503922, FAX 86-771-2503923, gxas@gxas.cn. Ed. Hai-peng Luo.

500 CHN ISSN 1673-8462
Q4
GUANGXI MINZU DAXUE XUEBAO (ZIRAN KEXUE BAN)/GUANGXI UNIVERSITY FOR NATIONALITIES. JOURNAL (NATURAL SCIENCE EDITION). Text in Chinese. 1995. q. CNY 8 per issue (effective 2010). **Document type:** *Journal, Academic/Scholarly.*
Formerly (until 2006): Guangxi Minzu Xueyuan Xuebao (Ziran Kexue Ban) (1007-0311)
Related titles: Online - full text ed.
Indexed: ESPM, PollutAb, RefZh, SWRA, Z02.
—East View.
Published by: Guangxi Minzu Xueyuan/Guangxi University for Nationalities, 188, Daxue Dong Lu, Nanning, 530006, China. TEL 86-771-3263361, FAX 86-771-3263361, http://www.gxun.edu.cn/.

500 CHN ISSN 1001-6600
GUANGXI SHIFAN DAXUE XUEBAO (ZIRAN KEXUE BAN)/GUANGXI NORMAL UNIVERSITY. JOURNAL (NATURAL SCIENCE EDITION). Text in Chinese. 1957. q. back issues avail. **Document type:** *Journal, Academic/Scholarly.*
Former titles (until 1983): Guangxi Shifan Xueyuan Xuebao (Ziran Kexue Ban); (until 1978): Guangxi Shiyuan (Ziran Kexue Ban); (until 1964): Kexue Lunwenji (Ziran Kexue Ban)
Related titles: Online - full text ed.
Indexed: A22, A28, A34, A35, A37, A38, APA, AgBio, AgrForAb, B21, BA, BP, BrCerAb, C&ISA, C25, C30, CA/WCA, CABA, CCMJ, CIA, CerAb, CivEngAb, CorrAb, E&CAJ, E11, E12, EEA, EMA, ESPM, EntAb, EnvEAb, F08, F12, FCA, G11, GH, H15, H16, I11, LT, M&TEA, M09, MBF, METADEX, MSN, MathR, N02, N03, N04, NSA, O01, P32, P33, P40, PGegResA, PGrRegA, PHN&I, PN&I, PollutAb, R07, R08, R12, R13, RA&MP, RM&VM, RRTA, RefZh, S12, S13, S16, SSciA, SolStAb, T04, T05, TAR, VS, W10, W11, WAA, Z01, Z02.
—BLDSC (4757.656500), IE, Ingenta, Linda Hall.
Published by: Guangxi Shifan Daxue/Guangxi Normal University, 15, Yucai Lu, Guilin, 541004, China. FAX 86-773-5817343, http://www.gxnu.edu.cn. Ed. Hong Liang.

500 CHN
GUANGXI SHIFAN XUEYUAN XUEBAO (ZIRAN KEXUE BAN)/GUANGXI TEACHERS COLLEGE. JOURNAL (NATURAL SCIENCE EDITION). Text in Chinese. 1983. q. CNY 24 domestic; USD 6 in Hong Kong, Macau & Taiwan; USD 12 elsewhere (effective 2007). **Document type:** *Journal, Academic/Scholarly.*
Formerly: Guangxi Shiyuan Xuebao (Ziran Kexue Ban) (1001-8743)
Related titles: Online - full text ed.
Published by: Guangxi Shifan Xueyuan, 175, Mingxiu Dong Lu, Nanning, 530001, China. **Dist. by:** China International Book Trading Corp, 35 Chegongzhuang Xilu, Haidian District, PO Box 399, Beijing 100044, China. TEL 86-10-68412045, FAX 86-10-68412023, cibtc@mail.cibtc.com.cn, http://www.cibtc.com.cn.

500 300 CHN ISSN 1674-3083
GUANGXI ZHIYE JISHU XUEYUAN XUEBAO/GUANGXI VOCATIONAL AND TECHNICAL COLLEGE. JOURNAL. Text in Chinese. 2008. bi-m. **Document type:** *Journal, Academic/Scholarly.*
Published by: Guangxi Zhiye Jishu Xueyuan/Guangxi Vocational and Technical College, Jiangnan Mingyang Gongye-qu, Nanning, Guangxi 530226, China. TEL 86-771-4213111.

500 CHN ISSN 1671-4229
GUANGZHOU DAXUE XUEBAO (ZIRAN KEXUE BAN). Text in Chinese. 1987. bi-m. USD 37.20 (effective 2009). **Document type:** *Journal, Academic/Scholarly.*
Formerly (until 2001): Guangzhou Daxue Xuebao/Guangzhou University. Journal (1008-9861)
Indexed: A28, APA, BrCerAb, C&ISA, CA/WCA, CCMJ, CIA, CerAb, CivEngAb, CorrAb, E&CAJ, E11, EEA, EMA, ESPM, EnvEAb, H15, M&TEA, M09, MBF, METADEX, MSN, MathR, SolStAb, T04, WAA, Z01, Z02.
—Linda Hall.
Published by: Guangzhou Daxue, Daxuecheng Wai Huanxi Lu #230, A213 Xinxiang, Guangzhou, 510006, China. TEL 86-20-39366068, FAX 86-20-39366066.

508 ESP ISSN 1988-7485
GUIAS PARA ENSENANZAS MEDIAS. CIENCIAS DE LA NATURALEZA. Text in Spanish. 2007. m. **Document type:** *Monographic series, Academic/Scholarly.*
Media: Online - full text.
Published by: Wolters Kluwer Espana - Educacion (Subsidiary of: Wolters Kluwer N.V.), C Collado Mediano 9, Las Rozas, Madrid, 28230, Spain. TEL 34-902-250510, FAX 34-902-250515, cleintes@wkeducacion.es, http://www.wkeducacion.es/index.asp. Ed. Joaquin Gairin.

500 CHN ISSN 1000-5269
GUIZHOU DAXUE XUEBAO (ZIRAN KEXUE BAN)/GUIZHOU UNIVERSITY. JOURNAL (NATURAL SCIENCE EDITION). Text in Chinese. 1974. bi-m. **Document type:** *Journal, Academic/Scholarly.*
Related titles: Online - full text ed.: (from WanFang Data Corp.).
—BLDSC (4230.235000), East View.
Published by: Guizhou Daxue/Guizhou University, Huaqi-qu, Bei Xiao-qu, 2/F, Chubanshe Lou, Guizhou, 550025, China. TEL 86-851-8292182, FAX 86-851-3621708. Ed. Jian-shi Li. **Dist. by:** China International Book Trading Corp, 35 Chegongzhuang Xilu, Haidian District, PO Box 399, Beijing 100044, China. TEL 86-10-68412045, FAX 86-10-68412023, cibtc@mail.cibtc.com.cn, http://www.cibtc.com.cn.

500 CHN ISSN 1003-6563
Q4
GUIZHOU KEXUE/GUIZHOU SCIENCE. Text in Chinese. 1983. q. USD 14.40 (effective 2009). 72 p./no.; **Document type:** *Academic/Scholarly.* **Description:** Covers mathematics, earth sciences, biology as well as natural resources of Guizhou Province.
Related titles: Online - full text ed.
—East View.
Published by: Guizhou Kexueyuan, 40 Yan an Donglu, Guiyang, Guizhou 550001, China. **Dist. overseas by:** China International Book Trading Corp, 35 Chegongzhuang Xilu, Haidian District, PO Box 399, Beijing 100044, China.

500 CHN ISSN 1004-5570
GUIZHOU SHIFAN DAXUE XUEBAO (ZIRAN KEXUEBAN)/GUIZHOU NORMAL UNIVERSITY. JOURNAL (NATURAL SCIENCE). Text in Chinese. 1960. q. USD 14.40 (effective 2009). **Document type:** *Journal, Academic/Scholarly.*
Related titles: Online - full text ed.
Indexed: Z02.
—East View.
Published by: Guizhou Shifan Daxue/Guizhou Normal University, 116, Baoshan Bei Lu, Guiyang, 550001, China. TEL 86-851-6762237, FAX 86-851-6771335.

500.9 JPN ISSN 0017-5668
Q4 CODEN: GDSHAU
GUNMA DAIGAKU KYOIKUGAKUBU KIYO. SHIZEN KAGAKU HEN/GUNMA UNIVERSITY. FACULTY OF EDUCATION. SCIENCE REPORTS. Text in English, Japanese; Summaries in English. 1950. a. per issue exchange basis.
Indexed: ChemAb, JPI, RefZh, Z02.
—CASDDS.
Published by: Gunma University, Faculty of Education/Gunma Daigaku Kyoikugakubu, Library, 4-2 Aramaki-Machi, Maebashi-shi, Gunma-ken 371-0044, Japan.

500 JPN ISSN 1342-4092
GUNMA MUSEUM OF NATURAL HISTORY. BULLETIN/GUNMA KENRITSU SHIZENSHI HAKUBUTSUKAN KENKYU HOKOKU. Text in English. 1996. a. **Document type:** *Bulletin, Academic/Scholarly.*
Indexed: Z01.
Published by: Gunma Kenritsu Shizenshi Hakubutsukan, 1674-1 Kamikuroiwa, Gunma-ken, Tomioka-shi, 370-2345, Japan. TEL 81-274-601200, FAX 81-274-601250, http://www.gmnh.pref.gunma.jp/.

500 600 TWN ISSN 1028-5636
GUOLI BINGDONG KEJI DAXUE XUEBAO. Text in Chinese. 1991. q. **Document type:** *Journal, Academic/Scholarly.*
Formerly (until 1997): Guoli Bindong Jishu Xueyuan Xuebao/National Pingtung Polytechnic Institute. Bulletin (1021-6081)
Indexed: CPEI, Englnd, SCOPUS.
Published by: Guoli Bingdong Keji Daxue/National Pingtung University of Science and Technology, No.1, Shuehfu Rd., Neipu, Pingtung, 91201, Taiwan. TEL 886-8-7703202, http://www.npust.edu.tw/.

507.1 GUY
GUYANA SCIENCE TEACHERS' ASSOCIATION. NEWSLETTER. Text in English. 3/yr. membership.
Published by: Guyana Science Teachers' Association, c/o Honorary Secretary, Mr. B.N. Kumar, Unity Village, East Coast Demerara, Guyana.

500 KOR ISSN 1228-3401
GWAHAG DONG'A/DONGA SCIENCE. Text in Korean. 1986. m. **Document type:** *Magazine, Consumer.* **Description:** Provides news and information on all science-related topics and a variety of creative educational programs and events.
Related titles: Online - full text ed.
Published by: Dong-A Ilbo, 139, Chungjongno 3-Ga Seodaemun-Gu, Seoul, 120-715, Korea, S. TEL 82-2-67492562, FAX 82-2-67492600, http://www.donga.com/.

500 DEU ISSN 1617-5239
Q143.H9
H I N - ALEXANDER VON HUMBOLDT IM NETZ. Text in English, German, Spanish. 2000. s-a. free (effective 2011). **Document type:** *Journal, Academic/Scholarly.*
Media: Online - full content.
Indexed: MLA-IB.
Published by: Universitaet Potsdam, Institut fuer Romanistik, Am Neuen Palais 10, Potsdam, 14415, Germany. Eds. Eberhard Knobloch, Ottmar Ette. **Co-publisher:** Humboldt Forschungsstelle der Berlin, Alexander von.

500.01 USA ISSN 1544-9912
H O P O S NEWSLETTER. (History of Philosophy of Science) Text in English. 1993. s-a. free (effective 2011). back issues avail. **Document type:** *Newsletter, Consumer.* **Description:** Promotes scholarly research on the history of the philosophy of science and related topics in the history of the natural and social sciences, logic, philosophy and mathematics.
Former titles (until 2003): History of Philosophy of Science Working Group. Newsletter (1527-9332); (until 199?): H O P O S Newsletter
Media: Online - full text.
Address: Department of Philosophy, Virginia Tech University, Blacksburg, VA 24061. krieger@mail.uri.edu, http://www.hopos.org. Ed. Rose-Mary Sargent.

500 NLD ISSN 1876-1704
H Z DISCOVERY. Text in Dutch. 2007. s-a.
Published by: Hogeschool Zeeland, Postbus 364, Vlissingen, 4380 AJ, Netherlands. TEL 31-118-489000, FAX 31-118-489200, info@hz.nl. Ed. Anja de Groene TEL 31-118-489224.

508 333.72 NLD ISSN 1879-7490
HAAGWINDE. Text in Dutch. 2008. q. EUR 10 (effective 2010).
Published by: Algemene Vereniging voor Natuurbescherming voor 's Gravenhage en Omstreken, Badhuisstraat 175, The Hague, 2584 HH, Netherlands. TEL 31-70-3388100, info@avn.nl, http://www.avnnatuurbescherming.nl. Circ: 5,000.

HACETTEPE JOURNAL OF BIOLOGY AND CHEMISTRY/HACETTEPE BULLETIN OF NATURAL SCIENCES AND ENGINEERING. SERIES A: BIOLOGY AND CHEMISTRY. *see* BIOLOGY

500 600 CHN ISSN 1007-2683
HAERBIN LIGONG DAXUE XUEBAO/HARBIN UNIVERSITY OF SCIENCE AND TECHNOLOGY. JOURNAL. Text in Chinese. 1996. bi-m. USD 18 (effective 2009). **Document type:** *Journal, Academic/Scholarly.*
Related titles: Online - full text ed.
—BLDSC (4757.879600).
Published by: Ha'erbin Ligong Daxue/Harbin University of Science and Technology, 23, Sandongli Lu, Ha'erbin, 150040, China. TEL 86-451-86396391.

500 CHN ISSN 1672-0946
HAERBIN SHANGYE DAXUE XUEBAO (ZIRAN KEXUE BAN)/HARBIN UNIVERSITY OF COMMERCE. JOURNAL (NATURAL SCIENCE EDITION). Text in Chinese. 1984. bi-m. CNY 10 newsstand/cover (effective 2005). **Document type:** *Journal, Academic/Scholarly.*
Indexed: A28, A32, APA, BrCerAb, C&ISA, CA/WCA, CIA, CerAb, CivEngAb, CorrAb, E&CAJ, E11, EEA, EMA, ESPM, EnvEAb, H15, M&TEA, M09, MBF, METADEX, PollutAb, RefZh, SWRA, SolStAb, T04, WAA.
—BLDSC (4262.515500), Linda Hall.
Published by: Ha'erbin Shangye Daxue/Harbin University of Commerce, 138 Tongda Street, Daoli District, Ha'erbin, 150076, China. Ed. Yu-bin Ji.

500 CHN ISSN 1004-1729
HAINAN DAXUE XUEBAO (ZIRAN KEXUE BAN)/NATURAL SCIENCE JOURNAL OF HAINAN UNIVERSITY. Text in Chinese. 1983. q. USD 20.80 (effective 2009). **Document type:** *Journal, Academic/Scholarly.*
Related titles: Online - full text ed.
—East View.
Published by: Hainan Daxue/Hainan University, Renmin Dadao, Haikou, 570228, China. TEL 86-898-66279237, FAX 86-898-66187920. Ed. Wen-shen Xu.

500 CHN ISSN 1674-4942
HAINAN SHIFAN DAXUE XUEBAO (ZIRAN KEXUE BAN)/HAINAN NORMAL UNIVERSITY. JOURNAL (NATURAL SCIENCE). Text in Chinese. 1987. q. **Document type:** *Journal, Academic/Scholarly.*
Formerly (until 2007): Hainan Shifan Xueyuan Xuebao (Ziran Kexue Ban) (1671-8747); Which superseded in part (in 2000): Hainan Shifan Xueyuan Xuebao
Related titles: Online - full text ed.
Indexed: Z02.
Published by: Hainan Shifan Daxue, 99, Longkun Nan Lu, Haikou, 571158, China. TEL 86-898-65882380, FAX 86-898-65881326, http://www.hainnu.edu.cn/.

HAIXIA KEJI YU CHANYE/TECHNOLOGIES AND INDUSTRIES ON BOTH SIDES OF THE STRAITS. *see* BUSINESS AND ECONOMICS

500 JPN ISSN 0289-4092
HAKUBUTSUKAN DAYORI/SAITO HO-ON KAI MUSEUM OF NATURAL HISTORY. NEWS. Text in Japanese. 1981. q. free. **Document type:** *Newsletter, Academic/Scholarly.*
Published by: Saito Ho-on Kai/Saito Gratitude Foundation, 20-2 Hon-cho 2-chome, Aoba-ku, Sendai-shi, Miyagi-ken 980-0014, Japan. TEL 81-222-262-5506, FAX 81-222-262-5508. Ed. Sadako Takeuti.

509 101 NLD ISSN 1878-9846
HANDBOOK OF THE PHILOSOPHY OF SCIENCE. Text in English. 2007. irreg., latest 2008. price varies. **Document type:** *Monographic series, Academic/Scholarly.* **Description:** Covers philosophical issues in the sciences, both basic and applied.
Published by: Elsevier BV, North-Holland (Subsidiary of: Elsevier Science & Technology), Sara Burgerhartstraat 25, Amsterdam, 1055 KV, Netherlands. TEL 31-20-4853911, FAX 31-20-4852457, JournalsCustomerServiceEMEA@elsevier.com, http://www.elsevier.com. Eds. Dov M Gabbay, John Woods, Paul Thagard.

500 CHN ISSN 1674-232X
HANGZHOU SHIFAN DAXUE XUEBAO (ZIRAN KEXUE BAN)/HANGZHOU NORMAL UNIVERSITY. JOURNAL (NATURAL SCIENCES EDITION). Text in Chinese; Abstracts in Chinese, English. 1979. bi-m. CNY 60, USD 60; CNY 10 per issue (effective 2011 & 2012). **Document type:** *Journal, Academic/Scholarly.* **Description:** Covers mainly research in organic chemistry, inorganic chemistry, analytical chemistry and environmental science, biomedical, molecular biology, and phytoecology, etc.
Formerly (until 2008): Hangzhou Shifan Xueyuan Xuebao (Ziran Kexue Ban); Which superseded in part (in 2000): Hangzhou Jiaoyu Xueyuan Xuebao/Hangzhou Educational Institute. Journal (1008-9403); Which was formed by the merger of (1979-1987): Hangzhou Shiyuan Xuebao (Ziran Kexue Ban) (1000-2146); (1982-1987): Hangzhou Shiyuan Xuebao (Shehui Kexue Ban)
Related titles: Online - full text ed.
Indexed: RefZh, Z02.
Published by: Hangzhou Shifan Xueyuan Xueshu Jikanshe/Hangzhou Teachers College, 16, Xuelin Jie, Xiasha Gaojiaoyuan, Hangzhou, 310036, China. TEL 86-571-28865872, FAX 86-571-28865871. Circ: 2,000.

500 CHN ISSN 1000-5897
CODEN: HKJXET
HARBIN KEXUE JISHU DAXUE XUEBAO/HARBIN UNIVERSITY OF SCIENCE AND TECHNOLOGY. JOURNAL. Text in Chinese. q. **Document type:** *Academic/Scholarly.*
Indexed: CIN, ChemAb, ChemTitl.
—CASDDS.
Published by: Harbin Kexue Jishu Daxue, Xuebao Bianjibu, 22, Xuefu Lu, Nangang-qu, Harbin, Heilongjiang 150080, China. TEL 61081. Ed. Ren Shanzhi.

500 CHN ISSN 1000-5617
HARBIN SHIFAN DAXUE ZIRAN KEXUE XUEBAO/NATURAL SCIENCES JOURNAL OF HARBIN UNIVERSITY. Text in Chinese. 1984. bi-m. USD 24.60 (effective 2009). **Document type:** *Academic/Scholarly.*
Related titles: Online - full text ed.
Indexed: CCMJ, MSN, MathR, Z02.
Published by: Ha'erbin Shifan Daxue, Xuebao Bianjibu, 24, Hexing Lu, Nangang-qu, Harbin, Heilongjiang 150080, China. TEL 86-451-6304889. Ed. Xuan-zhang Wang.

500 USA
HARVARD SCIENCE NEWS. Text in English. q. **Document type:** *Newsletter.* **Description:** Features short, fast-paced articles to keep you up-to-date on the latest scientific discoveries.
Media: Online - full text.

S

Published by: Harvard University, 4 University Hall, Cambridge, MA 02138.

500 USA

HARVARD SCIENCE REVIEW. Text in English. 1988. q. **Description:** Brings in-depth articles on contemporary issues in science to readers at Harvard and MIT.
Media: Online - full text.
Published by: Harvard University, 4 University Hall, Cambridge, MA 02138. http://www.hcs.harvard.edu. Ed. Imrad Javaid.

THE HASTINGS & EAST SUSSEX NATURALIST. *see* CONSERVATION

500 USA

HAWKHILL NEWS; a newsletter of scientific and civic literacy. Text in English. irreg. **Document type:** *Newsletter, Consumer.* **Description:** Explores the philosophic and social aspects of a variety of scientific issues, many of them controversial, and presents them to the general reader. Informs teachers in the sciences where they can obtain free or low-cost materials.
Formerly (until 2006): Hawkhill Science Newsletter
Media: E-mail.
Published by: Hawkhill Science Associates, Inc., 125 E Gilman St, Madison, WI 53701-1029. TEL 800-422-4295, FAX 608-251-3924, order@hawkhill.com, http://www.hawkhill.com. Ed. Bill Stonebarger.

500 JPN ISSN 1345-7225

HAYASHIBARA MUSEUM OF NATURAL SCIENCES RESEARCH BULLETIN. Text in Japanese. 2000. irreg. **Document type:** *Monographic series, Academic/Scholarly.*
Indexed: Z01.
Published by: Hayashibara Museum of Natural Sciences, 1-2-3 Shimoishii, Okayama, 700-0907, Japan. TEL 81-86-2244311, FAX 81-86-2333363, http://www.hayashibaramuseum.jp/.

500 060 ARM ISSN 1026-6496
CODEN: DANAAW

HAYASTANY GUITOUTYUNNERY AZGAYIN ACADEMIA ZEKUYTS'NER/AKADEMIYA NAUK ARMENII. DOKLADY. Text in Armenian, Russian. 1944. 10/yr. AMD 400. **Document type:** *Academic/Scholarly.*
Formerly (until 1991): Akademiya Nauk Armyanskoi S.S.R. Doklady (0321-1339)
Indexed: CCMJ, CIN, CIS, ChemAb, ChemTitl, GeoRef, INIS AtomInd, MSN, MathR, RASB, SpeleolAb, Z01, Z02.
—CASDDS, East View, INIST, Linda Hall. **CCC.**
Published by: Hayastany Guitoutyunnery Azgayin Academia/National Academy of Sciences of the Republic of Armenia, Marshal Bagramyan Ave 24b, Erevan, 375019, Armenia. TEL 52-45-80. Ed. Sergey Ambartsumian.

500 ARM ISSN 1029-7901
CODEN: IAAZAT

HAYASTANY HANRAPETUTYAN TITUTYUNNERI AZGAYIN AKADEMIA TEGHEKAGIR. GITUTYUNNER ERKRI MASIN. Text in Armenian. irreg. **Document type:** *Journal, Academic/Scholarly.*
Former titles (until 1993): Akademiya Nauk Armenii. Izvestiya. Nauki o Zemle (1029-7898); (until 1990): Akademiya Nauk Armyanskoi S.S.R. Izvestiya. Nauki o Zemle (0515-961X); (until 1964): Akademiya Nauk Armyanskoi S.S.R. Izvestiya. Geologicheskie i Geograficheskie Nauki (0367-6668)
Indexed: GeoRef, INIS AtomInd, Z01.
—East View, INIST. **CCC.**
Published by: Hayastany Guitoutyunnery Azgayin Academia/National Academy of Sciences of the Republic of Armenia, Marshal Bagramyan Ave 24b, Erevan, 375019, Armenia.

500 CHN ISSN 1673-1492

HEBEI BEIFANG XUEYUAN XUEBAO (ZIRAN KEXUE BAN)/HEBEI NORTH UNIVERSITY. JOURNAL (NATURAL SCIENCE EDITION). Text in Chinese. 1984. bi-m. USD 24.60 (effective 2009). **Document type:** *Journal, Academic/Scholarly.*
Supersedes in part (in 2004): Zhangjiakou Yixueyuan Xuebao/Zhangjiakou Medical College. Journal (1005-8796)
Related titles: Online - full text ed.
—East View.
Published by: Hebei Beifang Xueyuan/Hebei North University, 14, Changqing Lu, Zhangjiakou, 075000, China. TEL 86-313-8041719.

500 CHN ISSN 1000-1565
CODEN: HDXKEB

➤ **HEBEI DAXUE XUEBAO (ZIRAN KEXUE BAN)/HEBEI UNIVERSITY. JOURNAL (NATURAL SCIENCES EDITION).** Text in Chinese. 1962. bi-m. CNY 60, USD 60; USD 10 per issue (effective 2011 & 2012). **Document type:** *Journal, Academic/Scholarly.* **Description:** Covers mathematics, physics, chemistry, biology, and computer science.
Related titles: Online - full text ed.
Indexed: CCMJ, CIN, ChemAb, ChemTitl, MSN, MathR, RefZh, Z01.
—BLDSC (4757.985000), CASDDS, East View, IE, Ingenta.
Published by: Hebei Daxue/Hebei University, no.108, 54 Dong Lu, Baoding, Hebei 071002, China. TEL 86-312-5079413, FAX 86-312-5079712. Ed. Hanwen Sun. Circ: 1,300.

500 CHN ISSN 1673-9469
CODEN: HGDXD4

HEBEI GONGCHENG DAXUE XUEBAO (ZIRAN KEXUE BAN)/HEBEI UNIVERSITY OF ENGINEERING. JOURNAL (NATURAL SCIENCE EDITION). Text in Chinese. 1984. q. CNY 40, USD 40; CNY 10 newsstand/cover (effective 2010). **Document type:** *Journal, Academic/Scholarly.*
Formerly (until 2007): Hebei Jianzhu Keji Xueyuan Xuebao/Hebei Institute of Architectural Science and Technology. Journal (1007-6743); Which superseded in part (in 1996): Hebei Meitan Jianzhu Gongcheng Xueyuan Xuebao/Hebei Mining and Civil Engineering Institute. Journal (1004-5317)
Related titles: Online - full text ed.
Indexed: RefZh.
Published by: Hebei Jianzhu Keji Xueyuan/Hebei Institute of Architectural Science and Technology, 199, Guangming Nan Dajie, Handan, 056038, China. TEL 86-310-8579120, FAX 86-310-8579120. Circ: 1,000.

500 600 CHN ISSN 1008-1542

HEBEI KEJI DAXUE XUEBAO/HEBEI UNIVERSITY OF SCIENCE AND TECHNOLOGY. JOURNAL. Text in Chinese. 1980. q. CNY 500 newsstand/cover domestic. **Document type:** *Academic/Scholarly.*
Related titles: Online - full content ed.; Online - full text ed.
Indexed: A22, ESPM, Inspec, RefZh, SWRA.
—BLDSC (4757.986000), IE, Ingenta.
Published by: Hebei Keji Daxue, 186 Yuhua Dong Lu, Shijiazhuang, Hebei 050018, China. TEL 86-311-8632141. **Dist. by:** China National Publishing and Foreign Trade Co., PO Box 782, Beijing, China.

500 300 CHN ISSN 1673-2022

HEBEI RUANJIAN ZHIYE JISHU XUEYUAN XUEBAO/HEBEI SOFTWARE INSTITUTE. JOURNAL. Text in Chinese. 1999. q. CNY 6 newsstand/cover (effective 2006). **Document type:** *Journal, Academic/Scholarly.*
Former titles (until 2004): Hebei Gongcheng Jishu Zhiye Xueyuan Xuebao/Hebei Engineering & Technology Vocational College. Journal (1671-718X); (until 2001): Hebei Zhigong Daxue Xuebao/Hebei Staff and Workers University. Journal (1008-6277)
Related titles: Online - full text ed.
Published by: Hebei Ruanjian Zhiye Jishu Xueyuan, 1, Zhiye Da Lu, Baoding, 071000, China. TEL 86-312-5999817.

500 CHN ISSN 1001-9383
Q111 CODEN: HKXUEM

HEBEI-SHENG KEXUEYUAN XUEBAO/HEBEI ACADEMY OF SCIENCES. JOURNAL. Text in English. 1984. q. **Document type:** *Journal, Academic/Scholarly.*
Related titles: Online - full text ed.
—BLDSC (4757.982700).
Published by: Hebei-sheng Kexueyuan/Hebei Academy of Sciences, 46 Youyi Nan Dajie, Shijiazhuang, 050081, China. TEL 86-311-83019546, FAX 86-311-83032060. Ed. De-qiang Zhang.

500 CHN ISSN 1000-5854
CODEN: HSDKEG

HEBEI SHIFAN DAXUE XUEBAO (ZIRAN KEXUE BAN)/HEBEI NORMAL UNIVERSITY. JOURNAL (NATURAL SCIENCE EDITION). Text in Chinese. 1977. q. USD 31.20 (effective 2009). **Document type:** *Journal, Academic/Scholarly.*
Related titles: CD-ROM ed.; Online - full text ed.
Indexed: A28, APA, BrCerAb, C&ISA, CA/WCA, CCMJ, CIA, CIN, CerAb, ChemAb, ChemTitl, CivEngAb, CorrAb, E&CAJ, E11, EEA, EMA, ESPM, EnvEAb, GeoRef, H15, M&TEA, M09, MBF, METADEX, MSN, MathR, SolStAb, T04, WAA, Z01, Z02.
—BLDSC (4757.984800), CASDDS, IE, Ingenta, Linda Hall.
Published by: Hebei Shifan Daxue/Hebei Normal University, 265, Yuhua Dong Lu, Shijiazhuang, Hebei 050016, China. TEL 86-311-6049941, FAX 86-311-6049413. Ed. Jin Shixun. Circ: 1,500. **Dist overseas by:** China International Book Trading Corp, 35 Chegongzhuang Xilu, Haidian District, PO Box 399, Beijing 100044, China.

508 639.9 GBR ISSN 0953-4342

THE HEBRIDEAN NATURALIST. Text in English. 1978. a. free to members (effective 2009). adv. **Document type:** *Magazine, Trade.* **Description:** Contains articles, notes, letters or reviews, either in gaelic or in english.
Published by: Curracag (Western Isles Natural History Society), c o Lyn Lowe, Membership Secretary, Tigh na Mara, Cnoc-a-Lin, Isle of North Uist, Outer Hebrides, Western Isles, HS6 5DZ, United Kingdom. TEL 44-1876-510725, http://www.western-isles-wildlife.co.uk/curracag.htm.

500 CHN ISSN 1003-5060

HEFEI GONGYE DAXUE XUEBAO (ZIRAN KEXUE BAN)/HEFEI UNIVERSITY OF TECHNOLOGY. JOURNAL (NATURAL SCIENCE EDITION). Text in Chinese. 1956. m. **Document type:** *Journal, Academic/Scholarly.*
Related titles: Online - full text ed.
Indexed: A28, APA, BrCerAb, C&ISA, CA/WCA, CCMJ, CIA, CerAb, CivEngAb, CorrAb, E&CAJ, E11, EEA, EMA, ESPM, EnvEAb, H15, M&TEA, M09, MBF, METADEX, MSN, MathR, RefZh, SolStAb, T04, WAA, Z02.
—BLDSC (4283.265000), Linda Hall.
Published by: Hefei Gongye Daxue, 193, Tunxi Lu, Hefei, 230009, China. TEL 86-551-2901306, FAX 86-551-2901306. Ed. Er-ren Qu.

500 CHN ISSN 1673-162X

HEFEI XUEYUAN XUEBAO (ZIRAN KEXUE BAN). Text in Chinese. 1991. q. **Document type:** *Journal, Academic/Scholarly.*
Formerly (until 2004): Hefei Lianhe Daxue Xuebao/Hefei Union University. Journal (1008-6056)
Related titles: Online - full text ed.
Published by: Hefei Xueyuan, 373, Huangshan Lu, Hefei, 230022, China.

500 DEU ISSN 0341-2865
AS182

HEIDELBERGER AKADEMIE DER WISSENSCHAFTEN. JAHRBUCH. Text in German. 1964. a. **Document type:** *Journal, Academic/Scholarly.*
Indexed: GeoRef, MLA-IB.
—Linda Hall.
Published by: Heidelberger Akademie der Wissenschaften, Karlstr 4, Heidelberg, 69117, Germany. TEL 49-6221-543265, FAX 49-6221-543355, haw@baden-wuerttemberg.de, http://www.haw.baden-wuerttemberg.de.

500 DEU
AS182 CODEN: SHWMAL

HEIDELBERGER AKADEMIE DER WISSENSCHAFTEN. MATHEMATISCH - NATURWISSENSCHAFTLICHE KLASSE. SCHRIFTEN. Text in German. 1948. irreg., latest vol.21, 2010. price varies. reprints avail. **Document type:** *Monographic series, Academic/Scholarly.*
Formerly (until 1997): Heidelberger Akademie der Wissenschaften. Mathematisch - Naturwissenschaftliche Klasse. Sitzungsberichte (0371-0165)
Indexed: BibLing, GeoRef, IBR, IBZ, P30, SpeleolAb, Z02.
—CASDDS, GNLM. **CCC.**
Published by: Springer (Subsidiary of: Springer Science+Business Media), Tiergartenstr 17, Heidelberg, 69121, Germany. TEL 49-6221-4870, FAX 49-6221-345229, subscriptions@springer.com.

500 USA ISSN 0073-1641
AS181 CODEN: HDJBAC

HEIDELBERGER JAHRBUECHER. Text in English. 1819. irreg., latest vol.53, 2009. price varies. back issues avail.; reprints avail. **Document type:** *Monographic series, Academic/Scholarly.*
Former titles (until 1957): Neue Heidelberger Jahrbuecher (0179-0773); (until 1891): Heidelberger Jahrbuecher der Literatur (0179-0781)
Indexed: B24, CA, DIP, IBR, IBZ, MLA-IB, P30, RILM, T02.
—Infotrieve. **CCC.**
Published by: (Universitaets-Gesellschaft Heidelberg DEU), Springer New York LLC (Subsidiary of: Springer Science+Business Media), 233 Spring St, New York, NY 10013. TEL 212-460-1500, FAX 212-460-1575, service-ny@springer.com.

500 DEU ISSN 0935-6576

HEIDELBERGER STUDIEN ZUR NATURKUNDE DER FRUEHEN NEUZEIT. Text in German. 1989. irreg., latest vol.6, 1998. price varies. **Document type:** *Monographic series, Academic/Scholarly.*
Published by: Franz Steiner Verlag GmbH, Birkenwaldstr 44, Stuttgart, 70191, Germany. TEL 49-711-25820, FAX 49-711-2582290, service@steiner-verlag.de, http://www.steiner-verlag.de.

HEIHE XUEYUAN XUEBAO. *see* SOCIAL SCIENCES: COMPREHENSIVE WORKS

500 CHN ISSN 1001-7011

HEILONGJIANG DAXUE ZIRAN KEXUE XUEBAO/HEILONGJIANG UNIVERSITY. JOURNAL OF NATURAL SCIENCES. Text in Chinese. 1978. bi-m. USD 18 (effective 2009). **Document type:** *Journal, Academic/Scholarly.*
Related titles: Online - full text ed.
Indexed: CCMJ, M&GPA, MSN, MathR, RASB, Z02.
—East View.
Published by: Heilongjiang Daxue/Heilongjiang University, 74, Xuefu Lu, Nangang-qu, Ha'erbin, 150080, China. TEL 86-451-86608818.

500 CHN ISSN 1671-4679

HEILONGJIANG GONGCHENG XUEYUAN XUEBAO (ZIRAN KEXUE BAN)/HEILONGJIANG INSTITUTE OF TECHNOLOGY. JOURNAL. Text in Chinese. 1987. q. CNY 6 newsstand/cover (effective 2006). **Document type:** *Journal, Academic/Scholarly.*
Former titles (until 2000): Heilongjiang Jiaotong Gaodeng Zhuanke Xuexiao Xuebao/Heilongjiang Communications College. Journal (1008-7230); Jiaotong Jiaoyu Yanjiu
Related titles: Online - full text ed.
Published by: Heilongjiang Gongcheng Xueyuan/Heilongjiang Institute of Technology, 999, Hongqi Dajie, Harbin, 150050, China. TEL 86-451-88028495, FAX 86-451-88028496.

500 CHN ISSN 1673-1328

HEILONGJIANG KEJI XINXI/HEILONGJIANG SCIENCE AND TECHNOLOGY INFORMATION. Text in Chinese. 3/w. **Document type:** *Journal, Academic/Scholarly.*
Related titles: Online - full text ed.
Published by: Heilongjiang Kexue Jishu Xiehui/Heilongjiang Association for Science and Technology, Nangang-qu, 15 Xuanxin Jie, Shengzhengfu Zonghe Lou 526-shi, Ha'erbin, 150008, China. TEL 86-451-82634744, FAX 86-451-82613440, caih@ems.dragon.net.cn, http://www.hljkx.cn/.

500 CHN ISSN 1671-0118
CODEN: HLCKAQ

HEILONGJIANG KEJI XUEYUAN XUEBAO/HEILONGJIANG INSTITUTE OF SCIENCE AND TECHNOLOGY. JOURNAL. Text in Chinese; Abstracts in Chinese, English. 1991. bi-m. CNY 6, USD 10 newsstand/cover (effective 2009). **Document type:** *Journal, Academic/Scholarly.*
Formerly (until 2000): Heilongjiang Kuangye Xueyuan Xuebao/Heilongjiang Mining Institute. Journal (1006-303X)
Related titles: Online - full text ed.
Indexed: A28, APA, BrCerAb, C&ISA, CA/WCA, CIA, CerAb, CivEngAb, CorrAb, E&CAJ, E11, EEA, EMA, ESPM, EnvEAb, H15, M&TEA, M09, MBF, METADEX, RefZh, SolStAb, T04, WAA.
—Linda Hall.
Published by: Heilongjiang Keji Xueyuan, 1, Tangchang St., Songbei District, Harbin, 150027, China. TEL 86-451-88036032, FAX 86-451-88036078.

500 CHN ISSN 1004-1842

HEILONGJIANG SHANGXUEYUAN XUEBAO (ZIRAN KEXUEBAN)/HEILONGJIANG COMMERCIAL COLLEGE. JOURNAL. Text in Chinese. 1984. q. **Document type:** *Academic/Scholarly.*
Formerly (until 1992): Heilongjiang Shangxueyuan Xuebao (1001-6066)
Related titles: Online - full content ed.; Online - full text ed.
Published by: Heilongjiang Shangxueyuan, 50, Tongda Jie, Daoli-qu, Harbin, Heilongjiang 150076, China. Ed. Lin-de Tang.

505 AUS ISSN 1033-3096

HELIX. Text in English. 1989. bi-m. AUD 26 (effective 2008). back issues avail. **Document type:** *Magazine, Consumer.* **Description:** Provides science fun facts, stories and experiments for children aged 10 and over.
Formed by the merger of (1986 -1988): Double Helix News (0817-2463); (1977 -1988): Scifile (0314-4461)
Published by: (C S I R O), C S I R O Publishing, 150 Oxford St, PO Box 1139, Collingwood, VIC 3066, Australia. TEL 61-3-96627500, FAX 61-3-96627555, publishing@csiro.au, http://www.publish.csiro.au/home.htm.

HELMHOLTZZENTRUM MUENCHEN - DEUTSCHES FORSCHUNGSZENTRUM FUER GESUNDHEIT UND UMWELT. JAHRESBERICHT. *see* ENVIRONMENTAL STUDIES

HELWAN UNIVERSITY. SCIENCE & ARTS. RESEARCH STUDIES/MAGALLAT ULUM WA FONOUN. DIRASAT WA BEHOUTH. *see* LITERATURE

500 CHN ISSN 1003-4978
CODEN: HDAXE3

HENAN DAXUE XUEBAO (ZIRAN KEXUE BAN)/HENAN UNIVERSITY. JOURNAL (NATURAL SCIENCE EDITION). Text in Chinese. 1934. q. USD 31.20 (effective 2009). bk.rev. **Document type:** *Journal, Academic/Scholarly.* **Description:** Covers geography, mathematics, physics, chemistry and biology.
Related titles: Online - full text ed.
Indexed: RASB, Z02.
—BLDSC (4295.106000), CASDDS, East View.
Published by: Henan Daxue/Henan University, 85 Minglun Jie, Kaijeng, Henan 475001, China. TEL 86-378-2860394, http://www.henu.edu.cn. Ed. Guan Aihe. Circ: 1,500.

500 CHN ISSN 1674-330X

HENAN GONGCHENG XUEYUAN XUEBAO (ZIRAN KEXUE BAN)/HENNAN INSTITUTE OF ENGINEERING. JOURNAL (NATURAL SCIENCE EDITION). Text in Chinese. 1989. q. **Document type:** *Journal, Academic/Scholarly.*
Formerly: He'nan Fangzhi Gaodeng Zhuanke Xuexiao Xuebao/He'nan Textile College. Journal (1008-8385)
Related titles: Online - full text ed.

Published by: Henan Gongcheng Xueyuan/Henan Institute of Engineering, 62, Tongbai Lu, Zhengzhou, 450007, China. TEL 86-371-67718781.

500 CHN ISSN 1673-2383
HENAN GONGYE DAXUE XUEBAO (ZIRAN KEXUE BAN)/HENAN UNIVERSITY OF TECHNOLOGY. JOURNAL (NATURAL SCIENCE EDITION). Text in Chinese. 1980. bi-m. CNY 5 newsstand/cover (effective 2006). **Document type:** *Journal, Academic/Scholarly.*
Former titles: Zhengzhou Gongcheng Xueyuan Xuebao/Zhengzhou Institute of Technology. Journal (1671-1629); (until 1999): Zhengzhou Liangshi Xueyuan Xuebao/Zhengzhou Grain College. Journal (1000-2332)
Related titles: Online - full text ed.
Indexed: A28, APA, BrCerAb, C&ISA, CA/WCA, CIA, CerAb, CivEngAb, CorrAb, E&CAJ, E11, EEA, EMA, ESPM, EnvEAb, FS&TA, H15, M&TEA, M09, MBF, METADEX, RefZh, SolStAb, T04, WAA.
—BLDSC (4295.106850).
Published by: Henan Gongye Daxue/Henan University of Technology, 140, Songshan Lu, Zhengzhou, 450052, China. TEL 86-371-67789805, http://www2.haut.edu.cn/xuebaobianjibu/.

500 CHN ISSN 1007-0834
HE'NAN JIAOYU XUEYUAN XUEBAO (ZIRAN KEXUE BAN)/HENAN INSTITUTE OF EDUCATION. JOURNAL (NATURAL SCIENCE). Text in Chinese. 1982. q. USD 16.40 (effective 2009). **Document type:** *Journal, Academic/Scholarly.*
Formerly: Henan Jiaoyu Xueyuan Xuebao/Henan Collage of Education. Journal (1006-2920)
Related titles: Online - full text ed.
Published by: He'nan Jiaoyu Xueyuan, 21, Wei-Wu Lu, Zhengzhou, 450014, China. TEL 86-371-65682637.

500 CHN ISSN 1003-5168
HENAN KEJI. Variant title: Henan Keji (Keji Shidai Ban). Text in Chinese. 1981. m. **Document type:** *Journal, Academic/Scholarly.*
Related titles: Online - full text ed.
Published by: Henan Sheng Kexue Jishu Xinxi Yanjiuyuan/Henan Institute of Sci & Tech Information, 3, Zhengliu Jie, Jinshui-qu, Zhengzhou, 450003, China. TEL 86-371-65954220, FAX 86-371-65954220, qbsinfo@163.com, http://www.hnsti.cn/.

500 CHN ISSN 1672-3910
HENAN KEJI DAXUE XUEBAO (SHEHUI KEXUE BAN)/HENAN UNIVERSITY OF SCIENCE & TECHNOLOGY. JOURNAL (SOCIAL SCIENCE). Text in Chinese. 1964. bi-m. CNY 6 newsstand/cover (effective 2007). **Document type:** *Journal, Academic/Scholarly.*
Formerly: Luoyang Gongxueyuan Xuebao/Luoyang Institute of Technology. Journal (1000-5080)
Related titles: Online - full text ed.
Published by: Henan Keji Daxue, 48, Xiyuan Jie, PO Box 54, Luoyang, 471003, China. TEL 86-379-64231475, FAX 86-379-64231475, http://www.haust.edu.cn/.

500 CHN ISSN 1004-3918
Q4
HENAN KEXUE/HENAN SCIENCE. Text in English. 1985. q. USD 62.40 (effective 2009). **Document type:** *Journal, Academic/Scholarly.*
Related titles: Online - full content ed.; Online - full text ed.
—East View.
Published by: Henan-sheng Kexueyuan, 58 Hongzhuan Lu, Zhengzhou, 450002, China. TEL 86-371-5727639. Ed. Song-Lin Zhang.

500 CHN
HENAN LIGONG DAXUE XUEBAO (ZIRAN KEXUE BAN). Text in English. 1981. bi-m. CNY 8 newsstand/cover (effective 2006). **Document type:** *Journal, Academic/Scholarly.*
Former titles: Jiaozuo Gongxueyuan Xuebao/Jiaozuo Institute of Technology. Journal (1007-7332); Jiaozuo Kuangye Xueyuan Xuebao/Jiaozuo Mining Institute. Journal (1001-9103)
Related titles: Online - full text ed.
Indexed: APA, C&ISA, CorrAb, E&CAJ, EEA, SolStAb, WAA.
Published by: Henan Ligong Daxue, 2001, Shiji Dadao, Jiaozuo, 454000, China. TEL 86-391-3987068, FAX 86-391-2923353.

500 CHN ISSN 1000-2367
CODEN: HESKER
HENAN SHIFAN DAXUE XUEBAO (ZIRAN KEXUE BAN)/HENAN NORMAL UNIVERSITY. JOURNAL (NATURAL SCIENCE EDITION). Text in Chinese. 1960. bi-m. CNY 12 per issue (effective 2011). **Document type:** *Journal, Academic/Scholarly.*
Formerly (until 1985): Xinxiang Shifan Xueyuan Xuebao (Ziran Kexue Ban); Which superseded in part (in 1983): Xinxiang Shifan Xueyuan Xuebao/Xinxiang Normal College. Journal
Related titles: Online - full text ed.
Indexed: CCMJ, MSN, MathR, Z02.
—East View.
Published by: Henan Shifan Daxue, Jianshe Dong Lu, Xinxiang, Henan 453007, China. TEL 86-373-3326282, FAX 86-373-3329103, http://www.htu.cn/xuebao/. Ed. Zhu-dong Yang.

500.9 DEU ISSN 0018-0637
QK1 CODEN: HERCAS
➤ **HERCYNIA;** Beitraege zur Erforschung und Pflege der Natuerlichen Ressourcen. Text in German; Summaries in English. N.S. 1963. 2/yr. EUR 12.50 per issue (effective 2006). bk.rev. bibl.; charts; illus.; maps. 300 p./no.; back issues avail. **Document type:** *Journal, Academic/Scholarly.* **Description:** Covers biosciences, geography, plant life, and ecology.
Indexed: A34, A35, A38, B25, BIOSIS Prev, C25, C30, CABA, ChemAb, D01, E12, F08, F12, FCA, FR, G11, GEOBASE, GeoRef, H16, I11, IBR, IBZ, KWIWR, LT, MycolAb, P30, P32, P33, P39, P40, PGegResA, R07, R08, R12, R13, RRTA, RefZh, S13, S16, S17, SCOPUS, SpeleolAb, VS, W08, W10, Z01.
—CASDDS, INIST, Linda Hall. **CCC.**
Published by: (Martin-Luther-Universitaet Halle-Wittenberg, Mathematisch-Naturwissenschaftliche Fakultaet), Universitaets- und Landesbibliothek Sachsen-Anhalt, August Bebel Str 13, Halle, 06098, Germany. TEL 49-345-5522000, FAX 49-345-5527140, direktion@bibliothek.uni-halle.de, http://www.bibliothek.uni-halle.de.

500 AUT ISSN 1817-020X
HEUREKA; Die Welt der Naturwissenschaften. Text in German. 1996. 4/yr. EUR 10; EUR 3 newsstand/cover (effective 2005). **Document type:** *Journal, Academic/Scholarly.*
Published by: Verband der Chemielehrer Oesterreichs, Duernbergstr 71, Seeham-Salzburg, 5164, Austria. TEL 43-6217-75981, FAX 43-6217-75984, office@vcoe.or.at.

500.9 JPN ISSN 0389-5491
HIBA KAGAKU/HIBA SOCIETY OF NATURAL HISTORY. JOURNAL. Text in Japanese. 1947. 3/yr. USD 30. adv. bk.rev. **Document type:** *Bulletin.* **Description:** Contains original articles as well as reviews and commentary.
Indexed: Z01.
Published by: Hiba Science Educational Foundation/Hiba Kagaku Kyoiku Shinkokai, 1-1-7 Nishi-Hon-Machi, Shobara-shi, Hiroshima-ken 727-0013, Japan. TEL 08247-2-3234. Ed. S Nakamura. R&P Hibakagaku Shinkokai.

500 JPN ISSN 0917-0502
Q179.9
HIMEIJI KOGYO DAIGAKU RIGAKUBU KENKYU HOKOKU/HIMEIJI INSTITUTE OF TECHNOLOGY. FACULTY OF SCIENCE. REPORTS. Text in English, Japanese. 1990. a.
Published by: Himeiji Kogyo Daigaku, Rigakubu, 2167 Shoshiya, Himeji-shi, Hyogo-ken 671-2201, Japan.

500 JPN ISSN 1344-2139
Q4 CODEN: HUSRAK
HIROSAKI UNIVERSITY. FACULTY OF SCIENCE AND TECHNOLOGY. BULLETIN/HIROSAKI DAIGAKU RIKA HOKOKU. Text in English, Japanese. 1954. 2/yr. free. **Document type:** *Bulletin, Academic/Scholarly.* **Description:** Contains research reports written by members of the Faculty of Science and College of General Arts, Hirosaki University.
Former titles (until 1998): Hirosaki University. Faculty of Science. Science Reports (0367-6439); (until 1965): Hirosaki University. Faculty of Literature and Science. Science Reports (0371-2591)
Indexed: A22, ASFA, B21, CCMJ, ChemAb, ChemTitl, ESPM, MSN, MathR, Z02.
—BLDSC (2508.925000), CASDDS, IE, Ingenta.
Published by: Hirosaki Daigaku, Rikogakubu/Hirosaki University, Faculty of Science & Technology, 1 bunkyo-cho,, Hirosaki, Aomori 036-8224, Japan. http://www.st.hirosaki-u.ac.jp. Circ: 500.

500 FRA ISSN 0073-2362
HISTOIRE DE LA PENSEE. Text in French. 1960. irreg. price varies.
Indexed: CCMJ.
Published by: Editions Hermann, 293 rue Lecourbe, Paris, 75015, France. TEL 33-1-45574540, FAX 33-1-40601293.

509 FRA ISSN 1258-116X
HISTOIRE DES SCIENCES. Text in French. 1994. irreg. back issues avail. **Document type:** *Monographic series, Academic/Scholarly.*
Published by: Presses Universitaires du Septentrion, Rue du Barreau, BP 30199, Villeneuve d'Ascq, Cedex 59654, France. TEL 33-3-20416693, FAX 33-3-20416690, septentrion@septentrion.com, http://www.septentrion.com.

509 FRA ISSN 1779-7985
HISTOIRES DE SCIENCES. Text in French. 2006. irreg. back issues avail. **Document type:** *Monographic series.*
Published by: Editions Vuibert, 5 Allee de la 2e DB, Paris, 75015, France. TEL 33-1-42794400, FAX 33-1-42794680, http://www.vuibert.com.

HISTORIA, CIENCIAS, SAUDE - MANGUINHOS. *see* HISTORY

500 PRT ISSN 1647-7790
HISTORIA E FILOSOFIA DA CIENCIA. Text in Portuguese. 2003. irreg. **Document type:** *Monographic series, Academic/Scholarly.*
Published by: Porto Editora, Ld, Rua da Restauracao 365, Oporto, 4099-023, Portugal. TEL 351-22-6088300, FAX 351-22-6088301, http://www.portoeditora.pt.

508 ARG ISSN 0326-1778
CODEN: HINAEY
HISTORIA NATURAL. Text in Spanish. 1979. irreg.
Indexed: WildRev.
Address: Casilla de Correos 26, Corrientes, 3400, Argentina.

508 BGR ISSN 0205-3640
HISTORIA NATURALIS BULGARICA. Text in English. 1989. a. USD 29 (effective 2001). bk.rev. **Document type:** *Journal, Academic/Scholarly.*
Indexed: Z01.
Published by: (National Musem of Natural History), Akademichno Izdatelstvo Prof. Marin Drinov/Prof. Marin Drinov Academic Publishing House, Akad G Bonchev 6, Sofia, 1113, Bulgaria. Ed. P Beron. **Dist. by:** Pensoft Publishers, Akad G Bonchev 6, Sofia 1113, Bulgaria. TEL 359-2-716451, FAX 359-2-704508, info@pensoft.net, http://www.pensoft.net.

509 JPN ISSN 0285-4821
Q124.6
HISTORIA SCIENTIARUM. Text in English, French, German. 1962. 3/yr. free to members (effective 2005). bk.rev. back issues avail. **Document type:** *Journal, Academic/Scholarly.*
Formerly (until 1980): Japanese Studies in the History of Science (0090-0176)
Indexed: BAS, CCMJ, CIS, DIP, FR, HistAb, I14, IBR, IBZ, MSN, MathR, P30, RASB, SCOPUS, Z02.
—Ingenta, INIST, Linda Hall. **CCC.**
Published by: Nihon Kagakushi Gakkai/History of Science Society of Japan, c/o International AcademicPrinting Co., Ltd., 3-8-8, Takadanobaba, Shinjuku-ku, Tokyo, 169-0075, Japan. jshs@wwwsoc.nii.ac.jp, http://wwwsoc.nii.ac.jp/jshs/index-j.html.

500 AUS ISSN 0727-3061
Q93 CODEN: HRASEI
➤ **HISTORICAL RECORDS OF AUSTRALIAN SCIENCE;** the history of science, pure and applied, in Australia and the southwest Pacific. Text in English. 1966. s-a. USD 225 combined subscription (print & online eds.) (effective 2012). adv. Index. back issues avail. **Document type:** *Journal, Academic/Scholarly.* **Description:** Covers the history of science and scientists in Australia and the southwest Pacific, biographical memoirs of deceased Fellows of the Academy, and an annual bibliography of the history of Australian science.
Formerly (until 1980): Australian Academy of Science. Records (0067-155X)
Related titles: Online - full text ed.: ISSN 1448-5508.
Indexed: A01, A03, A08, A20, A22, AESIS, Agr, ArtHuCI, AusPAIS, CA, E01, FR, GeoRef, HistAb, P30, RASB, SCOPUS, SpeleolAb, T02, W07.
—IE, Infotrieve, Ingenta, INIST, Linda Hall. **CCC.**
Published by: (Australian Academy of Science), C S I R O Publishing, 150 Oxford St, PO Box 1139, Collingwood, VIC 3066, Australia. TEL 61-3-96627500, FAX 61-3-96627555, publishing@csiro.au, http://www.publish.csiro.au/home.htm. Ed. Rod W Home TEL 61-3-83446556. R&P Carla Flores. Adv. contact Wendy Wild TEL 61-3-96627606.

500 600 900 IRL
HISTORICAL STUDIES IN IRISH SCIENCE AND TECHNOLOGY. Text in English. 1980. irreg. price varies. back issues avail. **Document type:** *Monographic series, Academic/Scholarly.*
Indexed: SpeleolAb.
Published by: Royal Dublin Society, Ballsbridge, Dublin, 4, Ireland. TEL 353-1-6680866, FAX 353-1-6604014. Ed. R Carol Power. R&P Carol Power.

509 USA ISSN 1939-1811
CODEN: HSPSEW
➤ **HISTORICAL STUDIES IN THE NATURAL SCIENCES.** Abbreviated title: H S N S. Text in English. 1948. q. USD 244 combined subscription to institutions (print & online eds.) (effective 2012). adv. 200 p./no.; back issues avail.; reprint service avail. from PSC. **Document type:** *Journal, Academic/Scholarly.* **Description:** Examines the economic, social and intellectual environment in which the physical and biological sciences and allied subjects have been practiced since 1700.
Former titles (until 2008): Historical Studies in the Physical and Biological Sciences (0890-9997); (until 1986): Historical Studies in the Physical Sciences (0073-2672); Which superseded (in 1969): Chymia (0095-9367)
Related titles: Microform ed.: USD 82.80 to institutions (effective 2002 - 2003) (from PQC); Online - full text ed.: ISSN 1939-182X. USD 196 to institutions (effective 2012); Dutch ed.: Federatie der Chemische Nyverheid van Belgie.
Indexed: A01, A02, A03, A08, A20, A22, A26, ABS&EES, ASCA, AmH&L, ArtHuCI, B04, BRD, CA, ChemAb, CurCont, E01, E08, FR, G01, G03, G08, GSA, GSI, H04, HistAb, I05, IBR, IBZ, MLA-IB, MSN, P02, P10, P13, P15, P26, P30, P48, P52, P53, P54, P56, PCI, PQC, RASB, S01, S09, S10, SCI, SCOPUS, SSCI, T02, W03, W07.
—BLDSC (4317066000), CASDDS, IE, Infotrieve, Ingenta, INIST, Linda Hall. **CCC.**
Published by: University of California Press, Journals Division, 2000 Ctr St, Ste 303, Berkeley, CA 94704. TEL 510-643-7154, 877-262-4226, FAX 510-642-9917, customerservice@ucpressjournals.com, http://www.ucpressjournals.com. Adv. contact Jennifer Rogers TEL 510-642-6188. Circ: 413. **Subscr. to:** 149 5th Ave, 8th Fl, New York, NY 10010. participation@jstor.org.

500 BEL
HISTORISCHE DOCUMENTEN VAN DE WETENSCHAPPEN. Text in Dutch. 1966. irreg. price varies.
Related titles: French ed.
Published by: Belgisch Komitee voor de Geschiedenis der Wetenschappen, Koninklijke Bibliotheek - Bibliotheque Royale, Keizerslaan - Bd de l'Empereur 4, Brussels, 1000, Belgium.

500 GBR ISSN 1793-0820
HISTORY OF MODERN PHYSICAL SCIENCES. Text in English. 2003. irreg., latest vol.4, 2010. price varies. back issues avail. **Document type:** *Monographic series, Academic/Scholarly.* **Description:** Contains variety of books dealing with the development of physics, astronomy, chemistry and geology during the past two centuries.
Published by: Imperial College Press (Subsidiary of: World Scientific Publishing Co. Pte. Ltd.), 57 Shelton St, Covent Garden, London, WC2H 9HE, United Kingdom. TEL 44-20-78360888, FAX 44-20-78362020, edit@icpress.co.uk, http://www.icpress.co.uk/. **Subscr. to:** World Scientific Publishing Co. Pte. Ltd. series@wspc.com.sg. **Dist. by:** World Scientific Publishing Ltd.; World Scientific Publishing Co., Inc., 27 Warren St, Ste 401-402, Hackensack, NJ 07601. TEL 201-487-9655, 800-227-7562, FAX 201-487-9656, 888-977-2665, wspc@wspc.com.

500 507 GBR ISSN 0073-2753
Q125 CODEN: HISCAR
➤ **HISTORY OF SCIENCE.** Text in English. 1962. q. USD 84 to individuals in the Americas & Japan; GBP 42 elsewhere to individuals; USD 265 combined subscription to institutions in the Americas & Japan (print & online eds.); GBP 130 combined subscription elsewhere to institutions (print & online eds.); USD 28 per issue to individuals in the Americas & Japan; GBP 14 per issue elsewhere to individuals; USD 60 per issue to institutions in the Americas & Japan; GBP 30 per issue elsewhere to institutions (effective 2009). bk.rev. illus. index. back issues avail.; reprints avail. **Document type:** *Journal, Academic/Scholarly.* **Description:** Contains review of literature and research on the history of science, medicine and technology in its intellectual and social context.
Related titles: Online - full text ed.: ISSN 1753-8564 (from IngentaConnect).
Indexed: A01, A02, A03, A08, A20, A22, A26, ASCA, AmH&L, AmHI, ArtHuCI, B04, BRD, CA, CCMJ, CIS, CurCont, DIP, E08, EMBASE, ExcerpMed, FR, G01, G08, GeoRef, H05, H07, H08, H12, HAb, HistAb, HumInd, I05, I14, IBR, IBZ, IPB, ISR, MEDLINE, MSN, MathR, P10, P30, PCI, PQC, RASB, S09, SCI, SCOPUS, SSCI, SpeleolAb, T02, W03, W07, WBA, WMB.
—BLDSC (4318.460000), IE, Infotrieve, Ingenta, INIST, Linda Hall. **CCC.**
Published by: Science History Publications Ltd., 16 Rutherford Rd, Cambridge, CB2 8HH, United Kingdom. TEL 44-1638-605464, FAX 44-1638-605465, shp@shpltd.co.uk. Ed. Iwan Rhys Morus.

509 610.9 NLD ISSN 1872-0684
➤ **HISTORY OF SCIENCE AND MEDICINE LIBRARY.** Text in English. 2006. irreg., latest vol.7, 2008. price varies. **Document type:** *Monographic series.*
Indexed: IZBG.
Published by: Brill, PO Box 9000, Leiden, 2300 PA, Netherlands. TEL 31-71-5353500, FAX 31-71-5317532, cs@brill.nl.

500 900 USA ISSN 0739-4934
HISTORY OF SCIENCE SOCIETY NEWSLETTER (ONLINE). Text in English. 1972. q. free (effective 2010). adv. back issues avail.; reprints avail. **Document type:** *Newsletter, Academic/Scholarly.* **Description:** Reports on news of the society and contains notices of job openings, forthcoming meetings, awards, fellowships, and grants available.
Media: Online - full text.
—Linda Hall.

S

Published by: (History of Science Society), University of Chicago Press, 1427 E 60th St, Chicago, IL 60637. TEL 773-702-7700, FAX 773-702-9756, marketing@press.uchicago.edu, http://www.press.uchicago.edu. **Subscr. to:** PO Box 37005, Chicago, 60637, IL 60637. TEL 877-705-1878, FAX 877-705-1879, subscriptions@press.uchicago.edu.

700 500 JPN ISSN 0073-2788
AS551
➤ **HITOTSUBASHI JOURNAL OF ARTS AND SCIENCES.** Text in English, French, German. 1960. a., latest vol.14, no.1, 2000, Dec. JPY 1,900 (effective 2001). abstr.; bibl. cum.index. 80 p./no.; **Document type:** *Journal, Academic/Scholarly.*
Supersedes in part (1950-1960): Hitotsubashi Academy. Annals (0439-2841)
Indexed: BAS, CCMJ, FR, MLA, MLA-IB, MSN, MathR, P06, PCI, RASB.
—Ingenta, INIST, Linda Hall.
Published by: (Hitotsubashi Daigaku, Hitotsubashi Gakkai/Hitotsubashi University, Hitotsubashi Academy), Sanseido Publishing Company, Ltd., 2-22-14, Misakicho, Chiyoda-ku, Tokyo, 101-8371, Japan. FAX 81-3-3230-9569, info@sanseido-publ.co.jp, http://www.sanseido-publ.co.jp/. Ed. K Hashinuwa. Circ: 750. **Dist. by:** Japan Publications Trading Co., Ltd., Book Export II Dept, PO Box 5030, Tokyo International, Tokyo 101-3191, Japan. TEL 81-3-32923753, FAX 81-3-32920410, infoserials@jptco.co.jp, http://www.jptco.co.jp.

507.4 JPN ISSN 0285-5615
HIWA KAGAKU HAKUBUTSUKAN KENKYU HOKOKU/HIWA MUSEUM FOR NATURAL HISTORY. MISCELLANEOUS REPORTS. Text and summaries in Japanese, English. 1958. a. USD 20. **Document type:** *Bulletin.*
Indexed: Z01.
Published by: Hiwa Museum for Natural History/Hiwa Kagaku Hakubutsukan, Hiwa, Hiwa-cho, Hiba-gun, Hiroshima-ken 727-0301, Japan. TEL 082485-2111, FAX 082485-2421.

HOBSON'S CHOICE. *see* LITERATURE—Science Fiction, Fantasy, Horror

500 JPN ISSN 1344-2570
HOKKAIDO KYOIKU DAIGAKU KIYO. SHIZEN KAGAKU-HEN/HOKKAIDO UNIVERSITY OF EDUCATION. JOURNAL. NATURAL SCIENCES. Text in Japanese. 1998. s-a. **Document type:** *Journal, Academic/Scholarly.*
Formed by the merger of (1966-1998): Hokkaido Kyoiku Daigaku Kiyo. Dai 2-Bu, A. Sugaku, Butsurigaku, Kagaku, Kogaku-Hen/Hokkaido University of Education. Journal . Section 2, A. Mathematics, Physics, Chemistry and Engineering (0367-5939); Which was formerly (1960-1966): Hokkaido Gakugei Daigaku Kiyo. Dai 2-Bu, A. Sugaku, Butsurigaku, Kagaku, Kogaku-Hen/Hokkaido Gakugei University. Journal. Section 2, A (0386-4871); (1966-1998): Hokkaido Kyoiku Daigaku Kiyo. Dai 2-Bu, B. Seibutsugaku, Chigaku, Nogaku-Hen/Hokkaido University of Education. Journal. Section 2, B. Biology, Earth science and Agriculture (0018-3393); Which was formerly (1960-1966): Hokkaido Gakugei Daigaku Kiyo. Dai 2-Bu, B. Seibutsugaku, Chigaku, Nogaku-Hen/Hokkaido Gakugei University. Journal. Section 2, B (0386-488X); (1996-1998): Hokkaido Kyoiku Daigaku Kiyo. Dai 2-Bu, C. Katei, Yogo, Taiiku-Hen/Hokkaido University of Education. Journal. Section 2, C. Home Economics, School Health and Physical Education (0386-4901); Which was formerly (1960-1966): Hokkaido Gakugei Daigaku Kiyo. Dai 2-Bu, C. Katei, Taiiku-Hen/Hokkaido Gakugei University. Journal. Section 2, C. (0386-4898); Section 2 A, 2 B, 2C superseded in part (in 1959): Hokkaido Gakugei Daigaku Kiyo. Dai 2-Bu/Hokkaido Gakugei University. Journal. Section B. Natural Science (0367-6072); Which was formerly (until 1953): Gakugei. Dai 2-Bu
Indexed: CCMJ, MSN, MathR, Z01.
Published by: Hokkaido Kyoiku Daigaku/Hokkaido University of Education, 5-3-1 Ainosato, Kita-ku, Sapporo, Hokkaido 002-8502, Japan. http://www.hokkyodai.ac.jp/.

500 JPN ISSN 0386-4464
Q77
➤ **HOKKAIDO KYOIKU DAIGAKU TAISETSUZAN SHIZEN KYOIKU KENKYU SHISETSU KENKYU HOKOKU/HOKKAIDO UNIVERSITY OF EDUCATION. TAISETSUZAN INSTITUTE OF SCIENCE. REPORTS.** Text in Japanese; Summaries in English, Japanese. a. **Document type:** *Journal, Academic/Scholarly.*
Indexed: JPI.
Published by: Hokkaido University of Education, Taisetsuzan Institute of Science/Hokkaido Kyoiku Daigaku Taisetsuzan Shizen Kyoiku Kenkyu Shisetsu, 9 Hokumon-cho, Asahikawa-shi, Hokkaido 070-8621, Japan. TEL 81-166-59-1213, FAX 81-166-59-1220. Ed. Yukio Himiyama.

500 USA ISSN 2152-5188
▼ **HOPOS.** Text in English. forthcoming 2011. s-a. USD 129 combined subscription to institutions (print & online eds.) (effective 2012). adv. reprints avail. **Document type:** *Journal, Academic/Scholarly.* **Description:** Features articles concerning the history of philosophical discussions about science.
Related titles: Online - full text ed.: ISSN 2156-6240. forthcoming 2011. USD 115 to institutions (effective 2012).
Published by: (International Society for the History of Philosophy of Science), University of Chicago Press, 1427 E 60th St, Chicago, IL 60637. TEL 773-702-7600, FAX 773-702-0694, subscriptions@press.uchicago.edu. Eds. Don Howard, Menachem Fisch, Rose-Mary Sargent TEL 978-837-3478. **Subscr. to:** PO Box 370050, Chicago, IL 60637. TEL 773-753-3347, 877-705-1878, FAX 773-753-0811, 877-705-1879.

500 600 TWN ISSN 1680-2799
HORIZON/SHIYU. Text in Chinese. 2001. bi-w. free. Website rev. **Document type:** *Journal, Corporate.* **Description:** Contains up-to-date and cutting-edge S&T policies and innovation activities of over 20 nations and international organizations.
Published by: Xingzhengyuan Guojia Kexue Weiyuanhui, Kexue Jishu Ziliao Zhongxin/Science & Technology Information Center, 16F, 106, Hoping E. Rd., Sec. 2, Taipei, 106-36, Taiwan. TEL 886-2-27377835, FAX 886-2-27377838. Ed. Ms. Wei-Jen Wang.

500 GBR ISSN 2041-7322
▼ **HOW IT WORKS;** the magazine that feeds minds. Text in English. 2009. m. GBP 41 domestic; GBP 50 in Europe; GBP 60 elsewhere (effective 2010). adv. back issues avail.; reprints avail. **Document type:** *Magazine, Consumer.* **Description:** Provides guidance and knowledge for the sections dedicated to science, technology, transportation, space, history and the environment.
Published by: Imagine Publishing Ltd., Richmond House, 33 Richmond Hill, Bournemouth, Dorset BH2 6EZ, United Kingdom. TEL 44-1202-586200, imagine@servicehelpline.co.uk, http://www.imagine-publishing.co.uk. Ed. Dave Harfield TEL 44-1202-586229. Adv. contact Hang Deretz TEL 44-1202-586442. **Subscr. to:** 800 Guillat Ave, Kent Science Park, Sittingbourne ME9 8GU, United Kingdom. TEL 44-1795-592869.

HOW STUFF WORKS EXPRESS. *see* CHILDREN AND YOUTH—For

500 001.3 300 HRV ISSN 0352-9509
Q69.2
➤ **HRVATSKA AKADEMIJA ZNANOSTI I UMJETNOSTI. ZAVOD ZA ZNANSTVENI RAD U VARAZDINU. RADOVI.** Text in Croatian; Summaries in Croatian, English, French, German. 1986. irreg., latest vol.21, 2010. free to qualified personnel; exchange basis. back issues avail. **Document type:** *Monographic series, Academic/Scholarly.*
Related titles: Online - full text ed.: free (effective 2011).
Indexed: RILM.
Published by: Hrvatska Akademija Znanosti i Umjetnosti, Zavod za Znanstveni Rad u Varazdinu/Croatian Academy of Sciences and Arts, Institute for Scientific Research Work in Varazdin, Vladimira Nazora 14, Varazdin, 42000, Croatia. TEL 385-42-214503, FAX 385-42-214503, http://www.hazu.hr/Zzna_rad-Varazdin.html.

500 600 CHN ISSN 1672-7169
HUABEI KEJI XUEYUAN XUEBAO/NORTH CHINA INSTITUTE OF SCIENCE AND TECHNOLOGY. JOURNAL. Text in Chinese. 2004. q. **Document type:** *Journal, Academic/Scholarly.*
Formerly (until 2001): Huabei Kuangye Gaodeng Zhuanke Xuexiao Xuebao/North China Mining College. Journal (1008-8709)
Related titles: Online - full text ed.
Published by: Huabei Keji Xueyuan, Dongyanjiao, 206 Xinxiang, Beijing, 101601, China. TEL 86-10-61590321, FAX 86-10-61591452.

500 CHN ISSN 1006-8465
Q127.C5
HUADONG KEJI/EAST CHINA SCIENCE AND TECHNOLOGY. Text in Chinese. 1995. m. **Document type:** *Journal, Academic/Scholarly.*
Formerly (until 1996): Huadong Keji Guanli (1006-2688)
Related titles: Online - full text ed.
Published by: Huadong Keji Zazhishe, no.60, Rm. 408, Nandan Dong Lu, Shanghai, 200030, China. TEL 86-21-64688208, FAX 86-21-53084303.

500 CHN ISSN 1000-5641
Q4 CODEN: HSZKEO
HUADONG SHIFAN DAXUE XUEBAO (ZIRAN KEXUE BAN)/EAST CHINA NORMAL UNIVERSITY. JOURNAL (NATURAL SCIENCE EDITION). Text in Chinese. 1955. bi-m. CNY 84; CNY 14 per issue (effective 2011). **Document type:** *Journal, Academic/Scholarly.*
Related titles: Online - full text ed.
Indexed: A29, ASFA, B20, B21, CCMJ, E17, ESPM, INIS AtomInd, ImmunAb, M&GPA, MSN, MathR, RefZh, Z02.
—BLDSC (4735.108000), CASDDS, IE, Ingenta.
Published by: Huadong Shifan Daxue/East China Normal University, 3663 Zhongshan Beilu, Shanghai, 200062, China. TEL 86-21-62232305, FAX 86-21-62233702, http://www.ecnu.edu.cn.

500 CHN ISSN 1672-7177
HUAIBEI MEITAN SHIFAN XUEYUAN XUEBAO (ZIRAN KEXUE BAN)/HUAIBEI COAL INDUSTRY TEACHERS COLLEGE. JOURNAL (NATURAL SCIENCE EDITION). Text in Chinese. 1980. q. CNY 5 newsstand/cover (effective 2006). **Document type:** *Journal, Academic/Scholarly.*
Formerly (until 2003): Huaibei Mei-Shi-Yuan Xuebao (Ziran Kexue Ban)/Huaibei Teachers College. Journal (1000-2227)
Related titles: Online - full text ed.
Published by: Huaibei Meitan Shifan Xuyuan/Huabei Coal Industry Teachers College, 100, Dongshan Lu, Huaibei, 235000, China. TEL 86-561-3802261.

500 CHN ISSN 1672-6685
HUAIHAI GONGXUEYUAN XUEBAO (ZIRAN KEXUE BAN)/HUAIHAI INSTITUTE OF TECHNOLOGY. JOURNAL (NATURAL SCIENCES EDITION). Text in Chinese. 1985. q. USD 16.40 (effective 2009). **Document type:** *Journal, Academic/Scholarly.*
Incoporates: Lianyungang Huagong Gaodeng Zhuanke Xuexiao Xuebao/Lianyungang College of Chemical Technology. Journal (1008-3472); Supersded in part (in 2003): Huaihai Gongxueyuan Xuebao/Huaihai Institute of Technology. Journal (1008-3499)
Related titles: Online - full text ed.
Indexed: RefZh, Z02.
—BLDSC (4758.966550), East View.
Published by: Huaihai Gongxueyuan, 59, Cangwu Lu, Lianyungang, 222005, China.

HUAINAN ZHIYE JISHU XUEYUAN XUEBAO/HUAINAN VOCATIONAL & TECHNICAL COLLEGE. JOURNAL. *see* SOCIAL SCIENCES: COMPREHENSIVE WORKS

500 CHN ISSN 1671-6876
HUAIYIN SHIFAN XUEYUAN XUEBAO (ZIRAN KEXUE BAN)/HUAIYIN TEACHERS COLLEGE. JOURNAL (NATURAL SCIENCE EDITION). Text in Chinese. 2002. q. CNY 8 newsstand/cover (effective 2006). **Document type:** *Journal, Academic/Scholarly.*
Related titles: Online - full text ed.
Published by: Huaiyin Shifan Xueyuan, 71, Jiaotong Lu, Huai'an, 223001, China. TEL 86-517-3511053.

500 600 CHN ISSN 1000-565X
Q4 CODEN: HLDKEZ
HUANAN LIGONG DAXUE XUEBAO (ZIRAN KEXUE BAN)/SOUTH CHINA UNIVERSITY OF SCIENCE AND ENGINEERING. JOURNAL (NATURAL SCIENCE EDITION). Text in Chinese. 1957. m. USD 62.40 (effective 2009). **Document type:** *Journal, Academic/Scholarly.*
Formerly (until 1987): Huanan Gongxueyuan Xuebao (Ziran Kexue Ban) (0438-119X)
Related titles: Online - full text ed.
Indexed: A28, A32, APA, BrCerAb, C&ISA, CA/WCA, CIA, CIN, CPEI, CerAb, ChemAb, ChemTitl, CivEngAb, CorrAb, E&CAJ, E11, EEA, EMA, ESPM, EngInd, EnvEAb, H15, M&TEA, M09, MBF, METADEX, PollutAb, RefZh, SCOPUS, SolStAb, T04, WAA.
—BLDSC (4902.117000), CASDDS, East View, Linda Hall.
Published by: Huanan Ligong Daxue/South China University of Technology, Wushan Lu, Guangzhou, Guangdong 510641, China. TEL 86-20-87111794, FAX 86-20-87114699, http://www.scut.edu.cn/.

500 CHN ISSN 1000-5463
CODEN: HSDZER
HUANAN SHIFAN DAXUE XUEBAO (ZIRAN KEXUE BAN)/SOUTH CHINA NORMAL UNIVERSITY. JOURNAL (NATURAL SCIENCE EDITION). Text in Chinese; Abstracts in Chinese, English. 1956. q. USD 16.40 (effective 2009). bk.rev. **Document type:** *Journal, Academic/Scholarly.* **Description:** Reports the university's current achievements in scientific and educational researches.
Related titles: Online - full text ed.
Indexed: ASFA, B21, CCMJ, CIN, ChemAb, ChemTitl, ESPM, M&GPA, MSN, MathR, RefZh, SSciA, Z02.
—CASDDS.
Published by: Huanan Shifan Daxue/South China Normal University, Shipai, Guangzhou, 510631, China. TEL 86-20-85211440, http://www.scnu.edu.cn/. Circ: 1,500. **Dist. by:** China International Book Trading Corp, 35 Chegongzhuang Xilu, Haidian District, PO Box 399, Beijing 100044, China. TEL 86-10-68412045, FAX 86-10-68412023, cibtc@mail.cibtc.com.cn, http://www.cibtc.com.cn.

HUANGGANG ZHIYE JISHU XUEYUAN XUEBAO/HUANGGANG POLYTECHNIC. JOURNAL. *see* SOCIAL SCIENCES: COMPREHENSIVE WORKS

500 CHN ISSN 1008-5424
HUANGHE KEJI DAXUE XUEBAO/HUANGHE S & T UNIVERSITY. JOURNAL. Text in Chinese. 1999. bi-m. CNY 8 newsstand/cover (effective 2007). **Document type:** *Journal, Academic/Scholarly.*
Related titles: Online - full text ed.
Published by: Huanghe Keji Daxue/Huanghe S & T University, 94, Hanghai Zhong Lu, Zhengzhou, 450006, China. TEL 86-371-68951208, FAX 86-371-68951306.

500 CHN ISSN 1673-5153
HUANQIU KEXUE/SCIENTIFIC AMERICAN. Variant title: Global Science. Text in Chinese. 2006. m. CNY 180 (effective 2010). **Document type:** *Magazine, Consumer.*
Related titles: ◆ Regional ed(s).: Scientific American. ISSN 0036-8733.
Published by: (Zhongguo Kejibao Yanjiuhui/China Association for Science and Technology), Huanqiu Kexue Zazhishe, 3, Shuanggang Lu, Yuzhong-qu, Kexie Dasha 12/F, Chongqing, 400013, China.

500 CHN ISSN 1000-5013
QH7 CODEN: HDZIEF
HUAQIAO DAXUE XUEBAO (ZIRAN KEXUE BAN)/HUAQIAO UNIVERSITY. JOURNAL (NATURAL SCIENCE EDITION). Text in Chinese. 1980. q. USD 20.80 (effective 2009). **Document type:** *Journal, Academic/Scholarly.* **Description:** Carries scientific essays on theories of basic and applied sciences, new technologies, designs and products. Includes foreign news.
Related titles: Online - full text ed.
Indexed: CCMJ, CIN, ChemAb, ChemTitl, MSN, MathR, RefZh, SCOPUS.
—BLDSC (4758.966500), CASDDS, East View.
Published by: Huaqiao Daxue/Huaqiao University, 3/F, Yangsichun Kexueguan, Quanzhou, 362021, China.

500 600 CHN ISSN 1671-4512
Q4 CODEN: HKDXAT
HUAZHONG KEJI DAXUE XUEBAO (ZIRAN KEXUE BAN)/HUAZHONG UNIVERSITY OF SCIENCE AND TECHNOLOGY. JOURNAL (NATURE SCIENCE). Text in Chinese. 1973. m. USD 62.40 (effective 2009). **Document type:** *Journal, Academic/Scholarly.*
Former titles: Huazhong Keji Daxue Xuebao; Huazhong Ligong Daxue Xuebao (1000-8616); (until 1988): Huazhong Gongxueyuan Xuebao/Huazhong Institute of Technology. Journal (0253-4274)
Related titles: Online - full text ed.
Indexed: A22, A28, APA, BrCerAb, C&ISA, CA/WCA, CCMJ, CIA, CIN, CPEI, CerAb, ChemAb, ChemTitl, CivEngAb, CorrAb, E&CAJ, E11, EEA, EMA, ESPM, EngInd, EnvEAb, H15, Inspec, M&TEA, M09, MBF, METADEX, MSN, MathR, RefZh, SCOPUS, SolStAb, T04, WAA, Z02.
—BLDSC (4758.968500), AskIEEE, CASDDS, East View, IE, Ingenta, Linda Hall.
Published by: Huazhong Keji Daxue/Huazhong University of Science and Technology, 1037, Luoyu Lu, Wuhan, 430074, China. TEL 86-27-87543816, 86-27-87544294, http://www.hust.edu.cn/. **Dist. by:** China International Book Trading Corp, 35 Chegongzhuang Xilu, Haidian District, PO Box 399, Beijing 100044, China. TEL 86-10-68412045, FAX 86-10-68412023, cibtc@mail.cibtc.com.cn, http://www.cibtc.com.cn.

500 CHN ISSN 1000-1190
Q4 CODEN: HDZKEL
HUAZHONG SHIFAN DAXUE XUEBAO (ZIRAN KEXUE BAN)/CENTRAL-CHINA NORMAL UNIVERSITY. JOURNAL (NATURAL SCIENCE EDITION). Text in Chinese. 1955. q. USD 20.80 (effective 2009). **Document type:** *Journal, Academic/Scholarly.* **Description:** Covers mathematics, chemistry, physics, biology, and earth sciences.
Related titles: Online - full text ed.
Indexed: A28, APA, B25, BIOSIS Prev, BrCerAb, C&ISA, CA/WCA, CCMJ, CIA, CerAb, CivEngAb, CorrAb, E&CAJ, E11, EEA, EMA, ESPM, EnvEAb, H15, M&TEA, M09, MBF, METADEX, MSN, MathR, MycolAb, P30, SolStAb, T04, WAA, Z01, Z02.
—East View, Linda Hall.
Published by: Huazhong Shifan Daxue/Central China Normal University, Guizi-shan, Wuchang, 430079, China. TEL 86-27-67868127, FAX 86-27-87865407. **Dist. by:** China International Book Trading Corp, 35 Chegongzhuang Xilu, Haidian District, PO Box 399, Beijing 100044, China. TEL 86-10-68412045, FAX 86-10-68412023, cibtc@mail.cibtc.com.cn, http://www.cibtc.com.cn.

500 CHN ISSN 1000-2375
HUBEI DAXUE XUEBAO (ZIRAN KEXUE BAN)/HUBEI UNIVERSITY. JOURNAL (NATURAL SCIENCE EDITION). Text in Chinese. 1975. q. CNY 40; CNY 10 per issue (effective 2011). **Document type:** *Journal, Academic/Scholarly.*
Related titles: Online - full text ed.
Indexed: A22, Z02.

—BLDSC (4758.969000), East View, IE, Ingenta.
Published by: Hubei Daxue, 368, Youyi Dadao, Wuchang-qu, Wuhan, 430062, China. TEL 86-27-88663900, FAX 86-27-88663900. Ed. Chuan-xi Wu.

500 CHN ISSN 1008-8423
HUBEI MINZU XUEYUAN XUEBAO (ZIRAN KEXUE BAN)/HUBEI INSTITUTE FOR NATIONALITIES. JOURNAL (NATURAL SCIENCES EDITION). Text in Chinese. 1982. q. USD 20.80 (effective 2009). **Document type:** *Journal, Academic/Scholarly.*
Related titles: Online - full text ed.
Indexed: A34, A35, A37, AgBio, AgrForAb, B23, C25, C30, CABA, E12, F08, F12, FCA, GH, H16, I11, LT, MaizeAb, N02, O01, OR, P32, P40, PGegResA, PGrRegA, R07, R11, R12, RA&MP, RefZh, S13, S16, S17, TAR, VS, W10, W11, Z02.
—BLDSC (4758.968700), East View.
Published by: Hubei Minzu Xueyuan Xuebao/Hubei Institute for Nationalities, 20, Tuquiao Lu, Enshi, Hubei 445000, China. TEL 86-718-8430535, FAX 86-718-8430945.

500 CHN ISSN 1009-2714
HUBEI SHIFAN XUEYUAN XUEBAO (ZIRAN KEXUE BAN). Text in Chinese. 1982. q. USD 14.40 (effective 2009). **Document type:** *Journal, Academic/Scholarly.*
Related titles: Online - full text ed.
Published by: Hubei Shifan Xueyuan, 82, Chensha Lu, Huangshi, 435002, China. TEL 86-741-6573612.

HUIZHOU XUEYUAN XUEBAO/HUIZHOU UNIVERSITY. JOURNAL. *see* SOCIAL SCIENCES: COMPREHENSIVE WORKS

THE HUMAN NATURE REVIEW. *see* PSYCHOLOGY

500 001.3 POL ISSN 1234-4087
➤ **HUMANISTYKA I PRZYRODOZNAWSTWO.** Text in Polish; Summaries in English, Polish. 1995. a., latest vol.8, 2002. PLZ 20 per issue domestic; USD 20 per issue foreign (effective 2002 - 2003). abstr.; bibl. back issues avail. **Document type:** *Journal, Academic/Scholarly.*
Published by: (Uniwersytet Warminsko-Mazurski), Wydawnictwo Uniwersytetu Warminsko-Mazurskiego, ul J Heweliusza 14, Olsztyn, 10724, Poland. TEL 48-89-5233661, FAX 48-89-5233438, wydawca@uwm.edu.pl, http://www.uwm.edu.pl/wydawnictwo. Ed. Zbigniew Hull. Pub. Zofia Gawinek. Circ: 300 (paid and controlled).

➤ **HUMATICS**; Theorie der operablen Wissenseigenschaften. *see* SOCIAL SCIENCES: COMPREHENSIVE WORKS

500 CHN ISSN 1674-2974
CODEN: HDAXE3
HUNAN DAXUE XUEBAO (ZIRAN KEXUE BAN)/HUNAN UNIVERSITY. JOURNAL (NATURAL SCIENCE EDITION). Text in Chinese. 1956. m. **Document type:** *Academic/Scholarly.*
Supersedes in part (1989-1991): Hunan Daxue Xuebao (1674-716X); Which was formed by the 1989 merger of: Hunan Daxue Xuebao (Shehui Kexue Ban); Hunan Daxue Xuebao (Ziran Kexue Ban); Both of which superseded in part (1960-1987): Hunan Daxue Xuebao (1001-943X); Which was formerly: Hunan Gongxueyuan Xuebao
Related titles: Online - full text ed.
Indexed: CCMJ, CPEI, MSN, MathR, RefZh, SCOPUS.
Published by: Hunan Daxue Qikanshe/Hunan University Press, Yuelushan, Changsha, Hunan 410082, China. TEL 86-731-8821734, FAX 86-731-8821734, qks@hnu.cn, http://qks.hnu.cn/. Ed. Dao-ping Wang.

500 CHN ISSN 1673-9833
HUNAN GONGYE DAXUE XUEBAO/HUNAN UNIVERSITY OF TECHNOLOGY. JOURNAL. Text in Chinese. 1987. bi-m. CNY 8 newsstand/cover (effective 2009). **Document type:** *Journal, Academic/Scholarly.*
Former titles (until 2007): Zhuzhou Gongxueyuan Xuebao/Zhuzhou Institute of Technology. Journal (1008-2611); (until 1989): Baozhuang Xuebao; (until 1988): Zhuzhou Daxue Xuebao
Related titles: Online - full text ed.
Indexed: A28, APA, BrCerAb, C&ISA, CA/WCA, CIA, CerAb, CivEngAb, CorrAb, E&CAJ, E11, EEA, EMA, ESPM, EnvEAb, H15, M&TEA, M09, MBF, METADEX, SCOPUS, SociolAb, SolStAb, T04, WAA.
—BLDSC (4336.870200), Linda Hall.
Published by: Hunan Gongye Daxue/Hunan University of Technology, Tianyuan-qu, Taishan Lu, Zhuzhou, 412007, China. TEL 86-733-2622036.

500 CHN ISSN 1672-5298
HUNAN LIGONG XUEYUAN XUEBAO (ZIRAN KEXUE BAN)/HUNAN INSTITUTE OF SCIENCE AND TECHNOLOGY. JOURNAL (NATURAL SCIENCE). Text in Chinese. 1988. q. USD 20.80 (effective 2009). **Document type:** *Journal, Academic/Scholarly.*
Former titles (until 2003): Yueyang Shifan Xueyuan Xuebao (Ziran Kexue Ban) (1673-6494); (until 1999): Yueyang Daxue Xuebao (1008-620X)
Related titles: Online - full text ed.
Indexed: Z02.
—East View.
Published by: Hunan Ligong Xueyuan, Xueyuan Lu, Yueyang, 414006, China.

500 CHN
HUNAN NONGYE DAXUE XUEBAO (ZIRAN KEXUE BAN)/HUNAN AGRICULTURAL UNIVERSITY. JOURNAL (NATURAL SCIENCES). Text in Chinese. 1956. bi-m. USD 40.20 (effective 2009). **Document type:** *Journal, Academic/Scholarly.*
Former titles: Hunan Nongye Daxue Xuebao (1007-1032); (until 1994): Hunan Nongxueyuan Xuebao/Hunan Agricultural College. Journal (1000-5021)
Related titles: Online - full text ed.
Indexed: A22, A34, A35, A37, A38, AgBio, AgrForAb, B23, BA, BP, C25, C30, CABA, D01, E12, F08, F11, F12, FCA, G11, GH, H16, H17, I11, IndVet, LT, MaizeAb, N02, N03, N04, N05, O01, OR, P32, P33, P37, P38, P40, PGegResA, PGrRegA, PHN&I, PN&I, R07, R08, R11, R12, R13, RA&MP, RM&VM, RRTA, S12, S13, S16, S17, SoyAb, T05, TAR, TriticAb, VS, W10, W11, Z02.
—BLDSC (4759.156150), East View, IE, Ingenta.
Published by: Hunan Nongye Daxue/Hunan Agricultural University, Furong-qu, Changsha, 410128, China. TEL 86-731-4618035, FAX 86-731-4638380.

500 CHN
CODEN: HSXKEE
HUNAN SHIFAN DAXUE. ZIRAN KEXUE XUEBAO/ACTA SCIENTIARUM NATURALIUM/NATURAL SCIENCES JOURNAL OF HUNAN NORMAL UNIVERSITY/UNIVERSITATIS NORMALIS HUNANENSIS. Text in Chinese; Summaries in English. 1956. q. USD 24.80 (effective 2009). Index. back issues avail.; reprints avail. **Document type:** *Journal, Academic/Scholarly.* **Description:** Academic journal of scientific research in the natural sciences.
Formerly: Hunan Shifan Daxue Xuebao (Ziran Kexue Ban) (1000-2537)
Related titles: Online - full text ed.
Indexed: A34, A35, A37, A38, AgBio, B23, B25, BA, BIOSIS Prev, BP, C25, C30, CABA, CCMJ, ChemAb, D01, E12, EngInd, F08, F12, FCA, G11, GH, H16, H17, I11, IndVet, Inspec, LT, MSN, MathR, MycolAb, N02, O01, OR, P32, P33, P38, P40, PGegResA, PGrRegA, PHN&I, PN&I, R07, R08, R11, R12, R13, RA&MP, RM&VM, RRTA, RefZh, S12, S13, S16, S17, SCOPUS, T05, TAR, VS, W10, W11, Z01, Z02.
—AskIEEE, CASDDS, East View, IE, Ingenta.
Published by: Hunan Shifan Daxue/Hunan Normal University, Yuelushan, Changsha, Hunan 410081, China. TEL 86-731-8872473, FAX 86-731-8872209, http://www.hunnu.edu.cn/. **Dist. by:** China International Book Trading Corp, 35 Chegongzhuang Xilu, Haidian District, PO Box 399, Beijing 100044, China. TEL 86-10-68412045, FAX 86-10-68412023, cibtc@mail.cibtc.com.cn, http://www.cibtc.com.cn.

500 CHN ISSN 1672-6146
HU'NAN WENLI XUEYUAN XUEBAO (ZIRAN KEXUE BAN)/HUNAN UNIVERSITY OF ARTS AND SCIENCE. JOURNAL (NATURAL SCIENCE EDITION). Text in Chinese; Abstracts and contents page in English. 1987. q. CNY 9.80 newsstand/cover (effective 2011). **Document type:** *Journal, Academic/Scholarly.* **Description:** Covers all aspects of natural sciences studies.
Formerly (until 2003): Changde Shifan Xueyuan Xuebao (Ziran Kexue Ban)/Changde Teachers University. Journal (Natural Science Edition) (1009-3818)
Related titles: Online - full content ed.; Online - full text ed.
Indexed: B21, Z01, Z02.
—East View.
Published by: Hunan Wenli Xueyuan, 170, Dongting Dadao Xi-Duan, Changde, 415000, China. TEL 86-736-7186093, FAX 86-736-7186077.

HUZHOU ZHIYE JISHU XUEYUAN XUEBAO/HUZHOU VOCATIONAL AND TECHNOLOGICAL COLLEGE. JOURNAL. *see* SOCIAL SCIENCES: COMPREHENSIVE WORKS

500 USA ISSN 1542-3859
HYBRID VIGOR. Text in English. 1999 (Dec.). s-a.
Media: Online - full content.
Published by: Emory University, Science & Society Program, Dept. of Biology, Atlanta, GA 30322. TEL 404-727-6292, aeisen@emory.edu, http://www.emory.edu/COLLEGE/scienceandsociety.

500 JPN ISSN 1342-1646
HYOGO DAIGAKU RONSHU/HYOGO UNIVERSITY JOURNAL. Text in Japanese. 1996. a. **Document type:** *Journal, Academic/Scholarly.*
Indexed: CCMJ, MSN, MathR.
Published by: Hyogo Daigaku/Hyogo University, 2301 Shinzaike Hiraoka-cho, Kakogawa, 675-0195, Japan. http://www.hyogo-dai.ac.jp/.

500.9 USA ISSN 0264-5092
HYPOTENUSE. Text in English. 1980. q. free. **Document type:** *Newsletter.* **Description:** Covers RTI research in the areas of advanced technology, environmental protection, health and medicine, and public policy.
Indexed: EnvAb.
Published by: Research Triangle Institute, PO Box 12194, Research Triangle Park, NC 27709-2194. Ed., R&P Karen Lauterbach. Circ: 10,000.

500 NLD ISSN 1381-5652
HYPOTHESE (THE HAGUE). Text in Dutch. 1994. 5/yr. free (effective 2010). **Document type:** *Magazine, Trade.*
Published by: Nederlandse Organisatie voor Wetenschappelijk Onderzoek/Netherlands Organization for Scientific Research, PO Box 93138, The Hague, 2509 AC, Netherlands. TEL 31-70-3440640, FAX 31-70-3850971, nwo@nwo.nl. Ed. Caroline van Overbeeke.

500 IND ISSN 0970-0102
QA276.A1
➤ **I A P Q R TRANSACTIONS.** Text in English. 1976. s-a. free to members (effective 2011). bk.rev. cum.index: 1976-1989. 90 p./no.; **Document type:** *Journal, Academic/Scholarly.* **Description:** Covers theories and applications of productivity enhancing and regulatory techniques, with special reference to statistical quality control, reliability and life testing and production management.
Indexed: CCMJ, CIS, MSN, MathR, QC&AS, ST&MA, Z02.
—BLDSC (4359.536100), IE, Ingenta.
Published by: Indian Association for Productivity Quality and Reliability, AD-276, Sector-I, Salt Lake City, Kolkata, 700 064, India. TEL 91-33-23346233, FAX 91-33-23346234, iapqr@yahoo.co.in.

➤ **I A T U L PROCEEDINGS (CD-ROM).** *see* LIBRARY AND INFORMATION SCIENCES

500 GBR ISSN 1751-0724
➤ **I B SCIENTIFIC JOURNAL OF SCIENCE.** (Ibn Badis) Text in English. 2006. irreg. free (effective 2011). adv. back issues avail. **Document type:** *Journal, Academic/Scholarly.* **Description:** Features original research in a wide range of disciplines from science and engineering to the humanities.
Media: Online - full text.
Indexed: A39, C27, C29, D03, D04, E13, P30, R14, S14, S15, S18.
Published by: IBScientific Publishing Group, 14 Hilary Rd, London, W12 0QB, United Kingdom. info@ibscientific.net, http://www.ibscientific.net. Ed. Abdelkader Essafi. Adv. contact Elhadj Benkhelifa.

500 NLD ISSN 1381-1339
➤ **I C A S E - L A R C INTERDISCIPLINARY SERIES IN SCIENCE AND ENGINEERING.** (Institute for Computer Applications in Science and Engineering - Langley Research Center) Text in English. 1994. irreg., latest vol.10, 2004. price varies. **Document type:** *Monographic series, Academic/Scholarly.*
Indexed: CCMJ.
—BLDSC (4360.286700), IE, Ingenta. **CCC.**
Published by: (Institute for Computer Applications in Science and Engineering, Langley Research Center), Springer Netherlands (Subsidiary of: Springer Science+Business Media), Van Godewijckstraat 30, Dordrecht, 3311 GX, Netherlands. TEL 31-78-6576050, FAX 31-78-6576474. Ed. Manuel D Salas.

500 FRA ISSN 1029-0044
I C S U. ANNUAL REPORT. Text in English. 19??. a.
Related titles: Online - full text ed.: free.
Published by: International Council for Science/Conseil International pour la Science, 5 Rue Auguste Vacquerie, Paris, 75116, France. TEL 33-1-45250329, FAX 33-1-42889431, secretariat@icsu.org.

500 FRA
I C S U INSIGHT NEWSLETTER; science international. Text in English. 1964. q. free. **Document type:** *Newsletter, Academic/Scholarly.*
Former titles: I C S U AB News (0253-5572); (until 1980): I C S U Bulletin (0536-132X)
Media: Online - full text.
Indexed: RASB, SpeleolAb.
Published by: International Council for Science/Conseil International pour la Science, 5 Rue Auguste Vacquerie, Paris, 75116, France. TEL 33-1-45250329, FAX 33-1-42889431, secretariat@icsu.org. Ed. L Kohler. Circ: 5,000.

500 USA ISSN 2161-2641
▼ **I D.** (Ideas and Discoveries) Text in English. 2011. bi-m. USD 4.99 per issue (effective 2011). adv. **Document type:** *Magazine, Consumer.*
Published by: Bauer Publishing Group, 270 Sylvan Ave, Englewood Cliffs, NJ 07632. TEL 201-569-6699, info@bauerpublishing.com. Pub. Marc Richards TEL 212-994-4373. Adv. contact Audrey Robinson.

500 USA ISSN 2156-342X
▼ **I E E E TRANSACTIONS ON TERAHERTZ SCIENCE AND TECHNOLOGY.** (Institute of Electrical and Electronics Engineers) Text in English. 2011. s-a. USD 745; USD 930 combined subscription (print & online eds.) (effective 2012). adv.
Related titles: Online - full text ed.: ISSN 2156-3446. 2011. USD 675 (effective 2012).
—CCC.
Published by: I E E E, 445 Hoes Ln, Piscataway, NJ 08854. TEL 732-981-0060, 800-678-4333, FAX 732-562-6380, contactcenter@ieee.org, http://www.ieee.org. **Co-sponsor:** Microwave Theory and Techniques Society.

500.1 SEN ISSN 0018-9634
CODEN: BASNB7
I F A N BULLETIN. SERIE A: SCIENCES NATURELLES. Text in French; Text occasionally in English, Multiple languages. 1954. q. bk.rev. charts; illus. reprints avail.
Indexed: FR, GeoRef, SpeleolAb.
—INIST.
Published by: Institut Fondamental d'Afrique Noire/Cheikh Anta Diop, BP 206, Dakar, Senegal. Ed. Abdoulaye Bara Diop.

500 IND ISSN 0976-3104
▼ **THE I I O A B JOURNAL.** Text in English. 2010. bi-m. adv. bk.rev. **Document type:** *Journal, Academic/Scholarly.* **Description:** Covers multidisciplinary and translational researches on science, technology and biological sciences. Contains original research articles, short communications, findings in brief abstract/synopsis, reviews and mini-reviews, book reviews, meeting reports, commentaries, historical prospective, latest advances, letters to the editors, interviews, novel findings, case studies, market reports, industry trends, hottest topics in fast moving areas, news stories, IPR issues and conflicts, and various other upcoming issues in most advanced fields in life sciences.
Related titles: Online - full text ed.: free (effective 2011).
Indexed: A01, B21, CTA, NSA, PQC, T02.
Published by: Institute of Integrative Omics and Applied Biotechnology, Nonakuri, Purba Medinipur, West Bengal, 721172, India. info.iioab@gmail.com, http://www.iioab.webs.com/. Eds. George Perry, Greg Stephanopoulos.

500 FIN ISSN 1796-0363
I L E A P S. NEWSLETTER. (Intergrated Land Ecosystem-Atmosphere Processes Study) Text in English. 2005. biennial. **Document type:** *Newsletter, Trade.*
Related titles: Online - full text ed.: ISSN 1796-0401.
Published by: Intergrated Land Ecosystem-Atmosphere Processes Study. International Project Office, Gustaf Hallstrominkatu 2B, University of Helsinki, Hlsinki, 00014, Finland. TEL 358-9-19150571, FAX 358-9-19150717, ileaps-ipo@helsinki.fi, http://www.atm.helsinki.fi/ileaps. Ed. Anni Reissell. Circ: 1,000.

I N A S P NEWSLETTER. *see* LIBRARY AND INFORMATION SCIENCES

507.1 DEU ISSN 0179-5775
I P N - BLAETTER. Text in German. 1984. q. bk.rev. back issues avail. **Document type:** *Newsletter.*
Published by: Institut fuer die Paedagogik der Naturwissenschaften, Olshausenstr 62, Kiel, 24098, Germany. TEL 49-431-8803155, FAX 49-431-880-3100. Ed. Peter Nentwig. Circ: 7,500.

500 NZL ISSN 1179-6073
I R L SOLUTIONS. Text in English. 1991. q. free (effective 2010).
Description: Highlighting research and development undertaken at Industrial Research Ltd.
Formerly (until 2010): Innovate (1171-0152)
Related titles: Online - full text ed.: ISSN 1179-8165.
Published by: Industrial Research Ltd., 69 Gracefield Rd, Lower Hutt, PO Box 31310, Wellington, 5040, New Zealand. TEL 64-4-9313000, FAX 64-4-5666004. Ed. Mike Eng.

500 IDN ISSN 1978-3043
Q75
I T B JOURNAL OF SCIENCE. (Institut Teknologi Bandung) Text in Indonesian, English. 2003. s-a. **Document type:** *Journal, Academic/Scholarly.*
Related titles: Online - full text ed.: free (effective 2011).
Indexed: SCOPUS.
Published by: Institut Teknologi Bandung, Jalan Ganesha 10, Bandung, 40132, Indonesia. TEL 62-22-2534272, FAX 62-22-2506285. Ed. Bambang Riyanto Trilaksono.

S

500 TUR ISSN 1303-7021
Q4
I T U DERGISI C: FEN BILIMLERI/I T U MAGAZINE C: SCIENCE. Text in Turkish, English. 2002. s-a. **Document type:** *Journal, Academic/Scholarly.*
Related titles: Online - full text ed.: ISSN 1307-1661.
Indexed: A01, T02.
Published by: Istanbul Teknek Universitesi/Istanbul Technical University, Yeni Rektorluk Binasi, 5. kat Maslak, Istanbul, Turkey. TEL 90-212-2857126, FAX 90-212-2857126, itudergisi@itu.edu.tr. Ed. Can Fuat Delal.

500 600 IND
➤ **THE I U P JOURNAL OF SCIENCE AND TECHNOLOGY.** Text in English. 2005. q. INR 625 combined subscription domestic (print & online eds.); USD 32 combined subscription foreign (print & online eds.) (effective 2011). adv. back issues avail. **Document type:** *Journal, Academic/Scholarly.* **Description:** Provides an open forum to publish high quality research papers and review articles in the areas of science and engineering.
Formerly (until 2009): The I C F A I Journal of Science and Technology (0973-2268)
Related titles: Online - full text ed.
Indexed: C10, CA, T02.
Published by: (Institute of Chartered Financial Analysts of India), I C F A I University Press, Plot # 53, Nagarjuna Hills, Panjagutta, Hyderabad, 500 082, India. TEL 91-40-23430448, FAX 91-40-23430447, info@iupindia.in. Ed. E N Murthy. **Subscr. to:** Plot # 126, Maalaxmi Towers, Beside Nikhil Hospital, Srinagar Colony, Hyderabad 500 073, India. TEL 91-40-23423101, FAX 91-40-23423111, serv@iupindia.in.

500 JPN ISSN 0386-7668
➤ **IBARAKI DAIGAKU KYOIKUGAKUBU KIYO. SHIZEN KAGAKU/IBARAKI UNIVERSITY. FACULTY OF EDUCATION. BULLETIN. NATURAL SCIENCES.** Text in English, Japanese; Summaries in English. 1952. a. free. **Document type:** *Journal, Academic/Scholarly.*
Indexed: JPI.
Published by: Ibaraki Daigaku, Kyoikugakubu/Ibaraki University, Faculty of Education, 1-1 Bunkyo 2-chome, Mito, Ibaraki 310-8512, Japan. TEL 81-29-228-8111, FAX 81-29-228-8329. Ed. Hiroshi Yamamoto. Circ: 300 (controlled).

500 900 JPN ISSN 1343-0955
IBARAKI UNIVERSITY. NATURAL HISTORY BULLETIN. Text in English. 1997. a. **Document type:** *Journal, Academic/Scholarly.*
Indexed: B25, BIOSIS Prev, MycolAb.
Published by: Ibaraki University, Association for Natural History Studies, Natural History Laboratory, Faculty of Science, 2-1-1 Bunkyou, Mito, Ibaraki 310-8512, Japan. http://www.sci.ibaraki.ac.jp/~jkrte/nhbiu/top.html.

IBYKUS; Zeitschrift fuer Poesie, Wissenschaft und Staatskunst. *see* LITERATURE—Poetry

500 DEU ISSN 1433-2949
ICH TU WAS! AUSGABE 1. Text in German. 1990. m. EUR 20.40 for 6 mos.; EUR 2.90 newsstand/cover (effective 2009). **Document type:** *Magazine, Trade.* **Description:** Contains articles and information on the natural sciences for students in grades 1 through 3.
Formerly (until 2003): Tu was! Ausgabe 1 (1433-2922); Which superseded in part (in 1994): Tu was! (0943-7827)
Published by: Domino Verlag, Menzinger Str 13, Munich, 80638, Germany. TEL 49-89-179130, FAX 49-89-1783788, vertrieb@domino-verlag.de, http://www.domino-verlag.de.

500 DEU ISSN 1433-2957
ICH TU WAS! AUSGABE 2. Text in German. 1990. m. EUR 20.40 for 6 mos.; EUR 2.90 newsstand/cover (effective 2009). **Document type:** *Magazine, Trade.* **Description:** Contains articles and information on the natural sciences for students in grades 4 and up.
Formerly (until 2003): Tu was! Ausgabe 2 (1433-2930); Which superseded in part (in 1994): Tu was! (0943-7827)
Published by: Domino Verlag, Menzinger Str 13, Munich, 80638, Germany. TEL 49-89-179130, FAX 49-89-1783788, vertrieb@domino-verlag.de, http://www.domino-verlag.de.

500 GBR ISSN 2040-7319
ICONNECT. Text in English. 2008. w. free (effective 2011). back issues avail. **Document type:** *Newsletter, Consumer.*
Formerly (until 2009): Interfaith Seminary. Weekly Update (1759-8230)
Media: Online - full text.
Published by: Interfaith Foundation, Communications House, 26 York St, London, W1U 6PZ, United Kingdom.

500 MEX ISSN 0187-6015
Q23 CODEN: ICTEEB
ICYT. (Informacion Cientifica y Tecnologica) Text in Spanish. 1979. m. MXN 84; USD 48 in North America; USD 57 in Europe; USD 70 in Africa; USD 77 in Asia. adv. illus. **Document type:** *Academic/Scholarly.*
Formerly (until 1987): Informacion Cientifica y Tecnologica (0185-0261)
Indexed: Inspec.
Published by: Consejo Nacional de Ciencia y Tecnologia, Ave Insurgentes Sur 1582, Col Credito Constructor, Mexico, D.F., 03940, Mexico. TEL 52-55-53227700, http://www.conacyt.mx/. Ed. Clairette Ranc. Adv. contact Jose Luis Miranda Salgado. Circ: 39,000.

505 USA ISSN 0536-3012
CODEN: SPLCEU
➤ **IDAHO ACADEMY OF SCIENCE. JOURNAL.** Text in English. 1960. s-a. free to members (effective 2011). abstr. back issues avail.; reprints avail. **Document type:** *Journal, Academic/Scholarly.* **Description:** Covers on topics of specific Idaho interest.
Related titles: Online - full text ed.
Indexed: A01, A26, Agr, CA, E08, G08, GeoRef, I05, P30, S06, S09, SASA, SpeleolAb, T02, W08, WildRev.
Published by: (American Association for the Advancement of Science), Idaho Academy of Science, 909 Lucille Ave, Pocatello, ID 83201. TEL 208-234-7001, IdAcadSci@aol.com, http://www.isu.edu/ias/index.shtml.

➤ **IDAHO MUSEUM OF NATURAL HISTORY. OCCASIONAL PAPERS.** *see* MUSEUMS AND ART GALLERIES

500 NGA ISSN 0794-4896
➤ **IFE JOURNAL OF SCIENCE.** Text in English. s-a. **Document type:** *Journal, Academic/Scholarly.* **Description:** Aims to publish articles resulting from original research in the broad areas of chemical, biological, mathematical and physical sciences.
Related titles: Online - full text ed.
Indexed: A34, A38, B23, BP, C30, CABA, D01, E12, F08, F11, GH, H16, H17, I11, IndVet, N02, N03, N04, O01, P32, P33, P39, P40, PGegResA, PHN&I, R07, R08, R13, RA&MP, S13, S16, S17, T05, VS.
Published by: Obafemi Awolowo University, Faculty of Science, c/o Dr O O Jegede, Editor, Dept of Physics, Ile-Ife, Nigeria. TEL 234-803-4007146, oojegede@oauife.edu.ng. Ed. Dr. O O Jegede.

500 ESP ISSN 1130-7900
ILERDA. CIENCIES. Text in Spanish, Catalan. 1943. a.
Supersedes in part (in 1990): Ilerda (0212-565X)
Published by: Institut d'Estudis Ilerdencs, Placa Catedral, s-n, Lleida, 25002, Spain. TEL 34-973-271500, FAX 34-973-271538, publica@diputacionleida.es, http://www.fpiei.es/.

ILLINOIS NATURAL HISTORY SURVEY. REPORTS. *see* CONSERVATION

500 USA ISSN 0019-2252
Q11 CODEN: TISAAH
➤ **ILLINOIS STATE ACADEMY OF SCIENCE. TRANSACTIONS.** Text in English. 1907. q. free to members (effective 2011). bk.rev. charts; illus. back issues avail. **Document type:** *Proceedings, Academic/Scholarly.*
Related titles: Microform ed.: (from PQC); Supplement(s):.
Indexed: A22, A26, A34, A35, AgBio, Agr, B21, B23, B25, BA, BIOSIS Prev, C25, C30, CA, CABA, CIN, ChemAb, ChemTitl, E08, E12, ESPM, F08, F12, FCA, G11, GH, GeoRef, H16, H17, I05, I11, IndVet, KWIWR, MaizeAb, MathR, MycolAb, N02, N03, N04, O01, OR, P30, P32, P33, P37, P40, PGegResA, R07, R08, R11, R13, RA&MP, RASB, RefZh, S06, S09, S12, S13, S16, S17, SASA, SWRA, SoyAb, SpeleolAb, T02, TAR, VS, VirolAbstr, W08, W10, W11, WildRev, Z01, Z02.
—CASDDS, Ingenta, INIST, Linda Hall.
Published by: Illinois State Academy of Sciences, c/o Robyn Myers, Illinois State Museum, 502 South Spring St, Springfield, IL 62706. TEL 217-782-6436, FAX 217-782-1254, rmyers@museum.state.il.us.

➤ **ILLINOIS STATE MUSEUM. INVENTORY OF THE COLLECTIONS.** *see* MUSEUMS AND ART GALLERIES

500 USA ISSN 0360-0297
➤ **ILLINOIS STATE MUSEUM. POPULAR SCIENCE SERIES.** Key Title: Popular Science Series. Text in English. 1939. irreg. price varies. illus. back issues avail. **Document type:** *Monographic series, Academic/Scholarly.*
Indexed: GeoRef, SpeleolAb.
Published by: Illinois State Museum, 502 S Spring St, Springfield, IL 62706. TEL 217-782-7386, FAX 217-782-1254, info@museum.state.il.us.

500 USA ISSN 0360-0270
CODEN: ISRIB
ILLINOIS. STATE MUSEUM. REPORTS OF INVESTIGATIONS. Key Title: Reports of Investigations - Illinois State Museum. Text in English. 1948. irreg. price varies. bibl.; charts; illus. back issues avail. **Document type:** *Monographic series, Academic/Scholarly.*
Indexed: GeoRef, SpeleolAb, Z01.
Published by: Illinois State Museum, 502 S Spring St, Springfield, IL 62706. TEL 217-782-7386, FAX 217-782-1254, info@museum.state.il.us.

557 970 570 USA ISSN 0445-3395
➤ **ILLINOIS STATE MUSEUM. SCIENTIFIC PAPERS SERIES.** Text in English. 1940. irreg. price varies. illus. back issues avail. **Document type:** *Monographic series, Academic/Scholarly.*
Indexed: GeoRef, SpeleolAb.
—Linda Hall.
Published by: Illinois State Museum, 502 S Spring St, Springfield, IL 62706. TEL 217-782-7386, FAX 217-782-1254, info@museum.state.il.us.

500 600 610 DNK ISSN 0281-9341
ILLUSTRERAD VETENSKAP. Text in Swedish. 1984. 18/yr. SEK 756 (effective 2008). adv. illus. 84 p./no. 4 cols./p.; back issues avail. **Document type:** *Magazine, Consumer.*
Incorporates (1957-1999): Natur och Vetenskap (1403-3062); Which was formerly (until 1997): Polulaer Vetenskap (1403-8102); Which superseded in part (1957-1994): Roester i Radio TV (0035-7839)
Related titles: ◆ Danish ed.: Illustreret Videnskab. ISSN 0109-2456; ◆ Norwegian ed.: Illustrert Vitenskap. ISSN 0800-3955; ◆ German ed.: Illustrierte Wissenschaft. ISSN 0942-7090; Finnish ed.: Tieteen Kuvalehti. ISSN 0903-5583.
Published by: Bonnier Publications AS, Strandboulevarden 130, Copenhagen OE, 2100, Denmark. TEL 45-39-172000, FAX 45-39-290199, bp@bp.bonnier.dk, http://www.bonnierpublications.com. Ed. Jens Erik Matthiesen. Adv. contact Michael Sjoegren TEL 46-8-7539601. Circ: 146,700 (paid and controlled).

500 DNK ISSN 0109-2456
ILLUSTRERET VIDENSKAB. Text in Danish. 1984. 18/yr. DKK 829 (effective 2008). adv. illus. back issues avail. **Document type:** *Magazine, Consumer.* **Description:** Examines the natural sciences and social sciences: psychology, biology, astronomy, geography, medicine, anthropology, geology and archaeology; also deals with new technology.
Related titles: ◆ Swedish ed.: Illustrerad Vetenskap. ISSN 0281-9341; ◆ Norwegian ed.: Illustrert Vitenskap. ISSN 0800-3955; ◆ German ed.: Illustrierte Wissenschaft. ISSN 0942-7090; Finnish ed.: Tieteen Kuvalehti. ISSN 0903-5583.
Published by: Bonnier Publications AS, Strandboulevarden 130, Copenhagen OE, 2100, Denmark. TEL 45-39-172000, FAX 45-39-290199, bp@bp.bonnier.dk, http://www.bonnierpublications.com. Ed. Jens Erik Matthiesen. Adv. contact Janne Egelund Schmidt. color page DKK 47,200. Circ: 67,863 (paid).

500 NOR ISSN 0800-3955
ILLUSTRERT VITENSKAP. Text in Norwegian. 1984. 18/yr. NOK 839 (effective 2007). adv. back issues avail. **Document type:** *Magazine, Consumer.*
Incorporates (1994-1997): Facts og Fenomener (0805-3561); (1987-1992): Fakta (0801-6712)
Related titles: ◆ Danish ed.: Illustreret Videnskab. ISSN 0109-2456; ◆ Swedish ed.: Illustrerad Vetenskap. ISSN 0281-9341; ◆ German ed.: Illustrierte Wissenschaft. ISSN 0942-7090; Finnish ed.: Tieteen Kuvalehti. ISSN 0903-5583.
Published by: Bonnier Publications International AS (Subsidiary of: Bonnier Publications AS), Kirkegata 20, PO Box 433, Sentrum, Oslo, 0103, Norway. TEL 47-22-401200, FAX 47-22-401201, http://www.bonnierpublications.com. Ed. Ane Thurid Brudi. adv.: page NOK 53,000; 205 x 276. Circ: 67,000.

500 VEN ISSN 1856-5042
➤ **IMPACTO CIENTIFICO.** Text in Spanish. 2006. s-a. **Document type:** *Journal, Academic/Scholarly.*
Published by: Universidad del Zulia, Nucleo Luz - Col, Urb Las 40, entre calles 4 y 5, Cabimas, Venezuela. Ed. Ana Teresa Prieto.

500 GBR ISSN 1352-3368
IMPERIAL COLLEGE OF SCIENCE, TECHNOLOGY AND MEDICINE. CALENDAR. Text in English. 1908. a. membership. **Description:** Provides information on the governing body and staff, introductions to departments and centers, and general information about the college.
Formerly (until 1988): Imperial College of Science and Technology. Calendar (0305-4578)
Published by: Imperial College of Science, Technology and Medicine (Subsidiary of: University of London), Wye, Ashford, Kent TN25 5AH, United Kingdom. TEL 44-20-75942617, FAX 44-20-75942754, http://www.wye.ic.ac.uk. Circ: 3,000.

500.071 DNK ISSN 1904-2000
IMPROVING UNIVERSITY SCIENCE TEACHING AND LEARNING - PEDAGOGICAL PROJECTS. Text in English. 2008. irreg., latest vol.2, 2009. **Document type:** *Monographic series, Academic/Scholarly.*
Related titles: Online - full text ed.: ISSN 1904-2019.
Published by: Koebenhavns Universitet, Institut for Naturfagenes Didaktel/University of Copenhagen, Department of Science Education, Universitetsparken 15, Copenhagen OE, 2100, Denmark. TEL 45-35-320420, FAX 45-35-320110, ind@ind.ku.dk.

500.9 USA ISSN 1051-4546
AM101.C58
IN THE FIELD. Text in English. 1930. bi-m. free to members (effective 2010). illus. index. reprints avail. **Document type:** *Magazine, Academic/Scholarly.*
Supersedes in part (in Jun.1990): Field Museum of Natural History Bulletin (0741-2967); Which was formerly (until 1972): Field Museum of Natural History. Bulletin (0015-0703); (until 1966): Chicago Natural History Museum. Bulletin (1043-1616); (until 1944): Field Museum News (1049-7706); Field Museum of Natural History Bulletin incorporated (in 1980): Field Museum of Natural History. Biennial Report (0730-2819); Which was formerly (until 1980): Field Museum of Natural History. Report (1046-3135); (until 1968): Field Museum of Natural History. Annual Report (0735-3499); (until 1965): Chicago Natural History Museum. Annual Report (0095-8824); (until 1964): Chicago Natural History Museum. Report of the Director to the Board of Trustees (1067-2486)
Related titles: Microfiche ed.: (from BHP).
Indexed: AICP, GeoRef, SPPI, SpeleolAb.
—Ingenta, Linda Hall. **CCC.**
Published by: Field Museum, 1400 S Lake Shore Dr, Chicago, IL 60605. TEL 312-922-9410, membership@fieldmuseum.org, http://www.fieldmuseum.org.

500 600 AUS ISSN 1442-8121
INCITES; Australian science and technology online's innovations citations. Text in English. 1999. m. **Document type:** *Journal, Academic/Scholarly.*
Media: Online - full text.
Published by: Science Media, PO Box 4599, Kingston, ACT 2604, Australia. TEL 61-2-62478177, FAX 61-2-62470998, editorial@asto.com.au.

500 USA
INCREASE & DIFFUSION. Text in English. 1996. m. free. **Description:** Fosters the Smithsonian Institution's mission, the increase and diffusion of knowledge, and discusses aspects of the museums and collections.
Media: Online - full text.
Published by: Smithsonian Institution, SI Bldg, Washington, DC 20560-0010. TEL 202-357-2700, FAX 202-357-1729, info@info.si.edu.

500 BRA
INCRIVEL. Text in Portuguese. 1992. m. USD 33. **Document type:** *Consumer.*
Published by: Bloch Editores S.A., Edificio Manchete, Rua do Russel, 766-804, Gloria, Rio De Janeiro, RJ 22210010, Brazil. TEL 021-5554000, FAX 021-2059998. Ed. Janir Hollanda. Circ: 80,000.

500 600 IND ISSN 0085-1779
INDIA. DEPARTMENT OF SCIENCE & TECHNOLOGY. ANNUAL REPORT. Text in English. 1969. a. free (effective 2011). charts; stat. back issues avail. **Document type:** *Report, Government.*
Formerly: India. Committee on Science and Technology. Annual Report
Related titles: Online - full text ed.
Published by: Ministry of Science and Technology, Department of Science & Technology, Technology Bhavan, New Mehrauli Rd, New Delhi, 110 016, India. TEL 91-11-26567373, FAX 91-11-26864570, dstinfo@nic.in.

500 IND ISSN 0970-4140
Q1 CODEN: JIISAD
➤ **INDIAN INSTITUTE OF SCIENCE. JOURNAL.** Text in English. 1914-1924; resumed 1960 (resumed). q. INR 2,000 domestic; USD 400 foreign; INR 500 per issue domestic; USD 100 per issue foreign (effective 2012). adv. bk.rev. abstr.; bibl.; charts; illus. index. back issues avail.; reprints avail. **Document type:** *Journal, Academic/Scholarly.*
Formed by the 1960 merger of: Indian Institute of Science. Journal. Section A (0368-2668); Indian Institute of Science. Journal. Section B (0368-2676); Indian Institute of Science. Journal. Section C (0368-2684); All of which superseded in part (in 1925): Indian Institute of Science. Journal (0019-4964)
Related titles: Microfilm ed.: (from PQC); Online - full text ed.: free (effective 2011).
Indexed: A22, A28, A35, A36, A37, APA, AgBio, ApMecR, ApicAb, BrCerAb, C&ISA, CA/WCA, CABA, CCMJ, CIA, CIN, CIS, CPEI, CerAb, ChemAb, ChemTitl, CivEngAb, CorrAb, E&CAJ, E11, E12, EEA, EMA, EngInd, G11, GH, H15, H16, I11, Inspec, M&TEA, M09, MBF, METADEX, MSN, MathR, N02, P32, P40, PN&I, RASB, S13, S16, SCOPUS, ST&MA, SolStAb, T04, W11, WAA, Z01, Z02.
—AskIEEE, CASDDS, Ingenta, INIST, Linda Hall. **CCC.**

Published by: Indian Institute of Science, The Registrar, Bangalore, Karnataka 560 012, India. TEL 91-80-23600757, FAX 91-80-23600683, regr@admin.iisc.ernet.in, http://www.iisc.ernet.in. Ed. T N Guru Row.

509 IND ISSN 0019-5235
Q125 CODEN: IJHSA4
INDIAN JOURNAL OF HISTORY OF SCIENCE. Abbreviated title: I J H S. Text in English. 1966. bi-m. INR 500, USD 160 to individuals; INR 700, USD 210 to institutions (effective 2011). bk.rev. illus. index. **Document type:** *Journal, Academic/Scholarly.* **Description:** Brings together the results of studies and research in various fields of history of science from prehistoric period to modern times.
Indexed: A&ATA, BAS, CCMJ, FR, GeoRef, IBR, IBZ, MSN, MathR, P30, RASB, SpeleolAb, Z02.
—BLDSC (4414.700000), IE, Infotrieve, Ingenta, INIST, Linda Hall.
Published by: Indian National Science Academy, Bahadur Shah Zafar Marg, New Delhi, 110 002, India. TEL 91-11-23221931, FAX 91-11-23235648, esoffice@insa.nic.in. Ed. A K Bag.

500 IND ISSN 0973-2225
➤ **INDIAN JOURNAL OF MULTIDISCIPLINARY RESEARCH.** Text in English. 2005. q. INR 750 domestic to individuals; INR 800 domestic to institutions; USD 50 foreign (effective 2010). Index. back issues avail.; reprints avail. **Document type:** *Journal, Academic/Scholarly.*
Published by: Centre For Multidisciplinary Research and Action, Cheriyil Bldgs., PB No: 55, Thodupuzha, Kerala 685 584, India. TEL 91-9447-612913. Ed. C. A. Ninan. R&P, Adv. contact Stephen Joseph.

➤ **INDIAN JOURNAL OF PHYSICS.** *see* PHYSICS

500 600 IND ISSN 0974-6846
➤ **INDIAN JOURNAL OF SCIENCE AND TECHNOLOGY.** Text in English. 2007. m. INR 3,500, USD 400 (effective 2010). adv. **Document type:** *Journal, Academic/Scholarly.*
Related titles: Online - full text ed.: ISSN 0974-5645. free (effective 2011).
Indexed: A01, P52, P56.
Published by: Indian Society for Education and Environment, 23 (New) Neelkamal Apt, 3d Main Rd, Gandhi Nagar, Adyar, Chennai, 600 020, India. TEL 91-44-24421010, http://www.isee-adyar.org. Ed., Pub. Natarajan Gajendran. adv.: B&W page INR 1,000, color page INR 20,000; trim 85 x 110. Circ: 500.

500 IND ISSN 0976-2876
▼ ➤ **INDIAN JOURNAL OF SCIENTIFIC RESEARCH.** Abbreviated title: I J S R. Text in English. 2010 (Jul.). s-a. INR 400 domestic to individuals; USD 80 foreign to individuals; INR 1,500 domestic to institutions; USD 200 foreign to institutions (effective 2011). adv. bk.rev. abstr. Index. back issues avail.; reprints avail. **Document type:** *Journal, Academic/Scholarly.* **Description:** Publishes selected original research articles, reviews, short communication and book reviews in the fields of botany, zoology, chemistry, physics, mathmatics, medical sciences, agricultural sciences, enviornmental sciences, natural sciences, technological sciences and any other branch of related sciences. It covers recent discoveries in structural and functional principles of scientific research.
Related titles: E-mail ed.
Published by: Global Academic Society, S-24/20-25, Taktakpur, Cantt., Varanasi, 221 002, India. TEL 91-9415370131, ijsr2010@gmail.com. Ed., Pub., R&P, Adv. contact Dr. Deepak Kumar Srivastava. Circ: 175.

➤ **INDIAN NATIONAL SCIENCE ACADEMY. BIOGRAPHICAL MEMOIRS OF FELLOWS.** *see* BIOGRAPHY

500 IND
INDIAN NATIONAL SCIENCE ACADEMY. PROCEEDINGS; original research papers, review articles, short notes, commentaries. Text in English. 2006. 3/yr. back issues avail. **Document type:** *Proceedings, Academic/Scholarly.*
Formed by the 2006 merger of: Indian National Science Academy. Proceedings. Part A: Physical Sciences (0370-0046); Indian National Science Academy. Proceedings. Part B: Biological Sciences (0073-6600)
Related titles: Online - full text ed.
Published by: Indian National Science Academy, Bahadur Shah Zafar Marg, New Delhi, 110 002, India. TEL 91-11-23221931, FAX 91-11-23235648, esoffice@insa.nic.in, http://www.insaindia.org.

500 IND ISSN 0073-6619
Q73
INDIAN NATIONAL SCIENCE ACADEMY. YEAR BOOK. Text in English. 1960. a. **Document type:** *Yearbook, Consumer.*
Former titles (until 1971): National Institute of Sciences of India. Yearbook (0375-5193); National Institute of Sciences of India, Calcutta. Year Book
Indexed: GeoRef, SpeleolAb.
—Linda Hall.
Published by: Indian National Science Academy, Bahadur Shah Zafar Marg, New Delhi, 110 002, India. TEL 91-11-23221931, FAX 91-11-23235648, esoffice@insa.nic.in, http://www.insaindia.org.

500 600 IND ISSN 0373-0786
Q73.I39 CODEN: PISCAD
INDIAN SCIENCE CONGRESS ASSOCIATION. PROCEEDINGS. Text in English. 1914. a. index. **Document type:** *Proceedings, Corporate.*
Indexed: GeoRef, SpeleolAb, Z01.
—BLDSC (6844.220000), INIST.
Published by: Indian Science Congress Association, c/o Dr. Vijay Laxmi Saxena, General Secretary, 14 Dr Biresh Guha St, Kolkata, West Bengal 700 017, India. TEL 91-33-22874530, FAX 91-33-22872551, iscacal@vsnl.net, www.sciencecongress.nic.in.

500 IND ISSN 0970-4256
➤ **INDIAN SCIENCE CRUISER.** Text in English. 1985. 5/yr. INR 500 to institutions; free to members (effective 2011). bk.rev. 52 p./no. 2 cols./p.; back issues avail. **Document type:** *Journal, Academic/Scholarly.* **Description:** Disseminates knowledge of science and scientific information.
Formerly (until 1987): Science & Society (0970-4248)
Published by: Institute of Science Education and Culture, 42-B Syed Amir Ali Ave., Kolkata, West Bengal 700 017, India. TEL 91-33-22801798, iseckol@vsnl.net.

500 USA ISSN 0073-6767
Q11 CODEN: PIACAP
➤ **INDIANA ACADEMY OF SCIENCE. PROCEEDINGS.** Text in English. 1891. s-a. cum.index: 1891-1980, vols.1-90. back issues avail. **Document type:** *Proceedings, Academic/Scholarly.* **Description:** Publishes information dedicated to promote scientific research and the diffusion of scientific information, to encourage communication and cooperation among scientists, and to improve education in the sciences.
Related titles: Online - full text ed.
Indexed: A01, A26, A29, A34, A38, AgrForAb, B20, B21, B23, B25, BIOSIS Prev, C25, CA, CABA, CIN, CTA, ChemAb, ChemTitl, ChemoAb, DIP, E08, E12, E17, ESPM, EntAb, F08, F12, G08, G11, GH, GeoRef, H16, I05, I10, I11, IBR, IBZ, IndVet, LT, MaizeAb, MycolAb, N02, N04, NSA, O01, P33, P37, R07, R08, RA&MP, RM&VM, RefZh, S06, S09, S13, S16, SASA, SWRA, SoyAb, SpeleolAb, T02, T05, VS, VirolAbstr, W08, W10, W11, WildRev, Z01.
—CASDDS, Ingenta, INIST, Linda Hall.
Published by: Indiana Academy of Science, c/o Delores Brown, 650 W Washington, Indianapolis, IN 46204. TEL 317-974-0827, FAX 317-974-0783, ExecDir@indianaacademyofscience.org.

500 600 ESP ISSN 1988-8155
INFO R U V I D. (Red de Universidades Valencianas para el Fomento de la Investigacion, el Desarrollo y la Innovacion) Text in Spanish. 2007. m. back issues avail. **Document type:** *Bulletin, Academic/Scholarly.*
Media: Online - full text.
Published by: Red de Universidades Valencianas, Camino de Vera, s-n, Edif. 6G 3a. Planta, Valencia, 46022, Spain. TEL 34-96-3877067, FAX 34-96-3877949, ruvid@ruvid.org, http://www.ruvid.org/inforuvid.php.

500 CHL ISSN 0716-8756
CODEN: ITECFG
➤ **INFORMACION TECNOLOGICA.** Text in Spanish; Summaries in English, Spanish. 1990. bi-m. USD 500 in the Americas; USD 750 elsewhere. adv. bibl. 2 cols./p.; back issues avail.; reprints avail. **Document type:** *Journal, Academic/Scholarly.* **Description:** Presents original papers in 7 areas: energy and environment; minerals and metallurgy; applied computers; materials and natural resources; food and biotechnology; industrial processes and process equipment; and industrial management.
Related titles: Online - full text ed.: ISSN 0718-0764. 2004. free (effective 2011) (from SciELO).
Indexed: A01, A28, APA, BrCerAb, C&ISA, CA, CA/WCA, CIA, CPEI, CerAb, ChemAb, CivEngAb, CorrAb, E&CAJ, E11, EEA, EMA, EngInd, F03, F04, FS&TA, H15, Inspec, M&TEA, M09, MBF, METADEX, MinerAb, R18, SCOPUS, SolStAb, T02, T04, WAA.
—CASDDS, IE, Ingenta, Linda Hall.
Published by: Centro de Informacion Tecnologica, Monsenor Subercaseaux 667, La Serena, Chile. citchile@entelchile.net, http://citchile.8m.com. Eds. Carlos J Rojas, Jose O Valderrama. Adv. contact Jose O Valderrama.

500 CUB
INFORMACIONES ESPECIALES. Text in Spanish. fortn.
Published by: Academia de Ciencias de Cuba, Instituto de Documentacion e Informacion Cientifico-Tecnica (I D I C T), Capitolio Nacional, Prado y San Jose, Habana, 2, Cuba.

500 JPN ISSN 1343-4500
INFORMATION/XINXI/YOHO. Text in Chinese, English, Japanese. 1998. q. JPY 6,000 to individuals; JPY 16,000 to institutions (effective 2003).
Related titles: Online - full text ed.: ISSN 1344-8994.
Indexed: CCMJ, MSN, MathR, SCI, W07.
—BLDSC (4481.410000), IE, Ingenta.
Published by: International Information Institute, LI Lab, Faculty of Engineering, Hosei University, Koganei, Tokyo, 184-8584, Japan. office@information-iii.org. Ed. Lei Li.

060 POL ISSN 0537-667X
AS256.P7
INFORMATOR NAUKI POLSKIEJ. Text in Polish. 1958. a. USD 50 in Europe; USD 70 elsewhere. adv.
Published by: Osrodek Przetwarzania Informacji/Information Processing Centre, Redakcja Wydawnictw, PO Box 355, Warsaw, 00950, Poland. FAX 25-33-19, TELEX 813716 CINT PL. Ed. Mieczyslaw Stanczyk. Circ: 7,200. **Co-sponsor:** Polska Akademia Nauk, Komitet Badan Naukowych/Polish Academy of Sciences, Committee for Scientific Research.

658.4 USA
HD29 CODEN: TIMBD
INFORMS. Text in English. 1976. s-a. USD 25. adv. abstr. back issues avail. **Document type:** *Bulletin.*
Formerly: T I M S - O R S A Meeting Bulletin (0161-0295); Which superseded (1957-1975): Operations Research Society of America. Meeting Bulletin (0030-3666)
Indexed: ApMecR, GeoRef, Inspec, RASB.
—AskIEEE, IE, Ingenta, INIST, Linda Hall. **CCC.**
Address: 290 Westminster St, Providence, RI 02903. TEL 401-274-2525. Adv. contact Sandra S Owens. Circ: 3,000.

500 620 CHL ISSN 0718-073X
INGENIERIA AL DIA. Text in Spanish. 2003. s-a. **Document type:** *Journal, Academic/Scholarly.*
Published by: Universidad Central de Chile, Toesca 1783, Santiago, Chile. TEL 56-2-5826000, http://www.ucentral.cl.

INGENIERIA Y CIENCIA. *see* ENGINEERING

500 600 MEX ISSN 1405-0676
TA4
INGENIERIAS. Text in Spanish, English. 1993. q. **Document type:** *Journal, Academic/Scholarly.*
Related titles: Online - full text ed.: free (effective 2011).
Indexed: C01.
Published by: Universidad Autonoma de Nuevo Leon, Facultad de Ingenieria Mecanica y Electrica, Edificio 7, 1er Piso, Ala Norte, San Nicolas de los Garza, Nuevo Leon, Mexico. http://www.uanl.mx.

500 BRA ISSN 1518-1243
➤ **INICIACAO CIENTIFICA CESUMAR.** (Centro Universitario de Maringa) Text in Portuguese; Summaries in Portuguese, English. 1999. s-a. free (effective 2007). bk.rev. **Document type:** *Journal, Academic/Scholarly.* **Description:** Publishes scientific works of the researches at the Centro Universitario de Maringa.
Related titles: Online - full text ed.
Published by: Centro Universitario de Maringa (C E S U M A R), Av Guedner 1610, Maringa, Parana 87050-390, Brazil. TEL 55-44-2276360, FAX pesquisa@cesumar.br, 55-44-2275395. Ed. Ludhiana Bertoncello. Circ: 2,000.

➤ **INNER ASIA.** *see* HUMANITIES: COMPREHENSIVE WORKS

➤ **INNOVACION TECNOLOGICA.** *see* TECHNOLOGY: COMPREHENSIVE WORKS

500 COL ISSN 0121-5140
T4
INNOVACION Y CIENCIA. Text in Spanish. 1992. q. COP 21,000 domestic; USD 45 foreign (effective 2001). adv. bk.rev. biennial index. **Document type:** *Journal, Academic/Scholarly.* **Description:** Includes short articles on recent news and innovative projects and main articles on biology, physics, math, astronomy, medicine and social sciences.
Indexed: A01, CA, F03, F04, T02.
Published by: Asociacion Colombiana para el Avance de la Ciencia, CRA 50 No.27-70 Unidad Camilo Torres, Bloque C Modulo 3, Bogota, Colombia. TEL 57-1-3150734, FAX 57-1-2216950, acac@col.net.co. Ed. Eduardo Posada Florez. Pub. Rosario Martinez. Circ: 5,000 (controlled).

INNOVACORP. ANNUAL REPORT. *see* TECHNOLOGY: COMPREHENSIVE WORKS

500 SGP ISSN 0219-4023
T173.8 CODEN: ISSNB6
➤ **INNOVATION;** the magazine of research and technology. Abbreviated title: I N N. Text in English. 2000. 3/yr. SGD 34, USD 19, EUR 19 to institutions (effective 2012). adv. back issues avail. **Document type:** *Journal, Academic/Scholarly.* **Description:** Covers the research activities of the National University of Singapore and its related organisations.
Related titles: Online - full text ed.
Indexed: A01, A02, A03, A08, A09, A10, C23, CA, Inspec, L04, LISTA, T02, V03, V04.
Published by: World Scientific Publishing Co. Pte. Ltd., 5 Toh Tuck Link, Singapore, 596224, Singapore. TEL 65-6466-5775, FAX 65-6467-7667, wspc@wspc.com.sg, http://www.worldscientific.com. Ed. Candace Lim TEL 65-6516-4811. Adv. contact Sok Ching Lim TEL 65-6466-5775. **Dist. by:** World Scientific Publishing Co., Inc., 27 Warren St, Ste 401-402, Hackensack, NJ 07601. TEL 201-487-9655, 800-227-7562, FAX 201-487-9656, 888-977-2665, wspc@wspc.com; World Scientific Publishing Ltd., 57 Shelton St, London WC2H 9HE, United Kingdom. TEL 44-207-8360888, FAX 44-207-8362020, sales@wspc.co.uk.

➤ **INNOVATION POLICY AND THE ECONOMY.** *see* BUSINESS AND ECONOMICS

500 600 CAN
INNOVATIONS. Text in English. 1989. a. **Description:** Nova Scotia's magazine of science and technology. Features issues, events, profiles and news of the province's science and technology communities.
Related titles: Online - full text ed.
Published by: Stephen Kimber Associates, 2533 Beech St, Halifax, NS B3L 2X9, Canada. Ed. Stephen Kimber.

500 MYS ISSN 2180-2157
▼ ➤ **INNOVATIVE STUDIES.** Text in English. 2010. bi-m. MYR 3,700 domestic to individuals; USD 1,200 foreign to individuals; MYR 4,642 domestic to institutions; USD 1,500 foreign to institutions (effective 2011). bk.rev. abstr.; bibl. Index. back issues avail. **Document type:** *Journal, Academic/Scholarly.* **Description:** Publishes scholarly and practitioner-oriented papers, books, case studies, review essays, and book reviews related to innovation, creativity, change management, case studies, technology strategy and planning, etc.
Related titles: Online - full text ed.
Published by: Computer Science Journals, M-3-19 Plaza Damas, Sri Hartamas, Kuala Lumpur, 50480, Malaysia. TEL 60-3-62071607, FAX 60-3-62071697, info@cscjournals.org. Ed. James E. Smith. Pub. M.N. Tahir.

500 GBR
INSIDE SCIENCE. Text in English. 2008 (Jun.). s-a. **Document type:** *Magazine, Corporate.* **Description:** Aims to give its readers a better understanding of the people behind the work of the Royal Society and illustrate the huge breadth of projects and activities that the Society is engaged in.
Related titles: Online - full text ed.: free.
Published by: The Royal Society Publishing, 6-9 Carlton House Terr, London, SW1Y 5AG, United Kingdom. TEL 44-20-74512500, FAX 44-20-79302170, http://royalsocietypublishing.org. Ed. Charlotte Marling.

500 USA
Q179.9 CODEN: SIRRDL
INSIDE SMITHSONIAN RESEARCH. Text in English. 1972. q. free to members (effective 2009). illus. back issues avail.; reprints avail. **Document type:** *Magazine, Consumer.* **Description:** Publishes features and columns on research projects.
Formerly (until 2003): Smithsonian Institution. Research Reports (0364-0175)
Related titles: Online - full text ed.: ISSN 1946-6722.
Indexed: BiolDig, EnvAb, GeoRef, IUSGP, SpeleolAb.
—Linda Hall. **CCC.**
Published by: Smithsonian Institution, Office of Public Affairs, c o Becky Haberacker, Smithsonian Castle, Rm 354, PO Box 37012, Washington, DC 20013. TEL 202-633-5183, info@si.edu. Circ: 67,000.

500 FRA ISSN 1248-8577
LES INSOLITES DE LA RECHERCHE. Key Title: Les Insolites de la Science. Text in French. 1993. irreg. price varies. **Document type:** *Monographic series, Academic/Scholarly.*
Published by: Centre National de la Recherche Scientifique, Campus Gerard-Megie, 3 Rue Michel-Ange, Paris, 75794, France. TEL 33-1-44964000, FAX 33-1-44965390, http://www.cnrseditions.fr.

508 ESP ISSN 1133-6889
QH7
INSTITUCIO CATALANA D'HISTORIA NATURAL. BUTLLETI. Text in Spanish, Catalan. 1994. a., latest vol.74, 2008. EUR 12. **Document type:** *Journal, Academic/Scholarly.*

S

Formed by the merger of (1974-1991): Institucio Catalana d'Historia Natural. Butlleti. Seccio de Botanica (0210-6205); (1976-1989): Institucio Catalana d'Historia Natural. Butlleti. Seccio de Geologi (0210-6213); (1975-1992): Institucio Catalana d'Historia Natural. Butlleti. Seccio de Zoologia (0210-6191)
Related titles: Online - full text ed.: ISSN 2013-3987. 1994.
Indexed: GeoRef, IECT, Z01.
—INIST.
Published by: (Institucion Catalana de Historia Natural), Institut d'Estudis Catalans, Carrer del Carme 47, Barcelona, 08001, Spain. TEL 34-932-701620, FAX 34-932-701180, informacio@iecat.net, http://www2.iecat.net.

500 IND ISSN 0971-3107
Q2 CODEN: TSSTA8
INSTITUT FRANCAIS DE PONDICHERY. DEPARTEMENT D'ECOLOGIE. PUBLICATIONS. Text and summaries in English, French. 1957. irreg. price varies. index. **Document type:** *Academic/Scholarly.*
Formed by the merger of (1969-1991): Institut Francais de Pondichery. Section Scientifique et Technique. Travaux (0073-8336); (1969-1991): Institut Francais de Pondichery. Section Scientifique et Technique. Travaux. Hors Serie (0073-8344)
Indexed: GeoRef, SpeleolAb.
—INIST.
Published by: Institut Francais de Pondichery/French Institute of Pondicherry, PO Box 33, Pondicherry, Tamil Nadu 605 001, India. TEL 91-413-2334168, ifpinfo@ifpindia.org. Circ: 500.

500 600 FRA ISSN 0767-2896
INSTITUT FRANCAIS DE RECHERCHE SCIENTIFIQUE POUR LE DEVELOPPEMENT EN COOPERATION. COLLOQUES ET SEMINAIRES. Text in French. 1985. irreg. **Document type:** *Monographic series.*
Indexed: ASFA, B21, ESPM, GeoRef.
Published by: Institut de Recherche pour le Developpement (IRD), 911 Av. Agropolis, B.P. 64501, Montpellier, Cedex 5 34394, France. editions@ird.fr.

500 MAR ISSN 0253-3243
QH3 CODEN: BSMAAT
INSTITUT SCIENTIFIQUE. BULLETIN. Text in Multiple languages. 1920. a. **Document type:** *Journal, Academic/Scholarly.*
Former titles (until 1975): Societe des Sciences Naturelles et Physiques du Maroc. Bulletin (0037-9255); (until 1952): Societe des Sciences Naturelles du Maroc. Bulletin (0366-3450)
Indexed: GeoRef, SpeleolAb.
—INIST.
Published by: Institut Scientifique, Avenue Ibn Batouta, Rabat, 10106, Morocco. TEL 212-37-774548, FAX 212-37-774540, http://www.israbat.ac.ma.

500 AGO ISSN 0020-3912
Q127.A42 CODEN: IANBBN
INSTITUTO DE INVESTIGACAO CIENTIFICA DE ANGOLA. BOLETIM. Text in Portuguese; Summaries in English, French, German. 1962. s-a. bibl.; charts.
Indexed: GeoRef, MLA-IB, SpeleolAb.
Published by: Instituto de Investigacao Cientifica de Angola, Departamento de Documentacao e Informacao, CP 3244, Luanda, Angola.

500 600 AGO ISSN 0074-0098
INSTITUTO DE INVESTIGACAO CIENTIFICA DE ANGOLA. MEMORIAS E TRABALHOS. Text in Portuguese; Summaries in English, French, German. 1960. irreg., latest vol.8, 1971. price varies. abstr.
Related titles: Microform ed.
Indexed: GeoRef, SpeleolAb.
Published by: Instituto de Investigacao Cientifica de Angola, Departamento de Documentacao e Informacao, CP 3244, Luanda, Angola.

500 600 AGO ISSN 0003-343X
Q180.A58 CODEN: RCIAA5
INSTITUTO DE INVESTIGACAO CIENTIFICA DE ANGOLA. RELATORIOS E COMUNICACOES. Text in Portuguese. 1962. irreg., latest vol.25, 1973.
Indexed: GeoRef, SpeleolAb.
Published by: Instituto de Investigacao Cientifica de Angola, Departamento de Documentacao e Informacao, CP 3244, Luanda, Angola.

500 PRT ISSN 0870-001X
CODEN: EEDUDG
INSTITUTO DE INVESTIGACAO CIENTIFICA TROPICAL. ESTUDOS, ENSAIOS E DOCUMENTOS. Text in Portuguese. 1950. irreg., latest vol.161. back issues avail. **Document type:** *Monographic series, Academic/Scholarly.*
Formerly (until 1983): Junta de Investigacoes do Ultramar. Estudos, Ensaios e Documentos (0554-775X)
Indexed: BIOSIS Prev, GeoRef, MycolAb, SpeleolAb.
—INIST.
Published by: Instituto de Investigacao Cientifica Tropical, Rua da Junqueira 86, Lisbon, 1300-344, Portugal. TEL 351-21-3616340, FAX 351-21-3631460, iict@iict.pt. Circ: 1,000.

500 PRT ISSN 0870-0036
CODEN: MIITEJ
INSTITUTO DE INVESTIGACAO CIENTIFICA TROPICAL. MEMORIAS. Text in Portuguese. 1943; N.S. 19??. irreg., latest vol.71. back issues avail. **Document type:** *Monographic series, Academic/Scholarly.*
Formerly: Junta de Investigacoes Cientificas do Ultramar. Memorias (0870-6212)
Indexed: GeoRef, SpeleolAb.
Published by: Instituto de Investigacao Cientifica Tropical, Rua da Junqueira 86, Lisbon, 1300-344, Portugal. TEL 351-21-3616340, FAX 351-21-3631460, iict@iict.pt. Circ: 1,000.

508 ECU ISSN 0010-7972
INSTITUTO ECUATORIANO DE CIENCIAS NATURALES. CONTRIBUCIONES. Text in English, Spanish. 1937. s-a. per issue exchange basis.
Indexed: SpeleolAb.
Published by: Instituto Ecuatoriano de Ciencias Naturales/Ecuadorian Institute of Natural Sciences, Center, Apdo 408, Quito, Pichincha, Ecuador. Ed. M Acosta Solis. Circ: 2,500.

610 500 551.5 BOL ISSN 1561-8374
INSTITUTO MEDICO SUCRE. REVISTA. Text in Spanish. 1905. s-a. MXN 250 in Latin America; USD 90 elsewhere (effective 2006). back issues avail. **Document type:** *Journal, Academic/Scholarly.*
Published by: Instituto Medico Sucre, Arzobispado San Alberto 30, Sucre, Bolivia. TEL 591-4-6442909, inmedsuc@mara.scr.entelnet.bo, http://www.inmedsuc.com.mx. Ed. Manuel Cuellar.

500 PRT ISSN 1647-6530
▼ **INSTITUTO POLITECNICO DE CASTELO BRANCO. NEWSLETTER.** Text in Portuguese. 2010. m. **Document type:** *Newsletter, Consumer.*
Published by: Instituto Politecnico de Castelo Branco, Av Pedro Alvares Cabral, Castelo Branco, 6000-084, Portugal. TEL 351-272-339600, FAX 351-272-339601, http://www.ipcb.pt.

500 578.77 PRT ISSN 0872-9123
QH173
INSTITUTO PORTUGUES DE INVESTIGACAO MARITIMA. RELATORIOS CIENTIFICOS E TECNICOS. Text in Portuguese. 1989. irreg.
Formerly (until 1993): Instituto Nacional de Investigacao das Pescas. Relatorios Tecnicos e Cientificos (0871-3103)
Indexed: ASFA, B21, ESPM.
Published by: Instituto Nacional de Investigacao Agraria (I N I A) (Subsidiary of: Instituto Nacional dos Recursos Biologicos (I N R B)), Rua Barata Salgueiro 37, Lisbon, 1250-042, Portugal.

500 DOM ISSN 0378-956X
T173.S2497
INSTITUTO TECNOLOGICO DE SANTO DOMINGO. DOCUMENTOS. Text in Spanish. 1976. irreg., latest vol.6, 1981. free. **Document type:** *Monographic series.*
Published by: Instituto Tecnologico de Santo Domingo, Apdo Postal 342-9, Santo Domingo, Dominican Republic. Ed. Antonio Fernandez.

400 300 ROM
INSTITUTUL POLITEHNIC DIN IASI. BULETINUL. Text in English. 1946. q. **Document type:** *Journal, Academic/Scholarly.* **Description:** Contains a series of 10 titles that covers: Math, physic, chemistry, engineering, automation, electronics, machine manufacturing, architecture, hydrotechnics, textiles, social sciences and humanities.
Related titles: ◆ Series: Institutul Politehnic din Iasi. Buletinul. Sectia Matematica, Mecanica, Fizica; ◆ Institutul Politehnic din Iasi. Buletinul. Sectia Constructii de Masini; ◆ Institutul Politehnic din Iasi. Buletinul. Sectia Textile, Pielarie; ◆ Institutul Politehnic din Iasi. Buletinul. Sectia Hidrotehnica; ◆ Institutul Politehnic din Iasi. Buletinul. Sectia Electrotehnica, Energetica, Electronica; ◆ Institutul Politehnic din Iasi. Buletinul. Sectia Chimie si Inginerie Chimica; ◆ Institutul Politehnic din Iasi. Buletinul. Sectia Automatica si Calculatoare; ◆ Institutul Politehnic din Iasi. Buletinul. Sectia Constructii. Arhitectura. ISSN 1224-3884.
Published by: Universitatea Tehnica "Gheorghe Asachi" Iasi. Editura Politehnium/"Gheorghe Asachi" Technical University of Iasi. Politehnium Publishing House, Strada Prof.dr.doc. D, Mangeron nr.67, Iasi, 700050, Romania. TEL 40-232-231343, FAX 40-232-231343, simonasimionescu@yahoo.uk.co, http://www.tuiasi.ro.

INTEGRATION. *see* POLITICAL SCIENCE—International Relations

500 AUS ISSN 1834-304X
INTEGRATION INSIGHTS. Text in English. 2006. bi-m. **Document type:** *Journal, Academic/Scholarly.*
Media: Online - full text.
Published by: Australian National University, A N U College of Medicine and Health Sciences. National Centre for Epidemiology and Population Health, Cnr of Eggleston and Mills Rds, Canberra, ACT 0200, Australia. TEL 61-2-6125-2378, FAX 61-2-6125-0740, http://nceph.anu.edu.au.

500 NGA ISSN 1597-488X
INTER-WORLD JOURNAL OF SCIENCE AND TECHNOLOGY. Text in English. 2001.
Published by: R. Durson Associates, PO Box 581, Owerri, Imo State, Nigeria. TEL 234-803-7513519, FAX 234-803-3631624, info@rdurson.com, http://www.rdurson.com.

500 VEN ISSN 0378-1844
Q4 CODEN: ITRCDB
➤ **INTERCIENCIA**; journal of science and technology of the Americas. Text and summaries in English, Portuguese, Spanish. 1976. m. USD 90 worldwide to individuals; USD 120 to institutions in Latin America & Caribbean; USD 150 in North America to institutions; USD 160 in Europe to institutions; USD 180 in Asia to institutions (effective 2005). adv. bk.rev. back issues avail. **Document type:** *Journal, Academic/Scholarly.* **Description:** Interdisciplinary approach to the study of science and technology.
Related titles: Online - full text ed.: free (effective 2011).
Indexed: A20, A22, A29, A34, A35, A36, A37, A38, ASCA, ASFA, AgBio, AgrForAb, B&BAb, B19, B20, B21, B23, B25, BA, BIOSIS Prev, BP, C01, C25, C30, CABA, ChPerI, CurCont, D01, E12, E17, EIA, ESPM, EnerInd, EnvAb, F08, F11, F12, FCA, G11, GH, GeoRef, H16, H17, H21, I04, I05, I10, I11, IBR, IBZ, INIS AtomInd, ISR, IndVet, LT, MaizeAb, MycolAb, N02, N03, N04, N05, O01, OR, P08, P11, P30, P32, P33, P37, P38, P39, P40, P48, P52, P56, PGegResA, PGrRegA, PHN&I, PN&I, PQC, R07, R08, R11, R12, R13, RA&MP, RASB, RM&VM, RRTA, RefZh, Repind, S12, S13, S16, S17, SCI, SCOPUS, SSciA, SWRA, SoyAb, SpeleolAb, T05, TAR, TriticAb, VITIS, VS, VirolAbstr, W07, W10, W11, WildRev, Z01.
—BLDSC (4533.080000), CASDDS, IE, Infotrieve, Ingenta, INIST, Linda Hall. **CCC.**
Published by: Interciencia Association, Apdo 51842, Caracas, DF 1050-A, Venezuela. TEL 58-212-9917525, FAX 58-212-9923224. Ed. Miguel Laufer. R&P Pamela Navarro. Adv. contact Ana Raquel Picon. Circ: 1,200 (paid).

➤ **INTERCOM (NEW YORK, 1973).** *see* RELIGIONS AND THEOLOGY—Judaic

500 GBR ISSN 0308-0188
Q1 CODEN: ISCRD8
➤ **INTERDISCIPLINARY SCIENCE REVIEWS.** Abbreviated title: I S R. Text in English. 1976. q. GBP 559 combined subscription to institutions (print & online eds.); USD 968 combined subscription in United States to institutions (print & online eds.) (effective 2012). adv. bk.rev. 80 p./no.; back issues avail.; reprint service avail. from PSC. **Document type:** *Journal, Academic/Scholarly.* **Description:** Examines the advances arising from interaction among tue various scientific or engineering disciplines and the effect of science and technology on society, including such areas as global warming and public understanding of science.
Related titles: Online - full text ed.: ISSN 1743-2790. GBP 505 to institutions; USD 876 in United States to institutions (effective 2012) (from IngentaConnect).
Indexed: A01, A03, A08, A20, A22, A28, A29, APA, ASCA, B20, B21, BrCerAb, C&ISA, CA, CA/WCA, CIA, CLOSS, CTA, CerAb, ChemAb, ChemoAb, CivEngAb, CommAb, CorrAb, E&CAJ, E11, EEA, EMA, ESPM, EnvEAb, GenetAb, GeoRef, H15, I10, IBR, IBZ, Inspec, M&TEA, M09, MBF, METADEX, NSA, NucAcAb, P10, P11, P26, P30, P48, P52, P53, P54, P56, PQC, RASB, RILM, S10, SCI, SCOPUS, SSCI, SolStAb, SpeleolAb, T02, T04, VirolAbstr, W07, WAA.
—BLDSC (4533.357000), CASDDS, IE, Infotrieve, Ingenta, INIST, Linda Hall. **CCC.**
Published by: (Institute of Materials, Minerals and Mining), Maney Publishing, Ste 1C, Joseph's Well, Hanover Walk, Leeds, W Yorks LS3 1AB, United Kingdom. TEL 44-113-2432800, FAX 44-113-3868178, maney@maney.co.uk, http://www.maney.co.uk. Ed. Willard McCarty. **Subscr. in N. America to:** Maney Publishing, 875 Massachusetts Ave, 7th Fl, Cambridge, MA 02139. TEL 866-297-5154, FAX 617-354-6875, maney@maneyusa.com.

500 ISR ISSN 0334-1100
INTERFACE. Text in English. 1975. s-a. looseleaf. free (effective 2009). illus. back issues avail. **Description:** Contains reports on various scientific research projects conducted at the Weizmann Institute of Science.
Related titles: Online - full text ed.
Published by: Weizmann Institute of Science, Publications and Media Relations Dept. (Subsidiary of: Weizmann Institute of Science), P O Box 26, Rehovot, 76100, Israel. TEL 972-8-9343856, FAX 972-8-9344132, news@weizmann.ac.il, http://www.weizmann.ac.il. Ed. Yivsam Azgad. Circ: 20,000.

570.5 GBR ISSN 2042-8898
➤ **INTERFACE FOCUS.** Text in English. 2004. bi-m. EUR 1,404 combined subscription in Europe to institutions (print & online eds.); USD 1,934 combined subscription in US & Canada to institutions (print & online eds.); GBP 1,080 combined subscription to institutions in Europe & elsewhere (print & online eds.) (effective 2012). back issues avail. **Document type:** *Journal, Academic/Scholarly.* **Description:** Covers research articles, reports and reviews on scientific research.
Related titles: Online - full text ed.: ISSN 2042-8901. EUR 1,080 in Europe to institutions; USD 1,488 in US & Canada to institutions; GBP 831 to institutions in Europe & elsewhere (effective 2012); ◆ Supplement to: Journal of the Royal Society. Interface. ISSN 1742-5689.
—Linda Hall. **CCC.**
Published by: The Royal Society Publishing, 6-9 Carlton House Terr, London, SW1Y 5AG, United Kingdom. TEL 44-20-74512500, FAX 44-20-79761837, sales@royalsociety.org, http://royalsocietypublishing.org. Ed. Denis Noble. **Subscr. to:** Portland Customer Services, Commerce Way, Colchester CO2 8HP, United Kingdom. TEL 44-1206-796351, FAX 44-1206-799331, sales@portland-services.com, http://www.portlandpress.com.

500 570 USA ISSN 1081-3519
Q180.U5 CODEN: PMASAX
➤ **INTERMOUNTAIN JOURNAL OF SCIENCES.** Abbreviated title: I J S. Text in English. 1940. q. illus.; stat.; bibl.; charts. cum. index v.1-6 (1995-2000). back issues avail. **Document type:** *Journal, Academic/Scholarly.* **Description:** Encourages scientists, educators and students to submit their research, management applications or viewpoints concerning the sciences applicable to the intermountain region.
Supersedes (in 1995): Montana Academy of Sciences. Proceedings (0096-9206)
Indexed: B25, BIOSIS Prev, ChemAb, GeoRef, MycolAb, P30, SASA, SpeleolAb, W08, WildRev, Z01.
—CASDDS, Linda Hall.
Published by: (Montana Academy of Sciences), Intermountain Journal of Sciences, PO Box 3014, Bozeman, MT 59772. TEL 406-994-6362. **Co-sponsors:** American Fisheries Society, Montana Chapter; Wildlife Society, Montana Chapter.

500 600 IND ISSN 0976-4828
▼ ➤ **INTERNATIONAL ARCHIVE OF APPLIED SCIENCES AND TECHNOLOGY.** Abbreviated title: I A A S T. Text and summaries in English. 2010 (June). s-a. INR 500 domestic to individuals; USD 100 foreign to individuals; INR 2,000 domestic to institutions; USD 1,000 foreign to institutions (effective 2011). adv. bk.rev. tr.lit. Index. back issues avail.; reprints avail. **Document type:** *Journal, Academic/Scholarly.* **Description:** Publishes original research articles pertaining to the applied sciences, technology. It covers a wide range of interest in the fields of applied sciences.
Related titles: Online - full text ed.
Indexed: S13.
Published by: Society of Education, 27, B.N. Puram, Near Banshi Vihar Colony, Pascheem Puri Rd, Sikandra-Bodla, Agra, Uttar Pradesh 282 007, India. Ed. Deepmala Verma. Pub., R&P Dr. Manish Kumar.

500 JOR ISSN 1816-2509
➤ **INTERNATIONAL JOURNAL FOR SCIENCES AND TECHNOLOGY.** Text in Arabic, English. 2005. 3/yr. JOD 100 domestic to individuals; USD 250 foreign to individuals; JOD 200 domestic to institutions; USD 300 foreign to institutions (effective 2010). adv. back issues avail.; reprints avail. **Document type:** *Journal, Academic/Scholarly.* **Description:** Publishes original research papers on all aspects of science and technology including scientific disciplines of Microbiology, biotechnology, cell biology, ecology, entomology, environmental science, forestry, genomics, horticulture, animal science, plant sciences, proteomics, agricultural and food science, biostatistics, biological sciences and bioengineering, computer science and engineering and water resources.

Formerly (until 2010): Ibn Al-Haitham Journal for Science and Technology
Related titles: Online - full text ed.: free (effective 2010).
Published by: International Center for Advancement of Science and Technology, Bldg. 116 Wasfi Al tal St, PO Box 2793, Amman, 11953, Jordan. TEL 962-6-5602285, FAX 962-6-5602286, info.icast@yahoo.com, http://www.icast-jo.com/. Ed., Adv. contact Abdul Jabbar N. Al-Shammari. Pub. Baker Kiswani. Circ: 500.

▼ ➤ **INTERNATIONAL JOURNAL OF ACADEMIC RESEARCH.** *see* SOCIAL SCIENCES: COMPREHENSIVE WORKS

500 KOR ISSN 2005-4238
➤ **INTERNATIONAL JOURNAL OF ADVANCED SCIENCE AND TECHNOLOGY.** Text in Korean. 2008. m. Index. reprints avail. **Document type:** *Journal, Academic/Scholarly.* **Description:** Covers recent progress in the area of advanced science and technology, including: Communication and networking, computer science and its applications, ubiquitous multimedia computing, software engineering & its applications, security technology and information assurance, bio-science and bio-technology, u and eservice, science and technology, database theory and application, control and automation, signal processing, image processing and pattern recognition, grid and distributed computing, etc.
Related titles: Online - full text ed.: free (effective 2011).
Indexed: C10, T02.
Published by: Science and Engineering Research Support Society, Rm.402, Man-Je Bldg., 449-8 Ojung-Dong, Daedoek-Gu, Daejon, Korea, S. TEL 82-42-6242265, FAX 82-42-6242205. Eds. Tai-hoon Kim, Wai-Chi Fang.

500 600 USA ISSN 2221-0997
▼ **INTERNATIONAL JOURNAL OF APPLIED SCIENCE AND TECHNOLOGY.** Text in English. 2011. m. free. bk.rev. abstr.; bibl. back issues avail.; reprints avail. **Document type:** *Journal, Academic/Scholarly.* **Description:** Publishes original research, applied, and educational articles in all areas of science and technology. Topics include: Astronomy and astrophysics, chemistry, earth and atmospheric sciences, physics, biology in general, agriculture, biophysics and biochemistry, botany, environmental science, forestry, genetics, horticulture, husbandry, neuroscience, zoology, computer science, engineering, robotics and automation, materials science, mathematics, mechanics, statistics, health care & public health, nutrition and food science, pharmaceutical sciences, and more.
Related titles: Online - full text ed.: ISSN 2221-1004.
Indexed: I05.
Published by: Centre for Promoting Ideas, 432 Claremont Ave, New York, NY 10027. TEL 540-831-5888, info.cpi.usa@hotmail.com, http://www.cpinet.info. Ed. Jorge J. Santiago-Aviles. Pub., R&P Mamin Ullah.

500 MYS ISSN 2180-1258
▼ ➤ **INTERNATIONAL JOURNAL OF APPLIED SCIENCES.** Text in English. 2010 (May). bi-m. MYR 3,700 domestic to individuals; USD 1,200 foreign to individuals; MYR 4,742 domestic to institutions; USD 1,500 foreign to individuals (effective 2011). bk.rev. abstr.; bibl. Index. back issues avail. **Document type:** *Journal, Academic/Scholarly.* **Description:** Publishes multidisciplinary research articles reporting on original research across the fields of pure and applied sciences, including applied sciences, natural and social sciences industrial research materials science and technology, energy technology and society including impacts on the environment, climate, security, and economy, environmental sciences, physics of the games, creativity and new product development, professional ethics, hydrology and water resources, wind energy.
Related titles: Online - full text ed.
Published by: Computer Science Journals, M-3-19 Plaza Damas, Sri Hartamas, Kuala Lumpur, 50480, Malaysia. TEL 60-3-62071607, FAX 60-3-62071697, info@cscjournals.org. Ed. Rajab Challoo. Pub. M.N. Tahir.

➤ **INTERNATIONAL JOURNAL OF ARTS & SCIENCES.** *see* HUMANITIES: COMPREHENSIVE WORKS

500 PAK ISSN 2077-1223
▼ ➤ **INTERNATIONAL JOURNAL OF BASIC & APPLIED SCIENCES.** Text in English. 2009. bi-m. free. back issues avail. **Document type:** *Journal, Academic/Scholarly.*
Media: Online - full text.
Indexed: C10, T02.
Published by: I J E N S Publishers, Haider Rd., Saddar, Rawalpindi Cantt., Pakistan. publisher@ijens.org, http://www.ijens.org/index.htm.

500 IND ISSN 0975-5241
▼ ➤ **INTERNATIONAL JOURNAL OF CURRENT RESERACH AND REVIEW.** Text in English. 2009. m. free (effective 2011). **Document type:** *Journal, Academic/Scholarly.*
Media: Online - full text. **Related titles:** Print ed.: ISSN 2231-2196.
Published by: Radiance Bahu - Uddeshiya Sanstha http://www.ijcrr.com/.

▼ ➤ **INTERNATIONAL JOURNAL OF EDUCATION & ALLIED SCIENCES.** *see* EDUCATION

500 300 600 AUS ISSN 1835-8780
➤ **THE INTERNATIONAL JOURNAL OF EMERGING TECHNOLOGIES AND SOCIETY.** Abbreviated title: I J E T S. Text in English. 2003. s-a. free (effective 2011). back issues avail. **Document type:** *Journal, Academic/Scholarly.* **Description:** Focuses on the complex relationship between science and technology and their wider socio-cultural contexts.
Formerly (until 2008): Australian Journal of Emerging Technologies and Society (1449-0706)
Media: Online - full text. **Related titles:** Print ed.
Indexed: A01, A11, A12, A17, A39, ABIn, C27, C29, CA, D03, D04, E13, P46, P48, P51, P53, P54, PQC, R14, S02, S03, S14, S15, S18, SociolAb, T02.
Published by: Swinburne University of Technology, Faculty of Life & Social Sciences, H29, PO Box 218, Hawthorn, VIC 3122, Australia. TEL 61-3-86767002, FAX 61-3-98183648, international@swinburne.edu.au. Eds. Karen Farquharson, Mark Finn.

500 600 IND ISSN 0975-5462
TA1
▼ ➤ **INTERNATIONAL JOURNAL OF ENGINEERING SCIENCE AND TECHNOLOGY.** Text in English. 2009. m. free (effective 2011). **Document type:** *Journal, Academic/Scholarly.*
Media: Online - full text.
Indexed: A01.
Published by: Engg Journals Publications, 4/122, 2nd Fl., Perumal Naicker Complex, G.S.T. Road, Otteri, Vandalur, Chennai, 600048, India. TEL 91-44-22751131.

▼ ➤ **INTERNATIONAL JOURNAL OF ENGINEERING, SCIENCE AND TECHNOLOGY.** *see* ENGINEERING

➤ **INTERNATIONAL JOURNAL OF ENVIRONMENTAL AND SCIENCE EDUCATION.** *see* EDUCATION

➤ **INTERNATIONAL JOURNAL OF ENVIRONMENTAL RESEARCH AND PUBLIC HEALTH.** *see* ENVIRONMENTAL STUDIES

▼ ➤ **INTERNATIONAL JOURNAL OF GENDER, SCIENCE AND TECHNOLOGY.** *see* SOCIOLOGY

500 GBR ISSN 1757-2223
▼ ➤ **INTERNATIONAL JOURNAL OF INNOVATION SCIENCE.** Abbreviated title: I J I S. Text in English. 2009 (Feb.). q. GBP 272; GBP 283 combined subscription (print & online eds.) (effective 2012). **Document type:** *Journal, Academic/Scholarly.* **Description:** Contains articles on the study of function of the brain, exacting of designs, and perfection of the discovery process, pattern recognition, neuroscience, analytics, measurements, heuristic algorithms, optimization, and evaluation.
Related titles: Online - full text ed.: ISSN 1757-2231. 2009 (Feb.). GBP 253 (effective 2012).
Indexed: A01, T02.
Published by: Multi-Science Publishing Co. Ltd., 5 Wates Way, Brentwood, Essex CM15 9TB, United Kingdom. TEL 44-1277-244632, FAX 44-1277-223453, info@multi-science.co.uk. Ed. Dr. Praveen Gupta.

500 GBR ISSN 1741-6426
➤ **INTERNATIONAL JOURNAL OF LIABILITY AND SCIENTIFIC ENQUIRY.** Text in English. 2007. 4/yr. EUR 494 to institutions (print or online ed.); EUR 672 combined subscription to institutions (print & online eds.) (effective 2012). abstr.; bibl.; stat.; charts. **Document type:** *Journal, Academic/Scholarly.* **Description:** Aims establish an effective channel of communication between policy makers, the legal community, the expert community, risk and liability managers, government agencies, academic and research institutions and persons concerned with the resolution of complex disputes that are informed by science.
Related titles: Online - full text ed.: ISSN 1741-6434 (from IngentaConnect).
Indexed: A26, A28, APA, B02, B15, B17, B18, BrCerAb, C&ISA, CA/WCA, CIA, CerAb, CivEngAb, CorrAb, E&CAJ, E11, EEA, EMA, ESPM, EnvEAb, G04, H15, I05, M&TEA, M09, MBF, METADEX, RiskAb, SolStAb, T04, WAA.
—BLDSC (4542.319700), IE. **CCC.**
Published by: Inderscience Publishers, PO Box 735, Olney, Bucks MK46 5WB, United Kingdom. TEL 44-1234-240519, FAX 44-1234-240515, editorial@inderscience.com. Eds. Dr. M A Dorgham, Dr. Sylvia Mercado Kierkegaard. **Subscr. to:** World Trade Centre Bldg, 29 Rte de Pre-Bois, Case Postale 856, Geneva 15 1215, Switzerland. FAX 41-22-7910885, subs@inderscience.com.

500 620 GBR ISSN 2045-7057
▼ ➤ **INTERNATIONAL JOURNAL OF MULTIDISCIPLINARY SCIENCES AND ENGINEERING.** Abbreviated title: I J M S E. Text in English. 2010. m. free (effective 2010). back issues avail. **Document type:** *Journal, Academic/Scholarly.* **Description:** Designed for publication of novel ideas, state-of-the-art research results and fundamental advances in all aspects of theoretical and applied topics in science and engineering including areas in natural and social sciences.
Media: Online - full text.
Published by: Sysbase Solution, Ltd., 1 Granville Rd, London, E17 9BS, United Kingdom. TEL 44-7921-829134.

500 600 GBR ISSN 1752-8933
TA418.9.N35
➤ **INTERNATIONAL JOURNAL OF NANO AND BIOMATERIALS.** Text in English. 2007 (Dec.). 4/yr. EUR 494 to institutions (print or online ed.); EUR 672 combined subscription to institutions (print & online eds.) (effective 2012). **Document type:** *Journal, Academic/Scholarly.* **Description:** Aims at promoting and coordinating developments in the field of nano and biomaterials.
Related titles: Online - full text ed.: ISSN 1752-8941 (from IngentaConnect).
Indexed: A26, B&BAb, B19, B21, CPEI, CTA, E08, EMBASE, ExcerpMed, SCOPUS.
—BLDSC (4542.369020), IE. **CCC.**
Published by: Inderscience Publishers, PO Box 735, Olney, Bucks MK46 5WB, United Kingdom. TEL 44-1234-240519, FAX 44-1234-240515. Ed. Dr. M A Dorgham. **Subscr. to:** World Trade Centre Bldg, 29 Rte de Pre-Bois, Case Postale 856, Geneva 15 1215, Switzerland. FAX 41-22-7910885, subs@inderscience.com.

500 NGA ISSN 0794-4713
Q85.4
➤ **INTERNATIONAL JOURNAL OF NATURAL AND APPLIED SCIENCES.** Text in English. q. **Document type:** *Journal, Academic/Scholarly.* **Description:** Designed for academics, scholars, advanced students and reflective practitioners. Publishes scientific papers of significance in all areas of natural and applied sciences.
Published by: Tapas Institute of Scientific Research and Development, Ezeogidi Estate, Umunwanlo Irete, Owerri West Local Government Area, PO Box 2143, Owerri, Imo State, Nigeria. TEL 234-805-3127006, tapas-info@tapasinstitute.org, http://www.tapasinstitute.org.

500 620 TUR ISSN 1307-1149
Q1
➤ **INTERNATIONAL JOURNAL OF NATURAL AND ENGINEERING SCIENCES.** Abbreviated title: I J N E S. Text in English. 2007. 3/yr. EUR 75 to individuals; EUR 150 to institutions (effective 2009). **Document type:** *Journal, Academic/Scholarly.*
Related titles: Online - full text ed.
Indexed: A01, A34, A35, A36, A37, A38, AgBio, AgrForAb, B23, BP, C25, C30, CA, CABA, E12, F08, F11, F12, FCA, G11, GEOBASE, GH, H16, I11, IndVet, LT, MaizeAb, N02, N04, O01, OR, P32, P33, P37, P38, P39, P40, PGegResA, PGrRegA, PHN&I, R07, R12, R13, RA&MP, RM&VM, RRTA, S12, S13, S16, S17, T02, T05, TAR, TriticAb, VS, W11, Z01.
Published by: Nobel Publishing, Ivedik Organize Sanay, Agac Isleri Sitesi 521, Sok Nu 22-24 Ostim, Ankara, Turkey. TEL 90-312-3945264, FAX 90-312-3945268, nobel@nobel.gen.tr, nobeljournals@nobelonline.net. Ed. Dr. Mehmet Karatas.

500 IND ISSN 0975-3737
▼ ➤ **INTERNATIONAL JOURNAL OF OPERATIONAL RESEARCH & OPTIMIZATION.** Abbreviated title: I J O R O. Text and summaries in English. 2009. s-a. USD 40 to individuals; USD 70 to institutions (effective 2011). abstr.; bibl.; charts; illus.; stat.; tr.lit. cum. index. back issues avail.; reprints avail. **Document type:** *Journal, Academic/Scholarly.* **Description:** Publishes original papers, review papers, technical notes, and book reviews in the field of operational research and optimization.
Related titles: Online - full text ed.; Optical Disk - DVD ed.
Indexed: A01.
Published by: Association for the Advancement in Combinatorial Sciences, A-9 Gagan Enclave, Rohta Rd, Meerut, Uttar Pradesh, India. TEL 91-121-2682738, ultimateworld2050@gmail.com. Ed. Anubhav Pratab Singh. Pub., R&P S R Singh.

➤ **INTERNATIONAL JOURNAL OF POWER AND ENERGY SYSTEMS.** *see* ENERGY

500 IND ISSN 2229-6107
▼ ➤ **INTERNATIONAL JOURNAL OF PURE AND APPLIED SCIENCES AND TECHNOLOGY.** Text in English. 2010. m. free (effective 2011). **Document type:** *Journal, Academic/Scholarly.* **Description:** Covers all aspects of research relating to science, engineering and technology.
Media: Online - full text.
Address: c/o Hemen Dutta, Department of Mathematics, Gauhati University, Kokrajhar Campus, Kokrajhar, 783370, India. Ed., Pub. Hemen Dutta.

➤ **INTERNATIONAL JOURNAL OF RADIATION BIOLOGY.** *see* MEDICAL SCIENCES—Oncology

500 PAK ISSN 2076-734X
▼ ➤ **INTERNATIONAL JOURNAL OF RESEARCH AND REVIEWS IN APPLIED SCIENCES.** Text in English. 2009. q. USD 400 (effective 2011). Index. back issues avail. **Document type:** *Journal, Academic/Scholarly.* **Description:** Covers computer science, software engineering, mathematics, statistics, business, economics, applied physics, electronic engineering, applied chemistry, energy resources & research, environmental engineering, industrial engineering, mechanical engineering, mining engineering, nuclear engineering, bioinformatics, biotechnology and all other fields of engineering.
Related titles: Online - full text ed.: ISSN 2076-7366. free (effective 2011).
Indexed: A34, A37, C10, C25, CABA, D01, E12, F08, FCA, GH, H16, LT, N02, N03, N04, P33, P52, R08, S13, T02, T05, W11.
Published by: Academic Research Publishing Agency, Flat No.2, Block No.22, CAT-III, Sector G-10/2, Islamabad, 44000, Pakistan. TEL 92-300-5156970, arpapress@gmail.com, publisher@arpapress.com, editor@arpapress.com. Pub. Jawad Ahmed. R&P Awais Aziz Shah.

500 510 NLD ISSN 1571-0068
➤ **INTERNATIONAL JOURNAL OF SCIENCE AND MATHEMATICS EDUCATION.** Text in English. 2003. bi-m. EUR 334, USD 340 combined subscription to institutions (print & online eds.) (effective 2012). adv. reprint service avail. from PSC. **Document type:** *Journal, Academic/Scholarly.* **Description:** Publishes original articles on a variety of topics and research methods in both science and mathematics education.
Related titles: Online - full text ed.: ISSN 1573-1774 (from IngentaConnect).
Indexed: A22, A26, BRD, BibLing, CA, CPE, E01, E02, E03, E07, ERA, ERI, ERIC, EdA, EdI, M12, RefZh, S21, SCOPUS, T02, W03, W05, Z02.
—BLDSC (4542.543700), IE, Ingenta. **CCC.**
Published by: Springer Netherlands (Subsidiary of: Springer Science+Business Media), Van Godewijckstraat 30, Dordrecht, 3311 GX, Netherlands. TEL 31-78-6576050, FAX 31-78-6576474, http://www.springer.com. Ed. Fou-Lai Lin.

500 AUS ISSN 1832-1011
INTERNATIONAL JOURNAL OF SCIENCE AND RESEARCH. Text in English. 2005. s-a. **Document type:** *Journal, Academic/Scholarly.*
Indexed: B25, BIOSIS Prev, MycolAb, Z01.
Published by: International Research Association Inc., PO Box 472, Glen Waverley, VIC 3150, Australia. TEL 61-3-96532172, FAX 61-3-98334518, editors@international.org.au, http://www.international.org.au/index.htm.

500 IRN ISSN 1680-144X
INTERNATIONAL JOURNAL OF SCIENCE AND TECHNOLOGY OF THE UNIVERSITY OF KASHAN. Text in English. 2000. s-a.
Indexed: CCMJ, MSN, MathR.
Published by: University of Kashan Press, Kashan, Iran.

500 370 GBR ISSN 2154-8455
▼ ➤ **INTERNATIONAL JOURNAL OF SCIENCE EDUCATION. PART B: COMMUNICATION AND PUBLIC ENGAGEMENT.** Text in English. 2011. s-a. GBP 206 combined subscription in United Kingdom to institutions (print & online eds.); EUR 271, USD 340 combined subscription to institutions (print & online eds.) (effective 2012). **Document type:** *Journal, Academic/Scholarly.*
Related titles: Online - full text ed.: ISSN 2154-8463. 2011. GBP 185 in United Kingdom to institutions; EUR 244, USD 306 to institutions (effective 2012); ◆ Supplement to: International Journal of Science Education. ISSN 0950-0693.
Indexed: B29.
—**CCC.**
Published by: Routledge (Subsidiary of: Taylor & Francis Group), 4 Park Square, Milton Park, Abingdon, Oxon OX14 4RN, United Kingdom. subscriptions@tandf.co.uk, http://www.routledge.com.

S

500 GBR ISSN 1750-9823
INTERNATIONAL JOURNAL OF SPORTS SCIENCE AND ENGINEERING. Text in English. 2006. q. GBP 272 to institutions; GBP 40 to members; GBP 43 per issue (effective 2010). **Document type:** *Journal, Academic/Scholarly.* **Description:** Publishes original research and applied papers on sport science and sports engineering, including the application of system science and system engineering, mathematics and statistics, computer and information, mechanics and physics, material and textiles, operation research and management, modelling and simulation, medicine and biology, measurement and design, electric and machine engineering, etc. for sports, physical education, exercise, game and human movement.
Related titles: Online - full text ed.: ISSN 1750-9831. free (effective 2010).
—BLDSC (4542.681317), IE.
Published by: World Academic Union (World Academic Press), 113 Academic House, Mill Lane, Wavertree Technology Park, Liverpool, L13 4AH, United Kingdom. TEL 44-870-7779498, journals@worldacademicunion.com.

500 600 GBR ISSN 2040-4247
▼ ➤ **INTERNATIONAL JOURNAL OF SUDAN RESEARCH, POLICY AND SUSTAINABLE DEVELOPMENT.** Text in English. 2009 (4th q.). q. EUR 494 to institutions (print or online ed.); EUR 672 combined subscription to institutions (print & online eds.) (effective 2011). **Document type:** *Journal, Academic/Scholarly.* **Description:** Aims to provide a forum for practitioners, academics, and policymakers from around the world to exchange concepts, research, and best practices about Sudan.
Related titles: Online - full text ed.: ISSN 2040-4255.
—CCC.
Published by: Inderscience Publishers, PO Box 735, Olney, Bucks MK46 5WB, United Kingdom. TEL 44-1234-240519, FAX 44-1234-240515, editorial@inderscience.com. Ed. Dr. Allam Ahmed. **Subscr. to:** World Trade Centre Bldg, 29 Rte de Pre-Bois, Case Postale 856, Geneva 15 1215, Switzerland. FAX 41-22-7910885, subs@inderscience.com.

500 170 USA ISSN 1947-3451
BJ1
▼ ➤ **INTERNATIONAL JOURNAL OF TECHNOETHICS.** Text in English. 2010. q. USD 210 to individuals; USD 595 to institutions; USD 275 combined subscription to individuals (print & online eds.); USD 860 combined subscription to institutions (print & online eds.) (effective 2012). **Document type:** *Journal, Academic/Scholarly.* **Description:** Explores the impact of ethics in technological advances and applications in established and new areas of science.
Related titles: Online - full text ed.: ISSN 1947-346X. 2010. USD 140 to individuals; USD 595 to institutions (effective 2012).
Indexed: PAIS.
Published by: I G I Global, 701 E Chocolate Ave, Ste 200, Hershey, PA 17033. TEL 717-533-8845 ext 100, FAX 717-533-8661, cust@igi-global.com, http://www.igi-pub.com. Ed. Rocci Luppicini.

500 004 KOR ISSN 2005-4246
➤ **INTERNATIONAL JOURNAL OF U- AND E- SERVICE, SCIENCE AND TECHNOLOGY.** Text in English. 2008. q. bk.rev. Index. **Document type:** *Journal, Academic/Scholarly.* **Description:** Covers the adoption of standards and protocols for e- or u-business applications, B2B, B2C AND C2C architectures, case studies in industry and government, collaborative business systems, compression methodology, CRM and business solutions, data and knowledge engineering, e- or u-banking, e- or u-business systems for multiple platforms, e- or u-entertainment, e- or u-government, e- or u-learning, e- or u-marketing and consumer behavior, e- or u-negotiation and auction mechanisms, e- or u-payment systems, GPS applications and location-based services, grid computing for e- or u-business, healthcare and medical applications, intellectual rights, interoperability and integration, m-business and ubiquitous services, mobile services and architectures, mobility management in next generation networks, multi-agent systems and information integration, open source technologies in e- or u-business, quality of service (QOS) and metrics, security and privacy, semantic web applications and ontology sharing, service-oriented architectures, steganography technology, supply-chain management, systems development and evaluation, telematics and middleware platforms, trust and privacy issues in social networks, user interfaces and usability, virtual organizations, VPN technology and services, web data visualization, web personalization and decision making, web services, web site monitoring and optimization, workflow management systems, XML and domain mark-up languages, and others.
Related titles: Online - full text ed.: free (effective 2011).
Indexed: A01, T02.
Published by: Science and Engineering Research Support Society, Rm.402, Man-Je Bldg., 449-8 Ojung-Dong, Daedoek-Gu, Daejon, Korea, S. TEL 82-42-6242265, FAX 82-42-6242205. Eds. Hangbae Chang, Jianhua Ma.

➤ **INTERNATIONAL JOURNAL OF YOGA THERAPY.** *see* PHYSICAL FITNESS AND HYGIENE

500 PRT ISSN 1646-8945
INTERNATIONAL JOURNAL ON HANDS - ON SCIENCE. Text in English. 2008. irreg. **Document type:** *Magazine, Consumer.*
Published by: Associacao Hands - on Science Network, Rua 1o de Maio 2, Vila Verde, 4730-734, Portugal. contact@hsci.info, http://www.hsci.info.

500 GBR
INTERNATIONAL SOCIETY FOR THE SYSTEMS SCIENCES. PROCEEDINGS. Text in English. 1956. a. USD 125 per issue (effective 2009). back issues avail. **Document type:** *Proceedings, Academic/Scholarly.*
Formerly: Society for General Systems Research. Proceedings
Related titles: CD-ROM ed.: free to members (effective 2009); Online - full text ed.: ISSN 1999-6918.
Published by: International Society for the Systems Sciences, 47 Southfield Rd, Pocklington, York YO42 2XE, United Kingdom. TEL 44-1759-302718, FAX 44-1759-302718, isssoffice@dsl.pipex.com.

THE INTERNATIONAL SOROPTIMIST. *see* CLUBS

371.3 500 USA ISSN 2151-9587
▼ **INTERNATIONAL STUDIES OF NON-TRADITIONAL STUDENTS: CORRESPONDING PEDAGOGY IN SCIENCE EDUCATION.** Text in English. forthcoming 2010 (July). a. USD 25 per issue (effective 2010). **Document type:** *Academic/Scholarly.* **Description:** A guide for science teachers of non-traditional students.
Published by: International Consultation for Educators, LLC, 1015 Essex St, SE, Minneapolis, MN 55414. TEL 612-245-4471, publication@eduice.com, http://www.eduice.com/.

▼ **INTERNATIONAL TRANSACTION JOURNAL OF ENGINEERING, MANAGEMENT, & APPLIED SCIENCES & TECHNOLOGIES.** *see* ENGINEERING

500 IND ISSN 0974-7273
▼ ➤ **INTERNATIONAL TRANSACTIONS IN APPLIED SCIENCES.** Abbreviated title: I T A S. Text and summaries in English. 2009. q. USD 40 to individuals; USD 60 to institutions (effective 2011). abstr.; bibl.; charts; illus.; stat.; tr.lit. cum. index. back issues avail.; reprints avail. **Document type:** *Journal, Academic/Scholarly.* **Description:** Publishes research articles and reviews in the field of applied sciences. It provides information on the latest trends and developments.
Related titles: Online - full text ed.: ISSN 0975-3761; Optical Disk - DVD ed.
Published by: Association for the Advancement in Combinatorial Sciences, A-9 Gagan Enclave, Rohta Rd, Meerut, Uttar Pradesh, India. TEL 91-121-2682738, ultimateworld2050@gmail.com. Ed., Pub., R&P S R Singh.

500 DEU ISSN 0943-7207
Q101 CODEN: IWKLAL
INTERNATIONALES WISSENSCHAFTLICHES KOLLOQUIUM. Text in German. 1957. a. price varies. **Document type:** *Journal, Academic/Scholarly.*
Former titles (until 1992): Technische Hochschule Ilmenau. Internationales Wissenschaftliches Kolloquium (0374-3365); (until 1964): Internationales Kolloquium an der Hochschule fuer Elektrotechnik Ilmenau (0323-8091)
Indexed: CIN, ChemAb, ChemTitl.
—BLDSC (4557.190100), CASDDS, Linda Hall.
Published by: Technische Universitaet Ilmenau, Postfach 100565, Ilmenau, 98684, Germany. TEL 49-3677-692549, FAX 49-3677-691718, bettina.wegner@tu-ilmenau.de, http://www.tu-ilmenau.de. Ed. Andrea Schneider.

500 FRA ISSN 2108-5978
▼ **UNE INTRODUCTION A.** Text in French. 2010. irreg. price varies. **Document type:** *Monographic series, Academic/Scholarly.*
Published by: E D P Sciences, 17 Ave du Hoggar, Parc d'Activites de Courtaboeuf, BP 112, Cedex A, Les Ulis, F-91944, France. TEL 33-1-69187575, FAX 33-1-69860678, http://www.edpsciences.org.

500 608.7 IND ISSN 0970-0056
INVENTION INTELLIGENCE. Text in English. 1965. bi-m. bk.rev. abstr.; charts; illus.; tr.lit. **Document type:** *Magazine, Trade.* **Description:** Provides information on technology for industry and innovative works of individuals and institutions.
Indexed: FS&TA, ISA.
Published by: National Research Development Corporation, Kailash Colony Ext, 20-22 Zamroodpur Community Centre, New Delhi, 110 048, India. TEL 91-80-23341255, FAX 91-80-23347555, nrdc@bgl.vsnl.net.in, http://www.nrdcindia.com. Ed. R K Anthwal TEL 91-80-29240401 ext 344.

500 USA
INVENTOR'S NEWS. Text in English. 1935. bi-m. USD 50 domestic to members; USD 60 foreign to members (effective 2003). adv. bk.rev. back issues avail. **Document type:** *Newsletter, Trade.* **Description:** Introduces new inventions, and presents articles to help inventors.
Published by: Inventors Clubs of America, PO Box 450261, Atlanta, GA 30345. TEL 404-938-5089. Ed. Alexander T Marinaccio. Adv. contact Frank Davis. Circ: 6,000.

500 600 ESP ISSN 0210-136X
INVESTIGACION Y CIENCIA. Text in Spanish. 1976. m. EUR 65 domestic (effective 2010). adv. bk.rev. bibl.; charts; illus. index. 96 p./no.; back issues avail. **Document type:** *Journal, Academic/Scholarly.* **Description:** Includes articles on research in sciences and technology written by the researchers themselves.
Related titles: ◆ Italian ed.: Le Scienze. ISSN 0036-8083; ◆ English ed.: Scientific American. ISSN 0036-8733; ◆ German ed.: Spektrum der Wissenschaft. ISSN 0170-2971; ◆ Hungarian ed.: Tudomany. ISSN 0237-322X; ◆ French ed.: Pour la Science. ISSN 0153-4092; ◆ Chinese ed.: Ke Xue. ISSN 1002-1299; ◆ Japanese ed.: Nikkei Saiensu. ISSN 0917-009X; ◆ Arabic ed.: Majallat al-Ulum; ◆ Polish ed.: Swiat Nauki. ISSN 0867-6380; Turkish ed.: Bilim.
Indexed: A22, GeoRef, IECT, P30, SpeleolAb.
—IE, Infotrieve. **CCC.**
Published by: Prensa Cientifica S.A., Muntaner, 339, pral. 1a, Barcelona, 08021, Spain. TEL 34-93-414344, FAX 34-93-4145413. Circ: 25,600 (paid).

500 620 370 CHL ISSN 0717-0610
➤ **INVESTIGACION Y DESARROLLO.** Key Title: Revista de Investigacion y Desarrollo. Text in Spanish; Summaries in English, Spanish. 1994. a., latest vol.8, 2002. USD 10 (effective 2003). adv. abstr.; charts; illus.; stat. 70 p./no.; back issues avail. **Document type:** *Journal, Academic/Scholarly.* **Description:** Presents research in all areas completed by the university's faculty.
Published by: Universidad de La Serena, Facultad de Ciencias, Casilla 554, IV Region, La Serena, Coquimbo, Chile. TEL 56-51-204461, FAX 56-51-204391, http://www.uls.cl. Ed. Jorge Cepeda. R&P, Adv. contact Jose Valderrama.

500 620 MEX ISSN 1606-8165
INVESTIGACION Y DESARROLLO. Text in Spanish. 1998. m. **Document type:** *Newspaper, Consumer.*
Media: Online - full text. **Related titles:** ◆ Supplement to: La Jornada (Online). ISSN 1563-7476.
Published by: D E M O S - Desarrollo de Medios S.A. de C.V., Ave Cuauhtemoc 1236, Col Santa Cruz Atoyac, Mexico City, DF 03310, Mexico. TEL 52-5-262-4300, FAX 52-5-262-4356, jornada@condor.dgsca.unam.mx, http://unam.netgate.net/jornada/.

500 371.3 BRA ISSN 1518-9384
Q181.A1
➤ **INVESTIGACOES EM ENSINO DE CIENCIAS.** Text in Multiple languages. 1996. 3/yr. **Document type:** *Journal, Academic/Scholarly.*
Related titles: Online - full text ed.: ISSN 1518-8795. free (effective 2011).
Published by: Universidade Federal do Rio Grande do Sul, Instituto de Fisica, Campus do Vale, Porto Alegre, RS 91501-970, Brazil. ienci@if.ufrgs.br. Ed. Marco Antonio Moreira.

500 USA ISSN 1942-7794
▼ ➤ **THE INVESTIGATIVE SCIENCES JOURNAL.** Text in English. 2009. q. free (effective 2010). **Document type:** *Journal, Academic/Scholarly.* **Description:** Provides original research reports, evaluated practices, legal and policy analysis related to the investigative process.
Media: Online - full content.
Published by: James Adcock, Ed.& Pub., 1 Campbell Ave, No 54, West Haven, CT 06516. TEL 203-545-6546, isjournal@hotmail.com.

➤ **IO.** *see* ART

500 USA ISSN 0896-8381
Q11 CODEN: JIASEB
➤ **IOWA ACADEMY OF SCIENCE. JOURNAL.** Text in English. 1880. q. USD 22 domestic to non-members; USD 27 foreign to non-members; free to members (effective 2011). adv. charts; illus. back issues avail.; reprints avail. **Document type:** *Journal, Academic/Scholarly.* **Description:** Contains articles which covers all areas of science, and also on biological sciences, conservation, and Iowa related research.
Former titles (until 1988): Iowa Academy of Science. Proceedings (0085-2236); (until 1889): Iowa Academy of Science. Proceedings
Related titles: Microform ed.: (from PQC); Online - full text ed.
Indexed: A01, A03, A08, A22, A29, ASFA, Agr, B20, B21, B25, BIOSIS Prev, CA, CIN, ChemAb, ChemTitl, E17, EIP, ESPM, EntAb, GeoRef, I10, Inspec, MycolAb, SASA, SWRA, SpeleolAb, T02, VirolAbstr, WildRev, Z01.
—BLDSC (4802.529000), AskIEEE, CASDDS, IE, Ingenta, INIST, Linda Hall. **CCC.**
Published by: Iowa Academy of Science, 175 Baker Hall, University of Northern Iowa, 2607 Campus St, Cedar Falls, IA 50614. TEL 319-273-2021, FAX 319-273-2807, iascience@uni.edu. Ed. James Shiver TEL 641-628-5162.

500 IRN ISSN 1607-4033
CODEN: TUSQAD
➤ **IRANIAN INTERNATIONAL JOURNAL OF SCIENCE.** Text in English, French, German. 1984. s-a. IRR 5,000; USD 20 in Africa and Asia; USD 40 elsewhere. **Document type:** *Journal, Academic/Scholarly.* **Description:** Publishes papers dealing with different aspects of science, including biology, chemistry, geology, mathematics and computer science, and physics.
Formerly (until 2000): University of Tehran. Journal of Science (International Edition) (1026-5139); Supersedes in part: University of Tehran. Faculty of Science. Quarterly Bulletin (0042-0131)
Related titles: Online - full text ed.
Indexed: CCMJ, INIS AtomInd, Inspec, MSN, MathR, Z02.
—CASDDS, INIST.
Published by: (University of Tehran/Danishgah-i Tihran), University of Teheran Press Co., PO Box 14155-6455, Teheran, Iran. TEL 98-21-6113305, FAX 98-21-6405141, jsut@khayam.ut.ac.ir. Ed. M R Rezaee.

500 600 IRN ISSN 1028-6276
T1 CODEN: IJSTBT
➤ **IRANIAN JOURNAL OF SCIENCE AND TECHNOLOGY. TRANSACTION A: SCIENCE.** Text in English; Summaries in English, Persian, Modern. 1971. 2/yr. IRR 110,000, USD 120 to individuals; IRR 40,000 newsstand/cover (effective 2005). adv. bk.rev. abstr.; bibl.; charts. back issues avail.; reprints avail. **Document type:** *Journal, Academic/Scholarly.* **Description:** Publishes theoretical, fundamental and experimental research papers from the engineering disciplines and all areas of basic science.
Supersedes in part (in 1995): Iranian Journal of Science and Technology (0360-1307)
Related titles: CD-ROM ed.; E-mail ed.: (from PQC).
Indexed: A32, ApMecR, B21, B25, BIOSIS Prev, CCMJ, CIN, ChemAb, ChemTitl, ESPM, INIS AtomInd, ImmunAb, Inspec, MSN, MathR, MycolAb, OceAb, SCI, SCOPUS, SWRA, ToxAb, VirolAbstr, W07, Z01, Z02.
—BLDSC (4567.529500), AskIEEE, CASDDS, IE, Ingenta, Linda Hall.
Published by: Shiraz University, School of Engineering, Iranian Journal of Science & Technology, Shiraz, Iran. TEL 97-711-2282113, ijst_trans_a@susc.ac.ir. Ed. M. R. Eskandari. Circ: 1,000 (paid).

500.9 GBR ISSN 0021-1311
QH1 CODEN: INAJA4
➤ **THE IRISH NATURALISTS' JOURNAL.** Text in English. 1892. s-a. GBP 22, EUR 35 to individuals; GBP 40, EUR 55, USD 65 to institutions; GBP 8, EUR 12 to students (effective 2009). bk.rev. bibl.; illus. cum.index every 3 yrs. back issues avail. **Document type:** *Journal, Academic/Scholarly.* **Description:** Features short papers and notes on a wide range of topics relating to the natural environment of Ireland, including botany, zoology, geology rock, and obituaries.
Formerly (until 1925): Irish Naturalist (2009-2598)
Indexed: A22, A29, A34, A37, ASFA, B20, B21, B23, B25, BIOSIS Prev, BrGeoL, CABA, E12, E17, ESPM, EntAb, F08, F12, GeoRef, H16, H17, I10, IBR, IBZ, IndVet, LT, MycolAb, P32, P33, PGegResA, R07, R08, RM&VM, RRTA, S13, S16, SCOPUS, SpeleolAb, VS, VirolAbstr, W08, W10, Z01.
—BLDSC (4574.000000), IE, Ingenta, INIST, Linda Hall. **CCC.**
Published by: Irish Naturalists' Journal Ltd., c/o Mike Simms, Secretary, National Museums Northern Ireland, 153 Bangor Rd, Cultra, Holywood, Co. Down BT18 0EU, United Kingdom. michael.simms@nmni.com. Ed. Dr. Robin N Govier.

500 600 IRL ISSN 0791-878X
Q1
THE IRISH SCIENTIST. Text in English. 1994. a.
Indexed: INIS AtomInd.
Published by: Oldbury Publishing, 55 Kimmage Rd W, Dublin, 12, Ireland. TEL 353-1-4652310, FAX 353-1-4652311. Ed., Pub. Geraldine Van Esbeck.

509 USA ISSN 0021-1753
Q1 CODEN: ISISA4
➤ **ISIS;** international review devoted to the history of science and its cultural influences. Text in English. 1912. q. USD 475 combined subscription to institutions (print & online eds.) (effective 2012). adv. bk.rev. bibl.; charts; illus. Index. 212 p./no.; back issues avail.; reprint service avail. from PSC. **Document type:** *Journal, Academic/Scholarly.* **Description:** Features scholarly articles, research notes and commentary on the history of science, medicine, and technology, and their cultural influences.

Related titles: Microfiche ed.: (from PQC); Microfilm ed.: (from PMC, PQC); Online - full text ed.: ISSN 1545-6994. 2002 (Mar.). USD 402 to institutions (effective 2012).
Indexed: A01, A03, A06, A08, A20, A21, A22, A25, A26, A33, ABS&EES, Acal, AmH&L, AmHI, ArtHuCI, B04, B07, B14, BRD, BRI, BiolDig, CA, CBRI, CCMJ, CIS, ChemAb, CurCont, DIP, E08, EMBASE, ExcerpMed, FR, G03, G08, GSA, GSI, GeoRef, H07, H08, H09, H10, HAb, HistAb, HumInd, I05, I07, I14, IBR, IBSS, IBZ, IPB, ISR, IndMed, Inspec, MEDLINE, MLA-IB, MSN, MathR, P02, P10, P11, P13, P26, P30, P42, P48, P52, P53, P54, P56, PCI, PQC, PSA, PhilInd, R05, RI-1, RI-2, RefSour, S02, S03, S05, S08, S09, S10, S23, SCI, SCOPUS, SOPODA, SSA, SSCI, SociolAb, SpeleolAb, T02, W03, W04, W07, Z02.
—BLDSC (4583.000000), AskIEEE, CASDDS, GNLM, IE, Infotrieve, Ingenta, INIST, Linda Hall. **CCC.**
Published by: (University of Chicago, History of Science Society), University of Chicago Press, 1427 E 60th St, Chicago, IL 60637. TEL 773-702-7600, FAX 773-702-0694, subscriptions@press.uchicago.edu. Ed. Bernard Lightman TEL 416-650-8278. Adv. contact Cheryl Jones TEL 773-702-7361. **Subscr. to:** PO Box 370050, Chicago, IL 60637. TEL 773-753-3347, 877-705-1878, FAX 773-753-0811, 877-705-1879.

➤ **ISLAM & SCIENCE.** *see* RELIGIONS AND THEOLOGY—Islamic

500 PAK ISSN 0304-5218
Q1 CODEN: IJSCDE
ISLAMABAD JOURNAL OF SCIENCES. Text in English. 1974. irreg. **Document type:** *Journal, Academic/Scholarly.*
Formerly (until 1975): University of Islamabad. Journal of Mathematics and Sciences (0304-9906)
Indexed: Inspec, MathR.
—AskIEEE, CASDDS, Linda Hall.
Published by: Quaid-i-Azam University, Department of Physics, c/o Bookshop, Bookbank and Publication Cell, Islamabad, Pakistan. TEL 812563. Ed. Dr. Kamaluddin Ahmed.

500 610 TUR
Q80.T8
➤ **ISLAMIC ACADEMY OF SCIENCES. MEDICAL JOURNAL.** Text in English. 1988 (Aug.). q. adv. bk.rev.; Website rev. abstr.; charts; illus.; stat. back issues avail. **Document type:** *Journal, Academic/Scholarly.* **Description:** Presents results of original research in different scientific disciplines.
Formerly (until Aug. 2000): Islamic Academy of Sciences. Journal (1016-3360)
Related titles: CD-ROM ed.; Diskette ed.; E-mail ed.; Fax ed.; Microfilm ed.; Online - full text ed.: free (effective 2009).
Indexed: PerIslam.
Published by: (Islamic Academy of Sciences JOR), Anadolu Health and Research Foundation, Kizilay, Mithatpasa Caddesi 66-5, Ankara, 06420, Turkey. TEL 90-312-4250319, FAX 90-312-4259487. Ed. Naci M Bor. Circ: 1,000 (paid). **Co-sponsor:** Organization of Islamic Conference, Standing Committee on Scientific Cooperation.

➤ **ISLE OF MAN NATURAL HISTORY AND ANTIQUARIAN SOCIETY. PROCEEDINGS.** *see* HISTORY

500 RUS ISSN 1819-4192
ISSLEDOVANO V ROSSII/INVESTIGATED IN RUSSIA; elektronnyi mnogopredmetnyi nauchnyi zhurnal. Text in Russian. 1998. a. free. **Document type:** *Journal, Academic/Scholarly.*
Media: Online - full content.
Indexed: Z01.
Published by: Moskovskii Fiziko-Tekhnicheskii Institut, c/o Veselago Viktor, PO Box 70, Moscow, 119311, Russian Federation. http://www.mipt.ru. Ed. N N Kudryavtsev.

338.926 USA ISSN 0748-5492
Q124.6
➤ **ISSUES IN SCIENCE AND TECHNOLOGY.** Text in English. 1984. q. USD 48 domestic to individuals; USD 75 foreign to individuals; USD 126 domestic to institutions; USD 141 foreign to institutions; USD 12 newsstand/cover (effective 2012). adv. bk.rev. illus. Index. back issues avail.; reprints avail. **Document type:** *Journal, Academic/Scholarly.* **Description:** A journal of ideas and opinions, exploring the policy implications of developments in science, technology and health.
Related titles: Microform ed.: (from PQC); Online - full text ed.: ISSN 1938-1557.
Indexed: A01, A02, A03, A08, A09, A10, A11, A20, A22, A25, A26, A29, ABIPC, ARG, ASCA, ASIP, AbAn, Acal, Agr, B04, B20, B21, BRD, BiolDig, C05, C10, C12, CA, CADCAM, CCR, CPEI, CPerI, CTA, ChemoAb, CommAb, CompD, CurCont, E03, E07, E08, E11, EIA, ERI, ESPM, EnerInd, EngInd, EnvAb, EnvInd, FamI, FutSurv, G03, G05, G06, G07, G08, GSA, GSI, GeoRef, H&SSA, HPNRM, HRIS, I05, I06, I07, I10, IPARL, ISR, M&GPA, M01, M02, M06, MASUSE, MCR, MagInd, NSA, ORMS, P02, P04, P10, P11, P13, P15, P18, P26, P30, P34, P48, P52, P53, P54, P56, PAIS, PQC, PollutAb, QC&AS, R03, RGAb, RGPR, RI-1, RI-2, RefZh, RiskAb, S04, S06, S08, S09, S10, S23, SCI, SCOPUS, SSCI, SSciA, SWRA, SociolAb, SpeleolAb, T02, T04, TelAb, Telegen, V03, V04, VirolAbstr, W03, W05, W07, WBA, WMB.
—IE, Infotrieve, Ingenta, Linda Hall. **CCC.**
Published by: (National Academy of Sciences, National Academy of Engineering), University of Texas at Dallas, Cecil and Ida Green Center for the Study of Science and Society, 800 W Campbell Rd, Richardson, TX 75080-3021. TEL 972-883-6323, FAX 972-883-6327, http://www.utdallas.edu. Ed. Kevin Finneran.

500 ITA ISSN 0075-1499
ISTITUTO E MUSEO DI STORIA DELLA SCIENZA. BIBLIOTECA. Text in Italian. 1957. irreg., latest vol.8, 1970. price varies. **Document type:** *Monographic series, Academic/Scholarly.*
Published by: (Istituto e Museo di Storia della Scienza), Casa Editrice Leo S. Olschki, Viuzzo del Pozzetto 8, Florence, 50126, Italy. TEL 39-055-6530684, FAX 39-055-6530214, celso@olschki.it, http://www.olschki.it. Ed. Paolo Galluzzi. Circ: 1,000.

500 ITA ISSN 0392-9523
Q54 CODEN: RLMAAK
ISTITUTO LOMBARDO. ACCADEMIA DI SCIENZE E LETTERE. RENDICONTI. A: SCIENZE MATEMATICHE E APPLICAZIONI. Text in Multiple languages. 1868 (vol.107). a. price varies. **Document type:** *Monographic series, Academic/Scholarly.*
Formerly (until 1980): Istituto Lombardo Accademia di Scienze e Lettere. Rendiconti. A: Scienze Matematiche, Fisiche, Chimiche e Geologiche (0021-2504); Supersedes in part (in 1957): Istituto Lombardo di Scienze e Lettere. Rendiconti. Classe di Scienze Matematiche e Naturali. (0375-9164); Which was formerly (until 1943): Reale Istituto Lombardo di Scienze e Lettere. Classe di Scienze Matematiche e Naturali (0393-9286); (until 1936): Reale Istituto Lombardo di Scienze e Lettere. Rendiconti (0393-893X)
Indexed: ApMecR, BibLing, CCMJ, CIS, GeoRef, Inspec, MLA, MLA-IB, MSN, MathR, RASB, SpeleolAb, Z02.
—CASDDS, INIST.
Published by: Istituto Lombardo Accademia di Scienze e Lettere, Via Borgonuovo 25, Milan, 20121, Italy. TEL 39-02-864087, FAX 39-02-86461388, Istituto.lombardo@unimi.it, http://www.istitutolombardo.it.

500 ITA ISSN 0392-9531
CODEN: RILMEY
ISTITUTO LOMBARDO. ACCADEMIA DI SCIENZE E LETTERE. RENDICONTI. B: SCIENZE CHIMICHE E FISICHE, GEOLOGICHE, BIOLOGICHE E MEDICHE. Text in Multiple languages. 1868. a. price varies. **Document type:** *Monographic series, Academic/Scholarly.*
Formerly (until 1979): Istituto Lombardo. Accademia di Scienze e Lettere. Rendiconti. B: Scienze Biologiche e Mediche (0535-8582); Supersedes in part (in 1957): Istituto Lombardo di Scienze e Lettere. Rendiconti. Classe di Scienze Matematiche e Naturali (0375-9164); Which was formerly (until 1943): Reale Istituto Lombardo di Scienze e Lettere. Rendiconti. Classe di Scienze Matematiche e Naturali (0393-9286); (until 1936): Reale Istituto Lombardo di Scienze e Lettere. Rendiconti. (0393-893X)
Indexed: B25, BIOSIS Prev, MycolAb.
—INIST, Linda Hall.
Published by: Istituto Lombardo Accademia di Scienze e Lettere, Via Borgonuovo 25, Milan, 20121, Italy. TEL 39-02-864087, FAX 39-02-86461388, Istituto.lombardo@unimi.it, http://www.istitutolombardo.it.

500 ITA ISSN 0392-6680
Q54 CODEN: AIVNDZ
ISTITUTO VENETO DI SCIENZE, LETTERE ED ARTI. ATTI. CLASSE DI SCIENZE FISICHE, MATEMATICHE E NATURALI. Text in Multiple languages. 1935. a. **Document type:** *Monographic series, Academic/Scholarly.*
Former titles (until 1978): Istituto Veneto di Scienze, Lettere ed Arti. Classe di Scienze Matematiche e Naturali (0373-255X); (until 1949): Reale Istituto Veneto di Scienze, Lettere ed Arti. Parte Seconda. Classe di Scienze Matematiche e Naturali. Atti (0392-9434); (until 1938): Reale Istituto Veneto di Scienze, Lettere ed Arti. Parte Seconda. Scienze Matematiche e Naturali. Atti (0365-3528)
Indexed: GeoRef, Z02.
—INIST, Linda Hall.
Published by: Istituto Veneto di Scienze, Lettere ed Arti, Campo S Stefano 2945, Venezia, 30124, Italy. TEL 39-041-2407711, FAX 39-041-5210598, ivsla@istitutoveneto.it, http://www.istitutoveneto.it.

500 ITA ISSN 0373-2541
AS222.V495
ISTITUTO VENETO DI SCIENZE, LETTERE ED ARTI. ATTI. CLASSE SCIENZE MORALI, FISICHE E PARTE GENERALE E ATTI UFFICIALI. Text in Italian. 1951. every 3 mos. **Document type:** *Monographic series, Academic/Scholarly.*
—Linda Hall.
Published by: Istituto Veneto di Scienze, Lettere ed Arti, Campo S Stefano 2945, Venezia, 30124, Italy. TEL 39-041-2407711, FAX 39-041-5210598, http://www.istitutoveneto.it.

500 700 800 ITA ISSN 1122-3642
ISTITUTO VENETO DI SCIENZE, LETTERE ED ARTI. CLASSE DI SCIENZE FISICHE, MATEMATICHE E NATURALI. MEMORIE. Text in Italian. 1843. irreg. **Document type:** *Monographic series, Academic/Scholarly.*
Formerly (until 1990): Istituto Veneto di Scienze, Lettere ed Arti. Classe di Scienze Matematiche e Naturali. Memorie (1122-3634); Which superseded in part (in 1956): Reale Istituto Veneto di Scienze, Lettere ed Arti. Memorie (0393-8433); Which was formerly (until 1868): Imperiale Reale Istituto Veneto di Scienze Lettere ed Arti. Memorie (0393-957X)
Indexed: CCMJ, MSN, MathR.
—Linda Hall.
Published by: Istituto Veneto di Scienze, Lettere ed Arti, Campo S Stefano 2945, Venezia, 30124, Italy. TEL 39-041-2407711, FAX 39-041-5210598, ivsla@istitutoveneto.it, http://www.istitutoveneto.it.

500 ITA
ISTITUTO VENETO DI SCIENZE, LETTERE ED ARTI. SAGGI. Text in Italian. irreg. **Document type:** *Monographic series, Academic/Scholarly.*
Published by: Istituto Veneto di Scienze, Lettere ed Arti, Campo S Stefano 2945, Venezia, 30124, Italy. TEL 39-041-2407711, FAX 39-041-5210598, ivsla@istitutoveneto.it, http://www.istitutoveneto.it.

500 ITA
ISTITUTO VENETO DI SCIENZE, LETTERE ED ARTI. STORIA DELLA SCIENZE. SEMINARI. Text in Italian. irreg. **Document type:** *Monographic series, Academic/Scholarly.*
Published by: Istituto Veneto di Scienze, Lettere ed Arti, Campo S Stefano 2945, Venezia, 30124, Italy. TEL 39-041-2407711, FAX 39-041-5210598, ivsla@istitutoveneto.it, http://www.istitutoveneto.it.

509 RUS
ISTORIYA NAUKI I TEKHNIKI. Text in Russian. 2002. m. USD 168 foreign (effective 2006). **Document type:** *Journal.*
Published by: NauchTekhLitIzdat, Alymov per, dom 17, str 2, Moscow, 107258, Russian Federation. TEL 7-095-2690004, FAX 7-095-3239010, pribor@tgizdat.ru. **Dist. by:** East View Information Services, 10601 Wayzata Blvd, Minneapolis, MN 55305. TEL 952-252-1201, 800-477-1005, FAX 952-252-1202, info@eastview.com, http://www.eastview.com.

500 JPN ISSN 0287-3532
IWATANI NAOJI KINEN ZAIDAN KENKYU HOKOKUSHO/IWATANI NAOJI FOUNDATION. RESEARCH REPORT. Text in Japanese; Summaries in English, Japanese. 1977. a.
Published by: Iwatani Naoji Kinen Zaidan/Iwatani Naoji Foundation, TBR Bldg, 10-2 Nagata-cho 2-chome, Chiyoda-ku, Tokyo, 100-0014, Japan.

500 300 JPN ISSN 0385-4132
CODEN: KKNDDL
IWATE MEDICAL UNIVERSITY SCHOOL OF LIBERAL ARTS & SCIENCES. ANNUAL REPORT/IWATE IKA DAIGAKU KYOYOBU NENPO. Text in English, German, Japanese. 1966. a. free. back issues avail. **Document type:** *Bulletin.* **Description:** Reports of studies by faculty staff.
Related titles: Online - full text ed.
Indexed: RILM.
—CASDDS.
Published by: Iwate Ika Daigaku Kyoyobu/Iwate Medical University School of Liberal Arts & Sciences, 16-1 Honchi-Yodori 3-chome, Morioka-shi, Iwate-ken 020-0015, Japan. TEL 0196-51-5111, FAX 0196-25-5816. Ed., R&P Sadaaki Watanabe. Circ: 330 (controlled).

500 USA ISSN 1524-5047
CODEN: SJCREM
J C R SCIENCE EDITION. (Journal Citation Reports) Key Title: Journal Citation Reports on Microfiche (Science Edition). Text in English. 1975. a. **Document type:** *Journal, Academic/Scholarly.* **Description:** Contains feature articles in the areas of science, technology, and the social sciences.
Former titles (until 1997): S C I - J C R (Microform); (until 1989): S C I Journal Citation Reports (Print) (0161-3170); (until 1977): Journal Citation Reports (0361-1884)
Media: Microform. **Related titles:** CD-ROM ed.: Journal Citation Reports on CD-ROM (Science Edition). ISSN 1082-6661; Online - full text ed.: J C R Web Science Edition; ♦ Series: J C R Social Sciences Edition. ISSN 1524-5055.
—BLDSC (4958.369070), Linda Hall.
Published by: Thomson Reuters (Subsidiary of: Thomson Reuters Corp.), 1500 Spring Garden, 4th Fl, Philadelphia, PA 19130. TEL 215-386-0100, 800-336-4474, FAX 215-386-2911, general.info@thomson.com, http://science.thomsonreuters.com/.

500 FRA ISSN 1638-5705
J3EA; journal sur l'enseignement des sciences et technologies de l'information et des systemes. Text in French. irreg. free (effective 2012). **Document type:** *Journal, Academic/Scholarly.*
Media: Online - full text.
—Linda Hall.
Published by: E D P Sciences, 17 Ave du Hoggar, Parc d'Activites de Courtaboeuf, BP 112, Cedex A, Les Ulis, F-91944, France. TEL 33-1-69187575, FAX 33-1-69860678, subscribers@edpsciences.org, http://www.edpsciences.org.

508 NLD ISSN 1375-5692
JAARBOEK ECOLOGISCHE GESCHIEDENIS. Text in Dutch. 1998. a. EUR 14.90 (effective 2008). **Document type:** *Journal, Academic/Scholarly.*
Published by: Uitgeverij Verloren, Torenlaan 25, Hilversum, 1211 JA, Netherlands. TEL 31-35-6859856, FAX 31-35-6836557, info@verloren.nl.

500 PAK ISSN 0021-3888
JADEED SCIENCE. Text in Urdu; Summaries in English, German. 1956. bi-m. PKR 15, USD 3. adv. bk.rev. illus.
Indexed: RASB.
Published by: Scientific Society of Pakistan, University of Karachi, Dept. of Zoology, Karachi 32, Pakistan. Ed. Aftab Hassan. Circ: 2,000.

500 BGD ISSN 1012-2958
JAHANGIRNAGAR REVIEW. PART A, SCIENCE. Text in English. 1977. a.
Indexed: Inspec.
Published by: Jahangirnagar University, Savar, Dhaka, 1342, Bangladesh. FAX 880-2-7708478, registr@juniv.edu, http://www.juniv.edu/.

500 DEU ISSN 1860-7837
Q127.E85
JAHRBUCH FUER EUROPAEISCHE WISSENSCHAFTSKULTUR/ YEARBOOK FOR EUROPEAN CULTURE OF SCIENCE. Text in English, French, German, Italian. 2005. a. EUR 52; EUR 54 per issue (effective 2012). **Document type:** *Journal, Academic/Scholarly.*
Indexed: PhilInd.
Published by: Franz Steiner Verlag GmbH, Birkenwaldstr 44, Stuttgart, 70191, Germany. TEL 49-711-25820, FAX 49-711-2582290, service@steiner-verlag.de, http://www.steiner-verlag.de. Eds. Olaf Breidbach, Stefano Poggi.

500 DEU ISSN 0173-7600
HT391
➤ **JAHRBUCH FUER REGIONALWISSENSCHAFT**; review of regional research. Text in English, German. 1980. s-a. EUR 221, USD 239 combined subscription to institutions (print & online eds.) (effective 2012). back issues avail.; reprint service avail. from PSC. **Document type:** *Journal, Academic/Scholarly.* **Description:** Provides new contributions to theoretical as well as empirical issues in regional science.
Related titles: Online - full text ed.: ISSN 1613-9836 (from IngentaConnect).
Indexed: A22, A26, E01, EconLit, GEOBASE, IBR, IBSS, IBZ, JEL, SCOPUS.
—IE, Ingenta. **CCC.**
Published by: (Gesellschaft fuer Regionalforschung), Springer (Subsidiary of: Springer Science+Business Media), Tiergartenstr 17, Heidelberg, 69121, Germany. TEL 49-6221-4870, FAX 49-6221-345229, subscriptions@springer.com. Ed. Klaus Schoeler. Circ: 800. **Subscr. in the Americas to:** Springer New York LLC, Journal Fulfillment, PO Box 2485, Secaucus, NJ 07096. TEL 800-777-4643, 201-348-4033, FAX 201-348-4505, journals-ny@springer.com, http://www.springer.com; **Subscr. to:** Springer Distribution Center, Kundenservice Zeitschriften, Haberstr 7, Heidelberg 69126, Germany. TEL 49-6221-3454303, FAX 49-6221-3454229.

500 170 DEU ISSN 1430-9017
JAHRBUCH FUER WISSENSCHAFT UND ETHIK. Text in German, English. 1996. a. EUR 65, USD 98 to institutions; EUR 75, USD 113 combined subscription to institutions (print & online eds.) (effective 2012). reprint service avail. from SCH. **Document type:** *Journal, Academic/Scholarly.* **Description:** Provides a forum for interdisciplinary discussions on ethical questions arising from modern developments in science and technology.
Related titles: Online - full text ed.: ISSN 1613-1142. EUR 65, USD 98 to institutions (effective 2012).
Indexed: A01, A26, IBR, IBZ, PhilInd, T02.

S

—CCC.
Published by: Walter de Gruyter GmbH & Co. KG, Genthiner Str 13, Berlin, 10785, Germany. TEL 49-30-260050, FAX 49-30-26005251, info@degruyter.com.

500 DEU ISSN 0949-2364
Q49 CODEN: LEOPAS
JAHRBUCH LEOPOLDINA (REIHE 3). (Reihe 1: 1859-1923; Reihe 2: 1926-1930) Text in German. 1955. a. bk.rev. **Document type:** *Journal, Academic/Scholarly.*
Formerly (until 1992): Leopoldina (0323-4444)
Indexed: DIP, GeoRef, IBR, IBZ, P30, SpeleolAb.
—BLDSC (4619.506000), GNLM, Linda Hall. **CCC.**
Published by: Deutsche Akademie der Naturforscher Leopoldina, Emil-Abderhalden-Str 35, Halle, 06108, Germany. TEL 49-345-472390, FAX 49-345-4723919, leopoldina@leopoldina-halle.de, http://www.leopoldina-halle.de. Ed. Joachim Kaasch. Circ: 1,500.

500 JAM ISSN 1016-2054
Q29
➤ **JAMAICAN JOURNAL OF SCIENCE AND TECHNOLOGY.** Text in English. 1970. a. JMD 150 to individual members; USD 40 to individuals; JMD 150, USD 40 to institutions (effective 2001). adv. illus.; abstr.; charts; maps. 100 p./no.; **Document type:** *Journal, Academic/Scholarly.* **Description:** Publishes scientific research papers based on original data on research of interest and relevance to Jamaica.
Formerly (until 1989): Scientific Research Council of Jamaica. Journal (0036-8822); Supersedes: Scientific Research Council. Information
Indexed: ChemAb, GeoRef, SpeleolAb, Z01.
Published by: Scientific Research Council, PO Box 350, Kingston, 6, Jamaica. TEL 876-927-1771, FAX 876-927-1840, infosrc@cwjamaica.com. Ed. Tara P Dasgupta. R&P Tara Dasgupta. Adv. contact Andrews Woods. B&W page JMD 2,000. Circ: 2,500.

500 SAU ISSN 1319-1012
JAME'AT AL-MALIK 'ABDUL 'AZIZ. MAJALA. AL-'U'LUM/KING ABDUL AZIZ UNIVERSITY. JOURNAL. SCIENCE. Text in Arabic, English. 1989. a. **Document type:** *Journal, Academic/Scholarly.*
Related titles: Online - full text ed.: ISSN 1658-4252.
Indexed: A01.
Published by: King Abdulaziz University, Scientific Publishing Center/ Markaz al-Nashr al-'Ilmi Jami'at al-Malik 'Abd al-'Aziz, PO Box 80200, Jeddah21589, Saudi Arabia. TEL 966-26452017, publisher@kau.edu.sa, http://spc.kau.edu.sa/content.aspx?Site_ID=320&lng=EN&cid=2732&URL=www.kau.edu.sa.

500 JPN ISSN 0386-2208
QH301 CODEN: PJABDW
➤ **JAPAN ACADEMY. PROCEEDINGS. SERIES B: PHYSICAL AND BIOLOGICAL SCIENCES/NIPPON GAKUSHIIN KIYO B.** Text in English. 1912. 10/yr. **Document type:** *Journal, Academic/Scholarly.*
Supersedes in part (in 1977, vol.53): Japan Academy. Proceedings (0021-4280); Which was formerly (until 1945): The Imperial Academy. Proceedings (0369-9846)
Related titles: Microform ed.: (from PMC); Online - full text ed.: ISSN 1349-2896. free (effective 2011).
Indexed: A20, A22, A34, A35, A36, A38, A39, ASCA, ASFA, AgBio, B21, B25, BIOSIS Prev, C25, C27, C29, C30, CABA, CIN, CTA, ChemAb, ChemTitl, ChemoAb, CurCont, D01, D03, D04, E12, E13, EMBASE, ExcerpMed, F08, F12, GH, GeoRef, H16, I11, IBR, IBZ, INIS AtomInd, ISR, IndVet, Inpharma, Inspec, MEDLINE, MathR, MycolAb, N02, N03, NSA, O01, P30, P32, P33, P40, PGegResA, R07, R08, R10, R11, R13, R14, Reac, RefZh, S13, S14, S15, S16, S18, SCI, SCOPUS, SoyAb, SpeleolAb, T05, VS, W07, W10, WildRev, Z01.
—BLDSC (6742.100000), AskIEEE, CASDDS, IE, Ingenta, INIST, Linda Hall.
Published by: Nippon Gakushiin/Japan Academy, The, 7-32, Ueno Park, Taito-ku, Tokyo, 110-0007, Japan. TEL 81-3-38222101, FAX 81-3-38222105, http://www.japan-acad.go.jp/. Ed. Setsuro Ebashi. **Subscr. to:** Maruzen Co., Ltd., Import & Export Dept, PO Box 5050, Tokyo International, Tokyo 100-3191, Japan. http://www.maruzen.co.jp.

501 JPN ISSN 0453-0691
Q174
➤ **JAPAN ASSOCIATION FOR PHILOSOPHY OF SCIENCE. ANNALS.** Text in English, German, French. 1956. a. JPY 2,400 per issue (effective 2000). **Document type:** *Journal, Academic/Scholarly.* **Description:** Contains topics of articles confined to fields within logic, methodology and/or philosophy of science. They deal with basic problems of interest to specialists in the fields of science and philosophy.
Indexed: AmHI, CA, CCMJ, H07, Inspec, MSN, MathR, PsycholAb, T02, Z02.
—Ingenta, Linda Hall.
Published by: Japan Association for Philosophy of Science/Kagaku Kisoron Gakkai, c/o Dept of Philosophy, Keio University, 2-15-45 Mita, Minato-ku, Tokyo, 108-0073, Japan. TEL 81-3-3453-4511 ext 3084, FAX 81-3-3798-7480. Ed., Pub., R&P Yoichiro Murakami. Circ: 750.

508 USA ISSN 1061-1878
QH1
➤ **JEFFERSONIANA.** Text in English. 1992. irreg., latest 2010. back issues avail. **Document type:** *Monographic series, Academic/ Scholarly.* **Description:** Provides information about Virginia.
Related titles: Online - full text ed.: free (effective 2010).
Indexed: Z01.
Published by: Virginia Museum of Natural History, 21 Starling Ave, Martinsville, VA 24112. TEL 276-634-4141, FAX 276-634-4199, information@vmnh.virginia.gov.

500 CHN ISSN 1008-1402
JIAMUSI DAXUE XUEBAON (ZIRAN KEXUE BAN)/JIAMUSI UNIVERSITY. JOURNAL (NATURAL SCIENCE EDITION). Text in Chinese; Abstracts in Chinese, English. 1983. bi-m. CNY 60, USD 120; CNY 10 newsstand/cover (effective 2009). **Document type:** *Journal, Academic/Scholarly.*
Formerly (until 1998): Jiamusi Gongxueyuan Xuebao (1003-1626)
Related titles: Online - full text ed.
Indexed: ESPM, M&GPA, PollutAb, SWRA.
Published by: Jiamusi Daxue/Jiamusi University, 148, Xuefu Jie, Jiamusi, 154007, China. TEL 86-454-8618600, FAX 86-454-8618600. Ed. Dong-hai Li.

500 CHN ISSN 1673-0143
JIANGHAN DAXUE XUEBAO (ZIRAN KEXUE BAN)/JIANGHAN UNIVERSITY. JOURNAL (NATURAL SCIENCE EDITION). Text in Chinese. 1973. q. USD 20.80 (effective 2009). **Document type:** *Journal, Academic/Scholarly.*
Formerly: Jianghan Daxue Xuebao (Yixue Ban)
Related titles: Online - full text ed.
Published by: Jianghan Daxue, Jingji Kaifa-qu, Wuhan, 430056, China.

500 CHN ISSN 1671-7147
JIANGNAN DAXUE XUEBAO (ZIRAN KEXUE BAN)/JIANGNAN UNIVERSITY. JOURNAL (NATURAL SCIENCE EDITION). Text in Chinese. 1998. bi-m. **Document type:** *Journal, Academic/Scholarly.*
Formerly (until 2001): Jiangnan Xueyuan Xuebao/Jiangnan College. Journal (1008-8547)
Related titles: Online - full text ed.: (from WanFang Data Corp.).
Indexed: RefZh.
—BLDSC (4668.455500).
Published by: Jiangnan Daxue Zazhishe/Jiangnan University Magazines Agency, 1800, Lihu Dadao, Wuxi, 214122, China. TEL 86-510-85913516, FAX 86-510-85913523, zzs@jiangnan.edu.cn, http://zzs.jiangnan.edu.cn/index.asp. Ed. Wei-dong Gao.

500 CHN ISSN 1671-7775
Q4 CODEN: JDXZA6
➤ **JIANGSU DAXUE XUEBAO (ZIRAN KEXUE BAN)/JIANGSU UNIVERSITY. JOURNAL (NATURE SCIENCE EDITION).** Text in English; Abstracts in Chinese, English. 1980. bi-m. CNY 36, USD 72; CNY 6, USD 12 newsstand/cover (effective 2009). **Document type:** *Journal, Academic/Scholarly.* **Description:** Covers the latest developments of theoretical and applied researches in the fields of engineerings, including agricultural machinery, storage and process engineering of agricultural product, machinery of irrigation and drainage, tractor, automobile, internal-combustion engine, fluid machinery, thermal energy, design and manufacture of machinery, mechanical and electronics engineering, casting, metal materials and thermal treatment, computer science, telecommunications, electrical technology, industrial automation, electrical information, civil engineering, etc.
Formed by the merger of: Zhenjiang Nongye Jije Xueyuan Xuebao; (1994-2002): Jiangsu Ligong Daxue Xuebao (Ziran Kexue Ban)/of Jiangsu University of Science and Technology. Journal (Nature Science Edition) (1007-1741); Which was formerly (1982-1993): Jiangsu Gongxueyuan Xuebao/Jiangsu Institute of Technology. Journal (1000-2014)
Related titles: Online - full text ed.
Indexed: A28, A32, A34, A37, APA, BA, BrCerAb, C&ISA, C25, C30, CA/WCA, CABA, CCMJ, CIA, CPEI, CerAb, CivEngAb, CorrAb, D01, E&CAJ, E11, E12, EEA, EMA, ESPM, EngInd, EnvEAb, F08, F11, F12, FCA, G11, GH, H15, H16, I11, M&TEA, M09, MBF, METADEX, MSN, MathR, N02, N04, O01, P32, P33, P40, PGegResA, PHN&I, R07, R08, R11, R13, RefZh, S12, S13, S16, SCOPUS, SWRA, SolStAb, SoyAb, T04, TAR, WAA, Z02.
—BLDSC (4668.457000), East View, Linda Hall.
Published by: Jiangsu Daxue/Jiangsu University, No.30 Mengxiyuan Lane, Zhenjiang, Jiangsu 212003, China. TEL 86-511-84446612, FAX 86-511-84446464, http://www.ujs.edu.cn/. Ed. Shouqi Yuan. Circ: 1,500. **Dist. by:** China International Book Trading Corp, 35 Chegongzhuang Xilu, Haidian District, PO Box 399, Beijing 100044, China. TEL 86-10-68412045, FAX 86-10-68412023, cibtc@mail.cibtc.com.cn, http://www.cibtc.com.cn.

500 CHN ISSN 1673-4807
VM4
JIANGSU KEJI DAXUE XUEBAO (ZIRAN KEXUE BAN)/JIANGSU UNIVERSITY OF SCIENCE AND TECHNOLOGY. JOURNAL (NATURAL SCIENCE). Text in Chinese. 1986. bi-m. USD 24.60 (effective 2009). **Document type:** *Journal, Academic/Scholarly.*
Former titles (until 2004): Huadong Chuanbo Gongye Xueyuan Xuebao/East China Shipbuilding Institute. Journal (1006-1088); (until 1992): Zhenjiang Chuanbo Xueyuan Xuebao/Zhenjiang Shipbuilding Institute. Journal (1000-5765)
Related titles: Online - full text ed.
Indexed: ASFA, OceAb, RefZh, SCOPUS, Z02.
—BLDSC (4668.460500), East View.
Published by: Jiangsu Keji Daxue/Jiangsu Unviersity of Science and Technology, 2, Mengxi Lu, Zhenjiang, 212003, China. TEL 86-511-4401109, FAX 86-511-4401105.

500 CHN ISSN 1001-3679
➤ **JIANGXI KEXUE/JIANGXI SCIENCE.** Text in Chinese; Summaries in English. 1983. q. USD 40 (effective 2000 & 2001). adv. cum.index. back issues avail.; reprints avail. **Document type:** *Academic/ Scholarly.* **Description:** Covers various fields of natural sciences such as agriculture, biology, chemistry, engineering, environmental sciences, mathematics, physics, and veterinary microbiology.
Related titles: CD-ROM ed.; Online - full text ed.
Published by: Jiangxi Sheng Kexueyuan/Jiangxi Academy of Sciences, 108 Shangfang Rd, Nanchang, Jiangxi 330029, China. TEL 86-791-8331714, FAX 86-791-8333149, http://www.chinajournal.net.cn, http://www.chinainfo.gov.cn/periodical. Ed. Yanxiong Liao. R&P, Adv. contact Jiahai Lin. Circ: 3,000.

500 CHN ISSN 1000-2286
JIANGXI NONGYE DAXUE XUEBAO/ACTA AGRICULTURAE UNIVERSITATIS JIANGXIENSIS (NATURAL SCIENCES EDITION). Text in Chinese. 1979. bi-m. USD 24.60 (effective 2009). **Document type:** *Journal, Academic/Scholarly.*
Related titles: Online - full text ed.
Indexed: A29, A34, A35, A36, A37, A38, ASFA, AgBio, AgrForAb, B20, B21, B23, BA, BP, C25, C30, CABA, D01, E11, E12, E17, ESPM, F08, F11, F12, FCA, G11, GH, GenetAb, H16, H17, I11, ImmunAb, IndVet, LT, MaizeAb, N02, N03, N04, N05, O01, OR, P32, P33, P37, P38, P39, P40, PGegResA, PGrRegA, PHN&I, PN&I, PollutAb, R07, R08, R11, R12, R13, RA&MP, RM&VM, RRTA, S12, S13, S16, S17, SSciA, SWRA, SoyAb, T04, TAR, TriticAb, VS, W10, W11, Z01.
—BLDSC (0588.690000), East View.
Published by: Jiangxi Nongye Daxue, Nanchang, Jiangxi 330045, China. TEL 86-791-3813246, FAX 86-791-3813740. **Dist. by:** China International Book Trading Corp, 35 Chegongzhuang Xilu, Haidian District, PO Box 399, Beijing 100044, China. TEL 86-10-68412045, FAX 86-10-68412023, cibtc@mail.cibtc.com.cn, http://www.cibtc.com.cn.

500 CHN ISSN 1000-5862
Q4 CODEN: JSXKF3
JIANGXI SHIFAN DAXUE XUEBAO (ZIRAN KEXUE BAN)/JIANGXI NORMAL UNIVERSITY. JOURNAL (NATURAL SCIENCE EDITION). Text in Chinese. 1957. bi-m. USD 24.60 (effective 2009). adv. 96 p./no.; **Document type:** *Journal, Academic/Scholarly.*
Related titles: Online - full text ed.
Indexed: A28, A32, APA, B21, BrCerAb, C&ISA, CA/WCA, CCMJ, CIA, CerAb, CivEngAb, CorrAb, E&CAJ, E11, EEA, EMA, ESPM, EnvEAb, H15, M&TEA, M09, MBF, METADEX, MSN, MathR, PollutAb, RASB, RefZh, SWRA, SolStAb, T04, WAA, Z02.
—CASDDS, East View, Linda Hall.
Published by: Jiangxi Shifan Daxue/Jiangxi Normal University, 437 Beijing Xilu, Nanchang, Jiangxi 330027, China. TEL 86-791-8506814, FAX 86-791-8506185. **Dist. overseas by:** China International Book Trading Corp, 35 Chegongzhuang Xilu, Haidian District, PO Box 399, Beijing 100044, China.

JIAOZUO SHIFAN GAODENG ZHUANKE XUEXIAO XUEBAO/ JIAOZUO TEACHERS COLLEGE. JOURNAL. *see* HUMANITIES: COMPREHENSIVE WORKS

500 600 CHN ISSN 1009-3443
Q4
JIEFANGJUN LIGONG DAXUE XUEBAO (ZIRAN KEXUE BAN)/P L A UNIVERSITY OF SCIENCE AND TECHNOLOGY (NATURAL SCIENCE EDITION). JOURNAL. Text in Chinese. 2000. bi-m. CNY 48; CNY 8 per issue (effective 2010). 204 p./no.; **Document type:** *Journal, Academic/Scholarly.*
Formed by the merger of (1980-1999): Kongjun Qixiang Xueyuan Xuebao/Airforce Institute of Meteorology. Journal (1006-5121); (1992-1999): Tongxin Gongcheng Xueyuan Xuebao/Communications Engineeing Institute. Journal; (1985-1999): Gongchengbing Gongcheng Xueyuan Xuebao
Related titles: Online - full text ed.
Indexed: A28, APA, ASFA, B21, BrCerAb, C&ISA, CA/WCA, CIA, CPEI, CerAb, CivEngAb, CorrAb, E&CAJ, E11, EEA, EMA, ESPM, EnvEAb, H&SSA, H15, Inspec, M&GPA, M&TEA, M09, MBF, METADEX, PollutAb, RefZh, SCOPUS, SWRA, SolStAb, T04, WAA, Z02.
—BLDSC (4668.901250), East View, Linda Hall.
Published by: Jiefangjun Ligong Daxue Xuebao/P L A (People's Liberation Army) University of Science and Technology, 1, Haifuxiang, Nanjing, 210007, China. TEL 86-25-4873670. **Dist. by:** China International Book Trading Corp, 35 Chegongzhuang Xilu, Haidian District, PO Box 399, Beijing 100044, China. TEL 86-10-68412045, FAX 86-10-68412023, cibtc@mail.cibtc.com.cn, http://www.cibtc.com.cn.

500 CZE ISSN 0139-8172
JIHOCESKE MUZEUM V CESKYCH BUDEJOVICICH. PRIRODNI VEDY. SBORNIK. Text in Czech. 1960. a. price varies. **Document type:** *Academic/Scholarly.*
Indexed: A37, ASFA, AgrForAb, B21, B23, C25, CABA, E12, ESPM, EntAb, F08, F12, G11, GeoRef, H16, I11, O01, OR, P32, P33, P40, PGegResA, R07, R08, R13, RA&MP, S13, S16, W10, Z01.
Published by: Jihoceske Muzeum v Ceskych Budejovicich, Dukelska 1, Ceske Budejovice, 37051, Czech Republic. TEL 42-38-7929311, FAX 42-38-6356447, info@muzeumct.cz, http://www.muzeumct.cz. Ed. Petr Burger.

500 CHN ISSN 1671-5489
Q4
JILIN DAXUE XUEBAO (LIXUE BAN)/JILIN UNIVERSITY. JOURNAL (SCIENCE EDITION). Text in Chinese; Abstracts in Chinese, English. 1955. bi-m. **Document type:** *Journal, Academic/Scholarly.*
Former titles (until 2002): Jilin Daxue Ziran Kexue Xuebao/Jilin University. Journal of Natural Science/Acta Scientiarum Naturalium Universitatis Jilinensis (0529-0279); (until 1978): Jilin Daxue Xuebao (Ziran Kexue Ban); (until 1965): Jilin Daxue Ziran Kexue Xuebao; (until 1958): Dongbei Renmin Daxue Ziran Kexue Xuebao/Acta Scientiarum Naturalium
Related titles: Online - full text ed.
Indexed: A28, APA, BrCerAb, C&ISA, CA/WCA, CCMJ, CIA, CerAb, CivEngAb, CorrAb, E&CAJ, E11, EEA, EMA, ESPM, EnvEAb, H15, Inspec, M&TEA, M09, MBF, METADEX, MSN, MathR, RefZh, SolStAb, T04, WAA, Z02.
—BLDSC (4809.597870), East View, Linda Hall.
Published by: Jilin Daxue/Jilin University, 2699, Qianjin Dajie, Changchun, 130023, China.

500 CHN ISSN 1674-3873
JILIN SHIFAN DAXUE XUEBAO (ZIRAN KEXUE BAN)/JILIN NORMAL UNIVERSITY JOURNAL (NATURAL SCIENCE EDITION). Text in Chinese. 1973. q. CNY 8 newsstand/cover (effective 2007). **Document type:** *Journal, Academic/Scholarly.*
Former titles (until 2003): Songliao Xuekan (Ziran Kexue Ban) (1000-1840); (until 1979): Siping Shiyuan Xuebao; (until 1978): Siping Shiyuan; (until 1974): Jiaoge Fenglei
Related titles: Online - full text ed.
Published by: Jilin Shifan Xueyuan, 1301, Haifeng Dajie, Tiexi-qu, Siping, 136000, China. TEL 86-434-3292015.

500 CHN ISSN 1007-7405
QH7
JIMEI DAXUE XUEBAO (ZIRAN KEXUE BAN)/JIMEI UNIVERSITY. JOURNAL (NATURAL SCIENCE). Text in Chinese. 1981. q. USD 10.80 (effective 2009). **Document type:** *Journal, Academic/Scholarly.* **Description:** Covers the breeding of aquatic products, natural resources, fishing facilities and environmental protection.
Supersedes (in 1996): Xiamen Shuichan Xueyuan Xuebao/Xiamen Institute of Aquatic Products. Journal (1000-5196); Jimei Hanghai Xueyuan Xuebao/Jimei Navigation Institute. Journal (1005-0663)
Related titles: Online - full text ed.
Indexed: A32, ASFA, B21, CTA, ESPM, NSA, PollutAb.
—East View.
Published by: Jimei Daxue/Jimei University, 1, Jimeijicen Lu, Xiamen, 361021, China. TEL 86-592-6181045.

500 610 CHN ISSN 1000-9965
CODEN: JDXUET
JINAN DAXUE XUEBAO (ZIRAN KEXUE YU YIXUE BAN)/JOURNAL OF JINAN UNIVERSITY (NATURAL SCIENCE AND MEDICINE EDITION). (First and third issues cover natural science; second and fourth issues cover medical science.) Text in Chinese; Contents page in English. 1980. bi-m. USD 24.60 (effective 2009). **Document type:** *Journal, Academic/Scholarly.*

Formerly (until 1989): Jinan Li-yi Xuebao - Jinan University. Journal of Science and Medicine (1000-5064)
Related titles: Online - full text ed.
Indexed: A22, A32, B20, B21, CIN, ChemAb, ChemTitl, E17, ESPM, ImmunAb, OGFA, SWRA, ToxAb, Z01.
—BLDSC (4809.599000), CASDDS, East View, IE, Ingenta.
Published by: Ji'nan Daxue, Xuebao Bianjibu/Jinan University, Journal Editorial Department, Rm. 216, 2nd Fl, Bldg. 75, Shipai, Guangzhou, Guangdong 510632, China. TEL 86-20-85227865, FAX 86-20-85220281. Ed., R&P Weiliang Wang. **Dist. by:** China International Book Trading Corp, 35 Chegongzhuang Xilu, Haidian District, PO Box 399, Beijing 100044, China. TEL 86-10-68412045, FAX 86-10-68412023, cibtc@mail.cibtc.com.cn, http://www.cibtc.com.cn.

JINGMEN ZHIYE JISHU XUEYUAN XUEBAO/JINGMEN TECHNICAL COLLEGE. JOURNAL. *see* SOCIAL SCIENCES: COMPREHENSIVE WORKS

500 CHN ISSN 1672-755X
JINLING KEJI XUEYUAN XUEBAO/JINLING INSTITUTE OF TECHNOLOGY. JOURNAL. Text in Chinese. 1985. q. CNY 8 newsstand/cover (effective 2010). **Document type:** *Journal, Academic/Scholarly.*
Supersedes in part: Jinling Zhiye Daxue Xuebao/Nanjing Polytechnic College. Journal (1008-4932); Nanjing Nong-Zhuan Xuebao/Nanjing Agricultural Technology College. Journal (1008-1895)
Related titles: Online - full text ed.
—BLDSC (4669.043900).
Published by: Jinling Keji Xueyuan/Jinling Institute of Technology, 99, Hongjing Lu, Jiangning-qu, Nanjing, 211169, China. TEL 86-25-85393326, http://www.jit.edu.cn/. Ed. Chao-nian Feng.

500 600 CHN ISSN 1003-7438
JINRI KEJI/TODAY SCIENCE AND TECHNOLOGY. Text in Chinese. 1969. m. CNY 7 newsstand/cover (effective 2006). **Document type:** *Journal, Academic/Scholarly.*
Related titles: Online - full text ed.
Published by: Zhejiang Sheng Keji Qingbao Yanjiusuo/Zhejiang Provincial Institute of Science and Technology Information, 33, Huancheng Xilu, 4 Bldg., Shengxingzheng Zhongxin, Hangzhou, Zhejiang 310006, China. TEL 86-571-87054087, FAX 86-571-85214212.

500 600 FRA ISSN 0993-7064
J'INTEGRE. Text in French. 1987. irreg. price varies. **Document type:** *Monographic series, Academic/Scholarly.* **Description:** A collection of scientific texts for school high school students.
Published by: Dunod, 5 rue Laromiguiere, Paris, 75005, France. TEL 33-1-40463500, FAX 33-1-40464995, infos@dunod.com, http://www.dunod.com.

500 CHN ISSN 1007-2985
JISHOU DAXUE XUEBAO (ZIRAN KEXUE BAN)/JISHOU UNIVERSITY. JOURNAL (NATURAL SCIENCE EDITION). Text in Chinese. 1980. q. USD 64.20 (effective 2009). **Document type:** *Journal, Academic/ Scholarly.*
Related titles: Online - full text ed.
Indexed: B25, BIOSIS Prev, CCMJ, MSN, MathR, MycolAb, RefZh, SCOPUS, Z01.
—BLDSC (4809.599700), East View, IE, Ingenta.
Published by: Jishou Daxue/Jishou University, Daxue Xi-Xiao-Qu, Jishou, Hunan 416000, China. TEL 86-743-8563684. Ed. Haiping Zhong.

500 DEU ISSN 1435-9596
AS181
➤ **JOACHIM-JUNGIUS-GESELLSCHAFT DER WISSENSCHAFTEN, HAMBURG. VEROEFFENTLICHUNGEN.** Text in German. 1957. irreg., latest vol.98, 2005. price varies. **Document type:** *Monographic series, Academic/Scholarly.*
Published by: (Joachim-Jungius-Gesellschaft der Wissenschaften e.V., Hamburg), Vandenhoeck und Ruprecht, Theaterstr 13, Goettingen, 37073, Germany. TEL 49-551-508440, FAX 49-551-5084422, info@v-r.de, http://www.v-r.de.

500 JPN ISSN 0915-8162
AS552.J63A3 CODEN: JDKKE2
JOETSU KYOIKU DAIGAKU KENKYU KIYO/JOETSU UNIVERSITY OF EDUCATION. BULLETIN. Text and summaries in English, Japanese. a.
Published by: Joetsu University of Education/Joetsu Kyoiku Daigaku, 1 Yamayashiki-Machi, Joetsu-shi, Niigata-ken 943-0815, Japan.

500 DEU ISSN 0178-4757
JOHANNES GUTENBERG UNIVERSITAET MAINZ. FORSCHUNGSMAGAZIN. Text in German. 1985. s-a. EUR 4 newsstand/cover (effective 2006). adv. back issues avail. **Document type:** *Academic/Scholarly.* **Description:** Report on current research at the university.
Indexed: CEABA, IBR, IBZ, RASB.
Published by: Johannes Gutenberg Universitaet Mainz, Forum 2, Mainz, 55099, Germany. TEL 49-6131-3922369, FAX 49-6131-3924139. Ed. Bettina Leinauer. Circ: 4,000.

500 AUT
JOHANNES-KEPLER-UNIVERSITAET LINZ. SCHRIFTEN. REIHE C: TECHNIK UND NATURWISSENSCHAFTEN. Text in German. 1976. irreg., latest vol.59, 2009. price varies. **Document type:** *Monographic series, Academic/Scholarly.*
Supersedes in part (in 1993): Johannes-Kepler-Universitaet Linz. Dissertationen (0259-0689)
Published by: (Johannes Kepler Universitaet Linz), Trauner Verlag und Buchservice GmbH, Koeglstr 14, Linz, 4020, Austria. TEL 43-732-778241212, FAX 43-732-778241400, office@trauner.at.

600 JOR ISSN 1605-2587
Q80.J67
➤ **JORDAN JOURNAL OF APPLIED SCIENCE. NATURAL SCIENCE.** Text in English, Arabic; Summaries in English, Arabic. 1999. s-a. JOD 6 domestic to individuals; USD 20 foreign to individuals; JOD 12 domestic to institutions; USD 30 foreign to institutions (effective 2004). back issues avail. **Document type:** *Journal, Academic/ Scholarly.* **Description:** Devoted to the publication of experimental and theoretical original studies in pure and applied science.
Indexed: A22, A34, A38, B23, BP, CABA, D01, E12, EMBASE, ExcerpMed, F08, F11, F12, GH, H16, H17, N02, N03, N04, P33, P39, R07, R10, R13, RA&MP, RM&VM, Reac, S13, S16, SCOPUS, T05, VS, W10.
—BLDSC (4673.659700), IE, Ingenta.
Published by: Applied Science University/Jamiat Al-Ulum Al-Tatbikeyah, Deanship of Scientific Research, Amman, 11931, Jordan. TEL 962-6-5237181, FAX 962-6-5232899, vice_president@asu.edu.jo. Ed., R&P Naim Ismail. Pub. Odeh Al-Jayyousi.

➤ **JOSAI DAIGAKU KENKYU NENPO. SHIZEN KAGAKU HEN/JOSAI UNIVERSITY BULLETIN OF LIBERAL ARTS. NATURAL SCIENCE, HEALTH AND PHYSICAL EDUCATION.** *see* HUMANITIES: COMPREHENSIVE WORKS

500 JPN ISSN 0919-4614
JOSAI DAIGAKU RIGAKUBU KENKYU HOKOKU/JOSAI UNIVERSITY. SCIENCE BULLETIN. Text in Japanese. 1993. a. **Document type:** *Journal, Academic/Scholarly.*
Indexed: CCMJ, MSN, MathR, Z02.
Published by: Josai Daigaku, Rigakubu/Josai University, Faculty of Science, 1-1 Keyakidai, Sakado,, Saitama 350-0295, Japan.

500 SEN
JOURNAL DES SCIENCES POUR L'INGENIEUR. Text in French. 2001. a. **Document type:** *Journal, Academic/Scholarly.*
Published by: Ecole Superieure Polytechnique, BP 5085, Dakar, Senegal. TEL 221-8241388, FAX 221-8255594, http://esp.e-ucad.sn/.

501 NLD ISSN 0925-4560
Q3 CODEN: JGPSE4
➤ **JOURNAL FOR GENERAL PHILOSOPHY OF SCIENCE/ ZEITSCHRIFT FUER ALLGEMEINE WISSENSCHAFTSTHEORIE.** Text in English, German. 1969. s-a. EUR 467, USD 468 combined subscription to institutions (print & online eds.) (effective 2012). adv. bk.rev. bibl. index. back issues avail.; reprint service avail. from PSC. **Document type:** *Journal, Academic/Scholarly.* **Description:** Discusses issues relating to the philosophical, methodological, epistemological and ethical foundations of the sciences.
Formerly (until vol.21, 1990): Zeitschrift fuer Allgemeine Wissenschaftstheorie (0044-2216)
Related titles: Microform ed.: (from PQC); Online - full text ed.: ISSN 1572-8587 (from IngentaConnect).
Indexed: A01, A03, A08, A20, A22, A26, ArtHuCI, BibLing, CA, CCMJ, CIS, DIP, E01, E08, FR, G08, I05, IBR, IBRH, IBZ, IPB, Inspec, MSN, MathR, P30, PhilInd, RASB, S09, SCOPUS, T02, W07.
—BLDSC (4988.600000), AskIEEE, IE, Infotrieve, Ingenta, INIST, Linda Hall. **CCC.**
Published by: Springer Netherlands (Subsidiary of: Springer Science+Business Media), Van Godewijckstraat 30, Dordrecht, 3311 GX, Netherlands. TEL 31-78-6576050, FAX 31-78-6576474, http://www.springer.com. Eds. Gregor Schiemann, Helmut Pulte.

500 600 ZAF ISSN 1684-4998
JOURNAL FOR NEW GENERATION SCIENCE. Text in English. 2003. s-a. **Document type:** *Journal, Academic/Scholarly.*
Indexed: ISAP.
Published by: Central University of Technology, Free State, Private Bag X20539, Bloemfontein, 9300, South Africa. TEL 27-51-5073911, FAX 27-51-5073199, http://www.cut.ac.za. Ed. Laetus Lategan.

500 SYR ISSN 0379-2927
Q127.A5
JOURNAL FOR THE HISTORY OF ARABIC SCIENCE. Text in Arabic, English, French, German. 1977. s-a. SYP 15, USD 15. adv. bk.rev. illus. index, cum.index: 1977-1981 (vols.1-5). back issues avail. **Document type:** *Journal, Academic/Scholarly.*
Indexed: FR, I14, MEA&I, MathR, P30, RASB.
—INIST, Linda Hall.
Published by: University of Aleppo, Institute for the History of Arabic Science, Aleppo, Syria. TEL 963-21-236130, FAX 963-21-229184, TELEX 331018 SY ALUNIV. Ed. Dr Khaled Maghout. Circ: 1,500.

JOURNAL FOR THE SCIENTIFIC STUDY OF RELIGION. *see* RELIGIONS AND THEOLOGY

JOURNAL FUER U F O - FORSCHUNG. *see* AERONAUTICS AND SPACE FLIGHT

500 EGY ISSN 2090-1232
▼ ➤ **JOURNAL OF ADVANCED RESEARCH.** Text in English. 2009. q. **Document type:** *Journal, Academic/Scholarly.*
Related titles: Online - full text ed.: ISSN 2090-1224 (from ScienceDirect).
Indexed: SCOPUS, T02.
—CCC.
Published by: Cairo University, New Central Library/Jami'a Al-Qahira, Gamaa St, Giza, Cairo, Egypt. http://www.cu.edu.eg.

500 JPN ISSN 0915-5651
Q77 CODEN: JAVSEQ
➤ **JOURNAL OF ADVANCED SCIENCE.** Text in English, Japanese. 1989. q. **Document type:** *Journal, Academic/Scholarly.*
Indexed: A22.
—BLDSC (4918.947600), IE, Ingenta.
Published by: Haiteku Kyokai/Society of Advanced Science, c/o JAS Editorial Committee, Syounan Campas Tokai University, 1117 Kitakaname, Hiratsuka, Kanagawa, 259-1292, Japan. TEL 81-463-691960, FAX 81-463-691961, info@sas-jas.gr.jp.

➤ **JOURNAL OF AGRICULTURAL SCIENCES AND TECHNOLOGY.** *see* AGRICULTURE

➤ **JOURNAL OF ALGORITHMS & COMPUTATIONAL TECHNOLOGY.** *see* MATHEMATICS

500 USA ISSN 1545-1003
Q1
➤ **THE JOURNAL OF AMERICAN SCIENCE.** Text in English. 2005. m. adv. back issues avail. **Document type:** *Journal, Academic/Scholarly.* **Description:** Publishes research findings and reports, jobs and other information on a wide range of topics in the sciences, including natural sciences.
Related titles: Online - full text ed.
Indexed: A35, A37, A38, B23, C30, D01, S13, Z01.
Published by: Marsland Press, PO Box 21126, Lansing, MI 48909. TEL 347-321-7172, sciencepub@gmail.com, http://www.sciencepub.net. Ed. Hongbao Ma TEL 347-321-7172.

500 600 KOR ISSN 2093-3134
▼ ➤ **JOURNAL OF ANALYTICAL SCIENCE AND TECHNOLOGY.** Text in English. 2010. s-a. (Mar. & Sep.). back issues avail. **Document type:** *Journal, Academic/Scholarly.* **Description:** Publishes original research and review articles on all aspects of analytical principles, techniques, methods, procedures, and equipment.
Related titles: Online - full text ed.: ISSN 2093-3371. free (effective 2011).
Published by: Korea Basic Science Institute, Daedeok Headquarters 113 Gwahangno, 52 Eoeun-dong, Yusung-gu, Daejeon, 305-333, Korea, S. TEL 82-42-8653500, FAX 82-42-8653404. Ed. Chaejoon Cheong. **Co-sponsors:** Chungnam National University, Graduate School of Analytical Science and Technology; National Research Facilities & Equipment Center.

➤ **JOURNAL OF APPLIED SCIENCE & ENGINEERING TECHNOLOGY.** *see* ENGINEERING

500 ZWE ISSN 1019-7788
T28.A3555
➤ **JOURNAL OF APPLIED SCIENCE IN SOUTHERN AFRICA.** Short title: J A S S A. Text in English. 1994. s-a. ZWD 30 domestic; USD 15 in Africa; USD 20 elsewhere (effective 2004). bk.rev. **Document type:** *Journal, Academic/Scholarly.* **Description:** Multidisciplinary science journal specializing in applied research that is important to or deals with matters specific to the southern African region.
Related titles: Online - full text ed.
Indexed: SCOPUS.
Published by: University of Zimbabwe Publications, Mt Pleasant, Main Administration Bldg, 1st Fl, PO Box MP 203, Harare, Zimbabwe. TEL 263-04-303211, FAX 263-04-333407, uzpub@admin.uz.ac.zw, http://www.uz.ac.zw/publications. Ed. C F B Nhachi. R&P M S Mtetwa.

500 PAK ISSN 1812-5654
➤ **JOURNAL OF APPLIED SCIENCES.** Text in English. 2000. q. **Document type:** *Journal, Academic/Scholarly.* **Description:** Promotes and disseminate the knowledge by publishing original research findings, review articles and short communications in the fields of biology, chemistry, physics, environmental, business and economics, finance, mathematics and statistics, geology, engineering, computer science, social sciences, natural and technological sciences, linguistics, medicine, architecture, industrial, and all other applied and theoretical sciences.
Formerly (until 2004): Pakistan Journal of Applied Sciences (1607-8926)
Related titles: Online - full text ed.: ISSN 1812-5662. free (effective 2011).
Indexed: A28, A34, A35, A36, A37, A38, APA, ASFA, AgBio, AgrForAb, B21, B23, BA, BP, BrCerAb, C&ISA, C10, C25, C30, CA, CA/WCA, CABA, CIA, CerAb, CivEngAb, CorrAb, D01, E&CAJ, E11, E12, EEA, EMA, ESPM, EnvEAb, F08, F11, F12, FCA, G11, GH, H&SSA, H15, H16, H17, I11, IndVet, Inspec, LT, M&GPA, M&TEA, M09, MBF, METADEX, MaizeAb, N02, N03, N04, O01, OR, P32, P33, P37, P38, P39, P40, PGegResA, PGrRegA, PHN&I, R07, R08, R11, R12, R13, RA&MP, RM&VM, RRTA, S12, S13, S16, S17, SCOPUS, SSciA, SWRA, SolStAb, SoyAb, T02, T04, T05, TAR, TriticAb, VS, W10, W11, WAA, Z01.
Published by: A N S I Network, 308 Lasani Town, Sargodha Rd, Faisalabad, 38090, Pakistan. TEL 92-41-2001145, FAX 92-41-731433, http://www.ansijournals.com.

500 JOR ISSN 1819-544X
➤ **JOURNAL OF APPLIED SCIENCES RESEARCH.** Text in English. 2005. m. free. back issues avail. **Document type:** *Journal, Academic/ Scholarly.*
Media: Online - full text.
Indexed: A34, A35, A36, A37, A38, AgBio, Agr, AgrForAb, B23, BA, BP, C10, C25, C30, CA, CABA, D01, E12, F08, F11, F12, FCA, G11, GH, H16, H17, I11, IndVet, LT, MaizeAb, N02, N03, N04, N05, O01, OR, P32, P33, P37, P38, P39, P40, PGegResA, PGrRegA, PHN&I, PN&I, R07, R08, R11, R12, R13, RA&MP, RM&VM, RRTA, S12, S13, S16, S17, SCOPUS, SoyAb, T02, T05, TriticAb, VS, W10, W11.
Published by: American - Eurasian Network for Scientific Information, A E N S I Publications, c/o Dr. Abdel Rahman Mohammad Said Al-Tawaha, Al Hussein Bin Talal University, Biological Department, PO Box 20, Ma'an, Jordan. TEL 962-2-7305196. Eds. Abdel Rahman Al-Tawaha, Shaban D. Abou Hussein.

500 USA ISSN 1539-8714
➤ **JOURNAL OF ARTICLES IN SUPPORT OF THE NULL HYPOTHESIS.** Abbreviated title: J A S N H. Text in English. 2002. s-a. free (effective 2011). back issues avail. **Document type:** *Journal, Academic/Scholarly.* **Description:** Publishes original experimental studies in all areas of psychology where the null hypothesis is supported.
Media: Online - full text.
Indexed: A01, A03, A08, A26, A39, C27, CA, D03, D04, E08, E13, G08, I05, R14, S06, S09, S14, S15, S18, T02.
Published by: Reysen Group, Department of Psychology, Texas A&M-Commerce, Commerce, TX 75429. TEL 903-413-7026. Ed. Stephen Reysen.

500 PAK ISSN 2223-1331
▼ **JOURNAL OF ASIAN SCIENTIFIC RESEARCH.** Text in English. 2011. m. free. **Document type:** *Journal, Academic/Scholarly.* **Description:** Publishes research articles and reviews article; scientific commentaries in the fields of applied and theoretical sciences; biology; chemistry; physics; zoology; medical studies; environmental sciences; geology; engineering; short communications; computer science; social sciences; natural sciences; technological sciences; linguistics; medicine ; industrial; mathematics; statistics; and all other applied and theoretical sciences.
Media: Online - full content.
Published by: Asian Economic and Social Society, B 54 Block 2 Gulistan-e-Jauhar, Karachi, Pakistan. TEL 923146715528. Ed., Pub. Qazi Muhammad Adnan Hye.

500 IND ISSN 0976-9595
▼ ➤ **JOURNAL OF AVANCED SCIENTIFIC RESEARCH.** Text and summaries in English. 2010 (Aug.). q. Index. back issues avail. **Document type:** *Journal, Academic/Scholarly.* **Description:** Contains original research work, reviews, and short communications that contributes significantly to further the scientific knowledge in the subject areas pharmaceutical research, chemistry, chemical technology, biochemistry, microbiology, biotechnology, medicine, agro chemistry and applied biosciences.
Media: Online - full text.
Published by: Sciensage Publications, C-225, South City, Lucknow, Uttar Pradesh 226 016, India. TEL 91-581-2403860, editor@sciensage.info, info@sciensage.info. Ed., Pub., R&P, Adv. contact Pankaj Kumar.

S

500 IRN ISSN 1735-0611
JOURNAL OF BASIC SCIENCE/MAJALLAH-I 'ULUM-I PAYAH. Text in English. 2002. q. **Document type:** *Journal, Academic/Scholarly.*
Published by: The University of Mazandaran, Vice Chancellor in Charge of Research, PO Box 416, Babolsar, Iran. jbsum@umz.ac.ir, http://www.umz.ac.ir/en/index.asp.

500 610 570 USA ISSN 1747-5333
R31
JOURNAL OF BIOMEDICAL DISCOVERY AND COLLABORATION. Text in English. 2006. irreg. free (effective 2011). back issues avail. **Document type:** *Journal, Academic/Scholarly.* **Description:** Covers all aspects of scientific information management and studies of scientific practice.
Media: Online - full text.
Indexed: A01, A26, A39, B19, C27, C29, CA, D03, D04, E13, I05, P30, R14, S06, S14, S15, S18, SCOPUS, T02.
—CCC.
Published by: U I C Psychiatric Institute, c/o Neil R Smalheiser, UIC Psychiatric Institute MC912, 1601 W Taylor St, Rm 525, Chicago, IL 60612. TEL 312-413-4581, FAX 312-413-4569, discovery@psych.uic.edu. Ed. Neil Smalheiser.

133 USA ISSN 0897-0394
JOURNAL OF BORDERLAND RESEARCH. Text in English. 1945. q. adv. bk.rev. charts; illus.; pat.; stat. back issues avail. **Document type:** *Journal, Academic/Scholarly.* **Description:** Investigates into the realms normally beyond the range of basic human perception and physical measurement.
Formerly (until 1959): Meade Layne's Round Robin
Published by: Borderland Sciences Research Foundation, PO Box 6250, Eureka, CA 95502. TEL 707-497-6911, FAX 815-301-8655, info@borderlands.com, http://www.borderlands.com. adv.: page USD 600; trim 9.5 x 7.5. Circ: 5,000.

507.11 USA ISSN 0047-231X
Q183.U6 CODEN: JSCTBN
➤ **JOURNAL OF COLLEGE SCIENCE TEACHING.** Abbreviated title: J C S T. Text in English. 1971. bi-m. free to members (effective 2010). adv. bk.rev.; video rev. abstr.; tr.lit.; illus. index. back issues avail.; reprints avail. **Document type:** *Journal, Academic/Scholarly.* **Description:** Presents innovative techniques related to the teaching of science at the college level, principally in the introductory courses, and courses for nonscience majors.
Related titles: Microfilm ed.: (from PQC); Online - full text ed.: ISSN 1943-4898.
Indexed: A01, A02, A03, A08, A22, A25, A26, B04, BRD, CA, CPE, ChemAb, E02, E03, E06, E07, E08, E09, ERI, ERIC, EdA, EdI, G08, GeoRef, I05, Inspec, MRD, P02, P04, P07, P10, P18, P30, P48, P52, P53, P54, P55, P56, PQC, S04, S06, S08, S09, SpeleolAb, T02, W03, W05.
—BLDSC (4958.810000), CASDDS, IE, Infotrieve, Ingenta, Linda Hall. CCC.
Published by: National Science Teachers Association, 1840 Wilson Blvd, Arlington, VA 22201. TEL 703-243-7100, 800-722-6782, FAX 703-243-7177, pubinfo@nsta.org. Adv. contact Olenka Dobczanska TEL 703-312-9262. Circ: 6,000.

▼➤ **JOURNAL OF COMPREHENSIVE RESEARCH.** *see* HUMANITIES: COMPREHENSIVE WORKS

➤ **JOURNAL OF CONSCIOUSNESS STUDIES;** controversies in science & the humanities. *see* PSYCHOLOGY

➤ **JOURNAL OF CREATION.** *see* RELIGIONS AND THEOLOGY

➤ **JOURNAL OF EAST AFRICA NATURAL HISTORY.** *see* BIOLOGY

▼➤ **JOURNAL OF EMERGING TRENDS IN ENGINEERING AND APPLIED SCIENCES.** *see* ENGINEERING

➤ **JOURNAL OF ENGINEERING & APPLIED SCIENCES (FAISALABAD).** *see* ENGINEERING

➤ **JOURNAL OF ENGINEERING SCIENCE AND TECHNOLOGY REVIEW.** *see* ENGINEERING

500 620 USA ISSN 2159-5828
▼ **JOURNAL OF FOOD SCIENCE AND ENGINEERING.** Text in English. 2011. m. **Document type:** *Journal, Academic/Scholarly.*
Related titles: Online - full text ed.: ISSN 2159-581X.
Published by: David Publishing Co., Inc., 1840 Industrial Dr, Ste 160, Libertyville, IL 60048. TEL 847-281-9822, FAX 847-281-9855, order@davidpublishing.com, http://www.davidpublishing.com.

500 MYS ISSN 1823-626X
JOURNAL OF FUNDAMENTAL SCIENCES. Text in English. 2005. s-a. **Document type:** *Journal, Academic/Scholarly.*
Related titles: Online - full text ed.: free (effective 2011).
Published by: Universiti Teknologi Malaysia, Ibnu Sina Institute for Fundamental Science Studies, Johor Bahru, Johor 81310, Malaysia. Ed. Sugeng Triwahyono.

500 USA ISSN 0022-2038
Q167
JOURNAL OF IRREPRODUCIBLE RESULTS; the science humor magazine. Text in English. 1955. irreg. USD 39 in US & Canada to institutions; USD 51 in Mexico to institutions; USD 63 elsewhere to institutions (effective 2010). adv. bk.rev. illus. Index. 36 p./no.; back issues avail.; reprints avail. **Document type:** *Magazine, Consumer.* **Description:** Contains humorous articles of interest to scientists, doctors and the general public.
Indexed: A22, CIS, MEA&I.
—BLDSC (5008.400000), IE, Infotrieve, Ingenta, Linda Hall.
Address: 413 Poinsettia Ave, San Mateo, CA 94403-2803. TEL 650-573-7125. Ed. Norman Sperling. Circ: 2,000.

JOURNAL OF LIBERAL ARTS AND SCIENCES. *see* HUMANITIES: COMPREHENSIVE WORKS

JOURNAL OF MATHEMATICS AND STATISTICS. *see* MATHEMATICS

500 300 USA ISSN 1558-6898
➤ **JOURNAL OF MIXED METHODS RESEARCH.** Text in English. 2007 (Jan.). q. USD 508, GBP 299 combined subscription to institutions (print & online eds.); USD 498, GBP 293 to institutions (effective 2011). reprint service avail. from PSC. **Document type:** *Journal, Academic/Scholarly.* **Description:** Aims to publish empirical, methodological, and theoretical articles about mixed methods research.
Related titles: Online - full text ed.: ISSN 1558-6901. 2007 (Jan.). USD 457, GBP 269 to institutions (effective 2011).
Indexed: A22, CurCont, E01, ERIC, P30, PsycInfo, SCOPUS, SSCI, SocioIAb, W07.
—BLDSC (5020.540000), IE. CCC.
Published by: Sage Publications, Inc., 2455 Teller Rd, Thousand Oaks, CA 91320. TEL 805-499-9774, 800-818-7243, FAX 805-499-0871, 800-583-2665, info@sagepub.com, http://www.sagepub.com. Eds. Donna M Mertens, Manfred Max Bergman.

500 GBR ISSN 1756-9737
TA342
▼➤ **JOURNAL OF MULTISCALE MODELLING.** Abbreviated title: J M M. Text in English. 2009. q. SGD 653, USD 404, EUR 339 combined subscription to institutions (print & online eds.) (effective 2012). back issues avail. **Document type:** *Journal, Academic/Scholarly.* **Description:** Contains theoretical, computational and experimental original papers with a general emphasis on Multiscale issues.
Related titles: Online - full text ed.: ISSN 1756-9745. SGD 594, USD 367, EUR 308 to institutions (effective 2012).
Indexed: A22, E01.
Published by: Imperial College Press (Subsidiary of: World Scientific Publishing Co. Pte. Ltd.), 57 Shelton St, Covent Garden, London, WC2H 9HE, United Kingdom. TEL 44-20-78360888, FAX 44-20-78362020, edit@icpress.co.uk, http://www.icpress.co.uk/. Ed. M H Aliabadi. **Subscr. to:** World Scientific Publishing Co. Pte. Ltd., Farrer Rd, PO Box 128, Singapore 912805, Singapore. TEL 65-6467-7667, FAX 65-6466-5775, sales@wspc.com.sg. **Dist. by:** World Scientific Publishing Ltd. sales@wspc.co.uk.; World Scientific Publishing Co., Inc., 27 Warren St, Ste 401-402, Hackensack, NJ 07601. TEL 201-487-9655, 800-227-7562, FAX 201-487-9656, 888-977-2665, wspc@wspc.com.

570 IND ISSN 0970-3799
➤ **JOURNAL OF NATURAL & PHYSICAL SCIENCES.** Text in English, Hindi. 1987. s-a. bk.rev. **Document type:** *Journal, Academic/Scholarly.* **Description:** Covers biology, chemistry, physics, and mathematical sciences and computer science.
Indexed: CCMJ, MSN, MathR, Z02.
Published by: Gurukula Kangri University, PO Gurukula Kangri, Hardwar, Uttar Pradesh 249 404, India. TEL 91-1334-249013, registrargkv@yahoo.co.in.

500 JPN ISSN 0075-4307
JOURNAL OF NATURAL SCIENCE. Text in English, Japanese. 1952 (vol.2). a. avail. on exchange basis.
Published by: Tokushima Daigaku, Kyoikugakubu/Tokushima University, Faculty of Education, Tokushima-shi, Tokushima-ken 770, Japan.

500.1 510 PAK ISSN 0022-2941
Q1 CODEN: JNSMAC
JOURNAL OF NATURAL SCIENCES AND MATHEMATICS. Text in English. 1961. s-a. PKR 150, USD 15. bk.rev. index.
Indexed: CCMJ, CIS, ChemAb, ChemTitl, INIS AtomInd, Inspec, MSN, MathR, Z02.
—BLDSC (5021.300000), CASDDS, IE, Ingenta, Linda Hall.
Published by: Government College, Research Council, P O Box 1750, Lahore, 54000, Pakistan. Ed. M Zakria Butt. Circ: 250.

JOURNAL OF OPERATIONAL OCEANOGRAPHY. *see* EARTH SCIENCES—Oceanography

THE JOURNAL OF PHILOSOPHY, SCIENCE & LAW. *see* PHILOSOPHY

500 MYS ISSN 1675-3402
JOURNAL OF PHYSICAL SCIENCE. Text in English. 2007. irreg. **Document type:** *Journal, Academic/Scholarly.*
Related titles: Online - full text ed.: ISSN 1985-8337. free (effective 2011).
Published by: Penerbit Universiti Sains Malaysia/Universiti Sains Malaysia Press, Pulau Pinang, Pinang 11800, Malaysia. TEL 60-4-6534421, FAX 60-4-6575714, http://www.penerbit.usm.my. Ed. Ismail Ab Rahman.

500 USA ISSN 2159-5348
▼ **JOURNAL OF PHYSICAL SCIENCE AND APPLICATION.** Text in English. 2011. m. **Document type:** *Journal, Academic/Scholarly.*
Published by: David Publishing Co., Inc., 1840 Industrial Dr, Ste 160, Libertyville, IL 60048. TEL 847-281-9822, FAX 847-281-9855, order@davidpublishing.com, http://www.davidpublishing.com.

JOURNAL OF PSYCHOLOGY OF SCIENCE AND TECHNOLOGY (ONLINE). *see* PSYCHOLOGY

500 IND ISSN 0970-1990
QH301 CODEN: JRAAEK
JOURNAL OF RECENT ADVANCES IN APPLIED SCIENCES. Abbreviated title: J R A A S. Text in English. 1986. s-a. INR 300 domestic; USD 100 foreign (effective 2011). adv. **Document type:** *Journal, Academic/Scholarly.*
Related titles: Online - full text ed.: free (effective 2011).
Indexed: C10.
—Linda Hall.
Published by: Evoker Research Perfecting Company, c/o A. K. Srivastava, 20-A Vastavas, Triveni Nagar, Sitapur Rd, Lucknow 20, 226 020, India. mhcdr@rediff.com. Eds. Rama S Dwivedi, A K Srivastava.

507 USA ISSN 0022-4308
Q181.A1 CODEN: JRSTAR
➤ **JOURNAL OF RESEARCH IN SCIENCE TEACHING.** Text in English. 1963. 10/yr. GBP 997 in United Kingdom to institutions; EUR 1,261 in Europe to institutions; USD 1,744 in United States to institutions; USD 1,884 in Canada & Mexico to institutions; USD 1,954 elsewhere to institutions; GBP 1,147 combined subscription in United Kingdom to institutions (print & online eds.); EUR 1,452 combined subscription in Europe to institutions (print & online eds.); USD 2,006 combined subscription in United States to institutions (print & online eds.); USD 2,146 combined subscription in Canada & Mexico to institutions (print & online eds.); USD 2,216 combined subscription elsewhere to institutions (print & online eds.) (effective 2012). adv. bibl.; charts; illus. index. back issues avail.; reprint service avail. from PSC. **Document type:** *Journal, Academic/Scholarly.* **Description:** Features research articles related to the philosophy, historical perspective, teaching strategies, curriculum development and other topics relevant to science education.
Related titles: Microform ed.: (from PQC); Online - full text ed.: ISSN 1098-2736. GBP 890 in United Kingdom to institutions; EUR 1,126 in Europe to institutions; USD 1,744 elsewhere to institutions (effective 2012).
Indexed: A20, A22, AEI, ASCA, ASSIA, B04, BRD, CA, CDA, CPE, CPEI, CurCont, E-psyche, E02, E03, E06, EIA, ERI, ERIC, EdA, EdI, EnerInd, EngInd, FR, IBR, IBZ, MEA&I, P03, PsycInfo, PsycholAb, S02, S03, SCOPUS, SSCI, T02, W03, W07, W09.
—BLDSC (5052.030000), IE, Infotrieve, Ingenta, INIST. CCC.
Published by: (National Association for Research in Science Teaching), John Wiley & Sons, Inc., 111 River St, Hoboken, NJ 07030. TEL 201-748-6000, FAX 201-748-6088, info@wiley.com, http://www.wiley.com/WileyCDA/. Eds. Angelo Collins, J Randy McGinnis. Adv. contact Kim Thompkins TEL 212-850-6921. B&W page USD 1,241, color page USD 1,576; trim 6.875 x 10. **Subscr. outside the Americas to:** John Wiley & Sons Ltd., The Atrium, Southern Gate, Chichester, West Sussex PO19 8SQ, United Kingdom. TEL 44-1243-779777, FAX 44-1243-775878, cs-journals@wiley.com.

500 600 USA ISSN 1544-8053
TD767 CODEN: JRSTGX
➤ **JOURNAL OF RESIDUALS SCIENCE & TECHNOLOGY.** Abbreviated title: J R S T. Text in English. 2004 (Jan.). q. USD 219 (print or online ed.); USD 244 combined subscription (print & online eds.); USD 60 per issue (effective 2011). adv. 64 p./no.; back issues avail. **Document type:** *Journal, Academic/Scholarly.* **Description:** Provides a forum for scientific investigation and technical management of residuals. Presents work on municipal sludges, industrial sludges, and land application of biosolids.
Related titles: Online - full text ed.
Indexed: CPEI, CurCont, GEOBASE, SCI, SCOPUS, W07.
—BLDSC (5052.036100).
Published by: DEStech Publications, Inc., 439 N Duke St, Lancaster, PA 17602. TEL 717-290-1660, 877-500-4337, FAX 717-509-6100, info@destechpub.com. Ed. P Brent Duncan.

500 620 600 USA ISSN 1557-5284
Q183.3.A1
➤ **JOURNAL OF S T E M EDUCATION (ONLINE);** innovations and research. (Science Technology Engineering Math) Text in English. 2000. s-a. free (effective 2011). adv. bk.rev. abstr.; charts; illus. back issues avail.; reprints avail. **Document type:** *Journal, Academic/Scholarly.* **Description:** Promotes high-quality undergraduate education in science, mathematics, engineering and technology through peer reviewed articles.
Former titles (until Dec.2003): Journal of S T E M Education (Print) (1557-5276); (until Apr.2003): Journal of S M E T Education (1526-2367)
Media: Online - full text.
Indexed: A01, A03, A08, A39, C27, C29, CA, D03, D04, E03, E13, ERI, P02, P10, P26, P48, P52, P53, P54, PQC, R14, S10, S14, S15, S18, T02.
Published by: Institute for S T E M Education and Research, PO Box 4001, Auburn, AL 36831. TEL 334-821-4847, FAX 208-361-3381. Ed. P K Raju.

500 IRN ISSN 1016-1058
CODEN: TUSQAD
➤ **JOURNAL OF SCIENCE (NATIONAL EDITION).** Text in Persian, Modern; Summaries in English. 1968. s-a. IRR 2,500 to individuals; IRR 5,600 in Africa to individuals; IRR 5,600 in Asia to individuals; IRR 5,600 in Europe to individuals; IRR 6,640 in the Americas to individuals; IRR 6,640 in Australasia to individuals; IRR 2,700 to institutions; IRR 5,800 in Africa to institutions; IRR 5,800 in Asia to institutions; IRR 5,800 in Europe to institutions; IRR 6,840 in the Americas to institutions; IRR 6,840 in Australasia to institutions. **Document type:** *Journal, Academic/Scholarly.*
Supersedes in part: University of Tehran. Faculty of Science. Quarterly Bulletin (0042-0131)
Indexed: CCMJ, ChemAb, MSN, MathR, Z01.
—CASDDS, INIST.
Published by: (University of Tehran/Danishgah-i Tihran), University of Teheran Press Co., PO Box 14155-6455, Teheran, Iran. TEL 98-21-6113305, FAX 98-21-6405141. Circ: 1,000.

500 001.3 ROM ISSN 1844-9581
➤ **JOURNAL OF SCIENCE AND ARTS.** Text in English, Romanian. 2001. s-a. free. abstr.; charts; illus. Index. back issues avail. **Document type:** *Journal, Academic/Scholarly.* **Description:** Contains articles on mathematics, chemistry and physics.
Formerly (until 2002): Universitatea Valahia Targoviste. Anali. Serie Stiinte
Related titles: Online - full text ed.: free (effective 2011).
Published by: (Universitatea Valahia din Targoviste, University Press), Editura Bibliotheca/Bibliotheca Publishing House, Strada Nicolae Radian KB2/3, Targoviste, 130082, Romania. http://www.bibliotheca.ro. Ed. Ion Popescu. Pub. Cristiana Radulescu.

➤ **JOURNAL OF SCIENCE AND MATHEMATICS EDUCATION IN SOUTHEAST ASIA.** *see* EDUCATION—Teaching Methods And Curriculum

500 600 ZMB ISSN 1027-4928
Q91.Z33 CODEN: ZJSTDE
JOURNAL OF SCIENCE AND TECHNOLOGY. Text in English. 1976. 2/yr. adv. charts; stat. **Document type:** *Journal, Academic/Scholarly.* **Description:** Provides an outlet for research findings and reviews in areas of science and technology.
Formerly (until 1996): Zambia Journal of Science and Technology (0378-8857)
Related titles: Online - full text ed.
Indexed: ChemAb, FS&TA, GeoRef, INIS AtomInd, SpeleolAb.
—CASDDS.
Published by: University of Zambia, PO Box 32379, Lusaka, 10101, Zambia. Ed. G. Nkhowane. Circ: 2,500.

500 600 PAK ISSN 0250-5339
Q80.P3 CODEN: JSTPDU
➤ **JOURNAL OF SCIENCE AND TECHNOLOGY.** Text in English; Summaries in English. 1977. s-a. PKR 200 domestic; USD 35 foreign (effective 2007). bk.rev. abstr. back issues avail.; reprints avail. **Document type:** *Journal, Academic/Scholarly.* **Description:** Research articles in this journal are reporting original scientific research in the field of science and technology.
Indexed: A26, G08, I05, INIS AtomInd.
—CASDDS, Linda Hall.
Published by: University of Peshawar, National Centre of Excellence in Geology, c/o Dr. M. Tahir Shah, NCE in Geology, Peshawar, Pakistan. TEL 92-91-9218182, 92-91-9216471, FAX 92-91-9216736, 92-91-9218183, tahir_shah56@yahoo.com. Ed. M Javed Khan. Circ: 500.

500 GHA ISSN 0855-0395
T1 CODEN: JKUTDP
JOURNAL OF SCIENCE AND TECHNOLOGY. Text in English, French. 1959. s-a. GHC 80,000 domestic; USD 60 foreign (effective 2004). bk.rev.
Former titles: University of Science and Technology. Journal (0075-7225); (until no.6): Kumasitech
Indexed: INIS AtomInd.
Published by: Kwame Nkrumah University of Science and Technology, Kumasi, Ghana. TEL 233-51-60150. Ed. Stephen Owusu. Circ: 500.

500 NGA
➤ **JOURNAL OF SCIENCE AND TECHNOLOGY EDUCATION RESEARCH.** Text in English. m. free (effective 2010). adv. **Document type:** *Journal, Academic/Scholarly.*
Media: Online - full text.
Published by: Academic Journals, PO Box 73023, Victoria Island, Lagos, Nigeria. service@academicjournals.org. Eds. Dr. Christine Redman, Dr. Keith S Taber, S C Garg.

➤ **THE JOURNAL OF SCIENCE & TECHNOLOGY LAW.** *see* LAW

▼➤ **JOURNAL OF SCIENCE AND TECHNOLOGY OF THE ARTS/ REVISTA DE CIENCIA E TECNOLOGIA DAS ARTES.** *see* ART

500 600 GBR ISSN 1758-552X
▼➤ **JOURNAL OF SCIENCE AND TECHNOLOGY POLICY IN CHINA.** Abbreviated title: J S T P C. Text in English. 2010. 3/yr. EUR 359 combined subscription in Europe (print & online eds.); USD 509 combined subscription in the Americas (print & online eds.); GBP 329 combined subscription in the UK & elsewhere (print & online eds.); AUD 779 combined subscription in Australasia (print & online eds.) (effective 2012). back issues avail. **Document type:** *Journal, Academic/Scholarly.* **Description:** Aims to offer a fluid debate on science and technology issues in the hope of influencing the wider community of policy makers and contributors.
Related titles: Online - full text ed.: ISSN 1758-5538.
Indexed: P52.
—CCC.
Published by: Emerald Group Publishing Ltd., Howard House, Wagon Ln, Bingley, W Yorks BD16 1WA, United Kingdom. TEL 44-1274-777700, FAX 44-1274-785201, emerald@emeraldinsight.com, information@emeraldinsight.com, http://www.emeraldinsight.com. Ed. Dr. Jiang Yu.

➤ **JOURNAL OF SCIENCE COMMUNICATION.** *see* COMMUNICATIONS

500 COL ISSN 0124-5481
➤ **JOURNAL OF SCIENCE EDUCATION**; revista de edicacion en ciencias. Text and summaries in English, Spanish. 2000. s-a. COP 33,000 domestic; USD 44 foreign (effective 2006). bk.rev.; software rev. abstr.; illus. Index. back issues avail. **Document type:** *Journal, Academic/Scholarly.* **Description:** Publishes about science education for the high school and university levels.
Related titles: Online - full text ed.
Indexed: C01, CPE, ERA, P18, P48, P52, P53, P54, PQC, SCOPUS, V05.
Published by: Foundation Journal of Science Education, A.A.241 241, Bogota, Colombia.

507 NLD ISSN 1059-0145
Q183.3.A1 CODEN: JSEEEP
➤ **JOURNAL OF SCIENCE EDUCATION AND TECHNOLOGY.** Text in English. 1992. 6/yr. EUR 1,036, USD 1,121 combined subscription to institutions (print & online eds.) (effective 2012). adv. reprint service avail. from PSC. **Document type:** *Journal, Academic/Scholarly.* **Description:** Forum for the discussion of issues and policies relating to improvement of US science education at all levels, including legislative, administrative, and implementation issues.
Related titles: Online - full text ed.: ISSN 1573-1839 (from IngentaConnect).
Indexed: A01, A03, A08, A22, A26, BibLing, CA, CIN, CPE, ChemAb, ChemTitl, CurCont, E01, E03, E07, ERI, ERIC, SCI, SCOPUS, SSCI, T02, W07.
—BLDSC (5054.980000), CASDDS, IE, Infotrieve, Ingenta. **CCC.**
Published by: Springer Netherlands (Subsidiary of: Springer Science+Business Media), Van Godewijckstraat 30, Dordrecht, 3311 GX, Netherlands. TEL 31-78-6576050, FAX 31-78-6576474, http://www.springer.com. Ed. Karen C Cohen.

➤ **THE JOURNAL OF SCIENCE EDUCATION FOR PERSONS WITH DISABILITIES.** *see* EDUCATION

➤ **JOURNAL OF SCIENCE TEACHER EDUCATION.** *see* EDUCATION

500 IRN ISSN 1016-1104
Q80.I67 CODEN: JSIIEN
➤ **JOURNAL OF SCIENCES, ISLAMIC REPUBLIC OF IRAN.** Text in English. 1989. q. IRR 20,000 domestic to individuals; USD 80 foreign to individuals; IRR 40,000 domestic to institutions; USD 100 foreign to institutions; IRR 10,000 domestic to students; USD 30 foreign to students (effective 2003). **Document type:** *Journal, Academic/ Scholarly.* **Description:** Promotes the exchange of knowledge between scientific centers and scientists, researchers and international experts.
Indexed: AIDS&CR, ASFA, B21, B25, BIOSIS Prev, CCMJ, CIN, CTA, ChemAb, ChemTitl, ChemoAb, INIS AtomInd, MSN, MathR, MycolAb, NSA, VirolAbstr, Z01, Z02.
—CASDDS, IE, Ingenta.
Published by: National Center for Scientific Research, Enghelab Ave 1188, P O Box 13145-478, Tehran, 13158, Iran. TEL 98-21-8771578, FAX 98-21-8773352, office@ije-ir.info, http://www.ije-ir.info. Ed. Dr. Mohammad Reza Noori-Daloii. Adv. contact N. Nikpayam. Circ: 1,500.

500 IND ISSN 0022-4456
T1 CODEN: JSIRAC
➤ **JOURNAL OF SCIENTIFIC AND INDUSTRIAL RESEARCH.** Abbreviated title: J S I R. Text in English. 1942. m. USD 540 (effective 2009). bk.rev. back issues avail.; reprints avail. **Document type:** *Journal, Academic/Scholarly.* **Description:** Covers various facets of industrial development, industrial research and technology management, case studies, short debates and conference reports.
Related titles: Microform ed.: (from PQC); Online - full text ed.: ISSN 0975-1084. free (effective 2011).
Indexed: A20, A22, A34, A35, A36, A37, AIA, ASCA, ASFA, AgBio, AgrForAb, ApMecR, B21, B23, BA, BP, C25, C30, CABA, CADCAM, CBTA, CEA, CIN, CLOSS, CRIA, CRICC, Cadscan, ChemAb, ChemTitl, E12, EIA, EIP, ESPM, EnerInd, EnvAb, EnvInd, F08, F11, F12, FCA, FLUIDEX, FS&TA, GEOBASE, GH, GeoRef, H16, INIS AtomInd, ISA, ISR, IndVet, Inspec, LeadAb, N02, N03, OR, P30, P33, PHN&I, R07, R08, R11, R13, RA&MP, RM&VM, RoboAb, S12, S13, S16, S17, SCI, SCOPUS, SoyAb, SpeleolAb, TCEA, TOSA, TriticAb, VITIS, VS, W07, W11, Zincscan.
—BLDSC (5057.000000), AskIEEE, CASDDS, IE, Infotrieve, Ingenta, INIST, Linda Hall.
Published by: National Institute of Science Communication and Information Resources (N I S C A I R), Dr. K.S. Krishnan Marg, New Delhi, 110 012, India. TEL 91-11-25841647, FAX 91-11-25847062, http://www.niscair.res.in/. Ed. P D Tyagi.

500 IND ISSN 2231-4709
▼➤ **JOURNAL OF SCIENTIFIC AND TECHNOLOGICAL RESEARCH.** Abbreviated title: J S T R. Text and summaries in English, Hindi. 2011 (Mar.). s-a. INR 600 to individuals; INR 800 to institutions; free to qualified personnel (effective 2011). bk.rev. abstr.; bibl.; charts; maps; stat. back issues avail. **Document type:** *Journal, Academic/ Scholarly.*
Published by: Kunwar Educational Society for Research & Development, Agra, 87, R.S.Residency, Veshnodhan Colony, Phase-2, Near Radha Ballabh Inter College, Dayalbagh, Agra, Uttar Pradesh, India. TEL 91-562-4052262. Ed., Pub., R&P Rajnish Kunwar.

500 USA ISSN 1937-6456
Q11
➤ **JOURNAL OF SCIENTIFIC CONFERENCE PROCEEDINGS.** Abbreviated title: J C P. Text in English. 2008 (Oct.). 3/yr. USD 780; USD 1,480 combined subscription (print & online eds.) (effective 2010). adv. back issues avail. **Document type:** *Journal, Academic/ Scholarly.* **Description:** Provides a forum for dissemination of developments in microscopy techniques, as well as their applications in all areas of science, engineering, and medicine.
Related titles: Online - full text ed.: ISSN 1937-6464. USD 1,280 (effective 2010) (from IngentaConnect).
—BLDSC (5057.350000), IE.
Published by: American Scientific Publishers, 26650 The Old Rd, Ste 208, Valencia, CA 91381. TEL 661-799-7200, FAX 661-254-1207, order@aspbs.com. Ed. Dr. Hari Singh Nalwa. **Subscr. to:** 25650 N Lewis Way, Stevenson Ranch, CA 91381.

500 133 USA ISSN 0892-3310
Q180.55.M4
➤ **JOURNAL OF SCIENTIFIC EXPLORATION.** Abbreviated title: J S E. Text in English. 1987. q. free to members (effective 2010). bk.rev. illus. index. back issues avail.; reprints avail. **Document type:** *Journal, Academic/Scholarly.* **Description:** Features original research papers in areas falling outside the established scientific arena. Attempts to provide an unbiased, professional forum for discussion and debate about anomalous phenomena.
Related titles: Online - full text ed.: USD 55 to individuals (effective 2001).
Indexed: A01, CA, CPEI, DIP, EngInd, IBR, IBZ, IPsyAb, M&GPA, RASB, SCOPUS, SOPODA, SociolAb, T02.
—Ingenta, INIST. **CCC.**
Published by: Society for Scientific Exploration, c/o Mark Urban-Lurain, Michigan State University, 111 N Kedzie Lab, East Lansing, MI 48824. TEL 517-432-2152 ext 119, FAX 517-432-5653. Ed. Stephen E Braude TEL 410-455-2025. **Subscr. to:** Allen Press Inc., PO Box 1897, Lawrence, KS 66044. TEL 785-843-1235, FAX 785-843-1274, orders@allenpress.com, http://www.allenpress.com.

500 PAK ISSN 2070-0237
Q180.N33
▼➤ **JOURNAL OF SCIENTIFIC RESEARCH.** Text in English. 2009. q. **Document type:** *Journal, Academic/Scholarly.*
Related titles: Online - full text ed.: ISSN 2070-0245. free (effective 2011).
Indexed: A01.
—Linda Hall.
Published by: Rajshahi University, Faculty of Sciences, Rajshahi, 6205, Pakistan. TEL 92-880-721750041, FAX 92-880-721750064. Ed. A K M A Islam.

500 IND ISSN 0975-0754
▼➤ **JOURNAL OF SCIENTIFIC REVIEW.** Text in English. 2009. irreg. free (effective 2011). **Document type:** *Journal, Academic/Scholarly.*
Formerly (until 2009): S R B Mag
Media: Online - full text.
Published by: Scientific Review Board Ed. Sanjeev Kumar.

➤ **JOURNAL OF SOCIAL AND ECOLOGICAL BOUNDARIES.** *see* HUMANITIES: COMPREHENSIVE WORKS

570.5 GBR ISSN 1742-5689
Q179.9
➤ **JOURNAL OF THE ROYAL SOCIETY. INTERFACE.** Text in English. 2004. m. GBP 1,748, EUR 2,272 combined subscription in Europe to institutions (print & online eds.); USD 3,251 combined subscription in US & Canada to institutions (print & online eds.); GBP 1,851, USD 3,317 combined subscription elsewhere to institutions (print & online eds.) (effective 2012). back issues avail. **Document type:** *Journal, Academic/Scholarly.* **Description:** Promotes research at the interface between the physical and life sciences.
Related titles: Online - full text ed.: ISSN 1742-5662. GBP 1,345, EUR 1,748 in Europe to institutions; USD 2,501 in US & Canada to institutions; GBP 1,424, USD 2,552 elsewhere to institutions (effective 2012); ♦ Supplement(s): Interface Focus. ISSN 2042-8898.
Indexed: A20, A22, AnBeAb, B21, B25, B27, BIOSIS Prev, CPEI, CTA, CurCont, E01, E17, EMBASE, ESPM, EntAb, ExcerpMed, Inspec, MEDLINE, MycolAb, NSA, P30, R10, Reac, SCI, SCOPUS, W07, Z01.
—BLDSC (5052.120800), IE, Linda Hall. **CCC.**
Published by: The Royal Society Publishing, 6-9 Carlton House Terr, London, SW1Y 5AG, United Kingdom. TEL 44-20-74512500, FAX 44-20-79761837, sales@royalsociety.org, http://royalsocietypublishing.org. Ed. Leslie Dutton. **Subscr. to:** Portland Customer Services, Commerce Way, Colchester CO2 8HP, United Kingdom. TEL 44-1206-796351, FAX 44-1206-799331, sales@portland-services.com, http://www.portlandpress.com.

500 USA ISSN 1553-5975
➤ **JOURNAL OF THE SOUTH CAROLINA SCIENCE ACADEMY.** Abbreviated title: S C A S Journal. Text in English. 2003 (Fall). a. free (effective 2010). **Document type:** *Journal, Academic/Scholarly.*
Media: Online - full text.
Indexed: A01, A26, CA, E08, G08, I05, S06, S09, T02.
Published by: South Carolina Academy of Science, c/o Thomas Reeves, Science Department, Midlands Technical College, Columbia, SC 29202. TEL 803-822-3554, FAX 803-822-3422, reevest@midlandstech.edu. Ed. Hans-Conrad zur Loye.

500 371.3 TUR ISSN 1304-6020
➤ **JOURNAL OF TURKISH SCIENCE EDUCATION.** Abbreviated title: T U S E D. Text in English, Turkish. 2004 (July). 3/yr. free (effective 2011). **Document type:** *Journal, Academic/Scholarly.* **Description:** Covers all aspects of science education, including development and implementation of science curriculum, learning and teaching strategies, measurement and assessment and the use of information and communications technologies.
Media: Online - full text.
Indexed: CA, E03, ERA, ERI, S21, SCOPUS, T02.
Published by: Ekip Ltd. Sti., I. Pasa Mah. Deniz Sok. No. 4/1, Trabzon, Turkey. TEL 90-462-3233284, FAX 90-462-3211913, editortused@gmail.com, http://www.tused.org/internet/tused/ tufedmain1.htm. Ed. Salih Cepny.

500 USA ISSN 1948-5808
QC5.56
JOURNAL OF UNCONVENTIONAL THEORIES AND RESEARCH. Text in English. 2007. s-a. free (effective 2009). **Document type:** *Journal, Academic/Scholarly.*
Media: Online - full content.
Published by: Scientific Journals International (Subsidiary of: Global Commerce & Communication, Inc), 1407 33rd St S, Saint Cloud, MN 56301. TEL 320-217-6019, info@scientificjournals.org.

500 CAN ISSN 1911-8899
JOURNAL OF UNDERGRADUATE LIFE SCIENCES. Abbreviated title: J U L S. Text in English. 2007. a. **Document type:** *Journal, Academic/ Scholarly.*
Related titles: Online - full text ed.: free (effective 2011).
Published by: University of Toronto, Faculty of Arts & Science, 100 St. George St, Toronto, ON M5S 3G3, Canada. TEL 416-946-3118. Eds. Kirill Zaslavsky, Roy Yang.

JOURNAL OF WOMEN AND MINORITIES IN SCIENCE AND ENGINEERING. *see* ENGINEERING

500 USA ISSN 1539-4026
➤ **JOURNAL OF YOUNG INVESTIGATORS.** Abbreviated title: J Y I. Text in English. 1998. 3/yr. free (effective 2011). back issues avail. **Document type:** *Journal, Academic/Scholarly.* **Description:** Dedicated to the presentation of undergraduate research in science, mathematics, and engineering.
Formerly (until 2000): National Journal of Young investigators
Media: Online - full text.
Published by: Journal Of Young Investigators, Inc, 2762 N Randolph St, Arlington, VA 22207. TEL 703-243-3291. Ed. Selina Dobing.

➤ **JUNCTURES**; the journal for thematic dialogue. *see* ART

500 DEU ISSN 0179-8529
JUNGE WISSENSCHAFT/YOUNG RESEARCHER. Text in German. 1986. q. EUR 30; EUR 20 to students (effective 2010). adv. **Document type:** *Magazine, Consumer.*
Related titles: Online - full text ed.
Indexed: DIP, IBR, IBZ, TM.
Published by: Verlag Junge Wissenschaft, Athanasios Roussidis, Neuer Zollhof 3, Duesseldorf, 40221, Germany. TEL 49-211-38548912, FAX 49-211-38548929, info@verlag-jungewissenschaft.de, http:// www.verlag-jungewissenschaft.de. Ed. Sabine Walter. Pub. Paul Dobrinski. adv.: color page EUR 2,200.

500 IDN ISSN 1979-0880
T174.7
JURNAL NANOSAINS & NANOTEKNOLOGI. Text in English. 2008. s-a. **Document type:** *Journal, Academic/Scholarly.*
Related titles: Online - full text ed.: free (effective 2011).
Published by: Himpunan Riset Material Indonesia http://ijp.fi.itb.ac.id/ index.php/nano/index. Ed. Mikrajuddin Abdullah.

S

371.3 500 USA ISSN 1949-145X
▼➤ **K B M JOURNAL OF SCIENCE EDUCATION.** Text in English. 2010 (Jan.). q. free (effective 2010). **Document type:** *Journal, Academic/ Scholarly.* **Description:** Includes research and reviews in all areas of science education.
Media: Online - full content.
Published by: K B M Scientific Publishing, Ltd, 971 Pepperwood Dr, Fayetteville, NC 28331-9331. TEL 910-672-1114, info@kbm-scientific-publishing.org.

500 KWT
K I S R TECHNICAL REPORT. Text in English. irreg.
Published by: Kuwait Institute for Scientific Research, PO Box 24885, Safat, 13109, Kuwait. TEL 965-4836100, FAX 965-4830643, http://www.kisr.edu.kw/.

500 JPN ISSN 0022-7625
Q4 CODEN: KAGTAT
KAGAKU/SCIENCE JOURNAL KAGAKU. Text and summaries in Japanese. 1931. m. JPY 10,100. adv. bk.rev. charts; illus. index.
Indexed: ChemAb, INIS AtomInd, Inspec, JPI, P30.
—BLDSC (5080.000000), CASDDS, INIST, Linda Hall.
Published by: Iwanami Shoten, Publishers, 2-5-5 Hitotsubashi, Chiyoda-ku, Tokyo, 101-0003, Japan. FAX 81-3-239-9618. Ed. Shigeki Kobayashi. Circ: 20,000. **Dist. overseas by:** Japan Publications Trading Co., Ltd., Book Export II Dept, PO Box 5030, Tokyo International, Tokyo 101-3191, Japan. TEL 81-3-32923753, FAX 81-3-32920410, infoserials@jptco.co.jp, http://www.jptco.co.jp.

500 JPN ISSN 0368-4741
Q4 CODEN: KAASAU
KAGAKU ASAHI/SCIENTIFIC ASAHI. Text in Japanese. 1941. m. USD 119.
Indexed: JPI.

Published by: Asahi Shimbun Publishing Co., 5-3-2 Tsukiji, Chuo-ku, Tokyo, 104-8011, Japan. TEL 81-3-35450131. Ed. Takashi Iida. **Dist. by:** Japan Publications Trading Co., Ltd., Book Export II Dept, PO Box 5030, Tokyo International, Tokyo 101-3191, Japan. TEL 81-3-32923753, FAX 81-3-32920410, infoserials@jptco.co.jp, http://www.jptco.co.jp.

KAGAKU GIJUTSU HAKUSHO/WHITE PAPER OF SCIENCE AND TECHNOLOGY IN JAPAN. *see* TECHNOLOGY: COMPREHENSIVE WORKS

KAGAKU GIJUTSU HAKUSHO NO ARAMASHI. *see* TECHNOLOGY: COMPREHENSIVE WORKS

KAGAKU GIJUTSU SHINKO CHOSEIHI NYUSU. *see* TECHNOLOGY: COMPREHENSIVE WORKS

KAGAKU GIJUTSU SHINKO CHOSEIHI SHIKEN KENKYU JISSHI KEIKAKU. *see* TECHNOLOGY: COMPREHENSIVE WORKS

KAGAKU GIJUTSUCHO NENPO. *see* TECHNOLOGY: COMPREHENSIVE WORKS

500 JPN ISSN 0022-7668

➤ **KAGAKU KISORON KENKYU/JAPAN ASSOCIATION FOR PHILOSOPHY OF SCIENCE. JOURNAL.** Text in Japanese. 1954. s-a. JPY 800 per issue (effective 2000). bk.rev. **Document type:** *Academic/Scholarly.* **Description:** Articles relate to logic, and methodology or philosophy of science and deal with problems in the fields of science and philosophy.
Indexed: Inspec, PsycholAb.
Published by: Japan Association for Philosophy of Science/Kagaku Kisoron Gakkai, c/o Dept of Philosophy, Keio University, 2-15-45 Mita, Minato-ku, Tokyo, 108-0073, Japan. TEL 81-3-3453-4511 ext 3084, FAX 81-3-3798-7480. Ed., Pub., R&P Yoichiro Murakami. Circ: 700.

➤ **KAGAKU TO KOGYO (OSAKA)/SCIENCE AND INDUSTRY.** *see* TECHNOLOGY: COMPREHENSIVE WORKS

509 JPN ISSN 0022-7692
Q124.6 CODEN: KAGKA2

➤ **KAGAKUSHI KENKYU/JOURNAL OF HISTORY OF SCIENCE.** Text in Japanese; Summaries in Multiple languages. 1941. q. JPY 10,000. bk.rev. back issues avail. **Document type:** *Journal, Academic/Scholarly.*
Indexed: AmH&L, CA, ChemAb, ChemTitl, EMBASE, ExcerpMed, FR, HistAb, MEDLINE, P30, RILM, SCOPUS, T02.
—CASDDS, INIST, Linda Hall. **CCC.**
Published by: Nihon Kagakushi Gakkai/History of Science Society of Japan, West Pine Bldg, 201, 2-15-19 Hirakawa-cho, Chiyoda-ku, Tokyo, 102-0093, Japan. http://wwwsoc.nii.ac.jp/jshs/index-j.html. Ed. Masakatsu Yomazaki.

500 JPN ISSN 0389-6692
Q4 CODEN: KDSHA6

KAGOSHIMA DAIGAKU KYOIKUGAKUBU KENKYU KIYO. SHIZEN KAGAKU HEN/KAGOSHIMA UNIVERSITY. FACULTY OF EDUCATION. BULLETIN. NATURAL SCIENCE. Text and summaries in English, Japanese. 1949. a. **Document type:** *Academic/Scholarly.*
Indexed: CCMJ, ChemAb, ChemTitl, JPI, MSN, MathR.
—CASDDS.
Published by: Kagoshima Daigaku, Kyoikugakubu/Kagoshima University, Faculty of Education, 20-6 Korimo-To 1-chome, Kagoshima-shi, 890-0065, Japan.

500 JPN ISSN 1345-6938

KAGOSHIMA DAIGAKU RIGAKUBU KIYO/KAGOSHIMA UNIVERSITY. FACULTY OF SCIENCE. REPORTS. Text in Japanese. 1997. a. **Document type:** *Academic/Scholarly.*
Formed by the merger of (1969-1996): Kagoshima Daigaku Rigakubu Kiyo. Sugaku, Butsurigaku, Kagaku/Kagoshima University. Faculty of Science. Reports. Mathematics, Physics and Chemistry (0385-4027); (1969-1996): Kagoshima Daigaku Rigakubu Kiyo. Chigaku, Seibutsugaku/Kagoshima University. Faculty of Science. Reports. Earth Sciences and Biology (0385-4019); Both superseded (in 1968): Kagoshima Daigaku Rigakubu Kiyo/ Kagoshima University. Faculty of Science. Reports (0368-6728); Incorporated (1952-1996): Kagoshima Daigaku Rika Hokoku (0368-5136)
Indexed: CCMJ, GeoRef, MSN, MathR, Z02.
—BLDSC (7467.150000).
Published by: Kagoshima Daigaku, Rigakubu/Kagoshima University, Faculty of Science, 1-21-24 Korimoto, Kagoshima, 890-8580, Japan. TEL 81-99-2858025, FAX 81-99-2858029, http://www.sci.kagoshima-u.ac.jp/jhsrc/index.html.

KAGOSHIMA JOSHI TANKI DAIGAKU KIYO/KAGOSHIMA WOMEN'S JUNIOR COLLEGE. BULLETIN. *see* HUMANITIES: COMPREHENSIVE WORKS

500 JPN ISSN 0286-1208
CODEN: KTDHDC

KAGOSHIMA-KENRITSU TANKI DAIGAKU KIYO. SHIZEN KAGAKU HEN/KAGOSHIMA PREFECTURAL JUNIOR COLLEGE. BULLETIN. NATURAL SCIENCES. Text in Japanese, English; Summaries in English. 1950. a. **Document type:** *Bulletin.*
Indexed: JPI.
—CASDDS.
Published by: Kagoshima Prefectural College/Kagoshima-kenritsu Tanki Daigaku, 1-52-1 Shimo-Ishiki, Kagoshima-shi, 890-0005, Japan.

500 300 JPN ISSN 1345-0441

KAGOSHIMA UNIVERSITY. RESEARCH CENTER FOR THE PACIFIC ISLANDS. OCCASIONAL PAPERS. Text in English, Japanese. 1983. irreg. exchange basis. **Document type:** *Monographic series, Academic/Scholarly.* **Description:** Provides multi-disciplinary studies on the South Pacific region, from agriculture to zoology.
Formerly: Kagoshima University. Research Center for the South Pacific. Occasional Papers (0289-2707)
Indexed: Z01.
—BLDSC (6217.480790).
Published by: Kagoshima University, Research Center for the Pacific Islands, 1-21-24 Korimo-To, Kagoshima-shi, 890-8580, Japan. TEL 81-99-285-7394, FAX 81-99-285-6197, http://cpi.sci.kagoshima-u.ac.jp, http://cpi.sci.kagoshima-u.ac.jp. Circ: 700 (controlled).

500 IND ISSN 0022-7870

KALAIKATHIR. Text in Tamil. 1948. m. adv. bk.rev. charts; illus. index. **Document type:** *Magazine, Consumer.*
Published by: G R D Trust, Avanashi Rd, Neelambur, Coimbatore, 641 014, India. TEL 91-422-2626206, FAX 91-422-2625188, grdam@grd.org, http://www.grd.org.

508.074 JPN ISSN 0915-5074

KAMISHIHORO-CHO HIGASHI TAISETSU HAKUBUTSUKAN KENKYU HOKOKU/HIGASHI TAISETSU MUSEUM OF NATURAL HISTORY. BULLETIN. Text in Japanese; Summaries in English. 1975. irreg. JPY 1,000 per issue. **Document type:** *Bulletin.* **Description:** Contains original research papers.
Indexed: Z01.
Published by: Higashi Taisetsu Museum of Natural History/Kamishihoro-cho Higashi Taisetsu Hakubutsukan, Nukabira, Kato-gun, Kamishihoro-cho, Hokkaido 080-1403, Japan. TEL 81-1564-64-2323. Ed., R&P Momoki Kawabe.

507.4 JPN ISSN 0453-1906
QH188

KANAGAWA-KENRITSU HAKUBUTSUKAN KENKYU HOKOKU. SHIZEN KAGAKU/KANAGAWA PREFECTURAL MUSEUM OF NATURAL HISTORY. BULLETIN. NATURAL SCIENCE. Text and summaries in English, Japanese. 1968. a. **Document type:** *Bulletin.*
Indexed: GEOBASE, GeoRef, JPI, RefZh, SCOPUS, SpeleolAb, Z01.
—BLDSC (2597.965000).
Published by: Kanagawa-kenritsu Hakubutsukan/Kanagawa Prefectural Museum of Natural History, 499 Iriyuda, Odawara-shi, Kanagawa-ken 250-0031, Japan. TEL 81-465-211515, FAX 81-465-238846.

507.4 JPN ISSN 1342-8993

KANAGAWA-KENRITSU HAKUBUTSUKAN SHIRYO MOKUROKU. SHIZEN KAGAKU/KANAGAWA PREFECTURAL MUSEUM OF NATURAL HISTORY. CATALOGUE OF THE COLLECTION. Text in Japanese. 1996. a.
Indexed: GeoRef.
Published by: Kanagawa-kenritsu Hakubutsukan/Kanagawa Prefectural Museum of Natural History, 499 Iriyuda, Odawara-shi, Kanagawa-ken 250-0031, Japan. TEL 81-465-211515, FAX 81-465-238846, plan@pat-net.ne.jp.

KANAGAWA KOKA DAIGAKU KENKYU HOKOKU. B RIKOGAKU HEN/KANAGAWA INSTITUTE OF TECHNOLOGY. RESEARCH REPORTS. PART B. SCIENCE AND TECHNOLOGY. *see* TECHNOLOGY: COMPREHENSIVE WORKS

500.9 JPN ISSN 0388-9009

KANAGAWA SHIZENSHI SHIRYO/NATURAL HISTORY REPORT OF KANAGAWA. Text in Japanese; Summaries in English, Japanese. 1980. a.
Indexed: Z01.
Published by: Kanagawa-kenritsu Hakubutsukan/Kanagawa Prefectural Museum of Natural History, 499 Iriyuda, Odawara-shi, Kanagawa-ken 250-0031, Japan. TEL 81-465-211515, FAX 81-465-238846.

500 JPN ISSN 0387-0995
Q4 CODEN: KADSAB

KANAZAWA DAIGAKU KYOIKUGAKUBU KIYO. SHIZEN KAGAKU HEN/KANAZAWA UNIVERSITY. FACULTY OF EDUCATION. BULLETIN. NATURAL SCIENCES. Text in Japanese; Summaries in English. 1952. a.
Supersedes in part (1952-1962): Kanazawa Daigaku Kyoiku Gakubu Kiyo/Kanazawa University. Faculty of Education. Bulletin (0387-0901)
Indexed: CCMJ, GeoRef, JPI, MSN, SpeleolAb.
Published by: Kanazawa Daigaku, Kyoikugakubu/Kanazawa University, Faculty of Education, Kakuma-machi, Kanazawa-shi, 920-0937, Japan. TEL 81-76-2645555, info-edu@ed.kanazawa-u.ac.jp, http://www.ed.kanazawa-u.ac.jp/index-ed.html.

500 JPN ISSN 0302-0479
Q4

KANAZAWA DAIGAKU KYOYOBU RONSHU. SHIZEN KAGAKU HEN/KANAZAWA UNIVERSITY. COLLEGE OF LIBERAL ARTS. ANNALS OF SCIENCE. Text in English, Japanese; Summaries in English. 1965. a. illus.
Indexed: JPI, MathR.
Published by: Kanazawa Daigaku, Kyoyobu/Kanazawa University, College of Liberal Arts, 1-1 Marunouchi, Kanazawa-shi, Ishikawa-ken, 920, Japan.

500 JPN ISSN 0022-8338
Q4 CODEN: SRKAAT

KANAZAWA UNIVERSITY. SCIENCE REPORTS/KANAZAWA DAIGAKU RIKA HOKOKU. Text in English, French. 1951. s-a. per issue exchange basis. bibl.; charts; illus. index.
Indexed: CCMJ, ChemAb, GeoRef, INIS AtomInd, Inspec, JTA, MSN, MathR, MinerAb, RefZh, SpeleolAb, Z01, Z02.
—BLDSC (8155.000000), AskIEEE, CASDDS, INIST, Linda Hall.
Published by: Kanazawa Daigaku, Rigakubu/Kanazawa University, Faculty of Science, Kakuma-Machi, Kanazawa-shi, Ishikawa-ken 920-1164, Japan. TEL 0762-64-5620, FAX 0762-64-5737. Ed. Y Furuta. Circ: 500.

500 JPN ISSN 0285-3205

KANSAI SHIZEN KAGAKU. Text in Japanese. 1944. a. JPY 1,500. **Description:** Contains reviews, commentary, and news.
Published by: Kansai Natural Science Research Society/Kansai Shizen Kagaku Kenkyukai, Kinki Nihon Tetsudo K.K., 1-55 Uehon-Machi 6-chome, Tennoji-ku, Osaka-shi, 543-0001, Japan.

500 USA ISSN 0022-8443
Q11 CODEN: TSASAH

➤ **KANSAS ACADEMY OF SCIENCE. TRANSACTIONS.** Text in English. 1872. s-a. free (effective 2010). index. back issues avail. **Document type:** *Journal, Academic/Scholarly.* **Description:** Covers biological, physical and behavioral sciences, mathematics and computer science, history and philosophy of science.
Former titles (until 1903): Kansas Academy of Science. Transactions of the Annual Meetings (1933-0545); (until 1882): Kansas Academy of Science. Transactions (1933-0537)
Related titles: Online - full text ed.: ISSN 1938-5420.
Indexed: A22, A26, A37, ASFA, AgrForAb, AnBeAb, B21, B25, BIOSIS Prev, C25, C30, CABA, ChemAb, DentInd, E01, E08, E12, E17, ESPM, EntAb, F08, FCA, G08, GH, GeoRef, H16, I05, IBR, IBZ, IndMed, MaizeAb, MycolAb, N02, N03, P30, P32, RASB, S06, S09, S13, SASA, SpeleolAb, VITIS, W08, W10, WildRev, Z01.
—BLDSC (8976.000000), CASDDS, GNLM, IE, Infotrieve, Ingenta, INIST, Linda Hall. **CCC.**
Published by: (Kansas Academy of Sciences), Allen Press Inc., 810 E 10th St, PO Box 368, Lawrence, KS 66044. TEL 785-843-1234, FAX 785-843-1226, orders@allenpress.com. Eds. Michael J Everhart, Roy J Beckemeyer. Circ: 850.

508 USA ISSN 0022-877X
QH51

KANSAS SCHOOL NATURALIST. Abbreviated title: K S N. Text in English. 1954. irreg., latest vol.56, 2009. free to qualified personnel (effective 2010). bk.rev. charts; illus. back issues avail. **Document type:** *Monographic series, Academic/Scholarly.*
Related titles: Online - full text ed.: free (effective 2010).
Indexed: B25, BIOSIS Prev, MycolAb, WildRev, Z01.
—Ingenta, Linda Hall.
Published by: (Emporia State University, Division of Biology), Emporia State University Press, 1200 Commercial St, PO Box 4050, Emporia, KS 66801. TEL 620-341-1200, elemadvi@emporia.edu. Ed. John Richard Schrock.

500 PAK ISSN 0250-5363
Q80.P3 CODEN: KUJSDE

KARACHI JOURNAL OF SCIENCE. Text in English. 1972. s-a. PKR 100, USD 50. adv. bk.rev. abstr.; bibl.; charts. **Document type:** *Journal, Academic/Scholarly.*
Indexed: CCMJ, ChemAb, ChemTitl, INIS AtomInd, Inspec, MathR, Z02.
—BLDSC (5085.698300), AskIEEE, CASDDS.
Published by: University of Karachi, Department of Physics, Karachi, 75270, Pakistan. FAX 92-21-473-226. Ed. Viqar Uddin Ahmad. Circ: 500.

500 IND ISSN 0075-5168
Q1 CODEN: KUJSAB

KARNATAK UNIVERSITY, DHARWAD, INDIA. JOURNAL. SCIENCE. Key Title: Journal of the Karnatak University. Science. Text in English. 1959. a. **Document type:** *Journal, Academic/Scholarly.*
Supersedes in part (in 1959): Karnatak University. Journal
Indexed: BAS, ChemAb, GeoRef, SpeleolAb.
—CASDDS, Linda Hall.
Published by: Karnatak University, Pavate Nagar, Dharwad, Karnataka 580 003, India.

KARRIEREFUEHRER LIFE SCIENCES; Berufseinstieg fuer Hochschulabsolventen. *see* OCCUPATIONS AND CAREERS

KASHI SHIFAN XUEYUAN XUEBAO/KASHGAR TEACHERS COLLEGE. JOURNAL. *see* SOCIAL SCIENCES: COMPREHENSIVE WORKS

500 JPN ISSN 1346-5252

KASHIKA JOUHOU GAKKAI ROMBUNSHUU GAPPON/VISUALIZATION SOCIETY OF JAPAN. TRANSACTIONS. Text in Multiple languages. 1981. s-a. **Document type:** *Journal, Academic/Scholarly.*
Supersedes in part (in 2001): Kashika Joho Gakkaishi (0916-4731); Which was formerly (until 1990): Nagare no Kashika (0287-3605)
Related titles: Online - full text ed.: Kashika Jouhou Gakkai Rombunshuu. ISSN 1346-5260. free (effective 2011).
Indexed: A39, C27, C29, D03, D04, E13, INIS AtomInd, R14, S14, S15, S18.
—BLDSC (4912.557000). **CCC.**
Published by: Kashika Jouhou Gakkai/The Visualization Society of Japan, #103, 3-29-20, Kamijujo, Kita-ku, Tokyo, 114 0034, Japan. TEL 81-3-59935020, FAX 81-3-59935026, info@vsj.or.jp, http://www.ricoh.co.jp/net-messena/ACADEMIA/VISUAL/VISUALe.html.

571.3 JPN ISSN 0915-6089

➤ **KATACHI NO KAGAKKAIHO/SOCIETY FOR SCIENCE ON FORM. BULLETIN.** Text in Japanese. 1987. 3/yr. JPY 8,000 membership (effective 2002). bk.rev. 80 p./no.; back issues avail. **Document type:** *Journal, Academic/Scholarly.*
—**CCC.**
Published by: Society for Science on Form Japan/Katachi no Kagakkai, c/o Prof. Shu Matsuura, Faculty of Development Technology, Tokai University, Numazu, 410-0321, Japan. TEL 81-423-88-7224, 81-559-61-1111 ext 2306, FAX 81-423-85-7204, 81-559-68-1224. Ed., R&P Ryuji Takaki TEL 81-42-388-7224. Circ: 450 (paid).

500 600 NPL ISSN 1816-8752

➤ **KATHMANDU UNIVERSITY JOURNAL OF SCIENCE, ENGINEERING AND TECHNOLOGY.** Text in English. 2005. 2/yr. **Document type:** *Journal, Academic/Scholarly.* **Description:** Aims to facilitate researchers to publish their research findings, have a continued communication with peers and foster research in the fields of science, engineering and technology.
Media: Online - full text.
Published by: Kathmandu University, Dhulikhel Kavre, P B No.6250, Kathmandu, Nepal. TEL 977-11-661399, FAX 977-11-661443, kuset@ku.edu.np. Ed. Pushpa Raj Adhikary.

500 DEU ISSN 0941-8482
QH1

➤ **KAUPIA;** Darmstaedter Beitraege zur Naturgeschichte. Text in English, German; Summaries in English. 1992. irreg., latest vol.14, 2005. price varies. back issues avail. **Document type:** *Monographic series, Academic/Scholarly.*
Indexed: GeoRef, Z01.
—**CCC.**
Published by: Hessisches Landesmuseum Darmstadt, Friedensplatz 1, Darmstadt, 64283, Germany. TEL 49-6151-165703, FAX 49-6151-28942, info@hlmd.de, http://www.hlmd.de. Circ: 1,000.

500 IRN ISSN 1023-2079

KAYHAN ELMI. Text in Persian, Modern. 1989. m. USD 222 in North America. illus. **Document type:** *Consumer.*
Published by: Kayhan Publications, Ferdowsi Ave., P O Box 11365-9631, Tehran, Iran. TEL 98-21-3110251, FAX 98-21-3114228, TELEX 212467.

500 KAZ ISSN 1682-4296
AS262 CODEN: VANKAM

KAZAKSTAN RESPUBLIKASYNY GYLYM AKADEMIASYNYN BAANDAMALARY/REPUBLIC OF KAZAKHSTAN. MINISTRY OF SCIENCES AND HIGHER EDUCATION. NATIONAL ACADEMY OF SCIENCES. REPORTS. Text in Russian. 1944. m. adv. bk.rev. abstr.; bibl.; charts; illus.; stat. **Document type:** *Academic/Scholarly.*

Former titles (until 1999): Kazakstan Respublikasynyn Gylym Ministrligi Gylym Akademiiasynyn Baandamalary (1029-8665); (until 1996): Kazakstan Respublikasy Ulttyk Gylym Akademiasynyn Baandamalary (1025-9120); Which superseded in part (1944-1992): Akademiya Nauk Kazakhskoi S.S.R. Vestnik (0002-3213)
Indexed: C&ISA, CCMJ, ChemAb, CorrAb, E&CAJ, GeoRef, MSN, MathR, RASB, SolStAb, SpeleolAb, WAA, Z01, Z02.
—CASDDS, INIST, Linda Hall.
Published by: (Kazakhstan Respublikasy Gylym Zane Zogary Bilim Ministrliginn. Kazakhstan Respublikasy Ulttyk Gylym Akademiasynyn/ Ministry of Education and Science of the Republic of Kazakhstan, National Academy of Sciences of the Republic of Kazakhstan), Gylym, Pushkina 111-113, Almaty, 480100, Kazakstan. TEL 3272-611877. Ed. Sh E Esenov.

500 001.3 370 RUS ISSN 2072-6007
▼ ➤ **KAZANSKII GOSUDARSTVENNYI ENERGETICHESKII UNIVERSITET. VESTNIK/KAZAN STATE POWER ENGINEERING UNIVERSITY HERALD.** Text in Russian, English. 2009. q. abstr.; charts. 180 p./no.; back issues avail. **Document type:** *Journal, Academic/Scholarly.*
Related titles: Online - full text ed.
Published by: Kazanskii Gosudarstvennyi Energeticheskii Universitet/ Kazan State Power Engineering University, ul. Krasnoselskaia, 51, Kazan, 420066, Russian Federation. TEL 7-843-5194224, http:// www.kgeu.ru. Ed., Pub. Yurii N Petrushenko. Circ: 350 (paid); 150 (controlled).

500 600 CHN ISSN 1002-1299
Q4
KE XUE. Text in Chinese. 1978. m. CNY 118, USD 75 (effective 1996). adv. bk.rev. back issues avail. **Document type:** *Academic/Scholarly.*
Related titles: ◆ Italian ed.: Le Scienze. ISSN 0036-8083; ◆ English ed.: Scientific American. ISSN 0036-8733; ◆ German ed.: Spektrum der Wissenschaft. ISSN 0170-2971; ◆ Hungarian ed.: Tudomany. ISSN 0237-322X; ◆ French ed.: Pour la Science. ISSN 0153-4092; ◆ Spanish ed.: Investigacion y Ciencia. ISSN 0210-136X; ◆ Japanese ed.: Nikkei Saiensu. ISSN 0917-009X; ◆ Arabic ed.: Majallat al-Ulum; ◆ Polish ed.: Swiat Nauki. ISSN 0867-6380; Turkish ed.: Bilim.
Published by: I S T I C Chongqing, P.O. Box 2104, Chongqing, Sichuan, China. TEL 86-23-6351-7021, FAX 86-23-6350-2473. Ed., R&P Shide Wang. Pub. Yuanshu Chen. Adv. contact Wang Shide. Circ: 23,000 (paid).

500 JPN ISSN 0911-7237
KEIO GIJUKU DAIGAKU HIYOSHI KIYO. SHIZEN KAGAKU/HIYOSHI REVIEW OF NATURAL SCIENCE. Text in English, Japanese; Summaries in English. 1985. a. free to qualified personnel.
Indexed: CCMJ, MSN, MathR, Z01, Z02.
Published by: Keio Gijuku Daigaku, Hiyoshi Kiyo Kanko Iinkai, 1-1 Hiyoshi 4-chome, Kohoku-ku, Yokohama-shi, Kanagawa-ken 223-0061, Japan.

KEIO GIJUKU DAIGAKU RIKOGAKUBUHO. *see* TECHNOLOGY: COMPREHENSIVE WORKS

500 CHN ISSN 1004-8200
Q127.C5
KEJI CHAO/SCIENCE & CULTURE SCIENCE-TECH WAVES. Text in Chinese. 1989. m. illus. 64 p./no.; **Document type:** *Journal, Academic/Scholarly.*
Formerly: Keji Fazhan yu Gaige/Science and Technology Development and Reform
Related titles: Online - full text ed.
—East View.
Published by: (Beijing Shi Kexue Jishu Weiyuanhui. Beijing Gaojishu Chuangye Fuwu Zhongxin/Beijing Municipal Science & Technology Commission), Keji Chao Zazhishe, 11, Anxiang Beili, 5/F, Chuangye Dasha, Beijing, 100009, China. TEL 86-10-64860190, FAX 86-10-64862728. **Dist. by:** China International Book Trading Corp, 35 Chegongzhuang Xilu, Haidian District, PO Box 399, Beijing 100044, China. TEL 86-10-68412045, FAX 86-10-68412023, cibtc@mail.cibtc.com.cn, http://www.cibtc.com.cn.

500 600 CHN ISSN 1000-7857
Q127.C5
KEJI DAOBAO/SCIENCE & TECHNOLOGY REVIEW. Text in Chinese, English. bi-m. CNY 360 (effective 2009). **Document type:** *Journal, Academic/Scholarly.*
Related titles: Online - full text ed.
Indexed: A28, A34, A35, A36, A37, A38, APA, AgBio, AgrForAb, BA, BP, BrCerAb, C&ISA, C25, C30, CA/WCA, CABA, CIA, CerAb, CivEngAb, CorrAb, D01, E&CAJ, E11, E12, EEA, EMA, ESPM, EnvEAb, F08, F11, F12, FCA, G11, GH, H15, H16, H17, I11, IndVet, LT, M&GPA, M&TEA, M09, MBF, METADEX, MaizeAb, N02, N03, O01, OR, P32, P33, P37, P40, PGegResA, PHN&I, PN&I, R07, R08, R11, R12, R13, RA&MP, RM&VM, RefZh, S12, S13, S16, S17, SolStAb, SoyAb, T04, T05, TAR, TriticAb, VS, W10, W11, WAA.
—BLDSC (8134.282100), East View, Linda Hall.
Published by: (Zhongguo Kexue Jishu Xuehui/Chinese Association of Science and Technology), Keji Daobaoshe/Science & Technology Review Publishing House, 86 Xueyuan Nan Lu, Beijing, 100081, China. TEL 86-10-62118198. Ed. Changgen Feng.

500 600 TWN ISSN 1680-2314
➤ **KEJI FAZHAN BIAOGAN/BENCHMARKING SCI-TECH DEVELOPMENT.** Variant title: Guidepost for Science and Technology Development Quarterly. Text in Chinese. 2001. q. free. Website rev. abstr.; charts; bibl.; illus. 40 p./no.; reprints avail. **Document type:** *Journal, Academic/Scholarly.* **Description:** Covers current S&T development in Taiwan and provides reference sources of policy making.
Published by: Xingzhengyuan Guojia Kexue Weiyuanhui, Kexue Jishu Ziliao Zhongxin/Science & Technology Information Center, 16F, 106, Hoping E. Rd., Sec. 2, Taipei, 106-36, Taiwan. TEL 886-2-27377854, FAX 886-2-27377448. Ed. Ms. Chia-Jung Liang.

500 CHN ISSN 1000-7695
➤ **KEJI GUANLI YANJIU/SCIENCE AND TECHNOLOGY MANAGEMENT RESEARCH.** Text in Chinese. 1981. bi-m. USD 49.20 (effective 2009). adv. bk.rev.; software rev. **Document type:** *Journal, Academic/Scholarly.* **Description:** Covers management theories, management practices, science and technology development strategies, and personnel management.
Related titles: Online - full text ed.
—East View.
Published by: (Guangdong Association of Science & Technology Management Research), Keji Guanli Yanjiu, 171, Lianxin Road, Guangdong Guoji Keji Zhongxin 307, Guangzhou, Guangdong 510070, China. TEL 86-20-83568469, FAX 86-20-8777-5791. Ed. Huizhong Xu. Adv. contact Shengchu Liao. Circ: 5,000.
Co-sponsors: Guangdong Province Science and Technology Commission; Guangdong Province Academy of Science; Guangzhou City Science and Technology Commission.

500 600 330 371.2 CHN ISSN 1001-7348
➤ **KEJI JINBU YU DUICE/SCIENCE & TECHNOLOGY PROGRESS AND POLICY.** Text in Chinese; Summaries in English. 1984. m. CNY 144 domestic; USD 144 foreign (effective 2002). adv. bk.rev. abstr. 180 p./no.; back issues avail. **Document type:** *Journal, Academic/ Scholarly.*
Related titles: CD-ROM ed.; Diskette ed.; E-mail ed.; Fax ed.; Online - full text ed.
Published by: Hubei Sheng Kexue Jishu Weiyuanhui/Hubei Science and Technology Commission, Journal Office of Science and Technology Progress and Policy, Hubei Science and Technology Commission Bldg., Nan Yuan Cun 5-3, Shuiguohu Wuchang, Wuhan, 430071, China. TEL 86-27-87863110, FAX 86-27-87863110. Ed. Yong Yue. Adv. contact Chen Hongyu. Circ: 10,000. **Co-sponsor:** Wuhan Sheng Kexue Jishu Weiyuanhui.

500 600 CHN
KEJI RIBAO/SCIENCE & TECHNOLOGY DAILY. Text in Chinese. d. CNY 288, USD 104.40 (effective 2005). **Document type:** *Newspaper, Consumer.*
Address: 15, Fuxing Lu, Beijing, 100038, China. TEL 86-10-58884112, FAX 86-10-58884035. **Dist. by:** China International Book Trading Corp, 35 Chegongzhuang Xilu, Haidian District, PO Box 399, Beijing 100044, China. TEL 86-10-68412045, FAX 86-10-68412023, cibtc@mail.cibtc.com.cn, http://www.cibtc.com.cn.

500 CHN ISSN 1001-7119
KEJI TONGBAO/BULLETIN OF SCIENCE AND TECHNOLOGY. Text in Chinese. 1985. bi-m. USD 31.20 (effective 2009). **Document type:** *Journal, Academic/Scholarly.*
Related titles: Online - full text ed.
Published by: Zhejiang Sheng Kexue Jishu Xiehui, Wulin Guangchang Dongce, 3F, Zhejiang Kexie Dalou, Hangzhou, 310003, China. TEL 86-571-85107609. **Dist. by:** China International Book Trading Corp, 35 Chegongzhuang Xilu, Haidian District, PO Box 399, Beijing 100044, China. TEL 86-10-68412045, FAX 86-10-68412023, cibtc@mail.cibtc.com.cn, http://www.cibtc.com.cn.

509 TWN
KEJI, YILIAO YU SHEHUI/TAIWANESE JOURNAL OF STUDIES FOR SCIENCE, TECHNOLOGY, AND MEDICINE. Text in Chinese; Abstracts and contents page in Chinese, English. 1992. s-a. USD 15 to individuals; USD 30 to institutions; USD 10 to students (effective 2003). **Description:** Publishes on various topics in history and philosophy of science, with focus on Chinese science and mathematics.
Former titles (until 2001): Taiwanese Journal for Philosophy and History of Science; (until 1995): Philosophy and the History of Science (1022-4874)
Indexed: MSN, PhilInd.
Published by: Guoli Kexue Gongyi Tushuguan/National Science & Technology Museum, 720, Chiuju I Rd., Kaohsiung, 80765, Taiwan. TEL 886-7-3800089, FAX 886-7-3878748, http://www.nstm.gov.tw/.

KEJI YU FALU/SCIENCE, TECHNOLOGY AND LAW. *see* LAW

KENKYU GIJUTSU KEIKAKU/JOURNAL OF SCIENCE POLICY AND RESEARCH MANAGEMENT. *see* BUSINESS AND ECONOMICS—Management

500 001.3 NLD ISSN 1872-1869
KENNIS!. Text in Dutch. 1989. q. free (effective 2008).
Formerly (until 2006): Magazijn (0924-3798); Which incorporated: Indikator (0925-1820); Which was formerly (until 1990): Biologiewinkelkrant (0925-8299)
Published by: Utrechtse Kennispunten, Heidelberglaan 8, Utrecht, 3584 CS, Netherlands. TEL 31-30-2532539.

505 USA ISSN 1098-7096
Q11 CODEN: TKASAT
➤ **KENTUCKY ACADEMY OF SCIENCE. JOURNAL.** Text in English. 1923. s-a. bk.rev. charts; illus.; abstr.; bibl.; maps. index. 70 p./no. 2 cols./p.; back issues avail.; reprints avail. **Document type:** *Journal, Academic/Scholarly.* **Description:** Covers science from a(nthropolgy) to z(oology).
Formerly (until 1998): Kentucky Academy of Science. Transactions (0023-0081)
Related titles: Online - full text ed.: ISSN 1938-2960. free to members (effective 2011).
Indexed: A23, A24, ASFA, Agr, AnBeAb, B13, B21, B25, BIOSIS Prev, BibAg, ChemAb, E17, ESPM, EntAb, GeoRef, MycolAb, P30, PollutAb, SASA, SWRA, SpeleolAb, ToxAb, WildRev, Z01.
—CASDDS, Ingenta, Linda Hall. **CCC.**
Published by: Kentucky Academy of Science, PO Box 22579, Lexington, KY 40522. TEL 859-227-2837. Ed. David White TEL 270-474-2272. **Subscr. to:** Allen Press Inc.

500 600 KEN
QH301 CODEN: KSTSDG
KENYA JOURNAL OF SCIENCES. SERIES A: PHYSICAL AND CHEMICAL SCIENCES. Text and summaries in English. 1966. s-a. USD 140; USD 170 foreign (effective 1999). back issues avail. **Document type:** *Academic/Scholarly.*
Former titles: Kenya Journal of Science and Technology. Series A: Physical and Chemical Sciences (0250-8265); Kenya Science and Technology Journal
Indexed: ASFA, B21, ChemAb, ESPM.
—CASDDS.
Published by: Kenya National Academy of Sciences, PO Box 39450, Nairobi, Kenya. TEL 254-2-721345, FAX 254-2-721138. Ed. F N Onyango. Circ: 500 (paid).

500 600 KEN
KENYA NATIONAL ACADEMY FOR ADVANCEMENT OF ARTS AND SCIENCES. NEWSLETTER. Short title: K N A A S News. Text in English. 1977. a. **Document type:** *Newsletter.*
Published by: Kenya National Academy for Advancement of Arts and Sciences, PO Box 47288, Nairobi, Kenya. Ed. Francis Inganji.

500 KEN
KENYA NATIONAL ACADEMY OF SCIENCE. RESEARCH PAPERS. Text in English. a. **Document type:** *Journal, Academic/Scholarly.*
Former titles: Kenya National Academy of Science. Annual Report; Kenya National Academy for Advancement of Arts and Sciences. Annual Report
Published by: Kenya National Academy of Sciences, PO Box 39450, Nairobi, Kenya. Ed. Frederic N Onyango.

KENYA PAST AND PRESENT. *see* HISTORY—History Of Africa

600 CHN
KEPU WENZHAI/POPULAR SCIENCE DIGEST. Text in Chinese. 2003. m. CNY 57.60 (effective 2004). **Document type:** *Magazine, Academic/Scholarly.*
Related titles: Online - full content ed.
Published by: Hubei Kepu Wenzhai Zhazhishe, Wuchang-qu, 52-54, Wuchang Lu, Wuhan, Hubei 430060, China. TEL 86-27-88850170.

KERNCIJFERS ONDERWIJS CULTUUR EN WETENSCHAPPEN. *see* EDUCATION

500 CHN ISSN 0368-6396
Q4 CODEN: KEZAEV
KEXUE (SHANGHAI)/SCIENCE. Text in Chinese; Abstracts in English. 1915. bi-m. USD 18 (effective 2009). adv. **Description:** Introduces the frontiers of science and technology in the world and achievements by Chinese scientists.
Related titles: Online - full text ed.
Indexed: CMCI.
—CASDDS, East View.
Published by: Shanghai Keji Chubanshe, 450 Ruijin 2 Lu, Shanghai, 200020, China. TEL 86-21-473465, FAX 86-21-4730679. Ed. Zhou Guangchao. Circ: 4,000.

500 CHN ISSN 1002-7394
KEXUE 24 XIAOSHI/SCIENCE IN 24 HOURS. Text in Chinese. 1980. m. **Document type:** *Magazine, Consumer.*
Related titles: Online - full text ed.
Published by: Kexue 24 Xiaoshi Zazhishe, Wulin Guangchang Dongce, Shengkexie Dalou 309, Hangzhou, 310003, China. TEL 86-571-85172999, FAX 86-571-85101488. **Co-sponsors:** Zhejiang Jiaoyu Baokanshe; Zhejiang Keji Baoshe.

500 CHN ISSN 1003-1871
KEXUE DAGUANYUAN/GRAND GARDEN OF SCIENCE. Text in Chinese. 1981. bi-m. USD 96 (effective 2009).
Related titles: Online - full content ed.
Published by: Zhongguo Kepu, Haidian-qu, 16, Zhongguancu Nandajie, Beijing, 100081, China. TEL 86-10-62103154, FAX 86-10-62173819. **Dist. by:** China International Book Trading Corp, 35 Chegongzhuang Xilu, Haidian District, PO Box 399, Beijing 100044, China. TEL 86-10-68412045, FAX 86-10-68412023, cibtc@mail.cibtc.com.cn, http://www.cibtc.com.cn.

KEXUE DUI SHEHUI DE YINGXIANG/SCIENCE IMPACT ON SOCIETY. *see* SOCIAL SCIENCES: COMPREHENSIVE WORKS

500 TWN ISSN 0250-1651
Q4 CODEN: KHFKDF
➤ **KEXUE FAZHAN/SCIENCE DEVELOPMENT.** Text in Chinese. 1973. m. TWD 1,200 domestic; USD 50 (effective 2005). 80 p./no.; back issues avail.; reprints avail. **Document type:** *Journal, Academic/ Scholarly.*
Related titles: Online - full content ed.
—BLDSC (8142.470000), CASDDS, Linda Hall.
Published by: National Science Council/Xingzhengyuan Guojia Kexue Weiyuanhui, Rm 1701, 106 Ho-Ping E. Rd, Sec 2, Taipei, Taiwan. TEL 886-2-27377539, FAX 886-2-27377248, http://www.nsc.gov.tw. Circ: 3,500 (paid).

500 CHN ISSN 1674-6171
KEXUE FAZHAN/SCIENTIFIC DEVELOPMENT. Text in Chinese. 2008. m. CNY 20 (effective 2010). **Document type:** *Magazine, Government.*
Published by: Shanghai Fazhan Zhanlue Yanjiusuo, 3/F, 69, Yixueyuan Lu, Shanghai, 200032, China. TEL 86-21-64183007. **Co-sponsor:** Shanghai Shi Renmin Zhengfu Fazhan Yanjiu Zhongxin/Development Research Center of Shanghai Municipal People's Government.

500 600 CHN ISSN 1673-5668
KEXUE GUANCHA/SCIENCE FOCUS. Text in Chinese. 1988. bi-m. USD 30 (effective 2000). **Document type:** *Academic/Scholarly.*
Description: Reports on the new products and technologies developed by the 123 institutes and 400 high-tech companies of the Chinese Academy of Sciences.
Formerly (until 2005): Keji Kaifa Dongtai/R & D Information (1003-014X)
—East View.
Published by: Zhongguo Kexueyuan Wenxian Qingbao Zhongxin/ Chinese Academy of Sciences, Documentation and Information Center, 8 Kexueyuan Nanlu, Zhongguancun, Beijing, 100080, China. TEL 86-1-6256-6850, FAX 86-1-6256-6846, entref@las.ac.cn. Ed. Xia Yuan.

500 CHN ISSN 1000-8292
KEXUE HUABAO/SCIENCE PICTORIAL. Text in Chinese. 1926. m. USD 36 (effective 2009). **Document type:** *Journal, Academic/Scholarly.*
—East View.
Published by: Shanghai Shiji Jishu Chuban Gufen Youxian Gongsi, Kexue Jishu Chubanshe/Shanghai Scientific and Technical Publishers, 450 Ruijin Er Rd, Shanghai, 200020, China. TEL 86-21-64734639, FAX 86-21-64730679. Ed. Xu Fusheng. **Dist. by:** China International Book Trading Corp, 35 Chegongzhuang Xilu, Haidian District, PO Box 399, Beijing 100044, China. TEL 86-10-68412045, FAX 86-10-68412023, cibtc@mail.cibtc.com.cn, http://www.cibtc.com.cn.

500 600 CHN ISSN 1003-5680
Q174
KEXUE JISHU YU BIANZHENGFA/SCIENCE, TECHNOLOGY, AND DIALECTICS. Text in Chinese. 1984. bi-m. USD 23.40 (effective 2009). adv. bk.rev. **Document type:** *Academic/Scholarly.*
Description: Covers the philosophy of science, theory of technology, science and society, and the history of scientific development.
Related titles: Online - full text ed.
—East View.

S

Published by: Shanxi Sheng Ziran Bianzhengfa Yanjiuhui/Shanxi Institute of Dialectics of Nature, Bldg. 128, Shanxi University, 36 Wucheng Rd, Taiyuan, Shanxi 030006, China. TEL 0351-7074871. Ed. Zhang Jiazhi. Adv. contact Wang Hongqi. Circ: 2,500.
Co-sponsors: Taiyuan University of Engineering and Technology; Shanxi University.

500 600 620 CHN ISSN 1671-1815
KEXUE JISHU YU GONGCHENG. Abbreviated title: Science, Technology and Engineering. Text in Chinese. 2001. bi-m. **Document type:** *Journal, Academic/Scholarly.*
Related titles: Online - full text ed.
Published by: Zhongguo Jishu Jingji Yanjiuhui, No.86 Xueyuan South Road, Hai-Dian District, Beijing, 100081, China. Ed. Lijun Zhang.

KEXUE JISHU ZHEXUE/PHILOSOPHY OF SCIENCE AND TECHNOLOGY. *see* PHILOSOPHY

500 CHN
KEXUE SHIBAO/CHINESE SCIENCE NEWS. Text in Chinese. 6/w. CNY 180, USD 64.80 (effective 2005). **Document type:** *Magazine, Academic/Scholarly.*
Formerly: Zhongguo Kexue Bao
Related titles: Online - full content ed.
Address: Haidian District, Zhongguangcun South, Section 1, no.3, Beijing, 100080, China. TEL 86-10-82614600, FAX 86-10-82614609, mubin1@sina.com. **Dist. by:** China International Book Trading Corp, 35 Chegongzhuang Xilu, Haidian District, PO Box 399, Beijing 100044, China. TEL 86-10-68412045, FAX 86-10-68412023, cibtc@mail.cibtc.com.cn, http://www.cibtc.com.cn.

500 CHN ISSN 1003-1162
KEXUE SHIJIE/SCIENTIFIC WORLD. Text in Chinese. m. USD 74.40 (effective 2009). **Document type:** *Academic/Scholarly.* **Description:** Popular science magazine.
Published by: Kexue Chubanshe/Science Press, 16 Donghuang Cheng Genbei Jie, Beijing, 100717, China. TEL 86-10-64000246, FAX 86-10-64030255. **Dist. by:** China International Book Trading Corp, 35 Chegongzhuang Xilu, Haidian District, PO Box 399, Beijing 100044, China. TEL 86-10-68412045, FAX 86-10-68412023, cibtc@mail.cibtc.com.cn, http://www.cibtc.com.cn.

500 CHN ISSN 0023-074X
Q4 CODEN: KHTPAT
➤ **KEXUE TONGBAO.** Text in Chinese; Summaries in English. 1950. s-m. CNY 2,880; CNY 120 per issue (effective 2009). adv. **Document type:** *Journal, Academic/Scholarly.* **Description:** Presents concise reports on important recent results of scientific research in basic and applied sciences, reflecting the current level of development of science and technology in mainland China. Includes a letters column.
Related titles: Online - full content ed.; Online - full text ed.; ◆ English ed.: Chinese Science Bulletin. ISSN 1001-6538.
Indexed: CCMJ, CIS, ChemAb, GeoRef, ISR, Inspec, MOS, MSN, MathR, NPU, P30, RILM, SpeleolAb.
—BLDSC (5091.500000), CASDDS, East View, INIST, Linda Hall.
Published by: (Chinese Academy of Sciences/Zhongguo Kexueyuan), Kexue Chubanshe/Science Press, 16 Donghuang Cheng Genbei Jie, Beijing, 100717, China. TEL 86-10-64000246, FAX 86-10-64030255, http://www.sciencep.com/. Circ: 15,000. **Dist. in the Americas by:** Springer New York LLC, Journal Fulfillment, PO Box 2485, Secaucus, NJ 07096. TEL 201-348-4033, 212-473-6272, journals-ny@springer.com; **Dist. outside the Americas by:** Springer, Haber Str 7, Heidelberg 69126, Germany. subscriptions@springer.com.

➤ **KEXUE YANXI.** *see* EDUCATION

500 658 CHN ISSN 1003-8256
KEXUE YU GUANLI. Abbreviated title: Science and Management. Text in Chinese. 1981. bi-m. CNY 10 per issue (effective 2010). **Document type:** *Journal, Academic/Scholarly.*
Published by: Shandong Sheng Kexueyuan/Shandong Academy of Science, 19, Keyuan Lu, Ji'nan, 250014, China. TEL 86-531-82605310, http://www.sdas.org/.

500 CHN
KEXUE YU SHENGHUO/SCIENCE AND LIFE. Text in Chinese. bi-m.
Published by: Tianjin Kexue Jishu Chubanshe, 130 Chifeng Dao, Tianjin, 300041, China. TEL 706821. Ed. Kou Xiurong.

500 CHN ISSN 1000-3398
KEXUE YU WENHUA/SCIENCE AND CULTURE. Text in Chinese. 1980. m. USD 28.80 (effective 2009). **Document type:** *Journal, Academic/Scholarly.*
Related titles: Online - full text ed.
Indexed: BAS.
Published by: Fujian Sheng Kexue Jishu Xiehui/Fujiang Association For Science & Technology, 7, Fudong Lu, Fuzhou, 350003, China. TEL 86-591-87833041, http://www.fjkx.org/.

500 211.8 215 CHN ISSN 1008-9802
KEXUE YU WUSHENLUN/SCIENCE AND ATHEISM. Text in Chinese. 1997. bi-m. USD 18 (effective 2009). **Document type:** *Journal, Academic/Scholarly.*
Related titles: Online - full text ed.
—East View.
Published by: Zhongguo Shehui Kexueyuan, Shijie Zhongjiao Yanjiusuo/Chinese Academy of Social Sciences, Institution of World Religions, PO Box 1525, Beijing, 100005, China. **Dist. by:** China International Book Trading Corp, 35 Chegongzhuang Xilu, Haidian District, PO Box 399, Beijing 100044, China. TEL 86-10-68412045, FAX 86-10-68412023, cibtc@mail.cibtc.com.cn, http://www.cibtc.com.cn.

500 TWN ISSN 0250-331X
Q4 CODEN: KHYKD8
KEXUE YUEKAN/SCIENCE MONTHLY. Text in Chinese. 1970. m. TWD 1,400 domestic; USD 66 in Hong Kong & Macau; USD 70 elsewhere (effective 2005). **Document type:** *Magazine, Academic/Scholarly.*
Address: Section 3, no. 125, Roosevelt Road, 11th Fl, Room no. 4, Taipei, 106, Taiwan. TEL 886-2-23634910, FAX 886-2-23635999.

500 630 CHN ISSN 1001-4284
KEXUE ZHIFU YU SHENGHUO/SCIENCE PROSPERITY AND LIFE. Text in Chinese. 1978. m. CNY 1 per issue (effective 1999). adv. **Description:** Comprehensive popular science publication for rural areas of China. Covers agricultural techniques, rural architecture, energy resources, environmental protection, life and hygiene.
Former titles: Nongcun Kexue - Science in Countryside (1000-307X); Nongcun Kexue Shiyan

Published by: Kexue Chubanshe/Science Press, 16 Donghuang Cheng Genbei Jie, Beijing, 100717, China. TEL 86-10-64000246, FAX 86-10-64030255. Ed. Xu Tianxing. Circ: 100,000.

500 CHN ISSN 1673-3339
KEXUE ZHONG YANG. Text in Chinese. 2006. m. **Document type:** *Magazine, Consumer.*
Published by: Jindun Chubanshe/Jindun Publishing House, 5, Taiping Lu, Beijing, 100036, China. TEL 86-10-88229499, FAX 86-10-68152422.

500 CHN ISSN 1005-3573
DS775.2
KEXUE ZHONGGUOREN/SCIENTIFIC CHINESE. Text in Chinese. 1994. m. USD 80.40 (effective 2009). **Document type:** *Journal, Academic/Scholarly.*
Address: 11, Xueyuan Lu, Jimenli Bei Bing, Beijing, 100088, China. TEL 86-10-82076146, FAX 86-10-82074228. **Dist. by:** China International Book Trading Corp, 35 Chegongzhuang Xilu, Haidian District, PO Box 399, Beijing 100044, China. TEL 86-10-68412045, FAX 86-10-68412023, cibtc@mail.cibtc.com.cn, http://www.cibtc.com.cn.

500 CHN ISSN 1003-2053
Q174
KEXUEXUE YANJIU/STUDIES IN SCIENCE OF SCIENCE. Text in Chinese. 1983. q. USD 74.40 (effective 2009). **Document type:** *Journal, Academic/Scholarly.*
Related titles: Online - full text ed.
—East View.
Published by: Zhongguo Kexuexue Yu Ke-ji Zhengce Yanjiuhui/Chinese Association of Science of Science and S & T Policy Research, 55, Zhongguancun Dong Lu, Box 8712, Beijing, 100080, China. TEL 86-10-62622031, FAX 86-10-62542615.

KEY FIGURES EDUCATION, CULTURE AND SCIENCE. *see* EDUCATION

500 658 CHN ISSN 1000-2995
Q180.55.M3
KEYAN GUANLI/SCIENCE RESEARCH MANAGEMENT. Text in Chinese. 1980. bi-m. USD 48 (effective 2009). adv. **Document type:** *Academic/Scholarly.* **Description:** Explores the characteristics and laws of modern scientific development, theories and methods of science research management, scientific and technological policies, research systems, personnel training, and trends in newly emerging areas of research.
Related titles: Online - full text ed.
Published by: (Chinese Academy of Sciences/Zhongguo Kexueyuan), Kexue Chubanshe/Science Press, 16 Donghuang Cheng Genbei Jie, Beijing, 100717, China. TEL 86-10-64000246, FAX 86-10-64030255, http://www.sciencep.com/. Ed. Luo Wei. Circ: 21,000. **Dist. by:** China International Book Trading Corp, 35 Chegongzhuang Xilu, Haidian District, PO Box 399, Beijing 100044, China. TEL 86-10-68412045, FAX 86-10-68412023, cibtc@mail.cibtc.com.cn, http://www.cibtc.com.cn.

500 600 VNM
KHOA HOC KY THUAT KINH TE THE GIOI/WORLD SCIENCE, TECHNOLOGY AND ECONOMY. Text in Vietnamese. 1982. w.
Address: 5 Ly Thuong Kiet, Hanoi, Viet Nam. TEL 52931.

500 VNM ISSN 0866-7942
Q4
KHOA HOC VA DOI SONG/SCIENCE AND LIFE. Text in Vietnamese. 1959. fortn.
Address: 70 Tran Hung Dao St, Hanoi, Viet Nam. TEL 53427. Ed. Duong Hong Dat. Circ: 25,000. **Dist. abroad by:** Xunhasaba - Export and Import Revue Company, 32 Hai Ba Trung St, Hanoi, Viet Nam. TEL 252313.

500 NLD ISSN 0165-1390
KIJK. Text in Dutch. 1968. m. EUR 39.90; EUR 4.99 newsstand/cover (effective 2011). adv. bk.rev.; software rev. illus. index. back issues avail. **Document type:** *Magazine, Consumer.* **Description:** Informs readers of interesting and noteworthy topics in all the sciences, both natural and engineering.
Published by: Sanoma Men's Magazines, Haaksbergweg 75, Amsterdam (ZO), 1101 BR, Netherlands. TEL 31-20-7518000, FAX 31-20-7518301, sales@smm.nl, http://www.smm.nl. Ed. Vivianne Bendermacher.

KIMEN. *see* EDUCATION—Teaching Methods And Curriculum

500 SAU ISSN 1018-3647
Q80.S2 CODEN: JKSSED
➤ **KING SAUD UNIVERSITY JOURNAL. SCIENCE.** Key Title: Magallat Gami'at al-Malik Sa'ud, al-'Ulum. (Other sections avail.: Administrative Sciences, Agricultural Sciences, Architecture and Planning, Arts, Computer and Information Sciences, Educational Sciences and Islamic Studies, Engineering Sciences) Text in Arabic, English. 1969. m. charts; illus. **Document type:** *Journal, Academic/Scholarly.*
Former titles (until 1989): King Saud University. College of Science. Journal (0735-9799); University of Riyadh. Faculty of Sciences. Bulletin
Related titles: Online - full text ed.: (from ScienceDirect).
Indexed: B25, BIOSIS Prev, ChemAb, ChemTitl, FS&TA, GeoRef, INIS AtomInd, Inspec, MycolAb, SCOPUS, SpeleolAb, T02, Z02.
—BLDSC (4810.895000), CASDDS, IE, Ingenta, Linda Hall. **CCC.**
Published by: King Saud University, General Directorate for Academic Publishing and Press, PO Box 68953, Riyadh, 11537, Saudi Arabia. TEL 966-1-4672870, FAX 966-1-4672894, acksupress@ksu.edu.sa, http://printpress.ksu.edu.sa. Ed. Khalid A. Al-Hamoudi. R&P Dr. Sulaiman Saleh Al-Ogle. Circ: 2,000.

500 600 JPN ISSN 0386-4928
Q77 CODEN: KDRKBB
KINKI DAIGAKU RIKOGAKUBU KENKYU HOKOKU/KINKI UNIVERSITY. FACULTY OF SCIENCE AND TECHNOLOGY. JOURNAL. Text in English, Japanese; Summaries in English. 1966. a.
Indexed: CCMJ, ChemAb, INIS AtomInd, JPI, MSN, MathR, Z02.
Published by: Kinki Daigaku, Rikogakubu/Kinki University, Faculty of Science and Technology, 4-1 Kowakae 3-chome, Higashiosaka-shi, Osaka-fu 577-0818, Japan.

500.9 913 USA ISSN 0075-6245
QH1 CODEN: KIRTA4
KIRTLANDIA. Text in English. 1967. irreg., latest vol.47, 1985. price varies.

Indexed: B25, BIOSIS Prev, GeoRef, MycolAb, SpeleolAb, Z01.
Published by: Cleveland Museum of Natural History, One Wade Oval Dr, University Circle, Cleveland, OH 44106. TEL 216-231-4600, FAX 216-231-5919. Ed. Joseph Hannibal. Circ: 850.

507.4 JPN ISSN 0386-0655
KITAKAMI-SHIRITSU HAKUBUTSUKAN KENKYU HOKOKU/KITAKAMI CITY MUSEUM. BULLETIN. Text in Japanese. 1975. irreg. JPY 1,500. **Document type:** *Bulletin.* **Description:** Features comprehensive coverage on the humanities and natural sciences.
Published by: Kitakami-shiritsu Hakubutsukan/Kitakami City Museum, 14-59 Tachibana, Kitakami-shi, Iwate-ken 024-0043, Japan. TEL 81-197-64-1756, FAX 81-197-64-1860. Ed. Hisaichi Hondo.

500.9 JPN ISSN 1348-2653
QH7 CODEN: KHKHEW
KITAKYUUSHUU SHIRITSU SHIZENSHI, REKISHI HAKUBUTSUKAN KENKYUU HOUKOKU. ARUI, SHIZENSHI/KITAKYUSHU MUSEUM OF NATURAL HISTORY AND HUMAN HISTORY. BULLETIN. SERIES A, NATURAL HISTORY. Text in English, Japanese. 1979. a. **Document type:** *Bulletin, Academic/Scholarly.* **Description:** Covers original articles and short notes on natural history.
Supersedes in part (in 2002): Kitakyushu Shiritsu Shizenshi Hakubutsukan Kenkyu Hokoku/Kitakyushu Museum of Natural History. Bulletin (0387-964X)
Indexed: ASFA, B21, B25, BIOSIS Prev, ESPM, EntAb, GeoRef, MycolAb, RefZh, SSciA, SpeleolAb, WildRev, Z01.
—INIST.
Published by: Kitakyuushuu Shiritsu Shizenshi, Rekishi Hakubutsukan/Kitakyushu Museum of Natural History and Human History, 2-4-1, Higashida, Yahatahigashi-ku, Kitakyushu, 805-0071, Japan. TEL 81-93-6811011, FAX 81-93-6617503, info@kmnh.jp, http://www.kmnh.jp/. Circ: 1,200.

500 DEU ISSN 0341-4086
KLEINE SENCKENBERG REIHE. Text in German, English. 1971. irreg., latest vol.51, 2009. price varies. back issues avail. **Document type:** *Monographic series, Academic/Scholarly.* **Description:** Contains guides of exhibitions and projects.
Indexed: GeoRef, SpeleolAb.
Published by: (Senckenberg Gesellschaft fuer Naturforschung), E. Schweizerbart'sche Verlagsbuchhandlung, Johannesstr 3A, Stuttgart, 70176, Germany. TEL 49-711-3514560, FAX 49-711-35145699, order@schweizerbart.de. Ed. Volker Mosbrugger.

KNOW; the science magazine for curious kids. *see* CHILDREN AND YOUTH—For

KNOWLEDGE AND SOCIETY. *see* SOCIOLOGY

500 TWN ISSN 1606-9536
KNOWLEDGE BRIDGE/ZHISHI CHUANGXIN. Text in Chinese, English. 2000. m. free. Website rev. charts; illus.; pat. 8 p./no.; **Document type:** *Journal, Academic/Scholarly.* **Description:** Features the latest innovation and invention information from Taiwan's incubator centers and research institution.
Related titles: Online - full content ed.
Indexed: A28, APA, BrCerAb, C&ISA, CA/WCA, CIA, CerAb, CivEngAb, CorrAb, E&CAJ, E11, EEA, EMA, H15, M&TEA, M09, MBF, METADEX, SolStAb, T04, WAA.
Published by: Xingzhengyuan Guojia Kexue Weiyuanhui, Kexue Jishu Ziliao Zhongxin/Science & Technology Information Center, 16F, 106, Hoping E. Rd., Sec. 2, Taipei, 106-36, Taiwan. TEL 886-2-27377636, FAX 886-2-27377494, http://www.stic.gov.tw/. Ed. Ms. May-Huey Lee.

KNOWLEDGESPEAK. *see* PUBLISHING AND BOOK TRADE

500 JPN ISSN 0287-6515
Q179.9
KOBE DAIGAKU DAIGAKUIN SHIZEN KAGAKU KENKYUKA KIYO B/KOBE UNIVERSITY. GRADUATE SCHOOL OF SCIENCE AND TECHNOLOGY. MEMOIRS. SERIES B. Text in Japanese; Summaries in English, Japanese. 1983. a. abstr.
Published by: Kobe Daigaku, Daigakuin Shizen Kagaku Kenkyuka/Kobe University, Graduate School of Science and Technology, 1-1 Rokko-Dai-cho, Nada-ku, Kobe-shi, Hyogo-ken 657-0013, Japan.

KOBE SHOIN JOSHI GAKUIN DAIGAKU, KOBE SHOIN JOSHI GAKUIN TANKI DAIGAKU. GAKUJUTSU KENKYUKAI. KENKYU KIYO. JINBUN KAGAKU, SHIZEN KAGAKU-HEN. *see* HUMANITIES: COMPREHENSIVE WORKS

500 JPN ISSN 0389-9578
KOBE TOKIWA TANKI DAIGAKU KIYO/KOBE TOKIWA COLLEGE. BULLETIN. Text in English, Japanese. 1971. a. free. back issues avail. **Description:** Covers topics in the fields of liberal arts, pedagogy, medical science and technology.
Published by: Kobe Tokiwa Tanki Daigaku/Kobe Tokiwa College, 2-6-2 Otani-cho, Nagata-ku, Kobe-shi, Hyogo-ken 653-0838, Japan. TEL 078-611-1821, FAX 078-643-4361. Ed. Reiko Shimomura. Circ: 650.

500 JPN ISSN 0450-609X
VK4 CODEN: KDKRDX
KOBE UNIVERSITY OF MERCANTILE MARINE. REVIEW. PART 2. MARITIME STUDIES, AND SCIENCE AND ENGINEERING. Text in Japanese; Abstracts in English. 1953. a.
Formerly (until 1980): Kobe University of Mercantile Marine. Review. Part 2. Navigation, Marine Engineering, Nuclear Engineering and Scientific Section
Indexed: INIS AtomInd.
—CASDDS.
Published by: Kobe University of Mercantile Marine, 1-1 Fukaeminami-Machi 5-chome, Higashinada-ku, Kobe-shi, Hyogo-ken 658-0022, Japan.

500 JPN ISSN 0389-0244
Q4 CODEN: KDGAAR
KOCHI DAIGAKU GAKUJUTSU KENKYU HOKOKU. SHIZEN KAGAKU/KOCHI UNIVERSITY. RESEARCH REPORTS. NATURAL SCIENCE. Text in English, Japanese; Summaries in English. 1969. a.
Formed by the merger of part of (1961-1969): Kochi Daigaku Gakujutsu Kenkyu Hokoku. Shizen Kagaku 2 (0389-0236); (1961-1969): Kochi Daigaku Gakujutsu Kenkyu Hokoku. Shizen Kagaku 1 (0389-0228); Which superseded in part (1952-1960): Kochi Daigaku Gakujutsu Kenkyu Hokoku (0452-246X)
Indexed: CIN, ChemAb, ChemTitl, GeoRef, JPI, SpeleolAb.
—CASDDS.
Published by: Kochi Daigaku/Kochi University, 5-1 Akebono-cho 2-chome, Kochi-shi, Kochi-ken 780-8520, Japan.

500 JPN ISSN 0452-2486
CODEN: KJDSA6
KOCHI JOSHI DAIGAKU KIYO. SHIZEN KAGAKU HEN/KOCHI WOMEN'S UNIVERSITY. BULLETIN. SERIES OF NATURAL SCIENCES. Text and summaries in English, Japanese. 1952. a. **Document type:** *Bulletin.*
Indexed: ChemAb, JPI.
Published by: Kochi Joshi Daigaku/Kochi Women's University, 5-15 Eikokuji-cho, Kochi-shi, 780-0844, Japan. Ed. Katsuhiko Ikuta.

KODOMO NO KAGAKU. *see* CHILDREN AND YOUTH—For

500 JPN ISSN 0368-5098
T4 CODEN: KDKHAY
KOGAKUIN DAIGAKU. KENKYU HOKOKU/KOGAKUIN UNIVERSITY. RESEARCH REPORTS. Text in Japanese. 1954. irreg.
Indexed: INIS AtomInd, Inspec, RefZh.
—BLDSC (7762.400000), Linda Hall.
Published by: Kogakuin Daigaku/Kogakuin University, 1-24-2 Nishi-Shinjuku, Shinjuku-ku, Tokyo, 163-8677, Japan. TEL 03-3342-1211, http://naka2.cc.kogakuin.ac.jp.

KOKURITSU KAGAKU HAKUBUTSUKAN NENPO. *see* MUSEUMS AND ART GALLERIES

500 JPN ISSN 0082-4755
KOKURITSU KAGAKU HAKUBUTSUKAN SENPO/NATIONAL SCIENCE MUSEUM. MEMOIRS. Text in English, Japanese; Summaries in English. 1968. a. (4 issues in 2006). per issue exchange basis. **Document type:** *Monographic series, Academic/Scholarly.*
Indexed: B25, BIOSIS Prev, GeoRef, JPI, MycolAb, SpeleolAb, Z01.
—BLDSC (5627.700000), INIST.
Published by: Kokuritsu Kagaku Hakubutsukan/National Science Museum, Tokyo, 7-20 Ueno-Koen, Taito-ku, Tokyo, 110-0007, Japan. TEL 81-3-57778600, FAX 81-3-58149898, http://www.kahaku.go.jp/. Circ: 1,000 (controlled).

069 JPN ISSN 0288-7975
KOMATSU-SHIRITSU HAKUBUTSUKAN KENKYU KIYO/KOMATSU CITY MUSEUM. MEMOIRS. Text in Japanese. 1965. a. price varies.
Published by: Komatsu-shiritsu Hakubutsukan/Komatsu City Museum, Rojo Koen, Marunouchi Koen-machi, Komatsu-shi, Ishikawa-ken 923, Japan. Circ: 500.

500 JPN ISSN 0452-4160
Q1 CODEN: MKOUAS
KONAN DAIGAKU KIYO. RIGAKU HEN/KONAN UNIVERSITY. MEMOIRS. SCIENCE SERIES. Text and summaries in English, Japanese. 1955. a.
Indexed: ChemAb, INIS AtomInd, JPI, Z02.
—CASDDS.
Published by: Konan Daigaku/Konan University, 9-1 Okamo-To 8-chome, Higashinada-ku, Kobe-shi, Hyogo-ken 658-0072, Japan.

068.489 DNK ISSN 0368-7201
AS281
KONGELIGE DANSKE VIDENSKABERNES SELSKAB. OVERSIGT OVER SELSKABETS VIRKSOMHED/L'ACADEMIE ROYALE DES SCIENCES ET DES LETTRES DE DANEMARK. BULLETIN/ROYAL DANISH ACADEMY OF SCIENCES AND LETTERS. ANNUAL REPORT. Text in Danish; Summaries in English. 1814. a. price varies. illus. back issues avail. **Document type:** *Yearbook, Academic/Scholarly.*
Formerly (until 1932): Oversigt over det Kongelige Danske Videnskabernes Selskabs Forhandlinger (0369-7169)
Indexed: ChemAb, GeoRef, SpeleolAb.
—Linda Hall.
Published by: Det Kongelige Danske Videnskabernes Selskab/Royal Danish Academy of Sciences and Letters, H C Andersens Blvd 35, Copenhagen V, 1553, Denmark. TEL 45-33-435300, FAX 45-33-435301, kdvs@royalacademy.dk. **Subscr. to:** C.A. Reitzels Boghandel & Forlag A/S, Noerregade 20, Copenhagen K 1165, Denmark. TEL 45-33-122400, FAX 45-33-140270, info@careitzel.com, http://www.careitzel.com.

068 500 NOR ISSN 0803-1983
AS283 CODEN: KNSFA2
KONGELIGE NORSKE VIDENSKABERS SELSKAB. AARBOK FOR DKNVS AKADEMIET OG DKNVS STIFTELSEN. Text in Norwegian. 1926. a. **Document type:** *Corporate.* **Description:** Includes reports of meetings, selected lectures, and list of members.
Former titles (until 2004): Kongelige Norske Videnskabers Selskab. Forhandlinger (0368-6302); (until 1929): Kongelige Norske Videnskabers Selskab. Aarsberetning
Indexed: AICP, GeoRef, Inspec, MLA-IB, MathR, SpeleolAb, Z02.
—AskIEEE, INIST, Linda Hall.
Published by: Det Kongelige Norske Videnskabers Selskab/The Royal Norwegian Society of Sciences and Letters, Erling Skakkes Gate 47 C, Trondheim, 7491, Norway. TEL 47-73-592157, FAX 47-73-595895, postmaster@dknvs.no. Ed. Yngve Espmark.

001.3 500 NOR ISSN 0368-6310
AS283 CODEN: KNSSA7
➤ **KONGELIGE NORSKE VIDENSKABERS SELSKAB. SKRIFTER/ROYAL NORWEGIAN SOCIETY OF SCIENCES AND LETTERS. PUBLICATIONS.** Text in English, Norwegian. 1761. irreg. price varies. charts; illus.; stat. back issues avail. **Document type:** *Monographic series, Academic/Scholarly.*
Formerly (until 1768): Det Trondheimske Selskab. Skrifter (1504-3169)
Indexed: CCMJ, ChemAb, GeoRef, Inspec, MSN, MathR, SpeleolAb, Z02.
—AskIEEE, CASDDS, INIST, Linda Hall.
Published by: Det Kongelige Norske Videnskabers Selskab/The Royal Norwegian Society of Sciences and Letters, Erling Skakkes Gate 47 C, Trondheim, 7491, Norway. TEL 47-73-592157, FAX 47-73-595895, postmaster@dknvs.no. Ed. Yngve Espmark. **Dist. by:** Publications Expediting Inc., 200 Meacham Ave, Elmont, NY 11003.

500 CHN ISSN 1009-3516
KONGJUN GONGCHENG DAXUE XUEBAO (ZIRAN KEXUE BAN)/AIR FORCE ENGINEERING UNIVERSITY. JOURNAL (NATURAL SCIENCE EDITION). Text in Chinese. 2000. bi-m. USD 31.20 (effective 2009). **Document type:** *Journal, Academic/Scholarly.*
Related titles: Online - full text ed.
Indexed: A28, APA, BrCerAb, C&ISA, CA/WCA, CIA, CerAb, CivEngAb, CorrAb, E&CAJ, E11, EEA, EMA, ESPM, EnvEAb, H15, M&TEA, M09, MBF, METADEX, RefZh, SolStAb, T04, WAA.
—BLDSC (4682.480000), East View, Linda Hall.
Published by: Kongjun Gongcheng Daxue/Air Force Engineering University, 1, Changyue Donglu Jiazi, Xi'an, 710051, China. TEL 86-29-83686434, FAX 86-29-87685424.

500 300 DEU ISSN 0454-3335
KONSTANZER UNIVERSITAETSREDEN. Text in German. 1966. irreg., latest vol.240, 2011. price varies. **Document type:** *Monographic series, Academic/Scholarly.*
Published by: U V K Verlagsgesellschaft mbH, Schuetzenstr 24, Konstanz, 78462, Germany. TEL 49-7531-90530, FAX 49-7531-905398, nadine.ley@uvk.de, http://www.uvk.de.

500 300 DEU
KONSTANZER WISSENSCHAFTSFORUM. Text in German. 2008. irreg., latest vol.3, 2011. price varies. **Document type:** *Monographic series, Academic/Scholarly.*
Published by: U V K Verlagsgesellschaft mbH, Schuetzenstr 24, Konstanz, 78462, Germany. TEL 49-7531-90530, FAX 49-7531-905398, nadine.ley@uvk.de, http://www.uvk.de.

378.4 DEU ISSN 0171-1938
KONTAKT UND STUDIUM. Variant title: KontaktStudium. Text in German. 1974. irreg., latest vol.695, 2010. price varies. **Document type:** *Monographic series, Academic/Scholarly.*
Indexed: GeoRef, TM.
Published by: Expert Verlag GmbH, Wankelstr 13, Renningen, 71272, Germany. TEL 49-7159-92650, FAX 49-7159-926520, expert@expertverlag.de, http://www.expertverlag.de.

500 610 KOR ISSN 1229-814X
Q4
KOREAN ENGLISH SCIENCE AND TECHNOLOGY. Text in English. 2000. q. **Document type:** *Journal, Academic/Scholarly.*
Formed by the merger of: Korean Scientific Abstracts (0023-4052); Korean Medical Abstracts (0047-360X)
Media: CD-ROM.
Published by: Korea Institute for Industrial Economics and Trade/San-eob Yeon-gu-won, 66 Hoegiro, Dongdaemun-gu, Seoul, 130-742, Korea, S. TEL 82-2-32993114, webmaster@kiet.re.kr, http://www.kiet.re.kr/.

KOTONOURA. *see* MUSEUMS AND ART GALLERIES

502 POL ISSN 1427-3098
KULON. Text in Polish. 1996. s-a. **Document type:** *Journal.*
Indexed: AgrLib, Z01.
Published by: Radomsko-Kieleckie Towarzystwo Przyrodnicze, Pl Konstytucji 3 Maja 3, Pionki, 26670, Poland.

500 JPN ISSN 0454-6148
AS552.K93 CODEN: KDDSAW
KUMAMOTO DAIGAKU KYOIKUGAKUBU KIYO. SHIZEN KAGAKU/KUMAMOTO UNIVERSITY. FACULTY OF EDUCATION. MEMOIRS. NATURAL SCIENCE. Text and summaries in English, Japanese. 1953. a.
Indexed: B25, BIOSIS Prev, CCMJ, ChemAb, JPI, MSN, MathR, MycolAb, RILM, Z01, Z02.
—INIST.
Published by: Kumamoto Daigaku, Kyoikugakubu/Kumamoto University, Faculty of Education, 40-1 Kurokami 2-chome, Kumamoto-shi, 860-0862, Japan. FAX 096-343-1800. Circ: 300.

500 JPN ISSN 0286-5769
Q4
KUMAMOTO DAIGAKU KYOYOBU KIYO. SHIZEN KAGAKU HEN/KUMAMOTO UNIVERSITY. FACULTY OF GENERAL EDUCATION. MEMOIRS. NATURAL SCIENCES. Text and summaries in English, Japanese. 1966. a.
Indexed: JPI, Z02.
—Linda Hall.
Published by: Kumamoto Daigaku, Kyoyobu/Kumamoto University, Faculty of General Education, 40-1, Kurokami 2-chome, Kumamoto-shi, Kumamoto-ken 860, Japan.

500 060 SWE ISSN 0081-9956
KUNGLIGA VETENSKAPSAKADEMIEN. BIDRAG TILL KUNGLIGA VETENSKAPSAKADEMIENS HISTORIA. Text in Swedish. 1963. irreg., latest vol.37, 2003. **Document type:** *Monographic series, Academic/Scholarly.*
Indexed: GeoRef.
Published by: Kungliga Vetenskapsakademien/Royal Swedish Academy of Sciences, PO Box 50005, Stockholm, 10405, Sweden. TEL 46-8-6739500, FAX 46-8-155670, http://www.kva.se.

500 600 CHN
KUNMING LIGONG DAXUE XUEBAO (LIGONG BAN)/KUNMING UNIVERSITY OF SCIENCE AND TECHNOLOGY. JOURNAL (SCIENCE AND TECHNOLOGY). Text in Chinese. 1959. bi-m. USD 24.60 (effective 2009). **Document type:** *Journal, Academic/Scholarly.*
Former titles: Kunming Ligong Daxue Xuebao (1007-855X); Kunming Gongxueyuan Xuebao (1001-4896)
Related titles: Online - full text ed.
Indexed: A28, APA, BrCerAb, C&ISA, CA/WCA, CIA, CerAb, CivEngAb, CorrAb, E&CAJ, E11, EEA, EMA, ESPM, EnvEAb, H15, M&TEA, M09, MBF, METADEX, RefZh, SolStAb, T04, WAA.
—East View.
Published by: Kunming Ligong Daxue, 253, Xuefu Lu, Kunming, 650093, China. TEL 86-871-5192954, FAX 86-871-5130880.

KUNMING XUEYUAN XUEBAO/KUNMING UNIVERSITY. JOURNAL. *see* SOCIAL SCIENCES: COMPREHENSIVE WORKS

500 700 NLD ISSN 0927-3506
KUNST EN WETENSCHAP. Text in Dutch. 1992. 4/yr. EUR 14; EUR 5.75 newsstand/cover (effective 2009). adv. bk.rev. **Document type:** *Magazine, Trade.*
Published by: De Studenten Uitgeverij, Smidtstraat 12, Schraard, 8746 NG, Netherlands. TEL 31-517-531583, FAX 31-517-532042. Circ: 5,000.

500 700 AUT
KUNST UND WISSENSCHAFT AUS GRAZ. Text in German. 2007. irreg., latest vol.3, 2010. price varies. **Document type:** *Monographic series, Academic/Scholarly.*
Published by: Boehlau Verlag GmbH & Co.KG., Wiesingerstr 1, Vienna, W 1010, Austria. TEL 43-1-3302427, FAX 43-1-3302432, boehlau@boehlau.at, http://www.boehlau.at.

500 FIN ISSN 1237-8186
KUOPIA UNIVERSITY. OCCASIONAL PAPERS. C, NATURAL AND ENVIRONMENTAL SCIENCES/KUOPION YLIOPISTON SELVITYKSIAA. C, LUONNONTIETEET JA YMPARISTOTIETEET. Text in Multiple languages. 1992. irreg. back issues avail. **Document type:** *Monographic series, Academic/Scholarly.*
Formerly (until 1997): Kuopio University. Publications. C, Natural and Environmental Sciences (1235-0486)
Indexed: GeoRef.
Published by: Kuopion Yliopisto, Luonnontieteiden ja Ympaaristotieteiden Tiedekunta/University of Kuopia. Faculty of Natural Sciences and Environmental Sciences, PO Box 1627, Kuopio, 70211, Finland. TEL 358-17-162211.

508.074 JPN ISSN 0913-1566
KURASHIKI-SHIRITSU SHIZENSHI HAKUBUTSUKAN KENKYU HOKOKU/KURASHIKI MUSEUM OF NATURAL HISTORY. BULLETIN. Text in Japanese; Summaries in English, Japanese. 1986. a. JPY 430. abstr. back issues avail. **Description:** Contains mainly original papers.
Indexed: Z01.
Published by: Kurashiki-shiritsu Shizenshi Hakubutsukan/Kurashiki Museum of Natural History, 6-1 Chuo 2-chome, Kurashiki-shi, Okayama-ken 710-0046, Japan. TEL 0864-25-6037, FAX 0864-25-6038.

KURASHIKI-SHIRITSU SHIZENSHI HAKUBUTSUKANPO. *see* MUSEUMS AND ART GALLERIES

507.4 JPN ISSN 0912-1897
KUSHIRO-SHIRITSU HAKUBUTSUKAN KIYO/KUSHIRO CITY MUSEUM. MEMOIRS. Text in Japanese; Summaries in English, Japanese. 1972. a. 40 p./no.; back issues avail. **Document type:** *Bulletin.*
Published by: Kushiro-shiritsu Hakubutsukan/Kushiro City Museum, 1-7 Shiyunkodai, Kushiro-shi, Hokkaido 085-0822, Japan. TEL 81-154-41-5809, FAX 81-154-42-6000, ku610601@city.kushiro.hokkaido.jp, http://www.city.kushiro.hokkaido.jp/museum/index.html. Ed. Junichi Yamashiro. Pub. Tatsuo Shichita.

500 KWT ISSN 0250-4065
CODEN: ARKRDL
KUWAIT INSTITUTE FOR SCIENTIFIC RESEARCH. ANNUAL RESEARCH REPORT. Text in English. 1977. a. free. back issues avail. **Document type:** *Newsletter, Corporate.* **Description:** Contains articles meant to promote scientific and applied research in relation to industry, energy, environment, natural resources, food resources and economics.
Indexed: ASFA, B21, ChemAb, ESPM, GeoRef, SpeleolAb.
—CASDDS, INIST.
Published by: Kuwait Institute for Scientific Research, PO Box 24885, Safat, 13109, Kuwait. TEL 965-4836100, FAX 965-4846891, TELEX 22299 KISR KT. Circ: 2,000.

500 CAN ISSN 1025-7012
➤ **KUWAIT INTERNATIONAL JOURNAL OF CREATIVE ACHIEVEMENTS.** Text in Arabic, English, French. 1996. q. CAD 400 (effective 2006). adv. bk.rev. **Document type:** *Journal, Academic/Scholarly.* **Description:** Designed for concise, cooperative publication of simple low cost techniques and creative ideas.
Published by: M.I. Ismail, Ed. & Pub., 9 Finsh DDO, Montreal, PQ H9A 3G9, Canada. TEL 514-626-9800, ismail.csc@usa.net. Ed., Pub. M I Ismail TEL 965-918-9996.

500 KWT ISSN 1024-8684
Q80.K9 CODEN: JUKSD8
➤ **KUWAIT JOURNAL OF SCIENCE & ENGINEERING.** Text in English; Summaries in Arabic. 1974. s-a. USD 15 to individuals; USD 60 to institutions (effective 2004). **Document type:** *Journal, Academic/Scholarly.*
Formerly (until 1996): University of Kuwait. Journal (Science) (0376-4818)
Related titles: CD-ROM ed.
Indexed: A20, A22, A29, A34, A35, A37, AgBio, AgrForAb, B20, B21, B25, BIOSIS Prev, C25, C30, CABA, CCMJ, CIN, CIS, CTA, ChemAb, ChemTitl, ChemoAb, CurCont, D01, E12, ESPM, ExtraMED, F08, GH, GeoRef, H&SSA, H16, I10, I11, IMMAb, Inspec, M10, MSN, MathR, MycolAb, N02, N03, NSA, O01, P32, P33, P40, PetrolAb, PollutAb, R07, R13, RiskAb, S13, S16, SCI, SCOPUS, SWRA, SpeleolAb, T05, VirolAbstr, W07, W11, Z01, Z02.
—BLDSC (5131.934500), AskIEEE, CASDDS, IE, Ingenta, PADDS.
Published by: Academic Publication Council, University of Kuwait, Faculty of Science, PO Box 17225, Khaldiyah, 72453, Kuwait. TEL 965-4816261. Ed. Dr. Taher Ahmed Al-Sahhaf. Circ: 1,000.

500 510 RUS ISSN 0130-2221
QA1
KVANT. Text in Russian. 1970. bi-m. USD 119.95 in United States. adv. **Description:** Science and math magazine for children.
Indexed: RefZh.
—East View.
Published by: (Rossiiskaya Akademiya Nauk/Russian Academy of Sciences, Byro Kvantum/Quantum Bureau), Kvant Magazine, 1-ya Tverskaya-Yamskaya 2-1, Moscow, 103006, Russian Federation. Ed. Juri A Ossipyan. Adv. contact Irina Oleinik. **Dist. by:** East View Information Services, 10601 Wayzata Blvd, Minneapolis, MN 55305. TEL 952-252-1201, 800-477-1005, FAX 952-252-1202, info@eastview.com, http://www.eastview.com.

500 KOR
KWAHAK DONG-A. Text in Korean. 1986. m.
Published by: Dong-A Ilbo, 139, Chungjongno 3-Ga Seodaemun-Gu, Seoul, 120-715, Korea, S. TEL 02-721-7114. Ed. Kwon O Kie. Circ: 52,000.

500 PRK ISSN 1019-4223
KWAHAKWON TONGBO/KOREAN ACADEMY OF SCIENCES. BULLETIN. Text in Korean. bi-m.
Published by: Korean Academy of Sciences, Pyongyang, Korea, N.

KWANSEI GAKUIN DAIGAKU RIGAKUBU TSUSHIN. *see* COLLEGE AND ALUMNI

S

607 POL ISSN 0023-589X
Q4 CODEN: KHNTAB
KWARTALNIK HISTORII NAUKI I TECHNIKI/QUARTERLY JOURNAL OF THE HISTORY OF SCIENCE AND TECHNOLOGY. Text in Polish. 1956. q. EUR 69 foreign (effective 2006). bk.rev. abstr.; charts; illus. index, cum.index every 10 yrs. **Document type:** *Journal, Academic/Scholarly.*
Indexed: AgrLib, B22, CA, CIN, ChemAb, ChemTitl, EMBASE, ExcerpMed, FR, HistAb, IBR, IBZ, MEDLINE, MathR, P30, RASB, SCOPUS, T02.
—CASDDS, INIST, Linda Hall.
Published by: Polska Akademia Nauk, Instytut Historii Nauki, Palac Staszica, ul Nowy Swiat 72, pok 9, Warsaw, 00330, Poland. TEL 48-22-8268754, FAX 48-22-8266137, ihn@ihnpan.waw.pl. Ed. Stefan Zamecki. Circ: 740. **Dist. by:** Ars Polona, Obroncow 25, Warsaw 03933, Poland. TEL 48-22-5098609, FAX 48-22-5098610, arspolona@arspolona.com.pl, http://www.arspolona.com.pl.

500 UKR ISSN 1728-3817
KYIVS'KYI NATSIONAL'NYI UNIVERSYTET IMENI TARASA SHEVCHENKA. VISNYK. Text in Ukrainian. 1958. a. **Document type:** *Journal, Academic/Scholarly.*
Formerly (until 1998): Kyivs'kyi Universytet. Visnyk (0201-7601)
Related titles: Online - full text ed.; ◆ Series: Kyivs'kyi Natsional'nyi Universytet imeni Tarasa Shevchenka. Visnyk. Yurydychni Nauky. ISSN 1728-2195; ◆ Kyivs'kyi Natsional'nyi Universytet imeni Tarasa Shevchenka. Visnyk. Khimiya. ISSN 1728-2209; ◆ Kyivs'kyi Natsional'nyi Universytet imeni Tarasa Shevchenka. Visnyk. Fizyka. ISSN 1728-2411; ◆ Kyivs'kyi Natsional'nyi Universytet imeni Tarasa Shevchenka. Visnyk. Biolohiya. ISSN 1728-2748; ◆ Kyivs'kyi Natsional'nyi Universytet imeni Tarasa Shevchenka. Visnyk. Ekonomika. ISSN 1728-2667; ◆ Kyivs'kyi Natsional'nyi Universytet imeni Tarasa Shevchenka. Visnyk. Istoriya. ISSN 1728-2640; ◆ Kyivs'kyi Natsional'nyi Universytet imeni Tarasa Shevchenka. Visnyk. Kibernetyka. ISSN 1728-2276; ◆ Kyivs'kyi Natsional'nyi Universytet imeni Tarasa Shevchenka. Visnyk. Problemy Rehulyatsii Fiziolohichnyh Funktsii. ISSN 1728-2624; ◆ Kyivs'kyi Natsional'nyi Universytet imeni Tarasa Shevchenka. Visnyk. Radiofizyka ta Elektronika. ISSN 1728-2306; ◆ Kyivs'kyi Natsional'nyi Universytet imeni Tarasa Shevchenka. Visnyk. Filosofiya, Politolohiya. ISSN 1728-2632; ◆ Kyivs'kyi Natsional'nyi Universytet imeni Tarasa Shevchenka. Visnyk. Introduktsiya ta Zberezhennya Roslynnogo Riznomanittya. ISSN 1728-2284; ◆ Kyivs'kyi Natsional'nyi Universytet imeni Tarasa Shevchenka. Visnyk. Ukrainoznavstvo. ISSN 1728-2330; ◆ Kyivs'kyi Natsional'nyi Universytet imeni Tarasa Shevchenka. Visnyk. Sotsiolohiya, Psykholohiya, Pedahohika. ISSN 1728-2322; ◆ Kyivs'kyi Natsional'nyi Universytet imeni Tarasa Shevchenka. Visnyk. Literaturoznavstvo, Movoznavstvo, Fol'klorystyka. ISSN 1728-2659; ◆ Kyivs'kyi Natsional'nyi Universytet imeni Tarasa Shevchenka. Visnyk. Astronomiya. ISSN 1728-273X; ◆ Kyivs'kyi Natsional'nyi Universytet imeni Tarasa Shevchenka. Visnyk. Seriya: Fizyko-Matematychni Nauky. ISSN 1812-5409; ◆ Kyivs'kyi Natsional'nyi Universytet imeni Tarasa Shevchenka. Visnyk. Heohrafiya. ISSN 1728-2721; ◆ Kyivs'kyi Natsional'nyi Universytet imeni Tarasa Shevchenka. Visnyk. Heolohiya. ISSN 1728-2713; ◆ Kyivs'kyi Natsional'nyi Universytet imeni Tarasa Shevchenka. Visnyk. Zhurnalistyka. ISSN 1728-2705; ◆ Kyivs'kyi Natsional'nyi Universytet imeni Tarasa Shevchenka. Visnyk. Inozemna Filolohiya. ISSN 1728-2683; ◆ Kyivs'kyi Natsional'nyi Universytet imeni Tarasa Shevchenka. Visnyk. Shidni Movy ta Literatury. ISSN 1728-242X; ◆ Kyivs'kyi Natsional'nyi Universytet imeni Tarasa Shevchenka. Visnyk. Mizhnarodni Vidnosyny. ISSN 1728-2292; ◆ Kyivs'kyi Natsional'nyi Universytet imeni Tarasa Shevchenka. Visnyk. Matematyka ta Mekhanika. ISSN 1684-1565.
Indexed: RefZh.
—Linda Hall.
Published by: (Kyivs'kyi Natsional'nyi Universytet imeni Tarasa Shevchenka/National Taras Shevchenko University of Kyiv), Vydavnycho-Poligrafichnyi Tsentr Kyivs'kyi Universytet, bul'var Tarasa Shevchenko, 14, ofis 43, Kyiv, 01601, Ukraine. TEL 380-44-2393172.

500 JPN ISSN 0912-6449
KYODO TO KAGAKU/NATURE AND SCIENCE. Text in Japanese. 1954. s-a. JPY 1,000 (effective 2001). back issues avail. **Document type:** *Academic/Scholarly.* **Description:** Contains original papers, reviews, commentary, and news on nature and science.
Address: Hokkaido Kyoiku Daigaku, Sapporo Ko Chigaku Kyoshitsu, 1-5, 5-jo 3-chome, Ainosato, Kita-ku, Sapporo, Hokkaido 002-8502, Japan. FAX 81-11-778-0385. Ed. Masaichi Kimura. R&P M Kimura.

509 JPN ISSN 0023-6004
G575
KYOKUCHI/POLAR NEWS. Text in Japanese. 1965. s-a. JPY 5,000; JPY 2,500 newsstand/cover (effective 2001 & 2002). adv. bk.rev. charts; illus.; stat. 64 p./no.; back issues avail. **Document type:** *Newsletter, Trade.* **Description:** Contains Antarctic and Arctic information and relevant news on geoscience and polar-science.
Indexed: GeoRef, SpeleolAb.
—Linda Hall.
Published by: Japan Polar Research Association/Nihon Kyokuchi Kenkyu Shinkokai, 2-3-4 Hirakawa-cho, Chiyoda-ku, Tokyo, 102-0093, Japan. TEL 81-3-3239-7615, FAX 81-3-3239-7617. Ed. Takao Hoshiai. R&P, Adv. contact Tetsuya Torii. B&W page JPY 30,000; trim 160 x 240. Circ: 2,500.

505 605 JPN ISSN 0911-0305
Q77.K74 CODEN: MFETEC
KYOTO INSTITUTE OF TECHNOLOGY. FACULTY OF ENGINEERING AND DESIGN. MEMOIRS. Text in English, Multiple languages. 1952. a. per issue exchange basis.
Formerly: Kyoto Technical University. Faculty of Industrial Arts. Memoirs: Science and Technology (0453-0047)
Indexed: A28, APA, BrCerAb, C&ISA, CA/WCA, CCMJ, CIA, CerAb, ChemAb, ChemTitl, CivEngAb, CorrAb, E&CAJ, E11, EEA, EIA, EMA, EnvAb, GeoRef, H15, Inspec, M&TEA, M09, MBF, METADEX, MSN, MathR, SolStAb, SpeleolAb, T04, WAA, Z02.
—BLDSC (5593.345000), AskIEEE, CASDDS, Linda Hall.
Published by: Kyoto Institute of Technology, Faculty of Engineering and Design/Kyoto Kogei Sen'i Daigaku Kogeigakubu, Matsugasaki, Sakyo-ku, Kyoto-shi, 606, Japan. Circ: 790.

500 JPN ISSN 0287-7902
CODEN: KSRODS
KYOTO SANGYO DAIGAKU RONSHU. SHIZEN KAGAKU KEIRETSU/ ACTA HUMANISTICA ET SCIENTIFICA UNIVERSITATIS SANGIO KYOTIENSIS. NATURAL SCIENCE SERIES. Text and summaries in English, Japanese. 1972. a.
Indexed: ChemAb.
—CASDDS.
Published by: Kyoto Sangyo Daigaku/Kyoto Sangyo University, Motoyama, Kamigamo, Kita-ku, Kyoto-shi, Kyoto-Fu 603, Japan.

500.2 JPN ISSN 0368-9689
Q77 CODEN: MFKPAQ
➤ **KYOTO UNIVERSITY. FACULTY OF SCIENCE. MEMOIRS. SERIES OF PHYSICS, ASTROPHYSICS, GEOPHYSICS AND CHEMISTRY.** Text in English. 1903. s-a. per issue exchange basis. illus. **Document type:** *Journal, Academic/Scholarly.*
Supersedes in part (in 1967): University of Kyoto. College of Science. Memoirs. Series A (0369-2051); Which superseded in part (in 1924): Kyoto Imperial University. College of Science. Memoirs (0369-206X); Which superseded in part (in 1914): Kyoto Imperial University. College of Science and Engineering. Memoirs (0369-2078)
Indexed: ChemAb, ChemTitl, GeoRef, Inspec, JTA, SpeleolAb.
—BLDSC (5597.900000), AskIEEE, CASDDS, Ingenta, INIST, Linda Hall.
Published by: Kyoto University, Faculty of Science/Kyoto Daigaku Rigakubu, Kitashirakawa-Oiwake-cho, Sakyo-ku, Kyoto, 606-8502, Japan. Ed. Kenji Ueno. Circ: 800.

500 JPN
KYOUTO KYOUIKU DAIGAKU KIYOU/KYOTO UNIVERSITY OF EDUCATION. BULLETIN. (Issue number continues from merged titles.) Text in Japanese. 2002 (no.101). s-a. **Document type:** *Bulletin, Academic/Scholarly.*
Formed by the merger of (1966-2002): Kyoto Kyoiku Daigaku Kiyo. A: Jimbun, Shakai/Kyoto University of Education. Bulletin. Series A. Education, Social Sciences, Literature and Arts (0387-7833); Which was formerly (1951-1966): Kyoto Gakugei Daigaku Kiyo. A: Bunka/Kyoto Gakugei University. Bulletin. Series A. Education, Social Sciences, Literature and Arts (0453-0012); (1966-2002): Kyoto Kyoiku Daigaku Kiyo. B: Shizen Kagaku/Kyoto University of Education. Bulletin. Series B, Mathematics and Natural Science (0023-6101); Which was formerly (1951-1966): Kyoto Gakugei Daigaku Kiyo, B: Rika/Kyoto University of Education. Bulletin. Series B, Mathematics and Natural Science (0454-7934)
Related titles: Online - full text ed.
—Ingenta.
Published by: Kyoto Kyoiku Daigaku/Kyoto University of Education, 1 Fukakusa-Fujinomori-cho, Fushimi-ku, Kyoto-shi, 612-0863, Japan.

KYUSHU INSTITUTE OF TECHNOLOGY. BULLETIN: PURE & APPLIED MATHEMATICS. *see* MATHEMATICS

KYUSHU INSTITUTE OF TECHNOLOGY. BULLETIN: SCIENCE AND TECHNOLOGY/KYUSHU KOGYO DAIGAKU KENKYU HOKOKU: KOGAKU. *see* TECHNOLOGY: COMPREHENSIVE WORKS

500 USA
L B L CURRENTS WEEKLY NEWSLETTER. (Lawrence Berkeley Laboratory) Text in English. w. **Document type:** *Newsletter.*
Media: E-mail.
Published by: Ernest Orlando Lawrence Berkeley National Laboratory, Public Information Department, 1 Cyclotron Rd MS-65, Berkeley, CA 94720. TEL 510-486-5771, FAX 510-486-6641, http://www.lbl.gov. Ed. Pam Patterson.

LAB LINES; newsletter of the laboratory technicians' branch. *see* EDUCATION—Teaching Methods And Curriculum

LAB MANAGER; where science and management meet. *see* BUSINESS AND ECONOMICS—Management

LAB TALK. *see* EDUCATION—Teaching Methods And Curriculum

500 DEU ISSN 1864-2381
LAB TIMES. Text in English. 2006. bi-m. EUR 27 (effective 2009). adv. **Document type:** *Journal, Academic/Scholarly.* **Description:** Provides independent and investigative reporting as well as critical analysis of the European science and science policy.
Published by: L J Verlag Herfort und Sailer, Alte Str 1, Merzhausen, 79249, Germany. TEL 49-761-286869, FAX 49-761-35738, verlag@laborjournal.de. Ed. Ralf Neumann. Adv. contact Bernd Beutel. B&W page EUR 3,980, color page EUR 4,970. Circ: 21,800 (paid and controlled).

500 USA
LABORATORIO Y ANALISIS. Text in Spanish. 1975. q. free to qualified personnel (print or online ed.) (effective 2009). adv. **Document type:** *Magazine, Trade.* **Description:** Contains new laboratory products illustrated and described for export.
Related titles: Online - full text ed.
Published by: B2B Portales, Inc. (Subsidiary of: Carvajal International, Inc.), 6505 Blue Lagoon Dr, Ste 430, Miami, FL 33126. TEL 305-448-6875, FAX 305-448-9942, contactenos@b2bportales.com, http://www.b2bportales.com. Ed. Margarita Mejia TEL 54-11-49618246 ext 115. Pub. Terry Beirne TEL 305-448-6875 ext 47311. adv.: color page USD 7,950; 7 x 10. Circ: 22,519.

500 658 USA ISSN 1060-5118
LABORATORY INDUSTRY REPORT; the bi-monthly on lab management and marketing intelligence. Abbreviated title: L I R. Text in English. 1992. m. looseleaf. USD 474 combined subscription in US & Canada (print & online eds.); USD 574 combined subscription elsewhere (print & online eds.) (effective 2009). adv. back issues avail. **Document type:** *Newsletter, Trade.* **Description:** Features analysis of market trends, industry developments, and insights on evolving business arrangements. Aimed at lab industry executives, lab marketers, and lab directors.
Related titles: Online - full text ed.: USD 47 per issue (effective 2008).
—CCC.
Published by: Institute of Management & Administration, Inc., One Washington Park, Ste 1300, Newark, NJ 07102. TEL 973-718-4700, FAX 973-622-0595, subserve@ioma.com. Ed. Jondavid Klipp. Pub. Lee Rath. Circ: 1,000.

500 COL ISSN 2145-4086
▼ **LAMPSAKOS.** Text in English, Spanish. 2009. irreg. free (effective 2011). **Document type:** *Journal, Academic/Scholarly.*
Media: Online - full text.
Published by: Fundacion Universitaria Luis Amigo, Transversal 51 A, Medellin, 67B 90, Colombia. TEL 57-4-4487666, FAX 57-4-3849797, http://www.funlam.edu.com.

500 ITA ISSN 1971-1352
THE LANGUAGE OF SCIENCE. Text in English. 2007. irreg. **Document type:** *Monographic series, Academic/Scholarly.*
Media: Online - full text.
Published by: Polimetrica Publisher, Corso Milano 26, Monza, 20052, Italy. TEL 39-039-2301829, onlus@polimetrica.eu.

LANTERN; cultural journal. *see* EDUCATION

500 CHN ISSN 0455-2059
Q4 CODEN: LCTHAF
LANZHOU DAXUE XUEBAO (ZIRAN KEXUE BAN)/LANZHOU UNIVERSITY. JOURNAL (NATURAL SCIENCES). Text in Chinese. 1957. bi-m. USD 31.20 (effective 2009). **Document type:** *Journal, Academic/Scholarly.*
Related titles: Online - full text ed.
Indexed: A22, CCMJ, GeoRef, INIS AtomInd, Inspec, MSN, MathR, RASB, RefZh, SCOPUS, Z01, Z02.
—BLDSC (4812.961000), East View, IE, Ingenta, INIST, Linda Hall.
Published by: Lanzhou Daxue, 199, Donggang Xi Lu, Lanzhou, 730000, China. TEL 86-931-8912707, FAX 86-931-8625576. **Dist. by:** China International Book Trading Corp, 35 Chegongzhuang Xilu, Haidian District, PO Box 399, Beijing 100044, China. TEL 86-10-68412045, FAX 86-10-68412023, cibtc@mail.cibtc.com.cn, http://www.cibtc.com.cn.

500 CHN ISSN 1009-2269
LANZHOU GONGYE GAODENG ZHUANKE XUEXIAO XUEBAO/ LANZHOU POLYTECHNIC COLLEGE. JOURNAL. Text in Chinese. 1993. q. CNY 5 newsstand/cover (effective 2006). **Document type:** *Journal, Academic/Scholarly.*
Related titles: Online - full text ed.
Published by: Lanzhou Gongye Gaodeng Zhuanke Xuexiao, 1, Gongjiaping Dong Lu, Lanzhou, 730050, China.

500 CHN ISSN 1673-5196
LANZHOU LIGONG DAXUE XUEBAO/LANZHOU UNIVERSITY OF TECHNOLOGY. JOURNAL. Text in Chinese. 1975. bi-m. USD 21.60 (effective 2009). **Document type:** *Journal, Academic/Scholarly.*
Formerly: Gansu Gongye Daxue Xuebao/Gansu University of Technology. Journal (1000-5889)
Related titles: Online - full text ed.
Indexed: A22, A28, APA, BrCerAb, C&ISA, CA/WCA, CCMJ, CIA, CerAb, CivEngAb, CorrAb, E&CAJ, E11, EEA, EMA, ESPM, EnvEAb, H15, M&TEA, M09, MBF, METADEX, MSN, MathR, RefZh, SolStAb, T04, WAA, Z02.
—BLDSC (5155.830650), East View, IE, Ingenta, Linda Hall.
Published by: Lanzhou Ligong Daxue/Lanzhou University of Technology, 287, Langongping Lu, Lanzhou, 730050, China. TEL 86-931-2756301, FAX 86-931-2756815.

500 FIN ISSN 0788-7604
LAPIN YLIOPISTO. ACTA UNIVERSITATIS LAPPONIENSIS. Text in Multiple languages. 1991. irreg., latest vol.87, 2005. price varies. back issues avail. **Document type:** *Monographic series, Academic/ Scholarly.*
Published by: Lapin Yliopisto/University of Lapland, Yliopistonkatu 8, Rovaniemi, 9630, Finland. TEL 358-16-341341, FAX 358-16-3412207.

500 LVA ISSN 1407-009X
Q4 CODEN: PLABFE
➤ **LATVIAN ACADEMY OF SCIENCES. SECTION B. NATURAL SCIENCES. PROCEEDINGS/LATVIJAS ZINATNU AKADEMIJAS VETIS. B DALA. DABASZINATNES.** Text in Latvian, English. 1947. m. bk.rev. abstr.; bibl.; charts; illus. index. **Document type:** *Proceedings, Academic/Scholarly.*
Supersedes in part (in 1992): Latvijas Zinatnu Akademijas Vestis (0868-6556); Formerly (until 1990): Latvijas P.S.R. Zinatnu Akademijas Vestis (0132-6422)
Related titles: Online - full text ed.: free (effective 2011).
Indexed: ABIPC, B25, BIOSIS Prev, CCMJ, CIN, ChemAb, ChemTitl, DBA, HistAb, INIS AtomInd, Inspec, MLA, MLA-IB, MSN, MathR, MycolAb, NumL, P30, RASB, Z01, Z02.
—BLDSC (6746.880000), AskIEEE, CASDDS, IE, Ingenta, INIST, Linda Hall. **CCC.**
Published by: Latvijas Zinatnu Akademijas/Latvian Academy of Sciences, Akademijas Laukums 1, Riga, 1524, Latvia. TEL 371-7-223732, FAX 371-7-821153, http://www.lza.lv. Ed. Isaak Rashal. Circ: 1,400.

500 600 USA
LAWRENCE LIVERMORE NATIONAL LABORATORY. REPORT. Text in English. irreg.
Published by: University of California, Lawrence Livermore National Security LLC, 7000 East Ave, PO Box 808, Livermore, CA 94551-0808. TEL 925-422-1100, FAX 925-422-1370, http://www.llnl.gov.

500 LBN ISSN 1561-3410
➤ **LEBANESE SCIENCE JOURNAL/JOURNAL SCIENTIFIQUE LIBANAIS.** Text in English, French, Arabic. 1985. s-a. free (effective 2003). Index. 125 p./no.; reprints avail. **Document type:** *Journal, Academic/Scholarly.* **Description:** It is a forum for the presentation of research results, reports, studies, reviews and letters in all the fields of fundamental and applied sciences, biological, medical sciences and public health, food science, agriculture and environmental sciences that have a regional relevance.
Former titles (until 2000): Lebanese Scientific Research Reports (1027-9652); Lebanese Science Bulletin (0256-7482)
Indexed: ASFA, B21, ESPM, INIS AtomInd, Z01.
—BLDSC (5179.591300).
Published by: Lebanese National Council for Scientific Research, P O Box 11- 8281, Beirut, Lebanon. TEL 961-1-840260, FAX 961-1-822639, journal@cnrs.edu.lb, http://www.cnrs.edu.lb. Ed. Mouin Hamze.

500 SGP
▼ **LECTURES IN NANOSCIENCE AND TECHNOLOGY: ELECTRONICS FROM THE BOTTOM UP.** Text in English. forthcoming 2011. irreg. **Document type:** *Monographic series, Academic/Scholarly.* **Description:** Covers areas of nanoscience and technology which are related to electronics.

Published by: World Scientific Publishing Co. Pte. Ltd., 5 Toh Tuck Link, Singapore, 596224, Singapore. TEL 65-6466-5775, FAX 65-6467-7667, wspc@wspc.com.sg, http://www.worldscientific.com. Ed. Mark S Lundstrom. **Dist. by:** World Scientific Publishing Co., Inc., 27 Warren St, Ste 401-402, Hackensack, NJ 07601. TEL 201-487-9655, 800-227-7562, FAX 201-487-9656, 888-977-2665, wspc@wspc.com; World Scientific Publishing Ltd., 57 Shelton St, London WC2H 9HE, United Kingdom. TEL 44-207-8360888, FAX 44-207-8362020, sales@wspc.co.uk.

500.2 GBR ISSN 0260-1036
LEEDS NATURALISTS' CLUB AND SCIENTIFIC ASSOCIATION. NEWSLETTER. Text in English. 1976. a. GBP 5 to members (effective 2001). bk.rev. **Document type:** *Newsletter.*
Published by: Leeds Naturalists' Club and Scientific Association, c/o Mrs. M. Larner, 1 Ashleigh Rd, Leeds, LS16 5AX, United Kingdom. TEL 44-1132-775173. Eds. Mrs. M Larner, Mr. P Larner. Circ: 200.

500 DEU
LEIBNIZ. Text in German. 1994. q. **Document type:** *Journal, Academic/Scholarly.* **Description:** Presents articles and features on scientific research and innovations produced at the Gottfried Wilhelm Leibniz Institute.
Former titles: Wissenschaftsgemeinschaft Gottfried Wilhelm Leibniz. Journal (1435-8239); (until 1998): Wissenschaftsgemeinschaft Blaue Liste. Journal (0946-5138)
Indexed: GeoRef.
Published by: Wissenschaftsgemeinschaft Gottfried Wilhelm Leibniz e.V., Eduard-Pflueger-Str 55, Bonn, 53113, Germany. TEL 49-228-308150, FAX 49-228-30815255, info@leibniz-gemeinschaft.de. Circ: 5,000 (paid and controlled).

500 300 DEU ISSN 0947-5850
H15
LEIBNIZ-SOZIETAET. SITZUNGSBERICHTE. Text in German. 1994. irreg., latest vol.67, 2004. EUR 17.80 per issue (effective 2005). **Document type:** *Journal, Academic/Scholarly.* **Description:** Publishes scientific lectures given during sessions of the Leibniz Society, as well as announcements and information from this association of academics.
Formed by the merger of (1970-1994): Akademie der Wissenschaften in Berlin. Sitzungsberichte (0863-7652); Which was formerly (until 1991): Akademie der Wissenschaften der D D R. Gesellschaftswissenschaften. Sitzungsberichte (0138-4015); (1970-1994): Akademie der Wissenschaften der D D R. Mathematik, Naturwissenschaften, Technik. Sitzungsberichte (0138-3965); Both of which superseded in part (in 1975): Akademie der Wissenschaften der D D R. Sitzungsberichte (0323-5335); Which was formerly (until 1974): Akademie der Wissenschaften der D D R. Sitzungsberichte des Plenums und der Klassen (0138-2608); (until 1972): Deutschen Akademie der Wissenschaften zu Berlin. Sitzungsberichte des Plenums und der Problemgebundenen Klassen (0300-0699); Which was formed by the merger of (1922-1970): Deutsche Akademie der Wissenschaften zu Berlin. Klasse fuer Mathematik und Allgemeine Naturwissenschaften. Sitzungsberichte (0515-8877); Which was formerly (until 1950): Deutsche Akademie der Wissenschaften zu Berlin. Mathematisch-Naturwissenschaftliche Klasse. Sitzungsberichte (0233-0954); (until 1948): Preussische Akademie der Wissenschaften. Physikalisch-Mathematische Klasse. Sitzungsberichte (0371-2435); (1960-1970): Deutsche Akademie der Wissenschaften zu Berlin. Klasse fuer Bergbau, Huttenwesen und Montangeologie. Sitzungsberichte (0065-5082); (1956-1970): Deutsche Akademie der Wissenschaften zu Berlin. Klasse fuer Chemie, Geologie und Biologie. Sitzungsberichte (0065-5104); (1955-1970): Deutsche Akademie der Wissenschaften zu Berlin. Klasse fuer Mathematik, Physik und Technik. Sitzungsberichte (0065-5120); (1950-1970): Deutsche Akademie der Wissenschaften zu Berlin. Klasse fuer Sprachen, Literatur und Kunst. Sitzungsberichte (0011-9806); (1922-1970): Deutsche Akademie der Wissenschaften zu Berlin. Klasse fuer Philosophie, Geschichte, Staats-, Rechts- und Wirtschaftswissenschaften. Sitzungsberichte (0065-5155); Which was formerly (until 1955): Deutsche Akademie der Wissenschaften zu Berlin. Klasse fuer Gesellschaftswissenschaften. Sitzungsberichte (0515-8850); (1950-1970): Deutsche Akademie der Wissenschaften zu Berlin. Klasse fuer Medizin. Sitzungsberichte (0065-5139); Which was formerly (until 1959): Deutsche Akademie der Wissenschaften zu Berlin. Klasse fuer Medizinische Wissenschaften. Sitzungsberichte (0863-7660); (1954-1970): Deutsche Akademie der Wissenschaften zu Berlin. Klasse fuer Technische Wissenschaften. Sitzungsberichte (0515-8907)
Indexed: FR, GeoRef, MLA-IB, SCI.
—INIST. **CCC.**
Published by: (Leibniz-Sozietaet), Trafo Verlag, Finkenstr 8, Berlin, 12621, Germany. TEL 49-30-61299418, FAX 49-30-61299421, trafoberlin@gmx.de, http://www.trafoberlin.de. Ed. Dr. Herbert Hoerz. Pub., R&P, Adv. contact Dr. Wolfgang Weist.

LENAU-JAHRBUCH. *see* LITERATURE

LEONARDO & LEONARDO MUSIC JOURNAL. *see* ART

500 ROM ISSN 1583-0233
LEONARDO JOURNAL OF SCIENCES. Text in Multiple languages. 2002. s-a. **Document type:** *Journal, Academic/Scholarly.*
Related titles: Online - full text ed.: free (effective 2011).
Indexed: A01, A36, A37, AgrForAb, BA, C25, CA, CABA, E12, F08, F11, F12, FCA, GH, I11, N02, P32, P37, R12, S12, S13, S16, T02, T05, TAR, VS, W10, Z02.
Published by: AcademicDirect, 103-105 Muncii Bvd, Cluj-Napoca, Romania. TEL 40-766-239997. Ed. Lorentz Jantschi.

LEONARDO MUSIC JOURNAL. *see* MUSIC

LET'S FIND OUT. *see* EDUCATION—Teaching Methods And Curriculum

500 FRA ISSN 2100-2398
LETTRE INTERNATIONALE D'AGROPOLIS. Text in French, English. 2008. q. **Document type:** *Newsletter, Consumer.*
Published by: Agropolis International, Avenue Agropolis, Montpellier Cedex 5, 34394, France. TEL 33-4-67047575, FAX 33-4-67047599, agropolis@agropolis.fr, http://www.agropolis.fr/index.php.

LEVENDE NATUUR; tijdschrift voor natuurbehoud en natuurbeheer. *see* CONSERVATION

LIAISONS SCIENTIFIQUES. *see* EDUCATION—Teaching Methods And Curriculum

500 CHN ISSN 1672-6634
LIAOCHENG DAXUE XUEBAO (ZIRAN KEXUE BAN)/LIAOCHENG UNIVERSITY. JOURNAL (NATURAL SCIENCE EDITION). Text in Chinese. 1988. q. CNY 6 newsstand/cover (effective 2007). **Document type:** *Journal, Academic/Scholarly.*
Formerly (until 2002): Liaocheng Shi-Yuan Xuebao (Ziran Kexue Ban)/Liaocheng Teachers College. Journal (Natural Sciences Edition) (1007-8304)
Related titles: Online - full text ed.
Published by: Liaocheng Daxue, 34, Wenhua Lu, Liaocheng, 252059, China. TEL 86-635-8238412.

500 CHN ISSN 1008-2174
LIAODONG XUEYUAN XUEBAO (ZIRAN KEXUE BAN)/EASTERN LIAODONG UNIVERSITY. JOURNAL (NATURAL SCIENCE EDITION). Text in Chinese. 1988. q. CNY 3 newsstand/cover (effective 2007). **Document type:** *Journal, Academic/Scholarly.*
Formerly: Liaoning Cai-Zhuan Xuebao/Liaoning Financial College Journal (1008-2751)
Related titles: Online - full text ed.
Published by: Liaodong Xueyuan/Eastern Liaodong University, 116, Linjianghou Jie, Dandong, Liaoning 118001, China. TEL 86-415-3789074, http://www.ldxy.cn/.

500 CHN ISSN 1000-5846
Q4
LIAONING DAXUE XUEBAO (ZIRAN KEXUE BAN)/LIAONING UNIVERSITY. JOURNAL (NATURAL SCIENCES EDITION). Text in Chinese. 1974. q. USD 15.60 (effective 2009). **Document type:** *Journal, Academic/Scholarly.*
Related titles: Online - full text ed.
Indexed: CCMJ, ESPM, MSN, MathR, PollutAb, RefZh, RiskAb.
—BLDSC (4814.247000), East View.
Published by: Liaoning Daxue/Liaoning University, 66 Chongshanzhong Road, Huanggu District, Shenyang, 110036, China. TEL 86-24-86864173, FAX 86-24-62202048. Ed. Ming Wang.

500 CHN ISSN 1008-0562
TN4
LIAONING GONGCHENG JISHU DAXUE XUEBAO (ZIRAN KEXUE BAN)/LIAONING TECHNICAL UNIVERSITY. JOURNAL (NATURAL SCIENCE EDITION). Text in Chinese. 1979. bi-m. CNY 15 newsstand/cover (effective 2005). back issues avail. **Document type:** *Journal, Abstract/Index.*
Formerly (until 1998): Fuxin Kuangye Xueyuan Xuebao/Fuxin Mining Institute. Journal (1000-1662)
Related titles: Online - full text ed.
Indexed: A28, APA, BrCerAb, C&ISA, CA/WCA, CIA, CerAb, CivEngAb, CorrAb, E&CAJ, E11, EEA, EMA, ESPM, EngInd, EnvEAb, GeoRef, H15, M&TEA, M09, MBF, METADEX, RefZh, SCOPUS, SolStAb, T04, WAA.
—BLDSC (5186.247340), Linda Hall.
Published by: Liaoning Gongcheng Jishu Daxue, 47, Zhonghua Lu, Fuxin, 123000, China. TEL 86-418-3350453, FAX 86-418-6511388.

500 CHN ISSN 1674-3261
T4
LIAONING GONGYE DAXUE XUEBAO (ZIRAN KEXUE BAN)/LIAONING UNIVERSITY OF TECHNOLOGY. JOURNAL (NATURAL SCIENCE EDITION). Text in Chinese. 1982 (Aug). bi-m. CNY 1.60 per issue (effective 2009). back issues avail. **Document type:** *Journal, Academic/Scholarly.*
Former titles (until 2008): Liaoning Gongye Daxue Xuebao/Liaoning Institute of Technology. Journal (1005-1090); (until 1992): Jinzhou Gongxueyuan Xuebao/Jinzhou Institute of Technology. Journal (1001-4063)
Related titles: Online - full text ed.
Indexed: A28, APA, BrCerAb, C&ISA, CA/WCA, CIA, CerAb, CivEngAb, CorrAb, E&CAJ, E11, EEA, EMA, ESPM, EnvEAb, H15, M&TEA, M09, MBF, METADEX, RefZh, SolStAb, T04, WAA, Z02.
—Linda Hall.
Published by: Liaoning Gongye Daxue/Liaoning University of Technology, 169 Shiying Jie, Jinzhou, Liaoning 121001, China. TEL 86-416-4198696. Ed. Hui He.

500 600 CHN
LIAONING KEJI XUEYUAN XUEBAO/LIAONING INSTITUTE OF SCIENCE AND TECHNOLOGY. JOURNAL. Text in Chinese. 1999. q. CNY 7 newsstand/cover (effective 2007). **Document type:** *Journal, Academic/Scholarly.*
Formerly: Benxi Yejin Gaodeng Zhuanke Xuexiao Xuebao/Benxi College of Metallurgy. Journal (1008-3723)
Related titles: Online - full text ed.
Published by: Liaoning Keji Xueyuan, 42, Wenhua Lu, Benxi, 117022, China. TEL 86-414-2127183, FAX 86-414-4836532.

500 CHN ISSN 1008-5688
LIAONING SHI-ZHUANG XUEBAO (ZIRAN KEXUE BAN)/LIAONING TEACHERS COLLEGE. JOURNAL (NATURAL SCIENCE EDITION). Text in English. 1999. q. CNY 6 newsstand/cover (effective 2007). **Document type:** *Journal, Academic/Scholarly.*
Related titles: Online - full text ed.
Published by: Liaoning Shifan Gaodeng Zhuanke Xuexiao/Liaoning Teachers College, no.219, sec.4, Linghe Lu, Chaoyang, 122000, China. TEL 86-421-6681056, http://www.cysz.com.cn/.

500 CHN ISSN 1000-1735
Q4 CODEN: LSDKEQ
LIAONING SHIFAN DAXUE XUEBAO (ZIRAN KEXUE BAN)/LIAONING NORMAL UNIVERSITY. JOURNAL (NATURAL SCIENCE EDITION). Text in Chinese. 1978. q. USD 16.40 (effective 2009). **Document type:** *Journal, Academic/Scholarly.*
Related titles: Online - full text ed.
Indexed: A22, A28, A32, APA, B21, BrCerAb, C&ISA, CA/WCA, CCMJ, CIA, CerAb, ChemTitl, CivEngAb, CorrAb, E&CAJ, E11, EEA, EMA, ESPM, EnvEAb, H&SSA, H15, M&TEA, M09, MBF, METADEX, MSN, MathR, PollutAb, RefZh, RiskAb, SSciA, SolStAb, T04, WAA, Z01, Z02.
—BLDSC (4814.240000), CASDDS, East View, IE, Ingenta, Linda Hall.
Published by: Liaoning Shifan Daxue/Liaoning Normal University, 850 Huanghe Lu, Dalian, Liaoning 116029, China. TEL 86-411-84258277, FAX 86-411-84258913.

500 CHN ISSN 1674-0424
CODEN: LYXIAM
LIAONING YIXUEYUAN XUEBAO/LIAONING MEDICAL UNIVERSITY. JOURNAL. Text in Chinese; Abstracts in Chinese, English. 1980. bi-m. CNY 36, USD 36; CNY 6 per issue (effective 2009). **Document type:** *Journal, Academic/Scholarly.*
Formerly (until 2007): Jinzhou Yixueyuan Xuebao/Jinzhou Medical College. Journal (1000-5161)
Related titles: Online - full text ed.
Indexed: A34, A35, A36, A38, AgBio, B&BAb, B19, B20, B21, CABA, CTA, D01, ESPM, F08, F12, GH, H16, H17, I10, ImmunAb, IndVet, N02, N03, NSA, OGFA, P33, P37, PN&I, R12, RA&MP, RM&VM, T05, VS.
—BLDSC (5186.247790), East View.
Published by: Liaoning Yixueyuan/Liaoning Medical University, no.40, Sec. 3, Gongpo Rd., Jinzhou, 121001, China. TEL 86-416-4673258, FAX 86-416-4673173. Ed. Gang Lu. **Dist. by:** China International Book Trading Corp, 35 Chegongzhuang Xilu, Haidian District, PO Box 399, Beijing 100044, China. TEL 86-10-68412045, FAX 86-10-68412023, cibtc@mail.cibtc.com.cn, http://www.cibtc.com.cn.

500 LBY ISSN 0368-7481
Q1 CODEN: LBJSAP
LIBYAN JOURNAL OF SCIENCES; an international journal. Text in English; Summaries in Arabic. 1971. s-a. USD 3.50 to individuals; USD 5.25 to institutions. adv.
Indexed: ChemAb, GeoRef, MathR, PetrolAb, SpeleolAb, Z02.
—CASDDS, INIST.
Published by: Al-Fateh University, Faculty of Science, P O Box 13040, Tripoli, Libya. Ed. M J Salem. Circ: 400.

LIFE AND SCIENCE. *see* OCCUPATIONS AND CAREERS

500 SWE
LIFE SCIENCE NEWS. Text in English. q. free. **Document type:** *Journal, Academic/Scholarly.* **Description:** Contains articles about the newest products and applications in cell biology, applied genomics, proteomics and lab-scale separations.
Published by: Amersham Pharmacia Biotech AB, Uppsala, SE-751 84, Sweden. TEL 46-18-6120000, 44-870-6061921, communications@eu.apbiotech.com, http://www.apbiotech.com/.

500 USA ISSN 0024-3205
QH301 CODEN: LIFSAK
➤ **LIFE SCIENCES.** Text in English, French, German. 1973. 52/yr. EUR 6,340 in Europe to institutions; JPY 841,900 in Japan to institutions; USD 7,090 elsewhere to institutions (effective 2012). adv. charts; illus. index. back issues avail.; reprints avail. **Document type:** *Journal, Academic/Scholarly.* **Description:** Brings out articles that emphasize the molecular, cellular, and functional basis of therapy.
Formed by the merger of (1962-1973): Life Sciences. Part 1: Physiology and Pharmacology (0300-9653); (1962-1973): Life Sciences. Part 2: Biochemistry, General and Molecular (0300-9637); Both of which superseded in part (in 1970): Life Sciences (0161-5564)
Related titles: Microfiche ed.: (from MIM); Microfilm ed.: (from PQC); Online - full text ed.: ISSN 1879-0631 (from IngentaConnect, ScienceDirect).
Indexed: A01, A03, A08, A22, A26, A34, A35, A36, A38, AgBio, Agr, AgrForAb, B&AI, B04, B10, B21, B25, BA, BIOBASE, BIOSIS Prev, BP, C24, C25, C30, C33, CA, CABA, CIN, CTA, ChemAb, ChemTitl, ChemoAb, CurCR, CurCont, D01, DBA, DentInd, E-psyche, E12, EMBASE, ESPM, ExcerpMed, F08, F11, F12, FCA, FR, GH, GenetAb, H16, H17, I05, IABS, ISR, IndChem, IndMed, IndVet, Inpharma, Kidney, MEDLINE, MS&D, MaizeAb, MycolAb, N02, N03, N04, NRN, NSA, O01, P03, P30, P32, P33, P35, P37, P39, P40, PGegResA, PGrRegA, PHN&I, PN&I, PsycholAb, R07, R08, R10, R11, R12, R13, R16, RA&MP, RASB, RM&VM, Reac, S12, S17, SCI, SCOPUS, SSciA, SoyAb, T02, T05, TAR, THA, ToxAb, TriticAb, VITIS, VS, VirolAbstr, W07, W10, W11, WildRev.
—BLDSC (5208.930000), CASDDS, GNLM, IE, Infotrieve, Ingenta, INIST, Linda Hall. **CCC.**
Published by: Elsevier Inc. (Subsidiary of: Elsevier Science & Technology), 1600 John F Kennedy Blvd, Philadelphia, PA 19103. TEL 215-239-3900, FAX 215-238-7883, JournalCustomerService-usa@elsevier.com. Adv. contact Janine Castle TEL 44-1865-843844.

➤ **THE LIGHTBULB - INVENT!**; for the professional inventor/entrepreneur. *see* TECHNOLOGY: COMPREHENSIVE WORKS

500 600 TWN ISSN 1990-4401
LIGONG YANJIU XUEBAO/JOURNAL OF SCIENTIFIC AND TECHNOLOGICAL STUDIES. Text in Chinese, English. 1968. s-a. **Document type:** *Journal, Academic/Scholarly.*
Former titles (until 2005): Nan Daxue Bao (Shuli yu Kexue Lei)/National University Tainan. Journal (Mathematics, Science & Technology); (until 2004): Nan-Shi Xuebao (Shuli yu Kexue Lei)/National Tainan Teachers College. Journal (Mathematics, Science & Technology); Which superseded in part (in Oct. 2002): Nan-shi Xuebao; Which was formerly (until Jun. 2002): Tainan Shiyuan Xuebao/National University Tainan. Journal (1028-737X); (until 1987): Tainan Shizhuan Xuebao/Tainan Junior Teachers College. Bulletin; (until 1969): Tainan Shizhuan Jikan
Published by: Guoli Tainan Daxue/National University of Tainan, 33, Sec. 2, Shu-Lin St., Tainan, 700, Taiwan. TEL 886-6-2133111 ext 142, FAX 886-6-3017009, cathywu@mail.nutn.edu.tw, http://web.nutn.edu.tw/.

500 CHN ISSN 1671-8437
LIKE AIHAOZHE/SCIENCE FANS. Text in Chinese. 1998. s-a. **Document type:** *Magazine, Consumer.*
Published by: Chengdu Daxue, Jixu Jiaoyu Xueyuan/Chendu University, Adult Education College, Hongxin Lu Yi-Duan, 89, Zhaozhongci Jie, Chengdu, 610017, China. TEL 86-28-89955587, http://chengjiao.cdu.edu.cn/.

500 NZL ISSN 1178-0843
LINCOLN UNIVERSITY. RESEARCH PROFILE. Text in English. 2006. a.
Published by: Lincoln University, PO Box 94, Canterbury, New Zealand. TEL 64-3-3252811, FAX 64-3-3252965, http://www.lincoln.ac.nz.

500 DEU ISSN 1612-2224
TP242 CODEN: LIBEAQ
LINDE TECHNOLOGY (GERMAN EDITION). Text in German. 1957. s-a. free. **Document type:** *Journal, Trade.*
Former titles (until 2003): Berichte aus Technik und Wissenschaft (0942-332X); (until 1991): Linde Berichte aus Technik und Wissenschaft (0024-3728)
Related titles: English ed.: Linde Technology. ISSN 1612-2232. 1961.
Indexed: CIN, ChemAb, ChemTitl, Inspec, TM.

S

—BLDSC (5220.800000), CASDDS, Linda Hall. **CCC.**
Published by: Linde AG, Abraham-Lincoln-Str 21, Wiesbaden, 65189, Germany. TEL 49-611-7700, FAX 49-611-770269, http://www.linde.com. Ed. Volker R Leski.

LINKOEPING STUDIES IN ARTS AND SCIENCE. *see* HUMANITIES: COMPREHENSIVE WORKS

500 600 SWE ISSN 0345-7524
LINKOEPING STUDIES IN SCIENCE AND TECHNOLOGY; dissertations. Text in English, Swedish. 1974. irreg., latest 2010. **Document type:** *Monographic series, Academic/Scholarly.*
—IE, Ingenta.
Published by: Linkoepings Universitet, Institutionen foer Tema, Linkoeping, 58183, Sweden. TEL 46-13-282286, FAX 46-13-133630.

LIPPISCHE MITTEILUNGEN AUS GESCHICHTE UND LANDESKUNDE. *see* HISTORY—History Of Europe

508 ESP ISSN 2013-6951
LITHODORA. Text in Catalan. 2007. a. back issues avail. **Document type:** *Monographic series, Academic/Scholarly.*
Related titles: Online - full text ed.: ISSN 2013-696X. 2007.
Published by: Institut d'Estudis Catalans, Carrer del Carme 47, Barcelona, 08001, Spain. TEL 34-932-701620, FAX 34-932-701180, informacio@iecat.net, http://www2.iecat.net.

LIUZHOU ZHIYE JISHU XUEYUAN XUEBAO/LIUZHOU VOCATIONAL & TECHNICAL COLLEGE. JOURNAL. *see* SOCIAL SCIENCES: COMPREHENSIVE WORKS

LIVE (SAN FRANCISCO). *see* MUSEUMS AND ART GALLERIES

THE LIVING MUSEUM. *see* ART

500 ESP ISSN 0210-8615
Q124.6 CODEN: LLULEV
LLULL. Text in Spanish. 1977. s-m. EUR 27 (effective 2008). **Document type:** *Journal, Academic/Scholarly.*
Formerly (until 1978): Sociedad Espanola de Historia de las Ciencias. Boletin (1131-6055)
Indexed: CA, CCMJ, FR, HistAb, MSN, MathR, P09, P30, PCI, PhilInd, SCOPUS, T02, Z02.
—INIST, Linda Hall.
Published by: (Sociedad Espanola de Historia de las Ciencias y de las Tecnicas), Prensas Universitarias de Zaragoza, C/ Pedro Cerbuna 12, Edificio de Ciencias Geologicas, Zaragoza, 50009, Spain. TEL 34-976-761330, FAX 34-976-761063, puz@posta.unizar.es, http://puz.unizar.es.

LODZKIE TOWARZYSTWO NAUKOWE. SPRAWOZDANIA Z CZYNNOSCI I POSIEDZEN NAUKOWYCH. *see* HUMANITIES: COMPREHENSIVE WORKS

LOEWENZAHN. *see* CHILDREN AND YOUTH—For

LOGIC AND PHILOSOPHY OF SCIENCE. *see* PHILOSOPHY

508 FRA
LOIRET NATURE ENVIRONNEMENT. LA LETTRE. Text in French. 1966. q. **Document type:** *Newsletter.*
Former titles (until 2007): La Lettre des Naturalistes Orleanais (1952-367X); (until 2005): Loiret Nature (1167-6647); (until 1992): Naturalistes Orleanais (0291-8455); (until 1971): Association des Naturalistes Orleanais et de la Loire Moyenne. Bulletin (0374-2334); (until 1966): Association des Naturalistes Orleanais. Bulletin (0291-8447); Which superseded in part (in 1958): Naturalistes Orleanais (1151-2113)
Indexed: GeoRef.
—INIST.
Published by: Loiret Nature Environnement, 64 Route d'Olivet, Orleans, 45100, France. TEL 33-2-38566984, FAX 33-2-38563348, loiret.natureenvironnement@orange.fr.

500 300 CHN ISSN 1673-4629
LONGYAN XUEYUAN XUEBAO/LONGYAN UNIVERSITY. JOURNAL. Text in Chinese. 1983. bi-m. CNY 8 newsstand/cover (effective 2006). **Document type:** *Journal, Academic/Scholarly.*
Former titles (until 2005): Longyan Shi-Zhuan Xuebao/Longyan Teachers College. Journal (1672-044X); (until 1998): Longyan Shi-Zhuan Xuebao (Shehui kexue Ban) (1003-871X)
Related titles: Online - full text ed.
Published by: Longyan Xueyuan, 1, Fenghuang Bei Lu, Longyan, 364000, China.

500 EST ISSN 1406-5304
LOODUSEUURIJA KASIRAAMATUD/NATURALIST'S HANDBOOKS. Text in Estonian, English. 1999. irreg. **Document type:** *Monographic series, Academic/Scholarly.*
Published by: (Eesti Looduseuurijate Selts/Estonian Naturalists' Society), Teaduste Akadeemia Kirjastus/Estonian Academy Publishers, Kohtu 6, Tallinn, 10130, Estonia. TEL 372-6-454106, FAX 372-6-466026, asta@kirj.ee, http://www.kirj.ee.

500 USA ISSN 0096-9192
Q11 CODEN: PLAAA6
➤ **LOUISIANA ACADEMY OF SCIENCES. PROCEEDINGS.** Text in English. 1932. a. price varies. back issues avail. **Document type:** *Proceedings, Academic/Scholarly.*
Related titles: Online - full text ed.
Indexed: A26, ASFA, Agr, B21, CIN, CTA, ChemAb, ChemTitl, ChemoAb, E08, G08, I05, NSA, S06, S09, SASA, VirolAbstr, WildRev, Z01.
—CASDDS.
Published by: Louisiana Academy of Sciences, c/o Elisabeth Elder, Department of Biological Sciences, Louisiana State University, 8100 Hwy 71 S, Alexandria, LA 71115. jdujaili@lsue.edu, http://www.laacademy.org. Ed. Thomas Sasek. Circ: 400.

500 FIN ISSN 0355-3728
QH77.F55
LOUNAIS-HAMEEN LUONTO. Text in Finnish. 1955. a. **Document type:** *Yearbook.*
Indexed: GeoRef, Z01.
Published by: Lounais-Hameen Luonnonsuojeluyhdistys ry, c/o Forssan Luonnonhistoriallinen Museo, PO Box 46, Forssa, 30100, Finland. TEL 358-3-4354949, FAX 358-3-4355846.

LRABER HASARAKAKAN GITUT'YUNNERI/HERALD OF SOCIAL SCIENCES/VESTNIK OBSHCHESTVENNYKH NAUK. *see* HUMANITIES: COMPREHENSIVE WORKS

500 CHN ISSN 1673-8020
LUDONG DAXUE XUEBAO (ZIRAN KEXUE BAN)/LUDONG UNIVERSITY JOURNAL (NATURAL SCIENCE EDITION). Text in Chinese. 1985. q. **Document type:** *Journal, Academic/Scholarly.*
Formerly: Yantai Shifan Xueyuan Xuebao (Ziran Kexueban)/Yantai Normal University Journal (Natural Science Edition) (1004-4930)
Related titles: Online - full text ed.
Indexed: MSN, Z02.
Published by: Ludong Daxue/Ludong University, 184, Hongqi Zhonglu, Yantai, 264025, China. TEL 86-535-6672214, FAX 86-535-6014101.

LUOJIXUE YANJIU/STUDIES IN LOGIC. *see* SOCIAL SCIENCES: COMPREHENSIVE WORKS

509 SWE ISSN 0076-1648
Q64
➤ **LYCHNOS;** aarsbok foer ide- och laerdomshistoria. Text in Swedish; Summaries in English. 1936. a. price varies. bk.rev. index. back issues avail. **Document type:** *Academic/Scholarly.*
Indexed: DIP, FR, HistAb, IBR, IBZ, MLA-IB, P30, SCOPUS.
—INIST, Linda Hall.
Published by: Laerdomshistoriska Samfundet/Swedish History of Science Society, c/o Avd. foer Vetenskapshistoria, PO Box 2104, Uppsala, 75002, Sweden. Ed. Sven Widmalm.

➤ **M P O B TECHNOLOGY.** (Malaysian Palm Oil Board) *see* AGRICULTURE

➤ **M S U PROFESSIONAL PAPERS.** (Mindanao State University) *see* SOCIAL SCIENCES: COMPREHENSIVE WORKS

500 ITA ISSN 1591-3783
LA MACCHINA DEL TEMPO. Text in Italian. 2000. m. (11/yr.). **Document type:** *Magazine, Consumer.*
Published by: Arnoldo Mondadori Editore SpA, Via Mondadori 1, Segrate, 20090, Italy. TEL 39-02-66814363, FAX 39-030-3198412, http://www.mondadori.com.

500 IND ISSN 0085-2945
MADRAS. GOVERNMENT MUSEUM. BULLETIN. NEW SERIES. Variant title: Chennai. Government Museum. Bulletin. New Series. Text in English. 1931. irreg., latest 2005. price varies. back issues avail. **Document type:** *Monographic series, Government.*
Published by: Government Museum Chennai, Pantheon Rd, Egmore, Chennai, Tamil Nadu 600 008, India. TEL 91-44-28193238, FAX 91-44-28193035, govtmuse@tn.gov.in.

500 600 THA ISSN 1905-7873
Q1
➤ **MAEJO INTERNATIONAL JOURNAL OF SCIENCE AND TECHNOLOGY.** Text in English. 2007. s-a. **Document type:** *Journal, Academic/Scholarly.*
Related titles: Online - full text ed.: free (effective 2011).
Indexed: A34, A35, A36, A37, A38, AgrForAb, B23, C25, C30, CABA, D01, E12, F08, FCA, GH, H16, MaizeAb, N02, N03, N04, P32, P33, R07, R08, S13, SCI, SCOPUS, SoyAb, T05, W07, W10, W11, Z01.
Published by: Maejo University, Orchid Building, San Sai, Chiang Mai, 50290, Thailand. TEL 66-53-873880, FAX 66-53-873897. Ed. Duang Buddhasukh.

500 DEU ISSN 0949-5304
MAGDEBURGER WISSENSCHAFTSJOURNAL. Text in German; Summaries in English. 1996. s-a. **Document type:** *Journal, Academic/Scholarly.*
Related titles: Online - full text ed.
Indexed: A28, APA, BrCerAb, C&ISA, CA/WCA, CIA, CerAb, CivEngAb, CorrAb, E&CAJ, E11, EEA, EMA, H15, M&TEA, M09, MBF, METADEX, SolStAb, T04, WAA.
—Linda Hall.
Published by: Otto-von-Guericke-Universitaet Magdeburg, Universitatsplatz 2, Postfach 4120, Magdeburg, 39016, Germany. TEL 49-3-916718751, FAX 49-3-916711153.

500 HUN ISSN 0025-0325
AS205.M33
MAGYAR TUDOMANY/HUNGARIAN SCIENCE. Text in Hungarian, French, German, Russian; Contents page in English, French, German, Russian. 1890. m. USD 96 (effective 2000). adv. bk.rev. illus. index. **Document type:** *Academic/Scholarly.*
Related titles: Online - full text ed.: ISSN 1588-1245.
Indexed: BibLing, GeoRef, HL&ISA, HistAb, IBSS, MLA-IB, P30, RASB, RILM, SpeleolAb.
—Linda Hall.
Published by: Magyar Tudomanyos Akademia/Hungarian Academy of Sciences, Nador u. 7, Budapest, 1051, Hungary.

500 IRQ ISSN 1819-6489
MAJALLAT AL-MANSUR/MANSOUR JOURNAL. Text in Arabic, English. 2000. s-a. **Document type:** *Journal, Academic/Scholarly.*
Published by: Mansour University College, PO Box 69003, Baghdad, 69005, Iraq. info@muciraq.com, http://www.muciraq.com/home.html.

500 600 KWT
MAJALLAT AL-ULUM. Text in Arabic. m. USD 40 (effective 1992). adv.
Related titles: ◆ Italian ed.: Le Scienze. ISSN 0036-8083; ◆ English ed.: Scientific American. ISSN 0036-8733; ◆ German ed.: Spektrum der Wissenschaft. ISSN 0170-2971; ◆ Hungarian ed.: Tudomany. ISSN 0237-322X; ◆ French ed.: Pour la Science. ISSN 0153-4092; ◆ Chinese ed.: Ke Xue. ISSN 1002-1299; ◆ Spanish ed.: Investigacion y Ciencia. ISSN 0210-136X; ◆ Japanese ed.: Nikkei Saiensu. ISSN 0917-009X; ◆ Polish ed.: Swiat Nauki. ISSN 0867-6380; Turkish ed.: Bilim.
Address: P O Box 20856, Safat, Kuwait.

500 PSE ISSN 1810-6366
MAJALLAT JAMI'AT AL-AZHAR BI-GAZZAT. AL-'ULUM AL-TABI'IYAT/AZHAR UNIVERSITY, GAZA. NATURAL SCIENCE. JOURNAL. Text in English, Arabic. 1996. irreg., latest 2006. **Document type:** *Journal, Academic/Scholarly.*
Published by: Al-Azhar University in Gazza, Jamal Abdl Naser St, PO Box 1277, Gaza, Palestine. TEL 970-8-2824010, FAX 970-8-2823180, alazhar@alazhar-gaza.edu.

500 PSE ISSN 1992-8246
➤ **MAJALLAT JAMI'AT AL-HALIL LIL-BUHUTH/HEBRON UNIVERSITY RESEARCH JOURNAL.** Text in Arabic. 2005. a., latest 2006. **Document type:** *Journal, Academic/Scholarly.*
Related titles: Online - full text ed.: ISSN 1992-8254. 2002.
Published by: Jami'at al-Halil/Hebron University, PO Box 40, Hebron, Palestine. TEL 972-2-2220995.

500 PSE ISSN 1727-2114
MAJALLAT JAMI'AT AN-NAGAH AL-ABHATH. A, AL-'ULUM AL-TABI'IYYAT/AN-NAJAH UNIVERSITY JOURNAL FOR RESEARCH. A, NATURAL SCIENCES. Text in Arabic. 1983. bi-m. **Document type:** *Journal, Academic/Scholarly.*
Published by: Jami'at al-Najah al-Wataniyyat, Deanship of Scientific Research/An-Najah National University, PO Box 7, Nablus, Palestine. TEL 972-9-2345113, FAX 972-9-2345982, info@najah.edu, http://www.najah.edu/index.php.

500 FRA ISSN 1959-1519
MAKA; observatoire de la nature, de la terre et de l'espace. Text in French. 2007. bi-m. EUR 15.90 (effective 2008). **Document type:** *Magazine, Consumer.*
Published by: Editions Maka, 90 Bis Rue du Chemin-Neuf, Meltz-sur-Seine, 77171, France. http://www.maka-protected.com.

500 IDN ISSN 1693-6671
Q4.I5
MAKARA SERI SAINS. Text in Indonesian, English. 1997. 3/yr. **Document type:** *Journal, Academic/Scholarly.*
Related titles: Online - full text ed.: free (effective 2011).
Published by: Universitas Indonesia, Kamous Universitas Indonesia, Depok, 16424, Indonesia. http://www.ui.ac.id. Ed. Jarnuzi Gunlazuardi.

500 001.3 MKD ISSN 0580-4981
MAKEDONSKA AKADEMIJA NA NAUKITE I UMETNOSTITE. LETOPIS. Text in Macedonian. 1969. a. USD 20 foreign (effective 2001). **Document type:** *Yearbook.* **Description:** Report of activities in symposia and congresses with information on scientific projects, exhibitions, publications, and membership listings.
Indexed: SpeleolAb.
Published by: Makedonska Akademija na Naukite i Umetnostite, Bulevar Krste Misirkov 2, PO Box 428, Skopje, 91000, Macedonia. TEL 389-02-114200, FAX 389-02-115903, gde@manu.edu.mk, http://www.manu.edu.mk. Ed. Blaze Ristovski.

510 570 MKD ISSN 0351-3246
QA1 CODEN: PMANDL
MAKEDONSKA AKADEMIJA NA NAUKITE I UMETNOSTITE. ODDELENIE ZA MATEMATICKI I TEHNICKI NAUKI. PRILOZI/MACEDONIAN ACADEMY OF SCIENCES AND ARTS. SECTION OF MATHEMATICAL AND TECHNICAL SCIENCES. CONTRIBUTIONS. Text in Macedonian. 1969. s-a. USD 20 foreign (effective 2001). **Description:** Research in mathematics, physics, chemistry, earth sciences, engineering, energy.
Supersedes (in 1980): Makedonska Akademija na Naukite i Umetnostite. Oddelenie za Prirodno-Matematicki Nauki. Prilozi. (0581-0833)
Indexed: CCMJ, ChemAb, INIS AtomInd, MSN, MathR, Z02.
—CASDDS, Linda Hall.
Published by: (Oddelenie za Matematicki i Tehnicki Nauki), Makedonska Akademija na Naukite i Umetnostite, Bulevar Krste Misirkov 2, PO Box 428, Skopje, 91000, Macedonia. TEL 389-02-114200, FAX 389-02-115903, gde@manu.edu.mk, http://www.manu.edu.mk. Ed. Blagoj Popov.

507 UGA
MAKERERE UNIVERSITY. SCIENCE FACULTY. HANDBOOK. Text in English. irreg.
Published by: Makerere University, Science Faculty, PO Box 7062, Kampala, Uganda. Ed. A J Lutalo. Circ: 1,000.

500 370 ISR
HA MAKHON. Text in Hebrew. 1995. q. **Document type:** *Journal, Academic/Scholarly.*
Published by: Weizmann Institute of Science, Public Affairs Office, P O Box 26, Rehovot, 76100, Israel. TEL 972-8-934-2111, FAX 972-8-934-4107, http://wis-wander.weizmann.ac.il/site/HE/homepage.asp.

MAKING SENSE OF SCIENCE. *see* CHILDREN AND YOUTH—For

500 MWI
MALAWI JOURNAL OF SCIENCE. Text in English. 1972. a. adv. bk.rev. **Document type:** *Journal, Academic/Scholarly.*
Published by: Association for the Advancement of Science of Malawi, PO Box 280, Zomba, Malawi. Circ: 1,000.

MALAYSIAN NATURALIST. *see* CONSERVATION

500 PHL
➤ **MANILA JOURNAL OF SCIENCE.** Variant title: D L S U Journal of Science. Text in English. 1975. s-a. PHP 200, USD 30. bk.rev.; software rev. **Document type:** *Journal, Academic/Scholarly.* **Description:** Presents scientific research and reviews. Accepts full papers, communications, letters to editor, opinions in all areas of science and technology.
Formerly (until 1997): Agham (0115-5679)
Indexed: IPP.
—CASDDS.
Published by: De La Salle University, College of Science, 2401 Taft Ave, Manila, 1004, Philippines. FAX 632-526-5611. Ed., R&P, Adv. contact Eric Punzalan. page PHP 3,000. Circ: 300.

508 CAN ISSN 0823-2911
MANITOBA NATURALISTS SOCIETY BULLETIN. Text in English. 1975. m. (11/yr.). CAD 40 to members. adv. bk.rev. back issues avail. **Document type:** *Bulletin.* **Description:** Covers natural history topics, outdoor recreation activities, natural history lectures and workshops and environmental protection issues.
Published by: Manitoba Naturalists Society, 401 63 Albert St, Winnipeg, MB R3B 1G4, Canada. TEL 204-943-9029, FAX 204-943-9029. Ed. Margaret Kapinga. Adv. contact Paul Vonwichert. page CAD 200; trim 7.25 x 9.5. Circ: 1,500.

372.35 507.1 CAN ISSN 0315-9159
MANITOBA SCIENCE TEACHER. Text in English. 3/yr. membership. adv. bk.rev.
Indexed: C03, CEI, P48, PQC.
Published by: Science Teachers' Association of Manitoba, 155 Kingsway Ave, Winnipeg, MB R3R 0G3, Canada. Ed. Raj Goyal. Circ: 800.

500 EGY ISSN 1687-5109
MANSOURA JOURNAL OF GEOLOGY AND GEOPHYSICS. Text in English. 1974. s-a. **Document type:** *Journal, Academic/Scholarly.*
Formerly (until 2004): Mansoura Science Bulletin (1110-1326)
Published by: Mansoura University, Faculty of Science, PO Box 35516, Mansoura - Dakahlia, Egypt. TEL 20-50-2247055, FAX 20-50-2247330. Ed. Dr. T Z Sokkar.

500 EGY ISSN 1687-5095
MANSOURA JOURNAL OF PHYSICS/NASHRAT KOLIYYAT AL-'LUM G 'LUM TABI'YYAT. Text in English. 1976. q. USD 720; EGP 10 newsstand/cover. **Document type:** *Journal, Academic/Scholarly.*
Formerly (until 2004): Mansoura Science Bulletin. C, Natural Sciences (1110-4589)
Indexed: Inspec.
Published by: Mansoura University, Faculty of Science, PO Box 35516, Mansoura - Dakahlia, Egypt. TEL 20-50-2247055, FAX 20-50-2247330. Ed. Dr. T Z Sokkar.

MAOMING XUEYUAN XUEBAO/MAOMING COLLEGE. JOURNAL. *see* SOCIAL SCIENCES: COMPREHENSIVE WORKS

500.9 JPN
MARINE PARK RESEARCH STATIONS. BULLETIN/KAICHU KOEN KENKYUJO KENKYU HOKOKU. Text in English, Japanese. 1975. s-a. per issue exchange basis. illus.
Published by: Marine Parks Center of Japan, 1157 Arita, kushimo-To, Nishimuro-gun, Kushimoto-cho, Wakayama-ken 649-3503, Japan. Ed. Michitaka Uda. Circ: 600.

500 ROM
MARISIA: STUDII SI MATERIALE (STUDIA SCIENTIARIUM NATURAE). Text in Romanian. 1965. irreg., latest 2000. **Document type:** *Monographic series, Academic/Scholarly.*
Formerly (until 1983): Marisia (1016-9652); Which superseded in part (in 1974): Studii si Materiale - Muzeul Judetean Targu Mures (1224-2004); Which was formerly (until 1967): Studii si Materiale - Muzeul Regional Targu Mures (1220-1863)
Published by: Muzeul Judetean Mures/Mures County Museum, str. Marasti nr. 8A, Targu Mures, 540328, Romania. TEL 40-365-430021, FAX 40-365-430021, sberecki@yahoo.com, http://muzeumures.ro.

500 913 580 551 DEU ISSN 0931-5373
MARSCHENRAT ZUR FOERDERUNG DER FORSCHUNG IM KUESTENGEBIET DER NORDSEE. NACHRICHTEN. Text in German. 1962. a. free. **Document type:** *Journal, Academic/Scholarly.*
Formerly (until 1966): Marschenrat zur Foerderung der Forschung im Kuestengebiet der Nordsee. Mitteilungsblatt (0931-5365)
Indexed: GeoRef, SpeleolAb.
Published by: Marschenrat zur Foerderung der Forschung im Kuestengebiet der Nordsee, Viktoriastr 26, Wilhelmshaven, 26382, Germany. Circ: 1,200.

MARTIANUSCAPELLA.COM. *see* SOCIAL SCIENCES: COMPREHENSIVE WORKS

508 USA ISSN 0096-4158
QH1 CODEN: MNATAA
➤ **MARYLAND NATURALIST.** Text in English. 1930. s-a. USD 10 per issue (effective 2011). adv. bk.rev. back issues avail. **Document type:** *Journal, Academic/Scholarly.* **Description:** Covers research concerning the natural history and ecology of Maryland and adjacent states.
Former titles (until 1948): Maryland (0896-5587); (until 1944): Natural History Society of Maryland. Bulletin
Indexed: WildRev, Z01.
Published by: Natural History Society of Maryland, Inc., 6908 Belair Rd, PO Box 18750, Baltimore, MD 21206. nhsm@marylandnature.org, http://www.marylandnature.org/index.asp.

600 BRA ISSN 0102-3896
MATEMARICA FISICA. Text in Portuguese. 1982. **Document type:** *Journal, Academic/Scholarly.*
Related titles: ◆ Series of: Estudos Tecnologicos. ISSN 0101-5303.
Published by: Universidade do Vale do Rio dos Sinos (UNISINOS), Av Unisinos 950, Sao Leopoldo, RS 93022-000, Brazil. TEL 55-51-5908131, FAX 55-51-5908132, http://www.unisinos.br.

500 620.1 GBR ISSN 1432-8917
TA404.2 CODEN: MRINFV
➤ **MATERIALS RESEARCH INNOVATIONS.** Abbreviated title: M R I. Text in English. 1996. q. adv. back issues avail.; reprint service avail. from PSC. **Document type:** *Journal, Academic/Scholarly.* **Description:** Publishes papers in all core areas of materials research: metals, polymers, ceramics, composites, electronic materials, and biomaterials.
Formerly (until 1997): Innovations in Materials Research (0218-7566)
Related titles: ◆ Online - full text ed.: Materials Research Innovations (Online). ISSN 1433-075X.
Indexed: A28, APA, ASCA, BrCerAb, C&ISA, C33, CA/WCA, CIA, CPEI, CerAb, ChemAb, CivEngAb, CorrAb, CurCont, E&CAJ, E11, EEA, EMA, ESPM, EngInd, EnvEAb, H15, INIS AtomInd, ISR, Inspec, M&TEA, M09, MBF, METADEX, MSCI, SCI, SCOPUS, SolStAb, T04, W07, WAA.
—BLDSC (5396.411250), CASDDS, IE, Infotrieve, Ingenta, INIST, Linda Hall. **CCC.**
Published by: Maney Publishing, Ste 1C, Joseph's Well, Hanover Walk, Leeds, W Yorks LS3 1AB, United Kingdom. TEL 44-113-2432800, FAX 44-113-3868178, maney@maney.co.uk. Ed. Rustum Roy. **Subscr. in N. America to:** Maney Publishing, 875 Massachusetts Ave, 7th Fl, Cambridge, MA 02139. TEL 866-297-5154, FAX 617-354-6875, maney@maneyusa.com.

500 GBR ISSN 1433-075X
TA404.2
MATERIALS RESEARCH INNOVATIONS (ONLINE). Text in English. 1996. 6/yr. USD 908 in United States to institutions; GBP 453 elsewhere to institutions (effective 2012). **Document type:** *Journal, Academic/Scholarly.* **Description:** Publishes papers in all core areas of materials research: metals, polymers, ceramics, composites, electronic materials, and biomaterials.
Media: Online - full text (from IngentaConnect). **Related titles:** ◆ Print ed.: Materials Research Innovations. ISSN 1432-8917.
—**CCC.**
Published by: Maney Publishing, Ste 1C, Joseph's Well, Hanover Walk, Leeds, W Yorks LS3 1AB, United Kingdom. TEL 44-113-2432800, FAX 44-113-3868178, maney@maney.co.uk, http://www.maney.co.uk. Ed. Rustum Roy.

500 USA ISSN 1935-2441
TA401
MATERIALS SCIENCE RESEARCH JOURNAL. Text in English. 2007. q. USD 330 to institutions; USD 495 combined subscription to institutions (print & online eds.) (effective 2012). **Document type:** *Journal, Academic/Scholarly.* **Description:** Presents articles on those areas of chemistry and physics that deal with the properties of materials.
Related titles: Online - full text ed.: 2007. USD 330 to institutions (effective 2012).
Published by: Nova Science Publishers, Inc., 400 Oser Ave, Ste 1600, Hauppauge, NY 11788. TEL 631-231-7269, FAX 631-231-8175, main@novapublishers.com.

▼ **MATH + SCIENCE CONNECTION: INTERMEDIATE EDITION;** building understanding and excitement for children. *see* MATHEMATICS

THE MATH - SCIENCE CONNECTOR. *see* EDUCATION—Teaching Methods And Curriculum

MATHEMATICAL CONCEPTS AND METHODS IN SCIENCE AND ENGINEERING. *see* MATHEMATICS

MATHEMATICAL METHODS IN THE APPLIED SCIENCES. *see* MATHEMATICS

MATHEMATICAL MODELLING OF NATURAL PHENOMENA. *see* MATHEMATICS

MATHEMATICS APPLIED IN SCIENCE AND TECHNOLOGY. *see* MATHEMATICS

MATRIX 3000; neues Denken. *see* SOCIAL SCIENCES: COMPREHENSIVE WORKS

508.074 DEU ISSN 0233-173X
QH149 CODEN: MAUREH
MAURITIANA (ALTENBURG). Text in English, German. 1958. a. price varies. back issues avail. **Document type:** *Journal, Academic/Scholarly.* **Description:** Publishes articles relating to the natural sciences in Mauritania.
Formerly (until 1986): Naturkundliches Museum "Mauritianum" Altenburg. Abhandlungen und Berichte (0065-6631)
Indexed: GeoRef, IBR, IBZ, RefZh, SpeleolAb, Z01.
—INIST, Linda Hall.
Published by: Naturkundliches Museum Mauritianum, Postfach 1644, Altenburg, 04590, Germany. direktion@mauritianum.de, http://www.mauritianum.de. Ed. Norbert Hoeser. Circ: 900.

500 MUS ISSN 1694-0016
QH1 CODEN: MAUBA
MAURITIUS INSTITUTE BULLETIN. Text in English. 1937. a.?. **Document type:** *Bulletin, Academic/Scholarly.*
Indexed: AbAn, PLESA.
Published by: (Mauritius Institute), Mauritius Museums Council, Ministry of Arts & Culture, 7th Flr, Renganaden Seeneevassen Bldg, Port Louis, Mauritius. TEL 230-211-0681, FAX 230-212-9366, moac@mail.gov.mu, http:?/www.gov.mu/portal/site/mac/.

500 DEU ISSN 0341-0218
Q3 CODEN: MPJADF
➤ **MAX-PLANCK-GESELLSCHAFT. JAHRBUCH.** Text in German. 1951. a. bk.rev. index. back issues avail. **Document type:** *Journal, Academic/Scholarly.*
Formerly (until 1975): Max-Planck-Gesellschaft zur Foerderung der Wissenschaften. Jahrbuch (0076-5635)
Indexed: DIP, IBR, IBZ.
—INIST, Linda Hall.
Published by: Max-Planck-Gesellschaft zur Foerderung der Wissenschaften e.V., Hofgartenstr 8, Munich, 80539, Germany. TEL 49-89-21080, presse@gv.mpg.de.

500 600 DEU ISSN 1616-4172
Q49
MAXPLANCKFORSCHUNG. Text in German. 1972. q. free (effective 2011). adv. charts; illus. 84 p./no.; **Document type:** *Journal, Academic/Scholarly.* **Description:** Contains news for the public about research at the Max-Planck Society.
Former titles (until 1999): M P G Spiegel (0341-7727); (until 1973): M P G Monatsspiegel (0341-7697)
Related titles: English Translation: MaxPlanckResearch.
Indexed: BIOSIS Prev, CEABA, DIP, GeoRef, IBR, IBZ, INIS AtomInd, MycolAb, SpeleolAb, TM.
Published by: Max-Planck-Institut fuer Gesellschaft zur Foerderung der Wissenschaften, Hofgartenstr 8, Munich, 80539, Germany. TEL 49-89-21080, FAX 49-89-21081111, presse@gv.mpg.de. Ed. Christina Beck. Adv. contact Stefanie Beinl TEL 49-89-55241240. Circ: 50,000 (controlled).

500 CAN ISSN 1718-0775
Q21
➤ **MCGILL SCIENCE UNDERGRADUATE RESEARCH JOURNAL.** Short title: M S U R J. Text in English. 2006 (Feb.). s-a. **Document type:** *Journal, Academic/Scholarly.*
Related titles: Online - full text ed.: free (effective 2011).
Indexed: A01, CA, T02, Z01.
Published by: McGill University, Faculty of Science, Burnside Hall, Rm 1B21, 805 Sherbrooke St. W, Montreal, PQ H3A 2K6, Canada. TEL 514-398-6979, FAX 514-398-6766, mcgillsruj@gmail.com, http://www.msurj.mcgill.ca. Ed. Arij Riahi.

505.8 USA ISSN 0076-2016
Q121
MCGRAW-HILL YEARBOOK OF SCIENCE AND TECHNOLOGY. Text in English. 1962. a. USD 199 (effective 2008). 400 p./no.; back issues avail. **Document type:** *Yearbook, Academic/Scholarly.* **Description:** Features more than 7,000 concise articles covering all areas of science and technology.
—INIST. **CCC.**
Published by: McGraw-Hill Companies, Inc., 1221 Ave of the Americas, 43rd fl, New York, NY 10020. TEL 212-512-2000, FAX 212-426-7087, customer.service@mcgraw-hill.com, http://www.mcgraw-hill.com.

500 USA
➤ **MCNAIR RESEARCH JOURNAL.** Text in English. 2004. irreg., latest 2004. **Document type:** *Journal, Academic/Scholarly.*
Published by: Western Michigan University, Ronald E. McNair Post-Baccalaureate Scholars Program, 204A Ellworth Hall, Kalamazoo, MI 49008. TEL 616-387-3391, FAX 616-387-3390.

509 NLD ISSN 1567-8393
➤ **MEDIEVAL AND EARLY MODERN SCIENCE.** Text in English. 2001. irreg., latest vol.8, 2007. **Document type:** *Monographic series, Academic/Scholarly.*
Indexed: IZBG.
Published by: Brill, PO Box 9000, Leiden, 2300 PA, Netherlands. TEL 31-71-5353500, FAX 31-71-5317532, cs@brill.nl. Eds. Christoph H Luthy, J M M H Thijssen.

500 800 700 CHN
MEI YU SHIDAI (XUESHU BAN)/BEAUTY & TIMES (ACADEMICS EDITION). Text in Chinese. m. CNY 10 newsstand/cover (effective 2006). **Document type:** *Magazine, Consumer.*
Formerly (until 2002): Mei Yu Shidai/Beauty & Times (1003-2592)
—East View.
Published by: Zhengzhou Daxue* Meixue Yanjiusuo, 75, Daxue Lu, Zhengzhou, 450052, China.

MEIJI DAIGAKU KAGAKU GIJUTSU KENKYUJO HOKOKU. SOGO KENKYU/MEIJI UNIVERSITY. INSTITUTE OF SCIENCE AND TECHNOLOGY. REPORT. SPECIAL PROJECT. *see* TECHNOLOGY: COMPREHENSIVE WORKS

MEIJI DAIGAKU KAGAKU GIJUTSU KENKYUJO KIYO/MEIJI UNIVERSITY. INSTITUTE OF SCIENCE AND TECHNOLOGY. MEMOIRS. *see* TECHNOLOGY: COMPREHENSIVE WORKS

MEIJI DAIGAKU KAGAKU GIJUTSU KENKYUJO NENPO/MEIJI UNIVERSITY. INSTITUTE OF SCIENCE AND TECHNOLOGY. ANNUAL REPORT. *see* TECHNOLOGY: COMPREHENSIVE WORKS

500 620 JPN ISSN 0916-4944
MEIJI DAIGAKU RIKO GAKUBU KENKYU HOKOKU/MEIJI UNIVERSITY. SCHOOL OF SCIENCE AND TECHNOLOGY. RESEARCH REPORTS. Text in English, Japanese. 1950. a. **Document type:** *Monographic series, Academic/Scholarly.*
Formerly (until 1990): Meiji Daigaku Kogakubu Kenkyu Hokoku (0465-6075)
Indexed: A28, APA, BrCerAb, C&ISA, CA/WCA, CIA, CerAb, CivEngAb, CorrAb, E&CAJ, E11, EEA, EMA, GeoRef, H15, Inspec, M&TEA, M09, MBF, METADEX, SolStAb, T04, WAA.
—BLDSC (7762.570500), Linda Hall.
Published by: Meiji Daigaku, Kagaku Gijutsu Kenkyujo/Meiji University, Institute of Science and Technology, 1-1-1 Higashi-Mita, Tama-ku, Kawasaki-shi, Kanagawa-ken 214-0033, Japan. TEL 81-44-9347613, FAX 81-44-9347917, gi_ken@mics.meiji.ac.jp. **Co-sponsor:** Meiji Daigaku, Riko Gakubu/Meiji University, School of Science and Technology.

500 ITA ISSN 1971-5439
I MERCOLEDI DELL'ACCADEMIA. Text in Italian. 1993. a. **Document type:** *Monographic series, Academic/Scholarly.*
Published by: Accademia delle Scienze di Torino, Via Maria Vittoria 3, Turin, 10123, Italy. TEL 39-011-5620047, FAX 39-011-532619, info@accademia.csi.it, http://www.accademiadellescienze.it.

500 NLD ISSN 0815-0796
Q124.6
METASCIENCE; an international review journal for the history, philosophy and social studies of science. Text in English. 1984. 3/yr. EUR 299, USD 309 combined subscription to institutions (print & online eds.) (effective 2012). adv. bk.rev. reprint service avail. from PSC. **Document type:** *Journal, Academic/Scholarly.* **Description:** Publishes reviews of books in history and philosophy of science, science and technology studies, and related fields.
Related titles: Microfilm ed.: (from PQC); Online - full text ed.: ISSN 1467-9981 (from IngentaConnect).
Indexed: A01, A03, A08, A22, A26, BibLing, CA, CCMJ, E01, MSN, MathR, P52, P56, PCI, PhilInd, SCOPUS, T02.
—BLDSC (5701.810000), IE, Infotrieve, Ingenta, Linda Hall. **CCC.**
Published by: (Australasian Association for the History, Philosophy and Social Studies of Science AUS), Springer Netherlands (Subsidiary of: Springer Science+Business Media), Van Godewijckstraat 30, Dordrecht, 3311 GX, Netherlands. TEL 31-78-6576050, FAX 31-78-6576474, http://www.springer.com. Ed. Steven French.

500 ESP ISSN 1133-3987
Q4
METODE. Text in Catalan. 1992. q. **Document type:** *Journal, Academic/Scholarly.* **Description:** Aims at giving maximum exposure to university level scientific investigation.
Indexed: GeoRef.
Published by: Universitat de Valencia, Vice - Rectorat d'Investigacio, Jardi Botanic, C/ Quart 80, Valencia, 46008, Spain. TEL 34-96-3156828, FAX 34-96-3864067. Circ: 3,500.

▼ **METROPOLITAN MUSEUM STUDIES IN ART, SCIENCE AND TECHNOLOGY.** *see* ART

500 RUS ISSN 2076-9563
▼ ➤ **MEZHDUNARODNYE NAUCHNYE ISSLEDOVANIYA/ INTERNATIONAL SCIENTIFIC RESEARCHES.** Text in Russian, English. 2009. q. RUR 390 (effective 2010). back issues avail. **Document type:** *Journal, Academic/Scholarly.*
Published by: Sergey Gorin, PO Box 562, Moscow, 119619, Russian Federation. TEL 7-916-0724828, intereconom@intereconom.com, http://www.intereconom.com. Ed., Pub. Sergey Gorin.

➤ **MICHIGAN ACADEMICIAN.** *see* HUMANITIES: COMPREHENSIVE WORKS

➤ **MICROLOGUS;** natura, scienza e societa medievali - nature, science and medieval societies. *see* HISTORY—History Of Europe

500.0 GBR ISSN 0956-1021
MIDDLE EAST SCIENCE POLICY SERIES. Text in English. 1984. irreg., latest vol.13, 1994. price varies. **Document type:** *Monographic series, Academic/Scholarly.* **Description:** Features academic studies covering agricultural policy, development, the environment, and the use of natural resources in the Middle East.
—BLDSC (5761.401420).
Published by: (Overseas Development Institute), Ithaca Press (Subsidiary of: Garnet Publishing), 8 Southern Ct, South St, Reading, Berks RG1 4QS, United Kingdom. TEL 44-118-9597847, FAX 44-118-9597356, http://www.ithacapress.co.uk.

S

500 USA
MIDWEST RESEARCH INSTITUTE. ANNUAL REPORT. Text in English. 1945. a. free. **Description:** Reports on research performed at MRI in a varied spectrum, including chemical and biological sciences, engineering, economics, social and management sciences, and solar energy.
Published by: Midwest Research Institute, 425 Volker Blvd, Kansas City, MO 64110. TEL 816-753-7600, FAX 816-753-8420, TELEX 910-771-2128. Ed. Karen Alexander. Circ: 13,000.

MIKES INTERNATIONAL; Hungarian periodical for art, literature and science. *see* ART

500 363.7 DNK ISSN 1603-9254
MILJOENYT.DK. Text in Danish; Text occasionally in English. 2000. irreg. back issues avail. **Document type:** *Newsletter, Consumer.*
Formerly (until 2004): Ny Viden fra Miljoestyrelsen (1603-8843)
Media: Online - full content.
Published by: Miljoeministeriet, Miljoestyrelsen/Ministry of the Environment. Danish Environmental Protection Agency, Strandgade 29, Copenhagen K, 1401, Denmark. TEL 45-72-544000, FAX 45-33-322228, mst@mst.dk, http://www.mst.dk. Eds. Ida Amtoft TEL 45-32-660177, Lars Hindkjaer.

MINAMI KYUUSHUU DAIGAKU KENKYUU HOUKOKU. A, SHIZEN KAGAKU HEN/MINAMIKYUSHU UNIVERSITY. BULLETIN. A, NATURAL SCIENCE. *see* GARDENING AND HORTICULTURE

500 300 JPN ISSN 0916-0752
DU1 CODEN: MTKEER
➤ **MINAMI TAIHEIYO KENKYU/SOUTH PACIFIC STUDY.** Text in English, Japanese. 1980. s-a. exchange basis. **Document type:** *Journal, Academic/Scholarly.* **Description:** Provides multi-disciplinary studies on the South Pacific region. Covers a comprehensive range of fields from agriculture to zoology.
Formerly (until 1987): Nankaiken Kiyo (0389-5351)
Indexed: Z01.
—BLDSC (8352.127000).
Published by: Kagoshima University, Research Center for the Pacific Islands, 1-21-24 Korimo-To, Kagoshima-shi, 890-8580, Japan. TEL 81-99-285-7394, FAX 81-99-285-6197, sonda@cpi.kagoshima-u.ac.jp, http://cpi.sci.kagoshima-u.ac.jp. Eds. Kimihiko Oki, Norio Tabira, Shigeto Tominaga, Tetsushi Hidaka, Yasuhiro Tajima. Circ: 700 (controlled).

➤ **MINDANAO JOURNAL.** *see* SOCIAL SCIENCES: COMPREHENSIVE WORKS

507.11 NLD ISSN 0026-4695
AS121 CODEN: MINEFY
➤ **MINERVA**; a review of science, learning and policy. Text in English. 1962. q. EUR 448, USD 477 combined subscription to institutions (print & online eds.) (effective 2012). adv. bk.rev. charts. index. reprint service avail. from PSC. **Document type:** *Journal, Academic/Scholarly.* **Description:** Devoted to the study of ideas, traditions, cultures and institutions in science, higher education and research.
Related titles: Online - full text ed.: ISSN 1573-1871 (from IngentaConnect).
Indexed: A01, A03, A08, A20, A22, A26, AEI, AmH&L, B29, BibLing, CA, CPE, CommAb, CurCont, DIP, DRIE, E01, E03, E07, ERI, ERIC, FR, HECAB, HistAb, I13, IBR, IBSS, IBZ, MEA&I, P06, P30, P34, P42, PAIS, PSA, RASB, S02, S03, SCOPUS, SOPODA, SSA, SSCI, SociolAb, T02, W07, WSI, Z02.
—BLDSC (5793.920000), IE, Infotrieve, Ingenta, INIST, Linda Hall. **CCC.**
Published by: Springer Netherlands (Subsidiary of: Springer Science+Business Media), Van Godewijckstraat 30, Dordrecht, 3311 GX, Netherlands. TEL 31-78-6576050, FAX 31-78-6576474, http://www.springer.com. Ed. Peter Weingart.

500 001 USA ISSN 1076-500X
Q180.4
THE MINI-ANNALS OF IMPROBABLE RESEARCH. Text in English. 1994. m. free (effective 2007). **Document type:** *Newsletter, Consumer.* **Description:** Short humorous pieces about science and scientists.
Media: E-mail. **Related titles:** ◆ Supplement to: The Annals of Improbable Research. ISSN 1079-5146.
Published by: Annals of Improbable Research, PO Box 380853, Cambridge, MA 02238. TEL 617-491-4437, FAX 617-661-0927, info@improbable.com. Ed. Marc Abrahams.

500 USA ISSN 0026-539X
Q11 CODEN: JMNAAC
➤ **MINNESOTA ACADEMY OF SCIENCE. JOURNAL.** Text in English. 1964. s-a. free to members (effective 2011). bk.rev. charts; illus.; stat. back issues avail.; reprints avail. **Document type:** *Journal, Academic/Scholarly.*
Formed by the merger of (1936-1964): Minnesota Academy of Science. Proceedings (0096-9397); Which was formerly (until 1936): Minnesota Academy of Science. Annual Meeting; (1957-1964): Minnesota Journal of Science (0544-3598)
Related titles: Microform ed.: (from PQC); Online - full text ed.
Indexed: A22, Agr, ChemAb, ESPM, GeoRef, MLA-IB, SASA, SWRA, SpeleolAb, WildRev, Z01.
—Ingenta, Linda Hall.
Published by: Minnesota Academy of Science, 8700 W 36th St, Ste 114W, PO Box 25, St. Louis Park, MN 55426. contact@mnmas.org, http://www.mnmas.org.

500 USA ISSN 0026-5675
CODEN: MINSB4
MINNESOTA SCIENCE. Text in English. 1943. 3/yr. free. index. **Description:** Presents results of university research projects related to agriculture, forestry, human ecology, natural resources and the environment.
Media: Duplicated (not offset).
Indexed: Agr, P06, WildRev.
—Linda Hall.
Published by: University of Minnesota, Agricultural Experiment Station, 405 Coffey Hall, St. Paul, MN 55108. TEL 612-625-7290. Ed. David L Hansen. Circ: 24,000 (controlled).

MINNESOTA STUDIES IN THE PHILOSOPHY OF SCIENCE. *see* PHILOSOPHY

500 EGY ISSN 2090-1569
MINUFIYA UNIVERSITY. SCIENTIFIC JOURNAL OF FACULTY OF SCIENCE. BIOLOGY/GAMI'AT AL-MUNUFIYYAT. KULLIYYAT AL-'ULUM. AL-MAGALLAT AL-'ILLMIYYAT. AL-BIYULUGIYA. Text in English. 1987. a. **Document type:** *Journal, Academic/Scholarly.*
Supersedes in part (in 2007): Minoufia University. Scientific Journal of Faculty of Science (1110-2195)
Published by: Minoufia University, Faculty of Science, Shebin El-Kom, Munoufia, Egypt. TEL 20-48-2235690, FAX 20-48-2235689, science@menofia.edu.eg, http://www.menofia.edu.eg/en/faculty_generalInfo.asp?id=8. Ed. Dr. Muhammad Fatthi Farag.

500 USA ISSN 0076-9436
Q11 CODEN: JMSSAN
MISSISSIPPI ACADEMY OF SCIENCE. JOURNAL. Text in English. 1939. q. **Document type:** *Journal, Academic/Scholarly.*
Related titles: Microform ed.: (from PQC); Online - full text ed.
Indexed: A26, A34, A35, A37, AgBio, Agr, BA, CABA, ChemAb, E08, E12, F08, F11, F12, G08, G11, GH, GeoRef, H16, I05, IndVet, MSN, N02, P30, P32, P33, P40, PGegResA, PHN&I, R07, R08, S06, S09, S12, S13, S16, SASA, SpeleolAb, VS, WildRev, Z01.
—BLDSC (4828.200000), CASDDS.
Published by: Mississippi Academy of Sciences, Inc., PO Box 55907, Jackson, MS 39296. TEL 601-366-2995, FAX 601-366-2998, msacademyofscience@comcast.net, http://www.msacad.org.

505 USA
MISSOURI ACADEMY OF SCIENCE. BULLETIN. Text in English. 1972. m. free to members (effective 2010). **Document type:** *Bulletin, Trade.*
Published by: Missouri Academy of Science, W C Morris 206A, University of Central Missouri, Warrensburg, MO 64093. TEL 660-543-8734, FAX 660-543-4355, macy@ucmo.edu, http://www.moacadsci.org.

505 USA ISSN 0148-0944
CODEN: OPMSD4
MISSOURI ACADEMY OF SCIENCE. OCCASIONAL PAPER. Text in English. 1974. irreg. **Document type:** *Proceedings, Trade.*
—Linda Hall.
Published by: Missouri Academy of Science, W C Morris 206A, University of Central Missouri, Warrensburg, MO 64093. TEL 660-543-8734, FAX 660-543-4355, http://www.moacadsci.org.

505 USA ISSN 0544-540X
Q11 CODEN: MISTBW
➤ **MISSOURI ACADEMY OF SCIENCE. TRANSACTIONS.** Text in English. 1967. a. free to members (effective 2010). adv. 2 cols./p.; back issues avail. **Document type:** *Journal, Academic/Scholarly.*
Formerly (until 1967): Missouri Academy of Science. Proceedings (0891-236X)
Related titles: Online - full text ed.
Indexed: A01, A26, A37, Agr, B25, BIOSIS Prev, CA, E08, F12, G08, GeoRef, I05, I11, MLA-IB, MycolAb, P37, P40, R11, S06, S09, S13, S16, S17, SASA, SpeleolAb, T02, W08, WildRev, Z01.
—CASDDS, Ingenta, Linda Hall.
Published by: Missouri Academy of Science, W C Morris 206A, University of Central Missouri, Warrensburg, MO 64093. TEL 660-543-8734, FAX 660-543-4355, macy@ucmo.edu, http://www.moacadsci.org.

500 CHE ISSN 1420-4606
QH5
➤ **MITTEILUNGEN DER NATURFORSCHENDEN GESELLSCHAFTEN BEIDER BASEL.** Text in English, French, German. 1995. a. **Document type:** *Proceedings, Academic/Scholarly.*
Formed by the merger of (1854-1995): Naturforschende Gesellschaft in Basel. Verhandlungen (0077-6122); (1902-1995): Naturforschende Gesellschaft Baselland. Taetigkeitsberichte (1420-6471)
Indexed: ASFA, B21, B25, BIOSIS Prev, ESPM, GeoRef, IBR, IBZ, MycolAb, RefZh, Z01.
—Linda Hall.
Published by: (Naturforschende Gesellschaft in Basel), Birkhaeuser Verlag AG (Subsidiary of: Springer Science+Business Media), Viaduktstr 42, Postfach 133, Basel, 4051, Switzerland. TEL 41-61-2050707, FAX 41-61-2050792, birkhauser@springer.de, http://www.birkhauser.ch.

500 JPN ISSN 0285-8576
Q4 CODEN: MDKSAL
MIYAZAKI DAIGAKU KYOIKUGAKUBU KIYO. SHIZEN KAGAKU/ MIYAZAKI UNIVERSITY. FACULTY OF EDUCATION. MEMOIRS. NATURAL SCIENCE. Text in Japanese; Summaries in English, Japanese. 1955. 2/yr. **Document type:** *Academic/Scholarly.*
Indexed: ChemAb, JPI.
Published by: Miyazaki Daigaku, Kyoikugakubu/Miyazaki University, Faculty of Education, 1-1 Gakuen-Kibanadai-Nishi, Miyazaki-shi, 880-0000, Japan. TEL 81-985-58-2811, FAX 81-985-58-2892. Ed. Fijio Kawano.

605 CAN ISSN 1913-1844
➤ **MODERN APPLIED SCIENCE.** Text in English. 2007. m. CAD 20 (effective 2009). software rev. abstr.; bibl. Index. back issues avail. **Document type:** *Journal, Academic/Scholarly.* **Description:** Encourages and publishes research in all fields of applied science.
Related titles: Online - full text ed.: ISSN 1913-1852. free (effective 2011).
Indexed: A01, A17, A26, A34, A35, A36, A37, A38, A39, AgBio, AgrForAb, BA, C25, C27, C29, C30, CABA, CPerI, D01, D03, D04, E12, E13, F08, F11, F12, FCA, G11, GH, H16, I05, IndVet, LT, N02, N03, N04, O01, P10, P32, P33, P37, P40, P48, P51, P52, P53, P54, P56, PHN&I, PN&I, PQC, R07, R08, R11, R12, R13, R14, RA&MP, RM&VM, RRTA, S12, S13, S14, S15, S16, S18, SoyAb, T02, TAR, VS, W10, W11, Z02.
Published by: Canadian Center of Science and Education, 4915 Bathurst St, Unit 209-309, Toronto, ON M2R 1X9, Canada. TEL 416-208-4027, FAX 416-208-4028, info@ccsenet.org. Ed. Susan Sun. Circ: 200 (paid and controlled). **Subscr. to:** JournalBuy.com, Rm. 666, 118 Chongqing S. Rd., Qingdao 266032, China. TEL 86-532-86069259, FAX 86-532-95105198 ext 81082, order@journalbuy.com, http://www.journalbuy.com/.

➤ **MOKHTAREIN VA MOBTAKERIN.** *see* TECHNOLOGY: COMPREHENSIVE WORKS

500 LTU ISSN 2029-2341
▼ ➤ **MOKSLAS - LIETUVOS ATEITIS/SCIENCE - FUTURE OF LITHUANIA.** Text in English, Lithuanian. 2009. bi-m. EUR 210 (effective 2010). bk.rev. bibl. **Document type:** *Journal, Academic/Scholarly.*
Related titles: Online - full text ed.: ISSN 2029-2252.
Indexed: A01, A26, E08, I05.
Published by: (Vilniaus Gedimino Technikos Universitetas, Publishing House "Technika"/Vilnius Gediminas Technical University), Vilniaus Gedimino Technikos Universitetas, Leidykla Technika, Sauletekio aleja 11, Vilnius, 10223, Lithuania. TEL 370-5-2745038, FAX 370-5-2370602, books@vgtu.lt, http://leidykla.vgtu.lt. Ed. Raimundas Kirvatis.

500 600 LTU ISSN 2029-2430
➤ **MOKSLO IR TECHNIKOS RAIDA/EVOLUTION OF SCIENCE AND TECHNOLOGY.** Text in English, Lithuanian, German, Russian. 1996. s-a. EUR 60 (effective 2010). bk.rev. bibl. **Document type:** *Journal, Academic/Scholarly.* **Description:** Publishes original papers and review articles on all aspects of the history of science and technology.
Former titles (until 2009): Mokslo ir Technikos Raida Lietuvoje (2029-1566); (until 2001): Technikos Mokslu Raida Lietuvoje (1822-9956)
Related titles: Online - full text ed.: ISSN 2029-2449.
Indexed: A01, A26, E08, I05, S06.
Published by: (Vilniaus Gedimino Technikos Universitetas, Publishing House "Technika"/Vilnius Gediminas Technical University), Vilniaus Gedimino Technikos Universitetas, Leidykla Technika, Sauletekio aleja 11, Vilnius, 10223, Lithuania. TEL 370-5-2745038, FAX 370-5-2370602, books@vgtu.lt, http://leidykla.vgtu.lt. Ed. Romualdas Ginevicius.

500 ESP
MOLL MONOGRAFIES CIENTIFIQUES. Text in Catalan. irreg., latest vol.4. price varies. **Document type:** *Monographic series, Academic/Scholarly.*
Published by: Editorial Moll, Can Valero, 25, Poligon Can Valero, Palma de Mallorca, 07011, Spain. TEL 34-971-724176, FAX 34-971-726252, info@editorialmoll.es, http://www.editorialmoll.es/.

500 RUS ISSN 2072-0297
➤ **MOLODOY UCHENYI**; ezhemesyachnyi nauchnyi zhurnal. Text in Russian. 2008. m. RUR 3,780 domestic; USD 200 foreign (effective 2010). Index. back issues avail. **Document type:** *Journal, Academic/Scholarly.* **Description:** Aims to provide graduate students and doctoral candidates, job seekers, young professionals and scholars with an opportunity to publish the results of their research.
Related titles: Online - full text ed.: ISSN 2077-8295.
Indexed: RefZh.
Published by: Izdatel'skii Dom Molodoy Uchenyi, a/ya 417, Chita, Russian Federation. TEL 7-3022-398001, FAX 7-3022-396972. Ed. Olesya Shul'ga. Pub. Il'dar Ahmetov. Circ: 200 (paid); 100 (controlled).

500 COL ISSN 1692-5491
MOMENTOS DE CIENCIAS. Text in Spanish. 2001. s-a. **Document type:** *Journal, Academic/Scholarly.*
Published by: Universidad de la Amazonia, Calle 17 - Diagonal 17 con Carrera 3F, Barrio Porvenir, Florencia, Caqueta, Colombia. TEL 57-8-4358786, FAX 57-8-4352434, http://uniamazonia.edu.co/v8/. Ed. Cesar Estrada. Circ: 500.

500 ETH ISSN 2073-073X
MOMONA ETHIOPIAN JOURNAL OF SCIENCE. Text in English. 2008. s-a. **Document type:** *Journal, Academic/Scholarly.*
Related titles: Online - full text ed.: free (effective 2011).
Indexed: A35, AgrForAb, C25, C30, CABA, E12, F08, FCA, GH, H16, N02, P32, P33, R07, R08, S13, T05, W10, W11.
Published by: Mekelle University, College of Natural and Computational Sciences, PO Box 3037, Mekelle, Ethiopia. TEL 251-03-44407500, FAX 251-03-4409304. Ed. Tadesse Dejenie.

500 300 001.3 330 JPN ISSN 1346-048X
MOMOYAMA GAKUIN DAIGAKU SOGO KENKYUJO KIYO/ST. ANDREW'S UNIVERSITY.RESEARCH INSTITUTE. BULLETIN. Text in Japanese. 1975. 3/yr. **Document type:** *Bulletin, Academic/Scholarly.*
Former titles (until 1997): Sogo Kenkyujo Kiyo (0918-7758); (until 1972): Momoyama Gakuin Daigaku Sogo Kenkyujoho (0385-0811); Which was formed by the 1975 merger of: Kokusai Kankei Kenkyu; Momoyama Gakuin Daigaku Sangyo Boeki Kenkyujoho
Indexed: RILM.
Published by: Momoyama Gakuin Daigaku, Sogo Kenkyujo/St. Andrew's University, Research Institute, 1-1, Manabino, Izumi-shi, Osaka 594-1198, Japan. http://www.andrew.ac.jp/soken/soken1.html.

500 FRA ISSN 0221-0436
JV1802
MONDES ET CULTURES. Text in French. 1922. q. EUR 55 (effective 2008). adv. bk.rev. bibl.; charts. index. **Document type:** *Journal, Academic/Scholarly.*
Former titles (until 1977): Academie des Sciences d'Outre-Mer. Comptes Rendus Trimestriels (0221-0428); (until 1970): Academie des Sciences d'Outre-Mer. Comptes Rendus Mensuels (1257-645X); (until 1957): Academie des Sciences Coloniales. Comptes Rendus Trimestriels (1257-6441); (until 1946): Academie des Sciences Coloniales. Comptes Rendus des Seances (1257-6433)
Indexed: ASD, AmH&L, BAS, BibLing, CA, CCA, FR, HistAb, P30, RASB, T02.
Published by: Academie des Sciences d'Outre-Mer Paris, 15 rue la Perouse, Paris, 75116, France. TEL 33-1-47208793, FAX 33-1-47208972. Ed. Gilbert Mangin. Adv. contact Mme Sainctelette.

500 600 POL ISSN 0077-054X
MONOGRAFIE Z DZIEJOW NAUKI I TECHNIKI. Text in Polish. 1957. irreg., latest vol.151, 1995. price varies. adv. **Document type:** *Monographic series.*
Indexed: AgrLib, FR, MathR, RASB.
Published by: Polska Akademia Nauk, Instytut Historii Nauki, Palac Staszica, ul Nowy Swiat 72, pok 9, Warsaw, 00330, Poland. TEL 48-22-8268754, FAX 48-22-8266137. Ed. Stefan Zamecki. Adv. contact Jerzy Dobrzycki.

MONOGRAPHS-IN-DEBATE. *see* PHILOSOPHY

500 USA
MOSAIC MAGAZINE; science articles archive. Text in English. irreg.
Media: Online - full text. **Related titles:** E-mail ed.; Fax ed.
Address: PO Box 153, Garrett Park, MD 20896. FAX 301-942-0533. Ed. Adam Mickelson.

500 600 PER ISSN 1817-8391
MOSAICO CIENTIFICO. Text in Spanish. 2005. s-a. free (effective 2011). **Document type:** *Journal, Academic/Scholarly.*
Media: Online - full text.
Published by: Consejo Nacional de Ciencia, Tecnologia e Innovacion Tecnologica, Calle el Comercio 197, San Borja, Lima, 100, Peru. TEL 51-1-2251150, FAX 51-1-2240920. Ed. Naldo Balarezo Gerstein.

500 RUS ISSN 2078-6484
➤ **MOSKOVSKII GOSUDARSTVENNYI OTKRYTYI UNIVERSITET. VESTNIK.** Variant title: Vestnik M G O U. Moskva. Text in Russian. 2001. q. **Document type:** *Journal, Academic/Scholarly.*
Published by: Moskovskii Gosudarstvennyi Otkrytyi Universitet/Moscow State Open University, ul Pavla Korchagina 22, korpus 2, Moscow, 107996, Russian Federation. TEL 7-495-6836877, FAX 7-495-6836877, anna4k@mail.ru. Ed. E O Tsaturyan.

500 CHN ISSN 1008-8717
MUDANJIANG DAXUE XUEBAO/MUDANJIANG UNIVERSITY. JOURNAL. Text in Chinese. 1992. m. CNY 10 newsstand/cover (effective 2007). **Document type:** *Journal, Academic/Scholarly.*
Related titles: Online - full text ed.
Published by: Mudanjiang Daxue, 60, Xideming Jie, Mudanjiang, 157011, China. TEL 86-453-6592170.

500 CHN
MUDANJING SHIFAN XUEYUAN XUEBAO (ZIRAN KEXUE BAN)/ MUDANJING TEACHERS COLLEGE. JOURNAL (NATURAL SCIENCES EDITION). Text in Chinese. 1975. q. CNY 5.60 newsstand/cover (effective 2007). **Document type:** *Journal, Academic/Scholarly.*
Formerly: Mudanjiang Shi-Yuan Xuebao (Ziran Kexue Ban) (1003-6180)
Related titles: Online - full text ed.
Published by: Mudanjing Shifan Xueyuan/Mudanjing Teachers College, 19, Wenhua Jie, Mudanjiang, 157012, China. TEL 86-453-6511106.

MUENCHENER SCHRIFTEN ZUR DESIGN SCIENCE. *see* SOCIAL SCIENCES: COMPREHENSIVE WORKS

500 VEN ISSN 1317-2255
AS90.A1
➤ **MULTICIENCIAS.** Text in English, Spanish. 2000. 3/yr. VEB 45 domestic; USD 20 in Latin America; USD 30 in US & Canada; USD 40 elsewhere (effective 2008). abstr.; bibl.; illus.; maps. back issues avail.; reprints avail. **Document type:** *Journal, Academic/Scholarly.* **Description:** Publishes original papers on many scientific subjects.
Indexed: A32, ASFA, C01, ESPM.
Published by: Universidad del Zulia, Nucleo Luz Punto Fijo, Punto Fijo, Edo Falcon, Venezuela. TEL 58-269-2472158, FAX 58-269-2457587. Ed., R&P Blanquita Concepcion Garcia Garcia.

➤ **MULTIPHASE SCIENCE AND TECHNOLOGY.** *see* ENGINEERING

500 600 DEU ISSN 1612-9393
MUNDO. Text in German. 1985. s-a. adv. bibl.; illus. back issues avail. **Document type:** *Journal, Academic/Scholarly.* **Description:** News and essays concerning scientific and technological research.
Formerly (until 2003): Uni Report (Dortmund) (0179-7182)
Published by: Technische Universitaet Dortmund, Referat Hochschulkommunikation, Baroper Str 285, Dortmund, 44221, Germany. TEL 49-231-7555449, FAX 49-231-7554819, angelika.willers@tu-dortmund.de, http://www.tu-dortmund.de/uni/Medien/index.html. Ed. Angelika Willers.

508 ESP ISSN 0214-7688
QH7
MUNIBE CIENCIAS NATURALES. Text mainly in Spanish; Text occasionally in English, French. 1949. a. free to members. Supplement avail. **Document type:** *Bulletin, Academic/Scholarly.*
Supersedes in part (in 1984): Munibe (0027-3414)
Indexed: AICP, ChemAb, FR, GeoRef, IECT, SpeleolAb, Z01.
—BLDSC (5983.915010), INIST.
Published by: Sociedad de Ciencias Aranzadi/Zientzi Elkartea, Calle del Alto de Zorroaga 11, Donostia, San Sebastian 20014, Spain. TEL 34-943-466142, FAX 34-943-455811, idazkatitza@aranzadi-zientziak.org, http://www.aranzadi-zientziak.org. Circ: 2,500.

500 RUS ISSN 1560-9278
➤ **MURMANSKII GOSUDARSTVENNYI TEKHNICHESKII UNIVERSITET. VESTNIK.** Abbreviated title: Vestnik M G T U. Text in Russian. 1998. q. RUR 814 for 6 mos. (effective 2011). **Document type:** *Journal, Academic/Scholarly.*
Related titles: Online - full text ed.: ISSN 1997-4736. free (effective 2011).
Indexed: RefZh, Z01.
Published by: Murmanskii Gosudarstvennyi Tekhnicheskii Universitet/ Murmansk State Technical University, Sportivnaya 13, Murmansk, 183010, Russian Federation. TEL 7-152-236250, FAX 7-152-232492, redvst@mstu.edu.ru. Ed. A Namgaladze.

508 HUN ISSN 0521-4726
QH7 CODEN: AHMHAU
MUSEI NATIONALIS HUNGARICI. ANNALES HISTORICO-NATURALES/MAGYAR TERMESZETTUDOMANYI MUZEUM. EVKONYVE. Key Title: Annales Historico-Naturales Musei Nationalis Hungarici. Text in English, German. 1877. a. USD 48 (effective 2001). adv. charts; illus. back issues avail. **Document type:** *Journal, Academic/Scholarly.* **Description:** Contains papers written by museum staff members or based on materials deposited there. Covers mineralogy, paleontology, botany, entomology, zoology, anthropology and museology.
Formerly (until 1903): Termeszetrajzi Fuzetek
Indexed: B23, B25, BIOSIS Prev, C25, CABA, E12, F08, F12, G11, GeoRef, MycolAb, P32, P33, R07, R08, S13, S16, SpeleolAb, W10, Z01.
—CASDDS, Ingenta, INIST.
Published by: Magyar Termeszettudomanyi Muzeum, Baross utca 13, Budapest, 1088, Hungary. TEL 36-1-2677100, FAX 36-1-3171669. Ed. O Merkl. R&P, Adv. contact I Matskasi TEL 36-1-2677100. Circ: 600.

500 ARG ISSN 1514-5158
QH113 CODEN: RMACB8
MUSEO ARGENTINO DE CIENCIAS NATURALES. REVISTA. NUEVA SERIE. Text in Spanish. 1864; N.S. 1999. s-a. USD 30 to individuals; USD 50 to institutions (effective 2010). **Document type:** *Journal, Academic/Scholarly.*
Formerly (until 1999): Museo Argentino de Ciencias Naturales "Bernardino Rivadavia." Instituto Nacional de Investigacion de las Ciencias Naturales. Revista. Paleontologia (0524-9511); Which superseded in part (in 1964): Museo Argentino de Ciencias Naturales "Bernardino Rivadavia". Anales (0365-4206); Which was formerly (until 1931): Museo Nacional de Historia Natural de Buenos Aires. Anales (0326-9310); (until 1911): Museo Nacional de Buenos Aires. Anales (0326-534X); (until 1883): Museo Publico de Buenos Aires (0326-9302)
Indexed: ASFA, B21, B25, BIOSIS Prev, C01, ESPM, GeoRef, MycolAb, SCOPUS, SpeleolAb, Z01.
—INIST, Linda Hall.
Published by: Museo Argentino de Ciencias Naturales Bernardino Rivadavia, Instituto Nacional de Investigacion de las Ciencias Naturales, Avda. Angel Gallardo 470, Casilla de Correo 220-Sucursal 5, Buenos Aires, Argentina. TEL 54-11-49820306, FAX 54-11-49824494, macn@musbr.org.secyt.gov.ar. Circ: 1,000.

508 ITA ISSN 0393-8700
MUSEO CIVICO DI SCIENZE NATURALI "E.CAFFI". RIVISTA. Text in Italian. 1980. irreg. **Document type:** *Monographic series, Academic/Scholarly.*
Indexed: Z01.
Published by: Museo Civico di Scienze Naturali "E.Caffi", Piazza Cittadella 10, Bergamo, 24129, Italy. info@museoscienze.comune.bergamo.it, http://www.museoscienze.comune.bergamo.it.

500 ITA ISSN 1123-4806
MUSEO CIVICO DI STORIA NATURALE DI TRIESTE. CATALOGHI. Text in Italian. 1995. a. **Document type:** *Catalog, Consumer.*
Indexed: Z01.
Published by: Museo Civico di Storia Naturale di Trieste, Piazza Attilio Hortis 4, Trieste, 34123, Italy. TEL 39-040-301821, FAX 39-040-302563.

500.9 ITA ISSN 0392-0070
GN1
MUSEO CIVICO DI STORIA NATURALE DI VERONA. MEMORIE. SERIE 2, SEZIONE C: SCIENZE DELL'UOMO. Text in Multiple languages. 1976. irreg., latest vol.4, 1994. price varies. **Document type:** *Monographic series, Academic/Scholarly.*
Formerly: Museo Civico di Storia Naturale di Verona. Memorie. Serie 2, Part 3: Preistorica
Indexed: SpeleolAb.
—Linda Hall.
Published by: Museo Civico di Storia Naturale di Verona, Lungadige Porta Vittoria 9, Verona, VR 37129, Italy. TEL 39-045-8079400, FAX 39-045-8035639, mcsnat@comune.verona.it, http://www.museostorianaturaleverona.it.

500.9 ITA ISSN 0365-4389
QH7 CODEN: AMGDAN
MUSEO CIVICO DI STORIA NATURALE "GIACOMO DORIA", GENOA. ANNALI. Text in English, French, German, Italian, Spanish. 1870. biennial. per issue exchange basis only. **Document type:** *Journal, Academic/Scholarly.*
Related titles: ◆ Supplement(s): Doriana. ISSN 0417-9927.
Indexed: A34, ASFA, B21, B23, B25, BIOSIS Prev, CABA, E12, EntAb, F08, F11, GeoRef, H17, IBR, IBZ, MycolAb, P32, P33, P40, R07, R08, SpeleolAb, Z01.
—BLDSC (1008.400000), INIST.
Published by: Museo Civico di Storia Naturale "Giacomo Doria", Via Brigata Liguria 9, Genoa, 16121, Italy. http://www.museodoria.it.

500.9 ESP ISSN 0214-915X
QH7
➤ **MUSEO DE CIENCIAS NATURALES DE ALAVA. ESTUDIOS.** Text in Multiple languages. 1986. a., latest vol.16, 2001. abstr.; bibl.; illus.; maps. back issues avail.; reprints avail. **Document type:** *Journal, Academic/Scholarly.* **Description:** Contains original papers covering diverse aspects of life sciences and geosciences, including systematics, ecology, regional studies, and paleontology.
Formerly (until 1989): Instituto Alaves de la Naturaleza. Estudios (0214-8641)
Indexed: GeoRef, IECT, SpeleolAb, Z01.
Published by: Museo de Ciencias Naturales de Alava, Siervas de Jesus 24, Vitoria-Gasteiz, 01001, Spain. TEL 34-945-181924, FAX 34-945-181932. Circ: 1,300 (paid and controlled).

508 CHL ISSN 0716-0178
QH119 CODEN: AMHVEI
➤ **MUSEO DE HISTORIA NATURAL DE VALPARAISO. ANALES.** Text in Spanish. 1968. a. free. **Document type:** *Academic/Scholarly.*
Indexed: ASFA, B21, C01, ESPM, VITIS, WildRev, Z01.
—INIST.
Published by: Museo de Historia Natural de Valparaiso, Casilla 3208 Correo 3, Condell, 1546, Valparaiso, Chile. TEL 56-32-257441, FAX 56-32-220846. Ed. Sergio Zunino Tapia.

508 ITA ISSN 0393-3377
MUSEO DI STORIA NATURALE DI LIVORNO. QUADERNI. Text in Multiple languages. 1980. a. **Document type:** *Journal, Academic/Scholarly.*
Related titles: Supplement(s): Museo di Storia Naturale di Livorno. Quaderni. Supplemento. ISSN 1721-5803. 1980; Museo di Storia Naturale di Livorno. Quaderni. Serie Atti. ISSN 1126-7801. 1998.
Indexed: GeoRef, Z01.
Published by: Museo di Storia Naturale di Livorno, Via Roma 234, Rome, 57127, Italy.

508 ITA ISSN 1121-9548
MUSEO FRIULANO DI STORIA NATURALE. PUBBLICAZIONE. Text in Multiple languages. 1963. irreg. **Document type:** *Journal, Academic/Scholarly.*
Indexed: GeoRef, Z01.
Published by: Comune di Udine, Museo Friulano di Storia Naturale, Via Lionello 1, Udine, 33100, Italy. TEL 39-0432-584711, FAX 39-0432-584721, mfsn@comune.udine.it, http://www.comune.udine.it.

500.9 ARG ISSN 0375-1155
QH7
MUSEO MUNICIPAL DE HISTORIA NATURAL DE SAN RAFAEL. REVISTA. Text in Spanish. 1956. irreg. per issue exchange basis. bk.rev. charts; illus. index. **Document type:** *Academic/Scholarly.*
Former titles: Museo de Historia Natural de San Rafael. Revista; Museo de Historia Natural de San Rafael. Revista Cientifica de Investigaciones (0027-3902)
Indexed: AICP.
Published by: Museo Municipal de Historia Natural de San Rafael, Parque Mariano Moreno, San Rafael, Mendoza 5600, Argentina. FAX 54-0627-21244. Ed. Humberto A Lagiglia. Circ: 1,500.

508 CHL ISSN 0027-3910
QH7
MUSEO NACIONAL DE HISTORIA NATURAL. BOLETIN. Text in Spanish. 1908. irreg., latest vol.45, 1995. USD 20 (effective 1997). adv. **Document type:** *Bulletin.*
Indexed: ASFA, B21, B25, BIOSIS Prev, C01, ESPM, GeoRef, MycolAb, SpeleolAb, Z01.
Published by: Museo Nacional de Historia Natural, Casilla 787, Santiago, Chile. TEL 56-2-6814095, FAX 56-2-6817182. Ed. Daniel Frassinetti C. Adv. contact Luis Hidalgo.

508 CHL ISSN 0376-2041
MUSEO NACIONAL DE HISTORIA NATURAL. NOTICIARIO MENSUAL. Text in Spanish. 1956. m. USD 7 (effective 1998). adv. **Document type:** *Newsletter.*
Indexed: AICP, C01, GeoRef, SpeleolAb, Z01.
Published by: Museo Nacional de Historia Natural, Casilla 787, Santiago, Chile. TEL 56-2-6814095, FAX 56-2-6817182. Ed. Herman Nunez. Adv. contact Luis Hidalgo. Circ: 800.

508 ITA ISSN 1121-7553
CODEN: CMRNEW
MUSEO REGIONALE DI SCIENZE NATURALI TORINO. CATALOGHI. Text in Multiple languages. 1980. irreg. **Document type:** *Catalog, Academic/Scholarly.*
Indexed: GeoRef, Z01.
Published by: Museo Regionale di Scienze Naturali Torino, Redazione, Via Giovanni Giolitti, 36, Turin, TO 10123, Italy. TEL 39-011-4323063, FAX 39-011-4323331, redazione.mrsn@regione.piemonte.it, http://www.regione.piemonte.it/museodiscienzenaturali/museodiscienzenaturali.htm.

580 ITA ISSN 1590-6388
MUSEO REGIONALE DI SCIENZE NATURALI TORINO. GUIDE. Text in Italian. 2000. irreg. **Document type:** *Consumer.*
Published by: Museo Regionale di Scienze Naturali Torino, Redazione, Via Giovanni Giolitti, 36, Turin, TO 10123, Italy. TEL 39-011-4323063, FAX 39-011-4323331, redazione.mrsn@regione.piemonte.it, http://www.regione.piemonte.it/museodiscienzenaturali/museodiscienzenaturali.htm.

508 ITA ISSN 1121-7545
CODEN: MMRNE6
MUSEO REGIONALE DI SCIENZE NATURALI TORINO. MONOGRAFIE. Text in Multiple languages. 1983. irreg. **Document type:** *Monographic series, Academic/Scholarly.*
Indexed: GeoRef, Z01.
Published by: Museo Regionale di Scienze Naturali Torino, Redazione, Via Giovanni Giolitti, 36, Turin, TO 10123, Italy. TEL 39-011-4323063, FAX 39-011-4323331, redazione.mrsn@regione.piemonte.it, http://www.regione.piemonte.it/museodiscienzenaturali/museodiscienzenaturali.htm.

MUSEOSCIENZA. *see* MUSEUMS AND ART GALLERIES

508 PRT ISSN 0874-4416
MUSEU BOCAGE. PUBLICACOES AVULSAS. Text in Portuguese. 1990. irreg. **Document type:** *Monographic series, Academic/Scholarly.*
Indexed: Z01.
Published by: Universidade de Lisboa, Museu Nacional de Historia Natural (Museu Bocage), Rua da Escola Politecnica 58, Lisboa, 1250-102, Portugal. TEL 351-21-3921800, FAX 351-21-3970882, jb@fc.ul.pt, http://www.mnhn.pt.

500 600 BRA ISSN 0104-6969
Q105.B6
MUSEU DE CIENCIAS E TECNOLOGIA. DIVULGACOES. Text in Portuguese. 1994. irreg. **Document type:** *Monographic series, Academic/Scholarly.*
Indexed: Z01.
Published by: Pontificia Universidade Catolica do Rio Grande do Sul, Museu de Ciencias e Tecnologia, Av Ipiranga 6681, Predio 40, Porto Alegre, RS 90619-900, Brazil. TEL 55-51-33203597, mct@pucrs.br, http://www.mct.pucrs.br.

500 BRA ISSN 0102-4272
MUSEU DE HISTORIA NATURAL. ARQUIVOS. Text in Portuguese. 1974. irreg. **Document type:** *Monographic series, Academic/Scholarly.*
Published by: Universidade Federal de Minas Gerais, Av Antonio Carlos 6627, Belo Horizonte, MG 31270, Brazil. TEL 55-31-34994184, FAX 55-31-34994188, http://www.ufmg.br.

500.1 BRA ISSN 0365-4508
MUSEU NACIONAL. ARQUIVOS. Text in Portuguese, English. 1876. q. **Document type:** *Journal, Academic/Scholarly.*
Indexed: A34, AgrForAb, B23, B25, BA, BIOSIS Prev, C01, CABA, E12, F08, F12, G11, GH, GeoRef, H16, I11, LT, MaizeAb, MycolAb, N02, N03, P32, P33, P40, PGegResA, R07, R08, R12, RA&MP, RRTA, S13, S16, SpeleolAb, T05, TAR, VS, Z01.
Published by: Universidade Federal do Rio de Janeiro, Museu Nacional, Quinta da Boa Vista, Sao Cristovao, Rio de Janeiro, RJ 20940-040, Brazil. TEL 55-21-25688262, FAX 55-21-25681352, museu@mn.ufrj.br, http://www.acd.ufjr.br/~museuhp/homep.htm.

500.9 BRA ISSN 0100-6304
Q33 CODEN: PMNRAR
MUSEU NACIONAL. PUBLICACOES AVULSAS. Text in Multiple languages. 1945. irreg., latest vol.96, 2002. **Description:** These "Sundry Papers" of the National Museum of Rio de Janeiro cover in-depth a variety of scientific topics.
Indexed: B25, BIOSIS Prev, C01, GeoRef, MycolAb, SpeleolAb, Z01.
Published by: Universidade Federal do Rio de Janeiro, Museu Nacional, Quinta da Boa Vista, Sao Cristovao, Rio de Janeiro, RJ 20940-040, Brazil. TEL 55-21-25688262, FAX 55-21-25681352, museu@mn.ufrj.br, http://www.acd.ufjr.br/~museuhp/homep.htm.

500 069 BRA ISSN 0557-0689
AM101
MUSEU NACIONAL. RELATORIO ANUAL. Text in Portuguese. 1874. 3/w.

S

Published by: Universidade Federal do Rio de Janeiro, Museu Nacional, Quinta da Boa Vista, Sao Cristovao, Rio de Janeiro, RJ 20940-040, Brazil. TEL 55-21-25688262, FAX 55-21-25681352, museu@mn.ufrj.br, http://www.acd.ufjr.br/~museuhp/homep.htm.

508 BRA
MUSEU NACIONAL. SERIE LIVROS. Text in Portuguese. irreg.
Document type: *Monographic series, Academic/Scholarly.*
Indexed: SpeleolAb.
Published by: (Sociedade Brasileira de Mastozoologia), Universidade Federal do Rio de Janeiro, Museu Nacional, Quinta da Boa Vista, Sao Cristovao, Rio de Janeiro, RJ 20940-040, Brazil. museu@mn.ufrj.br, http://www.acd.ufjr.br/~museuhp/homep.htm.

500.9 FRA ISSN 1281-7139
➤ **MUSEUM NATIONAL D'HISTOIRE NATURELLE. ARCHIVES - NOUVELLE SERIE.** (7/02 Title history updated on the basis of detailed information from publisher.) Text in French. 1802-1970; N.S. 1997. irreg. (2-3/yr). price varies. adv. back issues avail. **Document type:** *Monographic series, Academic/Scholarly.* **Description:** Publishes scientific monographs on the scientists, historical buildings and development of science at the Museum National d'Histoire Naturelle and more generally in France.
Superseded (1926-1970): Museum National d'Histoire Naturelle. Archives (0078-9739); (1865-1914): Museum d'Histoire Naturelle. Nouvelles Archives (0766-7248); (1839-1861): Museum d'Histoire Naturelle. Archives (1256-2629); (1832-1835): Museum d'Histoire Naturelle. Nouvelles Archives ou Recueil de Memoires (1256-2610); (1815-1832): Museum d'Histoire Naturelle. Memoires (1256-2602); (1802-1827): Museum d'Histoire Naturelle. Annales (1256-2599)
Indexed: GeoRef, SpeleolAb.
—Linda Hall.
Published by: Museum National d'Histoire Naturelle, 57 Rue Cuvier, CP 39, Paris, 05 75231, France. TEL 33-1-40793777. Ed. Jean-Marc Drouin. Circ: 1,000.

508.44361 FRA ISSN 1243-4442
CODEN: MMNNEK
➤ **MUSEUM NATIONAL D'HISTOIRE NATURELLE. MEMOIRES.** Text in French, English; Summaries in English, French. 1936; N.S. 1950. irreg. (3-5/yr), latest vol.187. price varies. adv. back issues avail. **Document type:** *Monographic series, Academic/Scholarly.* **Description:** Covers zoology and animal taxonomy, biology and ecology, including entomology, ornithology and botany.
Formed by the 1993 merger of: Museum National d'Histoire Naturelle, Paris. Memoires. Nouvelle Serie. Serie A, Zoologie (0078-9747); Museum National d'Histoire Naturelle, Paris. Memoires. Nouvelle Serie. Serie B, Botanique (0078-9755); Museum National d'Histoire Naturelle, Paris. Memoires. Nouvelle Serie. Serie C, Sciences de la Terre (0246-1196); Museum National d'Histoire Naturelle, Paris. Memoires. Nouvelle Serie. Serie D, Sciences Physico-Chimiques (0078-9771); Which superseded (in 1950): Museum National d'Histoire Naturelle, Paris. Memoires (0246-0254)
Indexed: ASFA, B21, ESPM, FR, GeoRef, SpeleolAb.
—BLDSC (5558.950000), Ingenta, INIST, Linda Hall. **CCC.**
Published by: Museum National d'Histoire Naturelle, 57 Rue Cuvier, CP 39, Paris, 05 75231, France. TEL 33-1-40793777. Ed. Christian Erard. Circ: 450.

508 FRA ISSN 1158-422X
MUSEUM NATIONAL D'HISTOIRE NATURELLE. PATRIMOINES NATURELS. Text in French. 1991. irreg. (2-3/yr), latest vol.46, 2001. price varies. bibl. back issues avail. **Document type:** *Academic/Scholarly.* **Description:** Publishes documents and maps on faunistics and floristics of France and its overseas dependencies, such as Red Lists and documents on biodiversity management policies.
—INIST.
Published by: Museum National d'Histoire Naturelle, 57 Rue Cuvier, CP 39, Paris, 05 75231, France. TEL 33-1-40793777. Ed. Jacques Trouvilliez.

500 AUS ISSN 1833-0290
MUSEUM VICTORIA SCIENCE REPORTS. Text in English. 2002. irreg.
Indexed: A01, Z01.
Published by: Museum Victoria, GPO Box 666, Melbourne, VIC 3001, Australia. TEL 61-3-83417574, FAX 61-3-83417573, publications@museum.vic.gov.au, http://www.museum.vic.gov.au.

MUSEUMSNYTT. *see* MUSEUMS AND ART GALLERIES

500 JOR ISSN 1021-6812
Q80.J67
➤ **MU'TAH LIL-BUHUTH WAL-DIRASAT. AL-SILSILAH B: AL-'ULUM AL-TABI'IYYAH WAL-TATBIQIYYAH/SERIES B: NATURAL AND APPLIED SCIENCES.** Spine title: Mu'tah Journal for Research and Studies. Text in Arabic, English. 1986. 6/yr. JOD 9 domestic; USD 30 foreign (effective 2003). abstr.; bibl.; illus.; stat. index. **Document type:** *Journal, Academic/Scholarly.* **Description:** Publishes original research papers and articles on topics in agricultural sciences, engineering and technology, medical and biological sciences, and basic science.
Indexed: INIS AtomInd.
Published by: Mu'tah University, Deanship of Scientific Research/Jami'at Mu'tah, 'Imadat al-Bahth al-'Ilmi, P O Box 7, Mu'tah, 61710, Jordan. TEL 962-6-4629543, FAX 962-6-4654061, mutahlbd@mutah.edu.jo, http://www.mutah.edu.jo. Ed. Abdelrahim Hunaiti.

500 ESP ISSN 1130-4081
MUY INTERESANTE. Text in Spanish. 1981. m. EUR 30 domestic; EUR 66.40 in Europe; EUR 88.35 elsewhere. adv. **Document type:** *Magazine, Consumer.* **Description:** Covers scientific subjects, putting all the latest discoveries and new technologies within the reader's reach.
Related titles: ◆ Regional ed(s).: Muy Interesante. ISSN 0188-0659.
Indexed: A22.
—IE.
Published by: G y J Espana Ediciones S.L. (Subsidiary of: Gruner + Jahr AG & Co), Albasanz, 15 Edificio A, Madrid, 28037, Spain. TEL 34-91-4369800, FAX 34-91-5767881, http://www.grupogyj.es/. Ed. Jose Pardina. Adv. contact Elena Sanchez-Fabres. page EUR 17,000; bleed 224 x 285. Circ: 263,461 (paid).

500 MEX ISSN 0188-0659
MUY INTERESANTE. Text in Spanish. 1983. m. MXN 310 domestic (effective 2010). adv. **Document type:** *Magazine, Consumer.*
Related titles: Online - full text ed.; ◆ Regional ed(s).: Muy Interesante. ISSN 1130-4081; Supplement(s): Muy Interesante. Periodico Cientifico Semestral. ISSN 0188-0713. 1983.

Published by: Editorial Televisa, Vasco de Quiroga 2000, Edificio E, Colonia Santa Fe, Mexico City, DF 01210, Mexico. TEL 52-55-52612761, FAX 52-55-52612704, info@editorialtelevisa.com, http://www.esmas.com/editorialtelevisa/.

MUY INTERESANTE JUNIOR. *see* CHILDREN AND YOUTH—For

500 USA
MYNSF. Text in English. 19??. irreg. free (effective 2010). **Document type:** *Government.* **Description:** Provides email and RSS notifications about new NSF funding opportunities, news, official NSF documents, and more.
Formerly: National Science Foundation Custom News Service
Media: E-mail.
Published by: U.S. Department of Commerce, National Science Foundation, 4201 Wilson Blvd, Ste 245, Arlington, VA 22230. TEL 703-292-5111, 800-877-8339, info@nsf.gov.

500 600 AUS ISSN 0311-662X
N A T A NEWS. Text in English. 1974. q. AUD 59 domestic; AUD 80 foreign (effective 2009). adv. back issues avail. **Document type:** *Newsletter, Trade.* **Description:** Covers laboratory accreditation quality systems certification, environmental systems certification, inspaction, training, publications and other information related to NATA's activities.
Related titles: Online - full text ed.: free (effective 2009).
Published by: National Association of Testing Authorities, PO Box 7507, Silverwater, NSW 2128, Australia. TEL 61-2-97368222, FAX 61-2-97435311, corpcomm@nata.asn.au. Adv. contact Conan Elphicke TEL 61-2-97368222. color page AUD 858; 55 x 260. Circ: 4,500.

500 600 NLD ISSN 1383-7176
➤ **N A T O ADVANCED SCIENCE INSTITUTES SERIES. PARTNERSHIP SUB-SERIES 4: SCIENCE AND TECHNOLOGY POLICY.** (North Atlantic Treaty Organization) Text in English. 1995. irreg., latest vol.21, 2002. price varies. **Document type:** *Monographic series, Academic/Scholarly.*
—CCC.
Published by: (North Atlantic Treaty Organization (N A T O) BEL), Springer Netherlands (Subsidiary of: Springer Science+Business Media), Van Godewijckstraat 30, Dordrecht, 3311 GX, Netherlands. TEL 31-78-6576050, FAX 31-78-6576474.

500 USA ISSN 0730-9600
CODEN: NCMSD4
➤ **N A T O CHALLENGES OF MODERN SOCIETY.** (North Atlantic Treaty Organization) (Includes subseries: Air Pollution Modeling and its Applications) Text in English. 1981. irreg., latest vol.23, 1999. price varies. back issues avail. **Document type:** *Monographic series, Academic/Scholarly.*
Indexed: A22, CIN, ChemAb, ChemTitl, Inspec.
—CASDDS, IE, Ingenta. **CCC.**
Published by: (North Atlantic Treaty Organization (N A T O) BEL), Springer New York LLC (Subsidiary of: Springer Science+Business Media), 233 Spring St, New York, NY 10013. TEL 212-460-1500, FAX 212-460-1575, service-ny@springer.com.

500 600 NLD ISSN 1873-0337
N A T O SCIENCE SERIES. SERIES V: SCIENCE AND TECHNOLOGY POLICY. (North Atlantic Treaty Organization) Text in English. 1994 (Nov.). irreg., latest vol.51, 2006. price varies. **Document type:** *Monographic series, Academic/Scholarly.*
Formerly (until 2001): N A T O Science Partnership Sub-Series 4: Science and Technology Policy (1387-6708)
Related titles: Online - full text ed.: ISSN 1879-8403.
—BLDSC (6033.693340), IE, Ingenta. **CCC.**
Published by: (North Atlantic Treaty Organization, Scientific Affairs Division BEL), I O S Press, Nieuwe Hemweg 6B, Amsterdam, 1013 BG, Netherlands. TEL 31-20-6883355, FAX 31-20-6203419, info@iospress.nl.

500 BEL ISSN 0255-7134
N A T O SCIENTIFIC PUBLICATIONS. NEWSLETTER. (North Atlantic Treaty Organization) Text in English. 1980. q. free. adv. bk.rev. **Document type:** *Newsletter.*
Related titles: Online - full text ed.
Published by: (North Atlantic Treaty Organization, Scientific Affairs Division), North Atlantic Treaty Organization, Publication Coordination Office, Elcerlyclaan 2, Overijse, 3090, Belgium. TEL 32-2-6876636. Ed. B Kester. Circ: 25,000.

500 CAN ISSN 0047-9551
N B NATURALIST/NATURALISTE DU N B. (New Brunswick) Text in English, French. 1970. 4/yr. adv. bk.rev. **Document type:** *Newsletter, Consumer.* **Description:** Covers natural history of New Brunswick.
Published by: New Brunswick Federation of Naturalists, 924 Prospect St, Ste 110, Fredericton, NB E3B 2T9, Canada. TEL 506-532-3482, http://www.naturenb.ca/English/federation.htm. Ed., R&P Gart Bishop. Pub. Rose Alma Mallet. Circ: 500 (paid).

500 USA ISSN 1931-5775
QC39
➤ **N C S L INTERNATIONAL MEASURE.** (National Conference of Standards Laboratories) Text in English. 2006. q. **Document type:** *Journal, Trade.*
Published by: National Conference of Standards Laboratories (N C S L), 2995 Wilderness Pl, Ste 107, Boulder, CO 80301. TEL 303-440-3339, FAX 303-440-3384, info@ncsli.org, http://www.ncsli.org/.

➤ **N C S S S M S T NEWSLETTER.** *see* EDUCATION

500 JPN
N I M S NOW INTERNATIONAL. Text in English. 2003. m. **Document type:** *Newsletter, Academic/Scholarly.*
Formerly: N I M S now
Related titles: Online - full text ed.
Published by: National Institute for Materials Science/Busshitsu Zairyou Kenkyuu Kikou, 1-2-1 Sengen, Tsukuba, Ibaraki 305-0047, Japan. TEL 81-29-8592026, FAX 81-29-8592017, inquiry@nims.go.jp. Pub. Tomoaki Hyodo.

500 JPN
N I R A'S WORLD DIRECTORY OF THINK TANKS. Text in English. 1999. every 3 yrs., latest 2005. abstr. **Document type:** *Directory, Academic/Scholarly.* **Description:** Contains a list of think tanks from all over the world with brief explanations on their research activities.

Published by: National Institute for Research Advancement/Sogo Kenkyu Kaihatsu Kiko, 34F Yebisu Garden Place Tower, 4-20-3 Ebisu, Shibuya-ku, PO Box 5004, Tokyo, 150-6034, Japan. TEL 81-3-54481735, FAX 81-3-54481745, www@nira.go.jp, http://www.nira.go.jp.

N K H NAGAOKA-SHIRITSU KAGAKU HAKUBUTSUKANPO. *see* MUSEUMS AND ART GALLERIES

▼ **N P G ASIA MATERIALS.** (Nature Publishing Group) *see* ENGINEERING—Engineering Mechanics And Materials

N R G ONDERZOEKSMEMORANDA. (Nyenrode Research Group) *see* BUSINESS AND ECONOMICS

507 CAN ISSN 1493-1850
N S E R C AWARD HOLDER'S GUIDE FOR POSTGRADUATE SCHOLARSHIP (PGS) HOLDERS AT CANADIAN UNIVERSITIES. Text in English, French. 1999. a.
Related titles: Online - full text ed.: ISSN 1494-1961.
Published by: (Social Sciences and Humanities Research Council of Canada), Natural Sciences and Engineering Research Council of Canada/Conseil de Recherches en Sciences Naturelles et en Genie du Canada, 350 Albert St, Ottawa, ON K1A 1H5, Canada. TEL 613-995-4273, http://www.nserc-crsng.gc.ca.

507 USA ISSN 1946-2638
N S F CURRENT. (National Science Foundation) Text in English. 2005. m. free (effective 2009). back issues avail. **Document type:** *Newsletter, Trade.* **Description:** Highlights research and education efforts supported by the National Science Foundation.
Media: Online - full content.
Published by: National Science Foundation, 4201 Wilson Blvd, Arlington, VA 22230. TEL 703-292-5111, 800-877-8339, info@nsf.gov.

N S T A REPORTS. *see* EDUCATION

N T I S BIBLIOGRAPHIC DATABASE. (National Technical Information Service) *see* SCIENCES: COMPREHENSIVE WORKS—Abstracting, Bibliographies, Statistics

500.9 CHE
Q125
➤ **N T M JOURNAL OF HISTORY OF SCIENCES, TECHNOLOGY, AND MEDICINE/N T M ZEITSCHRIFT FUER GESCHICHTE DER WISSENSCHAFTEN, TECHNIK UND MEDIZIN.** (Natural Sciences, Technology & Medicine) Text in German. 1960. q. EUR 208, USD 235 combined subscription to institutions (print & online eds.) (effective 2012). adv. bk.rev. bibl.; charts; illus. index. back issues avail.; reprint service avail. from PSC. **Document type:** *Journal, Academic/Scholarly.* **Description:** Contains articles on the history and ethics of natural sciences, technology and medicine.
Former titles (until 2008): N T M International Journal of History and Ethics of Natural Sciences, Technology and Medicine (0036-6978); N T M Geschichte der Naturwissenschaften, Technik und Medizin. Schriftenreihe; Geschichte der Naturwissenschaften, Technik und Medizin. Schriftenreihe; Zeitschrift fuer Geschichte der Naturwissenschaften, der Technik und der Medizin
Related titles: Online - full text ed.: (from IngentaConnect).
Indexed: A20, A22, A26, ArtHuCI, CCMJ, CIS, DIP, E01, EMBASE, ExcerpMed, FR, IBR, IBZ, MEDLINE, MSN, MathR, P30, RASB, SCOPUS, W07, Z02.
—BLDSC (6180.606000), IE, Infotrieve, Ingenta, INIST, Linda Hall. **CCC.**
Published by: Birkhaeuser Verlag AG (Subsidiary of: Springer Science+Business Media), Viaduktstr 42, Postfach 133, Basel, 4051, Switzerland. TEL 41-61-2050707, FAX 41-61-2050799, info@birkhauser.ch. Ed. Sybilla Nikolow. **Subscr. in the Americas to:** Springer New York LLC, Journal Fulfillment, PO Box 2485, Secaucus, NJ 07096. TEL 201-348-4033, 800-777-4643, FAX 201-348-4505, journals@birkhauser.com; **Subscr. to:** Springer Distribution Center, Kundenservice Zeitschriften. birkhauser@springer.de. **Dist. in N. America by:** Springer.

500.9 NLD ISSN 0929-757X
N V O X; magazine voor onderwijs in natuurwetenschappen. Text in Dutch. 1984. 10/yr. EUR 85 (effective 2010). adv. bk.rev. charts; illus. index. **Document type:** *Magazine, Trade.*
Formerly (until 1994): N V O N Maandblad (0921-1713); Which was formed by the merger of (1975-1984): Nederlandse Vereniging voor het Onderwijs in de Natuurwetenschappen. Mededelingenblad (0166-6126); (1930-1984): Faraday (0014-7656)
—IE.
Published by: Nederlandse Vereniging voor het Onderwijs in de Natuurwetenschappen, Postbus 60047, Groningen, 9703 BA, Netherlands. TEL 31-50-8538517. Ed. W T W Vis. Circ: 3,650.

500 NLD ISSN 1874-8546
N W O-SPINOZAPREMIES. Text in Dutch. 1996. a.
Formerly (until 2004): Spinoza (1566-4872)
Published by: Nederlandse Organisatie voor Wetenschappelijk Onderzoek/Netherlands Organization for Scientific Research, PO Box 93138, The Hague, 2509 AC, Netherlands. TEL 31-70-3440640, FAX 31-70-3850971, nwo@nwo.nl, http://www.nwo.nl.

NAGAOKA COLLEGE OF TECHNOLOGY. RESEARCH REPORTS/ NAGAOKA KOGYO KOTO SENMON GAKKO KENKYU KIYO. *see* ENGINEERING

500 JPN ISSN 0285-6085
NAGAOKA-SHIRITSU KAGAKU HAKUBUTSUKAN KENKYU HOKOKU/NAGAOKA MUNICIPAL SCIENCE MUSEUM. BULLETIN. Text and summaries in Japanese. 1973. a. **Description:** Contains research reports from the museum.
Indexed: JPI, Z01.
Published by: Nagaoka-shiritsu Kagaku Hakubutsukan/Nagaoka Municipal Science Museum, 2-1 Yanagihara-Machi, Nagaoka-shi, Niigata-ken 940-0072, Japan. TEL 81-258-35-0184. Ed. Hisashi Watanabe.

500 JPN ISSN 1345-1359
Q4 CODEN: NADKBL
NAGASAKI DAIGAKU KYOIKU GAKUBU KIYO. SHIZEN KAGAKU/ NAGASAKI UNIVERSITY. FACULTY OF EDUCATION. BULLETIN: NATURAL SCIENCE. Text and summaries in English, Japanese. 1951. s-a. JPY 390 domestic; JPY 430 foreign (effective 2001); or exchange basis. **Document type:** *Bulletin, Academic/Scholarly.* **Description:** Covers multi-disciplines of science studies including but not exclusively chemistry, physics, machinery, spatial studies.

Formerly (until 1998): Nagasaki Daigaku Kyoikugakubu Shizen Kagaku Kenkyu Houkodu / Nagasaki University. Faculty of Education. Science Bulletin (0386-443X); (until 1966): Nagasaki Daigaku Gakugei Gakubu Shizen Kagaku Kenkyu Hokoku (0547-1419)
Indexed: A22, CCMJ, CIN, ChemAb, ChemTitl, JPI, MSN, MathR, Z02.
—BLDSC (2507.620000), IE, Ingenta.
Published by: Nagasaki Daigaku, Kyoikugakubu/Nagasaki University, Faculty of Education, 1-14 Bunkyo-Machi, Nagasaki-shi, 852-8521, Japan. TEL 81-95-847-1111, FAX 81-95-844-0401. Ed. Yoshimasa Hoshino. Circ: 260 (controlled).

500 JPN ISSN 0287-1319
Q4
NAGASAKI DAIGAKU KYOYOBU KIYO. SHIZEN KAGAKU HEN/ NAGASAKI UNIVERSITY. FACULTY OF LIBERAL ARTS. BULLETIN. Text in English, German, Japanese; Summaries in English, German. 1960. s-a. free.
Indexed: JPI, Z02.
Published by: Nagasaki Daigaku, Kyoyobu/Nagasaki University, Faculty of Liberal Arts, 1-14 Bunkyo-machi, Nagasaki-shi, Nagasaki-ken 852, Japan. Circ: 200.

500 JPN ISSN 1342-9329
CODEN: NSKKAB
NAGOYA CITY UNIVERSITY. INSTITUTE OF NATURAL SCIENCES. ANNUAL REVIEW (YEAR). Text in English, Japanese; Summaries in English. 1955. a. free. **Document type:** *Bulletin.* **Description:** Covers fundamental mathematics, computer science, analytical molecular science, photobiophysics, condensed matter theory, biomolecular science, cell function, health science and more.
Formerly (until 1997): Nagoya-Shiritsu Daigaku Kyoyobu Kiyo. Shizen Kagaku Hen - Nagoya City University. College of General Education. Bulletin. Natural Science Section (0465-7772)
Indexed: B25, BIOSIS Prev, ChemAb, JPI, MycolAb.
—CASDDS, Linda Hall.
Published by: Nagoya-shiritsu Daigaku, Kyoyobu/Nagoya City University, College of General Education, 1-1 Yamanohata-Mizuho-cho, Mizuho-ku, Nagoya-shi, Aichi-ken 467-0000, Japan. TEL 81-52-872-5791, FAX 81-52-872-5781. Ed. H Tatewaki. Circ: 300.

NAGOYA DAIGAKU HAKUBUSUKAN HOKOKU/NAGOYA UNIVERSITY MUSEUM. BULLETIN. *see* MUSEUMS AND ART GALLERIES

NAGOYA JOSHI DAIGAKU KIYO. KASEI, SHIZEN-HEN/NAGOYA WOMEN'S UNIVERSITY. JOURNAL. HOME ECONOMICS, NATURAL SCIENCE. *see* HOME ECONOMICS

500 JPN ISSN 0285-4538
CODEN: IGDKEB
NAGOYA KEIZAI DAIGAKU, ICHIMURA GAKUEN TANKI DAIGAKU SHIZEN KAGAKU KENKYUKAI KAISHI/NAGOYA ECONOMICS UNIVERSITY AND ICHIMURA GAKUEN JUNIOR COLLEGE. NATURAL SCIENTIFIC SOCIETY. JOURNAL. Text and summaries in English, Japanese. 1966. a.
—CASDDS.
Published by: Shizen Kagaku Kenkyukai, Ichimura Gakuen Tanki Daigaku, Inoya-shi, Aichi-ken 484, Japan. **Co-sponsor:** Nagoya Keizai Daigaku - Nagoya Economics University.

500 JPN ISSN 0911-971X
NAITO ZAIDAN JIHO. Text in Japanese. 1969. a. free. **Document type:** *Bulletin.* **Description:** Contains reviews, commentary, and news of the foundation.
Published by: Naito Kinen Kagaku Shinko Zaidan/Naito Foundation, 42-6 Hongo 3-chome, Bunkyo-ku, Tokyo, 113-0033, Japan. TEL 81-3-3813-3005, FAX 81-3-3811-2917. Ed. Yasuo Kumagai. Pub. Koji Naito.

500 300 NAM ISSN 1018-7677
Q85
NAMIBIA SCIENTIFIC SOCIETY. JOURNAL. Text in English, German. 1925. a. membership. adv. bk.rev. illus. **Document type:** *Journal, Academic/Scholarly.*
Formerly: South West Africa Scientific Society. Journal (0379-6051)
Indexed: ASD, GeoRef, ISAP, SpeleolAb, Z01.
—INIST.
Published by: Namibia Scientific Society, PO Box 67, Windhoek, Namibia. TEL 264-61-225372. Ed. A W Steffan.

500 NAM ISSN 1018-7685
Q85.8 CODEN: MNWGEH
NAMIBIA SCIENTIFIC SOCIETY. NEWSLETTER/NAMIBIA WISSENSCHAFTLICHE GESELLSCHAFT. MITTEILUNGEN. Text in Afrikaans, English, German. 1959. m. membership. **Document type:** *Newsletter, Academic/Scholarly.*
Formerly: South West Africa Scientific Society. Newsletter - S W A Wetenskaplike Vereniging. Nuusbrief - S W A Wissenschaftliche Gesellschaft. Mitteilungen (0036-2069); Incorporates (in 1983): Botanische Mitteilungen
Published by: Namibia Scientific Society, PO Box 67, Windhoek, Namibia. TEL 264-61-225372. Ed. I Demasius.

500 CHN ISSN 1006-0464
Q4
NANCHANG DAXUE XUEBAO (LIKE BAN)/NANCHANG UNIVERSITY. JOURNAL (NATURAL SCIENCES EDITION). Text in Chinese. 1963. bi-m. USD 24.60 (effective 2009). **Document type:** *Journal, Academic/Scholarly.*
Related titles: Online - full text ed.
Published by: Nanchang Daxue/Nanchang University, 235, Nanjing Dong Lu, Bei-qu, Nanchang, 330047, China. TEL 86-791-8305805.

500 CHN
NANCHANG HANGKONG GONGYE XUEYUAN XUEBAO (ZIRAN KEXUE BAN)/NANCHANG INSTITUTE OF AERONAUTICAL TECHNOLOGY. JOURNAL (NATURAL SCIENCES). Text in Chinese. 1987. q. USD 15.60 (effective 2009). back issues avail. **Document type:** *Academic/Scholarly.*
Formerly: Nanchang Hangkong Gongye Xueyuan Xuebao (1001-4926)
Related titles: Online - full text ed.
Published by: Nanchang Hangkong Daxue/Nanchang Hangkong University, 173, Shanghai lu, Nanchang, Zhejiang 330034, China. TEL 86-791-8223348.

500 620 CHN ISSN 1673-0062
NANHUA DAXUE XUEBAO (ZIRAN KEXUE BAN)/NANHUA UNIVERSITY. JOURNAL (SCIENCE & TECHNOLOGY). Text in Chinese. 1987. q. USD 16.40 (effective 2009). **Document type:** *Journal, Academic/Scholarly.*
Former titles: Nanhua Daxue Xuebao (Ligongban)/Nanhua University. Journal (Science & Engineering Edition) (1671-9239); (until 2001): Zhongnan Gongxueyuan Xuebao (1006-737X); (until 1995): Hengyang Gongxueyuan Xuebao (1000-5986)
Related titles: Online - full text ed.
Indexed: INIS AtomInd.
—BLDSC (6015.333340).
Published by: Nanhua Daxue/Nanhua University, Changcheng Xilu, Hengyang, Hunan 421001, China. TEL 86-734-8160781.

500 600 CHN ISSN 1007-7278
LA1133 CODEN: NCHPAZ
➤ **NANJING DAXUE XUEBAO (ZHEXUE RENWEN SHEHUI KEXUE)/ NANJING UNIVERSITY. JOURNAL (PHILOSOPHY, HUMANITIES AND SOCIAL SCIENCES).** Text in Chinese. 1955. bi-m. USD 17.80 (effective 2009). **Document type:** *Journal, Academic/Scholarly.*
Formerly: Nanjing Daxue Xuebao (Zhexue Shehui Kexue Ban) (0257-5892)
Related titles: Online - full text ed.
Indexed: CCMJ, CIN, ChemAb, ChemTitl, GeoRef, Inspec, MSN, MathR, SpeleolAb.
—CASDDS, East View, Ingenta.
Published by: (Nanjing Daxue), Nanjing Daxue Chubanshe, Hankou Lu, Nanjing, Jiangsu 210008, China. TEL 86-25-83592704. **Dist. by:** China International Book Trading Corp, 35 Chegongzhuang Xilu, Haidian District, PO Box 399, Beijing 100044, China. TEL 86-10-68412045, FAX 86-10-68412023, cibtc@mail.cibtc.com.cn, http://www.cibtc.com.cn.

500 CHN ISSN 0469-5097
NANJING DAXUE XUEBAO (ZIRAN KEXUE BAN)/NANJING UNIVERSITY. JOURNAL (NATURAL SCIENCES). Text in Chinese. 1955. bi-m. USD 53.40 (effective 2009). **Document type:** *Journal, Academic/Scholarly.*
Indexed: A22, CCMJ, GeoRef, MSN, MathR, RefZh, Z02.
—BLDSC (4828.680000), East View, IE.
Published by: Nanjing Daxue Chubanshe, Hankou Lu, Nanjing, Jiangsu 210008, China. TEL 86-25-83592704. **Dist. by:** China International Book Trading Corp, 35 Chegongzhuang Xilu, Haidian District, PO Box 399, Beijing 100044, China. TEL 86-10-68412045, FAX 86-10-68412023, cibtc@mail.cibtc.com.cn, http://www.cibtc.com.cn.

500 CHN ISSN 1672-2558
NANJING GONGCHENG XUEYUAN XUEBAO (ZIRAN KEXUE BAN). Text in Chinese. 2003. q. CNY 5 newsstand/cover (effective 2006). **Document type:** *Journal, Academic/Scholarly.*
Related titles: Online - full text ed.
Published by: Nanjing Gongcheng Xueyuan, Jiangning Kexueyuan, Hongjing Dadao #1, Nanjing, 211167, China. TEL 86-25-86118019.

NANJING GONGYE ZHIYE JISHU XUEYUAN XUEBAO/NANJING INSTITUTE OF INDUSTRY TECHNOLOGY. JOURNAL. *see* SOCIAL SCIENCES: COMPREHENSIVE WORKS

500 CHN ISSN 1001-4616
NANJING SHI-DAXUE BAO (ZIRAN KEXUE BAN)/NANJING NORMAL UNIVERSITY. JOURNAL (NATURAL SCIENCE EDITION). Text in Chinese. 1955. q. USD 16.40 (effective 2009). back issues avail. **Document type:** *Journal, Academic/Scholarly.*
Related titles: Online - full text ed.
Indexed: A28, APA, B25, BIOSIS Prev, BrCerAb, C&ISA, CA/WCA, CCMJ, CIA, CerAb, CivEngAb, CorrAb, E&CAJ, E11, EEA, EMA, H15, M&TEA, M09, MBF, METADEX, MSN, MathR, SolStAb, T04, WAA, Z02.
—BLDSC (6015.333742), Linda Hall.
Published by: Nanjing Shifan Daxue/Nanjing Normal University, 122 Ninghai Lu, Nanjing, Jiangsu 210097, China. TEL 86-25-83598632. Ed. Lingfu Chen.

500 CHN ISSN 1674-7070
CODEN: NXGDA5
▼ ➤ **NANJING XINXI GONGCHENG DAXUE XUEBAO (ZIRAN KEXUE BAN)/NANJING UNIVERSITY OF INFORMATION SCIENCE & TECHNOLOGY. JOURNAL (NATURAL SCIENCE EDITION).** Text in Chinese; Abstracts in Chinese, English. 2009. bi-m. CNY 72, USD 72; USD 12 per issue (effective 2011). **Document type:** *Journal, Academic/Scholarly.* **Description:** Publishes papers in atmospheric science and related subjects such as environmental science & technology, computer science & engineering, electronics, remote sensing, mathematics, information and control, etc.
Related titles: Online - full text ed.: (from WanFang Data Corp.).
Published by: Nanjing Xinxi Gongcheng Daxue/Nanjing University of Information Science & Technology, 219, Ningliu Rd., Nanjing, Jiangsu Province 210044, China. TEL 86-25-58731025, FAX 86-25-58731520, qks@nuist.edu.cn, http://www.nuist.edu.cn. Ed. Yi-ping Liu. Circ: 3,000.

500 CHN ISSN 1673-5439
NANJING YOUDIAN DAXUE XUEBAO (ZIRAN KEXUE BAN)/NANJING UNIVERSITY OF POSTS AND TELECOMMUNICATIONS. JOURNAL (NATURAL SCIENCE). Text in Chinese. 1960. bi-m. CNY 8 newsstand/cover (effective 2006). **Document type:** *Journal, Academic/Scholarly.*
Former titles: Nanjing Youdian Xueyuan Xuebao (Ziran Kexue Ban); Nanjing Youdian Xueyuan Xuebao (1000-1972)
Related titles: Online - full text ed.
Indexed: A28, APA, BrCerAb, C&ISA, CA/WCA, CIA, CerAb, CivEngAb, CorrAb, E&CAJ, E11, EEA, EMA, ESPM, EngInd, EnvEAb, H15, M&TEA, M09, MBF, METADEX, RefZh, SCOPUS, SolStAb, T04, WAA.
Published by: Nanjing Youdian Daxue, 66, Xinmofanma Lu, Nanjing, 210003, China. TEL 86-25-83492279, FAX 86-25-83492246.

500 CHN ISSN 0465-7942
Q4
NANKAI DAXUE XUEBAO/ACTA SCIENTIARUM NATURALIUM UNIVERSITATIS NANKAIENSIS (NATURAL SCIENCE EDITION). Text in Chinese. 1955. bi-m. USD 21.60 (effective 2009). **Document type:** *Journal, Academic/Scholarly.*
Related titles: Online - full text ed.
Indexed: RefZh, Z01, Z02.
—East View.
Published by: Nankai Daxue/Nankai University, 94, Weijin Lu, Tianjin, 300071, China. TEL 86-22-23501681, FAX 86-22-23508374, http://www.nankai.edu.cn/.

500 USA ISSN 2150-5551
T174.7
▼ ➤ **NANO-MICRO LETTERS.** Text in English. 2009. q. free. **Document type:** *Journal, Academic/Scholarly.* **Description:** Features research on nano and micro scale structures and systems, in the fields of physics, materials science, biology, chemistry, and engineering.
Media: Online - full text.
Indexed: A01, T02.
Published by: Open Access House of Science and Technology, 2840 N Boxwood Dr, Fayetteville, AR 72703. TEL 479-283-4354, http://oahost.org. Ed. Yafei Zhang.

500 CHN ISSN 1673-2340
NANTONG DAXUE XUEBAO (ZIRAN KEXUE BAN). Text in Chinese. 2002. q. CNY 5 newsstand/cover (effective 2007). **Document type:** *Journal, Academic/Scholarly.*
Formerly: Nantong Gongxueyuan Xuebao (Ziran Kexue Ban)/Nantong Institute of Technology. Journal (Natural Science) (1671-5314)
Related titles: Online - full text ed.
Indexed: ESPM, EnvEAb.
—BLDSC (6015.343201).
Published by: Nantong Daxue, 40, Qingnian Dong Lu, Nantong, 226007, China. TEL 86-513-85015388, FAX 86-513-85239312.

NANTONG FANGZHI ZHIYE JISHU XUEYUAN XUEBAO/NANTONG TEXTILE VOCATIONAL TECHNOLOGY COLLEGE. JOURNAL. *see* SOCIAL SCIENCES: COMPREHENSIVE WORKS

▼ **NANYANG LIGONG XUEYUAN XUEBAO/NANYANG INSTITUTE OF TECHNOLOGY. JOURNAL.** *see* SOCIAL SCIENCES: COMPREHENSIVE WORKS

500 300 CHN ISSN 1671-6132
NANYANG SHIFAN XUEYUAN XUEBAO. Text in Chinese. 1987. m. **Document type:** *Journal, Academic/Scholarly.* **Description:** Issues no.3, 6, 9, & 12 cover natural sciences, and the rest are social sciences.
Formerly (until 2002): Nanyang Jiaoyu Xueyuan Xuebao (1009-4628)
—BLDSC (6015.343450).
Published by: Nanyang Shifan Xueyuan Qikanbu/Nanyang Normal University, 1638, Wolong Lu, Nanyang, 473061, China. TEL 86-377-63523103, qikanbu@nynu.edu.cn, http://www2.nynu.edu.cn/xzbm/qk/.

500 JPN ISSN 0547-2407
Q4 CODEN: NKDSAC
NARA KYOIKU DAIGAKU KIYO. SHIZEN KAGAKU/NARA UNIVERSITY OF EDUCATION. BULLETIN. NATURAL SCIENCE. Text and summaries in English, Japanese. 1951. a.
Formerly (until 1965): Nara Gakugei Daigaku Kiyo. Shizen Kagaku (0369-3937)
Indexed: A34, A36, A37, C30, CABA, CCMJ, ChemAb, D01, E12, F08, F12, GH, GeoRef, H16, I11, JPI, LT, MSN, MathR, N02, N03, N04, O01, R07, RRTA, S13, S16, SpeleolAb, VS, W10.
—BLDSC (2629.150000).
Published by: Nara Kyoiku Daigaku/Nara University of Education, Takabatake-cho, Nara-shi, 630-8528, Japan. Circ: 600.

NARODNI MUZEUM V PRAZE. SBORNIK. RADA B: PRIRODNI VEDY/ACTA MUSEI NATIONALIS PRAGAE. SERIES B: HISTORIA NATURALIS. *see* MUSEUMS AND ART GALLERIES

500.05 DEU ISSN 0368-1254
Q49 CODEN: JANVAP
NASSAUISCHER VEREIN FUER NATURKUNDE. JAHRBUECHER. Text in German. 1844. a. EUR 36 (effective 2005). adv. bk.rev. **Document type:** *Journal, Academic/Scholarly.*
Indexed: GeoRef, IBR, IBZ, SpeleolAb, Z01.
—Linda Hall.
Published by: Nassauischer Verein fuer Naturkunde, Rheinstr 10, Wiesbaden, 65185, Germany. webmaster@naturkunde-online.de. Ed., R&P, Adv. contact Malte Fuhrmann.

500 DEU ISSN 0946-9427
NASSAUISCHER VEREIN FUER NATURKUNDE. MITTEILUNGEN. Text in German. 2/yr. EUR 26 membership (effective 2005). **Document type:** *Newsletter, Academic/Scholarly.*
Published by: Nassauischer Verein fuer Naturkunde, Rheinstr 10, Wiesbaden, 65185, Germany. webmaster@naturkunde-online.de. R&P Olaf Godmann.

S

500 620 USA ISSN 1534-8334
Q11
➤ **THE NATIONAL ACADEMIES IN FOCUS.** Text in English. 1951. 3/yr. USD 10 domestic; USD 12 foreign (effective 2012). bk.rev. bibl.; charts; illus. back issues avail.; reprints avail. **Document type:** *Magazine, Academic/Scholarly.* **Description:** Features activities of the National Academies, which serve as independent advisers to the federal government on scientific and technical questions of national importance.
Former titles (until 2001): The National Academies News Report; (until 1999): National Research Council. News Report (0027-8432)
Related titles: Microfilm ed.: (from PQC); Online - full text ed.: free (effective 2012).
Indexed: A15, A22, ABIn, Agr, GeoRef, IHD, P06, P15, P48, P51, P52, P56, PQC, SpeleolAb.
—CASDDS, Ingenta, Linda Hall. **CCC.**
Published by: (National Research Council), National Academy of Sciences, 500 Fifth St, NW, Washington, DC 20001. TEL 202-334-2000, 888-624-6242, FAX 202-334-2793, news@nas.edu, http://www.nationalacademies.org. Ed. Valerie Chase. **Co-sponsors:** National Research Council; Institute of Medicine; National Academy of Engineering.

➤ **NATIONAL ACADEMY OF SCIENCES. BIOGRAPHICAL MEMOIRS.** *see* BIOGRAPHY

500 530 IND ISSN 0369-8203
Q73 CODEN: PAIAA3
NATIONAL ACADEMY OF SCIENCES, INDIA. PROCEEDINGS. SECTION A. PHYSICAL SCIENCES. Text in English. 1930. q. INR 250 domestic; USD 100 foreign; INR 100 per issue (effective 2011). bibl.; charts. **Document type:** *Proceedings, Academic/Scholarly.*

Supersedes in part (in 1940): National Academy of Sciences, India. Proceedings (0369-3236); Which was formerly (until 1936): Academy of Sciences, United Provinces of Agra and Oudh, India. Proceedings (0370-1808); (until 1934): Academy of Sciences, United Provinces of Agra and Oudh, India. Bulletin (0366-3957)
Indexed: A22, CABA, CCMJ, CIN, ChemAb, ChemTitl, GH, INIS AtomInd, Inspec, MSN, MathR, SCI, SCOPUS, W07, Z02.
—BLDSC (6761.900000), AskIEEE, CASDDS, IE, Ingenta, INIST, Linda Hall.
Published by: National Academy of Sciences, 5 Lajpatrai Rd, New Katra, Allahabad, Uttar Pradesh 211 002, India. TEL 91-532-2640224, FAX 91-532-2641183. Ed. Suresh Chandra. **Subscr. to:** I N S I O Scientific Books & Periodicals.

500 IND ISSN 0250-541X
Q73 CODEN: NASLDX
NATIONAL ACADEMY OF SCIENCES, INDIA. SCIENCE LETTERS. Text in English. 1978. bi-m. INR 300 domestic; USD 125 foreign; INR 40 per issue domestic; USD 20 per issue foreign (effective 2011). back issues avail. **Document type:** *Journal, Academic/Scholarly.*
Indexed: A20, A22, A29, A34, A35, A36, A38, ASCA, AgBio, AgrForAb, B20, B21, B23, BA, BP, C25, C30, CABA, CCMJ, CIN, ChemAb, ChemTitl, CurCont, E12, ESPM, F08, F11, F12, FCA, G11, GH, H16, H17, I10, I11, INIS AtomInd, IndVet, Inspec, MSN, MaizeAb, MathR, N02, N03, N04, O01, OR, P32, P33, P37, P38, P39, P40, PGegResA, PGrRegA, PHN&I, R07, R08, R11, R12, R13, RA&MP, RM&VM, RefZh, S12, S13, S16, S17, SCI, SCOPUS, SoyAb, T05, TAR, TOSA, TriticAb, VS, VirolAbstr, W07, W10, W11, Z01, Z02.
—BLDSC (6015.756000), AskIEEE, CASDDS, IE, Ingenta, INIST, Linda Hall.
Published by: National Academy of Sciences, 5 Lajpatrai Rd, New Katra, Allahabad, Uttar Pradesh 211 002, India. TEL 91-532-2640224, FAX 91-532-2641183. **Subscr. to:** I N S I O Scientific Books & Periodicals.

505 USA ISSN 0027-8424
Q11 CODEN: PNASA6
➤ **NATIONAL ACADEMY OF SCIENCES. PROCEEDINGS.** Key Title: Proceedings of the National Academy of Sciences of the United States of America. Abbreviated title: P N A S. Variant title: Proceedings of the National Academy of Sciences. Text in English. 1914. w. USD 785 combined subscription domestic to institutions (print & online eds.); USD 1,140 combined subscription foreign to institutions (print & online eds.) (effective 2012). adv. charts; illus.; pat.; stat. Index. back issues avail.; reprints avail. **Document type:** *Proceedings, Academic/Scholarly.* **Description:** Publishes brief reports that describe the results of original research of exceptional importance.
Related titles: Microfilm ed.: (from PQC); Online - full text ed.: ISSN 1091-6490. 1977. USD 270 to institutions (effective 2012).
Indexed: A01, A02, A03, A08, A20, A22, A25, A26, A29, A33, A34, A35, A36, A37, A38, AIDS Ab, ASCA, ASFA, AgBio, Agr, AgrForAb, AnBeAb, B&AI, B04, B10, B20, B21, B23, B25, B27, BA, BIOBASE, BIOSIS Prev, BP, BRD, BibAg, BiolDig, C13, C25, C30, C33, CA, CABA, CBTA, CEABA, CIN, CIS, CMCI, CRFR, CTA, ChemAb, ChemTitl, ChemoAb, CurCont, D01, DBA, E08, E12, E17, EMBASE, ESPM, EntAb, ExcerpMed, F08, F11, F12, FCA, FR, FS&TA, G01, G03, G08, G11, GH, GSA, GSI, GenetAb, GeoRef, H09, H10, H16, H17, HGA, HPNRM, I05, I11, IABS, IBR, IBZ, INIS AtomInd, ISR, ImmunAb, IndMed, IndVet, Inpharma, Inspec, JW-D, JW-ID, Kidney, LT, M06, MEDLINE, MLA-IB, MS&D, MaizeAb, MathR, MycolAb, N02, N03, N04, N05, NRN, NSA, NucAcAb, O01, OGFA, OR, OceAb, P02, P03, P10, P11, P13, P26, P30, P32, P33, P34, P35, P37, P38, P39, P40, P48, P52, P53, P54, P56, PGegResA, PGrRegA, PHN&I, PN&I, PQC, PollutAb, PsycInfo, PsycholAb, R07, R08, R10, R11, R12, R13, RA&MP, RASB, RM&VM, RRTA, Reac, RefZh, S&MA, S01, S05, S06, S08, S09, S10, S12, S13, S16, S17, SCI, SCOPUS, SSciA, SoyAb, SpeleolAb, T02, T05, TAR, THA, Telegen, TriticAb, VITIS, VS, VirolAbstr, W03, W07, W08, W10, W11, WildRev, Z01, Z02.
—BLDSC (6762.000000), CASDDS, GNLM, IE, Infotrieve, Ingenta, INIST, Linda Hall. **CCC.**
Published by: National Academy of Sciences, 500 Fifth St, NW, Washington, DC 20001. TEL 202-334-2000, 888-624-6242, FAX 202-334-2793, subspnas@nas.edu. Ed. Randy R Schekman. Pub. Kenneth R Fulton. adv.: B&W page USD 1,840, color page USD 2,935; trim 7 x 10. Circ: 10,132.

500 USA ISSN 1071-8966
Q11
NATIONAL ASSOCIATION OF ACADEMIES OF SCIENCE. DIRECTORY, PROCEEDINGS AND HANDBOOK. Text in English. 1977. a. USD 15. back issues avail.
Former titles: National Association of Academies of Science. Proceedings, Directory and Handbook (0739-361X); Association of Academies of Science. Directory and Proceedings
Published by: National Association of Academies of Science, Science Division, Northeast Missouri State University, Kirksville, MO 63501. TEL 816-785-4618, FAX 816-785-4045. Ed. James H Shaddy. Circ: 500.

623 JPN ISSN 0388-4112
Q1 CODEN: MNDEDH
NATIONAL DEFENSE ACADEMY. MEMOIRS. MATHEMATICS, PHYSICS, CHEMISTRY AND ENGINEERING/BOEI DAIGAKKO KIYO RIKOGAKU-HEN. Text in English. 1956. 4/yr. free. abstr.; charts; illus. Index. back issues avail. **Document type:** *Journal, Academic/Scholarly.*
Formerly (until 1980): Defense Academy. Memoirs (0025-9136)
Indexed: CIS, ChemAb, ChemTitl, Inspec, MathR, Z02.
—BLDSC (5626.650000), AskIEEE, CASDDS, IE, Ingenta, INIST, Linda Hall.
Published by: National Defense Academy, Hashirimizu 1-10-20, Yokosuka, Kanagawa 239-8686, Japan. Circ: 700.

NATIONAL GEOGRAPHIC (THAI EDITION). *see* GEOGRAPHY

NATIONAL GEOGRAPHIC BRASIL. *see* GEOGRAPHY

500 028.5 USA ISSN 1930-8116
NATIONAL GEOGRAPHIC YOUNG EXPLORER. (Grades Kindergarten - 1) Text in English. 2006 (Sept.). 7/yr. USD 3.95 (effective 2009). back issues avail. **Document type:** *Magazine, Consumer.* **Description:** Provides the students of grades K-1 with curriculum-related topics in science and social studies that help them to develop their critical reading skills.
Related titles: Online - full text ed.: ISSN 1930-8124. 2006 (Sept.); Series: National Geographic Young Explorer (Pathfinder Edition); National Geographic Young Explorer (Pioneer Edition).
Indexed: P01.
Published by: National Geographic Society, PO Box 98199, Washington, DC 20090. TEL 800-647-5463, askngs@nationalgeographic.com.

500 JPN ISSN 0386-555X
➤ **NATIONAL INSTITUTE OF POLAR RESEARCH. MEMOIRS. SERIES F: LOGISTICS.** Text and summaries in English. 1964. irreg., latest vol.5, 1997. per issue exchange basis. **Document type:** *Monographic series, Academic/Scholarly.*
Supersedes: Japanese Antarctic Research Expedition, 1956-1962. Scientific Reports. Series F: Logistics (0075-3408)
—INIST, Linda Hall.
Published by: National Institute of Polar Research/Kokuritsu Kyokuchi Kenkyujo, Publications, 10-3, Midoricho, Tachikawa, Tokyo, 190-8518, Japan. FAX 81-3-39622225, publication402@nipr.ac.jp, http://www.nipr.ac.jp/. Ed. Okitsugu Watanabe. Circ: 1,000.

507 USA ISSN 1936-6035
NATIONAL PATTERNS OF R & D RESOURCES (ONLINE). Text in English. 1989. irreg., latest 2008. free (effective 2010). back issues avail. **Document type:** *Government.* **Description:** Contains information and analysis about the money and people devoted to research and development, including comparisons of U.S. performance with the efforts underway around the globe.
Media: Online - full text.
Published by: U.S. Department of Commerce, National Science Foundation, 4201 Wilson Blvd, Ste 245, Arlington, VA 22230. TEL 703-292-5111, 800-877-8339, info@nsf.gov.

500 600 EGY ISSN 1110-0591
Q1 CODEN: BNRCET
➤ **NATIONAL RESEARCH CENTRE. BULLETIN.** Text in English; Summaries in Arabic, English. 1976. 4/yr. USD 147 (effective 2002). reprint service avail. from IRC. **Document type:** *Journal, Academic/Scholarly.* **Description:** Original papers in chemistry and the physical and biological sciences.
Indexed: A34, A35, A36, A37, A38, AgBio, AgrForAb, B23, B25, BA, BIOSIS Prev, BP, C25, C30, CABA, CIN, ChemAb, ChemTitl, D01, E12, F08, F11, F12, FCA, G11, GH, GeoRef, H16, H17, I11, IndVet, LT, MaizeAb, MycolAb, N02, N03, N04, N05, O01, OR, P32, P33, P37, P38, P39, P40, PGegResA, PGrRegA, PHN&I, R07, R08, R11, R13, RA&MP, RM&VM, RRTA, S12, S13, S16, S17, SoyAb, SpeleolAb, T05, TriticAb, VS, W10.
—BLDSC (2641.770000), CASDDS.
Published by: (National Research Centre), National Information and Documentation Centre (NIDOC), Tahrir St., Dokki, Awqaf P.O., Giza, Egypt. TEL 20-2-3371696. Ed. Dr. Salah Muhammad Abdel-Dayem.

500 CAN ISSN 0842-6066
Q180.C2
NATIONAL RESEARCH COUNCIL OF CANADA. N R C ANNUAL REPORT - RAPPORT ANNUEL DU C N R C. Text in English, French. 1916. a. free. **Document type:** *Corporate.*
Former titles (until 1984): National Research Council. Annual Report (0823-5759); (until 1980): National Research Council of Canada. Report of the President - Rapport du President (0373-904X); (until 1968): National Research Council of Canada. Annual Report (0369-5484); (until 1967): National Research Council of Canada. Report (0228-6300); (until 1965): National Research Council of Canada. Annual Report (0228-6319); (until 1930): National Research Council of Canada. Report of the President and Financial Statement; (until 1924): Honourary Advisory Council for Science and Industrial Research of Canada. Report
Indexed: RASB.
—INIST. **CCC.**
Published by: National Research Council of Canada, Corporate Services, M 58, Ottawa, ON K1A 0R6, Canada. TEL 613-993-9101, FAX 613-952-9696. Circ: 6,000.

500 THA ISSN 0028-0011
CODEN: JRCTAF
➤ **NATIONAL RESEARCH COUNCIL OF THAILAND. JOURNAL.** Text in English, Thai. 1960. s-a. THB 100 domestic; USD 30 foreign (effective 2010). charts; illus.; stat. **Document type:** *Journal, Academic/Scholarly.* **Description:** Publishes research in many areas of the natural and social sciences.
Indexed: BAS, ChemAb, FS&TA, GeoRef, Inspec.
—BLDSC (4831.150000), AskIEEE, CASDDS, INIST, Linda Hall.
Published by: National Research Council of Thailand, 196 Phahonyothin Rd, Chatuchak, Bangkok, 10900, Thailand. TEL 66-2-579-7775, 66-2-940-7051, FAX 66-2-579-0455, TELEX 82213-NARECOU-TH, rrdt@email.nrct.go.th. Circ: 1,500 (paid and controlled).

500 TWN
Q72.5
NATIONAL SCIENCE COUNCIL REVIEW. Text in English. 1965. a. free. 170 p./no.; back issues avail.; reprints avail. **Document type:** *Government.*
Formerly (until 1990): N S C Review (0255-4399)
Related titles: Microfiche ed.; Online - full content ed.
Indexed: GeoRef, SpeleolAb.
—GNLM, Linda Hall.
Published by: National Science Council/Xingzhengyuan Guojia Kexue Weiyuanhui, Rm 1701, 106 Ho-Ping E. Rd, Sec 2, Taipei, Taiwan. TEL 886-2-27377594, FAX 886-2-27377248, ylchang@nsc.gov.tw, http://www.nsc.gov.tw. Circ: 3,200 (paid).

500 001.44 USA
NATIONAL SCIENCE FOUNDATION. ACTIVE FUNDING OPPORTUNITIES. Abbreviated title: N S F E-Bulletin. Text in English. 1998. irreg. free (effective 2010). back issues avail. **Document type:** *Government.* **Description:** Provides information on the due dates of NSF grants and other funding opportunities.
Formerly (until 2005): National Science Foundation. E-Bulletin
Media: Online - full text.
Published by: U.S. Department of Commerce, National Science Foundation, 4201 Wilson Blvd, Ste 245, Arlington, VA 22230. TEL 703-292-5111, 800-877-8339, info@nsf.gov.

500 LKA ISSN 1391-4588
Q4 CODEN: JNSFFU
NATIONAL SCIENCE FOUNDATION OF SRI LANKA. JOURNAL. Text in English. 1999. q. USD 80 (effective 2003). reprints avail.
Formerly (until 1999): National Science Council of Sri Lanka. Journal (0300-9254)
Indexed: A29, ASFA, B20, B21, B25, BIOSIS Prev, CIN, CTA, ChemAb, ChemTitl, ChemoAb, ESPM, FS&TA, GeoRef, I10, MycolAb, NSA, PST, SCI, SCOPUS, SLSI, SpeleolAb, VirolAbstr, W07, Z01, Z02.
—BLDSC (4831.175000), CASDDS, Linda Hall. **CCC.**
Published by: National Science Foundation of Sri Lanka, 47-5 Maitland Place, Colombo, 7, Sri Lanka. TEL 94-1-694170. Ed. Shyamalee Perera.

500 JPN ISSN 1342-9574
NATIONAL SCIENCE MUSEUM MONOGRAPHS. Text in English. 1994. irreg. (4-6/yr.). **Document type:** *Monographic series, Academic/Scholarly.*
Indexed: B25, BIOSIS Prev, GeoRef, MycolAb.
—Linda Hall.
Published by: Kokuritsu Kagaku Hakubutsukan/National Science Museum, Tokyo, 7-20 Ueno-Koen, Taito-ku, Tokyo, 110-0007, Japan. TEL 81-3-57778600, FAX 81-3-58149898, http://www.kahaku.go.jp/.

500 TWN ISSN 1607-5722
NATIONAL TAIWAN MUSEUM SPECIAL PUBLICATION SERIES. Text in English. 1983. irreg. **Document type:** *Monographic series, Academic/Scholarly.*
Formerly (until 1990): Taiwan Museum Special Publication Series (1010-1683)
Indexed: Z01.
—INIST.
Published by: National Taiwan Museum/Guoli Taiwan Bowuguan, No.2, Siangyang Rd., Taipei City, 100, Taiwan. TEL 886-2-23711052, FAX 886-2-23822684, http://www.ntm.gov.tw/.

500 BLR ISSN 1561-8323
Q60 CODEN: DBLRAC
➤ **NATSIYANAL'NAYA AKADEMIYA NAVUK BELARUSI. DOKLADY/ NATIONAL ACADEMY OF SCIENCES OF BELARUS. PAPERS.** Text in Russian, English. 1957. bi-m. bibl.; charts; illus. index. **Document type:** *Journal, Academic/Scholarly.* **Description:** Publishes short communications on new finished and previously not published original and especially prior experimental and theoretical investigations in the field of mathematics, informatics, physics, chemistry, biology, earth sciences and engineering.
Formerly (until 1992): Akademiya Navuk Belarusskai S.S.R. Doklady (0002-354X)
Indexed: CCMJ, CIN, CIS, ChemAb, ChemTitl, GeoRef, INIS AtomInd, Inspec, MSN, MathR, RASB, SpeleolAb, Z01, Z02.
—CASDDS, East View, INIST, Linda Hall. **CCC.**
Published by: (Natsiyanal'naya Akademiya Navuk Belarusi/National Academy of Sciences of Belarus), Vydavetstvo Belaruskaya Navuka/Publishing House Belaruskaya Navuka, ul F. Skaryny, 40, Minsk, 220141, Belarus. TEL 375-17-2633700, FAX 375-17-2637618, belnauka@infonet.by, http://www.belnauka.by. Ed. M V Myasnikovich. Circ: 400.

500 BLR
NATSIYANAL'NAYA AKADEMIYA NAVUK BELARUSI. SPRAVAZDACHA AB DZEINASTSI/NATIONAL ACADEMY OF SCIENCES OF BELARUS. ANNUAL REPORT. Text in Belorussian. a. **Document type:** *Academic/Scholarly.*
Published by: (Natsiyanal'naya Akademiya Navuk Belarusi/National Academy of Sciences of Belarus), Vydavetstvo Belaruskaya Navuka/Publishing House Belaruskaya Navuka, ul F. Skaryny, 40, Minsk, 220141, Belarus. TEL 375-17-2633700, FAX 375-17-2637618, belnauka@infonet.by. Ed. Fiodor Lakhvich.

500 BLR ISSN 1819-1444
NATSIYANAL'NAYA AKADEMIYA NAVUK BELARUSI. VEDY. Text in Russian, Belorussian. 1979. w. BYB 65,400 domestic to individuals; BYB 96,816 domestic to institutions (effective 2011). **Document type:** *Newspaper, Academic/Scholarly.* **Description:** Devoted to science in the Republic of Belarus. HIghlights the activities of research teams, organizations and educational institutions. Presents the achievements of scientists, news from the world of science, interviews with famous scientists, statesmen.
Former titles (until 1997): Natsiyanal'naya Akademiya Navuk Belarusi. Naviny; (until 1996): Belaruskaya Akademiya. Naviny; (until 1990): Za Peredovuyu Nauku
Published by: (Natsiyanal'naya Akademiya Navuk Belarusi/National Academy of Sciences of Belarus), Vydavetstvo Belaruskaya Navuka/Publishing House Belaruskaya Navuka, ul F. Skaryny, 40, Minsk, 220141, Belarus. TEL 375-17-2633700, FAX 375-17-2637618, belnauka@infonet.by. Ed. Sergey Dubovik.

508 ISL ISSN 0028-0550
NATTURUFRAEDINGURINN. Text in Icelandic; Summaries in English. 1930. q. ISK 3,500 (effective 2006). bk.rev. charts; illus. index. back issues avail. **Document type:** *Magazine, Academic/Scholarly.* **Description:** Research papers and reviews on the natural history of Iceland. Includes articles of more general interest.
Indexed: ASFA, B21, B25, BIOSIS Prev, ChemAb, ESPM, GeoRef, MycolAb, SpeleolAb, Z01.
Published by: Hid Islenska Natturufraedifelag/Icelandic Natural History Society, Hlemmur 3, Reykjavik, 105, Iceland. TEL 354-5900500, FAX 354-5900595, hin@hin.is, http://www.hin.is. Ed. Sigmundur Einarsson. Circ: 1,900.

508 ISL ISSN 1027-832X
NATTURUFRAEDISTOFNUN ISLANDS. FJOELRIT. Text in Icelandic; Summaries in English. 1985. irreg. (2-4/yr.). price varies. **Document type:** *Monographic series, Academic/Scholarly.*
Indexed: Z01.
—Linda Hall.
Published by: Natturufraedistofnun Islands/Icelandic Institute of Natural History, Hlemmur 3, PO Box 5320, Reykjavik, 125, Iceland. TEL 354-562-9822, 354-590-0500, FAX 354-590-0595. Ed. Erling Olafsson.

500 CHE ISSN 1018-2462
NATUR-MUSEUM LUZERN. VEROEFFENTLICHUNGEN. Text in German. 1991. irreg. **Document type:** *Monographic series, Academic/Scholarly.*
Indexed: Z01.
Published by: Natur-Museum Luzern, Kasernenplatz 6, Luzern, 6003, Switzerland. TEL 41-41-2285411, info@naturmuseum.ch, http://www.naturmuseum.ch.

505 DNK ISSN 0028-0585
QH7
NATUR OG MUSEUM. Text in Danish. 1951. q. DKK 198 (effective 2009). charts; illus. back issues avail. **Document type:** *Monographic series, Academic/Scholarly.* **Description:** Natural history with emphasis on Danish conditions and subjects.
Indexed: Z01.
Published by: Naturhistorisk Museum/Natural History Museum, Wilhelm Meyers Alle 210, Universitetsparken, Aarhus C, 8000, Denmark. TEL 45-86-129777, FAX 45-86-130882, nm@nathist.dk, http://www.naturhistoriskmuseum.dk.

500.9 DEU ISSN 0028-0593
QH5 CODEN: NTRHAA
NATUR UND HEIMAT. Text in German. 1934. 4/yr. bibl.; charts; illus.; maps. **Document type:** *Journal, Academic/Scholarly.*
Indexed: IBR, IBZ, RefZh, Z01.
Published by: Westfaelisches Landesmuseum mit Planetarium, Sentruper Str 285, Muenster, 48161, Germany. TEL 49-251-59105, FAX 49-251-5916098, naturkundemuseum@lwl.org, http://www.lwl.org/LWL/Kultur/WMfN. Ed. Dr. Bernd Tenbergen.

500.9 AUT ISSN 0028-0607
NATUR UND LAND; Zeitschrift des Oesterreichischen Naturschutzbundes. Text in German. 1913. q. EUR 16 domestic; EUR 21 foreign; EUR 3 newsstand/cover (effective 2005). adv. bk.rev.; music rev.; video rev.; Website rev. charts; illus.; stat. index. back issues avail.; reprints avail. **Document type:** *Magazine, Consumer.*
Formerly (until 1946): Blaetter fuer Naturkunde und Naturschutz Niederoesterreichs (1021-3554)
Indexed: EnvAb, IBR, IBZ.
Published by: Naturschutzbund Oesterreich, Museumsplatz 2, Salzburg, 5020, Austria. TEL 43-662-64290913, FAX 43-662-6437344, natur-land@naturschutzbund.at, http://www.naturschutzbund.at. Ed., Adv. contact Ingrid Hagenstein. Circ: 7,000 (paid and controlled).

500.9 DEU ISSN 0028-1301
QH5 CODEN: NAMUAR
NATUR UND MUSEUM. Text in German. 1867. bi-m. free to members (effective 2010). adv. bk.rev. charts; illus. index. back issues avail. **Document type:** *Journal, Academic/Scholarly.* **Description:** Contains papers of general interest on the entire field of natural sciences.
Indexed: ASFA, B21, ChemAb, ESPM, GeoRef, IBR, IBZ, P30, RefZh, SpeleolAb, W08, WildRev, Z01.
—Ingenta, INIST, Linda Hall. **CCC.**
Published by: Senckenbergische Naturforschende Gesellschaft/ Senckenberg Nature Research Society, Senckenberganlage 25, Frankfurt Am Main, 60325, Germany. TEL 49-69-75420, FAX 49-69-746238, sjessel@senckenberg.de. Ed., Adv. contact Thorsten Wenzel. Circ: 6,000.

500 ITA ISSN 0369-6243
QH7 CODEN: NTRMAP
NATURA; rivista di scienze naturali. Text in Italian. 1909. s-a. free to members (effective 2009). adv. bk.rev. index. back issues avail. **Document type:** *Monographic series, Academic/Scholarly.*
Indexed: B25, BIOSIS Prev, ChemAb, FR, GeoRef, MinerAb, MycolAb, P30, RefZh, SpeleolAb, WildRev, Z01.
—INIST, Linda Hall.
Published by: Societa Italiana di Scienze Naturali, Corso Venezia 55, Milan, MI 20121, Italy. TEL 39-02-795965, FAX 39-02-795965, http://www.scienzenaturali.org. Ed. Stefania Nosotti. **Co-sponsor:** Museo Civico di Storia Naturale di Milano.

500.9 VEN ISSN 0028-064X
QH7 CODEN: NTRCBU
NATURA; revista trimestral de divulgacion cientifica, tecnica y cultural. Text in Spanish. 1958. q. adv.
Indexed: ASFA, B21, C01, ESPM, GeoRef, IBR, IBZ, SpeleolAb.
Published by: Fundacion la Salle de Ciencias Naturales, Ave. Boyaca-Mariperez, Piso 5, Apdo 1930, Carcacas, 1010A, Venezuela. Ed. Jose A Monente. Circ: 1,200.

508 NLD ISSN 0028-0631
NATURA. Text in Dutch. 1906. bi-m. EUR 40 domestic; EUR 42 in Belgium; EUR 50 elsewhere; EUR 8 newsstand/cover (effective 2009). adv. bk.rev. charts; illus. index. **Description:** Covers all aspects of natural history.
Indexed: Z01.
—IE, Infotrieve.
Published by: Koninklijke Nederlandse Natuurhistorische Vereniging, Postbus 310, Zeist, 3707 BM, Netherlands. TEL 31-30-2314797, FAX 31-30-2368907, bureau@knnv.nl.

500 ITA ISSN 0391-156X
QH152
NATURA BRESCIANA. Text in Italian. 1965. a. **Document type:** *Journal, Academic/Scholarly.*
Indexed: B25, BIOSIS Prev, GeoRef, MycolAb, Z01.
—INIST.
Published by: Comune di Brescia, Museo Civico di Scienze Naturali, Via Ozanam 4, Brescia, Italy. TEL 39-030-2978672.

508 708.9 HRV ISSN 1330-0520
QH178.C73 CODEN: NACRE6
NATURA CROATICA; periodicum musei historiae naturalis Croatici - casopis Hrvatskoga prirodslovnog muzeja. Text in English; Summaries in English, Croatian. 1992. q. HRK 280 domestic; USD 35 foreign (effective 2000). bk.rev. charts; illus.; bibl.; maps; stat. index. back issues avail. **Document type:** *Bulletin.* **Description:** Includes articles, review papers, short communications, and checklists on zoology, botany, paleontology, and minerology (systematics, ecology, morphology, and biometry).
Related titles: ◆ Supplement(s): Natura Croatica. Supplementum. ISSN 1330-3430.
Indexed: A29, A34, A38, ASFA, AgrForAb, B20, B21, B25, BIOSIS Prev, C25, C30, CABA, E12, E17, ESPM, EntAb, F08, F12, FCA, G11, GEOBASE, GH, H16, H17, I10, I11, IndVet, MycolAb, O01, P32, P33, P37, P39, P40, P48, P52, P56, PGegResA, PN&I, PQC, R07, R08, RA&MP, S13, S16, SCOPUS, SoyAb, TAR, VS, VirolAbstr, W10, Z01.
Published by: Hrvatski Prirodoslovni Muzej/Croatian Natural History Museum, Demetrova 1, Zagreb, 10000, Croatia. TEL 385-1-4851700, FAX 385-1-4851644. Ed. Josip Balabanic.

508 ITA ISSN 1127-2716
NATURA MODENESE. Text in Italian. 1991. a. **Document type:** *Journal, Academic/Scholarly.*
Indexed: Z01.
Published by: Centro Italiano Studi Nidi Artificiali (C I S N I A R), Piazza Matteotti 28, Marano sul Panaro, MO 41054, Italy. museo.sc.nat@libero.it, http://www.cisniar.it.

500 ARG ISSN 0329-2177
➤ **NATURA NEOTROPICALIS**; revista de la Asociacion de Ciencias del Litoral. Text in Spanish; Summaries in English. 1970. a. (in 2 vol.), latest vol.32. USD 30 (effective 2010). adv. bk.rev. index, cum.index: 1970-1976; 1977-1981; 1982-1986; 1987-1995. 100 p./no.; back issues avail. **Document type:** *Journal, Academic/Scholarly.* **Description:** Publishes research papers, critical reviews and short notes on natural sciences.
Formerly (until 1997): Asociacion de Ciencias Naturales del Litoral. Revista (0325-2809)
Indexed: A29, ASFA, B20, B21, C01, ChemoAb, E17, ESPM, EntAb, GenetAb, HGA, I10, SCOPUS, SWRA, VirolAbstr, Z01.
—CCC.
Published by: Asociacion de Ciencias Naturales del Litoral, J Macia, 1933, Santo Tome, Santa Fe 3016, Argentina. TEL 54-342-4740723, FAX 54-342-4759394, acnlit@ceride.gov.ar. Ed., R&P Elly Cordiviola de Yuan. Adv. contact Raul D'Angelo. Circ: 600 (paid and controlled).

500 ITA ISSN 1826-3933
NATURA SEGRETA. Text in Italian. 2005. s-a. **Document type:** *Magazine, Consumer.*
Published by: Delta Editrice, Borgo Regale 21, Parma, PR 43100, Italy. TEL 39-0521-287883, FAX 39-0521-237546.

500.9 USA ISSN 0028-0712
QH1 CODEN: NAHIAX
NATURAL HISTORY. Text in English. 1900. 10/yr. USD 22 (effective 2009). adv. bk.rev. bibl.; illus. index. reprints avail. **Document type:** *Magazine, Consumer.* **Description:** Contains essays and articles written by professional scientists and scholars on the biological sciences, ecology, anthropology, archeology, earth sciences, astronomy.
Formerly (until 1919): The American Museum Journal (1049-1112); Incorporates (in 1960): Nature Magazine
Related titles: CD-ROM ed.; Microform ed.: (from PQC); Online - full text ed.
Indexed: A01, A02, A03, A06, A08, A11, A20, A21, A22, A25, A26, A28, A33, ABS&EES, AICP, APA, APD, ARG, AbAn, AcaI, Agr, B04, B05, B14, B21, BIOSIS Prev, BRD, BRI, BibAg, BiolDig, BrCerAb, C&ISA, C05, C12, CA, CA/WCA, CBRI, CIA, CPerI, CRFR, CerAb, ChLitAb, CivEngAb, CorrAb, CurCont, E&CAJ, E04, E05, E08, E11, EEA, EIA, EMA, ESPM, EnerInd, EnerRev, EnvAb, EnvEAb, EnvInd, FR, G01, G03, G05, G06, G07, G08, GSA, GSI, GardL, GeoRef, H05, H09, H10, H15, I05, I06, I07, ISR, JHMA, KWIWR, M&TEA, M01, M02, M06, M09, MASUSE, MBF, MEA&I, METADEX, MLA-IB, MagInd, MycolAb, P02, P10, P11, P13, P15, P19, P26, P30, P48, P52, P53, P54, P56, PQC, PRA, R03, R04, R06, RASB, RGAb, RGPR, RI-1, RI-2, RILM, S04, S05, S06, S08, S09, S10, S23, SCI, SCOPUS, SPPI, SolStAb, SpeleolAb, T02, T04, TOM, W03, W05, W07, W08, WAA, WBA, WMB, WildRev.
—BLDSC (6038.000000), IE, Infotrieve, Ingenta, INIST, Linda Hall.
Published by: (American Museum of Natural History), Natural History Magazine, Inc. (Subsidiary of: American Museum of Natural History), 36 W 25th St, 5th Fl, New York, NY 10010. TEL 646-356-6500, FAX 646-356-6511. Eds. Avis Lang, Peter Brown. Pub. Charles Harris. R&P Jennifer Evans. adv.: B&W page USD 13,500, color page USD 18,000; trim 8.125 x 10.5. Circ: 250,000 (paid). **Dist. in UK by:** Comag, Tavistock Rd, W Drayton, Middlesex UB7 7QE, United Kingdom. TEL 44-1895-433600, FAX 44-189-543-3606.

508 JPN ISSN 0915-9452
QH7
➤ **NATURAL HISTORY MUSEUM AND INSTITUTE, CHIBA. JOURNAL.** Text in English, Japanese. 1990. a. per issue exchange basis. back issues avail. **Document type:** *Journal, Academic/Scholarly.* **Description:** Contains original articles and reviews on natural history.
Indexed: B25, BIOSIS Prev, GeoRef, MycolAb, P30, SpeleolAb, Z01.
Published by: Natural History Museum and Institute Chiba, 955-2 Aoba-cho, Chuo-ku, Chiba-shi, 260-0852, Japan. TEL 81-43-265-3111, FAX 81-43-266-2481. Circ: 1,500 (controlled).

508.074 GBR ISSN 1746-1022
QH70.G72
NATURAL HISTORY MUSEUM. ANNUAL REVIEW. Text in English. 198?. a. free (effective 2009). back issues avail.; reprints avail. **Document type:** *Corporate.*
Formerly (until 2003): Natural History Museum. Annual Report (1368-1702); Which was formed by the merger of (1966-1997): Natural History Museum. Triennial Report (1360-0761); (1966-1997): British Museum (Natural History). Triennial Report (1359-0766); Both of which superseded in part (in 198?): British Museum (Natural History). Report (0524-6474)
Related titles: Online - full text ed.
Indexed: BrArAb, GeoRef, SpeleolAb.
—Linda Hall.
Published by: (Natural History Museum), Cambridge University Press, The Edinburgh Bldg, Shaftesbury Rd, Cambridge, CB2 8RU, United Kingdom. TEL 44-1223-312393, FAX 44-1223-315052, journals@cambridge.org, http://www.cambridge.org/uk.

505 USA ISSN 0076-0943
➤ **NATURAL HISTORY MUSEUM OF LOS ANGELES COUNTY. SCIENCE SERIES.** Text in English. 1930. irreg., latest vol.39, 2001. bk.rev. illus. index. **Document type:** *Proceedings, Academic/ Scholarly.* **Description:** Contains topics in science.
Related titles: Online - full text ed.: free (effective 2010).
Indexed: B25, BIOSIS Prev, GeoRef, MycolAb, SpeleolAb, Z01.
—Linda Hall.
Published by: Natural History Museum of Los Angeles County, 900 Exposition Blvd, Los Angeles, CA 90007. TEL 213-763-3426, FAX 213-763-3583, info@nhm.org.

508 CAN ISSN 0838-5971
NATURAL HISTORY OCCASIONAL PAPER. Text in English. 1976. irreg., latest vol.23, 1996. price varies. **Document type:** *Monographic series, Academic/Scholarly.*
Published by: Royal Alberta Museum, 12845-102 Ave, Edmonton, AB T5N 0M6, Canada. TEL 780-453-9100, FAX 780-454-6629, http://www.royalalbertamuseum.ca.

508 JPN ISSN 0915-9444
QH1 CODEN: NHREEN
➤ **NATURAL HISTORY RESEARCH.** Text in English. 1990. a. per issue exchange basis. back issues avail. **Document type:** *Journal, Academic/Scholarly.* **Description:** Contains original articles and reviews on natural history.
Indexed: B25, BIOSIS Prev, GeoRef, MycolAb, SCOPUS, SpeleolAb, Z01.
—Ingenta.
Published by: Natural History Museum and Institute Chiba, 955-2 Aoba-cho, Chuo-ku, Chiba-shi, 260-0852, Japan. TEL 81-43-265-3111, FAX 81-43-266-2481. Circ: 1,500 (controlled).

500.9 GBR ISSN 0144-221X
QH1 CODEN: TNHND5
➤ **NATURAL HISTORY SOCIETY OF NORTHUMBRIA. TRANSACTIONS.** Text in English. 1831. a. free to members (effective 2009). charts; illus. cum.index. back issues avail. **Document type:** *Proceedings, Academic/Scholarly.* **Description:** Covers all aspects of natural history of northern England.
Former titles (until 1974): Natural History Society of Northumberland, Durham and Newcastle upon Tyne. Transactions (0958-8280); (until 1904): Natural History Transactions of Northumberland, Durham and Newcastle; (until 1838): Natural History Society of Northumberland Durham and Newcastle upon Tyne. Transactions (0028-0720)
Indexed: A29, ASFA, B20, B21, B25, BIOSIS Prev, ESPM, GeoRef, I10, MycolAb, SCOPUS, SpeleolAb, VirolAbstr, Z01.
—BLDSC (8986.020000), INIST, Linda Hall.
Published by: Natural History Society of Northumbria, Great North Museum: Hancock, Newcastle upon Tyne, Northd NE2 4PT, United Kingdom. TEL 44-191-2326386, nhsn@ncl.ac.uk.

500 USA ISSN 2150-4091
Q1.A3
▼ **NATURAL SCIENCE.** Abbreviated title: N S. Text in English. 2009. q. USD 50 per issue (effective 2009). adv. back issues avail.; reprints avail. **Document type:** *Journal, Academic/Scholarly.* **Description:** Provides a platform for scientists and academicians all over the world to promote, share, and discuss various new issues and developments in different areas of natural sciences.
Related titles: Online - full text ed.: ISSN 2150-4105. free (effective 2011).
Indexed: A01, A26, A34, A35, A36, A38, AgrForAb, C25, C30, CABA, E08, E12, F08, FCA, GH, H16, I05, LT, N02, N04, P32, P33, R07, R08, S09, S13, T02, T05.
Published by: Scientific Research Publishing, Inc., 5005 Paseo Segovia, Irvine, CA 92603. service@scirp.org. Ed. Kuo-Chen Chou.

508 CHE ISSN 2076-0779
▼ ➤ **NATURAL SCIENCES.** Text in English. forthcoming 2011. q. free (effective 2011). **Document type:** *Journal, Academic/Scholarly.*
Media: Online - full text.
Published by: M D P I AG, Postfach, Basel, 4005, Switzerland. TEL 41-61-6837734, FAX 41-61-3028918, http://www.mdpi.org/.

507.11 CAN ISSN 1702-1359
CA1NS1
NATURAL SCIENCES AND ENGINEERING RESEARCH COUNCIL OF CANADA. ANNUAL REPORT. Variant title: N S E R C Annual Report. Text and summaries in English, French. 1978. a. free. adv. **Document type:** *Government.*
Former titles: Natural Sciences and Engineering Research Council of Canada. Highlights (1207-0734); (until 1992): Natural Sciences and Engineering Research Council of Canada. Report of the President (0225-2376)
Published by: Natural Sciences and Engineering Research Council of Canada/Conseil de Recherches en Sciences Naturelles et en Genie du Canada, 350 Albert St, Ottawa, ON K1A 1H5, Canada. TEL 613-995-5992, FAX 613-943-0742, http://www.nserc-crsng.gc.ca. Ed. Joyce French. R&P Victor Wallwark. Adv. contact Monique Martin. Circ: 4,000.

500 CAN ISSN 1910-460X
NATURAL SCIENCES AND ENGINEERING RESEARCH COUNCIL OF CANADA. CONTACT (ONLINE). Text in English. 1994. q. **Document type:** *Newsletter, Trade.*
Formerly (until 2004): N S E R C Contact (Online) (1493-6380)
Media: Online - full text. **Related titles:** ◆ Print ed.: Natural Sciences and Engineering Research Council of Canada. Contact (Print). ISSN 1714-7425; French ed.: Conseil de Recherches en Sciences Naturelles et en Genie du Canada. Contact. ISSN 1910-4618.
Published by: Natural Sciences and Engineering Research Council of Canada/Conseil de Recherches en Sciences Naturelles et en Genie du Canada, 350 Albert St, Ottawa, ON K1A 1H5, Canada. TEL 613-995-4273, http://www.nserc-crsng.gc.ca. Ed. Joyce French.

500 CAN ISSN 1714-7425
NATURAL SCIENCES AND ENGINEERING RESEARCH COUNCIL OF CANADA. CONTACT (PRINT)/CONSEIL DE RECHERCHES EN SCIENCES NATURELLES ET EN GENIE DU CANADA. CONTACT. Text in English. 1976. q.
Former titles (until 2004): N S E R C Contact (Print) (1188-066X); (until 1999): Natural Sciences and Engineering Research Council Canada. Contact (0225-5332); (until 1978): National Research Council Canada. Contact (0225-5324)
Related titles: ◆ Online - full text ed.: Natural Sciences and Engineering Research Council of Canada. Contact (Online). ISSN 1910-460X.
Published by: Natural Sciences and Engineering Research Council of Canada/Conseil de Recherches en Sciences Naturelles et en Genie du Canada, 350 Albert St, Ottawa, ON K1A 1H5, Canada. TEL 613-995-4273, http://www.nserc-crsng.gc.ca.

NATURAL SCIENCES AND ENGINEERING RESEARCH COUNCIL OF CANADA. LIST OF SCHOLARSHIPS AND GRANTS IN AID OF RESEARCH/CONSEIL DE RECHERCHES EN SCIENCES NATURELLES ET EN GENIE DU CANADA. LISTE DES BOURSES ET SUBVENTIONS DE RECHERCHE. *see* EDUCATION—Higher Education

NATURAL SCIENCES AND ENGINEERING RESEARCH COUNCIL OF CANADA. PROGRAM GUIDE FOR STUDENTS AND FELLOWS. *see* EDUCATION—Higher Education

508 ESP ISSN 2172-0525
▼ **NATURALAE MAGAZINE.** Text in Spanish. 2010. m. **Document type:** *Journal, Academic/Scholarly.*
Media: Online - full text.

S

Published by: Forum Natura, Gral. Martinex Campos, 15, Madrid, 28010, Spain. TEL 34-91-4466533, FAX 34-91-4476433, redaccion@forumnatura.org.

500.9 TTO
NATURALIST. Text in English. 1975. bi-m. USD 35. adv. bk.rev. illus.; stat. index. back issues avail.
Formerly: Trinidad Naturalist (0379-4016)
Published by: (Field Naturalists Club of Trinidad & Tobago), S.M. Publications Publishing House, 20 Collens Rd, Maraval, Port-of-Spain, Trinidad, Trinidad & Tobago. TEL 809 622-6625. Ed. Stephen Mohammed. Circ: 20,000.

500 AUS ISSN 1448-238X
THE NATURALIST NEWS. Text in English. 1960. 11/yr. **Document type:** *Newsletter.*
Published by: Western Australian Naturalists' Club Inc., PO Box 8257, Perth, W.A. 6849, Australia. TEL 61-8-92282495, FAX 61-8-92282496, wanats@iinet.net.au, http://www.wanats.iinet.net.au.

508 ITA ISSN 0394-0063
QH152
IL NATURALISTA SICILIANO. Text in Italian. 1881. q. **Document type:** *Journal, Academic/Scholarly.*
Indexed: A22, GeoRef, Z01.
—BLDSC (6042.500000), IE, Ingenta.
Published by: Societa Siciliana di Scienze Naturali, Via Archirafi 18, Palermo, 90123, Italy. TEL 39-091-6230133, mgup@unipa.it.

500.9 CAN ISSN 0028-0798
CODEN: NCANAS
➤ **LE NATURALISTE CANADIEN**; revue d'ecologie et de systematique. Text in English, French. 1868. q. free to members. bk.rev. charts; illus. index, cum.index: vols.1-96 (1868-1969). reprints avail. **Document type:** *Journal, Academic/Scholarly.*
Indexed: A33, APD, ChemAb, ESPM, GeoRef, PdeR, SWRA, SpeleolAb, WildRev, Z01.
—CASDDS, Ingenta, INIST, Linda Hall. **CCC.**
Published by: Societe Provancher d'Histoire Naturelle du Canada, 1400 Route de l'Aeroport, Quebec, PQ G2G 1G6, Canada. Ed. Michel Crete.

500 JPN ISSN 0914-028X
NATURALISTS. Text in Japanese. 1987. irreg.
Published by: Shizen Kagaku Kenkyukai, Shikoku Joshi Daigaku Seibutsugaku Kyoshitsu, 123-1 Ebisuno, Furukawa, Ojin-cho, Tokushima, 771-11, Japan.

508 GBR ISSN 0962-6360
NATURALISTS' HANDBOOKS. Text in English. 19??. irreg. price varies. back issues avail. **Document type:** *Monographic series, Academic/Scholarly.* **Description:** Provides what an investigator needs to make novel discoveries about local plants and animals.
—BLDSC (6044.265000).
Published by: The Company of Biologists Ltd., 140 Cowley Rd, Cambridge, CB4 0DL, United Kingdom. TEL 44-1223-426164, FAX 44-1223-423353, sales@biologists.com, http://www.biologists.org.

500 GBR ISSN 0028-0836
Q1 CODEN: NATUAS
➤ **NATURE**; international weekly journal of science. Text in English. 1869. w. EUR 2,609 in Europe to institutions; USD 3,280 in the Americas to institutions; GBP 1,685 to institutions in the UK & elsewhere (effective 2011). adv. bk.rev. abstr.; bibl.; charts; illus.; tr.lit. index. back issues avail.; reprints avail. **Document type:** *Journal, Academic/Scholarly.* **Description:** Provides research in all fields of science and technology. Also provides news and interpretation of topical and coming trends affecting science, scientists and the wider public.
Incorporates (1971-1973): Nature. Physical Science (0300-8746); (1971-1973): Nature. New Biology (0090-0028); Both of which superseded in part (in 1971): Nature (0028-0836)
Related titles: Braille ed.; CD-ROM ed.; Microform ed.: (from PMC, PQC); Online - full text ed.: ISSN 1476-4687; Talking Book ed.; ◆ Supplement(s): Nurture. ISSN 1746-4366; ◆ Nature Genetics. ISSN 1061-4036.
Indexed: A&ATA, A01, A02, A03, A08, A11, A20, A22, A25, A26, A28, A29, A32, A33, A34, A35, A36, A37, A38, ABC, ABIPC, AESIS, AIA, AICP, AIDS Ab, AMED, APA, APD, ASFA, AcaI, AgBio, Agr, AgrForAb, AnBeAb, ApMecR, B&AI, B03, B04, B07, B10, B14, B20, B21, B23, B25, BA, BAS, BDM&CN, BIOBASE, BIOSIS Prev, BP, BPRC&P, BRD, BRI, BibAg, BiolDig, Biostat, BrArAb, BrCerAb, BrGeoL, BrTechI, C&CR, C&ISA, C05, C13, C25, C30, C31, C33, CA, CA/WCA, CABA, CBRI, CBTA, CEABA, CIA, CIN, CIS, CISA, CPerI, CRFR, CTA, CTD, Cadscan, CerAb, ChemAb, ChemTitl, ChemoAb, CivEngAb, CorrAb, CurCR, CurCont, D01, DBA, DIP, DentInd, DiabCont, E&CAJ, E-psyche, E04, E05, E06, E08, E11, E12, E17, EEA, EIA, EMA, EMBASE, ESPM, EngInd, EntAb, EnvAb, EnvEAb, EnvInd, ExcerpMed, F08, F11, F12, FCA, FR, FS&TA, FoVS&M, FutSurv, G01, G03, G08, G10, G11, GEOBASE, GH, GSA, GSI, GenetAb, GeoRef, H04, H09, H10, H12, H15, H16, H17, HECAB, HGA, HPNRM, I05, I10, I11, IABS, IBR, IBZ, IMMAb, INI, ISMEC, ISR, IndChem, IndMed, IndVet, Inpharma, Inspec, JW-D, JW-ID, JW-N, JW-P, Kidney, L11, LT, LeadAb, M&GPA, M&TEA, M01, M02, M09, MASUSE, MBF, MEA&I, MEDLINE, METADEX, MLA-IB, MOS, MSN, MaizeAb, MathR, MinerAb, MycolAb, N02, N03, N04, N05, NPU, NRN, NSA, NucAcAb, NumL, O01, OR, OceAb, P02, P03, P10, P11, P13, P15, P20, P22, P24, P25, P26, P30, P32, P33, P34, P35, P37, P38, P39, P40, P43, P48, P52, P53, P54, P56, PGegResA, PGrRegA, PHN&I, PMR, PN&I, PQC, PRA, PetrolAb, PhilInd, PollutAb, PsycInfo, PsycholAb, R04, R07, R08, R10, R11, R12, R13, R16, RA&MP, RASB, RILM, RM&VM, RRTA, Reac, RefZh, S01, S02, S03, S05, S06, S08, S09, S10, S12, S13, S16, S17, SCI, SCOPUS, SPPI, SSciA, SWRA, SolStAb, SoyAb, SpeleolAb, T02, T04, T05, TAR, TM, Telegen, TriticAb, VITIS, VS, VirolAbstr, W03, W07, W08, W09, W10, W11, WAA, WBA, WMB, WildRev, Z01, Zincscan.
—BLDSC (6045.000000), AskIEEE, CASDDS, GNLM, IE, Infotrieve, Ingenta, INIST, Linda Hall, PADDS. **CCC.**
Published by: Nature Publishing Group (Subsidiary of: Macmillan Publishers Ltd.), The MacMillan Bldg, 4 Crinan St, London, N1 9XW, United Kingdom. TEL 44-20-78334000, FAX 44-20-78334640. Ed. Dr. Philip Campbell. Adv. contact Andy Douglas TEL 44-22-78434975.
Subscr. to: Brunel Rd, Houndmills, Basingstoke, Hamps RG21 6XS, United Kingdom. TEL 44-1256-329242, FAX 44-1256-812358, subscriptions@nature.com.

500 USA ISSN 1545-0740
QH1
➤ **NATURE AND SCIENCE.** Text in English. 2003 (Oct). m. free (effective 2010). back issues avail. **Document type:** *Journal, Academic/Scholarly.* **Description:** Contains original contributions, reviews and scientific opinions and debates in all scientific fields.
Related titles: Online - full text ed.
Indexed: A01.
Published by: Marsland Press, PO Box 21126, Lansing, MI 48909. TEL 347-321-7172, sciencepub@gmail.com. Ed. Hongbao Ma TEL 347-321-7172.

500 610 GBR ISSN 1751-5793
NATURE CHINA. Text in English. 2007. m. free (effective 2010). back issues avail. **Document type:** *Journal, Academic/Scholarly.* **Description:** Bring out the research being produced in Hong Kong and Mainland China in science and clinical medicine.
Media: Online - full text.
—CCC.
Published by: Nature Publishing Group (Subsidiary of: Macmillan Publishers Ltd.), The MacMillan Bldg, 4 Crinan St, London, N1 9XW, United Kingdom. TEL 44-20-78334000, FAX 44-20-78334640. Ed. Felix Man Ho Cheung.

500 GBR ISSN 2041-1723
QH301
▼ **NATURE COMMUNICATIONS.** Text in English. 2010 (Apr.). **Document type:** *Journal, Academic/Scholarly.* **Description:** Covers research across the biological, chemical and physical sciences.
Media: Online - full text.
Indexed: A22, B25, BIOSIS Prev, C33, CurCont, E01, MEDLINE, P30, SCI, SCOPUS, W07, Z01.
—CCC.
Published by: Nature Publishing Group (Subsidiary of: Macmillan Publishers Ltd.), The MacMillan Bldg, 4 Crinan St, London, N1 9XW, United Kingdom. TEL 44-20-78334000, FAX 44-20-78433601. Ed. Lesley Anson.

500 JPN ISSN 1880-0556
NATURE DIGEST. Text in Japanese. 2004. m. JPY 7,980 (effective 2008). **Document type:** *Journal, Academic/Scholarly.*
Formerly (until 2004): Nature Gekkan Daijesuto (1348-8449)
Related titles: Online - full text ed.: JPY 6,000 (effective 2008).
—CCC.
Published by: Neicha Japan Neicha ajia Pashifikku/N P G Nature Asia - Pacific Nature Japan (Nature Publishing Group), KK Chiyoda Bldg. 6F, 2-37 Ichigayatamachi, Shinjuku-ku, Tokyo, 162-0843, Japan. TEL 81-3-32678751, FAX 81-3-32678746, nature@naturejpn.com, http://www.natureasia.com/.

502 GBR
➤ **NATURE IN AVON.** Spine title: Proceedings of the Bristol Naturalists Society. Text in English. 1862. a., latest vol.66, 2006. adv. **Document type:** *Proceedings, Academic/Scholarly.* **Description:** Studies the natural history and geology of the Bristol area.
Former titles (until 1994): Bristol Naturalists' Society. Proceedings (0068-1040); (until 1935): Bristol Naturalists' Society. Annual Report and Proceedings
Indexed: GeoRef, SpeleolAb, Z01.
—BLDSC (6046.255000), INIST.
Published by: Bristol Naturalists' Society, c/o City Museum & Art Gallery, Queens Rd, Bristol, BS8 1RL, United Kingdom. info@bristolnats.org.uk, http://www.bristolnats.org.uk/. Circ: 600.

500 610 GBR ISSN 1755-3180
NATURE INDIA. Text in English. 2007. m. free (effective 2010). back issues avail. **Document type:** *Newsletter, Academic/Scholarly.*
Media: Online - full text.
—CCC.
Published by: Nature Publishing Group (Subsidiary of: Macmillan Publishers Ltd.), The MacMillan Bldg, 4 Crinan St, London, N1 9XW, United Kingdom. TEL 44-20-78434624, FAX 44-20-78433601, NatureReviews@nature.com. Ed. Subhra Priyadarshini.

500 GBR ISSN 1548-7091
QH319.A1 CODEN: NMAEA3
NATURE METHODS; techniques for life scientists and chemists. Text in English. 2004 (Oct.). m. EUR 2,297 in Europe to institutions; USD 2,890 in the Americas to institutions; GBP 1,481 to institutions in the UK & elsewhere (effective 2011). adv. back issues avail.; reprints avail. **Document type:** *Journal, Academic/Scholarly.* **Description:** Provides primary research papers as well as overviews of recent technical and methodological developments, and detailed descriptions of important established methods.
Related titles: Online - full text ed.: ISSN 1548-7105.
Indexed: A01, A20, A26, A29, A40, ASFA, B&BAb, B19, B20, B21, B25, B27, BIOBASE, BIOSIS Prev, BioEngAb, C33, CA, CurCont, EMBASE, ESPM, EntAb, ExcerpMed, GenetAb, H12, I05, IABS, MEDLINE, MycolAb, NSA, P11, P20, P22, P26, P30, P48, P52, P54, P56, PQC, R10, Reac, SCI, SCOPUS, T02, VirolAbstr, W07.
—IE, Ingenta. **CCC.**
Published by: Nature Publishing Group (Subsidiary of: Macmillan Publishers Ltd.), The MacMillan Bldg, 4 Crinan St, London, N1 9XW, United Kingdom. TEL 44-20-78334000, FAX 44-20-78334640. Ed. Daniel Evanko. Adv. contact Andy Douglas TEL 44-22-78434975.
Subscr. to: Brunel Rd, Houndmills, Basingstoke, Hamps RG21 6XS, United Kingdom. TEL 44-1256-329242, FAX 44-1256-812358, subscriptions@nature.com.

508 USA ISSN 0890-3735
NATURE SOCIETY NEWS; North America's backyard journal. Text in English. 1966. m. USD 15 domestic; USD 20 in Canada (effective 2000). bk.rev. illus. **Document type:** *Newspaper.*
Former titles: Purple Martin News; Purple Martin Capital News
Published by: Nature Society, PO Box 390, Griggsville, IL 62340. TEL 217-833-2323, FAX 217-833-2123, natsoc@adams.net, http://www.naturesociety.org. Ed., R&P Karen E Martin.

NATURE STRUCTURAL AND MOLECULAR BIOLOGY. *see* BIOLOGY

501 CAN
NATURE VIEWS. Text in English. 1963. 4/yr. CAD 30 foreign (effective 2001); Comes with membership & Blue Jay subscription. adv. Website rev. abstr.; illus. Not indexed. back issues avail. **Document type:** *Newspaper, Academic/Scholarly.* **Description:** Concerns society activities and current environmental and conservation issues in Saskatchewan.
Former titles: Blue Jay News (0822-9988); (until 1983): Saskatchewan Natural History Society Newsletter (0581-8443)
Published by: Nature Saskatchewan, 1860 Lorne St, Rm 206, Regina, SK S4P 2L7, Canada. TEL 306-780-9273, FAX 306-780-9263, http://www.nature.sask.com. Ed. Paule Hjertaas. adv.: B&W page CAD 400. Circ: 4,500.

500.9 NOR ISSN 0028-0887
Q4 CODEN: NTUNA9
NATUREN; populaervitenskapelig tidsskrift. Text in Norwegian, Danish, English, Swedish. 1877. bi-m. NOK 599 to individuals; NOK 599 to institutions; NOK 325 to students (effective 2010). bk.rev. charts; illus. index. back issues avail. **Document type:** *Journal, Academic/Scholarly.* **Description:** Covers all fields of natural sciences.
Incorporates (in 1996): Vaer og Klima (0803-3293); Which was formerly: Vaeret (0332-5040)
Related titles: Online - full text ed.: ISSN 1504-3118. 2004. NOK 699 (effective 2010).
Indexed: ChemAb, EnerRA, GeoRef, INIS AtomInd, NAA, SpeleolAb, Z01.
—CASDDS, INIST.
Published by: (Universitetet i Bergen/University of Bergen), Universitetsforlaget AS/Scandinavian University Press (Subsidiary of: Aschehoug & Co.), Sehesteds Gate 3, P O Box 508, Sentrum, Oslo, 0105, Norway. TEL 47-24-147500, FAX 47-24-147501, post@universitetsforlaget.no. Ed. Per Jakobsen. Circ: 1,100.

NATURFAG. *see* EDUCATION—Teaching Methods And Curriculum

500 CHE ISSN 1421-5551
NATURFORSCHENDE GESELLSCHAFT DES KANTONS SOLOTHURN. MITTEILUNGEN. Text in German. 1899. irreg. price varies. **Document type:** *Monographic series, Academic/Scholarly.*
Formerly (until 1963): Naturforschende Gesellschaft Solothurn. Mitteilungen (1421-5543)
Indexed: Z01.
Published by: Naturforschende Gesellschaft des Kantons Solothurn, Hofmatt 105, Bruegglen, 4582, Switzerland. TEL 41-32-6611377, p.berger@bluewin.ch, http://www.naturmuseum-so.ch/03_prog/3nfg.html#.

500 CHE ISSN 0373-384X
NATURFORSCHENDE GESELLSCHAFT GRAUBUENDEN. JAHRESBERICHT. Text in German. 1856. a. **Document type:** *Journal, Academic/Scholarly.*
Indexed: Z01.
—INIST.
Published by: Naturforschende Gesellschaft Graubuenden, Masanserstr 31, Chur, 7000, Switzerland. TEL 41-81-2572841, info@bnm.gr.ch, http://www.naturmuseum.gr.ch/index.php/ngg.

500 CHE ISSN 0077-6130
Q67 CODEN: MNGBAK
NATURFORSCHENDE GESELLSCHAFT IN BERN. MITTEILUNGEN. Text in German; Summaries in English, French. 1843. a. CHF 40 (effective 2000). adv. cum.index: 1944-1968 in no.26 (1969). **Document type:** *Bulletin, Academic/Scholarly.*
Indexed: B25, BIOSIS Prev, GeoRef, IBR, IBZ, MycolAb, RefZh, SpeleolAb, VITIS, Z01.
—INIST, Linda Hall.
Published by: Naturforschende Gesellschaft in Bern, c/o Stadt- und Universitaetsbibliothek, Muenstergasse 61, PO Box 958, Bern 7, 3000, Switzerland. TEL 41-31-3203211, FAX 41-31-3203299. Ed. Urs Brodbeck. Circ: 1,400.

500.9 CHE ISSN 0042-5672
Q67 CODEN: VNGZAL
NATURFORSCHENDE GESELLSCHAFT IN ZUERICH. VIERTELJAHRESSCHRIFT. Text in German. 1826. q. CHF 90 (effective 2010). adv. bk.rev. bibl.; charts; illus. index. **Document type:** *Journal, Academic/Scholarly.*
Former titles (until 1856): Naturforschende Gesellschaft in Zuerich. Mittheilungen (0257-2745); (until 1847): Naturforschende Gesellschaft. Bericht ueber die Verhandlungen (1421-8704)
Indexed: B25, BIOSIS Prev, ChemAb, GeoRef, IBR, IBZ, INIS AtomInd, MycolAb, SpeleolAb, Z01.
—BLDSC (9235.903000), CASDDS, INIST, Linda Hall. **CCC.**
Published by: Naturforschende Gesellschaft in Zuerich, Limmatstr 6, Vogelsang, 5300, Switzerland. TEL 41-56-3102647. Eds. Conradin Burga, Frank Kloetzli.

500 CHE ISSN 0373-3092
NATURFORSCHENDE GESELLSCHAFT SCHAFFHAUSEN. MITTEILUNGEN. Text in English, French, German. 1922. a. CHF 40 (effective 2000). bk.rev. illus. **Document type:** *Journal, Academic/Scholarly.* **Description:** Contains original articles concerning scientific subjects.
Indexed: SpeleolAb, Z01.
Published by: Naturforschende Gesellschaft Schaffhausen, Postfach, Schaffhausen, 8201, Switzerland. Ed. Ingo Rieger. Pub. Erich Hammer. Circ: 700 (paid).

500 DEU ISSN 0028-0917
Q49 CODEN: BEFBAZ
NATURFORSCHENDE GESELLSCHAFT ZU FREIBURG. BERICHTE. Text in German. 1855. a. EUR 22 per vol. (effective 2003). bk.rev. charts; illus. index, cum.index: 1855-1955. back issues avail. **Document type:** *Journal, Academic/Scholarly.* **Description:** Covers various natural sciences as they relate to the southwestern region of Germany.
Indexed: GeoRef, IBR, IBZ, SpeleolAb, VITIS, Z01.
—Linda Hall.
Published by: Naturforschende Gesellschaft Freiburg, Postfach 1629, Freiburg Im Breisgau, 79016, Germany. FAX 49-761-2033864, tausch@ub.uni-freiburg.de, http://www.naturforschende-gesellschaft.uni-freiburg.de. Ed. Dr. Hugo Genser. Circ: 800.

500 551 560 CHE
NATURHISTORISCHES MUSEUM BASEL. VEROEFFENTLICHUNGEN. Text in German. 1960. irreg. back issues avail. **Document type:** *Monographic series.*
Published by: Naturhistorisches Museum Basel, Augustinergasse 2, Basel, 4001, Switzerland. FAX 41-61-2665546. Circ: 2,500.

500.9 CHE ISSN 0253-4401
CODEN: JNMBEL
NATURHISTORISCHES MUSEUM BERN. JAHRBUCH. Text in English, French, German. 1960. triennial. CHF 75 (effective 2001). bk.rev. illus. back issues avail. **Document type:** *Corporate.* **Description:** Contains activity reports and miscellaneous articles (original papers and reports on collections) in the fields of mineralogy, palaeontology, invertebrate and vertebrate zoology and anthropology.
Indexed: GeoRef, KWIWR, SpeleolAb, WildRev, Z01.
Published by: Naturhistorisches Museum, Bernastr 15, Bern, 3005, Switzerland. TEL 41-31-3507111, FAX 41-31-3507499, contact@nmbe.ch. Ed. Marcel Guentert. Circ: 250.

500 AUT ISSN 0255-0091
QE1 CODEN: ANAPE6
➤ **NATURHISTORISCHES MUSEUM IN WIEN. ANNALEN. SERIE A, MINERALOGIE UND PETROGRAPHIE, GEOLOGIE UND PALAEONTOLOGIE, ANTHROPOLOGIE UND PRAEHISTORIE.** Text in English, French, German; Summaries in English, German. 1886. a. price varies. bk.rev. abstr.; illus.; maps. index. back issues avail. **Document type:** *Journal, Academic/Scholarly.*
Supersedes in part (in 1980): Naturhistorisches Museum in Wien. Annalen (0083-6133)
Indexed: ASFA, B21, B25, BIOSIS Prev, ESPM, GeoRef, MycolAb, RefZh, SPPI, SpeleolAb, Z01.
—INIST, Linda Hall. **CCC.**
Published by: Naturhistorisches Museum in Wien, Burgring 7, Postfach 417, Vienna, W 1014, Austria. TEL 43-1-52177-497, FAX 43-1-52177-229. Ed. Ortwin Schultz. Circ: 1,200.

570 AUT
NATURHISTORISCHES MUSEUM IN WIEN. KATALOGE DER WISSENSCHAFTLICHEN SAMMLUNGEN. Text and summaries in English, German. 1978. irreg., latest vol.15, 2000. price varies. adv. bk.rev. illus.; maps. back issues avail. **Document type:** *Catalog, Trade.* **Description:** Provides catalog of collections for scientists, taxonomists and museums.
Published by: Naturhistorisches Museum in Wien, Burgring 7, Postfach 417, Vienna, W 1014, Austria. TEL 43-1-52177-497, FAX 43-1-52177-229, http://www.nhm-wien.ac.at. Adv. contact Ernst Vitek.

500.9 AUT ISSN 0378-8202
NATURHISTORISCHES MUSEUM IN WIEN. VEROEFFENTLICHUNGEN. NEUE FOLGE. Text in German. 1958. irreg., latest vol.28, 2000. price varies. **Document type:** *Proceedings, Academic/Scholarly.*
Indexed: SpeleolAb, Z01.
Published by: Naturhistorisches Museum in Wien, Burgring 7, Postfach 417, Vienna, W 1014, Austria. TEL 43-1-52177-497, FAX 43-1-52177-229, http://www.nhm-wien.ac.at.

500 AUT ISSN 0470-3901
NATURKUNDLICHES JAHRBUCH DER STADT LINZ. Text in German; Abstracts in English. 1955. a. EUR 28 (effective 2008). illus. back issues avail. **Document type:** *Yearbook, Trade.* **Description:** Presents scientific papers of interest to professionals in the fields of biology and ecology.
Related titles: E-mail ed.; Fax ed.; Online - full text ed.
Indexed: KWIWR, SpeleolAb.
Published by: Amt fuer Natur- und Umweltschutz, Naturkundliche Station, Roseggerstr 20, Linz, 4020, Austria. TEL 43-732-70701862, FAX 43-732-7070541862, nast@mag.linz.at, http://www.linz.at/umwelt/3880.asp. Ed. Gerold Laister. Circ: 400.

NATURVITEREN. *see* LABOR UNIONS

500.9 DEU ISSN 0028-1042
Q3 CODEN: NATWAY
➤ **NATURWISSENSCHAFTEN.** Text in English. 1886. m. EUR 1,080, USD 1,311 combined subscription to institutions (print & online eds.) (effective 2012). adv. reprint service avail. from PSC. **Document type:** *Journal, Academic/Scholarly.* **Description:** Aims to inform those working in scientific fields, either as researchers or teachers, about what interests them outside their own fields.
Formerly (until 1913): Naturwissenschaftliche Rundschau (0178-1049); Which incorporated (1865-1909): Gaea (0178-1057); (1882-1890): Humboldt (0933-1921); Which incorporated (1877-1887): Kosmos (0933-1913)
Related titles: Microform ed.: (from PMC, PQC); Online - full text ed.: ISSN 1432-1904 (from IngentaConnect).
Indexed: A&ATA, A20, A22, A26, A29, A34, A35, A36, A38, ASCA, ASFA, AgBio, AgrForAb, AnBeAb, ApMecR, ApicAb, B20, B21, B23, B25, BA, BIOSIS Prev, BP, C25, C30, C33, CA, CABA, CEABA, CIN, CRFR, CTA, ChemAb, ChemTitl, ChemoAb, CurCR, CurCont, DBA, E01, E12, E17, EMBASE, ESPM, EntAb, ExcerpMed, F08, F11, F12, FCA, FS&TA, G11, GEOBASE, GH, GenetAb, GeoRef, H16, H17, I10, I11, IBR, IBZ, ISR, IndChem, IndMed, IndVet, Inpharma, Inspec, MEDLINE, MaizeAb, MycolAb, N02, N03, N04, N05, NSA, O01, OR, OceAb, P30, P32, P33, P37, P38, P39, P40, PGegResA, PGrRegA, PHN&I, PhilInd, PollutAb, R07, R08, R10, R11, R13, R16, RA&MP, RASB, RILM, RM&VM, Reac, S12, S13, S16, S17, SCI, SCOPUS, SWRA, SoyAb, SpeleolAb, T02, T05, TAR, TriticAb, VITIS, VS, VirolAbstr, W07, W08, W10, W11, WildRev, Z01.
—BLDSC (6049.000000), AskIEEE, CASDDS, GNLM, IE, Infotrieve, Ingenta, INIST, Linda Hall. **CCC.**
Published by: (Max-Planck-Institut fuer Gesellschaft zur Foerderung der Wissenschaften), Springer (Subsidiary of: Springer Science+Business Media), Tiergartenstr 17, Heidelberg, 69121, Germany. TEL 49-6221-4870, FAX 49-6221-345229. Ed. Sven Thatje. adv.: B&W page EUR 850, color page EUR 1,890. Circ: 600 (paid and controlled). **Subscr. in the Americas to:** Springer New York LLC, Journal Fulfillment, PO Box 2485, Secaucus, NJ 07096. TEL 800-777-4643, 201-348-4033, FAX 201-348-4505, journals-ny@springer.com, http://www.springer.com; **Subscr. to:** Springer Distribution Center, Kundenservice Zeitschriften, Haberstr 7, Heidelberg 69126, Germany. TEL 49-6221-3454303, FAX 49-6221-3454229, subscriptions@springer.com. **Co-sponsor:** Gesellschaft Deutscher Naturforscher und Aerzte.

580 DEU ISSN 0138-1636
NATURWISSENSCHAFTLICHE BEITRAEGE DES MUSEUMS DESSAU. Text in German. 1978. irreg. price varies. **Document type:** *Monographic series, Academic/Scholarly.*
Related titles: Supplement(s): Naturwissenschaftliche Beitraege des Museums Dessau. Sonderheft. ISSN 0863-646X. 1980.
Published by: Museum fuer Naturkunde und Vorgeschichte Dessau, Askanische Str 32, Dessau, 06842, Germany. TEL 49-340-214824, FAX 49-340-2303465, museum@naturkunde.dessau.de.

500 DEU ISSN 1435-6511
NATURWISSENSCHAFTLICHE FORSCHUNGSERGEBNISSE. Text in German. 1991. irreg., latest vol.78, 2008. price varies. **Document type:** *Monographic series, Academic/Scholarly.*
Published by: Verlag Dr. Kovac, Leverkusenstr 13, Hamburg, 22761, Germany. TEL 49-40-3988800, FAX 49-40-39888055, info@verlagdrkovac.de.

500.9 DEU ISSN 0028-1050
Q3 CODEN: NARSAC
➤ **NATURWISSENSCHAFTLICHE RUNDSCHAU.** Abbreviated title: N R. Text in German. 1948. m. EUR 158; EUR 96 to students; EUR 16 newsstand/cover (effective 2012). adv. bk.rev. bibl.; charts; illus. index. **Document type:** *Journal, Academic/Scholarly.* **Description:** Covers all fields of science: biology, medicine, pharmacy, chemistry, physics, astronomy and geography.
Indexed: A22, ASFA, B21, CIN, ChemAb, ChemTitl, DBA, DIP, ESPM, GeoRef, IBR, IBZ, P30, SCOPUS, SpeleolAb, VITIS.
—BLDSC (6049.275000), CASDDS, GNLM, IE, Infotrieve, INIST, Linda Hall. **CCC.**
Published by: Wissenschaftliche Verlagsgesellschaft mbH, Postfach 101061, Stuttgart, 70009, Germany. TEL 49-711-25820, FAX 49-711-2582290, service@wissenschaftliche-verlagsgesellschaft.de, http://www.wissenschaftliche-verlagsgesellschaft.de. Adv. contact Kornelia Wind TEL 49-711-2582245. Circ: 2,820 (paid).

500 DEU ISSN 0077-6165
Q49 CODEN: SNSHAS
➤ **NATURWISSENSCHAFTLICHER VEREIN FUER SCHLESWIG-HOLSTEIN. SCHRIFTEN.** Text in German, English. 1870. a. bk.rev. charts; illus. back issues avail. **Document type:** *Journal, Academic/Scholarly.* **Description:** Presents research on all aspects of natural history in the Schleswig-Holstein region of Germany.
Related titles: Online - full text ed.: ISSN 1867-7428. free (effective 2011).
Indexed: ASFA, B21, ESPM, GeoRef, RefZh, SpeleolAb, Z01.
—Linda Hall.
Published by: Naturwissenschaftlicher Verein fuer Schleswig-Holstein e.V., c/o Dr. Walter Doerfler, Olshausenstr 40, Kiel, 24098, Germany. TEL 49-431-8804059, FAX 49-431-8807300, wdoerfler@ufg.uni-kiel.de, http://www.nwvsh.uni-kiel.de. Ed. Elena Nikulina.

500.9 AUT ISSN 0369-1136
Q44 CODEN: MNVSAA
➤ **NATURWISSENSCHAFTLICHER VEREIN FUER STEIERMARK. MITTEILUNGEN.** Text in German. 1863. a. bk.rev. charts; illus. index, cum.index. back issues avail. **Document type:** *Journal, Academic/Scholarly.* **Description:** Covers such subjects as mineralogy, petrology, geology, paleontology, geography, climatology, biology, botany and zoology.
Indexed: GeoRef, RefZh, SpeleolAb, VITIS, WildRev, Z01.
—INIST.
Published by: Naturwissenschaftlicher Verein fuer Steiermark, Universitaetsbibliothek, Universitaetsplatz 3, Graz, St 8010, Austria. TEL 43-316-3805649, FAX 43-316-3809883, anton.drescher@kfunigraz.ac.at, karl.ettinger@ktunigraz.ac.at. Eds. A Drescher, K Stuewe. Pub., R&P Georg Hoinkes TEL 43-316-3805540. Circ: 600. **Dist. by:** Institute of Mineralogy, Universitaetsplatz 2, Graz, St 8010, Austria. TEL 43-316-3805552, FAX 43-316-9865.

508 NLD ISSN 0028-1107
NATUURHISTORISCH MAANDBLAD. Text occasionally in English, French, German; Summaries in English; Text mainly in Dutch. 1911. m. EUR 82.50 to institutions (effective 2010). bk.rev. illus. **Document type:** *Journal, Academic/Scholarly.* **Description:** Covers research in the biology and the geology of Limburg. Includes association news, reports, lists of events.
Indexed: B25, BIOSIS Prev, GeoRef, MycolAb, SpeleolAb.
Published by: (Natuurhistorisch Genootschap in Limburg), Publicatie Bureau N H G, Godsweerderstraat 2, Roemond, 6041 GH, Netherlands. TEL 31-475-386470, kantoor@nhgl.nl, http://www.nhgl.nl.

505 NLD ISSN 1573-6083
Q4 CODEN: NATTAP
NATUURWETENSCHAP & TECHNIEK. Text in Dutch. 1932. m. (11/yr.). EUR 81.25; EUR 7.45 newsstand/cover (effective 2009). adv. bk.rev. illus. index. **Document type:** *Consumer.*
Formerly (until 2003): Natuur en Techniek (0028-1093)
Indexed: CIN, CISA, ChemAb, ChemTitl, INIS AtomInd.
—BLDSC (6190.657000), CASDDS, IE, Infotrieve.
Published by: Veen Magazines, Postbus 256, Diemen, 1110 AG, Netherlands. TEL 31-20-5310900, FAX 31-20-5310950, http://www.veenmagazines.nl. Ed. Erwin van den Brink. Pub. Erno Eskens. adv.: B&W page EUR 2,100, color page EUR 3,335; trim 210 x 280. Circ: 21,407.

500 POL ISSN 1231-8515
AS261
NAUKA; czasopismo poswiecone rozwojowi nauki w Polsce. Text in Polish. 1953. q. EUR 86 foreign (effective 2005). bk.rev. charts; illus. index. **Document type:** *Journal, Academic/Scholarly.* **Description:** Devoted to the development and achievements of Polish science.
Formerly (until 1994): Nauka Polska (0028-1271)
Indexed: AgrLib, FR, HistAb, IBR, IBSS, IBZ, RASB.
—INIST, Linda Hall.
Published by: Polska Akademia Nauk/Polish Academy of Sciences, Palac Kultury i Nauki, Warsaw, 00901, Poland. TEL 48-22-6204970, FAX 48-22-6204910, http://www.pan.pl. Circ: 1,400. **Dist. by:** Ars Polona, Obroncow 25, Warsaw 03933, Poland. TEL 48-22-5098609, FAX 48-22-5098610, arspolona@arspolona.com.pl, http://www.arspolona.com.pl.

500 BGR
NAUKA. Text in Bulgarian. bi-m. USD 60 foreign (effective 2002). **Description:** Publishes materials about scientific researches in the field of natural, human, social, and technical sciences.
Published by: Union of Bulgarian Scientists, Ul. Madrid 39, Sofia, 1505, Bulgaria. TEL 359-2-9441157, FAX 359-2-9441590, science@bitex.com. **Dist. by:** Sofia Books, ul Silivria 16, Sofia 1404, Bulgaria. TEL 359-2-9586257, info@sofiabooks-bg.com, http://www.sofiabooks-bg.com.

500 POL ISSN 0077-6181
CODEN: NAWSD6
NAUKA DLA WSZYSTKICH/SCIENCE FOR EVERYONE. Text in Polish. 1966. irreg., latest vol.495, 2000. price varies. adv. **Document type:** *Academic/Scholarly.* **Description:** Popular-science publication. Presents the latest achievements of all domains of science.
Indexed: AgrLib.
—CASDDS.
Published by: (Uniwersytet Jagiellonski), Wydawnictwo Collegium Columbinum, Ul Fatimska 10-9, Krakow, 31831, Poland. TEL 48-12-6414254, FAX 48-12-6414254, http://www.filg.uj.edu.pl. Ed., R&P, Adv. contact Waclaw Walecki.

▼ **NAUKA I EKONOMIKA.** *see* BUSINESS AND ECONOMICS

500 BLR
➤ **NAUKA I INNOVATSII.** Text in Russian, Belorussian; Summaries in English. 2003. m. **Document type:** *Journal, Academic/Scholarly.* **Description:** Aims to cover the most important problems of development of science and technology, but also innovation movement in Belarus and abroad.
Related titles: Online - full text ed.
Published by: (Natsiyanal'naya Akademiya Navuk Belarusi/National Academy of Sciences of Belarus), Vydavetstvo Belaruskaya Navuka/Publishing House Belaruskaya Navuka, ul F. Skaryny, 40, Minsk, 220141, Belarus. TEL 375-17-2633700, FAX 375-17-2637618, belnauka@infonet.by, http://www.belnauka.by. Ed. Zhanna Komarova.

➤ **NAUKA I RELIGIYA.** *see* RELIGIONS AND THEOLOGY

500 RUS ISSN 0028-1263
Q4
➤ **NAUKA I ZHIZN';** nauchno-populyarnyi zhurnal. Text in Russian. 1934. m. USD 131 foreign; RUR 70 newsstand/cover domestic (effective 2004). adv. bk.rev. bibl.; charts; illus.; maps. index. 144 p./no.; back issues avail.; reprints avail. **Document type:** *Magazine, Academic/Scholarly.* **Description:** Presents information on domestic and world science and technology, including humanities, natural and health sciences. Provides materials for self-education.
Related titles: Online - full text ed.
Indexed: CDSP, GeoRef, RASB, SpeleolAb.
—BLDSC (0119.300000), East View, Linda Hall.
Address: Myasnitskaya ul 24, Moscow, 101877, Russian Federation. TEL 7-095-9241835, FAX 7-095-2002259, nauka.msk@g23.relcom.ru, http://nauka.relis.ru/. Ed., Pub., R&P Igor K Lagovsky. Adv. contact Anna Magomaeva. Circ: 44,550. **Dist. by:** East View Information Services, 10601 Wayzata Blvd, Minneapolis, MN 55305. TEL 952-252-1201, 800-477-1005, FAX 952-252-1202, info@eastview.com, http://www.eastview.com.

500 RUS ISSN 0869-706X
Q60 CODEN: NASRDH
NAUKA V ROSSII. Text in Russian. 1981. bi-m. RUR 250 for 6 mos. domestic (effective 2004). adv. bk.rev. **Document type:** *Journal, Academic/Scholarly.* **Description:** Topics covered include: ecology, discoveries and inventions, human environment, museums, astronomy, agronomy, medical research, geochemistry, space technology and more.
Formerly: Nauka v S.S.S.R. (0203-4425)
Related titles: Online - full text ed.; German ed.; Spanish ed.; English ed.
Indexed: ChemAb, RASB.
—CASDDS.
Published by: (Rossiiskaya Akademiya Nauk/Russian Academy of Sciences), Izdatel'stvo Nauka, Profsoyuznaya ul 90, Moscow, 117864, Russian Federation. TEL 7-095-3347151, FAX 7-095-4202220, secret@naukaran.ru, http://www.naukaran.ru. Circ: 110,000.

500 RUS
NAUKA V SIBIRI. Text in Russian. w. USD 249 in United States.
Indexed: RASB.
Address: Morskoi pr-t 2, Novosibirsk, 630090, Russian Federation. TEL 3832-34-31-58. Ed. I Glotov. **Dist. by:** East View Information Services, 10601 Wayzata Blvd, Minneapolis, MN 55305. TEL 952-252-1201, 800-477-1005, FAX 952-252-1202, info@eastview.com, http://www.eastview.com.

500 UKR
➤ **NAUKOVI VISTI;** naukovo-tekhnichnyi zhurnal. Text in Ukrainian. 1997. q. **Document type:** *Journal, Academic/Scholarly.*
Published by: Natsional'nyi Tekhnichnyi Universytet Ukrainy "Kyivs'kyi Politekhnichnyi Instytut", pr-kt Peremohy 37, Kyiv, 03056, Ukraine. TEL 380-44-2367989, http://www.ntu-kpi.kiev.ua. Ed. M Z Zhurovs'kyi.

507.1 USA
THE NAVIGATOR (ONLINE). Text in English. 1969. q. free (effective 2010). adv. back issues avail. **Document type:** *Newsletter, Trade.* **Description:** Contains articles to improve science education and safety.
Former titles: The Navigator (Print); (until 1994): National Science Supervisors Association. Newsletter
Media: Online - full text.
Published by: National Science Education Leadership Association, c/o Jeffrey Patterson, Science Coordinator, Norman Public Schools, 131 S Flood, Norman, OK 73069. TEL 405-366-5832, FAX 405-573-3505, jefferyp@norman.k12.ok.us.

500 USA ISSN 0163-9013
CODEN: TNASBH
➤ **NEBRASKA ACADEMY OF SCIENCES AND AFFILIATED SOCIETIES. TRANSACTIONS.** Text in English. 1972. a. free to members (effective 2010). back issues avail. **Document type:** *Journal, Academic/Scholarly.* **Description:** Contains reviewed scientific articles relating to the objectives of the academy.
Formerly (until 1976): Nebraska Academy of Sciences. Transactions (0077-6351)
Related titles: Online - full text ed.
Indexed: A01, A26, A29, ASFA, Agr, B20, B21, B25, BIOSIS Prev, E08, ESPM, EntAb, G08, GeoRef, I05, I10, MycolAb, RASB, RefZh, S06, S09, SASA, SWRA, SpeleolAb, VITIS, VirolAbstr, WildRev, Z01.
—Ingenta, Linda Hall.
Published by: Nebraska Academy of Sciences, 302 Morrill Hall, 14th & U St, Lincoln, NE 68588. TEL 402-472-2644, FAX 402-472-8899, nebacad@unl.edu.

S

500 USA ISSN 1529-1162
Q11 CODEN: PNBAAP
NEBRASKA ACADEMY OF SCIENCES. PROGRAM AND PROCEEDINGS. Text in English. 18??. a. free to members (effective 2010). back issues avail. **Document type:** *Proceedings, Academic/Scholarly.* **Description:** Contains the abstracts of all papers presented at the annual meeting, the annual meeting program, periodic newsletters and other material of scientific interest.
Former titles (until 1999): Nebraska Academy of Sciences. Proceedings (0077-6343); (until 1969): Nebraska Academy of Sciences. Proceedings of the Annual Meeting (0191-2755)
Indexed: SpeleolAb, VITIS, WildRev.
—Linda Hall.
Published by: Nebraska Academy of Sciences, 302 Morrill Hall, 14th & U St, Lincoln, NE 68588. TEL 402-472-2644, FAX 402-472-8899, nebacad@unl.edu, http://www.neacadsci.org.

508 NLD ISSN 0926-4264
CODEN: NTINEL
NEDERLANDS TIJDSCHRIFT VOOR NATUURKUNDE. Text in Dutch. m. adv. bk.rev. charts; illus. **Document type:** *Newsletter, Academic/Scholarly.*
Formed by the 1991 merger of: Nederlands Tijdschrift voor Natuurkunde. Part A (0378-6374); Nederlands Tijdschrift voor Natuurkunde. Part B (0166-5987); Both of which superseded (in 1977): Nederlands Tijdschrift voor Natuurkunde (0028-2189)
Indexed: A22, CIN, ChemAb, ChemTitl, IBR, IBZ, INIS AtomInd, Inspec, P30, SpeleolAb.
—AskIEEE, CASDDS, IE, Infotrieve, INIST, Linda Hall.
Published by: Nederlandse Natuurkundige Vereniging, Postbus 41882, Amsterdam, 1009 DB, Netherlands. TEL 31-20-5922211, FAX 31-20-5925155, bureau@nnv.nl, http://www.nnv.nl. Eds. Esger Brunner, Miriam Blaauboer. adv.: page EUR 1,500; trim 210 x 297. Circ: 4,000.

500 NLD ISSN 0925-5621
T177.N4
NEDERLANDSE ORGANISATIE VOOR TOEGEPAST NATUURWETENSCHAPPELIJK ONDERZOEK. JAARVERSLAG. Short title: T N O Jaarverslag. Text in Dutch. 1981. a. **Document type:** *Journal, Corporate.* **Description:** Provides an overview of the financial status and the technological products, services and solutions provided by TNO.
Formerly (until 1987): Centrale Organisatie voor Toegepast Natuurwetenschappelijk Onderzoek. Jaarverslag (0920-5365); Which was formed by the 1981 merger of: T N O. 5: Gezondheidsorganisatie. Jaarverslag (0165-1560); T N O. 4: Rijksverdedigingsorganisatie. Jaarverslag (0165-151X); T N O. 3: Voedingsorganisatie. Jaarverslag (0165-1463); T N O. 2: Nijverheidsorganisatie (0165-1412); T N O. 1: Centrale Organisatie. Jaarverslag (0165-1617); Which was formed by the 1972 merger of: T N O. 1-A: Central Organisatie. Algemeen Gedeelte. Jaaverslag (0165-1315); T N O. 1-B: Centrale Organisatie. Commissies en Instellingen. Jaarverslag (0165-1366); All merged titles superseded in part: Centrale Organisatie T N O en de Nijverheidsorganisatie T N O, de Voedingsorganisatie T N O, de Rijksverdedigingsorganisatie T N O, de Gezondheidsorganisatie T N O. Jaarverslag (0374-8677); Which was formerly: Centrale Organisatie T N O ende Bijzondere Organisaties T N O. Jaarverslag
Related titles: English ed.: Netherlands Organization for Applied Scientific Research. Annual Review. ISSN 1383-360X.
—Linda Hall.
Published by: Nederlandse Organisatie voor Toegepast Natuurwetenschappelijk Onderzoek (TNO)/Netherlands Organization for Applied Scientific Research, Postbus 6000, Delft, 2600 JA, Netherlands. TEL 31-15-2696900, FAX 31-15-2612403, infodesk@tno.nl, http://www.tno.nl.

500 NLD
NEDERLANDSE ORGANISATIE VOOR WETENSCHAPPELIJK ONDERZOEK. JAARBOEK/NETHERLANDS ORGANISATION FOR THE ADVANCEMENT OF PURE RESEARCH. YEARBOOK. Text in Dutch. 1955. a. **Document type:** *Yearbook.*
Formerly (until 1988): Nederlandse Organisatie voor Zuiver-Wetenschappelijk Onderzoek. Jaarboek (0167-6792)
—BLDSC (4601.200000).
Published by: Nederlandse Organisatie voor Wetenschappelijk Onderzoek/Netherlands Organization for Scientific Research, PO Box 93138, The Hague, 2509 AC, Netherlands. TEL 31-70-3440640, FAX 31-70-3850971, nwo@nwo.nl, http://www.nwo.nl.

500 JPN ISSN 0287-3052
NEEDS. Text in Japanese. 1975. a. **Description:** News of the foundation.
Published by: Iwatani Naoji Kinen Zaidan/Iwatani Naoji Foundation, TBR Bldg, 10-2 Nagata-cho 2-chome, Chiyoda-ku, Tokyo, 100-0014, Japan.

500 CHN ISSN 1000-1638
QK1 CODEN: NDZKEJ
NEI MENGGU DAXUE XUEBAO (ZIRAN KEXUE BAN)/ACTA SCIENTIARUM NATURALIUM UNIVERSITATIS NEIMONGOL. Text in Chinese. 1959. bi-m. USD 24.60 (effective 2009). Index. 120 p./no.; back issues avail. **Document type:** *Journal, Academic/Scholarly.* **Description:** Covers mathematics, physics, chemistry, biology, electronics and computer science.
Related titles: Online - full text ed.
Indexed: CCMJ, MSN, MathR, RefZh, Z01, Z02.
—BLDSC (0663.186000), CASDDS, East View.
Published by: Nei Menggu Daxue/Inner Mongolian University, Xincheng-qu, 235, Daxue Lu, Hohhot, 010021, China. TEL 86-471-43156, 86-471-4992006, FAX 86-471-611761. Circ: 300 (paid); 250 (controlled). **Subscr. to:** China International Book Trading Corp, 35 Chegongzhuang Xilu, Haidian District, PO Box 399, Beijing 100044, China. TEL 86-10-68412045, FAX 86-10-68412023, cibtc@mail.cibtc.com.cn, http://www.cibtc.com.cn.

500 MNG ISSN 1001-8735
QH7 CODEN: NSXKEC
NEI MENGGU SHIFAN DAXUE XUEBAO (ZIRAN KEXUE BAN)/INNER MONGOLIA NORMAL UNIVERSITY. JOURNAL (NATURAL SCIENCE EDITION). Text in Chinese. 1958. bi-m. USD 24.60 (effective 2009). **Document type:** *Journal, Academic/Scholarly.*
Related titles: Online - full text ed.; Mongol ed.
Indexed: A28, APA, BrCerAb, C&ISA, CA/WCA, CCMJ, CIA, CerAb, CivEngAb, CorrAb, E&CAJ, E11, EEA, EMA, ESPM, EnvEAb, H15, M&TEA, M09, MBF, METADEX, MSN, MathR, RefZh, SolStAb, T04, WAA, Z01, Z02.
—BLDSC (4769.774000), East View, Linda Hall.
Published by: Nei Menggu Shifan Daxue, 81, Zhaowuda Lu, Hohhot, Inner Mongolia 010022, Mongolia. TEL 86-471-4393042, FAX 86-471-4393043. Circ: 1,000.

500 JPN ISSN 0466-6089
QH7
NEICHA SUTADI/NATURE STUDY. Text in Japanese. 1955. m. JPY 3,000 (effective 2003). bk.rev. **Document type:** *Journal, Academic/Scholarly.* **Description:** Contains reviews, commentary, and news of the museum.
—BLDSC (6047.400000).
Published by: Oosaka-shiritsu Shizenshi Hakubutsukan/Osaka Museum of Natural History, 1-23 Nagaikoen, Higashisumiyoshi-ku, Osaka-shi, 546-0034, Japan. TEL 81-6-6697-6221, FAX 81-6-6697-6225. Ed. M Okamoto. Circ: 2,000.

500 CHN ISSN 1671-0185
Q4
NEIMENGGU MINZU DAXUE XUEBAO (ZIRAN KEXUE BAN)/INNER MONGOLIA UNIVERSITY FOR NATIONALITIES. JOURNAL (NATURAL SCIENCES). Text in English. 2001. bi-m. USD 18 (effective 2009). **Document type:** *Journal, Academic/Scholarly.*
Formed by the merger of (1990-2000): Neimenggu Minzu Shi-Yuan Xuebao (Ziran Kexue Hanwen Ban)/Inner Mongolia National Teacher's College. Journal (Natural Science Edition) (1001-7259); (1988-2000): Zhelimu Xumu Xueyuan Xuebao/Zhelimu Animal Husbandry College. Journal (1008-5149); Neimenggu Mengyixueyuan Xuebao
Related titles: Online - full text ed.; Mongol ed.: ISSN 1671-0193. 1988.
—East View.
Published by: Neimenggu Minzu Daxue, 16, Huolinhe Dajie, Tongliao, Inner Mongolia 028043, China. TEL 86-475-8314149.

500 NLD ISSN 1872-2407
NEMO NIEUWS. Text in Dutch. 2005. s-a.
Published by: Science Center NEMO, Postbus 421, Amsterdam, 1000 AK, Netherlands. TEL 31-20-5313233, FAX 31-20-5313535, info@e-nemo.nl, http://www.e-nemo.nl. Circ: 10,000.

500 600 NPL ISSN 1994-1412
➤ **NEPAL JOURNAL OF SCIENCE AND TECHNOLOGY.** Text in English. 1999. a. **Document type:** *Journal, Academic/Scholarly.* **Description:** Aims to accommodate all fields of science and technology viz. agriculture and animal science, biological science, engineering and technology, environment and nature conservation, forestry, health and medicine, physical science etc. It is envisaged to serve as a forum for the dissemination of the results and achievements of various research and development (R&D) programs carried out in Nepali context. It publishes original research papers, critical reviews, technical reports, and notes and comments.
Related titles: Online - full text ed.
Indexed: Z01.
Published by: Royal Nepal Academy of Science and Technology, G P O Box 3323, Kathmandu, Nepal. ronast@mos.com.np. Ed. Dayananada Bajracharya.

500 USA
NETSURFER SCIENCE. Text in English. 1998. w. back issues avail.
Media: Online - full text.
Published by: Netsurfer Communications, Inc., 333 Cobalt Way, Ste 107, Sunnyvale, CA 94086. TEL 408-249-6346. Ed., Pub. Arthur Bebak.

500 USA ISSN 1092-7360
HD9665.1 CODEN: NESCF2
NETWORK SCIENCE. Text in English. 1995. irreg. free (effective 2007).
Media: Online - full text.
Published by: Network Science Corporation, 1116 Miller Mountain Rd, Saluda, NC 28773. TEL 828-859-5036.

NETWORK WEEKLY NEWS. *see* COMPUTERS—Computer Networks

509 GRC ISSN 1106-5605
NEUSIS; the Greek journal for the history and philosophy of science and technology. Text in English, Greek. irreg. USD 40 (effective 2003).
Indexed: MSN.
Published by: Nefeli Publications, 6 Asclipiou Str, Athens, 106 80, Greece. TEL 30-21-3607744, FAX 30-21-3639962.

500 USA ISSN 0742-7514
Q162
NEW BOOK OF POPULAR SCIENCE ANNUAL; a science anthology with reviews of the year highlighting science news. Text in English. 1964. a. USD 27.90. charts; illus.; stat. index. **Description:** Contains special reports and summaries of the year's major events and trends in modern science.
Published by: Grolier Incorporated, Sherman Turnpike, Danbury, CT 06816. TEL 203-797-3500. Ed. Joseph M Castagno.

500 USA ISSN 0028-5455
Q11 CODEN: BJASAS
NEW JERSEY ACADEMY OF SCIENCE. BULLETIN. Text in English. 1955. s-a. USD 70 domestic; USD 76 foreign (effective 2003). abstr.; bibl.; illus.; maps; stat. back issues avail.; reprints avail. **Document type:** *Bulletin, Trade.* **Description:** Provides original paper and reviews in any field of science.
Related titles: Microform ed.: (from PQC); Online - full text ed.
Indexed: A01, A26, CA, ChemAb, E08, G08, H11, H12, I05, S06, S09, SASA, SpeleolAb, T02, Z01.
—BLDSC (2646.800000), Ingenta, Linda Hall.
Published by: New Jersey Academy of Science, 99 Avenue E, Beck Hall, Rm 215, Livingston Campus, Rutgers University, Piscataway, NJ 08854. njacadsc@rci.rutgers.edu, http://www.njas.org. Ed., R&P Michael C Kennish TEL 732-932-6555 ext 240. Circ: 300.

500 USA ISSN 0028-5463
CODEN: BJASAS
NEW JERSEY ACADEMY OF SCIENCE. NEWSLETTER. Text in English. 1966. 3/yr. membership. bk.rev. **Document type:** *Newsletter.*
Indexed: GeoRef, SpeleolAb.
—CASDDS.
Published by: New Jersey Academy of Science, 99 Avenue E, Beck Hall, Rm 215, Livingston Campus, Rutgers University, Piscataway, NJ 08854. njacadsc@rci.rutgers.edu, http://www.njas.org. Ed. Nancy Stevenson. Circ: 700.

500 USA ISSN 0028-6591
AS25
NEW RESEARCH CENTERS. Text in English. 1965. a. USD 578 per issue 37th ed. (effective 2009). cum.index in each issue. back issues avail. **Document type:** *Directory, Trade.* **Description:** Provides entries on newly formed, established, or discovered centers in the U.S., Canada, and internationally.
Related titles: ◆ Supplement to: Research Centers Directory. ISSN 0080-1518.
—Linda Hall.
Published by: Gale (Subsidiary of: Cengage Learning), 27500 Drake Rd, Farmington Hills, MI 48331. TEL 248-699-4253, 800-877-4253, FAX 248-699-8035, 800-414-5043, gale.customerservice@cengage.com, http://gale.cengage.com. Ed. Anthony L Gerring.

500 GBR ISSN 2042-9576
NEW SCIENCE. Text in English. 2008. a. free to qualified personnel (effective 2010). **Document type:** *Magazine, Trade.* **Description:** Explores the developments in the world of research without animals.
Related titles: Online - full text ed.: ISSN 2043-9881.
Published by: The Lord Dowding Fund, Millbank Tower, Millbank, London, SW1P 4QP, United Kingdom. TEL 44-20-76303340, FAX 44-20-78282179.

500 GBR ISSN 0262-4079
Q1 CODEN: NWSCAL
NEW SCIENTIST; the global science and technology weekly. Text in English. 1956. w. adv. bk.rev. charts; illus.; pat. q. index. back issues avail.; reprints avail. **Document type:** *Magazine, Consumer.* **Description:** Offers comprehensive coverage of a wide range of science-related fields and topics. Subjects of articles include botany, physics, evolution, nuclear power, mathematics and environmental studies.
Formerly (until 1971): New Scientist and Science Journal (0369-5808); Which was formed by the merger of (1956-1971): New Scientist (0028-6664); Which was formerly (until 1956): Atomic Scientists Journal (0365-6616); (until 1953): Atomic Scientists News (0365-6993); (1965-1971): Science Journal (0582-2092); Which incorporated (1920-1966): Discovery (London, 1920) (0366-9238); Which incorporated: Modern Science
Related titles: ◆ CD-ROM ed.: New Scientist on CD-ROM. ISSN 1356-1766; Online - full text ed.: New Scientist: Planet Science. ISSN 1364-8500. 1995 (from ScienceDirect).
Indexed: A&ATA, A01, A02, A03, A05, A08, A11, A15, A20, A21, A22, A23, A24, A25, A26, A29, A32, A33, ABC, ABIPC, ABIn, AESIS, AHCI, AIA, APD, AS&TA, AS&TI, ASCA, ASFA, AbAn, Acal, AcoustA, Agr, AnBeAb, ApMecR, B02, B04, B05, B07, B10, B13, B14, B15, B17, B18, B20, B21, B28, BAS, BIOSIS Prev, BMT, BRD, BRI, BioDAb, BiolDig, BldManAb, BrArAb, BrHumI, BrTechI, C04, C05, C06, C07, C08, C10, C13, CA, CADCAM, CBNB, CBRI, CBTA, CEA, CEABA, CIN, CINAHL, CISA, CPerI, CSNB, CTA, Cadscan, ChemAb, ChemTitl, ChemoAb, CoppAb, CurCont, E08, E11, E17, EIA, ESPM, EnerRev, EntAb, EnvAb, EnvInd, F&EA, F05, F06, F07, FR, FS&TA, FutSurv, G01, G02, G03, G04, G06, G07, G08, G10, GSA, GSI, GdIns, GenetAb, GeoRef, HECAB, HPNRM, HRIS, I05, I07, I10, IBR, IBZ, IMMAb, IPackAb, ISR, Inpharma, Inspec, JOF, KES, L04, L12, LISTA, LeadAb, M&GPA, M&MA, M01, M02, M06, MASUSE, MEA&I, MycolAb, NRN, NSA, NumL, P&BA, P02, P10, P11, P13, P15, P19, P26, P30, P34, P35, P48, P51, P52, P53, P54, P56, PAIS, PQC, PRA, PhilInd, R10, R18, RASB, RI-1, RICS, RILM, Reac, RefZh, RoboAb, S04, S06, S08, S09, S10, S23, SCI, SCOPUS, SPPI, SSciA, SWRA, SpeleolAb, T02, T04, Telegen, U01, ViroIAbstr, W03, W05, W07, W08, W09, WBA, WMB, WasteInfo, WildRev, Zincscan.
—BLDSC (6087.800000), AskIEEE, CASDDS, CIS, GNLM, IE, Infotrieve, Ingenta, INIST, Linda Hall, PADDS. **CCC.**
Published by: Reed Business Information Ltd. (Subsidiary of: Reed Business), Lacon House, 84 Theobald's Rd, London, WC1X 8NS, United Kingdom. TEL 44-20-76111200, FAX 44-20-76111250, rbi.subscriptions@qss-uk.com, http://www.reedbusiness.co.uk/. Ed. Roger Highfield TEL 44-20-76111201. Adv. contact Anna Garrard TEL 44-20-76111291. page GBP 7,945; trim 10.5 x 16. Circ: 151,324. **Subscr. to:** Quadrant Subscription Services, Rockwood House, 9-17 Perrymount Rd, Haywards Heath, W. Sussex RH16 3DH, United Kingdom. qss.customer.services@quadrantsubs.com, http://www.quadrantsubs.com.

500 600 AUS ISSN 1032-1233
NEW SCIENTIST (CHATSWOOD). Text in English. 1988. w. AUD 240 domestic; AUD 250 in New Zealand; AUD 260 elsewhere; AUD 6.95 newsstand/cover (effective 2008). adv. back issues avail. **Document type:** *Magazine, Consumer.* **Description:** Presents coverage of worldwide events and ground-breaking news on the major issues of today and tomorrow for both scientists and the general public.
Related titles: Online - full text ed.
Indexed: GeoRef, SD.
—CCC.
Published by: Reed Business Information Pty Ltd. (Subsidiary of: Reed Business Information International), Tower 2, 475 Victoria Ave, Locked Bag 2999, Chatswood, NSW 2067, Australia. TEL 61-2-94222999, FAX 61-2-94222922, customerservice@reedbusiness.com.au, http://www.reedbusiness.com.au. Pub. Sunita Harrington TEL 61-2-94222668. adv.: page AUD 5,500; trim 203 x 267. Circ: 26,571.

500 GBR ISSN 1356-1766
Q1
NEW SCIENTIST ON CD-ROM. Text in English. 199?. q. GBP 695; USD 795 in North America (effective 2000). **Document type:** *Magazine, Consumer.* **Description:** Provides a broad perspective of scientific developments in all fields and explores their effects on society.
Media: CD-ROM. **Related titles:** Online - full text ed.: New Scientist: Planet Science. ISSN 1364-8500. 1995 (from ScienceDirect); ◆ Print ed.: New Scientist. ISSN 0262-4079.
Published by: Reed Business Information Ltd. (Subsidiary of: Reed Business), Lacon House, 84 Theobald's Rd, London, WC1X 8NS, United Kingdom. TEL 44-20-76111200, FAX 44-20-76111250, rbi.subscriptions@qss-uk.com, http://www.reedbusiness.co.uk/.

500 USA ISSN 0077-8923
Q11 CODEN: ANYAA9

➤ **NEW YORK ACADEMY OF SCIENCES. ANNALS.** Text in English. 1823. 28/yr. GBP 3,173 combined subscription in United Kingdom to institutions (print & online eds.); EUR 4,027 combined subscription in Europe to institutions (print & online eds.); USD 5,710 combined subscription in the Americas to institutions (print & online eds.); USD 6,216 combined subscription elsewhere to institutions (print & online eds.) (effective 2012). adv. bibl.; charts; illus. index, cum.index: 1960-1974. back issues avail.; reprints avail. **Document type:** *Journal, Academic/Scholarly.*
Formerly (until 1877): Lyceum of Natural History of New York. Annals (0890-6564)
Related titles: Microfilm ed.: (from PMC); Online - full text ed.: ISSN 1749-6632. GBP 2,759 in United Kingdom to institutions; EUR 3,502 in Europe to institutions; USD 4,965 in the Americas to institutions; USD 5,405 elsewhere to institutions (effective 2012) (from IngentaConnect).
Indexed: A01, A20, A22, A23, A24, A26, A28, A29, A34, A35, A36, A37, A38, AESIS, AHCMS, APA, ASCA, ASFA, ASG, AbAn, AgBio, Agr, AgrForAb, B13, B20, B21, B23, BA, BIOSIS Prev, BP, BioDAb, BrCerAb, C&ISA, C06, C07, C08, C13, C25, C28, C30, CA, CA/WCA, CABA, CCMJ, CIA, CIN, CINAHL, CISA, CTA, Cadscan, CerAb, ChemAb, ChemTitl, ChemoAb, CivEngAb, CorrAb, CurCR, D01, DBA, DIP, E&CAJ, E01, E11, E12, E17, EEA, EMA, EMBASE, ESPM, EnvEAb, ExcerpMed, F08, F09, F11, F12, G11, GH, GenetAb, GeoRef, H&SSA, H09, H10, H12, H15, H16, H17, I10, I11, IBR, IBZ, ISR, ImmunAb, IndMed, IndVet, Inspec, LT, LeadAb, M&GPA, M&TEA, M09, MBF, MEDLINE, METADEX, MLA, MSN, MaizeAb, MathR, MycolAb, N02, N03, N04, N05, NSA, NucAcAb, O01, OR, OceAb, P30, P32, P33, P34, P37, P39, P40, PGegResA, PHN&I, PN&I, PhilInd, PollutAb, PsycholAb, R07, R08, R10, R11, R12, R13, R16, RA&MP, RM&VM, RRTA, Reac, RiskAb, S02, S03, S05, S12, S13, S16, S17, SCI, SCOPUS, SSciA, SolStAb, SoyAb, SpeleolAb, T02, T04, T05, TAR, THA, Telegen, ToxAb, TriticAb, VITIS, VS, VirolAbstr, W07, W08, W09, W10, W11, WAA, WildRev, Z01, Z02, Zincscan.
—BLDSC (1031.000000), CASDDS, GNLM, IE, Infotrieve, Ingenta, INIST, Linda Hall. **CCC.**
Published by: (New York Academy of Sciences), Wiley-Blackwell Publishing, Inc. (Subsidiary of: Wiley-Blackwell Publishing Ltd.), 111 River St, Hoboken, NJ 07030. TEL 201-748-6000, FAX 201-748-6088, info@wiley.com, http://www.wiley.com/.

500 USA ISSN 1554-0200
NEW YORK SCIENCE JOURNAL. Text in English. 2008. m. back issues avail. **Document type:** *Journal, Academic/Scholarly.*
Related titles: Online - full text ed.: free (effective 2011).
Published by: Marsland Press, PO Box 21126, Lansing, MI 48909. TEL 347-321-7172, sciencepub@gmail.com.

500 USA ISSN 0278-3355
Q11 CODEN: NYMBA2
NEW YORK STATE MUSEUM. BULLETIN. Text in English. 1887. irreg., latest vol.513, 2010. price varies. illus. back issues avail. **Document type:** *Monographic series, Government.* **Description:** Reports current research in the natural history of New York State.
Former titles (until 1976): New York State Museum and Science Service. Bulletin (0097-028X); (until 1956): New York State Museum. Bulletin
Related titles: Online - full text ed.
Indexed: AnthLit, GeoRef, SpeleolAb, WildRev.
—Linda Hall.
Published by: New York State Museum, Cultural Education Center, Rm 3023, Albany, NY 12230. TEL 518-474-5877, nysmpub@mail.nysed.gov.

500 USA
Q11
NEW YORK STATE MUSEUM. CIRCULAR. Text in English. 1928. irreg., latest vol.72, 2010. price varies. charts; illus. back issues avail. **Document type:** *Monographic series, Government.* **Description:** Research updates, short scientific reports and indices.
Former titles (until 19??): New York State Museum and Science Service. Circular (0271-4213); (until 1955): New York State Museum. Circular (1052-2018)
Related titles: Online - full text ed.: free (effective 2011).
Indexed: SpeleolAb.
—Linda Hall.
Published by: New York State Museum, Cultural Education Center, Rm 3023, Albany, NY 12230. TEL 518-474-5877, nysmpub@mail.nysed.gov.

500 USA ISSN 0735-4401
Q11
NEW YORK STATE MUSEUM. EDUCATIONAL LEAFLET SERIES. Variant title: Educational Leaflet. Text in English. 1948. irreg., latest vol.36, 2009. price varies. charts; illus. back issues avail. **Document type:** *Monographic series, Government.* **Description:** Popular and educational booklets covering topics in anthropology, biology, geology and history.
Former titles (until 199?): New York State Museum. Leaflet (0275-908X); (until 1979): New York State Museum and Science Service. Educational Leaflet; (until 1962): New York State Museum and Science Service. Educational Leaflet Series
Related titles: Online - full text ed.
Indexed: GeoRef, SpeleolAb.
Published by: New York State Museum, Cultural Education Center, Rm 3023, Albany, NY 12230. TEL 518-474-5877, nysmpub@mail.nysed.gov.

500 USA ISSN 0749-1158
CODEN: NYSMEZ
NEW YORK STATE MUSEUM. MEMOIR. Text in English. 1889. irreg., latest vol.28, 2009. price varies. charts; illus. back issues avail. **Document type:** *Monographic series, Government.* **Description:** Works on New York's natural history and prehistory.
Former titles (until 1976): New York State Museum. Memoir (0898-8846); (until 1974): New York State Museum and Science Service. Memoir (0548-8265); (until 1968): New York State Museum. Memoir; (until 1903): New York State Museum. Memoirs
Related titles: Online - full text ed.
Indexed: GeoRef, SpeleolAb.
—CASDDS, Linda Hall.
Published by: New York State Museum, Cultural Education Center, Rm 3023, Albany, NY 12230. TEL 518-474-5877, nysmpub@mail.nysed.gov.

500 NZL ISSN 0028-8667
Q1
NEW ZEALAND SCIENCE REVIEW. Text in English. 1957 (vol.15). q. free to members. adv. bk.rev. charts; illus.; stat. cum.index. **Document type:** *Journal, Academic/Scholarly.* **Description:** Reviews on science and science policy.
Indexed: A22, ChemAb, GeoRef, INIS AtomInd, RASB, SpeleolAb.
—Ingenta. **CCC.**
Published by: New Zealand Association of Scientists, PO Box 1874, Wellington, New Zealand. TEL 64-4-3895096 ext 825. Ed. Allen Petrey. Circ: 1,000.

500 GBR ISSN 1744-7933
Q1
NEWS@NATURE.COM. Text in English. 2004. w. includes subscr. with Nature. back issues avail. **Document type:** *Magazine, Consumer.*
Media: Online - full text.
—CCC.
Published by: Nature Publishing Group (Subsidiary of: Macmillan Publishers Ltd.), The MacMillan Bldg, 4 Crinan St, London, N1 9XW, United Kingdom. TEL 44-20-78334000, FAX 44-20-78334640. Ed. Mark Peplow.

NEWSRX HEALTH & SCIENCE. *see* MEDICAL SCIENCES

500 USA ISSN 1944-2610
NEWSRX SCIENCE. Text in English. 2008. w. USD 2,295 in US & Canada; USD 2,495 elsewhere; USD 2,525 combined subscription in US & Canada (print & online eds.); USD 2,755 combined subscription elsewhere (print & online eds.) (effective 2011). adv. back issues avail. **Document type:** *Newsletter, Trade.* **Description:** Covers research from major U.S. research centers and universities in geology, mathematics, astronomy, oceanography, archaeology, chemistry and physics.
Related titles: E-mail ed.; Online - full text ed.: ISSN 1944-2629. USD 2,295 combined subscription (online & e-mail eds.) (effective 2011).
Indexed: I05, P10, P26, P48, P52, P53, P54, PQC.
Published by: NewsRx, 2727 Paces Ferry Rd SE, Ste 2-440, Atlanta, GA 30339. TEL 770-435-8286, 800-726-4550, FAX 770-435-6800, pressrelease@newsrx.com, http://www.newsrx.com. Pub., Adv. contact Susan Hasty TEL 770-507-7777.

NEWTON. *see* CHILDREN AND YOUTH—For

500 600 JPN ISSN 0286-0651
Q4
NEWTON/NYUTON; graphic science magazine. Text in Japanese. 1981. m. JPY 12,000 to members (effective 2006). adv. **Document type:** *Magazine, Consumer.*
Related titles: Online - full content ed.
Published by: Newton Press Inc., 2-6-1, Nishi-shinjuku, Shinjuku-ku, Tokyo, 163-0207, Japan. TEL 81-3-53264671, FAX 81-3-33438184, http://www.newtonpress.co.jp/. Circ: 400,000.

500 ITA ISSN 1126-117X
NEWTON OGGI; lo spettacolo della scienza. Variant title: Newton. Text in Italian. 1997. m. adv. bk.rev.; film rev.; video rev. illus. **Document type:** *Magazine, Consumer.* **Description:** Explores the many fascinating worlds of science and makes them accessible to the general reader. Contains articles on technology, the human body, nature and the frontiers of science.
Related titles: CD-ROM ed.: Newton Oggi Multimedia. ISSN 1127-0608; Spanish ed.: Newton Hoy.
Published by: R C S Periodici (Subsidiary of: R C S Mediagroup), Via San Marco 21, Milan, 20121, Italy. TEL 39-2-25844111, FAX 39-2-25845444, info@periodici.rcs.it, http://www.rcsmediagroup.it/siti/periodici.php. Circ: 318,000 (paid).

508 NLD ISSN 1879-6001
▼ **NIEUWE VELUWE.** Text in Dutch. 2010. q. EUR 37.50; EUR 9.50 newsstand/cover (effective 2010). adv. **Document type:** *Magazine, Consumer.*
Published by: Grafisch Atelier Wageningen, Generaal Foulkesweg 72, Wageningen, 6703 BW, Netherlands. TEL 31-317-418128, FAX 31-317-425886, uitgever@nieuweveluwe.nl. Ed. Ria Dubbeldam. Pub. Jelie de Gruyter. adv.: color page EUR 750; trim 240 x 290. Circ: 1,000.

500.9 NGA ISSN 0029-0076
QH195.N5 CODEN: NIFIAC
➤ **THE NIGERIAN FIELD.** Text in English. 1931. s-a. NGN 500 domestic to individuals; GBP 10 foreign to individuals; NGN 2,000 domestic to institutions; GBP 25 foreign to institutions (effective 2003). adv. bk.rev. charts; illus.; maps. 88 p./no. 1 cols./p.; back issues avail. **Document type:** *Journal, Academic/Scholarly.* **Description:** Studies West African plants, animals and environment, and peoples and their cultures.
Indexed: ApicAb, BibInd, CABA, CCA, ChemAb, E12, F08, F12, G11, GH, GeoRef, H17, IBR, IBZ, MLA, MLA-IB, P33, R07, R08, R12, SpeleolAb, T05, WildRev, Z01.
Published by: Nigerian Field Society, Secretariat Post Office, PO Box 30385, Ibadan, Nigeria. jkladipo@mailskannet.com. Ed., R&P Pat Oyelola TEL 234-2-810-2138. Adv. contact A Jayeola. Circ: 1,000 (paid). **Subscr. to:** c/o Modupe Ladipo, Treasurer, Gerneral Outpatients Dept., University College Hospital, Ibadan, Oyo State, Nigeria.

500 NGA ISSN 0029-0114
Q1 CODEN: NJSCAW
NIGERIAN JOURNAL OF SCIENCE. Text in English. 1966. s-a. USD 35. adv. bk.rev. abstr.; charts; illus. index. back issues avail. **Document type:** *Journal, Academic/Scholarly.*
Formerly (until 1966): Science Association of Nigeria. Proceedings (0582-1983)
Indexed: ChemAb, MathR, SpeleolAb, Z02.
—Linda Hall.
Published by: Science Association of Nigeria, University of Ibadan, PO Box 4039, Ibadan, Oyo, Nigeria. Circ: 2,000.

500 JPN ISSN 0369-3562
G1 CODEN: NDBSAL
NIHON DAIGAKU BUNRIGAKUBU SHIZEN KAGAKU KENKYUJO KENKYU KIYO/NIHON UNIVERSITY. INSTITUTE OF NATURAL SCIENCES. PROCEEDINGS. Text in English, Japanese; Summaries in English. 1965. a. **Document type:** *Proceedings.*
Indexed: ChemAb, JPI, Z02.
Published by: Nihon Daigaku, Bunrigakubu Shizen Kagaku Kenkyujo/Nihon University, College of Humanities and Sciences, Institute of Natural Sciences, 25-40 Sakurajosui 3-chome, Setagaya-ku, Tokyo, 156-0045, Japan.

NIHON DAIGAKU RIKOGAKU KENKYUJO SHOHO/NIHON UNIVERSITY. RESEARCH INSTITUTE OF SCIENCE AND TECHNOLOGY. JOURNAL. *see* TECHNOLOGY: COMPREHENSIVE WORKS

NIHON JOSEI KAGAKUSHA NO KAI NYUSU/SOCIETY OF JAPANESE WOMEN SCIENTISTS. NEWS. *see* WOMEN'S INTERESTS

500 JPN ISSN 0919-1593
NIHON JOSHI DAIGAKU KIYO. RIGAKUBU/JAPAN WOMEN'S UNIVERSITY. FACULTY OF SCIENCE. JOURNAL. Text in Japanese. 1993. a. **Document type:** *Journal, Academic/Scholarly.*
—BLDSC (4808.490000). **CCC.**
Published by: Nihon Joshi Daigaku, Rigakubu/Japan Women's University, Faculty of Science, 2-8-1 Mejirodai, Bunkyo-ku, Tokyo, 112-8681, Japan.

NIHON KAGAKU GIJUTSU KANKEI CHIKUJI KANKOBUTSU SORAN (ONLINE)/DIRECTORY OF JAPANESE SCIENTIFIC PERIODICALS (ONLINE). *see* PUBLISHING AND BOOK TRADE—Abstracting, Bibliographies, Statistics

500 JPN
NIHON KAGAKUSHI GAKKAI NENKAI KENKYU HAPPYO KOEN YOSHISHU. Text in Japanese. a. JPY 1,500 (effective 2003). abstr. **Document type:** *Proceedings.* **Description:** Contains abstracts of the annual meeting of the society.
Published by: Nihon Kagakushi Gakkai/History of Science Society of Japan, West Pine Bldg, 201, 2-15-19 Hirakawa-cho, Chiyoda-ku, Tokyo, 102-0093, Japan. http://wwwsoc.nii.ac.jp/jshs/index-j.html.

NIHON KOKAI GAKKAI RONBUNSHU/JAPAN INSTITUTE OF NAVIGATION. JOURNAL. *see* TRANSPORTATION—Ships And Shipping

509.2 JPN ISSN 0029-0335
Q4
NIHON NO KAGAKUSHA/JOURNAL OF JAPANESE SCIENTISTS. Text in Japanese. 1966. m. JPY 600 per issue. adv. bk.rev. index.
Indexed: RASB.
Published by: Nihon Kagakusha Kaigi/Japan Scientists Association, 9-16 Yushima 1-chome, Bunkyo-ku, Tokyo, 113-0034, Japan. Ed. Harumi Kohara. Circ: 12,000.

500 600 JPN ISSN 0370-7024
T1 CODEN: RRITAV
NIHON UNIVERSITY. RESEARCH INSTITUTE OF SCIENCE AND TECHNOLOGY. REPORT. Text in English. 1952. s-a. per issue exchange basis.
Formerly (until 1966): Nihon University. Research Institute of Technology. Report (0549-2998)
Indexed: A28, APA, BrCerAb, C&ISA, CA/WCA, CCMJ, CIA, CerAb, CivEngAb, CorrAb, E&CAJ, E11, EEA, EMA, H15, Inspec, JCT, JTA, M&TEA, M09, MBF, METADEX, MSN, MathR, SolStAb, T04, WAA.
—BLDSC (7592.185000), Linda Hall. **CCC.**
Published by: Nihon Daigaku, Rikogaku Kenkyujo/Nihon University, Research Institute of Science and Technology, 1-8 Kanda-Surugadai, Chiyoda-ku, Tokyo, 101-0062, Japan.

500 JPN ISSN 0288-3422
Q4 CODEN: NDSKBF
NIIGATA DAIGAKU KYOIKUGAKUBU KIYO. SHIZEN KAGAKU HEN/NIIGATA UNIVERSITY. FACULTY OF EDUCATION. MEMOIRS. NATURAL SCIENCES. Text and summaries in English, Japanese. 1960. a.
Indexed: CIN, ChemAb, ChemTitl, JPI.
—CASDDS.
Published by: Niigata Daigaku, Kyoikugakubu/Niigata University, Faculty of Education, 8050 Igarashi Nino-cho, Niigata-shi, Niigata-ken 950-11, Japan.

NIIHAMA KOGYO KOTO SENMON GAKKO KIYO. RIKOGAKU HEN/NIIHAMA NATIONAL COLLEGE OF TECHNOLOGY. MEMOIRS. SCIENCE AND ENGINEERING. *see* TECHNOLOGY: COMPREHENSIVE WORKS

500 600 JPN ISSN 0917-009X
Q4
NIKKEI SAIENSU. Text in Japanese. 1971. m. JPY 10,753; JPY 13,393 foreign. adv. Supplement avail.
Formerly (until 1990): Saiensu (0386-4324)
Related titles: ◆ Italian ed.: Le Scienze. ISSN 0036-8083; ◆ English ed.: Scientific American. ISSN 0036-8733; ◆ German ed.: Spektrum der Wissenschaft. ISSN 0170-2971; ◆ Hungarian ed.: Tudomany. ISSN 0237-322X; ◆ French ed.: Pour la Science. ISSN 0153-4092; ◆ Chinese ed.: Ke Xue. ISSN 1002-1299; ◆ Spanish ed.: Investigacion y Ciencia. ISSN 0210-136X; ◆ Arabic ed.: Majallat al-Ulum; ◆ Polish ed.: Swiat Nauki. ISSN 0867-6380; Turkish ed.: Bilim.
Published by: Nikkei Science Inc. (Subsidiary of: Nihon Keizai Shimbun, Inc.), 2-2-1 Uchisaiwai-cho, Chiyoda-ku, Tokyo, 100-0011, Japan. TEL 03-5255-2125.

500 CHN ISSN 1001-5132
CODEN: NDXLEC
NINGBO DAXUE XUEBAO (LIGONG BAN)/NINGBO UNIVERSITY. JOURNAL (NATURAL SCIENCE AND ENGINEERING EDITION). Text in Chinese. 1988. q. USD 20.80 (effective 2009). **Document type:** *Journal, Academic/Scholarly.*
Related titles: Online - full text ed.
Indexed: Z01.
Published by: Ningbo Daxue/Ningbo University, 818 Fenghua Lu, Ningbo, Zhejiang 315211, China. TEL 86-574-87600816, FAX 86-574-87600291.

NINGBO JIAOYU XUEYUAN XUEBAO/NINGBO INSTITUTE OF EDUCATION. JOURNAL. *see* SOCIAL SCIENCES: COMPREHENSIVE WORKS

NINGBO ZHIYE JISHU XUEYUAN XUEBAO/NINGBO POLYTECHNIC. JOURNAL. *see* SOCIAL SCIENCES: COMPREHENSIVE WORKS

500 CHN ISSN 1004-2911
NINGDE SHI-ZHUAN XUEBAO (ZIRAN KEXUEBAN)/NINGDE TEACHERS COLLEGE. JOURNAL (NATURAL SCIENCE). Text in Chinese. 1982. q. CNY 4.60 newsstand/cover (effective 2007). **Document type:** *Journal, Academic/Scholarly.*

S

Published by: Ningde Shifan Gaodeng Zhuanke Xuexiao/Ningde Teachers College, Jiaocheng Nan Lu, Ningde, 352100, China. TEL 86-593-2977316, FAX 86-593-2954127.

NINGEN BUNKA RONSO/OCHANOMIZU UNIVERSITY. GRADUATE SCHOOL OF HUMANITIES AND SCIENCES. JOURNAL. *see* HUMANITIES: COMPREHENSIVE WORKS

NINGEN BUNKAKEI SIZEN KAGAKUKEI BUMON KIYOU/DOKKYO UNIVERSITY SCHOOL OF MEDICINE. BULLETIN OF HUMANITIES AND NATURAL SCIENCES. *see* HUMANITIES: COMPREHENSIVE WORKS

500 JPN ISSN 1345-2975
BP595.A1
NINGEN KAGAKU KENKYU/STUDIES IN HUMAN SCIENCES. Text in Japanese; Contents page in English. 1999. a. **Document type:** *Academic/Scholarly.*
Indexed: MLA-IB.
Published by: Oosaka Daigaku. Daigakuin, Ningen Kagaku Kenkyuka/Osaka University, Graduate School of Human Sciences, 1-2 Yamadaoka, Suita, Osaka 565-0871, Japan. TEL 81-6-6879-8015.

500 CHN ISSN 0253-2328
CODEN: NDXKD8
➤ **NINGXIA DAXUE XUEBAO. (ZIRAN KEXUE BAN)/NINGXIA UNIVERSITY. JOURNAL (NATURAL SCIENCE EDITION).** Text in Chinese; Summaries in Chinese, English. 1980. q. USD 20.80 (effective 2009). adv. **Document type:** *Journal, Academic/Scholarly.* **Description:** Contains articles on Agriculture, Biology, Chemistry, Computers, Electronics, Engineering, Mathematics, Medical Sciences and Physics.
Supersedes: Ningxia Gongxueyuan Xuebao/Ningxia Institute of Technology. Journal (1006-9054)
Related titles: CD-ROM ed.; Online - full text ed.
Indexed: CCMJ, MSN, MathR, Z02.
—East View.
Published by: Ningxia Daxue Xuebao Bianjibu, 217 Wencui Bei Lu, Yinchuan, Ningxia 750021, China. TEL 86-951-2061948. adv.: B&W page USD 179, color page USD 590; trim 179 x 210. Circ: 970. **Dist. by:** China International Book Trading Corp, 35 Chegongzhuang Xilu, Haidian District, PO Box 399, Beijing 100044, China. TEL 86-10-68412045, FAX 86-10-68412023, cibtc@mail.cibtc.com.cn, http://www.cibtc.com.cn.

➤ **NINGXIA SHIFAN XUEYUAN XUEBAO/NINGXIA TEACHERS UNIVERSITY. JOURNAL.** *see* SOCIAL SCIENCES: COMPREHENSIVE WORKS

500 JPN ISSN 1348-2904
NIOI KAORI KANKYOU GAKKAISHI/JAPAN ASSOCIATION ON ODOR ENVIRONMENT. JOURNAL. Text in Japanese. 1970. bi-m. **Document type:** *Journal, Academic/Scholarly.*
Former titles (until 2002): Shuki no Kenkyu/Journal of Odor Research and Engineering (0913-4883); (until 1986): Akushu no Kenkyu/Odor Control Association. Journal (0385-6828)
Related titles: Online - full text ed.: ISSN 1349-7847.
Indexed: B&BAb, B19, B21, ChemoAb, ESPM, NSA, PollutAb.
Published by: Nioi Kaori Kankyou Kyoukai/Japan Association on Odor Environment, Takara Bldg 4F, 2-6-2 Higashi-Kanda chiyoda-ku, Tokyo, 101-0031, Japan. TEL 81-3-58350315, FAX 81-3-58350316, nioi@orea.or.jp, http://www.orea.or.jp/.

NIPPON GAKUSHIIN KIYO/JAPAN ACADEMY. TRANSACTIONS. *see* SOCIAL SCIENCES: COMPREHENSIVE WORKS

600 JPN ISSN 0389-2514
NIPPON KOGYO DAIGAKU KNKYU HOKOKU/NIPPON INSTITUTE OF TECHNOLOGY. REPORT OF RESEARCHES. Text in Japanese. 1971. q. **Document type:** *Academic/Scholarly.*
Indexed: A22, Inspec, RILM, RefZh.
—BLDSC (7666.835000), IE, Ingenta.
Published by: Nippon Kogyo/Nippon Institute of Technology, 4-1 Gakuendai, Miyashiro-Machi, Minamisaitama-gun, Saitama-ken 345, Japan. TEL 81-480-344111, FAX 81-480-342941, http://www.nit.ac.jp/.

500 JPN ISSN 0914-1340
NISSAN KAGAKU SHINKO ZAIDAN JIGYO HOKOKUSHO/NISSAN SCIENCE FOUNDATION. ANNUAL REPORT. Text in Japanese. 1975. a. **Document type:** *Academic/Scholarly.*
Published by: Nissan Kagaku Shinko Zaidan/Nissan Science Foundation, 17-2 Ginza 6-chome, Chuo-ku, Tokyo, 104-0061, Japan. FAX 03-3543-5598.

500 JPN ISSN 0911-4572
NISSAN KAGAKU SHINKO ZAIDAN KENKYU HOKOKUSHO/NISSAN SCIENCE FOUNDATION. RESEARCH PROJECTS IN REVIEW. Text in Japanese; Summaries in English, Japanese. 1979. a. **Document type:** *Academic/Scholarly.*
—BLDSC (7755.727150).
Published by: Nissan Kagaku Shinko Zaidan/Nissan Science Foundation, 17-2 Ginza 6-chome, Chuo-ku, Tokyo, 104-0061, Japan. TEL 03-3543-5597, FAX 03-3543-5598.

NO D E A - NONLINEAR DIFFERENTIAL EQUATIONS AND APPLICATIONS. *see* MATHEMATICS

500 JPN ISSN 0078-0944
QR1 CODEN: RNIRAV
NODA INSTITUTE FOR SCIENTIFIC RESEARCH. REPORT/NODA SANGYO KAGAKU KENKYUJO KENKYU HOKOKU. Text in English. 1957. a. free or exchange. bk.rev. **Document type:** *Report, Academic/Scholarly.* **Description:** Technical journal specializing in microbiology and related fields.
Indexed: ChemAb, VITIS.
—INIST.
Published by: Noda Sangyo Kagaku Kenkyujo/Noda Institute for Scientific Research, 399 Noda, Noda-shi, Chiba-ken 278-0037, Japan. TEL 81-471-23-5585, FAX 81-471-23-5953, http://www.nisr.or.jp. Ed. Tsutomu Masuda. Circ: 500.

500 001.3 ESP ISSN 1887-0562
NOMINA DEL PERSONAL ACADEMIC I ANUARI DE LA CORPORACIO. Text in Spanish. a. **Document type:** *Directory, Corporate.*
Formerly (until 2005): Nomina del Personal Academico y Anuario de la Corporation (1137-2281)
Indexed: GeoRef, SpeleolAb.
—Linda Hall.
Published by: Real Academia de Ciencias y Artes de Barcelona, Rambla dels Estudis, 115, Barcelona, 08002, Spain. TEL 34-93-3170536, FAX 34-93-3011656, info@racab.es, http://www.racab.es/.

500 GBR ISSN 1386-288X
NONLINEAR PHENOMENA AND COMPLEX SYSTEMS. Text in English. 1996. a., latest vol.10, 2004. price varies. back issues avail. **Document type:** *Monographic series, Academic/Scholarly.*
—BLDSC (6117.316850), IE, Ingenta. **CCC.**
Published by: (The Centre for Nonlinear Physics and Complex Systems CHL), Springer U K (Subsidiary of: Springer Science+Business Media), 236 Gray's Inn Rd, Fl 6, London, WC1X 8HL, United Kingdom. TEL 44-20-31922000, postmaster@svl.co.uk. Ed. Martinez Servet.

NORDINA; nordic studies in science education. (Nordisk Didaktikk i Naturfag) *see* EDUCATION—Teaching Methods And Curriculum

001.3 500 600 DEU
Q49.C95 CODEN: RWAVAW
NORDRHEIN-WESTFAELISCHE AKADEMIE DER WISSENSCHAFTEN UND DER KUENSTE. VORTRAEGE. N - NATURWISSENSCHAFTEN UND MEDIZIN. Text in German. 1950. irreg., latest vol.476, 2010. price varies. **Document type:** *Monographic series, Academic/Scholarly.*
Former titles (until 2009): Nordrhein-Westfaelische Akademie der Wissenschaften. Vortraege N - Naturwissenschaften und Medizin; (until 1993): Nordrhein-Westfaelische Akademie der Wissenschaften. Vortraege Natur-, Ingenieur- und Wirtschaftswissenschaften (0944-8799); Rheinisch - Westfaelische Akademie der Wissenschaften. Vortraege Natur-, Ingenieur- und Wirtschaftswissenschaften; Rheinisch - Westfaelische Akademie der Wissenchaften. Veroeffentlichungen (0066-5754); (until 1970): Arbeitsgemeinschaft fuer Forschung des Landes Nordrhein-Westfalen. Veroeffentlichungen
Indexed: CCMJ, ChemAb, GeoRef, MSN, RASB, SpeleolAb, Z02.
—CASDDS, Linda Hall.
Published by: (Nordrhein-Westfaelische Akademie der Wissenschaften), Verlag Ferdinand Schoeningh GmbH, Postfach 2540, Paderborn, 33055, Germany. TEL 49-5251-1275, FAX 49-5251-127860, info@schoeningh.de.

NORSK SKOGBRUKSMUSEUM. AARBOK. *see* FORESTS AND FORESTRY

500 NOR ISSN 1890-3533
DET NORSKE VIDENSKAPS-AKADEMI. I. MAT.-NATURV. KLASSE. SKRIFTER OG AVHANDLINGER. Text mainly in Norwegian. 2006. irreg. price varies. back issues avail. **Document type:** *Monographic series, Academic/Scholarly.*
Formed by the merger of (1975-1995): Det Norske Videnskaps-Akademi. I. Mat.-Naturv. Klasse. Ny Serie. Avhandlinger (0801-2369); Which was formerly (until 1973): Det Norske Videnskaps-Akademi i Oslo. I. Matematisk-Naturvitenskapelig Klasse. Ny Serie. Avhandlinger (1502-8453); (until 1961): Det Norske Videnskaps-Akademi i Oslo. I. Mat.-Naturv. Klasse. Avhandlinger (0549-7019); Which superseded in part (1858-1924): Forhandlinger i Videnskapsselskapet i Kristiania (0332-6683); (1975-2000): Det Norske Videnskaps-Akademi. I. Mat.-Naturv. Klasse. Ny Serie. Skrifter (1502-0096); Which was formerly (until 1974): Det Norske Videnskaps-Akademi i Oslo. I. Mat.-Naturv. Klasse. Ny serie. Skrifter (0801-2385); (until 1960): Det Norske Videnskaps-Akademi i Oslo. I. Mat.-Naturv. Klasse. Skrifter (0029-2338); (1894-1926): Videnskapsselskapet i Kristiania. I. Matematisk-Naturvitenskapelig Klasse. Skrifter (0801-2083)
Indexed: Inspec.
—INIST, Linda Hall.
Published by: (Det Norske Videnskaps-Akademi/Norwegian Academy of Science and Letters), Novus Forlag AS, Herman Foss Gate 19, Oslo, 0171, Norway. TEL 47-22-717450, FAX 47-22-718107, novus@novus.no, http://www.novus.no. **Co-publisher:** Det Norske Videnskaps-Akademi/Norwegian Academy of Science and Letters.

500 USA
CODEN: JEMSA5
➤ **NORTH CAROLINA ACADEMY OF SCIENCE. JOURNAL.** Text in English. 1884. q. free to members (effective 2011). bibl.; charts; illus. index. back issues avail.; reprints avail. **Document type:** *Journal, Academic/Scholarly.* **Description:** Publishes papers in all scientific disciplines, as related to North Carolina and the Southeast.
Formerly (until 2002): Elisha Mitchell Scientific Society. Journal (0013-6220)
Related titles: Online - full text ed.: (from PQC).
Indexed: A22, B25, BIOSIS Prev, BiolDig, CIN, ChemAb, ChemTitl, GeoRef, MathR, MycolAb, P30, RASB, RefZh, SASA, SpeleolAb, VITIS, Z01, Z02.
—CASDDS, Ingenta, INIST, Linda Hall.
Published by: North Carolina Academy of Science, c/o Meredith College, Department of Biological Sciences, 3800 Hillsborough St, Raleigh, NC 27607. TEL 910-814-4365, guzman@campbell.edu, http://www.ncacadsci.org/NCAS/NCAS.html. Ed. Frank J Schwartz TEL 252-726-6841 ext 139.

506.2784 USA ISSN 0096-9214
Q11 CODEN: PNDAAZ
➤ **NORTH DAKOTA ACADEMY OF SCIENCE. PROCEEDINGS.** Text in English. 1947. a. USD 15 per issue; free to members (effective 2011). **Document type:** *Proceedings, Academic/Scholarly.*
Related titles: Online - full text ed.
Indexed: A01, A26, Agr, CA, ChemAb, E08, G08, GeoRef, I05, S06, S09, SASA, SpeleolAb, T02, WildRev.
—Ingenta, Linda Hall. **CCC.**
Published by: North Dakota Academy of Science, Minot State University, Department of Biology, 500 University Ave W, Minot, ND 58707. TEL 701-858-3508, ndas@ndacadsci.org, http://www.ndacadsci.org.

500 GBR ISSN 2044-057X
QH1 CODEN: NNHJAQ
NORTHAMPTONSHIRE NATURAL HISTORY SOCIETY. JOURNAL. Text in English. 1880. s-a. free to members (effective 2010). charts; illus. back issues avail. **Document type:** *Journal, Academic/Scholarly.*
Former titles (until 1985): Northamptonshire Natural History Society and Field Club. Journal (0144-0586); (until 1882): Northampton Natural History Society and Field Club. Journal
Indexed: BrArAb, GeoRef, SpeleolAb.
Published by: Northamptonshire Natural History Society, The Humfrey Rm, 10 Castilian Terr, Northampton, NN1 1LD, United Kingdom. http://www.nnhs.info.

500 001.3 CAN ISSN 1701-0004
NORTHERN LIGHTS SERIES. Text in English. 2002. irreg., latest vol.11, 2008. price varies. **Document type:** *Monographic series, Academic/Scholarly.* **Description:** Publishes works from all areas of northern scholarship, including natural sciences, social sciences, earth sciences, and the humanities.
Published by: University of Calgary Press, 2500 University Dr NW, Calgary, AB T2N 1N4, Canada. TEL 403-220-7578, FAX 403-282-0085, ucpmail@ucalgary.ca, http://www.uofcpress.com.

500 USA ISSN 0029-344X
Q1 CODEN: NOSCAX
➤ **NORTHWEST SCIENCE.** Text in English. 1927. q. USD 40 to individuals; USD 80 to institutions (effective 2011). charts; illus. cum.index: vols. 21-46. 88 p./no.; back issues avail.; reprints avail. **Document type:** *Journal, Academic/Scholarly.* **Description:** Publishes original research in the basic and applied sciences, with emphasis on the Pacific Northwest region of the United States and Canada.
Related titles: Microfilm ed.: (from PQC); Online - full text ed.: ISSN 2161-9859.
Indexed: A22, A34, A35, A37, A38, ASCA, ASFA, AbAn, AgBio, Agr, AgrForAb, B21, B23, B25, BIOBASE, BIOSIS Prev, BibAg, BiolDig, C25, C30, CABA, CIN, CRFR, ChemAb, ChemTitl, CurCont, E12, E17, ESPM, EntAb, F08, F11, F12, G11, GEOBASE, GH, GeoRef, H16, I11, IABS, ISR, IndVet, LT, M&GPA, MycolAb, N04, O01, OR, P32, P33, P37, P39, P40, PGegResA, PlantSci, PollutAb, R07, R08, R13, RRTA, S13, S16, S17, SCI, SCOPUS, SSciA, SWRA, SpeleolAb, VS, W07, W08, W10, W11, WildRev, Z01.
—BLDSC (6152.000000), CASDDS, IE, Ingenta, INIST, Linda Hall. **CCC.**
Published by: (Northwest Scientific Association), Washington State University Press, PO Box 645910, Pullman, WA 99164. TEL 509-335-3518, FAX 509-335-8568, wsupress@wsu.edu. Ed. Jeff Duda.

500 CUB
NOTICIERO DEL SISTEMA - INTERNACIONAL DE INFORMACION CIENTIFICO-TECNICA. Text in Spanish. 3/yr. USD 14 in North America; USD 16 in South America; USD 20 in Europe.
Published by: (Academia de Ciencias de Cuba, Instituto de Documentacion e Informacion Cientifico-Tecnica (I D I C T)), Ediciones Cubanas, Obispo 527, Havana, Cuba.

500.9 USA ISSN 0029-4608
Q111 CODEN: NONAA2
NOTULAE NATURAE. Text in English. 1939. irreg., latest vol.478. price varies. abstr.; bibl.; charts; illus.; stat. back issues avail. **Document type:** *Monographic series, Academic/Scholarly.*
Indexed: B25, BIOSIS Prev, ChemAb, GeoRef, IBR, IBZ, MycolAb, SpeleolAb, Z01.
—Linda Hall. **CCC.**
Published by: Academy of Natural Sciences of Philadelphia, 1900 Benjamin Franklin Pky, Philadelphia, PA 19103. TEL 215-299-1000, scipubseditor@ansp.org.

510 DEU ISSN 0369-5034
Q49 CODEN: NOALA4
NOVA ACTA LEOPOLDINA; Abhandlungen der Deutschen Akademie der Naturforscher Leopoldina. Text in English, German. 184?. irreg., latest vol.113, no.381, 2010. price varies. charts; illus.; stat. back issues avail. **Document type:** *Monographic series, Academic/Scholarly.*
Formerly (until 1933): Nova Acta (0323-8849)
Indexed: CCMJ, CIN, ChemAb, ChemTitl, DIP, GeoRef, IBR, IBZ, MSN, MathR, P30, RefZh, SpeleolAb, Z02.
—CASDDS, GNLM, Linda Hall. **CCC.**
Published by: Deutsche Akademie der Naturforscher Leopoldina, Emil-Abderhalden-Str 35, Halle, 06108, Germany. TEL 49-345-472390, FAX 49-345-4723919, leopoldina@leopoldina-halle.de, http://www.leopoldina-halle.de. Eds. Joachim Kaasch, Michael Kaasch.

500 DEU ISSN 0369-4771
Q49.D46 CODEN: NLPSBC
NOVA ACTA LEOPOLDINA. SUPPLEMENTUM. Text in German. 1968. irreg., latest vol.20, 2006. price varies. **Document type:** *Monographic series, Academic/Scholarly.*
—Linda Hall.
Published by: (Deutsche Akademie der Naturforscher Leopoldina), Wissenschaftliche Verlagsgesellschaft mbH, Postfach 101061, Stuttgart, 70009, Germany. TEL 49-711-25820, FAX 49-711-2582290, service@wissenschaftliche-verlagsgesellschaft.de, http://www.wissenschaftliche-verlagsgesellschaft.de.

500 510 520 SWE ISSN 0346-6523
NOVA ACTA REGIAE SOCIETATIS SCIENTIARUM UPSALIENSIS. A, ASTRONOMY AND MATHEMATICAL SCIENCES. Text in Multiple languages. 1973. irreg., latest vol.5, no.4, 1981. price varies. back issues avail. **Document type:** *Monographic series, Academic/Scholarly.*
Supersedes in part (1773-1973): Nova Acta Regiae Societatis Scientiarum Upsaliensis (0029-5000)
Related titles: ◆ Series of: Acta Universitatis Upsaliensis. ISSN 0346-5462.
—INIST, Linda Hall. **CCC.**
Published by: Uppsala Universitet, Acta Universitatis Upsaliensis/University Publications from Uppsala, PO Box 256, Uppsala, 75105, Sweden. TEL 46-18-4716804, FAX 46-18-4716804, acta@ub.uu.se, http://www.ub.uu.se/upu/auu/index.html. Ed. Bengt Landgren. **Dist. by:** Almqvist & Wiksell International.

500 SWE ISSN 0374-5929
NOVA ACTA REGIAE SOCIETATIS SCIENTIARUM UPSALIENSIS. C, BOTANY, GENERAL GEOLOGY, PHYSICAL GEOGRAPHY, PALAEONTOLOGY AND ZOOLOGY. Text in Multiple languages. 1773. irreg., latest vol.5, no.4, 1994. price varies. back issues avail. **Document type:** *Monographic series, Academic/Scholarly.*
Supersedes in part (in 1970): Nova Acta Regiae Societatis Scientiarum Upsaliensis (0029-5000)
Related titles: ◆ Series of: Acta Universitatis Upsaliensis. ISSN 0346-5462.
—Linda Hall.

Published by: Uppsala Universitet, Acta Universitatis Upsaliensis/ University Publications from Uppsala, PO Box 256, Uppsala, 75105, Sweden. TEL 46-18-4716804, FAX 46-18-4716804, acta@ub.uu.se, http://www.ub.uu.se/upu/auu/index.html. Ed. Bengt Landgren. **Dist. by:** Almqvist & Wiksell International.

500 001.3 MEX ISSN 2007-0705
➤ **NOVA SCIENTIA**; revista de investigacion de la Universidad De La Salle Bajio. Text in Spanish. 2008. s-a. free (effective 2011). Index. back issues avail. **Document type:** *Journal, Academic/Scholarly.*
Media: Online - full text.
Published by: Universidad De La Salle Bajio, Av. Universidad 602, Col. Lomas del Campestre, Leon, Guanajuato, Mexico. TEL 477-7-108500 ext 308, 608, FAX 477-7-185511. Pub. Jose Luis Alvarez Espinosa. R&P Maria Alicia Zavala Berbena.

500 CAN ISSN 0078-2521
Q21 CODEN: PNSIAW
➤ **NOVA SCOTIAN INSTITUTE OF SCIENCE. PROCEEDINGS.** Text in English. 1863. a., latest vol.42, 2002. price varies. bk.rev. **Document type:** *Proceedings, Academic/Scholarly.* **Description:** Reports of original scientific work and reviews of scientific topics with special reference to the natural history of the Atlantic Provinces of Canada and the Northeastern US.
Former titles (until 1930): Nova Scotian Institute of Science. Proceedings and Transactions (0370-2235); (until 1890): Nova Scotian Institute of Natural Science. Proceedings and Transactions (0700-8333)
Indexed: A34, A38, B25, BIOSIS Prev, CABA, E12, F08, G11, GH, GeoRef, IndVet, LT, MycolAb, N02, R07, RA&MP, RASB, S13, S16, SpeleolAb, VS, W11, WildRev, Z01.
—CASDDS, Ingenta, Linda Hall. **CCC.**
Published by: Nova Scotian Institute of Science, c/o Dr J E Stewart, Dept of Fisheries & Oceans, Bedford Institute of Oceanography, PO Box 1006, Dartmouth, NS B2Y 4A2, Canada. FAX 902-426-7827, stewartje@mar.dfo-mpo.gc.ca, http://www.chebucto.ns.ca/Science/NSIS/Home.html. Ed. Dr. James Stewart. Circ: 600.

500 GBR ISSN 1528-2511
CODEN: NFSYF7
NOVARTIS FOUNDATION SYMPOSIUM. Text in English. 1971. irreg., latest 2008. price varies. adv. back issues avail. **Document type:** *Monographic series, Academic/Scholarly.* **Description:** Covers information about series of information about Novartis Foundation.
Formerly (until 1998): Ciba Foundation Symposium (0300-5208)
Related titles: Online - full text ed.: ISSN 1935-4657.
Indexed: A20, A22, BIOSIS Prev, EMBASE, ExcerpMed, GeoRef, IMMAb, ISR, IndMed, MEDLINE, MycolAb, P30, R10, Reac, SCI, SCOPUS, SpeleolAb, W07, Z01.
—CASDDS, GNLM, IE, INIST. **CCC.**
Published by: (Novartis Foundation), John Wiley & Sons Ltd. (Subsidiary of: John Wiley & Sons, Inc.), 1-7 Oldlands Way, PO Box 808, Bognor Regis, West Sussex PO21 9FF, United Kingdom. TEL 44-1865-778315, FAX 44-1243-843232, cs-journals@wiley.com. **Subscr. in the Americas to:** John Wiley & Sons, Inc., 111 River St, Hoboken, NJ 07030. TEL 201-748-6645, subinfo@wiley.com; **Subscr. to:** 1-7 Oldlands Way, PO Box 809, Bognor Regis, West Sussex PO21 9FG, United Kingdom. TEL 44-1865-778054, cs-agency@wiley.com.

500 RUS ISSN 0868-4928
Q4
NOVITAS; new scientific ideas, hypotheses, conceptions. Text in Russian; Abstracts and contents page in English. 1995. a. free. **Description:** Publishes new scientific ideas, hypotheses, conceptions, suggestions concerning theoretical as well as practical aspects on different scientific branches.
Published by: Kazanskii Gosudarstvennyi Universitet/Kazan State University, 8/14 Galaktionova St, Kazan, 420015, Russian Federation. TEL 7-8432-361000, public.mail@ksu.ru, http://www.ksu.ru. Ed. Yu Sh Akhmerov.

500 BRA ISSN 1678-6602
NUCLEUS. Text in Portuguese. 2003. s-a. **Document type:** *Journal, Academic/Scholarly.*
Related titles: Online - full text ed.: ISSN 1982-2278. free (effective 2011).
Published by: Fundacao Educacional de Ituverava, Rua Flauzino Barbosa Sandoval 1259, Cidade Universitaria, Ituverava, 14500-000, Brazil. TEL 55-16-37299020, FAX 55-16-37299061. Ed. Vera Mariza Chaud de Paula.

500 NLD ISSN 0394-7394
Q127.I8
NUNCIUS; journal of the history of science. Text in English. 1976. s-a. EUR 175, USD 245 to institutions; EUR 191, USD 267 combined subscription to institutions (print & online eds.) (effective 2012). reprint service avail. from PSC. **Document type:** *Journal, Academic/Scholarly.*
Formerly (until 1985): Istituto e Museo di Storia della Scienza di Firenze. Annali (0391-3341)
Related titles: Online - full text ed.: ISSN 1825-3911. 2004. EUR 159, USD 223 to institutions (effective 2012).
Indexed: A20, A22, AmH&L, ArtHuCI, CA, CCMJ, DIP, EMBASE, ExcerpMed, FR, HistAb, I14, IBR, IBZ, MEDLINE, MSN, MathR, P30, PhilInd, RASB, SCI, SCOPUS, SSCI, T02, W07.
—BLDSC (6184.790000), IE, Infotrieve, Ingenta, INIST. **CCC.**
Published by: (Istituto e Museo di Storia della Scienza ITA), Brill, PO Box 9000, Leiden, 2300 PA, Netherlands. TEL 31-71-5353500, FAX 31-71-5317532, http://www.brill.nl.

500 ITA ISSN 1122-0910
NUNCIUS. BIBLIOTECA. Text in Italian. 1989. irreg., latest vol.42, 2001. price varies. **Document type:** *Monographic series, Academic/Scholarly.*
Indexed: CCMJ, IBR, IBZ, MSN, MathR, Z02.
Published by: Casa Editrice Leo S. Olschki, Viuzzo del Pozzetto 8, Florence, 50126, Italy. TEL 39-055-6530684, FAX 39-055-6530214, celso@olschki.it, http://www.olschki.it.

500 001.3 ITA ISSN 2037-7304
NUOVA ATLANTIDE. Text in Multiple languages. 1986. 3/yr. **Document type:** *Magazine, Consumer.*
Formerly (until 1993): Niovo Progetto (2037-7290)
Published by: Aracne Editrice, Via Raffaele Garofalo 133 A/B, Rome, 00173, Italy. info@aracneeditrice.it, http://store.aracneeditrice.com. Ed. Maria Rita Astolfi.

003 658.4 USA ISSN 1085-1038
➤ **O R - M S TODAY.** (Operations Research - Management Science) Text in English. 1971. bi-m. free (effective 2012). adv. bibl.; charts; illus. **Document type:** *Journal, Academic/Scholarly.* **Description:** Reports on the most recent developments in the field of operations research and management science, and covers applications to problems in all areas, including manufacturing, telecommunications, health care and defense.
Related titles: Online - full text ed.
Indexed: A12, A17, A22, A26, ABIn, B02, B15, B17, B18, CIS, CompD, E08, G04, G06, G07, G08, I05, ORMS, P11, P48, P51, P52, P53, P54, P56, PQC, QC&AS, S09.
—BLDSC (6277.415200), IE, Infotrieve, Ingenta. **CCC.**
Published by: Institute for Operations Research and the Management Sciences (I N F O R M S), 7240 Pky Dr, Ste 300, Hanover, MD 21076. TEL 443-757-3500, 800-446-3676, FAX 443-757-3515, informs@informs.org, http://www.informs.org. Ed., R&P Peter R. Horner TEL 770-431-0867. Pub. Patricia Shaffer. Circ: 12,000.

500 NLD ISSN 0928-2211
O T B WORKING PAPER. (Onderzoeksinstituut Technische Bestuurskunde) Text in Dutch. 1992. irreg. **Document type:** *Monographic series, Academic/Scholarly.*
Published by: (Onderzoeksinstituut OTB, Research Institute Policy Sciences and Information Systems), Delft University Press (Subsidiary of: I O S Press), Nieuwe Hemweg 6B, Amsterdam, 1013 BG, Netherlands. TEL 31-20-6883355, FAX 31-20-6870039, info.dupress@iospress.nl, http://www.dupress.nl.

500 NGA
OBAFEMI AWOLOWO UNIVERSITY. INAUGURAL LECTURE SERIES. Text in English. irreg., latest vol.95. **Document type:** *Monographic series.* **Description:** Each monograph covers a scientific, environmental, technological, political, or economic topic.
Published by: Obafemi Awolowo University, Ile Ife, Osun State, Nigeria. TEL 234-36-230290, oauife@oauife.edu.ng, http://www.oauife.edu.ng. **Dist. outside Africa by:** African Books Collective Ltd., The Jam Factory, 27 Park End St, Oxford, Oxon OX1 1HU, United Kingdom. TEL 44-1865-726686, FAX 44-1865-793298.

500 DEU ISSN 0340-4498
QH5 CODEN: ONZEDD
OBERHESSISCHE NATURWISSENSCHAFTLICHE ZEITSCHRIFT. Text in German. irreg., latest vol.61, 2002. price varies. **Document type:** *Monographic series, Academic/Scholarly.*
Formerly (until 1971): Oberhessische Gesellschaft fuer Natur- und Heilkunde, Giessen. Berichte (0078-2920)
Indexed: GeoRef, IBR, IBZ, SpeleolAb, VITIS.
—Linda Hall.
Published by: Oberhessische Gesellschaft fuer Natur- und Heilkunde, Giessen, c/o Universitaetsbibliothek, Otto-Behaghel-Str 8, Giessen, 35394, Germany. http://www.ohg-natur.de. Circ: 600.

500 600 IRL ISSN 0791-461X
OCCASIONAL PAPERS IN IRISH SCIENCE AND TECHNOLOGY. Text in English. 1985. irreg., latest vol.25, 2002. back issues avail. **Document type:** *Monographic series, Academic/Scholarly.*
Published by: Royal Dublin Society, Ballsbridge, Dublin, 4, Ireland. TEL 353-1-6680866, FAX 353-1-6604014, info@rds.ie, http://www.rds.ie.

500.1 JPN ISSN 0029-8190
Q77 CODEN: NASOA5
OCHANOMIZU JOSHI DAIGAKU SHIZEN KAGAKU HOKOKU/ OCHANOMIZU UNIVERSITY. NATURAL SCIENCE REPORT. Text in English, French, German, Japanese. 1951. s-a. per issue exchange basis only. charts; illus. Index. **Document type:** *Bulletin, Academic/Scholarly.*
Formerly: Ochanomizu Women's University. Natural Science Report
Indexed: ApMecR, CCMJ, ChemAb, GeoRef, INIS AtomInd, MSN, MathR, RefZh, SpeleolAb, Z01, Z02.
—Ingenta, Linda Hall.
Published by: Ochanomizu Joshi Daigaku/Ochanomizu University, 2-1-1 Otsuka, Bunkyo-Ku, Tokyo, 112-8610, Japan. TEL 81-3-5939-5839, FAX 81-3-5978-5849. Ed., R&P Hisako Watanabe. Circ: 900.

500 ROM ISSN 0253-1879
QH7 CODEN: OCRNAM
OCROTIREA NATURII SI A MEDIULUI INCONJURATOR. Text in Romanian; Summaries in English, French, German, Russian. 1955. s-a. bk.rev. charts; illus.; bibl. index, cum.index.
Formerly (until 1975): Ocrotirea Naturii (0029-8263)
Indexed: GeoRef, RASB, SpeleolAb, WildRev, Z01.
—INIST, Linda Hall.
Published by: (Academia Romana/Romanian Academy), Editura Academiei Romane/Publishing House of the Romanian Academy, Calea 13 Septembrie 13, Sector 5, Bucharest, 050711, Romania. TEL 40-21-3188146, FAX 40-21-3182444, edacad@ear.ro, http://www.ear.ro. Ed. Nicolae Botnariuc. **Dist. by:** Rodipet S.A., Piata Presei Libere 1, sector 1, PO Box 33-57, Bucharest 3, Romania. TEL 40-21-2224126, 40-21-2226407, rodipet@rodipet.ro.

ODYSSEY (PERU); adventures in science. *see* CHILDREN AND YOUTH—For

500 AUT ISSN 2218-4163
OE H Z. (Oesterreichische Hochschulzeitung) Text in German. 1949. 10/yr. EUR 77 (effective 2011). adv. **Document type:** *Journal, Academic/Scholarly.*
Former titles (until 2010): Campus (2218-3027); (until 2006): Oesterreichische Hochschulzeitung (0029-9197)
Indexed: MLA-IB, RASB.
Published by: Verlag Oesterreich GmbH, Baeckerstr 1, Vienna, 1010, Austria. TEL 43-1-610770, FAX 43-1-61077419, office@verlagoesterreich.at, http://www.jusline.at/verlagoesterreich/index.html.

500.9 AUT
OEKO.L; Zeitschrift fuer Oekologie. Natur- und Umwelt Schutz. Text in German. 1979. q. EUR 12 domestic; EUR 18 foreign (effective 2005). adv. bk.rev. charts; illus.; stat. 36 p./no.; back issues avail. **Document type:** *Magazine, Government.* **Description:** Contains articles on ecology, nature and conseration issues.
Formerly: Apollo (0003-6528)
Related titles: E-mail ed.; Fax ed.
Indexed: IBRH, KWIWR, RefZh, Z01.
Published by: Amt fuer Natur- und Umweltschutz, Naturkundliche Station, Roseggerstr 20, Linz, 4020, Austria. TEL 43-732-70702690, FAX 43-732-7070-2699, info@mag.linz.at. Ed. Gerold Laister. Circ: 5,000.

OESTERREICHISCHE AKADEMIE DER WISSENSCHAFTEN. ABTEILUNG 2: MATHEMATISCHE, PHYSIKALISCHE UND TECHNISCHE WISSENSCHAFTEN. SITZUNGSBERICHTE UND ANZEIGER. *see* MATHEMATICS

001.3 500 AUT ISSN 0378-8644
AS142 CODEN: OAWABT
OESTERREICHISCHE AKADEMIE DER WISSENSCHAFTEN. ALMANACH. Text in German. 1851. a. EUR 41.20 (effective 2011). 579 p./no.; back issues avail. **Document type:** *Monographic series, Academic/Scholarly.*
Indexed: BibLing, GeoRef, IBR, IBZ, RASB, SpeleolAb.
—Linda Hall.
Published by: (Oesterreichische Akademie der Wissenschaften), Verlag der Oesterreichischen Akademie der Wissenschaften, Postgasse 7/4, Vienna, W 1011, Austria. TEL 43-1-515813402, FAX 43-1-515813400, verlag@oeaw.ac.at, http://www.verlag.oeaw.ac.at.

500 510 610 AUT ISSN 1812-7991
OESTERREICHISCHE AKADEMIE DER WISSENSCHAFTEN. KOMMISSION FUER GESCHICHTE DER NATURWISSENSCHAFTEN, MATHEMATIK UND MEDIZIN. VEROEFFENTLICHUNGEN. Text in German. 1953. irreg., latest vol.61, 2010. price varies. **Document type:** *Monographic series, Academic/Scholarly.*
Published by: Verlag der Oesterreichischen Akademie der Wissenschaften, Postgasse 7/4, Vienna, W 1011, Austria. TEL 43-1-515813402, FAX 43-1-515813400, verlag@oeaw.ac.at, http://verlag.oeaw.ac.at.

OESTERREICHISCHE AKADEMIE DER WISSENSCHAFTEN. MATHEMATISCH-NATURWISSENSCHAFTLICHE KLASSE. DENKSCHRIFTEN. *see* MATHEMATICS

500 JPN ISSN 0386-8176
OGASAWARA KENKYU/OGASAWARA RESEARCH. Text in English; Summaries in Japanese. 1978. a. free. back issues avail. **Document type:** *Journal, Academic/Scholarly.*
Formerly: Ogasawara Research Committee. Publications
Indexed: FR, Z01.
Published by: Tokyo-toritsu Daigaku, Ogasawara Kenkyu Iinkai/Tokyo Metropolitan University, Ogasawara Research Committee, 1-1 Minami-Osawa, Hachioji-shi, Tokyo-to 192-0364, Japan. TEL 81-426-77-1111, FAX 81-426-77-1222. Ed. Nobuyuki Hori. Circ: 800.

500 JPN ISSN 0387-9844
OGASAWARA KENKYU NENPO/TOKYO METROPOLITAN UNIVERSITY. ANNUAL REPORT OF RESEARCH ON THE OGASAWARA (BONIN) ISLANDS. Text in Japanese. 1977. a. free. back issues avail. **Document type:** *Bulletin.*
Published by: Tokyo-toritsu Daigaku, Ogasawara Kenkyu Iinkai/Tokyo Metropolitan University, Ogasawara Research Committee, 1-1 Minami-Osawa, Hachioji-shi, Tokyo-to 192-0364, Japan. TEL 81-426-77-1111, FAX 81-426-77-1222. Ed. Nobuyuki Hori. Circ: 800.

500 USA ISSN 0030-0950
Q1 CODEN: OJSCA9
➤ **THE OHIO JOURNAL OF SCIENCE**; an international multidisciplinary publication. Text in English. 1900. q. USD 75 domestic; USD 90 foreign (effective 2011). bk.rev. abstr.; charts; illus. index. back issues avail. **Document type:** *Journal, Academic/Scholarly.* **Description:** Covers all branches of scientific research. Also publishes symposia on subjects of general scientific interest.
Former titles (until 1915): Ohio Naturalist and Journal of Science; (until 1914): Ohio Naturalist; (until 1901): O S U Naturalist
Related titles: Microfilm ed.: (from PMC); Online - full text ed.
Indexed: A01, A03, A06, A08, A20, A22, A26, A29, A34, A35, A36, A37, ASCA, ASFA, AgBio, Agr, AgrForAb, B20, B21, B25, BIOSIS Prev, C25, C30, CA, CABA, CIN, ChemAb, ChemTitl, CurCont, E08, E12, E17, ESPM, EntAb, EnvAb, EnvInd, F08, F12, FCA, G06, G07, G08, G11, GEOBASE, GH, GeoRef, H09, H10, H16, I05, I10, I11, ISR, IndVet, M&GPA, MaizeAb, MycolAb, N02, N03, O01, OR, P11, P30, P32, P33, P37, P40, P48, P52, P56, PN&I, PQC, PollutAb, R07, R08, S05, S06, S09, S13, S16, SASA, SCI, SCOPUS, SWRA, SoyAb, SpeleolAb, T02, TriticAb, VS, VirolAbstr, W08, W10, W11, WildRev, Z01.
—BLDSC (6247.000000), CASDDS, IE, Infotrieve, Ingenta, INIST, Linda Hall. **CCC.**
Published by: Ohio Academy of Science, 1500 W Third Ave, Ste 228, Columbus, OH 43212. TEL 614-488-2228, FAX 614-488-7629, oas@iwaynet.net.

500 551 551.5 USA
OHIO STATE UNIVERSITY. BYRD POLAR RESEARCH CENTER. MISCELLANEOUS SERIES. Text in English. 1958. irreg., latest vol.397, 1997. free or exchange basis. **Description:** Articles not appropriate to the Contribution Series (i.e. abstracts, letters to the editor, non-technical articles), published by members.
Formerly: Ohio State University. Institute of Polar Studies. Miscellaneous Series
Indexed: SpeleolAb.
Published by: Ohio State University, Byrd Polar Research Center, c/o Lynn Lay, Librarian, 1090 Carmack Rd, Columbus, OH 43210-1002. TEL 614-292-6715, FAX 614-292-4697, http://www.bprc.mps.ohio-state.edu.

500 551 USA ISSN 0896-2472
G575
OHIO STATE UNIVERSITY. BYRD POLAR RESEARCH CENTER. REPORT SERIES. Text in English. 1962. irreg., latest vol.18, 1998. price varies. **Description:** Scientific investigations that are too lengthy for regular journal articles.
Formerly: Ohio State University. Institute of Polar Studies. Report Series (0078-415X)
Indexed: GeoRef, SpeleolAb.
Published by: Ohio State University, Byrd Polar Research Center, c/o Lynn Lay, Librarian, 1090 Carmack Rd, Columbus, OH 43210-1002. TEL 614-292-6715, http://www.bprc.mps.ohio-state.edu. Circ: 500.

S

500 JPN ISSN 1345-0875
AS552.O35
OITA DAIGAKU KYOIKU FUKUSHI KAGAKUBU KENKYU KIYO/OITA UNIVERSITY. FACULTY OF EDUCATION AND WELFARE SCIENCE. RESEARCH BULLETIN. Text in English, Japanese; Summaries in English. 1952. s-a. **Document type:** *Bulletin, Academic/Scholarly.*
Formerly: Oita Daigaku Kyoikugakubu Kenkyu Kiyo/Oita University. Faculty of Education. Research Bulletin (0914-580X)
Indexed: CCMJ, JPI, MSN, MathR, RILM, Z02.
—BLDSC (7722.050000).
Published by: Oita Daigaku, Kyoiku Fukushi Kagakubu/Oita University, Faculty of Education and Welfare Science, Dannoharu 700, Oita, 870-1192, Japan. TEL 81-97-5547504, kykenkyu@ad.oita-u.ac.jp, http://www.ed.oita-u.ac.jp/.

500 JPN
OKAYAMA RIKA DAIGAKU KIYO. A, SHIZEN KAGAKU/OKAYAMA UNIVERSITY OF SCIENCE. A, NATURAL SCIENCE. BULLETIN. Text in Japanese. 1965. a. **Document type:** *Journal, Academic/ Scholarly.*
Supersedes in part (in 1981): Okayama Rika Daigaku Kiyo/Okayama University of Science. Bulletin (0285-6646)
Published by: Okayama Rika Daigaku/Okayama University of Science, 1-1 Ridai-cho, Okayama, 700-0005, Japan. TEL 81-86-2523161, FAX 81-86-2568413, http://www.ous.ac.jp/.

OKIDO. *see* CHILDREN AND YOUTH—For

OKINAWA KENRITSU HAKUBUTSUKAN KIYO/OKINAWA PREFECTURAL MUSEUM. BULLETIN. *see* MUSEUMS AND ART GALLERIES

500 USA ISSN 0078-4303
Q11 CODEN: POASAD
➤ **OKLAHOMA ACADEMY OF SCIENCE. PROCEEDINGS.** Text in English. 1920. a. free to members (effective 2010). abstr. cum.index every 10 yrs. back issues avail. **Document type:** *Proceedings, Academic/Scholarly.* **Description:** Publishes the results of original scientific investigations, including social, engineering, biological, biomedical, mathematical and computer sciences.
Related titles: CD-ROM ed.; Online - full text ed.
Indexed: A22, Agr, B25, BIOSIS Prev, CIN, ChemAb, ChemTitl, GeoRef, MycolAb, SASA, SpeleolAb, WildRev, Z01.
—BLDSC (6781.000000), CASDDS, IE, Ingenta, Linda Hall. **CCC.**
Published by: Oklahoma Academy of Science, University of Central Oklahoma, Campus Box 90, Edmond, OK 73034.

508.074 USA
OKLAHOMA MUSEUM OF NATURAL HISTORY. NEWSLETTER. Text in English. q.
Published by: Oklahoma University, Oklahoma Museum of Natural History, 2401 Chautauqua Ave, Norman, OK 73072.

508.074 USA
OKLAHOMA MUSEUM OF NATURAL HISTORY. SCIENTIFIC PUBLICATION. Text in English. irreg.
Published by: Oklahoma University, Oklahoma Museum of Natural History, 2401 Chautauqua Ave, Norman, OK 73072.

OMETECA. *see* HUMANITIES: COMPREHENSIVE WORKS

500 RUS
OMSKII UNIVERSITET. VESTNIK/OMSK UNIVERSITY. COMMUNICATIONS. Text in Russian. 1996. q. 100 p./no.;
Related titles: Online - full text ed.: 1998.
Published by: Omskii Gosudarstvennyi Universitet/Omsk State University, Prospekt Mira 55-a, Omsk, 644077, Russian Federation. TEL 7-3812-644492, vestnik@omsu.omskreg.ru. Ed. Vladimir I Matiushchenko.

ON NATURE. *see* CONSERVATION

363.7 500 FRA ISSN 1960-2995
ON SE BOUGE; une collection pour prendre conscience et agir. Text in French. 2007. irreg. **Document type:** *Monographic series, Consumer.*
Published by: Specifique Editions, 9 Passage Sainte-Avoye, Paris, 75003, France. TEL 33-1-40290329, FAX 33-1-40290249.

OOSAKA DENKI TSUSHIN DAIGAKU KENKYU RONSHU. SHIZEN KAGAKU HEN/OSAKA ELECTRO-COMMUNICATION UNIVERSITY. MEMOIRS. NATURAL SCIENCE. *see* COMMUNICATIONS

500 613.7 JPN ISSN 0289-8888
OOSAKA JOSHI DAIGAKU KIYO. KISO RIGAKU HEN, TAIIKUGAKU HEN/OSAKA WOMEN'S UNIVERSITY. BULLETIN. SERIES OF NATURAL SCIENCE, PHYSICAL EDUCATION. Text and summaries in English, Japanese. a. abstr.
Published by: Oosaka Joshi Daigaku, Kiso Rigakka/Osaka Women's University, 2-1 Daisen-cho, Sakai-shi, Osaka-fu 590-0035, Japan.

OOSAKA KOGYO DAIGAKU KIYO. RIKO HEN/OSAKA INSTITUTE OF TECHNOLOGY. MEMOIRS. SERIES A. SCIENCE & TECHNOLOGY. *see* TECHNOLOGY: COMPREHENSIVE WORKS

500 JPN ISSN 1340-4288
TA4 CODEN: OKHOEZ
OOSAKA KOGYO GIJUTSU KENKYUJO HOKOKU/OSAKA NATIONAL RESEARCH INSTITUTE. REPORT. Text in Japanese. 1953. a.
Former titles (until 1994): Osaka Kogyo Gijutsu Shikenjo Hokoku (0472-1438); Osaka Kogyo Shikenjo Hohoku
Indexed: INIS AtomInd, Inspec.
—INIST, Linda Hall.
Published by: Kogyo Gijutsuin, Oosaka Kogyo Gijutsu Kenkyujo/National Institute of Advanced Industrial Science and Technology, Osaka National Research Institute, 1-8-31 Midorigaoka, Ikeda, Osaka, 563-8577, Japan. TEL 81-727-519606, kanko@onri.go.jp, http://www.onri.go.jp.

500 JPN ISSN 1345-7209
CODEN: OKDSBO
OOSAKA KYOIKU DAIGAKU KIYO. DAI 3-BUMON, SHIZEN KAGAKU, OYO KAGAKU/OSAKA KYOIKU UNIVERSITY. MEMOIRS. SERIES 3: NATURAL SCIENCE AND APPLIED SCIENCE. Text and summaries in English, Japanese. 1952. s-a. free. **Document type:** *Academic/Scholarly.* **Description:** Compiles academic memoirs of natural science and applied science.
Former titles (until 1994): Osaka Kyoiku Daigaku Kiyo. 3 Shizen Kagaku (0373-7411); (until 1967): Osaka Gakugei Daigaku kiyo. B, Shizen Kagaku (0389-3413)
Indexed: A36, B25, BIOSIS Prev, CABA, CCMJ, ChemAb, E12, F08, F12, GH, INIS AtomInd, JPI, MSN, MathR, MycolAb, N02, N03, P32, P40, S13, S16, Z01.
—BLDSC (5629.540000), CASDDS, IE, Ingenta, INIST.
Published by: Oosaka Kyoiku Daigaku/Osaka Kyoiku University, 4-698-1 Asahigaoka, Kashiwara-shi, Osaka-fu 582-8582, Japan. TEL 81-729-78-3782, FAX 81-729-78-3803. Circ: 750.

500 JPN ISSN 0287-1394
OOSAKA SANGYO DAIGAKU RONSHU. SHIZEN KAGAKU HEN/OSAKA SANGYO UNIVERSITY. JOURNAL. NATURAL SCIENCES. Text in English, French, Japanese; Summaries in English. 1956. q. free.
Indexed: JPI.
Published by: Oosaka Sangyo Daigaku Gakkai/Society of Osaka Sangyo University, 1-1 Nakagai-To 3-chome, Daito-shi, Osaka-fu 574-0013, Japan. TEL 0720-75-3001, FAX 0720-75-6551. Circ: 1,500.

500.9 JPN ISSN 0078-6675
QH1 CODEN: OSSKAS
OOSAKA SHIRITSU-SHIZENSHI HAKUBUTSUKAN KENKYU HOKOKU/OSAKA MUSEUM OF NATURAL HISTORY. BULLETIN. Text in English, Japanese. 1954. a. JPY 1,200 (effective 2003); exchange basis. **Document type:** *Bulletin.*
Indexed: B23, B25, BIOSIS Prev, CABA, E12, F08, F12, GeoRef, I11, JPI, MycolAb, P32, P33, P40, R07, R08, RefZh, S13, S16, SpeleolAb, W10, Z01.
—BLDSC (2674.550000), IE, Ingenta, Linda Hall.
Published by: Oosaka-shiritsu Shizenshi Hakubutsukan/Osaka Museum of Natural History, 1-23 Nagaikoen, Higashisumiyoshi-ku, Osaka-shi, 546-0034, Japan. TEL 81-6-6697-6221, FAX 81-6-6697-6225. Ed. Ryohei Yamanishi. Circ: 1,000.

▼ **OPEN CONFERENCE PROCEEDINGS JOURNAL.** *see* MEDICAL SCIENCES

576.8 NLD ISSN 1874-4044
QH359
➤ **THE OPEN EVOLUTION JOURNAL.** Text in English. 2007. irreg. free (effective 2011). **Document type:** *Journal, Academic/Scholarly.*
Media: Online - full text.
Indexed: A01, A39, AnBeAb, C27, C29, D03, D04, E13, E17, ESPM, EntAb, GenetAb, NSA, R14, S14, S15, S18, Z01.
Published by: Bentham Open (Subsidiary of: Bentham Science Publishers Ltd.), PO Box 294, Bussum, AG 1400, Netherlands. TEL 31-35-6923800, FAX 31-35-6980150, subscriptions@bentham.org. Ed. Andres Moya.

➤ **THE OPEN NITRIC OXIDE JOURNAL.** *see* CHEMISTRY

➤ **THE OPEN SOCIETY**; serving New Zealand's non-religious community since 1927. *see* PHILOSOPHY

500 NLD ISSN 1875-399X
GV557
➤ **THE OPEN SPORTS SCIENCES JOURNAL.** Text in English. 2008. irreg. free (effective 2011). **Document type:** *Journal, Academic/ Scholarly.*
Media: Online - full text.
Indexed: A39, C27, C29, D03, D04, E13, ESPM, P30, PEI, R14, S14, S15, S18, SD.
Published by: Bentham Open (Subsidiary of: Bentham Science Publishers Ltd.), PO Box 294, Bussum, AG 1400, Netherlands. TEL 31-35-6923800, FAX 31-35-6980150, subscriptions@bentham.org. Ed. Jaime Sampaio.

003 NLD ISSN 0167-6377
T57.6.A1 CODEN: ORLED5
➤ **OPERATIONS RESEARCH LETTERS.** Text in English. 1981. 6/yr. EUR 811 in Europe to institutions; JPY 107,700 in Japan to institutions; USD 909 elsewhere to institutions (effective 2012). back issues avail.; reprints avail. **Document type:** *Journal, Academic/ Scholarly.* **Description:** Covers all aspects of operations research and the management and decision sciences.
Related titles: Microform ed.: (from PQC); Online - full text ed.: ISSN 1872-7468 (from IngentaConnect, ScienceDirect).
Indexed: A22, A26, ASCA, B01, B06, B07, B09, Biostat, C&ISA, C10, CA, CCMJ, CIS, CMCI, CPEI, CPM, CompAb, CompLI, CurCont, E&CAJ, ESPM, EngInd, I05, IAOP, ISMEC, ISR, Inspec, JCQM, MSN, MathR, ORMS, QC&AS, RefZh, RiskAb, SCI, SCOPUS, ST&MA, SolStAb, T02, W07, Z02.
—BLDSC (6269.363800), AskIEEE, IE, Infotrieve, Ingenta, INIST, Linda Hall. **CCC.**
Published by: Elsevier BV, North-Holland (Subsidiary of: Elsevier Science & Technology), Sara Burgerhartstraat 25, Amsterdam, 1055 KV, Netherlands. TEL 31-20-4853911, FAX 31-20-4852457, JournalsCustomerServiceEMEA@elsevier.com. Ed. Jan Karel Lenstra. **Subscr. to:** Elsevier BV, Radarweg 29, PO Box 211, Amsterdam 1000 AE, Netherlands. TEL 31-20-4853757, FAX 31-20-4853432.

500 300 DEU ISSN 1862-4642
ORANGE. Text in German. 1978. a. **Document type:** *Magazine, Trade.*
Formerly (until 2006): Fachhochschule Dortmund. Forschungsbericht (0930-2298)
Published by: (Fachhochschule Dortmund), V M M Wirtschaftsverlag GmbH & Co. KG, Kleine Grottenau 1, Augsburg, 86150, Germany. TEL 49-821-44050, FAX 49-821-4405409, info@vmm-wirtschaftsverlag.de, http://www.vmm-wirtschaftsverlag.de. Ed. Juergen Andrae.

500 FRA ISSN 0078-5601
ORDRE DES GEOMETRES-EXPERTS. ANNUAIRE. Text in French. 1956. a. price varies. adv. **Document type:** *Yearbook, Trade.*
Published by: (Ordre des Geometres-Experts), Editions Publi - Topex, 40 Avenue Hoche, Paris, 75008, France. TEL 33-1-53890080, FAX 33-1-53890089, edition@publi-topex.com, http://www.publi-topex.com. Circ: 3,000.

507.1 USA ISSN 0030-4794
OREGON SCIENCE TEACHER. Text in English. 1959. q. USD 30 membership (effective 2007). adv. bk.rev. illus. **Document type:** *Magazine, Academic/Scholarly.*
Published by: Oregon Science Teachers Association, PO Box 80456, Portland, OR 97280-1456. TEL 503-534-9112. Ed. Larry Enochs. Circ: 600.

500 001.3 RUS ISSN 1814-6457
➤ **ORENBURGSKII GOSUDARSTVENNYI UNIVERSITET. VESTNIK.** Text in Russian. 1999. m. **Document type:** *Journal, Academic/ Scholarly.*
Related titles: Online - full text ed.: ISSN 1814-6465.
Indexed: RefZh.
Published by: Orenburgskii Gosudarstvennyi Universitet/Orenburg State University, prospekt Pobedy 13, korpus 2, ofis 335, Orenburg, Russian Federation. TEL 7-3532-372778, FAX 7-3532-372778. Ed. V P Kovalevskii.

500 600 NGA ISSN 0474-6171
ORGANIZATION OF AFRICAN UNITY. SCIENTIFIC TECHNICAL AND RESEARCH COMMISSION. PUBLICATION. Text in English. 1951. irreg. price varies. **Document type:** *Newsletter, Trade.*
Published by: Organization of African Unity, Scientific Technical and Research Commission, PMB 2359, Lagos, Nigeria. TEL 234-1-26334300, FAX 234-1-2636093, TELEX 28786 TELCOAU NG.

509 POL ISSN 0078-6500
Q9
ORGANON. Text in English, French, German, Italian, Russian. 1963. irreg., latest vol.25, 1995. price varies. bibl.; illus. **Document type:** *Monographic series, Academic/Scholarly.* **Description:** Devoted to international research on the history and philosophy of science, culture and human civilization.
Indexed: EMBASE, ExcerpMed, FR, IBR, IBZ, MEDLINE, P30, PhilInd, RASB, SCOPUS.
—Linda Hall.
Published by: Polska Akademia Nauk, Instytut Historii Nauki, Palac Staszica, ul Nowy Swiat 72, pok 9, Warsaw, 00330, Poland. TEL 48-22-8268754, FAX 48-22-8266137. Ed. Andrzej Biernacki. Circ: 660. **Co-sponsor:** Division d'Histoire des Sciences de l'Union Internationale d'Histoire et de Philosophie des Sciences.

213.05 550 USA ISSN 0093-7495
BS651 CODEN: ORIGD
ORIGINS (LOMA LINDA). Text in English, French. 1974. irreg., latest vol.8, 2008. bk.rev. charts; illus. back issues avail. **Document type:** *Journal, Academic/Scholarly.*
Related titles: Online - full text ed.: free (effective 2010); free.
Indexed: CERDIC, GeoRef, SpeleolAb.
—BLDSC (6291.263850).
Published by: Geoscience Research Institute, 11060 Campus St, Loma Linda, CA 92350. TEL 909-558-4548, FAX 909-558-4314, info@grisda.org.

500 USA
ORIGINS DESIGN. Text in English. 4/yr. USD 15. **Description:** Considers aspects of the creation-evolution debate from a creationist viewpoint.
Formerly: Origins Research (0748-9919)
Indexed: CCR.
Published by: Access Research Network, PO Box 38069, Colorado Springs, CO 80937-8069.

508 GBR ISSN 0962-6468
THE ORKNEY NATURALIST. Variant title: Orkney Field Club. Bulletin. Text in English. 1985. a. free (effective 2009). back issues avail. **Document type:** *Bulletin, Trade.* **Description:** Contains the results of the study of Orkney wildlife, records and general articles on natural history.
Indexed: Z01.
Published by: Orkney Field Club, c/o Kirkwall Library, 44 Junction Rd, Orkney, KW15 1AG, United Kingdom. TEL 44-1856-879490, ray@rayhallam.co.uk. Ed. Ray Hallam.

500 900 USA ISSN 0369-7827
Q1 CODEN: OSIRE3
➤ **OSIRIS (CHICAGO)**; a research journal devoted to the history of science and its cultural influences. Text in English. 1936. a. included with subscr. to ISIS. adv. bibl.; charts; illus. back issues avail.; reprint service avail. from PSC. **Document type:** *Journal, Academic/ Scholarly.* **Description:** Deals with important emerging research in the history of science and its cultural influences.
Related titles: Online - full text ed.: ISSN 1933-8287.
Indexed: A01, A03, A08, A20, A22, A26, AmH&L, AmHI, ArtHuCI, B04, BRD, CA, CCMJ, CurCont, E08, EMBASE, ExcerpMed, FR, G03, G08, GSA, GSI, H07, HistAb, I05, ISR, Inspec, MEDLINE, MLA-IB, MSN, MathR, P06, P30, P42, PCI, PSA, RASB, S02, S03, S09, SCI, SCOPUS, SOPODA, SSCI, SociolAb, T02, W03, W04, W07, Z02.
—BLDSC (6301.000000), GNLM, IE, Infotrieve, Ingenta, INIST, Linda Hall. **CCC.**
Published by: (History of Science Society), University of Chicago Press, 1427 E 60th St, Chicago, IL 60637. TEL 773-702-7700, FAX 773-702-9756, marketing@press.uchicago.edu, http://www.press.uchicago.edu. Ed. Andrea Rusnock. Adv. contact Cheryl Jones TEL 773-702-7361.

500 DEU ISSN 0948-194X
➤ **OSNABRUECKER JAHRBUCH FRIEDEN UND WISSENSCHAFT.** Text in German. 1994. a. EUR 19.50 (effective 2010). **Document type:** *Journal, Academic/Scholarly.* **Description:** Presents reports, lectures, discussions and essays concerning all subjects of peace and conflict research.
Indexed: DIP, IBR, IBZ.
Published by: V & R Unipress GmbH (Subsidiary of: Vandenhoeck und Ruprecht), Robert-Bosch-Breite 6, Goettingen, 37079, Germany. TEL 49-551-5084303, FAX 49-551-5084333, info@vr-unipress.de, http://www.v-r.de/en/publisher/unipress.

500 DEU ISSN 0340-4781
QH5 CODEN: ONMIDS
➤ **OSNABRUECKER NATURWISSENSCHAFTLICHE MITTEILUNGEN.** Text in German; Summaries in English, German. 1873. a. EUR 20; EUR 10 to students (effective 2005). bk.rev. illus.; stat. **Document type:** *Proceedings, Academic/Scholarly.*
Formerly (until 1972): Naturwissenschaftlichen Vereins Osnabrueck. Veroeffentlichungen (0343-7914)
Indexed: GeoRef, IBR, IBZ, NumL, SpeleolAb, Z01.
—Linda Hall.
Published by: Naturwissenschaftlicher Verein Osnabrueck, Am Schoelerberg 8, Osnabrueck, 49082, Germany. TEL 49-541-560030, FAX 49-541-5600337, http://www.naturwissenschaftlicher-verein-os.de. Ed. Andreas Haenel. Circ: 820.

500 CAN ISSN 0710-4847
CODEN: OSPRE4
THE OSPREY. Text in English. q. CAD 20. **Description:** Covers natural history of Newfoundland.
Published by: Natural History Society of Newfoundland, P.O. Box 1013, St. John's, NF A1C 5M3, Canada.

OWL; the discovery magazine for kids . *see* CHILDREN AND YOUTH—For

508 GBR ISSN 0962-5305
OXFORD UNIVERSITY MUSEUM PUBLICATIONS. Text in English. 198?. irreg. price varies. **Document type:** *Monographic series, Academic/Scholarly.*
Published by: Oxford University Museum of Natural History, Parks Rd, Oxford, OX1 3PW, United Kingdom. TEL 44-1865-272950, FAX 44-1865-272970, info@oum.ox.ac.uk, http://www.oum.ox.ac.uk/.

500 GBR ISSN 0962-5313
OXFORDSHIRE MUSEUMS. OCCASIONAL PAPER. Text in English. 198?. irreg. **Document type:** *Monographic series, Academic/ Scholarly.*
Indexed: Z01.
Published by: Oxfordshire Museum, Fletcher's House, Park St, Woodstock, Oxon OX20 1SN, United Kingdom. TEL 44-1993-811456, FAX 44-1993-813239, www.oxfordshire.gov.uk/ oxfordshire_museums_service.

500 USA ISSN 1943-2429
➤ **OZEAN JOURNAL OF APPLIED SCIENCES.** Abbreviated title: O J A S. Text in English. 2008. q. back issues avail. **Document type:** *Journal, Academic/Scholarly.* **Description:** Brings out research papers and reviews in the fields of biology, chemistry, physics, environmental, business and economics, finance, mathematics and statistics, and geology.
Related titles: Online - full text ed.: ISSN 1943-2542. free (effective 2010).
Published by: Ozean Publication, 2141 Baneberry Ct, Columbus, OH 43235. infoozean@gmail.com, http://www.ozelacademy.com.

500 610 USA ISSN 1932-6203
Q179.9 CODEN: POLNCL
➤ **P L O S ONE.** Text in English. 2006. irreg. free (effective 2012). **Document type:** *Journal, Academic/Scholarly.* **Description:** Covers primary research from all disciplines within science and medicine.
Media: Online - full text.
Indexed: A01, A20, A29, A37, A38, A39, Agr, AnBeAb, B19, B20, B23, B25, BIOSIS Prev, C27, C29, C33, CA, D01, D03, D04, E13, E17, EMBASE, EntAb, ExcerpMed, F12, G11, GenetAb, H17, I11, MEDLINE, MycolAb, O01, P03, P30, P40, PsycInfo, R10, R11, R13, R14, Reac, S12, S13, S14, S15, S16, S18, SCI, SCOPUS, T02, VirolAbstr, W07, W08, Z01.
Published by: Public Library of Science, 1160 Battery St, Koshland Bldg E, Ste 100, San Francisco, CA 94111. TEL 415-624-1200, FAX 415-546-4090, plos@plos.org, http://www.plos.org. Ed. Damian Pattinson. Pub. Peter Binfield. Adv. contact Patric Donaghy TEL 415-948-9942.

500 DEU
P.M. FRAGEN UND ANTWORTEN. Text in German. 2000. m. EUR 43.20; EUR 3.80 newsstand/cover (effective 2010). adv. **Document type:** *Magazine, Consumer.* **Description:** Contains questions and answers on all aspects of knowledge and trivia.
Published by: Gruner + Jahr AG & Co, Weihenstephaner Str 7, Munich, 81673, Germany. TEL 49-89-41520, FAX 49-89-4152651, guj-redaktion@guj.de, http://www.brigitte.de. Adv. contact Christian Liesegang. page EUR 8,450. Circ: 70,000 (paid and controlled).

500 DEU ISSN 0935-9400
P.M. PERSPEKTIVE. Text in German. 1986. 4/yr. EUR 20; EUR 5 newsstand/cover (effective 2010). adv. back issues avail. **Document type:** *Magazine, Consumer.*
Published by: Gruner + Jahr AG & Co, Weihenstephaner Str 7, Munich, 81673, Germany. TEL 49-89-41520, FAX 49-89-4152651, guj-redaktion@guj.de, http://www.guj.de. Adv. contact Christian Liesegang. page EUR 8,350.

P O R I M OCCASIONAL PAPER. *see* AGRICULTURE

500 ITA ISSN 1824-8039
Q101
P O S - PROCEEDINGS OF SCIENCE. Text in English. 2005. irreg. free (effective 2011). **Document type:** *Journal, Academic/Scholarly.* **Description:** Publishes without charge the proceedings of scientific conferences.
Media: Online - full text.
Indexed: CCMJ, MSN, MathR.
Published by: Scuola Internazionale Superiore di Studi Avanzati (S I S S A)/International School of Advanced Studies, Via Beirut 2-4, Trieste, 34014, Italy. TEL 39-40-378711, FAX 39-40-3787528, http:// www.sissa.it.

500 CHE ISSN 1662-1719
P S I SCIENTIFIC REPORT. Text in English. 2006. a.
Formerly (until 2007): P S I Scientific Report. Vol. 1: Condensed Matter, Photons, Neutrons and Charged Particules (1661-7002); Which was formed by the merger of (1999-2006): P S I Scientific Report. Vol. 1: Particles and Matter (1423-7296); Which was formerly (until 1999): P S I Annual Report. Annex 1: PSI Nuclear and Particle Physics Muons in Solid-State Physics and Chemistry (1422-7002); (1988-1994): P S I Annual Report. Annex 1: PSI Nuclear and Particle Physics Newsletter (1422-6316); (1999-2006): P S I Scientific Report. Vol. 6: Large Research Facilities (1423-7350); (2003-2006): P S I Scientific Report. Vol. 7: Synchotron Radiation, Micro- and Nanotechnology (1660-4709); Which was formerly (1999-2003): P S I Scientific Report. Vol. 7: Swiss Light Source (1423-7369); (1999-2006): P S I Scientific Report. Vol. 3: Condensed Matter Research With Neutrons (1423-7326); Which was formed by the merger of (1995-1999): P S I Annual Report. Annex 3a: P S I Solid State Research at Large Facilities (1422-7010); Which was formerly (1988-1995): P S I Annual Report. Annex 3: P S I Condensed Matter Research and Materials Sciences Progress Report (1018-8738); (1992-1999): P S I Annual Report. Annex 3b: P S I Applied Solid State Physics (1422-6332)
Published by: Paul Scherrer Institut, Villigen Psi, 5232, Switzerland. TEL 41-56-3102111, FAX 41-56-3102199, info@psi.ch.

P T B BERICHTE. NEUTRONENPHYSIK. *see* TECHNOLOGY: COMPREHENSIVE WORKS

500 USA
GC1005.2
PACIFIC HIGH SCHOOL SCIENCE SYMPOSIUM. PROCEEDINGS. Text in English. 1976. a. free to qualified personnel. back issues avail. **Document type:** *Proceedings.* **Description:** Contains reports of student projects in science - all fields from grades 9-12.
Formerly (until 1998): Annual Student Symposium of Marine Affairs. Proceedings (0270-1480)
Published by: Hawaiian Academy of Science, 1776 University Ave., Honolulu, HI 96822-2463. TEL 808-956-7930, FAX 808-956-5183. Ed., R&P Katherine H Aratani. Circ: 200 (controlled).

500 600 USA ISSN 1551-7624
➤ **PACIFIC JOURNAL OF SCIENCE AND TECHNOLOGY (HILO).** Text in English. 2004. s-a. free (effective 2011). back issues avail. **Document type:** *Journal, Academic/Scholarly.* **Description:** Aims to provide a non-commercial platform for the dissemination of scientific research and theory across the academic disciplines.
Formerly (until 2004): Greenwhich Journal of Science and Technology (1444-1519)
Media: Online - full text.
Indexed: A39, C27, C29, D03, D04, E13, R14, S14, S15, S18.
Published by: Akamai University, 187 Kino 'ole St, Hilo, HI 96720. TEL 808-934-8793, FAX 808-443-0445, information@akamaiuniversity.us.

▼ ➤ **PACIFIC NORTHWEST JOURNAL OF UNDERGRADUATE RESEARCH AND CREATIVE ACTIVITIES.** *see* HUMANITIES: COMPREHENSIVE WORKS

570 USA ISSN 0030-8870
QH1 CODEN: PASCAP
➤ **PACIFIC SCIENCE**; a quarterly devoted to the biological and physical sciences of the Pacific Region. Abbreviated title: P S. Text in English. 1947. q. USD 40 domestic to individuals; USD 88 foreign to individuals; USD 90 domestic to institutions; USD 138 foreign to institutions; USD 20 per issue domestic to individuals; USD 32 per issue foreign to individuals; USD 30 per issue domestic to institutions; USD 42 per issue foreign to institutions (effective 2009). adv. bibl.; charts; illus. Index. 128 p./no.; back issues avail.; reprint service avail. from PSC. **Document type:** *Journal, Academic/Scholarly.* **Description:** Presents international and multidisciplinary reports on biological and physical sciences of the Pacific region.
Related titles: Microform ed.: (from PMC, PQC); Online - full text ed.: ISSN 1534-6188. 2001.
Indexed: A01, A02, A03, A08, A20, A22, A26, A29, A34, A35, A38, AESIS, ASFA, AgBio, AgrForAb, AnBeAb, B20, B21, B23, B25, BIOSIS Prev, BP, C25, C30, CA, CABA, ChemAb, ChemTitl, CurCont, DIP, E01, E04, E05, E08, E12, E17, ESPM, EntAb, F08, F11, F12, FCA, G08, G11, GEOBASE, GH, GeoRef, H16, H17, HPNRM, I05, I11, IBR, IBZ, IndVet, LT, MinerAb, MycolAb, N02, N03, O01, OR, OceAb, P10, P15, P26, P32, P33, P37, P39, P40, P48, P52, P53, P54, P56, PGegResA, PN&I, PQC, R07, R08, R12, R13, RA&MP, RASB, RRTA, S06, S09, S13, S16, S17, SCI, SCOPUS, SPPI, SSciA, SWRA, SpeleolAb, T02, T05, TAR, VS, VirolAbstr, W07, W08, W10, W11, WildRev, Z01.
—BLDSC (6331.000000), CASDDS, IE, Infotrieve, Ingenta, INIST, Linda Hall. **CCC.**
Published by: University of Hawaii Press, Journals Department, 2840 Kolowalu St, Honolulu, HI 96822. TEL 808-956-8255, FAX 808-988-6052, uhpbooks@hawaii.edu. Ed. Curtis C Daehler. R&P Joel Bradshaw TEL 808-956-6790. Adv. contact Norman Kaneshiro TEL 808-956-8833. page USD 200; 5.5 x 8. Circ: 525.

500 USA
PACIFIC SCIENCE ASSOCIATION. CONGRESS AND INTER-CONGRESS PROCEEDINGS. (Proceedings published by host country.) Text in English. 1920. biennial. price varies. **Document type:** *Proceedings.*
Formerly: Pacific Science Association. Congress Proceedings (0078-7647)
Indexed: SpeleolAb.
Published by: Pacific Science Association, 1525 Bernice St., Honolulu, HI 96817-2704. TEL 808-848-4139, FAX 808-841-8968.

PACT/RESEAU EUROPEEN DE SCIENCES ET TECHNIQUES APPLIQUEES AU PATRIMOINE CULTUREL. REVUE. *see* ARCHAEOLOGY

505 PAK ISSN 0377-2969
Q1 CODEN: PKSPAW
➤ **PAKISTAN ACADEMY OF SCIENCES. PROCEEDINGS.** Text in English. 1964. s-a. PKR 1,000 domestic to individuals; USD 100 foreign to individuals; PKR 2,000 domestic to institutions (effective 2010). adv. bk.rev. abstr.; bibl.; charts; illus. back issues avail. **Document type:** *Proceedings, Academic/Scholarly.* **Description:** Deals with different subjects such as agriculture, astronomy, biology, chemistry, computers, engineering, environmental studies, mathematics, medical sciences, physics and veterinary sciences. Aims at scientists, medical engineers, physicians and students and teachers interested in the areas.
Related titles: Fax ed.
Indexed: CCMJ, CIN, ChemAb, ChemTitl, INIS AtomInd, Inspec, MSN, MathR, SCOPUS.
—BLDSC (6784.000000), AskIEEE, CASDDS, IE, Ingenta, INIST, Linda Hall.
Published by: Pakistan Academy of Sciences, Constitution Ave, G-5/2, Islamabad, Pakistan. TEL 92-51-9207140, FAX 92-51-9206770, pasisb@yahoo.com. Ed., R&P, Adv. contact Dr. M A Hafeez. Pub. Dr. Khalid M Khan TEL 92-51-9206770. B&W page USD 200, color page USD 300. Circ: 250 (paid); 100 (controlled).

500 PAK
PAKISTAN ASSOCIATION FOR THE ADVANCEMENT OF SCIENCE. ANNUAL REPORT. Text in English. a. PKR 50, USD 8 (effective 1999 & 2000).
Published by: Pakistan Association for the Advancement of Science, 273 N. Model Town, Extension, Lahore, Pakistan. Ed. Muhammad Saleem Chaudhry.

500 607 PAK ISSN 0078-804X
PAKISTAN COUNCIL OF SCIENTIFIC AND INDUSTRIAL RESEARCH. ANNUAL REPORT. Abbreviated title: P C S I R Annual Report. Text in English. 1953. a. price varies. **Document type:** *Corporate.*
Published by: Pakistan Journal of Scientific and Industrial Research, Scientific Information Centre, PCSIR Laboratories Campus, Shahrah-e-Dr. Salimuzzaman Siddiqui, Karachi, 75280, Pakistan. TEL 92-21-34651739, FAX 92-21-34651738. Ed. A Rasheed Khan. Circ: 1,000.

PAKISTAN JOURNAL OF ENGINEERING AND APPLIED SCIENCES. *see* ENGINEERING

500 PAK ISSN 0030-9877
Q73 CODEN: PAJSAS
PAKISTAN JOURNAL OF SCIENCE. Text in English. 1949. q. PKR 100, USD 50 (effective 1999 & 2000). decennial index. **Document type:** *Journal, Academic/Scholarly.*
Indexed: A26, A34, A36, A37, A38, B23, BA, C25, C30, CABA, CIN, ChemAb, ChemTitl, D01, E12, F08, F12, FCA, FS&TA, G11, GH, GeoRef, H16, H17, I05, I11, INIS AtomInd, IndVet, Inspec, MaizeAb, N02, N03, N04, OR, P30, P32, P33, P39, P40, PGegResA, PHN&I, PST, R07, R08, R11, R12, RA&MP, S12, S13, S16, S17, SoyAb, SpeleolAb, T05, TAR, TriticAb, VS, W11.
—BLDSC (6342.000000), AskIEEE, CASDDS, Ingenta, Linda Hall.
Published by: Pakistan Association for the Advancement of Science, 273 N. Model Town, Extension, Lahore, Pakistan. Ed. Muhammad Saleem Chaudhry.

500 PAK ISSN 0030-9885
Q180.A1 CODEN: PSIRAA
➤ **PAKISTAN JOURNAL OF SCIENTIFIC AND INDUSTRIAL RESEARCH.** Text in English. 1958. bi-m. PKR 2,000 per vol. domestic to institutions; USD 400 per vol. foreign to institutions; PKR 350 newsstand/cover domestic to institutions; USD 70 newsstand/ cover foreign to institutions (effective 2011). adv. bk.rev. charts; illus.; abstr.; bibl.; maps. index. back issues avail.; reprints avail. **Document type:** *Journal, Academic/Scholarly.*
Related titles: Online - full text ed.: free (effective 2011) (from PQC).
Indexed: A22, A28, A29, A34, A35, A36, A37, A38, APA, ASFA, AgBio, AgrForAb, B20, B21, B23, B25, BA, BIOSIS Prev, BP, BrCerAb, C&ISA, C25, C30, CA/WCA, CABA, CIA, CTFA, CerAb, ChemAb, ChemTitl, CivEngAb, CorrAb, D01, E&CAJ, E11, E12, EEA, EMA, ESPM, EnvEAb, F08, F11, F12, FCA, FS&TA, G11, GEOBASE, GH, GeoRef, H15, H16, H17, I10, I11, I12, INIS AtomInd, IndVet, Inspec, LT, M&TEA, M09, MBF, METADEX, MaizeAb, MycolAb, N02, N03, N04, O01, OR, P30, P32, P33, P37, P39, P40, PGegResA, PGrRegA, PHN&I, PN&I, PollutAb, R07, R08, R11, R12, R13, RA&MP, RM&VM, RRTA, S&MA, S12, S13, S16, S17, SCOPUS, SolStAb, SoyAb, SpeleolAb, T04, T05, TOSA, TriticAb, VS, VirolAbstr, W10, W11, WAA, WildRev, Z01.
—BLDSC (6342.700000), CASDDS, IE, Infotrieve, Ingenta, INIST, Linda Hall.
Address: Scientific Information Centre, PCSIR Laboratories Campus, Shahrah-e-Dr. Salimuzzaman Siddiqui, Karachi, 75280, Pakistan. TEL 92-21-34651739, FAX 92-21-34651738, info@pjsir.org. Ed. Shoukat Parvez. R&P S M A Hai. Circ: 800.

500 PAK ISSN 0552-9050
Q180.P25 CODEN: PJSRAV
PAKISTAN JOURNAL OF SCIENTIFIC RESEARCH. Text in English. 1949. q. PKR 100, USD 50 (effective 1999). cum.index every 10 yrs. **Document type:** *Journal, Academic/Scholarly.*
Indexed: A34, A36, B23, C25, C30, CABA, CIN, ChemAb, ChemTitl, D01, FS&TA, GH, H16, H17, INIS AtomInd, IndVet, Inspec, N02, N04, OR, P32, P33, P38, P40, PGegResA, PHN&I, R07, R11, S13, S16, S17, SoyAb, SpeleolAb, TAR, VS.
—BLDSC (6343.000000), AskIEEE, CASDDS, INIST, Linda Hall.
Published by: Pakistan Association for the Advancement of Science, 273 N. Model Town, Extension, Lahore, Pakistan. Ed. Muhammad Saleem Chaudhry.

500 PAK ISSN 0078-8430
PAKISTAN SCIENCE CONFERENCE. PROCEEDINGS. Text in English. a. PKR 150, USD 60 (effective 1999 & 2000). index. **Document type:** *Proceedings.*
Indexed: GeoRef, SpeleolAb.
Published by: Pakistan Association for the Advancement of Science, 273 N. Model Town, Extension, Lahore, Pakistan. Ed. Muhammad Saleem Chaudhry.

PALM OIL DEVELOPMENTS. *see* AGRICULTURE

500 610 USA ISSN 1948-7843
▼ **PALO ALTO INSTITUTE. JOURNAL.** Variant title: Journal of the Palo Alto Institute. Text in English. 2009. q. **Document type:** *Journal, Academic/Scholarly.* **Description:** Contains articles on topics that receive little coverage in mainstream scientific and medical publications.
Related titles: Online - full text ed.: ISSN 1948-7851.
Published by: Palo Alto Institute, 470 University Ave, Palo Alto, CA 94301. TEL 650-470-3400, info@pa-institute.org, http:www.paloaltoinstitute.org.

508 IND
Q180.I5 CODEN: RBJUAT
PANJAB UNIVERSITY RESEARCH JOURNAL (SCIENCE). Text in English. 1950. s-a. back issues avail. **Document type:** *Journal, Academic/Scholarly.* **Description:** Multi-disciplinary studies of sciences, on both pre-doctoral and post-doctoral levels.
Former titles (until 2003): Panjab University Research Bulletin (Science) (0555-7631); (until 1954): East Panjab University. Research Bulletin (0555-7623)
Indexed: B25, BAS, BIOSIS Prev, CCMJ, CIN, ChemAb, ChemTitl, GeoRef, MSN, MathR, MycolAb, SpeleolAb, TOSA, WildRev, Z01, Z02.
—CASDDS, Ingenta, INIST.
Published by: (Panjab University), Publication Bureau (Subsidiary of: Panjab University), Chandigarh, 160 014, India. TEL 91-172-2784869, librarian@pu.ac.in, http://www.puchd.ac.in/.

500 GBR ISSN 1741-1572
THE PANTANETO FORUM; preliminaries to a science of the mind. Text in English. 2001. q. GBP 11.95 per issue (effective 2009). back issues avail. **Document type:** *Journal, Academic/Scholarly.* **Description:** Aims to promote debate on how scientists communicate, with particular emphasis on how such communication can be improved through education and a better philosophical understanding of science.
Related titles: Online - full text ed.: free (effective 2011).
Indexed: A39, C27, C29, D03, D04, E13, R14, S14, S15, S18.

S

Published by: The Pantaneto Press, 1st Fl, 3 Gordon St, Luton, LU1 2QP, United Kingdom. Ed. Nigel Sanitt.

PANYU ZHIYE JISHU XUEYUAN XUEBAO. *see* SOCIAL SCIENCES: COMPREHENSIVE WORKS

500 COL ISSN 1909-4302

➤ **PARADIGMAS.** Text in Spanish; Summaries in English, Portuguese. s-a. free. bk.rev. Index. back issues avail. **Document type:** *Journal, Academic/Scholarly.* **Description:** Publishes multidisciplinary analysis papers and thematic reviews in research topics with a methodological, epistemological, ethical and / or administrative focus, including: New methods and techniques developed within a project; research ethics; research methods; management and evaluation of research projects; philosophy of science; epistemology of science.
Related titles: Online - full text ed.: free.
Published by: Corporacion Universitaria Unitec, Centro de Publicaciones Academicas, Calle 76 #12-61, Bogota, Colombia. TEL 57-1-5939393 ext 3506, FAX 57-1-5939393 ext 1102, cpa@g.unitec.edu.co. Ed., Pub., R&P David Acosta. Circ: 200 (controlled).

500.9 FRA ISSN 0180-961X
QH147

PARC NATIONAL DE LA VANOISE. TRAVAUX SCIENTIFIQUES. Text in French; Summaries in English, German, Italian. 1970. irreg. bk.rev. **Document type:** *Monographic series, Academic/Scholarly.* **Description:** Covers the history, geography, geology, biology, botany, zoology, ornithology, culture, people, economy of the Vanoise region of the French Alps.
Indexed: FR, GeoRef, SpeleolAb.
—INIST.
Published by: France. Ministere de l'Ecologie, du Developpement Durable, des Transports et du Logement, 20 av. de Segur, Paris, Cedex 7 75302, France. http://www.developpement-durable.gouv.fr.

500.9 USA ISSN 0079-032X
QH1 CODEN: YUPBA8

PEABODY MUSEUM OF NATURAL HISTORY. BULLETIN. Text in English. 1925. s-a. USD 145 domestic; USD 175 foreign (effective 2011). back issues avail. **Document type:** *Bulletin, Academic/Scholarly.* **Description:** Dedicated to the dissemination of scholarly research and study of the world and its cultures.
Incorporates (1950-2004): Postilla (0079-4295); (1927-1967): Bulletin of Bingham Oceanographic Collection (0097-1375)
Related titles: Online - full text ed.: ISSN 2162-4135.
Indexed: A20, B25, BIOSIS Prev, CurCont, GeoRef, MycolAb, SCI, SpeleolAb, W07, Z01.
—Linda Hall. **CCC.**
Published by: Yale University, Peabody Museum of Natural History, PO Box 208118, New Haven, CT 06520. TEL 203-432-3786, FAX 203-432-5872, peabody.publications@yale.edu.

500 570 USA ISSN 1044-6753
CODEN: JPSCEY

➤ **PENNSYLVANIA ACADEMY OF SCIENCE. JOURNAL.** Text in English. 1924. 3/yr. bk.rev. abstr. back issues avail. **Document type:** *Journal, Academic/Scholarly.* **Description:** Presents papers from the natural, engineering and social sciences.
Formerly (until 1988): Pennsylvania Academy of Science. Proceedings (0096-9222)
Related titles: Online - full text ed.
Indexed: B25, BIOSIS Prev, CIN, ChemAb, ChemTitl, GeoRef, MycolAb, P30, SASA, SpeleolAb, VITIS, W08, WildRev, Z01.
—BLDSC (4839.645000), CASDDS, IE, Infotrieve, Ingenta, INIST, Linda Hall.
Published by: Pennsylvania Academy of Science, c/o Dr S K Majumdar, Ed, Department of Biology, Lafayette College, Easton, PA 18042.

500 COL ISSN 0120-1190
AS82.A1

PENSAMIENTO Y ACCION; revista internacional de ciencia y cultura. Text in Spanish. 1962. s-a. COP 30,000, USD 15; COP 15,000 newsstand/cover (effective 2001). adv. bk.rev.; play rev. charts; illus.
Formerly: Nueva Epoca
Published by: Universidad Pedagogica y Tecnologica de Colombia, Instituto de Investigaciones y Formacion Avanzada, Carretera Central del Norte, Tunja, BOY, Colombia. TEL 57-987-425268, FAX 57-987-425268, iifa@donato.uptc.edu.co. Ed. Edilberto Rodriguez Araujo. Circ: 1,000 (controlled).

500 GBR ISSN 2040-3968
Q175.4

PEOPLE AND SCIENCE. Text in English. 1986. q. GBP 60 domestic; GBP 70 in Europe; GBP 80 elsewhere (effective 2009). adv. software rev.; bk.rev.; Website rev.; tel.rev.; video rev. 32 p./no. 3 cols./p.; back issues avail. **Document type:** *Magazine, Academic/Scholarly.* **Description:** Aims to promote awareness of the importance of science, medicine, engineering and technology to our lives.
Formerly (until 2009): Science and Public Affairs (0268-490X)
Related titles: Online - full text ed.
Indexed: A22, BAS, E04, E05, P34, PAIS, PRA, PhilInd.
—BLDSC (6422.876130), IE, Infotrieve, Ingenta, Linda Hall. **CCC.**
Published by: The British Science Association, Welcome Wolfson Bldg, 165 Queen's Gate, London, SW7 5HE, United Kingdom. TEL 44-870-7707101, FAX 44-870-7707102. Ed. Wendy Barnaby. Circ: 5,200.

500 610 USA ISSN 1944-0065
Q1.A3

PERSPECTIVES (ARLINGTON). Text in English. 2001. w. free (effective 2009). back issues avail. **Document type:** *Journal, Academic/Scholarly.* **Description:** Summarizes current or emerging issues related to science or medicine.
Media: Online - full content.
Published by: Science Advisory Board, 2111 Wilson Blvd, Ste 250, Arlington, VA 22201. TEL 703-778-3080 ext 26, FAX 703-778-3081, questions@scienceboard.net.

500 USA ISSN 1063-6145
Q124.6 CODEN: PRSIEU

➤ **PERSPECTIVES ON SCIENCE**; historical, philosophical, social. Abbreviated title: P O S. Text in English. 1993. q. USD 248 combined subscription in US & Canada to institutions (print & online eds.); USD 62 per issue in US & Canada to institutions (effective 2012). adv. back issues avail.; reprints avail. **Document type:** *Journal, Academic/Scholarly.* **Description:** Devoted to studies of the sciences that integrate historical, philosophical, and sociological perspectives.
Related titles: Microfilm ed.: (from PQC); Online - full text ed.: ISSN 1530-9274. USD 215 in US & Canada to institutions (effective 2012).
Indexed: A01, A03, A08, A22, A26, AmH&L, BIOSIS Prev, CA, CCMJ, DIP, E01, E07, E08, G08, HistAb, I05, IBR, IBZ, MSN, MathR, MycolAb, P07, P30, PhilInd, RASB, S02, S03, S09, SCOPUS, SOPODA, SociolAb, T02.
—BLDSC (6428.163680), IE, Infotrieve, INIST, Linda Hall. **CCC.**
Published by: M I T Press, 55 Hayward St, Cambridge, MA 02142. TEL 617-253-2889, FAX 617-577-1545, journals-cs@mit.edu, http://mitpress.mit.edu. Eds. Mordechai Feingold, Roger Ariew TEL 813-974-0126.

➤ **PERSPECTIVES ON SCIENCE AND CHRISTIAN FAITH.** *see* RELIGIONS AND THEOLOGY

500 DEU ISSN 0933-1271
Q180.G3

PERSPEKTIVEN DER FORSCHUNG UND IHRER FORDERUNG. Text in German. 1961. irreg., latest 2008. price varies. **Document type:** *Monographic series, Academic/Scholarly.*
Formerly (until 1987): Deutsche Forschungsgemeinschaft. Aufgaben und Finanzierung (0418-8403)
Related titles: Online - full text ed.
Indexed: RASB.
Published by: (Deutsche Forschungsgemeinschaft), Wiley - V C H Verlag GmbH & Co. KGaA (Subsidiary of: John Wiley & Sons, Inc.), Postfach 101161, Weinheim, 69451, Germany. TEL 49-6201-606400, FAX 49-6201-606184, info@wiley-vch.de, http://www.wiley-vch.de.

500 600 MYS ISSN 1511-3701
CODEN: PERTDY

➤ **PERTANIKA JOURNAL OF SCIENCE AND TECHNOLOGY.** Text in English, Malay. irreg. (1-2/yr.), latest vol.10, 2002. USD 60 (effective 2002). **Document type:** *Journal, Academic/Scholarly.*
Supersedes in part (in 1993): Pertanika (0126-6128)
Indexed: A01, A29, B&BAb, B19, B20, B21, CA, E17, ESPM, FS&TA, I10, SCOPUS, T02.
—BLDSC (6428.183070), CASDDS, IE, Ingenta.
Published by: (Agricultural University of Malaysia/Universiti Pertanian Malaysia), Universiti Pertanian Malaysia Press, 43400 UPM, Serdang, Selangor, Malaysia. TEL 603-8946-8855, FAX 603-8941-6172. Ed. Abang Abdullah Abang Ali. Circ: 300.

500 BRA ISSN 0103-4049
Q180.A6

PESQUISA ANTARTICA BRASILEIRA. Text in English, Portuguese. 1989. irreg. 150 p./no.; back issues avail.
Indexed: ASFA, B21, C01, ESPM, GeoRef.
Published by: Academia Brasileira de Ciencias, Rua Anfilofio de Carvalho, 29-3A, Centro, Rio de Janeiro, RJ 20030-060, Brazil. TEL 55-21-2220-4794, FAX 55-21-2532-5807, aabc@abc.org.br, http://www.abc.org.br, http://www.scielo.br/aabc.

507.1025 USA ISSN 1093-8443
L901

PETERSON'S GRADUATE PROGRAMS IN THE PHYSICAL SCIENCES, MATHEMATICS, AGRICULTURAL SCIENCES, THE ENVIRONMENT & NATURAL RESOURCES. Text in English. 1966. a. USD 40.50 (effective 2008). **Document type:** *Directory, Academic/Scholarly.* **Description:** Covers more than 3,000 options for graduate study in chemistry, geosciences, marine sciences, physics, statistics, agricultural sciences, and natural resources, among others.
Former titles (until 1998): Peterson's Graduate and Professional Programs: The Physical Sciences, Mathematics, and Agricultural Sciences (Year) (Book 4) (1088-9426); Which superseded in part (in 1997): Peterson's Annual Guides to Graduate Study. Book 3, Peterson's Guide to Graduate Programs in the Biological and Agricultural Sciences (0894-9360); (until 1986): Peterson's Guide to Graduate Programs in the Physical Sciences and Mathematics (Year) (Book 4) (0894-9379); (until 1989): Peterson's Annual Guides to Graduate Study. Book 4. Graduate Programs in the Physical Sciences and Mathematics. (0887-8595); (until 1984): Peterson's Annual Guides to Graduate Study. Book 4. Physical Sciences and Mathematics (0887-8587); (until 1982): Peterson's Guides. Annual Guides to Graduate Study. Book 4: Physical Sciences (0887-8579)
Related titles: CD-ROM ed.; Online - full text ed.
Published by: Thomson Peterson's (Subsidiary of: Thomson Reuters Corp.), Princeton Pike Corporate Center, 2000 Lenox Dr, 3rd Fl, PO Box 67005, Lawrenceville, NJ 08648. TEL 609-896-1800, 800-338-3282 ext 54229, FAX 609-896-4531, custsvc@petersons.com, http://www.petersons.com.

500 DEU ISSN 1861-4035

PHAENOMENOLOGIE IN DER NATURWISSENSCHAFT. Text in German. 2005. irreg., latest vol.6, 2011. price varies. **Document type:** *Monographic series, Academic/Scholarly.*
Published by: Logos Verlag Berlin, Comeniushof, Gubener Str 47, Berlin, 10243, Germany. TEL 49-30-42851090, FAX 49-30-42851092, redaktion@logos-verlag.de. Eds. Johannes Grebe-Ellis, Lutz-Helmut Schoen.

500 001.3 600 300 GBR ISSN 1751-3030
Z286.S37

➤ **PHILICA**; where ideas are free. Text in English. 2006. irreg. free (effective 2011). **Document type:** *Journal, Academic/Scholarly.* **Description:** Features reviews of academic research.
Media: Online - full content.
Indexed: A01, A39, C27, C29, D03, D04, E13, R14, S14, S15, S18, T02.

500 PHL ISSN 0031-7683
Q75 CODEN: PJSCAK

PHILIPPINE JOURNAL OF SCIENCE. Text in English. 1906. q. PHP 260, USD 80. bk.rev. abstr.; bibl.; charts. index, cum.index: 1951-1970 (vols. 80-99), 1971-1975 (vols. 100-104).
Related titles: Microform ed.: (from PMC).
Indexed: A22, AESIS, ApMecR, BAS, ChemAb, ChemTitl, EIP, FS&TA, GeoRef, H09, H10, IBR, IBZ, INIS AtomInd, IPP, MLA-IB, S05, SCOPUS, SpeleolAb, WildRev, Z01.
—BLDSC (6456.000000), CASDDS, GNLM, IE, Ingenta, INIST, Linda Hall.
Published by: Industrial Technology Development Institute, P. Gil, Taft Ave, P.O. Box 744, Manila, Philippines. FAX 632-592275. Ed. Quintin L Kintanar. Circ: 1,300. **Subscr. to:** Science and Technology Information Institute, P.O. Box 3596, Manila, Philippines.

500 PHL ISSN 0079-1466
Q76 CODEN: PHISB5

➤ **PHILIPPINE SCIENTIST.** Text in English. 1964. a., latest vol.45, 2008. USD 15 (effective 2010). adv. bk.rev. cum.index: 1964-1993. 150 p./no.; back issues avail. **Document type:** *Journal, Academic/Scholarly.* **Description:** Deals with research in various natural science fields, emphasizing marine biology and entomology.
Formerly (until 1967): Junior Philippine Scientist (0115-2750)
Indexed: A29, ASFA, B20, B21, B25, BIOSIS Prev, CTA, ChemoAb, ESPM, EntAb, I10, IPP, MycolAb, NSA, OceAb, SWRA, ViroIAbstr, Z01.
—CASDDS.
Published by: San Carlos Publications, University of San Carlos, Cebu City, 6000, Philippines. TEL 63-32-2531000 ext 175, FAX 63-32-2554341, http://www.usc.edu.ph/administration/san_carlos_publication_contact_information.jsp. Ed. Patrick John Y. Lim. Circ: 200.

500 PHL

PHILIPPINE TECHNICAL INFORMATION SHEETS. Text in English. irreg. PHP 75 per issue; USD 10 per issue foreign. **Document type:** *Monographic series.* **Description:** Provides comprehensive information on the 15 Philippine S & T leading edges in the Science and Technology Master Plan (STMP).
Published by: (Department of Science and Technology), Science and Technology Information Institute, P.O. Box 3596, Manila, Philippines. TEL 822-0954. **Subscr. to:** Dept. of Science and Technology, Bicutan, Taguig, P.O. Box 2131, Manila, Philippines.

509 FRA ISSN 1281-2463
Q174

PHILOSOPHIA SCIENTIAE. Text in English, French, German; Abstracts in English, French. 1996. s-a. EUR 35 domestic; EUR 38 foreign (effective 2009). **Document type:** *Journal, Academic/Scholarly.*
Related titles: Online - full text ed.
Indexed: FR, PhilInd.
—BLDSC (6461.607000), INIST.
Published by: (Archives Henri Poincare), Editions Kime, 2 Impasse des Peintres, Paris, 75002, France. TEL 33-1-42213072, FAX 33-1-42213084, kime.editions@wanadoo.fr. Ed. Gerhard Heinzmann. **Dist. by:** Editions Les Belles Lettres, 25 Rue du General Leclerc, Kremlin Bicetre 94270, France. TEL 33-1-45151970, FAX 33-1-45151980.

500 IND ISSN 0974-4215

➤ **PHILOSOPHICAL NATURE.** Text in English. 2008. q. back issues avail. **Document type:** *Journal, Academic/Scholarly.* **Description:** Aims to cover conventional and cross-disciplinary ideas on mathematics, physics, chemical and molecular sciences, biomedicines and economics.
Related titles: CD-ROM ed.: ISSN 0974-4223; Online - full text ed.: ISSN 0974-4231. free (effective 2011).
Indexed: A01, T02.
Published by: Excogitation & Innovation Laboratory, 45/2 Atul Prasad Sarani, Hakimpara, PO Rabindra Sarani, Siliguri, WB 734 006, India. TEL 91-99336-77303, admin@eilab.org.

501 USA ISSN 0031-8248
Q1 CODEN: PHSCA6

➤ **PHILOSOPHY OF SCIENCE.** Text in English. 1934. 5/yr. USD 244 combined subscription to institutions (print & online eds.) (effective 2012). bk.rev. bibl.; illus. Index. back issues avail.; reprint service avail. from PSC. **Document type:** *Journal, Academic/Scholarly.* **Description:** Provides a forum for diverse philosophical perspectives on the sciences.
Incorporates (1970-1994): P S A (0270-8647)
Related titles: Microform ed.: (from PMC, PQC); Online - full text ed.: ISSN 1539-767X. USD 207 to institutions (effective 2012).
Indexed: A01, A02, A03, A08, A20, A21, A22, A25, A26, ASCA, AmHI, ArtHuCI, B04, B07, B25, BIOSIS Prev, BRD, CA, CCMJ, CIS, CLOSS, CurCont, DIP, E08, FR, G08, H07, H08, H09, H10, H14, HAb, HumInd, I05, I07, IBR, IBRH, IBSS, IBZ, IPB, ISR, Inspec, MLA-IB, MSN, MathR, MycolAb, P02, P10, P11, P13, P30, P48, P52, P53, P54, P56, PCI, PQC, PhilInd, PsycholAb, R05, RASB, RI-1, RI-2, S02, S03, S05, S08, S09, S23, SCI, SCOPUS, SOPODA, SSCI, SociolAb, T02, W03, W07.
—BLDSC (6465.000000), IE, Infotrieve, Ingenta, INIST, Linda Hall. **CCC.**
Published by: (University of Chicago, Philosophy of Science Association), University of Chicago Press, 1427 E 60th St, Chicago, IL 60637. TEL 773-702-7600, FAX 773-702-0694, subscriptions@press.uchicago.edu. Ed. Jeffrey Barrett. Adv. contact Cheryl Jones TEL 773-702-7361. **Subscr. to:** PO Box 370050, Chicago, IL 60637. TEL 773-753-3347, 877-705-1878, FAX 773-753-0811, 877-705-1879.

➤ **PHYSIKALISCH-TECHNISCHE BUNDESANSTALT. JAHRESBERICHT.** *see* TECHNOLOGY: COMPREHENSIVE WORKS

➤ **PHYSIKALISCH-TECHNISCHE BUNDESANSTALT. PRUEFREGELN.** *see* TECHNOLOGY: COMPREHENSIVE WORKS

530 ITA ISSN 0031-9414
Q54 CODEN: PYSSA3

PHYSIS; rivista internazionale di storia della scienza. Text in English, French, German, Italian, Spanish. 1959. s-a. EUR 130 combined subscription foreign to institutions (print & online eds.) (effective 2012). adv. bk.rev. illus. **Document type:** *Journal, Academic/Scholarly.*
Related titles: Online - full text ed.: ISSN 2038-6265.
Indexed: A22, AmH&L, CA, CCMJ, ChemAb, DIP, EMBASE, ExcerpMed, FR, HistAb, I14, IBR, IBZ, MEDLINE, MLA-IB, MSN, MathR, NumL, P30, RASB, SCOPUS, T02, Z02.
—IE, Infotrieve, Linda Hall.
Published by: Casa Editrice Leo S. Olschki, Viuzzo del Pozzetto 8, Florence, 50126, Italy. TEL 39-055-6530684, FAX 39-055-6530214, celso@olschki.it, http://www.olschki.it. Eds. Guido Cimino, Vincenzo Cappelletti. Circ: 1,000.

PINGDINGSHAN XUEYUAN XUEBAO/PINGDINGSHAN UNIVERSITY. JOURNAL. *see* SOCIAL SCIENCES: COMPREHENSIVE WORKS

PINNGORTITALERIFFIK. TEKNISK RAPPORT/GRONLANDS NATURINSTITUT. TEKNISK RAPPORT. *see* ENVIRONMENTAL STUDIES

500 GRL ISSN 1397-6109
PINNGORTITALERIFFIK. UKIUMOORTUMIK NALUNAARUSIAQ/ GROENLANDS NATURINSTITUT. AARSBERETNING. Text in Inuktitut, Danish. 1995. a. back issues avail. **Document type:** *Yearbook, Government.* **Description:** Annual report presenting scientific investigations, financial and employees issues.
Related titles: Online - full text ed.: ISSN 1604-0503. 1999.
Published by: Pinngortitaleriffik, Groenlands Naturinstitut/Greenland Institute of Natural Resources, PO Box 570, Nuuk, 3900, Greenland. TEL 299-361210, FAX 299-361212, info@natur.gl.

PITTSBURGH SERIES IN PHILOSOPHY & HISTORY OF SCIENCE. *see* PHILOSOPHY

500 POL ISSN 1230-2392
DK4121
POGRANICZE; studia spoleczne. Text in Polish. 1991. a., latest vol.11, 2003. PLZ 20 per vol. (effective 2005). **Document type:** *Academic/ Scholarly.*
Published by: Wydawnictwo Uniwersytetu w Bialymstoku, ul Marii Sklodowskiej-Curie 14, Bialystok, 15097, Poland. TEL 48-85-7457059, FAX 48-85-7457073, ac-dw@uwb.edu.pl.

500 600 ARG ISSN 1852-8791
▼ **POIESIS ACADEMICA.** Text in Spanish. 2009. a. back issues avail. **Document type:** *Monographic series, Academic/Scholarly.*
Published by: Universidad Catolica de Santa Fe, Secretaria de Ciencia y Tecnologia, Echague, 7151, Santa fe, S3004JBS, Argentina. TEL 54-342-4603030, secyt@ucsf.edu.ar, http://www.ucsf.edu.ar/ investigacion.html.

500 CZE ISSN 0032-2423
Q44.J3 CODEN: PMFAA4
POKROKY MATEMATIKY, FYZIKY A ASTRONOMIE/PROGRESS IN MATHEMATICS, PHYSICS AND ASTRONOMY. Text in Czech, Slovak. 1956. q. EUR 120.90 foreign (effective 2009). bk.rev. illus.; stat. cum.index: 1956-1985, 1985-2000. 88 p./no.; back issues avail. **Document type:** *Journal, Academic/Scholarly.* **Description:** Publishes articles concerning mathematics, physics and astronomy (expository papers, history, philosophy, science and society, modern trends in education) news and activities of the association.
Indexed: ChemAb, MathR, Z02.
—CASDDS, INIST, Linda Hall.
Published by: Jednota Ceskych Matematiku a Fyziku, Zitna 25, Prague, 11710, Czech Republic. TEL 420-2-22211100, jcmf@jcmf.cz. Ed. Michal Krizek. Circ: 1,700 (paid). **Dist. in Western countries by:** Kubon & Sagner Buchexport - Import GmbH, Hessstr 39-41, Munich 80798, Germany. TEL 49-89-542180, FAX 49-89-54218218, postmaster@kubon-sagner.de, http://www.kubon-sagner.de.

919.8 500 SWE ISSN 0800-0395
G575 CODEN: POREEQ
➤ **POLAR RESEARCH.** Text in English. 1982. 3/yr. free (effective 2011). bk.rev. bibl.; illus.; abstr.; charts. back issues avail.; reprint service avail. from PSC. **Document type:** *Journal, Academic/Scholarly.* **Description:** Treats various subjects within the field of polar research.
Related titles: Online - full text ed.: ISSN 1751-8369. 1982 (from IngentaConnect).
Indexed: A22, A33, A34, ASFA, B21, B25, BIOSIS Prev, C25, C30, CA, CABA, CurCont, E01, E04, E05, E12, ESPM, F08, F12, G11, GEOBASE, GH, GeoRef, I11, ISR, Inspec, KWIWR, LT, M&GPA, MycolAb, P30, P33, P37, R08, RRTA, S13, S16, SCI, SCOPUS, SpeleolAb, T02, VS, W07, W08, W11, WildRev, Z01.
—BLDSC (6542.300000), AskIEEE, IE, Ingenta, INIST, Linda Hall. **CCC.**
Published by: (Norsk Polarinstitutt/Norwegian Polar Institute NOR), Co-Action Publishing, Ripvaegen 7, Jaerfaella, 17564, Sweden. TEL 46-18-4951150, FAX 46-18-4951138, info@co-action.net, http:// www.co-action.net. Ed. Helle Valborg Goldman TEL 47-77-750618.

508 POL ISSN 1643-9953
QH301
➤ **POLISH JOURNAL OF NATURAL SCIENCES.** Text in English. 1985. irreg. **Document type:** *Journal, Academic/Scholarly.*
Formerly (until 2002): Natural Sciences (1505-4667); Which superseded in part (in 1998): Acta Academiae Agriculturae ac Technicae Olstenensis (1509-3727)
Related titles: Online - full text ed.: free (effective 2011).
Indexed: A34, A35, A36, A37, A38, AgBio, Agr, AgrAg, AgrLib, B23, B25, BA, BIOSIS Prev, BP, C25, C30, CABA, D01, E12, F08, F11, F12, FCA, G11, GH, H16, H17, I11, IndVet, LT, MaizeAb, MycolAb, N02, N03, N04, O01, OR, P32, P33, P37, P38, P39, P40, PGegResA, PGrRegA, PHN&I, PN&I, R07, R08, R11, R13, RA&MP, RM&VM, RRTA, S12, S13, S16, S17, SCOPUS, SoyAb, TAR, TriticAb, VS, W10, W11, Z01.
Published by: Uniwersytet Warminsko-Mazurski, ul Oczapowskiego 2, Olsztyn, 10719, Poland. TEL 48-89-5240310, FAX 48-89-5240408, http://www.uni.olsztyn.pl/.

500 POL ISSN 0860-097X
CODEN: MPKKEH
POLITECHNIKA KRAKOWSKA. MONOGRAFIE. Text in Polish; Summaries in English, French, German, Russian. 1985. irreg., latest vol.356, 2008. price varies. bibl.; charts; illus. **Document type:** *Monographic series, Academic/Scholarly.*
Related titles: Online - full text ed.; ◆ Series: Politechnika Krakowska. Monografie. Seria: Inzynieria i Technologia Chemiczna; ◆ Politechnika Krakowska. Monografie. Seria: Inzynieria Ladowa; ◆ Politechnika Krakowska. Monografie. Seria: Historyczno-Techniczna. ISSN 1232-9568; ◆ Politechnika Krakowska. Monografie. Seria: Inzynieria Elektryczna; ◆ Politechnika Krakowska. Monografie. Seria: Mechanika; ◆ Politechnika Krakowska. Monografie. Seria: Nauki Spoleczne i Ekonomiczne; ◆ Politechnika Krakowska. Monografie. Seria: Podstawowe Nauki Techniczne; ◆ Politechnika Krakowska. Monografie. Seria: Architektura; ◆ Politechnika Krakowska. Monografie. Seria: Inzynieria Sanitarna i Wodna.
Indexed: CCMJ, GeoRef, SpeleolAb, Z02.
—CASDDS, Linda Hall.
Published by: Politechnika Krakowska im. Tadeusza Kosciuszki/Tadeusz Kosciuszko Cracow University of Technology, ul Warszawska 24, Krakow, 31155, Poland. TEL 48-12-6282000, FAX 48-12-6282071, wydawnictwo@pk.edu.pl, http://www.pk.edu.pl. Ed. Elzbieta Nachlik. Adv. contact Ewa Malochleb. Circ: 200.

500 POL ISSN 0860-858X
POLITECHNIKA WARSZAWSKA. PRACE NAUKOWE. KONFERENCJE. Text in English, Polish. 1991. irreg., latest no.17, 1999. price varies. **Document type:** *Monographic series, Academic/ Scholarly.*
Indexed: B22.
—BLDSC (6590.827000).
Published by: Oficyna Wydawnicza Politechniki Warszawskiej/Publishing House of the Warsaw University of Technology, ul Polna 50, Warsaw, 00644, Poland. bgpw@bg.pw.edu.pl. Ed. Krzysztof Jemielniak.

500 POL ISSN 1230-1868
QA279.4 CODEN: BODEE6
➤ **POLITECHNIKA WROCLAWSKA. BADANIA OPERACYJNE I DECYZJE/WROCLAW UNIVERSITY OF TECHNOLOGY. OPERATIONS RESEARCH AND DECISIONS.** Text in Polish; Text occasionally in English. 1969. q. EUR 58 foreign (effective 2011). **Document type:** *Journal, Academic/Scholarly.*
Former titles (until 1991): Politechnika Wroclawska. Prace Naukoznawcze i Prognostyczne (0137-1215); (until 1972): Politechnika Wroclawska. Prace Naukoznawcze Politechniki (0137-1207)
Indexed: B01, B07, B22, CA, CCMJ, Inspec, MSN, MathR, T02.
—AskIEEE.
Published by: (Politechnika Wroclawska/Wroclaw University of Technology), Politechnika Wroclawska, Oficyna Wydawnicza/ Wroclaw University of Technology, Wybrzeze Wyspianskiego 27, Wroclaw, 50370, Poland. TEL 48-71-3202994, FAX 48-71-3282940, oficwyd@pwr.wroc.pl, http://www.oficyna.pwr.wroc.pl. Ed. Jacek Mercik. Circ: 450. **Dist. by:** Ars Polona, Obroncow 25, Warsaw 03933, Poland. TEL 48-22-5098609, FAX 48-22-5098610, arspolona@arspolona.com.pl, http://www.arspolona.com.pl.

➤ **POLITECNICA**; revista de informacion tecnico-cientifica. *see* ENGINEERING

500 620 TUR ISSN 1302-0900
POLITEKNIK DERGISI/GAZI UNIVERSITY. FACULTY OF TECHNICAL EDUCATION. JOURNAL OF POLYTECHNIC/JOURNAL OF POLYTECHNIC. Text in Turkish, English. 1998. q. **Document type:** *Journal, Academic/Scholarly.* **Description:** Contains research articles, short communications and review articles in various fields of science, technology and engineering at both national and international levels.
Related titles: Online - full text ed.
Address: Gazi Universitesi, Teknik Editim Fakultesi, Teknikokullar, Ankara, 06500, Turkey. TEL 90-312-2126820, FAX 90-312-2120059, politeknik@gazi.edu.tr. Ed. Dr. Cetin Elmas.

500 POL ISSN 0079-3531
AS262
POLSKA AKADEMIA NAUK. ODDZIAL W KRAKOWIE. ROCZNIK/ POLISH ACADEMY OF SCIENCES. KRAKOW BRANCH. THE ANNUAL. Text in Polish. 1959. a. price varies. **Document type:** *Journal, Academic/Scholarly.* **Description:** Information on the activity of the Cracow Branch of the Polish Academy of Sciences, list of members and bibliography of books published every year.
Indexed: RASB.
—Linda Hall.
Published by: Polska Akademia Nauk, Oddzial w Krakowie/Polish Academy of Sciences, Krakow Branch, ul sw Jana 28, Krakow, 31018, Poland. TEL 48-12-4224853, FAX 48-12-4222791, paniec@zdp.pan.krakow.pl, http://www.instytucja.pan.pl.

500 060 POL ISSN 0079-354X
AS262
POLSKA AKADEMIA NAUK. ODDZIAL W KRAKOWIE. SPRAWOZDANIA Z POSIEDZEN KOMISJI NAUKOWYCH/POLISH ACADEMY OF SCIENCES. KRAKOW BRANCH. SCIENTIFIC MEETING REPORTS. Text in Polish; Summaries in English, Polish. 1957. s-a. price varies. **Document type:** *Proceedings, Academic/ Scholarly.* **Description:** Contains summaries of papers presented and discussed at meetings of Scientific Commissions.
Formerly (until 1967): Polska Akademia Nauk. Oddzial w Krakowie. Sprawozdania z Posiedzen Komisji (0867-1699)
Indexed: BibLing, NumL, RASB, VITIS.
—INIST, Linda Hall.
Published by: Polska Akademia Nauk, Oddzial w Krakowie/Polish Academy of Sciences, Krakow Branch, ul sw Jana 28, Krakow, 31018, Poland. TEL 48-12-4224853, FAX 48-12-4222791, paniec@zdp.pan.krakow.pl, http://www.instytucja.pan.pl. Ed. Wladyslaw Sedzik.

▼ **POLYMATH.** *see* HUMANITIES: COMPREHENSIVE WORKS

500 VAT ISSN 0370-2138
PONTIFICIA ACADEMIA SCIENTIARUM. ACTA. Text in English, French. 1937. irreg. **Document type:** *Proceedings, Academic/Scholarly.*
Published by: Pontificia Academia Scientiarum, Casina Pio IV, 00120, Vatican City. academy.sciences@acdscience.va, http:// www.vatican.va/roman_curia/pontifical_academies/acdscien/ index_it.htm.

500 VAT ISSN 0554-6648
PONTIFICIA ACADEMIA SCIENTIARUM. COMMENTARII. Text in Italian. irreg. **Document type:** *Monographic series, Academic/Scholarly.*
—INIST.
Published by: Pontificia Academia Scientiarum, Casina Pio IV, 00120, Vatican City. academy.sciences@acdscience.va, http:// www.vatican.va/roman_curia/pontifical_academies/acdscien/ index_it.htm.

500 VAT ISSN 0377-9971
CODEN: PASVAE
PONTIFICIA ACADEMIA SCIENTIARUM. SCRIPTA VARIA. Text in English, French. irreg. Price varies. **Document type:** *Journal, Academic/Scholarly.*
Indexed: CCMJ.
—CASDDS, INIST.
Published by: Pontificia Academia Scientiarum, Casina Pio IV, 00120, Vatican City. academy.sciences@acdscience.va, http:// www.vatican.va/roman_curia/pontifical_academies/acdscien/ index_it.htm.

POPULAR MECHANICS EN ESPANOL. *see* TECHNOLOGY: COMPREHENSIVE WORKS

500 600 KEN ISSN 0253-5963
Q225 CODEN: POKEDO
POST; a magazine for the promotion of science and technology. Text in English. 3/yr.
Published by: Kenya National Academy for Advancement of Arts and Sciences, PO Box 47288, Nairobi, Kenya.

500 600 FRA ISSN 0153-4092
POUR LA SCIENCE. Text in French. 1977. m. EUR 56 combined subscription domestic print & online eds.; EUR 68 combined subscription in Europe print & online eds.; EUR 81 combined subscription elsewhere print & online eds. (effective 2009). bk.rev.; software rev.; video rev. bibl.; charts; illus.; maps; stat. back issues avail. **Document type:** *Magazine, Consumer.*
Related titles: CD-ROM ed.: ISSN 1766-0351; Online - full text ed.: ISSN 1625-9963; ◆ German ed.: Spektrum der Wissenschaft. ISSN 0170-2971; ◆ English ed.: Scientific American. ISSN 0036-8733; ◆ Italian ed.: Le Scienze. ISSN 0036-8083; ◆ Hungarian ed.: Tudomany. ISSN 0237-322X; ◆ Chinese ed.: Ke Xue. ISSN 1002-1299; ◆ Spanish ed.: Investigacion y Ciencia. ISSN 0210-136X; ◆ Japanese ed.: Nikkei Saiensu. ISSN 0917-009X; ◆ Arabic ed.: Majallat al-Ulum; ◆ Polish ed.: Swiat Nauki. ISSN 0867-6380; Turkish ed.: Bilim.
Indexed: A22, FR, GeoRef, INIS AtomInd, P30, PdeR, RILM, SpeleolAb.
—IE, INIST.
Published by: Groupe pour la Science, 8 rue Ferou, Paris, Cedex 6 75278, France. TEL 33-1-55428400, philippe.boulanger@pourlascience.fr, http://www.pourlascience.com. Ed. Herve This. Pub. Philippe Boulanger. R&P Oliver Brossollet. Adv. contact Jean-Francois Guillotin. Circ: 51,130.

POZNAN STUDIES IN THE PHILOSOPHY OF THE SCIENCES AND THE HUMANITIES. *see* PHILOSOPHY

509 CZE ISSN 1213-7928
AZ649.5
PRACE Z ARCHIVU AKADEMIE VED. RADA A, B, C, D/STUDIA HISTORIAE ACADEMIAE SCIENTARIUM. Text in Czech, English. 1995. irreg. price varies. **Document type:** *Monographic series, Academic/Scholarly.* **Description:** Focuses on the history of science, scientific institutions, and biographies of related personalities. Also covers other topics in Czech and Slovak history from the 18th century to the present.
Supersedes in part (in 2002): Prace z Dejin Akademie Ved. Serie A, B, C (1211-1813); Which was formed by the 1995 merger of: Prace z Dejin Ceskoslovenske Akademie Ved. Seria A (0862-4437); Prace z Dejin Ceske Akademie Ved. Seria B (1210-9878); Prace z Dejin Ceske Akademie Ved. Seria C (1210-9886)
Indexed: RASB.
Published by: Akademie Ved Ceske Republiky, Masarykuv Ustav a Archiv, Gabcikova ulice 2362/10, Prague 1, 18200, Czech Republic. TEL 420-2-286010110, FAX 420-2-284680150, mua@mua.cas.cz.

500 600 CZE ISSN 1801-0040
PRACE Z DEJIN TECHNIKY A PRIRODNICH VED. Text in Czech. 2000. irreg., latest vol.19, 2008. CZK 150 per vol. (effective 2009). **Document type:** *Monographic series, Academic/Scholarly.*
Published by: Spolecnost pro Dejiny Ved a Techniky/Society for the History of Science and Technology, Gabcikova 2362/10, Prague 8, 18200, Czech Republic. TEL 420-2-86010118.

500 001.3 CZE ISSN 1213-1199
PRACE Z DEJIN VED. Text in Czech. 2000. irreg. price varies. **Document type:** *Monographic series, Academic/Scholarly.*
Published by: Kabinet Dejin Vedy, Puskinovo Namesti 9, Prague 6, 160 00, Czech Republic. TEL 420-2-21990611, FAX 420-2-24943057, http://www.science.usd.cas.cz.

PRAIRIE FORUM. *see* ENVIRONMENTAL STUDIES

PREPA MAGAZINE. *see* EDUCATION—Higher Education

500 SVN ISSN 0351-6652
➤ **PRESEK**; list za mlade matematike, fizike, astronome in racunalnikarje. Text in Slovenian. 1971. bi-m. EUR 16.69 (effective 2007). adv. bk.rev.; software rev.; Website rev. charts; illus.; maps. 64 p./no. 1 cols./p.; back issues avail. **Document type:** *Journal, Academic/Scholarly.*
Related titles: Online - full content ed.
Published by: Drustvo Matematikov, Fizikov in Astronomov/Society of Mathematicians, Physicists and Astronomers, Jadranska ulica 19, pp 2964, Ljubljana, 1001, Slovenia. TEL 386-1-4766559, FAX 386-1-2517281, tajnik@dmfa.si, http://www.dmfa.si. Ed. Mrs. Maja Klavzar. Adv. contact Mr. Vladimir Bensa. Circ: 3,000.

S

➤ **PRIMARY SCIENCE.** *see* EDUCATION

➤ **PRIMARY SCIENCE AND TECHNOLOGY TODAY.** *see* EDUCATION—Teaching Methods And Curriculum

500 USA
PRINCETON SCIENCE LIBRARY. Text in English. 1946. irreg., latest 2008. price varies. illus. back issues avail. **Document type:** *Monographic series, Academic/Scholarly.* **Description:** Explores topics in all the natural sciences.
Indexed: CCMJ.
Published by: Princeton University Press, 41 William St, Princeton, NJ 08540. TEL 609-258-4900, 800-777-4726, FAX 609-258-6305, cpriday@pupress.co.uk. **Subscr. addr. in US:** California - Princeton Fulfillment Services, Inc., 1445 Lower Ferry Rd, Ewing, NJ 08618. TEL 609-883-1759, 800-777-4726, FAX 609-883-7413, 800-999-1958, orders@cpfsinc.com. **Dist. addr. in Canada:** University Press Group.; **Dist. addr. in UK:** John Wiley & Sons Ltd.

PRINCETON UNIVERSITY LIBRARY CHRONICLE. *see* HUMANITIES: COMPREHENSIVE WORKS

500 RUS ISSN 0032-874X
CODEN: PRIRA3
PRIRODA; populyarnyi estestvenno nauchnyi zhurnal. Text in Russian. 1912. m. USD 231 foreign (effective 2005). bk.rev. bibl.; illus.; maps. index. **Document type:** *Journal, Academic/Scholarly.*
Indexed: A&ATA, ASFA, B21, CCMJ, CDSP, ChemAb, ESPM, GeoRef, IBR, IBZ, Inspec, MSN, MathR, RASB, RefZh, SpeleolAb.
—BLDSC (0133.000000), CASDDS, East View, INIST, Linda Hall. **CCC.**

Published by: (Rossiiskaya Akademiya Nauk/Russian Academy of Sciences), Izdatel'stvo Nauka, Profsoyuznaya ul 90, Moscow, 117864, Russian Federation. TEL 7-095-3347151, FAX 7-095-4202220, secret@naukaran.ru, http://www.naukaran.ru. Circ: 62,000. **Dist. by:** M K - Periodica, ul Gilyarovskogo 39, Moscow 129110, Russian Federation. TEL 7-095-2845008, FAX 7-095-2813798, info@periodicals.ru, http://www.mkniga.ru.

500 BGR ISSN 0032-8731
Q4 CODEN: PRIRB4
PRIRODA/NATURE. Text in Bulgarian. 1952. 4/yr. BGL 6.80; USD 52 foreign (effective 2002). adv. bk.rev. abstr.; illus. index. reprint service avail. from IRC. **Document type:** *Journal.* **Description:** Covers problems of Bulgarian natural science.
Indexed: BSLBiol, CDSP, ChemAb, FR, RASB.
—CASDDS, INIST.
Published by: (Bulgarska Akademiya na Naukite/Bulgarian Academy of Sciences), Sofiiski Universitet Sv. Kliment Ohridski, Universitetsko Izdatelstvo/Sofia University St. Kliment Ohridski University Press, Akad G Bonchev 6, Sofia, 1113, Bulgaria. Circ: 2,200. **Dist. by:** Hemus, 6 Rouski Blvd., Sofia 1000, Bulgaria; **Dist. by:** Sofia Books, ul Silivria 16, Sofia 1404, Bulgaria. TEL 359-2-9586257, info@sofiabooks-bg.com, http://www.sofiabooks-bg.com.

500 370 600 700 DEU ISSN 0171-3604
PRISMA (KASSEL). Text in German. 1973. s-a. adv. back issues avail. **Document type:** *Academic/Scholarly.*
Published by: Universitaet Gesamthochschule Kassel, Moenchebergstr 19, Kassel, 34109, Germany. TEL 49-561-8042216, FAX 49-561-8047216, presse@hrz.uni-kassel.de. Ed. Jens Broemer. Circ: 4,500.

THE PRJ.COM. *see* MEDICAL SCIENCES

500 FIN ISSN 1459-6326
PROACADEMIA; news from the Academy of Finland. Text in English. 2003. 2/yr. free (effective 2005). **Document type:** *Magazine, Academic/Scholarly.*
Related titles: Online - full text ed.
Published by: Suomen Akatemia/The Academy of Finland, Vilhonvuorenkatu 6, PO Box 99, Helsinki, 00501, Finland. TEL 358-9-774881, FAX 358-9-77488299, keskus@aka.fi, http://www.aka.fi. Ed. Riitta Tirronen TEL 358-9-77488369. Circ: 3,000.

500 070 USA ISSN 1062-4155
PROBE (NEW YORK); David Zimmerman's newsletter on science, media, policy and health. Text in English. 1991. m. USD 65 to individuals; USD 75 foreign to individuals; USD 95 to institutions (effective 2000). bk.rev. back issues avail. **Document type:** *Newsletter.* **Description:** Explores the links between science, reason, and democracy.
Published by: Probe Newsletter, Inc., 139 W 13th St, 6, New York, NY 10011-7856. TEL 212-647-0200, FAX 212-463-8002. Ed., R&P David R Zimmerman. Circ: 750. **Subscr. to:** PO Box 1321, Cathedral Sta, New York, NY 10025-1321.

500 POL ISSN 0032-9487
PROBLEMY; miesiecznik popularno-naukowy. Text in Polish. 1945. m. USD 6.60. bk.rev. bibl.; charts; illus. index.
Indexed: AgrLib, MLA-IB.
Published by: Towarzystwo Wiedzy Powszechnej, Palac Kultury i Nauki, XII Fl., Warsaw, 00901, Poland. TEL 48-22-266404. Circ: 30,000. **Dist. by:** Ars Polona, Obroncow 25, Warsaw 03933, Poland.

500 620 RUS ISSN 1727-687X
TA329
PROBLEMY NELINEINOGO ANALIZA V INZHENERNYKH SISTEMAKH; mezhdunarodnyi sbornik. Text in Russian. 1995. s-a. (in 1 vol., 2 nos./vol.). USD 75 foreign (effective 2004). **Document type:** *Journal, Academic/Scholarly.* **Description:** Presents the works on non-linear problems in all areas of fundamental and applied sciences, including both natural and humanities disciplines.
Related titles: English ed.: Problems of Nonlinear Analysis in Engineering Systems; German ed.; French ed.
Indexed: RefZh.
—BLDSC (0133.473700), East View.
Published by: (International Federation of Nonlinear Analysts USA, Academy of Non-Linear Sciences), Kazanskii Gosudarstvennyi Tekhnicheskii Universitet im. A.N. Tupoleva/Tupolev Kazan Aviation Institute, Adamuck, 4-6, Kazan-15, 420015, Russian Federation. TEL 7-8432-361648, FAX 7-8432-367621, lyudmila.kuzmina@ksu.ru, http://www.kai.ru/kai/main.en.html. Ed. G L Degtyarev. **Co-publisher:** Academy of Non-Linear Sciences.

PROFESSIONAL ETHICS REPORT. *see* PHILOSOPHY

500 GBR ISSN 1002-0071
Q72 CODEN: PNASEA
➤ **PROGRESS IN NATURAL SCIENCE**; communication of state key laboratories of China. Text in English. 1991. m. EUR 635 in Europe to institutions; JPY 103,100 in Japan to institutions; USD 941 elsewhere to institutions (effective 2009). adv. back issues avail.; reprints avail. **Document type:** *Journal, Academic/Scholarly.* **Description:** Covers reviews of specialized subjects, theses, research news, and academic activities of state key laboratories in China.
Related titles: Online - full text ed.: ISSN 1745-5391 (from IngentaConnect); ◆ Chinese ed.: Ziran Kexue Jinzhan. ISSN 1002-008X.
Indexed: A01, A03, A08, A22, A28, A29, APA, B&BAb, B19, B20, B21, BrCerAb, C&ISA, CA, CA/WCA, CCMJ, CIA, CIN, CTA, CerAb, ChemAb, ChemTitl, ChemoAb, CivEngAb, CorrAb, CurCont, E&CAJ, E01, E11, E17, EEA, EMA, ESPM, EngInd, EnvEAb, GenetAb, GeoRef, H15, ImmunAb, M&TEA, M09, MBF, METADEX, MSN, MathR, NSA, S01, SCI, SCOPUS, SolStAb, T02, T04, VirolAbstr, W07, WAA, Z02.
—CASDDS, IE, Ingenta, Linda Hall. **CCC.**
Published by: (National Natural Science Foundation of China CHN), Elsevier Ltd (Subsidiary of: Elsevier Science & Technology), The Blvd, Langford Ln, Kidlington, Oxford, OX5 1GB, United Kingdom. TEL 44-1865-843434, FAX 44-1865-843970, journalscustomerserviceemea@elsevier.com. Ed. Z Zhu. **Co-sponsor:** Chinese Academy of Sciences/Zhongguo Kexueyuan.

➤ **PROGRESS IN NONLINEAR DIFFERENTIAL EQUATIONS AND THEIR APPLICATIONS.** *see* MATHEMATICS

500 330 CAN
PROGRESS RESEARCH & DEVELOPMENT. Text in English. 2005. 10/yr. **Document type:** *Magazine, Academic/Scholarly.* **Description:** Delivers the accomplishments of Atlantic Canadian universities, researchers and labs to the audience of business and government decision-makers. Targets entrepreneurs, CEOs, presidents, university leaders, granting institutions and research foundations, media, politicians, investors.
Published by: Progress Corp., 1660 Hollis St, Penthouse, Suite 1201, Halifax, NS B3J 1V7, Canada. TEL 902-494-0999, 800-565-9303, FAX 903-494-0997, progress@progresscorp.com, http://www.progresscorp.com. Pub. Neville J Gilfoy. Circ: 100,000.

PROMETEO; trimestrale di scienze e storia. *see* HUMANITIES: COMPREHENSIVE WORKS

500 BEL ISSN 0033-1082
PROMETHEE. Text in French. 1950. q. USD 2. adv. charts; illus.
Published by: Universite Libre de Bruxelles, Cercle des Sciences, Av Heger 22, Brussels, Belgium. Ed. David Pierre. Circ: 2,000.

500 600 PER ISSN 1990-2409
PROSPECTIVA UNIVERSITARIA. Text in Spanish. 2006. s-a. **Document type:** *Journal, Academic/Scholarly.*
Related titles: Online - full text ed.: ISSN 1990-7044.
Published by: Universidad Nacional del Centro del Peru, c/o Departamento de Publicaciones, Calle Real 160, Huancayo, Peru.

500 POL
PRZEGLAD EUREKA; serwis informacji naukowo-technicznej. Text in Polish. 2001. m.
Related titles: Online - full text ed.
Published by: Polska Akademia Nauk, Komitet Badan Naukowych/Polish Academy of Sciences, Committee for Scientific Research, Wspolna 1/3, Warszawa 53, 00529, Poland. TEL 48-22-5292718, FAX 48-22-6280922.

500 GBR ISSN 2045-3876
PUBLIC SERVICE REVIEW. EUROPEAN SCIENCE & TECHNOLOGY. Text in English. 2008. q. GBP 75 (effective 2011). adv. back issues avail. **Document type:** *Magazine, Trade.* **Description:** Covers major science questions facing the public sector, across the region and further afield.
Supersedes in part (in 2010): Public Service Review. Science & Technology (1757-2770)
Related titles: Online - full text ed.: ISSN 2046-5688. free (effective 2011).
Published by: P S C A International Ltd., Ebenezer House, Rycroft, Newcastle-under-Lyme, Staffs ST5 2UB, United Kingdom. TEL 44-1782-630200, FAX 44-1782-625533, subscriptions@publicservice.co.uk. Adv. contact Gerrod Mellor TEL 44-1782-630200.

500 GBR ISSN 2045-3884
PUBLIC SERVICE REVIEW. U K SCIENCE & TECHNOLOGY. (United Kingdom) Text in English. 2008. s-a. GBP 50 (effective 2011). adv. **Document type:** *Magazine, Trade.* **Description:** Addresses the key issues affecting the funding, application and success of the UK's science, research and technology base.
Supersedes in part (in 2010): Public Service Review. Science & Technology (1757-2770)
Related titles: Online - full text ed.: ISSN 2046-5696. free (effective 2011).
Published by: P S C A International Ltd., Ebenezer House, Rycroft, Newcastle-under-Lyme, Staffs ST5 2UB, United Kingdom. TEL 44-1782-630200, FAX 44-1782-625533, subscriptions@publicservice.co.uk. Adv. contact Gerrod Mellor TEL 44-1782-630200.

500 GBR ISSN 0963-6625
Q225 CODEN: PUNSEM
➤ **PUBLIC UNDERSTANDING OF SCIENCE.** Abbreviated title: P U S. Text in English. 1992. bi-m. USD 1,091, GBP 589 combined subscription to institutions (print & online eds.); USD 1,069, GBP 577 to institutions (effective 2011). adv. bk.rev. index. back issues avail.; reprint service avail. from PSC. **Document type:** *Journal, Academic/Scholarly.* **Description:** Provides a forum for the emerging interdisciplinary field of public understanding of science.
Related titles: Microfiche ed.: USD 221 in North America; GBP 127 elsewhere (effective 2003); Online - full text ed.: ISSN 1361-6609. USD 982, GBP 530 to institutions (effective 2011).
Indexed: A20, A22, A34, A35, A36, A38, AgBio, AgrForAb, ArtHuCI, C25, CA, CABA, CMM, CommAb, CurCont, E01, E12, E15, E16, EMBASE, ERA, ExcerpMed, F08, F12, FS&TA, G11, GH, GeoRef, IndVet, M12, MEDLINE, MaizeAb, N02, N03, P02, P10, P30, P32, P40, P48, P49, P52, P53, P54, P56, PAIS, PHN&I, PN&I, PQC, PRA, R07, R12, S02, S03, S10, S13, S16, S19, S20, S21, SCOPUS, SSCI, SociolAb, T02, V05, VS, W07, W11.
—BLDSC (6969.550000), IE, Infotrieve, Ingenta, INIST, Linda Hall. **CCC.**
Published by: (Institute of Physics), Sage Publications Ltd. (Subsidiary of: Sage Publications, Inc.), 1 Oliver's Yard, 55 City Rd, London, EC1Y 1SP, United Kingdom. TEL 44-20-73248500, FAX 44-20-73248600, info@sagepub.co.uk, http://www.uk.sagepub.com/home.nav. Ed. Martin Bauer. adv.: B&W page GBP 450; 140 x 210. **Subscr. in the Americas to:** Sage Publications, Inc., 2455 Teller Rd, Thousand Oaks, CA 91320. TEL 805-499-9774, FAX 805-499-0871, journals@sagepub.com.

500 300 AGO
PUBLICACOES CULTURAIS DA COMPANHIA. (Alternating series: biology, geology, climatology, history, archaeology and ethnology) Text in English, French, Portuguese. irreg.
Published by: Museu de Dundo, Dundo, Luanda, Angola.

500 620 630 BRA ISSN 1676-8477
Q4
PUBLICATIO U E P G. CIENCIAS EXATAS E DA TERRA, CIENCIAS AGRARIAS E ENGENHARIAS. (Universidade Estadual de Ponta Grossa) Text in Portuguese. 1993. 3/yr. BRL 10 per issue (effective 2006). **Document type:** *Journal, Academic/Scholarly.*
Supersedes in part (in 199?): Publicatio U E P G (0104-8570)
Indexed: C01.
Published by: Universidade Estadual de Ponta Grossa, Editora, Av Carlos Cavalcanti 4748, Campus Universitario de Uvaranas, Ponta Grossa, PR 84030-900, Brazil. TEL 55-42-32203744, http://www.uepg.br/editora/.

500 PRK ISSN 0555-781X
QD71 CODEN: PUHWAY
PUNSOK HWAHAK. Text in Korean. 1962. q.
—CASDDS.
Published by: Korean Academy of Sciences, Central Analytical Institute, Pyongyang, Korea, N.

PURSUIT - S I T U. *see* PARAPSYCHOLOGY AND OCCULTISM

500 QAT ISSN 1023-8948
➤ **QATAR UNIVERSITY SCIENCE JOURNAL.** Text in English; Summaries in Arabic, English. 1981. s-a. free. abstr. back issues avail.; reprints avail. **Document type:** *Journal, Academic/Scholarly.* **Description:** Publishes scholarly research in all the sciences.
Formerly (until 1991): Qatar University Science Bulletin (0255-6677)
Indexed: A34, A35, A38, AgBio, AgrForAb, B25, BIOSIS Prev, C25, C30, CABA, CCMJ, E12, F08, FCA, G11, GH, GeoRef, H16, IndVet, MSN, MathR, MycolAb, N02, N03, P32, P33, P39, P40, PGegResA, PHN&I, R07, R08, S12, S13, S16, S17, TriticAb, VS, W10, Z01.
—BLDSC (7163.585150).
Published by: Qatar University, Faculty of Science (Subsidiary of: Qatar University), PO Box 2713, Doha, Qatar. Qatar.Univ.Sci@qu.edu.qa, http://www.qu.edu.qa. Ed. Shoaa Al-Yousuf. Circ: 250 (controlled).

➤ **QIANNAN MINZU SHIFAN XUEYUAN XUEBAO/QIANNAN UNIVERSITY OF NATIONALITIES. JOURNAL.** *see* SOCIAL SCIENCES: COMPREHENSIVE WORKS

500 600 CHN ISSN 1006-9798
T4
QINGDAO DAXUE XUEBAO (GONGCHENG JISHU BAN)/QINGDAO UNIVERSITY. JOURNAL (ENGINEERING & TECHNOLOGY EDITION). Text in Chinese. 1986. q. USD 16.40 (effective 2009). back issues avail. **Document type:** *Journal, Academic/Scholarly.*
Formerly (until 1994): Shandong Fangzhi Gongxueyuan Xuebao/Shandong Textile Engineering College. Journal (1000-5927)
Related titles: Online - full text ed.
Indexed: A28, APA, BrCerAb, C&ISA, CA/WCA, CIA, CerAb, CivEngAb, CorrAb, E&CAJ, E11, EEA, EMA, ESPM, EnvEAb, H15, M&TEA, M09, MBF, METADEX, RefZh, SCOPUS, SolStAb, T04, WAA.
—BLDSC (4843.849000), East View, Linda Hall.
Published by: Qingdao Daxue/Qingdao University, 308, Ningxialu, Qingdao, Shandong 266071, China. TEL 86-532-5953597, http://www.qdu.edu.cn/.

500 CHN ISSN 1006-1037
QH7
QINGDAO DAXUE XUEBAO (ZIRAN KEXUE BAN)/QINGDAO UNIVERSITY. JOURNAL (NATURAL SCIENCE EDITION). Text in Chinese. 1988. q. USD 16.40 (effective 2009). **Document type:** *Journal, Academic/Scholarly.*
Related titles: Online - full text ed.
Indexed: A28, APA, B21, BrCerAb, C&ISA, CA/WCA, CCMJ, CIA, CerAb, CivEngAb, CorrAb, E&CAJ, E11, EEA, EMA, ESPM, EntAb, EnvEAb, H15, Inspec, M&TEA, M09, MBF, METADEX, MSN, MathR, RefZh, SolStAb, T04, WAA.
—BLDSC (4843.850000), Linda Hall.
Published by: Qingdao Daxue/Qingdao University, 308, Ningxialu, Qingdao, Shandong 266071, China. TEL 86-532-5953597, http://www.qdu.edu.cn/.

500 CHN ISSN 1672-6987
QINGDAO KEJI DAXUE XUEBAO (ZIRAN KEXUE BAN)/QINGDAO UNIVERSITY OF SCIENCE AND TECHNOLOGY. JOURNAL (NATURAL SCIENCE EDITION). Text in Chinese. 1980. bi-m. USD 24.60 (effective 2009). **Document type:** *Journal, Academic/Scholarly.*
Formerly (until 2003): Qingdao Huagong Xueyuan Xuebao (Ziran Kexue Ban); Which superseded in part: Qingdao Huagong Xueyuan Xuebao (1001-4764); Which was formerly (until 1981): Shandong Huagong Xueyuan Xuebao
Related titles: Online - full text ed.
Indexed: A28, APA, BrCerAb, C&ISA, CA/WCA, CIA, CerAb, CivEngAb, CorrAb, E&CAJ, E11, EEA, EMA, ESPM, EnvEAb, H15, Inspec, M&TEA, M09, MBF, METADEX, RefZh, SolStAb, T04, WAA.
—BLDSC (7163.635500), Linda Hall.
Published by: Qingdao Keji Daxue/Qingdao University of Science and Technology, 53, Zhengzhou Lu, Qingdao, 266042, China. TEL 86-532-4022843.

500 CHN ISSN 1673-4602
QINGDAO LIGONG DAXUE XUEBAO/QINGDAO TECHNOLOGICAL UNIVERSITY. JOURNAL. Text in Chinese. 1980. bi-m. (q. until 2005). CNY 48; CNY 8 newsstand/cover (effective 2009). **Document type:** *Journal, Academic/Scholarly.*
Former titles (until 2005): Qingdao Jianzhu Gongcheng Xueyuan Xuebao/Qingdao Institute of Architecture and Engineering. Journal (1000-5706); (until 1986): Shangdong Yejin Gongye Xueyuan Xuebao
Related titles: Online - full text ed.
Indexed: A28, APA, BrCerAb, C&ISA, CA/WCA, CIA, CerAb, CivEngAb, CorrAb, E&CAJ, E11, EEA, EMA, ESPM, EnvEAb, H15, M&TEA, M09, MBF, METADEX, SolStAb, T04, WAA.
—BLDSC (7163.636000).
Published by: Qingdao Ligong Daxue/Qingdao Technological University, 11, Fushun Lu, Qingdao, 266033, China. TEL 86-532-5071718, FAX 86-532-5071136. Ed. Chui-jie Yi.

500 CHN ISSN 1006-8996
QINGHAI DAXUE XUEBAO (ZIRAN KEXUE BAN)/QINGHAI UNIVERSITY. JOURNAL (NATURAL SCIENCE). Text in Chinese. 1983. bi-m. **Document type:** *Journal, Academic/Scholarly.*
Related titles: Online - full text ed.
Published by: Qinghai Daxue/Qinghai University, 97, Ningzhang Lu, Xining, 810016, China. TEL 86-971-5310411, http://www.qhu.cn/.

500 600 CHN ISSN 1005-9393
QINGHAI KEJI/QINGHAI SCIENCE AND TECHNOLOGY. Text in Chinese. 1994. bi-m. CNY 49 domestic; USD 12 in Hong Kong, Macau & Taiwan; USD 21 elsewhere (effective 2007). **Document type:** *Journal, Academic/Scholarly.*
Related titles: Online - full text ed.
Published by: Qinghai Sheng Kexue Jishuting, 2, Wu-Si Dajie, Xining, 810001, China. TEL 86-971-6166179, FAX 86-971-6145501. **Dist. by:** China International Book Trading Corp, 35 Chegongzhuang Xilu, Haidian District, PO Box 399, Beijing 100044, China. TEL 86-10-68412045, FAX 86-10-68412023, cibtc@mail.cibtc.com.cn, http://www.cibtc.com.cn.

500 CHN ISSN 1001-7542
QINGHAI SHIFAN DAXUE XUEBAO (ZIRAN KEXUE BAN)/QINGHAI NORMAL UNIVERSITY. JOURNAL (NATURAL SCIENCE EDITION). Text in Chinese. 1979. q. CNY 24 domestic; USD 6 in Hong Kong, Macau & Taiwan; USD 12 elsewhere (effective 2007). **Document type:** *Journal, Academic/Scholarly.*
Related titles: Online - full text ed.
Published by: Qinghai Shifan Daxue/Qinghai Normal University, 38, 54 Xi Lu, Xining, 810008, China. TEL 86-971-6307647, FAX 86-971-6302588. **Dist. by:** China International Book Trading Corp, 35 Chegongzhuang Xilu, Haidian District, PO Box 399, Beijing 100044, China. TEL 86-10-68412045, FAX 86-10-68412023, cibtc@mail.cibtc.com.cn, http://www.cibtc.com.cn.

500 CHN ISSN 1000-0054
Q4 CODEN: QDXKE8
➤ **QINGHUA DAXUE XUEBAO (ZIRAN KEXUE BAN)/JOURNAL OF TSINGHUA UNIVERSITY. SCIENCE AND TECHNOLOGY.** Text in Chinese; Abstracts in English. 1915. m. USD 106.80 (effective 2009). Index. **Document type:** *Journal, Academic/Scholarly.*
Formerly (until 1965): Ch'ing Hua Ta Hsueh Hsueh Pao/Journal of Tsinghua University (0577-9189)
Related titles: Online - full text ed.; ◆ English ed.: Tsinghua Science & Technology. ISSN 1007-0214.
Indexed: A22, A28, A32, APA, ApMecR, B21, BrCerAb, C&ISA, CA/WCA, CCMJ, CIA, CPEI, CerAb, CivEngAb, CorrAb, E&CAJ, E11, EEA, EMA, ESPM, EngInd, EnvAb, EnvEAb, H&SSA, H15, INIS AtomInd, Inspec, M&GPA, M&TEA, M09, MBF, METADEX, MSN, MathR, PollutAb, RefZh, SCOPUS, SolStAb, T04, WAA, Z02.
—BLDSC (4910.507000), AskIEEE, CASDDS, East View, IE, Ingenta, INIST, Linda Hall.
Published by: Qinghua Daxue, Xuebao Bianjibu/Tsinghua University, Editorial Board, Haidian-qu, Qinghuayuan, 100, Wenxi Lou, Beijing, 100084, China. TEL 86-10-62788108, FAX 86-10-62792976. Ed. Wentao Du. Circ: 2,150 (paid); 300 (controlled). **Dist. by:** China International Book Trading Corp, 35 Chegongzhuang Xilu, Haidian District, PO Box 399, Beijing 100044, China. TEL 86-10-68412045, FAX 86-10-68412023, cibtc@mail.cibtc.com.cn, http://www.cibtc.com.cn.

500 CHN ISSN 1007-984X
QIQIHAER DAXUE XUEBAO (ZIRAN KEXUE BAN)/QIQIHAR UNIVERSITY. JOURNAL (NATURAL SCIENCE EDITION). Text in Chinese. 1979. bi-m. CNY 10 newsstand/cover (effective 2007). **Document type:** *Journal, Academic/Scholarly.*
Formerly (until 1997): Qiqiha'er Qing-gong Xueyuan Xuebao/Qiqihar Institute of Light Industry. Journal (1001-4470)
Related titles: Online - full text ed.
Published by: Qiqihaer Daxue/Qiqihaer University, 30, Wenhua Dajie, Qiqihaer, 161006, China. TEL 86-452-2738213.

500 QAT ISSN 2223-506X
▼ ➤ **QSCIENCE CONNECT.** Text in English. forthcoming 2011. free (effective 2011). **Document type:** *Journal, Academic/Scholarly.*
Media: Online - full text.
Published by: Bloomsbury Qatar Foundation Journals, Villa 3, Education City, PO Box 5825, Doha, Qatar. info@qscience.com.

500 ITA ISSN 1974-7683
I QUADERNI DI FLAMINIA. Text in Italian. 1995. irreg., latest vol.6. price varies. **Document type:** *Monographic series, Academic/Scholarly.* **Description:** Contains studies on sciences.
Published by: (Universita degli Studi di Bologna, Fondazione Flaminia), Angelo Longo Editore, Via Paolo Costa 33, Ravenna, 48121, Italy. TEL 39-0544-217026, FAX 39-0544-217554, longo@longo-editore.it, http://www.longo-editore.it.

500 610 ITA
QUADERNI DI SCIENZA. Text in Italian. 1959. irreg., latest vol.5, 1976. price varies. **Document type:** *Monographic series, Academic/Scholarly.*
Published by: Fabrizio Serra Editore (Subsidiary of: Accademia Editoriale), c/o Accademia Editoriale, Via Santa Bibbiana 28, Pisa, 56127, Italy. TEL 39-050-542332, FAX 39-050-574888, accademiaeditoriale@accademiaeditoriale.it, http://www.libraweb.net.

500 600 CHN ISSN 1009-8623
QUANQIU KEJI JINGJI LIAOWANG/OUTLOOK ON GLOBAL SCIENCE, TECHNOLOGY AND ECONOMY. Text in Chinese. 1986. m. USD 49.20 (effective 2009). **Document type:** *Journal, Academic/Scholarly.* **Description:** Reports on the scientific, technical and economic development of advanced countries as well as newly industrialized countries.
Formerly: Guoji Keji Jiaoliu - International Science and Technology Exchange
Related titles: Online - full text ed.
Published by: (Zhongguo Kexue Jishu Xinxi Yanjiusuo/Institute of Scientific and Technical Information of China), Kexue Jishu Wenxian Chubanshe/Scientific and Technology Documents Publishing House, 15, Fuxin Lu, Beijing, 100038, China. TEL 86-10- 58882952, YouGou@kjwx.cn, http://www.stdph.com/.

500 ITA ISSN 1970-223X
QUANTUM BIOSYSTEMS. Text in English. 2007. bi-m. **Document type:** *Journal, Academic/Scholarly.* **Description:** Aims to promote a systematic, interdisciplinary vision of quantum concepts on the new fields of quantum computing, quantum logics, quantum biology, nanobiotechnology, cybernetics, robotics and other complex systems and on the more classical ones like the foundamental aspects of quantum mechanics.
Media: Online - full text.
Published by: Quantumbionet, c/o Prof Massimo Pregnolato, Dipartimento di Chimica Farmaceutica, Via Taramelli 12, Pavia, 27100, Italy. TEL 39-0382-987583, FAX 39-0382-987889.

500 610 ESP ISSN 1135-8521
QUARK; ciencia, medicina, comunicacion y cultura. Text in Spanish. 1995. q. back issues avail. **Document type:** *Journal, Academic/Scholarly.*
Related titles: Online - full text ed.
Published by: (Observatorio de la Comunicacion Cientifica), Rubes Editorial, S.L., Sicilia 236 Bis, 2-2, Barcelona, 08013, Spain. TEL 34-93-2311200, FAX 34-93-2311201, rubes.editorial@rubes.es. Ed. Cami Jordi.

500 SVK ISSN 1335-4000
QUARK. Text in Slovak. 1995. m. EUR 1.49, SKK 45 newsstand/cover (effective 2011). **Document type:** *Magazine, Consumer.*
Related titles: Online - full text ed.: ISSN 1337-8422. 2003.
Published by: Perfekt, a.s., Karpatska 7, Bratislava, 811 05, Slovakia. TEL 421-2-52499783, FAX 421-2-52499788, knihy@perfekt.sk, http://www.perfekt.sk. Ed. Jana Matejickova.

QUATERNARY SCIENCE REVIEWS. *see* EARTH SCIENCES—Geology

500 CAN ISSN 0021-6127
Q2J48
QUEBEC SCIENCE. Text in French. 1969. m. CAD 35.95; CAD 54 foreign (effective 1999). adv. bk.rev. bibl.; charts; illus. index. back issues avail.; reprints avail. **Description:** News and features on science and technology.
Supersedes: Jeune Scientifique
Related titles: Microform ed.: (from PQC); Online - full text ed.
Indexed: A22, A90, C03, CBCARef, CBPI, CPerI, ChemAb, P11, P52, P56, PQC, PdeR.
—BLDSC (7210.700000), IE, Ingenta, Linda Hall.
Published by: Presses de l'Universite du Quebec, Le Delta I, 2875 boul. Laurier, bureau 450, Ste Foy, PQ G1V 2M2, Canada. TEL 418-657-4075, FAX 418-657-2096, puq@puq.uquebec.ca, http://www.puq.ca. Ed. Jacki Dallaire. Pub. Carcle Martin. Circ: 20,000.

708.994 AUS ISSN 0079-8835
QH1 CODEN: MQUMA8
➤ **QUEENSLAND MUSEUM. MEMOIRS.** Text in English. 1891. irreg., latest vol.52, no.2, 2008. AUD 100 per issue (effective 2003). back issues avail. **Document type:** *Journal, Academic/Scholarly.* **Description:** Covers the natural sciences.
Formerly (until 1911): Queensland Museum. Annals (1321-9995)
Related titles: Online - full text ed.
Indexed: A29, A34, A38, AESIS, AICP, ASFA, ASI, AgrForAb, AnthLit, B20, B21, B23, B25, BIOSIS Prev, C25, CABA, E12, ESPM, EntAb, F08, F12, G11, GEOBASE, GH, GeoRef, H17, I10, I11, IBR, IBZ, IndVet, M&GPA, MycolAb, N05, OceAb, P32, P33, P40, PGegResA, PN&I, R07, R08, S13, S16, SCOPUS, SpeleolAb, T05, VS, VirolAbstr, Z01.
—BLDSC (5629.800000), IE, Ingenta, Linda Hall. **CCC.**
Published by: Queensland Museum, PO Box 3300, South Bank, QLD 4101, Australia. TEL 61-7-38407555, FAX 61-7-38461226, inquirycentre@qm.qld.gov.au. Ed., R&P Peter A Jell. Circ: 650.

➤ **THE QUEENSLAND SCIENCE TEACHER.** *see* EDUCATION—Teaching Methods And Curriculum

500 DEU
QUELLEN DER WISSENSCHAFTSGESCHICHTE. Text in German. 1991. irreg., latest vol.3, 2002. price varies. **Document type:** *Monographic series, Academic/Scholarly.*
Published by: G N T Verlag, Schlossstr. 1, Diepholz, 49356, Germany. TEL 49-5441-927129, FAX 49-5441-927127, service@gnt-verlag.de.

508 ESP ISSN 2013-7990
▼ **QUERA.** Text in Catalan. 2009. a. **Document type:** *Monographic series, Academic/Scholarly.*
Related titles: Online - full text ed.: ISSN 2013-8482. 2009.
Published by: Institucio Catalana d"Historia Natural, Carrer del Carme, 47, Barcelona, 08001, Spain. ichn@iec.cat, http://ichn.iec.cat/.

500 NLD ISSN 1573-4617
QUEST (DIEMEN). Text in Dutch. 2004. m. EUR 49.95; EUR 4.75 newsstand/cover (effective 2009). adv. **Document type:** *Magazine, Consumer.*
Related titles: ◆ Supplement(s): Quest. Special. ISSN 1871-8094.
Published by: G + J/R B A Publishing BV (Subsidiary of: Gruner + Jahr AG & Co), Gebouw Stede, Dalsteindreef 82 t/m 92, Diemen, 1112 XC, Netherlands. TEL 31-20-7943500, FAX 31-20-7943501, http://www.genj.nl. Ed. Karlijn van Overbeek. Adv. contact Niels Daviena TEL 31-20-7943564. color page EUR 10,900; trim 195 x 255. Circ: 197,461 (paid).

500 NLD ISSN 1871-8094
QUEST. SPECIAL. Text in Dutch. 2005. irreg. EUR 6.95 newsstand/cover (effective 2009).
Related titles: ◆ Supplement to: Quest (Diemen). ISSN 1573-4617.
Published by: G + J/R B A Publishing BV (Subsidiary of: Gruner + Jahr AG & Co), Gebouw Stede, Dalsteindreef 82 t/m 92, Diemen, 1112 XC, Netherlands. TEL 31-20-7943500, FAX 31-20-7943501, http://www.genj.nl.

LA QUESTIONE ROMANTICA; rivista internazionale di studi Romantici. *see* LITERATURE

500 300 CHN ISSN 1009-8879
QUJING SHIFAN XUEYUAN XUEBAO/QUJING NORMAL UNIVERSITY. JOURNAL. Text in Chinese. 1982. bi-m. USD 31.20 (effective 2009). **Document type:** *Journal, Academic/Scholarly.*
Formerly (until 2000): Qujing Shi-Zhuan Xuebao/Qujing Normal College. Journal (1008-2743)
Related titles: Online - full text ed.
—East View.
Published by: Qujing Shifan Xueyuan, Qujing, Yunnan 655011, China. TEL 86-874-8998687, FAX 86-874-8998697.

500 SGP ISSN 0217-6440
Q180.S5
R & D SURVEY. (Research and Development) Text in English. 1983. a. free. **Document type:** *Government.*
Published by: National Science and Technology Board, Singapore Science Park, 16 Science Park Dr, 01-03 The Pasteur, Singapore, 118227, Singapore. TEL 65-779-7066, FAX 65-777-1711.

R E C S A M NEWS. (Regional Centre for Education in Science and Mathematics) *see* EDUCATION—Teaching Methods And Curriculum

500 JPN
R I K E N FRONTIER RESEARCH SYSTEM. ANNUAL REPORT. (Rikagaku Kenkyujo) Text in English. a. **Document type:** *Corporate.*
Related titles: Online - full content ed.; Japanese ed.
Published by: R I K E N Frontier Research System/Rikagaku Kenkyusho, 2-1 Hirosawa, Wako, Saitama 351-0198, Japan. TEL 81-48-4621111, FAX 81-48-4658048, http://www.riken.jp/lab/frs/frontier/index.html.

500 JPN
R I K E N REVIEW. Text in English. 1993. irreg. **Document type:** *Corporate.*
Indexed: Inspec.
Published by: Rikagaku Kenkyusho/Institute of Physical and Chemical Research, 2-1 Hirosawa, Wako shi, Saitama ken 3510106, Japan. TEL 81-48-462-1111, FAX 81-48-462-4714, 81-48-465-8048, hensan@postman.riken.go.jp, http://www.riken.go.jp.

500 JPN ISSN 1343-8964
R I S T NEWS/RESEARCH ORGANIZATION FOR INFORMATION SCIENCE & TECHNOLOGY NEWS. Text in Japanese. 1995. s-a. **Document type:** *Journal, Academic/Scholarly.*
Formerly: N C C News
Indexed: INIS AtomInd.
Published by: Kodo Joho Kagaku Gijutsu Kenkyu Kiko/Research Organization for Information Science & Technology, 2-2-54, Nakameguro, Meguro-ku, Tokyo, 153-0061, Japan. TEL 81-3-37125321, FAX 81-3-37125552, info@tokyo.rist.or.jp.

500 DEU ISSN 0933-8535
R K W HANDBUCH FORSCHUNG, ENTWICKLUNG, KONSTRUKTION. (Rationalisierungs Kuratorium der Deutschen Wirtschaft) Text in German. 1976. irreg. looseleaf. price varies. **Document type:** *Monographic series, Trade.*
Published by: Erich Schmidt Verlag GmbH & Co. (Berlin), Genthiner Str 30 G, Berlin, 10785, Germany. TEL 49-30-2500850, FAX 49-30-250085305, esv@esvmedien.de, http://www.esv.info.

R N I B. SCIENTIFIC ENQUIRY. (Royal National Institute for the Blind) *see* HANDICAPPED—Visually Impaired

500 USA
R T P VIEWPOINTS. Text in English. 1990. q. looseleaf. free. **Document type:** *Newsletter.* **Description:** Reports events, new products and ongoing research projects in the research facilities and universities of Research Triangle Park.
Published by: Research Triangle Institute, 2 Hanes Dr., Box 12255, Research Triangle Park, NC 27709. TEL 919-549-8181, FAX 919-549-8246. Ed., R&P Jamie N Nunnelly. Circ: 3,500 (controlled).

500 DEU ISSN 0179-079X
AS181.R5
R W T H - THEMEN. Text in German. 1979. 2/yr. **Document type:** *Journal, Academic/Scholarly.*
Indexed: GeoRef, TM.
—CCC.
Published by: Rheinisch-Westfaelische Technische Hochschule Aachen, Templergraben 55, Aachen, 52056, Germany. TEL 49-241-8094327, FAX 49-241-8092324, pressestelle@zhv.rwth-aachen.de.

500 USA ISSN 0033-8222
QC798.D3 CODEN: RACAAT
➤ **RADIOCARBON;** an international journal of cosmogenic isotope research. Text in English. 1959. q. USD 140 to individuals; USD 280 to institutions (effective 2011). adv. bk.rev. bibl.; charts; illus.; abstr.; maps. cum.index: 1950-1965. 2 cols./p.; back issues avail. **Document type:** *Journal, Academic/Scholarly.* **Description:** Covers radiocarbon dating applications atmospheric sciences, archaeology, palynology, geophysics, geochemistry, oceanography, soil sciences, hydrology, and paleoclimatology.
Formerly (until 1961): American Journal of Science. Radiocarbon Supplement (1061-592X)
Related titles: Online - full text ed.: USD 70 to individuals; USD 180 to institutions (effective 2011).
Indexed: A&ATA, A01, A20, A22, A33, A34, A37, A38, AESIS, AICP, ASCA, AbAn, AnthLit, B21, BA, BrArAb, C25, C30, CABA, CIN, ChemAb, ChemTitl, CurCont, E12, F08, F11, F12, FR, G11, GEOBASE, GH, GeoRef, H16, I11, IBR, IBZ, ISR, LT, M&GPA, N02, NumL, P30, P32, P40, PGrRegA, R12, RRTA, S13, S16, SCI, SCOPUS, SPPI, SpeleolAb, TAR, TriticAb, W07, W11, Z01.
—BLDSC (7234.460000), CASDDS, IE, Infotrieve, Ingenta, INIST, Linda Hall. **CCC.**
Published by: (University of Arizona, Arizona Board of Regents), University of Arizona, Department of Geosciences, 4717 E Fort Lowell Rd, Tucson, AZ 85712. TEL 502-881-0857, FAX 502-881-0554, mdbarton@email.arizona.edu, http://www.geo.arizona.edu. Ed. A J T Jull.

500 016 IRN ISSN 1022-7792
Q101
RAHNAMA-YI SIMINARHA-YI IRAN/DIRECTORY OF SCIENTIFIC MEETINGS HELD IN IRAN. Text in Persian, Modern. 1993. q. USD 58 (effective 2003). 230 p./no.; back issues avail. **Document type:** *Directory.* **Description:** Contains a bibliography of papers and lectures presented in seminars held in Iran since 1989.
Published by: Iranian Information & Documentation Center (IRANDOC), 1188 Enqelab Ave., P O Box 13185-1371, Tehran, Iran. TEL 98-21-6494955, FAX 98-21-6462254, journal@irandoc.ac.ir, http://www.irandoc.ac.ir. Ed. Hussein Gharibi.

RAKUNO GAKUEN DAIGAKU KIYO. SHIZEN KAGAKU HEN/RAKUNO GAKUEN UNIVERSITY. JOURNAL: NATURAL SCIENCE. *see* AGRICULTURE—Dairying And Dairy Products

RAND CORPORATION. ANNUAL REPORT. *see* TECHNOLOGY: COMPREHENSIVE WORKS

081 500 600 USA
RAND PUBLICATIONS SERIES. Text in English. 1946. irreg. (approx. 200/yr.). USD 975 domestic; USD 1,250 foreign (effective 2001). **Document type:** *Monographic series.*
Former titles: Rand Corporation's Research Publications; Rand Report Series; Rand Paper Series (0092-2803); Rand Corporation. Paper
Indexed: LID&ISL, MCR, PopulInd.
—CCC.
Published by: Rand Corporation, Publications Department, 1776 Main St, PO Box 2138, Santa Monica, CA 90407-2138. TEL 310-451-7002, order@rand.org. Ed. Margaret Schumacher. R&P Judy Lewis.

500 BLR
RAZVITIYE NAUKI BELARUSI/BELARUS SCIENCE DEVELOPMENT. Text in Russian. a. **Document type:** *Monographic series, Academic/Scholarly.* **Description:** Publishes general estimations of scientific and technical potential of Belarus, its regional structure, organization and results of scientific and technical activity.
Published by: (Natsiyanal'naya Akademiya Navuk Belarusi/National Academy of Sciences of Belarus), Vydavetstvo Belaruskaya Navuka/Publishing House Belaruskaya Navuka, ul F. Skaryny, 40, Minsk, 220141, Belarus. TEL 375-17-2633700, FAX 375-17-2637618, belnauka@infonet.by. Ed. Viktor Gaisyonok.

S

500 ESP ISSN 0210-3648
REAL ACADEMIA DE CIENCIAS EXACTAS, FISICAS Y NATURALES. MEMORIA. SERIE DE CIENCIAS FISICAS Y QUIMICAS. Text in Spanish. 1974. irreg. price varies. **Document type:** *Monographic series, Academic/Scholarly.*
Indexed: IECT.
Published by: Real Academia de Ciencias Exactas Fisicas y Naturales, Valverde, 22, Madrid, 28004, Spain. TEL 34-91-7014230, FAX 34-91-7014232, secretaria@rac.es, http://www.rac.es/0/0_1.php.

500 ITA ISSN 1578-7303
QA1 CODEN: RCFNAT
REAL ACADEMIA DE CIENCIAS EXACTAS, FISICAS Y NATURALES. REVISTA. SERIE A, MATEMATICAS. Text in English, French, German, Spanish. 1849. q. EUR 120, USD 148 combined subscription to institutions (print & online eds.) (effective 2012). adv. bk.rev. **Document type:** *Journal, Academic/Scholarly.*
Former titles (until 2001): Real Academia de Ciencias Exactas, Fisicas y Naturales. Revista (1137-2141); (until 1995): Real Academia de Ciencias Exactas, Fisicas y Naturales de Madrid. Revista (0034-0596); (until 1904): Revista de los Progresos de la Ciencias Exactas, Fisicas y Naturales (1132-2977)
Related titles: Online - full text ed.: ISSN 1579-1505.
Indexed: A22, CCMJ, CIS, ChemAb, ChemTitl, GeoRef, IBR, IBZ, IECT, Inspec, MSN, MathR, RefZh, SCI, SCOPUS, SpeleolAb, W07, Z01, Z02.
—CASDDS, IE, INIST, Linda Hall. **CCC.**
Published by: (Real Academia de Ciencias Exactas Fisicas y Naturales ESP), Springer Italia Srl (Subsidiary of: Springer Science+Business Media), Via Decembrio 28, Milan, 20137, Italy. TEL 39-02-54259722, FAX 39-02-55193360, springer@springer.it. Ed. Giuliano Pizzini. Circ: 800.

500 001.3 ESP ISSN 0368-8283
CODEN: MACBAB
REAL ACADEMIA DE CIENCIAS Y ARTES DE BARCELONA. MEMORIAS. Text in Spanish. 1835. irreg., latest vol.57, no.10. **Document type:** *Monographic series.*
Formerly (until 1885): Real Academia de Ciencias Naturales y Artes de Barcelona. Memorias (0210-7783)
Indexed: CCMJ, FR, GeoRef, IECT, MSN, MathR, SpeleolAb, Z01.
—INIST, Linda Hall. **CCC.**
Published by: Real Academia de Ciencias y Artes de Barcelona, Rambla dels Estudis, 115, Barcelona, 08002, Spain. TEL 34-93-3170536, FAX 34-93-3011656, info@racab.es, http://www.racab.es/.

500 ESP ISSN 1135-5417
CODEN: RAGCEP
➤ **REAL ACADEMIA GALLEGA DE CIENCIAS. REVISTA.** Text in English, Spanish; Abstracts in English. 1982. a. price varies. adv. bk.rev. back issues avail. **Document type:** *Journal, Academic/Scholarly.*
Former titles (until 1994): Academia Galela de Ciencias. Revista (1132-6247); (until 1991): Academia Galega de Ciencias. Boletin (0212-9051)
Indexed: CIN, ChemAb, ChemTitl, GeoRef, IECT, SpeleolAb, Z01.
—BLDSC (7827.851000), CASDDS, IE, Ingenta. **CCC.**
Published by: Real Academia Gallega de Ciencias, San Roque 2, Santiago de Compostela, 15704, Spain. TEL 34-981-552235, FAX 34-981-552197, ragciencias@terra.es. Ed. L Cordero. Adv. contact Ernesto Vieitez. Circ: 250.

➤ **REAL ACADEMIA HISPANO-AMERICANA DE CIENCIAS Y ARTES. REVISTA DIGITAL.** *see* ART

508 ESP ISSN 1132-0869
REAL SOCIEDAD ESPANOLA DE HISTORIA NATURAL. MEMORIAS. Text in Spanish. 1903. irreg. **Document type:** *Monographic series, Academic/Scholarly.*
Supersedes in part (1872-1903): Sociedad Espanola de Historia Natural. Anales (0210-5160)
Indexed: ASFA, B21, GeoRef, IECT.
Published by: Real Sociedad Espanola de Historia Natural, Facultades de Biologia y Geologia, Universidad Complutense, Madrid, 28040, Spain. http://rshn.geo.ucm.es/.

500 UAE ISSN 2076-5061
Q1
▼ **RECENT RESEARCH IN SCIENCE AND TECHNOLOGY.** Text in English. 2009. irreg. free (effective 2011). **Document type:** *Journal, Academic/Scholarly.*
Media: Online - full text.
Indexed: A38, B23, F12, O01, R13, S12, S13.
Published by: Mohammad Abdul Mushin Agriculture and Engineering Consultants, Abu Dhabi, United Arab Emirates.

500 FRA ISSN 0029-5671
Q2 CODEN: RCCHBV
➤ **LA RECHERCHE.** Text in French; Summaries in English. 1970. 11/yr. EUR 58 to individuals; EUR 114 combined subscription to individuals print & online eds.; EUR 52 to students (effective 2011). adv. bk.rev. charts; illus. index. back issues avail.; reprints avail. **Document type:** *Journal, Academic/Scholarly.*
Incorporates (1946-1970): Atomes (0365-7515); (1871-1970): Nucleus (0550-3329); Which was formerly (until 1954): Revue Scientifique (0370-4556); (until 1884): Revue Scientifique de la France et de l'Etranger (0151-055X); (1873-1972): Science, Progres, Decouverte (0036-8490); Which was formerly (until 1969): Science Progres, La Nature (0371-2311); (until 1963): Nature, Science Progres (0369-5786); (until 1960): Nature (0369-3392)
Related titles: CD-ROM ed.; Online - full text ed.
Indexed: A20, A22, AIAP, ASCA, ApMecR, CBTA, CEABA, CIN, ChemAb, ChemTitl, EIA, EnerInd, FR, GeoRef, IBR, IBSS, IBZ, ILD, INIS AtomInd, Inspec, KES, MLA-IB, P30, PdeR, RASB, RefZh, SOPODA, SociolAb, SpeleolAb.
—BLDSC (7305.380000), AskIEEE, CASDDS, IE, Infotrieve, Ingenta, INIST, Linda Hall. **CCC.**
Published by: Sophia Publications, 74 Av. du Maine, Paris, 75014, France. TEL 33-1-44101010, FAX 33-1-44101394. Circ: 74,928.

371.3 500 FRA ISSN 2110-6460
▼ ➤ **RECHERCHES EN DIDACTIQUES DES SCIENCES ET DES TECHNOLOGIES.** Text in French. 2010. s-a. EUR 40 (effective 2011). back issues avail. **Document type:** *Journal, Academic/Scholarly.*
Description: Concentrates on the publishing of scientific and technical information as well as methods of teaching these subjects.
Formed by the merger of (1985-2010): Aster (0297-9373); (1993-2010): Didaskalia (1250-0739)
Related titles: Online - full text ed.
Published by: Institut National de Recherche Pedagogique, 19 Allee de Fontenay, BP 17424, Lyon, 69347 Cedex 07, France. TEL 33-4-72766100, FAX 33-4-72766110, publica@inrp.fr. Eds. Christian Orange, Ludovic Morge, Yves Girault.

500 ARG ISSN 0328-3186
H8.S7
➤ **REDES**; revista de estudios sociales de la ciencia. Text in Spanish; Abstracts in English, Spanish. 1994. 3/yr. ARS 40 domestic; ARS 60 foreign (effective 2010). **Document type:** *Academic/Scholarly.*
Description: Devoted to social studies of science and technology in developing countries. Focuses on empirical and theoretical investigation concerning science, technology and society relationships.
Indexed: C01.
Published by: (Instituto de Estudios Sociales de la Ciencia y la Tecnologia), Universidad Nacional de Quilmes, Avda. Rivadavia, 2358 Piso 6, Buenos Aires, 1034, Argentina. TEL 54-114-9518221, FAX 54-114-9512431, http://www.latbook.com. Eds. Mario Albornoz, Pablo Kreimer. Circ: 700.

508 USA ISSN 0034-2165
QL671 CODEN: RDSTAH
REDSTART. Text in English. 1933. q. USD 14 to non-members (effective 2000). bk.rev. charts; illus.; stat. index. back issues avail.
Description: Original papers in the field of natural history. Contains field and banding notes and reports of the Foray, Sortie, Christmas Count and other events.
Indexed: WildRev.
—Ingenta.
Published by: Brooks Bird Club, Inc., PO Box 4077, Wheeling, WV 26003. TEL 740-635-9246, http://www.brooksbirdclub.org. Ed. Albert R Buckelew Jr. Circ: 650.

500 DEU ISSN 1867-3198
RELATIONES. Text in German. 2008. irreg. price varies. **Document type:** *Monographic series, Academic/Scholarly.*
Published by: Shaker Verlag GmbH, Kaiserstr 100, Herzogenrath, 52134, Germany. TEL 49-2407-95960, FAX 49-2407-95969, info@shaker.de.

600 CHN ISSN 1671-3745
REN YU ZIRAN/HUMAN AND NATURE. Text in Chinese. 2001. m. CNY 180 (effective 2009). back issues avail. **Document type:** *Magazine, Academic/Scholarly.*
—East View.
Published by: Shanghai Yizhou Wenhua Chuanmei Youxian Gongsi (Subsidiary of: Shanghai Wenyi Chubanshe/Shanghai Literature & Art Publishing Group), 593, Yanan Xi Rd., Bldg.1, Rm.412, Shanghai, 200050, China. TEL 86-21-61229241, FAX 86-21-61229240.

RENDICONTI ACCADEMIA NAZIONALE DELLE SCIENZE DETTA DEI XL. MEMORIE DI SCIENZE FISICHE E NATURALI. *see* PHYSICS

500 ITA ISSN 2037-4631
QC1 CODEN: ANLNEL
➤ **RENDICONTI LINCEI. SCIENZE FISICHE E NATURALI.** Text in English, French, Italian; Summaries in English, Italian. 1847. 4/yr. EUR 56, USD 74 combined subscription to institutions (print & online eds.) (effective 2012). bibl.; charts; illus. index. back issues avail.; reprint service avail. from PSC. **Document type:** *Journal, Academic/Scholarly.* **Description:** Includes articles by academy fellows or by scholars presented by fellows.
Formerly (until 2008): Accademia Nazionale dei Lincei. Atti. Scienze Fisiche e Naturali. Rendiconti Lincei. Scienze Fisiche e Naturali (1120-6349); Which superseded in part (in 1989): Accademia Nazionale dei Lincei. Atti. Classe di Scienze Fisiche, Matematiche e Naturali. Rendiconti (0392-7881); Which was formerly (until 1944): Reale Accademia d'Italia. Atti. Classe di Scienze Fisiche, Matematiche e Naturali. Rendiconti (0365-5946); (until 1939): Reale Accademia dei Lincei. Atti. Classe di Scienze Fisiche, Matematiche e Naturali. Rendiconti (0001-4435)
Related titles: Online - full text ed.: ISSN 1720-0776 (from IngentaConnect); Supplement(s): ISSN 1121-3094.
Indexed: A22, A26, ApMecR, B25, BIOSIS Prev, CPEI, ChemAb, E01, E08, EngInd, GeoRef, Inspec, MathR, MinerAb, MycolAb, S09, SCI, SCOPUS, SpeleolAb, W07, Z01, Z02.
—AskIEEE, CASDDS, IE, Ingenta, INIST, Linda Hall. **CCC.**
Published by: (Accademia Nazionale dei Lincei), Springer Italia Srl (Subsidiary of: Springer Science+Business Media), Via Decembrio 28, Milan, 20137, Italy. TEL 39-02-54259722, FAX 39-02-55193360, springer@springer.it. Ed. Sandro Pignatti. Circ: 1,200.

500 CRI ISSN 1021-6294
REPERTORIO CIENTIFICO. Text in Spanish. 1993. 3/yr. USD 6. adv. **Document type:** *Academic/Scholarly.*
Published by: (Universidad Estatal a Distancia, Escuela de Ciencias Exactas y Naturales), Universidad Estatal a Distancia, San Pedro de Montes de Oca, San Jose, 2050, Costa Rica. TEL 506-253-8978, FAX 506-253-4990. R&P Gerardo Chaves. Adv. contact Cristina Pereira.

500 USA ISSN 1553-9873
▼ **REPORT AND OPINION.** Text in English. 2009. m. back issues avail. **Document type:** *Journal, Academic/Scholarly.*
Related titles: Online - full text ed.
Published by: Marsland Press, PO Box 21126, Lansing, MI 48909. TEL 347-321-7172, sciencepub@gmail.com.

500 IRL ISSN 0085-5545
RESEARCH AND DEVELOPMENT IN IRELAND. Text in English. 1967. irreg.
Published by: Forfas, Wilton Park House, Wilton Place, Dublin, 2, Ireland. TEL 353-1-6073000, FAX 353-1-6073030, info@forfas.ie, http://www.forfas.ie.

RESEARCH AND DEVELOPMENT IN JAPAN AWARDED THE OKOCHI MEMORIAL PRIZE. *see* TECHNOLOGY: COMPREHENSIVE WORKS

RESEARCH & REVIEWS IN BIOSCIENCES. *see* BIOLOGY

500 USA ISSN 0080-1518
AS25
RESEARCH CENTERS DIRECTORY; a guide to approximately 14,300 university-related & other non-profit research organizations. Text in English. 1962. s-a. USD 865 (effective 2009). index. **Document type:** *Directory, Trade.* **Description:** Details programs, facilities, publications, educational efforts and services of North America's university and nonprofit research institutes.
Formerly (until 1965): Directory of University Research Bureaus and Institutes
Related titles: ◆ Supplement(s): New Research Centers. ISSN 0028-6591.
—BLDSC (7734.700000).
Published by: Gale (Subsidiary of: Cengage Learning), 27500 Drake Rd, Farmington Hills, MI 48331. TEL 248-699-4253, 800-877-4253, FAX 877-363-4253, gale.customerservice@cengage.com, http://gale.cengage.com. Ed. Anthony L Gerring. Circ: 2,500.

500 600 ZWE ISSN 1818-3794
RESEARCH COUNCIL OF ZIMBABWE. SYMPOSIUM ON SCIENCE AND TECHNOLOGY. PROCEEDINGS. Text in English. 1988. biennial.
Published by: Research Council of Zimbabwe, PO Pox CY 294, Causeway, Zimbabwe. TEL 263-4-369407, FAX 263-4-369409, secretary@rcz.ac.zw.

RESEARCH DEVELOPMENT AND TECHNOLOGICAL INNOVATION. *see* STATISTICS

500 001.4 GBR ISSN 1366-9885
RESEARCH EUROPE. Text in English. 1996. fortn. EUR 845 combined subscription (print & online eds.) (effective 2009). adv. 12 p./no.; back issues avail. **Document type:** *Newsletter.* **Description:** Contains reports on research, funding and policy in Europe.
Related titles: Online - full text ed.
—CCC.
Published by: Research Research Ltd., Unit 111, 134-146 Curtain Rd, London, EC2A 3AR, United Kingdom. TEL 44-20-72166500, FAX 44-20-72166501, info@researchresearch.com, http://www.research-africa.net/. Ed. Colin Macilwain. Pub. William Cullerne Bown. Adv. contact Jon Thornton TEL 44-20-72166531. B&W page GBP 3,432, color page GBP 4,160.

500 GBR ISSN 0958-2029
Q180.55.E9 CODEN: REEVEW
➤ **RESEARCH EVALUATION.** Text in English. 1991. 5/yr. EUR 357 combined subscription in the European Union to institutions (print & online eds.); USD 386 combined subscription in North America to institutions (print & online eds.); USD 295, GBP 168 combined subscription in developing nations to institutions (print & online eds.); GBP 219 combined subscription elsewhere to institutions (print & online eds.); EUR 72 combined subscription per issue in the European Union to institutions (print & online eds.); USD 78 combined subscription per issue to institutions in developing nations & North America (print & online eds.); GBP 45 combined subscription per issue to institutions in developing nations & elsewhere (print & online eds.) (effective 2011). bk.rev. bibl.; abstr. index. 72 p./no. 2 cols./p.; back issues avail.; reprints avail. **Document type:** *Journal, Academic/Scholarly.* **Description:** Contains original research in various sciences.
Related titles: Online - full text ed.: ISSN 1471-5449. EUR 312 in the European Union to institutions; USD 337 in North America to institutions; USD 257, GBP 147 in developing nations to institutions; GBP 191 elsewhere to institutions (effective 2011) (from IngentaConnect).
Indexed: A01, A03, A08, A20, A22, CA, CMM, CurCont, ERA, H05, IBR, IBZ, L04, LISTA, SCOPUS, SSCI, T02, W07.
—BLDSC (7739.920000), IE, Infotrieve, Ingenta. **CCC.**
Published by: Beech Tree Publishing, 10 Watford Close, Guildford, Surrey GU1 2EP, United Kingdom. TEL 44-1483-824871, FAX 44-1483-567497, page@scipol.co.uk. Eds. Dr. Anton J Nederhof, Dr. Gretchen B Jordan. **Dist. by:** Turpin Distribution Services Ltd., Pegasus Dr, Stratton Business Park, Biggleswade, Bedfordshire SG18 8QB, United Kingdom. TEL 44-1767-604951, FAX 44-1767-601640, custserv@turpin-distribution.com, http://www.turpin-distribution.com/.

500 300 001.3 PHL ISSN 0119-6774
RESEARCH FOLIO. Text in English. 2000. q. PHP 80 domestic; USD 10 foreign (effective 2001). illus. back issues avail. **Document type:** *Newsletter, Academic/Scholarly.*
Published by: University of the Philippines, Office of the Vice Chancellor for Research and Development, Diliman, CP Garcia Ave, Quezon City, 1101, Philippines. TEL 632-927-2309, 632-927-2567, FAX 632-927-2568, rduo.ovcrd@up.edu.ph, http://www.ovcrd.upd.edu.ph/.

338.92 GBR ISSN 1358-1198
RESEARCH FORTNIGHT. Text in English. 1994. fortn. GBP 495 to individuals; GBP 895 combined subscription to individuals (print & online eds.) (effective 2009). adv. **Document type:** *Newsletter.* **Description:** Covers science and research policy and funding in the United Kingdom as well as news coming from government, the research councils and all other major players affecting researchers.
Related titles: Online - full text ed.
—CCC.
Published by: Research Research Ltd., Unit 111, 134-146 Curtain Rd, London, EC2A 3AR, United Kingdom. TEL 44-20-72166500, FAX 44-20-72166501, info@researchresearch.com, http://www.research-africa.net/. Ed. Colin Macilwain. Pub. William Cullerne Bown. Adv. contact Jon Thornton TEL 44-20-72166531. B&W page GBP 3,432, color page GBP 4,160.

RESEARCH HORIZONS. *see* ENGINEERING

▼ **RESEARCH IN EDUCATION ASSESSMENT AND LEARNING.** *see* EDUCATION—Teaching Methods And Curriculum

RESEARCH IN SCIENCE EDUCATION. *see* EDUCATION

500 371.3 USA ISSN 1537-3797
RESEARCH IN SCIENCE EDUCATION. Text in English. 2002. irreg. price varies. back issues avail. **Document type:** *Monographic series, Academic/Scholarly.*
Published by: Information Age Publishing, Inc., PO Box 79049, Charlotte, NC 28271. TEL 704-752-9125, FAX 704-752-9113, infoage@infoagepub.com. Eds. Dennis W Sunal, Emmett L Wright. Pub. George Johnson.

500 600 GBR ISSN 1744-8026
RESEARCH INFORMATION. Text in English. 2002. bi-m. GBP 95; GBP 16 per issue; free to qualified personnel (effective 2009). adv. back issues avail. **Document type:** *Journal, Academic/Scholarly.* **Description:** Features broad-ranging opinion, news, reviews and product-based articles addressing the latest developments in everything from scientific databases through electronic journal publishing to intellectual property legislation and debates about access.
Related titles: Online - full text ed.: free (effective 2009).
Indexed: L04, L13, LISTA, R02.
—IE. **CCC.**
Published by: Europa Science Ltd., The Spectrum Bldg, Michael Young Ctr, Purbeck Rd, Cambridge, CB2 8PD, United Kingdom. TEL 44-1223-211208, FAX 44-1223-211107, tom.wilkie@europascience.com, http://www.europascience.com. Ed. Sian Harris. Adv. contact Joe Galvin TEL 44-1223-211180.

500 FRA
RESEARCH INFRASTRUCTURES STUDIES. Text in English. irreg.
Related titles: Online - full text ed.
Published by: European Science Foundation, 1 Quai Lezay Marnesia, Strasbourg, 67080 Cedex, France. TEL 33-3-88767100, FAX 33-3-88370532, esf@esf.org, http://www.esf.org.

500 600 620 GBR ISSN 2040-7459
▼ **RESEARCH JOURNAL OF APPLIED SCIENCE, ENGINEERING AND TECHNOLOGY.** Text in English. 2009. bi-m. **Document type:** *Journal, Academic/Scholarly.*
Related titles: Online - full text ed.: ISSN 2040-7467. free (effective 2011).
Indexed: A34, A37, A38, AgrForAb, C25, C30, CABA, E12, F08, FCA, GH, H16, LT, MaizeAb, N02, N03, N04, O01, P32, P33, P39, P40, R07, R08, R11, R12, R13, S13, S16, T05, TAR, W10, W11, Z01.
Published by: Maxwell Science Publications http://maxwellsci.com.

500 PAK ISSN 1815-932X
RESEARCH JOURNAL OF APPLIED SCIENCES. Text in English. 2006. 4/yr. USD 900 to individuals; USD 1,200 to institutions; USD 150 newsstand/cover (effective 2007). **Document type:** *Journal, Academic/Scholarly.*
Related titles: Online - full text ed.: ISSN 1993-6079. free (effective 2007).
Indexed: SCOPUS.
Published by: Medwell Journals, ANSInet Bldg, 308-Lasani Town, Sargodha Rd, Faisalabad, 38090, Pakistan. TEL 92-41-5010004, 92-41-5004000, FAX 92-21-5206789, medwellonline@gmail.com, http://www.medwellonline.net.

▼ **RESEARCH JOURNAL OF CHEMICAL SCIENCES.** *see* CHEMISTRY

500 600 IND ISSN 0975-4393
▼ ➤ **RESEARCH JOURNAL OF SCIENCE AND TECHNOLOGY.** Abbreviated title: R J S T. Text in English. 2009. bi-m. INR 1,000 domestic; USD 200 foreign (effective 2011). **Document type:** *Journal, Academic/Scholarly.* **Description:** Publishes original research articles, short communications, review articles in all areas of science and technology.
Related titles: Online - full text ed.: INR 500 domestic; USD 100 foreign (effective 2011).
Published by: A & V Publications, E-282 Saikripa Sector-4, Pt. Deendayal Upadhya Nagar, Raipur, Chattisgarh 492 010, India. TEL 91-9406051618, avpublications@gmail.com. Ed. Daharwal S Monika.

616.8 610 200 500 USA ISSN 1530-6410
RESEARCH NEWS & OPPORTUNITIES IN SCIENCE AND THEOLOGY. Text and summaries in English. 2000. m. (except Jul.-Aug. combined). USD 10 domestic; USD 15 foreign (effective 2001). adv. bk.rev.; film rev.; Website rev. abstr.; illus.; stat.; tr.lit. 36 p./no.; back issues avail. **Document type:** *Newspaper, Consumer.*
Published by: Research News & Opportunities in Science and Theology, Inc., 415 Clarion Dr, Durham, NC 27705. jgodfrey@nc.rr.com. Ed. Karl Giberson. Pub. Harold Koenig. R&P Janet Calhoun TEL 617-745-3931. Adv. contact Jocelyn Godfrey TEL 919-309-7775. B&W page USD 1,200, color page USD 1,560; trim 9.75 x 12.125. Circ: 2,100 (paid); 25,900 (controlled).

300 500 CAN ISSN 1915-0091
RESEARCH PERSPECTIVES/PERSPECTIVES SUR LA RECHERCHE. Text in English, French. 1998. q. **Document type:** *Journal, Academic/Scholarly.*
Related titles: Online - full text ed.: free.
Published by: University of Ottawa, 550 Cumberland, Ottawa, ON K1N 6N5, Canada. TEL 613-562-5700, http://www.uottawa.ca.

600 658 NLD ISSN 0048-7333
CODEN: REPYBP
➤ **RESEARCH POLICY.** Text in Dutch. 1972. 10/yr. EUR 2,260 in Europe to institutions; JPY 300,100 in Japan to institutions; USD 2,527 elsewhere to institutions (effective 2012). adv. bk.rev. charts; illus. index. back issues avail.; reprints avail. **Document type:** *Journal, Academic/Scholarly.* **Description:** Multidisciplinary journal examining policy problems posed by research and development activities.
Related titles: Microform ed.: (from PQC); Online - full text ed.: (from IngentaConnect, ScienceDirect).
Indexed: A12, A13, A17, A20, A22, A26, ABIn, APEL, ASCA, B01, B02, B06, B07, B08, B09, B17, B18, BPIA, C12, CA, CPEI, CPM, CurCont, E08, EIA, EconLit, Emerald, EnerInd, EngInd, FR, G04, G06, G07, G08, HECAB, I05, I13, IBR, IBSS, IBZ, JEL, KES, P34, P42, P48, P51, P53, P54, PQC, RASB, S09, SCOPUS, SSCI, T02, W07.
—BLDSC (7755.076000), IE, Infotrieve, Ingenta, INIST, Linda Hall. **CCC.**
Published by: Elsevier BV (Subsidiary of: Elsevier Science & Technology), Radarweg 29, PO Box 211, Amsterdam, 1000 AE, Netherlands. TEL 31-20-4853911, FAX 31-20-4852457, JournalsCustomerServiceEMEA@elsevier.com. Eds. L Fleming, M Bell, M Callon.

▼ ➤ **RESEARCHERS WORLD**; journal of arts science and commerce. *see* ART

507 IND ISSN 0971-8044
CODEN: RESOFE
➤ **RESONANCE - JOURNAL OF SCIENCE EDUCATION.** Text in English. 1996. m. EUR 194, USD 236 combined subscription to institutions (print & online eds.) (effective 2012). bk.rev.; Website rev. 100 p./no. 1 cols./p.; back issues avail.; reprint service avail. from PSC. **Document type:** *Journal, Academic/Scholarly.* **Description:** Constitutes a medium of communication among students, teachers and practising scientists. Enriches the processes of teaching and learning science.
Related titles: Online - full text ed.: ISSN 0973-712X (from IngentaConnect).
Indexed: A22, A26, BiolDig, CA, E01, E03, E08, ERI, S09, SCOPUS, T02.
—BLDSC (7777.579000), CASDDS, IE. **CCC.**
Published by: Indian Academy of Sciences, C.V. Raman Ave, Sadashivanagar, PO Box 8005, Bangalore, Karnataka 560 080, India. TEL 91-80-22661200, FAX 91-80-23616094, http://www.ias.ac.in. Ed. S Mahadevan. Circ: 8,000. **Subscr. to:** I N S I O Scientific Books & Periodicals, PO Box 7234, Indraprastha HPO, New Delhi 110 002, India. iihm@ap.nic.in, http://iihm.ap.nic.in/. **Co-publisher:** Springer (India) Private Ltd.

500 GBR ISSN 1473-7841
RESOURCE; th newsletter of Scotland's National Academy. Text in English. 1993. q. free (effective 2003). 16 p./no. 3 cols./p.; back issues avail. **Document type:** *Newsletter.*
Formerly (until 2001): R S E News (1352-3325)
Related titles: Online - full text ed.
—**CCC.**
Published by: Royal Society of Edinburgh, 22-26 George St, Edinburgh, Midlothian EH2 2PQ, United Kingdom. TEL 44-131-2405000, FAX 44-131-2405024, publications@royalsoced.org.uk, http://www.royalsoced.org.uk/. R&P Vicki Ingpen. Circ: 1,500 (controlled).

RESOURCE DIRECTORY OF SCIENTISTS AND ENGINEERS WITH DISABILITIES. *see* BIOGRAPHY

500 600 LBN ISSN 1020-7392
T174.5
REVIEW OF SCIENCE AND TECNOLOGY IN ECONOMIC AND SOCIAL COMMISSION FOR WESTERN ASIA MEMBER COUNTRIES. Variant title: Review of Science and Tecnology in E S C W A Member Countries. Text in English. a.
Published by: United Nations, Economic and Social Commission for Western Asia, PO Box 11-8575, Beirut, Lebanon. TEL 961-1-981301, FAX 961-1-981510, webmaster-eswa@un.org, http://www.escwa.org.lb/.

500 SGP ISSN 1793-6268
REVIEWS OF ACCELERATOR SCIENCE AND TECHNOLOGY. Abbreviated title: R A S T. Text in English. 2008. a. SGD 289, USD 191, EUR 141 combined subscription to institutions (print & online eds.) (effective 2012). adv. back issues avail. **Document type:** *Journal, Academic/Scholarly.* **Description:** Covers linear and circular accelerators, high beam power accelerators, high brightness accelerators, synchrotron light sources, free electron lasers, medical accelerators, accelerators for industrial applications, advanced accelerator technologies as well as promising new breakthroughs (such as laser, plasma, wakefield acceleration, and beam physics).
Related titles: Online - full text ed.: ISSN 1793-8058. SGD 263, USD 174, EUR 128 to institutions (effective 2012).
Indexed: A22, E01.
—IE.
Published by: World Scientific Publishing Co. Pte. Ltd., 5 Toh Tuck Link, Singapore, 596224, Singapore. TEL 65-6466-5775, FAX 65-6467-7667, wspc@wspc.com.sg, http://www.worldscientific.com. Eds. Alexander W Chao, Weiren Chou. **Dist. by:** World Scientific Publishing Ltd., 57 Shelton St, London WC2H 9HE, United Kingdom. TEL 44-207-8360888, FAX 44-207-8362020, sales@wspc.co.uk; World Scientific Publishing Co., Inc., 27 Warren St, Ste 401-402, Hackensack, NJ 07601. TEL 201-487-9655, 800-227-7562, FAX 201-487-9656, 888-977-2665, wspc@wspc.com.

REVISTA BRASILEIRA DE INOVACAO. *see* TECHNOLOGY: COMPREHENSIVE WORKS

500 BRA ISSN 1806-5104
REVISTA BRASILEIRA DE PESQUISA EM EDUCACAO EM CIENCIAS. Text in Multiple languages. 2001. 3/yr. **Document type:** *Journal, Academic/Scholarly.*
Published by: Associacao Brasileira de Pesquisa em Educacao em Ciencias (A B R A P E C), Av Eng Luiz Edmundo Carrijo Coube s/n, Bauru, SP 17033-360, Brazil. abrapec@fc.unesp.br, http://www.fc.unesp.br/abrapec/.

500 CHL ISSN 0717-2664
REVISTA C & T. (Ciencia y Tecnologia) Variant title: Revista Conicyt. Text in Spanish. 1996. m. back issues avail.
Media: Online - full text.
Published by: Comision Nacional de Investigacion Cientifica y Tecnologica, Canada 308, Piso 2, Providencia, Santiago de Chile, Chile. TEL 56-2-3654459, FAX 56-2-6551396, http://www.conicy.cl.

500 CHL ISSN 0717-9618
REVISTA CHILENA DE EDUCACION CIENTIFICA. Text in Spanish. 2002. s-a. **Document type:** *Journal, Academic/Scholarly.*
Published by: Universidad Metropolitana de Ciencias de la Educacion, Avenida Jose Pedro Alessandri 774, Nunoa, Santiago, Chile. TEL 56-2-412400, FAX 56-2-412723, prensa@umce.cl, http://www.umce.cl.

500 620 COL ISSN 0124-8170
➤ **REVISTA CIENCIA E INGENIERIA NEOGRANADINA.** Text in English, Portuguese, Spanish; Summaries in English, Spanish. 1993. s-a. free. **Document type:** *Journal, Academic/Scholarly.* **Description:** Contains original articles and reviews on all areas of science and engineering research by the faculty, staff, and students of the university.
Former titles (until 2000): Facultad de Ingenieria. Revista; (until 1998): Facultad de Ingenieria Civil. Revista (0121-960X)
Related titles: Online - full text ed.: ISSN 1909-7735. 2007.
Indexed: F04, P52, T02.
Published by: Universidad Militar Nueva Granada. Facultad de Ingenieria. Centro de Investigacion, Carrera 11 No 101-80, Bogota, 49300, Colombia. TEL 57-1-2757300 ext 328, 57-1-6343200 ext 328. Ed. Luz Elena Santaella Valencia. Circ: 1,000.

508 BRA ISSN 1518-0352
Q4
REVISTA CIENCIAS EXACTAS E NATURAIS. Text in Portuguese. 1999. s-a. **Document type:** *Journal, Academic/Scholarly.*
Indexed: C01, Z01.
Published by: Universidade Estadual do Centro-Oeste, Editora, Rua Presidente Zacarias, 875, Guarapuava, PR 3010, Brazil. TEL 55-42-36211000, http://www.unicentro.br/editora/.

500 600 COL ISSN 0124-2253
LA565
REVISTA CIENTIFICA. Text in Spanish. 1999. a. back issues avail. **Document type:** *Journal, Academic/Scholarly.*
Published by: Universidad Distrital Francisco Jose de Caldas, Centro de Investigacion y Desarrollo Cientifico, Carrera 7 No. 40-53, Bogota, Colombia. TEL 57-1-3491512, centroi@udistrital.edu.co, http://cidc.udistrital.edu.co/index_1_1.html.

500 CHL ISSN 0716-0127
QE1 CODEN: CCTEDC
REVISTA CONTRIBUCIONES CIENTIFICAS Y TECNOLOGICAS. Text in Spanish; Summaries in English. 1971. irreg., latest 2001, May. USD 5 (effective 2001). bk.rev. illus.; abstr.; maps. back issues avail. **Document type:** *Journal, Academic/Scholarly.*
Indexed: CIN, ChemAb, ChemTitl.
—CASDDS, Linda Hall.
Published by: Universidad de Santiago de Chile, Departamento de Investigaciones Cientificas y Tecnologicas, Casilla 442 Correo 2, Alameda, 3363, Santiago, Chile. TEL 56-2-6812243, FAX 56-2-6813083, http://www.usach.cl/. Ed. Cristian Parker. Circ: 1,000.

500 CRI ISSN 1409-150X
Q25
REVISTA CRISOL. Text in Spanish. 1996. s-a.
Indexed: INIS AtomInd.
Published by: Universidad de Costa Rica, Oficina de Divulgacion e Informacion, Edificio Administrativo C, Primer Piso, Ciudad Universitaria Rodrigo Facio, San Pedro de Montes de Oca, San Jose, Costa Rica. TEL 506-207-5090, FAX 506-207-5152. Ed. Luis Mora.

500 600 BRA ISSN 0103-8575
Q33 CODEN: RCTEF9
REVISTA DE CIENCIA & TECNOLOGIA. Text in Portuguese; Summaries in English. 1991. s-a. bk.rev. back issues avail. **Document type:** *Journal, Academic/Scholarly.* **Description:** Covers technology, biology and computer sciences.
Indexed: C01, Weldasearch.
—CASDDS.
Published by: (Universidade Metodista de Piracicaba (U N I M E P)), Associacao Brasileira de Engenharia de Producao (A B E P R O), Av Prof Almeida Prado 531, 1o Andar, Sala 102, Sao Paulo, 05508-900, Brazil. TEL 55-11-30915363, FAX 55-11-30915399, http://abepro.locaweb.com.br. Ed. Heitor Amilcar da Dilveira Neto. Circ: 900 (controlled).

500 ARG ISSN 0329-8922
REVISTA DE CIENCIA Y TECNOLOGIA. Text in Spanish. 1998. a. **Document type:** *Monographic series, Academic/Scholarly.*
Related titles: Online - full text ed.
Indexed: A34, A35, A36, A37, A38, AgBio, AgrForAb, BP, C25, CABA, D01, E12, F08, F11, F12, GH, H16, H17, LT, N02, N03, N04, P32, P33, P40, PGegResA, PHN&I, R07, R08, R12, R13, RA&MP, RM&VM, RRTA, S13, S16, T05, VS, W10, W11.
Published by: Universidad Nacional de Misiones, Facultad de Ciencias Exactas, Quimicas y Naturales, Ave. Feliz de Azara, 1552, Posadas, Misiones, N3300LQH, Argentina. TEL 54-3752-427498, cidet@fcegn.unam.edu.ar. Ed. Maria Cristina Area. Circ: 500.

500 600 COL ISSN 1794-631X
REVISTA DE INVESTIGACIONES. Text in Spanish. 1985. a. **Document type:** *Monographic series, Academic/Scholarly.*
Published by: Universidad del Quindio, Cerrada 15 C11 12 N, Armenia, Quindio, Colombia. TEL 57-6-7460100, FAX 57-6-7460284, http://www.uniquindio.edu.co/uniquindio/index.html.

REVISTA ELECTRONICA DE INVESTIGACION EN EDUCACION EN CIENCIAS. *see* EDUCATION

507 607 ARG ISSN 1852-852X
▼ **REVISTA ELECTRONICA IBEROAMERICANA DE EDUCACION EN CIENCIAS Y TECNOLOGIA.** Text in Spanish. 2009. 3/yr. back issues avail. **Document type:** *Magazine, Academic/Scholarly.*
Media: Online - full text.
Published by: Universidad Nacional de Catamarca, Facultad de Ciencias Exactas y Naturales, Ave Belgrado, P., San Fernando del Valle, Catamarca, 47000, Argentina. TEL 54-3833-420900.

REVISTA ESPANOLA DE DOCUMENTACION CIENTIFICA. *see* LIBRARY AND INFORMATION SCIENCES

537.02 ESP ISSN 1697-011X
Q181.A1
➤ **REVISTA EUREKA SOBRE ENSENANZA Y DIVULGACION DE LAS CIENCIAS.** Text in Spanish. 2004. 3/yr. free (effective 2011). back issues avail. **Document type:** *Journal, Academic/Scholarly.* **Description:** Maintains a special commitment to improve ways to teach and to communicate science education in order to develop better attitudes in students and regular citizens towards the sciences in general.
Media: Online - full content.
Indexed: A01, CA, F03, F04, T02.
—IE. **CCC.**
Published by: Asociacion de Profesores Amigos de la Ciencia Eureka, c/Batalla del Salado s/n, Cadiz, 11011, Spain. TEL 34-956-292374, http://www.apac-eureka.org. Ed., Pub., R&P Jose Maria Oliva.

➤ **REVISTA EXPLORATORIS: EXPLORATORIO DE LA REALIDAD GLOBAL.** *see* SOCIAL SCIENCES: COMPREHENSIVE WORKS

500 COL ISSN 0123-5591
REVISTA NOOS. Text in Spanish. 1988. s-a.
Indexed: INIS AtomInd.
Published by: Universidad Nacional de Colombia, Facultad de Ciencias y Administracion, Carrera 27, No 64-60, Manizales, Colombia. FAX 57-968-863220.

▼ **REVISTA UMBRAL.** *see* HUMANITIES: COMPREHENSIVE WORKS

REVUE DE l'INFORMATION SCIENTIFIQUE ET TECHNIQUE. *see* EDUCATION

S

509 BEL ISSN 0035-2160
Q2 CODEN: RQSCAN
➤ **REVUE DES QUESTIONS SCIENTIFIQUES.** Text in French, English; Summaries in English. 1877. 4/yr. EUR 42.40 domestic; EUR 54 foreign (effective 2003). adv. bk.rev. abstr.; charts; illus. index. 112 p./no.; back issues avail. **Document type:** *Journal, Academic/Scholarly.* **Description:** Covers general scientific topics, with historical and philosophical concerns.
Indexed: A22, CCMJ, ChemAb, DIP, GeoRef, IBR, IBZ, INIS AtomInd, IPB, MSN, MathR, P30, RASB, RILM, RefZh, SpeleolAb, Z02.
—BLDSC (7945.000000), CASDDS, IE, Ingenta, INIST, Linda Hall.
Published by: Societe Scientifique de Bruxelles, Rue de Bruxelles 61, Namur, 5000, Belgium. TEL 32-81-724464, FAX 32-81-724465. Ed. D Lambert. Pub., R&P C Courtoy. Circ: 700.

500 600 FRA ISSN 0151-4105
Q2
REVUE D'HISTOIRE DES SCIENCES; la revue pluridisciplinaire de l'histoire des sciences. Text in French. 1972. s-a. EUR 59 combined subscription domestic to individuals (print & online eds.); EUR 69 combined subscription foreign to individuals (print & online eds.); EUR 89 combined subscription domestic to institutions (print & online eds.); EUR 99 combined subscription foreign to institutions (print & online eds.) (effective 2008). bk.rev. illus. index, cum.index. reprints avail. **Document type:** *Journal, Academic/Scholarly.* **Description:** For those interested in the evolution of scientific ideas and the history of scientific techniques.
Formed by the merger of (1947-1972): Revue d'Histoire des Sciences et de Leurs Applications (0048-7996); (1947-1972): Thales (0398-7817)
Related titles: Online - full text ed.
Indexed: A22, AmH&L, BAS, CA, CCMJ, DIP, FR, HistAb, I14, IBR, IBZ, IPB, MLA-IB, MSN, MathR, P30, PCI, RASB, RefZh, SCOPUS, T02, Z02.
—BLDSC (7919.998000), IE, Infotrieve, INIST, Linda Hall. **CCC.**
Published by: (Centre International de Synthese), Armand Colin, 21 Rue du Montparnasse, Paris, 75283 Cedex 06, France. TEL 33-1-44395447, FAX 33-1-44394343, infos@armand-colin.fr. Circ: 800.

500 FRA ISSN 0766-6314
REVUE PERIODIQUE DE LA PHYSIOPHILE. Key Title: Revue de la Physiophile. Text in French. 1924. s-m. **Document type:** *Journal, Academic/Scholarly.* **Description:** La Phisiophile (which means "the friend of nature") is dedicated to the natural sciences.
Formerly (until 1971): Revue Periodique de Vulgarisation des Sciences Naturelles et Prehistoriques de la Physiophile (0996-259X)
Indexed: FR.
—INIST.
Published by: La Physiophile, 23 Rue Jules Guesde, Montceau-les-Mines, Saone-&-Loire 71300, France. http://la.physiophile.free.fr/www/site/main.html.

500 FRA ISSN 1298-9800
Q180.F7
LA REVUE POUR L'HISTOIRE DU C N R S. (Centre Nationale de la Recherche Scientifique) Text in French; Summaries in English. 1999. s-a. EUR 8.55 newsstand/cover (effective 2011). back issues avail. **Document type:** *Journal, Academic/Scholarly.*
Related titles: Online - full text ed.: ISSN 1955-2408.
Published by: Centre National de la Recherche Scientifique, 15 Rue Malebranche, Paris, 75005, France. TEL 33-1-53102700, FAX 33-1-53102727.

508 ITA ISSN 1120-1371
REVUE VALDOTAINE D'HISTOIRE NATURELLE. Text in Multiple languages. 1902. a. **Document type:** *Journal, Academic/Scholarly.*
Former titles (until 1974): Societe de la Flore Valdotaine. Bulletin (1120-1355); (until 1941): Societa della Flora Valdostana. Bollettino (1120-1347); (until 1941): Societe de la Flore Valdotaine. Bulletin (1120-1339)
Indexed: Z01.
Published by: Societe de la Flore Valdotaine, Via J B de Tillier 3, Aosta, 11100, Italy. socflore@tiscali.it.

500 ITA ISSN 1126-795X
RICERCA E FUTURO. Text in Italian. 1996. q. **Document type:** *Journal, Academic/Scholarly.*
Related titles: Online - full text ed.: ISSN 1593-4985.
Published by: Consiglio Nazionale delle Ricerche (C N R)/Italian National Research Council, Piazzale Aldo Moro 7, Rome, 00185, Italy. TEL 39-06-49931, FAX 39-06-4461954, http://www.cnr.it.

RIDAI KAGAKU FORAMU. see TECHNOLOGY: COMPREHENSIVE WORKS

530 540 550 JPN ISSN 0287-718X
CODEN: RIGAD6
RIKAGAKKAISHI/JOURNAL OF PHYSICS, CHEMISTRY AND EARTH SCIENCE. Text in Japanese. 1958. a. JPY 500 to members.
—CASDDS.
Published by: Toyama-ken Rikagakkai, Toyama-ken Sogo Kyoiku Senta, Shotakata, Toyama-shi, Toyama-ken 930, Japan.

600 JPN ISSN 0919-3405
RIKEN REVIEW. Text in English. 1993. q. **Document type:** *Journal, Academic/Scholarly.*
Indexed: GeoRef, INIS AtomInd, Inspec.
—IE, Ingenta, Linda Hall.
Published by: Institute of Physical and Chemical Research/Rikagaku Kenkyujo, 2-1 Hirosawa, Wako, Saitama 351-0198, Japan. TEL 81-48-4621111, FAX 81-48-4621554.

500 FRA ISSN 0395-0395
QH3 CODEN: RSCQAX
RIVIERA SCIENTIFIQUE. Text in French. 1914. a. **Document type:** *Journal, Academic/Scholarly.*
Indexed: GeoRef, Z01.
—INIST.
Published by: Association des Naturalistes de Nice et des Alpes-Maritimes (A N N A M), 12 Ave de la Republique, Nice, 06300, France.

500 ITA ISSN 1125-114X
RIZA SCIENZE; scienza dell'uomo. Variant title: Scienze. Text in Italian. 1983. m. EUR 34 (effective 2010). **Document type:** *Magazine, Consumer.*
Published by: Edizioni Riza, Via Luigi Anelli 1, Milan, 20122, Italy. TEL 39-02-5845961, info@riza.it, http://www.riza.it. Circ: 18,000.

500 USA ISSN 0096-4166
Q11 CODEN: PROSA2
ROCHESTER ACADEMY OF SCIENCE. PROCEEDINGS. Text in English. 1889. irreg. price varies. **Document type:** *Proceedings.*
Indexed: A23, A24, B13, GeoRef, H09, H10, IBR, IBZ, S05, Z01.
—Linda Hall.
Published by: Rochester Academy of Science, P O Box 92642, Rochester, NY 14692-0642. TEL 585-234-8163, http://www.rasny.org.

ROCKEFELLER FOUNDATION. ANNUAL REPORT. see SOCIAL SERVICES AND WELFARE

508 USA ISSN 1050-9461
ROGER TORY PETERSON INSTITUTE'S FIELD GUIDE TO NATURAL HISTORY. Text in English. 19??. q. **Document type:** *Guide, Trade.*
Formerly (until 1989): Roger Tory Peterson Institute of Natural History. Field Guide
Indexed: GeoRef, Z01.
Published by: The Roger Tory Peterson Institute of Natural History, 311 Curtis St, Jamestown, NY 14701. TEL 716-665-2473, 800-758-6841, jberry@rtpi.org, http://www.rtpi.org.

500 RUS ISSN 0869-5652
AS262 CODEN: DAKNEQ
➤ **ROSSIISKAYA AKADEMIYA NAUK. DOKLADY**; svodnyi vypusk. Text in Russian; Contents page in English. 1933. 36/yr. RUR 1,560 for 6 mos. domestic; USD 1,112 foreign (effective 2004). charts; illus. index. reprints avail. **Document type:** *Journal, Academic/Scholarly.* **Description:** Includes material from the areas of mathematics, physics, computer science, and control theory. Publishes important new research in mathematics and its applications.
Formerly (until no.4, 1992): Akademiya Nauk S.S.S.R. Doklady (0002-3264)
Related titles: Microform ed.: (from BHP); Online - full text ed.; ◆ Partial English translation(s): Doklady Biochemistry and Biophysics. ISSN 1607-6729; ◆ Doklady Physical Chemistry. ISSN 0012-5016; ◆ Doklady Mathematics. ISSN 1064-5624; ◆ Doklady Physics. ISSN 1028-3358; ◆ Doklady Biological Sciences. ISSN 0012-4966; ◆ Doklady Earth Sciences. ISSN 1028-334X; ◆ Doklady Chemistry. ISSN 0012-5008.
Indexed: A&ATA, A20, ASFA, B25, BIOSIS Prev, C&ISA, CCMJ, CIS, CTFA, ChemAb, CompR, CorrAb, CybAb, DentInd, E&CAJ, FR, GeoRef, GeotechAb, INIS AtomInd, IndMed, Inspec, MSN, MathR, MycolAb, P30, PetrolAb, PsycholAb, RefZh, SCI, SCOPUS, SolStAb, SpeleolAb, WAA, Z01, Z02.
—BLDSC (0053.900000), AskIEEE, CASDDS, East View, GNLM, INIST, Linda Hall, PADDS. **CCC.**
Published by: (Rossiiskaya Akademiya Nauk/Russian Academy of Sciences), Izdatel'stvo Nauka, Profsoyuznaya ul 90, Moscow, 117864, Russian Federation. TEL 7-095-3347151, FAX 7-095-4202220, secret@naukaran.ru, http://www.naukaran.ru. Circ: 5,250. **Dist. by:** M K - Periodica, ul Gilyarovskogo 39, Moscow 129110, Russian Federation. TEL 7-095-2845008, FAX 7-095-2813798, info@periodicals.ru, http://www.mkniga.ru.

500 RUS ISSN 0869-5873
AS262 CODEN: VRANEL
ROSSIISKAYA AKADEMIYA NAUK. VESTNIK. Text in Russian. 1931. m. RUR 200 for 6 mos. domestic (effective 2004). bk.rev. bibl.; charts; illus. index. **Document type:** *Journal, Academic/Scholarly.* **Description:** Publishes the major work, speeches, and discussions presented to the Academy by the most eminent Russian and foreign scientists, presenting the viewpoints of various disciplines on many important subjects related to the natural, technical, and social sciences.
Formerly (until 1992): Akademiya Nauk S.S.S.R. Vestnik (0002-3442)
Related titles: Online - full text ed.: ISSN 1531-8435; ◆ English Translation: Russian Academy of Sciences. Herald. ISSN 1019-3316.
Indexed: A20, A22, ASCA, ASFA, B21, CCMJ, ChemAb, ESPM, FR, GeoRef, MSN, MathR, P30, PsycholAb, RASB, SCOPUS, SOPODA, SpeleolAb.
—BLDSC (0032.754000), CASDDS, East View, GNLM, IE, Ingenta, INIST, Linda Hall. **CCC.**
Published by: (Rossiiskaya Akademiya Nauk/Russian Academy of Sciences), Izdatel'stvo Nauka, Profsoyuznaya ul 90, Moscow, 117864, Russian Federation. TEL 7-095-3347151, FAX 7-095-4202220, secret@naukaran.ru, http://www.naukaran.ru. Circ: 5,125.

500 330 RUS
ROSSIISKII FOND FUNDAMENTAL'NYKH ISSLEDOVANII. INFORMATSIONNYI BULLETIN. Text in Russian. 1993. a., latest vol.9, 2001. **Description:** Lists grants of the Russian Fondation for Basic Research for the current year for all areas of the fundamental sciences.
Related titles: Online - full content ed.
Published by: Rossiiskii Fond Fundamental'nykh Issledovanii, Leninskii pr-t 32-a, Moscow, 117334, Russian Federation. TEL 7-095-9385417, FAX 7-095-9381931. Ed. M V Alfimov.

500 GBR
ROYAL INSTITUTION OF GREAT BRITAIN. REPORT & FINANCIAL STATEMENTS. Text in English. 1799. a. **Document type:** *Corporate.*
Former titles (until 2003): Royal Institution of Great Britain. Annual Record; (until 2000): Royal Institution of Great Britain. Record of the Year
Published by: Royal Institution of Great Britain, 21 Albemarle St, London, W1X 4BS, United Kingdom. TEL 44-20-74092992, FAX 44-20-76702920, ri@ri.ac.uk, http://www.rigb.org/. Circ: 3,000 (controlled).

500 GBR
ROYAL INSTITUTION OF GREAT BRITAIN. ROYAL INSTITUTION LECTURES. Text in English. 1853. 3/yr. **Document type:** *Journal, Academic/Scholarly.*
Published by: Royal Institution of Great Britain, 21 Albemarle St, London, W1X 4BS, United Kingdom. TEL 44-20-74092992, FAX 44-20-76702920, ri@ri.ac.uk, http://www.rigb.org/. Circ: 4,000 (controlled).

500 CAN ISSN 0317-3631
ROYAL SOCIETY OF CANADA. CALENDAR/SOCIETE ROYALE DU CANADA. ANNUAIRE. Text in English. a. CAD 15 (effective 2002).
Published by: Royal Society of Canada, 283 Sparks St., Ottawa, ON K1R 7X9, Canada. TEL 613-991-6990, FAX 613-991-6996, adminrsc@rsc.ca, http://www.rsc.ca.

500 CAN ISSN 1710-2863
CODEN: PRYCA4
ROYAL SOCIETY OF CANADA. PROCEEDINGS (ONLINE). Text in English, French. 1882. a. reprints avail. **Document type:** *Proceedings, Academic/Scholarly.*
Former titles (until 2001): Royal Society of Canada. Proceedings (Print) (0080-4517); (until 1963): Royal Society of Canada. Minutes of Proceedings (0316-4624); Which incorporated: Royal Society of Canada. Report of Council (1180-4130); Which superseded in part: Royal Society of Canada. Proceedings and Transactions (0316-4616)
Media: Online - full content. **Related titles:** Microfilm ed.: (from BHP); Microform ed.: (from BHP, PQC).
Indexed: A26, C03, CBCARef, CPerl, E08, G08, GeoRef, MLA-IB, MathR, PQC, S09, SpeleolAb.
—INIST, Linda Hall. **CCC.**
Published by: Royal Society of Canada, 283 Sparks St., Ottawa, ON K1R 7X9, Canada. TEL 613-991-6990, FAX 613-991-6996. Eds. D Hayne, P Smart.

500 CAN
ROYAL SOCIETY OF CANADA. PROCEEDINGS OF SYMPOSIA. Text in English. a.
Published by: Royal Society of Canada, 283 Sparks St., Ottawa, ON K1R 7X9, Canada. TEL 613-991-6990, FAX 613-991-6996, adminrsc@rsc.ca, http://www.rsc.ca.

500 CAN
ROYAL SOCIETY OF CANADA. REPORTS. Text in English. irreg.
Published by: Royal Society of Canada, 283 Sparks St., Ottawa, ON K1R 7X9, Canada. TEL 613-991-6990, FAX 613-991-6996, adminrsc@rsc.ca, http://www.rsc.ca.

500 CAN
ROYAL SOCIETY OF CANADA. REPORTS OF EXPERT PANELS. Text in English. irreg.
Published by: Royal Society of Canada, 283 Sparks St., Ottawa, ON K1R 7X9, Canada. TEL 613-991-6990, FAX 613-991-6996, adminrsc@rsc.ca, http://www.rsc.ca.

500 CAN
ROYAL SOCIETY OF CANADA. SOCIETY NEWS. Text in English, French. 1991. 4/yr. free. **Document type:** *Newsletter.*
Formerly (until 1998): Profile - Profil (1183-5001)
Published by: Royal Society of Canada, 283 Sparks St., Ottawa, ON K1R 7X9, Canada. TEL 613-991-6990, FAX 613-991-6996, adminrsc@rsc.ca, http://www.rsc.ca.

500 CAN
ROYAL SOCIETY OF CANADA. SPECIAL PUBLICATIONS. Text in English. irreg.
Published by: Royal Society of Canada, 283 Sparks St., Ottawa, ON K1R 7X9, Canada. TEL 613-991-6990, FAX 613-991-6996, adminrsc@rsc.ca, http://www.rsc.ca.

500 CAN ISSN 0035-9122
AS42S622 CODEN: TRSCAI
➤ **ROYAL SOCIETY OF CANADA. TRANSACTIONS.** Text and summaries in English, French. 1882. a., latest vol.3, 2003, Seventh series. CAD 20. bibl.; charts; illus. cum.index: 1882-1992 (in several vols.). reprints avail. **Document type:** *Proceedings, Academic/Scholarly.*
Supersedes in part: Royal Society of Canada. Proceedings and Transactions (0316-4616)
Related titles: Microfilm ed.: (from BHP); Microform ed.: (from MML, PMC).
Indexed: Agr, AmH&L, C03, CBCARef, CBPI, CPerl, ChemAb, FR, GeoRef, IBR, IBZ, Inspec, L09, MLA-IB, MathR, P11, P30, P48, P52, P56, PQC, PetrolAb, RASB, SCOPUS, SpeleolAb.
—AskIEEE, INIST, Linda Hall. **CCC.**
Published by: Royal Society of Canada, 283 Sparks St., Ottawa, ON K1R 7X9, Canada. TEL 613-991-6990, FAX 613-991-6996, adminrsc@rsc.ca. Ed. Patricia Demers. Circ: 800.

500 GBR ISSN 1476-4334
Q41 CODEN: RSEYAX
ROYAL SOCIETY OF EDINBURGH. DIRECTORY. Text in English. 1941. a. back issues avail. **Document type:** *Directory, Academic/Scholarly.* **Description:** Contains a complete listing of the Fellowship and all committees, plus information on the structure and activities of the Society for the current session.
Supersedes in part (in 2002): Royal Society of Edinburgh. Year Book (0080-4576)
Indexed: SpeleolAb.
—Linda Hall. **CCC.**
Published by: The R S E Scotland Foundation (Subsidiary of: Royal Society of Edinburgh), 22-26 George St, Edinburgh, EH2 2PQ, United Kingdom. TEL 44-131-2405000, FAX 44-131-2405024, publications@royalsoced.org.uk, http://www.royalsoced.org.uk/. R&P Vicki Ingpen. Circ: 1,500.

500 GBR ISSN 1476-4342
Q41
ROYAL SOCIETY OF EDINBURGH. REVIEW. Text in English. 1941. a. back issues avail. **Document type:** *Yearbook, Academic/Scholarly.* **Description:** Reports on the activities of the Society during the previous session.
Supersedes in part (in 2002): Royal Society of Edinburgh. Year Book (0080-4576)
—Linda Hall. **CCC.**
Published by: The R S E Scotland Foundation (Subsidiary of: Royal Society of Edinburgh), 22-26 George St, Edinburgh, EH2 2PQ, United Kingdom. TEL 44-131-2405000, FAX 44-131-2405024, http://www.royalsoced.org.uk/. R&P Vicki Ingpen.

500 GBR ISSN 0035-9149
Q41 CODEN: NOREAY
➤ **ROYAL SOCIETY OF LONDON. NOTES AND RECORDS.** Variant title: Royal Society. Notes and Records. Text in English. 19??. q. GBP 170, EUR 219 combined subscription in Europe to institutions (print & online eds.); USD 309 combined subscription in US & Canada to institutions (print & online eds.); GBP 178, USD 318 combined subscription elsewhere to institutions (print & online eds.) (effective 2012). bk.rev. bibl.; illus. index, cum.index: vols.1-20 (1938-1965). back issues avail. **Document type:** *Journal, Academic/Scholarly.* **Description:** Brings out research in the history of science, technology and medicine up to and including the 21st century.
Formerly (until 1938): Royal Society of London. Occasional Notices

Related titles: Online - full text ed.: ISSN 1743-0178. GBP 131, EUR 169 in Europe to institutions; USD 238 in US & Canada to institutions; GBP 137, USD 245 elsewhere to institutions (effective 2012).
Indexed: A20, A22, ASCA, ArtHuCI, BrArAb, CA, CCMJ, CurCont, E01, EMBASE, ExcerpMed, GeoRef, HistAb, MEDLINE, MLA-IB, MSN, MathR, P30, PCI, SCI, SCOPUS, SpeleolAb, T02, W07, Z02.
—BLDSC (6165.075000), IE, Infotrieve, Ingenta, Linda Hall. **CCC.**
Published by: The Royal Society Publishing, 6-9 Carlton House Terr, London, SW1Y 5AG, United Kingdom. TEL 44-20-74512500, FAX 44-20-79761837, sales@royalsociety.org, http://royalsocietypublishing.org. Ed. Robert Fox. **Subscr. to:** Portland Customer Services, Commerce Way, Colchester CO2 8HP, United Kingdom. TEL 44-1206-796351, FAX 44-1206-799331, sales@portland-services.com, http://www.portlandpress.com.

➤ **ROYAL SOCIETY OF LONDON. PROCEEDINGS A. MATHEMATICAL, PHYSICAL AND ENGINEERING SCIENCES.** *see* MATHEMATICS

500 GBR
ROYAL SOCIETY OF LONDON. REPORTS AND STATEMENTS. Text in English. irreg. price varies. **Document type:** *Monographic series, Academic/Scholarly.*
Published by: The Royal Society Publishing, 6-9 Carlton House Terr, London, SW1Y 5AG, United Kingdom. TEL 44-20-74512500, FAX 44-20-79302170, sales@royalsociety.org. **Orders to:** Portland Customer Services, Commerce Way, Colchester CO2 8HP, United Kingdom. TEL 44-1206-796351, FAX 44-1206-799331, sales@portland-services.com, http://www.portland-services.com.

506 GBR ISSN 0080-4673
Q41
ROYAL SOCIETY OF LONDON. YEAR BOOK. Variant title: Royal Society. Year Book. Text in English. 1898. a. GBP 39, EUR 50 per issue in Europe to institutions; USD 74 per issue in US & Canada to institutions; GBP 43, USD 78 per issue elsewhere to institutions (effective 2012). **Document type:** *Yearbook, Trade.* **Description:** Contains the Society's workings including details of the Royal Society's research grant schemes plus biographical notes on every fellow.
Former titles (until 1996): Royal Society. Annual Report (1367-3416); (until 1979): Royal Society. Report of Council (0268-2206)
Indexed: SCOPUS.
—BLDSC (9399.000000), Linda Hall. **CCC.**
Published by: The Royal Society Publishing, 6-9 Carlton House Terr, London, SW1Y 5AG, United Kingdom. TEL 44-20-74512500, FAX 44-20-79761837, sales@royalsociety.org. **Subscr. to:** Portland Customer Services, Commerce Way, Colchester CO2 8HP, United Kingdom. TEL 44-1206-796351, FAX 44-1206-799331, sales@portland-services.com, http://www.portlandpress.com.

500 AUS ISSN 0035-9173
Q93 CODEN: JPRSA5
➤ **ROYAL SOCIETY OF NEW SOUTH WALES. JOURNAL AND PROCEEDINGS.** Text in English. 1862. a. exchange basis. bk.rev. abstr.; bibl.; charts; illus.; maps. cum.index: 1862-1865, 1867-1916. 100 p./no.; back issues avail. **Document type:** *Proceedings, Academic/Scholarly.* **Description:** Features scientific research within an Australian context as well as contains abstracts of post-graduate theses.
Former titles (until 1877): Royal Society of New South Wales. Transactions and Proceedings; (until 1876): Royal Society of New South Wales. Transactions; (until 1865): Philosophical Society of New South Wales. Transactions
Related titles: Microform ed.: (from PMC); Online - full text ed.: free (effective 2009).
Indexed: AESIS, B25, BIOSIS Prev, ChemAb, GeoRef, IBR, IBZ, Inspec, MathR, MycolAb, PetrolAb, RASB, RefZh, SCOPUS, SSciA, SpeleolAb, Z01, Z02.
—AskIEEE, CASDDS, Ingenta, INIST, Linda Hall, PADDS. **CCC.**
Published by: Royal Society of New South Wales, Bldg H47, University of Sydney, Sydney, NSW 2006, Australia. TEL 61-2-90365282, FAX 61-2-90365309, info@nsw.royalsoc.org.au. Ed., R&P P A Williams. Circ: 900.

500 NZL ISSN 1176-1865
QE348.2 CODEN: RNZBAY
ROYAL SOCIETY OF NEW ZEALAND BULLETIN. Text in English. 1910. irreg. **Document type:** *Magazine, Academic/Scholarly.* **Description:** Presents specialist scientific and technical monographs.
Former titles (until 1998): Royal Society of New Zealand. Bulletin Series (0370-6559); New Zealand Institute. Bulletin
Indexed: AESIS, GeoRef, SpeleolAb.
—CASDDS, INIST, Linda Hall. **CCC.**
Published by: (Royal Society of New Zealand), R S N Z Publishing, PO Box 598, Wellington, 6001, New Zealand. TEL 64-4-4727421, FAX 64-4-4731841, sales@rsnz.org, http://www.rsnz.org.

500 SGP ISSN 0303-6758
Q1 CODEN: JRNZAK
➤ **ROYAL SOCIETY OF NEW ZEALAND. JOURNAL.** Text in English. 1971. q. GBP 250 combined subscription in United Kingdom to institutions (print & online eds.); EUR 276, AUD 451, USD 401 combined subscription to institutions (print & online eds.) (effective 2012). adv. bibl.; charts; illus.; maps. cum.index: 1869-1971, 1976, 1981. back issues avail.; reprint service avail. from PSC. **Document type:** *Journal, Academic/Scholarly.* **Description:** Covers indigenous natural history and environmental sciences including conservation, ecology, evolution, archaeology, paleontology, meteorology, soil sciences, palynology, and history of science.
Formed by the merger of (1962-1971): Royal Society of New Zealand. Transactions. General (0372-1965); Which was formerly (1952-1962): Royal Society of New Zealand. Transactions (0035-9181); (1961-1971): Royal Society of New Zealand. Transactions. Zoology (0372-1396); (1961-1971): Royal Society of New Zealand. Transactions. Botany (0372-1361); (1969-1971): Royal Society of New Zealand. Transactions. Earth Sciences (0370-8136); Which was formerly (1961-1969): Royal Society of New Zealand. Transactions. Geology (0372-137X); (1968-1971): Royal Society of New Zealand. Transactions. Biological Sciences (0557-417X)
Related titles: Online - full text ed.: ISSN 1175-8899. GBP 225 in United Kingdom to institutions; EUR 248, AUD 407, USD 360 to institutions (effective 2012).
Indexed: A01, A20, A22, A29, A34, A35, A37, A38, ASCA, ASFA, AgBio, B20, B21, B25, BIOSIS Prev, C25, CA, CABA, CTA, ChemAb, ChemoAb, CurCont, D01, E12, E17, ESPM, EntAb, EnvAb, EnvInd, F08, F11, F12, FCA, G11, GEOBASE, GH, GenetAb, GeoRef, H16, HPNRM, I10, I11, INIS AtomInd, ISR, IndVet, LT, MycolAb, N03, N04, N05, NSA, P32, P33, P37, P39, P40, P52, P56, PGegResA, PN&I, PetrolAb, R07, R08, R12, S13, S16, SCI, SCOPUS, SPPI, SSciA, SWRA, SpeleolAb, T02, TAR, VS, VirolAbstr, W07, W11, Z01.
—BLDSC (4864.630000), CASDDS, IE, Ingenta, INIST, Linda Hall, PADDS. **CCC.**
Published by: (Royal Society of New Zealand NZL), Taylor & Francis Asia Pacific (Singapore) (Subsidiary of: Taylor & Francis Group), 240 MacPherson Rd. #08-01, Pines Industrial Bldg., Singapore, 348574, Singapore. TEL 65-6741-5166, FAX 65-6742-9356, info@tandf.com.sg, http://www.taylorandfrancis.com.sg/. Ed. Anna Meyer. Circ: 300.

500 NZL ISSN 0111-3895
CODEN: MSRZEG
ROYAL SOCIETY OF NEW ZEALAND. MISCELLANEOUS SERIES. Text in English. 1977. irreg. price varies. **Document type:** *Proceedings, Academic/Scholarly.* **Description:** Presents scientific and technical conference proceedings and discussion documents.
Related titles: Online - full text ed.: ISSN 1178-1483.
Indexed: GeoRef, SpeleolAb.
—BLDSC (5827.500000).
Published by: (Royal Society of New Zealand), R S N Z Publishing, PO Box 598, Wellington, 6001, New Zealand. TEL 64-4-4727421, FAX 64-4-4731841, sales@rsnz.org, http://www.rsnz.org.

506 AUS ISSN 0080-469X
Q93 CODEN: PRSQAG
➤ **ROYAL SOCIETY OF QUEENSLAND. PROCEEDINGS.** Text in English. 1859. a. free to members (effective 2009). back issues avail.; reprints avail. **Document type:** *Proceedings, Academic/Scholarly.* **Description:** Contains research papers on various aspects of natural science including topics such as environmental conservation, management, restoration or policy.
Formerly (until 1885): Philosophical Society of Queensland. Transactions
Related titles: Online - full text ed.
Indexed: A01, A29, AESIS, ASFA, AgrForAb, B20, B21, B25, BIOSIS Prev, C25, C30, CA, CABA, CTA, ChemoAb, E12, ESPM, F08, F12, G11, GH, GeoRef, I10, I11, IBR, IBZ, MycolAb, NSA, OceAb, P32, S13, S16, S17, SWRA, SpeleolAb, T02, TAR, VirolAbstr, W10, W11, WildRev, Z01.
—IE, Ingenta, INIST, Linda Hall.
Published by: Royal Society of Queensland, PO Box 6021, St. Lucia, QLD 4067, Australia. admin@royalsocietyqld.org, http://royalsocietyqld.org. Ed. Julie Robins.

500 GBR ISSN 0035-919X
Q85 CODEN: TRSAAC
➤ **ROYAL SOCIETY OF SOUTH AFRICA. TRANSACTIONS.** Text in English. 1877. 3/yr. GBP 201 combined subscription in United Kingdom to institutions (print & online eds.); EUR 267, USD 333 combined subscription to institutions (print & online eds.) (effective 2012). bibl.; charts; illus. cum.index: 1878-1909, 1909-1955, 1956-1985. **Document type:** *Journal, Academic/Scholarly.*
Related titles: Microfilm ed.: (from PQC); Online - full text ed.: ISSN 2154-0098. 2010. GBP 181 in United Kingdom to institutions; EUR 240, USD 300 to institutions (effective 2012).
Indexed: A01, A20, A22, A29, ASCA, ASFA, B20, B21, B25, BIOSIS Prev, CA, CTA, ChemAb, ChemoAb, E01, ESPM, GeoRef, I10, IBR, IBZ, INIS AtomInd, ISAP, ISR, Inspec, MathR, MycolAb, NSA, SCOPUS, SWRA, SpeleolAb, T02, VirolAbstr, W08, Z01.
—BLDSC (9001.000000), IE, Ingenta, INIST, Linda Hall. **CCC.**
Published by: (Royal Society of South Africa ZAF), Taylor & Francis Ltd. (Subsidiary of: Taylor & Francis Group), 4 Park Sq, Milton Park, Abingdon, Oxfordshire OX14 4RN, United Kingdom. TEL 44-1235-828600, FAX 44-20-70176336, info@tandf.co.uk. Ed., R&P Johann R E Lutjeharms. Circ: 800.

500 AUS ISSN 0372-1426
Q93 CODEN: TSAUAN
➤ **ROYAL SOCIETY OF SOUTH AUSTRALIA. TRANSACTIONS.** Text in English. 18??. s-a. AUD 180 domestic to institutions; AUD 255 foreign to institutions; AUD 210 combined subscription domestic to institutions (print & online eds.); AUD 225 combined subscription foreign to institutions (print & online eds.); free to members (effective 2009). index. back issues avail. **Document type:** *Journal, Academic/Scholarly.* **Description:** Covers a wide variety of physical and biological topics from geology, to oceanography, fringing mangroves and salt marshes, and fauna and flora from plankton to dolphins, whales and seabirds.
Incorporates (1918-2003): South Australian Museum. Records (0376-2750); Former titles (until 1938): Royal Society of South Australia. Transactions and Proceedings (0372-0888); (until 1912): Royal Society of South Australia. Transactions and Proceedings and Report (1324-1796); (until 1904): Royal Society of South Australia. Transactions (1324-1788); (until 1890): Royal Society of South Australia. Transactions and Proceedings and Report (1324-177X); (until 1880): Philosophical Society of Adelaide, South Australia. Transactions and Proceedings and Report (1324-1761); (until 1878): Adelaide Philosophical Society. Annual Report and Transactions
Related titles: Online - full text ed.: AUD 160 domestic to institutions; AUD 185 foreign to institutions (effective 2009) (from IngentaConnect).
Indexed: A20, A29, A34, A38, AESIS, AbAn, B20, B21, B25, BIOSIS Prev, CABA, CurCont, E12, ESPM, F08, F12, G11, GH, GeoRef, H16, H17, I10, I11, IndVet, MinerAb, MycolAb, N05, O01, P32, P33, P37, P39, R07, S13, S16, SCI, SCOPUS, SpeleolAb, VS, VirolAbstr, W07, W10, Z01.
—INIST.
Published by: Royal Society of South Australia Inc., c/o SA Museum, North Terr, Adelaide, SA 5000, Australia. TEL 61-8-82077590, FAX 61-8-82077222, roysocsa@gmail.com. Ed. Scoresby Shepherd.

506 AUS ISSN 0080-4703
Q93 CODEN: PPRTA6
➤ **ROYAL SOCIETY OF TASMANIA, HOBART. PAPERS AND PROCEEDINGS.** Text in English. 1848. a. 80 p./no.; **Document type:** *Proceedings, Academic/Scholarly.* **Description:** Publishes papers on geology, geomorphology, botany, zoology, history and, from time to time, anthropology and other topics. Most articles concern Tasmania.
Incorporates (in 1914): Report of the Royal Society of Tasmania for the Year ..; Former titles (until 1855): Royal Society of Van Diemen's Land. Papers and Proceedings (1834-5816); (until 1849): The Tasmanian Journal of Natural Science, Agriculture, Statistics, etc (1440-0642)
Indexed: AESIS, ASFA, B21, B25, BIOSIS Prev, ESPM, FR, GeoRef, IBR, IBZ, MathR, MycolAb, SCOPUS, SpeleolAb, VITIS, Z01.
—BLDSC (6396.000000), IE, Ingenta, INIST, Linda Hall.
Published by: Royal Society of Tasmania, PO Box 1166, Hobart, TAS 7001, Australia. TEL 61-3-6211-4177, FAX 61-3-6211-4112. Ed., R&P Vivienne Mawson.

500 AUS ISSN 0035-9211
Q93 CODEN: PRSVAV
➤ **ROYAL SOCIETY OF VICTORIA. PROCEEDINGS.** Text in English. 18??. s-a. charts; illus.; maps. index. back issues avail. **Document type:** *Proceedings, Academic/Scholarly.* **Description:** Covers conservation, earth sciences, environmental studies, meetings, congresses and meterology.
Supersedes in part (in 1989): Transactions and Proceedings of the Royal Society of Victoria During the Years ..; Which was formerly (until 1964): Royal Society of Victoria. Transactions; (until 1960): Transactions of the Philosophical Institute of Victoria from January to December .
Indexed: A34, AESIS, ASFA, AgrForAb, B21, B25, BIOSIS Prev, C25, CABA, ChemAb, E12, ESPM, EntAb, F08, GEOBASE, GH, GeoRef, H16, IBR, IBZ, Inspec, M&GPA, MycolAb, P32, P33, S13, SCOPUS, SpeleolAb, W10, W11, Z01.
—BLDSC (6807.000000), AskIEEE, IE, Ingenta, INIST, Linda Hall. **CCC.**
Published by: Royal Society of Victoria, 9 Victoria St, Melbourne, VIC 3000, Australia. TEL 61-3-96635259, FAX 61-3-96632301, rsv@sciencevictoria.org.au.

500 AUS ISSN 0035-922X
Q93 CODEN: JRSUAU
➤ **ROYAL SOCIETY OF WESTERN AUSTRALIA. JOURNAL.** Text in English. 1915. a., latest vol.91, 2008. charts; illus. index. 36 p./no.; **Document type:** *Journal, Academic/Scholarly.* **Description:** Promotes science in Western Australia and counteracts the effects of specialization.
Formerly (until 1925): Royal Society of Western Australia. Journal and Proceedings (0368-3907)
Indexed: A29, A34, A37, A38, AESIS, ASFA, ASI, Agr, AgrForAb, B20, B21, B25, BA, BIOSIS Prev, C25, C30, CABA, ChemAb, E12, ESPM, F08, F11, F12, FCA, G11, GEOBASE, GeoRef, H16, I10, I11, IBR, IBZ, MycolAb, P30, P32, P33, P40, P52, P56, PGegResA, R07, R08, R13, RA&MP, RASB, S13, S16, S17, SCOPUS, SpeleolAb, TAR, W08, W10, WildRev, Z01.
—CASDDS, Ingenta, INIST, Linda Hall.
Published by: Royal Society of Western Australia Inc., c/o Western Australian Museum, Locked Bag 49, Welshpool DC, W.A. 6986, Australia. TEL 61-8-92123771, FAX 61-8-92123882, rswa@museum.wa.gov.au. Ed. Kathy Meney. Circ: 600.

500 GBR ISSN 1793-1827
ROYAL SOCIETY SERIES ON ADVANCES IN SCIENCE. Text in English. 2005. irreg., latest vol.3, 2007. price varies. 420 p./no.; back issues avail. **Document type:** *Monographic series, Academic/Scholarly.* **Description:** Contains articles based on contributions to the Royal Society journal philosophical transactions A, rewritten by their authors to broaden their scientific appeal and to reach general audience.
Published by: (The Royal Society Publishing), Imperial College Press (Subsidiary of: World Scientific Publishing Co. Pte. Ltd.), 57 Shelton St, Covent Garden, London, WC2H 9HE, United Kingdom. TEL 44-20-78360888, FAX 44-20-78362020, edit@icpress.co.uk, http://www.icpress.co.uk/. Ed. J Michael T Thompson. **Subscr. to:** World Scientific Publishing Co. Pte. Ltd. **Dist. by:** World Scientific Publishing Co., Inc., 27 Warren St, Ste 401-402, Hackensack, NJ 07601. TEL 201-487-9655, 800-227-7562, FAX 201-487-9656, 888-977-2665, wspc@wspc.com.; World Scientific Publishing Ltd.

500 600 POL
ROZPRAWY Z DZIEJOW NAUKI I TECHNIKI. Text in Polish. irreg. price varies. **Document type:** *Monographic series, Academic/Scholarly.*
Published by: Polska Akademia Nauk, Komitet Historii Nauki i Techniki, ul Nowy Swiat 72, Palac Staszica, Warsaw, 00330, Poland. TEL 48-22-6572730. Ed. Irena Stasiewicz-Jasiukowa.

500 CHN ISSN 1001-8409
RUAN KEXUE/SOFT SCIENCE. Text in Chinese; Summaries in Chinese, English. 1987. q. USD 31.20 (effective 2009). adv. **Document type:** *Academic/Scholarly.* **Description:** Covers the applications of science and technology to Chinese economics and agriculture.
Related titles: Online - full text ed.
Published by: Sichuan Keji Cujin Fazhan Yanjiu Zhongxin/Sichuan Provincial Research Center of Science and Technology Promoting Development, No 11 Renmin Nanlu 4 Duan, 7th Fl, Chengdu, Sichuan 610041, China. TEL 581835, FAX 028-582972. Ed. Xu Wenbin. Adv. contact Jinghui Zhang. Circ: 3,500.

RUBIN (BOCHUM). *see* COLLEGE AND ALUMNI

500 620 TWN ISSN 1028-5679
RUREN XUEZHI. LIGONG LEI/FU JEN STUDIES (SCIENCE AND ENGINEERING). Text in Chinese. 1996. a. **Document type:** *Journal, Academic/Scholarly.*
—BLDSC (4047.751200).
Published by: Fu Jen Catholic University, College of Science and Engineering/Furen Daxue, Ligong Xueyuan, 510 Chung Cheng Rd, Hsinchung, Taipei, 242, Taiwan. TEL 886-2-29031111 ext 2411, FAX 886-2-29014749, http://www.se.fju.edu.tw/.

500 600 RUS ISSN 1025-1820
Q127.R8
RUSSIA AND WORLD: SCIENCE AND TECHNOLOGY/ROSSIYA I MIR: NAUKA I TECHNOLOGIYA. Variant title: Ecolink. Text in Russian, English. 1994. q. USD 100 foreign (effective 2005). abstr. 40 p./no.; **Document type:** *Journal, Academic/Scholarly.*
Related titles: E-mail ed.; Fax ed.
Indexed: RASB.
Published by: Firma FiD/F&F Consulting Co., ul Raspletina, 15-16, Moscow, 123060, Russian Federation. info@fid-tech.com, http://www.fid-tech.com. Ed. Vladimir Fokin. Circ: 1,250 (paid).
Co-sponsor: Ministerstvo Obrazovaniya i Nauki Rossiiskoi Federatsii/Ministry of Education and Science of the Russian Federation.

S

500 RUS ISSN 1019-3316
Q60 CODEN: HRUSEG
RUSSIAN ACADEMY OF SCIENCES. HERALD. Text in English. 1931. bi-m. EUR 3,649, USD 4,420 combined subscription to institutions (print & online eds.) (effective 2012). **Document type:** *Journal, Academic/Scholarly.* **Description:** Publishes the major work, speeches, and discussions presented to the Academy by the most eminent Russian and foreign scientists, presenting the viewpoints of various disciplines on many important subjects related to the natural, technical, and social sciences.
Formerly (until 1992): U S S R Russian Academy of Sciences. Herald (1057-509X)
Related titles: Online - full text ed.: ISSN 1555-6492 (from IngentaConnect); ◆ Translation of: Rossiiskaya Akademiya Nauk. Vestnik. ISSN 0869-5873.
Indexed: A20, A22, A26, A28, APA, BrCerAb, C&ISA, CA/WCA, CIA, CerAb, CivEngAb, CorrAb, CurCont, E&CAJ, E01, E11, EEA, EMA, ESPM, EnvEAb, H15, M&GPA, M&TEA, M09, MBF, METADEX, OceAb, SCI, SCOPUS, SolStAb, T04, W07, WAA.
—BLDSC (0412.076000), East View, IE, Ingenta, Linda Hall. **CCC.**
Published by: (Rossiiskaya Akademiya Nauk/Russian Academy of Sciences), M A I K Nauka - Interperiodica (Subsidiary of: Pleiades Publishing, Inc.), Profsoyuznaya ul 90, Moscow, 117997, Russian Federation. TEL 7-095-3347420, FAX 7-095-3360666, compmg@maik.ru, http://www.maik.ru. Ed. Yurii S Osipov. **Dist. by:** Springer, Haber Str 7, Heidelberg 69126, Germany. TEL 49-6221-3454303, FAX 49-6221-3454229; Springer New York LLC, Journal Fulfillment, PO Box 2485, Secaucus, NJ 07096. TEL 212-460-1500, FAX 201-348-4505.

THE RUTHERFORD JOURNAL; the New Zealand journal for the history and philosophy of science and technology. *see* PHILOSOPHY

500.896872073 USA
S A C N A S NEWS. Text in English. q. membership. back issues avail. **Document type:** *Bulletin.*
Related titles: Online - full text ed.
Published by: Society for Advancement of Chicanos and Native Americans in Science, PO Box 8526, Santa Cruz, CA 95061-8526. TEL 831-459-0170. Ed. Rachel Barron. adv.: B&W page USD 1,200, color page USD 2,050; trim 10 x 7.5.

500 600 IND ISSN 0973-4007
S A T I JOURNAL OF SCIENCE AND TECHNOLOGY. Text in English. 2005. q. INR 100 domestic to individuals; USD 50 foreign to individuals; INR 500 domestic to institutions; USD 100 foreign to institutions; INR 50 per issue domestic; USD 40 per issue foreign (effective 2011). **Document type:** *Journal, Academic/Scholarly.*
Published by: Samrat Ashok Technological Institute, Civil Lines, Vidisha, 464 001, India. TEL 91-7592-250296, FAX 91-7592-250124, support@satiengg.org. Ed. R C Jain.

500 600 PHL
S & T POST. (Science and Technology) Text in English. m. free. **Description:** Official publication of the Department of Science and Technology.
Published by: (Department of Science and Technology), Science and Technology Information Institute, P.O. Box 3596, Manila, Philippines. TEL 822-0954.

500 ARG ISSN 0325-6146
S C A R BOLETIN. Text in Spanish. 1959. 4/yr. abstr.; bibl.; charts; illus.; stat. index. **Document type:** *Bulletin.*
Published by: (Scientific Committee on Antarctic Research), Direccion Nacional del Antartico, Instituto Antartico Argentino, Cerrito, 1248, Buenos Aires, 1010, Argentina. TEL 54-11-48120071, FAX 54-11-48137807, diriaa@dna.gov.ar, http://www.dna.gov.ar. Circ: 750. **Co-sponsor:** International Council of Scientific Unions.

S E S D NEWSLETTER. (Science Education for Students with Disabilities) *see* EDUCATION

S I I A S NEWS. *see* HUMANITIES: COMPREHENSIVE WORKS

S S E R C BULLETIN. *see* EDUCATION—Teaching Methods And Curriculum

S S M A CLASSROOM ACTIVITIES MONOGRAPH SERIES. *see* EDUCATION—Teaching Methods And Curriculum

S S M A TOPICS FOR TEACHERS MONOGRAPH SERIES. *see* EDUCATION—Teaching Methods And Curriculum

S T A: ITS ROLES AND ACTIVITIES. (Science and Technology Agency) *see* TECHNOLOGY: COMPREHENSIVE WORKS

S T E MTRENDS; science, technology, engineering, mathematics. (Science, Technology, Engineering, Mathematics) *see* OCCUPATIONS AND CAREERS

500 DEU
S Z WISSEN. (Sueddeutsche Zeitung) Text in German. 2004. bi-m. EUR 27; EUR 5 newsstand/cover (effective 2007). adv. **Document type:** *Magazine, Consumer.*
Published by: Sueddeutsche Zeitung GmbH (Subsidiary of: Sueddeutscher Verlag GmbH), Hultschiner Str 8, Munich, 81677, Germany. TEL 49-89-21830, FAX 49-89-21839777, verlag@sueddeutsche.de. adv.: page EUR 9,200. Circ: 105,548 (paid and controlled).

509 ARG ISSN 0328-6584
Q124.6
➤ **SABER Y TIEMPO**; revista de historia de la ciencia. Text in Spanish, Portuguese; Summaries in Spanish. 1996. s-a. ARS 20; ARS 40 foreign (effective 2001). bk.rev. abstr.; bibl.; illus. cum.index: 1997-1999. back issues avail.; reprints avail. **Document type:** *Journal, Academic/Scholarly.* **Description:** Covers the history of science and technology worldwide for students and researchers in the field.
Published by: Asociacion Biblioteca Jose Babini, Av. Santa Fe 1145, 3er piso, Buenos Aires, 1059, Argentina. TEL 54-11-48114826, FAX 54-11-49626174, babini@netex.com.ar, http://www.historiadelaciencia.org. Ed., Pub. Nicolas Babini. Circ: 200.

➤ **SACRED HEART UNIVERSITY REVIEW.** *see* HUMANITIES: COMPREHENSIVE WORKS

500 IND ISSN 0256-2499
Q73 CODEN: SAPSER
➤ **SADHANA**; academy proceedings in engineering sciences. Text in English. 1978. bi-m. EUR 194, USD 236 combined subscription to institutions (print & online eds.) (effective 2012). abstr.; bibl.; illus. 100 p./no. 1 cols./p.; back issues avail.; reprint service avail. from PSC. **Document type:** *Proceedings, Academic/Scholarly.* **Description:** Contains wide-ranging, original papers and reviews of interest to engineering scientists.
Former titles (until 1984): Indian Academy of Sciences. Proceedings. Engineering Sciences (0253-4096); (until 1979): Indian Academy of Sciences. Proceedings. Section C. Engineering Sciences (0250-5444)
Related titles: Microform ed.: (from PQC); Online - full text ed.: ISSN 0973-7677 (from IngentaConnect).
Indexed: A01, A20, A22, A26, A28, APA, ASCA, BrCerAb, C&ISA, CA, CA/WCA, CCMJ, CIA, CPEI, CerAb, ChemAb, ChemTitl, CivEngAb, CorrAb, CurCont, E&CAJ, E01, E08, E11, EEA, EIA, EMA, ESPM, EnerInd, EngInd, EnvEAb, H15, IBR, IBZ, INIS AtomInd, Inspec, M&TEA, M09, MBF, METADEX, MSN, MathR, RefZh, S09, SCI, SCOPUS, SolStAb, T02, T04, W07, WAA, Z02.
—BLDSC (8062.798000), AskIEEE, CASDDS, IE, Ingenta, INIST, Linda Hall. **CCC.**
Published by: Indian Academy of Sciences, C.V. Raman Ave, Sadashivanagar, PO Box 8005, Bangalore, Karnataka 560 080, India. TEL 91-80-22661200, FAX 91-80-23616094, http://www.ias.ac.in. Ed. R N Iyengar. Circ: 800. **Subscr. to:** I N S I O Scientific Books & Periodicals, PO Box 7234, Indraprastha HPO, New Delhi 110 002, India. iihm@ap.nic.in, http://iihm.ap.nic.in/. **Co-publisher:** Springer (India) Private Ltd.

507.4 JPN
SADO HAKUBUTSUKAN KENKYU HOKOKU/PUBLICATIONS FROM THE SADO MUSEUM. Text in English, Japanese; Summaries in English. 1957. irreg. **Description:** Contains research reports.
Published by: Sado Hakubutsukan/Sado Museum, Nakae, Yahata, Sado-gun, Sawata-machi, Niigata-ken 952-1311, Japan.

500 DEU ISSN 0080-5262
AS182
SAECHSISCHE AKADEMIE DER WISSENSCHAFTEN, LEIPZIG. JAHRBUCH. Text in German. 1955 (covering 1949-53). irreg., latest 2007, for the year 2005-2006. price varies. **Document type:** *Monographic series, Academic/Scholarly.*
Indexed: GeoRef, IBR, IBZ, RASB.
—Linda Hall.
Published by: (Saechsische Akademie der Wissenschaften, Leipzig), S. Hirzel Verlag, Postfach 101061, Stuttgart, 70009, Germany. TEL 49-711-25820, FAX 49-711-2582290, service@hirzel.de, http://www.hirzel.de. Ed. Heinz Penzlin.

500 510 DEU ISSN 0365-6470
CODEN: ASAWAO
SAECHSISCHE AKADEMIE DER WISSENSCHAFTEN, LEIPZIG. MATHEMATISCH-NATURWISSENSCHAFTLICHE KLASSE. ABHANDLUNGEN. Text in German. 1896. irreg., latest vol.64, no.3, 2007. price varies. **Document type:** *Monographic series, Academic/Scholarly.*
Formerly (until 1944): Saechsische Akademie der Wissenschaften. Mathematisch-Physische Klasse. Abhandlungen (0323-8741)
Indexed: CCMJ, DIP, GeoRef, IBR, IBZ, MSN, MathR, SpeleolAb, Z02.
—CASDDS, INIST, Linda Hall.
Published by: (Saechsische Akademie der Wissenschaften, Leipzig, Mathematisch-Naturwissenschaftliche Klasse), S. Hirzel Verlag, Postfach 101061, Stuttgart, 70009, Germany. TEL 49-711-25820, FAX 49-711-2582290, service@hirzel.de, http://www.hirzel.de.

510 500 DEU ISSN 0371-327X
AS182 CODEN: SSWMAU
SAECHSISCHE AKADEMIE DER WISSENSCHAFTEN, LEIPZIG. MATHEMATISCH-NATURWISSENSCHAFTLICHE KLASSE. SITZUNGSBERICHTE. Text in German. 1896. irreg., latest vol.128, 2003. price varies. **Document type:** *Proceedings, Academic/Scholarly.*
Indexed: CCMJ, GeoRef, IBR, IBZ, MSN, MathR, SpeleolAb, Z02.
—CASDDS, INIST, Linda Hall.
Published by: (Saechsische Akademie der Wissenschaften, Leipzig, Mathematisch-Naturwissenschaftliche Klasse), S. Hirzel Verlag, Postfach 101061, Stuttgart, 70009, Germany. TEL 49-711-25820, FAX 49-711-2582290, service@hirzel.de, http://www.hirzel.de.

500 JPN ISSN 0916-7676
SAGAMI JOSHI DAIGAKU KIYO. B, SHIZEN-KEI/SAGAMI WOMEN'S UNIVERSITY. JOURNAL. B (NATURAL SCIENCES). Text in Japanese. 1956. a. **Document type:** *Journal, Academic/Scholarly.*
Supersedes in part (in 1989): Sagami Joshi Daigaku Kiyo/Sagami Women's University. Journal (0286-6250)
—BLDSC (8069.213820).
Published by: Sagami Joshi Daigaku/Sagami Women's University, 2-1-1 Bunkyo, Sagamihara, Kanagawa 228-8533, Japan. TEL 81-42-742-1411, http://www.sagami-wu.ac.jp/.

500 MYS ISSN 0126-6039
Q1 CODEN: SAMADP
SAINS MALAYSIANA. Text in English, Malay. 1972. bi-m. MYR 25 per issue domestic; USD 25 per issue foreign (effective 2010). charts. Index. back issues avail. **Document type:** *Journal, Academic/Scholarly.* **Description:** Contains articles on earth sciences, health sciences, life sciences, mathematical sciences and physical sciences.
Indexed: BAS, ChemAb, GeoRef, SCI, SCOPUS, SpeleolAb, W07, Z01, Z02.
—CASDDS, INIST.
Published by: (Universiti Kebangsaan Malaysia. Fakulti Sains dan Teknologi/National University of Malaysia. Faculty of Science and Technology), Perbit Universiti Kebangsaan Malaysia/National University of Malaysia Press, Bangi, Selangor 43600, Malaysia. TEL 60-3-89215180, FAX 60-3-89254575, penerbit@ukm.my, http://pkukmweb.ukm.my/~penerbit/. Ed. R. Abd-Shukor. Circ: 5,000.

SAINT LOUIS UNIVERSITY RESEARCH JOURNAL; an interdisciplinary journal in the sciences and the humanities. *see* HUMANITIES: COMPREHENSIVE WORKS

600 JPN ISSN 0916-6394
SAITAMA DAIGAKU KIYO. KOGAKUBU/SCIENCE AND ENGINEERING REPORTS OF SAITAMA UNIVERSITY. Text in Japanese. 1967. a.
Formerly (until 1975): Saitama Daigaku Kiyo. Riko Gakubu. Kogaku-kei/Science and Engineering Reports of Saitama University. Series C (0586-7266)
Indexed: Inspec.
Published by: Saitama Daigaku/Saitama University, 255, Shimo-Okubo, Sakura-Ku, Saitama City, Saitama 338-8570, Japan. info@post.saitama-u.ac.jp, http://www.saitama-u.ac.jp.

500 JPN ISSN 0581-3662
SAITAMA DAIGAKU KIYO. SHIZEN KAGAKU HEN/SAITAMA UNIVERSITY. JOURNAL. NATURAL SCIENCE. Text in Japanese; Summaries in English. 1965. a.
Indexed: GeoRef, JPI, SpeleolAb.
—Linda Hall.
Published by: Saitama Daigaku, Kyoyobu/Saitama University, College of Liberal Arts, 255 Shimo-Okubo, Urawa-shi, Saitama-ken 338, Japan.

508.074 JPN ISSN 0288-5611
QH7
SAITAMA-KENRITSU SHIZENSHI HAKUBUTSUKAN KENKYU HOKOKU/SAITAMA MUSEUM OF NATURAL HISTORY. BULLETIN. Text in Japanese; Summaries in English. 1983. a. adv. **Document type:** *Bulletin.*
Indexed: GeoRef, SpeleolAb, Z01.
Published by: Saitama-kenritsu Shizenshi Hakubutsukan/Saitama Museum of Natural History, 1417-1 Nagatoro, Chichibu-gun, Nagatoro-machi, Saitama-ken 369-1305, Japan. TEL 81-494-660404, FAX 81-494-691002, sizensi@po.kumagaya.or.jp, http://www.kumagaya.or.jp/~sizensi. Ed. Kozo Yoshida. R&P Takuo Umezawa. Adv. contact Shuichi Takayanagi.

507.4 JPN ISSN 1346-079X
SAITAMA-KENRITSU SHIZENSHI HAKUBUTSUKAN SHUZO SHIRYO MOKUROKU/SAITAMA MUSEUM OF NATURAL HISTORY. CATALOGUE OF THE MATERIALS. Text in Japanese. a. **Document type:** *Abstract/Index.*
Indexed: Z01.
Published by: Saitama-kenritsu Shizenshi Hakubutsukan/Saitama Museum of Natural History, 1417-1 Nagatoro, Chichibu-gun, Nagatoro-machi, Saitama-ken 369-1305, Japan. TEL 81-494-660404, FAX 81-494-691002.

508.074 JPN ISSN 0375-1821
CODEN: SHMRBL
SAITO HO-ON KAI MUSEUM OF NATURAL HISTORY. RESEARCH BULLETIN. Text in English. 1934. a. free. **Document type:** *Bulletin, Academic/Scholarly.*
Indexed: GeoRef, SpeleolAb, Z01.
—INIST.
Published by: Saito Ho-on Kai/Saito Gratitude Foundation, 20-2 Hon-cho 2-chome, Aoba-ku, Sendai-shi, Miyagi-ken 980-0014, Japan. TEL 81-222-262-5506, FAX 81-222-262-5508. Ed. Tsunemasa Saito.

SALARIES OF SCIENTISTS, ENGINEERS AND TECHNICIANS; a summary of salary surveys. *see* OCCUPATIONS AND CAREERS

508.074 USA ISSN 1526-3614
QH1
SAM NOBLE OKLAHOMA MUSEUM OF NATURAL HISTORY. OCCASIONAL PAPER. Text in English. 1995. irreg.
Formerly (until 2000): Oklahoma Museum of Natural History. Occasional Paper (1080-7004)
Indexed: Z01.
—Linda Hall.
Published by: Oklahoma University, Oklahoma Museum of Natural History, 2401 Chautauqua Ave, Norman, OK 73072.

500 001.3 RUS ISSN 1810-5378
SAMARSKII GOSUDARSTVENNYI UNIVERSITET. VESTNIK. Text in Russian. 1995. bi-m. **Document type:** *Journal, Academic/Scholarly.*
Indexed: MSN, Z02.
Published by: (Samarskii Gosudarstvennyi Universitet), Izdatel'stvo Samarskii Universitet/Publishing House of Samara State University, ul Akademika Pavlova 1, k 209, Samara, 443011, Russian Federation. TEL 7-846-3345406, FAX 7-846-3345406, university-press@ssu.samara.ru, http://publisher.samsu.ru. Ed. Dr. I A Noskov.

508 USA ISSN 1059-8707
QH1 CODEN: PSDHER
➤ **SAN DIEGO SOCIETY OF NATURAL HISTORY. PROCEEDINGS.** Text in English. 1990. irreg., latest no.42, 2010. price varies. index. back issues avail. **Document type:** *Proceedings, Academic/Scholarly.* **Description:** Publishes papers in the biological and geological sciences.
Formed by the merger of (1931-1990): San Diego Society of Natural History. Memoir (0080-5920); (1905-1990): San Diego Society of Natural History. Transactions (0080-5947); Which incorporates: San Diego Society of Natural History. Occasional Papers (0080-5939)
Indexed: ASFA, B21, B25, BIOSIS Prev, ESPM, GeoRef, IBR, IBZ, MycolAb, SWRA, SpeleolAb, WildRev, Z01.
—Ingenta, INIST, Linda Hall.
Published by: San Diego Society of Natural History, San Diego Natural History Museum Library, PO Box 121390, San Diego, CA 92112. TEL 619-232-3821, FAX 619-232-0248, customerservice@sdnhm.org.

500 USA
SANDIA NATIONAL LABORATORIES. REPORT. Text in English. irreg.
Published by: Sandia National Laboratories, PO Box 5800, Albuquerque, NM 87185-0165. http://www.sandia.gov. **Subscr. to:** U.S. Department of Commerce, National Technical Information Service, 5301 Shawnee Rd, Alexandria, VA 22312. orders@ntis.fedworld.gov, http://www.ntis.gov/ordering.htm.

SANDNATS. *see* CONSERVATION

500 JPN ISSN 1349-6913
SANGAKU RENKEIGAKU/JAPAN SOCIETY FOR INTELLECTUAL PRODUCTION. JOURNAL. Text in Japanese. 2004. s-a. **Document type:** *Journal, Academic/Scholarly.*
Related titles: Online - full text ed.: ISSN 1881-8706.
Published by: Sangaku Renkei Gakkai/Japan Society for Intellectual Production, 4-23-17 Higashiikebukuro, Toshima-ku, Tamura Bldg 6F, Tokyo, 170-0013, Japan. TEL 81-3-59538575, FAX 81-88-6567593, h19-office@j-sip.org, http://www.j-sip.org/.

500 CHE
SANKT GALLISCHE NATURWISSENSCHAFTLICHE GESELLSCHAFT. BERICHTE. Text in German. 1860. irreg., latest vol.89, 2000. USD 30. **Document type:** *Academic/Scholarly.*

Formerly: Sankt Gallische Naturwissenschaftliche Gesellschaft. Bericht ueber die Taetigkeit (0080-6056)
Published by: Sankt Gallische Naturwissenschaftliche Gesellschaft, Myrtenstr 9, St. Gallen, 9010, Switzerland. TEL 41-71-2453470. Circ: 1,000.

500 JPN ISSN 1880-0041
HC465.H53
SANSOUKEN TODAY. Text in Japanese. 2001. q. **Document type:** *Journal, Academic/Scholarly.*
Formerly (until 2005): A I S T Today (Nihongo-Ban) (1346-5805)
Related titles: ◆ English ed.: A I S T Today (English Edition). ISSN 1346-602X.
Indexed: A28, APA, BrCerAb, C&ISA, CA/WCA, CIA, CerAb, CivEngAb, CorrAb, E&CAJ, E11, EEA, EMA, ESPM, EnvEAb, GeoRef, H15, M&TEA, M09, MBF, METADEX, SolStAb, T04, WAA.
—BLDSC (8075.303000), Linda Hall.
Published by: National Institute of Advanced Industrial Science and Technology/Sangyou Gijutsu Sougou Kenkyuujo, 1-1-1 Umezono, Tsukuba Central 2, Tsukuba, Ibaraki 305-8563, Japan. TEL 81-29-8626217, FAX 81-29-8626212, prpub@m.aist.go.jp.

500 USA
SANTA FE INSTITUTE. WORKING PAPERS. Text in English. 19??. irreg. free (effective 2010). back issues avail. **Document type:** *Monographic series, Academic/Scholarly.*
Related titles: Online - full content ed.
Published by: Santa Fe Institute, 1399 Hyde Park Rd, Santa Fe, NM 87501. TEL 505-984-8800, FAX 505-982-0565, email@santafe.edu.

500 CHN ISSN 1672-948X
SANXIA DAXUE XUEBAO (ZIRAN KEXUE BAN)/CHINA THREE GORGES UNIVERSITY. JOURNAL (NATURAL SCIENCES). Text in Chinese. 1979. bi-m. **Document type:** *Journal, Academic/Scholarly.*
Former titles (until 2000): Wuhan Shuili Dianli Daxue Xuebao (Yichang)/ University of Hydraulic and Electric Engineering. Journal (Yichang) (1007-7081); (until 1996): Gezhouba Shuidian Gongcheng Xueyuan Xuebao/Gezhouba Institute of Hydro-Electric Engineering. Journal (1005-9970)
Related titles: Online - full text ed.: (from WanFang Data Corp.).
Indexed: RefZh.
—BLDSC (8075.371750), East View.
Published by: Sanxia Daxue, 8, Daxue Lu, Yichang, 443002, China. TEL 86-717-6392057.

500 ITA ISSN 0036-4681
SAPERE. Text in Italian. 1935; N.S. 1974; N.S. 1983. bi-m. EUR 44 domestic; EUR 88 foreign (effective 2009). adv. bk.rev. bibl.; charts; illus.; tr.lit. back issues avail. **Document type:** *Journal, Academic/ Scholarly.* **Description:** Deals with contemporary scientific culture, from physics to medicine, computer science to ecology, examined by experts.
Indexed: IBR, IBZ, RASB.
Published by: Edizioni Dedalo, Viale Luigi Jacobini 5, Bari, BA 70123, Italy. TEL 39-080-5311413, FAX 39-080-5311414, info@edizionidedalo.it, http://www.edizionidedalo.it. Circ: 48,000.

SAPPORO IKA DAIGAKU IGAKUBU JINBUN SHIZEN KAGAKU KIYO/SAPPORO MEDICAL UNIVERSITY. SCHOOL OF MEDICINE. JOURNAL OF LIBERAL ARTS AND SCIENCES. *see* HUMANITIES: COMPREHENSIVE WORKS

500 JPN ISSN 0914-2401
SAPPORO-SHI SEISHONEN KAGAKUKAN KIYO. Text in Japanese. 1984. a. free.
Published by: Sapporo-shi Seishonen Kagakukan/Sapporo Science Center, 2-20 Atsubetsu-Chuo 1-Jo 5-chome, Atsubetsu-ku, Sapporo-shi, Hokkaido 004-0000, Japan. FAX 011-894-5445. Circ: 1,000.

500 CAN ISSN 0080-6587
T177.C2
SASKATCHEWAN RESEARCH COUNCIL. ANNUAL REPORT. Text in English. 1947. a. free. **Document type:** *Corporate.*
Indexed: GeoRef, SpeleolAb.
Published by: Saskatchewan Research Council, 15 Innovation Blvd, Saskatoon, SK S7N 2X8, Canada. TEL 306-933-5400, FAX 306-933-7446. Ed., R&P Gerald L Brown TEL 306-933-5490. Circ: 200,000 (controlled).

500 FRA ISSN 0989-3334
SAVOIRS ACTUELS. Text in French. 1987. irreg. price varies. **Document type:** *Monographic series, Academic/Scholarly.*
Published by: Centre National de la Recherche Scientifique, Campus Gerard-Megie, 3 Rue Michel-Ange, Paris, 75794, France. TEL 33-1-44964000, FAX 33-1-44965390, http://www.cnrseditions.fr.

SCANDINAVIAN JOURNAL OF MEDICINE & SCIENCE IN SPORTS. *see* MEDICAL SCIENCES—Sports Medicine

SCANFILE. *see* BUSINESS AND ECONOMICS—Management

500 600 610 USA ISSN 1687-8299
➤ **SCHOLARLY RESEARCH EXCHANGE.** Text in English. 2008. q. **Document type:** *Journal, Academic/Scholarly.* **Description:** Brings a number of important innovations to the traditional scholarly journal publishing system.
Related titles: Online - full text ed.: ISSN 1687-8302.
Indexed: A01, A26, CA, E08, H12, I05, S09, SCOPUS, T02.
Published by: Hindawi Publishing Corporation, 410 Park Ave, 15th Fl, PMB 287, New York, NY 10022. FAX 215-893-4392, hindawi@hindawi.com, http://www.hindawi.com.

500 001.3 300 BEL ISSN 1918-8722
▼ **SCHOOL OF DOCTORAL STUDIES JOURNAL.** Text in English. 2009. a. **Document type:** *Journal, Academic/Scholarly.*
Related titles: Online - full text ed.: ISSN 1918-8730. free (effective 2011).
Published by: I I U Press and Research Centre, 9 Boulevard de France, Batiment A, Braine-L'Alleud, 1420, Belgium. iiupress@iiuedu.eu.

507 IND ISSN 0036-679X
SCHOOL SCIENCE. Text in English. 1962. q. INR 220 (effective 2011). bk.rev. illus. index. back issues avail. **Document type:** *Journal, Academic/Scholarly.*
Published by: (Department of Education in Science and Mathematics), National Council of Educational Research and Training, Sri Aurbindo Marg, New Delhi, 110 016, India. TEL 91-11-26562708, pd.ncert@nic.in.

SCHOOL SCIENCE AND MATHEMATICS. *see* EDUCATION—Teaching Methods And Curriculum

507.1 GBR ISSN 0036-6811
Q1 CODEN: SSCRAD
➤ **SCHOOL SCIENCE REVIEW.** Abbreviated title: S S R. Text in English. 1919. q. GBP 112 domestic to libraries; GBP 127 in Europe to libraries; GBP 144 elsewhere to libraries; GBP 28 per issue domestic to libraries; GBP 31.75 per issue in Europe to libraries; GBP 36 per issue elsewhere to libraries; free to members (effective 2010). adv. bk.rev. charts; illus. cum.index: vols.48-57 (1967-1977). back issues avail.; reprints avail. **Document type:** *Journal, Academic/Scholarly.* **Description:** Aims to inform readers about the innovations and developments in science education.
Related titles: Microform ed.: (from PQC); Online - full text ed.
Indexed: A22, A26, AEI, B29, CA, CPE, ChemAb, ChemTitl, E03, E07, ERA, ERI, EnvAb, EnvInd, FR, G08, HECAB, I05, Inspec, P07, P30, RASB, S21, T02.
—BLDSC (8093.000000), CASDDS, IE, Infotrieve, Ingenta, INIST. **CCC.**
Published by: Association for Science Education, College Ln, Hatfield, Herts AL10 9AA, United Kingdom. TEL 44-1707-283000, FAX 44-1707-266532, info@ase.org.uk. Adv. contact Rebecca Dixon-Watmough. Circ: 19,000.

508 AUT
SCHRIFTENREIHE GESCHICHTE DER NATURWISSENSCHAFTEN UND DER TECHNIK. Text in German. 2003. irreg., latest vol.16, 2009. price varies. **Document type:** *Monographic series, Academic/ Scholarly.*
Published by: (Johannes Kepler Universitaet Linz), Trauner Verlag und Buchservice GmbH, Koeglstr 14, Linz, 4020, Austria. TEL 43-732-778241212, FAX 43-732-778241400, office@trauner.at, http://www.trauner.at.

500 CHE ISSN 1022-3495
➤ **SCHWEIZERISCHE AKADEMIE DER NATURWISSENSCHAFTEN. DENKSCHRIFTEN.** Text in English, French, German. 1829. irreg. price varies. **Document type:** *Monographic series, Academic/ Scholarly.*
Formerly: Schweizerische Naturforschende Gesellschaft. Denkschriften
Indexed: GeoRef, SpeleolAb.
Published by: (Schweizerische Akademie der Naturwissenschaften), Birkhaeuser Verlag AG (Subsidiary of: Springer Science+Business Media), Viaduktstr 42, Postfach 133, Basel, 4051, Switzerland. TEL 41-61-2050730, FAX 41-61-2050792, info@birkhauser.ch, http://www.birkhauser.ch/journals. **Subscr. in the Americas to:** Springer New York LLC, Journal Fulfillment, PO Box 2485, Secaucus, NJ 07096. TEL 201-348-4033, FAX 201-348-4505, journals@birkhauser.com; **Subscr. to:** Springer Distribution Center, Kundenservice Zeitschriften. TEL 49-6221-345-0, FAX 49-6221-345-4229, birkhauser@springer.de.

500 CHE ISSN 1421-4482
QH5
➤ **SCHWEIZERISCHE AKADEMIE DER NATURWISSENSCHAFTEN. JAHRBUCH.** Text in English, French, German; Summaries in English. 1960. a. price varies. index. back issues avail. **Document type:** *Proceedings, Academic/Scholarly.*
Former titles (until 1990): Schweizerische Akademie der Naturwissenschaften. Jahrbuch. Administrativer Teil (1421-4474); (until 1988): Schweizerischen Naturforschenden Gesellschaft. Jahrbuch (0252-2969); (until 1978): Verhandlungen der Schweizerischen Naturforschenden Gesellschaft (1017-2130)
Indexed: GeoRef, SpeleolAb, VITIS.
—INIST.
Published by: (Bern. Schweizerische Naturforschende Gesellschaft), Birkhaeuser Verlag AG (Subsidiary of: Springer Science+Business Media), Viaduktstr 42, Postfach 133, Basel, 4051, Switzerland. TEL 41-61-2050707, FAX 41-61-2050792, birkhauser@springer.de, http://www.birkhauser.ch. Circ: 600.

500 CHE
SCHWEIZERISCHER WISSENSCHAFTSRAT. JAHRESBERICHT/ CONSEIL SUISSE DE LA SCIENCE. RAPPORT ANNUEL. Text in French, German. 1965. a. free. **Document type:** *Yearbook, Government.*
Indexed: RASB.
Published by: Schweizerischer Wissenschafts- und Technologierat, Birkenweg 61, Bern, 3003, Switzerland. TEL 41-31-3229666, FAX 41-31-3228070, marianne.klein@swr.admin.ch, http://www.admin.ch/ swtr.

500 028.5 GBR ISSN 1362-7996
SCI-JOURNAL. Text in English. 1995. q. **Description:** Offers junior and senior high school students the chance to publish work done in science classes.
Media: Online - full text.
Indexed: GeoRef, SpeleolAb.
Published by: University of Southampton, Research and Graduate School of Education, Highfield, Southampton, Hants SO17 1BJ, United Kingdom. http://www.soton.ac.uk/~plf/Sci-Journal/index.htm.

500 600 TWN ISSN 1605-9395
SCI-TECH FOCUS. Text in English. 2000. m. free. bk.rev.; Website rev. 6 p./no.; back issues avail. **Document type:** *Newsletter, Academic/ Scholarly.* **Description:** Covers major ongoing sci-tech activities in the Pacific Rim.
Related titles: Online - full content ed.
Indexed: APA, C&ISA, CorrAb, E&CAJ, EEA, SolStAb, WAA.
—Linda Hall.
Published by: Xingzhengyuan Guojia Kexue Weiyuanhui, Kexue Jishu Ziliao Zhongxin/Science & Technology Information Center, 14-16F, 106 Hoping E Rd, Sec 2, Taipei, 106-36, Taiwan. TEL 886-2-27377649, FAX 886-2-27377664, http://www.stic.gov.tw/. Ed. Ms. Sophie Tsai.

500 ZMB ISSN 1609-4859
T28.Z33
SCI-TECH NEWSLETTER. Text in English. 1996. q.
Indexed: INIS AtomInd.
Published by: National Institute for Scientific and Industrial Research, PO Box 310158, Lusaka, 15302, Zambia. TEL 260-1-2810816, FAX 260-1-283533, nisiris@zamnet.zm, http://www.nisir.org.zm.

509 JPN
SCIAMUS; sources and commentaries in exact sciences. Text in English. 2000. a. USD 65 to individuals; USD 95 to institutions (effective 2005). **Description:** Covers the history of the exact sciences before A.D. 1600, especially as applies to Asian and Arabic science.
Formerly: S C I A M V S (1345-4617)
Indexed: CCMJ, I14, MSN, MathR, Z02.
—BLDSC (8127.927000), IE, Ingenta.
Address: c/o Prof. Michio Yano, Kyoto Sangyo University, Faculty of Cultural Studies, Kamigamo, Kita-ku, Kyoto, 603-8555, Japan. Ed. Michio Yano. **Dist. by:** Portico Librerias, S.A., Munoz Seca, 6, PO Box 503, Zaragoza 50080, Spain. FAX 34-976-353226, portico@zaragoza.net.

500 330 GBR ISSN 1945-3477
SCIBX. (Science Business Exchange) Text in English. 2008. w. back issues avail. **Document type:** *Journal, Academic/Scholarly.* **Description:** Provides analysis of the scientific content and commercial potential of the important translational research papers from across the life science literature.
Media: Online - full text.
—CCC.
Published by: Nature Publishing Group (Subsidiary of: Macmillan Publishers Ltd.), The MacMillan Bldg, 4 Crinan St, London, N1 9XW, United Kingdom. TEL 44-20-78334000, FAX 44-20-78334640. Eds. Susan Schaeffer, Tracey Bass, Karen Bernstein. **Subscr. to:** Brunel Rd, Houndmills, Basingstoke, Hamps RG21 6XS, United Kingdom. TEL 44-1256-329242, FAX 44-1256-812358, subscriptions@nature.com.

500 SWE ISSN 1652-3202
SCIECOM INFO. Text in English, Swedish. 2004. 6/yr. **Document type:** *Magazine, Academic/Scholarly.*
Media: Online - full content.
Published by: Svenskt Resurscentrum foer Vetenskaplig Kommunikation/Swedish Resource Centre for Scientific Communication, PO Box 134, Lund, 22100, Sweden. TEL 46-46-2220000, FAX 46-46-2223682. Ed. Ingegerd Rabow TEL 46-46-2229375.

500 600 CHE ISSN 0048-9557
SCIENCA REVUO. Text in Spanish. 1950. s-a. EUR 20 (effective 2002).
Indexed: Inspec, MLA-IB.
—Linda Hall.
Published by: Internacia Scienca Asocio Esperantista/International Association of Esperantist Scientists, c/o Rudi Hauger, Ringstrasse 13, Niederglatt, 8172, Switzerland.

500 USA ISSN 0036-8075
CODEN: SCIEAS
➤ **SCIENCE.** Text in English. 1880. w. USD 835 domestic to institutions; USD 934.50 in Canada to institutions; USD 890 in Mexico to institutions; USD 920 elsewhere to institutions; USD 10 per issue (effective 2009). adv. bk.rev. abstr.; bibl.; illus.; tr.lit. Index. back issues avail.; reprints avail. **Document type:** *Journal, Academic/ Scholarly.* **Description:** Provides news of recent international developments and research in all fields of science. Publishes original research results, reviews and short features.
Incorporates (1915 -1957): The Scientific Monthly (0096-3771)
Related titles: CD-ROM ed.; Microform ed.: (from PMC, PQC); Online - full text ed.: ISSN 1095-9203. Price varies.
Indexed: A&ATA, A01, A02, A03, A05, A06, A08, A11, A20, A21, A22, A23, A24, A25, A26, A28, A29, A33, A34, A35, A36, A37, A38, ABC, ABIPC, ABS&EES, AESIS, AIA, AIDS Ab, AJEE, AMED, APA, APD, AS&TA, AS&TI, ASFA, AbAn, AcaI, AgBio, Agr, AgrForAb, AnBeAb, B&AI, B04, B05, B07, B10, B13, B14, B20, B21, B23, B25, BA, BIOBASE, BIOSIS Prev, BP, BRD, BRI, BiolDig, Biostat, BrArAb, BrCerAb, C&ISA, C10, C11, C12, C13, C25, C30, C31, C33, CA, CA/WCA, CABA, CBRI, CBTA, CCMJ, CDA, CIA, CIS, CLFP, CMCI, CTA, CerAb, ChemAb, ChemoAb, CivEngAb, CompLI, CompR, CorrAb, CurCR, CurCont, CybAb, D01, DBA, DIP, DentInd, E&CAJ, E-psyche, E03, E04, E05, E06, E07, E08, E11, E12, E17, EEA, EMA, EMBASE, ERA, ERI, ESPM, EnerRev, EngInd, EntAb, EnvAb, EnvEAb, EnvInd, ExcerpMed, F08, F11, F12, FCA, FR, FS&TA, FoVS&M, FutSurv, G01, G03, G05, G06, G07, G08, G10, G11, GEOBASE, GH, GSA, GSI, GenetAb, GeoRef, GeotechAb, H04, H12, H15, H16, H17, HECAB, HGA, HPNRM, I05, I06, I07, I10, I11, IABS, IBR, IBZ, IDIS, INI, INIS AtomInd, ISMEC, ISR, IndChem, IndMed, IndVet, Inpharma, Inspec, JW, JW-D, JW-ID, JW-N, JW-P, L09, L11, LT, M&GPA, M&TEA, M01, M02, M06, M09, M12, MASUSE, MBF, MCR, MEA&I, MEDLINE, METADEX, MLA, MLA-IB, MSN, MagInd, MaizeAb, MathR, MycolAb, N02, N03, N04, N05, NRN, NSA, NucAcAb, NumL, O01, OR, OceAb, P02, P03, P04, P07, P10, P11, P13, P15, P18, P19, P20, P22, P26, P30, P32, P33, P34, P37, P38, P39, P40, P43, P48, P52, P53, P54, P56, PAIS, PGegResA, PGrRegA, PHN&I, PMR, PN&I, PQC, PRA, PersLit, PetrolAb, PhilInd, PollutAb, PopulInd, PsycInfo, PsycholAb, R03, R04, R06, R07, R08, R11, R12, R13, R16, RA&MP, RASB, RGAb, RGPR, RI-1, RILM, RM&VM, RRTA, RefZh, RepInd, S01, S02, S03, S08, S09, S10, S12, S13, S16, S17, S19, S23, SCI, SCOPUS, SOPODA, SPPI, SSCI, SSciA, SWRA, SociolAb, SolStAb, SoyAb, SpeleolAb, T02, T04, T05, TAR, TM, TOM, TelAb, Telegen, TriticAb, V05, VITIS, VS, VirolAbstr, W03, W07, W08, W09, W10, W11, WAA, WBA, WMB, WildRev, Z01.
—BLDSC (8130.000000), AskIEEE, CASDDS, GNLM, IE, Infotrieve, Ingenta, INIST, Linda Hall, PADDS. **CCC.**
Published by: American Association for the Advancement of Science, 1200 New York Ave, NW, Washington, DC 20005. TEL 202-326-6550, FAX 202-289-7562, membership@aaas.org, http://www.scienceonline.org. Ed. Bruce Alberts. Pub. Beth Rosner. Circ: 131,286 (paid).

➤ **SCIENCE (WAYVILLE).** *see* EDUCATION

500 USA ISSN 1931-3950
SCIENCE 101. Text in English. 2006. irreg. price varies. back issues avail. **Document type:** *Monographic series, Academic/Scholarly.* **Description:** Addresses emerging security threats and concerns posed by nations such as the proliferation of nuclear weapons, promoting terrorist activities, drug and weapons trafficking, and other transnational crimes.
Published by: Greenwood Publishing Group Inc. (Subsidiary of: A B C - C L I O), 88 Post Rd W, PO Box 5007, Westport, CT 06881. TEL 203-226-3571, 800-225-5800, FAX 877-231-6980, sales@greenwood.com, http://www.greenwood.com.

S

507.1 USA ISSN 0036-8121
Q181.A1
➤ **SCIENCE ACTIVITIES**; classroom projects and curriculum ideas. Text in English. 1969. q. GBP 107 combined subscription in United Kingdom to institutions (print & online eds.); EUR 141, USD 177 combined subscription to institutions (print & online eds.) (effective 2012). adv. bk.rev.; film rev. charts; illus.; stat. index. back issues avail.; reprint service avail. from PSC. **Document type:** *Journal, Academic/Scholarly.* **Description:** Covers a wide range of topics in the biological, physical, environmental, chemical, earth, and behavioral sciences.
Related titles: CD-ROM ed.; Microform ed.: (from PQC); Online - full text ed.: ISSN 1940-1302. GBP 97 in United Kingdom to institutions; EUR 127, USD 159 to institutions (effective 2012).
Indexed: A01, A02, A03, A08, A22, A26, B04, BRD, C05, CA, CPerI, DIP, E01, E02, E03, E07, E08, ERI, ERIC, EdA, EdI, G01, G05, G06, G07, G08, I05, I06, I07, I09, IBR, IBZ, M01, M02, MagInd, P04, P07, P10, P11, P18, P26, P30, P48, P52, P53, P54, P55, P56, PQC, S01, S04, S06, S09, S10, S23, T02, W03, W05.
—Ingenta. **CCC.**
Published by: (Helen Dwight Reid Educational Foundation), Routledge (Subsidiary of: Taylor & Francis Group), 325 Chestnut St, Ste 800, Philadelphia, PA 19106. TEL 215-625-8900, FAX 215-625-2940, journals@routledge.com, http://www.routledge.com.

372.35 USA ISSN 0036-8148
LB1585
➤ **SCIENCE AND CHILDREN.** Abbreviated title: S & C. Text in English. 1952. 9/yr. free to members (effective 2010). adv. bk.rev.; film rev. charts; illus. Index. back issues avail.; reprints avail. **Document type:** *Journal, Academic/Scholarly.* **Description:** Presents ideas and activities for science educators from preschool through middle school.
Formerly (until 1963): Elementary School Science Bulletin (0424-8767)
Related titles: Online - full text ed.: ISSN 1943-4812.
Indexed: A22, A26, B04, B14, BRD, C28, CA, CPE, ChLitAb, E02, E03, E06, E07, E08, E09, ECER, ERI, ERIC, EdA, EdI, G08, GeoRef, I05, MRD, P10, P11, P18, P48, P52, P53, P54, P55, P56, PQC, RASB, S04, S06, S09, SpeleolAb, T02, W03, W05, WSA.
—BLDSC (8131.800000), IE, Infotrieve, Ingenta. **CCC.**
Published by: National Science Teachers Association, 1840 Wilson Blvd, Arlington, VA 22201. TEL 703-243-7100, 800-722-6782, FAX 703-243-7177, pubinfo@nsta.org. Adv. contact Olenka Dobczanska TEL 703-312-9262. Circ: 21,000.

500 IND ISSN 0036-8156
QH1 CODEN: SCINAL
➤ **SCIENCE AND CULTURE.** Text in English. 1935. bi-m. bk.rev. charts; illus.; bibl. chemical abstracts, biological abstracts. 60 p./no. 2 cols./p.; back issues avail.; reprints avail. **Document type:** *Journal, Academic/Scholarly.* **Description:** Focus on research and development in science, society and culture, national issues and events.
Related titles: Online - full text ed.: free (effective 2011).
Indexed: A22, AbAn, B21, ChemAb, FS&TA, GeoRef, Inspec, P30, RASB, SpeleolAb, VirolAbstr, Z01.
—BLDSC (8132.000000), CASDDS, IE, Infotrieve, Ingenta, INIST.
Published by: Indian Science News Association, 92 Acharya Prafulla Chandra Rd, Kolkata, West Bengal 700 009, India. TEL 91-33-23502224, scie2224@dataone.in. **Subscr. to:** I N S I O Scientific Books & Periodicals, PO Box 7234, Indraprastha HPO, New Delhi 110 002, India.

371 NLD ISSN 0926-7220
Q181.A1 CODEN: SCEDE9
➤ **SCIENCE & EDUCATION**; contributions from history, philosophy & sociology of science and mathematics. Text in English. 1992. 10/yr. EUR 1,182, USD 1,234 combined subscription to institutions (print & online eds.) (effective 2012). adv. bk.rev. back issues avail.; reprint service avail. from PSC. **Document type:** *Journal, Academic/Scholarly.* **Description:** Promotes research seeking to improve teaching, learning and curricula in science and mathematics.
Related titles: Microform ed.: (from PQC); Online - full text ed.: ISSN 1573-1901 (from IngentaConnect).
Indexed: A20, A22, A26, AEI, ArtHuCI, B29, BibLing, CA, CPE, CurCont, DIP, E01, E03, E07, ERA, ERI, ERIC, FamI, IBR, IBZ, RASB, S02, S03, S21, SCI, SCOPUS, SOPODA, SSCI, SociolAb, T02, W07.
—BLDSC (8132.140000), IE, Infotrieve, Ingenta. **CCC.**
Published by: (International History, Philosophy and Science Teaching Group), Springer Netherlands (Subsidiary of: Springer Science+Business Media), Van Godewijckstraat 30, Dordrecht, 3311 GX, Netherlands. TEL 31-78-6576050, FAX 31-78-6576474, http://www.springer.com. Ed. Michael R Matthews.

502.1 USA ISSN 1934-1334
SCIENCE AND ENGINEERING DEGREES; a source book. Text in English. 1980. a. back issues avail. **Document type:** *Journal, Academic/Scholarly.* **Description:** Provides information on the number and types of bachelor's, master's and doctoral degrees awarded by U.S. institutions.
Related titles: Online - full text ed.: ISSN 1938-033X.
Published by: National Science Foundation, 4201 Wilson Blvd, Arlington, VA 22230. TEL 703-292-5111, 800-877-8339, FAX 703-292-9092, info@nsf.gov.

500 174 NLD ISSN 1353-3452
Q175.35 CODEN: SEETF4
➤ **SCIENCE AND ENGINEERING ETHICS.** Text in English. 1995. q. EUR 340, USD 413 combined subscription to institutions (print & online eds.) (effective 2012). adv. bk.rev.; video rev. abstr.; bibl.; charts; illus.; stat. 144 p./no. 1 cols./p.; back issues avail.; reprint service avail. from PSC. **Document type:** *Journal, Academic/Scholarly.* **Description:** Explores ethical issues of direct concern to scientists and engineers covering professional education, research, practice and the effect of innovations on society.
Related titles: Online - full text ed.: ISSN 1471-5546. 2001 (from IngentaConnect).
Indexed: A01, A03, A08, A20, A22, A26, AmHI, BrHumI, CA, CurCont, DIP, E01, E08, EMBASE, ESPM, ExcerpMed, FS&TA, H07, IBR, IBZ, IPB, ISR, IndMed, MEDLINE, P11, P20, P26, P30, P34, P48, P52, P54, P56, PQC, PhilInd, R10, Reac, RiskAb, S01, S09, SCI, SCOPUS, SOPODA, SSCI, SociolAb, T02, W07.
—BLDSC (8133.023800), IE, Infotrieve, Ingenta, Linda Hall. **CCC.**
Published by: Springer Netherlands (Subsidiary of: Springer Science+Business Media), Van Godewijckstraat 30, Dordrecht, 3311 GX, Netherlands. TEL 31-78-6576050, FAX 31-78-6576474, http://www.springer.com. Eds. R Spier, S J Bird.

500 USA ISSN 0892-9882
UA12.5 CODEN: SGSEE8
➤ **SCIENCE & GLOBAL SECURITY**; the technical basis for arms control and environmental policy initiatives. Text in English. 1989. 3/yr. GBP 596 combined subscription in United Kingdom to institutions (print & online eds.); EUR 710, USD 893 combined subscription to institutions (print & online eds.) (effective 2012). adv. bk.rev. reprint service avail. from PSC. **Document type:** *Journal, Academic/Scholarly.* **Description:** Covers scientific and technical studies relating to arms control, disarmament, and nonproliferation policy.
Related titles: Microform ed.; Online - full text ed.: ISSN 1547-7800. GBP 537 in United Kingdom to institutions; EUR 640, USD 804 to institutions (effective 2012) (from IngentaConnect).
Indexed: A22, A28, APA, BrCerAb, C&ISA, CA, CA/WCA, CIA, CPEI, CerAb, CivEngAb, CorrAb, E&CAJ, E01, E11, EEA, EMA, ESPM, EnvEAb, H15, I02, Inspec, LID&ISL, M&TEA, M09, MBF, METADEX, P11, P26, P42, P47, P52, P54, P56, PAIS, PCI, PQC, R02, RiskAb, SCOPUS, SolStAb, T02, T04, WAA.
—IE, Infotrieve, Ingenta. **CCC.**
Published by: (Princeton University, Program on Science & Global Security), Taylor & Francis Inc. (Subsidiary of: Taylor & Francis Group), 325 Chestnut St, Ste 800, Philadelphia, PA 19106. TEL 215-625-2940, 800-354-1420, orders@taylorandfrancis.com, http://www.taylorandfrancis.com. Eds. Harold A Feiveson, Stanislav N Rodionov.

500 USA
➤ **SCIENCE AND ITS CONCEPTUAL FOUNDATIONS.** Text in English. 1985. irreg., latest 1997. price varies. **Document type:** *Monographic series, Academic/Scholarly.*
Indexed: CCMJ.
Published by: University of Chicago, 5801 S Ellis Ave, Chicago, IL 60637. TEL 773-702-7899. Ed. David L Hull.

501 NLD ISSN 0924-4697
➤ **SCIENCE AND PHILOSOPHY.** Text in English. 1984. irreg., latest vol.10, 2000. price varies. **Document type:** *Monographic series, Academic/Scholarly.* **Description:** Forum for contemporary analysis of philosophical problems arising in connection with the construction of theories in the physical and biological sciences, reflecting the belief that the philosophy of science must be firmly rooted in an examination of actual scientific practice.
Indexed: CCMJ.
—**CCC.**
Published by: Springer Netherlands (Subsidiary of: Springer Science+Business Media), Van Godewijckstraat 30, Dordrecht, 3311 GX, Netherlands. TEL 31-78-6576050, FAX 31-78-6576474. Ed. Nancy J Nersessian.

500 600 IND ISSN 0973-0206
SCIENCE & SOCIETY. Text in English. 2003. s-a. INR 200 domestic to individuals; USD 50 foreign to individuals; INR 400 domestic to institutions; USD 100 foreign to institutions (effective 2011). back issues avail. **Document type:** *Journal, Academic/Scholarly.* **Description:** Provides a forum to discuss developments in science and its impact on modern society.
Published by: Nirmala College, Muvattupuzha PO, Ernakulam District, Kerala, 686 661, India. TEL 91-485-2832361, FAX 91-485-2836300, nirmalacollege@vsnl.com.

SCIENCE & TECHNOLOGY BULLETIN. *see* EDUCATION—Teaching Methods And Curriculum

500 CAN ISSN 1484-5830
CA1C1-4
SCIENCE AND TECHNOLOGY DATA. Text in English, French. 1995. a.
Related titles: Online - full text ed.: ISSN 1719-6485. 2001; Ed.: Donnees en Sciences et Technologie. ISSN 1719-6493. 2001.
Published by: Industry Canada, Innovation Secretariat (Subsidiary of: Industry Canada/Industrie Canada), 235 Queen St, Ottawa, ON K1A 0H5, Canada. TEL 613-946-5414, FAX 613-946-0167, secretariat.innovation@ic.gc.ca.

500 600 USA
SCIENCE AND TECHNOLOGY DESK REFERENCE. Text in English. 1992. irreg., latest 1996, 2nd ed. USD 95 per vol. (effective 2004). charts; illus.; maps. **Document type:** *Monographic series, Academic/Scholarly.* **Description:** Subject-arranged compendium of 1700 inquiries in science and technology. Includes citations for locating further information.
Published by: (Carnegie Library of Pittsburgh), Gale (Subsidiary of: Cengage Learning), 27500 Drake Rd, Farmington Hills, MI 48331. TEL 248-699-4253, 800-877-4253, FAX 877-363-4253, gale.galeord@thomson.com, http://gale.cengage.com.

SCIENCE AND TECHNOLOGY FACILITIES COUNCIL. ANNUAL REPORT. *see* TECHNOLOGY: COMPREHENSIVE WORKS

SCIENCE AND TECHNOLOGY FOR CULTURAL HERITAGE. *see* SOCIAL SCIENCES: COMPREHENSIVE WORKS

SCIENCE AND TECHNOLOGY IN CONGRESS (ONLINE). *see* PUBLIC ADMINISTRATION

500 PHL
SCIENCE AND TECHNOLOGY INFORMATION INSTITUTE. DEPARTMENT OF SCIENCE AND TECHNOLOGY. ANNUAL REPORT. Short title: D O S T Annual Report. Text in English. a. charts; illus.
Former titles: Philippines. National Science and Technology Authority. Annual Report; Philippines. National Science Development Board. Annual Report
Published by: (Department of Science and Technology), Science and Technology Information Institute, P.O. Box 3596, Manila, Philippines.

600 USA ISSN 1092-3055
Q180.U5 CODEN: STREFR
SCIENCE & TECHNOLOGY REVIEW. Text in English. 1975. 10/yr. free. illus. online index. back issues avail.; reprints avail. **Document type:** *Government.* **Description:** Communicates the laboratory's scientific and technical accomplishments.
Formerly (until July 1995): Energy and Technology Review (0884-5050)
Related titles: Online - full text ed.
Indexed: B04, BRD, BiolDig, M&GPA, R03, RGAb, RGPR, W03, W05.
—Ingenta, Linda Hall.
Published by: University of California, Lawrence Livermore National Security LLC, 7000 East Ave, PO Box 808, Livermore, CA 94551-0808. TEL 925-422-8961, FAX 925-422-8803. Ed. Sam Hunter. Circ: 27,000.

500 GBR ISSN 0950-5431
Q175.4
➤ **SCIENCE AS CULTURE.** Text in English. 1974. q. GBP 314 combined subscription in United Kingdom to institutions (print & online eds.); EUR 414, USD 519 combined subscription to institutions (print & online eds.) (effective 2012). adv. bk.rev. abstr.; bibl. index. back issues avail.; reprint service avail. from PSC. **Document type:** *Journal, Academic/Scholarly.* **Description:** Explores all the ways in which science, technology and medicine are involved in shaping society's values and priorities.
Former titles (until 1987): Radical Science Series (0952-410X); (until 1985): Radical Science; (until 1984): Radical Science Journal (0305-0963)
Related titles: Microform ed.: (from PQC); Online - full text ed.: ISSN 1470-1189. GBP 282 in United Kingdom to institutions; EUR 373, USD 468 to institutions (effective 2012) (from IngentaConnect).
Indexed: A01, A03, A08, A20, A22, AltPI, ArtHuCI, CA, CurCont, DIP, E01, FR, IBR, IBSS, IBZ, LeftInd, MLA-IB, P30, RASB, S02, S03, SCOPUS, SOPODA, SSCI, SociolAb, T02, W07.
—IE, Infotrieve, Ingenta. **CCC.**
Published by: Routledge (Subsidiary of: Taylor & Francis Group), 4 Park Sq, Milton Park, Abingdon, Oxon OX14 4RN, United Kingdom. TEL 44-20-70176000, FAX 44-20-70176336, subscriptions@tandf.co.uk, http://www.routledge.com. Ed. Les Levidow. Adv. contact Linda Hann TEL 44-1344-779945. **Subscr. to:** Taylor & Francis Ltd., Journals Customer Service, Sheepen Pl, Colchester, Essex CO3 3LP, United Kingdom. TEL 44-20-70175544, FAX 44-20-70175198, tf.enquiries@tfinforma.com.

500 USA ISSN 1941-2819
SCIENCE@A S U. Text in English. 2006. a. free (effective 2011). back issues avail. **Document type:** *Magazine, Trade.*
Related titles: Online - full text ed.: ISSN 1941-286X.
Published by: Alabama State Universtiy, Department of Mathematics and Science, PO Box 271, Montgomery, AL 36101. TEL 334-229-4100, admissions@alasu.edu. Ed. Shree Singh.

372.35 USA
SCIENCE AT HOME; connecting science to your home and community. Text in English. q. USD 17.75 domestic; USD 23.75 in Canada; USD 27.75 elsewhere (effective 2004). **Document type:** *Magazine, Consumer.* **Description:** Aims to introduce various aspects of science and mathematics to elementary school age children in a manner that will help increase their sense of wonder.
Published by: Family Creativity Corp., 100 Beekman St, New York, NY 10038. TEL 212-571-6237.

500 FRA ISSN 1296-7564
LA SCIENCE AU PRESENT. Text in French. 1996. a. EUR 110 newsstand/cover (effective 2009). **Document type:** *Consumer.*
Published by: Encyclopaedia Universalis, 18 Rue de Tilsitt, Paris, 75017, France.

500 TWN ISSN 0250-4189
SCIENCE BULLETIN. Text in English. 1969. m. TWD 25, USD 1 (effective 2001). **Document type:** *Bulletin, Academic/Scholarly.*
Related titles: Microfiche ed.; Online - full content ed.: ISSN 1607-3509.
Indexed: GeoRef, SpeleolAb.
—INIST.
Published by: National Science Council/Xingzhengyuan Guojia Kexue Weiyuanhui, Rm 1701, 106 Ho-Ping E. Rd, Sec 2, Taipei, Taiwan. TEL 886-2-27377594, FAX 886-2-27377248, ylchang@nsc.gov.tw, http://www.nsc.gov.tw.

331.1 USA
SCIENCE CAREER MAGAZINE. Text in English. 19??. w. free to members (effective 2009). adv. back issues avail.; reprints avail. **Document type:** *Magazine, Trade.* **Description:** Features articles on original scientific research.
Formerly (until 1996): Science's Next Wave
Related titles: Online - full text ed.
Published by: American Association for the Advancement of Science, 1200 New York Ave, NW, Washington, DC 20005. TEL 202-326-6550, FAX 202-289-4950, scienceonline@aaas.org, http://www.aaas.org. Ed. Jim Austin TEL 207-712-5445. Adv. contact Bill Moran TEL 202-326-6438.

SCIENCE COMMUNICATION. *see* SOCIOLOGY

500 300 PHL ISSN 0115-7809
Q1 CODEN: SCDIEJ
➤ **SCIENCE DILIMAN.** Text in English, Tagalog. 1980. s-a. abstr.; bibl.; charts; maps. back issues avail. **Document type:** *Journal, Academic/Scholarly.* **Description:** Covers pure and applied sciences.
Related titles: Online - full text ed.: free (effective 2011).
Indexed: AnBeAb, B21, BAS, CTA, ChemoAb, E17, ESPM, EntAb, GenetAb, IPP, NSA.
—CASDDS.
Published by: University of the Philippines, Office of the Vice Chancellor for Research and Development, Diliman, CP Garcia Ave, Quezon City, 1101, Philippines. TEL 632-927-2567, 632-927-2309, FAX 632-927-2568, rduo.ovcrd@up.edu.ph, http://www.ovcrd.upd.edu.ph/. Ed. Maricor N Soriano.

507.1 USA ISSN 0036-8326
Q1 CODEN: SEDUAV
➤ **SCIENCE EDUCATION.** Text in English. 1916. bi-m. GBP 892 in United Kingdom to institutions; EUR 1,128 in Europe to institutions; USD 1,622 in United States to institutions; USD 1,706 in Canada & Mexico to institutions; USD 1,748 elsewhere to institutions; GBP 1,027 combined subscription in United Kingdom to institutions (print & online eds.); EUR 1,298 combined subscription in Europe to institutions (print & online eds.); USD 1,866 combined subscription in United States to institutions (print & online eds.); USD 1,950 combined subscription in Canada & Mexico to institutions (print & online eds.); USD 1,992 combined subscription elsewhere to institutions (print & online eds.) (effective 2012). adv. bk.rev. charts; illus.; stat. index. back issues avail.; reprint service avail. from PSC. **Document type:** *Journal, Academic/Scholarly.* **Description:** Features original articles on the latest issues and trends occurring internationally in science curriculum, instruction, learning, policy and preparation of science teachers with the aim to advance the knowledge of science education theory and practice.

Incorporates (1973-1976): A Summary of Research in Science Education (0360-2907); Formerly (until 1929): General Science Quarterly (0097-0352)
Related titles: Microform ed.: (from PQC); Online - full text ed.: ISSN 1098-237X. 1996. GBP 828 in United Kingdom to institutions; EUR 1,047 in Europe to institutions; USD 1,622 elsewhere to institutions (effective 2012).
Indexed: A01, A02, A03, A08, A20, A22, A26, ASCA, B04, BAS, BRD, CA, CPE, ChPerI, CurCont, E-psyche, E02, E03, E06, E07, E08, E09, ERI, ERIC, EdA, EdI, FR, FamI, G08, I05, IBR, IBZ, L09, M01, M02, P02, P03, P04, P07, P10, P18, P30, P48, P53, P54, P55, PQC, PsycInfo, PsycholAb, S02, S03, S09, SCOPUS, SSCI, T02, W03, W07.
—BLDSC (8142.800000), IE, Ingenta, INIST, Linda Hall. **CCC.**
Published by: John Wiley & Sons, Inc., 111 River St, Hoboken, NJ 07030. TEL 201-748-6000, FAX 201-748-6088, info@wiley.com, http://www.wiley.com/WileyCDA/. Ed. Gregory J Kelly. Pub., Adv. contact Kim Thompkins TEL 212-850-6921. B&W page USD 1,241, color page USD 1,576; trim 6.875 x 10. **Subscr. outside the Americas to:** John Wiley & Sons Ltd., The Atrium, Southern Gate, Chichester, West Sussex PO19 8SQ, United Kingdom. TEL 44-1243-779777, FAX 44-1243-775878, cs-journals@wiley.com.

507.1 TUR ISSN 2077-2327
SCIENCE EDUCATION INTERNATIONAL. Abbreviated title: S E I. Text in English. 1990. q. free (effective 2011). **Document type:** *Journal, Academic/Scholarly.*
Formerly (until 2008): Science Education International (Print) (1450-104X)
Media: Online - full text.
Indexed: CA, E03, ERA, T02.
Published by: International Council of Associations for Science Education, c/o Dokuz Eyul Universitesi, Buca Egytim Fakultesi, Buca, Izmir, 35150, Turkey. Ed. Nicos Valanides.

500 371.3 GBR ISSN 0266-7665
SCIENCE EDUCATION NEWSLETTER. Text in English. 1966. bi-m. **Document type:** *Newsletter, Trade.*
Related titles: Online - full text ed.
Published by: British Council, 10 Spring Gardens, London, SW1A 2BN, United Kingdom. general.enquiries@britishcouncil.org. **Co-sponsor:** Shell International.

SCIENCE EDUCATOR. see EDUCATION—Teaching Methods And Curriculum

SCIENCE ET BIOMEDECINE. see MEDICAL SCIENCES

500 BEL ISSN 0773-3429
SCIENCE ET CULTURE. Text in French. 19??. bi-m. adv. **Document type:** *Bulletin.*
Formerly (until 1954): T.V. (0041-4476)
Indexed: ChemAb.
Published by: Institut de Physique, Sart Tilman, B-5, Liege, 4000, Belgium. TEL 32-41-663858, FAX 32-41-662355. Ed. Roger Moreau. Pub. F X Neve de Mevergnies.

500 CAN ISSN 1188-4290
SCIENCE ET TECHNOLOGIE AU QUEBEC. Text in English. biennial. CAD 44.95 (effective 2001). **Document type:** *Directory.* **Description:** Contains listings of research centers, scientific associations, and specialized publications in Quebec.
Published by: Quebec dans le Monde, C P 8503, Sainte Foy, PQ G1V 4N5, Canada. TEL 418-659-5540, FAX 418-659-4143.

500 FRA ISSN 0036-8369
T2
SCIENCE & VIE. Text in French. 1913. m. EUR 29.95 (effective 2008). bk.rev. illus. back issues avail. **Document type:** *Magazine, Consumer.*
Related titles: ◆ Supplement(s): Science et Vie Economie. ISSN 0765-0027; ◆ S V M. ISSN 1634-426X.
Indexed: A22, GeoRef, PdeR, RASB.
—IE, Infotrieve. **CCC.**
Published by: Mondadori France, 1 Rue du Colonel Pierre-Avia, Paris, Cedex 15 75754, France. TEL 33-1-46484848, contact@mondadori.fr, http://www.mondadori.fr. Circ: 344,049 (paid).

SCIENCE & VIE DECOUVERTES. see CHILDREN AND YOUTH—For

500 028.5 FRA ISSN 0992-5899
SCIENCE & VIE JUNIOR. Text in French. 1989. m. EUR 45.80 (effective 2008). adv. **Document type:** *Magazine, Consumer.* **Description:** Explores scientific and technical progress. For teen-agers.
Indexed: PdeR.
Published by: Mondadori France, 1 Rue du Colonel Pierre-Avia, Paris, Cedex 15 75754, France. TEL 33-1-46484848, contact@mondadori.fr, http://www.mondadori.fr. Circ: 174,218 (paid).

500 ZAF ISSN 1999-575X
SCIENCE FOR SOCIETY. Text in English. 2008. q. **Document type:** *Newsletter.*
Published by: Academy of Science of South Africa, PO Box 72135, Lynnwood Ridge, 0040, South Africa. TEL 27-12-8436482, admin@assaf.org.za.

505 CHN ISSN 1005-0841
Q127.C5
SCIENCE FOUNDATION IN CHINA. Text in English. 1993. s-a. **Document type:** *Journal, Academic/Scholarly.*
Related titles: Online - full text ed.
Published by: (National Natural Science Foundation of China), Kexue Jijin Zazhibu (Subsidiary of: Guojia Ziran Kexue Jijin Weiyuanhui/ National Natural Science Foundation of China), 83, Shuangqing Rd., Haidian District, Beijing, 100085, China. TEL 86-10-62327204, FAX 86-10-62326921.

500 USA ISSN 1094-8325
SCIENCE FRONTIERS. Text in English. 1976. bi-m. USD 7 domestic; GBP 5 (effective 2000). adv. bk.rev. back issues avail. **Document type:** *Newsletter.* **Description:** Digests articles dealing with scientific anomalies and appearing in the current literature.
Related titles: Online - full text ed.
Published by: Sourcebook Project, PO Box 107, Glen Arm, MD 21057. TEL 410-668-6047, ian@knoledge.com.uk. Ed., Pub., Adv. contact William R Corliss. Circ: 1,200.

500 610 USA ISSN 0897-8581
Q162
SCIENCE ILLUSTRATED. Text in English. 1987. bi-m. USD 24 domestic; USD 29.97 in Canada; USD 39.97 elsewhere (effective 2011). adv. bk.rev. illus. back issues avail. **Document type:** *Magazine, Consumer.* **Description:** Gateway to cutting-edge science, covering a tremendous range of subjects, from paleontology to space exploration, from medical breakthroughs to the latest environmental insights.
Indexed: G08, I05.
Published by: Bonnier Corp. (Subsidiary of: Bonnier Group), 2 Park Ave, 9th Fl, New York, NY 10016. TEL 212-779-5047, FAX 212-779-5108, http://www.bonniercorp.com. Ed. Mark Jannot. **Subscr. to:** PO Box 420235, Palm Coast, FL 32142. TEL 386-246-3402, 866-436-2461.

500 DEU
▼ **SCIENCE ILLUSTRATED.** Text in German. 2009. bi-m. EUR 4.50 newsstand/cover (effective 2010). adv. **Document type:** *Magazine, Consumer.*
Published by: Family Media GmbH & Co. KG, Schnewlinstr 6, Freiburg, 79098, Germany. TEL 49-761-705780, FAX 49-761-70578651, redaktion@familie.de, http://www.kinderzeit.com. Adv. contact Sabine Mecklenburg. Circ: 100,000 (controlled).

500 AUS ISSN 1836-5175
▼ **SCIENCE ILLUSTRATED.** Text in English. 2009. bi-m. AUD 9.95 newsstand/cover (effective 2010). adv. back issues avail. **Document type:** *Magazine, Trade.* **Description:** Designed for curious men and women with a passion for science and discovery and a desire to share that passion with their families.
Published by: Australian Media Properties, Ste 102, 19A Boundary St, Rushcutters Bay, NSW 2011, Australia. TEL 61-2-93321493, FAX 61-2-93321521, enquiries@wwmedia.net.au. Ed. Rhiannon Elston. Pub. Marijcke Thomson. Adv. contact Kate Pacey. page AUD 4,750.

500 ZAF
SCIENCE IN AFRICA; Africa's first online science magazine. Text in English. irreg. back issues avail. **Description:** Promotes local and international awareness of science conducted in Africa to give young scientists the opportunity to showcase their research to Africa and beyond.
Media: Online - full text.
Address: Box 696, Grahamstown, 6140, South Africa. Ed. Janice Limson.

500 GBR ISSN 0269-8897
Q175.4 CODEN: SCCOEW
➤ **SCIENCE IN CONTEXT.** Text in English. 1987. q. GBP 189, USD 339 to institutions; GBP 197, USD 354 combined subscription to institutions (print & online eds.) (effective 2012). adv. bk.rev. back issues avail.; reprint service avail. from PSC. **Document type:** *Journal, Academic/Scholarly.* **Description:** Studies the history, philosophy, sociology and epistemology of science.
Related titles: Online - full text ed.: ISSN 1474-0664. GBP 180, USD 316 to institutions (effective 2012).
Indexed: A20, A22, ASCA, AmH&L, ArtHuCI, BAS, CA, CCMJ, CIS, CurCont, DIP, E01, EMBASE, ExcerpMed, HistAb, IBR, IBZ, IPB, MEDLINE, MSN, MathR, P02, P10, P11, P26, P30, P48, P52, P53, P54, P56, PCI, PQC, PhilInd, R10, RASB, Reac, S02, S03, S10, SCI, SCOPUS, SSCI, SociolAb, T02, W07, Z02.
—BLDSC (8141.820000), IE, Infotrieve, Ingenta, Linda Hall. **CCC.**
Published by: Cambridge University Press, The Edinburgh Bldg, Shaftesbury Rd, Cambridge, CB2 8RU, United Kingdom. TEL 44-1223-312393, FAX 44-1223-315052, journals@cambridge.org, http://www.cambridge.org/uk. Eds. Alexandre Metraux, Asaf Goldschmidt, Jurgen Renn. R&P Linda Nicol TEL 44-1223-325702. adv.: page GBP 445, page USD 845. Circ: 450. **Subscr. to:** Cambridge University Press, 32 Ave of the Americas, New York, NY 10013. TEL 212-337-5000, FAX 212-691-3239, journals_subscriptions@cup.org.

500 PNG ISSN 0310-4303
➤ **SCIENCE IN NEW GUINEA.** Text in English. 1949. a. PGK 20 domestic to individuals; PGK 35 domestic to institutions; USD 35 in Asia & the Pacific; USD 40 elsewhere (effective 2002). adv. bk.rev. back issues avail. **Document type:** *Journal, Academic/Scholarly.* **Description:** Presents original research in basic and applied science with special reference to the Pacific Islands.
Supersedes (in 1972): Papua New Guinea Scientific Society. Annual Report and Proceedings (0085-4697)
Indexed: A34, A38, AESIS, CABA, ChemAb, E12, F08, F11, F12, FS&TA, GEOBASE, GH, GeoRef, H16, I11, MinerAb, N02, N03, O01, P32, P40, R12, S12, S13, S16, SCOPUS, SpeleolAb, T05, W11, Z01.
—Ingenta, Linda Hall.
Published by: University of Papua New Guinea, Faculty of Science, University of Papua New Guinea, PO Box 320, Port Moresby, Papua New Guinea. TEL 675-3267396, FAX 675-3267187, TELEX NE 22366. Ed. Ray Kumar. Circ: 250 (paid).

500 GBR ISSN 0263-6271
Q127.G7
SCIENCE IN PARLIAMENT. Text in English. 1982. q. GBP 16.70 per issue (effective 2009). bk.rev. back issues avail. **Document type:** *Journal, Academic/Scholarly.* **Description:** Covers scientific, technological and industrial matters before the UK Parliament and the European Union.
Indexed: CA, Cadscan, L04, L13, LISTA, LeadAb, P34, RASB, T02, Zincscan.
—BLDSC (8150.600000), IE, Infotrieve, Ingenta. **CCC.**
Published by: (Parliamentary and Scientific Committee), Westminster Publishing Ltd., PO Box 50253, London, EC2P 2WZ, United Kingdom. TEL 44-207-5881098, FAX 44-207-5881098, info@westminsterpublishing.org, http:// www.westminsterpublishing.org. Ed. Peter Simpson.

500 RUS ISSN 0869-7078
SCIENCE IN RUSSIA. Text in Russian. bi-m. **Document type:** *Journal, Academic/Scholarly.*
Related titles: Online - full text ed.
Indexed: A22, A33, GeoRef, SpeleolAb.
—East View, Infotrieve, Linda Hall. **CCC.**
Published by: M A I K Nauka - Interperiodica (Subsidiary of: Pleiades Publishing, Inc.), Profsoyuznaya ul 90, Moscow, 117997, Russian Federation. TEL 7-095-3347420, FAX 7-095-3360666, compmg@maik.ru, http://www.maik.ru. **Dist. by:** East View Information Services, 10601 Wayzata Blvd, Minneapolis, MN 55305. TEL 952-252-1201, 800-477-1005, FAX 952-252-1202, info@eastview.com, http://www.eastview.com.

SCIENCE IN SCHOOL. see EDUCATION—Teaching Methods And Curriculum

500 GBR ISSN 1754-9655
SCIENCE IN SOCIETY SERIES. Text in English. 200?. irreg. **Document type:** *Monographic series, Academic/Scholarly.*
Published by: Earthscan Ltd., Dunstan House, 14a St Cross St, London, EC1N 8XA, United Kingdom. TEL 44-20-78411930, FAX 44-20-72421474, earthinfo@earthscan.co.uk, http://www.earthscan.co.uk/.

500 UKR
SCIENCE INSIGHT. Text in Ukrainian. irreg. **Document type:** *Monographic series, Academic/Scholarly.* **Description:** Comprises a selection of news items drawn from a wide range of periodicals, newspapers, journals and press releases.
Media: Online - full text.
Published by: British Council, Science Policy Research Unit, Besarabska pl 9-1, Kiev, 252004, Ukraine. TEL 380-44-247-7235, FAX 380-44-247-7280, http://www.britcoun.org/science/insight/. Ed. June Rollinson.

500 PAK ISSN 1013-5316
➤ **SCIENCE INTERNATIONAL.** Text in English. 1988. q. USD 100 foreign (effective 2007). adv. back issues avail. **Document type:** *Journal, Academic/Scholarly.*
Indexed: A34, A35, A36, A37, A38, AgBio, AgrForAb, B23, BA, BP, C25, C30, CABA, D01, E12, F08, F11, F12, FCA, FS&TA, G11, GH, H16, H17, I11, INIS AtomInd, IndVet, LT, MaizeAb, N02, N03, N04, O01, OR, P32, P33, P37, P39, P40, PGegResA, PHN&I, R07, R08, R11, R12, R13, RA&MP, RRTA, S12, S13, S16, S17, SoyAb, T05, TAR, TriticAb, VS, W10, W11, Z01.
—BLDSC (8147.240000), IE, Ingenta.
Published by: Publications International, 11 D, Sabzazar Wahdat Rd, Lahore, 54590, Pakistan. TEL 92-42-5865863, sciint@gmail.com, sciint@sci-int.com. Pub., R&P M Azam Sheikh. adv.: B&W page USD 100, color page USD 150; trim 10 x 7. Circ: 400 (paid).

500 USA ISSN 1538-9111
SCIENCE LETTER. Text in English. 2003. w. USD 2,595 in US & Canada; USD 2,795 elsewhere; USD 2,825 combined subscription in US & Canada print & online eds.; USD 3,055 combined subscription elsewhere print & online eds. (effective 2007). **Document type:** *Newsletter, Academic/Scholarly.* **Description:** Contains the latest news and discoveries from the world of science.
Related titles: CD-ROM ed.: USD 2,295 (effective 2008); Online - full text ed.: ISSN 1538-9162. USD 2,595 (effective 2007).
Indexed: A26, E08, G08, H11, H12, H13, I05, I07, I09, P10, P19, P20, P48, P52, P53, P54, PQC, S09, S23.
Published by: NewsRx, 2727 Paces Ferry Rd SE, Ste 2-440, Atlanta, GA 30339. TEL 770-435-8286, 800-726-4550, FAX 770-435-6800, pressrelease@newsrx.com, http://www.newsrx.com. Pub. Susan Hasty TEL 770-507-7777.

500 USA ISSN 1529-7276
SCIENCE LETTERS. Text in English, French. 1999. irreg. free (effective 2004).
Media: Online - full text.
Published by: Moroccan Association of Researchers and Scholars science@mars-net.org. Ed. Abdelali Haoudi.

500 FRA ISSN 1777-0173
SCIENCE MAGAZINE. Text in French. 2005. q. EUR 38 for 2 yrs. (effective 2010). **Document type:** *Magazine, Consumer.*
Published by: Lafont Presse, 53 Rue du Chemin Vert, Boulogne-Billancourt, 92100, France. TEL 33-1-46102121, FAX 33-1-45792211.

500 USA
SCIENCE MUSEUM OF MINNESOTA. MONOGRAPH. Text in English. 1972. irreg., latest vol.4, 1998. **Document type:** *Monographic series.*
Indexed: SpeleolAb, Z01.
Published by: Science Museum of Minnesota, 120 W Kellogg Blvd, St. Paul, MN 55102. TEL 651-221-9444, 800-221-9444, science@smm.org.

500 USA ISSN 0161-4452
Q11 CODEN: SCSPBA
SCIENCE MUSEUM OF MINNESOTA. SCIENTIFIC PUBLICATIONS, NEW SERIES. Key Title: Scientific Publications of the Science Museum of Minnesota. Text in English. 1966. irreg.
Supersedes: Science Museum of Minnesota. Scientific Bulletin; Formerly: Science Museum of Minnesota. Scientific Publications (0080-5521)
Indexed: GeoRef, SpeleolAb, Z01.
—Linda Hall.
Published by: Science Museum of Minnesota, 120 W Kellogg Blvd, St. Paul, MN 55102. TEL 651-221-9444, 800-221-9444, science@smm.org.

500 CHE
➤ **SCIENCE NETWORKS HISTORICAL STUDIES.** Text in English. 1989. irreg., latest vol.24, 2000. price varies. back issues avail. **Document type:** *Monographic series, Academic/Scholarly.* **Description:** Covers various topics in the history of science.
Indexed: CCMJ.
Published by: Birkhaeuser Verlag AG (Subsidiary of: Springer Science+Business Media), Viaduktstr 42, Postfach 133, Basel, 4051, Switzerland. TEL 41-61-2050730, FAX 41-61-2050792. **Orders in N. America to:** Springer New York LLC, Journal Fulfillment, PO Box 2485, Secaucus, NJ 07096. TEL 201-348-4033, FAX 201-348-4505, orders@springer-ny.com. **Dist. by:** Springer Distribution Center, Kundenservice Zeitschriften, Haberstr 7, Heidelberg 69126, Germany. TEL 49-6221-3454324, FAX 49-6221-345229.

500 USA ISSN 0036-8423
Q1 CODEN: SCNEBK
SCIENCE NEWS; magazine of the society for science and the public. Text in English. 1922. bi-w. GBP 127 combined subscription in United Kingdom to institutions (print & online eds.); EUR 149 combined subscription in Europe to institutions (print & online eds.); USD 207 combined subscription elsewhere to institutions (print & online eds.) (effective 2012). adv. bk.rev. illus. Index. 16 p./no. 3 cols./p.; back issues avail.; reprints avail. **Document type:** *Magazine, Consumer.* **Description:** Publishes reports on new research findings, developments and issues in all disciplines of science, for a non-specialist audience. Includes short reports from major conferences and congresses, reviews of results published in scientific journals and coverage of legislative and political events relevant to scientific policy.

S

Former titles (until 1966): Science News Letter (0096-4018); Science News Bulletin
Related titles: Braille ed.; CD-ROM ed.; Microform ed.: (from PQC); Online - full text ed.: ISSN 1943-0930. GBP 110 in United Kingdom to institutions; EUR 129 in Europe to institutions; USD 180 elsewhere to institutions (effective 2012).
Indexed: A01, A02, A03, A08, A09, A10, A11, A15, A20, A22, A25, A26, A33, ABIPC, ABIn, AIA, ARG, ASCA, Acal, Agr, B04, B07, BPIA, BRD, BiolDig, C03, C04, C05, C11, C12, CADCAM, CBCARef, CBPI, CPerl, ChemAb, E03, E04, E05, E07, E08, E09, ERI, EnerRev, EnvAb, EnvInd, G01, G03, G05, G06, G07, G08, GSA, GSI, GardL, GeoRef, H03, HlthInd, I05, I06, I07, JHMA, M01, M02, M04, M06, MASUSE, MagInd, NRN, P02, P07, P10, P11, P18, P19, P26, P30, P34, P48, P51, P52, P53, P54, P56, PQC, R03, R04, R06, RASB, RGAb, RGPR, S04, S06, S08, S09, S23, SCOPUS, SpeleolAb, T02, TOM, Telegen, U01, V02, V03, V04, W03, W05, W08, WBA, WMB, WildRev.
—BLDSC (8150.010000), CASDDS, IE, Ingenta, INIST, Linda Hall. **CCC.**
Published by: Science Service, 1719 N St, NW, Washington, DC 20036. TEL 202-785-2255, FAX 202-785-3751, subnews@sciserv.org. Ed. Tom Siegfried. Pub. Elizabeth Marincola. R&P Christina Smith TEL 202-785-2255. Adv. contact Rick Bates. B&W page USD 6,408, color page USD 8,973. Circ: 133,000 (paid). **Subscr. to:** John Wiley & Sons, Inc., 111 River St, Hoboken, NJ 07030. TEL 201-748-6645, subinfo@wiley.com, http://www.wiley.com/WileyCDA/.

500 USA
SCIENCE NOTES. Text in English. a. free (effective 2010). **Document type:** *Journal, Academic/Scholarly.* **Description:** Consists of articles and illustrations by students in the Science Communication Program.
Media: Online - full text.
Published by: University of California, Santa Cruz, Science Communication Program, Crown Faculty Services, Santa Cruz, CA 95064. TEL 408-459-4475, scicom@cats.ucsc.edu, http://natsci.ucsc.edu/acad/.

507.1 JAM
SCIENCE NOTES AND NEWS. Text in English. irreg.
Published by: Association of Science Teachers of Jamaica, c/o Honorary Secretary Olive Baxter, 46 Paddington Terrace, Kingston, 6, Jamaica.

500 FRA
SCIENCE POLICY STUDIES. Text in French. 1965. irreg. price varies. **Document type:** *Monographic series, Academic/Scholarly.*
Formerly (until 2003): Science Policy Studies and Documents (0080-7591)
Related titles: French ed.: Etudes et Documents de Politique Scientifique. ISSN 0251-5695.
Published by: UNESCO, 7 Place de Fontenoy, Paris, 75352, France. TEL 33-1-45681000, FAX 33-1-45671690, bpi@unesco.org.

500 351 USA ISSN 1943-4502
Q127.U6
SCIENCE PROGRESS. Text in English. 2008. s-a. back issues avail. **Document type:** *Magazine, Trade.* **Description:** Aims to improve the understanding of science among policymakers and other leaders with the goal of developing exciting, progressive ideas about innovation in science and technology for the United States.
Related titles: Online - full text ed.
Published by: Center for American Progress, 1333 H St NW, 10th Fl, Washington, DC 20005. TEL 202-682-1611, FAX 202-682-1867, progress@americanprogress.org, http://www.americanprogress.org. Eds. Jonathan Moreno, Ed Paisley.

500 GBR ISSN 0036-8504
Q1 CODEN: SCPRAY
➤ **SCIENCE PROGRESS**; a review journal of current scientific advance. Text in English. 1896. q. GBP 290, USD 580, EUR 470 (print & online eds.) (effective 2011). adv. bk.rev. illus. index. back issues avail.; reprints avail. **Document type:** *Journal, Academic/Scholarly.*
Former titles (until 1916): Science Progress in the Twentieth Century (0302-1785); (until 1906): Science Progress
Related titles: Online - full text ed.: GBP 205, USD 410, EUR 265 (effective 2011) (from IngentaConnect).
Indexed: A20, A22, A26, ASCA, BIOSIS Prev, CIN, ChemAb, ChemTitl, E08, E10, EMBASE, ExcerpMed, G08, GeoRef, H09, H10, I05, IndMed, Inspec, MEDLINE, MycolAb, P30, RASB, S05, S06, S09, SCOPUS, SpeleolAb, T02.
—BLDSC (8151.000000), AskIEEE, CASDDS, GNLM, IE, Infotrieve, Ingenta, INIST, Linda Hall. **CCC.**
Published by: Science Reviews 2000 Ltd., PO Box 314, St Albans, Herts AL1 4ZG, United Kingdom. scilet@scilet.com. Ed. T J Kemp. **Dist. addr.:** Turpin Distribution Services Ltd., Pegasus Dr, Stratton Business Park, Biggleswade, Bedfordshire SG18 8QB, United Kingdom. TEL 44-1767-609451, FAX 44-1767-601640, custserv@turpin-distribution.com, http://www.turpin-distribution.com/.

500 IND ISSN 0036-8512
Q1 CODEN: SCRPA4
SCIENCE REPORTER. Text in English. 1964. m. **Document type:** *Magazine, Trade.*
Indexed: ASFA, B21, ESPM, ISA.
—Linda Hall.
Published by: Ministry of Science & Technology, Council of Scientific & Industrial Research, Anusandhan Bhavan, 2, Rafi Marg, New Delhi, 110001, India. TEL 91-11-23713011, FAX 91-11-23710618, headrdpd@csir.res.in. **Subscr. to:** I N S I O Scientific Books & Periodicals.

500 JPN ISSN 1340-8364
QE1 CODEN: HDSKEK
SCIENCE REPORTS. Text in English, Japanese; Summaries in English. 1992. a. per issue exchange basis. **Document type:** *Report, Academic/Scholarly.*
Formed by the merger of (1983-1991): Joho Kodo Kagaku Kenkyu (0385-1478); (1983-1991): Hoken Taiikugaku Kenkyu (0289-3002); (1980-1991): Kiso Kankyo Kagaku Kenkyu (0285-6905); Which was formerly (until 1980): Kankyo Kagaku Kenkyu; Which superseded in part: Hiroshima Daigaku Kyoyobu Kiyo
Indexed: JPI.
—CASDDS.
Published by: Hiroshima Daigaku, Sogo Kagakubu/Hiroshima University, Faculty of Integrated Arts and Sciences, 1-7-1 Kagazmiyama, Higashi Hiroshima, 739-8521, Japan. TEL 81-82-4227111, FAX 81-82-4240751, http://home.hiroshima-u.ac.jp/souka/.

500 GBR ISSN 2042-1397
▼ **SCIENCE REUTERS.** Text in English. 2009. m. adv. back issues avail. **Document type:** *Journal, Trade.* **Description:** Provides a forum to the researchers to publish their research findings in shape of research papers, reviews, mini-reviews, commentary and essays.
Related titles: Online - full text ed.: ISSN 2042-1400.
Address: 26 York St, London, W1U 6PZ, United Kingdom. FAX 44-20-33573194.

500 NZL ISSN 2230-3200
▼ **SCIENCE REVIEW.** Text in English. 2010. a. **Document type:** *Academic/Scholarly.*
Related titles: Online - full text ed.: ISSN 2230-3219. free (effective 2011).
Published by: AgResearch Limited, 5th Fl, Tower Block, Ruakura Research Ctr, E St, Private Bag 3123, Hamilton, 3240, New Zealand. TEL 64-7-8346600, FAX 64-7-8346640, corporate-affairs-secretary@agresearch.co.nz.

500 FRA ISSN 1621-9066
SCIENCE REVUE. Text in French. 2000. q. EUR 38 for 2 yrs. (effective 2010). **Document type:** *Magazine, Consumer.*
Published by: Lafont Presse, 53 Rue du Chemin Vert, Boulogne-Billancourt, 92100, France. TEL 33-1-46102121, FAX 33-1-45792211. Ed. Bernard Pace.

507.1 USA ISSN 0887-2376
LB1585.3
➤ **SCIENCE SCOPE.** Text in English. 1978. 9/yr. free to members (effective 2010). adv. bk.rev. charts; illus.; tr.lit. Index. back issues avail.; reprints avail. **Document type:** *Journal, Academic/Scholarly.* **Description:** Designed for middle level and junior high school science teachers.
Formerly (until 19??): Middle Jr. High Science Bulletin (0160-306X)
Related titles: Microform ed.; Online - full text ed.: ISSN 1943-4901.
Indexed: A22, A26, B04, BRD, CA, E02, E03, E07, E08, E09, ERI, ERIC, EdA, EdI, G08, GeoRef, I05, MRD, P10, P11, P18, P48, P52, P53, P54, P55, P56, PQC, S04, S06, S09, S10, SpeleolAb, T02, W03, W05.
—BLDSC (8164.237000), IE, Infotrieve, Ingenta, Linda Hall. **CCC.**
Published by: National Science Teachers Association, 1840 Wilson Blvd, Arlington, VA 22201. TEL 703-243-7100, 800-722-6782, FAX 703-243-7177, pubinfo@nsta.org. Adv. contact Olenka Dobczanska TEL 703-312-9262. Circ: 18,000.

500 USA ISSN 1945-0877
QP517.C45
➤ **SCIENCE SIGNALING.** Text in English. 1999. w. USD 409 combined subscription domestic to non-members (print & online eds.); USD 464 combined subscription in Mexico to non-members (print & online eds.); USD 487.20 combined subscription in Canada to non-members (print & online eds.); USD 539 combined subscription elsewhere to non-members (print & online eds.); USD 369 combined subscription domestic to members (print & online eds.); USD 424 combined subscription in Mexico to members (print & online eds.); USD 445.20 combined subscription in Canada to members (print & online eds.); USD 499 combined subscription elsewhere to members (print & online eds.) (effective 2009). adv. back issues avail.; reprints avail. **Document type:** *Journal, Academic/Scholarly.* **Description:** Aims to enable the experts and novices in cell signaling to find, organize, and utilize information relevant to processes of cellular regulation.
Formerly (until 2008): Signal Transduction Knowledge Environment (1525-8882)
Related titles: Online - full text ed.: ISSN 1937-9145. USD 109 domestic to non-members; USD 114.45 foreign to non-members; USD 69 domestic to members; USD 72.45 foreign to members (effective 2009).
Indexed: A29, B20, B21, CTA, EMBASE, ESPM, GenetAb, ImmunAb, NSA, NucAcAb, P30, SCOPUS.
—Infotrieve. **CCC.**
Published by: American Association for the Advancement of Science, 1200 New York Ave, NW, Washington, DC 20005. TEL 202-326-6550, FAX 202-289-7562, scienceonline@aaas.org, http://www.aaas.org. Eds. Nancy R Gough, Michael B Yaffe TEL 617-452-2442. Pub. Michael Keller.

500 300 BEL
SCIENCE, SOCIETY SECURITY NEWS. Text in English. q. **Document type:** *Newsletter, Consumer.*
Formerly (until 2003): N A T O Science and Society Newsletter
Indexed: EnvAb.
Published by: (North Atlantic Treaty Organization, Scientific Affairs Division), North Atlantic Treaty Organization (N A T O), Office of Information and Press, Blvd Leopold III, Brussels, 1110, Belgium. Ed. Jacques Ducuing. **Co-sponsors:** North Atlantic Treaty Organization, Committee on the Challenges of Modern Society; North Atlantic Treaty Organization, Science Committee.

500 600 FIN ISSN 0786-3012
➤ **SCIENCE STUDIES**; an interdisciplinary journal for science and technology studies. Text in English. 1988. 2/yr. adv. bk.rev. 80 p./no. 2 cols./p.; back issues avail. **Document type:** *Journal, Academic/Scholarly.* **Description:** Presents a forum for international contributors in the field of science and technology studies to analyze the restructuring of the knowledge production, of the scientific and technological system, and of science and technology policy.
Related titles: Online - full text ed.: free (effective 2011).
Indexed: A01, A03, A08, CA, P30, P42, PSA, RASB, S02, S03, SCOPUS, SOPODA, SSA, SociolAb, T02.
—BLDSC (8164.287000).
Published by: Finnish Society for Science and Technology Studies, PO Box 259, Tampere, 33101, Finland. TEL 358-3-7226065, novaco@novaco.fi, http://pro.tsv.fi/stts/english/index.html. Eds. Sampsa Hyysalo, Tarja Knuuttila.

500 370 USA ISSN 1933-3102
SCIENCE STUDIES WEEKLY. CHALLENGER. Text in English. 2001. 28/yr. USD 9.98 combined subscription to students 1-9 students (print & online eds.); USD 4.99 combined subscription to students 10 or more students (print & online eds.) (effective 2010 - 2011). **Document type:** *Newspaper, Consumer.* **Description:** Contains biographical spotlights on scientists both modern and historic, labs which contain experiments that reinforce the scientific principles of the lesson etc.
Formerly (until 2006): Science Studies Weekly (1534-8229)
Related titles: Online - full text ed.
Indexed: P01, T02.
Published by: American Legacy Publishing, 1922 W 200 N, Lindon, UT 84042. TEL 866-311-8734, FAX 866-531-5589, service@studiesweekly.com. Ed. Nicole Hefner. Pub. Edward Rickers.

500 370 USA ISSN 1933-3110
SCIENCE STUDIES WEEKLY. DISCOVERY; a weekly newspaper for young students of science. Text in English. 2003. 24/yr. USD 9.98 combined subscription to students 1-9 students (print& online eds.); USD 4.99 combined subscription to students 10 or more students (print & online eds.) (effective 2010). adv. **Document type:** *Newspaper, Consumer.* **Description:** Contains a standards-based science lesson, a current event article which parallels the weekly topic with current events which are scientifically related etc.
Formerly (until 2006): Science Studies Weekly, 3rd Grade (1544-0214)
Related titles: Online - full text ed.
Indexed: P01, T02.
Published by: American Legacy Publishing, 1922 W 200 N, Lindon, UT 84042. TEL 866-311-8734, FAX 866-531-5589, service@studiesweekly.com. Ed. Nicole Hefner. Pub. Edward Rickers. Circ: 39,953.

500 370 USA ISSN 1947-8399
▼ **SCIENCE STUDIES WEEKLY. ENDEAVOR.** Text in English. 2009. 28/yr. USD 24.95 to students; USD 10 to students (2-9 copies); USD 5 to students (10 or more copies) (effective 2009). **Document type:** *Newspaper, Consumer.* **Description:** Articles and activities on science for sixth grade students.
Published by: American Legacy Publishing, PO Box 264, American Fork, UT 84003. TEL 866-311-8734, FAX 801-785-4587.

500 USA ISSN 1934-9238
SCIENCE STUDIES WEEKLY. EXPLORATION. Text in English. 2006. 28/yr. USD 9.98 combined subscription to students 1-9 students (print & online eds.); USD 4.99 combined subscription to students 10 or more students (print & online eds.) (effective 2010 - 2011). **Document type:** *Newspaper, Academic/Scholarly.* **Description:** Contains articles about related technology, crossword puzzles, movie science etc.
Related titles: Online - full text ed.
Indexed: P01, T02.
Published by: American Legacy Publishing, 1922 W 200 N, Lindon, UT 84042. TEL 866-311-8734, FAX 866-531-5589, service@studiesweekly.com. Ed. Nicole Hefner. Pub. Edward Rickers.

500 370 USA ISSN 1937-1942
SCIENCE STUDIES WEEKLY. FOOTPRINTS. Text in English. 2007. 24/yr. USD 9.98 to students 1-9 students; USD 4.99 to students 10 or more students (effective 2010). **Document type:** *Magazine, Consumer.* **Description:** Features science education for kindergarten-level classes.
Published by: American Legacy Publishing, 1922 W 200 N, Lindon, UT 84042. TEL 866-311-8734, FAX 866-531-5589, service@studiesweekly.com. Ed. Kathy Hoover. Pub. Edward Rickers.

500 370 USA ISSN 1937-1969
SCIENCE STUDIES WEEKLY. TRAILBLAZER. Text in English. 2007. 24/yr. USD 9.98 to students 1-9 students; USD 4.99 to students 10 or more students (effective 2010 - 2011). **Document type:** *Magazine, Consumer.* **Description:** Features science education for second grade students, including age-appropriate concepts, hands-on labs and illustrations.
Published by: American Legacy Publishing, 1922 W 200 N, Lindon, UT 84042. TEL 866-311-8734, FAX 866-531-5589, service@studiesweekly.com. Pub. Edward Rickers.

THE SCIENCE TEACHER. *see* EDUCATION—Teaching Methods And Curriculum

SCIENCE TEACHER EDUCATION (ONLINE). *see* EDUCATION—Teaching Methods And Curriculum

500 CAN ISSN 1911-690X
SCIENCE, TECHNOLOGIE ET INNOVATION EN BREF. Text in English. 2006. irreg. **Document type:** *Newsletter.*
Published by: Institut de la Statistique du Quebec, 200 chemin Ste Foy, Quebec, PQ G1R 5T4, Canada. TEL 418-691-2401, 800-463-4090, FAX 418-643-4129, direction@stat.gouv.qc.ca, http://www.stat.gouv.qc.ca.

170 600 USA ISSN 0162-2439
Q175.4
➤ **SCIENCE, TECHNOLOGY & HUMAN VALUES.** Text in English. 1972. bi-m. USD 748, GBP 440 combined subscription to institutions (print & online eds.); USD 733, GBP 431 to institutions (effective 2011). bk.rev. bibl.; abstr.; illus. index. back issues avail.; reprint service avail. from PSC. **Document type:** *Journal, Academic/Scholarly.* **Description:** Takes an international and multidisciplinary approach to the study of science and technology, including their involvement in politics, society, and culture.
Former titles (until 1978): Science, Technology & Human Values. Newsletter (0738-2618); (until 1976): Program on Public Conceptions of Science. Newsletter (1546-315X); Incorporated (in 1988): Science and Technology Studies (0886-3040); Which was formerly (until 1986): 4S Review (0738-0526); (until 1983): 4S. Society for Social Studies of Science (0146-1435); (until 1976): SSSS. Newsletter of the Society for Social Studies of Science (0146-1427)
Related titles: Microform ed.; Online - full text ed.: ISSN 1552-8251. USD 673, GBP 396 to institutions (effective 2011).
Indexed: A01, A02, A03, A08, A20, A22, A25, A26, ASCA, B01, B06, B07, B09, BibInd, CA, CMM, CommAb, CurCont, DIP, E-psyche, E01, E03, E07, E08, ERI, EnvAb, EnvInd, FR, FamI, G08, H04, H14, I05, I13, IBR, IBSS, IBZ, IPARL, P02, P04, P07, P10, P13, P18, P26, P30, P34, P42, P48, P53, P54, PAIS, PCI, PQC, PSA, PerIslam, PhilInd, RASB, RI-1, RI-2, RILM, S02, S03, S08, S09, S10, S23, SCOPUS, SOPODA, SSCI, SociolAb, T02, Telegen, V02, W07.
—BLDSC (8164.850000), IE, Infotrieve, Ingenta, INIST, Linda Hall. **CCC.**
Published by: (Society for Social Studies of Science), Sage Publications, Inc., 2455 Teller Rd, Thousand Oaks, CA 91320. TEL 805-499-9774, 800-818-7243, FAX 805-499-0871, 800-583-2665, info@sagepub.com. Eds. Geoffrey C Bowker, Susan Leigh Star. Circ: 1,900. **Subscr. outside of the Americas to:** Sage Publications Ltd., 1 Oliver's Yard, 55 City Rd, London EC1Y 1SP, United Kingdom. TEL 44-20-73248701, FAX 44-20-73248733, subscription@sagepub.co.uk.

500 300 IND ISSN 0971-7218
T14.5
➤ **SCIENCE, TECHNOLOGY & SOCIETY**; an international journal devoted to the developing world. Text in English; Abstracts in French, Spanish. 1996. s-a. USD 344, GBP 191 combined subscription to institutions (print & online eds.); USD 337, GBP 187 to institutions (effective 2011). adv. bk.rev. index. reprint service avail. from PSC. **Document type:** *Journal, Academic/Scholarly.* **Description:** Devoted to the understanding of the interface between science, technology and development policies as applied to developing nations.
Related titles: Online - full text ed.: ISSN 0973-0796. USD 310, GBP 172 to institutions (effective 2011).
Indexed: A22, B07, CA, CMM, E01, GEOBASE, IBSS, S02, S03, SCOPUS, SOPODA, SSA, SociolAb, T02.
—IE. **CCC.**
Published by: (Society for the Promotion of S & T Studies), Sage Publications India Pvt. Ltd. (Subsidiary of: Sage Publications, Inc.), M-32 Market, Greater Kailash-I, PO Box 4215, New Delhi, 110 048, India. TEL 91-11-6444958, FAX 91-11-6472426, editors@indiasage.com, http://www.indiasage.com/. Eds. Leela Kasturi, Roland Waast, V V Krishna. Adv. contact Sunanda Ghosh. page USD 75. Circ: 500. **Subscr. to:** Sage Publications Ltd., 1 Oliver's Yard, 55 City Rd, London EC1Y 1SP, United Kingdom. TEL 44-207-3248701, FAX 44-207-3248733, subscription@sagepub.co.uk; Sage Publications, Inc., 2455 Teller Rd, Thousand Oaks, CA 91320. TEL 805-499-9774, FAX 805-499-0871, journals@sagepub.com.

500 IND ISSN 0975-6175
➤ **SCIENCE VISION.** Text in English. 2001 (Mar.). q. **Document type:** *Journal, Academic/Scholarly.* **Description:** Aims to provide a forum for the reporting and discussion of news and issues concerning science, and to disseminate the information to the public.
Related titles: Print ed.: ISSN 2229-6026. free (effective 2011).
Published by: Mizo Post-Graduate Science Society, D-63, Sikulpuikawn, Aizawl, Mizoram, 796 001, India. TEL 91-389-2312659, scivismipo@gmail.com. Ed. K Lalchhandama. Pub., R&P H Lalthanzara.

500 PAK ISSN 1027-961X
T170.3
SCIENCE VISION. Variant title: Vision. Text in English. 1995. q. PKR 200 domestic; USD 20 foreign (effective 2005). **Document type:** *Journal, Academic/Scholarly.* **Description:** Contains scientific articles and news on the latest advances and developments in scientific and technological research and development.
Indexed: INIS AtomInd.
Published by: Commission on Science and Technology for Sustainable Development in the South, Shahrah-e-Jamhuriat, 4th Flr., G-5/2, Islamabad, Pakistan. TEL 92-51-9204900, FAX 92-51-9216539, http://www.comsats.org.pk. Ed. M M Qureshi.

500 USA ISSN 1047-8043
CODEN: SCWAEM
SCIENCE WATCH. Text in English. 1990. bi-m. back issues avail. **Document type:** *Newsletter, Academic/Scholarly.* **Description:** Analyzes the scientific journal literature and provides science policymakers, research administrators, science journalists, and others with concise overviews of key developments in today's scientific research.
Related titles: Online - full text ed.
Indexed: A22, RASB.
—BLDSC (8165.079000), CASDDS, GNLM, IE, Infotrieve, Ingenta.
Published by: Thomson Reuters (Subsidiary of: Thomson Reuters Corp.), 1500 Spring Garden, 4th Fl, Philadelphia, PA 19130. TEL 215-386-0100, 800-336-4474, FAX 215-386-2911, general.info@thomson.com, http://science.thomsonreuters.com/.

500 371.3 USA ISSN 1529-1472
Q1
SCIENCE WEEK. Text in English. 1997. 3/w. free. **Document type:** *Journal, Trade.* **Description:** Devoted to the improvement of communication between the scientific disciplines, and between scientists, science educators, and science policy makers.
Media: Online - full content.
Published by: Spectrum Press, Inc., PMB 109, 3023 N Clark St, Chicago, IL 60657-5205. haller@scienceweek.com. Ed. D P Agin.

SCIENCE WEEKLY. *see* CHILDREN AND YOUTH—For

SCIENCE WEEKLY. LEVEL A. *see* CHILDREN AND YOUTH—For

SCIENCE WEEKLY. LEVEL B. *see* CHILDREN AND YOUTH—For

SCIENCE WEEKLY. LEVEL C. *see* CHILDREN AND YOUTH—For

SCIENCE WEEKLY. LEVEL D. *see* CHILDREN AND YOUTH—For

SCIENCE WEEKLY. LEVEL E. *see* CHILDREN AND YOUTH—For

SCIENCE WEEKLY. LEVEL PRE-A. *see* CHILDREN AND YOUTH—For

SCIENCE WORLD. *see* EDUCATION—Teaching Methods And Curriculum

500 NGA ISSN 1597-6343
➤ **SCIENCE WORLD JOURNAL.** Text in English. 2006. irreg. free (effective 2011). **Document type:** *Journal, Academic/Scholarly.* **Description:** Covers original research in the natural and physical sciences and their applications.
Media: Online - full text.
Indexed: A01, A37, F12, H17, I11, S13, S16, Z01.
Published by: Kaduna State University, Faculty of Science, PMB 2339, Kaduna, Nigeria.

➤ **SCIENCE YEAR.** *see* ENCYCLOPEDIAS AND GENERAL ALMANACS

500 THA ISSN 1513-1874
Q80.T5 CODEN: VKSTDB
➤ **SCIENCEASIA.** Text in Thai. 1975. q. THB 1,600 domestic to institutions; USD 120 foreign to institutions (effective 2010). Index. back issues avail. **Document type:** *Journal, Academic/Scholarly.* **Description:** Publishes original research in science and mathematics.
Formerly (until 1999): Science Society of Thailand. Journal (0303-8122)
Related titles: Online - full text ed.: free (effective 2011).
Indexed: A20, A34, A35, A36, A37, A38, AIT, AgrForAb, B23, B25, BIOSIS Prev, C25, C30, CABA, CIN, ChemAb, ChemTitl, E12, F08, FCA, GH, H16, Inspec, JOF, MaizeAb, MycolAb, N02, N03, N04, P30, P32, R07, S13, SCI, SCOPUS, SoyAb, T05, W07, W10, Z01.
—AskIEEE, CASDDS, Ingenta, Linda Hall.
Published by: Science Society of Thailand under the Patronage of His Majesty the King, Chulalongkorn University, Faculty of Science, Phyathai Rd., Bangkok, Pathumwan 10330, Thailand. TEL 66-2-252-7987, FAX 66-2-252-7987, scisoc.thailand@gmail.com, http://www.scisoc.or.th/. Ed. Worachart Sirawaraporn. Circ: 1,000.

507 USA
SCIENCEDAILY. Text in English. 1995. d. free (effective 2010); /. adv. **Document type:** *Magazine, Consumer.* **Description:** Covers news about the latest discoveries and hottest researching projects in everything from astrophysics to zoology.
Media: Online - full text.
Published by: Science Daily, 1 Research Ct, Ste 450, Rockville, MD 20850. TEL 240-454-9600, FAX 240-454-9600, sales@sciencedaily.com. Ed. Dan Hogan. Adv. contact Michele Hogan.

500 USA
SCIENCEDIRECT CONNECTIONS NEWSLETTER. Text in English. 1997. m. back issues avail. **Document type:** *Newsletter, Trade.*
Media: E-mail. **Related titles:** Online - full text ed.
Published by: ScienceDirect (Subsidiary of: Elsevier Science & Technology), 360 Park Ave S, PO Box 945, New York, NY 10010-1710. TEL 212-633-3730, 888-437-4636, FAX 212-462-1974, usinfo@scidirect.com, http://www.sciencedirect.com/.

500 USA ISSN 1947-8062
SCIENCENOW. Text in English. 1996. d. free to members (effective 2009). adv. back issues avail. **Document type:** *Magazine, Trade.* **Description:** Provides gateway to items of news interest on the Science sites.
Media: Online - full content.
Published by: American Association for the Advancement of Science, PO Box 96178, Washington, DC 20090. TEL 202-326-6417, 866-434-2227, FAX 202-842-1065, scienceonline@aaas.org, http://www.aaas.org. Ed. David Grimm.

500 JPN
SCIENCEPEDIA/SAIENSUPEDIA. Text in Japanese. 1982. 2/yr.
Published by: Obunsha Publishing Co. Ltd., 55 Yokotera-Machi, Shinjuku-ku, Tokyo, 1620831, Japan.

500 FRA ISSN 0151-0304
Q2
SCIENCES. Text in French. 1952-1979; resumed 1980. irreg. (1-2/yr). **Document type:** *Journal, Academic/Scholarly.*
Formerly (until 1969): Association Francaise pour l'Avancement des Sciences. Bulletin. Revue Generale des Sciences pures et Appliquees (0370-7431); Which was formed by the merger of (1936-1952): Sciences (0376-1231); Which was formerly (1904-1936): Association Francaise pour l'Avancement des Sciences. Bulletin Mensuel (1164-6543); (1896-1904): Association Francaise pour l'Avancement des Sciences. Bulletin (1164-6535); (1872-1896): Association Francaise pour l'Avancement des Sciences. Documents et Informations Divers (0988-2545); (1948-1952): Societe Philomathique. Bulletin. Revue Generale des Sciences pures et Appliquees (0370-520X); Which was formed by the merger of (1890-1947): Revue Generale des Sciences pures et Appliquees (0370-5196); (1864-1945): Societe Philomathique de Paris. Bulletin (0366-3515); Which was formerly (1836-1863): Societe Philomathique de Paris. Extraits des Proces-verbaux des Seances (0986-1904); (1825-1833): Nouveau Bulletin des Sciences (1164-6527); (1814-1824): Bulletin des Sciences (1164-6519); (1807-1814): Nouveau Bulletin des Sciences (1164-6500); (1797-1805): Bulletin des Sciences (1153-6489); (1791-1797): Societe Philomathique. Bulletin (1153-6470)
Related titles: Online - full text ed.
Indexed: FR, GeoRef, SpeleolAb.
—INIST, Linda Hall. **CCC.**
Published by: Association Francaise pour l'Avancement des Sciences, 1 place Aristide Briand, Meudon, 92195, France. afas@orange.fr. Ed. Alain Foucault.

500 FRA ISSN 0246-5558
SCIENCES D'AUJOURD'HUI. Text in French. 1979. irreg. back issues avail. **Document type:** *Monographic series, Consumer.*
Published by: Editions Albin Michel, 22 rue Huyghens, Paris, 75014, France. TEL 33-1-42791000, FAX 33-1-43272158, http://www.albin-michel.fr.

SCIENCES DE LA VIE ET DE LA TERRE. PREPARATION AUX CONCOURS. *see* EDUCATION—Higher Education

500 FRA ISSN 0036-8636
SCIENCES ET AVENIR. Text in French. 1948. m. EUR 45 domestic; EUR 55 in the European Union; EUR 63 in US & Canada; EUR 74 elsewhere (effective 2009). bk.rev. illus. **Document type:** *Magazine, Consumer.* **Description:** Articles covering all areas of science in a general sense: Environmental issues, technology, space explorations, medicine, with an insight into future implications.
Formerly (until 1949): Sciences et Avenir et Terre, Air, Mer (0295-950X); Which was formed by the merger of (1947-1948): Sciences et Avenir (0295-9526); (1946-1948): Terre, Air, Mer (0295-9518)
Indexed: A22, GeoRef, IBR, IBZ, INIS AtomInd, P30, PdeR, RASB, RILM, SpeleolAb.
—BLDSC (8165.850000), IE, Infotrieve, Ingenta. **CCC.**
Published by: Le Nouvel Observateur, 12 place de la Bourse, Paris, 75002, France. TEL 33-1-44883434, quotidien@nouvelobs.com. Ed., Pub. Georges Goldberine. Adv. contact Catherine Gardin. Circ: 320,000.

500 LAO ISSN 1021-2442
SCIENCES & TECHNIQUES. Text in Laotian. 1991. q. USD 35. adv.
Published by: C N D I S T - Science Technology and Environment Organization, PO Box 2279, Vientiane, Laos. TEL 213470. Ed. Sisavanh Boupha. Adv. contact Viengsavanh Dounagsavanh.

500 DJI
SCIENCES & TECHNIQUES. Text in French. 1989. 2/yr. USD 30.
Indexed: PLESA.
Published by: Institut Superieur d'Etudes et de Recherches Scientifiques et Techniques, BP 486, Djibouti, Djibouti. TEL 253-35-27-95, FAX 253-35-48-12.

SCIENCES ET TECHNIQUES EN PERSPECTIVE/SCIENCES AND TECHNOLOGY IN PERSPECTIVE. *see* HISTORY

500 600 BEL
SCIENCES ET TECHNIQUES EN PERSPECTIVES. Text in French. 1996. s-a. EUR 56 in the European Union; EUR 61 elsewhere (effective 2007). **Document type:** *Journal, Academic/Scholarly.*
Published by: (Societe Francaise d'Histoire des Sciences et des Techniques FRA), Brepols Publishers, Begijnhof 67, Turnhout, 2300, Belgium. TEL 32-14-448030, FAX 32-14-428919, periodicals@brepols.net, http://www.brepols.net.

500 CHN ISSN 1674-3822
SCIENCES IN COLD AND ARID REGIONS. Text in English. bi-m. 96 p./no.; **Document type:** *Journal, Academic/Scholarly.*
Related titles: Online - full text ed.
Published by: (Zhongguo Kexueyuan Hanquhanqu Huanjing yu Gongcheng Yanjiusuo/Chinese Academy of Sciences, Cold and Arid Regions Environmental and Engineering Research Institute), Kexue Chubanshe/Science Press, 16 Donghuang Cheng Genbei Jie, Beijing, 100717, China. Ed. Guodong Cheng.

500 PER ISSN 1681-7230
SCIENDO; ciencia para el desarrollo. Text in Spanish. a. **Document type:** *Monographic series, Academic/Scholarly.*
Published by: Universidad Nacional de Trujillo, Apdo Postal 315, Trujillo, Peru. TEL 51-44-205448, FAX 51-44-256629, http://www.unitru.edu.pe/. Ed. Cesar Augusto Jara.

500 CHL ISSN 0036-8679
QA1 CODEN: SCNTAU
SCIENTIA; revista cientifica y tecnologica. Text in Spanish; Summaries in English. 1934. 2/yr. USD 10. charts; illus. cum.index: 1934-1958, 1959-1968.
Related titles: ♦ Series: Scientia. Series A: Mathematical Sciences. ISSN 0716-8446.
Indexed: ASCA, C01, ChemAb, GeoRef, Inspec, MathR, Repind, SpeleolAb, Z02.
—AskIEEE, CASDDS, INIST.
Published by: Universidad Tecnica Federico Santa Maria, Casilla 110-V, Valparaiso, Chile. TEL 56-32-654246, FAX 56-32-654443, consulta@utfsm.cl, http://www.utfsm.cl. Ed. Carlos Gonzalez. Circ: 2,000.

500 BRA ISSN 0104-1770
SCIENTIA. Text in Portuguese. 1990. s-a. USD 20 or exchange basis. bibl. index, cum.index. back issues avail. **Document type:** *Journal, Academic/Scholarly.*
Published by: Universidade do Vale do Rio dos Sinos (UNISINOS), Av Unisinos 950, Sao Leopoldo, RS 93022-000, Brazil. TEL 55-51-5908131, FAX 55-51-5908132, http://www.unisinos.br. Circ: 250.

500 PAN ISSN 0258-9702
Q4
SCIENTIA. Text in Spanish. 1986. s-a. PAB 8, USD 8 (effective 1998). bk.rev. bibl.; illus.; maps; stat. biennial index. back issues avail. **Document type:** *Monographic series, Academic/Scholarly.* **Description:** Publishes results of research in biology, mathematics, physics and chemistry.
Published by: Universidad de Panama, Vicerrectoria de Investigacion y Postgrado, Estafeta Universitaria, Panama City, Panama. TEL 264-4242, FAX 264-4450. Pub., R&P Cesar A Villarreal. Circ: 500.

500 CAN ISSN 0829-2507
➤ **SCIENTIA CANADENSIS.** Text in English. 1976. 2/yr. USD 35.85 membership (effective 2009). bk.rev. bibl. back issues avail. **Document type:** *Journal, Academic/Scholarly.* **Description:** Covers history of science, technology, and medicine.
Formerly (until 1984): H S T C Bulletin (History of Science and Technology of Canada) (0228-0086)
Indexed: AmH&L, C03, CA, CBCARef, EMBASE, ExcerpMed, MEDLINE, P11, P30, P48, P52, P56, PQC, RASB, SCOPUS, T02.
Published by: Canadian Science and Technology Historical Association/Association pour l'Histoire de la Science et de la Technologie au Canada, Box 8502, Stn. T, Ottawa, ON K1G 3H9, Canada. TEL 416-483-7282, FAX 416-489-1713. Ed. Stephane Castonguay.

500 ESP ISSN 0213-5930
Q4 CODEN: ASCGDN
SCIENTIA GERUNDENSIS; annals de la seccio de ciencies. Text in Spanish. 1976. a. **Document type:** *Journal, Academic/Scholarly.*
Former titles (until 1985): Collegi Universitari de Girona. Seccio de Ciencies. Annals (0213-5922); (until 1983): Colegio Universitario de Gerona. Seccion de Ciencias. Anales (0378-9543)
Indexed: GeoRef, IECT, SpeleolAb, Z01.
—CASDDS.
Published by: Universitat de Girona, Facultat de Ciencies, Pza. Hospital 6, Gerona, 17071, Spain.

500 300 DEU ISSN 1868-7172
SCIENTIA GRAECO-ARABICA. Text in English, French, German, Italian. 2008. irreg., latest vol.8, 2012. price varies. **Document type:** *Monographic series, Academic/Scholarly.*
Indexed: MSN.
Published by: Walter de Gruyter GmbH & Co. KG, Genthiner Str 13, Berlin, 10785, Germany. TEL 49-30-260050, FAX 49-30-26005251, info@degruyter.com, http://www.degruyter.de. Ed. Marwan Rashed.

500 VEN ISSN 0798-1120
➤ **SCIENTIA GUAIANAE**; a series on natural sciences of the Guayana region. Text in English, Portuguese, Spanish. 1990. irreg., latest vol.11, 2000. price varies. abstr.; bibl.; illus.; maps. back issues avail. **Document type:** *Monographic series, Academic/Scholarly.* **Description:** Publishes original papers and monographs dealing with any aspect of the physical and biological sciences of the Guayana region in its widest geographical sense.
Indexed: Z01.
Address: Apdo 21827, Caracas, DF 1020-A, Venezuela. Ed., Pub. Otto Huber. Circ: 500. **Dist. by:** Koeltz Scientific Books.

500 CHN ISSN 1556-6706
QA241
➤ **SCIENTIA MAGNA.** Text mainly in English. 2005 (Oct.). a. **Document type:** *Journal, Academic/Scholarly.* **Description:** Publishes papers in science and includes mathematics, physics, philosophy, psychology, sociology, linguistics.
Related titles: Microfilm ed.; Online - full text ed.: free (effective 2011).
Indexed: A01, A26, A28, APA, BrCerAb, C&ISA, CA/WCA, CCMJ, CIA, CerAb, CivEngAb, CorrAb, E&CAJ, E08, E11, EEA, EMA, ESPM, EnvEAb, G08, H15, I05, M&TEA, M09, MBF, METADEX, MSN, MathR, P11, P17, P26, P48, P52, P53, P54, P56, PQC, RefZh, S09, SolStAb, T02, T04, WAA, Z02.

S

—Linda Hall.
Published by: Xi'an University, Department of Mathematics, Northwest University, Xi'an, Shaanxi, China. Ed. Dr. Zhang Wenpeng.

➤ **SCIENTIA POETICA.** *see* LITERATURE

500 MEX ISSN 1405-8723
SCIENTIAE NATURAE. Text in Spanish. 1998. s-a. **Document type:** *Journal, Academic/Scholarly.*
Indexed: C01.
Published by: Universidad Autonoma de Aguascalientes, Centro de Ciencias Basicas, Ave Universidad 940, Ciudad Universitaria, Aguascalientes, Aguascalientes, 20100, Mexico. TEL 52-449-9107400, http://www.uaa.mx/centros/ccbas/.

500 BEL
SCIENTIFIC AMERICAN. Text in Dutch. 2002. 6/yr. EUR 30; EUR 18 to students; EUR 5.90 newsstand/cover (effective 2009). adv. **Document type:** *Magazine, Consumer.*
Published by: Uitgeverij Cascade, Katwilgweg 2 bus 5, Antwerpen, 2050, Belgium. TEL 32-36-802561, FAX 32-36-802564. adv.: page EUR 3,100; trim 215 x 285. Circ: 9,019.

500 USA ISSN 0036-8733
CODEN: SCAMAC
SCIENTIFIC AMERICAN. Text in English. 1845. m. USD 24.97 domestic; CAD 39 in Canada; USD 44 elsewhere (effective 2009). adv. bk.rev. charts; illus. Index. 100 p./no.; back issues avail.; reprints avail. **Document type:** *Magazine, Consumer.* **Description:** Features the latest trends in science and technology.
Incorporates (1920-1921): Scientific American Monthly (0740-6495); Which superseded (in 1920): Scientific American Supplement (0096-3763); (1853-1854): People's Journal
Related titles: Microform ed.: (from PMC, PQC); Online - full text ed.: ISSN 1946-7087. USD 39.95 (effective 2009); ◆ Chinese ed.: Ke Xue. ISSN 1002-1299; ◆ Polish ed.: Swiat Nauki. ISSN 0867-6380; ◆ Arabic ed.: Majallat al-Ulum; ◆ Japanese ed.: Nikkei Saiensu. ISSN 0917-009X; ◆ Spanish ed.: Investigacion y Ciencia. ISSN 0210-136X; ◆ Italian ed.: Le Scienze. ISSN 0036-8083; ◆ German ed.: Spektrum der Wissenschaft. ISSN 0170-2971; ◆ Hungarian ed.: Tudomany. ISSN 0237-322X; ◆ French ed.: Pour la Science. ISSN 0153-4092; Turkish ed.: Bilim; International ed.: Scientific American (International Edition); ◆ Regional ed(s).: Huanqiu Kexue. ISSN 1673-5153; Scientific American (European Edition); ◆ Supplement(s): Scientific American Special. ISSN 1946-990X.
Indexed: A01, A02, A03, A05, A06, A08, A09, A10, A11, A12, A13, A17, A20, A21, A22, A24, A25, A26, A28, A29, A32, ABIPC, ABIn, ABS&EES, AESIS, AIA, APA, APD, ARG, AS&TA, AS&TI, ASCA, ASFA, AbAn, Acal, Agr, AnBeAb, ApMecR, B&AI, B01, B04, B05, B06, B07, B08, B09, B10, B13, B20, B21, B28, BAS, BDM&CN, BIOSIS Prev, BMT, BRD, BiolDig, Biostat, BrArAb, BrCerAb, BrRB, BrTechI, C&ISA, C03, C04, C05, C06, C07, C08, C10, C11, C13, CA, CA/WCA, CADCAM, CBCARef, CBPI, CBRI, CBTA, CCR, CIA, CINAHL, CIS, CLFP, CPerI, CTA, Cadscan, CerAb, ChemAb, ChemTitl, ChemoAb, CivEngAb, CorrAb, CurCont, DentAb, E&CAJ, E-psyche, E04, E05, E07, E08, E11, EEA, EIA, EMA, EMBASE, ESPM, EngInd, EntAb, EnvAb, EnvEAb, EnvInd, ExcerpMed, F09, FR, FS&TA, FutSurv, G01, G03, G05, G06, G07, G08, G09, GALA, GSA, GSI, GardL, GasAb, GdIns, GenetAb, GeoRef, H03, H04, H12, H15, HECAB, HPNRM, I05, I07, I10, I13, IBR, IBZ, IDIS, IHTDI, IPackAb, ISR, IndMed, Inpharma, Inspec, JOF, KWIWR, L09, LID&ISL, LeadAb, M&GPA, M&MA, M&TEA, M01, M02, M05, M06, M09, MASUSE, MBF, MCR, MEA&I, MEDLINE, METADEX, MLA-IB, MS&D, MSN, MagInd, MathR, MycolAb, NAA, NRN, NSA, NucAcAb, NumL, ORMS, P02, P10, P11, P13, P15, P18, P24, P26, P30, P34, P43, P47, P48, P51, P52, P53, P54, P56, PAIS, PEI, PQC, PRA, PhilInd, PopulInd, QC&AS, R03, R04, R06, R10, RASB, RGAb, RGPR, RI-1, RILM, Reac, RefZh, RoboAb, S01, S04, S06, S08, S09, S10, S23, SCI, SCOPUS, SPPI, SSciA, SWRA, SolStAb, SpeleolAb, T02, T04, TOM, Telegen, U01, V02, V03, V04, ViroIAbstr, W03, W05, W07, W08, WAA, WBA, WMB, WildRev, Zincscan.
—BLDSC (8175.000000), AskIEEE, CASDDS, GNLM, IE, Infotrieve, Ingenta, INIST, Linda Hall, PADDS. **CCC.**
Published by: Scientific American, Inc., 75 Varick St, 9th Fl, New York, NY 10013. TEL 212-451-8200, comments@sciam.com. Ed. Mariette DiChristina. Adv. contact Bruce Brandfon TEL 212-451-8561. B&W page USD 50,800, color page USD 76,100. Circ: 732,617 (paid). **Dist. by:** MarketForce UK Ltd.

500 USA ISSN 1946-990X
T1
SCIENTIFIC AMERICAN SPECIAL. Text in English. 1988. irreg., latest 2009. USD 10.95 per issue domestic; USD 13.95 per issue foreign (effective 2009). adv. bk.rev. illus. back issues avail. **Document type:** *Magazine, Consumer.* **Description:** Examines single topic or trends in contemporary science.
Former titles: Scientific American. Special Edition (1551-2991); (until 200?): Scientific American Presents (1524-0223); (until 1998): Scientific American. Special Issue (1048-0943)
Related titles: Online - full text ed.: USD 7.95 per issue (effective 2009); ◆ Supplement to: Scientific American. ISSN 0036-8733.
Indexed: CA, MASUSE.
—INIST. **CCC.**
Published by: Scientific American, Inc., 75 Varick St, 9th Fl, New York, NY 10013. TEL 212-451-8200, editors@sciam.com.

500 600 JPN
SCIENTIFIC AND TECHNICAL INFORMATION IN FOREIGN COUNTRIES/KAIGAKI KAGAKU GIJUTSU JOHO SHIRYO. Text in Japanese. irreg. **Document type:** *Government.*
Published by: (Japan. Keikaku-kyoku), Kagaku Gijutsucho/Science and Technology Agency, Planning Bureau, 2-1 Kasumigaseki 2-chome, Chiyoda-ku, Tokyo, 100-0013, Japan.

500 LBY
SCIENTIFIC BULLETIN. Text in English. m.
Published by: Jamahiriya News Agency, Sharia al-Fateh, P O Box 2303, Tripoli, Libya. TEL 37106.

500 200 USA ISSN 2153-831X
QC6.4.C57
▼ ➤ **SCIENTIFIC GOD JOURNAL.** Text in English. 2010. q. free (effective 2010). **Document type:** *Journal, Academic/Scholarly.* **Description:** Features scientific inquiries on the nature and origins of life, mind, physical laws and mathematics and their possible connections to a scientifically approachable transcendental ground of existence.
Media: Online - full text.
Published by: Scientific GOD, Inc., PO Box 267, Stony Brook, NY 11790-0267. TEL 631-678-1864, hupinghu@quantumbrain.org.

500 SDN
SCIENTIFIC INFORMATION BULLETIN. Text in English. 1977. m.
Published by: Industrial Research and Consultancy Institute, Department of Documentation and Technical Information, P O Box 268, Khartoum, Sudan.

500 USA ISSN 1552-1222
➤ **SCIENTIFIC INQUIRY.** Text in English. 19??. s-a. free (effective 2011). back issues avail. **Document type:** *Journal, Academic/Scholarly.* **Description:** Forum of the professional quality for both scientists and nonscientists alike to exchange ideas and publish new discoveries on a vast array of topics and issues.
Formerly (until 2006): Science Exploration
Media: Online - full text.
Published by: International Institute for General Systems Studies, Inc. (Subsidiary of: International Institute for General Systems Studies), 23 Kings Lane, Grove City, PA 16127. iigss@iigss.net. Ed. Jeffrey Forrest.

500 PRI ISSN 1548-9639
HV40
➤ **SCIENTIFIC INTERNATIONAL JOURNAL.** Text in English, Spanish. 2004 (May/Jun). bi-m. USD 60 to individuals; USD 180 to institutions; USD 40 to students (effective 2004). **Document type:** *Journal, Academic/Scholarly.* **Description:** It is a forum for the dissemination of information about relevant issues on the areas of health, education, and social sciences.
Related titles: Online - full text ed.: ISSN 1554-6349. free (effective 2011).
Published by: Non-Profit Evaluation & Resource Center, Inc., 53 Esmerelda Ave P M B 010, Guaynabo, 00969-4429, Puerto Rico. TEL 787-464-4644, FAX 787-780-1851, nperci@nperci.org, http://www.nperci.org. Ed. Lizzette Rojas.

➤ **SCIENTIFIC MEETINGS.** *see* MEETINGS AND CONGRESSES

500 GBR ISSN 2045-2322
▼ ➤ **SCIENTIFIC REPORTS.** Text in English. 2011 (Jun.). irreg. free (effective 2011). **Document type:** *Journal, Academic/Scholarly.* **Description:** Provides for the rapid publication of research covering all areas of the natural sciences - biology, chemistry, physics and earth sciences.
Media: Online - full text.
—CCC.
Published by: Nature Publishing Group (Subsidiary of: Macmillan Publishers Ltd.), The MacMillan Bldg, 4 Crinan St, London, N1 9XW, United Kingdom. TEL 44-20-78334000, FAX 44-20-78334640, NatureReviews@nature.com.

500 NGA ISSN 1992-2248
Q179.9
➤ **SCIENTIFIC RESEARCH AND ESSAYS.** Text in English. 2006. bi-m. free (effective 2011). adv. back issues avail.; reprints avail. **Document type:** *Journal, Academic/Scholarly.* **Description:** Covers science, medicine, agriculture and engineering.
Media: Online - full text.
Indexed: A34, A35, A36, A37, A38, AgBio, AgrForAb, B21, B23, BA, BP, C25, C30, CABA, D01, E12, ESPM, EntAb, F08, F11, F12, FCA, G11, GH, H16, H17, I11, IndVet, LT, MaizeAb, N02, N03, N04, O01, OR, P32, P33, P37, P38, P39, P40, PGegResA, PGrRegA, PHN&I, PN&I, R07, R08, R11, R12, R13, RA&MP, RM&VM, RRTA, S12, S13, S16, S17, SCI, SCOPUS, SSciA, SoyAb, T05, TAR, TriticAb, VS, W07, W10, W11.
Published by: Academic Journals, PO Box 73023, Victoria Island, Lagos, Nigeria. service@academicjournals.org. Eds. Dr. M Sivakumar, Dr. N J Tonukari.

500 MYS ISSN 1675-7009
SCIENTIFIC RESEARCH JOURNAL. Text in English. 2003. s-a. back issues avail. **Document type:** *Journal, Academic/Scholarly.*
Related titles: Online - full text ed.
Published by: M A R A University of Technology, Research Management Institute/Universiti Teknologi M A R A, Institut Pengurusan Penyelidikan, Shah Alam, Selangor 40450, Malaysia. TEL 60-3-55442095, FAX 60-3-55442096.

500 NPL ISSN 1996-8949
➤ **SCIENTIFIC WORLD/VAIJNANIKA JAGAT.** Text in English. 1999. a. **Document type:** *Journal, Academic/Scholarly.* **Description:** A multidisciplinary journal of science and technology.
Related titles: Online - full text ed.
Address: B.P. Koirala Memorial Planetarium, Observatory and Science Museum Development Board, Singha Durbar, Kathmandu, Nepal. TEL 977-1-4211971, FAX 977-1-4211897, sanatsharma@most.gov.np. Ed. Sanat Kumar Sharma.

500 GBR ISSN 2043-6963
▼ **SCIENTIFIC WORLD (LONDON).** Text in English. 2010. m. adv. back issues avail. **Document type:** *Journal, Academic/Scholarly.*
Related titles: Online - full text ed.: ISSN 2043-6971.
Published by: Scientific World, 26 York St, London, W1U 6PZ, United Kingdom. FAX 44-20-33573194.

500 GBR ISSN 1537-744X
➤ **THE SCIENTIFIC WORLD JOURNAL.** Abbreviated title: T S W J. Text in English. 2001. irreg. includes subscriptions to: TSW Development & Embryology, TSW Holistic Health & Medicine and TSW Urology. adv. abstr. back issues avail. **Document type:** *Journal, Academic/Scholarly.* **Description:** Offers a unified environment for the publication of all science drawn from over a hundred networked scientific domains within the life, biomedical and environmental sciences.
Formerly (until 2001): The Scientific World (1532-2246)
Media: Online - full text.
Indexed: A20, B21, B25, BIOSIS Prev, C06, C07, CTA, E-psyche, EMBASE, ESPM, ExcerpMed, F09, GenetAb, H&SSA, M&GPA, MEDLINE, MycolAb, NSA, NucAcAb, OceAb, P30, PollutAb, R10, Reac, RiskAb, SCI, SCOPUS, SSciA, W07, Z01.
—Infotrieve.
Published by: The ScientificWorld Ltd. sales@thescientificworld.com.

500 USA ISSN 0890-3670
CODEN: SCIEEW
THE SCIENTIST; magazine of the life sciences. Text in English. 1986. m. USD 210 domestic to institutions (academic); GBP 125, EUR 165 foreign to institutions (academic); USD 1,203 combined subscription domestic to institutions (print & online eds.); GBP 692, EUR 905 combined subscription foreign to institutions (print & online eds.); USD 602 combined subscription domestic to institutions academic (print & online eds.); GBP 344, EUR 460 combined subscription foreign to institutions academic (print & online eds.) (effective 2009); Subscr. rates based on 1-20 users. adv. illus. reprints avail. **Document type:** *Newspaper, Trade.* **Description:** News and commentary on business, policy and politics of science. Also includes profiles of laboratory equipment and services.
Related titles: Online - full text ed.: ISSN 1547-0806.
Indexed: A20, A22, A26, ABIPC, ASCA, Agr, B04, BIOSIS Prev, BiolDig, CurCont, E08, EnvAb, G03, G06, G07, G08, GSA, GSI, GeoRef, I05, I06, I07, ISR, Inpharma, MycolAb, P11, P15, P19, P26, P30, P48, P52, P54, P56, PQC, RASB, S06, S09, S23, SCI, SCOPUS, SSCI, SpeleolAb, TelAb, Telegen, W03, W05, W07.
—BLDSC (8205.010000), CASDDS, GNLM, IE, Infotrieve, Ingenta, INIST, Linda Hall. **CCC.**
Published by: The Scientist, Inc., 3600 Market St, Ste 450, Philadelphia, PA 19104-2645. TEL 215-386-9601, FAX 215-387-7542. Ed. Richard Gallagher. Pub. Alexander M Grimwade. R&P Alexander Grimwade. Adv. contact Diana Smith. Circ: 53,000 (controlled). **Subscr. to:** The Scientist, PO Box 15937, N Hollywood, CA 91615-5937.

SCIENTISTS, ENGINEERS, AND TECHNICIANS IN THE UNITED STATES. *see* POPULATION STUDIES

500 HUN ISSN 0138-9130
CODEN: SCNTDX
➤ **SCIENTOMETRICS;** an international journal for all quantitative aspects of the science of science, communication in science and science policy. Text in English. 1978. 4/yr. EUR 3,227, USD 3,326 combined subscription to institutions (print & online eds.) (effective 2012). adv. bk.rev. abstr.; bibl. 160 p./no.; back issues avail.; reprint service avail. from PSC. **Document type:** *Journal, Academic/Scholarly.* **Description:** Publishes original studies, short communications, preliminary reports, review papers on scientometrics.
Incorporates (in 1982): Journal of Research Communication Studies (0378-5939)
Related titles: Microform ed.: (from PQC); Online - full text ed.: ISSN 1588-2861 (from IngentaConnect).
Indexed: A20, A22, A26, ABS&EES, ASCA, B25, BIOSIS Prev, BibLing, C06, C07, C08, C10, CA, CINAHL, CIS, CLOSS, CMCI, CurCont, E01, FR, GeoRef, H12, ISTA, Inspec, L04, L13, LISTA, LT&LA, MycolAb, P30, PAIS, RASB, RefZh, S02, S03, SCI, SCOPUS, SOPODA, SSCI, SociolAb, SpeleolAb, T02, W07.
—BLDSC (8205.080000), CASDDS, IE, Infotrieve, Ingenta, INIST, Linda Hall. **CCC.**
Published by: (Eotvos Lorand Tudomanyegyetem, Institute of Inorganic & Analytical Chemistry/Eotvos Lorand University), Akademiai Kiado Rt. (Subsidiary of: Wolters Kluwer N.V.), Prielle Kornelia u 19/D, Budapest, 1117, Hungary. TEL 36-1-4648222, FAX 36-1-4648221, info@akkrt.hu. Ed. Tibor Braun. **Co-publisher:** Springer Netherlands.

500 AUS ISSN 1442-2212
SCIENTRIFFIC MAGAZINE. Text in English. 1999. bi-m. AUD 26 (effective 2008). back issues avail. **Document type:** *Magazine, Consumer.* **Description:** Entertains and educates children about science with articles, fun and easy to do experiments, puzzle pages, comics, competitions and crosswords.
Published by: (C S I R O), C S I R O Publishing, 150 Oxford St, PO Box 1139, Collingwood, VIC 3066, Australia. TEL 61-3-96627500, FAX 61-3-96627555, publishing@csiro.au, http://www.publish.csiro.au/home.htm. Ed. Tanya Patrick.

500 ITA ISSN 1720-9986
SCIENZA E CONOSCENZA. Text in Italian. 2002. bi-m. EUR 28 (effective 2009). **Document type:** *Magazine, Consumer.*
Published by: Macro Edizioni, Via Savona 70, Diegaro di Cesena, FC 47023, Italy. TEL 39-0547-346290, http://www.macroedizioni.it.

500 796 ITA ISSN 2039-0726
▼ **SCIENZA & SPORT.** Text in Italian. 2009. q. **Document type:** *Journal, Trade.*
Published by: Editoriale Sport Italia, Via Masaccio 12, Milan, MI 20149, Italy. TEL 39-02-4815396, FAX 39-02-4690907, editoriale@sportivi.it, http://www.sportivi.it.

500 945 ITA ISSN 1122-3693
SCIENZA E STORIA; saggi, interventi, recensioni. Text in Italian. 1983. s-a. adv. bk.rev. abstr. 130 p./no.; **Document type:** *Journal, Academic/Scholarly.*
Formerly (until 1986): Centro Internazionale A. Beltrame di Storia dello Spazio e del Tempo. Bollettino (1122-3685)
Indexed: FR.
—INIST.
Published by: Centro Internazionale di Storia della Nozione e della Misura dello Spazio e del Tempo, Via Roma 86-A, Brugine, PD 35020, Italy. TEL 39-049-586768, cisst@tin.it. Ed. Giampiero Bozzolato.

500 ITA ISSN 0582-2580
SCIENZA E TECNICA. Text in Italian. 1937-1951; N.S. 1957-1963; N.S. 1970. m. **Document type:** *Journal, Academic/Scholarly.*
Published by: Societa Italiana per il Progresso delle Scienze (S I P S), Via dell'Universita 11, Rome, 00185, Italy. TEL 39-06-4440515, sips@sipsinfo.it, http://www.sipsinfo.it.

500 100 ITA ISSN 2036-2927
Q174
▼ **SCIENZAEFILOSOFIA.IT.** Abbreviated title: S & F. Text in Italian, English. 2009. s-a. free (effective 2011). **Document type:** *Journal, Academic/Scholarly.*
Media: Online - full text.
Published by: Scienzaefilosofia

500 ITA ISSN 0036-8083
LE SCIENZE; edizione italiana di Scientific American. Text in Italian. 1968. m. EUR 39 (effective 2009). adv. bk.rev. bibl.; charts; illus. index. back issues avail. **Document type:** *Magazine, Consumer.*

Related titles: Online - full text ed.; ◆ German ed.: Spektrum der Wissenschaft. ISSN 0170-2971; ◆ Hungarian ed.: Tudomany. ISSN 0237-322X; ◆ French ed.: Pour la Science. ISSN 0153-4092; ◆ English ed.: Scientific American. ISSN 0036-8733; ◆ Chinese ed.: Ke Xue. ISSN 1002-1299; ◆ Spanish ed.: Investigacion y Ciencia. ISSN 0210-136X; ◆ Japanese ed.: Nikkei Saiensu. ISSN 0917-009X; ◆ Arabic ed.: Majallat al-Ulum; ◆ Polish ed.: Swiat Nauki. ISSN 0867-6380; Turkish ed.: Bilim.
Indexed: IBR, IBZ, Inspec.
Published by: Gruppo Editoriale l' Espresso SpA, Via Cristoforo Colombo 149, Rome, RM 00147, Italy. TEL 39-06-84781, FAX 39-06-8845167, espresso@espressoedit.it, http://www.espressoedit.it.

500 ITA ISSN 1825-2311
LO SCIENZIATO. Text in Italian. 2005. w. **Document type:** *Magazine, Consumer.*
Published by: R C S Libri (Subsidiary of: R C S Mediagroup), Via Mecenate 91, Milan, 20138, Italy. TEL 39-02-5095-2248, FAX 39-02-5095-2975, http://rcslibri.corriere.it/libri/index.htm.

SCIOS. *see* EDUCATION—Teaching Methods And Curriculum

THE SCITECH LAWYER. *see* LAW

SEARCH (WASHINGTON DC); science, religion, culture. *see* RELIGIONS AND THEOLOGY

500 AUT ISSN 1991-1750
SEE-SCIENCE.EU. Text in English. 2006. q. **Document type:** *Journal, Academic/Scholarly.* **Description:** Provides information on issues of science and technology policy in the region.
Media: Online - full content.
Published by: Information Office of the Steering Platform on Research for the Western Balkan Countries, c/o Centre for Social Innovation, Linke Wienzeile 246, Vienna, 1150, Austria. TEL 43-1-495044262, FAX 43-1-495044240, office@see-science.eu. Eds. Elke Dall, Florian Gruber.

500 USA ISSN 1499-0679
Q1
SEED (NEW YORK). Text in English. 2001-2004; resumed 2005. bi-m. USD 14.95 in US & Canada; USD 29.95 elsewhere (effective 2006). adv. illus. **Document type:** *Magazine, Consumer.* **Description:** Seeks out the ideas, trends and celebrities that are influencing science's place in culture and culture's place in science.
Indexed: ASIP, C03, CBCARef, P11, P48, P52, P56, PQC.
Published by: Seed Media Group, 12 W. 21st St., 7th Fl., New York, NY 10010. TEL 212-404-1920, FAX 212-404-1450, http://www.seedmediagroup.com/. Ed. Adam Bly. Circ: 150,000.

500 TUR ISSN 1300-4905
SELCUK UNIVERSITESI. FEN-EDEBIYAT FAKULTESI. FEN DERGISI/ SELCUK UNIVERSITY. SCIENCE AND ART FACULTY. JOURNAL OF SCIENCE. Text in English. 1984. a. **Document type:** *Journal, Academic/Scholarly.*
Related titles: Online - full text ed.
Published by: Selcuk Universitesi, Fen-Edebiyat Fakultesi, Fen Dergisi Editorlugu, Kampus / Konya, 42075, Turkey. TEL 90-332-2410107, FAX 90-332-2410106, fen@selcuk.edu.tr. Ed. Dr. Abdurrahman Aktumsek.

500 USA
SELECTED RESEARCH IN MICROFICHE. Abbreviated title: S R I M. Text in English. 1975. s-m. USD 4 per issue (effective 2011). cum.index. back issues avail. **Document type:** *Government.* **Description:** Provides subscribers with microfiche copies of the full text of reports. There are reports from within 350 existing subject areas; new subject areas may be created to meet the needs of particular individuals.
Media: Microfiche.
Published by: U.S. Department of Commerce, National Technical Information Service, 5301 Shawnee Rd, Alexandria, VA 22312. TEL 703-605-6000, info@ntis.gov.

500 BRA ISSN 1676-5451
SEMINA. CIENCIAS EXATAS E TECNOLOGICAS. Text in Portuguese. 1987. a. **Document type:** *Journal, Academic/Scholarly.*
Related titles: Online - full text ed.: ISSN 1679-0375. free (effective 2011).
Indexed: A35, A37, B23, BA, C01, C25, CABA, E12, F08, FCA, GH, H16, I11, N02, P32, P40, R13, S13, S16, SoyAb, W10.
Published by: Universidade Estadual de Londrina, Pro - Reitoria de Pesquisa e Pos - Graduacao, Campus Universitario, Londrina, Parana 86051-990, Brazil. Eds. Henrique de Santana, Marcos Moraes.

500 DEU ISSN 0341-4108
SENCKENBERG BUECHER. Text in German, English. 1926. irreg., latest vol.77, 2004. price varies. back issues avail. **Document type:** *Monographic series, Academic/Scholarly.* **Description:** Constitutes a scientific and popular-scientific book.
Indexed: GeoRef, SpeleolAb.
Published by: (Senckenberg Gesellschaft fuer Naturforschung), E. Schweizerbart'sche Verlagsbuchhandlung, Johannesstr 3A, Stuttgart, 70176, Germany. TEL 49-711-3514560, FAX 49-711-35145699, order@schweizerbart.de. Ed. Volker Mosbrugger.

500 JPN ISSN 0386-5827
SENSHU SHIZEN KAGAKU KIYO/SENSHU UNIVERSITY. ASSOCIATION OF NATURAL SCIENCE. BULLETIN. Text in English, Japanese; Summaries in English. 1969. a. JPY 3,000. **Document type:** *Bulletin.*
Published by: Senshu Daigaku, Shizen Kagaku Kenkyukai/Senshu University, Association of Natural Science, 1-1 Higashi-Mita 2-chome, Tama-ku, Kawasaki-shi, Kanagawa-ken 214-0033, Japan. TEL 81-44-911-0588, FAX 81-44-911-1243. Ed. Masakatsu Hirose. Circ: 350 (controlled).

500 SRB
SERBIAN ACADEMY OF SCIENCES AND ARTS. DEPARTMENT OF TECHNICAL SCIENCES. SCIENTIFIC MEETINGS. Text in English, Hungarian. irreg.
Indexed: Inspec.
Published by: Srpska Akademija Nauka i Umetnosti/Serbian Academy of Arts and Sciences, Knez Mihailova 35, Belgrade, 11000. TEL 381-11-2027154, FAX 381-11-2027178, izdavacka@sanu.ac.rs, http://www.sanu.ac.rs.

500 SGP
SERIES IN POPULAR SCIENCE. Text in English. 1996. irreg., latest vol.5, 2006. price varies. back issues avail. **Document type:** *Monographic series, Academic/Scholarly.*
Published by: World Scientific Publishing Co. Pte. Ltd., 5 Toh Tuck Link, Singapore, 596224, Singapore. TEL 65-6466-5775, FAX 65-6467-7667, wspc@wspc.com.sg, http://www.worldscientific.com. Ed. Richard J Weiss. **Dist. by:** World Scientific Publishing Co., Inc., 27 Warren St, Ste 401-402, Hackensack, NJ 07601. TEL 201-487-9655, 800-227-7562, FAX 201-487-9656, 888-977-2665, wspc@wspc.com; World Scientific Publishing Ltd., 57 Shelton St, London WC2H 9HE, United Kingdom. TEL 44-207-8360888, FAX 44-207-8362020, sales@wspc.co.uk.

500 600 SGP
SERIES ON THE FOUNDATIONS OF NATURAL SCIENCE AND TECHNOLOGY. Text in English. 1994. irreg., latest vol.6, 2003. price varies. back issues avail. **Document type:** *Monographic series, Academic/Scholarly.*
Published by: World Scientific Publishing Co. Pte. Ltd., 5 Toh Tuck Link, Singapore, 596224, Singapore. TEL 65-6466-5775, FAX 65-6467-7667, wspc@wspc.com.sg, http://www.worldscientific.com. Eds. C Politis, W Schommers TEL 49-7247-822432. **Dist. by:** World Scientific Publishing Ltd., 57 Shelton St, London WC2H 9HE, United Kingdom. TEL 44-207-8360888, FAX 44-207-8362020, sales@wspc.co.uk; World Scientific Publishing Co., Inc., 27 Warren St, Ste 401-402, Hackensack, NJ 07601. TEL 201-487-9655, 800-227-7562, FAX 201-487-9656, 888-977-2665, wspc@wspc.com.

SERVICE D'INFORMATION SCIENTIFIQUE ET TECHNIQUE. RAPPORT D'ACTIVITE. *see* TECHNOLOGY: COMPREHENSIVE WORKS

500 NZL ISSN 1177-3456
SETTING FUTURE DIRECTIONS. Variant title: Foundation for Research, Science and Technology. Summary of Initiatives. Text in English. 2006. a. **Description:** Provides a summary of key initiatives set out in the Statement of Intent.
Published by: Foundation for Research, Science and Technology, Level 11, AT&T Tower, 15-17 Murphy St, PO Box 12240, Thorndon, Wellington, 6144, New Zealand. TEL 64-4-9177800, FAX 64-4-9177850.

500 CHN
SHAANXI KEJI DAXUE XUEBAO (ZIRAN KEXUE BAN)/SHAANXI UNIVERSITY OF SCIENCE & TECHNOLOGY. JOURNAL (NATURAL SCIENCE EDITION). Text in Chinese. 1982. bi-m. USD 24.60 (effective 2009). **Document type:** *Journal, Academic/Scholarly.*
Formerly (until 2003): Xibei Qinggongye Xueyuan Xuebao (1000-5811)
Related titles: Online - full text ed.
—BLDSC (4874.705000), East View.
Published by: Shaanxi Keji Daxue/Shaanxi University of Science & Technology, PO Box 22, Xianyang, 710021, China. TEL 86-29-86168067. **Dist. by:** China International Book Trading Corp, 35 Chegongzhuang Xilu, Haidian District, PO Box 399, Beijing 100044, China. TEL 86-10-68412045, FAX 86-10-68412023, cibtc@mail.cibtc.com.cn, http://www.cibtc.com.cn.

500 CHN ISSN 1673-2944
SHAANXI LIGONG XUEYUAN XUEBAO (ZIRAN KEXUE BAN)/ SHAANXI INSTITUTE OF TECHNOLOGY. JOURNAL. Text in Chinese. q. **Document type:** *Journal, Academic/Scholarly.*
Supersedes in part: Hanzhong Shifan Xueyuan Xuebao/Hanzhong Teacher's College. Journal (1007-0842); Shaanxi Gongxueyuan Xuebao (1002-3410)
Related titles: Online - full text ed.
Published by: Shaanxi Ligong Xueyuan, Hedongdian, Hanzhong, 723003, China. TEL 86-916-2291064.

500 CHN ISSN 1672-4291
SHAANXI SHIFAN DAXUE XUEBAO (ZIRAN KEXUE BAN)/SHANXI NORMAL UNIVERSITY. JOURNAL (NATURAL SCIENCE EDITION). Text in Chinese. 1960. q. USD 24.60 (effective 2009). **Document type:** *Journal, Academic/Scholarly.*
Formerly (until 1996): Shaanxi Shi-da Xuebao (Ziran Kexue Ban)/Shaanxi Normal University (Natural Sciences Edition) (1001-3857)
Related titles: Online - full text ed.
Indexed: CCMJ, MSN, MathR, RefZh, Z01, Z02.
—BLDSC (4874.700000), East View.
Published by: Shaanxi Shifan Daxue/Shaanxi Normal University, Chang'an Nanlu, Box 66, Xi'an, 710062, China. TEL 86-29-85308734, FAX 86-29-85303859. **Dist. by:** China International Book Trading Corp, 35 Chegongzhuang Xilu, Haidian District, PO Box 399, Beijing 100044, China. TEL 86-10-68412045, FAX 86-10-68412023, cibtc@mail.cibtc.com.cn, http://www.cibtc.com.cn.

500 CHN ISSN 1671-9352
QH7 CODEN: SDXKEU
SHANDONG DAXUE XUEBAO (LIXUE BAN)/SHANDONG UNIVERSITY. JOURNAL (NATURAL SCIENCE EDITION). Text in Chinese. 1951. m. CNY 120 (effective 2009). **Document type:** *Journal, Academic/Scholarly.*
Formerly (until 2002): Shandong Daxue Xuebao (Ziran Kexue Ban) (0559-7234)
Related titles: Online - full text ed.
Indexed: B&BAb, B19, B20, B21, CCMJ, CIN, ChemAb, ChemTitl, E17, ESPM, EntAb, I10, MSN, MathR, SSciA, Z02.
—BLDSC (4874.730200), CASDDS, East View.
Published by: Shandong Daxue, 73, Jingshi Lu, Jinan, 250061, China. TEL 86-531-88396917, FAX 86-531-88392495.

500 CHN ISSN 1002-4026
SHANDONG KEXUE/SHANDONG SCIENCE. Text in Chinese; Abstracts in Chinese, English. 1984. bi-m. CNY 36 (effective 2010). back issues avail. **Document type:** *Journal, Academic/Scholarly.* **Description:** Publishes original papers and letters reflecting creative and inovative achievements in natrural sciences as well as review papers about important accomplishment in frontier science, especailly in oceanographic Instrumentation and computer science.
Formerly (until 1989): Shandong Sheng Kexueyuan Yuankan/Shandong Academy of Sciences. Journal
Related titles: Online - full text ed.: (from WanFang Data Corp.).
Indexed: A32, B21, ESPM, SWRA.
Published by: Shandong Sheng Kexueyuan/Shandong Academy of Science, 19, Keyuan Lu, Ji'nan, 250014, China. TEL 86-531-82605310, http://www.sdas.org/. Ed. Tian-yi Wang. Circ: 1,000.

500 600 CHN ISSN 1672-6197
SHANDONG LIGONG DAXUE XUEBAO (ZIRAN KEXUE BAN)/ SHANDONG UNIVERSITY OF TECHNOLOGY. JOURNAL (SCIENCE AND TECHNOLOGY). Text in Chinese. 1985. bi-m. USD 31.20 (effective 2009). **Document type:** *Journal, Academic/Scholarly.*
Supersedes (1999-2002): Zibo Xueyuan Xuebao (Ziran Kexue yu Gongcheng Ban)/Zibo University. Journal (Natural Sciences and Engineering) (1009-0452); (1991-2002): Shandong Gongcheng Xueyuan Xuebao (1007-1857); Which was formerly (until 1991): Shandong Nongye Jixie Huaxueyuan Xuebao
—East View.
Published by: Shandong Ligong Daxue/Shandong University of Technology, 12, Zhangzhou Lu, Zibo, 255049, China. TEL 86-533-2780711.

500 CHN
SHANDONG NONGYE DAXUE XUEBAO (ZIRAN KEXUE BAN)/ SHANDONG AGRICULTURAL UNIVERSITY. JOURNAL (NATURAL SCIENCE). Text in Chinese. 1955. q. USD 16.40 (effective 2009). **Document type:** *Journal, Academic/Scholarly.*
Formerly: Shandong Nongye Daxue Xuebao (1000-2324)
Related titles: Online - full text ed.
Indexed: A22, A34, A35, A37, AgBio, AgrForAb, C25, C30, CABA, E12, F08, F12, FCA, GH, H16, IndVet, N04, N05, O01, P32, P37, P40, R07, R12, R13, S13, S16, S17, VS, W11.
—BLDSC (4874.724000), IE, Ingenta.
Published by: Shandong Nongye Daxue, 61, Daizong Dajie, Taian, 271018, China. TEL 86-538-8242751.

500 CHN ISSN 1004-4280
Q4
➤ **SHANDONG QINGGONGYE XUEYUAN XUEBAO/SHANDONG LIGHT INDUSTRY INSTITUTE. JOURNAL.** Text in English. 1987. q. USD 14.40 (effective 2009). 80 p./no.; **Document type:** *Journal, Academic/Scholarly.* **Description:** Contains research and new theory articles relating to such light industry fields as paper and pulp engineering, leather engineering, fermentation and food engineering, inorganic materials engineering and mechanical and electrical engineering.
Related titles: Online - full text ed.
—East View.
Published by: Shandong Qinggongye Xueyuan, 23 Huangtai Beilu, Jinan, Shandong 250100, China. TEL 86-531-8964221. Ed., Adv. contact Liu Fuxiang. Circ: 300 (paid); 700 (controlled). **Dist. overseas by:** China International Book Trading Corp, 35 Chegongzhuang Xilu, Haidian District, PO Box 399, Beijing 100044, China.

500 CHN
SHANDONG SHIFAN DAXUE XUEBAO (ZIRAN KEXUE BAN)/ SHANDONG NORMAL UNIVERSITY. JOURNAL (NATURAL SCIENCE). Text in Chinese. 1986. q. CNY 12 newsstand/cover (effective 2007). **Document type:** *Journal, Academic/Scholarly.*
Formerly: Shandong Shi-da Xuebao (Ziran Kexue Ban) (1001-4748)
Related titles: Online - full text ed.
—BLDSC (4874.729400), IE, Ingenta.
Published by: Shandong Shifan Daxue, 88, Wenhua Donglu, Jinan, Shandong 250014, China.

500 CHN ISSN 1007-2861
CODEN: SDXKFV
SHANGHAI DAXUE XUEBAO (ZIRAN KEXUE BAN)/SHANGHAI UNIVERSITY. JOURNAL (NATURAL SCIENCE EDITION). Text in Chinese; Abstracts in Chinese, English. 1978. bi-m. CNY 8 per issue (effective 2010). back issues avail. **Document type:** *Journal, Academic/Scholarly.*
Merged with part of (1979-1994): Shanghai Gongye Daxne Xuebao (1000-5129); (1978 -1994): Shanghai Keji Daxue Xuebao/Shanghai University of Science and Technology. Journal (0258-7041)
Related titles: Online - full text ed.; ◆ English ed.: Shanghai University. Journal. ISSN 1007-6417.
Indexed: A28, APA, BrCerAb, C&ISA, CA/WCA, CCMJ, CIA, CIN, CerAb, ChemAb, ChemTitl, CivEngAb, CorrAb, E&CAJ, E11, EEA, EMA, ESPM, EnvEAb, H15, Inspec, M&TEA, M09, MBF, METADEX, MSN, MathR, RefZh, SolStAb, T04, WAA, Z02.
—BLDSC (4874.819000), CASDDS, IE, Linda Hall.
Published by: Shanghai Daxue/Shanghai University, 99, Shangda Lu, PO Box 126, Shanghai, 200444, China. TEL 86-21-66135508, FAX 86-21-66132736. **Dist. by:** China International Book Trading Corp, 35 Chegongzhuang Xilu, Haidian District, PO Box 399, Beijing 100044, China. TEL 86-10-68412045, FAX 86-10-68412023, cibtc@mail.cibtc.com.cn, http://www.cibtc.com.cn.

500 CHN ISSN 1001-4543
SHANGHAI DI-ER GONGYE DAXUE XUEBAO/SHANGHAI SECOND POLYTECHNIC UNIVERSITY. JOURNAL. Text in Chinese. 1984. q. CNY 6 newsstand/cover (effective 2006). **Document type:** *Journal, Academic/Scholarly.*
Related titles: Online - full text ed.
Indexed: Z02.
Published by: Shanghai Di-2 Gongye Daxue, 260, Pudong Jinhai Lu, Shanghai, 201209, China. TEL 86-21-50686814.

SHANGHAI JIAOTONG DAXUE XUEBAO. *see* TECHNOLOGY: COMPREHENSIVE WORKS

SHANGHAI JIAOTONG UNIVERSITY. JOURNAL. *see* TECHNOLOGY: COMPREHENSIVE WORKS

500 CHN ISSN 1000-5137
SHANGHAI SHIFAN DAXUE XUEBAO (ZIRAN KEXUE BAN)/ SHANGHAI TEACHERS UNIVERSITY. JOURNAL (NATURAL SCIENCES). Text in Chinese. 1958. bi-m. USD 24.60 (effective 2009). **Document type:** *Journal, Academic/Scholarly.*
Related titles: Online - full text ed.
Indexed: Z02.
—East View.
Published by: Shanghai Shifan Daxue/Shanghai Normal University, 100, Guilin Lu, Shanghai, 200234, China. TEL 86-21-64324387, FAX 86-21-64322304. **Dist. by:** China International Book Trading Corp, 35 Chegongzhuang Xilu, Haidian District, PO Box 399, Beijing 100044, China. TEL 86-10-68412045, FAX 86-10-68412023, cibtc@mail.cibtc.com.cn, http://www.cibtc.com.cn.

S

500 CHN ISSN 1007-6417
Q1 CODEN: JSUNFV
SHANGHAI UNIVERSITY. JOURNAL/SHANGHAI DAXUE XUEBAO (YINGWEN BAN). Text and summaries in English. 1977. bi-m. EUR 645, USD 787 combined subscription to institutions (print & online eds.) (effective 2011). back issues avail.; reprint service avail. from PSC. **Document type:** *Journal, Academic/Scholarly.* **Description:** Covers natural science and engineering technology.
Supersedes in part (in 1997): Shanghai Gongye Daxne Xuebao/ Shanghai University of Technology. Journal (1000-5129)
Related titles: Online - full text ed.: ISSN 1863-236X; ◆ Chinese ed.: Shanghai Daxue Xuebao (Ziran Kexue Ban). ISSN 1007-2861.
Indexed: A22, A26, A28, APA, ASFA, ApMecR, BrCerAb, C&ISA, CA/WCA, CCMJ, CIA, CerAb, CivEngAb, CorrAb, E&CAJ, E01, E08, E11, EEA, EMA, ESPM, EngInd, EnvEAb, H15, Inspec, M&TEA, M09, MBF, METADEX, MSN, MathR, RefZh, SCOPUS, SolStAb, T04, WAA, Z02.
—BLDSC (4874.818800), East View, IE, Ingenta, Linda Hall. **CCC.**
Published by: Shanghai Daxue/Shanghai University, 99, Shangda Lu, PO Box 124, Shanghai, 200444, China. TEL 86-21-66135510, FAX 86-21-66132736. **Dist. by:** China International Book Trading Corp, 35 Chegongzhuang Xilu, Haidian District, PO Box 399, Beijing 100044, China. TEL 86-10-68412045, FAX 86-10-68412023, cibtc@mail.cibtc.com.cn, http://www.cibtc.com.cn. **Co-publisher:** Springer.

500 CHN ISSN 1671-7333
SHANGHAI YINGYONG JISHU XUEYUAN XUEBAO (ZIRAN KEXUE BAN). Text in Chinese. 2001. q. **Document type:** *Journal, Academic/ Scholarly.*
Formed by the merger of (1985-2000): Shanghai Qinggongye Gaodeng Zhuanke Xuexiao Xuebao/Shanghai Light Industry College. Journal (1008-8210); (1982-2000): Shanghai Yejin Zhuanke Xuexiao Xuebao/Shanghai Technical College of Metallurgy. Journal (1005-6815)
Related titles: Online - full text ed.
Published by: Shanghai Yingyong Jishu Xueyuan, 120, Caobao Lu, Shanghai, 200235, China. TEL 86-21-64941184, FAX 86-21-34140102.

SHANGQIU ZHIYE JISHU XUEYUAN XUEBAO/SHANGQIU VOCATIONAL AND TECHNICAL COLLEGE. JOURNAL. *see* SOCIAL SCIENCES: COMPREHENSIVE WORKS

500 CHN ISSN 1001-4217
SHANTOU DAXUE XUEBAO (ZIRAN KEXUE BAN)/SHANTOU UNIVERSITY. JOURNAL (NATURAL SCIENCE EDITION). Text in Chinese. 1986. q. CNY 6, USD 2.50 per issue (effective 2008). **Document type:** *Journal, Academic/Scholarly.*
Related titles: Online - full text ed.
—BLDSC (8254.600900).
Published by: Shantou Daxue/Shantou University, Daxue Lu, Shantou, 515063, China. TEL 86-754-2903827. Ed. Xiao-hu Xu.

500 CHN ISSN 0253-2395
Q4 CODEN: SDXKDT
SHANXI DAXUE XUEBAO (ZIRAN KEXUE BAN)/SHANXI UNIVERSITY. JOURNAL (NATURAL SCIENCE EDITION). Text in Chinese. 1947. q. USD 16.40 (effective 2009). **Document type:** *Journal, Academic/ Scholarly.*
Related titles: Online - full text ed.
Indexed: A22, CIN, ChemAb, ChemTitl, RefZh, Z01.
—BLDSC (4874.825000), IE, Ingenta.
Published by: Shanxi Daxue, 92, Wucheng Lu, Bangong 1/F, Taiyuan, 030006, China. **Dist. by:** China International Book Trading Corp, 35 Chegongzhuang Xilu, Haidian District, PO Box 399, Beijing 100044, China. TEL 86-10-68412045, FAX 86-10-68412023, cibtc@mail.cibtc.com.cn, http://www.cibtc.com.cn.

500 CHN
SHANXI KEJI BAO/SHANXI SCIENCE AND TECHNOLOGY GAZETTE. Text in Chinese. 1980. 3/w. CNY 57.60 (effective 2004). **Document type:** *Newspaper, Academic/Scholarly.*
Address: 119, Yaowangdong, Xi'an, 710003, China. TEL 86-29-7347875, FAX 86-29-7345429. **Dist. by:** China International Book Trading Corp, 35 Chegongzhuang Xilu, Haidian District, PO Box 399, Beijing 100044, China. TEL 86-10-68412045, FAX 86-10-68412023, cibtc@mail.cibtc.com.cn, http://www.cibtc.com.cn.

500 CHN ISSN 1671-8151
SHANXI NONGYE DAXUE XUEBAO (ZIRAN KEXUE BAN)/SHANXI UNIVERSITY OF AGRICULTURE. JOURNAL (NATURAL SCIENCE EDITION). Text in Chinese. 1957. q. CNY 8 newsstand/cover (effective 2006). **Document type:** *Journal, Academic/Scholarly.*
Supersedes in part (until 2001): Shanxi Nongye Daxue Xuebao/Shanxi University of Agriculture. Journal (1000-162X)
Related titles: Online - full text ed.
Published by: Shanxi Nongye Daxue/Shanxi University of Agriculture, 6/F, Shiyan Dalou, Taigu, Shanxi 030801, China.

500 CHN ISSN 1009-4490
SHANXI SHIFAN DAXUE XUEBAO (ZIRAN KEXUE BAN)/SHANXI TEACHER'S UNIVERSITY. JOURNAL (NATURAL SCIENCE EDITION). Text in Chinese. 1986. q. USD 16.40 (effective 2009). **Document type:** *Journal, Academic/Scholarly.*
Related titles: Online - full text ed.
—East View.
Published by: Shanxi Shifan Daxue/Shanxi Teachers University, 1, Gongyuan Jie, Linfen, Shanxi 041004, China. TEL 86-357-2051149, FAX 86-357-2051149 ext 6.

SHAONIAN KEXUE/SCIENCE FOR JUVENILE. *see* CHILDREN AND YOUTH—For

SHAONIAN KEXUE HUABAO/JUVENILE SCIENTIFIC PICTORIAL. *see* CHILDREN AND YOUTH—For

SHAOXING WELI XUEYUAN XUEBAO/SHAOXING UNIVERSITY. JOURNAL. *see* SOCIAL SCIENCES: COMPREHENSIVE WORKS

500 CHN ISSN 1672-7010
SHAOYANG XUEYUAN XUEBAO (ZIRAN KEXUE BAN)/SHAOYANG UNIVERSITY. JOURNAL (NATURAL SCIENCE). Text in Chinese. 2004. q. CNY 10 newsstand/cover (effective 2007). **Document type:** *Journal, Academic/Scholarly.*
Supersedes in part (until 2004): Shaoyang Xueyuan Xuebao/Shaoyang University. Journal (1672-1012); Which was formed by the merger of (1998-2002): Shaoyang Shifan Gaodeng Zhuanke Xuexiao Xuebao/Shaoyang Teachers College. Journal (1008-1674); (1999-2002): Shaoyang Gaodeng Zhuanke Xuexiao Xuebao/ Shaoyang College. Journal (1009-2439); Which was formed by the merger of: Shaoyang Gaozhuan Xuebao; Hunan Shaoyang Gongzhuan Xuebao
Related titles: Online - full text ed.
Published by: Shaoyang Xueyuan, Liziyuan, Shaoyang, 422000, China. TEL 86-739-5431304, FAX 86-739-5305663.

SHENYANG DAXUE XUEBAO/SHENYANG UNIVERSITY. JOURNAL. *see* SOCIAL SCIENCES: COMPREHENSIVE WORKS

600 CHN ISSN 1000-1646
T4 CODEN: SGDXEO
SHENYANG GONGYE DAXUE XUEBAO/SHENYANG UNIVERSITY OF TECHNOLOGY. JOURNAL. Text in Chinese. 1964. q. USD 31.20 (effective 2009). **Document type:** *Journal, Academic/Scholarly.*
Supersedes in part: Shenyang Gongye Xueyuan Xuebao/Shenyang Institute of Technology. Journal (1003-1251)
Related titles: Online - full text ed.
Indexed: A28, APA, BrCerAb, C&ISA, CA/WCA, CIA, CPEI, CerAb, CivEngAb, CorrAb, E&CAJ, E11, EEA, EMA, ESPM, EnvEAb, H15, Inspec, M&TEA, M09, MBF, METADEX, RefZh, SCOPUS, SolStAb, T04, WAA.
—East View, IE, Linda Hall.
Published by: Shenyang Gongye Daxue, 1, Nan 13 Lu, Shenyang, 110023, China. TEL 86-24-25691039, FAX 86-24-25691041.

600 CHN ISSN 1004-4639
TP1
SHENYANG HUAGONG XUEYUAN XUEBAO/SHENYANG INSTITUTE OF CHEMICAL TECHNOLOGY. JOURNAL. Text in Chinese. 1986. q. USD 12 (effective 2009). **Document type:** *Journal, Academic/ Scholarly.*
Related titles: Online - full text ed.
—BLDSC (4874.935500), East View.
Published by: Shenyang Huagong Xueyuan/Shenyang Institute of Chemical Technology, Jingji Jizhu Kaifaqu, no.11 Street, Shenyang, 110142, China. TEL 86-24-98383908, http://www.syict.edu.cn/. **Dist. by:** China International Book Trading Corp, 35 Chegongzhuang Xilu, Haidian District, PO Box 399, Beijing 100044, China. TEL 86-10-68412045, FAX 86-10-68412023, cibtc@mail.cibtc.com.cn, http://www.cibtc.com.cn.

500 CHN
SHENYANG LIGONG DAXUE XUEBAO/SHENYANG LIGONG UNIVERSITY. TRANSACTIONS. Text in Chinese. 1982. bi-m. CNY 8 per issue (effective 2009). **Document type:** *Journal, Academic/ Scholarly.*
Supersedes in part: Shenyang Gongye Xueyuan Xuebao/Shenyang Institute of Technology. Journal (1003-1251)
Related titles: Online - full text ed.
—IE, Ingenta.
Published by: Shenyang Ligong Daxue, 6, Nanping Zhong Lu, Shenyang, 110168, China. **Dist. by:** China International Book Trading Corp, 35 Chegongzhuang Xilu, Haidian District, PO Box 399, Beijing 100044, China. TEL 86-10-68412045, FAX 86-10-68412023, cibtc@mail.cibtc.com.cn, http://www.cibtc.com.cn.

500 CHN ISSN 1673-5862
Q4 CODEN: SSDXC4
➤ **SHENYANG SHIFAN DAXUE XUEBAO (ZIRAN KEXUE BAN)/ SHENYANG NORMAL UNIVERSITY. JOURNAL (NATURAL SCIENCE EDITION).** Text in Chinese; Abstracts in Chinese, English. 1983. q. CNY 40, USD 10; CNY 10 per issue (effective 2009). **Document type:** *Journal, Academic/Scholarly.* **Description:** Covers the latest developments of theoretical and applied researches in the fields of natural science and engineering.
Formerly: Shenyang Shifan Xueyuan Xuebao (Ziran Kexue Ban) (1008-374X)
Related titles: Online - full text ed.
Indexed: ESPM, EnvEAb, RefZh, Z01, Z02.
—BLDSC (4874.936700).
Published by: Shenyang Shifan Xueyuan/Shenyang Normal University, 253, Northern Huanghe St., Huanggu District, Shenyang, Liaoning 110034, China. TEL 86-24-86592564, FAX 86-24-86592466. Eds. Hui Zhang, Hong-wei Liu. Circ: 1,000.

500 600 CHN ISSN 1000-2618
Q4 CODEN: SDXLEX
SHENZHEN DAXUE XUEBAO (LIGONG BAN)/SHENZHEN UNIVERSITY. JOURNAL (SCIENCE & ENGINEERING EDITION). Text in Chinese. 1984. q. CNY 40 domestic; USD 10 in Hong Kong, Macau & Taiwan; USD 17.60 elsewhere (effective 2007). 96 p./no.; **Document type:** *Journal, Academic/Scholarly.* **Description:** Contains academic papers. Aims to reflect research results and promote academic exchange.
Related titles: Online - full text ed.
Indexed: A22, A28, APA, BrCerAb, C&ISA, CA/WCA, CCMJ, CIA, CPEI, CerAb, CivEngAb, CorrAb, E&CAJ, E11, EEA, EMA, ESPM, EngInd, EnvEAb, H15, Inspec, M&TEA, M09, MBF, METADEX, MSN, MathR, RefZh, SCOPUS, SolStAb, T04, WAA, Z02.
—BLDSC (4874.939500), IE, Ingenta, Linda Hall.
Published by: Shenzhen Daxue, Rm 419, Xingzheng Lou, Shenzhen, Guangdong 518060, China. TEL 86-755-26536133, FAX 86-755-26538263, http://www.szu.edu.cn/. Ed. Weixin Xie. Adv. contact Chengzhen Zhang. **Dist. by:** China International Book Trading Corp, 35 Chegongzhuang Xilu, Haidian District, PO Box 399, Beijing 100044, China. TEL 86-10-68412045, FAX 86-10-68412023, cibtc@mail.cibtc.com.cn, http://www.cibtc.com.cn.

500 CHN ISSN 1672-0318
SHENZHEN ZHIYE JIEZHU XUEYUAN XUEBAO/SHENZHEN POLYTECHNIC. JOURNAL. Text in Chinese. 2002. q. **Document type:** *Journal, Academic/Scholarly.*
Related titles: Online - full text ed.
Indexed: Inspec.
—BLDSC (8256.423930).
Published by: Shenzhen Zhiye Jiezhu Xueyuan/Shenzhen Polytechnic, Institute for Technical & Vocational Education, nanshan-qu, Xilihu, Shenzhen, 518055, China. TEL 86-755-26731000, FAX 86-755-26731712.

500 USA ISSN 1556-3359
B808.9
SHIFT. Text in English. 19??. q. USD 4.99 per issue (effective 2010). bk.rev.; Website rev. illus. 48 p./no.; back issues avail. **Document type:** *Magazine, Trade.* **Description:** Contains articles, interviews, research updates, and review essays on the people and ideas in the forefront of consciousness research.
Former titles (until 2004): I O N S. Noetic Sciences Review (1541-9673); (until 1996): Noetic Sciences Review (0897-1005); (until 1986): Institute of Noetic Science. Newsletter (0888-3432); (until 197?): Noetic News
Related titles: Online - full text ed.
Indexed: A04, C11, CA, T02.
—Ingenta. **CCC.**
Published by: Institute of Noetic Sciences, 101 San Antonio Rd, Petaluma, CA 94952. TEL 707-775-3500, FAX 707-781-7420, info@noetic.org.

500 JPN ISSN 1342-9272
CODEN: SDKGAH
SHIGA DAIGAKU KYOIKU GAKUBU KIYO. SHIZEN KAGAKU/SHIGA UNIVERSITY. FACULTY OF EDUCATION. MEMOIRS. NATURAL SCIENCE. Text and summaries in English, French, Japanese. 1952. a. free. **Document type:** *Academic/Scholarly.*
Supersedes in part (in 1995): Shiga Daigaku Kyoiku Gakubu Kiyo. Shizen Kagaku, Kyoiku Kagaku/Shiga University. Faculty of Education. Memoirs. Natural Science and Pedagogic Science (1340-7953); Which was formerly (until 1987): Shiga Daigaku Kyoikugakubu Kiyo. Shizen Kagaku/Shiga University. Faculty of Education. Memoirs. Natural Sciences (0488-6291); (until 1953): Shiga Daigaku Gakugei Gakubu Kenkyu Ronshu, Shizen Kagaku/ Shiga University. Faculty of Liberal Arts and Education. Bulletin. Part 2. Natural Science (0488-6283)
Indexed: B25, BIOSIS Prev, CCMJ, CIS, ChemAb, JPI, MSN, MathR, MycolAb, Z01, Z02.
—BLDSC (5593.327000), CASDDS.
Published by: Shiga Daigaku, Kyoikugakubu/Shiga University, Faculty of Education, 5-1 Hiratsu 2-chome, Otsu-shi, Shiga-ken 520-0862, Japan. FAX 81-77-537-7840. Ed. Michiko Tachibana.

500 CHN ISSN 1007-7383
SHIHEZI DAXUE XUEBAO (ZIRAN KEXUE BAN)/SHIHEZI UNIVERSITY. JOURNAL (NATURAL SCIENCE). Text in Chinese. 1983. bi-m. USD 28.20 (effective 2009). **Document type:** *Journal, Academic/Scholarly.*
Formerly (until 1996): Shihezi Nongxueyuan Xuebao (1000-2855)
Related titles: Online - full text ed.
—BLDSC (8256.492900), East View.
Published by: Shihezi Daxue, Beixi Lu 31 Xiao-qu, Shihezi, Xinjiang 832003, China. TEL 86-993-2058977, FAX 86-993-2058050.

500 CHN ISSN 1006-6055
SHIJIE KEJI YANJIU YU FAZHAN/WORLD RESEARCH AND DEVELOPMENT ON SCIENCE AND TECHNOLOGY. Variant title: World Sci-Tech R & D. Text in Chinese. 1993. bi-m. CNY 90 domestic; USD 22.80 in Hong Kong, Macau & Taiwan; USD 33.60 elsewhere (effective 2007). **Document type:** *Journal, Academic/Scholarly.*
Formerly: Shijie Yanjiu yu Fazhan/World R & D Report (1005-1449)
Related titles: Online - full text ed.
—BLDSC (9359.920000).
Published by: Zhongguo Kexueyuan Chengdu Wenxian Qingbao Zhongxin, no.9, Sect. 4, Renmin Nan Lu, Chengdu, 610041, China. TEL 86-28-85223853, FAX 86-28-85210304. **Dist. by:** China International Book Trading Corp, 35 Chegongzhuang Xilu, Haidian District, PO Box 399, Beijing 100044, China. TEL 86-10-68412045, FAX 86-10-68412023, cibtc@mail.cibtc.com.cn, http:// www.cibtc.com.cn.

500 CHN ISSN 1000-0968
SHIJIE KEXUE. Text in Chinese. 1978. m. USD 43.20 (effective 2009). **Document type:** *Journal, Academic/Scholarly.*
Related titles: Online - full text ed.
—East View.
Address: no.622, Alley no.7, Huaihai Zhong Rd., 303/F Changyue Bldg., Shanghai, 200020, China. TEL 86-21-63844297, FAX 86-21-63844297. **Dist. by:** China International Book Trading Corp, 35 Chegongzhuang Xilu, Haidian District, PO Box 399, Beijing 100044, China. TEL 86-10-68412045, FAX 86-10-68412023, cibtc@mail.cibtc.com.cn, http://www.cibtc.com.cn.

500 600 CHN ISSN 1003-1898
RS180.C5
SHIJIE KEXUE JISHU/WORLD SCIENCE AND TECHNOLOGY. Text in Chinese, Esperanto. 1985. q. USD 106.80 (effective 2009). adv. **Document type:** *Academic/Scholarly.*
Related titles: Online - full text ed.: ISSN 1876-3553 (from ScienceDirect).
—East View.
Published by: Chinese High-Tech Industry Promotion Society, Zhongguo Kexueyuan, No 1, A, Nansijie, Zhongguanchun, Haidian District, Beijing, 100080, China. TEL 86-1-62616352, 86-1-68577557, FAX 86-1-62616352, wst@public.sti.ac.cn. Ed. Zhang Zhihua. Adv. contact Wenkai Cheng.

500 JPN ISSN 0919-1801
SHIKOKU DAIGAKU KIYO. SHIZEN KAGAKU-HEN/SHIKOKU UNIVERSITY. BULLETIN. SERIES B. Text in Japanese. 1965. a. **Document type:** *Journal, Academic/Scholarly.*
Supersedes in part (in 1992): Shikoku Joshi Daigaku Kiyo/Shikoku Women's University. Bulletin (0286-9527); Which was formerly (until 1981): Shikoku Joshi Daigaku Kenkyu Kiyo (0286-9918)
Indexed: Z01.
Published by: Shikoku Daigaku, Ojin-cho, Tokushima-shi, Tokushima 771-1192, Japan.

500 JPN ISSN 0586-9943
➤ **SHIMANE DAIGAKU KYOIKUGAKUBU KIYO. SHIZEN KAGAKU/ SHIMANE UNIVERSITY. FACULTY OF EDUCATION. MEMOIRS. NATURAL SCIENCE.** Text in English, Japanese; Summaries in English. 1972. a. **Document type:** *Journal, Academic/Scholarly.*
Indexed: JPI.
Published by: Shimane Daigaku, Kyoikugakubu/Shimane University, Faculty of Education, 1060 Nishi-Kawatsu-cho, Matsue-shi, Shimane-ken 690-8504, Japan. FAX 81-852-32-6259. Circ: 340.

➤ **SHIMANE IKA DAIGAKU KIYO/SHIMANE MEDICAL UNIVERSITY. BULLETIN.** *see* MEDICAL SCIENCES

500.9 JPN
SHIMANE NO SHIZEN. Text in Japanese. 1976. a. **Description:** Contains news about the association, and about natural parks in Shimane Prefecture.
Published by: Shimane-ken Shizen Koen Kyokai, Shimane-ken Kankyo Seikatsubu Keikan Shizenka, 1 Tono-Machi, Matsue-shi, Shimane-ken 690-8501, Japan. TEL 81-852-22-5348, FAX 81-852-26-2142.

500 MNG
SHINJLEH UHAANY AKADEMIYN MEDEE/ACADEMY OF SCIENCES NEWS. Text in Mongol. 1961. q.
Indexed: BibLing.
Published by: Mongolian Academy of Sciences, PO Box 48 17, Ulan Bator, Mongolia. Ed. S Norovsambuu.

505 JPN ISSN 0583-063X
Q77 CODEN: JFSSB9
SHINSHU UNIVERSITY. FACULTY OF SCIENCE. JOURNAL/SHINSHU DAIGAKU RIGAKUBU KIYO. Text in Japanese, Multiple languages. 1966. s-a. per issue exchange basis.
Indexed: CCMJ, ChemAb, GeoRef, MSN, MathR, SpeleolAb, Z02.
—CASDDS, INIST.
Published by: Shinshu University, Faculty of Science/Shinshu Daigaku Rigakubu, 1-1 Asahi 3-chome, Matsumoto-shi, Nagano-ken 390-8621, Japan. FAX 81-263-37-2438. Ed. Yasuo Matsugu.

069 JPN ISSN 0387-8716
SHIRETOKO HAKUBUTSUKAN KENKYU HOKOKU/SHIRETOKO MUSEUM. BULLETIN. Text in Japanese; Summaries in English, Japanese. 1979. a. per issue exchange basis. **Document type:** *Bulletin.* **Description:** Publishes area studies of the northeast region of Hokkaido, including the coastal areas and the Sea of Okhotsk, including geology, ecology, zoology, botany, archaeology and history.
Indexed: Z01.
Published by: Shari-choritsu Shiretoko Hakubutsukan/Shiretoko Museum, 49 Hon-Machi, Shiyari-gun, shiyari-cho, Hokkaido 099-4113, Japan. TEL 81-1522-3-1256, FAX 81-1522-3-1257, sirehaku@ohotuku26.or.jp. Ed., R&P Hajime Nakagawa. Circ: 1,000.

500 IND ISSN 0250-5347
CODEN: JSUSDA
SHIVAJI UNIVERSITY. JOURNAL (SCIENCE & TECHNOLOGY). Text in English. 1968. a. **Document type:** *Journal, Academic/Scholarly.*
Supersedes in part (in 1976): Shivaji University. Journal (0368-4199)
—CASDDS.
Published by: Shivaji University, c/o D V Muley, Registrar, Vidyanagar, Kolhapur, Maharashtra 416 004, India. TEL 91-231-2609000, FAX 91-231-2692333, registrar@unishivaji.ac.in.

SHIYAN JIAOXUE YU YIQI/EXPERIMENT TEACHING AND APPARATUS. *see* EDUCATION

500 JPN ISSN 0914-6385
Q77
SHIZEN KAGAKU KENKYU (TOKUSHIMA)/UNIVERSITY OF TOKUSHIMA. FACULTY OF INTEGRATED ARTS AND SCIENCES. NATURAL SCIENCE RESEARCH. Text in Japanese; Summaries in English. 1988. a.
Indexed: CCMJ, MSN, MathR, Z01, Z02.
Published by: Tokushima Daigaku, Sogo Kagakubu/University of Tokushima, Faculty of Integrated Arts and Sciences, 1-1 Minami-Josanjima-cho, Tokushima-shi, 770-0814, Japan.

500 JPN ISSN 0441-0017
Q4 CODEN: SZKKAD
SHIZEN KAGAKU KENKYU (TOKYO)/HITOTSUBASHI UNIVERSITY RESEARCH SERIES. SCIENCES. Text in Japanese. 1959. a. **Document type:** *Academic/Scholarly.*
Indexed: JPI.
—CASDDS.
Published by: Hitotsubashi Daigaku/Hitotsubashi University, 2-1 Naka, Kunitachi-shi, Tokyo, 186, Japan. FAX 81-42-580-8914. Ed. Naomichi Yamada. Circ: 620.

500 JPN ISSN 1341-402X
QD1 CODEN: KHHDD4
SHIZEN KAGAKU KENKYUJO KENKYU HOKOKU/RESEARCH INSTITUTE OF NATURAL SCIENCE. BULLETIN. Text and summaries in English, Japanese. 1975. a. **Document type:** *Academic/Scholarly.* **Description:** Contains original papers.
Formerly (until 1994): Hiruzen Kenkyujo Kenkyu Hokoku (0385-2776)
—BLDSC (2696.025000), CASDDS.
Published by: Okayama Rika Daigaku, Shizen Kagaku Kenkyujo/Okayama University of Science, Research Institute of Natural Science, 1-1 Ridai-cho-Okayama, Okayama, 700-0005, Japan. TEL 81-86-2523161, FAX 81-86-2568480, itaya@rins.ous.ac.jp.

500 JPN ISSN 0285-8150
SHIZEN KAGAKU RONSO. Text in Japanese. 1969. a.
Indexed: JPI.
Published by: Kyoto Joshi Daigaku, Shizen Kagaku Hoken Taiiku Kenkyushitsu/Kyoto Women's University, Society of Natural Science and Physical Education, 35 Imagumano-Kitahiyoshi-cho, Higashiyama-ku, Kyoto-shi, 605-0926, Japan.

SHIZEN KANSATSUKAI KAIHO. *see* ENVIRONMENTAL STUDIES

500 JPN ISSN 0385-759X
SHIZEN KYOIKUEN HOKOKU/JAPAN. MINISTRY OF EDUCATION. NATIONAL SCIENCE MUSEUM. INSTITUTE FOR NATURE STUDY. MISCELLANEOUS REPORTS. Text and summaries in English, Japanese. 1969. a. **Document type:** *Government.*
Published by: Monbusho Kokuritsu Kagaku Hakubutsukan, Fuzoku Shizen Kyoikuen/Ministry of Education, National Science Museum, Institute for Nature Study, 21-5 Shirokanedai 5-chome, Minato-ku, Tokyo, 108-0071, Japan. TEL 03-3441-7176, FAX 03-3441-7012.

500.9 JPN ISSN 0078-6683
SHIZENSHI KENKYU/OSAKA MUSEUM OF NATURAL HISTORY. OCCASIONAL PAPERS. Text in English, Japanese; Summaries in English. 1968. irreg. (1-3/yr.). price varies. **Document type:** *Monographic series, Academic/Scholarly.*
Indexed: CABA, E12, P32, P40, SpeleolAb, W10, Z01.
—BLDSC (8267.370000), Linda Hall.
Published by: Oosaka-shiritsu Shizenshi Hakubutsukan/Osaka Museum of Natural History, 1-23 Nagaikoen, Higashisumiyoshi-ku, Osaka-shi, 546-0034, Japan. TEL 81-6-6697-6221, FAX 81-6-6697-6225, http://www.mus-nh.city.osaka.jp. Ed. Ryohei Yamanishi. Circ: 1,000.

500 JPN ISSN 0286-7311
SHIZUOKA DAIGAKU KYOIKUGAKUBU KENKYU HOKOKU. SHIZEN KAGAKU HEN/SHIZUOKA UNIVERSITY. FACULTY OF EDUCATION. BULLETIN. NATURAL SCIENCES SERIES. Text and summaries in English, Japanese. 1950. a. not commercially avail. **Document type:** *Academic/Scholarly.*
Indexed: JPI, Z01.
—BLDSC (2507.630000).
Published by: Shizuoka Daigaku, Kyoikugakubu, 836 Oya, shizuoka-shi, 422-8017, Japan. TEL 81-54-238-4572, FAX 81-54-238-5422.

505 JPN ISSN 0583-0923
Q77 CODEN: RFSSBT
SHIZUOKA UNIVERSITY. FACULTY OF SCIENCE. REPORTS/SHIZUOKA DAIGAKU RIGAKUBU KENKYU HOKOKU. Text in Multiple languages. 1965. a. per issue exchange basis. **Description:** Contains original papers on mathematics, physics, chemistry, radiochemistry, biology, and geoscience.
Indexed: B25, BIOSIS Prev, CCMJ, CIN, ChemAb, ChemTitl, GeoRef, INIS AtomInd, Inspec, MSN, MathR, MycolAb, SpeleolAb, Z01, Z02.
—CASDDS, IE, Ingenta, INIST.
Published by: Shizuoka Daigaku, Rigakubu/Shizuoka University, Faculty of Science, 836 Oya, Shizuoka, 422-8529, Japan. TEL 81-54-237-1111, FAX 81-54-237-9895. Circ: 500.

500 CHN ISSN 1004-9398
SHOUDU SHIFAN DAXUE XUEBAO (ZIRAN KEXUE BAN)/CAPITAL NORMAL UNIVERSITY. JOURNAL (NATURAL SCIENCE EDITION). Text in Chinese. 1976. q. USD 24.60 (effective 2009).
Formerly (until 1992): Beijing Shifan Xueyuan Xuebao (Ziran Kexue Ban)/Beijing Normal Institute. Journal (Natural Science Edition) (1000-5366)
Related titles: Online - full text ed.
Indexed: Z02.
—East View.
Published by: Shoudu Shifan Daxue/Capital Normal University, 105, Xisanhuanbei, Beijing, 100037, China. Ed. Mei Xiangming. **Dist. by:** China International Book Trading Corp, 35 Chegongzhuang Xilu, Haidian District, PO Box 399, Beijing 100044, China. TEL 86-10-68412045, FAX 86-10-68412023, cibtc@mail.cibtc.com.cn, http://www.cibtc.com.cn.

500.9 THA ISSN 0080-9462
QH1 CODEN: NHSAAC
➤ **SIAM SOCIETY. NATURAL HISTORY BULLETIN.** Text in English. 1913. s-a. free to members (effective 2005). bk.rev. bibl.; charts; illus.; maps. back issues avail. **Document type:** *Journal, Academic/Scholarly.*
Indexed: B25, BAS, BIOSIS Prev, GeoRef, MycolAb, SCOPUS, WildRev, Z01.
—BLDSC (6039.000000), Linda Hall.
Published by: Siam Society, 131 Soi Asoke, Sukhumvit 21, Bangkok, 10110, Thailand. TEL 662-661-6470-7, FAX 662-258-3491, http://www.siam-society.org. Ed. Warren Y Brockelman.

500 CHN ISSN 1009-3087
Q4 CODEN: SXGKFI
➤ **SICHUAN DAXUE XUEBAO (GONGCHENG KEXUE BAN).** Text in Chinese; Abstracts and contents page in Chinese, English. 1957. bi-m. CNY 15 per issue (effective 2011). 118 p./no.; **Document type:** *Journal, Academic/Scholarly.* **Description:** Covers the academic papers and research notes in the fields of hydraulic and civil engineering, chemistry and chemical engineering, material science and engineering, mechanical engineering, electrical engineering, applied physics, information engineering, etc.
Formerly (until Jan. 2000): Chengdu Keji Daxue Xuebao/Chengdu University of Science and Technology. Journal (0253-2263)
Related titles: Online - full text ed.; English ed.: Sichuan University. Journal (Engineering Science Edition). CNY 6 newsstand/cover domestic (effective 2000).
Indexed: A22, A28, APA, BrCerAb, C&ISA, CA/WCA, CCMJ, CIA, CIN, CPEI, CerAb, ChemAb, ChemTitl, CivEngAb, CorrAb, E&CAJ, E11, EEA, EMA, ESPM, EngInd, EnvEAb, H15, M&TEA, M09, MBF, METADEX, MSN, MathR, RASB, RefZh, SCOPUS, SolStAb, T04, WAA, Z02.
—BLDSC (4876.273000), CASDDS, East View, IE, Ingenta, Linda Hall.
Published by: Sichuan Daxue, No.24, South Section, 1st Ring Rd, Chengdu, Sichuan 610065, China. TEL 86-28-85401005, FAX 86-28-85401005. Ed. Heping Xie. **Dist. by:** China International Book Trading Corp, 35 Chegongzhuang Xilu, Haidian District, PO Box 399, Beijing 100044, China. TEL 86-10-68412045, FAX 86-10-68412023, cibtc@mail.cibtc.com.cn, http://www.cibtc.com.cn/.

500 CHN ISSN 0490-6756
QH7 CODEN: SCTHAO
SICHUAN DAXUE XUEBAO (ZIRAN KEXUE BAN)/SICHUAN UNIVERSITY. JOURNAL (NATURAL SCIENCE EDITION). Text in Chinese, English. 1955. bi-m. USD 31.20 (effective 2009). **Document type:** *Journal, Academic/Scholarly.*
Related titles: Online - full text ed.
Indexed: A22, B25, BIOSIS Prev, CCMJ, CIN, ChemAb, ChemTitl, INIS AtomInd, MSN, MathR, MycolAb, Z01, Z02.
—BLDSC (4876.275000), CASDDS, IE, Ingenta.
Published by: Sichuan Daxue, Xuebao Bianjibu, 29, Wangjiang Lu, Wenkelou, 156-shi, Chengdu, Sichuan 610064, China. TEL 86-28-85410396, FAX 86-28-85412393. Ed. Liu Yingming. Circ: 2,000. **Dist. by:** China International Book Trading Corp, 35 Chegongzhuang Xilu, Haidian District, PO Box 399, Beijing 100044, China. TEL 86-10-68412045, FAX 86-10-68412023, cibtc@mail.cibtc.com.cn, http://www.cibtc.com.cn.

500 CHN ISSN 1673-1549
SICHUAN LIGONG XUEYUAN XUEBAO (ZIRAN KEXUE BAN)/SICHUAN UNIVERSITY OF SCIENCE & ENGINEERING. JOURNAL (NATURAL SCIENCE EDITION). Text in Chinese. 1988. bi-m. USD 24.60 (effective 2009).
Formerly: Sichuan Qing-Huagong Xueyuan Xuebao/Sichuan Institute of Light Industry and Chemical Technology. Journal (1008-438X)
Related titles: Online - full text ed.
Published by: Sichuan Ligong Xueyuan, 180, Huixin Lu Xueyuan Jie, Zigong, 643000, China. TEL 86-813-5505839, FAX 86-813-3930085.

500 CHN ISSN 1001-8395
QH7
SICHUAN SHIFAN DAXUE XUEBAO (ZIRAN KEXUE BAN)/SICHUAN NORMAL UNIVERSITY. JOURNAL (NATURAL SCIENCE EDITION). Text in Chinese. 1978. bi-m. USD 21.60 (effective 2009). **Document type:** *Journal, Academic/Scholarly.*
Related titles: Online - full text ed.
Indexed: A22, CCMJ, MSN, MathR, RefZh, Z02.
—BLDSC (4876.269300), East View, IE, Ingenta.
Published by: Sichuan Shifan Daxue, Xuebao Bianjibu/Sichuan Normal University, 5, Jingan Lu, Chengdu, Sichuan 610066, China. TEL 86-28-4760704, FAX 86-28-4761284, http://www.sicnu.edu.cn/. **Dist. by:** China International Book Trading Corp, 35 Chegongzhuang Xilu, Haidian District, PO Box 399, Beijing 100044, China. TEL 86-10-68412045, FAX 86-10-68412023, cibtc@mail.cibtc.com.cn, http://www.cibtc.com.cn.

SICHUAN ZHIYE JISHU XUEYUAN XUEBAO/SICHUAN VOCATIONAL AND TECHNICAL COLLEGE. JOURNAL. *see* SOCIAL SCIENCES: COMPREHENSIVE WORKS

500 CHL ISSN 0716-8136
SIGLO XXI CIENCIA AND TECNOLOGIA. Text in Spanish. 1990. w. USD 360 in North America; USD 410 in Europe. adv. bk.rev. **Document type:** *Newspaper.* **Description:** Covers computers, info-sciences, and technology for youth and young adults.
Related titles: Online - full text ed.
Published by: El Mercurio S.A.P., Ave. Santa Maria, 5542, Apartado Postal 13 D, Las Condes, Santiago, Chile. TEL 562-3301461, FAX 562-2421128, TELEX 341635. Ed., R&P Nicolas Luco TEL 56-2-3301526. Pub. Agustin Edwards. Adv. contact Macarena Marchant. Circ: 90,000.

500 USA
SIGMA XI NEWSLETTER. Text in English. 1991. m. membership. **Document type:** *Newsletter.* **Description:** Contains society news and announcements.
Published by: Sigma XI, Scientific Research Society, PO Box 13975, Research Triangle Park, NC 27709-9890. TEL 919-549-4691.

506 USA ISSN 0080-9578
SIGMA ZETAN. Text in English. 1927. a. free to members (effective 2008).
Published by: Sigma Zeta, c/o Jim Hall, Our Lady of the Lake University, Department of Biology, 411 SW 24th St, San Antonio, TX 78207-4689. TEL 210-434-6711, ext 2245.

500 PHL ISSN 0037-5284
AS540
➤ **SILLIMAN JOURNAL.** Text and summaries in English. 1954. s-a. bk.rev. illus.; abstr.; bibl.; maps; stat. Index. back issues avail.; reprints avail. **Document type:** *Journal, Academic/Scholarly.* **Description:** Covers humanities and sciences with an emphasis on Negros, Cebu, and the Visayan region.
Related titles: Microform ed.: (from PQC).
Indexed: BAS, ChemAb, IPP, MLA, MLA-IB, Z01.
—Ingenta.
Published by: Silliman University, Dumaguete City, 6200, Philippines. TEL 63-35-4227208, FAX 63-35-4227208. Ed. Margaret Helen Udarbe-Alvarez.

500 600 THA ISSN 1905-9159
Q127.I43
SILPAKORN UNIVERSITY. SCIENCE AND TECHNOLOGY JOURNAL. Text in English. 2007. irreg. free (effective 2011). **Document type:** *Journal, Academic/Scholarly.*
Media: Online - full text.
Indexed: A34, A36, Agr, BP, C25, C30, CABA, E12, F08, F11, F12, FCA, G11, GH, H16, I11, IndVet, N02, N03, N04, P32, P33, P40, PGrRegA, PHN&I, R11, R13, RA&MP, RM&VM, S13, S16, VS.
Published by: Silpakorn University, Sanamchandra Palace, Campus, Nakhom Pathom, 73000, Thailand. Ed. Onoomar Poobrasert Toyama.

SIMON STEVIN GEZEL. *see* TECHNOLOGY: COMPREHENSIVE WORKS

500 PAK ISSN 1813-1743
SINDH UNIVERSITY RESEARCH JOURNAL (SCIENCE SERIES). Text in English. 1964. s-a. **Document type:** *Journal, Academic/Scholarly.*
Related titles: Online - full text ed.
Indexed: A34, A37, A38, AgrForAb, B23, B25, BA, BIOSIS Prev, BP, C25, C30, CABA, D01, E12, F08, F12, FCA, G11, GH, H16, H17, I11, MaizeAb, N02, N03, N04, N05, P32, P33, P37, P39, P40, R08, R11, R12, R13, S12, S13, S16, SoyAb, T05, TAR, W11.
Published by: University of Sindh, Faculty of Natural Sceicnes, Allama I.I.Kazi Campus, Sindh, 76080, Pakistan. TEL 92-22-2771681 ext 2091, dean@science.usindh.edu.pk. Ed. Tahir Rajput.

500 ETH ISSN 0379-2897
Q91.E84 CODEN: SINTD7
➤ **SINET**; an Ethiopian journal of science. Text in English. 1978. 2/yr. ETB 20 domestic to individuals; USD 20 foreign to individuals; ETB 50 domestic to institutions; USD 50 foreign to institutions (effective 2004). **Document type:** *Journal, Academic/Scholarly.* **Description:** Features review articles, research papers or short notes in science and technology and related disciplines.
Related titles: Online - full text ed.: (from IngentaConnect).
Indexed: A34, A35, A37, A38, AgBio, AgrForAb, B23, C25, C30, CABA, CCMJ, CIS, D01, E12, F08, F12, FCA, GH, GeoRef, H16, I11, INIS AtomInd, IndVet, MSN, MaizeAb, MathR, N02, N03, N04, P32, P33, P37, P40, PGegResA, PGrRegA, R07, R08, R13, S&MA, S13, S16, S17, SoyAb, SpeleolAb, T05, TriticAb, VS, W10, W11, Z01.
—BLDSC (8285.410000), CASDDS, Ingenta.
Published by: Addis Ababa University, Faculty of Science, PO Box 31226, Addis Ababa, Ethiopia. TEL 251-1-125110, FAX 251-1-552350, TELEX 21205. Ed. Masresha Fetene.

500 ETH ISSN 1011-9507
Q1 CODEN: SINNEO
SINET NEWSLETTER. Text in English. 1978. m. **Document type:** *Newsletter.*
Indexed: SpeleolAb.
Published by: Addis Ababa University, Faculty of Science, PO Box 31226, Addis Ababa, Ethiopia. TEL 251-1-125110, FAX 251-1-552350. Ed. Eshetu Wencheko.

S

500 ETH
SINET: PROCEEDINGS OF ANNUAL PROGRAMMES REVIEW CONFERENCE. Text in English. 1978. a. **Document type:** *Proceedings.*
Published by: Addis Ababa University, Faculty of Science, PO Box 31226, Addis Ababa, Ethiopia. TEL 251-1-553177, FAX 251-1-552112. Ed. Masresha Fetene.

500 SGP
SINGAPORE. NATIONAL SCIENCE AND TECHNOLOGY BOARD. ANNUAL REPORTS. Text in English. 1972. a. free. charts; illus.; stat.
Formerly: Singapore. Science Council. Annual Reports
Published by: National Science and Technology Board, Singapore Science Park, 16 Science Park Dr, 01-03 The Pasteur, Singapore, 118227, Singapore. TEL 7797066, FAX 7771711.

500 KOR ISSN 1738-9895
SINLOESEONG EUNG'YONG YEON'GU/JOURNAL OF THE APPLIED RELIABILITY. Text in Korean. 2000. q. membership. **Document type:** *Journal, Academic/Scholarly.*
—BLDSC (4947.005000), IE.
Published by: Korean Reliability Society, Ajou University, Department of Industrial Information Systems Engineering, San 5 Wonchon-Dong, Youngtong-Gu, Suwon 443-749, Suwon, 443-749, Korea, S. TEL 86-31-2192957, FAX 86-31-2192982, koras@koras.or.kr. Ed. Hwan Jung Kim TEL 82-63-2901521.

500 USA ISSN 2153-0963
▼ **SINO SCIENCE REVIEW: SERIES A, GENERAL SCIENCES.** Text in English. 2010 (Feb.). bi-m. free (effective 2011). **Document type:** *Journal, Academic/Scholarly.* **Description:** Features Chinese research in the general sciences.
Media: Online - full text.
Published by: MJS USA, LLC, 4413 Grand Ave, Western Springs, IL 60558. TEL 708-246-7870, martin.stroka@gmail.com, http://www.mjschina.com/.

500 600 ECU ISSN 0253-5033
Q224.3.E2
SISTEMA NACIONAL DE INFORMACION CIENTIFICA Y TECNOLOGIA. BOLETIN. Key Title: Boletin S I N I C Y T. Text in Spanish. 1982. s-a. free. bk.rev. charts; illus. **Document type:** *Bulletin.* **Description:** Covers themes related to the development of scientific and technological information in Ecuador and Latin America.
Published by: Fundacion para la Ciencia y la Tecnologia, Edificio Banco de Prestamos, piso 9, Ave. Patria, 850, y 10 de Agosto, Casilla 17-12-00404, Quito, Pichincha, Ecuador. TEL 593-2-509027, FAX 593-2-509054, TELEX 22027 FUNCYT DE. Circ: 1,200.
Co-sponsor: Programa Regional de Desarrollo Cientifico y Tecnologico de la Organizacion de los Estados Americanos.

500 333.72 DNK ISSN 1602-1908
SKOV OG NATUR; nyhedsbrev. Text in Danish. 1996. s-m. back issues avail. **Document type:** *Newsletter, Consumer.*
Formerly (until 2002): Essens (1396-1209)
Media: Online - full content.
Published by: Miljoeministeriet, Skov- og Naturstyrelsen/Ministry of the Environment. Danish Forest & Nature Agency, Haraldsgade 53, Copenhagen OE, 2100, Denmark. TEL 45-39-472000, FAX 45-39-279899, sns@sns.dk.

SLOVENSKA AKADEMIJA ZNANOSTI IN UMETNOSTI. LETOPIS/ SLOVENIAN ACADEMY OF SCIENCES AND ARTS. YEARBOOK. *see* ART

508 SVN ISSN 0352-5090
Q69
SLOVENSKA AKADEMIJA ZNANOSTI IN UMETNOSTI. RAZRED ZA NARAVOSLOVNE VEDE. RAZPRAVE/ACADEMIA SCIENTIARUM ET ARTIUM SLOVENICA. CLASSIS 4: HISTORIA NATURALIS. DISSERTATIONES. Text in English, Slovenian. irreg. **Document type:** *Monographic series, Academic/Scholarly.*
Former titles (until 1982): Slovenska Akademija Znanosti in Umetnosti. Razred za Prirodoslovne Vede. Razprave (0351-9791); (until 1975): Slovenska Akademija Znanosti in Umetnosti. Razred za Prirodoslovne in Medicinske Vede. Oddelek za Prorodoslovne Vede. Razprave (0583-6107)
Indexed: A34, ASFA, B21, CABA, E12, ESPM, F08, F12, G11, GeoRef, IBR, IBZ, IndVet, P32, P40, R07, RefZh, S13, S16, S17, VS, W10.
—INIST, Linda Hall.
Published by: Slovenska Akademija Znanosti in Umetnosti/Slovenian Academy of Sciences and Arts, Novi trg 3-5, Ljubljana, 1000, Slovenia. TEL 386-1-4706100, FAX 386-1-4253462, sazu@sazu.si, http://www.sazu.si. Eds. Earnest Mayer, Matjaz Godala, Milan Herak, Mitja Zupancic. Pub. Dusan Merhar.

SMITHSONIAN. *see* SOCIAL SCIENCES: COMPREHENSIVE WORKS

500 USA ISSN 0093-8335
Q11.S8
SMITHSONIAN OPPORTUNITIES FOR RESEARCH AND STUDY IN HISTORY, ART, SCIENCE. Variant title: Smithsonian Research Opportunities. Text in English. 1964. a. index. **Document type:** *Journal, Academic/Scholarly.*
Former titles (until 1972): Smithsonian Institution. Opportunities for Research and Advanced Study (0191-3158); (until 1971): Smithsonian Institution. Office of Academic Programs. Smithsonian Research Opportunities
Published by: Smithsonian Institution, Office of Fellowships and Grants, SI Bldg, Rm 153, MRC 010, PO Box 37012, Washington, DC 20013. TEL 202-633-1000, info@si.edu, http://www.si.edu.

▼ **SOCIAL AND NATURAL SCIENCES JOURNAL.** *see* SOCIAL SCIENCES: COMPREHENSIVE WORKS

500 GBR ISSN 0306-3127
Q1
➤ **SOCIAL STUDIES OF SCIENCE**; an international review of research in the social dimensions of science and technology. Abbreviated title: S S S. Text in English. 1971. bi-m. USD 1,594, GBP 862 combined subscription to institutions (print & online eds.); USD 1,562, GBP 845 to institutions (effective 2011). adv. bk.rev. illus. index. back issues avail.; reprint service avail. from PSC. **Document type:** *Journal, Academic/Scholarly.* **Description:** Deals with the crucial issues in the relationship between science and society. It covers a range of topics, publishing important papers on new concepts, new methods and new research results. The journal is multidisciplinary, publishing work from a range of fields including political science, sociology, economics, history, philosophy, psychology, social anthropology and legal and educational disciplines.
Formerly (until 1975): Science Studies (0036-8539)
Related titles: Online - full text ed.: ISSN 1460-3659. USD 1,435, GBP 776 to institutions (effective 2011).
Indexed: A01, A02, A03, A08, A20, A22, A34, A35, A36, A38, ASCA, AgBio, AmH&L, ArtHuCI, B01, B06, B07, B09, C25, CA, CABA, CPE, CurCont, DIP, E01, E03, E12, EMBASE, ERI, ExcerpMed, F08, F12, FR, GH, GeoRef, H04, H16, HECAB, HistAb, I13, IBR, IBSS, IBZ, IPB, ISR, IndVet, Inpharma, LT, MEA&I, MEDLINE, MaizeAb, N02, P02, P04, P10, P11, P30, P32, P33, P34, P37, P39, P40, P42, P48, P52, P53, P54, P56, PCI, PQC, PSA, R07, R08, R12, RA&MP, RASB, RRTA, S02, S03, S10, S13, S16, SCI, SCOPUS, SD, SOPODA, SSA, SSCI, SociolAb, SoyAb, SpeleolAb, T02, T05, TAR, V02, VS, W07, W10, W11.
—BLDSC (8318.214100), IE, Infotrieve, Ingenta, INIST. **CCC.**
Published by: Sage Publications Ltd. (Subsidiary of: Sage Publications, Inc.), 1 Oliver's Yard, 55 City Rd, London, EC1Y 1SP, United Kingdom. TEL 44-20-73248500, FAX 44-20-73248600, info@sagepub.co.uk, http://www.uk.sagepub.com/home.nav. Ed. Michael J Lynch. adv.: B&W page GBP 450; 130 x 205. **Subscr. in the Americas to:** Sage Publications, Inc., 2455 Teller Rd, Thousand Oaks, CA 91320. TEL 805-499-9774, FAX 805-499-0871, journals@sagepub.com.

500 ARG ISSN 0037-8437
Q33 CODEN: ASCAA2
➤ **SOCIEDAD CIENTIFICA ARGENTINA. ANALES.** Text in English, Spanish; Summaries in English. 1876. a. USD 50. adv. bk.rev. bibl.; charts; illus. index. **Document type:** *Journal, Academic/Scholarly.*
Indexed: ChemAb, FR, GeoRef, SpeleolAb, Z02.
—CASDDS, INIST, Linda Hall.
Published by: Sociedad Cientifica Argentina, Comision de Cursos y Conferencias, Avda. Santa Fe, 1145, Buenos Aires, 1059, Argentina. TEL 54-114-8164745. Ed. Eduardo A Castro. Circ: 3,000 (controlled).

500.9 VEN ISSN 0037-8518
Q4 CODEN: SCNSAR
SOCIEDAD DE CIENCIAS NATURALES LA SALLE. MEMORIA. Text in Spanish. 1940. s-a. adv. charts; illus. index, cum.index: 1940-1990. reprint service avail. from PSC. **Document type:** *Journal.*
Incorporates: Novedades Cientificas Serie Zoologia
Related titles: Microfilm ed.: (from PQC).
Indexed: ASFA, B21, C01, ChemAb, ESPM, GeoRef, IBR, IBZ, SpeleolAb.
—INIST.
Published by: Fundacion la Salle de Ciencias Naturales, Ave. Boyaca-Mariperez, Piso 5, Apdo 1930, Carcacas, 1010A, Venezuela. Ed. Carlos Lasso. Circ: 1,300.

509 600 COL ISSN 0185-5107
SOCIEDAD LATINOAMERICANA DE HISTORIA DE LA CIENCIA Y LA TECNOLOGIA. BOLETIN INFORMATIVO. Text in English, Spanish. 1983. 3/yr. USD 5. bk.rev.
Published by: Sociedad Latinoamericana de Historia de la Ciencia y la Tecnologia, c/o Colciencias, Tranversal 9a 133-28, Bogota, DE, Colombia. Ed. Luis Carlos Arboleda.

500 BRA ISSN 0103-1899
SOCIEDADE BRASILEIRA DE HISTORIA DA CIENCIA. BOLETIM. Text in Portuguese. 1984. s-a. USD 20 to members. bk.rev. bibl. **Document type:** *Newsletter.* **Description:** Presents news of recent, past and future events related to history of science.
Published by: Sociedade Brasileira de Historia da Ciencia, c/o Centro Simao Mathias de Estudos em Historia da Ciencia, Potificia Universidade Catolica de Sao Paulo, Rua Marques de Paranagua, Predio 1, Sala 2, Sao Paulo, SP 01303-050, Brazil. TEL 55-11-2561622, FAX 55-11-8225771. Eds. Ana Maria Goldfarb, Vera Cecilia Mavellique.

500 BRA ISSN 0103-7188
Q124.6
SOCIEDADE BRASILEIRA DE HISTORIA DA CIENCIA. REVISTA. Text in Portuguese. 1985. irreg. **Document type:** *Journal, Academic/Scholarly.*
Published by: Sociedade Brasileira de Historia da Ciencia, c/o Centro Simao Mathias de Estudos em Historia da Ciencia, Potificia Universidade Catolica de Sao Paulo, Rua Marques de Paranagua, Predio 1, Sala 2, Sao Paulo, SP 01303-050, Brazil. TEL 55-11-2561622, FAX 55-11-8225771, cesimach@exactas.pucsp.br.

SOCIETA DEI NATURALISTI E MATEMATICI DI MODENA. ATTI. *see* MATHEMATICS

508 ITA ISSN 0037-8844
Q54 CODEN: ASIMAY
SOCIETA ITALIANA DI SCIENZE NATURALI E DEL MUSEO CIVICO DI STORIA NATURALE. ATTI. Text in Italian, English. 1856. s-a. free to members. bk.rev. charts; illus. index. back issues avail. **Document type:** *Proceedings, Academic/Scholarly.*
Former titles (until 1895): Societa Italiana di Scienze Naturali. Atti (1124-3643); (until 1859): Societa Geologica Residente in Milano. Atti (1124-3635)
Indexed: ChemAb, FR, GeoRef, RefZh, SpeleolAb, WildRev, Z01.
—CASDDS, INIST, Linda Hall.
Published by: Societa Italiana di Scienze Naturali, Corso Venezia 55, Milan, MI 20121, Italy. TEL 39-02-795965, FAX 39-02-795965, http://www.scienzenaturali.org.

500.9 ITA ISSN 0376-2726
Q54 CODEN: MINSA3
SOCIETA ITALIANA DI SCIENZE NATURALI E DEL MUSEO CIVICO DI STORIA NATURALE. MEMORIE. Text in Italian. 1865. irreg. price varies. back issues avail. **Document type:** *Monographic series, Academic/Scholarly.*
Indexed: GeoRef, RefZh, SpeleolAb, WildRev, Z01.
—Linda Hall.
Published by: Societa Italiana di Scienze Naturali, Corso Venezia 55, Milan, MI 20121, Italy. TEL 39-02-795965, FAX 39-02-795965, http://www.scienzenaturali.org.

500 ITA ISSN 0371-0424
SOCIETA ITALIANA PER IL PROGRESSO DELLE SCIENZE. ATTI DELLA RIUNIONE. Text in Italian. 1907. biennial. **Document type:** *Proceedings, Academic/Scholarly.*
Published by: Societa Italiana per il Progresso delle Scienze (S I P S), Via dell'Universita 11, Rome, 00185, Italy. TEL 39-06-4440515, sips@sipsinfo.it, http://www.sipsinfo.it.

508 ITA ISSN 0392-6710
CODEN: BSNTDQ
SOCIETA SARDA DI SCIENZE NATURALI. BOLLETTINO. Text in English, French, Italian; Summaries in English, Italian. 1967. a. bk.rev. index. back issues avail. **Document type:** *Journal, Academic/ Scholarly.*
Indexed: B25, BIOSIS Prev, MycolAb.
—INIST.
Published by: Societa Sarda di Scienze Naturali, Via Muroni 25, Sassari, SS 07100, Italy. TEL 39-079-237087. Ed., R&P, Adv. contact Bruno Corrias.

508 CHE ISSN 0379-1254
SOCIETA TICINESE DI SCIENZE NATURALI. BOLLETTINO. Variant title: Bollettino della Societa Ticinese di Scienze Naturali. Text in Italian. 1904. s-a. CHF 30 domestic; CHF 40 foreign. **Document type:** *Bulletin, Academic/Scholarly.* **Description:** Contains scientific articles and features relating to the southern slope of the Swiss Alps.
Indexed: SpeleolAb, Z01.
Published by: Societa Ticinese di Scienze Naturali, c/o Museo Cantonale Storia Naturale, Viale C Cattaneo 4, Lugano, 6900, Switzerland. TEL 41-91-9115380, FAX 41-91-9115389, pia.giorgetti@ti.ch.

508 CHE ISSN 1421-5586
SOCIETA TICINESE DI SCIENZE NATURALI. MEMORIE. Variant title: Memorie della Societa Ticinese di Scienze Naturali. Text in Italian. 1987. irreg. CHF 30 per vol. domestic; CHF 40 per vol. foreign. **Document type:** *Monographic series, Abstract/Index.* **Description:** Contains scientific articles and features concerning the southern slope of the Swiss Alps.
Indexed: Z01.
Published by: Societa Ticinese di Scienze Naturali, c/o Museo Cantonale Storia Naturale, Viale C Cattaneo 4, Lugano, 6900, Switzerland. TEL 41-91-9115380, FAX 41-91-9115389, pia.giorgetti@ti.ch.

500 ITA ISSN 0365-7655
QH7 CODEN: ATVAA2
SOCIETA TOSCANA DI SCIENZA NATURALI. ATTI. SERIE A (ABIOLOGICA). Text in Italian. 1875. a. EUR 25 domestic; EUR 40 foreign (effective 2009). **Document type:** *Proceedings, Academic/ Scholarly.*
Supersedes in part (in 1948): Societa Toscana di Scienze Naturali Residente in Pisa. Atti e Memorie (0365-7108); Which was formerly (until 1880): Societa Toscana di Scienze Naturali Residente in Pisa. Atti (0394-7165)
Related titles: Online - full text ed.
Indexed: GeoRef, SpeleolAb, Z01.
—CASDDS, Linda Hall.
Published by: (Societa Toscana di Scienze Naturali), Edizioni Plus - Universita di Pisa (Pisa University Press), Lungarno Pacinotti 43, Pisa, Italy. TEL 39-050-2212056, FAX 39-050-2212945, http://www.edizioniplus.it. Ed. Rodolfo Carosi.

408 500 ITA ISSN 0392-9450
SOCIETA VENEZIANA DI SCIENZE NATURALI. LAVORI. Text in Italian, English. 1976. a. EUR 30 to individuals; EUR 32 to institutions (effective 2003). illus. 100 p./no.; back issues avail. **Document type:** *Journal, Academic/Scholarly.* **Description:** Covers topics dealing with various natural aspects of northeastern Italy.
Indexed: A29, ASFA, B21, B25, BIOSIS Prev, ChemoAb, ESPM, EntAb, MycolAb, VirolAbstr, Z01.
—BLDSC (5160.870800).
Published by: Societa Veneziana di Scienze Naturali (S V S N), c/o Museo Civico di Storia Naturale, Fontego dei Turchi, S. Croce 1730, Venice, VE 30135, Italy. TEL 39-041-2750206, FAX 39-041-721000. Circ: 400.

508 ESP ISSN 0212-260X
QH171.2 CODEN: BSHBEB
SOCIETAT D'HISTORIA NATURAL DE LES BALEARS. BOLLETI. Text in Catalan, English, French, German, Italian, Spanish. 1955. a. bk.rev. **Document type:** *Journal, Trade.*
Formerly (until 1979): Sociedad de Historia Natural de Baleares. Boletin (0583-7405)
Indexed: A34, A35, AgBio, CABA, E12, F08, F12, G11, GEOBASE, GH, GeoRef, H16, IECT, IndVet, LT, O01, P32, P37, P40, PGegResA, R07, RA&MP, RRTA, S13, S16, SCOPUS, SpeleolAb, VS, W10, Z01.
Published by: Societat d'Historia Natural de les Balears, Sant Roc 4, Palma de Mallorca, 07001, Spain. FAX 34-971-719667, http://www.shnb.org/societat.htm. Circ: 1,000.

509 CHE ISSN 0252-7960
Q67
SOCIETE DE PHYSIQUE ET D'HISTOIRE NATURELLE DE GENEVE. MEMOIRES. Text in English. 1821. irreg.
Indexed: GeoRef.
—Linda Hall.
Published by: Societe de Physique et d'Histoire Naturelle de Geneve, Museum d'Histoire Naturelle, Case Postale 6434, Geneva 6, 1211, Switzerland.

500 800 POL ISSN 0459-6854
AS262.L6 CODEN: BSSEA3
SOCIETE DES SCIENCES ET DES LETTRES DE LODZ. BULLETIN. Text in English, French, German, Russian. 1960. irreg., latest vol.58, 2008. price varies. bibl.; illus. **Document type:** *Journal, Academic/ Scholarly.*

Formed by the merger of (19??-1960): Societe des Sciences et des Lettres de Lodz. Bulletin. Classe 1, de Linguistique, de Litterature et de Philosophie (0860-9136); (1950-1960): Societe des Sciences et des Lettres de Lodz. Bulletin. Classe 3, de Sciences Mathematiques et Naturelles (0376-0472); (1952-1960): Societe des Sciences et des Lettres de Lodz. Bulletin. Classe 4, de Sciences Medicales (0458-1652)
Indexed: CCMJ, GeoRef, MSN, MathR, RefZh, SpeleolAb, Z02.
—INIST, Linda Hall.
Published by: Lodzkie Towarzystwo Naukowe/Lodz Scientific Society, ul. M. Sklodowskiej-Curie 11, Lodz, 90-505, Poland. TEL 48-42-6655459, FAX 48-42-6655464, biuro@ltn.lodz.pl, http://www.ltn.lodz.pl. Ed. Julian Lawrynowicz. Circ: 500.

500 FRA ISSN 1154-7472
SOCIETE DES SCIENCES HISTORIQUES & NATURELLES DE LA CORSE. BULLETIN. Text in French. 1961. q. EUR 56 (effective 2010). **Document type:** *Bulletin.*
Supersedes in part (in 1961): Etudes Corses (0421-5893); Which was formed by the 1954 merger of: La Societe des Sciences Historiques et Naturelles de la Corse. Bulletin (0755-1932); Corse Historique (0574-1653)
Indexed: Z01.
Published by: Societe des Sciences Historiques & Naturelles de la Corse, 1, Place Vincenti, Bastia, 20200, France. infos@societesciencescorse.com, http://www.societesciencescorse.fr/php.

500 570 FRA ISSN 0153-9361
SOCIETE D'ETUDES SCIENTIFIQUES DE L'ANJOU. BULLETIN. Text in French. 1872. a. EUR 15 per issue (effective 2009). **Document type:** *Bulletin, Academic/Scholarly.*
Formerly (until 1961): Societe d'Etudes Scientifiques d'Angers. Bulletin (1145-7317)
Indexed: GeoRef, Z01.
—INIST.
Published by: Societe d'Etudes Scientifiques de l'Anjou, Arboretum, 9 rue du Chateau d'Orgemont, Angers, 49000, France. http://www.sauvegarde-anjou.org/quisommesnous/sesa/sesaindex.htm.

500 FRA ISSN 0750-6473
SOCIETE D'ETUDES SCIENTIFIQUES DE L'ANJOU. MEMOIRES. Text in French. 1972. irreg., latest vol.17, 2005. **Document type:** *Monographic series, Academic/Scholarly.*
Indexed: GeoRef, Z01.
—INIST.
Published by: Societe d'Etudes Scientifiques de l'Anjou, Arboretum, 9 rue du Chateau d'Orgemont, Angers, 49000, France. http://www.sauvegarde-anjou.org/quisommesnous/sesa/sesaindex.htm.

500.9 FRA ISSN 0753-4655
SOCIETE D'HISTOIRE NATURELLE DU DOUBS. BULLETIN. Text in French; Abstracts occasionally in English. 1900; N.S. 1968. a., latest vol.91, 2007. EUR 15 to non-members; EUR 5 to members (effective 2009). adv. bk.rev. bibl.; charts. cum.index. **Document type:** *Bulletin, Academic/Scholarly.*
Former titles (until 1978): Federation des Societes d'Histoire Naturelle de Franche-Comte. Bulletin (0376-1681); (until 1968): Societe d'Histoire Naturelle du Doubs. Bulletin (0366-3280); Which incorporated (1955-1959): La Societe d'Histoire Naturelle du Doubs. Bulletin. Supplement (1149-459X); (until 1917): Societe d'Histoire Naturelle du Doubs (0014-9357)
Indexed: VITIS.
—INIST.
Published by: Societe d'Histoire Naturelle du Doubs, UFR des Sciences, La Bouloie, 16, route de Gray, Besancon, Cedex 25030, France. presidente@shnd.fr, http://www.shnd.fr. Ed. Bernard Bonnet. Circ: 500.

500.9 FRA ISSN 0291-8390
QH3
SOCIETE D'HISTOIRE NATURELLE ET DES AMIS DU MUSEUM D'AUTUN. BULLETIN TRIMESTRIEL. Text in French; Summaries in English, French. 1888. q. back issues avail. **Document type:** *Bulletin.*
Former titles (until 1968): L'Eduen (0992-9487); (until 1949): Societe d'Histoire Naturelle d'Autun. Bulletin (1256-8996)
Indexed: GeoRef, RefZh, Z01.
—INIST.
Published by: Societe d'Histoire Naturelle et des Amis du Museum d'Autun, 15 rue St Antoine, Autun, 71400, France. TEL 33-3-85523407. Pub. Robert Pillon. Circ: 500.

500 630 FRA ISSN 0373-8701
QK1
SOCIETE D'HORTICULTURE ET D'HISTOIRE NATURELLE DE L'HERAULT. ANNALES. Text in French. 1861.
Indexed: GeoRef, Z01.
—INIST. **CCC.**
Published by: Societe d'Horticulture et d'Histoire Naturelle de l'Herault, Institut de Botanique, 163 rue Auguste Broussonnet, Montpellier, 34070, France.

502 CHE ISSN 0366-3256
Q67 CODEN: BSFNAX
SOCIETE FRIBOURGEOISE DES SCIENCES NATURELLES. BULLETIN. Text in French. 1880. s-a. free to members (effective 2009). **Document type:** *Journal, Academic/Scholarly.*
Incorporated (1904-1948): Societe Fribourgeoise des Sciences Naturelles. Memoires. Mathematique et Physique (0369-1985); (1900-1947): Societe Fribourgeoise des Sciences Naturelles. Memoires. Geologie et Geographie (0369-1993); (1907-1941): Societe Fribourgeoise des Sciences Naturelles. Memoires. Zoologie (0369-2019); (1901-1929): Societe Fribourgeoise des Sciences Naturelles. Memoires. Botanique (0369-1969); (1900-1928): Societe Fribourgeoise des Sciences Naturelles. Memoires. Chimie (0369-1977); (1908-1923): Societe Fribourgeoise des Sciences Naturelles. Memoires. Physiologie, Hygiene, Bacteriologie (0369-2000)
Indexed: GeoRef, RefZh, Z01.
—INIST.
Published by: Societe Fribourgeoise des Sciences Naturelles, Universite de Fribourg, Faculte des Sciences, Fribourg, 1700, Switzerland. TEL 41-26-3008970, http://www.unifr.ch/sfsn.

500 BEL ISSN 0037-9565
Q56 CODEN: BSRSA6
SOCIETE ROYALE DES SCIENCES DE LIEGE. BULLETIN. Text in English, French. 1931. 6/yr. charts. 500 p./no.; **Document type:** *Journal, Academic/Scholarly.*
Indexed: A22, ApMecR, CCMJ, CIN, ChemAb, ChemTitl, EngInd, FR, GeoRef, IBR, IBZ, Inspec, MSN, MathR, RASB, SCOPUS, SpeleolAb, Z01, Z02.
—BLDSC (2751.000000), AskIEEE, CASDDS, IE, Infotrieve, Ingenta, INIST, Linda Hall. **CCC.**
Published by: Societe Royale des Sciences de Liege, Univesite de Liege, Institut de Mathematique, Grande Traverse 12, Bat B37, Liege, 4000, Belgium. FAX 32-4-3669547, jaghion@ulg.ac.be, http://www.srsl-ulg.net. Ed., Pub., R&P J Aghion TEL 32-04-3663841. Circ: 24 (paid); 550 (controlled).

500 300 FRA ISSN 0995-9181
LA SOCIETE SCIENTIFIQUE ET LITTERAIRE DE CANNES ET DE L'ARRONDISSEMENT DE GRASSE. ANNALES. Text in French. 1869; N.S. 1929. a., latest vol.53, 2008. **Document type:** *Journal, Academic/Scholarly.*
Formerly (until 1879): Memoires de la Societe des Sciences Naturelles, des Lettres et des Beaux-arts de Cannes et de l'Arrondissement de Grasse (0995-9173)
Indexed: FR, GeoRef.
—INIST.
Published by: Societe Scientifique et Litteraire de Cannes et de l'Arrondissement de Grasse, Bibliotheque Municipale, Avenue Jean-de-Noailles, Cannes, 06400, France.

500.1 CHE ISSN 0037-9603
Q67 CODEN: BSVAA6
➤ **SOCIETE VAUDOISE DES SCIENCES NATURELLES. BULLETIN.** Text in French; Summaries in English, German, Italian. 1844. s-a. bk.rev. bibl.; charts; illus. index, cum.index: vols.1-50, 51-60. reprints avail. **Document type:** *Journal, Academic/Scholarly.* **Description:** Explores various issues in the natural sciences, including biology, geology, and environmental studies, as well as botany, physics, and mathematics.
Indexed: B21, B25, BIOSIS Prev, ChemAb, ESPM, EntAb, FR, GEOBASE, GeoRef, IBR, IBZ, Inspec, MycolAb, SCOPUS, SWRA, SpeleolAb, Z01.
—INIST, Linda Hall.
Published by: Societe Vaudoise des Sciences Naturelles, Palais de Rumine, Lausanne, 1005, Switzerland. TEL 41-21-312-4334. Ed. Jerome Pellet.

500.1 CHE ISSN 0037-9611
Q67 CODEN: MSVNAU
SOCIETE VAUDOISE DES SCIENCES NATURELLES. MEMOIRES. Text in French; Summaries in English, German, Italian. 1922. irreg. price varies. adv. bibl.; charts; illus.; maps. index, cum.index: vols.1-17. reprints avail. **Document type:** *Academic/Scholarly.* **Description:** Scientific studies in geology, paleontology, botany, zoology, physiology, agronomy, chemistry, ecology, ethnology, mathematics, medicine, meteorology, and physics.
Indexed: ASFA, B21, B25, BIOSIS Prev, ChemAb, GeoRef, MycolAb, SCOPUS, SpeleolAb, Z01.
—INIST, Linda Hall.
Published by: Societe Vaudoise des Sciences Naturelles, Palais de Rumine, Lausanne, 1005, Switzerland. TEL 021-3124334. Ed. Piere Gex.

SOCIETY FOR COMMON INSIGHTS. JOURNAL. *see* RELIGIONS AND THEOLOGY

500 MWI ISSN 0037-993X
DT858 CODEN: SMJODY
SOCIETY OF MALAWI JOURNAL. Text in English. 1970 (vol.23). s-a. USD 20 (effective 1992). bk.rev. charts; illus.; stat. index. **Document type:** *Journal, Academic/Scholarly.*
Formerly (until 1965): Nyasaland Journal
Indexed: A01, AICP, ASD, HistAb, MLA-IB, P30, PLESA, RASB.
Published by: Society of Malawi, PO Box 125, Blantyre, Malawi. TEL 265-630375. Ed. T Hopper. Circ: 500.

▼ **SOCIOLOGIA Y TECNOCIENCIA**; revista digital de sociologia del sistema tecnocientifico. *see* SOCIAL SCIENCES: COMPREHENSIVE WORKS

SOCIOLOGY OF THE SCIENCES LIBRARY. *see* SOCIOLOGY

301 NLD ISSN 0167-2320
➤ **SOCIOLOGY OF THE SCIENCES. YEARBOOK.** Key Title: Sociology of the Sciences. Text in English. 1977. a., latest vol.26, 2007. price varies. **Document type:** *Monographic series, Academic/Scholarly.*
Indexed: A22, RASB.
—BLDSC (8319.696700), IE, Ingenta. **CCC.**
Published by: Springer Netherlands (Subsidiary of: Springer Science+Business Media), Van Godewijckstraat 30, Dordrecht, 3311 GX, Netherlands. TEL 31-78-6576050, FAX 31-78-6576474. Ed. Peter Weingart.

500 USA ISSN 1539-445X
TA401 CODEN: SMOAAE
SOFT MATERIALS. Text in English. 2003. q. GBP 639 combined subscription in United Kingdom to institutions (print & online eds.); EUR 844, USD 1,058 combined subscription to institutions (print & online eds.) (effective 2012). adv. back issues avail.; reprint service avail. from PSC. **Document type:** *Journal, Academic/Scholarly.* **Description:** Covers theory, simulation, and experimental research in this rapidly expanding and interdisciplinary field.
Related titles: Online - full text ed.: ISSN 1539-4468. GBP 575 in United Kingdom to institutions; EUR 759, USD 952 to institutions (effective 2012) (from IngentaConnect).
Indexed: A01, A22, A28, APA, BrCerAb, C&ISA, CA, CA/WCA, CCI, CIA, CPEI, CerAb, CivEngAb, CorrAb, CurCont, E&CAJ, E01, E11, EEA, EMA, ESPM, EngInd, EnvEAb, H15, M&TEA, M09, MBF, METADEX, MSCI, SCI, SCOPUS, SolStAb, T02, T04, W07, WAA.
—BLDSC (8321.418000), IE, Ingenta, Linda Hall. **CCC.**
Published by: Taylor & Francis Inc. (Subsidiary of: Taylor & Francis Group), 325 Chestnut St, Ste 800, Philadelphia, PA 19106. TEL 215-625-2940, 800-354-1420, orders@taylorandfrancis.com, http://www.taylorandfrancis.com. Ed. Florian Mueller-Plathe. Adv. contact Linda Hann TEL 44-1344-779945.

500 600 JPN ISSN 0913-6584
SOGO GAKUJUTSU KENKYU SHUKAI. Text in Japanese. 1976. irreg. **Description:** Contains research reports of the association.
Published by: Nihon Kagakusha Kaigi/Japan Scientists Association, 9-16 Yushima 1-chome, Bunkyo-ku, Tokyo, 113-0034, Japan.

SOGO KENKYUJO HOKOKU. *see* TECHNOLOGY: COMPREHENSIVE WORKS

IL SOLE 24 ORE. BIBLIOTECA DEL SAPERE. *see* HUMANITIES: COMPREHENSIVE WORKS

SOMERSET ARCHAEOLOGY AND NATURAL HISTORY. *see* ARCHAEOLOGY

500 600 THA
SONGKLANAKARIN JOURNAL OF SCIENCE AND TECHNOLOGY. Text in English, Thai. 1979. bi-m. THB 200 domestic; USD 45 foreign (effective 2005). **Document type:** *Journal, Academic/Scholarly.* **Description:** Covers advances in science and technology.
Formerly: Warasan Wichakan Songkhlanakharin (0125-3395)
Related titles: Online - full text ed.: 2002. free (effective 2011).
Indexed: A01, A34, A35, A36, A37, A38, AgrForAb, B23, C25, C30, CA, CABA, D01, E12, F08, FCA, GH, H16, INIS AtomInd, LT, N02, N03, N04, P32, P33, R07, R08, S13, SCOPUS, SoyAb, T02, T05, W10, W11, Z01.
—IE.
Published by: Prince of Songkla University, 15 Kanchanavanich Rd, Hat Yai, 90110, Thailand. TEL 66-74-282159, FAX 66-74-212837, http://www.psu.ac.th/. Ed. Chakrit Tongurai.

500.9 USA ISSN 0277-4887
SONORENSIS. Text in English. 1972. a. membership. bibl.; illus. **Document type:** *Newsletter.*
Formerly (until 1978): A S D M Newsletter (0044-8850)
Indexed: WildRev.
Published by: Arizona-Sonora Desert Museum, Inc., 2021 N Kinney Rd, Tucson, AZ 85743. TEL 520-833-1380, FAX 520-883-2500. Ed., R&P Steven Phillips TEL 520-883-3028.

SOOCHOW JOURNAL OF MATHEMATICS. *see* MATHEMATICS

500.9 GBR ISSN 0038-1551
SORBY NATURAL HISTORY SOCIETY. NEWSLETTER. Text in English. 1964. m. free to members (effective 2009). adv. bk.rev. bibl. **Document type:** *Newsletter, Trade.* **Description:** Keeps members up to date with the latest news from Sorbyland.
Published by: Sorby Natural History Society, 159 Bell Hagg Rd, Sheffield, S Yorks S6 5DA, United Kingdom. secretary@sorby.org.uk.

500.9 GBR ISSN 0260-2245
THE SORBY RECORD; a journal of natural history for the Sheffield area. Text in English. 1958. a., latest vol.43, 2007. GBP 5 per issue to non-members; free to members (effective 2009). back issues avail. **Document type:** *Journal, Academic/Scholarly.* **Description:** Contains articles on all aspects of natural history in the Sheffield area.
Indexed: Z01.
Published by: Sorby Natural History Society, 159 Bell Hagg Rd, Sheffield, S Yorks S6 5DA, United Kingdom. secretary@sorby.org.uk.

500 AUS ISSN 1836-6627
THE SOURCE DOCUMENT. Text in English. 1985. bi-m. free to members (effective 2011). adv. back issues avail. **Document type:** *Newsletter, Trade.* **Description:** Aims to support scientists involved in the development of therapeutic products and also promotes education to enhance the professional competency of its members.
Formerly (until 2009): A R C S Australia. Newsletter (1448-5923)
Related titles: Online - full text ed.: free (effective 2011).
Published by: Association of Regulatory & Clinical Scientists, Ste 802, 28 Clarke St, Crows Nest, NSW 2065, Australia. TEL 61-2-89050829, FAX 61-2-89050830, arcs@arcs.com.au.

500 ZAF ISSN 0038-2353
Q85 CODEN: SAJSAR
➤ **SOUTH AFRICAN JOURNAL OF SCIENCE/SUID-AFRIKAANSE TYDSKRIF VIR WETENSKAP.** Text mainly in English; Text occasionally in Afrikaans. 1903. bi-m. ZAR 470 domestic to individuals; USD 190 foreign to individuals; ZAR 800 domestic to institutions; USD 220 foreign to institutions (effective 2010). adv. bk.rev. bibl.; charts; illus.; stat. index. reprints avail. **Document type:** *Journal, Academic/Scholarly.* **Description:** Publishes original research results and short communications in all fields of scientific endeavor. Also discusses science policy issues relevant to the South African and international scientific communities.
Incorporates (1968-1984): Scientific Progress - Wetenskaplike Vordering (0036-8814); (1947-1949): South African Science (0370-8438); (1903-1908): South African Association for the Advancement of Science. Report (0370-7121)
Related titles: Microform ed.: (from PQC); Online - full text ed.: ISSN 1996-7489. free (effective 2011); Supplement(s): South African Association for the Advancement of Science. Special Publication. ISSN 0370-8462.
Indexed: A01, A02, A03, A08, A20, A22, A29, A34, A35, A36, A37, A38, AICP, ASFA, AbAn, AgBio, AgrForAb, AnBeAb, B20, B21, B23, B25, BA, BIOBASE, BIOSIS Prev, BP, C25, C30, CA, CABA, CIN, CRFR, ChemAb, ChemTitl, CurCont, D01, E04, E05, E11, E12, E17, EIA, ESPM, EnerInd, EntAb, F08, F11, F12, FCA, FR, FS&TA, G11, GEOBASE, GH, GeoRef, GeotechAb, H&SSA, H16, H17, HGA, HPNRM, I10, I11, IABS, IBR, IBZ, IIBP, INIS AtomInd, ISAP, ISR, IndVet, Inpharma, Inspec, L09, LT, MaizeAb, MycolAb, N02, N03, N04, N05, O01, OR, P06, P30, P32, P33, P34, P37, P38, P39, P40, PGegResA, PGrRegA, PHN&I, PN&I, PollutAb, R07, R08, R12, R13, RA&MP, REE&TA, RM&VM, RRTA, S01, S12, S13, S16, S17, SCI, SCOPUS, SSciA, SWRA, SoyAb, SpeleolAb, T02, T04, T05, TAR, TOSA, TriticAb, VITIS, VS, VirolAbstr, W07, W08, W10, W11, WBA, WMB, Z01.
—BLDSC (8340.000000), CASDDS, GNLM, IE, Infotrieve, Ingenta, INIST, Linda Hall.
Published by: A O S I S Pty. Ltd., Postnet Ste #55, Private Bag X22, Tygervalley, 7536, South Africa. TEL 27-21-9145105, FAX 27-21-4204874, orders@openjournals.net. Ed. Michael Cherry. Adv. contact Robyn Arnold. B&W page ZAR 2,900, color page ZAR 4,400; trim 210 x 297. Circ: 1,000. **Subscr. to:** Foundation for Education Science and Technology, PO Box 1758, Pretoria 0001, South Africa. TEL 27-12-3226404, FAX 27-12-3207803.

500 AUS ISSN 1035-7939
SOUTH AUSTRALIAN MUSEUM. RECORDS. MONOGRAPH SERIES. Text in English. 1991. irreg. **Document type:** *Monographic series, Academic/Scholarly.*

S

Published by: South Australian Museum, North Terr., Adelaide, SA 5000, Australia. TEL 61-8-82077500, FAX 61-8-82077430, http://www.samuseum.sa.gov.au/page/default.asp?site=1&page=Home.

508 AUS ISSN 0038-2965
QH1 CODEN: SANAAR
SOUTH AUSTRALIAN NATURALIST. Text in English. 1919. s-a. bk.rev. charts; illus.; maps. back issues avail. **Document type:** *Journal, Academic/Scholarly.*
Indexed: AESIS, ASI, GeoRef, SpeleolAb, WildRev, Z01.
Published by: Field Naturalists' Society of South Australia Inc., GPO Box 1594, Adelaide, SA 5001, Australia. TEL 61-4-28188318, gillbrig@ozemail.com.au. Ed. Mrs. Pam Catcheside. Circ: 300.

500 USA ISSN 0096-414X
Q11 CODEN: BSCAAD
SOUTH CAROLINA ACADEMY OF SCIENCE. BULLETIN. Text in English. 1935. a., latest 2007. abstr. index. back issues avail. **Document type:** *Bulletin, Trade.* **Description:** Contains annual reports and membership list.
Related titles: Online - full text ed.
Indexed: A01, A26, E08, G08, GeoRef, I05, S09, SASA, SpeleolAb, WildRev.
Published by: South Carolina Academy of Science, c/o John L Safko, Treas, Department of Physics & Astronomy, University of South Carolina, Columbia, SC 29208. TEL 803-777-6466, FAX 803-777-3065, reevest@midlandstech.edu. Ed. G T Cowley.

500 USA ISSN 0096-378X
Q11 CODEN: PSDAA2
SOUTH DAKOTA ACADEMY OF SCIENCE. PROCEEDINGS. Text in English. 1916. a. USD 20 (effective 2005). abstr.; charts; illus.; stat. **Document type:** *Proceedings.* **Description:** Presents lectures and papers submitted at the proceedings.
Indexed: A29, A32, ASFA, Agr, AnBeAb, B20, B21, CA, ChemAb, E17, ESPM, EntAb, GeoRef, ImmunAb, PollutAb, SASA, SSciA, SWRA, SpeleolAb, T02, W08, WildRev.
—CASDDS, Ingenta, Linda Hall.
Published by: South Dakota Academy of Science, c/o Donna Hazelwood, Dakota State University, College of Natural Science, Madison, SD 57042. TEL 605-256-5187, http://acadsci.sdstate.org/. Ed. Steven R Chipps. Circ: 350 (controlled).

500 AUS ISSN 1838-8388
SOUTH PACIFIC JOURNAL OF NATURAL AND APPLIED SCIENCES (ONLINE). Text in English. 2001. a. **Document type:** *Journal, Academic/Scholarly.*
Formerly (until 2010): South Pacific Journal of Natural Science (Online) (1726-0787)
Media: Online - full text. **Related titles:** ◆ Print ed.: South Pacific Journal of Natural and Applied Sciences (Print). ISSN 1838-837X.
Published by: (University of the South Pacific, Faculty of Science and Technology FJI), C S I R O, 150 Oxford St, PO Box 1139, Collingwood, VIC 3066, Australia. TEL 61-3-96627500, FAX 61-3-96627555, publishing@csiro.au.

500 AUS ISSN 1838-837X
QH198.A1 CODEN: SPJSEY
➤ **SOUTH PACIFIC JOURNAL OF NATURAL AND APPLIED SCIENCES (PRINT).** Text in English. 1980. a. back issues avail.; reprints avail. **Document type:** *Journal, Academic/Scholarly.* **Description:** Covers all areas of natural science, engineering and mathematics.
Formerly (until 2010): South Pacific Journal of Natural Science (Print) (1013-9877)
Related titles: ◆ Online - full text ed.: South Pacific Journal of Natural and Applied Sciences (Online). ISSN 1838-8388.
Indexed: A35, A37, AgrForAb, C25, C30, CABA, E12, F08, H16, MLA-IB, P32, R07, S13, Z01.
Published by: (University of the South Pacific, Faculty of Science and Technology FJI), C S I R O Publishing, 150 Oxford St, PO Box 1139, Collingwood, VIC 3066, Australia. TEL 61-3-96627500, FAX 61-3-96627555, publishing@csiro.au, http://www.publish.csiro.au/home.htm. Eds. Sushil Kumar TEL 679-3232144, Anand Tyagi TEL 679-323-2066.

500 620 CHN ISSN 1003-7985
T1 CODEN: JSUOAT
SOUTHEAST UNIVERSITY. JOURNAL. Text in English. 1984. q. USD 20.80 (effective 2009). back issues avail. **Document type:** *Journal, Academic/Scholarly.* **Description:** Covers various branches of science and engineering.
Related titles: Online - full text ed.
Indexed: A28, APA, BrCerAb, C&ISA, CA/WCA, CCMJ, CIA, CPEI, CerAb, CivEngAb, CorrAb, E&CAJ, E11, EEA, EMA, ESPM, EngInd, EnvEAb, H15, Inspec, M&TEA, M09, MBF, METADEX, MSN, MathR, RefZh, SCOPUS, SolStAb, T04, WAA, Z02.
—East View, Linda Hall.
Published by: Dongnan Daxue/Southeast University, 2, Sipailou, Nanjing, Jiangsu 210096, China. TEL 86-25-83792627, FAX 86-25-57712719. Ed. Shan-feng Mao.

500 USA ISSN 0038-3872
Q11 CODEN: BCASAD
SOUTHERN CALIFORNIA ACADEMY OF SCIENCES. BULLETIN. Text in English. 1902. 3/yr. free to members. adv. bibl.; charts; illus. index. back issues avail. **Document type:** *Bulletin, Consumer.* **Description:** Seeks articles in any field of science documenting research relevant to the southern California area and Baja, Mexico, as the official bulletin of the Southern California Academy of Sciences.
Related titles: Online - full text ed.
Indexed: A22, A26, ASFA, Agr, B21, B25, BIOSIS Prev, E08, ESPM, G08, GeoRef, I05, MycolAb, PollutAb, S06, S09, SASA, SSciA, SpeleolAb, Z01.
—BLDSC (2763.000000), IE, Ingenta, INIST, Linda Hall.
Published by: Southern California Academy of Sciences, c/o Natural History Museum, 900 Exposition Blvd., Los Angeles, CA 90007. TEL 909-607-2836, 800-627-0629, FAX 913-843-1274, 909-621-8588, http://www.allenpress.com. Ed. Daniel A Guthrie. Circ: 500.

500 USA
SOUTHERN RESEARCH INSTITUTE. ANNUAL REPORT. Text in English. 1945. a. free. **Document type:** *Corporate.*
Published by: Southern Research Institute, PO Box 55305, Birmingham, AL 35255-5305. TEL 205-581-2000, FAX 205-581-2201. R&P Rhonda Jung TEL 205-581-2317.

500 CHN ISSN 1005-2429
AS451 CODEN: JSJUEU
➤ **SOUTHWEST JIAOTONG UNIVERSITY. JOURNAL.** Text in English. 1993. q. CNY 12 per issue (effective 2010). adv. **Document type:** *Journal, Academic/Scholarly.*
Related titles: Online - full text ed.; ◆ Chinese ed.: Xinan Jiaotong Daxue Xuebao. ISSN 0258-2724.
Indexed: A28, APA, BrCerAb, C&ISA, CA/WCA, CIA, CerAb, CivEngAb, CorrAb, E&CAJ, E11, EEA, EMA, H15, Inspec, M&TEA, M09, MBF, METADEX, SolStAb, T04, WAA, Z02.
—BLDSC (4902.257000), East View.
Published by: Xinan Jiaotong Daxue/Southwest Jiaotong University, 111, Er-Huan Lu Bei-Yi-Duan, Chengdu, Sichuan 610031, China. TEL 86-28-87600847, FAX 85-28-87600552. **Dist. overseas by:** China International Book Trading Corp, 35 Chegongzhuang Xilu, Haidian District, PO Box 399, Beijing 100044, China. TEL 86-10-68412045, FAX 86-10-68412023, cibtc@mail.cibtc.com.cn, http://www.cibtc.com.cn.

508 USA ISSN 0038-4909
QH1 CODEN: SWNAAB
➤ **SOUTHWESTERN NATURALIST.** Text in English, Spanish. 1953. q. free to members (effective 2011). bk.rev. bibl.; charts; illus. Bibl.& Ind.Geol. back issues avail.; reprints avail. **Document type:** *Journal, Academic/Scholarly.* **Description:** Contains articles on scientific investigations on plants and animals (living and fossil) endemic to the southwestern U.S., Mexico, and Central America.
Related titles: Microform ed.: (from PQC); Online - full text ed.: ISSN 1943-6262.
Indexed: A01, A22, A26, A29, A34, A35, A37, A38, ASCA, ASFA, AgBio, Agr, AgrForAb, B20, B21, B23, B25, BIOBASE, BIOSIS Prev, C25, C30, CA, CABA, CurCont, E08, E12, E17, ESPM, EntAb, F08, F12, FCA, G11, GH, GeoRef, H16, H17, I05, I10, I11, IABS, IndVet, KWIWR, LT, MaizeAb, MycolAb, N04, O01, P30, P32, P33, P37, P39, P40, PGegResA, PHN&I, PN&I, PlantSci, R07, R08, R11, R12, RA&MP, RRTA, RefZh, S09, S13, S16, S17, SCI, SCOPUS, SSciA, SWRA, SpeleolAb, T02, TAR, TriticAb, VS, VirolAbstr, W07, W08, W10, W11, WildRev, Z01.
—BLDSC (8357.280000), IE, Ingenta, INIST, Linda Hall. **CCC.**
Published by: Southwestern Association of Naturalists, c/o Robert C. Dowler, Department of Biology, Angelo State University, San Angelo, TX 76909. swan03@ou.edu. Ed. Troy L Best TEL 334-844-9260.

500.5 NOR ISSN 0801-9517
SPACE RESEARCH IN NORWAY (YEAR). Text in English. 1963. a. free. bk.rev. bibl.; illus. back issues avail. **Document type:** *Journal, Academic/Scholarly.* **Description:** Presents an overview of all space science projects in Norway, with description of infrastructure and organizations.
Former titles (until 1982): Space Activity in Norway (0801-9525); (until 1970): Norway. Komite for Romforskning. N.S.C. Report (0452-3687)
Published by: Norsk Romsenter/Norwegian Space Centre, PO Box 113, Skoeyen, Oslo, 0212, Norway. TEL 45-22-511800, FAX 45-22-511801. Ed. Bo N Andersen. Circ: 1,500.

SPECTRUM; natural science journal for teachers and lecturers. *see* EDUCATION—Teaching Methods And Curriculum

500 DEU ISSN 1864-0133
SPEKTRUM (MONSHEIM). Text in German. 1998. s-a. **Document type:** *Magazine, Trade.*
Published by: (Hochschule Esslingen), V M K - Verlag fuer Marketing und Kommunikation GmbH & Co. KG, Faberstr 17, Monsheim, 67590, Germany. TEL 49-6243-9090, FAX 49-6243-909400, info@vmk-verlag.de.

500 DEU ISSN 0170-2971
CODEN: SPEKDI
SPEKTRUM DER WISSENSCHAFT. Text in German. 1978. m. EUR 79.20 (effective 2009). adv. bk.rev. index. back issues avail. **Document type:** *Magazine, Consumer.*
Incorporates: Academie Spectrum (0940-225X); Spektrum (0049-1861)
Related titles: Online - full text ed.; ◆ English ed.: Scientific American. ISSN 0036-8733; ◆ Hungarian ed.: Tudomany. ISSN 0237-322X; ◆ French ed.: Pour la Science. ISSN 0153-4092; ◆ Italian ed.: Le Scienze. ISSN 0036-8083; ◆ Chinese ed.: Ke Xue. ISSN 1002-1299; ◆ Spanish ed.: Investigacion y Ciencia. ISSN 0210-136X; ◆ Japanese ed.: Nikkei Saiensu. ISSN 0917-009X; ◆ Arabic ed.: Majallat al-Ulum; ◆ Polish ed.: Swiat Nauki. ISSN 0867-6380; Turkish ed.: Bilim.
Indexed: A22, CEABA, DIP, GeoRef, IBR, IBZ, INIS AtomInd, MLA-IB, RASB, SpeleolAb, TM.
—CASDDS, GNLM, IE, Infotrieve, Linda Hall. **CCC.**
Published by: Spektrum der Wissenschaft Verlagsgesellschaft mbH (Subsidiary of: Verlagsgruppe Georg von Holtzbrinck GmbH), Slevogtstr 3-5, Heidelberg, 69126, Germany. TEL 49-6221-9126600, FAX 49-6221-9126751. Ed. Carsten Koenneker. Adv. contact Karin Schmidt. Circ: 86,784 (paid).

500 DEU ISSN 0176-3008
Q49 CODEN: SPFOE2
SPIEGEL DER FORSCHUNG. Text in German. 1983. s-a. free. adv. **Document type:** *Academic/Scholarly.*
Indexed: CABA, D01, DIP, GH, IBR, IBZ, N02, N03, P32, P33, T05, W11.
—**CCC.**
Published by: Justus-Liebig-Universitaet, Ludwigstr 23, Giessen, 35390, Germany. TEL 49-641-9912040, FAX 49-641-9912049. Ed. Christel Lauterbach. Circ: 10,000.

333.72 CAN ISSN 0381-4459
TD427.P4
SPILL TECHNOLOGY NEWSLETTER/BULLETIN DE LA LUTTE CONTRE LES DEVERSEMENTS. Text in English. 1976. q. free. illus. **Document type:** *Newsletter, Trade.* **Description:** A forum for the exchange of information on spill counter measures and related matters.
Indexed: EIA, EnvAb, EnvInd, Inspec, SCOPUS.
—BLDSC (8413.840000), IE, Ingenta, Linda Hall. **CCC.**
Published by: Environment Canada, Technology Development and Technical Services Branch (Subsidiary of: Environment Canada/Environnement Canada), 351 St. Joseph Blvd, Hull, PQ K1A 0H3, Canada. TEL 613-990-7297, FAX 613-991-9485. Ed., R&P Merv Fingas TEL 613-998-9622. Pub. Jennifer Charles. Circ: 2,500.

500 LKA ISSN 0081-3745
CODEN: SPZEAY
SPOLIA ZEYLANICA/NATIONAL MUSEUMS OF SRI LANKA. BULLETIN. Text in English. 1904. a. price varies.
Indexed: GeoRef, SpeleolAb.
—Linda Hall.
Published by: Department of National Museums, Sir Marcus Fernando Mawatha, P O Box 854, Colombo, 7, Sri Lanka.

SPORTS ENGINEERING. *see* SPORTS AND GAMES

SPORTSCIENCE. *see* SPORTS AND GAMES

500 POL ISSN 1230-1647
Q225.2.P7
SPRAWY NAUKI. Text in Polish. 1991. bi-m. **Document type:** *Bulletin, Academic/Scholarly.*
Formerly (until 1992): Komitet Badan Naukowych. Biuletyn (0867-8065)
Published by: Polska Akademia Nauk, Komitet Badan Naukowych/Polish Academy of Sciences, Committee for Scientific Research, Wspolna 1/3, Warszawa 53, 00529, Poland. TEL 48-22-5292718, FAX 48-22-6280922. Ed. Anna Leszkowska TEL 48-22-8251240 ext 42.

500 USA ISSN 0172-7389
CODEN: SSSYDF
SPRINGER SERIES IN SYNERGETICS. Text in English. 1978. irreg., latest 2010. price varies. back issues avail. **Document type:** *Monographic series.*
Indexed: A22, CCMJ, CIN, CIS, ChemAb, ChemTitl, Inspec, MSN, MathR, Z02.
—CASDDS, INIST. **CCC.**
Published by: Springer New York LLC (Subsidiary of: Springer Science+Business Media), 233 Spring St, New York, NY 10013. TEL 212-460-1500, FAX 212-460-1575, service-ny@springer.com.

500 LKA ISSN 1391-023X
SRI LANKA ASSOCIATION FOR THE ADVANCEMENT OF SCIENCE. PROCEEDINGS. PART 1: ABSTRACTS. Text in English. 1945. a. **Document type:** *Proceedings.*
Supersedes in part: Sri Lanka Association for the Advancement of Science. Proceedings of the Annual Session (0253-6374); Which was formerly (until 1975): Ceylon Association for the Advancement of Science. Proceedings of the Annual Session (0366-516X)
Indexed: INIS AtomInd, SLSI, SpeleolAb.
Published by: Sri Lanka Association for the Advancement of Science, 120/10 Vidya Mawatha, Colombo, 7, Sri Lanka. TEL 94-1-688740, FAX 94-1-691681, slaas@itmin.com, http://www.nsf.ac.lk/slaas/. Ed. C L M Nethsingha. Circ: 2,000.

500 LKA ISSN 1391-0248
SRI LANKA ASSOCIATION FOR THE ADVANCEMENT OF SCIENCE. PROCEEDINGS. PART 2: PRESIDENTIAL ADDRESSES, GUEST LECTURES. Text in English. 1945. a. **Document type:** *Proceedings.*
Supersedes in part: Sri Lanka Association for the Advancement of Science. Proceedings of the Annual Session (0253-6374); Which was formerly (until 1975): Ceylon Association for the Advancement of Science. Proceedings of the Annual Session (0366-516X)
Indexed: INIS AtomInd, SLSI, SpeleolAb.
Published by: Sri Lanka Association for the Advancement of Science, 120/10 Vidya Mawatha, Colombo, 7, Sri Lanka. TEL 691681. R&P C L M Nethsingha. Circ: 2,000.

509 SRB ISSN 0351-4765
AS346
SRPSKA AKADEMIJA NAUKA I UMETNOSTI. ODELJENJE ISTORIJSKIH NAUKA. GLAS/ACADEMIE SERBE DES SCIENCES ET DES ARTS. CLASSE DES SCIENCES HISTORIQUES. BULLETIN. Text in Serbo-Croatian. 1974. irreg.
Indexed: DIP, IBR, IBZ.
Published by: Srpska Akademija Nauka i Umetnosti/Serbian Academy of Arts and Sciences, Knez Mihailova 35, Belgrade, 11000. TEL 381-11-2027154, FAX 381-11-2027178, izdavacka@sanu.ac.rs, http://www.sanu.ac.rs.

509 SRB ISSN 0352-6194
SRPSKA AKADEMIJA NAUKA I UMETNOSTI. ODELJENJE ISTORIJSKIH NAUKA. NAUCNI SKUPOVI/ACADEMIE SERBE DES SCIENCES ET DES ARTS. CLASSE DES SCIENCES HISTORIQUES. CONFERENCES SCIENTIFIQUES. Text in Serbo-Croatian. irreg.
Indexed: DIP, IBR, IBZ.
Published by: Srpska Akademija Nauka i Umetnosti/Serbian Academy of Arts and Sciences, Knez Mihailova 35, Belgrade, 11000. TEL 381-11-2027154, FAX 381-11-2027178, izdavacka@sanu.ac.rs, http://www.sanu.ac.rs.

509 SRB ISSN 0354-1479
SRPSKA AKADEMIJA NAUKA I UMETNOSTI. ODELJENJE ISTORIJSKIH NAUKA. SPOMENIK. Text in Serbo-Croatian. irreg.
Indexed: IBR, IBZ.
Published by: Srpska Akademija Nauka i Umetnosti/Serbian Academy of Arts and Sciences, Knez Mihailova 35, Belgrade, 11000. TEL 381-11-2027154, FAX 381-11-2027178, izdavacka@sanu.ac.rs, http://www.sanu.ac.rs.

500 SRB ISSN 0374-7956
Q69.2 CODEN: GSAKAK
SRPSKA AKADEMIJA NAUKA I UMETNOSTI. ODELJENJE PRIRODNO-MATEMATICKIH NAUKA. GLAS. Text in Serbo-Croatian; Summaries in English, French, German, Russian. 1950. irreg., latest vol.39, 1972. Price varies.
Related titles: ◆ French ed.: Academie Serbe des Sciences et des Arts. Classe des Sciences Mathematiques et Naturelles. Bulletin Sciences Naturelles. ISSN 0352-5740.
Indexed: CCMJ, ChemAb, IBR, IBZ, SpeleolAb, Z02.
—INIST.
Published by: Srpska Akademija Nauka i Umetnosti/Serbian Academy of Arts and Sciences, Knez Mihailova 35, Belgrade, 11000. TEL 381-11-2027154, FAX 381-11-2027178, izdavacka@sanu.ac.rs, http://www.sanu.ac.rs. Circ: 500. **Dist. by:** Prosveta, Terazije 16, Belgrade, Serbia, Yugoslavia.

060 500 SRB
SRPSKA AKADEMIJA NAUKA I UMETNOSTI. POVREMENA IZDANJA. Text in Serbo-Croatian. irreg.
Published by: Srpska Akademija Nauka i Umetnosti/Serbian Academy of Arts and Sciences, Knez Mihailova 35, Belgrade, 11000. TEL 381-11-2027154, FAX 381-11-2027178, izdavacka@sanu.ac.rs, http://www.sanu.ac.rs.

SRPSKA AKADEMIJA NAUKA I UMETNOSTI. SPOMENICA. *see* HUMANITIES: COMPREHENSIVE WORKS

500 600 352.491 IRL
STATE EXPEDITURE ON SCIENCE & TECHNOLOGY. Text in English. irreg. **Description:** Acknowledges the progress made on some of the actions recommended to Government in and draws attention to a number of public investment priorities which remain outstanding.
Related titles: Online - full text ed.
Published by: Forfas, Wilton Park House, Wilton Place, Dublin, 2, Ireland. TEL 353-1-6073000, FAX 353-1-6073030, info@forfas.ie.

500 600 352.491 IRL
STATE INVESTMENT IN SCIENCE & TECHNOLOGY (YEAR). Text in English. a. **Description:** Covers financial allocations by government to institutions engaged in any activity related to Science and technology.
Related titles: Online - full text ed.
Published by: Forfas, Wilton Park House, Wilton Place, Dublin, 2, Ireland. TEL 353-1-6073000, FAX 353-1-6073030, info@forfas.ie.

STEINI. *see* CHILDREN AND YOUTH—For

STEVENS INDICATOR. *see* COLLEGE AND ALUMNI

500 600 DEU
STIFTERVERBAND FUER DIE DEUTSCHE WISSENSCHAFT. TAETIGKEITSBERICHT. Text in German. 1950. a. membership. **Document type:** *Journal, Trade.*
Supersedes: Stifterverband fuer die Deutsche Wissenschaft. Jahrbuch (0081-5551)
Published by: Stifterverband fuer die Deutsche Wissenschaft, Barkhovenallee 1, Essen, 45239, Germany. TEL 49-201-8401-0, FAX 49-201-8401301, mail@stifterverband.de, http://www.stifterverband.org. Circ: 10,000.

500 ROM ISSN 1220-6555
STIINTA SI TEHNICA. Text in Romanian. 1949. m. ROL 48,000; USD 30 foreign. adv. bk.rev.; software rev. illus.; pat. back issues avail. **Document type:** *Consumer.*
Published by: Stiinta & Tehnica S.A., Piata Presei Libere 1, Bucharest, 79781, Romania. TEL 40-1-6175833, FAX 40-1-2228494. Ed. Voichita Domaneanto. Pub., Adv. contact Albescu Ioan. B&W page USD 300, color page USD 500; trim 250 x 170. Circ: 15,000.

STRANGE MAGAZINE. *see* BIOLOGY—Zoology

500 RUS ISSN 2218-1881
▼➤ **STUDENCHESKII NAUCHNYI ZHURNAL/UNDERGRADUATE ACADEMIC JOURNAL.** Text in Russian. 2010. bi-m. free (effective 2011). **Document type:** *Journal, Academic/Scholarly.*
Media: Online - full text. Ed. Aleksandr Malakhov.

501 215 ITA
STUDI CRITICI SULLE SCIENZE. Text in Italian. 1961. irreg., latest vol.6, 1996. price varies. **Document type:** *Monographic series, Academic/Scholarly.*
Published by: (Pontificia Universita Gregoriana/Pontifical Gregorian University, Pontificia Universita Gregoriana, Facolta di Filosofia), Gregorian University Press/Editrice Pontificia Universita Gregoriana, Piazza della Pilotta 35, Rome, 00187, Italy. TEL 39-06-6781567, FAX 39-06-6780588, periodicals@biblicum.com, http://www.paxbook.com.

500 PRT ISSN 1647-6468
➤ **STUDIA.** Text in Portuguese. 2000. a. **Document type:** *Journal, Academic/Scholarly.*
Formerly (until 2009): INUAF Studia (0874-8608)
Published by: Instituto Superior Dom Afonso III, Convento Espirito Santo, Loule, 8100-641, Portugal. TEL 351-289-420480, FAX 351-289-420488, inuaf-academicos@mail.telepac.pt.

509 POL ISSN 0081-6701
QB36.C8
STUDIA COPERNICANA. Text in English, French, German, Latin, Polish. 1970. irreg., latest vol.36, 1997. price varies. illus. **Document type:** *Monographic series.*
Indexed: MathR.
Published by: Polska Akademia Nauk, Instytut Historii Nauki, Palac Staszica, ul Nowy Swiat 72, pok 9, Warsaw, 00330, Poland. TEL 48-22-8268754, FAX 48-22-8266137. Ed. Pawel Czartoryski. **Dist. by:** Ars Polona, Obroncow 25, Warsaw 03933, Poland.

STUDIA LEIBNITIANA; Zeitschrift fuer Geschichte der Philosophie und der Wissenschaften. *see* PHILOSOPHY

500 708.39 HUN ISSN 1215-5365
STUDIA NATURALIA. Text in Hungarian. 1992. irreg., latest vol.15, 2005. **Document type:** *Monographic series, Academic/Scholarly.*
Indexed: GeoRef, Z01.
Published by: Magyar Termeszettudomanyi Muzeum, Baross utca 13, Budapest, 1088, Hungary. http://www.nhmus.hu.

STUDIA SPINOZANA; an international & interdisciplinary series. *see* PHILOSOPHY

500 ROM ISSN 1584-2363
QH301
STUDIA UNIVERSITATIS "VASILE GOLDIS" ARAD. SERIE STIINTELE VIETII/LIFE SCIENCES SERIES. Text in Multiple languages. 2002. a. **Document type:** *Journal, Academic/Scholarly.*
Related titles: Online - full text ed.: ISSN 1842-7863. free (effective 2011).
Indexed: A01, A34, A35, A36, A38, AgBio, B23, C25, C30, CA, CABA, D01, E12, F08, F12, FCA, G11, GH, H16, H17, I11, MaizeAb, N02, N03, N04, O01, P32, P33, P39, P40, P52, P56, PGegResA, PGrRegA, R07, R13, RA&MP, S12, S13, S16, S17, SCOPUS, T02, W10.
Published by: Universitatea de Vest "Vasile Goldis"/"Vasile Goldis" University Press, B dul Revolutiei 94-96, Arad, 310025, Romania. http://uvvg.ro/editura/.

STUDIEN ZUR GESCHICHTE DER DEUTSCHEN FORSCHUNGSGEMEINSCHAFT. *see* HISTORY—History Of Europe

500 DEU ISSN 1867-2744
GB457.5
STUDIEN ZUR LANDSCHAFTS- UND SIEDLUNGSGESCHICHTE IM SUEDLICHEN NORDSEEGEBIET. Text in German. 1940. irreg., latest 2010. price varies. **Document type:** *Monographic series, Academic/Scholarly.*
Former titles (until 2010): Probleme der Kuestenforschung im Suedlichen Nordseegebiet (0343-7965); (until 1964): Probleme der Kuestenforschung im Gebiet der Suedlichen Nordsee (0343-7973)
Indexed: GeoRef, SpeleolAb.
Published by: (Niedersaechsisches Institut fuer Historische Kuestenforschung), Verlag Marie Leidorf GmbH, Stellerloh 65, Rahden, 32369, Germany. TEL 49-5771-951074, FAX 49-5771-951075, info@vml.de.

800 500 100 IRL ISSN 0039-3495
AP4
➤ **STUDIES**; an Irish quarterly review. Text in English. 1912. q. EUR 35 domestic; EUR 40 in Europe to individuals; EUR 45 elsewhere to individuals (effective 2005). adv. bk.rev. illus. cum.index: vols.1-50. reprints avail. **Document type:** *Journal, Academic/Scholarly.*
Related titles: Microform ed.: (from PQC).
Indexed: A22, AES, AmHI, BEL&L, CA, CERDIC, CPL, H07, HistAb, IBR, IBZ, MEA&I, MLA-IB, P06, P30, PCI, RASB, RILM, T02.
—BLDSC (8484.250000), IE, Infotrieve, Ingenta.
Address: 35 Lower Leeson St., Dublin, 2, Ireland. TEL 353-1-6766785, FAX 353-1-6762984. Ed. Thomas Layden. Adv. contact Fergus O'Donoghue. Circ: 1,300.

501 NLD ISSN 1871-7381
➤ **STUDIES IN HISTORY AND PHILOSOPHY OF SCIENCE.** Text in English. 1982. irreg., latest vol.23, 2009. price varies. **Document type:** *Monographic series, Academic/Scholarly.*
Former titles (until 2005): Australasian Studies in History and Philosophy of Science (0929-6425); Australasian Studies in History and Philosophy
—BLDSC (8490.652150). **CCC.**
Published by: Springer Netherlands (Subsidiary of: Springer Science+Business Media), Van Godewijckstraat 30, Dordrecht, 3311 GX, Netherlands. TEL 31-78-6576050, FAX 31-78-6576474. Ed. Steven Gaukroger.

509 GBR ISSN 0039-3681
Q125 CODEN: SHPSB5
➤ **STUDIES IN HISTORY AND PHILOSOPHY OF SCIENCE PART A.** Text in English. 1970. 4/yr. EUR 623 in Europe to institutions; JPY 82,800 in Japan to institutions; USD 697 elsewhere to institutions (effective 2012). bk.rev. charts; illus. Index. back issues avail.; reprints avail. **Document type:** *Journal, Academic/Scholarly.* **Description:** Covers with the historical, social and intellectual contexts of the sciences and with their methodology and epistemology.
Related titles: Microfilm ed.: (from PQC); Online - full text ed.: ISSN 1879-2510 (from IngentaConnect, ScienceDirect).
Indexed: A01, A02, A03, A08, A20, A22, A26, ASCA, AmH&L, AmHI, ArtHuCI, B04, BRD, CA, CCMJ, CIS, CurCont, DIP, E08, EMBASE, ExcerpMed, G08, GeoRef, H07, H08, H09, H10, H14, HAb, HistAb, HumInd, I05, IBR, IBSS, IBZ, IPB, ISR, Inspec, MEDLINE, MLA-IB, MSN, MathR, P02, P10, P11, P30, P48, P52, P53, P54, P56, PCI, PQC, PhilInd, RASB, S02, S03, S09, S10, SCI, SCOPUS, SOPODA, SSCI, SociolAb, SpeleolAb, T02, W03, W07, Z02.
—BLDSC (8490.652000), IE, Infotrieve, Ingenta, INIST, Linda Hall. **CCC.**
Published by: Pergamon (Subsidiary of: Elsevier Science & Technology), The Blvd, Langford Ln, East Park, Kidlington, Oxford OX5 1GB, United Kingdom. TEL 44-1865-843000, FAX 44-1865-843010, JournalsCustomerServiceEMEA@elsevier.com. Eds. Marina Frasca-Spada, Nicholas Jardine. **Subscr. to:** Elsevier BV, Radarweg 29, PO Box 211, Amsterdam 1000 AE, Netherlands. TEL 31-20-4853757, FAX 31-20-4853432, JournalsCustomerServiceEMEA@elsevier.com.

➤ **STUDIES IN HISTORY AND PHILOSOPHY OF SCIENCE PART B: STUDIES IN HISTORY AND PHILOSOPHY OF MODERN PHYSICS.** *see* PHYSICS

➤ **STUDIES IN LOCATIONAL ANALYSIS.** *see* HOUSING AND URBAN PLANNING

500 NLD ISSN 1571-0831
STUDIES IN MULTIDISCIPLINARITY. Text in English. 2003. irreg., latest vol.4, 2007. price varies. **Document type:** *Monographic series, Academic/Scholarly.*
Related titles: Online - full text ed.
Indexed: SCOPUS.
—**CCC.**
Published by: Elsevier BV (Subsidiary of: Elsevier Science & Technology), Radarweg 29, PO Box 211, Amsterdam, 1000 AE, Netherlands. TEL 31-20-4853911, FAX 31-20-4852457, JournalsCustomerServiceEMEA@elsevier.com, http://www.elsevier.com. Eds. Laura McNamara, Mary Meyer.

STUDIES IN REGIONAL AND URBAN PLANNING. *see* HOUSING AND URBAN PLANNING

STUDIES IN SCIENCE EDUCATION. *see* EDUCATION—Teaching Methods And Curriculum

STUDIUM INTEGRALE JOURNAL. *see* BIOLOGY

500 DEU ISSN 0341-0161
STUTTGARTER BEITRAEGE ZUR NATURKUNDE. SERIE C. ALLGEMEINVERSTAENDLICHE AUFSAETZE. Text in German. irreg. **Document type:** *Monographic series, Academic/Scholarly.*
Indexed: EntAb, GeoRef, RefZh, VirolAbstr, Z01.
—Linda Hall.
Published by: Staatliches Museum fuer Naturkunde Stuttgart, Rosenstein 1, Stuttgart, 70191, Germany. TEL 49-711-89360, FAX 49-711-8936200.

354 SDN
SUDAN. NATIONAL COUNCIL FOR RESEARCH. SCIENCE POLICY AND ANNUAL REPORT. Text in English. a. per issue exchange basis. **Document type:** *Corporate.*
Published by: National Centre for Research, Documentation and Information Centre, P O Box 2404, Khartoum, Sudan. TEL 249-11-770776, FAX 249-11-770701, TELEX BUHTH. Ed. Farida A Hamad.

SUDAN RESEARCH INFORMATION BULLETIN. *see* HUMANITIES: COMPREHENSIVE WORKS

500 DEU ISSN 1610-4196
SUDETENDEUTSCHE AKADEMIE DER WISSENSCHAFTEN UND KUENSTE. SCHRIFTEN. Text in German. 1980. irreg. **Document type:** *Monographic series, Academic/Scholarly.*
Indexed: CCMJ, MSN, MathR, Z02.
Published by: Sudetendeutsche Akademie der Wissenschaften und Kuenste e.V., Hochstr 8-III, Munich, 81669, Germany. TEL 49-89-48000348, FAX 49-89-48000374.

500 DEU ISSN 0039-4564
Q3 CODEN: SUARAH
➤ **SUDHOFFS ARCHIV**; Zeitschrift fuer Wissenschaftsgeschichte. Text in English, French, German. 1908. s-a. EUR 173.80; EUR 139 to members; EUR 89 per issue (effective 2012). adv. bk.rev. bibl.; illus. index. back issues avail.; reprint service avail. from SCH. **Document type:** *Journal, Academic/Scholarly.*
Former titles (until 1966): Sudhoffs Archiv fuer Geschichte der Medizin und der Naturwissenschaften (0365-2610); (until 1934): Sudhoffs Archiv fuer Geschichte der Medizin
Related titles: ◆ Supplement(s): Sudhoffs Archiv. Beihefte. ISSN 0341-0773.
Indexed: A22, AmH&L, CA, CCMJ, ChemAb, DIP, EMBASE, ExcerpMed, FR, HistAb, I14, IBR, IBZ, INI, IndMed, MEDLINE, MSN, MathR, P30, R10, RASB, Reac, SCOPUS, T02.
—GNLM, IE, Infotrieve, INIST, Linda Hall. **CCC.**
Published by: Franz Steiner Verlag GmbH, Birkenwaldstr 44, Stuttgart, 70191, Germany. TEL 49-711-25820, FAX 49-711-2582290, service@steiner-verlag.de. R&P Sabine Koerner. Adv. contact Susanne Szoradi. Circ: 500.

500 610 DEU ISSN 0341-0773
SUDHOFFS ARCHIV. BEIHEFTE. Text in German. 1961. irreg., latest vol.59, 2010. price varies. **Document type:** *Monographic series, Academic/Scholarly.*
Formerly (until 1966): Sudhoffs Archiv fuer Geschichte der Medizin und der Naturwissenschaften. Beihefte (0931-9425)
Related titles: ◆ Supplement to: Sudhoffs Archiv. ISSN 0039-4564.
Indexed: EMBASE, ExcerpMed, FR, IndMed, MEDLINE, P30, R10, Reac, SCOPUS, SpeleolAb.
—INIST.
Published by: Franz Steiner Verlag GmbH, Birkenwaldstr 44, Stuttgart, 70191, Germany. TEL 49-711-25820, FAX 49-711-2582290, service@steiner-verlag.de, http://www.steiner-verlag.de.

509 510 ESP ISSN 1576-9372
Q127.I742
SUHAYL; journal for the history of the exact and natural sciences in Islamic civilization. Text in Arabic, English. 2000. a. **Document type:** *Journal, Academic/Scholarly.*
Indexed: CCMJ, I14, MSN, MathR, Z02.
Published by: (Universitat de Barcelona, Departament d'Arab), Universitat de Barcelona, Servei de Publicacions, Gran Via Corts Catalanes 585, Barcelona, 08007, Spain. TEL 34-93-4021100, http://www.publicacions.ub.es. Ed. Juan Vernet. **Dist. by:** Portico Librerias, S.A., Munoz Seca, 6, PO Box 503, Zaragoza 50080, Spain. TEL 34-976-557039, FAX 34-976-353226, portico@zaragoza.net.

500 ZAF ISSN 0039-4807
SUID-AFRIKAANSE AKADEMIE VIR WETENSKAP EN KUNS. NUUSBRIEF. Text in English. 1961. q. looseleaf. ZAR 71.86 (effective 2000). adv. bibl.; illus. **Document type:** *Newsletter.*
Published by: Suid-Afrikaanse Akademie vir Wetenskap en Kuns/South African Academy of Science and Arts, Private Bag X11, Arcadia, 0007, South Africa. TEL 27-12-328-5082, FAX 27-12-328-5091, publikasies@akademie.co.za. Ed. J B Z Louw. Circ: 2,000.

500 ZAF ISSN 0254-3486
Q85 CODEN: SATTDF
SUID AFRIKAANSE TYDSKRIF VIR NATUURWETENSKAP EN TEGNOLOGIE. Text in Afrikaans; Summaries in Afrikaans, English. 1982. q. ZAR 162.04 (effective 2000). adv. bk.rev. charts; illus.; stat. index. back issues avail. **Document type:** *Academic/Scholarly.*
Indexed: A01, B25, BIOSIS Prev, CA, CIN, ChemAb, ChemTitl, INIS AtomInd, ISAP, Inspec, MycolAb, T02, Z02.
—AskIEEE, CASDDS.
Published by: Suid-Afrikaanse Akademie vir Wetenskap en Kuns/South African Academy of Science and Arts, Private Bag X11, Arcadia, 0007, South Africa. TEL 27-12-328-5082, FAX 27-12-328-5091, publikasies@akademie.co.za. Ed. J D van Wyk. R&P J B Z Louw. Circ: 900.

500 TUR ISSN 1306-7575
➤ **SULEYMAN DEMIREL UNIVERSITESI. FEN DERGISI/S D U JOURNAL OF SCIENCE.** Text in English, Turkish. 2006. s-a. free (effective 2011). **Document type:** *Journal, Academic/Scholarly.* **Description:** Publishes original research articles in the areas of biology, physics, chemistry and mathematics.
Media: Online - full text.
Indexed: A01, A32, A34, B23, C25, C30, CA, CABA, E12, ESPM, F08, F12, FCA, GH, H16, I11, IndVet, MSN, N02, O01, OR, P33, P37, PGrRegA, PollutAb, R07, R08, R13, RA&MP, RM&VM, S12, S13, S16, S17, SWRA, T02, T05, TriticAb, VS, W10, Z02.
Published by: Suleyman Demirel Universitesi, Fen-Edebiyat Fakultesi Adina, Isparta, 32260, Turkey. TEL 90-246-2113801, FAX 90-246-2371106, fendergisi@sdu.edu.tr, http://www.sdu.edu.tr/dergi/fendergisi/. Ed. Ali Gok.

▼➤ **SULEYMAN DEMIREL UNIVERSITESI. TEKNIK BILIMLER DERGISI/S D U JOURNAL OF TECHNICAL SCIENCES.** *see* TECHNOLOGY: COMPREHENSIVE WORKS

➤ **SULEYMAN DEMIREL UNIVERSITESI. ULUSLARARASI TEKNOLOJIK BILIMLER DERGISI/S D U INTERNATIONAL JOURNAL OF TECHNOLOGICAL SCIENCES.** *see* TECHNOLOGY: COMPREHENSIVE WORKS

500 FIN ISSN 0356-6927
Q60.2
SUOMALAINEN TIEDEAKATEMIA. VUOSIKIRJA/ACADEMIA SCIENTIARUM FENNICA. YEARBOOK. Text in English, Finnish; Text and summaries in English, French, German. 1977. a. index. back issues avail.; reprints avail. **Document type:** *Yearbook, Academic/Scholarly.*
Incorporates (1994-2000): Academia Scientiarum Fennica. Yearbook (1238-9137); Formed by the merger of (1908-1977): Suomalainen Tiedeakatemia - Esitelmt ja Pytkirjat (0371-3423); (1908-1977): Finnische Akademie der Wissenschaften - Sitzungsberichte (0065-0501)
Related titles: ◆ English ed.: Academia Scientiarum Fennica. Yearbook. ISSN 1238-9137.
Indexed: BibLing, GeoRef, MLA-IB, RASB, SpeleolAb.
—Linda Hall.

S

Published by: Suomalainen Tiedeakatemia/Academia Scientiarum Fennica, Mariankatu 5, Helsinki, 00170, Finland. TEL 358-9-636800, FAX 358-9-660117, acadsci@acadsci.fi, http://www.acadsci.fi. Ed. Pentti Kauranen. Circ: 500. **Dist. by:** Bookstore Tiedekirja, Kirkkokatu 14, Helsinki 00170, Finland. TEL 358-9-635177, FAX 358-9-635017, tiedekirja@pp.kolumbus.fi, http://www.tsv.fi/tkirja/tiekirj.html.

500 FIN ISSN 0358-9153
SUOMEN AKATEMIA. JULKAISUJA/ACADEMY OF FINLAND. PUBLICATIONS. Text in English, Finnish. 1977. irreg. free (effective 2005). back issues avail. **Document type:** *Monographic series, Academic/Scholarly.*
Related titles: Online - full text ed.
Indexed: GeoRef.
Published by: Suomen Akatemia/The Academy of Finland, Vilhonvuorenkatu 6, PO Box 99, Helsinki, 00501, Finland. TEL 358-9-774881, FAX 358-9-77488299, keskus@aka.fi. Ed. Riitta Tirronen TEL 358-9-77488369.

500 PRT
SUPERINTERESSANTE (PORTUGAL). Text in Portuguese. 199?. m. EUR 26.55 (effective 2011). **Document type:** *Magazine, Consumer.*
Published by: Motorpress Lisboa, SA (Subsidiary of: Gruner + Jahr AG & Co), Rua Policarpio Anjos No. 4, Cruz Quebrada, Dafundo 1495-742, Portugal. TEL 351-21-4154500, FAX 351-21-4154501, http://www.mpl.pt.

SUPERSCIENCE. *see* EDUCATION—Teaching Methods And Curriculum

500 FRA ISSN 1993-3800
➤ **SURVEYS AND PERSPECTIVES INTEGRATING ENVIRONMENT AND SOCIETY.** Variant title: SAPIENS. Text in English. 2008. irreg. **Document type:** *Journal, Academic/Scholarly.*
Related titles: Online - full text ed.: ISSN 1993-3819. free (effective 2011).
Indexed: CABA, E12, F08, F12, GH, R12, S13, S16, T05, W11.
Published by: Institut Veolia Environnement, 15 Rue des Sablons, Paris, 75016, France.

500 JPN ISSN 1862-4065
SUSTAINABILITY SCIENCE. Text in English. 2006. q. EUR 258, USD 326 combined subscription to institutions (print & online eds.) (effective 2012). reprint service avail. from PSC. **Document type:** *Journal, Academic/Scholarly.* **Description:** Designed to provide a platform for sustainability science and the way to a sustainable global society.
Related titles: Online - full text ed.: ISSN 1862-4057 (from IngentaConnect).
Indexed: A12, A22, A26, ABIn, Agr, CurCont, E01, ESPM, P10, P11, P26, P48, P51, P52, P53, P54, P56, PQC, S10, SCI, SCOPUS, SSciA, W07.
—IE, Ingenta. **CCC.**
Published by: Springer Japan KK (Subsidiary of: Springer Science+Business Media), No 2 Funato Bldg, 1-11-11 Kudan-kita, Chiyoda-ku, Tokyo, 102-0073, Japan. TEL 81-3-68317000, FAX 81-3-68317001, orders@springer.jp, http://www.springer.jp. Ed. Kazuhiko Takeuchi.

500 NLD ISSN 1871-2711
SUSTAINABILITY SCIENCE AND ENGINEERING. Text in English. 2006. irreg. **Document type:** *Monographic series, Academic/Scholarly.*
Indexed: SCOPUS.
—**CCC.**
Published by: Elsevier BV (Subsidiary of: Elsevier Science & Technology), Radarweg 29, PO Box 211, Amsterdam, 1000 AE, Netherlands. TEL 31-20-4853911, FAX 31-20-4852457, JournalsCustomerServiceEMEA@elsevier.com, http://www.elsevier.com. Ed. Martin Abraham.

500 USA ISSN 1548-7733
QH75.A1
➤ **SUSTAINABILITY: SCIENCE, PRACTICE, & POLICY.** Abbreviated title: S S P P. Text in English. 2005 (Spring). s-a. free (effective 2011). back issues avail. **Document type:** *Journal, Academic/Scholarly.* **Description:** Provides a platform for the dissemination of new practices and for dialogue emerging out of the field of sustainability.
Media: Online - full text.
Indexed: A34, A35, A37, A38, A39, AgBio, AgrForAb, B21, C27, C29, CA, CABA, D03, D04, E12, E13, E17, ESPM, F08, F12, G02, GH, H16, I11, LT, N02, P10, P11, P33, P39, P42, P48, P52, P56, PAIS, PQC, PSA, R12, R14, S02, S03, S12, S13, S14, S15, S16, S18, SCOPUS, SSciA, SociolAb, T02, T05, TAR, W11.
Published by: (National Biological Information Infrastructure, National Program Office), ProQuest LLC (Bethesda) (Subsidiary of: Cambridge Information Group), 789 E Eisenhower Pky, Ann Arbor, MI 48103. TEL 734-761-4700, FAX 734-997-4222, journals@csa.com, http://www.csa.com. Ed. Maurie Cohen.

500 CHN ISSN 1000-2073
SUZHOU DAXUE XUEBAO (ZIRAN KEXUE BAN)/SUZHOU UNIVERSITY. JOURNAL (NATURAL SCIENCE EDITION). Text in Chinese. 1960. q. USD 14.40 (effective 2009). **Document type:** *Journal, Academic/Scholarly.*
Related titles: Online - full text ed.
—BLDSC (4904.800000), East View, IE, Ingenta.
Published by: Suzhou Daxue Chubanshe/Suzhou University Press, 200, Ganjian Dong Rd, 5th Fl, Rm 515, Suzhou, 215021, China. TEL 86-512-67480078, FAX 86-512-67258875, sdcbs@suda.edu.cn, http://sudapress.com/.

500 CHN ISSN 1672-0687
SUZHOU KEJI XUEYUAN XUEBAO (ZIRAN KEXUE BAN)/ UNIVERSITY OF SCIENCE AND TECHNOLOGY OF SUZHOU. JOURNAL (NATURAL SCIENCE). Text in Chinese. 1984. q. **Document type:** *Journal, Academic/Scholarly.*
Formerly (until 2002): Tiedao Shi-Yuan Xuebao (Ziran Kexueban)/ Suzhou Railway Teachers College. Journal (1004-5201)
Related titles: Online - full text ed.
Indexed: RefZh, Z02.
Published by: Suzhou Keji Xueyuan, 1701, Binhe Lu, Suzhou, 215011, China. TEL 86-512-68087489, FAX 86-512-68242298.

500 300 CHN ISSN 1673-2006
SUZHOU XUEYUAN XUEBAO. Text in Chinese. 1998. bi-m. **Document type:** *Journal, Academic/Scholarly.*
Formerly (until 2004): Suzhou Shi-Zhuan Xuebao (1009-041X)
Related titles: Online - full text ed.
Published by: Suzhou Xueyuan/Suzhou University, 55, Bianhe Lu, Suzhou, 234000, China. TEL 86-557-3680407.

500 JPN ISSN 0389-5025
QH188 CODEN: SJTKBF
➤ **SUZUGAMINE JOSHI TANDAI KENKYU SHUHO. SHIZEN KAGAKU/SUZUGAMINE WOMEN'S COLLEGE. BULLETIN. NATURAL SCIENCE.** Text in English, Japanese. 1954. a., latest vol.33, 1992. **Document type:** *Journal, Academic/Scholarly.* **Description:** Contains original researches in the broad field of natural science.
Indexed: B25, BIOSIS Prev, JPI, MycolAb.
—CASDDS.
Published by: Suzugamine Joshi Tanki Daigaku/Suzugamine Women's College, 6-8 Inokuchi 4-chome, Nishi-ku, Hiroshima-shi, 733-0842, Japan. TEL 082-278-1103, FAX 082-277-0301. Ed. Yoshikazu Kondo. Circ: 300.

500 600 SWZ ISSN 1012-5957
SWAZILAND JOURNAL OF SCIENCE AND TECHNOLOGY. Text in English. 1982. 2/yr. **Document type:** *Journal, Academic/Scholarly.*
Formerly (until 1988): Royal Swaziland Society for Science and Technology. Journal
Indexed: PLESA.
Published by: Royal Swaziland Society for Science and Technology, c/o University of Swaziland, Private Bag, Kwaluseni, Swaziland.

500 600 POL ISSN 0867-6380
SWIAT NAUKI. Text in Polish. 1991. m. adv. **Document type:** *Magazine, Consumer.* **Description:** For those who are interested in science and wish to folllow the latest scientific discoveries and technologies.
Related titles: ◆ Italian ed.: Le Scienze. ISSN 0036-8083; ◆ English ed.: Scientific American. ISSN 0036-8733; ◆ German ed.: Spektrum der Wissenschaft. ISSN 0170-2971; ◆ Hungarian ed.: Tudomany. ISSN 0237-322X; ◆ French ed.: Pour la Science. ISSN 0153-4092; ◆ Chinese ed.: Ke Xue. ISSN 1002-1299; ◆ Spanish ed.: Investigacion y Ciencia. ISSN 0210-136X; ◆ Japanese ed.: Nikkei Saiensu. ISSN 0917-009X; ◆ Arabic ed.: Majallat al-Ulum; Turkish ed.: Bilim.
Indexed: AgrLib.
Published by: Wydawnictwa Szkolne i Pedagogiczne, Pl Dabrowskiego 8, Warsaw, 00950, Poland. TEL 48-22-8279280, wsip@wsip.com.pl, http://www.wsip.com.pl. Circ: 58,133.

500 USA
SYMMETRIES IN SCIENCE. Text in English. 1990 (vol.4). irreg., latest vol.11, 2004. price varies. back issues avail. **Document type:** *Proceedings.*
Published by: Springer New York LLC (Subsidiary of: Springer Science+Business Media), 233 Spring St, New York, NY 10013. TEL 212-460-1500, FAX 212-460-1575, service-ny@springer.com, http://www.springer.com/.

300 500 HUN ISSN 0865-4824
Q172.5.S95
➤ **SYMMETRY;** culture and science. Text in English. 1990. q. USD 78 to members; USD 100 to non-members (effective 2002). adv. bk.rev. abstr.; bibl.; illus. 112 p./no. 1 cols./p.; back issues avail. **Document type:** *Journal, Academic/Scholarly.* **Description:** Publishes original papers on symmetry and related issues such as asymmetry, dissymetry and antisymmetry.
Indexed: RILM, Z02.
Published by: International Society for the Interdisciplinary Study of Symmetry, c/o Symmetrion, PO Box 994, Budapest, 1245, Hungary. http://www.us.geocities.com/isis_symmetry. Ed. Szaniszlo Berczi. R&P, Adv. contact Gyorgy Darvas. **Co-sponsor:** International Symmetry Foundation.

500 CHE ISSN 2073-8994
Q172.5.S95 CODEN: SYMMAM
▼ **SYMMETRY.** Text in English. 2009. q. free (effective 2011). **Document type:** *Journal, Academic/Scholarly.*
Media: Online - full text.
Indexed: A01, T02.
Published by: M D P I AG, Postfach, Basel, 4005, Switzerland. TEL 41-61-6837734, FAX 41-61-3028918, http://www.mdpi.org/. Ed. Joe Rosen.

500 ZWE
SYMPOSIUM ON SCIENCE AND TECHNOLOGY. PROCEEDINGS. Text in English. 1992. biennial. USD 40. **Document type:** *Proceedings.*
Published by: Scientific Liaison Office, Causeway, PO Box CY 294, Harare, Zimbabwe. TEL 263-4-700573, FAX 263-4-728799.

500 SGP ISSN 0218-3188
SYNERGY. Text in English. bi-m. free. **Document type:** *Newsletter.* **Description:** Covers national science and technology policies and news of research and development projects.
Published by: National Science and Technology Board, Singapore Science Park, 16 Science Park Dr, 01-03 The Pasteur, Singapore, 118227, Singapore. TEL 65-779-7066, FAX 65-777-1711.

500 170 USA ISSN 2153-3679
▼ ➤ **SYNESIS.** Text in English. 2010 (Mar.). s-a. free (effective 2011). **Document type:** *Journal, Academic/Scholarly.* **Description:** Features research on science, technology, ethics and policy.
Media: Online - full text.
Published by: (Potomac Institute for Policy Studies), Potomac Institute Press, 901 N Stuart St, Arlington, VA 22203. TEL 703-525-0770, jgiordano@potomacinstitute.org, http://www.potomacinstitute.org/index.php?option=com_content&view=article&id=406&Itemid=37. Ed. James Giordano.

508.68 ZWE ISSN 1011-7881
SYNTARSUS. Text and summaries in English. 1956; N.S. 1983. irreg., latest 1991. price varies. illus. index. back issues avail. **Document type:** *Academic/Scholarly.* **Description:** Theses and surveys discussing research in natural history in southern Africa.
Former titles: Smithersia (0250-300X); National Museums and Monuments Administration. Occasional Papers. Series B: Natural Sciences; National Museums and Monuments of Rhodesia. Occasional Papers. Series B: Natural Sciences (0304-5315); Which superseded in part: National Museums and Monuments of Rhodesia. Occasional Papers (0027-9730)
Indexed: ISAP, SpeleolAb, WildRev.
Published by: (Natural History Museum of Zimbabwe), National Museums and Monuments of Zimbabwe, PO Box 240, Bulawayo, Zimbabwe. TEL 60045. Ed. A Kumarai. Circ: 400.

SYNTHESE; an international journal for epistemology, methodology and philosophy of science. *see* PHILOSOPHY

500 NLD ISSN 1873-9148
SYNTHESE (THE HAGUE). Running title: N W O Jaaroverzicht. Variant title: N W O Synthese. Text in Dutch. 2006. a. free (effective 2009).
Published by: Nederlandse Organisatie voor Wetenschappelijk Onderzoek/Netherlands Organization for Scientific Research, PO Box 93138, The Hague, 2509 AC, Netherlands. TEL 31-70-3440640, FAX 31-70-3850971, nwo@nwo.nl, http://www.nwo.nl. Ed. Caroline van Overbeeke. Circ: 13,000.

500 JPN ISSN 1883-0978
T177.J3
SYNTHESIOLOGY (ENGLISH EDITION). Text in English. 2008. q. **Document type:** *Journal, Academic/Scholarly.* **Description:** Contains some of the articles translated from the Japanese edition of Synthesiology with an estimated 4 months delay after the initial publiction. Covers all aspects of science and technology with the focus in societal value and integration.
Related titles: ◆ Translation of: Synthesiology (Japanese Edition). ISSN 1882-6229.
Indexed: ESPM, EnvEAb, RefZh, SCOPUS.
—BLDSC (8586.782000), IE, Linda Hall.
Published by: National Institute of Advanced Industrial Science and Technology/Sangyou Gijutsu Sougou Kenkyuujo, 1-1-1 Umezono, Tsukuba Central 2, Tsukuba, Ibaraki 305-8563, Japan. TEL 81-29-8626217, FAX 81-29-8626212, prpub@m.aist.go.jp. Ed. A. Ono.

500 JPN ISSN 1882-6229
T177.J3
SYNTHESIOLOGY (JAPANESE EDITION)/KOUSEIGAKU. Text in Chinese. 2008. q. back issues avail. **Document type:** *Journal, Academic/Scholarly.* **Description:** Covers all aspects of science and technology with the focus in societal value and integration.
Related titles: Online - full text ed.: ISSN 1882-7365; ◆ English Translation: Synthesiology (English Edition). ISSN 1883-0978.
Published by: National Institute of Advanced Industrial Science and Technology/Sangyou Gijutsu Sougou Kenkyuujo, 1-1-1 Umezono, Tsukuba Central 2, Tsukuba, Ibaraki 305-8563, Japan. TEL 81-29-8626217, FAX 81-29-8626212, prpub@m.aist.go.jp. Ed. A. Ono.

500 POL ISSN 1427-275X
Q295 CODEN: SSTEFU
➤ **SYSTEMS;** journal of transdisciplinary systems sciences. Text in English. 1997. s-a. USD 22 foreign (effective 2011). **Document type:** *Journal, Academic/Scholarly.* **Description:** Covers systems analysis and synthesis, systems design and informationscience, systems and education, socio-technological systems research, bio- and ecological systems evolution, systems methodology and informatics, cybernetics and theory in mathematics, human organizations and management systems, communication processing systems design.
Indexed: A01, B22, CA, Inspec, T02.
—Linda Hall.
Published by: (Politechnika Wroclawska/Wroclaw University of Technology, Polskie Towarzystwo Systemowe/Polish Systems Society), Politechnika Wroclawska, Oficyna Wydawnicza/Wroclaw University of Technology, Wybrzeze Wyspianskiego 27, Wroclaw, 50370, Poland. TEL 48-71-3202994, FAX 48-71-3282940, oficwyd@pwr.wroc.pl, http://www.oficyna.pwr.wroc.pl. Ed. Mieczyslaw Bazewicz.

500 600 POL ISSN 0082-1241
SZCZECINSKIE TOWARZYSTWO NAUKOWE. SPRAWOZDANIA. Text in Polish. 1960. irreg. price varies.
Published by: Szczecinskie Towarzystwo Naukowe, ul Wojska Polskiego 96, Szczecin, 71481, Poland. wtarc@univ.szczecin.pl.

500 POL ISSN 0137-5326
DK4600.L43
SZKICE LEGNICKIE. Text in Polish. 1962. irreg., latest vol.13, 1987. price varies. **Description:** Studies in the history, culture and social life of Legnica region.
Indexed: AgrLib.
Published by: Legnickie Towarzystwo Przyjaciol Nauk, Ul Zamkowa 2, Legnica, 59920, Poland. Ed. Tadeusz Guminski. **Dist. by:** Ars Polona, Obroncow 25, Warsaw 03933, Poland.

500 CHE
T A - SWISS NEWSLETTER. (Technology Assessment) Text in French, German. 1996. q. free. bk.rev.; Website rev. **Document type:** *Journal, Academic/Scholarly.*
Published by: Schweizerischer Wissenschafts- und Technologierat, Birkenweg 61, Bern, 3003, Switzerland. TEL 41-31-3229963, FAX 41-31-3228070, ta@swtr.admin.ch, http://www.admin.ch/swtr. Ed., R&P Walter Grossenbacher-Mansuy.

T I M S S AUSTRALIA MONOGRAPH. (Third International Mathematics and Science Study) *see* EDUCATION

500 THA
T I S T R RESEARCH NEWS. Text in Thai. m. **Document type:** *Newsletter.*
Formerly: A S R C T Research News
Published by: Thailand Institute of Scientific and Technological Research, 196 Phahonyothin Rd, Chatuchak, Bangkok, 10900, Thailand. TEL 579-8594, FAX 662-579-8594. Circ: 1,000.

500 NLD ISSN 1386-5447
T N O MAGAZINE (INTERNATIONAL EDITION); a quarterly technology update. (Toegepast Natuurwetenschappelijk Onderzoek) Text in English. 1983; N.S. 1997. q. free (effective 2009). illus. **Document type:** *Magazine, Trade.* **Description:** Covers research and development and technology applications at TNO.
Formerly (until 1997): Applied Research (0929-0702)
Indexed: A28, APA, BrCerAb, C&ISA, CA/WCA, CIA, CerAb, CivEngAb, CorrAb, E&CAJ, E11, EEA, EMA, FS&TA, H15, M&TEA, M09, MBF, METADEX, SolStAb, T04, WAA.
—Infotrieve, Linda Hall.
Published by: Nederlandse Organisatie voor Toegepast Natuurwetenschappelijk Onderzoek (TNO)/Netherlands Organization for Applied Scientific Research, Postbus 6000, Delft, 2600 JA, Netherlands. TEL 31-15-2696900, FAX 31-15-2612403, infodesk@tno.nl, http://www.tno.nl. Ed. Jan van den Brink.

500 BIH ISSN 1840-1503
➤ **T T E M TECHNICS TECHNOLOGIES EDUCATION MANAGEMENT.** Text in English. 2006. s-a. **Document type:** *Journal, Academic/ Scholarly.*

Published by: D R U N P P, Bolnicka bb, Sarajevo, 71000, Bosnia Herzegovina.

500 200 DEU

T T N - AKZENTE. (Technik Theologie Naturwissenschaften) Text in German. 1994. irreg., latest vol.19, 2008. price varies. **Document type:** *Monographic series, Academic/Scholarly.*
Formerly (until 2006): Akzente
Published by: (Ludwig-Maximilians-Universitaet Muenchen, Institut Technik-Theologie-Naturwissenschaften), Herbert Utz Verlag GmbH, Adalbertstr 57, Munich, 80799, Germany. TEL 49-89-27779100, FAX 49-89-27779101, utz@utzverlag.com.

TAISHAN XUEYUAN XUEBAO/TAISHAN UNIVERSITY. JOURNAL. *see* SOCIAL SCIENCES: COMPREHENSIVE WORKS

500 TWN ISSN 1023-442X

TAIWAN, REPUBLIC OF CHINA. NATIONAL SCIENCE COUNCIL. ANNUAL REPORT. Text in Chinese. 1963. a. TWD 300, USD 10 (effective 2001). 300 p./no.; back issues avail.; reprints avail. **Document type:** *Government.*
Related titles: Microfiche ed.; Online - full content ed.
Published by: National Science Council/Xingzhengyuan Guojia Kexue Weiyuanhui, Rm 1701, 106 Ho-Ping E. Rd, Sec 2, Taipei, Taiwan. TEL 886-2-27377594, FAX 886-2-27377248, ylchang@nsc.gov.tw, http://www.nsc.gov.tw. Circ: 2,200 (paid).

500 CHN ISSN 1673-2057

TAIYUAN KEJI DAXUE XUEBAO/TAIYUAN UNIVERSITY OF SCIENCE AND TECHNOLOGY. JOURNAL. Text in Chinese. 1980. q. USD 31.20 (effective 2009). **Document type:** *Journal, Academic/Scholarly.*
Formerly: Taiyuan Zhongxing Jixie Xueyuan Xuebao/Taiyuan Heavy-Machinery Institute. Journal (1000-159X)
Related titles: Online - full text ed.
Published by: Taiyuan Keji Daxue, 66, Waliu Lu, Taiyuan, 030024, China. TEL 86-351-6998047. **Dist. by:** China International Book Trading Corp, 35 Chegongzhuang Xilu, Haidian District, PO Box 399, Beijing 100044, China. TEL 86-10-68412045, FAX 86-10-68412023, cibtc@mail.cibtc.com.cn, http://www.cibtc.com.cn.

500 CHN ISSN 1672-2027

TAIYUAN SHIFAN XUEYUAN XUEBAO (ZIRAN KEXUE BAN). Text in Chinese. 2002. q. CNY 9 newsstand/cover (effective 2007). **Document type:** *Journal, Academic/Scholarly.*
Related titles: Online - full text ed.
Published by: Taiyuan Shifan Xueyuan/Taiyuan Normal University, 189, Nanneihuan Jie, Taiyuan, 030012, China. TEL 86-351-2279449, FAX 86-351-4198720.

500 300 CHN ISSN 1671-0142

TAIZHOU ZHIYE JISHU XUEYUAN XUEBAO/TAIZHOU POLYTECHNICAL INSTITUTE. JOURNAL. Text in Chinese. 2001. bi-m. CNY 6 newsstand/cover (effective 2006). **Document type:** *Journal, Academic/Scholarly.*
Related titles: Online - full text ed.
Published by: Taizhou Zhiye Jishu Xueyuan, 2, Binguan Lu, Taizhou, 225300, China. TEL 86-523-6665582, FAX 86-523-6662914.

500 JPN ISSN 0386-6890

TAKAYAMA TANKI DAIGAKU KENKYU KIYO/TAKAYAMA JUNIOR COLLEGE. MEMOIRS. Text in Japanese; Summaries in English. 1978. a.
Published by: Takayama Tanki Daigaku/Takayama Junior College, 1155 Shimo-Bayashi-Machi, Takayama-shi, Gifu-ken 506-0059, Japan.

500 CHN ISSN 1009-0568

TALIMU NONGKEN DAXUE XUEBAO/TARIM UNIVERSITY. JOURNAL. Text in Chinese. 1978. q. CNY 4 newsstand/cover (effective 2006). **Document type:** *Journal, Academic/Scholarly.*
Related titles: Online - full text ed.
Published by: Talimu Nongken Daxue, Aral, Xinjiang 843300, China. TEL 86-997-4681392, FAX 86-997-4681202.

TAMKANG JOURNAL OF SCIENCE AND ENGINEERING. *see* TECHNOLOGY: COMPREHENSIVE WORKS

500 TZA ISSN 0856-1761
CODEN: TJSCEY

➤ **TANZANIA JOURNAL OF SCIENCE.** Text in English. 1975. a. USD 30 in Africa; USD 50 elsewhere (effective 2004). bk.rev. **Document type:** *Journal, Academic/Scholarly.*
Formerly: University of Dar es Salaam. University Science Journal (0250-5592)
Indexed: A34, A35, A37, AgBio, AgrForAb, BA, C25, C30, CABA, ChemAb, E12, F08, F11, F12, FCA, G11, GH, H16, I11, MaizeAb, N02, O01, OR, P32, P33, P40, PGegResA, PHN&I, PN&I, R07, R08, R11, R12, R13, RA&MP, S12, S13, S16, S17, T05, W11.
—BLDSC (8602.704350), CASDDS.
Published by: University of Dar es Salaam, Faculty of Science, PO Box 35065, Dar Es Salaam, Tanzania. TEL 255-51-410465, TELEX 41327 UNISCIE TZ. Ed. R B M Senzota.

➤ **TAXILA INSTITUTE OF ASIAN CIVILIZATIONS. QUAID-I-AZAM UNIVERSITY. PUBLICATIONS.** *see* HISTORY—History Of Asia

➤ **TECBAHIA**; revista baiana de tecnologia. *see* TECHNOLOGY: COMPREHENSIVE WORKS

▼ ➤ **TECHNAI.** *see* ARCHAEOLOGY

➤ **TECHNICAL COMMUNICATION QUARTERLY.** *see* EDUCATION—Teaching Methods And Curriculum

➤ **TECHNICAL SCIENCES.** *see* TECHNOLOGY: COMPREHENSIVE WORKS

500 GRC ISSN 0040-4764

TECHNIKA CHRONIKA/ANNALES TECHNIQUES. Text in Greek; Summaries in English. 1932. q. USD 100 per issue. bk.rev. charts; illus. index.
Indexed: EIP, Inspec.
Published by: Technical Chamber of Greece, 4 Karageorgi Servias, Athens, 125 62, Greece. TEL 3222-466, FAX 3221772, TELEX 218374. Ed. D Rokos. Circ: 12,000.

500 ZAF ISSN 1017-4966
Q1

TECHNOBRIEF. Text in English. 1991. m. free. **Document type:** *Newsletter.* **Description:** Highlights CSIR's achievements in scientific and technological research, development and implementation, focusing on technology transfer partnership with industry, and environmental impact issues.
Supersedes (1959-1991): Scientiae (0036-8717)
Indexed: F&EA, ISAP.
Published by: Council for Scientific and Industrial Research (C S I R), PO Box 395, Pretoria, 0001, South Africa. TEL 27-12-8412911, FAX 27-12-3491153, http://www.csir.co.za. Circ: 16,000.

TECHNOLOGIA; historical and social studies in science, technology and industry. *see* TECHNOLOGY: COMPREHENSIVE WORKS

500 USA ISSN 1099-274X
T171

TECHNOLOGY REVIEW. Text in English. 1899. bi-m. (m. until 2006). USD 24.95 (print or online ed.) (effective 2011). bk.rev. illus. Index. reprints avail. **Document type:** *Magazine, Consumer.* **Description:** Helps readers to understand emerging technologies, their impact and how they are introduced in the market. Topics explored include human-computer interaction, intelligence in everday objects, digital privacy, intellectual property, and technology and popular culture. Also contains information on new products and prototypes, as well as a column explaining how a new technology works and its expected impact.
Former titles (until 1998): M I T's Technology Review (1096-3715); (until 1997): Technology Review (0040-1692)
Related titles: Microform ed.: (from PQC); Online - full text ed.: ISSN 2158-9186; Italian ed.; German ed.; French ed.; Dutch ed.; Chinese ed.
Indexed: A01, A02, A03, A05, A08, A09, A10, A11, A12, A13, A14, A17, A20, A22, A23, A24, A25, A26, A28, ABIPC, ABIn, ABS&EES, AIA, APA, AS&TA, AS&TI, ASCA, Acal, Agr, B01, B02, B04, B06, B07, B08, B09, B13, B15, B17, B18, B21, BIOSIS Prev, BPI, BPIA, BRD, BiolDig, BrCerAb, BusI, C&ISA, C04, C05, C10, C23, CA, CA/WCA, CADCAM, CBRI, CIA, CPEI, CPerI, CerAb, ChemAb, CivEngAb, CommAb, CompB, CompD, CompLI, CorrAb, CurCont, E&CAJ, E04, E05, E07, E08, E11, EEA, EIA, EMA, ESPM, EnerRev, EngInd, EnvAb, EnvEAb, EnvInd, F01, F02, FR, FutSurv, G01, G03, G04, G05, G06, G07, G08, GSA, GSI, GSS&RPL, GeoRef, H&SSA, H01, H02, H15, HECAB, HlthInd, I05, I07, ISR, Inspec, KES, L09, M&TEA, M01, M02, M05, M06, M09, MASUSE, MBF, METADEX, MagInd, Microcompind, MycolAb, N06, P02, P06, P07, P10, P13, P15, P17, P21, P26, P29, P30, P34, P47, P48, P51, P52, P53, P54, PAIS, PQC, R03, R04, R06, RASB, RGAb, RGPR, RoboAb, S01, S04, S06, S08, S09, S10, S23, SCI, SCOPUS, SSciA, SolStAb, SpeleolAb, T&II, T02, T04, TelAb, Telegen, U01, V02, V03, V04, W01, W02, W03, W05, W07, WAA, WBA, WMB.
—BLDSC (8761.000000), CASDDS, IE, Infotrieve, Ingenta, INIST, Linda Hall. **CCC.**
Published by: (Massachusetts Institute of Technology), Technology Review (Subsidiary of: Massachusetts Institute of Technology), One Main St, 7th Fl, Cambridge, MA 02142. TEL 800-877-5230.

500 DEU ISSN 1613-0138

TECHNOLOGY REVIEW; das M.I.T. Magazin fuer Innovation. Text in German. 2003. m. EUR 89.50 domestic; EUR 99 foreign; EUR 8.50 newsstand/cover (effective 2010). adv. **Document type:** *Magazine, Trade.*
—**CCC.**
Published by: Heise Zeitschriften Verlag GmbH und Co. KG, Helstorfer Str 7, Hannover, 30625, Germany. TEL 49-511-53520, FAX 49-511-5352129, kontakt@heise.de. Adv. contact Michael Hanke TEL 49-511-5352167.

500 USA ISSN 1528-431X

TECHNOLOGY TODAY. Text in English. 1949. 3/yr. free to qualified personnel. illus. **Document type:** *Corporate.* **Description:** Discusses some of the technologically-oriented research and development projects underway at Southwest Research Institute.
Formerly (until 1978): Tomorrow Through Research (0040-9146)
Indexed: A28, APA, BrCerAb, C&ISA, CA/WCA, CIA, CerAb, CivEngAb, CorrAb, E&CAJ, E11, EEA, EMA, H15, M&TEA, M09, MBF, METADEX, SolStAb, T04, WAA.
—IE, Linda Hall.
Published by: Southwest Research Institute, 6220 Culebra Rd, Drawer 28510, San Antonio, TX 78228-0510. TEL 210-522-3305, FAX 210-522-3547, TELEX 244846. Ed., R&P Maria I Martinez. Circ: 14,000.

500 600 MEX ISSN 1665-983X

TECNOINTELECTO. Text in Spanish. 2004. s-a. **Document type:** *Journal, Academic/Scholarly.*
Related titles: Online - full text ed.
Indexed: C01.
Published by: Instituto Tecnologico de Ciudad Victoria, Blvd. Emilio Portes Gil No. 1301 Pte., Apdo. Postal 175, Ciudad Victoria, Tamaulipas, 87010, Mexico. TEL 52-8343-130662, FAX 52-8343-133646.

500 600 MEX ISSN 0186-6036

TECNOLOGIA, CIENCIA, EDUCACION. Text in Spanish. 1985. s-a. **Document type:** *Journal, Academic/Scholarly.*
Related titles: Online - full text ed.: 2000. free (effective 2011).
Indexed: C01.
Published by: Instituto Mexicano de Ingenieros Quimicos (I M I Q), Horacio 124-1101, Col Polanco, Mexico City, DF 11560, Mexico. TEL 52-55-52504857, FAX 52-55-55455817, http://www.imiq.org. Ed. Ruth Pedroza Islas.

500 790.13 ROM

TEHNIUM. Text in Romanian. 1970. m. ROL 500. adv. bk.rev.
Address: Piata Presei Libere 1, Bucharest, 79784, Romania. TEL 40-0-2223374. Ed. Ilie Mihaescu. Circ: 50,000.

TEKSTILEC; glasilo Slovenskih tekstilcev. *see* TEXTILE INDUSTRIES AND FABRICS

TELOS; revista de estudios interdisciplinarios en ciencias sociales. *see* HUMANITIES: COMPREHENSIVE WORKS

500 USA ISSN 0040-313X
Q11 CODEN: JTASAG

➤ **TENNESSEE ACADEMY OF SCIENCE. JOURNAL.** Text in English. 1913. q. free to members (effective 2010). bk.rev. abstr.; charts; illus. index. back issues avail. **Document type:** *Journal, Academic/Scholarly.* **Description:** Contains research articles, information about the Tennessee Academy of Science, budget information, minutes of executive committee meetings, abstracts of papers presented at annual meetings, and collegiate abstracts.
Formerly (until 1926): Tennessee Academy of Science. Transactions
Related titles: Online - full text ed.
Indexed: A01, A22, A26, ASFA, Agr, B21, B25, BIOSIS Prev, CA, CIN, ChemAb, ChemTitl, E08, ESPM, G08, GeoRef, I05, MycolAb, P30, S06, S09, SASA, SWRA, SpeleolAb, T02, VITIS, VirolAbstr, W08, WildRev, Z01, Z02.
—CASDDS, Ingenta, INIST, Linda Hall.
Published by: Tennessee Academy of Science, c/o Kim Cleary Sadler, Biology Department, Middle Tennessee State University, Murfreesboro, TN 37132. TEL 615-904-8283, FAX 615-217-7870, ksadler@mtsu.edu, http://www.tnacadsci.org/.

301 100 CZE ISSN 1210-0250
Q44

➤ **TEORIE VEDY/THEORY OF SCIENCE.** Text in Czech, Slovak, English; Summaries in English. 1969. q. EUR 40 (effective 2008). bk.rev. bibl.; charts; stat. **Document type:** *Journal, Academic/Scholarly.* **Description:** Focuses on issues concerning the relation of science, technology, and society.
Formerly (until 1990): Teorie Rozvoje Vedy (0139-987X); Supersedes (in 1977): Teorie a Metoda (0322-9416)
Indexed: RASB.
Published by: Akademie Ved Ceske Republiky, Filozoficky Ustav, Kabinet pro Studium Vedy Techniky a Spolecnosti/Academy of Sciences of Czech Republic, Institute of Philosophy, Centre for Science, Technology and Society Studies, Jilska 1, Prague 1, 11000, Czech Republic. TEL 420-2-22220107, FAX 420-2-22220725, stsscz@cesnet.cz. Ed. Jiri Loudin. Circ: 530.

500 USA ISSN 1941-7411
TA165

TERAHERTZ SCIENCE & TECHNOLOGY; the international journal of THz. Abbreviated title: T S T. Text in English. 2008. q. free (effective 2009). back issues avail. **Document type:** *Journal, Trade.* **Description:** Features significant articles on THz science and technology.
Media: Online - full content.
Published by: Scinco, Inc., PO Box 6982, Williamsburg, VA 23188. TEL 757-941-7875, FAX 757-564-0238, scinco@cox.net, http://www.scincoauto.com.

500 HUN ISSN 0040-3717
Q44 CODEN: TEVIAS

TERMESZET VILAGA. Text in Hungarian. 1869. m. bk.rev. charts; illus. index.
Formerly: Termeszettudomanyi Kozlony
Related titles: Online - full content ed.: ISSN 1417-393X.
Indexed: CIN, ChemAb, ChemTitl, RASB.
—CASDDS, Linda Hall.
Published by: Tudomanyos Ismeretterjeszto Tarsulat, Pf. 176, Budapest, 1431, Hungary. TEL 36-1-4832540, FAX 36-1-4832549, titlap@telc.hu, http://www.titnet.hu. Ed. Staar Gyula. Circ: 17,500.

508.1 ROM ISSN 0373-9570

TERRA. Text in Romanian; Summaries in English. 1949. m. charts; illus.; maps. **Document type:** *Magazine, Academic/Scholarly.*
Formerly (until 1969): Natura. Serie Geografie - Geologie (0470-3693); Which superseded in part (in 1961): Natura (0369-6235)
Indexed: ChemAb, FR, GeoRef.
—INIST.
Published by: C D Press, Bd. Mircea Voda nr. 42, bl. M14, sc.2, ap.42, sector 3, Bucharest, Romania. TEL 40-21-3211131, FAX 40-21-3211131.

500 USA ISSN 0040-4403
Q1 CODEN: TJSCAU

➤ **TEXAS JOURNAL OF SCIENCE.** Text in English. 1941. q. charts; illus. index. back issues avail.; reprints avail. **Document type:** *Journal, Academic/Scholarly.*
Formerly (until 1949): Texas Academy of Science. Proceedings and Transactions (0099-4138); Which was formed by the merger of (1892-1941): Texas Academy of Science. Transactions; (193?-1941): Texas Academy of Science. Proceedings
Related titles: Microform ed.: (from PQC); Online - full text ed.
Indexed: A20, A22, A26, A34, ASCA, AbAn, Agr, B25, BIOBASE, BIOSIS Prev, C25, CABA, CIN, CIS, CRFR, ChemAb, ChemTitl, CurCont, E08, E12, F08, F12, FCA, G08, G11, GeoRef, H16, H17, I05, IABS, IndVet, Inspec, MSN, MathR, MycolAb, P32, P33, P37, P39, P40, PGegResA, S06, S09, S13, S16, SASA, SCI, SCOPUS, SpeleolAb, TAR, VS, W07, W08, WildRev, Z01.
—BLDSC (8799.000000), AskIEEE, CASDDS, IE, Ingenta, INIST, Linda Hall. **CCC.**
Published by: Texas Academy of Science, c/o Allan D. Nelson, Department of Biological Sciences, Tarleton State University, PO Box T-0100, Stephenville, TX 76402.

➤ **TEXTE UND STUDIEN ZUR WISSENSCHAFTSGESCHICHTE.** *see* PHILOSOPHY

500 JPN ISSN 0286-5092

TEZUKAYAMA TANKI DAIGAKU KIYO. SHIZEN KAGAKU HEN/TEZUKAYAMA COLLEGE. JOURNAL. NATURAL SCIENCE. Text and summaries in English, Japanese. 1963. a.
Published by: Tezukayama Tanki Daigaku/Tezukayama Junior College, 3-1 Gakuen-Minami, Nara-shi, 631-0034, Japan. FAX 0742-41-2941.

500 600 THA ISSN 0859-4074
Q1

THAMMASAT INTERNATIONAL JOURNAL OF SCIENCE AND TECHNOLOGY. Abbreviated title: T I J S A T. Text in English. 1996. q. **Document type:** *Journal, Academic/Scholarly.*
Related titles: Online - full text ed.: free (effective 2011).
Published by: Thammasat University, Office of the Rector Bldg, Rangsit Campus, Klongluang Pathum-Thani, 12121, Thailand. TEL 66-2-5644440, FAX 66-2-5644435.

500 600 CHL ISSN 0718-2562

THEAETETO ATHENIENSI MATHEMATICA; revista latinoamericana de ciencias e ingenieria. Text in Spanish. 2005. q. back issues avail. **Document type:** *Journal, Academic/Scholarly.*
Related titles: Online - full text ed.: ISSN 0718-2139. 2005.
Published by: Universidad de Valparaiso, Facultad de Ciencias Economicas y Administrativas, Las Heras No. 6, Valparaiso, Chile. tmat@uv.cl. Eds. Esteban Sefair, Cruzat Prince.

THEOLOGY AND SCIENCE. *see* RELIGIONS AND THEOLOGY

500 USA ISSN 1933-9577

▼ **THEORETICAL SCIENCE.** Text in English. forthcoming 2011 (Nov.). m. free (effective 2009). **Document type:** *Journal, Academic/Scholarly.* **Description:** Covers topics in theoretical science.

S

Media: Online - full content.
Published by: Science Observer, 414-3 Galleria Dr, San Jose, CA 95134. TEL 408-772-5658, derek_cunningham@scienceobserver.com.

500 POL ISSN 0867-4159
Q174
THEORIA ET HISTORIA SCIENTIARUM. Text in Polish. 1991. irreg., latest vol.7, no.2, 2003. price varies. **Document type:** *Monographic series, Academic/Scholarly.*
Indexed: CCMJ, MSN, MathR.
Published by: (Uniwersytet Mikolaja Kopernika/Nicolaus Copernicus University), Wydawnictwo Naukowe Uniwersytetu Mikolaja Kopernika/Nicolaus Copernicus University Press, ul Gagarina 39, Torun, 87100, Poland. TEL 48-56-6114295, FAX 48-56-6114705, dwyd@uni.torun.pl, http://www.wydawnictwo.umk.pl. Eds. Tomasz Komendzinski, Wieslaw Mincer.

THEORY & SCIENCE. *see* SOCIOLOGY

500 CHN
Q4 CODEN: TCHHA9
➤ **TIANJIN DAXUE XUEBAO (ZIRAN KEXUE BAN)/TIANJIN UNIVERSITY. JOURNAL.** Text in Chinese; Abstracts in Chinese, English. 1955. m. 128 p./no.; **Document type:** *Journal, Academic/Scholarly.*
Former titles (until 2003): Tianjin Daxue Xuebao (Ziran Kexue yu Gongcheng Jishu Ban)/Tianjin University. Journal (Sciences and Technology Edition); (until 1998): Tianjin Daxue Xuebao/Tianjin University. Journal (0493-2137)
Related titles: Online - full text ed.: (from WanFang Data Corp.).
Indexed: A28, APA, ASFA, BrCerAb, C&ISA, CA/WCA, CCMJ, CIA, CIN, CPEI, CerAb, ChemAb, ChemTitl, CivEngAb, CorrAb, E&CAJ, E11, EEA, EMA, ESPM, EngInd, EnvEAb, H15, INIS AtomInd, M&TEA, M09, MBF, METADEX, MSN, MathR, RASB, RefZh, SCOPUS, SWRA, SolStAb, T04, WAA, Z02.
—CASDDS, East View, Linda Hall.
Published by: Tianjin Daxue Jikan Zhongxin/Academic Journals Publishing Center of Tianjin University, 92, Weijin Lu NanKai, Tianjin, 300072, China. TEL 86-22-87402145, FAX 86-22-27403448, http://www2.tju.edu.cn/orgs/journal/default.htm. Circ: 2,000. **Dist. overseas by:** China International Book Trading Corp, 35 Chegongzhuang Xilu, Haidian District, PO Box 399, Beijing 100044, China. TEL 86-10-68412045, FAX 86-10-68412023, cibtc@mail.cibtc.com.cn, http://www.cibtc.com.cn.

500 CHN ISSN 1671-1114
TIANJIN SHIFAN DAXUE XUEBAO (ZIRAN KEXUE BAN)/TIANJIN NORMAL UNIVERSITY. JOURNAL (NATURAL SCIENCE EDITION). Text in Chinese. 1981. q. USD 12 (effective 2009). **Document type:** *Journal, Academic/Scholarly.*
Formerly (until 2000): Tianjin Shida Xuebao (Ziran Kexue Ban) (1001-7720)
Related titles: Online - full text ed.
Indexed: CCMJ, MSN, MathR, RefZh, Z02.
—BLDSC (4908.629000), East View.
Published by: Tianjin Shifan Daxue/Tianjin Normal University, 40, Gansu Road, Heping District, Tianjin, 300020, China. TEL 86-22-27232797, FAX 86-22-27217311. Ed. Gui-lin Wang. **Dist. by:** China International Book Trading Corp, 35 Chegongzhuang Xilu, Haidian District, PO Box 399, Beijing 100044, China. TEL 86-10-68412045, FAX 86-10-68412023, cibtc@mail.cibtc.com.cn, http://www.cibtc.com.cn.

TIANSHUI SHIFAN XUEYUAN XUEBAO. *see* HUMANITIES: COMPREHENSIVE WORKS

500 FIN ISSN 1457-9030
TIEDE. Text in Finnish. 1980. 13/yr. EUR 87 (effective 2009). bk.rev. **Document type:** *Magazine, Consumer.* **Description:** Contains articles and news relating to science in general.
Formerly (until 2001): Tiede 2000 (0358-1039)
Indexed: GeoRef, RASB, SpeleolAb.
Published by: Sanoma Magazines Finland Corporation, Lapinmaentie 1, Helsinki, 00350, Finland. TEL 358-9-1201, FAX 358-9-1205171, info@sanomamagazines.fi, http://www.sanomamagazines.fi. Circ: 49,816 (paid).

500 MEX ISSN 0186-5730
Q23
TIEMPOS DE CIENCIA; revista de difusion cientifica. Text in Spanish. 1985. q. USD 20. adv. bk.rev.
Indexed: C01.
Published by: Universidad de Guadalajara, Coordinacion de Difusion Cientifica, Av. Juarez y Enrique Diaz de Leon, 8 piso, Guadalajara, Jalisco 44170, Mexico. Ed. Javier Garcia de Alba Garcia.

500 FIN ISSN 0781-7916
TIETEESSA TAPAHTUU. Text in Finnish. 8/yr. EUR 480 (effective 2005). adv. back issues avail. **Document type:** *Newsletter.* **Description:** Information on events, publications and current issues within the learned societies and the academic community.
Related titles: Online - full text ed.: ISSN 1239-6540.
Published by: Tieteellisten Seurain Valtuuskunta/Federation of Finnish Learned Societies, Mariankatu 5, Helsinki, 00170, Finland. TEL 358-9-228691, tsv@tsv.fi. Ed. Jan Rydman. adv.: page EUR 420.

051 USA ISSN 0748-9579
F491
TIMELINE. Text in English. 1984. q. USD 55 to members (effective 2007). 72 p./no.; back issues avail. **Document type:** *Magazine, Consumer.* **Description:** Contains articles in history, prehistory and the natural sciences for a general audience.
Indexed: AmH&L, P30, RILM.
—BLDSC (8852.630000), IE, Infotrieve, Ingenta.
Published by: Ohio Historical Society, 1982 Velma Ave, Columbus, OH 43211-2497. TEL 614-297-2360, FAX 614-297-2367, ohiohistory@ohiohistory.org. Ed. David A Simmons. Circ: 7,000 (paid and free).

500 NLD ISSN 2211-2448
TNOTIME. Variant title: T N O Time. Toegepast Natuurwetenschappelijk Onderzoek Time. Text in Dutch. 1985. 5/yr. free (effective 2011). **Document type:** *Magazine, Trade.*
Formerly (until 2011): T N O Magazine (1877-7279); Which was formed by the 2009 merger of: T N O Magazine. T N O Defensie en Veiligheid (1871-0840); T N O Magazine. T N O Industrie en Techniek (1871-0824); T N O Magazine. T N O Informatie- en Communicatietechnologie (1871-0859); T N O Magazine. T N O Kwaliteit van Leven (1871-0832); T N O Magazine. T N O Ruimte en Infrastructuur (1871-0816); All of which superseded in part (in 2005): T N O Magazine (Dutch Edition) (1566-1725); Which was formerly (until 1999): Toegepaste Wetenschap (0920-4571); Which was formed by the 1985 merger of: Innovatie (0167-3475); T N O Project (0376-6993); Which was formerly (until 1973): T N O Nieuws (0039-8446)
Related titles: Online - full text ed.: ISSN 2211-2456.
—IE, INIST, Linda Hall.
Published by: Nederlandse Organisatie voor Toegepast Natuurwetenschappelijk Onderzoek (TNO)/Netherlands Organization for Applied Scientific Research, Postbus 6000, Delft, 2600 JA, Netherlands. TEL 31-15-2696900, FAX 31-15-2612403, infodesk@tno.nl. Ed. W J van den Brink.

507.4 JPN ISSN 0910-4100
TOCHIGI-KENRITSU HAKUBUTSUKAN KENKYU HOKOKUSHO/TOCHIGI PREFECTURAL MUSEUM. MEMOIRS. Text in Japanese; Summaries in English, Japanese. 1983. a. free. **Document type:** *Academic/Scholarly.* **Description:** Covers zoology, botany, geology, and related subjects.
Published by: Tochigi-kenritsu Hakubutsukan/Tochigi Prefectural Museum, 2-2 Mutsumi-cho, Utsunomiya-shi, Tochigi-ken 320-0865, Japan. TEL 81-28-634-1314, FAX 81-28-634-1310. Ed., R&P Terutake Hayashi. Circ: 100.

TOHOKU GAKUIN DAIGAKU KOGAKUBU KENKYU HOKOKU/TOHOKU GAKUIN UNIVERSITY. SCIENCE AND ENGINEERING REPORTS. *see* ENGINEERING

500 JPN ISSN 0910-7177
TOHOKU NO SHIZEN/NATURE OF TOHOKU. Text in Japanese. 1985. m.
Published by: Tohoku no Shizensha, Bunanoki Shuppan, 5-11 Tori-Machi 5-chome, Yonezawa-shi, Yamagata-ken 992-0025, Japan.

500 JPN ISSN 0919-5025
Q77 CODEN: PSCUER
TOKAI UNIVERSITY. SCHOOL OF SCIENCE. PROCEEDINGS. Text in English, German; Summaries in English. 1966. a. **Document type:** *Proceedings, Academic/Scholarly.*
Formerly (until 1993): Tokai University. Faculty of Science. Proceedings (0563-6795)
Indexed: CCMJ, CIN, ChemAb, ChemTitl, INIS AtomInd, MSN, MathR, Z02.
—BLDSC (6811.120000), CASDDS, INIST.
Published by: Toukai Daigaku Shuppansha/Tokai University Press, Tokai University Alumni Association Hall, 3-10-35 Minamiyana, Hadano, Kanagawa 257-0003, Japan. TEL 81-463-793921, FAX 81-463-695087, http://www.press.tokai.ac.jp/.

TOKUSHIMA DAIGAKU SOGO KAGAKUBU NINGEN SHAKAI BUNKA KENKYU/TOKUSHIMA UNIVERSITY. FACULTY OF INTEGRATED ARTS AND AND SCIENCES. JOURNAL. *see* HUMANITIES: COMPREHENSIVE WORKS

509 JPN ISSN 0912-0599
TOKUSHIMA KAGAKUSHI ZASSHI/TOKUSHIMA SOCIETY FOR THE HISTORY OF SCIENCE. JOURNAL. Text in Japanese. 1982. a. JPY 200. bk.rev.
Published by: Tokushima Kagakushi Kenkyukai, c/o Mr Toshimi Saijo, 651-4 Kamiura-Urasho, Myozai-gun, Ishii-cho, Tokushima-ken 779-3200, Japan. Ed. Toshimi Saijo.

500 JPN ISSN 0386-4006
Q4 CODEN: SRTUDZ
TOKYO JOSHI DAIGAKU KIYO. RONSHU. KAGAKU BUMON HOKOKU/TOKYO WOMAN'S CHRISTIAN UNIVERSITY. SCIENCE REPORTS. Text and summaries in English, Japanese. 1950. a.
Indexed: CIS, RILM.
—CASDDS.
Published by: Tokyo Joshi Daigaku Gakkai/Tokyo Woman's Christian University, Academic Society, 2 Zenpuku-Ji, Suginami-ku, Tokyo, 167-0041, Japan.

500 JPN
TOKYO KASEI DAIGAKU KENKYU KIYO. 2 SHIZEN KAGAKU/TOKYO KASEI UNIVERSITY. BULLETIN. NATURAL SCIENCES. Text in Japanese. 1985. a. **Document type:** *Journal, Academic/Scholarly.*
Supersedes in part (in 1989): Tokyo Kasei Daigaku Kenkyu Kiyo/Tokyo Kasei University. Bulletin; Which was formerly (until 1988): Tokyo Kasei Daigaku Kenkyu Kiyo. Jinbun Kagaku, Shizen Kagaku/Tokyo Kasei University. Bulletin. Cultural, Social and Natural Science; Which was formed by the merger of (1956-1985): Tokyo Kasei Daigaku Kenkyu Kiyo. 1 Jinbun Kagaku/Tokyo Kasei University. Bulletin. 1, Cultural and Social Science (0385-1206); (1956-1985): Tokyo Kasei Daigaku Kenkyu Kiyo. 2 Shizen Kagaku/Tokyo Kasei University. Bulletin. 2, Natural Science (0385-1214); Both of which superseded in part (in 1975): Tokyo Kasei Daigaku Kenkyu Kiyo/Tokyo College of Domestic Science. Bulletin (0371-831X)
Published by: Tokyo Kasei Daigaku/Tokyo Kasei University, 1-18-1 Kaga, Itabashi, Tokyo, 173-0003, Japan. TEL 81-3-39615226, http://www.tokyo-kasei.ac.jp/.

508 JPN ISSN 0918-3760
QL468
➤ **TOKYO METROPOLITAN UNIVERSITY BULLETIN OF NATURAL HISTORY.** Text in English. 1992. irreg. **Document type:** *Journal, Academic/Scholarly.*
Indexed: B21, EntAb.
Published by: Tokyo Toritsu Daigaku, Rigakubu, Shizenshi Koza/Metropolitan University, Graduate School of Science, Department of Natural History, 1-1 Minami-Osawa, Hachioji-shi, Tokyo, 192-0397, Japan. Ed. Tsukane Yamasaki.

500 JPN ISSN 0918-0753
TOKYO RIKA DAIGAKU KENKYU RONBUNSHU/SCIENCE UNIVERSITY OF TOKYO. COLLECTED PAPERS. Text and summaries in English, German, Japanese. 1958. a. per issue exchange basis only. **Document type:** *Academic/Scholarly.*
Published by: Tokyo Rika Daigaku/Tokyo University of Science, 1-3, Kagurazaka, Shinjuku Ku, Tokyo, 162-8601, Japan. http://www.sut.ac.jp/. Circ: 200.

500 387.5 JPN ISSN 0493-4474
TOKYO SHOSEN DAIGAKU KENKYU HOKOKU. SHIZEN KAGAKU/TOKYO UNIVERSITY OF MERCANTILE MARINE. JOURNAL. NATURAL SCIENCES. Text and summaries in English, Japanese. 1951. a., latest vol.51, 2000. **Document type:** *Journal, Academic/Scholarly.*
Indexed: JPI.
—BLDSC (4909.030000).
Published by: Tokyo Shosen Daigaku/Tokyo University of Mercantile Marine, 1-6 Ecchujima 2-chome, Koto-ku, Tokyo, 135-8533, Japan.

500 JPN ISSN 0288-2329
TOKYO-TO NO SHIZEN. Text in Japanese. 1973. a. **Document type:** *Bulletin.*
Published by: Tokyo-to Takao Shizen Kagaku Hakubutsukan/Takao Museum of Natural History, 2436 Takao-Machi, Hachioji-shi, Tokyo-to 193-0844, Japan. TEL 81-426-61-0305, FAX 81-426-62-9407, takaohaku@mwb.biglobe.ne.jp, http://www1.biz.biglobe.ne.jp/~takahaku/. Ed. Jiro Arai.

507.4 JPN ISSN 0286-8768
TOKYO-TO TAKAO SHIZEN KAGAKU HAKUBUTSUKAN KENKYU HOKOKU/TAKAO MUSEUM OF NATURAL HISTORY. SCIENCE REPORT. Text in Japanese; Summaries in English, Japanese. 1970. irreg. **Document type:** *Bulletin, Academic/Scholarly.*
Published by: Tokyo-to Takao Shizen Kagaku Hakubutsukan/Takao Museum of Natural History, 2436 Takao-Machi, Hachioji-shi, Tokyo-to 193-0844, Japan. TEL 81-426-61-0305, FAX 81-426-62-9407, takaohaku@mwb.biglobe.ne.jp, http://www1.biz.biglobe.ne.jp/~takahaku/. Ed. Jiro Arai.

500 808.83876 USA ISSN 2151-9838
▼ **TOME OF SORCERY AND SCIENCE.** Text in English. 2009. q. free (effective 2010). **Document type:** *Magazine, Consumer.* **Description:** Includes articles on science as well as science fiction and fantasy short stories.
Media: Online - full text.
Published by: Codex Publishing, Inc., PO Box 850707, Mesquite, TX 75185. tracya@codexpublishinginc.com.

500 CHN
Q4 CODEN: TTHPDJ
TONGJI DAXUE XUEBAO (ZIRAN KEXUE BAN)/TONGJI UNIVERSITY. JOURNAL (NATURAL SCIENCE). Text in Chinese. 1956. m. (bi-m. until 2001). USD 62.40 (effective 2009). **Document type:** *Journal, Academic/Scholarly.*
Former titles (until 1997): Tongji Daxue Xuebao (0253-374X); (until 1980): Tongji Daxue Xuebao (0494-190X)
Related titles: Online - full text ed.
Indexed: A22, A28, APA, ASFA, B21, BrCerAb, C&ISA, CA/WCA, CCMJ, CIA, CPEI, CerAb, CivEngAb, CorrAb, E&CAJ, E11, EEA, EMA, ESPM, EngInd, EnvEAb, GeoRef, H15, Inspec, M&TEA, M09, MBF, METADEX, MSN, MathR, RefZh, SCOPUS, SolStAb, T04, WAA, Z02.
—BLDSC (4909.200000), East View, IE, Ingenta, Linda Hall.
Published by: Tongji Daxue/Tongji University, 1239, Siping Lu, Di-3 Jiaxue Bldg., Rm. 423, Shanghai, 200092, China. **Dist. by:** China International Book Trading Corp, 35 Chegongzhuang Xilu, Haidian District, PO Box 399, Beijing 100044, China. TEL 86-10-68412045, FAX 86-10-68412023, cibtc@mail.cibtc.com.cn, http://www.cibtc.com.cn.

TOPLUM VE BILIM. *see* SOCIOLOGY

500 JPN
TORAY KAGAKU SHINKOKAI JIGYO HOKOKUSHO/TORAY SCIENCE FOUNDATION. ANNUAL REPORT. Text mainly in Japanese; Section in English. 1960. a. free. abstr.
Published by: Toray Kagaku Shinkokai/Toray Science Foundation, Toray Bldg 8-1 Mihama, Urayasu-shi, Chiba-ken 279-0011, Japan. TEL 86-47-3506103, FAX 86-47-3506082, jdp00117@nifty.ne.jp, http://www.toray.co.jp/tsf/index.html. Circ: 700.

500 JPN
TORAY KAGAKU SHINKOKAI KAGAKU KOENKAI KIROKU. Text in Japanese. 1963. a. free. **Document type:** *Proceedings, Academic/Scholarly.* **Description:** Contains proceedings from the lecture meetings sponsored by the foundation.
Published by: Toray Kagaku Shinkokai/Toray Science Foundation, Toray Bldg 8-1 Mihama, Urayasu-shi, Chiba-ken 279-0011, Japan. TEL 86-47-3506103, FAX 86-47-3506082, jdp00117@nifty.ne.jp, http://www.toray.co.jp/tsf/index.html. Circ: 2,000.

500 JPN
TORAY RIKA KYOIKUSHO JUSHO SAKUHINSHU. Text in Japanese. 1969. a. free. **Document type:** *Academic/Scholarly.* **Description:** Publishes works which have received the Toray Science Education Prize.
Indexed: ChemAb.
Published by: Toray Kagaku Shinkokai/Toray Science Foundation, Toray Bldg 8-1 Mihama, Urayasu-shi, Chiba-ken 279-0011, Japan. TEL 86-47-3506103, FAX 86-47-3506082, jdp00117@nifty.ne.jp, http://www.toray.co.jp/tsf/index.html. Circ: 15,000.

500.9 GBR ISSN 0082-5344
TORQUAY NATURAL HISTORY SOCIETY. TRANSACTIONS AND PROCEEDINGS. Text in English. 1909. a. GBP 1.25 per issue (effective 1999). **Document type:** *Proceedings, Academic/Scholarly.*
Indexed: BrArAb.
—BLDSC (9020.000000).
Published by: Torquay Natural History Society, The Museum, Torquay, 529, Babbacombe Rd, Torquay, TQ1 1HG, United Kingdom. TEL 44-1803-293975, FAX 44-1803-294186. Ed. M S Ackland. R&P M.S. Ackland. Circ: 600.

500 800 ITA ISSN 1827-4919
TORRICELLIANA. Text in Italian. 1948. a. **Document type:** *Journal, Academic/Scholarly.*
Published by: Societa Torricelliana di Scienze e Lettere, Corso Garibaldi 2, Faenza, 48018, Italy. TEL 39-0521-905882, FAX 39-0521-905705, medri@me.unipr.it.

507.4 JPN ISSN 0287-1688
TOTTORI-KENRITSU HAKUBUTSUKAN KENKYU HOKOKU/TOTTORI PREFECTURAL MUSEUM. BULLETIN. Text in Japanese; Summaries in English, Japanese. 1962. a.
Published by: Tottori-kenritsu Hakubutsukan/Tottori Prefectural Museum, 2-124 Higashi-Machi, Tottori-shi, 680-0011, Japan. FAX 0857-26-8041. Circ: 1,000.

500 JPN ISSN 1345-3335
TOTTORI UNIVERSITY. FACULTY OF EDUCATION AND REGIONAL SCIENCES. JOURNAL. Text in English, Japanese; Summaries in English. 1950. s-a. **Document type:** *Bulletin, Academic/Scholarly.*
Former titles (until 1999): Tottori Daigaku Kyoikugakubu Kenkyu Hokoku. Shizen Kagaku - Tottori University. Faculty of Education. Journal: Natural Science (0371-5965); (until 1965): Tottori Daigaku Gakugei Gakubu Kenkyu Hokoku, Shizen Kagaku (0493-5608)
Indexed: JPI.
Published by: Tottori Daigaku, Kyoiku Chiiki Kagakubu/Tottori University, Faculty of Education and Regional Sciences, 4-101 Minami-Koyama-cho, Tottori-shi, 680-8551, Japan. TEL 81-857-31-5498, FAX 81-857-31-5076, http://www.fed.tottori-u.ac.jp.

500 POL ISSN 0079-4805
TOWARZYSTWO NAUKOWE W TORUNIU. PRACE POPULARNONAUKOWE. Text in Polish; Summaries in English, German. 1961. irreg., latest vol.68, 2003. price varies. **Document type:** *Monographic series, Academic/Scholarly.*
Related titles: ◆ Series: Prace Popularnonaukowe. Biblioteczka Prawnicza. ISSN 0138-0508; ◆ Prace Popularnonaukowe. Zabytki Polski Polnocnej. ISSN 0138-0516.
Published by: Towarzystwo Naukowe w Toruniu, ul Wysoka 16, Torun, 87100, Poland. TEL 48-56-6223941, tnt.biuro@wp.pl. Ed. Cecylia Iwaniszewska. Circ: 6,500.

TOYAMA DAIGAKU KYOUIKUGAKUBU KENKYUROSHU/TOYAMA UNIVERSITY. FACULTY OF EDUCATION. BULLETIN. *see* EDUCATION

500 JPN ISSN 0387-9089
Q4
TOYAMA-SHI KAGAKU BUNKA SENTA KENKYU HOKOKU/TOYAMA SCIENCE MUSEUM. BULLETIN. Text and summaries in English, Japanese. 1979. a. **Document type:** *Bulletin.* **Description:** Contains research papers.
Indexed: GeoRef, SpeleolAb, Z01.
Published by: Toyama-shi Kagaku Bunka Senta/Toyama Science Museum, 1-8-31 Nishi-Nakano-Machi, Toyama-shi, 939-0000, Japan. TEL 0764-91-2123, FAX 0764-21-5950. Ed. Hisao Nanbu.

TOYAMA TO SHIZEN. *see* MUSEUMS AND ART GALLERIES

500 JPN ISSN 0372-0330
Q4 CODEN: TODKBF
TOYO DAIGAKU KIYO. KYOYO KATEI HEN. SHIZEN KAGAKU/TOYO UNIVERSITY. JOURNAL. GENERAL EDUCATION. NATURAL SCIENCE. Text in Japanese; Summaries in English. a.
Indexed: JPI.
—CASDDS.
Published by: Toyo Daigaku/Toyo University, 28-20 Hakusan 5-chome, Bunkyo-ku, Tokyo, 112-0000, Japan.

508 JPN ISSN 0919-1526
TOYOHASHI MUSEUM OF NATURAL HISTORY. MISCELLANEOUS REPORT/TOYOHASHI-SHI SHIZENSHI HAKUBUTSUKAN SHIRYOSHU. Text in Japanese. 1993. a. charts; stat. back issues avail. **Document type:** *Academic/Scholarly.* **Description:** Contains catalogue of the stored speciments of the Toyohashi Museum of Natural History.
Indexed: A29, ASFA, B20, B21, ESPM, EntAb, GeoRef, I10, OceAb, SpeleolAb, VirolAbstr, Z01.
Published by: Toyohashi Museum of Natural History/Toyohashi-shi Shizenshi Hakubutsukan, 1-238 Oana, Oiwa-cho, Toyohashi, 441-3147, Japan. TEL 81-532-41-4747, FAX 81-532-41-8020, http://mediazone.tcp-net.ad.jp/tzb/tmnh. Circ: 700.

508 JPN ISSN 0917-1703
QH7 CODEN: TSHHEN
TOYOHASHI MUSEUM OF NATURAL HISTORY. SCIENCE REPORT/TOYOHASHI-SHI SHIZENSHI HAKUBUTSUKAN KENKYU HOKOKU. Text in Japanese; Summaries in Japanese, English. 1991. a. charts; illus.; maps. back issues avail. **Document type:** *Bulletin, Academic/Scholarly.* **Description:** Covers the research activities under the theme of evolution of life and nature around Toyohashi.
Indexed: ASFA, B21, EntAb, GeoRef, SpeleolAb, Z01.
Published by: Toyohashi Museum of Natural History/Toyohashi-shi Shizenshi Hakubutsukan, 1-238 Oana, Oiwa-cho, Toyohashi, 441-3147, Japan. TEL 81-532-41-4747, FAX 81-532-41-8020, http://www.tcp-net.ad.jp/tzb/tmnh. Circ: 700.

500 600 GBR
TRAFODION Y GYMDEITHAS WYDDONOL GENEDLAETHOL. Text in Welsh. 1978. a. GBP 2. back issues avail.
Published by: Y Gymdeithas Wyddonol Genedlaethol, Talafon, Golan, Garndolbenmaen, LL51 9YU, United Kingdom. TEL 01766-75224. Ed. J S Davies. Circ: 300.

500 BGR ISSN 1312-1723
TRAKIA JOURNAL OF SCIENCES. Text in English. 2003. 3/yr. **Document type:** *Journal, Academic/Scholarly.*
Related titles: Online - full text ed.: free (effective 2011).
Indexed: A01, CA, T02, Z01.
Published by: Trakiiski Universitet/Trakia University, Student's Campus, Stara Zagora, 6000, Bulgaria. TEL 359-42-79012, FAX 4274112, tjs@uni-sz.bg.

▼ **TRANSDISCIPLINARY JOURNAL OF ENGINEERING & SCIENCE.** *see* ENGINEERING

508 ZAF ISSN 0041-1752
QH1 CODEN: ATVMA4
TRANSVAAL MUSEUM. ANNALS/TRANSVAAL MUSEUM. ANNALE. Text in English. 1908. irreg., latest vol.38, 2001. price varies. illus.; abstr.; bibl. index. back issues avail. **Document type:** *Monographic series, Academic/Scholarly.* **Description:** Original research articles in the field of zoology. Includes information on systematics and taxonomy.
Indexed: B25, BIOSIS Prev, GeoRef, IBR, IBZ, ISAP, MycolAb, SpeleolAb, WildRev, Z01.
—BLDSC (1034.000000), INIST.
Published by: Transvaal Museum, PO Box 413, Pretoria, 0001, South Africa. TEL 27-12-3227632, FAX 27-12-3227939, http://www.nfi.co.za/tmpage.html. Ed., R&P Anita Dreyer. Circ: 350.

500 SRB ISSN 0354-9682
TRECE OKO. Text in Serbian. 1989. fortn. adv. **Document type:** *Magazine, Consumer.*
Published by: Kompanija Novosti, Trg Nikole Pasica 7, Belgrade, 11000. TEL 381-11-3398202, FAX 381-11-3398337, redakcija@novosti.co.yu, http://www.novosti.co.yu. Ed. Dragan Vicanovic. Circ: 45,000 (paid).

500 USA ISSN 1819-3579
➤ **TRENDS IN APPLIED SCIENCES RESEARCH.** Text in English. 2006. q. **Document type:** *Journal, Academic/Scholarly.* **Description:** Contains research papers, reviews, and short communications in the fields of biology, chemistry, physics, environmental sciences, business and economics, finance, mathematics and statistics, geology, engineering, computer science, social sciences, natural and technological sciences, linguistics, medicine, architecture, industrial, and all other applied and theoretical sciences.
Related titles: Online - full text ed.: ISSN 2151-7908. free (effective 2009).
Indexed: A29, A32, A34, A35, A36, A37, A38, AgBio, AgrForAb, B&BAb, B19, B20, B21, BA, BP, C10, C25, C30, CA, CABA, D01, E12, ESPM, EntAb, F08, F11, F12, FCA, G11, GH, H16, I10, I11, IndVet, MaizeAb, N02, N03, N04, O01, P30, P32, P33, P38, P39, P40, PGegResA, PHN&I, PN&I, R07, R08, R11, R12, R13, RA&MP, RM&VM, S12, S13, S16, S17, SWRA, SoyAb, T02, T05, TAR, TriticAb, VS, W10, W11, Z01.
Published by: Academic Journals Inc., 224, 5th Ave, No 2218, New York, NY 10001. FAX 888-777-8532, support@scialert.com, http://www.academicjournalsinc.com/.

500 COL
TRIANEA. Text in Spanish. 1988. irreg.
Published by: Instituto Nacional de los Recursos Naturales, Renovables y del Ambiente, Apartado Aereo 13458, Bogota, Colombia. TEL 57-1-2860601, FAX 57-1-2868643.

500 UAE ISSN 1019-6919
QH193.U5 CODEN: TBULEF
➤ **TRIBULUS.** Text in Arabic, English. 1991. s-a. USD 30 (effective 2001). bk.rev. Index. back issues avail. **Document type:** *Journal, Academic/Scholarly.* **Description:** Publishes original research in archaeology and natural history in the United Arab Emirates.
Formerly (until 1991): Jam'iyyat al-Tarikh al-Tabi'i. Nashrat - Emirates Natural History Group Bulletin
Indexed: WildRev, Z01.
Published by: Emirates Natural History Group, PO Box 45553, Abu Dhabi, United Arab Emirates. TEL 971-2-4414441, FAX 971-2-4450458. Ed., R&P Peter Hellyer. Circ: 750.

508 NOR ISSN 0332-6195
TROMURA. NATURVITENSKAP. Variant title: Tromsoe Museum. Rapportserie, Naturvitenskap. Text in Norwegian, English. 1978. irreg., latest vol.85, 2000. price varies. back issues avail. **Document type:** *Monographic series, Academic/Scholarly.*
Indexed: GeoRef.
—INIST.
Published by: Tromsoe Museum - Universitesmuseet, Lars Thoeringsvei 10, Tromsoe, 9037, Norway. TEL 47-77-645000, FAX 47-77-645520, museumspost@uit.no, http://www2.uit.no/ikbViewer/page/tmu?p_lang=2.

500 600 CHN ISSN 1007-0214
Q1 CODEN: TSTEF7
TSINGHUA SCIENCE & TECHNOLOGY. Text in English. 1996. 6/yr. **Document type:** *Journal, Academic/Scholarly.*
Related titles: Online - full text ed.: USD 250 (effective 2012) (from ScienceDirect); ◆ Chinese ed.: Qinghua Daxue Xuebao (Ziran Kexue Ban). ISSN 1000-0054.
Indexed: A26, A28, APA, BrCerAb, C&ISA, CA, CA/WCA, CCMJ, CIA, CPEI, CerAb, CivEngAb, CorrAb, E&CAJ, E11, EEA, EMA, ESPM, EngInd, EnvAb, EnvEAb, H15, I05, INIS AtomInd, Inspec, M&TEA, M09, MBF, METADEX, MSN, MathR, P30, RefZh, SCOPUS, SolStAb, T02, T04, WAA, Z02.
—BLDSC (9067.617000), IE, Ingenta, Linda Hall. **CCC.**
Published by: Qinghua Daxue, Xuebao Bianjibu/Tsinghua University, Editorial Board, Haidian-qu, Qinghuayuan, 100, Wenxi Lou, Beijing, 100084, China. TEL 86-10-62788108, FAX 86-10-62792976.

500 JPN ISSN 0287-7805
AS552.T76
TSUDAJUKU DAIGAKU KIYO/TSUDA COLLEGE. JOURNAL. Text in Japanese. 1969. a. **Document type:** *Journal, Academic/Scholarly.*
Indexed: CCMJ, MSN, MathR.
Published by: Tsudajuku Daigaku/Tsuda College, 2-1-1 Tsuda-machi, Kodaira-shi, Tokyo, 187-8577, Japan. http://www.tsuda.ac.jp/.

500 600 HUN ISSN 0237-322X
TUDOMANY. Text in Hungarian. 1985. m. HUF 1,176, USD 40. adv. bk.rev. bibl.; charts; illus. back issues avail.
Related titles: ◆ Italian ed.: Le Scienze. ISSN 0036-8083; ◆ English ed.: Scientific American. ISSN 0036-8733; ◆ German ed.: Spektrum der Wissenschaft. ISSN 0170-2971; ◆ French ed.: Pour la Science. ISSN 0153-4092; ◆ Chinese ed.: Ke Xue. ISSN 1002-1299; ◆ Spanish ed.: Investigacion y Ciencia. ISSN 0210-136X; ◆ Japanese ed.: Nikkei Saiensu. ISSN 0917-009X; ◆ Arabic ed.: Majallat al-Ulum; ◆ Polish ed.: Swiat Nauki. ISSN 0867-6380; Turkish ed.: Bilim.
Address: PO Box 338, Budapest, 1536, Hungary. Eds. Futasz Dezso, Jonathan Piel. Circ: 25,000. **Subscr. to:** Kultura, PO Box 149, Budapest 1389, Hungary.

500 RUS ISSN 2071-6168
➤ **TUL'SKII GOSUDARSTVENNYI UNIVERSITET. IZVESTIYA. TEKHNICHESKIE NAUKI.** Text in Russian. 2008. q. **Document type:** *Journal, Academic/Scholarly.*
Indexed: RefZh.
Published by: (Tul'skii Gosudarstvennyi Universitet), Izdatel'stvo TulGU, ul Boldina 151, Tula, 300600, Russian Federation. TEL 7-4872-352506, 7-4872-353620, FAX 7-4872-353620, press@tsu.tula.ru, http://publishing.tsu.tula.ru. Ed. V V Preis.

500 FIN ISSN 0082-7002
AS262.T84 CODEN: AUTUAP
TURUN YLIOPISTO. JULKAISUJA. SARJA A. I. ASTRONOMICA - CHEMICA - PHYSICA - MATHEMATICA/ANNALES UNIVERSITATIS TURKUENSIS. Text in English, Finnish, French, German. 1922. irreg. price varies. **Document type:** *Monographic series, Academic/Scholarly.* **Description:** Studies astronomy, chemistry, physical sciences and mathematics.
Indexed: CIS, INIS AtomInd, Inspec, Z02.
—BLDSC (0963.345000), AskIEEE, CASDDS, INIST, Linda Hall.
Published by: Turun Yliopiston Kirjasto/University of Turku, Turku, 20500, Finland. FAX 358-2-3335050.

500.9 NLD ISSN 1877-0169
TWENTSEWELLE MAGAZINE. Variant title: T W-Magazine. Text in Dutch. 2003. s-a. bk.rev. **Document type:** *Bulletin, Consumer.*
Formerly (until 2008): Typisch Twente (1572-0837); Which was formed by the merger of (1968-2003): Inschrien (0166-3984); (1957-2003): d'ENVIronde (1572-2171); Which was formerly (until 2002): NatuurMuseumJannink (1389-739X); (until 1998): Natuur en Museum (0028-1085)
Published by: Stichting TwentseWelle, Het Rozendaal 11, Enschede, 7523 XG, Netherlands. TEL 31-53-4807680, info@twentsewelle.nl, http://www.twentsewelle.nl.

U-MAIL; Regensburger Universitaetszeitung. *see* COLLEGE AND ALUMNI

U N U - M E R I T WORKING PAPER SERIES. (United Nations University, Maastricht Economic Research Institute on Innovation and Technology) *see* BUSINESS AND ECONOMICS

300 500 GTM ISSN 1015-339X
F1430
U S A C. Text in Spanish. 1983. q. GTQ 825, USD 10.20. bk.rev. bibl.; charts; stat.
Formerly (until 1987): Perspectiva (0257-7356)
Indexed: C01, H21, P08.
Published by: (Direccion General de Extension Universitaria), Universidad de San Carlos de Guatemala, Ciudad Universitaria, zona 12, Edificio de Rectoria, Of. 307, Guatemala, Guatemala. Ed. Maldonado Eduardo.

U.S. NATIONAL COMMITTEE FOR MAN AND THE BIOSPHERE. BULLETIN. *see* CONSERVATION

338.973 USA ISSN 1936-2366
U.S. NATIONAL SCIENCE FOUNDATION. FEDERAL FUNDS FOR RESEARCH AND DEVELOPMENT (ONLINE). Text in English. 1952. a. free (effective 2010). charts; stat. back issues avail. **Document type:** *Government.* **Description:** Provides information and analysis on funding available for research and development from federal agencies.
Former titles (until 2001): U.S. National Science Foundation. Federal Funds for Research and Development (Print) (0198-8700); (until 1979): U.S. National Science Foundation. Federal Funds for Research, Development, and Other Scientific Activities (0083-2359); (until 1964): U.S. National Science Foundation. Federal Funds for Science
Media: Online - full text. **Related titles:** ◆ Series of: U.S. National Science Foundation. Surveys of Science Resources Series. ISSN 0083-2405.
Indexed: SpeleolAb.
—Linda Hall.
Published by: U.S. Department of Commerce, National Science Foundation, 4201 Wilson Blvd, Ste 245, Arlington, VA 22230. TEL 703-292-5111, 800-877-8339, info@nsf.gov.

500 USA
U.S. NAVAL RESEARCH LABORATORY. REPORT. Text in English. irreg.
Published by: U.S. Department of the Navy, Naval Research Laboratory, 4555 Overlook Ave, Washington, DC 20375. reports@library.nrl.navy.mil, http://www.nrl.navy.mil. **Subscr. to:** U.S. Department of Commerce, National Technical Information Service, 5301 Shawnee Rd, Alexandria, VA 22312. orders@ntis.fedworld.gov, http://www.ntis.gov/ordering.htm.

500 USA
U T S A DISCOVER; research, scholarship and creative achievement at UTSA. (University of Texas at San Antonio) Text in English. 2007. a. **Document type:** *Journal, Academic/Scholarly.* **Description:** Covers the research and creative activity in the University's Colleges and Research Centers.
Related titles: Online - full content ed.
Published by: (University of Texas at San Antonio, Office of the Vice President for Research), University of Texas at San Antonio, Office of University Publications, One UTSA Circle, San Antonio, TX 78249-1644. http://vpr.utsa.edu/index.php. **Co-sponsor:** University of Texas at San Antonio, Office of University Advancement.

500 THA ISSN 1906-9294
Q1
▼ **UBON RATCHATHANI UNIVERSITY. SCIENCE JOURNAL.** Text in English. 2010. irreg. free (effective 2011). **Document type:** *Journal, Academic/Scholarly.*
Published by: Ubon Ratchathani University, Faculty of Science, 85 Sthollmark Rd, Warinchamrap Ubon Ratchathani, 3419, Thailand. TEL 66-0-45353401.

001.3 500 RUS ISSN 1810-5505
➤ **UDMURTSKII UNIVERSITET. VESTNIK.** Text in Russian. 1991. m. RUR 200 per issue (effective 2010). **Document type:** *Journal, Academic/Scholarly.*
Related titles: Online - full text ed.: ISSN 1999-8597.
Indexed: RefZh.
Published by: Udmurtskii Gosudarstvennyi Universitet/Udmurt State University, Universitetskaya Str., 1, Izhevsk, 426034, Russian Federation. TEL 7-341-682061, ob@uni.udm.ru, http://v4.udsu.ru. Ed. Nikolai Leonov.

500.9 DEU
UEBERSEE-MUSEUM BREMEN. VEROEFFENTLICHUNGEN. SERIES NATURAL SCIENCE. Text in German. irreg. price varies. **Document type:** *Monographic series.*
Formed by the merger of (1978-199?): Uebersee-Museum Bremen. Veroeffentlichungen. Reihe E: Human-Oekologie (0170-2416); (1949-199?): Uebersee-Museum Bremen. Veroeffentlichungen. Naturwissenschaften (0944-4602); Which was formerly (until 1993): Uebersee-Museum Bremen. Veroeffentlichungen. Reihe A: Naturwissenschaften (0068-0885)
Indexed: GeoRef, SpeleolAb.
Published by: Uebersee-Museum Bremen, Bahnhofsplatz 13, Bremen, 28195, Germany. TEL 49-421-3619324, FAX 49-421-3619291.

S

500 IND ISSN 0970-9150
CODEN: SPSCEV
➤ **ULTRA SCIENTIST OF PHYSICAL SCIENCES**; international journal of physical sciences. Text in English. 1978. 3/yr. INR 300 domestic to individuals; USD 30 foreign to individuals; INR 900 domestic to institutions; USD 75 foreign to institutions (effective 2011). adv. **Document type:** *Journal, Academic/Scholarly.* **Description:** Publishes original research papers in pure and applied physical sciences.
Former titles (until 1991): Scientist of Physical Sciences; (until 1989): Journal of Scientific Research
Indexed: CCMJ, CIN, ChemAb, Inspec, MSN, MathR, Z02.
—BLDSC (9082.780623), AskIEEE, CASDDS, IE, Ingenta.
Published by: Ansari Education and Research Society, PO Box 93, Bhopal, Madhya Pradesh 462 001, India. TEL 91-755-2533437. Ed. A H Ansari.

➤ **ULUSLARARASI INSAN BILIMLERI DERGISI/INTERNATIONAL JOURNAL OF HUMAN SCIENCES.** *see* SOCIAL SCIENCES: COMPREHENSIVE WORKS

500 600 COL ISSN 1692-3375
UMBRAL UNIVERSITARIO. Text in Spanish. 2002. a. back issues avail. **Document type:** *Monographic series, Academic/Scholarly.*
Related titles: Online - full text ed.
Indexed: C01, F04, T02.
Published by: Universidad Manuela Beltral, Bogota Campus Universitario, Ave Circunvalar no. 60, Bogota, Colombia. TEL 57-1-5460600, umbralcientifico@umb.edu.co, http://www.umb.edu.co/Home.html?z=1&w=5. Ed. Luz Miryam Berrero de Gonzalez.

600 500 KEN ISSN 1020-5535
Q10
UNESCO NAIROBI BULLETIN. Text in English. 1969. 2/yr. USD 15; USD 5 newsstand/cover (effective 2000). bk.rev. bibl. **Document type:** *Bulletin, Academic/Scholarly.*
Formerly: UNESCO. Regional Office for Science and Technology for Africa. Bulletin (0503-4434)
Related titles: French ed.: Bulletin - Bureau de l'Unesco a Nairobi. ISSN 1020-5578.
Published by: UNESCO, Nairobi Office/Bureau de l'UNESCO a Nairobi, PO Box 30592, Nairobi, Kenya. TEL 254-2-621234, FAX 254-2-215991, TELEX 22275 NAIROBI. Ed. Dr. Paul B Vitta. Circ: 1,500.

500 FRA
UNESCO SCIENCE REPORT. Text in French. biennial. EUR 33.54 newsstand/cover (effective 2003). **Description:** Reviews the state of science and technology in various regions of the world and describes the recent orientations and trends in education and research, as well as the specific problems faced by each region.
Formerly (until 2005): World Science Report (1020-6892)
Related titles: French ed.: Rapport Mondial sur la Science. ISSN 1564-1805.
Indexed: IIS.
Published by: UNESCO Publishing, 7 place de Fontenoy, Paris, 75352, France. TEL 33-1-45684300, FAX 33-1-45685737, http://publishing.unesco.org/default.aspx. Ed. Howard Moore. **Dist. in U.S. by:** Bernan Associates, Bernan, 4611-F Assembly Dr., Lanham, MD 20706-4391. TEL 800-274-4447, FAX 800-865-3450.

▼ **UNIABEU. REVISTA.** *see* HUMANITIES: COMPREHENSIVE WORKS

500 CRI ISSN 1011-0275
➤ **UNICIENCIA.** Text in English, Spanish. 1984. a. CRC 1,500, USD 7 (effective 2000). adv. bk.rev. bibl.; charts; illus.; stat. back issues avail. **Document type:** *Journal, Academic/Scholarly.* **Description:** Covers basic and applied research in biology, chemistry, physics and mathematics, with emphasis on natural bioresources.
Indexed: ASFA, B21, C01, ESPM, INIS AtomInd.
Published by: Universidad Nacional, Facultad de Ciencias Exactas y Naturales, Apdo 86, Heredia, 3000, Costa Rica. TEL 506-2375230, FAX 506-2773485. Ed., R&P, Adv. contact Jorge Gunther. Circ: 400 (paid and controlled).

➤ **UNION LIST OF SCIENTIFIC AND TECHNICAL PERIODICALS IN ZAMBIA.** *see* BIBLIOGRAPHIES

500 CHE ISSN 1664-8552
UNIPRESS. Text in German. 1978. q. free (effective 2011). **Document type:** *Magazine, Consumer.*
Related titles: Online - full text ed.: ISSN 1664-8560.
Published by: Universitaet Bern, Abteilung Kommunikation, Hochschulstr 4, Bern, 3012, Switzerland. TEL 41-31-6318044, FAX 41-31-6314562, kommunikation@unibe.ch. Circ: 20,000 (controlled).

500 USA
UNISCI. Text in English. 1995. d. **Description:** Covers news of university scientific research.
Media: Online - full text.
Address: 3907 S E Second Ave, Cape Coral, FL 33904. TEL 239-549-7048, FAX 239-945-3002. Ed. Don Radler.

500 AUS
UNISERVE SCIENCE. ANNUAL REPORT. Text in English. a. back issues avail. **Document type:** *Corporate.*
Media: Online - full text.
Published by: UniServe Science, Carslaw Bldg F07, University of Sydney, Sydney, NSW 2006, Australia. TEL 61-2-93512960, FAX 61-2-93512175, uniserve@mail.usyd.edu.au, http://science.uniserve.edu.au.

500 AUS ISSN 1329-1645
UNISERVE SCIENCE NEWS (ONLINE). Text in English. 1995. 3/yr. back issues avail. **Document type:** *Newsletter, Consumer.* **Description:** Provides information about UniServe Science.
Media: Online - full text.
Published by: UniServe Science, Carslaw Bldg F07, University of Sydney, Sydney, NSW 2006, Australia. TEL 61-2-93512960, FAX 61-2-93512175, uniserve@mail.usyd.edu.au, http://science.uniserve.edu.au.

500 600 AUS
UNISERVE SCIENCE. SYMPOSIUM PROCEEDINGS. Text in English. irreg., latest 2008. **Document type:** *Monographic series, Academic/Scholarly.*
Formerly: UniServe Science. Workshop Proceedings
Media: Online - full text.
Published by: UniServe Science, Carslaw Bldg F07, University of Sydney, Sydney, NSW 2006, Australia. TEL 61-2-93512960, FAX 61-2-93512175, uniserve@mail.usyd.edu.au. Ed. Anne Fernandez.

UNITAS; a quarterly review for the arts and sciences. *see* ART

500 UAE ISSN 1021-0806
UNITED ARAB EMIRATES UNIVERSITY. FACULTY OF SCIENCE. JOURNAL/JAMI'AT AL-IMARAT AL-ARABIYYAH AL-MUTTAHIDAH. KULLIYYAT AL-ULUM. MAJALLAH. Text in Arabic, English. 1988. a. per issue exchange basis. **Document type:** *Journal, Academic/Scholarly.* **Description:** Publishes papers in mathematics, computer science, physics, chemistry, geology and the life sciences.
Indexed: ESPM, GeoRef, MycolAb, PollutAb, SSciA, Z02.
—INIST.
Published by: United Arab Emirates University, Faculty of Science, P.O. Box 17551, Al-ain, United Arab Emirates. TEL 677280, TELEX 33521 JAMEAH EM. Ed. Saleh El Nahwy. Circ: 500.

500 FRA ISSN 0083-3673
UNIVERS HISTORIQUE. Text in French. 1970. irreg. price varies.
—CCC.
Published by: Editions du Seuil, 27 Rue Jacob, Paris, 75006, France. TEL 33-1-40465050, FAX 33-1-40464300, contact@seuil.com, http://www.seuil.com. Eds. Jacques Julliard, Michel Winock.

500 AUT
AM101
UNIVERSALMUSEUM JOANNEUM. JAHRESBERICHT. Text in German. 1929. a. **Document type:** *Journal, Academic/Scholarly.*
Formerly (until 2009): Landesmuseum Joanneum Graz. Jahresbericht (0378-6862)
Indexed: FR, GeoRef, Z01.
Published by: Universalmuseum Joanneum, Mariahilferstr 2-4, Graz, St 8020, Austria. TEL 43-316-80179660, FAX 43-316-80179669, post@museum-joanneum.at, http://www.museum-joanneum.at.

500 MEX ISSN 0188-3976
UNIVERSIDAD; ciencia y tecnologia. Text in Spanish. 1990. q.
Published by: Universidad Autonoma del Estado de Morelos, Coordinacion de Investigacion Cientifica, Av Universidad, 1001, Colonia Chamilpa, Cuernavaca, Morelos 62209, Mexico. http://www.uaem.mx.

502 DOM
UNIVERSIDAD AUTONOMA DE SANTO DOMINGO. DIRECCION DE INVESTIGACIONES. D I C BOLETIN. Cover title: D I C Boletin. Text in Spanish. 1974 (vol.2). m.
Published by: Universidad Autonoma de Santo Domingo, Ciudad Universitaria, Santo Domingo, Dominican Republic.

508 COL ISSN 0123-3068
UNIVERSIDAD DE CALDAS. MUSEO DE HISTORIA NATURAL. BOLETIN CIENTIFICO. Text in Spanish. s-a. **Document type:** *Bulletin, Academic/Scholarly.*
Related titles: Online - full text ed.: (from SciELO).
Indexed: A26, I04, I05, Z01.
Published by: Universidad de Caldas, Museo de Historia Natural, Cerrada 23, No 58-65, Edif. Palogrande, Centro de Museos, Manizalez, Colombia. TEL 57-6-8851374, FAX 57-6-8850034, http://www.ucaldas.edu.co. Ed. Julian Adolfo Salazar. Circ: 300.

500 ARG ISSN 0328-6312
UNIVERSIDAD DE MORON. FACUTLAD DE CIENCIAS EXACTAS, QUIMICAS Y NATURALES. REVISTA. Text in Spanish. 1996. s-a. back issues avail. **Document type:** *Journal, Academic/Scholarly.*
Published by: Universidad de Moron, Facultad de Ciencias Exactas, Quimicas y Naturales, Edif. Central UM, Cabildo, 134, Moron, Buenos Aires, B1708JPD, Argentina. TEL 54-11-56272000, exactas@unimoron.edu.ar, http://www.unimoron.edu.ar/.

500 ESP ISSN 0559-6645
CODEN: AUHCAD
UNIVERSIDAD DE SEVILLA. PUBLICACIONES. Text in Spanish. 1953. irreg., latest vol.64, 2001. price varies. charts; illus. **Document type:** *Journal, Academic/Scholarly.*
Indexed: GeoRef, IECT, SpeleolAb.
—CASDDS. **CCC.**
Published by: Universidad de Sevilla, Secretariado de Publicaciones, Calle Porvenir 27, Sevilla, 41013, Spain. TEL 34-95-4487444, FAX 34-95-4487443, secpub10@us.es, http://www.us.es/publius/inicio.html.

500 COL
UNIVERSIDAD DEL NORTE. DIVISION DE INVESTIGACIONES Y PROYECTOS. ANUARIO CIENTIFICO. Text in Spanish. a. **Document type:** *Academic/Scholarly.* **Description:** Discusses scientific research and its impact on all facets of civil society and national development.
Published by: (Universidad del Norte, Division de Investigaciones y Proyectos), Universidad del Norte, Ediciones Uninorte, Km 5 Via a Puerto Colombia, Barranquilla, Colombia. TEL 57-5-3509218, FAX 57-5-3509489, ediciones@uninorte.edu.co.

505 VEN ISSN 1315-2076
Q33 CODEN: CENCEP
➤ **UNIVERSIDAD DEL ZULIA. FACULTAD EXPERIMENTAL DE CIENCIAS. CIENCIAS.** Text in English, Spanish. 1993. q. VEB 60, USD 80 (effective 2009). **Document type:** *Journal, Academic/Scholarly.* **Description:** International journal devoted to publishing original research papers in biology, chemistry, computer sciences, mathematics, and physics.
Indexed: A28, AESIS, APA, ASFA, B21, BrCerAb, C&ISA, CA/WCA, CIA, CerAb, CivEngAb, CorrAb, E&CAJ, E11, EEA, EMA, ESPM, EntAb, EnvEAb, FS&TA, GeoRef, H15, M&TEA, M09, MBF, METADEX, PollutAb, SWRA, SolStAb, SpeleolAb, T04, WAA, Z01, Z02.
—BLDSC (3193.900000), IE, Ingenta, Linda Hall.
Published by: Universidad del Zulia, Facultad Experimental de Ciencias, A.P. 15071, Las Delicias, Maracaibo 4003-A, Venezuela. TEL 58-61-598098, FAX 58-261-7598098, nmarquez@solidos.ciens.luz.ve, humberto@solidos.ciens.luz.ve.

500 300 VEN ISSN 1315-4109
UNIVERSIDAD METROPOLITANA. ANALES. Text in Spanish, English. 1994. s-a. **Document type:** *Journal, Academic/Scholarly.*
Indexed: A26, C01, E07, I04, I05.
Published by: Universidad Metropolitana, Autopista Petare-Guarenas, Urb Terrazas del Avila, Caracas, Venezuela. TEL 58-212-2403523, http://www.unimet.edu.ve. Ed. Laura Febres.

500 600 MEX
UNIVERSIDAD NACIONAL AUTONOMA DE MEXICO. INSTITUTO DE INVESTIGACIONES HISTORICAS. SERIE HISTORIA DE LA CIENCIA Y LA TECNOLOGIA. Text in Spanish. 198?. irreg., latest vol.6, 1994. price varies. **Document type:** *Monographic series.*
Published by: Universidad Nacional Autonoma de Mexico, Instituto de Investigaciones Historicas, Mtro. Mario de la Cueva, Zona Cultural, Ciudad Universitaria, Mexico City, DF 04511, Mexico. TEL 52-5-6227515, FAX 52-5-665-0070, coral@servidor.unam.mx, http://www.unam.mx/iih/instituto.

500 PRY
➤ **UNIVERSIDAD NACIONAL DE ASUNCION. FACULTAD DE CIENCIAS EXACTAS Y NATURALES. MEMORIA.** Text in Spanish. 1966. irreg. per issue exchange basis. **Document type:** *Academic/Scholarly.*
Formerly: Universidad Nacional de Asuncion. Instituto de Ciencias. Memoria
Published by: Universidad Nacional de Asuncion, Facultad de Ciencias Exactas y Naturales, Casilla de Correos 1039, Asuncion, Paraguay. TEL 595-21-585601, FAX 595-21-585600. Ed. Oscar Esquivel. Circ: 300.

500 ESP ISSN 1137-9537
UNIVERSIDAD NACIONAL DE EDUCACION A DISTANCIA. CIENCIAS. Key Title: 100cias@uned. Variant title: Ciencias a U N E D. Text in Spanish. 1997. a. **Document type:** *Journal, Academic/Scholarly.*
Published by: Universidad Nacional de Educacion a Distancia, Bravo Murillo 38, Madrid, Spain. TEL 34-91-3986000, FAX 34-91-3986600, infouned@adm.uned.es.

500 MEX ISSN 0186-2979
UNIVERSIDAD Y CIENCIA. Text in English, Spanish. 1984. s-a. MXN 80 domestic; USD 10 foreign (effective 2002).
Indexed: A26, ASFA, B21, C01, CA, ESPM, F04, H21, I04, I05, P08, P11, P48, P52, P56, PQC, T02.
Published by: (Universidad Juarez Autonoma de Tabasco, Direccion de Investigacion y Posgrado), Universidad Juarez Autonoma de Tabasco, Av Universidad s/n Zona de la Cultura, Villahermosa, Tabasco 2002, Mexico. TEL 52-993-3140698.

500 600 PRT ISSN 1647-4023
▼ **UNIVERSIDADE PORTUCALENSE. DEPARTAMENTO DE INOVACAO. CIENCIA E TECNOLGIA. REVISTA.** Text in Portuguese. 2009. a. **Document type:** *Journal, Academic/Scholarly.*
Published by: Univerdsidade Portucalense, Departamento de Inovacao, Ciencia e Tecnologia, Rua Dr. Antonio Bernardino de Almeida 541, Porto, 4200-072, Portugal. TEL 351-225-572000, FAX 351-225-572010, http://www.uportu.pt.

500 ITA ISSN 0370-727X
Q54 CODEN: RSFSAK
UNIVERSITA DEGLI STUDI DI CAGLIARI. FACOLTA DI SCIENZE. SEMINARIO. RENDICONTI. Text in English, Italian. 1931. irreg. bibl.; charts; illus. **Document type:** *Proceedings, Academic/Scholarly.*
Formerly (until 1945): Universita di Cagliari. Facolta di Scienze. Seminario. Rendiconti (1590-8496)
Indexed: CCMJ, ChemAb, GeoRef, MSN, MathR, Z01.
—INIST.
Published by: Universita degli Studi di Cagliari, Facolta di Scienze, Via Nicolo' Canelles, 15, Cagliari, CA 09124, Italy. Ed. Giovanni Floris.

500 ITA
UNIVERSITA DEGLI STUDI DI NAPOLI PARTHENOPE. FACOLTA DI SCIENZE E TECNOLOGIE. ANNALI. Text in Multiple languages. 1932. a., latest vol.66, 2002. **Document type:** *Journal, Academic/Scholarly.* **Description:** Covers a variety of disciplines related to naval and earth sciences.
Formerly (until 2003): Istituto Universitario Navale. Facolta di Scienze Nautiche, Naples. Annali (1590-9093); Which supersedes in part (in 1969): Istituto Universitario Navale, Napoli. Annali (0368-0649); Which was formerly (until 1939): Reale Istituto Superiore Navale. Annali (1590-9115)
Published by: Universita degli Studi di Napoli "Parthenope", Facolta di Scienze e Tecnologie, Via Amm. F. Acton 38, Naples, 80133, Italy. TEL 39-081-5475111, FAX 39-081-5521485, http://www.uniparthenope.it.

500 ITA ISSN 1973-5219
UNIVERSITA DEGLI STUDI DI PAVIA. SCIENTIFICA ACTA. Text in Italian. 1986. q. **Document type:** *Journal, Academic/Scholarly.*
Formerly (until 2006): Universita degli Studi di Pavia. Scientifica Acta. Quaderni del Dottorato (0394-2309)
Related titles: Online - full text ed.: ISSN 1973-5227.
Indexed: Z01.
Published by: (Universita degli Studi di Pavia), Pavia University Press, Via Ferrata 1, Pavia, 27100, Italy. TEL 39-0382-987743, FAX 39-0382-987262, unipress@unipv.it, http://www.paviauniversitypress.it. Ed. Sergio P Ratti.

001.3 500 DEU ISSN 0512-1523
UNIVERSITAET FRANKFURT. WISSENSCHAFTLICHE GESELLSCHAFT. SITZUNGSBERICHTE. Text in German. 1962. irreg., latest vol.46, no.2, 2008. price varies. **Document type:** *Monographic series, Academic/Scholarly.*
Published by: (Universitaet Frankfurt, Wissenschaftliche Gesellschaft), Franz Steiner Verlag GmbH, Birkenwaldstr 44, Stuttgart, 70191, Germany. TEL 49-711-25820, FAX 49-711-2582290, service@steiner-verlag.de, http://www.steiner-verlag.de.

500 600 DEU ISSN 0940-9475
UNIVERSITAET KIEL. FORSCHUNGS- UND TECHNOLOGIEZENTRUM WESTKUESTE. BERICHTE. Cover title: Bericht - Forschungs- und Technologiezentrum Westkuste, Christian-Albrechts-Universitaet zu Kiell. Text in English. 1991. irreg., latest vol.43, 2007. **Document type:** *Monographic series, Academic/Scholarly.*
Indexed: ASFA, B21, ESPM, GeoRef.
Published by: Christian-Albrechts-Universitaet zu Kiel, Forschungs- und Technologiezentrum Westkueste, Hafentoern, Buesum, 25761, Germany. TEL 49-4834-604-0, FAX 49-4834-604-299, office@ftz-west.uni-kiel.de, http://www.uni-kiel.de/ftzwest/.

500 AUT ISSN 0259-0700
UNIVERSITAET SALZBURG. DISSERTATIONEN. Text in German. 1970. irreg., latest vol.59, 1996. price varies. **Document type:** *Academic/Scholarly.*
Published by: (Universitaet Salzburg), Oesterreichischer Kunst- und Kulturverlag, Freundgasse 11, Vienna, 1040, Austria.

UNIVERSITAIRE DE DJIBOUTI. REVUE. *see* SOCIAL SCIENCES: COMPREHENSIVE WORKS

500 700 800 DEU ISSN 0041-9079
AP30 CODEN: UNIVA8
UNIVERSITAS; Orientierung in der Wissenschaft. Text in German. 1946. m. EUR 146.40; EUR 102 to students; EUR 14 newsstand/cover (effective 2011). adv. bk.rev.; film rev.; play rev. abstr.; bibl. index. **Document type:** *Journal, Academic/Scholarly.*
Indexed: A20, A22, BAS, ChemAb, DIP, EIP, FR, GeoRef, IBR, IBZ, MLA-IB, PhilInd, RASB, RILM, SpeleolAb.
—IE, Infotrieve, Ingenta, INIST. **CCC.**
Published by: Heidelberger Lese-Zeiten Verlag, Happelstr 12, Heidelberg, 69120, Germany. Circ: 3,000 (paid and controlled).

500 BRA ISSN 0102-6054
L45
UNIVERSITAS. CIENCIA. Text in Portuguese. 1968. q. bk.rev. illus. cum.index.
Supersedes in part (in 1985): Universitas (0041-9052)
Published by: Universidade Federal da Bahia, Centro Editorial e Didatico, Rua Augusto Viana s-n, Canela, Salvador, BA 40110-060, Brazil. TEL 071-245-2811. Circ: 500 (controlled).

500 COL ISSN 0122-7483
UNIVERSITAS SCIENTIARUM; revista de la Facultad de Ciencias de la Pontificia Universidad Javeriana. Text in Spanish, English. 1996. s-a. **Document type:** *Monographic series, Academic/Scholarly.*
Related titles: Online - full text ed.: free (effective 2011).
Indexed: C01, I04, I05, SCOPUS, Z01.
Published by: Pontificia Universidad Javeriana, Facultad de Ciencias, Cra 7a No 43-82, Bogota, Colombia. FAX 57-1-2850503, yorlik@javeriana.edu.co, http://www.javeriana.edu.co. Ed. Yuri Orlik.

500 ROM ISSN 1582-540X
UNIVERSITATEA DIN BACAU. STUDII SI CERTERARI STIINTIFICE. SERIA CHIMIE SI INGINERIE CHIMICA, BIOTEHNOLOGII, INDUSTRIE ALIMENTARA/UNIVERSITY OF BACAU. SCIENTIFIC STUDY AND RESEARCH. CHEMISTRY AND CHEMICAL ENGINEERING, BIOTECHNOLOGY, FOOD INDUSTRY. Text in Multiple languages. 2000. s-a. **Document type:** *Journal, Academic/Scholarly.*
Related titles: Online - full text ed.: free (effective 2011).
Indexed: B&BAb, B21, ESPM, RefZh.
Published by: Universitatea "Vasile Alecsandri" din Bacau, Calea Marasesti 157, Bacau, 600115, Romania. TEL 40-0234-534712, FAX 40-0234-545753, http://www.ub.ro.

509 ROM
UNIVERSITATEA TIBISCUS. SERIA STIINTELE NATURII. Text in Romanian; Summaries in German. a.
Published by: Universitatea Tibiscus din Timisoara, 4-6 Lascar Catargiu Str, Timisoara, 300559, Romania.

UNIVERSITATII MARITIME CONSTANTA. ANALELE/NAVIGATION AND MARITIME TRANSPORT. *see* TRANSPORTATION—Ships And Shipping

500 CIV ISSN 0251-4214
UNIVERSITE D'ABIDJAN. ANNALES. SERIE C. SCIENCES. Text in French. 1965. irreg. **Document type:** *Journal, Academic/Scholarly.*
Indexed: GeoRef.
—INIST, Linda Hall.
Published by: Universite Nationale de Cote d'Ivoire, 22 BP 535, Abidjan 22, Ivory Coast. TEL 225-439000, FAX 225-353635.

500 TGO
Q91.T6
UNIVERSITE DE LOME. JOURNAL DE LA RECHERCHE SCIENTIFIQUE. Text in French. 1990. s-a. back issues avail. **Document type:** *Journal, Academic/Scholarly.*
Former titles: Universite du Benin. Journal de la Recherche Scientifique (1027-1988); (until 1995): Actes des Journees Scientifiques de l'U.B. (1019-7060)
Related titles: Online - full text ed.
Published by: Universite de Lome, BP 1515, Lome, Togo. TEL 228-255094, FAX 228-258795, http://www.ub.tg. Ed. Mawulikplimi Edee.

500 510 MDG ISSN 0374-549X
Q91.M27
UNIVERSITE DE MADAGASCAR. ETABLISSEMENT D'ENSEIGNEMENT SUPERIEUR DES SCIENCES. ANNALES: SERIE SCIENCES DE LA NATURE ET MATHEMATIQUES. Text in French. 1966 (no.4). a.
Formerly (until 1966): Universite de Madagascar. Annales: Serie Sciences et Techniques (1011-0542)
Published by: Universite de Madagascar, Etablissement d'Enseignement Superieur des Sciences, BP 138, Antananarivo, Madagascar.

505 CMR ISSN 0566-201X
UNIVERSITE DE YAOUNDE. FACULTE DES SCIENCES. ANNALES. Text in French. 1968. irreg. USD 50. illus.
Continues: Universite Federale du Cameroun. Faculte des Sciences. Annales
Published by: (Universite De Yaounde, Faculte des Sciences), Universite de Yaounde, BP 337, Yaounde, Cameroon. FAX 237-23-53-88, TELEX 8384 KN. **Dist. by:** Service Central des Bibliotheques, Services des Publications, BP 1312, Yaounde, Cameroon.

500 300 ZAF ISSN 1018-0761
AS613.S8 CODEN: AUSBDY
➤ **UNIVERSITEIT VAN STELLENBOSCH. ANNALE.** Text in English, Afrikaans. 1989. s-a. price varies. back issues avail. **Document type:** *Journal, Academic/Scholarly.* **Description:** Presents publications of high quality by staff and postgraduate students which are too long for regular journals (20 - 150 pages).
Formed by the 1989 merger of (1923-1988): Universiteit van Stellenbosch. Annale. Serie B (0365-8058); (1979-1980): Universiteit van Stellenbosch. Annale. Serie A4, Bosbou (0254-1882); (1979-1988): Universiteit van Stellenbosch. Annale. Serie A3, Landbou (1012-0653); (1978-1984): Universiteit van Stellenbosch. Annale. Serie A2, Sologie (1012-0645); (1975-1988): Universiteit van Stellenbosch. Annale. Serie A1, Geologie (1013-218X)
Indexed: GeoRef, SpeleolAb.
—CASDDS.
Published by: Universiteit Stellenbosch/Stellenbosch University, Stellenbosch, 7600, South Africa. Circ: 400.

570.711 550.711 FRA ISSN 1292-1459
UNIVERSITES. SCIENCES DE LA VIE ET DE LA TERRE. Text in French. 1998. irreg. back issues avail. **Document type:** *Monographic series, Academic/Scholarly.*
Related titles: ◆ Series of: Universites. ISSN 1258-195X.
Published by: Editions Ellipses, 8-10 Rue de La Quintinie, Paris, 75740 Cedex 15, France. TEL 33-1-56566410, FAX 33-1-45310767, edito@editions-ellipses.fr.

500 NOR
UNIVERSITETET FOR MILJOE- OG BIOVITENSKAP. INSTITUTT FOR MATEMATISKE REALFAG OG TEKNOLOGI. I M T- RAPPORT. Text in Norwegian; Summaries in English. 1953. irreg. effective 1999. back issues avail. **Document type:** *Monographic series, Academic/Scholarly.*
Former titles (until 2005): Norges Landbrukshoegskole. Institutt for Tekniske Fag. I M T - Rapport (1503-9196); (until 2004): Norges Landbrukshoegskole. Institutt for Tekniske Fag. I T F Rapport (0805-7257); (until 1991): Norges Landbrukshoegskole. Institutt for Tekniske Fag. Melding (0802-8532); Which superseded in part (in 1990): Landbruksteknisk Institutt. Forsoeksmelding (0800-5788); (in 1990): Norges Landbrukshoegskole. Institutt for Bygningsteknikk. Melding (0065-0234); (in 1990): Landbruksteknisk Institutt. Rapport (0800-7691); Which was formerly (1955-1985): Orientering (0505-9402); (in 1990): Norges Landbrukshoegskole. Institutt for Hydroteknikk. Melding (0801-0501); Which was formerly (1962-1976): Norges Landbrukshogskole. Institutt for Kulturteknikk. Melding (0567-4751)
Published by: Universitetet for Miljoe- og Biovitenskap, Institutt for Matematiske Realfag og Teknologi/Norwegian University of Life Sciences, Department of Mathematics and Technology, PO Box 5003, Aas, 1432, Norway. TEL 47-64-965400, FAX 47-64-965401, imt@umb.no, http://www.umb.no/?avd=1.

500 EGY ISSN 0568-9619
Q87 CODEN: BFSAA2
➤ **UNIVERSITY OF ALEXANDRIA. FACULTY OF SCIENCE. BULLETIN.** Text in Arabic. 1968. s-a. charts. **Document type:** *Journal, Academic/Scholarly.* **Description:** Publishes original research papers and preliminary communications in various fields in the pure and applied sciences.
Indexed: CCMJ, Inspec, MSN, MathR.
—CASDDS.
Published by: University of Alexandria, Faculty of Science, 22 El-Geish Ave., El-Shatby, Alexandria, Egypt. TEL 20-3-4922919, 20-3-4922918, admin@sci.alex.edu.eg, http://www.sci.alex.edu.eg. Ed. Dr. Mamdouh S Masaoud.

507.11 ZAF
UNIVERSITY OF CAPE TOWN. COMMITTEE FOR UNDERGRADUATE EDUCATION IN SCIENCE. COLLOQUIUM SERIES. Variant title: C U E S Colloquium. Text in English. 1993. a. free. **Document type:** *Proceedings.*
Published by: University of Cape Town, Committee for Undergraduate Education in Science, Rondebosch, 7700, South Africa.

550 919.8 USA ISSN 0069-6145
CODEN: CAAOA
➤ **UNIVERSITY OF COLORADO. INSTITUTE OF ARCTIC AND ALPINE RESEARCH. OCCASIONAL PAPERS.** Text in English. 1971. irreg., latest vol.59, 2009. USD 10 per issue (effective 2010). **Document type:** *Monographic series, Academic/Scholarly.* **Description:** Contains miscellaneous work performed by institute personnel and associates.
Related titles: Online - full text ed.: free (effective 2010) (from NTI).
Indexed: ASFA, B21, GeoRef, RefZh, SCOPUS, SpeleolAb.
—Linda Hall.
Published by: University of Colorado, Institute of Arctic and Alpine Research, Campus Box 450, Boulder, CO 80309. TEL 303-492-6387, FAX 303-492-6388, instaar@colorado.edu.

500 600 MUS ISSN 1694-0342
UNIVERSITY OF MAURITIUS RESEARCH JOURNAL. SCIENCE & TECHNOLOGY. Text in English, French; Summaries in English. 1979. a. MUR 60.
Supersedes in part (in 1998): University of Mauritius. Journal
Published by: University of Mauritius, Reduit, Mauritius. TEL 230-454-1041. Circ: 250.

UNIVERSITY OF NEBRASKA STATE MUSEUM. MUSEUM NOTES. *see* MUSEUMS AND ART GALLERIES

UNIVERSITY OF OSAKA PREFECTURE. BULLETIN. SERIES A: ENGINEERING AND NATURAL SCIENCES/OSAKA-FURITSU DAIGAKU KIYO, A. KOGAKU, SHIZEN KAGAKU. *see* ENGINEERING

500 PAK ISSN 0080-9624
Q1.A1 CODEN: SURJAA
UNIVERSITY OF SIND. RESEARCH JOURNAL. SCIENCE SERIES. Text in English. 1965. a. PKR 25, USD 4.
Indexed: CIN, ChemAb, ChemTitl, INIS AtomInd, Z01.
—CASDDS.
Published by: University of Sind, Faculty of Science, Jamshoro, Hyderabad 6, Pakistan. Ed. M Rais Ahmed.

500 JPN ISSN 0910-481X
Q1 CODEN: BUTMDF
UNIVERSITY OF TOKYO. UNIVERSITY MUSEUM. BULLETIN. Text in English. 1970. irreg., latest 1999. **Document type:** *Bulletin, Academic/Scholarly.* **Description:** Contains original research papers.
Indexed: GeoRef, SpeleolAb.
—INIST.
Published by: University of Tokyo, University Museum, 3-1 Hongo 7-chome, Bunkyo-ku, Tokyo, 1130033, Japan. FAX 86-3-5841-8451, shomu@um.u-tokyo.ac.jp, http://www.um.u-tokyo.ac.jp.

500 POL ISSN 1640-1395
➤ **UNIWERSYTET WARMINSKO-MAZURSKI W OLSZTYNIE. BIULETYN NAUKOWY.** Text in Polish; Summaries in English, Polish. 1985. irreg. PLZ 20 domestic; USD 20 foreign (effective 2002 - 2003). abstr.; bibl.; charts; illus. back issues avail. **Document type:** *Journal, Academic/Scholarly.*
Former titles (until 2000): Akademia Rolniczo-Techniczna im. Michala Oczapowskiego w Olsztynie. Biuletyn Naukowy (1641-585X); (until 1999): Olsztyn University of Agriculture and Technology. Biuletyn Naukowy (1505-4705); Which superseded in part (in 1998): Acta Academiae Agriculturae ac Technicae Olstenensis (1509-3727)
Indexed: AgrLib.
Published by: (Uniwersytet Warminsko-Mazurski), Wydawnictwo Uniwersytetu Warminsko-Mazurskiego, ul J Heweliusza 14, Olsztyn, 10724, Poland. TEL 48-89-5233661, FAX 48-89-5233438, wydawca@uwm.edu.pl, http://www.uwm.edu.pl/wydawnictwo. Pubs. Tadeusz Rotkiewicz, Zofia Gawinek. Circ: 300 (paid and controlled).

500 001.3 POL ISSN 1509-3018
UNIWERSYTET WARMINSKO-MAZURSKI W OLSZTYNIE. ROZPRAWY I MONOGRAFIE. Text in Polish, English. 1985. irreg. **Document type:** *Monographic series, Academic/Scholarly.*
Former titles (until 1999): Akademia Rolniczo-Techniczna im. Michala Oczapowskiego. Rozprawy i Monografie (1506-2724); (until 1998): Akademia Rolniczo-Techniczna w Olsztynie im. Michala Oczapowskiego. Rozprawy Habilitacyjne i Monografie (1505-4691); Which superseded in part (in 1998): Acta Academiae Agriculturae ac Technicae Olstenensis (1509-3727)
Indexed: AgrAg.
Published by: (Uniwersytet Warminsko-Mazurski), Wydawnictwo Uniwersytetu Warminsko-Mazurskiego, ul J Heweliusza 14, Olsztyn, 10724, Poland. TEL 48-89-5233661, FAX 48-89-5233438, wydawca@uwm.edu.pl, http://www.uwm.edu.pl/wydawnictwo.

500 ARG ISSN 1515-5005
UNLAR CIENCIA. (Universidad Nacional de la Rioja) Text in Spanish. 2000. q. back issues avail. **Document type:** *Journal, Academic/Scholarly.*
Related titles: Online - full text ed.
Published by: Universidad Nacional de la Rioja, Ave Laprida y Ave Dr. Rene Favalara, La Rioja, 5300, Argentina. unlarciencia@unlar.edu.ar. Circ: 250.

089.959 THA ISSN 0858-6934
UP-DATE (BANGKOK, 1978); up to date reading material for modern people. Variant title: Update. Text and summaries in English, Thai. 1978. m. THB 720; THB 60 newsstand/cover. adv. bk.rev.; film rev.; software rev.; video rev. bibl.; charts; illus.; mkt.; maps; stat.; tr.lit. Index. back issues avail. **Document type:** *Consumer.* **Description:** Provides information about the latest developments in the world of science and technology.
Published by: Se - Education Public Company Ltd., Asok-Dindang Rd, Dindang, 800-43-45 Soi Trakulsuk, Bangkok, 10320, Thailand. TEL 66-2-6428900, FAX 66-2-6429866. Ed. Jumpol Hayakirin. Adv. contact Kriangkrai Cheepcharoenrath.

500 600 SWE ISSN 0284-9682
UPPFINNAREN & KONSTRUKTOEREN. Text in Swedish. 1985. 6/yr. SEK 300 (effective 1999). adv. 56 p./no. 4 cols./p.;
Formerly (until 1987): Uppfinnaren (0283-0809)
Published by: Teknikfoerlaget Facktidnings T F A B, Fack 104, Halmstad, 30104, Sweden. TEL 46-35-10-41-50, FAX 46-35-18-65-09. Ed. K V Bengtsson. Adv. contact Murgarela Sundberg. B&W page SEK 9,500, color page SEK 12,300; trim 265 x 186. Circ: 8,000.

500 SWE ISSN 1104-2516
Z7401
UPPSALA DISSERTATIONS FROM THE FACULTY OF SCIENCE AND TECHNOLOGY. Text in Multiple languages. 1970. irreg., latest vol.43, 2002. price varies. back issues avail. **Document type:** *Monographic series, Academic/Scholarly.*
Formerly (until 1993): Uppsala Dissertations from the Faculty of Science (0346-6485)
Related titles: ◆ Series of: Acta Universitatis Upsaliensis. ISSN 0346-5462.
Published by: Uppsala Universitet, Acta Universitatis Upsaliensis/University Publications from Uppsala, PO Box 256, Uppsala, 75105, Sweden. TEL 46-18-4716804, FAX 46-18-4716804, acta@ub.uu.se, http://www.ub.uu.se/upu/auu/index.html. Ed. Bengt Landgren. **Dist. by:** Almqvist & Wiksell International.

500 JPN ISSN 0287-2900
UTAN. Text in Japanese. 1982. m. JPY 5,400.
Published by: Gakken Co. Ltd., 1-17-15, Nakaikegami, Otaku, Tokyo, 145-0064, Japan. Ed. Nobuhiro Masuda.

500 JPN ISSN 0385-2415
AS552.U86 CODEN: UDKKBI
UTSUNOMIYA DAIGAKU KYOIKUGAKUBU KIYO. DAI-2-BU/UTSUNOMIYA UNIVERSITY. FACULTY OF EDUCATION. BULLETIN. SECTION 2. Text and summaries in English, Japanese. 1950. a. **Document type:** *Bulletin.*
Indexed: A22, CCMJ, CIN, ChemAb, ChemTitl, INIS AtomInd, JPI, MSN, MathR.
—BLDSC (2507.670000), CASDDS, IE, Ingenta.
Published by: Utsunomiya Daigaku, Kyoikugakubu/Utsunomiya University, Faculty of Education, 350 Mine-Machi, Utsunomiya-shi, Tochigi-ken 321-0943, Japan.

507 DEU
V H W MITTEILUNGEN. Text in German. q. free. adv. **Document type:** *Newsletter, Trade.*
Formerly (until 1982): Verband Hochschule und Wissenschaft: V H W
Published by: Verband Hochschule und Wissenschaft, Bundesvorsitzende, Gartenstrasse 6, Hirschberg, 69493, Germany. TEL 49-6201-51133, FAX 49-6201-58297, elke.platz-waury@vhw-bund.de, http://www.vhw-bund.de. adv.: B&W page EUR 790, color page EUR 1,390. Circ: 5,000 (controlled).

V R B - INFORMATIE. *see* LIBRARY AND INFORMATION SCIENCES

500 331.8 FRA ISSN 0338-1889
V R S. (Vie de la Recherche Scientifique) Text in French. 1960. q. adv. charts. **Document type:** *Magazine, Consumer.*
Formerly (until 1971): Vie de la Recherche Scientifique (0042-5427)
Indexed: RASB.
Published by: Syndicat National des Chercheurs Scientifiques, 1 Place Aristide Briand, Meudon, 92195, France. TEL 33-1-45075870, FAX 33-1-45075851.

500 600 DEU ISSN 0083-5080
VADEMECUM DEUTSCHER LEHR- UND FORSCHUNGSSTAETTEN. STAETTEN DER FORSCHUNG. Text in German. 1954. a. adv. **Document type:** *Monographic series, Academic/Scholarly.*
Related titles: CD-ROM ed.; Online - full text ed.
Published by: Dr. Josef Raabe Verlags GmbH, Rotebuehlstr 77, Stuttgart, 70178, Germany. TEL 49-711-629000, FAX 49-711-6290010, info@raabe.de, http://www.raabe.de. Circ: 5,000.

S

505 SWE ISSN 0346-4873
➤ **VAERLD OCH VETANDE**; populaer- och tvaervetenskaplig tidsskrift. Variant title: VoV. (Was not published in 1968, 1988, 1991, 1997, 1999, 2000) Text in Swedish; Summaries in English. 1951. irreg. SEK 350; EUR 200 foreign. adv. bk.rev. cum index: 1953-1992, 1996. back issues avail. **Document type:** *Magazine, Academic/Scholarly.* **Description:** Covers topics dealing with philosophy, political science, technology and history.
Published by: Vaerld och Vetande Ekonomisk Foerening, Sandbyvaeg 20, Borrby, 27630, Sweden. Ed. Rolf Ejvegaard. Circ: 1,000 (controlled).

500 SWE ISSN 2000-6942
▼ **VAERLDENS VETENSKAP!.** Text in Swedish. 2010. m. SEK 695 (effective 2011). **Document type:** *Magazine, Consumer.*
Related titles: Online - full text ed.
Published by: I D G AB (Subsidiary of: I D G Communications Inc.), Karlbergsvaegen 77-81, Stockholm, 10678, Sweden. TEL 46-8-4536000, FAX 46-8-4536005, kundservice@idg.se, http://www.idg.se. Ed. Andreas Leijon TEL 47-8-4536248.

500 600 ROM ISSN 2065-2828
VALAHIA UNIVERSITY OF TARGOVISTE. ANNALS. FOOD SCIENCE AND TECHNOLOGY. Text in English. 2000. s-a. free (effective 2011). **Document type:** *Journal, Academic/Scholarly.*
Media: Online - full text.
Indexed: A34, A35, A36, A37, A38, AgrForAb, C25, C30, CABA, D01, E12, F08, FCA, GH, H16, MaizeAb, N02, N03, N04, P32, P33, S13, SoyAb, T05, W10, W11.
Published by: Universitatea Valahia din Targoviste, University Press, 5 Moldovei St, Targoviste, 130024, Romania. FAX 40-245-213684, http://www.valahia.ro. Ed. Stefania Iordache.

500 600 FIN ISSN 1235-0621
QC790.95 CODEN: VTTPEY
➤ **VALTION TEKNILLINEN TUTKIMUSKESKUS. V T T PUBLICATIONS.** Text in English, Finnish. 1981. irreg., latest vol.496, 2003. price varies. back issues avail.; reprints avail. **Document type:** *Monographic series, Academic/Scholarly.*
Formerly (until 1992): Technical Research Centre of Finland. Publications (0358-5069); Incorporates (1981-2002): V T T Julkaisuja (1235-0613); Which was formerly (until 1992): Tutkimuksia - Valtion Teknillinen Tutkimuskeskus (0358-5077)
Related titles: Online - full text ed.: Valtion Teknillinen Tutkimuskeskus. V T T Publications (Online). ISSN 1455-0849.
Indexed: A28, A37, APA, ASFA, B21, BA, BrCerAb, C&ISA, CA/WCA, CABA, CIA, CIN, CerAb, ChemAb, CivEngAb, CorrAb, E&CAJ, E11, E12, EEA, EMA, ESPM, EngInd, EnvEAb, F08, F11, F12, FS&TA, GeoRef, H15, Inspec, M&TEA, M09, MBF, METADEX, S13, S16, SCOPUS, SolStAb, SpeleolAb, T04, TM, WAA.
—BLDSC (9258.906930), CASDDS, IE, Ingenta, Linda Hall.
Published by: (Information Service), Valtion Teknillinen Tutkimuskeskus/Technical Research Centre of Finland, Vuorimiehentie 5, PO Box 2000, Espoo, 02044, Finland. TEL 358-2-722111, FAX 358-2-7227001, inf@vtt.fi. R&P Pirjo Sutela.

500.1 GBR
QH1
➤ **VASCULUM (ONLINE).** Text in English. 1915. q. bk.rev. back issues avail. **Document type:** *Journal, Academic/Scholarly.*
Formerly (until 2006): Vasculum (Print) (0049-5891)
Media: Online - full text.
Indexed: GeoRef, SpeleolAb, Z01.
Published by: Northern Naturalists Union, c/o M Birtle, 10, Avon Grove, Billingham, Durham TS22 5BH, United Kingdom. Ed. M Birtle.

500 NLD ISSN 1872-1729
VECTOR. Text in Dutch. 2005. q.
Published by: Technische Universiteit Eindhoven, TU/e Innovation Lab, De Horsten 1, MultiMediaPaviljoen 0.01, Eindhoven, 5612 AX, Netherlands. TEL 31-40-2474822, FAX 31-40-2466712, innovationlab@tue.nl, http://www.tue.nl/ondernemen. Ed. Dr. Han Konings TEL 31-40-2473330.

500 BEL ISSN 0770-7665
CODEN: VKKWAB
VERHANDELINGEN. KLASSE VAN DE NATUURWETENSCHAPPEN. Text in Dutch. 1941. irreg., latest vol.174, 1986. **Document type:** *Monographic series.*
Formerly (until 1972): Koninklijke Vlaamse Academie voor Wetenschappen, Letteren en Schone Kunsten. Verhandeling. Klasse der Wetenschappen (0372-6916)
Indexed: GeoRef, Inspec, RASB, SpeleolAb.
—CASDDS, INIST, Linda Hall.
Published by: Koninklijke Vlaamse Academie van Belgie voor Wetenschappen en Kunsten/The Royal Flemish Academy of Belgium for Science and the Arts, Hertogsstraat 1, Brussels, 1000, Belgium.

VERKOERPERUNGEN; Perspektiven empirischer Wissenschaftsforschung. *see* SOCIAL SCIENCES: COMPREHENSIVE WORKS

500 BRA ISSN 1415-2843
VERTICES. Text in Portuguese, Spanish. 1997. 3/yr. **Document type:** *Journal, Academic/Scholarly.*
Related titles: Online - full text ed.: ISSN 1809-2667. free (effective 2011).
Published by: Instituto Federal de Educacao, Ciencia e Tecnica Fluminense, Rua Dr Siqueira 273, Bloco A, Sala 28, Parque Dom Bosco, Campos dos Goytacazes, RJ 28030-130, Brazil. TEL 55-22-27262882, FAX 55-22-27333079, essentia@iff.edu.br, http://www.essentiaeditora.iff.edu.br. Ed. Inez Barcellos de Andrade.

500 SWE ISSN 2000-530X
▼ **VETENSKAP & HISTORIA**; tidningen ned allt om det mest spaennande. Text in Swedish. 2010. bi-m. SEK 298 (effective 2010). adv. **Document type:** *Magazine, Consumer.*
Published by: L R F Media AB, Gaevlegatan 22, Stockholm, 11392, Sweden. TEL 46-8-58836600, FAX 46-8-58836989, lrfmedia@lrfmedia.lrf.se, http://www.online.lrf.se. Ed. Lars Bjoerkvall. Adv. contact Lars Dinell TEL 46-8-58836777.

500 ITA ISSN 2038-9108
▼ **VIAGGIO NELLA SCIENZA.** Text in Italian. 2010. w. **Document type:** *Magazine, Consumer.*
Published by: Poligrafici Editoriale (Subsidiary of: Monrif Group), Via Enrico Mattei 106, Bologna, BO 40138, Italy. TEL 39-051-6006111, FAX 39-051-6006266, http://www.monrifgroup.net.

500 LKA ISSN 1391-0302
VIDURAVA. Text in English, Singhalese. 1976. q. USD 8 (effective 2000). reprints avail.
Published by: National Science Foundation of Sri Lanka, 47-5 Maitland Place, Colombo, 7, Sri Lanka. Ed. K Ramasamy.

500 IND ISSN 0505-4753
CODEN: VIBBDS
VIDYA. Variant title: Vidya. B. Sciences. Text in English, Gujarati. 1973 (vol.16). s-a. bibl.; charts; illus. back issues avail. **Document type:** *Journal, Academic/Scholarly.*
Related titles: Online - full text ed.
Indexed: CIS, ChemAb.
—CASDDS.
Published by: Gujarat University, PO Box 4010, Ahmedabad, Gujarat 380 009, India. TEL 91-79-26301341, FAX 91-79-26302654.

509 GBR ISSN 1751-8261
VIEWPOINT (FLEET). Text in English. 1980. 3/yr. GBP 10 to non-members; free to members (effective 2010). adv. back issues avail. **Document type:** *Newsletter, Trade.* **Description:** Reports on developments in history of science, reports of meetings, and forthcoming meetings.
Formerly (until 2006): B S H S Newsletter (0144-6347)
Related titles: Online - full text ed.
Indexed: FR, RASB.
—INIST.
Published by: British Society for the History of Science, PO Box 3401, Norwich, NR7 7JF, United Kingdom. TEL 44-1603-516236, FAX 44-1603-208563, membership@bshs.org.uk. Ed. Rosemary Wall TEL 44-20-78483962.

500 USA ISSN 0042-658X
Q1 CODEN: VJSCAI
➤ **VIRGINIA JOURNAL OF SCIENCE.** Text in English. 1923. q. USD 35 (effective 2011). bk.rev. charts; illus. Index. Supplement avail.; back issues avail. **Document type:** *Journal, Academic/Scholarly.*
Supersedes (in 1940): Claytonia
Related titles: Microform ed.: (from PQC).
Indexed: A22, ASFA, B21, B25, BIOSIS Prev, CIS, ChemAb, E17, ESPM, EntAb, GeoRef, IBR, IBZ, MSN, MathR, MycolAb, P30, SASA, SpeleolAb, VirolAbstr, W08, WildRev, Z01.
—BLDSC (9239.000000), CASDDS, IE, Ingenta, INIST, Linda Hall.
Published by: Virginia Academy of Science, c/o Hillary Stewart, Science Museum of Virginia, 2500 W Broad St, Richmond, VA 23220. FAX 804-864-1488, vas@smv.org.

500 ISL ISSN 1010-7193
VISINDAFELAG ISLENDINGA - RADSTEFNURIT. Text in Icelandic. 1987. irreg., latest vol.5, 1996. **Document type:** *Proceedings.*
Published by: Visindafelag Islendinga/Societas Scientiarum Islandica (Icelandic Scientific Society), Landsbokasafn Islands - Haskolabokasafn, Arngrimsgoetu 3, Reykjavik, 107, Iceland. TEL 354-525-5600, FAX 354-525-5615.

500 ISL ISSN 0376-2599
Q62 CODEN: VIISA9
VISINDAFELAG ISLENDINGA. RIT/ICELANDIC SCIENTIFIC SOCIETY. OCCASIONAL PAPERS. Text in English. 1923. irreg., latest vol.45, 1988. price varies. **Document type:** *Monographic series.*
Indexed: GeoRef, SpeleolAb.
—INIST.
Published by: Visindafelag Islendinga/Societas Scientiarum Islandica (Icelandic Scientific Society), Landsbokasafn Islands - Haskolabokasafn, Arngrimsgoetu 3, Reykjavik, 107, Iceland. TEL 354-525-5600, FAX 354-525-5615. Circ: 1,000. **Subscr. to:** Bokaverslun Sigfusar Eymundssonar, Austurstraeti 18, Reykjavik 101, Iceland; Bokabud Mals og Menningar, Laugavegi 18, Reykjavik 101, Iceland.

500 CHE ISSN 1420-2468
Q180.S9
VISION; das Schweizer Magazin fuer Wissenschaft und Innovation. Text in German, French, English. 1972. 4/yr. (plus 2 to 4 special thematic nos.). CHF 45 domestic; CHF 55 in Europe; CHF 65 elsewhere; CHF 12.50, EUR 8 newsstand/cover (effective 2003 & 2004). adv. bibl. index. 64 p./no.; back issues avail. **Document type:** *Magazine, Academic/Scholarly.* **Description:** Publishes information on Swiss science policy and national and international higher education policy activities.
Formerly (until 1993): Politique de la Science (0085-4980)
Related titles: English ed.: ISSN 1420-5246; French ed.: ISSN 1420-2506.
Indexed: RASB.
—CCC.
Published by: (Switzerland. Office Federal de l'Education et de la Science/Bundesamt fuer Bildung und Wissenschaft - Ufficio Federale dell'Educazione e della Scienza - Federal Office for Education and Science), Science Com AG, Thunstr 5, Bern, 3005, Switzerland. TEL 41-31-3565353, FAX 41-31-3565350. Ed. Philippe Ganebin. Pub. Urs Aeberhard. Adv. contacts Michele Berner, Ursula Zingg. Circ: 25,400.

500 CHL ISSN 0716-677X
VISIONES CIENTIFICAS. Text in Spanish. 1985. a. **Document type:** *Journal, Academic/Scholarly.*
Indexed: F04, T02.
Published by: Universidad de Playa Ancha de Ciencias de la Educacion, Avenida Playa Ancha 850, Valparaiso, Chile. TEL 56-32-281758, FAX 56-32-285041, http://www.upa.cl.

500 RUS ISSN 0132-3776
DF501
VIZANTIJSKIJ VREMENNIK. Text in Russian. 1894. irreg. **Document type:** *Academic/Scholarly.*
Indexed: B24, IBR, IBZ.
—INIST.
Published by: Russian Academy of Science/Rossijskaa Akademia Nauk, 14 Leninskii pr, Moscow, 119991, Russian Federation. TEL 7-095-938-0309, http://www.ras.ru/.

500 947 RUS ISSN 0205-9606
Q124.6
VOPROSY ISTORII ESTESTVOZNANIYA I TEKHNIKI. Text in Russian. 1956. q. RUR 250 for 6 mos. domestic; USD 160 foreign (effective 2004). bk.rev. illus.; bibl. **Document type:** *Journal, Academic/Scholarly.*
Related titles: Online - full text ed.
Indexed: CA, CCMJ, FR, HistAb, MSN, MathR, P30, RASB, RefZh, SCOPUS, T02, Z02.
—East View, INIST, Linda Hall. **CCC.**
Published by: (Institut Istorii Estestvoznaniya i Tekhniki), Izdatel'stvo Nauka, Profsoyuznaya ul 90, Moscow, 117864, Russian Federation. TEL 7-095-3347151, FAX 7-095-4202220, secret@naukaran.ru, http://www.naukaran.ru. **Dist. by:** M K - Periodica, ul Gilyarovskogo 39, Moscow 129110, Russian Federation. TEL 7-095-2845008, FAX 7-095-2813798, info@periodicals.ru, http://www.mkniga.ru.

500 RUS ISSN 0234-5439
➤ **VORONEZHSKII GOSUDARSTVENNYI UNIVERSITET. VESTNIK.** Text in Russian. 1993. irreg. **Document type:** *Journal, Academic/Scholarly.*
Related titles: Online - full text ed.
Indexed: RefZh.
Published by: Voronezhskii Gosudarstvennyi Universitet, Universitetskaya pl 1, Voronezh, 394693, Russian Federation. TEL 7-4732-207521, FAX 7-4732-208755, http://www.vsu.ru.

500 USA ISSN 1942-2121
W R SCIENCE. (Weekly Reader) Text in English. 2007. 8/yr. USD 6.95 (effective 2007). **Document type:** *Magazine, Academic/Scholarly.* **Description:** Designed to help the students learn about their world by exploring science news.
Published by: Weekly Reader Corporation (Subsidiary of: W R C Media Inc.), 3001 Cindel Dr, PO Box 8037, Delran, NJ 08075. TEL 800-446-3355, FAX 856-786-3360, customerservice@weeklyreader.com. Ed. Chris Jozefowicz.

W S E A S TRANSACTIONS ON INFORMATION SCIENCE AND APPLICATIONS. *see* COMPUTERS—Information Science And Information Theory

500 CAN ISSN 1923-757X
▼ ➤ **W U R J: HEALTH AND NATURAL SCIENCES.** (Western Undergraduate Research Journal) Text in English. 2009. irreg., latest vol.1, no.1, 2010. free (effective 2010). **Document type:** *Journal, Academic/Scholarly.* **Description:** Publishes original research, review articles and research progress reports within the fields of biology, chemistry and the health sciences.
Media: Online - full text.
Published by: University of Western Ontario, Western Libraries, 1151 Richmond St, London, ON N6A 3K7, Canada. TEL 519-661-2111, FAX 519-661-3493, wufsfilm@hotmail.com, http://www.lib.uwo.ca. Eds. Alexander Yan, Soniya Sharma.

500 USA ISSN 1940-0659
Q11
WADE RESEARCH FOUNDATION. REPORTS. Text in English. 2004. irreg. free (effective 2011). **Document type:** *Report, Academic/Scholarly.* **Description:** Features scientific articles of international interest on a wide variety of topics.
Related titles: Online - full text ed.: ISSN 1940-2910.
Indexed: A01, CA, T02.
Published by: Wade Research Foundation, PO Box 257, Princeton, NJ 08542. http://www.wade-research.com/.

500 JPN ISSN 1342-4645
CODEN: WDKSAT
WAKAYAMA DAIGAKU KYOIKUGAKUBU KIYO. SHIZEN KAGAKU/WAKAYAMA UNIVERSITY. FACULTY OF EDUCATION. BULLETIN: NATURAL SCIENCE. Text in English, Japanese; Summaries in English. 1950. a.
Indexed: CCMJ, ChemAb, JPI, MSN, MathR, Z02.
Published by: Wakayama Daigaku, Kyoikugakubu/Wakayama University, Faculty of Education, 930 Sakaedani, Wakayama-shi, 640-8441, Japan. **Co-sponsor:** Wakayama Daigaku Gakugei Gakkai - Wakayama University, Liberal Arts Society.

500 USA
WAKE-ROBIN. Text in English. 1970. a. USD 15 to individuals; USD 100 to corporations; USD 10 to students. bk.rev. back issues avail. **Document type:** *Newsletter.* **Description:** Focuses on nature-oriented and conservation essays, as well as news of the association.
Published by: John Burroughs Association, 15 W 77th St, New York, NY 10024. TEL 212-769-5169, FAX 212-769-5329. Ed. Ralph Blazk. Circ: 480.

WAKOU. *see* CHILDREN AND YOUTH—For

400 500 THA ISSN 1686-9664
WARASAN WITTHAYASAT LAE THEKNOLOYI MAHAWITTHAYALAI MAHASARAKHAM. Text in Thai. 2005. q. **Document type:** *Journal, Academic/Scholarly.*
Related titles: Online - full text ed.: free (effective 2011).
Indexed: A37, B23, C30, D01, S13.
Published by: Mahawitthayalai Mahasarakham/Mahasarakham University, Silk Innovation Center Bldg., Khamriang Sub-District, Kantarawichai District, Maha Sarakham, 44150, Thailand. TEL 66-43-754416, FAX 66-43-754416, http://www.msu.ac.th/.

500 USA ISSN 0043-0439
Q11 CODEN: JWASA3
➤ **WASHINGTON ACADEMY OF SCIENCES. JOURNAL.** Key Title: Journal of the Washington Academy of Sciences. Text in English. 1899-1993; resumed 1996. q. USD 25 in US & Canada to non-members; USD 30 elsewhere to non-members; USD 10 per issue in US & Canada to non-members; USD 15 per issue elsewhere to non-members; free to members (effective 2011). bk.rev. bibl.; charts; illus. **Document type:** *Journal, Academic/Scholarly.* **Description:** Publishes original scientific research, critical reviews, historical articles, proceedings of scholarly meetings of its affiliated societies, reports of the academy, and other items of interest to academy members.
Supersedes (in 1911): Washington Academy of Sciences. Proceedings (0363-1095)
Indexed: A06, A22, ASFA, B21, BibLing, CIS, CTA, ChemAb, ChemoAb, GeoRef, H09, H10, Inspec, MLA-IB, MathR, NSA, P30, RASB, S05, SASA, SpeleolAb, VirolAbstr, WildRev.
—CASDDS, IE, Ingenta, INIST, Linda Hall.
Published by: Washington Academy of Sciences, 1200 New York Ave, Rm 631, Washington, DC 20005. was@washacadsci.org.

500 USA ISSN 0740-0535
CODEN: SIRAE5
WASHINGTON FEDERAL SCIENCE NEWSLETTER. Text in English. 1989. s-m. (m. Jan. and Aug.). USD 410 in North America; USD 500 elsewhere (effective 2000). bk.rev. bibl.; stat.; tr.lit. back issues avail. **Document type:** *Newsletter.* **Description:** Covers science and technology research being undertaken by all U.S. agencies. Includes programs, budgets, and personnel.
Published by: Felsher Publishing Co., P O Box 20, Germantown, DC 20875-0020. TEL 202-393-3640, FAX 301-428-0557. Ed., Pub. Murray Felsher. **Subscr. to:** PO Box 2075, Washington, DC 20013.

500.9 JPN ISSN 0389-6951
WATASHITACHI NO SHIZENSHI/NATURAL HISTORY. Text in Japanese. 1979. 4/yr. JPY 3,000 (effective 2001). 24 p./no.; back issues avail. **Document type:** *Bulletin.*
Published by: Kitakyushu-Shiritsu Shizenshi Hakubutsukan Tomo no Kai, Kitakyushu Shizenshi Hakubutsukan, Yahataeki Bldg, 3-6 Nishi-Hon-Machi, Yahatahigashi-ku, Kitakyushu-shi, Fukuoka-ken 805-0061, Japan. TEL 81-93-661-7308, FAX 81-93-661-7503. Ed. Takayoshi Harada. Circ: 2,000.

WEIFANG XUEYUAN XUEBAO/WEIFANG UNIVERSITY. JOURNAL. *see* SOCIAL SCIENCES: COMPREHENSIVE WORKS

500 600 ISR ISSN 0083-7849
Q80.I78
WEIZMANN INSTITUTE OF SCIENCE, REHOVOT, ISRAEL. SCIENTIFIC ACTIVITIES. Text in English. 1949. a., latest 2007. free.
Related titles: Online - full text ed.
—GNLM, Linda Hall.
Published by: Weizmann Institute of Science, Publications and Media Relations Dept. (Subsidiary of: Weizmann Institute of Science), P O Box 26, Rehovot, 76100, Israel. TEL 972-8-9343852, FAX 972-8-9344132, news@weizmann.ac.il, http://www.weizmann.ac.il. Circ: 3,000.

500 DEU
WELT DER WUNDER. Text in German. 2005. m. EUR 42; EUR 3.50 newsstand/cover (effective 2010). adv. **Document type:** *Magazine, Consumer.*
Published by: Bauer Media Group, Burchardstr 11, Hamburg, 20077, Germany. TEL 49-40-30190, FAX 49-40-30191043, kommunikation@bauermedia.com, http://www.bauermedia.com. Ed. Uwe Bokelmann. Adv. contact Tim Lammek. page EUR 15,014. Circ: 316,495 (paid).

500 DEU
WELTWISSEN SACHUNTERRICHT. Text in German. 2006. 4/yr. EUR 68 to institutions (effective 2010). adv. **Document type:** *Journal, Academic/Scholarly.*
Published by: Westermann Schulbuchverlag GmbH, Georg-Westermann-Allee 66, Braunschweig, 38104, Germany. TEL 49-531-7080, FAX 49-531-708209, schulservice@westermann.de, http://www.westermann.de. adv.: B&W page EUR 950, color page EUR 1,520. Circ: 3,500 (paid and controlled).

500 GBR ISSN 1475-536X
CODEN: WGCSA
➤ **WENNER - GREN INTERNATIONAL SYMPOSIUM SERIES.** Variant title: Wenner-Gren International Series. Text in English. 1962. irreg., latest 2010. price varies. back issues avail. **Document type:** *Monographic series, Academic/Scholarly.* **Description:** These symposia affirm the worth of anthropology and its capacity to address the nature of humankind from a wide variety of perspectives.
Former titles (until 2002): Wenner - Gren International Series (1356-0409); (until 1992): Wenner - Gren Center International Symposium Series (0083-7989)
Indexed: CIN, ChemAb.
—BLDSC (9295.160000), CASDDS, IE, Ingenta, INIST. **CCC.**
Published by: (Wenner-Gren Foundation for Anthropological Research USA), Berg Publishers (Subsidiary of: Oxford International Publishers Ltd.), 1st Fl Angel Ct, 81 St Clements St, Oxford, Berks OX4 1AW, United Kingdom. TEL 44-1865-245104, FAX 44-1865-791165, enquiry@bergpublishers.com. Ed. Richard G Fox.

500 CHN ISSN 1674-3563
➤ **WENZHOU DAXUE XUEBAO (ZIRAN KEXUE BAN)/WENZHOU UNIVERSITY. JOURNAL (NATURAL SCIENCES).** Text in Chinese; Summaries in Chinese, English. 1963. bi-m. CNY 15 newsstand/cover (effective 2009). Index. back issues avail. **Document type:** *Journal, Academic/Scholarly.* **Description:** Publishes original articles on science and technology and reviews.
Supersedes in part (1988 -2006): Wenzhou Daxue Xuebao/Wenzhou University. Journal (1008-309X); (1987-2006): Wenzhou Shifan Xueyuan Xuebao/Wenzhou Normal College. Journal (1006-0375); Which was formerly (1980-1986): Wenzhou Shi-Zhuan Xuebao
Related titles: Online - full text ed.
Published by: Wenzhou Daxue, Chashan, Xingzheng Bldg. 516, Wenzhou, 325035, China. TEL 86-577-86598068, http://www.wzu.edu.cn/. Ed., Pub., R&P Xiaowei Zhao. Circ: 2,000.

➤ **WENZHOU ZHIYE JISHU XUEYUAN XUEBAO/WENZHOU VOCATIONAL AND TECHNICAL COLLEGE. JOURNAL.** *see* SOCIAL SCIENCES: COMPREHENSIVE WORKS

500 NGA ISSN 0043-3020
Q85
WEST AFRICAN SCIENCE ASSOCIATION. JOURNAL. Text in English. 1958. irreg. **Document type:** *Journal, Academic/Scholarly.*
Published by: West African Science Association, University of Ibadan, PO Box 4039, Ibadan, Oyo, Nigeria. TEL 234-22-400550.

500 USA ISSN 0096-4263
Q11 CODEN: PWVAAI
➤ **WEST VIRGINIA ACADEMY OF SCIENCE. PROCEEDINGS.** Text in English. 1925. s-a. abstr. cum.index: 1925-1975. back issues avail. **Document type:** *Proceedings, Academic/Scholarly.* **Description:** Publishes papers in all areas of science especially dealing with regional ecological or biological issues.
Indexed: A34, A35, AgBio, C25, C30, CABA, E12, F08, F12, FCA, G11, GH, GeoRef, H16, IndVet, LT, MLA-IB, MathR, P32, P33, P37, P40, PGegResA, PGrRegA, PN&I, R07, R08, RRTA, S13, S16, SASA, SpeleolAb, VS, W10, W11, WildRev, Z01, Z02.
—Linda Hall.
Published by: West Virginia University, West Virginia Academy of Science, 395 Evansdale Dr, Morgantown, WV 26506-6103. TEL 304-293-4024, http://www.marshall.edu/wvas/. Ed. John Warner.

500 AUS ISSN 0726-9609
CODEN: WAUNA9
➤ **THE WESTERN AUSTRALIAN NATURALIST.** Text in English. 19??. s-a. free to members (effective 2009). back issues avail. **Document type:** *Journal, Academic/Scholarly.* **Description:** Covers natural sciences of Western Australia.
Formerly (until 1947): Western Australian Naturalist
Indexed: B25, BIOSIS Prev, MycolAb, WildRev, Z01.
—BLDSC (9300.192000), IE, Ingenta.
Published by: Western Australian Naturalists' Club Inc., PO Box 8257, Perth, W.A. 6849, Australia. TEL 61-8-92282495, FAX 61-8-92282496, wanats@iinet.net.au. Ed., R&P John Dell. Circ: 550.

➤ **THE WESTERN ONTARIO SERIES IN PHILOSOPHY OF SCIENCE.** *see* PHILOSOPHY

500.9 DEU ISSN 0175-3495
WESTFAELISCHEN MUSEUM FUER NATURKUNDE. ABHANDLUNGEN. Text in German. 1930. 4/yr. price varies. charts; illus. index. **Document type:** *Journal, Academic/Scholarly.*
Formerly: Landesmuseum fuer Naturkunde zu Muenster in Westfalen. Abhandlungen (0023-7906)
Indexed: GeoRef, IBR, IBZ, RefZh, SpeleolAb, Z01.
—Linda Hall.
Published by: Westfaelisches Landesmuseum mit Planetarium, Sentruper Str 285, Muenster, 48161, Germany. TEL 49-251-59105, FAX 49-251-5916098, naturkundemuseum@lwl.org, http://www.lwl.org/LWL/Kultur/WMfN. Ed. Dr. Bernd Tenbergen.

500 300 NLD ISSN 1504-8144
WETENSCHAP IN BEELD. Text in Dutch. 2007. m. EUR 34.95 (effective 2011). adv. **Document type:** *Magazine, Consumer.*
Published by: Vipmedia Publishing en Services, Takkebijsters 57a, Breda, 4817 BL, Netherlands. TEL 31-76-5301721, FAX 31-76-5144531, info@vipmedia.nl, http://www.vipmedia.nl. Adv. contact Ilse Groeneveld.

500 NLD ISSN 1574-5813
WETENSCHAPS- EN TECHNOLOGIE-INDICATOREN/SCIENCE AND TECHNOLOGY INDICATORS. Text in Dutch. 1994. biennial.
Published by: (United Nations University, Maastricht Economic Research Institute on Innovation and Technology, Ministerie van Onderwijs, Cultuur en Wetenschap, Directie Onderzoek en Wetenschapsbeleid), Universiteit Leiden, Centrum voor Wetenschaps en Technologie-Studies, Postbus 9555, Leiden, 2300 RB, Netherlands. TEL 31-71-5273960, FAX 31-71-5273911, http://www.nowt.nl. **Co-publisher:** United Nations University, Maastricht Economic Research Institute on Innovation and Technology.

500 DEU ISSN 0340-4390
WETTERAUISCHE GESELLSCHAFT FUER DIE GESAMTE NATURKUNDE ZU HANAU. JAHRESBERICHT. Text in German. 18??. a. EUR 10 per vol. (effective 2010). **Document type:** *Yearbook, Academic/Scholarly.*
Indexed: B25, BIOSIS Prev, MycolAb, RefZh.
Published by: Wetterauische Gesellschaft fuer die Gesamte Naturkunde zu Hanau e.V., Stresemannstrasse 9, Hanau, 63450, Germany. TEL 49-6181-31576, FAX 49-6181-31576, wetterauischegesellschaft@t-online.de, http://home.t-online.de/home/g.m.e.b.schuster/j_wetter.htm.

500 AUS ISSN 1448-1065
WHAT'S NEW IN LABORATORY TECHNOLOGY. Text in English. 1990. bi-m. free to qualified personnel (effective 2008). adv. back issues avail. **Document type:** *Magazine, Trade.* **Description:** Contains new product information for laboratory management.
Formerly (until 2003): What's New in Scientific & Laboratory Technology (1034-7658)
Related titles: Online - full text ed.
Published by: Westwick-Farrow Pty. Ltd., Locked Bag 1289, Wahroonga, NSW 2076, Australia. TEL 61-2-94872700, FAX 61-2-94891265, admin@westwick-farrow.com.au. Ed. Janette Woodhouse. Pub. Adrian Farrow. adv.: color page AUD 4,526, B&W page AUD 4,076. Circ: 9,489.

590 580 579 AUS ISSN 0812-423X
WHIRRAKEE. Text in English. 1980. m. (except Jan.). free to members (effective 2008). back issues avail. **Document type:** *Newsletter, Consumer.* **Description:** Contains short natural history articles in addition to information on club meetings, excursions, and community conservation activities.
Supersedes (in 1980): Bendigo Naturalist
Published by: Bendigo Field Naturalist Club Inc., PO Box 396, Bendigo, VIC 3552, Australia. TEL 61-7-54322380, wholsworth@bigpond.com, http://communitysites.impulse.net.au/bendigofieldnaturalists/fnats.html. Ed. T Burton. Circ: 170.

WHITE PAPER ON SCIENCE AND TECHNOLOGY (YEAR). *see* TECHNOLOGY: COMPREHENSIVE WORKS

500 ZAF
WHO-DOES-WHAT: REGISTER OF GRANT HOLDERS. Text in English. 1992. a. free.
Published by: Foundation for Research Development, Communications/Stigting vir Navorsingsontwikkeling, Kommunikasie, PO Box 2600, Pretoria, 0001, South Africa. TEL 27-012-481-4000, FAX 27-012-349-1179.

WHO'S WHO IN SCIENCE AND ENGINEERING. *see* BIOGRAPHY

500 KEN ISSN 1015-4957
Q85.2
WHYDAH. Text in English. 1987. q. KES 50; USD 10 foreign. **Document type:** *Newsletter.* **Description:** Provides a forum for scientists and policy makers throughout Africa.
Indexed: ASD.
Published by: (African Academy of Sciences), Academy Science Publishers, PO Box 14798, Nairobi, Kenya. TEL 254-2-884401, FAX 254-2-884406, TELEX 25446 AFACS, asp@africaonline.co.ke. Ed. Maggie Anaminyi.

WILLI WILLS WISSEN. *see* CHILDREN AND YOUTH—For

WILTSHIRE ARCHAEOLOGICAL AND NATURAL HISTORY MAGAZINE. *see* ARCHAEOLOGY

500 600 PER ISSN 1726-3182
WINAY YACHAY. Text in Spanish. 1997. s-a. back issues avail. **Document type:** *Journal, Academic/Scholarly.*
Published by: Universidad Nacional Federico Villareal, Oficina Central de Investigacion, Paseo Villareal 285, Maranga, San Miguel, Lima, 32, Peru. TEL 51-1-4519255, http://www.unfv.edu.pe/site/ocinv/index.aspx. Ed. Florita Pinto Herrera.

500 DEU ISSN 0943-5123
WIRTSCHAFT UND WISSENSCHAFT. Text in German. 1976. bi-m. free. **Document type:** *Journal, Academic/Scholarly.*
Formerly (until 1993): Forum (Essen) (0937-8316)
Indexed: RILM.
Published by: Gemeinnuetzige Verwaltungsgesellschaft fuer Wissenschaftspflege mbH, Postfach 164460, Essen, 45224, Germany. TEL 49-201-7221-0, FAX 49-201-714968. Ed. Norbert Schuergers. Circ: 7,000.

500 DEU
WISSEN PLUS; das Wissens-Magazin exklusiv fuer Kunden der inmediaONE. Text in German. 1994. 4/yr. adv. **Document type:** *Magazine, Consumer.*
Formerly (until 2005): Bertelsmann Lexikothek Plus (1439-9024)
Published by: Medienfabrik Guetersloh GmbH, Carl-Bertelsmann-Str 33, Guetersloh, 33311, Germany. TEL 49-5241-2348010, FAX 49-5241-2348022, kontakt@medienfabrik-gt.de, http://www.medienfabrik-gt.de. Circ: 250,000 (controlled).

500 300 AUT
WISSENSCHAFT - BILDUNG - POLITIK. Text in German. 1997. irreg., latest vol.14, 2011. price varies. **Document type:** *Monographic series, Academic/Scholarly.*
Published by: Boehlau Verlag GmbH & Co.KG., Wiesingerstr 1, Vienna, W 1010, Austria. TEL 43-1-3302427, FAX 43-1-3302432, boehlau@boehlau.at, http://www.boehlau.at.

500 DEU ISSN 0948-9096
WISSENSCHAFT OHNE GRENZEN. Text in German. 1996. bi-m. EUR 5 newsstand/cover (effective 2007). adv. **Document type:** *Magazine, Consumer.*
Published by: Mediengruppe Koenig, Aeussere Zeulenrodaer Str 11, Greiz, 07973, Germany. TEL 49-3661-674213, FAX 49-3661-674214, verlag-koenig@t-online.de, http://www.mediengruppe-koenig.de. Adv. contact Uwe Hilke. B&W page EUR 810, color page EUR 1,075. Circ: 23,125 (paid and controlled).

500 DEU ISSN 0935-6908
WISSENSCHAFT UND FORSCHUNG. Text in German. 1986. irreg., latest vol.10, 1997. price varies. **Document type:** *Monographic series, Academic/Scholarly.*
Published by: Weidler Buchverlag Berlin, Luebecker Str 8, Berlin, 10559, Germany. TEL 49-30-3948668, FAX 49-30-3948698, weidler_verlag@yahoo.de.

500 DEU ISSN 0947-3971
WISSENSCHAFT UND FRIEDEN. Text in German. 1993. q. EUR 30 domestic; EUR 35 foreign (effective 2010). **Document type:** *Journal, Academic/Scholarly.*
Formed by merger of (1992-1993): Frieden (0942-5721); (1983-1993): Informationsdienst Wissenschaft und Frieden (0177-1213); Which incorporated (198?-1990): M Oe P - Rundbrief (0933-7369)
Related titles: Online - full text ed.
Indexed: RASB.
Published by: (Wissenschaft und Frieden e.V.), BdWi - Verlag, Gisselberger Str 7, Marburg, 35037, Germany. TEL 49-6421-21395, FAX 49-6421-24654, bdwi@bdwi.de, http://www.bdwi.de. Ed. Fabian Virchow. Circ: 3,000.

500 DEU ISSN 1862-6998
WISSENSCHAFT UND OEFFENTLICHKEIT. Text in German. 2006. irreg. price varies. **Document type:** *Monographic series, Academic/Scholarly.*
Published by: Waxmann Verlag GmbH, Steinfurter Str 555, Muenster, 48159, Germany. TEL 49-251-265040, FAX 49-251-2650426, info@waxmann.com. Ed. Rainer Bromme.

500 BIH ISSN 0350-0012
WISSENSCHAFTLICHE MITTEILUNGEN DES BOSNISCH-HERZEGOWINISCHEN LANDESMUSEUMS. NATURWISSENSCHAFT. Text in English, German. 1971 (no.5). irreg. **Document type:** *Monographic series, Academic/Scholarly.*
Published by: Zemaljski Muzej Bosne i Hercegovine/National Museum of Bosnia and Herzegovina, Zmaja od Bosne 3, Sarajevo, 71000, Bosnia Herzegovina. Ed. Svjetoslav Obratil.

500 DEU ISSN 1613-673X
WISSENSCHAFTSKULTUR UM 1900. Text in German. 2004. irreg., latest vol.7, 2010. price varies. **Document type:** *Monographic series, Academic/Scholarly.*
Published by: Franz Steiner Verlag GmbH, Birkenwaldstr 44, Stuttgart, 70191, Germany. TEL 49-711-25820, FAX 49-711-2582290, service@steiner-verlag.de, http://www.steiner-verlag.de.

507 DEU ISSN 0947-9546
WISSENSCHAFTSMANAGEMENT; Zeitschrift fuer Innovation. Text in German. 1995. bi-m. EUR 114.50; EUR 19.80 newsstand/cover (effective 2011). adv. **Document type:** *Journal, Academic/Scholarly.* **Description:** Provides a forum for the study of innovation and efficiency in scientific research.
—IE, Infotrieve.
Published by: Lemmens Verlags- und Mediengesellschaft mbH, Matthias-Gruenewald-Str 1-3, Bonn, 53175, Germany. TEL 49-228-421370, FAX 49-228-4213729, info@lemmens.de. Circ: 2,000 (paid and controlled).

507 DEU
WISSENSCHAFTSMANAGEMENT SPECIAL. Text in German. 1999. irreg. EUR 2.50 per issue (effective 2011). adv. **Document type:** *Journal, Trade.*
Published by: Lemmens Verlags- und Mediengesellschaft mbH, Matthias-Gruenewald-Str 1-3, Bonn, 53175, Germany. TEL 49-228-421370, FAX 49-228-4213729, info@lemmens.de.

WOMEN AI KEXUE/WE LOVE SCIENCE. *see* CHILDREN AND YOUTH—For

WOMEN, MINORITIES, AND PERSONS WITH DISABILITIES IN SCIENCE AND ENGINEERING (ONLINE). *see* SOCIOLOGY

500 CAN ISSN 0049-7886
WOOD DUCK. Text in English. 1947. 9/yr. membership. bk.rev. **Document type:** *Newsletter.*

S

Published by: Hamilton Naturalists' Club, P O Box 89052, Hamilton, ON L8S 4R5, Canada. TEL 905-664-8796, FAX 905-664-8796. Ed. Don McLean. Circ: 600.

500 600 USA ISSN 0897-926X
T14.5
WORCESTER POLYTECHNIC INSTITUTE - STUDIES IN SCIENCE, TECHNOLOGY AND CULTURE. Text in English. 1989. irreg., latest vol.24, 2007. price varies. back issues avail. **Document type:** *Monographic series, Academic/Scholarly.* **Description:** Contains essays on the interrelationship of science, technology, and culture.
—IE.
Published by: Peter Lang Publishing, Inc. (Subsidiary of: Peter Lang Publishing Group), 29 Broadway, New York, NY 10006. TEL 212-647-7706, 212-647-7700, 800-770-5264, FAX 212-647-7707, customerservice@plang.com, http://www.peterlang.com. Eds. Francis C Lutz, Lance Schachterle. Pub. Christopher Myers. R&P Stephanie Archer. Adv. contact Patricia Mulrane.

500 PAK ISSN 1818-4952
➤ **WORLD APPLIED SCIENCES JOURNAL.** Text in English. 2006. 2/yr. USD 150 to individuals; USD 200 to institutions; USD 75 newsstand/cover (effective 2006). **Document type:** *Journal, Academic/Scholarly.*
Indexed: A34, A35, A36, A37, A38, AgBio, AgrForAb, B23, BA, BP, C25, C30, CABA, D01, E12, F08, F11, F12, FCA, G11, GH, H16, H17, I11, IndVet, LT, MaizeAb, N02, N03, N04, N05, O01, OR, P32, P33, P37, P39, P40, PGegResA, PGrRegA, PHN&I, PN&I, R07, R08, R11, R12, R13, RA&MP, RM&VM, RRTA, S12, S13, S16, S17, SoyAb, T05, TAR, TriticAb, VS, W10, W11, Z01.
Published by: International Digital Organization for Scientific Information (I D O S I), P-100, St# 7, Sohailabad, Peoples Colony # 2, Faisalabad, Pakistan. TEL 92-41-8542906, idosi@idosi.org. Ed. Abdel Rahman M Al-Tawaha.

500 016 USA ISSN 1946-7567
CB158
➤ **WORLD FUTURE REVIEW**; a journal of strategic foresight. Text in English. 1967. bi-m. USD 330 to institutions; free to members (effective 2009). adv. bk.rev. bibl.; illus. back issues avail.; reprints avail. **Document type:** *Journal, Academic/Scholarly.* **Description:** Aims to promote public understanding and education in the methods and applications of futures research.
Formed by the merger of (1985-2009): Futures Research Quarterly (8755-3317); Which was formerly (until 1985): World Future Society. Bulletin (0049-8092); (1979-2009): Future Survey (0190-3241); Which was formerly (until 1979): Public Policy Book Forecast (0197-9035)
Related titles: Microform ed.: (from PQC); Online - full text ed.
Indexed: A01, A03, A08, A22, CA, FutSurv, T02.
—BLDSC (9356.025400), IE, Infotrieve, Ingenta. **CCC.**
Published by: World Future Society, 7910 Woodmont Ave, Ste 450, Bethesda, MD 20814. TEL 301-656-8274, FAX 301-951-0394, info@wfs.org. Ed. Timothy C Mack. Adv. contact Jeff Cornish.

500 011 DEU
WORLD GUIDE TO SCIENTIFIC ASSOCIATIONS AND LEARNED SOCIETIES. Text in German. irreg., latest vol.10, 2006. EUR 318 base vol(s). (effective 2009). **Document type:** *Directory, Trade.* **Description:** Provides descriptions of more than 17,000 national and international societies involved in science, culture and technology. Includes a subject index arranged by country, name index, and publication index cross-referenced to the main section entries.
Published by: De Gruyter Saur (Subsidiary of: Walter de Gruyter GmbH & Co. KG), Mies-van-der-Rohe-Str 1, Munich, 80807, Germany. TEL 49-89-769020, FAX 49-89-76902150, info@degruyter.com.

▼ **WORLD JOURNAL OF ENGINEERING AND PURE & APPLIED SCIENCES.** *see* ENGINEERING

500 ZAF ISSN 1991-1343
WORLD JOURNAL OF RESEARCH AND SCIENCES. Text in English. 2006. q. USD 120 in Africa to individuals; USD 180 elsewhere to individuals; USD 350 in Africa to institutions; USD 450 elsewhere to institutions; USD 85 in Africa to students; USD 100 elsewhere to students (effective 2007). **Description:** Aims to broaden the international debate about the best research practices for young children, students and in higher education by representing a wide range of perspectives from different countries, different disciplines, and different research methodologies.
Published by: (World Research Organization), Isis Press, PO Box 1919, Cape Town, 8000, South Africa. TEL 27-21-4471574, FAX 27-86-6219999, orders@unwro.org, http://www.unwro.org/isispress.html.

500 GBR ISSN 2042-5945
▼ **WORLD JOURNAL OF SCIENCE, TECHNOLOGY AND SUSTAINABLE DEVELOPMENT.** Abbreviated title: W J S T S D. Text in English. 2010. q. **Document type:** *Journal, Trade.* **Description:** Provides information about science, technology and sustainable development.
Related titles: Online - full text ed.: ISSN 2042-5953. free (effective 2010).
Published by: World Association for Sustainable Development, PO Box 64607, London, SW8 9AT, United Kingdom. allam@worldsustainable.org. Ed. Allam Ahmed.

WORLD JOURNAL OF SCIENCES AND EDUCATIONAL ADMINISTRATION. *see* EDUCATION—School Organization And Administration

500 IND
▼ ➤ **WORLD JOURNAL OF YOUNG RESEARCHERS.** Abbreviated title: W J Y R. Text in English; Summaries in English, French. 2011. m. free (effective 2011). bk.rev.; tel.rev. abstr.; bibl.; charts; illus.; maps; mkt.; pat.; tr.lit. back issues avail. **Document type:** *Journal, Academic/Scholarly.* **Description:** Publishes research and review articles (and various other forms of articles, such as technical note, pictorial essay, case report, commentary, etc) in all fields where research is possible. In this note, articles from the broad and/or specialized fields of sciences, engineering, medicine, social-sciences, arts, etc would be considered to be fit for this WJYR.
Media: Online - full text.
Published by: Research Reviews Publications, School of Public Health, SRM University, Kattankulathur, Tamil Nadu, India. editor@rrpjournals.com, rrpjournals@gmail.com, http://www.rrpjournals.com/home.html. Ed. Salawu Emmanuel O. Circ: 1,000.

500 600 GBR ISSN 1741-2242
HC79.E5
➤ **WORLD REVIEW OF SCIENCE, TECHNOLOGY AND SUSTAINABLE DEVELOPMENT.** Abbreviated title: W R S T S D. Text in English. 2004. 4/yr. EUR 494 to institutions (print or online ed.); EUR 672 combined subscription to institutions (print & online eds.) (effective 2012). abstr.; bibl.; charts; illus. back issues avail. **Document type:** *Journal, Academic/Scholarly.*
Related titles: Online - full text ed.: ISSN 1741-2234 (from IngentaConnect).
Indexed: A26, A28, A35, A36, A37, APA, AgBio, B02, B15, B17, B18, BA, BrCerAb, C&ISA, C25, C30, CA/WCA, CABA, CIA, CerAb, CivEngAb, CorrAb, E&CAJ, E08, E11, E12, EEA, EMA, ESPM, EconLit, EnvAb, EnvEAb, F08, F12, FCA, G04, G08, GH, H15, H16, I05, I11, Inspec, JEL, LT, M&TEA, M09, MBF, METADEX, N02, N03, O01, OR, P32, P33, P40, PGegResA, PHN&I, PollutAb, R11, R12, RA&MP, RM&VM, RRTA, S09, S13, S16, SCOPUS, SSciA, SolStAb, T04, T05, TAR, W11, WAA.
—BLDSC (9359.252000), IE, Ingenta, Linda Hall. **CCC.**
Published by: Inderscience Publishers, PO Box 735, Olney, Bucks MK46 5WB, United Kingdom. TEL 44-1234-240519, FAX 44-1234-240515, editorial@inderscience.com. Ed. Dr. M A Dorgham. **Subscr. to:** World Trade Centre Bldg, 29 Rte de Pre-Bois, Case Postale 856, Geneva 15 1215, Switzerland. FAX 41-22-7910885, subs@inderscience.com.

➤ **WOT-STUDIES.** (Wettelijke Onderzoekstaken) *see* ENVIRONMENTAL STUDIES

➤ **WRITING SCIENCE.** *see* JOURNALISM

500 POL ISSN 0371-4756
WROCLAWSKIE TOWARZYSTWO NAUKOWE. SPRAWOZDANIA. SERIA A. Text in Polish. irreg., latest vol.39, 1986. price varies. **Document type:** *Proceedings.* **Description:** Reports of activities and sessions of the Humanistic Section of the Wroclaw Scientific Society. Summaries of dissertations.
Indexed: BibLing.
Published by: Wroclawskie Towarzystwo Naukowe, Ul Parkowa 13, Wroclaw, 50616, Poland. TEL 48-71-484-061. Ed. A Galos.

500.9 POL ISSN 0043-9592
➤ **WSZECHSWIAT/UNIVERSE.** Text in Polish. 1882. q. PLZ 54, USD 16 (effective 2003). adv. bk.rev. charts; illus. index. **Document type:** *Journal, Academic/Scholarly.*
Indexed: AgrLib.
Published by: Polskie Towarzystwo Przyrodnikow im. Kopernika/Polish Copernicus Society of Naturalists, Podwale 1/2, Krakow, 31118, Poland. TEL 48-12-4222924. Ed. Jacek Rajchel. Adv. contact Jerzy Vetulani. Circ: 1,500. **Dist. by:** Ars Polona, Obroncow 25, Warsaw 03933, Poland.

500 300 CHN ISSN 1671-8100
WUHAN CHUANBO ZHIYE JISHU XUEYUAN XUEBAO. Text in Chinese. 2002. bi-m. CNY 5 newsstand/cover (effective 2006). **Document type:** *Journal, Academic/Scholarly.*
Related titles: Online - full text ed.
Published by: Wuhan Chuanbo Zhiye Jishu Xueyuan, Longdengdi, Wuhan, 430050, China. TEL 86-27-84804358, FAX 86-27-84804571.

500 CHN ISSN 1671-8836
CODEN: WTHPDI
WUHAN DAXUE XUEBAO (LIXUE BAN)/WUHAN UNIVERSITY. JOURNAL (NATURAL SCIENCE EDITION). Text in Chinese. 1930. bi-m. USD 31.20 (effective 2009). **Document type:** *Academic/Scholarly.*
Former titles (until 2001): Wuhan Daxue Xuebao (Ziran Kexue Ban) (0253-9888); (until 1973): Wuhan Daxue Ziran Kexue Xuebao (0509-397X); (until 1956): Guoli Wuhan Daxue Like Jikan
Related titles: Online - full text ed.
Indexed: A22, A28, APA, BrCerAb, C&ISA, CA/WCA, CCMJ, CIA, CIN, CIS, CerAb, ChemAb, CivEngAb, CorrAb, E&CAJ, E11, EEA, EMA, ESPM, EnvEAb, H15, INIS AtomInd, M&TEA, M09, MBF, METADEX, MSN, MathR, SCOPUS, SolStAb, T04, WAA, Z01, Z02.
—BLDSC (4917.469300), CASDDS, East View, IE, Ingenta, Linda Hall.
Published by: (Xuebao Bianjibu), Wuhan Daxue, Luojiashan, Wuchang-qu, Wuhan, Hubei 430072, China. TEL 027-7882712, FAX 027-7882661. Eds. Li Weihua, Yang Yugao. **Dist. outside China by:** China International Book Trading Corp, 35 Chegongzhuang Xilu, Haidian District, PO Box 399, Beijing 100044, China.

500 CHN ISSN 1009-4881
WUHAN GONGYE XUEYUAN XUEBAO/WUHAN POLYTECHNIC UNIVERSITY. JOURNAL. Text in Chinese. 1982. q. USD 20.80 (effective 2009). **Document type:** *Journal, Academic/Scholarly.*
Former titles (until 1998): Wuhan Shipin Gongye Xueyuan Xuebao/Wuhan Food Industry College. Journal (1007-4341); (until 1992): Wuhan Liangshi Gongye Xueyuan Xuebao/Wuhan Grain Industry College. Journal (1001-6899)
Related titles: Online - full text ed.
Indexed: FS&TA.
—East View.
Published by: Wuhan Gongye Xueyuan/Wuhan Polytechnic University, Changqing Huayuan, 1 Zhonghuan Xilu, Wuhan, 430023, China. TEL 81-27-83956210, FAX 81-27-83955611.

500 CHN ISSN 1674-3644
CODEN: WGAXEJ
WUHAN KEJI DAXUE XUEBAO/WUHAN UNIVERSITY OF SCIENCE AND TECHNOLOGY. JOURNAL. Text in Chinese. 1982. bi-m. CNY 10 per issue (effective 2010). **Document type:** *Journal, Academic/Scholarly.*
Former titles (until 2008): Wuhan Keji Daxue Xuebao (Ziran Kexue Ban)/Wuhan University of Science and Technology. Journal (Natural Science Edition) (1672-3090); (until 2000): Wuhan Yejin Ke-Ji Daxue Xuebao/Wuhan Yejin University of Science and Technology. Journal (1007-5445); (until 1996): Wuhan Gangtie Xueyuan Xuebao/Wuhan Iron and Steel University. Journal (1001-4985)
Related titles: Online - full text ed.
Indexed: A28, APA, BrCerAb, C&ISA, CA/WCA, CIA, CerAb, CivEngAb, CorrAb, E&CAJ, E11, EEA, EMA, H15, M&TEA, M09, MBF, METADEX, SCOPUS, SolStAb, T04, WAA.
—BLDSC (4917.469350), East View.
Published by: Wuhan Keji Daxue/Wuhan University of Science and Technology, Jianshe 1 Lu, 947, Heping Dadao, Wuhan Keji Daxue Zhulou, 1313, Wuhan, Hubei 430081, China. TEL 86-27-68862620, FAX 86-27-68862317.

500 620 CHN ISSN 1009-5160
WUHAN KEJI XUEYUAN XUEBAO/WUHAN UNIVERSITY OF SCIENCE AND ENGINEERING. JOURNAL. Text in Chinese. 1988. m. CNY 10 newsstand/cover (effective 2007). **Document type:** *Journal, Academic/Scholarly.*
Formerly (until 1999): Wuhan Fangzhi Gongxueyuan Xuebao/Wuhan Textile Science and Technology Institute. Journal (1005-4790)
Related titles: Online - full text ed.
Published by: Wuhan Keji Xueyuan, 1, Fangzhi Lu, Wuhan, 430073, China. TEL 86-27-87181260 ext 9626.

600 620 CHN ISSN 1671-4431
CODEN: WLDXAV
➤ **WUHAN LIGONG DAXUE XUEBAO/WUHAN UNIVERSITY OF TECHNOLOGY. JOURNAL.** Text in Chinese. 1979. m. CNY 216; CNY 18 per issue (effective 2011). **Document type:** *Journal, Academic/Scholarly.*
Former titles (until 2001): Wuhan Gongye Daxue Xuebao (1000-2405); (until 1986): Wuhan Jiancai Xueyuan Xuebao/Wuhan Institute of Building Materials. Journal
Related titles: Online - full text ed.
Indexed: A28, APA, BrCerAb, C&ISA, CA/WCA, CIA, CerAb, CivEngAb, CorrAb, E&CAJ, E11, EEA, EMA, ESPM, EngInd, EnvEAb, H15, M&TEA, M09, MBF, METADEX, RefZh, SolStAb, T04, WAA.
—BLDSC (4917.469400), East View, Linda Hall.
Published by: Wuhan Ligong Daxue/Wuhan University of Technology, 122, Luoshi Road, Wuhan, Hubei 430070, China. TEL 86-27-87651953, FAX 86-27-87397739, http://www.whut.edu.cn/index.html. **Dist. by:** China International Book Trading Corp, 35 Chegongzhuang Xilu, Haidian District, PO Box 399, Beijing 100044, China. TEL 86-10-68412045, FAX 86-10-68412023, cibtc@mail.cibtc.com.cn, http://www.cibtc.com.cn.

500 CHN ISSN 1007-1202
QH7
WUHAN UNIVERSITY JOURNAL OF NATURAL SCIENCES. Text in Chinese. 1996. q. EUR 1,417, USD 1,719 combined subscription to institutions (print & online eds.) (effective 2012). reprint service avail. from PSC. **Document type:** *Journal, Academic/Scholarly.*
Related titles: Online - full text ed.: ISSN 1993-4998.
Indexed: A22, A26, A28, A34, A35, A36, A37, A38, AIDS&CR, APA, ASFA, AgBio, AgrForAb, B21, BA, BP, BrCerAb, C&ISA, C25, C30, CA/WCA, CABA, CCMJ, CIA, CerAb, CivEngAb, CorrAb, E&CAJ, E01, E08, E11, E12, EEA, EMA, ESPM, EngInd, EnvAb, EnvEAb, F08, F11, F12, FCA, G11, GH, H15, H16, I11, IndVet, Inspec, LT, M&TEA, M09, MBF, METADEX, MSN, MaizeAb, MathR, MycolAb, N02, O01, OR, P32, P33, P37, P38, P40, PGegResA, PGrRegA, PHN&I, R07, R08, R11, R12, R13, RA&MP, RM&VM, RRTA, RefZh, S09, S12, S13, S16, SCOPUS, SSciA, SolStAb, SoyAb, T04, T05, TAR, TriticAb, VS, W10, W11, WAA, Z01, Z02.
—BLDSC (9365.160005), CASDDS, East View, IE, Ingenta, Linda Hall. **CCC.**
Published by: (Editorial Department), Wuhan Daxue, Luojiashan, Wuchang-qu, Wuhan, Hubei 430072, China. TEL 86-27-68754846, FAX 86-27-68752560, http://www.whu.edu.cn/. Ed. Li Weihua. **Co-publisher:** Springer.

WUNDERWELT WISSEN; entertain your brain. *see* SOCIAL SCIENCES: COMPREHENSIVE WORKS

500 CHN ISSN 1006-7302
QH7
WUYI DAXUE XUEBAO (ZIRAN KEXUE BAN)/WUYI UNIVERSITY. JOURNAL (NATURAL SCIENCE EDITION). Text in Chinese. 1987. q. CNY 8 newsstand/cover (effective 2007). **Document type:** *Journal, Academic/Scholarly.*
Related titles: Online - full text ed.
Published by: Wuyi Daxue, 22, Dongchengcun, Jiangmen, 529020, China. TEL 86-750-3296183, FAX 86-750-3354323.

500 CHN ISSN 0438-0479
Q4 CODEN: HMHHAF
XIAMEN DAXUE XUEBAO (ZIRAN KEXUE BAN)/XIAMEN UNIVERSITY. JOURNAL (NATURAL SCIENCE EDITION). Text in Chinese; Abstracts in English. 1931. bi-m. USD 31.20 (effective 2009). **Document type:** *Journal, Academic/Scholarly.*
Formerly (until 1966): Xiamen Daxue Xuebao (Shehui Kexue Ban)/Universitatis Amoiensis Acta Scientiarum Socialium (1001-845X)
Related titles: Online - full text ed.
Indexed: A22, ASFA, B21, B25, BIOSIS Prev, CCMJ, CIN, ChemAb, ChemTitl, ESPM, Inspec, MSN, MathR, MycolAb, PollutAb, RefZh, SSciA, SWRA, Z01, Z02.
—BLDSC (4917.469600), AskIEEE, CASDDS, East View, IE, Ingenta, Linda Hall.
Published by: Xiamen Daxue/Xiamen University, Rm 218-221, Nangying, Xiamen, Fujian 361005, China. **Dist. outside China by:** China International Book Trading Corp, 35 Chegongzhuang Xilu, Haidian District, PO Box 399, Beijing 100044, China.

500 CHN ISSN 1673-4432
XIAMEN LIGONG XUEYUAN XUEBAO/XIAMEN UNIVERSITY OF TECHNOLOGY. JOURNAL. Text in Chinese. 1992. q. USD 12 (effective 2009). **Document type:** *Journal, Academic/Scholarly.*
Formerly: Lujiang Zhiye Daxue Xuebao/Lujiang University. Journal (1008-3804)
Related titles: Online - full text ed.
Published by: Xiamen Ligong Xueyuan, 394, Ximing Nan Lu, Xiamen, 361005, China. TEL 86-592-2189127.

500 CHN ISSN 1673-9965
➤ **XI'AN GONGYE DAXUE XUEBAO/XIAN TECHNOLOGICAL UNIVERSITY. JOURNAL.** Text in Chinese. 1981. bi-m. CNY 48, USD 48; CNY 8 newsstand/cover (effective 2011). **Document type:** *Journal, Academic/Scholarly.* **Description:** Publishes engineering articles in optics, mechanical, electronics, computer, material, and civil. Also includes topics in environmental protection, equipment testing, management, and other engineering research applications.
Formerly (until 2006): Xi'an Gongye Xueyuan Xuebao/Xi'an Institute of Technology. Journal (1000-5714)
Related titles: Online - full text ed.
Published by: Xi'an Gongye Daxue/Xian Technological University, 4, Jinhua Bei Lu, Xi'an, 710032, China. TEL 86-29-83208163, FAX 86-29-83208163, http://www.xait.edu.cn/index.jsp. Ed. Liu Wei-guo. Circ: 1,000.

500 CHN ISSN 0253-987X
TA4 CODEN: HCTPDW
XI'AN JIAOTONG DAXUE XUEBAO/XI'AN JIAOTONG UNIVERSITY. JOURNAL. Text in Chinese. 1960. bi-m. USD 62.40 (effective 2009). **Document type:** *Journal, Academic/Scholarly.*
Related titles: Online - full text ed.
Indexed: A22, A28, APA, BrCerAb, C&ISA, CA/WCA, CCMJ, CIA, CPEI, CerAb, CivEngAb, CorrAb, E&CAJ, E11, EEA, EMA, ESPM, Englnd, EnvEAb, H15, INIS AtomInd, Inspec, M&TEA, M09, MBF, METADEX, MSN, MathR, RefZh, SCOPUS, SolStAb, T04, WAA, Z02.
—BLDSC (4917.470000), East View, IE, Ingenta, Linda Hall.
Published by: Xi'an Jiaotong Daxue, 28, Xi'an Road, Xi'an, 710049, China. TEL 86-29-82668073, http://unit.xjtu.edu.cn/xjnet/xb/.

500 CHN ISSN 1671-8267
XI'AN JIATONG UNIVERSITY. ACADEMIC JOURNAL. Text in English. s-a. USD 12 (effective 2009). **Document type:** *Journal, Academic/Scholarly.*
Formerly (until 2001): Xi'an Medical University. Journal (1000-923X)
Related titles: Online - full text ed.
Indexed: A28, APA, BIOBASE, BrCerAb, C&ISA, CA/WCA, CIA, CerAb, CivEngAb, CorrAb, E&CAJ, E11, EEA, EMA, EMBASE, ESPM, EnvEAb, ExcerpMed, H15, IABS, M&TEA, M09, MBF, METADEX, P30, R10, Reac, SCOPUS, SolStAb, T04, WAA, Z02.
—BLDSC (0570.512550), East View, IE, Ingenta, Linda Hall.
Published by: Xi'an Jiatong University/Xi'an Jiatong Daxue, 76, Yanta Xi Lu, Xi'an, 710061, China. TEL 86-29-82655412, http://www.xjtu.edu.cn.

500 CHN ISSN 1672-9315
XI'AN KEJI DAXUE XUEBAO/XI'AN UNIVERSITY OF SCIENCE AND TECHNOLOGY. JOURNAL. Text in Chinese. 1981. q. USD 20.80 (effective 2009). **Document type:** *Journal, Academic/Scholarly.*
Former titles (until 2004): Xi'an Ke-Ji Xueyuan Xuebao (1671-1912); (until 1999): Xi'an Kuangye Xueyuan Xuebao (1001-7127)
Related titles: Online - full text ed.
—East View.
Published by: Xi'an Keji Daxue, 58, Yanta Lu Zhong-duan, Xi'an, 710054, China. TEL 86-29-85583054, FAX 86-29-85583138.

600 CHN ISSN 1673-064X
CODEN: XSDXBO
➤ **XI'AN SHIYOU DAXUE XUEBAO (ZIRAN KEXUE BAN)/XI'AN PETROLEUM UNIVERSITY. JOURNAL (NATURAL SCIENCE EDITION).** Text in Chinese; Abstracts in Chinese, English. 1986. bi-m. CNY 60, USD 60; CNY 10 per issue (effective 2009). **Document type:** *Journal, Academic/Scholarly.* **Description:** Covers the latest developments of theoretical and applied researches in the fields of petroleum industry.
Formerly (until 2003): Xi'an Shiyou Xueyuan Xuebao (Ziran Kexue Ban)/Xi'an Petroleum Institute. Journal (Natural Science Edition) (1001-5361)
Related titles: Online - full text ed.
Indexed: Englnd, PetrolAb, SCOPUS.
—BLDSC (9367.036320), IE, Ingenta, PADDS.
Published by: Xi'an Shiyou Daxue/Xi'an Petroleum University, No.18 Second Dianzi Rd., Xi'an, 710065, China. TEL 86-29-88382359, FAX 86-29-88216407, http://www.xsyu.edu.cn/. Ed. Zhan Qu. Circ: 600. **Dist. by:** China International Book Trading Corp, 35 Chegongzhuang Xilu, Haidian District, PO Box 399, Beijing 100044, China. TEL 86-10-68412045, FAX 86-10-68412023, cibtc@mail.cibtc.com.cn, http://www.cibtc.com.cn.

500 CHN
XI'AN WENLI XUEYUAN XUEBAO (ZIRAN KEXUE BAN). Text in Chinese. 1986. q. **Document type:** *Journal, Academic/Scholarly.*
Formerly: Xi'an Jiaoyu Xueyuan Xuebao/Xi'an College of Education. Journal (1008-5564)
Related titles: Online - full text ed.
Published by: Xi'an Wenli Xueyuan, 168, Taibai Nan Lu, Xi'an, 710065, China. TEL 86-29-88241039, FAX 86-29-88229951.

500 CHN ISSN 1000-5900
CODEN: XDZXEW
XIANGTAN DAXUE ZIRAN KEXUE XUEBAO/NATURAL SCIENCE JOURNAL OF XIANGTAN UNIVERSITY. Text in Chinese. 1978. q. USD 16.40 (effective 2009). **Document type:** *Journal, Academic/Scholarly.*
Related titles: Online - full text ed.
Indexed: A22, CCMJ, MSN, MathR, RefZh, SCOPUS, Z02.
—BLDSC (6041.017000), East View, IE, Ingenta.
Published by: Xiangtan Daxue/Xiangtan University, 5F, Chuban Dalou, Xiangtan, 411105, China. http://www.xtu.edu.cn/. **Dist. by:** China International Book Trading Corp, 35 Chegongzhuang Xilu, Haidian District, PO Box 399, Beijing 100044, China. TEL 86-10-68412045, FAX 86-10-68412023, cibtc@mail.cibtc.com.cn, http://www.cibtc.com.cn.

500 CHN ISSN 1671-0231
XIANGTAN SHIFAN XUEYUAN XUEBAO (ZIRAN KEXUE BAN). Text in Chinese. 1980. q. CNY 8 newsstand/cover (effective 2007). **Document type:** *Journal, Academic/Scholarly.*
Supersedes in part (in 2000): Xiangtan Shifan Xueyuan Xuebao/Xiangtan Teachers College. Journal (1005-1287)
Related titles: Online - full text ed.
Published by: Xiangtan Shifan Xueyuan, Xiangtan, 411201, China. TEL 86-732-8290354, FAX 86-732-8290509.

XIAOGAN XUEYUAN XUEBAO/XIAOGAN UNIVERSITY. JOURNAL. *see* SOCIAL SCIENCES: COMPREHENSIVE WORKS

500.028.5 CHN
XIAOXUE KEJI/ELEMENTARY SCHOOL SCIENCE AND TECHNOLOGY. Text in Chinese. m. adv. **Document type:** *Academic/Scholarly.*
Published by: Shanghai Keji Jiaoyu Chubanshe/Shanghai Science and Technology Education Publishing House, 393 Guanshengyuan Lu, Shanghai, 200235, China. TEL 86-21-4367970, FAX 86-21-4702835. Ed. Hong Rubhui. Adv. contact Yang Wang.

500 CHN ISSN 1000-274X
Q4
XIBEI DAXUE XUEBAO (ZIRAN KEXUE BAN)/NORTHWEST UNIVERSITY. JOURNAL (NATURAL SCIENCE EDITION). Text in Chinese. 1957. bi-m. USD 31.20 (effective 2009). **Document type:** *Journal, Academic/Scholarly.*
Related titles: Online - full text ed.
Indexed: CCMJ, GeoRef, MSN, MathR, Z02.
—BLDSC (4834.410900), East View.
Published by: Xibei Daxue/Northwest University, 229, Taibai Beilu, Xi'an, 710069, China. **Dist. by:** China International Book Trading Corp, 35 Chegongzhuang Xilu, Haidian District, PO Box 399, Beijing 100044, China. TEL 86-10-68412045, FAX 86-10-68412023, cibtc@mail.cibtc.com.cn, http://www.cibtc.com.cn.

500 CHN
XIBEI MINZU DAXUE XUEBAO (ZIRAN KEXUE BAN)/NORTHWEST UNIVERSITY NATIONALITIES. JOURNAL (NATURAL SCIENCE). Text in Chinese. 1980. q. USD 14.40 (effective 2009). **Document type:** *Journal, Academic/Scholarly.*
Formerly: Xibei Minzu Xueyuan Xuebao (Ziran Kexue Ban) (1009-2102)
Related titles: Online - full text ed.
—East View.
Published by: Xibei Minzu Daxue/Northwest University for Nationalities, No 1, Xibei Xincun, Lanzhou, Gansu 730030, China. TEL 86-931-2938091. **Dist. by:** China International Book Trading Corp. cibtc@mail.cibtc.com.cn, http://www.cibtc.com.cn.

500 CHN ISSN 1671-9387
XIBEI NONG-LIN KEJI DAXUE XUEBAO (ZIRAN KEXUE BAN)/NORTHWEST SCI-TECH UNIVERSITY OF AGRICULTURE AND FORESTRY. JOURNAL (NATURAL SCIENCE). Text in Chinese. 1936. m. USD 62.40 (effective 2009). **Document type:** *Journal, Academic/Scholarly.*
Former titles (until 2000): Xibei Nongye Daxue Xuebao/Acta Universitatis Septentrionali Occidentali Agriculturae (1000-2782); (until 1985): Hsi Pei Nung Hsueh Yuan Hsueh Pao/Northwest China College of Agriculture. Journal (0439-7010)
Related titles: Online - full text ed.
Indexed: A34, A35, A36, A37, A38, AgBio, AgrForAb, B23, BA, BP, C25, C30, CABA, D01, E12, F08, F11, F12, FCA, G11, GH, H16, H17, I11, IndVet, LT, MaizeAb, N02, N03, N04, N05, O01, OR, P32, P33, P37, P38, P39, P40, PGegResA, PGrRegA, PHN&I, PN&I, R07, R08, R11, R12, R13, RA&MP, RM&VM, RRTA, RefZh, S12, S13, S16, S17, SoyAb, T05, TAR, TriticAb, VS, W10, W11.
—BLDSC (4834.409000).
Published by: Xibei Nong-Lin Keji Daxue, 40 Xinxiang, Yangling, Shaanxi 712100, China. TEL 86-29-87092511, FAX 86-29-87091552.

500 CHN ISSN 1001-988X
Q4 CODEN: XDXKEH
XIBEI SHIFAN DAXUE XUEBAO (ZIRAN KEXUE BAN)/NORTHWEST NORMAL UNIVERSITY. JOURNAL (NATURAL SCIENCES EDITION). Text in Chinese. 1942. bi-m. USD 31.20 (effective 2009). **Document type:** *Journal, Academic/Scholarly.* **Description:** Includes academic papers of mathematics, physics, chemistry, biology, physical culture, geology, and computer science.
Related titles: Online - full text ed.
Indexed: A28, APA, B25, BIOSIS Prev, BrCerAb, C&ISA, CA/WCA, CCMJ, CIA, CIN, CerAb, ChemAb, CivEngAb, CorrAb, E&CAJ, E11, EEA, EMA, ESPM, EnvEAb, H15, M&TEA, M09, MBF, METADEX, MSN, MathR, MycolAb, RefZh, SolStAb, T04, WAA, Z01, Z02.
—BLDSC (4834.407500), CASDDS, East View, Linda Hall.
Published by: Xibei Shifan Daxue/Northwest Normal University, 697, Anning Dong Lu, Lanzhou, Gansu Province 730070, China. TEL 86-931-7971692, FAX 86-931-7971459. Ed. Gengji Zhao. Circ: 1,500. **Dist. by:** China International Book Trading Corp, 35 Chegongzhuang Xilu, Haidian District, PO Box 399, Beijing 100044, China.

500 CHN ISSN 1673-1891
XICHANG XUEYUAN XUEBAO (ZIRAN KEXUE BAN)/XICHANG COLLEGE. JOURNAL (NATURAL SCIENCE EDITION). Text in Chinese. 1986. q. CNY 10 newsstand/cover (effective 2010). **Document type:** *Journal, Academic/Scholarly.*
Former titles (until 2005): Xichang Nongye Gaodeng Zhuanke Xuexiao Xuebao (1008-4169); (until 1996): Xichang Nongye Zhuanke Xuexiao Xuebao
Related titles: Online - full text ed.
Published by: Xichang Xueyuan, Mapingba, Xichang, 615013, China. TEL 86-834-2580091.

500 CHN ISSN 1673-159X
T4
XIHUA DAXUE XUEBAO (ZIRAN KEXUE BAN)/XIHUA UNIVERSITY. JOURNAL (NATURAL SCIENCE EDITION). Text in Chinese. 1982. bi-m. USD 24.60 (effective 2009). **Document type:** *Journal, Academic/Scholarly.*
Formerly: Sichuan Gongye Xueyuan Xuebao/Sichuan Institute of Technology. Journal (1000-5722)
Related titles: Online - full text ed.
Indexed: A28, APA, BrCerAb, C&ISA, CA/WCA, CIA, CerAb, CivEngAb, CorrAb, E&CAJ, E11, EEA, EMA, ESPM, EnvEAb, H15, M&TEA, M09, MBF, METADEX, SolStAb, T04, WAA.
—East View, Linda Hall.
Published by: Xihua Daxue/Xihua University, Jinniu-qu, Chengdu, 610039, China. TEL 86-28-87720163, FAX 86-28-87720200.

500 CHN
XIHUA SHIFAN XUEYUAN XUEBAO (ZIRAN KEXUE BAN)/CHINA WEST NORMAL UNIVERSITY. JOURNAL (NATURAL SCIENCE EDITION). Text in Chinese. 1980. q. CNY 6 newsstand/cover (effective 2007). **Document type:** *Journal, Academic/Scholarly.*
Formerly (until Apr.2003): Sichuan Shifan Xueyuan Xuebao (Ziran Kexue Ban)/Sichuan Teachers College. Journal (Natural Science Edition) (1001-8220)
Related titles: Online - full text ed.
Indexed: CCMJ, MSN.
Published by: Xihua Shifan Xueyuan/China West Normal University, 44, Renmin Xilu, Nanchong, Sichuan 637002, China. TEL 86-817-2314311, http://www.sctc.edu.cn/. Ed. Tang Zesheng. **Dist. by:** China International Book Trading Corp, 35 Chegongzhuang Xilu, Haidian District, PO Box 399, Beijing 100044, China. TEL 86-10-68412045, FAX 86-10-68412023, cibtc@mail.cibtc.com.cn, http://www.cibtc.com.cn.

500 CHN ISSN 1673-9868
CODEN: XNDXEQ
XINAN DAXUE XUEBAO (ZIRAN KEXUE BAN)/SOUTHWEST UNIVERSITY. JOURNAL (NATURAL SCIENCE EDITION). Text in Chinese. 1951. m. CNY 10 newsstand/cover (effective 2009). **Document type:** *Journal, Academic/Scholarly.*
Former titles: Xinan Nongye Daxue Xuebao (Ziran Kexue Ban)/Southwest Agricultural University. Journal (Natural Science Edition); Xinan Nongye Daxue Xuebao/Southwest Agricultural University (1000-2642)
Related titles: Online - full text ed.
Indexed: A34, A35, A36, A37, A38, AgBio, B23, BP, C25, C30, CABA, D01, E12, F08, F12, FCA, G11, GH, H16, I11, IndVet, MaizeAb, N02, N03, N04, O01, OR, P32, P33, P37, P38, P39, P40, PGegResA, PGrRegA, PHN&I, PN&I, R07, R08, R11, R12, R13, RA&MP, S12, S13, S16, S17, SoyAb, T05, TAR, TriticAb, VS, W10, W11, Z01.
—BLDSC (9367.055400).
Published by: Xinan Daxue/Southwest University, no.2, Tiansheng Lu, Beibei-qu, Chongqing, 400715, China. TEL 86-23-68254576, FAX 86-23-68252538.

500 CHN ISSN 0258-2724
AS451 CODEN: XJDXEW
➤ **XINAN JIAOTONG DAXUE XUEBAO.** Text in Chinese; Abstracts in English. 1919. bi-m. 112 p./no.; **Document type:** *Journal, Academic/Scholarly.*
Former titles (until 1977): Tangshan Tiedao Xueyuan Xuebao; (until 196?): Jiaoda Tangyuan Jikan; (until 1919): Tangshan Gongye Zhuanmen Xuexiao ZazhiTangshan Engineering College Magazine
Related titles: Online - full text ed.: (from WanFang Data Corp.); ♦ English ed.: Southwest Jiaotong University. Journal. ISSN 1005-2429.
Indexed: A28, APA, BrCerAb, C&ISA, CA/WCA, CCMJ, CIA, CIN, CPEI, CerAb, ChemAb, CivEngAb, CorrAb, E&CAJ, E11, EEA, EMA, Englnd, H15, M&TEA, M09, MBF, METADEX, SCOPUS, SolStAb, T04, WAA, Z02.
—BLDSC (4902.300000), East View, Linda Hall.
Published by: Xinan Jiaotong Daxue/Southwest Jiaotong University, 111, Er-Huan Lu Bei-Yi-Duan, Chengdu, Sichuan 610031, China. TEL 86-28-87600550. Circ: 1,000. **Dist. overseas by:** China International Book Trading Corp, 35 Chegongzhuang Xilu, Haidian District, PO Box 399, Beijing 100044, China. TEL 86-10-68412045, FAX 86-10-68412023, cibtc@mail.cibtc.com.cn, http://www.cibtc.com.cn.

500 CHN
XINAN MINZU DAXUE XUEBAO (ZIRAN KEXUE BAN)/SOUTHWEST UNIVERSITY FOR NATIONALITIES. JOURNAL (NATURAL SCIENCE EDITION). Text in Chinese. 1975. bi-m. CNY 25 newsstand/cover (effective 2010). **Document type:** *Journal, Academic/Scholarly.*
Formerly (until 2003): Xinan Minzu Xueyuan Xuebao (Ziran Kexue Ban) (1003-2843)
Related titles: Online - full text ed.: (from WanFang Data Corp.).
Indexed: ESPM, EnvEAb, RefZh.
—BLDSC (9367.055555).
Published by: Xinan Minzu Daxue, 21, Ximianqiao Heng Jie, Chengdu, Sichuan 610041, China. TEL 86-28-85522104.

500 CHN ISSN 1000-5471
CODEN: XSDKEM
XI'NAN SHIFAN DAXUE XUEBAO (ZIRAN KEXUE BAN)/SOUTHWEST NORMAL UNIVERSITY. JOURNAL (NATURAL SCIENCES EDITION). Text in Chinese. 1957. bi-m. USD 31.20 (effective 2009). **Document type:** *Journal, Academic/Scholarly.*
Related titles: Online - full text ed.
Indexed: CCMJ, MSN, MathR.
—East View.
Published by: Xinan Shifan Daxue, Xuebao Bianjibu, No.1, Tiansheng Road, Beibei District, Chongqing, Sichuan 400715, China. TEL 86-23-68254576, 86-23-68252540, FAX 86-23-68252538. Ed. Qiu Yuhui. Circ: 7,000.

300 CHN ISSN 1674-5086
Q4 CODEN: XSXUEG
XINAN SHIYOU DAXUE XUEBAO (ZIRAN KEXUE BAN)/SOUTHWEST PETROLEUM UNIVERSITY. JOURNAL (SEIENCE & TECHNOLOGY EDITION). Text in Chinese. 1960. bi-m. CNY 180; CNY 30 per issue (effective 2010). back issues avail. **Document type:** *Journal, Academic/Scholarly.*
Formerly (until 2008): Xinan Shiyou Xueyuan Xuebao/Southwestern Petroleum Institute. Journal (1000-2634)
Related titles: Online - full text ed.
Indexed: APIAb, ASFA, ESPM, Englnd, GeoRef, PetrolAb, RefZh, SCOPUS, SWRA.
—East View, IE, PADDS.
Published by: Xinan Shiyou Daxue/Southwest Petroleum University, Xindu-qu, Chengdu, Sichuan 610500, China. TEL 86-28-83032341, FAX 86-817-2603362, swpuxuebao@yahoo.com.cn.

500 CHN ISSN 1673-3371
XINFAXIAN. Text in Chinese. 2005. m. CNY 132 (effective 2009). **Document type:** *Magazine, Consumer.*
Published by: Shanghai Yizhou Wenhua Chuanmei Youxian Gongsi (Subsidiary of: Shanghai Wenyi Chubanshe/Shanghai Literature & Art Publishing Group), 593, Yanan Xi Rd., Bldg.1, Rm.512, Shanghai, 200050, China. TEL 86-21-61229190, FAX 86-21-61229062.

XINHUA SHUMUBAO. KEJI XINSHU MUBAN/XINHUA CATALOGUE, SCIENCE & TECHNOLOGY. *see* ABSTRACTING AND INDEXING SERVICES

500 CHN ISSN 1000-2839
XINJIANG DAXUE XUEBAO (ZIRAN KEXUE BAN)/XINJIANG UNIVERSITY. JOURNAL (NATURAL SCIENCE EDITION). Text in Chinese. 1975. q. USD 16.40 (effective 2009). **Document type:** *Journal, Academic/Scholarly.*
Related titles: Online - full text ed.
Indexed: CCMJ, MSN, MathR, Z02.
Published by: Xinjiang Daxue/Xinjiang University, 14, Shengli Lu, Urumqi, Xinjiang 830046, China. TEL 86-991-8583071.

500 CHN ISSN 1008-9659
XINJIANG SHIFAN DAXUE XUEBAO (ZIRAN KEXUE BAN)/XINJIANG NORMAL UNIVERSITY. JOURNAL (NATURAL SCIENCES EDITION). Text in Chinese. 1982. q. CNY 8 newsstand/cover (effective 2007). **Document type:** *Journal, Academic/Scholarly.*
Related titles: Online - full text ed.
Published by: Xinjiang Shifan Daxue, 19, Xinyi Lu, Urumqi, 830054, China. TEL 86-991-4332658, 86-991-4332974.

S

500 CHN ISSN 1003-0972
XINYANG SHIFAN XUEYUAN XUEBAO (ZIRAN KEXUEBAN)/XINYANG NORMAL UNIVERSITY. JOURNAL (NATURAL SCIENCE EDITION). Text in Chinese. 1981. q. CNY 5 newsstand/cover (effective 2007). **Document type:** *Journal, Academic/Scholarly.*
Related titles: Online - full text ed.
Indexed: A28, A34, A35, A36, A37, A38, APA, AgBio, B23, BA, BrCerAb, C&ISA, C25, C30, CA/WCA, CABA, CIA, CerAb, CivEngAb, CorrAb, E&CAJ, E11, E12, EEA, EMA, ESPM, EnvEAb, F08, F11, F12, FCA, G11, GH, H15, H16, I11, IndVet, LT, M&TEA, M09, MBF, METADEX, N02, N03, N04, O01, OR, P32, P33, P40, PGegResA, PN&I, R07, R08, R11, R12, R13, RA&MP, RRTA, RefZh, S12, S13, S16, S17, SolStAb, SoyAb, T04, T05, TAR, TriticAb, VS, W10, W11, WAA, Z01, Z02.
—BLDSC (9367.092965).
Published by: Xinyang Shifan Xueyuan, Xuebao Bianjibu, 237, Changan Lu, Xinyang, Henan 464000, China. TEL 86-376-6390837 ext 7, FAX 86-376-6390857.

XINYU GAO-ZHUAN XUEBAO/XINYU COLLEGE. JOURNAL. *see* SOCIAL SCIENCES: COMPREHENSIVE WORKS

500 CHN ISSN 1007-6573
XUZHOU SHIFAN DAXUE XUEBAO (ZIRAN KEXUE BAN)/XUZHOU NORMAL UNIVERSITY. JOURNAL (NATURAL SCIENCE EDITION). Text in Chinese. 1983. q. USD 13.20 (effective 2009). **Document type:** *Journal, Academic/Scholarly.*
Formerly: Xuzhou Shifan Xueyuan Xuebao (Ziran Kexue Ban) (1005-863X)
Related titles: Online - full text ed.
Indexed: CCMJ, MSN, MathR, RefZh, Z02.
—BLDSC (4917.479000), IE, Ingenta.
Published by: Xuzhou Shifan Daxue/Xuzhou Normal University, 57, Heping Lu, Xuzhou, 221009, China. TEL 86-516-83867155, FAX 86-516-83867175.

500 001.3 COM ISSN 1019-9039
DT469.C7
YA MKOBE. Text in French; Text occasionally in Arabic. 1984. s-a. **Document type:** *Academic/Scholarly.*
Related titles: Online - full text ed.: ISSN 2072-6767. 2002.
Indexed: PLESA.
Published by: Centre National de Documentation et de Recherche Scientifique, B.P. 169, Moroni, Comoros. **Co-sponsors:** Archives Nationales; Musee National des Sciences de l'Homme et des Sciences de la Nature; Bibliotheque Nationale.

500 USA ISSN 0091-0287
Q1
➤ **YALE SCIENTIFIC.** Text in English. 1927. q. USD 5 per issue domestic; USD 10 per issue foreign (effective 2010). adv. bk.rev. charts; illus.; stat. index. back issues avail.; reprints avail. **Document type:** *Magazine, Academic/Scholarly.* **Description:** Provides a forum for both science and non-science majors to get a taste of the fascinating research found at Yale University.
Formerly (until 1958): Yale Scientific Magazine (0044-0140)
Related titles: Microfilm ed.: 1894 (from PQC).
Indexed: A22, BiolDig, ChemAb, P30.
—Ingenta, Linda Hall.
Published by: Yale University Press, PO Box 209040, New Haven, CT 06520. TEL 203-432-0960, 800-405-1619, FAX 203-432-0948, customer.care@triliteral.org, http://yalepress.yale.edu/home.asp. Ed. Ilana Yurkiewicz. Pub. Sameer Gupta.

➤ **YAMA TO HAKUBUTSUKAN/MOUNTAIN AND MUSEUM.** *see* MUSEUMS AND ART GALLERIES

500 JPN
YAMADA CONFERENCE. PROCEEDINGS. Text and summaries in English. 1979. irreg. **Document type:** *Proceedings.*
Published by: Yamada Kagaku Shinko Zaidan/Yamada Science Foundation, Roto Seiyaku, 8-1 Tatsumi-Nishi 1-chome, Ikuno-ku, Osaka-shi, 544-0012, Japan.

500 JPN
YAMADA KAGAKU SHINKO ZAIDAN JIGYO HOKOKUSHO/YAMADA SCIENCE FOUNDATION ANNUAL REPORT. Text in English, Japanese; Summaries in English. 1977. a.
Published by: Yamada Kagaku Shinko Zaidan/Yamada Science Foundation, Roto Seiyaku, 8-1 Tatsumi-Nishi 1-chome, Ikuno-ku, Osaka-shi, 544-0012, Japan.

500 JPN ISSN 0912-2354
YAMADA KAGAKU SHINKO ZAIDAN NYUSU/YAMADA SCIENCE FOUNDATION NEWS. Text in English, Japanese. 1974. s-a.
Published by: Yamada Kagaku Shinko Zaidan/Yamada Science Foundation, Roto Seiyaku, 8-1 Tatsumi-Nishi 1-chome, Ikuno-ku, Osaka-shi, 544-0012, Japan.

500 JPN ISSN 0513-1693
YAMAGUCHI DAIGAKU KYOIKUGAKUBU KENKYU RONSO. DAI-2-BU. SHIZEN KAGAKU/YAMAGUCHI UNIVERSITY. FACULTY OF EDUCATION. BULLETIN, PART 2. Text and summaries in English, Japanese. 1951. a. free. **Document type:** *Academic/Scholarly.*
Indexed: INIS AtomInd, JPI.
—BLDSC (2507.700000).
Published by: Yamaguchi Daigaku, Kyoikugakubu/Yamaguchi University, Faculty of Education, 1677-1 Yoshida, Yamaguchi-shi, 753-0841, Japan. FAX 81-839-33-5304. Circ: 300.

500 JPN ISSN 0387-4087
YAMAGUCHI DAIGAKU KYOYOBU KIYO. SHIZEN KAGAKU HEN/YAMAGUCHI UNIVERSITY. FACULTY OF LIBERAL ARTS. JOUNAL: NATURAL SCIENCE. Text and summaries in English, Japanese. 1967. a.
Indexed: JPI.
Published by: Yamaguchi Daigaku, Kyoyobu, 1677-1 Yoshida, Yamaguchi-shi, Yamaguchi-ken 753, Japan.

500 JPN ISSN 0385-2946
YAMAGUCHI JOSHI DAIGAKU KENKYU HOKOKU. DAI-2-BU. SHIZEN KAGAKU/YAMAGUCHI WOMEN'S UNIVERSITY. BULLETIN. SECTION 2, NATURAL SCIENCE. Text and summaries in English, Japanese. 1975. 2/yr. **Document type:** *Bulletin.*
Indexed: JPI.
Published by: Yamaguchi Joshi Daigaku/Yamaguchi Women's University, 2-1 Sakurabatake 3-chome, Yamaguchi-shi, 753-0021, Japan.

507.4 JPN ISSN 0288-4232
AM101.Y2858
YAMAGUCHI KENRITSU YAMAGUCHI HAKUBUTSUKAN KENKYU HOKOKU/YAMAGUCHI MUSEUM. BULLETIN. Text in English, Japanese; Abstracts in English. 1970. a. **Document type:** *Bulletin.* **Description:** Contains research reports from the museum.
Published by: Yamaguchi Kenritsu Yamaguchi Hakubutsukan/Yamaguchi Museum, 8-2 Kasuga-cho, Yamaguchi-shi, 753-0073, Japan. TEL 81-839-22-0294, FAX 81-839-22-0353.

500 JPN ISSN 0288-4240
YAMAGUCHIKEN NO SHIZEN. Text in Japanese. 1959. a. **Document type:** *Academic/Scholarly.* **Description:** Publishes articles on the natural history of Yamaguchi Prefecture.
Indexed: CIN, ChemAb, ChemTitl.
Published by: Yamaguchi Kenritsu Yamaguchi Hakubutsukan/Yamaguchi Museum, 8-2 Kasuga-cho, Yamaguchi-shi, 753-0073, Japan. TEL 81-839-22-0294, FAX 81-839-22-0353.

500 JPN ISSN 0385-8766
Q4 CODEN: MLMSDM
YAMANASHI DAIGAKU KYOIKU GAKUBU KENKYU HOKOKU. DAI 2 - BUNSATSU SHIZEN KAGAKU-KEI. Text and summaries in English, Japanese. 1966. a. **Document type:** *Academic/Scholarly.*
Supersedes in part (in 1972): Yamanashi Daigaku Kyoiku Gakubu Kenkyu Hokoku (1345-0549)
Indexed: CIN, ChemAb, ChemTitl, JPI.
—CASDDS.
Published by: Yamanashi Daigaku, Kyoikugakubu/Yamanashi University, Faculty of Liberal Arts & Education, 4-37 Takeda 4-chome, Kofu-shi, Yamanashi-ken 400-0016, Japan.

500 CHN ISSN 1004-602X
YAN'AN DAXUE XUEBAO (ZIRAN KEXUE BAN)/YANAN UNIVERSITY. JOURNAL (NATURAL SCIENCE EDITION). Text in Chinese. 1982. q. USD 14.40 (effective 2009). **Document type:** *Journal, Academic/Scholarly.*
Related titles: Online - full text ed.
Published by: Yan'an Daxue/Yan'an University, Yangjialing, Yan'an, Shaanxi 716000, China. TEL 86-911-2332076.

600 CHN ISSN 1004-4353
YANBIAN DAXUE XUEBAO (ZIRAN KEXUE BAN)/YANBIAN UNIVERSITY. JOURNAL (NATURAL SCIENCE EDITION). Text in Chinese. 1962. q. USD 14.40 (effective 2009). **Document type:** *Journal, Academic/Scholarly.*
Related titles: Online - full text ed.
—BLDSC (4917.508500), East View.
Published by: Yanbian Daxue/Yanbian University, 977, Gongyuan Lu, Yanji, 133002, China. TEL 86-433-2732196, http://www.ybu.edu.cn/en/frm.html. **Dist. by:** China International Book Trading Corp, 35 Chegongzhuang Xilu, Haidian District, PO Box 399, Beijing 100044, China. TEL 86-10-68412045, FAX 86-10-68412023, cibtc@mail.cibtc.com.cn, http://www.cibtc.com.cn.

500 CHN
YANCHENG GONGXUEYUAN XUEBAO/YANCHENG INSTITUTE OF TECHNOLOGY. JOURNAL. Text in Chinese. q. CNY 6 newsstand/cover (effective 2006). **Document type:** *Journal, Academic/Scholarly.*
Former titles (until 2002): Yancheng Gongxueyuan Xuebao (Ziran Kexue Ban) (1671-5322); (until 2001): Yancheng Gongxueyuan Xuebao (1008-5092)
Related titles: Online - full text ed.
Published by: Yancheng Gongxueyuan, 20, Huanhai Zhong Lu, 802 Xinxiang, Yancheng, 224003, China. TEL 86-515-8328388 ext 2113.

500 CHN ISSN 1007-824X
YANGZHOU DAXUE XUEBAO (ZIRAN KEXUE BAN)/YANGZHOU UNIVERSITY. JOURNAL (NATURAL SCIENCE EDITION). Text in Chinese. 1959. q. USD 13.20 (effective 2009). **Document type:** *Journal, Academic/Scholarly.*
Formerly: Yangzhou Shi-yuan Xuebao (Ziran Kexue Ban)/Yangzhou Teachers College. Jouranl (Natural Science Edition) (1001-6562)
Related titles: Online - full text ed.
Indexed: A22, B25, BIOSIS Prev, CCMJ, CIS, MSN, MathR, MycolAb, RefZh, Z02.
—BLDSC (4917.510000), East View, IE, Ingenta.
Published by: Yangzhou Daxue/Yangzhou University, 88, Daxue Nanlu, Yangzhou, 225009, China. TEL 86-514-7971607.

YANJIU YU FAZHAN GUANLI/R & D MANAGEMENT. *see* BUSINESS AND ECONOMICS—Management

500 620 CHN ISSN 1004-8820
YANTAI DAXUE XUEBAO (ZIRAN KEXUE YU GONGCHENG BAN)/YANTAI UNIVERSITY. JOURNAL (NATURAL SCIENCE AND ENGINEERING EDITION). Text in Chinese. 1988. q. CNY 6 newsstand/cover (effective 2007). **Document type:** *Journal, Academic/Scholarly.*
Related titles: Online - full text ed.
Indexed: A28, APA, BrCerAb, C&ISA, CA/WCA, CCMJ, CIA, CerAb, CivEngAb, CorrAb, E&CAJ, E11, EEA, EMA, ESPM, EnvEAb, H15, HPNRM, M&TEA, M09, MBF, METADEX, MSN, MathR, RefZh, SSciA, SolStAb, T04, WAA, Z02.
—Linda Hall.
Published by: Yantai Daxue/Yantai University, Laishan-qu, Yantai, 264005, China. TEL 86-535-6904913.

500 CHE ISSN 1660-1084
B105.R4
YEARBOOK OF THE ARTIFICIAL; nature, culture & technology. Text in English. 2002. irreg., latest vol.5, 2008. price varies. **Document type:** *Monographic series, Academic/Scholarly.* **Description:** Covers all disciplines that are involved with the reproduction of natural objects and processes.
Published by: Peter Lang AG (Subsidiary of: Peter Lang Publishing Group), Hochfeldstr 32, Postfach 746, Bern 9, 3000, Switzerland. TEL 41-31-3061717, FAX 41-31-3061727, info@peterlang.com, http://www.peterlang.com. Ed. Massimo Negrotti.

YEON'GU GWAHAG DONG'A/JUNIOR SCIENCE DONGA. *see* CHILDREN AND YOUTH—For

YES MAG; the science magazine for adventurous minds. *see* CHILDREN AND YOUTH—For

YICHUN XUEYUAN XUEBAO/YICHUN UNIVERSITY. JOURNAL. *see* SOCIAL SCIENCES: COMPREHENSIVE WORKS

500 MNG
YINGSHAN XUEKAN (ZIRAN KEXUE BAN)/YINSHAN ACADEMIC JOURNAL (NATURAL SCIENCE EDITION). Text in Chinese. 2006. q.
Published by: Baotou Shifan Xueyuan/Baotou Teacher's College, 3, Kexue Lu, Baotou, 014030, Mongolia. TEL 86-472-5184498, FAX 86-472-3993408.

600 620 CHN ISSN 1005-0930
YINGYONG JICHU YU GONGCHENG KEXUE XUEBAO/JOURNAL OF BASIC SCIENCE AND ENGINEERING. Text in Chinese. 1993. q. CNY 10 newsstand/cover (effective 2005). **Document type:** *Journal, Academic/Scholarly.*
Related titles: Online - full text ed.
Indexed: CPEI, EngInd, SCOPUS.
Published by: Zhongguo Guanli Kexue Yanjiuyuan, Yingyong Jichu Yu Gongcheng Kexue Yanjiusuo, Beijing Daxue, 110, Laodixue Lou, Beijing, 100871, China. TEL 86-10-62753153, FAX 86-10-62751184.

500 CHN ISSN 0255-8297
T4 CODEN: YKXUD4
YINGYONG KEXUE XUEBAO/JOURNAL OF APPLIED SCIENCES: ELECTRONICS AND INFORMATION ENGINEERING. Text mainly in Chinese; Section in English; Abstracts in English. 1983. bi-m. (q. until 2005). CNY 15 per issue (effective 2010). **Document type:** *Journal, Academic/Scholarly.*
Related titles: Online - full text ed.
Indexed: A28, APA, BrCerAb, C&ISA, CA, CA/WCA, CIA, CIN, CPEI, CerAb, ChemAb, CivEngAb, CorrAb, E&CAJ, E11, EEA, EMA, ESPM, EnvEAb, H15, Inspec, M&TEA, M09, M10, MBF, METADEX, RefZh, SCOPUS, SolStAb, T02, T04, WAA.
—BLDSC (4947.075000), CASDDS, East View, IE, Linda Hall.
Published by: (Shanghai Daxue/Shanghai University), Shanghai Kexue Jishu Chubanshe/Shanghai Scientific & Technical Publishers, 71 Qinzhou Rd. S., Shanghai, 200235, China. Ed. Hung-chia Huang.

YOGA AND TOTAL HEALTH. *see* PHILOSOPHY

500 JPN ISSN 1344-4646
Q4
YOKOHAMA KOKURITSU DAIGAKU KYOIKU NINGEN KAGAKUBU KIYO. IV, SHIZEN KAGAKU/YOKOHAMA NATIONAL UNIVERSITY. FACULTY OF EDUCATION AND HUMAN SCIENCES. JOURNAL (NATURAL SCIENCES). Text in Japanese. 1998. a. **Document type:** *Academic/Scholarly.*
Formed by the merger of (1952-1996): Yokohama Kokuritsu Daigaku Rika Kiyo. Dai-2-rui. Seibutsugaku, Chigaku (0513-5613); (1952-1997): Science Reports of the Yokohama National University. Section 1. Mathematics, Physics, Chemistry (0085-8366)
Related titles: Online - full text ed.
Indexed: CCMJ, MathR, RefZh, Z01.
—BLDSC (6041.415000), Linda Hall.
Published by: Yokohama Kokuritsu Daigaku, Kyoiku Ningen Kagakubu/Yokohama National University, Faculty of Education and Human Sciences, 79-2 Tokiwadai, Hodogaya-ku, Yokohama, 240-8501, Japan. http://www.ed.ynu.ac.jp/index.html.

500 JPN ISSN 0913-9664
YOKOHAMA-SHIRITSU DAIGAKU KIYO. SHIZEN KAGAKU HEN/YOKOHAMA CITY UNIVERSITY. JOURNAL. SERIES OF NATURAL SCIENCE. Text and summaries in English, Japanese. 1986. a.
Published by: Yokohama-shiritsu Daigaku/Yokohama City University, 4646 Mutsura-cho, Kanazawa-ku, Yokohama-shi, Kanagawa-ken 236-0032, Japan.

500 JPN ISSN 0911-7733
QH7 CODEN: YDRSAI
YOKOHAMA-SHIRITSU DAIGAKU RONSO. SHIZEN KAGAKU KEIRETSU/YOKOHAMA CITY UNIVERSITY. BULLETIN. NATURAL SCIENCE. Text in Japanese. 1949. s-a. **Document type:** *Bulletin.*
Indexed: ChemAb, JPI.
Published by: Yokohama-shiritsu Daigaku, Gakujutsu Kenkyukai/Yokohama City University, Arts and Science Society, 22-2 Se-To, Kanazawa-ku, Yokohama-shi, Kanagawa-ken 236-0027, Japan.

069 JPN ISSN 0513-2622
CODEN: SRYMAX
YOKOSUKA-SHI HAKUBUTSUKAN KENKYU HOKOKU. SHIZEN KAGAKU/YOKOSUKA CITY MUSEUM. SCIENCE REPORT. Text and summaries in English, Japanese. 1956. irreg. USD 5. back issues avail.
Indexed: B25, BIOSIS Prev, GeoRef, JPI, MycolAb, SpeleolAb, Z01.
—INIST.
Published by: Yokosuka-shi Shizen Hakubutsukan/Yokosuka City Museum, 95 Fukadadai, Yokosuka-shi, Kanagawa-ken 238-0000, Japan. Ed. N Onba. Circ: 1,000.

507.4 JPN ISSN 0386-4286
AM101.Y58
YOKOSUKA-SHI HAKUBUTSUKAN SHIRYOSHU/YOKOSUKA CITY MUSEUM. MISCELLANEOUS REPORT. Text in Japanese; Summaries in English. 1978. a.
Indexed: Z01.
Published by: Yokosuka-shi Shizen Hakubutsukan/Yokosuka City Museum, 95 Fukadadai, Yokosuka-shi, Kanagawa-ken 238-0000, Japan.

YOKOSUKA-SHI HAKUBUTSUKANPO/YOKOSUKA CITY MUSEUM. ANNUAL REPORT. *see* MUSEUMS AND ART GALLERIES

YOSHIDA KAGAKU GIJUTSU ZAIDAN NYUSU/YOSHIDA FOUNDATION FOR SCIENCE AND TECHNOLOGY. NEWS. *see* TECHNOLOGY: COMPREHENSIVE WORKS

400 300 CHN ISSN 1001-5817
YOUJIANG MINZU YIXUEYUAN XUEBAO/YOUJIANG MEDICAL UNIVERSITY FOR NATIONALITIES. JOURNAL. Text in Chinese. 1979. bi-m. bk.rev.; software rev.; Website rev. abstr. 168 p./no.; back issues avail. **Document type:** *Journal, Academic/Scholarly.*
Former titles (until 1979): Yixue Ziliao Xuanbian
Related titles: Online - full text ed.
—East View.
Published by: Youjiang Minzu Yixueyuan, 98, Chengxiang Lu, Baise, Guangxi 533000, China. TEL 86-776-2843414. Ed. Bo Jiao Song.

500 IND ISSN 0974-6102
YOUNG SCIENTISTS JOURNAL. Text in English. 2008. s-a. INR 600 domestic to individuals; USD 10 foreign to individuals; INR 1,500 domestic to institutions; USD 50 foreign to institutions (effective 2011). adv. bk.rev. abstr. reprints avail. **Document type:** *Journal, Academic/Scholarly.*
Related titles: Online - full text ed.: ISSN 0975-2145. free to qualified personnel (effective 2011).
Indexed: A01, A26, E08, H12, I05, P10, P48, P53, P54, PQC, S09, T02.
—CCC.
Published by: (Butrous Foundation GBR), Medknow Publications and Media Pvt. Ltd., B-9, Kanara Business Ctr, Off Link Rd, Ghatkopar (E), Mumbai, Maharastra 400 075, India. TEL 91-22-66491816, FAX 91-22-66491817, http://www.medknow.com.

YOUR BIG BACKYARD. *see* ENVIRONMENTAL STUDIES

YOUSE JINSHU KEXUE YU GONGCHENG/NONFERROUS METALS SCIENCE AND ENGINEERING. *see* METALLURGY

500 600 CHN ISSN 1007-6093
YUNCHOUXUE XUEBAO/OPERATIONS RESEARCH TRANSACTIONS. Text in Chinese. 1982. q. USD 26.80 (effective 2009). **Document type:** *Journal, Academic/Scholarly.*
Formerly (until 1996): Yunchouxue Xazhi/Chinese Journal of Operations Research (1001-6120)
Related titles: Online - full text ed.
Indexed: MSN, Z02.
—BLDSC (9421.869000), IE.
Published by: (Zhongguo Yunchou Xuehui/Operations Research Society of China), Shanghai Daxue/Shanghai University, 99, Shangda Lu, Shanghai, 200444, China. TEL 86-21-66132412. Ed. Min-yi Yue.

600 CHN ISSN 0258-7971
Q4
YUNNAN DAXUE XUEBAO (ZIRAN KEXUE BAN)/YUNNAN UNIVERSITY. JOURNAL (NATURAL SCIENCES EDITION). Text in Chinese. 1938. bi-m. CNY 30; CNY 5 newsstand/cover (effective 2011). **Document type:** *Journal, Academic/Scholarly.*
Related titles: Online - full text ed.
Indexed: A22, A28, A34, A35, A36, A37, A38, APA, AgBio, AgrForAb, BrCerAb, C&ISA, C25, C30, CA/WCA, CABA, CCMJ, CIA, CerAb, CivEngAb, CorrAb, D01, E&CAJ, E11, E12, EEA, EMA, ESPM, EnvEAb, F08, F11, F12, FCA, G11, GH, H15, H16, I11, IndVet, M&GPA, M&TEA, M09, MBF, METADEX, MSN, MaizeAb, MathR, N02, N03, N04, N05, O01, P32, P33, P38, P40, PN&I, R07, R11, R12, R13, RefZh, S13, S16, SolStAb, SoyAb, T04, T05, TAR, VS, W10, W11, WAA, Z02.
—BLDSC (4918.142000), IE, Ingenta, Linda Hall.
Published by: Yunnan Daxue/Yunnan University, 2, Cuihu Bei Lu, Kunming, 650091, China. TEL 86-871-5033829, http://www.ynu.edu.cn/. Ed. Ke-qin Zhang. **Dist. by:** China International Book Trading Corp, 35 Chegongzhuang Xilu, Haidian District, PO Box 399, Beijing 100044, China. TEL 86-10-68412045, FAX 86-10-68412023, cibtc@mail.cibtc.com.cn, http://www.cibtc.com.cn.

500 CHN
YUNNAN KEJI BAO. Text in Chinese. 1958. s-m. CNY 28.80 (effective 2004). **Document type:** *Academic/Scholarly.*
Published by: Yunnan Ribao Baoye Jituan, 209, Dongfeng Donglu, Kunming, 650041, China. **Dist. by:** China International Book Trading Corp, 35 Chegongzhuang Xilu, Haidian District, PO Box 399, Beijing 100044, China. TEL 86-10-68412045, FAX 86-10-68412023, cibtc@mail.cibtc.com.cn, http://www.cibtc.com.cn.

500 CHN ISSN 1672-8513
YUNNAN MINZU DAXUE XUEBAO (ZIRAN KEXUE BAN)/YUNNAN UNIVERSITY OF THE NATIONALITIES. JOURNAL (NATURAL SCIENCES EDITION). Text in Chinese. 1983. q. CNY 8 newsstand/cover (effective 2007). **Document type:** *Journal, Academic/Scholarly.*
Formerly (until 2002): Yunnan Minzu Xueyuan Xuebao (Ziran Kexue Ban) (1005-7188); Which superseded in part: Yunnan Minzu Xueyuan Xuebao/Yunnan Nationalities Institute. Journal (1001-8913)
Related titles: Online - full text ed.
Indexed: ESPM, RiskAb, Z02.
—BLDSC (9421.878200), East View, Ingenta.
Published by: Yunnan Minzu Daxue/Yunnan University of the Nationalities, 134, 121 Dajie, Kunming, Yunnan 650031, China. TEL 86-871-5132114, FAX 86-871-5137493.

500 CHN ISSN 1007-9793
YUNNAN SHIFAN DAXUE XUEBAO (ZIRAN KEXUE BAN)/YUNAN NORMAL UNIVERSITY. JOURNAL (NATURAL SCIENCES EDITION). Text in Chinese. bi-m. CNY 4 newsstand/cover (effective 2006). **Document type:** *Journal, Academic/Scholarly.*
Related titles: Online - full text ed.
Published by: Yunnan Shifan Daxue/Yunan Normal University, 158, 121 Dajie, Kunming, 650092, China. TEL 86-871-5516038.

500 POL
ZAGADNIENIA METODOLOGICZNE NAUK PRAKTYCZNYCH. Text in Polish. irreg. **Document type:** *Monographic series, Academic/Scholarly.*
Published by: (Polska Akademia Nauk, Komitet Naukoznawstwa), Polska Akademia Nauk, Instytut Filozofii i Socjologii, Nowy Swiat 72, Warsaw, 00330, Poland. TEL 48-22-8267181, FAX 48-22-8267823, secretar@ifispan.waw.pl, http://www.ifispan.waw.pl. Ed. Wojciech Gasparski.

500 POL ISSN 0044-1619
ZAGADNIENIA NAUKOZNAWSTWA. Text in Polish; Summaries in English, Russian. 1965. q. PLZ 72 (effective 2003). bk.rev. index. **Document type:** *Journal, Academic/Scholarly.* **Description:** Modern achievements in science.
Indexed: FR, IBR, IBZ, RASB.
—INIST.
Published by: (Polska Akademia Nauk, Komitet Naukoznawstwa), Polska Akademia Nauk, Biblioteka w Warszawie, Palac Kultury i Nauki, VI p., Warsaw, 00901, Poland. TEL 48-22-6566590, FAX 48-22-6566639, biblwaw@pan.pl, http://www.pan.pl. Ed. Salomea Kowalewska. Circ: 1,000.

500 378 EGY ISSN 1110-1555
ZAGAZIG UNIVERSITY. FACULTY OF SCIENCE. BULLETIN. Text in English. 1979. s-a. **Document type:** *Bulletin, Academic/Scholarly.*
Published by: Zagazig University, Faculty of Science, Center of Scientific Studies and Researches, Zagazig, Egypt. TEL 20-55-345618, 20-55-323252. Ed. Dr. Mohamed G Abdel-Wahed.

500 ZMB ISSN 0084-4950
Q180.Z3
ZAMBIA. NATIONAL COUNCIL FOR SCIENTIFIC RESEARCH. ANNUAL REPORT. Text in English. 1968. a. **Document type:** *Government.*
Published by: National Council for Scientific Research, Chelston, PO Box CH 158, Lusaka, Zambia.

ZAPADOCESKE MUZEUM V PLZNI. SBORNIK. PRIRODA. *see* MUSEUMS AND ART GALLERIES

500 JOR
➤ **ZARQA JOURNAL FOR RESEARCH AND STUDIES.** Text in English. s-a. **Document type:** *Journal, Academic/Scholarly.* **Description:** Publishes original research papers.
Published by: Zarqa Private University, Deanship of Scientific Research, PO Box 2000, Zarqa, 13110, Jordan. TEL 962-5-3821100 ext 1990, FAX 962-5-3821120.

500 SRB ISSN 0352-4906
➤ **ZBORNIK MATICE SRPSKE ZA PRIRODNE NAUKE.** Text in Serbian. 1984. s-a. EUR 10 per issue (effective 2007). **Document type:** *Journal, Academic/Scholarly.*
Related titles: Online - full text ed.: free (effective 2011).
Indexed: A01, A34, A36, A38, AgrForAb, C25, C30, CABA, D01, E12, F08, FCA, GH, H16, MaizeAb, N02, N03, N04, P32, P33, P40, R11, R13, S13, S16, SoyAb, T02, T05, W11, Z01.
Published by: Matica Srpska, Matice Srpske 1, Novi Sad, 21000. TEL 381-21-527622, FAX 381-21- 528901, ms@maticasrpska.org.yu, http://www.maticasrpska.org.yu. Ed. Rudolf Kastori.

502 NLD ISSN 0926-3497
ZEEPAARD. Text in Dutch. 1941. bi-m. EUR 10 domestic to members; EUR 17.50 foreign to members; EUR 12.50 to institutions (effective 2009).
Indexed: Z01.
Published by: (Koninklijke Nederlandse Natuurhistorische Vereniging, Strandwerkgemeenschap), Koninklijke Nederlandse Natuurhistorische Vereniging, Postbus 310, Zeist, 3707 BM, Netherlands. bureau@knnv.nl, http://www.knnv.nl. Ed. Frank Perk.

500 DEU
ZEIT WISSEN. Text in German. 2004. bi-m. EUR 31.80; EUR 5.90 newsstand/cover (effective 2011). adv. **Document type:** *Magazine, Consumer.*
Published by: Zeitverlag Gerd Bucerius GmbH & Co. KG, Pressehaus, Eingang Speersort 1, Hamburg, 20095, Germany. TEL 49-40-32800, FAX 49-40-3280472, kontakt@zeit.de. Ed. Jan Schweitzer. Adv. contact Maren Henke. Circ: 80,000 (paid).

ZEITSCHRIFT FUER DIDAKTIK DER NATURWISSENSCHAFTEN. *see* EDUCATION

ZEITSCHRIFT FUER GESCHICHTE DER ARABISCH-ISLAMISCHEN WISSENSCHAFTEN. *see* ASIAN STUDIES

ZEITSCHRIFT FUER KULTURPHILOSOPHIE. *see* PHILOSOPHY

500 BIH ISSN 0581-7528
QH7 CODEN: GZMND5
ZEMALJSKI MUZEJ BOSNE I HERCEGOVINE. GLASNIK. PRIRODNE NAUKE. Text in Bosnian; Summaries in English, French, German. 1945. irreg. EUR 10 per issue (effective 2011). illus. **Document type:** *Academic/Scholarly.*
Formerly: Zemaljski Muzej u Sarajevu. Glasnik. Prirodne Nauke
Indexed: B21, CABA, E12, EntAb, F08, F12, P32, P40, R07.
—CASDDS.
Published by: Zemaljski Muzej Bosne i Hercegovine/National Museum of Bosnia and Herzegovina, Zmaja od Bosne 3, Sarajevo, 71000, Bosnia Herzegovina. TEL 387-33-262710, z.muzej@zemaljskimuzej.ba, http://www.zemaljskimuzej.ba. Ed. Sulejman Redzic.

500 600 SVK ISSN 0862-1845
ZENIT. Text in Slovak. 1986. fortn.
Formerly: Zenit Pionierov
Published by: Smena Publishing House, Prazska 11, Bratislava, 81284, Slovakia. Ed. Ladislav Gyorffy. Circ: 45,000. **Subscr. to:** PNS, Gottwaldovo nam 6, Bratislava 81384, Slovakia.

ZERNIKE INSTITUTE PH.D.-THESIS SERIES. *see* MATHEMATICS

ZEYLANICA. *see* BIOLOGY

500 CHN ISSN 1008-7826
ZHANGZHOU SHIFAN XUEYUAN XUEBAO (ZIRAN KEXUE BAN)/ZHANGZHOU TEACHERS COLLEGE. JOURNAL (NATURAL SCIENCE EDITION). Text in Chinese. 1983. q. USD 16.40 (effective 2009). **Document type:** *Journal, Academic/Scholarly.*
Related titles: Online - full text ed.
Indexed: Z02.
Published by: Zhangzhou Shifan Xueyuan, 36, Xianqian Jie, Chuangye Lou 204, Zhangzhou, 363000, China. TEL 86-596-2527190.

500 CHN
ZHANGZHOU ZHIYE JISHU XUEYUAN XUEBAO/ZHANGZHOU TECHNICAL INSTITUTE. JOURNAL. Text in Chinese. 1999. q. CNY 5 newsstand/cover (effective 2006). **Document type:** *Journal, Academic/Scholarly.*
Formerly: Zhangzhou Zhiye Daxue Xuebao/Zhangzhou Vocational University. Journal (1008-2913)
Related titles: Online - full text ed.
Published by: Zhangzhou Zhiye Jishu Xueyuan, 1, Maanshan Lu, Zhangzhou, 363000, China. TEL 86-596-2660200, FAX 86-596-2594339.

500 CHN ISSN 1008-9497
➤ **ZHEJIANG DAXUE XUEBAO (LIXUE BAN).** Text in Chinese; Abstracts in English. 1956. bi-m. USD 31.20 (effective 2009). 120 p./no.; back issues avail. **Document type:** *Journal, Academic/Scholarly.*
Incorporates (1956-1999): Hangzhou Daxue Xuebao (Lixue Ban)/Hangzhou University. Journal (Natural Science Edition) (0253-3618); Formerly: Zhejiang Daxue Xuebao (Ziran Kexue Ban)/Zhejiang University. Journal (Natural Sciences Edition) (0253-9861)
Related titles: Online - full text ed.
Indexed: A29, A35, A37, ASFA, B21, C25, C30, CCMJ, E12, ESPM, F08, H16, Inspec, MSN, MathR, OceAb, P32, RefZh, S13, SWRA, T05, W10, W11, Z02.
—BLDSC (4918.150510), East View, IE, Ingenta, Linda Hall.
Published by: Zhejiang Daxue Chubanshe/Zhejiang University Press, 148, Tianmushan Rd, No 4 West Bldg, Rm 515, Hangzhou, 310028, China. TEL 86-571-88272803. **Dist. by:** China International Book Trading Corp, 35 Chegongzhuang Xilu, Haidian District, PO Box 399, Beijing 100044, China. TEL 86-10-68412045, FAX 86-10-68412023, cibtc@mail.cibtc.com.cn, http://www.cibtc.com.cn.

➤ **ZHEJIANG GONG-SHANG ZHIYE JISHU XUEYUAN XUEBAO/ZHEJIANG BUSINESS TECHNOLOGY INSTITUTE. JOURNAL.** *see* BUSINESS AND ECONOMICS

500 CHN ISSN 1008-830X
ZHEJIANG HAIYANG XUEYUAN XUEBAO (ZIRAN KEXUE BAN)/ZHEJIANG OCEAN UNIVERSITY. JOURNAL (NATURE SCIENCE EDITION). Text in Chinese. 1982. quadrennial. CNY 6 newsstand/cover (effective 2006).
Formerly: Zhejiang Shuichan Xueyuan Xuebao (1000-212X)
Related titles: Online - full text ed.
Indexed: ASFA, B21, ESPM.
—BLDSC (4918.150060).
Published by: Zhejiang Haiyang Xueyuan, 105, Wenhua Lu, Zhoushan, 316004, China. TEL 86-580-2550077, FAX 86-580-2551319.

500 CHN ISSN 1671-8798
ZHEJIANG KEJI XUEYUAN XUEBAO/ZHEJIANG UNIVERSITY OF SCIENCE AND TECHNOLOGY. JOURNAL. Text in Chinese. 1980. q. CNY 5 newsstand/cover (effective 2007). **Document type:** *Journal, Academic/Scholarly.*
Formerly (until 2001): Hangzhou Yingyong Gongcheng Jishu Xueyuan Xuebao/Hangzhou Institute of Applied Engineering. Journal (1008-7680)
Related titles: Online - full text ed.
Indexed: A28, APA, BrCerAb, C&ISA, CA/WCA, CIA, CerAb, CivEngAb, CorrAb, E&CAJ, E11, EEA, EMA, ESPM, EnvEAb, H15, M&TEA, M09, MBF, METADEX, RefZh, SolStAb, T04, WAA.
—Linda Hall.
Published by: Zhejiang Keji Xueyuan/Zhejiang University of Science and Technology, 318, Liuxia Liuhe Lu, Hangzhou, 310023, China.

500 CHN ISSN 1001-5051
Q4
ZHEJIANG SHIFAN DAXUE XUEBAO (ZIRAN KEXUE BAN)/ZHEJIANG NORMAL UNIVERSITY. JOURNAL (NATURAL SCIENCES). Text in Chinese. 1960. q. **Document type:** *Journal, Academic/Scholarly.*
Related titles: Online - full text ed.
Indexed: Z02.
—BLDSC (4918.150055).
Published by: Zhejiang Shifan Daxue/Zhejiang Normal University, PO Box 33, Jinhua, Zhejiang 321004, China. TEL 86-579-2282750, FAX 86-579-2282327.

500 CHN ISSN 1673-565X
Q1 CODEN: JZUSFR
➤ **ZHEJIANG UNIVERSITY. JOURNAL. SCIENCE A: APPLIED PHYSICS & ENGINEERING.** Text in English. 2000. m. EUR 1,711, USD 2,065 combined subscription to institutions (print & online eds.) (effective 2012). 120 p./no.; back issues avail.; reprint service avail. from PSC. **Document type:** *Journal, Academic/Scholarly.*
Supersedes in part (in 2010): Zhejiang University. Journal (Science) (1009-3095)
Related titles: Online - full text ed.: ISSN 1862-1775.
Indexed: A20, A22, A28, A29, APA, B21, BrCerAb, C&ISA, CA/WCA, CIA, CPEI, CerAb, CivEngAb, CorrAb, E&CAJ, E01, E11, EEA, EMA, ESPM, EnvEAb, H15, Inspec, M&TEA, M09, MBF, METADEX, OceAb, PollutAb, RefZh, SCI, SCOPUS, SWRA, SolStAb, T04, W07, WAA, Z01, Z02.
—BLDSC (4918.150526), East View, IE, Ingenta, Linda Hall. **CCC.**
Published by: Zheijiang University Press, Editorial Bd. of Journals of Zhejiang University - Science (A/B/C), 38 Zheda Rd., Hangzhou, Zhejiang 310027, China. TEL 86-571-87952276. **Subscr. outside China to:** Maney Publishing, China Journal Distribution Services, Hudson Rd, Leeds LS9 7DI, United Kingdom. TEL 44-113-2497481, FAX 44-113-2486983, subscriptions@maney.co.uk. **Co-publisher:** Springer.

➤ **ZHEJIANG WANLI XUEYUAN XUEBAO/ZHEJIANG WANLI UNIVERSITY. JOURNAL.** *see* SOCIAL SCIENCES: COMPREHENSIVE WORKS

500 CHN ISSN 1671-6841
CODEN: ZDXLA4
ZHENGZHOU DAXUE XUEBAO (LIXUE BAN)/ZHENGZHOU UNIVERSITY. JOURNAL (NATURAL SCIENCE EDITION). Text in Chinese; Abstracts in English. 1962. q. USD 20.80 (effective 2009). **Document type:** *Journal, Academic/Scholarly.*
Formerly (until 2001): Zhengzhou Daxue Xuebao (Ziran Kexue Ban)/Zhengzhou University. Journal (Natural Science Edition) (1001-8212)
Related titles: Online - full text ed.
Indexed: A28, APA, BrCerAb, C&ISA, CA/WCA, CCMJ, CIA, CIS, CerAb, CivEngAb, CorrAb, E&CAJ, E11, EEA, EMA, H15, M&TEA, M09, MBF, METADEX, MSN, MathR, RefZh, SCOPUS, SolStAb, T04, WAA, Z02.
—BLDSC (4918.163000), CASDDS, East View, IE, Ingenta, Linda Hall.
Published by: Zhengzhou Daxue/Zhengzhou University, 100, Kexue Dadao, Zhengzhou, 450001, China. TEL 86-371-67781272, FAX 86-371-67781273. Ed. Xin Shijun.

500 CHN ISSN 1006-2432
ZHISHI CHUANG/KNOWLEDGE WINDOW. Text in Chinese. 1979. bi-m. USD 25.20 (effective 2009). **Document type:** *Magazine, Consumer.* **Description:** General interest science articles.
Related titles: Online - full text ed.
—East View.
Published by: Jiangxi Kexue Jishu Chubanshe, 2-1, Luzhou Jie, Nanchang, 330009, China. TEL 86-791-6616450, FAX 86-791-6632592. **Dist. by:** China International Book Trading Corp, 35 Chegongzhuang Xilu, Haidian District, PO Box 399, Beijing 100044, China. TEL 86-10-68412045, FAX 86-10-68412023, cibtc@mail.cibtc.com.cn, http://www.cibtc.com.cn.

500 CHN ISSN 0529-150X
ZHISHI JIUSHI LILIANG/KNOWLEDGE IS POWER. Text in Chinese. 1956. m. USD 56.40 (effective 2009). **Document type:** *Magazine, Consumer.*
Related titles: Online - full text ed.
—East View.

S

Published by: Zhishi Jiushi Liliang Zazhishe, 16, Zhongguancun Nan Dajie, Beijing, 100081, China. TEL 86-10-62173819. **Dist. by:** China International Book Trading Corp, 35 Chegongzhuang Xilu, Haidian District, PO Box 399, Beijing 100044, China. TEL 86-10-68412045, FAX 86-10-68412023, cibtc@mail.cibtc.com.cn, http://www.cibtc.com.cn.

500 600 CHN ISSN 1673-4793
ZHONGGUO CHUANMEI DAXUE (ZIRAN KEXUE BAN)/ COMMUNICATION UNIVERSITY OF CHINA. JOURNAL (SCIENCE AND TECHNOLOGY). Text in Chinese. 1994. q. CNY 8 newsstand/cover (effective 2007). **Document type:** *Journal, Academic/Scholarly.*
Related titles: Online - full text ed.
Published by: Zhongguo Chuanmei Daxue/Communication University of China, PO Box 30, Beijing, 100024, China.

500 CHN ISSN 1004-1540
ZHONGGUO JILIANG XUEYUAN XUEBAO/CHINA JILIANG UNIVERSITY. JOURNAL. Text in Chinese. 1990. q. USD 20.80 (effective 2009). **Document type:** *Journal, Academic/Scholarly.*
Related titles: Online - full text ed.
Indexed: A28, APA, ASFA, B&BAb, B21, BioEngAb, BrCerAb, C&ISA, CA/WCA, CIA, CerAb, CivEngAb, CorrAb, E&CAJ, E11, EEA, EMA, ESPM, EnvEAb, H15, M&TEA, M09, MBF, METADEX, RefZh, SolStAb, T04, WAA.
—East View, Linda Hall.
Published by: Zhongguo Jiliang Xueyuan, Xiasha Gaojiaoyuan Xueyuan Jie, Hangzhou, 310018, China.

500 600 CHN ISSN 1002-6711
ZHONGGUO KEJI LUNTAN/FORUM ON SCIENCE AND TECHNOLOGY IN CHINA. Text in Chinese. 1985. m. USD 80.40 (effective 2009). **Document type:** *Journal, Academic/Scholarly.*
Related titles: Online - full text ed.
Published by: Zhongguo Keji Cujin Fazhan Zhongxin, 8, Yuyuantan Nan Lu, PO Box 3814, Beijing, 100038, China. TEL 86-10-58884590, FAX 86-10-58884592, http://www.nrcstd.org.cn/.

500 CHN ISSN 1673-7180
CODEN: ZKLZB2
➤ **ZHONGGUO KEJI LUNWEN ZAIXIAN/SCIENCEPAPER ONLINE.** Text in Chinese; Abstracts in Chinese, English. 2006. m. CNY 180; CNY 15 newsstand/cover (effective 2008). **Document type:** *Journal, Academic/Scholarly.*
Related titles: Online - full text ed.
Indexed: A28, A32, APA, BrCerAb, C&ISA, CA/WCA, CIA, CerAb, CivEngAb, CorrAb, E&CAJ, E11, EEA, EMA, ESPM, EnvEAb, H15, M&TEA, M09, MBF, METADEX, SolStAb, T04, WAA.
Address: No.35, Zhongguancun Ave, Haidian Region, Beijing, 100080, China. TEL 86-10-62514339, FAX 86-10-62514378. Ed. Qing-chun Chu.

500 600 CHN
ZHONGGUO KEJI SHILIAO/CHINA HISTORICAL MATERIALS OF SCIENCE AND TECHNOLOGY. Text in Chinese; Abstracts and contents page in English. q. bibl.; illus. **Document type:** *Academic/Scholarly.*
Published by: (Zhongguo Kexue Jishu Xiehui/China Association for Science and Technology), Zhongguo Kexue Jishu Chubanshe, 32, Baishiqiao Lu, Wei Gong Cun, Haidian-qu, Beijing, China. **Dist. outside China by:** China International Book Trading Corp, 35 Chegongzhuang Xilu, Haidian District, PO Box 399, Beijing 100044, China.

ZHONGGUO KEJI SHUYU/CHINA TERMINOLOGY. *see* LINGUISTICS

500 600 CHN
ZHONGGUO KEJISHI ZAZHI/HISTORICAL MATERIAL OF CHINESE SCIENCE AND TECHNOLOGY. Text in Chinese. q. USD 26.80 (effective 2009). **Document type:** *Academic/Scholarly.*
Supersedes: Zhongguo Keji Shiliao (1673-1441)
Related titles: Online - full text ed.
Indexed: CA, HistAb, T02.
Published by: Zhongguo Kexue Jishu Xiehui/Chinese Association of Science and Technology, 137 Chaoyangmennei Dajie, Beijing, 100010, China. TEL 89-10-896731. Ed. Wang Dezhao.

500 CHN ISSN 1006-9240
QD1
➤ **ZHONGGUO KEXUE. B JI: HUAXUE.** Text in Chinese; Summaries in English. 1950. m. CNY 960; CNY 80 per issue (effective 2009). adv. reprints avail. **Document type:** *Journal, Academic/Scholarly.* **Description:** Covers chemistry, biology, earth science, medical science, and agronomy. Contains mainly academic papers on scientific work.
Formerly: Zhongguo Kexue. B Ji: Huaxue, Shengwuxue, Nongxue, Yixue, Dixue (1000-3134); Which superseded in part (in 1981): Zhongguo Kexue (0301-9632); Which superseded in part: Scientia Sinica
Related titles: Online - full content ed.: USD 50 (effective 2003); Online - full text ed.; ◆ English ed.: Science China Chemistry. ISSN 1674-7291.
Indexed: AESIS, BMT, ChemAb, IndMed, MathR, RASB, WSCA.
—East View, INIST.
Published by: (Chinese Academy of Sciences/Zhongguo Kexueyuan), Zhongguo Kexue Zazhishe/Science in China Press, 16 Donghuangchenggen North Street, Beijing, 100717, China. TEL 86-10-64016732, FAX 86-10-64016350, sale@scichina.com, http://www.scichina.com/. Ed. Le-Min Li. **Dist. in the Americas by:** Springer New York LLC, Journal Fulfillment, PO Box 2485, Secaucus, NJ 07096. TEL 212-460-1500, FAX 201-348-4505, journals-ny@springer.com; **Dist. outside of the Americas by:** Springer, Haber Str 7, Heidelberg 69126, Germany. TEL 49-6221-3454303, FAX 49-6221-3454229, subscriptions@springer.com, http://www.springer.de. **Co-sponsor:** Chinese Medical Association.

500 CHN ISSN 1006-9259
QH301
➤ **ZHONGGUO KEXUE. C JI: SHENGMING KEXUE.** Text in Chinese. m. CNY 960; CNY 80 per issue (effective 2009). **Document type:** *Journal, Academic/Scholarly.*
Related titles: Online - full content ed.: USD 50 (effective 2003); Online - full text ed.; ◆ English ed.: Science China Life Sciences. ISSN 1674-7305.
—East View.
Published by: (Chinese Academy of Sciences/Zhongguo Kexueyuan), Zhongguo Kexue Zazhishe/Science in China Press, 16 Donghuangchenggen North Street, Beijing, 100717, China. TEL 86-10-64015399, sale@scichina.com, http://www.scichina.com/. Ed. Da-Cheng Wang. **Dist. outside the Americas by:** Springer, Haber Str 7, Heidelberg 69126, Germany. subscriptions@springer.com; **Dist. by:** Springer New York LLC, Journal Fulfillment, PO Box 2485, Secaucus, NJ 07096. TEL 212-460-1500, FAX 201-348-4505, journals-ny@springer.com.

500 CHN ISSN 1006-9267
QE1
ZHONGGUO KEXUE. D JI: DIQIU KEXUE. Text in Chinese. m. CNY 1,440; CNY 120 per issue (effective 2009). **Document type:** *Journal, Academic/Scholarly.*
Related titles: Online - full content ed.: USD 90 (effective 2003); Online - full text ed.; ◆ English ed.: Science China Earth Sciences. ISSN 1674-7313.
—East View, Ingenta.
Published by: (Chinese Academy of Sciences/Zhongguo Kexueyuan), Zhongguo Kexue Zazhishe/Science in China Press, 16 Donghuangchenggen North Street, Beijing, 100717, China. TEL 86-10-64019820, FAX 86-10-64031816, sale@scichina.com, http://www.scichina.com/. Ed. Shu Sun. **Dist. in the Americas by:** Springer New York LLC, Journal Fulfillment, PO Box 2485, Secaucus, NJ 07096. TEL 212-460-1500, FAX 201-348-4505, journals-ny@springer.com; **Dist. outside of the Americas by:** Springer, Haber Str 7, Heidelberg 69126, Germany. subscriptions@springer.com, http://www.springer.de.

500 CHN ISSN 1006-9275
➤ **ZHONGGUO KEXUE. E JI: JISHU KEXUE.** Text in Chinese. m. CNY 1,440; CNY 120 per issue (effective 2009). **Document type:** *Journal, Academic/Scholarly.*
Related titles: Online - full content ed.: USD 90 (effective 2003); Online - full text ed.; ◆ English ed.: Science China Technological Sciences. ISSN 1674-7321.
—East View.
Published by: (Chinese Academy of Sciences/Zhongguo Kexueyuan), Zhongguo Kexue Zazhishe/Science in China Press, 16 Donghuangchenggen North Street, Beijing, 100717, China. TEL 86-10-64010631, sale@scichina.com, http://www.scichina.com/. Ed. Luguang Yan. **Dist. in the Americas by:** Springer New York LLC, Journal Fulfillment, PO Box 2485, Secaucus, NJ 07096. TEL 212-460-1500, FAX 201-348-4505, journals-ny@springer.com; **Dist. outside the Americas by:** Springer, Haber Str 7, Heidelberg 69126, Germany.

500 CHN ISSN 1000-8217
Q127.C5
ZHONGGUO KEXUE JIJIN/SCIENCE FOUNDATION IN CHINA. Text in Chinese; Summaries in English. 1987. s-a. adv. **Document type:** *Bulletin, Academic/Scholarly.* **Description:** Publishes academic papers, science foundation policies, and technology trends and developments.
Related titles: Online - full text ed.
Published by: (Guojia Ziran Kexue Jijin Weiyuanhui/National Natural Science Foundation of China), Kexue Jijin Zazhibu (Subsidiary of: Guojia Ziran Kexue Jijin Weiyuanhui/National Natural Science Foundation of China), 83, Shuangqing Rd., Haidian District, Beijing, 100085, China. TEL 86-10-62327204, FAX 86-10-62326921. Circ: 5,000.

500 600 CHN ISSN 0253-2778
Q4 CODEN: CKHPD7
ZHONGGUO KEXUE JISHU DAXUE XUEBAO/UNIVERSITY OF SCIENCE AND TECHNOLOGY OF CHINA. JOURNAL. Text in Chinese, English. 1965. m. USD 80.40 (effective 2009). **Document type:** *Journal, Academic/Scholarly.*
Related titles: Online - full text ed.
Indexed: A28, APA, BrCerAb, C&ISA, CA/WCA, CCMJ, CIA, CIN, CerAb, ChemAb, ChemTitl, CivEngAb, CorrAb, CybAb, E&CAJ, E11, EEA, EMA, ESPM, EnvEAb, GeoRef, H15, INIS AtomInd, Inspec, M&TEA, M09, MBF, METADEX, MSN, MathR, RefZh, SolStAb, SpeleolAb, T04, WAA, Z02.
—BLDSC (4912.140000), CASDDS, East View, IE, Ingenta, Linda Hall.
Published by: Zhongguo Kexue Jishu Daxue/China University of Science and Technology, 96 Jinxiang Lu, Hefei, Anhui 230026, China. TEL 86-551-3600717, FAX 86-551-3606707. **Dist. by:** China International Book Trading Corp, 35 Chegongzhuang Xilu, Haidian District, PO Box 399, Beijing 100044, China. TEL 86-10-68412045, FAX 86-10-68412023, cibtc@mail.cibtc.com.cn, http://www.cibtc.com.cn.

500 CHN ISSN 1000-3045
ZHONGGUO KEXUEYUAN YUANKAN/CHINESE ACADEMY OF SCIENCES. BULLETIN. Text in Chinese; Abstracts and contents page in English. 1985. bi-m. USD 53.40 (effective 2009). adv. **Document type:** *Journal, Academic/Scholarly.* **Description:** Publicizes mainland China's policies on science and technology, and shows trends and directions in the development of science in China. Also introduces the work and achievements of the Academia Sinica and its scientists.
Related titles: Online - full content ed.; Online - full text ed.; ◆ English ed.: Chinese Academy of Sciences. Bulletin. ISSN 1003-3572.
—East View.
Published by: (Zhongguo Kexueyuan/Chinese Academy of Sciences), Kexue Chubanshe/Science Press, 16 Donghuang Cheng Genbei Jie, Beijing, 100717, China. TEL 86-10-64000246, FAX 86-10-64030255, http://www.sciencep.com/. Ed. Yu Zhihua. Circ: 7,000. **Dist. by:** China International Book Trading Corp, 35 Chegongzhuang Xilu, Haidian District, PO Box 399, Beijing 100044, China. TEL 86-10-68412045, FAX 86-10-68412023, cibtc@mail.cibtc.com.cn, http://www.cibtc.com.cn.

500 CHN ISSN 1000-1964
TN4 CODEN: ZKDXER
ZHONGGUO KUANGYE DAXUE XUEBAO. Text in Chinese; Abstracts in English. 1955. bi-m. CNY 15 per issue (effective 2009). **Document type:** *Journal, Academic/Scholarly.* **Description:** Covers the fields of coal geology and exploration, mine construction, coal mining, rock mechanics, civil engineering and architecture, safety science, coal chemistry, applied mathematics and mechanics, industrial automation, mining machinery, etc.
Formerly (until 1978): Pei Ching K'uang Yeh Hsueh Yuan Hsueh Pao (0476-028X)
Related titles: CD-ROM ed.; Online - full text ed.; ◆ English ed.: Mining Science and Technology. ISSN 1674-5264.
Indexed: A22, A28, APA, ApMecR, B21, BrCerAb, C&ISA, CA/WCA, CIA, CPEI, CerAb, CivEngAb, CorrAb, E&CAJ, E11, EEA, EMA, ESPM, EngInd, EnvEAb, GeoRef, H&SSA, H15, M&TEA, M09, MBF, METADEX, RefZh, SCOPUS, SolStAb, SpeleolAb, T04, WAA.
—BLDSC (4729.219350), East View, IE, Ingenta, Linda Hall.
Published by: Zhongguo Kuangye Daxue/China University of Mining and Technology, Jiefang Nan Lu, Xuzhou, Jiangsu 221008, China. TEL 86-516-3995897, FAX 86-516-3885569, http://www.cumt.edu.cn/. Ed. Qitai Chen.

ZHONGGUO NONGYE KEJI DAOBAO/REVIEW OF CHINA AGRICULTURAL SCIENCE AND TECHNOLOGY. *see* AGRICULTURE

500 600 CHN ISSN 1007-1784
ZHONGGUO RENMIN JINGGUAN DAXUE XUEBAO (ZIRAN KEXUE BAN)/CHINESE PEOPLE'S PUBLIC SECURITY UNIVERSITY. JOURNAL (SCIENCE AND TECHNOLOGY). Text in Chinese. 2000. q. CNY 12 newsstand/cover (effective 2007). **Document type:** *Journal, Academic/Scholarly.*
Related titles: Online - full text ed.
Published by: Zhongguo Renmin Jingguan Daxue/Chinese People's Public Security University, Muxidi Nan Li, Beijing, 100038, China. TEL 86-10-83903107, FAX 86-10-83903269.

500 CHN ISSN 1005-0566
ZHONGGUO RUANKEXUE/CHINA SOFT SCIENCE. Text in Chinese. 1986. m. USD 117.60 (effective 2009). **Document type:** *Journal, Academic/Scholarly.*
Formerly: Runkexue Yanjiu/Soft Science Research (1002-9753)
Related titles: Online - full text ed.
—East View.
Address: 54, SanliHe Lu, Rm. 270, Beijing, 100045, China. TEL 86-10-68598270, FAX 86-10-68598286.

ZHONGGUO SHIYOU DAXUE XUEBAO (ZIRAN KEXUE BAN)/CHINA UNIVERSITY OF PETROLEUM. JOURNAL (NATURAL SCIENCE EDITION). *see* PETROLEUM AND GAS

500 CHN ISSN 1674-5663
ZHONGKAI NONGYE GONGCHENG XUEYUAN XUEBAO/ZHONGKAI UNIVERSITY OF AGRICULTURE AND ENGINEERING. JOURNAL. Text in Chinese. 1988. q. **Document type:** *Journal, Academic/Scholarly.*
Formerly (until 2009): Zhongkai Nongye Jishu Xueyuan Xuebao/Zhongkai University of Agriculture and Technology. Journal (1006-0774)
Related titles: Online - full text ed.
Published by: Zhongkai Nongye Gongcheng Xueyuan/Zhongkai University of Agriculture and Engineering, 24, Fangzhi Lu Dong Sha Jie, Guangzhou, 510225, China. TEL 86-20-32293720, FAX 86-20-89003055, http://www.zhku.edu.cn/.

500 CHN ISSN 1672-4321
ZHONGNAN MINZU DAXUE XUEBAO (ZIRAN KEXUE BAN)/SOUTH-CENTRAL UNIVERSITY FOR NATIONALITIES. JOURNAL (NATURAL SCIENCE EDITION). Text in Chinese. 1982. q. USD 14.40 (effective 2009). **Document type:** *Journal, Academic/Scholarly.*
Formerly: Zhongnan Minzu Xueyuan Xuebao (Ziran Kexue Ban)/South-Central College for Nationalities. Journal (1005-3018)
Related titles: Online - full text ed.
Indexed: ESPM, RefZh, SSciA.
—BLDSC (9512.844487).
Published by: Zhongnan Minzu Daxue/South-Central University for Nationalities, No 5, Minyuan Lu, Wuhan, Hubei 430074, China. TEL 86-27-67842094.

500 CHN ISSN 0529-6579
Q4 CODEN: CHTHAJ
ZHONGSHAN DAXUE XUEBAO (ZIRAN KEXUE BAN)/ACTA SCIENTIARUM NATURALIUM UNIVERSITATIS SUNYATSENI. Text in Chinese. 1955. bi-m. USD 31.20 (effective 2009). **Document type:** *Journal, Academic/Scholarly.*
Related titles: Online - full text ed.; ◆ Supplement(s): Luojixue Yanjiu. ISSN 1674-3202.
Indexed: A34, A35, A36, A38, ASFA, AgBio, AgrForAb, B21, B23, C25, C30, CABA, CCMJ, CIN, CIS, ChemAb, ChemTitl, D01, E12, ESPM, EngInd, F08, F11, F12, FCA, G11, GH, GeoRef, H16, H17, I11, IndVet, Inspec, LT, MSN, MaizeAb, MathR, N02, N03, N04, N05, O01, OR, P32, P33, P38, P39, P40, PGegResA, PGrRegA, R07, R08, R11, R12, R13, RA&MP, RM&VM, RRTA, RefZh, S13, S16, S17, SCOPUS, SoyAb, SpeleolAb, T05, TAR, TOSA, TriticAb, VS, W10, W11, Z01, Z02.
—BLDSC (0663.200000), AskIEEE, CASDDS, East View, INIST, Linda Hall.
Published by: Zhongshan Daxue/Sun Yatsen University, 135, Xinkong Xilu, Guangzhou, Guangdong 510275, China. TEL 86-20-84111990, FAX 86-20-84038740.

ZHONGXUE KEJI/MIDDLE SCHOOL SCIENCE & TECHNOLOGY. *see* EDUCATION

500 CHN ISSN 1005-8036
ZHONGYANG MINZU DAXUE XUEBAO (ZIRAN KEXUE BAN)/ CENTRAL UNIVERSITY FOR NATIONALITIES. JOURNAL (NATURAL SCIENCES EDITION). Text in Chinese. 1992. q. CNY 6 newsstand/cover (effective 2006). **Document type:** *Journal, Academic/Scholarly.*
Related titles: Online - full text ed.
Published by: Zhongyang Minzu Xueyuan, Xuebao Bianjibu, 27, Zhongguancun Nan Dajie, Beijing, 100081, China. TEL 86-10-68932398, 86-10-68933635.

500 300 620 CHN ISSN 1008-3715
ZHONGZHOU DAXUE XUEBAO/ZHONGZHOU UNIVERSITY. JOURNAL. Text in Chinese. 1984. q. USD 20.80 (effective 2009). **Document type:** *Journal, Academic/Scholarly.*
Related titles: Online - full text ed.
Published by: Zhongzhou Daxue, 77, Hanghai Zhong Lu, Zhengzhou, 450015, China. TEL 86-371-68732814, FAX 86-371-68739690.

500 CHN ISSN 1003-3882
PL2464.Z7
ZHOUYI YANJIU/STUDIES OF ZHOUYI. Text in Chinese. 1988. bi-m. USD 21.60 (effective 2009). **Document type:** *Journal, Academic/Scholarly.*
Related titles: Online - full text ed.

Indexed: MLA-IB.
—East View.
Published by: Shandong Daxue, 27, Shanda Nanlu, Jinan, Shandong 250100, China. TEL 86-531-8906961 ext 2829. **Dist. by:** China International Book Trading Corp, 35 Chegongzhuang Xilu, Haidian District, PO Box 399, Beijing 100044, China. TEL 86-10-68412045, FAX 86-10-68412023, cibtc@mail.cibtc.com.cn, http://www.cibtc.com.cn.

500 001.3 UKR ISSN 2076-6173
➤ **ZHYTOMYRS'KYI DERZHAVNYI UNIVERSYTET IMENI IVANA FRANKA. VISNYK.** Text in Ukrainian; Summaries in English, Russian, Ukrainian. 1998. bi-m. bk.rev. abstr.; bibl.; charts. back issues avail. **Document type:** *Journal, Academic/Scholarly.* **Description:** Publishes scientific articles dealing with experimental and theoretical research in psychological, pedagogical, philosophical, historical and scientific spheres. Aims to disseminate research results thoughout Ukraine meant for scientists, scholars, post-graduate students and graduates.
Related titles: Online - full text ed.
Published by: Zhytomyrs'kyi Derzhavnyi Universytet imeni Ivana Franka, vul Velyka Berdychivs'ka, 40, Zhytomyr, 10008, Ukraine. TEL 380-412-372763, FAX 380-412-372763, zu@zu.edu.ua, http://www.zu.edu.ua. Ed. Petro Saukh. Pub. Viktor Zakharchuk.

500 ZWE ISSN 1016-1503
Q1 CODEN: ZSNED7
THE ZIMBABWE SCIENCE NEWS. Text in English. 1967. q. ZWD 300 domestic; USD 17.50 foreign (effective 2004). adv. bk.rev.; Website rev. abstr.; bibl.; charts; illus. index. 24 p./no. 2 cols./p.; back issues avail. **Document type:** *Journal, Academic/Scholarly.*
Former titles (until 1980): Zimbabwe Rhodesia Science News (0253-049X); (until 1979): Rhodesia Science News (0035-4732)
Related titles: Online - full content ed.; Online - full text ed.
Indexed: AbAn, B25, BIOSIS Prev, GeoRef, ISAP, KWIWR, MycolAb, PLESA, SpeleolAb.
—IE, Ingenta.
Published by: Zimbabwe Scientific Association, Causeway, PO Box CY 124, Harare, Zimbabwe. TEL 263-4-570336, FAX 263-4-335143, husseing@ecoweb.co.zw, http://www.zarnet.ac.zw, http:/www.inasp.org.uk/ajol/. Ed. J Hussen. Circ: 820.

500 ZWE ISSN 0254-2765
Q180.55.M4 CODEN: TZASDZ
➤ **ZIMBABWE SCIENTIFIC ASSOCIATION. TRANSACTIONS.** Text in English. 1901. irreg., latest vol.73, 1999. ZWD 300 domestic to members; USD 17.50, GBP 8, ZAR 80 elsewhere to members (effective 2004). bk.rev. 50 p./no. 2 cols./p.; back issues avail. **Document type:** *Monographic series, Academic/Scholarly.* **Description:** Refereed journal, multi-disciplinary. Publishes original research and authorative reviews. For universities, colleges, research developers, institutions and private subscribers.
Former titles (until vol.60, no.1, 1980): Rhodesia Scientific Association. Transactions (0379-9638); (until vol.56, 1974): Rhodesia Scientific Association. Proceedings and Transactions (0370-2294)
Related titles: Online - full content ed.; Online - full text ed.
Indexed: AICP, ASFA, B21, B25, BIOSIS Prev, ESPM, GeoRef, ISAP, Inspec, M&GPA, MycolAb, SpeleolAb.
—AskIEEE.
Published by: Zimbabwe Scientific Association, PO Box 978, Harare, Zimbabwe. TEL 263-4-335143, husseing@ecoweb.co.zw, http://www.zarnet.ac.zw. Ed. Brian Marshall. Circ: 600.

500 CHN ISSN 1002-008X
QH7
ZIRAN KEXUE JINZHAN/PROGRESS IN NATURAL SCIENCE. Text in Chinese. 1991. m. CNY 780; CNY 65 per issue (effective 2009). **Document type:** *Journal, Academic/Scholarly.*
Related titles: ◆ English ed.: Progress in Natural Science. ISSN 1002-0071.
—East View.
Published by: (Guojia Ziran Kexue Jijin Weiyuanhui/National Natural Science Foundation of China), Kexue Jijin Zazhibu (Subsidiary of: Guojia Ziran Kexue Jijin Weiyuanhui/National Natural Science Foundation of China), 83, Shuangqing Rd., Haidian District, Beijing, 100085, China. TEL 86-10-62327204, FAX 86-10-62326921.

500.9 CHN ISSN 1000-0224
ZIRAN KEXUESHI YANJIU/STUDIES IN THE HISTORY OF NATURAL SCIENCES. Text in Chinese; Summaries in English. 1982. q. USD 35.60 (effective 2009). adv. bk.rev. **Document type:** *Academic/Scholarly.* **Description:** Contains articles on theories of the history of science, biographies of scientists, and historical records of important scientific events in China and the world.
Related titles: Online - full text ed.
Indexed: CA, CCMJ, HistAb, MSN, MathR, P30, T02, Z02.
—East View, Linda Hall.
Published by: (Zhongguo Kexueyuan Ziran Kexueshi Yanjiusuo/Chinese Academy of Sciences, Institute for the History of Natural Science), Kexue Chubanshe/Science Press, 16 Donghuang Cheng Genbei Jie, Beijing, 100717, China. TEL 86-10-64000246, FAX 86-10-64030255, http://www.sciencep.com/. Circ: 6,000. **Dist. by:** China International Book Trading Corp, 35 Chegongzhuang Xilu, Haidian District, PO Box 399, Beijing 100044, China. TEL 86-10-68412045, FAX 86-10-68412023, cibtc@mail.cibtc.com.cn, http://www.cibtc.com.cn.

ZIRAN YU REN/NATURE AND MAN. see HISTORY

500 CHN ISSN 0253-9608
Q4 CODEN: TJTCD4
ZIRAN ZAZHI/CHINESE JOURNAL OF NATURE. Text in Chinese. 1978. bi-m. CNY 48; CNY 8 per issue (effective 2010). back issues avail. **Document type:** *Journal, Academic/Scholarly.*
Related titles: Online - full text ed.
Indexed: A&ATA, ChemAb.
—BLDSC (6046.650000), CASDDS, East View, IE, Linda Hall.
Published by: Shanghai Daxue/Shanghai University, 99, Shangda Lu, PO Box 121, Shanghai, 200444, China. TEL 86-21-66135618, FAX 86-21-66132736. Ed. Yuan-da Dong. **Dist. by:** China International Book Trading Corp, 35 Chegongzhuang Xilu, Haidian District, PO Box 399, Beijing 100044, China. TEL 86-10-68412045, FAX 86-10-68412023, cibtc@mail.cibtc.com.cn, http://www.cibtc.com.cn.

500 ESP ISSN 0213-4306
ZUBIA; revista de ciencias. Text in Spanish. 1983. a. EUR 15 domestic; EUR 20 foreign (effective 2011). illus. **Document type:** *Monographic series, Academic/Scholarly.* **Description:** Presents research in natural sciences, experimental science, and mathematics, especially dealing with local themes.
Formerly (until 1985): Berceo. Ciencias (0213-4292)
Related titles: ◆ Supplement(s): Zubia. Monografico. ISSN 1131-5423.
Indexed: GeoRef, IECT, SpeleolAb.
Published by: Instituto de Estudios Riojanos (I E R), Portales, 2, Lograno, 26001, Spain. TEL 34-941-29118, publicaciones.ier@larioja.org, http://www.larioja.org/.

500 ESP ISSN 1131-5423
ZUBIA. MONOGRAFICO. Text in Spanish. 1989. a. **Document type:** *Monographic series, Academic/Scholarly.*
Related titles: ◆ Supplement to: Zubia. ISSN 0213-4306.
Indexed: GeoRef, IECT, SpeleolAb.
Published by: Instituto de Estudios Riojanos (I E R), C. Muro de la Mata, 8 principal, Logrono, 26071, Spain. TEL 34-941-262064, FAX 34-941-246667, publicaciones.ier@larioja.org, http://www.larioja.org/.

500 DEU
ZUR GESCHICHTE DER WISSENSCHAFTEN. Text in German. 1997. irreg., latest vol.4, 2001. price varies. **Document type:** *Monographic series, Academic/Scholarly.*
Indexed: SpeleolAb.
Published by: (T U Braunschweig), Georg Olms Verlag, Hagentorwall 7, Hildesheim, 31134, Germany. TEL 49-5121-15010, FAX 49-5121-150150, info@olms.de. Eds. Herbert Mehrtens, Peter Albrecht.

ZYGON; journal of religion and science. see RELIGIONS AND THEOLOGY

347 CZE ISSN 1214-1097
21. STOLETI. Text in Czech. 2003. m. CZK 444; CZK 37 newsstand/cover (effective 2009). adv. **Document type:** *Magazine, Consumer.*
Published by: R F Hobby s.r.o., Bohdalecka 6, Prague 10, 110 00, Czech Republic. TEL 420-281-090610, FAX 420-281-090623, sekretariat@rf-hobby.cz, http://www.rf-hobby.cz. Ed. Pavel Preucil. Adv. contact Petr Doul. Circ: 85,000.

21. STOLETI JUNIOR. see CHILDREN AND YOUTH—For

500 600 USA
Q1
21ST CENTURY SCIENCE & TECHNOLOGY (ONLINE). Text in English. 1988. q. USD 25 for 6 issues (effective 2006). adv. bk.rev. cum.index. back issues avail. **Document type:** *Magazine, Consumer.* **Description:** Features comprehensive coverage of advanced technologies and science policy, as well as historical development of science and technology.
Formerly (until 2006): 21st Century Science & Technology (Print) (0895-6820)
Indexed: A10, A22, BiolDig, P30, V03.
—IE, Infotrieve, Ingenta, Linda Hall. **CCC.**
Published by: 21st Century Science Associates, PO Box 16285, Washington, DC 20041. TEL 703-777-6943, FAX 703-777-9214, tcs@mediasoft.net. Ed. Laurence Hecht. R&P Marjorie Hecht. Adv. contact Marsha Freeman. Circ: 23,000 (paid).

1000 WORLD LEADERS OF SCIENTIFIC INFLUENCE. see BIOGRAPHY

SCIENCES: COMPREHENSIVE WORKS—Abstracting, Bibliographies, Statistics

016.500 USA ISSN 1557-0444
Q11
A A A S ANNUAL MEETING. Text in English. 1992. a. USD 35 per issue to non-members; USD 30 per issue to members (effective 2009). adv. index. back issues avail.; reprints avail. **Document type:** *Abstract/Index.* **Description:** Covers the latest developments in the areas of science, technology, engineering, education, and policy-making.
Former titles (until 2003): A A A S Annual Meeting and Science Innovation Exposition; (until 1995): A A A S Annual Meeting Program - Abstracts of Papers; Which was formed by the merger of (1978-1992): American Association for the Advancement of Science. Abstracts of Papers of the National Meeting (0196-2922); Which was formerly (until 1978): A A A S. Contributed Papers of the National Meeting; (1983-1992): A A A S Annual Meeting Program (0272-4189); Which was formerly (until 1983): American Association for the Advancement of Science. National Meeting Program; (until 1976): American Association for the Advancement of Science. Annual Meeting (0361-1833); (until 1975): American Association for the Advancement of Science. Annual Meeting Program; (until 1972): American Association for the Advancement of Science. Meeting Program; (until 1967): American Association for the Advancement of Science. General Program of the Meeting; (until 1959): American Association for the Advancement of Science. General Program - Directory of the Meeting; (until 19??): American Association for the Advancement of Science. General Program of the (Year) Meeting
Indexed: GeoRef, SpeleolAb.
Published by: American Association for the Advancement of Science, 1200 New York Ave, NW, Washington, DC 20005. TEL 202-326-6450, FAX 202-289-4021, membership@aaas.org.

016.5 CAN
A S T I S BIBLIOGRAPHY. Text in English. base vol. plus d. updates. free (effective 2004). **Document type:** *Bibliography.* **Description:** Contains over 52,000 records describing publications and research projects about northern Canada.
Media: Online - full text.
Published by: Arctic Science & Technology Information System, Arctic Institute of North America, University of Calgary, 2500 University Dr N W, Calgary, AB T2N 1N4, Canada. TEL 403-220-7515, FAX 403-282-4609. Ed. C Ross Goodwin.

016.5 IRN ISSN 1026-7190
Q80.I67
THE ABSTRACT OF SCIENTIFIC AND TECHNICAL PAPERS/CHIKIDAH - I MAQALAT - I ILMI VA FANNI. Text in Persian, Modern; Summaries in English. 1994. q. USD 115 (effective 2003). 310 p./no.; back issues avail. **Document type:** *Abstract/Index.* **Description:** Contains abstract and index of scientific and technical articles in Iranian periodicals.
Related titles: Diskette ed.
Published by: Iranian Information & Documentation Center (IRANDOC), 1188 Enqelab Ave., P O Box 13185-1371, Tehran, Iran. TEL 98-21-6494955, FAX 98-21-6462254, journal@irandoc.ac.ir, http://www.irandoc.ac.ir. Ed. Hussein Gharibi. Circ: 500.

ABSTRACTS OF SCIENTIFIC AND TECHNOLOGICAL PUBLICATIONS. see TECHNOLOGY: COMPREHENSIVE WORKS—Abstracting, Bibliographies, Statistics

016.5 USA
ACADEMIC PAPERS DATABASE. Text in English. 2008. base vol. plus m. updates. **Document type:** *Database, Abstract/Index.*
Media: Online - full text.
Published by: Addleton Academic Publishers, 30-18 50th St, Woodside, NY 11377. TEL 718-626-6017, sales@addletonacademicpublishers.com, http://www.addletonacademicpublishers.com/.

016 KEN ISSN 1018-2136
AFRICAN URBAN AND REGIONAL SCIENCE INDEX. Text in English. 1999. a. USD 200 domestic; USD 220 foreign; USD 20 newsstand/cover (effective 1999). adv. back issues avail. **Document type:** *Abstract/Index.* **Description:** Covers all publications on Urban and Regional Sciences.
Related titles: Online - full text ed.
Published by: African Urban Quarterly Ltd., Private Bag 51336, Nairobi, Kenya. TEL 254-2-2-449229, FAX 254-2-2-444110. Ed. R A Ohuelho.

016.5 016.6 016.33 USA
APPLIED SCIENCE & BUSINESS PERIODICALS RETROSPECTIVE: 1913-1983. Text in English. base vol. plus d. updates. **Document type:** *Database, Abstract/Index.*
Media: Online - full text.
Published by: H.W. Wilson, 950 University Ave, Bronx, NY 10452. TEL 718-588-8400, 800-367-6770, FAX 718-590-1617, 800-590-1617, custserv@hwwilson.com.

APPLIED SCIENCE & TECHNOLOGY ABSTRACTS. see ENGINEERING—Abstracting, Bibliographies, Statistics

016.5 016.6 USA ISSN 1529-9759
Z7913
APPLIED SCIENCE & TECHNOLOGY FULL TEXT. Text in English. 1997. base vol. plus d. updates. USD 5,570 (effective 2011). **Document type:** *Database, Abstract/Index.* **Description:** Contains information from a wide variety of applied science specialties-acoustics to aeronautics, neural networks to nuclear engineering-from leading trade and industrial journals, professional and technical society journals, specialized subject periodicals, buyers' guides, directories, and conference proceedings.
Media: Online - full text. **Related titles:** ◆ Print ed.: Applied Science & Technology Index (Print). ISSN 0003-6986.
Published by: H.W. Wilson, 950 University Ave, Bronx, NY 10452. TEL 718-588-8400, 800-367-6770, FAX 718-590-1617, 800-590-1617, custserv@hwwilson.com.

APPLIED SCIENCE & TECHNOLOGY INDEX (PRINT). see ENGINEERING—Abstracting, Bibliographies, Statistics

016.5 016.6 USA
APPLIED SCIENCE & TECHNOLOGY INDEX RETROSPECTIVE: 1913-1983. Text in English. 2007. base vol. plus irreg. updates. USD 1,775 (effective 2011). **Document type:** *Database, Abstract/Index.*
Media: Online - full text.
Published by: H.W. Wilson, 950 University Ave, Bronx, NY 10452. TEL 718-588-8400, 800-367-6770, FAX 718-590-1617, 800-590-1617, custserv@hwwilson.com.

BAZTECH. see TECHNOLOGY: COMPREHENSIVE WORKS—Abstracting, Bibliographies, Statistics

500 USA ISSN 0145-0379
BERKELEY PAPERS IN HISTORY OF SCIENCE. Text in English. 1977. irreg., latest vol.21, 2005. price varies. bk.rev. back issues avail. **Document type:** *Monographic series, Academic/Scholarly.* **Description:** Bibliographies of works by and about scientists, and of inventories of their published and unpublished correspondence.
Indexed: MathR.
Published by: University of California, Berkeley, Office for History of Science and Technology, 543 Stephens Hall, 2350, Berkeley, CA 94720. TEL 510-642-4581, FAX 510-643-5321, ohst@berkeley.edu.

016.5 ESP ISSN 1575-0183
Z7403
BIBLIOGRAFIA ESPANOLA DE REVISTAS CIENTIFICAS DE CIENCIA Y TECNOLOGIA. Text in Spanish. 1980. a. **Document type:** *Abstract/Index.* **Description:** Offers bibliographic references to articles dealing with topics in science and technology in Spanish publications.
Formerly (until 1998): Indice Espanol de Ciencia y Tecnologia (0210-9409)
Media: CD-ROM. **Related titles:** Diskette ed.; Online - full text ed.
Indexed: RASB.
Published by: Instituto de Estudios Documentales sobre Ciencia y Tecnologia (I E D C Y T), Ciencia y Tecnologia, Joaquin Costa 22, Madrid, 28002, Spain. TEL 34-91-5635482, FAX 34-91-5642644, http://www.cindoc.csic.es. Circ: 450.

500 015 CHE ISSN 0067-6829
BIBLIOGRAPHIA SCIENTIAE NATURALIS HELVETICA. Text in French, German. 1927. a. CHF 45 (effective 2003). back issues avail. **Document type:** *Bibliography.*
Former titles (until 1950): Bibliographie der Schweizerischen Naturwissenschaftlichen und Geographischen Literatur (0257-683X); (until 1941): Bibliographie der Schweizerischen Naturwissenschaftlichen Literatur (1421-1580)
Indexed: CABA, E12, F08, F12, GeoRef, P32, S13, S16, SpeleolAb.
—Linda Hall.
Published by: Schweizerische Landesbibliothek/Bibliotheque Nationale Suisse, Hallwylstr 15, Bern, 3003, Switzerland. TEL 41-31-3228911, FAX 41-31-3228463, info@nb.admin.ch, http://www.snl.ch. Ed. Anton Caflisch. Circ: 800 (controlled).

500 600 TTO ISSN 1011-4866
CARINDEX: SCIENCE & TECHNOLOGY. Text in English. 1987. s-a. USD 45 (effective 1998). **Document type:** *Abstract/Index.* **Description:** Guide to science and technology literature (excluding medicine) published in the English-speaking Caribbean.
Published by: University of the West Indies, Main Library, St. Augustine, W I, Trinidad & Tobago. TEL 809-662-2002, FAX 809-662-9238, TELEX 24-520 UWI-WG. Ed. Sharida Hosein.

S

502.1 620.0021 USA ISSN 1936-1386
Q149.U5
CHARACTERISTICS OF DOCTORAL SCIENTISTS AND ENGINEERS IN THE UNITED STATES: DETAILED STATISTICAL TABLES (ONLINE). Text in English. 1973. biennial. free (effective 2010). back issues avail. **Document type:** *Government.*
Former titles (until 1997): Characteristics of Doctoral Scientists and Engineers in the United States: Detailed Statistical Tables (Print) (0734-6468); (until 1979): Characteristics of Doctoral Scientists and Engineers in the United States. Technical Notes and Detailed Statistical Tables; (until 1977): Characteristics of Doctoral Scientists and Engineers in the United States. Detailed Statistical Tables. Appendix B
Media: Online - full text.
Published by: U.S. Department of Commerce, National Science Foundation, 4201 Wilson Blvd, Ste 245, Arlington, VA 22230. TEL 703-292-5111, 800-877-8339, info@nsf.gov.

016 CHN ISSN 0254-5179
QA1
CHINESE SCIENCE ABSTRACTS. PART A; mathematics, mechanics, astronomy and space science, physics, technical sciences. Text in English. 1982. 6/yr. USD 335.95 domestic to individuals; USD 395.95 foreign to individuals; USD 504 domestic to institutions; USD 564 foreign to institutions. adv. 88 p./no.; **Document type:** *Abstract/Index.* **Description:** Publishes abstracts from more than 120 of China's leading scientific journals.
Related titles: Online - full text ed.; Chinese ed.: Zhongguo Kexue Wenzhai A.
—Ingenta.
Published by: Kexue Chubanshe/Science Press, 16 Donghuang Cheng Genbei Jie, Beijing, 100717, China. TEL 86-10-64000246, FAX 86-10-64030255. Circ: 5,000.

016 CHN ISSN 0254-4903
QD1
CHINESE SCIENCE ABSTRACTS. PART B; chemistry, life sciences, earth sciences. Text in English. 1982. 6/yr. USD 335.95 domestic to individuals; USD 395.95 foreign to individuals; USD 504 domestic to institutions; USD 564 foreign to institutions (effective 1999). adv. 88 p./no.; **Document type:** *Abstract/Index.* **Description:** Publishes abstracts from more than 120 of China's leading scientific journals.
Related titles: Microfilm ed.: (from PQC); Online - full text ed.; Chinese ed.: Zhongguo Kexue Wenzhai B.
Published by: Kexue Chubanshe/Science Press, 16 Donghuang Cheng Genbei Jie, Beijing, 100717, China. TEL 86-10-64000246, FAX 86-10-64030255. Circ: 5,000.

500 015 BGR ISSN 1310-9146
CHUZHDESTRANNI PERIODICHNI IZDANIIA V BULGARIA. Text in Bulgarian. 1963. a. price varies. **Document type:** *Bulletin, Bibliography.* **Description:** Lists foreign-language periodicals in the larger scientific libraries.
Formerly (until 1996): Chuzhdestranni Periodichni Izdaniia v Po-golemite Nauchni Biblioteki (0861-9700)
Published by: Narodna Biblioteka Sv. sv. Kiril i Metodii/Cyril and Methodius National Library, 88 Levski Blvd, Sofia, 1504, Bulgaria. TEL 359-2-9881600, FAX 359-2-435495, dipchikova@nationallibrary.bg. Ed., R&P T Nikolova TEL 359-2-9882811 ext 220. Circ: 400 (paid).

CLASE AND PERIODICA. *see* SOCIAL SCIENCES: COMPREHENSIVE WORKS—Abstracting, Bibliographies, Statistics

500 015 ECU
COLECCION BIBLIOGRAFICA CIENTIFICA ECUATORIANA. Text in Spanish. irreg., latest vol.2, 1997. ECS 30,000.
Published by: Casa de la Cultura Ecuatoriana, Avenida 6 de Diciembre 332, Quito, Ecuador. Circ: 1,500.

500 016 SWE ISSN 1104-232X
COMPREHENSIVE SUMMARIES OF UPPSALA DISSERTATIONS FROM THE FACULTY OF SCIENCE AND TECHNOLOGY. Text in English. 1961. irreg., latest vol.687, 2002. price varies. index. back issues avail. **Document type:** *Monographic series, Abstract/Index.*
Former titles (until 1993): Comprehensive Summaries of Uppsala Dissertations from the Faculty of Science (0282-7468); (until 1985): Abstracts of Uppsala Dissertations from the Faculty of Science (0345-0058); (until 1970): Abstracts of Uppsala Dissertations in Science (0001-3676)
Related titles: ◆ Series of: Acta Universitatis Upsaliensis. ISSN 0346-5462.
Indexed: ChemAb, GeoRef, Inspec, SpeleolAb.
—Ingenta.
Published by: (Uppsala University Library), Uppsala Universitet, Acta Universitatis Upsaliensis/University Publications from Uppsala, PO Box 256, Uppsala, 75105, Sweden. TEL 46-18-4716804, FAX 46-18-4716804, acta@ub.uu.se, http://www.ub.uu.se/upu/auu/index.html. Ed. Bengt Landgren. **Dist. by:** Almqvist & Wiksell International, PO Box 614, Soedertaelje 15127, Sweden. TEL 46-8-5509497, FAX 46-8-55016710.

CONFERENCE PAPERS INDEX. *see* MEETINGS AND CONGRESSES—Abstracting, Bibliographies, Statistics

016.5 USA
CONTEMPORARY RESEARCH INDEX. Text in English. 2008. base vol. plus m. updates. **Document type:** *Database, Abstract/Index.*
Media: Online - full text.
Published by: Addleton Academic Publishers, 30-18 50th St, Woodside, NY 11377. TEL 718-626-6017, sales@addletonacademicpublishers.com, http://www.addletonacademicpublishers.com/.

500 016 GBR ISSN 0309-8591
CROYDON BIBLIOGRAPHIES FOR REGIONAL SURVEY. Text in English. 1968. irreg. bibl. **Document type:** *Bibliography.* **Description:** Contains bibliographic details of the individual articles in periodicals with a very short indication as to their content if the title is not self-explanatory.
Published by: Croydon Natural History & Scientific Society Ltd., 96a Brighton Rd, South Croydon, Surrey CR2 6AD, United Kingdom. Ed. Brain Lancanster TEL 44-20-86686909. Circ: 100.

016.5 USA
CURRENT INDEX TO SCHOLARLY JOURNALS. Text in English. 2008. base vol. plus m. updates. **Document type:** *Database, Abstract/Index.*
Media: Online - full text.
Published by: Addleton Academic Publishers, 30-18 50th St, Woodside, NY 11377. TEL 718-626-6017, sales@addletonacademicpublishers.com, http://www.addletonacademicpublishers.com/.

500 JPN ISSN 0288-6022
Q77
CURRENT SCIENCE AND TECHNOLOGY RESEARCH IN JAPAN. Text in English. 1980. biennial. USD 427. abstr. index.
Related titles: Online - full text ed.
Published by: Japan Science and Technology Agency/Kagaku Gijutsu Shinko Jigyodan, 5-3, Yonbancho, Chiyoda-ku, Tokyo, Saitama 102-8666, Japan. TEL 81-3-52148401, FAX 81-3-52148400, http://www.jst.go.jp/. Circ: 600.

016.5 016.6 RUS ISSN 0202-6120
Z7409
DEPONIROVANNYE NAUCHNYE RABOTY. BIBLIOGRAFICHESKII UKAZATEL'; estestvennye i tochnye nauki, tekhnika. Text in Russian. 1963. m. USD 177.60 foreign (effective 2011). **Document type:** *Journal, Abstract/Index.*
Former titles (until 1986): Vsesoyuznyi Institut Nauchno-Tekhnicheskoi Informatsii. Deponirovannye Nauchnye Raboty; (until 1983): Vsesoyuznyi Institut Nauchno-Tekhnicheskoi Informatsii. Deponirovannye Rukopisi (0135-0617)
—East View.
Published by: VINITI RAN, ul Usievicha 20, Moscow, 125190, Russian Federation. TEL 7-499-1526113, FAX 7-499-9430060, http://www.viniti.ru. **Dist. by:** Informnauka Ltd., Ul Usievicha 20, Moscow 125190, Russian Federation. alfimov@viniti.ru.

016.5 USA
DIGITAL JOURNALS DATABASE. Text in English. 2008. base vol. plus m. updates. **Document type:** *Database, Abstract/Index.*
Media: Online - full text.
Published by: Addleton Academic Publishers, 30-18 50th St, Woodside, NY 11377.

016.5 600 ESP
DIRECTORIO DE REVISTAS ESPANOLAS DE CIENCIA Y TECNOLOGIA (ONLINE EDITION). Text in Spanish. 1990. a. free (effective 2009). **Document type:** *Directory, Abstract/Index.* **Description:** Lists more than 550 scientific and technical magazines and journals from Spain. In 3 sections: I. Alphabetical journal index; II. Alphabetical index of ceased journals; III. Indexes by subject, publisher, ISSN, & geographical region.
Formerly (until 1998): Directorio de Revistas Espanolas de Ciencia y Tecnologia (Print Edition) (1132-6654)
Media: Online - full text.
Published by: Consejo Superior de Investigaciones Cientificas (C S I C), Instituto de Estudios Documentales sobre Ciencia y Tecnologia, Joaquin Costa 22, Madrid, 28002, Spain. TEL 34-91-5635482, FAX 34-91-5642644, sdi@cindoc.csic.es, http://www.cindoc.cisc.es. Ed. Carmen Urdin.

016.5 USA
DIRECTORY OF ACADEMIC RESOURCES. Text in English. 2008. base vol. plus m. updates. **Document type:** *Database, Abstract/Index.*
Media: Online - full text.
Published by: Addleton Academic Publishers, 30-18 50th St, Woodside, NY 11377.

016 PAK
DIRECTORY OF SCIENTIFIC PERIODICALS OF PAKISTAN. Text in English. irreg. PKR 50, USD 5 (effective 1999).
Related titles: Microfilm ed.
Published by: Pakistan Scientific and Technological Information Centre, Quaid-i-Azam University Campus, P O Box 1217, Islamabad, Pakistan. Ed. Aejaz Ahmed Malik. Circ: 500.

016.5 016.6 USA ISSN 0419-4217
Z5053 CODEN: DABBBA
DISSERTATION ABSTRACTS INTERNATIONAL. SECTION B: THE SCIENCES AND ENGINEERING. Text in English. 1938. m. index. reprints avail. **Document type:** *Abstract/Index.*
Formerly (until 1969): Dissertation Abstracts. Section B: The Sciences and Engineering (0420-073X); Which superseded in part (in 1966): Dissertation Abstracts (0099-3123); Which was formerly (until 1951): Microfilm Abstracts (0099-4375); Dissertation Abstracts incorporated (1939-1961): Abstracts of Field Studies for the Degree of Doctor of Education
Related titles: CD-ROM ed.; Magnetic Tape ed.; Microfiche ed.: (from PQC); Online - full text ed.
Indexed: ABIPC, APICat, APIH&E, APIOC, APIPR, APIPS, APITS, ASFA, ArtlAb, B21, CIN, ChemAb, ChemTitl, E&PHSE, ESPM, F09, FS&TA, FaBeAb, GP&P, GeoRef, GeotechAb, KWIWR, L&LBA, MLA-IB, OceAb, OffTech, P03, PST, PetrolAb, PsycInfo, PsycholAb, RASB, S&MA, SociolAb, SpeleolAb, TOSA, W08, W09, WildRev.
—BLDSC (3599.040000), CASDDS, Infotrieve, INIST, Linda Hall, PADDS.
Published by: ProQuest (Subsidiary of: Cambridge Information Group), 789 E Eisenhower Pky, PO Box 1346, Ann Arbor, MI 48106. TEL 734-761-4700, 800-521-0600, FAX 734-997-4040, 888-241-5612, info@proquest.com.

DISSERTATION ABSTRACTS ON DISC. *see* HUMANITIES: COMPREHENSIVE WORKS—Abstracting, Bibliographies, Statistics

500 CHE
DOKUMENTATIONSSTELLE FUER WISSENSCHAFTSPOLITIK. NEUANSCHAFFUNGEN/CENTRE DE DOCUMENTATION DE POLITIQUE DE LA SCIENCE. NOUVELLES ACQUISITIONS. Text in English, French, German, Italian. 1992. 4/yr. free. **Document type:** *Bibliography.*
Published by: Schweizerischer Wissenschaftsrat, Dokumentationsstelle fuer Wissenschaftspolitik, Inselgasse 1, Bern, 3003, Switzerland. TEL 41-31-3229655, FAX 41-31-3228070. Ed. E Imhof.

016.5 USA
ELITE SCIENTIFIC JOURNALS ARCHIVE. Text in English. 2008. base vol. plus m. updates. **Document type:** *Database, Abstract/Index.*
Media: Online - full text.
Published by: Addleton Academic Publishers, 30-18 50th St, Woodside, NY 11377.

502.1 FIN ISSN 1457-4101
FINLAND. TILASTOKESKUS. TUTKIMUS- JA KEHITTAMISTOIMINTA SUOMESSA/FINLAND. CENTRAL STATISTICAL OFFICE. RESEARCH ACTIVITY/FINLAND. STATISTIKCENTRALEN. FORSKNINGSVERKSAMHETEN. (Section XXXVIII of Official Statistics of Finland) Text in English, Finnish, Swedish. 1988. a. EUR 37 (effective 2008). **Document type:** *Government.*
Formerly (until 1999): Finland. Tilastokeskus. Tutkimus- ja kehittamistoiminta (0785-0727); Which was formed by the merger of (1974-1988): Finland. Suomen Virallinen Tilasto. 38, Tutkimustoiminta (0355-2233); (1968-1988): Tilastokeskus. Sarja KO, Koulutus ja tutkimus (0355-2268)
Related titles: Online - full text ed.; ◆ Series of: Finland. Tilastokeskus. Tiede, Teknologia ja Tietoyhteiskunta. ISSN 1795-536X.
Published by: Tilastokeskus/Statistics Finland, Tyopajakatu 13, Statistics Finland, Helsinki, 00022, Finland. TEL 358-9-17341, FAX 358-9-17342279.

016.5 016.6 GBR
FOOD INDUSTRY UPDATES. SCIENCE. Text in English. 1947. m. GBP 605, EUR 730.90, USD 1,096.32 to non-members; GBP 470, EUR 567.81, USD 851.69 to members (effective 2009). pat. back issues avail. **Document type:** *Abstract/Index.* **Description:** Contains approximately 2,000 industry-oriented abstracts with full bibliographic details of recently published documents.
Former titles (until 2010): Food Industry Updates. Science & Technology (1478-7946); (until 2002): Science & Technology Abstracts (0950-1789); (until 1986): Abstracts from Current Scientific and Technical Literature (0001-3439)
Indexed: IPackAb.
Published by: Leatherhead Food Research, Randalls Rd, Leatherhead, Surrey KT22 7RY, United Kingdom. TEL 44-1372-376761, FAX 44-1372-386228, help@leatherheadfood.com.

500 DEU
FORSCHUNGSZENTRUM JUELICH. SCHRIFTEN. REIHE BIBLIOTHEK. Text in German. 1963. irreg., latest vol.10, 2001. **Document type:** *Monographic series, Academic/Scholarly.*
Former titles (until 1997): Forschungszentrum Juelich. Bibliographien (0938-6513); (until 1990): Kernforschungsanlage Juelich. Bibliographische Reihe (0451-7709)
—INIST.
Published by: Forschungszentrum Juelich GmbH, Leo-Brandt-Str, Juelich, 52428, Germany. TEL 49-2461-615220, FAX 49-2461-616103, info@fz-juelich.de.

016.5 USA
GENERAL SCIENCE ABSTRACTS. Text in English. 1996. base vol. plus d. updates. USD 3,300 in US & Canada (effective 2011). **Document type:** *Database, Abstract/Index.* **Description:** Contains full text articles, article abstracts, and indexing form science periodicals.
Media: Online - full text. **Related titles:** CD-ROM ed.: ISSN 1092-1443. 1997. price varies.
Published by: H.W. Wilson, 950 University Ave, Bronx, NY 10452. TEL 718-588-8400, 800-367-6770, FAX 718-590-1617, 800-590-1617, custserv@hwwilson.com.

016.5 USA
GENERAL SCIENCE COLLECTION. Text in English. base vol. plus w. updates. **Document type:** *Database, Abstract/Index.*
Media: Online - full text.
Published by: EBSCO Publishing (Subsidiary of: EBSCO Industries, Inc.), 10 Estes St, PO Box 682, Ipswich, MA 01938. TEL 978-356-6500, 800-653-2726, FAX 978-356-6565, information@ebscohost.com.

016.5 016.61 USA
GENERAL SCIENCE FULL TEXT. Text in English. 1996. base vol. plus d. updates. USD 3,445 in US & Canada (effective 2011). **Document type:** *Database, Abstract/Index.*
Media: Online - full text.
Published by: H.W. Wilson, 950 University Ave, Bronx, NY 10452. TEL 718-588-8400, 800-367-6770, FAX 718-590-1617, 800-590-1617, custserv@hwwilson.com.

016.5 USA
GENERAL SCIENCE INDEX. Text in English. 1995. (OCLC updated weekly)). base vol. plus d. updates. USD 2,470 in US & Canada (effective 2011). **Document type:** *Database, Abstract/Index.*
Media: Online - full text. **Related titles:** CD-ROM ed.: ISSN 1076-7096; Magnetic Tape ed.; ◆ Print ed.: General Science Index (Print). ISSN 0162-1963.
Published by: H.W. Wilson, 950 University Ave, Bronx, NY 10452. TEL 718-588-8400, 800-367-6770, FAX 718-590-1617, 800-590-1617, custserv@hwwilson.com.

016.5 USA ISSN 0162-1963
GENERAL SCIENCE INDEX (PRINT). Text in English. 1978. 10/yr. USD 685 (effective 2011). **Document type:** *Abstract/Index.* **Description:** Features graphs, charts, diagrams, photos, and illustrations that convey an abundance of scientific information.
Related titles: CD-ROM ed.: ISSN 1076-7096; Magnetic Tape ed.; ◆ Online - full text ed.: General Science Index.
Indexed: RASB.
—BLDSC (4111.196000), Linda Hall.
Published by: H.W. Wilson, 950 University Ave, Bronx, NY 10452. TEL 718-588-8400, 800-367-6770, FAX 718-590-1617, 800-590-1617, custserv@hwwilson.com.

011 DEU
GERMANY. DEUTSCHER BUNDESTAG. WISSENSCHAFTLICHE DIENSTE. NEUE BUECHER UND AUFSAETZE IN DER BIBLIOTHEK. Text in German. 1962. 6/yr. index. **Document type:** *Government.*
Former titles (until 2007): Germany. Deutscher Bundestag. Wissenschaftliche Dienste. Neue Aufsaetze in der Bibliothek (0931-8593); (until 1988): Germany. Deutscher Bundestag. Wissenschaftliche Dienste. Aufsaetze aus Zeitschriften und Sammelwerken (0931-3400); (until 1974): Germany. Deutscher Bundestag. Wissenschaftliche Dienste. Bibliothek des Bundestages. Zeitschriftenaufsaetze (0433-7638)
—CCC.
Published by: Deutscher Bundestag, Abteilung Wissenschaftliche Dienste, Platz der Republik 1, Berlin, 11011, Germany. TEL 49-30-2270, FAX 49-30-22736878, mail@bundestag.de, http://www.bundestag.de.

016 500 GHA ISSN 0855-0115
GHANA SCIENCE ABSTRACTS. Text in English. q. free domestic to institutions (effective 2003). abstr.; bibl. **Document type:** *Abstract/Index.*
Published by: Council for Scientific and Industrial Research, PO Box M32, Accra, Ghana. http://www.csir.org.gh.

500 600 HUN ISSN 0237-0808
T4
HUNGARIAN R AND D ABSTRACTS. SCIENCE AND TECHNOLOGY. Text in Hungarian. 1985. q. USD 80. index. **Document type:** *Abstract/Index.* **Description:** Covers all fields of science and technology,indexing articles by author and subject.
Supersedes: Hungarian Technical Abstracts (0018-7771)
Indexed: CRIA, CRICC, RASB, WSCA.
Published by: Orszagos Muszaki Informacios Kozpont es Konyvtar/ National Technical Information Centre and Library, Muzeum utca 17, PO Box 12, Budapest, 1428, Hungary. TEL 36-1-1185852. Ed. Zsuzsanna Bana.

500 HUN ISSN 1419-9033
HUNGARY. KOZPONTI STATISZTIKAI HIVATAL. TUDOMANYOS KUTATAS ES FEJLESZTES. Text in Hungarian. 1969. a. HUF 230. stat. **Document type:** *Government.*
Former titles (until 1997): Hungary. Kozponti Statisztikai Hivatal. Tudomanyos Kutatas es Kiserleti Fejlesztes (0866-0107); (until 1988): Hungary. Kozponti Statisztikai Hivatal. Todomanyos Kutatas es Fejlesztes (0230-7359); (until 1980): Hungary. Kozponti Statisztikai Hivatal. Tudomanyos Kutatas (0302-2226); (until 1970): Hungary. Kozponti Statisztikai Hivatal. Todomanyos Kutatas es Fejlesztes (0324-3192)
Indexed: RASB.
Published by: Kozponti Statisztikai Hivatal, Marketing Oszta'ly, Keleti Karoly utca 5-7, Budapest, 1024, Hungary. TEL 36-1-345-6000, FAX 36-1-345-6699, TELEX HUNGA. Circ: 1,000.

500 011 AGO ISSN 0018-9863
I I C A DOCUMENTACAO; boletim bibliografico. Text in Portuguese. 1969. s-m. free to qualified personnel.
Published by: Instituto de Investigacao Cientifica de Angola, Departamento de Documentacao e Informacao, CP 3244, Luanda, Angola.

500 016 USA ISSN 0149-8088
Z7403
INDEX TO SCIENTIFIC & TECHNICAL PROCEEDINGS. Short title: I S T P. Text in English. 1978. m. (plus a. cumulation). Index. **Document type:** *Abstract/Index.* **Description:** Indexes bibliographic information from scientific and technical conference proceedings.
Related titles: CD-ROM ed.: Index to Scientific & Technical Proceedings CD-ROM. ISSN 1076-9773. 1994; Magnetic Tape ed.; Online - full text ed.
Indexed: RASB.
—CASDDS, GNLM, Linda Hall.
Published by: Thomson Reuters (Subsidiary of: Thomson Reuters Corp.), 1500 Spring Garden, 4th Fl, Philadelphia, PA 19130. TEL 215-386-0100, 800-336-4474, FAX 215-386-2911, general.info@thomson.com, http://science.thomsonreuters.com/.

011 USA ISSN 0360-0661
Z7403
INDEX TO SCIENTIFIC REVIEWS. Short title: I S R. Text in English. 1974. s-a. (plus a. cumulation). Index. **Document type:** *Abstract/Index.* **Description:** Indexes review articles and surveys of scientific literature internationally.
Related titles: Magnetic Tape ed.
Indexed: RASB.
—BLDSC (4385.670000).
Published by: Thomson Reuters (Subsidiary of: Thomson Reuters Corp.), 1500 Spring Garden, 4th Fl, Philadelphia, PA 19130. TEL 215-386-0100, 800-336-4474, FAX 215-386-2911, general.info@thomson.com, http://science.thomsonreuters.com/.

500 600 IND
INDIA. DEPARTMENT OF SCIENCE AND TECHNOLOGY. RESEARCH AND DEVELOPMENT STATISTICS. Text in English. 19??. biennial. charts; stat. **Document type:** *Report, Government.*
Formerly: National Committee on Science and Technology. Research and Development Statistics
Related titles: Online - full text ed.: free (effective 2011).
Published by: Department of Science and Technology, Technology Bhavan, New Mehrauli Rd, New Delhi, 110 016, India. TEL 91-11-26567373, FAX 91-11-26864570, dstinfo@nic.in, http://www.dst.gov.in.

016.5 IND ISSN 0019-6339
Q1 CODEN: IDSAAV
INDIAN SCIENCE ABSTRACTS. Abbreviated title: I S A. Text in English. 1949. s-m. INR 5,300, USD 1,100; INR 265, USD 55 per issue (effective 2011). abstr. index. back issues avail. **Document type:** *Journal, Abstract/Index.*
Former titles (until 1965): Bibliography of Scientific Publications of South & South-East Asia (0409-4166); (until 1955): Bibliography of Scientific Publications of South Asia
Related titles: Online - full text ed.
—INIST, Linda Hall.
Published by: National Institute of Science Communication and Information Resources (N I S C A I R), Dr. K.S. Krishnan Marg, New Delhi, 110 012, India. TEL 91-11-25841647, FAX 91-11-25847062, sales@niscair.res.in. Ed. Dr. R K Verma. **Subscr. to:** I N S I O Scientific Books & Periodicals.

500 010 AGO ISSN 0074-008X
INSTITUTO DE INVESTIGACAO CIENTIFICA DE ANGOLA. BIBLIOGRAFICAS TEMATICAS. Text in Portuguese. 1969. irreg., latest vol.19, 1973. free to qualified personnel.
Indexed: ATA.
Published by: Instituto de Investigacao Cientifica de Angola, Departamento de Documentacao e Informacao, CP 3244, Luanda, Angola.

016.5 DEU ISSN 1617-9110
Z5051
INTERNATIONALE BIBLIOGRAPHIE DER REZENSIONEN GEISTES- UND SOZIALWISSENSCHAFTLICHER LITERATUR (PRINT)/ INTERNATIONAL BIBLIOGRAPHY OF BOOK REVIEWS OF SCHOLARLY LITERATURE. Short title: I B R. Text in Multiple languages. 1971. 2/yr. (in 2 vols., 3 nos./vol.). EUR 1,584 (effective 2008); CHF 2,726 (effective 2009). **Document type:** *Bibliography.* **Description:** Universal bibliography of book reviews with German and English keywords.
Former titles (until 1997): I B R. Internationale Bibliographie der Rezensionen Wissenschaftlicher Literatur (0177-8765); (until 1984): Internationale Bibliographie der Rezensionen Wissenschaftlicher Literatur (0020-918X)
Related titles: CD-ROM ed.: EUR 1,508 (effective 2005); Online - full text ed.: Internationale Bibliographie der Rezensionen Geistes- und Sozialwissenschaftlicher Literatur. ISSN 1865-0228. EUR 1,508 (effective 2005).
Indexed: RASB.
—BLDSC (4554.082000), Linda Hall.
Published by: De Gruyter Saur (Subsidiary of: Walter de Gruyter GmbH & Co. KG), Mies-van-der-Rohe-Str 1, Munich, 80807, Germany. TEL 49-89-769020, FAX 49-89-76902150, info@degruyter.com.

500 CHE
INTERNATIONALE WISSENSCHAFTSPOLITIK: PRESSESCHAU/ INTERNATIONAL SCIENCE POLICY: PRESS REVIEW/REVUE DE PRESSE. Text in English, French, German. 1991. 5/yr. free. **Document type:** *Abstract/Index.*
Published by: Schweizerischer Wissenschaftsrat, Dokumentationsstelle fuer Wissenschaftspolitik, Inselgasse 1, Bern, 3003, Switzerland. TEL 41-31-3229655, FAX 41-31-3228070. Ed. Janna Manz.

KAGAKU GIJUTSU FORAMU HOKOKUSHO. *see* TECHNOLOGY: COMPREHENSIVE WORKS—Abstracting, Bibliographies, Statistics

500 JPN
KANAZAWA DAIGAKU RIGAKUBU RONBUN OYOBI CHOSHO MOKUROKU/KANAZAWA UNIVERSITY. FACULTY OF SCIENCE. LIST OF PUBLICATIONS. Text in English, German, French, Japanese. 1961. quinquennial. bibl.
Published by: Kanazawa Daigaku, Rigakubu/Kanazawa University, Faculty of Science, Kakuma-Machi, Kanazawa-shi, Ishikawa-ken 920-1164, Japan. TEL 0762-64-5620, FAX 0762-64-5737.

KATAB: INDEX ANALYTIQUE BIBLIOGRAPHIQUE. *see* BUSINESS AND ECONOMICS—Abstracting, Bibliographies, Statistics

KUNI NO SHIKEN KENKYU GYOMU KEIKAKU. *see* TECHNOLOGY: COMPREHENSIVE WORKS—Abstracting, Bibliographies, Statistics

500 USA ISSN 0090-5232
Z7401
L C SCIENCE TRACER BULLET. Text in English. 1972. irreg. free (effective 2011). back issues avail. **Document type:** *Monographic series, Government.* **Description:** Contains research guides that help you locate information on science and technology subjects.
Related titles: Online - full text ed.
Published by: (Science and Technology Division), U.S. Library of Congress, 101 Independence Ave, SE, Washington, DC 20540. TEL 202-707-5000.

500 015 THA ISSN 0125-4537
LIST OF SCIENTIFIC AND TECHNICAL LITERATURE RELATING TO THAILAND. Text in English. 1964. irreg. USD 5 per issue. **Document type:** *Bibliography.*
Related titles: Online - full text ed.
Published by: (Thai National Documentation Centre), Thailand Institute of Scientific and Technological Research, 196 Phahonyothin Rd, Chatuchak, Bangkok, 10900, Thailand. TEL 579-8594, FAX 662-579-8594. Circ: 500.

016.5 UKR
LITOPYS AVTOREFERATIV DYSSERTATSII. Text in Ukrainian. 1999. q. USD 119 foreign (effective 2005). **Document type:** *Bibliography.* **Description:** Bibliography of authors' abstracts of dissertations defended in Ukraine.
Published by: Knyzhkova Palata Ukrainy imeni Ivana Fedorova/Ivan Fedorov Book Chamber of Ukraine, Pr Gagarina 27, Kyiv, 02094, Ukraine. TEL 380-44-5520134, ukrbook@ukr.net, http://www.ukrbook.net. **Dist. by:** East View Information Services, 10601 Wayzata Blvd, Minneapolis, MN 55305. TEL 952-252-1201, 800-477-1005, FAX 952-252-1202, info@eastview.com, http://www.eastview.com.

500 015 HUN ISSN 0133-8862
MAGYAR TUDOMANYOS AKADEMIA KONVYTARANAK KOZLEMENYEI/PUBLICATIONES BIBLIOTHECAE ACADEMIAE SCIENTIARUM HUNGARICAE. Variant title: Magyar Tudomanyos Akademia Konvytaranak Kiadvanyai. Text in Hungarian; Summaries in English, French, German. 1956. irreg. per issue exchange basis. **Document type:** *Monographic series.* **Description:** Monographs dealing with the history of the academy and the library. Collections of data and general studies on the history of science and library science.
Indexed: FR.
—INIST.
Published by: Magyar Tudomanyos Akademia, Konyvtara, Arany Janos utca 1, PO Box 1002, Budapest, 1245, Hungary. TEL 36-1-338-2344, FAX 36-1-331-6954. Eds. G Fekete, L Vekerdi.

500 600 MWI ISSN 1019-7079
Q91.M3 CODEN: MJSTF9
MALAWI JOURNAL OF SCIENCE AND TECHNOLOGY. Text in English. 1992. s-a. MWK 70 to individuals; USD 8 foreign to individuals; MWK 110 to institutions; USD 15 foreign to institutions. adv. bk.rev. bibl.; charts; illus. back issues avail. **Document type:** *Journal, Academic/Scholarly.*
Formed by the merger of (1980-1992): Luso (0251-0154); (1970-1992): Bunda Journal of Agricultural Research (1011-7830); Which was formerly (until 1989): Bunda College of Agriculture. Research Bulletin (0253-827X)
Indexed: A37, AgrForAb, BA, C25, CABA, CIN, ChemAb, ChemTitl, E12, F08, F11, F12, G11, GH, GeoRef, I11, MaizeAb, OR, R11, R12, S13, S16, SpeleolAb, T05, W11.
—CASDDS.
Published by: (University of Malawi, Bunda College of Agriculture, Research and Publication Committee), Chancellor College Publications, PO Box 219, Zomba, Malawi. TEL 265-522-222, FAX 265-522-046. Ed. P. Munyenyembe. Pub. P Munyenyembe. Circ: 500.

500 011 IRN
MARKAZ-I NASHARIYAT-I 'ILMI VA FARHANGI. FIHRIST-I MUNDARIJAT-I MAJALLAH-HA-YI JARI-I/CENTER FOR SCIENTIFIC AND CULTURAL PERIODICALS. TABLE OF CONTENTS OF CURRENT JOURNALS. Text in English, Persian, Modern. 1991. m. IRR 250 per issue.
Published by: Markaz-i Nahsariyat-i 'Ilmi va Farhangi/Center for Scientific and Cultural Periodicals, Irshad Islami int., Bldg. 1, Vali Asr Ave., Tehran, Iran. **Co-sponsor:** Vizarat-i Farhang va Irshad-i Islami - Ministry of Culture and Islamic Guidance.

016.5 USA ISSN 1064-0479
Z7401
N T I S BIBLIOGRAPHIC DATABASE. (National Technical Information Service) Text in English. 1983. q. index. **Document type:** *Database, Government.* **Description:** Multidisciplinary coverage of engineering, as well as research and development results of scientific and technical research of the U.S. government, its contractors and foreign governments.
Media: CD-ROM. **Related titles:** Online - full text ed.; Supplement(s): Subject Headings Booklet.
Published by: U.S. Department of Commerce, National Technical Information Service, 5301 Shawnee Rd, Alexandria, VA 22312. TEL 703-605-6000, info@ntis.gov.

500 RUS
NAUKA V SIBIRI I NA DAL'NEM VOSTOKE; ukazatel literaturi. Text in Russian. 1985. a. USD 30 foreign. **Description:** Covers books, articles, summaries, and reports of conferences and symposia on the problems of the history of science, industrial and higher educational science, organization and management of science, research staff, related to Siberia and the Far East.
Published by: Rossiiskaya Akademiya Nauk, Sibirskoe Otdelenie, Gosudarstvennaya Publichnaya Nauchno-Tekhnicheskaya Biblioteka/State Public Scientific and Technical Library of the Siberian Branch of the Russian Academy of Sciences, Ul Voskhod 15, Novosibirsk, 630200, Russian Federation. TEL 7-3832-661367, FAX 7-3832-663365, onb@spsl.nsc.ru, root@libr.nsk.su.

600 016 USA ISSN 0028-6869
CODEN: NTBOAJ
NEW TECHNICAL BOOKS; a selective list with descriptive annotations. Text in English. 1915. bi-m. USD 30; USD 35 foreign. bk.rev. index. **Document type:** *Bibliography.* **Description:** Provides an annotated listing of recently published science and technology monographs, monographic series and conference proceedings, predominantly at the undergraduate major, graduate and research level.
Indexed: A23, A24, ABIPC, B13, BRI, CBRI.
—CASDDS, Linda Hall.
Published by: New York Public Library, Science and Technology Research Center, Rm 120, Fifth Ave and 42nd St, New York, NY 10018. TEL 212-930-0920, FAX 212-869-7824. Ed. Gloria Rohmann. Circ: 1,700.

016.5 RUS
NOVAYA LITERATURA PO SOTSIAL'NYM I GUMANITARNYM NAUKAM. NAUKOVEDENIE; bibliograficheskii ukazatel'. Text in Russian. 1992. m. USD 399 in United States (effective 2004). **Document type:** *Bibliography.*
Formed by the merger of (1947-1992): Novaya Inostrannaya Literatura po Obshchestvennym Naukam. Naukovedenie (0134-2800); (1947-1992): Novaya Sovetskaya Literatura po Obshchestvennym Naukam. Naukovedenie (0134-2754)
Indexed: RASB.
Published by: Rossiiskaya Akademiya Nauk, Institut Nauchnoi Informatsii po Obshchestvennym Naukam, Nakhimovskii pr-t 51/21, Moscow, 117997, Russian Federation. TEL 7-095-1288930, FAX 7-095-4202261, info@inion.ru, http://www.inion.ru. Ed. N I Makeshin. **Dist. by:** East View Information Services, 10601 Wayzata Blvd, Minneapolis, MN 55305. TEL 952-252-1201, 800-477-1005, FAX 952-252-1202, info@eastview.com, http://www.eastview.com.

OUTSTANDING SCIENCE TRADE BOOKS FOR STUDENTS K-12. *see* CHILDREN AND YOUTH—Abstracting, Bibliographies, Statistics

500 016 PAK ISSN 0031-0085
PAKISTAN SCIENCE ABSTRACTS. Text in English. 1961. q. PKR 160, USD 30 (effective 1999). abstr.; pat. index. **Document type:** *Abstract/Index.*
Related titles: Microfilm ed.
Published by: Pakistan Scientific and Technological Information Centre, Quaid-i-Azam University Campus, P O Box 1217, Islamabad, Pakistan. Ed. Ghulam Hamid Khan. Circ: 500.

016.5 MEX
PERIODICA; indice de revistas latinoamericanas en ciencias. Text in Spanish. base vol. plus d. updates. MXN 150, USD 190 (effective 2000). **Document type:** *Database, Abstract/Index.*
Media: Online - full text. **Related titles:** ◆ Online - full text ed.: Clase and Periodica.
Published by: (Centro de Informacion Cientifica y Humanistica), Universidad Nacional Autonoma de Mexico, Direccion General de Bibliotecas, Apdo. Postal 70-392, Mexico City, DF 04510, Mexico. FAX 52-55-5550-8068, sinfo@dgb.unam.mx. Ed. Octavio Alonso Gamboa.

500 PHL ISSN 0116-3582
PHILIPPINE MEN OF SCIENCE. Text in English. 1967. a. PHP 250; USD 45 foreign. **Description:** Contains bio-bibliographic information of outstanding living Filipino scientists and technologists.
Published by: (Department of Science and Technology), Science and Technology Information Institute, P.O. Box 3596, Manila, Philippines. TEL 822-0954.

016.5 PHL
PHILIPPINE SCIENCE AND TECHNOLOGY ABSTRACTS. Text in English. 1960. q. PHP 200 (effective 2005). abstr. index. **Document type:** *Abstract/Index.*
Formerly: Philippine Science and Technology Abstracts Bibliography (0115-8724); Formed by the merger of: Philippine Abstracts (0031-7438); Philippine Science Index
—Linda Hall.

S

Published by: (Scientific Library and Documentation Division), Science and Technology Information Institute, DOST Complex, Gen Santos Ave, Bicutan, Taguig, Manila, Philippines. TEL 63-2-8377520. Circ: 500.

016.5 USA
PROQUEST NATURAL SCIENCE JOURNALS. Text in English. base vol. plus updates. **Document type:** *Database, Abstract/Index.*
Media: Online - full text.
Published by: ProQuest (Subsidiary of: Cambridge Information Group), 789 E Eisenhower Pky, PO Box 1346, Ann Arbor, MI 48106. TEL 734-761-4700, 800-521-0600, FAX 734-997-4040, 888-241-5612, info@proquest.com.

016.5 USA
PROQUEST SCIENCE JOURNALS. Text in English. base vol. plus d. updates. **Document type:** *Database, Abstract/Index.*
Media: Online - full text.
Published by: ProQuest (Subsidiary of: Cambridge Information Group), 789 E Eisenhower Pky, PO Box 1346, Ann Arbor, MI 48106. TEL 734-761-4700, 800-521-0600, FAX 734-997-4040, 888-241-5612, info@proquest.com, http://www.proquest.com.

016.5 016.6 USA
PROQUEST SCITECH JOURNALS. Text in English. base vol. plus updates. **Document type:** *Database, Abstract/Index.*
Media: Online - full text.
Published by: ProQuest (Subsidiary of: Cambridge Information Group), 789 E Eisenhower Pky, PO Box 1346, Ann Arbor, MI 48106. TEL 734-761-4700, 800-521-0600, FAX 734-997-4040, 888-241-5612, info@proquest.com.

016.5 USA
RECENT SCIENCE INDEX. Text in English. 2008. base vol. plus m. updates. **Document type:** *Database, Abstract/Index.*
Media: Online - full text.
Published by: Addleton Academic Publishers, 30-18 50th St, Woodside, NY 11377.

502.1 NZL ISSN 1177-0295
RESEARCH AND DEVELOPMENT IN NEW ZEALAND. Text in English. 2002. biennial. NZD 35 per issue (effective 2008). **Description:** Presents a statistical picture of research and development (R&D) in New Zealand.
Published by: Statistics New Zealand/Te Tari Tatau, Statistics House, The Blvd, Harbour Quays, PO Box 2922, Wellington, 6140, New Zealand. TEL 64-4-9314600, FAX 64-4-9314610, info@stats.govt.nz. **Co-sponsor:** Ministry of Research, Science & Technology.

500 JPN
RIKA NENPYO/SCIENCE ALMANAC. Text in Japanese. 1924. a. stat.
Published by: (University of Tokyo/Tokyo Daigaku Soryushi Butsuri Kokusai Kenkyu Senta, Tokyo Astronomical Observatory), Maruzen Co., Ltd./Maruzen Kabushikikaisha, 3-10 Nihonbashi 2-chome, Chuo-ku, Tokyo, 103-0027, Japan. TEL 81-3-3272-7211, FAX 81-3-3274-3238.

500 016 USA ISSN 1533-5046
Z7403
S B & F; your guide to science resources for all ages. (Science Books & Films) Text in English. 1965. bi-m. USD 45 combined subscription domestic to non-members (print & online eds.); USD 55 combined subscription in Canada to non-members (print & online eds.); USD 60 combined subscription elsewhere to non-members (print & online eds.); USD 35 combined subscription domestic to members (print & online eds.); USD 45 combined subscription in Canada to members (print & online eds.); USD 50 combined subscription elsewhere to members (print & online eds.) (effective 2009). adv. bk.rev. illus. index. back issues avail.; reprints avail. **Document type:** *Magazine, Trade.* **Description:** Contains reviews of print, film, and software materials in all sciences for all age levels, for librarians and educators.
Former titles (until 1999): Science Books & Films (0098-342X); (until 1975): A A A S Science Books (0036-8253); (until 1973): Science Books
Related titles: Microform ed.: (from PQC); Online - full text ed.
Indexed: A22, B05, B14, BRI, CBRI, ChLitAb, G08, I05, MRD.
—Linda Hall.
Published by: American Association for the Advancement of Science, 1200 New York Ave, NW, Washington, DC 20005. TEL 202-326-6670, FAX 202-371-9849, http://www.aaas.org. Eds. Heather Malcomson, Maria Sosa.

500 600 PHL
S E A ABSTRACTS. Text in English. q. PHP 200; USD 45 foreign. **Document type:** *Abstract/Index.* **Description:** Abstracts and summarizes the latest scientific and technical studies in Asia, excluding the Philippines.
Published by: (Department of Science and Technology), Science and Technology Information Institute, P.O. Box 3596, Manila, Philippines. TEL 822-0954. **Subscr. to:** Dept. of Science and Technology, Bicutan, Taguig, P.O. Box 2131, Manila, Philippines.

016.5 USA
SCHOLARLY JOURNALS INDEX. Text in English. 2008. base vol. plus m. updates. **Document type:** *Database, Abstract/Index.*
Media: Online - full text.
Published by: Addleton Academic Publishers, 30-18 50th St, Woodside, NY 11377. TEL 718-626-6017, sales@addletonacademicpublishers.com, http://www.addletonacademicpublishers.com/.

500 600 016 USA ISSN 0036-8059
CODEN: STNWAM
SCI-TECH NEWS. Text in English. 1947. q. USD 20 to non-members (effective 2005). adv. bk.rev. bibl. **Document type:** *Magazine, Consumer.*
Indexed: A22, A28, APA, B04, BrCerAb, C&ISA, CA/WCA, CIA, CerAb, CivEngAb, CorrAb, E&CAJ, E11, EEA, EMA, ESPM, EnvEAb, H15, Inspec, L04, L07, L08, L09, LISTA, LibLit, M&TEA, M09, MBF, METADEX, SolStAb, T02, T04, WAA.
—CASDDS, Ingenta, Linda Hall. **CCC.**
Published by: Special Libraries Association, Science and Technology Division, 331 S Patrick St, Alexandria, VA 22314-3501. TEL 703-647-4900, FAX 703-647-4901, sla@sla.org, http://www.sla.org. Ed. Susan Fingerman. Circ: 1,800.

016.5 016.6 USA
SCIENCE AND TECHNOLOGY. Text in English. base vol. plus w. updates. **Document type:** *Database, Abstract/Index.*
Media: Online - full text.
Published by: EBSCO Publishing (Subsidiary of: EBSCO Industries, Inc.), 10 Estes St, PO Box 682, Ipswich, MA 01938. TEL 978-356-6500, 800-653-2726, FAX 978-356-6565, information@ebscohost.com.

016.5 USA ISSN 0036-827X
Z7401 CODEN: SCIXAH
SCIENCE CITATION INDEX. Short title: S C I. Text in English. 1961. 6/yr. (plus a. cumulation). Index. reprints avail. **Document type:** *Abstract/Index.* **Description:** Indexes the world's science and technology literature. Provides cited reference searching and related records.
Related titles: CD-ROM ed.: ISSN 1044-6052; ◆ Online - full text ed.: Science Citation Index Expanded.
Indexed: RASB.
—INIST, Linda Hall.
Published by: Thomson Reuters (Subsidiary of: Thomson Reuters Corp.), 1500 Spring Garden, 4th Fl, Philadelphia, PA 19130. TEL 215-386-0100, 800-336-4474, FAX 215-386-2911, general.info@thomson.com, http://science.thomsonreuters.com/.

016.5 USA
SCIENCE CITATION INDEX EXPANDED. Text in English. base vol. plus w. updates. **Document type:** *Database, Abstract/Index.*
Media: Online - full text. **Related titles:** CD-ROM ed.: ISSN 1044-6052; ◆ Print ed.: Science Citation Index. ISSN 0036-827X.
Published by: Thomson Reuters (Subsidiary of: Thomson Reuters Corp.), 1500 Spring Garden, 4th Fl, Philadelphia, PA 19130. TEL 215-386-0100, 800-336-4474, FAX 215-386-2911, general.info@thomson.com, http://science.thomsonreuters.com/.

016.5 016.61 USA
SCIENCE FULL TEXT SELECT. Text in English. 1994. base vol. plus d. updates. USD 2,905 (effective 2011). **Document type:** *Database, Abstract/Index.*
Media: Online - full text.
Published by: H.W. Wilson, 950 University Ave, Bronx, NY 10452. TEL 718-588-8400, 800-367-6770, FAX 718-590-1617, 800-590-1617, custserv@hwwilson.com.

016.5 USA
SCIENCE IN CONTEXT. Text in English. base vol. plus d. updates. **Document type:** *Database, Abstract/Index.*
Formerly: Science Resource Center
Media: Online - full text.
Published by: Gale (Subsidiary of: Cengage Learning), 27500 Drake Rd, Farmington Hills, MI 48331. TEL 248-699-4253, 800-877-4253, FAX 248-699-8035, 877-363-4253, gale.customerservice@cengage.com, http://gale.cengage.com.

600.21 CAN ISSN 1209-1278
SCIENCE STATISTICS (ONLINE). Text in Multiple languages. 1974. irreg. free (effective 2006). stat. **Document type:** *Government.*
Formerly (until vol.22, no.1): Science Statistics (Print) (0706-0793); Which superseded in part (in 1979): Education Science and Culture (0317-5391); Which was formerly (1971-1974): Canada. Statistics Canada. Education Division. Service Bulletin (0317-5383)
Media: Online - full text.
Indexed: C04, C05, CA, T02.
Published by: (Statistics Canada, Education, Science and Culture Division), Statistics Canada/Statistique Canada, Publications Sales and Services, Ottawa, ON K1A 0T6, Canada. TEL 613-951-8116, 800-267-6677, infostats@statcan.ca, http://www.statcan.gc.ca.

502.1 602.1 LUX ISSN 1830-754X
SCIENCE, TECHNOLOGY AND INNOVATION IN EUROPE. Text in English. a. **Document type:** *Trade.*
Published by: (European Commission, Statistical Office of the European Communities (E U R O S T A T)), European Commission, Office for Official Publications of the European Union, 2 Rue Mercier, Luxembourg, L-2985, Luxembourg. TEL 352-29291, FAX 352-29291, info@publications.europa.eu, http://publications.europa.eu.

016.5 USA
SCIENCES MODULE. Text in English. base vol. plus d. updates. **Document type:** *Database, Abstract/Index.*
Media: Online - full text.
Published by: ProQuest (Subsidiary of: Cambridge Information Group), 789 E Eisenhower Pky, PO Box 1346, Ann Arbor, MI 48106. TEL 734-761-4700, 800-521-0600, FAX 734-997-4040, 888-241-5612, info@proquest.com, http://www.proquest.com.

500 600 BGR
SCIENTIFIC AND TECHNICAL PUBLICATIONS IN BULGARIA. Text in English. q. USD 33. **Description:** Contains abstracts of selected articles, published in prestigious Bulgarian journals, proceedings of scientific institutes and universities.
Published by: National Centre for Information and Documentation (N A C I D), 52A G M Dimitrov Blvd, Sofia, 1125, Bulgaria. Ed. Kamen Markov.

016.5 USA ISSN 1949-6508
▼ **SCIENTIFIC CONFERENCE ABSTRACT INDEX.** Abbreviated title: S C A I. Text in English. 2010 (Jan.). q. free (effective 2011). **Document type:** *Abstract/Index.* **Description:** Includes scientific abstracts that have been presented in local, regional, national, and international scientific meetings, conferences, and symposia since 2000. Also includes abstracts from conferences in business, social sciences and education.
Media: Online - full content.
Published by: Bio Tech System, PO Box 31932, Edmond, OK 73003. editorial@btsjournals.com.

016.5 USA
SCIENTIFIC PUBLICATIONS INDEX. Text in English. 2008. base vol. plus m. updates. **Document type:** *Database, Abstract/Index.*
Media: Online - full text.
Published by: Addleton Academic Publishers, 30-18 50th St, Woodside, NY 11377. TEL 718-626-6017, sales@addletonacademicpublishers.com, http://www.addletonacademicpublishers.com/.

016.5 USA
SCIENTIFIC RESOURCES DATABASE. Text in English. 2008. base vol. plus m. updates. **Document type:** *Database, Abstract/Index.*
Media: Online - full text.
Published by: Addleton Academic Publishers, 30-18 50th St, Woodside, NY 11377.

500 016 THA ISSN 0125-4529
SCIENTIFIC SERIALS IN THAI LIBRARIES. Text in English. 1968. a. THB 2,000, USD 80. **Document type:** *Bibliography.* **Description:** Lists over 13,800 journals and report series on science, technology, and socio-economic aspects of the sciences received by 148 libraries in Bangkok.
Related titles: Online - full text ed.
Published by: Thailand Institute of Scientific and Technological Research, 196 Phahonyothin Rd, Chatuchak, Bangkok, 10900, Thailand. TEL 579-8594, FAX 662-579-8594.

016.5 016.6 016.3 NLD
SCOPUS. Text in English. 2004. base vol. plus d. updates. **Document type:** *Database, Abstract/Index.* **Description:** Covers peer-reviewed titles from international publishers. Coverage includes open access journals, conference proceedings, trade publications, and book series.
Media: Online - full text.
Published by: Elsevier BV (Subsidiary of: Elsevier Science & Technology), Radarweg 29, PO Box 211, Amsterdam, 1000 AE, Netherlands. TEL 31-20-4853911, FAX 31-20-4852457, http://www.elsevier.com.

016 USA ISSN 0037-1343
AS36 CODEN: SRABAG
SELECTED RAND ABSTRACTS; a semiannual guide to publications of the Rand Corporation. Text in English. 1946. 2/yr. free to institutions. abstr. cum.index: 1946-1962; 1963-1972. **Document type:** *Bulletin, Abstract/Index.*
Formerly (until 1962): Rand Corporation. Index of Selected Publications (0485-9790)
Indexed: AMB, LID&ISL, RehabLit.
—CASDDS, Linda Hall. **CCC.**
Published by: Rand Corporation, Publications Department, 1776 Main St, PO Box 2138, Santa Monica, CA 90407-2138. TEL 310-451-7002, FAX 310-451-6996, TELEX 9103436878. R&P Judy Lewis. Circ: 1,000.

500 600 JPN ISSN 0917-7574
SHINKU TANKU NENPO/ALMANAC OF THINK TANKS IN JAPAN. Text in Japanese. 1976. a. JPY 5,000 (effective 2001). abstr. **Document type:** *Directory, Academic/Scholarly.* **Description:** Introduces the results of research conducted at Japanese think tanks and research institutes.
Published by: Sogo Kenkyu Kaihatsu Kiko/National Institute for Research Advancement, 34F Yebisu Garden Place Tower, 4-20-3 Ebisu, Shibuya-ku, Tokyo, 150-6034, Japan. TEL 03-5448-1735, FAX 03-5448-1745. Circ: 1,000.

016.5 RUS
SOTSIAL'NYE I GUMANITARNYE NAUKI. OTECHESTVENNAYA I ZARUBEZHNAYA LITERATURA. NAUKOVEDENIE; referativnyi zhurnal. Text in Russian. 1973. q. USD 159 in United States (effective 2004). **Document type:** *Abstract/Index.* **Description:** Contains abstracts of foreign and Russian books devoted to studies of Russian and foreign books on science about science acquired lately by INION.
Formerly: Obshchestvennye Nauki za Rubezhom. Naukovedenie (0202-2141)
Indexed: RASB.
—East View.
Published by: Rossiiskaya Akademiya Nauk, Institut Nauchnoi Informatsii po Obshchestvennym Naukam, Nakhimovskii pr-t 51/21, Moscow, 117997, Russian Federation. TEL 7-095-1288930, FAX 7-095-4202261, info@inion.ru, http://www.inion.ru. Ed. A M Kul'kin. **Dist. by:** East View Information Services, 10601 Wayzata Blvd, Minneapolis, MN 55305. TEL 952-252-1201, 800-477-1005, FAX 952-252-1202, info@eastview.com, http://www.eastview.com.

016.5 USA ISSN 1527-7178
➤ **STATE ACADEMIES OF SCIENCE ABSTRACTS.** Text in English. 1995. base vol. plus m. updates. USD 420 to individuals must complete a license agreement (effective Jan. 2005). **Document type:** *Database, Abstract/Index.* **Description:** Provides abstracts of proceedings of 41 of the 42 state academies of science. Covers 1946 to present.
Media: Online - full content. **Related titles:** CD-ROM ed.: ISSN 1089-5698.
Address: PO Box 141, Cumberland City, TN 37050. TEL 630-220-1019, FAX 630-876-8890, 931-827-3003, info@acadsci.com.

500 338 KWT
STATISTICS ON SCIENTIFIC AND TECHNOLOGICAL ACTIVITIES/ IHSA'AT AL-ANSHITAH AL-'ILMIYYAH WAL-TEKNOLOJIYYAH FI DAWLAT AL-KUWAYT. Text in Arabic, English. 1977. irreg., latest 1984. **Document type:** *Government.* **Description:** Provides statistical data on economic input (labor force and expenditures) deriving from scientific and technical activity in Kuwait.
Published by: Central Statistical Office/Al-Idarah al-Markaziyyah lil-Ihsa', P O Box 26188, Safat, 13122, Kuwait. TEL 965-2428200, FAX 965-2430464.

500 016 SDN ISSN 0255-4054
Q89.5
SUDAN SCIENCE ABSTRACTS. Text in English. 1980. a., latest vol.21, 1997. **Document type:** *Abstract/Index.* **Description:** Includes the scientific, technical, social, and economic literature of Sudan.
Published by: National Centre for Research, Documentation and Information Centre, P O Box 2404, Khartoum, Sudan. TEL 249-11-770776, FAX 249-11-770701.

016 THA ISSN 0125-0000
Q1
THAI ABSTRACTS, SERIES A. SCIENCE AND TECHNOLOGY. Text in English. 1974. s-a. THB 100, USD 5 per issue. author and subject indexes. **Document type:** *Abstract/Index.*
Related titles: Online - full text ed.
Published by: Thailand Institute of Scientific and Technological Research, 196 Phahonyothin Rd, Chatuchak, Bangkok, 10900, Thailand. TEL 579-8594, FAX 662-579-8594. Circ: 500.

U.S. NATIONAL SCIENCE FOUNDATION. DIVISION OF SCIENCE RESOURCES STATISTICS. GRADUATE STUDENTS AND POSTDOCTORATES IN SCIENCE AND ENGINEERING. *see* EDUCATION—Abstracting, Bibliographies, Statistics

500 016.016 RUS
UKAZATEL' BIBLIOGRAFICHESKYKH POSOBII PO SIBIRI I DAL'NEMU VOSTOKU; ezhegodnik. Text in Russian. 1969. a. USD 20 foreign. **Document type:** *Bibliography.* **Description:** Includes retrospective bibliographic handbooks and supplies, current bibliographic editions, literature listings, and other bibliographic resources relevant to science and Siberia and/or the Far East.
Indexed: RASB.
Published by: Rossiiskaya Akademiya Nauk, Sibirskoe Otdelenie, Gosudarstvennaya Publichnaya Nauchno-Tekhnicheskaya Biblioteka/State Public Scientific and Technical Library of the Siberian Branch of the Russian Academy of Sciences, Ul Voskhod 15, Novosibirsk, 630200, Russian Federation. TEL 7-3832-661367, FAX 7-3832-663365, onb@spsl.nsc.ru, root@libr.nsk.su. Ed. E B Soboleva.

061 005 UKR ISSN 1561-1086
H8.U45
UKRAINSKYI REFERATYVNYI ZHURNAL. SERIYA 1. PRYRODNYCHI NAUKY, MEDYTSYNA/UKRAINIAN JOURNAL OF ABSTRACTS. SER. 1. PRIRODNICI NAUKI, MEDICINE. Text and summaries in English, Russian, Ukrainian. 1995. q. UAK 250 domestic; USD 200 foreign (effective 2000). **Document type:** *Journal, Abstract/Index.*
Published by: Natsional'na Akademiya Nauk Ukrainy, Instytut Problem Reyestratsii Informatsii/National Academy of Sciences of Ukraine, Institute for Information Recording, Vul Shpaka 2, Kiev, 03113, Ukraine. TEL 380-44-4468389, FAX 380-44-2417233, djerelo@cki.ipri.kiev.ua, http://www.nbuv.gov.ua. Ed., Pub. V Petrov. Circ: 150 (paid); 100 (controlled).

UPPSALA DISSERTATIONS FROM THE FACULTY OF SCIENCE AND TECHNOLOGY. *see* SCIENCES: COMPREHENSIVE WORKS

WASEDA DAIGAKU DAIGAKUIN RIKOGAKU KENKYU IHO/WASEDA UNIVERSITY. GRADUATE SCHOOL OF SCIENCE AND ENGINEERING. SYNOPSES OF SCIENCE AND ENGINEERING PAPERS. *see* ENGINEERING—Abstracting, Bibliographies, Statistics

016.0013 016.3 016.5 USA
WEB OF SCIENCE. Text in English. base vol. plus irreg. updates. **Document type:** *Database, Abstract/Index.* **Description:** Contains bibliographic and citation information in the sciences, social sciences, arts, and humanities.
Media: Online - full text.
Published by: Thomson Reuters (Subsidiary of: Thomson Reuters Corp.), 1500 Spring Garden, 4th Fl, Philadelphia, PA 19130. TEL 215-386-0100, 800-336-4474, FAX 215-386-2911, general.info@thomson.com, http://science.thomsonreuters.com/.

500 ZMB
ZAMBIA. NATIONAL COUNCIL FOR SCIENTIFIC RESEARCH. N C S R BIBLIOGRAPHY. Short title: N C S R Bibliography. Text in English. 1976. irreg., latest 1979. ZMK 1.50. **Document type:** *Bibliography.*
Published by: National Council for Scientific Research, Chelston, PO Box CH 158, Lusaka, Zambia.

500 016 ZMB
ZAMBIA SCIENCE ABSTRACTS. Text in English. 1977. a. ZMK 5. **Document type:** *Abstract/Index.*
Published by: National Council for Scientific Research, Chelston, PO Box CH 158, Lusaka, Zambia. Ed. W C Mushipi.

310 CHN
ZHONGGUO KEJI TONGJI NIANJIAN/CHINA STATISTICAL YEARBOOK ON SCIENCE AND TECHNOLOGY. Text in Chinese. a.
Published by: Zhongguo Tongji Chubanshe/China Statistics Press, 6, Xi San Huan Nan Lu Jia, Beijing, 100073, China. TEL 8217162.

500 016 ZWE
ZIMBABWE RESEARCH INDEX; register of current research in Zimbabwe. Text in English. 1971. a. USD 40. index. **Document type:** *Abstract/Index.*
Formerly: Rhodesia Research Index
Media: Duplicated (not offset).
Published by: Scientific Liaison Office, Causeway, PO Box CY 294, Harare, Zimbabwe. TEL 263-4-700573, FAX 263-4-728799, TELEX 22141. Circ: 500 (controlled). **Subscr. to:** Government Printer, Causeway, PO Box CY 341, Harare, Zimbabwe.

SCIENCES: COMPREHENSIVE WORKS—Computer Applications

AR@CNE; revista electronica de recursos en Internet sobre geografia y ciencias. *see* GEOGRAPHY—Computer Applications

001.6 539.7 CHE ISSN 0304-2898
QC770
C E R N SCHOOL OF COMPUTING. PROCEEDINGS. Text in English. 1970. a. **Document type:** *Proceedings, Academic/Scholarly.*
Published by: C E R N - European Organization for Nuclear Research/ Organisation Europeenne pour la Recherche Nucleaire, C E R N, Geneva 23, 1211, Switzerland.

500 600 CAN ISSN 1482-5112
C I S T I NEWS (ONLINE). Text in English. 1994. q. free. **Document type:** *Newsletter.* **Description:** Contains information on developments and initiatives at CISTI. Serves as a reminder of its products and services.
Supersedes in part (in 2003): C I S T I News International (Online) (1482-5104)
Media: Online - full text.
Published by: (Canada Institute for Scientific and Technical Information), National Research Council Canada (N R C)/Conseil National de Recherches Canada (C N R C), NRC Communications & Corporate Relations, 1200 Montreal Rd, Bldg M-58, Ottawa, ON K1A 0R6, Canada. TEL 613-993-9101, FAX 613-952-9907, info@nrc-cnrc.gc.ca, http://www.nrc-cnrc.gc.ca. Ed. Tracie Taylor-Labonte.

502.85 NLD ISSN 2211-3568
▼➤ **COMPUTABILITY**; the journal of the Association CiE. Text in English. forthcoming 2012. s-a. USD 308 combined subscription in North America (print & online eds.); EUR 220 combined subscription elsewhere (print & online eds.) (effective 2012). **Document type:** *Journal, Academic/Scholarly.*
Related titles: Online - full text ed.: ISSN 2211-3576. forthcoming.
Published by: I O S Press, Nieuwe Hemweg 6B, Amsterdam, 1013 BG, Netherlands. TEL 31-20-6883355, FAX 31-20-6870019, info@iospress.nl, http://www.iospress.nl. Ed. Vasco Brattka.

502.85 GBR ISSN 1749-4680
COMPUTATIONAL SCIENCE & DISCOVERY. Text in English. 2007. q. back issues avail. **Document type:** *Journal, Academic/Scholarly.* **Description:** Focuses on scientific advances and discovery through computational science in physics, chemistry, biology and applied science.
Related titles: Online - full text ed.: ISSN 1749-4699.
Indexed: SCOPUS.
—**CCC.**
Published by: Institute of Physics Publishing Ltd., Dirac House, Temple Back, Bristol, BS1 6BE, United Kingdom. TEL 44-117-9297481, FAX 44-117-9301178, custserv@iop.org, http://publishing.iop.org/. Ed. Anthony Mezzacappa.

500 DEU ISSN 1432-9360
➤ **COMPUTING AND VISUALIZATION IN SCIENCE.** Text in English. 1997. q. EUR 635, USD 747 combined subscription to institutions (print & online eds.) (effective 2012). adv. reprint service avail. from PSC. **Document type:** *Journal, Academic/Scholarly.* **Description:** Aims to provide a platform for scientists from mathematics, computer science, physics, chemistry, environmental sciences, biosciences, and engineering willing to cooperate in solving challenging scientific and technological problems.
Related titles: Online - full text ed.: ISSN 1433-0369 (from IngentaConnect).
Indexed: A01, A03, A08, A22, A26, C10, CA, CCMJ, CPEI, CompAb, CompLI, E01, EngInd, Inspec, MSN, MathR, SCOPUS, T02.
—BLDSC (3395.020000), IE, Infotrieve, Ingenta, INIST. **CCC.**
Published by: Springer (Subsidiary of: Springer Science+Business Media), Tiergartenstr 17, Heidelberg, 69121, Germany. TEL 49-6221-4870, FAX 49-6221-345229. Ed. Gabriel Wittum. **Subscr. in the Americas to:** Springer New York LLC, Journal Fulfillment, PO Box 2485, Secaucus, NJ 07096. TEL 800-777-4643, 201-348-4033, FAX 201-348-4505, journals-ny@springer.com, http://www.springer.com; **Subscr. to:** Springer Distribution Center, Kundenservice Zeitschriften, Haberstr 7, Heidelberg 69126, Germany. TEL 49-6221-3454303, FAX 49-6221-3454229, subscriptions@springer.com.

➤ **DATA HANDLING IN SCIENCE AND TECHNOLOGY.** *see* COMPUTERS—Data Base Management

502.85 600 004 DEU ISSN 1863-2122
E A S S T ELECTRONIC COMMUNICATIONS. (European Association of Software Science and Technology) Text in English. 2006. irreg. free (effective 2011). **Document type:** *Journal, Academic/Scholarly.*
Media: Online - full text.
Published by: European Association of Software Science and Technology (E A S S T), Technische Universitaet Berlin, Sekr FR 6-1, FranklinStrasse 28-29, Berlin, 10587, Germany. Ed. Tiziana Margaria.

621.3 GBR ISSN 0266-1616
CODEN: IMTTAK
INSPEC MATTERS. Text in English. 1974. irreg. free (effective 2010). adv. back issues avail. **Document type:** *Newsletter, Trade.* **Description:** Keeps researchers up to date with changes, improvements, and events of interest related to the INSPEC services.
Related titles: Online - full text ed.: free (effective 2010).
Indexed: GALA.
—BLDSC (4518.380000), CASDDS, INIST. **CCC.**
Published by: The Institution of Engineering and Technology, Michael Faraday House, Stevenage, Herts SG1 2AY, United Kingdom. TEL 44-1438-313311, FAX 44-1438-765526, journals@theiet.org.

502.85 IND ISSN 0976-5875
➤ **INTERNATIONAL JOURNAL OF COMPUTATIONAL PHYSICAL SCIENCES.** Abbreviated title: I J C P S. Text in English. 2008. s-a. INR 3,500 domestic to libraries; USD 320 foreign to libraries; USD 360 combined subscription foreign to libraries (print & online eds.) (effective 2011). back issues avail. **Document type:** *Journal, Academic/Scholarly.* **Description:** Devoted to original research in most areas of sciences with an emphasis on computational and theoretical research.
Related titles: Online - full text ed.: 2008. USD 300 to libraries (effective 2011).
Published by: Research India Publications, D1/71, Top Fl, Rohini Sec-16, New Delhi, 110 089, India. TEL 91-11-65394240, FAX 91-11-27297815, info@ripublication.com. Ed. Jai Singh.

➤ **INTERNATIONAL JOURNAL OF MODERN PHYSICS C**; computational physics and physical computation. *see* PHYSICS

➤ **JOURNAL OF COMPUTERS IN MATHEMATICS AND SCIENCE TEACHING.** *see* MATHEMATICS—Computer Applications

500 620 USA ISSN 0925-5001
QA402.5 CODEN: JGOPEO
➤ **JOURNAL OF GLOBAL OPTIMIZATION**; an international journal dealing with theoretical and computational aspects of seeking global optima and their applications in science, management, and engineering. Text in English. 1991. m. EUR 2,269, USD 2,470 combined subscription to institutions (print & online eds.) (effective 2012). adv. back issues avail.; reprint service avail. from PSC. **Document type:** *Journal, Academic/Scholarly.* **Description:** Publishes carefully refereed papers dealing with every theoretical, computational and applicational aspect of global optimization. In a global optimization problem, global optima are sought, although local optima different from the global one exist.
Related titles: Microform ed.: (from PQC); Online - full text ed.: ISSN 1573-2916 (from IngentaConnect).
Indexed: A12, A17, A20, A22, A26, ABIn, ASCA, BibLing, C10, CA, CCMJ, CIS, CMCI, CPEI, CurCont, E01, ESPM, EngInd, I05, IBR, IBZ, ISR, MSN, MathR, P10, P17, P26, P48, P49, P51, P52, P53, P54, PQC, RefZh, RiskAb, S10, SCI, SCOPUS, ST&MA, T02, W07, Z02.
—BLDSC (4996.302000), IE, Infotrieve, Ingenta, Linda Hall. **CCC.**
Published by: Springer New York LLC (Subsidiary of: Springer Science+Business Media), 233 Spring St, New York, NY 10013. TEL 212-460-1500, FAX 212-460-1575, journals-ny@springer.com, http://www.springer.com. Ed. Panos M Pardalos.

500 USA ISSN 0885-7474
Q183.9 CODEN: JSCOEB
➤ **JOURNAL OF SCIENTIFIC COMPUTING.** Text in English. 1986. 10/yr. EUR 1,593, USD 1,649 combined subscription to institutions (print & online eds.) (effective 2012). adv. back issues avail.; reprint service avail. from PSC. **Document type:** *Journal, Academic/Scholarly.* **Description:** Discusses developments in the field of supercomputers.
Related titles: Microfilm ed.: (from PQC); Online - full text ed.: ISSN 1573-7691 (from IngentaConnect).
Indexed: A22, A26, ApMecR, BibLing, C&ISA, C10, CA, CCMJ, CMCI, CPEI, CompAb, CompLI, CompR, E&CAJ, E01, EngInd, ISMEC, Inspec, MSN, MathR, P30, RefZh, SCI, SCOPUS, SolStAb, W07, Z02.
—BLDSC (5057.250000), AskIEEE, IE, Infotrieve, Ingenta, INIST, Linda Hall. **CCC.**
Published by: Springer New York LLC (Subsidiary of: Springer Science+Business Media), 233 Spring St, New York, NY 10013. TEL 212-460-1500, FAX 212-460-1575, service-ny@springer.com, http://www.springer.com/. Ed. Chi-Wang Shu.

500 USA ISSN 1930-5753
CODEN: SCOAEG
SCIENTIFIC COMPUTING; information technology for science. Text in English. 1984. m. USD 121 domestic; USD 135 in Canada & Mexico; USD 226 elsewhere (effective 2007). adv. tr.lit. reprints avail. **Document type:** *Magazine, Trade.* **Description:** Covers computer technology for the scientific community and features technical software, computer systems and related hardware, as well as the latest applications and techniques that aid in scientific research.
Former titles (until Oct. 2005): Scientific Computing & Instrumentation (1524-2560); (until Jan. 1999): Scientific Computing and Automation (0891-9003)
Related titles: Online - full text ed.: ISSN 1930-6156. free to qualified personnel (effective 2008).
Indexed: A01, A03, A08, A09, A10, A15, A26, ABIn, B01, B06, B07, B09, C23, CPEI, CompD, CompLI, E08, EngInd, G06, G07, G08, I05, Inspec, Microcompind, P17, P26, P48, P49, P51, P53, P54, PQC, S09, SCOPUS, SoftBase, T02, V03, V04.
—AskIEEE, CASDDS, IE, Ingenta, Linda Hall. **CCC.**
Published by: Advantage Business Media, 100 Enterprise Dr, Ste 600, PO Box 912, Rockaway, NJ 07886. TEL 973-920-7000, FAX 973-920-7531, AdvantageCommunications@advantagemedia.com, http://www.advantagebusinessmedia.com. Ed. Suzanne Tracy TEL 973-920-7065. Pub. Matt Lally TEL 973-920-7132. adv.: color page USD 9,855; trim 7.875 x 10.5. Circ: 53,000 (controlled).

SHIMYURESHON/JAPAN SOCIETY FOR SIMULATION TECHNOLOGY. JOURNAL. *see* COMPUTERS—Computer Simulation

500 510 CHN ISSN 1000-3266
QA297
➤ **SHUZHI JISUAN YU JISUANJI YINGYONG/JOURNAL ON NUMERICAL METHODS AND COMPUTER APPLICATIONS.** Text in Chinese. 1979. q. USD 26.80 (effective 2009). adv. **Document type:** *Journal, Academic/Scholarly.* **Description:** Contains articles on mathematic modules and calculation methods in the solution of problems through the use of the computer in various scientific and technical spheres.
Related titles: Online - full text ed.
Indexed: CCMJ, MSN, MathR, Z02.
—East View, Linda Hall.
Published by: (Zhongguo Kexueyuan Jisuan Shuxue yu Kexue Gongcheng Jisuan Yanjiusuo/Chinese Academy of Sciences, Institute of Computational Mathematics and Scientific/Engineering Computing), Kexue Chubanshe/Science Press, 16 Donghuang Cheng Genbei Jie, Beijing, 100717, China. TEL 86-10-64000246, FAX 86-10-64030255, http://www.sciencep.com/. Circ: 12,000. **Dist. by:** China International Book Trading Corp, 35 Chegongzhuang Xilu, Haidian District, PO Box 399, Beijing 100044, China. TEL 86-10-68412045, FAX 86-10-68412023, cibtc@mail.cibtc.com.cn, http://www.cibtc.com.cn.

➤ **YAOGAN XUEBAO/JOURNAL OF REMOTE SENSING.** *see* GEOGRAPHY

SECURITY

see CRIMINOLOGY AND LAW ENFORCEMENT—Security

SHIPS AND SHIPPING

see TRANSPORTATION—Ships And Shipping

SHOES AND BOOTS

see also LEATHER AND FUR INDUSTRIES

685.31029 USA ISSN 0146-6437
TS945
AMERICAN SHOEMAKING DIRECTORY OF SHOE MANUFACTURERS. Cover title: American Shoemaking Directory. Text in English. 1901. a. USD 60 per issue (effective 2003). adv. back issues avail. **Document type:** *Directory, Trade.* **Description:** Lists every footwear manufacturing plant in the United States, Canada, and Puerto Rico. In addition to the company name, address, and telephone number, the directory delineates the number of shoes made in that factory within some 30 categories, and more.
Published by: Shoe Trades Publishing Co., 271, Swampscott, MA 01907-0471. TEL 781-648-8160. Ed. James D Sutton. Pub., R&P John Moynihan. Circ: 2,000.

ARS ARPEL WEEK; fashion and economy news on footwear and leather field. *see* LEATHER AND FUR INDUSTRIES

685.5 ITA ISSN 0004-265X
ARS SUTORIA; Italian & International Footwear Fashion Magazine. Text in English, French, German, Italian, Spanish. 1947. 8/yr. adv. **Document type:** *Magazine, Trade.*
Published by: Ars Arpel Group srl, Via Ippolito Nievo 33, Milan, 20145, Italy. TEL 39-02-319121, FAX 39-02-33611619, arsarpel@arsarpel.it, http://www.arsarpel.it. Circ: 49,000.

S

685.31 ITA
BAMBINO. Text in Italian, English. s-a. **Document type:** *Magazine, Trade.* **Description:** Specializes in children leather shoes.
Published by: Editoriale di Foto Shoe s.r.l., Via Leonardo da Vinci 43, Trezzano sul Naviglio, MI 20900, Italy. TEL 39-02-4459091, FAX 39-02-48402959, central@fotoshoe.com, http://www.fotoshoe.com.

BOR- ES CIPOTECHNIKA, -PIAC/LEATHER AND SHOE TECHNIQUE, -MARKET. *see* LEATHER AND FUR INDUSTRIES

685.31 GBR ISSN 1473-7337
BUSINESS RATIO REPORT. THE FOOTWEAR INDUSTRY. Text in English. 1974. a., latest no.27, 2008, Apr. GBP 365 per issue (effective 2010). back issues avail. **Document type:** *Report, Trade.* **Description:** Covers companies active in the footwear industry.
Former titles (until 2001): Business Ratio. The Footwear Industry (1470-6822); (until 2000): Business Ratio Plus. The Footwear Industry (1355-896X); (until 1994): Business Ratio Report. The Footwear Industry (1467-5102); (until 1992): Business Ratio Report. Footwear Manufacturers (0261-8141)
Published by: Key Note Ltd. (Subsidiary of: Bonnier Business Information), Harlequin House, 5th Fl, 7 High St, Teddington, Richmond upon Thames, TW11 8EE, United Kingdom. TEL 44-845-5040452, FAX 44-845-5040453, sales@keynote.co.uk.

CANADIAN FOOTWEAR & LEATHER DIRECTORY. *see* BUSINESS AND ECONOMICS—Trade And Industrial Directories

685.31 675 CAN ISSN 0705-1433
CANADIAN FOOTWEAR JOURNAL. (Annual Directory Number avail.) Text in English. 1888. 8/yr. CAD 40 domestic; USD 55 in United States; USD 120 foreign (effective 2004). adv. illus.; stat. index. reprints avail. **Document type:** *Journal, Trade.* **Description:** Edited to meet the specialized needs of those engaged in all aspects of the footwear business and its allied trades. Features on fashion, business management, efficient buying and stock control, store design and new developments in technology, materials and manufacturing processes.
Formerly: Shoe and Leather Journal (0037-4032)
Related titles: Microfiche ed.: (from MML).
Indexed: C03, CBCABus, CBPI, P48, PQC.
Published by: Shoe Trades Publications, 241 Senneville Rd, Senneville, PQ H9X 3X5, Canada. TEL 514-457-8787, 800-973-7463, info@shoetrades.com, http://www.shoetrades.com. Ed., R&P Barbara McLeish. Pub. George McLeish. Circ: 9,000.

685.31 FRA ISSN 0151-4040
CHAUSSER MAGAZINE. Text in French. 1946. m. (11/yr). EUR 88 domestic; EUR 98 in Europe; EUR 120 elsewhere (effective 2010). adv. illus. **Document type:** *Magazine, Trade.*
Former titles (until 1968): Nouveau Chausser (0151-4032); (until 1967): Chausser (0151-4024)
Published by: Infocuir S.a.r.l., 14 rue de la Folie Regnault, Paris, 75011, France. TEL 33-1-40095009, FAX 33-1-40240484, infocuir@free.fr. Ed. Jean-Pierre Bidegain.

CLEO EN LA MODA. *see* LEATHER AND FUR INDUSTRIES

CUOIO PELLI MATERIE CONCIANTI. *see* LEATHER AND FUR INDUSTRIES

685.31 GBR
CUTTING EDGE (NEWARK); for today's shoe repairer. Text in English. 2002. q. free to members. **Document type:** *Journal, Trade.*
Incorporates (1963-2008): Saint Crispin's Boot Trades Association. Shoe Service
Published by: The MultiService Assocation Ltd., PO Box 9378, Newark, NG24 9FE, United Kingdom. TEL 44-1400-281298, FAX 44-1400-282326, info@msauk.biz, http://www.msauk.biz/.

685.3 DEU ISSN 0947-2630
EDITION SCHUHE. Variant title: Schuhe. Text in German. 1995. a. EUR 10 per issue (effective 2011). adv. **Document type:** *Magazine, Trade.*
Published by: Verlag Otto Sternefeld GmbH, Oberkasseler Str 100, Duesseldorf, 40545, Germany. TEL 49-211-577080, FAX 49-211-5770812, sk.vertrieb@sternefeld.de. Ed. Petra Salewski. adv.: color page EUR 4,050. Circ: 18,000 (controlled).

685.31 IRL
FOOTWEAR IN IRELAND. Text in English. 2/yr. adv. **Document type:** *Magazine, Trade.*
Published by: Futura Communications Ltd., 5 Main St., Blackrock, Co. Dublin, Ireland. TEL 353-1-2836782, FAX 353-1-2836784. adv.: B&W page EUR 1,263, color page EUR 1,759; trim 210 x 297. Circ: 5,000 (controlled).

685.31 USA
FOOTWEAR INDUSTRIES OF AMERICA. STATISTICAL REPORTER. Text in English. 1981. q. USD 100 (effective 1999). **Document type:** *Newsletter, Trade.* **Description:** Provides data on production, foreign trade, marketing, labor, prices, consumer expenditures and quarterly trends in the footwear industry.
Formerly: Footwear Industries of America. Quarterly Report (0742-2555)
Related titles: Microfiche ed.: (from CIS).
Indexed: SRI.
Published by: Footwear Industries of America, 1601 N Kent St Ste 1200, Arlington, DC 22209-2105. TEL 202-789-1420, 800-688-7653, FAX 202-789-4058.

685.31 USA ISSN 0162-914X
TS989
FOOTWEAR NEWS. Abbreviated title: F N. Text in English. 1945. w. USD 72 domestic; USD 149 in Canada & Mexico; USD 295 elsewhere; USD 10 per issue (effective 2008). adv. bk.rev. illus.; mkt. Supplement avail.; back issues avail.; reprints avail. **Document type:** *Magazine, Trade.* **Description:** Provides an inside perspective on news, fashion trends and business strategies.
Related titles: Online - full text ed.: USD 49 (effective 2008).
Indexed: A10, A15, ABIn, B01, B02, B03, B07, B11, B15, B17, B18, BusI, CWI, G04, G06, G07, G08, I05, KES, P34, P48, P51, PQC, S22, T&II, T02, V03.
—CCC.
Published by: Fairchild Publications, Inc. (Subsidiary of: Advance Publications, Inc.), 750 3rd Ave, 3rd Fl, New York, NY 10017. TEL 212-630-4900, FAX 212-630-4919, customerservice@fairchildpub.com, http://www.fairchildpub.com. Pub. Jay Spaleta. adv.: B&W page USD 14,060, color page USD 17,570; trim 10.1875 x 12.75. Circ: 17,189.

685.31 USA ISSN 1054-898X
FOOTWEAR PLUS. Text in English. 1990. 10/yr. free to qualified personnel (effective 2009). adv. Supplement avail.; back issues avail. **Document type:** *Magazine, Trade.* **Description:** Designed for footwear retailers. Covers the entire footwear market: dress, casual and athletic footwear, as well as hosiery and accessories.
Formerly: Earnshaw's Footwear Plus
Indexed: A10, B02, G04, G06, G07, G08, I05, P16, P48, P53, P54, PQC, V03.
Published by: Symphony Publishing LLC, 8 W 38th St, Ste 201, New York, NY 10018. TEL 646-278-1550, 800-731-5852, FAX 646-278-1553, http://www.symphonypublishing.com. Pub. Caroline Diaco TEL 646-278-1518. Adv. contact Jennifer Craig TEL 646-278-1519. B&W page USD 9,800, color page USD 11,900; trim 9 x 10.875. Circ: 17,051 (controlled).

685.31 GBR ISSN 1942-4280
TS940
▼ ➤ **FOOTWEAR SCIENCE.** Text in English. 2009 (Apr.). 3/yr. GBP 231 combined subscription in United Kingdom to institutions (print & online eds.); EUR 368, USD 461 combined subscription to institutions (print & online eds.) (effective 2012). **Document type:** *Journal, Academic/Scholarly.* **Description:** Contains reports of original research in the disciplines of biomechanics, ergonomics, physiology, clinical science, kinanthropometry, physics, engineering and mathematics.
Related titles: Online - full text ed.: ISSN 1942-4299. 2009. GBP 208 in United Kingdom to institutions; EUR 332, USD 415 to institutions (effective 2012) (from IngentaConnect).
Indexed: A01, CA, T02.
—IE. **CCC.**
Published by: (Footwear Biomechanics Group), Taylor & Francis Ltd. (Subsidiary of: Taylor & Francis Group), 4 Park Sq, Milton Park, Abingdon, Oxfordshire OX14 4RN, United Kingdom. TEL 44-20-70176000, FAX 44-20-70176336, subscriptions@tandf.co.uk. Ed. Edward C Frederick.

391.413 685.31 GBR ISSN 1475-8601
FOOTWEAR TODAY. Text in English. 1998. m. GBP 50 domestic; GBP 75 in Europe; GBP 95 elsewhere; free to qualified personnel (effective 2009). adv. back issues avail. **Document type:** *Magazine, Trade.* **Description:** Contains the latest industry news, developments and product information, plus news and previews of forthcoming UK and European trade exhibitions.
Formerly (until 2001): Footwear & Leather Goods Today
Related titles: Online - full text ed.: free to qualified personnel (effective 2009).
—CCC.
Published by: Datateam Publishing Ltd, 15a London Rd, Maidstone, Kent ME16 8LY, United Kingdom. TEL 44-1622-687031, FAX 44-1622-757646, info@datateam.co.uk, http://www.datateam.co.uk. Ed. Cheryl Taylor TEL 44-1622-862962. Pub. Paul Ryder TEL 44-1622-699105. Adv. contact John Andrews TEL 44-1622-699135. B&W page GBP 850, color page GBP 1,350; trim 229 x 306.

685 ITA
FOTO SHOE. Text in English, Italian; Text occasionally in French, German, Spanish. 1969. 8/yr. adv. bk.rev. illus. **Document type:** *Magazine, Trade.* **Description:** Covers the shoe fashion industry, distribution and commercialization of footwear, and trade fairs held worldwide.
Supersedes in part: Foto Shoe
Published by: Editoriale di Foto Shoe s.r.l., Via Leonardo da Vinci 43, Trezzano sul Naviglio, MI 20900, Italy. TEL 39-02-4459091, FAX 39-02-48402959, central@fotoshoe.com, http://www.fotoshoe.com. Circ: 20,000.

685 ITA
FOTO SHOE 15; il nuovo corriere della calzatura. Text in Italian, English. 1963. 6/yr. adv. charts; illus. **Document type:** *Magazine, Trade.* **Description:** Covers technical information about footwear production: materials, technologies, accessories and component parts.
Former titles: Foto Shoe 15-3 Nuovo Corriere della Calzatura; Nuovo Corriere della Calzatura
Published by: Editoriale di Foto Shoe s.r.l., Via Leonardo da Vinci 43, Trezzano sul Naviglio, MI 20900, Italy. TEL 39-02-4459091, FAX 39-02-48402959, central@fotoshoe.com, http://www.fotoshoe.com. Circ: 14,000.

685.31 CHE
FUSS UND SCHUH. Text in German. 11/yr. **Document type:** *Trade.*
Published by: (Schweizer Schuhmacher- und Orthopaedieschuhmachermeister-Verband), Kretz AG, General Wille-Str 147, Postfach, Feldmeilen, 8706, Switzerland. TEL 41-1-9237656, FAX 41-1-9237657, info@kretzag.ch. Circ: 1,460.

FUTURA. *see* CLOTHING TRADE—Fashions

685.31 HKG
HONG KONG FOOTWEAR. Text in English. 1997. s-a. adv. **Document type:** *Magazine, Trade.* **Description:** Covers Hong Kong footwear industry.
Related titles: Online - full content ed.
Published by: Hong Kong Trade Development Council, 38th Fl Office Tower, Convention Plaza, 1 Harbour Rd, Wanchai, Hong Kong. TEL 852-1830668, FAX 852-28240249, publications@tdc.org.hk, http://www.tdc.org.hk. adv.: color page HKD 13,000; 213 x 280. Circ: 30,000.

THE INTERNATIONAL DIRECTORY OF LEATHER GOODS, FOOTWEAR AND TRAVEL ACCESSORIES IMPORTERS. *see* BUSINESS AND ECONOMICS—Trade And Industrial Directories

685.31 FIN ISSN 0021-4078
JALKINE. Text in Finnish. 1933. q. adv. illus. **Document type:** *Magazine, Trade.*
Published by: Suutariliikkeiden Liitto, Kauppakatu 2-4, Kuusankeski, 45700, Finland. pallaute@suutari.info, http://www.suutari.info. Ed. Pertti Loennqvist. adv.: B&W page EUR 250, color page EUR 340; 170 x 265. Circ: 500 (controlled).

688.76 ITA
JOGGING; sports shoes collection. Text in Italian. 2/yr. adv. **Document type:** *Magazine, Trade.*
Published by: Ars Arpel Group srl, Via Ippolito Nievo 33, Milan, 20145, Italy. TEL 39-02-319121, FAX 39-02-33611619, arsarpel@arsarpel.it, http://www.arsarpel.it.

685.31 ITA
JOLLY; men's shoes collection. Text in Italian. 2/yr. **Document type:** *Magazine, Trade.*
Formerly: Professional
Published by: Ars Arpel Group srl, Via Ippolito Nievo 33, Milan, 20145, Italy. TEL 39-02-319121, FAX 39-02-33611619, arsarpel@arsarpel.it, http://www.arsarpel.it.

685.31 ITA
JULIA; women's shoes collection. Text in Italian. 4/yr. **Document type:** *Magazine, Trade.*
Published by: Ars Arpel Group srl, Via Ippolito Nievo 33, Milan, 20145, Italy. TEL 39-02-319121, FAX 39-02-33611619, arsarpel@arsarpel.it, http://www.arsarpel.it.

685.31 ITA
JUNIOR; children's shoes collection. Text in Italian. 2/yr. adv. **Document type:** *Magazine, Trade.*
Published by: Ars Arpel Group srl, Via Ippolito Nievo 33, Milan, 20145, Italy. TEL 39-02-319121, FAX 39-02-33611619, arsarpel@arsarpel.it, http://www.arsarpel.it. Ed. Laura Muggiani Sancini. Adv. contact Alberto Clima.

685.31 POL ISSN 1640-9485
KATALOG RYNEK OBUWNICZY. Text in Polish. 2000. a. PLZ 19.90 (effective 2011). adv. **Document type:** *Catalog, Trade.*
Formerly (until 2001): Katalog Buty (1508-5058)
Published by: Unit Wydawnictwo Informacje Branzowe Sp. z o.o., ul Kierbedzia 4, Warsaw, 00-728, Poland. TEL 48-22-3201500, FAX 48-22-3201506, info@unit.com.pl, http://www.unit.com.pl. Ed. Joanna Banakiewicz-Brzozowska. Adv. contact Mariola Cynalewska.

KAWA TO HAKIMONO/LEATHER & FOOTWEARS. *see* LEATHER AND FUR INDUSTRIES

KEY NOTE PLUS MARKET REPORT. FOOTWEAR. *see* BUSINESS AND ECONOMICS—Production Of Goods And Services

KIDS MAGAZINE; het vakblad voor kindermode en -schoenen in de Benelux. *see* CLOTHING TRADE—Fashions

KOZARSTVI/LEATHER INDUSTRY; odborny casopis pro prumysl kozedelny, obuvnicky galanterni a kozesnicky. *see* LEATHER AND FUR INDUSTRIES

685.31 RUS ISSN 0023-4354
CODEN: KOOPAJ
KOZHEVENNO-OBUVNAYA PROMYSHLENNOST'. Text in Russian. 1959. bi-m. USD 194 foreign (effective 2005). adv. bibl.; illus. **Document type:** *Journal, Trade.* **Description:** Presents scientific and technical, economic and social development of the leather, fur and footwear industry.
Indexed: CIN, CISA, ChemAb, ChemTitl, RASB, RefZh.
—CASDDS, East View, INIST. **CCC.**
Address: B Kommunisticheskaya 6-a, Moscow, 109004, Russian Federation. TEL 7-095-9119469, FAX 7-095-9112776. **Dist. by:** East View Information Services, 10601 Wayzata Blvd, Minneapolis, MN 55305. TEL 952-252-1201, 800-477-1005, FAX 952-252-1202, info@eastview.com, http://www.eastview.com.

685 ITA
LEATHER TECHNOLOGY. Text in Italian, English. 1963. s-a. illus. **Document type:** *Magazine, Trade.*
Published by: Editoriale di Foto Shoe s.r.l., Via Leonardo da Vinci 43, Trezzano sul Naviglio, MI 20900, Italy. TEL 39-02-4459091, FAX 39-02-48402959, central@fotoshoe.com, http://www.fotoshoe.com. Ed. G Fossati. Circ: 18,200.

685.31 ESP ISSN 0211-7827
MODAPIEL. Text in English, Spanish. 1969. q. EUR 82 domestic; EUR 210 in Europe; EUR 226 elsewhere (effective 2010). adv. illus. **Document type:** *Magazine, Trade.*
Related titles: Online - full text ed.
Published by: Prensa Tecnica S.A., Caspe 118-120, 6o, Barcelona, 08013, Spain. TEL 34-93-2455190, FAX 34-93-2322773, http://www.prensa-tecnica.com. Ed. F Canet Tomas.

685.31 ITA
NEWS - FOOTWEAR & LEATHER NEWS JOURNAL. Text in English. adv.
Published by: Ars Arpel Group srl, Via Ippolito Nievo 33, Milan, 20145, Italy. TEL 39-02-319121, FAX 39-02-33611619, arsarpel@arsarpel.it, http://www.arsarpel.it.

685.31 DEU ISSN 0344-6026
ORTHOPAEDIE-SCHUHTECHNIK; Die Zeitschrift fuer Fussexperten. Text in German. 1949. 11/yr. EUR 114.80 domestic; EUR 116.70 foreign; EUR 11 newsstand/cover (effective 2009). adv. bk.rev. illus. index. **Document type:** *Magazine, Trade.*
Formerly (until 1978): Orthopaedieschuhmachermeister (0030-5871)
Published by: (Bundesinnungsverband fuer Orthopaedie-Technik), C. Maurer Druck und Verlag, Schubartstr 21, Geislingen, 73312, Germany. TEL 49-7331-9300, FAX 49-7331-930190, info@maurer-online.de, http://www.maurer-online.de. Ed., R&P Wolfgang Best. Adv. contact Sybille Lutz. B&W page EUR 1,850, color page EUR 3,200; trim 185 x 262. Circ: 3,912 (paid and controlled).

ORTHOPEDISCHE TECHNIEK. *see* MEDICAL SCIENCES—Orthopedics And Traumatology

685.31 USA
PRICE LINE: IMPORTS AND EXPORTS. Text in English. m. USD 175 to members; USD 350 to non-members. **Description:** Presents detailed monthly reports chart the global trade on U.S. footwear. Tables include footwear trade by country, price point, gender catagories and upper materials.
Published by: Footwear Industries of America, 1601 N Kent St Ste 1200, Arlington, DC 22209-2105. TEL 202-789-1420, 800-688-7653, FAX 202-789-4058.

685.31 646.4 NLD ISSN 1876-813X
THE RIGHT SIZE; vakblad voor de schoenenbranche in de Benelux. Text in Dutch. 2008. bi-m. EUR 45 (effective 2011). adv. **Document type:** *Magazine, Trade.*
Related titles: Online - full text ed.: ISSN 1876-8148.
Published by: Maruba b.v., Winthontlaan 200, Utrecht, 3526 KV, Netherlands. TEL 31-30-2891073, FAX 31-30-2887415, maruba@maruba.com, http://www.maruba.nl. Pub., Adv. contact Maas H van Drie. Circ: 3,500.

685.31 ZAF
S & V; the journal for southern Africa's footwear and accessories industries. (Shoes and Views) Text in English. 1935. bi-m. ZAR 342 domestic; ZAR 495 in Africa; EUR 150 elsewhere (effective 2008); subscr. includes S & V Trade Directory. adv. illus. **Document type:** *Magazine, Trade.*
Formerly: Shoes and Views
Published by: Shoe Search CC, PO Box 47197, Greyville, Durban, KwaZulu-Natal 4023, South Africa. TEL 27-31-2097505, FAX 27-31-2097506, tony@svmag.co.za, http://www.sv-directories.co.za. Ed., Pub., R&P Tony Dickson. Adv. contact Pierre Lailvaux. B&W page ZAR 3,758, color page ZAR 5,498. Circ: 2,200.

685.31 ZAF
S & V TRADE DIRECTORY. (Shoes and Views) Text in English. 1977. a. ZAR 342 domestic; ZAR 495 in Africa; EUR 150 elsewhere (effective 2008); includes subscr. to S & V magazine. adv. **Document type:** *Directory, Trade.* **Description:** Lists manufacturers, wholesalers, suppliers, institutions, retailers, agents and brand names throughout southern Africa and many neighboring states.
Former titles: Shoes and Views Trade Directory; Shoes and Views Telephone and Telex Directory; (until 1983): Shoes and Leather Trades Directory of Southern Africa
Published by: Shoe Search CC, PO Box 47197, Greyville, Durban, KwaZulu-Natal 4023, South Africa. TEL 27-31-2097505, FAX 27-31-2097506, tony@svmag.co.za, http://www.sv-directories.co.za. Ed., Pub., R&P Tony Dickson. Adv. contact Joanne Dickson.

685.31 ITA
SAFETY. Text in English, Italian. s-a. **Document type:** *Magazine, Trade.* **Description:** Dedicated to safety shoes and related matters.
Published by: Editoriale di Foto Shoe s.r.l., Via Leonardo da Vinci 43, Trezzano sul Naviglio, MI 20900, Italy. TEL 39-02-4459091, FAX 39-02-48402959, central@fotoshoe.com, http://www.fotoshoe.com.

685.31 NLD ISSN 0036-6269
SCHOEN - VISIE; vakblad voor schoenhandel en schoenindustrie. Short title: S V. Text in Dutch. 1959. 10/yr. EUR 115.80; EUR 60.32 to students (effective 2010). adv. charts; illus.; stat.; tr.lit. **Document type:** *Trade.* **Description:** Covers all aspects of shoes: manufacture, import, sales and repair.
Indexed: KES.
Published by: MYbusinessmedia b.v., Joan Muyskensweg 22, Amsterdam, 1096 CJ, Netherlands. TEL 31-20-4602201, FAX 31-20-4602244, info@mybusinessmedia.nl, http://www.mybusinessmedia.nl. Ed. Rosanne Loffeld. Pub. Hein Bronk. adv.: page EUR 2,750; trim 230 x 300.

685.31 DEU ISSN 0036-7044
HD9780.G3
SCHUH-KURIER. Text in German. 1946. w. EUR 188 domestic; EUR 247 foreign (effective 2008). adv. bibl.; mkt.; pat.; tr.mk. index. **Document type:** *Magazine, Trade.*
Indexed: KES.
Published by: Verlag Otto Sternefeld GmbH, Oberkasseler Str 100, Duesseldorf, 40545, Germany. TEL 49-211-577080, FAX 49-211-5770812, sk.vertrieb@sternefeld.de. Ed. Petra Salewski. Adv. contact Sabine Peters. B&W page EUR 2,498, color page EUR 4,328; 210 x 297. Circ: 8,830 (paid and controlled).

685.31 AUT
SCHUH-REVUE UND LEDERWAREN. Text in German. 1946. 16/yr. EUR 46; EUR 2.40 newsstand/cover (effective 2005). adv. **Document type:** *Magazine, Trade.*
Former titles: Schuh-Revue; Oesterreichische Schuhhaendler (0029-9456)
Related titles: Online - full text ed.: ISSN 1605-1343.
Published by: Springer Business Media Austria GmbH (Subsidiary of: Springer Science+Business Media), Inkustr 16, Klosterneuburg, 3403, Austria. TEL 43-2243-301110, FAX 43-2243-30111222, office@springer-sbm.at, http://www.springer-sbm.at. Ed. Ute Held. Adv. contact Renate Greiter. B&W page EUR 2,164, color page EUR 3,059. Circ: 4,000 (paid and controlled).

685.31 DEU
SCHUHMACHER FACHREPORT. Text in German. 4/yr. free. **Document type:** *Trade.*
Published by: Ingo Geisler Verlag, Am Brueckfeld 10, Willmering, 93497, Germany. TEL 49-9971-40506, FAX 49-9971-40504. Circ: 21,400.

685.31 DEU ISSN 0036-7079
SCHUHMARKT. Text in German. 1891. 27/yr. EUR 199; EUR 99.50 to students (effective 2010). adv. **Document type:** *Journal, Trade.*
Incorporates (1942-1982): Schuh-Wirtschaft (0036-7087); Which incorporated (1952-1978): Schuh im Bild (0036-7036)
—CCC.
Published by: (Bundesverband des Deutschen Schuheinzelhandels), Verlag Chmielorz GmbH und Co., Marktplatz 13, Wiesbaden, 65183, Germany. TEL 49-611-360980, FAX 49-611-301303, info@chmielorz.de, http://www.chmielorz.de. Ed. Peter Skop. Adv. contact Ilona Kirmes. Circ: 8,273 (controlled).

685.31 DNK ISSN 1602-2076
SHOE & BAG TRENDS. Text in Danish. 1985. q. adv. **Document type:** *Magazine, Trade.*
Former titles (until 2000): Laedervarer (1601-3026); (until 1998): Laedervarer i Glostrup (0906-6462); Which superseded in part (in 1992): Sko & Laedervarer (0901-0114); Which was formed by the merger of (1952-1985): Skomagasinet (0037-6388); (1961-1985): Laedervare-nyt (0901-1102)
Published by: Scandinavian Shoe Centre A/S, Center Boulevard 5, Copenhagen S, 2300, Denmark. TEL 45-32-473727, FAX 45-32-473787, ssc@shoe-centre.dk, http://www.shoe-centre.dk. Ed. Susanne Nonboe Jacobsen. Adv. contact Ellen Bak. color page DKK 4,500; 210 x 297.

685.31 AUT
SHOE & STYLE. Text in German. q. adv. **Document type:** *Magazine, Consumer.*
Published by: (Stiefelkoenig), D+R Verlagsgesellschaft mbH, Leberstr 122, Vienna, 1110, Austria. TEL 43-1-740770, FAX 43-1-74077841, office@d-r.at. Ed. Uschi Korda. Adv. contact Alexander Bechstein. B&W page EUR 5,395.96, color page EUR 7,194.61; trim 225 x 300. Circ: 100,000 (controlled).

685.31029 CAN
THE SHOE FACTORY BUYER'S GUIDE; directory of suppliers to the shoe manufacturing industry. Text in English. a. USD 59 per issue (effective 2002). adv. back issues avail. **Document type:** *Directory, Trade.* **Description:** Lists the suppliers to the American footwear and related industries, classified according to goods and services. Over 600 companies are listed with more than 400 classifications.
Published by: Shoe Trades Publications, 241 Senneville Rd, Senneville, PQ H9X 3X5, Canada. TEL 514-457-8787, 800-973-7463, FAX 514-457-5832. Circ: 2,000.

685.31 USA ISSN 0886-0963
SHOE RETAILING TODAY. Text in English. 1912. bi-m. USD 35 domestic to non-members; USD 50 foreign to non-members (effective 2006). adv. bk.rev. **Document type:** *Magazine, Trade.* **Description:** Covers trends in the shoe retailing industry.
Formerly: N S R A News
Published by: National Shoe Retailers Association, 7150 Columbia Gateway Dr, Ste G, Columbia, MD 21046-1151. TEL 410-381-8282, FAX 410-381-1167, info@nsra.org. Ed. Nancy Hultquist. Pub. William Boettge. R&P, Adv. contact Lauren McCray. Circ: 6,000 (paid).

338 USA
HD9787.U4
SHOE STATS. Text in English. 1975. a. (plus Statistical Reporter). USD 350 to non-members; USD 225 to libraries (effective 1999). stat. **Document type:** *Report, Trade.* **Description:** Analysis of today's industry including marketing, consumption, manufacturing, and international trade.
Formerly: Footwear Manual (0095-1048); Supersedes: Facts and Figures on Footwear (0362-3890)
Related titles: Microfiche ed.: (from CIS).
Indexed: SRI.
Published by: Footwear Industries of America, 1601 N Kent St Ste 1200, Arlington, DC 22209-2105. TEL 202-789-1420, 800-688-7653, FAX 202-789-4058. Circ: 300.

685.3 CAN
SHOEMAKING INTERNATIONAL. Text in English. 1901. bi-m. CAD 60 domestic; USD 40 in United States; USD 70 elsewhere (effective 2005). adv. charts; illus.; mkt.; stat. **Document type:** *Magazine, Trade.* **Description:** Examines shoe manufacturing, suggesting better shoemaking techniques.
Formerly (until 2003): American Shoemaking (0003-1038)
—CCC.
Published by: Shoe Trades Publications, 241 Senneville Rd, Senneville, PQ H9X 3X5, Canada. TEL 514-457-8787, 800-973-7463, FAX 514-457-5832, info@shoetrades.com, http://www.shoetrades.com. Ed. Inta Huns. Circ: 3,000 (paid).

685.3 DEU
SHOEZ; Was in der Branche laeuft. Text in German. 14/yr. EUR 39.90; EUR 4 newsstand/cover (effective 2008). adv. **Document type:** *Magazine, Trade.*
Published by: Profashional Media GmbH, Im Westpark 15, Wettenberg, 35435, Germany. TEL 49-641-795080, FAX 49-641-7950815. Ed., Adv. contact Manfred Willsch. B&W page EUR 3,890, color page EUR 4,900. Circ: 12,840 (paid and controlled).

685.31 NOR ISSN 0802-653X
SKO (NORWAY). Text in Norwegian. 1972. 6/yr. NOK 590 (effective 2002). adv. charts; illus.
Formerly (until 1980): Skotoey (0049-0679); Which was formed by the merger of (1928-1971): Norsk Skotoey (0029-2133); (1930-1971): Skotoidetaljisten (0037-6574)
Published by: Skoforlaget AS, Drammensvn 154, Oslo, 0277, Norway. TEL 47-22-56-39-10, FAX 47-22-56-31-76. Ed. Tove T. Riiser-Larsen TEL 47-22-56-39-11. Adv. contact Sigrun Boehn TEL 47-22-40-45-41. B&W page NOK 6,300, color page NOK 10,900; 185 x 260. Circ: 1,034.

685.31 SWE ISSN 1653-7793
SKO & MODE. Text in Swedish. 1942. 8/yr. SEK 650 (effective 2006). adv. bk.rev. **Document type:** *Magazine, Trade.*
Formerly (until 2006): Skohandlaren (0346-1300)
Published by: Skohandlarens Foerlags AB, Regeringsgatan 60, Stockholm, 10329, Sweden. TEL 46-8-7627620, FAX 46-8-7627622. Ed. Harriet Lindesmark. adv.: page SEK 15,900; 185 x 240. Circ: 4,000.

685.31 DNK ISSN 0909-3826
SKO - SHOES & MORE. Text in Danish. 1985. 9/yr. adv. illus.; stat. **Document type:** *Magazine, Trade.*
Formerly (until 1993): Sko og Laedervarer (0901-0114); Which was formed by the merger of (1952-1985): Skomagasinet (0037-6388); (1961-1985): Laedervare-Nyt (0901-1102)
Published by: Danmarks Skohandlerforening, Svanemoellevej 41, PO Box 34, Hellerup, 2900, Denmark. TEL 45-33-914607, FAX 45-33-914608, bm@skohandlerforening.dk, http://www.skohandlerforening.dk. Adv. contact Bente Mikkelsen. B&W page DKK 4,600; 262 x 183.

685.31 AUS
SNEAKER FREAKER. Text in English. 2003. 3/yr. free to members (effective 2009). adv. **Document type:** *Magazine, Consumer.* **Description:** Provides information about shoes.
Related titles: Online - full text ed.
Published by: Sneaker Freaker Magazine, PO Box 1571, Collingwood, VIC 3066, Australia. TEL 61-3-98269596, FAX 61-3-98266214, info@sneakerfreaker.com. Ed. Woody .

685.3 DEU
STEP FASHION. Text in German. 1996. 4/yr. EUR 46 domestic; EUR 56 foreign (effective 2011); includes Edition Schuhe. adv. **Document type:** *Magazine, Trade.* **Description:** Trade magazine for shoes with reports on fashion trends, stores and brands.
Published by: Verlag Otto Sternefeld GmbH, Oberkasseler Str 100, Duesseldorf, 40545, Germany. TEL 49-211-577080, FAX 49-211-5770812, sk.vertrieb@sternefeld.de. adv.: B&W page EUR 2,555, color page EUR 4,085. Circ: 15,500 (paid and controlled).

685.3 DEU
STEPTECHNIK. Text in German. 1999. 4/yr. EUR 40 domestic; EUR 45 foreign (effective 2011). adv. **Document type:** *Magazine, Trade.*
Published by: Verlag Otto Sternefeld GmbH, Oberkasseler Str 100, Duesseldorf, 40545, Germany. TEL 49-211-577080, FAX 49-211-5770812, sk.vertrieb@sternefeld.de. adv.: B&W page EUR 2,000, color page EUR 2,921; trim 179 x 270. Circ: 5,000 (paid and controlled).

STICHTING VRIENDENKRING VAN HET NEDERLANDS LEDER EN SCHOENEN MUSEUM. NIEUWSBRIEF. *see* LEATHER AND FUR INDUSTRIES

685.31 DEU
SUEDWESTDEUTSCHER EINZELHANDEL (STUTTGART). Text in German. m.
Published by: Verband des Schuh-Einzelhandels Baden-Wuerttemberg e.V., Neue Weinsteige 44, Stuttgart, 70180, Germany. TEL 603025.

685.31 POL ISSN 1428-3905
SWIAT BUTOW. Text in Polish. 1997. m. PLZ 70 (effective 2011). adv.
Published by: Unit Wydawnictwo Informacje Branzowe Sp. z o.o., ul Kierbedzia 4, Warsaw, 00-728, Poland. TEL 48-22-3201500, FAX 48-22-3201506, info@unit.com.pl. Ed. Joanna Banakiewicz-Brzozowska. Adv. contact Mariola Cynalewska.

685.31 ITA ISSN 0394-9796
TECNICA CALZATURIERA. Text in English, Italian. 1963. q. EUR 35 domestic; EUR 70 in Europe; EUR 90 elsewhere (effective 2011). adv. abstr.; illus. **Document type:** *Magazine, Trade.* **Description:** Features articles on manufacturing in the shoe industry. Covers machinery, fashion and materials.
Related titles: Online - full text ed.
Published by: Tecniche Nuove SpA, Via Eritrea 21, Milan, MI 201, Italy. TEL 39-02-390901, FAX 39-02-7570364, info@tecnichenuove.com. Ed. Stefania Parisi.

685.31 ESP ISSN 0211-3961
TECNICA DEL CALZADO. Text in Spanish, English. 1968. q. EUR 29 domestic; EUR 151 in Europe; EUR 167 elsewhere (effective 2010). adv. abstr.; bibl.; charts; illus.; pat.; stat.; tr.lit. **Document type:** *Magazine, Trade.*
Related titles: Online - full text ed.
Indexed: TM.
Published by: Prensa Tecnica S.A., Caspe 118-120, 6o, Barcelona, 08013, Spain. TEL 34-93-2455190, FAX 34-93-2322773, http://www.prensa-tecnica.com. Ed. F Canet Tomas.

685.31 NLD ISSN 0169-6173
TRED. Text in Dutch. 1981. m. EUR 89.90 domestic; EUR 97.25 in Belgium (effective 2008). adv. **Document type:** *Magazine, Trade.*
Published by: Blauw Media Uitgeverij B.V., Postbus 1043, Maarssen, 3600 BA, Netherlands. TEL 31-346-574040, FAX 31-346-576056, info@blauwmedia.com. Pub. Henk Louwmans. Adv. contact Jauke Louwmans. B&W page EUR 1,590, color page EUR 2,755; trim 235 x 322.

685.37 USA
TWO - TEN TODAY. Text in English. 1939. q. free to members. **Document type:** *Newsletter.* **Description:** Written for members of this charitable organization that provides human services to members of the footwear industry. Highlights programs and member news.
Formerly: Two - Ten Foundation Update
Published by: Two Ten International Footwear Foundation, 1466 Main St, Waltham, MA 02451-1623. TEL 781-736-1500, 800-346-3210, FAX 781-736-1555, pmeill@twoten.org, info@twoten.org, http://www.twoten.org. Ed. Carol Kennedy. Circ: 12,000 (controlled).

685.31 NLD ISSN 1570-520X
VAKNIEUWS. Text in Dutch. 1922. q. EUR 40 domestic; EUR 46 in Belgium (effective 2008). adv. illus. reprints avail. **Document type:** *Magazine, Trade.* **Description:** Covers national and international news of interest to members of the shoe manufacturing, sales and repair industries.
Formed by the 2002 merger of: Schoenwereld (0036-6307); Unie Info (1384-3796)
Indexed: SpeleolAb.
Published by: Advies en Secretariatenbureau Waldhober van Stuijvenberg VOF, Noordenseweg 1, Nieuwkoop, 2421 XW, Netherlands. TEL 31-172-575888, FAX 31-172-575266, info@asws.nl, http://www.asws.nl/. Eds. Elly van Stuijvenberg, Ruud Waldhober.

685.31 USA ISSN 1940-8269
W S A TODAY. (World Shoe Association) Text in English. 2006. m. free to qualified personnel (effective 2008). **Document type:** *Magazine, Trade.* **Description:** Features the latest and industry news and trends for buyers and retailers responsible for purchasing footwear and accessories.
Published by: W S A Global Holdings, 15821 Ventura Blvd, Ste 415, Encino, CA 91436. TEL 818-379-9400.

685.31 CAN ISSN 0894-3079
WORLD FOOTWEAR. Text in English. 1987. q. USD 95 (effective 2004). adv. **Document type:** *Magazine, Trade.* **Description:** Directed to shoe manufacturers worldwide.
—IE, Infotrieve. **CCC.**
Published by: Shoe Trades Publications, 241 Senneville Rd, Senneville, PQ H9X 3X5, Canada. TEL 514-457-8787, 800-973-7463, FAX 514-457-5832, info@shoetrades.com. adv.: B&W page USD 4,120. Circ: 10,985 (paid and controlled).

SHOES AND BOOTS—Abstracting, Bibliographies, Statistics

500.021 CAN ISSN 1192-3385
CANADA. STATISTICS CANADA. INDUSTRIAL RESEARCH AND DEVELOPMENT (YEAR) INTENTIONS/CANADA. STATISTIQUE CANADA. RECHERCHE ET DEVELOPPEMENT INDUSTRIELS (ANNEE) PERSPECTIVE. Text in English. 1983. a. CAD 78. **Document type:** *Government.*
Formerly (until 1992): Industrial Research and Development Statistics (0824-8133)
Published by: Statistics Canada, Operations and Integration Division (Subsidiary of: Statistics Canada/Statistique Canada), Circulation Management, 120 Parkdale Ave, Ottawa, ON K1A 0T6, Canada. TEL 613-951-7277, 800-267-6677, FAX 613-951-1584.

SINGLES' INTERESTS AND LIFESTYLES

051 USA ISSN 1553-7730
ACTIVE SINGLE'S LIFE. Text in English. 1973. m. USD 20 (effective 2003). adv. bk.rev.; film rev. **Document type:** *Newspaper, Consumer.* **Description:** Deals with the life-styles of single adults in the Northwest. Includes self-help articles, personal ads, and features on local well-known singles.

S

Published by: Voice Publishing, PO Box 98080, Des Moines, WA 98198-0080. TEL 206-243-8536, FAX 206-243-1956, http://www.nwasl.com. Ed., R&P Walt Briem. Adv. contact Stephanie Moore. Circ: 10,000.

051 917.93 USA ISSN 1041-4002
ALASKAMEN U S A. Text in English. 1990 (vol.3, no.2). bi-m. USD 49.95 domestic; USD 54.95 in Canada & Mexico; USD 63 elsewhere; USD 6.95 newsstand/cover domestic; USD 8.95 newsstand/cover in Canada (effective 2000). adv. illus. **Document type:** *Magazine, Consumer.* **Description:** Introduces single men in Alaska for interested single women.
Formerly: AlaskaMen
Published by: Alaska Quest Publisher, 205 E Dimond Blvd, 522, Anchorage, AK 99515-2099. TEL 907-522-1492, 907-522-1401, FAX 907-344-1493. Ed., Pub. Susie Carter Smutz.

790.1 USA ISSN 1075-6906
ALTERNATIVE LIFESTYLES DIRECTORY. Text in English. irreg., latest vol.2. USD 22; USD 20 in Canada; USD 24 elsewhere. **Document type:** *Directory.* **Description:** Lists more than 550 publications of interest to persons leading alternative life-styles. Contains sexually explicit material.
Published by: Winter Publishing Inc., PO Box 80667, Dartmouth, MA 02748. TEL 508-994-2908.

BOX. *see* SPORTS AND GAMES

BOYS TOYS. *see* MEN'S INTERESTS

051 USA
C T SINGLES CONNECTION; the magazine for sophisticated singles. (Connecticut) Text in English. 1997. m. free (effective 2000). adv. **Document type:** *Magazine, Consumer.* **Description:** Contains personal ads, list of singles clubs and singles activities in Connecticut.
Published by: M E A A Publishing, 30 Orchard Rd, East Haddam, CT 06423-0119. Ed. Shelley Kosky. Pub., R&P, Adv. contact Leland W Morgan. B&W page USD 200, color page USD 250; trim 7.25 x 9.75. Circ: 10,000 (free).

CHRISTIAN SINGLE; the magazine for successful single living. *see* RELIGIONS AND THEOLOGY—Protestant

051 USA
CHRISTIAN SINGLES; news and contacts. Text in English. 1987. m. USD 29.95 domestic membership; USD 44.95 foreign membership; USD 2 newsstand/cover (effective 1999). adv. bk.rev. illus. **Document type:** *Newspaper, Consumer.* **Description:** For Christian singles and churches. Contains articles on establishing and cultivating relationships, plus 600-700 Christian personal ads per issue.
Formerly: U S A Singles News
Published by: Christian Singles International, PO Box 100, Harrison, OH 45030. TEL 513-598-8900, FAX 513-598-8788. Ed., R&P James Lloyd Sloan. Adv. contact Carol Neal. Circ: 90,000.

051 USA
CONCERNED SINGLES NEWSLETTER. Text in English. 1984. bi-m. USD 60 domestic; USD 65 in Canada & Mexico; USD 70 elsewhere (effective 2000). adv. **Document type:** *Newsletter.* **Description:** Links compatible singles who care about peace, social justice, civil rights, gender equity, and the environment.
Published by: Concerned Singles, PO Box 444, Lenox, MA 01242-0444. TEL 413-445-6309, FAX 413-243-3066. Ed., Pub. Rodelinde Albrecht. Adv. contact Jack Handler.

051 USA
CONVERSELY. Text in English. 2000. m.
Published by: Conversely, Inc., 3053 Fillmore St., San Francisco, CA 94123-4009. Ed. Alejandro Gutierrez.

051 USA
COUNTRY CONNECTIONS (SUPERIOR). Text in English. 1986. m. USD 75 (effective 2007). 4 p./no. 2 cols./p.; back issues avail. **Document type:** *Magazine, Consumer.* **Description:** Provides information for country singles.
Published by: Superior Publishing Co., 148 E. Third St., Superior, NE 68978. TEL 402-879-3291, FAX 402-879-3463, bblauvelt@alltel.net, http://www.superiorne.com. Pub. Bill Blauvelt. Adv. contact Rita Blauvelt. Circ: 750 (paid).

051 USA
COUNTRYSINGLES.COM. Text in English. m. adv. **Description:** Covers North Dakota, South Dakota, Iowa, Nebraska, and Minnesota.
Formerly (until 2001): Solo R F D (Rural Free Delivery) (Print)
Media: Online - full text.
Published by: Country Singles, PO Box 2139, Sioux Falls, SD 57101. TEL 800-825-6632, FAX 605-335-6659, publisher@countrysingles.com.

790.1 USA
CUIR UNDERGROUND. Text in English. 10/yr. USD 20. illus. **Document type:** *Newspaper.* **Description:** Contains sexually explicit material for persons in the San Francisco Bay area interested in sadomasochism.
Address: 3288 21st St, 19, San Francisco, CA 94110.

052 GBR
DATELINE MAGAZINE. Text in English. 1977. 12/yr. GBP 24 in Europe; GBP 42 elsewhere (effective 1999); GBP 2 newsstand/cover. **Document type:** *Magazine, Consumer.* **Description:** Articles of interest to single people. Includes activities, meeting places, plus personal classified ads.
Former titles: Singles; (1982-1984): Select; Singles
Published by: Dateline, c/o John Patterson, 25 Abingdon Rd, London, W8 6AL, United Kingdom. TEL 44-1869-351525, FAX 071-937-3146. **Dist. by:** Tristar Distribution Ltd., PO Box 3954, Witham, Essex CM8 3UI, United Kingdom. TEL 44-1376-534555.

051 USA
FAIRY DUST. Text in English. 1996. m. free. **Description:** Articles regarding a wide array of topics, basically entertainment.
Media: Online - full text.
Address: fairydust@usa.net. Ed. Liz Shapiro.

051 600 USA ISSN 1061-6977
FUTURE SEX. Text in English. 1992. q. USD 18. adv. bk.rev. illus. **Document type:** *Magazine, Consumer.* **Description:** Covers the evolution of eroticism in the 90s, including cybersex and the impact of computer and information technology on sex.
Published by: Kundalini Publishing, Inc., 170 Columbus Ave, San Francisco, CA 94133. TEL 415-395-9488, FAX 415-621-4946. Ed. Lisa Palac. Adv. contact Brett Beutel.

051 USA ISSN 0882-8598
GET - TWO - GETHER. Text in English. 1981. m. USD 15. adv.
Published by: Get - Two - Gether Inc., PO Box 273344, Fort Collins, CO 80527-3344. TEL 303-221-4544, FAX 303-221-0234. Ed. Gary F Hirt. Circ: 4,500.

GETTING READY; a resource for independent living. *see* LIFESTYLE

GREAT RESTAURANTS OF LONG ISLAND. *see* FOOD AND FOOD INDUSTRIES

296 051 USA
JEWISH SINGLES MAGAZINE (BLOOMFIELD). Text in English. irreg. adv.
Address: PO Box 728, Bloomfield, CT 06002. TEL 203-243-1514.

296 051 USA
JEWISH SINGLES MAGAZINE (NEWTON). Text in English. 1983. m. USD 20. adv. bk.rev.
Formerly: Jewish Singles
Published by: Mark B. Golden, Ed. & Pub., PO Box 247, Newton, MA 02159-0002. TEL 617-278-4330. Circ: 50,000.

051 USA
LARGE ENCOUNTERS SINGLES. Text in English. 1990. bi-m. free (effective 2000). 24 p./no. 4 cols./p.; **Document type:** *Newspaper.* **Description:** Provides information for plus size women and men nationwide who would like to meet plus size women and men through personal ads and singles functions.
Published by: Large Encounters Inc., PO Box 1456, Seaford, NY 11783. TEL 576-409-1500, FAX 576-409-1828. R&P Mindy Watson TEL 516-409-1827. Circ: 35,000.

051 USA
LIFESTYLE SOUTHERN CALIFORNIA; single adults news & events. Text in English. 1967. bi-m. USD 7. adv. bk.rev.; film rev.; play rev. back issues avail. **Description:** Discusses relationships, medical issues, theater, wine and travel. Includes calendar of events, astrological forecasts and personals.
Formerly: Singles Critique
Published by: Gladys Smith & Associates, PO Box 5062, Sherman Oaks, CA 91413-5062. TEL 818-980-4786. Ed. R H Smith Jr. Circ: 40,000.

051 USA
LONG ISLAND SWINGERS MAGAZINE. Text in English. 1981. q. USD 12 per issue. **Description:** Provides Long Island sadomasochists with personal ads, many accompanied by photographs.
Published by: Bizzare Publishing Co., PO Box 25, Islip, NY 11752-0025. Ed. John Jay. adv.: B&W page USD 650. Circ: 10,000.

051 USA
LOVING ALTERNATIVES MAGAZINE. Text in English. 1990. bi-m. USD 20. bk.rev. back issues avail. **Description:** Dedicated to providing information for the swing community, including personal ads, reviews, editorials, lists of club addresses and events.
Formerly: S S C Magazine
Published by: Omnific Designs West, PO Box 459, San Dimas, CA 91773. TEL 909-593-6110, FAX 818-915-4715. Eds. Cindy Alderson, Ric Alderson. adv.: page USD 140. Circ: 8,000.

051 USA
MICHIGAN'S MOST ELIGIBLE BACHELORS AND BACHELORETTES. Text in English. 2004 (Feb.). irreg. USD 19.95 newsstand/cover (effective 2004). **Document type:** *Magazine, Consumer.*
Published by: JCBennett Company, 201114, Ferndale, MI 48220-9114.

MINI EXAMINER. *see* NEW AGE PUBLICATIONS

051 USA ISSN 1541-3136
ONE2ONE LIVING; making real connections. Text in English. 2002. bi-m. USD 29.99; USD 3.50 newsstand/cover (effective 2004). adv. **Document type:** *Magazine, Consumer.* **Description:** Aims to help single men and women attract and sustain fulfilling relationships.
Published by: One2One Magazine, 9903 Santa Monica Blvd, Ste 175, Beverly Hills, CA 90212. TEL 310-854-4255, editor@one2onemag.com. Ed. Ken Hatlestad.

796 USA
OUTDOOR SINGLES NETWORK. Text in English. 1989. q. USD 55 per issue; USD 75 print & online eds. (effective 2004). adv. **Document type:** *Newsletter, Consumer.* **Description:** Brings together outdoor-loving singles, ages 19-90. Includes personal ads and articles of interest to outdoor loving singles in US, Canada, and overseas.
Related titles: Online - full content ed.: USD 35 (effective 2004).
Published by: O S N - U, PO Box 781, Haines, AK 99827-0781. TEL 907-766-3517. Ed., Pub., R&P, Adv. contact Kathleen Menke.

790.1 793.2 USA
PALM BEACH YOUNG SOCIETY. Text in English. 1999. m. (Nov.-Apr.). USD 18; USD 3.50 newsstand/cover (effective 2007). adv. **Document type:** *Magazine, Consumer.* **Description:** Contains columns covering both public and private social and cultural events for young socialites. Includes photographs of the social, charitable, cultural and sports life of the area.
Published by: Palm Beach Society Companies, 240 Worth Ave, Palm Beach, FL 33480. TEL 561-659-5555, FAX 561-655-6209. Ed. James Jennings Sheeran. Pub., Adv. contact Joanne Cutner. B&W page USD 845, color page USD 1,450. Circ: 5,040 (paid).

051 USA
PARANOID BACHELOR GUY; random verbal violence for the young and jaded. Text in English. 1994. every 6 wks. USD 10. back issues avail.
Published by: Xeno - Vision, PO Box 109, Gardena, CA 90248-0109. TEL 310-324-5403.

051 USA
PHILIPPINE AMERICAN CHRISTIAN DATING & FRIENDSHIP SERVICE PEN-PAL BULLETIN; Phil-Am Christian Pen Pals. Text in English. 1995. 2/yr. USD 49.95 (effective 2000). adv. back issues avail. **Document type:** *Catalog.* **Description:** Contains Philippine ladies photographs, addresses and biodata for eligible single men.
Formerly (until 1996): Christian Contender (Navarre) (0893-8571)
Related titles: E-mail ed.; Fax ed.
Published by: American International Enterprises, Inc, 2949 E. Desert Inn Rd, Ste 1, Las Vegas, NV 89121. TEL 850-936-1175, 888-846-7309 ext 2367, johnhansen@mytalk.com, http://www.philippine-ladies.com. Ed., R&P, Adv. contact John P Hansen. B&W page USD 50, color page USD 100. Circ: 75 (paid).

057.87 SVK ISSN 1336-2925
RANDE EXTRA. Text in Slovak. 2003. bi-m. **Document type:** *Magazine, Consumer.*
Published by: Sander Media s.r.o., Bakalarska 2, Prievidza, 97101, Slovakia. TEL 421-46-5439184, FAX 421-46-5439186, sander@sander.sk, http://www.sander.sk.

051 SGP
SHIOK!. Text in English. irreg. **Document type:** *Newsletter, Consumer.* **Description:** Covers the single lifestyle in Singapore, including dating, restaurants, fashion and more.
Published by: Fletchers Communications Pte. Ltd., No.2 Tan Quee Lan St #02-01, Singapore, 188091, Singapore. TEL 65-3396014, FAX 65-3396044, editor@shiok.com.sg, http://www.shiok.com.sg/.

301.412 305.3 USA
SINGLE AGAIN. Text in English. 1976. 6/yr. adv. illus. **Document type:** *Magazine, Consumer.* **Description:** Directed to people who are divorced, separated, or widowed.
Address: 1237 Crescendo Dr, Roseville, CA 95678. Pub. Paul V Scholl. Circ: 10,000.

051 USA ISSN 1084-1040
SINGLE MAGAZINE AND ENTERTAINMENT GUIDE. Text in English. 1965. bi-m. USD 6.95. adv. **Document type:** *Magazine, Consumer.*
Address: PO Box 420966, San Diego, CA 92142-0966. TEL 619-296-6948, FAX 619-571-6136. Ed., Pub. L. Lutzke. R&P L Lutzke TEL 619-292-8049. Adv. contact J Reeve. Circ: 55,000.

051 USA
SINGLE SCENE - ARIZONA. Text in English. 1972. 6/yr. USD 9.50 (effective 2003). adv. bk.rev. stat. back issues avail. **Document type:** *Newspaper, Consumer.* **Description:** Presents a forum for single adults through news, self-help advice, and a calendar of events.
Formerly: Single Scene (0747-4350)
Related titles: Online - full text ed.
Address: PO Box 10159, Scottsdale, AZ 85271. http://www.primenet.com/~singles. Ed., R&P, Adv. contact Janet L Jacobsen. Pub. Harlan L Jacobsen. Circ: 5,000.

051 USA
SINGLE SCOOP CELEBRITY NEWS. Text in English. 1991. 10/yr. USD 12.95; USD 3.99 newsstand/cover. adv. bk.rev.; film rev.; music rev.; tel.rev.; video rev. **Document type:** *Magazine, Trade.* **Description:** Provides entertainment and news coverage for single people. Focuses on celebrity gossip, lifestyle, features, news and current events, and travel.
Related titles: Online - full text ed.
Published by: (SingleVision Television Network), GlobalComm 2000 Corp., 760 Skipper Dr N W, Atlanta, GA 30318-5922. TEL 404-756-9300, FAX 404-755-9407. Ed., R&P Nina Rich. Adv. contact Michael Wilson. page USD 1,600.

301.412 USA ISSN 0738-8578
SINGLE SOURCE NEWSLETTER. Text in English. 1987. a. looseleaf. USD 5 (effective 2007). adv. back issues avail. **Document type:** *Newsletter.* **Description:** Information on singles sources.
Published by: Bibliotheca Press, c/o Prosperity & Profits Unlimited, Distribution Services, Box 416, Denver, CO 80201-0416. TEL 303-575-5676, FAX 970-292-2136, prosperity@breadpudding.net, www.selfpublishing.bigstep.com. Ed. A Doyle. R&P A. Doyle. adv.: page USD 6,000. Circ: 1,500 (paid and controlled).

051 USA ISSN 1050-2998
SINGLE TODAY. Text in English. 1987. bi-m. USD 25 (effective 2000 & 2001). adv. bk.rev. **Document type:** *Newsletter.* **Description:** Allows singles in the Memphis area to meet other singles through an introduction service.
Formerly (until 1989): Memphis Singles
Published by: Septo Enterprises, Inc., 2121 Sycamore View Rd, 445, Memphis, TN 38134-5728. TEL 901-388-9099, FAX 901-388-9083. Ed., Pub., R&P, Adv. contact September Young. Circ: 30,000.

051 USA
SINGLES JOURNAL. Text in English. bi-m. USD 10. adv.
Address: 103 Cobblestone Ln, Cherry Hill, NJ 08003. TEL 609-424-3080.

051 USA
SINGLES LIFELINE. Text in English. 1983. bi-m. USD 7. adv. bk.rev.; film rev.
Published by: Singles Lifeline Co., PO Box 639, Randolph, MA 02368. TEL 617-341-8332, FAX 617-344-7207. Ed. Mark Snyder. Circ: 60,000.

051 USA
SINGLES LIFESTYLE & ENTERTAINMENT MAGAZINE. Text in English. 1997. bi-m.
Published by: Single Lifestyle Publishing Group, 7611 S Orange Blossom Trail #190, Orlando, FL 32809. Ed. Michael Orlando. Circ: 25,000.

051 USA
SINGLES NETWORK; of New York's Capital region. Text in English. 1983. m. USD 30 membership (effective 2003). adv. **Document type:** *Newsletter, Consumer.* **Description:** Covers educational and social activities for adult singles.
Former titles: Singles Outreach Services Newsletter; S O S Newsletter
Published by: Singles Outreach Services, 435 New Karner Rd, PO Box 12511, Albany, NY 12212. TEL 518-452-6883, http://www.singlesoutreach.org/. Ed. Gregg Kim. Circ: 5,500.

051 USA ISSN 1524-797X
SINGLES NETWORK NEWSLETTER. Text in English. 1996. m. USD 24 domestic; USD 40 in Canada; USD 5 to libraries; USD 3 newsstand/cover. adv. bk.rev.; film rev. back issues avail. **Document type:** *Newsletter, Consumer.* **Description:** Contains articles on health, well-being, positive improvement and recovery with source information, support groups, events calendars, books, and advertising geared to single adults.
Related titles: E-mail ed.
Address: PO Box 13, Springfield, VA 22150. TEL 703-690-1757, bonnietexas@mindspring.com, john100@erols.com. Ed., Pub., R&P Bonnie Stephens. Adv. contact Cathryn Crabb. Circ: 250 (paid and controlled). **Dist. by:** 8300 Brookvale Ct, Springfield, VA 22153.

051 USA
SINGLES NEWS MAGAZINE. Text in English. 1975. m. USD 9; USD 20 foreign (effective 1999). adv. bk.rev. **Document type:** *Newspaper.* **Description:** Focuses on singles' interests and lifestyles, including relationships, entertainment, products and services. Contains personal advertising for dating in the northern California area and a calender of events.

Address: PO Box 601061, Sacramento, CA 95860. TEL 916-486-1414, FAX 916-488-1931. Ed., R&P Betty Lu Moore. Pub. Michael P Moore. Adv. contact Mike Moore. Circ: 36,000.

261.26 USA
SINGLES SCENE - SPIRIT & LIFE. Text in English. 1981. m. USD 29.95 (effective 2003). adv. bk.rev. **Document type:** *Magazine, Consumer.* **Description:** Geared to Christian singles or those with traditional Judeo-Christian values.
Formerly: Singles Scene (Allardt) (0746-7982)
Published by: Sandra S. Turner, Ed. & Pub., PO Box 310, Allardt, TN 38504. TEL 615-879-4625, http://members.aol.com/spiritlif/homepage.html. Ed. Sandra Turner. Pub., Adv. contact Sandra S Turner. Circ: 5,500.

051 USA
SINGLES' SERENDIPITY. Text in English. 1985. bi-m. USD 12 (effective 2001). adv. **Document type:** *Magazine, Consumer.* **Description:** Lists activities and other single organizations. Includes articles and personal ads.
Address: PO Box 8117, Jacksonville, FL 32239-0117. TEL 904-731-7111. Ed. Judy Lanier. Pub., Adv. contact Ben Shear. Circ: 55,000.

051 USA
SINGLES TIMES. Text in English. 1984. m. USD 24 (effective 2000). adv. **Document type:** *Newspaper.* **Description:** Includes a monthly calendar, personals, movie reviews, classified ads, and editorials.
Address: PO Box 1015, Valley Stream, NY 11582. TEL 516-565-9100, FAX 516-565-9166. Pub. Greg Pelini.

070.48346 301.412 USA
SOUTHEAST SINGLES ASSOCIATION QUARTERLY PUBLICATION. Text in English. 1987. q. free. adv. bk.rev. back issues avail. **Document type:** *Directory.* **Description:** Offers advice and guidance for single adults and serves as a forum for their communications worldwide.
Former titles: Southeast Singles Association Bi-Monthly Publication; Southeast Singles Association Monthly Publication; (until 1991): Gulf Coast Singles Association Monthly Book
Published by: Southeast Singles Association, Inc., PO Box 267, Biloxi, MS 39533-0267. TEL 228-872-9555. Ed., R&P Glenda J Alba. Pub., Adv. contact Hugh B Jones. Circ: 3,000.

155.642 USA
SWEETHEART MAGAZINE. Text in English. 1988. m. USD 15 membership (effective 2008). adv. back issues avail. **Document type:** *Magazine, Consumer.* **Description:** Promotes healthy singles life and singles activities.
Formerly: Sweetheart Connection
Address: PO Box 514, St. Ignatius, MT 59865. TEL 406-745-4209. Ed. Katie R James. Pub., R&P Charlie L James. Adv. contact Lise James. Circ: 50,000.

367 USA ISSN 0748-7355
TODAY'S SINGLE; serving the singles of America. Text in English. 1980. q. USD 10. adv. bk.rev. **Document type:** *Magazine, Consumer.*
Published by: National Association of Christian Singles, 1933 W Wisconsin Ave, Milwaukee, WI 53233. TEL 414-344-7300. Ed. John M Fisco Jr. Circ: 12,000.

306.8 USA
TOUCHPOINT; network for the nonmonogamous. Text in English. 1988. USD 14. **Document type:** *Newsletter.* **Description:** Lists people, groups, organizations and publications exploring alternatives to monogamy. Seeks to create a network of these persons and entities.
Published by: Major Publications, PO Box 408 UD, Chloride, AZ 86431. Ed. Stanfield Major. Circ: 350 (paid).

TRAVEL COMPANIONS; North America's foremost newsletter for solo travelers. *see* TRAVEL AND TOURISM

051.059 USA
UNMARRIED AMERICA; news for unmarried workers, consumers, taxpayers and voters. Text in English. 1999. q. USD 10 to members (effective 2001).
Related titles: Online - full text ed.
Published by: American Association for Single People, PO Box 11030, Glendale, CA 91205. TEL (818) 230-5156, mail@unmarriedamerica.org. Ed. Tom Coleman.

052 USA
VEGGIE SINGLES NEWS; helping vegetarians (and those who want to be) meet & eat. Text in English. q. USD 18 for 6 issues. adv. bk.rev. back issues avail. **Document type:** *Magazine, Consumer.* **Description:** Provides a forum for vegetarian singles to meet others. Covers events and issues (e.g., animal rights, the environment, health) of interest to vegetarians.
Former titles: Veggie Social News; (until 1995): Vegetarian Singles News
Published by: Veggie Singles News Inc., 925 Newkirk Ave, Brooklyn, NY 11230. TEL 718-437-0190, FAX 718-633-9817. Ed., Pub., R&P, Adv. contact Arthur Goldberg. page USD 350; 10 x 7.25. Circ: 12,000. **Subscr. to:** 3307 W. Front St., Midland, TX 79701-7142. **Dist. by:** Healing Communications, 151 First Ave, Box 555, New York, NY 10003. TEL 718-488-7137.

SMALL BUSINESS

see BUSINESS AND ECONOMICS—Small Business

SOCIAL SCIENCES: COMPREHENSIVE WORKS

308 ESP ISSN 1699-8057
A C C E. Text in Spanish. 2005. q. free membership (effective 2008). **Document type:** *Bulletin, Academic/Scholarly.*
Related titles: Online - full text ed.: ISSN 1699-8065. 2005.
Published by: Asociacion Cultural Castillo de Embid, Ave de la Constitutcion 12-1o A, Molina de Aragon, Guadalajara, 19300, Spain. Ed. Juan Jose Fernandez Sanz.

A C W VISIE; weekblad van de christelijke arbeidersbeweging. *see* LABOR UNIONS

300 CHE ISSN 1660-7880
A CONTRARIO. Text in French. 2003. s-a. CHF 50 domestic to individuals; CHF 70 domestic to institutions; CHF 40 domestic to students; EUR 35 in Europe to individuals; EUR 55 in Europe to institutions; EUR 28 in Europe to students; CHF 55 elsewhere to individuals; CHF 90 elsewhere to institutions; CHF 50 elsewhere to students (effective 2007). **Document type:** *Journal, Academic/Scholarly.*
Related titles: Online - full text ed.
Indexed: CA, FR, IBSS, P42, PAIS, PSA, S02, S03, SCOPUS, SociolAb, T02.
—INIST.
Published by: A Contrario, Universite de Lausanne, Internef 80.1, Lausanne, 1015, Switzerland. TEL 41-21-6923141, FAX 41-21-6923145.

300 ESP ISSN 1887-1585
A D O Z. (Aisiazko Dokumentazio Zentruaren) Text in Basque, Spanish. 1994. 3/yr. EUR 15 domestic; EUR 35 foreign (effective 2010). back issues avail. **Document type:** *Journal, Academic/Scholarly.*
Formerly (until 2004): Centro de Documentacion en Ocio (A D O Z). Boletin (1134-6019)
Published by: Universidad de Deusto, Departamento de Publicaciones, Apdo 1/E, Bilbao, 48080, Spain. TEL 34-94-4139162, FAX 34-94-4456817, publicaciones@deusto.es, http://deusto-publicaciones.es/.

A F B INFO. *see* POLITICAL SCIENCE

A F E T VEROEFFENTLICHUNGEN. (Arbeitsgemeinschaft fuer Erziehungshilfe) *see* EDUCATION—Special Education And Rehabilitation

A F E T WISSENSCHAFTLICHE INFORMATIONSSCHRIFTEN. (Arbeitsgemeinschaft fuer Erziehungshilfe) *see* EDUCATION—Special Education And Rehabilitation

300 CAN ISSN 1910-3166
A I M S SPECIAL EQUALIZATION SERIES. (Atlantic Institute for Market Studies) Text in English. 2006. irreg. **Document type:** *Monographic series, Consumer.*
Published by: Atlantic Institute for Market Studies, 2000 Barrington St, Ste 1006, Cogswell Tower, Halifax, NS B3J 3K1, Canada. TEL 902-429-1143, FAX 902-425-1393, aims@aims.ca, http://www.aims.ca.

300 GBR ISSN 1747-9258
A L I S S QUARTERLY. Text in English. 1983. q. GBP 14 per issue; free to members (effective 2009). adv. bk.rev. back issues avail. **Document type:** *Journal, Academic/Scholarly.* **Description:** Contains information on activities, sources, and resources in the social sciences information field. Aims to provide in depth coverage of issues at an informal but scholarly level.
Formerly (until 2005): ASSIGnation (0265-2587)
Indexed: CA, L04, L13, LISTA, T02.
—BLDSC (0788.100000), IE, Ingenta. **CCC.**
Published by: A L I S S, c/o Heather Dawson, Secretary, British Library of Political and Economic Science, 10 Portugal St, London, WC2A 2HD, United Kingdom. TEL 44-20-79556806. Ed. Heather Dawson.

300 IND ISSN 0976-2744
▼ **A N U JOURNAL OF SOCIAL SCIENCES.** Text in English. 2009. s-a. **Document type:** *Journal, Academic/Scholarly.*
Published by: Acharya Nagarjuna University, Nagarjuna Nagar, Guntur, Andhra Pradesh 522 510, India. TEL 91-863-2293007, FAX 91-863-2293378, http://www.nagarjunauniversity.ac.in.

300 664 CHE
A PROPOS CULINA; Beitraege zur Kulturgeschichte des Essens und Trinkens. Text in German. q. CHF 54. **Document type:** *Consumer.*
Published by: A Propos Culina, Postfach 144, Zuerich, 8032, Switzerland. TEL 41-1-4220481, FAX 41-1-2625745. Ed. Rene Simmen.

A S E A S: AUSTRIAN JOURNAL OF SOUTH-EAST ASIAN STUDIES. *see* ASIAN STUDIES

A ST A - WIRTSCHAFTS- UND SOZIALSTATISTISCHES ARCHIV. *see* STATISTICS

300 USA
A W A I R'S MIDDLE EAST RESOURCES; a quarterly newsletter for social studies educators. Text in English, Spanish. q. **Document type:** *Newsletter.*
Published by: Arab World and Islamic Resources and School Services, 2095 Rose St, Ste 4, Berkeley, CA 94709. TEL 510-704-0517.

300 FIN ISSN 0358-5654
AABO AKADEMI. EKONOMISK-STATSVETENSKAPLIGA FAKULTETEN. MEDDELANDEN. Text in English, Finnish, Swedish. 1956. irreg. price varies. **Document type:** *Monographic series, Academic/Scholarly.*
Formerly: Aabo Akademi. Statsvetenskapliga Fakulteten. Meddelanden; Which was formed by the Jan. 1979 merger of: Aabo Akademi. Statsvetenskapliga Fakulteten. Meddelanden. Serie A (0355-4031); Aabo Akademi. Statsvetenskapliga Fakulteten. Meddelanden. Serie B (0355-4465)
Published by: Aabo Akademi, Statsvetenskapliga Institutionen/Aabo Akademi, Department of Political Science, Biskopsgatan 15, Truku, 20500, Finland. TEL 358-2-2154686, FAX 358-2-2154585. Ed. Marina Hamberg. Circ: 200.

300 FIN ISSN 0785-6822
AABO AKADEMI. INSTITUTET FOER FINLANDSSVENSK SAMHAELLSFORSKNING. FORSKNINGSRAPPORTER. Text in Swedish. 1966. irreg., latest 2002. price varies. back issues avail. **Document type:** *Monographic series, Academic/Scholarly.*
Former titles (until 1988): Institutet foer Finlandssvensk Samhaellsforskning vid Aabo Akademi. Forskningsrapporter (0781-5808); (until 1984): Svenska Litteratursaellskapet i Finland. Naemnd foer Samhaellsforskning. Forskningsrapporter (0355-3116)
Published by: Aabo Akademi, Institutet foer Finlandssvensk Samhaellsforskning, Strandgatan 2, Vasa, 65100, Finland. TEL 358-6-3247155, FAX 358-6-3247457.

300 DEU ISSN 0945-9251
AACHENER STUDIEN ZUR SOZIAL-OEKONOMISCHEN ENTWICKLUNGSFORSCHUNG. Text in German. 1994. irreg. **Document type:** *Monographic series, Academic/Scholarly.*
Published by: Shaker Verlag GmbH, Kaiserstr 100, Herzogenrath, 52134, Germany. TEL 49-2407-95960, FAX 49-2407-95969, info@shaker.de, http://www.shaker.de.

AACHENER STUDIEN ZUR WIRTSCHAFTS- UND SOZIALGESCHICHTE. *see* BUSINESS AND ECONOMICS

300 DNK ISSN 1902-4592
AALBORG UNIVERSITET. CENTER FOR DISKURSSTUDIER. DISCOURSE FILES. Text in English. 2007. irreg. **Document type:** *Monographic series, Academic/Scholarly.*
Media: Online - full content.
Published by: Aalborg Universitet, Center for Diskursstudier/University of Aalborg. Centre for Discourse Studies, Kroghstraede 3, Aalborg, 9220, Denmark. TEL 45-96-359195, FAX 45-98-157887, http://diskurs.hum.aau.dk/index.htm.

AB IMPERIO; studies of new imperial history and nationalism in the post-Soviet space. *see* HISTORY—History Of Europe

300 001.3 CHN ISSN 1008-4142
ABA SHIFAN GAODENG ZHUANKE XUEXIAO/ABA TEACHERS COLLEGE. JOURNAL. Text in Chinese. 1983. q. CNY 6.50 newsstand/cover (effective 2006). **Document type:** *Journal, Academic/Scholarly.*
Related titles: Online - full text ed.
Published by: Aba Shifan Gaodeng Zhuanke Xuexiao, Xianfengzhou Lu, Wenchuan, 623000, China.

300 ESP ISSN 0213-6252
D901
ABACO; revista de cultural y ciencias sociales. Text in Spanish. 1986. q. EUR 30 domestic to individuals; EUR 45 domestic to institutions; EUR 60 in Europe to institutions; EUR 80 in the Americas to institutions (effective 2008). cum. index 1986-1991. back issues avail. **Document type:** *Magazine, Consumer.* **Description:** Covers culture and social science. Endeavors to adopt a broad horizon, as universal as the very events and ideas about which it reflects and debates.
Related titles: Online - full text ed.
Published by: Centro de Estudios Economicos y Sociales, C. La Muralla 3 Bajo, Gijon, Asturias 33202, Spain. Ed. M A Alvarez Areces. **Dist. by:** Asociacion de Revistas Culturales de Espana, C Covarruvias 9 2o. Derecha, Madrid 28010, Spain. TEL 34-91-3086066, FAX 34-91-3199267, info@arce.es, http://www.arce.es/.

001.3 IND ISSN 0970-2385
HD70.I4
➤ **ABHIGYAN.** Text in English. 1983. q. bk.rev. back issues avail. **Document type:** *Journal, Academic/Scholarly.* **Description:** Expression of the changing management scenario and organization.
Indexed: A26, I05, IPsyAb, P03, PAA&I, PsycInfo, PsycholAb.
—BLDSC (0549.392000).
Published by: Foundation for Organisational Research and Education, FORE School of Management, B-18, Qutab Institutional Area, New Delhi, 110 016, India. TEL 91-11-41242424, FAX 91-11-26520509, admissions@fsm.ac.in.

➤ **ACADEMIA DE CIENCIAS POLITICAS Y SOCIALES. BOLETIN.** *see* POLITICAL SCIENCE

306 ESP ISSN 1130-426X
ACADEMIA DE CULTURA VALENCIANA. ANALES. Text in Spanish. 1928. a.
Formerly (until 1977): Centro de Cultura Valenciana. Anales (0210-8666)
Related titles: ◆ Supplement(s): Real Academia de Cultura Valenciana. Monografias. ISSN 1133-4320.
Indexed: FR, MLA-IB.
Published by: Real Academia de Cultura Valenciana, C. Avellanes, 26, Valencia, 46003, Spain. TEL 34-96-3916965, FAX 34-96-3915694, secretari@racv.es, http://www.racv.es/.

ACADEMIA. JINBUN, SHAKAI KAGAKU HEN/ACADEMIA. HUMANITIES, SOCIAL SCIENCES. *see* HUMANITIES: COMPREHENSIVE WORKS

ACADEMIA NACIONAL DE DERECHO Y CIENCIAS SOCIALES DE CORDOBA. ANALES. *see* LAW

▼ **ACADEMIC RESEARCH INTERNATIONAL.** *see* HUMANITIES: COMPREHENSIVE WORKS

300 001.3 CAN ISSN 0317-0179
ACADEMIE DES LETTRES ET DES SCIENCES HUMAINES. PRESENTATIONS. Text in French. 1943. a. CAD 10 (effective 1999). **Document type:** *Journal, Academic/Scholarly.*
Related titles: Online - full text ed.
Indexed: IBR, IBZ, RILM.
Published by: Royal Society of Canada, 283 Sparks St., Ottawa, ON K1R 7X9, Canada. TEL 613-991-6990, FAX 613-991-6996, adminrsc@rsc.ca, http://www.rsc.ca. Ed. Andree Desilets.

300 AUS ISSN 1328-5947
ACADEMY OF THE SOCIAL SCIENCES IN AUSTRALIA. ANNUAL REPORT. Text in English. 1971. a. **Document type:** *Corporate.*
Related titles: Online - full content ed.
Published by: Academy of the Social Sciences in Australia, GPO Box 1956, Canberra, ACT 2601, Australia. TEL 61-2-62491788, FAX 61-2-62474335, assa.secretariat@anu.edu.au. Circ: 1,500.

300 AUS ISSN 1441-8460
HN841
ACADEMY OF THE SOCIAL SCIENCES IN AUSTRALIA. DIALOGUE. Text in English. 1982. 3/yr. free. **Document type:** *Newsletter.* **Description:** Contains articles, as well as news from the academy, reports from workshops, overseas programs, and academy projects.
Former titles (until 1998): Academy of the Social Sciences in Australia. Newsletter (1038-7803); (until 1991): A S S A News (0727-6702)
Published by: Academy of the Social Sciences in Australia, GPO Box 1956, Canberra, ACT 2601, Australia. TEL 61-2-62491788, FAX 61-2-62474335, assa.secretariat@anu.edu.au. Ed. Peg Job. Circ: 1,550.

300 AUS ISSN 1323-7136
ACADEMY OF THE SOCIAL SCIENCES IN AUSTRALIA. OCCASIONAL PAPER SERIES. Text in English. s-a. free.
Related titles: Online - full content ed.
Published by: Academy of the Social Sciences in Australia, GPO Box 1956, Canberra, ACT 2601, Australia. TEL 61-2-62491788, FAX 61-2-62474335, assa.secretariat@anu.edu.au.

ACCESS; critical perspectives on communication, cultural & policy studies. *see* EDUCATION

S

056.1 PRY
HC222
ACCION; revista paraguaya de reflexion y dialogo. Text in Spanish. N.S. 1969. 10/yr. PYG 45,000 domestic; USD 35 foreign; PYG 5,000 newsstand/cover (effective 2000). adv. bk.rev. illus. **Document type:** *Academic/Scholarly.*
Incorporates: Dimension
Published by: Centro de Estudios Paraguayos "Antonio Guasch", Casilla 1072, Calle GUARANI, 2256, Asuncion, Paraguay. TEL 595-21-333962, FAX 595-21-211549. Ed. Bartomeu Melia S J. Pub. Jose Luis Caravias S J. R&P Bartomeu Melia. Adv. contact Andres Martin. Circ: 2,000. **Co-sponsor:** Society of Jesus.

300 ESP ISSN 1132-192X
ACCIONES E INVESTIGACIONS SOCIALES. Text in Spanish. 1991. a. free (effective 2008). **Document type:** *Journal, Academic/Scholarly.*
Related titles: Online - full text ed.: free (effective 2011).
Indexed: A39, C27, C29, CA, D04, E13, F04, S18, T02.
Published by: Universidad de Zaragoza, Escuela Universitaria de Estudios Sociales, Violante de Hundria, 23, Zaragoza, 50009, Spain. TEL 34-976-761028, FAX 34-976-761029, websociales@posta.unizar.es, http://www.unizar.es/.

ACTA ACADEMICA. *see* HUMANITIES: COMPREHENSIVE WORKS

ACTA ACADEMICA. SUPPLEMENTUM. *see* HUMANITIES: COMPREHENSIVE WORKS

300 NOR ISSN 0800-3831
DL421 CODEN: ABOAAB
ACTA BOREALIA; a Nordic journal of circumpolar societies. Text in English. 1878. s-a. GBP 56, EUR 73, USD 94 combined subscription to institutions (print & online eds.) (effective 2009). adv. reprint service avail. from PSC. **Document type:** *Journal, Academic/Scholarly.* **Description:** Presents results from multi-disciplinary cultural research on northern societies in areas such as history, archaeology, social anthropology, linguistics and geography.
Incorporates (1952-1979): Acta Borealia B. Humaniora (0065-1117); (1951-1975): Acta Borealia A. Scientia (0065-1109); Which was formerly (until 1947): Tromsoe Museums Aarshefter (0800-3998)
Related titles: Online - full text ed.: ISSN 1503-111X. GBP 53, EUR 69, USD 89 to institutions (effective 2009) (from IngentaConnect).
Indexed: A01, A03, A08, A20, A22, A33, AICP, AmHI, ArtHuCI, CA, E01, GeoRef, H07, NAA, P46, P48, P54, PCI, PQC, RASB, SCOPUS, SpeleolAb, T02, W07.
—IE, Ingenta. **CCC.**
Published by: (Tromsoe Museum - Universitetsmuseet), Taylor & Francis A S (Subsidiary of: Taylor & Francis Group), Biskop Gunnerusgate 14A, PO Box 12 Posthuset, Oslo, 0051, Norway. TEL 47-23-103460, FAX 47-23-103461, journals@tandf.no. Eds. Dikka Storm, Nels Petter Nielsen. **Subscr. to:** Taylor & Francis Ltd., Journals Customer Service, Sheepen Pl, Colchester, Essex CO3 3LP, United Kingdom. TEL 44-20-70175544, FAX 44-20-70175198, tf.enquiries@tfinforma.com.

300 DNK ISSN 0106-0937
ACTA JUTLANDICA. SAMFUNDSVIDENSKABELIG SERIE/ACTA JUTLANDICA. SOCIAL SCIENCES SERIES. Variant title: Samfundsvidenskabelig Serie. Text in Multiple languages. 1941. irreg. price varies. back issues avail. **Document type:** *Monographic series, Academic/Scholarly.*
Related titles: ◆ Series of: Acta Jutlandica. ISSN 0065-1354.
Published by: (Det Laerde Selskab i Aarhus), Aarhus Universitetsforlag/ Aarhus University Press, Langelandsgade 177, Aarhus N, 8200, Denmark. TEL 45-89-425370, FAX 45-89-425380, unipress@au.dk.

300 001.3 BRA ISSN 1679-7361
H8.P6
➤ **ACTA SCIENTIARUM. HUMAN AND SOCIAL SCIENCES.** Text in Multiple languages. 1974. q. **Document type:** *Journal, Academic/ Scholarly.*
Superseded in part (in 2003): Acta Scientiarum (1415-6814); Which was formerly (until 1998): Revista U N I M A R (0100-9354)
Related titles: Online - full text ed.: ISSN 1807-8656. free (effective 2011).
Indexed: A01, A26, C01, CA, I04, I05, L&LBA, MLA-IB, S02, S03, SCOPUS, SSA, SociolAb, T02.
Published by: Universidade Estadual de Maringa, Editora da Universidade - Eduem, Av Colombo, 5790 - Zona 7, Maringa, Parana 87020-900, Brazil. TEL 55-44-2614253, FAX 55-44-2222754, http://www.uem.br. Ed., R&P Alessandro de Lucca e Braccini.

300 ARG ISSN 1852-2874
ACTAS DE LAS JORNADAS DE DISCUSION. ARTE, POLITICA Y SOCIEDAD. Text in Spanish. 2008. a. **Document type:** *Proceedings, Academic/Scholarly.*
Published by: Universidad Nacional de General de Sarmiento, Instituto del Desarrollo Humano, Juan Maria Gutierrez, 1150, Buenos Aires, B1613GSX, Argentina. TEL 54-11-44697701, FAX 5411-44697734, idh@ungs.edu.ar, http://www.ungs.edu.ar/.

300 FRA ISSN 0335-5322
H3
➤ **ACTES DE LA RECHERCHE EN SCIENCES SOCIALES.** Text in French; Summaries in English, German, Spanish. 1975. q. bibl.; illus. **Document type:** *Journal, Academic/Scholarly.* **Description:** Discusses leading research in the social sciences - sociology, ethnology, social psychology, psychology, social history, sociolinguistics, the economics of consumption and symbolic goods, etc.
Related titles: Online - full text ed.: ISSN 1955-2564.
Indexed: A20, A22, ASCA, BAS, CA, CJA, CurCont, DIP, FR, HistAb, I13, IBR, IBSS, IBZ, MLA-IB, P30, P42, PAIS, PCI, PSA, RASB, RILM, S02, S03, SCOPUS, SOPODA, SSA, SSCI, SociolAb, T02, W07.
—BLDSC (0675.315000), IE, Infotrieve, Ingenta, INIST. **CCC.**
Published by: (Editions de la Maison des Sciences de l'Homme), Editions du Seuil, 27 Rue Jacob, Paris, 75006, France. TEL 33-1-40465050, FAX 33-1-40464300, contact@seuil.com, http:// www.seuil.com. Ed. Pierre Bourdieu. **Subscr. to:** Axime-Direct, La Vigne-aux-Loups, 55 route de Longjumeau, Chilly Mazarin Cedex 91388, France.

300 USA
▼ **ADVANCES IN PEOPLE-ENVIRONMENT STUDIES.** Text in English. 2010. irreg., latest vol.2, 2010. price varies. **Document type:** *Monographic series, Academic/Scholarly.*
Published by: Hogrefe Publishing Corp., 875 Massachusetts Ave, 7th Fl, Cambridge, MA 02139. TEL 866-823-4726, FAX 617-354-6875, publishing@hogrefe.com, http://www.hogrefe.com. Eds. David Uzzell, Gabriel Moser.

300 USA
▼ **ADVANCES IN SOCIAL SCIENCE.** Text in English. 2010 (Sep.). q. USD 60; USD 15 newsstand/cover (effective 2010). **Document type:** *Journal, Academic/Scholarly.* **Description:** Contains theoretical or speculative as well as statistical and mathematical papers on social sciences.
Published by: American Society for Education Science Research, 4301 E Valley Blvd #D2, Los Angeles, CA 90032. TEL 323-9088-554, FAX 323-2278-581, office@asesr.org.

ADVERTISING & SOCIETY REVIEW. *see* ADVERTISING AND PUBLIC RELATIONS

300 500 USA ISSN 1066-5145
AEON; a journal of interdisciplinary science. Text in English. 1988. 3/yr. USD 40 in North America; USD 55 elsewhere (effective 2011). adv. bk.rev. 100 p./no. 2 cols./p.; back issues avail.; reprints avail. **Document type:** *Journal, Academic/Scholarly.* **Description:** Explores the relationship between myth and science, particularly as it applies to the possibility of a synthesis between ancient myth and history.
Address: PO Box 1092, Ames, IA 50014. FAX 515-292-2603, ev@aeonJournal.com. Ed. Dwardu Cardona. Circ: 1,000.

AESTHESIS; international journal of art and aesthetics in management and organizational life. *see* BUSINESS AND ECONOMICS—Management

300 DEU
AESTHETIK UND BILDUNG. Text in German. 2007. irreg., latest vol.4, 2010. price varies. **Document type:** *Monographic series, Academic/ Scholarly.*
Published by: Transcript, Muehlenstr 47, Bielefeld, 33607, Germany. TEL 49-521-63454, FAX 49-521-61040, live@transcript-verlag.de.

300 UAE ISSN 1607-2081
DS36.85
AFAQ AL-TAQAFAH WA-AL-TURATH. Text in Arabic. 1993. q.
Published by: Department of Researches and Studies, Juma Al Majed Centre for Culture and Heritage, P O Box 15551, Dubai, United Arab Emirates. TEL 9713-7514336, FAX 9713-7641226, sultan.alolama@uaeu.ac.ae.

300 001.3 ZAF ISSN 1019-2182
HN800.S59
AFRICA 2001; dialogue with the future. Text in Afrikaans, English. 1974. s-a. ZAR 20. **Document type:** *Journal, Academic/Scholarly.* **Description:** Publishes conference papers and academic articles on topics relating to development issues in Africa.
Former titles (until 1993): R S A 2000 (1011-1913); R S A: Dialogue with the Future
Indexed: ASD, ISAP.
Published by: (Centre for Science Development), Human Sciences Research Council/Raad vir Geesteswetenskaplike Navorsing. Sentrum vir Wetenskapontwikkeling, Private Bag X41, Pretoria, 0001, South Africa. TEL 27- 12-302-2999, FAX 27- 12-326-5362. Ed. Marilyn Farquharson. Circ: 4,000.

960 NLD ISSN 1872-5457
DT16.5
AFRICAN DIASPORA. Text and summaries in French, English. 2008. 2/yr. EUR 176, USD 246 to institutions; EUR 176, USD 246 combined subscription to institutions (print & online eds.) (effective 2012). reprint service avail. from PSC. **Document type:** *Journal, Academic/ Scholarly.* **Description:** Covers various transnational movements, locations and intersections of subjectivity within the African diaspora.
Related titles: Online - full text ed.: ISSN 1872-5465 (from IngentaConnect).
Indexed: A22, CA, E01, IZBG, S02, S03, SCOPUS, T02.
—IE. **CCC.**
Published by: Brill, PO Box 9000, Leiden, 2300 PA, Netherlands. TEL 31-71-5353500, FAX 31-71-5317532, cs@brill.nl. Eds. Abebe Zegeye, Fassil Demissie, Sandra Jackson.

AFRICAN SECURITY. *see* POLITICAL SCIENCE

300 ZMB ISSN 0002-0168
HN771 CODEN: ASREDO
➤ **AFRICAN SOCIAL RESEARCH.** Text in English. 1944. s-a. ZMK 20,000, USD 35 (effective 2001). adv. bk.rev. charts. cum.index. **Document type:** *Monographic series, Academic/Scholarly.* **Description:** Contains articles in social research, with emphasis on sociology, economics, history and related disciplines.
Supersedes: Rhodes-Livingstone Journal
Indexed: A20, AICP, ASD, CCA, FR, HistAb, MEA&I, MLA-IB, P06, P30, PCI, PsycholAb, RASB, T02.
Published by: Unza Press (Subsidiary of: University of Zambia), PO Box 32379, Lusaka, Zambia. TEL 260-1-290409, FAX 260-1-253952, TELEX 44370. Eds. Stephen Banda, Mubanga E Kashoki. Pub. S Kasankha. R&P S. Kasankha TEL 260-1-290740. Circ: 500.

300 NLD ISSN 1876-018X
AFRICAN STUDIES COLLECTION. Text in English. 2007. irreg., latest vol.23, 2010. price varies. **Document type:** *Monographic series, Academic/Scholarly.*
Related titles: Online - full text ed.: ISSN 1876-0198.
Published by: Afrika-Studiecentrum, PO Box 9555, Leiden, 2300 RB, Netherlands. TEL 31-71-5273372, FAX 31-71-5273344, asc@ascleiden.nl.

960 USA ISSN 2152-2448
➤ **AFRICAN STUDIES QUARTERLY**; the online journal of African studies. Abbreviated title: A S Q. Text in English. 1997. q. free (effective 2011). adv. bk.rev. illus. back issues avail.; reprints avail. **Document type:** *Journal, Academic/Scholarly.* **Description:** Presents manuscripts of African studies from every discipline.
Media: Online - full text. **Related titles:** E-mail ed.
Indexed: A01, AmHI, B04, BRD, CA, HAb, HumInd, IIBP, P10, P27, P45, P46, P48, P53, P54, PQC, SCOPUS, SociolAb, W03.
Published by: University of Florida, Center for African Studies, 427 Grinter Hall, PO Box 115560, Gainesville, FL 32611. TEL 352-392-2183, FAX 352-392-2435, www@africa.ufl.edu. Ed. R Hunt Davis.

300 PRT ISSN 0871-2336
D1
AFRICANA. Text in Spanish. 1987. a. **Document type:** *Journal, Academic/Scholarly.*
Published by: Universidade Portucalense, Centro de Estudos Africanos, Rua Dr Antonio Bernardino de Almedia, 541-619, Porto, 4200-072, Portugal. TEL 351-22-5572000, http://www.uportu.pt/site-scripts/. Ed. Joaquim Da Silva Cunha. Circ: 750.

300 POL ISSN 0002-029X
DT19.9.P6
AFRICANA BULLETIN. Text in English, French. 1962. irreg., latest vol.50, 2002. price varies. bk.rev. abstr.; charts; illus.; stat. **Document type:** *Bulletin, Academic/Scholarly.*
Indexed: AICP, ASD, BibLing, CA, CCA, DIP, FR, HistAb, IBR, IBZ, MLA, MLA-IB, PAIS, RASB, T02.
—BLDSC (0735.150000).
Published by: (Uniwersytet Warszawski, Instytut Krajow Rozwijajacych sie), Wydawnictwa Uniwersytetu Warszawskiego, ul Nowy Swiat 4, Warsaw, 00497, Poland. TEL 48-22-5531319, FAX 48-22-5531318, wuw@uw.edu.pl. R&P Jolanta Okonska. Circ: 1,000. **Dist. by:** Ars Polona, Obroncow 25, Warsaw 03933, Poland. TEL 48-22-5098609, FAX 48-22-5098610, arspolona@arspolona.com.pl, http:// www.arspolona.com.pl.

960 PRT ISSN 0874-2375
DT1
AFRICANA STUDIA/INTERNATIONAL JOURNAL OF AFRICAN STUDIES; revista internacional de estudos africanos. Text in Portuguese, Spanish. 1999. a. **Document type:** *Journal, Academic/ Scholarly.*
Indexed: A01, CA, F04, T02.
Published by: Universidade do Porto, Centro de Estudos Africanos, Via Panoramica, s-n, Porto, 4150-564, Portugal. TEL 351-22-6077141, FAX 351-22-6091610, http://www.letras.up.pt/ceaup/. Ed. Antonio Custodio Goncalves. Circ: 500.

300 TUR ISSN 1302-2407
H8.T87
AFYON KOCATEPE UNIVERSITESI SOSYAL BILIMLER ENSTITUSU DERGISI/AFYON KOCATEPE UNIVERSITY. INSTITUTE OF SOCIAL SCIENCES. JOURNAL. Text in Turkish. 1999. a. **Document type:** *Journal, Academic/Scholarly.*
Indexed: MLA-IB.
Published by: Afyon Kocatepe Universitesi/Afyon Kocatepe University, Ahmet Necdet Sezer Kampusu, Gazligol Yolu, Afyon, 03200, Turkey. TEL 90-272-2281213, FAX 90-272-2281417, ogrenis@aku.edu.tr, http://www.aku.edu.tr.

▼ **AGATHOS**; an international review of the humanities and social sciences. *see* HUMANITIES: COMPREHENSIVE WORKS

AGEING AND SOCIETY. *see* GERONTOLOGY AND GERIATRICS

300 052 GBR ISSN 1464-7613
DA700
AGENDA (CARDIFF). Text in English. 1994. 3/yr. GBP 5 per issue to non-members; free to members (effective 2009). charts; stat. 76 p./no.; back issues avail.; reprints avail. **Document type:** *Journal, Academic/Scholarly.* **Description:** Features in-depth analysis of the issues affecting Wales today, focusing on the economy, education, culture, and Welsh society and how its changing profile fits into the UK, European, and worldwide perspectives.
Formerly: Welsh Agenda
Published by: Institute of Welsh Affairs/Sefydliad Materion Cymreig, Second Fl, 4 Cathedral Rd, Cardiff, CF11 9LJ, United Kingdom. TEL 44-29-20660820, wales@iwa.org.uk.

300 ITA ISSN 0002-094X
HN475.5
AGGIORNAMENTI SOCIALI. Text in Italian. 1950. m. EUR 32 domestic; EUR 50 foreign (effective 2009). adv. bk.rev.; software rev.; Website rev. bibl.; charts; stat. index, cum.index: 1950-1979, 1980-1989, 1950-1999. 80 p./no.; **Document type:** *Magazine, Consumer.*
Related titles: CD-ROM ed.; Diskette ed.; Online - full content ed.
Indexed: CA, ELLIS, FR, I13, IBR, IBZ, ILD, P34, P42, PSA, RASB, S02, S03, SCOPUS, SociolAb, T02.
—INIST.
Published by: (Istituto Aggiornamenti Sociali), San Fedele Edizioni s.r.l., Piazza San Fedele 4, Milan, 20121, Italy. TEL 39-02-86352, FAX 39-02-8635282. Ed. Bartolomeo Sorge. R&P Mario Reguzzoni TEL 39-02-86352406. Circ: 25,000.

300 VEN ISSN 1316-7790
H1
➤ **AGORA TRUJILLO.** Text in Spanish. 1998. s-a. VEB 10 domestic; USD 20 foreign (effective 2009). **Document type:** *Journal, Academic/ Scholarly.*
Related titles: Online - full text ed.: 1998. free (effective 2011).
Indexed: A26, I04, I05.
Published by: Universidad de los Andes, Trujillo, Nucleo Universitario Rafael Rangel, Trujillo, Venezuela.

➤ **AGRUPACIO BORRIANENCA DE CULTURA. ANUARI.** *see* HUMANITIES: COMPREHENSIVE WORKS

300 DEU
AISTHESIS-STUDIENBUCH. Text in German. 2001. irreg., latest vol.7, 2010. price varies. **Document type:** *Monographic series, Academic/ Scholarly.*
Published by: Aisthesis Verlag, Oberntorwall 21, Bielefeld, 33602, Germany. TEL 49-521-172604, FAX 49-521-172812, info@aisthesis.de.

AJIKEN WORLD TRENDS. *see* BUSINESS AND ECONOMICS

AJKAL. *see* LITERATURE

300 DEU ISSN 0940-2233
AKADEMIE GEMEINNUETZIGER WISSENSCHAFTEN ZU ERFURT. GEISTESWISSENSCHAFTLICHEN KLASSE. SITZUNGSBERICHTE. Text in German. 1992. irreg., latest vol.4, 2000. price varies. **Document type:** *Monographic series, Academic/ Scholarly.*
Published by: Akademie Gemeinnuetziger Wissenschaften zu Erfurt e.V., Gotthardtstr 24, Erfurt, 99051, Germany. TEL 49-3641-937792, FAX 49-3641-937796, sekretariat@akademie-erfurt.de, http:// www.akademie-erfurt.de.

300 BIH ISSN 0350-0039
AKADEMIJA NAUKA I UMJETNOSTI BOSNE I HERCEGOVINE. ODJELJENJE DRUSTVENIH NAUKA. RADOVI. Text in Serbo-Croatian. 1954. irreg., latest vol.84, no.23, 1989. price varies. **Document type:** *Academic/Scholarly.*
—INIST.
Published by: Akademija Nauka i Umjetnosti Bosne i Hercegovine, Odjeljenje Drustvenih Nauka/Academy of Sciences and Arts of Bosnia and Herzegovina, Department of Social Sciences, Bistrik 7, Sarajevo, 7100, Bosnia Herzegovina. TEL 387-33-206034, FAX 387-33-206033. Circ: 600.

AKADEMIK ARASTIRMALAR DERGISI/JOURNAL OF ACADEMIC STUDIES. *see* EDUCATION

001 300 MYS ISSN 0126-5008
AKADEMIKA; journal of Southeast Asia social sciences and humanities. Text and summaries in English, Malay. 1972. 3/yr. MYR 20 in ASEAN; USD 20 elsewhere (effective 2011). back issues avail. **Document type:** *Journal, Academic/Scholarly.* **Description:** Contains contributions from geographers as well as other scholars from the humanities, social sciences and environmental sciences with a research interest in the developing world. Publishes theoretical and empirical articles that deal with the environment, society and development of the developing countries from interrelated disciplinary viewpoints.
Formerly (in 1972): Humanisma (0126-6950)
Related titles: Online - full text ed.: free (effective 2011).
Indexed: BAS, PSA, SociolAb.
Published by: (Universiti Kebangsaan Malaysia. Fakulti Sains Sosial dan Kemanusiaan/National University of Malaysia. Faculty of Social Sciences and Humanities), Perbit Universiti Kebangsaan Malaysia/ National University of Malaysia Press, Bangi, Selangor 43600, Malaysia. TEL 60-3-89215180, FAX 60-3-89254575, penerbit@ukm.my, http://pkukmweb.ukm.my/~penerbit/. Ed. Rahimah Abdul Aziz.

300 TKM
AKADEMIYA NAUK TURKMENISTANA. IZVESTIYA. SERIYA OBSHCHESTVENNYKH NAUK. Text in Russian. bi-m.
Formerly (until 1992): Akademiya Nauk Turkmenskoi S.S.R. Izvestiya. Seriya Obshchestvennykh Nauk
Published by: Turkmenistan Ylymlar Akademiasynyn/Academy of Sciences of Turkmenistan, Gogolya ul 15, Ashkhabad, 744000, Turkmenistan. Circ: 500.

300 IND ISSN 0975-9263
▼ **AKSHAYA INTERNATIONAL JOURNAL OF DEVELOPMENT STUDIES.** Abbreviated title: A I J D S. Text in English. 2010. bi-m. **Document type:** *Journal, Academic/Scholarly.* **Description:** Provides a forum for rigorous and critical analysis of conventional theories and to provide on a regular and sustainable basis, a scholarly journal for reporting empirical research findings, topical issues, theoretical concerns and reviews on development-related fields of study. It covers a number of disciplines related to development, including economics, history, politics, anthropology and sociology, and will publish quantitative papers as well as surveys of literature.
Published by: Akshaya Educational Charitable Trust, S.F.No. 209, Myleripalayam Village, Premier Nagar Rd, Othakkalmandapam Post, Coimbatore, 641 032, India. TEL 91-422-2610230, FAX 91-422-2610122.

300 DEU ISSN 0937-1761
AKTUELLE BEITRAEGE ZUR SOZIALWISSENSCHAFTLICHEN FORSCHUNG. Text in German. 1989. irreg., latest vol.6, 1993. price varies. **Document type:** *Monographic series, Academic/Scholarly.*
Published by: Centaurus Verlag & Media KG, Kaiser-Joseph-Str 267, Freiburg, 79098, Germany. TEL 49-761-1525861, FAX 49-761-1525868, info@centaurus-verlag.de, http://www.centaurus-verlag.de.

300 DEU ISSN 1867-609X
▼ **AKTUELLE PROBLEME MODERNER GESELLSCHAFTEN.** Text in German. 2010. irreg., latest vol.3, 2010. price varies. **Document type:** *Monographic series, Academic/Scholarly.*
Published by: Peter Lang GmbH (Subsidiary of: Peter Lang Publishing Group), Eschborner Landstr 42-50, Frankfurt Am Main, 60489, Germany. TEL 49-69-7807050, FAX 49-69-78070550, zentrale.frankfurt@peterlang.com. Eds. Corinna Onnen-Isemann, Peter Nitschke.

300 DEU ISSN 0930-9489
AKTUELLE WISSENSCHAFT. Text in German. 1986. irreg., latest vol.3, 1997. price varies. **Document type:** *Monographic series, Academic/ Scholarly.*
Published by: Centaurus Verlag & Media KG, Kaiser-Joseph-Str 267, Freiburg, 79098, Germany. TEL 49-761-1525861, FAX 49-761-1525868, info@centaurus-verlag.de, http://www.centaurus-verlag.de.

300 CAN ISSN 1207-4977
F1075
ALBERTA COMMUNITY DEVELOPMENT. ANNUAL REPORT. Text in English. 1976. a. free. **Document type:** *Government.*
Former titles (until 1993): Alberta Culture and Multiculturalism. Annual Report (0848-2128); (until 1987): Alberta Culture. Annual Report (0702-9659)
Indexed: CPE.
Published by: Alberta Community Development, Communications Branch, Standard Life Centre, 7th Fl, 10405 Jasper Ave, Edmonton, AB T5J 3N4, Canada. TEL 403-427-6530, FAX 403-427-1496. Circ: 500.

300 VEN ISSN 1316-6727
HC236
➤ **ALDEA MUNDO.** Text in Spanish. 1997. s-a. adv. **Document type:** *Journal, Academic/Scholarly.* **Description:** Dedicated to the theoretical and empirical analysis of issues related to borders, regional integration and globalization.
Related titles: Online - full text ed.: free (effective 2011).
Indexed: C01, IBSS.
Published by: Universidad de los Andes, Tachira, C.E.F.I., Ave ULA, Sector Santa Cecilia, San Cristobal, 5001, Venezuela. TEL 58-276-3405056, FAX 58-276-3405149, info@saber.ula.ve. Ed., R&P, Adv. contact Jose Briceno Ruiz. Circ: 500 (paid and controlled).

300 MEX ISSN 0187-5973
K1
ALEGATOS. Text in Spanish. 1992 (no.22). 3/yr. MXN 25. bk.rev. **Document type:** *Academic/Scholarly.*
Related titles: Online - full text ed.
Indexed: A01, C01, CA, F03, F04, T02.
Published by: Universidad Autonoma Metropolitana - Azcapotzalco, Departamento de Derecho, Av. San Pablo 180, Mexico City, DF 02200, Mexico. Circ: 1,000.

ALERO. *see* LITERATURE

300 FRA ISSN 1267-3625
ALINEA; revue de sciences sociales et humaines. Text in French. 1992. s-a.
Indexed: FR.
—INIST.
Published by: Association Trapezes, Departement de Sociologie, Universite Pierre Mendes, BP 47, Grenoble, 38040 Cedex 09, France. TEL 33-4-38128651.

300 DEU ISSN 0176-9251
ALLENSBACHER BERICHTE. Text in German. 1949. irreg. (2-3/mo.). EUR 1 per issue (effective 2010). back issues avail. **Document type:** *Newsletter, Academic/Scholarly.* **Description:** Newsletter presenting current survey research findings from the areas of politics, economics and society.
Related titles: Online - full text ed.
Published by: (Institut fuer Demoskopie Allensbach), Verlag fuer Demoskopie, Radolfzellerstr 8, Allensbach, 78472, Germany. Eds. Edgar Piel, Elisabeth Noelle Neumann. Circ: 1,000.

980.1 PER ISSN 0252-8835
F3429
ALLPANCHIS. Variant title: Allpanchis Phuturinga. Text in Spanish. 1969. s-a. PEN 25 domestic; USD 21 in United States; USD 22 in Europe (effective 2001). adv. bk.rev. bibl.; charts. **Document type:** *Academic/ Scholarly.*
Indexed: A21, AICP, AnthLit, H21, IBR, IBZ, MLA-IB, P08, RI-1, RI-2.
Published by: (Instituto de Pastoral Andina, Area de Cultura Andina y Sociedad), Centro de Estudios y Publicaciones, Camilo Carrillo 479, Jesus Maria, Apdo Postal 11 0107, Lima, 11, Peru. TEL 51-14-4336453, FAX 51-14-4331078, cepu@amauta.rcp.net.pe, http:// www.cep.com.pe. Circ: 2,500.

300 DEU
ALTE UND NEUE UNGLEICHHEITEN; Transformationen und Perspektiven von Geschlechterverhaeltnissen in unterschiedlichen gesellschaftlichen Bereichen. Text in German. 2004. irreg., latest vol.2, 2005. price varies. **Document type:** *Monographic series, Academic/Scholarly.*
Published by: Wissenschaftlicher Verlag Berlin, Koertestr 10, Berlin, 10967, Germany. TEL 49-30-89379899, FAX 49-30-6185021, verlag@wvberlin.de, http://www.wvberlin.de.

301 CAN ISSN 0702-8865
HM1.A6
➤ **ALTERNATE ROUTES**; a journal of critical social research. Text in English. 1977. a. CAD 12 to individuals; CAD 21.50 to institutions; CAD 6 to students (effective 2002). adv. bk.rev. back issues avail. **Document type:** *Journal, Academic/Scholarly.* **Description:** Multidisciplinary journal of the social sciences; focuses on contemporary theoretical issues within sociology.
Related titles: Online - full text ed.
Indexed: CA, LeftInd, PerIslam, S02, S03, SCOPUS, SOPODA, SSA, SociolAb, T02.
Address: c/o Department of Sociology Anthropology, Carleton University, Ottawa, ON K1S 5B6, Canada. TEL 613-520-2582, FAX 613-520-4062, altroutes@ccs.carleton.ca. Circ: 250.

➤ **ALTERNATIVE PRESS INDEX (PRINT)**; access to movements, news, policy, theory. *see* POLITICAL SCIENCE—Abstracting, Bibliographies, Statistics

➤ **ALTERNATIVES JOURNAL.** *see* ENVIRONMENTAL STUDIES

300 PRI
EL AMAUTA; revista de estudios iberoamericanos. Text in Spanish. 2003. a. back issues avail. **Document type:** *Journal, Academic/Scholarly.*
Related titles: Online - full text ed.
Published by: Universidad de Puerto Rico, Departamento de Ciencias Sociales, PO Box 4010, Arecibo, 00614-4010, Puerto Rico. TEL 787-815-0000 ext 3900, FAX 787-878-5712, http://www.upra.edu/. Ed. Jaime Colon.

300 BRA ISSN 1414-753X
GF1
AMBIENTE & SOCIEDADE. Text in Portuguese. 1997. s-a. BRL 35 (effective 2005). back issues avail. **Document type:** *Journal, Academic/Scholarly.*
Related titles: Online - full text ed.: free (effective 2011).
Indexed: C01, C25, CA, CABA, E12, F08, F12, G11, GH, H16, I11, IBSS, P42, PSA, R12, S02, S03, S13, S16, SCOPUS, SSA, SociolAb, T02, T05, TAR, W10, W11.
Published by: Universidade Estadual de Campinas, Nucleo de Estudos e Pesquisas Ambientais, Caixa Postal 6166, Campinas, SP 13081-970, Brazil. TEL 55-19-37887631, FAX 55-19-37887690, revista@nepam.unicamp.br, http://www.ic.unicamp.br. Ed. Lucia de Costa Ferreira.

300 ESP ISSN 1130-2887
JL951.A1
AMERICA LATINA HOY; revista de ciencas sociales. Text in Spanish. 1991. 3/yr. EUR 12 (effective 2009). back issues avail. **Document type:** *Journal, Academic/Scholarly.*
Related titles: Online - full text ed.: free (effective 2011).
Indexed: A26, H21, I04, I05, I13, P08, P42, PAIS, PSA, SociolAb.
Published by: Universidad de Salamanca, Ediciones, Apartado 325, Salamanca, 37080, Spain. TEL 34-923-294598, FAX 34-923-262579, pedidos@universitas.usal.es, http://www.eusal.es/. Ed. Flavia Freidenber.

THE AMERICAN (ONLINE). *see* POLITICAL SCIENCE

AMERICAN ACADEMY OF POLITICAL AND SOCIAL SCIENCE. ANNALS. *see* POLITICAL SCIENCE

320 300 USA ISSN 0002-7642
H1
➤ **AMERICAN BEHAVIORAL SCIENTIST.** Abbreviated title: A B S. Text in English. 1957. m. USD 1,967, GBP 1,157 to institutions; USD 2,007, GBP 1,181 combined subscription to institutions (print & online eds.) (effective 2012). adv. index. back issues avail.; reprint service avail. from PSC. **Document type:** *Journal, Academic/Scholarly.* **Description:** Focuses, in theme-organized issues prepared under guest editors, on emerging cross-disciplinary interests, research and problems in the social and behavioral sciences.
Formerly (until 1960): Political Research, Organization and Design (1930-2665)
Related titles: Microform ed.: (from PQC); Online - full text ed.: ISSN 1552-3381. USD 1,806, GBP 1,063 to institutions (effective 2012).
Indexed: A01, A02, A03, A08, A12, A17, A18, A20, A22, A25, A26, A36, ABCPolSci, ABIn, AC&P, AMHA, ASCA, ASG, AcaI, AmH&L, B01, B04, B06, B07, B08, B09, BAS, BEL&L, BRD, CA, CABA, CMM, CPM, ChPerI, Chicano, CurCont, DIP, E-psyche, E01, E02, E03, E07, E08, EAA, EIP, ERI, EdA, EdI, F08, F09, F12, FamI, FutSurv, G08, G10, GH, H04, H09, H10, HRA, HistAb, I05, I13, I14, IBR, IBSS, IBZ, L09, LT, MEA&I, MLA-IB, N02, N03, P02, P03, P04, P06, P30, P34, P37, P42, P48, P51, P53, P54, PAIS, PCI, PQC, PRA, PSA, PersLit, PsycInfo, PsycholAb, R12, RASB, RRTA, RefZh, S02, S03, S05, S08, S09, SCOPUS, SFSA, SPAA, SRRA, SSA, SSAI, SSAb, SSCI, SSI, SUSA, SociolAb, T02, T05, TAR, THA, UAA, V&AA, V02, VS, W01, W02, W03, W07, W09, W11.
—BLDSC (0810.780000), IE, Infotrieve, Ingenta, INIST. **CCC.**
Published by: Sage Publications, Inc., 2455 Teller Rd, Thousand Oaks, CA 91320. TEL 800-818-7243, FAX 800-583-2665, info@sagepub.com, http://www.sagepub.com. Ed. Laura Lawrie. **Subscr. overseas to:** Sage Publications Ltd., 1 Oliver's Yard, 55 City Rd, London EC1Y 1SP, United Kingdom. TEL 44-207-3248701, FAX 44-207-3248733, subscription@sagepub.co.uk.

➤ **AMERICAN, BRITISH AND CANADIAN STUDIES.** *see* POLITICAL SCIENCE—International Relations

▼ ➤ **AMERICAN INTERNATIONAL JOURNAL OF CONTEMPORARY RESEARCH.** *see* SCIENCES: COMPREHENSIVE WORKS

▼ ➤ **AMERICAN JOURNAL OF ACADEMIC RESEARCH.** *see* SCIENCES: COMPREHENSIVE WORKS

➤ **AMERICAN JOURNAL OF ECONOMICS AND SOCIOLOGY.** *see* BUSINESS AND ECONOMICS

300 658 USA ISSN 1098-2140
H1
➤ **AMERICAN JOURNAL OF EVALUATION.** Abbreviated title: A J E. Text in English. 1980. q. USD 606, GBP 357 to institutions; USD 618, GBP 364 combined subscription to institutions (print & online eds.) (effective 2012). adv. bk.rev. index. back issues avail.; reprint service avail. from PSC. **Document type:** *Journal, Academic/Scholarly.* **Description:** Contains articles on techniques and methods of evaluation to assist evaluators to improve the theory and practice of their profession, to develop their skills, to encourage dialogue, and to improve their knowledege base.
Former titles (until 1998): Evaluation Practice (0886-1633); (until 1986): Evaluation News (0191-8036)
Related titles: Online - full text ed.: ISSN 1557-0878. USD 556, GBP 328 to institutions (effective 2012) (from IngentaConnect).
Indexed: A01, A02, A03, A08, A22, AEI, ASCA, AddicA, C28, CA, CLFP, CurCont, E-psyche, E01, E03, ERI, ERIC, FamI, H01, P03, P04, P18, P30, P34, P53, P54, P55, PAIS, PQC, PsycInfo, PsycholAb, S02, S03, SCOPUS, SOPODA, SSA, SSCI, SociolAb, T02, W07.
—BLDSC (0824.607000), IE, Infotrieve, Ingenta. **CCC.**
Published by: (American Evaluation Association), Sage Publications, Inc., 2455 Teller Rd, Thousand Oaks, CA 91320. TEL 800-818-7243, FAX 800-583-2665, info@sagepub.com, http://www.sagepub.com. Ed. Thomas A Schwandt. **Subscr. outside the US to:** Sage Publications Ltd.

➤ **AMERICAN JOURNAL OF ISLAMIC SOCIAL SCIENCES.** *see* RELIGIONS AND THEOLOGY—Islamic

➤ **THE AMERICAN JOURNAL OF SEMIOTICS.** *see* HUMANITIES: COMPREHENSIVE WORKS

300 USA ISSN 0272-2011
F1008
➤ **AMERICAN REVIEW OF CANADIAN STUDIES.** Abbreviated title: A R C S. Text in English. 1971. q. GBP 200 combined subscription in United Kingdom to institutions (print & online eds.); EUR 288, USD 360 combined subscription to institutions (print & online eds.) (effective 2012). bk.rev. bibl. back issues avail.; reprint service avail. from PSC. **Document type:** *Journal, Academic/Scholarly.* **Description:** Contains articles which explores Canada's arts, cultures, economics, politics, history, and society, recognizing Canada's position in the world.
Formerly (until 1973): A C S U S Newsletter (0193-6093)
Related titles: Microfiche ed.: (from MML); Microfilm ed.: (from MML, PQC); Online - full text ed.: ISSN 1943-9954. GBP 180 in United Kingdom to institutions; EUR 259, USD 323 to institutions (effective 2012).
Indexed: A01, A03, A08, A22, A26, A33, ABS&EES, AmH&L, AmHI, B04, B24, BEL&L, BNNA, BibInd, C03, C04, CA, CBCARef, CBPI, CLitI, CPerI, CWPI, DIP, E08, G08, GEOBASE, H07, HistAb, I05, IBR, IBSS, IBZ, L05, L06, MLA-IB, P30, P34, P42, P45, P48, PAIS, PCI, PQC, PSA, RASB, RILM, S02, S03, S09, SCOPUS, SSAI, SSAb, SSI, SociolAb, T02, W03, W05.
—BLDSC (0853.590000), CIS, IE, Infotrieve, Ingenta. **CCC.**
Published by: (Association for Canadian Studies in the United States), Routledge (Subsidiary of: Taylor & Francis Group), 325 Chestnut St, Ste 800, Philadelphia, PA 19106. TEL 215-625-8900, FAX 215-625-2940, journals@routledge.com, http://www.routledge.com. Ed. John L Purdy.

800 POL ISSN 0209-1232
AMERICAN STUDIES. Text in English. 1981. irreg., latest vol.19, 2001. price varies. **Document type:** *Monographic series, Academic/ Scholarly.*
Indexed: AmH&L, MLA-IB.

S

Published by: (Uniwersytet Warszawski, Osrodek Studiow Amerykanskich), Wydawnictwa Uniwersytetu Warszawskiego, ul Nowy Swiat 4, Warsaw, 00497, Poland. TEL 48-22-5531319, FAX 48-22-5531318, wuw@uw.edu.pl. Ed. Michal Rozbicki. R&P Jolanta Okonska. Circ: 300. **Dist. by:** Ars Polona, Obroncow 25, Warsaw 03933, Poland. TEL 48-22-5098609, FAX 48-22-5098610, arspolona@arspolona.com.pl, http://www.arspolona.com.pl.

970 300 USA ISSN 0026-3079
E169.1

➤ **AMERICAN STUDIES.** Text in English. 1957. q. USD 35 to individuals; USD 50 to institutions (effective 2010). adv. bk.rev. charts; illus.; maps. Index. 200 p./no.; back issues avail.; reprints avail. **Document type:** *Journal, Academic/Scholarly.* **Description:** Crosses academic disciplines to explore the society and culture of the United States.
Former titles (until 1971): Midcontinent American Studies Journal (0544-0335); (until 1962): Central Mississippi Valley American Studies Association. Journal; (until 1960): Central Mississippi Valley American Studies Association. Bulletin; Incorporates (1975-2004): American Studies International (0883-105X); Which was formerly (until 1975): American Studies (0003-1321); (until 1970): American Studies News; American Studies International Incorporated (1983-1996): American Studies International Newsletter (0883-1068)
Related titles: Microform ed.: (from PQC); Online - full text ed.: ISSN 2153-6856.
Indexed: A01, A02, A03, A08, A22, A26, AES, AmH&L, AmHI, B04, B14, BRD, CA, ChLitAb, DIP, E01, E08, G08, H07, H08, H09, H10, HAb, HistAb, HumInd, I05, IBR, IBZ, ICR, MLA, MLA-IB, P02, P06, P10, P30, P34, P48, P53, P54, PAIS, PCI, PQC, RASB, RILM, S02, S03, S09, S11, SCOPUS, T02, W03, W05.
—BLDSC (0857.657600), IE, Ingenta. **CCC.**
Published by: (Mid-America American Studies Association), University of Kansas, American Studies Department, 213 Bailey Hall, Lawrence, KS 66045. amerst@ku.edu, http://americanstudies.ku.edu. Eds. David Katzman, Randal M Jelks, Sherrie J Tucker. adv.: page USD 150; 5 x 7.25. Circ: 1,200 (paid).

970 GBR ISSN 1661-4712
AMERICAN STUDIES; culture, society & the arts. Text in English. 2006. irreg., latest vol.3, 2010. price varies. **Document type:** *Monographic series, Academic/Scholarly.* **Description:** Covers American studies in culture, society and the arts.
Published by: Peter Lang Ltd. (Subsidiary of: Peter Lang Publishing Group), Evenlode Ct, Main Rd, Long Hanborough, Oxfordshire OX29 8SZ, United Kingdom. TEL 44-1993-880088, FAX 44-1993-882040, info@peterlang.com. Ed. Zamir Shamoon.

306 USA ISSN 0740-0489
AMERICAN UNIVERSITY STUDIES. SERIES 11. ANTHROPOLOGY AND SOCIOLOGY. Variant title: Anthropology and Sociology. Text in English. 1984. irreg., latest vol.72, 2007. price varies. **Document type:** *Monographic series, Academic/Scholarly.* **Description:** Explores the culture and ways of societies throughout the world.
—BLDSC (0858.078500).
Published by: Peter Lang Publishing, Inc. (Subsidiary of: Peter Lang Publishing Group), 29 Broadway, New York, NY 10006. TEL 212-647-7700, 212-647-7706, 800-770-5264, FAX 212-647-7707, customerservice@plang.com.

300 MEX
AMERISTICA. Text in Spanish. 1998. s-a. MXN 70 domestic; USD 10 foreign (effective 2005). **Document type:** *Journal, Academic/Scholarly.*
Published by: Debora Publicaciones, Apdo Postal 22-235, Mexico, D.F., Mexico. Ed. Gustavo Vargas Martinez.

300 NLD ISSN 2210-2310
AMSTERDAM SOCIAL SCIENCE. Text in English. 2008. q. EUR 25 (effective 2010). **Document type:** *Journal, Academic/Scholarly.*
Published by: Universiteit van Amsterdam, Graduate School of Social Sciences, Prins Hendrikkade 189-B, Amsterdam, 1011 TD, Netherlands. TEL 31-20-5253777, FAX 31-20-5253778, gsss@uva.nl. Eds. Jonathan Mijs, Thomas Franssen.

300 TUR ISSN 1303-0876
H8.T87
➤ **ANADOLU UNIVERSITESI SOSYAL BILIMLER DERGISI/ANADOLU UNIVERSITY JOURNAL OF SOCIAL SCIENCES.** Text in English, French, German, Turkish. 2001. s-a. bk.rev. **Document type:** *Journal, Academic/Scholarly.*
Related titles: Online - full text ed.: free (effective 2011).
Indexed: A01, CA, EconLit, SociolAb, T02.
Published by: Anadolu Universitesi, Sosyal Bilimler Enstitusu/Anadolu University, Social Sciences Institute, c/o Sosyal Bilimler Dergisi Sekretaryasi, Eskisehir, 26470, Turkey. TEL 90-222-3350580 ext 3243, 3250, FAX 90-222-3353616, sosbilder@anadolu.edu.tr, http://www.anadolu.edu.tr/akademik/ens_sosbil/index.htm. Ed. Ramazan Geylan.

➤ **ANALES DE CIENCIAS POLITICAS Y SOCIALES.** *see* POLITICAL SCIENCE

306 ESP ISSN 0211-2175
ANALISI; quaderns de comunicacio i cultura. Text in Spanish, Catalan. 1980. irreg. price varies. **Document type:** *Journal, Academic/Scholarly.*
Related titles: Online - full text ed.: free (effective 2011).
Published by: (Universitat Autonoma de Barcelona, Facultat de Ciencies de la Comunicacio), Universitat Autonoma de Barcelona, Servei de Publicacions, Edifici A, Bellaterra, Cardanyola del Valles, Barcelona, 08193, Spain. TEL 34-93-5811022, FAX 34-93-5813239, sp@uab.es, http://www.uab.es/publicacions/.

300 PER ISSN 1682-4407
ANALISIS & PROPUESTAS. Text in Spanish. 2000. irreg.
Media: Online - full text.
Published by: Grupo de Analisis para el Desarrollo, Ave del Ejercito No. 1870, Lima, 27, Peru. TEL 51-1-2641780, FAX 51-12641882.

ANALISIS POLITICO; revista de estudios politicos y relaciones internacionales. *see* POLITICAL SCIENCE

300 URY
ANALISIS Y DESAFIOS. Text in Spanish. 1991. m.?. UYP 6,000 per issue. **Document type:** *Consumer.*
Published by: (Instituto "Liberalis" Centro de Investigacion y Analisis de la Sociedad), Laster S.A., Ciudadela, 1432 Piso 2 Of. 202, Montevideo, 11101, Uruguay. TEL 98-56-69. Ed. Jorge O Casella.

300 DEU ISSN 0171-5860
H1
➤ **ANALYSE & KRITIK**; Zeitschrift fuer Sozialtheorie. Text in English, German. 1979. s-a. EUR 62 to individuals; EUR 78 to libraries; EUR 42 to students (effective 2011). adv. abstr. back issues avail.; reprint service avail. from SCH. **Document type:** *Journal, Academic/Scholarly.* **Description:** Devoted to the fundamental issues of empirical and normative social theory.
Related titles: Online - full text ed.
Indexed: A22, CA, DIP, FR, IBR, IBSS, IBZ, IPB, P02, P27, P42, P46, P48, P54, PCI, PQC, PSA, RASB, S02, S03, SCOPUS, SSA, SociolAb, T02.
—BLDSC (0890.880000), IE, Infotrieve. **CCC.**
Published by: Lucius und Lucius Verlagsgesellschaft mbH, Gerokstr 51, Stuttgart, 70184, Germany. TEL 49-711-242060, FAX 49-711-242088, lucius@luciusverlag.com, http://www.luciusverlag.com. Eds. Anton Leist, Michael Baurmann. Pub. Wulf von Lucius. Circ: 220 (paid).

300 DEU
ANALYSE UND FORSCHUNG. Text in German. 1999. irreg., latest vol.70, 2011. price varies. **Document type:** *Monographic series, Academic/Scholarly.*
Published by: U V K Verlagsgesellschaft mbH, Schuetzenstr 24, Konstanz, 78462, Germany. TEL 49-7531-90530, FAX 49-7531-905398, nadine.ley@uvk.de, http://www.uvk.de.

300 AUT
ANALYSEN ZU GESELLSCHAFT UND POLITIK. Text in German. 1998. irreg., latest vol.3, 2006. price varies. **Document type:** *Monographic series, Academic/Scholarly.*
Published by: Trauner Verlag und Buchservice GmbH, Koeglstr 14, Linz, 4020, Austria. TEL 43-732-778241212, FAX 43-732-778241400, office@trauner.at, http://www.trauner.at.

ANCILLA IURIS. *see* LAW

300 MEX ISSN 1870-0063
H8.S7
➤ **ANDAMIOS**; revista de investigacion social. Text in Spanish. 2004. 2/yr. MXN 210 domestic; USD 22.50 foreign; MXN 80 newsstand/cover (effective 2010). **Document type:** *Journal, Academic/Scholarly.* **Description:** Aims to encourage the production, exchange and spread of ideas in social sciences and humanities.
Related titles: Online - full text ed.
Indexed: A01, B04, BRD, C01, CA, F03, F04, IBSS, P42, PSA, S02, S03, SCOPUS, SSAI, SSAb, SSCI, SSI, SociolAb, T02, W03, W05, W07.
—INIST.
Published by: Universidad Autonoma de la Ciudad de Mexico, Colegio de Humanidades y Ciencias Sociales, Av Division del Norte num 906, 8 piso, Col Narvarte Poniente, Delegacion Benito Juarez, CP 03020, Mexico DF, Mexico. TEL 52-55-430538 ext 16811, FAX 52-55-30921211. Ed. Eduardo Mosches Nitkin. Circ: 1,000 (paid and controlled).

➤ **ANGELAKI**; journal of the theoretical humanities. *see* HUMANITIES: COMPREHENSIVE WORKS

300 AUT
ANGEWANDTE KULTURWISSENSCHAFTEN WIEN. Text in German. 2005. irreg., latest vol.17, 2010. price varies. **Document type:** *Monographic series, Academic/Scholarly.*
Published by: Praesens VerlagsgesmbH, Wehlistr 154/12, Vienna, W 1020, Austria. TEL 43-1-720703506, FAX 43-1-25330334660, m.ritter@praesens.at, http://www.praesens.at.

300 CHN ISSN 1001-5019
AS452.H553
ANHUI DAXUE XUEBAO (ZHEXUE SHEHUI KEXUE BAN)/ANHUI UNIVERSITY. JOURNAL (PHILOSOPHY AND SOCIAL SCIENCES). Text in Chinese. 1960. bi-m. adv. **Document type:** *Journal, Academic/Scholarly.* **Description:** Covers philosophy and other aspects of social sciences.
Related titles: Online - full text ed.: (from WanFang Data Corp.).
—East View.
Published by: Anhui Daxue Xuebao Bianjibu, 3, Feixi Lu, Longhe Xiao-qu, Xingzheng Bei Lou 325, Hefei, Anhui 230039, China. TEL 86-551-5107157, http://xuebao.ahu.edu.cn/. Circ: 3,000. **Dist. overseas by:** China International Book Trading Corp, 35 Chegongzhuang Xilu, Haidian District, PO Box 399, Beijing 100044, China.

300 001.3 500 CHN ISSN 1671-802X
ANHUI DIANZI XINXI ZHIYE JISHU XUEYUAN XUEBAO/ANHUI VOCATIONAL COLLEGE OF ELECTRONICS & INFORMATION TECHNOLOGY. JOURNAL. Text in Chinese. 2002. bi-m. **Document type:** *Journal, Academic/Scholarly.*
Related titles: Online - full text ed.
Published by: Anhui Dianzi Xinxi Zhiye Jishu Xueyuan/Anhui Vocational College of Electronics & Information Technology, 1000, Caoshan Lu, Bengbu, 233030, China. TEL 86-552-3172958.

300 CHN ISSN 1671-9247
ANHUI GONGYE DAXUE XUEBAO (SHEHUI KEXUE BAN)/ANHUI UNIVERSITY OF TECHNOLOGY. JOURNAL (SOCIAL SCIENCES EDITION). Text in Chinese. 1984. bi-m. CNY 8 newsstand/cover (effective 2006). **Document type:** *Journal, Academic/Scholarly.*
Formerly (until 2000): Huadong Yejin Xueyuan Xuebao. Journal (Shehui Kexue Ban)/East China University of Metallurgy. Journal (Social Sciences) (1008-7494)
Related titles: Online - full text ed.
Published by: Anhui Gongye Daxue/Anhui University of Technology, Hudong Lu #59, Ma'anshan, 243002, China. TEL 86-555-2400674, FAX 86-555-2471263, http://www.ahut.edu.cn.

300 CHN ISSN 1672-1101
ANHUI LIGONG DAXUE XUEBAO (SHEHUI KEXUE BAN). Text in Chinese. 1999. q.
Formerly (until 2003): Huainan Gongye Xueyuan Xuebao (Shehui Kexue Ban)/Huainan Institute of Technology. Journal (Social Sciences) (1671-0533)
Published by: Anhui Ligong Daxue/Anhui University of Science and Technology, Journal Editorial Board, Huainan, Anhui 232001, China. TEL 86-554-6668044.

300 CHN ISSN 1009-2463
ANHUI NONGYE DAXUE XUEBAO (SHEHUI KEXUE BAN)/ANHUI AGRICULTURAL UNIVERSITY. JOURNAL (SOCIAL SCIENCES EDITION). Text in Chinese. 1991. bi-m. CNY 5 newsstand/cover (effective 2006). **Document type:** *Journal, Academic/Scholarly.*
Related titles: Online - full text ed.
Published by: Anhui Nongye Daxue, 675 Xinxiang, Hefei, 230036, China. TEL 86-551-2823795 ext 3465.

ANHUI SHIFAN XUEYUAN XUEBAO (RENWEN SHEHUI KEXUE BAN)/ANHUI NORMAL UNIVERSITY. JOURNAL (HUMANITIES & SOCIAL SCIENCES EDITION). *see* HUMANITIES: COMPREHENSIVE WORKS

300 500 CHN ISSN 1672-9994
ANHUI YEJIN KEJI ZHIYE XUEYUAN XUEBAO/ANHUI VOCATIONAL COLLEGE OF METALLURGY AND TECHNOLOGY. JOURNAL. Text in Chinese. 1990. q. **Document type:** *Journal, Academic/Scholarly.*
Formerly (until 2004): Magang Zhigong Daxue Xuebao/Magang Staff and Workers' University. Journal (1009-5136)
Related titles: Online - full text ed.
Published by: Anhui Yejin Keji Zhiye Xueyuan/Anhui Vocational College of Metallurgy and Technology, 555, Huxi Nan Lu, Maanshan, 243011, China. TEL 86-555-8325000, FAX 86-555-8325034.

300 CHN ISSN 1672-9536
ANHUI ZHIYE JISHU XUEYUAN XUEBAO/ANHUI VOCATIONAL TECHNICAL COLLEGE. JOURNAL. Text in Chinese. 2002. q. **Document type:** *Journal, Academic/Scholarly.*
Formerly (until 2004): Anhui Fangzhi Zhiye Jishu Xueyuan Xuebao/Anhui Textile Vocational Technical Institute. Journal (1671-7279)
Related titles: Online - full text ed.
Published by: Anhui Zhiye Jishu Xueyuan/Anhui Vocationcal Technical College, 268, Baohe Dadao, Hefei, 230051, China. TEL 86-551-3440097, http://www.ahtu.ah.cn/.

300 DEU ISSN 0517-8401
ANMERKUNGEN ZUR ZEIT. Text in German. 1956. irreg., latest vol.39, 2007. price varies. **Document type:** *Monographic series, Academic/Scholarly.*
Published by: Akademie der Kuenste, Pariser Platz 4, Berlin, 10117, Germany. TEL 49-30-200570, info@adk.de, http://www.adk.de.

300 FRA ISSN 1952-8108
L'ANNEE DU MAGHREB. Text in French. 1962. a. price varies. adv. bk.rev. index. back issues avail. **Document type:** *Journal, Academic/Scholarly.*
Formerly (until 2006): Annuaire de l'Afrique du Nord (0066-2607)
Indexed: A22, ASD, BibLing, CCA, DIP, FR, I14, IBR, IBZ, MLA-IB, P30, PCI, RASB.
—BLDSC (1049.143000), IE, Ingenta, INIST.
Published by: (Institut de Recherches et d'Etudes sur le Monde Arabe et Musulman (I R E M A M)), Centre National de la Recherche Scientifique, 15 Rue Malebranche, Paris, 75005, France. TEL 33-1-53102700, FAX 33-1-53102727. Circ: 1,500 (controlled).

ANNOTATIONS (YEAR); a guide to the independent critical press. *see* JOURNALISM

969.005 910 FRA ISSN 0247-400X
DT468
ANNUAIRE DES PAYS DE L'OCEAN INDIEN. Text in French; Summaries in English. 1974. a. price varies. adv. bk.rev. illus. index. **Document type:** *Academic/Scholarly.*
Indexed: ASD, CCA, FR, IBR, IBSS, IBZ, P30.
—INIST.
Published by: Centre National de la Recherche Scientifique, Campus Gerard-Megie, 3 Rue Michel-Ange, Paris, 75794, France. TEL 33-1-44964000, FAX 33-1-44965390, http://www.cnrseditions.fr. Eds. J Benoit, L Favoreu. Circ: 1,500. **Co-sponsor:** Universite d'Aix-Marseille III (Universite de Droit, d'Economie et des Sciences).

ANNUAL REVIEW OF LAW AND SOCIAL SCIENCE. *see* LAW

300 CHN
ANQING SHIFAN XUEYUAN XUEBAO (SHEHUI KEXUE BAN)/ ANQING TEACHERS COLLEGE. JOURNAL (SOCIAL SCIENCE EDITION). Text in English. 1981. m. back issues avail. **Document type:** *Journal, Academic/Scholarly.*
Former titles (until 1999): Anqing Shi-Yuan Shehui Kexue Xuebao; (until 1990): Anqing Shi-Yuan Xuebao (Shehui Kexue Ban) (1003-4730)
Related titles: Online - full text ed.
Published by: Anqing Shifan Xueyuan, 128, Hunan Lu, Anqing, 246011, China. TEL 86-556-5500129, FAX 86-556-5500148, http://www.aqtc.edu.cn/.

300 CHN ISSN 1008-2441
AS452.A5263
ANSHAN SHIFAN XUEYUAN XUEBAO/ANSHAN NORMAL UNIVERSITY. JOURNAL. Text in Chinese. bi-m. **Document type:** *Journal, Academic/Scholarly.*
Formerly (until 1993): Anshan Shizhuan Xuebao
Related titles: Online - full text ed.
Published by: Anshan Shifan Xueyuan/Anshan Normal University, 43, Pingan Jie, Anshan, 114007, China. TEL 86-412-2960892, FAX 86-412-2960891.

300 001.3 CHN ISSN 1673-9507
ANSHUN XUEYUAN XUEBAO/ANSHUN COLLEGE. JOURNAL. Text in Chinese. 1983. bi-m. CNY 10 per issue (effective 2009). **Document type:** *Journal, Academic/Scholarly.*
Former titles (until 2007): Anshun Shifan Gaodeng Zhuanke Xuexiao Xuebao/Anshun Teachers College. Journal (1672-3694); (until 2001): Anshun Shi-Zhuan Xuebao (1009-4334)
Related titles: Online - full text ed.
Published by: Anshun Xueyuan, 25, Xueyuan Lu, Anshun, 561000, China. TEL 86-853-2214795, FAX 86-853-3413582, http://www.asu.edu.cn/.

ANTHOLOGY; a social studies journal. *see* EDUCATION—Teaching Methods And Curriculum

300 986.1 COL ISSN 0120-2456
ANUARIO COLOMBIANO DE HISTORIA SOCIAL Y DE LA CULTURA. Text in Spanish; Summaries in English, Spanish. 1963. irreg. USD 24 domestic; USD 70 in the Americas; USD 135 elsewhere (effective 2011). adv. bk.rev. abstr.; bibl.; charts; maps; illus.; stat. **Document type:** *Journal, Academic/Scholarly.* **Description:** Aims to disseminate research on Colombian history and publishes comparative articles on Latin America and the world, as well as historiographic and theoretical analysis.
Related titles: Online - full text ed.
Indexed: CA, F04, H21, P08, P09, PCI, T02.

Published by: Universidad Nacional de Colombia, Departemento de Historia, Cra.30, No.45-03, Bldg. 224, Manuel Ancizar, Office 3064, Bogota, Colombia. TEL 57-1-3165000 ext 16486, FAX 57-1-3165000 ext 16477, dephistoria_bog@unal.edu.co, http://www.humanas.unal.edu.co/historia/. Ed., Pub. Mauricio Archila-Neira. R&P Adriana Rodriguez-Franco. Circ: 300. **Dist. by:** Siglo del Hombre Editores, Cra. 32 No.25-46/50, Bogota, D.C., Colombia. TEL 57-1-3377700, FAX 57-1-3377665, info@siglodelhombre.com, http://www.siglodelhombre.com.

300 572 ESP ISSN 0210-5810
F1401
ANUARIO DE ESTUDIOS AMERICANOS. Text in English, Portuguese, Spanish. 1944. s-a. bk.rev. back issues avail.; reprints avail. **Document type:** *Journal, Academic/Scholarly.*
Incorporates (in 1993): Anuario de Estudios Americanos. Suplemento. Seccion Historiografia y Bibliografia (0214-2252); Which was formerly (until 1987): Historiografia y Bibliografia Americanista (0439-2477)
Related titles: CD-ROM ed.: ISSN 1576-2912. 1997; Online - full text ed.: ISSN 1988-4273. 2000. free (effective 2011).
Indexed: A20, AICP, AmH&L, ArtHuCI, BibInd, CA, FR, H21, HistAb, IBR, IBZ, MLA-IB, P08, P09, P30, PCI, RILM, SCOPUS, T02, W07.
—INIST. **CCC.**
Published by: (Consejo Superior de Investigaciones Cientificas (C S I C), Escuela de Estudios Hispano-Americanos), Consejo Superior de Investigaciones Cientificas (C S I C), Departamento de Publicaciones, Vitruvio 8, Madrid, 28006, Spain. publ@csic.es, http://www.publicaciones.csic.es.

300 CRI ISSN 0377-7316
F1421
ANUARIO DE ESTUDIOS CENTROAMERICANOS. Text in Spanish. 1974. 2/yr. adv. bk.rev. **Document type:** *Journal, Academic/Scholarly.*
Related titles: Online - full text ed.
Indexed: A26, C01, H21, HistAb, I04, I05, IBR, IBSS, IBZ, P08, P30, PAIS, RASB.
Published by: Universidad de Costa Rica, Editorial, Sede Rodrigo Facio Brenes, Montes de Oca, San Jose, Costa Rica. TEL 506-207-4000, FAX 506-224-8214, direccion@editorial.ucr.ac.cr, http://editorial.ucr.ac.cr. Ed. Ronald Solano. Circ: 1,000.

300 ESP ISSN 1130-8966
HD3528.A3
ANUARIO DE ESTUDIOS COOPERATIVOS/KOOPERATIBA IKASKUNTZEN URTEKARIA. Text in Multiple languages. 1985. a. EUR 13 (effective 2010). back issues avail. **Document type:** *Journal, Academic/Scholarly.*
Published by: (Universidad de Deusto, Instituto de Estudios Cooperativos), Universidad de Deusto, Departamento de Publicaciones, Apdo 1/E, Bilbao, 48080, Spain. TEL 34-94-4139162, FAX 34-94-4456817, publicaciones@deusto.es, http://deusto-publicaciones.es/. Ed. Aitziber Mugarra Elorriana.

300 VEN ISSN 1316-7162
F1401
ANUARIO SOCIAL Y POLITICO DE AMERICA LATINA Y EL CARIBE. Text in Spanish. 1994. a., latest vol.2, 1998. adv. bk.rev. **Document type:** *Academic/Scholarly.*
Former titles (until 1994): Anuario Latinoamericana de Ciencias Sociales; Revista Latinoamericana de Ciencias Sociales (0188-7661)
Published by: (Facultad Latinoamericana de Ciencias Sociales CRI), Editorial Nueva Sociedad Ltda., Chacao, Apdo 61712, Caracas, DF 1060-A, Venezuela. Circ: 4,000.

300 JPN ISSN 0286-3901
H8
AOYAMA JOURNAL OF SOCIAL SCIENCES/AOYAMA SHAKAI KAGAKU KIYO. Text in Japanese. 1973. s-a.
—BLDSC (1567.732000).
Published by: Aoyama-Gakuin University/Aoyama Gakuin Daigaku, 4-4-25 Shibuya, Shibuya-ku, Tokyo, 150-0002, Japan.

300 DEU ISSN 1862-801X
APELIOTES; Studien zur Kulturgeschichte und Theologie. Text in German. 2007. irreg., latest vol.7, 2010. price varies. **Document type:** *Monographic series, Academic/Scholarly.*
Published by: Peter Lang GmbH (Subsidiary of: Peter Lang Publishing Group), Eschborner Landstr 42-50, Frankfurt Am Main, 60489, Germany. TEL 49-69-7807050, FAX 49-69-78070550, zentrale.frankfurt@peterlang.com. Ed. Rainer Kampling.

300 ESP ISSN 1696-7348
H8.S7
APOSTA; revista de ciencias sociales. Text in Spanish. 2003. m. free (effective 2011). back issues avail. **Document type:** *Journal, Academic/Scholarly.*
Media: Online - full text.
Indexed: F04, T02.

300 302 NLD ISSN 1871-2584
HN25
APPLIED RESEARCH IN QUALITY OF LIFE. Text in English. 2006. q. EUR 680, USD 846 combined subscription to institutions (print & online eds.) (effective 2012). reprint service avail. from PSC. **Document type:** *Journal, Academic/Scholarly.* **Description:** Focuses on applied research by targeting professionals in the applied social and behavioral science disciplines.
Related titles: Online - full text ed.: ISSN 1871-2576 (from IngentaConnect).
Indexed: A22, A26, E01, P03, P30, PsycInfo, SCOPUS.
—IE, Ingenta. **CCC.**
Published by: Springer Netherlands (Subsidiary of: Springer Science+Business Media), Van Godewijckstraat 30, Dordrecht, 3311 GX, Netherlands. TEL 31-78-6576050, FAX 31-78-6576474, http://www.springer.com. Eds. Alex C Michalos, Richard J Estes, M Joseph Sirgy.

300 USA
APPLIED SOCIAL RESEARCH. Text in English. 19??. irreg., latest 2001. price varies. back issues avail. **Document type:** *Monographic series, Academic/Scholarly.* **Description:** The intent of this series is to advance both theory-focused empirical work and empirically-grounded theoretical developments in all areas of applied social research, including consumer, political, organizational, legal, health, and other domains.
Related titles: Online - full text ed.
Published by: Psychology Press (Subsidiary of: Taylor & Francis Inc.), 325 Chestnut St, Ste 800, Philadelphia, PA 19106. TEL 800-354-1420, FAX 215-625-2940, orders@taylorandfrancis.com. Adv. contact Linda Hann TEL 44-1344-779945.

300 USA
APPLIED SOCIAL RESEARCH METHODS. Text in English. 1984. irreg., latest 2009. price varies. back issues avail. **Document type:** *Monographic series, Academic/Scholarly.* **Description:** Provides professionals and students with inexpensive texts describing the major methods used in applied social research. Includes focused summaries of the individual methods most used by applied researchers; are quick reference and offer practical exercises.
Published by: Sage Publications, Inc., Books (Subsidiary of: Sage Publications, Inc.), 2455 Teller Rd, Thousand Oaks, CA 91320. TEL 800-818-7243, FAX 800-583-2665, books.claim@sagepub.com. Pub. Sara Miller McCune.

300 PER ISSN 0252-1865
H8
APUNTES; revista semestral de ciencias sociales. Text in Spanish. 1973. s-a. adv. bk.rev. back issues avail. **Document type:** *Journal, Academic/Scholarly.*
Indexed: H21, IBR, IBSS, IBZ, P08, P09, PAIS, PCI.
Published by: Universidad del Pacifico, Ave Salaverry 2020, Jesus Maria, Lima, 11, Peru. TEL 51-1-2190100, http://www.up.edu.pe. Ed. Jose Luis Sardon. Circ: 1,000. **Subscr. to:** Libreria de la Universidad del Pacifico, Apdo. 4683, Lima 100, Peru.

300 ARG ISSN 0329-2142
H8.S7
APUNTES DE INVESTIGACION DEL CECYP. Text in Spanish. 1997. s-a. ARS 24 domestic; USD 20 foreign (effective 2010). bk.rev. **Document type:** *Journal, Academic/Scholarly.*
Related titles: Online - full text ed.: ISSN 1851-9814. 2008. free (effective 2011).
Published by: Fundacion del Sur, Centro de Estudios en Cultura y Politica, Cochabamba 449, Buenos Aires, 1150, Argentina. TEL 54-11-43618549, FAX 54-11-43070545, fundasur@fundasur.org.ar, http://www.fundasur.org.ar/. Ed. Lucas Rubinich.

300 COL ISSN 1657-5997
AQUICHAN. Text in Spanish. 2002. a. free (effective 2011). back issues avail. **Document type:** *Monographic series, Academic/Scholarly.*
Media: Online - full text.
Indexed: A01, C01, CA, F03, F04, H21, P08, P27, P48, P54, PQC, SCI, SSCI, T02, W07.
Published by: Universidad de la Sabana, Campus Universitario. Puente del Comun, Km. 21 Autopista Norte de Bogota, Chia, Cundinamarca, Colombia. TEL 57-1-8615555, FAX 57-1-8618517, usmail@unisabana.edu.co, http://www.unisabana.edu.co. Ed. Laureano Felipe Gomez Duenas.

ARANZADI SOCIAL. *see* LAW
ARANZADI SOCIAL (QUARTERLY EDITION). *see* LAW
ARANZADI SOCIAL. INDICES AUXILIARES. *see* LAW

300 ESP ISSN 1575-6823
JA26
ARAUCARIA. Text in Spanish. 1999. s-a. **Document type:** *Journal, Academic/Scholarly.*
Related titles: Online - full text ed.: 2003. free (effective 2011).
Indexed: CA, F04, T02.
—**CCC.**
Published by: Universidad de Sevilla, Secretariado de Publicaciones, Calle Porvenir 27, Sevilla, 41013, Spain. TEL 34-95-4487444, FAX 34-95-4487443, secpub10@us.es, http://www.us.es/publius/inicio.html. Ed. Antonio Hermosa Andujar.

300 DEU ISSN 0941-5025
ARBEIT; Zeitschrift fuer Arbeitsforschung, Arbeitsgestaltung und Arbeitspolitik. Text in German. 1992. q. EUR 69 to individuals; EUR 82 to libraries; EUR 46 to students; EUR 26 newsstand/cover (effective 2011). adv. abstr. 80 p./no.; back issues avail. **Document type:** *Journal, Academic/Scholarly.*
Related titles: Online - full text ed.
Indexed: A12, ABIn, CA, DIP, IBR, IBSS, IBZ, P48, P51, P53, P54, PAIS, PQC, S02, S03, SociolAb, T02.
Published by: Lucius und Lucius Verlagsgesellschaft mbH, Gerokstr 51, Stuttgart, 70184, Germany. TEL 49-711-242060, FAX 49-711-242088, lucius@luciusverlag.com. Circ: 460 (paid and controlled). **Dist. by:** Brockhaus Commission, Kreidlerstr 9, Kornwestheim 70806, Germany. TEL 49-7154-13270, FAX 49-7154-132713.

300 DEU ISSN 1861-647X
ARBEIT, BILDUNG UND GESELLSCHAFT/LABOUR, EDUCATION & SOCIETY. Text in German, English. 2006. irreg., latest vol.19, 2009. price varies. **Document type:** *Monographic series, Academic/Scholarly.*
Published by: Peter Lang GmbH (Subsidiary of: Peter Lang Publishing Group), Eschborner Landstr 42-50, Frankfurt Am Main, 60489, Germany. TEL 49-69-7807050, FAX 49-69-78070550, zentrale.frankfurt@peterlang.com.

300 DEU ISSN 0946-8811
ARBEIT - TECHNIK - ORGANISATION - SOZIALES. Text in German. 1996. irreg., latest vol.33, 2006. price varies. **Document type:** *Monographic series, Academic/Scholarly.*
Published by: Peter Lang GmbH (Subsidiary of: Peter Lang Publishing Group), Eschborner Landstr 42-50, Frankfurt Am Main, 60489, Germany. TEL 49-69-7807050, FAX 49-69-78070550, zentrale.frankfurt@peterlang.com. Ed. Wiking Ehlert.

300 DEU ISSN 0170-8775
ARBEITEN ZUR AESTHETIK, DIDAKTIK, LITERATUR- UND SPRACHWISSENSCHAFT. Text in German. 1975. irreg., latest vol.20, 1996. price varies. **Document type:** *Monographic series, Academic/Scholarly.*
Published by: Peter Lang GmbH (Subsidiary of: Peter Lang Publishing Group), Eschborner Landstr 42-50, Frankfurt Am Main, 60489, Germany. TEL 49-69-7807050, FAX 49-69-78070550, zentrale.frankfurt@peterlang.com.

300 AUT ISSN 1027-7269
ARBEITS- UND SOZIALRECHTSKARTEI. Text in German. 1997. m. EUR 173.80 (effective 2005). back issues avail. **Document type:** *Journal, Consumer.*
Published by: Linde Verlag Wien GmbH, Scheydgasse 24, Vienna, W 1211, Austria. TEL 43-1-246300, FAX 43-1-2463023, office@lindeverlag.at, http://www.lindeverlag.at. Circ: 5,000 (paid).

ARBEITSMATERIALIEN WIRTSCHAFTSGEOGRAPHIE REGENSBURG. *see* GEOGRAPHY

300 DEU ISSN 1432-5543
ARBEITSPAPIERE GEMEINSCHAFTEN. Text in German. 1997. irreg., latest vol.21, 1999. price varies. **Document type:** *Monographic series, Academic/Scholarly.*
Published by: Humboldt-Universitaet zu Berlin, Nordeuropa-Institut, Unter den Linden 6, Berlin, 10099, Germany. TEL 49-30-20939625, FAX 49-30-20935325, marzena.debska-buddenhagen@rz.hu-berlin.de, http://www.ni.hu-berlin.de.

300 ESP ISSN 0210-1963
AP60
ARBOR; revista general de investigacion y cultura. Text in Spanish. 1944. m. EUR 13.24 domestic; EUR 19.86 foreign (effective 2009). back issues avail. **Document type:** *Journal, Academic/Scholarly.* **Description:** Expresses the view that scientific and technological industries must be sensitive and responsible to the needs of the society that supports them.
Related titles: Online - full text ed.: ISSN 1988-303X. 2006. free (effective 2011).
Indexed: A20, A22, ASCA, ArtHuCI, BEL&L, CERDIC, CurCont, FR, HistAb, I14, IBR, IBZ, IECT, MLA, MLA-IB, P09, P30, PCI, PhilInd, RASB, SCOPUS, W07.
—IE, Infotrieve, INIST. **CCC.**
Published by: Consejo Superior de Investigaciones Cientificas (C S I C), Departamento de Publicaciones, Vitruvio 8, Madrid, 28006, Spain. publ@csic.es, http://www.publicaciones.csic.es.

ARCHAEOLOGY IN MONTANA. *see* ARCHAEOLOGY
ARCHIV FUER WISSENSCHAFT UND PRAXIS DER SOZIALEN ARBEIT. *see* SOCIAL SERVICES AND WELFARE
ARCHIVAL ISSUES. *see* LIBRARY AND INFORMATION SCIENCES
ARCHIVES DE SCIENCES SOCIALES DES RELIGIONS. *see* RELIGIONS AND THEOLOGY
ARCHIWUM HISTORII FILOZOFII I MYSLI SPOLECZNEJ. *see* PHILOSOPHY

300 ESP ISSN 1886-6530
AREA 3 (ONLINE); cuadernos de temas grupales e institucionales. Variant title: Area Tres. Text in Spanish. 1994. s-a. back issues avail. **Document type:** *Magazine, Consumer.*
Formerly (until 2005): Area 3 (Print) (1134-9999)
Media: Online - full text.
Published by: Centro de Estudios Sociosanitarios, Sauco, 1, 2o - 3, Madrid, 28039, Spain. revista@area3.org.es.

300 ESP ISSN 0211-6707
➤ **AREAS;** revista internacional de ciencias sociales. Text in Spanish. 1981. a., latest vol.20, 2000. **Document type:** *Monographic series, Academic/Scholarly.*
Indexed: DIP, IBR, IBZ.
Published by: Universidad de Murcia, Servicio de Publicaciones, Edificio Saavedra Fajardo, C/ Actor Isidoro Maiquez 9, Murcia, 30007, Spain. TEL 34-968-363887, FAX 34-968-363414, vgm@um.es, http://www.um.es/publicaciones/.

300 001.3 VEN ISSN 0254-1637
H8.S7
➤ **ARGOS.** Text in Spanish. 1980. bi-m. VEB 30 (effective 2009). **Document type:** *Journal, Academic/Scholarly.* **Description:** Features research-based, unpublished and original articles that scientifically study topics of social sciences and humanities: anthropology, architecture, plastic arts, political sciences, economics, education, cultural studies, philosophy, management and administration, history, languages, linguistics, literature, psychology, sociology and urban studies.
Related titles: Online - full text ed.
Indexed: A20, ArtHuCI, C01, MLA-IB, SCOPUS, SSCI, W07.
Published by: Universidad Simon Bolivar, Division de Ciencias Sociales y Humanidades, Edificio EGE, piso 1, Apartado 89000, Caracas, 1080-A, Venezuela. TEL 58-212-9063723, FAX 58-212-9063806.

053.1 DEU ISSN 0004-1157
HM5
DAS ARGUMENT; Zeitschrift fuer Philosophie und Sozialwissenschaften. Text in German. 1959. bi-m. EUR 52.50; EUR 11 newsstand/cover (effective 2008). adv. bk.rev. index. **Document type:** *Journal, Academic/Scholarly.*
Indexed: A20, A22, DIP, FR, IBR, IBZ, IPB, MLA-IB, P30, PCI, PRA, PhilInd, RASB, RILM, SOPODA, SociolAb.
—BLDSC (1664.355000), IE, Infotrieve, Ingenta, INIST.
Published by: Argument-Verlag GmbH, Glashuettenstr 28, Hamburg, 20357, Germany. TEL 49-40-4018000, FAX 49-40-40180020, verlag@argument.de, http://www.argument.de. Ed. Wolfgang Fritz Haug. adv.: B&W page EUR 400. Circ: 2,000 (paid and controlled).

300 BRA
ARGUMENTO; uma publicacao interdisciplinar. Text in Portuguese. 1992. s-a. adv. **Document type:** *Academic/Scholarly.*
Published by: Faculdades Integradas Candido Mendes, Rua Joana Angelica, 63, Ipanema, RJ 22420-030, Brazil. TEL 021-267-7141, FAX 021-267-7495. Ed. Monica Grin.

300 FRA ISSN 2107-7045
▼ **ARPES.** Text in French. 2010. irreg. **Document type:** *Journal, Academic/Scholarly.*
Media: Online - full text.
Published by: College Cooperatif en Bretagne, Universite Rennes 2 - Campus La Harpe, Av Charles Tillon - CS 24414, Rennes, 35 044, France. TEL 33-2-99141441, FAX 33-2-99141444, ccb@uhb.fr.

ARQUITECTONICS; mind, land and society. *see* ARCHITECTURE

300 BRA ISSN 1413-6597
HD8281
ARQUIVO EDGARD LEUENROTH. CADERNOS. Text in Portuguese. s-a. **Description:** Publishes scholarly research concerning the main subjects found in the archive's holdings, which include labor movement, history of industrialization, history of the left, human rights, political history, cultural and intellectual history, social movements and agrarian history.
Formerly (until 1992): Arquivo Edgard Leuenroth. Guia

S

Published by: Instituto de Filosofia e Ciencias Humanas, Centro de Pesquisa e Documentacao Social, Cidade Universitaria Zeferino Vaz, C Universitaria, Caixa Postal 6110, Campinas, SP 13083-970, Brazil. TEL 55-19-7887566, FAX 55-19-2893327. **Co-sponsor:** Associacao Cultural do Arquivo Edgard Leuenroth.

300 CHE ISSN 1661-4941
H1
ARTICULO.CH. Key Title: www.articulo.ch. Text in French. 2005. a. free (effective 2011). **Document type:** *Journal, Academic/Scholarly.*
Media: Online - full text.
Published by: Articulo. ch info@articulo.ch.

300 USA ISSN 2151-6200
H1.A3
▼ **ARTS AND SOCIAL SCIENCES JOURNAL.** Text in English. 2010. irreg. free (effective 2012). **Document type:** *Journal, Academic/Scholarly.*
Media: Online - full text.
Indexed: I05, S02, S03.
Published by: Aston Journals, 2026 NE Blue Heron Dr, Portland, OR 97211. contact@astonjournals.com.

▼ **ARTS MARKETING**; an international journal. *see* BUSINESS AND ECONOMICS—Marketing And Purchasing

300 GTM
ASI ES. Text in Spanish. 1991 (no.5). irreg. **Document type:** *Bulletin, Academic/Scholarly.*
Indexed: RASB.
Published by: Asociacion de Investigacion y Estudios Sociales, Apdo. Postal 1005 A, Guatemala City, Guatemala. Ed. Raquel Zelaya.

300 USA ISSN 1522-0966
HC411
➤ **ASIA - PACIFIC ISSUES.** Text in English. 1992. irreg., latest vol.95, 2010. USD 2.50 per issue (effective 2010). back issues avail. **Document type:** *Monographic series, Trade.* **Description:** Addresses topics of interest and significant impact relevant to current and emerging policy debates.
Related titles: Online - full text ed.: free (effective 2010).
Indexed: A01, CA, ESPM, GEOBASE, HPNRM, SCOPUS, SSciA, T02.
Published by: East-West Center, 1601 EW Rd, Honolulu, HI 96848. TEL 808-944-7111, FAX 808-944-7376, ewcbooks@eastwestcenter.org. Ed. Linda Kay Quintana.

300 IND ISSN 2229-5801
▼ ➤ **ASIA-PACIFIC JOURNAL OF SOCIAL SCIENCES.** Text and summaries in English. 2009 (Jun.). 2/yr. free (effective 2011). a. index. back issues avail. **Document type:** *Journal, Academic/Scholarly.* **Description:** Offers information relating to social issues and thereby disseminate the advanced knowledge of the social science-disciplines.
Related titles: Online - full text ed.: ISSN 0975-5942. free (effective 2011).
Published by: International Society for Asia Pacific Society, 18-8-99/1A, Madura Nagar, Sri Venkateswara University, Tirupati, Andhra Pradesh 517 502, India. TEL 91-9989258403, FAX 91-877-2248380, secretary@isapsindia.org, http://www.isapsindia.org. Ed., Pub. G Jayachandra Reddy.

300 PHL ISSN 0119-8386
H1
➤ **ASIA-PACIFIC SOCIAL SCIENCE REVIEW.** Text in English. 2000. s-a. **Document type:** *Journal, Academic/Scholarly.*
Indexed: CA, S02, S03, SCOPUS, T02.
Published by: De La Salle University, 2401 Taft Ave, Malate, Manila, 1004, Philippines. TEL 63-2-5244611, http://www.dlsu.edu.ph. Ed. Alfredo C Robles Jr.

300 GBR ISSN 2042-6143
▼ ➤ **ASIA PACIFIC WORLD.** Text in English. 2010. s-a. GBP 112, EUR 130, USD 190 combined subscription to institutions (print & online eds.) (effective 2011). **Document type:** *Journal, Academic/Scholarly.* **Description:** Focuses on the social, political, cultural and economic development of the Asia Pacific region and discusses issues of current and future concern for the Asia Pacific, and its relations with the rest of the world.
Related titles: Online - full text ed.: ISSN 2042-6151. GBP 101, EUR 117, USD 171 to institutions (effective 2011) (from IngentaConnect).
Published by: (International Association for Asia Pacific Studies JPN), Berghahn Books Ltd, 3 Newtec Pl, Magdalen Rd, Oxford, OX4 1RE, United Kingdom. TEL 44-1865-250011, FAX 44-1865-250056, journals@berghahnbooks.com, http://www.berghahnbooks.com. Ed. Malcolm J M Cooper.

307.14 THA
ASIAN INSTITUTE OF TECHNOLOGY. H S D RESEARCH PAPERS AND REPORTS. Text in English. 1982. irreg. price varies. **Document type:** *Report, Academic/Scholarly.*
Published by: (Human Settlements Development Program), Asian Institute of Technology, School of Environment, Resources and Development, Klong Luang, PO Box 4, Pathum Thani, 12120, Thailand. TEL 66-2-524-5610, FAX 66-2-524-5610, vpaa@ait.ac.th, http://www.ait.ac.th.

300 NLD ISSN 1568-4849
HN651 CODEN: AJSSA5
➤ **ASIAN JOURNAL OF SOCIAL SCIENCE.** Text in English. 1968. 5/yr. EUR 534, USD 747 to institutions; EUR 582, USD 815 combined subscription to institutions (print & online eds.) (effective 2012). adv. bk.rev. illus. Index. back issues avail.; reprint service avail. from PSC. **Document type:** *Journal, Academic/Scholarly.* **Description:** Provides a forum for exploring issues in Southeast Asian societies, including anthropology, economics, geography, history, language and literature, political science, psychology and sociology.
Formerly (until 2001): Southeast Asian Journal of Social Science (0303-8246); Which incorporated: Southeast Asia Ethnicity and Development Newsletter; Which was formerly: South-East Asian Journal of Sociology
Related titles: Online - full text ed.: ISSN 1568-5314. EUR 485, USD 679 to institutions (effective 2012) (from IngentaConnect).
Indexed: A01, A03, A08, A22, APEL, AbAn, BAS, BibLing, CA, CABA, E01, FR, GEOBASE, IBSS, IZBG, LT, M10, MLA-IB, P34, P42, PAIS, PCI, PSA, PerIslam, RASB, RRTA, S02, S03, SCOPUS, SOPODA, SSA, SSCI, SociolAb, T02, W07, W11.
—IE, Ingenta. **CCC.**

Published by: Brill, PO Box 9000, Leiden, 2300 PA, Netherlands. TEL 31-71-5353500, FAX 31-71-5317532, cs@brill.nl. Eds. Syed F Alatas, Vineeta Sinha. **Dist. by:** Turpin Distribution Services Ltd., Pegasus Dr, Stratton Business Park, Biggleswade, Bedfordshire SG18 8QB, United Kingdom. TEL 44-1767-604800, FAX 44-1767-601640, custserv@turpin-distribution.com, http://www.turpin-distribution.com/.

➤ **ASIAN PROFILE.** *see* ASIAN STUDIES

300 CAN ISSN 1911-2017
➤ **ASIAN SOCIAL SCIENCE.** Text in English. 2005. m. CAD 20 (effective 2009). Index. back issues avail. **Document type:** *Journal, Academic/Scholarly.* **Description:** Covers arts, sociology, politics, culture, history, philosophy, economics, education, laws, linguistics and psychology, for encouraging and publishing research in the field of social science, and the audiences are professional scholars and researchers.
Related titles: Online - full text ed.: ISSN 1911-2025. free (effective 2011).
Indexed: A01, A26, A39, C27, C29, CPerI, D03, D04, E13, I05, P02, P10, P14, P27, P48, P53, P54, PQC, R14, S14, S15, S18, T02.
Published by: Canadian Center of Science and Education, 4915 Bathurst St, Unit 209-309, Toronto, ON M2R 1X9, Canada. TEL 416-208-4027, FAX 416-208-4028, info@ccsenet.org. Ed. Wenwu Zhao. Circ: 200.

300 AUS ISSN 1753-1403
HV376
ASIAN SOCIAL WORK AND POLICY REVIEW. Text in English. 2007. 3/yr. GBP 249 in United Kingdom to institutions; EUR 287 in Europe to institutions; USD 352 elsewhere to institutions (effective 2012). **Document type:** *Journal, Academic/Scholarly.*
Related titles: Online - full text ed.: ISSN 1753-1411. GBP 249 in United Kingdom to institutions; EUR 287 in Europe to institutions; USD 352 elsewhere to institutions (effective 2012).
Indexed: A22, CA, E01, P34, S02, S03, SCOPUS, T02.
—IE. **CCC.**
Published by: (Korean Academy of Social Welfare KOR), Wiley-Blackwell Publishing Asia (Subsidiary of: Wiley-Blackwell Publishing Ltd.), 155 Cremorne St, Richmond, VIC 3121, Australia. TEL 61-3-92743100, FAX 61-3-92743101, subs@blackwellpublishingasia.com, http://www.wiley.com/WileyCDA/. Eds. Martha N Ozawa, Sang Kyun Kim.

300 DEU ISSN 1865-8768
E175.8
ASPEERS; American voices in American studies. Text in German. 2008. irreg. free (effective 2011). **Document type:** *Journal, Academic/Scholarly.* **Description:** Seeks to give emerging scholars a voice, a platform to showcase their work beyond the graduate classroom and a forum for discussion on research in American studies.
Media: Online - full text.
Indexed: AmH&L, CA, HistAb, T02.
Published by: American Studies Leipzig, Beethovenstr 15, Leipzig, 04107, Germany.

300 DEU ISSN 1439-0051
ASPEKTE DER FREIRE-PAEDAGOGIK. Text in German. 1999. irreg., latest vol.143. price varies. **Document type:** *Monographic series, Academic/Scholarly.*
Published by: Paulo Freire Verlag, Unterm Berg 65a, Oldenburg, 26123, Germany. TEL 49-441-381674, FAX 49-441-9330056, pfv@freire.de.

300 004 BRA ISSN 0102-5813
ASSOCIACAO BRASILEIRA DE CIBERNETICA SOCIAL. REVISTA. Text in Portuguese. 1986. 3/yr.
Published by: Associacao Brasileira de Cibernetica Social, Avenida L2 Norte, Quadra 601-B, Brasilia, DF 70830-000, Brazil. TEL 55-11-5491144.

ASSOCIATION FOR THE STUDY OF PLAY NEWSLETTER. *see* PSYCHOLOGY

EL ASTROLABIO. *see* SCIENCES: COMPREHENSIVE WORKS

300 ESP ISSN 1578-8946
ATHENEA DIGITAL. Text in Spanish. 2001. s-a. free (effective 2011). **Document type:** *Journal, Academic/Scholarly.*
Media: Online - full text.
Indexed: A01, CA, F03, F04, S02, S03, SCOPUS, SociolAb, T02.
—**CCC.**
Published by: (Universitat Autonoma de Barcelona, Departament de Psicologia de la Salut), Universitat Autonoma de Barcelona, Servei de Publicacions, Edifici A, Bellaterra, Cardanyola del Valles, Barcelona, 08193, Spain. TEL 34-93-5811022, FAX 34-93-5813239, sp@uab.es, http://www.uab.es/publicacions/.

300 VEN ISSN 0004-6876
ATLANTIDA. Text in Spanish. 1974. irreg. free to qualified personnel. bk.rev. **Document type:** *Journal, Academic/Scholarly.* **Description:** Includes articles in basic sciences, engineering and the humanities.
Indexed: MLA-IB, RASB, RILM.
Published by: Universidad Simon Bolivar, Division Ciencias Sociales y Humanidades, Valle de Sartenejas, Caracas, DF 1080, Venezuela. TEL 58-2-9063422, FAX 58-2-9063402. Ed. Dr. Patricio Hevia. Circ: 1,000.

303.842 DEU
ATLANTISCHE TEXTE. Text in German. 1997. irreg., latest vol.35, 2010. price varies. **Document type:** *Monographic series, Academic/Scholarly.*
Published by: Wissenschaftlicher Verlag Trier, Bergstr 27, Trier, 54295, Germany. TEL 49-651-41503, FAX 49-651-41504, wvt@wvttrier.de, http://www.wvttrier.de.

300 DEU
AUF DER SUCHE NACH DER VERLORENEN ZUKUNFT. Text in German. 1995. irreg., latest vol.17, 2004. price varies. **Document type:** *Monographic series, Academic/Scholarly.*
Published by: Trafo Verlag, Finkenstr 8, Berlin, 12621, Germany. TEL 49-30-61299418, FAX 49-30-61299421, info@trafoberlin.de, http://www.trafoberlin.de.

300 DEU ISSN 0934-0327
AUSLEGUNGEN. Text in German. 1990. irreg., latest vol.4, 1994. price varies. **Document type:** *Monographic series, Academic/Scholarly.*
Published by: Peter Lang GmbH (Subsidiary of: Peter Lang Publishing Group), Eschborner Landstr 42-50, Frankfurt Am Main, 60489, Germany. TEL 49-69-7807050, FAX 49-69-78070550, zentrale.frankfurt@peterlang.com. Ed. Alphons Silbermann.

300 AUS ISSN 1440-4842
➤ **AUSTRALIAN SOCIAL MONITOR.** Text in English. 1998. 4/yr. 12 p./no.; back issues avail. **Document type:** *Journal, Academic/Scholarly.* **Description:** Aims to monitor and analyze important social, political and economic trends and attitudes.
Indexed: AEI, AusPAIS, ERO.
Published by: International Survey Center, c/o Melbourne Institute of Applied Economic and Social Research, Parkville, VIC 3052, Australia. TEL 61-3-93445325, FAX 61-3-93445630, info@international-survey.org. Ed. Bruce Headey.

300 BRA ISSN 1678-345X
AUTOPOESIS. Text in Portuguese. 2002. s-a. **Document type:** *Journal, Academic/Scholarly.*
Published by: Faculdade Estacio de Sa de Santa Catarina, Ave Leoberto Leal, 431, Sao Jose, 88117-001, Brazil. http://www.sc.estacio.br/.

300 FRA ISSN 1243-6003
AUTREMENT DIT. Text in French. 1993. w. adv. **Document type:** *Newspaper.*
Published by: Europe Medias, 13 rue Jeanne d'Arc, BP 1353, Lille, Cedex 59015, France. TEL 33-3-20152737, FAX 33-3-20152636. Ed., R&P Jean-Claude Branquart. Pub. Jean Claude Branquart. Adv. contact Dominique Roman. Circ: 25,000.

AUTREMENT JUNIOR. SERIE SOCIETE. *see* CHILDREN AND YOUTH—For

500 FRA ISSN 1278-3986
D880
AUTREPART; revue des sciences sociales au Sud. Text in French; Summaries in English. 1963. q. EUR 59 combined subscription domestic to individuals (print & online eds.); EUR 69 combined subscription foreign to individuals (print & online eds.); EUR 89 combined subscription domestic to institutions (print & online eds.); EUR 99 combined subscription foreign to institutions (print & online eds.) (effective 2008). back issues avail. **Document type:** *Journal, Academic/Scholarly.*
Former titles (until 1997): Cahiers des Sciences Humaines (0768-9829); (until 1985): Cahiers O R S T O M Serie Sciences Humaines (0008-0403)
Related titles: Online - full text ed.
Indexed: A22, ASD, BibInd, BibLing, CA, CCA, EIP, FR, I14, IBSS, ILD, MLA-IB, P30, P34, P42, PAIS, PCI, PSA, PopulInd, RASB, S02, S03, SCOPUS, SociolAb, T02.
—BLDSC (1835.630800), IE, Ingenta, INIST.
Published by: (France. Institut de Recherche pour le Developpement), Armand Colin, 21 Rue du Montparnasse, Paris, 75283 Cedex 06, France. TEL 33-1-44395447, FAX 33-1-44394343, infos@armand-colin.fr. Circ: 1,000.

AVANZADA CIENTIFICA. *see* SCIENCES: COMPREHENSIVE WORKS

AWRAQ; estudios sobre el mundo arabe e islamico contemporaneo. *see* HISTORY—History Of Europe

AZTLAN; a journal of Chicano studies. *see* ETHNIC INTERESTS

301 GBR ISSN 1351-5667
B A C S NEWSLETTER. Text in English. 19??. a. free to members (effective 2009). back issues avail. **Document type:** *Newsletter, Trade.* **Description:** Covers various facets of Canadian studies: literature, history, geography, and political science.
Formerly (until 1988): British Association for Canadian Studies. Newsletter (0262-2718)
Published by: (Liverpool University Press), British Association for Canadian Studies, Rm 220, S Block, Senate House, University of London, Malet St, London, WC1E 7HU, United Kingdom. TEL 44-20-78628687, FAX 44-20-71171875, bacs@canadian-studies.org. **Subscr. to:** Marstons Book Services Ltd, PO Box 269, Abingdon, Oxfordshire OX14 4YN, United Kingdom. TEL 44-1235-465500, FAX 44-1235-465555, subscriptions@marston.co.uk, http://www.marston.co.uk/.

300 CAN ISSN 0005-2949
➤ **B C STUDIES**; the British Columbian quarterly. Text in English. 1969. q. CAD 40 domestic to individuals; USD 52 foreign to individuals; CAD 55 domestic to institutions; USD 67 foreign to institutions; CAD 25 domestic to students; USD 37 foreign to students (effective 2008). adv. bk.rev. bibl.; charts; illus. Index. back issues avail.; reprint service avail. from PSC. **Document type:** *Journal, Academic/Scholarly.* **Description:** Journal of informed writing on the political, economic and cultural life of British Columbia, past and present.
Related titles: Microfiche ed.: (from MML); Microform ed.: (from MML, PQC); Online - full text ed.
Indexed: A01, A03, A08, A26, AbAn, AmH&L, B04, B24, BNNA, BRD, BibInd, C03, C05, CA, CBCARef, CBPI, CPerI, E08, HistAb, I05, IBSS, P18, P27, P30, P48, P53, P54, P55, PQC, RASB, S09, SRRA, SSAI, SSAb, SSI, T02, W01, W02, W03, W04, W05.
—Ingenta. **CCC.**
Published by: University of British Columbia, Buchanan E162, 1866 Main Mall, Vancouver, BC V6T 1Z1, Canada. TEL 604-822-3727, FAX 604-822-0606, write_us@bcstudies.com, http://www.interchange.ubc.ca/bcstudie. Ed. Graeme Wynn. Pub., R&P, Adv. contact Leanne Coughlin. Circ: 600.

300 NZL ISSN 1177-2360
B R C S S OCCASIONAL PAPER SERIES. Text in English. 2005. irreg., latest vol.3, 2006. **Document type:** *Monographic series, Academic/Scholarly.*
Published by: Building Research Capability in the Social Sciences Network, Private Box 756, Wellington, 6140, New Zealand. TEL 64-4-8015799 ext 62178, FAX 64-4-8010805.

B R I D G E REPORT. (Briefings on Development & Gender) *see* BUSINESS AND ECONOMICS—International Development And Assistance

LE BAC EN TETE. SCIENCES ECONOMIQUES ET SOCIALES. *see* EDUCATION

300 DEU
BAIRE. Text in German. 2003. irreg., latest vol.2, 2005. price varies. **Document type:** *Monographic series, Academic/Scholarly.*
Published by: Wissenschaftlicher Verlag Berlin, Koertestr 10, Berlin, 10967, Germany. TEL 49-30-89379899, FAX 49-30-6185021, verlag@wvberlin.de, http://www.wvberlin.de.

300 TUR ISSN 1301-5265
H8.T87
BALIKESIR UNIVERSITESI. SOSYAL BILIMER ENSTITUSU. DERGISI. Text in Multiple languages. 1998. s-a. **Document type:** *Journal, Academic/Scholarly.*
Related titles: Online - full text ed.: free (effective 2011).
Indexed: A01, MLA-IB, SociolAb, T02.
Published by: Balikesir Universitesi, Sosyal Bilimer Enstitusu, Cagis Yerleskesi, Balikesir, 10145, Turkey. http://www.balikesir.edu.tr.

BALKAN STUDIES. *see* HISTORY—History Of Europe

BALKANISTIC FORUM. *see* HISTORY—History Of Europe

BANG. *see* WOMEN'S STUDIES

BANWA. *see* HUMANITIES: COMPREHENSIVE WORKS

BAODING XUEYUAN XUEBAO/BAODING UNIVERSITY. JOURNAL. *see* SCIENCES: COMPREHENSIVE WORKS

300 CHN ISSN 1008-4193
BAOJI WENLI XUEYUAN XUEBAO (SHEHUI KEXUE BAN)/BAOJI UNIVERSITY OF ARTS AND SCIENCE. JOURNAL (SOCIAL SCIENCE EDITION). Text in Chinese. 1979. bi-m. back issues avail. **Document type:** *Journal, Academic/Scholarly.*
Former titles (until 1993): Baoji Shiyuan Xuebao (Zhexue Shehui Kexue Ban); (until 1985): Jiaoxue yu Yanke (Zhexue Shehui Kexue Ban); Which superseded in part (in 1984): Jiaoxue yu Keyan (Zonghe Ban); Which was formerly (until 1982): Baoji Shiyuan Xuebao
Related titles: Online - full text ed.
Published by: Baoji Wenli Xueyuan/Baoji College of Arts and Sciences, 44, Baoguang Lu, Baoji, Shaanxi 721007, China. TEL 86-917-3364287.

300 001.3 MNG ISSN 1671-1440
BAOTOU ZHI-DA XUEBAO/STAFF AND WORKER'S UNIVERSITY. JOURNAL. Text in Chinese. 1989. q. **Document type:** *Journal, Academic/Scholarly.*
Formerly (until 1999): Zi Daxue Kan
Related titles: Online - full text ed.
Published by: Baotou Shi Zhigong Daxue/Staff and Worker's University, 20, Gangtie Dajie, Qingshan-qu, Baotou, 014030, Mongolia. TEL 86-472-5131546, FAX 86-472-5131546.

300 CHN ISSN 1672-0903
BAOTOU ZHIYE JISHU XUEYUAN XUEBAO/BAOTOU VOCATIONAL & TECHNICAL COLLEGE. JOURNAL. Text in Chinese. 2000. q. **Document type:** *Journal, Academic/Scholarly.*
Related titles: Online - full text ed.
Published by: Baotou Zhiye Jishu Xueyuan/Baotou Vocational & Technical College, 12, Hudemulin Dajie, Baotou, 014030, China. TEL 86-472-6918463, http://btzy.nm.edu.cn/.

300 BRA ISSN 0104-6578
BARBAROI. Text in Portuguese. 1994. s-a. BRL 18 (effective 2006).
Related titles: Online - full text ed.
Indexed: AmHI, SociolAb.
Published by: (Universidade de Santa Cruz do Sul, Departamento de Ciencias Humanas, Universidade de Santa Cruz do Sul, Departamento de Psicologia), Editora da Universidade de Santa Cruz do Sul, Av Independencia 2293, Barrio Universitario, Santa Cruz do Sul, RS 96815-900, Brazil. TEL 55-51-37177461, FAX 55-51-37177402, editora@unisc.br. Eds. Renato Nunes, Silvia Coutinho Areosa.

BASIC AND APPLIED SOCIAL PSYCHOLOGY. *see* PSYCHOLOGY

300 DEU
BASIS-INFO. Text in German. 9/yr. **Document type:** *Newsletter, Consumer.* **Description:** Presents background information on German politics, economics and social welfare.
Formed by the merger of: Sozial Report (0171-8738); Which was formerly (until 1974): Sozialpolitische Informationen (0171-869X); Sonderthema; Which was formerly: Sonderdienst
Related titles: English ed.; Spanish ed.; French ed.
Published by: Goethe-Institut, Frankenstr 13, Bonn, 53175, Germany. info@goethe.de, http://www.goethe.de.

300 DEU
▼ **BASIS-SCRIPTE. READER KULTURWISSENSCHAFTEN.** Text in German. 2010. irreg. price varies. **Document type:** *Monographic series, Academic/Scholarly.*
Published by: Transcript, Muehlenstr 47, Bielefeld, 33607, Germany. TEL 49-521-63454, FAX 49-521-61040, live@transcript-verlag.de.

BAU- UND KUNSTDENKMALER IM OESTLICHEN MITTELEUROPA. *see* HISTORY—History Of Europe

300 DEU ISSN 0932-5352
BECK'SCHE REIHE. Text in German. 1965. irreg. price varies. **Document type:** *Monographic series, Academic/Scholarly.*
Formerly (until 198?): Beck'sche Schwarze Reihe (0930-973X)
Indexed: GeoRef.
Published by: Verlag C.H. Beck oHG, Wilhelmstr 9, Munich, 80801, Germany. TEL 49-89-381890, FAX 49-89-38189398, bestellung@beck.de, http://www.beck.de.

300 USA
BEDOUIN. Text in English. irreg. **Description:** Seeks to investigate the way the culture interacts with everyday life.
Media: Online - full text.
Address: opinion@thebedouin.net.

300 CHN ISSN 1009-5101
BEIHUA DAXUE XUEBAO (SHEHUI KEXUE BAN)/JILIN TEACHERS COLLEGE. JOURNAL. Text in Chinese. 2000. bi-m. USD 40.20 (effective 2009). **Document type:** *Journal, Academic/Scholarly.*
Incorporated (in 1999): Jilin Shifan Xueyuan Xuebao/Jilin Teachers College. Journal (1006-7701)
—East View.
Published by: Beihua Daxue/Beihua University, 15, Jilin Dajie, Jilin, 132033, China. TEL 81-432-4602730, FAX 81-432-4602731.

BEIHUA HANGTIAN GONGYE XUEYUAN XUEBAO/NORTH CHINA INSTITUTE OF ASTRONAUTIC ENGINEERING. JOURNAL. *see* SCIENCES: COMPREHENSIVE WORKS

300 001.3 CHN ISSN 1673-4513
BEIJING CHENGSHI XUEYUAN XUEBAO/BEIJING CITY UNIVERSITY. JOURNAL. Text in Chinese. 1988. bi-m.
Formerly: Haidian Zoudu Daxue Xuebao/Haidian University Journal (1008-4851)
Published by: Beijing Chengshi Xueyuan/Beijing City University, 269, Bei Si Huan Zhong Lu, Haidian-qu, Beijing, 100083, China. TEL 86-10-62322830.

300 CHN
BEIJING DIANLI GAODENG ZHUANKE XUEXIAO XUEBAO (SHEHUI KEXUE BAN)/BEIJING ELECTRIC POWER COLLEGE. JOURNAL. (SOCIAL SCIENCE EDITION). Text in Chinese. 1992. m. back issues avail. **Document type:** *Journal, Academic/Scholarly.*
Supersedes in part: Beijing Dianli Gaodeng Zhuanke Xuexiao Xuebao (1009-0118)
Related titles: Online - full text ed.
Published by: Beijing Dianli Gaodeng Zhuanke Xuexiao, 42, Fucheng Lu, Beijing, 100036, China. TEL 86-10-86931100.

300 500 CHN ISSN 1672-464X
BEIJING DIANZI KEJI XUEYUAN XUEBAO/BEIJING ELECTRONIC SCIENCE AND TECHNOLOGY INSTITUTE. JOURNAL. Text in Chinese. 1993. q. **Document type:** *Journal, Academic/Scholarly.*
Related titles: Online - full text ed.
Published by: Beijing Dianzi Keji Xueyuan/Beijing Electronic Science and Technology Institute, 7, Fufeng Lu, Zhulou 420, Fengtai-qu, Beijing, 100070, China. TEL 86-10-63742714, FAX 86-10-68177273, http://www.besti.edu.cn/.

300 CHN ISSN 1009-6116
BEIJING GONGSHANG DAXUE XUEBAO (SHEHUI KEXUE BAN)/ BEIJING TECHNOLOGY AND BUSINESS UNIVERSITY. JORUNAL (SOCIAL SCIENCE EDITION). Text in Chinese. 1981. bi-m. USD 18 (effective 2009). **Document type:** *Journal, Academic/Scholarly.*
Formerly (until 2000): Beijing Shangxueyuan Xuebao/Beijing Institute of Business. Journal (1002-4018)
Related titles: Online - full text ed.
—East View.
Published by: Beijing Gongshang Daxue/Beijing Technology and Business University, 33, Fucheng Lu, Haidian-qu, Beijing, 100037, China. TEL 86-10-68984614.

300 CHN ISSN 1671-0398
BEIJING GONGYE DAXUE XUEBAO (SHEHUI KEXUE BAN)/BEIJING UNIVERSITY OF TECHNOLOGY. JOURNAL (SOCIAL SCIENCES EDITION). Text in Chinese. 2001. q. CNY 5 newsstand/cover (effective 2006). **Document type:** *Journal, Academic/Scholarly.*
Related titles: Online - full text ed.
Indexed: A28, APA, BrCerAb, C&ISA, CA, CA/WCA, CIA, CerAb, CivEngAb, CorrAb, E&CAJ, E11, EEA, EMA, ESPM, EnvEAb, H15, M&TEA, M09, MBF, METADEX, PSA, SociolAb, SolStAb, T04, WAA.
Published by: Beijing Gongye Daxue/Beijing University Of Technology, 100, Pingyueyuan, Zhixinyuan 317-shi, Beijing, 100022, China. TEL 86-10-67392534, http://www.bjpu.edu.cn/.

300 CHN ISSN 1671-6558
BEIJING GONGYE ZHIYE JISHU XUEYUAN XUEBAO/BEIJING VOCATIONAL & TECHNICAL INSTITUTE OF INDUSTRY. JOURNAL. Text in Chinese. 2002. q. **Document type:** *Journal, Academic/Scholarly.*
Related titles: Online - full text ed.
Published by: Beijing Gongye Zhiye Jishu Xueyuan/Beijing Vocational & Technical Institute of Industry, 368, Shimen Lu, Shijingshan-qu, Beijing, 100042, China. TEL 86-10-51511007, FAX 86-10-88907196, http://www.bgy.org.cn/.

300 CHN ISSN 1008-7648
BEIJING GUANGBO DIANSHI DAXUE XUEBAO/BEIJING OPEN UNIVERSITY. JOURNAL. Text in Chinese. 1996. q. **Document type:** *Journal, Academic/Scholarly.*
Related titles: Online - full text ed.
Published by: Beijing Guangbo Dianshi Daxue, 4, Zaojunmiao Jia, Haidian-qu, Beijing, 100081, China. TEL 86-10-82192162, FAX 86-10-66117647.

500 CHN ISSN 1008-2204
BEIJING HANGKONG HANGTIAN DAXUE XUEBAO (SHEHUI KEXUE BAN)/BEIJING UNIVERSITY OF AERONAUTICS AND ASTRONAUTICS. JOURNAL (SOCIAL SCIENCES EDITION). Text in Chinese. 1988. q. CNY 6 newsstand/cover (effective 2006). **Document type:** *Journal, Academic/Scholarly.*
Related titles: Online - full text ed.
Indexed: ESPM, M&GPA, SSciA.
Published by: Beijing Hangkong Hangtian Daxue/Beijing University of Aeronautics and Astronautics, 37, Xueyuan Lu, Beijing, 100083, China. TEL 86-10-82338013, FAX 86-10-82317850.

300 CHN ISSN 1671-6639
BEIJING HUAGONG DAXUE XUEBAO (SHEHUI KEXUE BAN)/ BEIJING UNIVERSITY OF CHEMICAL TECHNOLOGY. JOURNAL (SOCIAL SCIENCES EDITION). Text in Chinese. 1985. q. USD 12 (effective 2009). **Document type:** *Journal, Academic/Scholarly.*
Related titles: Online - full text ed.
Published by: Beijing Huagong Daxue/Beijing University of Chemical Technology, 15, Beisanhuan Dong Lu, Beijing, 100029, China. TEL 86-10-64452738.

300 CHN ISSN 1672-8106
BEIJING JIAOTONG DAXUE XUEBAO (SHEHUI KEXUE BAN)/ BEIJING JIAOTONG UNIVERSITY. JOURNAL (SOCIAL SCIENCES EDITION). Text in Chinese. 2002. q. CNY 8 newsstand/cover (effective 2006). **Document type:** *Journal, Academic/Scholarly.*
Formerly (until 2004): Beifang Jiaotong Daxue Xuebao (Shehui Kexue Ban) (1671-9514)
Related titles: Online - full text ed.
Published by: Beijing Jiaotong Daxue, Xizhimen Wai, 3, Shangyuancun, Beijing, 100044, China. TEL 86-10-51682711.

300 CHN ISSN 1008-228X
BEIJING JIAOYU XUEYUAN XUEBAO/BEIJING INSTITUTE OF EDUCATION. JOURNAL. Text in Chinese. 1987. bi-m. CNY 36; CNY 6 per issue (effective 2010). **Document type:** *Journal, Academic/Scholarly.*
Incorporates (1999-2000): Beijing Shi Chengren Jiaoyu Xueyuan Xuebao/Journal of Beijing Adult Educational College (1008-2212); Formerly (until 1990): Beijing Jiaoyu Xueyuan Xuekan
Related titles: Online - full text ed.
Published by: Beijing Jiaoyu Xueyuan/Beijing Institute of Education, 2, Dewai Shenfeng Jie, Zhonghe Lou Rm.602, Beijing, 100011, China. TEL 86-10-82089136.

300 CHN ISSN 1008-2689
BEIJING KEJI DAXUE XUEBAO (SHEHUI KEXUE BAN)/UNIVERSITY OF SCIENCE AND TECHNOLOGY BEIJING. JOURNAL (SOCIAL SCIENCES EDITION). Text in Chinese. 1985. q. CNY 8 newsstand/cover (effective 2006). **Document type:** *Journal, Academic/Scholarly.*
Related titles: Online - full text ed.
Published by: Beijing Keji Daxue/Beijing University of Science and Technology, Editorial Board of Journal of University of Science & Technology Beijing, 30 Xueyuan Lu, Haidian-qu, Beijing, 100083, China. TEL 86-10-62334089, http://www.ustb.edu.cn/.

BEIJING LAODONG BAOZHANG ZHIYE XUEYUAN XUEBAO. *see* SOCIAL SERVICES AND WELFARE

BEIJING LIANHE DAXUE XUEBAO (RENWEN SHEHUI KEXUE BAN)/BEIJING UNION UNIVERSITY. JOURNAL (HUMANITIES AND SOCIAL SCIENCES EDITION). *see* HUMANITIES: COMPREHENSIVE WORKS

300 CHN ISSN 1009-3370
BEIJING LIGONG DAXUE XUEBAO (SHEHUI KEXUE BAN)/BEIJING INSTITUTE OF TECHNOLOGY. JOURNAL (SOCIAL SCIENCES EDITION). Text in Chinese. 1999. bi-m. **Document type:** *Journal, Academic/Scholarly.*
Related titles: Online - full text ed.
Indexed: CA, PAIS, PSA, SociolAb.
Published by: Beijing Ligong Daxue/Beijing Institute of Technology, 5, Zhongguancun Nan Dajie, Haidian-qu, Beijing, 100081, China. TEL 86-10-68915605, http://www.bit.edu.cn/.

300 CHN ISSN 1671-6116
BEIJING LINYE DAXUE XUEBAO (SHEHUI KEXUE BAN)/BEIJING FORESTRY UNIVERSITY. JOURNAL (SOCIAL SCIENCS). Text in Chinese. 2002. q. USD 53.20 (effective 2009). **Document type:** *Journal, Academic/Scholarly.*
Related titles: Online - full text ed.
Published by: Beijing Linye Daxue/Beijing Forestry University, 35, Qinghua Dong Lu, Beijing, 100083, China. TEL 86-10-62337919, FAX 86-10-62337605.

300 CHN ISSN 1002-3054
H8.C47
BEIJING SHEHUI KEXUE/BEIJING SOCIAL SCIENCES. Text in Chinese. 1986. q. USD 31.20 (effective 2009). back issues avail. **Document type:** *Journal, Academic/Scholarly.*
Related titles: Online - full text ed.
Indexed: RASB.
—East View.
Published by: Beijing Shi Shehui Kexueyuan/Beijing Academy of Social Sciences, Zhaoyang-qu, 33, Bei Si Huan Zhong Lu, Beijing, 100101, China. TEL 86-10-64870591, FAX 86-10-64870897, bassic@263.net.cn, http://www.bass.gov.cn/. Ed. Zhou Yixing. **Dist. by:** China International Book Trading Corp, 35 Chegongzhuang Xilu, Haidian District, PO Box 399, Beijing 100044, China. TEL 86-10-68412045, FAX 86-10-68412023, cibtc@mail.cibtc.com.cn, http://www.cibtc.com.cn.

300 CHN ISSN 1673-0240
BEIJING SHI GONGHUI GANBU XUEYUAN XUEBAO/BEIJING FEDERATION OF TRADE UNIONS CADRE COLLEGE. JOURNAL. Text in Chinese. 1986. q. **Document type:** *Journal, Academic/Scholarly.*
Former titles (until 2004): Beijing Shi Zonggonghui Zhigong Daxue Xuebao/Beijing Federation of Trade Unions College Journal (1009-3648); (until 19??): Zhigong Gaodeng Jiaoyu; Zhigong Gaojiao Yanjiu
Related titles: Online - full text ed.
Published by: Beijing Shi Gonghui Ganbu Xueyuan/Beijing Federation of Trade Unions Cadre College, 53, Taoranting Lu, Xuanwu-qu, Beijing, 100054, China. TEL 86-10-83515527 ext 605, FAX 86-10-83517504, http://www.ghgy.com.cn/.

300 CHN ISSN 1002-0209
AS452.P25
BEIJING SHIFAN DAXUE XUEBAO (SHEHUI KEXUE BAN)/BEIJING NORMAL UNIVERSITY. JOURNAL (SOCIAL SCIENCE EDITION). Text in Chinese; Contents page in English. 1975. bi-m. USD 40.20 (effective 2009).
Related titles: Online - full text ed.
Indexed: CA, P42, SociolAb, T02.
—East View, Ingenta.
Published by: Beijing Shifan Daxue/Beijing Normal University, 19, Xinjiekouwai Dajie, Beijing, 100875, China. TEL 2012288. Ed. Bai Shouyi. **Dist. overseas by:** China Publication Foreign Trade Company, PO Box 782, Beijing 100011, China.

300 CHN ISSN 1008-7729
BEIJING YOUDIAN DAXUE XUEBAO (SHEHUI KEXUE BAN)/BEIJING UNIVERSITY OF POSTS AND TELECOMMUNICATIONS. JOURNAL (SOCIAL SCIENCES EDITION). Text in Chinese. 1999. q. USD 37.20 (effective 2009). **Document type:** *Journal, Academic/Scholarly.*
Related titles: Online - full text ed.
—East View.
Published by: Beijing Youdian Daxue/Beijing University of Posts and Telecommunications, 10, Xi Tucheng Lu, Haidian-qu, Beijing, 100876, China. TEL 86-10-62282143, FAX 86-10-62283573.

300 DEU ISSN 0937-7360
H5
BEITRAEGE AUS DER FORSCHUNG. Text in German. 1984. irreg., latest vol.125, 2001. **Document type:** *Monographic series, Academic/Scholarly.*
Published by: Sozialforschungsstelle Dortmund, Evinger Platz 17, Dortmund, 44339, Germany. TEL 49-231-8596-0, FAX 49-231-8596100, sfs@sfs-dortmund.de, http://www.sfs-dortmund.de.

301 DEU ISSN 0408-8352
BEITRAEGE ZUR GESCHICHTE DER SOZIALWISSENSCHAFTEN. Text in German. 1959. irreg., latest vol.3, 1975. price varies. **Document type:** *Monographic series, Academic/Scholarly.*
Published by: Duncker und Humblot GmbH, Carl-Heinrich-Becker-Weg 9, Berlin, 12165, Germany. TEL 49-30-7900060, FAX 49-30-79000631, info@duncker-humblot.de.

303 DEU ISSN 0177-2740
BEITRAEGE ZUR GESELLSCHAFTSWISSENSCHAFTLICHEN FORSCHUNG. Text in German. 1985. irreg., latest vol.24, 2005. price varies. **Document type:** *Monographic series, Academic/Scholarly.*

S

Published by: Centaurus Verlag & Media KG, Kaiser-Joseph-Str 267, Freiburg, 79098, Germany. TEL 49-761-1525861, FAX 49-761-1525868, info@centaurus-verlag.de, http://www.centaurus-verlag.de.

300 DEU
BEITRAEGE ZUR RECHTS-, GESELLSCHAFTS- UND KULTURKRITIK. Text in German. 2001. irreg., latest vol.9, 2009. price varies. **Document type:** *Monographic series, Academic/Scholarly.*
Formerly (until 2008): Salecina - Beitraege zur Gesellschafts- und Kulturkritik
Published by: Trafo Verlag, Finkenstr 8, Berlin, 12621, Germany. TEL 49-30-61299418, FAX 49-30-61299421, info@trafoberlin.de, http://www.trafoberlin.de. Eds. Gisela Engel, Malte-C Gruber.

300 DEU ISSN 0177-2759
BEITRAEGE ZUR RECHTSSOZIOLOGISCHEN FORSCHUNG. Text in German. 1985. irreg., latest vol.13, 1999. price varies. **Document type:** *Monographic series, Academic/Scholarly.*
Published by: Centaurus Verlag & Media KG, Kaiser-Joseph-Str 267, Freiburg, 79098, Germany. TEL 49-761-1525861, FAX 49-761-1525868, info@centaurus-verlag.de, http://www.centaurus-verlag.de.

300 DEU ISSN 1611-1893
BEITRAEGE ZUR SOZIALAESTHETIK. Text in German. 2003. irreg., latest vol.10, 2009. price varies. **Document type:** *Monographic series, Academic/Scholarly.*
Published by: (Carl-Richard-Montag-Stiftung fuer Jugend und Gesellschaft), Projekt Verlag GbR, Oskar-Hoffmann-Str 25, Bochum, 44789, Germany. TEL 49-234-3251570, FAX 49-234-3251571, lektorat@projektverlag.de.

300 CHE
BEITRAEGE ZUR SOZIALARBEIT. Text in German. 1994. irreg. **Document type:** *Monographic series.*
Published by: Philosophisch - Anthroposophischer Verlag am Goetheanum, Postfach 134, Dornach, 4143, Switzerland. TEL 41-61-7064464, FAX 41-61-7064465.

BEITRAEGE ZUR SOZIALGESCHICHTE BREMEN. *see* HISTORY—History Of Europe

300 DEU ISSN 1438-9525
BEITRAEGE ZUR SOZIALWISSENSCHAFTLICHEN PRAXIS UND ANALYSE. Text in German. 1999. irreg., latest vol.12, 2009. price varies. **Document type:** *Monographic series, Academic/Scholarly.*
Published by: Institut fuer Sozialwissenschaftliche Praxis und Analyse e.V., Parochialstr 1-3, Berlin, 10179, Germany. info@ispa-ev.de. Ed. Martin Eckert.

BEITRAEGE ZUR UNIVERSALGESCHICHTE UND VERGLEICHENDEN GESELLSCHAFTSFORSCHUNG. *see* HISTORY

BEITRAEGE ZUR WIRTSCHAFTSGEOGRAPHIE REGENSBURG. *see* GEOGRAPHY

BELIZE SOCIAL INDICATORS REPORT. *see* SOCIAL SCIENCES: COMPREHENSIVE WORKS—Abstracting, Bibliographies, Statistics

300 BLR
BELORUSSKII GOSUDARSTVENNYI UNIVERSITET. VESTNIK. SERIYA 3. ISTORIYA, FILOSOFIYA, PSIKHOLOGIYA, SOTSIOLOGIYA, POLITOLOGIYA, EKONOMIKA, PRAVO/ BELORUSSIAN STATE UNIVERSITY. PROCEEDINGS. SERIES 3. HISTORY, PHILOSOPHY, PSYCHOLOGY, SOCIOLOGY, POLITOLOGY, ECONOMICS, LAW. Text in Belorussian. 1969. 4/yr. USD 206 foreign (effective 2006). bk.rev.
Former titles: Belorusskii Gosudarstvennyi Universitet. Vestnik. Seriya 3. Gystoriya, Filasofiya, Palitologiya, Sotsiyalogiya, Ekanomika, Prava; Belaruski Dziarzhauny Universitet. Vesnik. Seryia 3: Historiya, Filosofiya, Navukovy Kamunism, Ekanomika, Prava (0321-0359)
Indexed: RASB.
Published by: Belorusskii Gosudarstvennyi Universitet/Belorussian State University, Vul Babruiskaya 5a, Minsk, Belarus. Ed. V Grigor'evich. **Dist. by:** East View Information Services, 10601 Wayzata Blvd, Minneapolis, MN 55305. TEL 952-252-1201, 800-477-1005, FAX 952-252-1202, info@eastview.com, http://www.eastview.com.

▼ **BERG NEW MEDIA SERIES.** *see* COMMUNICATIONS

300 DEU ISSN 0945-0998
BERICHTE AUS DER SOZIALWISSENSCHAFT. Text in German. 1994. irreg., latest 2008. price varies. **Document type:** *Monographic series, Academic/Scholarly.*
Published by: Shaker Verlag GmbH, Kaiserstr 100, Herzogenrath, 52134, Germany. TEL 49-2407-95960, FAX 49-2407-95969, info@shaker.de.

300 USA ISSN 2159-8053
▼ ➤ **BERKELEY JOURNAL OF SOCIAL SCIENCES.** Text in English. 2011. m. free (effective 2011). back issues avail. **Document type:** *Journal, Academic/Scholarly.* **Description:** Provides a forum where the scholars and academicians can carry on the integrated and collaborated efforts to promote the research in specific areas of social sciences.
Media: Online - full text.
Published by: Khawaja Ashraf, Ed. kashraf@ix.netcom.com.

300 DEU ISSN 1867-3953
BERLINER AUFKLAERUNG; kulturwissenschaftliche Studien. Text in German. 1999. irreg., latest vol.3, 2007. price varies. **Document type:** *Monographic series, Academic/Scholarly.*
Published by: Wehrhahn Verlag, Am Mittelfelde 1, Hannover, 30519, Germany. TEL 49-511-8988906, FAX 49-511-8988245, info@wehrhahn-verlag.de, http://www.wehrhahn-verlag.de.

300 DEU ISSN 1610-5834
BERLINER BEITRAEGE ZUR FAMILIENSOZIOLOGIE. Text in German. 2002. irreg., latest vol.2, 2007. price varies. **Document type:** *Monographic series, Academic/Scholarly.*
Published by: Weissensee Verlag e.K., Simplonstr 59, Berlin, 10245, Germany. TEL 49-30-29049192, FAX 49-30-27574315, mail@weissensee-verlag.de.

300 DEU ISSN 1867-920X
BERLINER BEITRAEGE ZUR WISSENS- UND WISSENSCHAFTSGESCHICHTE. Text in German. 1998. irreg., latest vol.13, 2010. price varies. **Document type:** *Monographic series, Academic/Scholarly.*
Formerly (until 2010): Berliner Beitraege zur Wissenschaftsgeschichte (0949-7897)

Published by: Peter Lang GmbH (Subsidiary of: Peter Lang Publishing Group), Eschborner Landstr 42-50, Frankfurt Am Main, 60489, Germany. TEL 49-69-7807050, FAX 49-69-78070550, zentrale.frankfurt@peterlang.com. Eds. Lutz Danneberg, Ralf Klausnitzer.

300 DEU ISSN 1863-4346
BERLINER KULTURANALYSEN. Text in German. 2006. irreg. price varies. **Document type:** *Monographic series, Academic/Scholarly.*
Published by: Frank und Timme GmbH, Wittelsbacherstr 27a, Berlin, 10707, Germany. TEL 49-30-88667911, FAX 49-30-86398731, info@frank-timme.de.

BEST STUDY SERIES FOR G E D. SOCIAL STUDIES. (General Education Development) *see* EDUCATION

300 DEU ISSN 1863-1029
BEWEGUNGSKULTUR. Text in German. 2006. irreg., latest vol.6, 2009. price varies. **Document type:** *Monographic series, Academic/Scholarly.*
Published by: Verlag Dr. Kovac, Leverkusenstr 13, Hamburg, 22761, Germany. TEL 49-40-3988800, FAX 49-40-39888055, info@verlagdrkovac.de.

300 IND ISSN 0972-8775
H1
BHARATIYA SAMAJIK CHINTAN. Text in English. 19??. q. INR 200 domestic to individuals (effective 2011); INR 300 domestic to libraries (effective 2010); USD 80 foreign (effective 2011). bk.rev. back issues avail. **Document type:** *Journal, Academic/Scholarly.* **Description:** Analyzes contemporary Indian social reality in its historical perspective.
Published by: Indian Academy of Social Sciences, c/o Prof. M.G.S. Narayanan, 'MAITRY' M-6/7, Malaparamba Housing Society, Calicut, Kerala 673 009, India. TEL 91-495-2370328, mgsnarayanan@yahoo.com.

300 DEU ISSN 0933-372X
BIBLIOGRAPHIEN ZUR RECHTS- UND SOZIALWISSENSCHAFT. Text in German. 1990. irreg. price varies. **Document type:** *Monographic series, Academic/Scholarly.*
Published by: Centaurus Verlag & Media KG, Kaiser-Joseph-Str 267, Freiburg, 79098, Germany. TEL 49-761-1525861, FAX 49-761-1525868, info@centaurus-verlag.de, http://www.centaurus-verlag.de.

300 ARG
BIBLIOTECA DE CIENCIAS SOCIALES. Text in Spanish. irreg., latest vol.2, 1982.
Published by: Consejo Latinoamericano de Ciencias Sociales, Avda Callao 875, Piso 3, Buenos Aires, 1023, Argentina. TEL 54-11-48142301, erol@clacso.edu.ar, http://www.clacso.org.

300 PRY
BIBLIOTECA DE ESTUDIOS PARAGUAYOS. Text in Spanish. 1981. irreg., latest vol.58, 1998. price varies. adv. back issues avail.
Published by: Universidad Catolica Nuestra Senora de la Asuncion, Centro de Estudios Antropologicos, Casilla de Correos 1718, Asuncion, Paraguay. TEL 595-21-446251, FAX 595-21-445245. Ed. Adriano Irala Burgos. Circ: 1,000.

300 RUS
BIBLIOTECHKA PROFSOYUZNOGO AKTIVA I PREDPRINIMATELEI. Text in Russian. 1961. s-m. USD 273 in United States (effective 2007).
Formerly: Bibliotechka Profsoyuznogo Aktivista (0201-7636)
—East View.
Published by: Profizdat, Myasnitskaya ul 13, stroenie 18-18a, Moscow, 101000, Russian Federation. TEL 7-495-6245740, FAX 7-495-6752329, profizdat@profizdat.ru, http://profizdat.ru. Ed. V B Fursova. **Dist. by:** East View Information Services, 10601 Wayzata Blvd, Minneapolis, MN 55305. TEL 952-252-1201, 800-477-1005, FAX 952-252-1202, info@eastview.com, http://www.eastview.com.

300 FRA ISSN 2116-7966
▼ **BIBLIOTHEQUE DES SCIENCES SOCIALES.** Text in French. 2011. irreg. **Document type:** *Monographic series, Academic/Scholarly.*
Published by: Editions Classiques Garnier, BP 93, Conde-sur-Noireau, 14110, France. TEL 33-2-31592500, FAX 33-2-31694435, contact@classiques-garnier.com, http://www.classiques-garnier.com.

500 001.3 FIN ISSN 0067-8481
Q60
BIDRAG TILL KAENNEDOM AV FINLANDS NATUR OCH FOLK. Text in Finnish, Swedish. 1857. irreg. price varies.
Indexed: FR, GeoRef, NAA, RefZh.
—Linda Hall.
Published by: Suomen Tiedeseura/Finnish Society of Sciences and Letters, Mariagatan 5, Helsinki, 00170, Finland. TEL 358-9-633005, FAX 358-9-661065. Ed. Paul Fogelberg. Circ: 500. **Co-sponsor:** Finnish Academy of Sciences and Letters.

BIGAKU GEIJUTSUGAKU KENKYU. *see* HUMANITIES: COMPREHENSIVE WORKS

300 ITA ISSN 1826-8226
BILANS, ECHANGES, PROJECTS. Text in Multiple languages. irreg. **Document type:** *Magazine, Consumer.*
Published by: Ecole Francaise de Rome, Piazza Navona 62, Rome, 00186, Italy. TEL 39-06-686011, FAX 39-06-6874834, http://www.ecole-francaise.it.

300 TUR ISSN 1301-0549
DR401
➤ **BILIG;** Turk dunyasi sosyal bilimler dergisi. Variant title: Journal of Social Sciences of the Turkish World. Text in Turkish; Text occasionally in English. 199?. q. TRY 80 domestic; USD 100 foreign (effective 2011). **Document type:** *Journal, Academic/Scholarly.*
Related titles: Online - full text ed.
Indexed: CA, IBSS, L&LBA, MLA-IB, P42, PAIS, PSA, S02, S03, SCOPUS, SSCI, SociolAb, T02, W07.
Published by: Ahmet Yesevi Universitesi, Mutevelli Heyet Baskanligi Yayinidir/Ahmet Yesevi University, Board of Trustees, Taskent Caddesi 10, Sokak No 30, Bahcelievler, Ankara, 06490, Turkey. TEL 90-312-2152206, FAX 90-312-2152209. Ed. Dr. Nurettin Demir.

300 CHN ISSN 1009-0274
BINGTUAN DANGXIAO XUEBAO/PARTY SCHOOL OF X P C C OF C.P.C. JOURNAL. Text in Chinese. 1989. bi-m. **Document type:** *Journal, Academic/Scholarly.*
Formerly: Bingtuan Dang-jiao Luntan

Published by: Xinjiang Bingtuan Dangxiao, Wujiaqu, 831300, China. TEL 86-994-5822987.

300 001.3 CHN ISSN 1009-1548
BINGTUAN JIAOYU XUEYUAN XUEBAO/BINGTUAN EDUCATION INSTITUTE. JOURNAL. Text in Chinese. 1991. bi-m. **Document type:** *Journal, Academic/Scholarly.*
Formerly (until 1992): Silu Xuekan
Related titles: Online - full text ed.
Published by: Bingtuan Jiaoyu Xueyuan/Bingtuan Education Institute, PO Box 1420, Shihezi, 832003, China. TEL 86-993-2058097.

300 CHN ISSN 1673-2618
BINZHOU XUEYUAN XUEBAO/BINZHOU UNIVERSITY. JOURNAL. Text in Chinese. 2005. bi-m. **Document type:** *Journal, Academic/Scholarly.*
Formed by the merger of (1995-2005): Binzhou Jiaoyu Xueyuan Xuebao (1009-0738); (1991-2005): Binzhou Shi-Zhuan Xuebao/Binzhou Teachers College. Journal (1008-2980); Which was formed by the merger of (1985-1991): Binzhou Shi-Zhuan Xuebao (Zhexue Shehui Kexue Ban); (1985-1991): Binzhou Shi-Zhuan Xuebao (Ziran Kexue Ban)
Related titles: Online - full text ed.
Published by: Binzhou Xueyuan/Binzhou University, 391, Huanghe Wu-Lu, Binzhou, 256603, China. TEL 86-543-3190158, FAX 86-543-3190000.

300 GBR ISSN 1745-8552
H1
➤ **BIOSOCIETIES.** Text in English. 2006. q. USD 476 in North America to institutions; GBP 264 elsewhere to institutions (effective 2012). adv. bk.rev. back issues avail.; reprint service avail. from PSC. **Document type:** *Journal, Academic/Scholarly.* **Description:** Dedicated to advancing analytic understanding of the social, ethical, legal, economic, public and policy aspects of current and emerging developments in the life sciences.
Related titles: Online - full text ed.: ISSN 1745-8560.
Indexed: A01, A22, A34, A35, A38, AgBio, CABA, CurCont, E01, E12, GH, IBSS, IndVet, LT, N02, N03, P20, P21, P27, P48, P52, P54, P56, PQC, R12, RA&MP, RRTA, S02, S03, SSCI, SociolAb, T02, T05, VS, W07.
—BLDSC (2089.615860), IE, Ingenta. **CCC.**
Published by: (London School of Economics and Political Science), Palgrave Macmillan Ltd. (Subsidiary of: Macmillan Publishers Ltd.), Houndmills, Basingstoke, Hants RG21 6XS, United Kingdom. TEL 44-1256-329242, FAX 44-1256-479476, orders@palgrave.com, http://www.palgrave.com. Eds. Adele Clarke, Ilina Singh, Nikolas Rose. **Subscr. to:** Subscription Department, Brunel Rd, Houndmills, Basingstoke, Hants RG21 2XS, United Kingdom. TEL 44-1256-357893, FAX 44-1256-812358, subscriptions@palgrave.com.

➤ **THE BLACK SCHOLAR;** journal of black studies and research. *see* ETHNIC INTERESTS

300 DEU ISSN 1613-3277
BLICKWECHSEL. Text in German. 2004. irreg., latest vol.9, 2011. price varies. **Document type:** *Monographic series, Academic/Scholarly.*
Published by: Franz Steiner Verlag GmbH, Birkenwaldstr 44, Stuttgart, 70191, Germany. TEL 49-711-25820, FAX 49-711-2582290, service@steiner-verlag.de, http://www.steiner-verlag.de.

BLUEPRINT FOR SOCIAL JUSTICE. *see* POLITICAL SCIENCE—Civil Rights

300 GBR ISSN 1357-034X
HM110
➤ **BODY & SOCIETY.** Text in English. 1995. q. USD 922, GBP 498 combined subscription to institutions (print & online eds.); USD 904, GBP 488 to institutions (effective 2011). adv. bk.rev. back issues avail.; reprint service avail. from PSC. **Document type:** *Journal, Academic/Scholarly.* **Description:** Caters for the upsurge of interest in the social and cultural analysis of the human body. Dedicated to the publication of contemporary empirical and theoretical work from a wide range of disciplines.
Related titles: Online - full text ed.: ISSN 1460-3632. USD 830, GBP 448 to institutions (effective 2011).
Indexed: A01, A03, A08, A20, A22, AltPI, B07, CA, CurCont, DIP, E01, H04, IBR, IBSS, IBZ, IBibSS, PEI, PerIslam, S02, S03, SCOPUS, SOPODA, SSA, SSCI, SociolAb, T02, V02, W07.
—BLDSC (2117.200200), IE, Infotrieve, Ingenta. **CCC.**
Published by: Sage Publications Ltd. (Subsidiary of: Sage Publications, Inc.), 1 Oliver's Yard, 55 City Rd, London, EC1Y 1SP, United Kingdom. TEL 44-20-73248500, FAX 44-20-73248600, info@sagepub.co.uk, http://www.uk.sagepub.com/home.nav. Eds. Lisa Blackman, Mike Featherstone. **Subscr. in the Americas to:** Sage Publications, Inc., 2455 Teller Rd, Thousand Oaks, CA 91320. TEL 805-499-9774, FAX 805-499-0871, journals@sagepub.com.

300 DEU ISSN 1867-6243
▼ **BODY-FEELING UND BODY-BILDUNG.** Text in German. 2009. irreg., latest vol.2, 2010. price varies. **Document type:** *Monographic series, Academic/Scholarly.*
Published by: Ibidem Verlag, Melchiorstr 15, Stuttgart, 70439, Germany. TEL 49-711-9807954, FAX 49-711-9807952, ibidem@ibidem-verlag.de, http://www.ibidem-verlag.de.

300 TUR ISSN 1300-9583
➤ **BOGAZICI JOURNAL: REVIEW OF SOCIAL, ECONOMIC AND ADMINISTRATIVE SCIENCES.** Text in English. 1973. s-a. TRY 10,000 domestic; USD 10 to individuals; USD 20 to institutions (effective 2009). adv. bk.rev. bibl.; stat. back issues avail. **Document type:** *Journal, Academic/Scholarly.* **Description:** Publishes research from a variety of social science disciplines including economics, management studies, political science and international studies, sociology, social anthropology, social demography and social psychology. Major attention is given to Turkey's domestic transformation and external relations with Europe, the Balkans, the Black Sea region and Central Asia as well as the Middle East.
Former titles (until 1993): Journal of Economics and Administrative Studies; (until 1987): Bogazici University Journal: Management, Economic and Social Sciences
Indexed: GEOBASE, SCOPUS.

Published by: Bogazici Universitesi, Faculty of Economics and Administrative Sciences, Bebek, Istanbul, 80815, Turkey. TEL 90-212-3595400, FAX 90-212-2877851, bjournal@boun.edu.tr. Eds. Fikret Adaman, Kemal Kirsci, Muzaffer Bodur. Circ: 1,000 (paid); 150 (controlled). **Subscr. to:** Price Waterhouse Coopers, Spor Caddesi 92, BJK Plaza B Blok Kat 9, Besiktas Istanbul 80680, Turkey. TEL 90-212-2594980, FAX 90-212-2594902, figen.kulak@tr.pwcglobal.com.

300 100 CHN ISSN 1672-8254
BOHAI DAXUE XUEBAO (ZHEXUE SHEHUI KEXUE BAN)/BOHAI UNIVERSITY. JOURNAL (PHILOSOPHY AND SOCIAL SCIENCE EDITION). Text in Chinese. 1979. bi-m. USD 31.20 (effective 2009). **Document type:** *Journal, Academic/Scholarly.*
Formerly: Jinzhou Shi-yuan Xuebao (Zhexue Shehui Kexue Ban)/Jinzhou Teachers' College Journal (Philosophy and Social Science Edition) (1001-6333)
Related titles: Online - full text ed.
Indexed: CA, P42, S02, S03, SCOPUS, SociolAb, T02.
—BLDSC (2118.250000).
Published by: Bohai Daxue/Bohai University, No. 27, Section 5, Jiefang Road, Linghe District, Jinzhou, Liaoning 121000, China. TEL 86-416-2849092, FAX 86-416-2849093, http://www.bhu.edu.cn/. Ed. Huan-Ping Liu.

300 IRQ
➤ **BOHOTH MUSTAQBALIYA/JOURNAL OF PROSPECTIVE RESEARCH.** (JPR) Text in Arabic, English. 1999 (Oct.). s-a. IQD 8,000 in Iraq to individuals; IQD 18,000 elsewhere to individuals; IQD 15,000 in Iraq to institutions; IQD 15,000 elsewhere to institutions (effective 2001). bk.rev. 250 p./no.; back issues avail.; reprints avail. **Document type:** *Journal, Academic/Scholarly.* **Description:** Publishes research papers in the fields of administration, economics, accountancy, law, politics, general and social affairs, quantitative methods, and computer sciences.
Related titles: CD-ROM ed.
Published by: Al Hadba'a University College/Kuliyat al-Hadba'a al-Jami'a, P O Box 1085, Mosul, 1085, Iraq. TEL 964-60-811276, 964-60-810137, FAX 964-60-009641, 964-60-8170285. Ed. Dr. Basman F Mahjoob.

➤ **BOLETIM CULTURAL.** *see* SCIENCES: COMPREHENSIVE WORKS

300 ARG ISSN 1515-6184
BOLETIN DE COYUNTURA TRIMESTRAL. Key Title: Boletin de Coyuntura Trimestral. La Nueva Cuestion Social en Argentina. Text in Spanish. 2000. q. back issues avail.
Related titles: Online - full text ed.: ISSN 1515-6192. 2000.
Published by: Universidad de Ciencias Empresariales y Sociales, Departamento de Investigacion, Paraguay, 1401 9o. Piso, Buenos Aires, 1061, Argentina. TEL 54-114-8130228, informes@uces.edu.ar.

300 COL ISSN 2011-2017
BOLETIN DEL OBSERVATORIO SOBRE DESARROLLO HUMANO. Text in Spanish. 2007. bi-m.
Published by: Universidad Autonoma de Colombia, Fundacion, Calle 12 No. 4 - 30 y Calle 13 No. 4 - 31, Bogota, Colombia. TEL 57-1-3414628, http://www.fuac.edu.co/?.

300 ARG ISSN 0497-0292
HC171
BOLETIN INFORMATIVO TECHINT. Text in Spanish. 1959. q. free.
Formerly: Organizacion Techint. Boletin Informativo
Indexed: PAIS.
Published by: Organizacion Techint, Avda. Cordoba, 320 Piso 3, Buenos Aires, 1054, Argentina. TEL 54-114-3185660, FAX 54-114-3110888. Ed. Jorge Lattes. Circ: 4,000.

300 BOL
BOLETIN POSGRADOS. Text in Spanish. bi-w.
Media: Online - full text. **Related titles:** E-mail ed.
Published by: Centro Boliviano de Estudios Multidisciplinarios, Ave. Ecuador no. 2330, esq. C. Rosendo Gutierrez, La Paz, Bolivia. TEL 591-2-2415324, FAX 591-2-2414726, cebem@cebem.com, http://www.cebem.com/. Ed. Fabiana Larranza.

300 DEU ISSN 0176-6546
BONNER AMERIKANISTISCHE STUDIEN. Text in English, Spanish, German. 1971. irreg., latest vol.45, 2008. price varies. **Document type:** *Monographic series, Academic/Scholarly.*
Published by: Shaker Verlag GmbH, Kaiserstr 100, Herzogenrath, 52134, Germany. TEL 49-2407-95960, FAX 49-2407-95969, info@shaker.de.

BONNER ZENTRUM FUER RELIGION UND GESELLSCHAFT. STUDIEN. *see* RELIGIONS AND THEOLOGY

300 PRI
▼ **EL BORICUA.** Text in English, Spanish. 2011. m. USD 15 (effective 2011). **Document type:** *Magazine, Consumer.*
Media: Online - full text.
Published by: El Boricua http://www.elboricua.com.

300 DEU
BORNO SAHARA AND SUDAN SERIES; studies in the humanities and social sciences. Text in English. 2006. irreg., latest vol.4, 2010. price varies. **Document type:** *Monographic series, Academic/Scholarly.*
Published by: Ruediger Koeppe Verlag, Wendelinstr 73-75, Cologne, 50933, Germany. TEL 49-221-4911236, FAX 49-221-4994336, info@koeppe.de. Eds. Gisela Seidensticker-Brikay, Kyari Tijani.

300 DEU ISSN 1864-287X
BRAUNSCHWEIGER BEITRAEGE ZUR KULTURGESCHICHTE. Text in German. 2007. irreg. price varies. **Document type:** *Monographic series, Academic/Scholarly.*
Published by: Peter Lang GmbH (Subsidiary of: Peter Lang Publishing Group), Eschborner Landstr 42-50, Frankfurt Am Main, 60489, Germany. TEL 49-69-7807050, FAX 49-69-78070550, zentrale.frankfurt@peterlang.com. Eds. Angela Klein, Gerd Biegel.

300 DEU ISSN 0935-6045
BREMER SOZIOLOGISCHE TEXTE. Text in German. 1988. irreg., latest vol.8, 2000. price varies. **Document type:** *Monographic series, Academic/Scholarly.*
Published by: Centaurus Verlag & Media KG, Kaiser-Joseph-Str 267, Freiburg, 79098, Germany. TEL 49-761-1525861, FAX 49-761-1525868, info@centaurus-verlag.de, http://www.centaurus-verlag.de.

300 DEU
▼ **BRENNPUNKT DOPING**; die Macht des Machbaren und der moderne Mensch. Text in German. 2010. irreg. price varies. **Document type:** *Monographic series, Academic/Scholarly.*
Published by: Transcript, Muehlenstr 47, Bielefeld, 33607, Germany. TEL 49-521-63454, FAX 49-521-61040, live@transcript-verlag.de.

301.094205 GBR ISSN 1756-0578
BRITAIN IN (YEAR). Text in English. 2007. a. GBP 4.95 newsstand/cover domestic (effective 2009). **Document type:** *Magazine, Consumer.* **Description:** Showcases the diversity of ESRC-funded research around the state of the nation. Contains a mixture of academic opinion pieces alongside informed journalistic writing, offering a concise analysis of research and topical issues concerning Britain today.
Formerly (until 2008): Britain Today (1753-1705)
—BLDSC (2286.151400).
Published by: Economic and Social Research Council, Polaris House, North Star Ave, Swindon, Wilts SN2 1UJ, United Kingdom. TEL 44-1793-413000, FAX 44-1793-413001, comms@esrc.ac.uk. Ed. Jacky Clake.

300 GBR ISSN 2047-1866
BRITISH ACADEMY. REVIEW. Text in English. 19??. irreg. **Document type:** *Report, Trade.*
Formerly (until 1999): British Academy. Annual Report
Related titles: Online - full text ed.: ISSN 2047-1874. free (effective 2011).
Published by: British Academy, 10-11 Carlton House Terr, London, SW1Y 5AH, United Kingdom. TEL 44-20-79695200, FAX 44-20-79695300, pubs@britac.ac.uk.

▼ **BRITISH IDENTITIES SINCE 1707.** *see* HISTORY—History Of Europe

300 GBR ISSN 2046-9578
▼ ➤ **BRITISH JOURNAL OF ARTS AND SOCIAL SCIENCES.** Text in English. 2011. m. abstr. back issues avail. **Document type:** *Journal, Academic/Scholarly.* **Description:** Publishes research articles, original research reports, reviews, short communications and scientific commentaries in the fields of social sciences.
Media: Online - full text. Ed. Jssica Sowaea. Pub., R&P Muhammad Naveed Khalid.

301 GBR ISSN 0269-9222
F1021
➤ **BRITISH JOURNAL OF CANADIAN STUDIES.** Abbreviated title: B J C S. Text in English, French. 1977. s-a. GBP 41, USD 69 combined subscription to individuals (print & online eds.); GBP 62, USD 110 combined subscription to institutions (print & online eds.); free to members (effective 2012). adv. bk.rev. index. back issues avail.; reprints avail. **Document type:** *Journal, Academic/Scholarly.* **Description:** Covers Canadian literature, history, geography, and political science.
Formerly (until 1986): Bulletin of Canadian Studies (0141-2639)
Related titles: Online - full text ed.: ISSN 1757-8078. GBP 34, USD 56 to individuals; GBP 49, USD 88 to institutions (effective 2012).
Indexed: A20, A26, AmH&L, ArtHuCI, BEL&L, C03, C05, CA, CBCARef, CBPI, CPerI, CurCont, E08, G08, HistAb, I05, IBSS, MLA-IB, P27, P48, P54, PQC, RILM, S09, T02, W07.
—BLDSC (2306.900000), IE, Ingenta. **CCC.**
Published by: (British Association for Canadian Studies), Liverpool University Press, 4 Cambridge St, Liverpool, L69 7ZU, United Kingdom. TEL 44-151-7942233, FAX 44-151-7942235, lup@liv.ac.uk. Ed. Heather Norris Nicholson. Adv. contact Janet Smith. **Subscr. to:** Marston Book Services Ltd., PO Box 269, Abingdon, Oxon OX14 4YN, United Kingdom. TEL 44-1235-465574, FAX 44-1235-465556, subscriptions@marston.co.uk, http://www.marston.co.uk/.

300 GBR ISSN 0265-6175
BRITISH PUBLIC OPINION. Text in English. 10/yr. GBP 100, USD 200 (effective 2000). index. back issues avail. **Document type:** *Report, Consumer.* **Description:** Review of surveys of public opinion.
Indexed: RASB.
Published by: Market & Opinion Research International, 32 Old Queen St, London, SW1H 9HP, United Kingdom. TEL 44-20-7222-0232, FAX 44-20-7222-1653. Ed. Robert Worcester. R&P Roger Mortimore.

300 GBR ISSN 0267-6869
HN400.P8
BRITISH SOCIAL ATTITUDES. Variant title: British Social Attitudes Survey Series. Text in English. 1984. a. USD 108 per issue (effective 2010). back issues avail. **Document type:** *Journal, Academic/Scholarly.* **Description:** Designed to chart changes in British social values over a period of time in relation to other changes in society.
Indexed: A22, RASB.
—BLDSC (2342.905800), IE, Ingenta. **CCC.**
Published by: Sage Publications Ltd. (Subsidiary of: Sage Publications, Inc.), 1 Oliver's Yard, 55 City Rd, London, EC1Y 1SP, United Kingdom. TEL 44-20-73248500, FAX 44-20-73248600, info@sagepub.co.uk, http://www.uk.sagepub.com/home.nav. Ed. Alison Park.

300 BEL ISSN 2031-0293
BRUSSELS STUDIES. Text in Multiple languages. 2006. m. free (effective 2011). **Document type:** *Journal, Academic/Scholarly.*
Media: Online - full text.
Published by: Facultes Universitaires Saint Louis, Institut de Recherches Interdisciplinaires sur Bruxelles (I R I B), Boulevard du Jardin Botanique 43, Brussels, 1000, Belgium. TEL 32-2-2117970, http://www.irib.be. Ed. Michel Hubert.

300 DEU ISSN 1861-6968
BUCHREIHE LAND-BERICHTE. Text in German. 1998. irreg., latest vol.3, 2008. price varies. **Document type:** *Monographic series, Academic/Scholarly.*
Formerly (until 2005): Land-Berichte (1436-8706)
Published by: Shaker Verlag GmbH, Kaiserstr 100, Herzogenrath, 52134, Germany. TEL 49-2407-95960, FAX 49-2407-95969, info@shaker.de.

300 SDN ISSN 0304-2561
BUHUTH. Text in Arabic. 1972. m. **Document type:** *Proceedings.*
Indexed: INIS AtomInd.
Published by: National Centre for Research, Documentation and Information Centre, P O Box 2404, Khartoum, Sudan. TEL 249-11-770776, FAX 249-11-770701. Ed. Farida A Hamad.

980 GBR ISSN 0261-3050
F1401 CODEN: BLARE9
BULLETIN OF LATIN AMERICAN RESEARCH. Text in English. 19??. q. GBP 568 in United Kingdom to institutions; EUR 722 in Europe to institutions; USD 1,047 in the Americas to institutions; USD 1,221 elsewhere to institutions; GBP 652 combined subscription in United Kingdom to institutions (print & online eds.); EUR 830 combined subscription in Europe to institutions (print & online eds.); USD 1,204 combined subscription in the Americas to institutions (print & online eds.); USD 1,404 combined subscription elsewhere to institutions (print & online eds.) (effective 2012). adv. bk.rev. abstr. back issues avail.; reprint service avail. from PSC. **Document type:** *Journal, Academic/Scholarly.* **Description:** Contains original research papers on topics of current interest on Latin America from all academic disciplines of the social sciences and humanities.
Former titles (until 1981): Society for Latin American Studies. Bulletin (0308-1540); (until 1967): Society for Latin America Studies. Information Bulletin (0583-9092)
Related titles: Online - full text ed.: ISSN 1470-9856. GBP 568 in United Kingdom to institutions; EUR 722 in Europe to institutions; USD 1,047 in the Americas to institutions; USD 1,221 elsewhere to institutions (effective 2012) (from IngentaConnect).
Indexed: A01, A02, A03, A08, A20, A21, A22, A26, ABCPolSci, AICP, AmH&L, AmHI, B01, B07, BibInd, BrHumI, CA, CurCont, E01, ESPM, FR, GEOBASE, H07, H14, H21, HistAb, I05, I08, IBR, IBSS, IBZ, MLA-IB, P02, P08, P10, P30, P34, P42, P48, P53, P54, PAIS, PCI, PQC, PSA, RASB, RI-1, RI-2, RILM, RiskAb, S02, S03, S11, SCOPUS, SOPODA, SSA, SSCI, SSciA, SociolAb, T02, W07.
—BLDSC (2865.440000), IE, Infotrieve, Ingenta. **CCC.**
Published by: (Society for Latin American Studies), Wiley-Blackwell Publishing Ltd. (Subsidiary of: John Wiley & Sons, Inc.), 9600 Garsington Rd, Oxford, OX4 2DQ, United Kingdom. TEL 44-1865-776868, FAX 44-1865-714591, customerservices@blackwellpublishing.com. Eds. David Howard, Dr. Geoffrey Kantaris. Adv. contact Craig Pickett TEL 44-1865-476267. B&W page USD 823; 145 x 230. Circ: 865.

BULLETIN OF SCIENCE, TECHNOLOGY & SOCIETY. *see* SCIENCES: COMPREHENSIVE WORKS

▼ **BUSINESS AND SOCIAL SCIENCES REVIEW.** *see* BUSINESS AND ECONOMICS

300 BOL
BUSQUEDA; revista semestral de ciencias sociales. Text in Spanish. 1959. s-a. per issue exchange basis.
Supersedes (in 1990): Universidad Boliviana Mayor de San Simon. Instituto de Estudios Sociales y Economicos. Revista (0041-8617)
Published by: (Instituto de Estudios Sociales y Economicos), Universidad Mayor de "San Simon", Facultad de Ciencias Economicas y Sociologia, Casilla 992, Cochabamba, Bolivia. TEL 32540 ext. 314, TELEX 6363 UMSS BV. Circ: 1,000.

960 CHE ISSN 1663-3059
▼ **C E A U P STUDIES ON AFRICA.** (Centro de Estudos Africanos da Universidade do Porto) Text in English. 2010. irreg. price varies. **Document type:** *Monographic series, Academic/Scholarly.*
Published by: (Centro de Estudos Africanos da Universidade do Porto PRT), Peter Lang AG (Subsidiary of: Peter Lang Publishing Group), Hochfeldstr 32, Postfach 746, Bern 9, 3000, Switzerland. TEL 41-31-3061717, FAX 41-31-3061727, info@peterlang.com.

980 300 NLD ISSN 1572-6401
C E D L A LATIN AMERICA STUDIES. Abbreviated title: C L A S. Text in English, Spanish. 1985. irreg., latest vol.97, 2009. price varies. back issues avail. **Document type:** *Monographic series, Academic/Scholarly.*
Indexed: IZBG.
—BLDSC (5160.149000), IE.
Published by: (Centrum voor Studie en Documentatie van Latijns Amerika/Center for Latin American Research and Documentation - Centro de Estudios y Documentacion Latinoamericanos), Brill, PO Box 9000, Leiden, 2300 PA, Netherlands. TEL 31-71-5353500, FAX 31-71-5317532, cs@brill.nl.

304.2 SWE ISSN 1654-8744
C E M U S. SKRIFTSERIE. (Centrum foer Miljoe- och Utvecklingsstudier) Text in Swedish. 2007. irreg. **Document type:** *Monographic series, Academic/Scholarly.*
Published by: Centrum foer Miljoe- och Utvecklingsstudier/Centre for Environmental and Development Studies, c/o Uppsala Universitet, Villavaegen 16, Uppsala, 75236, Sweden. TEL 46-18-4717294, FAX 46-18-4712796, info@cemus.uu.se, http://www.cemus.uu.se.

300 BRA ISSN 1516-2664
➤ **C E S U M A R. REVISTA.** (Centro Universitario de Maringa) Text in Portuguese. 1997. s-a. free (effective 2007). Index. **Document type:** *Journal, Academic/Scholarly.*
Indexed: CA, HPNRM, P42, PAIS, S02, S03, SSciA, SociolAb, T02.
Published by: Centro Universitario de Maringa (C E S U M A R), Av Guedner 1610, Maringa, Parana 87050-390, Brazil. TEL 55-44-2276360, FAX pesquisa@cesumar.br, 55-44-2275395. Ed. Leone Barzotto. Circ: 1,000.

300 FRA ISSN 0395-5621
C F D T MAGAZINE. Text in French. 1976. m. (11/yr.). bk.rev.; film rev. illus. **Document type:** *Magazine, Trade.*
Formerly: Syndicalisme Magazine
Indexed: RASB.
Published by: Confederation Francaise Democratique du Travail, 4 bd. de la Villette, Paris, Cedex 19 75955, France. TEL 33-1-42038140, FAX 33-1-42038148, gestionpresse@cfdt.fr, http://www.cfdt.org. Ed. Henri Israel.

C N K I WEB. (China National Knowledge Infrastructure) *see* SCIENCES: COMPREHENSIVE WORKS

C Q RESEARCHER. (Congressional Quarterly) *see* POLITICAL SCIENCE

300 BRA ISSN 0103-4979
H53.B7 CODEN: CACRFM
C R H. CADERNO. (Centro de Recursos Humanos) Text in Portuguese, Spanish. 1987. 3/yr. **Document type:** *Journal, Academic/Scholarly.* **Description:** Addresses social change and the cultural and political processes.
Related titles: Online - full text ed.: ISSN 1983-8239. 2007. free (effective 2011).
Indexed: C01, CA, P42, PSA, S02, S03, SCOPUS, SSA, SociolAb, T02.

S

Published by: Universidade Federal da Bahia, Centro de Recursos Humanos, Rua Caetano Moura, 99, 1 sub-solo, Salvador, Bahia 40210-340, Brazil. http://www.ufba.br/~crh/. Ed. Anete Brito Leal Ivo.

300 ZAF
C S D S WORKING PAPERS. Text in English. 1992 (no.2). irreg., latest vol.14, 1997. price varies. **Document type:** *Monographic series, Academic/Scholarly.*
Published by: University of KwaZulu-Natal, Centre for Social and Development Studies, Private Bag X10, Dalbridge, 4014, South Africa. TEL 27-31-2602525, FAX 27-31-2602813.

C S R C RESEARCH REPORT. (Chicano Studies Research Center) *see* ETHNIC INTERESTS

300 COL ISSN 2011-4281
CABECERA. Text in Spanish. 2007. m.
Published by: La Cabecera, Calle 100 No. 36-39 El Girasol No. 149, Bogota, Colombia. TEL 57-1-6362227, lacabecera@gmail.com, http://www.lacabecera.com. Ed. Manuel Fernando Acella.

300 BRA ISSN 0104-0782
CADERNOS DE CIENCIAS SOCIAIS. Text in Portuguese. 1991. s-a. **Document type:** *Journal, Academic/Scholarly.*
Indexed: P42, S02, S03, SociolAb.
Published by: Pontificia Universidade Catolica de Minas Gerais, Av Dom Jose Gaspar 500, Coracao Eucaristico, Belo Horizonte, MG 30535-610, Brazil. TEL 55-31-33194444, FAX 55-31-33194225, central@pucminas.br, http://www.pucminas.br.

300 PRT ISSN 0871-0945
CADERNOS DE CIENCIAS SOCIAIS. Text in Portuguese. 1984. irreg., latest vol.19, 2000. EUR 8.50 (effective 2005).
Published by: Edicoes Afrontamento, Lda., Rua de Costa Cabral, 859, Porto, 4200-225, Portugal. TEL 351-22-5074220, FAX 351-22-5074229, editorial@edicoesafrontamento.pt, http://www.edicoesafrontamento.pt. Ed. Jose Madureira Pinto.

CADERNOS DE DIVULGACAO CULTURAL. *see* MEDICAL SCIENCES

360 BRA ISSN 0102-4248
HC186
CADERNOS DE ESTUDOS SOCIAIS. Text in Portuguese; Summaries in English. 1985. s-a. BRL 2.92 per issue. bibl.
Indexed: AICP, C01.
Published by: (Fundacao Joaquim Nabuco), Editora Massangana, Rua Dois Irmaos, 15, Apipucos, Recife, PE 52071-440, Brazil. TEL 55-81-268-4611, FAX 55-81-268-9600. Circ: 1,000.

CADERNOS DE LINGUAGEM E SOCIEDADE. *see* LINGUISTICS

300 BRA ISSN 1516-0440
CADERNOS DE PESQUISA (CAXIAS DO SUL). Text in Portuguese. 1998. irreg.
Indexed: SociolAb.
Published by: Universidade de Caxias do Sul, Rua Francisco Getulio Vargas, 1130, Caxias do Sul, RS 95070-560, Brazil. informa@ucs.tce.br.

300 BRA
CADERNOS DO PATRIMONIO CULTURAL. Text in Portuguese. 1991. 4/yr. free. **Document type:** *Government.* **Description:** Publishes articles dealing with cultural heritage preservation in its various aspects: architectural, historic and social.
Published by: Secretaria Municipal de Cultura, Departamento Geral do Patrimonio Cultural, Rua Afonso Cavalcanti, 455 sala 207, C Nova, Rio De Janeiro, RJ 20211-110, Brazil. TEL 55-21-2734095, FAX 55-21-5032158. Circ: 1,000 (controlled).

300 ITA ISSN 2038-5242
▼ **CADMUS**; promoting leadership in thought that leads to action. Text in English. 2010. s-a. **Document type:** *Journal, Academic/Scholarly.*
Related titles: Online - full text ed.: ISSN 2038-5250. free (effective 2011).
Published by: The Risk Institute/L' Istituto del Rischio, Via della Torretta 10, Trieste, 34121, Italy. Ed. Orio Giarini.

300 FRA ISSN 1270-9247
DS327
CAHIERS D'ASIE CENTRALE. Text in French. 1996. s-a. EUR 20.20 (effective 2003). adv. **Document type:** *Monographic series, Consumer.*
Indexed: DIP, I14, IBR, IBZ.
Published by: Editions Edisud, 30 Av. des Ecoles Militaires, Le Vieux Lavoir, Aix-en-Provence, 13100, France. TEL 33-4-42216144, FAX 33-4-42215620. Ed. Vincent Fourniau. Pub. Mr. C Y Chaudoreille. Adv. contact Ms. Sibylle de Maisonseul.

300 FRA ISSN 1635-3544
LB1028
CAHIERS DE LA RECHERCHE SUR L'EDUCATION ET LES SAVOIRS. Text in French. 1998. a. **Document type:** *Monographic series, Academic/Scholarly.*
Formerly (until 2001): Atelier de Recherche sur l'Education et les Savoirs. Cahiers (1296-2023)
Published by: (Association de Recherche sur l'Education et les Savoirs (A R E S)), Editions de la Maison des Sciences de l'Homme, 54 Blvd Raspail, Paris, Cedex 6 75270, France. TEL 33-1-49542000, FAX 33-1-49542133, http://www.msh-paris.fr.

980 300 FRA ISSN 1141-7161
CAHIERS DES AMERIQUES LATINES. Text in French. 1968. 2/yr. abstr.; bibl. **Document type:** *Monographic series, Academic/Scholarly.*
Formerly (until 1984): Cahiers des Ameriques Latines. Serie - Sciences de l'Homme (0008-0020)
Indexed: AICP, CA, DIP, FR, H21, HistAb, I13, IBR, IBSS, IBZ, P08, P30, P42, PAIS, PCI, RASB, RILM, T02.
—BLDSC (2948.616400), INIST.
Published by: Institut des Hautes Etudes de l'Amerique Latine (I H E A L) (Subsidiary of: Centre National de la Recherche Scientifique), 28 rue Saint-Guillaume, Paris, 75007, France. http://www.credal.univ-paris3.fr. **Dist. by:** Documentation Francaise, 29-31 Quai Voltaire, Paris Cedex 7 75344, France. TEL 33-1-40157000.

CAHIERS D'ETUDES SUR LA MEDITERRANEE ORIENTALE ET LE MONDE TURCO-IRANIEN. *see* POLITICAL SCIENCE

LES CAHIERS RUSSIE/RUSSIA PAPERS. *see* HISTORY—History Of Europe

CAHIERS ZAIROIS D'ETUDES POLITIQUES ET SOCIALES. *see* POLITICAL SCIENCE

306 USA ISSN 1053-2285
DS646.67
CAKELELE: MALUKU RESEARCH JOURNAL. Text in English. 1990. s-a. USD 25 to individuals; USD 40 to institutions. bk.rev.
Description: Publishes the results of research in and about Maluku, as well as the Maluku communities scattered through Indonesia and the Netherlands.
Indexed: AICP, IBSS.
—Ingenta.
Published by: University of Hawaii, Center for Southeast Asian Studies, 1890 East West Rd, Moore 416, Honolulu, HI 96822. TEL 808-956-2688, FAX 808-956-2682. Ed. James T Collins. R&P Flo Lamoureux. Circ: 100 (paid).

300 MEX ISSN 1405-7107
CALEIDOSCOPIO; revista semestral de ciencias sociales y humanidades. Text in Spanish. 1997. s-a. MXN 120 domestic; USD 20 foreign (effective 2006). **Document type:** *Journal, Academic/ Scholarly.*
Indexed: C01.
Published by: Universidad Autonoma de Aguascalientes, Ave Universidad 940, Aguascalientes, 20100, Mexico. TEL 52-449-9108490, FAX 52-449-9108479, jgomez@correo.uaa.mx. Ed. Jesus Gomez Serrano.

300 ITA ISSN 0393-3741
IL CALENDARIO DEL POPOLO. Text in Italian. 1945. m. adv. **Document type:** *Newspaper, Consumer.*
Indexed: RASB.
Published by: Teti & C Editore Srl, Via Simone d'Orsenigo 21, Milan, MI 20135, Italy. TEL 39-02-55015584, FAX 39-02-55015595, teti@teti.it, http://www.teti.it. Circ: 25,000.

300 USA ISSN 1933-7051
CALIFORNIA INSTITUTE OF TECHNOLOGY. DIVISION OF THE HUMANITIES AND SOCIAL SCIENCES. SOCIAL SCIENCE WORKING PAPER. Text in English. 1997. irreg. free (effective 2010). **Document type:** *Monographic series, Academic/Scholarly.*
Formerly (until 1997): California Institute of Technology. Division of the Humanities and Social Sciences. Social Science Working Paper
Media: Online - full text.
Published by: California Institute of Technology, Division of the Humanities and Social Sciences. (Subsidiary of: California Institute of Technology), 1200 E California Blvd, Pasadena, CA 91125. TEL 626-395-4065, FAX 626-405-9841.

300 USA
CALIFORNIA STUDIES IN FOOD AND CULTURE. Text in English. 2002. irreg., latest vol.30, 2010. price varies. back issues avail. **Document type:** *Monographic series, Academic/Scholarly.* **Description:** Covers the relationship between food and culture from a range of disciplines and approaches including anthropology, sociology, history, economics, philosophy and women's studies and seeks to broaden the audience for serious scholarship as well as to celebrate food as a means of understanding the world.
Published by: University of California Press, Book Series, 2120 Berkeley Way, Berkeley, CA 94704. TEL 510-642-4247, FAX 510-643-7127, foundation@ucpress.edu. Ed. Darra Goldstein. **Subscr. to:** California - Princeton Fulfillment Services, Inc., 1445 Lower Ferry Rd, Ewing, NJ 08618. TEL 609-883-1759, 800-777-4726, FAX 800-999-1958, orders@cpfsinc.com.

302 CUB ISSN 1682-2463
CALLE B. Text in Spanish. 2001. q. back issues avail.
Related titles: Online - full text ed.: ISSN 1682-7368. 2001.
Published by: Direccion Municipal de Cultura de Cumanayagua, C. Antonio Machado, No. 76 y, Rafael Trejo y Artime, Cumanayagua, Cienfuegos, Cuba. TEL 53-78-09433566, cumanayagua@azurina.cult.cu, http://www.zurina.cult.cu/. Ed. Pepe Sanchez.

300 ARG ISSN 1851-3301
CAMBIOS Y CONTINUIDADES. Text in Spanish. 2001. a. **Document type:** *Monographic series, Academic/Scholarly.*
Published by: Universidad Autonoma de Entre Rios, Facultad de Humanidades, Artes y Ciencias Sociales, Jornada 50 Piso 1, Concepcion del Uruguay, Entre Rios 3260, Argentina. TEL 54-3442-429163, http://www.fhaycs-uader.edu.ar/. Ed. Celia Gladis Lopez.

300 PRT ISSN 1645-9857
▼ **CAMPUS SOCIAL**; revista lusofona de ciencias sociais. Text in Portuguese. 2010. s-a. **Document type:** *Journal, Academic/ Scholarly.*
Related titles: Online - full text ed.: ISSN 1646-3749.
Published by: Universidade Lusofona de Humanidades e Tecnologia, Edicoes Universitarias, Campo Grande 376, Lisbon, 1749-024, Portugal. TEL 351-217-515500, FAX 351-217-577006, http://ulusofona.pt.

300 001.3 ESP ISSN 1887-4657
F1001
CANADARIA; revista canaria de estudios canadienses. Text in Spanish, English. 2005. s-a. EUR 12 to individuals; EUR 15 to institutions (effective 2008). **Document type:** *Journal, Academic/Scholarly.*
Description: Focuses on Canadian literature, critical theory and cultural studies.
Indexed: IBR, IBZ, MLA-IB.
Published by: Universidad de La Laguna, Centro de Estudios Canadienses, Nivel 1, Campus de Guajara, La Laguna - Tenerife, 38071, Spain. TEL 34-922-317276, FAX 34-922-317611, cecanad@ull.es, http://webpages.ull.es/users/cecanad/. Ed. Juan Ignacio Oliva.

CANADIAN - AMERICAN SLAVIC STUDIES/REVUE CANADIENNE - AMERICAINE D'ETUDES SLAVES. *see* HUMANITIES: COMPREHENSIVE WORKS

CANADIAN ASSOCIATION OF SLAVISTS NEWSLETTER. *see* HUMANITIES: COMPREHENSIVE WORKS

CANADIAN ISSUES/THEMES CANADIENS. *see* HUMANITIES: COMPREHENSIVE WORKS

960 305.896 CAN ISSN 0008-3968
DT19.9.C3
➤ **CANADIAN JOURNAL OF AFRICAN STUDIES/REVUE CANADIENNE DES ETUDES AFRICAINES.** Abbreviated title: C J A S. Text in English, French. 1963. 3/yr. CAD 125 to individuals; CAD 150 to institutions; CAD 300 combined subscription to institutions (print & online eds.) (effective 2010). bk.rev. bibl.; illus. back issues avail.; reprints avail. **Document type:** *Journal, Academic/Scholarly.*
Description: Covers African political economy, history, development, and literature. Includes papers on agriculture, rural economy and medicine.
Formerly (until 1967): Bulletin of African Studies in Canada (0525-1370)
Related titles: Online - full text ed.: CAD 100 to individuals; CAD 200 to institutions (effective 2010).
Indexed: A20, A21, A22, A36, ABCPolSci, AICP, ARDT, ASCA, ASD, AbAn, AmH&L, B04, BibInd, BibLing, C03, C04, CA, CABA, CBCARef, CERDIC, FR, GH, HRIR, HistAb, IBR, IBZ, IIBP, ILD, LT, MEA&I, MLA, MLA-IB, P06, P30, PAIS, PCI, PQC, PdeR, R12, RASB, RI-1, RI-2, RILM, RRTA, S02, S03, SCOPUS, SOPODA, SSAI, SSAb, SSI, SociolAb, T02, T05, TAR, W03, W05, W11.
—BLDSC (3027.900000), IE, Infotrieve, Ingenta. **CCC.**
Published by: Canadian Association of African Studies, c/o Roger Fodjo, 4-17E Old Arts Bldg, University of Alberta, Edmonton, AB T6G 2E6, Canada. FAX 780-492-9125, http://www.arts.ualberta.ca/~caas. Ed. E Ann McDougall TEL 780-492-6695.

300 GBR ISSN 0225-5189
➤ **CANADIAN JOURNAL OF DEVELOPMENT STUDIES/REVUE CANADIENNE D'ETUDES DU DEVELOPPEMENT.** Text in English, French, Spanish. 1980. q. GBP 204 combined subscription in United Kingdom to institutions (print & online eds.); EUR 269, USD 337 combined subscription to institutions (print & online eds.) (effective 2012). adv. bk.rev. back issues avail.; reprint service avail. from PSC. **Document type:** *Journal, Academic/Scholarly.* **Description:** Provides an interdisciplinary forum for the discussion of a wide range of development issues. Open to all theoretical and development strategy orientations and publishes contributions dealing with all regions and countries of the developing world.
Related titles: Online - full text ed.: ISSN 2158-9100. GBP 183 in United Kingdom to institutions; EUR 242, USD 304 to institutions (effective 2012).
Indexed: A20, A22, A26, ABCPolSci, APEL, ARDT, ASCA, AgrForAb, AmH&L, BAS, C03, C25, CA, CABA, CBCARef, CBPI, CPerI, CurCont, E08, E12, EconLit, F08, F12, G08, GEOBASE, GH, H16, HistAb, I11, I13, I14, IBR, IBSS, IBZ, ILD, JEL, LT, N02, OR, P30, P32, P34, P42, P48, PAIS, PCI, PGegResA, PQC, PSA, PerIslam, R12, RA&MP, REE&TA, RRTA, S02, S03, S09, S12, S13, S16, SCOPUS, SSCI, SociolAb, T02, T05, TAR, W07, W11.
—BLDSC (3031.135000), IE, Infotrieve, Ingenta. **CCC.**
Published by: (Institute for International Development and Cooperation/ Institut de Developpement International et de Cooperation CAN), Routledge (Subsidiary of: Taylor & Francis Group), 4 Park Sq, Milton Park, Abingdon, Oxon OX14 4RN, United Kingdom. TEL 44-20-70176000, FAX 44-20-70176336, subscriptions@tandf.co.uk. Ed. John Harriss.

300 330 360 323.4 CAN ISSN 1705-3498
CANADIAN JOURNAL OF QUANTUUM ECONOMICS; the journal of academic research and current affairs on quality-of-life issues. Text in English. 2003 (Oct.). m. USD 89 per issue (effective 2003). bk.rev. **Document type:** *Journal, Academic/Scholarly.* **Description:** Covers the academic research and current affairs on quality-of-life issues, associated with critical exploration of a rejuvenated approach to economic development considerations that integrates economics, ecology, healthcare, civil rights and human rights, social justice, philosophy, social psychology, and democracy.
Published by: Agora Cosmopolitan, 300 Eagleson Rd, BP 24191, Ottawa, ON K2M 2C3, Canada. TEL 888-377-2222, FAX 888-849-2665, agoracosmopolite@on.aibn.com, http://www.agorapublishing.com. Ed. H. Raymond Samuels II.

300 CAN
CANADIAN JOURNAL OF SOCIAL RESEARCH. Text in English. 2008. q. CAD 5 per issue (effective 2009). **Document type:** *Journal, Academic/Scholarly.*
Indexed: CA, S02, S03.
Published by: Association for Canadian Studies, 1822-A Sherbrooke W, Montreal, PQ H3H 1E4, Canada. TEL 514-925-3094, FAX 514-925-3095, sarah.kooi@acs-aec.ca, http://www.acs-aec.ca.

CANADIAN SLAVONIC PAPERS/REVUE CANADIENNE DES SLAVISTES; an interdisciplinary journal devoted to Central and Eastern Europe. *see* HUMANITIES: COMPREHENSIVE WORKS

300 CAN ISSN 1712-8056
CANADIAN SOCIAL SCIENCE. Text in French, English. 2005. bi-m. USD 384; USD 80 per issue (effective 2011). back issues avail. **Document type:** *Journal, Academic/Scholarly.*
Related titles: Online - full text ed.: ISSN 1923-6697. free (effective 2011).
Indexed: A01, A03, A12, A17, A26, ABIn, C03, C04, C05, CA, CBCABus, CPerI, E08, I05, P10, P21, P27, P48, P51, P53, P54, PQC, S02, S03, S09, SSAI, SSAb, SSI, T02, W03, W05.
Published by: Canadian Academy of Oriental and Occidental Culture (C A O O C), 3-265 Melrose, Montreal, PQ H4H 1T2, Canada. caooc@hotmail.com. Eds. Jenny Ding, Alexey Kiselev.

CANADIAN SOCIAL STUDIES; the history and social science teacher. *see* EDUCATION—Teaching Methods And Curriculum

CANADIAN STUDIES. *see* HUMANITIES: COMPREHENSIVE WORKS

300 500 CHN ISSN 1008-4762
CANGZHOU SHIFAN ZHUANKE XUEXIAO XUEBAO/CANGZHOU TEACHERS' COLLEGE. JOURNAL. Text in Chinese. 1985. q. **Document type:** *Journal, Academic/Scholarly.*
Formerly (until 1998): Bohai Xuekan
Related titles: Online - full text ed.
Published by: Cangzhou Shifan Zhuanke Xuexiao/Cangzhou Teachers' College, 26, Nanhuan Xi Lu, Cangzhou, 061001, China. TEL 86-317-2159849.

300 BRA ISSN 1517-6916
CAOS. Text in Portuguese. 1999. s-a. back issues avail. **Document type:** *Journal, Academic/Scholarly.*
Media: Online - full text.

Published by: Universidade Federal da Paraiba, Centro de Ciencias Humanas, Letras y Artes, Cidade Universitaria, Joao Pessoa, Paraiba 58051-900, Brazil. TEL 55-83-32167204. Ed. Aecio Amaral.

CAPITALISM, NATURE, SOCIALISM; a journal of socialist ecology. *see* POLITICAL SCIENCE

327.172 USA
CARDOZO JOURNAL OF CONFLICT RESOLUTION. Text in English. 1998. s-a. USD 35 (effective 2009). back issues avail. **Document type:** *Journal, Academic/Scholarly.* **Description:** Features topics in alternative dispute resolution and mediation.
Formerly (until 2003): Cardozo Online Journal of Conflict Resolution
Related titles: Online - full text ed.: free (effective 2009).
Published by: Yeshiva University, Benjamin N. Cardozo School of Law, 55 Fifth Ave, Ste 527, New York, NY 10003. TEL 212-790-0443, lawinfo@yu.edu, http://www.cardozo.yu.edu. Ed. Jordan Walerstein.

972.9 300 PRI ISSN 0008-6533
F2161
CARIBBEAN STUDIES/ESTUDES DES CARAIBES/ESTUDIOS DEL CARIBE. Text in English, French, Spanish. 1961. s-a. USD 50 to institutions (effective 2010). adv. bk.rev. bibl.; charts; illus. index. back issues avail. **Document type:** *Journal, Academic/Scholarly.* **Description:** Designed for anyone interested in keeping up with the ongoing research and writing in the field of Caribbean studies.
Related titles: Online - full text ed.: ISSN 1940-9095.
Indexed: A01, A02, A03, A08, A22, A26, AmHI, B04, BAS, C01, C32, CA, DIP, E01, FR, H07, H09, H21, I04, I05, IBR, IBSS, IBZ, IIBP, M01, M02, MLA-IB, P08, P09, P30, P34, P42, PAIS, PCI, RASB, RILM, S02, S03, S05, SSAI, SSAb, SSI, SociolAb, T02, W01, W02, W03, W05.
—BLDSC (3053.130000), IE, Ingenta.
Published by: Universidad de Puerto Rico a Rio Piedras, Instituto de Estudios del Caribe/University of Puerto Rico at Rio Piedras, Institute of Caribbean Studies, PO Box 23361, San Juan, 00931-3361, Puerto Rico. TEL 787-764-0000, FAX 787-764-3099, http://www.uprrp.edu.

972.9 USA ISSN 1098-4186
CARIBBEAN STUDIES. Text in English. 1999. irreg., latest vol.26, 2010. price varies. **Document type:** *Monographic series, Academic/Scholarly.* **Description:** Covers all aspects of Caribbean culture and society, including literatures, history, film, music, art, geography, politics, languages, and social sciences.
Indexed: MLA-IB.
Published by: Peter Lang Publishing, Inc. (Subsidiary of: Peter Lang Publishing Group), 29 Broadway, New York, NY 10006. TEL 212-647-7700, 800-770-5264, FAX 212-647-7707, customerservice@plang.com.

CARIBBEAN STUDIES (LEWISTON). *see* HUMANITIES: COMPREHENSIVE WORKS

300 GBR ISSN 1757-1898
▼ ➤ **CATALAN JOURNAL OF COMMUNICATION & CULTURAL STUDIES.** Abbreviated title: C J C S. Text in English. 2009. s-a. GBP 36, USD 68 to individuals; GBP 180, USD 290 to institutions (effective 2012). adv. back issues avail. **Document type:** *Journal, Academic/Scholarly.* **Description:** Aims to disseminate research that will inform and stimulate scholarly interest in Catalonia as a complex society with a growing international profile.
Related titles: Online - full text ed.: ISSN 1757-1901. GBP 147, USD 220 (effective 2012).
Indexed: CA, CMM, CommAb, T02.
Published by: Intellect Ltd., The Mill, Parnall Rd, Fishponds, Bristol, BS16 3JG, United Kingdom. TEL 44-117-9589910, FAX 44-117-9589911, info@intellectbooks.com. Pub. Masoud Yazdani. **Subscr. to:** Turpin Distribution Services Ltd., Pegasus Dr, Stratton Business Park, Biggleswade, Bedfordshire SG18 8QB, United Kingdom. TEL 44-1767-604951, FAX 44-1767-601640, custserv@turpin-distribution.com, http://www.turpin-distribution.com/.

➤ **CATEDRA**; revista de ciencia, cultura y educacion. *see* SCIENCES: COMPREHENSIVE WORKS

300 BOL
CEBEM.COM. Text in Spanish. bi-w.
Media: Online - full text. **Related titles:** E-mail ed.
Published by: Centro Boliviano de Estudios Multidisciplinarios, Ave. Ecuador no. 2330, esq. C. Rosendo Gutierrez, La Paz, Bolivia. TEL 591-2-2415324, FAX 591-2-2414726, cebem@cebem.com, http://www.cebem.com/. Ed. Jose Blanes.

CEIBA. *see* LITERATURE

300 ESP ISSN 0528-3647
DP302.S71
CELTIBERIA. Text in Spanish. 1951. s-a. back issues avail. **Document type:** *Monographic series, Academic/Scholarly.*
Related titles: ◆ Supplement(s): Coleccion Biblioteca Soriana. ISSN 0577-2486.
Indexed: RILM.
Published by: Centro de Estudios Sorianos, Nicolas Rabal, 21, Soria, Castilla y Leon 42003, Spain, celtiberia-ces@jet.es. Ed. Emilio Ruiz.

301 BRA ISSN 1517-2643
F2510
CENARIOS. Text in Portuguese. 1999. a. back issues avail. **Document type:** *Monographic series, Academic/Scholarly.*
Indexed: C01, CA, DIP, IBR, IBZ, P42, PSA, S02, S03, SCOPUS, SociolAb, T02.
Published by: Universidade Estadual Paulista "Julio De Mesquita Filho", Faculdade de Ciencias e Letras, Campus de Araraquara, Rod Araraquara- Jau Km 1, Araraquara, SP 14800-901, Brazil. TEL 55-16-33016275, laboratorioeditorial@fclar.unesp.br, http://seer.fclar.unesp.br.

CENTER FOR MIGRATION STUDIES. GIOVANNI SCHIAVO COLLECTION. *see* POPULATION STUDIES

CENTER FOR RURAL POLICY AND DEVELOPMENT. NEWSLETTER. *see* BUSINESS AND ECONOMICS—Economic Situation And Conditions

CENTRAL ASIA; journal of area study centre (Russia, China & Central Asia). *see* ASIAN STUDIES

300 GBR ISSN 1479-0963
DAW1001
➤ **CENTRAL EUROPE.** Text in English. 1997. s-a. GBP 169 combined subscription to institutions (print & online eds.); USD 317 combined subscription in United States to institutions (print & online eds.) (effective 2012). adv. reprint service avail. from PSC. **Document type:** *Journal, Academic/Scholarly.* **Description:** Publishes original research articles on the history, languages, literature, political culture, music, arts and society of those lands once part of the Habsburg Monarchy and Poland-Lithuania from the Middle Ages to the present.
Formerly (until 2003): Masaryk Journal (1466-0032)
Related titles: Online - full text ed.: ISSN 1745-8218. 2005. GBP 152 to institutions; USD 293 in United States to institutions (effective 2012) (from IngentaConnect).
Indexed: AmHI, ArtHuCI, CA, CurCont, H05, H07, HistAb, IBSS, L&LBA, MLA-IB, P42, PSA, S02, S03, SCOPUS, SociolAb, T02, W07.
—BLDSC (3106.133940), IE, Ingenta. **CCC.**
Published by: Maney Publishing, Ste 1C, Joseph's Well, Hanover Walk, Leeds, W Yorks LS3 1AB, United Kingdom. TEL 44-113-2432800, FAX 44-113-3868178, maney@maney.co.uk, http://www.maney.co.uk. Ed. Richard Butterwick. **Subscr. in N. America to:** Maney Publishing, 875 Massachusetts Ave, 7th Fl, Cambridge, MA 02139. TEL 866-297-5154, FAX 617-354-6875, maney@maneyusa.com

300 HUN ISSN 1586-6335
CENTRAL EUROPEAN LIBRARY OF IDEAS. Text in English. 2000. irreg. price varies. **Document type:** *Monographic series, Academic/Scholarly.*
Published by: Central European University Press, Oktober 6 utca 14, Budapest, 1051, Hungary. TEL 36-1-3273000, FAX 36-1-3273183, ceupress@ceu.hu, http://www.ceupress.com.

CENTRE FOR POLICY ON AGEING. REPORTS. *see* GERONTOLOGY AND GERIATRICS

CENTRE FOR SOCIAL AND ECONOMIC RESEARCH ON THE GLOBAL ENVIRONMENT. WORKING PAPER. POLICY ANALYSIS. *see* BUSINESS AND ECONOMICS

300 AUS ISSN 1833-6493
CENTRE FOR SOCIAL SCIENCE RESEARCH WORKING PAPERS. Text in English. 2006. irreg. **Document type:** *Monographic series, Academic/Scholarly.*
Media: Online - full text.
Published by: Central Queensland University, Centre for Social Science Research, Bldg 18, Bruce Hwy, Rockhampton, QLD 4702, Australia. TEL 61-7-49306751, FAX 61-7-49309820.

300 BRA ISSN 0101-3300
F2501
➤ **CENTRO BRASILEIRO DE ANALISE E PLANEJAMENTO. NOVOS ESTUDOS.** Key Title: Novos Estudos C E B R A P. Text in Portuguese. 1971. 3/yr. BRL 45 domestic; USD 70 foreign (effective 2006). adv. bk.rev. back issues avail. **Document type:** *Journal, Academic/Scholarly.* **Description:** The journal aims to publish relevant studies and to present contributions to the intellectual debate in a wide variety of subjects, from art criticism to the implementation of economic and social policies.
Formerly (until 1981): Estudos C E B R A P (0100-7025)
Related titles: Online - full text ed.: free (effective 2011).
Indexed: A01, BibInd, C01, CA, DIP, F03, F04, FR, IBR, IBZ, P42, PSA, S02, S03, SCOPUS, SOPODA, SSA, SociolAb, T02.
—INIST.
Published by: (Centro Brasileiro de Analise e Planejamento), Editora Brasileira de Ciencias, Ltda., Rua Morgado de Mateus 615, Sao Paulo, SP 04015-902, Brazil. TEL 55-11-5740399, FAX 55-11-5745928. Ed. Flavio Moura. Pub. Francisco de Oliveira. R&P Omar R Thomaz. Adv. contact Omar Riberiro Thomaz. Circ: 2,000.

300 ARG ISSN 0328-185X
H8.S7
➤ **CENTRO DE ESTUDIOS AVANZADOS. ESTUDIOS.** Text in Spanish. 1993. s-a. USD 24 domestic; USD 40 foreign; USD 12 newsstand/cover foreign (effective 2000). bk.rev. bibl. back issues avail. **Document type:** *Academic/Scholarly.* **Description:** Presents intellectual works of the university on contemporary civilization issues.
Published by: Universidad Nacional de Cordoba, Centro de Estudios Avanzados, Ave. Velez Sarsfield, 153, Cordoba, 5000, Argentina. TEL 54-351-4332086, FAX 54-351-4332087. Ed. Hector Schmucler. Circ: 1,000. **Dist. in US by:** Fernando Garcia Cambeiro, Skyway USA Ste 100, 7225 NW 25th St, P O Box 014, Miami, FL 33122.

300 ESP ISSN 1887-1747
CENTRO DE ESTUDIOS "PEDRO SUAREZ." BOLETIN; estudios sobre las comarcas de Guadix, Baza y Huescar. Text in Spanish; Summaries in English, Spanish. 1988. a. EUR 15 domestic to individuals; EUR 20 foreign to individuals; free to institutions (effective 2009). bk.rev. illus. Index. **Document type:** *Journal, Academic/Scholarly.* **Description:** Covers research in all aspects of cultural patrimony.
Formerly (until 2003): Instituto de Estudios "Pedro Suarez." Boletin (1130-4049)
Indexed: P09.
Published by: Centro de Estudios "Pedro Suarez", Apartado 92, Guadix, 18500, Spain. Ed. Ana Maria Gomez Roman.

300 URY
CENTRO DE INFORMACIONES Y ESTUDIOS DEL URUGUAY. SERIE DOCUMENTOS DE TRABAJO. Text in Spanish. irreg., latest vol.177, 1991.
Published by: Centro de Informaciones y Estudios del Uruguay, Casilla 10587, Montevideo, 11100, Uruguay. TEL 48-3205, FAX 5982-48-0762.

300 URY
CENTRO DE INFORMACIONES Y ESTUDIOS DEL URUGUAY. SERIE ESTUDIOS. Text in Spanish. irreg., latest vol.12, 1989.
Published by: Centro de Informaciones y Estudios del Uruguay, Casilla 10587, Montevideo, 11100, Uruguay. TEL 48-3205, FAX 5982-48-0762.

300 URY
CENTRO DE INFORMACIONES Y ESTUDIOS DEL URUGUAY. SERIE INFORMES. Text in Spanish. irreg., latest vol.47, 1991.
Published by: Centro de Informaciones y Estudios del Uruguay, Casilla 10587, Montevideo, 11100, Uruguay. TEL 48-3205, FAX 5982-48-0762.

322.4 ARG ISSN 0325-1306
CENTRO DE INVESTIGACION Y ACCION SOCIAL. REVISTA. Text in Spanish. 1961. m. ARS 45, USD 50 (effective 2003). adv. bk.rev. 64 p./no.; **Document type:** *Bulletin.*
Former titles (until 1969): C I A S Centro de Investigacion y Accion Social (0007-8387); (until 1965): Centro de Investigacion y Accion Social. Boletin Mensual
Indexed: IBR, IBZ, RASB.
Published by: Centro de Investigacion y Accion Social, O'Higgins 1331, Buenos Aires, 1426, Argentina. Ed. Enrique E Fabbri. Circ: 1,000.

CENTRO JOURNAL. *see* HUMANITIES: COMPREHENSIVE WORKS

300 URY ISSN 0797-6062
HC121
CENTRO LATINOAMERICANO DE ECONOMIA HUMANA. CUADERNOS. Text in Spanish. 1958; N.S. 1976. 4/yr. UYP 55,000, USD 19. adv. bk.rev. charts; tr.lit. index, cum.index.
Former titles (until 1984): Centro Latinoamericano de Economia Humana. Publicaciones (0797-6070); (until 1967): Cuadernos Latinoamericanos de Economia Humana (0797-6089)
Indexed: A01, CA, F03, F04, H21, IBR, IBZ, P08, P34, PAIS, RASB, T02.
Published by: Centro Latinoamericano de Economia Humana, Zelmar Michelini, 1220, Casilla de Correos 5021, Montevideo, 11113, Uruguay. FAX 598-2-921127. Circ: 2,000.

300 500 HND
CENTRO UNIVERSITARIO DE ESTUDIOS GENERALES. REVISTA. Text in Spanish. 1991. s-a.?. per issue exchange basis. **Document type:** *Academic/Scholarly.* **Description:** Presents research work from the university in the areas of social sciences, natural sciences and physical-mathematical sciences.
Published by: Universidad Nacional Autonoma de Honduras, Centro Universitario de Estudios Generales, Blvd. Morazan, Tegucigalpa DC, Honduras.

300 DEU ISSN 1865-2255
CENTRUM FUER INTERKULTURELLE UND EUROPAEISCHE STUDIEN. INTERDISZIPLINAERE SCHRIFTENREIHE/CENTRE FOR INTERCULTURAL AND EUROPEAN STUDIES. INTERDISCIPLINARY SERIES. Text in English, German. 2007. irreg., latest vol.4, 2009. price varies. **Document type:** *Monographic series, Academic/Scholarly.*
Published by: (Centrum fuer Interkulturelle und Europaeische Studien/ Centre for Intercultural and European Studies), Ibidem Verlag, Melchiorstr 15, Stuttgart, 70439, Germany. TEL 49-711-9807954, FAX 49-711-9807952, ibidem@ibidem-verlag.de, http://www.ibidem-verlag.de.

300 CHN ISSN 1005-6718
CHAIDAMU KAIFA YANJIU/STUDIES OF DEVELOPING CHAIDAMU. Text in Chinese. 1987. bi-m. USD 18 (effective 2009). **Document type:** *Journal, Academic/Scholarly.*
Related titles: Online - full text ed.
—East View.
Address: 14, Honghe Lu, Delingha, Qinghai 817000, China. TEL 86-977-8201281. **Dist. by:** China International Book Trading Corp, 35 Chegongzhuang Xilu, Haidian District, PO Box 399, Beijing 100044, China. TEL 86-10-68412045, FAX 86-10-68412023, cibtc@mail.cibtc.com.cn, http://www.cibtc.com.cn.

CHALLENGE (ATLANTA); a journal of research on African American men. *see* ETHNIC INTERESTS

300 355 FRA ISSN 1253-1871
LES CHAMPS DE MARS. Text in French. 1996. s-a. **Document type:** *Journal, Government.*
Indexed: FR, IBSS.
—INIST.
Published by: (Centre d'Etudes en Sciences Sociales de la Defense), Documentation Francaise, 29-31 Quai Voltaire, Paris, Cedex 7 75344, France. Ed. Philippe Forget TEL 33-1-53696983.

300 CHN ISSN 1003-5478
CHANGBAI XUEKAN/CHANGBAI JOURNAL. Text in Chinese. 1985. bi-m. CNY 10 per issue (effective 2010).
Related titles: Online - full text ed.
Published by: Zhonggong Jilinsheng Weidangjiao, 1299, Qianjin Dajie, Changchun, 130012, China. TEL 86-431-85885094, FAX 86-431-85885092.

300 CHN ISSN 1009-8976
CHANGCHUN GONGCHENG XUEYUAN XUEBAO (SHEHUI KEXUE BAN)/CHANGCHUN INSTITUTE OF TECHNOLOGY. JOURNAL (SOCIAL SCIENCE EDITION). Text in Chinese. 2000. q. CNY 6.50 newsstand/cover (effective 2006).
Related titles: Online - full text ed.
Published by: Changchun Gongcheng Xueyuan, 395, Shangping Da Lu, Changchun, 130012, China. TEL 86-431-85955991 ext 2555, FAX 86-431-85940805.

300 CHN
CHANGCHUN GONGYE DAXUE XUEBAO (SHEHUI KEXUE BAN)/ CHANGCHUN UNIVERSITY OF TECHNOLOGY. JOURNAL (SOCIAL SCIENCE EDITION). Text in Chinese. 1988. bi-m. **Document type:** *Journal, Academic/Scholarly.*
Formerly (until 2003): Jilin Gongxueyuan Xuebao (Shehui Kexue Ban)
Related titles: Online - full text ed.
Published by: Changchun Gongye Daxue/Changchun Univeristy of Technology, 2055, Yanan Dajie, Changchun, 130012, China. TEL 86-431-85716508, http://www.jlit.edu.cn/.

300 CHN
CHANGCHUN LIGONG DAXUE XUEBAO (SHEHUI KEXUE BAN)/ CHANGCHUN UNIVERSITY OF SCIENCE AND TECHNOLOGY. JOURNAL (SOCIAL SCIENCES). Text in Chinese. 1999. bi-m. ('). CNY 90; CNY 15 per issue (effective 2010). **Document type:** *Journal, Academic/Scholarly.*
Formerly (until 2002): Changchun Guangxue Jingmi Jixie Xueyuan Xuebao (Shehui Kexue Ban)/Changchun Institute of Optics and Fine Mechanics. Journal (Social Science Edition) (1009-1068)
Related titles: Online - full text ed.
Published by: Changchun Ligong Daxue, 7186, Weixing Lu, Changchun, 130022, China. TEL 86-431-85582590.

300 CHN ISSN 1008-8466
CHANGCHUN SHI-WEI DANGXIAO XUEBAO/PARTY SCHOOL OF C P C OF CHANGCHUN MUNICIPAL COMMITTEE. JOURNAL. Text in Chinese. 1999. bi-m.

S

Former titles: Changchun Shi Dangxiao Xuebao; Zhonggong Changchun Shi-Wei Dangxiao
Related titles: Online - full text ed.
Published by: Zhonggong Changchun Shi-Wei Dangxiao/Party School of C P C of Changchun Municipal Committee, 912, Pingyang Jie, Changchun, 130022, China. TEL 86-431-8615337, FAX 86-431-8610390.

300 DEU ISSN 1863-8716
CHANGING EUROPE. Text in English. 2007. irreg., latest vol.7, 2010. price varies. **Document type:** *Monographic series, Academic/ Scholarly.*
Published by: Ibidem Verlag, Melchiorstr 15, Stuttgart, 70439, Germany. TEL 49-711-9807954, FAX 49-711-9807952, ibidem@ibidem-verlag.de, http://www.ibidem-verlag.de.

300 500 CHN ISSN 1008-4681
CHANGSHA DAXUE XUEBAO/CHANGSHA UNIVERSITY. JOURNAL. Text in Chinese. 1987. bi-m. CNY 5 newsstand/cover (effective 2006). **Document type:** *Journal, Academic/Scholarly.*
Related titles: Online - full text ed.
Published by: Changsha Daxue, 98, Hongshan Lu, Changsha, 410003, China. TEL 86-731-4261487, FAX 86-731-4250583.

300 CHN ISSN 1672-934X
CHANGSHA LIGONG DAXUE XUEBAO (SHEHUI KEXUE BAN)/ CHANGSHA UNIVERSITY OF SCIENCE AND TECHNOLOGY. JOURNAL (SOCIAL SCIENCE EDITION). Text in Chinese. 1986. q. **Document type:** *Journal, Academic/Scholarly.*
Former titles: Changsha Dianli Xueyuan Xuebao (Shehui Kexue Ban)/Changsha University of Electric Power. Journal (Social Science) (1007-6271); (until 1997): Changsha Shuidian Shi-Yuan Xuebao (Shehui Kexue Ban) (1004-8839)
Related titles: Online - full text ed.
Published by: Changsha Ligong Daxue/Changsha University of Science and Technology, Yuhua-qu, Yiwanjia Li 2-duan #960, Changsha, 410004, China. TEL 86-731-85258187, http://www.cscu.edu.cn/.

300 500 CHN ISSN 1673-2014
CHANGZHI XUEYUAN XUEBAO/CHANGZHI UNIVERSITY. JOURNAL. Text in Chinese. 1984. bi-m. **Document type:** *Journal, Academic/ Scholarly.*
Formerly (until 2005): Jindongnan Shifan Zhuanke Xuexiao Xuebao/ Jindongnan Teachers College. Journal (1009-0266)
Related titles: Online - full text ed.
Published by: Changzhi Xueyuan/Changzhi University, 73, Chengbei Dong Jie, Changzhi, 046011, China. TEL 86-355-2178466.

300 CHN ISSN 2095-042X
➤ **CHANGZHOU DAXUE XUEBAO (SHEHUI KEXUE BAN)/ CHANGZHOU UNIVERSITY. JOURNAL (SOCIAL SCIENCE EDITION).** Text in Chinese; Abstracts in Chinese, English. 2000. q. CNY 40, USD 40; CNY 10 per issue (effective 2011 & 2012). **Document type:** *Journal, Academic/Scholarly.*
Former titles (until 2009): Jiangsu Gongye Xueyuan Xuebao(Shehui Kexue Ban)/Jiangsu Polytechnic University. Journal (Social Sciences Edition) (1672-9048); (until 2004): Jiangsu Shiyou Huagong Xueyuan Xuebao(Shehui Kexue Ban)/Jiangsu Institute of Petrochemical Technology. JOurnal (Social Sciences Edition) (1009-7775)
Related titles: Online - full text ed.
Published by: Changzhou Daxue/Changzhou University, CZSET, Changzhou, 213164, China. TEL 86-519-86330175, FAX 86-519-86330175, http://www.cczu.edu.cn/. Ed. Guo-dong Shi. Circ: 2,200. **Dist. by:** China International Book Trading Corp, 35 Chegongzhuang Xilu, Haidian District, PO Box 399, Beijing 100044, China. TEL 86-10-68412045, FAX 86-10-68412023, cibtc@mail.cibtc.com.cn, http://www.cibtc.com.cn.

300 CHN ISSN 1673-0887
CHANGZHOU GONGXUEYUAN XUEBAO (SHEKE BAN)/ CHANGZHOU INSTITUTE OF TECHNOLOGY. JOURNAL (SOCIAL SCIENCE EDITION). Text in Chinese. 1993. bi-m. **Document type:** *Journal, Academic/Scholarly.*
Former titles (until 2005): Changzhou Shifan Zhuanke Xuexiao Xuebao/Changzhou Teachers' College Journal (1672-3082); (until 2003): Changzhou Shi-Zhuan Xuebao
Related titles: Online - full text ed.
Published by: Changzhou Gongxueyuan/Changzhou Institute of Technology, 299, Tongjiang Nan Lu, Changzhou, 213002, China. TEL 86-519-85217535, FAX 86-519-85217535.

300 CHN ISSN 1672-2868
CHAOHU XUEYUAN XUEBAO/CHAOHU COLLEGE. JOURNAL. Text in Chinese. 1987. bi-m. **Document type:** *Journal, Academic/Scholarly.*
Formerly (until 2002): Chaohu Shi-Zhuan Xuebao/Chaohu Teachers College Journal (1009-0835)
Related titles: Online - full text ed.
Published by: Chaohu Xueyuan/Chaohu College, 1, Bantang Lu Yucaixincun, Chaohu, 238000, China. TEL 86-565-2361424, FAX 86-565-2361424.

300 CHN ISSN 1004-342X
AS452.C46164
CHENGDU DAXUE XUEBAO (SHEHUI KEXUE BAN)/CHENGDU UNIVERSITY. JOURNAL (SOCIAL SCIENCE EDITION). Text in Chinese. 1981. bi-m. USD 24.60 (effective 2009). **Document type:** *Journal, Academic/Scholarly.* **Description:** Publishes research papers. Includes regular columns on Song dynasty literature, Sichuanese humanities, local literature and history, the Three Kingdoms and Zhuge Liang, political theses, economic and social development, library and information science, and Sichuan writers and their works.
Related titles: Online - full text ed.
—East View.
Published by: Chengdu Daxue/Chengdu University, Waidongshiling Zhen, Chengdu, 610106, China. TEL 86-28-84616023.

300 CHN ISSN 1672-0539
CHENGDU LIGONG DAXUE XUEBAO (SHEHUI KEXUE BAN). Text in Chinese. 1993. q. CNY 6 newsstand/cover (effective 2006). **Document type:** *Journal, Academic/Scholarly.*
Formerly (until 2003): Sichuan Shangye Gaodeng Zhuanke Xuexiao Xuebao/Sichuan Business College Journal (1008-5335)
Published by: Chengdu Ligong Daxue/Chengdu University of Technology, 1, Erxianqiao Dongsan Lu, Chengdu, 610059, China. TEL 86-28-84079524, FAX 86-28-84079523.

300 CHN ISSN 1008-5947
CHENGDU XINGZHENG XUEYUAN XUEBAO/CHENGDU INSTITUTE OF PUBLIC ADMINISTRATION. JOURNAL. Text in Chinese. 1984. bi-m.
Formerly (until 1999): Dangdai Chengdu
Related titles: Online - full text ed.
Published by: Chengdu Xingzheng Xueyuan/Chengdu Institute of Public Administration, Longquanyi-qu, 1492, Damianyidou Xi Lu, Chengdu, 610110, China. TEL 86-28-65983052, FAX 86-28-65983000, http://www.cddx.gov.cn/.

300 CHN ISSN 1002-2031
HT169.C6
CHENGSHI WENTI/URBAN PROBLEMS. Text in Chinese. 1983. bi-m. USD 62.40 (effective 2009). back issues avail. **Document type:** *Journal, Academic/Scholarly.*
Related titles: Online - full text ed.
—East View.
Published by: Beijing Shi Shehui Kexueyuan/Beijing Academy of Social Sciences, Zhaoyang-qu, 33, Bei Si Huan Zhong Lu, Beijing, 100101, China. TEL 86-10-64870894, bassic@263.net.cn. **Dist. by:** China International Book Trading Corp, 35 Chegongzhuang Xilu, Haidian District, PO Box 399, Beijing 100044, China. TEL 86-10-68412045, FAX 86-10-68412023, cibtc@mail.cibtc.com.cn, http:// www.cibtc.com.cn.

300 CHN
CHENGSHI YANJIU/URBAN STUDIES. Text in Chinese. bi-m.
Published by: Taiyuan Shi Shehui Yanjiusuo, 20, Hanxiguan, Taiyuan, Shanxi 030002, China. TEL 345483. Ed. Yang Guangliang.

CHIFENG XUEYUAN XUEBAO (MENGWEN ZHEXUE SHEHUI KEXUE BAN)/CHIFENG COLLEGE. JOURNAL. (PHILOSOPHY AND SOCIAL SCIENCE MONGOLIAN EDITION). *see* PHILOSOPHY

CHIFENG XUEYUAN XUEBAO (ZHEXUE SHEHUI KEXUE BAN)/ CHIFENG UNIMERSITY. JOURNAL (PHILOSOPHY AND SOCIAL SCIENCE CHINESE EDITION). *see* PHILOSOPHY

300 JPN ISSN 0385-1451
CHIIKI BUNKA KENKYU/HIROSHIMA UNIVERSITY. FACULTY OF INTEGRATED ARTS AND SCIENCES. BULLETIN. I, STUDIES IN AREA CULTURE. Text in Japanese. 1975. a. **Document type:** *Journal, Academic/Scholarly.*
Formerly: Hiroshima Daigaku Kyoyobu Kiyo
Indexed: RILM.
Published by: Hiroshima Daigaku, Sogo Kagakubu/Hiroshima University, Faculty of Integrated Arts and Sciences, 1-7-1 Kagazmiyama, Higashi Hiroshima, 739-8521, Japan. TEL 81-82-4227111, FAX 81-82-4240751, souka@ipc.hiroshima-u.ac.jp, http://home.hiroshima-u.ac.jp/souka/.

CHILD INDICATORS RESEARCH. *see* CHILDREN AND YOUTH—About

300 SGP ISSN 0219-7472
DS701
➤ **CHINA: AN INTERNATIONAL JOURNAL.** Abbreviated title: C I J. Text in English. 2003. s-a. SGD 35 to individuals; USD 25 to institutions in Asean countries & China; USD 30 elsewhere to institutions; SGD 60 combined subscription to institutions (print & online eds.); USD 44 combined subscription to institutions in Asean countries & China, (print & online eds.); USD 56 combined subscription elsewhere to institutions (print & online eds.) (effective 2011). adv. back issues avail. **Document type:** *Journal, Academic/Scholarly.* **Description:** Focuses on contemporary China, including Hong Kong, Macau and Taiwan, covering the fields of politics, economics, society, law, culture and international relations.
Related titles: Online - full content ed.: ISSN 0219-8614. SGD 45 to institutions; USD 32 to institutions in Asean countries & China; USD 40 elsewhere to institutions (effective 2011).
Indexed: A22, A26, CurCont, E01, EconLit, I05, IBSS, JEL, SCOPUS, SSCI, W07.
—BLDSC (3180.080050), IE, Ingenta. **CCC.**
Published by: World Scientific Publishing Co. Pte. Ltd., 5 Toh Tuck Link, Singapore, 596224, Singapore. TEL 65-6466-5775, FAX 65-6467-7667, wspc@wspc.com.sg, http://www.worldscientific.com. Eds. Yang Dali, Yongnian Zheng. **Dist. by:** World Scientific Publishing Co., Inc., 27 Warren St, Ste 401-402, Hackensack, NJ 07601. TEL 201-487-9655, 800-227-7562, FAX 201-487-9656, 888-977-2665, wspc@wspc.com; World Scientific Publishing Ltd., 57 Shelton St, London WC2H 9HE, United Kingdom. TEL 44-207-8360888, FAX 44-207-8362020, sales@wspc.co.uk. **Co-publisher:** N U S Press Pte Ltd.

➤ **THE CHINA JOURNAL.** *see* ASIAN STUDIES

➤ **CHINA PERSPECTIVES.** *see* POLITICAL SCIENCE—International Relations

➤ **CHINA REPORT**; a journal of East Asian studies. *see* POLITICAL SCIENCE—International Relations

300 CHN ISSN 1007-807X
CHINESE ACADEMIC JOURNALS FULL-TEXT DATABASE. ECONOMICS, POLITICS & LAWS. Text in Chinese, English. base vol. plus m. updates. USD 4,510 (effective 2003). **Document type:** *Database, Academic/Scholarly.* **Description:** Includes 1,498,039 full-text articles from over 722 academic journals, covering economics, commerce trading, finance, insurance, politics, foreign affairs, military affairs, laws.
Media: CD-ROM. **Related titles:** ◆ Online - full content ed.: C N K I Web.
Published by: Tsinghua Tongfang Optical Disc Co., Ltd., Room 1300, Huaye Building, Tsing Hua University, PO BOX 84-48, Beijing, 100084, China. TEL 86-1-62791819, FAX 86-1-62791944, Beijing@cnki.net, http://www.cnki.net. **Co-sponsor:** Tsinghua University, School of Law.

CHINESE ACADEMIC JOURNALS FULL-TEXT DATABASE. EDUCATION & SOCIAL SCIENCES. *see* EDUCATION

300 CHN ISSN 1671-6035
CHIZI/LOYAL SOLDIER MAGAZINE. Text in Chinese. m. USD 106.80 (effective 2009). **Document type:** *Journal, Academic/Scholarly.*
—East View.
Published by: Zhongguo Shehui Jingji Wenhua Jialiu Xiehui, Haidian-qu, 36, Beisanhuan Zhonglujia, 210-shi, Beijing, 100088, China. sjwjxh@public.gb.com.cn. **Dist. by:** China International Book Trading Corp, 35 Chegongzhuang Xilu, Haidian District, PO Box 399, Beijing 100044, China. TEL 86-10-68412045, FAX 86-10-68412023, cibtc@mail.cibtc.com.cn, http://www.cibtc.com.cn.

300 CHN ISSN 1008-5831
AS452.C477
CHONGQING DAXUE XUEBAO (SHEHUI KEXUE BAN)/CHONGQING UNIVERSITY. JOURNAL (SOCIAL SCIENCES EDITION). Text in Chinese. 1995. bi-m. CNY 120; CNY 10 per issue (effective 2010). **Document type:** *Journal, Academic/Scholarly.*
Related titles: Online - full text ed.
—East View.
Published by: Chongqing Daxue/Chongqing University, 174, Shapingba Zheng Jie, Chongqing, Sichuan 400044, China. TEL 86-23-65102306, 86-23-65111861, http://qks.cqu.edu.cn/qkscn/ch/ index.aspx.

300 CHN ISSN 1672-0598
CHONGQING GONGSHANG DAXUE XUEBAO (SHEHUI KEXUE BAN)/CHONGQING TECHNOLOGY AND BUSINESS UNIVERSITY. JOURNAL (SOCIAL SCIENCES EDITION). Text in Chinese. 1983. bi-m. USD 24.60 (effective 2009). **Document type:** *Journal, Academic/Scholarly.*
Formerly (until 2003): Yuzhou Daxue Xuebao (Zhexue Shehui Kexue Ban)/Yuzhou University. Journal (Philosophy and Social Sciences Edition) (1008-424X)
Related titles: Online - full text ed.
Published by: Chongqing Gongshang Daxue, 58, Xuefu Dadao, Chongqing, 400067, China. TEL 86-23-62769249, FAX 86-23-62769479.

CHONGQING JIAOTONG DAXUE XUEBAO (SHEHUI KEXUE BAN)/CHONGQING JIAOTONG UNIVERSITY. JOURNAL (SOCIAL SCIENCES EDITION). *see* POLITICAL SCIENCE

300 500 001.3 CHN ISSN 1008-6390
CHONGQING JIAOYU XUEYUAN XUEBAO/CHONGQING COLLEGE OF EDUCATION. JOURNAL. Text in Chinese. 1988. bi-m.
Related titles: Online - full text ed.: (from WanFang Data Corp.).
Published by: Chongqing Jiaoyu Xueyuan/Chongqing College of Education, Nanan-qu, 9, Xuefu Dadao, Chongqing, 400067, China. TEL 86-23-86380032.

300 CHN ISSN 1673-1999
CHONGQING KEJI XUEYUAN XUEBAO (SHEHUI KEXUE BAN)/ CHONGQING UNIVERSITY OF SCIENCE AND TECHNOLOGY. JOURNAL (SOCIAL SCIENCES EDITION). Text in Chinese. 1992. m. **Document type:** *Journal, Academic/Scholarly.*
Former titles: Chongqing Gongye Gaodeng Zhuanke Xuexiao Xuebao (1009-3494); (until 1999): Chongqing Gangtie Gaodeng Zhuanke Xuexiao Xuebao (1008-6420)
Related titles: Online - full text ed.
Published by: Chongqing Keji Xueyuan/Chongqing University of Science and Technology, 419, Xingzheng Lou, Chongqing, 401331, China. TEL 86-23-65023856, http://www.cqust.cn/default.htm.

300 CHN ISSN 1009-8135
CHONGQING SANXIA XUEYUAN XUEBAO/CHONGQING THREE GORGES UNIVERSITY. JOURNAL. Text in Chinese. 1985. bi-m. USD 24.60 (effective 2009). **Document type:** *Journal, Academic/ Scholarly.*
Formerly (until 2000): Sichuan Sanxia Xueyuan Xuebao/Sichuan Three-Gorges University. Journal (1008-4347)
Related titles: Online - full text ed.
—East View.
Published by: Chongqing Sanxia Xueyuan, 780, Shalong Lu, Chongqing, 404000, China. TEL 86-23-58105721, FAX 86-23-58102357.

300 CHN ISSN 1673-0186
CHONGQING SHEHUI KEXUE/CHONGQING SOCIAL SCIENCES. Text in Chinese. 1983. m. **Document type:** *Journal, Academic/Scholarly.*
Published by: (Chongqing Shi Shehui Kexuejie Lianhehui), Gaige Zazhishe, 270, Jiangbei-qu Qiaobei-cun, Chongqing, 400020, China. TEL 86-23-86856487.

300 CHN ISSN 1673-0429
B8.C5
CHONGQING SHIFAN DAXUE XUEBAO (ZHEXUE SHEHUI KEXUE BAN)/CHONGQING NORMAL UNIVERSITY. JOURNAL (SOCIAL SCIENCES EDITION). Text in Chinese. 1980. bi-m. **Document type:** *Journal, Academic/Scholarly.*
Former titles (until 2003): Chongqing Shi-Yuan Xuebao (Zhexue Shehui Kexue Ban) (1001-9936); (until 1983): Chongqing Shifan Xueyuan Xuebao (Zhexue Shehui Kexue Ban)
Related titles: Online - full text ed.
Published by: Chongqing Shifan Daxue/Chongqing Normal University, 12, Tianchen Road, Shapingba District, Chongqing, 400047, China. TEL 86-23-65362785, http://www.cqnu.edu.cn.

300 500 CHN ISSN 1671-8224
➤ **CHONGQING UNIVERSITY. JOURNAL.** Text in English. 2002. q. Index. back issues avail. **Document type:** *Journal, Academic/ Scholarly.*
Related titles: Online - full text ed.
Indexed: A05, A28, APA, AS&TA, AS&TI, B10, BRD, BrCerAb, C&ISA, C10, CA, CA/WCA, CCMJ, CIA, CerAb, CivEngAb, CorrAb, E&CAJ, E11, EEA, EMA, ESPM, EnvEAb, H15, M&TEA, M09, MBF, METADEX, MSN, MathR, SolStAb, T04, W03, W05, WAA, Z02.
—Linda Hall. **CCC.**
Published by: Chongqing Daxue/Chongqing University, 174, Shapingba Zheng Jie, Chongqing, Sichuan 400044, China. TEL 86-23-65112204, FAX 86-23-65120544. Ed. Xiao Hong Li. Circ: 500 (paid and controlled).

300 CHN ISSN 1673-8004
CHONGQING WENLI XUEYUAN XUEBAO (SHEHUI KEXUE BAN)/ CHONGQING UNIVERSITY OF ARTS AND SCIENCES. JOURNAL (SOCIAL SCIENCE EDITION). Text in Chinese. 1985. bi-m. CNY 6.50 newsstand/cover (effective 2006). **Document type:** *Journal, Academic/Scholarly.*
Former titles: Yuxi Xueyuan Xuebao (Shehui Kexue Ban)/Western Chongqing University. Journal (Social Sciences Edition) (1671-7546); (until 2001): Chongqing Shi-Zhuan Xuebao/Chongqing Teachers College. Journal (1008-6501)
Related titles: Online - full text ed.
Published by: Chongqing Wenli Xueyuan, Yongchuan, Chongqing, 402168, China. TEL 86-23-49891884, http://www.cqwu.net/.

300 CHN ISSN 1673-8268
CHONGQING YOUDIAN DAXUE XUEBAO (SHEHUI KEXUE BAN)/ CHONGQING UNIVERSITY OF POSTS AND TELECOMMUNICATIONS. JOURNAL (SOCIAL SCIENCE EDITION). Text in Chinese. 1986. bi-m. **Document type:** *Journal, Academic/Scholarly.*
Formerly (until 2006): Chongqing Youdian Xueyuan Xuebao (Shehui Kexue Ban) (1009-1289)
Indexed: PSA, SociolAb.
Published by: Congqing Youdian Daxue/Chongqing University of Posts and Telecommunications, Nanan-qu, Huangjiaoping, Chongqing, 400065, China. TEL 86-23-62461032, FAX 86-23-62471771, cyjournal@126.com, http://www.cqupt.edu.cn/.

300 323 NOR ISSN 0805-505X
HC59.69
CHR. MICHELSEN INSTITUTE. REPORT. Variant title: C M I Report Series. Text in Multiple languages. 1987. irreg., latest vol.15, 2002. back issues avail. **Document type:** *Monographic series.*
Formerly (until 1993): Chr. Michelsens Institutt. Avdeling for Samfunnsvitenskag og Utvikling. Rapport (0803-0030); Which superseded in part (in 1990): Chr. Michelsens Institutt. Programme of Human Rights Studies. Publications (0801-5856)
Related titles: Online - full text ed.
Indexed: A34, A38, CABA, E12, GH, LT, N02, P37, R12, RRTA, S13, S16, SCOPUS, T05, TAR, VS, W11.
—BLDSC (7397.645150).
Published by: Chr. Michelsen Institute, PO Box 6033 Postterminalen, Bergen, 5892, Norway. TEL 47-55-574000, FAX 47-55-574166, cmi@cmi.no.

300 323 NOR ISSN 0804-3639
HC59.69
CHR. MICHELSEN INSTITUTE. WORKING PAPER. Text in Multiple languages. 1963. irreg., latest vol.4, 2002. back issues avail. **Document type:** *Monographic series.*
Supersedes in part (1983-1993): Chr. Michelsen Institute. Programme of Human Rights Studies. Working Papers (0800-4234); (1963-1993): D E R A P. Working Papers (0800-2045)
Related titles: Online - full text ed.
Indexed: CABA, E12, F08, F12, GEOBASE, GH, R12, S13, S16, SCOPUS, T05, TAR, W11.
Published by: Chr. Michelsen Institute, PO Box 6033 Postterminalen, Bergen, 5892, Norway. TEL 47-55-574000, FAX 47-55-574166, cmi@cmi.no.

CHRONIQUE INTERNATIONALE DE L'I R E S. (Institut de Recherches Economiques et Sociales) *see* BUSINESS AND ECONOMICS

300 FRA ISSN 0242-7540
CHRONIQUES DE L'ANNUAIRE DE L'AFRIQUE DU NORD. Key Title: Collection Etudes de l'Annuaire de l'Afrique du Nord. Text in French. 1978. irreg. price varies. **Document type:** *Monographic series, Academic/Scholarly.*
Indexed: FR, IBSS.
Published by: Centre National de la Recherche Scientifique, Campus Gerard-Megie, 3 Rue Michel-Ange, Paris, 75794, France. TEL 33-1-44964000, FAX 33-1-44965390, http://www.cnrseditions.fr.

CHRONIQUES YEMENITES. *see* ARCHAEOLOGY

300 BOL
CHUQUISACA HOY. Text in Spanish. 1993. q.?.
Published by: Centro de Estudios para el Desarrollo Chuquisaca, Casilla 196, Calle Colon, 350, Sucre, Bolivia. TEL 591-64-25008, FAX 591-64-32628. Ed. Vladimir Gutierrez Perez.

300 CHN ISSN 1671-7406
CHUXIONG SHIFAN XUEYUAN XUEBAO/CHUXIONG NORMAL UNIVERSITY. JOURNAL. Text in Chinese. 1986. m. CNY 8 newsstand/cover (effective 2006). **Document type:** *Journal, Academic/Scholarly.*
Formerly (until 2001): Chuxiong Shi-Zhuan Xuebao/Chuxiong Teachers' College. Journal (1008-5068)
Related titles: Online - full text ed.
Published by: Chuxiong Shifan Xueyuan, Lucheng Nan Lu, Chuxiong, 675000, China. TEL 86-878-3120042.

300 CHN ISSN 1673-1794
CHUZHOU XUEYUAN XUEBAO. Text in Chinese. 1982. bi-m. CNY 8 newsstand/cover (effective 2006). **Document type:** *Journal, Academic/Scholarly.*
Formerly: Chuzhou Shi-Zhuan Xuebao (1009-1556)
Published by: Chuzhou Xueyuan, 80, Fengyue Nan Lu, Chuzhou, 239000, China.

300 320 COL ISSN 0121-3385
F2279
CIEN DIAS. Text in Spanish. 1988. q.
Published by: Centro de Investigacion y Educacion Popular (Cinep), Carrera 5 No.33A-08, Bogota, Colombia. TEL 57-1-2858977, info@cinep.org.co, http://www.cinep.org.co.

CIENCIA. *see* SCIENCES: COMPREHENSIVE WORKS

300 BRA ISSN 0304-2685
HN281
CIENCIA & TROPICO. Text in Portuguese; Abstracts in English, French. 1952. s-a. BRL 2.92 per issue. bk.rev. abstr.; bibl.; charts; illus.; stat.
Formerly (until 1971): Instituto Joaquim Nabuco de Pesquisas Sociais. Boletim (0074-0241)
Indexed: AICP, BibInd, C01, MLA-IB, RILM.
Published by: (Fundacao Joaquim Nabuco), Editora Massangana, Rua Dois Irmaos, 15, Apipucos, Recife, PE 52071-440, Brazil. TEL 55-81-268-4611, FAX 55-81-268-9600. Circ: 2,000.

CIENCIA, DOCENCIA Y TECNOLOGIA. *see* SCIENCES: COMPREHENSIVE WORKS

CIENCIA ERGO SUM; scientific multi-disciplinary journal. *see* HUMANITIES: COMPREHENSIVE WORKS

CIENCIA Y CULTURA. *see* SCIENCES: COMPREHENSIVE WORKS

300 BRA ISSN 1806-5821
BF311
CIENCIAS & COGNICAO. Text in Portuguese. 2004. 3/yr. free (effective 2011). **Document type:** *Journal, Academic/Scholarly.*
Media: Online - full text.
Indexed: MLA-IB.
Published by: Universidade Federal do Rio de Janeiro, Instituto de Ciencias Cognitivas http://br.geocities.com/icc_brasil/.

300 PER
CIENCIAS SOCIALES; revista de investigacion analisis y debate. Text in Spanish. 1993. irreg.?.
Published by: Universidad Nacional del Altiplano, Facultad de Ciencias Sociales, Ave. El Ejercito, 329, Puno, Peru. Ed. Jorge Adan Villegas Montoya.

300 COL ISSN 0134-5494
CIENCIAS SOCIALES. Text in Spanish. 1976. q.
Published by: (Akademiya Nauk S.S.S.R. SUN, Social Sciences Section RUS), Centro de Estudios e Investigaciones Sociales, Calle 21, 17-42, Apartado Aereo 11968, Bogota, CUND, Colombia. Ed. Alvaro Delgado Guzman.

300 PER ISSN 2079-3669
▼ **CIENCIAS SOCIALES (LIMA).** Text in Spanish. 2010. a. **Document type:** *Monographic series, Academic/Scholarly.*
Published by: Universidad Nacional Mayor de San Marcos, Facultad de Ciencias Sociales, Ciudad Universitaria, Ave. Venezuela, s-n, Lima, 1, Peru. informacion@sociales.unmsm.pe, http://sociales.unmsm.edu.pe/index.php.

300 CHL ISSN 0718-1671
H8
CIENCIAS SOCIALES ONLINE; revista electronica. Text in Spanish. 2004. s-a. free (effective 2011). **Document type:** *Journal, Academic/ Scholarly.*
Media: Online - full text.
Published by: Universidad de Vina del Mar, Escuela de Ciencias Sociales, Agua Santa, 7255, Sector Rodelio, Vina del Mar, Santiago, Chile. TEL 56-2-462600, http://www.uvm.cl/sociales/. Ed. Jorge Gibert.

300 BRA
CIENCIAS SOCIAS HOJE (YEAR). Text in Portuguese. irreg.
Published by: Associacao Nacional de Pos-Graduacao e Pesquisa em Ciencias Sociais, Ave. Prof. Luciano Gualberto 315, Sala 116, Butanta - Cidade Universitaria, Sao Paulo, SP 05508-900, Brazil. TEL 55-11-8184664, FAX 55-11-8185043.

CINTA DE MOEBIO; revista electronica de epistemologia de ciencias sociales. *see* PHILOSOPHY

300 LKA
CINTANA DHARA. Text in Singhalese. 1977. q. LKR 3.50.
Published by: Pushparama Institute, Delkanda, Nugegoda, Sri Lanka.

300 ESP ISSN 1696-1277
H8.S7
➤ **CIRCUNSTANCIA**; revista de ciencias sociales. Text in Spanish. 2003. 3/yr. free (effective 2011). back issues avail. **Document type:** *Journal, Academic/Scholarly.*
Media: Online - full text.
Published by: Instituto Universitario de Investigacion Ortega y Gasset, C Fortuny, 53, Madrid, 28010, Spain. TEL 34-91-7004149, FAX 34-91-7003530, jefatura.estudios@fog.es, http://www.ortegaygasset.edu/iuoyg/principal.htm. Ed. Maria Josefa Garcia Grande.

300 USA ISSN 1084-6832
CITIZEN (COLORADO SPRINGS). Variant title: Focus on the Family Citizen. Text in English. 198?. m. USD 24 (effective 2008). reprints avail. **Document type:** *Magazine, Consumer.* **Description:** Contains stories that set the record straight on various issues that affects the reader's family, neighborhood and church - plus stories of local heroes.
Indexed: ChrPI.
Published by: Focus on the Family, 8605 Explorer Dr, Colorado Springs, CO 80920. TEL 719-531-3400, 800-232-6459, FAX 719-531-3424, http://www.family.org. Ed. Tom Hess. Circ: 50,000.

307.76097471 USA
HN79.N43
CITY LIMITS (ONLINE); New York's urban affairs news magazine. Text in English. 1976. w. free (effective 2007). adv. bk.rev. illus. back issues avail.; reprints avail. **Document type:** *Magazine, Trade.* **Description:** Provides news, investigative reports and analysis of current urban issues.
Formerly (until 2006): City Limits (Print) (0199-0330)
Media: Online - full content. **Related titles:** Microform ed.: (from PQC).
Indexed: AIAP, APW, AltPI, CWI, G06, G07, G08, I05.
—CIS, Ingenta.
Published by: City Limits Community Information Service, Inc., 120 Wall St, 20th Fl, New York, NY 10005-4001. TEL 212-479-3344, FAX 212-344-6457. Eds. Carl Vogel, Glenn Thrush. Pub., Adv. contact Kim Nauer. R&P Kemba Johnson. B&W page USD 500. Circ: 3,000 (paid); 1,000 (controlled).

353.13 USA ISSN 1937-4127
CITY LIMITS INVESTIGATES. Text in English. 2007. q. USD 25 (effective 2007). adv. **Document type:** *Magazine, Trade.*
Related titles: Online - full text ed.: ISSN 1937-4135. 2007.
Indexed: APW, G06, G07, G08, I05.
Published by: City Limits Community Information Service, Inc., 120 Wall St, 20th Fl, New York, NY 10005-4001. TEL 212-479-3344, FAX 212-344-6457, citylimits@citylimits.org.

304 ESP ISSN 1132-3094
CIUTAT. Text in Catalan. 1992. s-a. back issues avail.
Published by: Amics de les Arts i Joventuts Musicals de Terrassa, C. Teatre, 2, Terrassa, Spain. TEL 34-93-7859231, FAX 34-93-7316043, amicsajjmm@ilimit.es, http://amics.terassa.net/.

300 001.3 COL ISSN 1657-8953
H8.S6
CIVILIZAR; ciencias sociales y humanas. Text in Spanish. 2001. s-a. **Document type:** *Journal, Academic/Scholarly.*
Related titles: Online - full text ed.: free (effective 2011) (from SciELO).
Indexed: F04, T02.
Published by: Universidad Sergio Arboleda, Calle 74. No 14-14, Bogota, Colombia. TEL 57-1-3257500, FAX 57-1-5452924.

300 ITA ISSN 1120-9860
CIVILTA DEL MEDITERRANEO. Text in Italian. 1991. s-a. **Document type:** *Journal, Academic/Scholarly.*
Published by: Universita degli Studi di Napoli "Federico II", Facolta di Lettere e Filosofia, Via Porta di Massa 1, Naples, 80133, Italy. dipfil@unina.it, http://www.filosofia.unina.it.

300 BRA ISSN 1519-6089
H8.P8
CIVITAS; revista de ciencias sociais. Text in Multiple languages. 2001. s-a. **Document type:** *Journal, Academic/Scholarly.*
Related titles: Online - full text ed.: free (effective 2011).
Indexed: C01, CA, T02.
Published by: (Pontificia Universidade Catolica do Rio Grande do Sul, Faculdade de Ciencias Sociais), Editora da P U C R S, Avenida Ipiranga 6681, Predio 33, Porto Alegre, RS 90619-900, Brazil. http://www.pucrs.br/edipucrs/.

305 ARG ISSN 1666-1842
CLAROSCURO. Text in Spanish. 2001. a. **Document type:** *Monographic series, Academic/Scholarly.*
Published by: Universidad Nacioanl de Rosario, Centro de Estudios sobre la Diversidad Cutltural, Entre Rios 758, Rosario, Santa Fe, 2000, Argentina. claroscuro.cedcu@gmail.com. Ed. Cristina De Bernardi.

301 616.89 USA ISSN 1566-7847
➤ **CLINICAL SOCIOLOGY**; research and practice. Text in English. 1996. irreg., latest 2009. price varies. back issues avail. **Document type:** *Monographic series, Academic/Scholarly.* **Description:** Contains ethical and legal aspects, the nature of client relationships, methods of intervention and evaluation, and the role of clinical sociology in specific settings.
Indexed: E-psyche.
Published by: Springer New York LLC (Subsidiary of: Springer Science+Business Media), 233 Spring St, New York, NY 10013. TEL 212-460-1500, FAX 212-460-1575, service-ny@springer.com. Ed. John G Bruhn.

300 MEX
CODIGOS: CUADERNOS DE COMUNICACION. Text in Spanish. 1991. q.
Published by: Universidad de las Americas, Puebla, Santa Catarina Martir, Cholula, Puebla, 72820, Mexico. TEL 52-22-293166, http://www.udlap.mx.

300 DEU ISSN 1869-9782
▼ **COINCIDENTIA**; Zeitschrift fuer europaeische Geistesgeschichte. Text in German. 2010. 2/yr. EUR 39.80; EUR 24.80 per issue (effective 2011). **Document type:** *Journal, Academic/Scholarly.*
Published by: Kueser Akademie fuer Europaeische Geistesgeschichte e.V., Gestade 6, Bernkastel-Kues, 54470, Germany. TEL 49-6531-9734288, FAX 49-6531-9734289, info@kueser-akademie.de.

300 ESP ISSN 0577-2486
COLECCION BIBLIOTECA SORIANA. Text in Spanish. 1956. irreg.
Related titles: ◆ Supplement to: Celtiberia. ISSN 0528-3647.
Published by: Centro de Estudios Sorianos, Nicolas Rabal, 21, Soria, Castilla y Leon 42003, Spain. celtiberia-ces@jet.es. Ed. Emilio Ruiz.

306 ESP
COLECCION CULTURA VIVA. Text in Spanish. 1995. irreg., latest vol.16, 2000. price varies. back issues avail. **Document type:** *Monographic series, Academic/Scholarly.*
Published by: Universidad de Sevilla, Secretariado de Publicaciones, Calle Porvenir 27, Sevilla, 41013, Spain. TEL 34-95-4487444, FAX 34-95-4487443, secpub10@us.es, http://www.us.es/publius/inicio.html.

300 CHL
COLECCION FE E HISTORIA. Text in Spanish. 1977. irreg.
Published by: Georgetown University, I L A D E S, Almirante Barroso 6, Santiago, Chile.

COLECION DERECHO, CULTURA Y SOCIEDAD. *see* LAW

300 COL ISSN 0120-3975
COLEGIO MAYOR DE NUESTRA SENORA DEL ROSARIO. REVISTA. Cover title: Nova et Vetera. Text in Spanish. 1905. q. **Document type:** *Academic/Scholarly.* **Description:** Covers economics, philosophy, and issues related to the social sciences.
Indexed: C01, IBR, IBZ, MLA-IB.
Published by: Colegio Mayor de Nuestra Senora del Rosario, Calle 14 no 6-25, Torre 1, Piso 4, Bogota, Colombia. TEL 57-1-282-0088, FAX 57-1-281-0494.

300 MEX ISSN 0185-0539
AS63
EL COLEGIO NACIONAL. MEMORIA. (Index avail. 1946-1993) Text in Spanish. 1946. a. Index. back issues avail. **Document type:** *Monographic series, Academic/Scholarly.*
Indexed: P30, PAIS.
Published by: El Colegio Nacional, Luis Gonzalez Obregon, 23, Centro Historico, Mexico, 06020, Mexico. TEL 52-55-57894330, FAX 52-55-57021779, colnal@mx.inter.net, http://www.colegionacional.org.mx/.

300 FRA ISSN 1951-5472
COLLECTION MIROIRS DU MONDE. Variant title: Miroirs du Monde. Text in French. 200?. irreg. back issues avail. **Document type:** *Monographic series, Consumer.*
Published by: Editions Miroirs du Sud, 33 Rond-Point Mirasouleou, Toulon, 83100, France. TEL 33-6-73399174, miroirsdusud83@orange.fr, http://www.miroirsdusud.fr/.

300 FRA ISSN 1285-9389
COLLECTION MONDE. Variant title: Monde. Text in French. 1983. irreg. **Document type:** *Monographic series.*
Former titles (until 1995): Autrement. Serie Monde (Paris, 1989) (1169-8039); (until 1988): Autrement. Hors - Serie (0763-6504); (until 1983): Autrement. Serie Monde (Paris, 1983) (0751-0152)
Indexed: FR, RILM.
—BLDSC (1835.630050), INIST.
Published by: Editions Autrement, 77 Rue du Faubourg St Antoine, Paris, 75011, France. TEL 33-1-44738000, FAX 33-1-44730012, contact@autrement.com.

300 FRA ISSN 1290-7332
COLLECTION MUTATIONS. Text in French. 1975. 14/yr. **Document type:** *Monographic series, Consumer.*
Former titles (until 1995): Autrement. Serie Mutations (1164-737X); (until 1988): Autrement (0763-6490); (until 1983): Autrement. Serie Mutations (0751-0144); Which supersedes in part (in 1982): Autrement (0336-5816); Which was formerly (1951-1974): Preuves (0032-7980)
Indexed: FR, MLA-IB, PRA, RASB, RILM.
—BLDSC (1835.630070), IE, Ingenta, INIST. **CCC.**

S

Published by: Editions Autrement, 77 Rue du Faubourg St Antoine, Paris, 75011, France. TEL 33-1-44738000, FAX 33-1-44730012, contact@autrement.com. Circ: 20,000.

300 FRA ISSN 1286-9686
COLLECTION NAISSANCE D'UN DESTIN. Text in French. 1998. irreg.
Document type: *Monographic series.*
Published by: Editions Autrement, 77 Rue du Faubourg St Antoine, Paris, 75011, France. TEL 33-1-44738000, FAX 33-1-44730012, contact@autrement.com, http://www.autrement.com.

300 FIN ISSN 1796-2986
AS9
➤ **COLLEGIUM.** Text in English. 2006. a. free (effective 2011).
Document type: *Journal, Academic/Scholarly.*
Media: Online - full text.
Indexed: A39, C27, C29, D03, D04, E13, R14, S14, S15, S18.
Published by: Helsingin Yliopisto, Tutkijakollegium, University of Helsinki, PO Box 4, Helsinki, 00014, Finland.

300 DEU
COLLEGIUM EUROPAEUM JENENSE. GERETTETE TEXTE. Text in German. 2000. irreg., latest vol.3, 2000. price varies. **Document type:** *Monographic series, Academic/Scholarly.*
Published by: Collegium Europaeum Jenense, Schillers Gartenhaus, Schillergaesschen 2, Jena, 07745, Germany. TEL 49-3641-931186, FAX 49-3641-931187, mail@cej-jena.eu.

300 DEU
COLLEGIUM EUROPAEUM JENENSE. KULTURWISSENSCHAFTLICHE REIHE. Text in German. 2000. irreg., latest vol.5, 2003. price varies. **Document type:** *Monographic series, Academic/Scholarly.*
Published by: Collegium Europaeum Jenense, Schillers Gartenhaus, Schillergaesschen 2, Jena, 07745, Germany. TEL 49-3641-931186, FAX 49-3641-931187, mail@cej-jena.eu.

300 DEU
COLLEGIUM EUROPAEUM JENENSE. SCHRIFTENREIHE. Text in German. 1991. irreg., latest vol.41, 2010. price varies. **Document type:** *Monographic series, Academic/Scholarly.*
Formerly (until 2004): Collegium Europaeum Jenense. Schriften
Published by: (Collegium Europaeum Jenense), I K S Garamond, Leutragraben 1, Jena, 07743, Germany. TEL 49-3641-460850, FAX 49-3641-460855, garamond@iks-jena.de, http://garamond.iks-jena.de.

300 DEU ISSN 1867-058X
▼ **COLLEGIUM PONTES. SCHRIFTEN.** Text in German. 2009. irreg., latest vol.4, 2009. price varies. **Document type:** *Monographic series, Academic/Scholarly.*
Published by: Peter Lang GmbH (Subsidiary of: Peter Lang Publishing Group), Eschborner Landstr 42-50, Frankfurt Am Main, 60489, Germany. TEL 49-69-7807050, FAX 49-69-78070550, zentrale.frankfurt@peterlang.com, http://www.peterlang.com.

300 BRA
COLLOR. Text in Portuguese. 1991. a.
Published by: Instituto Brasileiro de Analises Sociais e Economicas, Rua Vincente de Souza 29, Botafogo, Rio De Janeiro, RJ 22251, Brazil. TEL 021-286-0348.

305.8 FRA ISSN 1777-585X
COMBATS MAGAZINE; an international journal on literature and politics. Text in French. 2003. irreg. free (effective 2009). **Document type:** *Magazine, Consumer.* **Description:** Explores social, political and personal views and experiences stemming from cultural diversity.
Media: Online - full text.
Published by: Observatoire Multilateral sur la Diversite Culturelle, 16 rue de Bellevue, Les Lilas, 93260, France. TEL 33-1-871766093, fulvio.caccia@free.fr. Ed. Robert Richard.

300 FIN ISSN 0355-256X
COMMENTATIONES SCIENTIARUM SOCIALIUM. Text in English, Finnish. 1972. irreg. price varies. **Document type:** *Monographic series, Academic/Scholarly.*
Indexed: RASB, RefugAb.
Published by: Suomen Tiedeseura/Finnish Society of Sciences and Letters, Mariagatan 5, Helsinki, 00170, Finland. TEL 358-9-633005, FAX 358-9-661065. Ed. Per Schybergson. Circ: 600. **Co-sponsor:** Finnish Academy of Sciences and Letters.

COMMUNICATION AND MEDICINE. *see* MEDICAL SCIENCES

301 361 GBR ISSN 1366-8803
HD6050
➤ **COMMUNITY, WORK & FAMILY.** Text in English. 1998. q. GBP 561 combined subscription in United Kingdom to institutions (print & online eds.); EUR 745, USD 935 combined subscription to institutions (print & online eds.) (effective 2012). adv. back issues avail.; reprint service avail. from PSC. **Document type:** *Journal, Academic/Scholarly.* **Description:** Provides a forum for social scientists and practitioners to share experiences and ideas relating to the links between community, work, and family. Includes articles on theory, research, policy and practice.
Related titles: Online - full text ed.: ISSN 1469-3615. GBP 504 in United Kingdom to institutions; EUR 670, USD 841 to institutions (effective 2012) (from IngentaConnect).
Indexed: A01, A03, A08, A22, B01, B06, B07, B09, B21, CA, E-psyche, E01, E17, ESPM, F09, FamI, P03, P30, P42, PAIS, PSA, PsycInfo, PsycholAb, RiskAb, S02, S03, SCOPUS, SSA, SSciA, SociolAb, T02, W09.
—IE, Infotrieve, Ingenta. **CCC.**
Published by: Routledge (Subsidiary of: Taylor & Francis Group), 4 Park Sq, Milton Park, Abingdon, Oxon OX14 4RN, United Kingdom. TEL 44-20-70176000, FAX 44-20-70176336, subscriptions@tandf.co.uk, http://www.routledge.com. Eds. Carolyn Kagan, Suzan Lewis. Adv. contact Linda Hann TEL 44-1344-779945. **Subscr. in N. America to:** Taylor & Francis Inc., Customer Services Dept, 325 Chestnut St, 8th Fl, Philadelphia, PA 19106. TEL 215-625-8900, 800-354-1420, FAX 215-625-2940, customerservice@taylorandfrancis.com; **Subscr. to:** Taylor & Francis Ltd., Journals Customer Service, Sheepen Pl, Colchester, Essex CO3 3LP, United Kingdom. TEL 44-20-70175544, FAX 44-20-70175198.

300 BEL ISSN 1780-4515
COMPARATISME ET SOCIETE/COMPARATISM AND SOCIETY. Text in French, English. 2004. irreg., latest vol.11, 2010. price varies. **Document type:** *Monographic series, Academic/Scholarly.*
Published by: P I E - Peter Lang SA, 1 avenue Maurice, 6e etage, Brussels, 1050, Belgium. TEL 32-2-3477236, FAX 32-2-3477237, pie@peterlang.com, http://www.peterlang.net. Ed. Hubert Roland.

COMPARATIV; Leipziger Beitraege zur Universalgeschichte und vergleichenden Gesellschaftsforschung. *see* HISTORY

300 GBR ISSN 1477-5700
E175.8
COMPARATIVE AMERICAN STUDIES. Abbreviated title: C A S. Text in English. 2003 (Mar.). q. GBP 438 combined subscription to institutions (print & online eds.); USD 779 combined subscription in United States to institutions (print & online eds.) (effective 2012). adv. back issues avail.; reprint service avail. from PSC. **Document type:** *Journal, Academic/Scholarly.* **Description:** Extends scholarly debates about American Studies beyond the geographical boundaries of the United States, repositioning discussions about American culture explicitly within an international, comparative framework.
Related titles: Online - full text ed.: ISSN 1741-2676. GBP 398 to institutions; USD 719 in United States to institutions (effective 2012) (from IngentaConnect).
Indexed: A22, AmH&L, AmHI, CA, CMM, DIP, E01, FR, H07, IBR, IBSS, IBZ, L06, MLA-IB, S02, S03, SCOPUS, SRRA, SociolAb, T02.
—BLDSC (3363.742500), IE, Ingenta, INIST. **CCC.**
Published by: Maney Publishing, Ste 1C, Joseph's Well, Hanover Walk, Leeds, W Yorks LS3 1AB, United Kingdom. TEL 44-113-2432800, FAX 44-113-3868178, maney@maney.co.uk, http://www.maney.co.uk. Ed. Nick Selby.

300 VEN ISSN 1317-6099
COMPENDIUM; revista de investigacion cientifica. Text in Spanish. 1995. s-a. **Document type:** *Journal, Academic/Scholarly.*
Related titles: Online - full text ed.: free (effective 2011).
Indexed: A01, CA, F04, P42, S02, S03, T02.
Published by: Universidad Centroccidental, Decanato de Administracion y Contaduria, Calle 8 entre Carreras 19 y 20, Edif Extension, Investigacion Postrado 1er Piso, Barquisimento, Estado Lara, Venezuela. TEL 58-251-2591419, FAX 58-251-2591461, compedium@ucla.edu.ve, http://www.ucla.edu.ve/fac/. Ed. Pedro Reyes. Circ: 300.

300 FRA ISSN 1639-5875
COMPRENDRE ET AGIR. Text in French. 2003. irreg. back issues avail. **Document type:** *Monographic series, Consumer.*
Published by: (Institut de Recherches Historiques, Economiques, Sociales, Culturelles), Editions Syllepse, 69 rue des Rigoles, Paris, 75020, France. TEL 33-1-44620889.

COMPUTERS, COGNITION AND WORK. *see* COMPUTERS

COMUNICACAO E EDUCACAO. *see* EDUCATION

COMUNICACION. *see* EDUCATION

COMUNICAR; revista cientifica iberoamericana de comunicacion y educacion. *see* EDUCATION

CON - CIENCIA SOCIAL. *see* EDUCATION

CONCEPTOS BOLETIN. *see* SOCIOLOGY

300 DEU ISSN 2190-3433
▼ **CONCEPTS FOR THE STUDY OF CULTURE.** Text in English. 2010. irreg., latest vol.2, 2011. price varies. **Document type:** *Monographic series, Academic/Scholarly.*
Published by: Walter de Gruyter GmbH & Co. KG, Genthiner Str 13, Berlin, 10785, Germany. TEL 49-30-260050, FAX 49-30-26005251, info@degruyter.com, http://www.degruyter.de.

CONEXION 2000 ARTE Y CULTURA EN EL NUEVO MILENIO. *see* ART

300 PRT ISSN 1646-5075
DP702.E21
CONFIGURACOES. Text in Portuguese, English. 1986. s-a. **Document type:** *Journal, Academic/Scholarly.*
Formerly (until 2004): Cadernos do Noroeste (0870-9874)
Related titles: Online - full text ed.
Published by: Universidade do Minho, Instituto de Ciencias Sociais, Lago do Paco, Braga, 4700-320, Portugal. TEL 351-253604280, FAX 351-253676966, sec@ics.uminho.pt, http://www.uminho.pt/.

327.172 NLD ISSN 1877-8682
▼ **CONFLICTINZICHT.** Text in Dutch. 2009. 3/yr. EUR 22.50; EUR 7.50 newsstand/cover (effective 2011). adv. **Document type:** *Magazine, Trade.*
Published by: Uitgeverij Stili Novi, Postbus 690, Utrecht, 3512 NV, Netherlands. TEL 31-30-2331363, info@uitgeverijstilinovi.nl, http://www.uitgeverijstilinovi.nl. Pub. Simone Siemons. Circ: 5,000.

▼ **THE CONFLUENCE.** *see* HISTORY

▼ **CONGRESO DE INVESTIGACION. PROCEEDINGS.** *see* HUMANITIES: COMPREHENSIVE WORKS

300 COL
CONGRESO INTERNACIONAL DE VIVIENDA POPULAR. Text in Spanish. irreg., latest vol.3, 1974. COP 90. **Document type:** *Academic/Scholarly.*
Published by: (Servicio Latino-Americano y Asiatico de Vivienda Popular), Centro de Investigacion y Educacion Popular (Cinep), Carrera 5 No.33A-08, Bogota, Colombia. TEL 57-1-2858977.

CONHISREMI. *see* EDUCATION

300 CAN ISSN 0827-5548
JL241.A1
CONJONCTURES. Text in English. 1982. s-a. CAD 30, USD 33. bk.rev. back issues avail.
Indexed: PdeR.
Address: 4076 St Hubert, Montreal, PQ H2L 4A8, Canada. TEL 514-523-4724, FAX 514-525-0967.

300 USA ISSN 0226-1766
➤ **CONNECTIONS (ALHAMBRA).** Text in English. 1977. s-a. USD 50 to individuals; USD 60 to institutions (effective 2011). back issues avail. **Document type:** *Journal, Academic/Scholarly.* **Description:** Aims to support network analysis in general and INSNA members in particular by providing a method of pooling and sharing news about the membership, tools for teaching and research, data for analysis and results of scientific investigations.
Indexed: P30, SSAI, SSAb, SSI, W03, W05.
—BLDSC (3417.663610).
Published by: International Network for Social Network Analysis, University of Southern California, Dept of Preventive Medicine, 1000 Fremont Ave, Unit #8, Bldg A, Rm 5133, Alhambra, CA 91803. socnet@insna.org. Ed. Tom Valente.

300 170 330 ITA ISSN 1825-3946
IL CONSAPEVOLE. Text in Italian. 2004. bi-m. (8/yr.). EUR 24 (effective 2009). **Document type:** *Magazine, Consumer.*
Published by: Macro Edizioni, Via Savona 70, Diegaro di Cesena, FC 47023, Italy. TEL 39-0547-346290, http://www.macroedizioni.it. Ed. Giorgio Gustavo Rosso.

300 ARG
CONSEJO LATINOAMERICANO DE CIENCIAS SOCIALES. CARTA. Text in Spanish. m. **Document type:** *Newsletter.* **Description:** Informs of activities, trends, accomplishments and opportunities in the social sciences.
Published by: Consejo Latinoamericano de Ciencias Sociales, Avda Callao 875, Piso 3, Buenos Aires, 1023, Argentina. TEL 54-11-48142301, erol@clacso.edu.ar, http://www.clacso.org. Ed. Jorge Fraga.

300 PER ISSN 1680-3817
AS88.L67
CONSENSUS. Text in Spanish. 1995. a. **Document type:** *Journal, Academic/Scholarly.*
Indexed: CA, F04, T02.
Published by: Universidad Femenina del Sagrado Corazon, Ave Los Frutales 954, Urb Santa Magdalena Sofia, La Molina, Lima, 41, Peru. TEL 51-1-4364641, FAX 51-1-4350853, cinv@unife.edu.pe, http://www.unife.edu.pe. Ed. Rosanna Cordano Ripamonti.

300 IND ISSN 1817-4604
H1
➤ **CONTEMPORARY ISSUES AND IDEAS IN SOCIAL SCIENCES.** Abbreviated title: C I I S S. Text in English. 2005. irreg., latest vol.6, no.1, 2010. free (effective 2011). back issues avail. **Document type:** *Journal, Academic/Scholarly.* **Description:** Aims at encouraging research on neglected but important problems, whether theoretical or empirical, in social sciences.
Media: Online - full text.
Indexed: CA, S02, S03, T02.
Published by: Jawaharlal Nehru University, School of Social Sciences, Centre for Economic Studies and Planning, New Delhi, 110067, India. http://www.jnu.ac.in/main.asp?sendval=SchoolOfSocialSciences.

306.85 GBR ISSN 1530-3535
HQ1
CONTEMPORARY PERSPECTIVES ON FAMILY RESEARCH. Text in English. 2000. irreg., latest vol.5, 2004. price varies. back issues avail. **Document type:** *Monographic series, Academic/Scholarly.*
Related titles: Online - full text ed.
Indexed: SCOPUS, SSA, SociolAb.
—BLDSC (3425.198000). **CCC.**
Published by: Emerald Group Publishing Ltd., Howard House, Wagon Ln, Bingley, W Yorks BD16 1WA, United Kingdom. TEL 44-1274-777700, FAX 44-1274-785201, emerald@emeraldinsight.com. Ed. Felix M Berardo. **Dist. by:** Turpin Distribution Services Ltd., Pegasus Dr, Stratton Business Park, Biggleswade, Bedfordshire SG18 8QB, United Kingdom. TEL 44-1767-604951, FAX 44-1767-601640, custserv@turpin-distribution.com, http://www.turpin-distribution.com/.

300 GBR
➤ **CONTEMPORARY SOCIAL SCIENCE.** Text in English. 2006 (Jun.). 3/yr. GBP 292 combined subscription in United Kingdom to institutions (print & online eds.); EUR 387, USD 487 combined subscription to institutions (print & online eds.) (effective 2012). adv. back issues avail.; reprint service avail. from PSC. **Document type:** *Journal, Academic/Scholarly.* **Description:** Aims to promote the social sciences and synthesise, reflect and advance global public debates.
Formerly (until 20??): Twenty-First Century (1745-0144)
Related titles: Online - full text ed.: GBP 263 in United Kingdom to institutions; EUR 348, USD 439 to institutions (effective 2012).
Indexed: A22, CA, E01, PAIS, S02, S03, SCOPUS, SociolAb, T02.
—IE, Ingenta. **CCC.**
Published by: (Academy of Social Sciences), Routledge (Subsidiary of: Taylor & Francis Group), 4 Park Sq, Milton Park, Abingdon, Oxon OX14 4RN, United Kingdom. TEL 44-20-70176000, FAX 44-20-70176336, subscriptions@tandf.co.uk, http://www.routledge.com. Eds. Miriam David TEL 44-20-76126825, Philip Davies. Adv. contact Linda Hann TEL 44-1344-779945. **Subscr. to:** Taylor & Francis Ltd., Journals Customer Service, Sheepen Pl, Colchester, Essex CO3 3LP, United Kingdom. TEL 44-20-70175544, FAX 44-20-70175198, tf.enquiries@tfinforma.com.

➤ **CONTEXTS**; understanding people in their social worlds. *see* SOCIOLOGY

300 NGA ISSN 2141-4165
CONTINENTAL JOURNAL OF SOCIAL SCIENCES. Text in English. 2008. a. NGN 2,500 domestic to individuals; USD 120 foreign to individuals; NGN 5,000 domestic to institutions; USD 200 foreign to institutions (effective 2010). back issues avail.; reprints avail. **Document type:** *Journal, Academic/Scholarly.* **Description:** Focusesn theories, methods and applications in social sciences and humanities research.
Related titles: Online - full text ed.
Indexed: P10, P48, P53, P54, PQC.
Published by: Wilolud Journals, 2 Church Ave, Oke Eri qrt, Oba Ile, Ondo State 340001, Nigeria. TEL 234-803-4458674, managingeditor.olawale71@gmail.com. Ed. E.O. Ogunleye.

300 ESP ISSN 1988-7833
CONTRIBUCIONES A LAS CIENCIAS SOCIALES. Text in Spanish, Portuguese. 2008. m. **Document type:** *Journal, Academic/Scholarly.*
Media: Online - full text.
Published by: Universidad de Malaga, Eumed.net, Avenida Cervantes 2, Malaga, 29071, Spain. TEL 34-952-131000.

300 MEX ISSN 1870-0365
CONTRIBUCIONES DESDE COATEPEC. Text in Spanish. 1998. s-a. **Document type:** *Journal, Academic/Scholarly.*
Related titles: Online - full text ed.: free (effective 2011).
Indexed: C01.

Published by: Universidad Autonoma del Estado de Mexico, Facultad de Humanidades, Paseo de la Universidad s-n, esq Ave Tollocan, Ciudad Universitaria, Estado de Mexico, 50100, Mexico. concoatepec@uaemex.mx, http://www.uaemex.mx/. Ed. Gloria Camacho Pichardo. Circ: 500.

300 BRA
CONTRIBUICOES EM CIENCIAS SOCIAIS. Text in Portuguese. irreg. **Document type:** *Monographic series.*
Published by: Editora Campus Ltda. (Subsidiary of: Elsevier Science & Technology), Rua Sete de Setembro 111-16 andar, Rio De Janeiro, RJ 20150-002, Brazil. TEL 55-21-509-5340, FAX 55-21-507-1991.

CONTRIBUTIONS IN LATIN AMERICAN STUDIES. *see* HISTORY—History Of North And South America

CONTRIBUTIONS TO THE HISTORY OF CONCEPTS. *see* HISTORY

300 FRA ISSN 1779-2355
JA75.7
CONTROVERSES. Text in French. 2006. 3/yr. EUR 60 domestic; EUR 75 foreign (effective 2009). back issues avail. **Document type:** *Journal, Academic/Scholarly.*
Indexed: IBSS.
Published by: Editions de L' Eclat, 4 Av. Hoche, Paris, 75008, France. TEL 33-1-45770404, FAX 33-1-45759251, infos@lyber-eclat.net.

300 USA ISSN 1058-2029
AP2
➤ **COSMOS**; a journal of emerging issues and insights. Text in English. 1991. a. free to members (effective 2010). bk.rev. back issues avail. **Document type:** *Journal, Academic/Scholarly.*
Related titles: Online - full text ed.
Published by: Cosmos Club, 2121 Massachusetts Ave, NW, Washington, DC 20008. TEL 202-387-7783, FAX 202-234-6817, clubservices@cosmosclub.org, http://www.cosmos-club.org.

300 USA ISSN 0742-8995
HS2725.W3
COSMOS CLUB BULLETIN. Text in English. 1947. m. free to members (effective 2010). **Document type:** *Bulletin, Trade.* **Description:** Instructs the Cosmos Club members about the activities of the club. Provides cultural programs including evening lectures, noon forums, musical concerts, book and author dinners.
Indexed: P30.
Published by: Cosmos Club, 2121 Massachusetts Ave, NW, Washington, DC 20008. TEL 202-387-7783, FAX 202-234-6817, clubservices@cosmosclub.org, http://www.cosmos-club.org.

300 TZA
COUNCIL FOR THE SOCIAL SCIENCES IN EAST AFRICA. SOCIAL SCIENCE CONFERENCE. PROCEEDINGS. Text in English. a. TZS 200, USD 29. charts; stat. **Document type:** *Proceedings.*
Published by: Council for the Social Sciences in East Africa, c/o University of Dar-es-Salaam, Faculty of Arts and Social Science, PO Box 35091, Dar-Es-Salaam, Tanzania.

THE COUNCILOR. *see* EDUCATION

300 371.3 AUS ISSN 1835-9442
➤ **CREATIVE APPROACHES TO RESEARCH.** Text in English. 2008. 2/yr. **Document type:** *Journal, Academic/Scholarly.* **Description:** Reflects the convergences between epistemology, pedagogy and technology.
Media: Online - full text.
Indexed: A01, CA, T02.
Published by: R M I T, Publishing, A'Beckett St, PO Box 12058, Melbourne, VIC 8006, Australia. TEL 61-3-99258100, FAX 61-3-99258134, info@rmitpublishing.com.au. Ed. Laura Brearley.

300 ESP ISSN 1887-7370
CREATIVIDAD Y SOCIEDAD (ONLINE). Text in Spanish. 2001. a. back issues avail. **Document type:** *Monographic series, Academic/Scholarly.*
Formerly (until 2007): Creatividad y Sociedad (Print) (1578-214X)
Media: Online - full text.
Published by: Asociacion para la Creatividad, Passeig de la Vall de 'Hebron, 171, Barcelona, 08035, Spain. info@asocrea.com.

300 USA ISSN 1068-4689
CRITIC OF INSTITUTIONS. Text in English. 1994. irreg., latest vol.16, 2008. price varies. **Document type:** *Monographic series, Academic/Scholarly.*
Published by: Peter Lang Publishing, Inc. (Subsidiary of: Peter Lang Publishing Group), 29 Broadway, New York, NY 10006. TEL 212-647-7706, 212-647-7700, 800-770-5264, FAX 212-647-7707, customerservice@plang.com.

300 PER
CRITICA ANDINA. Text in Spanish. 1978. irreg. USD 12 to individuals; USD 18 to institutions. adv. bk.rev.
Published by: Instituto de Estudios Sociales, Director de Publicaciones, Apdo Postal 790, Cuzco, Peru. Ed. Marco Villasante. Circ: 2,000.

300 ARG
CRITICA DE NUESTRO TIEMPO; revista internacional de teoria y politica. Text in Spanish. 1991. 3/yr. USD 20 to individuals; USD 35 to institutions. adv. bk.rev. **Document type:** *Academic/Scholarly.*
Published by: (Centro de Estudios Marxistas Pedro Milesi), Busqueda de Nuestro Tiempo Editorial, Casilla de Correo 3509, Buenos Aires, 1000, Argentina. TEL 54-114-3046847. Ed. Luis Bilbao. Pub. Carlos Beacon. Adv. contact Juan Gandolfo. Circ: 2,000.

300 GBR ISSN 1740-5904
➤ **CRITICAL DISCOURSE STUDIES**; an interdisciplinary journal for the social sciences. Abbreviated title: C D S. Text in English. 2004. 3/yr. GBP 386 combined subscription in United Kingdom to institutions (print & online eds.); EUR 512, USD 642 combined subscription to institutions (print & online eds.) (effective 2012). adv. back issues avail.; reprint service avail. from PSC. **Document type:** *Journal, Academic/Scholarly.* **Description:** An international and interdisciplinary journal for the social sciences the relevant areas and disciplines, which include anthropology, communication, linguistics, sociology, politics, political economy, education, psychology, media studies, geography, urban studies, cultural studies, management studies, literary studies, history, technology studies, legal studies, philosophy, gender studies, migration studies, ethnic studies and others.
Related titles: Online - full text ed.: ISSN 1740-5912. GBP 347 in United Kingdom to institutions; EUR 461, USD 577 to institutions (effective 2012) (from IngentaConnect).
Indexed: A22, AmHI, CA, CMM, CommAb, E01, H07, IBSS, L&LBA, L11, MLA-IB, P42, PSA, S02, S03, SociolAb, T02.
—BLDSC (3487.451802), IE, Ingenta. **CCC.**
Published by: Routledge (Subsidiary of: Taylor & Francis Group), 4 Park Square, Milton Park, Abingdon, Oxon OX14 4RN, United Kingdom. subscriptions@tandf.co.uk, http://www.routledge.com. Eds. Norman Fairclough TEL 44-1524-593030, Phil Graham TEL 61-7-31388186. Adv. contact Linda Hann TEL 44-1344-779945. **Subscr. to:** Taylor & Francis Ltd., Journals Customer Service, Sheepen Pl, Colchester, Essex CO3 3LP, United Kingdom. TEL 44-20-70175544, FAX 44-20-70175198, tf.enquiries@tfinforma.com.

330 USA ISSN 1933-0987
CRITICAL PERSPECTIVES IN SOCIAL THEORY. Text in English. 1983. irreg. price varies. **Document type:** *Monographic series.*
Published by: Praeger Publishers (Subsidiary of: Greenwood Publishing Group Inc.), 88 Post Rd W, Westport, CT 06881. TEL 800-368-6868, tech.support@greenwood.com, http://www.greenwood.com.

CRITICAL PERSPECTIVES ON HISTORIC ISSUES. *see* HISTORY

300 MNE ISSN 0350-5472
H8
CRNOGORSKA AKADEMIJA NAUKA I UMJETNOSTI. ODJELJENJE DRUSTVENIH NAUKA. GLASNIK. Text in Serbian. 1979. a. EUR 5 per issue (effective 2007). **Document type:** *Journal, Academic/Scholarly.*
Published by: Crnogorska Akademija Nauka i Umjetnosti, Odjeljenje Drustvenih Nauka, Rista Stijovica 5, Podgorica, 81000. TEL 381-81-621121, FAX 381-81-655451, canu@cg.yu, http://www.canu.cg.yu.

300 ESP ISSN 1696-4063
CRONICAS ANAGRAMA. Text in Spanish. 1987. irreg. **Document type:** *Monographic series, Academic/Scholarly.*
Published by: Editorial Anagrama S.A., Pedro de la Creu, 58, Barcelona, 08034, Spain. anagrama@anagrama-ed.es, http://www.anagrama-ed.es/.

300 USA ISSN 1069-3971
H1 CODEN: CRCRE4
➤ **CROSS-CULTURAL RESEARCH**; the journal of comparative social science. Text in English. 1966. q. USD 638, GBP 375 combined subscription to institutions (print & online eds.); USD 625, GBP 368 to institutions (effective 2011). adv. bk.rev. bibl.; charts; illus. index. back issues avail.; reprint service avail. from PSC. **Document type:** *Journal, Academic/Scholarly.* **Description:** Studies cross-cultural or comparative issues in the social and behavioral sciences. Examines topics that span societies, nations and cultures, providing strategies for the systematic testing of theories about human society and behavior. Research reports, review articles, methodological studies, bibliographies and discussion pieces offer a wealth of information on cross-cultural issues providing a global perspective.
Former titles (until 1993): Behavior Science Research (0094-3673); Behavior Science Notes (0005-7886)
Related titles: Microform ed.: (from PQC); Online - full text ed.: ISSN 1552-3578. USD 574, GBP 338 to institutions (effective 2011).
Indexed: A01, A02, A03, A08, A12, A13, A17, A20, A22, A26, ABIn, ABS&EES, AICP, AbAn, AnthLit, B04, B07, BAS, BRD, CA, CMM, CPE, CommAb, CurCont, DIP, E-psyche, E01, E08, EI, ESPM, FR, FamI, G08, H04, I13, IBR, IBSS, IBZ, IPsyAb, L&LBA, MLA-IB, P02, P03, P06, P10, P25, P27, P30, P42, P48, P51, P53, P54, PCI, PQC, PSA, PsycInfo, PsycholAb, RiskAb, S02, S03, S09, S11, SCOPUS, SOPODA, SSA, SSAI, SSAb, SSCI, SSI, SSciA, SociolAb, T02, V02, W03, W07.
—BLDSC (3488.825000), IE, Infotrieve, Ingenta, INIST. **CCC.**
Published by: (Society for Cross-Cultural Research), Sage Publications, Inc., 2455 Teller Rd, Thousand Oaks, CA 91320. TEL 805-499-9774, 800-818-7243, FAX 805-499-0871, 800-583-2665, info@sagepub.com. Ed. Melvin Ember. Circ: 550 (paid and free). **Subscr. overseas to:** Sage Publications Ltd., 1 Oliver's Yard, 55 City Rd, London EC1Y 1SP, United Kingdom. TEL 44-207-3248701, FAX 44-207-3248733, subscription@sagepub.co.uk. **Co-sponsor:** Human Relations Area Files, Inc.

➤ **CROSS-THINKING FOR DISCOVERY AND CREATIVITY.** *see* SCIENCES: COMPREHENSIVE WORKS

300 COL ISSN 2011-0324
CS. (Ciencias Sociales) Text in Spanish. 2007. s-a. **Document type:** *Journal, Academic/Scholarly.*
Published by: Universidad Icesi, Calle 18, No 122-135, Pance, Santiago de Cali, Colombia. TEL 57-2-5552334, FAX 57-2-5551441, http://www.icesi.edu.co/.

300 ESP ISSN 1130-2569
JL951.A1
CUADERNOS AFRICA - AMERICA LATINA; revista de analisis sur-norte para una cooperacion solidaria. Text in Spanish. 1990. q. **Document type:** *Magazine, Consumer.* **Description:** Devoted to the analysis of the problems of the South and of the evil called under-development, focusing its approach from an angle of international cooperation and solidarity.
Indexed: IIBP, RILM.
Published by: Solidaridad para el Desarrollo y la Paz, C La Palma 69, Madrid, 28015, Spain. FAX 34-91-5323029, http://sodepaz.es.

CUADERNOS AMERICANOS; nueva epoca. *see* LITERATURE

CUADERNOS CRITICOS DE COMUNICACION Y CULTURA. *see* COMMUNICATIONS

300 PER
CUADERNOS DE CAPACITACION POPULAR. Text in Spanish. 1975. irreg., latest 1996. price varies. **Document type:** *Monographic series.*
Former titles: Cuadernos de Capacitacion Campesina; Cuadernos de Capacitacion Popular
Published by: Centro de Estudios Regionales Andinos "Bartolome de Las Casas", Pampa de la Alianza 164, Cusco, Peru. TEL 51-14-429992, FAX 51-14-427894. Pub. Andres Chirinos Rivera.

300 ESP ISSN 0210-847X
DP302.G11
CUADERNOS DE ESTUDIOS GALLEGOS. Text in Spanish. 1944. a. EUR 28.92 domestic; EUR 41.08 foreign (effective 2009). illus. back issues avail. **Document type:** *Monographic series, Academic/Scholarly.* **Description:** Includes thematic articles of archaeology, geography, ethnography, history and literature.
Related titles: Online - full text ed.: ISSN 1988-8333.
Indexed: FR, IBR, IBZ, MLA-IB, P09, P30, PCI.
—INIST.
Published by: Consejo Superior de Investigaciones Cientificas (C S I C), Departamento de Publicaciones, Vitruvio 8, Madrid, 28006, Spain. publ@csic.es, http://www.publicaciones.csic.es.

300 ARG ISSN 0326-6060
F2801
CUADERNOS DE HISTORIA REGIONAL. Text in Spanish. 1984. 4/yr. per issue exchange basis. bk.rev.
Indexed: IBR, IBZ.
Published by: (Universidad Nacional de Lujan, Departamento de Ciencias Sociales, Universidad Nacional de Lujan), Editorial Universitaria de Buenos Aires, Casilla de Correos 221, Lujan, Buenos Aires 6700, Argentina.

CUADERNOS DE HISTORIA. SERIE ECONOMIA Y SOCIEDAD. *see* HISTORY

300 ARG ISSN 0327-8115
AZ208.S62
CUADERNOS DE HUMANIDADES. Text in Spanish. 1989. a. **Document type:** *Monographic series, Academic/Scholarly.*
Published by: Universidad Nacional de Salta, Facultad de Humanidades, Av Bolivia 5150, Salta, 4400, Argentina. TEL 54-387-4255560, FAX 54-387-4255458, cdhum@unsa.edu.ar, http://www.unsa.edu.ar/humani/. Circ: 210.

300 COL ISSN 1794-7715
CUADERNOS DEL C I P E. (Centro de Investigaciones y Proyectos Especiales) Text in Spanish. irreg. **Document type:** *Monographic series, Academic/Scholarly.*
Published by: Universidad Externado de Colombia, Centro de Investigaciones y Proyectos Especiales, Calle 12 No. 1-17 Este, Bogota, Colombia.

300 MEX ISSN 1405-1966
CUADERNOS DEL SUR. Text in Spanish. 1992. q.
Indexed: AICP, AnthLit, BibLing, IPB, MLA-IB, SOPODA, SociolAb.
Published by: Instituto Nacional de Antropologia e Historia (I N A H), Cordoba 45, Mexico City 7, DF 06700, Mexico. TEL 52-50-619100, administracion.dg@inah.gob.mx, http://www.inah.gob.mx. **Co-sponsor:** Universidad Autonoma Benito Juarez de Oaxaca.

309 ESP ISSN 1889-9285
▼ **CUADERNOS KORE**; revista de historia y pensamiento de genero. Text in Spanish. 2009. s-a. back issues avail. **Document type:** *Journal, Academic/Scholarly.*
Related titles: Online - full text ed.: ISSN 1989-7391. 2009.
Published by: Grupo Kore de Estudios de Genero, C Madrid, 126, Getafe, Madrid, 28903, Spain. TEL 34-91-6249336, grupo.kore@gmail.com, http://www.grupokore.es/.

300 VEN ISSN 1315-4176
➤ **CUADERNOS LATINOAMERICANOS.** Text in Spanish; Summaries in English, Spanish. 1990. s-a. bibl.; charts; stat. **Document type:** *Monographic series, Academic/Scholarly.* **Description:** Contains information and analysis about Latin-American realities: social, political, historical and more.
Related titles: Diskette ed.
Published by: Universidad del Zulia, Centro Experimental de Estudios Latinoamericanos, Sector Grano de Oro, entre DPF y DIMO, Maracaibo, Venezuela. TEL 61-596752, FAX 61-596753. Pub. Italo Oliveros. Circ: 1,000.

➤ **CUADERNOS MEDICO SOCIALES.** *see* MEDICAL SCIENCES

➤ **CULTURA NACIONAL**; revista bimestrale de politica y ciencias sociales. *see* POLITICAL SCIENCE

300 BRA ISSN 0104-222X
AP66
CULTURA VOZES. Cover title: Vozes Cultura. Text in Portuguese. 1907. bi-m. **Document type:** *Magazine, Consumer.*
Former titles (until 1992): Revista de Cultura Vozes (0100-7076); (until 1969): Vozes de Petropolis (1413-6287)
Indexed: H21, MLA-IB, OTA, P08, RASB.
Published by: Editora Vozes Ltda., Rua Mexico 174, Rio de Janeiro, RJ 20031 143, Brazil. TEL 55-21-22156386, FAX 55-21-25338358, vozes42@uol.com.br, http://www.editoravozes.com.br.

300 DEU ISSN 1868-8713
▼ **CULTURAE.** Text in German. 2009. irreg., latest vol.3, 2010. price varies. **Document type:** *Monographic series, Academic/Scholarly.*
Published by: Harrassowitz Verlag, Kreuzberger Ring 7b-d, Wiesbaden, 65205, Germany. TEL 49-611-5300, FAX 49-611-530560, verlag@harrassowitz.de, http://www.harrassowitz.de.

300 001.3 USA ISSN 1530-9568
CULTURAL CRITIQUE (NEW YORK). Text in English. 2002. irreg., latest vol.6, 2006. price varies. **Document type:** *Monographic series, Academic/Scholarly.* **Description:** Creates a space for the study of those global cultural practices and cultural forms that shape the meanings of self, identity, race, ethnicity, class, nationality, and gender in the contemporary world.
Published by: Peter Lang Publishing, Inc. (Subsidiary of: Peter Lang Publishing Group), 29 Broadway, New York, NY 10006. TEL 212-647-7700, 800-770-5264, FAX 212-647-7707, customerservice@plang.com, http://www.peterlangusa.com. Ed. Norm Denzin.

CULTURAL IDENTITY STUDIES. *see* LITERATURE

300 GBR ISSN 1662-0364
CULTURAL INTERACTIONS; studies in the relationship between the arts. Text in English. 2007. irreg., latest vol.20, 2010. price varies. **Document type:** *Monographic series, Academic/Scholarly.*
Published by: Peter Lang Ltd. (Subsidiary of: Peter Lang Publishing Group), Evenlode Ct, Main Rd, Long Hanborough, Oxfordshire OX29 8SZ, United Kingdom. TEL 44-1993-880088, FAX 44-1993-882040, info@peterlang.com. Ed. J Bullen.

CULTURAL POLITICS. *see* POLITICAL SCIENCE

CULTURAL POLITICS SERIES. *see* POLITICAL SCIENCE

300 AUS ISSN 1836-0416
➤ **CULTURAL SCIENCE.** Text in English. 2008. irreg. (2/yr. in 2008). free (effective 2009). bk.rev. Index. back issues avail. **Document type:** *Journal, Academic/Scholarly.*
Media: Online - full content.
Address: Queensland University of Technology, Creative Industries Precinct, Z1-515, Musk Avenue, Kelvin Grove, QLD 4059, Australia. TEL 61-7-31385605, FAX 61-7-31383723.

S

399 DEU
CULTURAL STUDIES. Text in German. 2001. irreg., latest vol.35, 2011. price varies. **Document type:** *Monographic series, Academic/ Scholarly.*
Published by: Transcript, Muehlenstr 47, Bielefeld, 33607, Germany. TEL 49-521-63454, FAX 49-521-61040, live@transcript-verlag.de.

CULTURAL STUDIES - CRITICAL METHODOLOGIES. *see* LITERATURE

300 800 AUS ISSN 1837-8692
➤ **CULTURAL STUDIES REVIEW (ONLINE).** Text in English. 1995. s-a. free (effective 2011). adv. back issues avail. **Document type:** *Journal, Academic/Scholarly.* **Description:** Provides a forum for the critical discussion of academic and creative writing on cultural studies, with a regionalist perspective.
Media: Online - full text.
Published by: (Melbourne University Publishing Ltd.), University of Technology, Sydney, PO Box 123, Broadway, NSW 2007, Australia. TEL 61-2-95142000, publications@uts.edu.au, http://www.uts.edu.au. Eds. John Frow, Katrina Schlunke.

300 DEU ISSN 1613-902X
CULTURE AND KNOWLEDGE. Text in English. 2005. irreg., latest vol.12, 2010. price varies. **Document type:** *Monographic series, Academic/ Scholarly.*
Published by: Peter Lang GmbH (Subsidiary of: Peter Lang Publishing Group), Eschborner Landstr 42-50, Frankfurt Am Main, 60489, Germany. TEL 49-69-7807050, FAX 49-69-78070550, zentrale.frankfurt@peterlang.com. Ed. Friedrich Wallner.

300 GBR ISSN 1475-9551 CODEN: SCOSF3
➤ **CULTURE AND ORGANIZATION.** Text in English. 1995. q. GBP 318 combined subscription in United Kingdom to institutions (print & online eds.); EUR 340, USD 425 combined subscription to institutions (print & online eds.) (effective 2012). adv. back issues avail.; reprint service avail. from PSC. **Document type:** *Journal, Academic/Scholarly.* **Description:** Features articles that offers papers which employ ethnographic, critical and interpretive approaches, as practised in such disciplines as communication, media and cultural studies, which go beyond description and use data to advance theoretical reflection.
Formerly (until 2002): Studies in Cultures, Organizations & Societies (1024-5286)
Related titles: Online - full text ed.: ISSN 1477-2760. GBP 286 in United Kingdom to institutions; EUR 306, USD 383 to institutions (effective 2012) (from IngentaConnect).
Indexed: A01, A03, A08, A22, B01, B06, B07, B09, CA, CurCont, E01, IBSS, S02, S03, SCOPUS, SSCI, SociolAb, T02, W07.
—IE, Ingenta. **CCC.**
Published by: Routledge (Subsidiary of: Taylor & Francis Group), 4 Park Sq, Milton Park, Abingdon, Oxon OX14 4RN, United Kingdom. TEL 44-20-70176000, FAX 44-20-70176336, subscriptions@tandf.co.uk, http://www.routledge.com/journals/. Eds. Peter Case, Simon Lilley. Adv. contact Linda Hann TEL 44-1344-779945. **Subscr. to:** Taylor & Francis Ltd., Journals Customer Service, Sheepen Pl, Colchester, Essex CO3 3LP, United Kingdom. TEL 44-20-70175544, FAX 44-20-70175198.

300 DEU
CULTURE AREA KARAKORUM. Text in English, German. 1998. irreg., latest vol.12, 2008. price varies. **Document type:** *Monographic series, Academic/Scholarly.*
Published by: Ruediger Koeppe Verlag, Wendelinstr 73-75, Cologne, 50933, Germany. TEL 49-221-4911236, FAX 49-221-4994336, info@koeppe.de. Ed. Irmtraud Stellrecht.

300 DEU ISSN 1864-4120
CULTURE - DISCOURSE - HISTORY. Text in German. 2008. irreg. price varies. **Document type:** *Monographic series, Academic/Scholarly.*
Published by: Logos Verlag Berlin, Comeniushof, Gubener Str 47, Berlin, 10243, Germany. TEL 49-30-42851090, FAX 49-30-42851092, redaktion@logos-verlag.de. Eds. Jan Standke, Thomas Duello.

300 USA ISSN 1544-3159
➤ **CULTURE, SOCIETY & PRAXIS.** Text in English. 2002. s-a. free (effective 2011). back issues avail. **Document type:** *Journal, Academic/Scholarly.*
Media: Online - full text.
Indexed: A39, C27, C29, D03, D04, E13, R14, S02, S03, S14, S15, S18.
Published by: California State University, Monterey Bay, Social and Behavioral Sciences Institute, 100 Campus Ctr Dr, Seaside, CA 93955. TEL 831-582-3000, FAX 831-582-3566, http://sbsi.csumb.edu. Eds. Juan J Gutierrez, Mehni Gonzalez, Paul R Alexander.

300 001.3 GBR ISSN 1473-5784
AS121
➤ **CULTURE, THEORY AND CRITIQUE.** Text in English. 1957. 3/yr. GBP 330 combined subscription in United Kingdom to institutions (print & online eds.); EUR 430, USD 539 combined subscription to institutions (print & online eds.) (effective 2012). adv. back issues avail.; reprint service avail. from PSC. **Document type:** *Journal, Academic/ Scholarly.* **Description:** Aims to critique and reconstruct theories by interfacing them with one another and by relocating them in new sites and conjunctures.
Formerly (until 2002): Renaissance and Modern Studies (0486-3720)
Related titles: Online - full text ed.: ISSN 1473-5776. GBP 296 in United Kingdom to institutions; EUR 387, USD 485 to institutions (effective 2012) (from IngentaConnect).
Indexed: A01, A03, A08, A22, AmHI, CA, E01, FR, H07, HistAb, I14, IBR, IBSS, IBZ, MLA-IB, P30, PCI, RILM, T02.
—BLDSC (3491.669438), IE, Infotrieve, Ingenta, INIST. **CCC.**
Published by: Routledge (Subsidiary of: Taylor & Francis Group), 4 Park Square, Milton Park, Abingdon, Oxon OX14 4RN, United Kingdom. subscriptions@tandf.co.uk, http://www.routledge.com. Adv. contact Linda Hann TEL 44-1344-779945. **Subscr. to:** Taylor & Francis Ltd., Journals Customer Service, Sheepen Pl, Colchester, Essex CO3 3LP, United Kingdom. TEL 44-20-70175544, FAX 44-20-70175198, tf.enquiries@tfinforma.com.

302 ESP ISSN 1130-7749
CULTURES. Text in Spanish. 1991. s-a. back issues avail.
Published by: Academia de la Llingua Asturiana/Academy of the Asturian Language, C L'Aguila, 10, Asturias, 33080, Spain. TEL 34-985-211837, FAX 34-985-226816, alla@asturnet.es, http://www.academiadelallingua.com.

CULTURES IN AMERICA IN TRANSITION. *see* LITERATURE

300 AUS ISSN 1323-191X
CULTURESCOPE. Text in English. 1994. 3/yr. free to members. **Document type:** *Journal, Academic/Scholarly.*
Published by: Society & Culture Association, PO Box 577, Leichhardt, NSW 2040, Australia. TEL 61-2-95643322, FAX 61-2-95642342, culturescope@hotmail.com.

300 USA
CURRENT ISSUES: REFERENCE SHELF PLUS. Text in English. 2006. d. USD 670 (effective 2011). **Document type:** *Abstract/Index.*
Published by: H.W. Wilson, 950 University Ave, Bronx, NY 10452. TEL 718-588-8400, 800-367-6770, FAX 718-590-1617, 800-590-1617, custserv@hwwilson.com, http://www.hwwilson.com.

300 GBR ISSN 2041-3238
▼ **CURRENT RESEARCH JOURNAL OF SOCIAL SCIENCE.** Text in English. 2009. bi-m. **Document type:** *Journal, Academic/Scholarly.*
Related titles: Online - full text ed.: ISSN 2041-3246. free (effective 2011).
Published by: Maxwell Science Publications Ed. Afshan Akbar.

300 AUS ISSN 1037-728X
CURRENT SOCIAL ISSUES. Text in English. 1992. 20/yr. AUD 135 (effective 2009). Index. back issues avail. **Document type:** *Journal, Trade.* **Description:** Features informative news articles on civil rights, road safety, terrorism, biotechnology and poverty.
Related titles: Online - full text ed.: free (effective 2009).
Published by: Current Information Services, PO Box 274, Curtin, ACT 2605, Australia. info@currentinformation.com.au.

300 CYP ISSN 1015-2881
DS54.A2 CODEN: CYREEL
THE CYPRUS REVIEW; a journal of social, economic and political issues. Text in English. 1989. s-a. adv. bk.rev. **Document type:** *Journal, Academic/Scholarly.* **Description:** Deals exclusively with issues concerning social, economic, and political issues of Cyprus life.
Related titles: Online - full text ed.
Indexed: A12, A17, ABIn, CA, DIP, EconLit, FR, I13, IBR, IBSS, IBZ, IBibSS, JEL, L11, M10, P10, P27, P34, P42, P48, P51, P53, P54, PAIS, PCI, PQC, PRA, PSA, S02, S03, SCOPUS, SOPODA, SSA, SociolAb, T02.
—BLDSC (3506.733300), IE, Ingenta, INIST.
Published by: Intercollege - Research and Development Center, University of Nicosia, 46 Makedonitissas Ave, P O Box 24005, Nicosia, 1700, Cyprus. TEL 357-22-841555, FAX 357-22-353682, cy_review@unic.ac.cy, research@unic.ac.cy. Ed. Hubert Faustmann. adv.: B&W page USD 200.

300 POL ISSN 0239-3271
H8
➤ **CZLOWIEK I SPOLECZENSTWO.** Text in Polish; Text occasionally in English. 1984. irreg., latest vol.29, 2009. price varies. bk.rev. back issues avail. **Document type:** *Journal, Academic/Scholarly.* **Description:** Covers psychology, sociology and education.
Indexed: E-psyche.
Published by: (Uniwersytet im. Adama Mickiewicza w Poznaniu, Instytut Socjologii/Institute of Sociology), Wydawnictwo Naukowe Uniwersytetu im. Adama Mickiewicza/Adam Mickiewicz University Press, ul Fredry 10, Poznan, 61701, Poland. TEL 48-61-8294646, FAX 48-61-8294647, press@amu.edu.pl, http://press.amu.edu.pl. Ed. Grzegorz Dziamski. Circ: 300.

➤ **D L S U DIALOGUE.** *see* HUMANITIES: COMPREHENSIVE WORKS

▼➤ **D O C T - U S.** *see* HUMANITIES: COMPREHENSIVE WORKS

300 BRA ISSN 0011-5258
H8
➤ **DADOS;** revista de ciencias sociais. Text in Portuguese; Summaries in English, French. 1966. q. BRL 25 to individuals; BRL 50 to institutions (effective 1999). bk.rev. bibl.; charts. index, cum.index: 1966-1972. back issues avail.; reprints avail. **Document type:** *Academic/ Scholarly.*
Related titles: Online - full text ed.: free (effective 2011).
Indexed: A20, ASCA, BibInd, C01, CA, CurCont, FR, H21, I13, IBR, IBZ, P08, P42, PSA, RASB, S02, S03, SCOPUS, SOPODA, SSA, SSCI, SociolAb, T02, W07.
Published by: Instituto Universitario de Pesquisas do Rio de Janeiro, Rua da Matriz, 82, Botafogo, Rio De Janeiro, RJ 22260-100, Brazil. TEL 55-21-5378020, FAX 55-21-2867146. Eds. Amaury de Souza, Charles Pessanha. Circ: 4,000.

300 CHN
DALIAN DAXUE XUEBAO/DALIAN UNIVERSITY. JOURNAL. Text in Chinese. 1980. bi-m. CNY 4 newsstand/cover (effective 2006). **Document type:** *Journal, Academic/Scholarly.*
Related titles: Online - full text ed.
Published by: Dalian Daxue, Jingji Jishu Kaifa-qu, Dalian, 116622, China. TEL 86-411-87402179.

300 CHN ISSN 1671-7031
AS452.D34
DALIAN HAISHI DAXUE XUEBAO (SHEHUI KEXUE BAN)/DALIAN MARITIME UNIVERSITY. JOURNAL. Variant title: Dalian Haishi Daxue Wenke Xuebao. Text in Chinese. 1957. q. **Document type:** *Journal, Academic/Scholarly.*
Related titles: Online - full text ed.
Published by: Dalian Haishi Daxue Qikanshe, 7, Gangwan St., Rm.401, Times Bldg., Dalian, 116001, China. TEL 82-411-84726982, FAX 86-411-84729692.

300 CHN ISSN 1008-407X
AS452.D34
DALIAN LIGONG DAXUE XUEBAO (SHEHUI KEXUE BAN)/DALIAN UNIVERSITY OF TECHNOLOGY. JOURNAL (SOCIAL SCIENCES). Text in Chinese. 1980. q. CNY 5 newsstand/cover (effective 2004). **Document type:** *Journal, Academic/Scholarly.*
Related titles: Online - full text ed.
Indexed: CA, L&LBA, P42, PSA, S02, S03, SCOPUS, SociolAb, T02.
Published by: Dalian Ligong Daxue/Dalian University of Technology, No.2 Linggong Road, Ganjingzi District, Dalian City, Liaoning Province 116024, China. TEL 86-411-4708405, http://www.dlut.edu.cn/.

300 AUT
DAMIT ES NICHT VERLORENGEHT. Text in German. 1983. irreg., latest vol.65, 2011. price varies. **Document type:** *Monographic series, Academic/Scholarly.*
Published by: Boehlau Verlag GmbH & Co.KG., Wiesingerstr 1, Vienna, W 1010, Austria. TEL 43-1-3302427, FAX 43-1-3302432, boehlau@boehlau.at, http://www.boehlau.at.

DAOJIANG XUEBAO. *see* TECHNOLOGY: COMPREHENSIVE WORKS

300 CHN ISSN 1002-2341
DAQING SHEHUI KEXUE/DAQING SOCIAL SCIENCES. Text in Chinese. 1982. bi-m. CNY 36 domestic; USD 17.40 foreign (effective 2005). **Document type:** *Journal, Academic/Scholarly.*
Related titles: Online - full text ed.
Published by: Daqing Shi Shehui Kexue Lianhehui, Zhengfulou 3407-shi, Daqing, 163002, China. TEL 86-459-4666175, FAX 86-459-4666883. **Dist. by:** China International Book Trading Corp, 35 Chegongzhuang Xilu, Haidian District, PO Box 399, Beijing 100044, China. TEL 86-10-68412045, FAX 86-10-68412023, cibtc@mail.cibtc.com.cn, http://www.cibtc.com.cn.

300 500 CHN ISSN 2095-0063
➤ **DAQING SHIFAN XUEYUAN XUEBAO/DAQING NORMAL UNIVERSITY. JOURNAL.** Text in Chinese. 1988. bi-m. CNY 90, USD 90; USD 15 per issue (effective 2011 & 2012). abstr.; charts; stat. 112 p./no.; back issues avail.; reprints avail. **Document type:** *Journal, Academic/Scholarly.* **Description:** Issues 1, 2 & 4 covers philosophy and social sciences, including political science, social science, economics, law, literature, linguistics, history and cultural studies. Issues 3 & 6 covers natural sciences, including engineering, mathematics, physics, chemistry, material science, geography, environmental science, physical and life sciences.
Former titles (until 2010): Daqing Gaodeng Zhuanke Xuexiao Xuebao/ Daqing Advanced College. Journal (1006-2165); (until 1993): Daqing Shi-zhuan Xuebao/Daqing Teacher's College. Journal (1001-0246); Which was formed by the merger of (1982-1988): Daqing Shi-zhuan Xuebao (Zhexue Shehue Kexue Ban)/Daqing Teacher's College. (Philosophy and Social Sciences Edition). Journal; (1982-1988): Daqing Shi-zhuan Xuebao (Ziran Kexue Ban)/Daqing Teacher's College. (Natural Science Edition). Journal; Both of which superseded in part (1980-1982): Shifan Xuekan
—East View.
Published by: Daqing Shifan Xueyuan Xuebao Bianjibu, Xibin Xi Lu, Ranghulu-qu, Daqing, Heilongjiang 163712, China. TEL 86-459-5510135, FAX 86-459-5510135. Ed. Li Sui. Circ: 1,000. **Dist. overseas by:** China International Book Trading Corp, 35 Chegongzhuang Xilu, Haidian District, PO Box 399, Beijing 100044, China. TEL 86-10-68412045, FAX 86-10-68412023, cibtc@mail.cibtc.com.cn, http://www.cibtc.com.cn.

300 CHN ISSN 1009-9883
DASHIYE/BIG VIEW. Text in Chinese. 2001. m. **Document type:** *Journal, Academic/Scholarly.*
Published by: Hu'nan Renmin Chubanshe/Hunan People's Publishing House, 3, Yingpan Dong Lu, Changsha, 410005, China. TEL 86-731-2683371, FAX 86-731-2683305, http://www.hnppp.com/index.asp.

300 USA
➤ **DEAR HABERMAS.** Text in English. 1998. w. free (effective 2010). **Document type:** *Journal, Academic/Scholarly.* **Description:** Provides forum for students and their faculty that provides sociological and philosophical discussions of law, gender, the privileging of subjectivity, forgiveness in the interest of good faith public discourse, intertextuality and our role in the creation of texts.
Media: Online - full text.
Published by: California State University, Department of Sociology, 6000 J St, Sacramento, CA 95819. TEL 916-278-6522, FAX 916-278-6281, soc-sc@csus.edu, http://www.csus.edu/soc.

300 VEN ISSN 1316-1296
HC236
DEBATES I E S A. Text in Spanish. bi-m. **Document type:** *Journal, Academic/Scholarly.*
Indexed: A01, B01, B07, CA, F03, F04, T02.
Published by: Instituto de Estudios Superiores de Administracion, San Bernardino, Caracas, 1010-A, Venezuela. Ed. Jose Malave.

300 HUN ISSN 1218-022X
DEBRECENI SZEMLE. Text in Hungarian. 1927-1989; N.S. 1993. q. HUF 300.
Indexed: RASB, RILM.
Published by: Debreceni Egyetem, Egyetem ter 1, Debrecen, 4032, Hungary. TEL 36-52-412177, FAX 36-52-410909. Ed. Peter Gunst.

300 900 400 IND ISSN 0045-9801
DECCAN COLLEGE. POSTGRADUATE & RESEARCH INSTITUTE. BULLETIN. Text in English. 1939. a., latest vol.69, 2009. free (effective 2011). bk.rev. back issues avail. **Document type:** *Bulletin, Trade.*
Related titles: Microfiche ed.: (from IDC).
Indexed: BAS, BibLing, DIP, IBR, IBZ, MLA-IB, RASB, SpeleolAb.
Published by: Deccan College, Postgraduate & Research Institute, Deccan College Rd, Yerwada, Pune, Maharashtra 411006, India. TEL 91-20-26513204, info@deccancollegepune.ac.in. Circ: 500.

300 ARG ISSN 0328-0101
HV6881
DELITO Y SOCIEDAD; revista de ciencias sociales. Text in Spanish. 1992. s-a. **Document type:** *Academic/Scholarly.*
Published by: Universidad de Buenos Aires, Facultad de Ciencias Sociales, Marcelo T. de Alvear, 2230, Buenos Aires, 1122, Argentina. TEL 54-11-45083800, http://www.fsoc.uba.ar. Ed. Juan S Pegoraro. **Co-sponsor:** Centro de Informatica Aplicada.

302 USA ISSN 1555-8967
➤ **DEMOCRATIC COMMUNIQUE.** Text in English. 1986. s-a. USD 25 to individuals; USD 65 to institutions; free to members (effective 2010). Index. back issues avail. **Document type:** *Journal, Academic/ Scholarly.* **Description:** Presents scholarly analyses of mass media institutions and social and communicative phenomena.
Formerly (until 2001): U D C Communique Newsletter
Indexed: CA, CMM, CommAb, P42, T02.
—**CCC.**
Published by: Union for Democratic Communications, School of Communication and Multimedia Studies, Florida Atlantic University, 777 Glades Rd, GCS 238, Boca Raton, FL 33431. Jennifer.Proffitt@comm.fsu.edu, http://www.democraticcommunications.org.

➤ **DEMOS COLLECTION.** *see* POLITICAL SCIENCE

➤ **DEMOS. PUBLICATIONS.** *see* POLITICAL SCIENCE

300 DEU ISSN 1867-6413
DENKSTROEME: Journal der Saechsischen Akademie der Wissenschaften. Text in German. 2008. 2/yr. EUR 30 (effective 2011). **Document type:** *Journal, Academic/Scholarly.*
Related titles: Online - full text ed.: ISSN 1867-7061. 2008. free (effective 2011).
Published by: Leipziger Universitaetsverlag GmbH, Oststr 41, Leipzig, 04317, Germany. TEL 49-341-9900440, FAX 49-341-9900440, info@univerlag-leipzig.de.

DERECHO Y CIENCIAS SOCIALES. *see* LAW

▼ **DERECHO Y CIENCIAS SOCIALES.** *see* LAW

300 GBR ISSN 1754-8500
➤ **DERRIDA TODAY.** Text in English. 2008. s-a. GBP 83 domestic to institutions; USD 163 in North America to institutions; GBP 88 elsewhere to institutions; GBP 104 combined subscription domestic to institutions (print & online eds.); USD 203 combined subscription in North America to institutions (print & online eds.); GBP 110 combined subscription elsewhere to institutions (print & online eds.) (effective 2012). adv. back issues avail.; reprints avail. **Document type:** *Journal, Academic/Scholarly.* **Description:** Focuses on what Derrida's thought offers to contemporary debates about politics, society and global affairs.
Related titles: Online - full text ed.: ISSN 1754-8519. USD 138 in North America to institutions; GBP 75 elsewhere to institutions (effective 2012).
Indexed: AmHI, CA, H07, L06, MLA-IB, T02.
—**CCC.**
Published by: Edinburgh University Press, 22 George Sq, Edinburgh, Scotland EH8 9LF, United Kingdom. TEL 44-131-6504218, FAX 44-131-6503286, journals@eup.ed.ac.uk. Eds. Nick Mansfield, Nicole Anderson. Adv. contact Ruth Allison TEL 44-131-6504220.

▼ ➤ **DESIGN AND CULTURE.** *see* ART

300 DEU ISSN 0944-3649
DEUTSCH-FRANZOESISCHE KULTURBIBLIOTHEK. Text in German. 1993. irreg., latest vol.28, 2009. price varies. **Document type:** *Monographic series, Academic/Scholarly.*
Published by: Leipziger Universitaetsverlag GmbH, Oststr 41, Leipzig, 04317, Germany. TEL 49-341-9900440, FAX 49-341-9900440, info@univerlag-leipzig.de, http://www.univerlag-leipzig.de.

300 AUT
DEUTSCHES HYGIENE-MUSEUM DRESDEN. SCHRIFTEN. Text in German. 2003. irreg., latest vol.9, 2011. price varies. **Document type:** *Monographic series, Academic/Scholarly.*
Published by: (Deutsches Hygiene-Museum Dresden DEU), Boehlau Verlag GmbH & Co.KG., Wiesingerstr 1, Vienna, W 1010, Austria. TEL 43-1-3302427, FAX 43-1-3302432, boehlau@boehlau.at, http://www.boehlau.at.

320 DEU ISSN 0012-1428
DD261
DEUTSCHLAND ARCHIV; Zeitschrift fuer das vereinigte Deutschland. Text in German. 1950. q. EUR 49 (effective 2011). adv. bk.rev. charts. index. **Document type:** *Journal, Academic/Scholarly.*
Former titles (until 1968): S B Z Archiv (0563-0894); (until 1952): P Z Archiv (0174-9471)
Indexed: CERDIC, DIP, IBR, IBSS, IBZ, MLA-IB, P30, PAIS, PRA, RASB.
Published by: W. Bertelsmann Verlag GmbH & Co. KG, Postfach 100633, Bielefeld, 33506, Germany. TEL 49-521-911010, FAX 49-521-9110179, service@wbv.de. Ed. Dr. Marc-Dietrich Ohse. Circ: 5,200 (paid and controlled).

300 DEU
▼ **DEUTSCHLAND UND FRANKREICH IM WISSENSCHAFTLICHEN DIALOG/DIALOGUE SCIENTIFIQUE FRANCO-ALLEMAND.** Text in German, French. 2009. irreg. price varies. **Document type:** *Monographic series, Academic/Scholarly.*
Published by: V & R Unipress GmbH (Subsidiary of: Vandenhoeck und Ruprecht), Robert-Bosch-Breite 6, Goettingen, 37079, Germany. TEL 49-551-5084303, FAX 49-551-5084333, info@vr-unipress.de, http://www.v-r.de/en/publisher/unipress.

DEVELOPMENT AND SOCIETY. *see* POPULATION STUDIES

300 AUS ISSN 1035-1132
HC59.69
DEVELOPMENT BULLETIN (CANBERRA). Text in English. 1976. q. AUD 88 domestic to individuals; AUD 100 foreign to individuals; AUD 220 to institutions; AUD 66 domestic to students; AUD 70 foreign to students; AUD 25 per issue domestic; AUD 35 per issue foreign (effective 2009). bk.rev. abstr.; bibl. back issues avail. **Document type:** *Journal, Academic/Scholarly.* **Description:** Provides information on development issues, development research, and development-related courses, summaries of national and international conferences, information on development-related organizations and recent publications and other resources.
Former titles (until 1989): Australian Development Studies Network. Newsletter; (until Nov.1985): Australian National University. National Centre for Development Studies. Newsletter (0815-6247); (until Jun.1985): Australian National University. Development Studies Centre. Newsletter (0313-9980)
Related titles: Online - full text ed.: free (effective 2009).
Indexed: A36, AICP, APEL, C25, CABA, E12, ESPM, F08, F11, F12, GH, H16, HPNRM, IBSS, LT, N02, PHN&I, R12, RRTA, SCOPUS, SSciA, T05, W11.
—Ingenta. **CCC.**
Published by: Development Studies Network Ltd., Australian National University, Research School of Pacific & Asian Studie, 7 Liversidge St, Canberra, ACT 0200, Australia. TEL 61-2-61252466, FAX 61-2-61259785, devnetwork@anu.edu.au, http://devnet.anu.edu.au.

300 338.91 FRA ISSN 1951-0012
DEVELOPPEMENT ET CIVILISATIONS. Text in French. 1960. m. (10/yr.). bk.rev. bibl. back issues avail. **Document type:** *Journal, Consumer.*
Formerly (until 2006): Foi et Developpement (0339-0462); (until 1973): Developpement et Civilisations (0012-1657)
Indexed: CERDIC, FR, P30.
Published by: Centre International Lebret - Irfed, 48 Rue de la Glaciere, Paris, 75013, France. TEL 33-1-47071007, FAX 33-1-47076866, http://www.lebret-irfed.org/fr. Ed. M Regazzoni.

DEZEME; revista de historia e ciencias sociais da Fundacion 10 de Marzo. *see* HISTORY

DHAKA UNIVERSITY STUDIES. PART A: ARTS, HUMANITIES, AND SOCIAL SCIENCE. *see* HUMANITIES: COMPREHENSIVE WORKS

300 MEX ISSN 0185-7770
DIALECTICA. Text in Spanish. 1976-1986; resumed 1987. 4/yr. MXN 75, USD 40. bk.rev. back issues avail. **Description:** Covers philosophy, social sciences, literature, culture and politics.
Indexed: AltPI, C01, RASB.
Published by: Benemerita Universidad Autonoma de Puebla, Facultad de Filosofia y Letras, 3 Oriente No 210, Puebla, 72000, Mexico. http://www.buap.mx. Circ: 3,000.

300 COL ISSN 2011-3501
DIALECTICA LIBERTADORA. Text in Spanish. 2007. a. **Document type:** *Journal, Academic/Scholarly.*
Published by: Fundacion Universitaria los Libertadores, Departamento de Formacion Humana y Social, Carrera 16 No. 63A-68, Bogota, Colombia. TEL 57-1-2544750, webmaster@libertadores.edu.co, http://www.ulibertadores.edu.co/.

300 AUT
DIALOG. BEITRAEGE ZUR FRIEDENSFORSCHUNG. Text in German. q. USD 51.50. **Document type:** *Academic/Scholarly.*
Published by: Oesterreichisches Studienzentrum fuer Frieden und Konfliktloesung, Burg, Stadtschlaining, B 7461, Austria.

DIALOG ERZIEHUNGSHILFE. *see* EDUCATION—Special Education And Rehabilitation

300 DEU ISSN 1860-7861
DIALOG UND DISKURS. Text in German. 2004. irreg., latest vol.13, 2008. price varies. **Document type:** *Monographic series, Academic/Scholarly.*
Published by: Paulo Freire Verlag, Unterm Berg 65a, Oldenburg, 26123, Germany. TEL 49-441-381674, FAX 49-441-9330056, pfv@freire.de, http://www.paulo-freire-verlag.de.

301 CHL ISSN 0716-2278
DIALOGO ANDINO. Text in Spanish; Summaries in English, Spanish. 1982. a. USD 10 (effective 2001). **Document type:** *Academic/Scholarly.* **Description:** Contains results of research involving the Andes in the areas of ethnography, anthropology and social sciences.
Related titles: Online - full text ed.
Indexed: H21, P08.
Published by: Universidad de Tarapaca, Facultad de Educacion y Humanidades, 18 de Septiembre No. 2222, Casilla 2-D, Arica, Chile. TEL 56-58-205257, FAX 56-58-205251, http://dialogoandino.8m.com. Ed., R&P Luis Alvarez. Circ: 100 (paid); 400 (controlled); 100 (free).

300 150 ARG ISSN 1852-8481
▼ **DIALOGOS**; revista cientifica de psicologia, ciencias sociales, humanidades y ciencias de la salud. Text in Spanish. 2009. irreg. **Document type:** *Monographic series, Academic/Scholarly.*
Related titles: Online - full text ed.
Published by: Universidad Nacional de San Luis, Facultad de Ciencias Humanas, Avenida Ejercito de los Andes 950, IV Bloque, San Luis, 5700, Argentina. TEL 54-652-30224, 54-652-435512, http://humanas.unsl.edu.ar/. Ed. Marcelo Munoz.

300 BRA ISSN 1677-6488
➤ **DIALOGOS.** Text in Portuguese; Summaries in English, Portuguese. 2002. s-a. BRL 20 (effective 2008). bk.rev. abstr.; bibl.; charts; illus.; maps; stat.; tr.lit. Index. back issues avail. **Document type:** *Journal, Academic/Scholarly.* **Description:** Contains multidisciplinary works on social sciences from researchers and educators.
Published by: Universidade do Oeste de Santa Catarina (UNOESC), Rua Getulio Vargas, 2125, Bairro Flor da Serra, Joacaba, Santa Catarina CEP 89600, Brazil. TEL 55-49-35512065, FAX 55-49-35512004, editora@unoesc.edu.br. Ed., Pub. Claudio Luiz Orco.

300 001.3 PAK ISSN 1819-6462
DS376
➤ **THE DIALOGUE.** Text in English. 2006. q. PKR 700 domestic; USD 40 foreign; free to qualified personnel (effective 2009). bk.rev. Index. back issues avail. **Document type:** *Journal, Academic/Scholarly.* **Description:** Covers various culture and society topics such as human rights, social justice, law, education, religion, and politics.
Related titles: Online - full text ed.
Indexed: A01, A26, I05, T02.
Published by: Qurtuba University of Science & Information Technology, K-1, Phase III, Hayatabad, Peshawar, North-West Frontier Province, Pakistan. TEL 92-91-5812117, FAX 92-91-5825837, info@qurtuba.edu.pk. Eds. Qadar Bakhsh Baloch, Muhammad Saleem. R&P Qadar Bakhsh Baloch. Circ: 700 (paid); 300 (controlled).

300 CHN
DIANZI KEJI DAXUE XUEBAO (SHEHUI KEXUE XUEBAO)/ UNIVERSITY OF ELECTRONIC SCIENCE AND TECHNOLOGY OF CHINA. JOURNAL (SOCIAL SCIENCES EDITION). Text in English. 1999. bi-m. CNY 6 newsstand/cover (effective 2006). **Document type:** *Journal, Academic/Scholarly.*
Related titles: Online - full text ed.
Published by: Dianzi Keji Daxue/University of Electronic Science and Technology of China, Main Bldg., Rm.219, No.4, Section 2, N. Jianshe Rd., Chengdu, Sichuan 610054, China. TEL 86-28-83201443, http://www.uestc.edu.cn.

300 325 CAN ISSN 1044-2057
JV6001.A1 CODEN: DIASFE
➤ **DIASPORA**; a journal of transnational studies. Text in English. 1990. 3/yr. USD 68 in North America to institutions; USD 88 elsewhere to institutions (effective 2011). adv. illus. 160 p./no.; reprint service avail. from PSC. **Document type:** *Journal, Academic/Scholarly.* **Description:** Publishes essays on diasporas and other transnational and infranational phenomena that challenge the homogeneity of the nation-state. Includes specific accounts of ancient and contemporary diasporal communities, of their relations with real and imagined homelands, as well as their literatures, cultural productions, social structures, politics, and history.
Related titles: Online - full text ed.: ISSN 1911-1568.
Indexed: A01, A03, A08, A22, ABS&EES, AltPI, BAS, BibInd, C03, C05, C32, CA, CBCARef, E01, I14, IBSS, MLA-IB, P34, P42, P47, P48, PAIS, PCI, PQC, PSA, RILM, S02, S03, SCOPUS, SOPODA, SSA, SociolAb, T02.
—BLDSC (3580.230000), IE, Ingenta. **CCC.**
Published by: (Zoryan Institute), University of Toronto Press, Journals Division, 5201 Dufferin St, Toronto, ON M3H 5T8, Canada. TEL 416-667-7810, FAX 416-667-7881, journals@utpress.utoronto.ca. Ed. Jeremy W Crampton. R&P Jessica Shulist TEL 416-667-7777 ext 7849. Adv. contact Audrey Greenwood TEL 416-667-7777 ext 7766. Circ: 407.

300 ESP ISSN 0214-4379
DIDACTICA DE LAS CIENCIAS EXPERIMENTALES Y SOCIALES. Text in Spanish. 1989. a. **Document type:** *Journal, Academic/Scholarly.*
Published by: Universitat de Valencia, Departamento de Didactica de las Ciencias Experimentales y Sociales, Apdo. de Correos, 22045, Valencia, 46071, Spain. TEL 34-963-864483, FAX 34-963-864487, didacien@uv.es, http://www.uv.es/~diciex/cast.htm.

305.8 FRA ISSN 0247-9095
DIFFERENCES; magazine contre le racisme pour l'amitie entre les peuples. Text in French. 1949. m. bk.rev. **Document type:** *Magazine, Consumer.* **Description:** Current information and comments on racial-ethnic conflicts and various forms of action to suppress racism (law, education, mutual understanding).
Related titles: Online - full text ed.
Indexed: HRIR, IBSS, PerIslam.
Published by: Mouvement contre le Racisme et pour l'Amitie entre les Peuples (MRAP), 43 boulevard Magenta, Paris, 75010, France. TEL 33-1-53389999, FAX 33-1-40409098.

300 SWE ISSN 1652-9030
H1
DIGITAL COMPREHENSIVE SUMMARIES OF UPPSALA DISSERTATIONS FROM THE FACULTY OF SOCIAL SCIENCES. Text in English. 1971. irreg., latest vol.116, 2002. price varies. back issues avail. **Document type:** *Monographic series, Abstract/Index.*
Former titles (until 2005): Comprehensive Summaries of Uppsala Dissertations from the Faculty of Social Sciences (Print Edition) (0282-7492); (until 1985): Abstracts of Uppsala Dissertations from the Faculty of Social Sciences (0346-6426)
Media: Online - full content. **Related titles:** ◆ Series of: Acta Universitatis Upsaliensis. ISSN 0346-5462.
Published by: Uppsala Universitet, Acta Universitatis Upsaliensis/ University Publications from Uppsala, PO Box 256, Uppsala, 75105, Sweden. TEL 46-18-4716800, FAX 46-18-4716804, acta@ub.uu.se, http://www.ub.uu.se/upu/auu/index.html. Ed. Bengt Landgren. **Dist. by:** Almqvist & Wiksell International.

300 001.3 ESP ISSN 1575-2275
AS301
➤ **DIGITHUM**; humanities in digital era. Text in Catalan, Spanish, English. 1999. a. free (effective 2011). abstr. back issues avail. **Document type:** *Journal, Academic/Scholarly.* **Description:** Analyses the transformations taking place in the digital age in terms of the humanities and social sciences.
Media: Online - full text.
Indexed: MLA-IB.
Published by: Universitat Oberta de Catalunya, Av Tibidabo 39-43, Barcelona, 08035, Spain. TEL 34-902-372373. Eds. Lluis Rius, Salvador Climent.

➤ **DILEMA.** *see* HISTORY—History Of Europe

300 GBR ISSN 0392-1921
AS4
➤ **DIOGENES (ENGLISH EDITION).** Text in English. 1952. q. USD 616, GBP 333 combined subscription to institutions (print & online eds.); USD 604, GBP 326 to institutions (effective 2011). adv. illus. index. back issues avail.; reprint service avail. from PSC. **Document type:** *Journal, Academic/Scholarly.* **Description:** Provides a forum for discussion in all areas of philosophy and humanistic studies.
Related titles: Microfiche ed.; Online - full text ed.: ISSN 1467-7695. USD 554, GBP 300 to institutions (effective 2011); ◆ French ed.: Diogene. ISSN 0419-1633; Portuguese ed.: Diogenes (Brazilian Edition). ISSN 0102-6984; Spanish ed.: Diogenes (Spanish Edition). ISSN 0012-3048; Chinese ed.: Di'ougenni. ISSN 1000-6575; Hindi ed.; Arabic ed.; Japanese ed.: Diogenesu. ISSN 0911-5404.
Indexed: A01, A02, A03, A08, A20, A22, A26, ABS&EES, ASCA, AmHI, ArtHuCI, B04, BRD, CA, CurCont, DIP, E01, E08, G06, G07, G08, H07, H08, H09, H10, H14, HAb, HumInd, I05, I14, IBR, IBZ, IPB, MLA, MLA-IB, P02, P10, P13, P30, P34, P42, P48, P53, P54, PQC, PhilInd, R05, S02, S03, S09, SCOPUS, SOPODA, SociolAb, T02, W03, W05, W07.
—BLDSC (3588.750000), IE, Infotrieve, Ingenta. **CCC.**
Published by: (UNESCO, International Council for Philosophy and Humanistic Studies FRA), Sage Publications Ltd. (Subsidiary of: Sage Publications, Inc.), 1 Oliver's Yard, 55 City Rd, London, EC1Y 1SP, United Kingdom. TEL 44-20-73248500, FAX 44-20-73248600, info@sagepub.co.uk, http://www.uk.sagepub.com/home.nav. Eds. Luca Maria Scarantino, Maurice Aymard. **Subscr. in the Americas to:** Sage Publications, Inc., 2455 Teller Rd, Thousand Oaks, CA 91320. TEL 805-499-9774, FAX 805-499-0871, journals@sagepub.com.

300 ITA ISSN 1827-7691
DIPARTIMENTO DI TEORIA DEI SISTEMI E DELLE ORGANIZZAZIONI. QUADERNI. Text in Italian. 2003. irreg. price varies. **Document type:** *Monographic series, Academic/Scholarly.*
Published by: (Universita degli Studi di Teramo, Dipartimento di Teorie e Politiche dello Sviluppo Sociale), Casa Editrice Dott. A. Giuffre (Subsidiary of: LexisNexis Europe and Africa), Via Busto Arsizio, 40, Milan, MI 20151, Italy. TEL 39-02-380891, FAX 39-02-38009582, giuffre@giuffre.it, http://www.giuffre.it.

300 JPN
(YEAR) DIRECTORY OF THINK TANKS IN JAPAN. Text in Japanese. a. JPY 5,250 (effective 2000). **Document type:** *Directory, Academic/Scholarly.*
Published by: National Institute for Research Advancement/Sogo Kenkyu Kaihatsu Kiko, 34F Yebisu Garden Place Tower, 4-20-3 Ebisu, Shibuya-ku, PO Box 5004, Tokyo, 150-6034, Japan. TEL 81-3-54481735, FAX 81-3-54481745, www@nira.go.jp, http://www.nira.go.jp.

DISABILITY STUDIES; Koerper - Macht - Differenz. *see* HANDICAPPED

S

363.7 USA
DISASTER RESEARCH. Abbreviated title: D R. (Related title: Natural Hazards Observer) Text in English. 1989. bi-w. free (effective 2010). adv. back issues avail.; reprints avail. **Document type:** *Newsletter.* **Description:** Serves as the Center's moderated e-mail newsletter. Includes articles as well as queries and messages from subscribers related to disaster management, hazards research, political and policy developments, conferences and publications. Includes extensive web site listings and links.
Media: E-mail. **Related titles:** Online - full text ed.
Published by: University of Colorado, Institute of Behavioral Science, Program on Environment and Behavior, Natural Hazards Center, 482 UCB, Boulder, CO 80309. TEL 303-492-6818, FAX 303-492-2151, hazctr@colorado.edu.

300 USA ISSN 1055-6133
H1
➤ **DISCLOSURE (LEXINGTON)**; a journal of social theory. Text in English. 1991. a. USD 7 per issue to individuals; USD 25 per issue to institutions (effective 2011). bk.rev. back issues avail. **Document type:** *Journal, Academic/Scholarly.* **Description:** Contains scholarly articles, artwork, creative writing, book reviews, and experimental verbal and visual works.
Related titles: Online - full text ed.
Indexed: A01, A03, A08, B04, BLI, CA, MLA-IB, P48, P53, P54, PQC, PhilInd, SSAI, SSAb, SSI, T02, W03, W05.
Published by: College of Arts and Sciences, disClosure (Subsidiary of: University of Kentucky), 213 Patterson Office Tower, Lexington, KY 40506. TEL 859-257-8354, FAX 859-323-1073, http://www.as.uky.edu/Pages/default.aspx. Eds. Jeffrey Zamostny, Rebecca Lane TEL 859-257-1771.

300 USA ISSN 0163-853X
P302 CODEN: DIPRDG
➤ **DISCOURSE PROCESSES**; a multidisciplinary journal. Abbreviated title: D P. Text in English. 1978. 8/yr. GBP 516 combined subscription in United Kingdom to institutions (print & online eds.); EUR 688, USD 865 combined subscription to institutions (print & online eds.) (effective 2012). adv. bk.rev. index. back issues avail.; reprint service avail. from PSC. **Document type:** *Journal, Academic/Scholarly.* **Description:** Provides a forum for cross-fertilization of ideas from diverse disciplines sharing a common interest in discourse - prose comprehension and recall, text grammar construction, cross-cultural comparisons of communicative competence, or related topics.
Related titles: Online - full text ed.: ISSN 1532-6950. GBP 464 in United Kingdom to institutions; EUR 620, USD 779 to institutions (effective 2012).
Indexed: A01, A03, A08, A20, A22, ASCA, AmHI, B07, CA, CMM, CPE, CommAb, CurCont, DIP, E-psyche, E01, E03, ERI, ERIC, FamI, H07, IBR, IBZ, Inspec, L&LBA, L11, LT&LA, MLA, MLA-IB, P02, P03, P10, P27, P30, P48, P53, P54, PCI, PQC, PsycInfo, PsycholAb, RASB, RILM, S02, S03, S11, SCOPUS, SOPODA, SSCI, SociolAb, T02, W07.
—BLDSC (3595.860000), AskIEEE, IE, Infotrieve, Ingenta. **CCC.**
Published by: (Society for Text and Discourse), Routledge (Subsidiary of: Taylor & Francis Group), 325 Chestnut St, Ste 800, Philadelphia, PA 19106. TEL 800-354-1420, FAX 215-625-2940, journals@routledge.com, http://www.routledge.com. Ed. Michael F Schober.

300 GBR
DISCUSSION PAPERS IN SOCIOLOGY. Text in English. 19??. irreg., latest 2000. **Document type:** *Monographic series, Academic/Scholarly.*
Published by: University of Leicester, Department of Sociology, University Rd, Leicester, Leics LE1 7RH, United Kingdom. TEL 44-116-2522739, FAX 44-116-2525259, sociology@leicester.ac.uk, http://www.le.ac.uk/so/.

DISKURS KINDHEITS- UND JUGENDFORSCHUNG. *see* CHILDREN AND YOUTH—About

300 DEU
DISKURSYS; Ressourcen zur Beratungspraxis. Text in German. 2004. irreg., latest vol.3, 2007. price varies. **Document type:** *Monographic series, Academic/Scholarly.*
Published by: Transcript, Muehlenstr 47, Bielefeld, 33607, Germany. TEL 49-521-63454, FAX 49-521-61040, live@transcript-verlag.de.

300 RUS
DISPUT; istoriko-filosofskii relogiovedcheskii zhurnal. Text in Russian. 1992. s-a. USD 85 in the Americas (effective 2000).
Indexed: RASB.
Published by: Rossiiskaya Akademiya Upravleniya, Pr. Vernadskogo, 84, Moscow, 117571, Russian Federation. TEL 7-095-4369130, FAX 7-095-4369833.

300 BEL ISSN 2031-0331
DIVERSITAS. Text in French, English. 2008. irreg., latest vol.5, 2010. price varies. **Document type:** *Monographic series, Academic/Scholarly.*
Published by: P I E - Peter Lang SA, 1 avenue Maurice, 6e etage, Brussels, 1050, Belgium. TEL 32-2-3477236, FAX 32-2-3477237, pie@peterlang.com, http://www.peterlang.net. Ed. Alain Gagnon.

300 DEU
DOCUMENTA AUGUSTANA. Text in German. 1999. irreg., latest vol.21, 2010. price varies. **Document type:** *Monographic series, Academic/Scholarly.*
Published by: Wissner Verlag, Im Tal 12, Augsburg, 86179, Germany. TEL 49-821-259890, FAX 49-821-594932, info@wissner.com.

300 ESP ISSN 0417-8106
DOCUMENTACION SOCIAL; revista de estudios sociales y de sociologia aplicada. Text in Spanish. 1958. q. EUR 29.70 (effective 2008). back issues avail. **Document type:** *Monographic series, Consumer.* **Description:** A forum for theoretical and applied social studies whose goal is the creation of a society with new values.
Indexed: RASB, SCIMP, SociolAb.
Published by: Caritas Espanola, San Bernardo, 99 bis 7a, Madrid, 28015, Spain. TEL 34-91-4441000, FAX 34-91-5934882, publicaciones@caritas-espa.org, http://www.caritas.es.

300 ARG ISSN 1851-8788
DOCUMENTOS DE INVESTIGACION SOCIAL. Text in Spanish. 2008. bi-m. back issues avail. **Document type:** *Monographic series, Academic/Scholarly.*
Media: Online - full text.
Published by: Universidad Nacional de San Martin, Instituto de Altos Estudios Sociales, Parana, 145, Piso 5, Buenos Aires, 1017, Argentina. TEL idaes@unsam.edu.ar.

300 TUR ISSN 1302-3284
➤ **DOKUZ EYLUL UNIVERSITESI SOSYAL BILIMLER ENSTITUSU DERGISI/DOKUZ EYLUL UNIVERSITY JOURNAL OF GRADUATE SCHOOL OF SOCIAL SCIENCES.** Text in Turkish; Abstracts in English, Turkish; Text occasionally in English, French, German. 1999. q. free. back issues avail.; reprints avail. **Document type:** *Journal, Academic/Scholarly.* **Description:** Publishes original theoretical and empirical articles in social sciences.
Related titles: Online - full text ed.: free (effective 2011).
Indexed: A01.
Published by: Dokuz Eylul Universitesi Sosyal Bilimler Enstitusu/Dokuz Eylul University Graduate School of Social Sciences, Buca, Izmir 35160, Turkey. TEL 90-232-4128760, FAX 90-232-4530266. Eds. Ethem Duygulu, Faruk Sapancali. Pub. Utku Utkulu. Circ: 400.

300 ITA ISSN 1972-0769
DOMINI. RAPPORTI DI RICERCA. Text in Italian. 1999. irreg.
Published by: Liguori Editore, Via Posillipo 394, Naples, 80123, Italy. TEL 39-081-7206111, FAX 39-081-7206244, liguori@liguori.it, http://www.liguori.it.

300 CHN ISSN 1008-3758
H8.C47
DONGBEI DAXUE XUEBAO (SHEHUI KEXUE BAN)/NORTHEASTERN UNIVERSITY. JOURNAL (SOCIAL SCIENCE). Text in Chinese. 1999. bi-m. USD 18 (effective 2009). **Document type:** *Journal, Academic/Scholarly.*
Related titles: Online - full text ed.
Indexed: CA, L&LBA, P42, PSA, S02, S03, SCOPUS, SociolAb, T02.
—BLDSC (3619.224247), East View.
Published by: Dongbei Daxue, Xuebao Bianjibu, PO Box 269, Shenyang, Liaoning 110004, China. TEL 86-24-83687253, FAX 86-24-83687228.

300 100 CHN
DONGBEI SHI-DAXUEBAO (ZHEXUE SHEHUI KEXUE BAN)/ NORTHEAST NORMAL UNIVERSITY. JOURNAL (PHILOSOPHY, SOCIAL SCIENCES EDITION). Text in Chinese. 1951. bi-m. USD 40.20 (effective 2009). **Document type:** *Journal, Academic/Scholarly.* **Description:** Publishes research results in philosophy, political science, economics, history, education, linguistics, and literature.
Formerly: Dongbei Shi-Daxuebao (1001-6201)
Related titles: Online - full text ed.
—East View.
Published by: (Xuebao Bianjibu), Dongbei Shifan Daxue/Northeast Normal University, 5268 Renmin Dajie, Changchun, 130024, China. TEL 86-431-5099325.

300 CHN
DONGHUA DAXUE XUEBAO (SHEHUI KEXUE BAN)/DONGHUA UNIVERSITY. JOURNAL (SOCIAL SCIENCE EDITION). Text in Chinese. 2001. q. CNY 5 newsstand/cover (effective 2006). **Document type:** *Journal, Academic/Scholarly.*
Related titles: Online - full text ed.
Published by: Donghua Daxue/Donghua University, 1882, Yanan Xilu, Shanghai, 200051, China. TEL 86-21-62373643, http://www.dhu.edu.cn/.

300 CHN ISSN 1674-3512
DONGHUA LIGONG DAXUE XUEBAO (SHEHUI KEXUE BAN)/EAST CHINA INSTITUTE OF TECHNOLOGY. JOURNAL (SOCIAL SCIENCE). Text in Chinese. 1982. q. CNY 10 per issue (effective 2011).
Former titles (until 2008): Donghua Ligong Xueyuan Xuebao (Shehui Kexue Ban)/East China Institute of Technology. Journal (Social Science Edition); (until 2003): Fuzhou Shi-zhuan Xuebao/Fuzhou Teachers College. Journal (1001-635X); (until 1983): Fuzhou Shi-zhuan Xuebkan
Related titles: Online - full text ed.
Published by: Donghua Ligong Daxue/East China Institute of Technology, 56, Xuefu Lu, Fuzhou, 344000, China. TEL 86-794-8258893, FAX 86-794-8250911.

300 CHN ISSN 1002-2007
DONGJIANG XUEKAN (ZHEXUE SHEHUI KEXUE BAN)/DONGJIANG JOURNAL. Text in Chinese. 1984. q. USD 20.80 (effective 2009). **Document type:** *Journal, Academic/Scholarly.*
Related titles: Online - full text ed.
—East View.
Published by: Yanbian Daxue/Yanbian University, 977, Gongyuan Lu, Yanji, 133002, China. TEL 86-433-2567233. **Dist. by:** China International Book Trading Corp, 35 Chegongzhuang Xilu, Haidian District, PO Box 399, Beijing 100044, China. TEL 86-10-68412045, FAX 86-10-68412023, cibtc@mail.cibtc.com.cn, http://www.cibtc.com.cn.

300 100 CHN ISSN 1671-511X
DONGNAN DAXUE XUEBAO (ZHEXUE SHEHUI KEXUE BAN)/ SOUTHEAST UNIVERSITY. JOURNAL (PHILOSOPHY AND SOCIAL SCIENCE). Text in Chinese. 1999. bi-m. USD 28.20 (effective 2009). **Document type:** *Journal, Academic/Scholarly.*
Formerly (until 1999): Dongnan Daxue Xuebao (Shehui Kexue Ban) (1008-441X)
Related titles: Online - full text ed.
—East View.
Published by: Dongnan Daxue/Southeast University, 2, Sipailou, Nanjing, Jiangsu 210096, China.

300 CHN ISSN 1008-1569
DONGNAN XUESHU/SOUTH EAST ACADEMIC RESEARCH. Text in Chinese. 1978. bi-m. USD 24.60 (effective 2009). adv. **Document type:** *Journal, Academic/Scholarly.* **Description:** Covers all aspects of social sciences such as politics, economy, philosophy, law, literature, history and education.
Formerly (until 1998): Fujian Xuekan (1003-370X)
Related titles: Online - full text ed.
—East View.
Published by: Fujian Sheng Shehui Kexue Lianhehui, No 18, Liuhe Rd, Fuzhou, Fujian 350001, China. TEL 86-591-3739507, FAX 86-591-3704540. Ed. Bixiu Wang. R&P, Adv. contact Xiaorong Xie. page USD 1,000. **Dist. by:** China International Book Trading Corp, 35 Chegongzhuang Xilu, Haidian District, PO Box 399, Beijing 100044, China. TEL 86-10-68412045, FAX 86-10-68412023, cibtc@mail.cibtc.com.cn, http://www.cibtc.com.cn.

300 CHN ISSN 1003-2479
DONGNANYA ZONGHENG/ALL-ROUND SOUTHEAST ASIA. Text in Chinese. m. USD 62.40 (effective 2009). **Document type:** *Journal, Academic/Scholarly.*
Related titles: Online - full text ed.
—East View.
Published by: Guangxi Shehui Kexueyuan, Dongnanya Yanjiusuo, 5, Xinzhu Lu, Nanning, 530022, China. **Dist. by:** China International Book Trading Corp, 35 Chegongzhuang Xilu, Haidian District, PO Box 399, Beijing 100044, China. TEL 86-10-68412045, FAX 86-10-68412023, cibtc@mail.cibtc.com.cn, http://www.cibtc.com.cn.

300 CHN
DONG'OU/EASTERN EUROPE. Text in Chinese. q.
Published by: Beijing Waiyu Xueyuan/Beijing Foreign Language Institute, No 2 Xisanhuan Beilu, Beijing, 100081, China. TEL 890351. Ed. Yang Yanjie.

300 CHN ISSN 1003-8353
AP95.C4
DONGYUE LUNCONG/DONGYUE TRIBUNE. Text in Chinese. 1980. bi-m. USD 74.40 (effective 2009). **Document type:** *Journal, Academic/Scholarly.*
Related titles: CD-ROM ed.; Online - full text ed.
—East View.
Published by: Shandong Sheng Shehui Kexueyuan/Shandong Academy of Social Sciences, 56, Shungeng Lu, Jinan, 250002, China. Ed. Jia Bingdi. Circ: 3,000. **Dist. by:** China International Book Trading Corp, 35 Chegongzhuang Xilu, Haidian District, PO Box 399, Beijing 100044, China. TEL 86-10-68412045, FAX 86-10-68412023, cibtc@mail.cibtc.com.cn, http://www.cibtc.com.cn.

300 DEU
DORTMUNDER BEITRAEGE ZUR SOZIAL- UND GESELLSCHAFTSPOLITIK. Text in German. 1995. irreg., latest vol.61, 2010. price varies. **Document type:** *Monographic series, Academic/Scholarly.*
Published by: (Sozialforschungsstelle Dortmund), Lit Verlag, Grevener Str/Fresnostr 2, Muenster, 48159, Germany. TEL 49-251-235091, FAX 49-251-231972, lit@lit-verlag.de.

300 DEU
DRESDNER STUDIEN ZUR KULTUR. Text in German. 2003. irreg., latest vol.6, 2010. price varies. **Document type:** *Monographic series, Academic/Scholarly.*
Published by: Leipziger Universitaetsverlag GmbH, Oststr 41, Leipzig, 04317, Germany. TEL 49-341-9900440, FAX 49-341-9900440, info@univerlag-leipzig.de.

DROIT ET SOCIETE. *see* LAW

DROIT SOCIAL. *see* LAW

300 HRV ISSN 1330-0288
HA1
➤ **DRUSTVENA ISTRAZIVANJA**; casopis za opca drustvan pitanja. Text and summaries in Croatian, English, German, Italian. 1992. bi-m. HRK 100 domestic to individuals; USD 30 foreign to individuals; HRK 250 domestic to institutions; USD 60 foreign to institutions (effective 2011). adv. bk.rev. **Document type:** *Journal, Academic/Scholarly.* **Description:** Publishes works in different social disciplines, including sociology, philosophy, psychology, political sciences, psychiatry, history, law, economics, demography, linguistics etc.
Related titles: Online - full text ed.: free (effective 2011).
Indexed: A20, A22, ASCA, CA, CurCont, IBSS, P42, PSA, RASB, RILM, S02, S03, SCOPUS, SOPODA, SSA, SSCI, SociolAb, T02, W07.
—BLDSC (3630.145500), IE, Ingenta.
Published by: Institut Drustvenih Znanosti Ivo Pilar/Institute of Social Sciences Ivo Pilar, Marulicev trg 19/I, pp 277, Zagreb, 10001, Croatia. TEL 385-1-4886815, FAX 385-1-4828296, http://www.pilar.hr. Ed. Renata Franc.

300 305.8 GBR ISSN 1742-058X
HT1501
➤ **DU BOIS REVIEW**; social science research on race. Text in English. 2003. s-a. GBP 127, USD 218 to institutions; GBP 133, USD 224 combined subscription to institutions (print & online eds.) (effective 2012). adv. back issues avail.; reprint service avail. from PSC. **Document type:** *Journal, Academic/Scholarly.* **Description:** Covers research and criticism on race in the social sciences. Provides a forum for discussion and increased understanding of race and society from a range of disciplines, including but not limited to economics, political science, sociology, anthropology, law, communications, public policy, psychology, and history.
Related titles: Online - full text ed.: ISSN 1742-0598. GBP 118, USD 192 to institutions (effective 2012).
Indexed: A22, CA, E01, IIBP, P10, P27, P42, P46, P48, P53, P54, PAIS, PQC, PRA, PSA, S02, S03, SCOPUS, SociolAb, T02.
—BLDSC (3630.557000), IE. **CCC.**
Published by: (W E B Du Bois Institute for Afro-American Research USA), Cambridge University Press, The Edinburgh Bldg, Shaftesbury Rd, Cambridge, CB2 8RU, United Kingdom. TEL 44-1223-312393, FAX 44-1223-315052, journals@cambridge.org, http://www.cambridge.org/uk. Eds. Lawrence Bobo, Michael Dawson. Adv. contact Rebecca Roberts TEL 44-1223-325083. **Subscr. to:** Cambridge University Press, 32 Ave of the Americas, New York, NY 10013. TEL 212-337-5000, FAX 212-691-3239, journals_subscriptions@cup.org.

300 AUS ISSN 1833-3613
DUNSTAN PAPERS. Text in English. 2006. q. AUD 30 to individuals; AUD 500 to institutions (effective 2008). back issues avail. **Document type:** *Monographic series, Academic/Scholarly.* **Description:** Covers information on human rights and indigenous people, and the pursuit of social justice, cultural diversity and inclusive governance.
Published by: Don Dunstan Foundation, Level 4, 230 North Terr, The University of Adelaide, Adelaide, SA 5000, Australia. TEL 61-8-83033364, FAX 61-8-83036309, dunstan.foundation@adelaide.edu.au. Ed. Lionel Orchard.

300 GBR ISSN 1746-7586
JZ5588
➤ **DYNAMICS OF ASYMMETRIC CONFLICT**; pathways toward terrorism and genocide. Text in English. 2008. 3/yr. GBP 220 combined subscription in United Kingdom to institutions (print & online eds.); EUR 345, USD 433 combined subscription to institutions (print & online eds.) (effective 2012). adv. back issues avail.; reprint service avail. from PSC. **Document type:** *Journal, Academic/Scholarly.* **Description:** Publishes original papers and reviews that contribute to understanding and ameliorating conflicts between states and non-state challengers.
Related titles: Online - full text ed.: ISSN 1746-7594. GBP 199 in United Kingdom to institutions; EUR 311, USD 389 to institutions (effective 2012).
Indexed: A01, CA, T02.
—IE. **CCC.**
Published by: Routledge (Subsidiary of: Taylor & Francis Group), 4 Park Sq, Milton Park, Abingdon, Oxon OX14 4RN, United Kingdom. TEL 44-20-70176000, FAX 44-20-70176336, subscriptions@tandf.co.uk, http://www.routledge.com/journals/. Ed. Clark McCauley. Adv. contact Linda Hann TEL 44-1344-779945. **Subscr. to:** Taylor & Francis Ltd., Journals Customer Service, Sheepen Pl, Colchester, Essex CO3 3LP, United Kingdom. TEL 44-20-70175544, FAX 44-20-70175198.

300 001.3 MYS ISSN 1823-884X
E - BANGI; journal of social sciences and humanities. Text in Malay, English. 2006. irreg. free (effective 2011). **Document type:** *Journal, Academic/Scholarly.*
Media: Online - full text.
Published by: Universiti Kebangsaan Malaysia/National University of Malaysia, 43600 UKM, Bangi, Selangor 43600, Malaysia. http://www.ukm.my.

E C M I JOURNAL ON ETHNOPOLITICS AND MINORITY ISSUES IN EUROPE. see ETHNIC INTERESTS

300 PRT ISSN 1647-9270
E - CADERNOS C E S. (Centro de Estudos Sociais) Text in Portuguese. 2008. q. **Document type:** *Journal, Academic/Scholarly.*
Related titles: Online - full text ed.: ISSN 1647-0737.
Published by: Universidade de Coimbra, Faculdade de Economia, Ave Das da Silva, 165, Coimbra, 3004-512, Portugal. TEL 351-239-790500, FAX 351-239-790514, notas-economicas@fe.uc.pt, http://notas-economicas.fe.uc.pt/.

300 AUT ISSN 1811-1696
E I P C P MULTILINGUAL WEBJOURNAL. Variant title: Transversal. Text in Multiple languages. 2001. irreg. **Document type:** *Journal, Academic/Scholarly.*
Media: Online - full text.
Published by: European Institute for Progressive Cultural Policies, Gumpendorfer Str 63b, Vienna, 1060, Austria. contact@eipcp.net, http://www.eipcp.net.

300 USA
E-JOURNAL OF SOLIDARITY, SUSTAINABILITY, AND NONVIOLENCE. Text in English. 2005. m. **Document type:** *Journal, Consumer.* **Description:** Provides commentary on recent news and emerging new research in sustainable development.
Media: Online - full content.
Address: pelican@pelicanweb.org, http://pelicanweb.org/solisust.html. Ed., Pub., R&P, Adv. contact Luis T Gutierrez.

300 ARG ISSN 1666-9606
HN110.5
E-L@TINA; revista electronica de estudios latinoamericanos. Text in Spanish. 2002. q. free (effective 2011). **Document type:** *Journal, Academic/Scholarly.*
Media: Online - full text.
Published by: Universidad de Buenos Aires, Facultad de Ciencias Sociales, Marcelo T. de Alvear, 2230, Buenos Aires, 1122, Argentina. TEL 54-11-45083800, http://www.fsoc.uba.ar.

300 001.3 GBR ISSN 1756-8226
➤ **E-PISTEME.** Text in English. 2008. s-a. free (effective 2011). **Document type:** *Journal, Academic/Scholarly.* **Description:** Focuses on themes that reach across disciplines, seeking to challenge traditionally defined ways of thinking and conducting research.
Media: Online - full text.
Published by: Newcastle University, Newcastle upon Tyne, Tyne and Wear NE1 7RU, United Kingdom. TEL 44-191-2226000, press.office@ncl.ac.uk, http://www.ncl.ac.uk/.

300 001.3 GBR ISSN 2042-9401
H62.5.G7
E S D S NEWS. (Economic and Social Data Service) Text in English. 1975. q. bk.rev. back issues avail. **Document type:** *Newsletter, Trade.* **Description:** Provides a forum for information and news. Contains news and articles on data analysis and management in the humanities and social sciences.
Former titles (until 2010): U K Databytes (1474-9149); (until 2001): Data Archive Bulletin (1366-6649); (until 1996): E S R C Data Archive Bulletin (1366-6630); (until 1984): S S R C Data Archive Bulletin; (until 1981): S S R C Survey Archive Bulletin (0307-1391)
Related titles: Online - full text ed.: ISSN 2042-941X. free (effective 2010).
Indexed: P30.
—BLDSC (3811.128600). **CCC.**
Published by: University of Essex, UK Data Archive, Wivenhoe Park, Colchester, CO4 3SQ, United Kingdom. TEL 44-1206-872143, FAX 44-1206-872003, help@esds.ac.uk.

300.71 GBR ISSN 0269-2554
E S R C STUDENTSHIP HANDBOOK; postgraduate studentships in the social sciences. Text in English. 1970. a. free. **Document type:** *Corporate.*
Former titles (until 1984): S S R C Studentship Handbook; Social Science Research Council (Gt. Brit.) Postgraduate Studentships in the Social Sciences
—BLDSC (3811.662800).
Published by: Economic and Social Research Council, Polaris House, North Star Ave, Swindon, Wilts SN2 1UJ, United Kingdom. TEL 44-1793-413000, FAX 44-1793-413001, http://www.esrcsocietytoday.ac.uk/. R&P Phil Sooben TEL 44-1793-413028.

E S R I ACCOUNTS AND BALANCE SHEET. see BUSINESS AND ECONOMICS

E U I PAPERS IN POLITICAL AND SOCIAL SCIENCES. see POLITICAL SCIENCE

EARTH QUARTERLY; living in harmony with the Earth and each other. see GENERAL INTEREST PERIODICALS—United States

300 USA
EARTH: WHERE DO WE GO FROM HERE?. Text in English. 1993. bi-m. looseleaf. USD 3 (effective 1993). adv. bk.rev. **Document type:** *Newsletter.* **Description:** Attempts to change-stimulate the reader's mind with information about the world we live in today. Challenges modern theories, tries to establish new, more effective ones.
Address: 2802 Shelley Rd, Philadelphia, PA 19152. TEL 215-677-8146. Ed. Joseph Olszewski Jr. Circ: 53.

EAST ASIAN SCIENCE, TECHNOLOGY AND SOCIETY; an international journal. see SCIENCES: COMPREHENSIVE WORKS

300 ETH ISSN 1027-1775
➤ **EASTERN AFRICA SOCIAL SCIENCE RESEARCH REVIEW.** Text in English. 1985. 2/yr. USD 23 in Africa; USD 35 elsewhere (effective 2004). bk.rev. back issues avail. **Document type:** *Journal, Academic/Scholarly.*
Related titles: Online - full text ed.: ISSN 1684-4173. 2002.
Indexed: A22, ASD, CA, E01, IIBP, M10, P42, PCI, PLESA, PSA, S02, S03, SociolAb, T02.
—BLDSC (3646.575500), IE, Infotrieve, Ingenta.
Published by: Organization for Social Science Research in Eastern Africa, PO Box 31971, Addis Ababa, Ethiopia. TEL 251-1-551163, FAX 251-1-551399, http://www.ossrea.net. Eds. Bahru Zewde, Mohamed Salih. Circ: 500.

➤ **EBISU.** see ASIAN STUDIES

330.972 MEX ISSN 1405-8421
GR516
ECONOMIA, SOCIEDAD Y TERRITORIO. Text in Spanish. 1997. q. MXN 240 domestic; USD 50 in the Americas; USD 60 elsewhere (effective 2007). back issues avail. **Document type:** *Journal, Academic/Scholarly.*
Indexed: A34, AgrForAb, C01, C25, CA, CABA, D01, E12, F08, F12, FCA, G11, GH, H16, H21, I11, LT, MaizeAb, N02, OR, P08, P42, PAIS, PSA, R12, RRTA, S02, S03, S13, S16, SCOPUS, SociolAb, T02, T05, TAR, VS, W11.
Published by: El Colegio Mexiquense, A.C., Ex-Hacienda Santa Cruz de los Patos, Zinacantepec, Edo de Mexico, 51350, Mexico. TEL 52-722-2799908 ext 183, FAX 52-722-2799908 ext 200, est@cmq.edu.mx.

ECONOMIA Y SOCIEDAD. see BUSINESS AND ECONOMICS—Economic Situation And Conditions

ECONOMIC AND SOCIAL RESEARCH INSTITUTE. ANNUAL REPORT AND REVIEW OF RESEARCH. see BUSINESS AND ECONOMICS

ECONOMIC AND SOCIAL RESEARCH INSTITUTE. GENERAL RESEARCH SERIES. see BUSINESS AND ECONOMICS

ECONOMIC AND SOCIAL RESEARCH INSTITUTE. MEMORANDUM SERIES. see BUSINESS AND ECONOMICS

ECONOMIC AND SOCIAL RESEARCH INSTITUTE. TECHNICAL SERIES. see BUSINESS AND ECONOMICS

ECONOMIC AND SOCIAL REVIEW. see BUSINESS AND ECONOMICS

300 USA
ECONOMIC STUDIES IN INEQUALITY, SOCIAL EXCLUSION AND WELL-BEING. Text in English. 2006. irreg., latest vol.7, 2009. price varies. back issues avail. **Document type:** *Monographic series, Academic/Scholarly.*
Published by: Springer New York LLC (Subsidiary of: Springer Science+Business Media), 233 Spring St, New York, NY 10013. TEL 212-460-1500, FAX 212-460-1575, service-ny@springer.com. Ed. Jacques Silber. **Co-sponsor:** International Development Research Center.

330.1 570 NLD ISSN 1570-677X
QP1
ECONOMICS AND HUMAN BIOLOGY. Text in English. 2003 (Jan.). 3/yr. EUR 465 in Europe to institutions; JPY 62,000 in Japan to institutions; USD 520 elsewhere to institutions (effective 2012). **Document type:** *Journal, Academic/Scholarly.* **Description:** Devoted to the exploration of the effect of socio-economic processes on human beings as biological organisms.
Related titles: Online - full text ed.: ISSN 1873-6130 (from IngentaConnect, ScienceDirect).
Indexed: A20, A26, A34, A36, CA, CABA, CurCont, D01, E12, EMBASE, ESPM, EconLit, ExcerpMed, GH, HPNRM, I05, JEL, LT, MEDLINE, N02, N03, P30, R10, R12, RA&MP, RRTA, Reac, RiskAb, SCI, SCOPUS, SSCI, SSciA, T02, T05, TAR, VS, W07, W11.
—BLDSC (3656.930360), IE, Ingenta. **CCC.**
Published by: Elsevier BV, North-Holland (Subsidiary of: Elsevier Science & Technology), Sara Burgerhartstraat 25, Amsterdam, 1055 KV, Netherlands. TEL 31-20-4853911, FAX 31-20-4852457, JournalsCustomerServiceEMEA@elsevier.com, http://www.elsevier.nl/homepage/about/us/regional_sites.htt. Ed. John Komlos TEL 49-89-2180-3168. **Subscr. to:** Elsevier BV, Radarweg 29, PO Box 211, Amsterdam 1000 AE, Netherlands. TEL 31-20-4853757, FAX 31-20-4853432.

320.531 GBR ISSN 0308-5147
H1
➤ **ECONOMY AND SOCIETY.** Text in English. 1972. q. GBP 368 combined subscription in United Kingdom to institutions (print & online eds.); EUR 486, USD 609 combined subscription to institutions (print & online eds.) (effective 2012). adv. bk.rev. illus. index. back issues avail.; reprint service avail. from PSC. **Document type:** *Journal, Academic/Scholarly.* **Description:** Covers the social sciences, history and philosophy with an emphasis on theoretical perspectives.
Related titles: Microform ed.: (from PQC); Online - full text ed.: ISSN 1469-5766. GBP 332 in United Kingdom to institutions; EUR 437, USD 548 to institutions (effective 2012) (from IngentaConnect).
Indexed: A12, A13, A17, A20, A22, A26, ABIn, APEL, ASCA, AltPI, B01, B02, B04, B06, B07, B09, B15, B17, B18, BAS, BRD, CA, CWI, CurCont, DIP, E01, E08, EconLit, FR, G04, G08, GEOBASE, HPNRM, I05, I13, IBR, IBSS, IBZ, JEL, LeftInd, MEA&I, P30, P34, P42, P48, P51, P53, P54, PCI, PQC, PSA, PerIslam, RI-1, RI-2, S02, S03, S09, SCOPUS, SOPODA, SSA, SSAI, SSAb, SSCI, SSI, SociolAb, T02, W03, W07, WBA.
—IE, Infotrieve, Ingenta, INIST. **CCC.**
Published by: Routledge (Subsidiary of: Taylor & Francis Group), 4 Park Square, Milton Park, Abingdon, Oxon OX14 4RN, United Kingdom. subscriptions@tandf.co.uk, http://www.routledge.com/journals/. Adv. contact Linda Hann TEL 44-1344-779945. **Subscr. in N America to:** Taylor & Francis Inc., Customer Services Dept, 325 Chestnut St, 8th Fl, Philadelphia, PA 19106. TEL 215-625-8900, 800-354-1420, FAX 215-625-2940; **Subscr. to:** Taylor & Francis Ltd., Journals Customer Service, Sheepen Pl, Colchester, Essex CO3 3LP, United Kingdom. TEL 44-20-70175544, FAX 44-20-70175198, tf.enquiries@tfinforma.com.

➤ **ECONOMY TRANSDISCIPLINARY COGNITION.** see BUSINESS AND ECONOMICS—Economic Systems And Theories, Economic History

300 DEU ISSN 0943-9021
EDITION DISCOURS; Klassische und zeitgenoessische Texte der franzoesischsprachigen Humanwissenschaften. Text in German. 1994. irreg., latest vol.45, 2009. price varies. **Document type:** *Monographic series, Academic/Scholarly.*
Published by: U V K Verlagsgesellschaft mbH, Schuetzenstr 24, Konstanz, 78462, Germany. TEL 49-7531-90530, FAX 49-7531-905398, nadine.ley@uvk.de, http://www.uvk.de.

300 DEU ISSN 1866-685X
EDITION KULTURELLE INFRASTRUKTUR. Text in German. 2008. irreg. price varies. **Document type:** *Monographic series, Academic/Scholarly.*
Published by: Peter Lang GmbH (Subsidiary of: Peter Lang Publishing Group), Eschborner Landstr 42-50, Frankfurt Am Main, 60489, Germany. TEL 49-69-7807050, FAX 49-69-78070550, zentrale.frankfurt@peterlang.com. Ed. Matthias Theodor Vogt.

300 DEU
▼ **EDITION KULTURWISSENSCHAFT.** Text in German. 2010. irreg., latest vol.6, 2011. price varies. **Document type:** *Monographic series, Academic/Scholarly.*
Published by: Transcript, Muehlenstr 47, Bielefeld, 33607, Germany. TEL 49-521-63454, FAX 49-521-61040, live@transcript-verlag.de.

300 DEU ISSN 1615-7869
EDITION SOZIALPOLITIK. Text in German. 2000. irreg., latest vol.5, 2004. price varies. **Document type:** *Monographic series, Academic/Scholarly.*
Published by: Rainer Hampp Verlag, Marktplatz 5, Mering, 86415, Germany. TEL 49-8233-4783, FAX 49-8233-30755, info@rhverlag.de, http://www.rhverlag.de.

300 AUT ISSN 2070-1802
▼ **EDITION SOZIALWISSENSCHAFTEN.** Text in German. 2009. irreg., latest vol.2, 2009. price varies. **Document type:** *Monographic series, Academic/Scholarly.*
Published by: Wilhelm Braumueller Universitaets-Verlagsbuchhandlung GmbH, Servitengasse 5, Vienna, 1090, Austria. TEL 43-1-3191159, FAX 43-1-3102805, office@braumueller.at. Eds. Hannes Haas, Rudolf Richter.

EDUCACION, LENGUAJE Y SOCIEDAD. see EDUCATION

EDUCACION Y CIENCIAS HUMANAS. see EDUCATION

▼ **EDUCATIONAL QUEST**; an international journal of educational and applied social science. see EDUCATION

▼ **EGODOCUMENTS AND HISTORY SERIES.** see PUBLISHING AND BOOK TRADE

EGYPTE - MONDE ARABE. see POLITICAL SCIENCE

300 DEU ISSN 0424-6985
DIE EINHEIT DER GESELLSCHAFTSWISSENSCHAFTEN. Text in German. 1964. irreg., latest vol.144, 2011. price varies. **Document type:** *Monographic series, Academic/Scholarly.*
Published by: Mohr Siebeck GmbH & Co. KG, Wilhelmstr 18, Tuebingen, 72074, Germany. TEL 49-7071-9230, FAX 49-7071-51104, info@mohr.de.

621.388 USA ISSN 1183-5656
P87
➤ **ELECTRONIC JOURNAL OF COMMUNICATION/REVUE ELECTRONIQUE DE COMMUNICATION.** Text in English; Summaries in English, French. 1990. q. USD 50 to individual members; USD 300 to institutional members (effective 2010). bk.rev. illus. back issues avail.; reprints avail. **Document type:** *Journal, Academic/Scholarly.* **Description:** A scholarly journal addressing human communication research and theory.
Media: Online - full text.
Published by: Communication Institute for Online Scholarship, PO Box 57, Rotterdam Junction, NY 12150. TEL 518-887-2443, FAX 518-887-5186. Ed. Teresa Harrison. Circ: 2,500,000 (controlled).

300 NZL ISSN 1173-6631
➤ **THE ELECTRONIC JOURNAL OF RADICAL ORGANISATION THEORY.** Text in English. 1995. irreg., latest 2007. free (effective 2011). bk.rev. **Document type:** *Journal, Academic/Scholarly.*
Media: Online - full text.
Indexed: A39, C27, C29, D03, D04, E13, R14, S14, S15, S18.
—**CCC.**
Published by: University of Waikato, Waikato Management School, Private Bag 3105, Hamilton, 3240, New Zealand. TEL 64-7-8384477, FAX 64-7-8384063, management@waikato.ac.nz, http://www.mngt.waikato.ac.nz/depts/sml/journal/ejrot.htm. Ed. Clive Gilson.

300 TUR ISSN 1304-0278
ELEKTRONIK SOSYAL BILIMLER DERGISI/ELECTRONIC JOURNAL OF SOCIAL SCIENCES/ELECTRONICHE ZEITSCHRIFT FUER SOZIALWISSENSCHAFTEN/REVUE ELECTRONIQUE DES SCIENCES SOCIALES. Text in Multiple languages. 2002. q. free (effective 2011).
Media: Online - full text.
Indexed: A01, CA.
Published by: Dicle Universitesi, Coordination and Publication Office, Diyarbakir, Turkey. TEL 90-412-2488141, FAX 90-4122488440, http://www.dicle.edu.tr.

300 AZE ISSN 0134-3386
Q4
ELM VE KHAYAT. Text in Azerbaijani. q. USD 155 in the Americas (effective 2000).

S

Published by: Redaktsiya Elm ve Khayat, A Babaev denkesi 5, Istiglaliit kuch, Baku, 370000, Azerbaijan. TEL 994-12-927664. Ed. F Mamedova. **Dist. by:** East View Information Services, 10601 Wayzata Blvd, Minneapolis, MN 55305. TEL 952-252-1201, 800-477-1005, FAX 952-252-1202, info@eastview.com, http://www.eastview.com.

300 BRA ISSN 1519-7611
EMANCIPACAO. Text in Portuguese, English, Spanish. 2001. a. **Document type:** *Journal, Academic/Scholarly.*
Related titles: Online - full text ed.: ISSN 1982-7814. free (effective 2011).
Published by: Universidade Estadual de Ponta Grossa, Editora, Av Carlos Cavalcanti 4748, Campus Universitario de Uvaranas, Ponta Grossa, PR 84030-900, Brazil. TEL 55-42-32203744, http://www.uepg.br/editora/. Ed. Selma Maria Schons.

300 NLD ISSN 1755-4586
BF531
➤ **EMOTION, SPACE AND SOCIETY.** Text in English. 2008. s-a. EUR 225 in Europe to institutions; JPY 36,700 in Japan to institutions; USD 319 elsewhere to institutions (effective 2012). **Document type:** *Journal, Academic/Scholarly.* **Description:** Provides a forum for interdisciplinary debate on theoretically informed research on the emotional intersections between people and places.
Related titles: Online - full text ed.: (from ScienceDirect).
Indexed: CA, SCOPUS, T02.
—IE. **CCC.**
Published by: Elsevier BV (Subsidiary of: Elsevier Science & Technology), Radarweg 29, PO Box 211, Amsterdam, 1000 AE, Netherlands. TEL 31-20-4853911, FAX 31-20-4852457, JournalsCustomerServiceEMEA@elsevier.com, http://www.elsevier.nl.

300 DEU ISSN 0172-1739
EMPIRISCHE UND METHODOLOGISCHE BEITRAEGE ZUR SOZIALWISSENSCHAFT. Text in German. 1986. irreg., latest vol.26, 2009. price varies. **Document type:** *Monographic series, Academic/Scholarly.*
Published by: Peter Lang GmbH (Subsidiary of: Peter Lang Publishing Group), Eschborner Landstr 42-50, Frankfurt Am Main, 60489, Germany. TEL 49-69-7807050, FAX 49-69-78070550, zentrale.frankfurt@peterlang.com. Ed. Juergen Maier.

300 DEU ISSN 0935-0365
EMPIRISCHE WIRTSCHAFTS- UND SOZIALFORSCHUNG. Text in German. 1989. irreg., latest vol.16, 1996. price varies. **Document type:** *Monographic series, Academic/Scholarly.*
Published by: Centaurus Verlag & Media KG, Kaiser-Joseph-Str 267, Freiburg, 79098, Germany. TEL 49-761-1525861, FAX 49-761-1525868, info@centaurus-verlag.de, http://www.centaurus-verlag.de.

306 COL ISSN 2011-4559
EN CLAVE JOVEN LA REVISTA. Text in Spanish. 2008. s-a. **Document type:** *Magazine, Consumer.*
Published by: Gobernacion de Cundinamarca, Calle 26 No. 51-53, Bogota, Colombia. TEL 57-1-4260000.

EN-CLAVES DEL PENSAMIENTO JOURNAL. *see* HUMANITIES: COMPREHENSIVE WORKS

300 NIC ISSN 0424-9674
F1401
➤ **ENCUENTRO**; revista de la Universidad Centroamericana. Variant title: Revista Encuentro. Text in Spanish. 1968. q. NIC 120 domestic; USD 20 in Central America; USD 35 in US & Canada; USD 40 elsewhere (effective 2002). adv. bk.rev. bibl.; charts; stat. back issues avail. **Document type:** *Academic/Scholarly.* **Description:** Covers the natural, economical and social sciences research in Nicaragua.
Indexed: H21, IBR, IBZ, ILD, MLA-IB, P08.
Published by: Universidad Centroamericana, Apdo A-194, Managua, 70352, Nicaragua. TEL 505-2-2783923, FAX 505-2-670106. Ed. Marcos Membreno Idiaquez. Pub. Alejandro Brovo. Adv. contact Roxana Guerrero. B&W page USD 360, color page USD 520. Circ: 1,400.

306 ESP ISSN 1136-6389
F1788
ENCUENTRO DE LA CULTURA CUBANA. Text in Spanish. 1996. q. EUR 24.04 domestic; EUR 47.78 foreign (effective 2002). back issues avail. **Document type:** *Magazine, Consumer.*
Related titles: Online - full text ed.
Indexed: MLA-IB.
Published by: Asociacion Encuentro de la Cultura Cubana, Infanta Mercedes 43-1A, Madrid, 28020, Spain. TEL 34-91-4250404, FAX 34-91-5717316, asociacion@encuentro.net. Ed. Jesus Diaz.

ENCYCLOPAEDIA AFRICANA. INFORMATION REPORT. *see* HISTORY—History Of Africa

ENERGY EDUCATION SCIENCE & TECHNOLOGY, PART B: SOCIAL AND EDUCATIONAL STUDIES. *see* ENERGY

ENHANCING LEARNING IN THE SOCIAL SCIENCES. *see* EDUCATION

ENJEUX INTERNATIONAUX (BRUSSELS, 2003); revue de promotion humaine et chretienne en Afrique et dans le monde. *see* POLITICAL SCIENCE—International Relations

300 DEU ISSN 2172-8569
ENSAYOS DE TEORIA CULTURAL/ESSAYS ON CULTURAL THEORY. Text in Spanish. 2008. irreg. price varies. **Document type:** *Monographic series, Academic/Scholarly.*
Published by: Vervuert Verlag, Elisabethenstr 3-9, Frankfurt Am Main, 60594, Germany. TEL 49-69-5974617, FAX 49-69-5978743, info@iberoamericanalibros.com.

300 370 ESP ISSN 1579-2617
ENSENANZA DE LAS CIENCIAS SOCIALES. Text in Multiple languages. 2002. a. **Document type:** *Journal, Academic/Scholarly.*
Published by: (Universitat Autonoma de Barcelona, Institut de Ciencies de l'Educacio), Universitat Autonoma de Barcelona, Servei de Publicacions, Edifici A, Bellaterra, Cardanyola del Valles, Barcelona, 08193, Spain. TEL 34-93-5811022, FAX 34-93-5813239, sp@uab.es, http://www.uab.es/publicacions/.

300 320 ESP ISSN 1885-6985
H8.S6
ENTELEQUIA; revista interdisciplinar. Text in Spanish. 2005. s-a. free (effective 2011). **Document type:** *Journal, Academic/Scholarly.*
Media: Online - full text.
Published by: Universidad de Malaga, Eumed.net, Avenida Cervantes 2, Malaga, 29071, Spain. TEL 34-952-131000. Ed. Rafael Gomez Sanchez.

300 PRT ISSN 1646-1223
HD66
ENTERPRISE AND WORK INNOVATION STUDIES. Abbreviated title: E W I S. Text in English. 2005. irreg. free (effective 2011). **Document type:** *Journal, Academic/Scholarly.*
Media: Online - full text.
Indexed: S02, S03.
Published by: Universidade Nova de Lisboa, Faculdade de Ciencias e Tecnologia, Centro de Investigacao em Inovacao Empresarial, Caparica, 2829-526, Portugal. Ed. Jose Miquel Cabecas.

ENTERTEXT. *see* HUMANITIES: COMPREHENSIVE WORKS

300 COL ISSN 0124-7905
ENTORNOS. Text in Spanish. 1987. a. **Document type:** *Monographic series, Academic/Scholarly.*
Published by: Universidad Surcolombiana, Ave Pastrana Borrego Carrera 1, Neiva, Huila, Colombia. TEL 57-87-58889, FAX 57-87-54753, http://www.usco.edu.co. Ed. Miguel Angel Mahecha Bermudez.

300 MEX
ENTRE LINEAS. Text in Spanish. 1993. 3/yr. (3/yr.?).
Published by: Centro de Estudios Interdisciplinarios de la Frontera, Prol. Ave. Tecnologico s-n, Nogales, SONORA, Mexico. TEL 45970. Ed. Rual Almogabar S.

300 COL ISSN 1900-3803
ENTREMANDO. Text in Spanish. 2005. s-a. back issues avail. **Document type:** *Journal, Academic/Scholarly.*
Published by: Universidad Libre de Colombia, Diagonal 37- 3-29, Valle del Cauca, Bogota, Colombia. TEL 57-2-5240007, FAX 57-2-5241088, http://www.unilibre.edu.co/. Ed. Arnoldo Rios Alvarado.

300 GBR ISSN 1473-2866
HM711
EPHEMERA; theory & politics in organization. Text in English. 2001. q. free (effective 2011). **Document type:** *Journal, Academic/Scholarly.* **Description:** Forum for developing and extending discussions of critical perspectives on a range of issues relating to organizations and organizing in their widest senses.
Media: Online - full text.
Indexed: A01, A39, C27, C29, D03, D04, E13, R14, S14, S15, S18, T02.
Published by: University of Leicester, University Rd, Leicester, LE1 7RH, United Kingdom. TEL 44-116-2522522, FAX 44-116-2522200, http://www.le.ac.uk.

300 BIH ISSN 1840-3719
H1.A3
➤ **EPIPHANY.** Text in English. 2008. s-a. free (effective 2011). **Document type:** *Journal, Academic/Scholarly.*
Media: Online - full text.
Published by: International University of Sarajevo, Paromlinska 66, Sarajevo, 71000, Bosnia Herzegovina. TEL 387-33-720600. Ed. Mustafa Bal.

300 CHE ISSN 1013-6002
AS322.L35
EQUINOXE. Text in French. 1989. s-a. **Document type:** *Journal, Academic/Scholarly.*
Indexed: MLA-IB.
Published by: (Association Arches), Editions Medecine et Hygiene, Chemin de la Mousse 46, CP 475, Chene-Bourg 4, 1225, Switzerland. TEL 41-22-7029311, FAX 41-22-7029355, abonnements@medhyg.ch, http://www.medhyg.ch.

300 DEU ISSN 1619-9464
ERFAHRUNG - WISSEN - IMAGINATION; Schriften zur Wissenssoziologie. Text in German. 2002. irreg., latest vol.17, 2008. price varies. **Document type:** *Monographic series, Academic/Scholarly.*
Published by: U V K Verlagsgesellschaft mbH, Schuetzenstr 24, Konstanz, 78462, Germany. TEL 49-7531-90530, FAX 49-7531-905398, nadine.ley@uvk.de, http://www.uvk.de.

300 001.3 USA ISSN 2153-5345
▼ **ERKLAREN**; social sciences and humanities. Text mainly in Spanish. 2010 (May). s-a. **Document type:** *Journal, Academic/Scholarly.* **Description:** An intercultural, multilingual journal dedicated to multidisciplinary works in social sciences and humanities related to global citizenship.
Related titles: Online - full text ed.: free (effective 2011).
Published by: Carlson & Ortiz Publishing, 4065 Gravenstein Hwy S, No 5, Sebastopol, CA 95472. TEL 630-390-9507, longbeachfrog@yahoo.com.

300 DEU ISSN 0423-3433
ERLANGER FORSCHUNGEN. REIHE A: GEISTESWISSENSCHAFTEN. Text in German. 1954. irreg., latest vol.104, 2003. price varies. **Document type:** *Monographic series, Academic/Scholarly.*
—BLDSC (3810.480000).
Published by: Universitaetsbibliothek Erlangen-Nuernberg, Universitaetsstr. 4, Erlangen, 91054, Germany. TEL 49-9131-8522160, FAX 49-9131-8529309, direktion@bib.uni-erlangen.de, http://www.ub.uni-erlangen.de.

300 DEU ISSN 1610-3696
CODEN: ETSOE9
ERWAEGEN, WISSEN, ETHIK; Streitforum fuer Erwaegungskultur. Text in German; Summaries in English. 1990. q. EUR 82 to individuals; EUR 98 to institutions; EUR 57 to students; EUR 28 per issue (effective 2011). adv. index. 150 p./no. 2 cols./p.; back issues avail. **Document type:** *Journal, Academic/Scholarly.*
Formerly (until 2002): Ethik und Sozialwissenschaften (0937-938X)
Indexed: A12, ABIn, CA, DIP, FR, IBR, IBZ, P48, P51, P53, P54, PCI, PQC, S02, S03, SCOPUS, SOPODA, SociolAb, T02.
Published by: Lucius und Lucius Verlagsgesellschaft mbH, Gerokstr 51, Stuttgart, 70184, Germany. TEL 49-711-242060, FAX 49-711-242088, lucius@luciusverlag.com. Ed. Werner Loh. Circ: 550 (paid and controlled). **Dist. by:** Brockhaus Commission, Kreidlerstr 9, Kornwestheim 70806, Germany. TEL 49-7154-13270, FAX 49-7154-132713, info@brocom.de.

ERZIEHUNG, SCHULE, GESELLSCHAFT. *see* CHILDREN AND YOUTH—About

306 BOL ISSN 1609-6797
ESCARMENEAR; revista boliviana de estudios culturales. Text in Spanish. s-a. back issues avail.
Media: Online - full text.
Published by: Plural Editores, Rosendo Gutierrez 595 esq. Ecuador, Casilla 5097, La Paz, Bolivia. TEL 591-2-411018, FAX 591-2-411528, plural@caoba.entelnet.bo.

ESCUELA DE ADMINISTRACION DE NEGOCIOS. REVISTA. *see* BUSINESS AND ECONOMICS—Management

ESHARP. *see* HUMANITIES: COMPREHENSIVE WORKS

300 FRA ISSN 1953-8316
ESPACE KINSHASA. Text in French. 2003. irreg. **Document type:** *Monographic series, Academic/Scholarly.*
Published by: L' Harmattan, 5 Rue de l'Ecole Polytechnique, Paris, 75005, France. TEL 33-1-43257651, FAX 33-1-43258203.

300 MEX ISSN 2007-0608
ESPACIO TIEMPO. Variant title: Revista Latinoamericana de Ciencias Sociales y Humanidades. Text in Spanish. 2008. s-a. **Document type:** *Journal, Academic/Scholarly.*
Published by: Universidad Autonoma de San Luis Potosi, Coordinacion de Ciencias Sociales y Humanidades, Ave Industrias 101-A, Fracc. Talleres, San Luis Potosi, 78494, Mexico. TEL 52-444-8182475, FAX 52-444-8186453, http://sociales.uaslp.mx.

300 ARG ISSN 1515-9485
ESPACIOS EN BLANCO. SERIE INDAGACIONES. Text in Spanish. 1994. a. ARS 10 (effective 2010). **Document type:** *Monographic series, Academic/Scholarly.*
Published by: Universidad Nacional del Centro de la Provincia de Buenos Aires, Nucleo de Estudios Educacionales y Sociales, Campus Universitario, Paraje Arrollo Seco s-n, Tandil, 7000, Argentina. TEL 54-2293-439751, FAX 54-2293-439759, nees@fch.unicen.edu.ar, http://www.fch.unicen.edu.ar/. Ed. Hugo Russo. Circ: 700.

ESPRIT CRITIQUE; revue internationale de sociologie et des sciences sociales. *see* SOCIOLOGY

ESSAYS ON THE ECONOMY AND SOCIETY OF THE SUDAN. *see* BUSINESS AND ECONOMICS—Economic Situation And Conditions

300 HND
ESTIQUIRIN; arte-ciencia-literatura. Text in Spanish. bi-m.
Published by: Editorial Guaymuras S.A., Apartado Postal 1843, Tegucigalpa D.C., Honduras.

960 ESP ISSN 0214-2309
DT14
ESTUDIOS AFRICANOS; revista de la asociacion espanola de africanistas. Text in Spanish. 1985. s-a. **Document type:** *Journal, Academic/Scholarly.*
Indexed: P09, PCI, RILM.
Published by: Asociacion Espanola de Africanistas, Ramiro de Maetzu, s-n, Madrid, 28040, Spain.

300 CHL ISSN 0718-5022
ESTUDIOS AVANZADOS. Text in Spanish. 2002. s-a. back issues avail. **Document type:** *Journal, Academic/Scholarly.*
Formerly (until 2006): Estudios Avanzados Interactivos (0718-4999)
Related titles: Online - full text ed.: ISSN 0718-5014. 2007.
Published by: Universidad de Santiago de Chile, Instituto de Estudios Avanzados, Roman Diaz 89, Providencia, Santiago, Chile. TEL 56-2-7181360, FAX 56-2-7181358.

918.503 PER
ESTUDIOS AYMARAS BOLETIN DE IDEA. Text in Spanish. 1978. s-a. USD 16 (effective 2001). back issues avail.
Formerly (until 1997): Instituto de Estudios Aymaras. Boletin (0258-8536)
Indexed: AICP, AnthLit.
Published by: Instituto de Estudios Aymaras, Apdo Postal 295, Puno, Peru. Ed. Diego Irarrazaval.

972.8 300 SLV ISSN 0014-1445
AP63 CODEN: ESCEES
➤ **ESTUDIOS CENTROAMERICANOS.** Cover title: E C A. Estudios Centroamericanos. Text in Spanish. 1946. m. SVC 170 domestic; USD 40 in Central America; USD 70 in North America; USD 80 elsewhere (effective 2005). adv. bk.rev. charts; illus. Index. back issues avail. **Document type:** *Magazine, Academic/Scholarly.* **Description:** Covers economics, politics and society in national aspects.
Related titles: Online - full text ed.
Indexed: A22, C01, CA, DIP, H21, HistAb, IBR, IBZ, P08, P09, P34, P42, PAIS, PCI, PSA, RILM, S02, S03, SCOPUS, SOPODA, SSA, SociolAb, T02.
—IE, Infotrieve. **CCC.**
Published by: Universidad Centroamericana Jose Simeon Canas, U C A Editores, Apartado Postal 01-168, San Salvador, El Salvador. TEL 503-210-6600, FAX 503-210-6655, correo@www.uca.edu.sv. Circ: 3,000.

300 ESP ISSN 0423-4847
AP60
ESTUDIOS DE DEUSTO. Text in Spanish. 1953. s-a. EUR 41 domestic; EUR 50 elsewhere (effective 2010). bk.rev. index. back issues avail. **Document type:** *Journal, Academic/Scholarly.*
Indexed: CERDIC, DIP, IBR, IBZ, P09, PAIS, PCI.
Published by: Universidad de Deusto, Departamento de Publicaciones, Apdo 1/E, Bilbao, 48080, Spain. TEL 34-94-4139162, FAX 34-94-4456817, publicaciones@deusto.es, http://deusto-publicaciones.es/.

300 ESP ISSN 2172-2854
ESTUDIOS DE PROGRESO. Text in Spanish. 199?. irreg. **Document type:** *Monographic series, Academic/Scholarly.*
Published by: Fundacion Alternativas, Zurbano 29, 3o. Izq., Madrid, 28010, Spain. TEL 34-91-3199860, FAX 34-91-3192298.

ESTUDIOS FILOSOFICOS; revista de investigacion y critica. *see* PHILOSOPHY

300 CHL ISSN 0718-9230
▼ **ESTUDIOS HEMISFERICOS Y POLARES.** Text in Spanish, English. 2010. q. back issues avail. **Document type:** *Journal, Academic/Scholarly.*
Media: Online - full text.
Published by: Centro de Estudios Hemisfericos y Polares, Calle Roma, 115, Caleta Abarca, Vina del Mar, Chile. Ed. Maria Consuelo Leon Woppke.

300 001.3 ESP ISSN 1699-311X
DA900
➤ **ESTUDIOS IRLANDESES.** Text in Spanish, English. 2005. a. bk.rev.; film rev. back issues avail. **Document type:** *Monographic series, Academic/Scholarly.* **Description:** Publishes original research in the field of Irish studies.
Media: Online - full text.
Indexed: A01, A26, CA, I05, MLA-IB, T02.
Published by: Spanish Association for Irish Studies Ed. Rosa Gonzalez.

971 CHL ISSN 0717-3350
ESTUDIOS NORTEAMERICANOS. Text in Spanish. 1995. s-a. CLP 5,000 domestic; USD 15 foreign (effective 2010). back issues avail. **Document type:** *Journal, Academic/Scholarly.*
Published by: Asociacion Chilena de Estudios Norteamericanos, Balmaceda 37 Dept. 121, Recreo, Cina del Mar, Chile. TEL 56-32-2482831, achenchile@gmail.com, http://www.estudiosnorteamericanos.cl/. Ed. Consuelo Leon. Circ: 150.

300 PRY ISSN 0251-2483
F2661
ESTUDIOS PARAGUAYOS. Text in Spanish. 1973. s-a. (in 1 vol.). PYG 18,000, USD 30 (effective 1998). adv. bk.rev. cum.index. back issues avail.
Indexed: C01, H21, IBR, IBZ, P08, P30.
Published by: Universidad Catolica Nuestra Senora de la Asuncion, Centro de Estudios Antropologicos, Casilla de Correos 1718, Asuncion, Paraguay. TEL 595-21-446251, FAX 595-21-445245. Ed. Adriano Irala Burgos. Circ: 1,000.

330 CHL ISSN 0716-1115
HC191
ESTUDIOS PUBLICOS. Text in Spanish. 1980. q. CLP 9,000 domestic; USD 95 foreign (effective 2010). adv. bk.rev. **Document type:** *Journal, Academic/Scholarly.* **Description:** Contains articles covering a wide variety of interdisciplinary issues.
Related titles: Online - full text ed.: ISSN 0718-3089. 2006.
Indexed: CA, H21, I13, IBR, IBZ, P08, P09, P42, PAIS, PCI, PSA, RILM, S02, S03, SCOPUS, SociolAb, T02.
—BLDSC (3812.800800).
Published by: Centro de Estudios Publicos, Monsenor Sotero Sanz 162, Providencia, Santiago 9, Chile. TEL 56-2-3282400, FAX 56-2-3282440. Ed. Arturo Fontaine Talavera. Pub., R&P, Adv. contact Maria Teresa Miranda. Circ: 2,500.

300 MEX ISSN 0188-4557
H53.M6
➤ **ESTUDIOS SOCIALES**; revista de investigacion cientifica. Text in English, Spanish, Portuguese. 1990. s-a. MXN 200 domestic; USD 18 elsewhere (effective 2011). bk.rev. illus. reprints avail. **Document type:** *Journal, Academic/Scholarly.* **Description:** Focuses on the politics, economics, historical and sociological aspects of the Mexican American borderlands region.
Related titles: Online - full text ed.: free (effective 2011).
Indexed: A01, C01, CA, EconLit, F03, F04, H21, P08, S02, S03, T02.
Published by: Centro de Investigacion en Alimentacion y Desarrollo, Carretera a La Victoria, km 0.6, La Victoria, Mexico. TEL 52-662-2892400, FAX 52-662-2800055, http://www.ciad.mx/. R&P Sergio Sandoval Godoy. Circ: 750.

300 ARG ISSN 0327-4934
ESTUDIOS SOCIALES; revista universitaria semestral. Text in Spanish. 1991. s-a. ARS 25 (effective 2010). **Document type:** *Academic/Scholarly.*
Indexed: H21, P08.
Published by: Universidad Nacional del Litoral, Bv Pellegrini 2750, Santa Fe, S3000, Argentina. TEL 54-342-4571110, http://www.unl.edu.ar. Ed. Dario Macor. Circ: 250.

378 CHL ISSN 0716-0321
HC191
ESTUDIOS SOCIALES. Text in Spanish; Abstracts in English. 1973. s-a. CLP 2,500 domestic; USD 40 in South America; USD 50 in Central America; USD 50 in North America; USD 60 in Europe (effective 2001). bk.rev.; Website rev. abstr.; charts; stat. 270 p./no.; back issues avail. **Document type:** *Journal, Academic/Scholarly.* **Description:** Scholarly articles on employment, education, politics and social sciences.
Indexed: AICP, C01, FR, H21, IBR, IBZ, P08, P09, PAIS, PCI.
Published by: Corporacion de Promocion Universitaria, Casilla 42 Correo 22, Ave. Miguel Claro, 1460, Santiago, Chile. TEL 562-2043418, FAX 562-2741828, cpu@cpu.tie.cl, http:www.cpu.cl. Ed., R&P Eduardo Hill. Circ: 600. **Co-sponsor:** Fundacion Konrad Adenauer.

300 ARG ISSN 1850-6747
ESTUDIOS SOCIALES CONTEMPORANEOS. Text in Spanish. 2006. a. **Document type:** *Monographic series, Academic/Scholarly.*
Published by: Universidad Nacional del Cuyo, Facultad de Filosofia y Letras, 5o Piso Parque General San Martin, Mendoza, 5500, Argentina. TEL 54-261-4135000, FAX 54-261-4494138, cifot@uncu.edu.ar, http://ffyl.uncu.edu.ar/.

300 PER
ESTUDIOS Y DEBATES REGIONALES ANDINOS. Text in Spanish. irreg., latest 1996. **Document type:** *Monographic series.*
Formerly: Debates Andinos
Published by: Centro de Estudios Regionales Andinos "Bartolome de Las Casas", Pampa de la Alianza 164, Cusco, Peru. TEL 51-14-429992, FAX 51-14-427894. Pub. Andres Chirinos Rivera.

300 ARG ISSN 0327-5841
G155.L3
ESTUDIOS Y PERSPECTIVAS EN TURISMO. Text in Spanish. 1991. q. ARS 15 newsstand/cover (effective 2010). back issues avail. **Document type:** *Journal, Academic/Scholarly.*
Formerly (until 1992): Revista Latinoamericana de Turismo (0327-3865)
Related titles: Online - full text ed.: ISSN 1851-1732. 2007. free (effective 2011) (from SciELO).
Indexed: ESPM, F04, SSciA, T02.
Published by: Centro de Investigaciones y Estudios Turisticos, Ave Libertador 774 Piso 6 "W", Buenos Aires, C1001ABU, Argentina. TEL 54-11-45223222, FAX 54-11-48153222. Ed. REgina G Schluter. Circ: 700.

300 PRT ISSN 1647-4376
ESTUDOS. Text in Portuguese. 1998. irreg. **Document type:** *Monographic series, Academic/Scholarly.*
Published by: Universidade Nova de Lisboa, Faculdade de Ciencias Sociais e Humanas, Avenida de Berna 26, Lisbon, 1069-061, Portugal. http://www.cham.fcsh.unl.pt.

300 BRA ISSN 0101-546X
➤ **ESTUDOS AFRO-ASIATICOS.** Text in Portuguese; Abstracts in English, French. 1978. 2/yr. USD 30 domestic; USD 40 foreign; or exchange basis. adv. bk.rev. **Document type:** *Academic/Scholarly.* **Description:** Publishes relevant articles in the field of African and Asian studies. Specializes in race relations and Afro-Brazilian studies.
Related titles: Online - full text ed.: ISSN 1678-4650. 2000.
Indexed: H21, MLA-IB, P08, P42, PerIslam, S02, S03, SociolAb.
Published by: Sociedade Brasileira de Instrucao, Centro de Estudos Afro-Asiaticos, Rua da Assembleia, 10 Conj 501, Centro, Rio De Janeiro, RJ 20011-000, Brazil. TEL 55-21-5312636, FAX 55-21-5312155. Ed. Carlos Hasenbalg. Adv. contact Candido Mendes. Circ: 1,000 (controlled).

300 BRA ISSN 0103-4014
F2510
ESTUDOS AVANCADOS. Text in Multiple languages. 1987. 3/yr. BRL 50 domestic; USD 80 foreign (effective 2005). **Document type:** *Journal, Academic/Scholarly.*
Related titles: Online - full text ed.: ISSN 1806-9592. 2003. free (effective 2011).
Indexed: CA, H21, MLA-IB, P08, P42, PAIS, PSA, S02, S03, SCOPUS, SociolAb, T02.
Published by: Universidade de Sao Paulo, Instituto de Estudos Avancados, Av Professor Luciano Gualberto, Trav J - 374, Sao Paulo, 05508-900, Brazil. TEL 55-11-30913919, FAX 55-11-30914306, estavan@edu.usp.br. Ed. Alfredo Bosi.

300 BRA
ESTUDOS BRASILEIROS. Text in Portuguese. 199?. m. adv. **Document type:** *Newsletter.*
Published by: Universidade de Sao Paulo, Instituto de Estudos Brasileiros, Av. Prof. Mello Moraes, Travessa 8, No. 140, Sao Paulo, SP 05508-900, Brazil. TEL 55-11-2102429, FAX 55-11-8183143. Ed. Neuma Cavalcante. Adv. contact Marta Rossetti Batista.

300 869 BRA ISSN 0103-1821
PQ9000
➤ **ESTUDOS PORTUGUESES E AFRICANOS.** Text in Portuguese, French, Spanish. 1983. s-a. per issue exchange basis. bk.rev. abstr. **Document type:** *Journal, Academic/Scholarly.* **Description:** Presents studies in Portuguese culture and literature and Portuguese culture and literature in African countries.
Indexed: MLA-IB.
Published by: Universidade Estadual de Campinas, Instituto de Estudos da Linguagem, C Universitaria, Caixa Postal 6045, Campinas, SP 13084-976, Brazil. spublic@iel.unicamp.br, http://www.unicamp.br/iel. Eds. Adma Muhana, Haquira Osakabe. R&P Adma Muhana.

300 NGA ISSN 1595-6180
AS633.A1
➤ **ETHIOPE RESEARCH.** Text in English. 2000. 2/yr. USD 8; USD 5 per issue (effective 2004). **Document type:** *Journal, Academic/Scholarly.* **Description:** Contains well-researched articles in the humanities, law and social sciences.
Published by: Kraft Books Ltd., 6 Polytechnic Rd, Sango, Ibadan, Nigeria. Ed., R&P Simon Obikpeko Umukoro. Circ: 1,000 (paid and controlled).

001.3 300 ETH ISSN 1810-4487
HN789
➤ **ETHIOPIAN JOURNAL OF THE SOCIAL SCIENCES AND HUMANITIES.** Text in English. 2003. s-a. USD 15 per issue (effective 2007). **Document type:** *Journal, Academic/Scholarly.*
Indexed: IIBP.
Published by: Addis Ababa University, College of Social Sciences, PO Box 1176, Addis Ababa, Ethiopia. setargew@phil.aau.edu.et. Ed. Setargew Kenaw TEL 251-1-239747.

305.8 GBR ISSN 0141-9870
HT1501
➤ **ETHNIC AND RACIAL STUDIES.** Text in English. 1978. 10/yr. GBP 618 combined subscription in United Kingdom to institutions (print & online eds.); EUR 817, USD 1,021 combined subscription to institutions (print & online eds.) (effective 2012). adv. bk.rev. illus. index. back issues avail.; reprint service avail. from PSC. **Document type:** *Journal, Academic/Scholarly.* **Description:** Provides an interdisciplinary academic forum for the presentation of research and theoretical analysis, drawing on sociology, social policy, anthropology, political science, economics, international relations, history and social psychology.
Related titles: Online - full text ed.: ISSN 1466-4356. GBP 556 in United Kingdom to institutions; EUR 735, USD 919 to institutions (effective 2012) (from IngentaConnect).
Indexed: A01, A02, A03, A08, A20, A22, A25, A26, ABCPolSci, AEI, AICP, AMHA, APEL, ASCA, ASD, AbAn, AmH&L, B04, B05, BAS, BNNA, BRD, CA, CBRI, CJPI, CWI, Chicano, CurCont, DIP, E01, E07, E08, EI, ESPM, FR, FamI, G08, GEOBASE, H09, HPNRM, HRIR, HistAb, I02, I05, I13, IBR, IBSS, IBZ, IIBP, L&LBA, M08, M10, P02, P03, P10, P27, P30, P34, P42, P48, P53, P54, PAIS, PCI, PQC, PRA, PSA, PerIslam, PsycInfo, PsycholAb, R02, R05, RI-1, RI-2, S02, S03, S05, S08, S09, SCOPUS, SOPODA, SRRA, SSA, SSAI, SSAb, SSCI, SSI, SSciA, SWR&A, SociolAb, T02, V&AA, W01, W02, W03, W07, W09, WBA, WMB.
—CIS, IE, Infotrieve, Ingenta, INIST. **CCC.**
Published by: Routledge (Subsidiary of: Taylor & Francis Group), 4 Park Square, Milton Park, Abingdon, Oxon OX14 4RN, United Kingdom. subscriptions@tandf.co.uk, http://www.routledge.com. Ed. Martin Bulmer. Adv. contact Linda Hann TEL 44-1344-779945. Circ: 1,550. **Subscr. to:** Taylor & Francis Ltd., Journals Customer Service, Sheepen Pl, Colchester, Essex CO3 3LP, United Kingdom. TEL 44-20-70175544, FAX 44-20-70175198.

300 GBR ISSN 1468-7968
GN495.6
➤ **ETHNICITIES.** Text in English. 2001 (Apr.). q. USD 831, GBP 449 combined subscription to institutions (print & online eds.); USD 814, GBP 440 to institutions (effective 2011). adv. bk.rev. back issues avail.; reprint service avail. from PSC. **Document type:** *Journal, Academic/Scholarly.* **Description:** New cross-disciplinary journal, centred on sociology and politics, that will provide a critical, interdisciplinary dialogue on questions of ethnicity, nationalism and related issues such as identity politics and minority rights.
Related titles: Online - full text ed.: ISSN 1741-2706. USD 748, GBP 404 to institutions (effective 2011).
Indexed: A01, A03, A08, A20, A22, CA, CurCont, DIP, E01, ERA, ESPM, FR, I13, I14, IBR, IBSS, IBZ, L&LBA, M10, P34, P42, PAIS, PSA, PhilInd, RiskAb, S02, S03, SCOPUS, SRRA, SSCI, SSciA, SociolAb, T02, W07.
—BLDSC (3814.839000), IE, Ingenta, INIST. **CCC.**
Published by: Sage Publications Ltd. (Subsidiary of: Sage Publications, Inc.), 1 Oliver's Yard, 55 City Rd, London, EC1Y 1SP, United Kingdom. TEL 44-20-73248500, FAX 44-20-73248600, info@sagepub.co.uk, http://www.uk.sagepub.com/home.nav. Eds. Stephen May, Tariq Modood. **Subscr. in the Americas to:** Sage Publications, Inc., 2455 Teller Rd, Thousand Oaks, CA 91320. TEL 805-499-9774, FAX 805-499-0871, journals@sagepub.com.

➤ **ETHOS (CARLTON)**; ideas for the classroom discussions & reviews. *see* EDUCATION—Teaching Methods And Curriculum

➤ **ETHOS: DIALOGUES IN PHILOSOPHY AND SOCIAL SCIENCE.** *see* PHILOSOPHY

➤ **ETUDES CANADIENNES/CANADIAN STUDIES.** *see* HUMANITIES: COMPREHENSIVE WORKS

371 BEL ISSN 1781-3867
ETUDES CANADIENNES/CANADIAN STUDIES. Text in French. 2005. irreg., latest vol.21, 2010. price varies. **Document type:** *Monographic series, Academic/Scholarly.*
Published by: P I E - Peter Lang SA, 1 avenue Maurice, 6e etage, Brussels, 1050, Belgium. TEL 32-2-3477236, FAX 32-2-3477237, pie@peterlang.com, http://www.peterlang.net. Ed. Serge Jaumain.

EUROBALKANS. *see* HISTORY—History Of Europe

300 BEL ISSN 0944-2294
EUROCLIO. ETUDES ET DOCUMENTS. Text in French. 1993. irreg., latest vol.55, 2010. price varies. **Document type:** *Monographic series, Academic/Scholarly.*
Published by: P I E - Peter Lang SA, 1 avenue Maurice, 6e etage, Brussels, 1050, Belgium. TEL 32-2-3477236, FAX 32-2-3477237, pie@peterlang.com, http://www.peterlang.net. Eds. Eric Bussiere, Michel Dumoulin.

300 BEL ISSN 0946-9737
EUROCLIO. REFERENCES. Text in French. 1994. irreg., latest vol.2, 1995. price varies. **Document type:** *Monographic series, Academic/Scholarly.*
Published by: P I E - Peter Lang SA, 1 avenue Maurice, 6e etage, Brussels, 1050, Belgium. TEL 32-2-3477236, FAX 32-2-3477237, pie@peterlang.com, http://www.peterlang.net.

EUROHEALTH. *see* PUBLIC HEALTH AND SAFETY

EUROLIMES. *see* POLITICAL SCIENCE—International Relations

943 HUN ISSN 1215-4504
D1050
EUROPA FORUM. Text in Hungarian. 1991. q.
Related titles: English ed.: ISSN 1416-0161.
Published by: Orszagos Muszaki Informacios Kozpont es Konyvtar/ National Technical Information Centre and Library, Muzeum utca 17, PO Box 12, Budapest, 1428, Hungary. TEL 36-1-1382300, FAX 36-1-1180109.

300 DEU ISSN 0721-3409
EUROPAEISCHE HOCHSCHULSCHRIFTEN. REIHE 23: THEOLOGIE/ EUROPEAN UNIVERSITY STUDIES. SERIES 23: THEOLOGY/ PUBLICATIONS UNIVERSITAIRES EUROPEENNES. SERIE 23: THEOLOGIE. Text in English. 1970. irreg., latest vol.901, 2010. price varies. **Document type:** *Monographic series, Academic/Scholarly.*
Published by: Peter Lang GmbH (Subsidiary of: Peter Lang Publishing Group), Eschborner Landstr 42-50, Frankfurt Am Main, 60489, Germany. TEL 49-69-7807050, FAX 49-69-78070550, zentrale.frankfurt@peterlang.com, http://www.peterlang.com.

300 DEU ISSN 0721-3573
EUROPAEISCHE HOCHSCHULSCHRIFTEN. REIHE 29: SOZIALOEKONOMIE. Text in German. 1974. irreg., latest vol.18, 2004. price varies. **Document type:** *Monographic series, Academic/Scholarly.*
Published by: Peter Lang GmbH (Subsidiary of: Peter Lang Publishing Group), Eschborner Landstr 42-50, Frankfurt Am Main, 60489, Germany. TEL 49-69-7807050, FAX 49-69-78070550, zentrale.frankfurt@peterlang.com, http://www.peterlang.com.

EUROPAEISCHE HOCHSCHULSCHRIFTEN. REIHE 39: KONGRESSBERICHTE. *see* MEETINGS AND CONGRESSES

300 DEU
EUROPAEISCHE HORIZONTE. Text in German. 2004. irreg., latest vol.6, 2010. price varies. **Document type:** *Monographic series, Academic/Scholarly.*
Published by: Transcript, Muehlenstr 47, Bielefeld, 33607, Germany. TEL 49-521-63454, FAX 49-521-61040, live@transcript-verlag.de.

300 500 DEU ISSN 0948-7255
EUROPAEISCHE STUDIEN ZUR IDEEN- UND WISSENSCHAFTSGESCHICHTE/EUROPEAN STUDIES IN THE HISTORY OF SCIENCE AND IDEAS. Text in English, German. 1996. irreg., latest vol.16, 2009. price varies. **Document type:** *Monographic series, Academic/Scholarly.*
Published by: Peter Lang GmbH (Subsidiary of: Peter Lang Publishing Group), Eschborner Landstr 42-50, Frankfurt Am Main, 60489, Germany. TEL 49-69-7807050, FAX 49-69-78070550, zentrale.frankfurt@peterlang.com, http://www.peterlang.com. Eds. Georg Gimpl, Juha Manninen.

300 DEU
EUROPAEISCHE UND INTERNATIONALE STUDIEN. Text in German. 2001. irreg., latest vol.5, 2007. price varies. **Document type:** *Monographic series, Academic/Scholarly.*
Published by: Wissenschaftlicher Verlag Trier, Bergstr 27, Trier, 54295, Germany. TEL 49-651-41503, FAX 49-651-41504, wvt@wvttrier.de, http://www.wvttrier.de. Eds. Franz Knipping, Klaus Held.

300 DEU
EUROPAEISIERUNG DURCH KULTURELLE BILDUNG. Text in German. 2005. irreg., latest vol.2, 2005. price varies. **Document type:** *Monographic series, Academic/Scholarly.*
Published by: Waxmann Verlag GmbH, Steinfurter Str 555, Muenster, 48159, Germany. TEL 49-251-265040, FAX 49-251-2650426, info@waxmann.com.

S

300 BEL ISSN 2031-3519
▼ **EUROPE DES CULTURES.** Text in French. 2009. irreg., latest vol.2, 2010. price varies. **Document type:** *Monographic series, Academic/Scholarly.*
Published by: P I E - Peter Lang SA, 1 avenue Maurice, 6e etage, Brussels, 1050, Belgium. TEL 32-2-3477236, FAX 32-2-3477237, pie@peterlang.com, http://www.peterlang.net. Eds. Gabriel Fragniere, Mark Dubrulle.

EUROPEAN CENTRE FOR MINORITY ISSUES. WORKING PAPER. *see* ETHNIC INTERESTS

300 GBR ISSN 1749-4591
EUROPEAN DEVELOPMENT POLICY STUDY GROUP DISCUSSION PAPERS. Text in English. 1996. irreg. free (effective 2009). back issues avail. **Document type:** *Monographic series, Academic/Scholarly.*
Related titles: Online - full text ed.: ISSN 1749-4605.
Published by: (Development Studies Association), Manchester Metropolitan University, c/o Stephen Dearden, Department of Economics, Manchester Metropolitan University, Cavendish St, Manchester, M15 6BG, United Kingdom. FAX 44-161-2476302, s.dearden@mmu.ac.uk.

300 IRL ISSN 1028-5962
HD7260
EUROPEAN FOUNDATION FOR THE IMPROVEMENT OF LIVING AND WORKING CONDITIONS. BULLETIN FROM THE FOUNDATION. Text in English. 1986. bi-m. free. **Document type:** *Newsletter.*
Formerly (until 1996): E F News (0258-1965)
Published by: European Foundation for the Improvement of Living and Working Conditions/Fondation Europeenne pour l'Amelioration des Conditions de Vie et de Travail, Wyattville Rd, Loughlinstown, Co. Dublin 18, Ireland. TEL 353-1-2043100, FAX 353-1-2826456, information@eurofound.europa.eu, http://www.eurofound.europa.eu.

300 DEU ISSN 1863-4354
EUROPEAN INCLUSION STUDIES/STUDIUM EUROPAEISCHER INKLUSION. Text in English, German. 2006. irreg., latest vol.11, 2006. price varies. **Document type:** *Monographic series, Academic/Scholarly.*
Published by: Frank und Timme GmbH, Wittelsbacherstr 27a, Berlin, 10707, Germany. TEL 49-30-88667911, FAX 49-30-86398731, info@frank-timme.de.

300 HUN ISSN 1588-6735
JN26
EUROPEAN INTEGRATION STUDIES. Text in Multiple languages. 2002. s-a. **Description:** Publishes articles on the legal, economic, political, and cultural sides of the European integration process.
Published by: Miskolci Egyetem/University of Miskolc, Miskolc, 3515, Hungary. TEL 36-46-565036, FAX 36-46-365174. Ed. Pal Body.

EUROPEAN JOURNAL OF EPRACTICE. *see* LIBRARY AND INFORMATION SCIENCES

300 GBR ISSN 1450-2267
H1
➤ **THE EUROPEAN JOURNAL OF SOCIAL SCIENCES.** Text in English. 2005. q. **Document type:** *Journal, Academic/Scholarly.* **Description:** Covers scientific articles, original research reports, reviews, short communication and scientific commentaries on cultural studies rooted in lived experience.
Media: Online - full text.
Indexed: A01, SCOPUS, T02.
Published by: EuroJournals, 115 Ashby Rd., Leicestershire, LE153AB, United Kingdom. TEL 43-921-23113333, FAX 43-921-23113334, editor@eurojournals.com, http://www.eurojournals.com/. Ed. Michael J Donano.

980 300 NLD ISSN 0924-0608
F1401 CODEN: RELCEA
➤ **EUROPEAN REVIEW OF LATIN AMERICAN AND CARIBBEAN STUDIES/REVISTA EUROPEA DE ESTUDIOS LATINOAMERICANOS Y DEL CARIBE**; revista Europea de estudios Latinoamericanos y del Caribe. Text in English, Spanish. 1965. s-a. EUR 20 to individuals; EUR 45 to institutions (effective 2010). adv. bk.rev. bibl.; charts. back issues avail. **Document type:** *Journal, Academic/Scholarly.* **Description:** Addresses major debates in Latin America including problems of historical interpretations in social science research of the Caribbean and Latin America.
Former titles (until 1989): Boletin de Estudios Latinoamericanos y del Caribe (0304-2634); Boletin de Estudios Latinoamericanos; Boletin Informativo sobre Estudios Latinoamericanos en Europa (0006-6397)
Related titles: Microfiche ed.: (from IDC); Online - full text ed.: ISSN 1879-4750.
Indexed: A22, A26, A34, B01, B04, B07, C32, CA, CABA, DIP, E12, F08, F12, GH, H16, H21, HistAb, I05, IBR, IBSS, IBZ, ILD, KES, LT, MLA-IB, N02, O01, P06, P08, P09, P30, P34, P42, PAIS, PCI, PSA, R12, RASB, RRTA, S02, S03, S13, S16, SCOPUS, SSA, SSAI, SSAb, SSI, SociolAb, T02, T05, TAR, VS, W03, W05, W11.
—BLDSC (3829.951000), IE, Infotrieve, Ingenta.
Published by: Centrum voor Studie en Documentatie van Latijns Amerika/Center for Latin American Research and Documentation - Centro de Estudios y Documentacion Latinoamericanos, Keizersgracht 395-397, Amsterdam, 1016 EK, Netherlands. TEL 31-20-5253498, FAX 31-20-6255127, secretariat@cedla.nl. Ed. Kathleen Willingham.

➤ **EUROPEAN SEMIOTICS**; language, cognition, and culture. *see* LINGUISTICS

300 DEU ISSN 1615-2506
EUROPEAN SOCIAL INCLUSION/SOZIALGEMEINSCHAFT EUROPA. Text in English, German. 2000. irreg., latest vol.14, 2005. price varies. **Document type:** *Monographic series, Academic/Scholarly.*
Published by: Peter Lang GmbH (Subsidiary of: Peter Lang Publishing Group), Eschborner Landstr 42-50, Frankfurt Am Main, 60489, Germany. TEL 49-69-7807050, FAX 49-69-78070550, zentrale.frankfurt@peterlang.com.

EUROPEAN STUDIES. *see* HISTORY—History Of Europe

300 NLD ISSN 1871-1693
EUROPEAN STUDIES AMSTERDAM. WORKING PAPERS. Text in Dutch. 2005. irreg., latest vol.7, 2007.
Published by: Universiteit van Amsterdam, Opleiding Europese Studies, Spuistr 134, Amsterdam, 1012 VB, Netherlands. TEL 31-20-5252280, FAX 31-20-5254625, secr.es-fgw@uva.nl.

943 USA ISSN 0046-2802
D1050.82.U6
EUROPEAN STUDIES NEWSLETTER. Text in English. 1972. 3/yr. USD 40 to institutions (effective 2000). adv. bk.rev. bibl. 24 p./no.; **Document type:** *Newsletter.* **Description:** Carries notices of the council's programs, as well as announcements of conferences, grants and fellowships. Lists publications drawn from a wide range of sources in Europe and North America.
Published by: Council for European Studies, Columbia University, 808 809 International Affairs Bldg, New York, NY 10027. TEL 212-854-4172, FAX 212-854-8808. Ed. John K Glenn TEL 212-854-4172. R&P Ioannis Sinanoglou TEL 212-854-4727. Circ: 1,200 (paid).

EUROPEAN UNIVERSITY INSTITUTE. ROBERT SCHUMAN CENTRE FOR ADVANCED STUDIES. DISTINGUISHED LECTURES. *see* LAW

EUROPEAN UNIVERSITY INSTITUTE. ROBERT SCHUMAN CENTRE FOR ADVANCED STUDIES. POLICY PAPERS. *see* LAW

300 GBR ISSN 0969-7764
HT395.E85
➤ **EUROPEAN URBAN AND REGIONAL STUDIES.** Text in English. 1994. q. USD 890, GBP 481 combined subscription to institutions (print & online eds.); USD 872, GBP 471 to institutions (effective 2011). bk.rev. back issues avail.; reprint service avail. from PSC. **Document type:** *Journal, Academic/Scholarly.* **Description:** Provides a means of dialogue between different European traditions of intellectual enquiry on urban and regional development issues.
Related titles: Online - full text ed.: ISSN 1461-7145. USD 801, GBP 433 to institutions (effective 2011).
Indexed: A01, A03, A08, A22, A34, A35, A36, AgBio, B01, B06, B07, B09, BibInd, CA, CABA, CurCont, D01, E01, E12, ESPM, GEOBASE, GH, H04, I13, I14, IBSS, LT, N02, P02, P10, P30, P34, P42, P48, P53, P54, PAIS, PQC, PSA, R12, RRTA, RiskAb, S02, S03, S11, S13, S16, SCOPUS, SSCI, SSciA, SUSA, SociolAb, T02, V02, W07, W11, WBA.
—BLDSC (3830.370440), IE, Infotrieve, Ingenta. **CCC.**
Published by: Sage Publications Ltd. (Subsidiary of: Sage Publications, Inc.), 1 Oliver's Yard, 55 City Rd, London, EC1Y 1SP, United Kingdom. TEL 44-20-73248500, FAX 44-20-73248600, info@sagepub.co.uk, http://www.uk.sagepub.com/home.nav. Eds. Allan Williams, Judit Timar. **Subscr. in the Americas to:** Sage Publications, Inc. journals@sagepub.com.

300 NLD ISSN 1568-5926
EUROPEAN VALUES STUDIES. Text in English. 1993. irreg., latest vol.12, 2007. price varies. **Document type:** *Monographic series, Academic/Scholarly.* **Description:** Publishes interpretations and explanations of the quantitative survey data from the European Values Study.
Indexed: IZBG.
—BLDSC (3830.370606).
Published by: Brill, PO Box 9000, Leiden, 2300 PA, Netherlands. TEL 31-71-5353500, FAX 31-71-5317532, cs@brill.nl. Eds. Dr. Loek Halman, Dr. Paul de Graaf.

EUROPEAN YEARBOOK OF MINORITY ISSUES. *see* ETHNIC INTERESTS

300 AUT ISSN 1684-4637
EUROZINE; the netmagazine. Text in Multiple languages. 1998. irreg. **Document type:** *Academic/Scholarly.* **Description:** Publishes contemporary essays and literary texts on European cultural issues and links and promotes the leading cultural magazines from all over Europe.
Media: Online - full content.
Address: Rembrandtstr 31/10, Vienna, 1020, Austria. TEL 43-1-332669122, FAX 43-1-3332970. Ed. Carl Henrik Fredriksson. Adv. contact Stephanie Rhomberg.

300 GBR ISSN 1356-3890
HV41 CODEN: EVALFR
➤ **EVALUATION**; international journal of theory, research and practice. Text in English. 1995. q. USD 976, GBP 528 combined subscription to institutions (print & online eds.); USD 956, GBP 517 to institutions (effective 2011). adv. bk.rev. illus. Index. back issues avail.; reprint service avail. from PSC. **Document type:** *Journal, Academic/Scholarly.* **Description:** Publishes original evaluation research, both theoretical and empirical, as well as reviews of relevant literature and overviews of developments in evaluation policy and practice.
Related titles: Online - full text ed.: ISSN 1461-7153. USD 878, GBP 475 to institutions (effective 2011).
Indexed: A01, A03, A08, A22, ASSIA, B07, CA, E01, ERA, H04, HRA, HospAb, IBSS, P03, P34, P42, PAIS, PSA, PsycInfo, PsycholAb, S02, S03, SOPODA, SPAA, SSA, SociolAb, T02, V02.
—BLDSC (3830.559000), IE, Infotrieve, Ingenta. **CCC.**
Published by: (Tavistock Institute), Sage Publications Ltd. (Subsidiary of: Sage Publications, Inc.), 1 Oliver's Yard, 55 City Rd, London, EC1Y 1SP, United Kingdom. TEL 44-20-73248500, FAX 44-20-73248600, info@sagepub.co.uk, http://www.uk.sagepub.com/home.nav. Ed. Elliot Stern. adv.: B&W page GBP 400; 140 x 210. **Subscr. in the Americas to:** Sage Publications, Inc., 2455 Teller Rd, Thousand Oaks, CA 91320. TEL 805-499-9774, FAX 805-499-0871, journals@sagepub.com.

300 GBR ISSN 0149-7189
H62.A1
➤ **EVALUATION AND PROGRAM PLANNING.** Text in English. 1978. 4/yr. EUR 940 in Europe to institutions; JPY 124,500 in Japan to institutions; USD 1,047 elsewhere to institutions (effective 2012). adv. back issues avail.; reprints avail. **Document type:** *Journal, Academic/Scholarly.* **Description:** Provides articles based on the principle that the techniques and methods of evaluation and planning transcend the boundaries of specific fields and that relevant contributions to these areas come from people representing many different positions, intellectual traditions, and interests.
Related titles: Microfilm ed.: (from PQC); Online - full text ed.: ISSN 1873-7870 (from IngentaConnect, ScienceDirect).
Indexed: A20, A22, A26, A36, AHCMS, ASCA, ASSIA, B01, B06, B07, B09, CA, CABA, CIS, CJPI, CurCont, D01, E-psyche, E03, E12, EI, EMBASE, ERA, ERI, ERIC, ExcerpMed, FamI, GEOBASE, GH, HEA, I05, LT, M12, MCR, MEDLINE, N02, N03, P03, P30, P32, P34, P42, PAIS, PGegResA, PQC, PSA, PsycInfo, PsycholAb, R12, REE&TA, RRTA, S02, S03, S13, S16, S19, S21, SCOPUS, SOPODA, SPAA, SSA, SSCI, SociolAb, T02, T05, TAR, W07, W11.
—BLDSC (3830.565000), IE, Infotrieve, Ingenta. **CCC.**
Published by: Pergamon (Subsidiary of: Elsevier Science & Technology), The Blvd, Langford Ln, East Park, Kidlington, Oxford OX5 1GB, United Kingdom. TEL 44-1865-843000, FAX 44-1865-843010, JournalsCustomerServiceEMEA@elsevier.com. Ed. Jonathan A Morell. **Subscr. to:** Elsevier BV, Radarweg 29, PO Box 211, Amsterdam 1000 AE, Netherlands. TEL 31-20-4853757, FAX 31-20-4853432, http://www.elsevier.nl.

300 USA ISSN 0193-841X
HM1
➤ **EVALUATION REVIEW**; a journal of applied social research. Text in English. 1977. bi-m. USD 987, GBP 581 combined subscription to institutions (print & online eds.); USD 967, GBP 569 to institutions (effective 2011). bk.rev. abstr.; illus. index. back issues avail.; reprint service avail. from PSC. **Document type:** *Journal, Academic/Scholarly.* **Description:** Provides a forum for researchers, planners, and policymakers engaged in the development, implementation, and utilization of evaluation studies.
Formerly (until vol.4, Feb. 1980): Evaluation Quarterly (0145-4692)
Related titles: Microform ed.: (from PQC); Online - full text ed.: ISSN 1552-3926. USD 888, GBP 523 to institutions (effective 2011).
Indexed: A01, A02, A03, A08, A22, A26, AHCMS, AMHA, ASCA, AddicA, B07, BRD, CA, CIS, CLFP, CLI, CPE, CurCont, E-psyche, E01, E02, E03, E07, E08, EMBASE, ERA, ERI, ERIC, EdA, EdI, ExcerpMed, FamI, G08, H04, HRA, HRIS, I05, IBSS, LRI, MEA&I, MEDLINE, P02, P03, P04, P10, P18, P25, P27, P30, P34, P48, P53, P54, PAIS, PCI, PQC, PsycInfo, PsycholAb, R10, R17, Reac, S02, S03, S09, S11, S21, SCOPUS, SOPODA, SPAA, SSA, SSAI, SSAb, SSCI, SSI, SUSA, SWR&A, SociolAb, T02, V02, W01, W02, W03, W07.
—BLDSC (3830.618500), IE, Infotrieve, Ingenta. **CCC.**
Published by: Sage Publications, Inc., 2455 Teller Rd, Thousand Oaks, CA 91320. TEL 805-499-9774, 800-818-7243, FAX 805-499-0871, 800-583-2665, info@sagepub.com. Ed. Richard A Berk. Circ: 750 (paid). **Subscr. outside the Americas to:** Sage Publications Ltd., 1 Oliver's Yard, 55 City Rd, London EC1Y 1SP, United Kingdom. TEL 44-20-73248701, FAX 44-20-73248733, subscription@sagepub.co.uk.

300 GBR ISSN 1744-2648
H97
➤ **EVIDENCE AND POLICY**; a journal of research, debate and practice. Text in English. 2005 (Jan.). q. GBP 440, EUR 580 combined subscription in Europe to institutions (print & online eds.); USD 766 combined subscription in the Americas to institutions (print & online eds.); GBP 477 combined subscription elsewhere to institutions (print & online eds.) (effective 2012). **Document type:** *Journal, Academic/Scholarly.* **Description:** Addresses the needs of those who provide public services, and those who provide the research base for evaluation and development across a wide range of social and public policy issues from social care to education, from public health to criminal justice.
Related titles: Online - full text ed.: ISSN 1744-2656. EUR 522 in Europe to institutions; USD 651 in the Americas to institutions; GBP 373 to institutions in the UK & elsewhere (effective 2011) (from IngentaConnect).
Indexed: CA, CurCont, IBSS, P30, S02, S03, SCOPUS, SSCI, SociolAb, T02, W07.
—BLDSC (3831.036520), IE, Ingenta. **CCC.**
Published by: The Policy Press, University of Bristol, 4th Fl, Beacon House, Queen's Rd, Bristol, BS8 1QU, United Kingdom. TEL 44-117-3314054, FAX 44-117-3314093, tpp-info@bristol.ac.uk, http://www.policypress.org.uk. **Subscr. to:** Portland Customer Services, Commerce Way, Colchester CO2 8HP, United Kingdom. TEL 44-1206-796351, FAX 44-1206-799331, sales@portland-services.com, http://www.portland-services.com.

300 FRA ISSN 1158-4971
EXPLORATIONS ET DECOUVERTES EN TERRES HUMAINES. Text in French. 1990. irreg. back issues avail. **Document type:** *Monographic series, Consumer.*
Published by: Editions Syllepse, 69 rue des Rigoles, Paris, 75020, France. TEL 33-1-44620889.

302.23 300 USA ISSN 1539-7785
P87
EXPLORATIONS IN MEDIA ECOLOGY. Abbreviated title: E M E. Text in English. 2002. s-a. **Description:** Dedicated to extending our understanding of media and media environments.
Indexed: CA, CMM, CommAb, MLA-IB, T02.
Published by: (Media Ecology Association), Hampton Press, Inc., 23 Broadway, Cresskill, NJ 07626. TEL 201-894-1686, hamptonpr1@aol.com. Eds. Judith Y. Lee, Lance Strate.

300 VEN ISSN 1316-7480
F2301
EXTRAMUROS. Text in Spanish. 1990. s-a. looseleaf. bk.rev. abstr.; bibl.; illus.; stat. back issues avail. **Document type:** *Journal, Academic/Scholarly.* **Description:** Presents information on humanities and social science research for scholars, students and professionals.
Related titles: CD-ROM ed.
Indexed: C01.
Published by: Universidad Central de Venezuela, Facultad de Ciencias Juridicas y Politicas, Fondo Editorial de Humanidades y Educacion, Galpon Siete Frente a Fac. de Farmacia, Cuidad Universitaria, Los Chaguaramos, Caracas, 1041, Venezuela. TEL 58-2-6052938, FAX 58-2-6052937, extramurosfhe@yahoo.com. Ed., R&P Gustavo Hernandez Diaz. Pub. Benjamin Sanchez Mujica. Circ: 500.

300 NLD
F S W PUBLICATIEREEKS. (Faculteit Sociale Wetenschappen) Text in Dutch. irreg., latest 2008. price varies.
Published by: (Universiteit van Tilburg, Faculteit Sociale Wetenschappen/University of Tilburg, Faculty of Social Sciences), Rozenberg Publishers, Lindengracht 302 D&E, Amsterdam, 1015 KM, Netherlands. TEL 31-20-6255429, FAX 31-20-6203395, info@rozenbergps.com.

300 384 BRA ISSN 1415-0549
FACULDADE DOS MEIOS DE COMUNICACAO SOCIAL. REVISTA; midia, cultura e tecnologia. Text in Portuguese. 1994. 3/yr. BRL 38 (effective 2007). **Document type:** *Journal, Academic/Scholarly.*
Related titles: Online - full text ed.: free (effective 2011).
Indexed: A26, CA, CMM, H21, I04, I05, P08, P48, P51, P53, P54, PQC, T02.

Published by: (Pontificia Universidade Catolica do Rio Grande do Sul, Faculdade dos Meios de Comunicacao Social), Editora da P U C R S, Avenida Ipiranga 6681, Predio 33, Porto Alegre, RS 90619-900, Brazil. http://www.pucrs.br/edipucrs/.

300 ARG ISSN 1514-6227
H8.S6
FACULTAD DE CIENCIAS HUMANAS. ANUARIO. Text in Spanish. 1998. a. **Document type:** *Journal, Academic/Scholarly.*
Related titles: Online - full text ed.
Indexed: A01, CA, F03, F04, T02.
Published by: Universidad Nacional de la Pampa, Facultad de Ciencias Humanas, Coronel Gil 353 Piso 2, Santa Rosa, La Pampa, 6300, Argentina. TEL 54-2954-422581, FAX 54-2954-433037, anclajes@hotmail.com, http://www.unlpam.edu.ar/index.php. Ed. Maria Herminia Di Liscia. Circ: 500.

300 ARG
FACULTAD DE CIENCIAS SOCIALES. BOLETIN. Text in Spanish. 1998 (no.33). q. back issues avail.
Media: Online - full text.
Published by: Universidad de Buenos Aires, Facultad de Ciencias Sociales, Marcelo T. de Alvear, 2230, Buenos Aires, 1122, Argentina. TEL 54-11-45083800.

300 914.4 CHN ISSN 1002-0888
DC1
FAGUO YANJIU/RESEARCH ON FRANCE. Text in Chinese, French. 1983. s-a. USD 26.80 (effective 2009). bk.rev. **Document type:** *Journal, Academic/Scholarly.* **Description:** Covers French social sciences. Contains articles, translations, and original records on French language, literature, history, philosophy, politics, and economics. Includes columns on academic activities and personal profiles.
Related titles: Online - full text ed.
—East View.
Published by: Wuhan Daxue Faguo Wenti Yanjiusuo, Luojiashan, Wuhan, 430072, China. TEL 86-27-87682945, FAX 86-27-87686879. Circ: 2,000. **Dist. by:** China International Book Trading Corp, 35 Chegongzhuang Xilu, Haidian District, PO Box 399, Beijing 100044, China. TEL 86-10-68412045, FAX 86-10-68412023, cibtc@mail.cibtc.com.cn, http://www.cibtc.com.cn.

300 ITA ISSN 0392-2774
LA FAMIGLIA. Text in Italian. 1965. bi-m. EUR 50.50 domestic; EUR 80 in Europe; EUR 100 elsewhere (effective 2009). **Document type:** *Magazine, Consumer.*
Published by: Editrice La Scuola SpA, Via Luigi Cadorna 11, Brescia, BS 25124, Italy. TEL 39-030-29931, FAX 39-030-2993299, http://www.lascuola.it.

300 GBR ISSN 2046-7435
▼ **FAMILIES, RELATIONSHIPS AND SOCIETIES.** Text in English. forthcoming 2012. 3/yr. GBP 295, EUR 354 combined subscription in Europe to institutions (print & online eds.); USD 530 combined subscription in North America to institutions (print & online eds.); GBP 325 combined subscription elsewhere to institutions (print & online eds.) (effective 2012). **Document type:** *Journal, Academic/Scholarly.* **Description:** Explores family life, relationships and generational issues from interdisciplinary, social science perspectives, whilst maintaining a solid grounding in sociological theory and methods and a strong policy and practice focus.
Related titles: Print ed.: ISSN 2046-7443. forthcoming. EUR 319 in Europe to institutions; USD 430 in North America to institutions; GBP 266 to institutions in the UK & elsewhere (effective 2012).
Published by: The Policy Press, University of Bristol, 4th Fl, Beacon House, Queen's Rd, Bristol, BS8 1QU, United Kingdom. TEL 44-117-3314054, FAX 44-117-3314093, tpp-info@bristol.ac.uk, http://www.policypress.org.uk.

FANGZHI GAOXIAO JICHU KEXUE XUEBAO/BASIC SCIENCES JOURNAL OF TEXTILE UNIVERSITIES. *see* SCIENCES: COMPREHENSIVE WORKS

FAST CAPITALISM. *see* POLITICAL SCIENCE

300 305.4 USA ISSN 1070-549X
FEMINISM IN SOCIAL SCIENCES. Text in English. 2002. irreg., latest vol.2, 2002. price varies. 224 p./no.; **Document type:** *Monographic series, Academic/Scholarly.*
Published by: Peter Lang Publishing, Inc. (Subsidiary of: Peter Lang Publishing Group), 29 Broadway, New York, NY 10006. TEL 212-647-7700, 800-770-5264, FAX 212-647-7707, customerservice@plang.com, http://www.peterlangusa.com. Eds. Carol Brown, Renee G Kasinsky.

300 USA
FERNAND BRAUDEL CENTER. NEWSLETTER. Text in English. 1977. a. free (effective 2003). back issues avail.; reprints avail. **Document type:** *Newsletter.*
Media: E-mail. **Related titles:** Online - full content ed.
Published by: Fernand Braudel Center for the Study of Economies, Historical Systems, and Civilizations, Binghamton University, Fernand Braudel Center, P.O. Box 6000, Binghamton, NY 13902. TEL 607-777-4924, FAX 607-777-4315. Ed. Immanuel Wallerstein. R&P Donna DeVoist.

300 PER ISSN 1992-1330
FIAT LUX. Text in Spanish. 2001. s-a. PEN 50 domestic; USD 30 in the Americas; USD 50 elsewhere (effective 2006). back issues avail. **Document type:** *Journal, Academic/Scholarly.*
Published by: Universidad Nacional de Cajamarca, Escuela de Posgrado, Ave. Atahualpa 1050, Cajamarca, Peru. TEL 51-76-363263, FAX 51-76-362796, posgrafounc@yahoo.es, http://www.unc.edu.pe/paginas/postgradoweb/inicio.htm.

300 301 900 FJI
➤ **FIJIAN STUDIES**; a journal of contemporary Fiji. Text in English. 2003. s-a. (May & Nov.). bk.rev. **Document type:** *Journal, Academic/Scholarly.* **Description:** Contains scholarly articles on contemporary Fijian issues in the broad field of humanities and the social sciences. Also includes debates, commentaries and interviews with scholars, public figures and policy makers on issues relevant to contemporary Fiji.
Published by: Fiji Institute of Applied Studies, PO Box 7580, Lautoka, Fiji. ganesh@connect.com.fj. Ed. Ganesh Chand.

➤ **FILOSOFIA, STORIA, SCIENZE SOCIALI.** *see* PHILOSOPHY

➤ **THE FLAG & BANNER.** *see* GENEALOGY AND HERALDRY

300 DEU ISSN 0932-5859
FLENSBURGER HEFTE. Text in German. 1987. q. EUR 42 domestic; EUR 46 foreign (effective 2005). bk.rev. illus. back issues avail. **Document type:** *Journal, Academic/Scholarly.*
Published by: Flensburger Hefte Verlag GmbH, Holm 64, Flensburg, 24937, Germany. flensburgerhefte@t-online.de, http://www.flensburgerhefte.de. Eds. Klaus Dieter Neumann, Wolfgang Weirauch. Circ: 7,000 (paid).

300 DEU ISSN 0943-5549
FLENSBURGER HEFTE. SONDERHEFT. Text in German. 1987. irreg. **Document type:** *Monographic series, Academic/Scholarly.*
Published by: Flensburger Hefte Verlag GmbH, Holm 64, Flensburg, 24937, Germany. flensburgerhefte@t-online.de, http://www.flensburgerhefte.de.

FLORIDA ATLANTIC COMPARATIVE STUDIES. *see* HUMANITIES: COMPREHENSIVE WORKS

300 USA ISSN 2160-7486
▼ **FLORIDA STUDIES WEEKLY. 1 SOCIAL STUDIES.** Text in English. 2011. s-m. USD 9.98 1-9 students; USD 4.99 10 or more students (effective 2012). **Document type:** *Magazine, Consumer.*
Published by: American Legacy Publishing, 1922 W 200 N, Lindon, UT 84042. TEL 866-311-8734, FAX 866-531-5589, service@studiesweekly.com.

300 LKA
FOCUS. Text in English. 1977. m. LKR 36.
Published by: Collective, 26 Clifford Ave., Colombo, 3, Sri Lanka.

300 CAN ISSN 0838-5319
FOCUS NEWSLETTER. Text in English. 1972. irreg. free to members.
Formerly (until 1988): Focus (Edmonton) (0315-2227)
Published by: Alberta Teachers' Association, 11010 142 St NW, Edmonton, AB T5N 2R1, Canada. TEL 780-447-9400, FAX 780-455-6481, http://www.teachers.ab.ca. Circ: 1,114.

306.0971 CAN ISSN 0843-7548
FOCUS ON CULTURE. Text in Multiple languages. 1989. q.
Indexed: C03, CBCARef, P48, PQC.
Published by: Statistics Canada/Statistique Canada, Publications Sales and Services, Ottawa, ON K1A 0T6, Canada. TEL 613-951-8116, 800-267-6677, infostats@statcan.ca, http://www.statcan.gc.ca.

300 DEU ISSN 1861-4108
FOERMIG EDITION. Text in German. 2005. irreg., latest vol.6, 2009. price varies. **Document type:** *Monographic series, Academic/Scholarly.*
Published by: Waxmann Verlag GmbH, Steinfurter Str 555, Muenster, 48159, Germany. TEL 49-251-265040, FAX 49-251-2650426, info@waxmann.com.

300 330.1 POL ISSN 1506-1965
HD1401
➤ **FOLIA UNIVERSITATIS AGRICULTURAE STETINENSIS. OECONOMICA.** Text in Polish; Abstracts in English. 1976. irreg. price varies. bk.rev. **Document type:** *Journal, Academic/Scholarly.*
Former titles: Akademia Rolnicza w Szczecinie. Zeszyty Naukowe. Nauki Spoleczne i Ekonomiczne (1230-770X); Akademia Rolnicza w Szczecinie. Zeszyty Naukowe Nauk Spolecznych i Ekonomicznych (0208-7669); Akademia Rolnicza w Szczecinie. Zeszyty Naukowe. Ekonomika, Organizacja i Kierowanie (0137-2009)
Indexed: AgrAg, AgrLib, BA, CABA, ChemAb, GH, IndVet, LT, OR, P37, PHN&I, PN&I, REE&TA, RRTA, S17, TriticAb, VS.
Published by: Akademia Rolnicza w Szczecinie/Agricultural University of Szczecin, Dzial Wydawnictw, Ul Doktora Judyma 22, Szczecin, 71466, Poland. TEL 48-91-4541639, FAX 48-91-4541642, TELEX 0425494 AR, nauka@ar.szczecin.pl. Ed. Wieslaw F Skrzypczak.

300 COL ISSN 0123-4870
H8.S6
FOLIOS (BOGOTA). Text in Spanish. 1990. s-a.
Formerly (until 1990): Folios de Literatura e Idiomas (0120-2146)
Related titles: Online - full text ed.: (from SciELO).
Indexed: CPE, ERA, MLA-IB, S21.
Published by: (Universidad Pedagogica Nacional, Facultad de Artes y Humanidades), Universidad Pedagogica Nacional, Centro de Investigaciones, Calle 127 #12A-20, Bogota, DC, Colombia. TEL 57-1-6156531, FAX 57-1-6156512, investigaciones@pedagogica.edu.co, http://ciup.pedagogica.edu.co. Circ: 500.

301 945 ITA ISSN 0393-3954
HX15
FONDAZIONE GIANGIACOMO FELTRINELLI. ANNALI. Text in Italian. 1958. a. price varies. bk.rev. **Document type:** *Journal, Academic/Scholarly.*
Formerly (until 1973): Istituto Giangiacomo Feltrinelli. Annali (0544-1374)
Indexed: IBR, IBZ, P30.
Published by: Fondazione Giangiacomo Feltrinelli, Via Gian Domenico Romagnosi 3, Milan, 20121, Italy. TEL 39-02-874175, FAX 39-02-86461855, fondazione@feltrinelli.it, http://www.feltrinelli.it. Circ: 3,000.

300 ITA
FONDAZIONE GIUSEPPE DI VITTORIO. ANNALI. Text in Italian. 1993. irreg. **Document type:** *Yearbook, Corporate.*
Published by: Fondazione Giuseppe Di Vittorio, Via Donizzetti 7 B, Rome, 00198, Italy. TEL 39-06-85356715, FAX 39-06-85834227, http://www.fondazionedivittorio.it.

300 ITA ISSN 0531-9870
H17 CODEN: AFLEF7
FONDAZIONE LUIGI EINAUDI. ANNALI. Text in Italian. 1967. a., latest vol.38, 2004. EUR 98 combined subscription foreign to institutions (print & online eds.) (effective 2012). **Document type:** *Proceedings, Academic/Scholarly.* **Description:** Reports on the scientific activities of the foundation. Includes papers on the social sciences from grant recipients.
Related titles: Online - full text ed.: ISSN 2036-5667.
Indexed: AmH&L, CA, HistAb, IBR, IBSS, IBZ, P30, RASB, SOPODA, SociolAb, T02.
Published by: (Fondazione Luigi Einaudi), Casa Editrice Leo S. Olschki, Viuzzo del Pozzetto 8, Florence, 50126, Italy. TEL 39-055-6530684, FAX 39-055-6530214, celso@olschki.it, http://www.olschki.it. Ed. Terenzio Cozzi. Circ: 1,000.

300 USA ISSN 1063-7281
AS911.F6
FORD FOUNDATION REPORT. Text in English. 1970. 3/yr. free (effective 2005). bibl.; illus. index. back issues avail.; reprints avail. **Document type:** *Newsletter.* **Description:** Contains articles and reports on subjects related to the foundation's interests in the U.S. and abroad. Includes brief announcements of recent grants, publications and appointments.
Formerly: Ford Foundation Letter (0015-699X)
Related titles: Microform ed.: (from PQC); Online - full text ed.
Indexed: A01, A03, A08, A22, ABS&EES, BiolDig, C04, CA, HRIR, MLA-IB, P05, P06, P30, T02.
Published by: Ford Foundation, Office of Communications, 320 E 43rd St, New York, NY 10017. TEL 212-573-5000, FAX 212-351-3677, office-of-communications@fordfound.org. Ed. Thomas Quinn. Circ: 35,000.

FORESIGHT (CAMBRIDGE); the journal for future studies, strategic thinking and policy. *see* TECHNOLOGY: COMPREHENSIVE WORKS

300 320 ESP ISSN 1578-4576
JA26
➤ **FORO INTERNO.** Text in Spanish. 2001. a., latest vol.10, 2010. EUR 15 domestic to institutions; EUR 20 in Europe to institutions; EUR 24 elsewhere to institutions (effective 2011). **Document type:** *Journal, Academic/Scholarly.*
Related titles: CD-ROM ed.; Online - full text ed.: ISSN 1988-2920. free (effective 2011).
Indexed: H21, I04, I05, IBSS, P08, P27, P45, P48, P54, PQC, PhilInd.
Published by: (Universidad Complutense de Madrid, Facultad de Ciencias Politicas y Sociologia), Universidad Complutense de Madrid, Servicio de Publicaciones, C/ Obispo Trejo 2, Ciudad Universitaria, Madrid, 28040, Spain. TEL 34-91-3941127, FAX 34-91-3941126, servicio.publicaciones@rect.ucm.es, http://www.ucm.es/publicaciones. Ed. Javier Roiz Parra.

➤ **FORSCHUNG, STUDIUM UND PRAXIS.** *see* EDUCATION

300 DEU ISSN 0341-1508
FORTSCHRITTE DER SOZIALPAEDIATRIE. Text in German. 1973. irreg., latest vol.13, 1990. price varies. **Document type:** *Monographic series, Academic/Scholarly.*
—GNLM. **CCC.**
Published by: Hansisches Verlagskontor, Mengstr 16, Luebeck, 23552, Germany. TEL 49-451-703101, FAX 49-451-7031253, http://www.beleke.de/verlagsgruppe/ind_hvk.html. Ed. Dr. Theodor Hellbruegge.

504 AUT ISSN 1990-9748
FORUM EXKURSE. Text in German. 2006. q. EUR 3 newsstand/cover (effective 2007). **Document type:** *Journal, Academic/Scholarly.*
Published by: Forum Umweltbildung, Alser Str 21, Vienna, 1080, Austria. TEL 43-1-4024701, FAX 43-1-402470151, forum@umweltbildung.at, http://www.umweltbildung.at.

300 DEU ISSN 0947-1960
FORUM MIGRATION. Text in German. 1995. irreg., latest vol.10, 2007. price varies. **Document type:** *Monographic series, Academic/Scholarly.*
Published by: Lucius und Lucius Verlagsgesellschaft mbH, Gerokstr 51, Stuttgart, 70184, Germany. TEL 49-711-242060, FAX 49-711-242088, lucius@luciusverlag.com, http://www.luciusverlag.com.

300 001.3 USA ISSN 1556-763X
H96
➤ **FORUM ON PUBLIC POLICY.** Text in English. 2005. 5/yr. USD 74 domestic; USD 80 foreign; USD 30 per issue domestic; USD 37 per issue foreign (effective 2010). back issues avail. **Document type:** *Journal, Academic/Scholarly.*
Related titles: Online - full text ed.: ISSN 1938-9809. free (effective 2010).
Indexed: A26, CA, I05, P42, T02.
Address: 406 W Florida Ave, Urbana, IL 61801. TEL 217-344-0237, FAX 217-344-6963.

300 DEU ISSN 1436-2708
FORUM POLITIK UND GESCHLECHTERVERHAELTNISSE. Text in German. 1999. irreg. price varies. **Document type:** *Monographic series, Academic/Scholarly.*
Published by: Centaurus Verlag & Media KG, Kaiser-Joseph-Str 267, Freiburg, 79098, Germany. TEL 49-761-1525861, FAX 49-761-1525868, info@centaurus-verlag.de, http://www.centaurus-verlag.de.

300 DEU ISSN 1438-5627
H62.A1
➤ **FORUM QUALITATIVE SOZIALFORSCHUNG/FORUM: QUALITATIVE SOCIAL RESEARCH.** Abbreviated title: F Q S. Text in German, English, Spanish. 1999. 3/yr. free (effective 2011). bk.rev. abstr. back issues avail. **Document type:** *Journal, Academic/Scholarly.* **Description:** Fosters discussion among qualitative researchers from various nations and social science disciplines.
Media: Online - full content. **Related titles:** Online - full text ed.
Indexed: AEI, CA, CJA, E-psyche, E03, IBSS, LeftInd, P30, P42, PSA, S02, S03, SCOPUS, SSA, SociolAb, T02.
—**CCC.**
Published by: Freie Universitaet Berlin, Institut fuer Qualitative Forschung, Habelschwerdter Allee 45, Berlin, 14195, Germany. TEL 49-30-83855725, FAX 49-30-83852843, katja.mruck@fu-berlin.de, http://www.qualitative-forschung.de. **Co-publisher:** Zentrum fuer Qualitative Bildungs-, Geratungs- und Sozialforschung. **Co-sponsor:** Zentrum fuer Qualitative Bildungs-, Geratungs- und Sozialforschung.

300 DEU ISSN 1618-694X
FORUM SOZIALPOLITIK. Text in German. 1970. irreg. bk.rev. **Document type:** *Newsletter, Consumer.*
Former titles (until 1997): Forum der AG Spak (0943-7088); (until 1991): Arbeitsgemeinschaft Sozialpolitischer Arbeitskreise. Forum (0722-8198); (until 1981): Spak-Forum (0171-3159)
Published by: A G - S P A K, Dorfstr 25, Wasserburg, 88142, Germany. agspak@t-online.de, http://www.agspak.de. Ed. Dieter Koschek.

300 DEU ISSN 0942-0045
FORUM SUPERVISION. Text in German. 1993. s-a. EUR 14 newsstand/cover (effective 2010). adv. bk.rev. **Document type:** *Journal, Academic/Scholarly.*
Indexed: IBR, IBZ.

S

Published by: Fachhochschulverlag - Der Verlag fuer Angewandte Wissenschaften e.K., Kleiststr 10, Frankfurt, 60318, Germany. TEL 49-69-15332820, FAX 49-69-15332840, kontakt@fhverlag.de. Circ: 2,000.

323.4 UGA
FORWARD. Text in English. 1979-1985; resumed 1986. q. UGX 400, USD 10. adv. bk.rev.; play rev.
Published by: Forward Publications Ltd., PO Box 5160, Kampala, Uganda. Circ: 3,000.

300 CHN ISSN 1008-018X
FOSHAN KEXUE JISHU XUEYUAN XUEBAO (SHEHUI KEXUE BAN)/FOSHAN UNIVERSITY. JOURNAL (SOCIAL SCIENCE EDITION). Text in Chinese. 1983. bi-m. CNY 5 newsstand/cover (effective 2007). **Document type:** *Journal, Academic/Scholarly.*
Supersedes in part (in 1998): Foshan Daxue Xuebao/Foshan University. Journal (1004-2520); Which was formerly: Foshan Daxue Foshan Shi-zhuan Xuebao/Foshan University and Foshan Normal College. Journal (1001-8190)
Related titles: Online - full text ed.
Published by: Foshan Kexue Jishu Xueyuan/Foshan University, 18, Jiangwan Yi Lu, Foshan, Guangdong 528000, China.

FOURTH DOOR REVIEW. *see* ENVIRONMENTAL STUDIES

FRAMING FILM; the history and art of cinema. *see* MOTION PICTURES

300 DEU ISSN 1612-989X
FREIBERGER BEITRAEGE ZUR INTERKULTURELLEN UND WIRTSCHAFTSKOMMUNIKATION. Text in German. 2005. irreg., latest vol.5, 2009. price varies. **Document type:** *Monographic series, Academic/Scholarly.*
Published by: Peter Lang GmbH (Subsidiary of: Peter Lang Publishing Group), Eschborner Landstr 42-50, Frankfurt Am Main, 60489, Germany. TEL 49-69-7807050, FAX 49-69-7807050, zentrale.frankfurt@peterlang.com, http://www.peterlang.com. Ed. Michael Hinner.

300 DEU ISSN 1438-0277
FREIENWALDER HEFTE. Text in German. 1999. irreg., latest vol.7, 2006. price varies. **Document type:** *Monographic series, Academic/Scholarly.*
Published by: Akademische Verlagsanstalt AVA, Oststr 41, Leipzig, 04317, Germany. TEL 49-341-9900440, FAX 49-341-9900440, info@univerlag-leipzig.de.

300 DEU
FREMDE NAEHE; Wissenschaftliche Diskurse zu Politik, Gesellschaft und Wirtschaft in einer globalisierten Welt. Text in German. 2005. irreg., latest vol.8, 2006. price varies. **Document type:** *Monographic series, Academic/Scholarly.*
Published by: Wissenschaftlicher Verlag Berlin, Koertestr 10, Berlin, 10967, Germany. TEL 49-30-89379899, FAX 49-30-6185021, verlag@wvberlin.de, http://www.wvberlin.de.

300 IND
FRENCH INSTITUTE, PONDICHERRY. PONDY PAPERS IN SOCIAL SCIENCES. Text in English; Summaries in French. 1989. irreg., latest 1993. price varies. **Document type:** *Monographic series, Trade.*
Published by: Institut Francais de Pondichery/French Institute of Pondicherry, PO Box 33, Pondicherry, Tamil Nadu 605 001, India. TEL 91-413-2334168, ifpinfo@ifpindia.org. Circ: 250.

300 DEU ISSN 0947-2339
FRIEDENSAUER SCHRIFTENREIHE. REIHE B: GESELLSCHAFTSWISSENSCHAFTEN. Text in German. 1995. irreg., latest vol.12, 2007. price varies. **Document type:** *Monographic series, Academic/Scholarly.*
Published by: Peter Lang GmbH (Subsidiary of: Peter Lang Publishing Group), Eschborner Landstr 42-50, Frankfurt Am Main, 60489, Germany. TEL 49-69-7807050, FAX 49-69-78070550, zentrale.frankfurt@peterlang.com. Eds. Horst Rolly, Johann Gerhardt, Wolfgang Kabus.

300 DEU
FRITZ-HUESER-INSTITUT FUER DEUTSCHE UND AUSLAENDISCHE ARBEITERLITERATUR. SCHRIFTEN. Text in German. 2006. irreg., latest vol.19, 2009. price varies. **Document type:** *Monographic series, Academic/Scholarly.*
Formed by the merger of (1985-2006): Fritz-Hueser-Institut fuer Deutsche und Auslaendische Arbeiterliteratur. Reihe 1: Ausstellungskataloge zur Arbeiterkultur (1436-1965); (1995-2006): Fritz-Hueser-Institut fuer Deutsche und Auslaendische Arbeiterliteratur. Reihe 2: Forschungen zur Arbeiterliteratur (1436-1973)
Published by: (Fritz-Hueser-Institut fuer Deutsche und Auslaendische Arbeiterliteratur), Klartext Verlag GmbH, Hesslerstr 37, Essen, 45329, Germany. TEL 49-201-8620631, FAX 49-201-8620622, info@klartext-verlag.de, http://www.klartext-verlag.de.

300 MEX
FRONTERA INTERIOR; revista de ciencias sociales y humanidades. Text in Spanish. 1999. q. MXN 100; MXN 35 newsstand/cover (effective 2000).
Published by: Universidad Autonoma de Queretaro, Facultad de Ciencias Politicas y Sociales, Centro Universitario, Cerra de las Campanas, Queretaro, Queretaro, 76000, Mexico. TEL 52-42-167-526, herman@sunserver.uaq.mx.

FUDAN JOURNAL OF THE HUMANITIES AND SOCIAL SCIENCES. *see* HUMANITIES: COMPREHENSIVE WORKS

300 CHN ISSN 0257-0289
H8.C49
FUDAN XUEBAO (SHEHUI KEXUE BAN)/FUDAN JOURNAL (SOCIAL SCIENCES EDITION). Text in Chinese; Contents page in English. 1935. bi-m. 112 p./no.; **Document type:** *Journal, Academic/Scholarly.*
Formerly: Fudan Daxue Xuebao (Zhexue Shehui Kexue Ban)
Related titles: Online - full text ed.
Indexed: MLA-IB.
—East View.
Published by: Fudan Daxue/Fudan University, 220 Handan Lu, Shanghai, 200433, China. TEL 86-21-65642109, FAX 86-21-65642669. **Dist. outside China by:** China International Book Trading Corp, 35 Chegongzhuang Xilu, Haidian District, PO Box 399, Beijing 100044, China.

FUJIAN LUNTAN (RENWEN SHEHUI KEXUE BAN)/FUJIAN TRIBUNE (THE HUMANITIES & SOCIAL SCIENCES). *see* HUMANITIES: COMPREHENSIVE WORKS

300 100 CHN ISSN 1671-6922
FUJIAN NONG-LIN DAXUE XUEBAO (ZHEXUE SHEHUI KEXUE BAN)/FUJIAN AGRICULTURE AND FORESTRY UNIVERSITY. JOURNAL (PHILOSOPHY AND SOCIAL SCIENCES). Text in Chinese. 1998. q. CNY 5 newsstand/cover (effective 2006). **Document type:** *Journal, Academic/Scholarly.*
Formerly (until 2001): Fujian Nongye Daxue Xuebao (Shehui Kexue Ban)/Fujian Agricultural University. Journal (Social Science Edition) (1008-6854)
Related titles: Online - full text ed.
Published by: Fujian Nong-Lin Daxue, Jinshan, Fuzhou, 350002, China. TEL 86-591-83789314, FAX 86-591-83769237.

300 CHN ISSN 1007-550X
FUJIAN QINGFANG/LIGHT & TEXTILE INDUSTRIES OF FUJIAN. Text in Chinese. 1988. m. CNY 2.20 newsstand/cover (effective 2006). **Document type:** *Journal, Academic/Scholarly.*
Formerly: Fujian Qingfang Xinxi (1005-6394); Zouxiang Shijie (1001-2370)
Related titles: Online - full text ed.
Published by: Fujian Sheng QingFang Qingbao Yanjiusuo, 53, Baima Zhong Lu, Fujian, 350005, China. TEL 86-591-3338817, FAX 86-591-3362442.

300 500 CHN ISSN 1008-3421
FUJIAN SHI-DA FUQING FENXIAO XUEBAO/FUJIAN NORMAL UNIVERSITY. FUQING BRANCH. JOURNAL. Text in Chinese. 1981. bi-m. CNY 5 newsstand/cover (effective 2006). **Document type:** *Journal, Academic/Scholarly.*
Related titles: Online - full text ed.
Published by: Fujian Shifan Daxue, Fuqing Fenxiao, Fuqing, 350300, China. TEL 86-591-5260230.

300 CHN ISSN 1000-5285
AS452.F8314
FUJIAN SHIFAN DAXUE XUEBAO (SHEHUI KEXUE BAN)/FUJIAN NORMAL UNIVERSITY. JOURNAL (SOCIAL SCIENCE EDITION). Text in Chinese. q. USD 24.60 (effective 2009). **Description:** Covers research results in different fields of the social sciences, including philosophy, economics, linguistics, literature, history, education and the arts.
Related titles: Online - full text ed.
Published by: Fujian Shifan Daxue/Fujian Normal University, 137 Shangsan Lu, Cangshan-qu, Fuzhou, Fujian 350007, China. TEL 86-25-5410349. Ed. Chen Zheng. **Dist. overseas by:** Jiangsu Publications Import & Export Corp., 56 Gao Yun Ling, Nanjing, Jiangsu, China.

300 CHN ISSN 1009-4784
FUJIAN YIKE DAXUE XUEBAO (SHEHUI KEXUE BAN). Text in Chinese. 2000. q. CNY 5 newsstand/cover (effective 2006). **Document type:** *Journal, Academic/Scholarly.*
Related titles: Online - full text ed.
Published by: Fujian Yike Daxue/Fujian Medical University, Minghouxian Shang Jie, Zhenxueyuan Lu #1, Fuzhou, 350108, China. TEL 86-591-22862454, FAX 86-591-22862341.

300 JPN ISSN 0286-3227
H8.J3
FUKUOKA KYOIKU DAIGAKU KIYO. DAI 2-BUNSATSU, SHAKAIKA-HEN/FUKUOKA UNIVERSITY OF EDUCATION. BULLETIN. PART 2, SOCIAL SCIENCES. Text in Japanese. 1952. a. **Document type:** *Bulletin, Academic/Scholarly.*
Formerly (until 1966): Fukuoka Gakugei Daigaku Kiyo. Dai 2-bu, Shakaika-hen/Fukuoka Gakugei University. Bulletin. Part 2, Social Sciences (0286-5165); Which supersedes in part (1954-1966): Fukuoka Gakugei Daigaku Kiyo. Dai 1-bu, Bunka-hen (0286-5157); Which was superseded in part (in 1953): Fukuoka Gakugei Daigaku kiyo/Fukuoka Gakugei University. Bulletin (0286-4363)
Published by: Fukuoka Kyoiku Daigaku/Fukuoka University of Education, 1-1 Akamabunkyomachi, Munakata, Fukuoka 811-4192, Japan. http://www.fukuoka-edu.ac.jp/.

300 BRA
FUNDACAO JOAQUIM NABUCO. SERIE MONOGRAFIAS. Text in Portuguese. 1975. irreg., latest vol.31, 1989. USD 2.50 per issue. **Document type:** *Monographic series.*
Formerly: Instituto Joaquim Nabuco de Pesquisas Sociais. Serie Monografias
Published by: (Fundacao Joaquim Nabuco), Editora Massangana, Rua Dois Irmaos, 15, Apipucos, Recife, PE 52071-440, Brazil. TEL 081-268-4611, FAX 081-268-9600.

300 COL ISSN 0120-7075
FUNDACION ANTIOQUENA PARA LOS ESTUDIOS SOCIALES. ESTUDIOS SOCIALES. Text in Spanish. 1986. s-a. COP 12,000; USD 60 foreign. adv. bk.rev. **Document type:** *Academic/Scholarly.* **Description:** Presents research and studies in the social sciences.
Published by: Fundacion Antioquena para los Estudios Sociales, Carrera 45, 59-77, Apartado Aereo 8650, Medellin, ANT, Colombia. TEL 57-4-254-1792, FAX 57-4-254-4953. Ed. Hector Abad Faciolince. Pub., Adv. contact Juan Manuel Ospina Restrepo. Circ: 1,000 (paid).

300 ESP ISSN 0213-1404
AS301
FUNDACION JOAQUIN COSTA. ANALES. Text in Spanish. 1984. a. back issues avail. **Document type:** *Monographic series, Academic/Scholarly.*
Published by: Fundacion Joaquin Costa, Diego de Leon, 33, Madrid, 28006, Spain. TEL 34-974-294120, FAX 34-974-294122.

303 USA ISSN 1554-7744
CB161
➤ **FUTURE TAKES;** transcultural futurist magazine. Text in English. 1993. q. free to members (effective 2011). back issues avail. **Document type:** *Journal, Academic/Scholarly.* **Description:** Brings professions, disciplines, nations, ethnic groups, and cultures together to study the future from a non-partisan perspective.
Media: Online - full text.
Published by: Center for Transcultural Foresight, Inc., PO Box 42327, Washington, DC 20015. TEL 202-263-1140.

300 PHL ISSN 1022-7849
FUTURES BULLETIN. Text in English. q. USD 50 to non-members (effective 2000). **Document type:** *Bulletin.* **Description:** Serves as an information forum for WFSF members, subscribers and other interested persons, with regard to future-oriented studies and activities. Looks at futures of development, methods of social forecasting.
Formerly: World Futures Studies Federation Newsletter
Published by: World Futures Studies Federation, Secretariat, c/o Cesar Villanueva Ed., 2nd Fl. Main Administration B106, University of S. La Salle, La Salle Ave, PO Box 249, Bacolod City, Negros Occidental 6100, Philippines. TEL 63-34-4353857. Ed. Rayboy Pandan Jr. R&Ps Cesar Villanueva, Jean Lee Manayon TEL 63-2-435-3857.

▼ **EL FUTURO DEL PASADO;** revista electronica de historia. *see* HISTORY

FUTUROLOGY. *see* TECHNOLOGY: COMPREHENSIVE WORKS

300 CHN ISSN 1004-4310
FUYANG SHIFAN XUEYUAN XUEBAO (SHEHUI KEXUEBAN)/FUYANG TEACHERS COLLEGE. JOURNAL (SOCIAL SCIENCE EDITION). Text in Chinese. 1982. bi-m. CNY 8 newsstand/cover (effective 2006). **Document type:** *Journal, Academic/Scholarly.*
Related titles: Online - full text ed.
Published by: Fuyang Shifan Xueyuan/Fuyang Teachers College, 41, Qinghe Xi Lu, Fuyang, 236032, China. TEL 86-558-2596143.

300 CHN ISSN 1002-3321
FUZHOU DAXUE XUEBAO (ZHEXUE SHEHUI KEXUE BAN)/FUZHOU UNIVERSITY. JOURNAL (PHILOSOPHY AND SOCIAL SCIENCES EDITION). Text in Chinese. 1981-1984; resumed 1987. q. USD 31.20 (effective 2009). **Document type:** *Journal, Academic/Scholarly.*
Related titles: Online - full text ed.
Published by: Fuzhou Daxue/Fuzhou University, 523, Gongye Lu, Fuzhou, Fujian 350002, China. TEL 86-591-87892444, FAX 86-591-83799030. Ed. Chen Ziming.

G E F A M E; journal of African studies. *see* HISTORY—History Of Africa

300 CHN ISSN 1003-7543
GAIGE/REFORM. Text in Chinese. 1988. m. **Document type:** *Journal, Academic/Scholarly.*
Related titles: Online - full text ed.
Indexed: RASB.
—East View.
Published by: (Chongqing Shehui Kexueyuan/Chongqing Academy of Social Sciences), Gaige Zazhishe, 270, Jiangbei-qu Qiaobei-cun, Chongqing, 400020, China. TEL 86-23-86856491, FAX 86-23-86856491. **Dist. by:** China International Book Trading Corp, 35 Chegongzhuang Xilu, Haidian District, PO Box 399, Beijing 100044, China. TEL 86-10-68412045, FAX 86-10-68412023, cibtc@mail.cibtc.com.cn, http://www.cibtc.com.cn.

300 CHN ISSN 1004-7069
GAIGE YU KAIFANG/REFORM & OPENING. Text in Chinese. 1987. m. USD 49.20 (effective 2009). **Document type:** *Journal, Academic/Scholarly.*
—East View.
Published by: Nanjing Cubanshe/Nanjing Publishing House, 43-2, Beijing Donglu, Nanjing, 210008, China. TEL 86-25-57712866, FAX 86-25-57712866, http://www.njcbs.com. **Dist. by:** China International Book Trading Corp, 35 Chegongzhuang Xilu, Haidian District, PO Box 399, Beijing 100044, China. TEL 86-10-68412045, FAX 86-10-68412023, cibtc@mail.cibtc.com.cn, http://www.cibtc.com.cn.

300 CHN ISSN 1002-736X
HC427.92
GAIGE YU ZHANLUE/REFORM & STRATEGY. Text in Chinese. 1985. m. USD 80.40 (effective 2009). **Document type:** *Journal, Academic/Scholarly.*
Related titles: Online - full text ed.
Address: 5, Xinzhou Lu, Nanning, 530022, China. **Dist. by:** China International Book Trading Corp, 35 Chegongzhuang Xilu, Haidian District, PO Box 399, Beijing 100044, China. TEL 86-10-68412045, FAX 86-10-68412023, cibtc@mail.cibtc.com.cn, http://www.cibtc.com.cn.

GALILEI. *see* HUMANITIES: COMPREHENSIVE WORKS

306.4 GBR ISSN 1540-8493
GAMBLING ONLINE MAGAZINE. Abbreviated title: G O M. Text in English. 200?. m. GBP 13 domestic; GBP 39.99 in Europe; USD 59.99 elsewhere (effective 2009). adv. **Document type:** *Magazine, Consumer.* **Description:** Explains some of the more elusive aspects of gambling.
Related titles: Online - full text ed.
—CCC.
Published by: Players Publishing Ltd., 7 Chapel Pl, Rivington St, London, EC2A 3DQ, United Kingdom. TEL 44-20-77396999, FAX 44-20-77399918, info@playerspublishing.co.uk, http://www.playerspublishing.co.uk/. Ed. Chris Lines.

GAMI'AT QATAR. KULLIYYAT AL-INSANIYYAT WA-AL-'ULUM AL-IGTIMA'IYYAT. MAGALLAT/JOURNAL OF HUMANITIES AND SOCIAL SCIENCES. *see* HUMANITIES: COMPREHENSIVE WORKS

300 370 CHN ISSN 1004-8332
AS452.K354
GANNAN SHIFAN XUEYUAN XUEBAO/GANNAN TEACNER'S COLLEGE. JOURNAL. Text in Chinese. 1980. bi-m. CNY 7 newsstand/cover (effective 2006). **Document type:** *Journal, Academic/Scholarly.*
Related titles: Online - full text ed.
Published by: Gannan Shifan Xueyuan, Jingji Kaifa-qu, Ganzhou, 341000, China. TEL 86-797-8393677.

300 CHN ISSN 1672-707X
GANSU LIANHE DAXUE XUEBAO (SHEHUI KEXUE BAN). Text in Chinese. 1985. bi-m. USD 21.60 (effective 2009). **Document type:** *Journal, Academic/Scholarly.*
Formerly: Gansu Jiaoyu Xueyuan Xuebao (Shehui Kexue Ban) (1009-4938)
Related titles: Online - full text ed.
—East View.
Published by: Gansu Lianhe Daxue/Gansu Lianhe University, 400, Yantan Bei Mian Tan, Lanzhou, Gansu 730000, China. TEL 86-931-8685110, FAX 86-931-8685007.

300 CHN ISSN 1003-3637
AS452.L37
➤ **GANSU SHEHUI KEXUE/GANSU SOCIAL SCIENCE.** Text in Chinese. 1979. bi-m. USD 40.20 (effective 2009). adv. bk.rev. **Document type:** *Journal, Academic/Scholarly.*
Formerly (until 1990): Shehui Kexue (Lanzhou)
Related titles: Online - full text ed.

Published by: Gansu Sheng Shehui Kexueyuan/Gansu Academy of Social Sciences, Anning-qu, 143, Jiankang Lu, Lanzhou, Gansu 730070, China. TEL 86-931-7763141. Circ: 3,500 (paid). **Dist. overseas by:** China International Book Trading Corp, 35 Chegongzhuang Xilu, Haidian District, PO Box 399, Beijing 100044, China.

300 CHN ISSN 1007-2187
GAODENG HANSHOU XUEBAO (ZHEXUE SHEHUI KEXUE BAN)/ JOURNAL OF HIGHER CORRESPONDENCE EDUCATION (PHILOSOPHY AND SOCIAL SCIENCES EDITION). Text in Chinese. 1987. bi-m. CNY 5.80 newsstand/cover (effective 2006). **Document type:** *Journal, Academic/Scholarly.*
Related titles: Online - full text ed.
Published by: Huazhong Shifan Daxue, Chengren Jiaoyu Xueyuan, Wuhan, 430079, China. TEL 86-27-67867240.

300 CHN
GAOXIAO SHEHUI KEXUE/SOCIAL SCIENCES IN HIGHER EDUCATION. Text in Chinese. bi-m.
Published by: Zhongguo Jiaoyu Zazhishe, 35 Damucang Hutong, Xidan, Beijing, 100816, China. TEL 654921. Ed. Zhang Dimei.

300 CHN
GAOXIAO SHEKE DONGTAI/SOCIAL SCIENCES PERSPECTIVES IN HIGHER EDUCATION. Text in Chinese. bi-m. **Document type:** *Government.*
Formerly (until 2006): Gaoxiao Sheke Xinxi
Published by: Anhui Sheng Shehui Kexueyuan/Anhui Academy of Social Sciences, 131, Weigangmeiling Dadao, Hefei, 230053, China. TEL 86-551-3438358.

642.5 USA ISSN 1529-3262
TX631
GASTRONOMICA; the journal of food and culture. Text in English. 2001. q. USD 275 combined subscription to institutions (print & online eds.) (effective 2012). adv. illus. back issues avail.; reprints avail. **Document type:** *Journal, Academic/Scholarly.* **Description:** Presents a forum for ideas, discussion, and thoughtful reflection on the history, literature, representation, and cultural impact of food.
Related titles: Online - full text ed.: ISSN 1533-8622. USD 225 to institutions (effective 2012).
Indexed: A01, A22, AmHI, B04, B24, BRD, BrHumI, CA, E01, F10, FS&TA, G09, H&TI, H06, H07, P02, P10, P11, P26, P27, P48, P52, P53, P54, P56, PQC, S02, S03, SSAI, SSAb, SSI, T02, W03.
—BLDSC (4089.077500), IE, Ingenta. **CCC.**
Published by: University of California Press, Journals Division, 2000 Ctr St, Ste 303, Berkeley, CA 94704. TEL 510-643-7154, 877-262-4226, FAX 510-642-9917, customerservice@ucpressjournals.com, http://www.ucpressjournals.com. Ed. Darra Goldstein. Adv. contact Jennifer Rogers TEL 510-642-6188. Circ: 8,784.

300 AUS ISSN 1836-3393
LC189.8
GATEWAYS (SYDNEY); international journal of community research & engagement. Text in English. 2008. a. free (effective 2011). **Document type:** *Journal, Academic/Scholarly.* **Description:** It provides a forum for academics, practitioners and community representatives to pursue issues and reflect on practices related to interactions between tertiary institutions and community organizations, academic interventions in a community, community-based projects with links to the tertiary sector and community initiatives.
Media: Online - full text.
Indexed: A01, T02.
Published by: University of Technology, Sydney, ePress, PO Box 123, Broadway, NSW 2007, Australia. TEL 61-2-95141902, FAX 61-2-95141894.

GAVEA - BROWN; a bilingual journal of Portuguese-American studies and letters. *see* LITERATURE

371 FRA ISSN 0768-6374
GAZET SIFON BLE. Text in French. 1983. q. EUR 15 (effective 2007). **Document type:** *Journal, Academic/Scholarly.*
—CCC.
Published by: Institut d'Etudes Creoles, 9 Bd de la Republique, Aix-en-Provence, 13100, France. hazael@up.univ-mrs.fr, http://creoles.free.fr/association.htm.

GEARY LECTURE SERIES. *see* BUSINESS AND ECONOMICS

GENDER AND DEVELOPMENT. *see* WOMEN'S STUDIES

305.3 GBR ISSN 1742-870X
GENDER IN THE MIDDLE AGES. Text in English. 2004. irreg., latest vol.7, 2011. price varies. **Document type:** *Monographic series, Academic/Scholarly.*
Published by: Boydell & Brewer Ltd., Whitwell House, St Audrys Park Rd, Melton, Woodbridge, IP12 1SY, United Kingdom. TEL 44-1394-610600, FAX 44-1394-610316, editorial@boydell.co.uk, http://www.boydell.co.uk.

300 DOM
GENERO Y SOCIEDAD. Text in Spanish. 1993. 3/yr. USD 8 per issue. **Document type:** *Monographic series.*
Published by: (Centro de Estudio del Genero), Editora Taller, Apdo. 2190, Isabel la Catolica 260, Santo Domingo, Dominican Republic. TEL 809-682-9369, FAX 809-689-7259.

300 FRA ISSN 1155-3219
H3
GENESES. Text in French. 1990. q. EUR 60 domestic to individuals; EUR 70 foreign to individuals; EUR 70 domestic to institutions; EUR 80 foreign to institutions (effective 2006). **Document type:** *Journal, Academic/Scholarly.*
Related titles: Online - full text ed.: ISSN 1776-2944.
Indexed: AmH&L, CA, FR, HistAb, I14, IBSS, P30, P42, PSA, S02, S03, SCOPUS, SSA, SociolAb, T02.
—INIST.
Published by: (Institut de Recherche sur les Societes Contemporaines), Editions Belin, 8 Rue Ferou, Paris, 75278, France. TEL 33-1-55428400, FAX 33-1-43251829, http://www.editions-belin.com. Ed. Jean Leroy.

304.2 NOR ISSN 1503-2701
GEOGRAFI I BERGEN. Text in Multiple languages. 1966. irreg. back issues avail. **Document type:** *Monographic series, Academic/Scholarly.*
Former titles (until 1998): Universitetet i Bergen. Institutt for Geografi. Meddelelser. Geografi i Bergen. Serie A (Print) (0806-671X); (until 1987): Norges Handelshoejskole and Universitetet i Bergen. Geografisk Institutt. Meddelelser (0801-1168)
Media: Online - full content.
Published by: (Norges Handelshoeyskole/Norwegian School of Economics and Business Administration), Universitetet i Bergen, Institutt for Geografi/University of Bergen. Department of Geography, Fosswinckelsgate 6, Bergen, 5007, Norway. TEL 47-55-583062, FAX 47-55-583099, post@geog.uib.no. **Co-publisher:** Norges Handelshoeyskole/Norwegian School of Economics and Business Administration.

300 USA ISSN 1083-7523
JK468.P64
THE GEORGETOWN PUBLIC POLICY REVIEW. Abbreviated title: G P P R. Text in English. 1995 (Fall). s-a. back issues avail. **Document type:** *Journal, Academic/Scholarly.* **Description:** Presesnts articles that investigate current public policy issues and promote discourse among members of the policymaking community.
Published by: (Georgetown Public Policy Institute), Georgetown University, 37th and O St, NW, Washington, DC 20057. TEL 202-687-0100, lrh28@georgetown.edu, http://www.georgetown.edu.

300 USA ISSN 2160-7524
▼ **GEORGIA STUDIES WEEKLY. AMERICAN HEROES. 1 SOCIAL STUDIES.** Text in English. 2011. w. USD 9.98 1-9 students; USD 4.99 10 or more students (effective 2012). **Document type:** *Magazine, Consumer.*
Published by: American Legacy Publishing, 1922 W 200 N, Lindon, UT 84042. TEL 866-311-8734, FAX 866-531-5589, service@studiesweekly.com.

300 330 ITA ISSN 1970-7193
GEOSTORIA DEL TERRITORIO. Text in Italian. 2003. irreg. price varies. **Document type:** *Monographic series, Academic/Scholarly.*
Published by: Franco Angeli Edizioni, Viale Monza 106, Milan, 20127, Italy. TEL 39-02-2837141, FAX 39-02-26144793, redazioni@francoangeli.it, http://www.francoangeli.it.

300 PRT ISSN 1645-9369
GEOWORKING PAPERS. Text in Portuguese. 2004. irreg. **Document type:** *Monographic series, Academic/Scholarly.*
Published by: Universidade do Minho, Instituto de Ciencias Sociais, Lago do Paco, Braga, 4700-320, Portugal. http://www.uminho.pt/.

305.83 DEU ISSN 1439-3387
GERMANICA PACIFICA. Text in German. 2002. irreg., latest vol.5, 2010. price varies. **Document type:** *Monographic series, Academic/Scholarly.*
Published by: Peter Lang GmbH (Subsidiary of: Peter Lang Publishing Group), Eschborner Landstr 42-50, Frankfurt Am Main, 60489, Germany. TEL 49-69-7807050, FAX 49-69-78070550, zentrale.frankfurt@peterlang.com. Ed. James Bade.

300 900 DEU ISSN 0340-613X
H5
➤ **GESCHICHTE UND GESELLSCHAFT**; Zeitschrift fuer Historische Sozialwissenschaft. Text in German. 1975. q. EUR 69; EUR 41 to students; EUR 19.90 newsstand/cover (effective 2011). adv. index. **Document type:** *Journal, Academic/Scholarly.*
Indexed: A20, A22, ASCA, AmH&L, ArtHuCI, CA, CurCont, DIP, EI, FR, HistAb, IBR, IBSS, IBZ, P30, PCI, PRA, RASB, SCOPUS, T02, W07.
—BLDSC (4162.521000), IE, Infotrieve, Ingenta, INIST. **CCC.**
Published by: Vandenhoeck und Ruprecht, Theaterstr 13, Goettingen, 37073, Germany. TEL 49-551-508440, FAX 49-551-5084422, info@v-r.de. Circ: 1,900 (paid and controlled).

300 DEU
▼ **GESELLSCHAFT DER UNTERSCHIEDE.** Text in German. 2011. irreg., latest vol.3, 2011. price varies. **Document type:** *Monographic series, Academic/Scholarly.*
Published by: Transcript, Muehlenstr 47, Bielefeld, 33607, Germany. TEL 49-521-63454, FAX 49-521-61040, live@transcript-verlag.de.

304 DEU ISSN 0435-8287
GESELLSCHAFT FUER SOZIALEN FORTSCHRITT. SCHRIFTEN. Text in German. 1951. irreg., latest vol.26, 2008. price varies. **Document type:** *Monographic series, Academic/Scholarly.*
Published by: (Gesellschaft fuer Sozialen Fortschritt e.V.), Duncker und Humblot GmbH, Carl-Heinrich-Becker-Weg 9, Berlin, 12165, Germany. TEL 49-30-7900060, FAX 49-30-79000631, info@duncker-humblot.de.

300 DEU
GESELLSCHAFT - GESCHICHTE - GEGENWART. Text in German. 1995. irreg., latest vol.40, 2009. price varies. **Document type:** *Monographic series, Academic/Scholarly.*
Published by: Trafo Verlag, Finkenstr 8, Berlin, 12621, Germany. TEL 49-30-61299418, FAX 49-30-61299421, info@trafoberlin.de.

300 DEU ISSN 1862-037X
GESELLSCHAFT UND ERZIEHUNG; historische und systematische Perspektiven. Text in German. 2006. irreg., latest vol.7, 2010. price varies. **Document type:** *Monographic series, Academic/Scholarly.*
Published by: Peter Lang GmbH (Subsidiary of: Peter Lang Publishing Group), Eschborner Landstr 42-50, Frankfurt Am Main, 60489, Germany. TEL 49-69-7807050, FAX 49-69-78070550, zentrale.frankfurt@peterlang.com.

300 DEU
GESELLSCHAFT - WIRTSCHAFT - MEDIEN. Text in German. 2006. irreg. price varies. **Document type:** *Monographic series, Academic/Scholarly.*
Published by: V & R Unipress GmbH (Subsidiary of: Vandenhoeck und Ruprecht), Robert-Bosch-Breite 6, Goettingen, 37079, Germany. TEL 49-551-5084303, FAX 49-551-5084333, info@vr-unipress.de, http://www.v-r.de/en/publisher/unipress. Ed. Justine Suchanek.

300 DEU
GESUNDHEITS- UND INNOVATIONSMANAGEMENT. Text in German. 2006. irreg., latest vol.7, 2008. price varies. **Document type:** *Monographic series, Academic/Scholarly.*
Published by: Rainer Hampp Verlag, Marktplatz 5, Mering, 86415, Germany. TEL 49-8233-4783, FAX 49-8233-30755, info@rhverlag.de, http://www.rhverlag.de.

300 USA ISSN 1946-6838
GHANA STUDIES COUNCIL. NEWSLETTER. Variant title: G S C Newsletter. Text in English. 1989. a. free to members (effective 2009). back issues avail. **Document type:** *Newsletter.*
Formerly (until 1994): Akan Studies Council. Newsletter
Related titles: Online - full text ed.
Published by: Ghana Studies Council, c/o Dr. Dennis Laumann, Department of History, The University of Memphis, Memphis, TN 38152. ghanastudiescouncil@gmail.com.

300 DEU
GIESSEN CONTRIBUTIONS TO THE STUDY OF CULTURE. Text in English. 2008. irreg., latest vol.3, 2010. price varies. **Document type:** *Monographic series, Academic/Scholarly.*
Published by: Wissenschaftlicher Verlag Trier, Bergstr 27, Trier, 54295, Germany. TEL 49-651-41503, FAX 49-651-41504, wvt@wvttrier.de, http://www.wvttrier.de.

300 ISR ISSN 0793-4114
GITELSON PEACE PAPERS. Text in English. 1994. irreg., latest no.33, 2007. price varies.
Published by: Hebrew University of Jerusalem, Harry S. Truman Research Institute for the Advancement of Peace, Mount Scopus, Jerusalem, Israel. TEL 972-2-5882300, FAX 972-2-5828076, http://truman.huji.ac.il/default.asp. R&P Lisa Perlman TEL 972-2-5882315.

300 USA ISSN 1932-8060
JZ1318
GLOBAL-E; a global studies journal. Text in English. 2007. m. free (effective 2011). **Document type:** *Journal, Academic/Scholarly.* **Description:** Contains commentaries on global events, processes, and issues.
Media: Online - full text.
Published by: University of Illinois at Urbana-Champaign, Center for Global Studies, 302 International Studies Bldg, 910 S Fifth St, Champaign, IL 61820. TEL 217-265-5186, FAX 217-333-6270, global-studies@illinois.edu, http://cgs.illinois.edu/. **Co-sponsors:** University of North Carolina, Chapel Hill, Center for Global Initiatives; University of Wisconsin at Milwaukee, Center for International Education; University of Wisconsin at Madison, Global Studies.

362.509 NZL ISSN 1175-7655
GLOBAL ISSUES. Text in English. 2002. q. NZD 12 domestic individual teachers (effective 2008). **Document type:** *Magazine, Consumer.* **Description:** For secondary school students that provides information and ideas for exploring global issues.
Related titles: Online - full text ed.: ISSN 1178-5179.
Published by: (Development Resource Centre, Global Education Centre), Dev-Zone, Floor 2, James Smith Bldg., 49-55 Cuba St., PO Box 12440, Wellington, New Zealand. TEL 64-4-4729549, FAX 64-4-4969599, info@dev-zone.org, http://www.dev-zone.org.

300 NGA ISSN 1596-6216
H53.N6
➤ **GLOBAL JOURNAL OF SOCIAL SCIENCES.** Text in English. 2002. s-a. NGN 1,500 domestic; USD 50 foreign (effective 2007). bk.rev. back issues avail.; reprints avail. **Document type:** *Journal, Academic/Scholarly.* **Description:** Aimed at promoting research in all areas of sociology, anthropology, management sciences, geography, and regional planning.
Related titles: Online - full text ed.
Indexed: A34, A37, C25, CABA, D01, E12, GH, H16, I11, LT, MaizeAb, N02, OR, P27, P48, P54, PQC, R11, R12, S13, S16, T05, TAR, W11.
Published by: Global Journal Series, c/o Prof Barth N Ekwueme, University of Calabar, Unical Post Office, PO Box 3651, Calabar, Cross River State, Nigeria. bachudo@yahoo.com. Eds. J U Obot, Barth N Ekwueme.

300 AUS ISSN 1835-4432
➤ **THE GLOBAL STUDIES JOURNAL.** Text in English. 2008. irreg. USD 500 combined subscription (print & online eds.) (effective 2009). **Document type:** *Proceedings, Academic/Scholarly.* **Description:** Devoted to mapping and interpreting new trends and patterns in globalization.
Related titles: Online - full text ed.: USD 50 to individuals; USD 300 to institutions (effective 2009).
Indexed: A01.
Published by: Common Ground Publishing, PO Box 463, Altona, VIC 3018, Australia. TEL 61-3-93988000, FAX 61-3-93988088, mail@commongroundpublishing.com, http://commongroundpublishing.com. Eds. Dr. Bill Cope, Mary Kalantzis.

➤ **GLOBALISATION, SOCIETIES AND EDUCATION.** *see* EDUCATION

➤ **GLOBALIZACION**; revista web mensual de economia, sociedad y cultura. *see* BUSINESS AND ECONOMICS—Economic Situation And Conditions

300 CAN ISSN 1535-9794
➤ **GLOBALIZATION.** Text in English. 2001. q. free. **Document type:** *Journal, Academic/Scholarly.* **Description:** Covers social, political, economic, and technological globalization.
Media: Online - full content.
Indexed: A01, CA, T02.
Published by: International Consortium for Alternative Academic Publication (Subsidiary of: Athabasca University) icaap@athabascau.ca, http://www.icaap.org. Ed. Dennis M Ray.

➤ **GLOBULUS.** *see* SCIENCES: COMPREHENSIVE WORKS

301 SWE ISSN 0072-5099
GOETEBORGS UNIVERSITET. SOCIOLOGISKA INSTITUTIONEN. FORSKNINGS-RAPPORT. Text in Multiple languages. 1964. irreg. price varies.
Published by: Goeteborgs Universitet, Sociologiska Institutionen/ University of Gothenburg. Department of Sociology, Spraengkullsgatan 23, PO Box 40530, Goeteborg, 40530, Sweden. TEL 46-31-773 10 00, FAX 46-31-773 47 64.

300 DEU ISSN 1866-0711
GOETTINGER BEITRAEGE ZUR ETHNOLOGIE. Text in German. 1996. irreg., latest vol.3, 2009. price varies. **Document type:** *Monographic series, Academic/Scholarly.*
Formerly (until 2008): Goettinger Studien zur Ethnologie
Published by: Universitaetsverlag Goettingen, Platz der Goettinger Sieben 1, Goettingen, 37073, Germany. TEL 49-551-395243, FAX 49-551-3922457, pabst@sub.uni-goettingen.de.

300 DEU ISSN 1866-4903
GOETTINGER KULTURWISSENSCHAFTLICHE STUDIEN. Text in German. 2008. irreg., latest vol.3, 2009. price varies. **Document type:** *Monographic series, Academic/Scholarly.*

S

Formed by the merger of (1986-2008): Beitraege zur Volkskunde in Niedersachsen (0933-5404); (1991-2008): Goettinger Beitraege zu Politik und Zeitgeschichte (0941-2468)
Published by: Schmerse Verlag, Mittelbergring 26, Goettingen, 37085, Germany. TEL 49-551-46335, FAX 49-551-47550, mail@schmersemedia.com, http://www.schmersemedia.com.

300 NLD ISSN 1572-3763
H61
➤ **GRADUATE JOURNAL OF SOCIAL SCIENCE.** Text in English. 2004. s-a. free (effective 2011). bk.rev. **Document type:** *Journal, Academic/Scholarly.* **Description:** The journal aims at providing examples of and discussions over pluralism in methodology across the social sciences, thus building opportunities for progress through dialogue and reciprocal awareness.
Media: Online - full text.
Indexed: A39, C27, C29, CA, D03, D04, E13, R14, S02, S03, S14, S15, S18, T02.
Published by: Amsterdam University Press, Prinsengracht 747-751, Amsterdam, 1017 JX, Netherlands. TEL 31-20-420-0050, FAX 31-20-420-3214, info@aup.nl, http://www.aup.nl. Ed. Mia Liinason TEL 46-46-2210000.

➤ **GRADUATE PROGRAMS IN SOCIAL SCIENCES.** *see* EDUCATION—Guides To Schools And Colleges

300 FRA ISSN 1777-375X
AP20
LES GRANDS DOSSIERS DES SCIENCES HUMAINES. Text in French. 1993. m.
Formerly (until 2005): Sciences Humaines. Hors Serie (1252-3429)
Related titles: Online - full text ed.: ISSN 2108-6583. 200?; ◆ Supplement to: Sciences Humaines. ISSN 0996-6994.
Indexed: FR, IBSS.
—INIST.
Published by: Sciences Humaines, 38, rue Rantheaume, BP 256, Auxerre, Cedex 89004, France. TEL 33-3-86720700, FAX 33-3-86525326, communication@scienceshumaines.fr, http://www.scienceshumaines.com. Ed. Jean Francois Dortier. Pub. Jean Claude Ruano Borbalan.

300 GBR ISSN 0266-2043
H11
GREAT BRITAIN. ECONOMIC AND SOCIAL RESEARCH COUNCIL. ANNUAL REPORT. Text in English. 1966. a. **Document type:** *Corporate.*
Former titles (until 1984): Great Britain. Social Science Research Council. Annual Report (0262-5482); (until 1981): Great Britain. Social Science Research Council. Report (0081-0444)
Related titles: Online - full text ed.
—BLDSC (1241.048000). **CCC.**
Published by: Economic and Social Research Council, Polaris House, North Star Ave, Swindon, Wilts SN2 1UJ, United Kingdom. TEL 44-1793-413000, FAX 44-1793-413001, comms@esrc.ac.uk.

331.2 GBR
GREAT BRITAIN. THE PENSIONS REGULATOR. ANNUAL REPORT AND ACCOUNTS. Text in English. 19??. a. GBP 16.95 per issue (effective 2010). back issues avail.; reprints avail. **Document type:** *Government.* **Description:** Provides information about pension activities & reviews.
Former titles (until 2005): Great Britain. Occupational Pensions Regulatory Authority. Annual Report; Great Britain. Government Actuary. Occupational Pension Board. Annual Report
Related titles: Online - full text ed.: free (effective 2010).
Published by: (Great Britain. The Pensions Regulator), The Stationery Office, St Crispins, Duke St, Norwich, NR3 1PD, United Kingdom. TEL 44-1603-622211, customer.services@tso.co.uk, http://www.tso.co.uk. **Subscr. to:** PO Box 29, Norwich NR3 1GN, United Kingdom. TEL 44-870-6005522, FAX 44-870-6005533, subscriptions@tso.co.uk.

GREAT PLAINS RESEARCH. *see* SCIENCES: COMPREHENSIVE WORKS

300 GRC ISSN 0013-9696
H8
GREEK REVIEW OF SOCIAL RESEARCH/EPITHEORISIS KOINONIKON EREVNON. Text in Greek. 1969. q. USD 30. adv. bk.rev. bibl.; charts; stat. **Document type:** *Academic/Scholarly.*
Indexed: MLA-IB, P30.
—INIST.
Published by: National Center of Social Research, 1 Sofokleous St., Athens, 105 59, Greece. FAX 30-1-3216471. Ed. K Tsoukalas. Circ: 2,000.

300 GBR ISSN 1462-6179
GREGYNOG PAPERS. Text in English. 1996. irreg., latest 2005. GBP 7.99 per issue to non-members; free to members (effective 2009). back issues avail. **Document type:** *Monographic series, Academic/Scholarly.*
—BLDSC (4215.376000).
Published by: Institute of Welsh Affairs/Sefydliad Materion Cymreig, Second Fl, 4 Cathedral Rd, Cardiff, CF11 9LJ, United Kingdom. TEL 44-29-20660820, wales@iwa.org.uk.

300 AUS ISSN 1832-3715
GRIFFITH ASIA INSTITUTE. NEWSLETTER. Text in English. 1998. 3/yr. free (effective 2009). back issues avail. **Document type:** *Newsletter, Academic/Scholarly.* **Description:** Highlights the major developments in the politics, economics, societies and cultures of Asia and the South Pacific.
Formerly (until 2004): Griffith Asia Pacific (1441-3612)
Related titles: Online - full text ed.: free (effective 2009).
Published by: Griffith University, Griffith Asia Institute, Rm 1.41, Business 1 Building (N50), Griffith University, 170 Kessels Rd, Nathan, QLD 4111, Australia. TEL 61-7-37353730, FAX 61-7-37353731, gai@griffith.edu.au.

GROWTH STRATEGIES. *see* BUSINESS AND ECONOMICS—Economic Situation And Conditions

300 500 DEU ISSN 1619-3490
GRUNDLAGENPROBLEME UNSERER ZEIT. Text in German. 2002. irreg., latest vol.5, 2006. price varies. **Document type:** *Monographic series, Academic/Scholarly.*
Published by: Leipziger Universitaetsverlag GmbH, Oststr 41, Leipzig, 04317, Germany. TEL 49-341-9900440, FAX 49-341-9900440, info@univerlag-leipzig.de.

300 CHN ISSN 1008-8512
GUANCHA YU SIKAO/STUDY AND THINK. Text in Chinese. 1983. s-m. USD 72 (effective 2009). **Document type:** *Journal, Academic/Scholarly.*
Formerly (until 1999): Xuexi yu Sikao (1003-6091)
Related titles: Online - full text ed.
Published by: Zhejiang Sheng Shehui Kexueyuan, 1, Miduqiao, Baima Gongyu 2-701, Hangzhou, 310006, China. TEL 86-571-85812324, FAX 86-571-85812677. **Dist. by:** China International Book Trading Corp, 35 Chegongzhuang Xilu, Haidian District, PO Box 399, Beijing 100044, China. TEL 86-10-68412045, FAX 86-10-68412023, cibtc@mail.cibtc.com.cn, http://www.cibtc.com.cn.

300 CHN ISSN 1671-623X
GUANGDONG GONGYE DAXUE XUEBAO (SHEHUI KEXUE BAN)/GUANGDONG UNIVERSITY OF TECHNOLOGY. JOURNAL. Text in Chinese. 1984. q. CNY 5 newsstand/cover (effective 2006). **Document type:** *Journal, Academic/Scholarly.*
Related titles: Online - full text ed.
Published by: Guangdong Gongye Daxue/Guangdong Institute of Technology, 729, Dongfeng Donglu, Guangzhou, Guangdong 510090, China.

300 500 CHN ISSN 1672-402X
➤ **GUANGDONG JISHU SHIFAN XUEYUAN XUEBAO/GUANGDONG POLYTECHNIC NORMAL UNIVERSITY. JOURNAL.** Text in Chinese. 1980. bi-m. (in 2 vols.). CNY 10 newsstand/cover (effective 2006). adv. bk.rev. 112 p./no.; **Document type:** *Journal, Academic/Scholarly.* **Description:** Contains 3 issues on social sciences (no.1,2 &3) and 1 issue on natural science (no.4). Social science editions are mostly about vocational education, economics, ethnology, sociology, literature, history, philosophy and linguistics, as well as the pop problems such as vocational education research and economic research of Guangdong. Also includes topics such as historical national problems research of southern China. It is characterized by polytechnic normal education, temporariness, ethnocentrism, and localisms. The natural science edition focuses on research about electronic engineering, computer, mathematics, physics, etc.
Former titles: Guangdong Zhiye Jishu Shifan Xueyuan Xuebao (1009-2803); Guangdong Minzu Xueyuan Xuebao
Related titles: Online - full text ed.
Published by: Guangdong Jishu Shifan Xueyuan/Guangdong Polytechnic Normal University, 293, Zhongshan Dadao, Guangdong, 510665, China. Circ: 1,200.

300 CHN ISSN 1009-931X
GUANGDONG NONG-GONG-SHANG ZHIYE JISHU XUEYUAN XUEBAO/GUANGDONG A I B POLYTECHNIC COLLEGE. JOURNAL. Text in Chinese. 1985. q. CNY 5 newsstand/cover (effective 2006). **Document type:** *Journal, Academic/Scholarly.*
Formerly (until 2000): Guangdong Nong-Gong-Shang Guanli Ganbu Xueyuan Xuebao/Guangdong A I B Management College. Journal (1009-2668)
Related titles: Online - full text ed.
Published by: Guangdong Nong-Gong-Shang Zhiye Jishu Xueyuan, 198, Yueken Lu, Guangzhou, 510507, China. TEL 86-20-85230586, FAX 86-20-85230563.

500 300 CHN ISSN 1672-1950
GUANGDONG QINGGONG ZHIYE JISHU XUEYUAN XUEBAO/GUANGDONG INDUSTRY TECHNICAL COLLEGE. JOURNAL. Text in Chinese. 2002. q. CNY 3 newsstand/cover (effective 2006). **Document type:** *Journal, Academic/Scholarly.*
Related titles: Online - full text ed.
Published by: Guangdong Qinggong Zhiye Jishu Xueyuan, 152, Xingang Xi Lu, Guangzhou, 510300, China.

300 CHN ISSN 1009-5446
GUANGDONG QINGNIAN GANBU XUEYUAN XUEBAO/GUANGDONG COLLEGE OF YOUNG CADRES. JOURNAL. Text in Chinese. 1987. q. CNY 10 newsstand/cover (effective 2006). **Document type:** *Journal, Academic/Scholarly.*
Related titles: Online - full text ed.
Published by: Guangdong Qingnian Ganbu Xueyuan, Tianping Jiashatai Lu, Guangzhou, 510507, China. TEL 86-20-37251134, FAX 86-20-87226959.

300 CHN ISSN 1000-114X
AS452.C366
GUANGDONG SHEHUI KEXUE/GUANGDONG SOCIAL SCIENCE. Text in Chinese. 1984. bi-m. USD 24.60 (effective 2009). **Document type:** *Journal, Academic/Scholarly.*
Related titles: Online - full text ed.
Indexed: RASB.
—East View.
Published by: Guangdong Sheng Shehui Kexueyuan/Guangdong Academy of Social Sciences, 369, Tianhe Bei Lu, Guangdong, 510610, China. TEL 86-20-38801447, FAX 86-20-38846258. **Dist. by:** China International Book Trading Corp, 35 Chegongzhuang Xilu, Haidian District, PO Box 399, Beijing 100044, China. TEL 86-10-68412045, FAX 86-10-68412023, cibtc@mail.cibtc.com.cn, http://www.cibtc.com.cn.

300 CHN ISSN 1672-0962
GUANGDONG WAIYU WAIMAO DAXUE XUEBAO/GUANGDONG UNIVERSITY OF FOREIGN STUDIES. JOURNAL. Text in Chinese. 2002. q. USD 24.60 (effective 2009). **Document type:** *Journal, Academic/Scholarly.*
Related titles: Online - full text ed.
Published by: Guangdong Waiyu Waimao Daxue/Guangdong University of Foreign Studies, 2, Baiyun Dadao Bei, Guangzhou, Guangdong 510420, China. TEL 86-20-36204656, FAX 86-20-36207367, http://www.gdufs.edu.cn/.

300 100 CHN ISSN 1001-8182
GUANGXI DAXUE XUEBAO (ZHEXUE SHEHUI KEXUE BAN)/GUANGXI UNIVERSITY. JOURNAL (PHILOSOPHY AND SOCIAL SCIENCES). Text in Chinese; Abstracts and contents page in Chinese, English. 1979. bi-m. **Document type:** *Journal, Academic/Scholarly.*
Related titles: Online - full text ed.
Indexed: Z02.
—East View.
Published by: Guangxi Daxue/Guangxi University, 75, Xiuling Lu, Nanning, Guangxi 530005, China. TEL 86-771-3239230.

GUANGXI MINZU DAXUE XUEBAO (ZHEXUE SHEHUI KEXUE BAN)/GUANGXI UNIVERSITY FOR NATIONALITIES. JOURNAL (PHILOSOPHY AND SOCIAL SCIENCE EDITION). *see* PHILOSOPHY

300 CHN ISSN 1001-6597
AP95.C4
GUANGXI SHIFAN DAXUE XUEBAO (ZHEXUE SHEHUI KEXUE BAN)/GUANGXI NORMAL UNIVERSITY. JOURNAL (PHILOSOPHY AND SOCIAL SCIENCES EDITION). Text in Chinese. 1957. q. USD 28.20 (effective 2009). **Document type:** *Journal, Academic/Scholarly.*
Related titles: Online - full text ed.
Indexed: PSA, SociolAb.
Published by: Guangxi Shifan Daxue/Guangxi Normal University, 15, Yucai Lu, Guilin, 541004, China. TEL 86-773-5822213, FAX 86-773-5817343, http://www.gxnu.edu.cn.

GUANGXI ZHIYE JISHU XUEYUAN XUEBAO/GUANGXI VOCATIONAL AND TECHNICAL COLLEGE. JOURNAL. *see* SCIENCES: COMPREHENSIVE WORKS

300 CHN ISSN 1671-394X
GUANGZHOU DAXUE XUEBAO (SHEHUI KEXUE BAN)/GUANGZHOU UNIVERSITY. JOURNAL (SOCIAL SCIENCE EDITION). Text in Chinese. 1987. m. USD 74.40 (effective 2009). **Document type:** *Journal, Academic/Scholarly.*
Supersedes in part (in 2001): Guangzhou Daxue Xuebao (1008-9861)
Published by: Guangzhou Daxue, Daxuecheng Wai Huanxi Lu #230, A213 Xinxiang, Guangzhou, 510006, China. TEL 86-20-39366068.

GUIDE TO SOCIAL SCIENCE AND RELIGION. *see* RELIGIONS AND THEOLOGY—Abstracting, Bibliographies, Statistics

300 CHN ISSN 1000-5099
AS452.K777
GUIZHOU DAXUE XUEBAO (SHEHUI KEXUE BAN)/GUIZHOU UNIVERSITY. JOURNAL (SOCIAL SCIENCE). Text in Chinese. 1942. bi-m. **Document type:** *Journal, Academic/Scholarly.*
Related titles: Online - full text ed.: (from WanFang Data Corp.).
—East View.
Published by: Guizhou Daxue/Guizhou University, Huaqi-qu, Bei Xiao-qu, 2/F, Chubanshe Lou, Guizhou, 550025, China. TEL 86-851-8292182, FAX 86-851-3621708.

500 CHN ISSN 1002-6924
H53.C55
GUIZHOU SHEHUI KEXUE/SOCIAL SCIENCES IN GUIZHOU. Text in Chinese. 1980. m. USD 49.20 (effective 2009). **Document type:** *Journal, Academic/Scholarly.*
Formed by the merger of: Guizhou Shehui Kexue (Wen-Shi-Zhe Ban); Guizhou Shehui Kexue (Jingji Ban)
Related titles: Online - full text ed.
Indexed: RILM.
—East View.
Published by: Guizhou Sheng Shehui Kexueyuan/Guizhou Academy of Social Sciences, 95, Suoshixiang, Guiyang, Guizhou 550002, China. TEL 86-851-5928568, 28566.

300 CHN ISSN 1001-733X
AS452.K76
GUIZHOU SHIFAN DAXUE XUEBAO (SHEHUI KEXUE BAN)/GUIZHOU NORMAL UNIVERSITY. JOURNAL (SOCIAL SCIENCE EDITION). Text in Chinese. 1960. bi-m. USD 21.60 (effective 2009). **Document type:** *Journal, Academic/Scholarly.*
Related titles: Online - full text ed.
—East View.
Published by: Guizhou Shifan Daxue/Guizhou Normal University, 116, Baoshan Bei Lu, Guiyang, 550001, China. TEL 86-851-6702106.

300 CHN ISSN 1002-4913
GUOJI SHEHUI KEXUE ZAZHI/INTERNATIONAL SOCIAL SCIENCE JOURNAL. Text in Chinese. 1984. q. USD 44.40 (effective 2009). **Document type:** *Journal, Academic/Scholarly.*
—East View.
Published by: Zhongguo Shehui Kexue Zazhishe, 158, Gulouxi Dajie, Beijing, 100720, China. http://ssic.cass.cn. **Dist. by:** China International Book Trading Corp, 35 Chegongzhuang Xilu, Haidian District, PO Box 399, Beijing 100044, China. TEL 86-10-68412045, FAX 86-10-68412023, cibtc@mail.cibtc.com.cn, http://www.cibtc.com.cn.

300 CHN ISSN 1000-4777
➤ **GUOWAI SHEHUI KEXUE/SOCIAL SCIENCE ABROAD.** Text in Chinese. 1980. bi-m. USD 48 (effective 2009). bk.rev. **Document type:** *Academic/Scholarly.* **Description:** Covers new theories, new methodologies, and the latest developments in various fields of the social sciences in countries other than China, including Marxism studies, political science, economics, philosophy, law, history, education, arts, ethnology, religion, and sinology.
Related titles: Online - full text ed.
—East View.
Published by: Zhongguo Shehui Kexueyuan/Chinese Academy of Social Sciences, 5 Jianguomennei Dajie, Beijing, 100732, China. TEL 86-10-6513-7749, FAX 86-10-6512-6393. Ed. Yufu Huang. R&P, Adv. contact Yanbin Yang. Circ: 3,000 (controlled). **Co-sponsor:** Wenxian Xinxi Zhongxin/Center for Documentation & Information.

300 CHN ISSN 1009-3923
H8.C47
GUOWAI SHEHUI KEXUE WENZHAI. Text in Chinese. 1958. m. USD 45.60 (effective 2009). **Document type:** *Journal, Academic/Scholarly.*
Related titles: Online - full text ed.
Published by: Shanghai Shehui Kexueyuan Xinxi Yanjiusuo, 1610, Zhongshan Xi Lu, Shanghai, 200235, China. TEL 86-21-64862266 ext 2302.

300 001.3 CHN ISSN 1674-6643
▼ **GUOXUE XUEKAN.** Text in Chinese. 2009. q. CNY 100; CNY 25 per issue (effective 2011). **Document type:** *Journal, Academic/Scholarly.*
Published by: Zhongguo Renmin Daxue Shubao Ziliao Zhongxin/Renmin University of China, Information Center for Social Sciences, Dongcheng-qu, 3, Zhangzizhong Lu, Beijing, 100007, China. center@zlzx.org.

GYPSY LORE SOCIETY. NEWSLETTER. *see* ANTHROPOLOGY

300 ITA ISSN 1974-1952
H D C P - I R C. WORKING PAPERS SERIES. (Human Development, Capability and Poverty International Research Centre) Text in Multiple languages. 2008. irreg. **Document type:** *Monographic series, Academic/Scholarly.*
Published by: Istituto Universitario di Studi Superiori, Human Development, Capability and Poverty International Research Centre, Viale Lungo Ticino Sforza 56, Pavia, 27100, Italy. TEL 39-0382-516911, FAX 39-0382-529131, http://www.iusspavia.it.

H-NET REVIEWS IN THE HUMANITIES AND SOCIAL SCIENCES. *see* HUMANITIES: COMPREHENSIVE WORKS

H W W A - REPORT. (Hamburgisches Welt Wirtschafts Archiv) *see* BUSINESS AND ECONOMICS

300 TUR ISSN 1301-5737
HACETTEPE UNIVERSITESI. EDEBIYAT FAKULTESI. DERGISI/ HACETTEPE UNIVERSITY. FACULTY OF LETTERS. JOURNAL. Text in Turkish. 1983. s-a. free (effective 2009). **Document type:** *Journal, Academic/Scholarly.* **Description:** Publishes national and international research articles on a wide variety of disciplines in the humanities and social sciences.
Related titles: Online - full text ed.
Indexed: AmHI, CA, H07, MLA-IB, T02.
Published by: Hacettepe Universitesi, Edebiyat Fakultesi/Hacettepe University, Faculty of Letters, Beytepe, Ankara, 06800, Turkey. TEL 90-312-2976810, FAX 90-312-2992085, http://www.edebiyat.hacettepe.edu.tr. Ed. Ufuk Ozdag.

300 CHN ISSN 1009-1971
HAERBIN GONGYE DAXUE XUEBAO (SHEHUI KEXUE BAN)/HARBIN INSTITUTE OF TECHNOLOGY. JOURNAL (SOCIAL SCIENCES EDITION). Text in Chinese. 1999. bi-m. USD 37.20 (effective 2009). **Document type:** *Journal, Academic/Scholarly.*
Related titles: Online - full text ed.
Indexed: CA, L&LBA, PSA, S02, S03, SCOPUS, SSA, SociolAb, T02.
—East View.
Published by: Ha'erbin Gongye Daxue/Ha'erbin Institute of Technology, Nangang-qu, 92, Xidazhijie, 247 Xinxiang, Ha'erbin, 150001, China. TEL 86-451-86414389, FAX 86-451-86416920.

300 ISR ISSN 1565-3323
H1
➤ **HAGAR**; international social science review. Text in English. 1983. irreg. USD 25 to individuals; USD 50 to institutions (effective 2002). bk.rev.; film rev.; play rev. back issues avail. **Document type:** *Journal, Academic/Scholarly.* **Description:** A forum for critical, analytical, and comparative studies on issues related to social science in Israel.
Formerly (until Nov. 2000): Israel Social Science Research (0334-133X)
Indexed: B04, CA, E-psyche, IBSS, M10, P10, P27, P30, P42, P48, P54, PQC, PSA, PsycholAb, S02, S03, SCOPUS, SOPODA, SSAI, SSAb, SSI, SociolAb, T02, W03, W05.
—BLDSC (4238.149000).
Published by: Hubert H. Humphrey Institute for Social Research, Ben-Gurion University of the Negev, P O Box 653, Beersheba, 84105, Israel. TEL 972-8-646-1429, FAX 972-8-647-2938. Ed. Oren Yiftachel. R&P Hila Levinson. Circ: 750 (controlled). **Co-sponsor:** Israel Sociological Society.

300 001.3 CHN ISSN 1674-5531
HAIJUN GONGCHENG DAXUE XUEBAO (ZONGHE BAN)/NAVAL UNIVERSITY OF ENGINEERING. JOURNAL (COMPREHENSIVE EDITION). Text in Chinese. 2004. q. **Document type:** *Journal, Academic/Scholarly.*
Published by: Haijun Gongcheng Daxue/Naval University of Engineering, 717, Jiefang Dadao, Wuhan, 430033, China.

HAINAN DAXUE XUEBAO (RENWEN SHEHUI KEXUEBAN)/ HUMANITIES & SOCIAL SCIENCES JOURNAL OF HAINAN UNIVERSITY. *see* HUMANITIES: COMPREHENSIVE WORKS

300 CHN ISSN 1674-5310
HAINAN SHIFAN DAXUE XUEBAO (SHEHUI KEXUE BAN)/HAINAN NORMAL UNIVERSITY. JOURNAL (HUMANITIES AND SOCIAL SCIENCES). Text in Chinese. 1987. bi-m. **Document type:** *Journal, Academic/Scholarly.*
Former titles (until 2008): Hainan Shifan Xueyuan Xuebao (Shehui Kexue Ban) (1672-223X); (until 2002): Hainan Shifan Xueyuan Xuebao (Renwen Shehui Kexue Ban) (1006-1053); Which superseded in part (in 2000): Hainan Shifan Xueyuan Xuebao
Related titles: Online - full text ed.
—East View.
Published by: Hainan Shifan Daxue, 99, Longkun Nan Lu, Haikou, 571158, China. TEL 86-898-65883414, FAX 86-898-65881326, http://www.hainnu.edu.cn/.

HALLESCHE DISKUSSIONSBEITRAEGE ZUR WIRTSCHAFTS- UND SOZIALGEOGRAPHIE. *see* GEOGRAPHY

300 DEU ISSN 1862-3921
H5
➤ **HAMBURG REVIEW OF SOCIAL SCIENCES.** Text in German, English. 2006. 3/yr. free (effective 2011). **Document type:** *Journal, Academic/Scholarly.* **Description:** Covers topics within the broad field of social sciences.
Media: Online - full text.
Indexed: A01, CA, T02.
Address: c/o Kolja Raube, IPW, Allende Platz 1, Hamburg, 20146, Germany. TEL 49-040-428383233, FAX 49-040-428383534. Eds. Annika Frisch, Katja Marjanen, Stephan Hensell.

330 DEU ISSN 0936-3084
HANDLUNGSBEDINGUNGEN UND HANDLUNGSSPIELRAEUME FUER ENTWICKLUNGSPOLITIK/CONDITIONS AND SCOPES OF ACTION IN DEVELOPMENT POLICY. Text in English, German. 1989. irreg., latest vol.2, 1991. price varies. **Document type:** *Monographic series, Academic/Scholarly.*
Published by: Lit Verlag, Grevener Str/Fresnostr 2, Muenster, 48159, Germany. TEL 49-251-235091, FAX 49-251-231972, lit@lit-verlag.de.

300 CHN ISSN 1674-2338
AS452.H29
HANGZHOU SHIFAN DAXUE XUEBAO (SHEHUI KEXUE BAN)/ HANGZHOU TEACHERS COLLEGE. JOURNAL (SOCIAL SCIENCE EDITION). Text in Chinese. 1987. bi-m. CNY 6 per issue (effective 2010). adv. bk.rev. **Document type:** *Journal, Academic/Scholarly.*
Former titles (until 2008): Hangzhou Shifan Xueyuan Xuebao (Shehui Kexue Ban); (until 2001): Hangzhou Jiaoyu Xueyuan Xuebao (Renwen Kexue Ban)/Hangzhou Educational Institute. Journal (Humanities and Social Sciences Edition); Which superseded in part (in 2000): Hangzhou Jiaoyu Xueyuan Xuebao/Hangzhou Educational Institute. Journal (1008-9403); Which was formed by the merger of (1979-1987): Hangzhou Shiyuan Xuebao (Ziran Kexue Ban) (1000-2146); (1982-1987): Hangzhou Shiyuan Xuebao (Shehui Kexue Ban)
Related titles: Online - full text ed.
Indexed: CA, PSA, RASB, SociolAb, T02.
Published by: Hangzhou Shifan Xueyuan Xueshu Jikanshe/Hangzhou Teachers College, 16, Xuelin Jie, Xiasha Gaojiaoyuan, Hangzhou, 310036, China. TEL 86-571-28865870, FAX 86-571-28865871, http://qks.hznu.edu.cn/. Ed. Shumeng Huang. R&P, Adv. contact Xing Cheng. Circ: 2,000.

300 DEU
▼ **HANNOVERSCHE BEITRAEGE ZU KULTURVERMITTLUNG UND DIDAKTIK.** Text in German. 2010. irreg. price varies. **Document type:** *Monographic series, Academic/Scholarly.*
Published by: Aisthesis Verlag, Oberntorwall 21, Bielefeld, 33602, Germany. TEL 49-521-172604, FAX 49-521-172812, info@aisthesis.de.

300 CHN ISSN 1007-6883
HANSHAN SHIFAN XUEYUAN XUEBAO/HANSHAN TEACHERS COLLEGE. JOURNAL. Text in English. 1980. bi-m. CNY 7 newsstand/cover (effective 2006). **Document type:** *Journal, Academic/Scholarly.*
Formerly: Hanshan Shi-Zhuan Xuebao (1004-6798)
Related titles: Online - full text ed.
Published by: Hanshan Shifan Xueyuan, Chaozhou, 521041, China. TEL 86-768-2318786.

HARYANA AGRICULTURAL UNIVERSITY. JOURNAL OF RESEARCH. *see* AGRICULTURE

300 AUS ISSN 1833-136X
HAWKE RESEARCH INSTITUTE. POSTGRADUATE WORKING PAPER SERIES (ONLINE). Text in English. 2005. irreg., latest no.38, 2008. free (effective 2009). back issues avail. **Document type:** *Monographic series, Academic/Scholarly.* **Description:** Presents the work of University of South Australia researchers relating to the institute's central themes, including sustainable societies, the effects of globalization, equity, participation and citizenship, and questions of cultural identity. From paper No. 22 they appear online only.
Formerly: Hawke Research Institute. Postgraduate Working Paper Series (Print)
Media: Online - full text.
Published by: University of South Australia, Hawke Research Institute, Magill Campus, St Bernards Rd, Magill, SA 5072, Australia. TEL 61-8-83026611, FAX 61-8-83024723. Ed. Kate Leeson.

HAWLIYYAT KULLIYYAT AL-ADAB/ANNALS OF THE ARTS AND SOCIAL SCIENCES. *see* HUMANITIES: COMPREHENSIVE WORKS

HEALTH, RISK & SOCIETY. *see* PUBLIC HEALTH AND SAFETY

HEALTH SERVICES AND OUTCOMES RESEARCH METHODOLOGY; an international journal devoted to quantitative methods for the study of the utilization, quality, cost and outcomes of health care. *see* MEDICAL SCIENCES

300 100 CHN ISSN 1005-6378
AS452.P234
➤ **HEBEI DAXUE XUEBAO (SHEHUI ZHEXUE BAN)/HEBEI UNIVERSITY. JOURNAL (PHILOSOPHY & SOCIAL SCIENCES).** Text in Chinese. 1960. bi-m. USD 31.20 (effective 2009). **Document type:** *Journal, Academic/Scholarly.*
Related titles: Online - full text ed.
Indexed: RASB.
—East View.
Published by: Hebei Daxue/Hebei University, no.108, 54 Dong Lu, Baoding, Hebei 071002, China. TEL 86-312-5079412. Circ: 2,000. **Dist. by:** China International Book Trading Corp, 35 Chegongzhuang Xilu, Haidian District, PO Box 399, Beijing 100044, China. TEL 86-10-68412045, FAX 86-10-68412023, cibtc@mail.cibtc.com.cn, http://www.cibtc.com.cn.

300 CHN ISSN 1008-9896
HEBEI JIANZHU KEJI XUEYUAN XUEBAO (SHE-KE BAN)/HEBEI INSTITUTE OF ARCHITECTURAL SCIENCE AND TECHNOLOGY. JOURNAL (SOCIAL SCIENCE). Text in Chinese. 1996. q. CNY 10 newsstand/cover (effective 2006). **Document type:** *Journal, Academic/Scholarly.*
Supersedes in part: Hebei Meitan Jianzhu Gongcheng Xueyuan Xuebao/Hebei Mining and Civil Engineering Institute. Journal (1004-5317)
Related titles: Online - full text ed.
Published by: Hebei Jianzhu Keji Xueyuan/Hebei Institute of Architectural Science and Technology, 199, Guangming Nan Dajie, Handan, 056038, China. TEL 86-22-23973378.

300 CHN ISSN 1671-1653
HEBEI KEJI DAXUE XUEBAO (SHEHUI KEXUE BAN)/HEBEI UNIVERSITY OF SCIENCE AND TECHNOLOGY. JOURNAL (SOCIAL SCIENCES). Text in Chinese. 2001. q. CNY 8 newsstand/cover (effective 2006). **Document type:** *Journal, Academic/Scholarly.*
Formerly: Gaodeng Jiaoyu Yanjiu (Shijiazhuang)
Related titles: Online - full text ed.
Published by: Hebei Keji Daxue, 186 Yuhua Dong Lu, Shijiazhuang, Hebei 050018, China. TEL 86-311-8632071.

300 CHN
HEBEI LIGONG DAXUE XUEBAO (SHEHUI KEXUE BAN)/HEBEI POLYTECHNIC UNIVERSITY. JOURNAL (SOCIAL SCIENCE EDITION). Text in Chinese. 2001. q. CNY 10 newsstand/cover (effective 2006). **Document type:** *Journal, Academic/Scholarly.*
Formerly: Hebei Ligong Xueyuan Xuebao (Shehui Kexue Ban)/Hebei Institute of Technology. Journal (Social Science Edition) (1671-1068)
Published by: Hebei Ligong Daxue/Hebei Institute of Technology, 46 Xinhua-dao, Tangshan, 063009, China. TEL 86-315-2592093, http://www.heut.edu.cn/.

HEBEI RUANJIAN ZHIYE JISHU XUEYUAN XUEBAO/HEBEI SOFTWARE INSTITUTE. JOURNAL. *see* SCIENCES: COMPREHENSIVE WORKS

300 CHN ISSN 1000-5587
AS452.S543
HEBEI SHIFAN DAXUE XUEBAO (SHEHUI KEXUE BAN)/HEBEI NORMAL UNIVERSITY. JOURNAL (SOCIAL SCIENCE EDITION). Text in Chinese. 1963. q. USD 37.20 (effective 2009).
Related titles: CD-ROM ed.; Online - full text ed.
Published by: Hebei Shifan Daxue/Hebei Normal University, 265, Yuhua Dong Lu, Shijiazhuang, Hebei 050016, China. TEL 86-311-6049941, FAX 86-311-6049413. Eds. Chunming Feng, Guifang Cao. Circ: 2,000. **Dist. overseas by:** China International Book Trading Corp, 35 Chegongzhuang Xilu, Haidian District, PO Box 399, Beijing 100044, China.

300 CHN ISSN 1003-7071
AS451
HEBEI XUEKAN/HEBEI ACADEMIC JOURNAL. Text in Chinese; Contents page in English. 1981. bi-m. USD 40.20 (effective 2009). adv. 112 p./no.; reprints avail.
Related titles: Online - full text ed.
—East View.
Published by: Hebei Sheng Shehui Kexueyuan/Hebei Academy of Social Sciences, No 423 Yuhua Xilu, Shijiazhuang, Hebei 050051, China. TEL 86-311-3035767. Ed., Adv. contact Chen Yaobin. Circ: 3,000.

THE HEDGEHOG REVIEW; critical reflections on contemporary culture. *see* HUMANITIES: COMPREHENSIVE WORKS

300 CHN ISSN 1008-3634
H8
HEFEI GONGYE DAXUE XUEBAO (SHEHUI KEXUE BAN)/HEFEI UNIVERSITY OF TECHNOLOGY. JOURNAL (SOCIAL SCIENCES). Text in Chinese. 1985. bi-m. CNY 72; CNY 12 per issue (effective 2010). **Document type:** *Journal, Academic/Scholarly.*
Formerly: Hefei Gongye Daxue Xuebao (Wenke Ban)
Related titles: Online - full text ed.
Indexed: CA, L&LBA, PSA, SCOPUS, SociolAb.
—BLDSC (4283.264900), East View.
Published by: Hefei Gongye Daxue, 193, Tunxi Lu, Hefei, 230009, China. TEL 86-551-2901307, FAX 86-551-2901307.

300 CHN ISSN 1672-920X
HEFEI XUEYUAN XUEBAO (SHEHUI KEXUE BAN)/HEFEI UNIVERSITY. JOURNAL (SOCIAL SCIENCES). Text in Chinese. 1984. q. CNY 8 newsstand/cover (effective 2006). **Document type:** *Journal, Academic/Scholarly.*
Formerly: Hefei Jiaoyu Xueyuan Xuebao/Hefei Institute of Education. Journal (1009-1297)
Published by: Hefei Xueyuan, 373, Huangshan Lu, Hefei, 230022, China. TEL 86-551-2158516, FAX 86-551-3635969.

300 100 CHN ISSN 1671-4970
HEHAI DAXUE XUEBAO (ZHEXUE SHEHUI KEXUE BAN)/HOHAI UNIVERSITY. JOURNAL (PHILOSOPHY AND SOCIAL SCIENCES EDITION). Text in Chinese. 1999. q. CNY 5 newsstand/cover (effective 2006). **Document type:** *Journal, Academic/Scholarly.*
Formerly (until 2000): Hehai Daxue Xuebao (Shehui Kexue Ban)/Hohai University. Journal (Social Sciences) (1008-3316)
Published by: Hehai Daxue, 1 Xikang Rd, Nanjing, Jiangsu 210098, China. TEL 86-25-83786376, FAX 86-25-83787381.

300 500 001.3 CHN ISSN 1674-9499
HEIHE XUEYUAN XUEBAO. Text in Chinese. bi-m. **Document type:** *Journal, Academic/Scholarly.*
Related titles: Online - full text ed.
Published by: Heihe Xueyuan, 1, Xueyuan Lu, Jiaoyu Keji-qu, Heilongjiang, 164300, China. TEL 86-456-6842083, FAX 86-456-6842083.

300 USA
HELEN KELLOGG INSTITUTE FOR INTERNATIONAL STUDIES. WORKING PAPER. Text in Multiple languages; Abstracts in English, Portuguese, Spanish. 1983. irreg., latest vol.306, 2003.
Published by: University of Notre Dame, Helen Kellogg Institute for International Studies, 130 Hesburgh Ctr., Notre Dame, IN 46556-5677. TEL 574-631-6580, FAX 574-631-6717, kellogg@nd.edu.

300 CHN ISSN 1673-1751
HENAN GONGYE DAXUE XUEBAO (SHEHUI KEXUE BAN)/HENAN UNIVERSITY OF TECHNOLOGY. JOURNAL (SOCIAL SCIENCE EDITION). Text in Chinese. 1985. q. CNY 5 newsstand/cover (effective 2006).
Related titles: Online - full text ed.
Published by: Henan Gongye Daxue/Henan University of Technology, 140, Songshan Lu, Zhengzhou, 450052, China. TEL 86-371-67789954, http://www2.haut.edu.cn/xuebaobianjibu/.

300 CHN
HENAN LIGONG DAXUE XUEBAO (SHEHUI KEXUE BAN)/HENAN POLYTECHNIC UNIVERSITY. JOURNAL (SOCIAL SCIENCES). JOURNAL. Text in Chinese. 2000. q. CNY 8 newsstand/cover (effective 2006). **Document type:** *Journal, Academic/Scholarly.*
Formerly: Jiaozuo Gongxueyuan Xuebao (Shehui Kexue Ban) (1009-3893)
Related titles: Online - full text ed.
Published by: Henan Ligong Daxue, 2001, Shiji Dadao, Jiaozuo, 454000, China. TEL 86-391-3987069.

300 CHN ISSN 1000-2359
AS452.H7964
HENAN SHIFAN DAXUE XUEBAO (ZHEXUE SHEHUI KEXUE BAN)/HENAN NORMAL UNIVERSITY. JOURNAL (SOCIAL SCIENCE EDITION). Text in Chinese. 1960. bi-m. CNY 12 per issue (effective 2011). **Document type:** *Journal, Academic/Scholarly.*
Supersedes in part (in 1983): Xinxiang Shifan Xueyuan Xuebao/ Xinxiang Normal College. Journal
Related titles: Online - full text ed.
Indexed: RASB.
—East View.
Published by: Henan Shifan Daxue, Jianshe Dong Lu, Xinxiang, Henan 453007, China. TEL 86-373-3326281, FAX 86-373-3326374, http://www.htu.cn/xuebao/.

300 CHN ISSN 1008-9276
HE'NAN ZHIGONG YIXUEYUAN XUEBAO/HENAN MEDICAL COLLEGE FOR STAFF AND WORKERS. JOURNAL. Text in Chinese. 1994. bi-m. CNY 7 newsstand/cover (effective 2007). **Document type:** *Journal, Academic/Scholarly.*
Related titles: Online - full text ed.
—BLDSC (4295.134000).

S

Published by: Henan Zhigong Yixueyuan, 8, Weiwu Lu, Zhengzhou, 450003, China. TEL 86-371-65585453.

300 TUR ISSN 1307-5942
HER YONUYLE DERNEKLER. Text in Turkish; Summaries in English, Turkish. 2007 (Jul.). q. TRY 50 domestic to individuals; USD 50 foreign to individuals; TRY 100 for 3 yrs. domestic to institutions; USD 100 for 3 yrs. foreign to institutions; TRY 15 newsstand/cover domestic; USD 15 newsstand/cover foreign (effective 2009). adv. bk.rev.; software rev. abstr.; charts; maps; bibl.; illus.; stat. back issues avail. **Document type:** *Journal, Academic/Scholarly.*
Related titles: Online - full text ed.
Published by: Uluslararasi Sivil Toplumu Destekleme ve Gelistirme Dernegi (USIDER)/International Association of Supporting and Development of Civil Society, 1324. Cad no.24 Asagi Ovecler Cankaya, Ankara, Turkey. TEL 90-312-4726475, FAX 90-312-4723791, info@usider.org, http://www.usider.org/. Ed. Gokhan Bacik. Pub. Yusuf Atalay. Adv. contact Halit Hakan Edig. color page TRY 7,500. Circ: 3,500.

300 GBR ISSN 1740-3790
HERALD OF EUROPE; the magazine of European culture, politics and development. Text in English. 2004. bi-m. GBP 6.60 per issue domestic; EUR 10.75 per issue in Europe, Russia & CIS countries; EUR 15.40 per issue elsewhere (effective 2009). adv. back issues avail. **Document type:** *Magazine, Consumer.* **Description:** Designed to examine, for readers from Europe and elsewhere, aspects of the development of Europe and its role in the world.
—BLDSC (4296.071100).
Address: 29 Curzon St, London, W1J 7TL, United Kingdom. TEL 44-20-74954007, FAX 44-20-74954008. Eds. Victor Yaroshenko, Michael Borshchevsky. Pub. Michael Borshchevsky. adv.: B&W page GBP 1,100, color page GBP 1,300.

300 GBR ISSN 1756-4832
HERITAGE MATTERS. Text in English. 2008. irreg., latest vol.6, 2011. price varies. **Document type:** *Monographic series, Academic/Scholarly.*
Published by: Boydell & Brewer Ltd., Whitwell House, St Audrys Park Rd, Melton, Woodbridge, IP12 1SY, United Kingdom. TEL 44-1394-610600, FAX 44-1394-610316, editorial@boydell.co.uk, http://www.boydell.co.uk.

300 167 168 FRA ISSN 0767-9513
P87
HERMES. Text in French. 1984. 3/yr. price varies. back issues avail. **Document type:** *Journal, Academic/Scholarly.*
Formerly (until 1988): Cahiers S T S (0762-5332)
Indexed: A20, ArtHuCI, CurCont, FR, I13, IBSS, L&LBA, PAIS, PSA, RILM, SSCI, SociolAb, W07.
—INIST.
Published by: Centre National de la Recherche Scientifique, Campus Gerard-Megie, 3 Rue Michel-Ange, Paris, 75794, France. TEL 33-1-44964000, FAX 33-1-44965390, http://www.cnrs.fr. Ed. Dominique Wolton.

500 JPN ISSN 1882-7756
HIGASHIAJIA BUNKA KOUSHOU KENKYUU. BESSATSU/JOURNAL OF EAST ASIAN CULTURAL INTERACTION STUDIES. Text in Japanese. 2008. s-a. **Document type:** *Journal, Academic/Scholarly.*
Published by: Kansai Daigaku, Bunka Koushougaku Kyouiku Kenkyuu Kyoten/Kansai University, Institute for Cultural Interaction Studies, 3-3-35 Yamate-cho, Suita-shi, Osaka, 564-8680, Japan. TEL 81-6-63680256, FAX 81-6-63680235, icis@jm.kansai-u.ac.jp.

300 JPN ISSN 1341-1659
CODEN: HSBUF3
HIKAKU SHAKAI BUNKA/KYUSHU UNIVERSITY. GRADUATE SCHOOL OF SOCIAL AND CULTURAL STUDIES. BULLETIN. Variant title: Kyushu Daigaku Daigakuin Hikaku Shakai Bunka Kenkyuka Kiyo. Text in English, Japanese. 1995. a. **Document type:** *Bulletin, Academic/Scholarly.*
Indexed: BAS, GeoRef, SpeleolAb, Z01.
Published by: Kyushu Daigaku Daigakuin, Hikaku Shakai Bunka Kenkyuka, 4-2-1 Ropponmatsu, Chuo-ku, Fukuoka-shi, 810-0044, Japan. TEL 81-92-771-4161.

300 DEU ISSN 0947-2436
HILDESHEIMER SCHRIFTEN ZUR SOZIALPAEDAGOGIK UND SOZIALARBEIT. Text in German. 1992. irreg., latest vol.18, 2009. price varies. **Document type:** *Monographic series, Academic/Scholarly.*
Published by: Georg Olms Verlag, Hagentorwall 7, Hildesheim, 31134, Germany. TEL 49-5121-15010, FAX 49-5121-150150, info@olms.de.

HISPANIC STUDIES; culture and ideas. *see* LITERATURE

HISTORIA SOCIAL. *see* HISTORY—History Of Europe

HISTORIA Y GRAFIA. *see* HISTORY

HISTORIA Y SOCIEDAD. *see* HISTORY

300 GRC ISSN 1790-3572
➤ **THE HISTORICAL REVIEW/REVUE HISTORIQUE.** Text in English, French. 2007. a. **Document type:** *Journal, Academic/Scholarly.*
Related titles: Online - full text ed.: ISSN 1791-7603. free (effective 2011).
Indexed: A20, AmH&L, ArtHuCI, HistAb, T02, W07.
Published by: National Hellenic Research Foundation, Institute for Neohellenic Research, 48 Vas Constantinou Ave, Athens, 116 35, Greece. TEL 30-210-7273554, FAX 30-210-7246212, http://www.eie.gr/nhrf/institutes/inr/contact-en.html. Ed. Paschalis M Kitromilides.

300 DEU
HISTORISCH-VERGLEICHENDE SOZIALISATIONS- UND BILDUNGSFORSCHUNG. Text in German. 1997. irreg., latest vol.9, 2010. price varies. **Document type:** *Monographic series, Academic/Scholarly.*
Published by: Waxmann Verlag GmbH, Steinfurter Str 555, Muenster, 48159, Germany. TEL 49-251-265040, FAX 49-251-2650426, info@waxmann.com.

HISTORISCHE ANTHROPOLOGIE; Kultur - Gesellschaft - Alltag. *see* HISTORY

▼ **HISTORISCHE LEBENSWELTEN IN POPULAEREN WISSENSKULTUREN/HISTORY IN POPULAR CULTURES.** Text in German. 2009. irreg., latest vol.4, 2010. price varies. **Document type:** *Monographic series, Academic/Scholarly.*
Published by: Transcript, Muehlenstr 47, Bielefeld, 33607, Germany. TEL 49-521-63454, FAX 49-521-61040, live@transcript-verlag.de.

300 FRA
HISTORY OF HUMANITY. Text in French. 1994. biennial, latest 2008. EUR 122 per issue (effective 2010). **Document type:** *Monographic series.* **Description:** Aims to provide an account of the history of humanity in terms of its cultural and scientific achievements.
Published by: UNESCO Publishing, 7 place de Fontenoy, Paris, 75352, France. TEL 33-1-45684300, FAX 33-1-45685737, http://publishing.unesco.org/default.aspx. **Dist. in the U.S. by:** Bernan Associates, Bernan, 4611-F Assembly Dr., Lanham, MD 20706-4391. TEL 800-274-4447, FAX 800-865-3450. **Co-publisher:** Routledge.

306.8 GBR ISSN 1081-602X
HQ503 CODEN: HFAMFJ
➤ **THE HISTORY OF THE FAMILY.** Text in English. 1996. 4/yr. EUR 414 in Europe to institutions; JPY 55,000 in Japan to institutions; USD 463 elsewhere to institutions (effective 2012). back issues avail.; reprint service avail. from PSC. **Document type:** *Journal, Academic/Scholarly.* **Description:** Features articles and research reflecting new developments in scholarship and new directions in the historical study of the family.
Related titles: Online - full text ed.: ISSN 1873-5398 (from IngentaConnect, ScienceDirect).
Indexed: A01, A02, A03, A08, A22, A26, CA, CurCont, F09, FamI, HistAb, I05, IBSS, M01, M02, P30, PopulInd, S02, S03, SCOPUS, SOPODA, SSA, SSCI, SociolAb, T02, W04, W07, W09.
—BLDSC (4318.139000), IE, Infotrieve, Ingenta. **CCC.**
Published by: Pergamon (Subsidiary of: Elsevier Science & Technology), The Blvd, Langford Ln, East Park, Kidlington, Oxford OX5 1GB, United Kingdom. TEL 44-1865-843000, FAX 44-1865-843010, JournalsCustomerServiceEMEA@elsevier.com. Eds. J Kok, T Engelen. **Subscr. to:** Elsevier BV, Radarweg 29, PO Box 211, Amsterdam 1000 AE, Netherlands. http://www.elsevier.nl.

300 301 GBR ISSN 0952-6951
H1
➤ **HISTORY OF THE HUMAN SCIENCES.** Abbreviated title: H H S. Text in English. 1988. 5/yr. USD 1,368, GBP 740 combined subscription to institutions (print & online eds.); USD 1,341, GBP 725 to institutions (effective 2011). adv. bk.rev. illus. index. back issues avail.; reprint service avail. from PSC. **Document type:** *Journal, Academic/Scholarly.* **Description:** Provides a forum for contemporary social science research that examines its own historical origins and interdisciplinary influences in an effort to review current practice.
Related titles: Online - full text ed.: ISSN 1461-720X. USD 1,231, GBP 666 to institutions (effective 2011).
Indexed: A01, A02, A03, A08, A20, A22, A26, ASCA, AmH&L, AmHI, ArtHuCI, B04, B07, BRD, BrHumI, CA, CurCont, DIP, E-psyche, E01, E08, FamI, G08, H04, H07, HistAb, I05, I13, IBR, IBSS, IBZ, IPB, ISR, MLA-IB, P02, P03, P10, P25, P27, P30, P42, P48, P53, P54, PCI, PQC, PSA, PhilInd, PsycInfo, PsycholAb, RASB, S02, S03, S09, S11, SCI, SCOPUS, SOPODA, SSA, SSAI, SSAb, SSCI, SSI, SociolAb, T02, V02, W03, W07.
—BLDSC (4318.143000), IE, Infotrieve, Ingenta. **CCC.**
Published by: Sage Publications Ltd. (Subsidiary of: Sage Publications, Inc.), 1 Oliver's Yard, 55 City Rd, London, EC1Y 1SP, United Kingdom. TEL 44-20-73248500, FAX 44-20-73248600, info@sagepub.co.uk, http://www.uk.sagepub.com/home.nav. Ed. James Good. adv.: B&W page GBP 400; 130 x 205. **Subscr. in the Americas to:** Sage Publications, Inc., 2455 Teller Rd, Thousand Oaks, CA 91320. TEL 805-499-9774, FAX 805-499-0871, journals@sagepub.com.

300 JPN ISSN 0073-280X
H1
➤ **HITOTSUBASHI JOURNAL OF SOCIAL STUDIES.** Text in English, German, French. 1950. s-a. JPY 5,000 (effective 2000). 55 p./no.; **Document type:** *Journal, Academic/Scholarly.*
Supersedes in part (in 1960): Hitotsubashi Academy. Annals (0439-2841)
Indexed: BAS, CA, FR, IBSS, P06, P42, PAIS, PCI, PSA, RASB, S02, S03, SociolAb, T02.
—BLDSC (4318.970000), IE, Ingenta, INIST.
Published by: (Hitotsubashi Daigaku, Hitotsubashi Gakkai/Hitotsubashi University, Hitotsubashi Academy), Sanseido Publishing Company, Ltd., 2-22-14, Misakicho, Chiyoda-ku, Tokyo, 101-8371, Japan. FAX 81-3-3230-9569, info@sanseido-publ.co.jp, http://www.sanseido-publ.co.jp/. Ed. N Banzai. Circ: 750. **Dist. by:** Japan Publications Trading Co., Ltd., Book Export II Dept, PO Box 5030, Tokyo International, Tokyo 101-3191, Japan. TEL 81-3-32923753, FAX 81-3-32920410, infoserials@jptco.co.jp, http://www.jptco.co.jp.

➤ **HITOTSUBASHI REVIEW/HITOTSUBASHI RONSO.** *see* BUSINESS AND ECONOMICS

➤ **HOKKAIDO KYOIKU DAIGAKU KIYO. JIMBUN KAGAKU, SHAKAI KAGAKU-HEN/HOKKAIDO UNIVERSITY OF EDUCATION. JOURNAL. HUMANITIES AND SOCIAL SCIENCES.** *see* HUMANITIES: COMPREHENSIVE WORKS

300 GBR ISSN 1740-6315
NA2543.S6
➤ **HOME CULTURES**; the journal of architecture, design & domestic space. Text in English. 2004 (Mar.). 3/yr. USD 353 combined subscription in US & Canada to institutions (print & online eds.); GBP 181 combined subscription elsewhere to institutions (print & online eds.) (effective 2011). adv. bk.rev. back issues avail.; reprint service avail. from PSC. **Document type:** *Journal, Academic/Scholarly.* **Description:** Dedicated to the critical understanding of the domestic sphere across timeframes and cultures.
Related titles: Online - full text ed.: ISSN 1751-7427. USD 300 in US & Canada to institutions; GBP 154 elsewhere to institutions (effective 2011) (from IngentaConnect).
Indexed: A01, A03, A07, A08, A20, A26, A30, A31, AA, ABM, AICP, ArtHuCI, ArtInd, B04, BRD, BrHumI, CA, CurCont, D05, G08, I05, IBR, IBSS, IBZ, P42, PSA, S02, S03, SCOPUS, SociolAb, T02, W03, W05, W07.
—BLDSC (4326.015200), IE, Ingenta.
Published by: Berg Publishers (Subsidiary of: Oxford International Publishers Ltd.), 1st Fl Angel Ct, 81 St Clements St, Oxford, Berks OX4 1AW, United Kingdom. TEL 44-1865-245104, FAX 44-1865-791165, enquiry@bergpublishers.com. Eds. Alison Clarke, Setha Low, Victor Buchli. **Dist. addr.:** Turpin Distribution Services Ltd., Pegasus Dr, Stratton Business Park, Biggleswade, Bedfordshire SG18 8QB, United Kingdom. TEL 44-1767-604800, FAX 44-1767-601640, custserv@turpin-distribution.com, http://www.turpin-distribution.com/.

300 PRI ISSN 0252-8908
H8.S7 CODEN: HOMIER
HOMINES; revista latinoamericana de ciencias sociales. Text in Spanish. 1977. s-a. USD 15 domestic; USD 22 in North America; USD 25 elsewhere (effective 2005). bk.rev. cum.index: 1977-1992. back issues avail. **Document type:** *Academic/Scholarly.*
Indexed: C01, CA, DIP, H21, IBR, IBZ, IBibSS, MLA-IB, P08, P42, PSA, PerIslam, RASB, RILM, S02, S03, SCOPUS, SOPODA, SociolAb, T02.
Published by: Universidad Interamericana de Puerto Rico, Departamento de Ciencias Sociales, Apdo 191293, Hato Rey, Puerto Rico. http://coqui.metro.inter.edu/. Ed. Aline Frambes-Buxeda. Circ: 7,000.

300 AUT ISSN 1012-5825
HOMOLOGIE-STUDIEN ZUR GERMANISCHEN KULTURMORPHOLOGIE. Text in German. 1980. irreg. price varies. **Document type:** *Monographic series, Academic/Scholarly.*
Published by: Verlag der Oesterreichischen Akademie der Wissenschaften, Postgasse 7/4, Vienna, W 1011, Austria. TEL 43-1-515813402, FAX 43-1-515813400, verlag@oeaw.ac.at.

300 HKG ISSN 1021-3619
H8.C47
HONG KONG JOURNAL OF SOCIAL SCIENCES. Key Title: Xianggang Shehui Kexue Xuebao. Text in English, Chinese. 1993. s-a.
Related titles: Online - full text ed.
Indexed: CA, E08, HistAb, I05, PSA, SociolAb, T02.
—BLDSC (4326.385950).
Published by: City University of Hong Kong Press, 83 Tat Chee Ave, Kowloon Tong, Hong Kong. TEL 852-2788-7327, FAX 852-2788-7328, rckjsc@cityu.edu.hk. Eds. Joseph Cheng, Law Kam-Yee.

HOOVER DIGEST; research and opinion on public policy. *see* POLITICAL SCIENCE

300 GBR ISSN 2042-7913
▼ **HOSPITALITY & SOCIETY.** Text in English. forthcoming 2011. 3/yr. GBP 132 domestic to institutions; GBP 141 in the European Union to institutions; USD 144 in US & Canada to institutions; GBP 144 elsewhere to institutions (effective 2011). adv. **Document type:** *Journal, Academic/Scholarly.* **Description:** Aims to provide a forum to expand frontiers of knowledge and contributions to the literature on hospitality social science.
Related titles: Online - full text ed.: ISSN 2042-7921. forthcoming. USD 114 in US & Canada to institutions; GBP 99 elsewhere to institutions (effective 2011).
Published by: Intellect Ltd., The Mill, Parnall Rd, Fishponds, Bristol, BS16 3JG, United Kingdom. TEL 44-117-9589910, FAX 44-117-9589911, info@intellectbooks.com. Eds. Alison McIntosh, Paul Lynch. Pub. Masoud Yazdani.

HRVATSKA AKADEMIJA ZNANOSTI I UMJETNOSTI. ZAVOD ZA ZNANSTVENI RAD U VARAZDINU. RADOVI. *see* SCIENCES: COMPREHENSIVE WORKS

300 SGP ISSN 1793-7248
▼ **HUA REN YAN JIU GUO JI XUE BAO/INTERNATIONAL JOURNAL OF DIASPORIC CHINESE STUDIES.** Abbreviated title: I J D C S. Text in Chinese. 2009. s-a. SGD 74, USD 74, EUR 38 combined subscription to institutions (print & online eds.) (effective 2012). adv. back issues avail. **Document type:** *Journal, Academic/Scholarly.* **Description:** Aims to promote the study of Chinese originality and diversity.
Related titles: Online - full text ed.: ISSN 1793-9631. SGD 71, USD 71, EUR 36 to institutions (effective 2012).
Published by: World Scientific Publishing Co. Pte. Ltd., 5 Toh Tuck Link, Singapore, 596224, Singapore. TEL 65-6466-5775, FAX 65-6467-7667, wspc@wspc.com.sg, http://www.worldscientific.com. Eds. Lee Guan Kin, Liu Hong, Zeng Shaocong. **Dist. by:** World Scientific Publishing Co., Inc., 27 Warren St, Ste 401-402, Hackensack, NJ 07601. TEL 201-487-9655, 800-227-7562, FAX 201-487-9656, 888-977-2665, wspc@wspc.com; World Scientific Publishing Ltd., 57 Shelton St, London WC2H 9HE, United Kingdom. TEL 44-207-8360888, FAX 44-207-8362020, sales@wspc.co.uk.

300 CHN ISSN 1008-2603
HUABEI DIANLI DAXUE XUEBAO (SHEHUI KEXUE BAN)/NORTH CHINA ELECTRIC POWER UNIVERSITY. JOURNAL (SOCIAL SCIENCES). Text in Chinese. 1995. q. CNY 8 newsstand/cover (effective 2006). **Document type:** *Journal, Academic/Scholarly.*
Related titles: Online - full text ed.
Published by: Huabei Dianli Daxue, Zhuxinzhuang, Beijing, 102206, China. TEL 86-10-80798721, FAX 86-10-80791604.

300 CHN ISSN 1008-4444
HUABEI SHUILI SHUIDIAN XUEYUAN XUEBAO (SHE-KE BAN)/NORTH CHINA INSTITUTE OF WATER CONSERVANCY AND HYDROELECTRIC POWER. JOURNAL (SOCIAL SCIENCE). Text in Chinese. 1985. q. CNY 8 newsstand/cover (effective 2006). **Document type:** *Journal, Academic/Scholarly.*
Related titles: Online - full text ed.
Published by: Huabei Shuili Shuidian Xueyuan/North China Institute of Water Conservancy and Hydroelectric Power, 20, Zhenghua Lu, Zhengzhou, 450011, China. TEL 86-371-65727655 ext 3381, FAX 86-371-65790227.

300 100 CHN ISSN 1000-5579
AS452.S394
HUADONG SHIFAN DAXUE XUEBAO (ZHEXUE SHEHUI KEXUE BAN)/EAST CHINA NORMAL UNIVERSITY. JOURNAL (PHILOSOPHY AND SOCIAL SCIENCES). Text in Chinese. 1955. bi-m. CNY 84; CNY 14 per issue (effective 2011).
Related titles: Online - full text ed.
—East View, Ingenta.

Published by: Huadong Shifan Daxue/East China Normal University, 3663 Zhongshan Beilu, Shanghai, 200062, China. TEL 86-21-62232305, FAX 86-21-62233702, http://www.ecnu.edu.cn. Ed. Guo Yushi. **Dist. outside China by:** China International Book Trading Corp, 35 Chegongzhuang Xilu, Haidian District, PO Box 399, Beijing 100044, China.

300 100 CHN
HUAIBEI MEITAN SHIFAN XUYUAN XUEBAO (ZHEXUE SHEHUI KEXUE BAN)/HUABEI COAL INDUSTRY TEACHERS COLLEGE. JOURNAL (PHILOSOPHY AND SOCIAL SCIENCES). Text in Chinese. 1979. bi-m. CNY 6 newsstand/cover (effective 2006). **Document type:** *Journal, Academic/Scholarly.*
Formerly: Huaibei Mei Shi-Yuan Xuebao (Zhexue Shehui Kexue Ban)/North Anhui Coal Teachers College. Journal (Philosophy and Social Sciences) (1003-2134)
Related titles: Online - full text ed.
Published by: Huaibei Meitan Shifan Xuyuan/Huabei Coal Industry Teachers College, 100, Dongshan Lu, Huaibei, 235000, China. TEL 86-561-3802261.

300 CHN
HUAIHAI GONGXUEYUAN XUEBAO (SHEXUE KEXUE BAN). Text in Chinese. 1990. q. CNY 8 newsstand/cover (effective 2007). **Document type:** *Journal, Academic/Scholarly.*
Supersedes in part (in 2003): Huaihai Gongxueyuan Xuebao/Huaihai Institute of Technology. Journal (1008-3499)
Related titles: Online - full text ed.
—East View.
Published by: Huaihai Gongxueyuan, 59, Cangwu Lu, Lianyungang, 222005, China.

300 500 CHN ISSN 1671-4733
HUAINAN ZHIYE JISHU XUEYUAN XUEBAO/HUAINAN VOCATIONAL & TECHNICAL COLLEGE. JOURNAL. Text in Chinese. 2001. q. CNY 9.80 newsstand/cover (effective 2006). **Document type:** *Journal, Academic/Scholarly.*
Related titles: Online - full text ed.
Published by: Huainan Zhiye Jishu Xueyuan, Dongshanhuai, Huainan, 232001, China. TEL 86-554-6656907, FAX 86-554-7621927.

300 CHN ISSN 1007-8444
HUAIYIN SHIFAN XUEYUAN XUEBAO (ZHEXUE SHEHUI KEXUE BAN)/HUAIYIN TEACHERS COLLEGE. JOURNAL (SOCIAL SCIENCES EDIITON). Text in Chinese. 1979. bi-m. USD 31.20 (effective 2009). **Document type:** *Journal, Academic/Scholarly.*
Formerly: Huaiyin Shi-Zhuan Xuebao (1004-5724)
Related titles: Online - full text ed.
—East View.
Published by: Huaiyin Shifan Xueyuan, 71, Jiaotong Lu, Huai'an, 223001, China. TEL 86-517-3511053.

300 CHN ISSN 1009-055X
HUANAN LIGONG DAXUE XUEBAO (SHEHUI KEXUE BAN)/SOUTH CHINA UNIVERSITY OF TECHNOLOGY. JOURNAL (SOCIAL SCIENCE EDITION). Text in Chinese. 1999. bi-m. CNY 8 newsstand/cover (effective 2006). **Document type:** *Journal, Academic/Scholarly.*
Related titles: Online - full text ed.
Published by: Huanan Ligong Daxue/South China Unversity of Technology, Wushan Lu, Guangzhou, Guangdong 510641, China.

300 CHN ISSN 1000-5455
AS452.C364
HUANAN SHIFAN DAXUE XUEBAO (SHEHUI KEXUE BAN)/SOUTH CHINA NORMAL UNIVERSITY. JOURNAL (SOCIAL SCIENCE EDITION). Text in Chinese. 1956. bi-m. USD 24.60 (effective 2009). bk.rev. **Document type:** *Journal, Academic/Scholarly.* **Description:** Covers the scientific and educational researches in the areas of history, philosophy, education, economy, Chinese language and literature.
Related titles: Online - full text ed.
—East View.
Published by: Huanan Shifan Daxue/South China Normal University, Shipai, Guangzhou, 510631, China. TEL 86-20-85211440, http://www.scnu.edu.cn/. Circ: 1,500. **Dist. overseas by:** China International Book Trading Corp, 35 Chegongzhuang Xilu, Haidian District, PO Box 399, Beijing 100044, China.

300 CHN
HUANGGANG SHIFAN XUEYUAN XUEBAO/HUANGGANG NORMAL UNIVERSITY. JOURNAL. Text in Chinese. 1981. bi-m. CNY 8 newsstand/cover (effective 2006). **Document type:** *Journal, Academic/Scholarly.*
Formerly: Huanggang Shi-Zhuan Xuebao (1003-8078)
Related titles: Online - full text ed.
Published by: Huanggang Shifan Xueyuan/Huanggang Normal University, 146, Xingang Er-Lu, Huangzhou-qu, Huanggang, 438000, China. TEL 86-713-8621636.

300 500 CHN ISSN 1672-1047
HUANGGANG ZHIYE JISHU XUEYUAN XUEBAO/HUANGGANG POLYTECHNIC. JOURNAL. Text in Chinese. 1999. q. CNY 8 newsstand/cover (effective 2006). **Document type:** *Journal, Academic/Scholarly.*
Related titles: Online - full text ed.
Published by: Huanggang Zhiye Jishu Xueyuan, 109, Nanhu Taoyuan Jie, Huanggang, 438002, China. TEL 86-713-8345190, FAX 86-713-8345265.

300 CHN ISSN 1002-7289
HUANGPU/HUANG PU MILITARY ACADEMY GRADUATES. NEWSLETTER. Text in Chinese. 1988. bi-m. USD 18 (effective 2009). **Document type:** *Journal, Academic/Scholarly.*
—East View.
Published by: Huangpu Junxiao Tongxuehui, 20, Nansanhuan Zhong Lu, Zhaogongkou Xiao-qu, Beijing, 100075, China. http://www.huangpu.org.cn/. **Dist. by:** China International Book Trading Corp, 35 Chegongzhuang Xilu, Haidian District, PO Box 399, Beijing 100044, China. TEL 86-10-68412045, FAX 86-10-68412023, cibtc@mail.cibtc.com.cn, http://www.cibtc.com.cn.

300 CHN ISSN 1672-447X
HUANGSHAN XUEYUAN XUEBAO/HUANGSHAN UNIVERSITY. JOURNAL. Text in Chinese. 2002. bi-m. CNY 8 newsstand/cover (effective 2006). **Document type:** *Journal, Academic/Scholarly.*
Formerly (until 2001): Huangshan Gaodeng Zhuanke Xuexiao Xuebao/Huangshan College. Journal (1009-1149)
Related titles: Online - full text ed.
Published by: Huangshan Xueyuan, Tunqi-qu, Huangshan, 245021, China. TEL 86-559-2544687, FAX 86-559-2512066.

300 CHN ISSN 1006-1398
AS452.C6197
HUAQIAO DAXUE XUEBAO (ZHEXUE SHEHUI KEXUE BAN)/HUAQIAO UNIVERSITY. JOURNAL (PHILOSOPHY & SOCIAL SCIENCES). Text in Chinese. 1983. q. USD 16.40 (effective 2009). **Document type:** *Journal, Academic/Scholarly.*
Related titles: Online - full text ed.
—East View.
Published by: Huaqiao Daxue/Huaqiao University, Quanzhou, Fujian 362021, China. TEL 86-595-2692431. Ed. Chen Juewan.

300 CHN ISSN 1671-7023
HUAZHONG KEJI DAXUE XUEBAO (SHEHUI KEXUE BAN)/HUAZHONG UNIVERSITY OF SCIENCE AND TECHNOLOGY. JOURNAL (SOCIAL SCIENCE EDITION). Text in Chinese. 1987. bi-m. CNY 10 newsstand/cover (effective 2006). **Document type:** *Journal, Academic/Scholarly.*
Formerly (until 1999): Huazhong Ligong Daxue Xuebao (Shehui Kexue Ban)/Huazhong University of Science and Technology. Journal (1006-3889)
Related titles: Online - full text ed.
Published by: Huazhong Keji Daxue/Huazhong University of Science and Technology, 1037, Luoyu Lu, Wuhan, 430074, China. TEL 86-27-87543816.

300 CHN ISSN 1008-3456
HUAZHONG NONGYE DAXUE XUEBAO (SHEHUI KEXUE BAN)/HUAZHONG AGRICULTURAL UNIVERSITY. JOURNAL (SOCIAL SCIENCES EDITION). Text in Chinese. 1981. q. USD 31.20 (effective 2009). **Document type:** *Journal, Academic/Scholarly.*
Related titles: Online - full text ed.
—East View.
Published by: Huazhong Nongye Daxue, 1, Nanhu Shizishan Jie, Wuhan, Hubei 430070, China. TEL 86-27-87287256.

300 CHN
AS452.W84
HUAZHONG SHIFAN DAXUE XUEBAO (RENWEN SHEKE BAN)/HUAZHONG NORMAL UNIVERSITY. JOURNAL (HUMANITIES AND SOCIAL SCIENCES). Text in Chinese. 1955. bi-m. USD 37.20 (effective 2009). 128 p./no.; **Document type:** *Journal, Academic/Scholarly.*
Formerly: Huazhong Shifan Daxue Xuebao (Zhexue Shehui Kexue Ban)/Central China Normal University. Journal (Social Science Edition) (1000-2456)
Related titles: Online - full text ed.
Indexed: RASB.
—East View, Ingenta.
Published by: Huazhong Shifan Daxue/Central China Normal University, Guizi-shan, Wuchang, 430079, China. **Dist. by:** China International Book Trading Corp, 35 Chegongzhuang Xilu, Haidian District, PO Box 399, Beijing 100044, China.

300 CHN ISSN 1001-4799
AS452.W842
➤ **HUBEI DAXUE XUEBAO (ZHEXUE SHEHUI KEXUE BAN).** Text in Chinese. 1974. bi-m. CNY 60; CNY 10 per issue (effective 2011). **Document type:** *Journal, Academic/Scholarly.*
Related titles: Online - full text ed.
—East View.
Published by: Hubei Daxue, 11 Xueyuan Lu, Wuchang-qu, Wuhan, 430062, China.

300 100 CHN ISSN 1009-4733
HUBEI SHIFAN XUEYUAN XUEBAO (ZHEXUE SHEHUI KEXUE BAN)/HUBEI NORMAL UNIVERSITY. JOURNAL (PHILOSOPHY AND SOCIAL SCIENCES). Text in Chinese. 1981. bi-m. USD 24.60 (effective 2009). **Document type:** *Journal, Academic/Scholarly.*
Related titles: Online - full text ed.
Published by: Hubei Shifan Xueyuan, 82, Chensha Lu, Huangshi, 435002, China. TEL 86-741-6573612.

300 100 500 CHN ISSN 1671-5934
HUIZHOU XUEYUAN XUEBAO/HUIZHOU UNIVERSITY. JOURNAL. Text in Chinese. 1981. bi-m. CNY 8 newsstand/cover (effective 2006). **Document type:** *Journal, Academic/Scholarly.*
Former titles (until 2002): Huizhou Daxue Xuebao (1007-6107); (until 1994): Huiyang Shizhuan Xuebao
Related titles: Online - full text ed.
Published by: Huizhou Xueyuan, Jinshanhu, Huizhou, 516007, China. TEL 86-752-2527281.

303 SVK
CODEN: HUAFFZ
➤ **HUMAN AFFAIRS.** Text in English. 1991. s-a. **Document type:** *Journal, Academic/Scholarly.* **Description:** Covers a wide range of social sciences with humanistic and multidisciplinary orientation. Focuses on the whole spectrum of social sciences including their relation to arts and natural sciences.
Related titles: Online - full text ed.: free (effective 2011).
Indexed: AmH&L, CA, HistAb, PSA, PhilInd, S02, S03, SCOPUS, SociolAb, T02.
Published by: (Slovenska Akademia Vied, Historicky Ustav/Slovak Academy of Sciences, Institute of History), Slovak Academic Press Ltd., Nam Slobody 6, PO Box 57, Bratislava, 81005, Slovakia. TEL 421-2-55421729, FAX 421-2-55565862, sap@sappress.sk, http://www.sappress.sk. Ed. Emil Visnovsky.

301 USA ISSN 0969-4501
HD72
HUMAN DEVELOPMENT REPORT. Abbreviated title: H D R. Text in English. 1990. a. USD 40, GBP 24.99 per issue (effective 2010). back issues avail. **Document type:** *Report, Trade.*
Related titles: Spanish ed.: Informe sobre Desarrollo Humano. ISSN 1020-2528.
—BLDSC (4336.054000). **CCC.**
Published by: United Nations Development Programme, Human Development Report Office, 304 E 45th St, 12th Fl, New York, NY 10017. TEL 212-906-3661, FAX 212-906-5161, william.orme@undp.org.

301.3 USA ISSN 1530-7069
HM206
HUMAN ECOLOGY (ITHACA). Text in English. 1970. q. USD 20 domestic; USD 24 in Canada; USD 26 elsewhere (effective 2005). adv. charts; illus. back issues avail.; reprints avail. **Document type:** *Magazine, Consumer.* **Description:** Intended to inform alumni, legislators, and other key audiences about the activities, programs, and research of the college.
Formerly (until 2000): Human Ecology Forum (0018-7178)
Related titles: Online - full text ed.
Indexed: A01, A02, A03, A08, A22, A26, Agr, B04, BRD, C11, C12, CA, E04, E05, E07, E08, EnerRev, EnvAb, EnvInd, G06, G07, G08, H04, H09, H11, H12, I05, M01, M02, P02, P06, P10, P26, P27, P34, P43, P48, P52, P53, P54, P56, PAIS, PQC, S02, S03, S05, S09, S11, S23, SFSA, SSAI, SSAb, SSI, T02, W03.
—BLDSC (4336.054800), IE, Ingenta.
Published by: Cornell University, College of Human Ecology, Box HE, Ithaca, NY 14853-4401. gla2@cornell.edu, http://www.human.cornell.edu. Ed., Adv. contact Gret L Atkin. Circ: 5,000.

156 USA ISSN 1045-6767
GN365.9 CODEN: HNATER
➤ **HUMAN NATURE;** an interdisciplinary biosocial perspective. Text in English. 1990. q. EUR 354, USD 487 combined subscription to institutions (print & online eds.) (effective 2012). adv. charts; illus. back issues avail.; reprint service avail. from PSC. **Document type:** *Journal, Academic/Scholarly.* **Description:** Covers interdisciplinary investigation of the biological, social, and environmental factors that underlie human behavior.
Related titles: Online - full text ed.: ISSN 1936-4776 (from IngentaConnect).
Indexed: A01, A02, A03, A08, A20, A22, ASG, AnthLit, CA, CurCont, E-psyche, E01, ESPM, FamI, G10, HPNRM, IBSS, IPsyAb, P03, P10, P30, P43, P46, P48, P52, P53, P54, P56, PQC, PsycInfo, PsycholAb, RASB, S02, S03, SCOPUS, SOPODA, SSA, SSCI, SSciA, SociolAb, T02, W07.
—BLDSC (4336.223500), GNLM, IE, Infotrieve, Ingenta. **CCC.**
Published by: Springer New York LLC (Subsidiary of: Springer Science+Business Media), 233 Spring St, New York, NY 10013. TEL 212—460-1500, FAX 212-460-1575, service-ny@springer.com. Ed. Jane Lancaster. Circ: 250.

➤ **HUMAN ORGANIZATION.** *see* ANTHROPOLOGY

300 GBR ISSN 0018-7267
H1 CODEN: HUREAA
➤ **HUMAN RELATIONS.** Text in English. 1947. m. USD 2,114, GBP 1,143 combined subscription to institutions (print & online eds.); USD 2,072, GBP 1,120 to institutions (effective 2011). adv. bk.rev. bibl.; charts; illus. index. back issues avail.; reprint service avail. from PSC. **Document type:** *Journal, Academic/Scholarly.* **Description:** Provides an interdisciplinary forum for research into human relations among all the social sciences.
Related titles: Microfilm ed.: (from PQC); Online - full text ed.: ISSN 1741-282X. USD 1,903, GBP 1,029 to institutions (effective 2011) (from IngentaConnect).
Indexed: A12, A13, A17, A20, A22, A25, A26, ABIn, AC&P, AICP, ASCA, AbAn, B01, B02, B04, B07, B08, B09, B15, B17, B18, BPI, BPIA, BRD, BibLing, BusI, C06, C07, C08, C28, CA, CINAHL, CIS, CMM, CPE, CPM, ChPerI, CommAb, CurCont, DIP, E-psyche, E01, E02, E03, E07, E08, E10, EAA, ERI, EdA, EdI, Emerald, ErgAb, FR, FamI, G04, G06, G07, G08, H09, H12, HRA, I05, I14, IBR, IBSS, IBZ, ILD, IPsyAb, MEA&I, MReSA, ManagCont, P02, P03, P06, P30, P34, P42, P48, P51, P53, P54, PAIS, PCI, PQC, PRA, PSA, PersLit, PsycInfo, PsycholAb, RASB, RILM, S02, S03, S05, S08, S09, SCIMP, SCOPUS, SOPODA, SSA, SSAI, SSAb, SSCI, SSI, SociolAb, T02, V&AA, W01, W02, W03, W07, W09.
—BLDSC (4336.400000), IE, Ingenta, INIST. **CCC.**
Published by: (Tavistock Institute), Sage Publications Ltd. (Subsidiary of: Sage Publications, Inc.), 1 Oliver's Yard, 55 City Rd, London, EC1Y 1SP, United Kingdom. TEL 44-20-73248500, FAX 44-20-73248600, info@sagepub.co.uk, http://www.uk.sagepub.com/home.nav. Ed. Stephen Deery. adv.: B&W page GBP 400; 140 x 210. **Subscr. in the Americas to:** Sage Publications, Inc., 2455 Teller Rd, Thousand Oaks, CA 91320. TEL 805-499-9774, FAX 805-499-0871.

➤ **HUMAN SCIENCES RESEARCH COUNCIL. ANNUAL REPORT.** *see* HUMANITIES: COMPREHENSIVE WORKS

300 DEU ISSN 1432-8259
HUMANGEOGRAPHIE; Sozialoekonomische Strukturen in Europa. Text in German. 1998. irreg., latest vol.4, 2006. price varies. **Document type:** *Monographic series, Academic/Scholarly.*
Published by: Peter Lang GmbH (Subsidiary of: Peter Lang Publishing Group), Eschborner Landstr 42-50, Frankfurt Am Main, 60489, Germany. TEL 49-69-7807050, FAX 49-69-78070550, zentrale.frankfurt@peterlang.com. Ed. Karl Eckart.

300 200 DEU ISSN 1433-514X
HUMANISMUS AKTUELL; Zeitschrift fuer Kultur und Weltanschauung. Text in German. 1997. s-a. EUR 6.50 (effective 2006). adv. **Document type:** *Magazine, Academic/Scholarly.* **Description:** Covers all aspects of humanism, atheism, and the study and theory of culture and civilization.
Related titles: Online - full text ed.
Published by: Humanistische Akademie Berlin, Wallstr 65, Berlin, 10179, Germany. TEL 49-30-6139040, FAX 49-30-61390450, hvd-berlin@humanismus.de, http://www.humanismus.de. Ed., Pub. Horst Groschopp. Circ: 1,000 (paid).

▼ **HUMANITIES AND SOCIAL SCIENCES: INTERDISCIPLINARY APPROACH.** *see* HUMANITIES: COMPREHENSIVE WORKS

300 001.3 LVA ISSN 1022-4483
DK504.32
HUMANITIES AND SOCIAL SCIENCES. LATVIA. Text in English. 1993. q.
Published by: University of Latvia, 4a Visvalza Iela, Riga, 1011, Latvia. TEL 371-7-228877, FAX 371-7-227802. Ed. Viktors Ivbulis.

300 500 DEU ISSN 1612-8907
HUMATICS; Theorie der operablen Wissenseigenschaften. Text in German. 2003. irreg. price varies. **Document type:** *Monographic series, Academic/Scholarly.*
Published by: Weissensee Verlag e.K., Simplonstr 59, Berlin, 10245, Germany. TEL 49-30-29049192, FAX 49-30-27574315, mail@weissensee-verlag.de, http://www.weissensee-verlag.de.

301 USA ISSN 0160-4341
HN65 CODEN: HJSRAB
➤ **HUMBOLDT JOURNAL OF SOCIAL RELATIONS.** Abbreviated title: H J S R. Text in English. 1973. s-a. adv. bk.rev. illus. index. back issues avail.; reprints avail. **Document type:** *Journal, Academic/Scholarly.* **Description:** Publishes original research in the fields of sociology, anthropology, political science, economics, geography, history, philosophy and psychology.
Indexed: A22, ABS&EES, CA, ChPerI, E-psyche, FR, MEA&I, MLA-IB, P03, P30, PsycInfo, PsycholAb, RASB, RILM, S02, S03, SCOPUS, SOPODA, SSA, SWR&A, SociolAb, T02, W09.
—BLDSC (4336.595000), IE, Infotrieve, Ingenta.
Published by: Humboldt State University, Department of Sociology, Behavioral and Social Sciences Bldg 539C, 1 Harpst St, Arcata, CA 95521. TEL 707-826-4354, amc17@humboldt.edu, http://sorrel.humboldt.edu/~soc/. Ed. Jennifer Eichstedt TEL 707-826-4949.

300 CHN ISSN 1008-1763
AS452.C457
HUNAN DAXUE XUEBAO (SHEHUI KEXUE BAN). Text in Chinese. 1987. bi-m. **Document type:** *Journal, Academic/Scholarly.*
Formerly (until 1995): Hunan Daxue Shehui Kexue Xuebao; Which superseded in part (1989-1991): Hunan Daxue Xuebao (1674-716X); Which was formed by the 1989 merger of: Hunan Daxue Xuebao (Shehui Kexue Ban); Hunan Daxue Xuebao (Ziran Kexue Ban); Both of which superseded in part (1960-1987): Hunan Daxue Xuebao/ Hunan University. Journal (1001-943X); Which was formerly: Hunan Gongxueyuan Xuebao
Related titles: Online - full text ed.
Indexed: CCMJ, EngInd, MSN, MathR, SCOPUS.
—BLDSC (4759.170000), East View.
Published by: Hunan Daxue Qikanshe/Hunan University Press, Yuelushan, Changsha, Hunan 410082, China. TEL 86-731-8821734, FAX 86-731-8821734, qks@hnu.cn, http://qks.hnu.cn/.

300 CHN ISSN 1674-117X
HUNAN GONGYE DAXUE XUEBAO (SHEHUI KEXUE BAN)/HUNAN UNIVERSITY OF TECHNOLOGY. JOURNAL (SOCIAL SCIENCES EDITION). Text in Chinese. 1996. bi-m. **Document type:** *Journal, Academic/Scholarly.*
Former titles (until 2008): Zhuzhou Shifan Gaodeng Zhuanke Xuexiao Xuebao/Zhuzhou Teachers College. Journal (1009-1432); (until 1999): Zhuzhou Jiaoyu Xueyuan Xuebao
Related titles: Online - full text ed.
Published by: Hunan Gongye Daxue/Hunan University of Technology, Tianyuan-qu, Taishan Lu, Zhuzhou, 412007, China. TEL 86-733-2887111.

300 CHN ISSN 1009-5152
HUNAN GUANGBO DIANSHI DAXUE XUEBAO/HUNAN RADIO AND TELEVISION UNIVERSITY. JOURNAL. Text in Chinese. 2000. q. CNY 5 newsstand/cover (effective 2006). **Document type:** *Journal, Academic/Scholarly.*
Related titles: Online - full text ed.
Published by: Hunan Guangbo Dianshi Daxue, 168, Qingyuan Lu, Changsha, 410004, China. TEL 86-731-2821960, FAX 86-731-5582554.

300 CHN ISSN 1672-7835
HUNAN KEJI DAXUE XUEBAO (SHEHUI KEXUE BAN)/HUNAN UNIVERSITY OF SCIENCE & TECHNOLOGY. JOURNAL (SOCIAL SCIENCE EDITION). Text in Chinese. 1999. bi-m. CNY 8 newsstand/cover (effective 2007). **Document type:** *Journal, Academic/Scholarly.*
Formerly (until 2003): Xiangtan Gongxueyuan Xuebao (Shehui Kexue Ban)/Social Science Journal of Xiangtan Polytechnic University (1009-5357)
Related titles: Online - full text ed.
Published by: Hunan Keji Daxue Qikanshe, Xiangtan, 411201, China. TEL 86-731-58290354, xuebaoz@hnust.edu.cn, http://www.hnust.edu.cn/.

300 CHN ISSN 1009-2013
HUNAN NONGYE DAXUE XUEBAO (SHEHUI KEXUE BAN). Text in Chinese. 1999. bi-m. CNY 6 newsstand/cover (effective 2006). **Document type:** *Journal, Academic/Scholarly.*
Related titles: Online - full text ed.
Published by: Hunan Nongye Daxue/Hunan Agricultural University, Furong-qu, Changsha, 410128, China. TEL 86-731-4618538, FAX 86-731-4638380.

300 CHN ISSN 1000-2529
HUNAN SHIFAN DAXUE. SHEHUI KEXUE XUEBAO/SOCIAL SCIENCE JOURNAL OF HUNAN NORMAL UNIVERSITY. Text in Chinese. 1986. bi-m. USD 37.20 (effective 2009). **Document type:** *Journal, Academic/Scholarly.*
Related titles: Online - full text ed.
—East View, Ingenta.
Published by: Hunan Shifan Daxue/Hunan Normal University, Yuelushan, Changsha, Hunan 410081, China. TEL 86-731-8872471, xb@hunnu.edu.cn, http://www.hunnu.edu.cn/. Ed. Qinghua Bu.

HUNGARIAN STUDIES; a journal of the International Association for Hungarian Studies. *see* HUMANITIES: COMPREHENSIVE WORKS

300 500 CHN ISSN 1672-2388
HUZHOU ZHIYE JISHU XUEYUAN XUEBAO/HUZHOU VOCATIONAL AND TECHNOLOGICAL COLLEGE. JOURNAL. Text in Chinese. 2003. q. CNY 7 newsstand/cover (effective 2006). **Document type:** *Journal, Academic/Scholarly.*
Related titles: Online - full text ed.
Published by: Huzhou Zhiye Jishu Xueyuan, 299, Xuefu Lu, Huzhou, 313000, China.

320 USA
H62.A1
I C P S R BULLETIN (ONLINE). Text in English. 1980. 3/yr. free (effective 2010). back issues avail. **Document type:** *Bulletin, Academic/Scholarly.* **Description:** Contains report on research, data science, and developments at ICPSR.
Formerly (until 2008): I C P S R Bulletin (Print) (0198-6848)
Media: Online - full text.
Published by: (Inter-University Consortium for Political and Social Research), University of Michigan, Institute for Social Research, PO Box 1248, Ann Arbor, MI 48106. TEL 734-764-8354, FAX 734-647-4575, isr-info@isr.umich.edu, http://www.isr.umich.edu. Ed. Dan Meisler TEL 734-615-7904.

I C S CAHIERS. *see* RELIGIONS AND THEOLOGY

300 IND ISSN 0018-9049
H62.5.I5
I C S S R NEWSLETTER. (Indian Council of Social Science Research) Text in English. 1969. q. free (effective 2011). abstr.; stat. back issues avail. **Document type:** *Newsletter, Consumer.* **Description:** Lists all projects, fellowships, contingency and other grants given to social scientists. Includes other news of relevance to social scientists in India, featuring political implications of research.
Indexed: AICP, P30, WBSS.
—BLDSC (4362.093000).
Published by: Indian Council of Social Science Research, JNU Institutional Area, Aruna Asaf Ali Marg, New Delhi, 110 067, India. TEL 91-11-26741849, FAX 91-11-26741836, info@icssr.org. Eds. R R Prasad, Rachna Jain, Ranjit Sinha.

I D E RESEARCH SERIES/KENKYU-SOSHO. *see* BUSINESS AND ECONOMICS

300 ESP ISSN 2171-8571
▼ **I E S I. CADERNOS.** Text in Gaelic. 2010. s-a. **Document type:** *Journal, Academic/Scholarly.*
Media: Online - full text.
Published by: Instituto de Estudos Sociais e Internacionais, Apdo de Correos 2091, Santiago de Compostela, Coruna, Spain. info@iesigalicia.org.

303.842 FIN ISSN 1797-0695
I F; journal of italo-finnish studies. Text in English, Finnish, Italian. 2007. a. EUR 20 per issue (effective 2008). **Document type:** *Journal, Academic/Scholarly.* **Description:** For readers whose personal and/or professional interests are strongly related to the Italo-Finnish cultural relationship.
Published by: U M W E B, Topelinksenkatu 11 B 33, Helsinki, 00250, Finland. info@umweb.org, http://www.umweb.org. Ed. Dario Martinelli.

I F H P NEWSLETTER. *see* HOUSING AND URBAN PLANNING

300 FRA ISSN 2078-3493
L'I F P O. COLLECTIONS ELECTRONIQUES. (Institut Francais du Proche-Orient) Text in French. 2008. irreg. **Document type:** *Monographic series, Academic/Scholarly.*
Media: Online - full text.
Published by: Institut Francais du Proche-Orient, Ambassade de France a Damas, S/C valise diplomatique, 13, rue Louveau, Chatillon Cedex, 92438, France. TEL 963-11-33400111, FAX 963-11-33400112, http://www.ifporient.org.

300 550 570 SWE ISSN 1650-7770
I G B P SCIENCE. (International Geosphere - Biosphere Programme) Text in English. 1997. irreg. **Document type:** *Monographic series.*
Indexed: GeoRef.
Published by: Royal Swedish Academy of Sciences, International Geosphere-Biosphere Programme, IGBP Secretariat, Box 50005, Stockholm, 10405, Sweden. TEL 46-8-166448, FAX 46-8-166405, sec@igbp.kva.se, http://www.igbp.kva.se/.

551.588 DEU ISSN 1727-155X
I H D P UPDATE. Text in English. 2002. q. **Document type:** *Newsletter, Trade.*
Related titles: Online - full text ed.: ISSN 1727-6519. 1999.
—CCC.
Published by: International Human Dimensions Programme on Global Environmental Change, Hermann-Ehlers-Str 10, Bonn, 53113, Germany. TEL 49-228-8150602, FAX 49-228-8150620, ihdp@uni-bonn.de.

330 ARG ISSN 1852-6586
▼ **I I S E. REVISTA.** (Instituto de Investigaciones Socioeconomicas) Variant title: I I S E. Rev. Text in Spanish. 2009. s-a. **Document type:** *Journal, Academic/Scholarly.*
Published by: Universidad Nacional de San Juan, Facultad de Ciencias Sociales, Ave. Ignacio de la Roza Oeste 590, Complejo Universitario, Rivadavia, San Juan, Islas Malvinas, Argentina. http://www.facso.unsj.edu.ar/.

300 NLD ISSN 0927-4618
I I S G RESEARCH PAPERS. Text in English. 1989. irreg., latest vol.44, 2005. **Document type:** *Monographic series, Academic/Scholarly.*
Published by: Internationaal Instituut voor Sociale Geschiedenis/ Netherlands Institute of Social History, PO Box 2169, Amsterdam, 1000 CD, Netherlands. TEL 31-20-6685866, FAX 31-20-6654181, info@iisg.nl.

I N R A SCIENCES SOCIALES. *see* AGRICULTURE—Agricultural Economics

I S E A S SERIES ON JAPAN AND THE ASIA - PACIFIC. *see* HISTORY—History Of Asia

ZAF
I S E R FACT PAPER. (Institute for Social and Economic Research) Text in English. 1983. irreg., latest vol.6, 1986. back issues avail. **Document type:** *Monographic series, Academic/Scholarly.*
Published by: University of KwaZulu-Natal, Institute for Social and Economic Research, Private Bag X54001, Durban, KwaZulu-Natal 4000, South Africa. TEL 27-31-820-2298, FAX 27-31-820-2834. Ed. J J McCarthy.

300 ZAF
I S E R OCCASIONAL PAPER. (Institute for Social and Economic Research) Text in English. 1981. irreg., latest vol.24, 1989. per issue exchange basis. back issues avail. **Document type:** *Monographic series, Academic/Scholarly.*
Published by: University of KwaZulu-Natal, Institute for Social and Economic Research, Private Bag X54001, Durban, KwaZulu-Natal 4000, South Africa. TEL 27-31-820-2298, FAX 27-31-820-2834. Ed. J J McCarthy.

300 USA
I S E R OCCASIONAL PAPERS. (Institute of Social and Economic Research) Text in English. 1970. irreg. bibl. **Document type:** *Monographic series, Academic/Scholarly.*
Formerly (until 19??): I S E G R Occasional Papers
Related titles: Online - full text ed.: free (effective 2011).
Published by: University of Alaska, Institute of Social and Economic Research, 3211 Providence Dr, Anchorage, AK 99508t. TEL 907-786-7710, http://www.iser.uaa.alaska.edu/.

300 ZAF
I S E R REPORT. (Institute for Social and Economic Research) Text in English. 1976. irreg. back issues avail. **Document type:** *Monographic series, Academic/Scholarly.*
Published by: University of KwaZulu-Natal, Institute for Social and Economic Research, Private Bag X54001, Durban, KwaZulu-Natal 4000, South Africa. TEL 27-31-820-2298, FAX 27-31-820-2834. Ed. J J McCarthy.

300 ZAF
I S E R SPECIAL PUBLICATION. (Institute for Social and Economic Research) Text in English. 1985. irreg., latest vol.5, 1988. back issues avail. **Document type:** *Monographic series, Academic/Scholarly.*
Published by: University of KwaZulu-Natal, Institute for Social and Economic Research, Private Bag X54001, Durban, KwaZulu-Natal 4000, South Africa. TEL 27-31-820-2298, FAX 27-31-820-2834. Ed. J J McCarthy.

300 AUT
I S W - FORSCHUNGSARBEITEN. Text in German. 1979. irreg., latest vol.59, 2008. price varies. **Document type:** *Monographic series, Academic/Scholarly.*
Published by: Institut fuer Sozial- und Wirtschaftswissenschaften, Gruberstr 40-42, Linz, 4020, Austria. TEL 43-732-669273, FAX 43-732-6692732889, isw@ak-ooe.at.

300 TUR ISSN 1303-7013
I T U DERGISI B: SOSYAL BILIMLER/I T U MAGAZINE B: SOCIAL SCIENCES. Text in Turkish, English. 2002. a. **Document type:** *Journal, Academic/Scholarly.*
Related titles: Online - full text ed.: ISSN 1307-1653.
Indexed: S02, S03, T02.
Published by: Istanbul Teknek Universitesi/Istanbul Technical University, Yeni Rektorluk Binasi, 5. kat Maslak, Istanbul, Turkey. TEL 90-212-2857126, FAX 90-212-2857126, itudergisi@itu.edu.tr, http://www.itudergisi.itu.edu.tr. Ed. Ahsen Ozsoy.

300 001.3 PAK ISSN 1999-8880
➤ **I U B JOURNAL OF SOCIAL SCIENCES AND HUMANITIES.** (Islamia University of Bahawalpur) Text in English, Urdu; Abstracts in English. 2003. s-a. PKR 500 domestic; USD 30 in SAARC Countries; USD 50 elsewhere (effective 2011). abstr.; bibl.; charts; stat. back issues avail. **Document type:** *Journal, Academic/Scholarly.*
Published by: Islamia University of Bahawalpur, Faculty of Arts, Baghdad-ul-Jadeed Campus, Bhawalpur, Pakistan. Ed. Najeeb Jamal.

300 DEU ISSN 1610-6261
IABLIS; Jahrbuch fuer europaeische Prozess. Text in German. 2002. a. EUR 25 (effective 2006). **Document type:** *Journal, Academic/ Scholarly.*
Related titles: Online - full text ed.: ISSN 1610-6253. free (effective 2011).
—CCC.
Published by: Manutius Verlag, Eselspfad 2, Heidelberg, 69117, Germany. TEL 49-6221-163290, FAX 49-6221-167143, manutiusverlag@t-online.de, http://www.manutius-verlag.de. Ed. Renate Solbach.

300.71 ESP ISSN 1133-9810
IBER; didactica de las ciencias sociales, geografia e historia. Text in Spanish. 1994. q. EUR 58.50 domestic; EUR 61.50 foreign (effective 2009). bk.rev. index. **Document type:** *Monographic series, Academic/Scholarly.* **Description:** Covers the teaching of social sciences, history and geography on all levels.
Published by: Editoral Grao, C Hurtado, 29, Barcelona, 08022, Spain. TEL 34-93-4080464, FAX 34-93-3524337, web@grao.com, http://www.grao.com. Circ: 2,500 (paid).

300 JPN ISSN 0388-1237
DP1
➤ **IBEROAMERICANA.** Text in English, Japanese, Portuguese, Spanish. 1979. s-a. JPY 2,800 (effective 2003). bk.rev. 100 p./no.; back issues avail. **Document type:** *Journal, Academic/Scholarly.*
Published by: Universidad Sofia, Instituto Iberoamericano, 7-1 Kioi-cho, Chiyoda-ku, Tokyo, 102-8554, Japan. TEL 81-3-3238-3530, FAX 81-3-3238-3229, http://www.info.sophia.ac.jp/ibero/. Ed. Norkio Hataya. Pub. Keiko Imai.

300 MEX ISSN 2007-0675
IBEROFORUM. Text in Spanish. 2006. s-a. back issues avail. **Document type:** *Journal, Academic/Scholarly.*
Related titles: Online - full text ed.
Published by: Universidad Iberoamericana, Departamento de Ciencias Sociales y Politicas, Prolongacion Paseo de la Reforma 880, Edif. 1, Nivel 1, Lomas de Santa Fe, Mexico, D.F., 01219, Mexico. TEL 52-55-59504036, FAX 52-55-59504223, csp@uia.mx, http://www.iberosocialesypoliticas.info/.

300 ECU ISSN 1390-1249
JL3001
➤ **ICONOS**; revista de ciencias sociales. Text in Spanish. 1997. q. USD 20 domestic; USD 40 in Latin America; USD 50 elsewhere (effective 2007). **Document type:** *Journal, Academic/Scholarly.* **Description:** Aims to stimulate critical reflections on subjects of social, political, cultural and economic debate in Ecuador, the Andean region and the world in general.
Related titles: Online - full text ed.: free (effective 2011).
Indexed: A01, A26, C01, CA, F03, F04, H21, I04, I05, P08, P42, PSA, S02, S03, SociolAb, T02.
Published by: Facultad Latinoamericana de Ciencias Sociales - Sede Academica de Ecuador, Calle la Pradera E7-174 y Diego de Almagro, Quito, Ecuador. TEL 593-2-3238888, FAX 593-2-3237960, http://www.flacso.org.ec. Ed., R&P, Adv. contact Edison Hurtado. Pub. Eduardo Kingman Garces. Circ: 700 (paid and controlled).

306 USA ISSN 1523-1712
IDEA (CHICAGO); a journal of social issues. Text in English. 1996. a. free (effective 2011). back issues avail. **Document type:** *Journal, Academic/Scholarly.* **Description:** Covers the exchange of ideas related mainly, to cults, mass movements, autocratic power, war, genocide, democide, holocaust, and murder.
Media: Online - full text. **Related titles:** Print ed.: 1996.
Indexed: E13, P42, PSA, S02, S03, S18, SCOPUS, SociolAb.
Address: editor@ideajournal.com. Ed. Alan Jacobs.

300 ARG ISSN 0326-386X
H8.S7
IDEAS EN CIENCIAS SOCIALES. Text in Spanish. 1984. 3/yr. USD 30 domestic; USD 48 foreign. adv. bk.rev. bibl.; charts; stat. back issues avail. **Description:** Covers politics, law and sociology in Latin America.
Indexed: C01, IBR, IBZ, RASB.
Published by: Universidad de Belgrano, Teodoro Garcia, 2090, Buenos Aires, 1426, Argentina. TEL 54-114-7742133. Ed. Avelino J Porto. Circ: 1,000.

338.2 ESP ISSN 1887-2379
HC79.E5
IDE@SOSTENIBLE. Text in Spanish, Catalan. 2003. irreg. free (effective 2011). **Document type:** *Journal, Academic/Scholarly.*
Media: Online - full content.
Published by: Universidad Politecnica de Catalunya, Catedra UNESCO de Sostenibilitat, C/Colom 1, Terrassa, 08222, Spain. TEL 34-93-7398050, FAX 34-93-7398032, sostenible@catunesco.upc.es, http://www.catunesco.upc.es. Pub. Jordi Carres.

300 FRA ISSN 1778-6827
LES IDEES ET LES THEORIES A L'EPREUVE DES FAITS. Text in French. 2006. irreg. **Document type:** *Monographic series, Consumer.*
Published by: L' Harmattan, 5 Rue de l'Ecole Polytechnique, Paris, 75005, France. TEL 33-1-43257651, FAX 33-1-43258203.

711.4 ESP ISSN 1886-6840
IDENTIDADES. Text in English, Spanish. 2005. irreg. **Document type:** *Monographic series, Academic/Scholarly.*
Media: Online - full text.
Published by: Universitat Politecnica de Catalunya, Departament d'Urbanisme i Ordenacio del Territori, Av Diagonal, 649, Edifici A, 4a Planta, Barcelona, 08028, Spain. TEL 34-93-4016402, FAX 34-93-4016400, marta.sogas@upc.edu, http://www.etsab.upc.edu/web/frame2.htm?i=2&m=escuela&s=dep&c=740.

300 DEU
▼ **IMAGE (BIELEFELD).** Text in German. 2009. irreg., latest vol.14, 2011. **Document type:** *Monographic series, Academic/Scholarly.*
Published by: Transcript, Muehlenstr 47, Bielefeld, 33607, Germany. TEL 49-521-63454, FAX 49-521-61040, live@transcript-verlag.de.

300 PHL ISSN 0300-4155
DS1
IMPACT; Asian magazine for human transformation. Text in English. 1967. m. PHP 550 domestic; USD 30 in Hong Kong, Japan, Australia, New Zealand, Pacific Isles & Middle East; USD 25 in Korea, Taiwan & Singapore; USD 20 elsewhere in Asia; USD 55 elsewhere (effective 2004). adv. bk.rev. illus. index. reprints avail. **Description:** Covers social development issues in Asia.
Related titles: Microfiche ed.: 1967 (from IDC); Microform ed.: 1967 (from PQC).
Indexed: A22, ARDT, BAS, EIP, EnvAb, HRIR, ICUIS, IPP, SOPODA, SociolAb.
Published by: Social Impact Foundation Inc., PO Box 2950, Manila, 1099, Philippines. TEL 63-2-6500188, FAX 63-2-6500388. Ed. Cornelius G Breed. adv.: page PHP 3,000; trim 10.75 x 8.25. Circ: 1,400 (paid); 300 (controlled).

300 DEU
▼ **IMPULSE. VILLA VIGONI IM GESPRAECH.** Text in German. 2011. irreg., latest vol.3, 2011. price varies. **Document type:** *Monographic series, Academic/Scholarly.*
Published by: Franz Steiner Verlag GmbH, Birkenwaldstr 44, Stuttgart, 70191, Germany. TEL 49-711-25820, FAX 49-711-2582290, service@steiner-verlag.de, http://www.steiner-verlag.de.

300 BRA ISSN 0103-7676
Q180.B7
IMPULSO; revista de ciencias sociais e humanas. Text in Portuguese; Summaries in English. 1987. q. bk.rev. **Document type:** *Journal, Academic/Scholarly.* **Description:** Focuses on social sciences and the humanities.
Indexed: A01, AmHI, C01, CA, F03, F04, H07, H21, P08, P42, PSA, PhilInd, S02, S03, SCOPUS, SociolAb, T02.
Published by: Universidade Metodista de Piracicaba (U N I M E P), Rodovia do Acucar Km 156, Piracicaba, SP 13400-911, Brazil. TEL 55-19-31241560, FAX 55-19-31241560, editora@unimep.br, http://www.unimep.br. Ed. Heitor Amilcar de Silveira Neto. Circ: 700 (controlled).

300 001.3 ZAF
HF5549.5.M3
IN FOCUS FORUM. Text in Afrikaans, English. 1969. m. free. **Document type:** *Newsletter.* **Description:** Discusses HSRC services, products, expertise and other activities.
Formerly (until 1996): H S R C - R G N in Focus (1018-726X); Which superseded: Human Sciences Research Council. Newsletter - Raad vir Geesteswetenskaplike Navorsing. Nuusbrief (0256-6796)
Indexed: ISAP.
Published by: (Group: Corporate Communications), Human Sciences Research Council/Raad vir Geesteswetenskaplike Navorsing, Sentrum vir Wetenskapontwikkeling, Private Bag X41, Pretoria, 0001, South Africa. TEL 27- 12-302-2999, FAX 27- 12-326-5362. Ed. Maryna Swarts. Circ: 4,000 (controlled).

300 USA ISSN 1047-7969
H96
THE INDEPENDENT. Text in English. 1988. q. free to members (effective 2010). bk.rev. 12 p./no. 2 cols./p.; back issues avail. **Document type:** *Newsletter, Academic/Scholarly.* **Description:** Publishes research findings, publications conferences and media programs pertaining to the social sciences and public policy research.
Related titles: Online - full text ed.: free (effective 2010).
Indexed: A01, A03, A08, LeftInd, P05, P34, T02.
—CCC.
Published by: Independent Institute, 100 Swan Way, Oakland, CA 94621. TEL 510-632-1366, 800-927-8733, FAX 510-568-6040, info@independent.org.

THE INDEPENDENT REVIEW; a journal of political economy. *see* POLITICAL SCIENCE

300 011 THA ISSN 0125-5827
AI19.T47
INDEX TO THAI PERIODICAL LITERATURE. Text in Thai. 1964. a. USD 30. **Document type:** *Abstract/Index.*
Published by: (Publication and Dissemination of Information Division), National Institute of Development Administration, Library and Information Center, Klongjan, Bangkapi, Bangkok, 10240, Thailand. FAX 66-2-375-9026. Ed. Suntaree Rossudhadham. Circ: 100.

300 IND ISSN 0256-4491
H62.5.I5
INDIAN COUNCIL OF SOCIAL RESEARCH. ANNUAL REPORT. Text in English. 1970. a. free (effective 2011). **Document type:** *Report, Trade.* **Description:** Bulletin of the Indian Council of Social Science Research.
Related titles: Hindi ed.
Published by: (National Social Science Documentation Centre), Indian Council of Social Science Research, JNU Institutional Area, Aruna Asaf Ali Marg, New Delhi, 110 067, India. TEL 91-11-26741849, FAX 91-11-26741836, info@icssr.org.

330 300 IND ISSN 0019-4646
HC431
➤ **INDIAN ECONOMIC AND SOCIAL HISTORY REVIEW.** Text in English. 1963. q. USD 453, GBP 245 combined subscription to institutions (print & online eds.); USD 444, GBP 240 to institutions (effective 2011). adv. bk.rev. cum.index: 1963-1969. back issues avail.; reprint service avail. from PSC. **Document type:** *Journal, Academic/Scholarly.* **Description:** Covers the histories, economies, and societies of India and South Asia and includes comparative studies of world development.
Related titles: Microform ed.: (from PQC); Online - full text ed.: ISSN 0973-0893. USD 408, GBP 221 to institutions (effective 2011); Special ed(s).: Demographic History of India.
Indexed: A20, A22, ASCA, ArtHuCI, B07, BAS, CA, CurCont, DIP, E01, EconLit, FamI, HistAb, I14, IBR, IBSS, IBZ, JEL, NumL, P30, P42, PCI, PSA, RASB, S02, S03, SCOPUS, SOPODA, SSA, SociolAb, T02, W07, W09.
—BLDSC (4396.320000), IE, Infotrieve, Ingenta. **CCC.**
Published by: (Indian Economic and Social History Association), Sage Publications India Pvt. Ltd. (Subsidiary of: Sage Publications, Inc.), M-32 Market, Greater Kailash-I, PO Box 4215, New Delhi, 110 048, India. TEL 91-11-6444958, FAX 91-11-6472426, editors@indiasage.com. Eds. Sanjay Subrahmanyam, Sunil Kumar. adv.: page USD 75. Circ: 900. **Subscr. in Europe, Middle East, Africa & Australasia to:** Sage Publications Ltd., 1 Oliver's Yard, 55 City Rd, London EC1Y 1SP, United Kingdom. TEL 44-207-3248701, FAX 44-207-3248733, subscription@sagepub.co.uk; **Subscr. in the Americas to:** Sage Publications, Inc., 2455 Teller Rd, Thousand Oaks, CA 91320. TEL 805-499-9774, FAX 805-499-0871, journals@sagepub.com.

300 IND ISSN 0046-9017
HT395.I5
INDIAN JOURNAL OF REGIONAL SCIENCE. Text in English. 1968. s-a. INR 200 to non-members; free to members (effective 2011). bk.rev. charts; illus.; maps; stat. index. 132 p./no. 1 cols./p.; back issues avail. **Document type:** *Journal, Academic/Scholarly.*
Related titles: E-mail ed.; Fax ed.; Online - full text ed.: 1968. INR 200 per vol. domestic; USD 25 per vol. SAARC (effective 2001).
Indexed: A34, A37, A38, BA, C25, CABA, D01, E12, F08, F12, GH, H16, I11, IBSS, LT, N02, OR, P38, PHN&I, R12, RRTA, S13, S16, T05, TAR, TriticAb, VS, W11.
—BLDSC (4421.030000).
Published by: Regional Science Association India, CK-134 Salt Lake City Sect. II, Kolkata, West Bengal 700 009, India. TEL 91-33-23583927.

300 IND ISSN 0019-5626
CODEN: IJTPAL
➤ **INDIAN JOURNAL OF SOCIAL RESEARCH.** Text in English. 1960. q. USD 280 (effective 2011). adv. bk.rev. abstr.; bibl.; charts; illus.; stat. index, cum.index. 80 p./no.; back issues avail.; reprints avail. **Document type:** *Journal, Academic/Scholarly.*
Indexed: BAS, F09, FR, GIPL, P06, P30, PAIS, RASB, S02, S03, SSA, SociolAb.
—BLDSC (4421.170000), IE, Ingenta.
Published by: Academic & Law Serials, F-22, B/3, Laxmi Nagar, Delhi, 110 092, India. TEL 91-11-23282663. Pub. S K Puri.

➤ **INDIAN JOURNAL OF SOCIAL WORK.** *see* SOCIAL SERVICES AND WELFARE

➤ **INDIVIDUAL DIFFERENCES RESEARCH.** *see* PSYCHOLOGY

➤ **INDOCHINA UNIT SERIES.** *see* HISTORY—History Of Asia

300 658 PAK ISSN 1992-8319
➤ **INDUS JOURNAL OF MANAGEMENT AND SOCIAL SCIENCE.** Text in English. 2007. s-a. PKR 450 domestic; USD 200 foreign; free to qualified personnel (effective 2011). **Document type:** *Journal, Academic/Scholarly.*
Related titles: Online - full text ed.: ISSN 2075-6844. free (effective 2011).
Published by: Indus Institute of Higher Education, ST-2D, Block 17, Adjacent to National Stadium, Karachi, Pakistan. indus@indus.edu.pk, Http://www.indus.edu.pk. Ed., R&P Gobind M Herani. Pub. Khalid Amin. Circ: 1,000 (free).

➤ **INDUSTRY AND INNOVATION.** *see* BUSINESS AND ECONOMICS

300 PER ISSN 2078-4031
▼ **INFANCIA Y CIENCIA SOCIAL.** Text in Spanish. 2010. a. **Document type:** *Journal, Academic/Scholarly.*
Published by: Universidad Nacional Mayor de San Carlos, Facultad de Ciencias Sociales, Ave Venezuelas s-n, Ciudad Universitarias, Lima, 1, Peru. TEL 51-1-6197000, http://sociales.unmsm.edu.pe/.

INFORMACIJOS MOKSLAI/INFORMATION SCIENCES. *see* COMPUTERS—Information Science And Information Theory

300 USA
INFORMATION PLUS REFERENCE SERIES. Text in English. 2005. biennial. USD 1,596 38 vol. set (effective 2006). **Document type:** *Monographic series, Academic/Scholarly.*
Formerly (until 2000): Information Series on Current Topics
Related titles: Online - full content ed.; ◆ Series: Information Plus Reference Series. Genetics and Genetic Engineering. ISSN 1546-6426; ◆ Information Plus Reference Series. The Health Care System. ISSN 1543-2556; ◆ Information Plus Reference Series. Abortion. ISSN 1538-6643; ◆ Information Plus Reference Series. Homeless in America. ISSN 1536-5204; ◆ Information Plus Reference Series. Alcohol, Tobacco, and Illicit Drugs. ISSN 1938-8896; ◆ Information Plus Reference Series. Immigration and Illegal Aliens. ISSN 1536-5263; ◆ Information Plus Reference Series. Minorities. ISSN 1532-1185; ◆ Information Plus Reference Series. National Security. ISSN 1543-5407; ◆ Information Plus Reference Series. Crime, Prisons, and Jails. ISSN 1938-890X; ◆ Information Plus Reference Series. Social Welfare. ISSN 1532-1177; ◆ Information Plus Reference Series. Space Exploration. ISSN 1551-210X; ◆ Information Plus Reference Series. Violent Relationships. ISSN 1534-1615; ◆ Information Plus Reference Series. Water. ISSN 1536-5212; ◆ Information Plus Reference Series. Weight in America. ISSN 1551-2118; ◆ Information Plus Reference Series. Women in American Society. ISSN 1557-6302; ◆ Information Plus Reference Series. Health and Wellness. ISSN 1549-0971; ◆ Information Plus Reference Series. Gun Control. ISSN 1534-1909; ◆ Information Plus Reference Series. Growing Up in America. ISSN 1534-1631; ◆ Information Plus Reference Series. Growing Old in America. ISSN 1538-6686; ◆ Information Plus Reference Series. Gambling. ISSN 1543-4915; ◆ Information Plus Reference Series. The Environment. ISSN 1532-270X; ◆ Information Plus Reference Series. Energy. ISSN 1534-1585; ◆ Information Plus Reference Series. Endangered Species. ISSN 1930-3319; ◆ Information Plus Reference Series. Education: Meeting America's Needs?. ISSN 1557-7201; ◆ Information Plus Reference Series. AIDS / HIV. ISSN 1549-599X; ◆ Information Plus Reference Series. Alcohol and Tobacco. ISSN 1536-5239; ◆ Information Plus Reference Series. Capital Punishment. ISSN 1538-6678; ◆ Information Plus Reference Series. Careers & Occupations. ISSN 1532-1169; ◆ Information Plus Reference Series. Child Abuse, Betraying a Trust. ISSN 1534-1607; ◆ Information Plus Reference Series. Crime. ISSN 1532-2696; ◆ Information Plus Reference Series. Death and Dying. ISSN 1532-2726; ◆ Information Plus Reference Series. World Poverty. ISSN 1930-3300; ◆ Information Plus Reference Series. Animal Rights. ISSN 1546-6736.
Published by: Gale (Subsidiary of: Cengage Learning), 27500 Drake Rd, Farmington Hills, MI 48331. TEL 248-699-4253, 800-877-4253, FAX 877-363-4253, gale.customerservice@cengage.com, http://www.galegroup.com.

INFORMATION PLUS REFERENCE SERIES. MINORITIES; race and ethnicity in America. *see* POLITICAL SCIENCE—Civil Rights

300 GBR ISSN 1756-1078
➤ **INFORMATION, SOCIETY AND JUSTICE.** Abbreviated title: I S J. Text in English. 2007. s-a. free (effective 2011). back issues avail. **Document type:** *Journal, Academic/Scholarly.* **Description:** Publishes debates, reflections, book and film reviews, reports and briefings on varied issues and from and diverse range of institutions and individuals.
Media: Online - full text. **Related titles:** CD-ROM ed.: ISSN 1756-3712.
Published by: London Metropolitan University, Faculty of Applied Social Sciences, 62-66 Highbury Grove, London, N5 2AD, United Kingdom. TEL 44-20-71335107, FAX 44-20-71335203, socialscience@londonmet.ac.uk.

➤ **INFORMATION SOURCES IN DEVELOPMENT STUDIES.** *see* HUMANITIES: COMPREHENSIVE WORKS

300 DEU ISSN 0935-218X
INFORMATIONSDIENST SOZIALE INDIKATOREN. Abbreviated title: I S I. Text in German. 1989. s-a. **Document type:** *Journal, Academic/Scholarly.*
Related titles: Online - full text ed.: free (effective 2011).
Indexed: A39, C27, C29, D03, D04, E13, R14, S14, S15, S18.
Published by: Gesellschaft Sozialwissenschaftlicher Infrastruktureinrichtungen e.V., Postfach 122155, Mannheim, 68072, Germany.

300 020 RUS ISSN 1606-1330
INFORMATSIONNOE OBSHCHESTVO. Text in Russian. 1989. bi-m. USD 194 in United States (effective 2004). **Document type:** *Journal, Academic/Scholarly.*
Formerly (until 1997): Vsesoyuznoe Obshchestvo Informatiki i Vychislitel'noi Tekhniki. Vestnik (0236-2244)
Related titles: Online - full text ed.: ISSN 1605-9921.
Indexed: RASB, RefZh.
—East View.
Published by: Institut Razvitiya Informatsionnogo Obshchestva, a/ya 189, Moscow, 125009, Russian Federation. info@iis.ru. Ed. Yu Khokhlov. **Dist. by:** East View Information Services, 10601 Wayzata Blvd, Minneapolis, MN 55305. TEL 952-252-1201, 800-477-1005, FAX 952-252-1202, info@eastview.com, http://www.eastview.com.

300 ARG
INICIATIVAS PARA EL DESARROLLO DE ESPACIOS SOLIDARIOS. Text in Spanish. 1992. q. USD 12.
Published by: Fundacion Generacion 2000, Agrelo 3356, Piso 1, Buenos Aires, 1224, Argentina. TEL 54-114-938842. Ed. Roderto Di Lorenzo.

▼ **INKANYISO**; journal of humanities and social sciences. *see* HUMANITIES: COMPREHENSIVE WORKS

300 600 GBR ISSN 1351-1610
H1
➤ **INNOVATION (ABINGDON)**; the European journal of social sciences. Text in English. 1988. q. GBP 704 combined subscription in United Kingdom to institutions (print & online eds.); EUR 942, USD 1,184 combined subscription to institutions (print & online eds.) (effective 2012). adv. bk.rev. index. back issues avail.; reprint service avail. from PSC. **Document type:** *Journal, Academic/Scholarly.* **Description:** Publishes articles on all aspects of European developments that contribute to the improvement of social science knowledge and to the setting of a policy-focused European research agenda.
Formerly (until 1994): Innovation in Social Sciences Research (1012-8050)
Related titles: Online - full text ed.: ISSN 1469-8412. GBP 633 in United Kingdom to institutions; EUR 848, USD 1,065 to institutions (effective 2012) (from IngentaConnect).
Indexed: A01, A02, A03, A08, A22, ASSIA, B01, B06, B07, B08, B09, B21, C12, CA, CPE, E01, E17, ESPM, GEOBASE, I13, IBSS, P02, P10, P34, P41, P42, P46, P48, P53, P54, PAIS, PQC, PSA, S02, S03, S11, SCOPUS, SOPODA, SSA, SSCI, SociolAb, T02, W07.
—IE, Infotrieve, Ingenta. **CCC.**

S

Published by: (Interdisciplinary Centre for Comparative Research in the Social Sciences (ICCR) AUT), Routledge (Subsidiary of: Taylor & Francis Group), 4 Park Sq, Milton Park, Abingdon, Oxon OX14 4RN, United Kingdom. TEL 44-20-70176000, FAX 44-20-70176336, subscriptions@tandf.co.uk, http://www.routledge.com. Eds. Liana Giorgi, Ronald J Pohoryles. Adv. contact Linda Hann TEL 44-1344-779945. **Subscr. to:** Taylor & Francis Ltd., Journals Customer Service, Sheepen Pl, Colchester, Essex CO3 3LP, United Kingdom. TEL 44-20-70175544, FAX 44-20-70175198.

300 ROM ISSN 2065-8389
▼ **INOVATIA SOCIALA/SOCIAL INNOVATION.** Variant title: Revista Inovatia Sociala. Text in Romanian, English. 2009. s-a. free (effective 2011). **Document type:** *Journal, Academic/Scholarly.*
Media: Online - full text.
Published by: Academia Romana, Institutul de Cercetare a Calitatii Vietii/Romanian Academy, Research Institute for Quality of Life, Calea 13 Septembrie 13, Bucharest, 010071, Romania. Ed. Simona Stanescu.

INQUIRY; an interdisciplinary journal of philosophy. *see* PHILOSOPHY

300 CAN ISSN 1188-746X
F1001
INROADS; a journal of opinion. Text in English. 1992. s-a. CAD 48 for 2 yrs. to individuals; CAD 60 for 2 yrs. to institutions; CAD 36 for 2 yrs. to students (effective 2003).
Related titles: Online - full text ed.
Indexed: A26, C03, C05, CBCARef, CPerI, G08, H12, I05, P02, P10, P13, P48, P53, P54, PQC, S11, S23, SSAI, SSAb, SSI, W03, W05.
Published by: Inroads Journal Publishing, Inc., 3777 Kent Ave, Ste A, Montreal, PQ H3S 1N4, Canada. TEL 514-731-2691, FAX 514-731-8256, inroads@canada.com, http://www.inroadsjournal.ca. Eds. Henry Milner, John Richards.

300 USA ISSN 1550-1574
JZ6.5
➤ **INSIGHTS TO A CHANGING WORLD.** Text in English. 1992. q. USD 285 domestic; USD 320 foreign; USD 80 per issue domestic; USD 92 per issue foreign (effective 2010). bk.rev. back issues avail. **Document type:** *Journal, Academic/Scholarly.* **Description:** Covers issues about the complex nature of today's society.
Indexed: A01.
Published by: Franklin Publishing Company, 2723 Steamboat Cir, Arlington, TX 76006. TEL 817-548-1124, FAX 817-369-2689. Pub. Dr. Ludwig Otto.

300 IND ISSN 0971-3085
INSTITUT FRANCAIS DE PONDICHERY. DEPARTEMENT DE SCIENCES SOCIALES. PUBLICATIONS. Text and summaries in English, French. 1991. irreg. price varies. index. **Document type:** *Trade.*
Published by: Institut Francais de Pondichery/French Institute of Pondicherry, PO Box 33, Pondicherry, Tamil Nadu 605 001, India. TEL 91-413-2334168, ifpinfo@ifpindia.org. Circ: 500.

300 550 PER ISSN 0303-7495
F2212 CODEN: BIFEB5
INSTITUT FRANCAIS D'ETUDES ANDINES. BULLETIN/INSTITUTO FRANCES DE ESTUDIOS ANDINOS. BOLETIN. Text in English, French, Spanish. 1972. 3/yr. USD 10 per issue (effective 2006). adv. illus. **Document type:** *Journal, Academic/Scholarly.* **Description:** Covers many areas in earth and social sciences, including anthropology, agriculture, archaeology, ethnic history, sociology, biology, linguistics, geology and paleontology.
Related titles: Online - full text ed.: free (effective 2011).
Indexed: AICP, AnthLit, BibInd, FR, GeoRef, H21, IBR, IBSS, IBZ, P08, SCOPUS, SOPODA, SociolAb, SpeleolAb.
—BLDSC (2570.100000), INIST.
Published by: Institut Francais d'Etudes Andines, Casilla 18-1217, Miraflores, Lima 18, Peru. TEL 5114-476070, FAX 5114-457650. Ed. Anne-Marie Brougere. R&P Georges Pratlong. Adv. contact Zaida Lanning de Sanchez. Circ: 850.

300 550 PER ISSN 0768-424X
INSTITUT FRANCAIS D'ETUDES ANDINES. TRAVAUX. Text in French, Spanish. 1949. irreg. price varies. **Document type:** *Monographic series.*
Indexed: AICP, FR.
—INIST.
Published by: Institut Francais d'Etudes Andines, Casilla 18-1217, Miraflores, Lima 18, Peru. TEL 5114-476070, FAX 5114-457650. Ed. Anne-Marie Brougere. R&P Georges Pratlong.

300 JPN ISSN 0563-8186
AS552.T7166
INSTITUTE FOR COMPARATIVE STUDIES OF CULTURE. ANNALS. Text in Japanese. 1955. a. JPY 1,500 (effective 2000). title index.
Formerly: Institute for Comparative Studies of Culture. Publications
Published by: Institute for Comparative Studies of Culture, c/o Tokyo Woman's Christian University, 2-6-1 Zenpuku-Ji, Suginami-ku, Tokyo, 167-8585, Japan. Circ: 600.

300 CAN ISSN 0834-1729
H62.A1
INSTITUTE FOR SOCIAL RESEARCH NEWSLETTER. Text in English. 1985. 3/yr. free. **Document type:** *Newsletter.* **Description:** Presents articles on findings of research studies of interest to academics and government agencies - housing, health, gender issues, politics, education, ethnocultural studies, law, progam and policy evaluation, quality of life, research methodology.
Published by: Institute for Social Research, York University, 4700 Keele St, Toronto, ON M3J 1P3, Canada. TEL 416-736-5061, FAX 416-736-5749. Ed. John Pollard. Circ: 3,000 (controlled).

300 GHA ISSN 0855-4412
➤ **INSTITUTE OF AFRICAN STUDIES RESEARCH REVIEW.** Text in English. 1997. s-a. GHC 20,000 domestic; USD 35 foreign (effective 2004). back issues avail. **Document type:** *Journal, Academic/Scholarly.* **Description:** Aims as an inter-disciplinary scholarly journal of the humanities and social sciences in Africa.
Related titles: Online - full text ed.
Indexed: IIBP.
Published by: University of Ghana, Institute of African Studies, PO Box 73, Legon, Ghana.

➤ **INSTITUTE OF SOCIAL AND ECONOMIC RESEARCH. REPORTS.** *see* BUSINESS AND ECONOMICS

300 SGP ISSN 0217-7099
INSTITUTE OF SOUTHEAST ASIAN STUDIES. FIELD REPORTS SERIES. Text in English. 1973. irreg., latest FR 29. price varies. **Document type:** *Monographic series.* **Description:** Field reports of research on southeast Asian economics, politics and social issues.
Published by: Institute of Southeast Asian Studies, 30 Heng Mui Keng Terrace, Pasir Panjang, Singapore, 119614, Singapore. TEL 65-6870-2447, FAX 65-6775-6259, pubsunit@iseas.edu.sg, http://www.iseas.edu.sg/. Ed., R&P Mrs. Triena Ong TEL 65-6870-2449.

300 SGP
INSTITUTE OF SOUTHEAST ASIAN STUDIES. MONOGRAPHS SERIES. Text in English. 1973. irreg., latest vol.244, 2003. price varies. **Document type:** *Monographic series, Academic/Scholarly.* **Description:** Major works on Southeast Asia, particularly current economics, political and social issues.
Published by: Institute of Southeast Asian Studies, 30 Heng Mui Keng Terrace, Pasir Panjang, Singapore, 119614, Singapore. TEL 65-6870-2447, FAX 65-6775-6259, pubsunit@iseas.edu.sg, http://www.iseas.edu.sg/. Ed., R&P Mrs. Triena Ong TEL 65-6870-2449.

300 SGP ISSN 0073-9731
HC441.A1
INSTITUTE OF SOUTHEAST ASIAN STUDIES. OCCASIONAL PAPER. Text in English. 1970. irreg., latest vol.93, 1996. price varies. bibl. back issues avail. **Document type:** *Monographic series, Academic/Scholarly.* **Description:** Studies on Southeast Asia, particularly current economic, political and social issues.
—BLDSC (4582.832500).
Published by: Institute of Southeast Asian Studies, 30 Heng Mui Keng Terrace, Pasir Panjang, Singapore, 119614, Singapore. TEL 65-6870-2447, FAX 65-6775-6259, pubsunit@iseas.edu.sg, http://www.iseas.edu.sg/. Ed., R&P Mrs. Triena Ong TEL 65-6870-2449.

300 SGP ISSN 0129-8828
INSTITUTE OF SOUTHEAST ASIAN STUDIES. RESEARCH NOTES AND DISCUSSION SERIES. Text in English. 1976. irreg., latest vol.75, 1992. price varies. bibl.; charts; stat. back issues avail. **Document type:** *Monographic series, Academic/Scholarly.* **Description:** Short papers on current research on Southeast Asia, particularly economic, political and social issues.
Published by: Institute of Southeast Asian Studies, 30 Heng Mui Keng Terrace, Pasir Panjang, Singapore, 119614, Singapore. TEL 65-6870-2447, FAX 65-6775-6259, pubsunit@iseas.edu.sg, http://www.iseas.edu.sg/. Ed., R&P Mrs. Triena Ong TEL 65-6870-2449.

300 COL ISSN 0121-7194
NX535.A1
INSTITUTO COLOMBIANO DE CULTURA. GACETA; revista internacional de cultura. Text in Spanish. 1975. bi-m. USD 60. adv. bk.rev.; film rev. **Document type:** *Government.* **Description:** Contains literary essays and contemporary poetry.
Published by: Instituto Colombiano de Cultura, Calle 11 no. 5-16, Apartado Aereo 43617, Bogota, CUND, Colombia. TEL 57-1-3410675, FAX 57-1-2820854. Ed. Ruben Sierra Mejia. Adv. contact Martha Traslavina. B&W page USD 62.50, color page USD 87.50; 240 x 340. Circ: 5,000.

300 BRA ISSN 0104-1525
➤ **INSTITUTO DE CIENCIAS HUMANAS. CADERNOS.** Key Title: Cadernos do I C H. Text in Portuguese. 1992. a., latest no.8, 1998. BRL 20 (effective 1999). abstr.; bibl.; maps. **Document type:** *Magazine, Academic/Scholarly.* **Description:** Discloses the academic production of the Human Sciences Institute of PUC Campinas University, with special attention to the fields of geography, history, anthropology, sociology and political science.
Published by: Pontificia Universidade Catolica de Campinas, Instituto de Ciencias Humanas, Rod. D. Pedro I - Km 136, CP 317, Campinas, SP 13020-904, Brazil. TEL 55-19-7567238. Ed. Lilia Ines Z de Medrano.

300 BRA
➤ **INSTITUTO DE CIENCIAS HUMANAS. HUMANITAS.** Cover title: Humanitas. Revista do ICH. Text in Portuguese, English, Spanish; Summaries in Portuguese, English. 1997. a., latest vol.2, no.2, 1998. BRL 40 domestic; USD 20 foreign (effective 1999). bk.rev. abstr.; bibl.; maps. **Document type:** *Magazine, Academic/Scholarly.* **Description:** Offers a mulitdisciplinary perspective of the human sciences, especially those related to the fields of history, geography, and the social sciences, for academics and professionals.
Published by: Pontificia Universidade Catolica de Campinas, Instituto de Ciencias Humanas, Rod. D. Pedro I - Km 136, CP 317, Campinas, SP 13020-904, Brazil. TEL 55-19-7567238, agfarias@correionet.com.br. Ed., Pub. Agenor Jose T Pinto Farias. Circ: 500.

300 ESP ISSN 2172-1041
INSTITUTO DE ESTUDIOS ALMERIENSES. TEXTOS Y ENSAYOS. Text in Spanish. 1997. irreg. **Document type:** *Monographic series, Academic/Scholarly.*
Published by: Instituto de Estudios Almerienses, Pl Julio Alfredo Egea, 3, Almeria, 0971, Spain. TEL 34-950281854, FAX 34-950281287, iea@dipalme.org, http://www.iealmerienses.es/.

300 PER ISSN 1019-4479
INSTITUTO DE ESTUDIOS PERUANOS. COLECCION MINIMA. Text in Spanish. 1973. irreg., latest vol.38, 1999. price varies. back issues avail. **Document type:** *Monographic series, Academic/Scholarly.*
Published by: (Instituto de Estudios Peruanos), I E P Ediciones (Subsidiary of: Instituto de Estudios Peruanos), Horacio Urteaga 694, Jesus Maria, Lima, 11, Peru. TEL 51-14-3326194, FAX 51-14-3326173, libreria@iep.org.pe, http://iep.perucultural.org.pe.

300 PER ISSN 1022-0356
INSTITUTO DE ESTUDIOS PERUANOS. DOCUMENTOS DE TRABAJO. Text in Spanish. 1985. irreg., latest vol.110, 1999. price varies. back issues avail. **Document type:** *Monographic series, Academic/Scholarly.*
Related titles: ◆ Series: Instituto de Estudios Peruanos. Documentos de Trabajo. Serie Antropologia. ISSN 1022-0364; ◆ Instituto de Estudios Peruanos. Documentos de Trabajo. Serie Economia. ISSN 1022-0399; ◆ Instituto de Estudios Peruanos. Documentos de Trabajo. Serie Documentos de Politica. ISSN 1022-0372; ◆ Instituto de Estudios Peruanos. Documentos de Trabajo. Serie Talleres. ISSN 1022-0437; ◆ Instituto de Estudios Peruanos. Documentos de Trabajo. Serie Historia. ISSN 1022-0402; ◆ Instituto de Estudios Peruanos. Documentos de Trabajo. Serie Linguistica. ISSN 1022-0410; ◆ Instituto de Estudios Peruanos. Documentos de Trabajo. Serie Sociologia, Politica. ISSN 1022-0429; ◆ Instituto de Estudios Peruanos. Documentos de Trabajo. Serie Etnohistoria. ISSN 1022-0380.
Published by: (Instituto de Estudios Peruanos), I E P Ediciones (Subsidiary of: Instituto de Estudios Peruanos), Horacio Urteaga 694, Jesus Maria, Lima, 11, Peru. TEL 51-14-3326194, FAX 51-14-3326173, libreria@iep.org.pe, http://iep.perucultural.org.pe.

300 CHL ISSN 0716-6478
F3186 CODEN: APSOE5
➤ **INSTITUTO DE LA PATAGONIA. ANALES. SERIE CIENCIAS SOCIALES.** Text in Spanish; Summaries in English. 1970. a., latest vol.30. CLP 7,000, USD 15 (effective 2003). adv. bk.rev. bibl.; charts; illus. back issues avail. **Document type:** *Academic/Scholarly.* **Description:** Publishes original papers by researchers of the institute in the area of social sciences referring to Patagonia, Tierra del Fuego, Antarctica, adjacent islands and the southeastern Pacific Ocean.
Supersedes in part (vol.21, 1992): Instituto de la Patagonia. Anales (0085-1922)
Indexed: GeoRef.
Published by: Universidad de Magallanes, Instituto de la Patagonia, Casilla de Correos 13 D, Punta Arenas, Magallanes, Chile. TEL 56-61-207058, FAX 56-61-212973, xsilva@aoniken.fc.umag.cl. Ed. Mateo Martinic. Circ: 500.

300 ROM ISSN 1223-1088
AP86
INSTITUTUL DE CERCETARI SOCIO-UMANE -SIBIU. ANUARUL. Text in Romanian. 1993. a.
Indexed: AICP.
Published by: Editura Academiei Romane/Publishing House of the Romanian Academy, Calea 13 Septembrie 13, Sector 5, Bucharest, 050711, Romania. TEL 40-21-3188146, FAX 40-21-3182444, edacad@ear.ro, http://www.ear.ro. Ed. Eugen Onu. **Dist. by:** Rodipet S.A., Piata Presei Libere 1, sector 1, PO Box 33-57, Bucharest 3, Romania. TEL 40-21-2226407, 40-21-2224126, rodipet@rodipet.ro.

300 ROM
INSTITUTUL DE SUBINGINERI ORADEA. LUCRARI STIINTIFICE: SERIA STIINTE SOCIALE. Text in Romanian; Text occasionally in English, French; Summaries in English, French, German, Romanian. 1973. a. **Document type:** *Academic/Scholarly.*
Formerly: Institutul Pedagogica Oradea. Lucrari Stiintifice: Seria Stiinte Sociale; Which superseded in part (in 1973): Institutul Pedagogica Oradea. Lucrari Stiintifice: Seria Istorie, Stiinte Sociale, Pedagogie; Which superseded in part (in 1971): Institutul Pedagogic Oradea. Lucrari Stiintifice: Seria A si Seria B; Which was formerly (until 1969): Institutul Pedagogic Oradea, Lucrari Stiintifice
Published by: Universitatea din Oradea, Facultatea de Inginerie Electrica si Tehnologia Informatiei, Strada Universitatii 1, Oradea, 410087, Romania.

INSTITUTUL POLITEHNIC DIN IASI. BULETINUL. *see* SCIENCES: COMPREHENSIVE WORKS

300 001.3 ROM ISSN 1224-5860
INSTITUTUL POLITEHNIC DIN IASI. BULETINUL. SECTIA STIINTE SOCIO-UMANE/POLYTECHNIC INSTITUTE OF IASI. BULLETIN. SOCIAL-HUMAN SCIENCES. Text in English. 1996. q. free to qualified personnel.
Published by: Universitatea Tehnica "Gheorghe Asachi" Iasi. Editura Politehnium/"Gheorghe Asachi" Technical University of Iasi. Politehnium Publishing House, Strada Prof.dr.doc. D, Mangeron nr.67, Iasi, 700050, Romania. TEL 40-232-231343, FAX 40-232-231343, simonasimionescu@yahoo.uk.co, http://www.tuiasi.ro. **Dist. by:** Universitatea Tehnica "Gheorghe Asachi" Iasi Biblioteca, B-dul Carol I, nr.11, Iasi 700506, Romania. diatan@library.tuiasi.ro, http://www.tuiasi.ro/index.php?page=1145.

300 301 FRA ISSN 1021-0814
INSULA; international journal of island affairs. Text in English. 1992. s-a. EUR 70 to individuals; EUR 190 to institutions (effective 2010). **Document type:** *Journal, Academic/Scholarly.* **Description:** A scientific review that focuses on islands. It provides highlights on the everyday life and debates over crucial issues of their development.
—BLDSC (4531.302000), IE, Ingenta.
Published by: UNESCO, International Scientific Council for Island Development, 1 Rue de Miollis, Paris, 75015, France. TEL 33-1-46684056, FAX 33-1-45685804, insula@unesco.org.

300 ESP ISSN 1697-9818
HD28
INTANGIBLE CAPITAL. Text in Spanish. 2004. m. free (effective 2011). **Document type:** *Journal, Academic/Scholarly.*
Media: Online - full text.
Indexed: SCOPUS. Ed. Pep Simo Guzman.

300 USA ISSN 1553-3069
HM101
➤ **INTEGRAL REVIEW.** Short title: I R. Text in English. 2005. s-a. free (effective 2011). **Document type:** *Journal, Academic/Scholarly.*
Media: Online - full text.
Indexed: A39, AmHI, C27, C29, CA, D03, D04, E13, H07, MLA-IB, R14, S14, S15, S18, T02.
Published by: A R I N A, Inc., 3109 State Rte 222, Bethel, OH 45106. info@global-arina.org. Ed. Jonathan Reams.

➤ **INTER-UNIVERSITY CONSORTIUM FOR POLITICAL AND SOCIAL RESEARCH. ANNUAL REPORT.** *see* POLITICAL SCIENCE

➤ **INTERACCOES.** *see* HUMANITIES: COMPREHENSIVE WORKS

300 BRA ISSN 1518-7012
HN110.5.Z9
INTERACOES (CAMPO GRANDE). Text in Portuguese, Spanish, French. 2000. irreg. **Document type:** *Journal, Academic/Scholarly.*
Related titles: Online - full text ed.: free (effective 2011).
Indexed: C01, IBSS.
Published by: Universidade Catolica Dom Bosco. Editora, Ave Tamandare 6000, Jd Seminario, Campo Grande, Mato Grosso do Sul 79117-900, Brazil. TEL 55-67-33123594, FAX 55-67-33123727, editora@ucdb.br, http://www.editora.ucdb.br. Ed. Maria Augusta Castilho.

300 DEU ISSN 1868-8063
▼ ➤ **INTERACTION.** Text in English. 2009. s-a. **Document type:** *Journal, Academic/Scholarly.*
Related titles: Online - full text ed.: ISSN 2191-8961.
Published by: Association for the Quality Development of Solution Focused Consulting and Training, Gluckensteinweg 10-14, Bad Homburg, 61350, Germany. info@asfct.org.

300 370 USA ISSN 1548-3320
➤ **INTERACTIONS (OAKLAND)**; UCLA journal of education and information studies. Text in English. 2004. s-a. free (effective 2011). charts; illus.; maps. back issues avail. **Document type:** *Journal, Academic/Scholarly.* **Description:** Aims to promote scholarship that examines education and information studies through interdisciplinary perspectives.
Media: Online - full text.
Indexed: A39, C27, C29, CA, D03, D04, E03, E13, ERI, MLA-IB, R14, S14, S15, S18, T02.
Published by: (University of California, Los Angeles, Graduate School of Education and Information Studies), eScholarship (Subsidiary of: California Digital Library), 300 Lakeside Dr, 7th Fl, Oakland, CA 94612. TEL 510-587-6439, FAX 510-987-0243, info@escholarship.org, http://www.escholarship.org. Eds. Amy Liu, Andrew Lau, Melissa L Millora.

➤ **INTERAKTIONISTISCHER KONSTRUKTIVISMUS.** *see* PHILOSOPHY

➤ **INTERCOLLEGIATE REVIEW**; a journal of scholarship and opinion. *see* LITERARY AND POLITICAL REVIEWS

300 DEU
▼ **INTERCULTURAL KNOWLEDGE.** Text in English. 2009. irreg. price varies. **Document type:** *Monographic series, Academic/Scholarly.*
Published by: Wissenschaftlicher Verlag Trier, Bergstr 27, Trier, 54295, Germany. TEL 49-651-41503, FAX 49-651-41504, wvt@wvttrier.de, http://www.wvttrier.de. Eds. Brendan Dooley, Immacolata Amodeo.

300 DEU ISSN 1610-7217
INTERCULTURE JOURNAL; online zeitschrift fuer interkulturelle studien. Variant title: Inteculture Online. Text in German, English. 2002. irreg. free (effective 2011). **Document type:** *Journal, Academic/Scholarly.*
Media: Online - full text.
Published by: Friedrich-Schiller-Universitaet Jena, Fachgebiet Interkulturelle Wirtschaftskommunikation, Ernst-Abbe Platz 8, Jena, 07743, Germany. TEL 49-3641-944377, http://www.uni-jena.de. Eds. Juergen Bolten, Stephanie Rathje.

INTERDISCIPLINARIA; revista de psicologia y ciencias afines/journal of psychology and related sciences. *see* PSYCHOLOGY

300 GBR ISSN 1661-8645
INTERDISCIPLINARY COMMUNICATION STUDIES. Text in English. 2008. irreg., latest vol.4, 2010. price varies. **Document type:** *Monographic series, Academic/Scholarly.* **Description:** Features research (monographs and edited volumes) in the field of interdisciplinary communication studies.
Published by: Peter Lang Ltd. (Subsidiary of: Peter Lang Publishing Group), Evenlode Ct, Main Rd, Long Hanborough, Oxfordshire OX29 8SZ, United Kingdom. TEL 44-1993-880088, FAX 44-1993-882040, info@peterlang.com. Ed. Colin B Grant.

INTERDISCIPLINARY DESCRIPTION OF COMPLEX SYSTEMS. *see* ENVIRONMENTAL STUDIES

INTERDISCIPLINARY STUDIES IN ECONOMICS AND MANAGEMENT. *see* BUSINESS AND ECONOMICS

300 001.3 FIN ISSN 1799-2702
▼ ➤ **INTERDISCIPLINARY STUDIES JOURNAL.** Text in English. 2010. q. free. Index. back issues avail.; reprints avail. **Document type:** *Journal, Academic/Scholarly.* **Description:** Publish papers on diverse subjects related but not limited to business management, tourism, leadership and development of preventive welfare work, health promotion, social services, business information technology, regional development, beauty care, correctional services, and nursing.
Related titles: Online - full text ed.
Published by: Laurea University of Applied Sciences/Laurea Ammattikorkeakoulu, Ratatie 22, Vantaa, FI-01300, Finland. TEL 358-40-5074599, http://www.laurea.fi/internet/en/index.jsp. Ed. Minna Mattila. R&P, Adv. contact Mr. Timo Riihelae.

911 CHE ISSN 1661-1349
INTERDISCIPLINARY STUDIES ON CENTRAL AND EASTERN EUROPE. Text in English. 2005. irreg., latest vol.6, 2009. price varies. **Document type:** *Monographic series, Academic/Scholarly.* **Description:** Focuses on political, economic and cultural changes in Eastern, East-Central and South-Eastern Europe.
Published by: Peter Lang AG (Subsidiary of: Peter Lang Publishing Group), Hochfeldstr 32, Postfach 746, Bern 9, 3000, Switzerland. TEL 41-31-3061717, FAX 41-31-3061727, info@peterlang.com, http://www.peterlang.com. Eds. Nicolas Hayoz, Rolf Fieguth.

▼ **INTERFACING SCIENCE, LITERATURE, AND THE HUMANITIES.** *see* HUMANITIES: COMPREHENSIVE WORKS

300 DEU ISSN 2191-4915
▼ **INTERKULTURALITAET UND WIRTSCHAFT.** Text in German. 2010. irreg., latest vol.2, 2011. **Document type:** *Monographic series, Academic/Scholarly.*
Published by: Logos Verlag Berlin, Comeniushof, Gubener Str 47, Berlin, 10243, Germany. TEL 49-30-42851090, FAX 49-30-42851092, redaktion@logos-verlag.de, http://www.logos-verlag.de.

305 USA ISSN 2152-5137
▼ **THE INTERNATIONAL.** Text in English. 2009. m. USD 4.95 per issue (print or online ed.) (effective 2010). adv. **Document type:** *Journal, Trade.* **Description:** Aims to raise awareness about important world issues.
Related titles: Online - full text ed.: ISSN 2152-5145.
Published by: The International Journal, Inc., 3-622 W 137th St, New York, NY 10031. TEL 800-733-6515.

300 NLD ISSN 1568-4474
INTERNATIONAL COMPARATIVE SOCIAL STUDIES. Text in English. 2001. irreg., latest vol.18, 2008. price varies. **Document type:** *Monographic series, Academic/Scholarly.* **Description:** Focuses on comparative research by anthropologists, sociologists, political scientists and other social scientists in the areas of migration, violence, urbanization, trust and social capital.
Indexed: IZBG.
—BLDSC (4538.725200).
Published by: Brill, PO Box 9000, Leiden, 2300 PA, Netherlands. TEL 31-71-5353500, FAX 31-71-5317532, cs@brill.nl. Ed. Mehdi P Amineh.

300 GBR ISSN 2159-8282
▼ ➤ **INTERNATIONAL CRITICAL THOUGHT.** Text in English. 2011. 4/yr. GBP 187 combined subscription in United Kingdom to institutions (print & online eds.); EUR 248, USD 309 combined subscription to institutions (print & online eds.) (effective 2012). **Document type:** *Journal, Academic/Scholarly.* **Description:** Aims to cultivate, encourage and facilitate the development and dissemination of thinking and scholarship responding to the profound social, political, cultural and economic changes taking place in the world today.
Related titles: Online - full text ed.: ISSN 2159-8312. 2011. GBP 168 in United Kingdom to institutions; EUR 223, USD 278 to institutions (effective 2012).
—CCC.
Published by: Routledge (Subsidiary of: Taylor & Francis Group), 4 Park Sq, Milton Park, Abingdon, Oxon OX14 4RN, United Kingdom. TEL 44-20-70176000, FAX 44-20-70176336, subscriptions@tandf.co.uk. Eds. Cheng Enfu, David Schweickart, Tony Andreani.

300 GBR ISSN 1744-8212
INTERNATIONAL JOURNAL FOR THE APPLIED STUDY OF PUBLIC ORDER. Text in English. 200?. 3/yr. GBP 24.95 to members (effective 2009). **Document type:** *Journal, Academic/Scholarly.* **Description:** Features articles concerned with the identification, analysis and regulation of risks to public order.
Media: Online - full text.
Published by: International Management Journals info@managementjournals.com. Ed. Bob Haigh.

300 500 001.3 AZE ISSN 2075-4124
▼ ➤ **INTERNATIONAL JOURNAL OF ACADEMIC RESEARCH.** Text in English. 2009. bi-m. USD 120 domestic to individuals; USD 240 foreign to individuals; USD 240 domestic to institutions; USD 360 foreign to institutions (effective 2010). bk.rev.; rec.rev. abstr.; bibl.; charts; illus.; maps; stat.; tr.lit. Index. back issues avail.; reprints avail. **Document type:** *Journal, Academic/Scholarly.* **Description:** Covers research in all fields of science and provides news and interpretation of topical and coming trends affecting science, scientists and the wider public.
Related titles: CD-ROM ed.; Online - full text ed.: ISSN 2075-7107. free (effective 2011).
Indexed: A01, RefZh, T02, Z01.
Published by: Progress Press Inc., M.Mushfig 4B, Apt.107, Baku, 1006, Azerbaijan. TEL 994-050-6691364, subijar@gmail.com. Eds. Nigar Babakhanova, Javid Jafarzade. Pub. Javid Jafarzade. Circ: 1,000.

▼ ➤ **INTERNATIONAL JOURNAL OF ACADEMIC RESEARCH IN BUSINESS AND SOCIAL SCIENCES.** *see* BUSINESS AND ECONOMICS

300 DEU ISSN 1861-1303
H62
➤ **INTERNATIONAL JOURNAL OF ACTION RESEARCH.** Text in English. 2005. 3/yr. EUR 60 to individuals; EUR 150 combined subscription to institutions (print & online eds.) (effective 2010). **Document type:** *Journal, Academic/Scholarly.* **Description:** Provides a forum for an open and non-dogmatic discussion about action research, both its present situation and future perspectives.
Related titles: Online - full text ed.
Indexed: A12, ABIn, CA, P27, P48, P51, P53, P54, PQC, S02, S03, SCOPUS, T02.
Published by: Rainer Hampp Verlag, Marktplatz 5, Mering, 86415, Germany. TEL 49-8233-4783, FAX 49-8233-30755, info@rhverlag.de, http://www.rhverlag.de. Eds. Richard Ennals, Werner Fricke.

➤ **INTERNATIONAL JOURNAL OF ARTS & SCIENCES.** *see* HUMANITIES: COMPREHENSIVE WORKS

▼ ➤ **INTERNATIONAL JOURNAL OF BUSINESS AND SOCIAL SCIENCE.** *see* BUSINESS AND ECONOMICS

300 GBR ISSN 1756-5669
▼ ➤ **INTERNATIONAL JOURNAL OF CULTURAL MANAGEMENT.** Text in English. forthcoming 2011. 4/yr. EUR 494 to institutions (print or online ed.); EUR 672 combined subscription to institutions (print & online eds.) (effective 2011). **Document type:** *Journal, Academic/Scholarly.* **Description:** Fosters cooperation and encourages dissemination of information that is related to cultural management, culture and all its manifestations.
Related titles: Online - full text ed.: ISSN 1756-5677. forthcoming.
—CCC.
Published by: Inderscience Publishers, PO Box 735, Olney, Bucks MK46 5WB, United Kingdom. TEL 44-1234-240519, FAX 44-1234-240515, editorial@inderscience.com. Ed. Dr. Alexandros Apostolakis. **Subscr. to:** World Trade Centre Bldg, 29 Rte de Pre-Bois, Case Postale 856, Geneva 15 1215, Switzerland. FAX 41-22-7910885, subs@inderscience.com.

306.4 GBR ISSN 1028-6632
CODEN: JCPOEW
➤ **THE INTERNATIONAL JOURNAL OF CULTURAL POLICY.** Text in English. 1994. q. GBP 607 combined subscription in United Kingdom to institutions (print & online eds.); EUR 607, USD 763 combined subscription to institutions (print & online eds.) (effective 2012). adv. back issues avail.; reprint service avail. from PSC. **Document type:** *Journal, Academic/Scholarly.* **Description:** Aims to provide an outlet for an interdisciplinary and international exploration of the nature, function and impact of cultural policies.
Formerly (until 1997): The European Journal of Cultural Policy (1074-6897)
Related titles: Online - full text ed.: ISSN 1477-2833. GBP 547 in United Kingdom to institutions; EUR 547, USD 687 to institutions (effective 2012) (from IngentaConnect).
Indexed: A01, A03, A08, A22, ABM, B21, BrHumI, CA, CABA, CMM, D05, E01, E17, ESPM, IBSS, LT, N02, P32, P34, P42, P47, PAIS, PQC, PSA, R12, RRTA, S02, S03, SCOPUS, SD, SociolAb, T02, W11.
—BLDSC (4542.180700), IE, Ingenta. **CCC.**
Published by: Routledge (Subsidiary of: Taylor & Francis Group), 4 Park Sq, Milton Park, Abingdon, Oxon OX14 4RN, United Kingdom. TEL 44-20-70176000, FAX 44-20-70176336, subscriptions@tandf.co.uk, http://www.routledge.com. Ed. Oliver Bennett. Adv. contact Linda Hann TEL 44-1344-779945. **Subscr. to:** Taylor & Francis Ltd., Journals Customer Service, Sheepen Pl, Colchester, Essex CO3 3LP, United Kingdom. TEL 44-20-70175544, FAX 44-20-70175198, tf.enquiries@tfinforma.com.

➤ **INTERNATIONAL JOURNAL OF DYNAMICAL SYSTEMS AND DIFFERENTIAL EQUATIONS.** *see* MATHEMATICS

▼ ➤ **INTERNATIONAL JOURNAL OF EDUCATION AND SOCIAL SCIENCES.** *see* EDUCATION

➤ **THE INTERNATIONAL JOURNAL OF EDUCATIONAL AND PSYCHOLOGICAL ASSESSMENT.** *see* EDUCATION

▼ ➤ **INTERNATIONAL JOURNAL OF EMERGENCY SERVICES.** *see* FIRE PREVENTION

➤ **THE INTERNATIONAL JOURNAL OF EMERGING TECHNOLOGIES AND SOCIETY.** *see* SCIENCES: COMPREHENSIVE WORKS

➤ **INTERNATIONAL JOURNAL OF ENVIRONMENTAL STUDIES.** *see* ENVIRONMENTAL STUDIES

➤ **INTERNATIONAL JOURNAL OF ENVIRONMENTAL STUDIES.** *see* ENVIRONMENTAL STUDIES

300 440 GBR ISSN 1368-2679
P35.5.F7
➤ **INTERNATIONAL JOURNAL OF FRANCOPHONE STUDIES.** Abbreviated title: I J F S. Text in English. 1998. q. GBP 300 domestic to institutions; GBP 319 in the European Union to institutions; USD 480 in US & Canada to institutions; GBP 322 elsewhere to institutions (effective 2011). adv. back issues avail. **Document type:** *Journal, Academic/Scholarly.* **Description:** Features scholars, teachers and students whose focus is on French-speaking areas of the world. Articles discuss English linguistic dominance, post-colonial migration, oppression, resistance, representation, identity, race and gender.
Related titles: Online - full text ed.: ISSN 1758-9142. USD 400 in US & Canada to institutions; GBP 267 domestic to institutions (effective 2011).
Indexed: A01, A02, A03, A08, A22, CA, E01, MLA-IB, S02, S03, SociolAb, T02.
—IE. **CCC.**
Published by: Intellect Ltd., The Mill, Parnall Rd, Fishponds, Bristol, BS16 3JG, United Kingdom. TEL 44-117-9589910, FAX 44-117-9589911, info@intellectbooks.com. Ed. Kamal Salhi TEL 44-113-2333501. Pub. Masoud Yazdani. **Subscr. to:** Turpin Distribution Services Ltd., Pegasus Dr, Stratton Business Park, Biggleswade, Bedfordshire SG18 8QB, United Kingdom. TEL 44-1767-604951, FAX 44-1767-601640, custserv@turpin-distribution.com, http://www.turpin-distribution.com/.

➤ **INTERNATIONAL JOURNAL OF HUMAN AND SOCIAL SCIENCES.** *see* HUMANITIES: COMPREHENSIVE WORKS

▼ ➤ **INTERNATIONAL JOURNAL OF HUMANITIES AND SOCIAL SCIENCE.** *see* HUMANITIES: COMPREHENSIVE WORKS

➤ **INTERNATIONAL JOURNAL OF HUMANITY AND SOCIAL SCIENCES.** *see* HUMANITIES: COMPREHENSIVE WORKS

➤ **THE INTERNATIONAL JOURNAL OF INCLUSIVE DEMOCRACY.** *see* POLITICAL SCIENCE

➤ **INTERNATIONAL JOURNAL OF INFORMATION MANAGEMENT.** *see* COMPUTERS—Information Science And Information Theory

300 AUS ISSN 1833-1882
➤ **THE INTERNATIONAL JOURNAL OF INTERDISCIPLINARY SOCIAL SCIENCES.** Text in English. 2006. irreg., latest vol.3, no.11, 2009. USD 750 combined subscription (print & online eds.) (effective 2009). Index. back issues avail. **Document type:** *Journal, Academic/Scholarly.* **Description:** Examines the nature of disciplinary practices and the interdisciplinary practices that arise in the context of 'real world' applications.
Related titles: Online - full text ed.: USD 50 to individuals; USD 300 to institutions (effective 2009).
Indexed: A01.
—BLDSC (4542.311050).
Published by: Common Ground Publishing, PO Box 463, Altona, VIC 3018, Australia. TEL 61-3-93988000, FAX 61-3-93988088, mail@commongroundpublishing.com, http://commongroundpublishing.com. Ed. Dr. Bill Cope.

➤ **INTERNATIONAL JOURNAL OF PUBLIC THEOLOGY.** *see* RELIGIONS AND THEOLOGY

001.42 CAN ISSN 1609-4069
H1
➤ **INTERNATIONAL JOURNAL OF QUALITATIVE METHODS.** Text in Multiple languages. 2002. q. free (effective 2011). back issues avail. **Document type:** *Journal, Academic/Scholarly.*
Media: Online - full content. **Related titles:** Online - full text ed.
Indexed: A01, A03, A08, A39, C27, C29, CA, D03, D04, E13, IBSS, R14, S01, S02, S03, S14, S15, S18, SSA, SociolAb, T02.
—CCC.
Published by: University of Alberta, International Institute for Qualitative Methodology, 6-10 University Extension Centre, 8303 112 Ste, Edmonton, AB T6G 2T4, Canada. TEL 780-492-9041, FAX 780-492-9040, ijqm@ualberta.ca, http://www.ualberta.ca/~iiqm/. Ed. Dan Given.

➤ **THE INTERNATIONAL JOURNAL OF REGIONAL AND LOCAL STUDIES.** *see* HISTORY—History Of Europe

300 AUS ISSN 2094-1420
➤ **THE INTERNATIONAL JOURNAL OF RESEARCH AND REVIEW.** Text in English. 2008. 2/w. free. bk.rev. abstr. cum.index. back issues avail. **Document type:** *Journal, Academic/Scholarly.* **Description:** Publish empirical reports in the various fields of arts, sciences, education, psychology, nursing, computer science, and business.
Related titles: Online - full text ed.
Indexed: A01, T02.
Published by: Time Taylor International, The MLC Centre, Castlereagh St., Sydney, NSW 2000, Australia. http://www.time-taylor.com/index.php. Ed., R&P, Adv. contact Carlo Magno. Pub. Paul Robertson.

S

300 IND ISSN 2249-2496
▼ ➤ **INTERNATIONAL JOURNAL OF RESEARCH IN SOCIAL SCIENCES.** Abbreviated title: I J R S S. Text and summaries in English. 2011. q. free (effective 2011). charts; maps; pat.; illus.; mkt.; tr.lit. back issues avail. **Document type:** *Journal, Academic/Scholarly.* **Description:** Focuses on theories, methods and applications of social sciences. It provides an intellectual platform for the international scholars & promotes interdisciplinary studies in the society.
Media: Online - full text.
Published by: (Radha Krishna Educational Society), International Journals of Multidisciplinary Research Academy, Radha Krishna Educational Society, #1459, Sec 17 HUDA Jagadhri, Yamuna Nagar, Haryana 135 001, India. TEL 91-9034872290, FAX 91-1732-231167, info@ijmra.us, http://www.ijmra.us/. Ed. Mr Vishal. Pub., R&P Shyam Sunder. Circ: 15,000.

300 GBR ISSN 1752-6124
➤ **INTERNATIONAL JOURNAL OF SOCIAL AND HUMANISTIC COMPUTING.** Text in English. 2008 (Sep.). 4/yr. EUR 494 to institutions (print or online ed.); EUR 672 combined subscription to institutions (print & online eds.) (effective 2012). charts; illus.; abstr.; bibl. **Document type:** *Journal, Academic/Scholarly.* **Description:** Aims at leading multidisciplinary research and practice on the critical themes of the human and society. It investigates computing approaches to humanity's and society's agendas, and provides a publication outlet for a new emerging discipline which stands in the converging domains of high tech technologies, intelligent systems and human-sensitive, context-aware experiences.
Related titles: Online - full text ed.: ISSN 1752-6132 (from IngentaConnect).
Indexed: A26, A28, APA, BrCerAb, C&ISA, CA/WCA, CIA, CerAb, CivEngAb, CorrAb, E&CAJ, E08, E11, EEA, EMA, ESPM, EnvEAb, H15, M&TEA, M09, MBF, METADEX, SolStAb, T04, WAA.
—CCC.
Published by: Inderscience Publishers, PO Box 735, Olney, Bucks MK46 5WB, United Kingdom. TEL 44-1234-240519, FAX 44-1234-240515, editorial@inderscience.com. Eds. Ambjorn Naeve, John M Caroll, Dr. Miltiadis Lytras, Walt Scacchi. **Subscr. to:** World Trade Centre Bldg, 29 Rte de Pre-Bois, Case Postale 856, Geneva 15 1215, Switzerland. FAX 41-22-7910885, subs@inderscience.com.

300 NOR ISSN 1504-8446
➤ **INTERNATIONAL JOURNAL OF SOCIAL AND MANAGEMENT SCIENCES.** Variant title: I J O S A M S. Text in English. 2007. q. **Document type:** *Journal, Academic/Scholarly.*
Media: Online - full content.
Published by: D-Net Communications, Teienvejen 19, Hommersaak, 4310, Norway. TEL 47-51-680353. Ed. Dimeji Togunde.

300 USA ISSN 0889-0293
H1
➤ **INTERNATIONAL JOURNAL OF SOCIAL EDUCATION.** Abbreviated title: I J S E. Text in English. 1945. s-a. USD 14 domestic to individuals; USD 17 foreign to individuals; USD 16 per issue to institutions; USD 7, USD 8.50 per issue to individuals; USD 8 per issue to institutions (effective 2011). adv. back issues avail.; reprints avail. **Document type:** *Journal, Academic/Scholarly.*
Former titles (until 1986): Indiana Social Studies Quarterly (0019-6746); (until 1946): Social Studies Quarterly
Related titles: Microform ed.: (from PQC); Online - full text ed.
Indexed: A22, A26, AmH&L, BRD, CA, CPE, E02, E03, E07, ERI, ERIC, EdA, EdI, HistAb, MLA-IB, P18, P27, P30, P48, P53, P54, PCI, PQC, S02, S03, T02, W05.
—BLDSC (4542.556000), IE, Infotrieve, Ingenta.
Published by: (Indiana Council for the Social Studies), Ball State University, Department of History, 2000 W University Ave, Muncie, IN 47306. TEL 765-289-1241, FAX 800-382-8540, askus@bsu.edu, http://cms.bsu.edu. Ed. John M Glen.

300 USA ISSN 2156-5767
▼ **INTERNATIONAL JOURNAL OF SOCIAL ISSUES.** Text in English. 2010. q. USD 295 to institutions; USD 442 combined subscription to institutions (print & online eds.) (effective 2011). **Document type:** *Journal, Academic/Scholarly.*
Related titles: Online - full text ed.: USD 295 to institutions (effective 2011).
Published by: Nova Science Publishers, Inc., 400 Oser Ave, Ste 1600, Hauppauge, NY 11788. TEL 631-231-7269, FAX 631-231-8175, journals@novapublishers.com, https://www.novapublishers.com.

300.72 GBR ISSN 1364-5579
➤ **INTERNATIONAL JOURNAL OF SOCIAL RESEARCH METHODOLOGY.** Text in English. 1998. 5/yr. GBP 485 combined subscription in United Kingdom to institutions (print & online eds.); EUR 643, USD 805 combined subscription to institutions (print & online eds.) (effective 2012). adv. back issues avail.; reprint service avail. from PSC. **Document type:** *Journal, Academic/Scholarly.* **Description:** Aims to provide a focus for the on-going and emerging methodological debates across a wide range of social science disciplines and substantive interests.
Related titles: Online - full text ed.: ISSN 1464-5300. GBP 436 in United Kingdom to institutions; EUR 578, USD 725 to institutions (effective 2012) (from IngentaConnect).
Indexed: A01, A03, A08, A20, A22, B01, B06, B07, B09, B21, CA, CJA, CurCont, E01, E17, ESPM, IBSS, P03, P30, P34, P42, PSA, PsycInfo, PsycholAb, S02, S03, S21, SCOPUS, SSA, SSCI, SociolAb, T02, W07.
—IE, Infotrieve, Ingenta. **CCC.**
Published by: (Social Research Association), Routledge (Subsidiary of: Taylor & Francis Group), 4 Park Sq, Milton Park, Abingdon, Oxon OX14 4RN, United Kingdom. TEL 44-20-70176000, FAX 44-20-70176336, subscriptions@tandf.co.uk, http://www.routledge.com. Adv. contact Linda Hann. **Subscr. in N. America to:** Taylor & Francis Inc., Customer Services Dept, 325 Chestnut St, 8th Fl, Philadelphia, PA 19106. TEL 215-625-8900, 800-354-1420, FAX 215-625-2940, customerservice@taylorandfrancis.com; **Subscr. to:** Taylor & Francis Ltd., Journals Customer Service, Sheepen Pl, Colchester, Essex CO3 3LP, United Kingdom. TEL 44-20-70175544, FAX 44-20-70175198, tf.enquiries@tfinforma.com.

▼ ➤ **INTERNATIONAL JOURNAL OF SOCIAL ROBOTICS.** *see* COMPUTERS—Robotics

300 CAN ISSN 1192-2664
➤ **INTERNATIONAL JOURNAL OF SOCIAL SCIENCES.** Text in Arabic, English, French. 1993. 4/yr. CAD 400 (effective 2006). adv. bk.rev. **Document type:** *Journal, Academic/Scholarly.* **Description:** Designed for concise, cooperative publication of simple and creative ideas.
Published by: M.I. Ismail, Ed. & Pub., 9 Finsh DDO, Montreal, PQ H9A 3G9, Canada. TEL 514-626-9800, ismail.csc@usa.net. Ed., Pub. M I Ismail TEL 965-918-9996.

300 370 PAK ISSN 2223-4934
▼ **INTERNATIONAL JOURNAL OF SOCIAL SCIENCES AND EDUCATION.** Text in English. 2011. q. free. **Document type:** *Journal, Academic/Scholarly.* **Description:** Covers all subjects of social sciences reports of original educational research, reviews of recent research in all educational areas or discussion articles on research topics.
Media: Online - full text.
Published by: Federal College of Education, Department of Education, H9, Islamabad, Pakistan. TEL 92-51-9257484, FAX 92-51-9257131. Ed. Aijaz Ahmed Gujjar.

300 001.3 TUR
▼ ➤ **THE INTERNATIONAL JOURNAL OF SOCIAL SCIENCES AND HUMANITY STUDIES.** Abbreviated title: I J S S H S. Text and summaries in English. 2009. s-a. EUR 20 to individuals; EUR 40 to institutions (effective 2011). back issues avail. **Document type:** *Journal, Academic/Scholarly.* **Description:** Aims to publish research studies in all sub-areas of social sciences, including economics, business, management, law, political science, sociology, philosophy, ethics etc.
Related titles: Online - full text ed.: ISSN 1309-8063. free (effective 2011).
Published by: The Social Sciences Research Society, Gazi Bulvari No.66/602, Gazi Ishani, Cankaya-Izmir, 35230, Turkey. TEL 90-232-3424750, FAX 90-232-3424750, sobiad@sobiad.org, editor@sobiad.org. Ed. Coskun Can Aktan. Pub., R&P Dilek Dileyici.

300 GBR ISSN 1756-2511
➤ **INTERNATIONAL JOURNAL OF SOCIETY SYSTEMS SCIENCE.** Abbreviated title: I J S S S. Text in English. 2008. 4/yr. EUR 494 to institutions (print or online ed.); EUR 672 combined subscription to institutions (print & online eds.) (effective 2012). abstr.; bibl.; illus.; charts. back issues avail. **Document type:** *Journal, Academic/Scholarly.* **Description:** Aims to call for attention to the interdisciplinary principles, architectures, techniques, methodologies, models, as well as the appropriate strategies, that can solve the various society-related dilemmas.
Related titles: Online - full text ed.: ISSN 1756-252X (from IngentaConnect).
Indexed: A26, E08.
—CCC.
Published by: Inderscience Publishers, PO Box 735, Olney, Bucks MK46 5WB, United Kingdom. TEL 44-1234-240519, FAX 44-1234-240515, editorial@inderscience.com. Ed. John Wang. **Subscr. to:** World Trade Centre Bldg, 29 Rte de Pre-Bois, Case Postale 856, Geneva 15 1215, Switzerland. FAX 41-22-7910885, subs@inderscience.com.

➤ **INTERNATIONAL JOURNAL OF TRANSDISCIPLINARY RESEARCH.** *see* BUSINESS AND ECONOMICS

307.76 GBR
INTERNATIONAL JOURNAL OF URBAN LABOUR AND LEISURE. Text in English. 1998. s-a. free (effective 2009). adv. bk.rev. back issues avail. **Document type:** *Directory, Academic/Scholarly.* **Description:** Focuses on on-going and emerging debates across a wide range of social science disciplines.
Formerly (until 2001): The Journal of Urban Labour and Leisure (1465-1270)
Media: Online - full content.
Indexed: CABA, GH, LT, N02, N03, R12, RRTA.
Published by: University of Leicester, Department of Sociology, University Rd, Leicester, Leics LE1 7RH, United Kingdom. TEL 44-116-2522739, FAX 44-116-2525259, sociology@leicester.ac.uk, http://www.le.ac.uk/so/.

INTERNATIONAL MIGRATION REVIEW; a quarterly studying sociological, demographic, economic, historical, and legislative aspects of human migration movements and ethnic group relations. *see* POPULATION STUDIES

361 USA ISSN 0160-0176
HT390
➤ **INTERNATIONAL REGIONAL SCIENCE REVIEW.** Abbreviated title: I R S R. Text in English. 1975. q. USD 539, GBP 317 to institutions; USD 550, GBP 323 combined subscription to institutions (print & online eds.) (effective 2012). adv. bibl.; charts. back issues avail.; reprint service avail. from PSC. **Document type:** *Journal, Academic/Scholarly.* **Description:** Multidisciplinary journal designed to strengthen the regional and spatial aspects of theoretical and quantitative research in the social sciences - particularly economics, geography and demography - and to improve the analytical foundations of urban and regional planning.
Related titles: Online - full text ed.: ISSN 1552-6925. USD 495, GBP 291 to institutions (effective 2012).
Indexed: A01, A02, A03, A08, A12, A17, A22, A34, A38, ABCPolSci, ABIn, AIAP, ASCA, B01, B06, B07, B09, BAS, C25, CA, CABA, CurCont, D01, E01, E12, EIA, ESPM, EconLit, EnerInd, F08, F12, G11, GEOBASE, GH, H04, H16, IBR, IBSS, IBZ, JEL, LT, N02, P30, P48, P51, P53, P54, PAIS, PCI, PQC, PopulInd, R12, RASB, RRTA, RiskAb, S13, S16, SCOPUS, SSCI, SSciA, SUSA, T02, T05, TriticAb, V02, VS, W07, W11.
—BLDSC (4545.785000), IE, Infotrieve, Ingenta. **CCC.**
Published by: Sage Publications, Inc., 2455 Teller Rd, Thousand Oaks, CA 91320. TEL 805-499-9774, 800-818-7243, FAX 805-499-0871, 800-583-2665, info@sagepub.com, http://www.sagepub.com. Eds. Alan T Murray, Luc Anselin, Sergio J Rey. **Subscr. outside of N. America to:** Sage Publications Ltd., 1 Oliver's Yard, 55 City Rd, London EC1Y 1SP, United Kingdom. TEL 44-207-3248701, FAX 44-207-3248733, subscription@sagepub.co.uk.

300 USA ISSN 1940-8447
R853.Q34
➤ **INTERNATIONAL REVIEW OF QUALITATIVE RESEARCH.** Abbreviated title: I R Q R. Text in English. 2008 (May). q. USD 199 to institutions; USD 279 combined subscription to institutions (print & online eds.) (effective 2010). adv. back issues avail. **Document type:** *Journal, Academic/Scholarly.*
Related titles: Online - full text ed.: ISSN 1940-8455.
Published by: Left Coast Press, Inc., 1630 N Main St, Ste 400, Walnut Creek, CA 94596. TEL 925-935-3380, FAX 925 935-2916, Explore@LCoastPress.com. Ed. Norman K Denzin TEL 217-333-0795.

300 001.3 IND ISSN 2248-9010
▼ **INTERNATIONAL REVIEW OF SOCIAL SCIENCES AND HUMANITIES.** Abbreviated title: I R S S H. Text in English. 2011 (Apr.). q. free (effective 2011). **Document type:** *Journal, Academic/Scholarly.*
Media: Online - full text.
Address: Bargandubii Village, Bangaon Post, Barpeta District, Assam, India. TEL 91-9401352185, hemen_dutta08@ijopaasat.in. Ed., Pub. Hemen Dutta.

300 GBR ISSN 0020-8701
H1
➤ **INTERNATIONAL SOCIAL SCIENCE JOURNAL.** Text in English. 1949. q. GBP 228 in United Kingdom to institutions; EUR 290 in Europe to institutions; USD 501 in the Americas to institutions; USD 585 elsewhere to institutions; GBP 252 combined subscription in United Kingdom to institutions (print & online eds.); EUR 333 combined subscription in Europe to institutions (print & online eds.); USD 576 combined subscription in the Americas to institutions (print & online eds.); USD 643 combined subscription elsewhere to institutions (print & online eds.) (effective 2012). adv. bibl.; charts; illus. index. back issues avail.; reprint service avail. from PSC. **Document type:** *Journal, Academic/Scholarly.* **Description:** Provides a forum for review, reflection and discussion informed by the results of recent and ongoing research.
Formerly (until 1959): International Social Science Bulletin (1014-5508)
Related titles: Microform ed.: (from MIM, PQC); Online - full text ed.: ISSN 1468-2451. GBP 228 in United Kingdom to institutions; EUR 290 in Europe to institutions; USD 501 in the Americas to institutions; USD 585 elsewhere to institutions (effective 2012) (from IngentaConnect); ◆ French ed.: Revue Internationale des Sciences Sociales. ISSN 0304-3037.
Indexed: A01, A02, A03, A08, A20, A22, A25, A26, ABCPolSci, AICP, APEL, ARDT, ASCA, AbAn, AmH&L, B02, B04, B15, B17, B18, BAS, BNNA, BRD, BibLing, CA, CPM, DIP, E01, E02, E03, E07, E08, EAA, EI, ERA, ERI, ERIC, ESPM, EconLit, EdA, EdI, F09, FutSurv, G04, G08, GEOBASE, GeoRef, H09, H10, HECAB, HistAb, I05, I13, IBR, IBSS, IBZ, ILD, JEL, M10, MEA&I, MLA, MLA-IB, P02, P03, P06, P10, P27, P30, P34, P42, P48, P52, P53, P54, P56, PAIS, PCI, PQC, PRA, PSA, PerIslam, PsycInfo, PsycholAb, RASB, S02, S03, S05, S08, S09, S11, S21, SCOPUS, SOPODA, SPAA, SSA, SSAI, SSAb, SSCI, SSI, SSciA, SociolAb, SpeleolAb, T02, W03, W09.
—BLDSC (4549.450000), IE, Infotrieve, Ingenta. **CCC.**
Published by: (UNESCO, Social and Human Science FRA), Wiley-Blackwell Publishing Ltd. (Subsidiary of: John Wiley & Sons, Inc.), 9600 Garsington Rd, Oxford, OX4 2DQ, United Kingdom. TEL 44-1865-776868, FAX 44-1865-714591, customerservices@blackwellpublishing.com. Ed. John Crowley TEL 33-1-45683828. Adv. contact Craig Pickett TEL 44-1865-476267.

300 USA ISSN 0278-2308
H1
➤ **INTERNATIONAL SOCIAL SCIENCE REVIEW.** Abbreviated title: I S S R. Text in English. 1925. s-a. bk.rev. index. cum.index: vols.21-25 (1946-1950). **Document type:** *Journal, Academic/Scholarly.* **Description:** Publishes historical and modern, quantitative and qualitative studies in all social sciences, humanities, and related fields.
Formerly (until Jan.1982): Social Science (0037-7848)
Related titles: Online - full text ed.
Indexed: A01, A02, A03, A08, A20, A22, A26, ABS&EES, AmH&L, B01, B06, B07, B08, B09, C12, CA, DIP, E08, G08, HistAb, I05, IBR, IBZ, IBibSS, KES, M01, M02, MEA&I, P02, P06, P10, P27, P30, P34, P42, P45, P48, P53, P54, PAIS, PCI, PQC, PRA, PSA, PerIslam, RASB, RILM, S02, S03, S09, S11, SCOPUS, SOPODA, SSAI, SSAb, SSI, SWR&A, SociolAb, T02, W03, W05, WBSS.
—BLDSC (4549.459000), IE, Infotrieve, Ingenta. **CCC.**
Published by: Pi Gamma Mu, Social Sciences Honor Society, 1001 Millington, Ste B, Winfield, KS 67156. TEL 620-221-3128, FAX 620-221-7124, pgm@sckans.edu. Ed. Dean J Fafoutis TEL 410-546-6004.

300 POL ISSN 1641-4233
JA66
➤ **INTERNATIONAL STUDIES**; interdisciplinary political and cultural journal. Text in English. 2000. s-a. PLZ 18 per issue domestic (effective 2011). bk.rev. back issues avail. **Document type:** *Journal, Academic/Scholarly.* **Description:** Covers international relations, communication, anthropology, social and political geography, philosophy, literature, cultural studies, journalism, and some areas of media studies.
Indexed: IBSS.
Published by: (Uniwersytet Lodzki, Wydzial Studiow Miedzynarodowych i Politologicznych, Zaklad Studiow Brytyjskich i Krajow Wspolnoty Brytyjskiej/University of Lodz, Department of International an Political studies, British and Commonwealth Studies Department), Wydawnictwo Uniwersytetu Lodzkiego/Lodz University Press, ul Lindleya 8, Lodz, 90-131, Poland. FAX 48-42-6655861, wdwul@uni.lodz.pl, http://www.wydawnictwo.uni.lodz.pl.

➤ **INTERNATIONAL STUDIES IN SOCIOLOGY AND SOCIAL ANTHROPOLOGY.** *see* SOCIOLOGY

371.3 300 USA ISSN 2152-6893
▼ **INTERNATIONAL STUDIES OF NON-TRADITIONAL STUDENTS: CORRESPONDING PEDAGOGY IN SOCIAL SCIENCE EDUCATION.** Text in English. forthcoming 2010 (Jul.). a. USD 25 per issue (effective 2010). **Document type:** *Academic/Scholarly.* **Description:** A guide for social science teachers of non-traditional students.
Published by: International Consultation for Educators, LLC, 1015 Essex St, SE, Minneapolis, MN 55414. TEL 612-245-4471, publication@eduice.com, http://www.eduice.com/.

▼ **INTERNATIONAL TRANSACTIONS IN HUMANITIES AND SOCIAL SCIENCES.** *see* HUMANITIES: COMPREHENSIVE WORKS

300 DEU ISSN 2192-0281
▼ ➤ **INTERNATIONAL YEARBOOK OF FUTURISM STUDIES.** Text in English. 2011 (Oct.). a. EUR 99.95 (effective 2012). **Document type:** *Journal, Academic/Scholarly.* **Description:** Contains new research on all aspects of futurism within diverse fields such as literature, fine arts, music, theater, and design.
Related titles: Online - full text ed.: ISSN 2192-029X. 2011.
Published by: Walter de Gruyter GmbH & Co. KG, Genthiner Str 13, Berlin, 10785, Germany. TEL 49-30-260050, FAX 49-30-26005251, info@degruyter.com. Ed. Guenter Berghaus.

300.711 DEU ISSN 0932-4763
➤ **INTERNATIONALE HOCHSCHULSCHRIFTEN/INTERNATIONAL UNIVERSITY STUDIES.** Text in German. 1987. irreg., latest vol.554, 2011. price varies. **Document type:** *Monographic series, Academic/Scholarly.* **Description:** Presents a series of postdoctoral theses and dissertations carrying the honorary titles summa cum laude, magna cum laude or their equivalents.
Published by: Waxmann Verlag GmbH, Steinfurter Str 555, Muenster, 48159, Germany. TEL 49-251-265040, FAX 49-251-2650426, info@waxmann.com.

304 DEU ISSN 0720-6895
INTERNATIONALE INSTITUT FUER EMPIRISCHE SOZIALOEKONOMIE. SCHRIFTEN. Text in German. 1978. irreg., latest vol.10, 1990. price varies. **Document type:** *Monographic series, Academic/Scholarly.*
Published by: (Internationale Institut fuer Empirische Sozialoekonomie), Duncker und Humblot GmbH, Carl-Heinrich-Becker-Weg 9, Berlin, 12165, Germany. TEL 49-30-7900060, FAX 49-30-79000631, info@duncker-humblot.de.

300 GBR ISSN 0379-0282
INTERNATIONALE REVUE FUER SOZIALE SICHERHEIT. Text in German. 1967. q. **Document type:** *Journal, Academic/Scholarly.*
Related titles: Online - full text ed.: ISSN 1752-1726. 2007. GBP 158 in United Kingdom to institutions; EUR 201 in Europe to institutions; USD 265 in the Americas to institutions; USD 310 elsewhere to institutions (effective 2010) (from IngentaConnect); ◆ English ed.: International Social Security Review. ISSN 0020-871X; ◆ French ed.: Revue Internationale de Securite Sociale. ISSN 0379-0312; ◆ Spanish ed.: Revista Internacional de Seguridad Social. ISSN 0250-605X.
Indexed: A22, B01, B07, CA, E01, IBR, IBZ, SCOPUS, T02.
—IE. **CCC.**
Published by: Wiley-Blackwell Publishing Ltd. (Subsidiary of: John Wiley & Sons, Inc.), 9600 Garsington Rd, Oxford, OX4 2DQ, United Kingdom. TEL 44-1865-776868, FAX 44-1865-714591, customerservices@blackwellpublishing.com, http://www.wiley.com/WileyCDA/.

304 DEU ISSN 0417-9978
INTERNATIONALE TAGUNGEN DER SOZIALAKADEMIE DORTMUND. Text in German. 1959. irreg., latest vol.23, 2002. price varies. **Document type:** *Monographic series, Academic/Scholarly.*
Published by: Duncker und Humblot GmbH, Carl-Heinrich-Becker-Weg 9, Berlin, 12165, Germany. TEL 49-30-7900060, FAX 49-30-79000631, info@duncker-humblot.de.

300 DEU ISSN 1862-6106
INTERNATIONALE UND INTERKULTURELLE KOMMUNIKATION. Text in German. 2005. irreg., latest vol.6, 2008. price varies. **Document type:** *Monographic series, Academic/Scholarly.*
Published by: Frank und Timme GmbH, Wittelsbacherstr 27a, Berlin, 10707, Germany. TEL 49-30-88667911, FAX 49-30-86398731, info@frank-timme.de.

300 BRA ISSN 1517-6088
H8.P8
INTERSECOES; revista de estudios interdisciplinares. Text in Portuguese. 1999. s-a. **Document type:** *Journal, Academic/Scholarly.*
Indexed: CA, P42, PSA, S02, S03, SociolAb, T02.
Published by: Universidade do Estado do Rio de Janeiro, Programa de Pos-Graduacao em Ciencias Sociais, Rua Sao Francisco Xavier, 524, 9o. Andar, Bloco F, Sala 9037, Maracana, RJ, Brazil. TEL 55-21-25698049, FAX 55-21-25877746, http://www.uerj.br/.

300 URY
INTERSTICIOS; de la socio-cultura. Text in Spanish. 1990. m.?. **Document type:** *Consumer.*
Address: Apto. 103, Ituzaingo, 1522, Montevideo, 11003, Uruguay. TEL 95-81-70. Eds. Basilio Munoz, Gabriela Delsignore.

300 ARG ISSN 0329-3475
AS78.A1
INVENIO. Text in Spanish. 1997. s-a. ARS 24 domestic; USD 24 foreign (effective 2010). **Document type:** *Journal, Academic/Scholarly.*
Related titles: Online - full text ed.: free (effective 2011).
Indexed: MLA-IB.
Published by: Universidad del Centro Educativo Latinoamericano, Ave Pellegrini 1332, Rosario, Santa Fe 2000, Argentina. TEL 54-341-4499292, FAX 54-341-4261241, informaes@ucel.edu.ar, http://www.ucel.edu.ar/. Ed. Rogelio Ponzon. Circ: 1,000.

300 COL ISSN 0121-3261
H8.S7
➤ **INVESTIGACION & DESARROLLO.** Text in Spanish. 1990. s-a. **Document type:** *Journal, Academic/Scholarly.*
Related titles: Online - full text ed.: ISSN 2011-7574. 2006. free (effective 2011) (from SciELO).
Indexed: A01, A26, CA, F03, F04, I04, I05, SociolAb, T02.
Published by: Universidad del Norte, Ediciones Uninorte, Km 5 Via a Puerto Colombia, Barranquilla, Colombia. TEL 57-5-3509218, FAX 57-5-3509489, ediciones@uninorte.edu.co, http://www.uninorte.edu.co. Circ: 300.

300 MEX ISSN 1665-4412
AS63.A42
INVESTIGACION Y CIENCIA. Text in Spanish. 1990. s-a. back issues avail. **Document type:** *Journal, Academic/Scholarly.*
Related titles: Online - full text ed.: free (effective 2011).
Indexed: C01.
Published by: Universidad Autonoma de Aguascalientes, Direccion General de Investigacion y Posgrado, Ave Universidad No. 940, Aguascalientes, Aguascalientes 20100, Mexico. investigacion@correo.uaa.mx, http://www.uaa.mx/iniciosa.htm. Ed. Rosa del Carmen Zapata.

300 VEN ISSN 1316-0087
LB2371.6.V46
➤ **INVESTIGACIONES Y POSTGRADO.** Text in Spanish; Abstracts in English, Spanish. 1985. s-a. VEB 5 per issue (effective 2009). **Document type:** *Journal, Academic/Scholarly.*
Related titles: Online - full text ed.: free (effective 2011).
Indexed: C01, CA, F04, T02.
Published by: Universidad Pedagogica Experimental Libertador, Av Sucre, Parque del Oeste, Caracas, 1010, Venezuela. TEL 58-212-8647822, FAX 58-212-8607227. Ed. Sonia Bustamante. Circ: 5,000 (paid and controlled).

300 USA
➤ **IOWA JOURNAL OF CULTURAL STUDIES.** Text in English. 197?. s-a. USD 30 to individuals; USD 50 to institutions (effective 2011). adv. back issues avail. **Document type:** *Journal, Academic/Scholarly.* **Description:** Aims to present the best in contemporary cultural studies criticism while fostering conversations across disciplinary and ideological divides.
Formerly (until 2001): Iowa Journal of Literary Studies (0743-2747)
Related titles: Online - full text ed.
Indexed: AmHI, H07, H08, HAb, HumInd, MLA-IB, P02, P10, P27, P48, P53, P54, PQC, T02, W03, W05.
Address: c/o English Department, 308 English-Philosophy Bldg, University of Iowa, Iowa City, IA 52242. Adv. contact Sara Sullivan.

300 IRL ISSN 1393-4945
THE IRISH JOURNAL OF SOCIAL WORK RESEARCH. Text in English. 1980. bi-m. **Document type:** *Journal, Academic/Scholarly.*
Former titles (until 1997): Irish Social Worker (0332-4583); (until 1981): Irish Social Work Journal (0332-4575)
—Ingenta.
Published by: Irish Association of Social Workers, 114-116 Pearse St, Dublin, 2, Ireland. TEL 353-1-6774838, FAX 353-1-6715734, iasw@iol.ie. Ed. Sarah Blackmore.

300 DEU
ISA LOHMANN-SIEMS STIFTUNG. SCHRIFTENREIHE. Text in German. 2007. irreg., latest vol.2, 2007. price varies. **Document type:** *Monographic series, Academic/Scholarly.*
Published by: (Isa Lohmann-Siems Stiftung), Dietrich Reimer Verlag GmbH, Berliner Str 53, Berlin, 10713, Germany. TEL 49-30-700138850, FAX 49-30-700138855, vertrieb-kunstverlage@reimer-verlag.de, http://www.dietrichreimerverlag.de.

302 297.092 USA ISSN 1541-0552
ISLAMIC DISCOURSE; a magazine of muslims in america. Text in English. 2001. q.
Published by: Islamic Educational Center of Orange County, 3194-B Airport Loop Dr., Costa Mesa, CA 92626. TEL 714-432-0060, FAX 714-432-0070, info@iecoc.org, http://www.iecoc.org. Ed. Fatma Saleh.

300 USA ISSN 1084-9513
DS101
➤ **ISRAEL STUDIES.** Text in English. 1996. 3/yr. USD 150.75 combined subscription to institutions (print & online eds.) (effective 2012). adv. back issues avail.; reprint service avail. from PSC. **Document type:** *Journal, Academic/Scholarly.* **Description:** Presents multidisciplinary scholarship on Israeli history, politics, society, and culture.
Related titles: Online - full text ed.: ISSN 1527-201X. 1999. USD 99.50 to institutions (effective 2012).
Indexed: A01, A02, A03, A08, A22, A26, AmH&L, B04, BRD, CA, E01, E08, ENW, G06, G07, G08, HistAb, I02, I05, I06, I07, I13, IBSS, IJP, J01, M10, MLA-IB, P10, P27, P28, P30, P34, P42, P48, P53, P54, PAIS, PQC, PSA, R02, R05, S02, S03, S09, S23, SCOPUS, SSAI, SSAb, SSI, SociolAb, T02, W03, W05.
—BLDSC (4583.914800), IE, Ingenta. **CCC.**
Published by: (Ben-Gurion University of the Negev, The Ben-Gurion Research Center ISR), Indiana University Press, 601 N Morton St, Bloomington, IN 47404. TEL 812-855-9449, FAX 812-855-8507, http://iup.journals.org/. Ed. Dr. S Ilan Troen. Circ: 500.

300 331 PHL ISSN 0117-4800
HC451
ISSUES AND LETTERS. Text in English. 1989. bi-m. PHP 250 domestic; USD 30 foreign (effective 2000). **Document type:** *Newsletter, Consumer.* **Description:** Aims to provide timely and clear-cut analyses of current public issues from a progressive viewpoint. it reaches out to public decision-makers, mass leaders, and educators who need quick and authoritative assessments of controversial topics.
Related titles: Online - full text ed.
Indexed: A12, A17, ABIn, IPP, P14, P48, P51, P53, P54, PQC.
Published by: Phillipine Center for Policy Studies, UP Post Office, Diliman, PO Box 6, Quezon City Mm, 1144, Philippines. TEL 63-2-920-5457, FAX 63-2-920-5458, http://www.pcps.ph. Eds. Emmanuel F. Esgurerra, Emmanuel S. de Dios, Germelino M Bautsita, Ricardo D Rerrer, Temario C Rivera. Circ: 250.

ISSUES CURRENT IN THE SOCIAL STUDIES. *see* EDUCATION

ISSUES IN NIGERIAN DEVELOPMENT SERIES. *see* GENERAL INTEREST PERIODICALS—Nigeria

300 ITA ISSN 1824-1255
ISTITUTO DI SCIENZE AMMINISTRATIVE E SOCIALI. COLLANA. Abbreviated title: I S A S Collana. Text in Italian. 1983. irreg. price varies. **Document type:** *Monographic series, Academic/Scholarly.*
Published by: Istituto di Scienze Amministrative e Sociali (I S A S), Via della Ferrovia 54, Palermo, 30146, Italy. TEL 39-091-6713840, FAX 39-091-6713823.

300 ITA
ISTITUTO UNIVERSITARIO ORIENTALE. DIPARTIMENTO DI SCIENZE SOCIALI. QUADERNI. Text in Italian. 1988. irreg., latest vol.10, 1997. price varies. adv. **Document type:** *Monographic series, Academic/Scholarly.*
Published by: Liguori Editore, Via Posillipo 394, Naples, 80123, Italy. TEL 39-081-7206111, FAX 39-081-7206244, liguori@liguori.it, http://www.liguori.it. Pub. Guido Liguori. Adv. contact Maria Liguori.

300 USA ISSN 1549-4942
H62.A1
ITEMS & ISSUES. Text in English. 1947. q. free (effective 2010). bk.rev. illus. back issues avail.; reprints avail. **Document type:** *Newsletter, Academic/Scholarly.* **Description:** Advances the quality and usefulness of research in the social sciences. Also provides news of Council programs and fellowship opportunities.
Formerly (until 2000): Social Science Research Council. Items (0049-0903)
Related titles: Microform ed.; Online - full text ed.
Indexed: A22, ABS&EES, AICP, AmH&L, MEA&I, MLA-IB, P06, P30.
—BLDSC (4588.610000), Ingenta, INIST.
Published by: Social Science Research Council, One Pierrepont Plz, 15th Fl, Brooklyn, NY 11201. TEL 212-377-2700, FAX 212-377-2727, info@ssrc.org, http://www.ssrc.org. Eds. Alyson Metzger, Paul Price.

IWATE MEDICAL UNIVERSITY SCHOOL OF LIBERAL ARTS & SCIENCES. ANNUAL REPORT/IWATE IKA DAIGAKU KYOYOBU NENPO. *see* SCIENCES: COMPREHENSIVE WORKS

300 MEX ISSN 0185-4259
H8.S7 CODEN: IZTAFP
IZTAPALAPA; revista de ciencias sociales y humanidades. Text in Spanish. 1979. s-m. **Document type:** *Monographic series.*
Indexed: C01, FR, PAIS, SCOPUS, SociolAb.
Published by: Universidad Autonoma Metropolitana - Iztapalapa, Division de Ciencias Sociales y Humanidades, Departamento de Antropologia, Ave San Rafael Atlixco # 186, Col Vicentina, Del Iztapalapa, Mexico City, 09340, Mexico. TEL 52-55-7724-4760, cedit@xanum.uam.mx, http://www.iztapalapa.uam.mx/.

300 RUS
IZVESTIYA VYSSHIKH UCHEBNYKH ZAVEDENII. SEVERO-KAVKAZSKII REGION. SERIYA OBSHCHESTVENNYE NAUKI/ BULLETIN OF HIGHER EDUCATIONAL INSTITUTIONS. NORTH CAUCASUS REGION.SERIES OF SOCIAL SCIENCES; nauchno-obrazovatel'nyi i prikladnoi zhurnal. Text in Russian. 1973. q. USD 110 in United States. **Description:** Covers all aspects of theoretical and experimental researches in social sciences in the North Caucuses region of the Russian Federation.
Published by: Rostovskii Gosudarstvennyi Universitet, B Sadovaya 105, Rostov-on-Don, 344006, Russian Federation. TEL 7-8632-640500. Ed. Yu. Zhdanov. **Dist. by:** East View Information Services, 10601 Wayzata Blvd, Minneapolis, MN 55305. TEL 952-252-1201, 800-477-1005, FAX 952-252-1202, info@eastview.com, http://www.eastview.com.

J A S T. (Journal of American Studies of Turkey) *see* HISTORY—History Of North And South America

J I S R MANAGEMENT AND SOCIAL SCIENCES & ECONOMICS. (Journal of Independent Studies and Research) *see* BUSINESS AND ECONOMICS—Management

300 DEU ISSN 0941-8563
DS145
➤ **JAHRBUCH FUER ANTISEMITISMUSFORSCHUNG.** Text in German. 1992. a. bk.rev. **Document type:** *Journal, Academic/Scholarly.*
Indexed: DIP, IBR, IBSS, IBZ, MLA-IB.
Published by: (Technische Universitaet Berlin, Zentrum fuer Antisemitismusforschung), Metropol Verlag, Ansbacher Str 70, Berlin, 10777, Germany. TEL 49-30-2618460, FAX 49-30-2650518, veitl@metropol-verlag.de, http://www.metropol-verlag.de. Circ: 2,000.

300 DEU
JAHRBUCH FUER HANDLUNGS- UND ENTSCHEIDUNGSTHEORIE. Text in German. 2000. a. EUR 49.95 (effective 2010). **Document type:** *Journal, Academic/Scholarly.* **Description:** Contains research on various aspects of social institutions and interactions.
Published by: V S - Verlag fuer Sozialwissenschaften (Subsidiary of: Springer Fachmedien Wiesbaden GmbH), Abraham-Lincoln-Str 46, Wiesbaden, 65189, Germany. TEL 49-611-78780, FAX 49-611-7878400, springerfachmedien-wiesbaden@springer.com, http://www.vs-verlag.de.

300 DEU
JAHRBUCH FUER KULTURMANAGEMENT. Text in German. 2005. a. **Document type:** *Journal, Academic/Scholarly.*
Formerly (until 2009): Spiel-Plan (1661-1241)
Published by: Transcript, Muehlenstr 47, Bielefeld, 33607, Germany. TEL 49-521-63454, FAX 49-521-61040, live@transcript-verlag.de.

300 943 DEU ISSN 0936-465X
HM435 CODEN: JASOFY
JAHRBUCH FUER SOZIOLOGIEGESCHICHTE. Text in German. 1990. irreg., latest 2007. price varies. bk.rev. **Document type:** *Journal, Academic/Scholarly.*
Indexed: CA, FR, S02, S03, SCOPUS, SOPODA, SociolAb, T02.
—INIST.
Published by: V S - Verlag fuer Sozialwissenschaften (Subsidiary of: Springer Fachmedien Wiesbaden GmbH), Abraham-Lincoln-Str 46, Wiesbaden, 65189, Germany. TEL 49-611-78780, FAX 49-611-7878400, springerfachmedien-wiesbaden@springer.com, http://www.vs-verlag.de. Ed. Carsten Klingemann.

300 FIN ISSN 1235-7812
HN1 CODEN: JANUFR
JANUS. Text in Finnish. 1992. q. EUR 35 to individual members; EUR 205 to institutional members; EUR 18 to students (effective 2006). **Document type:** *Journal, Academic/Scholarly.*
Indexed: CA, HistAb, S02, S03, SSA, SociolAb, T02.
Published by: (Sosiaalityon Tutkimuksen Seura/Finnish Society of Social Work Research), Sosiaalipoliittinen Yhdistys ry, PO Box 127, Turku, 20521, Finland. TEL 358-2-2501909, FAX 358-2-4690502, http://www.sosiaalipoliittinenyhdistys.fi/index.htm. Ed. Susan Kuivalainen.

300 SVN ISSN 1318-3222
HM1.A1 CODEN: JAVNFC
➤ **JAVNOST/PUBLIC.** Text in English. 1994. q. USD 45 to individuals; USD 90 to institutions (effective 2011). bk.rev. **Document type:** *Journal, Academic/Scholarly.* **Description:** Addresses problems of the public sphere on international and interdisciplinary levels, stimulates the development of theory and research in the field of social sciences and helps understand the bridges between different cultures.
Related titles: Online - full text ed.: ISSN 1854-8377.

S

Indexed: A01, A20, CA, CMM, CommAb, CurCont, DIP, IBR, IBSS, IBZ, P34, P42, PRA, PSA, S02, S03, SCOPUS, SPAA, SSA, SSCI, SociolAb, T02, W07.
—BLDSC (4663.422750), IE, Ingenta.
Published by: European Institute for Communication and Culture (Euricom), Euricom, c/o University of Ljubljana, Faculty of Social Sciences, PO Box 2511, Ljubljana, 1001, Slovenia. FAX 386-61-721193, slavko.splichal@uni-lj.si. Ed. Slavko Splichal.

300 USA ISSN 2154-6355
▼ **JFORWARD.** Text in English. 2010 (June). s-a. free (effective 2011). **Document type:** *Journal, Academic/Scholarly.* **Description:** Features research from undergraduate and graduate students in all areas of social sciences.
Media: Online - full text.
Published by: Prescott Institute, 16B Brookline St, Pepperell, MA 01463. TEL 617-418-1802, c.bagby@jforward.org. Ed. Caitlin Bagby.

300 IND ISSN 0973-8444
JHARKAND JOURNAL OF DEVELOPMENT AND MANAGEMENT STUDIES. Text in English. 2002. q. INR 500 domestic to individuals; USD 75 in Asia to individuals; USD 100 elsewhere to individuals; INR 600 domestic to institutions; USD 100 in Asia to institutions; USD 150 elsewhere to institutions (effective 2010). bk.rev. **Document type:** *Journal, Academic/Scholarly.*
Published by: Xavier Institute of Social Service, Dr Camil Bulcke Path, PO Box 7, Ranchi, Jharkhand 834 001, India. TEL 91-651-2200873, FAX 91-651-2315381, xiss@xiss.ac.in. Ed. Alex Ekka.

300 CHN ISSN 1000-856X
AS452.N35924
JIANGHAI XUEKAN/JIANGHAI ACADEMIC JOURNAL. Text in Chinese; Contents page in English. 1958. bi-m. USD 40.20 (effective 2009). adv. bk.rev. **Document type:** *Journal, Academic/Scholarly.* **Description:** Contains high quality academic papers in the fields of philosophy, economics, political science, law, sociology, history and literature.
Formed by the 1988 merger of: Jianghai Xuekan (Wen-Shi-Zhe Ban) (1000-601X); Jianghai Xuekan (Jingji Shehui Ban) (1000-6001)
Related titles: Online - full text ed.
Indexed: RASB.
—East View, Ingenta.
Published by: Jiangsu Sheng Shehui Kexueyuan/Jiangsu Academy of Social Sciences, 12, Huju Belu, Nanjing, Jiangsu 210013, China. TEL 86-25-83715429. Ed. Gongzheng Wu. Adv. contact Peng Li. Circ: 3,200. **Dist. by:** China International Book Trading Corp, 35 Chegongzhuang Xilu, Haidian District, PO Box 399, Beijing 100044, China. TEL 86-10-68412045, FAX 86-10-68412023, cibtc@mail.cibtc.com.cn, http://www.cibtc.com.cn. **Co-sponsor:** Jiangsu Sheng Zhexue Shehui Kexue Lianhehui.

300 CHN
JIANGHAN DAXUE XUEBAO (SHEHUI KEXUE BAN)/JIANGHAN UNIVERSITY. JOURNAL (SOCIAL SCIENCES). Text in Chinese. 1983. q. USD 20.80 (effective 2009). **Document type:** *Journal, Academic/Scholarly.*
Formerly: Jianghan Daxue Xuebao (1006-639X)
Related titles: Online - full text ed.
—East View.
Published by: Jianghan Daxue, Jingji Jishu Kaifa-qu, Wuhan, 430056, China.

300 CHN ISSN 1003-854X
AP95.C4
JIANGHAN LUNTAN/JIANGHAN FORUM. Text in Chinese. 1959. m. USD 74.40 (effective 2009). **Document type:** *Magazine, Consumer.*
Related titles: Online - full text ed.
Indexed: RASB.
—East View, Ingenta.
Published by: Hubei Sheng Shehui Kexueyuan/Hubei Academy of Social Sciences, 165, Wuchang Donhu Lu, Wuchang, Hubei 430077, China. TEL 86-27-86789435. **Dist. by:** China International Book Trading Corp, 35 Chegongzhuang Xilu, Haidian District, PO Box 399, Beijing 100044, China. TEL 86-10-68412045, FAX 86-10-68412023, cibtc@mail.cibtc.com.cn, http://www.cibtc.com.cn.

300 CHN ISSN 1001-862X
AS452.H553
JIANGHUAI LUNTAN/JIANGHUAI TRIBUNE. Text in Chinese. 1979. bi-m. **Document type:** *Journal, Academic/Scholarly.*
Related titles: Online - full text ed.
Indexed: RASB.
—East View.
Published by: Anhui Sheng Shehui Kexueyuan/Anhui Academy of Social Sciences, 131, Weigangmeiling Dadao, Hefei, 230053, China. TEL 86-551-3438358. **Dist. by:** China International Book Trading Corp, 35 Chegongzhuang Xilu, Haidian District, PO Box 399, Beijing 100044, China. TEL 86-10-68412045, FAX 86-10-68412023, cibtc@mail.cibtc.com.cn, http://www.cibtc.com.cn.

JIANGHUAI - WENZHAI. *see* PUBLIC ADMINISTRATION

JIANGNAN DAXUE XUEBAO (RENWEN SHEHUI KEXUE BAN)/SOUTHERN YANGTZE UNIVERSITY. JOURNAL (HUMANITIES & SOCIAL SCIENCES EDITION). *see* HUMANITIES: COMPREHENSIVE WORKS

300 CHN ISSN 1673-1026
JIANGNAN SHEHUI XUEYUAN XUEBAO/JIANGNAN SOCIAL UNIVERSITY. JOURNAL. Text in Chinese. 1999. q.
Related titles: Online - full text ed.
Published by: Jiangnan Shehui Xueyuan/Jiangnan Social University, Editorial Dept., Suzhou, 215124, China. TEL 86-512-65272348, FAX 86-512-65272348.

300 CHN ISSN 1671-6604
JIANGSU DAXUE XUEBAO (SHEHUI KEXUE BAN)/JIANGSU UNIVERSITY. JOURNAL (SOCIAL SCIENCE EDITION). Text in Chinese. 1985. bi-m. USD 24.60 (effective 2009). **Document type:** *Journal, Academic/Scholarly.* **Description:** Contains scholarly articles in such fields as politics, philosophy, society, history, law, ethics, economy, management, literature, art, language, with Study of Chinese Modern History, Chinese Culture and Poetics, Study of Pearl S. Buck, Study of Liu Xie and Literary Mind and Carving of Dragon, Study of Overseas Chinese Literature, Study of Jin and Yuan Literature, Study of Reform and Development of SME, and Study of Regional Economy of Jiangsu Province as its permanent columns.
Formerly (until 2002): Jiangsu Ligong Daxue Xuebao (Shehui Kexue Ban)/of Jiangsu University of Science and Technology. Journal (Social Sciences Edition) (1008-1917)
Related titles: Online - full text ed.
—East View.
Published by: Jiangsu Daxue/Jiangsu University, No.30 Mengxiyuan Lane, Zhenjiang, Jiangsu 212003, China. TEL 86-511-4446186, http://www.ujs.edu.cn/. Ed. Ji-chang Yang. **Dist. by:** China International Book Trading Corp, 35 Chegongzhuang Xilu, Haidian District, PO Box 399, Beijing 100044, China. TEL 86-10-68412045, FAX 86-10-68412023, cibtc@mail.cibtc.com.cn, http://www.cibtc.com.cn.

300 CHN ISSN 1674-8522
JIANGSU JISHU SHIFAN XUEYUAN XUEBAO/JIANGSU TEACHERS UNIVERSITY OF TECHNOLOGY. JOURNAL (NATURAL SCIENCE EDITION). Text in Chinese. 1995. m. **Document type:** *Journal, Academic/Scholarly.*
Formerly (until 2010): Jiangsu Jishu Shifan Xueyuan Xuebao (Ziran Kexue Ban) (1674-2222); Which superseded in part (in 2008): Jiangsu Jishu Shifan Xueyuan Xuebao/Teachers University of Technology. Journal (1672-7401); Which was formerly (until 2002): Changzhou Jishu Shifan Xueyuan Xuebao/Changzhou Teachers College of Technology. Journal
Published by: Jiangsu Jishu Shifan Xueyuan/Jiangsu Teachers University of Technology, 1801, Zhongwu Da Dao, Changzhou, 213001, China. TEL 86-519-86999550, http://www.jstu.edu.cn/.

300 CHN ISSN 1673-0453
JIANGSU KEJI DAXUE XUEBAO (SHEHUI KEXUE BAN)/JIANGSU UNIVERSITY OF SCIENCE AND TECHNOLOGY. JOURNAL (SOCIAL SCIENCE). Text in Chinese. 2001. q. CNY 5 newsstand/cover (effective 2006). **Document type:** *Journal, Academic/Scholarly.*
Formerly: Huadong Chuanbo Gongye Xueyuan Xuebao (Shehui Kexue Ban)/East China Shipbuilding Institute. Journal (Social Science Edition) (1009-7082)
Related titles: Online - full text ed.
Published by: Jiangsu Keji Daxue/Jiangsu Unviersity of Science and Technology, 2, Mengxi Lu, Zhenjiang, 212003, China. TEL 86-511-4407610, FAX 86-511-4421823.

300 CHN ISSN 1672-3163
JIANGSU SHENG SHEHUI ZHUYI XUEYUAN XUEBAO/JIANGSU INSTITUTE OF SOCIALISM. JOURNAL. Text in Chinese. bi-m. CNY 8 newsstand/cover (effective 2006). **Document type:** *Journal, Academic/Scholarly.*
Related titles: Online - full text ed.
Published by: Jiangsu Sheng Shehui Zhuyi Xueyuan, 51, Muleiyuan Dajie, Nanjing, 210007, China. TEL 86-25-84287232, FAX 86-25-84287218.

300 CHN ISSN 1009-8860
JIANGSU XINGZHENG XUEYUAN XUEBAO/JOURNAL OF JIANGSU ADMINISTRATION INSTITUTE. Text in Chinese. 2001. bi-m. USD 31.20 (effective 2009). **Document type:** *Journal, Academic/Scholarly.*
Related titles: Online - full text ed.
—East View.
Published by: Jiangsu Sheng Xingzheng Xueyuan, 168, Jiangye Lu, Nanjing, 210004, China. TEL 86-25-84200709, FAX 86-25-84466172. **Dist. by:** China International Book Trading Corp, 35 Chegongzhuang Xilu, Haidian District, PO Box 399, Beijing 100044, China. TEL 86-10-68412045, FAX 86-10-68412023, cibtc@mail.cibtc.com.cn, http://www.cibtc.com.cn.

300 CHN ISSN 1671-6523
JIANGXI NONGYE DAXUE XUEBAO (SHEHUI KEXUE BAN)/JIANGXI AGRICULTURAL UNIVERSITY. JOURNAL (SOCIAL SCIENCES EDITION). Text in Chinese. 2002. q. CNY 8 newsstand/cover (effective 2006). **Document type:** *Journal, Academic/Scholarly.*
Related titles: Online - full text ed.
Published by: Jiangxi Nongye Daxue, Nanchang, Jiangxi 330045, China. TEL 86-791-3813246.

300 CHN ISSN 1004-518X
H8.C47
JIANGXI SHEHUI KEXUE/JIANGXI SOCIAL SCIENCES. Text in Chinese. 1980. m. CNY 10 per issue (effective 2009). **Document type:** *Journal, Academic/Scholarly.*
Related titles: Online - full text ed.
Published by: (Jiangxi Sheng Shehui Kexueyuan), Jiangxi Shehui Kexue Zazhishe, no.649, Hongdu North Ave, Nanchang, 330077, China. TEL 86-791-8596531, FAX 86-791-8596531.

300 CHN ISSN 1000-579X
AS452.N352
JIANGXI SHIFAN DAXUE XUEBAO (ZHEXUE SHEHUI KEXUE BAN)/JIANGXI NORMAL UNIVERSITY. JOURNAL (PHILOSOPHY AND SOCIAL SCIENCES EDITION). Text in Chinese. 1957. bi-m. USD 24.60 (effective 2009). adv. **Document type:** *Journal, Academic/Scholarly.*
Related titles: Online - full text ed.
—East View.
Published by: Jiangxi Shifan Daxue/Jiangxi Normal University, 437 Beijing Xilu, Nanchang, Jiangxi 330027, China. TEL 86-791-8506814, FAX 86-791-8506185.

300 CHN
JIATING - YU'ER. Text in Chinese. m.
Published by: Tianjin Shi Kexue Jishu Xiehui, 287 Heping Lu, Tianjin 300041, China. TEL 311552. Ed. Zhou Xiuping.

300 CHN ISSN 1006-642X
JIAYING DAXUE XUEBAO/JIAYING UNIVERSITY. JOURNAL. Text in Chinese. 1983. bi-m. CNY 5 newsstand/cover (effective 2006). **Document type:** *Journal, Academic/Scholarly.*
Related titles: Online - full text ed.
Published by: Jiaying Daxue, Meizigang, Meizhou, 514015, China. TEL 86-753-2186639.

300 CHN ISSN 0257-2834
AS451
JILIN DAXUE SHEHUI KEXUE XUEBAO/JILIN UNIVERSITY JOURNAL (SOCIAL SCIENCE EDITION). Text in Chinese. 1955. bi-m. USD 37.20 (effective 2009). **Document type:** *Journal, Academic/Scholarly.*
Published by: Jilin Daxue/Jilin University, 2699, Qianjin Dajie, Changchun, 130023, China. TEL 86-431-5166970, FAX 86-431-5168748.

JILIN SHIFAN DAXUE XUEBAO (RENWEN SHEHUI KEXUE BAN)/JILIN NORMAL UNIVERSITY JOURNAL (HUMANITIES AND SOCIAL SCIENCES EDITION). *see* HUMANITIES: COMPREHENSIVE WORKS

JIMBUN GAKUHO/JOURNAL OF SOCIAL SCIENCES AND HUMANITIES. *see* HUMANITIES: COMPREHENSIVE WORKS

300 100 CHN ISSN 1008-889X
JIMEI DAXUE XUEBAO (ZHEXUE SHEHUI KEXUE BAN)/JIMEI UNIVERSITY. JOURNAL (PHILOSOPHY AND SOCIAL SCIENCES). Text in Chinese. 1998. q. USD 10.80 (effective 2009). **Document type:** *Journal, Academic/Scholarly.*
Related titles: Online - full text ed.
—East View.
Published by: Jimei Daxue/Jimei University, 1, Jimeijicen Lu, Xiamen, 361021, China. TEL 86-592-6181348.

300 CHN ISSN 1671-3842
HN731
JI'NAN DAXUE XUEBAO (SHEHUI KEXUE BAN)/JI'NAN UNIVERSITY. JOURNAL (SOCIAL SCIENCES EDITION). Text in Chinese. 1990. bi-m. USD 31.20 (effective 2009). **Document type:** *Journal, Academic/Scholarly.*
Related titles: Online - full text ed.
—East View.
Published by: Ji'nan Daxue/Ji'nan University, 106, Jiwei Lu, Ji'nan, Shandong 250022, China. TEL 86-531-2769171, 86-531-2765454.

JINAN XUEBAO (ZHEXUE SHEHUI KEXUE BAN)/JINAN UNIVERSITY. JOURNAL (PHILOSOPHY & SOCIAL SCIENCES EDITION). *see* PHILOSOPHY

JINBUN SHIZEN KAGAKU RONSHU/JOURNAL OF HUMANITIES AND NATURAL SCIENCES. *see* HUMANITIES: COMPREHENSIVE WORKS

300 CHN ISSN 1674-5078
JINCHENG ZHIYE JISHU XUEYUAN XUEBAO/JINCHENG INSTITUTE OF TECHNOLOGY. JOURNAL. Text in Chinese. 2008. bi-m. **Document type:** *Journal, Academic/Scholarly.*
Related titles: Online - full text ed.
Published by: Jincheng Zhiye Jishu Xueyuan/Jincheng Institute of Technology, 1658, Fengtai Dong Jie, Jincheng, 048026, China. TEL 86-356-2190612.

JINGJI YU SHEHUI FAZHAN (NANNING)/ECONOMIC AND SOCIAL DEVELOPMENT. *see* BUSINESS AND ECONOMICS—Economic Situation And Conditions

300 CHN ISSN 1008-4657
JINGMEN ZHIYE JISHU XUEYUAN XUEBAO/JINGMEN TECHNICAL COLLEGE. JOURNAL. Text in Chinese. 1986. bi-m. CNY 8 newsstand/cover (effective 2007). **Document type:** *Journal, Academic/Scholarly.*
Formerly: Jingmen Daxue Xuebao
Related titles: Online - full text ed.
Published by: Jingmen Zhiye Jishu Xueyuan, 23, Xiangshan Dadao, Jingmen, 448000, China.

300 CHN ISSN 1673-131X
JINLING KEJI XUEYUAN XUEBAO (SHEHUI KEXUE BAN)/JINLING INSTITUTE OF TECHNOLOGY. JOURNAL (SOCIAL SCIENCE). Text in Chinese. 1986. q. **Document type:** *Journal, Academic/Scholarly.*
Supersedes in part: Nanjing Nong-Zhuan Xuebao/Nanjing Agricultural Technology College. Journal (1008-1895); Jinling Zhiye Daxue Xuebao/Nanjing Polytechnic College. Journal (1008-4932)
Published by: Jinling Keji Xueyuan/Jinling Institute of Technology, 314, Baisha Lu, Nanjing, 210001, China. TEL 86-25-84557814, FAX 86-25-84557775.

300 CHN ISSN 1000-2987
AS452.T379
JINYANG XUEKAN/ACADEMIC JOURNAL OF JINYANG. Text in Chinese. 1980. bi-m. USD 24.60 (effective 2009). adv. bk.rev. back issues avail. **Document type:** *Journal, Academic/Scholarly.*
Related titles: Online - full text ed.
Indexed: RASB.
—East View.
Published by: Shanxi Sheng Shehui Kexueyuan/Shanxi Academy of Social Sciences, 282, Beingzhou Nanlu, Taiyuan, 030006, China. TEL 86-351-5691856, FAX 86-351-7069477. Circ: 2,000. **Dist. by:** China International Book Trading Corp, 35 Chegongzhuang Xilu, Haidian District, PO Box 399, Beijing 100044, China. TEL 86-10-68412045, FAX 86-10-68412023, cibtc@mail.cibtc.com.cn, http://www.cibtc.com.cn.

300 CHN ISSN 1007-4074
JISHOU DAXUE XUEBAO (SHEHUI KEXUE BAN)/JISHOU UNIVERSITY. JOURNAL (SOCIAL SCIENCES EDITION). Text in Chinese. 1980. q. USD 66.60 (effective 2009). **Document type:** *Journal, Academic/Scholarly.*
Related titles: Online - full text ed.
Published by: Jishou Daxue/Jishou University, Daxue Xi-Xiao-Qu, Jishou, Hunan 416000, China. TEL 86-743-8563684.

300 CHN ISSN 1673-4580
JIUJIANG XUEYUAN XUEBAO (SHEHUI KEXUE BAN). Text in Chinese. 1989. q. **Document type:** *Journal, Academic/Scholarly.*
Formerly (until 2004): Jiujiang Shi-Zhuan Xuebao/Jiujiang Teachers College. Journal (1005-6882); Which was formed by the merger of (1985-1989): Jiujiang Shi-Xhuan Xuebao (Zhexue Shehui Kexue Ban); (1985-1989): Jiujiang Shi-Xhuan Xuebao (Ziran Kexue Ban); Both of which superseded in part (in 1984): Jiujiang Shi-Xhuan Xuebao; Which was formed by the 1982 merger of: Yuwen Jiaoxue (Wenke Ban); Jiaoxue yu Keyan (Like Ban)
Related titles: Online - full text ed.
Published by: Jiujiang Xueyuan, 551, Qianjin Donglu, Jiujiang, 332005, China.

300 DEU ISSN 0942-5020
JOHANN-BECKMANN-JOURNAL. Text in German. 1987. irreg., latest vol.12, 1998. price varies. **Document type:** *Monographic series, Academic/Scholarly.*
Published by: (Johann-Beckmann-Gesellschaft e.V.), G N T Verlag, Schlossstr. 1, Diepholz, 49356, Germany. TEL 49-5441-927129, FAX 49-5441-927127, service@gnt-verlag.de, http://www.gnt-verlag.de.

300 DEU ISSN 0512-1507
JOHANN WOLFGANG GOETHE UNIVERSITAET FRANKFURT AM MAIN. WISSENSCHAFTLICHE GESELLSCHAFT. SCHRIFTEN. Text in German. irreg., latest vol.22, 2008. price varies. **Document type:** *Monographic series, Academic/Scholarly.*
Published by: (Johann Wolfgang Goethe Universitaet Frankfurt am Main, Wissenschaftliche Gesellschaft), Franz Steiner Verlag GmbH, Birkenwaldstr 44, Stuttgart, 70191, Germany. TEL 49-711-25820, FAX 49-711-2582290, service@steiner-verlag.de, http://www.steiner-verlag.de.

JOHANNES-KEPLER-UNIVERSITAET LINZ. SCHRIFTEN. REIHE B: WIRTSCHAFTS- UND SOZIALWISSENSCHAFTEN. *see* BUSINESS AND ECONOMICS

331 DEU ISSN 1619-4020
JOURNAL ARBEIT. Text in German. 2001. s-a. **Document type:** *Journal, Academic/Scholarly.*
Published by: (Sozialforschungsstelle Dortmund), Lit Verlag, Grevener Str/Fresnostr 2, Muenster, 48159, Germany. TEL 49-251-235091, FAX 49-251-231972, lit@lit-verlag.de. Ed. Olaf Katenkamp.

306 USA ISSN 1531-0485
HM623
➤ **JOURNAL FOR EARLY MODERN CULTURAL STUDIES.** Abbreviated title: J E M C S. Text in English. 2001. s-a. USD 35 to individuals (effective 2010); USD 20 to students; USD 52 to institutions (effective 2011). adv. back issues avail.; reprint service avail. from PSC. **Document type:** *Journal, Academic/Scholarly.* **Description:** Provides an interdisciplinary forum for the study of the period from the late fifteenth to the late nineteenth centuries.
Related titles: Online - full text ed.: ISSN 1553-3786. USD 30 to individuals; USD 44.50 to institutions (effective 2011).
Indexed: A22, AmHI, B04, BRD, CA, E01, E08, G08, H07, H08, HAb, HumInd, I05, MLA-IB, P02, P10, P27, P48, P53, P54, PQC, S11, T02, W03, W05.
—BLDSC (4970.707000), IE. **CCC.**
Published by: (Group for Early Modern Cultural Studies, Florida State University, Department of English), University of Pennsylvania Press, 3905 Spruce St, Philadelphia, PA 19104. TEL 215-898-6261, FAX 215-898-0404, custserv@pobox.upenn.edu, http://www.upenn.edu/pennpress. Circ: 450.

300 AUS
JOURNAL FOR STUDENTS OF V C E INTERNATIONAL STUDIES. Text in English. 19??. s-a. AUD 46 per issue (effective 2009).
Former titles (until 19??): V C E International Studies Papers; (until 1994): Journal for Students of V C E International Studies; Journal for Students of V C E Political and International Studies; (until 1991): Journal for Students of Year 12 Politics
Published by: Social Education Victoria Inc., 150 Palmerston St, Carlton, VIC 3053, Australia. TEL 61-3-93494957, FAX 61-3-93492050, admin@sev.asn.au.

JOURNAL FOR THE ACADEMIC STUDY OF MAGIC. *see* PARAPSYCHOLOGY AND OCCULTISM

JOURNAL FOR THE STUDY OF BRITISH CULTURES. *see* HUMANITIES: COMPREHENSIVE WORKS

JOURNAL FOR THE THEORY OF SOCIAL BEHAVIOUR. *see* PSYCHOLOGY

JOURNAL OF AFRICAN STUDIES AND DEVELOPMENT. *see* HISTORY—History Of Africa

JOURNAL OF AGRICULTURE AND SOCIAL SCIENCES. *see* AGRICULTURE

301 USA ISSN 1944-1088
➤ **JOURNAL OF ALTERNATIVE PERSPECTIVES IN THE SOCIAL SCIENCES.** Text in English. 2008. irreg. **Document type:** *Journal, Academic/Scholarly.*
Related titles: Online - full text ed.: ISSN 1944-1096. free (effective 2011).
Indexed: A01, T02.
Published by: Guild of Independent Scholars, 1420 High Point Way SW, Ste B, Delray Beach, FL 33445.

303.48273059 NLD ISSN 1058-3947
DS518.8
JOURNAL OF AMERICAN - EAST ASIAN RELATIONS. Text in English. 1992-1999; resumed 2000. q. EUR 184, USD 256 to institutions; EUR 200, USD 280 combined subscription to institutions (print & online eds.) (effective 2012). adv. **Document type:** *Journal, Academic/Scholarly.*
Related titles: Online - full text ed.: ISSN 1876-5610. EUR 167, USD 233 to institutions (effective 2012) (from IngentaConnect).
Indexed: A01, A02, A03, A08, A22, A25, A26, APEL, AmH&L, B04, BAS, BRD, CA, E01, E08, G08, HistAb, I02, I05, P02, P10, P47, P48, P53, P54, PCI, PQC, S02, S03, S08, S09, S11, SSAI, SSAb, SSI, T02, W01, W02, W03.
—IE, Ingenta. **CCC.**
Published by: Brill, PO Box 9000, Leiden, 2300 PA, Netherlands. TEL 31-71-5353500, FAX 31-71-5317532, http://www.brill.nl.

300 974 USA ISSN 1082-7161
F106 CODEN: JAPSFV
➤ **JOURNAL OF APPALACHIAN STUDIES.** Text in English. 1989. s-a. USD 50 to individuals; USD 45 to institutions (effective 2010). bk.rev. bibl. **Document type:** *Journal, Academic/Scholarly.* **Description:** Publishes articles in the areas of history, sociology and anthropology, political science, economics, literary criticism, creative arts and other disciplines.
Formerly (until 1995): Appalachian Studies Association. Journal (1048-6143)
Related titles: Online - full text ed.
Indexed: A01, A03, B04, BibInd, CA, E02, E03, ERI, ERIC, EdA, EdI, MLA-IB, RILM, S02, S03, SCOPUS, SOPODA, SSA, SSAI, SSAb, SSI, SociolAb, T02, W03, W05.
Published by: (Appalachian Studies Association), Marshall University, One John Marshall Dr, Huntington, WV 25755. http://www.marshall.edu.

➤ **JOURNAL OF APPLIED SOCIAL PSYCHOLOGY.** *see* PSYCHOLOGY

➤ **JOURNAL OF ASIAN BUSINESS.** *see* BUSINESS AND ECONOMICS—Economic Situation And Conditions

▼ ➤ **JOURNAL OF BEHAVIOR, HEALTH & SOCIAL ISSUES.** *see* PSYCHOLOGY

300 305.896 USA ISSN 0021-9347
E185.5
➤ **JOURNAL OF BLACK STUDIES.** Text in English. 1970. bi-m. USD 1,085, GBP 638 combined subscription to institutions (print & online eds.); USD 1,063, GBP 625 to institutions (effective 2011). adv. bk.rev. illus. index. back issues avail.; reprint service avail. from PSC. **Document type:** *Journal, Academic/Scholarly.* **Description:** Sustains full analytical discussion of economic, political, sociological, historical, literary, and philosophical issues related to African-Americans.
Related titles: Microform ed.: (from PQC); Online - full text ed.: ISSN 1552-4566. USD 977, GBP 574 to institutions (effective 2011).
Indexed: A01, A02, A03, A08, A20, A22, A25, A26, ASCA, ASSIA, AmH&L, AmHI, B04, B07, B14, BRD, BRI, BrArAb, CA, CBRI, CCA, ChPerI, CurCont, E-psyche, E01, E02, E03, E07, E08, ERI, ESPM, EdA, EdI, FamI, G06, G07, G08, H04, H07, H09, HEA, HRA, HistAb, I05, I13, I14, IBR, IBSS, IBZ, IIBP, L&LBA, M08, MLA-IB, P02, P03, P04, P06, P10, P13, P18, P25, P27, P30, P34, P42, P48, P53, P54, PAIS, PCI, PQC, PSA, PsycInfo, PsycholAb, RILM, RiskAb, S02, S03, S05, S08, S09, S21, SCOPUS, SOPODA, SRRA, SSA, SSAI, SSAb, SSCI, SSI, SUSA, SWR&A, SociolAb, T02, V02, W03, W07, W09.
—BLDSC (4954.200000), IE, Infotrieve, Ingenta. **CCC.**
Published by: (Association of Black Psychologists), Sage Publications, Inc., 2455 Teller Rd, Thousand Oaks, CA 91320. TEL 805-499-9774, 800-818-7243, FAX 805-499-0871, 800-583-2665, info@sagepub.com. Ed. Molefi Kete Asante. adv.: color page USD 775, B&W page USD 385; 4.5 x 7.5. Circ: 900 (paid). **Subscr. outside the Americas to:** Sage Publications Ltd., 1 Oliver's Yard, 55 City Rd, London EC1Y 1SP, United Kingdom. TEL 44-20-73248701, FAX 44-20-73248733, subscription@sagepub.co.uk.

➤ **JOURNAL OF CANADIAN STUDIES/REVUE D'ETUDES CANADIENNES.** *see* HUMANITIES: COMPREHENSIVE WORKS

300 ARG ISSN 1851-6599
JOURNAL OF CENTRUM CATHEDRA. Text in English. 2008. 3/yr.
Indexed: A12, A17, A26, ABIn, E08, EconLit, H21, I04, I05, P08, P27, P48, P51, P53, P54, PQC, S09.
Published by: Cengage Learning Argentina, Rojas 2128, Buenos Aires, C1416, Argentina. TEL 54-11-45820601, http://www.cegage.com.ar/, clinetes.conosur@cengage.com. Ed. Fernando D'Alessio.

305.8951 NLD ISSN 1793-0391
DS732
JOURNAL OF CHINESE OVERSEAS. Text in English. 2005. s-a. EUR 154, USD 216 to institutions; EUR 168, USD 235 combined subscription to institutions (print & online eds.) (effective 2012). reprint service avail. from PSC. **Document type:** *Journal, Academic/Scholarly.* **Description:** Publishes research articles, reports and book reviews on Chinese overseas throughout the world, and the communities from which they trace their origins.
Related titles: Online - full text ed.: ISSN 1793-2548. EUR 140, USD 196 to institutions (effective 2012) (from IngentaConnect).
Indexed: A01, A22, CA, E01, IZBG, MLA-IB, SCOPUS, T02.
—IE. **CCC.**
Published by: Brill, PO Box 9000, Leiden, 2300 PA, Netherlands. cs@brill.nl, http://www.brill.nl.

THE JOURNAL OF COMPARATIVE ASIAN DEVELOPMENT. *see* BUSINESS AND ECONOMICS—International Development And Assistance

▼ **JOURNAL OF COMPREHENSIVE RESEARCH.** *see* HUMANITIES: COMPREHENSIVE WORKS

327.172 USA ISSN 0022-0027
JX1901 CODEN: JCFRAL
➤ **JOURNAL OF CONFLICT RESOLUTION**; research on war and peace between and within nations. Text in English. 1957. bi-m. USD 1,110, GBP 653 combined subscription to institutions (print & online eds.); USD 1,088, GBP 640 to institutions (effective 2011). adv. bk.rev. charts; illus. Index. back issues avail.; reprint service avail. from PSC. **Document type:** *Journal, Academic/Scholarly.* **Description:** Takes an interdisciplinary approach in analyzing the causes, prevention, and solution of international, domestic, and interpersonal conflicts.
Formerly: Conflict Resolution (0731-4086)
Related titles: Microfilm ed.: (from PQC); Online - full text ed.: ISSN 1552-8766. USD 999, GBP 588 to institutions (effective 2011).
Indexed: A01, A02, A03, A08, A12, A17, A18, A20, A22, A25, A26, ABCPolSci, ABIn, ABS&EES, AMB, ASCA, AcaI, AmH&L, B01, B04, B06, B07, B08, B09, BAS, BRD, CA, CMM, CurCont, DIP, E-psyche, E01, E02, E03, E07, E08, EAA, EI, ERI, ERIC, ESPM, EconLit, EdA, EdI, FamI, G08, H04, H09, H10, HistAb, I02, I05, I13, IBR, IBSS, IBZ, IPARL, JEL, LID&ISL, MEA&I, P02, P03, P04, P06, P07, P30, P34, P42, P48, P51, P53, P54, PAIS, PCI, PQC, PRA, PSA, PsycInfo, PsycholAb, RASB, RiskAb, S02, S03, S05, S08, S09, SCOPUS, SOPODA, SPAA, SSA, SSAI, SSAb, SSCI, SSI, SWR&A, SociolAb, T02, V&AA, V02, W01, W02, W03, W07.
—BLDSC (4965.130000), IE, Infotrieve, Ingenta, INIST. **CCC.**
Published by: (Peace Science Society), Sage Publications, Inc., 2455 Teller Rd, Thousand Oaks, CA 91320. TEL 805-499-9774, 800-818-7243, FAX 805-499-0871, 800-583-2665, info@sagepub.com. Ed. Paul Huth. Circ: 2,200. **Subscr. in Europe to:** Sage Publications Ltd., 1 Oliver's Yard, 55 City Rd, London EC1Y 1SP, United Kingdom. TEL 44-207-3248701, FAX 44-207-3248733, subscription@sagepub.co.uk.

300 GBR ISSN 0258-9001
DT1 CODEN: JCASF4
➤ **JOURNAL OF CONTEMPORARY AFRICAN STUDIES.** Abbreviated title: J C A S. Text in English. 1981-199?; resumed 1995. q. GBP 672 combined subscription in United Kingdom to institutions (print & online eds.); EUR 890, USD 1,117 combined subscription to institutions (print & online eds.) (effective 2012). adv. bk.rev. illus. index. back issues avail.; reprint service avail. from PSC. **Document type:** *Journal, Academic/Scholarly.* **Description:** Takes an interdisciplinary approach to foster a better understanding of African politics, sociology, geography, and literature.
Related titles: Online - full text ed.: ISSN 1469-9397. GBP 604 in United Kingdom to institutions; EUR 801, USD 1,006 to institutions (effective 2012) (from IngentaConnect).
Indexed: A01, A03, A08, A22, ASD, ASSIA, B21, BibLing, CA, CABA, DIP, E01, E17, ESPM, GEOBASE, HistAb, I02, I13, IBR, IBSS, IBZ, IIBP, ISAP, M10, MLA-IB, P30, P34, P42, PAIS, PSA, R02, R12, RASB, S02, S03, SCOPUS, SOPODA, SSA, SSciA, SociolAb, T02, TAR, W04, W11.
—IE, Infotrieve, Ingenta. **CCC.**
Published by: Routledge (Subsidiary of: Taylor & Francis Group), 4 Park Sq, Milton Park, Abingdon, Oxon OX14 4RN, United Kingdom. TEL 44-20-70176000, FAX 44-20-70176336, subscriptions@tandf.co.uk, http://www.routledge.com. Adv. contact Linda Hann TEL 44-1344-779945. Circ: 2,000. **Subscr. to:** Taylor & Francis Ltd., Journals Customer Service, Sheepen Pl, Colchester, Essex CO3 3LP, United Kingdom. TEL 44-20-70175544, FAX 44-20-70175198.

➤ **JOURNAL OF CONTEMPORARY EUROPEAN STUDIES (ONLINE EDITION).** *see* POLITICAL SCIENCE

➤ **JOURNAL OF CONTEMPORARY EUROPEAN STUDIES (PRINT EDITION).** *see* POLITICAL SCIENCE

300 330 GBR ISSN 1753-0350
➤ **JOURNAL OF CULTURAL ECONOMY.** Text in English. 2008. 3/yr. GBP 398 combined subscription in United Kingdom to institutions (print & online eds.); EUR 623, USD 779 combined subscription to institutions (print & online eds.) (effective 2012). adv. reprint service avail. from PSC. **Document type:** *Journal, Academic/Scholarly.* **Description:** Seeks to provide a forum for debating the relations between culture, economy and the social in all their various manifestations.
Related titles: Online - full text ed.: ISSN 1753-0369. GBP 359 in United Kingdom to institutions; EUR 561, USD 701 to institutions (effective 2012).
Indexed: A22, CA, E01, S02, S03, T02.
—IE. **CCC.**
Published by: (The University of Manchester, Centre for Research on Socio-Cultural Change), Routledge (Subsidiary of: Taylor & Francis Group), 4 Park Sq, Milton Park, Abingdon, Oxon OX14 4RN, United Kingdom. TEL 44-20-70176000, FAX 44-20-70176336, subscriptions@tandf.co.uk, http://www.routledge.com. Eds. Liz McFall, Michael Pryke, Tony Bennett. **Subscr. to:** Taylor & Francis Ltd., Journals Customer Service, Sheepen Pl, Colchester, Essex CO3 3LP, United Kingdom. TEL 44-20-70175544, FAX 44-20-70175198.

300 001.3 NGA ISSN 1595-0956
DT30.5
➤ **JOURNAL OF CULTURAL STUDIES.** Text in English. 1999. s-a. NGN 1,400 in Nigeria to individuals; USD 30 in Africa to individuals; USD 50 elsewhere to individuals; NGN 2,000 in Nigeria to institutions; USD 50 in Africa to institutions; USD 70 elsewhere to institutions (effective 2003). bk.rev. **Document type:** *Journal, Academic/Scholarly.*
Related titles: Online - full text ed.
Indexed: A01, IBSS, IIBP, MLA-IB, P27, P46, P54, SCOPUS, SociolAb.
Published by: African Cultural Initiatives, 346 Herbert Macaulay Rd, Yaba, Lagos, Nigeria. **Subscr. to:** c/o Anthonia Makwemoisa, PO Box 909, Marina, Lagos, Nigeria. makwemoisa@yahoo.com.

300 AZE ISSN 2078-0311
▼ ➤ **JOURNAL OF CULTURAL STUDIES.** Text in English, French, Spanish, Russian. forthcoming 2011. 4/yr. **Document type:** *Journal, Academic/Scholarly.*
Related titles: Online - full text ed.: forthcoming.
Indexed: AmHI, H07.
Published by: Progress Press Inc., M.Mushfig 4B, Apt.107, Baku, 1006, Azerbaijan. TEL 994-050-6691364, subijar@gmail.com.

800 TUR ISSN 1303-2925
DS54.A2
➤ **JOURNAL OF CYPRUS STUDIES/KIBRIS ARASTIRMALARI DERGISI**; research pioneer on Cyprus studies. Text in English, Turkish. 2001. s-a. **Document type:** *Journal, Academic/Scholarly.* **Description:** Covers social, cultural, historical, political and legal matters relevant to the past, present or future of the island of Cyprus.
Indexed: A01, A26, CA, E08, G08, HistAb, I05, S09, T02.
Published by: Eastern Mediterranean University, Center for Cyprus Studies, Famagusta, Northern Cyprus, Mersin, 10, Turkey. TEL 90-392-6301327, FAX 90-392-6302865, jcs@emu.edu.tr. Eds. Mehmet M Erginel, Ozlem Caykent.

300 001.3 GBR ISSN 1745-2546
HC59.69 CODEN: PGDTA9
JOURNAL OF DEVELOPING SOCIETIES (ONLINE). Text in English. q. USD 505, GBP 273 to institutions (effective 2011). **Document type:** *Journal, Academic/Scholarly.*
Formerly: Contributions to Asian Studies (Online) (2212-2753)
Media: Online - full text. **Related titles:** ◆ Print ed.: Journal of Developing Societies (Print). ISSN 0169-796X.
—**CCC.**
Published by: Sage Publications Ltd. (Subsidiary of: Sage Publications, Inc.), 1 Oliver's Yard, 55 City Rd, London, EC1Y 1SP, United Kingdom. TEL 44-20-73248500, FAX 44-20-73248600, info@sagepub.co.uk, http://www.uk.sagepub.com/home.nav.

300 001.3 IND ISSN 0169-796X
DS1 CODEN: JDSOEK
➤ **JOURNAL OF DEVELOPING SOCIETIES (PRINT)**; a forum on issues of development and change in all societies. Text in English. 1971. q. USD 561, GBP 303 combined subscription to institutions (print & online eds.); USD 550, GBP 297 to institutions (effective 2011). adv. back issues avail.; reprint service avail. from PSC. **Document type:** *Journal, Academic/Scholarly.* **Description:** Interdisciplinary, international analysis of all aspects of the processes of development and change in all times and places, including research in contemporary societies, as well as historical, theoretical and applied studies.
Formerly (until 1985): Contributions to Asian Studies (0304-2693)
Related titles: ◆ Online - full text ed.: Journal of Developing Societies (Online). ISSN 1745-2546.
Indexed: A01, A03, A08, A21, A22, APEL, BAS, BibInd, CA, DIP, E01, EI, ESPM, GEOBASE, HPNRM, HistAb, IBR, IBSS, IBZ, P30, P34, P42, PAIS, PCI, PSA, RI-1, RI-2, RiskAb, S02, S03, SCOPUS, SOPODA, SSciA, SociolAb, T02.
—BLDSC (4969.202000), IE, Ingenta. **CCC.**
Published by: Sage Publications India Pvt. Ltd. (Subsidiary of: Sage Publications, Inc.), M-32 Market, Greater Kailash-I, PO Box 4215, New Delhi, 110 048, India. TEL 91-11-6444958, FAX 91-11-6472426, sage@vsnl.com, http://www.indiasage.com/. Ed. Richard Harris. adv.: B&W page GBP 300; 130 x 200. **Subscr. in the Americas to:** Sage Publications, Inc., 2455 Teller Rd, Thousand Oaks, CA 91320. TEL 805-499-9774, FAX 805-499-0871, journals@sagepub.com.

S

300 USA ISSN 1651-9728
HC59.69
➤ **JOURNAL OF DEVELOPMENT ALTERNATIVES AND AREA STUDIES.** Text in English. 19??. q. bk.rev. Index. 150 p./no.; back issues avail. **Document type:** *Journal, Academic/Scholarly.* **Description:** Devoted to the studies of genuine development related to basic human needs satisfaction such as socio-economic problems, conflict and peace, human rights, migration, environment, North-South relations and anthropological views.
Former titles (until 2001): Scandinavian Journal of Development Alternatives and Area Studies; (until 1996): Scandinavian Journal of Development Alternatives (0280-2791); (until 1983): Scandinavian Journal of Developing Countries; (until 198?): Scandinavian Journal on the Developing Countries
Related titles: CD-ROM ed.
Indexed: A22, ASD, B04, CA, DIP, I13, IBR, IBZ, ILD, P30, PAIS, PCI, PerIslam, RASB, S02, S03, SCOPUS, SOPODA, SSAI, SSAb, SSI, SociolAb, T02, W03, W05.
—BLDSC (4969.214000), IE, Ingenta.
Address: 136 Antler Cir, San Antonio, TX 78232. journalstudies@aol.com.

967 KEN ISSN 0251-0405
DT365.A2
➤ **JOURNAL OF EASTERN AFRICAN RESEARCH & DEVELOPMENT.** Text in English. 1971-1976; resumed 1979. a. USD 45 (effective 2001). adv. bk.rev. illus. reprints avail. **Document type:** *Journal, Academic/Scholarly.* **Description:** Focuses on research and development in Africa and aims at promoting an interdisciplinary approach to the study of society.
Indexed: ASD, AbAn, Agr, CCA, HistAb, ILD, MLA-IB, P30, PAIS, PLESA, PerIslam.
Published by: Gideon S. Were Press, PO Box 10622, Nairobi, Kenya. TEL 254-2-740819, FAX 254-2-740819, gswere@insightkenya.com. Ed. M B K Darkoh. Pub., R&P Naomi Lina Were. Circ: 200.

300 GBR ISSN 1753-1055
DT365
JOURNAL OF EASTERN AFRICAN STUDIES. Text in English. 2007. 3/yr. GBP 553 combined subscription in United Kingdom to institutions (print & online eds.); EUR 735, USD 917 combined subscription to institutions (print & online eds.) (effective 2012). adv. back issues avail.; reprint service avail. from PSC. **Document type:** *Journal, Academic/Scholarly.* **Description:** Aims to promote fresh scholarly enquiry on the region from within the humanities and the social sciences, and to encourage work that communicates across disciplinary boundaries.
Related titles: Online - full text ed.: ISSN 1753-1063. GBP 498 in United Kingdom to institutions; EUR 661, USD 826 to institutions (effective 2012).
Indexed: A22, A34, A35, AgBio, CA, CABA, CurCont, D01, E01, E12, F08, F11, F12, G11, GH, H16, IBR, IBSS, IBZ, LT, N02, N03, P32, P33, P39, P42, P46, P48, P54, PAIS, PQC, PSA, R08, R12, RA&MP, RRTA, S02, S03, S13, S16, SCOPUS, SSCI, SociolAb, T02, T05, TAR, W07, W11.
—IE. **CCC.**
Published by: (The British Institute in Eastern Africa KEN), Routledge (Subsidiary of: Taylor & Francis Group), 4 Park Sq, Milton Park, Abingdon, Oxon OX14 4RN, United Kingdom. TEL 44-20-70176000, FAX 44-20-70176336, subscriptions@tandf.co.uk, http://www.routledge.com. **Subscr. to:** Taylor & Francis Ltd., Journals Customer Service, Sheepen Pl, Colchester, Essex CO3 3LP, United Kingdom. TEL 44-20-70175544, FAX 44-20-70175198.

300 BRB ISSN 1028-8813
JOURNAL OF EASTERN CARIBBEAN STUDIES. Text in English. 1975. q. BBD 96 domestic; USD 68 in the Caribbean; USD 88 elsewhere (effective 2010).
Formerly (until 1997): Bulletin of Eastern Caribbean Studies (0254-7406)
Related titles: Online - full text ed.
Indexed: A01, A03, A12, A17, ABIn, C01, C32, CA, FR, H05, H21, IBSS, IIBP, P08, P10, P27, P48, P51, P53, P54, PAIS, PQC, T02.
Published by: University of the West Indies, Institute of Social and Economic Research, PO Box 64, Bridgeton, Barbados.

JOURNAL OF ECONOMIC AND SOCIAL RESEARCH. *see* BUSINESS AND ECONOMICS—Economic Systems And Theories, Economic History

JOURNAL OF ETHIOPIAN STUDIES. *see* HISTORY—History Of Africa

300 USA ISSN 1879-3665
DK1
▼ **THE JOURNAL OF EURASIAN STUDIES.** Text in English. 2010. s-a. USD 275 to institutions (effective 2010). **Document type:** *Journal, Academic/Scholarly.*
Related titles: Online - full text ed.: ISSN 1879-3673 (from ScienceDirect).
Indexed: SCOPUS, SSAI, SSAb, SSI, T02, W03.
—**CCC.**
Published by: Elsevier Inc. (Subsidiary of: Elsevier Science & Technology), 360 Park Ave S, New York, NY 10010. TEL 212-633-3100, FAX 212-633-3140, http://www.elsevier.com.

170 GBR ISSN 1744-9626
➤ **JOURNAL OF GLOBAL ETHICS.** Text in English. 2005 (June). 3/yr. GBP 269 combined subscription in United Kingdom to institutions (print & online eds.); EUR 356, USD 448 combined subscription to institutions (print & online eds.) (effective 2012). adv. back issues avail.; reprint service avail. from PSC. **Document type:** *Journal, Academic/Scholarly.* **Description:** Covers all aspects of the theory and practice of global ethics as well as ethics in the context of globalization.
Related titles: Online - full text ed.: ISSN 1744-9634. GBP 242 in United Kingdom to institutions; EUR 320, USD 404 to institutions (effective 2012).
Indexed: A22, CA, E01, IBSS, P34, P42, PAIS, PSA, PhilInd, SociolAb, T02.
—IE, Ingenta. **CCC.**
Published by: Routledge (Subsidiary of: Taylor & Francis Group), 4 Park Sq, Milton Park, Abingdon, Oxon OX14 4RN, United Kingdom. TEL 44-20-70176000, FAX 44-20-70176336, subscriptions@tandf.co.uk, http://www.routledge.com. Eds. Christien van den Anker, Sirkku Hellsten. Adv. contact Linda Hann TEL 44-1344-779945. **Subscr. to:** Taylor & Francis Ltd., Journals Customer Service, Sheepen Pl, Colchester, Essex CO3 3LP, United Kingdom. TEL 44-20-70175544, FAX 44-20-70175198.

➤ **JOURNAL OF GLOBAL HISTORY.** *see* HISTORY

300 305.8 320 USA ISSN 1930-3009
D860
➤ **JOURNAL OF GLOBAL INITIATIVES.** Abbreviated title: J G I. Text in English. 2006. s-a. USD 30 to individuals; USD 50 to institutions (effective 2010). **Document type:** *Journal, Academic/Scholarly.* **Description:** Covers diversity issues, globalization, global learning, the intersections of local and global issues, international politics and policies, and multicultural studies.
Published by: Kennesaw State University, 1000 Chastain Rd, English Bldg. #27/Ste 220, Kennesaw, GA 30144. TEL 678-797-2169, FAX 678-797-2215, kspress@kennesaw.edu. Ed. Akanmu Adebayo.

300 USA ISSN 1540-2126
HV6773.52
JOURNAL OF HATE STUDIES. Text in English. 2001. a. USD 25 per issue (effective 2010). **Document type:** *Journal, Academic/Scholarly.* **Description:** Aims to promote the sharing of interdisciplinary ideas and research relating to the study of hate, where hate comes from, and how to combat it.
Related titles: Online - full text ed.
Indexed: A01, A02, A03, A08, C04, CA, CJA, I02, P05, S02, S03, T02.
Published by: Gonzaga Institute for Action Against Hate, Gonzaga University, AD Box 43, 502 E Boone Ave, Spokane, WA 99258. TEL 509-323-3665, againsthate@gonzaga.edu. Ed. Joanie Eppinga.

THE JOURNAL OF HUMANITIES AND SOCIAL SCIENCES. *see* HUMANITIES: COMPREHENSIVE WORKS

JOURNAL OF HUMANITIES AND SOCIAL SCIENCES. *see* HUMANITIES: COMPREHENSIVE WORKS

JOURNAL OF HUMANITIES & SOCIAL SCIENCES. *see* HUMANITIES: COMPREHENSIVE WORKS

300 USA ISSN 0092-2323
CB201
➤ **JOURNAL OF INDO-EUROPEAN STUDIES.** Text in English. 1973. q. USD 49.50 to individuals; USD 128 to institutions; USD 208 combined subscription to institutions (print & online eds.) (effective 2010). bk.rev. **Document type:** *Journal, Academic/Scholarly.* **Description:** Serves as a medium for the exchange and synthesis of information relating to the anthropology, archaeology, mythology, philology, and general cultural history of the Indo-European speaking peoples.
Related titles: Online - full text ed.: USD 148 (effective 2010).
Indexed: A20, A21, A22, ABS&EES, AICP, ASCA, AbAn, AnthLit, ArtHuCI, BEL&L, BibInd, BibLing, BrArAb, CurCont, DIP, FR, IBR, IBSS, IBZ, L11, MEA&I, MLA, MLA-IB, NAA, NumL, P48, PCI, PQC, RASB, RI-1, RI-2, SCOPUS, SOPODA, W07.
—BLDSC (5005.380000), IE, Infotrieve, Ingenta, INIST.
Published by: Institute for the Study of Man, 1133 13th St, NW, Ste C2, Washington, DC 20005. j.mallory@qub.ac.uk. Ed. James Mallory.

300 USA ISSN 0895-7258
JOURNAL OF INDO-EUROPEAN STUDIES. MONOGRAPH SERIES. Text in English. 1975. irreg., latest vol.58. price varies. **Document type:** *Monographic series, Academic/Scholarly.* **Description:** Monographs of interest to Indo-Europeanists in the areas of philology, historical linguistics, mythology, archeology, and anthropology.
Indexed: DIP, IBR, IBZ, NAA, SCOPUS, SOPODA.
—BLDSC (5005.381900).
Published by: Institute for the Study of Man, 1133 13th St, NW, Ste C2, Washington, DC 20005. TEL 202-371-2700, FAX 202-371-1523, j.mallory@qub.ac.uk.

300 001.3 NLD ISSN 1979-8431
H92.5.I6
JOURNAL OF INDONESIAN SOCIAL SCIENCES AND HUMANITIES. Text in Indonesian. 2008. s-a. **Document type:** *Journal, Academic/Scholarly.*
Related titles: Online - full text ed.: free (effective 2011).
Indexed: S02, S03.
Published by: Igitur, Utrecht Publishing & Archiving Services, Postbus 80124, Utrecht, 3508 TC, Netherlands. TEL 31-30-2536635, FAX 31-30-2536959, info@igitur.uu.nl, http://www.igitur.uu.nl.

300 USA ISSN 1942-1052
▼ ➤ **JOURNAL OF INTEGRATED SOCIAL SCIENCES.** Abbreviated title: J I S S. Text in English. 2009. s-a. free (effective 2010). back issues avail. **Document type:** *Journal, Academic/Scholarly.* **Description:** Features scholarly articles for investigation of social phenomena.
Media: Online - full text.
Published by: Rainer Diriwaechter, Ed. & Pub. Ed. Rainer Diriwaechter.

300 001.3 GBR ISSN 1747-5759
P87
➤ **JOURNAL OF INTERCULTURAL COMMUNICATION RESEARCH.** Abbreviated title: J I C R. Text in English. 1972. 3/yr. GBP 249 combined subscription in United Kingdom to institutions (print & online eds.); EUR 349, USD 438 combined subscription to institutions (print & online eds.) (effective 2012). adv. back issues avail.; reprint service avail. from PSC. **Document type:** *Journal, Academic/Scholarly.* **Description:** Publishes qualitative and quantitative research that focuses on interrelationships between culture and communication.
Former titles (until 2002): World Communication (1818-8087); (until 1985): Communication (0882-4088)
Related titles: Online - full text ed.: ISSN 1747-5767. GBP 224 in United Kingdom to institutions; EUR 314, USD 394 to institutions (effective 2012).
Indexed: A22, CA, CMM, CommAb, E01, L&LBA, S02, S03, SCOPUS, T02.
—IE, Ingenta. **CCC.**
Published by: (World Communication Association USA), Routledge (Subsidiary of: Taylor & Francis Group), 4 Park Sq, Milton Park, Abingdon, Oxon OX14 4RN, United Kingdom. TEL 44-20-70176000, FAX 44-20-70176336, subscriptions@tandf.co.uk, http://www.routledge.com. Ed. Jerry L Allen. Adv. contact Linda Hann TEL 44-1344-779945. **Subscr. to:** Taylor & Francis Ltd., Journals Customer Service, Sheepen Pl, Colchester, Essex CO3 3LP, United Kingdom. TEL 44-20-70175544, FAX 44-20-70175198.

➤ **JOURNAL OF INTERCULTURAL STUDIES.** *see* ETHNIC INTERESTS

➤ **JOURNAL OF INTERDISCIPLINARY STUDIES (PASADENA)**; an international journal of interdisciplinary and interfaith dialogue. *see* HUMANITIES: COMPREHENSIVE WORKS

306 USA ISSN 1948-5786
GN345.7
JOURNAL OF INTERNATIONAL AND CROSS-CULTURAL STUDIES. Text in English. 2007. s-a. free (effective 2009). **Document type:** *Journal, Academic/Scholarly.*
Media: Online - full content.
Published by: Scientific Journals International (Subsidiary of: Global Commerce & Communication, Inc), 1407 33rd St S, Saint Cloud, MN 56301. TEL 320-217-6019, info@scientificjournals.org.

JOURNAL OF INTERNATIONAL POLITICAL THEORY. *see* POLITICAL SCIENCE

300 TUR ISSN 1307-9581
H1
➤ **JOURNAL OF INTERNATIONAL SOCIAL RESEARCH/ ULUSLARARASI SOSYAL ARASTIRMALAR DERGISI.** Text in English, Turkish. 2007. 4/yr. free (effective 2011). **Document type:** *Journal, Academic/Scholarly.*
Media: Online - full text.
Indexed: AmHI, CA, H07, L&LBA, MLA-IB, P42, PAIS, PSA, S02, S03, SociolAb, T02. Ed. Dr. Muhammet Kuzubas.

300 KOR ISSN 1226-881X
GB471
JOURNAL OF ISLAND STUDIES. Text in English. 1998. q. **Document type:** *Journal, Academic/Scholarly.*
Published by: World Association for Island Studies, 66 Jejudaehakno, Jeju, Jeju Special Self-Governing Province 690-756, Korea, S. TEL 82-64-7542936, FAX 82-64-7562968, ko.changhoon@gmail.com.

323 300 320 BEL ISSN 1370-7205
THE JOURNAL OF KURDISH STUDIES. Text in English. 1995. a., latest vol.5, 2005. EUR 40 combined subscription (print & online eds.) (effective 2011). **Document type:** *Journal, Academic/Scholarly.* **Description:** Seeks to make known to both specialists and a wider audience of scholars and interested persons the results of original research in Kurdish studies and new interpretations of significant issues.
Related titles: Online - full text ed.: ISSN 1783-1539.
Indexed: BibLing, CA, HistAb, P30, P42, PSA, SociolAb, T02.
—IE.
Published by: Peeters Publishers, Bondgenotenlaan 153, Leuven, 3000, Belgium. TEL 32-16-235170, FAX 32-16-228500, peeters@peeters-leuven.be, http://www.peeters-leuven.be. Ed. Keith Hitchins.

JOURNAL OF LATIN AMERICAN CULTURAL STUDIES. *see* HISTORY—History Of North And South America

JOURNAL OF LAW AND SOCIETY. *see* LAW

300 USA ISSN 2159-7855
▼ **JOURNAL OF METHODS AND MEASUREMENT IN THE SOCIAL SCIENCES.** Abbreviated title: J M M. Text in English. 2010. s-a. free (effective 2011). **Document type:** *Journal, Trade.* **Description:** Focuses on methodology and research design, measurement, and data analysis.
Media: Online - full text.
Published by: University of Arizona Libraries, Department of Psychology, 1503 E University Blvd, PO Box 210068, Tucson, AZ 85721. TEL 520-621-6406, FAX 520-621-9733, http://www.library.arizona.edu/. Ed. Melinda F Davis.

JOURNAL OF MIXED METHODS RESEARCH. *see* SCIENCES: COMPREHENSIVE WORKS

JOURNAL OF MODERN JEWISH STUDIES. *see* HUMANITIES: COMPREHENSIVE WORKS

300 USA ISSN 1947-2900
▼ ➤ **JOURNAL OF MULTIDISCIPLINARY RESEARCH.** Abbreviated title: J M R. Text in English. 2009. s-a. free (effective 2011). **Document type:** *Journal, Academic/Scholarly.* **Description:** Articles on leadership as well as other current research topics.
Related titles: Online - full text ed.: ISSN 1947-2919. 2009.
Indexed: P02, P10, P48, P53, P54, PQC.
Published by: Saint Thomas University, 16401 NE 37th Ave, Miami Gardens, FL 33054. TEL 305-628-6627. Ed. Hagai Gringarten.

300 NLD ISSN 2211-792X
▼ ➤ **JOURNAL OF MUSLIMS IN EUROPE.** Text in English. forthcoming 2012. 2/yr. EUR 175, USD 245 to institutions; EUR 191, USD 267 combined subscription to institutions (print & online eds.) (effective 2012). **Document type:** *Journal, Academic/Scholarly.*
Related titles: Online - full text ed.: forthcoming 2012. EUR 159, USD 223 to institutions (effective 2012).
Published by: Brill, PO Box 9000, Leiden, 2300 PA, Netherlands. TEL 31-71-5353500, FAX 31-71-5317532, cs@brill.nl, http://www.brill.nl.

300 GBR ISSN 2046-6749
▼ ➤ **JOURNAL OF ORGANIZATIONAL ETHNOGRAPHY.** Text in English. forthcoming 2012. s-a. EUR 409 combined subscription in Europe (print & online eds.); USD 519 combined subscription in the Americas (print & online eds.); AUD 589 combined subscription in Australasia (print & online eds.); GBP 309 combined subscription in the UK & elsewhere (print & online eds.) (effective 2012). **Document type:** *Journal, Academic/Scholarly.*
Related titles: Online - full text ed.: forthcoming 2012.
Published by: Emerald Group Publishing Ltd., Howard House, Wagon Ln, Bingley, W Yorks BD16 1WA, United Kingdom. TEL 44-1274-777700, FAX 44-1274-785201, information@emeraldinsight.com. Eds. Dr. Frank Worthington, Dr. Matthew Brannan, Dr. Mike Rowe.

300 FJI ISSN 1011-3029
DU1
JOURNAL OF PACIFIC STUDIES. Text in English. 1975. a. USD 6.50. bk.rev. back issues avail.
Indexed: APEL, INZP, SPPI.
—Ingenta.
Published by: University of the South Pacific, School of Social and Economic Development, PO Box 1168, Suva, Fiji. TEL 313-900. Ed. Nii K Plange. Circ: 250.

JOURNAL OF POLITENESS RESEARCH; language, behavior, culture. *see* LINGUISTICS

300 USA ISSN 1073-0451
JA75.8
➤ **JOURNAL OF POLITICAL ECOLOGY**; case studies in history and society. Text in English, French, Spanish. 1994. a. free (effective 2010). **Document type:** *Journal, Academic/Scholarly.* **Description:** Encourages research into the linkages between political economy and human environmental impacts.
Related titles: Online - full text ed.: free (effective 2011).
Indexed: A39, C27, C29, D03, D04, E13, ESPM, HPNRM, PAIS, R14, S14, S15, S18, SSciA.
Published by: University of Arizona, Bureau of Applied Research in Anthropology, Anthropology Bldg, Rm 316, PO Box 210030, Tucson, AZ 85721. TEL 520-621-6282, FAX 520-621-9608, http://bara.arizona.edu/. Eds. James Greenberg, Simon Batterbury, Tad Park.

300 USA ISSN 1555-7359
JK1
➤ **JOURNAL OF POLITICS & SOCIETY.** Text in English. 1989. a. USD 7.95 per issue (effective 2009). adv. **Document type:** *Journal, Academic/Scholarly.* **Description:** Provides a forum for young scholars to contribute to the global discussion of a diverse range of issues, including problems of economics, public policy, international relations, and law.
Formerly (until 1990): Columbia Undergraduate Journal of Law and Public Policy
Related titles: Online - full text ed.
Published by: The Helvidius Group, 515 Alfred Lerner Hall, 2920 Broadway, MC 2601, New York, NY 10027. Ed. Josh Mathew. Circ: 3,000 (paid and controlled).

▼ ➤ **JOURNAL OF POSTCOLONIAL CULTURES AND SOCIETIES.** *see* HUMANITIES: COMPREHENSIVE WORKS

300 GBR ISSN 1754-0291
BD438
➤ **JOURNAL OF POWER.** Text in English. 2008. 3/yr. GBP 223 combined subscription in United Kingdom to institutions (print & online eds.); EUR 349, USD 438 combined subscription to institutions (print & online eds.) (effective 2012). adv. back issues avail.; reprints avail. **Document type:** *Journal, Academic/Scholarly.* **Description:** Details for empirical analysis of the process whereby globalization, ethnicity, nationalism, war and gender are central to the constitution of power, whether conceptualised as domination or empowerment.
Related titles: Online - full text ed.: ISSN 1754-0305. GBP 201 in United Kingdom to institutions; EUR 314, USD 394 to institutions (effective 2012).
Indexed: A22, CA, E01, I02, P42, PSA, T02.
—IE. **CCC.**
Published by: Routledge (Subsidiary of: Taylor & Francis Group), 4 Park Sq, Milton Park, Abingdon, Oxon OX14 4RN, United Kingdom. TEL 44-20-70176000, FAX 44-20-70176336, subscriptions@tandf.co.uk, http://www.routledge.com. Ed. Mark Haugaard. Adv. contact Linda Hann TEL 44-1344-779945. **Subscr. to:** Taylor & Francis Ltd., Journals Customer Service, Sheepen Pl, Colchester, Essex CO3 3LP, United Kingdom. TEL 44-20-70175544, FAX 44-20-70175198, tf.enquiries@tfinforma.com.

300 GBR ISSN 0143-814X
H96
➤ **JOURNAL OF PUBLIC POLICY.** Text in English. 1981. 3/yr. GBP 186, USD 310 to institutions; GBP 200, USD 342 combined subscription to institutions (print & online eds.) (effective 2012). adv. bk.rev. back issues avail.; reprint service avail. from PSC. **Document type:** *Journal, Academic/Scholarly.* **Description:** Social scientists and policymakers analyze the problems facing contemporary governments in their social, economic and political contexts.
Related titles: Microform ed.: (from PQC); Online - full text ed.: ISSN 1469-7815. GBP 172, USD 292 to institutions (effective 2012).
Indexed: A22, A26, ABCPolSci, B21, BRD, CA, E01, E08, ESPM, G08, GEOBASE, H&SSA, I05, I13, IBR, IBSS, IBZ, L10, MEA&I, P02, P10, P27, P30, P34, P42, P45, P47, P48, P53, P54, PAIS, PCI, PQC, PSA, RiskAb, S02, S03, S09, SCOPUS, SOPODA, SPAA, SSA, SSAI, SSAb, SSI, SociolAb, T02, W03.
—BLDSC (5043.640000), IE, Infotrieve, Ingenta. **CCC.**
Published by: Cambridge University Press, The Edinburgh Bldg, Shaftesbury Rd, Cambridge, CB2 8RU, United Kingdom. TEL 44-1223-312393, FAX 44-1223-315052, journals@cambridge.org, http://www.cambridge.org/uk. Ed. Richard Rose. R&P Linda Nicol TEL 44-1223-325702. Adv. contact Rebecca Roberts TEL 44-1223-325083. page GBP 405, page USD 705. Circ: 800. **Subscr. to:** Cambridge University Press, 32 Ave of the Americas, New York, NY 10013. TEL 212-337-5000, FAX 212-691-3239, journals_subscriptions@cup.org.

954.5 USA
DS485.P88 CODEN: IJPSFF
➤ **JOURNAL OF PUNJAB STUDIES.** Text in English. 1994. s-a. bk.rev. index. back issues avail.; reprints avail. **Document type:** *Journal, Academic/Scholarly.* **Description:** Provides a forum for an authoritative analysis on the Punjab region, both Indian and Pakistani, with contributions from a wide range of disciplines, including history, political science, economics, sociology, anthropology, geography, theology, literature, and linguistics.
Formerly (until 2004): International Journal of Punjab Studies (0971-5223)
Related titles: CD-ROM ed.; Online - full text ed.
Indexed: HistAb, P30, PerIslam, SCOPUS, SOPODA, SociolAb.
—**CCC.**
Published by: University of California, Center for Sikh and Punjab Studies, Santa Barbara, CA 93106. TEL 805-893-5115, FAX 805-893-2059.

001.42 THA ISSN 0857-2933
➤ **JOURNAL OF RESEARCH METHODOLOGY.** Text in English, Thai; Abstracts in English. 1989. 3/yr. THB 180 (effective 2002). abstr.; bibl.; charts; stat. **Document type:** *Journal, Academic/Scholarly.* **Description:** Covers research methodology, statistics, measurement and evaluation and research results in education and social sciences.
Published by: (Chulalongkorn University, Department of Educational Research), Chulalongkorn University Press, Phyathai Rd, Bangkok, 10330, Thailand. TEL 66-2-2153626, psomwung@chul.ac.th. Circ: 1,000.

300 USA ISSN 2151-4178
HD1405
➤ **JOURNAL OF RURAL SOCIAL SCIENCES.** Text in English. 1975. s-a. free (effective 2011). **Document type:** *Journal, Academic/Scholarly.* **Description:** Includes research on Southern rural issues and social change.
Formerly (until 2010): Southern Rural Sociology (1940-4662)
Media: Online - full text.
Indexed: A34, A38, A39, C25, C27, C29, D03, D04, E12, E13, H16, R14, S14, S15, S18, SSA, SociolAb, W11.
Published by: Southern Rural Sociological Association, G W Carver Agricultural Experiment Station, T M Campbell Hall, Tuskegee University, Tuskegee, AL 36088. http://www.ag.auburn.edu/srs/.

300 330 GBR ISSN 1748-538X
HC257.S4
➤ **JOURNAL OF SCOTTISH HISTORICAL STUDIES.** Abbreviated title: J S H S. Text in English. 1981. s-a. GBP 99 domestic to institutions; USD 198 in North America to institutions; GBP 109 elsewhere to institutions; GBP 124 combined subscription domestic to institutions (print & online eds.); USD 250 combined subscription in North America to institutions (print & online eds.); GBP 137 combined subscription elsewhere to institutions (print & online eds.) (effective 2012). bk.rev. back issues avail.; reprints avail. **Document type:** *Journal, Academic/Scholarly.* **Description:** Features articles, essays, and reviews on issues relating to Scottish economic and social history.
Formerly (until 2005): Scottish Economic and Social History (0269-5030)
Related titles: Online - full text ed.: ISSN 1755-1749. USD 163 in North America to institutions; GBP 89 elsewhere to institutions (effective 2012).
Indexed: A01, A03, A08, A12, A17, ABIn, B01, B06, B07, B09, CA, HistAb, P30, P48, P51, P53, P54, PQC, SCOPUS, T02, W04.
—BLDSC (5062.070000), IE, Ingenta. **CCC.**
Published by: (Economic and Social History Society of Scotland), Edinburgh University Press, 22 George Sq, Edinburgh, Scotland EH8 9LF, United Kingdom. TEL 44-131-6504218, FAX 44-131-6503286, journals@eup.ed.ac.uk. Eds. Gordon Pentland, Katie Stevenson. Adv. contact Ruth Allison TEL 44-131-6504220.

➤ **JOURNAL OF SOCIAL AFFAIRS/SHU'UN IJTIMA'IYYAH.** *see* HUMANITIES: COMPREHENSIVE WORKS

300 150 UAE ISSN 2221-1152
➤ **JOURNAL OF SOCIAL AND DEVELOPMENT SCIENCES.** Text in English. m. free (effective 2011). adv. bk.rev. abstr.; bibl.; charts; illus.; stat. Index. back issues avail. **Document type:** *Journal, Academic/Scholarly.* **Description:** Publishes original research paper, conceptual paper, case studies, and technical report in the disciplines of social and development sciences, addressing emerging issues and developments in sociology, psychology, anthropology, economics, political science, international relations, linguistics, and history.
Media: Online - full text.
Published by: International Foundation for Research and Development, PO Box 93181, Daira, Dubai, United Arab Emirates. info@ifrnd.org. Ed. Nek Kamal Yeop Yunus. Pub., Adv. contact N T Ran.

301 GBR ISSN 1756-7483
JOURNAL OF SOCIAL AND PSYCHOLOGICAL SCIENCES. Abbreviated title: J S P S. Text in English. 2008. s-a. GBP 40 to institutions; GBP 180 combined subscription to institutions (print & online eds.) (effective 2009). back issues avail. **Document type:** *Journal, Academic/Scholarly.*
Related titles: Online - full text ed.: ISSN 1756-7491. 2008. GBP 110 to institutions (effective 2009).
Indexed: A26, CA, E08, H11, H12, I05, S02, S03, S09, T02.
—**CCC.**
Published by: Oxford Mosaic Publications, 291b Iffley Rd, Oxford, Oxfordshire OX4 4AQ, United Kingdom. TEL 44-844-3091487, FAX 44-871-7146590, enquiries@oxford-mosaic.co.uk, http://www.oxford-mosaic.co.uk. Eds. Mauro Ramos Pereira, Phithizela Ngcobo, Shadreck Mwale.

300 USA ISSN 1948-3260
R853.I53
➤ **JOURNAL OF SOCIAL, BEHAVIORAL AND HEALTH SCIENCES.** Abbreviated title: J S B H S. Text in English. 2007. a. free (effective 2009). back issues avail. **Document type:** *Journal, Academic/Scholarly.* **Description:** Focuses on research findings that address contemporary national and international issues.
Media: Online - full content.
Published by: Walden University http://www.waldenu.edu. Ed. Daniel Weigand.

300 ROM ISSN 2067-2640
▼ ➤ **JOURNAL OF SOCIAL RESEARCH AND POLICY.** Text in English, French, German; Summaries in English. 2010 (Jul.). s-a. ROL 60 domestic to individuals; USD 30 foreign to individuals; ROL 100 domestic to institutions; USD 50 foreign to institutions (effective 2010). bk.rev. **Document type:** *Journal, Academic/Scholarly.* **Description:** Contains articles based on policy research and methodological approaches of policy topics from anthropologists, psychologists, statisticians, economists, historians and political scientists.
Related titles: Online - full text ed.: free (effective 2011).
Indexed: P10, P45, P46, P48, P53, P54, PQC.
Published by: Editura Universitatii din Oradea/University of Oradea Publishing House, Str Universitatii 1, Geotermal Bldg., 2nd Fl., Oradea, Jud.Bihor 410087, Romania. TEL 40-259-408642, editura@uoradea.ro, http://webhost.uoradea.ro/editura/. R&P Adrian Hatos. Circ: 200 (controlled).

300 ISL ISSN 1670-7788
JOURNAL OF SOCIAL SCIENCE. Text in English, Icelandic. 2007. irreg. **Document type:** *Journal, Academic/Scholarly.*
Related titles: Online - full text ed.: ISSN 1670-7796. free (effective 2011).
Indexed: A01, A39, C27, C29, D03, D04, E13, R14, S14, S15, S18, T02.
Published by: Bifrost University, Borgarnes, 311, Iceland. Ed. Ian Watson.

300 JPN ISSN 0454-2134
H8
➤ **JOURNAL OF SOCIAL SCIENCE.** Text in English, Japanese. 1960. 2/yr. not for sale or subscription. bk.rev. reprints avail. **Document type:** *Journal, Academic/Scholarly.*
Indexed: BAS, IBR, IBZ, MLA-IB, RASB.
Published by: International Christian University, Social Science Research Institute/Kokusai Kiristokyo Daigaku, 3-10-2 Osawa, Mitaka-shi, Tokyo-to 181-8585, Japan. TEL 81-422-33-3224, FAX 81-422-33-3489, ssri@icu.ac.jp. Circ: 600.

300 DEU ISSN 1618-5293
JOURNAL OF SOCIAL SCIENCE EDUCATION/JOURNAL FUER SOZIALWISSENSCHAFTLICHE STUDIEN UND DIDAKTIK. Text in German, English. 2000. irreg. free (effective 2011). **Document type:** *Journal, Academic/Scholarly.*
Formerly (until 2001): Sowi - Onlinejournal (1439-6246)
Media: Online - full text.
Published by: Universitaet Bielefeld, Faculty of Sociology, Postbox 100 131, Bielefeld, 33501, Germany.

300 IND ISSN 0970-1087
JOURNAL OF SOCIAL SCIENCE INTERNATIONAL. Text in English. 1971. s-a. INR 750 domestic (print or online ed.); USD 75 foreign (print or online ed.); INR 1,250 combined subscription domestic (print & online eds.); USD 125 combined subscription foreign (print & online eds.) (effective 2010). **Document type:** *Journal, Academic/Scholarly.* **Description:** Encompasses various disciplines of humanities and social sciences such as psychology, sociology, economics, management, education, home science, environment and political science.
Related titles: Online - full text ed.
Indexed: P03, PsycInfo.
—BLDSC (8318.161800), IE.
Published by: M D Publications Pvt Ltd, 11 Darya Ganj, New Delhi, 110 002, India. TEL 91-11-41563325, FAX 91-11-23275542, contact@mdppl.com. Ed. Pravash Kumar Mishra.

300 PAK ISSN 1812-0687
H1
➤ **JOURNAL OF SOCIAL SCIENCES.** Text in English. 2004. a. USD 10 (effective 2007). **Document type:** *Journal, Academic/Scholarly.* **Description:** Seeks to foster original research in the various fields of social sciences including sociology, geography, political science, history, education, international relations, social theory, political economy, anthropology, urban studies, globalization and other knowledge disciplines.
Published by: G C University, Faisalabad, Faisalabad, Pakistan. TEL 92-041-9200670, FAX 92-041-9200671, gcuf@gcuf.edu.pk, http://www.gcuf.edu.pk. Ed., R&P Ghulam Ghous. Circ: 1,000 (paid and controlled).

300 USA ISSN 1549-3652
H1
➤ **JOURNAL OF SOCIAL SCIENCES.** Text in English. 2005. q. USD 1,600 (effective 2009). adv. **Document type:** *Journal, Academic/Scholarly.* **Description:** Presents the results and conclusions of social science research to an international reading audience.
Related titles: Online - full text ed.: ISSN 1558-6987. free (effective 2011).
Indexed: A01, A26, A39, C27, C29, CA, D03, D04, E08, E13, FamI, G08, I05, Inspec, R14, S06, S09, S14, S15, S18, T02.
—BLDSC (5064.912655), IE.
Published by: Science Publications, 244, 5th Ave, Ste 207, New York, NY 10001. TEL 845-510-3028, FAX 866-250-7082, support@scipub.org, http://www.thescipub.com. adv.: B&W page USD 200, color page USD 500. Circ: 149 (paid).

300 IND ISSN 0971-8923
H1
➤ **JOURNAL OF SOCIAL SCIENCES**; interdisciplinary reflection of contemporary society. Text in English. 1997. m. USD 400 (effective 2012). bk.rev. 80 p./no. 2 cols./p.; back issues avail. **Document type:** *Journal, Academic/Scholarly.* **Description:** Aims at disseminating knowledge which may serve as a forum for social scientists, especially those who share common interests in understanding of various issues related to contemporary society.
Related titles: Online - full text ed.: 2004. free (effective 2012).
Indexed: CA, IBSS, P34, P42, PAIS, PSA, S02, S03, SCOPUS, SSA, SociolAb, T02.
Published by: Kamla-Raj Enterprises, 2273 Gali Bari Paharwali, Chawri Bazar, New Delhi, 110 006, India. TEL 91-11-23284126, kre@airtelmail.in. Circ: 300. **Subscr. to:** I N S I O Scientific Books & Periodicals.

300 001.3 PAK ISSN 1994-7046
➤ **JOURNAL OF SOCIAL SCIENCES AND HUMANITIES.** Text in English. 1994. s-a. PKR 120 domestic; PKR 180 in SAARC Countries; USD 18 elsewhere; PKR 80 to students (effective 2009). bk.rev. back issues avail.; reprints avail. **Document type:** *Journal, Academic/Scholarly.* **Description:** Covers contemporary social sciences with particular reference to Pakistan.
Published by: Allama Iqbal Open University, Department of History, Block-9, Islamabad, Pakistan. Eds. Samina Awan, Samina Awan, Inam-ul-Haq Javeid. Pub. Mahmood H. Butt.

300 USA ISSN 1529-1227
HM403
➤ **JOURNAL OF SOCIAL STRUCTURE.** Abbreviated title: J o S S. Text in English. 2000. irreg. free (effective 2011). back issues avail. **Document type:** *Journal, Academic/Scholarly.*
Media: Online - full text.
Indexed: CA, S02, S03, SociolAb, T02.
Published by: (International Network for Social Network Analysis), Carnegie Mellon University, H. John Heinz III School of Public Policy and Management, Pittsburgh, PA 15213. TEL 412-268-4758, FAX 412-268-7902. Ed. James W Moody.

300 BGD ISSN 1012-7844
JOURNAL OF SOCIAL STUDIES. Text in English. 1978. q. BDT 152 domestic to individuals; USD 40 foreign to individuals; BDT 172 domestic to institutions; USD 48 foreign to institutions (effective 1999). adv. bk.rev. cum.index: vols.1-58 (1978-1992). **Document type:** *Journal, Academic/Scholarly.* **Description:** Covers the socio-economic problems of the world in general, focusing on Bangladesh.
Related titles: ◆ Bengali ed.: Samaj Nirikkhon.
Indexed: BAS, P30.
—BLDSC (5064.913700), IE, Infotrieve, Ingenta.
Published by: Centre for Social Studies/Samaj Nirikkhon Kendro, Rm 1107 Arts Bldg, Dhaka University, Dhaka, 1000, Bangladesh. Ed. B.K. Jahangir. R&P B K Jahangir. Adv. contact Hasina Ahmed. Circ: 500.

300 370 TUR ISSN 1309-9108
▼➤ **JOURNAL OF SOCIAL STUDIES EDUCATION RESEARCH/ SOSYAL BILGILER EGITIMI ARASTIRMALARI DERGISI.** Text in English, Turkish. 2010. s-a. free (effective 2011). **Document type:** *Journal, Academic/Scholarly.* **Description:** Serves as a forum for social studies educators from Turkey and around the world to present and discuss common concerns in local, national, global, international and transnational issues in social studies education.
Media: Online - full text.
Published by: Association for Social Studies Educators/Sosyal Bilgiler Egitimcileri Birligi, Ataturk Mah. Kutsal Sok, 6/27 Sincan, Ankara, Turkey. TEL 90-507-3104933, FAX 90-332-3245510, http://www.sosyalbilgiler.org/. Ed. Cemil Ozturk. Pub., R&P Bulent Tarman.

300.71 USA ISSN 0885-985X
➤ **JOURNAL OF SOCIAL STUDIES RESEARCH.** Text in English. 1977. s-a. USD 55 domestic; USD 60 foreign (effective 2009). back issues avail. **Document type:** *Journal, Academic/Scholarly.* **Description:** Designed to foster the dissemination of ideas and research findings related to the social studies.
Related titles: Microfilm ed.; Online - full text ed.
Indexed: A26, B04, BRD, CA, E02, E03, E07, ERI, ERIC, EdA, EdI, P10, P18, P27, P46, P48, P53, P54, PQC, S02, S03, T02, W03, W05.
—BLDSC (5064.914000), IE, Ingenta.
Published by: The International Society for the Social Studies, University of Central Florida, 4000 Central Florida Blvd, Orlando, FL 32816-1250. TEL 407-823-4345, FAX 407-823-1776, ISSS@mail.ucf.edu, http://www.TheJSSR.com. Ed. William B Russell III. Circ: 200.

300 GBR ISSN 0305-7070
DT727
➤ **JOURNAL OF SOUTHERN AFRICAN STUDIES.** Text in English. 1974. q. GBP 476 combined subscription in United Kingdom to institutions (print & online eds.); EUR 678, USD 851 combined subscription to institutions (print & online eds.) (effective 2012). adv. bk.rev. illus. index. back issues avail.; reprint service avail. from PSC. **Document type:** *Journal, Academic/Scholarly.* **Description:** Provides a scholarly inquiry and exposition in the fields of economics, sociology, geography, demography, social anthropology, administration, law, political science, international relations, history, and natural sciences, as they relate to the human condition.
Related titles: Microform ed.: (from PQC); Online - full text ed.: ISSN 1465-3893. GBP 428 in United Kingdom to institutions; EUR 610, USD 765 to institutions (effective 2012) (from IngentaConnect).
Indexed: A01, A02, A03, A08, A20, A22, A34, A36, ABCPolSci, AICP, ARDT, ASCA, ASD, AmHI, BrHumI, CA, CABA, CCA, CurCont, DIP, E01, E12, ESPM, F08, F12, FamI, G10, GEOBASE, GH, H07, H16, HistAb, I02, I08, I13, IBR, IBSS, IBZ, IIBP, ILD, ISAP, IndVet, L&LBA, L05, L06, LT, MLA-IB, P02, P10, P13, P30, P33, P34, P42, P45, P48, P53, P54, PAIS, PCI, PQC, PSA, R08, R12, RASB, RILM, RRTA, S02, S03, S11, S13, S16, SCOPUS, SOPODA, SSA, SSCI, SSciA, SociolAb, T02, T05, TAR, VS, W04, W07, W09, W10, W11.
—IE, Infotrieve, Ingenta. **CCC.**
Published by: Routledge (Subsidiary of: Taylor & Francis Group), 4 Park Sq, Milton Park, Abingdon, Oxon OX14 4RN, United Kingdom. TEL 44-20-70176000, FAX 44-20-70176336, subscriptions@tandf.co.uk, http://www.routledge.com. Adv. contact Linda Hann TEL 44-1344-779945. Circ: 900. **Subscr. to:** Taylor & Francis Ltd., Journals Customer Service, Sheepen Pl, Colchester, Essex CO3 3LP, United Kingdom. TEL 44-20-70175544, FAX 44-20-70175198.

➤ **JOURNAL OF THE DOCUMENTATION AND HUMANITIES RESEARCH CENTRE.** *see* HUMANITIES: COMPREHENSIVE WORKS

300 KWT ISSN 0253-1097
H8.A7
➤ **JOURNAL OF THE SOCIAL SCIENCES/MAJALLAT AL-ULUM AL-IJTIMA'IYAH.** Text in Arabic, English. 1973. q. KWD 3 domestic to individuals; USD 15 foreign to individuals; KWD 15 domestic to institutions; USD 60 foreign to institutions (effective 2003). abstr. 250 p./no.; **Document type:** *Journal, Academic/Scholarly.* **Description:** Includes theoretical articles in the fields of social sciences.
Indexed: AmH&L, CA, DIP, E-psyche, EconLit, GEOBASE, HistAb, I13, IBR, IBZ, JEL, M10, P03, P42, PSA, PerIslam, PsycholAb, S02, S03, SCOPUS, SSA, SociolAb, T02.
Published by: Academic Publication Council, Kuwait University/Majliss an-Nushir al-Elmi, P O Box 13411, Keifan, 71955, Kuwait. ajoas@ku.edu.kw, http://www.pubcouncil.kuniv.edu.kw. Ed. Ahmad Abdel-Khalek. Circ: 3,000.

153.4 USA ISSN 0022-5231
➤ **JOURNAL OF THOUGHT.** Text in English. 1966. q. USD 50 to individuals; USD 100 to institutions (effective 2010). bk.rev. illus. index. 96 p./no. 1 cols./p.; back issues avail.; reprints avail. **Document type:** *Journal, Academic/Scholarly.* **Description:** Features interdisciplinary articles with a focus on philosophy of education.
Related titles: Microform ed.: (from PQC); Online - full text ed.
Indexed: A20, A22, A26, B04, CA, CPE, DIP, E02, E03, E07, E08, ERI, EdA, EdI, G08, GSS&RPL, I05, IBR, IBZ, P02, P06, P18, P27, P30, P48, P53, P54, PCI, PQC, PerIslam, PhilInd, S09, S21, SOPODA, SociolAb, T02, W03, W05.
—BLDSC (5069.300000), IE, Infotrieve, Ingenta.
Published by: (Texas Tech University, College of Education), Caddo Gap Press, 3145 Geary Blvd, PMB 275, San Francisco, CA 94118. TEL 415-666-3012, FAX 415-666-3552, info@caddogap.com, http://www.caddogap.com. Ed. Douglas J Simpson. Pub. Alan H Jones.

300 001.3 USA ISSN 1940-0764
E175.8
▼➤ **JOURNAL OF TRANSNATIONAL AMERICAN STUDIES.** Text in English. 2009. irreg. free (effective 2011). **Document type:** *Journal, Academic/Scholarly.* **Description:** Seeks to broaden the interdisciplinary study of American cultures in a transnational context.
Media: Online - full text.
Indexed: AmH&L, CA, HistAb, MLA-IB, T02.
Published by: eScholarship (Subsidiary of: California Digital Library) http://www.escholarship.org.

➤ **JOURNAL OF UKRAINIAN STUDIES.** *see* LITERATURE

300 ROM ISSN 2067-4082
▼ **JOURNAL OF URBAN AND REGIONAL ANALYSIS.** Text in English. 2010. s-a. **Document type:** *Journal, Academic/Scholarly.*
Related titles: Online - full text ed.: ISSN 2068-9969. free (effective 2011).
Indexed: PQC.
Published by: Editura Universitatii din Bucuresti, Soseaua Panduri 90-92, Sector 5, Bucharest, Romania. TEL 40-21-4102384, FAX 40-21-2317418, editura_unibuc@yahoo.com, http://editura.unibuc.ro.

▼ **JOURNAL OF WORLD DEVELOPMENT.** *see* POLITICAL SCIENCE—International Relations

300 USA ISSN 1076-156X
HN1
➤ **JOURNAL OF WORLD-SYSTEMS RESEARCH.** Text in English. 1995. irreg. free (effective 2011). bk.rev. back issues avail. **Document type:** *Journal, Academic/Scholarly.* **Description:** Dedicated to scholarly research on the modern world systems and societies.
Media: Online - full text.
Indexed: A39, AltPI, C27, C29, CA, D03, D04, E13, LeftInd, P42, PRA, PSA, R14, S02, S03, S14, S15, S18, SSA, SociolAb, T02.
Published by: University of California, Riverside, Institute for Research on World-Systems, College Bldg S, Riverside, CA 92521. TEL 909-787-2062, FAX 909-787-3330, chriscd@ucr.ed, http://www.irows.ucr.edu. Eds. Andrew K Jorgenson, Edward Kick.

➤ **JOURNAL ON CHAIN AND NETWORK SCIENCE.** *see* BUSINESS AND ECONOMICS

➤ **JUDICATURE.** *see* LAW—Judicial Systems

300 CHN ISSN 1003-5419
HC427.92
JUECE TANSUO/POLICY RESEARCH. Text in Chinese. 1987. s-a. USD 61.20 (effective 2009). **Document type:** *Journal, Academic/Scholarly.*
Related titles: Online - full text ed.
—East View.
Published by: Henan Sheng Renmin Zhengfu Fazhan Yanjiu Zhongxin, 5, Zheng Yi Jie, Zhengzhou, 450003, China. TEL 86-371-67215331, FAX 86-371-65738108. **Dist. by:** China International Book Trading Corp, 35 Chegongzhuang Xilu, Haidian District, PO Box 399, Beijing 100044, China. TEL 86-10-68412045, FAX 86-10-68412023, cibtc@mail.cibtc.com.cn, http://www.cibtc.com.cn.

JUNCTURES; the journal for thematic dialogue. *see* ART

300 CAN ISSN 1705-1436
HD4802
➤ **JUST LABOUR**; a Canadian journal of work and society. Text in English, French. 2002. irreg. free (effective 2011). **Document type:** *Journal, Academic/Scholarly.* **Description:** Explores the complex ways new technologies, subcontracting, new management strategies, and the emerging self-employment are undermining the traditional employee-employer relationships and disciplining workers.
Media: Online - full text.
Indexed: A39, C27, C29, D03, D04, E13, R14, S14, S15, S18.
—CCC.
Published by: York University, Centre for Research on Work and Society, 4700 Keele St, Toronto, ON M3J 1P3, Canada. TEL 416-736-5612, FAX 416-736-5912, crws@yorku.ca. Ed. Gil Levine.

➤ **K D C SCRIPTA.** *see* RELIGIONS AND THEOLOGY—Roman Catholic

➤ **KAGOSHIMA JOSHI TANKI DAIGAKU KIYO/KAGOSHIMA WOMEN'S JUNIOR COLLEGE. BULLETIN.** *see* HUMANITIES: COMPREHENSIVE WORKS

➤ **KAGOSHIMA UNIVERSITY. RESEARCH CENTER FOR THE PACIFIC ISLANDS. OCCASIONAL PAPERS.** *see* SCIENCES: COMPREHENSIVE WORKS

300 CHN ISSN 1008-343X
KAIFENG DAXUE XUEBAO/KAIFENG UNIVERSITY. JOURNAL. Text in Chinese. 1987. q. USD 16.40 (effective 2009). **Document type:** *Journal, Academic/Scholarly.*
Related titles: Online - full text ed.
Published by: Kaifeng Daxue, Daliang Lu, Kaifeng, 475004, China. TEL 86-378-3810004, FAX 86-378-3857112.

300 ARG ISSN 1514-9331
KAIROS. Text in Spanish. 1997. s-a. back issues avail.
Media: Online - full text.
Indexed: A26, I04, I05.
Published by: Universidad Nacional de San Luis, Facultad de Ingenieria y Ciencias Economico-Sociales, Ave. 25 de Mayo, 384, Villa Mercedes, San Luis, 5730, Argentina. http://www.fices.unsl.edu.ar/kairos/index.html. Ed. Graciela Yolanda Castro.

KALYANI; journal of humanities and social sciences of the University of Kelaniya. *see* HUMANITIES: COMPREHENSIVE WORKS

KANAGAWA KOKA DAIGAKU KENKYU HOKOKU. A, JINBUN SHAKAI KAGAKU-HEN/KANAGAWA INSTITUTE OF TECHNOLOGY. RESEARCH REPORTS. PART A, HUMANITIES AND SOCIAL SCIENCE. *see* HUMANITIES: COMPREHENSIVE WORKS

300 TUR ISSN 1308-6200
H8.T87
KARADENIZ/BLACK SEA. Text in English, Russian, Turkish. 2008. q. TMM 40 domestic; USD 60, EUR 50 foreign (effective 2011). bk.rev. back issues avail. **Document type:** *Journal, Academic/Scholarly.* **Description:** Covers all aspects of social sciences with a particular focus on the Black Sea Region and a global perspective.
Related titles: Online - full text ed.
Published by: Kultur Ajans, Giresun University, Faculty of Arts and Sciences, Department of Turkish Language & Literature, Giresun, 28049, Turkey. TEL 90-454-2161255 ext 196, FAX 90-454-2164518. Eds. Erdogan Altinkaynak, Mustafa Aca. R&P Hayrettin Ivgin. Circ: 1,000.

300 940 TUR ISSN 1304-6918
➤ **KARADENIZ ARASTIRMALARI/BLACK SEA STUDIES**; journal of studies on the Balkans, the Caucasus, Eastern Europe & Anatolia. Text in English, Russian, Turkish. 2004. q. TRY 40 domestic; USD 50 foreign (effective 2010). adv. bk.rev. bibl.; charts; illus.; maps. back issues avail. **Document type:** *Journal, Academic/Scholarly.* **Description:** Covers studies in social sciences on the regions around the Black Sea.
Related titles: Online - full text ed.: free (effective 2011).
Indexed: A01, MLA-IB, P02, P10, P27, P48, P53, P54, PQC, T02.
Published by: Karadeniz Arastirmalari Merkezi, Mithat Pasa Cad. Kivanc Apt. 54/18 Kizilay, Ankara, Turkey. TEL 90-312-4315395. Ed. Yahya Kemal Tastan. Pub. Bilgehan A. Gokdag.

300 DEU ISSN 1610-479X
KARL POPPER FOUNDATION KLAGENFURT. SCHRIFTENREIHE. Text in German. 2003. irreg., latest vol.5, 2008. price varies. **Document type:** *Monographic series, Academic/Scholarly.*
Published by: (Karl Popper Foundation Klagenfurt AUT), Peter Lang GmbH (Subsidiary of: Peter Lang Publishing Group), Eschborner Landstr 42-50, Frankfurt Am Main, 60489, Germany. TEL 49-69-7807050, FAX 49-69-78070550, zentrale.frankfurt@peterlang.com. Ed. Reinhard Neck.

360 DEU ISSN 1868-033X
▼ **KARLSRUHER SCHRIFTENREIHE WOHNUNGSSICHERUNG AM ANGESPANNTEN WOHNUNGSMARKT.** Text in German. 2009. irreg., latest vol.3, 2009. price varies. **Document type:** *Monographic series, Academic/Scholarly.*
Published by: Cuvillier Verlag, Nonnenstieg 8, Goettingen, 37075, Germany. TEL 49-551-547240, FAX 49-551-5472421, info@cuvillier.de.

300 IND ISSN 0075-5176
HN681
KARNATAK UNIVERSITY, DHARWAD, INDIA. JOURNAL. SOCIAL SCIENCES. Text in English. 1965. a. **Document type:** *Journal, Academic/Scholarly.*
Indexed: BAS, DIP, IBR, IBZ.
Published by: Karnatak University, Pavate Nagar, Dharwad, Karnataka 580 003, India.

300 500 001.3 CHN ISSN 1006-432X
KASHI SHIFAN XUEYUAN XUEBAO/KASHGAR TEACHERS COLLEGE. JOURNAL. Text in Chinese. 1980. bi-m. USD 31.20 (effective 2009). **Document type:** *Journal, Academic/Scholarly.*
Related titles: Online - full text ed.
—East View.
Published by: Kashi Shifan Xueyuan/Kashi Teachers College, 463, Kuonanaizeerbage Lu, Kashi, Xinjiang 844007, China. TEL 86-998-2892218, FAX 86-998-2892555.

300 POL
KATOLICKI UNIWERSYTET LUBELSKI. WYDZIAL NAUK SPOLECZNYCH. ROZPRAWY. Text in Polish; Summaries in English, French. 1947. irreg. price varies. index.
Published by: Katolicki Uniwersytet Lubelski, Towarzystwo Naukowe, ul Gliniana 21, Lublin, 20616, Poland. Circ: 1,025.

500 KAZ
KAZAKHSTAN AIELDERI. Text in Kazakh. m. USD 171 in North America (effective 2000).
Address: Ul M Makataeve 53 ofis 102, Almaty, 480002, Kazakstan. TEL 3272-330623. Ed. A Zhafanova. **Dist. by:** East View Information Services, 10601 Wayzata Blvd, Minneapolis, MN 55305. TEL 952-252-1201, 800-477-1005, FAX 952-252-1202, info@eastview.com, http://www.eastview.com.

300 KAZ ISSN 1029-8657
KAZAKSTAN RESPUBLIKASYNYN GYLYM MINISTRLIGI. GYLYM AKADEMIASYNYN KHABARLARY. SERIYA OBSHCHESTVENNYKH NAUK. Text in Russian. 1963. 6/yr. **Document type:** *Academic/Scholarly.*
Former titles (until 1996): Akademiya Nauk Kazakhstana. Izvestiya. Seriya Obshchestvennykh Nauk (1025-9139); (until 1993): Akademiya Nauk Kazakhskoi S.S.R. Izvestiya. Seriya Obshchestvennykh Nauk (0132-6163)
Indexed: AICP, IBibSS.
Published by: (Kazakhstan Respublikasy Gylym Zane Zogary Bilim Ministrliginn. Kazakhstan Respublikasy Ulttyk Gylym Akademiasynyn/ Ministry of Education and Science of the Republic of Kazakhstan, National Academy of Sciences of the Republic of Kazakhstan), Gylym, Pushkina 111-113, Almaty, 480100, Kazakstan. TEL 3272-611877. Ed. R B Suleimenov. **Subscr. to:** G.R. Kondubayeva, Ul Shevchenko 28, Almaty 480021, Kazakstan.

300 JPN ISSN 0916-328X
HQ682
KAZOKU SHAKAIGAKU KENKYU/JAPANESE JOURNAL OF FAMILY SOCIOLOGY. Text in Japanese. 1989. a. **Document type:** *Journal, Academic/Scholarly.*
Related titles: Online - full text ed.
Indexed: SCOPUS, SSA, SociolAb.
—BLDSC (5088.211000). **CCC.**
Published by: Nihon Kazoku Shakaigaku Gakkai/Japan Society of Family Sociology, 4-4-19 Takadanobaba, Shinjuku-ku, Tokyo, 169-0075, Japan. jsfs-hp@bunken.co.jp.

302.23 JPN ISSN 0388-7596
P87
KEIO COMMUNICATIONS REVIEW. Text in English. 1980. a. **Document type:** *Journal, Academic/Scholarly.*
Indexed: MLA-IB.
Published by: Keio Gijuku Daigaku, Shinbun Kenkyujo/Keio University. Institute for Media and Communications Research, 2-15-45 Mita Ninato-ku, Tokyo, 108-8345, Japan. TEL 81-3-3453-4511, FAX 81-3-5427-1636, http://www.mediacom.keio.ac.jp/. Ed. Minoru Sugaya.

KENYA JOURNAL OF SCIENCES. SERIES C: HUMANITIES AND SOCIAL SCIENCES. *see* HUMANITIES: COMPREHENSIVE WORKS

300 USA ISSN 0748-8815
JK1
KETTERING REVIEW; a journal of ideas and activities dedicated to improving the quality of public life in the American democracy. Text in English. 1983. s-a. free (effective 2010). back issues avail. **Document type:** *Journal, Academic/Scholarly.*
Related titles: Online - full text ed.
Published by: Charles F. Kettering Foundation, 200 Commons Rd, Dayton, OH 45459. TEL 937-434-7300, 800-221-3657. Ed. Robert J Kingston.

300 CHN ISSN 0254-8763
KEXUE DUI SHEHUI DE YINGXIANG/SCIENCE IMPACT ON SOCIETY. Text in Chinese. q. USD 20.80 (effective 2009).
Related titles: Online - full text ed.
—East View.
Published by: Zhongguo Kexueyuan Keji Zhengce yu Guanli Kexue Yanjiusuo/Chinese Academy of Sciences, Research Institute of Science and Technology Policy and Management, PO Box 8712, Beijing, 100080, China. TEL 289831. Ed. Shen Chenru.

300 CHN ISSN 1002-1493
KEXUE SHEHUI ZHUYI/SCIENTIFIC SOCIALISM. Text in Chinese. bi-m. USD 40.20 (effective 2009).
Formerly (until 1990): Kexue Shehui Zhuyi (Beijing, 1978) (1001-3210)
Related titles: Online - full text ed.
Published by: Zhongyang Dangjiao, Jiaoyang Bu, 100, Dayouzhuang, Beijing, 100091, China. TEL 86-10-62809964, FAX 86-10-62805245.

THE KEY CONCEPTS. *see* HUMANITIES: COMPREHENSIVE WORKS

KHAZAR JOURNAL OF HUMANITIES AND SOCIAL SCIENCES. *see* HUMANITIES: COMPREHENSIVE WORKS

300 DEU ISSN 1860-8647
KLASSIKER DER WISSENSSOZIOLOGIE. Text in German. 2006. irreg., latest vol.12, 2011. price varies. **Document type:** *Monographic series, Academic/Scholarly.*
Published by: U V K Verlagsgesellschaft mbH, Schuetzenstr 24, Konstanz, 78462, Germany. TEL 49-7531-90530, FAX 49-7531-905398, nadine.ley@uvk.de, http://www.uvk.de.

300 DEU ISSN 1865-7095
KLOSTERMANN ROTEREIHE. Variant title: Seminar Klostermann. Text in German. 2004. irreg., latest vol.37, 2010. price varies. **Document type:** *Monographic series, Academic/Scholarly.*
Formerly (until 2007): KlostermannSeminar (1612-4545)
Indexed: MSN.
Published by: Vittorio Klostermann, Frauenlobstr 22, Frankfurt Am Main, 60487, Germany. TEL 49-69-9708160, FAX 49-69-708038, verlag@klostermann.de.

300 NLD ISSN 1877-9220
KNOWLEDGE AND SPACE. Text in English. 2008. irreg., latest vol.4, 2011. price varies. **Document type:** *Monographic series, Academic/Scholarly.* **Description:** Covers topics dealing with the production, application, spatial distribution and diffusion of knowledge.
Published by: (Klaus Tschira Symposia), Springer Netherlands (Subsidiary of: Springer Science+Business Media), Van Godewijckstraat 30, Dordrecht, 3311 GX, Netherlands. TEL 31-78-6576050, FAX 31-78-6576474. Ed. Peter Meusburger.

300 USA ISSN 1936-2188
HD30.2
➤ **KNOWLEDGE ECOLOGY STUDIES.** Variant title: K E Studies. Text in French, English. 2007 (May). a. free (effective 2011). back issues avail. **Document type:** *Journal, Academic/Scholarly.* **Description:** Covers knowledge specialties such as sciences, technologies, public policies, the laws of intellectual property, business, free speech and privacy, telecommunications and other related knowledge disciplines.
Media: Online - full text.
Indexed: A39, C27, C29, D03, D04, E13, R14, S14, S15, S18.
Published by: Knowledge Ecology International, 1621 Connecticut Ave NW, Ste 500, Washington, DC 20009. TEL 202-332-2670, FAX 202-332-2673, http://www.keionline.org.

300 GBR ISSN 1947-4199
HD30.2
➤ **KNOWLEDGE MANAGEMENT FOR DEVELOPMENT JOURNAL.** Abbreviated title: K M 4 D. Text in English. 2005. q. GBP 226 combined subscription in United Kingdom to institutions (print & online eds.); EUR 326, USD 407 combined subscription to institutions (print & online eds.) (effective 2012). **Document type:** *Journal, Academic/Scholarly.* **Description:** Covers knowledge management, information management, international development, organizational learning, information and communication technologies, knowledge sharing.
Related titles: Online - full text ed.: ISSN 1871-6342. GBP 203 in United Kingdom to institutions; EUR 293, USD 366 to institutions (effective 2012).
Indexed: A01, A36, GH, T02, W11.
—CCC.
Published by: Taylor & Francis Ltd. (Subsidiary of: Taylor & Francis Group), 4 Park Sq, Milton Park, Abingdon, Oxfordshire OX14 4RN, United Kingdom. TEL 44-1235-828600, FAX 44-1235-829000, info@tandf.co.uk.

➤ **KOBE UNIVERSITY OF MERCANTILE MARINE. REVIEW. PART 1. STUDIES IN HUMANITIES AND SOCIAL SCIENCE.** *see* HUMANITIES: COMPREHENSIVE WORKS

300 DEU ISSN 1866-2129
KOELNER BEITRAEGE ZU EINER GEISTESWISSENSCHAFTLICHEN FACHINFORMATIK. Text in German. 2008. irreg., latest vol.3, 2009. price varies. **Document type:** *Monographic series, Academic/Scholarly.*
Published by: Verlag Dr. Kovac, Leverkusenstr 13, Hamburg, 22761, Germany. TEL 49-40-3988800, FAX 49-40-39888055, info@verlagdrkovac.de. Ed. Manfred Thaller.

300 DEU
KOERPER, ZEICHEN, KULTUR. Text in German. 1998. irreg., latest vol.20, 2008. price varies. **Document type:** *Monographic series, Academic/Scholarly.*
Published by: Weidler Buchverlag Berlin, Luebecker Str 8, Berlin, 10559, Germany. TEL 49-30-3948668, FAX 49-30-3948698, weidler_verlag@yahoo.de.

300 DEU ISSN 1434-274X
KOINON; sozialwissenschaftliche interdisziplinaere Studien. Text in German. 1999. irreg., latest vol.7, 2002. price varies. **Document type:** *Monographic series, Academic/Scholarly.*
Published by: Peter Lang GmbH (Subsidiary of: Peter Lang Publishing Group), Eschborner Landstr 42-50, Frankfurt Am Main, 60489, Germany. TEL 49-69-7807050, FAX 49-69-78070550, zentrale.frankfurt@peterlang.com. Ed. Savvas Katsikides.

KOKKA GAKKAI ZASSHI/ASSOCIATION OF POLITICAL AND SOCIAL SCIENCES. JOURNAL. *see* POLITICAL SCIENCE

300 DEU ISSN 0941-9381
KOLLEGIUM; Schriften der Paedagogischen Hochschule St. Gallen. Text in German. 1995. irreg., latest vol.4, 1997. price varies. **Document type:** *Monographic series, Academic/Scholarly.*
Published by: U V K Verlagsgesellschaft mbH, Schuetzenstr 24, Konstanz, 78462, Germany. TEL 49-7531-90530, FAX 49-7531-905398, nadine.ley@uvk.de, http://www.uvk.de.

301 DEU ISSN 1616-2617
HM742
KOMMUNIKATION@GESELLSCHAFT; soziologie - telematik - kulturwissenschaft. Text in German. 2000. irreg. free (effective 2011). **Document type:** *Journal, Academic/Scholarly.* **Description:** Explores the use of various communications techniques and technologies in society, both old and new.
Media: Online - full text.
Indexed: A39, C27, C29, D03, D04, E13, R14, S14, S15, S18.
—CCC.
Address: c/o Dr Christian Stegbauer, Universitaet Frankfurt, Institut fuer Gesellschafts und Politikanalyse, Frankfurt, 60054, Germany. TEL 49-69-554392, stegbauer@soz.uni-frankfurt.de. Eds. Christian Stegbauer, Jan Schmidt, Klaus Schoenberger.

300 DEU ISSN 0947-0352
KOMMUNIKATION UND BERATUNG. Text in German. 1994. irreg., latest vol.90, 2009. price varies. **Document type:** *Monographic series, Academic/Scholarly.*
Published by: Margraf Publishers, Kanalstr 21, Weikersheim, 97990, Germany. TEL 49-79-343071, FAX 49-79-348156, info@margraf-verlag.de, http://www.margraf-verlag.de.

300 384.0285 DEU ISSN 1860-8353
KOMMUNIKATIONSWISSENSCHAFT. Text in German. 2005. irreg., latest vol.4, 2008. price varies. **Document type:** *Monographic series, Academic/Scholarly.*
Published by: Frank und Timme GmbH, Wittelsbacherstr 27a, Berlin, 10707, Germany. TEL 49-30-88667911, FAX 49-30-86398731, info@frank-timme.de.

300 DEU ISSN 0934-0858
LB43
KOMPARATISTISCHE BIBLIOTHEK/BIBLIOTHEQUE D'ETUDES COMPARATIVES/COMPARATIVE STUDIES SERIES. Text in German. 1988. irreg., latest vol.18, 2008. price varies. **Document type:** *Monographic series, Academic/Scholarly.*
—BLDSC (5105.524000).
Published by: Peter Lang GmbH (Subsidiary of: Peter Lang Publishing Group), Eschborner Landstr 42-50, Frankfurt Am Main, 60489, Germany. TEL 49-69-7807050, FAX 49-69-78070550, zentrale.frankfurt@peterlang.com, http://www.peterlang.com. Ed. Juergen Schriewer.

300 DEU
▼ **KONGLOMERATIONEN**; Studien zu Alltagspraktiken subjektiver Absicherung. Text in German. 2009. irreg., latest vol.2, 2011. price varies. **Document type:** *Monographic series, Academic/Scholarly.*
Published by: Transcript, Muehlenstr 47, Bielefeld, 33607, Germany. TEL 49-521-63454, FAX 49-521-61040, live@transcript-verlag.de.

300 DEU ISSN 0933-1204
KONSTANZER BIBLIOTHEK. Text in German. 1985. irreg., latest vol.24, 1998. price varies. **Document type:** *Monographic series, Academic/Scholarly.*
Published by: U V K Verlagsgesellschaft mbH, Schuetzenstr 24, Konstanz, 78462, Germany. TEL 49-7531-90530, FAX 49-7531-905398, nadine.ley@uvk.de, http://www.uvk.de.

300 DEU ISSN 0936-8868
KONSTANZER SCHRIFTEN ZUR SOZIALWISSENSCHAFT. Text in German. 1989. irreg., latest vol.73, 2007. price varies. **Document type:** *Monographic series, Academic/Scholarly.*
Published by: Hartung-Gorre Verlag, Konstanz, 78465, Germany. TEL 49-7533-97227, FAX 49-7533-97228, Hartung.Gorre@t-online.de.

KONSTANZER UNIVERSITAETSREDEN. *see* SCIENCES: COMPREHENSIVE WORKS

KONSTANZER WISSENSCHAFTSFORUM. *see* SCIENCES: COMPREHENSIVE WORKS

KOREA FOUNDATION NEWSLETTER. *see* HUMANITIES: COMPREHENSIVE WORKS

300 KOR ISSN 1225-0368
HN730.5
➤ **KOREAN SOCIAL SCIENCE JOURNAL.** Text in English. 1973. s-a. bibl.; stat. **Document type:** *Journal, Academic/Scholarly.*
Formerly (until 1983): Social Science Journal (0302-976X)
Indexed: APEL, BAS, IBSS, MEA&I, P06, PAIS, PCI, PsycholAb.
—Ingenta.
Published by: Korean Social Science Research Council, 304 428, Sajick-dong, Chongno-ku, Seoul, 110-054, Korea, S. TEL 82-2-73552159, FAX 82-2-73773264, kossrec@chol.com. Ed. Dai-Yeun Jeong.

300 AUS ISSN 1177-083X
H1
➤ **KOTUITUI**; New Zealand journal of social sciences online. Text in English. 2006. s-a. free (effective 2011). bk.rev. **Document type:** *Journal, Academic/Scholarly.* **Description:** Inquiries and research across all social science disciplines.
Media: Online - full text.
Indexed: A39, C27, C29, CA, D03, D04, E13, R14, S02, S03, S14, S15, S18, SCOPUS, T02.
—CCC.
Published by: (Royal Society of New Zealand NZL), Routledge (Subsidiary of: Taylor & Francis Group), Level 2, 11 Queens Rd, Melbourne, VIC 3004, Australia. TEL 61-03-90098134, FAX 61-03-98668822, http://www.informaworld.com. Eds. Dr. Nick Lewis, Paul Spoonley.

300 DEU
KRITISCHE HUMANFORSCHUNG. Text in German. 1996. irreg., latest vol.3, 1999. price varies. **Document type:** *Monographic series, Academic/Scholarly.*
Published by: Holos Verlag, Breite Str 47, Bonn, 53111, Germany. TEL 49-228-263020, FAX 49-228-212435, info@holos-verlag.de, http://www.holos-verlag.de.

KRONOSCOPE (ONLINE); journal for the study of time. *see* HUMANITIES: COMPREHENSIVE WORKS

300 DEU ISSN 1864-9386
KULTUR - BILDUNG - GESELLSCHAFT. Text in German. 2007. irreg., latest vol.4, 2008. price varies. **Document type:** *Monographic series, Academic/Scholarly.*
Published by: Ibidem Verlag, Melchiorstr 15, Stuttgart, 70439, Germany. TEL 49-711-9807954, FAX 49-711-9807952, ibidem@ibidem-verlag.de, http://www.ibidem-verlag.de.

300 DEU ISSN 1869-5884
▼ **KULTUR - KOMMUNIKATION - KOOPERATION.** Text in German. 2010. irreg., latest vol.5, 2010. price varies. **Document type:** *Monographic series, Academic/Scholarly.*
Published by: Ibidem Verlag, Melchiorstr 15, Stuttgart, 70439, Germany. TEL 49-711-9807954, FAX 49-711-9807952, ibidem@ibidem-verlag.de, http://www.ibidem-verlag.de.

300 DEU
▼ **KULTUR UND KONFLIKT.** Text in German. 2009. irreg., latest vol.3, 2011. price varies. **Document type:** *Monographic series, Academic/Scholarly.*
Published by: Transcript, Muehlenstr 47, Bielefeld, 33607, Germany. TEL 49-521-63454, FAX 49-521-61040, live@transcript-verlag.de.

300 DEU ISSN 1866-6884
KULTUR- UND SOZIALWISSENSCHAFTLICHE STUDIEN. Text in German. 2008. irreg., latest vol.6, 2010. price varies. **Document type:** *Monographic series, Academic/Scholarly.*
Published by: Harrassowitz Verlag, Kreuzberger Ring 7b-d, Wiesbaden, 65205, Germany. TEL 49-611-5300, FAX 49-611-530560, verlag@harrassowitz.de, http://www.harrassowitz.de.

KULTURA; Russland-Kulturanalysen. *see* POLITICAL SCIENCE—International Relations

300 DEU ISSN 1868-405X
▼ **KULTURALITAET UND SUBJEKT.** Text in German. 2010 (Jun.). irreg. price varies. **Document type:** *Monographic series, Academic/Scholarly.*
Published by: Peter Lang GmbH (Subsidiary of: Peter Lang Publishing Group), Eschborner Landstr 42-50, Frankfurt Am Main, 60489, Germany. TEL 49-69-7807050, FAX 49-69-78070550, zentrale.frankfurt@peterlang.com.

300 DEU ISSN 0936-4366
KULTURANALYSEN (BERLIN). Text in German. 1989. irreg., latest vol.10, 2009. price varies. back issues avail. **Document type:** *Monographic series, Academic/Scholarly.*
Published by: Dietrich Reimer Verlag GmbH, Berliner Str 53, Berlin, 10713, Germany. TEL 49-30-700138850, FAX 49-30-700138855, vertrieb-kunstverlage@reimer-verlag.de, http://www.dietrichreimerverlag.de. R&P Beate Behrens.

300 DEU ISSN 1867-769X
KULTURANALYSEN (MARBURG). Text in German. 2006. irreg., latest vol.11, 2009. price varies. **Document type:** *Monographic series, Academic/Scholarly.*
Published by: Tectum Wissenschaftsverlag Marburg, Biegenstr 4, Marburg, 35037, Germany. TEL 49-6421-481523, FAX 49-6421-43470, email@tectum-verlag.de. Ed. Ulrike Prokop.

300 DEU ISSN 1863-219X
KULTURELLE IDENTITAETEN; Studien zur Entwicklung der europaeischen Kulturen der Neuzeit. Text in German. 2007. irreg., latest vol.3, 2008. price varies. **Document type:** *Monographic series, Academic/Scholarly.*
Published by: Peter Lang GmbH (Subsidiary of: Peter Lang Publishing Group), Eschborner Landstr 42-50, Frankfurt Am Main, 60489, Germany. TEL 49-69-7807050, FAX 49-69-78070550, zentrale.frankfurt@peterlang.com. Ed. Sonja Fielitz.

300 AUT ISSN 1810-4541
KULTURELLE MOTIVSTUDIEN. Text in German. 2001. irreg., latest vol.10, 2009. price varies. **Document type:** *Monographic series, Academic/Scholarly.*
Published by: Praesens VerlagsgesmbH, Wehlistr 154/12, Vienna, W 1020, Austria. TEL 43-1-720703506, FAX 43-1-25330334660, m.ritter@praesens.at, http://www.praesens.at.

300 DEU ISSN 1864-0249
KULTURELLE UND SPRACHLICHE KONTAKTE. Text in German. 2004. irreg., latest vol.3, 2008. price varies. **Document type:** *Monographic series, Academic/Scholarly.*
Published by: Ergon Verlag, Keesburgstr 11, Wuerzburg, 97074, Germany. TEL 49-931-280084, FAX 49-931-282872, service@ergon-verlag.de, http://www.ergon-verlag.de.

300 DEU
▼ **KULTUREN DER GESELLSCHAFT.** Text in German. 2011 (Mar.). irreg., latest vol.2, 2011. price varies. **Document type:** *Monographic series, Academic/Scholarly.*
Published by: Transcript, Muehlenstr 47, Bielefeld, 33607, Germany. TEL 49-521-63454, FAX 49-521-61040, live@transcript-verlag.de.

300 DEU
▼ **KULTUREN - KOMMUNIKATION - KONTAKTE.** Text in German. 2009. irreg., latest vol.2, 2009. price varies. **Document type:** *Monographic series, Academic/Scholarly.*
Published by: Frank und Timme GmbH, Wittelsbacherstr 27a, Berlin, 10707, Germany. TEL 49-30-88667911, FAX 49-30-86398731, info@frank-timme.de.

300 CHE ISSN 0171-7332
KULTURHISTORISCHE VORLESUNGEN. Text in German. 1972. irreg., latest vol.107, 2009. price varies. **Document type:** *Monographic series, Academic/Scholarly.*
Published by: Peter Lang AG (Subsidiary of: Peter Lang Publishing Group), Hochfeldstr 32, Postfach 746, Bern 9, 3000, Switzerland. TEL 41-31-3061717, FAX 41-31-3061727, info@peterlang.com.

300 AUT ISSN 1818-1694
KULTURRISSE; Zeitschrift fuer radikaldemokratische Kulturpolitik. Text in German. 1996. q. EUR 22; EUR 17 to students; EUR 6 newsstand/cover (effective 2011). **Document type:** *Journal, Academic/Scholarly.*
Related titles: Online - full text ed.: ISSN 1990-3545.
Published by: IG Kultur Oesterreich, Gumpendorfer Str 63b, Vienna, 1060, Austria. TEL 43-1-5037120, FAX 43-1-503712015, office@igkultur.at, http://igkultur.at.

300 DEU ISSN 1438-8944
KULTURTRANSFER UND GESCHLECHTERFORSCHUNG. Text in German. 2002. irreg., latest vol.6, 2010. price varies. **Document type:** *Monographic series, Academic/Scholarly.*
Published by: Peter Lang GmbH (Subsidiary of: Peter Lang Publishing Group), Eschborner Landstr 42-50, Frankfurt Am Main, 60489, Germany. TEL 49-69-7807050, FAX 49-69-78070550, zentrale.frankfurt@peterlang.com. Eds. Sibylle Penkert, Sigrid Bauschinger.

S

300 DEU ISSN 1862-6092
KULTURWISSENSCHAFTEN (BERLIN). Text in German. 2005. irreg., latest vol.8, 2009. price varies. **Document type:** *Monographic series, Academic/Scholarly.*
Published by: Frank und Timme GmbH, Wittelsbacherstr 27a, Berlin, 10707, Germany. TEL 49-30-88667911, FAX 49-30-86398731, info@frank-timme.de.

300 DEU ISSN 1431-2573
KULTURWISSENSCHAFTEN (FRANKFURT AM MAIN). Text in German. 2001. irreg., latest vol.4, 2008. price varies. **Document type:** *Monographic series, Academic/Scholarly.*
Published by: Peter Lang GmbH (Subsidiary of: Peter Lang Publishing Group), Eschborner Landstr 42-50, Frankfurt Am Main, 60489, Germany. TEL 49-69-7807050, FAX 49-69-78070550, zentrale.frankfurt@peterlang.com. Eds. Hartmut Salzwedel, Ingeborg Siggelkow.

300 DEU
KULTURWISSENSCHAFTLICHE BEITRAEGE; Quellen und Forschungen. Text in German. 2002. irreg., latest vol.6, 2009. price varies. **Document type:** *Monographic series, Academic/Scholarly.*
Published by: J.H. Roell, Wuerzburgerstr 16, Dettelbach, 97337, Germany. TEL 49-9324-99770, FAX 49-9324-99771, info@roell-verlag.de, http://www.roell-verlag.de.

300 DEU ISSN 1860-8809
B2523
KULTURWISSENSCHAFTLICHE STUDIEN. Text in German. 1996. irreg., latest vol.10, 2002. price varies. **Document type:** *Monographic series, Academic/Scholarly.*
Published by: Philo und Philo Fine Arts GmbH, c/o Europaeische Verlagsanstalt, Bei den Muehren 70, Hamburg, 20457, Germany. TEL 49-40-4501940, FAX 49-40-45019450, info@europaeische-verlagsanstalt.de, http://www.philo-verlag.de.

300 CHN ISSN 1671-1254
KUNMING LIGONG DAXUE XUEBAO (SHEHUI KEXUE BAN)/ KUNMING UNIVERSITY OF SCIENCE AND TECHNOLOGY. JOURNAL (SOCIAL SCIENCES). Text in Chinese. 2001. q. CNY 8 newsstand/cover (effective 2006). **Document type:** *Journal, Academic/Scholarly.*
Related titles: Online - full text ed.
Published by: Kunming Ligong Daxue, 253, Xuefu Lu, Kunming, 650093, China. TEL 86-871-5190023 ext 354.

300 001.3 500 CHN ISSN 1674-5639
KUNMING XUEYUAN XUEBAO/KUNMING UNIVERSITY. JOURNAL. Text in Chinese. 1979. bi-m.
Formerly (until 2008): Kunming Shifan Gaodeng Zhuanke Xuexiao Xuebao/Kunming Teachers College. Journal (1008-7958)
Related titles: Online - full text ed.
Published by: Kunming Xueyuan/Kunming University, 2, Kunshi Lu, Kunming, 650031, China. TEL 86-871-5359436, FAX 86-871-5329599.

300 NLD ISSN 1385-1535
KWALON. Variant title: Kwaliatief Onderzoek in Nederland. Text in Dutch. 1996. 3/yr. EUR 60 combined subscription (print & online eds.); EUR 21 newsstand/cover (effective 2010). adv. **Document type:** *Journal, Trade.*
Related titles: Online - full text ed.: ISSN 1875-7324. EUR 48 (effective 2010).
Published by: (Kwaliatief Sociaal-Wetenschappelijk Onderzoek in Nederland), Boom Lemma Uitgeverij, Postbus 85576, The Hague, 2508 CG, Netherlands. TEL 31-70-3307033, FAX 31-70-3307030, infodesk@lemma.nl, http://www.lemma-tijdschriften.nl. Ed. Harrie Jansen. adv.: B&W page EUR 536, color page EUR 1,400; trim 160 x 240. Circ: 183.

300 JPN ISSN 0452-9456
H8.J3
KWANSEI GAKUIN DAIGAKU SHAKAI GAKUBU KIYO/KWANSEI GAKUIN UNIVERSITY. SCHOOL OF SOCIOLOGY AND SOCIAL WORK. JOURNAL. Text in Japanese. 1960. s-a. **Document type:** *Journal, Academic/Scholarly.*
Indexed: RILM.
—Ingenta.
Published by: Kwansei Gakuin Daigaku, Shakai Gakubu/School of Sociology and Social Work, 1-1-155 Uegahara, Nishinomiya, 662-8501, Japan. http://www-soc.kwansei.ac.jp/index.html.

300 JPN ISSN 1342-8861
H1
KWANSEI GAKUIN UNIVERSITY SOCIAL SCIENCES REVIEW. Text in English. 1996. a.
Indexed: MLA-IB.
Published by: Kwansei Gakuin University/Kwansei Gakuin Daigaku, 1-155 Uegahara-Ichiban-cho, Nishinomiya-shi, Hyogo-ken 662-0000, Japan.

KYOTO FURITSU DAIGAKU GAKUJUTSU HOKOKU. JIMBUN SHAKAI/KYOTO PREFECTURAL UNIVERSITY. SCIENTIFIC REPORTS: HUMANITIES AND SOCIAL SCIENCES. *see* HUMANITIES: COMPREHENSIVE WORKS

KYUSHU INSTITUTE OF TECHNOLOGY. BULLETIN: HUMANITIES, SOCIAL SCIENCES/KYUSHU KOGYO DAIGAKU KENKYU HOKOKU: JINBUN-SHAKAI-KAGAKU. *see* HUMANITIES: COMPREHENSIVE WORKS

980 USA ISSN 0890-7218
F1401
L A S A FORUM. Text in English. 1969. q. free to members (effective 2010). adv. **Document type:** *Newsletter, Trade.* **Description:** Provides information about LASA activities, including how to propose panels and papers for the LASA congress, and serves as an important source of information on employment, grant opportunities and conferences of interest.
Formerly (until 1983): L A S A Newsletter (0023-8805)
Related titles: Online - full text ed.: free (effective 2010).
Indexed: PAIS.
—INIST. **CCC.**
Published by: Latin American Studies Association, 416 Bellefield Hall, University of Pittsburgh, Pittsburgh, PA 15260. TEL 412-648-7929, FAX 412-624-7145, lasa@pitt.edu. Ed. John Coatsworth.

300 PRT ISSN 1646-5237
HF5549.A2
LABOREAL. Text in Portuguese, Spanish. 2005. s-a. free (effective 2011). **Document type:** *Journal, Academic/Scholarly.*
Media: Online - full text.
Indexed: T02.
Published by: Universidade do Porto, Praca Gomes Teixeira, Porto, 4099-002, Portugal.

918 980 CHN ISSN 1002-6649
KFT1207
LADING MEIZHOU YANJIU/LATIN AMERICAN STUDIES. Text in Chinese. 1979. bi-m. USD 40.20 (effective 2009). bk.rev. **Document type:** *Academic/Scholarly.*
Related titles: Online - full text ed.
—East View.
Published by: Zhongguo Shehui Kexueyuan, Lading Meizhou Yanjiusuo/ Chinese Academy of Social Sciences, Institute on Latin America, 3 Zhangzizhong Lu, PO Box 1113, Beijing, 100007, China. TEL 86-10-403-5588. Ed. Zhenxing Su. Circ: 1,000. **Dist. overseas by:** China International Book Trading Corp, 35 Chegongzhuang Xilu, Haidian District, PO Box 399, Beijing 100044, China.

300 CHN ISSN 1008-7141
LAIYANG NONGXUEYUAN XUEBAO (SHEHUI KEXUE BAN). Text in Chinese. 1987. q. CNY 8 newsstand/cover (effective 2006). **Document type:** *Journal, Academic/Scholarly.*
Related titles: Online - full text ed.
Published by: Laiyang Nongxueyuan/Laiyang Agricultural College, Changyang-qu, Chunyang Lu, Qingdao, Shandong 266109, China. TEL 86-532-86080472.

300 DEU ISSN 1868-2545
LAND-BERICHTE. SOZIALWISSENSCHAFTLICHES JOURNAL. Text in German. 2006. 3/yr. EUR 10 per issue (effective 2011). **Document type:** *Journal, Academic/Scholarly.*
Formerly (until 2009): Sozialwissenschaftliches Journal (1862-9695)
Published by: Shaker Verlag GmbH, Kaiserstr 100, Herzogenrath, 52134, Germany. TEL 49-2407-95960, FAX 49-2407-95969, info@shaker.de, http://www.shaker.de.

300 CHN ISSN 1674-3210
LANGFANG SHIFAN XUEYUAN XUEBAO (SHEHUI KEXUE BAN)/ LANGFANG TEACHERS COLLEGE. JOURNAL (SOCIAL SCIENCES EDITION). Text in Chinese. 1985. q. **Document type:** *Journal, Academic/Scholarly.*
Former titles (until 2008): Langfang Shifan Xueyuan Xuebao/Langfang Teachers College. Journal (1671-1416); (until 2001): Langfang Shi-Zhuan Xuebao/Langfang Junior Teachers' College. Journal (1008-9616)
Related titles: Online - full text ed.
Published by: Langfang Shifan Xueyuan, 100, Ai-Ming Xi Dao, Langfang, 065000, China. TEL 86316-2188440, http://www.lfsfxy.edu.cn/.

300 600 CHN ISSN 1674-3229
LANGFANG SHIFAN XUEYUAN XUEBAO (ZIRAN KEXUE BAN)/ LANGFANG TEACHERS COLLEGE. JOURNAL (NATURAL SCIENCE EDITION). Text in Chinese. 2001. bi-m. **Document type:** *Journal, Academic/Scholarly.*
Formerly (until 2008): Hebei Zhiye Jishu Xueyuan Xuebao/Hebei Polytechnic College. Journal (1671-1017)
Related titles: Online - full text ed.
Published by: Langfang Shifan Xueyuan, 100, Ai-Ming Xi Dao, Langfang, 065000, China. TEL 86-316-7933671, http://www.lfsfxy.edu.cn/.

LANGUAGE, CULTURE AND SOCIETY. *see* LINGUISTICS

IL LANTERNINO; bimestrale di storia della medicina e medicina sociale. *see* MEDICAL SCIENCES

300 CHN ISSN 1000-2804
H8.C47
LANZHOU DAXUE XUEBAO (SHEHUI KEXUE BAN)/LANZHOU UNIVERSITY. JOURNAL (SOCIAL SCIENCES). Text in Chinese. 1957. bi-m. USD 31.20 (effective 2009). **Document type:** *Journal, Academic/Scholarly.*
Related titles: Online - full text ed.
Indexed: MLA-IB.
—East View.
Published by: Lanzhou Daxue, 298, Tianshui Lu, Lanzhou, 730000, China. FAX 86-391-8912706.

LAPIS (ONLINE EDITION). *see* HUMANITIES: COMPREHENSIVE WORKS

LATIN AMERICA; interdisciplinary studies. *see* LITERATURE

LATIN AMERICA IN TRANSLATION/EN TRADUCCION/EM TRADUCAO. *see* HUMANITIES: COMPREHENSIVE WORKS

300 001.3 USA
LATIN AMERICAN MONOGRAPH AND DOCUMENT SERIES. Text in English. irreg., latest vol.13, 2005. price varies. back issues avail.; reprints avail. **Document type:** *Monographic series, Academic/ Scholarly.*
Published by: University of Pittsburgh, Center for Latin American Studies, 4200 Wesley W Posvar Hall, Pittsburgh, PA 15260. TEL 412-648-7392, FAX 412-648-2199, clas@pitt.edu.

320 USA ISSN 0094-582X
F1401
➤ **LATIN AMERICAN PERSPECTIVES**; a journal on capitalism and socialism. Text in English. 1974. bi-m. USD 648, GBP 381 combined subscription to institutions (print & online eds.); USD 635, GBP 373 to institutions (effective 2011). bk.rev. illus. back issues avail.; reprint service avail. from PSC. **Document type:** *Journal, Academic/ Scholarly.* **Description:** Discusses critical issues relating to capitalism, imperialism, and socialism as they affect individuals, societies, and nations.
Related titles: Microfiche ed.; Microform ed.: (from PQC); Online - full text ed.: ISSN 1552-678X. USD 583, GBP 343 to institutions (effective 2011).
Indexed: A12, A17, A20, A22, A25, A26, ABCPolSci, ABIn, ASCA, AltPI, AmH&L, B04, BRD, CA, ChPerI, Chicano, CurCont, DIP, E01, E07, E08, ESPM, FamI, G08, GEOBASE, H21, HistAb, I05, I13, IBR, IBSS, IBZ, ILD, LeftInd, M08, P02, P06, P07, P08, P10, P13, P27, P30, P34, P42, P48, P51, P53, P54, PAIS, PCI, PQC, PRA, PSA, RASB, RILM, RiskAb, S02, S03, S08, S09, SCOPUS, SSAI, SSAb, SSCI, SSI, SSciA, SociolAb, T02, W01, W02, W03, W07, W09.
—BLDSC (5160.085000), IE, Infotrieve, Ingenta. **CCC.**
Published by: (Latin American Perspective Collective), Sage Publications, Inc., 2455 Teller Rd, Thousand Oaks, CA 91320. TEL 805-499-9774, 800-818-7243, FAX 805-499-0871, 800-583-2665, info@sagepub.com, http://www.sagepub.com. Ed. Ronald H Chilcote. Circ: 750 (paid). **Subscr. outside the Americas to:** Sage Publications Ltd., 1 Oliver's Yard, 55 City Rd, London EC1Y 1SP, United Kingdom. TEL 44-20-73248701, FAX 44-20-73248733, subscription@sagepub.co.uk.

980 300 USA ISSN 0023-8791
F1401
➤ **LATIN AMERICAN RESEARCH REVIEW.** Abbreviated title: L A R R. Text in English, Spanish. 1965. 3/yr. free to members (effective 2010). adv. bk.rev. bibl.; charts; illus. cum.index. 248 p./no.; back issues avail.; reprints avail. **Document type:** *Journal, Academic/Scholarly.* **Description:** Publishes scholarly articles, research reports and notes, and review essays to promote and expound studies of Latin American culture, politics, and economics.
Related titles: CD-ROM ed.; Microfilm ed.: (from PQC); Online - full text ed.: ISSN 1542-4278.
Indexed: A01, A02, A03, A08, A12, A20, A22, A25, A26, ABCPolSci, ABIn, ABS&EES, ASCA, AcaI, AmH&L, AmHI, B01, B04, B07, BRD, C12, C32, CA, ChPerI, Chicano, CurCont, E01, E08, ESPM, FR, G06, G07, G08, H07, H09, H21, HistAb, I04, I05, I07, I13, IBR, IBSS, IBZ, IIBP, ILD, M01, M02, M05, M06, M08, MLA-IB, P02, P06, P08, P10, P13, P27, P30, P34, P42, P45, P46, P47, P48, P51, P53, P54, PAIS, PCI, PQC, PSA, RASB, RILM, S02, S03, S05, S08, S09, S23, SCOPUS, SSAI, SSAb, SSCI, SSI, SSciA, SociolAb, T02, W03, W04, W05, W07, W09.
—BLDSC (5160.120000), IE, Infotrieve, Ingenta, INIST. **CCC.**
Published by: Latin American Studies Association, 416 Bellefield Hall, University of Pittsburgh, Pittsburgh, PA 15260. TEL 412-648-7929, FAX 412-624-7145, lasa@pitt.edu. Ed. Philip Oxhorn.

300 016 USA
LATIN AMERICAN STUDIES WORKING PAPERS. Text in English, Spanish. 1972. irreg., latest vol.9, 1999. price varies. back issues avail. **Document type:** *Monographic series.*
Published by: Indiana University, Center for Latin American & Caribbean Studies, 1125 E Atwater Ave, Bloomington, IN 47401. TEL 812-855-9097, FAX 812-855-5345, clacs@indiana.edu. Ed. Jeffrey Gould.

303.868 USA ISSN 1529-2452
▼ **LATINA/O STUDIES.** Text in English. 2010. irreg. price varies. **Document type:** *Monographic series, Academic/Scholarly.*
Published by: Peter Lang Publishing, Inc. (Subsidiary of: Peter Lang Publishing Group), 29 Broadway, New York, NY 10006. TEL 212-647-7700, 800-770-5264, FAX 212-647-7707, customerservice@plang.com.

300 PER ISSN 0254-203X
F1414.2
LATINAMERICA PRESS. Text in English. 1969. w. (48/yr.). USD 55 Latin America and Caribbean; USD 65 rest of world; USD 110 to institutions (effective 2000). adv. bk.rev. index, cum.index. back issues avail. **Document type:** *Bulletin.* **Description:** Focuses on issues involving human rights, the church, women's rights, grassroots organizations, indigenous issues, the environment, politics and economics in Latin America and the Caribbean.
Related titles: E-mail ed.; Online - full text ed.; ◆ Spanish ed.: Noticias Aliadas.
Indexed: HRIR, ICUIS, RASB.
Published by: Noticias Aliadas/Latinamerica Press, Apdo Postal 18 0964, Miraflores, Lima 18, Peru. TEL 511-261-9469, FAX 511-261-4753. Ed. Elsa Chanduvi Jana. Pub., R&P Barbara Fraser. Adv. contact Lucian Chauvin. Circ: 650.

LATINO POLICY & ISSUES BRIEF. *see* ETHNIC INTERESTS

300 303.868 USA ISSN 2160-0821
➤ **LATINO(A) RESEARCH REVIEW.** Abbreviated title: L R R. Text in English. 1995. s-a. USD 20 domestic to individuals; USD 25 foreign to individuals; USD 35 to institutions; USD 7 per issue (effective 2011). adv. film rev.; bk.rev. illus. back issues avail.; reprints avail. **Document type:** *Journal, Academic/Scholarly.* **Description:** Publishes research notes, scholarly articles, and review articles focusing on the Latino experience in the U.S. and that of populations in their Latin American and Carribean countries of origin. Aims to stimulate critical thought and dialogue about the linkages between the Americas, both North and South.
Formerly (until 1999): The Latino Review of Books (1088-3851)
Related titles: Online - full text ed.: free (effective 2011).
Indexed: Chicano, MLA-IB, SSAI, SSAb, SSI, W05.
Published by: State University of New York at Albany, Center for Latino, Latin American, and Caribbean Studies (CELAC), Social Sciences, Rm 247, 1400 Washington Ave, University at Albany, Albany, NY 12222. TEL 518-442-4890, FAX 518-442-4790, c.bose@albany.edu. Ed. Edna Acosta-Belen TEL 518-442-4719. **Co-sponsor:** Department of Latin American and Caribbean Studies (LACS).

300 MEX
LATINOAMERICA; anuario de estudios latinoamericanos. Text in Spanish. 1968. a. MXN 30 per issue (effective 2000). bk.rev. **Document type:** *Academic/Scholarly.* **Description:** Contains studies on South and Central America: politics, history, culture, education, biography, art, literature, geography, philosophy.
Published by: Universidad Nacional Autonoma de Mexico, Centro Coordinador y Difusor de Estudios Latinoamericanos, Torre I de Humanidades, 1o piso, Ciudad Universitaria, Mexico City, DF 04510, Mexico. TEL 52-5-6221901, FAX 52-5-6221910. Ed. Patricia Escandon. Circ: 1,000.

LATITUD SUR. *see* LAW

LATVIJAS ZINATNU AKADEMIJAS VETIS. A DALA. HUMANITARAS ZINATNES/LATVIAN ACADEMY OF SCIENCES. SECTION A. HUMAN AND SOCIAL SCIENCES. PROCEEDINGS. *see* HUMANITIES: COMPREHENSIVE WORKS

300 ARG ISSN 1852-4435
LAVBORATORIO. Text in Spanish. 1999. s-a. back issues avail. **Document type:** *Journal, Academic/Scholarly.*
Media: Online - full text. **Related titles:** E-mail ed.: ISSN 1852-4427. 1999.
Published by: Universidad de Buenos Aires, Facultad de Ciencias Sociales, Marcelo T. de Alvear, 2230, Buenos Aires, 1122, Argentina. TEL 54-11-45083800, http://www.fsoc.uba.ar. Ed. Astor Massetti.

300 074 FRA ISSN 1776-0771
L'AVISE. Text in French. 2006. m. free (effective 2010). back issues avail. **Document type:** *Magazine, Consumer.* **Description:** Aims to inform through in-depth studies of social or political topics.
Media: Online - full text.
Address: 170 Av. de La Resistance, Le Plessis Robinson, 92350, France.

LAW AND SOCIAL INQUIRY. *see* LAW

LAW & SOCIETY REVIEW. *see* LAW

300 GBR ISSN 1755-2273
H62.A1
➤ **LEARNING AND TEACHING**; the international journal of higher education in the social sciences. Text in English. 2004-2006 (vol.3, no.3); N.S. 2008. 3/yr. GBP 150 combined subscription domestic to institutions (print & online eds.); EUR 216 combined subscription in Europe to institutions (print & online eds.); USD 274 combined subscription elsewhere to institutions (print & online eds.) (effective 2011). adv. reprint service avail. from PSC. **Document type:** *Journal, Academic/Scholarly.* **Description:** Aims to use the disciplines of sociology, anthropology, politics, international relations and social policy to reflect critically on learning and teaching practices in higher education and to analyse their relationship to changes in higher education policies and institutions.
Formerly (until 2008): Learning and Teaching in the Social Sciences (1740-5866)
Related titles: Online - full text ed.: ISSN 1755-2281. GBP 135 domestic to institutions; EUR 195 in Europe to institutions; USD 246 elsewhere to institutions (effective 2011) (from IngentaConnect).
Indexed: A22, B04, CA, E01, E02, E03, EdA, EdI, S02, S03, T02, W03, W05.
—BLDSC (5179.326013), IE. **CCC.**
Published by: Berghahn Books Ltd, 3 Newtec Pl, Magdalen Rd, Oxford, OX4 1RE, United Kingdom. TEL 44-1865-250011, FAX 44-1865-250056, journals@berghahnbooks.com, http://www.berghahnbooks.com. Eds. Penny Welch, Susan Wright. **Dist. in Europe by:** Turpin Distribution Services Ltd., Pegasus Dr, Stratton Business Park, Biggleswade, Bedfordshire SG18 8QB, United Kingdom. TEL 44-1767-604951, FAX 44-1767-601640, berghahnjournalsuk@turpin-distribution.com, http://www.turpin-distribution.com/; **Dist. outside of Europe by:** Turpin Distribution Services Ltd., The Bleachery, 143 W St, New Milford, CT 06776. TEL 860-350-0041, FAX 860-350-0039, berghahnjournalsus@turpin-distribution.com.

300 DEU ISSN 0935-4271
LEBENSFORMEN (BERLIN). Text in German. 1987. irreg., latest vol.17, 2005. price varies. back issues avail. **Document type:** *Monographic series, Academic/Scholarly.*
Published by: Dietrich Reimer Verlag GmbH, Berliner Str 53, Berlin, 10713, Germany. TEL 49-30-700138850, FAX 49-30-700138855, vertrieb-kunstverlage@reimer-verlag.de, http://www.dietrichreimerverlag.de.

300 DEU ISSN 1612-2739
LEBENSFORMEN (FREIBURG). Text in German. 2003. irreg., latest vol.56, 2010. price varies. **Document type:** *Monographic series, Academic/Scholarly.*
Published by: Centaurus Verlag & Media KG, Kaiser-Joseph-Str 267, Freiburg, 79098, Germany. TEL 49-761-1525861, FAX 49-761-1525868, info@centaurus-verlag.de, http://www.centaurus-verlag.de.

300 DEU
LEBENSWISSENSCHAFTEN IM DIALOG. Text in German. 2006. irreg., latest vol.7, 2009. price varies. **Document type:** *Monographic series, Academic/Scholarly.*
Published by: Verlag Karl Alber, Hermann-Herder-Str 4, Freiburg, 79104, Germany. TEL 49-761-2717436, FAX 49-761-2717212, info@verlag-alber.de. Eds. Kristian Koechy, Stefan Majetschak.

LEGETE. ESTUDIOS DE COMUNICACION Y SOCIEDAD. *see* COMMUNICATIONS

LEIBNIZ-SOZIETAET. SITZUNGSBERICHTE. *see* SCIENCES: COMPREHENSIVE WORKS

LEIPZIGER BEITRAEGE ZUR SOZIALMEDIZIN. *see* MEDICAL SCIENCES

300 DEU ISSN 1435-3040
LEIPZIGER STUDIEN ZUR ERFORSCHUNG VON REGIONENBEZOGENEN IDENTIFIKATIONSPROZESSEN. Text in German. 1998. irreg., latest vol.10, 2003. price varies. **Document type:** *Monographic series, Academic/Scholarly.*
Published by: Leipziger Universitaetsverlag GmbH, Oststr 41, Leipzig, 04317, Germany. TEL 49-341-9900440, FAX 49-341-9900440, info@univerlag-leipzig.de, http://www.univerlag-leipzig.de.

LER HISTORIA. *see* HISTORY—History Of Europe

300 CHN ISSN 1009-8666
LESHAN SHIFAN XUEYUAN XUEBAO. Text in Chinese. 1985. m. CNY 8.20 newsstand/cover (effective 2006). **Document type:** *Journal, Academic/Scholarly.*
Formerly (until 2000): Leshan Shifan Gaodeng Zhuanke Xuexiao Xuebao/Leshan Teachers College. Journal (1008-6595)
Related titles: Online - full text ed.
Published by: Leshan Shifan Xueyuan, Limatou, Leshan, 614004, China. TEL 86-833-2276365, FAX 86-833-2276022.

300 DEU ISSN 1864-4031
➤ **LETTERS IN SPATIAL AND RESOURCE SCIENCES.** Text in English. 2008. 3/yr. EUR 209, USD 277 combined subscription to institutions (print & online eds.) (effective 2010). reprint service avail. from PSC. **Document type:** *Journal, Academic/Scholarly.* **Description:** Publishes short papers on new theoretical or empirical results, models and methods in social sciences that contain a spatial dimension.
Related titles: Online - full text ed.: ISSN 1864-404X. 2008.
Indexed: A22, Agr, E01, EconLit, SCOPUS.
—IE. **CCC.**
Published by: Springer (Subsidiary of: Springer Science+Business Media), Tiergartenstr 17, Heidelberg, 69121, Germany. TEL 49-6221-4870, FAX 49-6221-345229, subscriptions@springer.com. Eds. Henk Folmer TEL 31-50-3633875, Luc Anselin TEL 480-965-7533, Roberta Capello TEL 39-2-23992751.

300 DEU ISSN 0340-0425
H5
LEVIATHAN; Berliner Zeitschrift fuer Sozialwissenschaft. Text in German. 1973. q. EUR 231.78, USD 285 combined subscription to institutions (print & online eds.) (effective 2012). adv. bk.rev. reprint service avail. from PSC. **Document type:** *Journal, Academic/Scholarly.*
Related titles: Online - full text ed.: ISSN 1861-8588.
Indexed: A22, A26, CA, DIP, E01, FR, I13, IBR, IBSS, IBZ, P10, P34, P42, P46, P48, PAIS, PCI, PQC, PRA, PSA, RASB, S02, S03, SCOPUS, SociolAb, T02.
—BLDSC (5185.590000), IE, Infotrieve, Ingenta, INIST. **CCC.**
Published by: V S - Verlag fuer Sozialwissenschaften (Subsidiary of: Springer Fachmedien Wiesbaden GmbH), Abraham-Lincoln-Str 46, Wiesbaden, 65189, Germany. TEL 49-611-78780, FAX 49-611-7878400, springerfachmedien-wiesbaden@springer.com, http://www.vs-verlag.de. Ed. Bodo von Greiff. Circ: 980 (paid and controlled).

300 CHN ISSN 1672-1217
LIAOCHENG DAXUE XUEBAO (SHEHUI KEXUE BAN)/LIAOCHENG UNIVERSITY. JOURNAL (SOCIAL SCIENCES EDITION). Text in Chinese. 1982. bi-m. CNY 8 newsstand/cover (effective 2006). **Document type:** *Journal, Academic/Scholarly.*
Formerly: Liaocheng Daxue Xuebao (Zhexue Shehui Kexue Ban)
Related titles: Online - full text ed.
Published by: Liaocheng Daxue, 34, Wenhua Lu, Liaocheng, 252059, China. TEL 86-635-8238158.

300 CHN ISSN 1672-8572
HN731
LIAODONG XUEYUAN XUEBAO (SHEHUI KEXUE BAN)/EASTERN LIAODONG UNIVERSITY. JOURNAL (SOCIAL SCIENCES). Text in Chinese. 1999. bi-m. CNY 20 newsstand/cover (effective 2007). **Document type:** *Journal, Academic/Scholarly.*
Supersedes in part: Liaoning Cai-Zhuan Xuebao (1008-2751)
Related titles: Online - full text ed.
Indexed: L&LBA, PSA, SociolAb.
Published by: Liaodong Xueyuan/Eastern Liaodong University, 116, Linjianghou Jie, Dandong, Liaoning 118001, China. FAX 86-415-4151172, http://www.ldxy.cn/.

300 100 CHN ISSN 1002-3291
AS451
LIAONING DAXUE XUEBAO (ZHEXUE SHEHUI KEXUE BAN)/ LIAONING UNIVERSITY. JOURNAL (PHILOSOPHY AND SOCIAL SCIENCES EDITION). Text in Chinese. 1959. bi-m. USD 37.20 (effective 2009). **Document type:** *Journal, Academic/Scholarly.*
Related titles: Online - full text ed.
—East View.
Published by: Liaoning Daxue/Liaoning University, 66 Chongshanzhong Road, Huanggu District, Shenyang, 110036, China. TEL 86-24-86864173, FAX 86-24-62202048.

300 CHN ISSN 1008-391X
AS452.F895
LIAONING GONGCHENG JISHU DAXUE XUEBAO (SHEHUI KEXUE BAN)/LIAONING TECHNICAL UNIVERSITY. JOURNAL (SOCIAL SCIENCE EDITION). Text in Chinese. 1999. bi-m. USD 31.20 (effective 2009). **Document type:** *Journal, Academic/Scholarly.*
Related titles: Online - full text ed.
—East View.
Published by: Liaoning Gongcheng Jishu Daxue, 47, Zhonghua Lu, Fuxin, 123000, China. TEL 86-418-3350452.

300 CHN ISSN 1674-327X
LIAONING GONGYE DAXUE XUEBAO (SHEHUI KEXUE BAN)/ LIAONING UNIVERSITY OF TECHNOLOGY. JOURNAL (SOCIAL SCIENCE EDITION). Text in Chinese. 1999. bi-m. CNY 4 newsstand/cover (effective 2009). **Document type:** *Journal, Academic/Scholarly.*
Formerly (until 2008): Liaoning Gongxueyuan Xuebao (Shehui Kexue Ban)/Liaoning Institute of Technology. Journal (Social Science Edition) (1008-3391)
Related titles: Online - full text ed.
Published by: Liaoning Gongye Daxue/Liaoning University of Technology, 169 Shiying Jie, Jinzhou, Liaoning 121001, China. TEL 86-416-4199543, http://www.lnut.edu.cn/.

300 CHN ISSN 1000-1751
AS452.T294
LIAONING SHIFAN DAXUE XUEBAO (SHEHUI KEXUE BAN)/ LIAONING NORMAL UNIVERSITY. JOURNAL (SOCIAL SCIENCES EDITION). Text in Chinese. 1978. bi-m. USD 24.60 (effective 2009). **Document type:** *Journal, Academic/Scholarly.*
Related titles: Online - full text ed.
Indexed: CA, P42, PSA, S02, S03, SCOPUS, SociolAb, T02.
—East View.
Published by: Liaoning Shifan Daxue/Liaoning Normal University, 850 Huanghe Lu, Dalian, Liaoning 116029, China. TEL 86-411-84258277, FAX 86-411-84258913.

300 CHN ISSN 1674-0416
LIAONING YIXUEYUAN XUEBAO (SHEHUI KEXUE BAN)/LIAONING MEDICAL UNIVERSITY. JOURNAL (SOCIAL SCIENCE EDITION). Text in Chinese. q. **Document type:** *Journal, Academic/Scholarly.*
Formerly (until 2007): Jinzhou Yixueyuan Xuebao (Shehui Kexue Ban)/Jinzhou Medical College. Journal (Social Science Edition) (1672-4569)
Related titles: Online - full text ed.
Published by: Liaoning Yixueyuan/Liaoning Medical University, no.40, Sec. 3, Gongpo Rd., Jinzhou, 121001, China. TEL 86-416-4673515, FAX 86-416-4673126, http://www.jzmu.edu.cn/.

966.6 USA ISSN 0024-1989
DT621
➤ **LIBERIAN STUDIES JOURNAL.** Text in English. 1968. s-a. free (effective 2010). bk.rev. bibl. back issues avail. **Document type:** *Journal, Academic/Scholarly.*
Indexed: ASD, AmH&L, BibInd, BibLing, CA, CCA, HistAb, I13, IBSS, MLA, MLA-IB, P30, P42, RILM, T02.
—BLDSC (5186.740000), IE, Infotrieve, Ingenta.
Published by: Liberian Studies Association, c/o Mary Moran, Secretary Treasurer, Department of Sociology and Anthropology, Colgate University, Hamilton, NY 13346. TEL 315-228-7538, mmoran@mail.colgate.edu, http://faculty.uncfsu.edu/doyler/lsapg.htm.

966.6 300 USA
LIBERIAN STUDIES MONOGRAPH SERIES. Text in English. 1972. irreg. price varies. charts; illus. back issues avail. **Document type:** *Monographic series, Academic/Scholarly.*
Published by: Liberian Studies Association, c/o Mary Moran, Secretary Treasurer, Department of Sociology and Anthropology, Colgate University, Hamilton, NY 13346. TEL 315-228-7538, mmoran@mail.colgate.edu, http://faculty.uncfsu.edu/doyler/lsapg.htm.

LIBERTARIAN ALLIANCE. SCIENTIFIC NOTES. *see* POLITICAL SCIENCE

300 001.3 PER ISSN 1683-6197
F3410
LIBROS & ARTES; revista de cultura de la Biblioteca Nacional del Peru. Text in Spanish. 2002. bi-m. bk.rev. bibl.; illus. 25 p./no.; back issues avail. **Document type:** *Magazine, Academic/Scholarly.*
Published by: Biblioteca Nacional del Peru, Ave. Abancay 4ta. Cuadra, Lima, 01, Peru. TEL 51-14-287690, FAX 51-14-277331, dn@binape.gob.pe, http://www.binape.gob.pe. Ed. Luis Valera Diaz.

300 RUS ISSN 1606-951X
HM621
➤ **LICHNOST', KULTURA, OBSHCHESTVO/PERSONALITY, CULTURE, SOCIETY.** Text in Russian; Summaries in English. 1999. q. **Document type:** *Journal, Academic/Scholarly.* **Description:** Publishes papers on the analysis on interdiscipline problems of the social theory and social practice.
Published by: (Natsiyanal'naya Akademiya Navuk Belarusi/National Academy of Sciences of Belarus BLR), Nezavisimyi Institut Grazhdanskogo Obshchestva, ul Volkhonka 14/1, str 5, Moskow, 119992, Russian Federation. TEL 7-095-2039067, FAX 7-095-2039169. Ed. Yurii M Reznik.

➤ **THE LIGHTHOUSE.** *see* POLITICAL SCIENCE

300 CHN ISSN 1000-8594
HX9.C5
LILUN TANTAO/THEORETICAL INVESTIGATION. Text in Chinese. 1984. bi-m. USD 31.20 (effective 2009). **Document type:** *Journal, Academic/Scholarly.*
Related titles: Online - full text ed.
—East View.
Published by: Zhong-Gong Heilongjiang Sheng-Wei Dangxiao, 74, Qingbin Lu, Ha'erbin, 150080, China. TEL 86-451-86358606, FAX 86-451-86358761. **Dist. by:** China International Book Trading Corp, 35 Chegongzhuang Xilu, Haidian District, PO Box 399, Beijing 100044, China. TEL 86-10-68412045, FAX 86-10-68412023, cibtc@mail.cibtc.com.cn, http://www.cibtc.com.cn.

300 CHN ISSN 1003-1502
LILUN YU XIANDAIHUA/THEORY AND MODERNIZATION. Text in Chinese. 1989. bi-m. CNY 6 newsstand/cover (effective 2006). **Document type:** *Journal, Academic/Scholarly.*
Related titles: Online - full text ed.
Published by: Tianjin Shi Shehui Kexuejie Lianhehui, 52, Chengdu Dao, Tianjin, 300051, China. TEL 86-22-23398649, FAX 86-22-23307884.

LIMINAR. *see* HISTORY—History Of North And South America

300 SWE ISSN 1654-2029
LINKOEPING STUDIES IN BEHAVIOURAL SCIENCE. Text in English. 1992. irreg. **Document type:** *Monographic series, Academic/Scholarly.*
Formerly (until 2007): Linkoeping Studies in Education and Psychology (1102-7517); Which was formed by the merger of (1973-1992): Linkoeping Studies in Education. Dissertations (0345-7516); (1973-1982): Linkoeping Studies in Education. Reports (0347-1780)
Published by: Linkoepings Universitet, Institutionen foer Beteendevetenskap och Laerande/University of Linkoeping, Department of Behavioural Sciences and Learning, Campus Valla, Linkoeping, 58183, Sweden. TEL 46-13-281000, FAX 46-13-282145, http://www.ibl.liu.se.

300 AUT
LINZER SCHRIFTENREIHE FUER ENTWICKLUNGSZUSAMMENARBEIT. Variant title: LISEZ. Text in German. 1993. irreg., latest vol.10, 2007. price varies. **Document type:** *Monographic series, Academic/Scholarly.*
Published by: Trauner Verlag und Buchservice GmbH, Koeglstr 14, Linz, 4020, Austria. TEL 43-732-778241212, FAX 43-732-778241400, office@trauner.at, http://www.trauner.at.

300 DEU
LITERALITAET UND LIMINALITAET. Text in German. 2007. irreg., latest vol.13, 2010. price varies. **Document type:** *Monographic series, Academic/Scholarly.*
Published by: Transcript, Muehlenstr 47, Bielefeld, 33607, Germany. TEL 49-521-63454, FAX 49-521-61040, live@transcript-verlag.de.

LITERATURA E SOCIEDADE. *see* LITERATURE

300 500 CHN ISSN 1671-1084
LIUZHOU ZHIYE JISHU XUEYUAN XUEBAO/LIUZHOU VOCATIONAL & TECHNICAL COLLEGE. JOURNAL. Text in Chinese. 2001. q. CNY 8 newsstand/cover (effective 2006). **Document type:** *Journal, Academic/Scholarly.*
Related titles: Online - full text ed.
Published by: Liuzhou Zhiye Jishu Xueyuan, 28, Shewan Lu, Liuzhou, 545006, China. TEL 86-772-3946701.

970 GBR
LIVERPOOL LATIN AMERICAN STUDIES. Text in English. 19??. irreg. price varies. back issues avail. **Document type:** *Monographic series, Academic/Scholarly.* **Description:** Aims to showcase cutting edge research in the field of Latin American Studies from a variety of approaches.
Supersedes (in 1999): Latin American Monographs
Published by: Liverpool University Press, 4 Cambridge St, Liverpool, L69 7ZU, United Kingdom. TEL 44-151-7942233, FAX 44-151-7942235, lup@liv.ac.uk. Eds. John Fisher, Steve Rubenstein.

300 AUS ISSN 1832-6919
➤ **LOCAL GLOBAL**; identity, security, community. Text in English. 2005. irreg., latest vol.6, 2009. back issues avail. **Document type:** *Journal, Academic/Scholarly.* **Description:** Concerned with the resilience and difficulties of contemporary community life.
Related titles: Online - full text ed.: free (effective 2009).

S

Published by: R M I T, Globalism Research Centre, Level 5, Bldg 37, 411 Swanston St, GPO Box 2476V, Melbourne, VIC 3001, Australia. TEL 61-3-99251921, FAX 61-3-99253049, globalism@rmit.edu.au, http://www.communitysustainability.info. Eds. Martin Mulligan, Paul James.

300 FRA ISSN 1778-4808
LOGIQUES SOCIALES. SERIE LITTERATURES ET SOCIETE. Text in French. 2005. irreg. **Document type:** *Monographic series.*
Related titles: ◆ Series of: Logiques Sociales. ISSN 0295-7736.
Published by: L' Harmattan, 5 Rue de l'Ecole Polytechnique, Paris, 75005, France. TEL 33-1-43257651, FAX 33-1-43258203. Ed. Florent Gaudez.

300 NLD ISSN 0924-4905
CODEN: TGLBD8
➤ **LONGITUDINAL RESEARCH IN THE BEHAVIORAL, SOCIAL AND MEDICAL SCIENCES.** Text in English. 1981. irreg., latest vol.5, 1985. price varies. **Document type:** *Monographic series, Academic/ Scholarly.*
Published by: Springer Netherlands (Subsidiary of: Springer Science+Business Media), Van Godewijckstraat 30, Dordrecht, 3311 GX, Netherlands. TEL 31-78-6576050, FAX 31-78-6576474.

300 USA ISSN 1574-1001
LONGITUDINAL RESEARCH IN THE SOCIAL AND BEHAVIORAL SCIENCES; an interdisciplinary series. Text in English. 1995. irreg., latest 2006. price varies. back issues avail. **Document type:** *Monographic series.* **Description:** Focuses on key topics in the growing field of research methodology.
Indexed: E-psyche.
Published by: Springer New York LLC (Subsidiary of: Springer Science+Business Media), 233 Spring St, New York, NY 10013. TEL 212-460-1500, FAX 212-460-1575, service-ny@springer.com. Eds. Adele Eskeles Gottfried, Allen W Gottfried, Howard B Kaplan. **Dist. by:** Journal Fulfillment, PO Box 2485, Secaucus, NJ 07096.

LONGYAN XUEYUAN XUEBAO/LONGYAN UNIVERSITY. JOURNAL. *see* SCIENCES: COMPREHENSIVE WORKS

300 IND ISSN 0971-4960
H62.5.I5
➤ **LOYOLA JOURNAL OF SOCIAL SCIENCES.** Text in English. 1987. s-a. INR 300 combined subscription domestic to institutions (print & online eds.); USD 50 combined subscription foreign to institutions (print & online eds.) (effective 2011). back issues avail. **Document type:** *Journal, Academic/Scholarly.* **Description:** Covers recent trends and developments in research in the fields of sociology, social psychology, anthropology, politics, management, rural development and allied branches.
Related titles: Online - full text ed.
Indexed: CA, IBSS, P42, PSA, S02, S03, SCOPUS, SSA, SociolAb, T02.
Published by: Loyola College of Social Sciences, Sreekariyam PO, Thiruvananthapuram, Kerala 695 017, India. TEL 91-471-2591018, FAX 91-471-2591760, lcsstvm@asianetindia.com, http://www.loyolacollegekerala.edu.in. Eds. R Sooryamoorthy, Joye James.

300 CHN ISSN 1673-8039
LUDONG DAXUE XUEBAO (ZHESHE BAN)/LUDONG UNIVERSITY JOURNAL (PHILOSOPHY AND SOCIAL SCIENCES EDITION). Text in Chinese. 1984. q. USD 37.20 (effective 2009). **Document type:** *Journal, Academic/Scholarly.*
Formerly (until 2007): Yantai Shifan Xueyuan Xuebai (Zhexue Shehui Kexueban)/Yantai Normal University Journal (Philosophy and Social Sciences Edition) (1003-5117)
Related titles: Online - full text ed.
—East View.
Published by: Ludong Daxue/Ludong University, 184, Hongqi Zhonglu, Yantai, 264025, China. TEL 86-535-6672716, FAX 86-535-6014101. **Dist. by:** China International Book Trading Corp, 35 Chegongzhuang Xilu, Haidian District, PO Box 399, Beijing 100044, China. TEL 86-10-68412045, FAX 86-10-68412023, cibtc@mail.cibtc.com.cn, http://www.cibtc.com.cn.

300 DEU
▼ **LUEBECKER BEITRAEGE ZUR ETHNOLOGIE.** Text in German. 2010. irreg. price varies. **Document type:** *Monographic series, Academic/Scholarly.*
Published by: Max Schmidt-Roemhild KG, Mengstr 16, Luebeck, 23552, Germany. TEL 49-451-703101, FAX 49-451-7031253, info@schmidt-roemhild.de, http://www.beleke.de/unternehmen/verlage/schmidtroemhild/index.html.

300 CHN ISSN 1008-7834
LULIANG GAODENG ZHUANKE XUEXIAO XUEBAO/LULIANG HIGHER COLLEGE. JOURNAL. Text in Chinese. 1985. q. CNY 6 newsstand/cover (effective 2006). **Document type:** *Journal, Academic/Scholarly.*
Related titles: Online - full text ed.
Published by: Luliang Gaodeng Zhuanke Xuexiao, 38, Binhe Bei Dong Lu, Lishi, 033000, China. TEL 86-358-8248730, FAX 86-358-8221435.

306 SWE ISSN 1101-9948
LUND MONOGRAPHS IN SOCIAL ANTHROPOLOGY. Text in English, Swedish. 1991. irreg. price varies. **Document type:** *Monographic series, Academic/Scholarly.*
Published by: Sociologiska Institutionen, Box 114, Lund, 22100, Sweden. FAX 46-46-2224100, allmaent@soc.lu.se, http://www.soc.lu.se.

300 610 500 CHN ISSN 1674-3202
LUOJIXUE YANJIU/STUDIES IN LOGIC. Text in Chinese. 1981. q. CNY 25 newsstand/cover (effective 2010). **Document type:** *Journal, Academic/Scholarly.*
Formerly: Zhongshan Daxue Xuebao Luncong/Sun Yatsen University Forum (1007-1792)
Related titles: Online - full text ed.; ◆ Supplement to: Zhongshan Daxue Xuebao (Ziran Kexue Ban). ISSN 0529-6579; ◆ Supplement to: Zhongshan Daxue Xuebao (Yixue Kexue Ban). ISSN 1672-3554; ◆ Supplement to: Zhongshan Daxue Xuebao (Shehui Kexue Ban). ISSN 1000-9639.
Published by: Zhongshan Daxue/Sun Yatsen University, 135, Xinkong Xilu, Guangzhou, Guangdong 510275, China. **Co-sponsor:** Zhongguo Luoji Xuehui/Chinese Association of Logic.

300 CHN ISSN 1008-8814
LUOYANG GONGYE GAODENG ZHUANKE XUEXIAO XUEBAO/ LUOYANG TECHNOLOGY COLLEGE. JOURNAL. Text in Chinese. 1986. q. CNY 8 newsstand/cover (effective 2006). **Document type:** *Journal, Academic/Scholarly.*
Related titles: Online - full text ed.
Published by: Luoyang Gongye Gaodeng Zhuanke Xuexiao, Niudu Xi Lu, Luoyang, 471003, China. TEL 86-379-64882290.

300 CHN ISSN 1007-113X
LUOYANG UNIVERSITY. JOURNAL. Text in Chinese. 1986. q. **Document type:** *Journal, Academic/Scholarly.*
Related titles: Online - full text ed.
Indexed: Z02.
—BLDSC (5307.376000).
Published by: Luoyang Ligong Xueyuan/Luoyang Institute of Science and Technology, 1, Daxue Lu, Luoyang, 471023, China. TEL 86-379-65620258, FAX 86-379-65620799. **Dist. by:** China International Book Trading Corp, 35 Chegongzhuang Xilu, Haidian District, PO Box 399, Beijing 100044, China. TEL 86-10-68412045, FAX 86-10-68412023, cibtc@mail.cibtc.com.cn, http://www.cibtc.com.cn.

300 500 PHL
➤ **M S U PROFESSIONAL PAPERS.** (Mindanao State University) Text in English. 1981. irreg., latest no.14, series 2000. USD 5 (effective 2002). **Document type:** *Monographic series, Academic/Scholarly.*
Formerly: Mindanao State University. U R C Professional Papers (0115-7329)
Published by: (Mamitua Saber Research Center), Mindanao State University, Office of the Vice Chancellor for Research & Extension, PO Box 5594, Iligan City, Lanao Del Norte 9200, Philippines. Ed. Raymond Llorca.

300 FRA ISSN 1633-8901
MA PART DE VERITE. Text in French. 2001. irreg. back issues avail. **Document type:** *Monographic series, Consumer.*
Published by: Editions Chemineuments, 1 Chemin des Pieces - Bron, Le Coudray-Macouard, 49260, France. TEL 33-2-41677454, FAX 33-2-41677406, jgiard@cheminements.fr.

300 CHL ISSN 0718-0209
MAGALLANIA. Text in Spanish; Abstracts in English, Spanish. 1992. s-a. **Document type:** *Journal, Academic/Scholarly.* **Description:** Its principal aim is the publication of works written preferably by investigators of the University of Magallanes in the fields of social sciences and humanities with reference to Patagonia, Tierra del Fuego, adjacent Antarctica and islands of the Southeastern Pacific Ocean.
Formerly (until 2002): Instituto de la Patagonia. Anales. Serie Ciencias Humanas (0717-2478)
Related titles: Online - full text ed.: ISSN 0718-2244. 2005. free (effective 2011) (from SciELO).
Indexed: AICP, H21, P08, P27, P48, P54, PQC, SCOPUS, SSCI, W07, Z01.
Published by: Universidad de Magallanes, Instituto de la Patagonia, Casilla de Correos 13 D, Punta Arenas, Magallanes, Chile. TEL 56-61-207058, FAX 56-61-212973, magallania@aoniken.fc.umag.cl. Ed. Mateo Martinic.

MAGHREB MACHREK. *see* POLITICAL SCIENCE

300 ITA ISSN 1721-9809
H7
M@GM@. Text in Multiple languages. 2002. q. free (effective 2011). **Document type:** *Journal, Academic/Scholarly.*
Media: Online - full text.
Published by: Osservatorio Processi Educativi, Via Pietro Mascagni 20, Catania, 95131, Italy. Ed. Orazio Maria Valastro.

300 DEU
▼ **MAINZER HISTORISCHE KULTURWISSENSCHAFTEN.** Text in German. 2010. irreg., latest vol.4, 2010. price varies. **Document type:** *Monographic series, Academic/Scholarly.*
Published by: Transcript, Muehlenstr 47, Bielefeld, 33607, Germany. TEL 49-521-63454, FAX 49-521-61040, live@transcript-verlag.de.

MAISON FRANCO-JAPONAISE. BULLETIN. *see* ASIAN STUDIES

300 GBR ISSN 0959-7646
MAJORITY MINORITY REVIEW. Text in English. 1989. irreg. **Document type:** *Journal, Academic/Scholarly.*
Published by: University of Ulster, Centre for the Study of Conflict, Coleraine, Londonderry BT52 1SA, United Kingdom. TEL 0265-44141, FAX 0265-40917.

300 IDN
MAKARA SERI SOSIAL HUMANIORA. Text in English, Indonesian. 1997. s-a. **Document type:** *Journal, Academic/Scholarly.*
Related titles: Online - full text ed.: free (effective 2011).
Published by: Universitas Indonesia, Kamous Universitas Indonesia, Depok, 16424, Indonesia. http://www.ui.ac.id. Ed. Ali Nina Liche Seniati.

300 MKD ISSN 0350-1698
H8
MAKEDONSKA AKADEMIJA NA NAUKITE I UMETNOSTITE. ODDELENIE ZA OPSTESTVENI NAUKI. PRILOZI/MACEDONIAN ACADEMY OF SCIENCES AND ARTS. SECTION OF SOCIAL SCIENCES. CONTRIBUTIONS. Text in Macedonian. 1970. s-a. USD 20 foreign (effective 2001). **Description:** Research in economy, law, education, history, sociology and philosophy.
Indexed: RASB.
Published by: (Oddelenie za Opstestveni Nauki), Makedonska Akademija na Naukite i Umetnostite, Bulevar Krste Misirkov 2, PO Box 428, Skopje, 91000, Macedonia. TEL 389-02-114200, FAX 389-02-115903, gde@manu.edu.mk, http://www.manu.edu.mk. Ed. Cvetan Grozdonov.

300 MWI
MALAWI JOURNAL OF SOCIAL SCIENCE. Text in English. 1972. a. MWK 70 domestic to individuals; USD 5 in Africa to individuals; USD 8 elsewhere to individuals; MWK 110 domestic to institutions; USD 15 foreign to institutions. bk.rev. back issues avail. **Document type:** *Journal, Academic/Scholarly.* **Description:** Devoted to the study of social science in its broadest sense.
Formerly: Chancellor College. Journal of Social Science (0302-3060)
Indexed: ASD.
Published by: (University of Malawi, Chancellor College, Chancellor College, Faculty of Social Science), Chancellor College Publications, PO Box 280, Zomba, Malawi. TEL 265-522-222, FAX 265-522-0346. Ed. W. Chirwa. Pub. W Chirwa. Circ: 500.

300 DEU
MANAGEMENTCONVENT DER UNIVERSITAET PASSAU - NEUBURGER GESPRAECHSKREIS. SCHRIFTENREIHE. Text in German. 200?. irreg. **Document type:** *Monographic series, Academic/Scholarly.*
Formerly: Schriftenreihe des Neuburger Gespraechkreises (1614-3469)
Published by: ManagementConvent der Universitaet Passau - Neuburger Gespraechskreis e.V., Innstr 41, Passau, 94032, Germany. TEL 49-851-5091003, FAX 49-851-5091102, managementconvent@uni-passau.de, http://www.managementconvent.uni-passau.de.

300 GBR ISSN 1753-7762
MANCHESTER PAPERS IN ECONOMIC AND SOCIAL HISTORY. Text in English. 1990. irreg., latest vol.64, 2008. back issues avail. **Document type:** *Monographic series, Academic/Scholarly.* **Description:** Provides information about social, cultural and economic history.
Formerly (until 2007): University of Manchester. School of Arts, Histories and Cultures. Working Papers in Economic and Social History
Related titles: Online - full text ed.: ISSN 1753-7770. free (effective 2009).
Published by: University of Manchester, School of Arts, Histories and Cultures, Oxford Rd, Manchester, M13 9PL, United Kingdom. TEL 44-161-3061240, FAX 44-161-3061241. Ed. Dr. Peter Kirby.

THE MANCHESTER SCHOOL. *see* BUSINESS AND ECONOMICS—Economic Systems And Theories, Economic History

MANITOBA SOCIAL SCIENCE TEACHER. *see* EDUCATION—Teaching Methods And Curriculum

MANSHOLT STUDIES (ONLINE). *see* BUSINESS AND ECONOMICS

300 500 CHN ISSN 1671-6590
MAOMING XUEYUAN XUEBAO/MAOMING COLLEGE. JOURNAL. Text in Chinese. 1991. bi-m. CNY 8 newsstand/cover (effective 2006). **Document type:** *Journal, Academic/Scholarly.*
Related titles: Online - full text ed.
Published by: Maoming Xueyuan, 139, Guandu Er-Lu, Maoming, 525000, China. TEL 86-668-2923438.

300 DEU
MARBURGER ARBEITSGRUPPE FUER TIEFENHERMENEUTIK UND KULTURANALYSE. SCHRIFTENREIHE. Text in German. 2008. irreg., latest vol.2, 2010. price varies. **Document type:** *Monographic series, Academic/Scholarly.*
Published by: (Marburger Arbeitsgruppe fuer Tiefenhermeneutik und Kulturanalyse), Tectum Wissenschaftsverlag Marburg, Biegenstr 4, Marburg, 35037, Germany. TEL 49-6421-481523, FAX 49-6421-43470, email@tectum-verlag.de.

300 DEU
MARBURGER WISSENSCHAFTLICHE BEITRAEGE. Text in German. 1992. irreg., latest vol.10, 1996. price varies. **Document type:** *Monographic series, Academic/Scholarly.*
Published by: Tectum Wissenschaftsverlag Marburg, Biegenstr 4, Marburg, 35037, Germany. TEL 49-6421-481523, FAX 49-6421-43470, email@tectum-verlag.de.

MARE BALTICUM. *see* POLITICAL SCIENCE—International Relations

954.93 300 LKA ISSN 0047-5912
HC424.A1
MARGA. Text in English. 1972. q. USD 30. adv. bk.rev. **Document type:** *Bulletin.* **Description:** Touches on social and economic problems.
Indexed: BAS, HRIR, IBSS, ILD, P30, SLSI.
Published by: (Sri Lanka Centre for Development Studies), Marga Institute, 61 Isipathana Mawatha, P O Box 601, Colombo, 5, Sri Lanka. TEL 941-585186, FAX 941-580585, TELEX 21642-MARGA-CE. Ed. Godfrey Gunatilleke. Circ: 2,000.

300 LKA ISSN 0304-7709
H62.5.C4
MARGA INSTITUTE. ANNUAL REPORT. Text in English. 1973. a.
Published by: Marga Institute, 61 Isipathana Mawatha, P O Box 601, Colombo, 5, Sri Lanka. TEL 941-585186, FAX 941-580585, TELEX 21643-MARGA-CE.

300 BRA ISSN 0103-8915
H8.P8 CODEN: MARGE3
➤ **MARGEM.** Text in Portuguese; Summaries in Portuguese, English. 1992. bi-w. BRL 60, USD 25 (effective 2001 - 2002). adv. bk.rev. abstr.; illus.; charts. back issues avail. **Document type:** *Academic/ Scholarly.* **Description:** Presents essays on the humanities, history and social sciences.
Indexed: SCOPUS, SOPODA, SociolAb.
Published by: Pontificia Universidade Catolica de Sao Paulo, Faculdade de Ciencias Sociais, Rua Monte Alegre, 984, sala S-21, Perdizes, Sao Paulo, SP 05014-001, Brazil. TEL 55-11-36708113, FAX 55-11-36708109, margem@pucsp.br, http://www.pucsp.br/~margem. Ed. Edgard de Assis Carvalho. Pubs. Maria Elisa Mazzilli-Pereira, Mario Do Carno Guebes. Adv. contact Silvia Borelu. Circ: 800 (paid).

300 DEU ISSN 1864-838X
▼ **MARIE JAHODA SOZIALWISSENSCHAFTLICHE STUDIEN.** Text in German. 2009. irreg., latest vol.3, 2009. price varies. **Document type:** *Monographic series, Academic/Scholarly.*
Published by: Peter Lang GmbH (Subsidiary of: Peter Lang Publishing Group), Eschborner Landstr 42-50, Frankfurt Am Main, 60489, Germany. TEL 49-69-7807050, FAX 49-69-78070550, zentrale.frankfurt@peterlang.com, http://www.peterlang.com.

MARKET FORCES; journal of management thought. *see* BUSINESS AND ECONOMICS—Management

300 500 CAN
MARTIANUSCAPELLA.COM. Text in English. 2000. w. adv. **Document type:** *Journal, Academic/Scholarly.* **Description:** Promotes cross-disciplinary research, open discussion and synthesis, as well as providing an easy way to search through multiple documents for specific keywords and topics.
Media: Online - full text.
Address: 4 Sherman St, Thamesville, ON N0P 2KO, Canada. advertising@martianuscapella.com. Ed., Pub. C K Clarke.

300 DEU
MASSE UND MEDIUM. Text in German. 2000. irreg., latest vol.9, 2011. price varies. **Document type:** *Monographic series, Academic/Scholarly.*
Published by: Transcript, Muehlenstr 47, Bielefeld, 33607, Germany. TEL 49-521-63454, FAX 49-521-61040, live@transcript-verlag.de.

300 ESP ISSN 1989-9610
▼ **MASTER EN METODOLOGIA DE LA INVESTIGACION EN CIENCIAS SOCIALES, INNOVACIONES Y APLICACIONES. DOCUMENTO DE TRABAJO.** Text in Spanish. 2009. irreg. **Document type:** *Monographic series, Academic/Scholarly.*
Media: Online - full text.
Published by: Universidad Complutense de Madrid, Facultad de Ciencias Politicas y Sociologia, Campus de Somosaguas, s-n, Pozuelo de Alarcon, Madrid, 28223, Spain. TEL 34-91-3942671, FAX 34-91-394-2673, infrpys@cps.ucm.es, http://www.ucm.es/centros/webs/fpolisoc/.

300 IDN ISSN 0125-9989
H8
MASYARAKAT INDONESIA: MAJALAH ILMU - ILMU SOSIAL INDONESIA. Text in English, Indonesian. 1974. s-a. IDR 10,000, USD 15. index. **Document type:** *Magazine, Academic/Scholarly.*
Indexed: APEL, BAS.
Published by: Indonesian Institute of Sciences/Lembaga Ilmu Pengetahuan Indonesia, Jalan Jenderal Gatot Subroto 10, PO Box 250 JKT, Jakarta, 10002, Indonesia. TEL 62-21-525-1542. Ed. Mochtar Pabottingi. Circ: 1,500. **Subscr. to:** Yayasan Memajukan Jasa Informasi, Gedung PDII-LIPI Lt.V, Jl. Jend.Gatot Subroto 10, Jakarta 12710, P.O. Box 4509, Jakarta 12045, Indonesia.

300 DEU ISSN 0937-7379
MATERIALIEN AUS DER FORSCHUNG. Text in German. 1984. irreg., latest vol.34, 1997. **Document type:** *Monographic series, Academic/Scholarly.*
Published by: Sozialforschungsstelle Dortmund, Evinger Platz 17, Dortmund, 44339, Germany. TEL 49-231-8596-0, FAX 49-231-8596100, sfs@sfs-dortmund.de.

MATERIALIEN UND STUDIEN ZUR OSTMITTELEUROPA. *see* HISTORY—History Of Europe

300 DEU
MATERIALITAETEN. Text in German. 2006. irreg., latest vol.17, 2011. price varies. **Document type:** *Monographic series, Academic/Scholarly.*
Published by: Transcript, Muehlenstr 47, Bielefeld, 33607, Germany. TEL 49-521-63454, FAX 49-521-61040, live@transcript-verlag.de.

MATHEMATICAL SOCIAL SCIENCES. *see* MATHEMATICS

MATHEMATIQUES ET SCIENCES HUMAINES/MATHEMATICS AND SOCIAL SCIENCES. *see* MATHEMATICS

300 500 DEU ISSN 1439-4154
MATRIX 3000; neues Denken. Text in German. 1999. bi-m. EUR 6.50 newsstand/cover (effective 2010). adv. **Document type:** *Magazine, Consumer.*
Published by: Michaels Verlag und Vertrieb GmbH, Ammergauer Str 80, Peiting, 86971, Germany. TEL 49-8861-59018, FAX 49-8861-67091, info@michaelsverlag.de, http://www.michaelsverlag.de.

MAX-PLANCK-GESELLSCHAFT. JAHRBUCH. *see* SCIENCES: COMPREHENSIVE WORKS

300 GBR ISSN 1470-8078
HM479.W42
MAX WEBER STUDIES. Text in English. 2000. s-a. USD 55 in the Americas to individuals; GBP 25 elsewhere to individuals; USD 160 in the Americas to institutions; GBP 80 elsewhere to institutions (effective 2010). adv. back issues avail. **Document type:** *Journal, Academic/Scholarly.* **Description:** Features articles devoted to the development, application and dissemination of Max Weber's idea.
Related titles: Online - full text ed.
Indexed: A01, A02, A03, A08, CA, P42, PSA, S02, S03, SCOPUS, SociolAb, T02.
—BLDSC (5413.302100), IE, Ingenta.
Address: London Metropolitan University, Calcutta House, DASS, Old Castle St, London, E1 7NT, United Kingdom. TEL 44-20-73201044, FAX 44-20-73201034, office@maxweberstudies.org. Ed. Sam Whimster. adv.: page GBP 225.

059.96 TZA ISSN 0025-6234
MBIONI. Text in English. 1964. m. USD 4.20. bk.rev. index.
Published by: Kivukoni College, PO Box 9193, Dar Es Salaam, Tanzania. Circ: 4,000.

MEASUREMENT METHODS FOR THE SOCIAL SCIENCES. *see* METROLOGY AND STANDARDIZATION

MEDDELELSER OM GROENLAND. MAN & SOCIETY/MONOGRAPHS ON GREENLAND, MAN AND SOCIETY. *see* ANTHROPOLOGY

300 DEU ISSN 1613-8961
MEDIA AND CULTURAL MEMORY/MEDIEN UND KULTURELLE ERINNERUNG. Text in German. 2004. irreg., latest vol.12, 2010. price varies. **Document type:** *Monographic series, Academic/Scholarly.* **Description:** Aims to promote a cross-national and cross-cultural dialogue on memory research in cultural studies.
—CCC.
Published by: Walter de Gruyter GmbH & Co. KG, Genthiner Str 13, Berlin, 10785, Germany. TEL 49-30-260050, FAX 49-30-26005251, info@degruyter.com, http://www.degruyter.de. Eds. Ansgar Nuenning, Astrid Erll.

300 DEU ISSN 2172-8895
MEDIAMERICANA; kultur- und medienwissenschaftliche Studien zu Lateinamerika. Text in German, Spanish. 2004. irreg., latest vol.5, 2010. price varies. **Document type:** *Monographic series, Academic/Scholarly.*
Published by: Vervuert Verlag, Elisabethenstr 3-9, Frankfurt Am Main, 60594, Germany. TEL 49-69-5974617, FAX 49-69-5978743, info@iberoamericanalibros.com.

681.3 FRA ISSN 1626-1429
MEDIAMORPHOSES. Text in French. 2001. 3/yr. EUR 49 combined subscription domestic to individuals (print & online eds.); EUR 59 combined subscription foreign to individuals (print & online eds.); EUR 59 combined subscription domestic to institutions (print & online eds.); EUR 69 combined subscription foreign to institutions (print & online eds.) (effective 2008). **Document type:** *Journal, Academic/Scholarly.*
Related titles: Online - full text ed.
Indexed: IBSS.
—IE, INIST.
Published by: Armand Colin, 21 Rue du Montparnasse, Paris, 75283 Cedex 06, France. TEL 33-1-44395447, FAX 33-1-44394343, infos@armand-colin.fr. Ed. Genevieve Jacquinot-Delaunay.

MEDIATED YOUTH. *see* CHILDREN AND YOUTH—About

300 ARG ISSN 1852-6322
▼ **MEDIOS Y ENTEROS.** Text in Spanish. 2009. 3/yr. back issues avail. **Document type:** *Journal, Academic/Scholarly.*
Media: Online - full text.
Published by: Universidad Nacional de Rosario, Escuela de Comunicacion Social, Riobamba y Berutti, Rosario, Santa Fe, 2000, Argentina. TEL 54-341-4808521, http://www.bdp.org.ar/facultad/comunicacion/. Ed. Silvana Comba.

300 GBR ISSN 1354-358X
➤ **MEDITERRANEA SERIES.** Text in English. 1994. irreg., latest 2000. price varies. back issues avail. **Document type:** *Monographic series, Academic/Scholarly.* **Description:** Features ethnographic monographs and collected works on theoretical approaches to aspects of life and culture in the areas bordering the Mediterranean sea.
Published by: Berg Publishers (Subsidiary of: Oxford International Publishers Ltd.), 1st Fl Angel Ct, 81 St Clements St, Oxford, Berks OX4 1AW, United Kingdom. TEL 44-1865-245104, FAX 44-1865-791165, enquiry@bergpublishers.com. Ed. Jackie Waldren.

300 ITA ISSN 2039-2117
▼ ➤ **MEDITERRANEAN JOURNAL OF SOCIAL SCIENCES.** Text in English, Italian; Summaries in English. 2010. q. free (effective 2011). Index. back issues avail. **Document type:** *Journal, Academic/Scholarly.* **Description:** Publishes research papers in the fields of mediterranean and world culture, sociology, philosophy, linguistics, education, history, history of religion, anthropology, statistics, politics, laws, psychology and economics.
Media: Online - full text.
Published by: Mediterranean Center of Social and Educational Research, Piazza s Giovanni in Laterano 18/B, Rome, 00183, Italy. TEL 39-6-92913868, FAX 39-6-92913868, contact@mcser.org. Ed. Andrea Carteny.

306.42 FRA ISSN 1771-3757
HM258
MEDIUM. Text in French. 1996. q. EUR 40 domestic; EUR 50 in Europe; EUR 52 in US & Canada (effective 2007). **Document type:** *Journal, Academic/Scholarly.*
Formerly (until 2004): Les Cahiers de Mediologie (1270-0665)
Related titles: Online - full text ed.: 1997.
Indexed: IBSS.
—CCC.
Published by: Editions Babylone, 4 Rue de Commaille, Paris, 75007, France. TEL 33-1-42221125, FAX 33-1-45481501, infos@editions-babylone.com.

300 610 DEU
MEDIZINSOZIOLOGIE. Text in German. 1991. irreg., latest vol.20, 2009. price varies. **Document type:** *Monographic series, Academic/Scholarly.*
Indexed: RASB.
Published by: Lit Verlag, Chausseestr 128/129, Berlin, 10115, Germany. TEL 49-30-28040880, FAX 49-30-28040882, lit@lit-verlag.de.

300 CHN ISSN 1002-8986
E175.8
➤ **MEIGUO YANJIU/AMERICAN STUDIES QUARTERLY.** Text in Chinese. 1987. q. USD 28.40 (effective 2009). bk.rev. abstr. 160 p./no.; **Document type:** *Journal, Academic/Scholarly.* **Description:** Contains articles on American political, economic, diplomatic and military affairs and policies, sciences and technology, literature and arts.
Related titles: Online - full text ed.
Indexed: AmH&L, CA, HistAb, P42, T02.
—East View.
Published by: Zhongguo Shehui Kexueyuan, Meiguo Yanjiusuo/Chinese Academy of Social Sciences, Institute of American Studies, No 3 Zhangzizhong Rd, Beijing, 100007, China. TEL 86-10-6400-0071, FAX 86-10-6400-0021. Ed. Wang Jisi. Circ: 1,600.

300 330 CAN ISSN 1204-833X
MEMORIAL UNIVERSITY OF NEWFOUNDLAND. INSTITUTE OF SOCIAL AND ECONOMIC RESEARCH. ANNUAL REPORT. Text in English. 1971. a.
Formerly (until 199?): Memorial University of Newfoundland. Institute of Social and Economic Research. Report (1204-8321); Which superseded in part (in 1989): Memorial University of Newfoundland. Institute of Social and Economic Research. Report and Bibliography (1204-8313); Which was formerly (until 1974): I S E R Report (0840-9927)
Published by: Memorial University of Newfoundland, Institute of Social and Economic Research, Arts and Administration Bldg, St. John's, NF A1C 5S7, Canada. TEL 709-737-8156, FAX 709-737-2041, iser@mun.ca, http://www.mun.ca/iser/.

364 GBR ISSN 1465-2927
➤ **THE MENAI PAPERS.** Text in English; Abstracts in English, Welsh. 1998. irreg. **Document type:** *Monographic series, Academic/Scholarly.* **Description:** Provides opportunities for members of the School to disseminate their work for discussion and comment.
Related titles: Online - full text ed.: free.
—BLDSC (5678.427700).
Published by: Bangor University, School of Social Sciences, Bangor, Gwynedd LL57 2DG, United Kingdom. TEL 44-1248-382007, socialsciences@bangor.ac.uk, http://www.bangor.ac.uk/so/index.php.en?menu=0&catid=0.

300 DEU ISSN 0930-939X
MENSCH UND GESELLSCHAFT; Schriftenreihe fuer Sozialmedizin, Sozialpsychiatrie und medizinische Anthropologie. Text in German. 1997. irreg., latest vol.16, 2009. price varies. **Document type:** *Monographic series, Academic/Scholarly.*
Published by: Peter Lang GmbH (Subsidiary of: Peter Lang Publishing Group), Eschborner Landstr 42-50, Frankfurt Am Main, 60489, Germany. TEL 49-69-7807050, FAX 49-69-78070550, zentrale.frankfurt@peterlang.com, http://www.peterlang.com. Ed. Erwin Riefler.

MENSCH UND UMWELT. *see* ENVIRONMENTAL STUDIES

300 DEU ISSN 0179-3705
MENSCHEN UND STRUKTUREN; historisch-sozialwissenschaftliche Studien. Text in German. 1986. irreg., latest vol.17, 2010. price varies. **Document type:** *Monographic series, Academic/Scholarly.*
Published by: Peter Lang GmbH (Subsidiary of: Peter Lang Publishing Group), Eschborner Landstr 42-50, Frankfurt Am Main, 60489, Germany. TEL 49-69-7807050, FAX 49-69-78070550, zentrale.frankfurt@peterlang.com, http://www.peterlang.com. Ed. Heiko Haumann.

300 DEU ISSN 1610-076X
MENSCHEN - WISSEN - MEDIEN. Text in German. 2007. irreg. price varies. **Document type:** *Monographic series, Academic/Scholarly.*
Published by: Peter Lang GmbH (Subsidiary of: Peter Lang Publishing Group), Eschborner Landstr 42-50, Frankfurt Am Main, 60489, Germany. TEL 49-69-7807050, FAX 49-69-78070550, zentrale.frankfurt@peterlang.com, http://www.peterlang.com.

300 DEU ISSN 1431-3553
MENSCHENARBEIT; Freiburger Studien. Text in German. 1996. irreg., latest vol.28, 2010. price varies. **Document type:** *Monographic series, Academic/Scholarly.*
Published by: Hartung-Gorre Verlag, Konstanz, 78465, Germany. TEL 49-7533-97227, FAX 49-7533-97228, Hartung.Gorre@t-online.de.

300 DEU ISSN 1861-4744
MENSCHENFORMEN PLATEAU. Text in German. 2005. irreg., latest vol.4, 2008. price varies. **Document type:** *Monographic series, Academic/Scholarly.*
Published by: Sine Causa Verlag, Droysenstr 11, Berlin, 10629, Germany. TEL 49-30-74788767, sine-causa@arcor.de.

MERIDIANA; rivista di storia e scienze sociali. *see* HISTORY

300 GTM ISSN 0252-9963
F1421
➤ **MESOAMERICA.** Text in English. 1980. 2/yr. GTQ 50, USD 20 (effective 2005). adv. bk.rev. cum.index. back issues avail. **Document type:** *Journal, Academic/Scholarly.*
Indexed: AICP, AbAn, AnthLit, CA, FR, H21, HistAb, IBR, IBSS, IBZ, IBibSS, MLA, MLA-IB, P08, P09, P30, PCI, PopulInd, RASB, RILM, T02.
Published by: Centro de Investigaciones Regionales de Mesoamerica (CIRMA), Plumsock Mesoamerican Studies, 5e. Calle Oriente No. 5, Antigua, Guatemala. http://www.cirma.org. Eds. Armando J Alfonzo, W George Lovell. Circ: 1,200.

➤ **METASCIENCE**; an international review journal for the history, philosophy and social studies of science. *see* SCIENCES: COMPREHENSIVE WORKS

300 GBR ISSN 1748-0612
HM24
➤ **METHODOLOGICAL INNOVATIONS ONLINE.** Text in English. 2006. 3/yr. free (effective 2011). **Document type:** *Journal, Academic/Scholarly.* **Description:** Publishes on research methods and methodology from all social science disciplines.
Media: Online - full content.
Indexed: A39, C27, C29, D03, D04, E13, P42, PSA, R14, S14, S15, S18, SociolAb.
Published by: University of Plymouth, Roland Levinsky Bldg, Drake Circus, Plymouth, Devon PL4 8AA, United Kingdom. TEL 44-1752-233283, malcolm.williams@plymouth.ac.uk, http://www.plymouth.ac.uk.

➤ **METHODOLOGY**; European journal of research methods for the behavioral and social sciences. *see* PSYCHOLOGY

300 ITA ISSN 1720-2892
MEZZOCIELO. Text in Italian. 19??. m. **Document type:** *Magazine, Consumer.*
Published by: Associazione Mezzocielo, Viale F Scaduto 14, Palermo, PA 90100, Italy. http://www.mezzocielo.it. Ed. Simona Mafai.

300 VIR ISSN 0147-7935
JC365
MICROSTATE STUDIES. Text in English. 1977. a.
Published by: College of the Virgin Islands, Caribbean Research Institute, St Thomas, 00801, Virgin Isl., US. Ed. Norwell Harrigan. Circ: 200.

MIDDLE EAST CULTURES SERIES. *see* HISTORY—History Of The Near East

300 FRA ISSN 2109-9618
▼ **MIDDLE EAST STUDIES/ETUDES DU MOYEN - ORIENT.** Text in English, French, Arabic. 2010. irreg. free (effective 2011). **Document type:** *Journal, Academic/Scholarly.*
Media: Online - full text. Ed. Hichem Karoui.

304.8 ESP ISSN 1138-5774
MIGRACIONES. Text in English. 1996. s-a. EUR 31 domestic; EUR 53 elsewhere (effective 2009). **Document type:** *Journal, Academic/Scholarly.*
Indexed: CA, ESPM, P42, PSA, S02, S03, SCOPUS, SSA, SSciA, SociolAb, T02.
Published by: Universidad Pontificia de Comillas, Instituto Universitario de Estudios sobre Migraciones, C Universidad Comillas, 3, Madrid, 28049, Spain. TEL 34-91-734-3950, FAX 34-91-734-4570, http://www.upco.es/.

304.8 MEX ISSN 1665-8906
JV6006
➤ **MIGRACIONES INTERNACIONALES.** Text in English, Spanish. s-a. **Document type:** *Journal, Academic/Scholarly.* **Description:** Publishes research in the form of articles, essays, and book reviews on international migration throughout the world.
Indexed: A01, A26, C01, CA, ESPM, F03, F04, H21, I04, I05, P08, P42, PSA, S02, S03, SCOPUS, SSciA, SociolAb, T02.
Published by: Colegio de la Frontera Norte, Publications Department, Blvd Abelardo L Rodriguez 2925, Zona del Rio, Tijuana, Baja California 22350, Mexico. TEL 664-631-6300, FAX 664-631-6342, publica@colef.mx. Ed. Juan de Dios Barajas.

325 AUT ISSN 1563-440X
MIGRATION AND DIFFUSION; an international journal. Text in English. 2000. q. EUR 150; EUR 40 newsstand/cover (effective 2006). **Document type:** *Journal, Academic/Scholarly.*
Published by: Odyssee-Verlag-Wien, Zehenthofgasse19/RH.1, Vienna, 1190, Austria. TEL 43-1-3205920, FAX 43-1-32059205, christine.pellech@chello.at. Ed. Christine Pellech.

S

300 DEU ISSN 1434-8896
MIGRATION - MINDERHEITEN - KULTUREN. Text in German. 1998. irreg., latest vol.4, 2008. price varies. **Document type:** *Monographic series, Academic/Scholarly.*
Published by: Centaurus Verlag & Media KG, Kaiser-Joseph-Str 267, Freiburg, 79098, Germany. TEL 49-761-1525861, FAX 49-761-1525868, info@centaurus-verlag.de, http://www.centaurus-verlag.de.

THE MILBANK QUARTERLY; a journal of public health and health care policy . *see* POLITICAL SCIENCE

300 150 BRA ISSN 0102-7484
F2501 CODEN: MIMEES
➤ **MIMESIS (BAURU)**; revista da area de ciencias humanas. Text in Portuguese; Abstracts in English. 1979. s-a. BRL 20, USD 10 per issue (effective 2003). bk.rev. stat.; abstr.; bibl.; charts; illus.; maps. back issues avail. **Document type:** *Journal, Academic/Scholarly.* **Description:** Contains original works of technical, didactic, and scientific character in the area of humanities. Promotes research directed to the academic community in general.
Related titles: Online - full text ed.
Indexed: A01, CA, F03, F04, S02, S03, SCOPUS, SociolAb, T02.
Published by: Universidade do Sagrado Coracao, Rua Irma Arminda, 10-50, Bauru, SP 17011-160, Brazil. TEL 55-14-2357111, FAX 55-14-2357219, edusc@edusc.com.br, http://www.usc.br. Ed. Jacinta Turolo Garcia. Pub. Luis Eugenio Vescio TEL 55-14-2357111. Circ: 500.

300 JPN ISSN 1348-6381
MINAMI KYUUSHUU DAIGAKU KENKYUU HOUKOKU. B, JIMBUN SHAKAI KAGAKU HEN/MINAMIKYUSHU UNIVERSITY. BULLETIN. B, CULTURAL AND SOCIAL SCIENCE. Text and summaries in English, Japanese. 1968. a. **Document type:** *Journal, Academic/Scholarly.*
Formerly (until 2003): Minami-Kyushu Daigaku Engeigakubu Kenkyu Hokoku. Jinbun Shakai Kagakukei/Minami Kyushu University. Faculty of Horticulture. Bulletin. Cultural and Social Sciences (1341-2116); Which superseded in part (in 1995): Minamikyushu Daigaku Engei Gakubu Kenkyu Hokoku. Shizen Kagaku, Jinbun Shakai Kagaku/ Miami Kyushu University. Faculty of Horticulture. Bulletin. Natural Science, Cultural Science, and Social Science (0285-211X); Which was formerly (until 1972): Minamikyushu Daigaku Engei Gakubu Kenkyu Hokoku/Minami Kyushu University. Faculty of Horticulture. Bulletin
Related titles: Online - full text ed.
Indexed: Agrind, JPI.
—BLDSC (5775.478950).
Published by: Minamikyushu Daigaku/Minamikyushu University, 11609 Minami Takanabe, Takanabe-cho, Miyazaki 884-0003, Japan. TEL 81-983-230793.

MINAMI TAIHEIYO KENKYU/SOUTH PACIFIC STUDY. *see* SCIENCES: COMPREHENSIVE WORKS

MIND AND HUMAN INTERACTION; windows between history, culture, politics, and psychoanalysis. *see* PSYCHOLOGY

300 001.3 GBR ISSN 1611-8812
RC321
➤ **MIND AND MATTER**; an international interdisciplinary journal of mind-matter research. Text in English. 2003. s-a. GBP 63, USD 126 combined subscription to institutions (print & online eds.) (effective 2009). adv. back issues avail. **Document type:** *Journal, Academic/ Scholarly.* **Description:** Aimed at an educated interdisciplinary readership interested in all aspects of mind-matter research from the perspectives of the sciences and humanities. It is devoted to the publication of empirical, theoretical, and conceptual research and the discussion of its results.
Related titles: Online - full text ed.: (from IngentaConnect).
—Ingenta.
Published by: (I G P P Theory and Data Analysis Department DEU), Imprint Academic, PO Box 200, Exeter, Devon EXS 5YX, United Kingdom. TEL 44-1392-851550, FAX 44-1392-851178, http:// www.imprint.co.uk. Ed. Harald Atmanspacher.

300 DEU ISSN 1593-7879
B63
➤ **MIND & SOCIETY.** Text in English. 2000. s-a. EUR 184, USD 229 combined subscription to institutions (print & online eds.) (effective 2012). reprint service avail. from PSC. **Document type:** *Journal, Academic/Scholarly.* **Description:** Features cognitive and epistemological studies on social economics.
Related titles: Online - full text ed.: ISSN 1860-1839 (from IngentaConnect).
Indexed: A22, A26, CA, E01, EconLit, P10, P48, P51, P53, P54, PQC, Phillnd, PsycInfo, S02, S03, SCOPUS, T02.
—IE, Ingenta. **CCC.**
Published by: Springer (Subsidiary of: Springer Science+Business Media), Tiergartenstr 17, Heidelberg, 69121, Germany. TEL 49-6221-4870, FAX 49-6221-345229, subscriptions@springer.com. Ed. Riccardo Viale.

300 USA ISSN 1074-9039
BF309 CODEN: MCACEM
➤ **MIND, CULTURE, AND ACTIVITY**; an international journal. Abbreviated title: M C A. Text in English. 1976. q. GBP 396 combined subscription in United Kingdom to institutions (print & online eds.); EUR 529, USD 665 combined subscription to institutions (print & online eds.) (effective 2012). adv. back issues avail.; reprint service avail. from PSC. **Document type:** *Journal, Academic/Scholarly.* **Description:** Provides an interdisciplinary and international journal devoted to the study of the human mind in its cultural and historical contexts.
Former titles (until 1994): Laboratory of Comparative Human Cognition. Quarterly Newsletter (0278-4351); (until 1978): Rockefeller University. Institute of Comparative Human Development. Quarterly Newsletter (0160-3361)
Related titles: Online - full text ed.: ISSN 1532-7884. GBP 357 in United Kingdom to institutions; EUR 476, USD 598 to institutions (effective 2012).
Indexed: A01, A03, A08, A22, CA, CurCont, E-psyche, E01, ERIC, Faml, L&LBA, P03, P20, P27, P43, P48, P54, PQC, PsycInfo, PsycholAb, S02, S03, SCOPUS, SOPODA, SSCI, SociolAb, T02, W07.
—BLDSC (5775.555400), IE, Infotrieve, Ingenta. **CCC.**
Published by: Routledge (Subsidiary of: Taylor & Francis Group), 325 Chestnut St, Ste 800, Philadelphia, PA 19106. TEL 800-354-1420, FAX 215-625-2940, journals@routledge.com, http:// www.routledge.com. Ed. Wolff-Michael Roth. Adv. contact Linda Hann TEL 44-1344-779945.

300 500 PHL ISSN 0115-2742
DS688.S9
MINDANAO JOURNAL. Text in English. 1974. s-a. USD 10 (effective 2001). **Document type:** *Journal, Academic/Scholarly.*
Indexed: BAS, IPP, MLA-IB.
—Ingenta.
Published by: (Mamitua Saber Research Center), Mindanao State University, Office of the Vice Chancellor for Research & Extension, PO Box 5594, Iligan City, Lanao Del Norte 9200, Philippines. Ed. Raymond Llorca. Circ: 500.

300 CHN ISSN 1009-7821
MINJIANG XUEYUAN XUEBAO/MINJIANG UNIVERSITY. JOURNAL. Text in Chinese. 1981. bi-m. CNY 5 newsstand/cover (effective 2006). **Document type:** *Journal, Academic/Scholarly.*
Former titles: Minjiang Zhiye Daxue Xuebao/Minjiang Vocational University Journal (1008-4770); Minjiang Daxue Xuebao
Related titles: Online - full text ed.
Published by: Minjiang Xueyuan, 59, Changdong Nan Lu, Fuzhou, 350011, China. TEL 86-591-83663234.

300 CHN ISSN 1002-4360
GR334
MINSU YANJIU/FOLKLORE STUDIES. Text in Chinese. 1985. q. USD 26 (effective 2009). adv. **Document type:** *Journal, Academic/Scholarly.*
Related titles: Online - full text ed.
Indexed: RASB.
Published by: Shandong Daxue, Hongjialou, Jinan, 250100, China. TEL 86-531-8903860. adv.: page USD 500. Circ: 3,018.

▼ **MIRIADA HISPANICA.** *see* LITERATURE

MISHU/SECRETARY. *see* POLITICAL SCIENCE

300 DEU ISSN 1435-9685
MOBILITY AND NORM CHANGE. Text in English. 1998. irreg., latest vol.7, 2008. price varies. **Document type:** *Monographic series, Academic/Scholarly.*
Published by: Galda und Leuchter GmbH, Franz-Schubert-Str 61, Glienicke, 16548, Germany. TEL 49-33056-88090, FAX 49-33056-80157, contact@galda.com, http://www.galda.com.

MODERN CHINA; an international quarterly of history and social science. *see* HISTORY—History Of Asia

MODERN CHINA STUDIES/DANGDAI ZHONGGUO YANJIU. *see* ASIAN STUDIES

MODERN INTELLECTUAL HISTORY. *see* LITERARY AND POLITICAL REVIEWS

300 LKA
MODERN SRI LANKA STUDIES; journal of the social sciences. Text in English. 1970. s-a. LKR 120, USD 20 (effective 2000). bk.rev.
Formerly: Modern Ceylon Studies
Indexed: BAS.
Published by: University of Peradeniya, P.O. Box 35, Peradeniya, Sri Lanka. Eds. Rarijith Amarasinghe, S Liyange. Circ: 500.

300 CHE ISSN 1619-358X
MODERNE - KULTUREN - RELATIONEN. Text in German. 2002. irreg., latest vol.10, 2009. price varies. **Document type:** *Monographic series, Academic/Scholarly.*
Published by: Peter Lang AG (Subsidiary of: Peter Lang Publishing Group), Hochfeldstr 32, Postfach 746, Bern 9, 3000, Switzerland. TEL 41-31-3061717, FAX 41-31-3061727, info@peterlang.com, http://www.peterlang.com. Eds. Gerhard Droesser, Stephan Schirm.

MOMOYAMA GAKUIN DAIGAKU SOGO KENKYUJO KIYO/ST. ANDREW'S UNIVERSITY.RESEARCH INSTITUTE. BULLETIN. *see* SCIENCES: COMPREHENSIVE WORKS

MONDAY PHENOMENON. *see* ETHNIC INTERESTS

300 954 FRA ISSN 1621-2843
MONDE INDIEN. SCIENCES SOCIALES, 15E - 20E SIECLE. Text in French. 2000. irreg. price varies. **Document type:** *Monographic series, Academic/Scholarly.*
Published by: Centre National de la Recherche Scientifique, 15 Rue Malebranche, Paris, 75005, France. TEL 33-1-53102700, FAX 33-1-53102727, http://www.cnrseditions.fr.

300 FRA ISSN 1777-4977
MONDES CONTEMPORAINS. Text in French. 2005. irreg. back issues avail. **Document type:** *Monographic series, Consumer.*
Published by: Aux Lieux d'Etre, 51 rue de Geneve, La Courneuve, 93120, France. TEL 33-1-48548181, FAX 33-1-48366224.

300 327 FRA ISSN 1961-1331
MONDES ET NATIONS. Text in French. 2002. irreg. back issues avail. **Document type:** *Monographic series, Consumer.*
Formerly (until 2008): Autrement - CERI (1637-1720)
Published by: Editions Autrement, 77 Rue du Faubourg St Antoine, Paris, 75011, France. TEL 33-1-44738000, FAX 33-1-44730012, contact@autrement.com.

300 BRA ISSN 1516-6392
MOSAICO; revista de ciencias sociais. Text in Portuguese. 1998. s-a. **Document type:** *Journal, Academic/Scholarly.*
Indexed: AICP, SCOPUS, SociolAb.
Published by: Universidade Federal do Espirito Santo, Campus Universitario, Avenida Fernando Ferrari, Goiabeiras, Vitoria, ES 29060-900, Brazil. TEL 55-27-3352244, FAX 55-27-3352210, http://www.ufes.br.

300 959 FRA ISSN 1620-3224
HN690.8
MOUSSONS; recherches en sciences humaines sur l'Asie du sud-est. Text in English, French. 1999. s-a. bk.rev.
Indexed: FR.
—INIST.
Published by: Editions Edisud, 30 Av. des Ecoles Militaires, Le Vieux Lavoir, Aix-en-Provence, 13100, France. TEL 33-4-42216144, FAX 33-4-42215620. Ed. Mr. Bernard Sellato.

300 FRA ISSN 1291-6412
HN1
MOUVEMENTS. Text in French. 1998. bi-m. **Document type:** *Journal, Academic/Scholarly.*
Related titles: Online - full content ed.: ISSN 1776-2995. 2005.
Indexed: FR, IBSS.
—CCC.
Published by: Editions La Decouverte, 9 bis rue Abel Hovelacque, Paris, 75013, France. TEL 33-1-44088401, FAX 33-1-44088417, http:// www.editionsladecouverte.fr.

300 CHN ISSN 1009-2323
MUDANJIANG JIAOYU XUEYUAN XUEBAO/MUDANJIANG COLLEGE OF EDUCATION. JOURNAL. Text in Chinese. 1983. bi-m. **Document type:** *Journal, Academic/Scholarly.*
Published by: Mudanjiang Jiaoyu Xueyuan, 86, Guanghua Jie, Mudanjiang, 157005, China. TEL 86-453-6955905, http:// www.mdjie.com/.

MUDOT; magazine for urban documentation, opinion and theory. *see* HOUSING AND URBAN PLANNING

300 DEU ISSN 0344-6840
MUENCHENER AKADEMIE-SCHRIFTEN. Text in German. 1958. irreg. price varies. **Document type:** *Monographic series, Academic/ Scholarly.*
Formerly (until 1969): Studien und Berichte der Katholischen Akademie in Bayern (0453-3798)
Published by: Koesel-Verlag GmbH und Co. (Subsidiary of: Verlagsgruppe Random House GmbH), Flueggenstr 2, Munich, 80639, Germany. TEL 49-89-178010, FAX 49-89-17801111, leserservice@koesel.de, http://www.koesel.de.

300 500 DEU ISSN 1865-6315
MUENCHENER SCHRIFTEN ZUR DESIGN SCIENCE. Text in German. 2007. irreg., latest vol.6, 2010. price varies. **Document type:** *Monographic series, Academic/Scholarly.*
Published by: Shaker Verlag GmbH, Kaiserstr 100, Herzogenrath, 52134, Germany. TEL 49-2407-95960, FAX 49-2407-95969, info@shaker.de, http://www.shaker.de.

MUSEE ROYAL DE L'AFRIQUE CENTRALE. ANNALES - SCIENCES HUMAINES. SERIE IN 8/KONINKLIJK MUSEUM VOOR MIDDEN-AFRIKA. ANNALEN - MENSELIJKE WETENSCHAPPEN. SERIE IN 8. *see* HUMANITIES: COMPREHENSIVE WORKS

MUSEO CIVICO DI STORIA NATURALE DI VERONA. BOLLETTINO. GEOLOGIA PALEONTOLOGIA PREISTORIA. *see* EARTH SCIENCES—Geology

300 708.1 USA ISSN 1559-6893
AM7
➤ **MUSEUMS & SOCIAL ISSUES.** Text in English. 2006. s-a. USD 40 to individuals; USD 159 to institutions; USD 89 museums (effective 2009). **Document type:** *Journal, Academic/Scholarly.* **Description:** Provides a forum for consideration of social issues and their engagement with museums. Each issue focuses on a specific theme, and including theoretical, philosophical and practical perspectives from within and outside of the museum field, explores the intersections between society and museums.
—BLDSC (5989.915500), IE. **CCC.**
Published by: Left Coast Press, Inc., 1630 N Main St, Ste 400, Walnut Creek, CA 94596. TEL 925-935-3380, FAX 925 935-2916, journals@lcoastpress.com. Ed. Kris Morrissey. Pub. Mitch Allen.

300 LBN ISSN 1024-9834
DS36
➤ **AL-MUSTAQBAL AL-ARABI/ARAB FUTURE.** Text in Arabic. 1978. m. USD 60 domestic to individuals; USD 80 in Europe to individuals; USD 90 elsewhere to individuals; USD 100 domestic to institutions; USD 120 foreign to institutions (effective 2000). adv. bk.rev. 200 p./no.; back issues avail. **Document type:** *Journal, Academic/ Scholarly.*
Indexed: P30.
Published by: Centre for Arab Unity Studies/Markaz Dirasat al-Wahdah al-Arabiyyah, Hamra, P O Box 113-6001, Beirut, 2034, Lebanon. TEL 961-1-801582, FAX 961-1-865548, info@caus.org.lb, http:// www.caus.org.lb. adv.: B&W page USD 500, color page USD 850; trim 17 x 24. Circ: 8,000.

300 KAZ ISSN 0130-7789
HX8
MYSL'. Text in Russian. m. USD 165 in North America (effective 2000).
Related titles: Microfiche ed.: (from EVP, IDC).
Indexed: RASB.
—East View.
Published by: Ministry of Information, Ul Zhybek Zholy 64, 4 etazh, Almaty, 480007, Kazakstan. TEL 3272-33-42-69. **Dist. by:** East View Information Services, 10601 Wayzata Blvd, Minneapolis, MN 55305. TEL 952-252-1201, 800-477-1005, FAX 952-252-1202, info@eastview.com, http://www.eastview.com.

N D U JOURNAL. (National Defence University) *see* POLITICAL SCIENCE—International Relations

300 NOR ISSN 0805-4460
N F - RAPPORT. (Nordlandsforskning) Text in Norwegian. 1993. irreg., latest 2011. price varies. **Document type:** *Monographic series, Academic/Scholarly.*
Formed by the merger of (1981-1993): N F - Rapport Nr 20 (0805-438X); (1981-1993): N F - Rapport Nr 40 (0805-4398); (1981-1993): N F - Rapport Nr 50 (0805-4428); (1981-1993): N F - Rapport Nr 60 (0805-4436); (1981-1993): N F - Rapport Nr 70 (0805-4444); (1981-1993): N F - Rapport Nr 75 (0805-4452); Which all superseded in part (in 1990): N F - Rapport (0802-765X); Which was formerly (until 1988): Nordlandsforskning. Rapport (0802-7641)
Related titles: Online - full text ed.
Indexed: ASFA, B21.
Published by: Nordlandsforskning/Nordland Research Institute, Moerkvedtraakket 30, PO Box 1490, Bodoe, 8049, Norway. TEL 47-75-517600, FAX 47-75-517234, nf@forsk.no, http:// www.nordlandsforskning.no.

053.1 DEU ISSN 1615-2468
N I K. (Nachrichten und Informationen zur Kultur) Text in German. 1999. irreg. **Document type:** *Magazine, Academic/Scholarly.*
Published by: Seminar fuer Ur- und Fruehgeschichte, Nikolausberger Weg 15, Goettingen, 37073, Germany. TEL 49-551-393868. Ed. Immo Heske.

300 IRL
N I R S A. WORKING PAPER SERIES. Text in English. 2001 (Nov). irreg. **Document type:** *Monographic series.*

Published by: National Institute for Regional and Spatial Analysis (Subsidiary of: National University of Ireland), National University of Ireland, Maynooth, Co. Kildare, Ireland. TEL 353-1-7083350, FAX 353-1-7083934, NIRSA@may.ie.

300 330 NGA
N I S E R OCCASIONAL PAPERS. Text in English. irreg. price varies. **Document type:** *Monographic series.*
Published by: Nigerian Institute of Social and Economic Research, University of Ibadan, PMB 5, Ibadan, Oyo, Nigeria. TEL 234-22-400501-5. Ed. Eddy C Ndekwu.

300 USA ISSN 1937-2469
H62.5.U5
N O R C UPDATE. Text in English. 2006. q. free (effective 2007). **Document type:** *Newsletter, Consumer.* **Description:** Reports information about studies and survey results of the the National Opinion Research Center. Studies and surveys typically cover topics relating to health and social welfare.
Media: Online - full content.
Published by: National Opinion Research Center, 1155 E 60th St, Chicago, IL 60637. TEL 773-256-6000, http://norc.org/homepage.htm.

300 PNG
N R I DISCUSSION PAPERS. Text in English. 1976. irreg. price varies. **Document type:** *Monographic series, Academic/Scholarly.*
Formerly: I A S E R Discussion Papers
Published by: National Research Institute, PO Box 5854, Boroko, Papua New Guinea. TEL 675-26-0300, FAX 675-26-0213. Ed. Jim Robbins.

300 PNG
N R I MONOGRAPHS. Text in English. 1976. irreg. price varies. **Document type:** *Monographic series, Academic/Scholarly.*
Formerly: I A S E R Monographs
Published by: National Research Institute, PO Box 5854, Boroko, Papua New Guinea. TEL 675-26-0300, FAX 674-26-0213. Ed. Jim Robbins.

300 PNG
N R I SPECIAL PUBLICATIONS. Text in English. 1981. irreg. price varies. **Document type:** *Monographic series, Academic/Scholarly.*
Formerly (until 1989): I A S E R Special Publications
Published by: National Research Institute, PO Box 5854, Boroko, Papua New Guinea. TEL 675-26-0300, FAX 675-26-0213. Ed. Jim Robbins. Circ: 350.

301 NLD ISSN 1382-2373
N W I G. (New West Indian Guide) Text in English. 1919. 2/yr. EUR 80 domestic to institutions; EUR 91.50 foreign to institutions (effective 2009). adv. bk.rev. bibl.; illus. index, cum.index. **Document type:** *Journal, Academic/Scholarly.* **Description:** Publishes articles in the social sciences and the humanities pertaining to the Caribbean, with an extensive review section on Caribbean books.
Formerly (until 1992): Nieuwe West Indische Gids (0028-9930); Which was formed by the merger of (1919-1959): De West-Indische Gids (0372-7289); (1954-1959): Vox Guyanae (0506-1164)
Indexed: AICP, BibInd, C32, CA, H21, HistAb, IBR, IBZ, IIBP, KES, L&LBA, MLA-IB, P08, P30, P42, PSA, RILM, S02, S03, SCOPUS, SOPODA, SociolAb, T02.
Published by: (Koninklijk Instituut voor Taal-, Land- en Volkenkunde), K I T L V Press, PO Box 9515, Leiden, 2300 RA, Netherlands. TEL 31-71-5272372, FAX 31-71-5272638, kitlvpress@kitlv.nl, http://www.kitlv.nl.

300 CHE
NACH FEIERABEND; Zuercher Jahrbuch fuer Wissensgeschichte. Text in German. 2005. a. CHF 39, EUR 24.90 (effective 2009). **Document type:** *Journal, Academic/Scholarly.*
Published by: Diaphanes, Kochstr 18, Zurich, 8004, Switzerland. TEL 41-43-3220783, FAX 41-43-3220784.

NAGOYA JOSHI DAIGAKU KIYO. JINBUN, SHAKAI-HEN/NAGOYA WOMEN'S UNIVERSITY. JOURNAL. HUMANITIES, SOCIAL SCIENCE. *see* HUMANITIES: COMPREHENSIVE WORKS

NAMIBIA SCIENTIFIC SOCIETY. JOURNAL. *see* SCIENCES: COMPREHENSIVE WORKS

300 DEU
NAMIBIAN AFRICAN STUDIES. Text in English. 199?. irreg., latest vol.8, 2004. price varies. **Document type:** *Monographic series, Academic/Scholarly.*
Formerly (until 1997): African Studies of the Academy
Published by: Ruediger Koeppe Verlag, Wendelinstr 73-75, Cologne, 50933, Germany. TEL 49-221-4911236, FAX 49-221-4994336, info@koeppe.de.

NANCHANG DAXUE XUEBAO (SHEHUI KEXUE BAN)/NANCHANG UNIVERSITY. JOURNAL (HUMANITIES AND SOCIAL SCIENCES). *see* HUMANITIES: COMPREHENSIVE WORKS

300 CHN ISSN 1009-1912
NANCHANG HANGKONG GONGYE XUEYUAN XUEBAO (SHEHUI KEXUE BAN)/NANCHANG INSTITUTE OF AERONAUTICAL TECHNOLOGY. JOURNAL (SOCIAL SCIENCE EDITION). Text in Chinese. 1999. q. CNY 5 newsstand/cover (effective 2006). **Document type:** *Journal, Academic/Scholarly.*
Related titles: Online - full text ed.
Published by: Nanchang Hangkong Daxue/Nanchang Hangkong University, 173, Shanghai lu, Nanchang, Zhejiang 330034, China. TEL 86-791-8223348.

NANDU XUETAN. *see* HUMANITIES: COMPREHENSIVE WORKS

300 CHN ISSN 1673-0755
NANHUA DAXUE XUEBAO (SHEHUI KEXUE BAN)/NANHUA UNIVERSITY. SOCIAL JOURNAL (SOCIAL SCIENCE EDITION). Text in Chinese. 1999. bi-m. **Document type:** *Journal, Academic/Scholarly.*
Formerly: Hengyang Yixueyuan Xuebao (Shehui Kexue Ban)/Hengyang Medical College. Journal (Social Science Edition) (1009-4504)
Related titles: Online - full text ed.
Published by: Nanhua Daxue/Nanhua University, Changcheng Xilu, Hengyang, Hunan 421001, China. TEL 86-734-8160521.

300 CHN
NANJING GONGCHENG XUEYUAN XUEBAO (SHEHUI KEXUE BAN)/NANJING INSTITUTE OF TECHNOLOGY. JOURNAL (SOCIAL SCIENCE EDITION). Text in Chinese. 2001. q. CNY 5 newsstand/cover (effective 2006). **Document type:** *Journal, Academic/Scholarly.*
Formerly: Nanjing Gongcheng Xueyuan Xuebao (1671-3753)
Published by: Nanjing Gongcheng Xueyuan, Jiangning Kexueyuan, Hongjing Dadao #1, Nanjing, 211167, China. TEL 86-25-86118016.

300 CHN ISSN 1671-7287
NANJING GONGYE DAXUE XUEBAO (SHEHUI KEXUE BAN)/NANJING UNIVERSITY OF TECHNOLOGY. JOURNAL (SOCIAL SCIENCE EDITION). Text in Chinese. 2002. q. CNY 10 newsstand/cover (effective 2006). **Document type:** *Journal, Academic/Scholarly.*
Formed by the 2002 merger of: Nanjing Jianzhu Gongcheng Xueyuan Xuebao (Shehui Kexue Ban); (1991-2002): Nanjing Huagong Daxue Xuebao (Zhexue Shehui Kexue Ban)/Nanjing University of Chemical Technology. Journal (Social Sciences Edition) (1008-9179)
Published by: Nanjing Gongye Daxue, 200, Zhongshan Lu, Nanjing, 210009, China. TEL 86-25-83239871.

300 500 CHN ISSN 1671-4644
NANJING GONGYE ZHIYE JISHU XUEYUAN XUEBAO/NANJING INSTITUTE OF INDUSTRY TECHNOLOGY. JOURNAL. Text in Chinese. 2001. q. CNY 8 newsstand/cover (effective 2006). **Document type:** *Journal, Academic/Scholarly.*
Related titles: Online - full text ed.
Published by: Nanjing Gongye Zhiye Jishu Xueyuan, 532-2, Zhongshan Dong Lu, Nanjing, 210016, China.

300 CHN ISSN 1008-2646
NANJING LIGONG DAXUE XUEBAO (SHEHUI KEXUE BAN)/NANJING UNIVERSITY OF SCIENCE AND TECHNOLOGY. JOURNAL (SOCIAL SCIENCES EDITION). Text in Chinese. 1988. bi-m. CNY 4 newsstand/cover (effective 2006). **Document type:** *Journal, Academic/Scholarly.*
Published by: Nanjing Ligong Daxue, 200, Xiaolingwei, Nanjing, 210094, China. TEL 86-25-84315745, FAX 86-25-84315134.

300 001.3 CHN ISSN 1671-1165
NANJING LINYE DAXUE XUEBAO (RENWEN SHEHUI KEXUE BAN)/NANJING FORESTRY UNIVERSITY. JOURNAL (HUMANITIES AND SOCIAL SCIENCES EDITION). Text in Chinese. 2001. q. CNY 6 newsstand/cover (effective 2006). **Document type:** *Journal, Academic/Scholarly.*
Related titles: Online - full text ed.
Published by: Nanjing Linye Daxue/Nanjing Forestry University, 159, Longpan Lu, Nanjing, 210037, China. TEL 86-25-85427018.

300 CHN ISSN 1671-7465
NANJING NONGYE DAXUE XUEBAO (SHEHUI KEXUE BAN)/NANJING AGRICULTURAL UNIVERSITY. JOURNAL. Text in Chinese. 1956. q. CNY 10 newsstand/cover (effective 2006). **Document type:** *Journal, Academic/Scholarly.*
Related titles: Online - full text ed.
Published by: Nanjing Nongye Daxue/Nanjing Agricultural University, Weigang #1, Nanjing, Jiangsu 210095, China. TEL 86-25-84395214, FAX 86-25-84434734.

300 CHN ISSN 1001-8263
H53.C55
NANJING SHEHUI KEXUE/SOCIAL SCIENCES IN NANJING. Text in Chinese. 1990. m. USD 62.40 (effective 2009). adv. bk.rev. Index. **Document type:** *Journal, Academic/Scholarly.* **Description:** Covers literature, history, philosophy, economics, law, sociology and other aspects of social sciences.
Related titles: ◆ CD-ROM ed.: Chinese Academic Journals Full-Text Database. Science & Engineering, Series A. ISSN 1007-8010; Online - full text ed.
Published by: Nanjing Shehui Kexuejie Lianhehui, 43, Chengxian Jie, Nanjing, Jiangsu 210018, China. TEL 86-25-83611547. adv.: color page USD 1,000. Circ: 2,000 (paid). **Dist. by:** China International Book Trading Corp, 35 Chegongzhuang Xilu, Haidian District, PO Box 399, Beijing 100044, China. TEL 86-10-68412045, FAX 86-10-68412023, cibtc@mail.cibtc.com.cn, http://www.cibtc.com.cn.

300 CHN ISSN 1001-4608
H8.C47 CODEN: CVEDDX
NANJING SHI-DAXUE BAO (SHEHUI KEXUE BAN)/NANJING NORMAL UNIVERSITY. JOURNAL (SOCIAL SCIENCE EDITION). Text in Chinese. 1955. bi-m. USD 37.20 (effective 2009). bk.rev. **Document type:** *Journal, Academic/Scholarly.* **Description:** Publishes academic articles on philosophy, economics, law, education, psychology, literature, linguistics, and history.
Formerly (until 1984): Nanjing Normal College. Academic Journal
Related titles: Online - full text ed.
Indexed: CA, P42, S02, S03, SCOPUS, SociolAb, T02.
—Ingenta.
Published by: Nanjing Shifan Daxue/Nanjing Normal University, 122 Ninghai Lu, Nanjing, Jiangsu 210097, China. Circ: 3,100.

300 CHN ISSN 1671-0479
NANJING YIKE DAXUE XUEBAO (SHEHUI KEXUE BAN)/ACTA UNIVERSITATIS MEDICINALIS NANJING (SOCIAL SCIENCE). Text in Chinese. 2000. q. USD 20.80 (effective 2009). **Document type:** *Journal, Academic/Scholarly.*
Related titles: Online - full text ed.
—East View.
Published by: Nanjing Yike Daxue/Nanjing Medical University, 140, Hanzhong Lu, Nanjing, 210029, China. TEL 86-25-86662862, FAX 86-25-86682738.

300 CHN ISSN 1009-3222
NANJING ZHONGYIYAO DAXUE XUEBAO (SHEHUI KEXUE BAN)/NANJING UNIVERSITY OF TRADITIONAL CHINESE MEDICINE. JOURNAL. (SOCIAL SCIENCE). Text in Chinese. 1999. q. CNY 5 newsstand/cover (effective 2006). **Document type:** *Journal, Academic/Scholarly.*
Related titles: Online - full text ed.
Published by: Nanjing Zhongyiyao Daxue, 282, Hanzhong Lu, Nanjing, 210029, China.

300 100 CHN ISSN 1001-4667
AS451
NANKAI XUEBAO. ZHEXUE SHEHUI KEXUE BAN/NANKAI UNIVERSITY. JOURNAL. PHILOSOPHY AND SOCIAL SCIENCES EDITION. Text in Chinese; Contents page in English. m. USD 24.60 (effective 2009). charts.
Related titles: Online - full text ed.
Indexed: CA, L&LBA, P42, PSA, S02, S03, SociolAb, T02.
—East View, Ingenta.
Published by: (Nankai Daxue/Nankai University), Nankai Xuebao Bianjibu, Balitai Nankai-qu, Tianjin 300071, China. TEL 34412-538. Ed. Zhu Guanghua. **Dist. outside China by:** China International Book Trading Corp, 35 Chegongzhuang Xilu, Haidian District, PO Box 399, Beijing 100044, China.

300 CHN ISSN 1009-3621
NANNING ZHIYE JISHU XUEYUAN XUEBAO/NANNING POLYTECHNIC. JOURNAL. Text in Chinese. 1993. q. CNY 8 newsstand/cover (effective 2006). **Document type:** *Journal, Academic/Scholarly.*
Related titles: Online - full text ed.
Published by: Nanning Zhiye Jishu Xueyuan, Wuliting, Nanning, 530003, China.

300 CHN ISSN 1673-2359
NANTONG DAXUE XUEBAO (SHEHUI KEXUE BAN)/NANTONG UNIVERSITY. JOURNAL (SOCIAL SCIENCE EDITION). Text in Chinese. 1985. bi-m. CNY 5 newsstand/cover (effective 2006). **Document type:** *Journal, Academic/Scholarly.*
Former titles: Nantong Shifan Xueyuan Xuebao (Zhexue Shehui Kexue Ban); Nantong Shi-Zhuan Xuebao (Shehui Kexue Ban) (1003-7489)
Related titles: Online - full text ed.
Published by: Nantong Daxue, 40, Qingnian Dong Lu, Nantong, 226007, China. TEL 86-513-85015557.

300 500 CHN ISSN 1671-6191
NANTONG FANGZHI ZHIYE JISHU XUEYUAN XUEBAO/NANTONG TEXTILE VOCATIONAL TECHNOLOGY COLLEGE. JOURNAL. Text in Chinese. 2001. q. CNY 5 newsstand/cover (effective 2006). **Document type:** *Journal, Academic/Scholarly.*
Related titles: Online - full text ed.
Published by: Nantong Fangzhi Zhiye Jishu Xueyuan, 69, Qingnan Dong Lu, Nantong, 226007, China. TEL 86-513-5238031.

300 500 CHN ISSN 1674-5132
▼ **NANYANG LIGONG XUEYUAN XUEBAO/NANYANG INSTITUTE OF TECHNOLOGY. JOURNAL.** Text in Chinese. 2009. bi-m. **Document type:** *Journal, Academic/Scholarly.*
Related titles: Online - full text ed.
Published by: Nanyang Ligong Xueyuan/Nanyang Institute of Technology, 80, Changjiang Lu, Nanyan, 473004, China. TEL 86-377-62076887, FAX 86-377-62076885.

NANYANG SHIFAN XUEYUAN XUEBAO. *see* SCIENCES: COMPREHENSIVE WORKS

300 DEU ISSN 0176-6023
NASSAUER GESPRAECHE DER FREIHERR-VOM-STEIN-GESELLSCHAFT. Text in German. 1985. irreg., latest vol.8, 2010. price varies. **Document type:** *Monographic series, Academic/Scholarly.*
Published by: (Freiherr-vom-Stein-Gesellschaft), Franz Steiner Verlag GmbH, Birkenwaldstr 44, Stuttgart, 70191, Germany. TEL 49-711-25820, FAX 49-711-2582290, service@steiner-verlag.de, http://www.steiner-verlag.de. R&P Sabine Koerner.

NATIONAL COUNCIL FOR THE SOCIAL STUDIES. BULLETINS. *see* EDUCATION—Teaching Methods And Curriculum

301 304.6 338.91 USA
NATIONAL HUMAN DEVELOPMENT REPORTS. Abbreviated title: N H D R. Text in English. 19??. irreg. free (effective 2010). back issues avail. **Document type:** *Report, Trade.* **Description:** Contains vital data and statistics on population studies on different nations with each report.
Related titles: Online - full text ed.
Published by: United Nations Development Programme, Human Development Report Office, 304 E 45th St, 12th Fl, New York, NY 10017. TEL 212-906-3661, FAX 212-906-5161, william.orme@undp.org.

300 GBR ISSN 0077-491X
H11
NATIONAL INSTITUTE OF ECONOMIC AND SOCIAL RESEARCH, LONDON. ANNUAL REPORT. Text in English. 1941. a. free to members (effective 2009). back issues avail. **Document type:** *Corporate.*
Formerly (until 1942): National Institute of Economic and Social Research. Report
Related titles: Online - full text ed.: free (effective 2009).
Indexed: AICP.
—BLDSC (1364.670000).
Published by: National Institute of Economic and Social Research, 2 Dean Trench St, Smith Sq, London, SW1P 3HE, United Kingdom. TEL 44-20-72227665, FAX 44-20-76541900, enquiries@niesr.ac.uk.

NATIONAL INSTITUTE OF ECONOMIC AND SOCIAL RESEARCH, LONDON. ECONOMIC AND SOCIAL STUDIES. *see* BUSINESS AND ECONOMICS

NATIONAL RESEARCH COUNCIL OF THAILAND. JOURNAL. *see* SCIENCES: COMPREHENSIVE WORKS

300 USA ISSN 2154-1736
H61
➤ **NATIONAL SOCIAL SCIENCE JOURNAL.** Text in English. 1986. q. free to members (effective 2010). back issues avail. **Document type:** *Journal, Academic/Scholarly.*
Related titles: Online - full text ed.: ISSN 2154-1744. free (effective 2010).
Indexed: S02, S03, T02.
Published by: National Social Science Association, 2020 Hills Lake Dr, El Cajon, CA 92020. TEL 619-448-4709, FAX 619-258-7636, natsocsci@aol.com.

300 TWN ISSN 0077-5835
H8.C47
NATIONAL TAIWAN UNIVERSITY. COLLEGE OF LAW. JOURNAL OF SOCIAL SCIENCE. Text in Chinese, English. 1950. irreg., latest vol.41, 1993.
Published by: National Taiwan University, College of Law, Taipei, Taiwan. FAX 02-3948914.

330 IRL
NATIONAL UNIVERSITY OF IRELAND, GALWAY. SOCIAL SCIENCES RESEARCH CENTRE. OCCASIONAL PAPER. Text in English. 1998. irreg. **Document type:** *Monographic series, Academic/Scholarly.*
Published by: National University of Ireland, Galway, Social Sciences Research Centre/Ollscoil nah Eireann, Gaillimh, Galway, Ireland.

S

300 320 GBR ISSN 0090-5992
DR24
➤ **NATIONALITIES PAPERS.** Text in English. 1972. bi-m. GBP 751 combined subscription in United Kingdom to institutions (print & online eds.); EUR 996, USD 1,245 combined subscription to institutions (print & online eds.) (effective 2012). adv. bk.rev. bibl.; illus. index. back issues avail.; reprint service avail. from PSC. **Document type:** *Journal, Academic/Scholarly.* **Description:** Focuses on nationality and minority questions in Eastern Europe and former USSR.
Related titles: Microfiche ed.; Online - full text ed.: ISSN 1465-3923. GBP 676 in United Kingdom to institutions; EUR 896, USD 1,120 to institutions (effective 2012) (from IngentaConnect).
Indexed: A01, A03, A08, A22, ABS&EES, AmHI, B21, CA, DIP, E01, E17, ESPM, GEOBASE, H07, HRIR, HistAb, I02, I08, I13, IBR, IBSS, IBZ, L&LBA, M10, MLA, MLA-IB, P10, P30, P34, P42, P45, P46, P48, P53, P54, PAIS, PQC, PSA, Perlslam, RASB, RILM, S02, S03, S21, SCOPUS, SOPODA, SSA, SociolAb, T02, W04.
—IE, Infotrieve, Ingenta. **CCC.**
Published by: (Association for the Study of Nationalities (Ex-U.S.S.R. and East Europe), Inc. USA), Routledge (Subsidiary of: Taylor & Francis Group), 4 Park Sq, Milton Park, Abingdon, Oxon OX14 4RN, United Kingdom. TEL 44-20-70176000, FAX 44-20-70176336, subscriptions@tandf.co.uk, http://www.routledge.com. Ed. Steve O Sabol TEL 704-687-4632. Adv. contact Linda Hann TEL 44-1344-779945. **Subscr. to:** Taylor & Francis Ltd., Journals Customer Service, Sheepen Pl, Colchester, Essex CO3 3LP, United Kingdom. TEL 44-20-70175544, FAX 44-20-70175198.

330 DNK ISSN 0028-0453
HB9
➤ **NATIONALOEKONOMISK TIDSSKRIFT/DANISH JOURNAL OF ECONOMICS.** Text in Danish; Text occasionally in Multiple languages, English; Summaries in English. 1873. 3/yr. DKK 445; DKK 220 to students (effective 2009). adv. bk.rev. bibl. index, cum.index every 25 yrs. reprints avail. **Document type:** *Journal, Academic/Scholarly.*
Related titles: Microfilm ed.: (from PQC).
Indexed: A20, ASCA, DIP, EconLit, IBR, IBZ, JEL, P06, P30, PCI, RASB.
Published by: Nationaloekonomisk Forening, c/o Peder Andersen, University of Copenhagen, Studiestraede 6, Copenhagen K, 1455, Denmark. TEL 45-35-324419, FAX 45-35-323000. Eds. Christian Hjorth-Andersen, Claus Thustrup Kreiner.

300 KAZ
NATSIONALNAYA AKADEMIYA NAUK RESPUBLIKI KAZAKHSTAN. IZVESTIYA. SERIYA OBSHCHESTVENNYKH NAUK. Text in Kazakh, Russian. bi-m. USD 245 in North America (effective 2000).
Published by: Academy of Sciences of Kazakhstan, Ul Kabanbai Batyra 69-a, Almaty, 480100, Kazakhstan. TEL 7-3732-615608, FAX 7-3272-615314, adm@geol.academ.alma-ata.su. **Dist. by:** East View Information Services, 10601 Wayzata Blvd, Minneapolis, MN 55305. TEL 952-252-1201, 800-477-1005, FAX 952-252-1202, info@eastview.com, http://www.eastview.com.

300 BLR
➤ **NATSIYANAL'NAYA AKADEMIYA NAVUK BELARUSI. VESTSI. SERYYA GUMANITARNYKH NAVUK/NATIONAL ACADEMY OF SCIENCES OF BELARUS. PROCEEDINGS. SERIES OF HUMANITARIAN SCIENCES/NATSIONAL'NAYA AKADEMIYA NAUK BELARUSI. IZVESTIYA. SERIYA GUMANITARNYKH NAUK.** Text in Belorussian; Summaries in Russian, English. 1956. q. bibl.; charts; illus. index. **Document type:** *Journal, Academic/Scholarly.* **Description:** Presents papers on problems of philosophy and law, sociology, economics, Byelorussian history, art, folklore, literature and linguistics.
Former titles (until 1998): Akademiya Navuk Belarusi. Vestsi. Seryya Gumanitarnykh Navuk (1024-5928); (until 1994): Akademiya Navuk Belarusskai S.S.R. Vestsi. Seryya Gramadskykh Navuk (0321-1649)
Indexed: AICP, BibLing, IBSS, MLA-IB, RASB.
Published by: (Natsiyanal'naya Akademiya Navuk Belarusi/National Academy of Sciences of Belarus), Vydavetstvo Belaruskaya Navuka/Publishing House Belaruskaya Navuka, ul F. Skaryny, 40, Minsk, 220141, Belarus. TEL 375-17-2633700, FAX 375-17-2637618, belnauka@infonet.by, http://www.belnauka.by. Ed. A A Kovalenya. Circ: 350.

300 363.3 USA
NATURAL HAZARDS CENTER. QUICK RESPONSE REPORTS. Text in English. 1986. irreg., latest vol.213, 2009. free (effective 2010). back issues avail.; reprints avail. **Document type:** *Report.* **Description:** Consists of reports presenting the results of research by social scientists conducted immediately following disasters. Covers immediate impact and response for a broad range of disasters - natural and caused by humans - in diverse settings, and affecting all types of human communities.
Media: Online - full text.
Published by: (Quick Response Program), University of Colorado, Institute of Behavioral Science, Program on Environment and Behavior, Natural Hazards Center, 482 UCB, Boulder, CO 80309. TEL 303-492-6818, FAX 303-492-2151, hazctr@colorado.edu. **Co-sponsor:** National Science Foundation.

363.7 USA
NATURAL HAZARDS CENTER. SPECIAL PUBLICATIONS (ONLINE). Text in English. 1981. irreg., latest vol.39, 2003. free (effective 2010). back issues avail.; reprints avail. **Document type:** *Proceedings, Academic/Scholarly.* **Description:** Consists of studies and analyses that do not fit into the Center's other series. Includes conference proceedings and other works that add to the body of knowledge on societal response to natural hazards.
Formerly (until 2000): Natural Hazards Center. Special Publications (Print)
Media: Online - full text.
Published by: University of Colorado, Institute of Behavioral Science, Program on Environment and Behavior, Natural Hazards Center, 482 UCB, Boulder, CO 80309. TEL 303-492-6818, FAX 303-492-2151, hazctr@colorado.edu.

300 363.3 USA ISSN 0082-5166
NATURAL HAZARDS RESEARCH WORKING PAPERS. Text in English. 1968. irreg., latest vol.109, 2004. free (effective 2010). back issues avail.; reprints avail. **Document type:** *Monographic series, Academic/Scholarly.*
Media: Online - full text.
Indexed: GeoRef, SpeleolAb.
Published by: University of Colorado, Institute of Behavioral Science, Program on Environment and Behavior, Natural Hazards Center, 482 UCB, Boulder, CO 80309. TEL 303-492-6818, FAX 303-492-2151, hazctr@colorado.edu.

NATURES SCIENCES SOCIETES. *see* EARTH SCIENCES

300 RUS
NAUCHNAYA MYSL' KAVKAZA. Text in Russian. 1995. q. USD 110 in North America (effective 2000).
Indexed: RASB.
Address: Ul Pushkinskaya 140, Rostov-na-Donu, 344006, Russian Federation. TEL 8632-643052. Ed. Yu A Zhdanov. **Dist. by:** East View Information Services, 10601 Wayzata Blvd, Minneapolis, MN 55305. TEL 952-252-1201, 800-477-1005, FAX 952-252-1202, info@eastview.com, http://www.eastview.com.

300 UKR ISSN 0130-7037
NAUKA I SUSPIL'STVO/SCIENCE AND SOCIETY. Text in Ukrainian. 1951. m. USD 184 foreign (effective 2005). **Document type:** *Journal, Academic/Scholarly.* **Description:** Popular science and literature magazine for family reading and self-education.
—BLDSC (0119.350000).
Published by: (Tovarystvo Znannia), Vydavnytstvo Presa Ukrainy, pr-kt Peremohy, Kyiv 47, 03047, Ukraine. TEL 380-44-4548272, FAX 380-44-4548810. Ed. B M Hychko. **Dist. by:** East View Information Services, 10601 Wayzata Blvd, Minneapolis, MN 55305. TEL 952-252-1201, 800-477-1005, FAX 952-252-1202, info@eastview.com, http://www.eastview.com.

300 305.8927 NLD ISSN 1877-6477
NEDERLANDS-ARABISCHE KRING. MAGAZINE. Variant title: N A K Magazine. Text in Dutch. 1992. s-a. EUR 5 newsstand/cover (effective 2011).
Published by: Nederlands-Arabische Kring, Hondsrug 889, Utrecht, 3524 BZ, Netherlands. info@nederlandsarabischekring.nl, http://www.nederlandsarabischekring.nl.

300 BEL ISSN 1780-9231
NEGOCIATIONS. Text in French. 2004. s-a. EUR 60 (effective 2011). back issues avail. **Document type:** *Journal, Academic/Scholarly.*
Related titles: Online - full text ed.: ISSN 1782-1452.
Published by: (Centre de Recherche et d'Intervention Sociologiques, Faculte d'Economie de Gestion et de Sciences Sociales), De Boeck Universite (Subsidiary of: Editis), Fond Jean-Paques 4, Louvain-la-Neuve, 1348, Belgium. TEL 32-10-482511, FAX 32-10-482519, info@superieur.deboeck.com.

300 CHN
AS452.H815
NEI MENGGU DAXUE XUEBAO (RENWEN - SHEHUI KEXUE BAN)/INNER MONGOLIA UNIVERSITY. JOURNAL (HUMANITIES & SOCIAL SCIENCES EDITION). Text in Chinese. 1959. bi-m. USD 24.60 (effective 2009). index. 120 p./no.; **Document type:** *Journal, Academic/Scholarly.* **Description:** Covers linguistics, literature, philosophy, Mongolian studies, religion, history, politics, economics and law.
Formerly: Nei Menggu Daxue Xuebao (Shehui Kexue Ban)/Inner Mongolian University. Journal (Social Science Edition) (1000-5218)
Related titles: Online - full text ed.
—East View.
Published by: Nei Menggu Daxue/Inner Mongolian University, Xincheng-qu, 235, Daxue Lu, Hohhot, 010021, China. TEL 86-471-43156, 86-471-4992006, FAX 86-471-611761. Circ: 450 (paid); 300 (controlled). **Subscr. to:** China International Book Trading Corp, 35 Chegongzhuang Xilu, Haidian District, PO Box 399, Beijing 100044, China. TEL 86-10-68412045, FAX 86-10-68412023, cibtc@mail.cibtc.com.cn, http://www.cibtc.com.cn.

300 CHN
NEI MENGGU SHEHUI KEXUE/INNER MONGOLIAN SOCIAL SCIENCES. Text in Chinese. 1985. bi-m. USD 31.20 (effective 2009). **Document type:** *Journal, Academic/Scholarly.*
Formerly: Neimenggu Shehui Kexue (Wen-Shi-Zheban) (1003-5281)
Related titles: Online - full text ed.; Mongol ed.: ISSN 1002-9265. 1981. CNY 34.80, USD 16.80 (effective 2005).
—East View, Ingenta.
Published by: Neimenggu Shehui Kexueyuan/Inner Mongolian Academy of Social Sciences, 19, Daxue Donglu, Huhhot, Inner Mongolia 010010, China. TEL 86-471-4963431. **Dist. by:** China International Book Trading Corp, 35 Chegongzhuang Xilu, Haidian District, PO Box 399, Beijing 100044, China. TEL 86-10-68412045, FAX 86-10-68412023, cibtc@mail.cibtc.com.cn, http://www.cibtc.com.cn.

NEI MENGGU SHIFAN DAXUE XUEBAO (ZHEXUE SHEHUI KEXUE HANWEN BAN)/INNER MONGOLIA NORMAL UNIVERSITY. JOURNAL (PHILOSOPHY & SOCIAL SCIENCE CHINESE EDITION). *see* PHILOSOPHY

300 CHN ISSN 1672-3473
NEIMENGGU DIAN-DAXUE KAN/INNER MONGOLIA RADIO & T V UNIVERSITY. JOURNAL. Text in Chinese. 1987. m. CNY 7 newsstand/cover (effective 2006). **Document type:** *Journal, Academic/Scholarly.*
Related titles: Online - full text ed.
Published by: Neimenggu Guangbo Dianshi Daxue, 34, Jichang Lu (Xinhua Dong Jie), Hohhot, Inner Mongolia 010011, China. TEL 86-471-4601487.

300 CHN ISSN 1671-0215
AS452.T786
NEIMENGGU MINZU DAXUE XUEBAO (SHEHUI KEXUE BAN)/INNER MONGOLIA UNIVERSITY FOR NATIONALITIES. JOURNAL (SOCIAL SCIENCES). Text in Chinese. 2001. bi-m. USD 18 (effective 2009). **Document type:** *Journal, Academic/Scholarly.*
Formed by the merger of (1990-2000): Neimenggu Minzu Shi-Yuan Xuebao (Zhexue Shehui Kexue Hanwen Ban)/ Inner Mongolia National Teacher's College. Journal (Social Science Edition) (1001-7267); (1998-2000): Zhelimu Xumu Xueyuan Xuebao/Zhelimu Animal Husbandry College. Journal (1008-5149); Neimenggu Mengyixueyuan Xuebao
Related titles: Online - full text ed.
—East View.
Published by: Neimenggu Minzu Daxue, 16, Huolinhe Dajie, Tongliao, Inner Mongolia 028043, China. TEL 86-475-8314149, FAX 86-475-8314247.

300 CHN ISSN 1009-4458
NEIMENGGU NONGYE DAXUE XUEBAO (SHEHUI KEXUE BAN)/INNER MONGOLIA AGRICULTURAL UNIVERSITY. JOURNAL (SOCIAL SCIENCE EDITION). Text in Chinese. 1999. q. CNY 8 newsstand/cover (effective 2006). **Document type:** *Journal, Academic/Scholarly.*
Formerly (until 1999): Neimenggu Linxueyuan Xuebao (Zhexue Shehui Kexue Ban)/Inner Mongolia Forestry College. Journal (Philosophy and Social Sciences Edition) (1008-7788)
Related titles: Online - full text ed.
Published by: Neimenggu Nongye Daxue/Inner Mongolia Agricultural University, 306, Zhaowuda Lu, Hohhot, Inner Mongolia 010018, China. TEL 86-471-4309309, FAX 86-471-4301530.

300 MNG ISSN 1674-2524
NEIMENGGU TONGZHAN LILUN YANJIU/INNER MONGOLIA THEORY RESEARCH OF UNITED FRONT. Text in Chinese. 1984. bi-m. CNY 24 (effective 2009). **Document type:** *Journal, Academic/Scholarly.*
Related titles: Online - full text ed.
Published by: Neimenggu Shehui Zhuyi Xueyuan, 80, Wulanchabu Dong Lu, Hohhot, 010010, Mongolia. TEL 86-471-4901619.

300 NPL ISSN 2071-3258
➤ **NEPALESE JOURNAL OF QUALITATIVE RESEARCH METHODS.** Text in English. 2007. a. **Document type:** *Journal, Academic/Scholarly.* **Description:** Publishes articles on theoretical aspects of qualitative research methods, uses and misuses of qualitative research techniques, methods and processes in different social science researches and book reviews on qualitative research.
Related titles: Online - full text ed.
Indexed: A01, T02.
Published by: Local Initiative Promotion Trust, c/o Bhanu Timseena, Exe. Dir., Lalitpur, Kathmandu, 13, Nepal. TEL 977-1-6915288, btimseena@ntc.net.np. Ed. Laya Prasad Uprety.

508 AUT ISSN 1016-605X
NEUE DENKSCHRIFTEN DES NATURHISTORISCHEN MUSEUMS IN WIEN. Text in German. irreg. price varies. **Document type:** *Monographic series, Academic/Scholarly.*
Formerly (until 1977): Denkschriften des Naturhistorischen Museums in Wien
Indexed: BIOSIS Prev, MycolAb, SpeleolAb, Z01.
Published by: Verlag Ferdinand Berger und Soehne GmbH, Wienerstr 21-23, Horn, N 3580, Austria. TEL 43-2982-4161332, FAX 43-2982-4161382, office@berger.at, http://www.berger.at. Eds. Friedrich Bachmayer, Ortwin Schultz. Circ: 500.

NEUE SOZIALE BEWEGUNGEN. *see* POLITICAL SCIENCE

390 DEU
NEUES JAHRBUCH DRITTE WELT. Text in English. 1983. a. **Document type:** *Journal, Academic/Scholarly.*
Formerly (until 2001): Jahrbuch Dritte Welt (0724-4762)
Indexed: PRA.
Published by: V S - Verlag fuer Sozialwissenschaften (Subsidiary of: Springer Fachmedien Wiesbaden GmbH), Abraham-Lincoln-Str 46, Wiesbaden, 65189, Germany. TEL 49-611-78780, FAX 49-611-7878400, springerfachmedien-wiesbaden@springer.com, http://www.vs-verlag.de.

THE NEW AMERICAN (APPLETON). *see* POLITICAL SCIENCE

300 DEU ISSN 0077-801X
➤ **NEW BABYLON: STUDIES IN THE SOCIAL SCIENCES.** Text in German. irreg., latest vol.50, 1994. price varies. back issues avail. **Document type:** *Monographic series, Academic/Scholarly.*
Indexed: E-psyche.
Published by: De Gruyter Mouton (Subsidiary of: Walter de Gruyter GmbH & Co. KG), Genthiner Str 13, Berlin, 10785, Germany. TEL 49-30-260050, FAX 49-30-26005251, mouton@degruyter.de.

➤ **THE NEW CENTENNIAL REVIEW;** interdisciplinary perspectives on the Americas. *see* HUMANITIES: COMPREHENSIVE WORKS

300 AUS ISSN 1833-7597
THE NEW CRITIC. Text in English. 2006. 3/yr. free (effective 2009). back issues avail. **Document type:** *Journal, Academic/Scholarly.* **Description:** Covers politics, the arts, international issues, sport, literature, science, history, ethics, reviews and a small amount of creative fiction.
Media: Online - full text.
Published by: University of Western Australia, Institute of Advanced Studies, 35 Stirling Hwy, Crawley, W.A. 6009, Australia. TEL 61-8-64881340, FAX 61-8-64881711, iasuwa@admin.uwa.edu.au. Ed. David Ritter. Pub. Terri-ann White TEL 61-8-64882114.

300 658 USA ISSN 1097-6736
H62.A1 CODEN: NDFEF4
NEW DIRECTIONS FOR EVALUATION. Text in English. 1979. q. GBP 190 in United Kingdom to institutions; EUR 240 in Europe to institutions; USD 295 in United States to institutions; USD 335 in Canada & Mexico to institutions; USD 369 elsewhere to institutions; GBP 219 combined subscription in United Kingdom to institutions (print & online eds.); EUR 277 combined subscription in Europe to institutions (print & online eds.); USD 342 combined subscription in United States to institutions (print & online eds.); USD 382 combined subscription in Canada & Mexico to institutions (print & online eds.); USD 416 combined subscription elsewhere to institutions (print & online eds.) (effective 2012). Index. back issues avail.; reprint service avail. from PSC. **Document type:** *Journal, Academic/Scholarly.* **Description:** Features empirical, methodological, and theoretical works on all aspects of evaluation.
Formerly (until 1995): New Directions for Program Evaluation (0164-7989)
Related titles: Microform ed.: (from PQC); Online - full text ed.: ISSN 1534-875X. GBP 152 in United Kingdom to institutions; EUR 192 in Europe to institutions; USD 295 elsewhere to institutions (effective 2012).
Indexed: A01, A02, A03, A08, A22, BRD, C12, CA, CPE, E-psyche, E01, E02, E03, ERI, ERIC, EdA, EdI, HEA, M01, M02, P04, P34, P42, PSA, S02, S03, SCOPUS, SOPODA, SSA, SociolAb, T02, W03.
—BLDSC (6083.364800), IE, Ingenta. **CCC.**
Published by: (American Evaluation Association), Jossey-Bass Inc., Publishers (Subsidiary of: John Wiley & Sons, Inc.), 111 River St, Hoboken, NJ 07030. TEL 201-748-6000, FAX 201-748-6088, info@wiley.com. Ed. Sandra Mathison.

NEW ENGLAND JOURNAL OF HISTORY. *see* HISTORY—History Of North And South America

300 GBR
NEW ETHNICITIES NEWSLETTER. Text in English. s-a. GBP 2.
Document type: *Newsletter.* **Description:** Reports on research in progress, discussion of intellectual perspectives, and background information about the Centre's other activities.
Published by: University of East London, Centre for New Ethnicities Research, East Building, 4-6 University Way, London, E16 2RD, United Kingdom. TEL 44-2082-232512, FAX 44-2082-232898.

NEW GENETICS AND SOCIETY. *see* BIOLOGY—Genetics

NEW HUMANIST. *see* PHILOSOPHY

NEW LABOR FORUM; a journal of ideas, analysis and debate. *see* LABOR UNIONS

300 AUS ISSN 1447-235X
NEW N A R U DISCUSSION PAPER SERIES (ONLINE). (North Australian Research Unit) Text in English. 1991. irreg., latest vol.19, 2000. free (effective 2008). back issues avail. **Document type:** *Monographic series, Academic/Scholarly.* **Description:** Covers issues on North Australia, including environmental management and planning, governance and policy making structures, and economic development and social equity. Also provides comparative studies and history information.
Formerly (until 1999): New N A R U Discussion Paper Series (1037-5112)
Media: Online - full content.
Published by: Australian National University, North Australia Research Unit, PO Box 41321, Casuarina, N.T. 0811, Australia. TEL 61-8-89209999, FAX 61-8-89209988, naru@anu.edu.au. Ed. Christine Fletcher.

300 GBR ISSN 1472-2895
➤ **NEW TECHNOLOGIES / NEW CULTURES.** Text in English. 2001. irreg., latest 2004. price varies. back issues avail. **Document type:** *Monographic series, Academic/Scholarly.* **Description:** Aims to draw together the best scholarship, across the social science disciplines, that addresses emergent technologies in relation to cultural transformation in the broadest sense.
Published by: Berg Publishers (Subsidiary of: Oxford International Publishers Ltd.), 1st Fl Angel Ct, 81 St Clements St, Oxford, Berks OX4 1AW, United Kingdom. TEL 44-1865-245104, FAX 44-1865-791165, enquiry@bergpublishers.com. Ed. Don Slater.

➤ **NEW ZEALAND GAZETTE TRADE LISTS. MARRIAGE CELEBRANTS.** *see* BUSINESS AND ECONOMICS—Trade And Industrial Directories

300 NZL ISSN 1172-1146
➤ **NEW ZEALAND JOURNAL OF SOCIAL STUDIES.** Text in English. 1968. s-a. adv. bk.rev. back issues avail. **Document type:** *Journal, Academic/Scholarly.* **Description:** Covers social studies education in elementary and secondary schools, teacher education in social studies, and curriculum design.
Formerly (until 1992): Social Studies Observer (0110-6031)
Indexed: A11, CA, INZP, T02.
Published by: New Zealand Federation of Social Studies Association, c/o School of Education, Univ. of Waikato, Private Bag 3105, Hamilton, New Zealand. TEL 64-7-8384500, FAX 64-7-8384555, hughbarr@waikato.ac.nz. Ed. Hugh R Barr. R&P Hugh Barr. adv.: page NZD 100.

➤ **NEW ZEALAND SLAVONIC JOURNAL.** *see* HUMANITIES: COMPREHENSIVE WORKS

051 300 CAN ISSN 1719-1726
➤ **NEWFOUNDLAND AND LABRADOR STUDIES.** Text in English, French. 1985. s-a. CAD 20 domestic to individuals; CAD 23 foreign to individuals; CAD 30 domestic to institutions; CAD 35 foreign to institutions (effective 2008). adv. bk.rev. illus. Index. reprints avail. **Document type:** *Journal, Academic/Scholarly.* **Description:** Publishes essays in the arts and sciences about the society and culture of Newfoundland.
Formerly (until 2003): Newfoundland Studies (0823-1737)
Indexed: A26, AmH&L, B04, C03, C04, CA, CBCARef, CBPI, CPerI, E08, G08, HistAb, I05, MLA-IB, P48, PQC, S09, SSAI, SSAb, SSI, T02, W01, W02, W03, W05.
Published by: Memorial University of Newfoundland, Department of English, Arts and Administration 3026, Elizabeth Ave, St. John's, NF A1C 5S7, Canada. TEL 709-737-2144, FAX 709-737-4342, irenew@plato.ucs.mun.can, http://www.ucs.mun.ca/~nflds/. Ed. Jeff Webb. Circ: 250.

300 001.3 ZAF
NEWS FOR THE HUMAN SCIENCES BULLETIN. Text in Afrikaans, English. 1971. 10/yr. ZAR 15. index. **Document type:** *Bulletin, Academic/Scholarly.* **Description:** Covers newsworthy developments in the human sciences for an academic audience.
Former titles: Human Sciences Research Council. Bulletin - News for the Human Sciences; Human Sciences Research Council. Institute for Research Development. Bulletin (1017-6136); (until 1988): Human Sciences Research Council. Research Bulletin - Raad vir Geesteswetenskaplike Navorsing. Navorsingsbulletin (1011-1816); Supersedes: Register of Research in the Human Sciences in South Africa - Register van Navorsing in die Geesteswetenskappe in Suid-Afrika
Published by: (Centre for Science Development), Human Sciences Research Council/Raad vir Geesteswetenskaplike Navorsing. Sentrum vir Wetenskapontwikkeling, Private Bag X41, Pretoria, 0001, South Africa. TEL 27- 12-302-2999, FAX 27- 12-326-5362. Ed. Marilyn Farquharson. Circ: 3,500.

306 USA
NEWS FROM THE WHITE HOUSE. Text in English. 1989. irreg. (2-4/yr.). USD 8; USD 10 in Canada & Mexico; USD 12 elsewhere. adv. bk.rev. illus. back issues avail. **Document type:** *Newsletter.* **Description:** Promotes the organization's philosophies (folkish revival-national socialism) through political action and cultural education.
Related titles: Portuguese ed.: 1989.
Published by: (White House Network), White House Press, PO Box 6088, Harrisburg, PA 17112-0088. wolfshook4@aol.com. Ed. Eric Lowe. Adv. contact Eric West. Circ: 3,000 (paid).

300 056.1 MEX ISSN 0185-1535
F1201
➤ **NEXOS**; sociedad, ciencia, y literatura. Text in Spanish. 1978. m. MXN 480 domestic; USD 75 in US & Canada; USD 95 in Europe; USD 114 elsewhere (effective 2005). adv. bk.rev. illus. back issues avail.; reprints avail. **Document type:** *Academic/Scholarly.* **Description:** Political and cultural magazine that deals with International and Mexican current affairs.
Related titles: CD-ROM ed.; Online - full text ed.: ISSN 1563-762X.
Indexed: A26, C01, H21, I04, I05, IBR, IBZ, MLA-IB, P08.
Published by: Nexos Sociedad Ciencia y Literatura S.A. de C.V., Mazatlan 119, Col Condesa, Del Cuahutemoc, Mexico City, DF 06140, Mexico. TEL 52-5-553-1374, FAX 52-5-211-5886, proyectosespeciales@nexos.com.mx. Ed. Roberto Pliego. Pub. Hector Aguilar Camin. R&P Jesus Garcia Ramirez TEL 52-5-2861305. Adv. contact Martha Gallegos. B&W page MXN 1,983,750, color page MXN 25,622; trim 250 x 200. Circ: 15,600.

300 ESP ISSN 1133-1453
NI HABLAR. Text in Spanish. 1993. bi-m. **Document type:** *Magazine, Consumer.* **Description:** Interprets the present and past state of affairs according to their significance as projects or as automatized responses.
Published by: Ediciones Caimar, Sagasta, 19, Madrid, 28004, Spain. TEL 34-1-4469798, FAX 34-1-4457619. Ed. Ignacio Pastor.

300 DEU ISSN 0722-2548
NIEDERSAECHSISCHE BEITRAEGE ZUR SOZIALPAEDAGOGIK UND SOZIALARBEIT. Text in German. 1984. irreg., latest vol.16, 2003. price varies. **Document type:** *Monographic series, Academic/ Scholarly.*
Published by: Peter Lang GmbH (Subsidiary of: Peter Lang Publishing Group), Eschborner Landstr 42-50, Frankfurt Am Main, 60489, Germany. TEL 49-69-7807050, FAX 49-69-78070550, zentrale.frankfurt@peterlang.com.

300 330 NGA ISSN 0078-074X
NIGERIAN INSTITUTE OF SOCIAL AND ECONOMIC RESEARCH. ANNUAL REPORT. Text in English. 1954. a. free. **Document type:** *Corporate.*
Formerly: West African Institute of Social and Economic Research. Annual Report
Published by: Nigerian Institute of Social and Economic Research, University of Ibadan, PMB 5, Ibadan, Oyo, Nigeria. TEL 234-22-400501-5, TELEX 31119 NISER G. Ed. Remi Lawal.

300 NGA ISSN 0189-0085
HC1055.A1
NIGERIAN INSTITUTE OF SOCIAL AND ECONOMIC RESEARCH. RESEARCH FOR DEVELOPMENT. Text in English. 1981. s-a. **Document type:** *Journal, Academic/Scholarly.*
Published by: Nigerian Institute of Social and Economic Research, University of Ibadan, PMB 5, Ibadan, Oyo, Nigeria. TEL 234-22-400501-5. Ed. Kunle Adeniji.

300 CHN ISSN 1001-5124
AS452.H314
NINGBO DAXUE XUEBAO (RENWEN KEXUE BAN)/NINGBO UNIVERSITY. JOURNAL (LIBERAL ARTS EDITION). Text in Chinese. q. USD 31.20 (effective 2009). **Document type:** *Academic/ Scholarly.*
Related titles: Online - full text ed.
Published by: Ningbo Daxue/Ningbo University, 818 Fenghua Lu, Ningbo, Zhejiang 315211, China. TEL 86-574-6694294, FAX 86-574-6694161. Ed. Jin Tao.

300 001.3 500 CHN ISSN 1009-2560
NINGBO JIAOYU XUEYUAN XUEBAO/NINGBO INSTITUTE OF EDUCATION. JOURNAL. Text in Chinese. 1999. q. CNY 8 newsstand/cover (effective 2006). **Document type:** *Journal, Academic/Scholarly.*
Related titles: Online - full text ed.
Published by: Ningbo Jiaoyu Xueyuan, 625, Huancheng Bei Lu Xi-duan, Ningbo, 315010, China. TEL 86-574-87217980.

300 500 CHN ISSN 1671-2153
NINGBO ZHIYE JISHU XUEYUAN XUEBAO/NINGBO POLYTECHNIC. JOURNAL. Text in Chinese. 2001. bi-m. CNY 8 newsstand/cover (effective 2006). **Document type:** *Journal, Academic/Scholarly.*
Related titles: Online - full text ed.
Published by: Ningbo Zhiye Jishu Xueyuan, 1069, Xin Da Lu, Ningbo, 315800, China.

NINGEN BUNKA KENKYU NEMPO. *see* HUMANITIES: COMPREHENSIVE WORKS

300 JPN
NINGEN KAIGI. Text in Japanese. 2001. s-a. JPY 1,900 (effective 2008). **Document type:** *Magazine, Consumer.*
Published by: Sendenkaigi Co. Ltd., 3-13-16, Minami-Aoyama, Minato-ku, Tokyo, 107-8335, Japan. info@sendenkaigi.co.jp.

300 CHN ISSN 1001-5744
AS452.Y55
➤ **NINGXIA DAXUE XUEBAO (SHEHUI KEXUE BAN)/NINGXIA UNIVERSITY JOURNAL (PHILOSOPHY AND SOCIAL SCIENCE EDITION).** Text in Chinese; Summaries in Chinese, English. 1979. q. USD 40.20 (effective 2009). adv. 96 p./no.; **Document type:** *Academic/Scholarly.* **Description:** Contains studies on languages, economy, cultural history, law, literature, education and more.
Related titles: CD-ROM ed.; Online - full text ed.
Indexed: RASB.
—East View.
Published by: (Ningxia University), Ningxia Daxue Xuebao Bianjibu, 217 Wencui Bei Lu, Yinchuan, Ningxia 750021, China. TEL 86-951-2077800, FAX 86-951-2077740. Ed. Chunbao Ma. adv.: B&W page USD 179, color page USD 590. Circ: 2,200. **Subscr. to:** China International Book Trading Corp, 35 Chegongzhuang Xilu, Haidian District, PO Box 399, Beijing 100044, China. TEL 86-10-68412045, FAX 86-10-68412023, cibtc@mail.cibtc.com.cn, http://www.cibtc.com.cn.

300 CHN ISSN 1002-0292
AS452.Y55
NINGXIA SHEHUI KEXUE/SOCIAL SCIENCE IN NINGXIA. Text in Chinese. 1982. bi-m. adv. bk.rev. **Document type:** *Journal, Academic/Scholarly.*
Related titles: Online - full text ed.
Indexed: RASB.
—East View.
Published by: Ningxia Shehui Kexueyuan/Ningxia Academy of Social Sciences, 8, Xinfeng Xiang, Xinshi-qu, Yinchuan, 750021, China. TEL 86-951-2074593, FAX 86-951-2093003. adv.: B&W page USD 500, color page USD 1,000.

300 500 CHN ISSN 1674-1331
NINGXIA SHIFAN XUEYUAN XUEBAO/NINGXIA TEACHERS UNIVERSITY. JOURNAL. Text in Chinese. 1980. bi-m.
Formerly (until 2007): Guyuan Shi-Zhuan Xuebao/Guyuan Teachers College. Journal (1001-0491)
Related titles: Online - full text ed.
Published by: Ningxia Shifan Xueyuan/Ningxia Teachers University, Guyuanxian Wenhuaxiang #161, Ningxia, 756000, China. TEL 86-954-2024821.

300 001.3 500 JPN ISSN 0388-0036
AS552.T7155
NIPPON GAKUSHIIN KIYO/JAPAN ACADEMY. TRANSACTIONS. Text in Japanese. 1942. 3/yr. **Document type:** *Academic/Scholarly.*
Formerly (until 1947): Teikoku Gakushiin Kiji (0387-9984)
Indexed: RILM.
Published by: Nippon Gakushiin/Japan Academy, The, 7-32, Ueno Park, Taito-ku, Tokyo, 110-0007, Japan. TEL 81-3-38222101, FAX 81-3-38222105.

300 MEX ISSN 0188-9834
F1261
NOESIS. REVISTA DE CIENCIAS SOCIALES Y HUMANIDADES. Text in Spanish. 1988. s-a. **Document type:** *Journal, Academic/Scholarly.*
Related titles: Online - full text ed.
Indexed: C01.
Published by: Universidad Autonoma de Ciudad Juarez, Instituto de Ciencias Sociales y Administracion, Heorico Colegio Militar y Ave Universidad s-n, Ciudad Juarez, Chihuahua, Mexico. TEL 52-656-6883800, noesis@uacj.mx, http://www.uacj.mx/ICSA/. Ed. Hector Padilla Delgado.

NOKOKO. *see* ETHNIC INTERESTS

300 CHL ISSN 0717-2761
HQ1460.5
NOMADIAS. Text in Spanish. 1996. irreg., latest vol.5. **Document type:** *Monographic series, Academic/Scholarly.*
Related titles: Online - full text ed.
Indexed: A01, A26, AmHI, CA, F03, F04, H07, H21, I04, I05, MLA-IB, P08, T02.
Published by: Universidad de Chile, Centro de Estudios de Genero y Cultura en America Latina, Avda Capitan Ignacio Carrera Pinto 1025, piso 3, Nunao, Santiago, Chile. TEL 56-2-6787098, FAX 56-2-2716823, genfil@abello.dic.uchile.cl, http://www.uchile.cl/facultades/filosofia/frameset.htm.

300 CHN ISSN 0546-9503
S471.C6
NONGCUN GONGZUO TONGXUN/CORRESPONDENCE OF COUNTRYSIDE AFFAIRS. Text in Chinese. m. USD 72 (effective 2009). adv. **Document type:** *Newsletter.* **Description:** Offers a comprehensive guidance on Chinese policies on rural work.
—East View.
Published by: Zhongguo Nongcun Zazhishe, 61 Fuxing Lu, Beijing, 100036, China. TEL 86-10-6821-5244. Ed. Hongfei Zhou. R&P Xiaochun Xu. Adv. contact Jing Yu. Circ: 300,000.

▼ **NONGYEBU GUANLI GANBU XUEYUAN XUEBAO/ AGRICULTURAL MANAGEMENT INSTITUTE OF MINISTRY OF AGRICULTURE. JOURNAL.** *see* AGRICULTURE

NONLINEAR DYNAMICS, PSYCHOLOGY, AND LIFE SCIENCES. *see* PSYCHOLOGY

NORDENS TIDNING. *see* GENERAL INTEREST PERIODICALS—Scandinavia

300 DEU ISSN 0942-0657
NORDEUROPAEISCHE BEITRAEGE AUS DEN HUMAN- UND GESELLSCHAFTSWISSENSCHAFTEN. Text in German. 1992. irreg., latest vol.29, 2010. price varies. **Document type:** *Monographic series, Academic/Scholarly.*
—CCC.
Published by: Peter Lang GmbH (Subsidiary of: Peter Lang Publishing Group), Eschborner Landstr 42-50, Frankfurt Am Main, 60489, Germany. TEL 49-69-7807050, FAX 49-69-78070550, zentrale.frankfurt@peterlang.com, http://www.peterlang.com. Ed. Hartmut Schroeder.

300 NOR ISSN 1890-0429
NORDFORSK MAGASIN. Text in Norwegian. 2006. s-a. **Document type:** *Magazine, Consumer.*
Published by: NordForsk/Nordic Research Board, Stensberggata 25, Oslo, 0170, Norway. TEL 47-476-14400, FAX 47-22-565565, nordforsk@nordforsk.org, http://www.nordforsk.org.

300 NOR ISSN 1504-8640
NORDFORSK POLICY BRIEFS/NORDFORSK. REPORT. Text in Multiple languages. 2006. irreg. **Document type:** *Monographic series, Consumer.*
Formerly (until 2007): NordForsk. Rapporter (1890-3258)
Related titles: Online - full text ed.
Published by: NordForsk/Nordic Research Board, Stensberggata 25, Oslo, 0170, Norway. TEL 47-476-14400, FAX 47-22-565565, nordforsk@nordforsk.org.

▼ **NORDIDACTICA**; journal of humanities and social science education. *see* EDUCATION—Teaching Methods And Curriculum

NORTEAMERICA; revista academica del C I S A N - U N A M. *see* POLITICAL SCIENCE—International Relations

NORTHERN REVIEW. *see* HUMANITIES: COMPREHENSIVE WORKS

500 600 USA
NORTHWEST SCIENCE & TECHNOLOGY (ONLINE). Text in English. 1999 (Mar.). s-a. free (effective 2011). **Document type:** *Magazine, Trade.* **Description:** Provides comprehensive coverage of science & technology in the Pacific Northwest while serving as a platform for an expanded science writing curriculum at the UW.
Formerly (until 2005): Northwest Science & Technology (Print)
Published by: University of Washington, Department of Technical Communication, c/o Deborah Illman, PO Box 353740, Seattle, WA 98195. TEL 206-616-4826. Ed. Deborah Illman.

S

300 ITA ISSN 1128-2401
BJ55
NOTIZIE DI POLITEIA. Text in Multiple languages. 1985. q. **Document type:** *Journal, Academic/Scholarly.*
Indexed: P30, PhilInd, SCOPUS.
Published by: Tipolito Subalpina, Via Genova 57, Cascine Vica, Rivoli, TO 10090, Italy. TEL 39-011-9576450, FAX 39-011-9575449, commerciale@subalpina.it, http://www.subalpina.net.

300 320 ESP ISSN 0213-1366
HX345.C3
NOUS HORITZONS. Text in Spanish, Catalan. 1960. q. back issues avail. **Document type:** *Magazine, Consumer.*
Formerly (until 1961): Horitzons (0213-1358)
Published by: Fundacio Nous Horitzons, Ciutat 7, Barcelona, 08002, Spain. TEL 34-93-3010612, FAX 34-93-4124252, fundacio@noushoritzons.cat, http://noushoritzons.cat.

300 DEU ISSN 0546-9104
NUERNBERGER ABHANDLUNGEN ZU DEN WIRTSCHAFTS- UND SOZIALWISSENSCHAFTEN. Text in German. 1952. irreg., latest vol.26, 1968. price varies. **Document type:** *Monographic series, Academic/Scholarly.*
Published by: Duncker und Humblot GmbH, Carl-Heinrich-Becker-Weg 9, Berlin, 12165, Germany. TEL 49-30-7900060, FAX 49-30-79000631, info@duncker-humblot.de.

NUEVA CACERES REVIEW. *see* ANTHROPOLOGY

300 ARG ISSN 0327-7437
AS78.U53
➤ **NUEVAS PROPUESTAS.** Text in Spanish, English, Portuguese. 2/yr. USD 20. abstr.; bibl.; illus.; maps; stat. **Document type:** *Journal, Academic/Scholarly.*
Formerly (until 1986): Propuestas
Published by: Universidad Catolica de Santiago del Estero, Ave. Alsina, Casilla de Correos 285, Santiago Del Estero, 4200, Argentina. TEL 54-385-4213820, ediciones@ucse.edu.ar, http://www.ucse.edu.ar. Ed., R&P Jose Hector Ludy TEL 54-385-4211777. Circ: 500.

➤ **NURSING RESEARCH.** *see* MEDICAL SCIENCES—Nurses And Nursing

300 ESP ISSN 1989-1385
H1
O B E T S. REVISTA; revista de ciencias sociales. (Observatorio Europeo de Tendencias Sociales) Text in Spanish, English, Italian. 2008. s-a. free (effective 2011). **Document type:** *Journal, Academic/Scholarly.*
Media: Online - full text.
Published by: Universidad de Alicante, Instituto Universitario de Desarrollo Social y Paz (I U D E S P)/Universitat d'Alacant, Institut Universitari de Desenvolupament i Pau, Aulari I, 3a Planta, Alicante, 03080, Spain.

300 362.1 FRA
O E C D ILIBRARY: QUESTIONS SOCIALES/MIGRATIONS/SANTE. (Organisation for Economic Cooperation and Development) Text in French. irreg., latest 2007. **Document type:** *Report, Trade.*
Formerly (until 2010): Source O C D E. Questions Sociales/Migrations/Sante (1683-2426)
Related titles: Online - full text ed.: EUR 980, GBP 775, USD 1,250 (effective 2011) (from IngentaConnect); ◆ English ed.: O E C D Social Issues/Migration/Health iLibrary.
—Ingenta.
Published by: Organisation for Economic Cooperation and Development (O E C D)/Organisation de Cooperation et de Developpement Economiques (O C D E), 2 Rue Andre Pascal, Paris, 75775 Cedex 16, France. TEL 33-1-45248200, FAX 33-1-45248500, http://www.oecd.org.

300 362.1 FRA
O E C D SOCIAL ISSUES/MIGRATION/HEALTH ILIBRARY. (Organisation for Economic Cooperation and Development) Text in English. irreg. **Document type:** *Report, Trade.*
Former titles (until 2010): Source O E C D. Social Issues/Migration/Health; (until 200?): Source O E C D. Social Issues & Migration (1608-0289)
Related titles: Online - full text ed.: EUR 980, GBP 775, USD 1,250 (effective 2011) (from IngentaConnect); ◆ French ed.: O E C D iLibrary: Questions Sociales/Migrations/Sante.
—IE, Ingenta.
Published by: Organisation for Economic Cooperation and Development (O E C D)/Organisation de Cooperation et de Developpement Economiques (O C D E), 2 Rue Andre Pascal, Paris, 75775 Cedex 16, France. TEL 33-1-45248200, FAX 33-1-45248500, http://www.oecd.org. **Dist. addr. in N. America:** O E C D Turpin North America, PO Box 194, Downingtown, PA 19335-0194. TEL 610-524-5361, 800-456-6323, FAX 610-524-5417, journalscustomer@turpinna.com; **Dist. addr. in the UK:** Turpin Distribution Services Ltd., Pegasus Dr, Stratton Business Park, Biggleswade, Bedfordshire SG18 8QB, United Kingdom. TEL 44-1767-604800, FAX 44-1767-601640, custserv@turpin-distribution.com, http://www.turpin-distribution.com/.

300 BEL ISSN 0779-3677
L'OBSERVATOIRE. Text in French. 1947. q. EUR 31 domestic to individuals; EUR 38 domestic to institutions; EUR 45 in Europe; EUR 55 elsewhere; EUR 10 per issue domestic; EUR 12 per issue in Europe; EUR 15 per issue elsewhere (effective 2005). back issues avail.
Former titles (until 1992): Revue d'Action Sociale (0772-1676); (until 1976): Centre d'Etudes et de Documentation Sociales. Bulletin (0303-9587)
Indexed: FR, WBSS.
Published by: Revue d'Action Sociale et Medicosociale asbl, 28-30 Bd d'Avroy, Liege, 4000, Belgium. TEL 32-4-232-3160, FAX 32-4-232-3179. Ed. Philippe Brogniet.

325.1 325.21 FRA ISSN 1769-521X
L'OBSERVATOIRE DE L'INTEGRATION. Text in French. 1975. 6/yr. EUR 1.50 newsstand/cover (effective 2009). back issues avail. **Document type:** *Newsletter.*
Former titles (until 2004): F T D A. La Lettre d'Information (1143-659X); (until 1989): F T D A. (France Terre d'Asile) (0338-5752)
Published by: France Terre d'Asile, 24 Rue Marc Seguin, Paris, 75018, France. TEL 33-1-53043999, infos@france-terre-asile.org.

300 RUS ISSN 2072-3156
OBSERVATORIYA KUL'TURY. Text in Russian. 2004. bi-m. **Document type:** *Journal, Academic/Scholarly.*
Published by: (Rossiiskaya Gosudarstvennaya Biblioteka/Russian State Library), Idatel'stvo Rossiiskoi Gosudarstvennoi Biblioteki Pashkov Dom/Pashkov Dom, Russian State Library Publishing House, Vozdizhenka 3/5, Moscow, 101000, Russian Federation. TEL 7-495-6955953, FAX 7-495-6955953, pashkov_dom@rsl.ru, http://www.rsl.ru/pub.asp. Ed. Tamara Lapteva. **Dist. by:** East View Information Services, 10601 Wayzata Blvd, Minneapolis, MN 55305. TEL 952-252-1201, 800-477-1005, FAX 952-252-1202, info@eastview.com, http://www.eastview.com.

300 RUS ISSN 0869-0499
OBSHCHESTVENNYE NAUKI I SOVREMENNOST'. Text in Russian. 1970. bi-m. RUR 290 for 6 mos. domestic (effective 2004). bk.rev. bibl. **Document type:** *Journal, Academic/Scholarly.*
Formerly (until 1991): Akademiya Nauk S.S.S.R. Obshchestvennye Nauki (0132-3458)
Related titles: Online - full text ed.; Spanish ed.; German ed.; Portuguese ed.; English ed.; French ed.
Indexed: IBSS, ILD, RASB.
—East View. **CCC.**
Published by: (Rossiiskaya Akademiya Nauk/Russian Academy of Sciences), Izdatel'stvo Nauka, Profsoyuznaya ul 90, Moscow, 117864, Russian Federation. TEL 7-095-3347151, FAX 7-095-4202220, secret@naukaran.ru, http://www.naukaran.ru.

300 UZB ISSN 0029-7763
OBSHCHESTVENNYE NAUKI V UZBEKISTANE. Text in Russian, Uzbek. 1956. m. RUR 21. bk.rev. bibl.; charts; illus.; stat.
Indexed: NumL, RASB.
Published by: O'zbekiston Respublikasi Fanlar Akademiyasi/Academy of Sciences of Uzbekistan, 70, Academician Yahyo, Gulamov St, Tashkent, 700047, Uzbekistan. Ed. P M Krumov. Circ: 1,420.

300 DEU ISSN 1866-1319
OEKONOMIE IN STAAT, KIRCHE UND GESELLSCHAFT. Text in German. 2008. irreg. price varies. **Document type:** *Monographic series, Academic/Scholarly.*
Published by: Verlag Dr. Kovac, Leverkusenstr 13, Hamburg, 22761, Germany. TEL 49-40-3988800, FAX 49-40-39888055, info@verlagdrkovac.de. Ed. Siegfried Schoppe.

300 170 VAT ISSN 1720-1691
OIKONOMIA; rivista di etica e scienze sociali/review of ethics & social sciences. Text in Italian, English. 2002 (June). q. **Document type:** *Journal, Academic/Scholarly.*
Media: Online - full text.
Published by: Pontificia Universita San Tommaso d'Aquino - Angelicum, Largo Angelicum 1, Vatican City, 00184, Vatican City. TEL 39-06-67021, FAX 39-06-6790407, http://www.angelicum.org.

300 947.9 001.3 NLD ISSN 1570-7121
DK502.3
➤ **ON THE BOUNDARY OF TWO WORLDS**; identity, freedom, and moral imagination in the Baltics. Text in English. 2004. irreg., latest vol.15, 2008. price varies. **Document type:** *Monographic series, Academic/Scholarly.*
Indexed: T02.
Published by: Editions Rodopi B.V., Tijnmuiden 7, Amsterdam, 1046 AK, Netherlands. TEL 31-20-6114821, FAX 31-20-4472979, info@rodopi.nl. Ed. Dr. Leonidas Donskis.

➤ **ONATI INTERNATIONAL SERIES IN LAW AND SOCIETY.** *see* LAW

300 VEN ISSN 1012-1587
AS90.M378
➤ **OPCION/OPTION**; revista de ciencias humanas y sociales. Text in Spanish; Summaries in English, Spanish. 1984. 3/yr. VEB 40 domestic; USD 25 in Latin America; USD 42 elsewhere (effective 2010). bk.rev. **Document type:** *Journal, Academic/Scholarly.* **Description:** Publishes results of fundamental research in the human and social sciences areas.
Related titles: Online - full text ed.: free (effective 2011).
Indexed: C01, SCOPUS.
Published by: Universidad del Zulia, Facultad Experimental de Ciencias, Apdo. 15.197, Las Delicias, Maracaibo, 4005-A, Venezuela. TEL 58-261-7598113, FAX 58-261-7598077, opcion38@yahoo.com, http://www.ciens.luz.ve. Ed. Jose Vicente Villalobos. Circ: 1,000 (paid).

300 NLD ISSN 1874-9453
H1
➤ **THE OPEN SOCIAL SCIENCE JOURNAL.** Text in English. 2008. irreg. free (effective 2011). **Document type:** *Journal, Academic/Scholarly.*
Media: Online - full text.
Indexed: ESPM, RiskAb, S02, S03, SSciA.
Published by: Bentham Open (Subsidiary of: Bentham Science Publishers Ltd.), PO Box 294, Bussum, AG 1400, Netherlands. TEL 31-35-6923800, FAX 31-35-6980150, subscriptions@bentham.org. Ed. Brij Mohan.

301.5 GBR ISSN 0142-5277
OPEN UNIVERSITY. FACULTY OF SOCIAL SCIENCES. URBAN RESEARCH GROUP. OCCASIONAL PAPER. Text in English. 1978. irreg. **Document type:** *Monographic series, Academic/Scholarly.*
—CCC.
Published by: Open University, Faculty of Social Sciences, Walton Hall, Milton Keynes, MK7 6AA, United Kingdom. TEL 44-1908-654431, FAX 44-1908-654488, http://www.open.ac.uk/socialsciences/contact-us/.

ORANGE. *see* SCIENCES: COMPREHENSIVE WORKS

ORD & BILD/WORDS AND PICTURES. *see* LITERARY AND POLITICAL REVIEWS

300 DEU ISSN 1869-6112
▼ **ORGANISATION, INTERVENTION, EVALUATION.** Text in German. 2010. irreg. price varies. **Document type:** *Monographic series, Academic/Scholarly.*
Published by: Rainer Hampp Verlag, Marktplatz 5, Mering, 86415, Germany. TEL 49-8233-4783, FAX 49-8233-30755, info@rhverlag.de, http://www.rhverlag.de.

300 GBR ISSN 0170-8406
HD28
➤ **ORGANIZATION STUDIES.** Abbreviated title: O S. Text in English. 1980. m. USD 1,915, GBP 1,036 combined subscription to institutions (print & online eds.); USD 1,877, GBP 1,015 to institutions (effective 2011). adv. bk.rev. illus. back issues avail.; reprint service avail. from PSC. **Document type:** *Journal, Academic/Scholarly.* **Description:** Aims to promote the understanding of organizations, organizing the organized, and the social relevance of that understanding. It encourages the interplay between empirical research, in the belief that they should be mutually informative.
Related titles: Online - full text ed.: ISSN 1741-3044. USD 1,724, GBP 932 to institutions (effective 2011).
Indexed: A12, A13, A17, A20, A22, A26, ABIn, ASCA, B01, B02, B06, B07, B08, B09, B15, B17, B18, BAS, BPIA, BibInd, BusI, CA, CABA, CLOSS, CMM, CPM, CommAb, CurCont, DIP, E-psyche, E01, E10, EI, ESPM, Emerald, F08, F11, F12, FR, G04, G06, G07, G08, I05, I13, IBR, IBSS, IBZ, LT, P03, P25, P42, P48, P51, P53, P54, PAIS, PMA, PQC, PSA, PSI, PsycInfo, PsycholAb, R12, RRTA, RefZh, RiskAb, S02, S03, SCIMP, SCOPUS, SOPODA, SSA, SSCI, SociolAb, T02, TAR, W07, W11.
—BLDSC (6290.730000), IE, Infotrieve, Ingenta. **CCC.**
Published by: (European Group for Organizational Studies DEU), Sage Publications Ltd. (Subsidiary of: Sage Publications, Inc.), 1 Oliver's Yard, 55 City Rd, London, EC1Y 1SP, United Kingdom. TEL 44-20-73248500, FAX 44-20-73248600, info@sagepub.co.uk, http://www.uk.sagepub.com/home.nav. Ed. David Courpasson. adv.: B&W page GBP 450; 140 x 210. **Subscr. in the Americas to:** Sage Publications, Inc., 2455 Teller Rd, Thousand Oaks, CA 91320. TEL 805-499-9774, FAX 805-499-0871, journals@sagepub.com.

300 DEU ISSN 0724-5246
CODEN: ORIEEP
➤ **ORIENTIERUNGEN ZUR GESELLSCHAFTS- UND WIRTSCHAFTSPOLITIK.** Text in German. 1979. q. EUR 38; EUR 11 per issue (effective 2011). back issues avail. **Document type:** *Journal, Academic/Scholarly.*
Indexed: B01, B07, CA, IBR, IBZ, S02, S03.
Published by: Lucius und Lucius Verlagsgesellschaft mbH, Gerokstr 51, Stuttgart, 70184, Germany. TEL 49-711-242060, FAX 49-711-242088, lucius@luciusverlag.com. Pub. Wulf von Lucius. Circ: 1,200 (paid). **Dist. by:** Brockhaus Commission, Kreidlerstr 9, Kornwestheim 70806, Germany. TEL 49-7154-13270, FAX 49-7154-132713, info@brocom.de.

300 IND ISSN 0970-0269
HC431
OSMANIA JOURNAL OF SOCIAL SCIENCES. Text in English. 1981. s-a. **Document type:** *Journal, Academic/Scholarly.*
Indexed: PAIS.
Published by: Osmania University, Faculty of Social Sciences, Hyderabad, 500 007, India. TEL 91-40-7096187, FAX 91-40-7096187, http://www.osmania.ac.in/.

300 DEU
OSNABRUECKER SOZIALWISSENSCHAFTLICHE SCHRIFTEN. Text in German. 1996. irreg., latest vol.2, 2001. price varies. **Document type:** *Monographic series, Academic/Scholarly.*
Published by: V & R Unipress GmbH (Subsidiary of: Vandenhoeck und Ruprecht), Robert-Bosch-Breite 6, Goettingen, 37079, Germany. TEL 49-551-5084303, FAX 49-551-5084333, info@vr-unipress.de, http://www.v-r.de/en/publisher/unipress.

301 DEU ISSN 0580-2008
OSTEUROPA-INSTITUT. VEROEFFENTLICHUNGEN. REIHE WIRTSCHAFT UND GESELLSCHAFT. Text in German. 1957. irreg., latest vol.25, 2003. price varies. **Document type:** *Monographic series, Academic/Scholarly.*
Published by: Duncker und Humblot GmbH, Carl-Heinrich-Becker-Weg 9, Berlin, 12165, Germany. TEL 49-30-7900060, FAX 49-30-79000631, info@duncker-humblot.de, http://www.duncker-humblot.de.

OSTMITTELEUROPA IN VERGANGENHEIT UND GEGENWART. *see* HISTORY—History Of Europe

940 339 CHN
OUZHOU YANJIU/CHINESE JOURNAL OF EUROPEAN STUDIES. Text in Chinese. 1983. bi-m. USD 37.20 (effective 2009). **Document type:** *Journal, Academic/Scholarly.*
Former titles: Ouzhou/Europe (1004-9789); (until 1993): Xi'ou Yanjiu/Western European Studies (1000-3576)
Related titles: Online - full text ed.
Published by: Zhongguo Shehui Kexueyuan, Ouzhou Yanjiusuo/Chinese Academy of Social Sciences, Institute of European Studies, 5, Jianguomennei Dajie, Beijing, 100732, China. TEL 86-10-65135017, FAX 86-10-65125818.

300 USA ISSN 1943-2577
H1
OZEAN JOURNAL OF SOCIAL SCIENCE. Abbreviated title: O J S S. Text in English. 2008. 3/yr. back issues avail. **Document type:** *Journal, Academic/Scholarly.* **Description:** Provides a unique forum for educators, researchers, and practitioners on all aspects of the social sciences.
Related titles: Online - full text ed.: ISSN 1943-2585. free (effective 2009).
Published by: Ozean Publication, 2141 Baneberry Ct, Columbus, OH 43235. infoozean@gmail.com, http://www.ozelacademy.com.

P.M. FRAGEN UND ANTWORTEN. *see* SCIENCES: COMPREHENSIVE WORKS

320 338 GBR ISSN 0954-3694
P S I DISCUSSION PAPERS. Text in English. 1980-1992; N.S. 2008. irreg., latest 2009. price varies. back issues avail. **Document type:** *Monographic series, Trade.*
Formerly (until 1987): Policy Studies Institute. Discussion Paper
Related titles: Online - full text ed.: free (effective 2010).
Published by: Policy Studies Institute, 50 Hanson St, London, W1W 6UP, United Kingdom. TEL 44-20-79117500, FAX 44-20-79117501, psi-admin@psi.org.uk.

300 PHL ISSN 0115-1169
H62.5.P47
P S S C SOCIAL SCIENCE INFORMATION. Text in English. 1973. q. USD 25 (effective 2008). bk.rev. **Document type:** *Journal, Academic/Scholarly.*
Indexed: BAS.

Published by: Philippine Social Science Council, PSSC Book Center/ Central Subscription Service, 2/F Philippine Social Science Center, Commonwealth Ave, Dilman, P.O. Box 655, Quezon City, 1101, Philippines. TEL 63-2-9929627, FAX 63-2-9292602, css@psscorg.ph, http://www.pssc.org.ph/. Circ: 1,500.

PACIFIC AFFAIRS; an international review of Asia and the Pacific. *see* POLITICAL SCIENCE—International Relations

▼ **PACIFIC NORTHWEST JOURNAL OF UNDERGRADUATE RESEARCH AND CREATIVE ACTIVITIES.** *see* HUMANITIES: COMPREHENSIVE WORKS

300 FJI ISSN 0379-525X

PACIFIC PERSPECTIVE. Text in English. 1972. 2/yr. USD 8 (effective 2001). adv. bk.rev.
Indexed: APEL, FR, RASB, SPPI.
Published by: University of the South Pacific, Institute of Pacific Studies, c/o IPS, USP, Suva, Fiji. TEL 679-212248, FAX 679-301594, ips@usp.ac.fj. Circ: 2,000.

301 USA ISSN 0275-3596
DU1

➤ **PACIFIC STUDIES.** Text in English. 1977. q. USD 39 (effective 2010). adv. bk.rev. back issues avail. **Document type:** *Journal, Academic/ Scholarly.*
Related titles: Online - full text ed.
Indexed: A21, A26, AICP, APEL, AbAn, AmH&L, AnthLit, CA, CBRI, DIP, E08, G08, HistAb, I05, I13, IBR, IBSS, IBZ, INZP, MLA-IB, P30, P42, PAIS, PCI, PSA, RI-1, RI-2, RILM, RefZh, S02, S03, S09, SCOPUS, SOPODA, SociolAb, T02.
—BLDSC (6331.520000), IE, Infotrieve, Ingenta.
Published by: Brigham Young University - Hawaii, The Pacific Institute, 55-220 Kulanui St, Laie, HI 96762. TEL 808-675-3211. Ed. Phillip McArthur.

320.95491 PAK ISSN 1990-6579

➤ **PAKISTAN.** Text in English. 1980. 2/yr. USD 3 per issue (effective 2007). **Document type:** *Journal, Academic/Scholarly.*
Published by: University of Peshawar, Pakistan Study Centre, University of Peshawar, Pakistan Study Centre, Peshawar, Pakistan. TEL 92-91-9216765, FAX 92-91-9216632, psc@upesh.edu.pk, http:// www.upesh.edu.pk/academics/researchcenter/psc/psc.html. Eds. Iftihar Hussain, Parvez Ahmad Khan. Circ: 500 (controlled).

338.9 PAK ISSN 0030-9729
HC440.5 CODEN: JGSIAJ

➤ **PAKISTAN DEVELOPMENT REVIEW.** Text in English. 1961. q. PKR 300 domestic to individuals; PKR 450 domestic to institutions; PKR 100 domestic to students; EUR 85 foreign to individuals; EUR 125 foreign to institutions; USD 100 foreign to individuals; USD 150 foreign to institutions; PKR 125 per issue domestic; EUR 35 per issue foreign (effective 2007). bk.rev. stat. back issues avail.; reprints avail. **Document type:** *Journal, Academic/Scholarly.* **Description:** Publishes theoretical and empirical research in the social sciences fields.
Indexed: A22, A26, A34, A35, A36, A37, APEL, ARDT, AgBio, BAS, BibInd, C25, CA, CABA, E12, EIP, EconLit, F08, F11, F12, G11, GEOBASE, GH, H16, I05, I11, IBSS, JEL, LT, M10, MaizeAb, N02, OR, P06, P30, P32, P33, P39, P40, PGegResA, PGrRegA, PHN&I, PerIslam, PopulInd, R07, R11, R12, REE&TA, RM&VM, RRTA, S13, S16, SCOPUS, T02, T05, TOSA, TriticAb, W10, W11.
—BLDSC (6340.680000), IE, Infotrieve, Ingenta.
Published by: Pakistan Institute of Development Economics, PO Box 1091, Islamabad, 44000, Pakistan. TEL 92-51-9209419, FAX 92-51-9210886, publications@pide.org.pk, http://www.pide.org.pk. Eds. Aurangzeb A Hashmi, Rashid Amjad. Circ: 1,500.

➤ **PAKISTAN JOURNAL OF COMMERCE AND SOCIAL SCIENCES.** *see* BUSINESS AND ECONOMICS

300 PAK ISSN 1683-8831
H53.P18

PAKISTAN JOURNAL OF SOCIAL SCIENCES (FAISALABAD). Text in English. 2007. 4/yr. EUR 900 to individuals; EUR 1,200 to institutions; EUR 150 newsstand/cover (effective 2007). **Document type:** *Journal, Academic/Scholarly.*
Related titles: Online - full text ed.: ISSN 1993-6052. free (effective 2007).
Published by: Medwell Journals, ANSInet Bldg, 308-Lasani Town, Sargodha Rd, Faisalabad, 38090, Pakistan. TEL 92-41-5010004, 92-41-5004000, FAX 92-21-5206789, medwellonline@gmail.com, http://www.medwellonline.net.

300 PAK ISSN 2074-2061

➤ **PAKISTAN JOURNAL OF SOCIAL SCIENCES (MULTAN).** Text in English. 1987. s-a. PKR 500 domestic; USD 50 foreign (effective 2009). **Document type:** *Journal, Academic/Scholarly.* **Description:** Disseminates new and advance research in all disciplines of social sciences.
Formerly (until 2008): Journal of Research. Humanities (1816-7853)
Indexed: S02, S03, T02.
Published by: Bahauddin Zakariya University, Faculty of Arts and Social Sciences, Multan, 60800, Pakistan. TEL 92-61-9210071, FAX 92-61-9210098, info@bzu.edu.pk, http://www.bzu.edu.pk/mca/. Eds. Imran Sharif Chaudhry, Azra Asghar Ali.

300 070 COL ISSN 0122-8285
P87

➤ **PALABRA CLAVE.** Text in Spanish, English; Summaries in Spanish, English. 1996. s-a. bk.rev. abstr.; bibl. back issues avail. **Document type:** *Journal, Academic/Scholarly.* **Description:** Publishes investigations, studies and opinions about themes related with social communications and journalism.
Related titles: Online - full text ed.: ISSN 2027-534X. 1996. free (effective 2011) (from SciELO).
Indexed: A01, C01, CA, F03, F04, H21, P08, P27, P48, P54, PQC, R15, T02.
Published by: Universidad de la Sabana, Campus Universitario. Puente del Comun, Km. 21 Autopista Norte de Bogota, Chia, Cundinamarca, Colombia. TEL 57-1-8615555, FAX 57-1-8618517, usmail@unisabana.edu.co, http://www.unisabana.edu.co. Circ: 500.

300 COL ISSN 1657-5083
H8.S7

PALIMPSESTUS. Text in Spanish. 2001. s-a. free. bk.rev.; film rev. **Document type:** *Journal, Academic/Scholarly.*
Published by: Universidad Nacional de Colombia, Facultad de Ciencias Humanas, Biblioteca Central, Division de Canje, Apartado Aereo 14490, Bogota, Colombia. Ed. Luis Bernardo Lopez Caicedo.

300 DEU ISSN 1439-9857

PALLAS ATHENE. Text in German. 2000. irreg., latest vol.37, 2011. price varies. **Document type:** *Monographic series, Academic/Scholarly.*
Published by: Franz Steiner Verlag GmbH, Birkenwaldstr 44, Stuttgart, 70191, Germany. TEL 49-711-25820, FAX 49-711-2582290, service@steiner-verlag.de, http://www.steiner-verlag.de.

PANJAB UNIVERSITY RESEARCH JOURNAL (ARTS). *see* HUMANITIES: COMPREHENSIVE WORKS

300 ESP ISSN 1699-6852
HN581

PANORAMA SOCIAL. Text in Spanish. 2005. s-a. EUR 25 (effective 2009). back issues avail. **Document type:** *Journal, Academic/ Scholarly.*
Published by: Fundacion de las Cajas de Ahorros Confederadas para la Investigacion Economica y Social, Edif. Foro C. Caballero de Gracia, 28, Madrid, 28013, Spain. TEL 34-91-5965718, FAX 34-91-5965796, publica@funcas.ceca.es, http://www.funcas.ceca.es.

300 500 CHN ISSN 1672-0997

PANYU ZHIYE JISHU XUEYUAN XUEBAO. Text in Chinese. 2002. q. USD 12 (effective 2009). **Document type:** *Journal, Academic/ Scholarly.*
Related titles: Online - full text ed.
—East View.
Published by: Panyu Zhiye Jishu Xueyuan, Shawan Qingshanhu, Panyu, 511483, China.

300 CHN ISSN 1672-0563

PANZHIHUA XUEYUAN XUEBAO (ZONGHE BAN)/PANZHIHUA UNIVERSITY. JOURNAL. Text in Chinese. 1984. bi-m. CNY 6 newsstand/cover (effective 2006). **Document type:** *Journal, Academic/Scholarly.*
Formerly: Panzhihua Daxue Xuebao (Zonghe Ban) (1006-4834)
Related titles: Online - full text ed.
Published by: Panzhihua Xueyuan, Xueyuan Lu, Panzhihua, 617000, China. TEL 86-812-3370630, FAX 86-812-3371009.

PAPELES DE TRABAJO. AMERICA LATINA. *see* HISTORY—History Of North And South America

338.2 ESP ISSN 1577-8819

PAPERS DE LA CATEDRA UNESCO. Text in Catalan, Spanish. 1999. irreg. free (effective 2009). **Document type:** *Journal, Academic/ Scholarly.*
Related titles: Online - full text ed.: ISSN 1887-3111.
Published by: Universidad Politecnica de Catalunya, Catedra UNESCO de Sostenibilitat, C/Colom 1, Terrassa, 08222, Spain. TEL 34-93-7398050, FAX 34-93-7398032, sostenible@catunesco.upc.es.

300 900 500 USA ISSN 1056-8190
HT390

➤ **PAPERS IN REGIONAL SCIENCE.** Text in English. 1955. q. USD 808 combined subscription in the Americas to institutions (print & online eds.); GBP 482 combined subscription in United Kingdom to institutions (print & online eds.); EUR 607 combined subscription in Europe to institutions (print & online eds.); USD 948 combined subscription elsewhere to institutions (print & online eds.) (effective 2010); subscr. includes Regional Science Policy and Practice. adv. back issues avail.; reprint service avail. from PSC. **Document type:** *Journal, Academic/Scholarly.* **Description:** Publishes papers that make a new contribution to the theory, methods and models related to urban and regional (or spatial) matters.
Former titles (until 1991): Regional Science Association. Papers (0486-2902); (until 1964): Regional Science Association. Meeting. Papers and Proceedings (1059-1575)
Related titles: Online - full text ed.: ISSN 1435-5957. USD 735 in the Americas to institutions; GBP 438 in United Kingdom to institutions; EUR 552 in Europe to institutions; USD 863 elsewhere to institutions (effective 2010) (from IngentaConnect).
Indexed: A01, A03, A08, A12, A20, A22, A26, ABIn, AIAP, ASCA, B01, B06, B07, B08, B09, CA, CREJ, CurCont, E01, ESPM, EconLit, FR, FamI, GEOBASE, IBSS, JEL, P10, P27, P30, P34, P48, P51, P53, P54, PCI, PQC, S02, S03, S11, SCOPUS, SSCI, SSciA, SUSA, SociolAb, T02, W07.
—BLDSC (6400.035000), IE, Infotrieve, Ingenta. **CCC.**
Published by: (Regional Science Association International), Wiley-Blackwell Publishing, Inc. (Subsidiary of: Wiley-Blackwell Publishing Ltd.), 111 River St, Hoboken, NJ 07030. TEL 201-748-6000, FAX 201-748-6088, info@wiley.com. Ed. Jouke van Dijk.

300 TWN

PAPERS IN SOCIAL SCIENCES. Text in Chinese. 1980 (no.80). irreg. **Document type:** *Academic/Scholarly.*
Indexed: PsycholAb.
Published by: Academia Sinica, Sun Yat-Sen Institute for Social Sciences and Philosophy/Chung Yang Yen Chiu Yuan, Chung Shan Ren Wen Sheh Hui Ko Sheyue Yen Chiu So, Nankang, Taipei, 11529, Taiwan. TEL 886-2-7821693, FAX 886-2-7854160. Ed. Yun Peng Chu.

300 HND

PARANINFO. Text in Spanish. 1992. s-a. HNL 15, USD 5 per issue (effective 2003). **Document type:** *Academic/Scholarly.* **Description:** Presents philosophical, historical and literary articles.
Published by: Instituto de Ciencias del Hombre, Apartado Postal 4260, Tegucigalpa, Honduras. TEL 504-237-6399, FAX 504-237-6395, paidos@itsnetworks.net. Ed. Augusto Serrano. Circ: 800 (paid).

PASOS. *see* RELIGIONS AND THEOLOGY—Protestant

300 DEU ISSN 1861-583X

PASSAGEM; estudos em ciencias culturais. Text in German, Portuguese. 2006. irreg., latest vol.2, 2007. price varies. **Document type:** *Monographic series, Academic/Scholarly.*
Published by: Peter Lang GmbH (Subsidiary of: Peter Lang Publishing Group), Eschborner Landstr 42-50, Frankfurt Am Main, 60489, Germany. TEL 49-69-7807050, FAX 49-69-78070550, zentrale.frankfurt@peterlang.com, http://www.peterlang.com. Eds. Marilia dos Santos Lopes, Peter Hanenberg.

300 DEU ISSN 1435-3520

PASSAUER DISKUSSIONSPAPIERE. VOLKSWIRTSCHAFTLICHE REIHE. Text in German. 1998. irreg., latest vol.55, 2008. **Document type:** *Monographic series, Academic/Scholarly.*
Published by: Universitaet Passau, Wirtschaftswissenschaftliche Fakultaet, Innstr 27, Passau, 94032, Germany. TEL 49-851-5092401, FAX 49-851-5091005, brigitte.paffenholz@uni-passau.de, http:// www.wiwi.uni-passau.de/2326.html?&L=0.

300 USA ISSN 2160-3928

THE PEACE MEMO. Text in English. 2007. bi-m. free (effective 2011). back issues avail. **Document type:** *Journal, Academic/Scholarly.*
Formerly (until 2009): I C S Peace Memo (2160-4002)
Media: Online - full text.
Published by: Peacebuilding Institute

PENNSYLVANIA GEOGRAPHER. *see* GEOGRAPHY

300 BRA ISSN 1982-2707
H8+

➤ **PENSAMENTO PLURAL.** Text in Portuguese; Text occasionally in English, Spanish. 2007. s-a. free. bk.rev. Index. back issues avail. **Document type:** *Journal, Academic/Scholarly.* **Description:** Presents academics articles and book reviews relating to issues in social sciences, including politics, sociology and antropology. The audience is for academic scholars and the public.
Media: Online - full text.
Published by: Universidade Federal de Pelotas, Instituto de Sociologia e Politica, Rua Alberto Rosa, 154, Centro de Pelotas, Rio Grande do Sul, Brazil. TEL 55-53-2845542, FAX 55-533-2845543, http:// www.ufpel.tche.br/isp/ppgcs/. Ed. Daniel de Mendonca.

300 NIC ISSN 1016-9628
HC146.A1

PENSAMIENTO PROPIO; revista bilingue de ciencias sociales del Gran Caribe. Text in English, Spanish. 1982. s-a. USD 31 in Latin America; USD 36 in Europe. adv. bk.rev. back issues avail. **Document type:** *Magazine, Academic/Scholarly.* **Description:** Covers globalization, integration and regional development.
Related titles: Online - full text ed.
Indexed: C01, RASB.
Published by: Coordinadora Regional de Investigaciones Economicas y Sociales, Apdo 3516, Managua, Nicaragua. TEL 505-222-5217, FAX 505-268-1565. Ed. Andres Serbin. Pub. Lillian Levi. Circ: 5,000.
Co-sponsor: Novib de Holanda.

PENSAMIENTO Y ACCION; revista internacional de ciencia y cultura. *see* SCIENCES: COMPREHENSIVE WORKS

300 BRA

PENSANDO O BRASIL; reflexoes e sugestoes para os problemas do Brasil. Text in Portuguese. 1993 (Jun., no.3). irreg.
Address: Rua Apinages, 1752, Apto. 83, Sumare, Sao Paulo, SP 01258-000, Brazil. TEL 55-11-262-2758.

300 BEL ISSN 1379-213X

PENSEE ET PERSPECTIVES AFRICAINES/AFRICAN THOUGHT AND PERSPECTIVES. Text in French, English. 2003. irreg., latest vol.4, 2006. price varies. **Document type:** *Monographic series, Academic/ Scholarly.* **Description:** Aims at a critical analysis of the various aspects of African thought.
Published by: P I E - Peter Lang SA, 1 avenue Maurice, 6e etage, Brussels, 1050, Belgium. TEL 32-2-3477236, FAX 32-2-3477237, pie@peterlang.com, http://www.peterlang.net. Ed. Semzara Kabuta Ngo.

300 MEX ISSN 0188-7653
H8.S7

➤ **PERFILES LATINOAMERICANOS.** Text in Spanish; Abstracts in English. 1992. s-a. MXN 140 domestic; USD 25 in Latin America; USD 35 elsewhere (effective 2010). adv. bk.rev. 200 p./no.; **Document type:** *Journal, Academic/Scholarly.* **Description:** Each issue addresses a different topic in the social and political sciences.
Related titles: Online - full text ed.: free (effective 2011).
Indexed: A26, C01, CA, H21, IBSS, P08, P30, P42, PAIS, PSA, S02, S03, SCOPUS, SSA, SSCI, SociolAb, T02, W07.
Published by: Facultad Latinoamericana de Ciencias Sociales, Camino al Ajusco 377, Col Heroes de Padierna, Mexico City, DF 14200, Mexico. TEL 52-5-631-7016, FAX 52-5-631-6609, rwinocur@flacso.flacso.mx, http://www.flacso.flacso.edu.mx.

300 DEU ISSN 1867-5301

PERILOG; Freiburger Beitraege zur Kultur- und Sozialforschung. Text in German. 2008. irreg., latest vol.5, 2011. price varies. **Document type:** *Monographic series, Academic/Scholarly.*
Published by: Logos Verlag Berlin, Comeniushof, Gubener Str 47, Berlin, 10243, Germany. TEL 49-30-42851090, FAX 49-30-42851092, redaktion@logos-verlag.de. Eds. Michael Schetsche, Renate-Berenike Schmidt.

PERIODICA POLYTECHNICA. SOCIAL AND MANAGEMENT SCIENCES. *see* BUSINESS AND ECONOMICS—Management

300 DEU

PERIPLUS PARERGA. Text in German. 1994. irreg., latest vol.9, 2010. price varies. **Document type:** *Monographic series, Academic/ Scholarly.*
Published by: Lit Verlag, Grevener Str/Fresnostr 2, Muenster, 48159, Germany. TEL 49-251-6203222, FAX 49-251-231972, lit@lit-verlag.de.

300 200 CHL ISSN 0716-730X
HN39.L3

PERSONA Y SOCIEDAD. Text in Spanish. 1987. 3/yr. CLP 15,000 to individuals; CLP 25,000 to institutions; USD 70 foreign (effective 2010). **Document type:** *Journal, Academic/Scholarly.* **Description:** Analyzes and discusses the problems of the relationship between faith and culture in Latin America.
Indexed: IBR, IBZ.
Published by: Georgetown University, I L A D E S, Almirante Barroso 6, Santiago, Chile. info@ilades.cl, http://www.ilades.cl. Ed. Jorge Larrain.

300 BRA ISSN 0101-3459
AS80.A1 CODEN: PRSVDY

➤ **PERSPECTIVAS**; revista de ciencias sociais. Text in Portuguese; Summaries in English, Portuguese. 1976-1977; resumed 1980. s-a. USD 30 per vol. (effective 2006); or exchange basis. bk.rev. abstr.; charts; bibl. back issues avail. **Document type:** *Journal, Academic/ Scholarly.* **Description:** Covers original articles and research in the social sciences.
Indexed: AbAn, C01, CA, DIP, I13, IBR, IBZ, P42, PCI, PSA, RASB, RILM, S02, S03, SOPODA, SSA, SociolAb, T02.

S

Published by: Universidade Estadual Paulista, Fundacao Editora U N E S P, Praca da Se 108, Sao Paulo, SP 01001-900, Brazil. TEL 55-11-32427171, cgb@marilia.unesp.br, http://www.unesp.br. Ed. Milton Lahuerta. Circ: 1,000.

300 CHL ISSN 0718-4468
PERSPECTIVAS. Text in Spanish. 2007. q.
Published by: Pontificia Universidad Catolica de Chile, Centro de Estudios de Emprendimientos Solidarios, Ave Vicuna Mackenna 4860, Macul, Santiago, Chile. TEL 56-7-6315988, FAX 56-2-3544637, cees@uc.cl, http://www.puc.cl/cienciassociales/cees/. Ed. Daniel Diaz.

300 ESP ISSN 1575-8443
R724
PERSPECTIVAS BIOETICAS. Text in Spanish. 1995. s-a. **Document type:** *Magazine, Consumer.*
Formerly (until 1998): Perspectivas Bioeticas en las Americas (0328-5634)
Indexed: F04, H05, T02.
Published by: (Facultad Latinoamericana de Ciencias Sociales (F L A C S O), Argentina ARG), Editorial Gedisa, Avel del Tibidabo, 12, Barcelona, 08022, Spain. TEL 34-93-2530904, FAX 34-93-2530905, informacion@gedisa.com, http://www.gedisa.com.

300 BRA ISSN 1980-0193
➤ **PERSPECTIVAS CONTEMPORANEAS**; revista de ciencias sociais aplicadas. Text in Portuguese; Summaries in English, Portuguese. 2006. s-a. free (effective 2011). bibl.; illus.; stat. back issues avail. **Document type:** *Journal, Academic/Scholarly.* **Description:** Publishes regional, national and international articles covering the field of applied social sciences.
Media: Online - full text.
—**CCC.**
Published by: Faculdade Integrado de Campo Mourao, Av Irmaos Pereira 670, Centro, Campo Mourao, PR 87303-010, Brazil. TEL 55-44-35231982, http://www.grupointegrado.br. Ed., Pub., R&P, Adv. contact Patricia Queiroz.

➤ **PERSPECTIVES CHINOISES.** *see* POLITICAL SCIENCE—International Relations

300 600 NLD ISSN 1569-1500
HC59.69 CODEN: PGDTA9
➤ **PERSPECTIVES ON GLOBAL DEVELOPMENT AND TECHNOLOGY.** Text in English. 1971. q. EUR 282, USD 394 to institutions; EUR 307, USD 430 combined subscription to institutions (print & online eds.) (effective 2012). bk.rev. back issues avail.; reprint service avail. from PSC. **Document type:** *Journal, Academic/Scholarly.* **Description:** Journal for the discussion of current social science research on diverse socioeconomic development issues that reflect the profoundly altered opportunities and threats wrought by the bipolar to global world order shift, the present monopoly of economic liberalization that constricts development options, and the new enabling technologies of the Information Age.
Supersedes in part (in 2002): Journal of Developing Societies (0169-796X); Which was formerly (until 1985): Contributions to Asian Studies (0304-2693)
Related titles: Online - full text ed.: ISSN 1569-1497. EUR 256, USD 358 to institutions (effective 2012) (from IngentaConnect).
Indexed: A01, A02, A03, A08, A12, A17, A22, A36, ABIn, ASSIA, B01, B06, B07, B08, B09, BA, C23, CA, CABA, E01, E12, ESPM, GEOBASE, GH, I13, IBR, IBSS, IBZ, IZBG, LT, LeftInd, M10, N02, P34, P42, P48, P51, P53, P54, PAIS, PQC, PSA, R12, RRTA, S02, S03, S13, S16, SCOPUS, SSA, SSciA, SociolAb, T02, T05, TAR, W11.
—BLDSC (6428.143050), IE, Ingenta. **CCC.**
Published by: Brill, PO Box 9000, Leiden, 2300 PA, Netherlands. TEL 31-71-5353500, FAX 31-71-5317532, cs@brill.nl. Ed. Rubin Patterson TEL 419-530-4953. **Dist. by:** Turpin Distribution Services Ltd., Pegasus Dr, Stratton Business Park, Biggleswade, Bedfordshire SG18 8QB, United Kingdom. TEL 44-1767-604954, FAX 44-1767-601640, custserv@turpin-distribution.com, http://www.turpin-distribution.com/.

300 NOR ISSN 1502-1408
PERSPEKTIV: 17 X 24. Variant title: Perspektiv: Sytten gaange Tjuefire. Text in Norwegian; Text occasionally in English. 2000. irreg., latest vol.30, 2006. price varies. back issues avail. **Document type:** *Monographic series, Academic/Scholarly.*
Published by: Unipub Forlag AS, Kristan Ottosens Hus, PO Box 33, Blindern, Oslo, 0313, Norway. TEL 47-22-853300, FAX 47-22-853039, post@unipub.no.

300 DEU
PERSPEKTIVENWECHSEL INTERKULTURELL. Text in German. 1996. irreg., latest vol.4, 2010. price varies. **Document type:** *Monographic series, Academic/Scholarly.*
Formerly (until 1999): Beitraege zur Sozialwissenschaftlichen Analyse Interkultureller Beziehungen
Published by: Weissensee Verlag e.K., Simplonstr 59, Berlin, 10245, Germany. TEL 49-30-29049192, FAX 49-30-27574315, mail@weissensee-verlag.de.

300 001.3 MYS ISSN 0128-7702
H1 CODEN: PERTDY
➤ **PERTANIKA JOURNAL OF SOCIAL SCIENCE AND HUMANITIES.** Text in English, Malay. irreg. (1-2/yr.), latest vol.10, 2002. USD 60 (effective 2002). **Document type:** *Journal, Academic/Scholarly.*
Supersedes in part (in 1993): Pertanika (0126-6128)
Indexed: APEL, AmHI, C25, CA, CABA, E12, F08, F11, F12, H07, LT, N02, R11, R12, S16, SCOPUS, SoyAb, T02, T05, W11.
—CASDDS.
Published by: (Agricultural University of Malaysia/Universiti Pertanian Malaysia), Universiti Pertanian Malaysia Press, 43400 UPM, Serdang, Selangor, Malaysia. TEL 603-8946-8855, FAX 603-8941-6172. Ed. Abdul Rahman Md Aroff. Circ: 200.

378 PAK ISSN 1608-7925
AS569.A1
➤ **PESHAWAR UNIVERSITY TEACHERS' ASSOCIATION. JOURNAL.** Text in English, Arabic, Pushto, Urdu. 1993 (Jun.). a. PKR 250 per issue to individuals (effective 2006). **Document type:** *Journal, Academic/Scholarly.* **Description:** Publishes researches in the areas of Humanities, Natural Sciences, Social Sciences, and Management Sciences for researchers and students in these areas.
Published by: University of Peshawar, Peshawar University Teachers' Association, Teachers' Community Centre, Peshawar, 25120, Pakistan. Ed. Dr. Muhammad Jahanzeb Khan. Pub. Dr. Nasir Jamal Khattak. R&P Dr. Muhammad Jahanzeb.

➤ **PETERSON'S GRADUATE PROGRAMS IN THE HUMANITIES, ARTS, AND SOCIAL SCIENCES.** *see* HUMANITIES: COMPREHENSIVE WORKS

➤ **PHILICA**; where ideas are free. *see* SCIENCES: COMPREHENSIVE WORKS

300 PHL ISSN 0116-7081
PHILIPPINE-AMERICAN STUDIES JOURNAL. Text in English. 1987. a. PHP 30, USD 3.20. adv. bk.rev. **Document type:** *Journal, Academic/Scholarly.* **Description:** Publishes scholarly articles reflecting significant quantitative or qualitative research. Includes speeches, research reports, and "state of the art" papers.
Indexed: IPP.
Published by: (De La Salle University), De La Salle University Press, 2401 Taft Ave, Manila, Philippines. Circ: 300.

PHILIPPINE SOCIAL SCIENCES REVIEW/REBYU NG AGHAM PANLIPUNAN NG PILIPINAS. *see* HUMANITIES: COMPREHENSIVE WORKS

PHILIPPINE STUDIES. *see* HUMANITIES: COMPREHENSIVE WORKS

PHILOSOPHICAL EXPLORATIONS; an international journal for the philosophy of mind and action. *see* PHILOSOPHY

PHILOSOPHICAL STUDIES IN CONTEMPORARY CULTURE. *see* PHILOSOPHY

300 IND ISSN 0377-2772
HN681
➤ **PHILOSOPHY & SOCIAL ACTION**; quarterly of philosophy, science and society. Variant title: Philos. soc. action. Text in English, Hindi. 1975. q. adv. bk.rev. back issues avail. **Document type:** *Journal, Academic/Scholarly.* **Description:** Discusses substantive socio-economic, political, legal and science and public policy issues that concern the people of India and the Third World in particular.
Related titles: E-mail ed.; Online - full text ed.: free (effective 2011).
Indexed: APW, B04, CA, DIP, FR, HRIR, IBR, IBZ, PhilInd, S02, S03, SCOPUS, SOPODA, SSAI, SSAb, SSI, SociolAb, T02, W03, W05.
—IE, Ingenta.
Published by: Committee of Concerned Indian Philosophers for Social Action, Nirmala-Nilaya, Dehra Dun, Uttaranchal 248 009, India. TEL 91-135-2735627, psand@vsnl.net. Ed. Dhirendra Sharma. **Subscr. to:** I N S I O Scientific Books & Periodicals.

➤ **PHILOSOPHY & SOCIAL CRITICISM**; an international, interdisciplinary journal. *see* PHILOSOPHY

300 NLD ISSN 2210-5433
T10.5 CODEN: KNPOEI
➤ **PHILOSOPHY & TECHNOLOGY.** Text in English. 1988. q. EUR 370, USD 496 combined subscription to institutions (print & online eds.) (effective 2012). adv. bk.rev. illus. Index. reprint service avail. from PSC. **Document type:** *Journal, Academic/Scholarly.* **Description:** Seeks to promote the development of an interdisciplinary science of knowledge transfer between technology and philosophy.
Former titles (until 2011): Knowledge, Technology and Policy (1946-4789); (until 1998): Knowledge and Policy (1053-8798); (until 1991): Knowledge in Society (0897-1986)
Related titles: Online - full text ed.: ISSN 2210-5441 (from IngentaConnect).
Indexed: A01, A02, A03, A08, A12, A22, A26, ABIn, C10, C12, CA, CompLI, DIP, E01, E03, E07, E08, ERI, G01, G08, I05, IBR, IBSS, IBZ, Inspec, L04, LISTA, M01, M02, P04, P27, P34, P41, P42, P46, P48, P51, P53, P54, PAIS, PQC, PSA, PerIslam, S01, S02, S03, S09, SCOPUS, SOPODA, SociolAb, T02.
—BLDSC (5100.460000), IE, Ingenta. **CCC.**
Published by: Springer Netherlands (Subsidiary of: Springer Science+Business Media), Van Godewijckstraat 30, Dordrecht, 3311 GX, Netherlands. TEL 31-78-6576050, FAX 31-78-6576474. Ed. Luciano Floridi.

300 USA ISSN 0048-3931
H1
➤ **PHILOSOPHY OF THE SOCIAL SCIENCES.** Text in English. 1971. q. USD 585, GBP 345 combined subscription to institutions (print & online eds.); USD 573, GBP 338 to institutions (effective 2011). bk.rev. illus. index. back issues avail.; reprint service avail. from PSC. **Document type:** *Journal, Academic/Scholarly.* **Description:** Publishes articles, discussions, symposia, literature surveys, translations, and reviews of interest to both philosophers concerned with the social sciences and social scientists concerned with the philosophical foundations of their subject.
Related titles: Online - full text ed.: ISSN 1552-7441. USD 527, GBP 311 to institutions (effective 2011).
Indexed: A01, A02, A03, A08, A20, A22, A26, AC&P, ASCA, ArtHuCI, B04, B07, BRD, C03, CA, CBCARef, CBPI, CPerI, CurCont, DIP, E-psyche, E01, E08, FR, G08, H04, H14, I05, I13, IBR, IBRH, IBSS, IBZ, IPB, MEA&I, P02, P10, P27, P30, P42, P48, P53, P54, PCI, PQC, PSA, PerIslam, PhilInd, R05, RASB, S02, S03, S09, SCOPUS, SOPODA, SSA, SSAI, SSAb, SSCI, SSI, SociolAb, T02, V02, W03, W07.
—BLDSC (6465.080000), IE, Ingenta, INIST. **CCC.**
Published by: Sage Publications, Inc., 2455 Teller Rd, Thousand Oaks, CA 91320. TEL 805-499-9774, FAX 805-499-0871, info@sagepub.com. Ed. Ian C Jarvie. Circ: 1,300. **Subscr. overseas to:** Sage Publications Ltd., 1 Oliver's Yard, 55 City Rd, London EC1Y 1SP, United Kingdom. TEL 44-207-3248701, FAX 44-207-3248733, subscription@sagepub.co.uk.

300 USA ISSN 0556-0152
E839.5
PHYLLIS SCHLAFLY REPORT. Text in English. 1967. m. USD 20 (effective 2005). back issues avail. **Document type:** *Newsletter.* **Description:** Commentary on women's issues, education, national defense, legal issues, privacy rights, economics and foreign policy.
Published by: Eagle Trust Fund, PO Box 618, Alton, IL 62002. TEL 618-462-5415. Ed. Phyllis Schlafly. Circ: 70,000.

300 BRA ISSN 0103-7331
RA421
PHYSIS. Text in Portuguese, Spanish. 1991. s-a. **Document type:** *Journal, Academic/Scholarly.*
Related titles: Online - full text ed.: 2004. free (effective 2011).
Indexed: S02, S03, SCOPUS, SociolAb.
Published by: Universidade do Estado do Rio de Janeiro, Instituto de Medicina Social, Rua Sao Francisco Xavier 524, Rio de Janeiro, 20550-900, Brazil. TEL 55-21-25877303, FAX 55-21-22641142, publicacoes@ims.uerj.br. Ed. Kenneth Rochel de Camargo.

300 500 CHN ISSN 1673-1670
PINGDINGSHAN XUEYUAN XUEBAO/PINGDINGSHAN UNIVERSITY. JOURNAL. Text in Chinese. 1986. bi-m. CNY 7 newsstand/cover (effective 2006). **Document type:** *Journal, Academic/Scholarly.*
Formerly (until 2004): Pingdingshan Shi-Zhuan Xuebao (1008-5211)
Related titles: Online - full text ed.
Published by: Pingdingshan Xueyuan, Pingdingshan, 467002, China.

300 CHN ISSN 1007-9149
PINGXIANG GAODENG ZHUANKE XUEXIAO XUEBAO/PINGXIANG COLLEGE. JOURNAL. Text in Chinese. 1984. bi-m. CNY 8 newsstand/cover (effective 2006). **Document type:** *Journal, Academic/Scholarly.*
Related titles: Online - full text ed.
Published by: Pingxiang Gaodeng Zhuanke Xuexiao/Pingxiang College, Wulipai, Pingxiang, 337000, China. TEL 86-799-6682112.

327 USA
PITT LATIN AMERICAN SERIES. Text in English. 1968. irreg. price varies. **Document type:** *Monographic series, Academic/Scholarly.* **Description:** Contains a wide array of distinguished books from a variety of disciplinary, ideological, and methodological perspectives on every aspect of Latin American politics, society, economics, and culture with particular strength in the disciplines of politics and history.
Related titles: ◆ Series: Cuban Studies. ISSN 0361-4441.
Published by: University of Pittsburgh Press, Eureka Bldg, 5th Fl, 3400 Forbes Ave, Pittsburgh, PA 15260. TEL 412-383-2456, FAX 412-383-2466, press@pitt.edu, http://www.upress.pitt.edu/upressIndex.aspx. Eds. Catherine M Conaghan, John Charles Chasteen.

300 AUS ISSN 1835-8799
➤ **PLACE.** Text in English. a. **Document type:** *Journal, Academic/Scholarly.* **Description:** Dedicated to the scholarly analysis of place from the point of view of such fields as philosophy, human and cultural geography, archaeology, anthropology, spatial history, the history of art and architecture, urban studies, architecture and planning, and musicology.
Media: Online - full content.
Published by: University of Western Australia, 35 Stirling Highway, Crawley, W.A. 6009, Australia. TEL 61-8-9383838, FAX 61-8-9381380, general.enquiries@uwa.edu.au, http://www.uwa.edu.au. Ed. Susan Broomhall. **Co-publisher:** Australians Studying Abroad.

300 USA ISSN 0192-5059
HN50
PLANTATION SOCIETY IN THE AMERICAS; an interdisciplinary journal of tropical and subtropical history and culture. Text in English. 1979. 3/yr. USD 20 to individuals; USD 40 to libraries. adv. bk.rev.
Indexed: BibInd, HistAb, MLA, MLA-IB.
Published by: Plantation Society, c/o Prof Edward Lazzerini, Man Ed, Department of History, University of New Orleans, New Orleans, LA 70148. TEL 504-286-6886. Ed. Thomas Fiehrer. Circ: 800.

300 FRA ISSN 0336-1721
HT1501
PLURIEL. Text in French. 1975. q. bk.rev.
Published by: Editions Pluriel, Mantilly, Passais la Conception, 61350, France. TEL 33-38-77-23. Ed. Jean Foucher.

POIESIS & PRAXIS; international journal of ethics of science and technology assessment. *see* TECHNOLOGY: COMPREHENSIVE WORKS

300 004.3 GBR ISSN 2154-896X
▼ **POLAR JOURNAL.** Text in English. forthcoming 2011 (June). s-a. GBP 198 combined subscription in United Kingdom to institutions (print & online eds.); EUR 261, USD 327 combined subscription to institutions (print & online eds.) (effective 2012). **Document type:** *Journal, Academic/Scholarly.* **Description:** Features multidisciplinary research in the social sciences and humanitites on the north and south poles.
Related titles: Online - full text ed.: ISSN 2154-8978. forthcoming 2011 (June). GBP 178 in United Kingdom to institutions; EUR 235, USD 294 to institutions (effective 2012).
—**CCC.**
Published by: Taylor & Francis Ltd. (Subsidiary of: Taylor & Francis Group), 4 Park Sq, Milton Park, Abingdon, Oxfordshire OX14 4RN, United Kingdom. TEL 44-20-70176000, FAX 44-20-70176336, info@tandf.co.uk, http://www.tandf.co.uk/journals.

300 GTM
POLEMICA; revista centroamericana de ciencias sociales. Text in Spanish.
Published by: Facultad Latinoamericana de Ciencias Sociales, Programa Guatemala, 13 Calle 11-42, Apdo. Postal 988 A, Guatemala City Zona, Guatemala. TEL 502-2-21683, FAX 502-2-80344. Ed. Roberto Diaz Castillo.

POLICY STUDIES. *see* POLITICAL SCIENCE

300 CHL ISSN 0717-6554
AS81.A1
POLIS; revista de la Universidad Bolivariana. Text in Spanish. 2001. s-a. **Document type:** *Journal, Academic/Scholarly.*
Related titles: Online - full text ed.: ISSN 0718-6568. 2008.
Indexed: CA, F04, T02.
Published by: Universidad Bolivariana, Huerfanos 2917, Santiago, Chile. TEL 56-1-6815095, http://www.ubolivariana.cl. Circ: 1,000.

300 CHE ISSN 2192-1822
▼ **POLISH STUDIES IN CULTURE, NATIONS AND POLITICS.** Text in English. forthcoming 2011. irreg. price varies. **Document type:** *Monographic series, Academic/Scholarly.*
Published by: Peter Lang AG (Subsidiary of: Peter Lang Publishing Group), Hochfeldstr 32, Postfach 746, Bern 9, 3000, Switzerland. TEL 41-31-3061717, FAX 41-31-3061727, info@peterlang.com. Eds. Joanna Kurczewska, Yasuko Shibata.

330.1 POL
POLITECHNIKA KRAKOWSKA. MONOGRAFIE. SERIA: NAUKI SPOLECZNE I EKONOMICZNE. Text in Polish; Summaries in English, French, German, Russian. 1985. irreg. price varies. bibl.; charts; illus. **Document type:** *Monographic series, Academic/Scholarly.*

Former titles: Politechnika Krakowska. Monografie. Seria: Ekonomia, Socjologia, Filozofia; Politechnika Krakowska. Monografie. Seria: Nauki Spoleczne i Ekonomiczne
Related titles: ◆ Series of: Politechnika Krakowska. Monografie. ISSN 0860-097X.
Published by: Politechnika Krakowska im. Tadeusza Kosciuszki/Tadeusz Kosciuszko Cracow University of Technology, ul Warszawska 24, Krakow, 31155, Poland. TEL 48-12-6374289, FAX 48-12-6374289. Ed. Elzbieta Nachlik. Adv. contact Ewa Malochleb. Circ: 200.

300 330 POL ISSN 0137-2599
POLITECHNIKA LODZKA. ZESZYTY NAUKOWE. ORGANIZACJA I ZARZADZANIE. Text in Polish; Summaries in English. 1975. irreg. price varies. **Document type:** *Monographic series, Academic/Scholarly.* **Description:** Covers organization and management in enterprise, human resources management, ergonomics, economics, marketing, production management, information system, occupational safety management, environment management system, total quality management, quality of life.
Indexed: B22.
Published by: (Politechnika Lodzka/Technical University of Lodz), Wydawnictwo Politechniki Lodzkiej, ul Wolczanska 223, Lodz, 93005, Poland. TEL 48-42-6312087. Ed., R&P Jerzy Lewandowski TEL 48-42-6370043. Circ: 226. **Dist. by:** Ars Polona, Obroncow 25, Warsaw 03933, Poland. TEL 48-22-5098609, FAX 48-22-5098610, arspolona@arspolona.com.pl, http://www.arspolona.com.pl.

300 POL ISSN 1230-2767
POLITECHNIKA POZNANSKA. ZESZYTY NAUKOWE. HUMANISTYKA I NAUKI SPOLECZNE. Text in Polish. 1975. irreg., latest vol.57, 2009. price varies. 100 p./no.; **Document type:** *Monographic series, Academic/Scholarly.* **Description:** Covers social philosophy, philosophy of science, methodology of science, general sociology, sociology of management, sociology of social changes, economics.
Former titles: Politechnika Poznanska. Instytut Nauk Ekonomicznych i Spolecznych. Zeszyty Naukowe (0239-9423); Politechnika Poznanska. Instytut Nauk Ekonomicznych i Spolecznych. Prace Naukowe (0239-0094)
Published by: (Politechnika Poznanska), Wydawnictwo Politechniki Poznanskiej, Pl M Sklodowskiej Curie 2, Poznan, 60965, Poland. TEL 48-61-6653516, FAX 48-61-6653583, office_ed@put.poznan.pl, http://www.ed.put.poznan.pl. Ed. Stanislaw Poplawski. Circ: 100.

300 POL ISSN 0072-4718
H35
POLITECHNIKA SLASKA. ZESZYTY NAUKOWE. NAUKI SPOLECZNE. Text in Polish; Summaries in English, German, Russian. 1964. irreg. price varies.
—Linda Hall.
Published by: Politechnika Slaska, ul Akademicka 5, Gliwice, 44100, Poland. wydawnictwo_mark@polsl.pl. Ed. Jozef Haber. Circ: 205. **Dist by:** Ars Polona, Obroncow 25, Warsaw 03933, Poland.

300 320 340 DNK ISSN 1601-3476
POLITIK, RET OG SAMFUND. Text in Danish. 2001. irreg., latest vol.6, 2010. price varies. **Document type:** *Monographic series, Academic/Scholarly.* **Description:** Focuses on politics and social sciences.
Related titles: Online - full text ed.: ISSN 1604-3022.
Published by: Museum Tusculanum Press, c/o University of Copenhagen, Njalsgade 126, Copenhagen S, 2300, Denmark. TEL 45-35-329109, FAX 45-35-329113, info@mtp.dk, http://www.mtp.dk. Ed. Anders Berg Sorensen. **Dist. in France by:** Editions Picard, Editions Picard, Paris 75006, France. TEL 33-1-43269778, FAX 33-1-43264264; **Dist. in UK by:** Gazelle Book Services Ltd., White Cross Mills, Hightown, Lancaster LA1 4UU, United Kingdom. TEL 44-1524-68765, FAX 44-1524-63232, sales@gazellebooks.co.uk, http://www.gazellebookservices.co.uk/; **Dist. in US & Canada by:** International Specialized Book Services Inc., 920 NE 58th Ave Ste 300, Portland, OR 97213. TEL 503-287-3093, 800-944-6190, FAX 503-280-8832, orders@isbs.com, http://www.isbs.com/.

POLSKA AKADEMIA NAUK. ODDZIAL W KRAKOWIE. SPRAWOZDANIA Z POSIEDZEN KOMISJI NAUKOWYCH/POLISH ACADEMY OF SCIENCES. KRAKOW BRANCH. SCIENTIFIC MEETING REPORTS. *see* SCIENCES: COMPREHENSIVE WORKS

300 GBR ISSN 0140-5918
POLYTECHNIC OF CENTRAL LONDON. FACULTY OF BUSINESS, MANAGEMENT AND SOCIAL STUDIES. RESEARCH WORKING PAPER. Text in English. 1976. irreg., latest vol.43, 1992. **Document type:** *Monographic series.*
Published by: Polytechnic of Central London, Faculty of Business, Management and Social Studies, 32-38 Wells St, London, W1P 3FG, United Kingdom.

300 DEU ISSN 1434-7407
POP UND GO; Schriften zur populaeren Kultur. Text in German. 1996. irreg., latest vol.2, 1997. price varies. **Document type:** *Monographic series, Academic/Scholarly.*
Published by: Peter Lang GmbH (Subsidiary of: Peter Lang Publishing Group), Eschborner Landstr 42-50, Frankfurt Am Main, 60489, Germany. TEL 49-69-7807050, FAX 49-69-78070550, zentrale.frankfurt@peterlang.com.

▼ **POPULAERE KULTUR UND THEOLOGIE.** *see* RELIGIONS AND THEOLOGY

300 GBR ISSN 1754-3819
➤ **POPULAR NARRATIVE MEDIA.** Abbreviated title: P N M. Text in English. 1997. s-a. USD 50 combined subscription in US & Canada to individuals (print & online eds.); GBP 25 combined subscription elsewhere to individuals (print & online eds.); USD 110 combined subscription in US & Canada to institutions (print & online eds.); GBP 55 combined subscription elsewhere to institutions (print & online eds.) (effective 2009). adv. **Document type:** *Journal, Academic/Scholarly.* **Description:** Features articles devoted to the study of the mass media and its cultural reception.
Formerly (until 2008): Diegesis (1471-1281)
Related titles: Online - full text ed.: ISSN 1754-3827. 2008.
Indexed: A26, AmHI, CA, H07, I05, T02.
—BLDSC (6550.768350). **CCC.**
Published by: Liverpool University Press, 4 Cambridge St, Liverpool, L69 7ZU, United Kingdom. TEL 44-151-7942233, FAX 44-151-7942235, lup@liv.ac.uk, http://www.liverpool-unipress.co.uk/. Eds. Joanne Knowles, Nickianne Moody. Adv. contact Janet Smith. **Subscr. to:** Marston Book Services Ltd., PO Box 269, Abingdon, Oxon OX14 4YN, United Kingdom. TEL 44-1235-465500, FAX 44-1235-465555.

➤ **POPULATION ET SOCIETES.** *see* POPULATION STUDIES

➤ **POPULATIONS ET SOCIETES (ONLINE)/POPULATIONS AND SOCIETIES.** *see* POPULATION STUDIES

➤ **LE PORTIQUE.** *see* PHILOSOPHY

300 GBR ISSN 1476-413X
H1
➤ **PORTUGUESE JOURNAL OF SOCIAL SCIENCE.** Abbreviated title: P J S S. Text in English. 2002. s-a. GBP 210 domestic to institutions; GBP 219 in the European Union to institutions; USD 330 in US & Canada to institutions; GBP 222 elsewhere to institutions (effective 2011), adv. bk.rev. abstr.; bibl.; charts; illus. back issues avail. **Document type:** *Journal, Academic/Scholarly.* **Description:** Introduces an international readership to work currently being produced by Portuguese scholarship in the social sciences.
Related titles: Online - full text ed.: ISSN 1758-9509. USD 265 in US & Canada to institutions; GBP 177 elsewhere to institutions (effective 2011).
Indexed: A01, A02, A03, A08, A22, CA, E01, IBSS, P42, PSA, S02, S03, SociolAb, T02.
—IE. **CCC.**
Published by: (Unidade de Investigacao em Ciencias Sociais, Instituto Superior de Ciencias do Trabalho e da Empresa PRT, Fundacao para a Ciencia e a Tecnologia PRT), Intellect Ltd., The Mill, Parnall Rd, Fishponds, Bristol, BS16 3JG, United Kingdom. TEL 44-117-9589910, FAX 44-117-9589911, info@intellectbooks.com. Ed., R&P Luisa Oliveira. Circ: 100. **Subscr. in US to:** Intellect Books, Ste.106E, King Hall, 601 S. College Rd., Wilmington, NC 28403. TEL 910-962-2609, USinfo@intellectbooks.com. **Subscr. to:** Turpin Distribution Services Ltd., Pegasus Dr, Stratton Business Park, Biggleswade, Bedfordshire SG18 8QB, United Kingdom. TEL 44-1767-604951, FAX 44-1767-601640, custserv@turpin-distribution.com, http://www.turpin-distribution.com/.

➤ **PORTUGUESE STUDIES REVIEW.** *see* HUMANITIES: COMPREHENSIVE WORKS

➤ **POSTCOLONIAL STUDIES**; culture, politics, economy. *see* HISTORY

➤ **POSTCOLONIAL STUDIES.** *see* HISTORY

300 DEU ISSN 1612-6602
POTSDAMER BEITRAGE ZUR SOZIALFORSCHUNG. Text in German. 1995. irreg., latest vol.27, 2006. price varies. **Document type:** *Monographic series, Academic/Scholarly.*
Related titles: Online - full text ed.: ISSN 0947-109X.
Published by: Universitaet Potsdam, Wirtschafts- und Sozialwissenschaftliche Fakultaet, Universitaetskomplex III, Haus 1, Zi 1-35, Potsdam, 14482, Germany. TEL 49-331-9773324, FAX 49-331-9773325, wisodek@uni-potsdam.de, http://www.uni-potsdam.de/fakultaeten/wiso.html.

300 CHN ISSN 1674-6848
▼ ➤ **POYANGHU XUEKAN/POYANG LAKE JOURNAL.** Text in Chinese; Summaries in Chinese, English. 2009. bi-m. CNY 90, USD 90, CNY 15, USD 15 (effective 2009). **Document type:** *Journal, Academic/Scholarly.* **Description:** Covers various interdisciplinary research achievement on both ecologist humanities and social sciences at home and aboard.
Indexed: PAIS, PSA, SSA, SociolAb.
Published by: (Jiangxi Sheng Shehui Kexueyuan), Jiangxi Shehui Kexue Zazhishe, no.649, Hongdu North Ave, Nanchang, 330077, China. TEL 86-791-8596012, FAX 86-791-8596531. Ed. Yue Yu.

➤ **PRATIQUE MAGAZINE.** *see* HOME ECONOMICS

300 RUS
PRAVOZASHCHITNIK. Text in Russian. 1994. q. USD 89 in North America (effective 2000).
Indexed: RASB.
Published by: Izdatel'stvo Prava Cheloveka, Zubovskii bul 17, k 30, Moscow, 119021, Russian Federation. TEL 7-495-2466700. Ed. V F Vedrashko. **Dist. by:** East View Information Services, 10601 Wayzata Blvd, Minneapolis, MN 55305. TEL 952-252-1201, 800-477-1005, FAX 952-252-1202, info@eastview.com, http://www.eastview.com.

300 BIH ISSN 0032-7271
DB231
PREGLED (SARAJEVO, 1910); casopis za drustvena pitanja. Text in Serbo-Croatian. 1910. m. **Document type:** *Journal, Academic/Scholarly.* **Description:** Discusses current social matters, mostly in the fields of sociology, history, economy and literature.
Indexed: CA, RASB, T02.
Published by: Univerzitet u Sarajevu/University of Sarajevo, Obala Kulina Bana 7/II, Sarajevo, 71000, Bosnia Herzegovina. Ed. Radovan Milanovic.

300 DEU ISSN 1868-9442
PREISTRAEGER DER SOCIETAS JABLONOVIANA. Text in German. 2001. irreg., latest 2007. price varies. **Document type:** *Monographic series, Academic/Scholarly.*
Published by: Leipziger Universitaetsverlag GmbH, Oststr 41, Leipzig, 04317, Germany. TEL 49-341-9900440, FAX 49-341-9900440, info@univerlag-leipzig.de.

PRINCETON UNIVERSITY LIBRARY CHRONICLE. *see* HUMANITIES: COMPREHENSIVE WORKS

PRO JUGEND. AUSGABE BAYERN. *see* CHILDREN AND YOUTH—About

300 DEU ISSN 1865-2204
PROBLEME UND CHANCEN DER GLOBALISIERUNG. Text in German. 2007. irreg., latest vol.3, 2009. price varies. **Document type:** *Monographic series, Academic/Scholarly.*
Published by: Verlag Dr. Kovac, Leverkusenstr 13, Hamburg, 22761, Germany. TEL 49-40-3988800, FAX 49-40-39888055, info@verlagdrkovac.de.

300 NLD ISSN 1877-0428
▼ ➤ **PROCEDIA: SOCIAL AND BEHAVIORAL SCIENCES.** Text in English. 2009 (Feb.). 6/yr. **Document type:** *Proceedings, Academic/Scholarly.* **Description:** Aims to rapidly publish high quality conference proceedings in the social and behavioral sciences.
Media: Online - full content. **Related titles:** Online - full text ed.: (from ScienceDirect).
Indexed: P30.
—**CCC.**
Published by: Elsevier BV (Subsidiary of: Elsevier Science & Technology), Radarweg 29, PO Box 211, Amsterdam, 1000 AE, Netherlands. TEL 31-20-4853911, FAX 31-20-4852457, JournalsCustomerServiceEMEA@elsevier.com.

300 ITA ISSN 2035-4045
PRODUZIONE E RIPRODUZIONE SOCIALE. RICERCHE. Text in Italian. 1992. irreg. **Document type:** *Monographic series, Academic/Scholarly.*
Published by: Franco Angeli Edizioni, Viale Monza 106, Milan, 20127, Italy. TEL 39-02-2837141, FAX 39-02-26144793, redazioni@francoangeli.it, http://www.francoangeli.it.

300 ITA ISSN 2035-4029
PRODUZIONE E RIPRODUZIONE SOCIALE. TEMATIZZAZIONI. Text in Italian. 1992. irreg. **Document type:** *Monographic series, Academic/Scholarly.*
Published by: Franco Angeli Edizioni, Viale Monza 106, Milan, 20127, Italy. TEL 39-02-2837141, FAX 39-02-26144793, redazioni@francoangeli.it, http://www.francoangeli.it.

300 USA ISSN 1933-8740
PROGRAM ON INTRASTATE CONFLICT REPORT. Text in English. 1989. irreg. **Document type:** *Monographic series, Academic/Scholarly.*
Formerly (until 2006): W P F Reports (1933-8775)
Related titles: Online - full text ed.: ISSN 1933-8759.
Published by: Harvard University, John F. Kennedy School of Government. Belfer Center for Science and International Affairs. Program on Intrastate Conflict, 79 John F Kennedy St, Cambridge, MA 02138. TEL 617-495-1400, FAX 617-495-8963, conflict@ksg.harvard.edu, http://www.belfercenter.org/project/52/intrastate_conflict_program.html.

225 FRA ISSN 0033-0884
HN37.C3
PROJET. Text in French. 1920. q. EUR 59 to individuals; EUR 45 to students (effective 2008). adv. bk.rev. bibl.; charts. index. **Document type:** *Journal.*
Former titles (until 1965): Revue de l'Action Populaire (1149-2678); (until 1950): Travaux de l'Action Populaire (1149-266X); (until 1940): Les Dossiers de l'Action Populaire (1149-2651)
Related titles: Online - full text ed.: ISSN 2108-6648. 2010.
Indexed: A22, BAS, CISA, DIP, FR, I13, IBR, IBSS, IBZ, ILD, PAIS, PdeR, PerIslam, RASB, WBSS.
—BLDSC (6924.930000), IE, Infotrieve, Ingenta, INIST.
Published by: Ceras, 4 Rue de la Croix Faron, La Plaine Saint-Denis, 93217, France. TEL 33-8-70406389, FAX 33-1-49983950. Circ: 5,200.

PROMETHEUS (LONDON). *see* HUMANITIES: COMPREHENSIVE WORKS

300 PRT ISSN 1647-5100
PROMONTORIA MONOGRAFICA. Text in Portuguese. 2004. irreg. **Document type:** *Monographic series, Academic/Scholarly.*
Published by: Universidade do Algarve, Faculdade de Ciencias Humanas e Sociais, Campus de Gambelas, Faro, 8005-139, Portugal. TEL 351-289-800914, FAX 351-289-800067, fchs@ualg.pt, http://www.fchs.ualg.pt.

PROYECCIONES. *see* EDUCATION—Higher Education

PRZEGLAD UNIWERSYTECKI. *see* HUMANITIES: COMPREHENSIVE WORKS

300 150 BRA ISSN 1807-0310
PSICOLOGIA E SOCIEDADE. Text in Multiple languages. 2002. s-a. free (effective 2011). **Document type:** *Journal, Academic/Scholarly.*
Media: Online - full text.
Indexed: IBSS.
Published by: Associacao Brasileira de Psicologia Social, Rua Ramiro Barcelos 2600, Sala 13, Porto Alegre, RS 90035-030, Brazil.

300 ITA ISSN 1827-2517
PSICOLOGIA SOCIALE. Text in Multiple languages. 2006. 3/yr. EUR 93 combined subscription domestic to institutions (print & online eds.); EUR 144.50 combined subscription foreign to institutions (print & online eds.) (effective 2009). **Document type:** *Journal, Academic/Scholarly.*
Related titles: Online - full text ed.
Indexed: P03, PsycInfo.
Published by: Societa Editrice Il Mulino, Strada Maggiore 37, Bologna, 40125, Italy. TEL 39-051-256011, FAX 39-051-256034, riviste@mulino.it. Ed. Augusto Palmonari.

PSICOPERSPECTIVAS (ONLINE); individuo y sociedad. *see* PSYCHOLOGY

PSYCHOLOGY TODAY; for a healthier life. *see* PSYCHOLOGY

300 USA ISSN 1937-2477
JK1118
PUBLIC INTEREST GROUP PROFILES. Text in English. 1978. biennial. USD 245 per issue (effective 2008). reprints avail. **Document type:** *Directory.* **Description:** Contains assessments of group effectiveness and group political orientation, contact information, mission statements, funding sources, leadership and membership information, publication lists and methods of advocacy.
Formerly (until 2004): Public Interest Profiles (1058-627X)
Related titles: Online - full text ed.
Published by: C Q Press, Inc. (Subsidiary of: Sage Publications, Inc.), 2300 N St, NW, Ste 800, Washington, DC 20037. TEL 202-729-1900, FAX 800-380-3810, customerservice@cqpress.com.

PUBLIC OPINION QUARTERLY. *see* POLITICAL SCIENCE

PUBLIC POLICY INSTITUTE OF CALIFORNIA. RESEARCH BRIEF. *see* POLITICAL SCIENCE

PUBLICACOES CULTURAIS DA COMPANHIA. *see* SCIENCES: COMPREHENSIVE WORKS

PUBLICAR EN ANTROPOLOGIA Y CIENCIAS SOCIALES. *see* ANTHROPOLOGY

PUBLICATIONES UNIVERSITATIS MISKOLCIENSIS. SECTIO PHILOSOPHICA. *see* HUMANITIES: COMPREHENSIVE WORKS

300 CHE ISSN 1422-7630
PUBLICATIONS D'HISTOIRE ECONOMIQUE ET SOCIALE INTERNATIONALE/INTERNATIONAL ECONOMIC AND SOCIAL HISTORY PUBLICATIONS. Text in French. 1985. irreg., latest vol.26, 2011. price varies. **Document type:** *Monographic series, Academic/Scholarly.*
Formerly (until 1998): Publications du Centre d'Histoire Economique Internationale de l'Universite de Geneve (1422-9471)

S

Published by: Librairie Droz S.A., 11 rue Firmin-Massot, Geneva 12, 1211, Switzerland. TEL 41-22-3466666, FAX 41-22-3472391, droz@droz.org, http://www.droz.org.

300 USA ISSN 1047-3726
E184.D6
PUNTO 7 REVIEW; a journal of marginal discourse. Text in English. 1992 (vol.2, no.2). a. **Description:** Encourages scholarly, intellectual, artistic and scientific discourse by and about the representatives of all sectors of our society.
Indexed: MLA-IB.
Published by: Council of Dominican Educators, Social Science Dept, LaGuardia Community College, 31 10 Thomson Ave, Long Island City, NY 11101. Eds. Ramona Hernandez, Silvio Torres Saillant.

PURUSHARTHA. *see* HISTORY—History Of Asia

300 RUS
PUTI K BEZOPASNOSTI. Text in Russian. 1993. irreg. USD 99 in North America (effective 2000).
Indexed: RASB.
Published by: Institut Mira Rossiiskoi Akademii Nauk, Profsoyuznaya ul 23, Moscow, 117418, Russian Federation. **Dist. by:** East View Information Services, 10601 Wayzata Blvd, Minneapolis, MN 55305. TEL 952-252-1201, 800-477-1005, FAX 952-252-1202, info@eastview.com, http://www.eastview.com.

300 CHN ISSN 1008-7885
PUTIAN GAODENG ZHUANKE XUEXIAO XUEBAO. Text in Chinese. 1994. bi-m. CNY 6 newsstand/cover (effective 2006). **Document type:** *Journal, Academic/Scholarly.*
Related titles: Online - full text ed.
Published by: Putian Gaodeng Zhuanke Xuexiao, 1133, Xueyuan Zhong Jie, Putian, 351100, China.

300 500 CHN ISSN 1674-2389
QIANNAN MINZU SHIFAN XUEYUAN XUEBAO/QIANNAN UNIVERSITY OF NATIONALITIES. JOURNAL. Text in Chinese. 1981. bi-m. **Document type:** *Journal, Academic/Scholarly.*
Formerly (until 2000): Qiannan Minzu Shizhuan Xuebao/Qiannan Teachers' College of Nationalities. Journal (1005-6769)
Related titles: Online - full text ed.
Published by: Qiannan Minzu Shifan Xueyuan/Qiannan Normal College of Nationalities, Editorial Department, Duyun, 558000, China. TEL 86-854-8737044, FAX 86-854-8254937.

300 CHN ISSN 1001-022X
AS452.C4783
QILU XUEKAN. Text in Chinese. 1974. bi-m. USD 28.20 (effective 2009). **Document type:** *Academic/Scholarly.* **Description:** Covers philosophy, literature, history, educational and social sciences.
Formerly (until 1980): Po yu Li
Related titles: Online - full text ed.
Indexed: MLA-IB.
—East View.
Published by: (Qilu Xuekan Bianjibu), Qufu Shifan Daxue/Qufu Normal University, 21, Jingxuan Xi Lu, Qufu, Shandong 273165, China. TEL 86-537-4424347. Ed. Wang Junlin.

300 100 CHN ISSN 1006-4133
QINGDAO DAXUE SHIFAN XUEYUAN XUEBAO/TEACHERS COLLEGE QINGDAO UNIVERSITY. JOURNAL. Text in Chinese. 1982. q. USD 20.80 (effective 2009). **Document type:** *Journal, Academic/Scholarly.*
Formerly (until 1993): Qingdao Shi-Zhuan Xuebao/Qingdao Teachers College. Journal (1001-9049)
Related titles: Online - full text ed.
Indexed: CA, E03, L&LBA, P42, PSA, S02, S03, SociolAb, T02.
Published by: Qingdao Daxue Shifan Xueyuan, 16, Qingda Yi Lu, Qingdao, 266071, China. TEL 86-532-5956640.

300 CHN ISSN 1671-8372
QINGDAO KEJI DAXUE XUEBAO (SHEHUI KEXUE BAN)/QINGDAO UNIVERSITY OF SCIENCE AND TECHNOLOGY. JOURNAL (SOCIAL SCIENCES EDITION). Text in Chinese. 1983. q. USD 16.40 (effective 2009).
Formerly (until 2001): Qingdao Huagong Xueyuan Xuebao (Shehui Kexue Ban)/Qingdao Institute of Chemical Technology. Journal (Social Sciences Edition) (1008-6773)
Related titles: Online - full text ed.
Indexed: CA, L&LBA, P42, PAIS, PSA, S02, S03, SCOPUS, SociolAb, T02.
Published by: Qingdao Keji Daxue/Qingdao University of Science and Technology, 53, Zhengzhou Lu, Qingdao, 266042, China.

QINGHAI MINZU DAXUE XUEBAO (SHEHUI KEXUE BAN)/QINGHAI NATIONALITIES UNIVERSITY. JOURNAL (SOCIAL SCIENCES). *see* ASIAN STUDIES

300 CHN
QINGHAI MINZU DAXUE XUEBAO (ZANGWEN BAN)/QINGHAI NATIONALITIES UNIVERSITY. JOURNAL (TIBETAN EDITION). Text in Chinese. 2003. s-a. **Document type:** *Journal, Academic/Scholarly.*
Formerly (until 2010): Qinghai Shi-Zhuan Xuebao (Zangwen Ban)/Qinghai Junior Normal College. Journal (Tibetan Edition)
Published by: Qinghai Minzu Daxue/QingHai Nationalities University, 72, Ba-Yi Zhong Lu, Qinghai, 810007, China. http://www.qhmu.edu.cn/.

300 CHN ISSN 1000-5102
H8.C47
➤ **QINGHAI SHIFAN DAXUE XUEBAO (ZHEXUE SHEHUI KEXUE BAN)/QINGHAI NORMAL UNIVERSITY. JOURNAL (PHILOSOPHY AND SOCIAL SCIENCE EDITION).** Text in Chinese. 1960. bi-m. USD 31.20 (effective 2009). adv. bk.rev. cum.index: 1960-2000. **Document type:** *Journal, Academic/Scholarly.* **Description:** Contains research papers on political science, business and economics, philosophy, literature, history, education, psychology, and art.
Related titles: ◆ CD-ROM ed.: Chinese Academic Journals Full-Text Database. Literature, History & Philosophy. ISSN 1007-8061; Online - full text ed.
Published by: Qinghai Shifan Daxue/Qinghai Normal University, 38, 54 Xi Lu, Xining, 810008, China. TEL 86-971-6307647, FAX 86-971-6302588. Ed., Pub., R&P, Adv. contact Guo Hongji. Circ: 2,500 (paid). **Dist. by:** China International Book Trading Corp, 35 Chegongzhuang Xilu, Haidian District, PO Box 399, Beijing 100044, China. TEL 86-10-68412045, FAX 86-10-68412023, cibtc@mail.cibtc.com.cn, http://www.cibtc.com.cn.

➤ **QINGHUA DAXUE XUEBAO (ZHEXUE SHEHUI KEXUE BAN)/TSINGHUA UNIVERSITY. JOURNAL (PHILOSOPHY AND SOCIAL SCIENCES).** *see* PHILOSOPHY

300 CHN ISSN 1674-4896
QINGYUAN ZHIYE JISHU XUEYUAN XUEBAO/QINGYUAN POLYTECHNIC. JOURNAL. Text in Chinese. 2003. bi-m.
Formerly (until 2008): Guangdong Jingji Guanli Xueyuan Xuebao/Guangdong Institute of Business Administration. Journal (1672-4100); Which was formed by the merger (1985-2003): Guangdong Sheng Cai-Mao Guanli Ganbu Xueyuan Xuebao/Guangdong Institute for Managers in Finance and Trade. Journal (1671-3192); (1999-2003): Guangdong Sheng Jingji Guanli Ganbu Xueyuan Xuebao/Guangdong Economic Management Cadre Institute. Journal (1009-0223)
Published by: Qingyuan Zhiye Jishu Xueyuan/Qingyuan Polytechnic, Qicheng-Qu, Dongcheng Jie, Panlongyuan, Qingyuan, 511510, China. TEL 86-763-3936229, wlzx3c208@qypt.com.cn, http://www.qypt.com.cn/.

300 CHN ISSN 1008-5629
QINZHOU SHIFAN GAODENG ZHUANKE XUEXIAO XUEBAO/QINZHOU TEACHERS COLLEGE. JOURNAL. Text in Chinese. 1986. bi-m. CNY 6 newsstand/cover (effective 2006). **Document type:** *Journal, Academic/Scholarly.*
Related titles: Online - full text ed.
Published by: Qinzhou Shifan Gaodeng Zhuanke Xuexiao, Nanzhu Xi Dajie, Qinzhou, 535000, China. TEL 86-777-2808106, FAX 86-777-2808633.

300 CHN ISSN 1008-6722
QIONGZHOU DAXUE XUEBAO/QIONGZHOU UNIVERSITY. JOURNAL. Text in English. 1994. bi-m. USD 18 (effective 2009). **Document type:** *Journal, Academic/Scholarly.*
Related titles: Online - full text ed.
—East View.
Published by: Qiongzhou Daxue, Tongshi, 572200, China. TEL 86-898-86622207.

300 CHN ISSN 1008-2638
QIQIHAER DAXUE XUEBAO (ZHEXUE SHEHUI KEXUE BAN)/QIQIHAR UNIVERSITY. JOURNAL (PHILOSOPHY & SOCIAL SCIENCE). Text in Chinese. 1972. bi-m. USD 31.20 (effective 2009). 110 p./no.; **Document type:** *Journal, Academic/Scholarly.* **Description:** Contains academic researches by college staff in the fields of philosophy, economics, politics, history, literature, linguistics, and education.
Formerly (until 1997): Qiqiha'er Shifan Xueyuan Xuebao/Qiqiha'er Teachers College. Journal (1001-473X)
Related titles: Online - full text ed.
—East View.
Published by: Qiqihaer Daxue/Qiqihaer University, 30, Wenhua Dajie, Qiqihaer, 161006, China. TEL 86-452-2738210.

300 100 CHN ISSN 1000-7504
AS452.H3196
QIUSHI XUEKAN/SEEKING TRUTH. Text in Chinese. 1974. bi-m. CNY 15 per issue. **Document type:** *Journal, Academic/Scholarly.*
Formerly (until 1980): Heilongjiang Daxue Xuebao (Zhexue Shehui Kexue Ban)
Related titles: Online - full text ed.
—East View.
Published by: Heilongjiang Daxue/Heilongjiang University, 74, Xuefu Lu, Nangang-qu, Ha'erbin, 150080, China. TEL 86-451-86608815, FAX 86-451-86608215. **Dist. by:** China International Book Trading Corp, 35 Chegongzhuang Xilu, Haidian District, PO Box 399, Beijing 100044, China. TEL 86-10-68412045, FAX 86-10-68412023, cibtc@mail.cibtc.com.cn, http://www.cibtc.com.cn.

300 CHN ISSN 1001-490X
AP95.C4
QIUSUO/SEEKER BIMONTHLY. Text in Chinese. 1981. bi-m. USD 117.60 (effective 2009). bk.rev. 128 p./no.; **Document type:** *Academic/Scholarly.* **Description:** Discusses the major theoretical and practical issues related to Chinese socialism. Also contains research on Chinese history and traditional culture.
Related titles: Online - full text ed.
—East View.
Published by: (Hunan Sheng Shehui Kexueyuan/Social Science Institute in Hunan Providence), Qiusuo Zazhishe, Deyacun, Changsha, Hunan 410003, China. TEL 86-731-4223870, qszzs@sina.com.cn. Ed. Li Huasheng. Pub. Zheng Jie. R&P Jie Zheng. Adv. contact Xiao Ou Sheng. Circ: 5,000. **Dist. overseas by:** China International Book Trading Corp, 35 Chegongzhuang Xilu, Haidian District, PO Box 399, Beijing 100044, China.

300 301 ITA ISSN 1824-4750
QUADERNI DI TEORIA SOCIALE. Text in Italian. 2001. a. **Document type:** *Journal, Academic/Scholarly.*
Published by: Morlacchi Editore, Piazza Morlacchi 7-9, Perugia, 06123, Italy. TEL 39-075-5716036, FAX 39-075-5725297, editore@morlacchilibri.com, http://www.morlacchilibri.com.

300 330 BRA ISSN 1677-4280
QUALIT@S. Text in Portuguese. 2002. s-a. free (effective 2011). **Document type:** *Journal, Academic/Scholarly.*
Media: Online - full text.
Published by: Universidade Estadual da Paraiba, Centro de Ciencias Sociais Aplicadas waleska.silveira@oi.com.br, http://www.uepb.edu.br. Ed. Waleska Silveira Lira.

301 USA ISSN 1077-8004
H61 CODEN: QUINFS
➤ **QUALITATIVE INQUIRY.** Text in English. 1995. 10/yr. USD 1,346, GBP 792 combined subscription to institutions (print & online eds.); USD 1,319, GBP 776 to institutions (effective 2011). bk.rev. bibl.; charts. back issues avail.; reprint service avail. from PSC. **Document type:** *Journal, Academic/Scholarly.* **Description:** Takes an interdisciplinary approach to examine qualitative methodology and related issues in the human sciences.
Related titles: Online - full text ed.: ISSN 1552-7565. USD 1,211, GBP 713 to institutions (effective 2011).
Indexed: A01, A02, A03, A08, A20, A22, A26, B07, CA, CommAb, CurCont, E01, E08, ERA, FR, FamI, G08, H04, I05, IBSS, P02, P10, P26, P30, P48, P53, P54, PQC, RILM, S02, S03, S09, S11, S19, S20, S21, SCOPUS, SOPODA, SSA, SSCI, SociolAb, T02, V02, W07, W09.
—BLDSC (7168.124300), IE, Infotrieve, Ingenta, INIST. **CCC.**
Published by: (Association for Research on Nonprofit Organizations and Voluntary Action), Sage Publications, Inc., 2455 Teller Rd, Thousand Oaks, CA 91320. TEL 805-499-9774, 800-818-7243, FAX 805-499-0871, 800-583-2665, info@sagepub.com. Eds. Norman K Denzin, Yvonna S Lincoln. **Subscr. outside of the Americas to:** Sage Publications Ltd., 1 Oliver's Yard, 55 City Rd, London EC1Y 1SP, United Kingdom. TEL 44-207-3248701, FAX 44-207-3248733, subscription@sagepub.co.uk. **Co-sponsor:** Yale University, Program on Non-profit Organizations.

300 USA ISSN 2160-3715
➤ **THE QUALITATIVE REPORT (ONLINE).** Abbreviated title: T Q R. Text in English. 1990. bi-m. free (effective 2011). back issues avail. **Document type:** *Journal, Academic/Scholarly.* **Description:** Provides a forum for researchers, scholars, and practitioners concerning qualitative inquiry in the social sciences.
Formerly (until 199?): The Qualitative Report (Print) (1052-0147)
Media: Online - full text.
Indexed: A26, A39, C27, C29, CA, D03, D04, E-psyche, E13, ERIC, FamI, I05, P10, P46, P48, P53, P54, PQC, R14, S02, S03, S14, S15, S18, SCOPUS, SSA, SociolAb, T02.
Published by: Nova Southeastern University, 3301 College Ave, Fort Lauderdale-Davie, FL 33314. TEL 800-541-6682, help@nova.edu. Ed. Dr. Ronald J Chenail TEL 954-262-5389.

300 GBR ISSN 1468-7941
H62.A1
➤ **QUALITATIVE RESEARCH.** Text in English. 2001 (Apr.). 6/yr. USD 1,012, GBP 547 combined subscription to institutions (print & online eds.); USD 992, GBP 536 to institutions (effective 2011). adv. bk.rev. back issues avail.; reprint service avail. from PSC. **Document type:** *Journal, Academic/Scholarly.* **Description:** Dedicated to promoting and debating qualitative research methods in a broad intellectual framework. It provides a forum for the publication of international and interdisciplinary research, in the form of articles, short communications and research notes, reports on new technologies and other innovations and review essays and book reviews.
Related titles: Online - full text ed.: ISSN 1741-3109. USD 911, GBP 492 to institutions (effective 2011).
Indexed: A01, A03, A08, A22, AICP, C06, C07, CA, CIS, CurCont, DIP, E01, FamI, IBR, IBSS, IBZ, P03, P30, P42, PSA, PsycInfo, PsycholAb, S02, S03, SCOPUS, SSCI, SociolAb, T02, W07.
—BLDSC (7168.124380), IE, Ingenta. **CCC.**
Published by: Sage Publications Ltd. (Subsidiary of: Sage Publications, Inc.), 1 Oliver's Yard, 55 City Rd, London, EC1Y 1SP, United Kingdom. TEL 44-20-73248500, FAX 44-20-73248600, info@sagepub.co.uk, http://www.uk.sagepub.com/home.nav. Eds. Paul A Atkinson, Sara Delamont. adv.: B&W page GBP 350; 140 x 210. **Subscr. in the Americas to:** Sage Publications, Inc., 2455 Teller Rd, Thousand Oaks, CA 91320. TEL 805-499-9774, FAX 805-499-0871, journals@sagepub.com.

300 AUS ISSN 1448-0980
➤ **QUALITATIVE RESEARCH JOURNAL.** Text in English. 2002. 2/yr. bk.rev. **Document type:** *Journal, Academic/Scholarly.* **Description:** Contains articles, book reviews, and essays on teaching qualitative research methodology.
Formerly (until 2001): Qualitative Research Journal (Print) (1443-9883)
Media: Online - full text.
Indexed: A26, B04, CA, H05, I05, P48, P51, P53, P54, PQC, S02, S03, SCOPUS, SSAI, SSAb, SSI, T02, W03, W05.
Published by: (Association for Qualitative Research), RMIT Publishing, Level 3, Swanston St, Melbourne, VIC, Australia. TEL 61-03-99258100, FAX 61-03-99258134, info@rmitpublishing.com.au. Ed. Jan Brace-Govan.

300 USA ISSN 0888-5397
QUALITATIVE RESEARCH METHODS SERIES. Text in English. 1986. irreg., latest 2008. price varies. back issues avail.; reprints avail. **Document type:** *Monographic series, Academic/Scholarly.* **Description:** Covers various aspects of the use of qualitative research methods in social sciences research.
Related titles: Online - full text ed.; ◆ Series of: Sage University Papers Series.
Indexed: A22.
—BLDSC (7168.124400), IE, Ingenta. **CCC.**
Published by: Sage Publications, Inc., Books (Subsidiary of: Sage Publications, Inc.), 2455 Teller Rd, Thousand Oaks, CA 91320. TEL 800-818-7243, FAX 800-583-2665, books.claim@sagepub.com. Pub. Sara Miller McCune. **Subscr. in Asia to:** Sage Publications India Pvt. Ltd.; **Subscr. in Europe to:** Sage Publications Ltd.

300 USA ISSN 0149-192X
QUANTITATIVE APPLICATIONS IN THE SOCIAL SCIENCES SERIES. Text in English. 1976. irreg., latest 2010. price varies. back issues avail.; reprints avail. **Document type:** *Monographic series, Academic/Scholarly.* **Description:** Covers series of concise and accessible papers on methodology in the social sciences is a publishing phenomenon, with over 115 titles currently in print and world-wide sales.
Related titles: Online - full text ed.; ◆ Series of: Sage University Papers Series.
Indexed: A22, CIS.
—BLDSC (8069.271900), IE, Ingenta. **CCC.**
Published by: Sage Publications, Inc., Books (Subsidiary of: Sage Publications, Inc.), 2455 Teller Rd, Thousand Oaks, CA 91320. TEL 800-818-7243, FAX 800-583-2665, books.claim@sagepub.com. Pub. Sara Miller McCune. **Subscr. in Asia to:** Sage Publications India Pvt. Ltd.; **Subscr. in Europe to:** Sage Publications Ltd.

300 CHN ISSN 1009-8224
QUANZHOU SHIFAN XUEYUAN XUEBAO. Text in Chinese. 1983. bi-m. CNY 5 newsstand/cover (effective 2006). **Document type:** *Journal, Academic/Scholarly.*
Formerly (until 2000): Quanzhou Shi-Zhuan Xuebao/Quanzhou Normal College. Journal (1008-4924)
Related titles: Online - full text ed.
Published by: Quanzhou Shifan Xueyuan, Donghai Jiao-qu, Quanzhou, 362000, China. TEL 86-595-22919659.

QUELLEN ZUR GESCHICHTE UND LANDESKUNDE OSTMITTELEUROPAS. *see* HISTORY—History Of Europe

300 GBR ISSN 1754-260X
QUESTIONING CITIES SERIES. Text in English. 200?. irreg., latest 2007. price varies. back issues avail. **Document type:** *Monographic series, Academic/Scholarly.* **Description:** Draws on contemporary social, urban and critical theory to explore different aspects of the city.
Published by: Routledge (Subsidiary of: Taylor & Francis Group), 4 Park Sq, Milton Park, Abingdon, Oxon OX14 4RN, United Kingdom. TEL 44-20-70176000, FAX 44-20-70176336, subscriptions@tandf.co.uk.

300 FRA ISSN 1778-3429
QUESTIONS CONTEMPORAINES. SERIE GLOBALISATION ET SCIENCES SOCIALES. Text in French. 2005. **Document type:** *Monographic series.*
Related titles: ◆ Series of: Questions Contemporaines. ISSN 1286-8698.
Published by: L' Harmattan, 5 Rue de l'Ecole Polytechnique, Paris, 75005, France. TEL 33-1-43257651, FAX 33-1-43258203, http://www.editions-harmattan.fr.

300 CHN ISSN 1001-5337
Q4 CODEN: QSDXEI
QUFU SHIFAN DAXUE XUEBAO (ZIRAN KEXUE BAN)/QUFU NORMAL UNIVERSITY. JOURNAL (NATURAL SCIENCE EDITION). Text in Chinese; Summaries in English. 1964. q. USD 16.40 (effective 2009). bk.rev. **Document type:** *Journal, Academic/Scholarly.* **Description:** Contains research papers on mathematics, physics, chemistry, biology, geography, philosophy and history.
Related titles: CD-ROM ed.; Online - full text ed.
Indexed: A22, CCMJ, CIS, MSN, MathR, RefZh, Z01, Z02.
—BLDSC (4844.200000), IE, Ingenta.
Published by: Qufu Shifan Daxue/Qufu Normal University, 21, Jingxuan Xi Lu, Qufu, Shandong 273165, China. TEL 86-537-4456260, FAX 86-537-4455344. **Dist. by:** China International Book Trading Corp, 35 Chegongzhuang Xilu, Haidian District, PO Box 399, Beijing 100044, China. TEL 86-10-68412045, FAX 86-10-68412023, cibtc@mail.cibtc.com.cn, http://www.cibtc.com.cn.

QUINTO SOL; revista de historia regional. *see* HISTORY

QUJING SHIFAN XUEYUAN XUEBAO/QUJING NORMAL UNIVERSITY. JOURNAL. *see* SCIENCES: COMPREHENSIVE WORKS

300 657 658 BRA ISSN 1983-6635
➤ **R G O. REVISTA GESTAO ORGANIZACIONAL.** Text in Portuguese; Summaries in English, Portuguese. 2004. s-a. Index. back issues avail. **Document type:** *Journal, Academic/Scholarly.* **Description:** Publishes articles in the areas of administration, management, accounting, and methodological issues in social sciences for professores, researches, and students in Brazil.
Media: Online - full content.
Indexed: CA, T02.
Published by: Universidade Comunitaria Regional de Chapeco (UNOCHAPECO), Avenida Senador Attilio Fontana, 591-E, Bairro Efapi, Caixa Postal: 1141, Chapeco, Santa Catarina 89809-000, Brazil. TEL 55-49-33218054. Ed. Leonardo Secchi.

300 FRA ISSN 1771-1347
B778
R H R. (Renaissance, Humanisme, Reforme) Text in French. 1975. irreg. **Document type:** *Journal, Academic/Scholarly.*
Formerly (until 1997): Association d'Etudes sur la Renaissance, l'Humanisme et la Reforme. Bulletin (0181-6799)
Indexed: PCI.
—IE.
Published by: Association d'Etudes sur la Renaissance, l'Humanisme et la Reforme, c/o Institut des Sciences de l'Homme, 14 Av. Berthelot, Lyon, 69006, France.

300 331.12 304.6 DEU ISSN 1612-3573
R W I: MATERIALIEN. (Rheinisch-Westfaelisches Institut) Text in German. irreg., latest vol.17, 2004. price varies. **Document type:** *Monographic series, Academic/Scholarly.*
Published by: Rheinisch-Westfaelisches Institut fuer Wirtschaftsforschung Essen, Hohenzollernstr 1-3, Essen, 45128, Germany. TEL 49-201-81490, FAX 49-201-8149200, rwi@rwi-essen.de.

300 MEX ISSN 1665-0441
➤ **RA XIMHAI**; revista cientifica de sociedad, cultura y desarrollo sustenable. Text in Spanish, English, French. 2005. 3/yr. free (effective 2011). **Document type:** *Journal, Academic/Scholarly.*
Media: Online - full text.
Indexed: C01, H21, P08.
Published by: Universidad Autonoma Indigena de Mexico, Juarez 39, Mochicahui, Sinaloa, 81890, Mexico.

300 USA ISSN 1867-1748
HT1501
▼ ➤ **RACE AND SOCIAL PROBLEMS.** Text in English. 2009. q. EUR 270, USD 405 combined subscription to institutions (print & online eds.) (effective 2012). back issues avail.; reprint service avail. from PSC. **Document type:** *Journal, Academic/Scholarly.* **Description:** Provides a forum for the publication of articles and discussion of issues germane to race and its enduring relationship to psychological, socioeconomic, political, and cultural problems.
Related titles: Online - full text ed.: ISSN 1867-1756. 2009 (from IngentaConnect).
Indexed: A22, E01, P10, P48, P51, P53, P54, PQC, PsycInfo, SSA, SociolAb.
—IE. **CCC.**
Published by: Springer New York LLC (Subsidiary of: Springer Science+Business Media), 233 Spring St, New York, NY 10013. TEL 212-460-1500, FAX 212-460-1575, service-ny@springer.com, http://www.springer.com. Ed. Gary F Koeske.

300 DEU ISSN 1615-0155
RAISONS D'AGIR. Text in German. 2000. irreg., latest vol.8, 2001. price varies. **Document type:** *Monographic series, Academic/Scholarly.*
Published by: U V K Verlagsgesellschaft mbH, Schuetzenstr 24, Konstanz, 78462, Germany. TEL 49-7531-90530, FAX 49-7531-905398, nadine.ley@uvk.de, http://www.uvk.de.

300 FRA ISSN 1150-1367
RAISONS PRATIQUES; epistemologie, sociologie, theorie sociale. Text in French. 1990. a. price varies. **Document type:** *Monographic series, Academic/Scholarly.*
Indexed: FR.
—INIST.
Published by: College de France, Ecole des Hautes Etudes en Sciences Sociales (E H E S S), 96 Boulevard Raspail, Paris, 75006, France. TEL 33-1-53635658, FAX 33-1-49542428, http://www.ehess.fr. **Dist. by:** Centre Interinstitutionnel pour la Diffusion de Publications en Sciences Humaines, 131 bd. Saint-Michel, Paris 75005, France. TEL 33-1-43544715, FAX 33-1-43548073.

300 USA ISSN 2158-5784
▼ **RAMIFY.** Text in English. 2010. a. USD 10 per issue (effective 2010). **Document type:** *Journal, Trade.* **Description:** Seeks to foster the involvement of scholars, teachers, and students in the ongoing dialogue within the Western tradition.
Published by: University of Dallas, 1845 E Northgate Dr, Irving, TX 75062. TEL 972-721-5000, FAX 972-721-5017, http://www.udallas.edu.

300 658 ITA ISSN 1826-0713
RASSEGNA ITALIANA DI VALUTAZIONE. Short title: R I V. Text in Italian. 1996. 3/yr. EUR 59 combined subscription domestic to institutions (print & online eds.); EUR 95.50 combined subscription foreign to institutions (print & online eds.) (effective 2009). **Document type:** *Journal, Academic/Scholarly.*
Related titles: Online - full text ed.: ISSN 1972-5027.
Indexed: A01, CA, T02.
Published by: (Associazione Italiana di Valutazione), Franco Angeli Edizioni, Viale Monza 106, Milan, 20127, Italy. TEL 39-02-2837141, FAX 39-02-26144793, redazioni@francoangeli.it, http://www.francoangeli.it.

300 ITA ISSN 2035-3871
RATIO SOCIOLOGICA. Variant title: Journal of Social Sciences: Theory and Applications. Text in Multiple languages. 2008. 3/yr. **Document type:** *Journal, Academic/Scholarly.*
Published by: Universita degli Studi di Chieti e Pescara "Gabriele d'Annunzio", Dipartimento di Scienze Sociali, Via dei Vestini 31, Chieti, 66013, Italy. http://www.unich.it.

300 GBR ISSN 1043-4631
H62.A1 CODEN: RTSOEG
➤ **RATIONALITY AND SOCIETY.** Text in English. 1989. q. USD 953, GBP 515 combined subscription to institutions (print & online eds.); USD 934, GBP 505 to institutions (effective 2011). adv. back issues avail.; reprint service avail. from PSC. **Document type:** *Journal, Academic/Scholarly.* **Description:** Focuses on the growing contributions of rational-action based theory, and the questions and controversies surrounding this growth.
Related titles: Microfilm ed.: (from PQC); Online - full text ed.: ISSN 1461-7358. USD 858, GBP 464 to institutions (effective 2011).
Indexed: A01, A02, A03, A08, A20, A22, ABCPolSci, ASCA, B07, CA, CurCont, DIP, E-psyche, E01, FR, FamI, H04, I13, IBR, IBSS, IBZ, IBibSS, MEA&I, MLA-IB, P02, P03, P10, P25, P34, P42, P48, P53, P54, PCI, PQC, PSA, PSI, PerIslam, PhilInd, PsycInfo, PsycholAb, S02, S03, S11, SCOPUS, SOPODA, SSA, SSCI, SociolAb, T02, V02, W07.
—BLDSC (7295.473000), IE, Infotrieve, Ingenta, INIST. **CCC.**
Published by: Sage Publications Ltd. (Subsidiary of: Sage Publications, Inc.), 1 Oliver's Yard, 55 City Rd, London, EC1Y 1SP, United Kingdom. TEL 44-20-73248500, FAX 44-20-73248600, info@sagepub.co.uk, http://www.uk.sagepub.com/home.nav. Ed. Douglas D Heckathorn. adv.: B&W page GBP 400; 105 x 185. **Subscr. in the Americas to:** Sage Publications, Inc., 2455 Teller Rd, Thousand Oaks, CA 91320. TEL 805-499-9774, FAX 805-499-0871, journals@sagepub.com.

➤ **READINGS DI FILOSOFIA SCIENZE UMANE E SOCIALI.** *see* HUMANITIES: COMPREHENSIVE WORKS

306 ESP ISSN 1133-4320
REAL ACADEMIA DE CULTURA VALENCIANA. MONOGRAFIAS. Text in Spanish. 1949-1961; resumed 1992. irreg. **Document type:** *Monographic series, Academic/Scholarly.*
Formerly (until 1992): Anales del Centro de Cultura Valenciana. Anejo (0490-2173)
Related titles: ◆ Supplement to: Academia de Cultura Valenciana. Anales. ISSN 1130-426X.
Published by: Real Academia de Cultura Valenciana, C. Avellanes, 26, Valencia, 46003, Spain. TEL 34-96-3916965, FAX 34-96-3915694, secretari@racv.es, http://www.racv.es/.

300 ESP ISSN 0211-111X
DP302.B41
REAL SOCIEDAD BASCONGADA DE LOS AMIGOS DEL PAIS. BOLETIN. Text in Spanish. 1945. q. cum.index: 1945-1992. **Document type:** *Bulletin, Academic/Scholarly.*
Related titles: ◆ Supplement(s): Egan. ISSN 0422-7328.
Indexed: HistAb, RILM.
Published by: Real Sociedad Bascongada de los Amigos del Pais/Euskalerriaren Adiskideen Elkartea, San Antonio 41, Vitoria - Gasteiz, 01001, Spain. TEL 34-945-147770, FAX 34-945-155015, info@bascongada.org, http://www.bascongada.org.

300 FRA ISSN 0034-124X
HM3
RECHERCHE SOCIALE. Text in French. 1948. q. EUR 42 domestic; EUR 47 foreign (effective 2009). bk.rev. bibl.; charts; tr.lit. back issues avail. **Document type:** *Journal, Academic/Scholarly.*
Former titles (until 1965): Centre de Recherches Economiques et Sociales. Etudes et Documents (0577-1579); (until 1952): Centre de Recherches Economiques et Sociales. Bulletin Hebdomadaire. (1245-6969)
Indexed: A22, BAS, CCA, FLP, FR, P30, PAIS, RASB.
—BLDSC (7307.500000), IE, Infotrieve, Ingenta, INIST.
Published by: Fondation pour la Recherche Sociale (FORS), 47 Rue Chabrol, Paris, 75010, France. TEL 33-1-48247900, FAX 33-1-48247901, http://www.fors-rs.com. Ed. Roger Benjamin. Circ: 1,600.

RECHERCHES D'HISTOIRE ET DE SCIENCES SOCIALES/STUDIES IN HISTORY AND THE SOCIAL SCIENCES. *see* HISTORY

340 DEU ISSN 0938-7277
RECHTS- UND SOZIALWISSENSCHAFTLICHE REIHE. Text in German. 1991. irreg., latest vol.34, 2009. price varies. **Document type:** *Monographic series, Academic/Scholarly.*
Published by: Peter Lang GmbH (Subsidiary of: Peter Lang Publishing Group), Eschborner Landstr 42-50, Frankfurt Am Main, 60489, Germany. TEL 49-69-7807050, FAX 49-69-78070550, zentrale.frankfurt@peterlang.com, http://www.peterlang.com. Ed. Wilhelm Brauneder.

300 ESP ISSN 1579-0185
HM741
➤ **REDES**; revista hispana para el analisis de redes sociales. Variant title: Revista Hispana para el Analisis de Redes Sociales. Text in Spanish. 2001. s-a. free (effective 2011). back issues avail. **Document type:** *Journal, Academic/Scholarly.*
Media: Online - full content. **Related titles:** ◆ English ed.: Social Networks. ISSN 0378-8733.
Indexed: CA, F04, T02.
—**CCC.**
Published by: (International Network for Social Network Analysis USA), Redes

300 CRI ISSN 1021-1209
REFLEXIONES. Text in Spanish. 1992. s-a. back issues avail. **Document type:** *Journal, Academic/Scholarly.*
Related titles: Online - full text ed.
Indexed: A01, C01, F03, F04, T02.
Published by: Universidad de Costa Rica, Facultad de Ciencias Sociales, Ciudad Universitaria Rodrigo Facio, 4o. Piso, San Pedro de Montes de Oca, Costa Rica. TEL 506-207-4697, FAX 506-234-7248, geobuzon@fcs.ucr.ac.cr, http://fcs.ucr.ac.cr/. Ed. Gilberth Vargas.

300 URY ISSN 0797-0005
REFLEXIONES DEL BATALLISMO. Text in Spanish. irreg.
Published by: Revista Reflexiones, Casa del Partido Colorado, Andres Martinez Trueba, 1271, Montevideo, 11216, Uruguay.

REGARDS SUR L'INTERNATIONAL/INTERNATIONAL INSIGHTS. *see* POLITICAL SCIENCE—International Relations

300 DEU
REGENSBURGER KULTURLEBEN. Text in German. 2002. irreg., latest vol.4, 2007. price varies. **Document type:** *Monographic series, Academic/Scholarly.*
Published by: Verlag Schnell und Steiner GmbH, Leibnizstr 13, Regensburg, 93055, Germany. TEL 49-941-787850, FAX 49-941-7878516, post@schnell-und-steiner.de.

300 UKR
REGION. Text in Ukrainian. w. USD 245 in United States.
Published by: Izdatel'skii Tsentr Region, Ul Belorusskaya 30, Kiev, 254050, Ukraine. TEL 380-44-213-8889, FAX 380-44-213-1831. Ed. Oleg Kolesnikov. Circ: 35,500. **Dist. by:** East View Information Services, 10601 Wayzata Blvd, Minneapolis, MN 55305. TEL 952-252-1201, 800-477-1005, FAX 952-252-1202, info@eastview.com, http://www.eastview.com.

300 RUS ISSN 0135-5538
➤ **REGION: EKONOMIKA I SOTSIOLOGIYA**; vserossiiskii nauchnyi zhurnal. Text in Russian. 1963. q. RUR 150 per issue; USD 12 per issue foreign (effective 2002). bk.rev. illus.; abstr.; bibl.; charts; maps; stat. 200 p./no. 1 cols./p.; **Document type:** *Journal, Academic/Scholarly.*
Former titles (until 1994): Rossiiskaya Akademiya Nauk. Sibirskoe Otdelenie. Izvestiya. Region: Ekonomika i Sotsiologiya; Akademiya Nauk S.S.S.R. Sibirskoe Otdelenie. Izvestiya. Ser: Ekonomika i Sotsiologiya (0868-5169); (until 1989): Akademiya Nauk S.S.S.R. Sibirskoe Otdelenie. Izvestiya. Seriya Ekonomiki i Prikladnoi Sotsiologii (0233-7606); (until 1984): Akademiya Nauk S.S.S.R. Sibirskoe Otdelenie. Izvestiya. Seriya Obshchestvennykh Nauk (0130-1748)
Indexed: GeoRef, IBSS, RASB, RefZh, SpeleolAb.
Published by: Rossiiskaya Akademiya Nauk, Sibirskoe Otdelenie, Institut Ekonomiki, Pr-t Akad Lavrent'eva 17, k 338, Novosibirsk, 630090, Russian Federation. TEL 7-3832-302438. Ed. V E Dr. Seliverstov. Pub. A. A. Dr. Kin. Circ: 500. **Dist. by:** East View Information Services, 10601 Wayzata Blvd, Minneapolis, MN 55305. TEL 952-252-1201, 800-477-1005, FAX 952-252-1202, info@eastview.com, http://www.eastview.com.

➤ **REGION Y SOCIEDAD.** *see* SOCIOLOGY

300 USA ISSN 1757-7802
HT390
▼ ➤ **REGIONAL SCIENCE POLICY AND PRACTICE.** Text in English. 2009. s-a. **Document type:** *Journal, Academic/Scholarly.* **Description:** Explores policy and practice issues in regional and local development.
Media: Online - full content.
Indexed: A22, CA, E01, P42, T02.
—**CCC.**
Published by: (Regional Science Association International), Wiley-Blackwell Publishing, Inc. (Subsidiary of: Wiley-Blackwell Publishing Ltd.), Commerce Pl, 350 Main St, Malden, MA 02148. TEL 800-835-6770, info@wiley.com, http://www.wiley.com/WileyCDA/. Ed. Michael C Carroll.

300 RUS
REGIONOLOGY; popular scientific magazine. Text in Russian; Summaries in English. 1992. q. **Document type:** *Academic/Scholarly.*
Published by: Scientific Research Institute of Regionology, Ul Proletarskaya 61, Saransk, Mordovia, 430000, Russian Federation. TEL 834-2-242694, FAX 834-2-173995, rri@moris.ru. Ed. Alexander Ivanovich Sukharev. Circ: 1,500 (paid).

REGULATION & GOVERNANCE. *see* LAW

300 DEU ISSN 1434-0798
REIHE PRAXIS SOZIALFORSCHUNG. Text in German. 1998. irreg., latest vol.6, 2006. price varies. **Document type:** *Monographic series, Academic/Scholarly.*
Published by: Rainer Hampp Verlag, Marktplatz 5, Mering, 86415, Germany. TEL 49-8233-4783, FAX 49-8233-30755, info@rhverlag.de, http://www.rhverlag.de.

RELIGION AND THE SOCIAL ORDER. *see* RELIGIONS AND THEOLOGY

RELIGION - STAAT - GESELLSCHAFT; Zeitschrift fuer Glaubensformen und Weltanschauungen. *see* RELIGIONS AND THEOLOGY

300 BRA ISSN 0103-183X
PN1
➤ **REMATE DE MALES.** Text in Portuguese, French, Spanish, English. 1980. a. per issue exchange basis. bk.rev. back issues avail. **Document type:** *Journal, Academic/Scholarly.* **Description:** Presents studies in Brazilian and Latin American culture and literature.
Indexed: L&LBA, MLA-IB, RASB.

S

Published by: Universidade Estadual de Campinas, Instituto de Estudos da Linguagem, C Universitaria, Caixa Postal 6045, Campinas, SP 13084-976, Brazil. spublic@iel.unicamp.br, http://www.unicamp.br/iel. Eds. Antonio Arnoni Prado, Maria Betania Amoroso, Vilma Areas.

➤ **RENCAI ZIYUAN KAIFA.** *see* BUSINESS AND ECONOMICS—Personnel Management

300 100 CHE
RENCONTRES INTERNATIONALES DE GENEVE. Text in French. 1947. biennial. CHF 50 (effective 1999). reprints avail. **Document type:** *Proceedings, Academic/Scholarly.*
Published by: Editions L'Age d'Homme, 10 rue de Geneve, Lausanne, 1003, Switzerland.

300 MEX ISSN 0186-4963
RENGLONES. Text in Spanish. 1989. 3/yr. **Document type:** *Journal, Academic/Scholarly.*
Published by: Universidad Jesuita de Guadalajara, Instituto Tecnologico y de Estudios Superiores de Occidente (I T E S O), Periferico Sur Manuel Gomez Morin 8585, Tlaquepaque, Jalisco 45090, Mexico. TEL 52-33-36693434, portal@iteso.mx, http://www.portal.iteso.mx.

RENOVATIO IMPERII; Zeitschrift fuer Tradition, Kunst und geistige Ueberlieferung. *see* ART

300 CHN ISSN 1003-5001
RENSHENG YU BANLU/LIFE AND COMPANIONS. Text in Chinese. 1985. m. USD 36 (effective 2009). **Document type:** *Consumer.* **Description:** Discusses family, marriage, love and related issues.
—East View.
Published by: Henan Sheng Shehui Kexue Lianhehui/Henan Society of Social Sciences, No 9 Fengchan Lu, Zhengzhou, Henan, 450002, China. TEL 86-371-3933739, FAX 86-371-3933739. Ed. Ren Shoushun. Circ: 500,000. **Dist. overseas by:** China International Book Trading Corp, 35 Chegongzhuang Xilu, Haidian District, PO Box 399, Beijing 100044, China.

RENWEN JI SHEHUI KEXUE JIKAN/JOURNAL OF SOCIAL SCIENCES AND PHILOSOPHY. *see* PHILOSOPHY

300 CHE ISSN 1422-7924
REPERE SOCIAL; revue d'information sociale. Text in French. 1995. bi-m. CHF 95 (effective 1999). bk.rev. **Document type:** *Bulletin.*
Formerly (until 1998): Reperes (1420-0368); Formed by the 1995 merger of: Social (1420-1542); Travail Social (0255-9641)
Published by: Hospice General, Case Postale 3360, Geneva 3, 1211, Switzerland. TEL 44-22-7875300, FAX 44-22-7875299. Ed. Paul Andre Berger. adv.: B&W page CHF 1,000; trim 270 x 180.

300 NOR ISSN 0806-8593
REPLIKK; tidsskrift for human- og samfunnsvitenskap. Text in Norwegian. 1995. s-a. NOK 200 to individuals; NOK 275 to institutions; NOK 60 per issue (effective 2006). back issues avail. **Document type:** *Journal, Academic/Scholarly.*
Related titles: Online - full text ed.: ISSN 0806-9689.
Indexed: RILM.
Address: Det Akademiske Kvarter, Olav Kyrresgate 53, Bergen, 5015, Norway. Ed. Finn I Birkeland.

300 CAN ISSN 1715-4731
H1
RESEARCH AND PRACTICE IN SOCIAL SCIENCES. Text in English. 2005. irreg. free (effective 2011). **Document type:** *Journal, Academic/Scholarly.*
Media: Online - full text.
Indexed: A39, C27, C29, D03, D04, E13, R14, S14, S15, S18.
Address: researchandpractice@gmail.com. Ed. Joe Kincheloe.

RESEARCH AND PRACTICE IN TECHNOLOGY ENHANCED LEARNING. *see* COMPUTERS

RESEARCH FOLIO. *see* SCIENCES: COMPREHENSIVE WORKS

RESEARCH IN THE SOCIAL SCIENTIFIC STUDY OF RELIGION. *see* RELIGIONS AND THEOLOGY

▼ **RESEARCH JOURNAL OF ARTS, MANAGEMENT AND SOCIAL SCIENCES.** *see* ART

RESEARCH JOURNAL OF HUMANITIES AND SOCIAL SCIENCES. *see* HUMANITIES: COMPREHENSIVE WORKS

RESEARCH JOURNAL OF INTERNATIONAL STUDIES. *see* POLITICAL SCIENCE

RESEARCH JOURNAL OF PHILOSOPHY AND SOCIAL SCIENCES. *see* PHILOSOPHY

300 570 IND ISSN 0973-3914
➤ **RESEARCH JOURNAL OF SOCIAL AND LIFE SCIENCES.** Text and summaries in English, Hindi. 2006. s-a. INR 400 (effective 2011). bk.rev. abstr.; bibl.; charts; maps; mkt.; stat. back issues avail. **Document type:** *Journal, Academic/Scholarly.* **Description:** Contains original unpublished research papers, summary of research projects/works and book review relating to all subjects of social and life sciences and to promote interdisciplinary research work.
Published by: Gayatri Publications, 41/42, Raghuwans Sadan, Shantikunj Bichhiya, Rewa, Madhya Pradesh 486 001, India. TEL 91-7662-255177, 91-9425186437, gayatripublicationsrewa@rediffmail.com, gresearchjournal@rediffmail.com. Ed. Braj Gopal. Pub. Gayatri Shukla. Circ: 300 (paid); 10 (controlled).

300 658 SGP ISSN 2010-457X
▼ ➤ **RESEARCH JOURNAL OF SOCIAL SCIENCE & MANAGEMENT.** Text in English. 2011. m. bk.rev. abstr. back issues avail. **Document type:** *Journal, Academic/Scholarly.*
Media: Online - full text.
Published by: International Journal Organisation, Blk 489, Jurong W. Ave.1, Singapore, Singapore. TEL 65-90528323. Ed., Pub. R V Pillai.

300 JOR
RESEARCH JOURNAL OF SOCIAL SCIENCES. Text in English. 1994. a. free. **Document type:** *Journal, Academic/Scholarly.*
Media: Online - full text. **Related titles:** Print ed.: ISSN 1815-9125.
Indexed: A01, CA, T02.
Published by: American - Eurasian Network for Scientific Information, A E N S I Publications, c/o Dr. Abdel Rahman Mohammad Saeb Al-Tawaha, Al Hussein Bin Talal University, Biological Department, PO Box 20, Ma'an, Jordan. TEL 962-2-7305196.

300 DEU ISSN 0940-2829
RESEARCH ON CASES AND THEORIES. Text in English, German. 1992. irreg., latest vol.12, 2008. price varies. **Document type:** *Monographic series, Academic/Scholarly.*
Published by: Rainer Hampp Verlag, Marktplatz 5, Mering, 86415, Germany. TEL 49-8233-4783, FAX 49-8233-30755, info@rhverlag.de, http://www.rhverlag.de.

RESEARCH PERSPECTIVES/PERSPECTIVES SUR LA RECHERCHE. *see* SCIENCES: COMPREHENSIVE WORKS

RESOURCES FOR FEMINIST RESEARCH/DOCUMENTATION SUR LA RECHERCHE FEMINISTE. *see* WOMEN'S STUDIES

300 USA
RESOURCES ON CONTEMPORARY ISSUES. Text in English. irreg., latest vol.7, 1993. USD 40. **Document type:** *Monographic series.* **Description:** Annotated bibliographies on contemporary issues of importance.
Published by: Pierian Press, PO Box 1808, Ann Arbor, MI 48106. TEL 313-434-5530, 800-678-2435, FAX 313-434-6409, pubinfo@pierianpress.com, http://www.pierianpress.com.

REVIEW JOURNAL OF PHILOSOPHY AND SOCIAL SCIENCE. *see* PHILOSOPHY

300 IND ISSN 0972-2661
REVIEW OF DEVELOPMENT AND CHANGE. Text in English. 1996. s-a. INR 100 to individuals India and SAARC Counties; GBP 20, USD 25 elsewhere to individuals; INR 150 to institutions India and SAARC Countries; GBP 40, USD 50 elsewhere to institutions (effective 2011). bk.rev. back issues avail. **Document type:** *Journal, Academic/Scholarly.*
Published by: Madras Institute of Development Studies, 79 Second Main Rd., Gandhi Nagar, Adyar, Chennai, Tamil Nadu 600 020, India. TEL 91-44-24412589, FAX 91-44-24910872, chairperson@mids.ac.in, director@mids.ac.in. Ed. R Maria Saleth.

300 GBR ISSN 1750-6816
HC79.E5
➤ **REVIEW OF ENVIRONMENTAL ECONOMICS AND POLICY.** Abbreviated title: R E E P. Text in English. 2007 (Mar.). s-a. GBP 123 in United Kingdom to institutions; EUR 185 in Europe to institutions; USD 206 in US & Canada to institutions; GBP 123 elsewhere to institutions; GBP 134 combined subscription in United Kingdom to institutions (print & online eds.); EUR 202 combined subscription in Europe to institutions (print & online eds.); USD 227 combined subscription in US & Canada to institutions (print & online eds.); GBP 134 combined subscription elsewhere to institutions (print & online eds.) (effective 2012). adv. back issues avail.; reprint service avail. from PSC. **Document type:** *Journal, Academic/Scholarly.* **Description:** Seeks to fill the gap between traditional academic journals and the general interest press by providing a widely accessible yet scholarly source for the latest thinking on environmental economics and related policy.
Related titles: Online - full text ed.: ISSN 1750-6824. GBP 112 in United Kingdom to institutions; EUR 168 in Europe to institutions; USD 189 in US & Canada to institutions; GBP 112 elsewhere to institutions (effective 2012) (from IngentaConnect).
Indexed: A22, CABA, CurCont, E01, E04, E05, E12, EconLit, F08, F12, GEOBASE, GH, I11, LT, R12, S13, S16, SCOPUS, SSCI, T02, T05, W07, W11.
—IE. **CCC.**
Published by: (Association of Environmental and Resource Economists USA), Oxford University Press, Great Clarendon St, Oxford, OX2 6DP, United Kingdom. TEL 44-1865-556767, FAX 44-1865-556646, enquiry@oup.co.uk, http://www.oxfordjournals.org. Ed. Robert Stavins. Adv. contact Linda Hann TEL 44-1344-779945.

300 JPN
REVIEW OF JAPANESE CULTURE AND SOCIETY. Text in English. 1986. a. **Document type:** *Monographic series, Academic/Scholarly.*
Published by: Josai University, Center for Inter-cultural Studies and Education/Josai Daigaku, Kokusai Bunka Kyoiku Senta, 1-1, Keyakidai, Sakado City, 350-0295, Japan. TEL 81-49-2717795, FAX 81-49-2717981, kokusai@stf.josai.ac.jp, http://mail.josai.ac.jp/%7Ekokusai/.

320 USA ISSN 2151-3481
DS41 CODEN: MESBEL
REVIEW OF MIDDLE EAST STUDIES. Text in English. 1967. s-a. (June & Dec.). USD 90 domestic membership; USD 105 foreign membership (effective 2000). adv. bk.rev. abstr.; bibl.; illus. Index. reprints avail. **Document type:** *Bulletin, Academic/Scholarly.*
Formerly (until 2009): Middle East Studies Association Bulletin (0026-3184)
Related titles: Online - full text ed.: 200?. free (effective 2010).
Indexed: A21, A22, ABS&EES, AICP, AmHI, B04, BRD, BibLing, CA, DIP, GEOBASE, H07, H08, HAb, HistAb, HumInd, I13, I14, IBR, IBSS, IBZ, L&LBA, M10, MEA&I, MLA-IB, P30, P42, PerIslam, RASB, RI-1, RI-2, RILM, SCOPUS, T02, W03.
—BLDSC (7793.095000), IE, Infotrieve, Ingenta.
Published by: Middle East Studies Association of North America, Inc., SUNY New Paltz, Department of History, JFT 916, New Paltz, NY 12561. TEL 845-257-2681, FAX 845-257-2735, bulletin@newpaltz.edu, mesabulletin@uncc.edu. Ed. John VenderLippe. Adv. contact Sara L Palmer. Circ: 2,200 (paid).

300 GBR
REVIEW OF NIGERIA AFFAIRS. Text in English. 2007. q. back issues avail. **Document type:** *Journal, Academic/Scholarly.* **Description:** Explores all aspects of the Nigerian society: its politics, economy, culture and development trajectory.
Related titles: Online - full text ed.
Published by: Adonis & Abbey Publishers Ltd., PO Box 43418, London, SE11 4XZ, United Kingdom. TEL 44-845-3887248, editor@adonis-abbey.com. Ed. Dr. Jideofor Adibe.

300 LSO ISSN 1024-4190
DT1001
REVIEW OF SOUTHERN AFRICAN STUDIES; a multidisplinary journal of arts, social and behavioural sciences. Text in English. 1995. s-a. LSL 30 domestic to individuals; USD 25 foreign to individuals; LSL 60 domestic to institutions; USD 50 foreign to institutions (effective 2004). back issues avail. **Document type:** *Journal, Academic/Scholarly.*
Related titles: Online - full text ed.
Indexed: IIBP.
Published by: Institute of Southern African Studies, PO 180, Roma, Lesotho. t.khalanyane@nul.lst, http://www.nul.ls/isas/index.htm.

918.503 PER ISSN 0259-9600
F2212
REVISTA ANDINA. Text in Spanish. 1983. s-a. USD 50 domestic to individuals; USD 60 foreign to individuals; USD 60 domestic to institutions; USD 75 foreign to institutions. adv. bk.rev. cum.index: 1983-1985. back issues avail. **Document type:** *Academic/Scholarly.*
Related titles: CD-ROM ed.; Online - full text ed.: ISSN 1609-9583. 1983.
Indexed: AICP, AnthLit, C01, H21, IBR, IBZ, MLA-IB, P08, RASB.
Published by: Centro de Estudios Regionales Andinos "Bartolome de Las Casas", Pampa de la Alianza 164, Cusco, Peru. TEL 51-14-223703, FAX 51-14-427894, http://www.cbc.org.pe. Ed. Juan Carlos Garcia. Pub. Andres Chirinos Rivera. R&P Beatriz Garland TEL 5114-429992. Circ: 1,000.

REVISTA ARGENTINA DE ECONOMIA Y CIENCIAS SOCIALES. *see* BUSINESS AND ECONOMICS

300 001.3 ARG ISSN 1669-1555
REVISTA ARGENTINA DE HUMANIDADES Y CIENCIAS SOCIALES (ONLINE). Text in Spanish. 2003. s-a. **Document type:** *Journal, Academic/Scholarly.*
Formerly (until 2003): Revista Argentina de Humanidades y Ciencias Sociales (Print) (1667-9318)
Media: Online - full text.
Published by: Sociedad Argentina de Informacion, Av Pueyrredon 854, 110 A, Buenos Aires, 1032, Argentina. http://www.sai.com.ar.

300 CHL ISSN 0717-3202
REVISTA AUSTRAL DE CIENCIAS SOCIALES. Text in Spanish. 1997. a. CLP 7,000 domestic; USD 15 foreign (effective 2010). back issues avail. **Document type:** *Monographic series, Academic/Scholarly.*
Indexed: C01, SCOPUS.
Published by: Universidad Austral de Chile, Facultad de Filosofia y Humanidades, Casilla 142, Valdivia, Chile. TEL 56-63-221476, http://www.uach.cl/efil/.

300 BOL
REVISTA BOLIVIANA DE INVESTIGACION. Text in Spanish. 4/yr. **Document type:** *Journal, Academic/Scholarly.*
Published by: Universidad Autonoma "Gabriel Rene Moreno", CP 702, Santa Cruz de la Sierra, Bolivia. TEL 591-2-372898, FAX 591-2-342160, http://www.uagrm.edu.bo.

300 BRA ISSN 0102-6909
H8.P8 CODEN: RBCSEQ
➤ **REVISTA BRASILEIRA DE CIENCIAS SOCIAIS.** Text in English, French, Portuguese. 1986. 3/yr. BRL 50 domestic; USD 70 foreign (effective 2006). adv. bk.rev.; film rev.; software rev. abstr.; bibl.; illus. back issues avail. **Document type:** *Journal, Academic/Scholarly.* **Description:** Publishes theoretical and empirical studies on social sciences.
Related titles: Online - full text ed.: ISSN 1806-9053. 1997. free (effective 2011).
Indexed: C01, CA, FR, H21, I13, P08, P42, PSA, RASB, S02, S03, SCOPUS, SOPODA, SSA, SSciA, SociolAb, T02.
—INIST.
Published by: Associacao Nacional de Pos-Graduacao e Pesquisa em Ciencias Sociais, Ave. Prof. Luciano Gualberto 315, Sala 116, Butanta - Cidade Universitaria, Sao Paulo, SP 05508-900, Brazil. TEL 55-11-8184664, FAX 55-11-8185043, http://www.scielo.br/, http://www.anpocs.org.br. R&P Argelina Cheibub Figueiredo TEL 55-11-815-7869. Adv. contact Miriam Dasilveira Pavanelli. **Co-sponsors:** Ministerio da Ciencia e Tecnologia, Financiadora de Estudos e Projetos (F I N E P); Conselho Nacional de Desenvolvimento Cientifico e Tecnologico.

▼ ➤ **REVISTA BRASILEIRA DE HISTORIA & CIENCIAS SOCIAIS.** *see* HISTORY

300 BRA ISSN 1679-1991
H8.P8
REVISTA CAPITAL CIENTIFICO. Text in Portuguese. 2003. a. **Document type:** *Monographic series, Academic/Scholarly.*
Published by: Universidade Estadual do Centro-Oeste, Editora, Rua Presidente Zacarias, 875, Guarapuava, PR 3010, Brazil. TEL 55-42-36211000, http://www.unicentro.br/editora/.

300 CHL ISSN 0718-4379
REVISTA CENTRAL DE SOCIOLOGIA. Text in Spanish. 2006. a. **Document type:** *Monographic series, Academic/Scholarly.*
Published by: Universidad Central de Chile, Facultad de Ciencias Sociales, Campus La Reina, Carlos Silva Vidosola, 9783, La Reina, Santiago, Chile. TEL 56-2-5826505, FAX 56-2-5826502, sdecano@ucentral.cl, http://www.fcscentral.cl/.

300 CHL ISSN 0716-4181
REVISTA CHILENA DE HUMANIDADES. Text in Spanish. 1982. irreg. **Document type:** *Journal, Academic/Scholarly.*
Related titles: Online - full text ed.
Indexed: A26, C01, I04, I05, IBR, IBZ.
Published by: Universidad de Chile, Facultad de Filosofia y Humanidades, Capitan Ignacio Carrerr Pinto 1025, Santiago, Chile. TEL 56-2-9787026, FAX 56-2-2716823.

300 BRA ISSN 1413-8999
REVISTA CIENCIAS SOCIAIS. Text in Portuguese. 1995. s-a. **Document type:** *Journal, Academic/Scholarly.* **Description:** Publishes articles about the social sciences by UGF professors and others.
Published by: Universidade Gama Filho, Rua Manoel Vitorino 625, Piedade, Rio de Janeiro, RJ 20748-900, Brazil. TEL 55-21-32137735, FAX 55-21-32137731, http://www.ugf.br.

300 ECU ISSN 0252-8681
REVISTA CIENCIAS SOCIALES. Text in Spanish. 1977. q. ECS 250, USD 20.
Published by: (Escuela de Sociologia), Universidad Central del Ecuador, Apdo 3291, Quito, Pichincha, Ecuador.

300 PRT ISSN 0254-1106
➤ **REVISTA CRITICA DE CIENCIAS SOCIAIS.** Text in Portuguese. 1978. 3/yr. EUR 23 domestic to individuals; USD 50 foreign to individuals; EUR 40 domestic to institutions; USD 80 foreign to institutions (effective 2002). adv. bk.rev. 220 p./no.; **Document type:** *Academic/Scholarly.*
Indexed: CA, F04, FR, HistAb, IBR, IBZ, P42, PSA, S02, S03, SCOPUS, SOPODA, SSA, SociolAb, T02.
—INIST.

Published by: Centro de Estudos Sociais, Faculdade de Economia, Aptdo 3087, Coimbra, 3001-401, Portugal. TEL 351-239-855570, FAX 351-239-855589, ces@fe.uc.pt. Ed. Boaventura de Sousa Santos. Circ: 1,500.

300 CUB ISSN 0138-6425
REVISTA CUBANA DE CIENCIAS SOCIALES. Text in Spanish. 1983. s-a. USD 12 in South America; USD 14 in North America; USD 16 elsewhere.
Indexed: AICP, C01, EIP, IBR, IBZ, RASB.
Published by: (Academia de Ciencias de Cuba, Academia de Ciencias de Cuba, Instituto de Filosofia), Ediciones Cubanas, Obispo 527, Havana, Cuba. Ed. Thalia Fung. Circ: 6,000.

300 BRA ISSN 0104-0111
AS80.C932
REVISTA DE CIENCIAS HUMANAS (CURITIBA). Text in Portuguese. 1992. a. per issue exchange basis. **Document type:** *Academic/Scholarly.*
Indexed: C01, S02, S03, SociolAb.
Published by: Universidade Federal do Parana, Sector de Ciencias Humanas, Letras e Artes, Rua Amintas de Barros 333, Curitiba, PARANA 80020240, Brazil. TEL 55-41-2634171. Ed. Maria Jose Justino. Pub. Roberto Gomes.

300 BRA ISSN 0101-9589
H8.P8 CODEN: RCHUFV
REVISTA DE CIENCIAS HUMANAS (FLORIANOPOLIS). Text in Portuguese. 1982. s-a.
Indexed: CA, L&LBA, P42, PAIS, PSA, S02, S03, SSA, SociolAb, T02.
Published by: Universidade Federal de Santa Catarina, Centro de Filosofia e Ciencias Humanas, Campus Universitario da Trindade, Florianopolis, SC 88040-970, Brazil.

300 BRA ISSN 1519-1974
REVISTA DE CIENCIAS HUMANAS (VICOSA). Text in Multiple languages. 2001. s-a. **Document type:** *Journal, Academic/Scholarly.*
Published by: Universidade Federal de Vicosa, Campus Universitario, Vicosa, MG 36570-000, Brazil. TEL 55-31-38991858, FAX 55-31-38992203, reitoria@mail.ufv.br, http://www.ufv.br.

300 100 BRA ISSN 0303-9862
H8
REVISTA DE CIENCIAS SOCIAIS (FORTALEZA). Text in Portuguese; Summaries in English, French. 1970. s-a. BRL 400, USD 12. adv. bk.rev. bibl.; charts. index, cum.index.
Indexed: AICP, C01, EIP, H21, P08, PsycholAb, RILM.
Published by: Universidade Federal do Ceara, Departamento de Ciencias Sociais e Filosofia, C.P. 1257, Fortaleza, Ceara, Brazil. Ed. Paulo Elpidio De Menezes Neto. Circ: 3,000.

300 BRA ISSN 0102-8200
REVISTA DE CIENCIAS SOCIAIS (PORTO ALEGRE). Text in Portuguese. 1986. s-a.
Indexed: PAIS.
Published by: Universidade Federal do Rio Grande do Sul, Departamento de Ciencias Sociais, Av Eento Goncalves 9500, Campus do Vale, Porto Alegre, 91546-000, Brazil.

300 CHL ISSN 0717-2257
H8.S7
REVISTA DE CIENCIAS SOCIALES. Text in Spanish. 1992. s-a. **Document type:** *Journal, Academic/Scholarly.*
Related titles: Online - full text ed.: ISSN 0718-3631.
Indexed: H21, P08.
Published by: Universidad Arturo Prat, Departamento de Ciencias Sociales, Canje y correspondencia a la Casilla 121, Iquique, Tarapaca 2120, Chile. http://www.unap.cl/sociales/. Circ: 300.

300 PRI ISSN 0034-7817
H8
REVISTA DE CIENCIAS SOCIALES. Text in Spanish, English. 1957. s-a. USD 18 to individuals; USD 30 to institutions (effective 2005). adv. bk.rev. bibl.; charts; illus. cum.index: 1957-1991. **Document type:** *Journal, Academic/Scholarly.*
Indexed: BibInd, C01, CIS, EIP, H21, HistAb, I13, IBSS, P08, PAIS, RI-1, RI-2, RILM, S02, S03, SOPODA, SociolAb.
Published by: Universidad de Puerto Rico, Centro de Investigaciones Sociales, Recinto de Rio Piedras, Apdo 23345, Estacion UPR, San Juan, 00931-3345, Puerto Rico. Ed. Ana Victoria Garcia. Circ: 1,000.

300 ARG ISSN 0328-2643
H8.S7
REVISTA DE CIENCIAS SOCIALES. Text in Spanish. 1994. s-a. ARS 160 to individuals; ARS 200 to institutions; USD 300 foreign. **Document type:** *Academic/Scholarly.*
Indexed: C01.
Published by: Universidad Nacional de Quilmes, Avda. Rivadavia, 2358 Piso 6, Buenos Aires, 1034, Argentina. FAX 54-114-2593091.

300 VEN ISSN 1315-9518
➤ **REVISTA DE CIENCIAS SOCIALES.** Text in Spanish. N.S. 1974. q. VEB 60 domestic; USD 30 in Latin America; USD 50 elsewhere (effective 2011). **Document type:** *Journal, Academic/Scholarly.* **Description:** Presents research in the social sciences field, including economics, sociology, politics, population, culture, religion, psychology, anthropology, administration, public finance, and more.
Formerly (until 1990): Universidad del Zulia. Facultad de Ciencias Economicas Sociales. Economia y Administracion (1315-9720)
Related titles: Online - full text ed.: 2003. free (effective 2011).
Indexed: C01, CA, P42, PAIS, PSA, RASB, S02, S03, SSCI, SociolAb, T02, W07.
Published by: Universidad del Zulia, Facultad de Ciencias Economicas y Sociales, Apdo 529, Maracaibo, Zulia 4011, Venezuela. TEL 58-61596595, FAX 58-61596546. Ed. Nelson Labarca. Circ: 1,000.

300 URY ISSN 0797-5538
REVISTA DE CIENCIAS SOCIALES. Text in Spanish. 1986. a. USD 23 (effective 1998).
Indexed: SociolAb.
Published by: Fundacion de Cultura Universitaria, 25 de Mayo 568, Montevideo, 11003, Uruguay. TEL 598-2-9161152, FAX 598-2-9152549.

300 CRI ISSN 0482-5276
K19
➤ **REVISTA DE CIENCIAS SOCIALES.** Text in Spanish. 1956. 4/yr. CRC 2,000 domestic; USD 60 foreign (effective 2005). adv. **Document type:** *Journal, Academic/Scholarly.*
Related titles: Online - full text ed.
Indexed: A01, A26, C01, CA, F03, F04, FR, H21, HistAb, I04, I05, IBR, IBZ, P08, P42, PAIS, PSA, RASB, RI-1, RI-2, S02, S03, SSA, SociolAb, T02.
—INIST.
Published by: Universidad de Costa Rica, Editorial, Sede Rodrigo Facio Brenes, Montes de Oca, San Jose, Costa Rica. TEL 506-207-4000, FAX 506-224-8214, direccion@editorial.ucr.ac.cr, http://editorial.ucr.ac.cr. Ed. Cecilia Arguedas.

➤ **REVISTA DE DERECHO U DE C.** (Universidad de Concepcion) *see* LAW

➤ **REVISTA DE DIREITO DO UNIFOA.** *see* LAW

➤ **REVISTA DE EDUCACION Y DESARROLLO SOCIAL.** *see* EDUCATION

300 ESP ISSN 1135-6618
➤ **REVISTA DE ESTUDIOS COOPERATIVOS.** Abbreviated title: REVESCO. Text in Spanish. 1963. irreg. **Document type:** *Journal, Academic/Scholarly.* **Description:** Publishes research works focused on introducing the latest contributions that deal with "participation companies".
Formerly (until 1987): Estudios Cooperativos (0425-3485)
Related titles: Online - full text ed.: ISSN 1885-8031. 2004. free (effective 2011).
Indexed: A12, A39, ABIn, C27, C29, D03, D04, E13, EconLit, H21, P08, P27, P48, P51, P53, P54, PQC, R14, S14, S15, S18.
Published by: (Universidad Complutense de Madrid, Facultad de Ciencias Economicas Empresariales. Asociacion de Estudios Cooperativos), Universidad Complutense de Madrid, Servicio de Publicaciones, C/ Obispo Trejo 2, Ciudad Universitaria, Madrid, 28040, Spain. TEL 34-91-3941127, FAX 34-91-3941126, servicio.publicaciones@rect.ucm.es, http://www.ucm.es/publicaciones. Ed. Sonia Martin Lopez.

➤ **REVISTA DE ESTUDIOS DE EGIPTOLOGIA.** *see* HISTORY—History Of Africa

300 ARG ISSN 0327-3032
F2911
➤ **REVISTA DE ESTUDIOS REGIONALES.** Text in Spanish. 1988. s-a. ARS 40, USD 40. back issues avail. **Document type:** *Academic/Scholarly.* **Description:** Presents works in the human and social sciences related to the region of Cuyo.
Media: Diskette.
Indexed: FR.
Published by: Universidad Nacional de Cuyo, Facultad de Filosofia y Letras, Centro Universitario, Parque Gral. San Martin, CC 345, Mendoza, 5500, Argentina. TEL 54-261-4494093, FAX 54-261-4380457, editor@logos.uncu.edu.ar, http://ffyl.uncu.edu.ar/. Ed. Adolfo Omar Cueto. Circ: 500.

300 COL ISSN 0123-885X
H8.S7
➤ **REVISTA DE ESTUDIOS SOCIALES/JOURNAL OF SOCIAL STUDIES.** Text in English; Text occasionally in English, Portuguese. 1998. q. adv. bk.rev. Index. 160 p./no.; back issues avail. **Document type:** *Journal, Academic/Scholarly.*
Related titles: Online - full text ed.: ISSN 1900-5180. 2005. free (effective 2011) (from SciELO).
Indexed: A01, A26, CA, F03, F04, H21, HistAb, I04, I05, IBSS, MLA-IB, P08, P10, P27, P42, P45, P46, P48, P54, PQC, PSA, S02, S03, SCOPUS, SSA, SSCI, SociolAb, T02, W07.
Published by: Universidad de los Andes, Facultad de Ciencias Sociales/Universidad de los Andes, Social Sciences Faculty, Carrera 1A No 18A -10 Edificio Franco, Bogota, Colombia. TEL 57-1-3324505, FAX 57-1-3324508, fahuciso@uniandes.edu.co, http://faciso.uniandes.edu.co/index.php?ac=inicio. Ed. Natalia Rubio. **Dist. by:** Siglo del Hombre Editores, Cra. 32 No.25-46/50, Bogota, D.C., Colombia. TEL 57-1-3377700, FAX 57-1-3377665, http://www.siglodelhombre.com; Libreria Universidad de los Andes, Cra. 1 No. 19-27 Ed AU106, Bogota, D. C., Colombia. libreria@uniandes.edu.co, http://libreria.uniandes.edu.co/.

➤ **REVISTA DE GESTAO SOCIAL E AMBIENTAL/ENVIRONMENTAL AND SOCIAL MANAGEMENT JOURNAL.** *see* ENVIRONMENTAL STUDIES

300 PER ISSN 2079-3650
H62.5P45
▼ **REVISTA DE GRADUADOS.** Text in Spanish. 2009. a. **Document type:** *Monographic series, Academic/Scholarly.*
Published by: Universidad Nacional Mayor de San Marcos, Facultad de Ciencias Sociales, Ciudad Universitaria, Ave. Venezuela, s-n, Lima, 1, Peru. informacion@sociales.unmsm.pe, http://sociales.unmsm.edu.pe/index.php.

REVISTA DE HISTORIA SOCIAL Y DE LAS MENTALIDADES. *see* HISTORY

300 BOL
REVISTA DE HUMANIDADES, CIENCIAS SOCIALES Y RELACIONES INTERNACIONALES. Text in Spanish. 2/yr. **Document type:** *Journal, Academic/Scholarly.*
Published by: Universidad Autonoma "Gabriel Rene Moreno", CP 702, Santa Cruz de la Sierra, Bolivia. TEL 591-2-372898, FAX 591-2-342160, http://www.uagrm.edu.bo.

300 ESP ISSN 1139-8205
REVISTA DE HUMANIDADES Y CIENCIAS SOCIALES. Text in Spanish. 1981. a.
Formerly (until 1998): Instituto de Estudios Almerienses. Boletin. Letras (1133-1496); Which was superseded in part (in 1986): Instituto de Estudios Almerisense. Boletin (0211-7541)
Published by: Instituto de Estudios Almerienses, Pl Julio Alfredo Egea, 3, Almeria, 0971, Spain. TEL 34-950281854, FAX 34-950281287, iea@dipalme.org, http://www.iealmerienses.es/.

REVISTA DE INDIAS. *see* HISTORY—History Of North And South America

REVISTA DE INDIAS. ANEXOS. *see* HISTORY—History Of North And South America

316 ROM ISSN 1584-384X
➤ **REVISTA DE INFORMATICA SOCIALA.** Text in English, French, Romanian. 2004. s-a. free. bk.rev.; software rev. abstr.; bibl.; charts; illus.; maps; stat. Index. back issues avail. **Document type:** *Journal, Academic/Scholarly.* **Description:** Publishes articles and papers connected to the social aspects of computerization.
Media: Online - full content.
Published by: Universitatea de Vest din Timisoara, Facultatea de Sociologie si Psihologie, Laborator de Informatica Sociala, Bv V Parvan nr 4, Cab 029, Timisoara, 300223, Romania. TEL 40-256-592266, FAX 40-256-592320, revistais@socio.uvt.ro. Eds. Gabriela Grosseck, Laura Malita. R&P Gabriela Grosseck.

➤ **REVISTA DE INTERNET, DERECHO Y POLITICA/REVISTA D'INTERNET, DRET I POLITICA.** *see* LAW

300 COL ISSN 1657-6772
REVISTA DE INVESTIGACION. Text in Spanish. 2002. s-a. COP 5,000 (effective 2006). back issues avail. **Document type:** *Journal, Academic/Scholarly.*
Indexed: C01.
Published by: Universidad de la Salle, Vicerrectoria Academica, Cra. 2 No. 10-70, Bogota, Colombia. TEL 57-1-2170885, FAX 57-1-2868391, http://investigaciones.lasalle.edu.co/index.php?option=com_frontpage&Itemid=1.

300 ROM ISSN 1453-5378
REVISTA DE ISTORIE SOCIALA. Text in Romanian. 1997. a.
Published by: Fundatia Culturala Romana, Aleea Alexandru 38, Bucharest, 71273, Romania. TEL 40-1-2301373, FAX 40-1-2307559, http://www.fcr.ro/romana.

300 600 ARG ISSN 1515-1026
➤ **REVISTA DE LA SECYT.** Variant title: Revista de la Secretaria de Ciencia y Tecnica. Text in Spanish, English, Portuguese. 1999. s-a. USD 20 (effective 2002). abstr.; bibl.; illus.; maps; stat. 130 p./no.; **Document type:** *Magazine, Academic/Scholarly.*
Published by: Universidad Catolica de Santiago del Estero, Ave. Alsina, Casilla de Correos 285, Santiago Del Estero, 4200, Argentina. TEL 54-385-4213820, ediciones@ucse.edu.ar, http://www.ucse.edu.ar. Ed., R&P Jose Hector Ludy TEL 54-385-4211777.

300 370 VEN ISSN 1316-9505
H62.A1
➤ **REVISTA DE TEORIA Y DIDACTICA DE LAS CIENCIAS SOCIALES.** Text in Spanish. 1996. a. free (effective 2011). **Document type:** *Journal, Academic/Scholarly.* **Description:** It aims at investigating the meaning of teaching and teaching what to whom, when and in what context.
Media: Online - full text.
Indexed: C01.
Published by: Universidad de los Andes, Facultad de Humanidades y Educacion, Av Las Americas, Complejo La Liria, Edif B, Piso 3, Merida, Venezuela. TEL 58-274-2401738.

➤ **REVISTA DE UNIVERSIDAD Y SOCIEDAD DEL CONOCIMIENTO.** *see* EDUCATION

300 ARG ISSN 1851-3263
➤ **LA REVISTA DEL C C C.** (Centro Cultural de la Cooperacion) Text in Spanish. 2007. q. free (effective 2008). bk.rev. illus.; charts. Index. back issues avail. **Document type:** *Journal, Academic/Scholarly.*
Media: Online - full content.
Published by: Centro Cultural de la Cooperacion Floreal Gorini, Corrientes 1543, Buenos Aires, Argentina. TEL 54-11-50778000, uninfo@centrocultural.coop. Ed., Pub. Jorge Testero.

300 URY ISSN 0797-4892
D880
REVISTA DEL SUR. Text in Spanish. 1990. m. USD 60; UYP 2,500 newsstand/cover. **Document type:** *Consumer.*
Related titles: English ed.: Third World Resurgence.
Published by: (Red del Tercer Mundo), Instituto del Tercer Mundo/Third World Institute, Juan D Jackson, 1136, Montevideo, 11200, Uruguay. TEL 598-2-49-61-92, TELEX 0402-6105926 GMA LU, http://www.item.org.uy. Ed. Alejandro Gomez.

300 ESP ISSN 1989-967X
▼ **REVISTA ELECTRONICA DE PENSAMIENTO, ECONOMIA Y SOCIEDAD;** o. Text in Spanish. 2009. bi-m. back issues avail. **Document type:** *Journal, Academic/Scholarly.*
Media: Online - full text.
Published by: Instituto Virtual de Ciencias Humanas http://www.ivch-cursos.es/index.php. Ed. Eloy Rodriguez Navarro.

300 URY ISSN 0797-9517
REVISTA ENCUENTROS. Text in Spanish. 1992. irreg., latest vol.5. USD 13 (effective 1999).
Published by: Fundacion de Cultura Universitaria, 25 de Mayo 568, Montevideo, 11003, Uruguay. TEL 598-2-9161152, FAX 598-2-9152549.

REVISTA ESPANOLA DE DESARROLLO Y COOPERACION. *see* LAW

300 917.1 ESP ISSN 1132-7839
F1001
➤ **REVISTA ESPANOLA DE ESTUDIOS CANADIENSES.** Text in English, French, Spanish. 1990. irreg. bk.rev. **Document type:** *Journal, Academic/Scholarly.* **Description:** Includes articles on any aspect of Canadiana.
Indexed: MLA-IB.
Published by: (Asociacion de Estudios Canadienses en Espana), Universitat de Barcelona, Servei de Publicacions, Gran Via Corts Catalanes 585, Barcelona, 08007, Spain. TEL 34-93-4021100, http://www.publicacions.ub.es.

300 500 USA ISSN 2153-3318
REVISTA EXPLORATORIS: EXPLORATORIO DE LA REALIDAD GLOBAL. Text in Spanish. a. free (effective 2010). **Document type:** *Journal, Academic/Scholarly.* **Description:** Features research about Hispanic countries and society, education, business, industry, technology information, communication and culture.
Media: Online - full text.
Published by: P D H Tech, LLC, 346 Grassmarket, San Antonio, TX 78259. TEL 210-415-3353, info@pdhtech.com, http://www.pdhtech.com.

300 BRA ISSN 1679-1851
REVISTA FACTUS. Text in Portuguese. 2003. a. back issues avail. **Document type:** *Monographic series, Academic/Scholarly.*
Related titles: Online - full text ed.: ISSN 1982-0445.
Published by: Faculdade Taboao da Serra, Rodovia Regis Bittencourt, 199, Taboa da Serra, Sao Paulo, 06768-001, Brazil. TEL 55-11-4787978, revistafactus@fts.com.br. Ed. Paulo Henrique Pereira.

306 COL ISSN 0121-2559
REVISTA FORO. Text in Spanish. 1986. q. USD 53 (effective 1997). **Document type:** *Academic/Scholarly.* **Description:** Reflects on contemporary ideas in the field of social science.

S

Indexed: H21, P08, PAIS.
Published by: Ediciones Foro Nacional por Colombia, Carrera 3a, 27-62, Apartado Aereo 10141, Bogota, CUND, Colombia. TEL 57-1-2835982, FAX 57-1-2836045. Ed. Pedro Santana. Circ: 4,000 (paid).

300 MEX ISSN 2007-123X
▼ **REVISTA FUENTE.** Text in Spanish. 2009. q. back issues avail. **Document type:** *Journal, Academic/Scholarly.*
Media: Online - full text.
Published by: Universidad Autonoma de Nayarit, Ciudad de la Cultura "Amado Nervo", Tepic, Nayarit, 63155, Mexico. TEL 52-311-2118800, http://www.uan.edu.mx/. Ed. Rosa Esthela Gonzalez Flores.

300 CHL ISSN 0717-1498
UA602.3
REVISTA FUERZAS ARMADAS Y SOCIEDAD. Text in Spanish. 1989. q. **Document type:** *Magazine, Consumer.*
Indexed: H21, LID&ISL, P08.
Published by: Facultad Latinoamericana de Ciencias Sociales (F L A C S O), Chile, Av Dag Hammerskjold 3269, Vitacura, Santiago de Chile, Chile. TEL 56-2-2900200, FAX 56-2-2900263, http://www.flacso.cl.

300 BRA ISSN 1982-257X
REVISTA I D E A S. (Interfaces em Desenvolvimento, Agricultura e Sociedade) Text in Spanish, Portuguese. 2007. s-a. **Document type:** *Journal, Academic/Scholarly.*
Related titles: Online - full text ed.: ISSN 1984-9834. free (effective 2011).
Published by: Universidade Federal Rural do Rio de Janeiro, Programa de Pos - Graduacao de Ciencias Sociais, Av Presidente Vargas 417, 6o Andar, Centro, Rio de Janeiro, 20071-003, Brazil.

300 COL ISSN 0121-5051
HD28
➤ **REVISTA INNOVAR;** revista de ciencias administrativas y sociales. Text in Spanish. 1991. 2/yr. COP 40,000 domestic; USD 30 in United States; EUR 35 in Europe (effective 2010). adv. **Document type:** *Journal, Academic/Scholarly.* **Description:** Aimed at students, researchers and teachers interested in theoretical, empirical and practical themes related to the social and administrative sciences.
Related titles: Online - full text ed.: free (effective 2011) (from SciELO).
Indexed: A26, C01, I04, I05, PAIS, SCOPUS, SSCI, SociolAb, W07.
Published by: Universidad Nacional de Colombia, Escuela de Administration de Empresas y Contaduria Publica, Carrera 30, no 45-03, Ciudad Universitaria, Edificio 310, of 116, Bogota, Colombia. Ed., R&P Edison Jair Duque Oliva. Circ: 2,000 (paid and controlled).

300 MEX ISSN 1405-3543
REVISTA INTERNACIONAL DE CIENCIAS SOCIALES Y HUMANIDADES. Text in Spanish. 1991. s-a. back issues avail. **Document type:** *Journal, Academic/Scholarly.*
Published by: Universidad Autonoma de Tamaulipas, Matamoros 8 y 9 Col. Centro, Victoria, Tamaulipas, 87000, Mexico. TEL 52-834-3181800, hmcappello@yahoo.com, http://portal.uat.edu.mx/portal/index.htm.

338.2 ESP ISSN 1988-0928
REVISTA INTERNACIONAL DE SOSTENIBILIDAD, TECNOLOGIA Y HUMANISMO. Text in Catalan, English, Spanish. 2006. a. free (effective 2009). **Document type:** *Journal, Academic/Scholarly.* **Description:** Deals with issues related to urban planning, regional planning, architecture, research in engineering and other fields related to economics, political and social sciences, philosophy and ethics.
Media: Online - full text.
Published by: Universidad Politecnica de Catalunya, Catedra UNESCO de Sostenibilitat, C/Colom 1, Terrassa, 08222, Spain. TEL 34-93-7398050, FAX 34-93-7398032, sostenible@catunesco.upc.es. Pub. Miquel Barcelo. Adv. contact Ana Andres.

300 BRA ISSN 1807-1384
HM401
➤ **REVISTA INTERNACIONAL INTERDISCIPLINAR INTERTHESIS.** Text in English, Portuguese, Spanish. 2004. 2/yr. free (effective 2011). back issues avail. **Document type:** *Journal, Academic/Scholarly.* **Description:** Provides a forum for interdisciplinary studies in the several areas of knowledge, especially in the field of human sciences.
Media: Online - full text.
Published by: Universidade Federal de Santa Catarina, Centro de Filosofia e Ciencias Humanas, Campus Universitario da Trindade, Florianopolis, SC 88040-970, Brazil. TEL 55-48-3319330, FAX 55-48-331975. Ed. Selvino Assmann. Pub., R&P Silmara Cimbalista.

300 COL ISSN 1692-715X
➤ **REVISTA LATINOAMERICANA DE CIENCIAS SOCIALES, NINEZ Y JUVENTUD.** Text in Spanish. 2003. 2/yr. COP 50,000 (effective 2008). adv. bk.rev. abstr.; bibl.; charts; illus.; maps. Index. back issues avail. **Document type:** *Journal, Academic/Scholarly.*
Related titles: Online - full text ed.: free (effective 2011).
Indexed: A26, C01, F04, H21, I04, I05, P08, P27, P48, P54, PQC, SSA, SociolAb.
Published by: Universidad de Manizales, Centro de Estudios Avanzados en Ninez y Juventud, Carrera 9 no 19-03, Manizales, Colombia. TEL 57-6-8849589, FAX 57-6-8849589. Ed. Hector Fabio Ospina. Circ: 500 (paid and controlled).

➤ **REVISTA LATINOAMERICANA DE ESTUDIOS EDUCATIVOS.** *see* EDUCATION

300 BRA ISSN 1414-0543
H53.B7
➤ **REVISTA MEDIACOES.** Spine title: Mediacoes. Text in Portuguese. 1996. s-a. **Document type:** *Journal, Academic/Scholarly.*
Related titles: Online - full text ed.: free (effective 2011).
Indexed: CA, P42, PSA, S02, S03, SCOPUS, SociolAb, T02.
Published by: Universidade Estadual de Londrina, Departamento de Ciencias Sociais, Caixa Postal 6001, Londrina, 86051-990, Brazil. TEL 55-43-33714456, FAX 55-43-33284440, csociais@uel.br. Ed. Renata Goncalves.

➤ **REVISTA MEXICANA DE ESTUDIOS CANADIENSES.** *see* HISTORY—History Of North And South America

300.972 MEX ISSN 1405-2962
F2155
➤ **REVISTA MEXICANA DEL CARIBE.** Text in English, Spanish. 1996. s-a. USD 15 domestic; USD 35 foreign (effective 1999 & 2000). adv. bk.rev. bibl.; illus.; stat. cum.index: 1996-1998. back issues avail. **Document type:** *Journal, Academic/Scholarly.* **Description:** Divulges the results of the research on the Caribbean. Gives priority to the analysis of comtemporary problems in the region such as history, social sciences and sustainable development.
Related titles: Diskette ed.; E-mail ed.; Online - full text ed.
Indexed: A01, A26, C01, C32, CA, F03, F04, H21, I04, I05, P08, PAIS, T02.
Published by: (Universidad de Quintana Roo), San Serif Editores, Blvd. BAHIA Y COMONFORT, Del Bosque, Chetumal, Q ROO 77010, Mexico. TEL 52-983-50342, FAX 52-983-29656, recaribe@balam.cuc.uqroo.mx, http://www.recaribe.uqroo.mx. Ed. Martin Ramos Diaz. Pub. Roberto Zavala. R&P Maria Eugenia. adv.: B&W page USD 1,000. Circ: 800 (paid); 200 (controlled).

300 BRA ISSN 1414-6304
REVISTA MULTIPLA. Text in Portuguese. 1996. s-a. back issues avail. **Document type:** *Journal, Academic/Scholarly.*
Related titles: Online - full text ed.
Published by: Faculdade Integradas da Uniao Pioneira de Integracao Social, SEP/Sul - EQ 712-912, Conjunto A, Brasilia, D.F., 70390-125, Brazil. TEL 55-61-3445-6715, contacto@upis.br. Ed. Mercedes G. Kothe.

300 CRI ISSN 1013-9060
REVISTA NACIONAL DE CULTURA. Text in Spanish. 1988. q. CRC 2,400, USD 24; USD 30 in Europe. adv. **Document type:** *Academic/Scholarly.*
Indexed: MLA-IB.
Published by: Universidad Estatal a Distancia, San Pedro de Montes de Oca, San Jose, 2050, Costa Rica. TEL 506-224-1766, FAX 506-2241766. Ed. Alberto Canas. Adv. contact Cristina Pereira.

300 BRA ISSN 1677-3942
REVISTA OMNIA. Text in Spanish. 1998. a. back issues avail. **Document type:** *Monographic series, Academic/Scholarly.*
Published by: Faculdades Adamantinenses Integradas, Rua Nove de Julho, 730-740, Adamantina, RJ 17800-000, Brazil. TEL 55-18-3522-1002, fai@fai.com.br. Ed. Roldao Simione.

300 ARG ISSN 1851-3123
REVISTA PILQUEN. SECCION CIENCIAS SOCIALES (ONLINE). Text in Spanish. 1998. a. back issues avail. **Document type:** *Monographic series, Academic/Scholarly.*
Formerly (until 2005): Revista Pilquen. Seccion Ciencias Sociales (Print) (1666-0579)
Media: Online - full text (from SciELO).
Published by: Universidad Nacional del Comahue, Centro Universitario Regional Zona Atlantica, Buenos Aires, 14000, Neuquen, 8300, Argentina. TEL 54-299-4490363, FAX 54-299-4490351, curza@uncoma.edu.ar, http://www.uncoma.edu.ar. Ed. Graciela Salto.

300 SLV ISSN 1019-9594
REVISTA SALVADORENA DE CIENCIAS SOCIALES. Text in Spanish. 1992. s-a. **Document type:** *Journal, Academic/Scholarly.*
Published by: Fundacion Dr. Guillermo Manuel Ungo, Avenida la Revolucion, Pasaje 6, Casa 147, Colonia San Benito, San Salvador, El Salvador. TEL 503-2430406, FAX 503-2438206, contacto@fundaungo.org.sv, http://www.fundaungo.org.sv.

300 BOL
REVISTA TEMAS ECONOMICOS Y SOCIALES. Text in Spanish. a. **Document type:** *Journal, Academic/Scholarly.*
Published by: Universidad Autonoma "Gabriel Rene Moreno", CP 702, Santa Cruz de la Sierra, Bolivia. TEL 591-2-372898, FAX 591-2-342160, http://www.uagrm.edu.bo.

REVISTA THEOMAI; estudios sobre sociedad, naturaleza y desarrollo. *see* ENVIRONMENTAL STUDIES

▼ **REVISTA UMBRAL.** *see* HUMANITIES: COMPREHENSIVE WORKS

300 ESP ISSN 1698-7446
HD3528.A3
REVISTA VASCA DE ECONOMIA SOCIAL/GIZARTE EKONOMIAREN EUSKAL ALDIZKARIA. Text in Spanish. 2004. a. **Document type:** *Journal, Academic/Scholarly.*
Published by: Universidad del Pais Vasco, Servicio Editorial, Apartado 1397, Bilbao, 48080, Spain. TEL 34-94-6015126, FAX 34-94-4801314, luxedito@lg.ehu.es, http://www.ehu.es/servicios/se_az/.

300 VEN ISSN 1316-4090
H8.S7
REVISTA VENEZOLANA DE CIENCIAS SOCIALES. Text in Spanish. 1997. s-a. VEB 30 domestic; USD 8 in Latin America; USD 10 in United States (effective 2009). **Document type:** *Journal, Academic/Scholarly.*
Related titles: CD-ROM ed.; Online - full text ed.: free (effective 2011).
Indexed: C01.
Published by: Universidad Nacional Experimental Rafael Maria Baralt, Avenida Intercomunal con Carretera H, Quinta Yoly 267, Cabimas, Zulia, Venezuela. TEL 58-264-2513010, FAX 58-264-2513505, http://www.unermb.edu.ve.

300 VEN ISSN 1317-5904
HQ1180
➤ **REVISTAS OTRAS MIRADAS.** Text in Spanish. 2001. s-a. free (effective 2011). **Document type:** *Journal, Academic/Scholarly.* **Description:** Open forum to foster critical reflection and debate about gender themes and questions.
Media: Online - full text.
Published by: Universidad de los Andes, Facultad de Humanidades y Educacion, Departamento de Antroplogia y Sociologia, Av Las Americas, La Liria, Edif A, Piso 1, Merida, 5101, Venezuela.

300 FRA ISSN 2101-048X
▼ **REVUE DE RECHERCHE EN CIVILISATION AMERICAINE.** Text in French, English. 2009. a. free (effective 2011). **Document type:** *Journal, Academic/Scholarly.*
Media: Online - full text.
Published by: Universite de Bordeaux IV (Montesquieu), Av. Leon Duguit, Bordeaux, 33608, France. TEL 33-5-56842924, FAX 33-5-56845477.

300 FRA ISSN 1623-6572
CODEN: RSSEED
➤ **REVUE DES SCIENCES SOCIALES.** Text in French. 1972. a., latest vol.42, 2009. EUR 18.30 (effective 2003). bk.rev. 200 p./no.; **Document type:** *Journal, Academic/Scholarly.* **Description:** Covers research in methodology and cultural anthropology and in demographic, economical, and social problems of the eastern region of France and of Europe.
Formerly (until 1999): Revue des Sciences Sociales de la France de l'Est (0336-1578)
Related titles: Online - full text ed.: ISSN 2107-0385. 200?.
Indexed: CA, FR, IBR, IBSS, IBZ, P30, S02, S03, SCOPUS, SOPODA, SSA, SociolAb, T02.
—INIST.
Published by: Universite de Strasbourg II (Marc Bloch/Sciences Humaines), 22 rue Descartes, Strasbourg, 67084, France.

➤ **REVUE D'ETUDES EN AGRICULTURE ET ENVIRONNEMENT.** *see* AGRICULTURE—Agricultural Economics

300 CHE ISSN 0048-8046
H1
REVUE EUROPEENNE DES SCIENCES SOCIALES. Variant title: R E S S. Text in English, French, German, Italian. 1963. 3/yr. price varies. bk.rev. **Document type:** *Journal, Academic/Scholarly.* **Description:** European studies of social sciences.
Formerly (until 1971): Cahiers Vilfredo Pareto (0008-0497)
Indexed: A20, A22, BibInd, DIP, FR, IBR, IBSS, IBZ, P30, PAIS, PCI, RASB.
—BLDSC (7900.180000), IE, Ingenta, INIST. **CCC.**
Published by: Librairie Droz S.A., 11 rue Firmin-Massot, Geneva 12, 1211, Switzerland. TEL 41-22-3466666, FAX 41-22-3472391, droz@droz.org, http://www.droz.org. Ed. Giovanni Busino. Circ: 2,000.

REVUE FRANCAISE DE CIVILISATION BRITANNIQUE. *see* SOCIOLOGY

300 FRA
LA REVUE INTERNATIONALE DES LIVRES & DES IDEES. Text in French. 2007. bi-m. EUR 25 domestic; EUR 33 in Europe; EUR 33 DOM-TOM; EUR 40 elsewhere (effective 2008). **Document type:** *Journal, Consumer.*
Published by: Revue Internationale des Livres et des Idees, 31 Rue Paul Fort, Paris, 75014, France. parutions@revuedeslivres.net, http://revuedeslivres.net.

300 FRA ISSN 0304-3037
H3
REVUE INTERNATIONALE DES SCIENCES SOCIALES. Text in French. 1949. q. EUR 44 in developing nations; EUR 68 elsewhere to individuals; EUR 72 elsewhere to institutions (effective 2011). adv. bibl.; charts. index. back issues avail. **Document type:** *Journal, Academic/Scholarly.* **Description:** Seeks to bridge communities of social scientists from different disciplines and from different regions of the world with contributions by panels of leading scholars on selected themes.
Formerly (until 1958): Bulletin International des Sciences Sociales (1011-114X)
Related titles: Microfilm ed.: (from PQC); Online - full text ed.: ISSN 2222-4610; ◆ English ed.: International Social Science Journal. ISSN 0020-8701.
Indexed: A22, ARDT, CERDIC, FR, I13, IBR, IBZ, ILD.
—IE, Infotrieve, INIST. **CCC.**
Published by: Editions Eres, 33 Av. Marcel Dassault, Toulouse, 31500, France. TEL 33-5-61751576, FAX 33-5-61735289, eres@edition-eres.com. Ed. John Crowley. Circ: 1,100. **Co-publisher:** UNESCO.

300 MDG
REVUE ITA. Text in French. 1985. m.
Published by: Ministry of Social Welfare, BP 681, Antananarivo, 101, Madagascar. TEL 23630. Ed. Paulin Rakotoarivony. Circ: 500.

300 TUN ISSN 0035-4333
H3
REVUE TUNISIENNE DES SCIENCES SOCIALES. Text in Arabic, French. q. TND 2,000. bk.rev. charts; stat. cum.index: 1964-1968.
Indexed: CCA, FR, IBR, IBSS, IBZ, ILD, MLA, MLA-IB, P30, PAIS, PopulInd.
—INIST.
Published by: Universite de Tunis, Centre d'Etudes et de Recherches Economiques et Sociales, 23 rue d'Espagne, Tunis, Tunisia.

300 CAN ISSN 1705-2165
HD2951 R48
REVUE UNIRCOOP. Text in Multiple languages. 2003. a. **Document type:** *Journal, Academic/Scholarly.* **Description:** Intends to make known the scientific output of the existing wealth of knowledge regarding cooperatives and associations.
Related titles: Online - full text ed.: free (effective 2011).
Indexed: A39, C27, C29, D03, D04, E13, R14, S14, S15, S18.
Published by: Universite de Sherbrooke, Faculte d'Administration, 2500 Boulevard de l'Universite, Sherbrooke, PQ J1K 2R1, Canada. http://www.usherbrooke.ca.

300 CHE ISSN 1664-9966
▼ **RHEINSPRUNG 11;** Zeitschrift fuer Bildkritik. Text in German. 2011. s-a. **Document type:** *Journal, Academic/Scholarly.*
Media: Online - full text.
Published by: Eikones - NFS Bildkritik, Rheinsprung 11, Basel, 4051, Switzerland. http://www.eikones.ch.

RHIZOMES; cultural studies in emerging knowledge. *see* HUMANITIES: COMPREHENSIVE WORKS

300 CHN ISSN 1008-1593
RIBENXUE LUNTAN/JAPANESE STUDIES FORUM. Text in Chinese. 1964. q. USD 28.40 (effective 2009). bk.rev. **Document type:** *Journal, Academic/Scholarly.* **Description:** Covers economics, politics, history, philosophy, education, and international relations in Northeast Asia.
Formerly (until 1998): Waiguo Wenti Yanjiu/Foreign Problem Research (1006-7809)
Related titles: Online - full text ed.
—East View.
Published by: (Riben Yanjiusuo), Dongbei Shifan Daxue/Northeast Normal University, 5268 Renmin Dajie, Changchun, 130024, China. TEL 86-431-5099741.

300 FRA ISSN 0035-5666
RIVAROL; quand les peuples cessent d'estimer, ils cessent d'obeir. Text in French. 1951. w. EUR 114 domestic; EUR 126 foreign (effective 2008). adv. bk.rev. **Document type:** *Newspaper, Consumer.*
Related titles: Microfiche ed.: 1951.
Published by: Editions des Tuileries, 1 Rue d'Hauteville, Paris, 75010, France. Ed. Camille Galic. Circ: 18,000.

300 ITA ISSN 1724-5389
HN371
LA RIVISTA DELLE POLITICHE SOCIALI. Text in Italian. 2004. q. EUR 60 (effective 2008). **Document type:** *Magazine, Consumer.*
Related titles: Online - full text ed.
Published by: Ediesse srl, Via dei Frentani 4A, Rome, 00185, Italy. TEL 39-06-44870283, FAX 39-06-44870335, ediesse@cgil.it, http://www.ediesseonline.it. Ed. Maria Luisa Mirabile.

300 POL ISSN 0137-4176
H9
ROCZNIKI NAUK SPOLECZNYCH. Text in Polish; Summaries in English. 1949. a. price varies. **Document type:** *Academic/Scholarly.*
Indexed: RASB.
Published by: Katolicki Uniwersytet Lubelski, Towarzystwo Naukowe, ul Gliniana 21, Lublin, 20616, Poland. Circ: 820.

300 NOR ISSN 1503-0946
ROKKANSENTERET-NOTAT. Text in Norwegian. 2000. irreg.
Formed by the merger of (1987-2000): L O S-Senter Notat (0802-3646); (1999-2000): S E F O S - Notat (1501-0651); Which was formerly: Senter for Samfunnsforskning. Notat (0802-0973); (1988-1989): S E F O S Serie B (0803-009X)
Indexed: ASFA, B21, ESPM.
Published by: Stein Rokkan Senter for Flerfaglige Samfunnsstudier/Stein Rokkan Centre for Social Studies, Nygaardsgaten 5, Bergen, 5015, Norway. TEL 47-55-58-97-10, FAX 47-55-58-97-11.

300 330 ROM ISSN 1843-8520
HT395.E85
ROMANIAN JOURNAL OF REGIONAL SCIENCE. Text in English. 2007. s-a. free (effective 2011). **Document type:** *Journal, Academic/Scholarly.*
Media: Online - full text.
Indexed: CA, T02.
Published by: Asociatia Romana de Stiinte Regionale/Romanian Regional Science Association, Bd Lascar Catargiu 16A, Ap 8, Sector 1, Bucharest, Romania. arsr@k.ro.

300 GBR
ROUTLEDGE STUDIES IN DEVELOPMENT AND SOCIETY. Text in English. 1996. irreg., latest 2009. price varies. back issues avail. **Document type:** *Monographic series, Academic/Scholarly.* **Description:** Incorporates a multidisciplinary approach to explore the impact of development theory and practice.
Published by: Routledge (Subsidiary of: Taylor & Francis Group), 4 Park Sq, Milton Park, Abingdon, Oxon OX14 4RN, United Kingdom. TEL 44-20-70176000, FAX 44-20-70176336, subscriptions@tandf.co.uk.

ROUTLEDGE STUDIES IN SOCIAL AND POLITICAL THOUGHT. *see* POLITICAL SCIENCE

300 GBR
ROUTLEDGE STUDIES ON CHINA IN TRANSITION. Text in English. 1996. irreg., latest 2009. price varies. back issues avail. **Document type:** *Monographic series, Academic/Scholarly.* **Description:** Focuses on social, political and cultural change in the China of the 1990s and beyond.
Former titles (until 2005): RoutledgeCurzon Studies on China in Transition; (until 2003): Routledge Studies in China in Transition
—BLDSC (8026.519252).
Published by: Routledge (Subsidiary of: Taylor & Francis Group), 2 Park Sq, Milton Park, Abingdon, Oxon OX14 4RN, United Kingdom. TEL 44-20-70176000, FAX 44-20-70176699, info@routledge.co.uk. Ed. David S. G Goodman.

300 GBR
ROYAL HOLLOWAY UNIVERSITY OF LONDON. DEPARTMENT OF SOCIAL & POLITICAL SCIENCE. OCCASIONAL PAPERS. Text in English. irreg. **Document type:** *Monographic series, Academic/Scholarly.*
Formerly: Royal Holloway University of London. Department of Social & Political Science. Discussion Paper
Published by: University of London, Royal Holloway, Department of Social & Political Science, Egham, Surrey TW20 0EX, United Kingdom. TEL 44-1784-443687, FAX 44-1784-434375.

300 POL ISSN 1505-1161
RUBIKON; studencki kwartalnik naukowy. Text in Polish. 1998. q. **Document type:** *Journal, Academic/Scholarly.* **Description:** Presents the working papers of various young international researchers on diverse subjects from social science.
Published by: Klub Dyskusyjny Kartoteka, ul Koszykowa 24 m.1, Warsaw, 00553, Poland. TEL 48-22-6254469. Ed. Lech M Nijakowski. Circ: 600.

300 DEU ISSN 1865-4215
RURAL. Text in German. 2007. irreg., latest vol.3, 2010. price varies. **Document type:** *Monographic series, Academic/Scholarly.*
Published by: Cuvillier Verlag, Nonnenstieg 8, Goettingen, 37075, Germany. TEL 49-551-547240, FAX 49-551-5472421, info@cuvillier.de.

300 630 370 USA
RURAL MINNESOTA JOURNAL. Abbreviated title: R M J. Text in English. 2006. s-a. free to members (effective 2010). back issues avail. **Document type:** *Journal, Academic/Scholarly.* **Description:** Covers a theme with each issue on rural MN issues, including demographic, economics, agriculture, education, and healthcare.
Related titles: Online - full content ed.: free.
Indexed: CA.
Published by: Center for Rural Policy and Development, 600 S Fifth St, Ste 211, Saint Peter, MN 56082. TEL 507-934-7700, 877-787-2566, FAX 507-934-7704, crpd@ruralmn.org, http://www.mnsu.edu/ruralmn/index.html.

RUSSELL SAGE FOUNDATION SERIES ON TRUST. *see* PSYCHOLOGY

RUSSIAN SOCIAL SCIENCE REVIEW. *see* POLITICAL SCIENCE

300 ITA ISSN 1128-6377
DK32
RUSSICA ROMANA. Text in Italian. 1994. a. EUR 345 domestic to institutions (print & online eds.); EUR 445 foreign to institutions (print & online eds.) (effective 2009). **Document type:** *Journal, Academic/Scholarly.*
Related titles: Online - full text ed.: ISSN 1724-1510.
Published by: Fabrizio Serra Editore (Subsidiary of: Accademia Editoriale), c/o Accademia Editoriale, Via Santa Bibbiana 28, Pisa, 56127, Italy. TEL 39-050-542332, FAX 39-050-574888, accademiaeditoriale@accademiaeditoriale.it, http://www.libraweb.net.

RUSSKOE ZARUBEZH'E: ISTORIYA I SOVREMENNOST'. *see* HISTORY—History Of Europe

300 GBR ISSN 1350-4649
S E I WORKING PAPERS. (Sussex European Institute) Text in English. 1993. irreg., latest vol.110, 2009. GBP 5 per issue (effective 2009). back issues avail. **Document type:** *Monographic series, Academic/Scholarly.* **Description:** Aims to make research results, accounts of work-in-progress and background information available to those concerned with contemporary European issues.
Related titles: Online - full text ed.: free (effective 2009).
Published by: University of Sussex, Sussex European Institute, Falmer, Brighton, E Sussex BN1 9RG, United Kingdom. TEL 44-1273-678578, FAX 44-1273-678571, sei@sussex.ac.uk.

300 GBR ISSN 2042-3586
▼ **S I R E FOCUS.** Text in English. 2009. irreg. back issues avail. **Document type:** *Monographic series, Academic/Scholarly.*
Related titles: Online - full text ed.: ISSN 2042-3594. free (effective 2010).
Published by: Scottish Institute for Research in Economics, The University of Edinburgh, First Fl - Rm 1.10, 31 Buccleuch Pl, Edinburgh, EH8 9JT, United Kingdom. TEL 44-131-6504066, info@sire.ac.uk.

355.1 DEU ISSN 1433-9390
S O W I ARBEITSPAPIERE. Text in German. 193?. irreg. **Document type:** *Monographic series, Academic/Scholarly.*
Published by: Sozialwissenschaftliches Institut der Bundeswehr, Proetzeler Chaussee 20, Strausberg, 15344, Germany. TEL 49-3341-581830, FAX 49-3341-581802.

300 NAM
S S D DISCUSSION PAPERS. (Social Sciences Division) Text in English. 1990. irreg. (3-5/yr.). price varies. **Document type:** *Monographic series, Academic/Scholarly.* **Description:** Covers legal, social, economic, gender, and development related issues affecting present-day Namibia.
Supersedes: Namibian Institute for Social and Economic Research. Discussion Papers
Published by: (Multi-Disciplinary Research Centre), University of Namibia, Social Sciences Division, Private Bag 13301, Windhoek, Namibia. TEL 264-61-2063051. R&P Lazarus Hangula.

300 NAM
S S D RESEARCH REPORTS. (Social Sciences Division) Text in English. 1990. irreg. price varies. **Document type:** *Report, Academic/Scholarly.* **Description:** Presents research in social, gender, and economic conditions affecting specific regions or population groups in present-day Namibia.
Supersedes: Namibian Institute for Social and Economic Research. Research Reports
Published by: (Multi-Disciplinary Research Centre), University of Namibia, Social Sciences Division, Private Bag 13301, Windhoek, Namibia. TEL 264-61-2063051. R&P Lazarus Hangula.

300 CAN ISSN 0839-4377
S S H R C NEWS/CONSEIL DE RECHERCHES EN SCIENCES HUMAINES DU CANADA. NOUVELLES. (Social Sciences and Humanities Research Council) Text in French, English. 1979. q.
Formerly (until 1985): Council Update (0225-1787)
Published by: Social Sciences and Humanities Research Council of Canada, 350 Albert St, PO Box 1610, Ottawa, ON K1P 6G4, Canada. TEL 613-992-0691, FAX 613-992-1787, http://www.sshrc-crsh.gc.ca.

300 AUT ISSN 1013-1469
HM261 CODEN: SRUNEK
➤ **S W S - RUNDSCHAU.** Text in German. 1961. q. EUR 23.30 to individuals; EUR 35.60 to institutions; EUR 13.10 to students (effective 2003). adv. bk.rev. charts; illus.; stat. index. back issues avail. **Document type:** *Journal, Academic/Scholarly.* **Description:** Quantitative and qualitative empirical research in political science, sociology and survey research.
Former titles: Journal fuer Sozialforschung (0253-3995); (until 1981): Journal fuer Angewandte Sozialforschung (0025-8822)
Indexed: A20, IBR, IBZ, P30, SCOPUS, SSCI, SocialAb, W07.
Published by: Sozialwissenschaftliche Studiengesellschaft, Maria-Theresien-Strasse 9, Vienna, W 1090, Austria. TEL 43-1-3173127, FAX 43-1-3102238. Ed. Christian Schaller. Adv. contact Gerlinde Pacholik. Circ: 2,500.

300 DEU ISSN 1862-314X
SACHSEN - MITTELEUROPA - OSTEUROPA. Text in German. 2006. irreg., latest vol.2, 2007. price varies. **Document type:** *Monographic series, Academic/Scholarly.*
Published by: Peter Lang GmbH (Subsidiary of: Peter Lang Publishing Group), Eschborner Landstr 42-50, Frankfurt Am Main, 60489, Germany. TEL 49-69-7807050, FAX 49-69-78070550, zentrale.frankfurt@peterlang.com.

SACHSEN UND ANHALT. *see* HISTORY—History Of Europe

SAGAMI JOSHI DAIGAKU KIYO. A, JINBUN, SHAKAI-KEI/SAGAMI WOMEN'S UNIVERSITY. JOURNAL. A. HUMANITIES - SOCIAL SCIENCES SECTION. *see* HUMANITIES: COMPREHENSIVE WORKS

301 USA
SAGE LIBRARY OF SOCIAL RESEARCH. Text in English. 1973. irreg., latest 1998. price varies. back issues avail.; reprints avail. **Document type:** *Monographic series, Academic/Scholarly.*
Published by: Sage Publications, Inc., Books (Subsidiary of: Sage Publications, Inc.), 2455 Teller Rd, Thousand Oaks, CA 91320. TEL 800-818-7243, FAX 800-583-2665, books.claim@sagepub.com. **Subscr. to:** Sage Publications India Pvt. Ltd.; Sage Publications Ltd.

▼ **SAGE OPEN.** *see* HUMANITIES: COMPREHENSIVE WORKS

300 USA
SAGE UNIVERSITY PAPERS SERIES. Text in English. 197?. irreg. back issues avail. **Document type:** *Monographic series.* **Description:** Discusses various aspects of research in the social sciences.
Related titles: ◆ Series: Qualitative Research Methods Series. ISSN 0888-5397; ◆ Quantitative Applications in the Social Sciences Series. ISSN 0149-192X.
Published by: Sage Publications, Inc., Books (Subsidiary of: Sage Publications, Inc.), 2455 Teller Rd, Thousand Oaks, CA 91320. TEL 805-499-0721, FAX 805-499-0871. **Subscr. in Asia to:** Sage Publications India Pvt. Ltd., M-32 Market, Greater Kailash-I, PO Box 4215, New Delhi 110 048, India; **Subscr. in Europe to:** Sage Publications Ltd., 1 Oliver's Yard, 55 City Rd, London EC1Y 1SP, United Kingdom.

SAINT ANTONY'S MIDDLE EAST MONOGRAPHS. *see* HISTORY—History Of The Near East

SALMAGUNDI; a quarterly of the humanities & social sciences. *see* HUMANITIES: COMPREHENSIVE WORKS

300 DEU ISSN 2192-1849
▼ **SALZBURGER INTERDISZIPLINAERE DISKURSE.** Text in German. forthcoming 2011. irreg. price varies. **Document type:** *Monographic series, Academic/Scholarly.*
Published by: Peter Lang GmbH (Subsidiary of: Peter Lang Publishing Group), Eschborner Landstr 42-50, Frankfurt Am Main, 60489, Germany. TEL 49-69-7807050, FAX 49-69-78070550, zentrale.frankfurt@peterlang.com. Ed. Franz Gmainer-Pranzl.

300 BGD
SAMAJ NIRIKKHON. Text in Bengali. 1978. q. BDT 152 domestic to individuals (effective 1999); USD 40 foreign to individuals; BDT 172 domestic to institutions; USD 48 foreign to institutions. cum.index: vols.1-58 (1978-1992). reprints avail. **Document type:** *Academic/Scholarly.* **Description:** Contains scholarly articles on the socio-economic problems of the world in general and of Bangladesh in particular.
Related titles: ◆ English ed.: Journal of Social Studies. ISSN 1012-7844.
Published by: Centre for Social Studies/Samaj Nirikkhon Kendro, Rm 1107 Arts Bldg, Dhaka University, Dhaka, 1000, Bangladesh. TEL 880-2-9661900, FAX 880-2-865583. R&P B K Jahangir.

SAMANYOLU; uc aylik egitim dergisi - quarterly magazine of the social sciences. *see* RELIGIONS AND THEOLOGY—Islamic

SAMMLUNGEN DES HERDER-INSTITUTS ZUR OSTMITTELEUROPA-FORSCHUNG. *see* HISTORY—History Of Europe

300 DNK ISSN 1600-8510
SAMTID. Text in Danish. 1975. irreg. back issues avail. **Document type:** *Newspaper, Consumer.* **Description:** News about events and their backgrounds in present day society aimed at young people.
Formerly (until 1998): Samtid (Print) (0105-1326)
Media: Online - full content. **Related titles:** CD-ROM ed.: ISSN 1601-5703.
Published by: Forlaget Hedeskov, Teglvaerksvej 1, Grenaa, 8500, Denmark. TEL 45-70-201864. Ed. Sven Skovmand TEL 45-86-381688.

SANCHO EL SABIO; revista de cultura e investigacion vasca. *see* ANTHROPOLOGY

300 CHN ISSN 1671-9123
SANMENXIA ZHIYE JISHU XUEYUAN XUEBAO/SANMENXIA POLYTECHNIC. JOURNAL. Text in English. 2002. q. back issues avail. **Document type:** *Journal, Academic/Scholarly.*
Related titles: Online - full text ed.
Published by: Sanmenxia Zhiye Jishu Xueyuan, 42, Yaoshan Lu, Xi-duan, Sanmenxia, 472000, China. TEL 86-398-2183589, FAX 86-398-2183533, http://www.smxpt.cn/smxptsite/.

300 CHN ISSN 1673-4343
SANMING XUEYUAN XUEBAO/SANMING COLLEGE. JOURNAL. Text in Chinese. 2000. bi-m. (q. until 2010).
Formerly (until 2005): Sanming Gaodeng Zhuanke Xuexiao Xuebao (1671-1343); Which was formed by the merger of (1998-2000): Sanming Shi-Zhuan Xuebao/Sanming Teachers College. Journal (1008-3413); (1989-2000): Sanming Zhiye Daxue Xuebao/Sanming Vocational University. Journal (1008-3227)
Related titles: Online - full text ed.
Published by: Sanming Xueyuan/Sanming University, 25, Jingdong Lu, Sanming, 365004, China. TEL 86-598-8399961, FAX 86-598-8399961.

SANXIA DAXUE XUEBAO (RENWEN SHEHUI KEXUE BAN)/CHINA THREE GORGES UNIVERSITY. JOURNAL (HUMANITIES & SOCIAL SCIENCES). *see* HUMANITIES: COMPREHENSIVE WORKS

300 BRA ISSN 0102-8839
HC188.S3
SAO PAULO EM PERSPECTIVA. Text in Portuguese. 1985. 4/yr. USD 76.10.
Formerly (until 1986): Fundacao S E A D E. Revista. Sao Paulo em Perspectiva (0102-3926)
Related titles: Online - full text ed.: ISSN 1806-9452. 2000. free (effective 2007).
Indexed: A26, C01, I04, I05.
Published by: Fundacao Sistema Estadual de Analise de Dados, Av Casper Libero, 464, Centro, Caixa Postal 8223, Sao Paulo, SP 01033-000, Brazil. FAX 011-229-5259, TELEX 011-31390. Circ: 2,000.

300 DEU ISSN 1865-0856
SCHOLA NOVA. Text in German. 2006. irreg. **Document type:** *Monographic series, Academic/Scholarly.*
Published by: Paulo Freire Verlag, Unterm Berg 65a, Oldenburg, 26123, Germany. TEL 49-441-381674, FAX 49-441-9330056, pfv@freire.de, http://www.paulo-freire-verlag.de.

▼ **SCHOOL OF DOCTORAL STUDIES JOURNAL.** *see* SCIENCES: COMPREHENSIVE WORKS

300 DEU
SCHRIFT UND BILD IN BEWEGUNG. Text in German. 2002. irreg., latest vol.16, 2009. price varies. **Document type:** *Monographic series, Academic/Scholarly.*
Published by: Aisthesis Verlag, Oberntorwall 21, Bielefeld, 33602, Germany. TEL 49-521-172604, FAX 49-521-172812, info@aisthesis.de.

S

▼ **SCHRIFTEN ZUM SOZIAL-, UMWELT- UND GESUNDHEITSRECHT.** *see* LAW

300 DEU ISSN 1438-1729
SCHRIFTEN ZUR HUMANITAETS- UND GLUECKSFORSCHUNG. Text in German. 2001. irreg., latest vol.3, 2008. price varies. **Document type:** *Monographic series, Academic/Scholarly.*
Published by: Peter Lang GmbH (Subsidiary of: Peter Lang Publishing Group), Eschborner Landstr 42-50, Frankfurt Am Main, 60489, Germany. TEL 49-69-7807050, FAX 49-69-78070550, zentrale.frankfurt@peterlang.com. Eds. Hans Lenk, Robert Weimar.

300 DEU ISSN 1862-7277
SCHRIFTEN ZUR KULTURGESCHICHTE. Text in German. 2006. irreg., latest vol.18, 2010. price varies. **Document type:** *Monographic series, Academic/Scholarly.*
Published by: Verlag Dr. Kovac, Leverkusenstr 13, Hamburg, 22761, Germany. TEL 49-40-3988800, FAX 49-40-39888055, info@verlagdrkovac.de.

300 DEU
▼ **SCHRIFTEN ZUR KULTURGESCHICHTE MITTELDEUTSCHLANDS.** Text in German. 2009. irreg. price varies. **Document type:** *Monographic series, Academic/Scholarly.*
Published by: Frank und Timme GmbH, Wittelsbacherstr 27a, Berlin, 10707, Germany. TEL 49-30-88667911, FAX 49-30-86398731, info@frank-timme.de.

300 DEU ISSN 1435-6589
SCHRIFTEN ZUR KULTURWISSENSCHAFT. Text in German. 1993. irreg., latest vol.84, 2010. price varies. **Document type:** *Monographic series, Academic/Scholarly.*
Published by: Verlag Dr. Kovac, Leverkusenstr 13, Hamburg, 22761, Germany. TEL 49-40-3988800, FAX 49-40-39888055, info@verlagdrkovac.de.

340 DEU ISSN 0936-4048
SCHRIFTEN ZUR RECHTS- UND SOZIALWISSENSCHAFTEN. Variant title: Konstanzer Schriften zur Rechts- und Sozialwissenschaft. Text in German. 1989. irreg., latest vol.14, 2004. price varies. **Document type:** *Monographic series, Academic/Scholarly.*
Published by: Hartung-Gorre Verlag, Konstanz, 78465, Germany. TEL 49-7533-97227, FAX 49-7533-97228, Hartung.Gorre@t-online.de.

300 CHE ISSN 0175-6990
SCHRIFTEN ZUR SYMBOLFORSCHUNG. Text in German. 1984. irreg., latest vol.15, 2005. price varies. **Document type:** *Monographic series, Academic/Scholarly.*
Published by: Theologischer Verlag Zurich, Badenerstr 73, Zurich, 8026, Switzerland. TEL 41-44-2993355, FAX 41-44-2993358, tvz@ref.ch, http://www.tvz-verlag.ch.

330 DEU ISSN 0582-0588
SCHRIFTEN ZUR WIRTSCHAFTS- UND SOZIALGESCHICHTE. Text in German. 1966. irreg., latest vol.83, 2006. price varies. **Document type:** *Monographic series, Academic/Scholarly.*
Published by: Duncker und Humblot GmbH, Carl-Heinrich-Becker-Weg 9, Berlin, 12165, Germany. TEL 49-30-7900060, FAX 49-30-79000631, info@duncker-humblot.de.

300 DEU
SCHRIFTENREIHE DES BEZIEHUNGS- UND FAMILIENPANELS. Text in German. 2008. irreg., latest vol.2, 2010. price varies. **Document type:** *Monographic series, Academic/Scholarly.*
Formerly (until 2010): Schriftenreihe des Beziehungs- und Familienentwicklungspanels
Published by: Ergon Verlag, Keesburgstr 11, Wuerzburg, 97074, Germany. TEL 49-931-280084, FAX 49-931-282872, service@ergon-verlag.de, http://www.ergon-verlag.de.

142.7 ROM ISSN 2067-0621
▼ ➤ **SCHUTZIAN RESEARCH**; a yearbook of worldly phenomenology and qualitative social science. Text in Chinese, English, Korean, Spanish; Abstracts in English. 2009 (Nov.). a. EUR 25 to individuals; EUR 65 to institutions (effective 2010). back issues avail. **Document type:** *Journal, Academic/Scholarly.* **Description:** Contains philosophical, cultural-scientific, or multidisciplinary papers based on the work of Alfred Schutz.
Related titles: Online - full text ed.: EUR 10 to individuals; EUR 150 to institutions (effective 2010).
Published by: Zeta Books, 51 B-dul Coposu, ap. 48, Bucharest, 030604, Romania. TEL 40-73-3046689, FAX 40-31-8166779, zeta@zetabooks.com. Ed. Michael Barber.

300 CHE
▼ **SCHWABE REFLEXE.** Variant title: Reflexe. Text in German. 2009 (Oct.). irreg., latest vol.13, 2011. price varies. **Document type:** *Monographic series, Academic/Scholarly.*
Published by: Schwabe und Co. AG, Steinentorstr 13, Basel, 4010, Switzerland. TEL 41-61-2789565, FAX 41-61-2789566, verlag@schwabe.ch, http://www.schwabe.ch.

500 600 300 ITA ISSN 1121-9122
CC135
SCIENCE AND TECHNOLOGY FOR CULTURAL HERITAGE. Text in English. 1992. s-a. EUR 445 combined subscription domestic to institutions (print & online eds.); EUR 595 combined subscription foreign to institutions (print & online eds.) (effective 2009). **Document type:** *Journal, Academic/Scholarly.* **Description:** Concerned with the diffusion of experimental results dealing with all aspects of science and technology applied to cultural heritage.
Related titles: Online - full text ed.: ISSN 1724-1847.
Indexed: A&ATA, AIAP, BibInd, GeoRef, SpeleolAb.
—BLDSC (8134.255620), IE, Ingenta.
Published by: (Comitato Nazionale per la Scienza e la Tecnologia dei Beni Culturali), Fabrizio Serra Editore (Subsidiary of: Accademia Editoriale), c/o Accademia Editoriale, Via Santa Bibbiana 28, Pisa, 56127, Italy. TEL 39-050-542332, FAX 39-050-574888, accademiaeditoriale@accademiaeditoriale.it, http://www.libraweb.net.

SCIENCE DILIMAN. *see* SCIENCES: COMPREHENSIVE WORKS

SCIENCE, SOCIETY SECURITY NEWS. *see* SCIENCES: COMPREHENSIVE WORKS

SCIENCE, TECHNOLOGY AND INNOVATION STUDIES. *see* TECHNOLOGY: COMPREHENSIVE WORKS

SCIENCE, TECHNOLOGY & SOCIETY; an international journal devoted to the developing world. *see* SCIENCES: COMPREHENSIVE WORKS

300 FRA ISSN 1777-4969
SCIENCES CONTEMPORAINES. Text in French. 2005. EUR 28.50 newsstand/cover (effective 2006). **Document type:** *Monographic series.*
Published by: Aux Lieux d'Etre, 51 rue de Geneve, La Courneuve, 93120, France. TEL 33-1-48548181, FAX 33-1-48366224. Ed. Julien Tenedos.

300 FRA ISSN 1168-1446
➤ **SCIENCES DE LA SOCIETE.** Text in French. 1983. 3/yr. EUR 51 to individuals; EUR 62 domestic to institutions; EUR 67 foreign to institutions; EUR 38.50 to students (effective 2008). adv. back issues avail. **Document type:** *Academic/Scholarly.* **Description:** Thematic issues deal with transformations of society and those of public and private organizations, which is then analyzed with interdisciplinary approaches.
Incorporates (1987-1993): Groupe de Recherches Socio-Economiques. Papiers (1149-0411); Formerly (until 1992): Cahiers du L E R A S S (0998-8262)
Indexed: CA, FR, IBSS, MLA-IB, P42, PAIS, S02, S03, SociolAb, T02.
—INIST. **CCC.**
Published by: Presses Universitaires du Mirail, Universite de Toulouse II (Le Mirail), 5, Allee Antonio Machado, Toulouse, 31058, France. TEL 33-05-61503810, FAX 33-05-61503800, pum@univ-tlse2.fr, http://www.univ-tlse2.fr. Ed. Robert Boure. Circ: 1,100.

300 FRA ISSN 0996-6994
AP20
SCIENCES HUMAINES. Text in French. 1989. 11/yr. EUR 48 domestic to individuals; EUR 58 foreign; EUR 58 foreign to institutions; EUR 41 to students (effective 2011). adv. back issues avail. **Document type:** *Journal, Academic/Scholarly.*
Related titles: Online - full text ed.: EUR 65 combined subscription domestic to individuals; EUR 82 combined subscription foreign; EUR 82 combined subscription to institutions; EUR 55 combined subscription to students (effective 2009); ◆ Supplement(s): Les Grands Dossiers des Sciences Humaines. ISSN 1777-375X.
Indexed: A22, FR, IBSS.
—IE, INIST.
Address: 38, rue Rantheaume, BP 256, Auxerre, Cedex 89004, France. TEL 33-3-86720700, FAX 33-3-86525326, communication@scienceshumaines.fr, http://www.scienceshumaines.com. Ed. Jean Francois Dortier. Pub. Jean Claude Ruano Borbalan. adv.: B&W page EUR 2,000; 210 x 297. Circ: 46,604.

SCIENTIA GRAECO-ARABICA. *see* SCIENCES: COMPREHENSIVE WORKS

SCIENZE REGIONALI/ITALIAN JOURNAL OF REGIONAL SCIENCE. *see* BUSINESS AND ECONOMICS—Economic Systems And Theories, Economic History

SCOTTISH LITERARY REVIEW. *see* LITERATURE

SCRIPTA HIEROSOLYMITANA; studies in Mishnaic Hebrew. *see* HUMANITIES: COMPREHENSIVE WORKS

300 001.2 PAK ISSN 0377-5143
➤ **SCRUTINY.** Text in English. 2007. irreg. **Document type:** *Journal, Academic/Scholarly.* **Description:** Publishes original (theoretical and empirical) contributions geography, economics, linguistics, anthropology, history, political science, demography and environment with reference to Pakistan.
Published by: Quaid-i-Azam University, National Institute of Pakistan Studies, Islamabad, Pakistan. FAX 92-51-2896004.

300 ITA
IL SECONDO RINASCIMENTO. Text in Italian. 1992. bi-m. (5/yr.). price varies. **Document type:** *Magazine, Consumer.*
Published by: Spirali Edizioni, Via Fratelli Gabba 3, Milan, 20121, Italy. TEL 39-02-8054417, FAX 39-02-8692631, redazione@spirali.com, http://www.spirali.com. Ed. Armando Verdiglione.

327.1 300 FRA ISSN 1959-6782
JZ5588
➤ **SECURITE GLOBALE.** Text in French. 2007. q. EUR 98 domestic to individuals; EUR 138 foreign to individuals; EUR 215 domestic to institutions; EUR 290 foreign to institutions (effective 2008). back issues avail. **Document type:** *Journal, Academic/Scholarly.*
Indexed: I02, IBSS, T02.
Published by: Choiseul Editions, 28 Rue Etienne Marcel, Paris, 75002, France. TEL 33-1-53340993, FAX 33-1-53340994.

300 ESP ISSN 1889-1152
DP302.C68
SEGLE XX. Text in Spanish. 2008. a. EUR 19 domestic to individuals; EUR 25 foreign to individuals; EUR 25 domestic to institutions; EUR 30 foreign to institutions (effective 2009). **Document type:** *Monographic series, Academic/Scholarly.*
Published by: Editorial Afers S.L., La Libertat, 12, Apartat de Correus 267, Catarroja, Valencia 46470, Spain. TEL 34-961-268654, FAX 34-961-272582, afers@provicom.com, http://www.editorialafers.cat/. Ed. Andreu Mayayo i Artal.

300 TUR ISSN 1302-1796
H8.T87
➤ **SELCUK UNIVERSITESI SOSYAL BILIMLER ENSTITUSU DERGISI/SELCUK UNIVERSITY. INSTITUTE OF SOCIAL SCIENCES. JOURNAL.** Text mainly in Turkish; Text occasionally in English, French, German. 1999. s-a. **Document type:** *Journal, Academic/Scholarly.*
Related titles: Online - full text ed.: ISSN 1304-8899. 2005 (Jan.). free (effective 2009).
Indexed: CA, MLA-IB, S02, S03, SociolAb, T02.
—IE.
Published by: Selcuk Universitesi, Sosyal Bilimler Enstitusu/Selcuk University, Institute of Social Sciences, C.U. Sosyal Bilimler Enstitusu Mudurlugu, Balcali, Adana, 01330, Turkey. TEL 90-322-3386574, FAX 90-322-3386574, sosbil@cu.edu.tr.

➤ **SEMIOTIC REVIEW OF BOOKS.** *see* HUMANITIES: COMPREHENSIVE WORKS

300 620 JPN ISSN 0386-4243
SENDAI DENPA KOGYO KOTO SENMON GAKKO KENKYU KIYO/ SENDAI NATIONAL COLLEGE OF TECHNOLOGY. RESEARCH REPORT. Text in Japanese; Summaries in English, French, Japanese. 1972. a. free. charts. index.
Published by: Sendai Denpa Kogyo Koto Senmon Gakko, 1, Kitahara, Kamiayashi, Aoba-ku, Sendai-shi, Miyagi-ken 989-21, Japan. TEL 03-581-6411. Circ: 270.

300 GBR ISSN 1745-8927
QP431
➤ **THE SENSES AND SOCIETY.** Text in English. 2006 (Mar.). 3/yr. USD 387 combined subscription in US & Canada to institutions (print & online eds.); GBP 198 combined subscription elsewhere to institutions (print & online eds.) (effective 2011). adv. reprint service avail. from PSC. **Document type:** *Journal, Academic/Scholarly.* **Description:** Covers groundbreaking work in the social sciences and incorporates cutting-edge developments in art, design and architecture.
Related titles: Online - full text ed.: ISSN 1745-8935. USD 329 in US & Canada; GBP 169 elsewhere (effective 2011) (from IngentaConnect).
Indexed: A01, A26, ABM, AICP, ArtHuCI, B04, BRD, BrHumI, CA, CurCont, I05, IBR, IBSS, IBZ, MLA-IB, S02, S03, SCOPUS, SSAI, SSAb, SSI, SociolAb, T02, W01, W02, W03, W05, W07.
—BLDSC (8241.643500), IE, Ingenta. **CCC.**
Published by: Berg Publishers (Subsidiary of: Oxford International Publishers Ltd.), 1st Fl Angel Ct, 81 St Clements St, Oxford, Berks OX4 1AW, United Kingdom. TEL 44-1865-245104, FAX 44-1865-791165, enquiry@bergpublishers.com. R&P Ms. Kathleen May. Adv. contacts Ms. Corina Kapinos TEL 44-1865-245104, Eleanor Graves. **Dist. addr.:** Turpin Distribution Services Ltd., Pegasus Dr, Stratton Business Park, Biggleswade, Bedfordshire SG18 8QB, United Kingdom. TEL 44-1767-604800, FAX 44-1767-601640, custserv@turpin-distribution.com, http://www.turpin-distribution.com/.

➤ **SETSUNAN UNIVERSITY. REVIEW OF HUMANITIES AND SOCIAL SCIENCES/SETSUDAI JINBUN KAGAKU.** *see* HUMANITIES: COMPREHENSIVE WORKS

300 CHN
SHAANXI LIGONG XUEYUAN XUEBAO (SHEHUI KEXUE BAN). Text in Chinese. q. CNY 5 newsstand/cover (effective 2006). **Document type:** *Journal, Academic/Scholarly.*
Supersedes in part: Hanzhong Shifan Xueyuan Xuebao/Hanzhong Teacher's College. Journal (1007-0842); Shaanxi Gongxueyuan Xuebao (1002-3410)
Related titles: Online - full text ed.
Published by: Shaanxi Ligong Xueyuan, Hedongdian, Hanzhong, 723003, China. TEL 86-916-2641545.

SHAANXI SHIFAN DAXUE XUEBAO (ZHEXUE SHEHUI KEXUE BAN)/SHANXI NORMAL UNIVERSITY. JOURNAL (PHILOSOPHY AND SOCIAL SCIENCES EDITION). *see* PHILOSOPHY

300 JPN ISSN 0419-6759
H8
SHAKAI KAGAKU/SOCIAL SCIENCES. Text in Japanese. 1965. a. **Document type:** *Journal, Academic/Scholarly.*
Indexed: RILM.
Published by: Doshisha Daigaku, Jinbun Kagaku Kenkyujo/Doshisha University, Institute for the Study of Humanities & Social Sciences, Karasuma-Higashi-iru, Imadegawa-dori, Kamigyo-ku, Kyoto, 602-8580, Japan. ji-jimbn@mail.doshisha.ac.jp, http://www.doshisha.ac.jp/academics/institute/jinbun/.

300 JPN ISSN 0387-3307
H8.J3
SHAKAI KAGAKU KENKYU/SOCIAL SCIENCES JOURNAL. Text in Japanese. 1948. bi-m. bk.rev. **Document type:** *Journal, Academic/Scholarly.*
Indexed: HistAb, SWR&A.
—BLDSC (5064.900000).
Published by: University Of Tokyo, Institute of Social Science/Shakai Kagaku Kenkyujo, 7-3-1 Hongo, Bunkyo-ku, Tokyo, 113-0033, Japan. TEL 81-3-58414931, FAX 81-3-58414905.

300 100 CHN ISSN 1001-9839
AS452.T778
SHANDONG DAXUE XUEBAO (ZHEXUE SHEHUI KEXUE BAN)/ SHANDONG UNIVERSITY. JOURNAL (PHILOSOPHY AND SOCIAL SCIENCES). Text in Chinese. 1951. bi-m. CNY 72 (effective 2009). **Document type:** *Journal, Academic/Scholarly.*
Related titles: Online - full text ed.
—East View.
Published by: (Xuebao Bianjibu), Shandong Daxue, 27, Shanda Nanlu, Jinan, Shandong 250100, China. TEL 86-531-88364638, FAX 86-531-88564645.

300 CHN ISSN 1000-5323
SHANDONG GONGYE DAXUE XUEBAO (SHEHUI KEXUE BAN)/ SHANDONG INDUSTRIAL UNIVERSITY. JOURNAL (SOCIAL SCIENCE EDITION). Text in Chinese. q. **Document type:** *Academic/Scholarly.*
Related titles: Online - full text ed.
—East View.
Published by: Shandong Gongye Daxue, Xuebao Bianjibu, No 33, Jing 10 Lu, Jinan, SHANDONG, China. TEL 615081. Ed. Wei Bingquan.

300 CHN
SHANDONG KEJI DAXUE XUEBAO (SHEHUI KEXUE BAN)/ SHANDONG UNIVERSITY OF SCIENCES & TECHNOLOGY. JOURNAL (SOCIAL SCIENCE EDITION). Text in Chinese. 1999. q. CNY 8 newsstand/cover (effective 2006). **Document type:** *Journal, Academic/Scholarly.*
Formerly: Shandong Kuangye Xueyuan Xuebao (Shehui Kexue Ban)/Shandong Institute of Mining and Technology. Journal (Social Science Edition) (1008-7699)
Related titles: Online - full text ed.
Published by: Shandong Keji Daxue/Shandong University of Science and Technology, 223, Daizong Dajie, Taian, 271019, China.

300 CHN ISSN 1672-0040
SHANDONG LIGONG DAXUE XUEBAO (SHEHUI KEXUE BAN). Text in Chinese. 1985. bi-m. CNY 10 newsstand/cover (effective 2006).
Formerly (until 2003): Zibo Xueyuan Xuebao (Shehui Kexue Ban)/Zibo University. Journal (Social Sciences) (1008-7435); (until 1999): Zibo Xueyuan Xuebao (Renwen Shehui Kexue Ban); (until 1998): Zibo Shi-Zhuan Xuebao/Zibo Normal College. Journal (1006-995X)
Indexed: SociolAb.
Published by: Shandong Ligong Daxue/Shandong University of Technology, 12, Zhangzhou Lu, Zibo, 255049, China. TEL 86-533-2782057.

300 CHN ISSN 1008-8091
SHANDONG NONGYE DAXUE XUEBAO (SHEHUI KEXUE BAN)/ SHANDONG AGRICULTURAL UNIVERSITY. JOURNAL (SOCIAL SCIENCE EDITION). Text in Chinese. 1999. q. CNY 10 newsstand/ cover (effective 2006). **Document type:** *Journal, Academic/Scholarly.*
Related titles: Online - full text ed.
Published by: Shandong Nongye Daxue, 61, Daizong Dajie, Taian, 271018, China. TEL 86-538-8242242, FAX 86-538-8226399.

300 CHN ISSN 1003-4145
SHANDONG SHEHUI KEXUE/SHANDONG SOCIAL SCIENCES. Text in Chinese. 1987. m. USD 62.40 (effective 2009). adv. bk.rev. **Document type:** *Journal, Academic/Scholarly.* **Description:** Deals with current research on literature, history, philosophy, economics, politics and law.
Related titles: Online - full text ed.
Published by: Shandong Sheng Shehui Kexue Lianhehui, 46, Shungeng Lu, Shandong, 250002, China. TEL 86-531-6915174. Circ: 10,000 (paid). **Dist. by:** China International Book Trading Corp, 35 Chegongzhuang Xilu, Haidian District, PO Box 399, Beijing 100044, China. TEL 86-10-68412045, FAX 86-10-68412023, cibtc@mail.cibtc.com.cn, http://www.cibtc.com.cn.

300 CHN
➤ **SHANDONG SHIFAN DAXUE XUEBAO (RENWEN SHEHUI KEXUE BAN)/SHANDONG NORMAL UNIVERSITY. JOURNAL (SOCIAL SCIENCE EDITION).** Text in Chinese. 1956. bi-m. USD 31.20 (effective 2009). bk.rev. **Document type:** *Journal, Academic/ Scholarly.* **Description:** Contains research papers on literature, history, philosophy, economics, education, and middle school teaching of social sciences and humanities.
Formerly: Shandong Shida Xuebao (Shehui Kexue Ban)/Shandong Normal University. Journal (Social Science Edition) (1001-5973)
Related titles: Online - full text ed.
Published by: Shandong Shifan Daxue, 88, Wenhua Donglu, Jinan, Shandong 250014, China. Circ: 1,200.

300 CHN ISSN 1000-5595
SHANDONG YIKE DAXUE XUEBAO (SHEHUI KEXUE BAN)/ SHANDONG UNIVERSITY OF MEDICAL SCIENCES. JOURNAL (SOCIAL SCIENCES EDITION). Text in Chinese. 1987. q. **Document type:** *Academic/Scholarly.* **Description:** Covers philosophy, political economy, history, social medicine, medical ethics, medical philosophy, health law, health economics, traditional Chinese medical science.
Related titles: Online - full text ed.
Published by: Shandong Yike Daxue, Xuebao Bianjibu, No 44 Wenhua Xilu, Jinan, Shandong, 250012, China. TEL 86-531-2942295, FAX 86-531-2953813, TELEX 390007 MED JN CN. Ed. Wu Xianglian. Circ: 8,000. **Dist. overseas by:** China International Book Trading Corp, 35 Chegongzhuang Xilu, Haidian District, PO Box 399, Beijing 100044, China.

300 CHN ISSN 1007-6522
SHANGHAI DAXUE XUEBAO (SHEHUI KEXUE BAN)/SHANGHAI UNIVERSITY. JOURNAL (SOCIAL SCIENCES EDITION). Text in Chinese. 1984. bi-m. CNY 84; CNY 12 per issue (effective 2010). **Document type:** *Journal, Academic/Scholarly.*
Related titles: Online - full text ed.
—BLDSC (8254.589086).
Published by: Shanghai Daxue/Shanghai University, 99, Shangda Lu, PO Box 125, Shanghai, 200444, China. TEL 86-21-66135506, http://www.shu.edu.cn/.

300 CHN
SHANGHAI JIAOTONG DAXUE XUEBAO (ZHEXUE SHEHUI KEXUE BAN)/SHANGHAI JIAOTONG UNIVERSITY. JOURNAL (PHILOSOPHY AND SOCIAL SCIENCES). Text in Chinese. 1993. bi-m. CNY 6 newsstand/cover (effective 2011). **Document type:** *Journal, Academic/Scholarly.*
Formerly: Shanghai Jiaotong Daxue Xuebao (Shehui Kexue Ban) (1008-7095)
Related titles: Online - full text ed.
Indexed: P42, S02, S03, SociolAb.
Published by: Shanghai Jiaotong Daxue/Shanghai Jiaotong University, 1954 Huasha Lu, Shanghai, 200030, China. TEL 86-21-62933089.

300 CHN ISSN 1009-895X
SHANGHAI LIGONG DAXUE XUEBAO (SHEHUI KEXUE BAN)/ UNIVERSITY OF SHANGHAI FOR SCIENCE AND TECHNOLOGY. JOURNAL (SOCIAL SCIENCE). Text in Chinese. 1979. q. CNY 5 newsstand/cover (effective 2006). **Document type:** *Journal, Academic/Scholarly.*
Related titles: Online - full text ed.
Published by: Shanghai Ligong Daxue/University of Shanghai for Science and Technology, 516, Jungong Lu, Shanghai, 200093, China. TEL 86-21-65684935, http://www.usst.edu.cn/.

300 100 CHN ISSN 1004-8634
SHANGHAI SHIFAN DAXUE XUEBAO (ZHEXUE SHEHUI KEXUE BAN)/SHANGHAI NORMAL UNIVERSITY. JOURNAL (PHILOSOPHY & SOCIAL SCIENCES). Text in Chinese. 1958. bi-m. USD 24.60 (effective 2009). **Document type:** *Journal, Academic/ Scholarly.*
Related titles: Online - full text ed.
—East View.
Published by: (Xuebao Bianjibu), Shanghai Shifan Daxue/Shanghai Normal University, 100, Guilin Lu, Shanghai, 200234, China. TEL 86-21-64322304, FAX 86-21-64324387. Circ: 6,000. **Dist. overseas by:** China International Book Trading Corp, 35 Chegongzhuang Xilu, Haidian District, PO Box 399, Beijing 100044, China. TEL 86-10-68412045, FAX 86-10-68412023, cibtc@mail.cibtc.com.cn, http://www.cibtc.com.cn.

300 320.532 CHN ISSN 1009-3176
SHANGHAI XINGZHENG XUEYUAN XUEBAO/SHANGHAI ADMINISTRATION INSTITUTE. JOURNAL. Text in Chinese. 2000. bi-m. CNY 10 newsstand/cover (effective 2006). **Document type:** *Journal, Academic/Scholarly.*
Related titles: Online - full text ed.
Published by: Shanghai Xingzheng Xueyuan, 200, Hongcao Nan Lu, Shanghai, 200233, China.

300 500 CHN ISSN 1671-8127
SHANGQIU ZHIYE JISHU XUEYUAN XUEBAO/SHANGQIU VOCATIONAL AND TECHNICAL COLLEGE. JOURNAL. Text in Chinese. 2002. bi-m. CNY 5 newsstand/cover (effective 2006). **Document type:** *Journal, Academic/Scholarly.*
Related titles: Online - full text ed.
Published by: Shangqiu Zhiye Jishu Xueyuan, 61, Gui-de Bei Lu, Shangqiu, 476000, China.

SHANTOU DAXUE XUEBAO (RENWEN KEXUE BAN)/SHANTOU UNIVERSITY. JOURNAL (HUMANITIES & SOCIAL SCIENCES EDITION). *see* HUMANITIES: COMPREHENSIVE WORKS

300 100 CHN ISSN 1000-5935
AS452.T38
SHANXI DAXUE XUEBAO (SHEHUI KEXUE BAN)/SHANXI UNIVERSITY. JOURNAL (SOCIAL SCIENCE EDITION). Text in Chinese; Contents page in English. 1947. bi-m. USD 31.20 (effective 2009). **Document type:** *Journal, Academic/Scholarly.* **Description:** Covers literature, history, philosophy, politics, economics, law, education, arts and other disciplines of social sciences.
Related titles: Online - full text ed.
Indexed: RASB.
—East View.
Published by: Shanxi Daxue, 92, Wucheng Lu, Bangong 1/F, Taiyuan, 030006, China. TEL 86-351-7018311. **Dist. overseas by:** China International Book Trading Corp, 35 Chegongzhuang Xilu, Haidian District, PO Box 399, Beijing 100044, China.

300 CHN ISSN 1008-6285
SHANXI GAODENG XUEXIAO SHEHUI KEXUE XUEBAO/SOCIAL SCIENCES JOURNAL OF COLLEGES OF SHANXI. Text in Chinese. 1989. m. CNY 10 newsstand/cover (effective 2006). **Document type:** *Journal, Academic/Scholarly.*
Related titles: Online - full text ed.
Published by: Shanxi Gaodeng Xuexiao, 53, Xikuang Jie, Taiyuan, 030024, China. TEL 86-351-6014499, FAX 86-351-6018979.

300 CHN ISSN 1671-816X
SHANXI NONGYE DAXUE XUEBAO (SHEHUI KEXUE BAN)/SHANXI AGRICULTURAL UNIVERSITY. JOURNAL (SOCIAL SCIENCE EDITION). Text in Chinese. 1957. q. CNY 8 newsstand/cover (effective 2006). **Document type:** *Journal, Academic/Scholarly.*
Supersedes in part (in 2001): Shanxi Nongye Daxue Xuebao/Shanxi Agricultural University. Journal (1000-162X)
Related titles: Online - full text ed.
Published by: Shanxi Nongye Daxue/Shanxi University of Agriculture, 6/F, Shiyan Dalou, Taigu, Shanxi 030801, China.

300 CHN ISSN 1001-5957
SHANXI SHI-DA XUEBAO (SHEHUI KEXUE BAN)/SHANXI TEACHERS UNIVERSITY. JOURNAL (SOCIAL SCIENCE EDITION). Text in Chinese. 1973. bi-m. USD 24.60 (effective 2009). **Document type:** *Journal, Academic/Scholarly.*
Related titles: Online - full text ed.
—East View.
Published by: Shanxi Shifan Daxue/Shanxi Teachers University, 1, Gongyuan Jie, Linfen, Shanxi 041004, China. TEL 86-357-2051149, FAX 86-357-2051149 ext 6.

300 CHN
SHAOGUAN XUEYUAN XUEBAO/SHAOGUAN UNIVERSITY. JOURNAL. Text in Chinese. 1980. m. USD 49.20 (effective 2009). **Document type:** *Journal, Academic/Scholarly.*
Supersedes (in 2000): Shaoguan Daxue Xuebao (1007-5348)
Related titles: Online - full text ed.
Published by: Shaoguan Daxue, Datang Lu, Shaoguan, 512005, China. TEL 86-751-8120092, FAX 86-751-8120025.

300 500 CHN ISSN 1008-293X
SHAOXING WELI XUEYUAN XUEBAO/SHAOXING UNIVERSITY. JOURNAL. Text in Chinese. 1981. m. USD 49.20 (effective 2009). **Document type:** *Journal, Academic/Scholarly.*
Supersedes: Shaoxing Shi-zhuan Xuebao/Shaoxing Teacher's College. Journal (1001-6554)
Related titles: Online - full text ed.
Indexed: Z02.
—East View.
Published by: Shaoxing Weli Xueyuan, 508, Huancheng Xi Lu, Shaoxing, 312000, China. TEL 86-575-8341516, FAX 86-575-8066543, http://www.zscas.edu.cn/.

300 CHN
SHAOYANG XUEYUAN XUEBAO (SHEHUI KEXUE BAN). Text in Chinese. 1983. bi-m. CNY 12 newsstand/cover (effective 2006).
Supersedes in part (in 2004): Shaoyang Xueyuan Xuebao/Shaoyang University. Journal (1672-1012); Which was formed by the merger of (1998-2002): Shaoyang Shifan Gaodeng Zhuanke Xuexiao Xuebao/Shaoyang Teachers College. Journal (1008-1674); (1999-2002): Shaoyang Gaodeng Zhuanke Xuexiao Xuebao/ Shaoyang College. Journal (1009-2439); Which was formed by the merger of: Shaoyang Gaozhuan Xuebao; Hunan Shaoyang Gongzhuan Xuebao
Related titles: Online - full text ed.
Published by: Shaoyang Xueyuan, Liziyuan, Shaoyang, 422000, China. TEL 86-739-5431304, FAX 86-739-5305663.

301 USA ISSN 1054-0695
SHAREDEBATE INTERNATIONAL; a ShareWare diskette magazine. Text in English. 1990. q. USD 60. adv. bk.rev. **Description:** Debate forum for PC users by PC users who are concerned about the present and the future.
Related titles: CD-ROM ed.: 1990; Online - full text ed.: 1990.
Published by: Applied Foresight, Inc., c/o Roleigh Martin, Ed., 5511 Malibu Dr, Edina, MN 55420. FAX 612-933-3092. Ed. R H Martin.

300 CHN ISSN 1004-8804
HM7
SHEHUI/CHINESE JOURNAL OF SOCIOLOGY. Text in Chinese; Summaries in Chinese, English. bi-m. CNY 72; CNY 12 per issue (effective 2010). adv. Index. **Document type:** *Journal, Academic/ Scholarly.* **Description:** Covers social theories, cultural and social changes, social psychology and behaviors.
Related titles: Online - full text ed.
Indexed: PAIS, RASB, SWR&A, SociolAb.
—BLDSC (8256.049900).
Published by: Shanghai Daxue/Shanghai University, 99, Shangda Lu, PO Box 32, Shanghai, 200444, China. TEL 86-21-66135633, FAX 86-21-66135633. adv.: page CNY 4,000.

300 CHN ISSN 0257-5833
AS451
SHEHUI KEXUE (SHANGHAI)/SOCIAL SCIENCES. Text in Chinese. 1979. m. USD 80.40 (effective 2009). **Document type:** *Journal, Academic/Scholarly.*
Incorporates: Shanghai Shehui Kexueyuan Xueshu Jikan/Shanghai Academy of Social Sciences. Quarterly Journal (1009-2226)
Related titles: Online - full text ed.
Indexed: RASB.
—East View.
Published by: Shanghai Shehui Kexueyuan/Shanghai Academy of Social Sciences, No. 7 Alley 622 Huaihai Zhonglu, Shanghai, 200020, China.

300 CHN ISSN 1001-6198
H8.C47
SHEHUI KEXUE JIKAN/SOCIAL SCIENCE JOURNAL. Text in Chinese, English. 1979. bi-m. USD 48 (effective 2009). adv. bk.rev. **Document type:** *Journal, Academic/Scholarly.* **Description:** Publishes academic papers on literature, history, philosophy, sociology and economics pertaining to Northeast China.
Related titles: Online - full text ed.
Indexed: RASB.
—Ingenta.
Published by: Liaoning Shehui Kexueyuan/Liaoning Academy of Social Sciences, 86, Taishan Lu, Huanggu-qu, Shenyang, Liaoning 110031, China. TEL 86-24-86120485, FAX 86-551-5107157. adv.: page CNY 10,000. Circ: 8,000. **Dist. by:** China International Book Trading Corp, 35 Chegongzhuang Xilu, Haidian District, PO Box 399, Beijing 100044, China.

300 CHN ISSN 1000-4769
AS452.C46165
SHEHUI KEXUE YANJIU/SOCIAL SCIENCE RESEARCH. Text in Chinese. 1979. bi-m. USD 31.20 (effective 2009). adv. bk.rev. **Document type:** *Academic/Scholarly.*
Related titles: Online - full text ed.
Indexed: RASB.
Published by: Sichuan Sheng Shehui Kexueyuan/Sichuan Academy of Social Science, Qingyang Gong, Chengdu, Sichuan 610072, China. TEL 769347-124. Ed. Liu Changguo. Circ: 3,600. **Dist. outside China by:** China International Book Trading Corp, 35 Chegongzhuang Xilu, Haidian District, PO Box 399, Beijing 100044, China.

300 CHN ISSN 0257-0246
AS451
SHEHUI KEXUE ZHANXIAN/SOCIAL SCIENCE FRONT. Text in Chinese. 1978. bi-m. USD 76.80 (effective 2009). adv. bk.rev. **Document type:** *Journal, Academic/Scholarly.*
Related titles: Online - full text ed.
Indexed: RASB, RILM.
—East View, Ingenta.
Published by: Jilin Sheng Shehui Kexueyuan/Jilin Academy of Social Sciences, 5399, Ziyou Dalu, Changchun, Jilin 130033, China. TEL 86-431-4638362, FAX 86-431-4638345. adv.: page USD 1,000. Circ: 5,000 (paid).

300 CHN ISSN 1001-3431
H8
SHEHUI KEXUE ZONGLUN/STUDIES IN SOCIAL SCIENCES. Text in Chinese. 1980. q. USD 22.10 (effective 2009). 64 p./no.; **Document type:** *Journal, Academic/Scholarly.*
Published by: Zhongguo Renmin Daxue Shubao Ziliao Zhongxin/Renmin University of China, Information Center for Social Sciences, Dongcheng-qu, 3, Zhangzizhong Lu, Beijing, 100007, China. TEL 86-10-64039458, FAX 86-10-64015080, center@zlzx.org, http:// www.zlzx.org/. **Dist. in US by:** China Publications Service, PO Box 49614, Chicago, IL 60649. TEL 312-288-3291, FAX 312-288-8570; **Dist. by:** China International Book Trading Corp, 35 Chegongzhuang Xilu, Haidian District, PO Box 399, Beijing 100044, China. TEL 86-10-68412045, FAX 86-10-68412023, cibtc@mail.cibtc.com.cn, http://www.cibtc.com.cn.

300 500 CHN ISSN 1008-9225
AS452.S5385
SHENYANG DAXUE XUEBAO/SHENYANG UNIVERSITY. JOURNAL. Text in Chinese. 1999. bi-m. CNY 10 newsstand/cover (effective 2006). **Document type:** *Journal, Academic/Scholarly.*
Related titles: Online - full text ed.
Published by: Shenyang Daxue, 54, Lianhe Lu, Shenyang, 110044, China. TEL 86-24-62268727.

S

300 CHN ISSN 1674-0823
HN731.
➤ **SHENYANG GONGYE DAXUE XUEBAO (SHEHUI KEXUE BAN)/SHENYANG INSTITUTE OF TECHNOLOGY. JOURNAL (SOCIAL SCIENCE EDITION).** Text in Chinese; Abstracts in Chinese, English. 2008. q. CNY 40, USD 32; CNY 10, USD 8 newsstand/cover (effective 2009). **Document type:** *Journal, Academic/Scholarly.* **Description:** Covers the latest developments of theoretical and applied researches in the fields of traditional social sciences.
Supersedes in part: Shenyang Gongye Xueyuan Xuebao/Shenyang Institute of Technology. Journal (1003-1251)
Related titles: Online - full text ed.
Indexed: PAIS, PSA, SociolAb.
—IE.
Published by: Shenyang Gongye Daxue, 1, Nan 13 Lu, Shenyang, 110023, China. TEL 86-24-25691039, FAX 86-24-25691041. Ed. Wei He.

300 CHN ISSN 1008-9713
HN731
SHENYANG NONGYE DAXUE XUEBAO (SHEHUI KEXUE BAN). Text in Chinese. 1999. q. USD 53.40 (effective 2009). **Document type:** *Journal, Academic/Scholarly.*
Related titles: Online - full text ed.
Published by: Shenyang Nongye Daxue/Shenyang Agricultural University, 120, Dongling Lu, Shenyang, 110161, China. TEL 86-24-88487082.

300 CHN ISSN 1674-5450
➤ **SHENYANG SHIFAN DAXUE XUEBAO (SHEHUI KEXUE BAN)/ SHENYANG NORMAL UNIVERSITY. JOURNAL. (SOCIAL SCIENCE EDITION).** Text in Chinese; Contents page in English. 1977. bi-m. adv. bk.rev. 112 p./no.; **Document type:** *Journal, Academic/Scholarly.* **Description:** Reflects the scientific research conducted by the faculties and students of the college.
Formerly (until 2003): Shenyang Shifan Xueyuan Xuebao (Shehui Kexue Ban) (1000-5226)
Related titles: Online - full text ed.
—East View.
Published by: Shenyang Shifan Xueyuan/Shenyang Normal University, 253, Northern Huanghe St., Huanggu District, Shenyang, Liaoning 110034, China. TEL 86-24-86574467, FAX 86-24-86592466. Ed. Sun Jiguo. Circ: 1,500. **Dist. outside China by:** China Publication Foreign Trade Company, PO Box 782, Beijing 100011, China.

➤ **SHIHEZI DAXUE XUEBAO (ZHEXUE SHEHUI KEXUE BAN)/ SHIHEZI UNIVERSITY. JOURNAL (PHILOSOPHY AND SOCIAL SCIENCE).** *see* PHILOSOPHY

300 CHN ISSN 1009-4873
SHIJIAZHUANG ZHIYE JISHU XUEYUAN XUEBAO/SHIJIAZHUANG VOCATIONAL TECHNOLOGY INSTITUTE. JOURNAL. Text in Chinese. 1989. bi-m. CNY 6 newsstand/cover (effective 2006). **Document type:** *Journal, Academic/Scholarly.*
Formerly (until 2000): Shijiazhuang Daxue Xuebao/Shijiazhuang University. Journal (1008-4568)
Related titles: Online - full text ed.
Published by: Shijiazhuang Zhiye Jishu Xueyuan, 12, Changxin Jie, Shijiazhuang, 050081, China. TEL 86-311-85333837.

SHIKOKU DAIGAKU KIYO. JINBUN, SHAKAI KAGAKU-HEN/ SHIKOKU UNIVERSITY. BULLETIN. SERIES A. *see* HUMANITIES: COMPREHENSIVE WORKS

300 JPN ISSN 0388-6859
SHIMANE DAIGAKU HOBUNGAKUBU KIYO. BUNGAKUKA HEN/ SHIMANE UNIVERSITY. FACULTY OF LAW AND LITERATURE. MEMOIRS. Text in English, Japanese. 1973. a. **Document type:** *Journal, Academic/Scholarly.*
Published by: Shimane Daigaku, Hobungakubu/Shimane University, Faculty of Law and Literature, 1060 Nishi-Kawazu-Machi, Matsue-shi, Shimane-ken 690-0000, Japan. Circ: 400.

SHISO (TOKYO)/THOUGHT. *see* HUMANITIES: COMPREHENSIVE WORKS

SHIZUOKA DAIGAKU KYOIKUGAKUBU KENKYU HOKOKU. JINBUN, SHAKAI KAGAKU HEN/SHIZUOKA UNIVERSITY. FACULTY OF EDUCATION. BULLETIN. LIBERAL ARTS AND SOCIAL SCIENCES SERIES. *see* HUMANITIES: COMPREHENSIVE WORKS

300 CHN ISSN 1004-9142
SHOUDU SHIFAN DAXUE XUEBAO (SHEHUI KEXUE BAN)/CAPITAL NORMAL UNIVERSITY. JOURNAL (SOCIAL SCIENCE EDITION). Text in Chinese. 1973. bi-m. USD 24.60 (effective 2009).
Formerly (until 1992): Beijing Shifan Xueyuan Xuebao (Shehui Kexue Ban) (1002-3836)
Related titles: Online - full text ed.
—East View.
Published by: Shoudu Shifan Daxue/Capital Normal University, 105, Xisanhuanbei, Beijing, 100037, China. Ed. Zhang Shoukang.

300 320.532 CHN
SI XING YUEKAN. Text in Chinese. 1986. m. **Document type:** *Journal, Academic/Scholarly.*
Formerly (until 2008): Si yu Xing (1002-7483)
Published by: Heilongjiang Sheng Chuban Zhongshe, 17-1, Jiejing Jie, Nangang-qu, Ha'erbin, 150001, China. TEL 86-451-87017989.

300 DEU
SIAM-JOURNAL; eine Zeitschrift fuer alle Freunde Thailands. Text in German. 1992. q. adv. **Document type:** *Bulletin.*
Address: Postfach 1227, Halver, 58542, Germany. TEL 49-2353-2005, FAX 49-2353-2006. Ed. Axel Ertelt.

300 THA ISSN 0304-226X
DS561
SIAM SOCIETY. JOURNAL. Text in English. 1904. s-a. USD 32 to individuals; USD 80 to institutions (effective 2001). adv. bk.rev. bibl.; charts; illus. cum.index: vols. 1-50. back issues avail.; reprint service avail. from PSC. **Document type:** *Journal, Academic/Scholarly.*
Indexed: BAS, BibLing, CA, EI, HistAb, MLA-IB, PCI, RASB, T02.
—BLDSC (4876.250000), IE, Ingenta.
Published by: Siam Society, 131 Soi Asoke, Sukhumvit 21, Bangkok, 10110, Thailand. TEL 662-661-6470-7, FAX 662-258-3491, info@siam-society.org. Ed. Ronald Renard. Circ: 1,500.

300 CHN ISSN 1006-0766
AS452.C462
SICHUAN DAXUE XUEBAO (ZHEXUE SHEHUI KEXUE BAN)/ SICHUAN UNIVERSITY. JOURNAL (SOCIAL SCIENCES EDITION). Text in Chinese; Contents page in English. 1955. bi-m. USD 24.60 (effective 2009). bibl. **Document type:** *Journal, Academic/Scholarly.*
Related titles: Online - full text ed.
Indexed: RASB.
—East View.
Published by: Sichuan Daxue, Xuebao Bianjibu, 29, Wangjiang Lu, Wenkelou, 156-shi, Chengdu, Sichuan 610064, China. TEL 86-28-85410396, FAX 86-28-85412393. Ed. Tian Zuwu. **Dist. by:** China International Book Trading Corp, 35 Chegongzhuang Xilu, Haidian District, PO Box 399, Beijing 100044, China. TEL 86-10-68412045, FAX 86-10-68412023, cibtc@mail.cibtc.com.cn, http://www.cibtc.com.cn.

300 CHN ISSN 1672-8580
SICHUAN LIGONG XUEYUAN XUEBAO (SHEHUI KEXUE BAN)/ SICHUAN UNIVERSITY OF SCIENCE & ENGINEERING. JOURNAL (SOCIAL SCIENCES EDITION). Text in Chinese. 1986. bi-m. CNY 10 newsstand/cover (effective 2006). **Document type:** *Journal, Academic/Scholarly.*
Formerly (until 2003): Zigong Shifan Gaodeng Zhuanke Xuexiao Xuebao/Zigong Teachers College Journal (1008-5459)
Related titles: Online - full text ed.
Indexed: L&LBA, PSA, SociolAb.
Published by: Sichuan Ligong Xueyuan, 180, Huixin Lu Xueyuan Jie, Zigong, 643000, China. TEL 86-813-5505932, FAX 86-813-5505800.

300 CHN ISSN 1000-5315
AS452.C4618
SICHUAN SHIFAN DAXUE XUEBAO (SHEHUI KEXUE BAN)/SICHUAN NORMAL UNIVERSITY. JOURNAL (PHILOSOPHY AND SOCIAL SCIENCES EDITION). Text in Chinese. 1985. bi-m. USD 24.60 (effective 2009). **Document type:** *Journal, Academic/Scholarly.* **Description:** Covers philosophy, political science, economics, literature, linguistics, history and law.
Related titles: Online - full text ed.
—East View.
Published by: Sichuan Shifan Daxue, Xuebao Bianjibu/Sichuan Normal University, Jinjiang District, 3, Shizhishan Road, Chengdu, Sichuan 610066, China. TEL 86-28-4760703, FAX 86-28-4762391, http://www.sicnu.edu.cn/. Ed., R&P Li Daming TEL 028-4760703.

300 500 CHN ISSN 1672-2094
SICHUAN ZHIYE JISHU XUEYUAN XUEBAO/SICHUAN VOCATIONAL AND TECHNICAL COLLEGE. JOURNAL. Text in Chinese. 1987. q. CNY 8 newsstand/cover (effective 2006). **Document type:** *Journal, Academic/Scholarly.*
Formerly (until 2002): Chuanbei Jiaoyu Xueyuan Xuebao/Northern Sichuan Education College. Journal (1009-4075)
Related titles: Online - full text ed.
Published by: Sichuan Zhiye Jishu Xueyuan, 243, Suizhou Zhong Lu, Suining, 629000, China. TEL 86-825-2290470, FAX 86-825-2290087.

305.85 USA ISSN 8755-6987
SICILIA PARRA. Text in English. 1983. s-a. free to members (effective 2010). adv. bk.rev. 20 p./no.; back issues avail. **Document type:** *Newsletter, Consumer.* **Description:** Highlights the activities of the Arba Sicula organization.
Related titles: Online - full text ed.: free (effective 2010).
Published by: Arba Sicula Inc., c/o Gaetano Cipolla, Languages and Literatures Department, St. John's University, 8000 Utopia Pky, Queens, NY 11439. TEL 718-990-5203, FAX 718-990-5954, cipollag@stjohns.edu, http://www.arbasicula.org. Ed. Gaetano Cipolla.

SIGNES DU PRESENT. *see* BUSINESS AND ECONOMICS

300 954.9 PAK
SINDH QUARTERLY. Text in English. 1973. q. PKR 1,000, USD 100 (effective 1999). bk.rev. back issues avail. **Document type:** *Journal, Academic/Scholarly.* **Description:** Covers the socio-political and economic history of Sindh, Pakistan, and India.
Published by: Sayid Ghulam Mustafa Shah, Ed. & Pub., 36-D Karachi Administration Co-operative Housing Society, Off Shaheed-e-Millat Rd., Karachi 8, Pakistan. TEL 92-21-4540248. Ed., Pub. Sayid Ghulam Mustafa Shah. Circ: 1,750.

300 320 SGP ISSN 1793-4338
SINGAPORE PERSPECTIVES. Text in English. 2007. irreg., latest 2010. price varies. back issues avail. **Document type:** *Monographic series, Academic/Scholarly.* **Description:** Provides analysis of emerging trends and issues Singapore faces in terms of social, economic and political development.
Published by: World Scientific Publishing Co. Pte. Ltd., 5 Toh Tuck Link, Singapore, 596224, Singapore. TEL 65-6466-5775, FAX 65-6467-7667, wspc@wspc.com.sg, http://www.worldscientific.com. Ed. Gillian Koh. **Dist. by:** World Scientific Publishing Ltd., 57 Shelton St, London WC2H 9HE, United Kingdom. TEL 44-207-8360888, FAX 44-207-8362020, sales@wspc.co.uk; World Scientific Publishing Co., Inc., 27 Warren St, Ste 401-402, Hackensack, NJ 07601. TEL 201-487-9655, 800-227-7562, FAX 201-487-9656, 888-977-2665, wspc@wspc.com. **Co-publisher:** Institute of Policy Studies.

300 USA ISSN 2153-0971
▼ **SINO SCIENCE REVIEW: SERIES B, SOCIAL SCIENCES.** Text in English. 2010 (Feb.). bi-m. free (effective 2011). **Document type:** *Journal, Academic/Scholarly.* **Description:** Features Chinese research in the social sciences.
Media: Online - full text.
Published by: MJS USA, LLC, 4413 Grand Ave, Western Springs, IL 60558. TEL 708-246-7870, martin.stroka@gmail.com, http://www.mjschina.com/.

SINTESE. *see* PHILOSOPHY

300 COL
SINTESIS (YEAR); anuario social, politico y economico de Colombia. Text in Spanish. a.
Published by: (Universidad Nacional de Colombia, Instituto de Estudios Politicos y Relaciones Internacionales), Tercer Mundo Editores, Tranversal 2a A 67-27, Bogota, CUND, Colombia. TEL 57-1-2551695. Ed. Luis Alberto Restrepo Moreno.

300 ESP ISSN 0210-0223
H8
SISTEMA. Text in Spanish. 1973. bi-m. EUR 48 domestic; EUR 88 in Europe; EUR 102 in the Americas (effective 2009). adv. bk.rev. index, cum.index every 20 nos. back issues avail. **Document type:** *Journal, Academic/Scholarly.* **Description:** Covers sociology, political science, philosophy, methodology, and social history.
Indexed: A22, CA, I13, IBR, IBSS, IBZ, P09, P42, PAIS, PCI, PSA, RASB, S02, S03, SCOPUS, SociolAb, T02.
—IE, Infotrieve.
Published by: (Instituto de Tecnicas Sociales de la Fundacion Fondo Social Universitario), Fundacion Sistema, Fuencarral 127, 1o, Madrid, 28010, Spain. TEL 34-91-4487319, FAX 34-91-4487339, info@fundacionsistema.com. Eds. Elias Diaz, Jose Felix Tezanos. Circ: 8,000. **Dist. by:** Asociacion de Revistas Culturales de Espana, C Covarruvias 9 2o. Derecha, Madrid 28010, Spain. TEL 34-91-3086066, FAX 34-91-3199267, info@arce.es, http://www.arce.es/.

300 POL ISSN 0208-5070
HM1 CODEN: SISYEE
SISYPHUS; social studies. Text in English. 1981. s-a. PLZ 25 (effective 2005).
Indexed: CA, FR, P42, S02, S03, SCOPUS, SociolAb, T02.
—BLDSC (8286.424390).
Published by: Polska Akademia Nauk, Instytut Filozofii i Socjologii, Nowy Swiat 72, Warsaw, 00330, Poland. TEL 48-22-8267181, FAX 48-22-8267823, secretar@ifispan.waw.pl.

300 ARG ISSN 0327-7909
HA943
SITUACION Y EVOLUCION SOCIAL - SINTESIS. Text in Spanish. 1992-1993; resumed 1995. a. ARS 12, USD 20. **Document type:** *Government.* **Description:** Presents social indicators: population, family, home, residence, health, education, work, income, social security and welfare.
Related titles: Diskette ed.
Published by: Instituto Nacional de Estadistica y Censos, Presidente Julio A Roca 615, Buenos Aires, 1067, Argentina. TEL 54-114-3499662, FAX 54-114-3499621, ces@indec.mecon.ar, http://www.indec.mecon.ar.

SITUATIONS; project of the radical imagination. *see* LITERARY AND POLITICAL REVIEWS

300 CHN ISSN 1006-3587
SIWEI YU ZHIHUI/THINKING AND WISDOM. Text in Chinese. 1982. m. CNY 50.40 (effective 2009). adv. 48 p./no.; **Document type:** *Journal, Academic/Scholarly.*
Formerly (until 1995): Luoji yu Yuyan Xuexi - Logic and Language Studies (1003-5044)
Related titles: Online - full text ed.
Published by: Hebei Shifan Daxue/Hebei Normal University, Xixiao-qu, Shijiazhuang, 050091, China. TEL 86-311-83826540, FAX 86-311-86263298. adv.: page CNY 12,000. **Dist. by:** China International Book Trading Corp, 35 Chegongzhuang Xilu, Haidian District, PO Box 399, Beijing 100044, China. TEL 86-10-68412045, FAX 86-10-68412023, cibtc@mail.cibtc.com.cn, http://www.cibtc.com.cn.

300 CHN ISSN 1001-778X
AS451
SIXIANG ZHANXIAN/IDEOLOGICAL FRONT. Text in Chinese; Summaries in English. 1975. bi-m. CNY 12 per issue. 96 p./no.; **Document type:** *Journal, Academic/Scholarly.*
Related titles: Online - full text ed.
—East View, Ingenta.
Published by: Yunnan Daxue/Yunnan University, 2, Cuihu Bei Lu, Kunming, 650091, China. TEL 86-871-5031473, http://www.ynu.edu.cn/. Ed. Qin Jiahua. **Dist. overseas by:** China International Book Trading Corp, 35 Chegongzhuang Xilu, Haidian District, PO Box 399, Beijing 100044, China.

300 USA ISSN 1754-1328
CB425
THE SIXTIES; a journal of history, politics and culture. Text in English. 2008. s-a. GBP 163 combined subscription in United Kingdom to institutions (print & online eds.); EUR 252, USD 316 combined subscription to institutions (print & online eds.) (effective 2012). bk.rev. reprint service avail. from PSC. **Document type:** *Journal, Academic/Scholarly.* **Description:** Features cross-disciplinary scholarship from academics and public intellectuals.
Related titles: Online - full text ed.: ISSN 1754-1336. GBP 147 in United Kingdom to institutions; EUR 227, USD 285 to institutions (effective 2012).
Indexed: AmH&L, CA, HistAb, T02.
—IE. **CCC.**
Published by: Routledge (Subsidiary of: Taylor & Francis Group), 325 Chestnut St, Ste 800, Philadelphia, PA 19106. TEL 215-625-8900, 800-354-1420, FAX 215-625-2940, orders@taylorandfrancis.com. Eds. Jeremy Varon, John McMillian, Michael S Foley.

SKRIBUAK; working paper. *see* EDUCATION

300 947 USA ISSN 0037-6779
D377.A1
➤ **SLAVIC REVIEW**; American quarterly of Russian, Eurasian and East European studies. Text in English. 1893. q. USD 240 combined subscription domestic to institutions (print & online eds.); USD 275 combined subscription foreign to institutions (print & online eds.) (effective 2012). adv. bk.rev.; film rev. bibl.; charts; illus. index, cum.index: 1941-1964, 1965-1979. back issues avail.; reprints avail. **Document type:** *Journal, Academic/Scholarly.* **Description:** Publishes scholarly articles, discussions, and essays on all areas of Russian, Eurasian and East European studies.
Former titles (until 1961): American Slavic and East European Review (1049-7544); (until 1945): Slavonic and East European Review. American Series (1535-0940); (until 1943): Slavonic Year-Book, American Series (1535-0959); (until 1940): The Slavonic and East European Review; (until 1928): The Slavonic Review (1471-7816); (until 1922): Anglo-Russian Literary Society. Proceedings
Related titles: Microform ed.; Online - full text ed.: USD 200 to institutions (effective 2012).
Indexed: A01, A02, A03, A08, A20, A22, A25, A26, ABCPolSci, ABS&EES, ASCA, AcaI, AmHI, ArtHuCI, B04, B14, B24, BRD, BRI, BibLing, CA, CBRI, CurCont, DIP, E08, FR, G08, H07, H08, H09, H10, HAb, HistAb, HumInd, I05, I13, IBR, IBSS, IBZ, M10, MLA, MLA-IB, P02, P06, P10, P27, P34, P42, P48, P53, P54, PAIS, PCI, PQC, PSA, RASB, RILM, RefSour, S02, S03, S05, S08, S09, S11, SCOPUS, SSAI, SSAb, SSCI, SSI, SociolAb, T02, W03, W07.
—BLDSC (8309.385000), IE, Infotrieve, Ingenta, INIST.
Published by: (University of Illinois at Urbana-Champaign), American Association for the Advancement of Slavic Studies, University of Illinois at Urbana-Champaign, 57 E Armory Ave, Champaign, IL 61820. aaass@fas.harvard.edu, http://www.fas.harvard.edu/~aaass. Ed. Mark D Steinberg. Adv. contact Jane T Hedges. page USD 425; 7.5 x 4.5. Circ: 5,000.

300 GBR ISSN 0954-6839
DK1
➤ **SLOVO (LONDON).** Text in English. 1988. s-a. USD 220 in United States to institutions; GBP 116 elsewhere to institutions (effective 2010). bk.rev.; film rev. reprint service avail. from PSC. **Document type:** *Journal, Academic/Scholarly.* **Description:** Aims to discuss and interpret Russian, Eurasian, Central and East European affairs, covering the fields of anthropology, economics, film, geography, history, international studies, linguistics, literature, media, politics and sociology.
Related titles: Online - full text ed.
Indexed: A01, A03, A08, A20, AmHI, ArtHuCI, CA, H07, IBSS, MLA-IB, P42, PCI, PSA, RILM, S02, S03, SCOPUS, SociolAb, T02, W07.
—BLDSC (8309.883300). **CCC.**

Published by: (University of London, School of Slavonic and East European Studies), Maney Publishing, Ste 1C, Joseph's Well, Hanover Walk, Leeds, W Yorks LS3 1AB, United Kingdom. TEL 44-113-2432800, FAX 44-113-3868178, maney@maney.co.uk, http://www.maney.co.uk. **Subscr. in N. America to:** Maney Publishing, 875 Massachusetts Ave, 7th Fl, Cambridge, MA 02139. TEL 866-297-5154, FAX 617-354-6875, maney@maneyusa.com.

300 DEU ISSN 1612-149X
SLOWAKISCHE AKADEMIE DER WISSENSCHAFTEN. SCHRIFTENREIHE. Text in English, German. 2005. irreg., latest vol.3, 2006. price varies. **Document type:** *Monographic series, Academic/Scholarly.*
Indexed: MSN.
Published by: (Slovenska Akademia Vied/Slovak Academy of Sciences SVK), Peter Lang GmbH (Subsidiary of: Peter Lang Publishing Group), Eschborner Landstr 42-50, Frankfurt Am Main, 60489, Germany. TEL 49-69-7807050, FAX 49-69-78070550, zentrale.frankfurt@peterlang.com.

001.4 USA ISSN 0037-7333
AS30 CODEN: SMSNA5
SMITHSONIAN. Text in English. 1970. m. USD 12 domestic; USD 25 in Canada; USD 38 elsewhere (effective 2009). adv. bk.rev. illus. index. back issues avail.; reprints avail. **Document type:** *Magazine, Consumer.* **Description:** Contains articles on history, natural history and the arts.
Related titles: Microform ed.: (from PQC); Online - full text ed.: Smithsonian Magazine Web. ISSN 1930-5508.
Indexed: A01, A02, A03, A08, A11, A20, A21, A22, A25, A26, A30, A31, A33, ABIPC, ABM, ABS&EES, AIAP, ARG, AbAn, Acal, AmH&L, AmHI, ArtHuCI, B04, B05, B07, BEL&L, BIOSIS Prev, BRD, BiolDig, C03, C05, C12, CA, CADCAM, CBCARef, CBPI, CBRI, CLFP, CPerl, ChLitAb, ChPerl, Chicano, CurCont, E04, E05, E08, EnvAb, EnvInd, F01, F02, G05, G06, G07, G08, G09, GardL, GeoRef, H05, H07, HistAb, I05, I06, I07, IBR, IBZ, JHMA, M01, M02, M04, M06, MASUSE, MLA-IB, MagInd, MycolAb, P02, P07, P10, P13, P15, P30, P34, P47, P48, P52, P53, P54, P56, PCI, PMR, PQC, R03, R04, R06, RASB, RGAb, RGPR, RGYP, RI-1, RI-2, RILM, S06, S08, S09, S23, SCOPUS, SpeleolAb, T02, TOM, Telegen, U01, W03, W04, W05, W07, WBA, WMB, WildRev.
—BLDSC (8311.450000), IE, Infotrieve, Ingenta, Linda Hall.
Published by: Smithsonian Magazine, Capital Gallery, Ste 6001, MRC 513, PO Box 37012, Washington, DC 20013. TEL 202-633-6090, MagazinePermissions@si.edu. Ed. Carey Winfrey. adv.: B&W page USD 89,845, color page USD 131,640; trim 8 x 10.875. **Subscr. to:** PO Box 420312, Palm Coast, FL 32142. TEL 800-766-2149.

370 IND ISSN 0037-7627
HN681 CODEN: SOACE2
SOCIAL ACTION; a quarterly review of social trends. Text in English. 1951. q. INR 175, USD 55 to non-members; INR 50 per issue to non-members; free to members (effective 2011). bk.rev. index. reprints avail. **Document type:** *Journal, Academic/Scholarly.*
Related titles: Microform ed.: 1951 (from PQC).
Indexed: A21, BAS, CABA, E-psyche, E12, IBSS, ILD, IPsyAb, P30, R12, REE&TA, RI-1, RI-2, S02, S03, S13, S16, SOPODA, SWR&A, SociolAb, TAR, W11.
—BLDSC (8318.040000), IE, Infotrieve, Ingenta.
Published by: Indian Social Institute, 10, Institutional Area, Lodi Rd, New Delhi, 110003, India. Ed. Christopher Lakra.

300 GBR ISSN 0264-5262
HN381
SOCIAL AFFAIRS UNIT. RESEARCH REPORTS. Text in English. 1983. irreg., latest vol.37, 2004. price varies. back issues avail. **Document type:** *Monographic series, Academic/Scholarly.*
—IE. **CCC.**
Published by: Social Affairs Unit, 314-322 Regent St, London, W1B 5SA, United Kingdom. TEL 44-20-76374356, FAX 44-20-74368530, info@socialaffairsunit.org.uk.

300 GBR ISSN 1464-9365
GF1
➤ **SOCIAL & CULTURAL GEOGRAPHY.** Text in English. 2000. 8/yr. GBP 781 combined subscription in United Kingdom to institutions (print & online eds.); EUR 1,036, USD 1,299 combined subscription to institutions (print & online eds.) (effective 2012). adv. bk.rev. abstr. 116 p./no. 2 cols./p.; back issues avail.; reprint service avail. from PSC. **Document type:** *Journal, Academic/Scholarly.* **Description:** Seeks to address topical issues relating to social and cultural geography and foster scholarly debate.
Related titles: Online - full text ed.: ISSN 1470-1197. GBP 703 in United Kingdom to institutions; EUR 932, USD 1,169 to institutions (effective 2012) (from IngentaConnect).
Indexed: A01, A03, A08, A20, A22, CA, CurCont, DIP, E01, ESPM, GEOBASE, IBR, IBSS, IBZ, P34, P42, PSA, RILM, S02, S03, SCOPUS, SSA, SSCI, SSciA, SociolAb, T02, W07.
—IE, Infotrieve, Ingenta. **CCC.**
Published by: Routledge (Subsidiary of: Taylor & Francis Group), 4 Park Sq, Milton Park, Abingdon, Oxon OX14 4RN, United Kingdom. TEL 44-20-70176000, FAX 44-20-70176336, subscriptions@tandf.co.uk, http://www.routledge.com. Adv. contact Linda Hann TEL 44-1344-779945. **Subscr. to:** Taylor & Francis Ltd., Journals Customer Service, Sheepen Pl, Colchester, Essex CO3 3LP, United Kingdom. TEL 44-20-70175544, FAX 44-20-70175198, tf.enquiries@tfinforma.com.

301 330 JAM ISSN 0037-7651
HN244
➤ **SOCIAL AND ECONOMIC STUDIES.** Text in English. 1953. 4/yr. USD 15 per issue (effective 2005). adv. bk.rev. charts; stat. index. reprints avail. **Document type:** *Journal, Academic/Scholarly.* **Description:** Brings information on the current social and economic thinking in the West Indies, Latin America and the rest of the Third World.
Related titles: Microform ed.: (from PQC); Online - full text ed.
Indexed: A12, A20, A22, A26, ABIn, AICP, ASCA, B04, BRD, C01, C32, CA, CREJ, E08, EconLit, FR, G08, H09, H21, I05, IBR, IBSS, IBZ, IIBP, IIMP, ILD, JEL, P06, P08, P10, P27, P30, P34, P42, P45, P48, P51, P53, P54, PAIS, PCI, PQC, PSA, PopulInd, PsycholAb, RASB, RILM, S02, S03, S05, S09, SCOPUS, SOPODA, SSA, SSAI, SSAb, SSI, SociolAb, T02, W03.
—BLDSC (8318.045000), IE, Infotrieve, Ingenta.
Published by: University of the West Indies, Sir Arthur Lewis Institute of Social and Economic Research, Mona Campus, Kingston, 7, Jamaica. TEL 876-927-1020, FAX 876-927-2409, TELEX 2123 JA, ses@uwimona.edu.jm. Eds. Annie Paul, Elsie Le Franc. adv.: page USD 250. Circ: 2,000.

300 500 CZE ISSN 1804-4158
▼ ➤ **SOCIAL AND NATURAL SCIENCES JOURNAL.** Text in English. 2010 (Dec.). q. adv. bk.rev. abstr.; bibl.; charts; illus.; stat. back issues avail. **Document type:** *Journal, Academic/Scholarly.* **Description:** Publishes social and all natural sciences related articles.
Published by: BARAR International Communications and Business Insitute s.r.o., Editorial and publishing department, Nam. Winstona Churchilla 2, Praha 3, 13000, Czech Republic. TEL 42-2-34462023, papers@journals.cz, http://www.journals.cz. Ed., R&P, Adv. contact Petr Hajek. Pub. Kholnazar Amonov. Circ: 200.

➤ **SOCIAL CHANGE.** *see* SOCIOLOGY

300 NLD ISSN 1879-9655
▼ ➤ **SOCIAL COSMOS.** Text in English. 2010. **Document type:** *Journal, Academic/Scholarly.*
Media: Online - full text.
Published by: Igitur, Utrecht Publishing & Archiving Services, Postbus 80124, Utrecht, 3508 TC, Netherlands. TEL 31-30-2536685, FAX 31-30-2536959, info@igitur.uu.nl, http://www.igitur.uu.nl. Eds. Dr. Elisabet Rasch TEL 31-30-2531064, O J Sadmin.

300 960 GBR ISSN 0253-3952
HM1
➤ **SOCIAL DYNAMICS**; a journal of african studies. Text in English. 1975. s-a. GBP 226 combined subscription in United Kingdom to institutions (print & online eds.); EUR 353, USD 440 combined subscription to institutions (print & online eds.) (effective 2012). adv. bk.rev. back issues avail.; reprint service avail. from PSC. **Document type:** *Journal, Academic/Scholarly.* **Description:** Publishes original multidisciplinary works on topics in African studies, with an emphasis on contemporary theoretical debate.
Related titles: Online - full text ed.: ISSN 1940-7874. GBP 203 in United Kingdom to institutions; EUR 317, USD 396 to institutions (effective 2012).
Indexed: A20, A22, ASCA, ASD, CA, CurCont, E01, IBSS, ISAP, LeftInd, MLA-IB, P30, P42, PSA, PerIslam, RASB, S02, S03, SCOPUS, SOPODA, SSA, SSCI, SociolAb, T02, W07.
—BLDSC (8318.081000), IE, Ingenta. **CCC.**
Published by: (University of Cape Town, Centre for African Studies ZAF), Routledge (Subsidiary of: Taylor & Francis Group), 4 Park Sq, Milton Park, Abingdon, Oxon OX14 4RN, United Kingdom. TEL 44-20-70176000, FAX 44-20-70176336, subscriptions@tandf.co.uk, http://www.routledge.com. Ed. Meg Samuelson. Adv. contact Linda Hann TEL 44-1344-779945. **Subscr. to:** Taylor & Francis Ltd., Journals Customer Service, Sheepen Pl, Colchester, Essex CO3 3LP, United Kingdom. TEL 44-20-70175544, FAX 44-20-70175198, tf.enquiries@tfinforma.com.

➤ **SOCIAL EDUCATION.** *see* EDUCATION—Teaching Methods And Curriculum

➤ **THE SOCIAL EDUCATOR.** *see* EDUCATION

➤ **SOCIAL EPISTEMOLOGY**; a journal of knowledge, culture and policy. *see* PHILOSOPHY

300 SWE ISSN 0283-202X
SOCIAL FORSKNING; inblick i SFRs verksamhetsomraade. Text in Swedish. 1986. q. free. adv. bk.rev. **Document type:** *Academic/Scholarly.*
Published by: Socialvetenskapliga Forskningsraadet - S F R, Fack 2220, Stockholm, 10315, Sweden. TEL 46-8-440-4110, FAX 46-8-440-4112. Ed., Adv. contact Bodil Gustavsson. Pub. Erland Bergman. Circ: 4,000.

300 DEU ISSN 1729-4274
GF1
➤ **SOCIAL GEOGRAPHY.** Text in English, German. 2003. s-a. **Document type:** *Journal, Academic/Scholarly.* **Description:** Aims to enhance and to accelerate communication amongst scientists working in social geography, including human geography, sociology, anthropology, architecture, ecology, cultural studies, history, politics, philosophy, or linguistics.
Related titles: Online - full text ed.: ISSN 1729-4312. 2005. free (effective 2011).
Indexed: A01, GEOBASE, P27, P52, P54, P56, SCOPUS, T02.
Published by: Copernicus GmbH, Bahnhofsallee 1e, Goettingen, 37081, Germany. TEL 49-551-9003390, FAX 49-551-90033970, info@copernicus.org, http://www.copernicus.org. Eds. Anthony Giddens, Benno Werlen, Matthew Hannah.

➤ **SOCIAL GEOGRAPHY DISCUSSIONS.** *see* GEOGRAPHY

300 GBR ISSN 0307-1022
HN1 CODEN: SOHSEH
➤ **SOCIAL HISTORY.** Text in English. 1976. q. GBP 402 combined subscription in United Kingdom to institutions (print & online eds.); EUR 529, USD 665 combined subscription to institutions (print & online eds.) (effective 2012). adv. bk.rev. illus. index. back issues avail.; reprint service avail. from PSC. **Document type:** *Journal, Academic/Scholarly.* **Description:** Presents articles, reviews and debates of high quality historical analysis without restrictions on place, period or viewpoint.
Related titles: Online - full text ed.: ISSN 1470-1200. GBP 362 in United Kingdom to institutions; EUR 476, USD 598 to institutions (effective 2012) (from IngentaConnect).
Indexed: A01, A02, A03, A08, A20, A22, A26, ABS&EES, AmH&L, AmHI, ArtHuCI, B04, B21, BRD, BrHumI, CA, CurCont, DIP, E01, E08, E17, ESPM, G08, G10, H05, H07, H08, H09, HAb, HistAb, HumInd, I05, IBR, IBSS, IBZ, MLA-IB, P02, P10, P30, P42, P48, P53, P54, PCI, PQC, PSA, RASB, S02, S03, S05, S09, S11, S21, SCOPUS, SOPODA, SSA, SSAI, SSAb, SSI, SociolAb, T02, W03, W04, W07, W09.
—IE, Infotrieve, Ingenta. **CCC.**
Published by: Routledge (Subsidiary of: Taylor & Francis Group), 4 Park Sq, Milton Park, Abingdon, Oxon OX14 4RN, United Kingdom. TEL 44-20-70176000, FAX 44-20-70176336, subscriptions@tandf.co.uk, http://www.routledge.com. Eds. Janet Blackman, Keith Nield. Adv. contact Linda Hann TEL 44-1344-779945. **Subscr. to:** Taylor & Francis Ltd., Journals Customer Service, Sheepen Pl, Colchester, Essex CO3 3LP, United Kingdom. TEL 44-20-70175544, FAX 44-20-70175198.

301 USA ISSN 1474-2918
SOCIAL ISSUES. Text in English. 2000. irreg., latest 2008. free (effective 2011). **Document type:** *Journal, Academic/Scholarly.*
Media: Online - full text.
Published by: White Horse Books

300 DNK ISSN 0904-3535
HV4
SOCIAL KRITIK; tidsskrift for social analyse og debat. Text in Danish. 1988. q. DKK 400 (effective 2009). bk.rev. back issues avail. **Document type:** *Magazine, Consumer.*
Indexed: PCI, RILM.
Published by: Selskabet til Fremme af Social Debat, Nansensgade 66, Copenhagen K, 1366, Denmark. TEL 45-33-939963, FAX 45-33-158076, http://www.socialkritik.dk. Ed. Benny Lihme.

300 GBR ISSN 1474-2837
➤ **SOCIAL MOVEMENT STUDIES**; journal of social, cultural and political protest. Text in English. 2002. q. GBP 446 combined subscription in United Kingdom to institutions (print & online eds.); EUR 591, USD 738 combined subscription to institutions (print & online eds.) (effective 2012). adv. back issues avail.; reprint service avail. from PSC. **Document type:** *Journal, Academic/Scholarly.* **Description:** Provides a forum for academic debate and analysis of extra-parliamentary political, cultural and social movements throughout the world.
Related titles: Online - full text ed.: ISSN 1474-2829. 2000. GBP 401 in United Kingdom to institutions; EUR 531, USD 665 to institutions (effective 2012) (from IngentaConnect).
Indexed: A01, A03, A08, A22, B21, CA, E01, E17, ESPM, IBSS, LeftInd, P34, P42, PSA, S02, S03, SCOPUS, SSciA, SociolAb, T02.
—IE, Ingenta. **CCC.**
Published by: Routledge (Subsidiary of: Taylor & Francis Group), 4 Park Sq, Milton Park, Abingdon, Oxon OX14 4RN, United Kingdom. TEL 44-20-70176000, FAX 44-20-70176336, subscriptions@tandf.co.uk, http://www.routledge.com. Adv. contact Linda Hann TEL 44-1344-779945. **Subsc. in N. America:** Taylor & Francis Inc., Customer Services Dept, 325 Chestnut St, 8th Fl, Philadelphia, PA 19106. TEL 215-625-8900, 800-354-1420, FAX 215-625-2940, customerservice@taylorandfrancis.com; **Subscr. to:** Taylor & Francis Ltd., Journals Customer Service, Sheepen Pl, Colchester, Essex CO3 3LP, United Kingdom. TEL 44-20-70175544, FAX 44-20-70175198.

300 NLD ISSN 0378-8733
HM73
➤ **SOCIAL NETWORKS.** Text in English. 1979. 4/yr. EUR 534 in Europe to institutions; JPY 70,900 in Japan to institutions; USD 597 elsewhere to institutions (effective 2012). adv. bk.rev. illus. Index. reprints avail. **Document type:** *Journal, Academic/Scholarly.* **Description:** Provides a common forum for representatives of anthropology, sociology, history, social psychology, political science, human geography, biology, economics, and communications science.
Related titles: Microform ed.: (from PQC); Online - full text ed.: (from IngentaConnect, ScienceDirect); ◆ Spanish ed.: Redes. ISSN 1579-0185.
Indexed: A22, A26, AICP, ASCA, CA, CIS, CommAb, CurCont, E-psyche, FR, FamI, I05, IBSS, JCQM, MEA&I, MathR, P03, P30, P42, PCI, PsycInfo, PsycholAb, RASB, S02, S03, SCOPUS, SOPODA, SSA, SSCI, SociolAb, T02, W07.
—BLDSC (8318.125300), IE, Infotrieve, Ingenta, INIST. **CCC.**
Published by: (International Network for Social Network Analysis USA), Elsevier BV (Subsidiary of: Elsevier Science & Technology), Radarweg 29, PO Box 211, Amsterdam, 1000 AE, Netherlands. TEL 31-20-4853911, FAX 31-20-4852457, JournalsCustomerServiceEMEA@elsevier.com. Eds. P Doreian, T Snijders. **Subscr.:** Radarweg 29, PO Box 211, Amsterdam 1000 AE, Netherlands. TEL 31-20-4853757, FAX 31-20-4853432.

361.2 USA ISSN 0037-7783
HN51
SOCIAL POLICY; organizing for social and economic justice. Text in English. 1970. q. USD 45 domestic to individuals; USD 50 in Canada & Mexico to individuals; USD 60 elsewhere to individuals; USD 185 domestic to institutions; USD 205 in Canada & Mexico to institutions; USD 225 elsewhere to institutions (effective 2010). adv. bk.rev. illus.; stat. 58 p./no. 2 cols./p.; back issues avail.; reprints avail. **Document type:** *Journal, Academic/Scholarly.* **Description:** Covers social movements and discusses contemporary social thought on policy issues and action.
Related titles: CD-ROM ed.; Microform ed.: (from PQC); Online - full text ed.: ISSN 1944-9216.
Indexed: A01, A02, A03, A08, A20, A22, A25, A26, ABCPolSci, ASCA, ASSIA, Acal, AltPI, AmH&L, B04, BRD, C12, CA, Chicano, DIP, E02, E03, E07, E08, ERI, EdA, EdI, FutSurv, G05, G06, G07, G08, G10, H01, H02, H09, HRA, I05, IBR, IBSS, IBZ, LeftInd, M01, M02, MCR, MEA&I, MEDSOC, MLA-IB, P02, P07, P10, P13, P18, P27, P30, P34, P42, P48, P53, P54, PAIS, PCI, PQC, PSA, PersLit, RASB, S02, S03, S05, S08, S09, S11, SOPODA, SRRA, SSA, SSAI, SSAb, SSI, SWR&A, SociolAb, T02, W03, W05, W09.
—BLDSC (8318.130100), IE, Infotrieve, Ingenta. **CCC.**
Published by: Labor Neighbor Research and Training Center, PO Box 3924, New Orleans, LA 70177. TEL 504-302-1238. adv.: page USD 400.

300 USA ISSN 0192-8686
HN1
SOCIAL PRACTICE. Text in English. 1978. q. USD 6.
Published by: Inter-University Consortium for Ethics and Aesthetics, PO Box 211, Winfield, IL 60190. Ed. D A Strickland.

320 USA ISSN 0037-783X
H1
➤ **SOCIAL RESEARCH**; an international quarterly of the social sciences. Text in English. 1934. q. USD 155 domestic to institutions; USD 177 foreign to institutions; USD 170 combined subscription domestic to institutions (print & online eds.); USD 192 combined subscription foreign to institutions (print & online eds.) (effective 2010). adv. illus. index. reprints avail. **Document type:** *Journal, Academic/Scholarly.*
Related titles: Microform ed.: (from PMC, PQC); Online - full text ed.: ISSN 1944-768X. USD 155 to institutions (effective 2010).

S

Indexed: A01, A02, A03, A08, A12, A20, A22, A25, A26, ABCPolSci, ABIn, ABS&EES, ASCA, AmH&L, B01, B02, B04, B06, B07, B09, B15, B17, B18, BAS, BRD, CA, CBRI, CMM, ChPerI, CommAb, CurCont, DIP, E07, E08, EI, EconLit, FR, FamI, G04, G05, G06, G07, G08, H09, H10, HistAb, I03, I05, I07, IBR, IBZ, IPB, JEL, M01, M02, MEA&I, MLA-IB, P02, P06, P07, P10, P13, P26, P27, P30, P34, P42, P43, P45, P46, P48, P51, P53, P54, PAIS, PCI, PQC, PRA, PSA, PerIslam, PhilInd, RASB, S02, S03, S05, S08, S09, S11, S23, SCOPUS, SOPODA, SSA, SSAI, SSAb, SSCI, SSI, SociolAb, T02, W03, W04, W05, W07, W09.
—BLDSC (8318.150000), IE, Infotrieve, Ingenta, INIST. **CCC.**
Address: The New School for Social Research, 65 Fifth Ave, Rm 240B, New York, NY 10003. TEL 212-229-5735, FAX 212-807-1669. Ed. Arien Mack. Circ: 3,000.

300 ROM ISSN 2066-6861
▼ **SOCIAL RESEARCH REPORTS.** Text in Romanian, English. 2009. irreg. **Document type:** *Journal, Academic/Scholarly.*
Related titles: Online - full text ed.: ISSN 2067-5941. free (effective 2011).
Published by: (Directia Generala de Asistenta Sociala si Protectia Copilului/General Directorate of Social Assistance and Child Protection), Expert Projects SRL, Str Voinesti 63, Iasi, 700615, Romania. Ed. Daniela Cojocaru.

301 GBR ISSN 1360-7898
➤ **SOCIAL RESEARCH UPDATE.** Text in English. 1993. q. free to individuals; GBP 180 to institutions (effective 2009). bk.rev. illus. back issues avail. **Document type:** *Journal, Academic/Scholarly.* **Description:** Covers methods of social research and statistical techniques in the social sciences.
Related titles: Online - full text ed.: free (effective 2009).
Indexed: CA, P02, P10, P27, P46, P48, P53, P54, PQC, S02, S03, SSAI, SSAb, SSI, SociolAb, T02, W03, W05.
—BLDSC (8318.151960). **CCC.**
Published by: University of Surrey, Department of Sociology, Faculty of Arts & Human Sciences, Guildford, GU2 7XH, United Kingdom. TEL 44-1483-259365, FAX 44-1483-259551, information@surrey.ac.uk, http://www.soc.surrey.ac.uk/. Eds. Gayle Letherby, Ross Coomber.

➤ **SOCIAL SCIENCE & MEDICINE.** *see* MEDICAL SCIENCES

➤ **SOCIAL SCIENCE COMPUTER REVIEW.** *see* EDUCATION—Computer Applications

300 PHL ISSN 1655-1524
H53.P45
➤ **SOCIAL SCIENCE DILIMAN.** Text in English. 2000. s-a. bk.rev. abstr.; bibl.; charts; maps; stat. back issues avail. **Document type:** *Journal, Academic/Scholarly.* **Description:** Covers multidisciplinary fields in the social sciences.
Related titles: Online - full text ed.: ISSN 2012-0796.
Published by: University of the Philippines, Office of the Vice Chancellor for Research and Development, Diliman, CP Garcia Ave, Quezon City, 1101, Philippines. TEL 632-927-2309, 632-927-2567, FAX 632-927-2568, rduo.ovcrd@up.edu.ph, http://www.ovcrd.upd.edu.ph/. Ed. Maria F Mangahas.

300 USA ISSN 0145-5532
H1
➤ **SOCIAL SCIENCE HISTORY.** Abbreviated title: S S H. Text in English. 1976. q. USD 70 to individuals; USD 167 to institutions; USD 172 combined subscription to institutions (print & online eds.); USD 42 per issue to institutions (effective 2012). adv. bk.rev. illus. Index. back issues avail.; reprint service avail. from PSC. **Document type:** *Journal, Academic/Scholarly.* **Description:** Provides articles that blend empirical research with theoretical work, undertake comparisons across time and space, or contribute to the development of quantitative and qualitative methods of analysis.
Related titles: Microform ed.; Online - full text ed.: ISSN 1527-8034. 1999. USD 144 to institutions (effective 2012).
Indexed: A01, A02, A03, A08, A20, A22, ABS&EES, ASCA, AmH&L, ArtHuCI, BAS, CA, CurCont, DIP, E01, FamI, HistAb, I13, IBR, IBSS, IBZ, P10, P30, P42, P46, P48, P53, P54, PCI, PQC, PSA, RASB, S02, S03, S21, SCOPUS, SOPODA, SSA, SSCI, SociolAb, T02, V&AA, W07.
—BLDSC (8318.160500), IE, Infotrieve, Ingenta. **CCC.**
Published by: Duke University Press, 905 W Main St, Ste 18 B, Durham, NC 27701. TEL 919-688-5134, 888-651-0122, FAX 919-688-2615, 888-651-0124, subscriptions@dukeupress.edu, http://www.dukeupress.edu. Ed. Douglas L Anderton.

306 GBR ISSN 0539-0184
H1 CODEN: SSCIBL
➤ **SOCIAL SCIENCE INFORMATION/INFORMATION SUR LES SCIENCES SOCIALES**; information sur les sciences sociales. Text in English, French. 1954; N.S. 1961. q. USD 904, GBP 489 combined subscription to institutions (print & online eds.); USD 886, GBP 479 to institutions (effective 2011). adv. illus. Index. back issues avail.; reprint service avail. from PSC. **Document type:** *Journal, Academic/Scholarly.* **Description:** Provides a forum for research in social anthropology, sociology of science, social psychology and sociological theory.
Formerly (until 1962): International Social Science Council. Information
Related titles: Online - full text ed.: ISSN 1461-7412. USD 814, GBP 440 to institutions (effective 2011).
Indexed: A20, A22, ABCPolSci, AICP, ARDT, ASCA, ASSIA, BAS, BibInd, C25, CA, CABA, CPM, CurCont, DIP, E01, E12, ESPM, FR, FamI, GH, H16, HistAb, I13, IBR, IBSS, IBZ, IPP, LT, MLA-IB, N02, N03, P02, P10, P30, P34, P42, P48, P53, P54, PAA&I, PAIS, PCI, PQC, PSA, PhilInd, PsycholAb, R12, RASB, RRTA, S02, S03, S11, S12, S13, S16, SCOPUS, SOPODA, SSA, SSCI, SSciA, SociolAb, T02, TAR, W07, W11.
—BLDSC (8318.161000), IE, Infotrieve, Ingenta, INIST. **CCC.**
Published by: (Editions de la Maison des Sciences de l'Homme FRA), Sage Publications Ltd. (Subsidiary of: Sage Publications, Inc.), 1 Oliver's Yard, 55 City Rd, London, EC1Y 1SP, United Kingdom. TEL 44-20-73248500, FAX 44-20-73248600, info@sagepub.co.uk, http://www.uk.sagepub.com/home.nav. Ed. Anna Rocha Perazzo. adv.: B&W page GBP 400; 130 x 205. **Subscr. in the Americas to:** Sage Publications, Inc., 2455 Teller Rd, Thousand Oaks, CA 91320. TEL 805-499-9774, FAX 805-499-0871, journals@sagepub.com.
Co-sponsor: Ecoles des Hautes en Sciences Sociales.

300 JPN ISSN 1340-7155
H62.A1
SOCIAL SCIENCE JAPAN. Text in English. 1994. s-a. **Document type:** *Newsletter, Academic/Scholarly.*
Related titles: Online - full text ed.
Indexed: IBSS.
Published by: University Of Tokyo, Institute of Social Science/Shakai Kagaku Kenkyujo, 7-3-1 Hongo, Bunkyo-ku, Tokyo, 113-0033, Japan. TEL 81-3-58414931, FAX 81-3-58414905. Circ: 1,400.

300 GBR ISSN 1369-1465
H62.5.J3
➤ **SOCIAL SCIENCE JAPAN JOURNAL.** Text in English. 1953. s-a. GBP 154 in United Kingdom to institutions; EUR 231 in Europe to institutions; USD 308 in US & Canada to institutions; GBP 154 elsewhere to institutions; GBP 168 combined subscription in United Kingdom to institutions (print & online eds.); EUR 252 combined subscription in Europe to institutions (print & online eds.); USD 336 combined subscription in US & Canada to institutions (print & online eds.); GBP 168 combined subscription elsewhere to institutions (print & online eds.) (effective 2012). adv. bk.rev. back issues avail.; reprint service avail. from PSC. **Document type:** *Journal, Academic/Scholarly.* **Description:** Provides a forum for solid information on, and analysis of, modern Japan. Publishes papers that focus on Japan in a comparative perspective as well as international issues that affect Japan.
Former titles (until 1996): University of Tokyo. Institute of Social Science. Annals (0563-8054); (until 1965): Social Science Abstracts
Related titles: Online - full text ed.: ISSN 1468-2680. GBP 140 in United Kingdom to institutions; EUR 210 in Europe to institutions; USD 280 in US & Canada to institutions; GBP 140 elsewhere to institutions (effective 2012) (from IngentaConnect).
Indexed: A12, A22, ABIn, AmH&L, B04, BAS, BRD, CA, E01, EconLit, GEOBASE, HistAb, I08, IBSS, JEL, P10, P42, P46, P48, P51, P53, P54, PAIS, PCI, PQC, PSA, S02, S03, SCOPUS, SSA, SSAI, SSAb, SSCI, SSI, SociolAb, T02, W01, W02, W03, W05, W07.
—BLDSC (8318.161920), IE, Infotrieve, Ingenta. **CCC.**
Published by: (University Of Tokyo, Institute of Social Science/Shakai Kagaku Kenkyujo JPN), Oxford University Press, Great Clarendon St, Oxford, OX2 6DP, United Kingdom. TEL 44-1865-556767, FAX 44-1865-556646, jnl.orders@oup.co.uk, http://www.oxfordjournals.org. Ed. Hiroshi Ishida. Pub. Martin Green. R&P Fiona Bennett. adv.: B&W page GBP 230, B&W page USD 380; 145 x 200. Circ: 900.

300 GBR ISSN 0362-3319
H1
➤ **THE SOCIAL SCIENCE JOURNAL.** Text in English. 1963. 4/yr. EUR 454 in Europe to institutions; JPY 60,300 in Japan to institutions; USD 512 elsewhere to institutions (effective 2012). adv. bk.rev. bibl.; charts; illus.; stat. index, cum.index: 1963-68, 1969-72. back issues avail.; reprint service avail. from PSC. **Document type:** *Journal, Academic/Scholarly.* **Description:** Covers scholarly work in the social sciences defined in the classical sense, that is in the social sciences, the humanities, and the natural sciences.
Formerly (until 1976): Rocky Mountain Social Science Journal (0035-7634)
Related titles: Online - full text ed.: ISSN 1873-5355. 2001 (from IngentaConnect, ScienceDirect).
Indexed: A01, A02, A03, A08, A20, A22, A25, A26, ABCPolSci, ABS&EES, ASCA, AbAn, AmH&L, B01, B04, B06, B07, B09, BRD, CA, ChPerI, Chicano, CommAb, CurCont, DIP, E-psyche, E08, ESPM, FamI, G05, G06, G07, G08, H09, HistAb, I05, I13, IBR, IBSS, IBZ, KES, M01, M02, P02, P03, P06, P10, P27, P30, P34, P42, P43, P48, P53, P54, PAIS, PQC, PRA, PSA, PsycInfo, PsycholAb, RASB, RiskAb, S02, S03, S05, S08, S09, S11, SCOPUS, SOPODA, SSA, SSAI, SSAb, SSCI, SSI, SWR&A, SociolAb, T02, V&AA, W03, W05, W07.
—BLDSC (8318.162000), IE, Infotrieve, Ingenta. **CCC.**
Published by: (Western Social Science Association USA), Pergamon (Subsidiary of: Elsevier Science & Technology), The Blvd, Langford Ln, East Park, Kidlington, Oxford OX5 1GB, United Kingdom. TEL 44-1865-843000, FAX 44-1865-843010, JournalsCustomerServiceEMEA@elsevier.com. Ed. N Prabha Unnithan.

300 CAN
➤ **SOCIAL SCIENCE PAPER PUBLISHER.** Text in Multiple languages. 1997. 3/yr. bk.rev. **Document type:** *Journal, Academic/Scholarly.* **Description:** Publishes papers from all ranks of the social sciences.
Media: Online - full content.
Published by: University of Western Ontario, Department of Sociology, Social Science Center, 5th Fl, London, ON N6A 5C2, Canada.

300 IND
SOCIAL SCIENCE PROBINGS. Text in English. 1984. q. INR 80, USD 25.
Indexed: RASB.
Published by: People's Publishing House Private Ltd., 5 E Rani Jhansi Rd., New Delhi, 110 055, India. Ed. R S Sharma. Circ: 1,000.

300 USA ISSN 0038-4941
H1
➤ **SOCIAL SCIENCE QUARTERLY.** Abbreviated title: S S Q. Text in English. 1920. 5/yr. GBP 295 in United Kingdom to institutions; EUR 375 in Europe to institutions; USD 327 in the Americas to institutions; USD 578 elsewhere to institutions; GBP 340 combined subscription in United Kingdom to institutions (print & online eds.); EUR 431 combined subscription in Europe to institutions (print & online eds.); USD 377 combined subscription in the Americas to institutions (print & online eds.); USD 665 combined subscription elsewhere to institutions (print & online eds.) (effective 2012). adv. bk.rev. abstr.; bibl.; illus. index. reprint service avail. from PSC. **Document type:** *Journal, Academic/Scholarly.* **Description:** Dedicated to developing communication across traditional disciplinary boundaries.
Former titles (until 1968): Southwestern Social Science Quarterly (0276-1742); (until 1931): Southwestern Political and Social Science Quarterly
Related titles: Microform ed.: (from PQC); Online - full text ed.: ISSN 1540-6237. GBP 295 in United Kingdom to institutions; EUR 375 in Europe to institutions; USD 327 in the Americas to institutions; USD 578 elsewhere to institutions (effective 2012) (from IngentaConnect).
Indexed: A01, A02, A03, A08, A12, A20, A21, A22, A25, A26, ABCPolSci, ABIn, ABS&EES, APEL, ASCA, AmH&L, B01, B04, B06, B07, B09, B21, BAS, BRD, C28, CA, CBRI, CIS, ChPerI, Chicano, CommAb, CurCont, DIP, E-psyche, E01, E02, E03, E07, E08, EAA, EIA, ERI, ESPM, EconLit, EdA, EdI, EnerInd, F09, FR, FamI, G06, G07, G08, G10, H&SSA, H09, H10, HRA, HistAb, I05, I13, IBR, IBSS, IBZ, JEL, MEA&I, MLA-IB, P02, P03, P04, P06, P07, P10, P13, P18, P25, P27, P30, P34, P42, P43, P48, P51, P53, P54, PAIS, PCI, PQC, PRA, PSA, PerIslam, PopulInd, PsycInfo, PsycholAb, R05, RASB, RI-1, RI-2, RiskAb, S02, S03, S05, S08, S09, S11, S21, SCOPUS, SFSA, SOPODA, SPAA, SRRA, SSA, SSAI, SSAb, SSCI, SSI, SSciA, SUSA, SociolAb, T02, W01, W02, W03, W07, W09.
—BLDSC (8318.167000), IE, Infotrieve, Ingenta, INIST. **CCC.**
Published by: (Southwestern Social Science Association), Wiley-Blackwell Publishing, Inc. (Subsidiary of: Wiley-Blackwell Publishing Ltd.), 111 River St, Hoboken, NJ 07030. TEL 201-748-6000, FAX 201-748-6088, info@wiley.com, http://www.wiley.com/WileyCDA/. Ed. Robert Lineberry. Adv. contact Kristin McCarthy TEL 201-748-7683.

300 USA ISSN 0049-089X
H1 CODEN: SSREBG
➤ **SOCIAL SCIENCE RESEARCH.** Text in English. 1972. bi-m. EUR 970 in Europe to institutions; JPY 101,300 in Japan to institutions; USD 756 elsewhere to institutions (effective 2012). adv. charts; stat.; illus. index. back issues avail.; reprints avail. **Document type:** *Journal, Academic/Scholarly.* **Description:** Designed to illustrate the use of quantitative methods in the empirical solution of substantive problems, and emphasizes those concerned with issues or methods that cut across traditional disciplinary lines.
Related titles: Online - full text ed.: ISSN 1096-0317 (from IngentaConnect, ScienceDirect).
Indexed: A01, A02, A03, A08, A20, A22, A26, ABCPolSci, AC&P, AMHA, ASCA, ASG, AmH&L, B04, BAS, BRD, CA, CIS, Chicano, CommAb, CurCont, DIP, E-psyche, E01, E08, EMBASE, ERA, ESPM, ExcerpMed, FamI, G08, H09, I05, IBR, IBSS, IBZ, M01, M02, MEA&I, MEDLINE, P02, P03, P10, P27, P30, P34, P42, P48, P53, P54, PCI, PQC, PSA, PopulInd, PsycInfo, PsycholAb, R10, RASB, Reac, RiskAb, S02, S03, S05, S09, S11, S21, SCOPUS, SOPODA, SSA, SSAI, SSAb, SSCI, SSI, SociolAb, T02, W03, W07, W09.
—BLDSC (8318.170100), IE, Infotrieve, Ingenta. **CCC.**
Published by: Academic Press (Subsidiary of: Elsevier Science & Technology), 3251 Riverport Ln, Maryland Heights, MO 63043. TEL 314-447-8010, FAX 314-447-8030, JournalCustomerService-usa@elsevier.com, http://www.elsevierdirect.com/imprint.jsp?iid=5. Ed. James D Wright.

300 USA ISSN 1546-8151
SOCIAL SCIENCE RESEARCH COUNCIL. PRESIDENT'S REPORT. Text in English. 1926. biennial. **Document type:** *Report.*
Former titles (until 2001): Social Science Research Council. Biennial Report; (until 1998): Social Science Research Council. Annual Report (0361-462X); (until 1927): Social Science Research Council. Annual Report of the Chairman (0740-655X)
Indexed: RASB.
Published by: Social Science Research Council, One Pierrepont Plz, 15th Fl, Brooklyn, NY 11201. TEL 212-377-2700, FAX 212-377-2727, info@ssrc.org, http://www.ssrc.org.

300 USA ISSN 1949-6516
▼ ➤ **SOCIAL SCIENCE RESEARCH GROUP, INC. QUARTERLY JOURNAL.** Text in English. 2010 (Jan.). q. USD 29.95 (effective 2011). **Document type:** *Journal, Academic/Scholarly.* **Description:** Presents scientific papers dealing with the varied disciplines of social science.
Related titles: Online - full text ed.: ISSN 1949-6524. 2010 (Jan.).
Published by: Social Science Research Group, Inc., 1400-134, Ste 333, Veteran's Memorial Hwy, Mableton, GA 30126. TEL 800-948-0769, info@ssrginc.org, http://ssrginc.org. Ed. Michael Tappler.

300 GBR
SOCIAL SCIENCE RESEARCH SERIES. Text in English. 1998. irreg. price varies. **Document type:** *Monographic series, Academic/Scholarly.*
Published by: Politeia, 22 Charing Cross Rd, London, WC2H 0H, United Kingdom. TEL 44-20-72405070, FAX 44-20-72405095.

300 LKA
SOCIAL SCIENCE REVIEW. Text in English. 1979. q. USD 10 to individuals; USD 15 to institutions.
Indexed: SLSI.
Published by: Social Science Association of Sri Lanka, 120-10 Wijerama Mawatha, Colombo, Sri Lanka.

300 ISSN 0134-5486
➤ **SOCIAL SCIENCES**; a quarterly journal of the Russian Academy of Sciences. Text in English. 1970. q. USD 435 to institutions; USD 479 combined subscription to institutions (print & online eds.) (effective 2009). bk.rev. Index. reprints avail. **Document type:** *Journal, Academic/Scholarly.* **Description:** Publishes translated articles in the disciplines of philosophy, history, economics, politics, sociology, law, philology, psychology, and ethnic studies.
Related titles: Online - full text ed.: USD 61 to individuals; USD 435 to institutions (effective 2009).
Indexed: A01, A02, A03, A08, A12, A22, ABIn, ABS&EES, CA, CMM, DIP, EIP, EconLit, HistAb, IBR, IBSS, IBZ, JEL, M02, P02, P10, P30, P34, P42, P45, P46, P48, P51, P53, P54, PAIS, PQC, PSA, RASB, S02, S03, S11, SCOPUS, SSA, SociolAb, T02.
—East View, IE, Ingenta. **CCC.**
Published by: (Rossiiskaya Akademiya Nauk/Russian Academy of Sciences RUS), East View Information Services, 10601 Wayzata Blvd, Minneapolis, MN 55305. TEL 952-252-1201, 800-477-1005, FAX 952-252-1202, info@eastview.com. Circ: 130 (paid).

300 CAN
SOCIAL SCIENCES/SCIENCES SOCIALES. Text in English. 1971. **Document type:** *Monographic series, Trade.* **Description:** Studies on various aspects of social sciences: the political economy and societies, the Canadian society in relation with social sciences and the justice and social problems.
Published by: University of Ottawa Press/Presses de l'Universite d'Ottawa, 542 King Edward, Ottawa, ON K1N 6N5, Canada. TEL 613-562-5246, FAX 613-562-5247. Ed. Marie Blanche Tanon.

300 PAK ISSN 1818-5800
H53.P18
THE SOCIAL SCIENCES. Text in English. 2007. 4/yr. EUR 900 to individuals; EUR 1,200 to institutions; EUR 150 newsstand/cover (effective 2007). **Document type:** *Journal, Academic/Scholarly.*
Related titles: Online - full text ed.: ISSN 1993-6125. free (effective 2007).
Published by: Medwell Journals, ANSInet Bldg, 308-Lasani Town, Sargodha Rd, Faisalabad, 38090, Pakistan. TEL 92-41-5010004, 92-41-5004000, FAX 92-21-5206789, medwellonline@gmail.com, http://www.medwellonline.net.

300 CHE ISSN 2076-0760
▼ ➤ **SOCIAL SCIENCES.** Text in English. forthcoming 2011. q. free (effective 2011). **Document type:** *Journal, Academic/Scholarly.*
Media: Online - full text.
Published by: M D P I AG, Postfach, Basel, 4005, Switzerland. TEL 41-61-6837734, FAX 41-61-3028918, http://www.mdpi.org/.

300 CAN ISSN 1910-4545
SOCIAL SCIENCES AND HUMANITIES RESEARCH COUNCIL OF CANADA. ANNUAL REPORT. Text in English. 2002. a. **Document type:** *Report, Trade.*
Media: Online - full text. **Related titles:** ◆ Print ed.: Social Sciences and Humanities Research Council of Canada. Annual Report. ISSN 0225-2384; French ed.: Conseil de Recherches en Sciences Humaines du Canada. Rapport Annuel. ISSN 1910-4553.
Published by: Social Sciences and Humanities Research Council of Canada, 350 Albert St, PO Box 1610, Ottawa, ON K1P 6G4, Canada. TEL 613-992-0691, FAX 613-992-1787, http://www.sshrc-crsh.gc.ca.

300 CAN ISSN 0225-2384
H62.5.C22
SOCIAL SCIENCES AND HUMANITIES RESEARCH COUNCIL OF CANADA. ANNUAL REPORT. Text in English, French. 1979. a.
Related titles: ◆ Online - full text ed.: Social Sciences and Humanities Research Council of Canada. Annual Report. ISSN 1910-4545.
Published by: Social Sciences and Humanities Research Council of Canada, 350 Albert St, PO Box 1610, Ottawa, ON K1P 6G4, Canada. TEL 613-992-0691, FAX 613-992-1787, http://www.sshrc-crsh.gc.ca.

SOCIAL SCIENCES IN ASIA. *see* ASIAN STUDIES

300 USA ISSN 0252-9203
HC426
➤ **SOCIAL SCIENCES IN CHINA.** Text in English. 1980. q. GBP 219 combined subscription in United Kingdom to institutions (print & online eds.); EUR 344, USD 433 combined subscription to institutions (print & online eds.) (effective 2012). adv. bk.rev. illus. Index. 224 p./no.; back issues avail.; reprint service avail. from PSC. **Document type:** *Journal, Academic/Scholarly.* **Description:** Focuses on recent important developments across the breadth of social sciences and humanities in China.
Related titles: Online - full text ed.: ISSN 1940-5952. GBP 198 in United Kingdom to institutions; EUR 310, USD 389 to institutions (effective 2012); ◆ Chinese ed.: Zhongguo Shehui Kexue. ISSN 1002-4921.
Indexed: A22, APEL, BAS, CA, IBSS, ILD, P30, PAIS, PSA, RASB, S02, S03, SCOPUS, SociolAb, T02.
—BLDSC (8318.187400), East View, IE, Infotrieve, Ingenta. **CCC.**
Published by: (Zhongguo Shehui Kexueyuan/Chinese Academy of Social Sciences CHN), Routledge (Subsidiary of: Taylor & Francis Group), 325 Chestnut St, Ste 800, Philadelphia, PA 19106. TEL 800-354-1420, FAX 215-625-2940, journals@routledge.com, http://www.routledge.com. Ed. Gao Xiang. Adv. contact Linda Hann TEL 44-1344-779945.

300 VNM
SOCIAL SCIENCES INFORMATION REVIEW. Text in English. 2007. q. **Document type:** *Journal, Academic/Scholarly.* **Description:** Covers the study of social science in Vietnam.
Related titles: Online - full text ed.: free.
Published by: Vietnamese Academy of Social Sciences, Institute of Social Sciences Information, Rm. 608, No.1 Lieu Giai Rd., Hanoi, Viet Nam.

300 IND ISSN 0251-348X
SOCIAL SCIENCES RESEARCH JOURNAL. Text in English. 1976. 3/yr. **Document type:** *Journal, Academic/Scholarly.*
Published by: Panjab University, Arts Block No. 3, Panjab University Campus, Chandigarh, Haryana 160 014, India. librarian@pu.ac.in, http://beta.puchd.ac.in.

▼ **SOCIAL SCIENTIFIC STUDIES IN REFORM ERA CHINA.** *see* ASIAN STUDIES

300 NGA ISSN 0081-0487
SOCIAL SCIENTIST. Text in English. 1965. a. price varies.
Published by: (Economics Society), Obafemi Awolowo University, Ile Ife, Osun State, Nigeria.

SOCIAL SEMIOTICS. *see* PHILOSOPHY

300 USA ISSN 0037-7996
D16.3
➤ **THE SOCIAL STUDIES;** a periodical for teachers and administrators. Text in English. 1909. bi-m. GBP 110 combined subscription in United Kingdom to institutions (print & online eds.); EUR 145, USD 181 combined subscription to institutions (print & online eds.) (effective 2012). bk.rev. bibl.; illus. index. back issues avail.; reprint service avail. from PSC. **Document type:** *Journal, Academic/Scholarly.* **Description:** Provides teachers with a forum to offer commentary and perspectives on current issues in social studies education.
Former titles (until 1953): Social Studies for Teachers and Administrators; (until 1951): The Social Studies; (until 1934): Historical Outlook (2155-2983); (until 1918): History Teacher's Magazine
Related titles: Microform ed.: (from PQC); Online - full text ed.: ISSN 2152-405X. GBP 99 in United Kingdom to institutions; EUR 130, USD 163 to institutions (effective 2012).
Indexed: A01, A02, A03, A08, A20, A22, A25, A26, Acal, AmH&L, B04, B14, BRD, BRI, CA, CBRI, CPE, DIP, E01, E02, E03, E06, E07, E08, E09, ENW, ERI, ERIC, EdA, EdI, G05, G06, G07, G08, HistAb, I05, I07, IBR, IBZ, L09, M01, M02, P02, P04, P06, P07, P10, P13, P18, P30, P34, P43, P48, P53, P54, P55, PAIS, PCI, PQC, PSI, RILM, S02, S03, S08, S09, S21, S23, SociolAb, T02, W03, W05.
—BLDSC (8318.209000), IE, Infotrieve, Ingenta. **CCC.**
Published by: (Helen Dwight Reid Educational Foundation), Routledge (Subsidiary of: Taylor & Francis Group), 325 Chestnut St, Ste 800, Philadelphia, PA 19106. TEL 215-625-8900, FAX 215-625-2940, journals@routledge.com.

➤ **SOCIAL STUDIES AND THE YOUNG LEARNER.** *see* EDUCATION—Teaching Methods And Curriculum

➤ **SOCIAL STUDIES JOURNAL.** *see* EDUCATION—Teaching Methods And Curriculum

➤ **SOCIAL STUDIES OF SCIENCE;** an international review of research in the social dimensions of science and technology. *see* SCIENCES: COMPREHENSIVE WORKS

➤ **THE SOCIAL STUDIES PROFESSIONAL.** *see* EDUCATION—Teaching Methods And Curriculum

300 USA ISSN 1056-6325
LB1584
➤ **SOCIAL STUDIES REVIEW.** Text in English. 1973. a. USD 15 per issue to non-members; free to members (effective 2011). adv. bk.rev. back issues avail.; reprints avail. **Document type:** *Journal, Academic/Scholarly.* **Description:** Offers cutting edge commentary and ideas for classroom teachers, curriculum consultants, and college-university educators.
Former titles (until 1973): California Council for the Social Studies Review (0575-5492); (until 1968): California Social Science Review; (until 1962): Southern California Social Science Review
Related titles: Microform ed.: (from PQC); Online - full text ed.
Indexed: A22, B04, ChPerI, E02, E03, ERI, EdA, EdI, P02, P18, P48, P53, P54, PQC, T02, W03, W05.
—BLDSC (8318.214000), IE.
Published by: California Council for Social Studies, PO Box 9319, Chico, CA 95927. TEL 530-809-0290, FAX 888-804-1662, info@ccss.org.

➤ **THE SOCIAL STUDIES TEXAN.** *see* EDUCATION—Teaching Methods And Curriculum

➤ **SOCIALARBEIT IN EUROPA/EUROPEAN INTERESTS.** *see* SOCIOLOGY

300 LTU ISSN 1392-0758
H62.A1
➤ **SOCIALINIAI MOKSLAI.** Text in Lithuanian, English. 1994. q. **Document type:** *Journal, Academic/Scholarly.*
Related titles: Online - full text ed.
Indexed: CA, S02, S03, SCOPUS, SociolAb, T02.
—BLDSC (8318.243712).
Published by: (Kauno Technologijos Universitetas, Edukologijos Institutas, Socialiniu Mokslu Fakultetas), Kauno Technologijos Universitetas/Kaunas University of Technology, K Donelaicio g 73, Kaunas, 44029, Lithuania. TEL 370-37-300000, FAX 370-37-324144, rastine@ktu.lt, http://www.ktu.lt. Ed. Palmira Juceviciene.

300 LTU ISSN 1648-4789
HV315.9
➤ **SOCIALINIS DARBAS/SOCIAL WORK.** Text in Lithuanian, German, English. 2002. s-a. EUR 52.13 (effective 2011). **Document type:** *Journal, Academic/Scholarly.* **Description:** Aims to promote dialogue between researchers from different branches of social science (social policy, social work, sociology, education, psychology, etc.) and to present interdisciplinary studies on social development and population problems in Lithuania, the EU, Eastern and Central European and other countries.
Related titles: Online - full text ed.: ISSN 2029-2775.
Indexed: CA, S02, S03, T02.
—BLDSC (8318.243713).
Published by: (Mykolo Romerio Universitetas, Socialinio Darbo Fakultetas/Mykolas Romeris University, Faculty of Sociology), Mykolo Romerio Universitetas/Mykolas Romeris University, Ateities g. 20, Vilnius, LT-08303, Lithuania. TEL 370-5-2714517, FAX 370-5-2714561, roffice@mruni.eu. Ed. Dr. Leta Dromantiene.

300 LTU ISSN 2029-2236
▼ ➤ **SOCIALINIU MOKSLU STUDIJOS.** Text in Lithuanian. 2009. q. **Document type:** *Journal, Academic/Scholarly.*
Related titles: Online - full text ed.: ISSN 2029-2244.
Published by: (Mykolo Romerio Universitetas, Leidybos Centras), Mykolo Romerio Universitetas/Mykolas Romeris University, Ateities g. 20, Vilnius, LT-08303, Lithuania. TEL 370-5-2714517, FAX 370-5-2714561, roffice@mruni.eu. Ed. Lora Tamosiuniene.

300 001.3 CAN ISSN 0830-9086
➤ **SOCIALIST STUDIES BULLETIN/BULLETIN D'ETUDES SOCIALISTES.** Text in English. 1985. q. CAD 20; free to members (effective 2004). 80 p./no. 1 cols./p.; back issues avail.; reprints avail. **Document type:** *Journal, Academic/Scholarly.*
Formerly: Socialist Studies (0712-1970)
Indexed: C03, CBCARef, LeftInd, PQC.
Published by: Society for Socialist Studies, University College, University of Manitoba, Winnipeg, MB R3T 2M8, Canada. TEL 204-474-9119, FAX 204-261-0021, slr@compusmart.ab.ca, http://www.ucs.mun.ca/~socwrk/sss.html. Ed. Sandra Rollings-Magnusson. Circ: 450.

➤ **SOCIAL'NYE I GUMANITARNYE NAUKI NA DAL'NEM VOSTOKE/HUMANITIES AND SOCIAL STUDIES IN THE FAR EAST;** research theoretical journal. *see* HUMANITIES: COMPREHENSIVE WORKS

300 ARG ISSN 0327-7712
H8.S7
SOCIEDAD. Text in Spanish. 1992. s-a. USD 20 to individuals; USD 30 to institutions. bk.rev. **Document type:** *Academic/Scholarly.*
Related titles: Online - full text ed.
Published by: Universidad de Buenos Aires, Facultad de Ciencias Sociales, Marcelo T. de Alvear, 2230, Buenos Aires, 1122, Argentina. TEL 54-11-45083800.

300 BRA ISSN 1415-8566
SOCIEDADE E CULTURA. Text in Portuguese. 1996. s-a. free.
Supersedes in part (in 1995): Ciencias Humanas em Revista (0104-3587); Which superseded in part (1981-1984): Revista do I C H L (0101-6938)
Related titles: Online - full text ed.: ISSN 1980-8194.
Published by: Universidade Federal de Goias, Faculdade de Ciencias Humanas e Filosofia, Caixa Postal 131, Goiania - GO, 74001-970, Brazil. TEL 55-62-35211314, FAX 55-62-35211128. Eds. Heloisa Dias Bezerra, Ivanilde Goncalves de Moura, Roberto Lima.

300 CHL
SOCIETAS. Text in Spanish. 1991. s-a.?. **Document type:** *Academic/Scholarly.*
Published by: Academia Chilena de Ciencias Sociales Politicas y Morales, Correo Central, Clasificador, 1349, Santiago, Chile. TEL 331902. Ed. Cristian Zegers Ariztia. Circ: 1,000.

300 913 FRA ISSN 0300-953X
➤ **SOCIETE DES OCEANISTES. JOURNAL.** Text in English, French. 1937. s-a. EUR 48 to members; EUR 80 to institutions (effective 2005). bk.rev. bibl.; illus.; abstr. cum.index: 1945-1960 in vol.16, 1960-1970 in vol.26. 230 p./no.; reprints avail. **Document type:** *Journal, Academic/Scholarly.*
Formerly (until 1938): Societe des Oceanistes. Bulletin (0995-7618)
Related titles: E-mail ed.; Fax ed.; Online - full text ed.: ISSN 1760-7256. 2008.
Indexed: AICP, AnthLit, BibLing, EI, FR, HistAb, IBR, IBSS, IBZ, P30, SPPI.
—IE, INIST. **CCC.**
Published by: Societe des Oceanistes, Musee du Quai Branly, 222, rue de l'Universite, Cedex 07, Paris, 75343, France. TEL 33-1-56617116, FAX 33-1-56615319. Ed., R&P Isabelle Leblic. Adv. contact Claire Moyse. Circ: 1,100.

300 FRA ISSN 0081-0894
SOCIETE DES OCEANISTES. PUBLICATIONS. Text in French. 1951. irreg., latest 2005. bk.rev. **Document type:** *Academic/Scholarly.*
Indexed: FR, RASB.
Published by: Societe des Oceanistes, Musee de l'Homme, Palais de Chaillot, Paris, 75116, France. Ed. Claire Moyse. Circ: 1,100.

LA SOCIETE SCIENTIFIQUE ET LITTERAIRE DE CANNES ET DE L'ARRONDISSEMENT DE GRASSE. ANNALES. *see* SCIENCES: COMPREHENSIVE WORKS

300 FRA ISSN 1262-2966
HM405
➤ **SOCIETES & REPRESENTATIONS.** Text in French; Abstracts in English. 1996. s-a. **Document type:** *Academic/Scholarly.* **Description:** Aims to address uncommon social issues, especially those that are rarely investigated by the media and which are seldom the object of research. Contains the work of a multidisciplinary team of researchers who bring together the humanities, medicine and exact sciences.
Indexed: BibInd, FR, IBSS.
—INIST.
Published by: Centre de Recherches et d'Etudes en Droit Histoire Economie et Sociologie du Social, Universite de Paris I, 17 rue de la Sorbonne, Paris, Cedex 5 75231, France. TEL 33-1-40462836, FAX 33-1-40463162. Eds. Myriam Tsikounas, Remi Lenoir. **Subscr. to:** G I S, BP 5, Vassy 14410, France.

300 CHE ISSN 2075-4698
▼ ➤ **SOCIETIES.** Text in English. 2011. q. free (effective 2011). **Document type:** *Journal, Academic/Scholarly.* **Description:** Provides an international and interdisciplinary forum for the study of all aspects of the social realm.
Media: Online - full text.
Published by: M D P I AG, Postfach, Basel, 4005, Switzerland. TEL 41-61-6837734, FAX 41-61-3028918, http://www.mdpi.org/. Ed. Madine VanderPlaat.

300 USA ISSN 0147-2011
H1
➤ **SOCIETY.** Text in English. 1963. bi-m. EUR 341, USD 427 combined subscription to institutions (print & online eds.) (effective 2012). bk.rev. abstr.; bibl.; charts; illus.; stat. index, cum.index: vols.1-5. back issues avail.; reprint service avail. from PSC. **Document type:** *Journal, Academic/Scholarly.* **Description:** Covers articles in social sciences, including sociology, political science, economics, psychology, and anthropology.
Formerly (until 1972): Trans-action (0041-1035)
Related titles: CD-ROM ed.; Microform ed.: (from PQC); Online - full text ed.: ISSN 1936-4725 (from IngentaConnect).
Indexed: A01, A02, A03, A08, A20, A21, A22, A25, A26, ABCPolSci, ABS&EES, AC&P, ARG, ASCA, Acal, AmH&L, B04, B05, B14, BAS, BRD, BRI, C12, C28, CA, CBRI, Chicano, CurCont, DIP, E-psyche, E01, E03, E07, E08, EAA, ERI, ESPM, FamI, FutSurv, G05, G06, G07, G08, GSS&RPL, HRA, HistAb, I05, IBR, IBSS, IBZ, JEL, M01, M02, M06, MASUSE, MCR, MEA&I, MEDSOC, MagInd, P02, P05, P06, P10, P13, P18, P27, P30, P34, P42, P46, P48, P51, P53, P54, PAIS, PCI, PMR, PQC, PRA, PSA, PSI, R03, R04, R05, RASB, RGAb, RGPR, RI-1, RI-2, RiskAb, S02, S03, S08, S09, S11, SCOPUS, SD, SOPODA, SPAA, SRRA, SSA, SSCI, SSciA, SUSA, SWR&A, SociolAb, T02, UAA, W03, W07, W09.
—BLDSC (8319.183000), IE, Infotrieve, Ingenta. **CCC.**
Published by: Springer New York LLC (Subsidiary of: Springer Science+Business Media), 233 Spring St, New York, NY 10013. TEL 212-460-1500, FAX 212-460-1575, service-ny@springer.com, http://www.springer.com. Ed. Jonathan B Imber.

➤ **SOCIETY & NATURAL RESOURCES.** *see* ENVIRONMENTAL STUDIES

300 800 USA ISSN 0891-7477
SOCIETY FOR THE ADVANCEMENT OF SCANDINAVIAN STUDY. NEWS AND NOTES. Text in English. 1973. q.
Published by: Ohio State University, Department of German, 314 Cunz Hall, 1841 Millikin Rd, Columbus, OH 43210. TEL 614-292-8687. Ed. Marilyn Johns Blackwell. Circ: 700 (controlled).

300.94105 GBR ISSN 1758-2121
SOCIETY NOW. Text in English. 2008 (Jul.). 3/yr. free. **Document type:** *Magazine, Consumer.* **Description:** Highlights research currently being undertaken by the UK's leading social scientists and demonstrates how social science research can contribute to better policymaking and, ultimately, a better society.
Formed by the merger of (1999-2008): The Edge (1753-2183); (1989-2008): Social Sciences (0957-4026)
Related titles: Online - full text ed.: ISSN 1758-213X.
—BLDSC (8319.392000).
Published by: Economic and Social Research Council, Polaris House, North Star Ave, Swindon, Wilts SN2 1UJ, United Kingdom. TEL 44-1793-413000, FAX 44-1793-413001, comms@esrc.ac.uk. Eds. Arild Foss, Jacky Clake.

SOCIO - ANTHROPOLOGIE. *see* ANTHROPOLOGY

SOCIO-LEGAL NEWSLETTER. *see* LAW

SOCIOLOGIA (ROME); rivista di scienze storiche e sociali. *see* SOCIOLOGY

S

300 ITA ISSN 0392-5048
HD6951
SOCIOLOGIA DEL LAVORO. Text in Italian. q. EUR 81 combined subscription domestic to institutions (print & online eds.); EUR 121 combined subscription foreign to institutions (print & online eds.) (effective 2009). **Document type:** *Journal, Academic/Scholarly.*
Formerly (until 1978): Analisi e Documenti
Related titles: Online - full text ed.: ISSN 1972-554X.
Indexed: CA, DIP, FR, IBR, IBSS, IBZ, ILD, P30, P42, PAIS, PSA, RASB, RILM, S02, S03, SCOPUS, SOPODA, SSA, SociolAb, T02.
—INIST.
Published by: (Universita degli Studi di Bologna, Centro Internazionale di Documentazione e Studi sui Problemi del Lavoro), Franco Angeli Edizioni, Viale Monza 106, Milan, 20127, Italy. TEL 39-02-2837141, FAX 39-02-26144793, redazioni@francoangeli.it, http://www.francoangeli.it.

300 500 ESP ISSN 1989-8487
▼ ➤ **SOCIOLOGIA Y TECNOCIENCIA**; revista digital de sociologia del sistema tecnocientifico. Text in English, Gallegan, Portuguese, Spanish. 2009. s-a. free (effective 2011). Index. back issues avail. **Document type:** *Journal, Academic/Scholarly.* **Description:** Aims to study, understand and analyze the social influence of the various scientific and technological or technoscientific activities. Hence, the politics, economics or ethics (among other disciplines of human knowledge) as well as the many concerns, factors, or imagined social impact generated by all activities of the techno-scientific system (biotechnology, information and communication technologies, cloning, politics, economics, drugs, technology risk, etc.).
Media: Online - full text.
Indexed: A12, A17, ABIn, P10, P27, P46, P48, P51, P53, P54, PQC.
Published by: Universidad de Valladolid, Departamento de Sociologia y Trabajo Social, Escuela Universitaria de Educacion, Campus de la Yutera, Palencia, 34004, Spain. Eds. Jesus A. Valero Matas, Juan R. Coca.

➤ **SOCIOLOGICAL STUDIES OF CHILDREN AND YOUTH.** *see* CHILDREN AND YOUTH—About

300 ROM ISSN 1220-5389
SOCIOLOGIE ROMANEASCA. Text in Romanian. 1972. q. **Document type:** *Journal, Academic/Scholarly.*
Incorporates (1994 -2003): Revista de Cercetari Sociale (1222-8125); Formerly (until 1990): Viitorul Social (0379-3745)
Related titles: Online - full text ed.
Indexed: S02, S03, SociolAb.
Published by: (Asociatia Romana de Sociologie/Romanian Sociological Association), Institutul European, Str. Grigore Ghica Voda nr.13 et.9, Universitatea Petre Andrei, Iasi, 700469, Romania. http://www.euroinst.ro/. Ed. Sergiu Baltatescu.

300 LTU ISSN 1392-3358
HM417.L58
➤ **SOCIOLOGIJA. MINTIS IR VEIKSMAS.** Text in Lithuanian. 1997. q. **Document type:** *Journal, Academic/Scholarly.*
Related titles: Online - full text ed.: free (effective 2011).
Indexed: CA, IBSS, S02, S03, SociolAb, T02.
—CCC.
Published by: Klaipedos Universiteto, Sociologijos Katedra, Minijos g 153, Klaipeda, 93185, Lithuania. TEL 370-8-46398664, sigitak@yahoo.com.

▼ ➤ **SOLIDARITY: THE JOURNAL OF CATHOLIC SOCIAL THOUGHT AND SECULAR ETHICS.** *see* RELIGIONS AND THEOLOGY—Roman Catholic

▼ ➤ **SOLUTIONS (BURLINGTON)**; for a sustainable and desirable future. *see* ENVIRONMENTAL STUDIES

300 TWN ISSN 1019-0449
HM7
SOOCHOW JOURNAL OF SOCIOLOGY/DONGWU SHEHUI XUEBAO. Text in Chinese. 1977. a. USD 21 per issue. reprints avail. **Document type:** *Academic/Scholarly.*
Supersedes in part (in 1992): Soochow Journal of Political Science and Sociology (0259-3785); Which was formerly: Soochow Journal of Social and Political Sciences
Published by: Soochow University, Wai Shuang Hsi, Shih Lin, Taipei, Taiwan. FAX 886-2-8837110.

SORTUZ; Onati journal of emergent socio-legal studies. *see* LAW

610 368.4 FIN ISSN 1238-5069
SOSIAALI- JA TERVEYSTURVAN KATSAUKSIA/SOCIAL SECURITY AND HEALTH REPORTS. Text in English, Finnish. 1995. irreg., latest 2007. back issues avail. **Document type:** *Monographic series, Academic/Scholarly.*
Formed by the merger of (1967-1995): Finland. Kansanelakelaitos. Julkaisuja. Sarja M (0355-4821); (1973-1995): Finland. Kansanelakelaitos. Julkaisuja. Sarja ML (0355-483X)
Related titles: Online - full text ed.
Published by: Kansanelakelaitos/Social Insurance Institution of Finland, PO Box 450, Helsinki, 00101, Finland. TEL 358-20-63411.

368.4 FIN ISSN 1238-5050
SOSIAALI- JA TERVEYSTURVAN TUTKIMUKSIA/STUDIES IN SOCIAL SECURITY AND HEALTH. Text in Finnish, English. 1995. irreg., latest 2007. price varies. bibl. **Document type:** *Monographic series, Academic/Scholarly.*
Formed by the merger of (1967-1995): Finland. Kansanelakelaitos. Julkaisuja. Sarja A (0430-5205); (1975-1995): Finland. Kansanelakelaitos. Julkaisuja. Sarja AL (0355-4813)
Related titles: Online - full text ed.
Published by: Kansanelakelaitos/Social Insurance Institution of Finland, PO Box 450, Helsinki, 00101, Finland. TEL 358-20-63411.

338.2 ESP ISSN 1139-966X
SOSTENIBLE?. Text in Catalan, English, Spanish. 1999. a. **Document type:** *Journal, Academic/Scholarly.* **Description:** Contains articles on sustainability, globalization and the current state of the world.
Related titles: Online - full text ed.: ISSN 1575-6688. free (effective 2011).
Published by: Universidad Politecnica de Catalunya, Catedra UNESCO de Sostenibilitat, C/Colom 1, Terrassa, 08222, Spain. TEL 34-93-7398050, FAX 34-93-7398032, sostenible@catunesco.upc.es, http://www.catunesco.upc.es. Pub. Miquel Barcelo.

300 TUR
SOSYAL BILIMLER DERGISI/JOURNAL OF SOCIAL SCIENCES. Text in Turkish. 1986. a. free (effective 2009). **Document type:** *Journal, Academic/Scholarly.* **Description:** Publishes scientific articles that contribute to the field of social sciences according to the referees' reports, evaluation criteria and ethics of publishing.
Formerly (until 2001): Ataturk Universitesi Fen-Edebiyat Fakultesi Edebiyat Bilimleri Arastirma Dergisi (1300-9389); Which superseded in part (in 1986): Edebiyat Fakultesi Arastirma Dergisi (0378-3847)
Indexed: MLA-IB.
Published by: Gaziantep Univeristesi, Sosyal Bilimler Enstitusu, University Campus, Gaziantep, 27310, Turkey. TEL 90-342-3171896, http://sbe.gantep.edu.tr, sdemir@gantep.edu.tr, aagir@gantep.edu.tr. Ed. Ahmet Agir.

300 001.3 TUR
▼ **SOSYAL VE BESERI BILIMLER DERGISI/JOURNAL OF SOCIAL SCIENCES AND HUMANITIES.** Text in Turkish; Some issues in English. 2009. s-a. **Document type:** *Journal, Academic/Scholarly.* **Description:** Contains articles in the areas of social and humanity sciences.
Related titles: Online - full text ed.: ISSN 1309-8012. free (effective 2011).
Published by: The Social Sciences Research Society, Gazi Bulvari No.66/602, Gazi Ishani, Cankaya-Izmir, 35230, Turkey. TEL 90-232-3424750, FAX 90-232-3424750, sobiad@sobiad.org, editor@sobiad.org. Ed. Coskun Can Aktan. Pub., R&P Dilek Dileyici.

300 RUS
SOTSIAL'NO-GUMANITARNYE ZNANIYA; nauchno-obrazovatel'noe izdanie. Text in Russian. 1973. 6/yr. USD 170 in United States (effective 2007). **Document type:** *Journal, Academic/Scholarly.*
Former titles (until 1998): Sotsial'no-Politicheskii Zhurnal (0869-8120); (until no.8, 1992): Sotsial'no-Politicheskie Nauki (0868-5797); (until 1990): Nauchno-Teoriticheskii Zhurnal. Nauchnyi Kommunizm (0235-1196); (until 1987): Vyssha Shkola. Nauchnei Doklady. Nauchnyi Kommunizm (0321-3153)
Indexed: IBSS, RASB.
—East View.
Address: B Nikitskaya 5, komn. 307, Moscow, 103009, Russian Federation. Ed. A V Mironov. Circ: 15,600. **Dist. by:** East View Information Services, 10601 Wayzata Blvd, Minneapolis, MN 55305. TEL 952-252-1201, 800-477-1005, FAX 952-252-1202, info@eastview.com, http://www.eastview.com.

SOTSIOLOGIYA MEDITSINY. *see* MEDICAL SCIENCES

SOTSIONIKA, MENTOLOGIYA I PSIKHOLOGIYA LICHNOSTI. *see* SOCIOLOGY

SOUNDINGS (PORTLAND); an interdisciplinary journal. *see* HUMANITIES: COMPREHENSIVE WORKS

SOURCE O E C D. EDUCATION & SKILLS. *see* EDUCATION

SOURCE O E C D. GENERAL ECONOMICS & FUTURE STUDIES. (Organisation for Economic Cooperation and Development) *see* BUSINESS AND ECONOMICS

300.95 FRA ISSN 1960-6060
HN670.3 .A1
➤ **SOUTH ASIA MULTIDISCIPLINARY ACADEMIC JOURNAL.** Text in English. 2007. s-a. **Document type:** *Journal, Academic/Scholarly.*
Related titles: Online - full text ed.: free (effective 2011).
Published by: Ecole des Hautes Etudes en Sciences Sociales, Centre d'Etudes de l'Inde et de l'Asie du Sud (Subsidiary of: Ecole des Hautes Etudes en Sciences Sociales), 54 Bd Raspail, Paris, 75006, France. TEL 33-9-52132547, samajonline@gmail.com. Eds. Amelie Blom, Nicolas Jaoul.

➤ **SOUTH ASIAN ANTHROPOLOGIST.** *see* ANTHROPOLOGY

300 LKA
SOUTH ASIAN REVIEWS AND ABSTRACTS. Text in English. 1987. 12/yr. USD 45; USD 75 in developing nations; USD 150 elsewhere. **Document type:** *Abstract/Index.*
Formerly: D E V I N S A Abstracts (1391-0035)
Published by: (Committee on Studies for Cooperation in Development in South Asia), Marga Institute, 61 Isipathana Mawatha, P O Box 601, Colombo, 5, Sri Lanka. TEL 941-585186, FAX 941-580585. Ed. Godfrey Gunatilleke.

300 PAK ISSN 1026-678X
DS331
➤ **SOUTH ASIAN STUDIES.** Text in English. 1984. 2/yr. PKR 175, USD 50; PKR 100, USD 30 per issue (effective 2010). bk.rev. abstr. back issues avail. **Document type:** *Journal, Academic/Scholarly.* **Description:** Publishes articles, chronologies of important events, and bibliographies pertaining to South Asia.
Related titles: Online - full text ed.
Indexed: A01, I05, P02, P10, P48, P53, P54, PQC.
Published by: Centre for South Asian Studies, University of the Punjab, Quaid-i-Azam Campus, Lahore, 54590, Pakistan. TEL 92-42-99231143, FAX 92-42-99232039. Ed., R&P Muhammad Saleem Mazhar.

➤ **SOUTH ASIAN STUDIES.** *see* ASIAN STUDIES

300 DEU
SOUTH BY MIDWEST. Text in English. 2008. irreg., latest vol.2, 2010. price varies. **Document type:** *Monographic series, Academic/Scholarly.*
Published by: Vervuert Verlag, Elisabethenstr 3-9, Frankfurt Am Main, 60594, Germany. TEL 49-69-5974617, FAX 49-69-5978743, info@iberoamericanalibros.com.

959 JPN ISSN 0563-8682
DS520 CODEN: TNAKAQ
➤ **SOUTH EAST ASIAN STUDIES/TONAN AJIA KENKYU.** Text in English, Japanese; Abstracts in English. 1963. q. bk.rev. **Document type:** *Journal, Academic/Scholarly.*
Related titles: Online - full text ed.: free (effective 2011).
Indexed: A22, AICP, CA, GEOBASE, GeoRef, HistAb, MLA-IB, P30, RILM, SCOPUS, T02.
—BLDSC (8351.900000), IE, Infotrieve, Ingenta.
Published by: Kyoto University, Centre for Southeast Asian Studies, 46 Shimoadachi-cho, Yoshida, Sakyo-ku, Kyoto, 606-8501, Japan. TEL 075-753-7302, FAX 075-753-7350, hp@cseas.kyoto-u.ac.jp.

300 DEU ISSN 1435-2869
HD6660.7
SOUTH EAST EUROPE REVIEW; for labour and social affairs. Abbreviated title: S E E R. Text in English. 1998. q. EUR 69 (effective 2011). reprint service avail. from SCH. **Document type:** *Journal, Academic/Scholarly.* **Description:** Stimulates the exchange of information among researchers, trade unionists, and people who have a special interest in the political, social and economic development of the region of south-east Europe.
Related titles: Online - full text ed.
Indexed: IBSS.
—BLDSC (8351.922250). **CCC.**
Published by: Hans-Boeckler-Stiftung, Hans-Boeckler-Str 39, Duesseldorf, 40476, Germany. TEL 49-211-77780, FAX 49-211-7778225, zentrale@boeckler.de. Eds. Bela Galgoczi, Calvin Allen.

300.71 USA ISSN 1047-7942
LB1585
➤ **SOUTHERN SOCIAL STUDIES JOURNAL.** Abbreviated title: S S S J. Text in English. 1975. s-a. USD 15 to institutions; free to members (effective 2011). bk.rev. back issues avail. **Document type:** *Journal, Academic/Scholarly.* **Description:** Publishes articles for and by people interested in social studies.
Formerly (until 1990): Southern Social Studies Quarterly (0741-143X)
Related titles: Online - full text ed.: free (effective 2011).
Indexed: CA, E03, T02.
—BLDSC (8355.644000), IE, Ingenta.
Published by: Morehead State University, 150 University Blvd, Morehead, KY 40351. TEL 606-783-2200, 800-585-6781, FAX 606-783-5037, library@moreheadstate.edu, http://www.moreheadstate.edu. Ed. David B Peterson. **Co-sponsor:** Kentucky Council for the Social Studies.

300 976.3 USA ISSN 0735-8342
F366
➤ **SOUTHERN STUDIES**; an interdisciplinary journal of the South. Text in English. 1961; N.S. 1990. q. USD 20 in US & Canada; USD 35 elsewhere (effective 2009). adv. bk.rev. bibl.; charts; illus. index, cum.index: 1962-1966. reprints avail. **Document type:** *Journal, Academic/Scholarly.* **Description:** Publishes original research in various fields contributing to a greater knowledge and understanding of the South.
Formerly (until 1977): Louisiana Studies (0024-693X)
Related titles: Microform ed.: N.S. (from PQC).
Indexed: A22, AES, AmH&L, CA, MLA, MLA-IB, P30, PCI, SSAI, SSAb, SSI, T02, W03, W05.
—BLDSC (8356.030000), Infotrieve, Ingenta.
Published by: Northwestern State University of Louisiana, Southern Studies Institute, School of Social Sciences, 203 Russell Hall, Natchitoches, LA 71497. TEL 318-357-6195, FAX 318-357-6153, http://www.nsula.edu/socialsciences/Facilities/SouthernStudies. Ed. Chad Long.

300 DEU ISSN 0931-279X
SOZIAL EXTRA; Zeitschrift fuer Soziale Arbeit und Sozialpolitik. Text in German. 1977. 10/yr. EUR 157.01, USD 194 combined subscription to institutions (print & online eds.) (effective 2012). adv. reprint service avail. from PSC. **Document type:** *Journal, Academic/Scholarly.*
Former titles (until 1985): Extra Sozialarbeit (0724-228X); (until 1982): Pad. Extra Sozialarbeit (0341-7107)
Related titles: Online - full text ed.: ISSN 1863-8953. 2005.
Indexed: A22, A26, E01, I05.
—IE, Ingenta. **CCC.**
Published by: V S - Verlag fuer Sozialwissenschaften (Subsidiary of: Springer Fachmedien Wiesbaden GmbH), Abraham-Lincoln-Str 46, Wiesbaden, 65189, Germany. TEL 49-611-78780, FAX 49-611-7878400, springerfachmedien-wiesbaden@springer.com, http://www.vs-verlag.de. Circ: 1,200 (paid).

300 AUT
SOZIAL- UND KULTURWISSENSCHAFTLICHE MATERIALIEN. Text in German. 1982. irreg., latest vol.45, 2008. price varies. **Document type:** *Monographic series, Academic/Scholarly.*
Formerly (until 2008): Sozialwissenschaftliche Materialien
Published by: Trauner Verlag und Buchservice GmbH, Koeglstr 14, Linz, 4020, Austria. TEL 43-732-778241212, FAX 43-732-778241400, office@trauner.at, http://www.trauner.at.

SOZIAL- UND WIRTSCHAFTSHISTORISCHE STUDIEN. *see* BUSINESS AND ECONOMICS—Economic Systems And Theories, Economic History

300 DEU
SOZIALE ARBEIT AKTUELL IN PRAXIS, FORSCHUNG UND LEHRE. Text in German. 1998. irreg., latest vol.4, 1999. price varies. **Document type:** *Monographic series, Academic/Scholarly.*
Published by: V W B - Verlag fuer Wissenschaft und Bildung, Postfach 110368, Berlin, 10833, Germany. TEL 49-30-2510415, FAX 49-30-2511136, info@vwb-verlag.com.

364 CHE ISSN 1661-6871
SOZIALE INNOVATION; Forschung und Entwicklung in der Sozialen Arbeit. Text in German. 2006. a. **Document type:** *Journal, Academic/Scholarly.*
Published by: Fachhochschule Nordwestschweiz, Hochschule fuer Soziale Arbeit, Riggenbachstr 16, Olten, 4600, Switzerland. TEL 41-848-821011, FAX 41-62-2860090, info.sozialearbeit@fhnw.ch, http://www.fhnw.ch/sozialearbeit/.

304 DEU ISSN 0720-6917
SOZIALE ORIENTIERUNG. Text in German. 1979. irreg., latest vol.19, 2007. price varies. **Document type:** *Monographic series, Academic/Scholarly.*
Published by: Duncker und Humblot GmbH, Carl-Heinrich-Becker-Weg 9, Berlin, 12165, Germany. TEL 49-30-7900060, FAX 49-30-79000631, info@duncker-humblot.de.

300 DEU ISSN 1867-0180
▼ **SOZIALE PASSAGEN.** Text in German. 2009. 2/yr. EUR 250.47, USD 308 combined subscription to institutions (print & online eds.) (effective 2012). adv. reprint service avail. from PSC. **Document type:** *Journal, Academic/Scholarly.*
Related titles: Online - full text ed.: ISSN 1867-0199. 2009.
—IE. **CCC.**

Published by: V S - Verlag fuer Sozialwissenschaften (Subsidiary of: Springer Fachmedien Wiesbaden GmbH), Abraham-Lincoln-Str 46, Wiesbaden, 65189, Germany. TEL 49-611-78780, FAX 49-611-7878400, springerfachmedien-wiesbaden@springer.com. Eds. Karin Bock, Karin Boellert, Werner Thole.

360 DEU ISSN 0038-609X
HN441 CODEN: SOFOFU
➤ **SOZIALER FORTSCHRITT**; Unabhaengige Zeitschrift fuer Sozialpolitik. Text in German. 1952. m. EUR 116 combined subscription to individuals (print & online eds.); EUR 208 combined subscription to institutions (print & online eds.); EUR 14.80 newsstand/cover (effective 2012). adv. bk.rev. index. **Document type:** *Journal, Academic/Scholarly.*
Related titles: Online - full text ed.: ISSN 1865-5386. 2008.
Indexed: A22, CA, DIP, IBR, IBZ, ILD, P34, P42, PAIS, S02, S03, SCOPUS, SOPODA, SociolAb, T02, WBSS.
—IE, Infotrieve. **CCC.**
Published by: (Gesellschaft fuer Sozialen Fortschritt e.V.), Duncker und Humblot GmbH, Carl-Heinrich-Becker-Weg 9, Berlin, 12165, Germany. TEL 49-30-7900060, FAX 49-30-79000631, info@duncker-humblot.de, http://www.duncker-humblot.de. Circ: 580 (paid and controlled).

300 911 DEU
SOZIALGEOGRAPHIE KOMPAKT. Text in German. 2007. irreg. price varies. **Document type:** *Monographic series, Academic/Scholarly.*
Published by: Franz Steiner Verlag GmbH, Birkenwaldstr 44, Stuttgart, 70191, Germany. TEL 49-711-25820, FAX 49-711-2582290, service@steiner-verlag.de, http://www.steiner-verlag.de.

300 DEU ISSN 1860-3955
SOZIALGEOGRAPHISCHE BIBLIOTHEK. Text in German. 2005. irreg., latest vol.15, 2010. price varies. **Document type:** *Monographic series, Academic/Scholarly.*
Published by: Franz Steiner Verlag GmbH, Birkenwaldstr 44, Stuttgart, 70191, Germany. TEL 49-711-25820, FAX 49-711-2582290, service@steiner-verlag.de, http://www.steiner-verlag.de.

300 DEU ISSN 0943-1462
DIE SOZIALGERICHTSBARKEIT; Zeitschrift fuer das aktuelle Sozialrecht. Text in German. 1992. m. EUR 297; EUR 30 newsstand/cover (effective 2012). back issues avail. **Document type:** *Journal, Academic/Scholarly.*
Formed by the merger of (1991-2992): Die Sozialgerichtsbarkeit. Ausgabe A (0939-8651); (1991-1992): Die Sozialgerichtsbarkeit. Ausgabe B (0939-866X); Both of which superseded in part (1954-1991): Die Sozialgerichtsbarkeit (0490-1657)
Related titles: Online - full text ed.: ISSN 1864-8029. EUR 297 (effective 2012).
Indexed: ELLIS, IBR, IBZ.
—**CCC.**
Published by: Erich Schmidt Verlag GmbH & Co. (Berlin), Genthiner Str 30 G, Berlin, 10785, Germany. TEL 49-30-2500850, FAX 49-30-250085305, vertrieb@esvmedien.de, http://www.erich-schmidt-verlag.de. Ed. Peter Becker. Adv. contact Peter Taprogge. Circ: 1,000 (paid).

300 DEU ISSN 1615-1151
SOZIALPAEDAGOGIK IN FORSCHUNG UND PRAXIS. Text in German. 2000. irreg., latest vol.23, 2009. price varies. **Document type:** *Monographic series, Academic/Scholarly.*
Published by: Verlag Dr. Kovac, Leverkusenstr 13, Hamburg, 22761, Germany. TEL 49-40-3988800, FAX 49-40-39888055, info@verlagdrkovac.de.

371 AUT ISSN 1023-6929
➤ **SOZIALPAEDAGOGISCHE IMPULSE.** Text in German. 1988. q. EUR 18; EUR 5 newsstand/cover (effective 2008). adv. back issues avail. **Document type:** *Journal, Academic/Scholarly.*
Published by: (Bundesinstitut fuer Sozialpaedagogik), Manfred Breindl Communications, Jahnstr 14-16, Hollabrunn, 2020, Austria. TEL 43-2952-56323, FAX 43-2952-56324, agentur@mbc.co.at, http://www.mbc.co.at. Pub., R&P Karin Lauermann.

➤ **SOZIALPOLITISCHE INFORMATIONEN.** *see* POLITICAL SCIENCE

300 DEU ISSN 0584-5998
SOZIALPOLITISCHE SCHRIFTEN. Text in German. 1956. irreg., latest vol.89, 2008. price varies. **Document type:** *Monographic series, Academic/Scholarly.*
Published by: Duncker und Humblot GmbH, Carl-Heinrich-Becker-Weg 9, Berlin, 12165, Germany. TEL 49-30-7900060, FAX 49-30-79000631, info@duncker-humblot.de.

300 DEU ISSN 1868-2596
▼ **SOZIALRAUM.DE.** Text in German. 2009. s-a. free (effective 2011). **Document type:** *Journal, Academic/Scholarly.*
Media: Online - full text.
Published by: Socialnet GmbH, Weidengarten 25, Bonn, 53129, Germany. http://www.socialnet.de.

300 DEU ISSN 0944-1239
SOZIALWISSENSCHAFTEN. Text in German. 1993. irreg., latest vol.21, 2005. price varies. **Document type:** *Monographic series, Academic/Scholarly.*
Published by: Peter Lang GmbH (Subsidiary of: Peter Lang Publishing Group), Eschborner Landstr 42-50, Frankfurt Am Main, 60489, Germany. TEL 49-69-7807050, FAX 49-69-78070550, zentrale.frankfurt@peterlang.com. Eds. Hartmut Salzwedel, Ingrid Reichart-Dreyer.

301 DEU ISSN 0724-3464
SOZIALWISSENSCHAFTEN UND BERUFSPRAXIS. Text in German. 1978. s-a. EUR 45 to individuals; EUR 58 to institutions; EUR 34 newsstand/cover (effective 2011). adv. bk.rev. back issues avail. **Document type:** *Journal, Academic/Scholarly.*
Indexed: CA, DIP, IBR, IBSS, IBZ, S02, S03, T02.
—**CCC.**
Published by: (Berufsverband Deutscher Soziologen e.V.), Lucius und Lucius Verlagsgesellschaft mbH, Gerokstr 51, Stuttgart, 70184, Germany. TEL 49-711-242060, FAX 49-711-242088, lucius@luciusverlag.com. Circ: 400.

300 DEU ISSN 1861-244X
SOZIALWISSENSCHAFTLICHE EVALUATIONSFORSCHUNG. Text in German. 2000. irreg., latest vol.9, 2009. price varies. **Document type:** *Monographic series, Academic/Scholarly.*
Published by: Waxmann Verlag GmbH, Steinfurter Str 555, Muenster, 48159, Germany. TEL 49-251-265040, FAX 49-251-2650426, info@waxmann.com. Ed. Reinhard Stockmann.

300 DEU
▼ **SOZIALWISSENSCHAFTLICHE FORSCHUNGSMETHODEN.** Text in German. 2010. irreg., latest vol.2, 2010. price varies. **Document type:** *Monographic series, Academic/Scholarly.*
Published by: Rainer Hampp Verlag, Marktplatz 5, Mering, 86415, Germany. TEL 49-8233-4783, FAX 49-8233-30755, info@rhverlag.de, http://www.rhverlag.de.

300 DEU ISSN 0175-6559
HM5
SOZIALWISSENSCHAFTLICHE LITERATURRUNDSCHAU; Sozialarbeit - Sozialpaedagogik - Sozialpolitik - Gesellschaftspolitik. Text in German. 1978. s-a. EUR 34; EUR 30 to students; EUR 19 newsstand/cover (effective 2011). adv. bk.rev. **Document type:** *Journal, Academic/Scholarly.*
Formerly (until 1983): Literatur Rundschau (0178-1960)
Indexed: DIP, IBR, IBZ.
Published by: Verlag Neue Praxis GmbH, Lahneckstr 10, Lahnstein, 56112, Germany. TEL 49-2621-187159, FAX 49-2621-187176, info@verlag-neue-praxis.de, http://www.verlag-neue-praxis.de. Ed. Hans-Uwe Otto. Adv. contact Ute Renda-Becker. Circ: 1,200 (paid).

300 DEU ISSN 0935-4808
SOZIALWISSENSCHAFTLICHE SCHRIFTEN. Text in German. 1981. irreg., latest vol.46, 2009. price varies. **Document type:** *Monographic series, Academic/Scholarly.*
Published by: Duncker und Humblot GmbH, Carl-Heinrich-Becker-Weg 9, Berlin, 12165, Germany. TEL 49-30-7900060, FAX 49-30-79000631, info@duncker-humblot.de.

300 DEU ISSN 0584-603X
SOZIALWISSENSCHAFTLICHE STUDIEN ZU INTERNATIONALEN PROBLEMEN/SOCIAL SCIENCE STUDIES ON INTERNATIONAL PROBLEMS. Text in German, English. 1966. irreg., latest vol.209, 2002. price varies. **Document type:** *Monographic series, Academic/Scholarly.*
Indexed: IBR, IBZ.
Published by: Verlag fuer Entwicklungspolitik Saarbruecken GmbH, Auf der Adt 14, Saarbruecken, 66130, Germany. TEL 49-6893-986094, FAX 49-6893-986095, vfe@verlag-entwicklungspolitik.de, http://www.verlag-entwicklungspolitik.de.

355.1 DEU ISSN 0177-9141
SOZIALWISSENSCHAFTLICHES INSTITUT DER BUNDESWEHR. VORTRAEGE. Text in German. 1982. irreg. **Document type:** *Monographic series, Academic/Scholarly.*
Published by: Sozialwissenschaftliches Institut der Bundeswehr, Proetzeler Chaussee 20, Strausberg, 15344, Germany. TEL 49-3341-581830, FAX 49-3341-581802.

330 DEU ISSN 1864-483X
SOZIO-OEKONOMISCHE PERSPEKTIVEN IN SUEDOSTEUROPA/ SOCIO-ECONOMIC PERSPECTIVES IN SOUTH-EASTERN EUROPE. Text in German. 2007. irreg. price varies. **Document type:** *Monographic series, Academic/Scholarly.*
Published by: Peter Lang GmbH (Subsidiary of: Peter Lang Publishing Group), Eschborner Landstr 42-50, Frankfurt Am Main, 60489, Germany. TEL 49-69-7807050, FAX 49-69-78070550, zentrale.frankfurt@peterlang.com.

300 CHE
SOZIOOEKONOMISCHE FORSCHUNGEN. Text in German, English. 1974. irreg., latest vol.42, 2000. price varies. **Document type:** *Monographic series, Academic/Scholarly.*
Published by: Paul Haupt AG, Falkenplatz 14, Bern, 3001, Switzerland. TEL 41-31-3012425, FAX 41-31-3014669, verlag@haupt.ch, http://www.haupt.ch.

300 100 RUS ISSN 1027-4359
SOZNANIE I FIZICHESKAYA REAL'NOST'. Text in Russian. 1996. bi-m. USD 111 in United States (effective 2004). **Document type:** *Journal, Academic/Scholarly.* **Description:** Presents a combination of Western scientific paradigm and Eastern sacral wisdom.
—East View.
Published by: Izdatel'stvo Folium, Dmitrovskoe shosse 58, Moscow, 127238, Russian Federation. TEL 7-095-4825544, 7-095-4825590, info@folium.ru. Ed. O P Burmistrova. Circ: 1,000. **Dist. by:** East View Information Services, 10601 Wayzata Blvd, Minneapolis, MN 55305. TEL 952-252-1201, 800-477-1005, FAX 952-252-1202, info@eastview.com, http://www.eastview.com.

SPACE AND POLITY. *see* POLITICAL SCIENCE

300 301 USA ISSN 1945-8673
HM146
SPACES FOR DIFFERENCE. Text in English. 2008. s-a. free (effective 2011). **Document type:** *Journal, Academic/Scholarly.*
Media: Online - full text.
Published by: eScholarship (Subsidiary of: California Digital Library)

SPEKTRUM (MONSHEIM). *see* SCIENCES: COMPREHENSIVE WORKS

300 POL ISSN 0867-0412
LA840
SPOLECZENSTWO OTWARTE. Text in Polish. 1969. 11/yr. USD 22. back issues avail. **Description:** Searches for new ideas, democratic ideas as a base of educational reform.
Supersedes: Wychowanie Obywatelskie (0512-4263)
Published by: (Poland. Ministerstwo Edukacji Narodowej), Centralny Osrodek Doskonalenia Nauczycieli, Al Ujazdowskie 28, pok. 204, Warsaw, 00478, Poland. TEL 48-22-6214800. Ed. Edward Wieczorek. Circ: 10,000. **Dist. by:** Ars Polona, Obroncow 25, Warsaw 03933, Poland.

SPORT COMMERCE AND CULTURE. *see* SPORTS AND GAMES

SPORT IN SOCIETY. *see* SPORTS AND GAMES

300 330 AUT ISSN 0937-6836
SPRINGERS KURZLEHRBUECHER DER WIRTSCHAFTSWISSENSCHAFTEN. Text in German. 1990. irreg., latest 2002. price varies. **Document type:** *Monographic series, Academic/Scholarly.*
Published by: Springer Wien (Subsidiary of: Springer Science+Business Media), Sachsenplatz 4-6, Vienna, W 1201, Austria. TEL 43-1-3302415-0, FAX 43-1-330242665, books@springer.at, http://www.springer.at. R&P Angela Foessl TEL 43-1-3302415517. **Subscr. in N. America to:** Springer New York LLC, 233 Spring St, New York, NY 10013. TEL 800-777-4643, FAX 201-348-4505.

SRI LANKA JOURNAL OF HISTORICAL AND SOCIAL STUDIES. *see* HISTORY

300 LKA ISSN 0258-9710
H1
SRI LANKA JOURNAL OF SOCIAL SCIENCES. Text in English. 1978. s-a. USD 8.50 (effective 2000). **Document type:** *Journal, Academic/Scholarly.*
Indexed: BAS, P30.
—Ingenta. **CCC.**
Published by: National Science Foundation of Sri Lanka, 47-5 Maitland Place, Colombo, 7, Sri Lanka. http://www.nsf.ac.lk. Ed. S T Hettige.

300 IND
SRIMANTA SANKARADEVA RESEARCH INSTITUTE JOURNAL. Text in English. 1990. a.
Published by: Srimanta Sankaradeva Research Institute, Batadrawa, Nagaon, Assam, India.

300 SRB ISSN 0081-394X
AS346.A1
SRPSKA AKADEMIJA NAUKA I UMETNOSTI. ODELJENJE DRUSTVENIH NAUKA. GLAS/ACADEMIE SERBE DES SCIENCES ET DES ARTS. CLASSE DES SCIENCES SOCIALES. BULLETIN. Text in Serbo-Croatian; Summaries in English, French, German, Russian. 1951. irreg. price varies.
Indexed: A&ATA, DIP, IBR, IBZ, RASB.
Published by: Srpska Akademija Nauka i Umetnosti/Serbian Academy of Arts and Sciences, Knez Mihailova 35, Belgrade, 11000. TEL 381-11-2027154, FAX 381-11-2027178, izdavacka@sanu.ac.rs, http://www.sanu.ac.rs. Circ: 1,000.

300 SRB ISSN 0354-4850
SRPSKA AKADEMIJA NAUKA I UMETNOSTI. ODELJENJE DRUSTVENIH NAUKA. NAUCNI SKUPOVI/ACADEMIE SERBE DES SCIENCES ET DES ARTS. CLASSE DES SCIENCES SOCIALES. CONFERENCES SCIENTIFIQUES. Text in Serbo-Croatian. irreg.
Indexed: DIP, IBR, IBZ.
Published by: Srpska Akademija Nauka i Umetnosti/Serbian Academy of Arts and Sciences, Knez Mihailova 35, Belgrade, 11000. TEL 381-11-2027154, FAX 381-11-2027178, izdavacka@sanu.ac.rs, http://www.sanu.ac.rs.

300 SRB ISSN 0354-4893
SRPSKA AKADEMIJA NAUKA I UMETNOSTI. ODELJENJE DRUSTVENIH NAUKA. POSEBNA IZDANJA. Text in Serbo-Croatian; Summaries in English, French, German, Russian. N.S. 1949. irreg. price varies.
Published by: Srpska Akademija Nauka i Umetnosti/Serbian Academy of Arts and Sciences, Knez Mihailova 35, Belgrade, 11000. TEL 381-11-2027154, FAX 381-11-2027178, izdavacka@sanu.ac.rs, http://www.sanu.ac.rs. Circ: 1,000. **Dist. by:** Prosveta, Terazije 16, Belgrade, Serbia, Yugoslavia.

300 913 720 SRB ISSN 0081-4059
SRPSKA AKADEMIJA NAUKA I UMETNOSTI. ODELJENJE DRUSTVENIH NAUKA. SPOMENIK. Text in Serbo-Croatian; Summaries in English, French, German, Russian. N.S. 1950. irreg. Price varies.
Indexed: IBR, IBZ.
Published by: Srpska Akademija Nauka i Umetnosti/Serbian Academy of Arts and Sciences, Knez Mihailova 35, Belgrade, 11000. TEL 381-11-2027154, FAX 381-11-2027178, izdavacka@sanu.ac.rs, http://www.sanu.ac.rs. Circ: 1,000. **Dist. by:** Prosveta, Terazije 16, Belgrade, Serbia, Yugoslavia.

SRPSKA AKADEMIJA NAUKA I UMETNOSTI. SPOMENICA. *see* HUMANITIES: COMPREHENSIVE WORKS

SRUCTURE AND DYNAMICS; eJournal of anthropological and related sciences. *see* ANTHROPOLOGY

SSU YU YEN/THOUGHT AND WORDS; journal of the humanities and social sciences. *see* HUMANITIES: COMPREHENSIVE WORKS

300 DEU
STADT RAND NOTIZEN; Bildung, Gesellschaft, Urbanitaet. Text in German. 2003. irreg., latest vol.5, 2007. price varies. **Document type:** *Monographic series, Academic/Scholarly.*
Published by: Edition Temmen, Hohenlohestr 21, Bremen, 28209, Germany. TEL 49-421-348430, FAX 49-421-348094, info@edition-temmen.de, http://www.edition-temmen.de.

300 DEU
STAEDTEFORSCHUNG. REIHE A: DARSTELLUNGEN. Text in German. 1976. irreg., latest vol.84, 2011. price varies. **Document type:** *Monographic series, Academic/Scholarly.*
Published by: Boehlau Verlag GmbH & Cie, Ursulaplatz 1, Cologne, 50668, Germany. TEL 49-221-913900, FAX 49-221-9139011, vertrieb@boehlau.de.

300 DEU
STAEDTEFORSCHUNG. REIHE B: HANDBUECHER. Text in German. 1986. irreg., latest vol.2, 1996. price varies. **Document type:** *Monographic series, Academic/Scholarly.*
Published by: Boehlau Verlag GmbH & Cie, Ursulaplatz 1, Cologne, 50668, Germany. TEL 49-221-913900, FAX 49-221-9139011, vertrieb@boehlau.de.

300 DEU
STAEDTEFORSCHUNG. REIHE C: QUELLEN. Text in German. 1990. irreg., latest vol.7, 1996. price varies. **Document type:** *Monographic series, Academic/Scholarly.*
Published by: Boehlau Verlag GmbH & Cie, Ursulaplatz 1, Cologne, 50668, Germany. TEL 49-221-913900, FAX 49-221-9139011, vertrieb@boehlau.de.

S

306.05 GBR ISSN 1757-1111
JA75.7
STANDPOINT. Text in English. 2008. m. GBP 37.80 domestic; GBP 55 in Europe; GBP 60 elsewhere (effective 2010). adv. back issues avail. **Document type:** *Magazine, Consumer.* **Description:** Aims to celebrate British civilization, its arts and its values in particular democracy, debate and freedom of speech at a time when they are under threat.
Published by: Social Affairs Unit, 11 Manchester Sq, London, W1U 3PW, United Kingdom. TEL 44-20-75639840, letters@standpointmag.co.uk, http://www.socialaffairsunit.org.uk. Ed. Daniel Johnson. Pub. Simon Tiffin. adv.: color page GBP 2,990; trim 297 x 450.

300 DNK ISSN 1395-3672
➤ **STATS- OG LIVSFORMER.** Text in Danish. 1995. irreg., latest vol.9, 2010. price varies. back issues avail. **Document type:** *Monographic series, Academic/Scholarly.*
Published by: Museum Tusculanum Press, c/o University of Copenhagen, Njalsgade 126, Copenhagen S, 2300, Denmark. TEL 45-35-329109, FAX 45-35-329113, info@mtp.dk, http://www.mtp.dk. Eds. Signe Mellemgaard, Thomas Hoejrup. **Dist. in France by:** Editions Picard, Editions Picard, Paris 75006, France. TEL 33-1-43269778, FAX 33-1-43264264; **Dist. in UK by:** Gazelle Book Services Ltd., White Cross Mills, Hightown, Lancaster LA1 4UU, United Kingdom. TEL 44-1524-68765, FAX 44-1524-63232, sales@gazellebooks.co.uk, http://www.gazellebookservices.co.uk/; **Dist. in US & Canada by:** International Specialized Book Services Inc., 920 NE 58th Ave Ste 300, Portland, OR 97213. TEL 503-287-3093, 800-944-6190, FAX 503-280-8832, orders@isbs.com.

301.364 USA ISSN 1081-9142
E185.93.G4 CODEN: TPFAE5
THE STATUS OF BLACK ATLANTA. Text in English. 1993. a. USD 15 (effective 2000). adv.
Published by: Southern Center for Studies in Public Policy, Clark Atlanta University, Atlanta, GA 30314. TEL 404-880-8085, FAX 404-880-8090. R&P Bob Holmes. Adv. contact Sharon Whipple.

300 USA ISSN 1547-2663
STAY FREE!. Text in English. 1993. 3/yr. USD 20.95; USD 10.95 to students (effective 2005). adv. bk.rev. **Document type:** *Magazine, Consumer.* **Description:** Explores the world of advertising, commercialism and pop culture.
Related titles: Online - full text ed.
Indexed: APW.
Address: 390 Butler St., Thrid Fl, New York, NY 11217. TEL 718-398-9324, stayfree@sunsite.unc.edu, http://sunsite.unc.edu/stayfree. Ed., Pub., R&P, Adv. contact Carrie McLaren. Circ: 5,000.

300 ITA ISSN 0392-1735
DG975.G673
STUDI GORIZIANI; rivista della Biblioteca Statale Isontina di Gorizia. Text in Italian. 1923. s-a. bk.rev. bibl.; illus. 200 p./no.; back issues avail. **Document type:** *Monographic series, Academic/Scholarly.*
Indexed: FR, MLA-IB, RILM.
Published by: Biblioteca Statale Isontina di Gorizia, Via Mameli, 12, Gorizia, GO 34170, Italy. TEL 39-0481-580210, FAX 39-0481-580260, isontina@librari.beniculturali.it. Ed. Marco Menato. Circ: 800.

300 ITA ISSN 1125-2057
AS222.U7
STUDI URBINATI. SERIE B: SCIENZE UMANE E SOCIALI. Text in Italian. N.S. 1950. a. price varies. bk.rev. charts; illus. index. **Document type:** *Monographic series, Academic/Scholarly.*
Former titles (until 1988): Studi Urbinati. Serie B: Letteratura, Storia, Filosofia (0039-3088); Studi Urbinati. Serie B: Letteratura
Indexed: A20, IPB, MLA-IB.
Published by: (Universita degli Studi di Urbino), Edizioni Quattroventi, Piazza Rinascimento 4, Urbino, PS 61029, Italy. TEL 39-072-22588, FAX 39-072-2320998, info@edizioniquattroventi.it, http://www.edizioniquattroventi.it.

300 ITA ISSN 1591-2965
HV286
STUDI ZANCAN. Variant title: Studi Zancan. Politiche e Servizi alle Persone. Text in Italian. 2000. bi-m. EUR 65 combined subscription (print & online eds.) (effective 2011). **Document type:** *Journal, Academic/Scholarly.*
Formed by the merger of (1979-1999): Servizi Sociali (1591-2981); (1996-1999): Politiche Sociali (1591-299X)
Related titles: Online - full text ed.: EUR 30 (effective 2007).
Published by: Fondazione Emanuela Zancan, Centro Studi e Formazione Sociale, via Vescovado, 66, Padova, 35141, Italy. TEL 39-49-663800, FAX 39-49-663013, fz@fondazionezancan.it, http://www.fondazionezancan.it/home/index.cfm.

300 ITA ISSN 1970-5395
STUDIA MEDITERRANEA. Text in Italian. 1981. irreg. **Document type:** *Monographic series, Academic/Scholarly.*
Published by: Gianni Iuculano Editore - Italian University Press, Piazza Petrarca 28, Pavia, 27100, Italy. TEL 39-0382-539830, FAX 39-0382-531693, info@iuculanoeditore.it, http://www.iuculanoeditore.it.

300 ITA ISSN 1970-5441
STUDIA MEDITERRANEA. SERIES HETHAEA. Text in Italian. 19??. irreg. **Document type:** *Monographic series, Academic/Scholarly.*
Published by: Gianni Iuculano Editore - Italian University Press, Piazza Petrarca 28, Pavia, 27100, Italy. TEL 39-0382-539830, FAX 39-0382-531693, info@iuculanoeditore.it, http://www.iuculanoeditore.it.

300 ITA
STUDIA SOCIALIA. Text in English, French, Italian, Spanish. 1957; N.S. 1985. irreg., latest vol.5, 1997. price varies. **Document type:** *Monographic series, Academic/Scholarly.* **Description:** Covers contemporary religious sociology: family, population, information about religions, theology and progress, church teaching on social problems and more.
Published by: (Pontificia Universita Gregoriana, Facolta di Scienze Sociali), Gregorian University Press/Editrice Pontificia Universita Gregoriana, Piazza della Pilotta 35, Rome, 00187, Italy. TEL 39-06-6781567, FAX 39-06-6780588, periodicals@biblicum.com, http://www.paxbook.com. Circ: 200.

300 ROM ISSN 1224-8746
D1
➤ **STUDIA UNIVERSITATIS BABES-BOLYAI. STUDIA EUROPAEA.** Text in English, French, German; Abstracts in English. 1996. q. exchange basis. abstr.; charts; illus. index. **Document type:** *Journal, Academic/Scholarly.*
Related titles: Online - full text ed.: ISSN 2065-9563.
Indexed: A26, B02, B15, B17, B18, CA, G04, G08, I05, IBSS, P10, P27, P42, P48, P54, PQC, PSA, S02, S03, SociolAb, T02.
Published by: Universitatea "Babes-Bolyai", Studia/Babes-Bolyai University, Studia, 51 Hasdeu Str, Cluj-Napoca, 400371, Romania. TEL 40-264-405352, FAX 40-264-591906, office@studia.ubbcluj.ro, http://www.studia.ubbcluj.ro. Eds. Ladislau Gyemant, Sergiu Miscoiu. **Dist by:** "Lucian Blaga" Central University Library, International Exchange Department, Clinicilor st no 2, Cluj-Napoca 400371, Romania. TEL 40-264-597092, FAX 40-264-597633, iancu@bcucluj.ro.

➤ **STUDIEN ZUR GESCHICHTE DER WISSENSCHAFTEN IN BASEL. NEUE FOLGE.** *see* HISTORY—History Of Europe

306.43 DEU ISSN 1612-2003
STUDIEN ZUR INTERNATIONAL UND INTERKULTURELL VERGLEICHENDEN ERZIEHUNGSWISSENSCHAFT. Text in German. 2003. irreg., latest vol.11, 2010. price varies. **Document type:** *Monographic series, Academic/Scholarly.*
—BLDSC (8483.653300).
Published by: Waxmann Verlag GmbH, Steinfurter Str 555, Muenster, 48159, Germany. TEL 49-251-265040, FAX 49-251-2650426, info@waxmann.com. Eds. Juergen Henze, Marianne Krueger-Potratz, Wilfried Bos.

320 DEU ISSN 1611-700X
STUDIEN ZUR KULTURPOLITIK. Text in German. 2003. irreg., latest vol.7, 2008. price varies. **Document type:** *Monographic series, Academic/Scholarly.*
Published by: Peter Lang GmbH (Subsidiary of: Peter Lang Publishing Group), Eschborner Landstr 42-50, Frankfurt Am Main, 60489, Germany. TEL 49-69-7807050, FAX 49-69-78070550, zentrale.frankfurt@peterlang.com, http://www.peterlang.com. Ed. Wolfgang Schneider.

300 DEU ISSN 0175-9868
STUDIEN ZUR TECHNIK-, WIRTSCHAFTS- UND SOZIALGESCHICHTE. Text in German. 1985. irreg., latest vol.15, 2009. price varies. **Document type:** *Monographic series, Academic/Scholarly.*
Published by: Peter Lang GmbH (Subsidiary of: Peter Lang Publishing Group), Eschborner Landstr 42-50, Frankfurt Am Main, 60489, Germany. TEL 49-69-7807050, FAX 49-69-78070550, zentrale.frankfurt@peterlang.com, http://www.peterlang.com. Ed. Hans-Joachim Braun.

300 DEU ISSN 1867-7622
STUDIEN ZUR UNTERHALTUNGSWISSENSCHAFT. Text in German. 2008. irreg., latest vol.2, 2009. price varies. **Document type:** *Monographic series, Academic/Scholarly.*
Published by: Tectum Wissenschaftsverlag Marburg, Biegenstr 4, Marburg, 35037, Germany. TEL 49-6421-481523, FAX 49-6421-43470, email@tectum-verlag.de.

300 DEU
STUDIEN ZUR VISUELLEN KULTUR. Text in German. 2006. irreg., latest vol.15, 2011. price varies. **Document type:** *Monographic series, Academic/Scholarly.*
Published by: Transcript, Muehlenstr 47, Bielefeld, 33607, Germany. TEL 49-521-63454, FAX 49-521-61040, live@transcript-verlag.de.

300 USA ISSN 0039-3606
H31
➤ **STUDIES IN COMPARATIVE INTERNATIONAL DEVELOPMENT.** Abbreviated title: S C I D. Text in English. 1964. q. EUR 443, USD 577 combined subscription to institutions (print & online eds.) (effective 2012). back issues avail.; reprint service avail. from PSC. **Document type:** *Journal, Academic/Scholarly.* **Description:** Addresses issues of political, social, economic, and environmental change in local, national, and international contexts.
Related titles: Microform ed.: (from PQC); Online - full text ed.: ISSN 1936-6167 (from IngentaConnect).
Indexed: A01, A02, A03, A08, A12, A17, A20, A22, A25, A26, A28, ABCPolSci, ABIn, ABS&EES, APA, APEL, ASCA, ASSIA, AmH&L, B01, B02, B06, B07, B08, B09, B15, B17, B18, BAS, BrCerAb, C&ISA, C12, CA, CA/WCA, CIA, CerAb, CivEngAb, CorrAb, CurCont, DIP, E&CAJ, E01, E08, E11, EEA, EMA, ESPM, EnvEAb, G04, G06, G07, G08, GEOBASE, H15, H21, HPNRM, HRA, HistAb, I02, I05, I13, IBR, IBSS, IBZ, ILD, M&TEA, M01, M02, M09, MBF, MEA&I, METADEX, P06, P08, P10, P27, P30, P34, P42, P45, P48, P51, P52, P53, P54, PAIS, PQC, PRA, PSA, R02, RASB, RiskAb, S02, S03, S08, S09, S11, SCOPUS, SOPODA, SSA, SSCI, SSciA, SociolAb, SolStAb, T02, T04, W07, WAA, WBA, WMB.
—BLDSC (8490.250000), IE, Infotrieve, Ingenta. **CCC.**
Published by: Springer New York LLC (Subsidiary of: Springer Science+Business Media), 233 Spring St, New York, NY 10013. TEL 212—460-1500, FAX 212-460-1575, service-ny@springer.com, http://www.springer.com. Ed. Barbara Stallings.

300 NLD ISSN 1573-4234
STUDIES IN CRITICAL SOCIAL SCIENCES. Text in English. 2004. irreg., latest vol.12, 2008. price varies. **Document type:** *Monographic series, Academic/Scholarly.*
Indexed: IZBG.
Published by: Brill, PO Box 9000, Leiden, 2300 PA, Netherlands. TEL 31-71-5353500, FAX 31-71-5317532, cs@brill.nl. Ed. David Fasenfest.

300 IND ISSN 0972-1401
➤ **STUDIES IN HUMANITIES AND SOCIAL SCIENCES.** Text in English. 1994. s-a. INR 200 domestic to individuals; USD 25 foreign to individuals; INR 300 domestic to institutions; USD 35 foreign to institutions (effective 2011). bk.rev. **Document type:** *Journal, Academic/Scholarly.* **Description:** Carries articles focusing on particular theme.
Published by: Indian Institute of Advanced Studies, Rashtrapati Nivas, Shimla, Himachal Pradesh 171 005, India. TEL 91-177-2832930, FAX 91-177-2831389, proiias@gmail.com. Ed. Manas Ray.

➤ **STUDIES IN PUBLIC POLICY.** *see* POLITICAL SCIENCE

300 001.4 GBR ISSN 1042-3192
H62.A1
STUDIES IN QUALITATIVE METHODOLOGY. Text in English. 1988. irreg., latest vol.10, 2008. price varies. back issues avail. **Document type:** *Monographic series, Academic/Scholarly.*
Related titles: Online - full text ed.
Indexed: CA, S02, S03, SCOPUS, SSA, SociolAb, T02.
—BLDSC (8491.308000). **CCC.**
Published by: Emerald Group Publishing Ltd., Howard House, Wagon Ln, Bingley, W Yorks BD16 1WA, United Kingdom. TEL 44-1274-777700, FAX 44-1274-785201, emerald@emeraldinsight.com. Ed. Christopher Pole. **Dist. by:** Turpin Distribution Services Ltd., Pegasus Dr, Stratton Business Park, Biggleswade, Bedfordshire SG18 8QB, United Kingdom. TEL 44-1767-604951, FAX 44-1767-601640, custserv@turpin-distribution.com, http://www.turpin-distribution.com/.

STUDIES IN SOCIAL CHANGE AND DEVELOPMENT. *see* SOCIOLOGY

300 FRA ISSN 1265-2067
➤ **SUD NORD**; folies et cultures - revue internationale. Text in French. 1994. a. EUR 36 for 2 yrs.; EUR 19 for 2 yrs. in developing nations; EUR 25 for 2 yrs. to students (effective 2011). back issues avail. **Document type:** *Journal, Academic/Scholarly.*
Related titles: Online - full text ed.: ISSN 1776-288X.
Published by: Editions Eres, 33 Av. Marcel Dassault, Toulouse, 31500, France. TEL 33-5-61751576, FAX 33-5-61735289, eres@edition-eres.com. Ed. Edmond Perrier. Circ: 700.

300 SDN
SUDAN. ECONOMIC AND SOCIAL RESEARCH COUNCIL. OCCASIONAL PAPER. Text in English. irreg., latest vol.7, 1976. bibl.
Published by: Economic and Social Research Council, P O Box 1166, Khartoum, Sudan.

330.9 SDN ISSN 0377-5828
HC591.S8
SUDAN JOURNAL OF ECONOMIC AND SOCIAL STUDIES. Text in English. 1974. s-a. USD 5.
Indexed: RASB.
Published by: (University of Khartoum, Faculty of Economic and Social Studies), Khartoum University Press, P O Box 321, Khartoum, Sudan. Ed. Ahmed A Ahmed.

300 SDN
SUDAN. NATIONAL COUNCIL FOR RESEARCH. ECONOMIC AND SOCIAL RESEARCH COUNCIL. BULLETIN. Text in Arabic, English. 1974. irreg., latest vol.152, 1990. **Description:** Presents papers on specific topics relating to agricultural, industrial, social and theoretical economics issues in the Sudan.
Published by: National Council for Research, Economic and Social Research Council, P O Box 1166, Khartoum, Sudan. TEL 78805.

300 338.91 SDN
SUDAN. NATIONAL COUNCIL FOR RESEARCH. ECONOMIC AND SOCIAL RESEARCH COUNCIL. RESEARCH METHODS. Text in Arabic, English. 1983. irreg., latest vol.3, 1989.
Published by: National Council for Research, Economic and Social Research Council, P O Box 1166, Khartoum, Sudan. TEL 78805.

300 SDN
SUDAN. NATIONAL COUNCIL FOR RESEARCH. ECONOMIC AND SOCIAL RESEARCH COUNCIL. RESEARCH REPORT. Text in Arabic, English. 1976. irreg., latest vol.42, 1989. **Description:** Presents reports on social and economic issues in the Sudan, with emphasis on the impact of modernization programs.
Published by: National Council for Research, Economic and Social Research Council, P O Box 1166, Khartoum, Sudan. TEL 78805.

SUDAN RESEARCH INFORMATION BULLETIN. *see* HUMANITIES: COMPREHENSIVE WORKS

360 GBR
SUDAN STUDIES SERIES. Text in English. 1980. irreg., latest vol.13, 1991. price varies. **Document type:** *Monographic series, Academic/Scholarly.* **Description:** Features academic studies on Sudan including topics such as political development, land law and use, the Danagla traders of Northern Sudan, the English language in the Sudan, etc.
Published by: Ithaca Press (Subsidiary of: Garnet Publishing), 8 Southern Ct, South St, Reading, Berks RG1 4QS, United Kingdom. TEL 44-118-9597847, FAX 44-118-9597356, http://www.ithacapress.co.uk.

300 TUR ISSN 1305-7774
➤ **SULEYMAN DEMIREL UNIVERSITESI. SOSYAL BILIMLER ENSTITUSU DERGISI/S D U INSTITUTE OF SOCIAL SCIENCES. JOURNAL.** Text in Turkish. s-a. **Document type:** *Journal, Academic/Scholarly.*
Related titles: Online - full text ed.: ISSN 1304-6373. free (effective 2011).
Indexed: A01.
Published by: Suleyman Demirel University, Sosyal Bilimler Enstitusu/Suleyman Demirel University, Institute of Social Sciences, Dogu Campus, Isparta, 32260, Turkey. TEL 90-246-2113850, sosyal@sdu.edu.tr.

300 IND
➤ **SUMMERHILL**; I I A S review. Text in English. 1994. s-a. INR 35 (effective 2011). bk.rev. **Document type:** *Journal, Academic/Scholarly.*
Published by: Indian Institute of Advanced Studies, Rashtrapati Nivas, Shimla, Himachal Pradesh 171 005, India. TEL 91-177-2832930, FAX 91-177-2831389, proiias@gmail.com. Ed. Satish Aikant.

300 TWN ISSN 0300-3302
AS455
SUN YAT-SEN CULTURAL FOUNDATION BULLETIN/CHUNG SHAN HSUEH SHU WEN HUA CH'I K'AN. Text in Chinese, English. 1968. s-a. TWD 250, USD 16 per issue. charts.
Published by: Sun Yat-sen Cultural Foundation, No 23, Ln 13, Yung Kang St, Taipei, Taiwan.

▼ **SURAKSHA CHINTAN**; an interdisciplinary journal of humanities and social sciences. *see* HUMANITIES: COMPREHENSIVE WORKS

300 GBR ISSN 1477-7487
TK7882.E2
➤ **SURVEILLANCE & SOCIETY.** Text in English. 2002. 4/yr. free (effective 2011). **Document type:** *Journal, Academic/Scholarly.* **Description:** Contains interdisciplinary papers on surveillance, politics, and policy across academic disciplines.
Media: Online - full text.
Indexed: CJA, IBSS, P30, P48, P54, PQC, S02, S03, SociolAb, T02.
—CCC.
Published by: Surveillance Studies Network, University of Newcastle upon Tyne, Global Urban Research Unit, Claremont Tower, Newcastle upon Tyne, NE1 7RU, United Kingdom. TEL 44191-2227801, FAX 44-191-2226008.

300.723 GBR ISSN 1363-4518
SURVEY METHODS CENTRE. NEWSLETTER. Variant title: Survey Methods Newsletter. Text in English. 1980. s-a. free (effective 2005). adv. back issues avail. **Document type:** *Newsletter.* **Description:** Discusses current issues in survey methodology and publishes articles disseminating survey methods research findings.
Media: Online - full content.
Published by: Survey Methods Centre, National Centre for Social Research, 35 Northampton Sq, London, EC1V 0AX, United Kingdom. TEL 44-20-72501866, FAX 44-20-72501524, info@netcen.ac.uk. Ed. Peter Lynn. Adv. contact Carol Lawrence.

310 300.723 GBR
SURVEY METHODS CENTRE. WORKING PAPERS. Text in English. irreg., latest vol.6. GBP 2 (effective 2000). **Document type:** *Monographic series.*
Published by: Survey Methods Centre, National Centre for Social Research, 35 Northampton Sq, London, EC1V 0AX, United Kingdom. TEL 44-20-7250-1866, FAX 44-20-7250-1524, info@netcen.ac.uk, http://www.natcen.ac.uk. Ed. Peter Lynn.

300 DEU ISSN 1864-3361
HA31.2
➤ **SURVEY RESEARCH METHODS.** Text in English. 2007. irreg. free (effective 2011). **Document type:** *Journal, Academic/Scholarly.* **Description:** Aims to assist researchers in all disciplines involved in the design, implementation and analysis of surveys.
Media: Online - full text.
Published by: European Survey Research Association, c/o Rainer Schnell, Universitaet Konstanz, Postfach D92, Konstanz, 78434, Germany. esra@sqp.nl, http://esra.sqp.nl/esra/. Ed. Peter Lynn.

300 HRV ISSN 1847-2397
H8.C76
▼ **SUVREMENE TEME/CONTEMPORARY ISSUES.** Text in Croatian, English. 2009. s-a. free (effective 2011). **Document type:** *Journal, Academic/Scholarly.*
Media: Online - full text.
Indexed: PSA, T02.
Published by: Centar za Politoloska Istrazivanja/Political Science Research Centre, Gupceva 14 A, Zagreb, 10090, Croatia. cpi@cpi.hr, http://www.cpi.hr. Ed. Vladimir Lay.

300 100 CHN ISSN 1001-4403
AS452.S917
➤ **SUZHOU DAXUE XUEBAO (ZHEXUE SHEHUI KEXUE BAN)/SUZHOU UNIVERSITY. JOURNAL (PHILOSOPHY AND SOCIAL SCIENCES).** Text in Chinese. 1906. q. USD 24.60 (effective 2009). adv. bk.rev. **Document type:** *Academic/Scholarly.* **Description:** Covers the studies of the Chinese language, Chinese and foreign literature, history, law, economics, philosophy, and psychology with special columns featuring the studies of poetry and prose of the Ming and Qing dynasties, Wu culture, and local history of Suzhou.
Formerly (until 1982): Dongwu Daxue. Xuebao
Related titles: Online - full text ed.
Published by: Suzhou Daxue/Soochow University, 1 Shizi Jie, Suzhou, Jiangsu 215006, China. TEL 86-512-5112857, FAX 86-512-5236257. Ed. Chen Shao Ying. R&P Shao Ying Chen. Adv. contact Shao-ying Chen. Circ: 2,500. **Dist. overseas by:** China Publication Foreign Trade Company, PO Box 782, Beijing 100011, China.

300 CHN
SUZHOU KEJI XUEYUAN XUEBAO (SHEHUI KEXUE BAN)/ UNIVERSITY OF SCIENCE AND TECHNOLOGY OF SUZHOU. JOURNAL (SOCIAL SCIENCE). Text in Chinese. 1984. q. **Document type:** *Journal, Academic/Scholarly.*
Former titles: Suzhou Keji Xueyuan Xuebao/University of Science and Technology of Suzhou. Journal (1672-0695); Which was formed by the merger of: Suzhou Tiedao Shifan Xueyuan Xuebao (Shehui Kexue Ban)/Suzhou Railway Teachers College. Journal (Social Science Edition) (1009-394X); Suzhou Chengshi Jianshe Huanjing Baohu Xueyuan Xuebao (She-ke Ban)/Suzhou Institute of Urban Construction and Environmental Protection. Journal (Social Science) (1009-2579)
Related titles: Print ed.
Published by: Suzhou Keji Xueyuan, Shihu Xiao-qu, Shangfangshan Tieshi Lu, Suzhou, 215009, China. TEL 86-512-68418315.

SUZHOU XUEYUAN XUEBAO. *see* SCIENCES: COMPREHENSIVE WORKS

307.1 CHE ISSN 1661-3082
SWISSFUTURE. Text in English, French, German. 1972. 4/yr. CHF 100 membership; CHF 30 to students (effective 2008). bk.rev. abstr.; bibl.; charts; stat. back issues avail. **Document type:** *Bulletin, Trade.* **Description:** Focuses on long-range planning, forecasts, strategic management and futures research.
Former titles (until 2003): Zukunftsforschung (1661-3074); (until 1982): S Z F-Bulletin
Published by: Swissfuture - Schweizerische Vereinigung fuer Zukunftsforschung/Swiss Association for Futures Research, Spitalgasse 24, Bern 7, 3000, Switzerland. TEL 41-31-3201912, FAX 41-31-3201910, future@swissfuture.ch, http://www.swissfuture.ch. Circ: 1,020.

300 USA ISSN 0195-6086
HM1
➤ **SYMBOLIC INTERACTION.** Abbreviated title: S I. Text in English. 1977. q. GBP 250 combined subscription in United Kingdom to institutions (print & online eds.); EUR 293 combined subscription in Europe to institutions (print & online eds.); USD 389 combined subscription elsewhere to institutions (print & online eds.) (effective 2012). adv. 170 p./no.; back issues avail.; reprint service avail. from PSC. **Document type:** *Journal, Academic/Scholarly.* **Description:** Emphasizes empirically grounded research based upon ethnographic and other qualitative methods.
Related titles: Microform ed.: USD 193.50 to institutions (effective 2002 - 2003) (from PQC); Online - full text ed.: ISSN 1533-8665. GBP 227 in United Kingdom to institutions; EUR 266 in Europe to institutions; USD 353 elsewhere to institutions (effective 2012) (from IngentaConnect).
Indexed: A01, A02, A03, A08, A20, A22, ABS&EES, ASCA, CA, CommAb, CurCont, E-psyche, E01, FamI, IBSS, MEA&I, P03, P10, P25, P46, P48, P50, P53, P54, PQC, PsycInfo, PsycholAb, S02, S03, S11, SCOPUS, SOPODA, SSA, SSCI, SociolAb, T02, W07.
—BLDSC (8582.080000), IE, Infotrieve, Ingenta. **CCC.**
Published by: (Society for the Study of Symbolic Interaction), Wiley-Blackwell Publishing, Inc. (Subsidiary of: Wiley-Blackwell Publishing Ltd.), 111 River St, Hoboken, NJ 07030. TEL 201-748-6000, FAX 201-748-6088, info@wiley.com, http://www.wiley.com/WileyCDA/. Ed. Carol Rambo. Circ: 596.

➤ **SYMMETRY**; culture and science. *see* SCIENCES: COMPREHENSIVE WORKS

300 USA
➤ **SYMPOSIUM SERIES.** Text in English. 1970. irreg., latest vol.79, 2004. price varies. back issues avail. **Document type:** *Monographic series, Academic/Scholarly.*
Indexed: ISR.
Published by: Edwin Mellen Press, 415 Ridge St, PO Box 450, Lewiston, NY 14092. TEL 716-754-2266, FAX 716-754-4056, cservice@mellenpress.com.

▼ ➤ **SYNERGIES CANADA.** *see* LINGUISTICS

300 401 ROM ISSN 1841-8333
SYNERGIES ROUMANIE. Text in French, Romanian. 2006. a. **Document type:** *Journal, Academic/Scholarly.*
Related titles: Online - full text ed.: free (effective 2011).
Published by: Centrul de Cercetari Literare si Enciclopedice, Str Horea 31, Cabinet 140, Cluj-Napoca, 400202, Romania. FAX 40-264-598343. Ed. Dorin Constantin Domuta.

SYNTHESE LIBRARY; studies in epistemology, logic, methodology and philosophy of science. *see* PHILOSOPHY

SYNTHESIS LECTURES ON ENGINEERS, TECHNOLOGY AND SOCIETY. *see* ENGINEERING

SYSTEM DYNAMICS REVIEW. *see* BUSINESS AND ECONOMICS—Management

300 GBR ISSN 0961-8309
➤ **THE SYSTEMIST.** Text in English. 1979. q. back issues avail. **Document type:** *Journal, Academic/Scholarly.* **Description:** Provides a platform for systems thinkers and practitioners to communicate their experiences of using systems ideas, and promotes the development of systems theory, concepts and practice.
Related titles: Online - full text ed.: eSystemist. free to members (effective 2009).
Indexed: Inspec.
—CCC.
Published by: U K Systems Society, 34 Stean Bridge Rd, Bristol, BS32 8AH, United Kingdom. TEL 44-117-9076124, FAX 44-117-9311590, http://www.ukss.org.uk/. Ed. Frank Stowell TEL 44-2392-846021.

300 POL ISSN 0860-2212
H8.P6
SZCZECINSKIE ROCZNIKI NAUKOWE, NAUKI SPOLECZNE. Variant title: Annales Scientiarum Stetinenses, Nauki Spoleczne. Text in Polish; Summaries in English, Russian. 1986. a. price varies. **Document type:** *Academic/Scholarly.* **Description:** Papers on different research fields by scientists from the region of Szczecin Pomerania.
Published by: Szczecinskie Towarzystwo Naukowe, ul Wojska Polskiego 96, Szczecin, 71481, Poland. wtarc@univ.szczecin.pl. Ed. Eugeniusz Mietkiewski.

300 POL ISSN 0082-1292
SZCZECINSKIE TOWARZYSTWO NAUKOWE. WYDZIAL NAUK SPOLECZNYCH. PRACE. Text in Polish; Summaries in English, German, Russian. 1959. irreg. price varies. **Document type:** *Academic/Scholarly.*
Published by: (Szczecinskie Towarzystwo Naukowe, Wydzial Nauk Spolecznych), Szczecinskie Towarzystwo Naukowe, ul Wojska Polskiego 96, Szczecin, 71481, Poland. TEL 48-91-4231862, wtarc@univ.szczecin.pl, http://www.stn.szc.pl. Circ: 400.

340 ARG ISSN 1850-972X
TABLAS DE CONTENIDOS EN CIENCIAS JURIDICAS Y CIENCIAS SOCIALES. Text in Spanish. 1998. bi-m. **Document type:** *Bulletin.*
Published by: Universidad del Salvador, Rodriguez Pena No. 770 2o, Buenos Aires, Argentina. TEL 54-11-48139630, FAX 54-11-48124625, rect@salvador.edu.ar, http://www.salvador.edu.ar/.

TAGUNGEN ZUR OSTMITTELEUROPA-FORSCHUNG. *see* HISTORY—History Of Europe

300 500 CHN ISSN 1672-2590
TAISHAN XUEYUAN XUEBAO/TAISHAN UNIVERSITY. JOURNAL. Text in Chinese. 1979. bi-m. CNY 6 newsstand/cover (effective 2006). **Document type:** *Journal, Academic/Scholarly.*
Formerly: Taian Shi-Zhuan Xuebao (1003-7888)
Related titles: Online - full text ed.
—BLDSC (8598.536300).
Published by: Taishan Xueyuan, Dongyue Dajie Xi Shou, Taian, 271021, China. TEL 86-538-6715561.

320.9 CHN ISSN 1006-6683
DS798.92
TAIWAN YANJIU/TAIWAN STUDY. Text in Chinese. 1988. bi-m. USD 36 (effective 2009). **Document type:** *Journal, Academic/Scholarly.* **Description:** Contains mainland Chinese studies of Taiwan society.
Published by: Zhongguo Shehui Kexueyuan, Taiwan Yanjiusuo, 15, Yiheyuan Beiposhangcun, Beijing, 100091, China. TEL 86-10-82864912. **Dist. by:** China International Book Trading Corp, 35 Chegongzhuang Xilu, Haidian District, PO Box 399, Beijing 100044, China. TEL 86-10-68412045, FAX 86-10-68412023, cibtc@mail.cibtc.com.cn, http://www.cibtc.com.cn.

300 CHN ISSN 1009-5837
TAIYUAN LIGONG DAXUE XUEBAO (SHEHUI KEXUE BAN)/TAIYUAN UNIVERSITY OF TECHNOLOGY. JOURNAL (SOCIAL SCIENCES EDITION). Text in Chinese. 1983. q. CNY 6 newsstand/cover (effective 2006). **Document type:** *Journal, Academic/Scholarly.*
Related titles: Online - full text ed.
Published by: Taiyuan Ligong Daxue, Yingze Xi Dajie Xinkuangyuan Lu #18, Taiyuan, 030024, China. TEL 86-351-6018486.

TAIZHOU ZHIYE JISHU XUEYUAN XUEBAO/TAIZHOU POLYTECHNICAL INSTITUTE. JOURNAL. *see* SCIENCES: COMPREHENSIVE WORKS

300 GBR ISSN 2040-3194
TAKING THE LONG VIEW. Text in English. 1991. a. free (effective 2010). back issues avail. **Document type:** *Journal, Academic/Scholarly.* **Description:** Provides an overview of the research and other activity undertaken by ISER in the past year.
Former titles (until 2000): I S E R Reports (1464-8350); (until 1998): E S R C Research Centre on Micro-social Change in Britain. Occasional Papers (0962-7790)
Related titles: Online - full text ed.: ISSN 2043-6823. free (effective 2010).
Published by: University of Essex, Institute for Social & Economic Research, Wivenhoe Park, Colchester, Essex CO4 3SQ, United Kingdom. TEL 44-1206-872957, FAX 44-1206-873151, iser@essex.ac.uk.

300 USA ISSN 1532-5555
➤ **TAMARA**; journal for critical organization inquiry. Text in English. 200?. q. USD 60 to individuals; USD 250 to institutions (effective 2010). adv. abstr. back issues avail.; reprints avail. **Document type:** *Journal, Academic/Scholarly.* **Description:** Aims to combine critical theory as well as postmodern theory and postcolonial theory and critical pedagogy with praxis.
Formerly (until 2002): Journal of Critical Postmodern Organization Science
Related titles: Online - full text ed.: ISSN 1545-6420.
Indexed: B01, B04, B06, B07, B09, CA, P10, P45, P48, P53, P54, PQC, S02, S03, SSAI, SSAb, SSI, T02, W03, W05.
—BLDSC (8601.538000).
Address: Department of Management, MSC 3DJ, New Mexico State University, PO Box 30001, Las Cruces, NM 88003. TEL 575-646-1001, FAX 575-646-1372. Ed. Heather Hopfl.

301 PHL ISSN 0117-6323
DS651
TAMBARA; Ateneo de Davao University journal. Text in English. 1984. a. PHP 250, USD 13 (effective 2000). bk.rev. **Document type:** *Journal, Academic/Scholarly.* **Description:** Covers community studies on socio-cultural, historical, and theological issues in Mindanao.
Indexed: BAS, IPP, MLA-IB.
Published by: Ateneo de Davao University, PO Box 13, Davao City, Davao Del Sur 8000, Philippines. TEL 63-221-2411. Ed., R&P Heidi K Gloria. Circ: 1,000 (paid).

300 972 PAN ISSN 0494-7061
F1561
➤ **TAREAS.** Text in Spanish. 1960. q. USD 12 domestic; USD 24 foreign (effective 2003). bk.rev. back issues avail. **Document type:** *Academic/Scholarly.*
Indexed: C01, IBR, IBSS, IBZ, RASB.
Published by: Centro de Estudios Latinoamericanos "Justo Arosemena", Apdo. 87-1918, Panama City, 7, Panama. TEL 507-2230028, FAX 507-2692032, celaja@pty.com. R&P M A Gandasegui. Circ: 1,500.

390 IND
➤ **TATTVADIPAH/ACADEMY OF SANSKRIT RESEARCH. JOURNAL.** Text in English. 1988. s-a. INR 240 per issue (effective 2011). **Document type:** *Journal, Academic/Scholarly.*
Published by: Academy of Sanskrit Research, Melkote, Mandya Dist., Karnataka 571 431, India. asrbng@vsnl.com. Circ: 1,997.

300 DEU
TECHNIK - KOERPER - GESELLSCHAFT. Text in German. 2008. irreg., latest vol.4, 2009. price varies. **Document type:** *Monographic series, Academic/Scholarly.*
Published by: Transcript, Muehlenstr 47, Bielefeld, 33607, Germany. TEL 49-521-63454, FAX 49-521-61040, live@transcript-verlag.de.

TECHNOLOGIES IDEOLOGIES PRATIQUES; revue d'anthropologie des connaissances. *see* ANTHROPOLOGY

TELOS; revista de estudios interdisciplinarios en ciencias sociales. *see* HUMANITIES: COMPREHENSIVE WORKS

300 PER
TEMAS DE ACTUALIDAD. Text in Spanish. irreg., latest no.120, 1995. price varies. **Document type:** *Monographic series.*
Published by: Centro de Estudios Regionales Andinos "Bartolome de Las Casas", Pampa de la Alianza 164, Cusco, Peru. TEL 51-14-229992, FAX 51-14-427894. Pub. Andres Chirinos Rivera.

600 VEN ISSN 1316-5003
HC236
TEMAS DE COYUNTURA. Text in Spanish. 1992. s-a. **Document type:** *Journal, Academic/Scholarly.*
Related titles: Online - full text ed.
Indexed: A01, A26, CA, F03, F04, I04, I05, T02.
Published by: Universidad Catolica Andres Bello, Instituto de Investigaciones Economicas y Sociales, Apdo 29068, Caracas, 1023-A, Venezuela. lespana@ucab.edu.ve, http://www.ucab.edu.ve/cai/index.htm#Contactos.

300 MEX ISSN 0188-9273
F1306
TEMAS SUBJECTIVIDAD Y PROCESOS SOCIALES. Text in Spanish. 1992. s-a. back issues avail. **Document type:** *Journal, Academic/Scholarly.*
Indexed: C01.
Published by: Universidad Autonoma Metropolitana - Xochimilco, Calz del Hueso 1100, Col Villa Quietud, Mexico City, DF 04960, Mexico. TEL 52-5-7245050, FAX 52-5-6716702, http://www.uam.mx/.

S

300 SVN ISSN 0040-3598
DR381.S6 CODEN: TEPRFU
➤ **TEORIJA IN PRAKSA**; revija za druzbena vprasanja. Text in Slovenian, English. 1964. bi-m. EUR 50 to individuals; EUR 100 to institutions (effective 2009). bk.rev. index. back issues avail. **Document type:** *Journal, Academic/Scholarly.*
Indexed: CA, DIP, I13, IBR, IBZ, MLA-IB, P42, PSA, RASB, S02, S03, SOPODA, SSA, SociolAb, T02.
Published by: Univerza v Ljubljani, Fakulteta za Druzbene Vede/University of Ljubljana, Faculty of Social Sciences, Kerdeljeva Poscad 5, Ljubljana, 1000, Slovenia. TEL 386-1-5805100, FAX 386-1-5805101, fdv.faculty@fdv.uni-lj.si, http://www.fdv.uni-lj.si. Ed. Anton Grizold. Circ: 4,500. **Co-sponsor:** Kulturna Skupnost Slovenije.

301 ESP ISSN 0210-3524
DP302.T31
TERUEL. Text in Spanish, English. 1949. s-a. EUR 5.40 newsstand/cover (effective 2009). back issues avail. **Document type:** *Journal, Academic/Scholarly.*
Indexed: GeoRef, MLA-IB.
Published by: Instituto de Estudios Turolenses, Amantes 15, 2a Planta, Teruel, 44001, Spain. TEL 34-978-617860, FAX 34-978-617861, ieturolenses@dpteruel.es, http://www.dpteruel.es/.

300 DEU
TEXTE DER FAKULTAET FUER STUDIUM GENERALE UND INTERDISZIPLINAERE STUDIEN DER HOCHSCHULE MUENCHEN. Text in German. 2002. irreg., latest vol.7, 2010. price varies. **Document type:** *Monographic series, Academic/Scholarly.*
Formerly (until 2008): Texte des Fachbereich Allgemeinwissenschaften (1614-0133)
Published by: Rainer Hampp Verlag, Marktplatz 5, Mering, 86415, Germany. TEL 49-8233-4783, FAX 49-8233-30755, info@rhverlag.de, http://www.rhverlag.de.

TEXTUAL STUDIES IN CANADA; Canada's journal of cultural literacy. *see* LITERARY AND POLITICAL REVIEWS

300 NLD ISSN 1570-7253
THAMYRIS / INTERSECTING; place, sex and race. Variant title: Thamyris Intersecting. Text in English. 1994. irreg., latest vol.19, 2008. price varies. **Document type:** *Monographic series, Academic/Scholarly.*
Formerly (until 2001): Thamyris (1381-1312)
Related titles: Online - full text ed.: ISSN 1879-5846 (from IngentaConnect).
Indexed: A01, A03, A08, CA, I14, MLA-IB, PAIS, S02, S03, T02.
—BLDSC (8814.230700), IE, Ingenta. **CCC.**
Published by: Editions Rodopi B.V., Tijnmuiden 7, Amsterdam, 1046 AK, Netherlands. TEL 31-20-6114821, FAX 31-20-4472979, info@rodopi.nl. Ed. Dr. Ernst van Alphen.

300 DEU ISSN 1610-4277
THEMATICON; Wissenschaftliche Reihe des Collegium Polonicum. Text in German. 2002. irreg., latest vol.15, 2010. price varies. **Document type:** *Monographic series, Academic/Scholarly.*
Published by: (Collegium Polonicum), Logos Verlag Berlin, Comeniushof, Gubener Str 47, Berlin, 10243, Germany. TEL 49-30-42851090, FAX 49-30-42851092, redaktion@logos-verlag.de.

300 DEU ISSN 1439-1805
THEODOR-LITT-JAHRBUCH. Text in German. 1999. irreg., latest vol.7, 2010. price varies. **Document type:** *Monographic series, Academic/Scholarly.*
Published by: Leipziger Universitaetsverlag GmbH, Oststr 41, Leipzig, 04317, Germany. TEL 49-341-9900440, FAX 49-341-9900440, info@univerlag-leipzig.de.

300 DEU ISSN 1868-274X
▼ **THEOPHRASTUS PARACELSUS STUDIEN.** Text in German. 2009. irreg., latest vol.3, 2011. price varies. **Document type:** *Monographic series, Academic/Scholarly.*
Published by: Walter de Gruyter GmbH & Co. KG, Genthiner Str 13, Berlin, 10785, Germany. TEL 49-30-260050, FAX 49-30-26005251, info@degruyter.com, http://www.degruyter.de.

THEORIA; a journal of social and political theory. *see* HUMANITIES: COMPREHENSIVE WORKS

300 DEU
THEORIE UND METHODE. Text in German. 1999. irreg., latest vol.58, 2011. price varies. **Document type:** *Monographic series, Academic/Scholarly.*
Published by: U V K Verlagsgesellschaft mbH, Schuetzenstr 24, Konstanz, 78462, Germany. TEL 49-7531-90530, FAX 49-7531-905398, nadine.ley@uvk.de, http://www.uvk.de.

300 100 USA ISSN 0040-5833
H61 CODEN: THDCBA
➤ **THEORY AND DECISION**; an international journal for multidisciplinary advances in decision sciences. Text in English. 1970. 8/yr. (in 2 vols., 4 nos./vol.). EUR 1,217, USD 1,361 combined subscription to institutions (print & online eds.) (effective 2012). adv. bk.rev. illus. Index. back issues avail.; reprint service avail. from PSC. **Document type:** *Journal, Academic/Scholarly.* **Description:** Features papers discussing issues related to the engineering of decision making, including intelligence, choice, uncertainty and conflict resolution.
Related titles: Microform ed.: (from PQC); Online - full text ed.: ISSN 1573-7187 (from IngentaConnect).
Indexed: A12, A13, A20, A22, A26, A28, ABIn, APA, ASCA, BibLing, BrCerAb, C&ISA, CA, CA/WCA, CCMJ, CIA, CIS, CPEI, CerAb, CivEngAb, CorrAb, CurCont, DIP, E&CAJ, E-psyche, E01, E11, EEA, EMA, ESPM, EconLit, EngInd, EnvEAb, FR, H15, IBR, IBSS, IBZ, IPB, JCQM, JEL, M&TEA, M09, MBF, METADEX, MSN, MathR, P03, P10, P13, P25, P27, P30, P42, P48, P51, P52, P53, P54, PCI, PQC, PSA, PhilInd, PsycInfo, PsycholAb, RASB, RefZh, RiskAb, S02, S03, S11, SCOPUS, SOPODA, SSA, SSCI, SociolAb, SolStAb, T02, T04, W07, WAA, Z02.
—BLDSC (8814.627000), IE, Infotrieve, Ingenta, INIST, Linda Hall. **CCC.**
Published by: Springer New York LLC (Subsidiary of: Springer Science+Business Media), 233 Spring St, New York, NY 10013. TEL 212-460-1500, FAX 212-460-1575, service-ny@springer.com. Ed. Mohammed Abdellaoui. **Subscr. to:** Journal Fulfillment, PO Box 2485, Secaucus, NJ 07096. TEL 201-348-4033, FAX 201-348-4505, journals-ny@springer.com.

300 100 NLD ISSN 0921-3384
➤ **THEORY AND DECISION LIBRARY. SERIES A: PHILOSOPHY AND METHODOLOGY OF THE SOCIAL SCIENCES.** Text in English. 1973; N.S. 1987. irreg., latest vol.46, 2009. price varies. back issues avail. **Document type:** *Monographic series, Academic/Scholarly.* **Description:** Covers the foundations, general methodology, and the criteria, goald and purpose of the social sciences.
Supersedes in part (in 1987): Theory and Decision Library (0921-3376)
Indexed: CIS.
—BLDSC (8814.628020). **CCC.**
Published by: Springer Netherlands (Subsidiary of: Springer Science+Business Media), Van Godewijckstraat 30, Dordrecht, 3311 GX, Netherlands. TEL 31-78-6576050, FAX 31-78-6576474. Ed. Julian Nida-Rumelin.

➤ **THEORY AND DECISION LIBRARY. SERIES B: MATHEMATICAL AND STATISTICAL METHODS.** *see* MATHEMATICS

➤ **THEORY AND DECISION LIBRARY. SERIES C: GAME THEORY, MATHEMATICAL PROGRAMMING AND OPERATIONS RESEARCH.** *see* MATHEMATICS—Computer Applications

➤ **THEORY AND DECISION LIBRARY. SERIES D: SYSTEM THEORY, KNOWLEDGE ENGINEERING AND PROBLEM SOLVING.** *see* COMPUTERS—Cybernetics

➤ **THEORY AND RESEARCH IN SOCIAL EDUCATION.** *see* EDUCATION—Teaching Methods And Curriculum

300 USA ISSN 1937-0229
H1
➤ **THEORY IN ACTION.** Text in English. 2008. q. USD 105 combined subscription to individuals (print & online eds.); USD 200 combined subscription to institutions (print & online eds.) (effective 2010). bk.rev. Index. back issues avail. **Document type:** *Journal, Academic/Scholarly.* **Description:** Provides a forum for the exchange of ideas and the discussion of current research (qualitative and quantitative) on the interconnections between theory and action aimed at promoting social justice.
Related titles: Online - full text ed.: ISSN 1937-0237.
Indexed: AltPI, AmHI, B04, CA, H07, MLA-IB, P42, PSA, SSAI, SSAb, SSI, SociolAb, T02, W03, W05.
Published by: Transformative Studies Institute, 39-09 Berdan Ave, Fair Lawn, NJ 07410. TEL 201-254-3595, orders@transformativestudies.org, http://www.transformativestudies.org. Eds. Ali Shehzad Zaidi, John Asimakopoulos.

300 RUS
THESIS. Text in Russian. irreg. USD 75 in United States.
Indexed: RASB.
Published by: Mezhdistsiplinarnyi Akademicheskii Tsentr Sotsyal'nykh Nauk, Ul M Dzhalilya 34, Moscow, 115573, Russian Federation. TEL 7-095-1281774. Ed. A V Poletaev. **Dist. by:** East View Information Services, 10601 Wayzata Blvd, Minneapolis, MN 55305. TEL 952-252-1201, 800-477-1005, FAX 952-252-1202, info@eastview.com, http://www.eastview.com.

300 AUS ISSN 1323-9163
➤ **THIRD SECTOR REVIEW.** Abbreviated title: T S R. Text in English. 1995. s-a. back issues avail. **Document type:** *Journal, Academic/Scholarly.* **Description:** Contains theoretical and empirical papers on the characteristics of the third sector or any aspect of its management, including governance, human resource management, the labor market, financial management, strategic management and managing change, community development, fund-raising, user rights, relations with government, legal issues, historical developments.
Indexed: A26, AusPAIS, E08, I05, N06, T02.
Published by: Australian and New Zealand Third Sector Research Inc., c/o Social Justice & Social Change Research Centre, College of Social & Health Sciences, University of Western Sydney, Bankstown Campus, Locked Bag 1797, Penrith South DC, NSW 1797, Australia. TEL 61-2-97726376, FAX 61-2-97726450, anztsr@uws.edu.au. Ed. Rosemary Leonard TEL 61-2-96787322. Pub. Rose Leonard. Circ: 300.

300 CHN ISSN 1004-0633
DS793.S8
TIANFU XINLUN/TIAN FU NEW IDEA. Text in Chinese. 1985. bi-m. USD 24.60 (effective 2009). **Document type:** *Journal, Academic/Scholarly.*
Related titles: Online - full text ed.
—East View.
Address: Dashi Xilu Kelian Jie 12, Chengdu, 610017, China. TEL 86-28-82973512, FAX 86-28-82973516.

300 CHN ISSN 1008-4339
TIANJIN DAXUE XUEBAO (SHEHUI KEXUE BAN)/TIANJIN UNIVERSITY. JOURNAL (SOCIAL SCIENCES EDITION). Text in Chinese. 1999. bi-m. **Document type:** *Journal, Academic/Scholarly.*
Related titles: Online - full text ed.: (from WanFang Data Corp.).
Published by: Tianjin Daxue Jikan Zhongxin/Academic Journals Publishing Center of Tianjin University, 92, Weijin Lu NanKai, Tianjin, 300072, China. TEL 86-22-27400282, FAX 86-22-27403448, tdxbeb@tju.edu.cn, http://www2.tju.edu.cn/orgs/journal/default.htm.

300 CHN ISSN 1002-3976
TIANJIN SHEHUI KEXUE/TIANJIN SOCIAL SCIENCES. Text in Chinese. bi-m. USD 29.40 (effective 2009). **Document type:** *Academic/Scholarly.*
Related titles: Online - full text ed.
Indexed: RASB.
—East View.
Published by: (Tianjin Shehui Kexueyuan), Tianjin Shehui Kexue Zazhishe, 7 Yingshuidao, Nankai-qu, Tianjin 300191, China. TEL 86-22-3369296. **Dist. overseas by:** China International Book Trading Corp, 35 Chegongzhuang Xilu, Haidian District, PO Box 399, Beijing 100044, China.

300 CHN ISSN 1671-1106
TIANJIN SHIFAN DAXUE XUEBAO (SHEHUI KEXUE BAN)/TIANJIN NORMAL UNIVERSITY. JOURNAL (SOCIAL SCIENCE). Text in Chinese. 1974. bi-m. USD 18 (effective 2009). **Document type:** *Journal, Academic/Scholarly.*
Former titles (until 2000): Tianjin Shi-Da Xuebao (Shehui Kexue Ban) (1001-7712); (until 1987): Tianjin Shi-Da Xuebao (1001-7704); (until 1982): Tianjin Shi-Yuan Xuebao (1001-7690)
Related titles: Online - full text ed.
—East View.
Published by: Tianjin Shifan Daxue/Tianjin Normal University, 40, Gansu Road, Heping District, Tianjin, 300020, China. TEL 86-22-27232792, FAX 86-22-27217311.

300 CHN ISSN 1006-5261
TIANZHONG XUEKAN/JOURNAL OF TIANZHONG. Text in Chinese. 1986. bi-m. USD 31.20 (effective 2009). **Document type:** *Journal, Academic/Scholarly.*
Related titles: Online - full text ed.
—East View.
Published by: Huanghuai Xueyuan/Huanghuai University, 599, Wenhua Lu, Zhumadian, 463000, China.

300 NOR ISSN 0040-716X
➤ **TIDSSKRIFT FOR SAMFUNNSFORSKNING**; Norwegian journal of social research. Text in Norwegian; Summaries in English. 1960. q. NOK 500 to individuals; NOK 1,030 to institutions; NOK 270 to students (effective 2010). bk.rev. bibl.; charts; stat. index. back issues avail.; reprints avail. **Document type:** *Journal, Academic/Scholarly.*
Related titles: Microfilm ed.; Online - full text ed.: ISSN 1504-291X. 2004. NOK 1,130 (effective 2010).
Indexed: A20, A22, ASCA, B21, CA, CurCont, HistAb, IBR, IBZ, MLA-IB, P30, P42, PSA, RASB, S02, S03, S21, SCOPUS, SOPODA, SSA, SSCI, SociolAb, T02, W07.
—IE, Infotrieve.
Published by: (Institutt for Samfunnsforskning/Institute for Social Research), Universitetsforlaget AS/Scandinavian University Press (Subsidiary of: Aschehoug & Co.), Sehesteds Gate 3, P O Box 508, Sentrum, Oslo, 0105, Norway. TEL 47-24-147500, FAX 47-24-147501, post@universitetsforlaget.no, http://www.universitetsforlaget.no. Ed. Karl Henrik Sivesind TEL 47-23-086127. Circ: 800.

300 VEN ISSN 0798-2968
TIERRA FIRME. Text in Spanish. 1983. q. VEB 20 domestic; USD 80 foreign (effective 2009). back issues avail. **Document type:** *Journal, Academic/Scholarly.*
Indexed: C01, CA, IBR, IBZ, PSA, SCOPUS, SociolAb.
Published by: Fundacion Tierra Firme, Ave Edison, Centro Comercial Los Chaguaramos, Piso 9 Ofic. No. 9-9, Caracas, 1041-1, Venezuela. TEL 58-212-6624517, FAX 58-212-6936950, serik@cantv.net, http://www2.bvs.org.ve/scielo.php?script=sci_serial&pid=0798-2968&lng=es.

TIJDSCHRIFT VOOR ECONOMISCHE EN SOCIALE GEOGRAFIE/ JOURNAL OF ECONOMIC AND SOCIAL GEOGRAPHY. *see* GEOGRAPHY

300 BOL ISSN 1990-7451
T'INKAZOS. Variant title: Revista Boliviana de Ciencias Sociales Tinkazos. Text in Spanish. 1997. 3/yr.
Related titles: Online - full text ed.: free (effective 2011) (from SciELO).
Published by: Fundacion para la Investigacion Estrategica en Bolivia, Edificio Fortaleza, Piso 6, Of 601, Av Arce 2700 Esq Cordero, La Paz, Bolivia. TEL 591-2-2432582, FAX 591-2-2431866.

300 363.7 CAN ISSN 1196-8206
TOK BLONG PASIFIK. Text in English. 1982. q. **Document type:** *Newsletter.*
Formerly (until 1993): Tok Blong S P P F (0828-9670)
Related titles: Online - full text ed.
Indexed: CPerI, CWI, G05, G06, G07, G08, I05.
Published by: South Pacific Peoples Foundation Of Canada, 1921 Fernwood Rd, Victoria, BC V8T 2Y6, Canada. TEL 250-381-4131, FAX 250-388-5258, sppf@sppf.org, http://www.sppf.org.

TOKAI DAIGAKU KIYO. BUNGAKUBU/TOKAI UNIVERSITY. FACULTY OF LETTERS. BULLETIN. *see* HUMANITIES: COMPREHENSIVE WORKS

300 JPN ISSN 0288-5530
TOKYO DENKI UNIVERSITY. FACULTY OF ENGINEERING. GENERAL EDUCATION. RESEARCH REPORTS. Text in Japanese; Summaries in English, Japanese. 1951. a. back issues avail. **Document type:** *Academic/Scholarly.* **Description:** Contains academic research reports of the faculty members in the field of general education, business and economics, humanities, social sciences, law, literature, linguistics and physical fitness and hygiene.
Published by: Tokyo Denki Daigaku, Kogakubu/Tokyo Denki University, Faculty of Engineering, 2-2 Kanda-Nishiki-cho, Chiyoda-ku, Tokyo, 101-0054, Japan. TEL 81-3-5280-3522, FAX 81-3-5280-3588. Ed. Hideki Hiroishi.

300 JPN
TOKYO KASEI DAIGAKU KENKYU KIYO. 1. JUNBUN SHAKAI KAGAKU/TOKYO KASEI UNIVERSITY. BULLETIN. 1. CULTURAL AND SOCIAL SCIENCE. Text and summaries in English, Japanese. 1985. a. **Document type:** *Bulletin, Academic/Scholarly.*
Supersedes in part (in 1989): Tokyo Kasei Daigaku Kenkyu Kiyo/Tokyo Kasei University. Bulletin; Which was formerly (until 1988): Tokyo Kasei Daigaku Kenkyu Kiyo. Jinbun Kagaku, Shizen Kagaku/Tokyo Kasei University. Bulletin. Cultural, Social and Natural Science; Which was formed by the merger of (1956-1985): Tokyo Kasei Daigaku Kenkyu Kiyo. 1 Jinbun Kagaku/Tokyo Kasei University. Bulletin. 1, Cultural and Social Science (0385-1206); (1956-1985): Tokyo Kasei Daigaku Kenkyu Kiyo. 2 Shizen Kagaku/Tokyo Kasei University. Bulletin. 2, Natural Science (0385-1214); Both of which superseded in part (in 1975): Tokyo Kasei Daigaku Kenkyu Kiyo/Tokyo College of Domestic Science. Bulletin (0371-831X)
Indexed: ChemAb, PsycholAb.
Published by: Tokyo Kasei Daigaku/Tokyo Kasei University, 1-18-1 Kaga, Itabashi, Tokyo, 173-0003, Japan. TEL 81-3-39615226, http://www.tokyo-kasei.ac.jp/.

300 CHN ISSN 1009-3060
TONGJI DAXUE XUEBAO (SHEHUI KEXUE BAN)/TONGJI UNIVERSITY. JOURNAL (SOCIAL SCIENCE SECTION). Text in Chinese. 1990. bi-m. USD 24.60 (effective 2009). **Document type:** *Journal, Academic/Scholarly.*
Related titles: Online - full text ed.
—East View.
Published by: Tongji Daxue/Tongji University, 1239, Siping Lu, Di-3 Jiaxue Bldg., Rm. 423, Shanghai, 200092, China.

300 CHN ISSN 1003-0484
DS777.75
TONGYI LUNTAN/UNITED TRIBUNE. Text in Chinese. 1989. bi-m. USD 31.20 (effective 2009). 56 p./no.; **Description:** Covers politics, current affairs, and social and cultural events.

Related titles: Online - full text ed.
—East View.
Published by: Tongyi Luntan Zazhishe, 74 Xishiku Daijie, Xichen, Beijing, 100034, China. TEL 86-10-6036916, FAX 86-10-6063320. Ed. Miu Qun. Circ: 10,000.

TOPIC (WASHINGTON); the Washington & Jefferson College review. *see* HUMANITIES: COMPREHENSIVE WORKS

300 DEU ISSN 0949-541X
TOPICOS; Deutsch-Brasilianische Hefte. Text and summaries in German, Portuguese. 1960. q. EUR 26 (effective 2009). adv. bk.rev. **Document type:** *Trade.* **Description:** News and background on Brazilian topics in all areas.
Formerly (until 1995): Deutsch-Brasilianische Hefte (0341-7239)
Indexed: DIP, IBR, IBZ.
Published by: Deutsch-Brasilianische Gesellschaft e.V., Kaiserstr 201, Bonn, 53113, Germany. TEL 49-228-210707, FAX 49-228-241658. Ed. Geraldo Hoffmann. Pubs. Helmut Hoffman, Uwe Kaestner. adv.: B&W page EUR 1,700; 210 x 297. Circ: 8,000.

300 DEU ISSN 2191-5806
▼ **TOPOI**; Berlin Studies of the Ancient World. Text in German. 2011. irreg., latest vol.10, 2012. price varies. **Document type:** *Monographic series, Academic/Scholarly.*
Published by: Walter de Gruyter GmbH & Co. KG, Genthiner Str 13, Berlin, 10785, Germany. TEL 49-30-260050, FAX 49-30-26005251, info@degruyter.com, http://www.degruyter.de.

TOUKYOU GAKUGEI DAIGAKU KIYOU. JIMBUN SHAKAI KAGAKUKEI. 1/TOKYO GAKUGEI UNIVERSITY. BULLETIN. HUMANITIES AND SOCIAL SCIENCES. 1. *see* HUMANITIES: COMPREHENSIVE WORKS

TOUKYOU GAKUGEI DAIGAKU KIYOU. JIMBUN SHAKAI KAGAKUKEI. 2/TOKYO GAKUGEI UNIVERSITY. BULLETIN. HUMANITIES AND SOCIAL SCIENCES. 2. *see* HUMANITIES: COMPREHENSIVE WORKS

300 PER ISSN 1022-0941
TRABAJOS DEL COLEGIO ANDINO. Text in Spanish. 1990. irreg., latest 1996. price varies. **Document type:** *Monographic series.*
Formerly (until 1991): Estudios Andinos (Cuzco)
Published by: Centro de Estudios Regionales Andinos "Bartolome de Las Casas", Pampa de la Alianza 164, Cusco, Peru. TEL 51-14-429992, FAX 51-14-427894. Pub. Andres Chirinos Rivera.

TRAJECTOIRES. *see* HUMANITIES: COMPREHENSIVE WORKS

300 001.3 EST ISSN 1406-0922
H1 CODEN: TRMSF7
➤ **TRAMES.** Text in English; Summaries in Estonian, German, Russian. 1997. q. EUR 110; EUR 28 per issue (effective 2010). adv. bk.rev. charts; illus.; maps; abstr. index. 96 p./no.; **Document type:** *Journal, Academic/Scholarly.* **Description:** Publishes papers from a wide range of subjects in the humanities and social sciences.
Former titles (until 1997): Eesti Teaduste Akadeemia. Toimetised. Humanitaar ja Sotsiaalteadused; Eesti Teaduste Akadeemia. Toimetised. Uhiskonnateadused (0373-6431)
Related titles: Online - full text ed.: ISSN 1736-7514.
Indexed: A01, A03, A08, A20, A26, AICP, ArtHuCI, B04, CA, E08, HistAb, I05, L&LBA, P10, P42, P46, P48, PQC, PSA, PhilInd, S02, S03, S09, SCOPUS, SOPODA, SSA, SSAI, SSAb, SSCI, SSI, SociolAb, T02, W03, W05, W07.
Published by: (Eesti Teaduste Akadeemia/Estonian Academy of Sciences, Tartu Ulikool/University of Tartu), Teaduste Akadeemia Kirjastus/Estonian Academy Publishers, Kohtu 6, Tallinn, 10130, Estonia. TEL 372-6-454106, FAX 372-6-466026, asta@kirj.ee, http://www.kirj.ee. Ed. Urmas Sutrop. Circ: 700.

➤ **TRANSATLANTIC PERSPECTIVES**; a series of interdisciplinary North American studies. *see* HISTORY—History Of North And South America

300 FRA ISSN 1765-2766
E151
TRANSATLANTICA; revue d;'etudes americaines. Text in English, French. 2001. s-a. free (effective 2011). **Document type:** *Journal, Academic/Scholarly.*
Media: Online - full text.
Published by: Association Francaise d'Etudes Americaines Eds. Veronique Beghain, Vincent Michelot.

TRANSATLANTISCHE STUDIEN ZU MITTELALTER UND FRUEHER NEUZEIT/TRANSATLANTIC STUDIES ON MEDIEVAL AND EARLY MODERN LITERATURE AND CULTURE. *see* HISTORY—History Of Europe

300 FRA ISSN 1950-1684
TRANSCONTINENTALES. Text in French. 2005. s-a. EUR 45 combined subscription domestic to individuals (print & online eds.); EUR 55 combined subscription foreign to individuals (print & online eds.); EUR 59 combined subscription domestic to institutions (print & online eds.); EUR 65 combined subscription foreign to institutions (print & online eds.) (effective 2008). **Document type:** *Journal, Academic/Scholarly.*
Related titles: Online - full text ed.
Indexed: IBSS.
Published by: Armand Colin, 21 Rue du Montparnasse, Paris, 75283 Cedex 06, France. TEL 33-1-44395447, FAX 33-1-44394343, infos@armand-colin.fr. Ed. Jean-Luc Racine.

300 DEU
▼ **TRANSCRIPT KLASSIKER.** Text in German. 2009. irreg. price varies. **Document type:** *Monographic series, Academic/Scholarly.*
Published by: Transcript, Muehlenstr 47, Bielefeld, 33607, Germany. TEL 49-521-63454, FAX 49-521-61040, live@transcript-verlag.de.

300 DEU ISSN 1613-8414
TRANSCRIPTION; Kulturen Konzepte Kontroversen - cultures concepts controversies. Text in English, German. 2006. irreg., latest vol.4, 2009. price varies. **Document type:** *Monographic series, Academic/Scholarly.* **Description:** Focuses on explorations of North American cultural practices.
Published by: Peter Lang GmbH (Subsidiary of: Peter Lang Publishing Group), Eschborner Landstr 42-50, Frankfurt Am Main, 60489, Germany. TEL 49-69-7807050, FAX 49-69-78070550, zentrale.frankfurt@peterlang.com, http://www.peterlang.com. Ed. Sabine Sielke.

300 USA ISSN 1930-6253
GN345.7
➤ **TRANSCULTURAL STUDIES**; a series in interdisciplinary research. Text in English. 2005. a. USD 15 per issue to individuals; USD 20 per issue to institutions (effective 2010). back issues avail. **Document type:** *Journal, Academic/Scholarly.*
Indexed: CA, S02, S03, T02.
—BLDSC (9020.580670).
Published by: Charles Schlacks, Jr., PO Box 1256, Idyllwild, CA 92512. TEL 951-659-4641, info@schlacks.com. Eds. Evert van der Zweerde, Slobodanka M Vladiv-Glover.

300 DEU ISSN 1862-6165
TRANSFER AUS DEN SOZIAL- UND KULTURWISSENSCHAFTEN. Text in German. 2006. irreg., latest vol.11, 2009. price varies. **Document type:** *Monographic series, Academic/Scholarly.*
Published by: Frank und Timme GmbH, Wittelsbacherstr 27a, Berlin, 10707, Germany. TEL 49-30-88667911, FAX 49-30-86398731, info@frank-timme.de.

300 ZAF ISSN 0258-7696
DT1756
TRANSFORMATION; critical perspectives on Southern Africa. Text in English. 1986. 3/yr. ZAR 120 in Africa to individuals; GBP 40 in United Kingdom to individuals; USD 60 in North America to individuals; ZAR 240 in Africa to institutions; GBP 50 in United Kingdom to institutions; USD 75 in North America to institutions (effective 2005). back issues avail. **Document type:** *Journal, Academic/Scholarly.*
Related titles: Online - full text ed.: ISSN 1726-1368. 2002.
Indexed: A22, A26, BibInd, E01, I05, IBSS, IIBP, ISAP, MLA-IB, PCI.
—BLDSC (9020.592500), IE, Ingenta. **CCC.**
Published by: University of KwaZulu-Natal, King George V Avenue, Glenwood, Durban, KwaZulu-Natal 4041, South Africa. TEL 27-31-2602212, http://www.ukzn.ac.za.

TRANSFORMATIONEN (BAD WALDSEE). *see* RELIGIONS AND THEOLOGY

300 AUS ISSN 1444-3775
HN841
➤ **TRANSFORMATIONS.** Text in English. 2000. irreg. free (effective 2011). **Document type:** *Journal, Academic/Scholarly.* **Description:** Dedicated to the exploration of ideas, issues and debates emerging out of contemporary global culture.
Media: Online - full text.
Indexed: A39, C27, C29, D03, D04, E13, R14, S14, S15, S18.
Published by: Central Queensland University, Faculty of Arts, Humanities and Education, University Drive, Bundaberg, QLD 4670, Australia. TEL 61-3-0741507142, FAX 61-3-0741507080. Ed. Warwick Mules.

300 AUT ISSN 0938-2062
AS181
TRANSIT; europaeische Revue. Text in German. 1990. s-a. **Document type:** *Academic/Scholarly.*
Indexed: IBR, IBSS, IBZ.
—CCC.
Published by: Institut fuer die Wissenschaften vom Menschen, Spittelauer Laende 3, Vienna, Austria. TEL 43-1-313580, FAX 43-1-3135830, iwm@iwm.at. Ed. Timothy Snyder.

300 GUY ISSN 1012-8263
TRANSITION. Text in English. 1978. a. USD 10. adv. **Document type:** *Journal, Academic/Scholarly.* **Description:** Progressive multidisciplinary journal of Third World scholarship.
Related titles: Online - full text ed.
Indexed: IBR, IBZ.
Published by: University of Guyana, Faculty of Social Sciences and the Institute of Development Studies, Georgetown, Guyana. TEL 592-22-5409. Circ: 500.

300 AUT ISSN 1614-4007
TRANSITION STUDIES REVIEW. Text in English. 2003. 3/yr. EUR 487, USD 571 combined subscription to institutions (print & online eds.) (effective 2012). adv. reprint service avail. from PSC. **Document type:** *Journal, Academic/Scholarly.* **Description:** Analyzes a wide range of transition issues, especially to economic, financial, social, cultural and strategic quantitative applied research, as it applies to Central and Southeast Europe, in Russia, CIS and in the Black Sea and Mediterranean region.
Related titles: Online - full text ed.: ISSN 1614-4015 (from IngentaConnect).
Indexed: A22, A26, E01, EconLit, JEL, SCOPUS.
—BLDSC (9020.864000), IE, Ingenta. **CCC.**
Published by: (Central and Eastern European University Network ITA), Springer Wien (Subsidiary of: Springer Science+Business Media), Sachsenplatz 4-6, Vienna, W 1201, Austria. TEL 43-1-33024150, FAX 43-1-3302426, journals@springer.at, http://www.springer.at. Ed. G Dominese. Adv. contact Irene Hofmann. B&W page EUR 1,290; trim 120 x 190. Circ: 1,100 (paid and controlled). **Subscr. to:** Springer Distribution Center, Kundenservice Zeitschriften, Haberstr 7, Heidelberg 69126, Germany. TEL 49-6221-3454303, FAX 49-6221-3454229, subscriptions@springer.com.

TRANSITIONS; ex-revue des pays de l'est. *see* POLITICAL SCIENCE—International Relations

300 DEU
TRANSKULTURELLE PERSPEKTIVEN. Text in German. 2004. irreg., latest vol.9, 2008. price varies. **Document type:** *Monographic series, Academic/Scholarly.*
Published by: V & R Unipress GmbH (Subsidiary of: Vandenhoeck und Ruprecht), Robert-Bosch-Breite 6, Goettingen, 37079, Germany. TEL 49-551-5084303, FAX 49-551-5084333, info@vr-unipress.de, http://www.v-r.de/en/publisher/unipress.

300 DEU ISSN 1860-6202
TRANSNATIONALISIERUNG UND REGIONALISIERUNG VOM 18. JAHRHUNDERT BIS ZUR GEGENWART. Text in German. 2005. irreg., latest vol.4, 2010. price varies. **Document type:** *Monographic series, Academic/Scholarly.*
Published by: Leipziger Universitaetsverlag GmbH, Oststr 41, Leipzig, 04317, Germany. TEL 49-341-9900440, FAX 49-341-9900440, info@univerlag-leipzig.de.

300 DEU ISSN 1860-868X
TRANSPEKTE; transdisziplinaere Perspektiven der Sozial- und Kulturwissenschaften. Text in English, German. 2005. irreg., latest vol.6, 2008. price varies. **Document type:** *Monographic series, Academic/Scholarly.*
Published by: Peter Lang GmbH (Subsidiary of: Peter Lang Publishing Group), Eschborner Landstr 42-50, Frankfurt Am Main, 60489, Germany. TEL 49-69-7807050, FAX 49-69-78070550, zentrale.frankfurt@peterlang.com, http://www.peterlang.com.

316 CHE ISSN 1424-5868
TRANSVERSALES; langues, societes, cultures et apprentissages. Text in French. 2000. irreg., latest vol.27, 2010. price varies. **Document type:** *Monographic series, Academic/Scholarly.*
Published by: Peter Lang AG (Subsidiary of: Peter Lang Publishing Group), Hochfeldstr 32, Postfach 746, Bern 9, 3000, Switzerland. TEL 41-31-3061717, FAX 41-31-3061727, info@peterlang.com, http://www.peterlang.com. Ed. Aline Gohard-Radenkovic.

TRANSVERSALITES; revue de l'Institut Catholique de Paris. *see* RELIGIONS AND THEOLOGY—Roman Catholic

LA TRAUMA DE LA COMUNICACION. *see* COMMUNICATIONS

304 BEL ISSN 1376-0955
TRAVAIL & SOCIETE/WORK AND SOCIETY. Text in French. 1986. irreg., latest vol.55, 2007. price varies. **Document type:** *Monographic series, Academic/Scholarly.*
—BLDSC (9348.092000).
Published by: P I E - Peter Lang SA, 1 avenue Maurice, 6e etage, Brussels, 1050, Belgium. TEL 32-2-3477236, FAX 32-2-3477237, pie@peterlang.com, http://www.peterlang.net. Ed. Philippe Pochet.

300 CHE ISSN 1424-6201
TRAVAUX DE SCIENCES SOCIALES. Text in English, French. 1963. irreg., latest vol.213, 2007. price varies. **Document type:** *Monographic series, Academic/Scholarly.* **Description:** Covers research on law, economics, political science and sociology.
Former titles (until 1999): Travaux de Droit d'Economie, de Sciences Politiques, de Sociologie et d'Anthropologie (0254-2838); (until 1982): Travaux de Droit, d'Economique de Sociologie et de Sciences Politiques (0082-6022)
—CCC.
Published by: Librairie Droz S.A., 11 rue Firmin-Massot, Geneva 12, 1211, Switzerland. TEL 41-22-3466666, FAX 41-22-3472391, droz@droz.org, http://www.droz.org. Ed. G Busino. Circ: 800.

300 ESP ISSN 1136-8780
TRAVESIAS; politica, cultura y sociedad en iberoamerica. Text in Spanish. 1996. s-a. **Document type:** *Journal, Academic/Scholarly.*
Published by: Universidad Internacional de Andalucia, Sede Iberoamericana Santa Maria de la Rabida, Paraje La Rabina, s-n, Palos de la Frontera, Huelva 21891, Spain. TEL 34-959-350452, FAX 34-959-350158, http://www.uniara.uia.es/.

300 330 320 MEX ISSN 1405-8928
TRAYECTORIAS; revista de ciencias sociales de la Universidad Autonoma de Nuevo Leon. Text in Spanish; Summaries in Spanish, English. 1999. s-a. MXN 190 domestic to institutions; USD 30 in North America to institutions and Caribbean; USD 40 in Europe to institutions and South America; USD 50 elsewhere to institutions and South America (effective 2011). adv. bk.rev. back issues avail. **Document type:** *Journal, Academic/Scholarly.*
Related titles: Online - full text ed.: ISSN 2007-1205. 1999.
Indexed: C01, CA, F04, H21, IBSS, P08, P42, PAIS, PSA, S02, S03, SCOPUS, SociolAb, T02.
Published by: Universidad Autonoma de Nuevo Leon, Av Alfonso Reyes 4000, Edificio de la Biblioteca Raul Rangel Frias, Monterrey, 64440, Mexico. TEL 52-81-83294237, FAX 52-81-83294237. Ed. Rosaura Gonzales de la Rosa. Circ: 1,000.

▼ **TRENDS IN APPLIED LINGUISTICS.** *see* LINGUISTICS

300 370 NLD ISSN 2211-3894
▼ **TRENDS IN BEELD.** Text in Dutch. 2010. a. EUR 25 (effective 2011). **Document type:** *Report, Government.*
Formed by the merger of (2005-2010): Bestel in Beeld (2211-3886); (2004-2010): Kennis in Kaart (1876-7281); Which was formerly (until 2007): H O O P (1872-2393)
Published by: Ministerie van Onderwijs, Cultuur en Wetenschap, Postbus 16375, The Hague, 2500 BJ, Netherlands. TEL 31-70-4123456, FAX 31-70-4123450, ocwinfo@postbus51.nl, http://www.minocw.nl/.

TRENN-STRICHE, BINDE-STRICHE; Beitraege zur Literatur- und Kulturwissenschaft. *see* LITERATURE

TRIVIUM. *see* HUMANITIES: COMPREHENSIVE WORKS

300 RUS ISSN 2071-6141
TUL'SKII GOSUDARSTVENNYI UNIVERSITET. IZVESTIYA. GUMANITARNYE NAUKI. Text in Russian. 2008. irreg. **Document type:** *Journal, Academic/Scholarly.*
Published by: (Tul'skii Gosudarstvennyi Universitet), Izdatel'stvo TulGU, ul Boldina 151, Tula, 300600, Russian Federation. TEL 7-4872-352506, 7-4872-353620, FAX 7-4872-353620, press@tsu.tula.ru, http://publishing.tsu.tula.ru. Ed. I A Batanina TEL 7-4872-354921.

TURK DUNYASI INCELEMELERI DERGISI/JOURNAL OF TURKIC WORLD STUDIES. *see* ETHNIC INTERESTS

300 001.3 TUR ISSN 1309-6591
H62.A1
▼ **TURKISH ONLINE JOURNAL OF QUALITATIVE INQUIRY.** Text in English. 2010. q. free (effective 2011). bk.rev. Index. back issues avail. **Document type:** *Journal, Academic/Scholarly.* **Description:** Publishes original research papers conducted with qualitative, mixed and action research methodology in social sciences and humanities. Also includes eligible works on theoretical and cognitive issues or book reviews related to qualitative research paradigm.
Media: Online - full text.
Indexed: E03.
Published by: Abdullah Kuzu, Ed. & Publ., Anadolu University, Faculty of Education, Department of Computer Education & Instructional Technology, Eskisehir, 26470, Turkey. akuzu@anadolu.edu.tr. Ed. Abdullah Kuzu.

300 TUR ISSN 1300-7874
➤ **TURKLUK BILIMI ARASTIRMALARI.** Variant title: T U B A R. Text in Turkish; Abstracts in English, Turkish. 1992. s-a. TRY 5 (effective 2010). bk.rev. abstr.; bibl. cum.index: 2008. back issues avail. **Document type:** *Journal, Academic/Scholarly.* **Description:** Publishes articles related with the Turkology Studies including culture, language, literature, political history, science and art history, sociology and philosophy.
Related titles: Online - full text ed.
Indexed: A01, L&LBA, MLA-IB, SociolAb, T02.

S

Address: Sira Sogutler Mah. Cevreyolu Aydogdu Apt. Kat 2 No 2, Bor, Nigde, Turkey. FAX 90-388-2250180. Eds. Bayram Unal TEL 202-569-1884, Nazim Hikmet Polat. Pub., R&P Nazim Hikmet Polat. Adv. contact Bayram Unal TEL 202-569-1884.

300 USA ISSN 0743-748X
THE TWINS LETTER. Text in English. 1984. q. USD 25 domestic membership; USD 30 foreign membership (effective 2000). adv. bk.rev. charts; illus. cum.index: 1984-1995. **Document type:** *Newsletter.* **Description:** Serves twins, their family, the media, medical and social scientists, and the general public with articles on multiple births.
Published by: Twins Foundation, PO Box 6043, Providence, RI 02940-6043. TEL 401-729-1000, FAX 401-751-4642. Ed., R&P Kay Cassill. Adv. contact Marilyn Holmes. Circ: 2,500.

300 ZAF ISSN 0041-4751
AS611
TYDSKRIF VIR GEESTESWETENSKAPPE. Text in Afrikaans; Summaries in English, French, German. 1961. q. bk.rev. bibl. index. **Document type:** *Journal, Academic/Scholarly.*
Related titles: Online - full text ed.: free (effective 2011).
Indexed: A01, ASD, BibLing, CA, ISAP, MLA, MLA-IB, P42, PAIS, PSA, S02, S03, SCOPUS, SOPODA, SSA, SSCI, SociolAb, T02, W07.
Published by: Suid-Afrikaanse Akademie vir Wetenskap en Kuns/South African Academy of Science and Arts, Private Bag X11, Arcadia, 0007, South Africa. publikasies@akademie.co.za. Ed. R C (Ina) Wolfaardt-Graebe.

300 004 MYS ISSN 1511-7219
H1
➤ **U N I T A R E-JOURNAL.** (Universiti Tun Abdul Razak) Text in English. 2005. irreg. **Document type:** *Journal, Academic/Scholarly.* **Description:** It covers topics in the social sciences, business and information technology.
Media: Online - full text.
Indexed: A01, CA, T02.
Published by: Universiti Tun Abdul Razak, Kelana Java Sudy Center 16-1, Jalan SS6/12, Petaling Java, Selangor Darul Ehsan 47301, Malaysia. TEL 60-3-78092100, crm@unitar.edu.my, http://www2.unitar.edu.my. Ed. Syed Abdul Hamid Aljunid.

300 CHE ISSN 1020-6825
HN978
U N R I S D NEWS. Text in English. 1963. biennial. free. bk.rev. back issues avail. **Document type:** *Newsletter, Consumer.* **Description:** Provides updated information on U.N.R.I.S.D. research work.
Former titles (until 1997): U N R I S D Social Development News (1020-0754); (until 1994): U N R I S D News (1014-8361); (until 1989): United Nations Research Institute for Social Development. Research Notes (0258-9834); United Nations Research Institute for Social Development. Report
Related titles: Online - full text ed.; Spanish ed.: U N R I S D informa. ISSN 1020-6841; French ed.: U N R I S D infos. ISSN 1020-6833.
Published by: United Nations Research Institute for Social Development, Reference Centre, Palais des Nations, Geneva 10, 1211, Switzerland. TEL 4122-917-3020, FAX 4122-917-0650, TELEX 412962 UNO CH, info@unrisd.org, http://www.unrisd.org/engindex/publisher. Eds. Jenifer Freedman, Nicolas Bovay. R&P Nicolas Bovay. Circ: 10,000.

300 CHE
HC59.69
➤ **U N R I S D PROGRAMME PAPER SERIES.** (United Nations Research Institute for Social Development) Text in English. 1987. bi-m. USD 8 newsstand/cover (effective 2002). back issues avail. **Document type:** *Journal, Academic/Scholarly.* **Description:** Preliminary documents circulated in a limited number to stimulate discussion and critical comment on topical and pressing social issues such as sustainable development, gender issues, ethnic conflict, political conflict, illicit drugs, crisis-adjustment and social change.
Formerly: U N R I S D Discussion Paper Series (1012-6511)
Indexed: FR.
—INIST.
Published by: United Nations Research Institute for Social Development, Reference Centre, Palais des Nations, Geneva 10, 1211, Switzerland. TEL 41-22-917-3020, FAX 41-22-917-0650, TELEX 41 29 62 UNO CH, info@unrisd.org, http://www.unrisd.org. R&P Nicolas Bovay.

300 384 ESP ISSN 1885-1541
HM851
➤ **U O C. PAPERS**; revista sobre la societat del coneixement. (Universitat Oberta de Catalunya) Text and summaries in Catalan, English, Spanish. 2005. s-a. free (effective 2011). abstr. back issues avail. **Document type:** *Journal, Academic/Scholarly.*
Media: Online - full text.
Published by: Universitat Oberta de Catalunya, Av Tibidabo 39-43, Barcelona, 08035, Spain. TEL 34-902-372373. Ed. Lluis Rius.

➤ **U S A C.** *see* SCIENCES: COMPREHENSIVE WORKS

300 DEU ISSN 1434-1905
U S A STUDIEN. Text in German. 1980. irreg., latest vol.15, 2008. price varies. **Document type:** *Monographic series, Academic/Scholarly.*
Formerly (until 1997): Von Deutschland nach Amerika (0173-1955)
Published by: Franz Steiner Verlag GmbH, Birkenwaldstr 44, Stuttgart, 70191, Germany. TEL 49-711-25820, FAX 49-711-2582290, service@steiner-verlag.de, http://www.steiner-verlag.de. R&P Sabine Koerner.

300 DEU ISSN 0178-1405
UEBERGAENGE; Texte und Studien zu Handlung, Sprache und Lebenswelt. Text in German. 1983. irreg., latest vol.58, 2010. price varies. **Document type:** *Monographic series, Academic/Scholarly.*
Published by: Wilhelm Fink Verlag, Juehenplatz 1-3, Paderborn, 33098, Germany. TEL 49-5251-1275, FAX 49-5251-127860, kontakt@fink.de, http://www.fink.de.

300 500 TUR ISSN 1303-5134
➤ **ULUSLARARASI INSAN BILIMLERI DERGISI/INTERNATIONAL JOURNAL OF HUMAN SCIENCES.** Text in English, Turkish. 2002. 2/yr. free (effective 2011). **Document type:** *Journal, Academic/Scholarly.*
Media: Online - full text.
Indexed: A01, CA, T02.
Published by: Sakarya Universitesi, Egitim Fakultesi, Hendek, Adapazari, Turkey. TEL 90-542-2722084, nakinci@sakarya.edu.tr, editor@insanbilimleri.com. Ed. Curreyt Birkok.

504 AUT ISSN 1818-7188
UMWELT UND BILDUNG. Text in German. 1998. 5/yr. EUR 5 newsstand/cover (effective 2007). **Document type:** *Journal, Academic/Scholarly.*
Published by: Forum Umweltbildung, Alser Str 21, Vienna, 1080, Austria. TEL 43-1-4024701, FAX 43-1-402470151, forum@umweltbildung.at, http://www.umweltbildung.at.

300 DEU
▼ **UMWELT UND GESELLSCHAFT.** Text in German. 2010. irreg., latest vol.2, 2010. price varies. **Document type:** *Monographic series, Academic/Scholarly.*
Published by: Vandenhoeck und Ruprecht, Theaterstr 13, Goettingen, 37073, Germany. TEL 49-551-508440, FAX 49-551-5084422, info@v-r.de.

300 FRA
UNESCO: RESOLUTIONS AND DECISIONS. Text in English, French, Spanish. 1997. irreg. EUR 38.11 (effective 2003). **Description:** Contains the full texts of all resolutions passed at UNESCO's General Conferences and of decisions made by the Executive Board since 1987.
Media: CD-ROM.
Published by: UNESCO Publishing, 7 place de Fontenoy, Paris, 75352, France. TEL 33-1-45684300, FAX 33-1-45685737, http://publishing.unesco.org/default.aspx. **Dist. in the U.S. by:** Bernan Associates, Bernan, 4611-F Assembly Dr., Lanham, MD 20706-4391. TEL 800-274-4888, FAX 800-865-3450.

UNITED NATIONS. ECONOMIC AND SOCIAL COUNCIL. ANNEXES. *see* BUSINESS AND ECONOMICS

UNITED NATIONS ECONOMIC AND SOCIAL COUNCIL. OFFICIAL RECORDS. SUPPLEMENTS AND SPECIAL SUPPLEMENTS. *see* BUSINESS AND ECONOMICS

UNITED NATIONS ECONOMIC AND SOCIAL COUNCIL. RESOLUTIONS AND DECISIONS. *see* BUSINESS AND ECONOMICS

UNITED NATIONS ECONOMIC AND SOCIAL COUNCIL. SUMMARY RECORDS OF PLENARY MEETINGS. *see* BUSINESS AND ECONOMICS

300 PER ISSN 1810-1100
UNIVERSALIA. Text in Spanish. 1993. s-a. **Document type:** *Journal, Academic/Scholarly.*
Published by: Universidad Nacional de Piura, Instituto de Investigacion y Promocion para el Desarrollo, Campus Universitario, Urb. Miraflores s-n, Castilla, Piura, Peru. http://www.unp.edu.pe/. Ed. Manuel Galvez Paredes.

UNIVERSIDAD DE SAN CARLOS. REVISTA; artes - literatura - ciencias humanas. *see* ART

UNIVERSIDAD DEL ACONCAGUA. FACULTAD DE ECONOMIA Y CIENCIAS COMERCIALES. REVISTA. *see* BUSINESS AND ECONOMICS

300 900 PRI
UNIVERSIDAD INTERAMERICANA DE PUERTO RICO. RECINTO DE SAN GERMAN. REVISTA DE CIENCIAS SOCIALES E HISTORIA. ANALES. Text in Spanish. 1984. a. USD 6.
Published by: Universidad Interamericana de Puerto Rico, Recinto San German/Inter American University of Puerto Rico, San German Campus, Av Interamericana, Carr 102, km 30.6, San Juan, 00683, Puerto Rico. TEL 787-264-1912, FAX 787-892-3090.

UNIVERSIDAD METROPOLITANA. ANALES. *see* SCIENCES: COMPREHENSIVE WORKS

300 ESP ISSN 1886-6611
UNIVERSIDAD MIGUEL HERNANDEZ. FACULTAD DE CIENCIAS SOCIALES Y JURIDICAS. REVISTA. Text in Spanish. 2006. s-a. free (effective 2011). **Document type:** *Monographic series, Academic/Scholarly.*
Media: Online - full text.
Published by: Universidad Miguel Hernandez, Facultad de Ciencias Sociales y Juridicas, Avenida de la Universidad s/n, Elche, Alicante 03202, Spain. TEL 34-96-6658681, FAX 34-96-6658680, http://www.umh.es.

300 HND ISSN 0252-8770
F1501
UNIVERSIDAD NACIONAL AUTONOMA DE HONDURAS. INSTITUTO DE INVESTIGACIONES ECONOMICAS Y SOCIALES. BOLETIN. Text in Spanish. 1971. m. bibl.
Published by: Universidad Nacional Autonoma de Honduras, Instituto de Investigaciones Economicas y Sociales, Ciudad Universitaria, Tegucigalpa DC, Honduras. Ed. Victor Meza.

300 ARG ISSN 0327-1471
F2801
➤ **UNIVERSIDAD NACIONAL DE JUJUY. FACULTAD DE HUMANIDADES Y CIENCIAS SOCIALES. CUADERNOS.** Text in Spanish. 1989. s-a. ARS 25 newsstand/cover (effective 2010). **Document type:** *Journal, Academic/Scholarly.*
Related titles: Online - full text ed.: ISSN 1668-8104. 1989 (from SciELO).
Published by: Universidad Nacional de Jujuy, Facultad de Humanidades y Ciencias Sociales, Otero 262, San Salvador del Jujuy, 4600, Argentina. http://www.unju.edu.ar. Circ: 250.

300 BRA ISSN 1413-3547
UNIVERSIDADE DE ALFENAS. REVISTA. Text in Portuguese. 1990. s-a. **Document type:** *Journal, Academic/Scholarly.*
Published by: Universidade de Alfenas, Rodovia MG 179 Km 0, Campus Universitario, Alfeinas, 37130-000, Brazil. TEL 55-35-32993000, unifemas@unifemas.br, http://www.unifemas.br/.

300 BRA ISSN 0020-3874
F2501
UNIVERSIDADE DE SAO PAULO. INSTITUTO DE ESTUDOS BRASILEIROS. REVISTA. Text in Portuguese. 1966. s-a. BRL 8 newsstand/cover. bk.rev. bibl.; charts; illus. **Document type:** *Academic/Scholarly.* **Description:** Publishes original articles related to Brazilian studies.
Indexed: C01, FR, H21, HistAb, P08, RILM.
Published by: Universidade de Sao Paulo, Instituto de Estudos Brasileiros, Av. Prof. Mello Moraes, Travessa 8, No. 140, Sao Paulo, SP 05508-900, Brazil. TEL 55-11-2102429, FAX 55-11-8183143, TELEX 011-36950 USPO BR. Ed. Yedda Dias Lima. Circ: 2,000.

300 BRA ISSN 0103-9024
AS80.U53
UNIVERSIDADE DO AMAZONAS. REVISTA. SERIE: CIENCIAS HUMANAS. Text in Portuguese. 1991. s-a. BRL 10,000, USD 50. **Document type:** *Academic/Scholarly.*
Published by: Universidade do Amazonas, Instituto de Ciencias Humanas e Letras, Campus Universitario, Estrada do Contorno, 3000, Manaus, AM 69077-000, Brazil.

300 100 BRA ISSN 0041-8870
UNIVERSIDADE FEDERAL DO CEARA. DEPARTAMENTO DE CIENCIAS SOCIAIS E FILOSOFIA. DOCUMENTOS. Text in English, Portuguese; Summaries in English. 1967. irreg., latest vol.8, no.2, 1977. BRL 5, USD 6. adv. bk.rev. **Document type:** *Journal, Academic/Scholarly.*
Published by: Universidade Federal do Ceara, Departamento de Ciencias Sociais e Filosofia, C.P. 1257, Fortaleza, Ceara, Brazil. Circ: 2,000.

300 PRT ISSN 0871-2778
UNIVERSIDADE NOVA DE LISBOA. FACULDADE DE CIENCIAS SOCIAIS E HUMANAS. REVISTA. Text in Portuguese. 1980. a.
Indexed: MLA-IB.
Published by: (Universidade Nova de Lisboa, Faculdade de Ciencias Sociais e Humanas), Edicoes Colibri, Apartado 42.001, Telheiras, Lisbon, 1601-801, Portugal. colibri@edi-colibri.pt, http://www.edi-colibri.pt.

UNIVERSITA DI FERRARA. ANNALI. SEZIONE 10: SCIENZE GIURIDICHE. *see* LAW

300 DEU ISSN 1437-2703
UNIVERSITAET AUGSBURG. INSTITUT FUER EUROPAEISCHE KULTURGESCHICHTE. MITTEILUNGEN. Text in German. 1997. irreg., latest vol.17, 2007. **Document type:** *Monographic series, Academic/Scholarly.*
—CCC.
Published by: Universitaet Augsburg, Institut fuer Europaeische Kulturgeschichte, Eichleitnerstr 30, Augsburg, 86159, Germany. TEL 49-821-5985840, FAX 49-821-5985850, Sekretariat@iek.uni-augsburg.de, http://www.uni-augsburg.de/institute/iek/html/haupt.html.

300 DEU ISSN 1614-3450
UNIVERSITAET PASSAU. SCHRIFTENREIHE. Text in German. 1986. irreg., latest vol.30, 2009. **Document type:** *Monographic series, Academic/Scholarly.*
Formerly (until 2004): Universitaet Passau. Nachrichten und Berichte. Sonderheft (0945-3008)
Published by: Universitaet Passau, Innstr 41, Passau, 94032, Germany. TEL 49-851-5090, FAX 49-851-5091005, praesident@uni-passau.de, http://www.uni-passau.de.

300 500 DJI ISSN 1997-4493
AS659.D5
UNIVERSITAIRE DE DJIBOUTI. REVUE. Text in French. 2003. biennial. **Document type:** *Journal, Academic/Scholarly.*
Published by: Universite de Djibouti, Centre de Recherches (C R U D), BP 1904, Djibouti City, Djibouti. TEL 253-250459, FAX 253-250474, Mel ud@univ.edu.dj, http://www.univ.edu.dj/universite/index_univ.html.

300 ITA ISSN 2070-6790
➤ **UNIVERSITAS FORUM**; international journal on human development and international cooperation. Text in English, Spanish, Italian, French. 2008. 3/yr. free (effective 2011). **Document type:** *Journal, Academic/Scholarly.*
Media: Online - full text.
Published by: United Nations, Office for Project Services (U N O P S), Viale delle Terme di Caracalla, Rome, 00153, Italy. TEL 39-06-57050214, FAX 39-06-57050297. Ed. Sara Swartz.

300 COL ISSN 0120-4807
LE41.B8
➤ **UNIVERSITAS HUMANISTICA.** Text in Spanish. 1971. s-a. back issues avail. **Document type:** *Journal, Academic/Scholarly.* **Description:** Expolores interesting and noteworthy issues and publishes scholarship in anthropology, history, literature, history, and sociology.
Related titles: Online - full text ed.
Indexed: A01, C01, CA, F03, F04, H21, HistAb, I04, I05, IBSS, MLA-IB, P08, RASB, SociolAb, T02.
—BLDSC (9101.380000).
Published by: Pontificia Universidad Javeriana, Facultad de Ciencias Sociales, Carrera 7 No 40-62, Edif 19, Jose Celestino Andrade, SJ, Bogota, Colombia. TEL 57-1-320-8320, http://www.javeriana.edu.co/Facultades/C_Sociales/Facultad/Facultad.html.

300 HUN ISSN 1215-1092
➤ **UNIVERSITAS LITTERARUM ET ARTIUM MISKOLCIENSIS. ANNALES.** Text in English, French, German, Hungarian; Contents page in English, Hungarian. 1991. a. HUF 2,000 (effective 2000). bk.rev. bibl. **Document type:** *Journal, Academic/Scholarly.* **Description:** Covers literature, history, sociology, psychology, linguistics, art history, philosophy and education.
Indexed: BibLing, RILM.
Published by: Miskolci Egyetem/University of Miskolc, Miskolc, 3515, Hungary. TEL 36-46-565036, FAX 36-46-365174, http://www.uni-miskolc.hu. Circ: 2,000.

300 ROM ISSN 1844-6051
➤ **UNIVERSITATEA "CONSTANTIN BRANCUSI" DIN TARGU JIU. ANALELE. SERIA LITERE SI STIINTE SOCIALE/UNIVERSITY "CONSTANTIN BRANCUSI" OF TARGU JIU. ANNALS. SERIES LETTERS AND SOCIAL SCIENCES.** Key Title: Analele Universitatii "Constantin Brancusi" din Targu Jiu. Seria Litere si Stiinte Sociale. Text in English, Romanian. 2008. s-a. **Document type:** *Journal, Academic/Scholarly.*
Related titles: Online - full text ed.: free (effective 2011).
Published by: (Universitatea "Constantin Brancusi" din Targu Jiu/University "Constantin Brancusi" of Targu Jiu), Editura Academica Brancusi, B-dul Republicii, 1, Targu Jiu, 210152, Romania. TEL 40-23-214307. Ed. Dr. Adrian Gorun.

300 340 ROM ISSN 1841-6594
➤ **UNIVERSITATEA PETROL - GAZE DIN PLOIESTI. SERIA STIINTE SOCIO-UMANE SI JURIDICE. BULETINUL.** Text in English, French. 1956. s-a. EUR 50; EUR 25 newsstand/cover (effective 2010). **Document type:** *Journal, Academic/Scholarly.* **Description:** Publishes original research papers that present important ideas in all fields of law, administration sciences, history, philosophy and sociology.
Supersedes in part (in 2005): Universitatea Petrol - Gaze Ploiesti. Buletinul (1221-9371); Which was formerly (until 1995): Institutului de Petrol si Gaze Ploiesti. Buletinul (0376-4516); (until 1974): Institutului de Petrol, Gaze si Geologie Ploiesti. Buletinul
Related titles: Online - full text ed.
Published by: Universitatea Petrol - Gaze din Ploiesti/Petroleum-Gas University of Ploiesti, Bd Bucuresti 39, Ploiesti, 100680, Romania. TEL 40-244-573171, FAX 40-244-575847. Ed. Dragos Radulescu. Pub. Serban Vasilescu. Adv. contact Dragos Grigorescu. Circ: 100 (paid).

300 150 ROM ISSN 1582-6635
➤ **UNIVERSITATII "SPIRU HARET". ANALELE. SERIA SOCIOLOGIE-PSIHOLOGIE/SPIRU HARET UNIVERSITY. ANNALS. SOCIOLOGY-PSYCHOLOGY STUDIES.** Text in Romanian, English; Abstracts in English. 2000. a. USD 10 per issue to individuals; USD 15 per issue to institutions (effective 2010). bk.rev. abstr.; bibl. back issues avail.; reprints avail. **Document type:** *Journal, Academic/Scholarly.* **Description:** Contains interdisciplinary contributions on scholarly research and theory, targeting both students, professors, researchers and professionals in sociology and social assistance, and those in the area of psychology, pedagogy and anthropology.
Indexed: MLA-IB.
Published by: (Universitatea Spiru Haret/Spiru Haret University), Editura Fundatiei "Romania de Maine", Splaiul Independentei nr. 313, Bucuresti Sector 6, Romania. TEL 40-21-3169786, FAX 40-21-3143908, difuzare@edituraromaniademaine.ro, http://www.edituraromaniademaine.ro/. Ed. Florian Tanasescu. Pub. Grigore Nicola. R&P Ancuta Plaesu. Circ: 300.

➤ **UNIVERSITEIT VAN STELLENBOSCH. ANNALE.** *see* SCIENCES: COMPREHENSIVE WORKS

300.72 NOR ISSN 0807-3139
UNIVERSITETET I OSLO. ARENA - CENTRE FOR EUROPEAN STUDIES. REPORT. (Advanced Research on the Europeanisation of the Nation State) Text in English. 1996. irreg. back issues avail. **Document type:** *Monographic series, Academic/Scholarly.*
Related titles: Online - full text ed.: ISSN 1504-8152. 2007; ♦ Includes: R E C O N Report. ISSN 1504-7253.
Published by: Universitetet i Oslo, ARENA - Senter for Europaforskning/ University of Oslo, ARENA - Centre for European Studies, PO Box 1143, Blindern, Oslo, 0318, Norway. TEL 47-22-858700, FAX 47-22-858710, arena@arena.uio.no, http://www.arena.uio.no.

300.72 NOR ISSN 1890-7733
UNIVERSITETET I OSLO. ARENA - CENTRE FOR EUROPEAN STUDIES. WORKING PAPERS. (Advanced Research on the Europeanisation of the Nation State) Text in English. 1994. irreg. **Document type:** *Monographic series, Academic/Scholarly.*
Formerly (until 2004): Universitetet i Oslo. ARENA - Advanced Research on the Europeanisation of the Nation State. Working Papers (0805-5130)
Related titles: Online - full text ed.: ISSN 1890-7741. 1997.
Published by: Universitetet i Oslo, ARENA - Senter for Europaforskning/ University of Oslo, ARENA - Centre for European Studies, PO Box 1143, Blindern, Oslo, 0318, Norway. TEL 47-22-858700, FAX 47-22-858710, arena@arena.uio.no, http://www.arena.uio.no.

300 NOR ISSN 1504-9272
UNIVERSITY OF AGDER. DOCTORAL DISSERTATIONS. Text in Multiple languages. 2005. irreg. **Document type:** *Monographic series, Academic/Scholarly.*
Formerly (until 2008): Hoegskolen i Agder. Doktoravhandlingar (0809-7682)
Published by: Universitetet i Agder/Agder University, PO Box 422, Kristiansand, 4604, Norway. TEL 47-38-141000, FAX 47-38-141001, post@uia.no, http://www.uia.no.

300 USA ISSN 2150-9069
▼ **UNIVERSITY OF ATLANTA MONOGRAPH SERIES IN APPLIED CRITICAL THEORY.** Text in English. 2010 (Jan.). irreg. **Document type:** *Monographic series, Academic/Scholarly.*
Related titles: Online - full text ed.: ISSN 2150-9077. 2010 (Jan.).
Published by: University of Atlanta, 6685 Peachtree Industrial Blvd, Atlanta, GA 30360. TEL 404-247-2809, rlebarnett@uofa.edu.

UNIVERSITY OF BIRMINGHAM. INSTITUTE FOR ADVANCED RESEARCH IN ARTS AND SOCIAL SCIENCES. OCCASIONAL PAPER. *see* HUMANITIES: COMPREHENSIVE WORKS

UNIVERSITY OF CENTRAL FLORIDA UNDERGRADUATE RESEARCH JOURNAL. *see* HUMANITIES: COMPREHENSIVE WORKS

300 ZAF ISSN 0377-8533
H64.U55
UNIVERSITY OF DURBAN-WESTVILLE. INSTITUTE FOR SOCIAL AND ECONOMIC RESEARCH. ANNUAL REPORT. Text in English. 1973. a. free. **Document type:** *Corporate.*
Published by: University of KwaZulu-Natal, Institute for Social and Economic Research, Private Bag X54001, Durban, KwaZulu-Natal 4000, South Africa. TEL 27-31-820-2298, FAX 27-31-820-2834. Ed. J J McCarthy. Circ: 250.

300 945 GBR
UNIVERSITY OF DURHAM. CENTRE FOR EUROPEAN STUDIES. WORKING PAPERS. Text in English. irreg., latest vol.4, 1993. **Document type:** *Monographic series, Academic/Scholarly.*
Published by: University of Durham, Centre for European Studies, University of Durham, Dept. of Geography, Science Laboratories, South Rd, Durham, DH1 3LE, United Kingdom. Ed. John Slatter.
Subscr. to: Mrs. J. Dresser, Centre for European Studies, Dept. of Geography, Science Laboratories, South Rd, Durham DH1 3LE, United Kingdom.

300 GBR ISSN 1756-7904
UNIVERSITY OF EAST ANGLIA. SCHOOL OF INTERNATIONAL DEVELOPMENT. WORKING PAPERS. Text in English. 1974. irreg., latest vol.18, 2009. free to members (effective 2009). back issues avail. **Document type:** *Monographic series, Academic/Scholarly.*
Former titles (until 2007): University of East Anglia. School of Development Studies. Working Papers (Print); (until 1981): Development Studies Discussion Paper (0951-2861)
Media: Online - full text.
—CCC.
Published by: University of East Anglia, School of International Development, Faculty of Social Sciences, Norwich, NR4 7TJ, United Kingdom. TEL 44-1603-592329, FAX 44-1603-451999, dev.general@uea.ac.uk.

300 GBR
UNIVERSITY OF EAST LONDON. CENTRE FOR NEW ETHNICITIES RESEARCH. WORKING PAPER. Text in English. irreg., latest vol.2, 1995. **Document type:** *Monographic series.*
Formerly: University of East London. New Ethnicities Unit. Working Paper
Published by: University of East London, Centre for New Ethnicities Research, East Building, 4-6 University Way, London, E16 2RD, United Kingdom. TEL 44-2082-232512, FAX 44-2082-232898.

300 GHA
UNIVERSITY OF GHANA. INSTITUTE OF STATISTICAL, SOCIAL AND ECONOMIC RESEARCH. DISCUSSION PAPERS. Text in English. 1977. irreg., latest vol.26, 1986. **Description:** Examines the dimensions of the problems of childhood survival.
Published by: University of Ghana, Institute of Statistical, Social and Economic Research, PO Box 74, Legon, Ghana.

UNIVERSITY OF HONG KONG. CENTRE OF ASIAN STUDIES. OCCASIONAL PAPERS AND MONOGRAPHS. *see* ASIAN STUDIES

UNIVERSITY OF KHARTOUM. DEVELOPMENT STUDIES AND RESEARCH CENTRE. DISCUSSION PAPERS. *see* BUSINESS AND ECONOMICS—International Development And Assistance

300 DEU
▼ **UNIVERSITY OF LEIPZIG. GLOBAL AND EUROPEAN STUDIES INSTITUTE. WORKING PAPER SERIES.** Text in English. 2009. irreg., latest vol.2, 2009. price varies. **Document type:** *Monographic series, Academic/Scholarly.*
Published by: Leipziger Universitaetsverlag GmbH, Oststr 41, Leipzig, 04317, Germany. TEL 49-341-9900440, FAX 49-341-9900440, info@univerlag-leipzig.de.

325.3 GBR ISSN 0076-0781
UNIVERSITY OF LONDON. INSTITUTE OF COMMONWEALTH STUDIES. ANNUAL REPORT. Text in English. 1949. biennial. free (effective 2009). **Document type:** *Report, Academic/Scholarly.* **Description:** Provides information about the Institute of Commonwealth Studies.
Published by: University of London, Institute of Commonwealth Studies, 2nd Fl, S Block, Senate House, Malet St, London, WC1E 7HU, United Kingdom. TEL 44-20-78628844, FAX 44-20-78628813, ics@sas.ac.uk, http://commonwealth.sas.ac.uk/. Ed. Troy Rutt.

300 GBR ISSN 0076-0773
UNIVERSITY OF LONDON. INSTITUTE OF COMMONWEALTH STUDIES. COLLECTED SEMINAR PAPERS. Text in English. 1967. irreg. price varies. **Document type:** *Monographic series, Academic/Scholarly.* **Description:** Papers presented to research seminars.
—CCC.
Published by: University of London, Institute of Commonwealth Studies, 2nd Fl, S Block, Senate House, Malet St, London, WC1E 7HU, United Kingdom. TEL 44-20-78628844, FAX 44-20-78628813, ics@sas.ac.uk, http://commonwealth.sas.ac.uk/.

UNIVERSITY OF MAURITIUS. JOURNAL: LAW, MANAGEMENT & SOCIAL SCIENCE. *see* LAW

300 ZAF
UNIVERSITY OF NATAL. CENTRE FOR SOCIAL AND DEVELOPMENT STUDIES. ANNUAL REPORT. Text in English. 1959. a. free. **Document type:** *Corporate.*
Former titles: University of Natal. Centre for Applied Social Research. Annual Report; University of Natal. Institute for Social Research. Annual Report (0070-7759)
Published by: University of KwaZulu-Natal, Centre for Social and Development Studies, Durban, KwaZulu-Natal 4041, South Africa. TEL 27-31-2601031, FAX 27-31-2602359, TELEX 6-21231 SA. Ed. S Bekker. Circ: 150.

300 ZAF
UNIVERSITY OF NATAL. CENTRE FOR SOCIAL AND DEVELOPMENT STUDIES. C S D S RESEARCH REPORTS. Text in English. 1990. irreg., latest vol.10, 1997. price varies.
Published by: University of KwaZulu-Natal, Centre for Social and Development Studies, Private Bag X10, Dalbridge, 4014, South Africa. TEL 27-31-2602525, FAX 27-31-2602813.

300 ZAF
UNIVERSITY OF NATAL. CENTRE FOR SOCIAL AND DEVELOPMENT STUDIES. PUBLICATION CATALOGUE. Text in English. a. free.
Published by: University of KwaZulu-Natal, Centre for Social and Development Studies, Durban, KwaZulu-Natal 4041, South Africa. TEL 27-31-2601031, FAX 27-31-2602359. Ed. S Bekker.

300 USA
UNIVERSITY OF NEW MEXICO. LATIN AMERICAN AND IBERIAN INSTITUTE. RESEARCH PAPER SERIES. Text in English. 1979. irreg. free (effective 2010). bibl.; charts; stat. index. **Document type:** *Monographic series, Academic/Scholarly.*
Former titles (until 1999): University of New Mexico. Latin American Institute. Research Paper Series (0734-5976); (until 1981): University of New Mexico. Latin American Institute. Working Paper (0737-2019)
Published by: University of New Mexico, Latin American and Iberian Institute, MSC 02 1690, 801 Yale N E, Albuquerque, NM 87131-1016. TEL 505-277-6839, 800-472-0888, FAX 505-277-5989, info@ladb.unm.edu, http://laii.unm.edu/.

UNIVERSITY OF PENNSYLVANIA. JOURNAL OF LAW AND SOCIAL CHANGE. *see* LAW

300 150 304.6 320 ROM ISSN 1582-1501
H1
➤ **UNIVERSITY OF PETROSANI. SOCIAL SCIENCES. ANNALS.** Text in English. 2001. a., latest vol.2, 2001. ROL 55,300, USD 4 (effective 2003). illus. **Document type:** *Journal, Academic/Scholarly.*
Published by: Universitatea din Petrosani, Str. Universitatii, nr 20, Petrosani, 332006, Romania. TEL 40-254-542994, FAX 40-254-543491, rector@upet.ro, http://www.upet.ro. Eds. Ioan-Lucian Bolundut, Septimiu Krausz. Circ: 150 (paid).

300 GBR ISSN 1753-7053
UNIVERSITY OF PLYMOUTH. FACULTY OF SOCIAL SCIENCE & BUSINESS. POSTGRADUATE SYMPOSIUM. PROCEEDINGS. Text in English. 2007. a. **Document type:** *Proceedings, Academic/Scholarly.*
Related titles: Online - full text ed.: ISSN 1753-7061.
Published by: University of Plymouth, Roland Levinsky Bldg, Drake Circus, Plymouth, Devon PL4 8AA, United Kingdom. TEL 44-1752-600600, prospectus@plymouth.ac.uk, http://www.plymouth.ac.uk.

300 001.3 PHL ISSN 0047-5742
AS539.5
UNIVERSITY OF SANTO TOMAS. GRADUATE SCHOOL. JOURNAL OF GRADUATE RESEARCH. Variant title: University of Santo Tomas Journal of Graduate Research. Text in English. 1971. s-a. bk.rev. bibl.; illus.; charts. **Document type:** *Journal, Academic/Scholarly.*
Indexed: BAS, IPP.
—Ingenta.
Published by: (University Of Santo Tomas, Graduate School), University of Santo Tomas Publishing House (U S T P H), Beato Angelico Bldg, Espana, Manila, Philippines. TEL 63-2-7313522 ext 8252/8278, FAX 63-2-7313522, http://www.ust.edu.ph. Circ: 1,500.

300 TTO
UNIVERSITY OF THE WEST INDIES, TRINIDAD. INSTITUTE OF SOCIAL & ECONOMIC RESEARCH. OCCASIONAL PAPERS: GENERAL SERIES. Text in English. 1977. irreg. price varies. charts; stat. back issues avail.
Published by: University of the West Indies, Institute of Social and Economic Research, St. Augustine, WI, Trinidad & Tobago. Ed. Jack Harewood. Circ: 220.

300 ZAF
➤ **UNIVERSITY OF THE WITWATERSRAND. INSTITUTE FOR ADVANCED SOCIAL RESEARCH. SEMINAR PAPERS.** Text in English. 1979. irreg. (20-24/yr.). ZAR 35, USD 65 to individuals; ZAR 110, USD 110 to institutions. **Document type:** *Monographic series, Academic/Scholarly.*
Published by: University of the Witwatersrand, Institute for Advanced Social Research, Private Bag 3, Wits, 2050, South Africa. FAX 27-11-716-8030. Circ: 150.

300 JPN
➤ **UNIVERSITY OF TOKUSHIMA. SOCIAL SCIENCE RESEARCH.** Text in English, Japanese. 1988. a. back issues avail. **Document type:** *Journal, Academic/Scholarly.* **Description:** Contains exclusive academic articles, coving comprehensive range of social sciences.
Published by: University of Tokushima, Faculty of Integrated Arts and Sciences, 1-1 Minami Josanjima, Tokushima, 770-8503, Japan. TEL 81-88-656-7021, FAX 81-88-656-7012. Circ: 600.

301.4 USA
UNIVERSITY OF WISCONSIN AT MADISON. INSTITUTE FOR RESEARCH ON POVERTY. SPECIAL REPORT SERIES (ONLINE). Text in English. 2002. irreg., latest 2003, Sep. free (effective 2010). back issues avail.; reprints avail. **Document type:** *Monographic series, Trade.*
Media: Online - full text.
Published by: University of Wisconsin at Madison, Institute for Research on Poverty, 3412 Social Science Bldg, 1180 Observatory Dr, Madison, WI 53706. TEL 608-262-6358, FAX 608-265-3119, irppubs@ssc.wisc.edu, http://www.ssc.wisc.edu/irp/.

301.4 USA
UNIVERSITY OF WISCONSIN, MADISON. INSTITUTE FOR RESEARCH ON POVERTY. DISCUSSION PAPERS. Text in English. 1967. irreg. price varies. back issues avail. **Document type:** *Monographic series, Academic/Scholarly.* **Description:** Features non-copyrighted papers dealing with issues related to poverty.
Related titles: Online - full text ed.: ISSN 1934-824X. free (effective 2010).
Published by: University of Wisconsin at Madison, Institute for Research on Poverty, 3412 Social Science Bldg, 1180 Observatory Dr, Madison, WI 53706. TEL 608-262-6358, FAX 608-265-3119, irppubs@ssc.wisc.edu, http://www.ssc.wisc.edu/irp/.

300.711 ZMB
UNIVERSITY OF ZAMBIA. SCHOOL OF HUMANITIES AND SOCIAL SCIENCES. ANNUAL REPORT. Text in English. 1968. a.
Published by: School of Humanities and Social Sciences, PO Box 2379, Lusaka, Zambia. TELEX ZA 44370.

300 ESP ISSN 1698-6083
P35.5.I24
UNIVERSOS; revista de lenguas indigenas y universos culturles. Text in Spanish. 2004. a. EUR 11 (effective 2009). **Document type:** *Journal, Academic/Scholarly.*
Indexed: L&LBA.
Published by: Universidad de Granada, Editorial, Antiguo Colegio Maximo, Campus de Cartuja, Granada, 18071, Spain. TEL 34-958-246220, FAX 34-958-243931, http://www.editorialugr.com.

300 001.3 CHL ISSN 0716-498X
UNIVERSUM; revista de humanidades y ciencias sociales. Text in Spanish. 1986. s-a. CLP 10,000 to individuals; CLP 18,000 to institutions (effective 2010). **Document type:** *Journal, Academic/Scholarly.* **Description:** Areas of interest include the humanities and social sciences as related to the historic, political, social, economic and cultural aspects of Latin America.
Related titles: Online - full text ed.: ISSN 0718-2376. 2005. free (effective 2011) (from SciELO).
Indexed: H21, P08, SCOPUS.
Published by: Universidad de Talca, 2 Norte 685, Talca, Chile. TEL 56-71-200200, FAX 56-71-200410. Ed. Francisco Javier Pinedo Castro. Circ: 1,000.

300 SVK
UNIVERZITA KOMENSKEHO. USTAV MARXIZMU-LENINIZMU. ZBORNIK: VEDECKY KOMUNIZMUS. Text in Slovak; Summaries in German, Russian. 1978. a. per issue exchange basis.
Indexed: RASB.
Published by: Univerzita Komenskeho, Ustav Marxizmu-Leninizmu, c/o Study and Information Center, Safarikovo nam 6, Bratislava, 81806, Slovakia. Ed. Peter Kulasik. Circ: 450.

S

300 POL ISSN 1427-6437
UNIWERSYTET OPOLSKI. ZESZYTY NAUKOWE. SERIA A. NAUKI SPOLECZNO-POLITYCZNE. Text in Polish; Summaries in English. 1985. irreg., latest vol.11, 1995. **Document type:** *Monographic series, Academic/Scholarly.*
Formerly (until 1994): Wyzsza Szkola Pedagogiczna, Opole. Zeszyty Naukowe. Seria A. Nauki Spoleczno-Polityczne (0239-670X)
Indexed: RASB.
Published by: Wyzsza Szkola Pedagogiczna Opole, Ul Sienkiewicza 33, Opole, 45037, Poland. TEL 48-77-538387. Ed. Jan Korbel.

▼ **UNOESC & CIENCIA. ACHS.** *see* HUMANITIES: COMPREHENSIVE WORKS

300 DEU ISSN 0170-1657
UNTERSUCHUNGEN ZUR WIRTSCHAFTS-, SOZIAL- UND TECHNIKGESCHICHTE. Text in German. 1973. irreg., latest vol.28, 2011. price varies. **Document type:** *Monographic series, Academic/Scholarly.*
Published by: Ardey-Verlag GmbH, An den Speichern 6, Muenster, 48157, Germany. TEL 49-251-41320, FAX 49-251-413220, grabowsky@ardey-verlag.de.

300 USA ISSN 2152-7474
▼ **UPSCALEHOUSTON ONLINE.** Text in English. 2009. m. free (effective 2010). adv. back issues avail. **Document type:** *Magazine, Consumer.* **Description:** Features articles on better living in the Houston area as well as commentary and blogs on stories and events impacting and affecting everyday life.
Media: Online - full text.
Published by: The Urban Equities Group, PO Box 311164, Houston, TX 77231.

URBAN AFFAIRS REVIEW. *see* HOUSING AND URBAN PLANNING

URBAN HISTORY. *see* HISTORY—History Of Europe

URBAN INSTITUTE. ANNUAL REPORT. *see* BUSINESS AND ECONOMICS

300 DEU
▼ **URBANE WELTEN;** Texte zur kulturwissenschaftlichen Stadtforschung. Text in German. 2009. irreg., latest vol.3, 2010. price varies. **Document type:** *Monographic series, Academic/Scholarly.*
Published by: Transcript, Muehlenstr 47, Bielefeld, 33607, Germany. TEL 49-521-63454, FAX 49-521-61040, live@transcript-verlag.de.

URBANI IZZIV. *see* HOUSING AND URBAN PLANNING

300 CHN ISSN 1009-3397
URUMQI ZHIYE DAXUE XUEBAO/URUMQI VOCATIONAL UNIVERSITY. JOURNAL. Text in Chinese. 1992. q. CNY 5 newsstand/cover (effective 2006). **Document type:** *Journal, Academic/Scholarly.*
Related titles: Online - full text ed.
Published by: Urumqi Zhiye Daxue, 72, Xingfu Lu, Urumqi, 830002, China. TEL 86-991-8858304, FAX 86-991-8819092.

UTAFITI; journal of the faculty of arts and social science. *see* LITERATURE

335.02 COL ISSN 0123-1952
H8
➤ **UTOPIA SIGLO XXI;** revista de la facultad de ciencias sociales y humanas. Text in Spanish. 1997. a. COP 20,000 domestic; USD 15 foreign; COP 15,000 domestic to students (effective 2003). adv. Index. **Document type:** *Journal, Academic/Scholarly.*
Indexed: A26, I04, I05.
Published by: (Universidad de Antioquia, Facultad de Ciencias Sociales y Humanas), Universidad de Antioquia, Departamento de Publicaciones, Calle 67, No 53-108, Bloque 28, Oficina 233, Medellin, Colombia. TEL 57-4-2105010, FAX 57-4-2105012, ediudea@catios.udea.edu.co. Ed. Jose Rosique Gracia. R&P, Adv. contact Angelica Maria Tobon. Circ: 1,000 (controlled).

303.3 RUS
V I P PREMIER. Text in Russian. 1991. m. RUR 300,000, USD 120. back issues avail. **Description:** Covers leadership phenomena in Russia and elsewhere.
Related titles: English ed.
Indexed: RASB.
Address: Ul Petrovka 26, k 2, Moscow, 103051, Russian Federation. TEL 7-095-2099958, FAX 7-095-2099704. Ed. Vladimir Marozov. Pub. Evgeni Kosov. adv.: page USD 7,000; trim 300 x 225. Circ: 200,000.

330 300 DEU ISSN 0340-8728
➤ **V S W G - VIERTELJAHRSCHRIFT FUER SOZIAL- UND WIRTSCHAFTSGESCHICHTE.** Text in English, German. 1893. q. EUR 209.80; EUR 167.80 to members; EUR 58.20 per issue (effective 2012). adv. bk.rev. cum.index: vols.21-50 (1928-1963). back issues avail.; reprint service avail. from SCH. **Document type:** *Journal, Academic/Scholarly.* **Description:** Contains research and articles on European and German social and economic history.
Former titles (until 1972): Vierteljahrschrift fuer Sozial- und Wirtschaftsgeschichte (0042-5699); (until 1900): Zeitschrift fuer Social- und Wirtschaftsgeschichte (1619-6104)
Related titles: Online - full text ed.: (from IngentaConnect); ◆ Supplement(s): Vierteljahrschrift fuer Sozial- und Wirtschaftsgeschichte. Beihefte. ISSN 0341-0846.
Indexed: CA, DIP, HistAb, IBR, IBSS, IBZ, P06, P30, PAIS, PCI, RASB, SCOPUS, T02.
—IE, Infotrieve. **CCC.**
Published by: Franz Steiner Verlag GmbH, Birkenwaldstr 44, Stuttgart, 70191, Germany. TEL 49-711-25820, FAX 49-711-2582290, service@steiner-verlag.de. R&P Sabine Koerner. Adv. contact Susanne Szoradi. Circ: 1,080 (paid and controlled).

300 ARG ISSN 0326-3398
VALORES EN LA SOCIEDAD INDUSTRIAL. Text in Spanish. 1983. q. USD 20 per issue (effective 2005). **Document type:** *Journal, Academic/Scholarly.*
Indexed: CA, F04, T02.
Published by: (Pontificia Universidad Catolica Argentina, Facultad de Ciencias Sociales y Economicas), Pontificia Universidad Catolica Argentina, E D U C A, Av Alicia M de Justo 1400, Buenos Aires, C1107AFD, Argentina. educa@uca.edu.ar, http://www.uca.edu.ar/educa.htm. Ed. Ludovico Videla.

300 GTM
VARIOUS. SERIE MONOGRAFICA. Text mainly in Spanish; Text occasionally in English. 1981. irreg. (1-2/yr.). price varies. **Document type:** *Monographic series.*
Formerly: Centro de Investigaciones Regionales de Mesoamerica. Serie Monografica (0252-9971)
Indexed: AICP, AbAn, IBibSS.
Published by: Centro de Investigaciones Regionales de Mesoamerica (CIRMA), Plumsock Mesoamerican Studies, 5e. Calle Oriente No. 5, Antigua, Guatemala. TEL 802-457-1199, FAX 802-457-2212, http://www.cirma.org. Eds. Armando J Alfonzo, Christopher H Lutz. Circ: 1,000.

300 DEU
VEREIN FUER SOCIALPOLITIK. SCHRIFTEN. Text in German. 1873. irreg., latest vol.322, 2009. price varies. **Document type:** *Monographic series, Academic/Scholarly.*
Formerly: Verein fuer Socialpolitik - Gesellschaft fuer Wirtschafts- und Sozialwissenschaften. Schriften (0505-2777)
Published by: (Verein fuer Socialpolitik), Duncker und Humblot GmbH, Carl-Heinrich-Becker-Weg 9, Berlin, 12165, Germany. TEL 49-30-7900060, FAX 49-30-79000631, info@duncker-humblot.de.

VERHALTENSTHERAPIE UND PSYCHOSOZIALE PRAXIS. *see* PSYCHOLOGY

300 USA
VERITAS; the world's best kept secrets. Text in English. 1988. q. free. **Document type:** *Newsletter.* **Description:** Provides a forum for specific solutions to economic and social problems.
Address: 10807 E Nolcrest Dr, Silver Spring, MD 20903. TEL 301-593-1686. Ed. Abraham H Kalish. Circ: 1,000.

300 500 DEU
VERKOERPERUNGEN; Perspektiven empirischer Wissenschaftsforschung. Text in German. 2008. irreg., latest vol.11, 2011. price varies. **Document type:** *Monographic series, Academic/Scholarly.*
Published by: Transcript, Muehlenstr 47, Bielefeld, 33607, Germany. TEL 49-521-63454, FAX 49-521-61040, live@transcript-verlag.de.

300 DEU ISSN 0930-8849
VEROEFFENTLICHUNGEN AUS DEN ARCHIVEN PREUSSISCHER KULTURBESITZ. Text in German. 1967. irreg., latest vol.66, 2010. price varies. **Document type:** *Monographic series, Academic/Scholarly.*
Published by: Boehlau Verlag GmbH & Cie, Ursulaplatz 1, Cologne, 50668, Germany. TEL 49-221-913900, FAX 49-221-9139011, vertrieb@boehlau.de. Eds. Dieter Heckmann, Juergen Kloosterhuis.

300 DEU
VEROEFFENTLICHUNGEN DER AG "MENSCHEN FORMEN". Text in German. 2000. irreg., latest vol.3, 2005. price varies. **Document type:** *Monographic series, Academic/Scholarly.*
Published by: Tectum Wissenschaftsverlag Marburg, Biegenstr 4, Marburg, 35037, Germany. TEL 49-6421-481523, FAX 49-6421-43470, email@tectum-verlag.de.

300 AUT ISSN 1990-9586
VEROEFFENTLICHUNGEN ZUR SOZIALANTHROPOLOGIE. Text in German. 1996. irreg., latest vol.24, 2010. price varies. **Document type:** *Monographic series, Academic/Scholarly.*
Published by: Verlag der Oesterreichischen Akademie der Wissenschaften, Postgasse 7/4, Vienna, W 1011, Austria. TEL 43-1-515813402, FAX 43-1-515813400, verlag@oeaw.ac.at, http://verlag.oeaw.ac.at.

VERTIGO; la revue electronique en sciences de l'environnement. *see* ENVIRONMENTAL STUDIES

VESTIGIUM. *see* HUMANITIES: COMPREHENSIVE WORKS

300 USA ISSN 1930-286X
DK1
➤ **VESTNIK.** Text in English. 2005. 3/yr. free (effective 2011). **Document type:** *Journal, Academic/Scholarly.* **Description:** Aims at encouraging the study of Russia and those states formerly a part of the Soviet Union.
Media: Online - full text.
Indexed: A39, C27, C29, D03, D04, E13, R14, S14, S15, S18.
Published by: The School of Russian and Asian Studies, 117 Marva Oaks Dr, Woodside, CA 94062. Ed. Joshua H Wilson.

➤ **VICTORIAN STUDIES;** a journal of the humanities, arts and sciences. *see* HUMANITIES: COMPREHENSIVE WORKS

300 LKA ISSN 1391-1937
HN670.8
VIDYODAYA JOURNAL OF SOCIAL SCIENCES. Text in English, Singhalese, Tamil. 1968. s-a. LKR 200, USD 10 (effective 1999). bk.rev. bibl.; charts; illus.; stat. index, cum.index. **Document type:** *Journal, Academic/Scholarly.*
Supersedes in part (in Jul. 1987): Vidyodaya (0042-532X)
Indexed: BAS, MLA-IB, SLSI.
Published by: University of Sri Jayewardenepura, Nugegoda, Sri Lanka. TEL 941-853-194, FAX 941-852-604. R&P P Vidanapathirana. Circ: 1,000.

330 300 DEU ISSN 0341-0846
VIERTELJAHRSCHRIFT FUER SOZIAL- UND WIRTSCHAFTSGESCHICHTE. BEIHEFTE. Text in German. 1923. irreg., latest vol.214, 2011. price varies. **Document type:** *Monographic series, Academic/Scholarly.*
Related titles: ◆ Supplement to: V S W G - Vierteljahrschrift fuer Sozial- und Wirtschaftsgeschichte. ISSN 0340-8728.
Indexed: CLT&T, PCI, RASB.
—**CCC.**
Published by: Franz Steiner Verlag GmbH, Birkenwaldstr 44, Stuttgart, 70191, Germany. TEL 49-711-25820, FAX 49-711-2582290, franz.steiner.verlag@t-online.de, http://www.steiner-verlag.de.

300 VNM ISSN 1013-4328
H62.5.V5
VIETNAM SOCIAL SCIENCES. Text in English. 1984. q. **Document type:** *Journal, Academic/Scholarly.*
Related titles: French ed.: Viet Nam Sciences Sociales. ISSN 1017-5423.
Indexed: APEL, BAS, FR, IBSS, PerIslam, RASB.
—INIST.
Published by: Viet-Nam Institute of Social Science, 27 Tran Xuan Soan, Hanoi, Viet Nam. TEL 84-52031. Ed. Nguyen Huu Thanh.

VIETNAMESE STUDIES. *see* HISTORY—History Of Asia

300 DEU ISSN 2191-7280
▼ **VIGONIANAE;** Deutsch-italienische Halbjahresschrift - rivista semestrale italo-tedesca. Text in German, Italian. 2010. 2/yr. EUR 69; EUR 39 newsstand/cover (effective 2012). **Document type:** *Journal, Academic/Scholarly.*
Published by: Franz Steiner Verlag GmbH, Birkenwaldstr 44, Stuttgart, 70191, Germany. TEL 49-711-25820, FAX 49-711-2582290, service@steiner-verlag.de, http://www.steiner-verlag.de.

VIRGINIA ISSUES & ANSWERS; a public policy forum. *see* PUBLIC ADMINISTRATION

VIRGINIA JOURNAL OF SOCIAL POLICY & THE LAW. *see* LAW

300 USA ISSN 0507-1305
H1 CODEN: VSSJF5
➤ **VIRGINIA SOCIAL SCIENCE JOURNAL.** Text in English. 1966. a. back issues avail. **Document type:** *Journal, Academic/Scholarly.* **Description:** Provides original research articles on social science issues.
Indexed: B04, CA, DIP, IBR, IBZ, P06, P42, PAIS, PSA, S02, S03, SCOPUS, SOPODA, SSAI, SSAb, SSI, SociolAb, T02, W03, W05.
Published by: Virginia Social Science Association, c/o Kimberly Kinsler, 180 Pinehurst Ave, New York, NY 10033 . kkinsler@hunter.cuny.edu. Eds. Mary Stegmaier, Tinni Sen.

300 001.3 BRA ISSN 1516-2982
➤ **VISAO GLOBAL.** Text in Portuguese; Summaries in English, Portuguese. 1997. s-a. BRL 20 (effective 2008). bk.rev. bibl.; charts; illus.; maps; stat.; tr.lit. Index. back issues avail. **Document type:** *Journal, Academic/Scholarly.* **Description:** Provides information for researchers, teachers and students of social sciences and humanities.
Published by: Universidade do Oeste de Santa Catarina (UNOESC), Rua Getulio Vargas, 2125, Bairro Flor da Serra, Joacaba, Santa Catarina CEP 89600, Brazil. TEL 55-49-35512065, FAX 55-49-35512004, editora@unoesc.edu.br. Ed., Pub. Roque Strieder. Adv. contact Debora Diersmann Silva Pereira TEL 55-49-35512065.

➤ **VISUAL COMMUNICATION.** *see* COMMUNICATIONS

➤ **VISUAL CULTURE & GENDER.** *see* ART

➤ **VITAL ISSUES;** the journal of African American speeches. *see* POLITICAL SCIENCE

300 DEU ISSN 1432-8739
VOLKSWIRTSCHAFTLICHE ANALYSEN. Text in German. 1998. irreg., latest vol.15, 2009. price varies. **Document type:** *Monographic series, Academic/Scholarly.*
Published by: Peter Lang GmbH (Subsidiary of: Peter Lang Publishing Group), Eschborner Landstr 42-50, Frankfurt Am Main, 60489, Germany. TEL 49-69-7807050, FAX 49-69-78070550, zentrale.frankfurt@peterlang.com, http://www.peterlang.com.

300 DEU ISSN 1435-6872
VOLKSWIRTSCHAFTLICHE FORSCHUNGSERGEBNISSE. Text in German. 1986. irreg., latest vol.157, 2010. price varies. **Document type:** *Monographic series, Academic/Scholarly.*
Published by: Verlag Dr. Kovac, Leverkusenstr 13, Hamburg, 22761, Germany. TEL 49-40-3988800, FAX 49-40-39888055, info@verlagdrkovac.de.

300 GBR ISSN 2040-8056
▼ ➤ **VOLUNTARY SECTOR REVIEW;** an international journal of third sector research, policy and practice. Text in English. 2010 (Mar.). 3/yr. GBP 323, EUR 387 combined subscription in Europe to institutions (print & online eds.); USD 530 combined subscription in the Americas to institutions (print & online eds.); GBP 355 combined subscription elsewhere to institutions (print & online eds.) (effective 2012). **Document type:** *Journal, Academic/Scholarly.* **Description:** Covers voluntary sector studies from a variety of disciplines, including sociology, social policy, politics, psychology, economics, business studies, social anthropology, philosophy and ethics.
Related titles: Online - full text ed.: ISSN 2040-8064 (from IngentaConnect).
Indexed: PAIS.
—IE.
Published by: (Voluntary Sector Studies Network), The Policy Press, University of Bristol, 4th Fl, Beacon House, Queen's Rd, Bristol, BS8 1QU, United Kingdom. TEL 44-117-3314054, FAX 44-117-3314093, tpp-info@bristol.ac.uk, http://www.policypress.org.uk. Ed. Peter Halfpenny. Pub. Alison Shaw. Adv. contact Kathryn King TEL 44-117-3314097. **Subscr. to:** Portland Customer Services, Commerce Way, Colchester CO2 8HP, United Kingdom. TEL 44-1206-796351, FAX 44-1206-799331, sales@portland-services.com, http://www.portland-services.com.

➤ **VORGAENGE;** Zeitschrift fuer Buergerrechte und Gesellschaftspolitik. *see* POLITICAL SCIENCE

300 BRA
VOZ LUSIADA. Text in Portuguese. s-a. **Document type:** *Academic/Scholarly.*
Published by: Academia Lusiada de Ciencias Letras e Artes, Edif. Casa de Portugal, Av da Liberdade, 602, Liberdade, Sao Paulo, SP 01502-001, Brazil. TEL 55-11-2704172.

300 SWE ISSN 2000-8023
▼ ➤ **VULNERABLE GROUPS & INCLUSION.** Text in English. 2011. free (effective 2011). **Document type:** *Journal, Academic/Scholarly.* **Description:** Contains research relating to the processes behind the inclusion of people who are either at risk of becoming marginalized or who are already marginalized.
Media: Online - full text.
Published by: Co-Action Publishing, Ripvaegen 7, Jaerfaella, 17564, Sweden. TEL 46-18-4951150, FAX 46-18-4951138, info@co-action.net, http://www.co-action.net. Ed. Bodil Landstad.

300 AUT ISSN 1012-3059
W I S O. (Wirtschafts- und Sozialpolitische) Variant title: Wirtschafts- und Sozialpolitische Zeitschrift des I S W. Text in German. 1978. q. EUR 22 domestic; EUR 28 foreign; EUR 13 to students (effective 2009). **Document type:** *Journal, Academic/Scholarly.*
Indexed: IBSS.
Published by: Institut fuer Sozial- und Wirtschaftswissenschaften, Gruberstr 40-42, Linz, 4020, Austria. TEL 43-732-669273, FAX 43-732-6692732889, isw@ak-ooe.at.

300 AUT
W I S O - DOKUMENTE. (Wirtschafts- und Sozialpolitische) Text in German. irreg., latest vol.51, 2006. price varies. **Document type:** *Monographic series, Academic/Scholarly.*
Published by: Institut fuer Sozial- und Wirtschaftswissenschaften, Gruberstr 40-42, Linz, 4020, Austria. TEL 43-732-669273, FAX 43-732-6692732889, isw@ak-ooe.at, http://www.isw-linz.at.

330 331.8 300 DEU ISSN 0342-300X
HC281
W S I MITTEILUNGEN. Text in German. 1948. m. EUR 79.80; EUR 8 newsstand/cover (effective 2009). adv. bk.rev. charts; stat. index. **Document type:** *Journal, Academic/Scholarly.*
Formerly (until 1972): W W I Mitteilungen (0042-9872)
Indexed: A22, DIP, ELLIS, IBR, IBZ, PAIS, RASB, WBSS. —BLDSC (9364.930000), IE, Infotrieve, Ingenta. **CCC.**
Published by: (Deutscher Gewerkschaftsbund), Bund-Verlag GmbH, Heddernheimer Landstr 144, Frankfurt Am Main, 60439, Germany. TEL 49-69-79501020, FAX 49-69-79501010, kontakt@bund-verlag.de, http://www.bund-verlag.de. Ed. Gudrun Trautwein-Kalms. Adv. contact Hartmut Griesbach. B&W page EUR 975; trim 180 x 260. Circ: 4,100 (paid and controlled).

300 600 DEU ISSN 1612-3468
➤ **W Z B DISCUSSION PAPERS.** Text in German, English. irreg. free. back issues avail. **Document type:** *Monographic series, Academic/ Scholarly.*
Formerly: W Z B Papers
Related titles: Online - full text ed.
Published by: Wissenschaftszentrum Berlin fuer Sozialforschung, Reichpietschufer 50, Berlin, 10785, Germany. TEL 49-30-254910, FAX 49-30-25491684, presse@wzb.eu.

320 DEU ISSN 0174-3120
W Z B - MITTEILUNGEN. Text in German. 1978. q. free. back issues avail. **Document type:** *Newsletter, Academic/Scholarly.*
Related titles: Online - full text ed.
Indexed: RASB.
Published by: Wissenschaftszentrum Berlin fuer Sozialforschung, Reichpietschufer 50, Berlin, 10785, Germany. TEL 49-30-254910, FAX 49-30-25491684, presse@wzb.eu. Ed. Dr. Jutta Allmendinger. Circ: 11,000.

300 AUT ISSN 1817-8944
WECHSELBEZIEHUNGEN OESTERREICH - NORDEN. Text in German. 2003. irreg., latest vol.10, 2006. price varies. **Document type:** *Monographic series, Academic/Scholarly.*
Published by: Praesens VerlagsgesmbH, Wehlistr 154/12, Vienna, W 1020, Austria. TEL 43-1-720703506, FAX 43-1-25330334660, http://www.praesens.at.

300 500 CHN ISSN 1671-4288
WEIFANG XUEYUAN XUEBAO/WEIFANG UNIVERSITY. JOURNAL. Text in Chinese. 2001. bi-m. CNY 8 newsstand/cover (effective 2006). **Document type:** *Journal, Academic/Scholarly.*
Formed by the merger of (1993-2001): Weifang Gaodeng Zhuanke Xuexiao Xuebao/Weifang College. Journal (1008-8237); (1998-2001): Changwei Shi-Zhuan Xuebao/Changwei Teachers College. Journal (1008-4150)
Related titles: Online - full text ed.
Published by: Weifang Xueyuan, 149, Dongfeng Dong Jie, Weifang, 261061, China. TEL 86-536-8785229.

300 DEU ISSN 1860-8639
WEIMARER STUDIEN ZUR KULTURPOLITIK UND KULTUROEKONOMIE. Text in German. 2005. irreg., latest vol.6, 2010. price varies. **Document type:** *Monographic series, Academic/ Scholarly.*
Published by: Leipziger Universitaetsverlag GmbH, Oststr 41, Leipzig, 04317, Germany. TEL 49-341-9900440, FAX 49-341-9900440, info@univerlag-leipzig.de.

300 AUT
WELSER UNIVERSITAERE SCHRIFTEN. Text in German. 2007. irreg. price varies. **Document type:** *Monographic series, Academic/ Scholarly.*
Published by: Trauner Verlag und Buchservice GmbH, Koeglstr 14, Linz, 4020, Austria. TEL 43-732-778241212, FAX 43-732-778241400, office@trauner.at, http://www.trauner.at.

942.9 USA ISSN 1543-7892
➤ **WELSH STUDIES.** Text in English. 1990. irreg., latest vol.18, 2004. price varies. back issues avail. **Document type:** *Monographic series, Academic/Scholarly.*
Published by: Edwin Mellen Press, 415 Ridge St, PO Box 450, Lewiston, NY 14092. TEL 716-754-2266, FAX 716-754-4056, cservice@mellenpress.com.

300 DEU ISSN 1438-9886
WELT - KOERPER - SPRACHE; Perspektiven kultureller Wahrnehmungs- und Darstellungsformen. Text in German. 2000. irreg., latest vol.8, 2010. price varies. **Document type:** *Monographic series, Academic/Scholarly.*
Published by: Peter Lang GmbH (Subsidiary of: Peter Lang Publishing Group), Eschborner Landstr 42-50, Frankfurt Am Main, 60489, Germany. TEL 49-69-7807050, FAX 49-69-78070550, zentrale.frankfurt@peterlang.com, http://www.peterlang.com. Ed. Eva Kimminich.

306 CHN ISSN 1001-2788
DS721
WENHUA YANJIU/CULTURAL RESEARCH. Text in Chinese. 1987. m. USD 79 (effective 2009). 128 p./no.; **Document type:** *Journal, Academic/Scholarly.*
Indexed: RASB.
Published by: Zhongguo Renmin Daxue Shubao Ziliao Zhongxin/Renmin University of China, Information Center for Social Sciences, Dongcheng-qu, 3, Zhangzizhong Lu, Beijing, 100007, China. TEL 86-10-64039458, FAX 86-10-64015080, center@zlzx.org, http://www.zlzx.org/. **Dist. in US by:** China Publications Service, PO Box 49614, Chicago, IL 60649. TEL 312-288-3291, FAX 312-288-8570; **Dist. by:** China International Book Trading Corp, 35 Chegongzhuang Xilu, Haidian District, PO Box 399, Beijing 100044, China. TEL 86-10-68412045, FAX 86-10-68412023, cibtc@mail.cibtc.com.cn, http://www.cibtc.com.cn.

300 CHN ISSN 1674-4608
WENHUA ZONGHENG/BEIJING CULTURAL REVIEW. Text in Chinese. 2008. bi-m. CNY 156 (effective 2010). **Document type:** *Journal, Academic/Scholarly.*
Related titles: Online - full text ed.
Published by: (Shoudu Qingnian Bianji Jizhe Xiehui/Capital Young Journalists Association), Wenhua Zongheng Zazhishe, 32, Baiziwan Lu, Pingguoshe-qu Bei-qu #3, A-303, Beijing, 100022, China. TEL 86-10-52097990 ext 809.

300 CHN ISSN 1004-8359
DS736
WENJIAO ZILIAO/DATA OF CULTURE AND EDUCATION. Text in Chinese. 1986. every 10 days. **Document type:** *Journal, Academic/ Scholarly.*
Related titles: Online - full text ed.
Published by: Nanjing Shifan Daxue/Nanjing Normal University, 122 Ninghai Lu, Nanjing, Jiangsu 210097, China. TEL 86-25-83951252, http://www.njnu.edu.cn/.

300 CHN ISSN 1674-9200
WENSHAN XUEYUAN XUEBAO/WENSHAN UNIVERSITY. JOURNAL. Text in Chinese. 1986. bi-m. CNY 8 newsstand/cover (effective 2006). **Document type:** *Journal, Academic/Scholarly.*
Former titles (until 2010): Wenshan Shifan Gaodeng Zhuanke Xuexiao Xuebao/Wenshan Teachers College. Journal (1671-3303); (until 2001): Wenshan Shizhuan Xuebao
Related titles: Online - full text ed.
Published by: Wenshan Xueyuan, 66, Xuefu Lu, Wenshan, 663000, China. TEL 86-876-8886216, FAX 86-876-2152077, http://www.wstc.net/.

300 895.1 CHN ISSN 1002-9869
WENSHI ZHISHI/KNOWLEDGE OF LITERATURE AND HISTORY. Text in Chinese. 1981. m. USD 43.20 (effective 2009). adv. bk.rev. abstr.; bibl.; charts; illus. Index. **Document type:** *Journal, Academic/ Scholarly.* **Description:** Concerns Chinese literature and history.
Related titles: Microfiche ed.
—East View.
Published by: Zhonghua Shuju, 36 Wangfujing Jie, Beijing, 100710, China. TEL 86-10-63458229. Ed. Xiong Guo Zhen. Adv. contact Wenshi Zhishi. Circ: 40,000.

300 CHN ISSN 1674-3555
➤ **WENZHOU DAXUE XUEBAO (SHEHUI KEXUE BAN)/WENZHOU UNIVERSITY. JOURNAL (SOCIAL SCIENCES).** Text in Chinese; Summaries in Chinese, English. 1988. bi-m. CNY 25 (effective 2009). bk.rev.; film rev.; play rev.; tel.rev.; video rev. Index. back issues avail. **Document type:** *Journal, Academic/Scholarly.* **Description:** Publishes original articles on philosophy, humanities and social sciences and reviews.
Supersedes in part (1988 -2006): Wenzhou Daxue Xuebao/Wenzhou University. Journal (1008-309X); (1987-2006): Wenzhou Shifan Xueyuan Xuebao/Wenzhou Normal College. Journal (1006-0375); Which was formerly (1980-1986): Wenzhou Shi-Zhuan Xuebao
Related titles: Online - full text ed.
Indexed: L&LBA, PSA, SSA, SociolAb.
Published by: Wenzhou Daxue, Chashan, Xingzheng Bldg. 516, Wenzhou, 325035, China. TEL 86-577-86598068, http://www.wzu.edu.cn/. Ed., Pub., R&P Xiaowei Zhao. Circ: 2,200.

300 500 CHN ISSN 1671-4326
WENZHOU ZHIYE JISHU XUEYUAN XUEBAO/WENZHOU VOCATIONAL AND TECHNICAL COLLEGE. JOURNAL. Text in Chinese. 2001. q. CNY 6 newsstand/cover (effective 2006). **Document type:** *Journal, Academic/Scholarly.*
Related titles: Online - full text ed.
Published by: Wenzhou Zhiye Jishu Xueyuan, Gaoke Lu, Wenzhou, 325035, China. TEL 86-577-86680067.

300 DEU ISSN 0942-704X
DD233 CODEN: GESCEQ
➤ **WERKSTATT GESCHICHTE.** Text in German. 1985. 3/yr. EUR 37; EUR 14 newsstand/cover (effective 2010). adv. **Document type:** *Journal, Academic/Scholarly.*
Formerly (until 1992): Geschichtswerkstatt (0933-5706)
Indexed: CA, DIP, HistAb, IBR, IBZ, P30, T02.
—CCC.
Published by: (Verein fuer Kritische Geschichtsschreibung e.V), Klartext Verlag GmbH, Hesslerstr 37, Essen, 45329, Germany. TEL 49-201-8620631, FAX 49-201-8620622, info@klartext-verlag.de, http://www.klartext-verlag.de. Ed. Sabine Horn.

➤ **THE WESTERN SCHOLAR.** *see* HUMANITIES: COMPREHENSIVE WORKS

➤ **WETENSCHAP IN BEELD.** *see* SCIENCES: COMPREHENSIVE WORKS

384.53 CAN ISSN 1918-2104
➤ **WI: JOURNAL OF MOBILE MEDIA.** Text in English. 2006. 3/yr. free (effective 2009). bk.rev.; dance rev.; film rev.; music rev.; play rev.; software rev.; tel.rev.; video rev. abstr.; bibl.; charts; illus.; maps; stat. Index. back issues avail. **Document type:** *Journal, Academic/ Scholarly.* **Description:** Aims to highlight and disseminate the on-going research results of collaboration amongst designers, theorists, artists, engineers, and software developers as a research network in mobile, wireless and gaming technologies.
Media: Online - full content.
Published by: Mobile Media Lab, c/o Barbara Crow, Graduate Program in Communication & Culture, York University, 4700 Keele St, Toronto, ON M3J 1P3, Canada. TEL 416-736-2100 ext 40549, FAX 416-736-5924, wieditors@gmail.com, http://wi.hexagram.ca.

300 CHE ISSN 1420-0945
HX6
WIDERSPRUCH; Beitraege zur sozialistischen Politik. Text in German. 1981. s-a. CHF 32, USD 35. **Document type:** *Academic/Scholarly.*
Indexed: DIP, IBR, IBZ.
Published by: Foerderverein Widerspruch, Postfach, Zuerich, 8026, Switzerland. TEL 41-1-2730302, FAX 41-1-2730302.

300 DEU
WIRTSCHAFTS- UND SOZIALPSYCHOLOGIE. Text in German. 2002. irreg., latest vol.3, 2005. price varies. **Document type:** *Monographic series, Academic/Scholarly.*
Published by: Herbert Utz Verlag GmbH, Adalbertstr 57, Munich, 80799, Germany. TEL 49-89-27779100, FAX 49-89-27779101, utz@utzverlag.com.

300 DEU
WIRTSCHAFTS-, UND SOZIALWISSENSCHAFTEN. Text in German. 1995. irreg., latest vol.50, 2009. price varies. **Document type:** *Monographic series, Academic/Scholarly.*
Published by: Herbert Utz Verlag GmbH, Adalbertstr 57, Munich, 80799, Germany. TEL 49-89-27779100, FAX 49-89-27779101, utz@utzverlag.com.

300 DEU
WIRTSCHAFTS- UND SOZIALWISSENSCHAFTLICHE OSTMITTELEUROPA-STUDIEN. Text in German. 1980. irreg., latest vol.21, 1996. price varies. **Document type:** *Monographic series, Academic/Scholarly.*
Published by: Herder Institut e.V., Gisonenweg 5-7, Marburg, 35037, Germany. TEL 49-6421-1840, FAX 49-6421-184139, mail@herder-institut.de, http://www.herder-institut.de.

WISSENSCHAFT - BILDUNG - POLITIK. *see* SCIENCES: COMPREHENSIVE WORKS

500 DEU ISSN 1863-7655
WISSENSCHAFT, POLITIK UND GESELLSCHAFT. Text in German. 2006. irreg., latest vol.7, 2010. price varies. **Document type:** *Monographic series, Academic/Scholarly.*
Published by: Franz Steiner Verlag GmbH, Birkenwaldstr 44, Stuttgart, 70191, Germany. TEL 49-711-25820, FAX 49-711-2582290, service@steiner-verlag.de, http://www.steiner-verlag.de.

300 DEU ISSN 1861-8049
WISSENSCHAFTLICHE BEITRAEGE AUS DEM TECTUM-VERLAG. REIHE SOZIALWISSENSCHAFTEN. Text in German. 1999. irreg., latest vol.37, 2010. price varies. **Document type:** *Monographic series, Academic/Scholarly.*
Published by: Tectum Wissenschaftsverlag Marburg, Biegenstr 4, Marburg, 35037, Germany. TEL 49-6421-481523, FAX 49-6421-43470, email@tectum-verlag.de.

300 DEU
WISSENSGESELLSCHAFT. Text in German. irreg. price varies. **Document type:** *Monographic series, Academic/Scholarly.*
Published by: Transcript, Muehlenstr 47, Bielefeld, 33607, Germany. TEL 49-521-63454, FAX 49-521-61040, live@transcript-verlag.de.

300 DEU ISSN 0342-8990
WOCHENSCHAU FUER POLITISCHE ERZIEHUNG, SOZIAL- UND GEMEINSCHAFTSKUNDE. AUSGABE FUER SEKUNDARSTUFE I. Text in German. 1949. 7/yr. EUR 150 (effective 2010). bk.rev. index. **Document type:** *Journal, Academic/Scholarly.*
Indexed: DIP, IBR, IBZ.
Published by: Wochenschau Verlag, Adolf Damaschke Str 10, Schwalbach, 65824, Germany. TEL 49-6196-86065, FAX 49-6196-86060, info@wochenschau-verlag.de, http://www.wochenschau-verlag.de. Ed. Bernward Debus.

300 DEU ISSN 0342-8974
WOCHENSCHAU FUER POLITISCHE ERZIEHUNG, SOZIAL- UND GEMEINSCHAFTSKUNDE. AUSGABE FUER SEKUNDARSTUFE II. Text in German. 1949. 7/yr. EUR 150 (effective 2010). adv. bk.rev. charts; illus.; stat. index. back issues avail. **Document type:** *Journal, Academic/Scholarly.*
Indexed: DIP, IBR, IBZ.
Published by: Wochenschau Verlag, Adolf Damaschke Str 10, Schwalbach, 65824, Germany. TEL 49-6196-86065, FAX 49-6196-86060, info@wochenschau-verlag.de, http://www.wochenschau-verlag.de. Ed. Bernward Debus.

WOMEN AND MUSIC; a journal of gender and culture. *see* MUSIC

▼ **WOOD CULTURE.** *see* FORESTS AND FORESTRY—Lumber And Wood

300 960 USA
GN643
WORKING PAPERS IN AFRICAN STUDIES (ONLINE). Text in English. 1978. irreg., latest vol.262, 2009. price varies. back issues avail. **Document type:** *Monographic series, Academic/Scholarly.*
Formerly (until 2008): Working Papers in African Studies (Print) (0281-6814)
Media: Online - full text.
Indexed: FR.
Published by: Boston University, African Studies Center, 232 Bay State Rd, Boston, MA 02215. TEL 617-353-7306, FAX 617-353-4975, ascpub@bu.edu. Ed. Michael DiBlasi.

300 USA ISSN 1931-3748
WORLD CULTURES (CD-ROM). Text in English. 1985. s-a. back issues avail. **Document type:** *Journal, Academic/Scholarly.*
Former titles (until 2006): World Cultures (Print) (1931-373X); (until 1999): World Cultures (Diskette) (1045-0564)
Media: CD-ROM. **Related titles:** Online - full text ed.
Published by: York College, Social Science Department, 94-20 Guy R, Brewer Blvd, Jamaica, NY 11451. TEL 718-262-2000, divale@york.cuny.edu, http://www.worldcultures.org/.

300 AUS ISSN 1838-3785
▼ **WORLD JOURNAL OF SOCIAL SCIENCES.** Abbreviated title: W J S S. Text in English. 2011. bi-m. back issues avail. **Document type:** *Journal, Academic/Scholarly.* **Description:** Covers topics relating to the broad field of banking, finance, economics, management, marketing, political science, sociology, and other disciplines related to social sciences.
Related titles: Online - full text ed.: ISSN 1839-1184.
Published by: World Business Institute, 31 Blake St, Berwick, Melbourne, VIC 3806, Australia. TEL 61-3-97022734, FAX 61-3-97020122, haqq50@wbint.org. Ed. Nicholas Koumbiadis.

300 SGP
▼ **WORLD SCIENTIFIC SERIES ON HUMAN SECURITY.** Text in English. 2010. irreg., latest vol.1, 2010. price varies. **Document type:** *Monographic series, Academic/Scholarly.* **Description:** Aims to publish book manuscripts that addresses human security issues in the contemporary world.
Published by: World Scientific Publishing Co. Pte. Ltd., 5 Toh Tuck Link, Singapore, 596224, Singapore. TEL 65-6466-5775, FAX 65-6467-7667, wspc@wspc.com.sg, http://www.worldscientific.com. Ed. Amitav Acharya. **Dist. by:** World Scientific Publishing Co., Inc., 27 Warren St, Ste 401-402, Hackensack, NJ 07601. TEL 201-487-9655, 800-227-7562, FAX 201-487-9656, 888-977-2665, wspc@wspc.com; World Scientific Publishing Ltd., 57 Shelton St, London WC2H 9HE, United Kingdom. TEL 44-207-8360888, FAX 44-207-8362020, sales@wspc.co.uk.

S

300 FRA
WORLD SOCIAL SCIENCE REPORT. Text in English. 1999. irreg., latest 1999. EUR 44.97 newsstand/cover (effective 2003). **Document type:** *Journal, Academic/Scholarly.*
Related titles: ◆ Series: World List of Social Science Periodicals. ISSN 0251-4877.
Published by: UNESCO Publishing, 7 place de Fontenoy, Paris, 75352, France. FAX 33-1-45685737, http://www.unesco.org/publishing.

WORLDMARK YEARBOOK. *see* POLITICAL SCIENCE

WORLDVIEWS; global religions, culture, and ecology. *see* ENVIRONMENTAL STUDIES

300 DEU
WUERZBURGER STUDIEN ZUR SPRACHE UND KULTUR. Text in German. 1989. irreg., latest vol.11, 2009. price varies. **Document type:** *Monographic series, Academic/Scholarly.*
Published by: J.H. Roell, Wuerzburgerstr 16, Dettelbach, 97337, Germany. TEL 49-9324-99770, FAX 49-9324-99771, info@roell-verlag.de, http://www.roell-verlag.de.

WUHAN CHUANBO ZHIYE JISHU XUEYUAN XUEBAO. *see* SCIENCES: COMPREHENSIVE WORKS

300 100 CHN ISSN 1672-7320
AS451
WUHAN DAXUE XUEBAO (ZHEXUE SHEHUI KEXUE BAN)/WUHAN UNIVERSITY. JOURNAL (PHILOSOPHY AND SOCIAL SCIENCE EDITION). Text in Chinese; Contents page in English. 1930. bi-m. USD 37.20 (effective 2009). bk.rev. **Document type:** *Journal, Academic/Scholarly.*
Formerly: Wuhan Daxue Xuebao (Shehui Kexue Ban) (1671-8828); Which superseded in part: Wuhan Daxue Xuebao (Renwen Shehui Kexue Ban); Which was formerly: Wuhan Daxue Xuebao (1000-5374); (until 1981): Wuhan Daxue Xuebao (Zhexue Shehui Kexue Ban) (1001-8441); Which was formed by the merger of: Guoli Wuhan Daxue Wen-Zhe Jiekan; Guoli Wuhan Daxue Shehui Kexue Jikan
Related titles: Online - full text ed.
Indexed: CA, L&LBA, P42, PSA, S02, S03, SCOPUS, SociolAb, T02.
—East View, Ingenta.
Published by: Wuhan Daxue, Meiyuan Yi-She, Wuhan, 430072, China. TEL 86-27-68754972, FAX 86-27-68752498, http://www.whu.edu.cn/. Ed. Tao Delin. **Dist. outside China by:** China International Book Trading Corp, 35 Chegongzhuang Xilu, Haidian District, PO Box 399, Beijing 100044, China.

300 CHN ISSN 1009-3699
WUHAN KEJI DAXUE XUEBAO (SHEHUI KEXUE BAN)/WUHAN UNIVERSITY OF SCIENCE AND TECHNOLOGY. JOURNAL (SOCIAL SCIENCE EDITION). Text in Chinese. 1999. q. **Document type:** *Journal, Academic/Scholarly.*
Related titles: Online - full text ed.
—East View.
Published by: Wuhan Keji Daxue/Wuhan University of Science and Technology, Jianshe 1 Lu, 947, Heping Dadao, Wuhan Keji Daxue Zhulou, 1319, Wuhan, 430081, China. TEL 86-27-68862627, FAX 86-27-68862317.

300 CHN ISSN 1671-6477
HN731
WUHAN LIGONG DAXUE XUEBAO (SHEHUI KEXUE BAN)/WUHAN UNIVERSITY OF TECHNOLOGY. JOURNAL (SOCIAL SCIENCE EDITION). Text in Chinese. 1988. bi-m. CNY 15 newsstand/cover (effective 2006). **Document type:** *Journal, Academic/Scholarly.*
Formerly (until 2000): Wuhan Jiaotong Keji Daxue Xuebao (Shehui Kexue Ban)/Wuhan Transportation University. Journal (Social Science Edition) (1009-0614)
Related titles: Online - full text ed.
Indexed: CA, L&LBA, PSA, S02, S03, SociolAb, T02.
Published by: Wuhan Ligong Daxue/Wuhan University of Technology, 1040, Heping Dadao, PO Box 50, Wuhan, 430063, China.

300 CHN ISSN 1674-9014
WULING XUEKAN. Text in Chinese. 1962. bi-m. CNY 10 per issue (effective 2011). **Document type:** *Journal, Academic/Scholarly.*
Former titles (until 2010): Hunan Wenli Xueyuan Xuebao (Shehui Kexue Ban) (1672-6154); (until 2002): Changde Shifan Xueyuan Xuebao (Shehui Kexue Ban) (1009-489X); (until 1999): Wuling Xuekan/Journal of Wuling (1007-0397)
Related titles: Online - full text ed.
Published by: Hunan Wenli Xueyuan, 170, Dongting Dadao Xi-Duan, Changde, 415000, China. TEL 86-736-7186179, FAX 86-736-7186077.

300 DEU
WUNDERWELT WISSEN; entertain your brain. Text in German. 2007. bi-m. EUR 18.60; EUR 3.30 newsstand/cover (effective 2010). adv. **Document type:** *Magazine, Consumer.*
Published by: Gruner + Jahr AG & Co, Am Baumwall 11, Hamburg, 20459, Germany. TEL 49-40-37030, FAX 49-40-37035601, info@gujmedia.de, http://www.guj.de. Ed. Hans Hermann Sprado. Adv. contact Christian Liesegang. color page EUR 9,250. Circ: 111,534 (paid).

500 CHN ISSN 1009-1513
WUYI DAXUE XUEBAO (SHEHUI KEXUE BAN)/WUYI UNIVERSITY. JOURNAL (SOCIAL SCIENCE EDITION). Text in Chinese. 1999. q. CNY 10 newsstand/cover (effective 2006). **Document type:** *Journal, Academic/Scholarly.*
Related titles: Online - full text ed.
Published by: Wuyi Daxue, 22, Dongchengcun, Jiangmen, 529020, China. TEL 86-750-3296184, FAX 86-750-3354323.

300 CHN ISSN 0438-0460
H8.C47
XIAMEN DAXUE XUEBAO (ZHEXUE SHEHUI KEXUE BAN)/XIAMEN UNIVERSITY. JOURNAL: A BIMONTHLY FOR STUDIES IN ARTS & SOCIAL SCIENCES. Variant title: Xiamen University. Journal (Natural Science). Text in Chinese; Contents page in English. 1926. bi-m. USD 21.60 (effective 2009). **Document type:** *Journal, Academic/Scholarly.*
Related titles: Online - full text ed.
—East View, Ingenta.
Published by: Xiamen Daxue/Xiamen University, Jiageng no.3 Bldg., Rm. 815, Xiamen, 361005, China. TEL 86-592-2182366. **Dist. outside China by:** China International Book Trading Corp, 35 Chegongzhuang Xilu, Haidian District, PO Box 399, Beijing 100044, China.

300 CHN ISSN 1008-472X
XI'AN DIANZI KEJI DAXUE XUEBAO (SHEHUI KEXUE BAN)/XIDIAN UNIVERSITY. JOURNAL (SOCIAL SCIENCE EDITION). Text in Chinese. 1985. q. USD 40.20 (effective 2009). **Document type:** *Journal, Academic/Scholarly.*
Supersedes in part: Xi'an Dianzi Keji Daxue Xuebao (1001-2400)
Related titles: Online - full text ed.
—BLDSC (4917.477500), East View.
Published by: Xi'an Dianzi Keji Daxue, 2, Taibai Nan LU, 354 Xiangxin, Xi'an, Shaanxi 710071, China. TELEX 86-29-88202922.

300 CHN ISSN 1008-7192
XI'AN JIANZHU KEJI DAXUE XUEBAO (SHEHUI KEXUE BAN)/XI'AN UNIVERSITY OF ARCHITECTURE & TECHNOLOGY. JOURNAL (SOCIAL SCIENCE EDITION). Text in Chinese. 1982. q. CNY 5 newsstand/cover (effective 2006). **Document type:** *Journal, Academic/Scholarly.*
Related titles: Online - full text ed.
Published by: Xi'an Jianzhu Keji Daxue/Xi'an University of Architecture and Technology, 13, Yanta Lu, Xi'an, 710055, China. TEL 86-29-82202167.

300 CHN ISSN 1008-245X
XI'AN JIAOTONG DAXUE XUEBAO (SHEHUI KEXUE BAN)/XI'AN JIAOTONG UNIVERSITY. JOURNAL (SOCIAL SCIENCES). Text in Chinese. 1981. q. USD 23.40 (effective 2009). **Document type:** *Journal, Academic/Scholarly.*
Related titles: Online - full text ed.
Published by: Xi'an Jiaotong Daxue, 28, Xi'an Road, Xi'an, 710049, China. TEL 86-29-82663982, FAX 86-29-82667978.

300 CHN
XI'AN SHIYOU DAXUE XUEBAO (SHEHUI KEXUE BAN)/XI'AN SHIYOU UNIVERSITY. JOURNAL (SOCIAL SCIENCES). Text in Chinese. 1992. q. CNY 6 newsstand/cover (effective 2005). **Document type:** *Journal, Academic/Scholarly.*
Formerly: Xi'an Shiyou Xueyuan Xuebao (Shehui Kexue Ban)/Xi'an Petroleum Institute. Journal (Social Sciences Edition) (1008-5645)
Related titles: Online - full content ed.; Online - full text ed.
Published by: Xi'an Shiyou Daxue/Xi'an Petroleum University, No.18 Second Dianzi Rd., Xi'an, 710065, China. TEL 86-29-88382662, FAX 86-29-88216407, http://www.xsyu.edu.cn/.

300 CHN ISSN 1009-2854
XIANGFAN XUEYUAN XUEBAO/XIANGFAN UNIVERSITY. JOURNAL. Text in Chinese. 1981. bi-m. USD 36 (effective 2009). **Document type:** *Journal, Academic/Scholarly.*
Related titles: Online - full text ed.
—East View.
Published by: Xiangfan Xueyuan, 7, Longzhong Lu, Xiangfan, 441053, China. TEL 86-710-3590704.

300 CHN ISSN 1672-8173
XIANGNAN XUEYUAN XUEBAO/XIANGNAN UNIVERSITY. JOURNAL. Text in Chinese. 2004. bi-m. CNY 10 newsstand/cover (effective 2006). **Document type:** *Journal, Academic/Scholarly.*
Supersedes (1998-2004): Chenzhou Shifan Gaodeng Zhuanke Xuexiao Xuebao/Chenzhou Teachers College. Journal (1008-2042); (2001-2004): Chenzhou Yixue Gaodeng Zhuanke Xuexiao Xuebao (1671-4105)
Related titles: Online - full text ed.
Published by: Xiangnan Xueyuan, 8, Suxian Bei Lu, Chenzhou, 423000, China. TEL 86-735-2865113.

300 CHN
XIANGTAN DAXUE XUEBAO (ZHEXUE SHEHUI KEXUE BAN)/XIANGTAN UNIVERSITY. JOURNAL (PHILOSOPHY AND SOCIAL SCIENCES EDITION). Text in Chinese. 1977. bi-m. USD 24.60 (effective 2009). **Document type:** *Journal, Academic/Scholarly.*
Formerly: Xiangtan Daxue Xuebao (Shehui Kexue Ban)/Xiangtan University. Journal (Social Sciences Edition) (1001-5981)
Related titles: Online - full text ed.
—East View.
Published by: Xiangtan Daxue/Xiangtan University, 5F, Chuban Dalou, Xiangtan, 411105, China. FAX 86-731-8292001, http://www.xtu.edu.cn/.

300 CHN
XIANNING XUEYUAN XUEBAO (YIXUE BAN)/XIANNING COLLEGE. JOURNAL (MEDICAL SCIENCES). Text in Chinese. 1979. bi-m. CNY 8 newsstand/cover (effective 2006). **Document type:** *Journal, Academic/Scholarly.*
Supersedes: Xianning Yixueyuan Xuebao/Xianning Medical College. Journal (1008-0635); Xianning Shi-Zhuan Xuebao/Xianning Teachers College. Journal (1006-5342)
Related titles: Online - full text ed.; Ed.
Published by: Xianning Xueyuan, 2, Yongan Shadao, Xianning, 437005, China.

300 500 100 CHN ISSN 1671-2544
XIAOGAN XUEYUAN XUEBAO/XIAOGAN UNIVERSITY. JOURNAL. Text in Chinese. 1981. bi-m. CNY 8 newsstand/cover (effective 2006). **Document type:** *Journal, Academic/Scholarly.* **Description:** Covers philosphy & social science in issues number 1, 2, 4 & 5. Number 3 & 6 covers natural science.
Formerly (until 2000): Xiaogan Shi-Zhuan Xuebao/Xiaogan Teachers College. Journal (1007-1075)
Related titles: Online - full text ed.
Published by: Xiaogan Xueyuan, 272, Jiaotong Dadao, Xiaogan, 432000, China.

300 CHN ISSN 1000-2731
AS451
XIBEI DAXUE XUEBAO (SHEHUI KEXUE BAN)/NORTHWEST UNIVERSITY. JOURNAL (SOCIAL SCIENCES EDITION). Text in Chinese; Contents page in English. 1913. bi-m. USD 31.20 (effective 2009). **Document type:** *Journal, Academic/Scholarly.*
Related titles: Online - full text ed.
Indexed: SpeleolAb.
—East View, Ingenta.
Published by: Xibei Daxue/Northwest University, 229, Taibai Beilu, Xi'an, 710069, China. **Dist. outside China by:** China International Book Trading Corp, 35 Chegongzhuang Xilu, Haidian District, PO Box 399, Beijing 100044, China.

300 CHN ISSN 1009-2447
XIBEI GONGYE DAXUE XUEBAO (SHEHUI KEXUE BAN)/NORTHWESTERN POLYTECHNICAL UNIVERSITY. JOURNAL (SOCIAL SCIENCES). Text in Chinese. 1991. q. CNY 5 newsstand/cover (effective 2006). **Document type:** *Journal, Academic/Scholarly.*
Related titles: Online - full text ed.
Published by: Xibei Gongye Daxue/Northwestern Polytechnical University, 127, Youyi Xilu, 647 Xinxiang, Xi'an, Shaanxi 710072, China.

300 CHN
XIBEI MINZU DAXUE XUEBAO (MENGWEN BAN)/NORTHWEST UNIVERSITY FOR NATIONALITIES. JOURNAL (MONGOLIAN EDITION). Text in Mongol. s-a. USD 6 (effective 2009). 82 p./no.; **Document type:** *Journal, Academic/Scholarly.* **Description:** Focuses on theoretical studies of social sciences.
Formerly: Xibei Minzu Xueyuan Xuebao (Mengwen Ban) (1002-9125)
Related titles: ◆ Tibetan ed.: Xibei Minzu Daxuebao (Zangwenban). ISSN 1002-9117; ◆ Chinese ed.: Xibei Minzu Daxue Xuebao (Zhexue Shehui Kexue Ban).
—East View.
Published by: Xibei Minzu Daxue/Northwest University for Nationalities, No 1, Xibei Xincun, Lanzhou, Gansu 730030, China. http://www.xbmu.edu.cn/shxx. **Dist. by:** China International Book Trading Corp, 35 Chegongzhuang Xilu, Haidian District, PO Box 399, Beijing 100044, China.

300 CHN
AS452.L34
XIBEI MINZU DAXUE XUEBAO (ZHEXUE SHEHUI KEXUE BAN)/NORTHWEST UNIVERSITY OF NATIONALIES. JOURNAL (PHILOSOPHY AND SOCIAL SCIENCE). Text in Chinese. 1979. bi-m. USD 24.60 (effective 2009). 128 p./no.; **Document type:** *Journal, Academic/Scholarly.* **Description:** Focuses on theoretical studies of social sciences.
Formerly: Xibei Minzu Xueyuan Xuebao (Zhexue Shehui Kexue Ban) (1001-5140)
Related titles: Online - full text ed.; ◆ Mongol ed.: Xibei Minzu Daxue Xuebao (Mengwen Ban); ◆ Tibetan ed.: Xibei Minzu Daxuebao (Zangwenban). ISSN 1002-9117.
—East View.
Published by: Xibei Minzu Daxue/Northwest University for Nationalities, No 1, Xibei Xincun, Lanzhou, Gansu 730030, China. TEL 86-931-2938091, http://www.xbmu.edu.cn/shxx. **Dist. overseas by:** China International Book Trading Corp, 35 Chegongzhuang Xilu, Haidian District, PO Box 399, Beijing 100044, China.

300 CHN ISSN 1002-9117
XIBEI MINZU DAXUEBAO (ZANGWENBAN)/NORTHWEST UNIVERSITY FOR NATIONALITIES. JOURNAL (TIBETAN EDITION). Text in Tibetan. s-a. USD 6 (effective 2009). 92 p./no.; **Document type:** *Journal, Academic/Scholarly.* **Description:** Focuses on theoretical studies of social sciences.
Related titles: ◆ Mongol ed.: Xibei Minzu Daxue Xuebao (Mengwen Ban); ◆ Chinese ed.: Xibei Minzu Daxue Xuebao (Zhexue Shehui Kexue Ban).
—East View.
Published by: Xibei Minzu Daxue/Northwest University for Nationalities, No 1, Xibei Xincun, Lanzhou, Gansu 730030, China. http://www.xbmu.edu.cn/shxx. **Dist. by:** China International Book Trading Corp, 35 Chegongzhuang Xilu, Haidian District, PO Box 399, Beijing 100044, China.

300 CHN ISSN 1009-9107
XIBEI NONG-LIN KEJI DAXUE XUEBAO (SHEHUI KEXUE BAN)/NORTHWEST SCI-TECH UNIVERSITY OF AGRICULTURE AND FORESTRY. JOURNAL. Text in Chinese. 2001. bi-m. USD 24.60 (effective 2009). **Document type:** *Journal, Academic/Scholarly.*
Related titles: Online - full text ed.
Published by: Xibei Nong-Lin Keji Daxue, 34 Xinxiang, Yangling, Shaanxi 712100, China. TEL 86-29-87092606.

300 CHN ISSN 1001-9162
AS451
XIBEI SHI-DA XUEBAO (SHEHUI KEXUE BAN). Text in Chinese. 1989. bi-m. USD 31.20 (effective 2009).
Related titles: Online - full text ed.
—East View.
Published by: Xibei Shifan Daxue/Northwest Normal University, 697, Anning Dong Lu, Lanzhou, Gansu Province 730070, China. TEL 86-931-7971692, FAX 86-931-7668159, mayh@nwnu.edu.cn.

300 CHN ISSN 1674-3687
XIBU FAXUE PINGLUN/WESTERN LAW REVIEW. Text in Chinese. 1990. bi-m. CNY 15 newsstand/cover (effective 2009). **Document type:** *Journal, Academic/Scholarly.*
Formerly (until 2008): Gansu Zheng-Fa Chengren Jiaoyu Xueyuan Xuebao/Journal of Adults Education of Gansu Political Science and Law Institute (1009-7759)
Related titles: Online - full text ed.
Published by: Gansu Zheng-Fa Xueyuan, 6, Anning Xi Lu, Lanzhou, 730070, China. TEL 86-931-7604500.

300 CHN ISSN 1673-1883
XICHANG XUEYUAN XUEBAO (SHEHUI KEXUE BAN)/XICHANG COLLEGE. JOURNAL (SOCIAL SCIENCE EDITION). Text in Chinese. 1989. q. CNY 10 newsstand/cover (effective 2010). **Document type:** *Journal, Academic/Scholarly.*
Formerly: Xichang Shifan Gaodeng Zhuanke Xuexiao Xuebao/Xichang Teachers College Journal (1008-6307)
Related titles: Online - full text ed.
Published by: Xichang Xueyuan, Mapingba, Xichang, 615013, China. TEL 86-834-2580091, FAX 86-834-2580091, http://www.xcc.sc.cn/.

300 CHN
XIHUA SHIFAN XUEYUAN XUEBAO (ZHEXUE SHEHUI KEXUE BAN)/SICHUAN NORMAL COLLEGE. JOURNAL. (PHILOSOPHY & SOCIAL SCIENCE EDITION). Text in Chinese. 1989. bi-m. **Document type:** *Journal, Academic/Scholarly.*
Formerly (until Apr.2003): Sichuan Shifan Xueyuan Xuebao (Zhexue Shehui Kexue Ban)/Sichuan Teachers College. Journal. (Philosophy Social Science Edition) (1005-1465)
Related titles: Online - full text ed.

Published by: Xihua Shifan Xueyuan/China West Normal University, 44, Renmin Xilu, Nanchong, Sichuan 637002, China. TEL 86-817-2314311, http://www.sctc.edu.cn/. Ed. Yan Zengye. **Dist. by:** China International Book Trading Corp, 35 Chegongzhuang Xilu, Haidian District, PO Box 399, Beijing 100044, China. TEL 86-10-68412045, FAX 86-10-68412023, cibtc@mail.cibtc.com.cn, http://www.cibtc.com.cn.

300 CHN ISSN 1673-9841
AS452.C5914
XINAN DAXUE XUEBAO (SHEHUI KEXUE BAN)/SOUTHWEST UNIVERSITY. JOURNAL (HUMANITIES AND SOCIAL SCIENCES EDITION). Text in Chinese; Abstracts in English. 1957. bi-m. USD 31.20 (effective 2009). **Document type:** *Journal, Academic/Scholarly.*
Former titles (until 2006): Xi'nan Daxue Xuebao (Renwen Shehui Kexue Ban)/Southwest University. Journal (Humanities and Social Sciences Edition); Xinan Shifan Daxue Xuebao (Zhexue Shehui Kexue Ban)/Southwest Normal University. Journal (Philosophy and Social Science Edition) (1000-2677); Xinan Shifan Daxue Xuebao (Shehui Kexue Ban)/Southwest Normal University. Journal (Social Science Edition)
Related titles: Online - full text ed.
Indexed: RASB.
—East View.
Published by: Xinan Shifan Daxue, Xuebao Bianjibu, No.1, Tiansheng Road, Beibei District, Chongqing, Sichuan 400715, China. TEL 86-23-68252540. Ed. Yang Guangyan.

300 CHN ISSN 1009-4474
XINAN JIAOTONG DAXUE XUEBAO (SHEHUI KEXUE BAN)/SOUTHWEST JIAOTONG UNIVERSITY. JOURNAL (SOCIAL SCIENCES). Text in Chinese. 2000. bi-m. **Document type:** *Journal, Academic/Scholarly.*
Related titles: Online - full text ed.: (from WanFang Data Corp.).
Published by: Xinan Jiaotong Daxue/Southwest Jiaotong University, 111, Er-Huan Lu Bei-Yi-Duan, Chengdu, Sichuan 610031, China. TEL 86-28-87600845.

300 CHN
AS452.C4815
➤ **XINAN MINZU DAXUE XUEBAO (ZHEXUE SHEHUI KEXUE BAN)/SOUTHWEST UNIVERSITY FOR NATIONALITIES. JOURNAL (PHILOSOPHY, SOCIAL SCIENCE EDITION).** Text in Chinese. 1979. bi-m. USD 159.60 (effective 2009). adv. bk.rev. **Document type:** *Journal, Academic/Scholarly.* **Description:** Contains academic papers mainly focusing on minority nationalities of southwestern China. Covers politics, philosophy, economics, education, linguistics, and literature.
Formerly (until 2003): Xinan Minzu Xueyuan Xuebao (Zhexue Shehui Kexue Ban) (1004-3926)
Related titles: Online - full text ed.
Indexed: RILM.
—East View.
Published by: Xinan Minzu Daxue, 21, Ximianqiao Heng Jie, Chengdu, Sichuan 610041, China. TEL 86-910-3755470. Ed. Wang Jue.

300 CHN ISSN 1672-5379
XI'NAN NONGYE DAXUE XUEBAO (SHEHUI KEXUE BAN)/SOUTHWEST AGRICULTURAL UNIVERSITY. JOURNAL (SOCIAL SCIENCE EDITION). Text in Chinese. 2003. q. CNY 8 newsstand/cover (effective 2006). **Document type:** *Journal, Academic/Scholarly.*
Supersedes in part (1987-2003): Sichuan Xumu Shouyi Xueyuan Xuebao/Sichuan Institute of Animal Husbandry and Veterinary Medicine. Journal (1009-0533)
Related titles: Online - full text ed.
Published by: Xinan Nongye Daxue, Beibei, Chongqing, 400716, China.

300 CHN ISSN 1674-5094
XINAN SHIYOU DAXUE XUEBAO (SHEHUI KEXUE BAN)/SOUTHWEST PETROLEUM UNIVERSITY. JOURNAL (SOCIAL SCIENCES EDITION). Text in Chinese. 2008. bi-m. CNY 90; CNY 15 per issue (effective 2010). back issues avail. **Document type:** *Journal, Academic/Scholarly.*
Related titles: Online - full text ed.
Published by: Xinan Shiyou Daxue/Southwest Petroleum University, Xindu-qu, Chengdu, Sichuan 610500, China. TEL 86-28-83032016, FAX 86-28-83035158, swpuxuebao@yahoo.com.cn.

XINHUA SHUMUBAO. SHEKE XINSHU MUBAN/XINHUA CATALOGUE, SOCIAL SCIENCE. *see* ABSTRACTING AND INDEXING SERVICES

300 100 001.3 CHN
XINJIANG DAXUE XUEBAO (ZHEXUE - RENWEN SHEHUI KEXUE BAN)/XINJIANG UNIVERSITY. JOURNAL (PHILOSOPHY,HUMANITIES & SOCIAL SCIENCE). Text in Chinese. 1973. bi-m. USD 31.20 (effective 2009). **Document type:** *Journal, Academic/Scholarly.*
Formerly: Xinjiang Daxue Xuebao (Zhexue Shehui Kexue Ban) (1000-2820)
Related titles: Online - full text ed.
—East View.
Published by: Xinjiang Daxue/Xinjiang University, 14, Shengli Lu, Urumqi, Xinjiang 830046, China. TEL 86-991-8585177.

300 CHN ISSN 1009-5330
HN740.S55
XINJIANG SHEHUI KEXUE (HANWEN BAN)/SOCIAL SCIENCE IN XINJIANG (CHINESE EDITION). Text in Chinese. 1981. bi-m. USD 22.80 (effective 2009). bibl. **Document type:** *Journal, Academic/Scholarly.*
Formerly (until 2001): Xinjiang Shehui Jingji (1002-4735); Which superseded in part (in 1991): Xinjiang Shehui Kexue (1000-4262)
Related titles: Online - full text ed.; Kazakh ed.: 1990; Uigur ed.: 1981.
Indexed: RASB.
—East View.
Published by: Xinjiang Shehui Kexueyuan/Xinjiang Academy of Social Sciences, 16, Beijing Nanlu, Urumqi, Xinjiang 830011, China. TEL 86-991-3837937, FAX 86-991-3835946, http://www.xjts.cn/qyjz/xjsky/.

300 100 CHN ISSN 1005-9245
XINJIANG SHIFAN DAXUE XUEBAO (ZHEXUE SHEHUI KEXUE BAN). Text in Chinese. 1980. q. USD 20.80 (effective 2009). **Document type:** *Journal, Academic/Scholarly.*
Related titles: Online - full text ed.
Published by: Xinjiang Shifan Daxue, 19, Xinyi Lu, Urumqi, 830054, China. TEL 86-991-4332658.

300 CHN ISSN 1009-7465
XINSILU/NEW THINKING. Text in Chinese. 1986. m. (q. until 2001). CNY 30 (effective 2004). 88 p./no.; **Document type:** *Journal, Academic/Scholarly.*
Formerly (until 2001): Xinxing Xueke (1001-3105)
Indexed: RASB.
Published by: Zhongguo Renmin Daxue Shubao Ziliao Zhongxin/Renmin University of China, Information Center for Social Sciences, Dongcheng-qu, 3, Zhangzizhong Lu, Beijing, 100007, China. TEL 86-10-64039458, FAX 86-10-64015080, center@zlzx.org, http://www.zlzx.org/. **Dist. in US by:** China Publications Service, PO Box 49614, Chicago, IL 60649. TEL 312-288-3291, FAX 312-288-8570; **Dist. by:** China International Book Trading Corp, 35 Chegongzhuang Xilu, Haidian District, PO Box 399, Beijing 100044, China. TEL 86-10-68412045, FAX 86-10-68412023, cibtc@mail.cibtc.com.cn, http://www.cibtc.com.cn/.

300 CHN ISSN 1674-3326
➤ **XINXIANG XUEYUAN XUEBAO (ZIRAN KEXUE BAN)/XINXING UNIVERSITY. JOURNAL (NATURAL SCIENCE EDITION).** Text in Chinese; Abstracts in Chinese, English. 1984. bi-m. CNY 60, USD 60; CNY 10 newsstand/cover (effective 2011). **Document type:** *Journal, Academic/Scholarly.*
Former titles (until 2007): Pingyuan Daxue Xuebao/Pingyuan University. Journal (1008-3944); (until 1986): Pingyuan Xuebao
Related titles: Online - full text ed.
Published by: Xinxiang Xueyuan/Xinxing University, Jinsui Dadao Dong Duan, Xinxiang, 453003, China. TEL 86-373-3041671, http://www.xxu.edu.cn/. Ed. Ai-xian Guo. Circ: 1,000.

300 CHN ISSN 1003-0964
XINYANG SHIFAN XUEYUAN XUEBAO (ZHEXUE SHEHUI KEXUEBAN)/XINYANG NORMAL UNIVERSITY. JOURNAL (PHILOSOPHY AND SOCIAL SCIENCES EDITION). Text in Chinese. 1981. bi-m. USD 31.20 (effective 2009). bk.rev. 128 p./no.; **Document type:** *Journal, Academic/Scholarly.* **Description:** Focuses on academic studies of philosophy and other social science disciplines.
Related titles: Online - full text ed.
—East View.
Published by: Xinyang Shifan Xueyuan, Xuebao Bianjibu, 237, Changan Lu, Xinyang, Henan 464000, China. TEL 86-376-6390837 ext 3, FAX 86-376-6390857. Ed. Shi Mingde. Circ: 1,000.

300 500 CHN ISSN 1008-6765
XINYU GAO-ZHUAN XUEBAO/XINYU COLLEGE. JOURNAL. Text in Chinese. 1996. bi-m. CNY 8 newsstand/cover (effective 2006). **Document type:** *Journal, Academic/Scholarly.*
Related titles: Online - full text ed.
Published by: Xinyu Gaodeng Zhuanke Xuexiao, 1, Wu-yi Lu, Xinyu, 338000, China.

300 CHN
XINZHIKU. Text in Chinese. 2001. m. **Document type:** *Newspaper.*
Formerly (until 2009): Sixiang Caifu
Published by: Ningxia Shehui Kexueyuan/Ningxia Academy of Social Sciences, 8, Xinfeng Xiang, Xinshi-qu, Yinchuan, 750021, China.

300 CHN
XIWANG/HOPE. Text in Chinese. bi-m.
Published by: Xin Shiji Chubanshe, No 10, 4 Malu, Dashatou, Guangzhou, Guangdong 510102, China. TEL 335210. Ed. Chen Sang.

300 CHN ISSN 1674-8077
▼ **XIXIA YANJIU/TANGUT RESEARCH.** Text in Chinese. 2009. q. **Document type:** *Journal, Academic/Scholarly.*
Related titles: Online - full text ed.
Published by: Ningxia Shehui Kexueyuan/Ningxia Academy of Social Sciences, 8, Xinfeng Xiang, Xinshi-qu, Yinchuan, 750021, China. TEL 86-951-2079025, FAX 86-951-2079025.

300 CHN ISSN 1002-7122
➤ **XIYA FEIZHOU/WEST ASIA AND AFRICA.** Text in Chinese; Summaries in English. 1980. m. USD 79.20 (effective 2009). bk.rev. abstr.; bibl.; mkt.; stat. 80 p./no.; back issues avail. **Document type:** *Academic/Scholarly.*
Related titles: Online - full text ed.
—East View.
Published by: Zhongguo Shehui Kexueyuan, Xiya Feizhou Yanjiusuo/Chinese Academy of Social Sciences, Institute of West-Asia and African Studies, 3 Zhangzizhong Lu, Dongcheng-qu, Beijing, 100007, China. TEL 86-10-64039172, FAX 86-10-64035718. Eds. Guang Yang, Lihua Yang, Zhibino Li. Pub. Guang Yang. R&P, Adv. contact Zhibino Li. **Dist. by:** China International Book Trading Corp, 35 Chegongzhuang Xilu, Haidian District, PO Box 399, Beijing 100044, China. TEL 86-10-68412045, FAX 86-10-68412023, cibtc@mail.cibtc.com.cn, http://www.cibtc.com.cn.

300 CHN ISSN 1002-4743
XIYU YANJIU/WESTERN REGIONS STUDIES. Text in Chinese. 1981. q. USD 16 (effective 2009).
Supersedes in part (in 1991): Xinjiang Shehui Kexue (1000-4262)
Related titles: Online - full text ed.
—East View.
Published by: Xinjiang Shehui Kexueyuan/Xinjiang Academy of Social Sciences, 16, Beijing Nanlu, Urumqi, Xinjiang 830011, China. TEL 86-991-3837937, http://www.xjts.cn/qyjz/xjsky/.

300 CHN ISSN 1005-5738
AS452.L47
XIZANG DAXUE XUEBAO/TIBET UNIVERSITY. JOURNAL. Text in Chinese. 1986. q. USD 21.60 (effective 2009). **Document type:** *Journal, Academic/Scholarly.*
Related titles: Online - full text ed.; Tibetan ed.: ISSN 1005-5746.
Published by: Xizang Daxue/Tibet University, 36, Jiangsu Lu, Lhasa, Tibet 850000, China. TEL 86-891-6322055.

300 CHN ISSN 1001-9790
XUE HAI/SEA OF KNOWLEDGE. Text in Chinese. 1990. bi-m. USD 40.20 (effective 2009). adv. bk.rev. **Document type:** *Journal, Academic/Scholarly.*
Formed by the merger of: Faxue Luncong; Jiangsu Shixue; Zhexue Tantao; Shehuixue Tansuo
Related titles: Online - full text ed.
—East View.
Published by: Jiangsu Sheng Shehui Kexueyuan/Jiangsu Academy of Social Sciences, 12 Huju Bei Lu, Nanjing, Jiangsu 210013, China. Circ: 1,500.

300 CHN ISSN 1004-4434
XUESHU LUNTAN. Text in Chinese. 1978. bi-m. USD 62.40 (effective 2009). 104 p./no.; **Document type:** *Academic/Scholarly.*
Related titles: Online - full text ed.
Indexed: RASB.
—East View.
Published by: (Guangxi Shehui Kexueyuan/Guangxi Academy of Social Sciences), Xueshu Luntan Bianjibu, 5 Xinzu Lu, Nanning, Guangxi 530022, China. TEL 560201. Eds. Yang Shaotao, Zhan Hongsong.

300 CHN ISSN 1000-7326
AS451.A1
XUESHU YANJIU/ACADEMIC RESEARCH. Text in Chinese. 1958. m. USD 80.40 (effective 2009). **Document type:** *Journal, Academic/Scholarly.*
Related titles: Online - full text ed.
—East View.
Published by: (Guangdong Sheng Shehui Kexue Xuehui Lianhehui), Xueshu Yanjiu Zazhishe, 4-2, Huanghua Lu, Guangzhou, 510050, China.

300 CHN ISSN 0439-8041
DS701
XUESHU YUEKAN/ACADEMIC MONTHLY. Text in Chinese. 1957. m. USD 80.40 (effective 2009). **Document type:** *Journal, Academic/Scholarly.* **Description:** Covers philosophy, political science, ethics, literature, history, economics, culture, aesthetics, important issues in China.
—East View.
Published by: Shanghai Shehui Kexue Jielianhehui/Shanghai Social Sciences Association, Lane 662, no.7, Huaihai Zhonglu, Room 402, Lianxin Dalou, Shanghai, 200020, China. TEL 86-21-53060399, xuesyka@public3.sta.com.cn, http://www.sssa.org.cn/. Circ: 6,500. **Dist. by:** China International Book Trading Corp, 35 Chegongzhuang Xilu, Haidian District, PO Box 399, Beijing 100044, China. TEL 86-10-68412045, FAX 86-10-68412023, cibtc@mail.cibtc.com.cn, http://www.cibtc.com.cn.

300 CHN ISSN 1002-462X
AP95.C4
XUEXI YU TANSUO/STUDY & EXPLORATION. Text and summaries in Chinese. 1979. bi-m. USD 50.40 (effective 2009). **Document type:** *Journal, Academic/Scholarly.*
Related titles: Online - full text ed.
—East View.
Published by: (Heilongjiang Sheng Shehui Kexueyuan/Heilongjiang Provincial Academy of Social Sciences), Xuexi yu Tansuo Zazhishe, 62, Lianfa Jie, Harbin, Heilongjiang 150006, China. Eds. Ji Kefei, Sun Qinglin. **Dist. by:** China International Book Trading Corp, 35 Chegongzhuang Xilu, Haidian District, PO Box 399, Beijing 100044, China.

300 100 CHN ISSN 1007-6425
AS452.H87
XUZHOU SHIFAN DAXUE XUEBAO (ZHEXUE SHEHUI KEXUE BAN)/XUZHOU NORMAL UNIVERSITY. JOURNAL (PHILOSOPHY AND SOCIAL SCIENCES EDITION). Text in Chinese. 1975. bi-m. USD 18 (effective 2009). **Document type:** *Journal, Academic/Scholarly.*
Formerly: Xuzhou Shifan Xueyuan Xuebao (Zhexue Shehui Kexue Ban)/Xuzhou Teachers college. Journal (Philosophy and Social Sciences Edition) (1005-8648)
—East View.
Published by: Xuzhou Shifan Daxue/Xuzhou Normal University, 57, Heping Lu, Xuzhou, 221009, China. TEL 86-516-83867156, FAX 86-516-83845087.

300 USA ISSN 0084-3326
YALE FASTBACK SERIES. Text in English. 1970. irreg., latest 1999. price varies. back issues avail. **Document type:** *Monographic series, Academic/Scholarly.*
Published by: Yale University Press, PO Box 209040, New Haven, CT 06520. TEL 203-432-0960, 800-405-1619, FAX 203-432-0948, customer.care@triliteral.org, http://yalepress.yale.edu/home.asp.

YALE SOUTHEAST ASIA STUDIES. MONOGRAPH SERIES. *see* ASIAN STUDIES

300 JPN ISSN 0513-4684
H8
YAMAGATA DAIGAKU KIYO (SHAKAI KAGAKU)/YAMAGATA UNIVERSITY. BULLETIN (SOCIAL SCIENCE). Text in Japanese. 1960. a. **Document type:** *Bulletin, Academic/Scholarly.*
—BLDSC (2821.920000).
Published by: Yamagata Daigaku/Yamagata University, Publicatin Committee, Library, Division of Information Processing & Management, 1-4-12, Kojirakawa, Yamagata, Yamagata 990-9585, Japan. TEL 81-23-6285054, FAX 81-23-6285059.

300 JPN
YAMANASHI UNIVERSITY. FACULTY OF EDUCATION & HUMAN SCIENCES. BULLETIN. Text in English, Japanese. 1966. q.
Formerly (until 1999): Yamanashi Daikaku Kyoiku Gakabu Kenkyu Hokoku. Dai 1 - Bunsatu Jinbun. Shakai Kagaku-kei (0385-8758); Which superseded in part (in 1972): Yamanashi Daigaku Kyoiku Gakubu Kenkyu Hokoku (1345-0549)
Published by: Yamanashi Daigaku, Kyoikugakubu/Yamanashi University, Faculty of Liberal Arts & Education, 4-37 Takeda 4-chome, Kofu-shi, Yamanashi-ken 400-0016, Japan.

300 CHN ISSN 1002-4077
YAN DU/CAPITAL OF YAN. Text in Chinese. bi-m.
Published by: Yanshan Chubanshe, No 36 Fuxue Hutong, Dongcheng-qu, Beijing, 100007, China. TEL 4014694. Ed. Song Tishui.

300 CHN ISSN 1004-9975
AS452.Y4627
YAN'AN DAXUE XUEBAO (SHEHUI KEXUEBAN)/YAN'AN UNIVERSITY. JOURNAL (SOCIAL SCIENCE EDITION). Text in Chinese. 1979. bi-m. USD 21.60 (effective 2009). **Document type:** *Journal, Academic/Scholarly.*
Related titles: Online - full text ed.
Indexed: SociolAb.
Published by: Yan'an Daxue/Yan'an University, Yangjialing, Yan'an, Shaanxi 716000, China. TEL 86-911-2332076.

S

300 CHN ISSN 1009-3311
AS452.Y4658
YANBIAN DAXUE XUEBAO (SHEHUI KEXUE BAN)/YANBIAN UNIVERSITY. JOURNAL (SOCIAL SCIENCE EDITION). Text in Chinese. 1958. q. CNY 6 newsstand/cover (effective 2006). **Document type:** *Journal, Academic/Scholarly.*
Related titles: Online - full text ed.
Published by: Yanbian Daxue/Yanbian University, 105 GongYuan Road, Yanji, Jilin 133002, China. TEL 86-433-2732197.

300 CHN
YANCHENG GONGXUEYUAN XUEBAO (SHEHUI KEXUE BAN)/ YANCHENG INSTITUTE OF TECHNOLOGY. JOURNAL (SOCIAL SCIENCE EDITION). Text in Chinese. 1987. q. CNY 6 newsstand/ cover (effective 2006). **Document type:** *Journal, Academic/Scholarly.*
Supersedes in part (in 2001): Yancheng Gongxueyuan Xuebao (1008-5092)
Related titles: Online - full text ed.
Published by: Yancheng Gongxueyuan, 20, Huanhai Zhong Lu, 802 Xinxiang, Yancheng, 224003, China. TEL 86-515-8328388 ext 2113.

300 CHN
YANCHENG SHIFAN XUEYUAN XUEBAO (RENWEN SHEHUI KEXUE BAN)/YANCHENG TEACHERS COLLEGE. JOURNAL (HUMANITIES & SOCIAL SCIENCES EDITION). Text in Chinese. 1981. q. CNY 8 newsstand/cover (effective 2006). **Document type:** *Journal, Academic/Scholarly.*
Formerly: Yancheng Shi-zhuan Xuebao (Shehui Kexueban) (1003-6873)
Related titles: Online - full text ed.
Published by: Yancheng Shifan Xueyuan, 50, Kaifang Dadao, Yancheng, 224002, China. TEL 86-515-8233090.

300 CHN ISSN 1007-7030
YANGZHOU DAXUE XUEBAO (RENWEN SHEHUI KEXUE BAN)/ YANGZHOU UNIVERSITY. JOURNAL (HUMANITIES AND SOCIAL SCIENCES EDITION). Text in Chinese. 1959. bi-m. USD 24.60 (effective 2009). **Document type:** *Journal, Academic/Scholarly.*
Formerly: Yangzhou Shi-yuan Xuebao (Shehui Kexue Ban)/Yangzhou Teachers College. Journal (Social Science Edition) (1001-6570)
Related titles: Online - full text ed.
—East View.
Published by: Yangzhou Daxue/Yangzhou University, 88, Daxue Nanlu, Yangzhou, 225009, China. TEL 86-514-7971607.

300 620 370 CHN ISSN 1008-3693
YANGZHOU ZHIYE DAXUE XUEBAO/YANGZHOU POLYTECHNIC COLLEGE. JOURNAL. Text in Chinese. 1994. q. CNY 4 newsstand/ cover (effective 2006). **Document type:** *Journal, Academic/Scholarly.*
Related titles: Online - full text ed.
Published by: Yangzhou Zhiye Daxue, Wenchang Xi Lu, Yangzhou, 225009, China. TEL 86-514-7624562.

300 CHN ISSN 1007-791X
T4
YANSHAN DAXUE XUEBAO/YANSHAN UNIVERSITY. JOURNAL. Text in Chinese. 1963. bi-m. USD 18 (effective 2009). **Document type:** *Journal, Academic/Scholarly.*
Formerly (until 1998): Dongbei Zhongxing Jixie Xueyuan Xuebao/ Northeast Institute of Heavey Machinery. Journal (1000-1867)
Related titles: Online - full text ed.
Indexed: A28, APA, BrCerAb, C&ISA, CA/WCA, CIA, CerAb, CivEngAb, CorrAb, E&CAJ, E11, EEA, EMA, ESPM, EnvEAb, H15, M&TEA, M09, MBF, METADEX, RefZh, SolStAb, T04, WAA.
—East View, Linda Hall.
Published by: Yanshan Daxue, 438, Hebei Dajie Xi-Duan, Qinhuangdao, 066004, China. TEL 86-335-8057043, FAX 86-335-8074648.

300 100 CHN ISSN 1009-2692
AS452.Q569
YANSHAN DAXUE XUEBAO (ZHEXUE SHEHUI KEXUE BAN). Text in Chinese. 2000. q. USD 20.80 (effective 2009). **Document type:** *Journal, Academic/Scholarly.*
Related titles: Online - full text ed.
—East View.
Published by: Yanshan Daxue, 438, Hebei Dajie Xi-Duan, Qinhuangdao, 066004, China. TEL 86-335-8047985, FAX 86-335-8074648.

300 100 CHN ISSN 1002-3194
YANTAI DAXUE XUEBAO (SHEHUI KEXUE BAN)/YANTAI UNIVERSITY. JOURNAL (PHILOSOPHY AND SOCIAL SCIENCE EDITION). Text in Chinese. 1988. q. USD 16.40 (effective 2009). **Document type:** *Journal, Academic/Scholarly.*
Related titles: Online - full text ed.
Published by: Yantai Daxue/Yantai University, Laishan-qu, Yantai, 264005, China. TEL 86-535-6902703.

YASAR UNIVERSITY. JOURNAL. *see* HUMANITIES: COMPREHENSIVE WORKS

300 USA ISSN 1089-6651
BP605.N48
YES!; a journal of positive futures. Text in English. 1980. q. USD 24 domestic; USD 29 in Canada & Mexico; USD 33 elsewhere (effective 2004). adv. bk.rev. illus. reprints avail. **Document type:** *Magazine, Consumer.* **Description:** Provides a balanced perspective on social and environmental issues, concentrating on creative solutions. Encourages direct participation in development of sustainable culture.
Formerly (until Dec. 1995): In Context (0741-6180)
Indexed: AltPI, CPerI, E04, E05, EnvAb, P34, T02.
—BLDSC (9418.332500).
Published by: Positive Futures Network, PO Box 10818, Bainbridge Is, WA 98110-0818. TEL 206-842-0216, 800-937-4551, FAX 206-842-5208, http://www.yesmagazine.org. Eds. Fran Korten, Sarah Ruth van Gelder. Pub. Fran Korten. R&P Carol Estes. Circ: 12,000 (paid). **Dist. by:** International Publishers Direct, 27500 Riverview Center Blvd, Bonita Springs, FL 34134. TEL 858-320-4563, FAX 858-677-3220.

300 FIN ISSN 1796-7996
YHTEISKUNTATIETEELLISIA JULKAISUJA. Text in Multiple languages. 1984. irreg., latest vol.78, 2007. back issues avail. **Document type:** *Monographic series, Academic/Scholarly.*
Formerly (until 2007): Joensuun Yliopisto. Yhteiskuntatieteellisia Julkaisuja (0781-0350)
Related titles: Online - full text ed.: ISSN 1796-8003. 2003.
Published by: Joensuun Yliopisto/University of Joensuu, PO Box 111, Joensuu, 80101, Finland. TEL 358-13-251111, FAX 358-13-2512050, intnl@joensuu.fi.

300 500 CHN ISSN 1671-380X
YICHUN XUEYUAN XUEBAO/YICHUN UNIVERSITY. JOURNAL. Text in Chinese. 1979. bi-m. CNY 8 newsstand/cover (effective 2006). **Document type:** *Journal, Academic/Scholarly.*
Formerly (until 2000): Yichun Shi-Zhuan Xuebao/Yichun Normal Institute. Journal (1006-2270)
Related titles: Online - full text ed.
Published by: Yichun Xueyuan, 576, Xueyuan Lu, Yichun, 336000, China. TEL 86-795-3201238.

300 MNG
YINGSHAN XUEKAN (SHEHUI KEXUE BAN)/YINSHAN ACADEMIC JOURNAL (SOCIAL SCIENCE EDITION). Text in Chinese. 1982. bi-m. USD 31.20 (effective 2009). **Document type:** *Journal, Academic/Scholarly.*
Formerly: Yingshan Xuekan (Zhexue Shehui Kexue Ban) (1004-1869)
Related titles: Online - full text ed.
Published by: Baotou Shifan Xueyuan/Baotou Teacher's College, 3, Kexue Lu, Baotou, 014030, Mongolia. TEL 86-472-5181481, FAX 86-472-3993408.

YIVO NEWS/YEDIES FUN YIVO. *see* HUMANITIES: COMPREHENSIVE WORKS

100 300 JPN ISSN 0513-5621
YOKOHAMA KOKURITSU DAIGAKU JINBUN KIYO DAI-1-RUI, TETSUGAKU, SHAKAI KAGAKU/YOKOHAMA NATIONAL UNIVERSITY. HUMANITIES. SECTION 1: PHILOSOPHY AND SOCIAL SCIENCES. Text in Japanese; Summaries in English. 1953. a. **Document type:** *Academic/Scholarly.*
Published by: Yokohama Kokuritsu Daigaku, Shakaigaku Kyoshitsu/ Yokohama National University, Department of Sociology, 156 Tokiwa-Dai, Hodogaya-ku, Yokohama-shi, Kanagawa-ken 240-0067, Japan.

300 JPN ISSN 1344-4638
H8.J3
YOKOHAMA KOKURITSU DAIGAKU KYOIKU NINGEN KAGAKUBU KIYO. III, SHAKAI KAGAKU/YOKOHAMA NATIONAL UNIVERSITY. FACULTY OF EDUCATION AND HUMAN SCIENCES. JOURNAL (SOCIAL SCIENCES). Text in Japanese. 1998. a. **Document type:** *Academic/Scholarly.*
Related titles: Online - full text ed.
Published by: Yokohama Kokuritsu Daigaku. Kyoiku Ningen Kagakubu/ Yokohama National University, Faculty of Education and Human Sciences, 79-2 Tokiwadai, Hodogaya-ku, Yokohama, 240-8501, Japan. http://www.ed.ynu.ac.jp/index.html.

300 GBR ISSN 1750-0974
➤ **THE YORKSHIRE AND HUMBER REGIONAL REVIEW.** Text in English. 1991. 3/yr. GBP 60 (effective 2009). **Document type:** *Journal, Academic/Scholarly.* **Description:** Designed to offer expert and objective commentary on all important social, economic, political and environmental trends within the region.
Formerly (until 2002): The Regional Review (0961-5334)
Published by: (Yorkshire and Humberside Regional Research Observatory), Yorkshire Futures, 1st Fl, Victoria House, 2 Victoria Pl, Leeds, LS11 5AE, United Kingdom. TEL 44-113-3949764, info@yorkshirefutures.com, http://www.yorkshirefutures.com. Circ: 150 (controlled).

➤ **YOUJIANG MINZU YIXUEYUAN XUEBAO/YOUJIANG MEDICAL UNIVERSITY FOR NATIONALITIES. JOURNAL.** *see* SCIENCES: COMPREHENSIVE WORKS

300 CAN ISSN 1196-6459
YOUTH ACTION FORUM/FORUM ACTION JEUNESSE; the future of youth in Canada. Text in English, French. 1992. q. back issues avail. **Description:** Educates youth on current issues and encourages them to act upon national and international concerns. Provides a listing of Action projects and activities across Canada.
Formerly (until 1994): World Affairs Canada Quarterly (1188-6870)
Published by: Youth Action Network/Action Jeunesse, 67 Richmond St W, Ste 410, Toronto, ON M5H 1Z5, Canada. TEL 416-368-2277, 800-618-LINK, FAX 416-368-8354. Eds. A Sud, S Rahmani. Pubs. Blaise Wigglesworth, Kenny Yum. Circ: 5,000.

300 CHN ISSN 1674-7089
▼ **YUEJIANG XUEKAN/YUEJIANG ACADEMIC JOURNAL.** Text in Chinese. 2009. bi-m. CNY 78; CNY 13 per issue (effective 2010).
Related titles: Online - full text ed.: (from WanFang Data Corp.).
Published by: Nanjing Xinxi Gongcheng Daxue/Nanjing University of Information Science & Technology, 219, Ningliu Rd., Nanjing, Jiangsu Province 210044, China. TEL 86-25-58731034, qks@nuist.edu.cn, http://www.nuist.edu.cn.

300 CHN
YUNCHENG XUEYUAN XUEBAO/YUNCHENG UNIVERSITY. JOURNAL. Text in Chinese. 1983. bi-m. CNY 8 newsstand/cover (effective 2006). **Document type:** *Journal, Academic/Scholarly.*
Formed by the merger of: Yuncheng Gaodeng Zhuanke Xuexiao Xuebao (1008-8008); Hedong Xuekan; Yuncheng Shizhuan Xuebao
Related titles: Online - full text ed.
Published by: Yuncheng Xueyuan, 333, Hedong Dong Jie, Yuncheng, 044000, China. TEL 86-359-2090304.

YUNMENG XUEKAN. *see* HUMANITIES: COMPREHENSIVE WORKS

300 CHN ISSN 1671-7511
YUNNAN DAXUE XUEBAO (SHEHUI KEXUE BAN)/YUNAN UNIVERSITY. JOURNAL (SOCIAL SCIENCE EDITION). Text in Chinese. 2002. bi-m. CNY 10 per issue (effective 2010). back issues avail. **Document type:** *Journal, Academic/Scholarly.*
Formerly: Yunnan Daxue Xuebao (Zhexue Shehui Kexue Ban)
Related titles: Online - full content ed.
—East View.
Published by: Yunnan Daxue/Yunnan University, 2, Cuihu Bei Lu, Wenjin Lou A-qu, 3/F, Kunming, 650091, China. TEL 86-871-5031238, FAX 86-871-5031238, http://www.ynu.edu.cn/.

300 100 CHN ISSN 1672-867X
B8.C5
➤ **YUNNAN MINZU DAXUE XUEBAO (ZHEXUE SHEHUI KEXUE BAN)/YUNNAN UNIVERSITY OF THE NATIONALITIES. JOURNAL (SOCIAL SCIENCES EDITION).** Text in Chinese. 1983. bi-m. USD 31.20 (effective 2009). adv. bk.rev. **Document type:** *Journal, Academic/Scholarly.* **Description:** Contains research papers and reports on political science, philosophy, economics, literature, history, and linguistics relating to ethnic groups in Yunnan Province.
Formerly (until 2002): Yunnan Minzu Xueyuan Xuebao. (Zhexue Shehui Kexue Ban) (1673-6419); Which superseded in part: Yunnan Minzu Xueyuan Xuebao/Yunnan Institute of Nationalities. Journal (1001-8913)
Related titles: Online - full text ed.
—East View, Ingenta.
Published by: Yunnan Minzu Daxue/Yunnan University of the Nationalities, 134, 121 Dajie, Kunming, Yunnan 650031, China. TEL 86-871-5137494, FAX 86-871-5137493. Ed. Huikun Huang. Circ: 2,500.

300 CHN ISSN 1000-8691
H8.C47
YUNNAN SHEHUI KEXUE/SOCIAL SCIENCE IN YUNNAN. Text in Chinese; Contents page in English. bi-m. USD 31.20 (effective 2009). **Document type:** *Journal, Academic/Scholarly.*
Related titles: Online - full text ed.
—East View.
Published by: Yunnan Shehui Kexueyuan/Yunnan Academy of Social Sciences, 45, Qixiang Lu, Kunming, Yunnan 650032, China. http://www.sky.yn.gov.cn/. **Dist. by:** China International Book Trading Corp, 35 Chegongzhuang Xilu, Haidian District, PO Box 399, Beijing 100044, China.

300 CHN ISSN 1005-7781
PL1009
YUWEN YUEKAN/CHINESE LANGUAGE MONTHLY. Text in Chinese. 1982. m. USD 28.80 (effective 2009). adv. 48 p./no.; **Document type:** *Journal, Academic/Scholarly.* **Description:** Covers all aspects of Chinese language, literature, and education at high school level.
—East View.
Published by: Huanan Shifan Daxue, Renwen Xueyuan/South China Normal University, School of Humanities, 6/F, Wenke Lou, Guangzhou, Guangdong 510631, China. TEL 86-20-85213337. Ed. Jiang Kaibo. Adv. contact Jiajun Hu. Circ: 100,000. **Dist. by:** China International Book Trading Corp, 35 Chegongzhuang Xilu, Haidian District, PO Box 399, Beijing 100044, China. TEL 86-10-68412045, FAX 86-10-68412023, cibtc@mail.cibtc.com.cn, http:// www.cibtc.com.cn.

300 ZWE ISSN 0379-0622
H1
➤ **ZAMBEZIA**; the journal of humanities of the University of Zimbabwe. Text in English. 1969. s-a. GBP 20 (effective 2005). adv. bk.rev. illus. Supplement avail.; back issues avail. **Document type:** *Journal, Academic/Scholarly.* **Description:** Multidisciplinary journal with a particular focus on southern Africa.
Formerly: Zambezia: A Journal of Social Studies in Southern and Central Africa (0514-5236); Which incorporated: University of Rhodesia. Series in Education. Occasional Paper; University of Rhodesia. Series in Humanities. Occasional Paper; University of Rhodesia. Series in Science. Occasional Paper; University of Rhodesia. Series in Social Studies. Occasional Paper
Related titles: Online - full text ed.: ISSN 1726-9091. 2000.
Indexed: AICP, ASD, BibLing, CA, HistAb, IIBP, ISAP, MLA, MLA-IB, P06, P30, PLESA.
—IE, Infotrieve, Ingenta.
Published by: University of Zimbabwe Publications, Mt Pleasant, Main Administration Bldg, 1st Fl, PO Box MP 203, Harare, Zimbabwe. TEL 263-04-303211, FAX 263-04-333407, http://www.uz.ac.zw/ publications. Ed. A S Mlambo. R&P M S Mtetwa. Adv. contact M Mutimbanyoka. Circ: 400.

300 SRB ISSN 0352-5732
AS346
➤ **ZBORNIK MATICE SRPSKE ZA DRUSTVENE NAUKE.** Text in Serbo-Croatian. 1915. a. EUR 10 per issue (effective 2007). **Document type:** *Journal, Academic/Scholarly.*
Former titles (until 1984): Zbornik za Drustvene Nauke (0044-1937); (until 1956): Matica Srpska. Naucni Zbornik. Serija Drustvenih Nauka (0353-6300)
Indexed: AICP, BibLing, HistAb, RASB, RILM.
Published by: Matica Srpska, Matice Srpske 1, Novi Sad, 21000. TEL 381-21-527622, FAX 381-21- 528901, ms@maticasrpska.org.yu. Ed. Milovan Mitrovich.

300 DEU ISSN 0044-2429
➤ **ZEITSCHRIFT FUER DAS GESAMTE GENOSSENSCHAFTSWESEN.** Text in German. 1950. q. EUR 69 to individuals; EUR 138 to institutions; EUR 49 to students; EUR 24.90 newsstand/cover (effective 2011). adv. bk.rev. bibl.; charts. index. reprints avail. **Document type:** *Journal, Academic/Scholarly.*
Indexed: BAS, DIP, IBR, IBZ, KES, PAIS.
—CCC.
Published by: Vandenhoeck und Ruprecht, Theaterstr 13, Goettingen, 37073, Germany. TEL 49-551-508440, FAX 49-551-5084422, info@v-r.de. Ed. Volker Peemoeller. Circ: 600 (paid and controlled).

300 940.53 DEU ISSN 1438-8332
HV6322.7
ZEITSCHRIFT FUER GENOZIDFORSCHUNG. Text in German. 1999. s-a. EUR 38 domestic; EUR 40.50 foreign; EUR 31 domestic to students; EUR 33.50 foreign to students; EUR 20 newsstand/cover (effective 2002). **Document type:** *Journal, Academic/Scholarly.*
—BLDSC (9462.458500).
Published by: Institut fuer Diaspora- und Genozidforschung, Universitaetstr 150, Bochum, 44801, Germany. TEL 49-234-3229702, FAX 49-234-3214770, idg@ruhr-uni-bochum.de, http://www.ruhr-uni-bochum.de.

300 DEU
ZEITSCHRIFT FUER KULTURWISSENSCHAFT. Text in German. 2007. 2/yr. EUR 8.50 newsstand/cover (effective 2011). **Document type:** *Journal, Academic/Scholarly.*
Published by: Transcript, Muehlenstr 47, Bielefeld, 33607, Germany. TEL 49-521-63454, FAX 49-521-61040, live@transcript-verlag.de.

ZEITSCHRIFT FUER OSTMITTELEUROPA-FORSCHUNG. *see* HISTORY—History Of Europe

300 DEU
HM571
➤ **ZEITSCHRIFT FUER QUALITATIVE FORSCHUNG.** Abbreviated title: Z Q F. Text in German. 1999. 2/yr. EUR 42 to individuals; EUR 45 to institutions; EUR 29.90 to students; EUR 22 per issue (effective 2011). **Document type:** *Journal, Academic/Scholarly.*
Formerly (until 2007): Zeitschrift fuer Qualitative Bildungs-, Beratungs- und Sozialforschung (1438-8324)

Indexed: CA, DIP, E03, ERI, IBR, IBSS, IBZ, T02.
—CCC.
Published by: Verlag Barbara Budrich, Stauffenbergstr 7, Leverkusen, 51379, Germany. TEL 49-2171-344594, FAX 49-2171-344693, info@budrich-verlag.de, http://www.budrich-verlag.de.

300 DEU ISSN 1610-2339
ZEITSCHRIFT FUER SOZIALPAEDAGOGIK. Text in German. 2003. q. EUR 58; EUR 46 to students; EUR 16.50 newsstand/cover (effective 2011). adv. **Document type:** *Journal, Academic/Scholarly.*
Indexed: DIP, IBR, IBZ.
Published by: Juventa Verlag GmbH, Ehretstr 3, Weinheim, 69469, Germany. TEL 49-6201-90200, FAX 49-6201-902013, juventa@juventa.de, http://www.juventa.de. Ed. Christian Niemeyer. Adv. contact Karola Weiss. Circ: 650 (paid and controlled).

ZEITSCHRIFT FUER UMWELTPOLITIK UND UMWELTRECHT. *see* ENVIRONMENTAL STUDIES

320.5322 DEU ISSN 0940-0648
ZEITSCHRIFT MARXISTISCHE ERNEUERUNG. Text in German. 1978. q. EUR 32 domestic; EUR 38 foreign (effective 2006). back issues avail. **Document type:** *Newsletter, Consumer.*
Formerly (until 1990): Marxistische Studien (0171-3698)
Indexed: RASB.
Published by: Institut fuer Marxistische Studien und Forschungen e.V., Postfach 500936, Frankfurt Am Main, 60397, Germany. Circ: 3,000.

300 IND ISSN 2231-5780
▼ ➤ **ZENITH**; international journal of multidisciplinary research. Text in English. 2011 (May). m. INR 3,000, USD 100 (effective 2011). **Document type:** *Journal, Academic/Scholarly.* **Description:** Publishes research work in a wide variety of disciplines including finance, accounting, marketing, human resource management, industrial relations, commerce, economics, computer science, information technology, tourism and hospitality management, political science, public administration, history, and psychology.
Media: Online - full text.
Published by: Zenith International Research & Academic Foundation, c/o R K Wadhwa, University Book Centre, Opp Third Gate, Kurukshetra University, Kurukshetra, India. TEL 91-9050141570, info@zenithresearch.org.in. Ed. Heera Sharma.

300 DEU ISSN 1614-6360
ZENTRUM UND PERIPHERIE. Text in German. 2004. irreg., latest vol.8, 2010. price varies. **Document type:** *Monographic series, Academic/Scholarly.*
Published by: Rainer Hampp Verlag, Marktplatz 5, Mering, 86415, Germany. TEL 49-8233-4783, FAX 49-8233-30755, info@rhverlag.de, http://www.rhverlag.de.

300 CHN ISSN 1009-8445
ZHAOQING XUEYUAN XUEBAO/ZHAOQING UNIVERSITY. JOURNAL. Text in Chinese. 1980. bi-m. **Document type:** *Journal, Academic/Scholarly.*
Former titles (until 2000): Xijiang Daxue Xuebao; (until 1990): Xijiang Daxue. Zhaoqing Shizuan Xuebao; (until 1985): Zhaoqing Shizhuan Xuebao
Related titles: Online - full text ed.
Published by: Zhaoqing Xueyuan, Zhaoqing, 526061, China. TEL 86-758-2716328, FAX 86-758-2716586.

300 CHN ISSN 1008-942X
➤ **ZHEJIANG DAXUE XUEBAO (RENWEN SHEHUI KEXUE BAN)/ ZHEJIANG UNIVERSITY. JOURNAL (HUMANITIES AND SOCIAL SCIENCES EDITION).** Text in Chinese; Abstracts in English. 1955. bi-m. USD 53.40 (effective 2009). 160 p./no.; **Document type:** *Journal, Academic/Scholarly.*
Formed by the 1998 merger of: Zhejiang Daxue Xuebao (Shehui Kexue Ban) (1003-8612); Hangzhou Daxue Xuebao (Zhexue Shehui Kexue Ban) (1000-2081)
Related titles: Online - full text ed.
Indexed: CA, L&LBA, MLA-IB, P42, PSA, S02, S03, SCOPUS, SociolAb, T02.
—East View, Ingenta.
Published by: Zhejiang Daxue Chubanshe/Zhejiang University Press, 148, Tianmushan Rd, No 4 West Bldg, Rm 515, Hangzhou, 310028, China. TEL 86-571-88273210. **Dist. by:** China International Book Trading Corp, 35 Chegongzhuang Xilu, Haidian District, PO Box 399, Beijing 100044, China. TEL 86-10-68412045, FAX 86-10-68412023, cibtc@mail.cibtc.com.cn, http://www.cibtc.com.cn.

➤ **ZHEJIANG GONG-SHANG ZHIYE JISHU XUEYUAN XUEBAO/ ZHEJIANG BUSINESS TECHNOLOGY INSTITUTE. JOURNAL.** *see* BUSINESS AND ECONOMICS

➤ **ZHEJIANG HAIYANG XUEYUAN XUEBAO (RENWEN SHEHUI KEXUE BAN)/ZHEJIANG OCEAN UNIVERSITY. JORUNAL (HUMANE SCIENCE).** *see* HUMANITIES: COMPREHENSIVE WORKS

300 CHN ISSN 1001-5035
AS452.C4753
ZHEJIANG SHIFAN DAXUE XUEBAO (SHEHUI KEXUE BAN)/ ZHEJIANG NORMAL UNIVERSITY. JOURNAL (SOCIAL SCIENCE EDITION). Text in Chinese. q. USD 21.60 (effective 2009). **Document type:** *Academic/Scholarly.*
Related titles: Online - full text ed.
—East View.
Published by: Zhejiang Shifan Daxue/Zhejiang Normal University, PO Box 33, Jinhua, Zhejiang 321004, China. Ed. Luo Xiangfa.

300 500 CHN ISSN 1671-2250
ZHEJIANG WANLI XUEYUAN XUEBAO/ZHEJIANG WANLI UNIVERSITY. JOURNAL. Text in Chinese. 1988. bi-m. CNY 8 newsstand/cover (effective 2006). **Document type:** *Journal, Academic/Scholarly.*
Related titles: Online - full text ed.
Published by: Zhejiang Wanli Xueyuan, 8 Qianhu Nan Lu, Ningbo, 315100, China. TEL 86-574-88222279, FAX 86-574-88357720.

300 CHN ISSN 1003-420X
AS451
ZHEJIANG XUEKAN/ZHEJIANG LEARNED JOURNAL. Text in Chinese. 1963. bi-m. USD 31.20 (effective 2009). 128 p./no.; **Document type:** *Journal, Academic/Scholarly.* **Description:** Studies theories of multiple social sciences disciplines.
Related titles: Online - full content ed.; Online - full text ed.
Indexed: RASB.
—East View.
Published by: Zhejiang Sheng Shehui Kexueyuan/Zhejiang Academy of Social Sciences, Shengfudayuan, no.2 Building, Hangzhou, Zhejiang 310006, China. TEL 86-571-87053176. Ed. Lin Shujian. **Dist. overseas by:** China International Book Trading Corp, 35 Chegongzhuang Xilu, Haidian District, PO Box 399, Beijing 100044, China. TEL 86-10-68412045, FAX 86-10-68412023, cibtc@mail.cibtc.com.cn, http://www.cibtc.com.cn.

300 CHN ISSN 1672-2795
ZHEJIANG YISHU ZHIYE XUEYUAN XUEBAO/ZHEJIANG VOCATIONAL ACADEMY OF ART. JOURNAL. Text in Chinese. 2003. q. CNY 15 newsstand/cover (effective 2006). **Document type:** *Journal, Academic/Scholarly.*
Related titles: Online - full text ed.
Indexed: RILM.
Published by: Zhejiang Yishu Zhiye Xueyuan, 518, Binwen Lu, Hangzhou, 310053, China. http://www.zj-art.com/.

300 100 CHN ISSN 1001-8204
AS452.C4613
ZHENGZHOU DAXUE XUEBAO (ZHEXUE SHEHUI KEXUE BAN)/ ZHENGZHOU UNIVERSITY. JOURNAL (PHILOSOPHY AND SOCIAL SCIENCE EDITION). Text in Chinese. 1960. bi-m. USD 40.20 (effective 2009). **Document type:** *Journal, Academic/Scholarly.*
Related titles: Online - full text ed.
—East View.
Published by: Zhengzhou Daxue/Zhengzhou University, 100, Kexue Dadao, Zhengzhou, 450001, China. TEL 86-371-67781275.

300 CHN ISSN 1009-1270
ZHENGZHOU GONGYE DAXUE XUEBAO (SHEHUI KEXUE BAN)/ ZHENGZHOU UNIVERSITY OF TECHNOLOGY. JOURNAL (SOCIAL SCIENCE EDITION). Text in Chinese. 1982. q. CNY 6 newsstand/cover (effective 2006). **Document type:** *Journal, Academic/Scholarly.*
Related titles: Online - full text ed.
Published by: Zhengzhou Gongye Daxue, 97, Wenhua Lu, Zhengzhou, 450002, China. TEL 86-371-3887128.

300 CHN ISSN 1009-1750
ZHENGZHOU HANGKONG GONGYE GUANLI XUEYUAN XUEBAO (SHEHUI KEXUE BAN)/ZHENGZHOU INSTITUTE OF AERONAUTICAL INDUSTRY MANAGEMENT. JOURNAL (SOCIAL SCIENCE EDITION). Text in Chinese. 1982. bi-m. CNY 10 newsstand/cover (effective 2006). **Document type:** *Journal, Academic/Scholarly.*
Related titles: Online - full text ed.
Published by: Zhengzhou Hangkong Gongye Guanli Xueyuan/ Zhengzhou Institute of Aeronautical Industry Management, 2, Daxue Zhong Lu, Zhengzhou, 450015, China. TEL 86-371-8252208, FAX 86-371-8894808, http://www.zzia.edu.cn/.

300 CHN ISSN 1009-3729
ZHENGZHOU QINGGONGYE XUEYUAN XUEBAO (SHEHUI KEXUE BAN)/ZHENGZHOU UNIVERSITY OF LIGHT INDUSTRY. JOURNAL (SOCIAL SCIENCE EDITION). Text in Chinese. 2000. bi-m. CNY 6 newsstand/cover (effective 2006). **Document type:** *Journal, Academic/Scholarly.*
Related titles: Online - full text ed.
Published by: Zhengzhou Qinggongye Xueyuan, 5, Dongfeng Lu, Zhengzhou, 450002, China.

300 CHN ISSN 1674-5000
ZHONG-GONG HEFEI SHI-WEI DANGXIAO XUEBAO/PARTY COLLEGE OF C.P.C HEFEI MUNICIPAL COMMITTEE. JOURNAL. Text in Chinese. 2002. q. **Document type:** *Journal, Academic/Scholarly.*
Published by: Zhong-Gong Hefei Shi-Wei Dangxiao/Party College of C.P.C Hefei Municipal Committee, Changjiang Xi Lu, Hefei, 230031, China.

300 CHN ISSN 1673-1646
ZHONGBEI DAXUE XUEBAO (SHEHUI KEXUE BAN)/NORTH UNIVERSITY OF CHINA. JOURNAL (SOCIAL SCIENCE EDITION). Text in Chinese. 1985. bi-m. CNY 10 newsstand/cover (effective 2008). **Document type:** *Journal, Academic/Scholarly.*
Related titles: Online - full text ed.
Published by: Zhongbei Daxue Chubanbu/Press of North University of China, Xueyuan Lu, Taiyuan, 030051, China. TEL 86-351-3942656, FAX 86-351-3922085, http://xuebao.nuc.edu.cn/.

300 CHN ISSN 1671-0169
ZHONGGUO DIZHI DAXUE XUEBAO (SHEHUI KEXUE BAN)/CHINA UNIVERSITY OF GEOSCIENCES. JOURNAL (SOCIAL SCIENCES EDITION). Text in Chinese. 2000. bi-m. CNY 10 newsstand/cover (effective 2006). **Document type:** *Journal, Academic/Scholarly.*
Related titles: Online - full text ed.
Indexed: ESPM, SSciA.
Published by: Zhongguo Dizhi Daxue/China University of Geosciences, Hongshan-qu, 388, Lumo Lu, Wuhan, Hubei 430074, China. TEL 86-27-67885186, FAX 86-27-87483461.

300 CHN ISSN 1672-335X
ZHONGGUO HAIYANG DAXUE XUEBAO (SHEHUI KEXUE BAN)/ OCEAN UNIVERSITY OF CHINA. JOURNAL (SOCIAL SCIENCES EDITION). Text in Chinese. 1988. bi-m. USD 18 (effective 2009).
Formerly (until 2003): Qingdao Haiyang Daxue Xuebao (Shehui Kexue Ban)/Ocean University of Qingdao. Journal (Social Sciences Edition) (1008-262X)
Related titles: Online - full text ed.
—East View.
Published by: Zhongguo Haiyang Daxue, 5, Yushan Lu, Qingdao, 266003, China. TEL 86-532-82032739.

300 CHN ISSN 1009-105X
ZHONGGUO KUANGYE DAXUE XUEBAO (SHEHUI KEXUE BAN)/ CHINA UNIVERSITY OF MINING & TECHNOLOGY. JOURNAL (SOCIAL SCIENCES). Text in Chinese. 1999. q. CNY 10 newsstand/ cover (effective 2009). **Document type:** *Journal, Academic/Scholarly.*
Related titles: Online - full text ed.
Published by: Zhongguo Kuangye Daxue/China University of Mining and Technology, Jiefang Nan Lu, Xuzhou, Jiangsu 221008, China. TEL 86-516-83884931, http://www.cumt.edu.cn/.

ZHONGGUO MINZU/CHINA ETHNICITY. *see* ETHNIC INTERESTS

300 CHN ISSN 1004-8111
HD2096
ZHONGGUO NONGCUN/RURAL CHINA. Text in Chinese. bi-m. CNY 4.20 newsstand/cover. **Description:** Covers new strategies and thoughts on China's rural reform, and trends in export-oriented development of Chinese rural economy.
Published by: Zhongguo Nongcun Zazhishe, 61 Fuxing Lu, Beijing, 100036, China. TEL 86-10-6821-1919. Ed. Hongfei Zhou. Circ: 50,000.

ZHONGGUO QINGNIAN YANJIU/CHINA YOUTH STUDY. *see* CHILDREN AND YOUTH—About

300 CHN ISSN 1000-5420
AS452.P4422
ZHONGGUO RENMIN DAXUE XUEBAO/CHINA PEOPLE'S UNIVERSITY. JOURNAL. Text in Chinese. 1950-1966; resumed 1978. bi-m. USD 40.20 (effective 2009). 128 p./no.; **Document type:** *Journal, Academic/Scholarly.*
Formerly: Renming Daxue Zhoubao
Related titles: Online - full content ed.; Online - full text ed.
—BLDSC (9512.795400), East View, Ingenta.
Published by: Zhongguo Renmin Daxue/Renmin University of China, Keyan Bangonglou, Donglou, Beijing, 100872, China. TEL 86-10-62511076, http://www.ruc.edu.cn/. Ed. Xinghua Wei. **Dist. overseas by:** China International Book Trading Corp, 35 Chegongzhuang Xilu, Haidian District, PO Box 399, Beijing 100044, China.

300 CHN
ZHONGGUO SHEHUI BAO/CHINA SOCIAL NEWS. Text in Chinese. 1985. d. (Mon.-Fri.). CNY 168 (effective 2004). **Document type:** *Newspaper, Government.*
Address: Zhaoyang-qu, 4, Dongdaqiaoxiajie, Beijing, 100020, China. TEL 86-10-65915616, FAX 86-10-65915726. **Dist. by:** China International Book Trading Corp, 35 Chegongzhuang Xilu, Haidian District, PO Box 399, Beijing 100044, China. TEL 86-10-68412045, FAX 86-10-68412023, cibtc@mail.cibtc.com.cn, http:// www.cibtc.com.cn.

300 CHN ISSN 1674-3857
ZHONGGUO SHEHUI GONGZUO/CHINA SOCIAL WORK. Text in Chinese. 1988. every 10 days. USD 136.80 (effective 2009). **Document type:** *Journal, Academic/Scholarly.*
Former titles: Zhongguo Shehui Daokan/China Society Periodical (1008-7206); (until 1998): Zhongguo Shehui Gongzuo (1007-2128); (until 1995): Shehui Gongzuo Yanjiu/Social Affairs Study (1001-8557)
Related titles: Online - full text ed.
—East View.
Published by: Zhongguo Shehui Xinwen Chuban Zongshe/China Society Press, 33, Erlong Lu Jia, Beijing, 100020, China. TEL 86-10-66063618, FAX 86-10-66063358.

ZHONGGUO SHEHUI JINGJISHI YANJIU/JOURNAL OF CHINESE SOCIAL AND ECONOMIC HISTORY. *see* HISTORY—History Of Asia

300 CHN ISSN 1002-4921
H8.C47
➤ **ZHONGGUO SHEHUI KEXUE/SOCIAL SCIENCES IN CHINA.** Text in Chinese. 1980. q. USD 74.40 (effective 2009). adv. bk.rev. back issues avail. **Document type:** *Academic/Scholarly.* **Description:** Reflects the highest level of current academic research in the social sciences in China. Includes articles on law, economy, demography, sociology, politics, philosophy and history.
Related titles: Online - full text ed.; ◆ English ed.: Social Sciences in China. ISSN 0252-9203.
Indexed: APEL, RASB.
—East View, Ingenta.
Published by: Zhongguo Shehui Kexue Zazhishe, 158, Gulouxi Dajie, Beijing, 100720, China. TEL 86-10-64033952. Ed. Li Xinda.

300 CHN ISSN 1000-2952
AS452.P443
ZHONGGUO SHEHUI KEXUEYUAN YANJIU SHENGYUAN XUEBAO/ CHINESE ACADEMY OF SOCIAL SCIENCES. GRADUATE SCHOOL. JOURNAL. Text in Chinese. 1985. bi-m. USD 31.20 (effective 2009). **Document type:** *Academic/Scholarly.*
Related titles: Online - full text ed.
Indexed: RASB.
—BLDSC (9512.797150), East View, Ingenta.
Published by: Zhongguo Shehui Kexueyuan, Yanjiushengyuan, No 131 Xibajianfang, Dongzhimenwai, Beijing, 100015, China. TEL 472019. Ed. Wang Haibo.

300 CHN ISSN 1672-3104
ZHONGNAN DAXUE XUEBAO (SHEHUI KEXUE BAN)/CENTRAL SOUTH UNIVERSITY. JOURNAL (SOCIAL SCIENCE). Text in Chinese. 1995. bi-m. CNY 12 newsstand/cover (effective 2006). **Document type:** *Journal, Academic/Scholarly.*
Formerly (until 2002): Zhongnan Gongye Daxue Xuebao (Shehui Kexue Ban) (1008-4061)
Related titles: Online - full text ed.
Published by: Zhongnan Daxue/Central South University, Lushan Nan Lu, Changsha, 410083, China. TEL 86-731-8830141, FAX 86-731-8877197.

ZHONGNAN MINZU DAXUE XUEBAO (RENWEN SHEHUI KEXUE BAN)/SOUTH-CENTRAL UNIVERSITY FOR NATIONALITIES. JOURNAL (HUMANITIES AND SOCIAL SCIENCES). *see* HUMANITIES: COMPREHENSIVE WORKS

300 CHN ISSN 1000-9639
AS451 CODEN: CHTHAJ
ZHONGSHAN DAXUE XUEBAO (SHEHUI KEXUE BAN)/SUN YAT-SEN UNIVERSITY. JOURNAL (SOCIAL SCIENCE EDITION). Text in Chinese; Contents page in English. 1955. bi-m. USD 31.20 (effective 2009). bk.rev. bibl. Index. **Document type:** *Journal, Academic/Scholarly.*
Formerly: Zhongshan Daxue Shehui Kexue Xuebao (0412-443X)
Related titles: Online - full text ed.; ◆ Supplement(s): Luojixue Yanjiu. ISSN 1674-3202.
Indexed: SpeleolAb.
—CASDDS, East View, Ingenta.
Published by: Zhongshan Daxue/Sun Yatsen University, 135, Xinkong Xilu, Guangzhou, Guangdong 510275, China. Eds. He Zhiping, Liao Wenhui.

S

300 100 CHN ISSN 1005-8575
DS730
ZHONGYANG MINZU DAXUE XUEBAO (ZHEXUE SHEHUI KEXUE BAN)/CENTRAL UNIVERSITY FOR NATIONALITIES. JOURNAL (PHILOSOPHY AND SOCIAL SCIENCES EDITION). Text in Chinese. 1974. bi-m. USD 24.60 (effective 2009). **Document type:** *Journal, Academic/Scholarly.*
Formerly: Zhongyang Minzu Xueyuan Xuebao/Central University for Nationalities. Journal (1000-8667)
Related titles: Online - full text ed.
Indexed: RILM.
—East View.
Published by: Zhongyang Minzu Xueyuan, Xuebao Bianjibu, 27, Zhongguancun Nan Dajie, Beijing, 100081, China. TEL 86-10-68933635, FAX 86-10-68932447.

ZHONGZHOU DAXUE XUEBAO/ZHONGZHOU UNIVERSITY. JOURNAL. *see* SCIENCES: COMPREHENSIVE WORKS

300 CHN ISSN 1003-0751
AS452.C4614
ZHONGZHOU XUEKAN/ACADEMIC JOURNAL OF ZHONGZHOU. Text in Chinese. 1979. bi-m. USD 37.20 (effective 2009). **Document type:** *Journal, Academic/Scholarly.*
Related titles: Online - full text ed.
Indexed: RILM.
—East View, Ingenta.
Published by: Henan Sheng Shehui Kexueyuan/Henan Academy of Social Science, 50 Wenhua Lu, Zhengzhou, Henan 450002, China. TEL 86-371-3936507. **Dist. by:** China International Book Trading Corp, 35 Chegongzhuang Xilu, Haidian District, PO Box 399, Beijing 100044, China. TEL 86-10-68412045, FAX 86-10-68412023, cibtc@mail.cibtc.com.cn, http://www.cibtc.com.cn.

300 RUS ISSN 1727-0634
HN1
➤ **ZHURNAL ISSLEDOVANII SOTSIAL'NOI POLITIKI/JOURNAL OF SOCIAL POLICY STUDIES.** Text in Russian. 2003. q. USD 125 in United States (effective 2008). adv. **Document type:** *Journal, Academic/Scholarly.* **Description:** Publishes major articles, disciplinary review essays, book reviews, and special sections, which involve various aspects of social policy including associated teaching and learning issues.
Related titles: Online - full text ed.
Indexed: CA, IBSS, P34, P42, P46, P48, PQC, S02, S03, SociolAb, T02.
—BLDSC (0060.834000), East View, IE.
Published by: Tsentr Sotsial'noi Politiki i Gendernykh Issledovanii/Center for Social Policy and Gender Studies, ul Politekhnicheskaya 77, korpus 5, Saratov, 410035, Russian Federation. TEL 7-8452-566755, FAX 7-8452-566818. Eds. Elena Yarskaya-Smirnova, Pavel Romanov. adv.: B&W page RUR 3,600, B&W page USD 120; 154 x 203. **Dist. by:** East View Information Services, 10601 Wayzata Blvd, Minneapolis, MN 55305. TEL 952-252-1201, 800-477-1005, FAX 952-252-1202, info@eastview.com, http://www.eastview.com.

300 100 900 CHN ISSN 1000-0763
B809.7.A1
➤ **ZIRAN BIANZHENGFA TONGXUN/JOURNAL OF DIALECTICS OF NATURE.** Text in Chinese. 1979. bi-m. USD 24.60 (effective 2009). abstr. 112 p./no.; **Document type:** *Journal, Academic/Scholarly.*
Related titles: Online - full text ed.
—East View.
Published by: (Zhongguo Kexueyuan/Chinese Academy of Sciences), Ziran Bianzhengfa Tongxun Zazhishe, Jia-19 Yuquan Lu, Beijing, 100039, China. Ed., R&P Xing-Min Li. Adv. contact Da-Ming Wang.

➤ **ZUKUENFTE.** *see* TECHNOLOGY: COMPREHENSIVE WORKS

300 DEU ISSN 1860-658X
ZUKUNFTSSTUDIEN. Text in German. 1991. irreg., latest vol.33, 2008. price varies. **Document type:** *Monographic series, Academic/Scholarly.*
Published by: Peter Lang GmbH (Subsidiary of: Peter Lang Publishing Group), Eschborner Landstr 42-50, Frankfurt Am Main, 60489, Germany. TEL 49-69-7807050, FAX 49-69-78070550, zentrale.frankfurt@peterlang.com, http://www.peterlang.com. Ed. Rolf Kreibich.

300 FRA ISSN 1636-8592
128. SCIENCES SOCIALES. Cover title: Collection 128. Sciences Sociales. Variant title: Cent-Vingt-Huit. Sciences Sociales. Text in French. 1992. irreg. **Document type:** *Monographic series.*
Formerly (until 1996): 128. Lettres et Sciences Sociales
Related titles: ◆ Series of: Collection 128. ISSN 1160-2422.
Published by: Armand Colin, 21 Rue du Montparnasse, Paris, 75283 Cedex 06, France. TEL 33-1-44395447, FAX 33-1-44394343, infos@armand-colin.fr, http://www.armand-colin.com.

300 DEU
▼ **1800 - 2000**; Kulturgeschichten der Moderne. Text in German. 2010. irreg., latest vol.4, 2011. price varies. **Document type:** *Monographic series, Academic/Scholarly.*
Published by: Transcript, Muehlenstr 47, Bielefeld, 33607, Germany. TEL 49-521-63454, FAX 49-521-61040, live@transcript-verlag.de.

300 AUS ISSN 1833-3338
➤ **10,000 STEPS WORKING PAPER SERIES.** Text in English. 2005. q. back issues avail. **Document type:** *Report, Academic/Scholarly.* **Description:** Contains series of brief reports explaining research conducted by 10,000 Steps.
Related titles: Online - full text ed.: ISSN 1835-3789. free (effective 2008).
Published by: Central Queensland University, Centre for Social Science Research, Bldg 18, Bruce Hwy, Rockhampton, QLD 4702, Australia. TEL 61-7-49306751, FAX 61-7-49309820, c.hooker@cqu.edu.au, http://cssr.cqu.edu.au.

SOCIAL SCIENCES: COMPREHENSIVE WORKS—Abstracting, Bibliographies, Statistics

016.3 USA
Z7163
A S S I A (ONLINE). (Applied Social Sciences Index & Abstracts) Text in English. 1987. base vol. plus m. updates. abstr.; illus. back issues avail.; reprints avail. **Document type:** *Database, Abstract/Index.* **Description:** Studies of social sciences, with emphasis on the needs of people and social work.
Supersedes (in 1999): A S S I A (Print) (0950-2238)
Media: Online - full text.
Published by: ProQuest LLC (Bethesda) (Subsidiary of: Cambridge Information Group), 789 E Eisenhower Pky, Ann Arbor, MI 48103. TEL 734-761-4700, FAX 734-997-4222, info@proquest.com.

ALTERNATIVE PRESS INDEX. *see* POLITICAL SCIENCE—Abstracting, Bibliographies, Statistics

306.021 AUS
AUSTRALIA. BUREAU OF STATISTICS. ATTENDANCE AT SELECTED CULTURAL VENUES, AUSTRALIA (ONLINE). Text in English. 1991. every 3 yrs. (every 4 yrs. until 1999), latest 2009-10. free (effective 2009). **Document type:** *Government.* **Description:** Contains details on characteristics of people who attend, and frequency of visits, a range of cultural venues including libraries, museums, various categories of music and performing arts, cinemas, botanic gardens and animal parks.
Formerly (until 2002): Australia. Bureau of Statistics. Attendance at Selected Cultural Venues, Australia (Print)
Media: Online - full text.
Published by: Australian Bureau of Statistics, Locked Bag 10, Belconnen, ACT 2616, Australia. TEL 61-2-62527037, FAX 61-2-92684654, client.services@abs.gov.au.

300.021 AUS ISSN 1321-1781
HN844
AUSTRALIA. BUREAU OF STATISTICS. AUSTRALIAN SOCIAL TRENDS. Text in English. 1994. a. AUD 60 per issue (effective 2009). charts; stat. **Document type:** *Government.* **Description:** Presents statistical analysis and commentary on a wide range of current social issues within the following broad areas of interest: population, families, health, education and training, work, income and housing.
Former titles (until 1994): Social Indicators Australia; (until 1980): Social Indicators
Related titles: Online - full text ed.: free (effective 2009).
Indexed: AEI, ERO.
Published by: Australian Bureau of Statistics, Locked Bag 10, Belconnen, ACT 2616, Australia. TEL 61-2-62527037, FAX 61-2-92684654, client.services@abs.gov.au, http://www.abs.gov.au.

300.021 AUS
AUSTRALIA. BUREAU OF STATISTICS. GENERAL SOCIAL SURVEY: SUMMARY RESULTS, AUSTRALIA (ONLINE). Text in English. 2002. irreg., latest 2006. free (effective 2009). stat. **Document type:** *Government.* **Description:** Presents results of the 2006 General Social Survey, which brings together a wide range of information to enable it to be linked across areas of social concern.
Formerly: Australia. Bureau of Statistics. General Social Survey: Summary Results, Australia (Print)
Media: Online - full text.
Published by: Australian Bureau of Statistics, Locked Bag 10, Belconnen, ACT 2616, Australia. TEL 61-2-92684909, 61-2-62527037, 300-135-070, FAX 61-2-62528103, client.services@abs.gov.au.

300.021 AUS
AUSTRALIA. BUREAU OF STATISTICS. STANDARDS FOR STATISTICS ON CULTURAL AND LANGUAGE DIVERSITY (ONLINE). Text in English. 199?. irreg., latest 1999. free (effective 2009). **Document type:** *Government.* **Description:** Includes first language spoken, religion, Australian citizenship, indigenous status and year of arrival in Australia.
Former titles: Australia. Bureau of Statistics. Standards for Statistics on Cultural and Language Diversity (Print); (until 19??): Australia. Bureau of Statistics. Standards for Statistics on Cultural Diversity
Media: Online - full text.
Published by: Australian Bureau of Statistics, Locked Bag 10, Belconnen, ACT 2616, Australia. TEL 61-2-62527037, 61-2-92684909, 300-135-070, FAX 61-2-62528103, client.services@abs.gov.au.

300 DEU ISSN 1430-3310
BAYERISCHES LANDESAMT FUER STATISTIK UND DATENVERARBEITUNG. STATISTISCHE BERICHTE P: VOLKSWIRTSCHAFTLICHE GESAMTRECHNUNGEN. Text in German. 1973. irreg. **Document type:** *Government.*
Formerly (until 1982): Bayerisches Statistisches Landesamt. Statistische Berichte P (1430-3140)
Published by: Bayerisches Landesamt fuer Statistik und Datenverarbeitung, Neuhauser Str 8, Munich, 80331, Germany. TEL 49-89-2119205, FAX 49-89-2119410, poststelle@statistik.bayern.de, http://www.statistik.bayern.de.

300 BLZ
BELIZE SOCIAL INDICATORS REPORT. Text in English. 1998. a. free. **Document type:** *Government.* **Description:** Analysis of social indicators. Includes definitions, formulas and data reliability.
Published by: Ministry of Finance, Central Statistical Office, Belmopan, Belize. TEL 501-8-22352, FAX 501-8-23206, csogob@btl.net.

016.3 ESP ISSN 1138-9796
G1
BIBLIO 3W; revista bibliografica de geografia y ciencias sociales. Text in Spanish. 1996. a. free (effective 2011). **Document type:** *Journal, Academic/Scholarly.*
Media: Online - full text.
Published by: (Universitat de Barcelona, Facultat de Geografia e Historia), Universitat de Barcelona, Servei de Publicacions, Gran Via Corts Catalanes 585, Barcelona, 08007, Spain. TEL 34-93-4021100, http://www.publicacions.ub.es.

016.3 016.001 ESP ISSN 1575-0175
Z7161
BIBLIOGRAFIA ESPANOLA DE REVISTAS CIENTIFICAS DE CIENCIAS SOCIALES Y HUMANIDADES/SPANISH BIBLIOGRAPHY OF SCIENTIFIC JOURNALS IN SOCIAL SCIENCES AND HUMANITIES. Text in Spanish. 1998. a., latest 2001. EUR 30.05 (effective 2003). cum.index: 1995-1998. **Document type:** *Abstract/Index.*
Formed by the merger of (1978-1998): Indice Espanol de Ciencias Sociales. Serie A, Psicologia y Ciencias de la Educacion (0213-019X); (1978-1998): Indice Espanol de Ciencias Sociales. Serie B, Economica, Sociologia y Ciencias Politicas (0213-0521); Which was formerly (until 1987): Indice Espanol de Ciencias Sociales. Serie B, Economia, Sociologia, Politica y Urbanismo (1575-0647); (1978-1998): Indice Espanol de Ciencias Sociales. Serie C, Derecho (0213-4683); (1978-1998): Indice Espanol de Ciencias Sociales. Serie D, Ciencia y Documentacion Cientifica (0214-1086); (1978-1998): Indice Espanol de Ciencias Sociales. Serie E, Geografia, Urbanismo y Arquitectura; Which was formerly (until 1989): Indice Espanol de Ciencias Sociales. Serie E, Urbanismo y Ordenacion del Territorio (1130-3700); All of which superseded in part (in 1984): Indice Espanol de Ciencias Sociales (0211-1373); (1978-1998): Indice Espanol de Humanidades. Serie A, Bellas Artes (0214-7548); (1978-1998): Indice Espanol de Humanidades. Serie B, Ciencias Historicas (1130-099X); (1978-1998): Indice Espanol de Humanidades. Serie C, Linguistica y Literatura (1130-1163); (1978-1998): Indice Espanol de Humanidades. Serie D, Filosofia (1130-9105); All of which superseded in part (in 1988): Indice Espanol de Humanidades (0210-8488)
Media: CD-ROM.
Published by: (Spain. Consejo Superior de Investigaciones Cientificas (C S I C)), Consejo Superior de Investigaciones Cientificas (C S I C), Instituto de Estudios Documentales sobre Ciencia y Tecnologia, Joaquin Costa 22, Madrid, 28002, Spain. TEL 34-91-5635482, FAX 34-91-5642644, sdi@cindoc.csic.es.

300 BEL ISSN 0773-3933
BIBLIOGRAPHIE DE L'AFRIQUE SUD-SAHARIENNE; sciences humaines et sociales. Text in French. 1932. biennial. back issues avail. **Document type:** *Bibliography.*
Former titles (until 1982): Bibliographie Ethnographique de l'Afrique Sud-Saharienne (0772-3741); (until 1962): Bibliographie Ethnographique du Congo Belge et des Regions Avoisinantes (0772-3725)
Indexed: AICP.
Published by: Musee Royal de l'Afrique Centrale/Koninklijk Museum voor Midden-Afrika, Steenweg op Leuven 13, Tervuren, 3080, Belgium. TEL 32-2-7695299, FAX 32-2-7670242. Eds. A M Bouttaiux, M d'Hertefelt.

016.3 BGR ISSN 0861-5683
BIULETIN ZA NOVONABAVENI KNIGI NA CHUZHDI EZTIZI. SERIIA A: OBSHTESTVENI I HUMANITARNI NAUKI. Text in Bulgarian. 1954. m. BGL 16.80 (effective 2003). **Document type:** *Bulletin, Bibliography.* **Description:** Lists newly acquired foreign-language books in the social sciences.
Published by: Narodna Biblioteka Sv. sv. Kiril i Metodii/Cyril and Methodius National Library, 88 Levski Blvd, Sofia, 1504, Bulgaria. TEL 359-2-9881600, FAX 359-2-435495, dipchikova@nationallibrary.bg. Ed., R&P T Nikolova TEL 359-2-9882811 ext 220. Circ: 40 (paid).

016.3 MEX
C L A S E. (Citas Latinoamericanas en Ciencias Sociales y Humanidades) Text in Spanish. base vol. plus d. updates. MXN 150, USD 190 (effective 2000). **Document type:** *Database, Abstract/Index.*
Media: Online - full text. **Related titles:** ◆ Online - full text ed.: Clase and Periodica.
Published by: Universidad Nacional Autonoma de Mexico, Direccion General de Bibliotecas, Apdo. Postal 70-392, Mexico City, DF 04510, Mexico. TEL 52-55-56223956, FAX 52-55-5550-8068, sinfo@dgb.unam.mx. Ed. Octavio Alonso Gamboa. R&P Octavio Alonso-Gamboa.

300 001.3 TTO ISSN 0250-7617
CARINDEX: SOCIAL SCIENCES AND HUMANITIES. Text in English. 1977. s-a. USD 45 (effective 1998). bk.rev. back issues avail. **Document type:** *Abstract/Index.* **Description:** Guide to the social sciences and humanities literature published in the English-speaking Caribbean. Covers periodical articles, as well as conference proceedings, reports, and theses presented to the university.
Formerly (until 1982): Carindex: Social Sciences
Published by: University of the West Indies, Main Library, St. Augustine, W I, Trinidad & Tobago. TEL 809-662-2002, FAX 809-662-9238. Ed. Hannah Francis. Circ: 100.

016.3 016.0013 016.5 016.6 MEX
CLASE AND PERIODICA. Text in English, French, Portuguese, Spanish. base vol. plus q. updates. **Document type:** *Database, Abstract/Index.*
Media: Online - full text. **Related titles:** ◆ Online - full text ed.: Periodica; ◆ C L A S E.
Published by: Universidad Nacional Autonoma de Mexico, Direccion General de Bibliotecas, Apdo. Postal 70-392, Mexico City, DF 04510, Mexico. TEL 52-55-56223956, FAX 52-55-5550-8068, sinfo@dgb.unam.mx, http://dgb.unam.mx.

304.6 CYP ISSN 0253-875X
CYPRUS. DEPARTMENT OF STATISTICS AND RESEARCH. STATISTICAL ABSTRACT. Text in English. 1955. a. bk.rev. **Document type:** *Government.* **Description:** Summarizes statistics concerning the economic and social conditions in Cyprus on a time-series basis.
Published by: Ministry of Finance, Department of Statistics and Research, 13 Andreas Araouzos St, Nicosia, 1444, Cyprus. TEL 357-2-309318, FAX 357-2-374830.

DIGITAL COMPREHENSIVE SUMMARIES OF UPPSALA DISSERTATIONS FROM THE FACULTY OF SOCIAL SCIENCES. *see* SOCIAL SCIENCES: COMPREHENSIVE WORKS

016.3 ESP
DIRECTORIO DE REVISTAS ESPANOLAS DE CIENCIAS SOCIALES Y HUMANAS (ONLINE EDITION). Text in Spanish. 1992. irreg. free (effective 2009). **Document type:** *Directory, Bibliography.* **Description:** Compiles the most relevant Spanish periodicals in these fields.

Former titles (until 1998): Directorio de Revistas Espanolas de Ciencias Sociales y Humanas (Print Edition) (1134-3338); (until 1994): Directorio de Revistas Espanolas de Humanidades y Ciencias Sociales (1133-0090)
Media: Online - full text.
Published by: Consejo Superior de Investigaciones Cientificas (C S I C), Instituto de Estudios Documentales sobre Ciencia y Tecnologia, Albasanz 26-28, Madrid, 28037, Spain. TEL 34-91-6022356, FAX 34-91-3045710, sci@cindoc.csic.es, http://www.cindoc.cisc.es. Ed. Angel Villagra.

DIRECTORY OF PUBLISHED PROCEEDINGS. SERIES S S H - SOCIAL SCIENCES - HUMANITIES. *see* HUMANITIES: COMPREHENSIVE WORKS—Abstracting, Bibliographies, Statistics

DISSERTATION ABSTRACTS INTERNATIONAL. SECTION A: HUMANITIES AND SOCIAL SCIENCES. *see* HUMANITIES: COMPREHENSIVE WORKS—Abstracting, Bibliographies, Statistics

300 016 BOL
EXTENSION BIBLIOGRAFICA. Text in Spanish. 1974. irreg., latest vol.10, 1984. price varies. **Document type:** *Monographic series, Academic/Scholarly.*
Published by: Centro de Investigaciones Sociales, Casilla 6931 - C.C., La Paz, Bolivia. TEL 591-2-352931. Ed. Antonio Cisneros.

F R A N C I S. *see* HUMANITIES: COMPREHENSIVE WORKS—Abstracting, Bibliographies, Statistics

016.3 IND ISSN 0017-5285
GUIDE TO INDIAN PERIODICAL LITERATURE. Text in English. 1964. q. USD 300 (effective 2009). adv. bk.rev. illus. reprints avail. **Document type:** *Abstract/Index.*
Indexed: RASB.
Published by: (Indian Documentation Service), Scientific Publishers, 5-A, New Pali Rd, PO Box 91, Jodhpur, Rajasthan 342 001, India. TEL 91-291-2433323, FAX 91-291-2624154, info@scientificpub.com, http://www.scientificpub.com. Ed. Satyaprakash.

300 016 USA
GUIDE TO LITERARY & ALTERNATIVE MAGAZINES. Text in English. 1980. a. price varies. adv. illus. **Document type:** *Bibliography.*
Published by: New Pages Press, PO Box 1580, Bay City, MI 48706. TEL 908-671-0081, newpagesonline@hotmail.com, http://www.newpages.com. Ed. Denise Hill. Pub. Casey Hill.

GUIDE TO SOCIAL SCIENCE AND RELIGION. *see* RELIGIONS AND THEOLOGY—Abstracting, Bibliographies, Statistics

HUMANITIES & SOCIAL SCIENCES INDEX RETROSPECTIVE; 1907-1984. *see* HUMANITIES: COMPREHENSIVE WORKS—Abstracting, Bibliographies, Statistics

310 IND ISSN 0970-9061
H62.5.I5
I A S S I QUARTERLY. Text in English. 1981. q. INR 550 combined subscription domestic (print & online eds.); USD 100 combined subscription foreign (print & online eds.) (effective 2011). **Document type:** *Journal, Academic/Scholarly.* **Description:** Seeks to draw upon all social sciences in the application of available social knowledge to the solution of outstanding national and other problems.
Former titles (until 1989): I A S S I Quarterly Bulletin (0970-5066); (until 1987): I A S S I Quarterly Newsletter (0970-5058)
Related titles: Online - full text ed.: ISSN 0974-018X. INR 400 domestic; USD 75 foreign (effective 2011).
Indexed: CA, S02, S03, T02.
Published by: Indian Association of Social Science Institutions, c/o A K Dasgupta, Member Secretary, IAMR, Indraprastha Estate, New Delhi, 110 002, India. TEL 91-11-3324851, FAX 91-11-3315284, stiassi@bol.net.in. Ed. A K Dasgupta. **Subscr. to:** Indianjournals.com, Divan Enterprises, B-9, Local Shopping Complex, A-Block, Naraina Vihar, Ring Rd, New Delhi 110 028, India. TEL 91-11-25770411, FAX 91-11-25778876, info@indianjournals.com, http://www.indianjournals.com.

I A S S I S T QUARTERLY (ONLINE). *see* LIBRARY AND INFORMATION SCIENCES

011 IND
I C S S R UNION CATALOGUE OF SOCIAL SCIENCE PERIODICALS. (Indian Council of Social Science Research) Text in English. 1973. irreg. bibl. index. **Document type:** *Catalog, Trade.* **Description:** Contains a catalogue of social science periodicals.
Formerly: I C S S R Union Catalogue of Social Science Periodicals - Serials
Published by: (National Social Science Documentation Centre), Indian Council of Social Science Research, JNU Institutional Area, Aruna Asaf Ali Marg, New Delhi, 110 067, India. TEL 91-11-26741849, FAX 91-11-26741836, info@icssr.org, http://www.icssr.org. Circ: 1,000.

IBERO - AMERICANA; Nordic journal of Latin American and Caribbean studies/revista nordica de estudios latinamericanos y del caribe. *see* HISTORY—Abstracting, Bibliographies, Statistics

300 001.3 USA ISSN 0191-0574
Z7163
INDEX TO SOCIAL SCIENCES & HUMANITIES PROCEEDINGS. Short title: I S S H P. Text in English. 1979. q. (plus a. cumulation). Index. reprints avail. **Document type:** *Proceedings.* **Description:** International multidisciplinary index of papers presented at social sciences and humanities professional meetings.
Related titles: CD-ROM ed.: ISSN 1076-9765.
Indexed: RASB.
—BLDSC (4386.400000).
Published by: Thomson Reuters (Subsidiary of: Thomson Reuters Corp.), 1500 Spring Garden, 4th Fl, Philadelphia, PA 19130. TEL 215-386-0100, 800-336-4474, FAX 215-386-2911, general.info@thomson.com, http://science.thomsonreuters.com/.

508 BRA ISSN 1516-4926
QH117
INSTITUTO PAU BRASIL DE HISTORIA NATURAL. PUBLICACOES AVULSAS. Text in Multiple languages. 1999. irreg. **Document type:** *Monographic series, Academic/Scholarly.*
Indexed: B25, BIOSIS Prev, C01, MycolAb, Z01.
—Linda Hall.
Published by: Instituto Pau Brasil de Historia Natural, Ave Benedito Manoel dos Santos, 369, Jardim Fazenda Rincao, Arujo, Sao Paulo, Brazil. TEL 55-11-46552731, FAX 55-11-46525262, http://www.institutopaubrasil.org.br/index.cfm. Eds. Ana Maria de Souza, Erika Schlenz. Circ: 1,000.

INTERNATIONAL AFRICAN BIBLIOGRAPHY; current books, articles and papers in African studies. *see* BIBLIOGRAPHIES

016.3 USA
INTERNATIONAL BIBLIOGRAPHY OF THE SOCIAL SCIENCES/ BIBLIOGRAPHIE INTERNATIONALE DES SCIENCES SOCIALES. Text in English. 1951. base vol. plus w. updates. price varies. **Document type:** *Database, Abstract/Index.*
Media: Online - full text. **Related titles:** ◆ Print ed.: International Bibliography of the Social Sciences. Economics. ISSN 0085-204X; ◆ International Bibliography of the Social Sciences. Anthropology; ◆ International Bibliography of the Social Sciences. Sociology. ISSN 0085-2066; ◆ International Bibliography of Political Science. ISSN 0085-2058.
Published by: ProQuest (Subsidiary of: Cambridge Information Group), 789 E Eisenhower Pky, PO Box 1346, Ann Arbor, MI 48106. TEL 734-761-4700, 800-521-0600, FAX 734-997-4040, 888-241-5612, info@proquest.com, http://www.proquest.com.

300 USA ISSN 1524-5055
➤ **J C R SOCIAL SCIENCES EDITION.** (Journal Citation Reports) Key Title: Journal Citation Reports on Microfiche (Social Science Edition). (Not avail. in printed format. Includes Journal Ranking, Reference Data, and Source Data Packages) Text in English. 1977. a. **Document type:** *Journal, Academic/Scholarly.* **Description:** Provides citation data of journals in the social sciences.
Former titles (until 199?): S S C I - J C R; (until 1989): S S C I Journal Citation Reports (0161-3162)
Media: Microfiche. **Related titles:** CD-ROM ed.: Journal Citation Reports on CD-ROM (Social Sciences Edition). ISSN 1082-6653; Online - full text ed.: J C R Web Social Science Edition; ◆ Series: J C R Science Edition. ISSN 1524-5047.
Published by: Thomson Reuters (Subsidiary of: Thomson Reuters Corp.), 1500 Spring Garden, 4th Fl, Philadelphia, PA 19130. TEL 215-386-0100, 800-336-4474, FAX 215-386-2911, general.info@thomson.com, http://science.thomsonreuters.com/.

➤ **JOURNAL OF QUANTITATIVE ANALYSIS IN SPORTS.** *see* SPORTS AND GAMES

➤ **KOKURITSU KOKKAI TOSHOKAN ZASSHI KIJI SAKUIN CD-ROM KARENTO-BAN/JAPANESE PERIODICAL INDEX ON CD.** *see* HUMANITIES: COMPREHENSIVE WORKS—Abstracting, Bibliographies, Statistics

306.021 NOR ISSN 0800-2959
HA1501
KULTURSTATISTIKK/CULTURAL STATISTICS. Text in English, Norwegian. 1976. irreg.
Related titles: Online - full text ed.; ◆ Series of: Norges Offisielle Statistikk. ISSN 0300-5585.
Published by: Statistisk Sentralbyraa/Statistics Norway, Kongensgate 6, P O Box 8131, Dep, Oslo, 0033, Norway. TEL 47-21-090000, FAX 47-21-094973, ssb@ssb.no.

300 RUS ISSN 0234-4491
Z3408.L5
LITERATURA, ISKUSSTVO SIBIRI I DAL'NEGO VOSTOKA; tekushchii ukazatel' literatury. Text in Russian. 1985. a. USD 55 foreign. **Document type:** *Bibliography.* **Description:** Covers books, articles, and summaries of reports and dissertations on the problems of modern Siberian and Far Eastern culture and arts.
Published by: Rossiiskaya Akademiya Nauk, Sibirskoe Otdelenie, Gosudarstvennaya Publichnaya Nauchno-Tekhnicheskaya Biblioteka/State Public Scientific and Technical Library of the Siberian Branch of the Russian Academy of Sciences, Ul Voskhod 15, Novosibirsk, 630200, Russian Federation. TEL 7-3832-661367, FAX 7-3832-663365, onb@spsl.nsc.ru, root@libr.nsk.su. Eds. L P Yakimova, V N Volkova.

300 HUN ISSN 0133-6894
AI19.H8
MAGYAR NEMZETI BIBLIOGRAFIA. IDOSZAKI KIADVANYOK REPERTORIUMA; tarsadalomtudomanyok, termeszettudomanyok. Text in Hungarian. 1946. m. HUF 2,400, USD 50.50. **Document type:** *Bibliography.* **Description:** Contains articles in the fields of social and exact sciences from scientific, literary and art periodicals, leading newspapers, and yearbooks published in Hungary.
Formerly: Magyar Folyoiratok Repertoriuma (0025-0112); Which supersedes in part (in 1977): Magyar Nemzeti Bibliografia (0373-1766)
Indexed: RASB.
Published by: Orszagos Szechenyi Konyvtar/National Szechenyi Library, Budavari Palota F epulet, Budapest, 1827, Hungary. TEL 36-1-2243788, FAX 36-1-2020804, kint@oszk.hu, http://www.ki.oszk.hu. Ed. Magda Wolf. **Subscr. to:** Nemzetkozi es Kulturalis Kapcsolatok Irodaja, Public Relations and Cultural Affairs, Budavari Palota F epulet, Budapest 1827, Hungary.

MARKAZ-I NASHARIYAT-I 'ILMI VA FARHANGI. FIHRIST-I MUNDARIJAT-I MAJALLAH-HA-YI JARI-I/CENTER FOR SCIENTIFIC AND CULTURAL PERIODICALS. TABLE OF CONTENTS OF CURRENT JOURNALS. *see* SCIENCES: COMPREHENSIVE WORKS—Abstracting, Bibliographies, Statistics

300.1 USA
METHODOLOGY IN THE SOCIAL SCIENCES. Text in English. 19??. irreg. price varies. back issues avail. **Document type:** *Monographic series, Academic/Scholarly.* **Description:** Provides applied researchers and students with analysis and research design books that emphasize the use of methods to answer research questions.
Related titles: Online - full text ed.
Published by: Guilford Publications, Inc., 72 Spring St, 4th Fl, New York, NY 10012. TEL 800-365-7006, FAX 212-966-6708, info@guilford.com. Ed. Todd D Little.

300 SVN ISSN 1854-0031
METODOLOSKI ZVEZKI. Text in Slovenian. 1987. s-a. USD 50 to individuals; USD 90 to institutions (effective 2008). **Document type:** *Monographic series, Academic/Scholarly.*
Formerly (until 2004): Methodoloski Zvezki
Indexed: A01, T02.
Published by: Univerza v Ljubljani, Fakulteta za Druzbene Vede/University of Ljubljana, Faculty of Social Sciences, Kerdeljeva Poscad 5, Ljubljana, 1000, Slovenia. TEL 386-1-5805100, FAX 386-1-5805101, fdv.faculty@fdv.uni-lj.si, http://www.fdv.uni-lj.si.

300 NGA ISSN 0078-0766
NIGERIAN INSTITUTE OF SOCIAL AND ECONOMIC RESEARCH. LIBRARY. LIST OF ACCESSIONS. Text in English. 1963. q. per issue exchange basis. **Document type:** *Bibliography.*
Published by: Nigerian Institute of Social and Economic Research, University of Ibadan, PMB 5, Ibadan, Oyo, Nigeria. TEL 234-22-400501-5. Ed. J A Akisanya.

300 011 NGA ISSN 0189-8671
NIGERIAN JOURNAL OF SOCIAL SCIENCE RESEARCH ABSTRACTS. Text in English. 1982. s-a. **Document type:** *Abstract/Index.*
Published by: Nigerian Institute of Social and Economic Research, University of Ibadan, PMB 5, Ibadan, Oyo, Nigeria. TEL 234-22-400501-5. Ed. Kunle Adeniji.

016.3 016.0285 USA
NOTABLE SOCIAL STUDIES TRADE BOOKS FOR YOUNG PEOPLE. Text in English. 1971. a. **Document type:** *Bibliography.* **Description:** Annotated committee-selected bibliography of the year's most notable social studies books, for kindergarten to eighth grade in American and world history and culture. Includes biographies, folktales, myths and legends.
Formerly: Notable Children's Trade Books in the Field of Social Studies
Published by: (National Council for the Social Studies), Children's Book Council, Inc., 54 W 39th St, 14 Fl, New York, NY 10018. cbc.info@cbcbooks.org.

PCI ESPANOL. *see* HUMANITIES: COMPREHENSIVE WORKS—Abstracting, Bibliographies, Statistics

016.3 016.0013 GBR
PIO - PERIODICALS INDEX ONLINE. Text in English. base vol. plus q. updates. price varies; segments of the index are offered as a permanent purchase, with pricing ranging from $3,000 to $12,000 each. Also offered as a subscription, with pricing ranging from $4,000 to $15,000 yearly. **Document type:** *Database, Abstract/Index.* **Description:** Indexes over 4,700 international periodicals in the humanities and social sciences, from their inception to 1995.
Formerly (until 2006): Periodicals Contents Index
Media: Online - full text. **Related titles:** CD-ROM ed.: Periodicals Content Index (CD-ROM Edition). ISSN 1462-2831.
Published by: ProQuest LLC, The Quorum, Barnwell Rd, Cambridge, CB5 8SW, United Kingdom. TEL 44-1223-215512, FAX 44-1223-215513, http://www.proquest.co.uk/. Ed., Pub. Stephen Brooks.

PRISMA (PUBLICACIONES Y REVISTAS SOCIALES Y HUMANISTICAS). *see* HUMANITIES: COMPREHENSIVE WORKS—Abstracting, Bibliographies, Statistics

016.3 USA
PROQUEST SOCIAL SCIENCE JOURNALS. Text in English. base vol. plus d. updates. **Document type:** *Database, Abstract/Index.*
Media: Online - full text.
Published by: ProQuest (Subsidiary of: Cambridge Information Group), 789 E Eisenhower Pky, PO Box 1346, Ann Arbor, MI 48106. TEL 734-761-4700, 800-521-0600, FAX 734-997-4040, 888-241-5612, info@proquest.com, http://www.proquest.com.

300 954 016 FRA ISSN 0080-2484
Z7059
REVUE BIBLIOGRAPHIQUE DE SINOLOGIE. Text in English, French. 1955; N.S. 1984. a. EUR 38 per issue (effective 2003). adv. bk.rev. **Document type:** *Journal, Abstract/Index.* **Description:** Aims at providing a quick survey of the most recent trends in Chinese studies. Each volume offers a number of abstracts of books and articles selected from various periodicals in different fields, from archaeology to history of science and technology.
Indexed: BAS, FR, RASB.
—INIST.
Published by: College de France, Ecole des Hautes Etudes en Sciences Sociales (E H E S S), 96 Boulevard Raspail, Paris, 75006, France. TEL 33-1-53635658, FAX 33-1-49542428, http://www.ehess.fr. Eds. Danielle Ellisseeff, Michel Cartier. Circ: 400. **Dist. by:** Centre Interinstitutionnel pour la Diffusion de Publications en Sciences Humaines, 131 bd. Saint-Michel, Paris 75005, France. TEL 33-1-43544715, FAX 33-1-43548073.

016.3 USA
S I R S GOVERNMENT REPORTER. (Social Issues Resources Series) Text in English. 1993. d. charts; illus.; maps. **Document type:** *Database, Abstract/Index.* **Description:** Reference database which brings together a wide range of information published by and about our federal government. Full-text government documents and graphics, information about federal bureaucracy and elected leaders, US Supreme Court decisions and more are easily accessible.
Media: Online - full text. **Related titles:** CD-ROM ed.
Published by: S I R S (Subsidiary of: ProQuest), 789 E Eisenhower Pky, PO Box 1346, Ann Arbor, MI 48106. TEL 734-761-4700, 800-521-0600, info@il.proquest.com.

016.3 USA
S I R S INTERACTIVE CITIZENSHIP. (Social Issues Resources Series) Text in English. 2002. d. **Document type:** *Database, Abstract/Index.* **Description:** A database utilizing interactive books that link to appropriate Web sites and information on government, world affairs and economics on SIRS databases.
Media: Online - full text.
Published by: S I R S (Subsidiary of: ProQuest), 789 E Eisenhower Pky, PO Box 1346, Ann Arbor, MI 48106. TEL 734-761-4700, 800-521-0600, info@il.proquest.com.

016.3 USA
S I R S RESEARCHER. (Social Issues Resources Series) Variant title: S I R S Issues Researcher. Text in English. 1989. d. charts; illus.; maps. **Document type:** *Database, Abstract/Index.* **Description:** General reference database containing thousands of full-text articles exploring social, scientific, health, historic, business, economic, political and global issues. Articles and graphics are from 1,500 domestic and international publications.
Media: Online - full text. **Related titles:** CD-ROM ed.
Published by: S I R S (Subsidiary of: ProQuest), 789 E Eisenhower Pky, PO Box 1346, Ann Arbor, MI 48106. TEL 734-761-4700, 800-521-0600, info@il.proquest.com.

SCITECH BOOK NEWS; an annotated bibliography of new books in science, technology, & medicine. *see* BIBLIOGRAPHIES

SCOPUS. *see* SCIENCES: COMPREHENSIVE WORKS—Abstracting, Bibliographies, Statistics

S

016.3 USA
SOCIAL SCIENCES ABSTRACTS. Text in English. 1995. (OCLC updated weekly)), base vol. plus d. updates. USD 3,990 (effective 2011). **Document type:** *Database, Abstract/Index.*
Media: Online - full text. **Related titles:** ◆ CD-ROM ed.: Social Sciences Abstracts (CD-ROM). ISSN 1092-1427.
Published by: H.W. Wilson, 950 University Ave, Bronx, NY 10452. TEL 718-588-8400, 800-367-6770, FAX 718-590-1617, 800-590-1617, custserv@hwwilson.com.

016.3 USA ISSN 1092-1427
H1
SOCIAL SCIENCES ABSTRACTS (CD-ROM). Text in English. 1995. m. price varies. **Document type:** *Abstract/Index.* **Description:** Contains article abstracts and indexing to periodicals in the social sciences.
Formerly (until 1997): Wilson Social Sciences Abstracts (1082-3557)
Media: CD-ROM. **Related titles:** ◆ Online - full text ed.: Social Sciences Abstracts.
Published by: H.W. Wilson, 950 University Ave, Bronx, NY 10452. TEL 718-588-8400, 800-367-6770, FAX 718-590-1617, 800-590-1617, custserv@hwwilson.com.

016.3 USA
SOCIAL SCIENCES CITATION INDEX. Text in English. base vol. plus w. updates. free (effective 2009). **Document type:** *Database, Abstract/Index.*
Media: Online - full text. **Related titles:** CD-ROM ed.: ISSN 1044-6044; ◆ Print ed.: Social Sciences Citation Index (Print). ISSN 0091-3707.
Published by: Thomson Reuters (Subsidiary of: Thomson Reuters Corp.), 1500 Spring Garden, 4th Fl, Philadelphia, PA 19130. TEL 215-386-0100, 800-336-4474, FAX 215-386-2911, general.info@thomson.com, http://science.thomsonreuters.com/.

016.3 USA ISSN 0091-3707
Z7161
SOCIAL SCIENCES CITATION INDEX (PRINT). Short title: S S C I. Text in English. 1969. 3/yr. (plus a. cumulation). illus. cum.index: 1956-1965, 1966-1970, 1971-1975, 1976-1980, 1981-1985, 1986-1990. reprints avail. **Document type:** *Abstract/Index.* **Description:** Multidisciplinary indexing of research in all fields of social sciences.
Related titles: CD-ROM ed.: ISSN 1044-6044; ◆ Online - full text ed.: Social Sciences Citation Index.
Indexed: RASB.
Published by: Thomson Reuters (Subsidiary of: Thomson Reuters Corp.), 1500 Spring Garden, 4th Fl, Philadelphia, PA 19130. TEL 215-386-0100, 800-336-4474, FAX 215-386-2911, general.info@thomson.com, http://science.thomsonreuters.com/.

016.3 USA
SOCIAL SCIENCES FULL TEXT. (Consists of: Social Sciences Abstracts and Social Sciences Index) Text in English. 1995. base vol. plus d. updates. USD 4,365 in US & Canada (effective 2011). **Document type:** *Database, Abstract/Index.* **Description:** Covers the latest concepts, trends, opinions, theories, and methods from both applied and theoretical aspects of the social sciences.
Media: Online - full text. **Related titles:** CD-ROM ed.: ISSN 1529-9937. 2000.
Published by: H.W. Wilson, 950 University Ave, Bronx, NY 10452. TEL 718-588-8400, 800-367-6770, FAX 718-590-1617, 800-590-1617, custserv@hwwilson.com.

016.3 USA
SOCIAL SCIENCES INDEX. Text in English. (OCLC updated weekly)), base vol. plus d. updates. USD 2,470 in US & Canada (effective 2011). **Document type:** *Database, Abstract/Index.*
Media: Online - full text. **Related titles:** CD-ROM ed.: ISSN 1063-3308. 198?; ◆ Print ed.: Social Sciences Index (Print). ISSN 0094-4920.
Published by: H.W. Wilson, 950 University Ave, Bronx, NY 10452. TEL 718-588-8400, 800-367-6770, FAX 718-590-1617, 800-590-1617, custserv@hwwilson.com.

016.3 USA ISSN 0094-4920
AI3
SOCIAL SCIENCES INDEX (PRINT). Text in English. 1913. m. USD 685 (effective 2011). **Document type:** *Abstract/Index.* **Description:** Author and subject index to periodicals in the fields of anthropology, community health and medicine, economics, geography, international relations, law, criminology and police science, political science, psychology and psychiatry, public administration, sociology, social work, and related subjects.
Supersedes in part (in 1974): Social Sciences and Humanities Index (0037-7899); Which was formerly (until 1966): International Index (0363-0382); (until 1958): International Index to Periodicals; (until 1923): Readers' Guide to Periodical Literature. Supplement
Related titles: CD-ROM ed.: ISSN 1063-3308. 198?; ◆ Online - full text ed.: Social Sciences Index Retrospective; ◆ Social Sciences Index.
—Linda Hall.
Published by: H.W. Wilson, 950 University Ave, Bronx, NY 10452. TEL 718-588-8400, 800-367-6770, FAX 718-590-1617, 800-590-1617, custserv@hwwilson.com.

016.3 USA
SOCIAL SCIENCES INDEX RETROSPECTIVE; 1907-1983. Text in English. base vol. plus irreg. updates. USD 1,775 in US & Canada (effective 2011). **Document type:** *Database, Abstract/Index.*
Media: Online - full text. **Related titles:** ◆ Print ed.: Social Sciences Index (Print). ISSN 0094-4920.
Published by: H.W. Wilson, 950 University Ave, Bronx, NY 10452. TEL 718-588-8400, 800-367-6770, FAX 718-590-1617, 800-590-1617, custserv@hwwilson.com.

016.3 USA
SOCIAL SCIENCES MODULE. Text in English. base vol. plus d. updates. **Document type:** *Database, Abstract/Index.*
Media: Online - full text.
Published by: ProQuest (Subsidiary of: Cambridge Information Group), 789 E Eisenhower Pky, PO Box 1346, Ann Arbor, MI 48106. TEL 734-761-4700, 800-521-0600, FAX 734-997-4040, 888-241-5612, info@proquest.com, http://www.proquest.com.

300 310 NGA ISSN 0189-6067
HN831
SOCIAL STATISTICS IN NIGERIA. Text in English. a. USD 10. **Document type:** *Government.*
Published by: Federal Office of Statistics, Dissemination Division, c/o Mrs. M.T. Osita, 36-38 Broad St, PMB 12528, Lagos, Nigeria. TEL 234-1-2601710-4.

SUDAN. NATIONAL COUNCIL FOR RESEARCH. ECONOMIC AND SOCIAL RESEARCH COUNCIL. BIBLIOGRAPHIES. *see* BUSINESS AND ECONOMICS—Abstracting, Bibliographies, Statistics

363 061 UKR ISSN 1561-1108
UKRAINSKYI REFERATYVNYI ZHURNAL. SERIYA 3. SOTSIAL'NI TA HUMANITARNI NAUKY, MYSTETSTVO/UKRAINIAN JOURNAL OF ABSTRACTS. SER. 3. SOCIAL SCIENCES AND HUMANITIES, ART. Text and summaries in English, Russian, Ukrainian. 1995. q. UAK 250 domestic; USD 200 foreign. **Document type:** *Abstract/Index.* **Description:** Covers social sciences, humanities and art.
Published by: Natsional'na Akademiya Nauk Ukrainy, Instytut Problem Reyestratsii Informatsii/National Academy of Sciences of Ukraine, Institute for Information Recording, Vul Shpaka 2, Kiev, 03113, Ukraine. TEL 380-44-4468389, FAX 380-44-2417233, http://www.nbuv.gov.ua. Pub. V Petrov. Circ: 150 (paid); 100 (controlled).
Co-publisher: Natsional'na Biblioteka Ukrainy im. V.I. Vernads'koho.

300 015 JAM
UNIVERSITY OF THE WEST INDIES. INSTITUTE OF SOCIAL AND ECONOMIC RESEARCH. OCCASIONAL BIBLIOGRAPHY SERIES. Text in English. 1974. irreg., latest vol.9.
Published by: University of the West Indies, Sir Arthur Lewis Institute of Social and Economic Research, Mona Campus, Kingston, 7, Jamaica. TEL 809-927-1020, FAX 809-927-2409.

WEB OF SCIENCE. *see* SCIENCES: COMPREHENSIVE WORKS—Abstracting, Bibliographies, Statistics

300 USA ISSN 0734-9033
HM206
WHOLE AGAIN RESOURCE GUIDE; periodical and resource directory. Text in English. 1982. irreg. (2nd ed. 1987). USD 26.95. bk.rev. bibl.; illus. index. back issues avail. **Document type:** *Directory.*
Incorporates: International Guide to Psi-Periodicals (0277-9870)
Published by: SourceNet, PO Box 6767, Santa Barbara, CA 93160. TEL 805-373-7123. Ed. Tim Ryan. Circ: 5,000.

SOCIAL SERVICES AND WELFARE

see also DRUG ABUSE AND ALCOHOLISM ; HANDICAPPED ; PUBLIC HEALTH AND SAFETY

360 USA
A A M C SURVEY OF HOUSESTAFF STIPENDS, BENEFITS, AND FUNDING. Text in English. 1969. a. **Document type:** *Report, Corporate.*
Former titles (until Aug.1996): Council of Teaching Hospitals and Health Systems Survey of Housestaff Stipends, Benefits, and Funding; Council of Teaching Hospitals Survey of Housestaff Stipends, Benefits, and Funding; (until 1990): C O T H Survey of House Staff Stipends, Benefits, and Funding (0272-9148); (until 1978): C O T H Survey of House Staff Policy and Related Information (0272-9156); (until 1977): C O T H Survey of House Staff Policy and Related Issues (0164-1573); (until 1975): C O T H Survey of House Staff Policy (0093-7045)
Related titles: Online - full text ed.
Published by: (Council of Teaching Hospitals), Association of American Medical Colleges, 2450 N St, NW, Washington, DC 20037. TEL 202-828-0400, FAX 202-828-1125, amcas@aamc.org, http://www.aamc.org.

A B P CONTACT. (Association Belge des Paralyses) *see* HANDICAPPED

A C A NEWS; the provincial newsletter for seniors. *see* GERONTOLOGY AND GERIATRICS

A C A R T S O D NEWSLETTER. *see* BUSINESS AND ECONOMICS—International Development And Assistance

360 AUS ISSN 1442-486X
A C O S S INFO. (Australian Council of Social Service) Text in English. 1999. irreg. **Document type:** *Monographic series, Consumer.* **Description:** Provides short information and policy statments on contemporary Australian issues in public policy.
Related titles: Online - full text ed.
Published by: Australian Council of Social Service, Locked Bag 4777, Strawberry Hills, NSW 2012, Australia. TEL 61-2-93106200, FAX 61-2-93104822, info@acoss.org.au, http://www.acoss.org.au.

362.5 FRA ISSN 2108-1751
A C T E D NEWS. (Agence d'Aide a la Cooperation Technique et au Developpement) Text in English, French. 2003. m. **Document type:** *Newsletter, Consumer.*
Published by: Agence d'Aide a la Cooperation Technique et au Developpement (A C T E D)/Agency for Technical Cooperation and Development, 33, Rue Godot de Mauroy, Paris, 75009, France. TEL 33-1-42653333, http://www.acted.org/en, http://www.acted.org/fr.

362.7 AUS ISSN 1327-2810
A C W A NEWS. (Association of Childrens Welfare Agencies) Text in English. 1996. bi-m. back issues avail. **Document type:** *Newsletter, Consumer.* **Description:** Provides services to non-governmental agencies that focus on children, young people and families.
Media: Online - full text. **Related titles:** Ed.
Published by: Association of Childrens Welfare Agencies, Inc., Locked Bag 13, Haymarket, NSW 1240, Australia. TEL 61-2-92818822, FAX 61-2-92818827, acwa@acwa.asn.au. Ed. Eric Scott TEL 61-2-92818822.

362.4 USA ISSN 1054-5948
KF480
A D A COMPLIANCE GUIDE. (Americans with Disabilities Act) Text in English. 1990. 2 base vols. plus m. updates. looseleaf. USD 399 (print or online ed.); USD 498 combined subscription (print & online eds.) (effective 2008); subscr. includes newsletter. adv. reprints avail. **Document type:** *Handbook/Manual/Guide, Trade.* **Description:** Explains the meaning of disability, reasonable accommodation, undue hardship, readily achievable barrier removal, program accessibility and the law's many other key terms.
Related titles: Online - full content ed.: USD 499 (effective 2008).
—CCC.
Published by: Thompson Publishing Group, 805 15th St, N W, 3rd Floor, Washington, DC 20005. TEL 800-677-3789, FAX 202-872-4000, service@thompson.com. Pub. Richard Thompson.

A F B ENEWS. *see* HANDICAPPED—Visually Impaired

614 USA ISSN 0279-1692
A H C A NOTES. Text in English. 1972. 10/yr. USD 150 to non-members (effective 2007). adv. illus. 8 p./no. 2 cols./p.; **Document type:** *Newsletter, Trade.*
Formerly: A H C A Weekly Notes (0146-6321)
—Ingenta.
Published by: American Health Care Association, 1201 L St, N W, Washington, DC 20005. TEL 202-842-4444, FAX 202-842-3860, http://www.ahca.org/. Eds. Lisa Gelhaus, Joanne Erickson TEL 202-898-2811. Circ: 10,000.

362.13 USA ISSN 1551-840X
A H P JOURNAL. Text in English. 1971. s-a. USD 50 to non-members; USD 25 to members (effective 2011). back issues avail. **Document type:** *Journal, Trade.* **Description:** Provides insight on the changing world of health care fundraising.
Former titles (until 2001): Association for Healthcare Philanthropy. Journal (1061-7655); (until 1991): National Association for Hospital Development. Journal (0196-4933)
Related titles: Online - full text ed.: ISSN 2162-2418.
Indexed: EMBASE, ExcerpMed, MEDLINE, P30, SCOPUS.
Published by: Association for Healthcare Philanthropy, 313 Park Ave, Ste 400, Falls Church, VA 22046. TEL 703-532-6243, FAX 703-532-7170, ahp@ahp.org.

A H R C CHRONICLE. (Association for the Help of Retarded Children) *see* MEDICAL SCIENCES—Psychiatry And Neurology

360 USA
A L M A SEARCHLIGHT. Text in English. 1974. q. membership.
Published by: Adoptees' Liberty Movement Association, PO Box 85, Denville, NJ 07834. TEL 973-586-1358. Ed. Florence Fisher.

A M S STUDIES IN MODERN SOCIETY; political and social issues. (Abrahams Magazine Service) *see* PUBLIC HEALTH AND SAFETY

362.8682 CUB
A N J U P E C. Text in Spanish. q.
Published by: Asociacion Nacional de Jubilados y Pensionados de Comunicaciones, Oquendo No. 751, Havana, 3, Cuba.

362 COL ISSN 2011-3455
A N P I S S INFORMATIVO. (Asociacion Nacional de Pensionados por el Instituto del Seguro Social) Text in Spanish. 2007. m.
Published by: Asociacion Nacional de Pensionados por el ISS, Carrera 27 No. 27-25, Bogota, Colombia. TEL 57-1-2885005.

A P I ACCOUNT. *see* BUSINESS AND ECONOMICS—Accounting

A P I AFFILIATE NEWSBRIEF. *see* BUSINESS AND ECONOMICS—Accounting

360 PAK ISSN 0001-2262
A P W A NEWSLETTER. Text in English. 1967. 3/yr. free. charts; illus. **Document type:** *Newsletter.*
Published by: All Pakistan Women's Association, Information and Research Bureau, 67-B Garden Rd., Karachi 3, Pakistan. Ed. Ishrat Aftab.

361.73 USA
A R N O V A NEWS. Text in English. q. membership. bk.rev. **Document type:** *Newsletter.* **Description:** Promotes multi-disciplinary, scholarly research on voluntary - non-profit organizations, volunteering and voluntary action, including philanthropy, charity and the common good.
Published by: Association for Research on Nonprofit Organizations and Voluntary Action, c/o Katherine M Finley, Exec Dir, 340 W. Michigan St., Canal Level, Ste. A, Indianapolis, IN 46202. TEL 317-684-2120, FAX 317-684-2128, exarnova@iupui.edu. Ed. Martha Golensky.

360 USA ISSN 0001-2335
A R S HAI SIRD. (Armenian Relief Society) Text in English. 1939. a. USD 10. adv. bk.rev.
Published by: Armenian Relief Society, Inc., 80 Bigelow Ave, Watertown, MA 02472-2021. TEL 617-926-5892, FAX 617-926-4855. Eds. T Sonentz Papazian, V Habeshian. Adv. contact O Gregorian. Circ: 1,000.

361.8 GBR ISSN 1755-1331
A R V A C BULLETIN (ONLINE). Text in English. 1978. q. looseleaf. free to members (effective 2009). bk.rev.; Website rev. bibl. Index. 24 p./no. 3 cols./p.; back issues avail. **Document type:** *Bulletin.* **Description:** Contains news and information about all aspects of research in the voluntary and community sector.
Formerly (until 2006): A R V A C Bulletin (Print) (0263-1873)
Media: Online - full text.
Published by: Association for Research in the Voluntary and Community Sector, c/o School of Business and Social Sciences, Roehampton University, Southlands College, 80 Roehampton Ln, London, SW15 5SL, United Kingdom. TEL 44-20-77042315, FAX 44-20-77049995, arvac@arvac.org.uk, http://www.arvac.org.uk/. Ed. Jurgen Grotz.

613 NLD ISSN 0168-2857
A S; maandblad voor de activiteitensector. (Activiteitensektor) Key Title: AS. Maandblad Aktiviteitensektor. Text in Dutch. 1981. 10/yr. EUR 87.25 to individuals; EUR 162.95 to institutions; EUR 43.50 to students (effective 2009). adv. bk.rev. **Document type:** *Journal, Trade.* **Description:** Provides social service leaders at various mental-health, rehabilitative, and gerontological agencies (both in- and out-patient) with news and professional advice.
Incorporates (1956-1982): Ligament (0024-3264)
—IE, Infotrieve.
Published by: (Y-Publicaties), Elsevier Gezondheidszorg bv (Subsidiary of: Reed Business bv), Planetenbaan 80-99, Maarssen, 3606 AK, Netherlands. TEL 31-346-577901, FAX 31-346-577371, http://www.elseviergezondheidszorg.nl. Ed. Ralf Beekveldt. Pub. Ben Konings. adv.: B&W page EUR 1,078, color page EUR 2,817; trim 215 x 285. Circ: 2,178 (controlled).

362 DEU ISSN 0939-9763
A S B MAGAZIN. Text in German. 1987. q. adv. **Document type:** *Magazine, Consumer.*
Formerly (until 1990): Der Arbeiter-Samariter (0933-8659); Which was formed by the merger of (1985-1987): Der Arbeiter-Samariter. Ausgabe A (0933-9566); (1985-1987): Der Arbeiter-Samariter. Ausgabe B (0933-9574); (1985-1987): Der Arbeiter-Samariter. Ausgabe C (0933-9582); (1985-1987): Der Arbeiter-Samariter. Ausgabe D (0933-9590); (1985-1987): Der Arbeiter-Samariter.

Ausgabe E (0933-9604); All of which superseded in part (1984-1985): Der Arbeiter-Samariter (0177-3801); Which was formed by the merger of (1983-1984): Der Samariter. Ausgabe A (0933-9523); (1983-1984): Der Samariter. Ausgabe B (0933-9531); (1983-1984): Der Samariter. Ausgabe C (0933-954X); All of which superseded in part (1982-1983): Der Samariter (0723-2306)
Published by: Arbeiter-Samariter-Bund Deutschland e.V., Suelzburgstr 140, Cologne, 50937, Germany. TEL 49-221-476050, FAX 49-221-47605288, asb-bv@asb-online.de, http://www.asb-online.de. adv.: color page EUR 12,437. Circ: 832,115 (controlled).

361.2071 ETH
A S W E A JOURNAL FOR SOCIAL WORK EDUCATION IN AFRICA. Text in English. 1974. s-a.
Supersedes: Association for Social Work Education in Africa. Bulletin
Related titles: French ed.
Published by: Association for Social Work Education in Africa, c/o College of Social Sciences, Addis Ababa University, PO Box 1176, Addis Ababa, Ethiopia.

A U F; Eine Frauenzeitschrift. (Aktion Unabhaengiger Frauen) *see* WOMEN'S INTERESTS

360 DEU
A W O - ECHO. Text in German. q. EUR 1.20 (effective 2009). adv. **Document type:** *Magazine, Consumer.*
Published by: (Arbeiterwohlfahrt Bezirksverband Baden e.V.), Druck und Verlagsgesellschaft Suedwest mbH Druckhaus Karlsruhe, Ostring 6, Karlsruhe, 76131, Germany. TEL 49-721-62830, FAX 49-721-628310, dhk@druckhaus-karlsruhe.de, http://www.druckhaus-karlsruhe.de. Ed. Ute Eisenacher. Adv. contact Christine Krueckl. Circ: 15,000 (controlled).

364.124 DEU
A W O HELFER. (Arbeiterwohlfahrt) Text in German. bi-m. EUR 5 newsstand/cover (effective 2006). adv. **Document type:** *Magazine, Consumer.*
Published by: S V Corporate Media GmbH (Subsidiary of: Sueddeutscher Verlag GmbH), Emmy-Noether-Str 2, Munich, 80992, Germany. TEL 49-89-5485201, FAX 49-89-54852192, info@sv-medien-service.de, http://www.sv-medien-service.de/svcm/. adv.: B&W page EUR 1,500, color page EUR 1,950. Circ: 13,000 (controlled).

360 DEU
A W O MAGAZIN. (Arbeiter Wohlfahrt) Text in German. 1973. bi-m. EUR 6 (effective 2008). adv. **Document type:** *Magazine, Trade.*
Formerly (until 1994): Sozialprisma
Published by: Arbeiterwohlfahrt Bundesverband e.V., Bluecherstr 62/63, Berlin, 10961, Germany. TEL 49-30-263090, FAX 49-30-2630932599, info@awo.org. Ed. Michael Blum. Adv. contact Volker Fritzemeier. B&W page EUR 3,420, color page EUR 5,985; trim 185 x 265. Circ: 63,000 (controlled).

360 DEU
A W O MITTEILUNGEN; Kreisverband Karlsruhe-Stadt e.V. Text in German. 1969. q. adv. bk.rev. bibl.; stat. back issues avail. **Document type:** *Newsletter.*
Formerly: A W Mitteilungen
Related titles: E-mail ed.
Published by: Kreisverband Karlsruhe-Stadt e.V., Kronenstr 15, Karlsruhe, 76133, Germany. TEL 49-721-350070, FAX 49-721-3500735. Ed. Erich Weichsel. Circ: 4,500.

361.609172 NOR ISSN 1890-310X
AARSRAPPORT OM NORSK BILATERAL BISTAND. Text in Norwegian. 2006. a. back issues avail. **Document type:** *Government.*
Related titles: Online - full text ed.; English ed.: Annual Report on Norwegian Bilateral Development Cooperation. ISSN 1890-3118.
Published by: Direktoratet for Utviklingssamarbeid/Norwegian Agency for Development Cooperation, PO Box 8034, Dep, Oslo, 0030, Norway. TEL 47-22-242030, FAX 47-22-242031, postmottag@norad.no.

361.6 USA
ABE'S DAILY GRANT REPORT. Text in English. 2000. d. USD 200 (effective 2006). **Document type:** *Newsletter.* **Description:** Lists grant opportunities the same day or soon after they appear in the Federal Register and other government documents. Includes requests for proposals from corporate, private and community foundations.
Media: E-mail.
Published by: Capitol City Publishers, 4416 East West Hwy, Ste 400, Bethesda, MD 20814-4568. TEL 301-916-1800, 800-523-4271, FAX 301-528-2497, inquiry@capitolcitypublishers.com, http://capitolcitypublishers.com.

ABILITIES. *see* HANDICAPPED—Hearing Impaired

ACCESS (ONLINE). *see* HANDICAPPED

360 AUS ISSN 1839-1362
ACCESS AND EQUITY IN GOVERNMENT SERVICES. Text in English. 1993. biennial. free (effective 2011). back issues avail. **Document type:** *Report, Government.*
Former titles (until 2008): Accessible Government Services for all .. Annual Report (1834-8319); (until 2006): Access and Equity Annual Report (1321-1048)
Related titles: Online - full text ed.: ISSN 1839-1370.
Published by: Australian Government, Department of Immigration and Citizenship, GPO Box 717, Canberra, ACT 2601, Australia. FAX 61-2-62480479.

361 PER ISSN 0258-2678
HV110.5
ACCION CRITICA. Text in Spanish. 1976. s-a. USD 6. bk.rev.
Indexed: C01, RASB.
Published by: Asociacion Latinoamericana de Escuelas de Servicio Social, Centro Latinoamericano de Trabajo Social, Jr. Jorge Vanderghen No. 351, Apdo. 348, Lima, Peru. Ed. Maria Cecilia Tobon.

360 FIN ISSN 1796-9352
ACTA WASAENSIA. SOSIAALI- JA TERVEYSHALLINTOTIEDE. Text in Finnish. 2006. irreg., latest vol.2, 2007. price varies. back issues avail. **Document type:** *Monographic series, Academic/Scholarly.*
Formerly (until 2007): Acta Wasaensia. Sosiaali- ja Terveyshallinto (1796-2285)
Related titles: Online - full text ed.; ◆ Series of: Acta Wasaensia. ISSN 0355-2667.
Published by: Vaasan Yliopisto/University of Vaasa, PO Box 700, Vaasa, 65101, Finland. TEL 358-6-3248111, FAX 358-6-3248187.

362.7 344.73 USA
ACTION (CINCINNATI). Text in English. 1987. bi-m. free. **Document type:** *Newsletter, Consumer.* **Description:** Reports news on legal developments related to illegal obscenity.
Formerly (until 199?): Standing Together
Published by: National Coalition for the Protection of Children and Families, 800 Compton Rd, Ste 9224, Cincinnati, OH 45231. TEL 513-521-6227 ext 111, FAX 513-521-6337, http://www.nationalcoalition.org. Ed. Franceska Jensen. Circ: 15,000.

ACTION (LONDON); questions. ideas. innovation. inspiration. *see* BUSINESS AND ECONOMICS—International Development And Assistance

360 IRL ISSN 1649-3796
ACTION ON POVERTY TODAY. Text in English. 1987. q. free. bk.rev. illus. **Document type:** *Newsletter, Government.* **Description:** Discusses public policy in regard to poverty.
Formerly (until 2003): Combat Poverty Agency. Resource Series (0791-0096)
Published by: Combat Poverty Agency, Bridgewater Centre, Conyngham Rd., Island Bridge, Dublin, 8, Ireland. TEL 353-1-670-6746, FAX 353-1-670-6760, info@cpa.ie, http://www.cpa.ie. Ed. Joan O'Flynn. Circ: 5,500.

360 FRA ISSN 1269-8377
ACTIONS SOCIALES. Text in French. 1996. irreg. back issues avail. **Document type:** *Monographic series, Consumer.*
Published by: E S F Editeur (Subsidiary of: Reed Business Information France), 2 rue Maurice Hartmann, Issy-les-Moulineaux, 92133 Cedex, France. TEL 33-1-46294629, FAX 33-1-46294633, info@esf-editeur.fr, http://www.esf-editeur.fr.

361 AUS ISSN 1837-5960
▼ **ACTIVE BULLETIN.** Text in English. 2009. m. free (effective 2010). back issues avail. **Document type:** *Newsletter, Trade.* **Description:** Designed for active people with Multiple Sclerosis in New South Wales.
Media: Online - full text.
Published by: Active MS NSW, PO Box 488, Glebe, NSW 2038, Australia. TEL 44-2-95664110, mail@activemsnsw.net.

362.5 NLD ISSN 1871-5885
ACTIVIST. Text in Dutch. 2005. q.
Related titles: Online - full text ed.: ISSN 1871-5893.
Published by: Stichting TEAR Fund Nederland, Laan van Vollenhove 2941, Postbus 981, Zeist, 3700 AZ, Netherlands. TEL 31-30-6969600, FAX 31-30-6969635, info@tear.nl, http://www.tear.nl.

361 MAR ISSN 1113-9536
ACTIVITE, EMPLOI ET CHOMAGE. Text in French. 1997. q. MAD 55 foreign (effective 2000). **Document type:** *Bulletin, Government.*
Published by: Morocco. Direction de la Statistique, B P 178, Rabat, Morocco. TEL 212-7-77-36-06, FAX 212-7-773042.

360 AUS ISSN 1030-7451
ACTIVNEWS. Text in English. 1953. bi-m. adv. bk.rev. back issues avail. **Document type:** *Newsletter, Academic/Scholarly.* **Description:** Promotes a wide range of services for adults and children with developmental disabilities in Western Australia.
Formerly: Our Children (0048-2382)
Published by: Activ Foundation Inc., PO Box 446, Wembley, W.A. 6913, Australia. TEL 61-8-93870555, FAX 61-8-93870599, records@activ.asn.au. Ed. Leanne Pitcher. Circ: 2,500.

360 FRA ISSN 1145-8690
ACTUALITES SOCIALES HEBDOMADAIRES. Text in French. 1955. w. EUR 69.50 (effective 2008). adv. bk.rev. **Document type:** *Journal.*
Related titles: Online - full text ed.: ISSN 2116-5823. 20??.
Indexed: FR.
Published by: (Actualites Sociales Hebdomadaires s.a.r.l.), Wolters Kluwer France (Subsidiary of: Wolters Kluwer N.V.), 1 Rue Eugene et Armand Peugeot, Rueil-Malmaison, Cedex 92856, France. Adv. contact Anne Mallet. B&W page EUR 1,800, color page EUR 2,300. Circ: 50,000.

360 AUS ISSN 1833-9972
ADELAIDE UPDATE. Text in English. 2005. s-a. donation. back issues avail. **Document type:** *Newsletter, Consumer.* **Description:** Provides information about the activities of UnitingCare Wesley organisation.
Media: Online - full text.
Published by: UnitingCare Wesley Adelaide Inc., 10 Pitt St, Adelaide, SA 5000, Australia. TEL 61-8-82025111, enquiries@ucwesleyadelaide.org.au, http://www.ucwesleyadelaide.org.au/default.htm. Eds. Diane Harris, Mark Henley TEL 61-8-82025135.

361 BGD ISSN 0042-1057
ADHUNA. Text in Bengali. 1974. q. USD 10 (effective 2000). adv. bk.rev. **Document type:** *Newsletter.* **Description:** Provides a creative means for exchanging opinion and expressions of the development organizations, especially the NGOs engaged in development activities.
Former titles (until 1991): A D A B Sangbad; Adab Sangbad; Adab
Published by: Association of Development Agencies in Bangladesh, 1-3 Block F, Lalmatia, Dhaka, 1207, Bangladesh. TEL 880-2-8122845, FAX 880-2-8113095, adab@bdonline.com. Circ: 7,000.

360 USA ISSN 0364-3107
HV1 CODEN: ASWODB
➤ **ADMINISTRATION IN SOCIAL WORK**; the quarterly journal of human services management. Abbreviated title: A S W. Text in English. 1977. q. GBP 772 combined subscription in United Kingdom to institutions (print & online eds.); EUR 1,003, USD 1,009 combined subscription to institutions (print & online eds.) (effective 2012). adv. bk.rev. illus. 120 p./no. 1 cols./p.; back issues avail.; reprint service avail. from PSC. **Document type:** *Journal, Academic/Scholarly.* **Description:** Provides current information to administrators, supervisors, managers and sub-executives in social work and related human services fields.
Related titles: Microfiche ed.: (from PQC); Microform ed.; Online - full text ed.: ISSN 1544-4376. GBP 695 in United Kingdom to institutions; EUR 903, USD 908 to institutions (effective 2012).
Indexed: A01, A02, A03, A08, A10, A12, A13, A17, A20, A22, A26, ABIn, AHCMS, ASCA, AbAn, B01, B02, B06, B07, B08, B09, B11, B15, B17, B18, BPIA, BRD, C06, C07, C08, C12, CA, CINAHL, CMM, CurCont, DIP, E-psyche, E01, E08, F09, FR, FamI, G04, G06, G07, G08, GSS&RPL, H12, H13, HRA, HospLI, I05, IBR, IBZ, M02, MEA&I, ManagAb, ManagCont, P02, P03, P10, P20, P27, P30, P34, P48, P51, P53, P54, PQC, PSI, PsycInfo, PsycholAb, S02, S03, S09, S11, SCOPUS, SOPODA, SPAA, SSA, SSAI, SSAb, SSCI, SSI, SWR&A, SociolAb, T02, V03, W03, W07.
—BLDSC (0696.270000), IE, Infotrieve, Ingenta, INIST. **CCC.**
Published by: (National Network for Social Work Managers), Routledge (Subsidiary of: Taylor & Francis Group), 325 Chestnut St, Ste 800, Philadelphia, PA 19106. TEL 215-625-8900, 800-354-1420, FAX 215-625-8914, http://www.routledge.com. Ed. Leon Ginberg. adv.: B&W page USD 315, color page USD 550; trim 4375 x 7.125. Circ: 972 (paid).

➤ **ADOLESCENCE EDUCATION NEWSLETTER.** *see* EDUCATION

362.82 ESP ISSN 2013-2956
▼ **ADOPCIONES, FAMILIAS, INFANCIA.** Text in Spanish. 2009. m. **Document type:** *Bulletin, Consumer.*
Media: Online - full text.
Published by: A F I N gestion@afin.org.es, http://www.afin.org/.

362.7 USA ISSN 0273-6497
ADOPTALK. Text in English. 1976. q. USD 45 domestic to individuals; USD 60 in Canada to individuals; USD 1,000 domestic to corporations; USD 1,200 in Canada to corporations (effective 2005); membership required. adv. bk.rev. **Document type:** *Newsletter, Consumer.* **Description:** Information and articles about special needs adoption, foster care, adoptive family support, resources, and federal and state legislation.
Supersedes (1965-1976): National Adoptalk (0027-8459)
Media: Duplicated (not offset).
Published by: North American Council on Adoptable Children (NACAC), 970 Raymond Ave, St Paul, MN 55114-1149. TEL 651-644-3036, FAX 651-644-9848, info@nacac.org. Ed., R&P Diane Riggs. Circ: 5,000 (controlled).

314.33 NLD ISSN 1388-3526
ADOPTIETIJDSCHRIFT. Variant title: Adoptie. Text in Dutch. 1998. q. EUR 40, USD 60 to institutions (effective 2009). adv. **Document type:** *Magazine, Trade.*
Published by: Bohn Stafleu van Loghum B.V. (Subsidiary of: Springer Science+Business Media), Postbus 246, Houten, 3990 GA, Netherlands. TEL 31-30-6383872, FAX 31-30-6383991, boekhandels@bsl.nl, http://www.bsl.nl. Ed. L Waanders. Circ: 4,434.

362.7 USA ISSN 1944-4990
HV873
ADOPTION & CULTURE. Text in English. 2007. a. USD 20 to individuals; USD 25 to libraries (effective 2010). **Document type:** *Journal, Academic/Scholarly.* **Description:** Publishes essays on aspects of adoption's intersection with culture, including scholarly examinations of adoption practice, literature, art, law, ethics and science.
Published by: Alliance for the Study of Adoption and Culture, University of West Georgia, Department of English and Philosophy, 1601 Maple St, Carrollton, GA 30118. Ed. Emily Hipchen.

362.7 GBR ISSN 0308-5759
HV875 CODEN: ADFOFR
➤ **ADOPTION AND FOSTERING.** Text in English. 1952. q. GBP 62 domestic to individuals; GBP 78 foreign to individuals; GBP 125 domestic to institutions; GBP 145 foreign to institutions; free to members (effective 2010). bk.rev.; video rev. stat.; abstr. cum.index. 96 p./no. 2 cols./p.; back issues avail. **Document type:** *Journal, Academic/Scholarly.* **Description:** Takes a multidisciplinary professional look at children in danger of separation from their families or needing foster care or adoption.
Formerly (until 1976): Child Adoption (0412-1007)
Related titles: Online - full text ed.: ISSN 1740-469X. GBP 50 to individuals; GBP 120 to institutions (effective 2010) (from IngentaConnect).
Indexed: A22, A26, ASSIA, B28, C06, C07, C08, C28, CA, CINAHL, DIP, ELJI, F09, FamI, H12, I05, IBR, IBZ, LJI, PsycholAb, S02, S03, SCOPUS, SSA, SWR&A, SociolAb, T02.
—BLDSC (0696.592000), IE, Infotrieve, Ingenta. **CCC.**
Published by: British Association for Adoption & Fostering, Saffron House, 6-10 Kirby St, London, EC1N 8TS, United Kingdom. TEL 44-20-74212600, FAX 44-20-74212601, mail@baaf.org.uk.

360 GBR
ADOPTION APPLICATIONS IN SCOTLAND. Text in English. 1994. a., latest 2004. back issues avail. **Document type:** *Bulletin, Government.* **Description:** Features statistics on the number of adoption and freeing order applications in Scotland.
Related titles: Online - full text ed.: free (effective 2010).
Published by: Social Work Services Group, Statistics Branch, Scottish Government, Education Directorate, Mail Point 1, 1-B (S), Victoria Quay, Edinburgh, EH6 6QQ, United Kingdom. TEL 44-131-2440313, FAX 44-131-2440354, children.statistics@scotland.gsi.gov.uk.

362.7 USA
ADOPTION FACTBOOK; United States data, issues, regulations and resources. Text in English. 1985. irreg., latest vol.2, 1989. USD 39.95. **Description:** Comprehensive U.S. statistics on adoption. Information sources for adoption and related services, especially services to young, single or troubled parents. Includes a hotline.
Published by: National Council for Adoption, Inc., 225 N Washington St, Alexandria, VA 22314-2561. ncfa@adoptioncouncil.org.

362.7 USA ISSN 1092-6755
HV875 CODEN: ADQUFW
➤ **ADOPTION QUARTERLY**; innovations in community and clinical practice, theory and research. Abbreviated title: A Q. Text in English. q. GBP 318 combined subscription in United Kingdom to institutions (print & online eds.); EUR 415, USD 420 combined subscription to institutions (print & online eds.) (effective 2012). adv. 120 p./no. 1 cols./p.; back issues avail.; reprint service avail. from PSC. **Document type:** *Journal, Academic/Scholarly.* **Description:** Offers a forum devoted to all aspects of adoption.
Related titles: Microform ed.; Online - full text ed.: ISSN 1544-452X. GBP 286 in United Kingdom to institutions; EUR 373, USD 379 to institutions (effective 2012).

S

Indexed: A01, A03, A22, C06, C07, C08, CA, CINAHL, DIP, E-psyche, E01, E03, ERI, ESPM, F09, FamI, IBR, IBZ, M02, P03, P30, PsycInfo, PsycholAb, RefZh, RiskAb, S02, S03, SCOPUS, SSA, SWR&A, SociolAb, T02.
—BLDSC (0696.593300), IE, Ingenta. **CCC.**
Published by: Routledge (Subsidiary of: Taylor & Francis Group), 325 Chestnut St, Ste 800, Philadelphia, PA 19106. TEL 215-625-8900, 800-354-1420, FAX 215-625-8914, journals@routledge.com, http://www.routledge.com. Ed. Scott Ryan. adv.: B&W page USD 315, color page USD 550; trim 4.375 x 7.125. Circ: 305 (paid).

362.7 USA
ADOPTION TODAY (ONLINE). Text in English. 1998. bi-m. USD 12; USD 2 per issue (effective 2010). back issues avail. **Document type:** *Magazine, Consumer.* **Description:** Presents a guide to the issues and answers surrounding international adoption.
Former titles (until 200?): Adoption Today (Print) (1527-8522); (until 2000): Chosen Child (1098-0911)
Media: Online - full text.
Published by: Louis & Company Publishing, 541 E Garden Dr, Unit N, Windsor, CO 80550-3150. TEL 970-686-7412, 888-924-6736, FAX 970-686-7412. Pub. Richard Fischer.

362.2 362.3 USA ISSN 0363-2733
ADVANCE (RICHMOND). Text in English. 1950. q. **Document type:** *Government.*
Formerly (until 1973): Mental Health in Virginia (0539-3485)
Published by: State Mental Health, Mental Retardation and Substance Abuse Services Board, PO Box 1797, Richmond, VA 23218. TEL 804-786-7945, marlene.butler@co.dmhmrsas.virginia.gov.

ADVANCES IN LIFE COURSE RESEARCH. *see* GERONTOLOGY AND GERIATRICS

361.3 USA
ADVANCES IN SOCIAL WORK (ONLINE). Text in English. s-a. free (effective 2011).
Media: Online - full text. **Related titles:** ◆ Print ed.: Advances in Social Work (Print). ISSN 1527-8565.
Published by: Indiana University, School of Social Work, 902 W New York St, Indianapolis, IN 46202. TEL 317-274-6705, FAX 317-274-8630, iussw@iupui.edu, http://socialwork.iu.edu/.

361.3 USA ISSN 1527-8565
HV1
➤ **ADVANCES IN SOCIAL WORK (PRINT).** Text in English. 2000 (Spr.). s-a. **Document type:** *Journal, Academic/Scholarly.* **Description:** Addresses current issues, challenges and responses facing social work practice and education.
Related titles: ◆ Online - full text ed.: Advances in Social Work (Online).
Indexed: CA, P30, S02, S03, SCOPUS, SSA, SWR&A, SociolAb, T02.
—BLDSC (0711.405850), IE, Ingenta.
Published by: Indiana University, School of Social Work, 902 W New York St, Indianapolis, IN 46202. TEL 317-274-6705, FAX 317-274-8630, iussw@iupui.edu, http://socialwork.iu.edu/. Ed. William Barton.

361.3 AUS ISSN 1329-0584
ADVANCES IN SOCIAL WORK AND WELFARE EDUCATION. Text in English. 19??. s-a. free to members (effective 2011). back issues avail. **Document type:** *Journal, Academic/Scholarly.*
Former titles (until 1996): Advances in Social Welfare Education (1035-011X); (until 1988): Advances in Social Work Education
Related titles: Online - full text ed.: free (effective 2011).
Published by: Australian Association for Social Work and Welfare Education, c/o Faculty of Education and Social Work, Education Bldg, A35, The University of Sydney, Sydney, NSW 2006, Australia. TEL 61-2-93516899. Eds. Karen Healy, Liz Beddoe.

362.28 NLD ISSN 0922-3061
➤ **ADVANCES IN SUICIDOLOGY.** Text in Dutch. 1989. irreg., latest vol.2, 1995. price varies. back issues avail. **Document type:** *Monographic series, Academic/Scholarly.* **Description:** Scholarly treatment of issues pertaining to the prevention of suicide.
Indexed: E-psyche, IZBG.
Published by: Brill, PO Box 9000, Leiden, 2300 PA, Netherlands. TEL 31-71-5353500, FAX 31-71-5317532, cs@brill.nl. R&P Elizabeth Venekamp. **Dist. in N. America by:** Brill, PO Box 605, Herndon, VA 20172-0605. TEL 703-661-1585, 800-337-9255, FAX 703-661-1501, cs@brillusa.com; **Dist. by:** Turpin Distribution Services Ltd., Pegasus Dr, Stratton Business Park, Biggleswade, Bedfordshire SG18 8QB, United Kingdom. TEL 44-1767-604954, FAX 44-1767-601640, custserv@turpin-distribution.com, http://www.turpin-distribution.com/.

361.73 AUS ISSN 1837-901X
▼ **ADVANCING FUNDRAISING.** Text in English. 2009. bi-m. AUD 50 to non-members; free to members (effective 2011). adv. back issues avail. **Document type:** *Magazine, Trade.* **Description:** Covers Fundraising Institute Australia's news, features, discussions of fundraising ethics and practical articles for fundraisers working in the sector today.
Related titles: Online - full text ed.: free (effective 2011).
Published by: Fundraising Institute Australia, PO Box 642, Chatswood, NSW 2753, Australia. TEL 61-2-94116644, FAX 61-2-94116655, members@fia.org.au. Ed., Adv. contact Gail Knox TEL 61-2-2 94105911.

361.73 USA ISSN 1077-2545
HG177
ADVANCING PHILANTHROPY. Text in English. 1993. bi-m. free to members. adv. bk.rev. 48 p./no.; back issues avail. **Document type:** *Magazine, Trade.* **Description:** Provides a forum for research and the presentation of practical new ideas in the fund-raising profession.
Former titles (until 1993): National Society of Fund Raising Executives. Journal (1056-2443); N S F R E Journal (0196-3295)
Published by: Association of Fundraising Professionals, 4300 Wilson Blvd, Ste 300, Arlington, VA 22203. TEL 703-684-0410, FAX 703-684-0540, http://www.afpnet.org. Adv. contact Todd McLaughlin. Circ: 23,000 (paid and free).

ADVANCING SUICIDE PREVENTION. *see* MEDICAL SCIENCES—Psychiatry And Neurology

363.5 GBR ISSN 0950-5458
ADVISER. Text in English. 1979. bi-m. GBP 33 (effective 2009). adv. bk.rev. index. back issues avail. **Document type:** *Magazine, Trade.* **Description:** Guide to social security, housing, employment. Includes consumer and money advice.
Former titles: Housing Aid; S N H A T News Bulletin (0262-4885)
Indexed: ELJI, LJI.
—BLDSC (0712.289400), IE, Ingenta.
Published by: National Association of Citizens Advice Bureau, Myddelton House, 115-123 Pentonville Rd, London, N1 9LZ, United Kingdom. corporate.communications@citizensadvice.org.uk. Ed. Alan Markey.

362.7 USA
ADVOCASEY. Text in English. 1999. a. **Document type:** *Magazine, Consumer.* **Description:** Highlights issues and policies that affect the lives of children and families in the United States.
Related titles: Online - full content ed.
Published by: Annie E. Casey Foundation, 701 St Paul St, Baltimore, MD 21202. TEL 410-547-6600, FAX 410-547-6624.

THE ADVOCATE (ALBANY). *see* HANDICAPPED

361.3 USA
➤ **ADVOCATE'S FORUM.** Text in English. 1994. a. free (effective 2010). back issues avail. **Document type:** *Journal, Academic/Scholarly.* **Description:** Provides students, alumni and other with an opportunity to debate and discuss relevant issues while also sharing news and resources for the benefit of anyone interested in issues of social work.
Media: Online - full text.
Published by: University of Chicago, School of Social Service Administration, 969 E 60th St, Chicago, IL 60637. TEL 773-702-1250, FAX 773-702-0874, info@ssa.uchicago.edu. Eds. Emily Oshima, Jennifer Baker.

360 305.4 USA ISSN 0886-1099
HV1442
➤ **AFFILIA**; journal of women and social work. Text in English. 1986. q. USD 667, GBP 393 to institutions; USD 681, GBP 401 combined subscription to institutions (print & online eds.) (effective 2012). adv. bk.rev. illus. back issues avail.; reprint service avail. from PSC. **Document type:** *Journal, Academic/Scholarly.* **Description:** Brings insight and knowledge to the field of social work from a feminist perspective and provides research and tools necessary to make large changes and improvements in the delivery of social services.
Related titles: Online - full text ed.: ISSN 1552-3020. USD 613, GBP 361 to institutions (effective 2012).
Indexed: A01, A02, A03, A08, A20, A22, A25, A26, ASCA, B07, C06, C07, C08, CA, CINAHL, CJPI, CMM, CurCont, E01, E07, E08, ERA, F09, FamI, FemPer, G08, G10, H04, H12, HRA, I05, P02, P03, P10, P13, P24, P30, P34, P48, P53, P54, PCI, PQC, PSI, PsycInfo, S02, S03, S08, S09, S21, SCOPUS, SFSA, SOPODA, SSA, SSCI, SWR&A, SociolAb, T02, V&AA, V02, W06, W07, W09, WSA, WSI.
—BLDSC (0731.720700), IE, Infotrieve, Ingenta. **CCC.**
Published by: Sage Publications, Inc., 2455 Teller Rd, Thousand Oaks, CA 91320. TEL 800-818-7243, FAX 800-583-2665, info@sagepub.com, http://www.sagepub.com. Eds. Christine Flynn Saulnier, Fariyal Ross-Sheriff. **Subscr. outside the Americas to:** Sage Publications Ltd., 1 Oliver's Yard, 55 City Rd, London EC1Y 1SP, United Kingdom. TEL 44-20-73248701, FAX 44-20-73248733, subscription@sagepub.co.uk.

360 ZAF
AFFORDABILITY. Text in English. 2/yr. free. **Document type:** *Newsletter.* **Description:** Covers initiatives and studies on subjects relating to affordable material provision, personal safety and social provision.
Published by: (Co-operative Programme: Affordable Social Security), Human Sciences Research Council/Raad vir Geesteswetenskaplike Navorsing. Sentrum vir Wetenskapontwikkeling, Private Bag X41, Pretoria, 0001, South Africa. TEL 27- 12-302-2999, FAX 27-12-326-5362, dbb@zeus.hsrc.ac.za, http://www.hsrc.ac.za. Ed. Ina Snyman. Circ: 1,200.

362.1 305.896 USA ISSN 1534-3855
THE AFRICAN AMERICAN HEALTHLINK. Text in English. q. **Document type:** *Newsletter.* **Description:** Provides healthcare workers a clearinghouse of information on critical issues, vital resources and successful; health initiatives that impact the health of African American.
Published by: Edge City Innovations, Inc., PO Box 704, Occoquan, VA 22125-9998. TEL 703-590-5207, FAX 703-590-6368. Ed. K L Ray.

362.5 330.9 KEN ISSN 1814-9642
AFRICAN INSTITUTE FOR CAPACITY DEVELOPMENT NEWS. Variant title: A I C A D News. Text in English. 2001. q.
Related titles: Online - full text ed.: ISSN 1814-9650. 2003.
Published by: African Institute for Capacity Development, PO Box 46179, Nairobi, 00100, Kenya. TEL 254-67-52221, FAX 254-67-52360, webmaster@aicad.or.ke.

361 ZWE ISSN 1563-3934
AFRICAN JOURNAL OF SOCIAL WORK. Text in English. 1999. a.
Indexed: CA, SociolAb.
Published by: Zimbabwe, National Association of Social Workers, P O Box 5369, Harare, Zimbabwe. TEL 263-4-771801, FAX 263-4-771802, nasw-z@mweb.co.zw. **Co-sponsor:** International Federation of Social Workers.

362.1 ZAF ISSN 1728-774X
AFRICAN SAFETY PROMOTION. Text in English. 2002. a. **Description:** Aims to be forum for discussion and debate among scholars, policy-makers and practitioners active in the field of injury prevention and safety promotion.
Related titles: Online - full text ed.
Indexed: A36, AgrForAb, CABA, E12, F08, F12, GH, LT, R12, RRTA, T05, TAR, W11.
Published by: University of South Africa, Institute for Social and Health Sciences and Centre for Peace Action, PO Box 1087, Lenasia, 1820, South Africa. TEL 27-11-8571142, FAX 27-11-8571770, lourilc@unisa.ac.za, http://www.unisa.ac.za. Ed. Mohamed Seedat.

AFRIKA ZAMANI. *see* BUSINESS AND ECONOMICS—International Development And Assistance

▼ **AFRO ASIAN JOURNAL OF ANTHROPOLOGY AND SOCIAL POLICY.** *see* ANTHROPOLOGY

362.1 NOR ISSN 1504-5250
AFRODITE. Text in Norwegian. 2002. q. **Document type:** *Magazine, Consumer.*
Formerly (until 2004): Nytt fra U K F (1504-5242)
Published by: Foreningen for Gynekologisk Kreftrammede/ Gynocological Cancer Volunteers Organization, PO Box 4, Sentrum, Oslo, 0101, Norway. Circ: 2,000.

AFYA. *see* MEDICAL SCIENCES

360 362.1 CAN ISSN 1719-8593
AGENCE DE DEVELOPPEMENT DE RESEAUX LOCAUX DE SERVICES DE SANTE ET DE SERVICES SOCIAUX DE LA CAPITALE NATIONALE. RAPPORT ANNUEL DE GESTION. Text in French. 1972. a. **Document type:** *Government.*
Former titles (until 2004): Regie Regionale de la Sante et des Services Sociaux de Quebec. Rapport Annuel des Activites (1486-6234); C R S S S de Quebec. Rapport Annuel (0710-2305)
Published by: Quebec, Agence de la Sante et des Services Sociaux de la Capitale-Nationale, 3725 Saint-Denis St, Montreal, PQ H2X 3L9, Canada. TEL 514-286-6500, FAX 514-286-5669, http://www.santemontreal.qc.ca/fr/index.html.

AGING MATTERS. *see* GERONTOLOGY AND GERIATRICS

AGING TRENDS. *see* PUBLIC HEALTH AND SAFETY

361.77 FRA ISSN 2108-3924
AGIR ENSEMBLE. Text in French. 1865. bi-m. adv. bk.rev. charts; illus.; stat. index.
Former titles (until 2010): Croix-Rouge Francaise (1294-2855); (until 1998): Presence Croix-Rouge (0301-0260); (until 1972): Vie et Bonte (0042-5486)
Related titles: Microform ed.
Published by: Croix-Rouge Francaise, 17 rue Quentin Bauchart, Paris, Cedex 8 75384, France. Ed. J Boulet. Circ: 30,000.

362.1 FRA ISSN 2108-8705
AIDE MEDICALE ET DEVELOPPEMENT. LE JOURNAL. Text in French. 1993. s-a. **Document type:** *Consumer.*
Former titles (until 2008): Action (1953-1567); (until 2000): Action Humanitaire (1251-0491)
Published by: Aide Medicale et Developpement, 14, Rue Colbert, Grenoble, 38000, France. amd@amd-france.org, http://www.amd-france.org.

616.97 360 CAN ISSN 1719-8208
AIDS COMMITTEE OF TORONTO REPORT TO DONORS. Text in English. 1999. a., latest 2005. **Document type:** *Report, Trade.*
Formerly (until 2004): AIDS Committee of Toronto. Annual Report (1719-8194)
Media: Online - full text.
Published by: AIDS Committee of Toronto, 399 Church St, 4th flr, Toronto, ON M5B 2J6, Canada. TEL 416-340-2437, FAX 416-340-8224, ask@actoronto.org, http://www.actoronto.org/website/home.nsf/pages/home!opendocument.

360 FIN ISSN 1236-9845
AIHEITA. Text in Finnish. 1992. irreg. back issues avail. **Document type:** *Government.*
Related titles: ◆ Series: Lastensuojelu. ISSN 0788-6101.
Published by: Sosiaali- ja Terveysalan Tutkimus- ja Kehittamiskeskus/ National Research and Development Centre for Welfare and Health, PO Box 220, Helsinki, 00531, Finland. TEL 358-9-39671, FAX 358-9-396761307, infolib@stakes.fi, http://www.stakes.fi.

362.6 CAN ISSN 1912-2349
LES AINES AU CANADA. Text in French. 2001. irreg. **Document type:** *Monographic series, Trade.*
Media: Online - full text. **Related titles:** Ed.: Seniors in Canada. ISSN 1912-2330.
Published by: National Advisory Council on Aging/Conseil Consultatif National sur le Troisieme Age, Box 1908A1, Ottawa, ON K1A 1B4, Canada. TEL 613-957-1968, FAX 613-957-9938, seniors@hc-sc.gc.ca, http://www.hc-sc.gc.ca.

360 CHN ISSN 1009-8100
AIREN/LOVE PEOPLE. Text in Chinese. 1993. s-m. **Document type:** *Magazine, Consumer.*
Published by: Shaanxi Sheng Chuban Zongshe, 124, Youyi East Rd., Cehui Keji Bldg. A, 7th Fl., Xi'an, 710054, China. TEL 86-29-87813581, FAX 86-29-87886413.

360 SWE ISSN 1652-9898
AKADEMIKERN; medlemstidning foer akademikerfoerbundet SSR. Text in Swedish. 1958. 10/yr. adv. bk.rev. illus. **Document type:** *Magazine, Trade.*
Formerly (until 2005): S S R - Tidningen (0283-1910); Which supersedes in part (in 1987): S S R - Tidningen Socionomen (0282-1001); Which was formerly (until 1984): Socionomen (0038-044X)
Related titles: Online - full text ed.: 2009.
Published by: Akademikerfoerbundet SSR, Mariedalsvaegen 4, PO Box 12800, Stockholm, 11296, Sweden. TEL 46-8-6174400, FAX 46-8-6174401, kansli@akademssr.se, http://www.akademssr.se. Ed. Margaretha Holmqvist TEL 46-8-7891171. Adv. contact Robin Zackrisson TEL 46-8-103920. Circ: 55,000.

360 DEU
AKTUELL JOSEFS-GESELLSCHAFT; katholischer Traeger von Einrichtungen zur Rehabilitation Koerperbehinderter. Text in German. 1986. q. free. **Document type:** *Bulletin, Consumer.*
Formerly (until 1990): Dankbrief
Published by: Josefs-Gesellschaft e.V., Alarichstr 40, Cologne, 50679, Germany. TEL 49-221-88998-0, FAX 49-221-8899860. Ed. Alfred Hovestaedt. Circ: 50,000.

ALABAMA COUNSELING ASSOCIATION. JOURNAL. *see* OCCUPATIONS AND CAREERS

362.7 CAN ISSN 1497-0457
HV745.A7
ALBERTA CHILDREN'S SERVICES ANNUAL REPORT. Text in English. 2000. a. **Document type:** *Government.*
Published by: Alberta Children's Services, 12th Fl., Sterling Pl., 9940-106 St., Edmonton, AB T5K 2N2, Canada. TEL 780-422-3004, FAX 780-422-3071, http://www.child.gov.ab.ca/.

ALERT; maandblad voor rampenbestrijding en crisisbeheersing. *see* CIVIL DEFENSE

ALERT (EWING); news on alcoholism and drug addiction services for persons who are hard of hearing. *see* DRUG ABUSE AND ALCOHOLISM

614 361.3 338.91 USA
ALERT (NEW YORK). Text in English. 1997. q. **Document type:** *Magazine, Consumer.* **Description:** Chronicles humanitarian and medical crises around the world and the health care workers who volunteer to assist those impacted by famine, war, and epidemics.
Related titles: Online - full text ed.: ISSN 1933-6861.
Published by: Doctors Without Borders, 333 7th Ave, 2nd Fl, New York, NY 10001. TEL 212-679-6800, FAX 212-679-7016. Ed. Jason Cone.

360 SWE ISSN 1404-8868
ALLA. Text in Swedish. 1993. q. free. back issues avail. **Document type:** *Magazine, Consumer.*
Former titles (until 2000): Fackjournalen (1104-1404); (until 1993): Fackjournalen med Social- och Foersaekringsnytt (1102-0504); Which was formed by the merger of (1987-1990): Fackjournalen med Foersaekringsnyheter (0284-2165); (1987-1990): Fackjournalen med Sociala Nyheter (0284-2181)
Related titles: Online - full text ed.
Published by: Landsorganisationen i Sverige/The Swedish Trade Union Confederation, Barnhusgatan 18, Stockholm, 10553, Sweden. TEL 46-8-7962500, FAX 46-8-200358, mailbox@lo.se, http://www.lo.se. Ed. Marja Korvisto.

360 USA
HV89
THE ALLIANCE FOR CHILDREN AND FAMILIES. DIRECTORY OF MEMBER AGENCIES IN THE UNITED STATES AND CANADA. Text in English. 1987. a. **Document type:** *Directory.* **Description:** Contains addresses, telephone numbers, chief executives and areas served for all members of the Alliance for Children and Families.
Formerly (until 1996): Family Service America. Directory of Member Agencies in the United States and Canada (1045-1684)
Published by: Alliance for Children and Families, 11700 W Lake Park Dr, Milwaukee, WI 53224. TEL 414-359-1040, FAX 414-359-1074, info@familiesinsociety.org, http://www.alliance1.org/. Ed., R&P Susan Hornung. Pub. Isabel Wrotkowski TEL 905-945-7221. Adv. contact Mr. Peter B Goldberg.

362.82 USA ISSN 1946-1305
ALLIANCE FOR CHILDREN & FAMILIES MAGAZINE. Text in English. 2001. q. USD 24 (effective 2009). adv. back issues avail. **Document type:** *Magazine, Consumer.* **Description:** Aims to target specialized national audience that includes senior management and leadership of nonprofit social service organizations, as well as volunteer board members, child and family advocates, and key elected officials throughout the nation who impact the future of children and families.
Related titles: Online - full text ed.: ISSN 1946-1321.
Published by: Alliance For Children and Families, 11700 W Lake Park Dr, Milwaukee, WI 53224. TEL 414-359-1040, FAX 414-359-1074. Adv. contact Malcolm McIntyre TEL 414-359-6570. Circ: 14,500.

361.8 USA ISSN 1945-7200
ALLIANCE FOR PROGRESS. Text in English. 2007. bi-m. free (effective 2008). **Document type:** *Newsletter, Consumer.*
Related titles: Online - full text ed.: ISSN 1945-7219.
Published by: Alliance for Progress, Inc., 1070 Ogden Ave, Ste CS-2, Bronx, NY 10452. TEL 718-992-6448, inquiry@allianceprogress.org.

360 GBR
ALMSHOUSE ASSOCIATION. ANNUAL REPORT (YEAR). Text in English. a. GBP 3 (effective 2010). stat. **Document type:** *Corporate.*
Former titles: Almshouse Association. Annual Report and Statement of Accounts; National Association of Almshouses. Yearbook and Statement of Accounts
Published by: Almshouse Association, Billingbear Lodge, Maidenhead Rd, Wokingham, Berks RG40 5RU, United Kingdom. TEL 44-1344-452922, FAX 44-1344-862062, naa@almshouses.org, http://www.almshouses.org/.

362.6 GBR
ALMSHOUSES GAZETTE. Text in English. 1950. q. GBP 2.50 (effective 2009). **Document type:** *Newsletter, Consumer.* **Description:** Contains items of news within the almshouse movement and also articles of general interest with a property bent.
—BLDSC (0801.803000).
Published by: Almshouse Association, Billingbear Lodge, Maidenhead Rd, Wokingham, Berks RG40 5RU, United Kingdom. TEL 44-1344-452922, FAX 44-1344-862062, naa@almshouses.org, http://www.almshouses.org/.

362 ESP ISSN 1133-0473
ALTERNATIVAS. Text in Spanish. 1992. a. back issues avail. **Document type:** *Monographic series, Academic/Scholarly.*
Related titles: Online - full text ed.: ISSN 1989-9971. 1992.
Published by: Universidad de Alicante, Departamento de Trabajo Social y Servicios Sociales, Ctra. San Vicente, s-n, San Vicente del Raspeig, Alicante, 03560, Spain. TEL 34-965-903983, FAX 334-965-903988, dtsss@ua.es, http://www.ua.es/dpto/dtsss/index.html.

362.6 CAN ISSN 1705-8848
ALZHEIMER GROUPE INC. Text in English. 1993. s-a. **Document type:** *Newsletter, Consumer.*
Formerly (until 2002): Alzheimer Newsletter (1912-1695)
Published by: Alzheimer Groupe Inc., 5800, boule Cavendish, Ste 311, Montreal, PQ H4W 2T5, Canada. TEL 514-485-7233, FAX 514-485-7946, admin@alzheimergroupe.org, http://www.alzheimergroupe.org/home.htm.

ALZHEIMER'S CARE GUIDE; published especially for those who care for people with Alzheimer's disease and related disorders. *see* GERONTOLOGY AND GERIATRICS

ALZHEIMER'S CARE TODAY; best practices in dementia care. *see* MEDICAL SCIENCES—Psychiatry And Neurology

ALZHEIMER'S RESEARCH REVIEW. *see* MEDICAL SCIENCES—Psychiatry And Neurology

AMBULATORY QUALITY AND COMPLIANCE INSIDER. *see* HEALTH FACILITIES AND ADMINISTRATION

362.6 USA ISSN 1063-3189
HQ1064.U5
AMERICAN ASSOCIATION OF RETIRED PERSONS. PUBLIC POLICY INSTITUTE. ISSUE BRIEF. Text in English. 1991. m.
Indexed: AgeL, P30, SCOPUS.
Published by: American Association of Retired Persons (A A R P), 601 E St, NW, Washington, DC 20049. TEL 202-434-3525, 888-687-2277, member@aarp.org, http://www.aarp.org.

AMERICAN BAR ASSOCIATION. COMMISSION ON LAWYER ASSISTANCE PROGRAMS. HIGHLIGHTS. *see* LAW

361.7 USA ISSN 1092-5414
HV27
THE AMERICAN BENEFACTOR. Text in English. 1997. q. USD 48; USD 52 in Canada; USD 60 elsewhere. **Description:** Designed for major philanthropists and covers everything from deserving causes to explaining the legal loopholes that can make giving a good thing for your bottom line.
Published by: Capital Publishing, 575 Lexington Ave, 17th Fl, New York, NY 10022. TEL 212-223-3100, 800-818-0724, FAX 212-838-8560. Ed. Larkin Warren. Pub. Bente Strong. Circ: 250,000. **Subscr. to:** 49 Richmondville Ave, Ste 302, Westport, CT 06880-2052.

AMERICAN FOUNDATION FOR THE BLIND. ANNUAL REPORT. *see* HANDICAPPED—Visually Impaired

361.7 USA ISSN 0071-9617
AMERICAN FRIENDS SERVICE COMMITTEE. ANNUAL REPORT. Text in English. 1917. a. back issues avail. **Document type:** *Report, Corporate.*
Related titles: Online - full text ed.: free (effective 2011).
—CCC.
Published by: American Friends Service Committee, Inc., 1501 Cherry St, Philadelphia, PA 19102. TEL 215-241-7000, FAX 215-241-7275, afscinfo@afsc.org.

362.1 614 USA ISSN 0888-0352
RA973.5
AMERICAN HEALTH CARE ASSOCIATION. PROVIDER. Variant title: Provider. Text in English. 1975. m. USD 48 domestic; USD 61 in Canada & Mexico; USD 85 elsewhere; free to qualified personnel (effective 2006). adv. illus. **Document type:** *Magazine, Trade.*
Formerly (until 1986): American Health Care Association. Journal (0360-4969)
Related titles: Online - full text ed.
Indexed: A22, AgeL, C06, C07, C08, CINAHL, EMBASE, ExcerpMed, F09, INI, MCR, MEDLINE, P30, R10, Reac, SCOPUS.
—BLDSC (6937.687000), GNLM, IE, Infotrieve, Ingenta.
Published by: American Health Care Association, 1201 L St, N W, Washington, DC 20005. TEL 202-842-4444, FAX 202-842-3860, http://www.ahca.org/. Ed., R&P Joanne Erickson TEL 202-898-2811. Pub. Linda Keegan. Adv. contact Mike Disanto. Circ: 36,000.

AMERICAN JOURNAL OF DISASTER MEDICINE. *see* MEDICAL SCIENCES

AMERICAN JOURNAL OF ORTHOPSYCHIATRY; interdisciplinary approaches to mental health and social justice. *see* PSYCHOLOGY

362.6 USA
AMERICAN PARKINSON DISEASE ASSOCIATION. NEWSLETTER. Text in English. 1965. q. free (effective 2010). **Document type:** *Newsletter, Trade.* **Description:** Informs recipients A.P.D.A. activities, how to cope with their disorder, and of developments in medical research.
Related titles: Online - full text ed.
Indexed: E-psyche.
Published by: American Parkinson Disease Association, Inc., 135 Parkinson Ave, Staten Island, NY 10305. TEL 718-981-8001, 800-223-2732, FAX 718-981-4399, apda@apdaparkinson.org. Eds. Kathryn G Whitford, Michele Popadynec.

361.6 USA ISSN 0163-8300
AMERICAN PUBLIC WELFARE ASSOCIATION. W - MEMO. Text in English. 1961. bi-m. index. **Document type:** *Bulletin.* **Description:** Covers national human service issues and policies aimed principally at state administrators.
Published by: American Public Human Services Association, 1133 19th St, NW, Ste 400, Washington, DC 20036. TEL 202-682-0100, FAX 202-289-6555, MemberServicesHelpDesk@aphsa.org, http://www.aphsa.org. Ed. Elaine Ryan.

361 USA ISSN 0894-5454
HV575
AMERICAN RED CROSS. ANNUAL REPORT. Text in English. 1901. a. free. **Document type:** *Corporate.*
Formerly: American National Red Cross. Annual Report (0080-0384)
Related titles: Microfilm ed.: (from BHP); Online - full text ed.
Published by: American National Red Cross, Creative Services, 8111 Gatehouse Rd, Falls Church, VA 22042. TEL 703-206-7542, FAX 703-206-7507. Ed. Joy Davis. R&P Gloria Lamb. Circ: 25,000.

AMERICAN VETERAN. *see* MILITARY

AMERICANS WITH DISABILITIES ACT: PUBLIC ACCOMMODATIONS AND COMMERCIAL FACILITIES. *see* HANDICAPPED

362.4 USA
AMERICANS WITH DISABILITIES ACT TECHNICAL ASSISTANCE MANUAL: TITLE I. Text in English. base vol. plus irreg. updates. looseleaf. USD 25; USD 31.25 foreign. **Document type:** *Government.* **Description:** Provides guidance on the practical application of legal requirements of the Americans with Disabilities Act of 1990, as established by the E.E.O.C.
Published by: (Office of Communications), U.S. Equal Employment Opportunity Commission, 1801 L St, N W, Washington, DC 20507. **Subscr. to:** U.S. Government Printing Office, Superintendent of Documents, PO Box 371954, Pittsburgh, PA 15250. TEL 202-512-1800, FAX 202-512-2250, orders@gpo.gov, http://www.access.gpo.gov.

362.4 USA
AMERICANS WITH DISABILITIES ACT TECHNICAL ASSISTANCE MANUAL: TITLE II. Text in English. base vol. plus irreg. updates. looseleaf. USD 24; USD 30 foreign. **Document type:** *Government.* **Description:** Shows how discrimination on the basis of disability in state and local governments is prohibited by the Americans with Disabilities Act of 1990.
Published by: U.S. Department of Justice, 10th St & Constitution Ave, N W, Washington, DC 20530. **Subscr. to:** U.S. Government Printing Office, Superintendent of Documents, PO Box 371954, Pittsburgh, PA 15250. TEL 202-512-1800, FAX 202-512-2250, orders@gpo.gov, http://www.access.gpo.gov.

362.4 USA
AMERICANS WITH DISABILITIES ACT TECHNICAL ASSISTANCE MANUAL: TITLE III. Text in English. base vol. plus irreg. updates. looseleaf. USD 25; USD 31.25 foreign. **Document type:** *Government.* **Description:** Shows how discrimination against persons with disabilities in commercial facilities and places of public accommodation is prohibited by the Americans with Disabilities Act of 1990.
Published by: U.S. Department of Justice, 10th St & Constitution Ave, N W, Washington, DC 20530. **Subscr. to:** U.S. Government Printing Office, Superintendent of Documents, PO Box 371954, Pittsburgh, PA 15250. TEL 202-512-1800, FAX 202-512-2250, orders@gpo.gov, http://www.access.gpo.gov.

360 USA ISSN 0886-1196
AMERICA'S SPIRIT. Text in English. 1941. q. free to qualified personnel. illus. **Document type:** *Newsletter.*
Formerly: Wherever They Go
Related titles: Microform ed.: (from PQC).
Published by: United Service Organizations, Inc., U S O World Headquarters, Washington Navy Yard, 901 M St, S E, Bldg 198, Washington, DC 20374-5096. TEL 202-610-5700, FAX 202-610-5701. Ed. Jennifer L Blanck. Circ: 10,000.

360 DEU
AMT FUER ARBEITSSCHUTZ HAMBURG. SCHRIFTEN. Text in German. 1993. irreg. **Document type:** *Trade.*
Published by: Behoerde fuer Arbeit, Gesundheit und Soziales der Freien und Hansestadt Hamburg, Billstr 80, Hamburg, 20539, Germany. TEL 49-40-428372112, FAX 49-40-428373100, arbeitnehmerschutz@bsg.hamburg.de, http://www.hamburg.de/arbeitsschutz/.

362.2 PRI ISSN 1542-7544
HV171
ANALISIS. Text in Spanish. 1999. a. USD 10 (effective 2006). **Document type:** *Monographic series, Academic/Scholarly.*
Published by: Universidad de Puerto Rico, Escuela Graduada de Trabajo Social, Apdo Postal 23345, San Juan, 00931-3345, Puerto Rico. TEL 787-764-0000 ext 5829, FAX 787-763-3725, http://www.upr.clu.edu/home1200.html. Ed. Nilsa Burgos Ortiz. Circ: 500.

360 NIC ISSN 1607-1425
ANGEL DE LA GUARDA. Text in Spanish. m.
Media: Online - full text. **Related titles:** English ed.: ISSN 1607-1433. 2000; English Translation:. Eds. Carlos Fonseca, Hebert Rodriguez.
Co-sponsor: Save the Children.

362.76 GBR ISSN 2046-2247
THE ANN CRAFT TRUST BULLETIN. Abbreviated title: A C T. Text in English. 1992. q. free to members (effective 2011). adv. bk.rev. **Document type:** *Bulletin, Trade.* **Description:** Contains articles regarding the protection from abuse of adults and children with learning disabilities.
Former titles (until 1998): N A P A C Bulletin; (until 1997): National Association for the Protection from Sexual Abuse of Adults and Children with Learning Disabilities. Bulletin (1362-6272)
—IE, Ingenta. **CCC.**
Published by: Ann Craft Trust (ACT), Centre for Social Work, University of Nottingham, University Park, Nottingham, NG7 2RD, United Kingdom. TEL 44-115-9515400, FAX 44-115-9515232, ann-craft-trust@nottingham.ac.uk.

360 ITA ISSN 0003-4568
ANNALI DELLA CARITA. Text in Italian. 1930. m. **Document type:** *Magazine, Consumer.*
Published by: (Centro Liturgico Vincenziano), C L V Edizioni Liturgiche, Via Pompeo Magno 21, Rome, 00192, Italy. TEL 39-06-3216114, FAX 39-06-3221078, http://www2.chiesacattolica.it/clv/. Circ: 3,000.

361 FRA ISSN 1772-3701
L'ANNEE DE L'ACTION SOCIALE (YEAR). Text in French. 2005. a. EUR 30 newsstand/cover (effective 2009). **Document type:** *Journal.*
Published by: Dunod, 5 rue Laromiguiere, Paris, 75005, France. TEL 33-1-40463500, FAX 33-1-40464995, infos@dunod.com, http://www.dunod.com.

360 USA ISSN 0272-4464
HN51
➤ **ANNUAL EDITIONS: SOCIAL PROBLEMS.** Text in English. 1973. a. USD 22.25 per issue (effective 2010). illus. back issues avail. **Document type:** *Journal, Academic/Scholarly.*
Formerly (until 19??): Annual Editions: Readings in Social Problems (0094-9183)
Related titles: Online - full text ed.
Published by: McGraw-Hill, Contemporary Learning Series (Subsidiary of: McGraw-Hill Companies, Inc.), 1221 Ave of the Americas, New York, NY 10020. TEL 212-904-2000, FAX 212-512-2000, customer.service@mcgraw-hill.com, http://www.mcgraw-hill.com.

362.5 USA ISSN 0364-0256
ANNUAL EVALUATION REPORT ON PROGRAMS ADMINISTERED BY THE U.S. OFFICE OF EDUCATION. Text in English. 1975. a.
Published by: U.S. Department of Health and Human Services, Assistant Secretary for Planning and Evaluation (A S P E), 200 Independence Ave SW, Washington, DC 20201. TEL 202-619-0257, FAX 877-696-6775, http://aspe.hhs.gov/index.shtml.

361.73 GBR ISSN 1369-5827
ANNUAL LECTURE ON PHILANTHROPY. Text in English. 1994. a.
—BLDSC (1087.117000).
Published by: Association for Charitable Foundations, 2 Plough Yard, Shoreditch High Street, London, EC2A 3LP, United Kingdom. TEL 44-20-74228600, FAX 44-20-74228606, acf@acf.org.uk, http://www.acf.org.uk.

361.9485 SWE ISSN 1653-5502
ANSVARSKOMMITTEN. SKRIFTSERIE. Text in Swedish. 2005. irreg. free. back issues avail. **Document type:** *Monographic series, Government.*
Published by: Ansvarskommitten, Vasagatan 8-10, Stockholm, 10333, Sweden. TEL 46-8-4051000, ansvar@finance.ministry.se.

ANSWERS (RICHMOND); the magazine for adult children of aging parents. *see* GERONTOLOGY AND GERIATRICS

360 NZL ISSN 1178-5527
HV515.5
AOTEAROA NEW ZEALAND SOCIAL WORK REVIEW. Text in English. 1965. q. members free. adv. bk.rev.
Former titles (until 2007): Social Work Review (0113-7662); (until 1988): New Zealand Social Work Journal (0111-7351); (until 1981): New Zealand Social Work (0110-3954); Which was formerly (until 1977): New Zealand Social Worker (0028-8691)
Related titles: Online - full text ed.
Indexed: A10, A11, CA, INZP, S02, S03, T02, V03.
—BLDSC (1567.727880), IE, Ingenta. **CCC.**

S

Published by: Aotearoa New Zealand Association of Social Workers, PO Box 14-230, Christchurch, 8544, New Zealand. TEL 64-3-3586920, FAX 64-3-3589503, admin@anzasw.org.nz, http://www.anzasw.org.nz.

361.76 NOR ISSN 0804-7758
APPELL. Text in Norwegian. 1941. q. NOK 200 membership (effective 2006). adv. **Document type:** *Magazine, Consumer.*
Former titles (until 1994): Magasinet Norsk Folkehjelp (0801-9681); (until 1987): Norsk Folkehjelp (0801-4779); (until 1986): Helse, Mijoe, Trivsel (0801-471X); (until 1973): Helse og Trivsel paa Arbeidsplassen og i Hjemmet (0801-4787); (until 1957): Helsa (0801-4833); (until 1950): Norsk Folkehjelp. Melding (0801-4841)
Related titles: Supplement(s): Appell, Medlem. ISSN 0809-974X. 2006.
Published by: Norsk Folkehjelp/Norwegian People's Aid, Storgate 33 A, Oslo, 0028, Norway. TEL 47-22-037700, FAX 47-22-200870, norsk.folkehjelp@npaid.org, http://otto.idium.no/folkehjelp.no. Ed. Are Stranden. Adv. contact Kirsti Knudsen. color page NOK 23,000; 268 x 180. Circ: 50,000.

▼ **APPLAUS PLUS.** *see* BUSINESS AND ECONOMICS—Labor And Industrial Relations

360 CAN ISSN 1910-9229
L'APPLICATION DE LA PROCEDURE D'EXAMEN DES PLAINTES EN MATIERE DE SANTE ET DE SERVICES SOCIAUX ET SUR L'AMELIORATION DE LA QUALITE DES SERVICES DISPENSES DANS LE RESEAU DE LA SANTE ET DES SERVICES SOCIAUX DE L'OUTAOUAIS. RAPPORT ANNUEL. Text in French. 2002. a. **Document type:** *Report, Trade.*
Former titles (until 2005): Le Regime d'Examen des Plaintes en Matiere de Sante et de Services Sociaux et sur l'Amelioration de la Qualite des Services Dispenses dans le Reseau de la Sante et des Services Sociaux de l'Outaouais. Rapport Annuel (1712-4948); (until 2004): Plaintes et de l'Amelioration de la Qualite des Services Dispenses dans le Reseau de la Sante et des Services Sociaux de l'Outaouais. Rapport (1716-4753); (until 2003): Plaintes de la Regie Regionale de l'Outaouais et du Reseau Regional de la Sante et des Services Sociaux. Rapport Annuel (1703-9401)
Published by: Agence de Developpement de Reseaux Locaux de Services de Sante et de Services Sociaux de l'Outaouais, 104, rue Lois, Gatineau, PQ J8Y 3R7, Canada. TEL 819-770-7747, FAX 819-771-8632, http://www.santeoutaouais.qc.ca, http://www.rrsss07.gouv.qc.ca/rrsss/RRSSS/index_f.aspx.

ARAFMI NEWS; providing support for carers of people with mental disorders. *see* MEDICAL SCIENCES—Psychiatry And Neurology

366 FRA ISSN 0991-7357
L'ARC BOUTANT; organe d'information des questions scolaires et familiales. Text in French. 1952. m. (10/yr). EUR 29 (effective 2008). charts; stat. **Document type:** *Newsletter, Trade.*
Formed by the 1952 merger of: Midi-Occident (0991-7365); Bulletin Regional de Liaison de L'A.P.E.L. (0991-7381)
Published by: Federation Nationale des Organismes de Gestion des Etablissements de l'Enseignement Catholique (F N O G E C), 277 Rue Saint Jacques, Paris, Cedex 5 75240, France. TEL 33-1-53737440, FAX 33-1-53737444.

362.3 USA
THE ARC INSIGHT. Text in English. 1952. q. free to members (effective 2006). adv. bk.rev. illus. reprints avail. **Document type:** *Newspaper, Consumer.*
Former titles: The Arc Today; A R C (0199-9435); Mental Retardation News (0009-4072); Children Limited
Related titles: Microform ed.: (from PQC).
Indexed: E-psyche.
Published by: Arc, National Headquarters, 1010 Wayne Ave, Ste 650, Silver Spring, MD 20910. TEL 3015653842, info@thearc.org. Ed. Chris Privett. R&P Liz Moore. Adv. contact Jim Humphrey. Circ: 95,000.

360 300 DEU ISSN 0340-3564
ARCHIV FUER WISSENSCHAFT UND PRAXIS DER SOZIALEN ARBEIT. Text in German. 1970. q. EUR 42.70 to non-members; EUR 25.90 to members (effective 2010). bk.rev. **Document type:** *Journal, Academic/Scholarly.*
Indexed: DIP, IBR, IBZ.
Published by: Deutscher Verein fuer Oeffentliche und Private Fuersorge, Michaelkirchstr 17-18, Berlin, 10179, Germany. TEL 49-30-629800, FAX 49-30-62980150, info@deutscher-verein.de. Ed. Dr. Sabine Schmitt. Circ: 800.

362.5 NLD ISSN 1571-7828
ARMOEDEBERICHT. Text in Dutch. biennial. EUR 10.70 per issue (effective 2010). **Document type:** *Report, Government.*
Supersedes in part (in 2002): Armoedemonitor (1387-7585)
Published by: (Netherlands. Sociaal en Cultureel Planbureau/Social and Cultural Planning Office), Centraal Bureau voor de Statistiek, Henri Faasdreef 312, The Hague, 2492 JP, Netherlands. TEL 31-70-3373800, FAX 31-70-62980150, infoserv@cbs.nl, http://www.cbs.nl.

362.5 NLD ISSN 2211-307X
▼ **ARMOEDESIGNALEMENT.** Text in Dutch. 2009. a. EUR 16.50 (effective 2011).
Formerly (until 2010): Lage Inkomens, Kans op Armoede en Uitsluiting (1879-758X)
Published by: (Netherlands. Sociaal en Cultureel Planbureau/Social and Cultural Planning Office), Centraal Bureau voor de Statistiek, Henri Faasdreef 312, The Hague, 2492 JP, Netherlands. TEL 31-70-3373800, FAX 31-70-3375994, infoserv@cbs.nl, http://www.cbs.nl. **Co-publisher:** Sociaal en Cultureel Planbureau/Social and Cultural Planning Office.

361.73 GBR ISSN 1369-9768
THE ARTS FUNDING GUIDE (YEAR). Text in English. 1989. a. GBP 22.95 per issue (effective 2009). **Document type:** *Directory, Consumer.* **Description:** Guide to sources of funding for the arts, covering the National Lottery, official sources in the UK and Europe and support from companies and trusts. Contains concise profile of each of the funders covered.
—CCC.
Published by: Directory of Social Change, 24 Stephenson Way, London, NW1 2DP, United Kingdom. TEL 44-20-73914800, FAX 44-20-73914808, publications@dsc.org.uk.

ARTS REACH. *see* ART

360 USA
AS THE SOUTH GOES. Text in English. irreg. **Document type:** *Newsletter.*
Related titles: Online - full text ed.
Published by: Project South: Institute for the Elimination of Poverty and Genocide, 9 Gammon Ave, Atlanta, GA 30315. TEL 404-622-0602, FAX 404-622-6618, general-info@projectsouth.org.

ASAHIGAWASO KENKYU NENPO/ASAHIGAWASO INSTITUTE OF MEDICAL WELFARE. ANNUAL REPORT. *see* MEDICAL SCIENCES

ASFALTER; die Strassenzeitung in Salzburg. *see* GENERAL INTEREST PERIODICALS—Austria

361.3 SGP ISSN 0218-5385
HV376
➤ **ASIA PACIFIC JOURNAL OF SOCIAL WORK.** Text in English. 1991. s-a. SGD 41.20 domestic to individuals; SGD 50 to individuals in ASEAN/HKSAR; USD 45 elsewhere to individuals; SGD 51.50 domestic to institutions; SGD 60 to institutions in ASEAN/HKSAR; USD 53 elsewhere to institutions (effective 2004). adv. abstr.; bibl.; charts; illus. 136 p./no.; back issues avail. **Document type:** *Journal, Academic/Scholarly.* **Description:** Serves as a forum for exchanging ideas and knowledge and discussing issues relevant to social work research, education and practice in the Asia-Pacific region.
Indexed: A20, CA, CurCont, DIP, FamI, IBR, IBZ, P30, S02, S03, SCOPUS, SSCI, SociolAb, T02, W07.
—Ingenta.
Published by: (National University Of Singapore, Department of Social Work and Psychology), Marshall Cavendish International (Singapore) Pte. Ltd., Academic Publishing Division, Times Centre, 1 New Industrial Rd, Singapore, 536196, Singapore. TEL 65-62139288, FAX 65-62849772, mca@sg.marshallcavendish.com, http://www.timesacademic.com/. Ed. S Vasoo.

➤ **ASIAN AMERICAN POLICY REVIEW.** *see* ETHNIC INTERESTS

360 305.895 USA ISSN 1944-6640
▼ **ASIAN SOCIETY FOR INTERNATIONAL RELATIONS AND PUBLIC AFFAIRS. JOURNAL.** Text in English. 2009. s-a. **Description:** Aims to collect, store and disseminate new and relevant information on Indonesian human resources, cultural, educational, economic and public welfare development.
Related titles: Print ed.: ISSN 1944-6659.
Published by: Asian Society for International Relations and Public Affairs, 26 Shady Dr, Indiana, PA 15705. TEL 724-549-2860. Ed. Kustim Wibowo.

360 DEU
ASME HUMANITAS BULLETIN. Text in German. 1974. s-a. free (effective 2008). back issues avail. **Document type:** *Bulletin, Trade.*
Published by: A S M E Humanitas - Humanitaere Gesellschaft fuer Soziale und Medizinische Hilfe e.V., Guettenbergstr 7, Marktleugast, 95352, Germany. TEL 49-9255-7970, FAX 49-9255-8257. Circ: 15,000.

ASPHALT MAGAZIN. *see* GENERAL INTEREST PERIODICALS—Germany

ASSESSING NEW FEDERALISM; issues and options for states. *see* PUBLIC ADMINISTRATION

360 CAN ISSN 1912-3795
ASSISTANCE-EMPLOI. AIDE SOCIALE. Text in French. 2004. a. **Document type:** *Journal, Consumer.*
Published by: Quebec, Ministere de l'Emploi et de la Solidarite Sociale, 425, rue Saint-Amable, RC, Quebec, PQ G1R 4Z1, Canada. TEL 418-643-4721, 888-643-4721, http://www.mess.gouv.qc.ca/index.asp.

ASSOCIATION OF GAY AND LESBIAN PSYCHIATRISTS. NEWSLETTER. *see* HOMOSEXUALITY

360 USA
ASSOCIATION OF GOSPEL RESCUE MISSIONS MEMBERSHIP DIRECTORY & RESOURCE GUIDE. Text in English. biennial. USD 20 (effective 2001). **Document type:** *Directory.* **Description:** Lists member organizations in the association with a breakdown of services provided.
Formerly (until 2000): International Union of Gospel Missions Membership Directory & Resource Guide
Published by: Association of Gospel Rescue Missions, 1045 Swift Ave, Kansas City, MO 64116-4127. TEL 816-471-8020, FAX 816-471-3718, agrm@agrm.org, http://rescuemissions.org. Ed. Stephen E Burger TEL 816-471-8020. R&P Phil Rydman.

360 CAN ISSN 1910-6661
ASSOCIATION QUEBECOISE D'ETABLISSEMENTS DE SANTE ET DE SERVICES SOCIAUX. REPERTOIRE DES ETABLISSEMENTS MEMBRES. Text in French. 2006. a. CAD 36.46 per issue to members; CAD 56.98 per issue to non-members (effective 2006). **Document type:** *Journal, Trade.*
Published by: Association Quebecoise d'Etablissements de Sante et de Services Sociaux, 505, boul. De Maisonneuve Ouest, bureau 400, Montreal, PQ H3A 3C2, Canada. TEL 514-842-4861, http://www.aqesss.qc.ca/fr/accueil.aspx.

362.7 USA ISSN 1941-9376
ATLANTIC REPORTS. Text in English. 2008. irreg., latest 2008. free (effective 2009). back issues avail. **Description:** A resource for organizations around the world, working to make lasting changes in the lives of disadvantaged people.
Related titles: Online - full text ed.: ISSN 1946-1593.
Published by: The Atlantic Philanthropies Inc., 125 Park Ave, 21st Fl, New York, NY 10017. TEL 212-916-7300, FAX 212-922-0360, USA@atlanticphilanthropies.org.

362.7 346.1 649 SWE ISSN 0347-6324
ATT ADOPTERA. Text in Swedish. 1970. bi-m. SEK 225 (effective 1994). adv. bk.rev. **Document type:** *Bulletin.*
Formerly (until 1975): Adoptionscentrum. Rapport
Published by: Adoptionscentrum (AC), Fack 1520, Sundbyberg, 17229, Sweden. TEL 46-8-627-44-00. Ed. Ingert Nilsson. Circ: 10,500.

AUF - INFO. *see* WOMEN'S INTERESTS

AUF - INFO ONLINE. *see* WOMEN'S INTERESTS

360 DEU ISSN 0933-2057
AUFSICHT IN DER SOZIALVERSICHERUNG. Text in German. 1979. base vol. plus a. updates. looseleaf. EUR 49.80 base vol(s).; EUR 47.80 per issue (effective 2009). **Document type:** *Monographic series, Trade.*
Published by: Erich Schmidt Verlag GmbH & Co. (Berlin), Genthiner Str 30 G, Berlin, 10785, Germany. TEL 49-30-2500850, FAX 49-30-250085305, vertrieb@esvmedien.de, http://www.erich-schmidt-verlag.de.

AUGUSTIN. *see* GENERAL INTEREST PERIODICALS—Austria

AUSSCHUSS VOLKSWIRTSCHAFT DES G D V. *see* INSURANCE

360 AUS ISSN 1833-4687
KU1456.A15
AUSTRALIA. DEPARTMENT OF FAMILIES, COMMUNITY SERVICES AND INDIGENOUS AFFAIRS. ANNUAL REPORT. Text in English. 199?. a. **Document type:** *Report, Trade.* **Description:** Provides strategic information about the achievements and policy directions for FaCSIA, the achievements and challenges faced by the department.
Formerly (until 2005): Australia. Department of Family and Community Services. Annual Report (1442-5238)
Related titles: Online - full content ed.
Published by: Australia. Department of Families, Community Services and Indigenous Affairs, GPO Box 7788, Canberra Mail Centre, ACT 2610, Australia. TEL 61-2-62445458, 300-653-227, FAX 61-2-62446589, enquiries@fahcsia.gov.au, http://www.facs.gov.au/internet/facsinternet.nsf.

361.994 AUS ISSN 1833-4415
AUSTRALIA. DEPARTMENT OF FAMILIES, COMMUNITY SERVICES AND INDIGENOUS AFFAIRS. OCCASIONAL PAPER. Text in English. 2001. irreg. free (effective 2008). **Document type:** *Monographic series, Government.* **Description:** Designed to disseminate data and analysis on a range of topics.
Formerly (until 2003): Australia. Department of Family and Community Services. Occasional Paper Series (1444-965X)
Published by: Australia. Department of Families, Community Services and Indigenous Affairs, GPO Box 7788, Canberra Mail Centre, ACT 2610, Australia. TEL 61-2-62445458, 300-653-227, FAX 61-2-62446589, enquiries@fahcsia.gov.au, http://www.facs.gov.au/internet/facsinternet.nsf.

AUSTRALIA. DEPTARTMENT OF PARLIAMENTARY SERVICES. PARLIAMENTARY LIBRARY. RESEARCH PAPER. *see* PUBLIC ADMINISTRATION

362 AUS ISSN 1442-696X
AUSTRALIA. SAFETY, REHABILITATION AND COMPENSATION COMMISSION. ANNUAL REPORT. Abbreviated title: S R C C Annual Report. Text in English. 1992. a. free (effective 2008). back issues avail. **Document type:** *Government.* **Description:** Provides information on the commission's overview, scheme trends and performance.
Former titles: Comcare Australia. Annual Report (1325-1031); Australia. Rehabilitation and Compensation of Commonwealth Employees. Commission for the Safety. Annual Report
Related titles: Online - full text ed.: ISSN 1832-0260. 2002.
Published by: Comcare, GPO Box 9905, Canberra, ACT 2601, Australia. TEL 300-366-979, FAX 61-2-62575634, ohs.help@comcare.gov.au.

AUSTRALIAN AND NEW ZEALAND JOURNAL OF FAMILY THERAPY; innovative and contextual approaches to human problems. *see* SOCIOLOGY

360 AUS ISSN 1326-7124
➤ **AUSTRALIAN COUNCIL OF SOCIAL SERVICE PAPERS.** Abbreviated title: A C O S S Papers. Text in English. 1986. irreg., latest series 13, no. 104. AUD 125 combined subscription domestic includes ACOSS INFO; AUD 160 combined subscription foreign includes ACOSS INFO (effective 2006). charts; stat. back issues avail. **Document type:** *Monographic series, Academic/Scholarly.* **Description:** Cover research & policy papers on contemporary issues in Australian public policy.
Published by: Australian Council of Social Service, Locked Bag 4777, Strawberry Hills, NSW 2012, Australia. TEL 61-2-93106200, FAX 61-2-93104822, acoss@acoss.org.au. Ed. Betty Hounslow. R&P Ian Wilson. Circ: 200.

360 AUS ISSN 0157-6321
HN841
➤ **AUSTRALIAN JOURNAL OF SOCIAL ISSUES.** Text in English. 1961. q. AUD 78.50 to individuals; AUD 112.50 to institutions (effective 2008). adv. bk.rev. abstr.; bibl. cum.index. **Document type:** *Journal, Academic/Scholarly.* **Description:** Provides articles that discuss specific social issues, reviews conceptual problems, presents empirical reports and debates on policy alternatives.
Supersedes in part: A C O S S Quarterly (0045-0391)
Related titles: E-mail ed.: AUD 61.50 to individuals; AUD 94.50 to institutions (effective 2004); Online - full text ed.: AUD 63 to individuals; AUD 97 to institutions (effective 2008).
Indexed: A01, A02, A03, A08, A11, A20, A22, A26, AEI, ASCA, ASG, AusPAIS, CA, CurCont, E08, FamI, G08, GdIns, I05, I07, ILD, P02, P10, P14, P30, P34, P42, P45, P46, P48, P50, P53, P54, PQC, S02, S03, S09, S11, S23, SCOPUS, SOPODA, SSA, SSCI, SWR&A, SociolAb, T02, W07, W09, WBA, WBSS, WMB.
—BLDSC (1812.550000), IE, Infotrieve, Ingenta. **CCC.**
Published by: (A C S P R I Centre for Social Research), Australian Council of Social Service, Locked Bag 4777, Strawberry Hills, NSW 2012, Australia. TEL 61-2-93106200, FAX 61-2-93104822, acoss@acoss.org.au. R&P, Adv. contact Ian Wilson. Circ: 900.

360 AUS ISSN 1325-8362
➤ **AUSTRALIAN JOURNAL ON VOLUNTEERING.** Abbreviated title: A J O V. Text in English. 1996. s-a. AUD 50 combined subscription to non-members (print & online eds.); AUD 70 combined subscription to non-profit organizations (print & online eds.); AUD 85 combined subscription to institutions (print & online eds.); AUD 40 combined subscription to individual members (print & online eds.) (effective 2009). adv. **Document type:** *Journal, Academic/Scholarly.* **Description:** Aims to encourage discussion, debate and research on contemporary issues of importance to volunteering in Australia.
Related titles: Online - full text ed.: ISSN 1836-0246.
Indexed: AusPAIS, CA, N06, S02, S03, SD, SociolAb, T02.
—Ingenta.
Published by: Volunteering Australia, 4th Fl, 247-251 Flinders Ln, Melbourne, VIC 3000, Australia. volaus@volunteeringaustralia.org.

362 AUS ISSN 1832-6390
AUSTRALIAN PEACEKEEPER AND PEACEMAKER. Text in English. 2005. 3/yr. AUD 5.50 newsstand/cover; free to members (effective 2008). adv. back issues avail. **Document type:** *Magazine, Trade.* **Description:** Provide information regarding the APPVA represents, addressing anomalies in the current compensation, rehabilitation and repatriation entitlements.
Related titles: Online - full text ed.: free (effective 2008).
Published by: (Australian Peacekeeper and Peacemaker Veterans' Association Inc.), Classic Printing Pty. Ltd., PO Box 362, Currumbin, QLD 4223, Australia. TEL 300-139-033, FAX 300-139-034, admin@peacekeepersmag.com.au. Ed. James Traill. Pub. Dan Bannister. Adv. contact Dough Walker.

336.249 AUS ISSN 1442-6331
HD7250
AUSTRALIAN SOCIAL POLICY (CANBERRA). Text in English. 1973. a. bk.rev. **Document type:** *Government.*
Former titles (until 1998): Social Security Journal (0726-1195); (until 1981): Australian Department of Social Security. Social Security (0159-6349); (until 1979): Australian Department of Social Security. Social Security Quarterly (0310-544X)
Indexed: A11, AEI, AusPAIS, CA, H05, PAIS, T02.
—Ingenta. **CCC.**
Published by: (Australia. Australian Department of Social Security), AusInfo, Parliament House, Canberra Mc, ACT 2600, Australia. TEL 61-2-6295-4512, FAX 61-2-6295-4455, TELEX AA62013. Ed. Rosemary Lynch. Circ: 10,000. **Orders to:** AusInfo Mail Order Sales, GPO Box 84, Canberra, ACT 2601, Australia. FAX 61-2-6295-4888.

360 AUS ISSN 0312-407X
➤ **AUSTRALIAN SOCIAL WORK.** Text in English. 1947. q. GBP 155 combined subscription in United Kingdom to institutions (print & online eds.); EUR 205, AUD 307, USD 258 combined subscription to institutions (print & online eds.) (effective 2012). adv. bk.rev. charts. index. back issues avail.; reprint service avail. from PSC. **Document type:** *Journal, Academic/Scholarly.* **Description:** Provides access to informed opinion on current social, political, economic and human relations, trends, and issues.
Formerly (until 1971): Australian Journal of Social Work (0004-9565)
Related titles: Online - full text ed.: ISSN 1447-0748. GBP 139 in United Kingdom to institutions; EUR 184, AUD 276, USD 231 to institutions (effective 2012) (from IngentaConnect).
Indexed: A01, A02, A03, A08, A11, A22, AEI, AusPAIS, C06, C07, C08, CA, CINAHL, E01, ESPM, F09, FamI, P03, P34, PAIS, PsycInfo, RiskAb, S02, S03, SCOPUS, SSA, SWR&A, SociolAb, T02.
—BLDSC (1820.600000), IE, Ingenta. **CCC.**
Published by: (Australian Association of Social Workers), Routledge (Subsidiary of: Taylor & Francis Group), Level 2, 11 Queens Rd, Melbourne, VIC 3004, Australia. TEL 61-03-90098134, FAX 61-03-98668822, http://www.informaworld.com. Adv. contact Ingrid Sjolund TEL 61-3-98672152. page AUD 600. Circ: 6,500 (paid). **Subscr. to:** Taylor & Francis Ltd., Journals Customer Service, Sheepen Pl, Colchester, Essex CO3 3LP, United Kingdom. TEL 44-20-70175544, FAX 44-20-70175198.

362 ITA ISSN 0392-2278
AUTONOMIE LOCALI E SERVIZI SOCIALI; vademecum a schede. Text in Italian. 1977. 3/yr. EUR 102 combined subscription domestic to institutions (print & online eds.); EUR 146.50 combined subscription foreign to institutions (print & online eds.) (effective 2009). adv. index. back issues avail. **Document type:** *Journal, Academic/Scholarly.*
Related titles: Online - full text ed.
Indexed: IBR, IBZ.
Published by: Societa Editrice Il Mulino, Strada Maggiore 37, Bologna, 40125, Italy. TEL 39-051-256011, FAX 39-051-256034, riviste@mulino.it. Ed. Michele La Rosa. Adv. contact M Luisa Vezzali. Circ: 4,000.

362.7 GBR ISSN 1461-9105
B A A F NEWS. Text in English. 1979. bi-m. free to members (effective 2010). back issues avail. **Document type:** *Newsletter, Trade.* **Description:** Includes news and information on publications, practice, policy, legislation, training events and seminars.
Former titles (until 1998): Adoption and Fostering News (0966-2103); (until 199?): B A A F News (0260-3888); (until 1981): A B A F A News (0143-2591)
Related titles: Online - full text ed.: free (effective 2010).
Published by: British Association for Adoption & Fostering, Saffron House, 6-10 Kirby St, London, EC1N 8TS, United Kingdom. TEL 44-20-74212600, FAX 44-20-74212601, mail@baaf.org.uk.

362.6 CAN ISSN 1910-6955
B C SENIORS' GUIDE. (British Columbia) Text in English. 1991. irreg. (8th ed.). **Document type:** *Handbook/Manual/Guide, Consumer.*
Formerly (until 2006): Information for Seniors (1189-0177)
Related titles: Online - full text ed.
Published by: British Columbia, Ministry of Community Services. Seniors Division, PO Box 9490, Stn Prov Govt, Victoria, BC V8W 9N7, Canada. TEL 800-465-4911, FAX 250-356-0542, Feedback@gov.bc.ca.

B I S S. (Buerger in Sozialen Schwierigkeiten) *see* GENERAL INTEREST PERIODICALS—Germany

352.4 362.6 GBR
B L E S M A G. Text in English. 1947. 3/yr. free membership. adv. bk.rev. back issues avail. **Document type:** *Magazine, Consumer.* **Description:** Promotes the welfare of those of either sex who have lost a limb or limbs, or one or both eyes as a result of service in any branch of Her Majesty's Forces.
Published by: British Limbless Ex-Servicemen's Association, 185-187 High Rd, Chadwell Heath, Romford, Essex RM6 6NA, United Kingdom. TEL 44-208-5901124, FAX 44-208-5992932, headquarters@blesma.org, http://www.blesma.org/. Circ: 11,000 (controlled).

B M C PALLIATIVE CARE. (BioMed Central) *see* MEDICAL SCIENCES

B.OPEN; supporting one parent families in Ireland. *see* SOCIOLOGY

THE B V A BULLETIN. (Blinded Veterans Association) *see* HANDICAPPED—Visually Impaired

THE BACKCARE JOURNAL. *see* MEDICAL SCIENCES—Orthopedics And Traumatology

362.7 BEL ISSN 1784-3405
BADJE INFO. Text in French. 2002. q.
Formerly (until 2002): Le Badje Bavard (1784-3391)
Published by: Bruxelles Accueil et Developpement pour la Jeunesse et l'Enfance (B A D J E), 22 Rue de Bosnie, Bruxelles, 1060, Belgium. TEL 32-2-2481729, FAX 32-2-2425172, info@badje.be.

361.77 DEU
BAFF. Text in German. 1970. q. bk.rev. **Document type:** *Magazine, Consumer.* **Description:** Contains information about Red Cross youth and youth activities for readers between the ages of 8 and 25.
Published by: Bayerisches Jugendrotkreuz, Volkartstr 83, Munich, 80636, Germany. TEL 49-89-92411342, FAX 49-89-92411210, info@jrk-bayern.de. Ed. Petra Dietz. Circ: 10,000 (controlled).

362 COL ISSN 2011-0588
BALANCE SOCIAL INTERNACIONAL DE SEGURIDAD. Text in Spanish. 2005. a.
Published by: Internacional de Seguridad, Avenida 5C Norte No. 47C-22, Cali, Colombia. TEL 57-800-165463, http://www.internacionaldeseguridad.com/.

BANKING AND COMMUNITY PERSPECTIVES. *see* BUSINESS AND ECONOMICS—Banking And Finance

360 AUT ISSN 0005-5999
BARMHERZIGKEIT; Blaetter fuer die Freunde des Hauses der Barmherzigkeit. Text in German. 1959. q. free. abstr. **Document type:** *Newsletter, Consumer.*
Published by: Institut Haus der Barmherzigkeit, Seeboeckgasse 30a, Vienna, W 1160, Austria. TEL 43-1-401990, FAX 43-1-401991308, info@hausderbarmherzigkeit.at, http://www.hausderbarmherzigkeit.at. Ed. Irene Brandstetter.

362.7 SWE ISSN 1404-8965
BARN; tidningen om barns raettigheter. Text in Swedish. 1942. 6/yr. SEK 200 (effective 2001). adv. **Document type:** *Magazine, Consumer.* **Description:** Children's rights.
Former titles: Barnen & Vi (0345-1305); (until 1962): Raedda Barnen
Related titles: Online - full content ed.
Published by: Raedda Barnens Riksfoerbund, Torsgatan 4, Stockholm, 10788, Sweden. TEL 46-8-698-90-00, FAX 46-8-698-90-14, info@rb.se. Ed. Lisbet Helleberg. Adv. contact Ann-Christin Widinghoff TEL 46-8-37-91-30. B&W page SEK 24,500, color page SEK 28,500; trim 180 x 263. Circ: 115,200 (paid and controlled).

362.7 346.1 SWE ISSN 0282-454X
BARNEN FRAMFOER ALLT/CHILDREN ABOVE ALL. Text in Swedish. 1980. q.
Published by: Barnen Framfoer Allt (BFA), Kronhusgatan 16, Goeteborg, 41105, Sweden. TEL 46-031-13-90-67, FAX 46-031-13-23-45.

362.7 GBR ISSN 1651-0534
➤ **BARNLAEKAREN.** Variant title: Barnlakaren. Text in Swedish. 1993. bi-m. GBP 27 in United Kingdom to institutions; EUR 34 in Europe to institutions; USD 45 in the Americas to institutions; USD 52 elsewhere to institutions (effective 2012). adv. back issues avail. **Document type:** *Journal, Academic/Scholarly.*
Formerly (until 2002): B L F - Nytt (0805-9721)
—BLDSC (1863.712270), IE.
Published by: (Svenska Barnlaekarfoereningen SWE), Wiley-Blackwell Publishing Ltd. (Subsidiary of: John Wiley & Sons, Inc.), 9600 Garsington Rd, Oxford, OX4 2DQ, United Kingdom. TEL 44-1865-776868, FAX 44-1865-714591, customerservices@blackwellpublishing.com, http://www.wiley.com/WileyCDA/. Ed. Goran Wennergren. adv.: B&W page SEK 6,500, color page SEK 12,500; trim 190 x 260.

362.7 332.3 ARG ISSN 1852-4052
BAROMETRO DE LA DEUDA SOCIAL ARGENTINA. Text in Spanish. 2004. a. **Document type:** *Report, Consumer.*
Published by: Universidad Catolica Argentina, Observatorio de la Deuda Social Argentina, Ave Alicia Moreau de Justo, 1500, Edif. San Alberto Magno Piso 4, Ofic. 462, Buenos Aires, Argentina. TEL 54-11-43380615, observatorio_deudasocial@uca.edu.ar, http://www.uca.edu.ar/. Ed. Carola Sanchez Bustamante.

362.7 332.3 ARG ISSN 1852-4176
▼ **BAROMETRO DE LA DEUDA SOCIAL DE LA INFANCIA.** Text in Spanish. 2009. a. back issues avail. **Document type:** *Report, Academic/Scholarly.*
Published by: Universidad Catolica Argentina, Observatorio de la Deuda Social Argentina, Ave Alicia Moreau de Justo, 1500, Edif. San Alberto Magno Piso 4, Ofic. 462, Buenos Aires, Argentina. TEL 54-11-43380615, observatorio_deudasocial@uca.edu.ar, http://www.uca.edu.ar/.

BASIMAN SHELANU/OUR REVIEW. *see* HANDICAPPED—Hearing Impaired

BASIN AND TOWEL. *see* RELIGIONS AND THEOLOGY—Protestant

BEDSIT BRIEFING. *see* REAL ESTATE

360 DEU ISSN 0171-9319
BEGEGNEN UND HELFEN. Text in German. 1912. q. EUR 10; EUR 3 newsstand/cover (effective 2005). adv. bk.rev. index. **Document type:** *Bulletin, Consumer.*
Published by: Verband der Caritas-Konferenzen Deutschlands, Blumenstr 20, Cologne, 50670, Germany. TEL 49-221-131131, FAX 49-221-138953, vinzenz@skmev.de, http://www.vinzenz-gemeinschaft.caritas.de. Ed. Elisabeth Goetz. Adv. contact Ingrid Huefner. Circ: 10,000. **Co-sponsor:** Gemeinschaft der Vinzenzkonferenzen Deutschlands.

▼ **BEHAVIORAL HEALTH AND DEVELOPMENTAL SERVICES LAWS OF VIRGINIA ANNOTATED.** *see* LAW

360 CHN ISSN 1674-0025
BEIJING LAODONG BAOZHANG ZHIYE XUEYUAN XUEBAO. Text in Chinese. 1991. q.
Formerly (until 2007): Beijing Shi Jihua Laodong Guanli Ganbu Xueyuan Xuebao/Beijing College of Management of Plan & Labor. Journal (1008-6684)
Related titles: Online - full text ed.
Published by: Beijing Laodong Baozhang Zhiye Xueyuan/Beijing Vocational College of Labour and Social Security, 5, Huixin Dong Jie, Chaoyang-qu, Beijing, 100029, China. TEL 86-10-64941713, http://www.bvclss.cn/.

360 DEU ISSN 0940-080X
BEITRAEGE ZUR MENTALITAETSGESCHICHTE. Text in German. 1993. irreg., latest vol.2, 1993. price varies. **Document type:** *Monographic series, Academic/Scholarly.*
Published by: Peter Lang GmbH (Subsidiary of: Peter Lang Publishing Group), Eschborner Landstr 42-50, Frankfurt Am Main, 60489, Germany. TEL 49-69-7807050, FAX 49-69-78070550, zentrale.frankfurt@peterlang.com.

349.3 DEU ISSN 0175-5994
BEITRAEGE ZUR SOZIALPOLITIK UND ZUM SOZIALRECHT. Text in German. 1982. irreg., latest vol.38, 2009. price varies. **Document type:** *Monographic series, Academic/Scholarly.*
Published by: Erich Schmidt Verlag GmbH & Co. (Berlin), Genthiner Str 30 G, Berlin, 10785, Germany. TEL 49-30-2500850, FAX 49-30-250085305, vertrieb@esvmedien.de.

BEKNOPT OVERZICHT VAN DE SOCIALE ZEKERHEID IN BELGIE/SURVEY OF SOCIAL SECURITY IN BELGIUM. *see* PUBLIC ADMINISTRATION

DE BELGISCH TIJDSCHRIFT VOOR SOCIALE ZEKERHEID/BELGIAN SOCIAL SECURITY JOURNAL. *see* PUBLIC ADMINISTRATION

BELGIUM. FEDERAAL MINISTERIE VAN SOCIALE ZAKEN, VOLKSGEZONDHEID EN LEEFMILIEU. ALGEMEEN VERSLAG OVER DE SOCIALE ZEKERHEID. *see* PUBLIC ADMINISTRATION

BELGIUM. FEDERAAL MINISTERIE VAN SOCIALE ZAKEN, VOLKSGEZONDHEID EN LEEFMILIEU. HANIDGIDS/GUIDE OF THE DISABLED PERSON. *see* HANDICAPPED

BELGIUM. FEDERAAL MINISTERIE VAN SOCIALE ZAKEN, VOLKSGEZONDHEID EN LEEFMILIEU. TEGEMOETKOMINGEN AAN GEHANDICAPTEN/BENEFITS FOR THE DISABLED. *see* HANDICAPPED

BELGIUM. MINISTERE FEDERAL DES AFFAIRES SOCIALES, DE LA SANTE PUBLIQUE ET DE L'ENVIRONNEMENT. RAPPORT GENERAL SUR LA SECURITE SOCIALE. *see* INSURANCE

360 NGA
BENDEL STATE. MINISTRY OF INFORMATION, SOCIAL DEVELOPMENT AND SPORTS. ESTIMATE. Text in English. a. NGN 5. **Document type:** *Government.*
Formerly: Bendel State. Ministry of Home Affairs and Information. Mid-Western State Estimates
Published by: Ministry of Information Social Development and Sports, PMB 1099, Benin City, Bendel, Nigeria. **Orders to:** Bendel State Government Printer, Government Press, Benin City, Bendel, Nigeria.

361.73 USA ISSN 2155-787X
▼ **BENEFIT AUCTION IDEAS.** Text in English. 2009. bi-w. free (effective 2010). **Document type:** *Magazine, Consumer.* **Description:** Includes how-to articles and tips for organizations to plan benefit auctions.
Formerly (until 2009): Red Apple Auctions E-Zine
Media: Online - full text.
Published by: Red Apple Auctions, PO Box 3602, Alexandria, VA 22302. TEL 888-474-0838, info@redappleauctions.com .

BENEFIT MAGAZINE. *see* LIFESTYLE

361.3 158 GBR ISSN 0268-2621
RC455.4.L67
➤ **BEREAVEMENT CARE**; an international journal for those who help bereaved people. Text in English. 1982. 3/yr. GBP 138 combined subscription in United Kingdom to institutions (print & online eds.); EUR 222, USD 279 combined subscription to institutions (print & online eds.) (effective 2012). adv. bk.rev.; music rev.; Website rev. abstr.; charts; illus. index. 16 p./no.; back issues avail.; reprint service avail. from PSC. **Document type:** *Journal, Academic/Scholarly.* **Description:** Contains articles of importance to those who help bereaved persons, including counsellors, psychotherapists, psychologists, social workers, the clergy, funeral directors, doctors, and nurses.
Related titles: Online - full text ed.: ISSN 1944-8279. GBP 125 in United Kingdom to institutions; EUR 200, USD 251 to institutions (effective 2012).
Indexed: A22, AMED, B28, C06, C07, C08, CINAHL, E-psyche, P30, P48, PQC.
—BLDSC (1893.880000), IE, Ingenta. **CCC.**
Published by: (Cruse Bereavement Care), Routledge (Subsidiary of: Taylor & Francis Group), 4 Park Sq, Milton Park, Abingdon, Oxon OX14 4RN, United Kingdom. info@routledge.co.uk, http://www.routledge.com.

360 DEU ISSN 1612-3530
BERLINER RATGEBER ZUR AUSLANDSTAETIGKEIT. Text in German. 2003. irreg. price varies. **Document type:** *Monographic series, Academic/Scholarly.*
Published by: Weissensee Verlag e.K., Simplonstr 59, Berlin, 10245, Germany. TEL 49-30-29049192, FAX 49-30-27574315, mail@weissensee-verlag.de.

362 USA ISSN 1933-4915
LB2824
BERNARD & AUDRE RAPOPORT FOUNDATION. ANNUAL REPORT. Text in English. 1990. a. **Document type:** *Report, Consumer.*
Media: Online - full text.
Published by: The Bernard & Audre Rapoport Foundation, 5400 Bosque Blvd., Ste 245, Waco, TX 76710. TEL 254-741-0510, FAX 254-741-0092, rapoport@rapoportfdn.org, http://www.rapoportfdn.org/index.php.

362.7 DEU
BERUFSAUSBILDUNG JUGENDARBEITSLOSIGKEIT. Text in German. 1976. m. **Document type:** *Bulletin, Trade.*
Published by: U. Kurz Verlag, Korallenweg 10, Stuttgart, 70619, Germany. TEL 49-711-442076, FAX 49-711-445644, heinzkurzverlag@t-online.de. Ed. Heinz Kurz. Circ: 450.

360 USA ISSN 1553-5703
HD6050
BEST FOR WOMEN. Text in English. 1921. q. USD 11 in US & Canada; USD 15 elsewhere; free to members (effective 2005). adv. bk.rev. illus. index. reprints avail. **Document type:** *Magazine, Consumer.* **Description:** Includes feature stories pertaining to women's issues, Soroptimist programs, and updates on the organizations efforts and accomplishments.
Formerly (until 2004): Soroptimist of the Americas (0097-9562)
Published by: Soroptimist International of the Americas, 1709 Spruce St, Philadelphia, PA 19103-6103. TEL 219-893-9000, FAX 219-893-9200. Ed., R&P Darlene Friedman. Circ: 30,820 (paid and free).

BETREUUNGSMANAGEMENT. *see* LAW—Legal Aid

S

BETREUUNGSRECHTLICHE PRAXIS; Zeitschrift fuer Sozialarbeit, gutachterliche Taetigkeit und Rechtsanwendung in der Betreuung. *see* LAW—Legal Aid

362.6 CAN ISSN 1718-7435
BEYOND 50 MAGAZINE. Text in English. 2006. q. free (effective 2007). adv. **Document type:** *Magazine, Consumer.*
Published by: Laurel D'Andrea, 1850 Ranchmont Crescent, Kelowna, BC V1V 1T4, Canada. FAX 250-869-1490, letters@beyond50mag.com, http://www.beyond50mag.com/index.cfm. Ed. Jeremy Hoemsen. Pub. Laurel D'Andrea.

362.7 CAN ISSN 1910-7234
BEYOND BORDERS NEWSLETTER. Text in English. 2002. s-a. **Document type:** *Newsletter, Consumer.*
Published by: Beyond Borders, 387 Broadway Ave., Winnipeg, MB R3C 0V5, Canada. TEL 204-284-6862, FAX 204-452-1333, rprober@beyondborders.org, http://www.beyondborders.org/index.shtml.

BIBLIOTECA DE EDUCACION. PEDAGOGIA SOCIAL Y TRABAJO SOCIAL. *see* EDUCATION

362.609 610.7365 FRA ISSN 1959-0601
BIEN VIEILLIR EN COTE D'OR. Text in French. 2002. s-a. free. **Document type:** *Bulletin, Consumer.*
Formerly (until 2006): Comite Departemental des Retraites et Personnes Agees. Bulletin (1775-7959)
Published by: Comite Departementale des Retraites et Personnes Agees de la Cote d'Or, 3 rue Jean-Renoir, Dijon, 21000, France.

BIG ISSUE. *see* GENERAL INTEREST PERIODICALS—Great Britain

362 NLD ISSN 2211-1778
DE BIJSTAND IN PRAKTIJK. Text in Dutch. 2007. a. EUR 53.10 (effective 2010).
Published by: Kluwer B.V. (Subsidiary of: Wolters Kluwer N.V.), Postbus 23, Deventer, 7400 GA, Netherlands. TEL 31-570-673449, FAX 31-570-691555, info@kluwer.nl, http://www.kluwer.nl.

360 DEU ISSN 0340-8574
BLAETTER DER WOHLFAHRTSPFLEGE; Deutsche Zeitschrift fuer Sozialarbeit. Text in German. 1848. bi-m. EUR 70 (effective 2011). adv. bk.rev. bibl. index. 44 p./no. 3 cols./p.; back issues avail. **Document type:** *Magazine, Trade.*
Indexed: DIP, IBR, IBZ.
Published by: (Baden-Wuerttemberg. Wohlfahrtswerk fuer Baden-Wuerttemberg), Nomos Verlagsgesellschaft mbH und Co. KG, Waldseestr 3-5, Baden-Baden, 76530, Germany. TEL 49-7221-21040, FAX 49-7221-210427, nomos@nomos.de, http://www.nomos.de. Ed. Gerhard Pfannendoerfer. Adv. contact Bettina Roos. Circ: 3,600 (paid and controlled).

360 AUT
BLAULICHT. Text in German. q.
Address: Pillergasse 24, Vienna, W 1150, Austria. TEL 01-89145. Circ: 52,000.

362.4 DEU ISSN 1614-2772
BLICKKONTAKT; Magazin der Christoffel-Blindenmission. Text in German. 1911. q. free (effective 2009). 12 p./no.; **Document type:** *Magazine, Consumer.* **Description:** Covers Christian missionary work and medical aid to the blind, the handicapped, and the hungry in Third World countries.
Former titles (until 2001): Lichtblicke (1615-1070); (until 1999): Weltweiten Christlichen Behindertendiakonie. Projekt-Berichte; (until 1997): Weltweiten Christlichen Behindertendiakonie. Berichte (0944-3118); Weltweiten Christlichen Armendiakonie. Bericht (0723-1539); (until 1979): Weltweiten Christlichen Behindertenhilfe. Bericht (0723-1512); Weltweiten Dienst Christlicher Blindennothilfe. Bericht (0723-1490); Evangelische Missionsarbeit an Blinden und Augenkranken in Asien und Afrika. Bericht (0723-1482); Evangelische Missionsarbeit an den Blinden in Asien und Afrika. Bericht (0723-1474); Evangelische Missionsarbeit an den Blinden Irans. Bericht (0723-1466); Christoffel-Blindenmission. Bericht (0009-580X)
Published by: Christoffel-Blindenmission e.V., Nibelungenstr 124, Bensheim, 64625, Germany. TEL 49-6251-1310, FAX 49-6251-131122, info@cbm.de, http://www.christoffel-blindenmission.de. Ed. Ulrike Loos. Circ: 400,000 (controlled).

BLINDESAGEN. *see* HANDICAPPED—Visually Impaired

362.1 NOR ISSN 1503-2728
BLOEDER-NYTT. Text in Norwegian. 1980. q. NOK 200 to individual members; NOK 300 to institutional members (effective 2011). **Document type:** *Newsletter, Consumer.*
Published by: Foreningen for Bloedere i Norge/Norwegian Hemophilia Society, c/o Turid Nymoen, Turubakken 6, Nesoddtangen, 1450, Norway. TEL 47-66-914637, fbin@fbin.no.

362.82 NZL ISSN 1177-3952
BLUE SKIES REPORT. Text in English. 2006. irreg. free (effective 2007). **Document type:** *Monographic series.* **Description:** Offered to researchers to examine contemporary and emerging family issues.
Related titles: Online - full text ed.: ISSN 1177-8261.
Published by: Families Commission, Level 6, Public Trust Bldg, 117-125 Lambton Quay, PO Box 2839, Wellington, New Zealand. TEL 64-4-9177040, FAX 64-4-9177059, enquiries@nzfamilies.org.nz.

BOARD MEMBER; the periodical for members of the National Center for Nonprofit Boards. *see* BUSINESS AND ECONOMICS—Management

362 JPN ISSN 0915-8634
BOBASU JANARU/JAPAN BOBATH ASSOCIATION. JOURNAL. Text in Japanese. s-a. JPY 4,000. **Document type:** *Academic/Scholarly.*
Formerly (until 1988): Nihon Bobath Kenkyukai Nyusu
Published by: Nihon Bobasu Kenkyukai/Japan Bobath Association, 6-5 Higashi-Naka-Hama 1-chome, Joto-ku, Osaka-shi, 536-0023, Japan. TEL 06-962-3131, FAX 06-963-2233. Ed. Masamichi Furusawa.

▼ **BOCHUMER STUDIEN ZUM STIFTUNGSWESEN.** *see* LAW—Corporate Law

361 362.1 KOR ISSN 1226-3648
BO'GEON BOGJI PO'REOM/HEALTH AND WELFARE POLICY FORUM. Text in Korean. 1996. m. membership. **Document type:** *Journal, Academic/Scholarly.*
Published by: Korea Institute for Health and Social Affairs/Hangug Bogeon Sahoe Yeonguweon, San 42-14 Bulgwang-Dong, Eunpyung-Ku, Seoul, 122-705, Korea, S. TEL 82-2-3808000, FAX 82-2-3529129, library@kihusa.re.kr, http://www.kihusa.re.kr.

304.6 KOR ISSN 1226-072X
HB3652.5.A3
➤ **BOGEON SAHOE YEONGU/HEALTH AND SOCIAL WELFARE REVIEW.** Text in English, Korean. 1981. s-a. membership. 200 p./no.; **Document type:** *Journal, Academic/Scholarly.*
Former titles (until 1995): Bogeon Sahoe Nonjib/Journal of Population, Health and Social Welfare (1226-0282); (until 1989): In-gu Bo-geon Nonjib/Journal of Population and Health Studies (0259-9112)
Indexed: ExtraMED, P30, PopulInd, SCOPUS.
Published by: Korea Institute for Health and Social Affairs/Hangug Bogeon Sahoe Yeonguweon, San 42-14 Bulgwang-Dong, Eunpyung-Ku, Seoul, 122-705, Korea, S. TEL 82-2-3808000, FAX 82-2-3529129, library@kihusa.re.kr, http://www.kihusa.re.kr. Ed. Hyun Ae Ahn. Circ: 500.

362.1 COL ISSN 2011-3870
BOLETIN INFORMATIVO GOBERNAR. Text in Spanish. 2008. m. **Document type:** *Bulletin, Consumer.*
Published by: Corporacion Colombiana de Secretarios Municipales y Distritales de Salud, Calle 32 No. 13-32, Torre 1 Ofic. 207, Parque Residencial Baviera, Bogota, Colombia. TEL 57-1-2324775, FAX 57-1-2875798, cosesam@cable.net.co, http://www.cosesam.org.co/.

BORDER CONNECTIONS. *see* BUSINESS AND ECONOMICS—International Development And Assistance

362.7 USA
BOYS TOWN JOURNAL. Text in English. 1976. 4/yr. free voluntary donation (effective 2009). illus. back issues avail. **Document type:** *Journal, Consumer.* **Description:** Aims to spread the message of hope and healing for the families of America.
Former titles: Girls and Boys Town Journal; (until 2004): Boys Town Journal; (until 1998): Boys Town Quarterly (0889-6828); Which supersedes: Boys Town Times
Related titles: Microform ed.: (from PQC); Online - full text ed.: free (effective 2009).
—CCC.
Published by: Boys Town, 14100 Crawford St, Boys Town, NE 68010. TEL 402-498-1300, 800-217-3700, FAX 402-498-1348.

BRAILLE MONITOR; voice of the nation's blind. *see* HANDICAPPED—Visually Impaired

BRAILLE SPORTING RECORD. *see* HANDICAPPED—Visually Impaired

361.6 BRA
BRASILIA. FUNDACAO DO SERVICO SOCIAL DO DISTRITO FEDERAL. RELATORIO ANUAL DAS ATIVIDADES. Text in Portuguese. a.
Published by: Fundacao do Servico Social do Distrito Federal, Brasilia, DF, Brazil.

360 BRA
BRAZIL. SERVICO SOCIAL DO COMERCIO. ADMINISTRACAO REGIONAL NO ESTADO DE SAO PAULO. RELATORIO ANUAL. Text in Portuguese. 1946. a. free. charts. **Document type:** *Corporate.*
Published by: Servico Social do Comercio, Administracao Regional no Estado de Sao Paulo, Ave. PAULISTA, 119, Centro, Caixa Postal 6643, Sao Paulo, SP 01064-970, Brazil. TEL 55-11-2842111, FAX 55-11-2886206, TELEX 1123423. Ed. Abram Szajman. Circ: 2,000.

362.8 USA ISSN 1045-1005
BREAD FOR THE WORLD NEWSLETTER. Variant title: Bread Newsletter. Text in English. 1989. 8/yr. free to members (effective 2010). back issues avail. **Document type:** *Newsletter, Consumer.* **Description:** Covers issues and legislation that affects hungry and poor people.
Formed by the merger of (1986-1989): Action Alert; (1986-1989): Bread; Both of which superseded (in 1986): Bread for the World (0198-6511)
Related titles: Online - full text ed.: free (effective 2010).
Published by: Bread for the World Institute, 50 F St, NW, Ste 500, Washington, DC 20001. TEL 202-639-9400, FAX 202-639-9401, bread@bread.org.

361 BWA ISSN 1017-6233
LA1600
BRIGADES BOPANG BOTSWANA. Text in English. 1978. q. free. **Document type:** *Newsletter, Government.* **Description:** Covers news of the brigades, Vocational Training Centres, and organizations involved in training for production and commercial services, community development, and extension work primarily in rural areas.
Published by: Department of Vocational Education and Training, Ministry of Education, Private Bag 0062, Gaborone, Botswana. TEL 267-352589, FAX 267-313191. Ed. Angela Schaeken. Circ: 4,000.

362.7 AUS ISSN 1834-8335
BRIGHTER FUTURES. Text in English. 2004. m. free (effective 2009). back issues avail. **Document type:** *Magazine, Trade.* **Description:** Contains the latest news about the services, programs, policies and initiatives of Queensland's lead child protection agency.
Formerly (until 2007): Building Blocks (1832-2387)
Related titles: Online - full text ed.
Published by: Queensland, Department of Child Safety, Corporate Communications Branch, GPO Box 806, Brisbane, QLD 4000, Australia. TEL 61-7-32248045, 800-811-810, FAX 61-7-34043570, info@childsafety.qld.gov.au.

361.30941 GBR
BRITISH ASSOCIATION OF SOCIAL WORKERS. ANNUAL REPORT AND FINANCIAL STATEMENTS. Text in English. 1970. a. free. adv. bk.rev. bibl.; tr.lit. **Document type:** *Corporate.*
Former titles (until 2008): British Association of Social Workers. Annual Report; (until 198?): British Association of Social Workers. Annual Report and Statement of Accounts
—BLDSC (1502.980280).
Published by: British Association of Social Workers, 16 Kent St, Birmingham, B5 6RD, United Kingdom. Circ: 14,000.

BRITISH COLUMBIA ALLIANCE CONCERNED WITH EARLY PREGNANCY AND PARENTHOOD. NEWSLETTER. *see* BIRTH CONTROL

361 GBR ISSN 0045-3102
HV1 CODEN: BJSWAS
➤ **THE BRITISH JOURNAL OF SOCIAL WORK.** Text in English. 1971. 8/yr. GBP 538 in United Kingdom to institutions; EUR 807 in Europe to institutions; USD 1,077 in US & Canada to institutions; GBP 538 elsewhere to institutions; GBP 587 combined subscription in United Kingdom to institutions (print & online eds.); EUR 881 combined subscription in Europe to institutions (print & online eds.); USD 1,175 combined subscription in US & Canada to institutions (print & online eds.); GBP 587 combined subscription elsewhere to institutions (print & online eds.) (effective 2012). adv. bk.rev. abstr.; illus. 148 p./no.; back issues avail.; reprint service avail. from PSC. **Document type:** *Journal, Academic/Scholarly.* **Description:** Publishes papers on the research and practice of every aspect of social work. Examines its principles and theories.
Formed by the merger of (1947-1970): British Journal of Psychiatric Social Work; (1939-1970): Social Work
Related titles: Microform ed.: (from PQC); Online - full text ed.: ISSN 1468-263X. 2000. GBP 489 in United Kingdom to institutions; EUR 734 in Europe to institutions; USD 979 in US & Canada to institutions; GBP 489 elsewhere to institutions (effective 2012) (from IngentaConnect).
Indexed: A20, A22, A26, AHCMS, AMHA, ASCA, ASG, B28, C06, C07, C08, C28, CA, CINAHL, CurCont, DIP, E-psyche, E01, E08, ERA, ESPM, F09, FamI, G08, H12, HRA, I05, IBR, IBSS, IBZ, MEA&I, P03, P10, P24, P25, P30, P46, P48, P50, P53, P54, PAIS, PCI, PQC, PsycInfo, PsycholAb, RiskAb, S02, S03, S09, S11, SCOPUS, SFSA, SOPODA, SSA, SSCI, SWR&A, SociolAb, T02, V&AA, W07, W09.
—BLDSC (2324.790000), IE, Infotrieve, Ingenta. **CCC.**
Published by: (British Association of Social Workers), Oxford University Press, Great Clarendon St, Oxford, OX2 6DP, United Kingdom. TEL 44-1865-556767, FAX 44-1865-556646, enquiry@oup.co.uk, http://www.oxfordjournals.org. Eds. Eric Blyth, Helen Masson. Adv. contact Linda Hann TEL 44-1344-779945.

➤ **BRITISH JOURNAL OF VISUAL IMPAIRMENT.** *see* HANDICAPPED—Visually Impaired

➤ **BRITISH POLIO FELLOWSHIP. BULLETIN.** *see* MEDICAL SCIENCES—Psychiatry And Neurology

362.5 AUS ISSN 1320-8632
BROTHERHOOD COMMENT; a newsletter of social policy and research. Text in English. 1991. 3/yr. AUD 20 to individuals; AUD 33 to institutions; AUD 5 to the unemployed (effective 2008). back issues avail. **Document type:** *Newsletter.*
Related titles: Online - full text ed.
Published by: Brotherhood of St. Laurence, 67 Brunswick St, Fitzroy, VIC 3065, Australia. TEL 61-3-94831183, FAX 61-3-94172691, info@bsl.org.au. Eds. Don Sieman, Mas Generis.

BROWN UNIVERSITY CHILD AND ADOLESCENT BEHAVIOR LETTER. *see* CHILDREN AND YOUTH—About

361.7 USA ISSN 2155-3262
TD370
HOWARD G. BUFFETT FOUNDATION. ANNUAL REPORT. Text in English. 199?. a. **Document type:** *Report, Trade.*
Published by: Howard G. Buffett Foundation, 158 W Prairie Ave, Ste 107, Decatur, IL 62523. TEL 217-423-9286.

362.5 AUS
BUILDING BETTER LIVES; a newsletter for our valued friends and supporters. Text in English. 1944. q. donation. bk.rev. back issues avail. **Document type:** *Newsletter.* **Description:** Publishes articles on the services of the Brotherhood and on advocacy of the disadvantaged.
Former titles (until 1989): Action (Fitzroy) (0300-4678); (until 1982): Brotherhood Action; (until 1969): Brotherhood News; (until 1963): B S L Notes; (until 1944): B S L Quarterly Notes
Related titles: Online - full content ed.
Published by: Brotherhood of St. Laurence, 67 Brunswick St, Fitzroy, VIC 3065, Australia. TEL 61-3-94831183, FAX 61-3-94172691, info@bsl.org.au. Ed. Dianne Clark. Circ: 42,000.

BUILDING BLOCKS. *see* CHILDREN AND YOUTH—About

362.7 FRA ISSN 1961-3636
LE BULLETIN DE LA PROTECTION DE L'ENFANCE. Text in French. 2007. m. (10/yr). EUR 39 to individuals; EUR 60 to institutions (effective 2008). **Document type:** *Bulletin, Trade.*
Published by: L' Action Sociale, 13 Bd. Saint Michel, Paris, 75005, France. TEL 33-1-53102410, FAX 33-1-53102412, http://www.lejas.com.

362 NLD ISSN 1871-8205
BULLETIN WERK EN DAGBESTEDING. Text in Dutch. 2005. bi-m. EUR 147, USD 220 to institutions (effective 2009).
Published by: Bohn Stafleu van Loghum B.V. (Subsidiary of: Springer Science+Business Media), Postbus 246, Houten, 3990 GA, Netherlands. TEL 31-30-6383872, FAX 31-30-6383991, boekhandels@bsl.nl, http://www.bsl.nl. Eds. Ernst Merhottein, Jacqueline Kremer.

BURN SUPPORT NEWS. *see* MEDICAL SCIENCES—Orthopedics And Traumatology

362 ESP ISSN 1988-7639
BUTLLETI DE LA DEPENDENCIA. Text in Catalan. 2007. irreg.
Media: Online - full text.
Published by: Generalitat de Catalunya, Departament de Accio Social i Ciutadania, Placa Pau Vila, 1, Barcelona, 08039, Spain. TEL 34-93-4831000, FAX 34-93-4831011.

361.73 USA
BY THE WAY. Text in English. 1994. q. free. **Document type:** *Newsletter.* **Description:** Reports on the social welfare agencies funded by this United Way chapter. Also contains Morris County, NJ, news about health and welfare.
Published by: United Way of Morris County, PO Box 1948, Morristown, NJ 07962-1948. TEL 973-993-1160. Ed., Pub. Tiffany Haworth.

C A E P R NEWS. (Centre for Aboriginal Economic Policy Research) *see* BUSINESS AND ECONOMICS

360 GBR ISSN 1350-9160
C A I P E BULLETIN. Text in English. 1990. 3/yr. free to members (effective 2009). **Document type:** *Bulletin, Trade.* **Description:** Contains articles about Centre for the Advancement of Interprofessional Education.
Related titles: Online - full text ed.: free (effective 2009).

—CCC.
Published by: Centre for the Advancement of Interprofessional Education, c/o Health Sciences and Practice Subject Ctr, Higher Education Academy, 3-12 Waterloo Bridge Wing, Franklin Wilkins Bldg, King's College, 150 Stamford St, London, SE1 9NH, United Kingdom. admin@caipe.org.uk, http://www.caipe.org.uk. Eds. Lesley Hughes, Siobhan Ni-Mhaolrunaigh.

361 CAN ISSN 1488-0296
HV101
C A S W BULLETIN. Text in English. 1932. s-a. free to members. adv. bk.rev. back issues avail. **Document type:** *Bulletin, Trade.*
Description: Keeps social workers informed of initiatives and activities of the CASW.
Supersedes in part (in 1999): Social Worker - Travailleur Social (0037-8089)
Related titles: Online - full text ed.; French ed.
—IE, Ingenta.
Published by: (Canadian Association of Social Workers), Myropen Publications Ltd., 383 Parkdale Ave, Ste 402, Ottawa, ON K1Y 4R4, Canada. Ed. Eugenia Repetur Moreno. Circ: 15,000.

360 AUS ISSN 1835-8454
C B E R S NETWORK. (Christian Brothers Ex-Residents and Students) Text in English. 1997. s-a. free (effective 2008). back issues avail. **Document type:** *Newsletter, Consumer.*
Formerly (until 2006): C B E R S Ex-press (1449-6992)
Related titles: Online - full text ed.: free (effective 2008).
Published by: C - B E R S Consultancy, 24 High St, Fremantle, W.A. 6160, Australia. TEL 61-8-94333644, FAX 61-8-93824114, welcome@cberss.org. Ed. Dr. Philippa White.

362.5 DEU ISSN 1615-1054
C B M FREUNDESBRIEF. Text in German. 1961. bi-m. free (effective 2009). **Document type:** *Bulletin, Consumer.*
Published by: Christoffel-Blindenmission e.V., Nibelungenstr 124, Bensheim, 64625, Germany. TEL 49-6251-1310, FAX 49-6251-131122, info@cbm.de. Circ: 500,000. **U.S. subscr. to:** Christian Blind Mission International Inc., 450 E Park Ave, Greenville, SC 29601. TEL 800-937-2264, info@cbmi-usa.org, AEskew@cbmi-usa.org, http://www.cbmi-usa.org.

361.7 CAN ISSN 0838-6803
C C C C BULLETIN. Text in English. 1984. irreg. (5-7/yr.). CAD 40 (effective 2006). adv. **Description:** Provides updates on legislative developments and information on services helpful to charities and churches.
Formerly (until 1987): Canadian Council of Christian Charities. Bulletin (0831-3164)
Published by: Canadian Council of Christian Charities, 1-21 Howard Ave, Elmira, ON N3B 2C9, Canada. TEL 519-669-5137, FAX 519-669-3291, mail@cccc.org, http://www.cccc.org.

C E N S I S NOTE E COMMENTI. *see* SOCIOLOGY

C I R I E C ESPANA; revista de economia publica, social y cooperativa. (Centro Internacional de Investigacion e Informacion sobre la Economia Publica, Social y Cooperativa) *see* BUSINESS AND ECONOMICS—Economic Situation And Conditions

362.609 FRA ISSN 1953-6828
C O D E R P A 59. (Comite Departemental des Retraites et Personnes Agees) Text in French. 1999. irreg. EUR 2 per issue (effective 2006). **Document type:** *Bulletin, Consumer.*
Former titles (until 2006): C O D E R P A du Nord (1774-9840); (until 2004): C O D E R P A Bulletin Trimestriel (1296-0179)
Published by: Comite Departemental des Retraites et Personnes Agees, 13 rue Faidherbe, B.P. 223, Lille, 59002 Cedex, France.

362.5 NZL ISSN 1177-4339
C P A G WORKING PAPER. Text in English. 2005. irreg. **Document type:** *Monographic series.*
Published by: Child Poverty Action Group, Dominion Rd, PO Box 56 150, Auckland, New Zealand. TEL 64-9-3039260.

362.4 336.2 363.5 GBR
C P A G'S HOUSING BENEFIT AND COUNCIL TAX BENEFIT LEGISLATION (YEAR). Text in English. 1988. latest 22th ed., base vol. plus a. updates. GBP 99 base vol(s). (effective 2010); subscr. includes Supplement. back issues avail. **Document type:** *Handbook/ Manual/Guide, Trade.* **Description:** Covers housing benefit and council tax benefit legislation as it applies in England, Wales and Scotland.
Published by: Child Poverty Action Group, 94 White Lion St, London, N1 9PF, United Kingdom. TEL 44-20-78377979, FAX 44-20-78376414, info@cpag.org.uk. Eds. C George, R Poynter, S Wright.

C T A JOURNAL. *see* TRANSPORTATION

C U B COMMUNICATOR. ADOPTION NEWSLETTER. *see* SOCIOLOGY

CAHIERS ALBERT SCHWEITZER. *see* PHILOSOPHY

LES CAHIERS DU SOCIAL. *see* POPULATION STUDIES

362.7 342 FRA ISSN 1276-3780
LES CAHIERS DYNAMIQUES. Text in French. 1995. q. EUR 40 domestic to individuals; EUR 60 foreign to individuals; EUR 50 domestic to institutions (effective 2011). back issues avail. **Document type:** *Journal, Academic/Scholarly.*
Related titles: Online - full text ed.: ISSN 2109-9545.
Published by: (Ecole nationale de protection judiciaire de la jeunesse (ENPJJ)), Editions Eres, 33 Av. Marcel Dassault, Toulouse, 31500, France. eres@edition-eres.com, http://www.edition-eres.com. Ed. Dominique Youf.

362.5 NLD ISSN 2211-2774
CALCUTTA RESCUE NEDERLAND. NIEUWSBRIEF. Text in Dutch. 1990. s-a. **Document type:** *Newsletter, Consumer.*
Published by: Calcutta Rescue Nederland, Frans Halslaan 34, Oegstgeest, 2443 EJ, Netherlands. TEL 31-71-5173432, FAX 31-84-7354502, info@calcuttarescue.nl.

CALIFORNIA FAMILY LAW MONTHLY. *see* LAW—Family And Matrimonial Law

360 USA
CALIFORNIA STATE PLAN FOR REHABILITATION FACILITIES. Text in English. a. free (effective 2008). **Document type:** *Government.*
Published by: Health and Welfare Agency, Department of Rehabilitation, PO Box 944222, Sacramento, CA 94244-2220. TEL 916-324-1313, publicaffairs@dor.ca.gov.

362 GBR
CAMBRIDGESHIRE COUNTY COUNCIL. SOCIAL SERVICES DEPARTMENT. CAMBRIDGESHIRE COMMUNITY CARE PLAN. Text in English. 1992. a., latest 2005. charts. back issues avail. **Document type:** *Government.* **Description:** Covers common objectives among social agencies in Cambridgeshire to address the needs of the county's most vulnerable citizens.
Related titles: Online - full content ed.
Published by: Cambridgeshire County Council. Social Care and Health Department, CC1313 Castle Ct, Castle Hill, Cambridge, CB3 0AP, United Kingdom. TEL 44-345-0455201, http://www.cambridgeshire.gov.uk/social.

362.7 351 GBR
CAMBRIDGESHIRE COUNTY COUNCIL. SOCIAL SERVICES DEPARTMENT. CHILDREN'S SERVICES PLAN. Text in English. 1993. triennial, latest 2001. charts. **Document type:** *Government.* **Description:** Covers child welfare social services in Cambridgeshire for the ensuing three years.
Related titles: Online - full text ed.
Published by: Cambridgeshire County Council. Social Care and Health Department, CC1313 Castle Ct, Castle Hill, Cambridge, CB3 0AP, United Kingdom. TEL 44-345-0455201, http://www.cambridgeshire.gov.uk/social.

362 GBR
CAMBRIDGESHIRE COUNTY COUNCIL. SOCIAL SERVICES DEPARTMENT. SOCIAL SERVICES SERVICE PLAN. Text in English. 19??. biennial, latest 2003. charts. back issues avail. **Document type:** *Government.* **Description:** Covers forth the challenges the Cambridgeshire County Council faces and sets priorities for acting on them.
Published by: Cambridgeshire County Council. Social Care and Health Department, CC1313 Castle Ct, Castle Hill, Cambridge, CB3 0AP, United Kingdom. TEL 44-345-0455201, http://www.cambridgeshire.gov.uk/social.

362.0965 GBR ISSN 1749-5466
CAMPAIGN NEWS (ONLINE); fighting skin disease. Text in English. 2002. q. free. **Document type:** *Newsletter, Trade.*
Media: Online - full text.
Published by: Skin Care Campaign (Subsidiary of: National Eczema Society), Hill House, Highgate Hill, London, N19 5NA, United Kingdom. Ed. Claire Moulds.

360 351 CAN ISSN 1912-5143
UB359.C2
CANADA. HOUSE OF COMMONS. STANDING COMMITTEE ON VETERANS AFFAIRS. MINUTES OF PROCEEDINGS. Text in English. 1989. irreg. **Document type:** *Government.*
Supersedes in part (in 2006): Standing Committee on National Defence and Veterans Affairs. Minutes of Proceedings (1204-5179); Which was formerly (until 1995): Standing Committee on National Defence and Veterans Affairs. Minutes of Proceedings and Evidence (0846-4928); Which was formed by the merger of (1986-1988): Standing Committee on National Defence. Minutes of Proceedings and Evidence (0846-4936); (195?-1988): Standing Committee on Veterans Affairs. Minutes of Proceedings and Evidence (0410-8388); Which was formerly (until 195?): Special Committee on Veterans Affairs. Minutes of Proceedings and Evidence (0226-837X); Standing Committee on Veterans Affairs. Minutes of Proceedings and Evidence incorporated (195?-1969): Comite permanent des Affaires des Anciens Combattants. Proces-Verbaux et Temoignages (0576-3703); Which was formerly (1945-195?): Comite Special des Affaires des Anciens Combattants. Proces-Verbaux et Temoignages (0226-8388)
Related titles: French ed.: Canada. Chambre des Communes. Comite Permanent des Affaires des Anciens Combattants. Proces-verbal. ISSN 1912-5151.
Published by: (Canada, House of Commons. Standing Committee on Veterans Affairs), Canada, House of Commons (Subsidiary of: Parliament), Information Service, Ottawa, ON K1A 0A9, Canada. TEL 613-992-4793, info@parl.gc.ca, http://www.parl.gc.ca.

360 CAN ISSN 1910-2704
CANADA PENSION PLAN / OLD AGE SECURITY REVIEW TRIBUNALS BIENNIAL REPORT/TRIBUNAUX DE REVISION DU REGIME DE PENSIONS DU CANADA ET DE LA SECURITE DE LA VIEILLESSE, RAPPORT BIENNAL. Text in English, French. 1998. biennial. **Document type:** *Government.*
Formerly (until 2002): Canada Pension Plan / Old Age Security Review Tribunals Annual Report (1497-3618)
Published by: Canada, Office of the Commissioner of Review Tribunals, Canada Pension Plan - Old Age Security, PO Box 8250, Station "T", Ottawa, ON K1G 5S5, Canada. TEL 613-946-0320, 800-363-0076, FAX 613-941-3348, 866-263-7918, info@ocrt-bctr.gc.ca, http://www.ocrt-bctr.gc.ca/index_e.html.

362.6 310 CAN ISSN 1719-3494
CANADA PENSION PLAN, OLD AGE SECURITY, STATISTICAL BULLETIN. Text in English. 1979. m. back issues avail. **Document type:** *Bulletin, Government.*
Former titles (until 1997): Canada Pension Plan, Old Age Security, Statistical Bulletin (Print) (1196-0205); (until 1993): Income Security Programs, Monthly Statistics (1196-0191); (until 1991): Monthly Statistics, Income Security Programs (0715-108X); Incorporates (in 1986): Canada Pension Plan Statistical Bulletin (0382-3334)
Media: Online - full text. **Related titles:** French ed.: Regime de Pensions du Canada, Securite de la Vieillesse, Bulletin Statistique.
Published by: Human Resources and Social Development Canada, Public Enquiries Centre, 140 Promenade du Portage, Phase IV, Level 0, Gatineau, PQ K1A 0J9, Canada. TEL 800-935-5555, FAX 819-953-7260, http://www.hrsdc.gc.ca.

360 CAN ISSN 0848-2691
CANADA. STANDING COMMITTEE ON HEALTH AND WELFARE, SOCIAL AFFAIRS, SENIORS AND THE STATUS OF WOMEN. MINUTES OF THE PROCEEDINGS AND EVIDENCE. Text in English. 1989. irreg. **Document type:** *Proceedings.*
Published by: Canadian Government Publishing Center, Supply and Services Canada, Ottawa, ON K1A 0S9, Canada.

301.1 362 CAN ISSN 1195-4027
CANADA. STATISTICS CANADA. MENTAL HEALTH STATISTICS. Text in English. 193?. a. **Document type:** *Government.*
Former titles (until 199?): Health Reports. Supplement. Mental Health Statistics (1180-3037); (until 1984): Mental Health Statistics (0835-6092); (until 1982): Mental Health Statistics. Mental and Psychiatric Hospitals (0828-7066); (until 1980): Mental Health Statistics. Volume 1, Institutional Admissions and Separations (0380-6510); Which superseded in part (in 1961): Mental Health Statistics (0590-7705); Which was formerly (until 1952): Mental Institutions (0318-7233); (until 194?): Annual Report of Mental Institutions (0829-6057)
—CCC.
Published by: Statistics Canada, Canadian Centre for Health Information (Subsidiary of: Statistics Canada/Statistique Canada), 1500 Rm, Main Bldg, Holland Ave, Ottawa, ON K1A 0T6, Canada. TEL 613-951-8116.

362.82 CAN ISSN 1701-9079
CANADA'S MISSING CHILDREN. ANNUAL REPORT. Variant title: Enfants Disparus au Canada. Rapport Annuel. Text in English, French. 1988. a.
Formerly (until 1994): Annual Report on Canada's Missing Children (1201-9046)
Related titles: Online - full text ed.: ISSN 1701-9109.
Published by: (Royal Canadian Mounted Police/Gendarmerie Royale du Canada), National Missing Children Services, c/o Royal Canadian Mounted Police, 1200 Vanier Pkwy, PO Box 8885, Ottawa, ON K1G 3M8, Canada. TEL 613-993-1525, 877-318-3576, FAX 613-993-5430.

361.7 CAN ISSN 0226-0409
CANADIAN BOOK OF CHARITIES. Text in English. 1979. a. USD 19.95 (effective 2006).
Published by: Mavora Publications Inc., 86 Kingsway Crescent, Toronto, ON M8X 2R6, Canada. TEL 416-233-5490, FAX 416-239-2757.

362.7 CAN ISSN 0835-5819
CANADIAN CHILD DAY CARE FEDERATION. INTERACTION. Text in English, French. 1987. q. CAD 50 (effective 2006). adv. back issues avail. **Document type:** *Magazine, Trade.*
Indexed: C03, CBCARef, P48, PQC.
—CCC.
Published by: Canadian Child Care Federation, 383 Parkdale Ave, Suite 201, Ottawa, ON K1Y 4R4, Canada. TEL 613-729-5289, 800-858-1412, FAX 613-729-3159, info@cccf-fcsge.ca. adv.: B&W page CAD 600, color page CAD 820; 7 x 9.5. Circ: 10,000.

300 CAN ISSN 0068-8584
CANADIAN COUNCIL ON SOCIAL DEVELOPMENT. ANNUAL REPORT - RAPPORT ANNUEL. Text in English, French. 1920. a. CAD 65 to individuals; CAD 100 to institutions (effective 1999).
Published by: Canadian Council on Social Development, 441 MacLaren, 4th Fl, Ottawa, ON K2P 2H3, Canada. TEL 613-236-8977, FAX 613-236-2750. Ed. Nancy Perkins. Circ: 5,000.

360 CAN ISSN 1719-5330
CANADIAN COUNCIL ON SOCIAL DEVELOPMENT. BOARD OF GOVERNORS/BUREAU DES GOUVERNEURS. Text in English, French. 1979. a. **Document type:** *Government.*
Formerly (until 1980): Canadian Council on Social Development. Board of Governors and Executive Committee (1719-5314)
Published by: Canadian Council on Social Development, 190 O'Connor St, 1st Flr, Ottawa, ON K2P 2R3, Canada. TEL 613-236-8977, FAX 613-236-2750, council@ccsd.ca, http://www.ccsd.ca.

361.73 CAN ISSN 1490-764X
AS911.A2
CANADIAN DIRECTORY TO FOUNDATIONS AND GRANTS. Text in English. 1986. a. CAD 295 (effective 2000). **Document type:** *Directory.* **Description:** Lists addresses and contact persons of Canadian foundations, a description of what the foundation supports, its current officers and directors, names and addresses of recipients, the dollar amount of grant and how-to information on researching and writing proposals.
Former titles (until 1997): Canadian Directory Foundations (0831-3369); (until 1985): Canadian Directory to Foundations and Other Granting Agencies (0820-7682)
Related titles: Online - full text ed.
Published by: Canadian Center for Philanthropy, 425 University Ave, Ste 700, Toronto, ON M5G 1T6, Canada. TEL 416-597-2293, general@ccp.ca, http://www.ccp.ca. Ed. Jason Taniguchi. Circ: 1,000.

361.73 CAN
CANADIAN DONOR'S GUIDE (YEAR)/GUIDE DES DONATEURS CANADIENS. Text in English. a. CAD 59.95 (effective 2000).
Description: Covers all fund raising organizations in Canada.
Published by: International Press Publications Inc, 90 Nolan Ct, Ste 21, Markham, ON L3R 4L9, Canada. TEL 905-946-9588, FAX 905-946-9590.

360 CAN
CANADIAN FACT BOOK ON POVERTY/DONNEES DE BASE SUR LA PAUVRETE AU CANADA. Text in English. 1975. irreg. price varies. **Document type:** *Handbook/Manual/Guide, Trade.*
Published by: Canadian Council on Social Development, 441 MacLaren, 4th Fl, Ottawa, ON K2P 2H3, Canada. TEL 613-236-8977, FAX 613-236-2750.

361.7 CAN ISSN 1183-8957
CANADIAN FUNDRAISER. Text in English. 1990. 30/yr. CAD 217 (effective 1999). adv. bk.rev. charts; stat.; tr.lit. back issues avail. **Document type:** *Newsletter, Trade.* **Description:** Covers News, legislation, tips, advice, trends and economic development affecting professional fund raisers in Canada.
Published by: Hilborn Group Ltd., 109 Vanderhoof Ave, Ste 205, Toronto, ON M4G 2H7, Canada. TEL 416-696-8146, FAX 416-424-3016. Ed., Pub., R&P James Hilborn. Adv. contact Nancy Collett.

360 CAN ISSN 1910-3603
CANADIAN INTERNATIONAL DEVELOPMENT AGENCY, MULTILATERAL PROGRAMS BRANCH. BRANCH PERFORMANCE REPORT/RAPPORT SUR LE RENDEMENT. Text in English, French. 2005. a. **Document type:** *Report, Trade.*
Published by: Canadian International Development Agency, Multilateral Programs Branch (Subsidiary of: Canadian International Development Agency/Agence Canadienne de Developpement International), 200 Promenade du Portage, Gatineau, PQ K1A 0G4, Canada. TEL 819-997-5006, 800-230-6349, FAX 819-953-6088, info@acdi-cida.gc.ca, http://www.acdi-cida.gc.ca/CIDAWEB/acdicida.nsf/En/NIC-5412921-LXW.

S

CANADIAN JOURNAL OF QUANTUUM ECONOMICS; the journal of academic research and current affairs on quality-of-life issues. *see* SOCIAL SCIENCES: COMPREHENSIVE WORKS

362.4 372.41 CAN ISSN 1719-6574
CANADIAN NATIONAL INSTITUTE FOR THE BLIND, MANITOBA - SASKATCHEWAN DIVISION. ANNUAL REVIEW. Text in English. 2005. a. **Document type:** *Journal, Trade.*
Formed by the merger of (199?-2005): Canadian National Institute for the Blind. Saskatchewan Division. Annual Report (1719-6558); Which was formerly (1991-199?): Canadian National Institute for the Blind. Saskatchewan Division. Annual Report and Division Highlights (1202-9750); (19??-1991): Canadian National Institute for the Blind. Saskatchewan Division. Annual Report (0706-6279); (1996-2005): Canadian National Institute for the Blind. Manitoba Division. Annual Report (1719-6566); Which was formerly (1990-1996): Canadian National Institute for the Blind. Manitoba Division. Division Report (1719-654X); (19??-1990): Canadian National Institute for the Blind. Manitoba Division. Annual Report (0706-6295)
Published by: Canadian National Institute for the Blind, Manitoba-Saskatchewan Division (Subsidiary of: Canadian National Institute for the Blind, National Office), 1080 Portage Ave, Winnipeg, MB R3G 3M3, Canada. TEL 204-774-5421, FAX 204-775-5090, manitoba@cnib.ca, http://www.cnib.ca.

CANADIAN NATIONAL INSTITUTE FOR THE BLIND. NATIONAL ANNUAL REVIEW. *see* HANDICAPPED—Visually Impaired

361.5 CAN ISSN 0821-3232
CANADIAN RED CROSS SOCIETY. ANNUAL REPORT. Text in English, French. 1914. a. free. **Document type:** *Corporate.*
Published by: Canadian Red Cross Society, National Headquarters, 5700 Cancross Court, Mississauga, ON L5R 3E9, Canada. TEL 416-890-1000. Circ: 60,000.

361 CAN ISSN 0836-303X
➤ **CANADIAN REVIEW OF SOCIAL POLICY/REVUE CANADIENNE DE POLITIQUE SOCIALE.** Text in English, French. 1979. s-a. USD 50 to individuals; USD 85 to institutions (effective 2011). **Document type:** *Journal, Academic/Scholarly.* **Description:** Promotes the exchange of ideas involving education, the public sector, and social movements in Canadian social policy and administration.
Former titles (until 1987): S P A N. Social Policy and Administration Network (0836-3080); (until 1984): S P A N Newsletter (0822-6407)
Related titles: Online - full text ed.
Indexed: A26, C03, CA, CBCARef, CPerI, E08, G08, P21, P48, P50, PAIS, PQC, S02, S03, S09, SCOPUS, SSA, SociolAb, T02.
—CCC.
Published by: York University, 4700 Keele St, Toronto, ON M3J 1P3, Canada.

360 CAN ISSN 1488-0318
HV101 CODEN: SOCWE4
➤ **CANADIAN SOCIAL WORK/TRAVAIL SOCIAL CANADIEN.** Text in English. 1932. a. free to members. adv. bk.rev. index. **Document type:** *Journal, Academic/Scholarly.* **Description:** Information about social work groups in Canada and current social welfare policy. Examines regional, national and international social issues.
Supersedes in part (in 1999): Social Worker - Travailleur Social (0037-8089)
Related titles: Microfiche ed.: (from MML); Microfilm ed.: (from MML); Microform ed.: (from MML); French ed.
Indexed: ASSIA, C03, CA, CBCARef, CBPI, P48, PQC, S02, S03, SCOPUS, SOPODA, SSA, SWR&A, SociolAb, T02.
—IE, Ingenta. **CCC.**
Published by: (Canadian Association of Social Workers), Myropen Publications Ltd., 383 Parkdale Ave, Ste 402, Ottawa, ON K1Y 4R4, Canada. Ed. Dr. Bill Rowe. Pub. Eugemis Moreno. Circ: 15,000.

360 CAN ISSN 0820-909X
HV11C35 CODEN: CSWRE9
➤ **CANADIAN SOCIAL WORK REVIEW/REVUE CANADIENNE DE SERVICE SOCIAL.** Text in English, French. 1983. s-a. CAD 65 domestic to institutions; USD 70 foreign to institutions; CAD 36 per issue domestic to institutions; USD 36 per issue foreign to institutions (effective 2012). adv. bk.rev. back issues avail. **Document type:** *Journal, Academic/Scholarly.* **Description:** Focuses a national perspective on Canadian social work. The purpose of this journal is to advance social work scholarship, practice and education in Canada by publishing original research and critical analysis which enriches or challenges existing knowledge.
Supersedes (in 1983): Canadian Journal of Social Work Education (0316-8565)
Indexed: C03, CA, CBCARef, CDA, CWPI, FamI, P21, P27, P30, P48, P50, P54, PAIS, PQC, S02, S03, SOPODA, SSA, SSAI, SSAb, SSI, SWR&A, SociolAb, T02, W03, W05.
—BLDSC (3044.741000), IE, Infotrieve, Ingenta. **CCC.**
Published by: (Canadian Association of Schools of Social Work/Societe Canadienne d'Anthropologie), Wilfrid Laurier University Press, 75 University Ave W, Waterloo, ON N2L 3C5, Canada. TEL 519-884-0710 ext 6124, FAX 519-725-1399, press@wlu.ca, http://www.wlupress.wlu.ca. Circ: 470 (paid and controlled).

➤ **CANTERBURY DISTRICT HEALTH BOARD. STATEMENT OF INTENT.** *see* PUBLIC HEALTH AND SAFETY

362.1 NZL ISSN 1177-6889
CANTERBURY DISTRICT HEALTH BOARD. WOMEN'S AND CHILDREN'S HEALTH. ANNUAL CLINICAL REPORT. Text in English. 2001. a.
Formerly (until 2005): Canterbury District Health Board. Women's Health Division. Annual Clinical Report (1176-2225)
Published by: Canterbury District Health Board, Women's and Children's Health, PO Box 1600, Christchurch, New Zealand. TEL 64-3-3644106, FAX 64-3-3644101, http://www.cdhb.govt.nz.

362.7 FRA ISSN 2106-3249
CAP ESPERANCE. Text in French. 1994. a. **Document type:** *Newsletter, Consumer.*
Formerly (until 2009): Suivre (1252-7106)
Address: 3, Rue Gabriel Peri, Montrouge, 92120, France. TEL 33-1-40503934.

THE CAPSTONE (TOWSON); news from the Council, and its accreditation and evaluation systems and ProLerna. *see* HANDICAPPED

362.428 NZL ISSN 1177-0783
CAPTIVATE. Text in English. s-a. **Document type:** *Magazine, Consumer.*
Formerly (until 2005): Word
Published by: TVNZ Captioning, PO Box 3819, Auckland, New Zealand. TEL 64-9-9167392, FAX 64-9-9167902, captioning@tvnz.co.nz, http://www.captioningnz.co.nz. Ed. Melissa Irvine.

360 NLD
CARE & WELFARE. Text in Dutch. irreg. price varies. **Document type:** *Monographic series.*
Published by: Amsterdam University Press, Herengracht 221, Amsterdam, 1016 BG, Netherlands. TEL 31-20-4200050, FAX 31-20-4203214, info@aup.nl, http://www.aup.nl.

362.6 GBR ISSN 0965-2914
CARE HOME BRIEFING. Variant title: Care Home Management. Care Home Management: Records & Procedures. Text in English. 1992. base vol. plus q. updates. GBP 385 base vol(s). (effective 2010). **Document type:** *Newsletter, Trade.*
Related titles: Online - full text ed.
Published by: Croner C C H Group Ltd. (Subsidiary of: Wolters Kluwer UK Ltd.), 145 London Rd, Kingston upon Thames, Surrey KT2 6SR, United Kingdom. TEL 44-20-85473333, FAX 44-20-85472638, info@croner.co.uk.

362.6 GBR
CARE HOME MANAGEMENT. Text in English. 1986. base vol. plus q. updates. looseleaf. EUR 331.96 (effective 2001). **Description:** For residential care home or nursing home owners and managers.
Formerly: Croner's Care Home Management Bulletin (0968-6649)
Related titles: Online - full text ed.
Published by: Croner C C H Group Ltd. (Subsidiary of: Wolters Kluwer UK Ltd.), 145 London Rd, Kingston upon Thames, Surrey KT2 6SR, United Kingdom. TEL 44-20-85473333, FAX 44-20-85472638, info@croner.co.uk, http://www.croner.co.uk/. Ed. Nick O'Connor.

362.6 GBR
CARE HOME MANAGEMENT: RECORDS & PROCEDURES. Abbreviated title: C R K. Text in English. base vol. plus q. updates. looseleaf. EUR 247.93 (effective 2001). **Document type:** *Handbook/Manual/Guide, Trade.*
Published by: Croner C C H Group Ltd. (Subsidiary of: Wolters Kluwer UK Ltd.), 145 London Rd, Kingston upon Thames, Surrey KT2 6SR, United Kingdom. TEL 44-20-85473333, FAX 44-20-85472638, info@croner.co.uk, http://www.croner.co.uk/.

362.7 NZL ISSN 1177-2573
CARE MATTERS; quarterly news for child, youth and family to caregivers. Text in English. 2004. q. free. **Document type:** *Newsletter, Consumer.*
Media: Online - full text.
Published by: Child, Youth and Family, PO Box 2620, Wellington, New Zealand. TEL 64-4-9189100.

361.5 USA
CARE WORLD REPORT. Text in English. 1972. q. donation. **Document type:** *Newsletter.* **Description:** Covers the relief work of CARE worldwide and provides information on world hunger and infant mortality.
Published by: CARE, Inc., 9731 S M-37, Baldwin, MI 49304. TEL 231-745-0500, FAX 231-745-9662, care1@triton.net, http://www.care1.org. Circ: 400,000.

360 USA ISSN 1559-4475
HQ1063.6
THE CAREGIVER RESOURCE GUIDE. Text in English. biennial. USD 14.95 per issue; USD 17.95 combined subscription per issue print & online eds. (effective 2007). **Document type:** *Guide, Consumer.*
Formerly (until 2004): Aging America Resource Guide
Related titles: Online - full text ed.: USD 8.95 per issue (effective 2007).
Published by: Aging America Resources, 11611 Kosine Lane, Ste 100, Loveland, OH 45140. TEL 888-500-7965, FAX 888-501-7965, http://www.agingamericaresources.com.

360 AUS ISSN 1445-6761
CARERS IN VICTORIA. Text in English. 1995. q. free to members (effective 2008). adv. charts; illus.; stat.; tr.lit. 16 p./no.; back issues avail. **Document type:** *Newsletter, Trade.* **Description:** Contains information on current issues, services and activities of interest to carers, as well as a selection of carers stories.
Formerly (until 2000): Victorian Carer (1440-5040)
Related titles: Online - full text ed.
Published by: Carers Association Victoria, Level 1, 37 Albert St, PO Box 2204, Footscray, VIC 3011, Australia. TEL 61-3-93969500, FAX 61-3-93969555, info@carersvic.org.au, http://www.carersvic.org.au/.

362.4 JAM ISSN 0799-1215
HV1
CARIBBEAN JOURNAL OF SOCIAL WORK. Text in English. 2002. irreg. **Document type:** *Journal, Academic/Scholarly.*
Indexed: A10, C32, CA, S02, S03, SCOPUS, SociolAb, T02, V03.
Published by: Arawak Publications, 17 Kensington Cres Unit 5, Kingston, 5, Jamaica. TEL 876-960-7538, FAX 876-960-8219, arawakpubl@cwjamaica.com.

362 USA
CARING; the holistic ministries of the Salvation Army. Text in English. 2000. q. USD 30; USD 7.50 per issue (effective 2005). adv. **Document type:** *Magazine, Consumer.* **Description:** Contains articles about the social services provided by the Salvation Army worldwide.
Published by: The Salvation Army New Frontier Publications, 180 E Ocean Blvd, 4th Fl, Long Beach, CA 90802. TEL 562-491-8329, FAX 562-491-8791. Eds. Dr. Robert Docter, Ms. Sue Schumann-Warner. R&P, Adv. contact Mr. Jeff Curnow. color page USD 1,400. Circ: 3,500 (paid).

CARING (WASHINGTON). *see* MEDICAL SCIENCES—Nurses And Nursing

360 CAN ISSN 1910-8443
HN110.Z9
CARING CANADIANS, INVOLVED CANADIANS; highlights from the Canada survey of giving, volunteering and participating. Text in English. 1997. irreg. **Document type:** *Government.*
Related titles: Online - full text ed.: ISSN 1704-6866; French ed.: Canadiens Devoues, Canadiens Engages. ISSN 1910-8451.
Published by: Statistics Canada/Statistique Canada, Communications Division, 3rd Fl, R H Coats Bldg, Ottawa, ON K1A 0A6, Canada. TEL 800-263-1136, infostats@statcan.gc.ca, http://www.statcan.gc.ca.

362.8 USA
CARING CONNECTION. Text in English. 1980. q. free to donors. **Document type:** *Newsletter, Consumer.* **Description:** Important information for customers (donors) of United Way of Summit County.
Formerly (until 1997, vol.17): Common Ground (Akron)
Published by: United Way of Summit County, 90 N Prospect St, Akron, OH 44309-1260. TEL 330-762-7601. Ed., R&P Janet Fashbaugh. Circ: 43,000 (controlled and free).

360 GBR ISSN 0953-4873
CARING TIMES; the management magazine for the long term care sector. Text in English. 1988. m. GBP 70; free to qualified personnel (effective 2009). adv. bk.rev.; software rev.; video rev.; Website rev. 36 p./no.; back issues avail. **Document type:** *Magazine, Trade.* **Description:** Contains information about residential, nursing home, and sheltered housing management.
Incorporates (in Mar.1993): Care Concern (0266-4933)
Related titles: Online - full text ed.
—CCC.
Published by: Hawker Publications Ltd., Culvert House, Culvert Rd, London, SW11 5DH, United Kingdom. TEL 44-20-77202108, FAX 44-20-74983023, suec@hawkerpublications.com. Eds. Geoff Hodgson, Dr. Richard Hawkins. Adv. contact Caroline Bowern TEL 44-20-77202108. B&W page GBP 1,925, color page GBP 2,485; trim 228 x 298. Circ: 16,780. **Subscr. to:** ESCO Business Services Ltd., Trinity House, Sculpins Ln, Wethersfield, Braintree, Essex CM7 4AY, United Kingdom. TEL 44-1371-810433, FAX 44-1371-851808, enquiries@esco.co.uk, http://www.esco.co.uk.

362.1 USA ISSN 1545-7133
CARING WITH CONFIDENCE. Text in English. 2003 (Mar.). m. USD 22.95 (effective 2003).
Published by: Mather LifeWays, 1603 Orrington Ave. Ste. 1800, Evanston, IL 60201. TEL 847-492-7500, FAX 847-492-6789, http://www.matherlifeways.com.

360 ESP ISSN 1138-2139
CARITAS. Text in Spanish. 1952. m. EUR 26.15 (effective 2008). back issues avail. **Document type:** *Magazine, Consumer.* **Description:** Provides information about Caritas' local and international activities and services.
Published by: Caritas Espanola, San Bernardo, 99 bis 7a, Madrid, 28015, Spain. TEL 34-91-4441000, FAX 34-91-5934882, publicaciones@caritas-espa.org, http://www.caritas.es.

361.7068109410 GBR ISSN 1756-4026
CARITAS; leadership & management for the third sector. Text in English. 2007. m. GBP 99 charities; GBP 145 non-charities (effective 2009). adv. **Document type:** *Magazine, Trade.* **Description:** Provides information and detailed coverage on all charity management issues.
—CCC.
Published by: CaritasData Ltd., 6-14 Underwood St, London, N1 7JQ, United Kingdom. TEL 44-20-73242362, FAX 44-20-75498677, enquiries@caritasdata.co.uk.

360 282 NZL ISSN 1174-6793
CARITAS UPDATE; the Catholic agency for justice, peace and development. Text in English. 1988. 3/yr. bk.rev. illus. **Document type:** *Newsletter.* **Description:** Provides a regular report on the activities both in New Zealand and throughout the world. Includes advocacy issues, long term human development & emergency relief responses.
Former titles (until 1998): Catholic Office for Social Justice Update (1172-8396); (until 1992): Share (1170-5558)
Related titles: Online - full content ed.: ISSN 1178-5721.
Published by: Caritas Aotearoa New Zealand, PO Box 12193, Wellington, 6144, New Zealand. caritas@caritas.org.nz. Ed. Martin de Jong. Pub. Edward Hodges. Circ: 19,000.

360 AUT
CARITAS-ZEITSCHRIFT. Text in German. 1947. q. free. adv. bk.rev. abstr.; bibl. **Document type:** *Bulletin.*
Former titles: Caritas; Oesterreichische Caritas Zeitschrift (0029-8980)
Published by: Caritas, Trauttmansdorffgasse 15, Vienna, W 1130, Austria. FAX 43-1-8767538. Ed., Pub., R&P Elisabeth Hotter. Adv. contact Bettina Fink. Circ: 12,000.

361.73 USA ISSN 0069-0635
HV97.C3
CARNEGIE CORPORATION OF NEW YORK ANNUAL REPORT. Text in English. 1921. a. free. **Document type:** *Corporate.* **Description:** Promotes the advancement and diffusion of knowledge and understanding; and the use of funds for the same purpose among the people of the United States and certain countries that are or have been members of the British overseas Commonwealth.
Formerly (until 1971): Carnegie Corporation of New York. Reports of the Officers
Related titles: Microfiche ed.: (from BHP).
Indexed: GeoRef, SpeleolAb.
—BLDSC (1137.600000).
Published by: Carnegie Corporation of New York, 437 Madison Ave, New York, NY 10022. TEL 212-371-3200, FAX 212-754-4073. Ed. Avery Russell. Circ: 10,000.

361.73 USA ISSN 1546-9883
LB2336
CARNEGIE REPORTER. Text in English. 1953. 2/yr. free. bk.rev. illus. reprints avail. **Description:** Promotes the advancement and diffusion of knowledge and understanding; and the use of funds for the same purpose among the people of the United States and in certain countries that are or have been members of the British overseas Commonwealth.
Former titles (until 2000): Carnegie Quarterly (0576-7954); Carnegie Corporation of New York Quarterly (0146-1613); Carnegie Corporation of New York. Quarterly Report (0146-1605)
Related titles: Microfilm ed.; Online - full text ed.
Indexed: A22, AbAn, ChPerI, IFP, P06, P30, PAIS.
Published by: Carnegie Corporation of New York, 437 Madison Ave, New York, NY 10022. TEL 212-371-3200, FAX 212-754-4073, TELEX US166776. Ed. Eleanor Lerman. Circ: 38,500.

360 CAN ISSN 1914-0584
CARREFOUR DU BENEVOLAT. Text in French. 1994. q. **Document type:** *Newsletter, Consumer.*
Published by: Centre d'Action Benevole de Quebec Inc., 245, rue Soumande, local 285, Quebec, PQ G1M 3H6, Canada. TEL 418-681-3501, FAX 418-681-6481, http://www.cabqinc.net/pages/cabqpag.html.

CARRYING THE TORCH (INDIANAPOLIS). *see* POLITICAL SCIENCE—Civil Rights

361.3 USA
CATALYST (BOTSFORD). Text in English. 1958. q. free to members (effective 2010). back issues avail. **Document type:** *Newsletter, Trade.* **Description:** Provides a forum for members to express their perspectives on a wide range of issues of interest to Christians in social work.
Related titles: Online - full text ed.
Published by: North American Association of Christians in Social Work, PO Box 121, Botsford, CT 06404. TEL 888-426-4712, FAX 888-426-4712, info@nacsw.org. Ed. Rick Chamiec-Case.

361 USA
CATHOLIC RELIEF SERVICES. ANNUAL REPORT. Text in English. a. **Document type:** *Corporate.* **Description:** Covers various types of information including financial statements, country updates, and headquarters information.
Published by: Catholic Relief Services, 209 W Fayette St, Baltimore, MD 21201-3443. TEL 410-625-2220, FAX 410-234-2983.

360 USA ISSN 0886-1811
CATHOLIC WAR VETERAN. Text in English. 1935. bi-m. **Description:** Covers veteran news, legislation and veteran administration policies.
Published by: Catholic War Veterans, U.S.A., 441 N Lee St, Alexandria, VA 22314. TEL 216-333-2951. Ed. William J Gill. Circ: 36,000.

CAYAPA; revista venezolana de economia social. *see* SOCIOLOGY

362.4 DNK ISSN 1395-4660
DET CENTRALE HANDICAPRAAD. AARSBERETNING. Text in Danish. 1981. a. free. **Document type:** *Consumer.*
Formerly (until 1994): Det Centrale Handicapraads Virksomhed (0108-9420)
Related titles: Audio CD ed.: ISSN 1901-6514; Audio cassette/tape ed.: ISSN 1901-6522; Online - full text ed.: ISSN 1398-2133.
Published by: Det Centrale Handicapraad/The Danish Disability Council, Bredgade 25 F, Copenhagen K, 1260, Denmark. TEL 45-33-111044, FAX 45-33-111082, dch@dch.dk. Ed. Mogens Wiederholt. Circ: 1,500.

360 CAN ISSN 1910-6475
CENTRE D'ACTION BENEVOLE DE QUEBEC. RAPPORT ANNUEL. Text in French. 19??. a. **Document type:** *Report, Trade.*
Published by: Centre d'Action Benevole de Quebec, Halles Fleur de Lys, 2 etage, 245 Rue Soumande, Local 285, Quebec, PQ G1M 3H6, Canada. TEL 418-861-3501, http://www.cabqinc.net/pages/cabqpag.html.

361.7 355 CAN ISSN 1912-1490
CENTRE DE LA FAMILLE VALCARTIER. RAPPORT ANNUEL. Text in French. 19??. a. **Document type:** *Report, Consumer.*
Formerly (until 2005): Centre de la Famille Valcartier. Rapport d'Activites (1497-2050)
Published by: Centre de la Famille Valcartier/Valcartier Family Centre, Case postale 1000, succursale Forces, Courcelette, PQ G0A 4Z0, Canada. TEL 418-844-6060, crv-valcartier@videotron.net, http://www.crfmv.com/index.htm.

CENTRE DE SANTE ET DE SERVICES SOCIAUX DE L'OUEST-DE-L'ILE. ANNUAL REPORT. *see* PUBLIC HEALTH AND SAFETY

CENTRE FOR CIVIL SOCIETY. INTERNATIONAL WORKING PAPER. *see* SOCIOLOGY

360 CAN ISSN 1719-3672
CENTRE REGIONAL DE SANTE ET DE SERVICES SOCIAUX DE LA BAIE - JAMES. RAPPORT SUR L'APPLICATION DE LA PROCEDURE D'EXAMEN DES PLAINTES ET L'AMELIORATION DE LA QUALITE DES SERVICES. Text in French. 2004. a. **Document type:** *Report, Trade.*
Published by: Centre Regional de Sante et de Services Sociaux de la Baie-James, 312, 3e Rue, Chibougamau, PQ G8P 1N5, Canada. TEL 418-748-3575, FAX 418-748-2081, julie_pelletier@ssss.gouv.qc.ca.

CENTREPIECES. *see* WOMEN'S INTERESTS

300 BRA
CENTRO DE ESTUDOS LATINO AMERICANOS. BOLETIM. Text in Portuguese. s-a.?.
Published by: Universidade de Sao Paulo, Faculdade de Historia, Direito, e Servico Social, Rua Major Claudiano, 1488, Centro, Caixa Postal 211, Franca, SP 14400-690, Brazil. TEL 55-16-7226222, FAX 55-16-7236645.

360 BGD
CHAKRA. Text in Bengali. w.
Address: 242 A Nakhalpara, PO Box 2682, Dhaka, 1215, Bangladesh. TEL 2-604568. Ed. Husneara Aziz.

CHANGING WELFARE STATES. *see* PUBLIC HEALTH AND SAFETY

360 CHN ISSN 1671-5136
CHANGSHA MINZHENG ZHIYE JISHU XUEYUAN XUEBAO/ CHANGSHA SOCIAL WORK COLLEGE. JOURNAL. Text in Chinese. 1994. q. **Document type:** *Journal, Academic/Scholarly.*
Related titles: Online - full text ed.
Published by: Changsha Minzheng Zhiye Jishu Xueyuan/Changsha Social Work College, 22, Xiangzhang Lu, Changsha, 410004, China. TEL 86-731-82625043.

CHARITABLE GIFT PLANNING NEWS. *see* BUSINESS AND ECONOMICS—Public Finance, Taxation

360 GBR ISSN 0590-9783
HV241
CHARITIES DIGEST (YEAR). Text in English. 1882. a. GBP 37.50 per issue (effective 2010). adv. **Document type:** *Directory.* **Description:** Lists major UK charities and other organizations with contact addresses and other details. Covers the histories of key local volunteer organizations.
Formerly (until 1970): Annual Charities Digest (0066-3867)
—BLDSC (3129.918000).
Published by: (Family Welfare Association), Waterlow Professional Publishing, 6-14 Underwood St, London, N1 7JQ, United Kingdom. TEL 44-20-74900049, FAX 44-20-72531308, legalweb@waterlow.com, http://www.waterlow.com/. Ed. Michael Chapman. Pub. Polly Avghennos. Adv. contact Ashley Adams.

361.7 GBR ISSN 0964-9093
CHARITIES MANAGEMENT. Text in English. 1991. bi-m. GBP 48 domestic for charities; GBP 56 domestic for non-charities; GBP 96 foreign (effective 2009). adv. back issues avail. **Document type:** *Journal, Trade.* **Description:** Designed to serve as a guide for those involved in the management and running of charities. Includes fundraising, investments, funds, legal and accountancy for voluntary sector and employment.
Indexed: N06.
—CCC.
Published by: Mitre House Publishing Ltd., PO Box 29, South Petherton, TA13 5WE, United Kingdom. TEL 44-1460-241106, FAX 44-1460-241091, richardblausten@btconnect.com, http://www.mitrehousepublishing.co.uk/. Ed. Richard Blausten. adv.: B&W page GBP 1,100, color page GBP 1,700. Circ: 5,000.

361.7 USA ISSN 0364-0760
HV530
CHARITIES U S A. Text in English. 1974. q. USD 25 domestic; USD 33 foreign (effective 2000). adv. bk.rev. illus. **Document type:** *Magazine, Trade.* **Description:** Focuses on social justice and social service issues of interest to Catholic Charities USA members, such as poverty, family counseling, aging issues, low-income housing, emergency service, teen pregnancy, and adoption.
Published by: Catholic Charities U S A, 1731 King St, Ste 200, Alexandria, VA 22314. TEL 703-549-1390, FAX 703-549-1656. Ed. Alexandra Peeler. Pub. Fred Kammer. R&P, Adv. contact Margaret Hagood. Circ: 3,000.

360 GBR ISSN 1460-115X
CHARITY BUYERS GUIDE. Text in English. 1998. a. GBP 39.95 per issue domestic; GBP 64 per issue foreign; GBP 65 combined subscription per issue (print & online eds.) (effective 2010). adv. Supplement avail. **Document type:** *Handbook/Manual/Guide, Trade.* **Description:** Offers a comprehensive reference source to the diverse businesses that play a crucial role in the day-to-day activities and management of charities.
Related titles: Online - full text ed.
—CCC.
Published by: Perspective Publishing Ltd., 3 London Wall Bldgs, 6th Fl, London, EC2M 5PD, United Kingdom. TEL 44-20-75622401, FAX 44-20-73742701, http://www.perspectivepublishing.com/. Adv. contact Cerys McLean TEL 44-77-66662610.

360 GBR ISSN 0953-6302
CHARITY CHOICE (UK EDITION); the encyclopaedia of charities. Text in English. 1988. a. GBP 84.95 per issue (effective 2009). adv. **Document type:** *Directory.* **Description:** Contains details of 7,000 charitable organizations, revealing the charity's aim, sphere of influence, and procedure for assistance.
Related titles: Online - full text ed.; Regional ed(s).: Charity Choice (Scotland Edition); Charity Choice (N. Ireland Edition).
—BLDSC (3129.918671). **CCC.**
Published by: Waterlow Professional Publishing, Paulton House, 8 Shepherdess Walk, London, N1 7LB, United Kingdom. legalweb@waterlow.com, http://www.waterlow.com/.

CHARITY FINANCE. *see* BUSINESS AND ECONOMICS—Investments

631.7632 AUS
CHARITY NEWS DAILY. Text in English. 2000. d. AUD 790 (effective 2001). adv. bk.rev.; Website rev. 1 p./no.; back issues avail. **Document type:** *Newsletter, Consumer.*
Media: E-mail.
Published by: Civic Chamber Australia, 19 Prospect St, Box Hill, VIC 3128, Australia. TEL 61-3-98993448, FAX 61-3-98993449, admin@civic-chamber.com.au, http://www.civic-chamber.com.au. adv.: page AUD 500; 180 x 250. Circ: 1,000.

CHARITY REWARDS. *see* BUSINESS AND ECONOMICS—Labor And Industrial Relations

360 GBR ISSN 1355-4573
CHARITY TIMES. Text in English. 1994. bi-m. GBP 119 domestic; GBP 127 in Europe; GBP 132 elsewhere (effective 2010). adv. **Document type:** *Magazine, Trade.* **Description:** Contains a wide range of written features and news analysis, coverage of all the financial, legal, fundraising, marketing and technology management issues facing charities, voluntary groups and non-profits.
Related titles: Online - full text ed.: Charity Times Online.
—CCC.
Published by: Perspective Publishing Ltd., 3 London Wall Bldgs, 6th Fl, London, EC2M 5PD, United Kingdom. TEL 44-20-75622401, FAX 44-20-73742701, http://www.perspectivepublishing.com/. Ed. Andrew Holt TEL 44-20-75622411. Adv. contact Cerys McLean TEL 44-77-66662610.

CHECKLISTS AND ILLUSTRATIVE FINANCIAL STATEMENTS FOR NONPROFIT ORGANIZATIONS. *see* BUSINESS AND ECONOMICS—Accounting

362.7 970.1 USA ISSN 0890-5185
CHEROKEE VOICE. Text in English. 1981. q. free. **Document type:** *Newsletter.* **Description:** Contains items of interest to the American Indian community.
Related titles: Online - full text ed.
Indexed: ENW.
Published by: Cherokee Center for Family Services, PO Box 507, Cherokee, NC 28719. TEL 704-497-5001, FAX 704-497-5818. Ed. Joy Evans-Widenhouse. R&P Joy Evans Widenhouse. Circ: 5,800.

360 JPN ISSN 1880-5523
CHIIKI RIHABIRITESHON. Text in Japanese. 2006. m. JPY 22,680; JPY 1,890 newsstand/cover (effective 2007). **Document type:** *Journal, Academic/Scholarly.*
Published by: Miwa-Shoten Ltd., 6-17-9 Hongo, Bunkyo-ku, Hongou Tsuna Bldg. 4F, Tokyo, 113-0033, Japan. TEL 81-3-38167796, FAX 81-3-38167756, info@miwapubl.com, http://www.miwapubl.com/.

362.76 USA ISSN 1935-1216
HV6626.52
CHILD ABUSE AND DOMESTIC VIOLENCE. Text in English. 2007 (Apr.). biennial. USD 49 per issue (effective 2008). back issues avail. **Document type:** *Monographic series, Academic/Scholarly.* **Description:** Contains essays and directory listings that describe the historical development of religious families and give factual information about each group within those families, including, when available, rubrics for membership figures, educational facilities and periodicals.
Formed by the merger of (1995-2005): Child Abuse, Betraying a Trust (1534-1607); (1995-2005): Violent Relationships (1534-1615); Both of which superseded in part (1981-1993): Domestic Violence
Related titles: Online - full text ed.
Published by: Gale (Subsidiary of: Cengage Learning), 27500 Drake Rd, Farmington Hills, MI 48331. TEL 248-699-4253, 800-877-4253, FAX 877-363-4253, gale.galeord@cengage.com.

CHILD ABUSE & NEGLECT. *see* CHILDREN AND YOUTH—About

362.76 AUS ISSN 1320-2871
CHILD ABUSE PREVENTION; national child protection clearing house newsletter. Text in English. 1994. s-a. free. bk.rev. abstr.; bibl. back issues avail. **Document type:** *Newsletter, Trade.* **Description:** Provides information bulletin of research, practice, and policy for professionals working in areas related to child abuse prevention.
Related titles: CD-ROM ed.
Published by: Australian Institute of Family Studies, Level 20, 485 La Trobe St, Melbourne, VIC 3000, Australia. TEL 61-3-92147888, FAX 61-3-92147839, fic@aifs.org.au, http://www.aifs.org.au. Ed. Judy Adams. Circ: 7,000.

302.76 AUS ISSN 1446-9995
CHILD ABUSE PREVENTION ISSUES. Text in English. 1994. s-a. free. bk.rev. abstr.; bibl. back issues avail. **Document type:** *Newsletter, Academic/Scholarly.* **Description:** Provides an information bulletin of research, practice, and policy for professionals working in areas related to child abuse prevention.
Formerly: Issues In Child Abuse Prevention (1321-2540)
Related titles: CD-ROM ed.; Online - full content ed.: ISSN 1447-0004.
Published by: Australian Institute of Family Studies, Level 20, 485 La Trobe St, Melbourne, VIC 3000, Australia. TEL 61-3-92147888, FAX 61-3-92147839, fic@aifs.org.au, http://www.aifs.org.au. Ed. Judy Adams. Circ: 7,000 (controlled).

362.7 155.4 GBR ISSN 0952-9136
HV6626.5 CODEN: CABEEB
CHILD ABUSE REVIEW. Text in English. 1992. bi-m. GBP 341 in United Kingdom to institutions; EUR 341 in Europe to institutions; USD 510 elsewhere to institutions; GBP 393 combined subscription in United Kingdom to institutions (print & online eds.); EUR 393 combined subscription in Europe to institutions (print & online eds.); USD 588 combined subscription elsewhere to institutions (print & online eds.) (effective 2012). adv. back issues avail.; reprint service avail. from PSC. **Document type:** *Journal, Academic/Scholarly.* **Description:** Reflects current child welfare issues and concerns.
Related titles: Online - full text ed.: ISSN 1099-0852. GBP 341 in United Kingdom to institutions; EUR 341 in Europe to institutions; USD 510 elsewhere to institutions (effective 2012) (from IngentaConnect).
Indexed: A01, A02, A03, A08, A22, B28, C06, C07, C08, C28, CA, CINAHL, CJA, CJPI, CurCont, E-psyche, F09, FamI, IBR, IBZ, IPsyAb, P03, P43, PAIS, PQC, PsycInfo, PsycholAb, S02, S03, SCOPUS, SSA, SSCI, SociolAb, T02, W07.
—GNLM, IE, Infotrieve, Ingenta. **CCC.**
Published by: (British Association for the Study and Prevention of Child Abuse and Neglect), John Wiley & Sons Ltd. (Subsidiary of: John Wiley & Sons, Inc.), 1-7 Oldlands Way, PO Box 808, Bognor Regis, West Sussex PO21 9FF, United Kingdom. TEL 44-1865-778315, FAX 44-1243-843232, cs-journals@wiley.com, http://eu.wiley.com/WileyCDA/. Eds. Jane V Appleton, Nicky Stanley. **Subscr. in the US to:** John Wiley & Sons, Inc., 111 River St, Hoboken, NJ 07030. TEL 201-748-6645, subinfo@wiley.com; **Subscr. to:** 1-7 Oldlands Way, PO Box 809, Bognor Regis, West Sussex PO21 9FG, United Kingdom. TEL 44-1865-778054, cs-agency@wiley.com.

CHILD & ADOLESCENT HEALTH CARE. *see* MEDICAL SCIENCES—Pediatrics

360 GBR ISSN 1356-7500
HV697 CODEN: CFSWFG
➤ **CHILD & FAMILY SOCIAL WORK.** Variant title: C F S. Text in English. 1996. q. GBP 457 in United Kingdom to institutions; EUR 580 in Europe to institutions; USD 847 in the Americas to institutions; USD 986 elsewhere to institutions; GBP 526 combined subscription in United Kingdom to institutions (print & online eds.); EUR 668 combined subscription in Europe to institutions (print & online eds.); USD 975 combined subscription in the Americas to institutions (print & online eds.); USD 1,135 combined subscription elsewhere to institutions (print & online eds.) (effective 2012). adv. reprint service avail. from PSC. **Document type:** *Journal, Academic/Scholarly.* **Description:** Provides a forum where researchers, practitioners, policy-makers and managers in the field exchange knowledge, increase understanding and develop notions of good practice.
Related titles: ◆ Online - full text ed.: Child & Family Social Work Online. ISSN 1365-2206.
Indexed: A01, A02, A03, A08, A22, A26, C06, C07, C08, C11, C28, CA, CINAHL, CMM, CurCont, E-psyche, E01, E07, ESPM, F09, FamI, H04, H12, IBSS, P02, P03, P18, P27, P34, P48, P53, P54, PQC, PsycInfo, PsycholAb, RiskAb, S02, S03, SCOPUS, SSA, SSCI, SWR&A, SociolAb, T02, W07.
—BLDSC (3172.915350), IE, Infotrieve, Ingenta. **CCC.**
Published by: Wiley-Blackwell Publishing Ltd. (Subsidiary of: John Wiley & Sons, Inc.), 9600 Garsington Rd, Oxford, OX4 2DQ, United Kingdom. TEL 44-1865-776868, FAX 44-1865-714591, customerservices@blackwellpublishing.com. Ed. Susan White. Pub. Elaine Stott. R&P Sophie Savage. Adv. contact Craig Pickett TEL 44-1865-476267. Circ: 425.

360 GBR ISSN 1365-2206
➤ **CHILD & FAMILY SOCIAL WORK ONLINE.** Text in English. 1997. q. GBP 457 in United Kingdom to institutions; EUR 580 in Europe to institutions; USD 847 in the Americas to institutions; USD 986 elsewhere to institutions (effective 2012). **Document type:** *Journal, Academic/Scholarly.* **Description:** Provides a forum where researchers, practitioners, policy-makers and managers in the field of child and family social work exchange knowledge, increase understanding and develop notions of good practice.
Media: Online - full text (from IngentaConnect). **Related titles:** ◆ Print ed.: Child & Family Social Work. ISSN 1356-7500.
—CCC.
Published by: Wiley-Blackwell Publishing Ltd. (Subsidiary of: John Wiley & Sons, Inc.), 9600 Garsington Rd, Oxford, OX4 2DQ, United Kingdom. TEL 44-1865-776868, FAX 44-1865-714591, customerservices@blackwellpublishing.com, http://www.wiley.com/. Ed. Susan White. Adv. contact Craig Pickett TEL 44-1865-476267.

S

362.7 USA ISSN 0145-935X
HV701 CODEN: CYSEDP
➤ **CHILD & YOUTH SERVICES.** Abbreviated title: C Y S. Text in English. 1977. 4/yr. GBP 502, EUR 650, USD 604 combined subscription to institutions (print & online eds.) (effective 2011). adv. bk.rev. abstr.; bibl.; illus. Index. 120 p./no. 1 cols./p.; back issues avail.; reprint service avail. from PSC. **Document type:** *Journal, Academic/Scholarly.* **Description:** Covers one particular topic regarding conditions of young people in our society.
Related titles: Microform ed.: (from PQC); Online - full text ed.: ISSN 1545-2298. GBP 452, EUR 585, USD 592 to institutions (effective 2011).
Indexed: A01, A03, A22, AC&P, AMHA, BehAb, C06, C07, C08, C28, CA, CDA, CINAHL, CPLI, DIP, E-psyche, E01, E03, ECER, ERI, FamI, IBR, IBZ, M02, P03, PC&CA, PSI, PsycInfo, PsycholAb, RehabLit, S02, S03, SCOPUS, SOPODA, SSA, SWR&A, SociolAb, T02, ViroIAbstr.
—BLDSC (3172.916000), IE, Infotrieve, Ingenta, INIST. **CCC.**
Published by: Routledge (Subsidiary of: Taylor & Francis Group), 325 Chestnut St, Ste 800, Philadelphia, PA 19106. TEL 215-625-8900, 800-354-1420, FAX 215-625-8914, journals@routledge.com, http://www.routledge.com. Ed. Doug Magnuson. adv.: B&W page USD 315, color page USD 550; trim 4.375 x 7.125. Circ: 234 (paid).

362.7 USA ISSN 2153-3555
CHILD AND YOUTH SERVICES SURVEY PREPARATION GUIDE. Text in English. 19??. a. USD 610 per issue (print & CD-ROM eds.) (effective 2010). back issues avail. **Document type:** *Guide, Trade.* **Description:** Contains the accreditation sourcebook (hard copy), standards manual (hard copy), and the electronic standards manual with survey preparation guide (on CD-ROM).
Related titles: CD-ROM ed.
Published by: C A R F International, 4891 E Grant Rd, Tucson, AZ 85712. TEL 520-325-1044, 888-281-6531, FAX 520-318-1129, bookstore@carf.org, http://www.carf.org.

CHILD CARE BRIDGES. *see* CHILDREN AND YOUTH—About

362.7 USA
CHILD CARE BULLETIN. Text in English. 1994. q. **Document type:** *Bulletin, Government.*
Related titles: Online - full text ed.
Indexed: A10.
Published by: U.S. Department of Health and Human Services, 220 Independence Ave, S W, Washington, DC 20201.

CHILD HEALTH TALK. *see* CHILDREN AND YOUTH—About

360 GBR
CHILD PROTECTION MANAGEMENT INFORMATION (YEAR). Text in English. 1995. a. GBP 2. **Document type:** *Bulletin, Government.*
Published by: Social Work Services Group, Statistics Branch, Rm 52, James Craig Walk, Edinburgh, EH1 3BA, United Kingdom. TEL 44-131-244-5431, FAX 44-131-244-5315. **Dist. by:** Her Majesty's Stationery Office Bookshop, 71 Lothian Rd, EH3 9AZ, Edinburgh, Midlothian EH3 9AZ, United Kingdom. TEL 44-131-228-4181.

CHILD SUPPORT HANDBOOK. *see* LAW—Family And Matrimonial Law

360 USA ISSN 0884-8076
HV741
CHILD SUPPORT REPORT. Text in English. 1979. irreg. back issues avail. **Document type:** *Government.*
Related titles: Online - full text ed.
Published by: (National Child Support Enforcement Center), U.S. Department of Health and Human Services, Office of Child Support Enforcement, 370 L'Enfant Promenade, S W, Mail Stop OCSE RC, Washington, DC 20447.

CHILD SUPPORT: THE LEGISLATION (YEAR). *see* LAW—Family And Matrimonial Law

362.7 JPN ISSN 0289-6842
CHILD WELFARE; quarterly news from Japan. Text in Japanese. q. free.
Formerly: Child Welfare Quarterly
Related titles: Online - full text ed.
Published by: Foundation for Children's Future, Maho Bldg, 3-11-18 Ginza, Chuo-ku, Tokyo, 104-0061, Japan. TEL 81-3-5550-0465, FAX 81-3-5550-0469.

362.7 USA ISSN 0009-4021
HV701 CODEN: CHWFA
➤ **CHILD WELFARE**; journal of policy, practice and program. Text in English. 1921. bi-m. USD 140 domestic to individuals; USD 210 foreign to individuals; USD 195 domestic to institutions; USD 265 foreign to institutions; free to members (effective 2009). adv. charts; illus.; abstr. index. 96 p./no. 1 cols./p.; back issues avail. **Document type:** *Journal, Academic/Scholarly.* **Description:** Designed to link the latest findings in child welfare and related research with the best practice, policy, and program development into one innovative resource equally indispensable to child welfare and associated professionals.
Formerly (until 1948): Child Welfare League of America. Bulletin
Related titles: Microform ed.: (from PQC); Online - full text ed.
Indexed: A01, A02, A03, A08, A09, A10, A20, A22, A25, A26, ABS&EES, AC&P, AMHA, AcaI, Agr, BRD, BibAg, C06, C07, C08, C11, C12, C22, C28, CA, CDA, CINAHL, CJA, CLFP, Chicano, CurCont, E-psyche, E02, E03, E06, E07, E08, ECER, EMBASE, ERI, ERIC, EdA, EdI, ExcerpMed, F09, FamI, G08, G10, H01, H02, H04, H09, H11, H12, HRA, HlthInd, I05, IBSS, INI, IndMed, L03, M01, M02, MEDLINE, P02, P03, P04, P06, P07, P10, P13, P16, P18, P19, P20, P22, P24, P25, P27, P30, P34, P43, P46, P48, P50, P53, P54, P55, PAIS, PQC, PSI, PsycInfo, PsycholAb, RI-1, RI-2, S02, S03, S05, S08, S09, S11, SCOPUS, SFSA, SOPODA, SSA, SSAI, SSAb, SSCI, SSI, SWR&A, SociolAb, T02, V&AA, V02, V03, V04, W03, W05, W07, W09.
—BLDSC (3172.950000), GNLM, IE, Infotrieve, Ingenta, INIST. **CCC.**
Published by: Child Welfare League of America, Inc., 2345 Crystal Dr, Ste 250, Arlington, VA 22202. TEL 703-412-2400, FAX 703-412-2401, journal@cwla.org. Adv. contact Karen Dunn TEL 703-412-2416. page USD 800; 4.625 x 7.625. Circ: 7,000. **Subscr. to:** P M D S, 9050 Jct Dr, PO Box 2019, Annapolis, MD 20701. TEL 301-617-7825, 800-407-6273, FAX 301-206-9789, cwla@pmds.com.

362.7 344.0327 USA ISSN 1073-5666
CHILD WELFARE REPORT. Text in English. 1993. m. USD 149 domestic; USD 162 foreign (effective 2006). **Document type:** *Newsletter, Consumer.* **Description:** Contains "insider" information in the areas of funding sources and resources, training, legal issues, parenting techniques, education, abuse prevention, medical issues, conference listings, informational web sites and more.
Published by: Impact Publications, Inc., E3430 Mountain View Lane, Box 322, Waupaca, WI 54981. TEL 715-258-2448, FAX 715-258-9048, info@impact-publications.com, http://www.impact-publications.com/. Ed. Mike Jacquart.

362.1 USA
➤ **CHILD WELFARE REVIEW**; the internet journal on child welfare. Text in English. 19??. m. back issues avail. **Document type:** *Journal, Academic/Scholarly.* **Description:** Covers issues related to the well-being of children, containing both links to articles related to child welfare and original articles.
Media: Online - full text.
Published by: Child Walfare Research Institute, 3250 Public Policy Bldg, Los Angeles, CA 90095. info@childwelfare.com. Ed. Duncan Linsey.

362.7 NZL ISSN 1170-7240
CHILDREN. Text in English. 1991. q. free (effective 2009). **Document type:** *Newsletter.*
Related titles: Online - full text ed.: ISSN 1178-3397.
Published by: Office of the Children's Commissioner, Level 12, 86-90 Lambton Quay, PO Box 5610, Wellington, New Zealand. TEL 64-4-4711410, FAX 64-4-4711418, children@occ.org.nz.

361.6 USA ISSN 1532-8759
LB3013.4 CODEN: SOWEEG
CHILDREN & SCHOOLS; a journal of social work practice. Text in English. 1978. q. GBP 78 in United Kingdom to institutions; EUR 118 in Europe to institutions; USD 149 in US & Canada to institutions; GBP 78 elsewhere to institutions; GBP 85 combined subscription in United Kingdom to institutions (print & online eds.); EUR 128 combined subscription in Europe to institutions (print & online eds.); USD 163 combined subscription in US & Canada to institutions (print & online eds.); GBP 85 combined subscription elsewhere to institutions (print & online eds.) (effective 2012). adv. bk.rev. illus. Index. 64 p./no.; back issues avail.; reprints avail. **Document type:** *Journal, Academic/Scholarly.* **Description:** Addresses practice issues faced by social workers employed in educational organizations and community agencies whose practice focuses on helping children and improving the conditions of children and schools.
Formerly (until 2000): Social Work in Education (0162-7961)
Related titles: Microform ed.: (from PQC); Online - full text ed.: ISSN 1545-682X. GBP 71 in United Kingdom to institutions; EUR 107 in Europe to institutions; USD 135 in US & Canada to institutions; GBP 71 elsewhere to institutions (effective 2012) (from IngentaConnect).
Indexed: A01, A02, A03, A08, A22, A26, AMHA, ASSIA, AbAn, B04, BRD, C06, C07, C08, C11, C28, CA, CINAHL, CMM, CPE, E02, E03, E07, E15, ECER, ERA, ERI, ERIC, EdA, EdI, H04, H12, M01, M02, M12, P02, P03, P04, P18, P19, P24, P30, P43, P46, P48, P50, P53, P54, P55, PQC, PSI, PsycInfo, PsycholAb, S02, S03, S19, S20, S21, SCOPUS, SOPODA, SSA, SWR&A, SociolAb, T02, W03.
—BLDSC (3172.961250), IE, Ingenta. **CCC.**
Published by: (National Association of Social Workers), Oxford University Press (Subsidiary of: Oxford University Press), 2001 Evans Rd, Cary, NC 27513. TEL 919-677-0977, 800-445-9714, FAX 919-677-1303, jnlorders@oup-usa.org, http://www.oxfordjournals.org. Ed. Melissa Jonson-Reid. adv.: B&W page USD 480. Circ: 3,700 (paid).

362.7094105 GBR ISSN 1755-8093
CHILDREN AND YOUNG PEOPLE NOW; for everyone working with children and young people. Text in English. 2007. w. (47/yr.). GBP 89 (effective 2009); subscr. includes Youth Work Now; InPractice. adv. back issues avail. **Document type:** *Magazine, Trade.* **Description:** Covers childcare and early years, education, health, social care, youth justice, and youth work.
Incorporates (1983-2009): Chilkdright (0265-1459); Formed by the merger of (1999-2007): Children Now (1465-9360); Which was formerly (until 1999): Children UK (1356-7020); (until 1994): Concern (0591-017X); (1989-2007): Young People Now (0956-2842); Which was formerly (1973-1989): Youth in Society (0307-1790); Which incorporated (1973-19??): Youth Social Work Bulletin (0307-3513)
Indexed: S02, S03.
—BLDSC (3172.961490), IE.
Published by: (The National Youth Agency), Haymarket Publishing Ltd. (Subsidiary of: Haymarket Media Group), 174 Hammersmith Rd, London, W6 7JP, United Kingdom. TEL 44-20-82675000, FAX 44-20-82674268, hpg@haymarketgroup.com, http://www.haymarket.com. Ed. Ravi Chandiramani TEL 44-20-82674707. Adv. contact Elliott Thomas TEL 44-20-82674667. Circ: 12,000. **Subscr. to:** 12-13 Cranleigh Gardens Industrial Estate, Southall UB1 2DB, United Kingdom. TEL 44-84-51557355, FAX 44-8451-948840, subscriptions@haymarket.com, http://www.haymarketbusinesssubs.com.

CHILDREN AND YOUTH SERVICES REVIEW. *see* CHILDREN AND YOUTH—About

362.70994 AUS ISSN 1035-0772
CHILDREN AUSTRALIA. Text in English. 1976. q. AUD 150 combined subscription domestic (print & online eds.); AUD 165 combined subscription foreign (print & online eds.) (effective 2011). back issues avail. **Document type:** *Journal, Academic/Scholarly.* **Description:** Aims to provide an opportunity for professional staff, academics and others concerned with children, youth and families, to report on research and practice in Australia and beyond.
Formerly (until 1990): Australian Child and Family Welfare (0312-8970)
Related titles: Online - full text ed.
Indexed: A11, AEI, AusPAIS, E03, ERO, PCI.
—Ingenta.
Published by: Australian Academic Press Pty. Ltd., 32 Jeays St, Bowen Hills, QLD 4006, Australia. TEL 61-7-32571176, FAX 61-7-32525908, info@australianacademicpress.com.au, http://www.australianacademicpress.com.au. Ed. Jennifer Lehmann.

362.7 FIN ISSN 0783-6244
CHILDREN IN FINLAND. Text in Finnish. irreg. **Document type:** *Magazine, Consumer.*
Related titles: ◆ Supplement to: Lapsen Maailma. ISSN 0786-0188.
Published by: Lastensuojelun Keskusliitto/Central Union for Child Welfare in Finland, Kauppakeskus Columbus, Vuotie 45, Helsinki, 00980, Finland. TEL 358-45-6361222, info@lapsenmaailma.fi. Ed. M Launis.

362.7 GBR
CHILDREN IN FOCUS. Text in English. 1881. 3/yr. free. bk.rev. **Document type:** *Magazine, Consumer.* **Description:** Discusses child welfare issues.
Former titles: Children in Form; (until 1993): Gateway
Published by: Children's Society, Edward Rudolph House 69-84, Margery St, London, WC1X 0JL, United Kingdom. TEL 44-207-8414436, FAX 44-207-8414500. Ed. Josephine Hocking. Circ: 300,000.

360 GBR
CHILDREN LOOKED AFTER. Text in English. 1979. a. back issues avail. **Document type:** *Bulletin, Government.* **Description:** Provides information on the characteristics of the children in care or under supervision in Scotland.
Formerly: Children in Care or Under Supervision (Year) (0260-5473); Which superseded in part (in 1979): Scottish Social Work Statistics (0307-9597)
Related titles: Online - full text ed.: free (effective 2010).
Published by: Social Work Services Group, Statistics Branch, Scottish Government, Education Directorate, Mail Point 1, 1-B (S), Victoria Quay, Edinburgh, EH6 6QQ, United Kingdom. TEL 44-131-2440313, FAX 44-131-2440354, info@statistics.gov.uk.

CHILDREN'S ADVOCATE. *see* CHILDREN AND YOUTH—About

362.7 USA
CHILDREN'S AID SOCIETY. ANNUAL REPORT. Text in English. 1854. a. free. **Document type:** *Newsletter, Corporate.*
Published by: Children's Aid Society, 105 East 22 St, New York, NY 10010. TEL 212-949-4933, FAX 212-477-3705. Ed. Truda C Jewett. Circ: 35,000.

362.7 USA
CHILDREN'S AID SOCIETY NEWS. Text in English. 1971. s-a. free. charts; illus. **Document type:** *Newsletter, Consumer.*
Former titles: Children's Aid Society Newsletter; Children's Aid Society News (0045-6667)
Published by: Children's Aid Society, 105 East 22 St, New York, NY 10010. TEL 212-949-4933, FAX 212-477-3705. Ed. Truda C Jewett. Circ: 35,000.

CHILDREN'S BUREAU EXPRESS. *see* CHILDREN AND YOUTH—About

CHILDREN'S GEOGRAPHIES; advancing interdisciplinary understanding of younger people's lives. *see* PSYCHOLOGY

362.7 USA ISSN 0273-9615
RJ242
➤ **CHILDREN'S HEALTH CARE.** Text in English. 1973. q. GBP 394 combined subscription in United Kingdom to institutions (print & online eds.); EUR 526, USD 661 combined subscription to institutions (print & online eds.) (effective 2012). adv. back issues avail.; reprint service avail. from PSC. **Document type:** *Journal, Academic/Scholarly.* **Description:** Features empirically-based articles addressing the theoretical, clinical, programmatic, training and professional practice issues relevant to the family-centered, developmental and psychosocial aspects of children's health care.
Former titles (until 1980): Association for the Care of Children's Health. Journal (0274-8916); (until 197?): Association for the Care of Children in Hospitals. Journal (0145-3351)
Related titles: Microform ed.: (from PQC); Online - full text ed.: ISSN 1532-6888. GBP 355 in United Kingdom to institutions; EUR 473, USD 595 to institutions (effective 2012).
Indexed: A01, A02, A03, A08, A22, ASCA, ASSIA, B21, C06, C07, C08, C11, C22, C28, CA, CINAHL, CurCont, E-psyche, E01, ECER, EMBASE, ESPM, ExcerpMed, F09, FamI, H&SSA, H04, H13, P02, P03, P10, P20, P24, P30, P43, P48, P53, P54, PQC, PsycInfo, PsycholAb, RiskAb, S11, SCOPUS, SSCI, T02, THA, W07.
—BLDSC (3172.990200), GNLM, IE, Infotrieve, Ingenta. **CCC.**
Published by: (Association for the Care of Children's Health (A C C H)), Routledge (Subsidiary of: Taylor & Francis Group), 325 Chestnut St, Ste 800, Philadelphia, PA 19106. TEL 800-354-1420, FAX 215-625-2940, journals@routledge.com, http://www.routledge.com. Ed. Kenneth J Tarnowski. Adv. contact Linda Hann TEL 44-1344-779945.

➤ **CHILDREN'S RIGHTS.** *see* POLITICAL SCIENCE—Civil Rights

362.7 USA ISSN 1057-736X
HV741
CHILDREN'S VOICE. Text in English. 1985. bi-m. USD 25 domestic; USD 40 foreign; USD 34.97 in North America to individuals; USD 64.97 elsewhere to individuals; USD 10 per issue domestic; USD 130 per issue foreign (effective 2009). adv. illus. 40 p./no.; back issues avail. **Document type:** *Magazine, Trade.* **Description:** Reports current program and policy developments in child welfare services.
Formed by the merger of (1976-1985): Child Welfare Planning Notes (0738-5986); (1971-1985): Child Welfare League Newsletter (0045-6659); (1979-1985): C W L A - Crittenton Reporter on School-Age Parenting
Related titles: Online - full text ed.: ISSN 1930-868X.
Indexed: A26, C06, C07, C08, CINAHL, E07, E09, H12, I05, P10, P18, P19, P24, P27, P48, P50, P53, P54, PQC, S02, S03.
—Ingenta. **CCC.**
Published by: Child Welfare League of America, Inc., 2345 Crystal Dr, Ste 250, Arlington, VA 22202. TEL 703-412-2400, FAX 703-412-2401, journal@cwla.org. Ed. Emily Shenk. Adv. contact Karen Dunn TEL 703-412-2416. **Subscr. to:** PO Box 932831, Atlanta, GA 31193. TEL 770-280-4164, 800-407-6273.

362.7 NLD ISSN 1879-5196
▼ **CHILDREN'S WELL-BEING.** Text in English. 2010. irreg., latest vol.4, 2010. price varies. **Document type:** *Monographic series, Academic/Scholarly.* **Description:** Explores how child indicators can be used to improve the development and well-being of children.
Related titles: Online - full text ed.: ISSN 1879-520X.
Published by: Springer Netherlands (Subsidiary of: Springer Science+Business Media), Van Godewijckstraat 30, Dordrecht, 3311 GX, Netherlands. TEL 31-78-6576050, FAX 31-78-6576474. Ed. Asher Ben-Arieh.

360 USA ISSN 1934-3868
HF3831
CHINA IN FOCUS. Text in English. 2005. bi-w. **Document type:** *Newsletter, Consumer.*
Media: Online - full text.
Published by: Asia America Initiative, 1523 16th St., NW, Washington, DC 20036. TEL 202-232-7020, FAX 202-232-7023, admin@asiaamerica.org, http://www.asiaamerica.org/index.html.

360 GBR ISSN 1752-5098
HV416
➤ **CHINA JOURNAL OF SOCIAL WORK.** Text in English; Abstracts in Chinese, English. 2008. 3/yr. GBP 217 combined subscription in United Kingdom to institutions (print & online eds.); EUR 337, USD 423 combined subscription to institutions (print & online eds.) (effective 2012). adv. back issues avail.; reprint service avail. from PSC. **Document type:** *Journal, Academic/Scholarly.* **Description:** Aims to provide a platform for scholars within and outside of the Chinese mainland to share research, teaching and practice experiences and to facilitate critical dialogue between Chinese social workers and their international peers.
Related titles: Online - full text ed.: ISSN 1752-5101. GBP 196 in United Kingdom to institutions; EUR 304, USD 381 to institutions (effective 2012).
Indexed: A22, CA, E01, PQC, S02, S03, T02.
—IE. **CCC.**
Published by: (Hong Kong Polytechnic University HKG), Routledge (Subsidiary of: Taylor & Francis Group), 4 Park Sq, Milton Park, Abingdon, Oxon OX14 4RN, United Kingdom. TEL 44-20-70176000, FAX 44-20-70176336, subscriptions@tandf.co.uk, http://www.routledge.com/journals/. Ed. Angelina W K Yuen. Adv. contact Linda Hann TEL 44-1344-779945. **Subscr. to:** Taylor & Francis Ltd., Journals Customer Service, Sheepen Pl, Colchester, Essex CO3 3LP, United Kingdom. TEL 44-20-70175544, FAX 44-20-70175198.

361 338.91 NLD ISSN 1876-5092
HD2769.2.C6
▼ ➤ **THE CHINA NONPROFIT REVIEW.** Text in English. 2009. s-a. EUR 163, USD 229 to institutions; EUR 178, USD 249 combined subscription to institutions (print & online eds.) (effective 2012). **Document type:** *Journal, Academic/Scholarly.*
Related titles: Online - full text ed.: ISSN 1876-5149. EUR 148, USD 208 to institutions (effective 2012) (from IngentaConnect).
Indexed: A22, CA, CABA, E01, IZBG, LT, N06, R12, RRTA, SCOPUS, T02, TAR, W11.
—**CCC.**
Published by: Brill, PO Box 9000, Leiden, 2300 PA, Netherlands. TEL 31-71-5353500, FAX 31-71-5317532, cs@brill.nl. Ed. Ming Wang.

➤ **CHRETIENS DE L'EST.** *see* RELIGIONS AND THEOLOGY—Roman Catholic

➤ **CHRIS**; Kinderzeitschrift der Christoffel-Blindenmission. *see* CHILDREN AND YOUTH—For

360 GBR
CHRONIC POVERTY RESEARCH CENTRE. WORKING PAPERS. Variant title: C P R C Working Paper. Text in English. 2001. irreg., latest vol.150, no.38, 2009. back issues avail. **Document type:** *Monographic series, Academic/Scholarly.*
Related titles: Online - full text ed.: free (effective 2009).
Published by: Chronic Poverty Research Centre, Institute for Development Policy and Management, School of Environment and Development, University of Manches, Humanities Bridgeford St, Manchester, M13 9PL, United Kingdom. TEL 44-161-2752810, FAX 44-161-2738829, cprc@manchester.ac.uk.

361.73 USA ISSN 1040-676X
THE CHRONICLE OF PHILANTHROPY; the newspaper of the non-profit world. Text in English. 1988. bi-w. USD 72 domestic; USD 99.75 in Canada; USD 135 elsewhere; USD 5.63 per issue; free to qualified personnel (effective 2009). adv. back issues avail.; reprints avail. **Document type:** *Newspaper, Trade.* **Description:** Provides news and information for fund raisers, professional employees of foundations, corporate grant makers and people who work for non-profit, tax-exempt organizations in health, education, religion, the arts, and social services.
Related titles: Online - full text ed.: ISSN 1943-3980. USD 52.50 domestic; USD 2.19 per issue (effective 2009).
Indexed: A01, A03, A08, A21, A22, A26, B02, B04, B07, B14, B15, B17, B18, BPI, BRD, BRI, CA, E08, G04, G06, G07, G08, I05, M02, N06, P34, PSI, RI-1, RI-2, S09, SRI, T02, W01, W02, W03, W05.
—Linda Hall. **CCC.**
Published by: Chronicle of Higher Education, Inc., 1255 23rd St, NW, Ste 700, 7th Fl, Washington, DC 20037. TEL 202-466-1200, FAX 202-452-1033, orders@allenpress.com, help@chronicle.com, http://chronicle.com. Eds. Jeffrey J Selingo TEL 202-466-1075, Philip Semas.

177.7 CHN ISSN 1008-0376
CISHAN/CHARITY. Text in Chinese. 1998. bi-m. USD 24 (effective 2009). **Document type:** *Journal, Academic/Scholarly.*
—East View.
Published by: Tianjin Shi Hepingqu Wenlian, Heping-qu, 10, Chengdudao Wenxingli, Tianjin, 300051, China. TEL 86-22-23306369, http://www.cswh.com.cn/. **Dist. by:** China International Book Trading Corp, 35 Chegongzhuang Xilu, Haidian District, PO Box 399, Beijing 100044, China. TEL 86-10-68412045, FAX 86-10-68412023, cibtc@mail.cibtc.com.cn, http://www.cibtc.com.cn.

360 USA ISSN 1535-6841
HT101
➤ **CITY & COMMUNITY.** Text in English. q. GBP 290 in United Kingdom to institutions; EUR 367 in Europe to institutions; USD 368 in the Americas to institutions; USD 503 elsewhere to institutions; GBP 323 combined subscription in United Kingdom to institutions (print & online eds.); EUR 410 combined subscription in Europe to institutions (print & online eds.); USD 410 combined subscription in the Americas to institutions (print & online eds.); USD 561 combined subscription elsewhere to institutions (print & online eds.) (effective 2012). reprint service avail. from PSC. **Document type:** *Journal, Academic/Scholarly.*
Related titles: Online - full text ed.: ISSN 1540-6040. GBP 290 in United Kingdom to institutions; EUR 367 in Europe to institutions; USD 368 in the Americas to institutions; USD 503 elsewhere to institutions (effective 2012) (from IngentaConnect).
Indexed: A01, A03, A08, A20, A22, A26, CA, CJA, CurCont, E01, ESPM, P02, P03, P10, P34, P48, P53, P54, PQC, PsycInfo, PsycholAb, RiskAb, S02, S03, S11, SCOPUS, SRRA, SSCI, SSciA, SUSA, SociolAb, T02, W07.
—BLDSC (3268.302500), IE, Ingenta. **CCC.**
Published by: (American Sociological Association), Wiley-Blackwell Publishing, Inc. (Subsidiary of: Wiley-Blackwell Publishing Ltd.), Commerce Pl, 350 Main St, Malden, MA 02148. TEL 781-388-8206, FAX 781-388-8232, info@wiley.com, http://www.wiley.com/WileyCDA/. Ed. Anthony M Orum.

360 614.8 USA ISSN 0898-6339
HV99.C55
CLEVELAND FOUNDATION. ANNUAL REPORT. Text in English. a. **Document type:** *Corporate.* **Description:** The foundation exists to enhance the quality of life for all residents of Greater Cleveland. Using funds entrusted to its stewardship by thousands of people of various means, the foundation makes grants to non-profit organizations and governmental agencies to address the community's needs and opportunities.
Published by: Cleveland Foundation, 1422 Euclid Ave, Ste 1300, Cleveland, OH 44115-2063. TEL 216-861-3810, FAX 216-861-1729, http://www.clevelandfoundation.org. Ed. Lynne E Woodman.

362 JPN
CLINIC BAMBOO. Text in Japanese. 1981. m. JPY 12,240 (effective 2007). **Document type:** *Journal, Academic/Scholarly.*
Formerly (until Mar. 2006): Banbu/Bamboo (0912-8662)
Published by: Nihon Iryo Kikaku/Japan Medical Planning, 4-14 Kanda-Iwamoto-cho, Chiyoda-ku, Tokyo, 101-0033, Japan. TEL 81-3-32562861, FAX 81-3-32562865.

CLINICAL CHILD PSYCHOLOGY & PSYCHIATRY. *see* CHILDREN AND YOUTH—About

CLINICAL GERONTOLOGIST; the journal of aging and mental health. *see* GERONTOLOGY AND GERIATRICS

361.3 USA ISSN 0091-1674
HV1 CODEN: CSWJBG
➤ **CLINICAL SOCIAL WORK JOURNAL.** Text in English. 1973. q. EUR 984, USD 1,018 combined subscription to institutions (print & online eds.) (effective 2012). adv. bk.rev. illus. index. back issues avail.; reprint service avail. from PSC. **Document type:** *Journal, Academic/Scholarly.* **Description:** Covers clinical social work theory and practice, and provides a cross-fertilization of ideas and concepts.
Related titles: Microform ed.: (from PQC); Online - full text ed.: ISSN 1573-3343 (from IngentaConnect).
Indexed: A01, A02, A03, A08, A20, A22, A25, A26, AC&P, AMHA, ASCA, B04, BRD, BibLing, C28, CA, CDA, CurCont, E-psyche, E01, E08, E15, E16, ERA, ESPM, F09, FR, FamI, G08, G10, HRA, I05, M12, MEA&I, P02, P03, P10, P25, P27, P30, P46, P48, P50, P53, P54, PQC, PsycInfo, PsycholAb, RiskAb, S02, S03, S08, S09, S11, S19, S20, S21, SCOPUS, SFSA, SOPODA, SSA, SSAI, SSAb, SSCI, SSI, SWR&A, SociolAb, T02, V&AA, V05, W03, W05, W07, W09.
—BLDSC (3286.381000), GNLM, IE, Infotrieve, Ingenta, INIST. **CCC.**
Published by: (Clinical Social Work Association), Springer New York LLC (Subsidiary of: Springer Science+Business Media), 233 Spring St, New York, NY 10013. TEL 212-460-1500, FAX 212-460-1575, service-ny@springer.com. Ed. Carol Tosone.

361 USA ISSN 0732-5223
RC336 CODEN: CLSUEH
➤ **THE CLINICAL SUPERVISOR**; the journal of supervision in psychotherapy and mental health. Text in English. 1982. s-a. GBP 651 combined subscription in United Kingdom to institutions (print & online eds.); EUR 844, USD 847 combined subscription to institutions (print & online eds.) (effective 2012). adv. bk.rev. 120 p./no. 1 cols./p.; back issues avail.; reprint service avail. from PSC. **Document type:** *Journal, Academic/Scholarly.* **Description:** Reflects the concerns, needs, and interests of supervisors in a variety of professional settings. Highlights current supervisory techniques and methods.
Formerly (until 1983): Journal of Social Work Supervision
Related titles: Microfiche ed.: (from PQC); Microform ed.; Online - full text ed.: ISSN 1545-231X. GBP 586 in United Kingdom to institutions; EUR 760, USD 762 to institutions (effective 2012).
Indexed: A01, A03, A22, B21, C06, C07, C08, CA, CINAHL, CPLI, E-psyche, E01, E03, E17, ERI, ESPM, FamI, HRA, M02, P03, P04, PC&CA, PsycInfo, PsycholAb, RehabLit, S02, S03, SCOPUS, SOPODA, SSA, SWR&A, SociolAb, T02, V&AA.
—BLDSC (3286.387000), GNLM, IE, Infotrieve, Ingenta, INIST. **CCC.**
Published by: Routledge (Subsidiary of: Taylor & Francis Group), 325 Chestnut St, Ste 800, Philadelphia, PA 19106. TEL 215-625-8900, 800-354-1420, FAX 215-625-8914, journals@routledge.com, http://www.routledge.com. Ed. Carlean Gilbert. adv.: B&W page USD 315, color page USD 550; trim 4.375 x 7.125. Circ: 334 (paid).

361.2 USA
CO-OP VOICES. Text in English. q. free. **Document type:** *Newsletter.* **Description:** Reports the most recent and pertinent news about the campus co-op movement.
Related titles: Online - full text ed.
Published by: North American Students of Cooperation, PO Box 7715, Ann Arbor, MI 48107. TEL 734-663-0889, FAX 734-663-5072.

362 617.087 USA ISSN 1936-0266
COACHING CLIPS. Text in English. 2006. bi-m. free (effective 2007). **Document type:** *Newsletter, Consumer.* **Description:** Provides tips for health care professionals, parents and others who work in support of people with Down syndrome and related disabilities to make healthy lifestyle choices.
Media: Online - full content.
Published by: Phronesis Publishing, 14535 Westlake Dr, Ste A-2, Lake Oswego, OR 97035. TEL 503-246-3849, FAX 503-443-4211, info@downsyndromenutrition.com, http://www.nutritioncoaching.net/index.htm. Ed. Joan Guthrie Medlen.

360 USA ISSN 1932-5398
HV4506.N7
COALITION FOR THE HOMELESS RESOURCE GUIDE. Text in English. 1993. irreg., latest 2002. **Document type:** *Guide, Consumer.*
Published by: Coalition for the Homeless, 129 Fulton St, New York, NY 10038. TEL 212-776-2000, FAX 212-964-1303, info@cfthomeless.org, http://www.coalitionforthehomeless.org.

360 340 BEL ISSN 1782-1908
CODEX O C M W - WETGEVING. Text in Dutch. 2002. irreg. **Document type:** *Monographic series, Academic/Scholarly.*
Published by: Die Keure NV, Kleine Pathoekeweg 3, Bruges, 8000, Belgium. TEL 32-50-471272, FAX 32-50-335154, juridische.uitgaven@diekeure.be, http://www.diekeure.be.

CODEX OPENBARE HULPVERLENING. HULPDIENSTEN. *see* PUBLIC ADMINISTRATION

CODEX OPENBARE HULPVERLENING. INTERVENTIE. *see* PUBLIC ADMINISTRATION

CODEX OPENBARE HULPVERLENING. PREVENTIE. *see* PUBLIC ADMINISTRATION

368.4 BEL ISSN 1783-8835
CODEX SOCIALE ZEKERHEID. Text in Dutch. 1984. a. EUR 81 (effective 2008). **Document type:** *Trade.*
Published by: Die Keure NV, Kleine Pathoekeweg 3, Bruges, 8000, Belgium. TEL 32-50-471272, FAX 32-50-335154, juridische.uitgaven@diekeure.be, http://www.diekeure.be.

360 IRL
COMBAT POVERTY AGENCY. POVERTY AND POLICY DISCUSSION PAPER. Text in English. 1993. irreg., latest vol.3, 1997. **Document type:** *Monographic series, Academic/Scholarly.*
Published by: Combat Poverty Agency, Bridgewater Centre, Conyngham Rd., Island Bridge, Dublin, 8, Ireland. TEL 353-1-670-6746, FAX 353-1-670-6760, info@cpa.ie, http://www.cpa.ie.

362.580982 ARG
COMITE EJECUTIVO DE LA POBREZA EN LA ARGENTINA. ESTUDIOS. Variant title: Estudios C E P A. Text in Spanish. 1993. irreg., latest vol.3, 1993. ARS 10, USD 15 (effective 1999). **Document type:** *Government.*
Published by: Instituto Nacional de Estadistica y Censos, Presidente Julio A Roca 615, Buenos Aires, 1067, Argentina. TEL 54-114-3499662, FAX 54-114-3499621.

360 AUS ISSN 1448-4749
COMMON GROUND. Text in English. 2003 (Jul.). s-a. back issues avail. **Document type:** *Magazine, Government.* **Description:** Designed to inform the indigenous population about government opportunities.
Published by: Northern Territory, Department of Chief Minister, PO Box 2605, Alice Springs, N.T. 0871, Australia. TEL 61-8-89995511, FAX 61-8-89996733, http://www.nt.gov.au/dcm/index.html.

COMMONWEALTH; politics, ideas and civic life in Massachusetts. *see* PUBLIC ADMINISTRATION

COMMUNICATION (LONDON, 1967); the magazine of the National Autistic Society. *see* EDUCATION—Special Education And Rehabilitation

361.8 GBR ISSN 0143-2168
COMMUNITY. Text in English. 1940. bi-m. GBP 15 to non-members; free to members (effective 2010). adv. bk.rev. **Document type:** *Magazine, Consumer.* **Description:** Carries news from community organizations around the country, updates on national matters relevant to community groups such as legislation, campaigns, funding and new government initiatives.
—BLDSC (3363.571970).
Published by: (The National Federation of Community Organisers), Community Matters, 12-20 Baron St, London, N1 9LL, United Kingdom. TEL 44-20-78377887, FAX 44-20-72789253, nfo@communitymatters.org.uk, http://www.communitymatters.org.uk/. Circ: 2,500.

361.8 CAN ISSN 0833-0816
COMMUNITY ACTION. Text in English. 1985. 22/yr. CAD 35.95 domestic to individuals; CAD 44.95 in United States to individuals; CAD 51.95 elsewhere to individuals. adv. bk.rev. **Document type:** *Newspaper.* **Description:** Provides news and information on health and social services in Canada.
Related titles: Online - full text ed.
Indexed: A26, C03, CBCARef, CPerI, G08, I05, P48, P50, PQC.
—CIS.
Published by: Community Action Publishers, P O Box 448, Don Mills, ON M3C 2T2, Canada. TEL 416-449-6766, FAX 416-444-5850. Ed., Pub. Leon Kumove. adv.: B&W page CAD 1,969, color page CAD 2,300; trim 17 x 11.38. Circ: 6,768 (paid).

361.3 GBR
COMMUNITY CARE (EDINBURGH). Text in English. 1991. a. back issues avail. **Document type:** *Government.* **Description:** Provides information covering the whole range of health and social care services for adults in Scotland.
Related titles: Online - full text ed.: free (effective 2010).
Published by: Social Work Services Group, Statistics Branch, Scottish Government, Education Directorate, Mail Point 1, 1-B (S), Victoria Quay, Edinburgh, EH6 6QQ, United Kingdom. TEL 44-131-2440313, FAX 44-131-2440354, info@statistics.gov.uk.

361 GBR ISSN 0307-5508
HV241
COMMUNITY CARE (SUTTON); for everyone in social care. Text in English. 1974. w. GBP 2.45 per issue; free to qualified personnel (effective 2010). bk.rev. s-a. index. back issues avail. **Document type:** *Magazine, Trade.* **Description:** Information for social care staff and other related professionals involved in the provision, organization and management of social welfare in the UK.
Incorporates (1970-1993): Social Work Today (0037-8070); Which was formed by the merger of (1970-1973): Residential Social Work (0308-7816); Which was formerly (until 1973): Child in Care; (1970-19??): Case conference and A S W News (0576-8551); Mental Welfare; Medical Social Work
Related titles: Online - full text ed.
Indexed: A01, A03, A08, A15, A22, A26, ABIn, AMED, ASG, ASSIA, B02, B15, B17, B18, B28, BRD, C06, C07, C08, CINAHL, E02, E03, ERI, EdA, EdI, F09, G04, G06, G07, G08, H01, H12, I05, P19, P21, P24, P27, P34, P48, P50, P51, P54, PQC, S02, S03, SCOPUS, SRRA, SSAI, SSAb, SSI, T02, W03, W05.
—BLDSC (3363.598000), IE, Infotrieve, Ingenta. **CCC.**
Published by: Reed Business Information Ltd. (Subsidiary of: Reed Business), Quadrant House, The Quadrant, Sutton, Surrey SM2 5AS, United Kingdom. TEL 44-20-86524214, FAX 44-20-86524739, http://www.reedbusiness.co.uk/. Ed. Gordon Carson TEL 44-20-86524717. Adv. contact James Frowde TEL 44-20-86528870. **Subscr. to:** Quadrant Subscription Services, Rockwood House, 9-17 Perrymount Rd, Haywards Heath, W. Sussex RH16 3DH, United Kingdom. TEL 44-1444-445566, FAX 44-1444-445447, qss.customer.services@quadrantsubs.com, http://www.quadrantsubs.com.

S

360 AUS
COMMUNITY CARE REVIEW NEWSLETTER. Text in English. 2000 (Feb. 18th, no.1). **Document type:** *Newsletter, Government.*
Related titles: Online - full content ed.
Published by: Victoria, Department Of Human Services, Community Care Division (Subsidiary of: Victoria, Department of Human Services), 50 Lonsdale St, Melbourne, VIC 3000, Australia. TEL 61-3-90960000, 300-650-172, http://www.dhs.vic.gov.au.

COMMUNITY CHANGE. *see* BUSINESS AND ECONOMICS—Economic Situation And Conditions

361.8 AUS
COMMUNITY CONNECT. Text in English. 2008. bi-m. free (effective 2009). back issues avail. **Document type:** *Magazine, Consumer.* **Description:** Provides reports on initiatives, policies, and programs and covers events that promote community partnerships and community-focused achievements.
Formed by the merger of (2005-2008): Community Spirit (1449-8421); (2004-2008): Connect (1449-4841); Which was formerly (until 2004): Disability Views (1448-9600)
Related titles: Online - full text ed.
Published by: (Queensland, Department of Disability Services), Queensland, Department of Communities, GPO Box 806, Brisbane, QLD 4001, Australia. TEL 61-7-32359999, 800-177-135, FAX 61-7-34043570, enquiries@communities.qld.gov.au.

COMMUNITY, CULTURE AND CHANGE. *see* PHILOSOPHY

354.35 USA ISSN 1557-5330
HN1
➤ **COMMUNITY DEVELOPMENT (COLUMBUS).** Text in English. 1970. q. GBP 242 combined subscription in United Kingdom to institutions (print & online eds.); EUR 301, USD 435 combined subscription to institutions (print & online eds.) (effective 2012). adv. bk.rev. abstr.; bibl.; charts. back issues avail.; reprint service avail. from PSC. **Document type:** *Journal, Academic/Scholarly.* **Description:** Devoted to improving knowledge and practice in the field of purposive community change by disseminating information on theory, research and practice.
Formerly (until 2005): Community Development Society. Journal (0010-3829)
Related titles: Microfilm ed.; Online - full text ed.: ISSN 1944-7485. 2005. GBP 217 in United Kingdom to institutions; EUR 271, USD 391 to institutions (effective 2012).
Indexed: A22, A26, Agr, BibAg, CA, E03, E07, E08, ERI, G08, I05, P06, P10, P11, P30, P48, P52, P53, P54, P56, PAIS, PCI, PQC, S02, S03, S09, S11, SCOPUS, SOPODA, SSciA, SWR&A, SociolAb, T02.
—BLDSC (3363.614000), IE, Infotrieve, Ingenta. **CCC.**
Published by: (Community Development Society), Routledge (Subsidiary of: Taylor & Francis Group), 325 Chestnut St, Ste 800, Philadelphia, PA 19106. TEL 215-625-8900, FAX 215-625-8914, journals@routledge.com, http://www.routledge.com. Ed. Rhonda Phillips.

360 GBR ISSN 0010-3802
HN1
➤ **COMMUNITY DEVELOPMENT JOURNAL**; an international forum. Text in English. 1949. q. GBP 198 in United Kingdom to institutions; EUR 296 in Europe to institutions; USD 394 in US & Canada to institutions; GBP 198 elsewhere to institutions; GBP 216 combined subscription in United Kingdom to institutions (print & online eds.); EUR 323 combined subscription in Europe to institutions (print & online eds.); USD 430 combined subscription in US & Canada to institutions (print & online eds.); GBP 216 combined subscription elsewhere to institutions (print & online eds.) (effective 2012). adv. bk.rev. illus. index, cum.index. 108 p./no.; back issues avail.; reprint service avail. from PSC. **Document type:** *Journal, Academic/Scholarly.* **Description:** Covers community work and development in industrial and developing nations.
Former titles (until 1996): Community Development Bulletin; (until 1951): Mass Education Bulletin
Related titles: Microform ed.: (from PQC); Online - full text ed.: ISSN 1468-2656. 2000. GBP 180 in United Kingdom to institutions; EUR 269 in Europe to institutions; USD 358 in US & Canada to institutions; GBP 180 elsewhere to institutions (effective 2012) (from IngentaConnect).
Indexed: A01, A03, A08, A12, A20, A22, A36, ABIn, APEL, ARDT, ASD, ASSIA, BAS, CA, CABA, CCA, CurCont, DIP, E01, E03, E12, ERI, ESPM, EconLit, F08, F11, F12, GEOBASE, GH, H09, I13, IBR, IBSS, IBZ, ILD, JEL, JOF, LT, MEA&I, MLA-IB, N02, P06, P10, P21, P30, P34, P42, P48, P50, P51, P53, P54, PAIS, PCI, PQC, PRA, PSA, PSI, R12, RASB, REE&TA, RRTA, RiskAb, S02, S03, S05, S11, S13, S16, SCOPUS, SOPODA, SPAA, SSA, SSCI, SSciA, SUSA, SWR&A, SociolAb, T02, T05, TAR, W07, W09, W11.
—BLDSC (3363.621000), IE, Infotrieve, Ingenta. **CCC.**
Published by: Oxford University Press, Great Clarendon St, Oxford, OX2 6DP, United Kingdom. TEL 44-1865-556767, FAX 44-1865-556646, enquiry@oup.co.uk, http://www.oup.co.uk/. Ed. Chris Miller. Pub. Martin Green. Adv. contact Linda Hann TEL 44-1344-779945. B&W page GBP 295, B&W page USD 490; 110 x 185. Circ: 1,250.

➤ **COMMUNITY FOCUS.** *see* ADVERTISING AND PUBLIC RELATIONS

060 USA
COMMUNITY FOUNDATION REPORT. Text in English. q. **Description:** Focuses on foundation news and local philanthropic activity.
Published by: Community Foundation for Southeastern Michigan, 333 W Fort St, Ste 2010, Detroit, MI 48226. TEL 313-961-6675, FAX 313-961-2886.

360 NZL ISSN 1172-5516
COMMUNITY HELP; the New Zealand directory of services. Text in English. 1992. a. NZD 55.95 domestic; NZD 70 in Australia; NZD 95 elsewhere (effective 2008). adv. back issues avail. **Document type:** *Directory, Trade.* **Description:** Describes the services that are provided by government and various organizations throughout the country. Lists contacts at local, regional and national levels.
Formerly (until 1994): Rural Help
Published by: C R McPhail Ltd., P.O. Box 2091, Palmerston North, New Zealand. TEL 64-6-3571644, FAX 64-6-3571648, http://www.crmcphail.co.nz. Ed., R&P, Adv. contact Ron McPhail.

360 GBR ISSN 0951-9815
COMMUNITY LIVING. Text in English. 1987. q. GBP 30 in Europe to individuals; GBP 36 elsewhere to individuals; GBP 48 in Europe to institutions; GBP 50 elsewhere to institutions (effective 2009). bk.rev. back issues avail. **Document type:** *Magazine, Consumer.*
Indexed: A22, A26, AMED, B28, C06, C07, C08, CINAHL, E08, G06, G07, G08, H11, H12, I05, P20, P48, P54, PQC, S09.
—BLDSC (3363.635300), IE, Ingenta. **CCC.**
Published by: The Elfrida Society, 34 Islington Park St, Islington, London, N1 1PX, United Kingdom. TEL 44-20-73597443, FAX 44-20-77041358, elfrida@elfrida.com, http://www.elfrida.com. Ed. Elinor Harbridge.

301.1 362 USA ISSN 0010-3853
RA790.A1 CODEN: CMHJAY
➤ **COMMUNITY MENTAL HEALTH JOURNAL.** Text in English. 1965. bi-m. EUR 1,153, USD 1,192 combined subscription to institutions (print & online eds.) (effective 2012). adv. bk.rev.; film rev. abstr.; bibl.; charts; illus. index. back issues avail.; reprint service avail. from PSC. **Document type:** *Journal, Academic/Scholarly.* **Description:** Coordinates emergent approaches to mental health and social well-being, covering crisis intervention, suicide prevention, family therapy, and social welfare.
Related titles: Microform ed.: (from PQC); Online - full text ed.: ISSN 1573-2789 (from IngentaConnect).
Indexed: A01, A02, A03, A08, A12, A13, A20, A22, A26, ABIn, AHCMS, AMED, AMHA, ASCA, ASSIA, B04, B21, BRD, BibLing, C06, C07, C08, CA, CERDIC, CINAHL, Chicano, CurCont, E-psyche, E01, E08, EMBASE, ERA, ESPM, ExcerpMed, F09, FR, FamI, G08, H&SSA, H09, H12, H13, HEA, HRA, HospLI, I05, INI, IndMed, MEA&I, MEDLINE, MRD, MRefA, P02, P03, P10, P13, P19, P20, P22, P24, P25, P27, P30, P34, P46, P48, P50, P51, P53, P54, PCI, PQC, PsycInfo, PsycholAb, R10, Reac, RiskAb, S02, S03, S05, S09, S11, S20, S21, SCOPUS, SFSA, SOPODA, SSA, SSAI, SSAb, SSCI, SSI, SWR&A, SociolAb, T02, V&AA, W01, W02, W03, W05, W07.
—BLDSC (3363.643000), GNLM, IE, Infotrieve, Ingenta, INIST. **CCC.**
Published by: (American Association of Community Psychiatrists, National Council of Community Mental Health Centers, Inc.), Springer New York LLC (Subsidiary of: Springer Science+Business Media), 233 Spring St, New York, NY 10013. TEL 212-460-1500, FAX 212-460-1575, service-ny@springer.com. Ed. Jacqueline M Feldman.

616.858 362.2 364.4 USA ISSN 1531-1848
RA790.6
COMMUNITY MENTAL HEALTH REPORT. Text in English. 2000. bi-m. USD 179.95 (effective 2008). **Document type:** *Newsletter.* **Description:** Provides information for professionals working with mentally disordered persons in the community.
—CCC.
Published by: Civic Research Insitute, 4478 US Rte 27, PO Box 585, Kingston, NJ 08528. TEL 609-683-4450, FAX 609-683-7291, order@civicresearchinstitute.com, http://www.civicresearchinstitute.com. Ed. Fred Cohen.

COMMUNITY, WORK & FAMILY. *see* SOCIAL SCIENCES: COMPREHENSIVE WORKS

361 PER
COMO ESTAMOS?; revista trimestral de analisis social. Text in Spanish. 1993. q.
Published by: Instituto Cuanto, Plaza De Ovalo, 203-B, San Isidro, Lima 27, Peru. TEL 51-14-423421, FAX 51-14-425460. Ed. Walter Cavero Dhaga.

360 150 371.3 CAN ISSN 1488-6782
➤ **COMPASS (VICTORIA)**; a magazine for peer assistance, mentorship and coaching. Text in English. 1999 (Winter). irreg., latest 2002, Winter. CAD 53.50 per issue domestic to individuals; USD 53.50 per issue foreign to individuals; CAD 107 per issue domestic to corporations; USD 107 foreign to corporations; CAD 21.40 domestic to students; USD 21.40 foreign to students; CAD 15 domestic to members (effective 2003). bk.rev.; Website rev. abstr.; bibl. back issues avail. **Document type:** *Journal, Academic/Scholarly.* **Description:** Shares insights and information about issues, innovations, research, resources, and practices related to mentorship, peer assistance, and coaching.
Formed by the merger of (1993-1999): Oddysey (1195-9975); (1982-1999): Peer Counsellor Journal (1194-8167); Which was formerly (until 1993): Peer Counsellor (1180-470X)
Related titles: Online - full content ed.
Published by: Peer Resources, 1052 Davie St, Victoria, BC V8S 4E3, Canada. TEL 250-595-3503, FAX 250-595-3504, info@peer.ca. Ed., R&P Dr. Rey A Carr. Circ: 150 (free); 2,000 (paid).

➤ **COMPASSION AND CHOICES MAGAZINE.** *see* MEDICAL SCIENCES

362.2 USA ISSN 1089-9871
COMPREHENSIVE ACCREDITATION MANUAL FOR BEHAVIORAL HEALTH CARE. Abbreviated title: C A M B H C. Text in English. 1998. biennial. USD 265 per issue (effective 2009). reprints avail. **Document type:** *Handbook/Manual/Guide, Trade.*
Formed by the merger of (1993-1995): Accreditation Manual for Mental Health, Chemical Dependency, and Mental Retardation/ Developmental Disabilities Services. Vol. 2, Scoring Guidelines (1077-5617); Which was formerly (until 1991): Joint Commission on Accreditation of Hospitals. Consolidated Standards Manual (1041-5238); (until 1985): Consolidated Standards Manual for Child, Adolescent, and Adult Psychiatric, Alcoholism, and Drug Abuse Facilities (1041-522X); (1993-1995): Accreditation Manual for Mental Health, Chemical Dependency, and Mental Retardation/ Developmental Disabilities Services. Vol.1, Standards (1077-5609)
—CCC.
Published by: Joint Commission on Accreditation of Healthcare Organizations, 1 Renaissance Blvd, Oakbrook Terrace, IL 60181. TEL 630-792-5000, FAX 630-792-5005, customerservice@jointcommission.org, http://www.jointcommission.org/.

361 610 USA
CONCERN NEWS. Text in English. 1961. q. free. illus. **Document type:** *Newsletter, Consumer.* **Description:** News of projects and people working to ensure the survival of children whose lives are at risk and the access to health care for those in need, reporting on medical assistance & malnutrition issues, and efforts to build self-reliant health care systems in countries throughout the world.
Former titles: Project Concern News (0033-0906); Project Concern Newsletter
Related titles: Online - full text ed.
Published by: Project Concern International, 5151 Murphy Canyon Rd, Ste 320, San Diego, CA 92123-4339. TEL 619-279-9690, FAX 619-694-0294, postmaster@ProjectConcern.org, http://www.projectconcern.org/. Ed. Charles Goldberg. Circ: 5,000.

361 ZAF ISSN 1561-9818
CONFLICT TRENDS MAGAZINE. Text in English. 2000. 3/yr. **Document type:** *Magazine, Consumer.* **Description:** Offers unique at-a-glance overviews of both developments in conflicts and positive steps towards renaissance on the continent of Africa. Also included are in-depth articles focusing on conflict analysis.
Related titles: Online - full text ed.
Indexed: IIBP.
Published by: African Centre for the Constructive Resolution or Disputes (A C C O R D), Private Bag X018, Umhlanga Rocks, 4320, South Africa. TEL 27-31-5023908, FAX 27-31-5024160, info@accord.org.za, http://www.accord.org.za.

CONNECT WYOMING. *see* HANDICAPPED

CONNECTIONS (BUNDANOON). *see* ALTERNATIVE MEDICINE

CONNECTIONS (DAYTON). *see* POLITICAL SCIENCE

360 USA ISSN 2152-6362
▼ **CONNECTIONS (HAVRE).** Text in English. 2009. q. free (effective 2010). back issues avail. **Document type:** *Newsletter, Trade.*
Related titles: Online - full text ed.: ISSN 2152-6370.
Published by: Opportunity Link, Inc, 2229 5th Ave, Ste 218-224, PO Box 80, Havre, MT 59501. TEL 406-265-3699, 877-332-3699, FAX 406-265-2075, ttucker@opportunitylinkmt.org.

362.6 ITA
CONQUISTE DEI PENSIONATI. Text in Italian. 1953. m. free to members. **Document type:** *Bulletin, Consumer.*
Published by: Federpensionati Srl, Via Castelfidardo 47, Rome, 00185, Italy. TEL 39-06-44881301, FAX 39-06-4460570.

361.06 CAN
CONTACT POINT BULLETIN. Text in English. 1997. q. free. adv. **Description:** Provides information and news for career counsellors and career development practitioners.
Media: Online - full text.
Published by: Counselling Foundation of Canada, 674 Markham St, Ste 200, Toronto, ON M6G 2L9, Canada. TEL 416-205-9543. Ed. Riz Ibrahim.

CONTINUING CARE NEWS; supporting the transition into post hospital care. *see* HEALTH FACILITIES AND ADMINISTRATION

CONTOURS. *see* TRAVEL AND TOURISM

361.74 USA ISSN 1559-6168
CONTRIBUTE NEW YORK; the people and ideas of giving. Text in English. 2006. bi-m. USD 85 domestic; USD 125 foreign (effective 2007). adv. **Document type:** *Magazine, Consumer.* **Description:** Geared toward the donor and dedicated to all things philanthropic. It provides the 'donor' community with engaging and responsible coverage of the philanthropic world to promote more effective giving.
Published by: Contribute Magazine, Inc., 630 5th Ave, Ste 1776, New York, NY 10111-1705. TEL 212-756-0041, FAX 646-349-3980, advertising@contributemedia.com. Ed. Marcia Stepanek TEL 917-535-1399. Pub. Lisa Gyselen. adv.: color page USD 9,800; trim 8.375 x 10.875. Circ: 65,000 (controlled).

361.73 USA ISSN 1070-9444
HG177.5.U6
CONTRIBUTIONS. Text in English. 1987. bi-m. USD 40 domestic (effective 2001). **Document type:** *Magazine, Trade.* **Description:** Covers fundraising issues of interest to nonprofit professionals.
Indexed: N06.
Published by: Cambridge Fund Raising Associates, P O Box 338, Medfield, MA 02052. TEL 508-359-0019, FAX 508-359-2703. Ed. Jerry Cianciolo. Pub. Kathleen Brennan.

361 USA ISSN 1552-9592
HV85
CONVERSATIONS ON PHILANTHROPY; emerging questions on liberality and social thought. Text in English. 2004. a. free in US & Canada; USD 15 per issue elsewhere to individuals; USD 50 per issue elsewhere to institutions (effective 2009). back issues avail. **Document type:** *Journal, Consumer.* **Description:** Aims to promote inquiry and reflection on the importance of liberality both in the sense of generosity and of the character befitting free individuals for the flourishing of local communities, political societies, and humanity in general.
Related titles: Online - full text ed.: ISSN 2150-0959. free (effective 2009).
Published by: Donors Trust, 109 N Henry St, Alexandria, VA 22314. TEL 703-535-3563, FAX 703-535-3564, https://www.donorstrust.org. Ed. Lenore T Ealy TEL 317-502-2735.

360 FRA ISSN 1962-8447
COOPERER AUJOURD'HUI. Text in French. 2008. irreg.
Published by: Groupe de Recherche et d'Echanges Technologiques, 45 bis Av de la Belle Gabrielle, Nogent-sur-Marne, 94736, France. TEL 33-1-70919200, FAX 33-1-70919201, gret@gret.org, http://www.gret.org/default.asp.

365 USA ISSN 1055-0623
HV97.A3
CORPORATE GIVING DIRECTORY; comprehensive profiles of American's major corporate foundations & corporate giving programs. Text in English. 1981. a. USD 629 (effective 2011). **Document type:** *Directory, Trade.* **Description:** Provides complete profiles of the 1,000 largest corporate foundations and corporate direct giving programs in the United States.
Former titles (until 1991): Taft Corporate Giving Directory (0882-7176); (until 1984): Taft Corporate Directory (0732-8958)
Published by: Information Today, Inc., 143 Old Marlton Pike, Medford, NJ 08055. TEL 609-654-6266, 800-300-9868, FAX 609-654-4309, custserv@infotoday.com, http://www.infotoday.com. Ed. Owen O'Donnell.

361.73 USA ISSN 0885-8365
CORPORATE PHILANTHROPY REPORT. Text in English. m. GBP 1,907 in United Kingdom to institutions; EUR 2,235 in Europe to institutions; USD 3,053 in United States to institutions; USD 3,101 in Canada & Mexico to institutions; USD 3,119 elsewhere to institutions; GBP 2,194 combined subscription in United Kingdom to institutions (print & online eds.); EUR 2,571 combined subscription in Europe to institutions (print & online eds.); USD 3,517 combined subscription in United States to institutions (print & online eds.); USD 3,565 combined subscription in Canada & Mexico to institutions (print & online eds.); USD 3,583 combined subscription elsewhere to institutions (print & online eds.) (effective 2012). **Document type:** *Newsletter.* **Description:** Explores why companies give, where and what they give, and which ones are setting the corporate giving pace. Also includes related news and articles.
Related titles: E-mail ed.; Online - full text ed.: ISSN 1949-3207. GBP 1,866 in United Kingdom to institutions; EUR 2,187 in Europe to institutions; USD 3,053 elsewhere to institutions (effective 2012).
Indexed: B01, N06.
—CCC.
Published by: Jossey-Bass Inc., Publishers (Subsidiary of: John Wiley & Sons, Inc.), 111 River St, Hoboken, NJ 07030. TEL 201-748-6000, FAX 201-748-6088, jbsubs@jbp.com, http://www.josseybass.com/WileyCDA/. Ed. Nicholas King. Pub. Sue Lewis.

361 USA ISSN 2154-641X
CORPORATION FOR NATIONAL AND COMMUNITY SERVICE. OFFICE OF INSPECTOR GENERAL. SEMIANNUAL REPORT TO THE CONGRESS. Text in English. 1994. s-a. free (effective 2010). back issues avail. **Document type:** *Journal, Government.* **Description:** Provides opportunities for Americans to serve their communities.
Related titles: Online - full text ed.
Published by: Corporation For National And Community Service, Office of Inspector General, 1201 New York Ave, NW, Ste 830, Washington, DC 20525. TEL 202-606-9390, 800-452-8210, FAX 202-606-9397, hotline@cncsig.gov.

362 616.21 ITA
CORRIERE DEI LARINGECTOMIZZATI. Text in Italian. 1957. q. adv. illus. **Document type:** *Newspaper, Consumer.* **Description:** Organizational news for laryngectomees and users of artificial speaking devices.
Published by: Associazione Italiana Laringectomizzati, Via Friuli 28, Milan, 20135, Italy. TEL 39-02-5510819, FAX 39-02-54122104, http://www.laringect.it.

360 CHE ISSN 0538-8295
HD7091
THE COST OF SOCIAL SECURITY. Text in English. irreg. price varies. **Document type:** *Bulletin.*
Related titles: Microform ed.: (from CIS).
Indexed: IIS.
Published by: I L O, 4 Route des Morillons, Geneva, 1211, Switzerland. TEL 41-22-7996111, FAX 41-22-7988655, ilo@ilo.org, http://www.ilo.org.

362.6 CAN ISSN 1910-8699
COUNCIL ON AGING OF OTTAWA. ANNUAL REPORT/CONSEIL SUR LE VIEILLISSEMENT D'OTTAWA. RAPPORT ANNUEL. Text in English, French. 199?. a. **Document type:** *Report, Trade.*
Formerly (until 2001): Council on Aging of Ottawa-Carleton. Annual Report (1495-1568)
Published by: Council on Aging of Ottawa, 101-1247 Kilborn Pl, Ottawa, ON K1H 6K9, Canada. TEL 613-789-3577, FAX 613-789-4406, coa@coaottawa.ca, http://www.coaottawa.ca.

360 USA ISSN 0277-4259
AS911.A2
COUNCIL ON FOUNDATIONS. ANNUAL REPORT. Text in English. 1964. a. back issues avail. **Document type:** *Report, Corporate.*
Related titles: Online - full text ed.: free (effective 2011).
Published by: Council on Foundations, Inc., 2121 Crystal Dr, Ste 700, Arlington, VA 22202.

362.5 336.2 GBR
COUNCIL TAX HANDBOOK. Text in English. 1993. irreg., latest 2009, 8th ed. GBP 17 per issue to non-members; free to members (effective 2009). back issues avail. **Document type:** *Handbook/Manual/Guide, Trade.* **Description:** Provides social services caseworkers with the updated knowledge on the council tax, as it applies in England, Wales, and Scotland, they need to counsel their clients.
Published by: Child Poverty Action Group, 94 White Lion St, London, N1 9PF, United Kingdom. TEL 44-20-78377979, FAX 44-20-78376414, info@cpag.org.uk. Ed. Alan Murdie.

CRIME, LAW AND SOCIAL CHANGE; an interdisciplinary journal. *see* CRIMINOLOGY AND LAW ENFORCEMENT

CRIMINAL JUSTICE FUNDING REPORT. *see* CRIMINOLOGY AND LAW ENFORCEMENT

360 BRA
CRITICA SOCIAL. Text in Portuguese. 1974. irreg.
Published by: Universidade Catolica de Minas Gerais, Escola de Servico Social, Av Dom Jose Gaspar, 500, C Eucaristico, Belo Horizonte, MG 30535-610, Brazil.

320.6 GBR ISSN 0261-0183
➤ **CRITICAL SOCIAL POLICY**; a journal of theory and practice in social welfare. Abbreviated title: C S P. Text in English. 1981. q. USD 665, GBP 359 combined subscription to institutions (print & online eds.); USD 652, GBP 352 to institutions (effective 2011). adv. bk.rev. illus. back issues avail.; reprint service avail. from PSC. **Document type:** *Journal, Academic/Scholarly.* **Description:** Provides an international forum to develop an understanding of welfare from socialist, feminist, antiracist and radical perspectives.
Related titles: Online - full text ed.: ISSN 1461-703X. USD 599, GBP 323 to institutions (effective 2011).
Indexed: A01, A03, A08, A20, A22, B07, B28, C06, C07, C08, CA, CINAHL, CJA, CurCont, DIP, E01, ERA, ESPM, FamI, GEOBASE, H04, IBR, IBSS, IBZ, P03, P34, P42, PAIS, PCI, PSA, PsycInfo, PsycholAb, RASB, RiskAb, S02, S03, SCOPUS, SD, SOPODA, SPAA, SSA, SSCI, SSciA, SociolAb, T02, V02, W07.
—BLDSC (3487.485500), IE, Infotrieve, Ingenta. **CCC.**
Published by: (Critical Social Policy Editorial Collective), Sage Publications Ltd. (Subsidiary of: Sage Publications, Inc.), 1 Oliver's Yard, 55 City Rd, London, EC1Y 1SP, United Kingdom. TEL 44-20-73248500, FAX 44-20-73248600, info@sagepub.co.uk, http://www.uk.sagepub.com/home.nav. Adv. contact Jenny Kirby. **Subscr. in the Americas to:** Sage Publications, Inc., 2455 Teller Rd, Thousand Oaks, CA 91320. TEL 805-499-9774, FAX 805-499-0871, journals@sagepub.com.

361.3 CAN ISSN 1543-9372
CRITICAL SOCIAL WORK. Text in English. 2000 (Spr.). s-a. free (effective 2005). **Document type:** *Journal, Academic/Scholarly.* **Description:** It aims at refining ideas about the individual and community, clarifying the relationship between interpersonal relations and institutional structures and identifying actions that promote both individual and community well-being.
Media: Online - full content.
—CCC.
Published by: University of Windsor, School of Social Work, 401 Sunset Ave, Winsor, ON N9B 3P4, Canada. TEL 519-253-3000 x3064. Ed. Brent Angell.

361.4 USA
THE CROPWALKER. Text in English. s-a. free. **Document type:** *Newsletter, Consumer.* **Description:** Reports on news, events, and issues of interest to participants in the annual CROP WALK, an event to raise funds to help the poor.
Formerly: CropWalk; Which supersedes in part: Harvest News (1034-5183); Which was formerly (until 1983): Service News (Elkhart) (0037-2617)
Published by: Church World Service, 28606 Phillips St, Elkhart, IN 46515. TEL 800-297-1516, FAX 219-262-0966. Ed. Ronda Hughes. R&P Ron Kaser. Circ: 140,000; 140,000 (controlled).

361 ESP ISSN 1575-2011
CRUZ ROJA. Text in Spanish. 1893. q. adv. illus. **Document type:** *Newsletter, Consumer.*
Former titles (until 1986): Cruz Roja Espanola (0210-4482); (until 1939): Cruz Roja (0210-4474); (until 1889): Caridad en la Guerra (1575-1864); (until 1896): Caridad (1575-1872)
Related titles: Online - full text ed.
Published by: Asociacion Cruz Roja Espanola, Ave Dr Federico Rubio y Gali No 3, Madrid, 28039, Spain. TEL 34-91-5334120. Ed. Octavio Cabeza. Circ: 700,000.

361.8 USA ISSN 2151-9595
▼ **CRYSTAL SPIRIT MAGAZINE.** Text in English. 2011 (Mar.). m. USD 24.95 (effective 2011). **Document type:** *Magazine, Trade.* **Description:** Highlights nonprofit organizations and best practices in the US. Includes calendar of events, fundraising tips and ideas, and grant writing information.
Related titles: Online - full text ed.: ISSN 2151-9609. 2010 (Apr.).
Published by: Crystal Spirit Publishing, Inc., PO Box 27041, Fayetteville, NC 28314. TEL 910-764-0760, crystalspiritinc@gmail.com.

361 CHL ISSN 0717-9391
CUADERNO DE TRABAJO SOCIAL. Text in Spanish. 2000. s-a. **Document type:** *Journal, Academic/Scholarly.*
Indexed: A01, F03, F04.
Published by: Universidad Tecnologica Metropolitana, Escuela de Trabajo Social, Padre Felipe Gomez de Vadurre, 1550, Santiago, Chile. TEL 56-2-7877502, http://www.utem.cl/oferta-academica/oferta-academica-diurna/trabajo-social/.

300 VEN ISSN 0798-0841
CUADERNOS DE ACTUALIDAD INTERNACIONAL. Text in Spanish. 1990. s-a. adv. back issues avail. **Description:** Selection of articles published by Documentation Francaise about different topics of the current world in an international perspective.
Published by: Universidad Central de Venezuela, Centro de Estudios del Desarrollo, Apartado Postal 6622, Caracas, DF 1010-A, Venezuela. TEL 4523266, FAX 7512691. Eds. B Preto Nelme, Pablo Harari. Circ: 1,000. **U.S. subscr. addr.:** Poba International, 151, Box 02 5255, Miami, FL 33102-5255. **Co-sponsor:** Editorial Trilce de Uruguay.

361 ESP ISSN 0214-0314
HV40
➤ **CUADERNOS DE TRABAJO SOCIAL.** Text in Spanish. 1987. a., latest vol.23, 2010. EUR 18 domestic; EUR 24 in Europe; EUR 28 elsewhere (effective 2011). back issues avail. **Document type:** *Journal, Academic/Scholarly.* **Description:** Presents a forum for social workers in Spain. Includes scientific articles as well as professional experiences written by experts in the field.
Related titles: CD-ROM ed.; Online - full text ed.: ISSN 1988-8295. free.
Indexed: A26, CA, H21, I04, I05, P08, P46, P48, PQC, S02, S03, SCOPUS, SSA, SociolAb, T02.
Published by: (Universidad Complutense de Madrid, Escuela Universitaria de Trabajo Social), Universidad Complutense de Madrid, Servicio de Publicaciones, C/ Obispo Trejo 2, Ciudad Universitaria, Madrid, 28040, Spain. TEL 34-91-3941127, FAX 34-91-3941126, servicio.publicaciones@rect.ucm.es, http://www.ucm.es/publicaciones. Eds. Alfonsa Rodriguez Rodriguez, Aurora Castillo Charfolet.

361.3 COL
➤ **CUADERNOS DEL CIDS.** (In 3 series) Text in Spanish. 1997. 6/yr. (2 per series). COP 135,000 domestic; USD 72 foreign (effective 2003). **Document type:** *Academic/Scholarly.* **Description:** Presents the results of field work by the Center for Research on Social Dynamics, which embraces the methodological research perspective.
Published by: Universidad Externado de Colombia, Departamento de Publicaciones, Calle 12, No 1-17 Este, Bogota, Colombia. TEL 57-1-3420288, publicaciones@uexternado.edu.co, http://www.uexternado.edu.co.

➤ **CURRENT ACTIVITIES IN LONGTERM CARE**; the activity professional's magazine. *see* GERONTOLOGY AND GERIATRICS

361.7632 USA ISSN 0162-5780
HV97.F62
CURRENT INTERESTS OF THE FORD FOUNDATION. Text in English. 1975. biennial. free (effective 2004).
Published by: Ford Foundation, Office of Communications, 320 E 43rd St, New York, NY 10017. TEL 212-573-5000, FAX 212-351-3677, office-of-communications@fordfound.org, http://www.fordfound.org.

362.5 USA
CURRENT POPULATION REPORTS. CONSUMER INCOME. INCOME, POVERTY, AND HEALTH INSURANCE COVERAGE IN THE UNITED STATES. Text in English. 1960. a. **Document type:** *Government.*
Formed by the 2002 merger of: Income in the United States; Which was formerly (until 2002): Money Income in the United States; (1995-2002): Poverty in the United States; Both Money Income in the United States & Poverty in the United States superseded in part (in 1994): Income, Poverty, and Valuation of Noncash Benefits; Which was formed by the merger of (19??-1992): Poverty in the United States; (198?-1992): Measuring the Effect of Benefits and Taxes on Income and Poverty; (1980-1992): Money Income of Households, Families, and Persons in the United States; Which was formerly: Money Income of Families and Persons in the United States; Money Income in (Year) of Families, Unrelated Individuals and Persons in the United States (0073-5698); (2002-2002): Health Insurance Coverage in the United States; Which was formerly (1994-2001): Health Insurance Coverage; (until 1994): Income and Poverty Statistics; (until 1992): Poverty in the United States
Related titles: Online - full content ed.
Published by: U.S. Census Bureau (Subsidiary of: U.S. Department of Commerce), 4600 Silver Hill Rd, Washington, DC 20233.

360 CAN ISSN 1499-6073
HV1
➤ **CURRENTS (CALGARY)**; new scholarship in the human services. Text in English. 2002 (Sep.). m. free (effective 2011). **Document type:** *Journal, Academic/Scholarly.* **Description:** Publishes critical and research work by current graduate students in the Human Services as well as articles by guest scholars.
Media: Online - full text.
Published by: (University of Calgary, Faculty of Social Work), University of Calgary Press, 2500 University Dr NW, Calgary, AB T2N 1N4, Canada. TEL 403-220-7578, FAX 403-282-0085, http://www.uofcpress.com. Eds. Michael Rothery, Rick Enns.

➤ **THE CUSAN.** *see* RELIGIONS AND THEOLOGY

➤ **CZAS SERCA**; dwumiesiecznik religijno-spoleczny. *see* RELIGIONS AND THEOLOGY—Roman Catholic

360 ESP ISSN 1699-8227
D A S. Variant title: Revista d'Accio Social. Text in Spanish, Gallegan. 2005. q.
Related titles: Print ed.: ISSN 1699-8235. 2005.
Published by: Diputacion Provincial de Castellon, Plaza de las Alas, 7, Castellon, 12001, Spain. TEL 34-964-359600.

363.348 USA ISSN 0164-1867
D R C HISTORICAL AND COMPARATIVE DISASTERS SERIES. (Disaster Research Center) Variant title: Historical & Comparative Series. Text in English. 1977. irreg., latest vol.12, 2000. price varies. back issues avail. **Document type:** *Monographic series, Academic/Scholarly.*
Published by: Disaster Research Center, University of Delaware, 166 Graham Hall, Newark, DE 19716. TEL 302-831-6618, FAX 302-831-2091, drc-mail@copland.udel.edu.

300 360 USA
D S S NEWSLETTER. (Department of Social Services) Text in English. 1960. m. free. **Document type:** *Newsletter.*
Published by: Maryland. Department of Social Services, Public Information Office, 1510 Guilford Ave, Baltimore, MD 21202. TEL 301-361-2002, FAX 301-361-3150. Ed. Sue Fitzsimmons. Circ: 4,000 (controlled).

362.82 AUS ISSN 1834-366X
D V I R C QUARTERLY. (Domestic Violence & Incest Resource Centre) Text in English. 1987. q. **Document type:** *Newsletter, Trade.* **Description:** Provides articles that address issues concerning domestic violence and sexual assault, providing updates on the law, current research and training, new print and internet resources, and a comprehensive listing of support groups in Victoria.
Former titles (until 2005): Domestic Violence and Incest Resource Centre. Newsletter (1445-436X); (until 1994): D V I R C Newsletter (1324-4264)
Published by: Domestic Violence & Incest Resource Centre (D V I R C), 292 Wellington St, Collingwood, VIC 3066, Australia. TEL 61-3-9486-9866, FAX 61-3-9486-9744, dvirc@dvirc.org.au, http://www.dvirc.org.au.

360 368.4 SWE ISSN 1652-9472
DAGENS SOCIALFOERSAEKRING; tidningen foer dig i foersaekringskassan. Variant title: D S. Text in Swedish. 2005. 9/yr. SEK 190 (effective 2011). adv. **Document type:** *Magazine, Trade.*
Formed by the merger of (1999-2005): rfv.se (1404-0980); (1971-2005): Socialfoersaekring (0346-1467); Which was formerly (1963-1970): Tidskrift foer Socialfoersaekring
Published by: Foersaekringskassan/Swedish Social Insurance Administration, Klara Vaestra Kyrkogata 11, Stockholm, 10351, Sweden. TEL 46-8-7869000, FAX 46-8-4112789, huvudkontoret@forsakringskassan.se, http://www.forsakringskassan.se. Ed. Sven-Erik Johansson.

325.21 DNK ISSN 1600-1729
DANSK FLYGTNINGEHJAELP. Text in Danish. 1982. 4/yr. free (effective 2003). illus. **Document type:** *Newsletter, Consumer.* **Description:** News about refugees in Denmark and other parts of the world.
Former titles (until 2000): Flygtninge (1396-2310); (until 1996): Flygtninge Nyt (0900-2537); (until 1995): Nyt om Flygtninge (0108-1845)
Related titles: Online - full text ed.
Address: Borgergade 10, PO Box 53, Copenhagen K, 1300, Denmark. TEL 45-33-735000, FAX 45-33-328448, drc@drc.dk, http://www.drc.dk., http://www.flygtning.dk. Ed. Mik Steenberger. Circ: 32,000.

THE DEAF - BLIND AMERICAN. *see* HANDICAPPED—Physically Impaired

DEAF - BLIND PERSPECTIVES. *see* HANDICAPPED—Visually Impaired

DEAF SAN DIEGAN (ONLINE EDITION). *see* HANDICAPPED—Hearing Impaired

360 BRA ISSN 0011-7242
DEBATES SOCIAIS. Text in Portuguese. 1965. s-a. per issue exchange basis. bk.rev. **Description:** Examines community development.
Indexed: C01.

S

Published by: Centro Brasileiro de Cooperacao e Intercambio de Servicos Sociais, Rua Santa Luzia 685, 2 andar, Rio De Janeiro, R.J. 20030, Brazil. Ed. Moacyr Velloso Cardoso de Oliveira. Circ: 5,000.

362.7 332.3 GBR
DEBT ADVICE HANDBOOK. Text in English. 1993. irreg., latest 2008, 8th ed. GBP 20 per issue to non-members; free to members (effective 2009). **Document type:** *Handbook/Manual/Guide, Trade.* **Description:** Contains all the essential information needed by advisers dealing with debt problems, and explains the key stages and issues in money advice.
Published by: Child Poverty Action Group, 94 White Lion St, London, N1 9PF, United Kingdom. TEL 44-20-78377979, FAX 44-20-78376414, info@cpag.org.uk.

362.734 346.017 USA ISSN 1092-0730
KF545.A15
DECREE. Text in English. 1980. q. USD 35 to members; USD 5 newsstand/cover to members (effective 1998). bk.rev.; film rev.; tel.rev.; video rev. stat. back issues avail. **Document type:** *Newsletter.* **Description:** Dedicated to exploring adoption issues and facilitating changes in attitudes and public policies which will provide adult adoptees with access to information on their ancestral, medical and social history.
Related titles: Online - full text ed.
Published by: American Adoption Congress, PO Box 42730, Washington, DC 20015. TEL 202-483-3399. Ed. Mary Zoller. Circ: 3,000.

362.82 NLD ISSN 1879-8861
▼ **DEFINITIEF ADVIES OVER HET W M O-BUDGET HUISHOUDELIJKE HULP.** (Wet Maatschappelijke Ondersteuning) Text in Dutch. 2009. a. EUR 14.90 (effective 2010). **Document type:** *Report, Government.*
Published by: Sociaal en Cultureel Planbureau/Social and Cultural Planning Office, Postbus 16164, The Hague, 2500 BD, Netherlands. TEL 31-70-3407000, FAX 31-70-3407044, info@scp.nl, http://www.scp.nl.

361 IRL ISSN 2009-1087
DEPARTMENT OF SOCIAL AND FAMILY AFFAIRS. ANNUAL REPORT. Text in English. 199?. a.
Formerly (until 2002): Department of Social, Community and Family Affairs. Annual Report (2009-1079)
Related titles: Irish ed.: Roinn Gnothai Soisialacha agus Teaghlaigh. Tuairisc Bhliantuil. ISSN 2009-1095.
Published by: Department of Social and Family Affairs/Roinn Gnothai Soisialacha agus Teaghlaigh, Store St, Dublin, 1, Ireland. TEL 353-1-7043000.

360 DEU ISSN 0012-1185
DEUTSCHER VEREIN FUER OEFFENTLICHE UND PRIVATE FUERSORGE. NACHRICHTENDIENST. Text in German. 1947. m. EUR 21.90; EUR 3.30 newsstand/cover (effective 2009). adv. bk.rev. index. **Document type:** *Journal, Trade.*
Incorporates (1951-1956): Auslaendische Sozialprobleme (0404-0589)
Indexed: A22, DIP, IBR, IBZ.
—IE, Infotrieve.
Published by: Deutscher Verein fuer Oeffentliche und Private Fuersorge, Michaelkirchstr 17-18, Berlin, 10179, Germany. TEL 49-30-629800, FAX 49-30-62980150, info@deutscher-verein.de, http://www.deutscher-verein.de. Ed. Ralf Mulot. Adv. contact Tatjana Hally. B&W page EUR 880. Circ: 6,300 (paid and controlled).

362.7 AUS ISSN 1445-6818
DEVELOPING PRACTICE; the child youth and family work journal. Text in English. 2001. 3/yr. AUD 49.50 domestic; AUD 55 foreign (effective 2008). back issues avail. **Document type:** *Journal, Consumer.* **Description:** Presents discussions on practices, programs, ideas and practical initiatives aimed at assisting vulnerable children, young people and families.
Related titles: Online - full text ed.
Indexed: C06, C07, C08, CINAHL.
—IE.
Published by: Association of Childrens Welfare Agencies, Inc., Locked Bag 13, Haymarket, NSW 1240, Australia. TEL 61-2-92818822, FAX 61-2-92818827, acwa@acwa.asn.au. **Co-sponsor:** N S W Family Services.

360 GBR
DEVELOPMENT DEPARTMENT RESEARCH PROGRAMME. RESEARCH FINDINGS. Text in English.
Published by: Great Britain. Scottish Office. Central Research Unit. Development Department Research Program, 2J Victori Quay, Edinburgh, EH6 6QQ, United Kingdom. TEL 44-131-244-7560, cru.admin@scotland.gov.uk, http://www.scotland.gov.uk/cru.

361.971 CAN ISSN 1488-6499
CA2PQCSD27
DEVELOPPEMENT SOCIAL. Text in French. 1999. a. **Document type:** *Journal, Trade.*
—CCC.
Published by: Quebec. Conseil de la Sante et du Bien-Etre, 1020, rte de l'Eglise, Bureau 700, Quebec, PQ G1V 3V9, Canada. TEL 418-643-3040, FAX 418-644-0654, csbe@msss.gouv.qc.ca, http://www.csbe.gouv.qc.ca.

DEVIANT; tijdschrift tussen psychiatrie en maatschappij. *see* MEDICAL SCIENCES—Psychiatry And Neurology

360 CHE
DEZIBEL; Zeitschrift fuer hoeren und erleben. Text in German. bi-m. CHF 32 domestic; CHF 47 foreign (effective 2008). adv. **Document type:** *Magazine, Consumer.*
Former titles: B S S V Monatsblatt; Monatsblatt der Hoerbehinderten
Published by: Pro Audito Schweiz, Feldeggstr 69, Postfach 1332, Zurich, 8032, Switzerland. TEL 41-44-3631200, FAX 41-44-3631303, info@pro-audito.ch. Ed. Karin Huber. adv.: B&W page CHF 1,300, color page CHF 2,020; trim 210 x 297. Circ: 8,800 (paid).

DIAKONIE MAGAZIN. *see* RELIGIONS AND THEOLOGY

360 DEU ISSN 1864-1660
DIAKONIE-MAGAZIN. Text in German. 2007. q. free (effective 2009). bk.rev. illus. **Document type:** *Magazine, Consumer.*
Incorporates (1950-2007): In Der Tat; Which was formerly (until 2001): Weltweite Hilfe (0043-2644); (until 1959): Mitteilungsblatt der Inneren Mission in Hessen und Nassau
Published by: Diakonisches Werk in Hessen und Nassau, Ederstr 12, Frankfurt am Main, 60486, Germany. TEL 49-69-79470, FAX 49-69-7947310, kontakt@dwhn.de, http://www.diakonie-hessen-nassau.de.

362.3 CAN ISSN 0383-8528
DIALECT. Text in English. 1977. bi-m. free. adv. bk.rev.; film rev. back issues avail. **Document type:** *Newsletter.* **Description:** Publishes writing that promotes the full inclusion, equality and dignity of people with intellectual disabilities.
Indexed: E-psyche.
Published by: Saskatchewan Association for Community Living, 3031 Louise St, Saskatoon, SK S7J 3L1, Canada. TEL 306-955-3344, FAX 306-373-3070, sacl.comm@home.com, http://www.members.home.net/sacl.com. Ed., R&P, Adv. contact Karin Melberg-Schwier. Circ: 5,900.

360 FIN ISSN 0789-0346
HV4
DIALOGI. Text in Finnish. 1991. bi-m. (6-9/yr.). free (effective 2005). **Document type:** *Journal, Academic/Scholarly.*
Formed by the merger of (1979-1990): Laakintohallitus Tiedottaa (0783-1900); (1981-1990): Sisiaaliviesti (0358-5166)
Related titles: Online - full content ed.: ISSN 1458-610X.
Published by: Sosiaali- ja Terveysalan Tutkimus- ja Kehittamiskeskus/National Research and Development Centre for Welfare and Health, PO Box 220, Helsinki, 00531, Finland. TEL 358-9-39671, FAX 358-9-396761307. Ed. Riitta Viialainen TEL 358-9-39672440. Circ: 30,000.

360 FRA ISSN 1161-2428
DICTIONNAIRE PERMANENT: ACTION SOCIALE. Text in French. 2 base vols. plus m. updates. looseleaf. EUR 395 base vol(s).; EUR 41 per month (effective 2009).
Published by: Editions Legislatives, 80 ave de la Marne, Montrouge, Cedex 92546, France. TEL 33-1-40923636, FAX 33-1-40923663, infocom@editions-legislatives.fr, http://www.editions-legislatives.fr. Pub. Michel Vaillant.

362 DEU
DIMENSIONEN SOZIALER ARBEIT UND DER PFLEGE. Text in German. 1996. irreg., latest vol.11, 2007. price varies. **Document type:** *Monographic series, Academic/Scholarly.*
Formerly (until 2000): Dimensionen Sozialer Arbeit (1430-4848)
Published by: Lucius und Lucius Verlagsgesellschaft mbH, Gerokstr 51, Stuttgart, 70184, Germany. TEL 49-711-242060, FAX 49-711-242088, lucius@luciusverlag.com, http://www.luciusverlag.com.

DIRECTORIO DE OBRAS SOCIALES. *see* BUSINESS AND ECONOMICS—Trade And Industrial Directories

DIRECTORY OF AL-ANON AND ALATEEN MEETINGS IN AUSTRALIA. *see* DRUG ABUSE AND ALCOHOLISM

261.7 USA ISSN 1062-6492
HG4027.65
DIRECTORY OF BUILDING AND EQUIPMENT GRANTS. Text in English. 1992. a. (4th ed. 1996). USD 59.50 (effective 1998). **Document type:** *Directory.* **Description:** Lists more than 600 funding sources for equipment, building, and renovation grants. Profiles foundations, corporations and associations.
Published by: Research Grant Guides, PO Box 1214, Loxahatchee, FL 33470. TEL 561-795-6129, FAX 561-495-7794. Ed. Richard M Eckstein.

363.348 CAN ISSN 1207-3644
HV551.5.C2
DIRECTORY OF CANADIAN SEARCH AND RESCUE ORGANIZATIONS. Text in English. 1993. irreg.
Published by: (Canada. National Search and Rescue Program), National Search and Rescue Secretariat/Secretariat National Recherche et Sauvetage, 400-275 Slater St, Ottawa, ON K1A 0K2, Canada. TEL 800-727-9414, FAX 613-996-3746, http://www.nss.gc.ca.

DIRECTORY OF COLLEGES AND UNIVERSITIES WITH ACCREDITED SOCIAL WORK DEGREE PROGRAMS. *see* EDUCATION—Guides To Schools And Colleges

360 USA
DIRECTORY OF COMMUNITY RESOURCES AND SERVICES. Text in English. 1943. irreg., latest vol.20, 1997-99. USD 40. index. **Document type:** *Directory.* **Description:** Lists nonprofit health and human services in the Greater Houston area and the surrounding counties.
Related titles: Diskette ed.
Published by: United Way of the Texas Gulf Coast, Information and Referral Services Department, 2200 North Loop West, Houston, TX 77018. TEL 713-950-4357, 800-833-5948, FAX 713-956-2868. Ed. Isabel Wanza. Circ: 1,800. **Subscr. to:** PO Box 924507, Houston, TX 77292.

361.6 CAN ISSN 0319-258X
HV110.M6
DIRECTORY OF COMMUNITY SERVICES OF GREATER MONTREAL/ REPERTOIRE DES SERVICES COMMUNAUTAIRES DU GRAND MONTREAL; welfare-health-recreation. Text in English, French. 1956. biennial. CAD 53 (effective 2000). adv. **Document type:** *Directory.*
Formerly: Directory of Health, Welfare and Recreation Services of Greater Montreal (0070-5640)
Published by: Information and Referral Centre of Greater Montreal/ Centre de Reference du Grand Montreal, 801 Sherbrooke St E, Ste 401, Montreal, PQ H2L 1K7, Canada. TEL 514-527-1375, FAX 514-527-9712. Ed., Pub. Laurent L'Ecuyer. R&P, Adv. contact Lorraine Lebeau. Circ: 3,000.

362.7 618 CAN ISSN 1715-4200
DIRECTORY OF FETAL ALCOHOL SPECTRUM DISORDER (F A S D) INFORMATION AND SUPPORT SERVICES IN CANADA/ REPERTOIRE CANADIEN DES SERVICES D'INFORMATION ET DE SOUTIEN SUR L'ENSEMBLE DES TROUBLES CAUSES PAR L'ALCOOLISME FOETALE (E T C A F). Text in English, French. 2004. irreg. **Document type:** *Directory, Trade.* **Description:** A listing of organizations and individuals.
Media: Online - full text. **Related titles:** Print ed.: ISSN 1715-4197. 199?.
Published by: Canadian Centre on Substance Abuse/Centre Canadien de Lutte Contre l'Alcoolisme et les Toxicomanies, 75 Albert St, Ste 500, Ottawa, ON K1P 5E7, Canada. TEL 613-235-4048, FAX 613-235-8101.

360 USA ISSN 1071-6726
HV97.A3
DIRECTORY OF OPERATING GRANTS. Text in English. 1992. biennial. USD 59.50 (effective 1998). **Document type:** *Directory.* **Description:** Profiles more than 640 foundations providing operating grants for nonprofit organizations.
Published by: Research Grant Guides, PO Box 1214, Loxahatchee, FL 33470. FAX 561-795-7794, http://www.researchgrant.com/.

364 CAN ISSN 0847-3668
DIRECTORY OF SERVICES FOR VICTIMS OF CRIME/REPERTOIRE DES SERVICES AUX VICTIMES D'ACTES CRIMINELS. Text in English. 1988. s-a. CAD 20 per issue to members; CAD 25 per issue to non-members (effective 2005). **Document type:** *Directory, Trade.* **Description:** Lists services for victims of crime in Canada, with addresses and phone numbers.
Published by: Canadian Criminal Justice Association/Association Canadienne de Justice Penale, 320 Parkdale Ave, Ste 301, Ottawa, ON K1Y 4X9, Canada. TEL 613-725-3715, FAX 613-725-3720, ccja@bellnet.ca. Circ: 320.

362 NZL ISSN 1177-2522
DIRECTORY OF SUPPORT SERVICES. Text in English. a. **Document type:** *Directory.*
Published by: North Shore Community Health Network Inc. - Raeburn House, PO Box 36-336, Northcote, Auckland, New Zealand. TEL 64-9-4418989.

362.4 615.82 IND ISSN 2211-5242
➤ **DISABILITY, C B R AND INCLUSIVE DEVELOPMENT.** (Community Based Rehabilitation) Abbreviated title: A P D R J. Text in English. 1990. 4/yr. free (effective 2010). bk.rev. **Document type:** *Journal, Academic/Scholarly.* **Description:** Covers policy development, concept clarification, development of methodology in areas of service delivery, training of manpower and programme evaluation, and development of technology related to rehabilitation.
Former titles (until Apr.2011): Asia Pacific Disability Rehabilitation Journal; Actionaid Disability News (0971-9601)
Related titles: Online - full text ed.: free (effective 2011).
Published by: (Shree Ramana Maharishi Academy for the Blind), Action for Disability Regional Rehabilitation Centre, J-124 Ushas Apartments, 16th Main, 4th Block, Jayanagar, Bangalore, Karnataka 560 011, India. thomasmaya@hotmail.com, m_thomas@rediffmail.com, http://www.mayathomas.in. Ed., Pub., R&P Dr. Maya Thomas. Circ: 2,000.

362.4 360 USA ISSN 1933-3854
K4
DISABILITY FUNDING NEWS; covering funding, programs and news on physical, mental and learning disabilities. Text in English. 1993. 24/yr. USD 427 (effective 2007). 2 cols./p.; **Document type:** *Newsletter, Trade.* **Description:** Provides details on public and private funding opportunities for a wide range of programs in areas such as emotional disabilities, physical handicaps, learning disabilities, visual impairment, autism, speech impairment, and multiple handicaps.
Former titles (until 2006): Disability Funding Week (1551-7896); (until 2004): Disability Funding News (1069-1359)
Related titles: Online - full text ed.: ISSN 1933-4346.
—CCC.
Published by: C D Publications, Inc., 8204 Fenton St, Silver Spring, MD 20910. TEL 301-588-6380, 800-666-6380, FAX 301-588-6385, subscriptions@cdpublications.com, http://www.cdpublications.com. Eds. Malcolm Spicer, John Reistrup. Pub. Mike Gerecht.

DISABILITY ISSUES. *see* HANDICAPPED

DISABILITY, PREGNANCY & PARENTHOOD INTERNATIONAL; journal for disabled parents and professionals to exchange information and experience. *see* HANDICAPPED

362.4 GBR
DISABILITY RIGHTS HANDBOOK. Text in English. 1975. a. GBP 25 per issue; GBP 10 per issue to qualified personnel (effective 2010). **Document type:** *Handbook/Manual/Guide, Consumer.* **Description:** Provides clear and concise information on the welfare benefits and tax credits systems, as well as other areas such as social and residential care and a range of other issues relevant to disabled people and their families.
Related titles: CD-ROM ed.: GBP 14.20 per vol.
Published by: Disability Alliance, Universal House, 88-94 Wentworth St, London, E1 7SA, United Kingdom. TEL 44-20-72478776, FAX 44-20-72478765, office.da@dial.pipex.com.

DISABILITY UPDATE. *see* HANDICAPPED

362.4 GBR
THE DISABLEMENT INCOME GROUP. NEWSLETTER. Text in English. 1993. q. **Document type:** *Newsletter, Academic/Scholarly.* **Description:** Keeps people informed about the campaigns and activities that are working to improve the financial circumstances of disabled people.
Formerly: The Disablement Income Group. Journal (1351-6191)
Published by: Disablement Income Group, PO Box 5743, Finchingfield, CM7 4PW, United Kingdom. TEL 44-01371-811621, FAX 44-01371-811633. Eds. Jean Macqueen, Pauline Thompson. Circ: 5,000 (paid).

DISASTER RESEARCH. *see* SOCIAL SCIENCES: COMPREHENSIVE WORKS

360 267 796.31 USA ISSN 8755-965X
DISCOVERY Y M C A. (Young Men's Christian Association) Text in English. 1982. q. USD 10; free to qualified personnel. adv. 32 p./no.; back issues avail. **Document type:** *Magazine, Consumer.* **Description:** Concentrates on challenges and accomplishments of more than 2,500 YMCAs in the U.S.A. and on issues facing the YMCA movement as a whole.
Published by: Y M C A of the U S A, 101 N Wacker Dr, Chicago, IL 60606-1718. TEL 312-977-0031, FAX 312-977-9063. Ed., R&P Kristi Turnbaugh. Adv. contact Wendy Gould TEL 312-419-8757. Circ: 70,000.

360 362 GBR ISSN 1759-1422
DIVERSITY IN HEALTH AND CARE. Text in English. 2004. q. GBP 445 to institutions (effective 2009). **Document type:** *Journal, Academic/Scholarly.* **Description:** Concerned with all aspects of diversity in health and social care.
Formerly (until 2009): Diversity in Health and Social Care (1743-1913)
Related titles: Online - full text ed.: ISSN 1743-4904 (from IngentaConnect).

Indexed: A22, ASSIA, B28, C06, C07, C08, CA, CINAHL, E01, H05, S02, S03, SSA, SociolAb, T02.
—BLDSC (9830.236000), IE, Ingenta. **CCC.**
Published by: Radcliffe Publishing Ltd., 18 Marcham Rd, Abingdon, Oxon OX14 1AA, United Kingdom. TEL 44-1235-528820, FAX 44-1235-528830, contact.us@radcliffemed.com. Eds. Mark Johnson TEL 44-116-2013906, Paula McGee TEL 44-121-3315340.

362 ESP ISSN 2013-3871
DIXIT. Text in Catalan. 2008. s-a. back issues avail. **Document type:** *Bulletin, Government.*
Media: Online - full text.
Published by: Generalitat de Catalunya, Departament de Benestar Social i Familia, Place Pau Vila, 1, Barcelona, 08039, Spain. TEL 34-93-5517699, http://www20.gencat.cat/portal/site/dasc/.

362.82 649.8 FRA ISSN 1952-8531
DOC' DOMICILE. Text in French. 2006. bi-m. EUR 39 domestic; EUR 44 in the European Union & DOM (effective 2009). back issues avail. **Document type:** *Magazine, Consumer.*
Published by: Doc Editions, 14 Rue Jean-Jaures, Revigny-sur-Ornain, 55800, France. TEL 33-3-29705241, FAX 33-3-29787880, doc.editions@wanadoo.fr.

362.42 948.9 DNK ISSN 1602-5768
DOEVEHISTORISK TIDSSKRIFT. Text in Danish. 1984. irreg. membership. illus. **Document type:** *Monographic series, Consumer.*
Former titles (until 2002): Doevehistorisk Selskab (0909-9514); (until 1988): Doeveforsorgens Historiske Selskab (0109-5021)
Published by: Doevehistorisk Selskab/Historical Society of the Deaf, Kastelsvej 58, Copenhagen OE, 2100, Denmark. FAX 45-35-385662, jwr.spk@ci.kk.dk, http://www.dovehistoriskselskab.dk.

362.4 ISL ISSN 1670-6013
DOFFBLADID. Text in Icelandic. 1989. 2/yr. **Document type:** *Magazine, Consumer.*
Formerly (until 1997): Felag Heymariausra. Frettabref
Published by: Felag Heymarlausra/Icelandic Association of the Deaf, Sudurlandsbraut 24, Reykjavik, 108, Iceland. TEL 354-561-3560, FAX 354-551-3567, deaf@deaf.is, http://www.deaf.is.

362.4 610.6 NLD ISSN 1877-3060
DOKTERS VAN DE WERELD. NIEUWSBRIEF. Text in Dutch. 199?. m. **Document type:** *Newsletter, Consumer.*
Published by: Dokters van de Wereld, Nieuwe Herengracht 20, Amsterdam, 1018 DP, Netherlands. TEL 31-20-4652866, FAX 31-20-4631775, info@doktersvandewereld.org, http://www.doktersvandewereld.org.

362.4 330.9 NLD ISSN 1878-8440
DOSSIER ARMOEDE IN NEDERLAND. Text in Dutch. 1996. triennial. EUR 10 per vol. (effective 2011).
Published by: (Dienst in de Industriele Samenleving Vanwege de Kerken), Werkgroep Arme Kant van Nederland - E V A, Luijbenstraat 17, 's-Hertogenbosch, 5211 BR, Netherlands. TEL 31-73-6121939, info@armekant-eva.nl, http://www.armekant.-eva.nl.

360 TWN
DOUJIA AIXIN BAO/DORCAS LOVE MISSION POST. Text in Chinese. 2006. bi-m. **Document type:** *Newsletter, Consumer.*
Published by: Lihebo Shehui Fuli Jijinghui/Rehoboth Welfare Foundation, 9F-1, No.167, Fu-hsing North Rd., Taipei, Taiwan. TEL 886-2-25448282, FAX 886-2-27185850.

362.4 DEU ISSN 1434-5129
DURCHBLICK V D A B. Text in German. 1993. q. EUR 22.60 (effective 2007). adv. **Document type:** *Magazine, Trade.*
Published by: Verband Deutscher Alten- und Behindertenhilfe e.V., Im Teelbruch 132, Essen, 45219, Germany. TEL 49-2054-95780, FAX 49-2054-957840, info@vdab.de, http://www.vdab.de. Ed. Nicole Jakobs. adv.: B&W page EUR 960. Circ: 1,200 (paid and controlled).

DYSTONIA DIALOGUE. *see* MEDICAL SCIENCES

E C H O NEWS. (European Community Humanitarian Office) *see* BUSINESS AND ECONOMICS—International Development And Assistance

361 GBR
E-INTERCHANGE. Text in English. 1980. q. free (effective 2009). adv. bk.rev. back issues avail. **Document type:** *Newsletter, Trade.* **Description:** Covers news of voluntary groups and contains listings on events, publications, and training for voluntary sector groups.
Formerly (until 2007): Interchange (0144-3488)
Media: Online - full text.
Published by: Glasgow Council for Voluntary Service, 11 Queen's Cres, Glasgow, G4 9AS, United Kingdom. TEL 44-141-3322444, FAX 44-141-3320175, information@gcvs.org.uk.

360 616.89 NOR ISSN 1892-4441
▼ **E M M-A**; tidsskrift for miljoearbeid. Text in Multiple languages. 2011. irreg. (1-2/yr). bk.rev. **Document type:** *Journal, Academic/Scholarly.*
Media: Online - full text.
Address: c/o Arvis Lone, Institutt for Sosialfag, Universitetet i Stavanger, Stavanger, 4036, Norway. Ed. Arvid Lone.

E S S EMPLOYMENT OPPORTUNITIES. (Executive Search Service) *see* OCCUPATIONS AND CAREERS

360 FRA
L'E-SSENTIEL. Variant title: L' Essentiel. Text in French. 1948. 10/yr. free. bk.rev. bibl.; charts; illus. **Document type:** *Newsletter.*
Supersedes: Caisse des Allocations Familiales. Lettre; Which was formerly: C A F Revue; C A F Bulletin Mensuel (0181-8929)
Media: Online - full text.
Published by: Caisse Nationale des Allocations Familiales, 32 Av. de la Sibelle, Paris, Cedex 14 75685, France. TEL 33-1-45655252, FAX 33-1-45655377, TELEX 201146. Ed. Daniel Bequignon. Circ: 7,500.

368.4 USA
EARNINGS AND EMPLOYMENT DATA FOR WORKERS COVERED UNDER SOCIAL SECURITY, BY STATE AND COUNTY. Text in English. 19??. a., latest 2008. free (effective 2011). charts; stat. **Document type:** *Journal, Government.* **Description:** Presents selected characteristics (age, gender, race) on the number of wage and salary workers and self-employed persons, the amount of their taxable earnings, and the amount they paid in Social Security and Medicare contributions.
Related titles: Online - full text ed.
Published by: U.S. Social Security Administration, Office of Research, Evaluation and Statistics, Office of Public Inquiries, Windsor Park Bldg, 6401 Security Blvd, Baltimore, MD 21235. TEL 800-772-1213, ores.publications@ssa.gov, http://www.ssa.gov/policy/about/ORES.html.

361 344.01 USA ISSN 1569-2949
K5
EAST WEST REVIEW OF LABOR LAW & SOCIAL POLICY. Text in English. 1995. 2/yr. USD 154 per vol. domestic; USD 178 per vol. foreign (effective 2008). 150 p./no. 1 cols./p.; back issues avail. **Document type:** *Journal, Trade.* **Description:** Designed to be a forum for contributions on labor law, social security law and general social policy issues.
Formerly (until 1998): East - West Review of Social Policy (1381-5709)
—BLDSC (3646.563200), IE, Ingenta.
Published by: Bookworld Publications/B W P - Bookcenter, PO Box 951361, Lake Mary, FL 32795. TEL 407-417-2470, FAX 407-321-7730, info@bwp-bookcenter.com. Eds. Andrzej Swiatkowski, Frans Pennings.

362.2 CAN ISSN 1914-072X
L'EBRUITEUR (ONLINE EDITION). Text in French. 2005. bi-m. **Document type:** *Newsletter, Trade.*
Media: Online - full text. **Related titles:** Print ed.: L' Ebruiteur (Print Edition). ISSN 1205-5751. 1985.
Published by: Association du Quebec pour l'Integration Sociale, 3958, Rue Dandurand, Montreal, PQ H1X 1P7, Canada. TEL 514-725-7245, FAX 514-725-2796.

360 FRA ISSN 1956-5429
ECHANGES, SANTE, SOCIAL. COLLECTION. Text in French. 1975. q. EUR 36.50 domestic; EUR 39 in the European Union; EUR 40 DOM-TOM; EUR 41 elsewhere (effective 2003). **Document type:** *Government.*
Former titles (until 2007): Echanges Sante Social (1253-8515); (until 1993): Echanges Sante (0760-8675); Which superseded in part (in 1984): Echanges (0337-6567)
Related titles: Microfiche ed.
Indexed: FR.
Published by: (France. Ministere du Travail, des Relations Sociales, de la Famille, de la Solidarite et de la Ville), Documentation Francaise, 29-31 Quai Voltaire, Paris, Cedex 7 75344, France. FAX 33-1-40157230, http://www.ladocumentationfrancaise.fr.

ECHO DE L'UNION. *see* GERONTOLOGY AND GERIATRICS

362.6 610.73 CAN ISSN 1718-8571
L'ECHO DU R I I R. (Regroupement des Infirmieres et Infirmiers Retraitees) Text in French. 1993. 3/yr. **Document type:** *Journal, Trade.*
Published by: Regroupement des Infirmieres et Infirmiers Retraitees, 405-1170, boul. Lebourgneuf, Quebec, PQ G2K 2E3, Canada. TEL 418-626-0861, 800-639-9519, FAX 418-626-0799, riir@globetrotter.net.

360 VEN ISSN 0013-0680
ECOS. Text in Spanish. 1945. bi-m. looseleaf. free. bk.rev. **Document type:** *Bulletin.*
Published by: (Asociacion Benefico - Social Hogar Virgen de los Dolores), Editorial Sucre, Monzon a Barcenas No. 135, Caracas, Venezuela. Ed. Hermann Gonzalez Oropeza. Circ: 18,000 (controlled).

052 GBR ISSN 1369-9318
THE EDUCATIONAL GRANTS DIRECTORY (YEAR). Text in English. 1988. irreg., latest 2009, 10th ed. GBP 50 per issue (effective 2009). **Document type:** *Directory, Consumer.* **Description:** Lists of educational charities which support children and students in need up to the first degree level. Covers over 260 national and general sources of help, giving a total of GPB32 million a year in educational grants to individuals.
Related titles: Online - full text ed.: free (effective 2009).
—BLDSC (3661.415200).
Published by: Directory of Social Change, 24 Stephenson Way, London, NW1 2DP, United Kingdom. TEL 44-20-73914800, FAX 44-20-73914808, publications@dsc.org.uk.

EEN OGENBLIK. *see* MEDICAL SCIENCES—Ophthalmology And Optometry

L'EGLISE DANS LE MONDE. *see* RELIGIONS AND THEOLOGY—Roman Catholic

EGYPTIAN JOURNAL OF BIOLOGICAL PEST CONTROL. *see* AGRICULTURE—Crop Production And Soil

362.6 340 USA ISSN 1551-5117
ELDER LAW WEEKLY. Text in English. 2005. w. USD 2,295 in US & Canada; USD 2,495 elsewhere; USD 2,525 combined subscription in US & Canada (print & online eds.); USD 2,755 combined subscription elsewhere (print & online eds.) (effective 2008). back issues avail. **Document type:** *Newsletter, Trade.*
Related titles: E-mail ed.; Online - full text ed.: ISSN 1551-5125. USD 2,295 combined subscription (online & email eds.); single user (effective 2008).
Indexed: L10, P10, P20, P27, P48, P50, P53, P54, PQC.
Published by: NewsRx, 2727 Paces Ferry Rd SE, Ste 2-440, Atlanta, GA 30339. TEL 770-435-8286, 800-726-4550, FAX 770-435-6800, pressrelease@newsrx.com. Ed. Donald Kennedy. Pub. Susan Hasty TEL 770-507-7777.

362 649.8 USA ISSN 1548-8829
ELI'S HOME CARE WEEK; news & analysis on reimbursement, regulations, finance, operations, & compliance. Text in English. 1992. w. USD 287 (effective 2009). back issues avail. **Document type:** *Newsletter, Trade.*
Former titles (until 200?): Eli's Home Health Care (1094-396X); (until 1997): Home Health Care (1068-9478)
Related titles: Online - full text ed.: ISSN 1948-1063.
Indexed: H01.
Published by: Eli Research, Inc., PO Box 90324, Washington, DC 20090. TEL 800-874-9180, FAX 800-789-3560, help@eliresearch.com, http://www.eliresearch.com. Ed. Mary Compton TEL 919-647-9569. **Subscr. to:** National Subscription Bureau, Inc., Dept 1380, Denver, CO 80291. TEL 800-472-0148, FAX 800-508-2592, subscribe@eliresearch.com.

ELSEVIER SOCIALE VERZEKERINGEN ALMANAK. *see* INSURANCE

360 BRA ISSN 1809-0842
HV191
EM DEBATE. Text in Portuguese. 2005. s-a. back issues avail. **Document type:** *Journal, Academic/Scholarly.*
Related titles: Online - full text ed.
Published by: Pontificia Universidade Catolica do Rio de Janeiro, Departamento de Servico Social, Rua Marques de Sao Vicente, 225, Rio de Janeiro, RJ 22453-900, Brazil. TEL 55-21-35271001, embates@ser.puc-rio.br, http://www.puc-rio.br/sobrepuc/depto/servicosocial/professores_rel.html. Ed. Luis Correa Lima.

361 NOR ISSN 0807-0628
EMBLA. Text in Norwegian. 1996. 9/yr. NOK 760 (effective 2005). adv. bk.rev. **Document type:** *Magazine, Trade.*
Formed by the merger of (1972-1996): Vernepleieren (0332-8473); (1976-1996): Barnevernpedagogen (0802-7625); (1968-1996): Sosionomen (0332-7191); Which was formerly (1956-1968): Kuratoren (0332-7833)
Related titles: Online - full text ed.
Published by: Fellesorganisasjonen for Barnevernpedagoger, Sosionomer og Vernepleiere/Norwegian Union of Social Educators and Social Workers, PO Box 231, Sentrum, Oslo, 0103, Norway. TEL 47-23-061333, FAX 47-23-061112, http://www.fobsv.no. Ed. Vibeke Liane. Adv. contact Bente Semb TEL 47-23-061162. color page NOK 14,900, B&W page NOK 8,200; 185 x 240. Circ: 20,237.

EMERGENCY MANAGEMENT (FOLSOM); strategy & leadership in critical times. *see* PUBLIC ADMINISTRATION

360 FRA ISSN 1152-3336
➤ **EMPAN**; prendre la mesure de l'humain. Text in French. 1990. q. EUR 48 domestic to individuals; EUR,60 domestic to institutions; EUR 65 foreign (effective 2011). back issues avail. **Document type:** *Journal, Academic/Scholarly.*
Related titles: Online - full text ed.: ISSN 1776-2812.
Indexed: FR, SCOPUS, SD.
Published by: (Association Regionale pour la Sauvegarde de l'Enfant, de l'Adolescent et de l'Adulte (A R S E A A)), Editions Eres, 33 Av. Marcel Dassault, Toulouse, 31500, France. TEL 33-5-61751576, FAX 33-5-61735289, eres@edition-eres.com. Ed. Remy Puyelo. Circ: 1,000.

362 340 GBR ISSN 0261-3573
ENCYCLOPEDIA OF SOCIAL SERVICES AND CHILD CARE LAW. Text in English. 1981. 5 base vols. plus updates 3/yr. looseleaf. GBP 887 base vol(s). domestic; EUR 1,172 base vol(s). in Europe; USD 1,525 base vol(s). elsewhere (effective 2011). **Document type:** *Handbook/Manual/Guide, Trade.* **Description:** Provides clear explanation of the law relating to the care of children and vulnerable adults and social services.
Published by: Sweet & Maxwell Ltd. (Subsidiary of: Thomson Reuters Corp.), 100 Avenue Rd, London, NW3 3PF, United Kingdom. TEL 44-20-73937000, FAX 44-20-74491144, sweetandmaxwell.customer.services@thomson.com. Ed. Richard Jones. **Subscr. to:** PO Box 1000, Andover SP10 9AF, United Kingdom. TEL 44-20-73938051, sweetandmaxwell.international.queries@thomson.com.

361 USA ISSN 0071-0237
HV35
ENCYCLOPEDIA OF SOCIAL WORK. Text in English. 1929. irreg. (in 4 vols.), latest 2007, 20th ed. USD 495 per issue (effective 2009). adv. **Description:** Accesses data on the entire range of activities in social work and social welfare.
Formerly: Social Work Year Book
Indexed: SWR&A.
—**CCC.**
Published by: (National Association of Social Workers), N A S W Press, 750 First St NE, Ste 700, Washington, DC 20002-4241. TEL 800-227-3590, FAX 202-336-8312, press@naswdc.org, http://www.naswpress.org. Circ: 25,000.

END-OF-LIFE LAW DIGEST. *see* PUBLIC HEALTH AND SAFETY

362.5 USA ISSN 1935-4835
HV4506
ENDING HOMELESSNESS IN NEW JERSEY EZINE. Text in English. 2006. irreg. free (effective 2007). **Document type:** *Magazine, Consumer.* **Description:** Chronicles events and news related to helping the homeless population in New Jersey.
Media: Online - full content.
Published by: Monarch Housing Associates, 15 Alden St, Ste 10, Cranford, NJ 07016. TEL 908-272-5363, FAX 908-382-6309.

362.7 FRA ISSN 0013-757X
ENFANTS DU MONDE. Text in French. 1965. q. bk.rev. charts; illus.; maps. **Document type:** *Magazine, Consumer.* **Description:** Aim is to promote assistance to deprived children worldwide, by exposing their unsatisfactory living conditions.
Related titles: Online - full text ed.: free.
Indexed: FR.
Published by: Fonds des Nations Unies pour l'Enfance (UNICEF), Comite Francais, 3 rue Duguay-Trouin, Paris, 75006, France. TEL 33-1-44397777, FAX 33-1-44397778, contact@unicef.fr. Ed., R&P, Adv. contact Josette Tagher Roche TEL 33-1-44397739. Pub. Jacques Hintzy. Circ: 15,000.

ENFANTS DU MONDE ACTIONS. *see* CHILDREN AND YOUTH—About

360 GBR ISSN 1759-9911
ENGAGE (LONDON, 1979). Text in English. 1979. bi-m. GBP 30 domestic to voluntary or community organizations; GBP 65 domestic to public and private sector orgainizations; GBP 80 foreign (effective 2009). adv. back issues avail. **Document type:** *Magazine, Trade.* **Description:** Information and ideas about ways in which voluntary agencies can improve their effectiveness.
Former titles (until 2008): Voluntary Sector (1472-3867); (until 2000): N C V O News (0955-2170); (until 1989): Voluntary Action (0143-5744)
Related titles: Online - full text ed.
—BLDSC (3747.918500). **CCC.**
Published by: (National Council for Voluntary Organisations), Think Publishing, The Pall Mall Deposit, 124-128 Barlby Rd, London, W10 6BL, United Kingdom. TEL 44-20-89623020, FAX 44-20-89628689. Ed. Caitlin Mackesy Davies. Pub. Ian McAuliffe. Adv. contact Andrew Lawston.

S

362.3 CAN ISSN 1922-0561
ENGAGE IN COMMUNITY LIVING. Text in English. 1967. irreg. free to members (effective 2010). bk.rev. bibl. back issues avail. **Document type:** *Newsletter, Trade.* **Description:** Provides information with intellectual disabilities in the areas of education, housing, recreation and employment for parents and caregivers.
Formerly (until 2009): The Trust (0381-9612)
Related titles: Online - full text ed.: free (effective 2010).
Published by: Regina and District Association for Community Living Inc., 2216 Smith St, Regina, SK S4P 2P4, Canada. TEL 306-790-5680, FAX 306-586-7899, mainrdacl@sasktel.net.

360 ESP ISSN 1138-218X
ENTRE CULTURAS. Text in Spanish. 1992. bi-m. free (effective 2008). back issues avail. **Document type:** *Bulletin, Consumer.*
Published by: Caritas Espanola, San Bernardo, 99 bis 7a, Madrid, 28015, Spain. TEL 34-91-4441000, FAX 34-91-5934882, publicaciones@caritas-espa.org, http://www.caritas.es.

362.178 DNK ISSN 1014-8485
HQ766
ENTRE NOUS (ENGLISH EDITION); the european magazine for sexual and reproductive health. Text in English. 1983. 3/yr. back issues avail. **Document type:** *Magazine, Consumer.* **Description:** Aims to inform about sexual and reproductive health initiatives, policy, projects and resources in Europe.Produced at the World Health Organization Regional Office for Europe in Copenhagen.
Supersedes in part (1983-1990): Entre Nous (Bilingual Edition) (1010-3120)
Related titles: Online - full text ed.; Bulgarian ed.; Portuguese ed.: ISSN 1014-983X. 19??; Hungarian ed.: ISSN 1217-3606. 1989; Russian ed.: ISSN 1020-6329. 1994; Spanish ed.: ISSN 1012-621X. 1984.
Indexed: FR, P30, SCOPUS.
Published by: World Health Organization, Regional Office for Europe, Scherfigsvej 8, Copenhagen OE, 2100, Denmark. TEL 45-39-171426, FAX 45-39-171818. Eds. Jeffrey V Lazarus TEL 45-39-171341, Lisa Avery. Circ: 3,000 (controlled and free).

EPILEPSIA-LEHTI. *see* MEDICAL SCIENCES—Psychiatry And Neurology

610 BGD
EQUITY DIALOGUE. Text in English. 2003. 3/yr. **Document type:** *Journal, Academic/Scholarly.* **Description:** Concerns with equitable health and development in Bangladesh.
Related titles: Online - full content ed.
Published by: International Centre for Diarrhoeal Disease Research Bangladesh, GPO Box 128, Dhaka, 1000, Bangladesh. TEL 880-2-8811751, FAX 880-2-8823116, info@icddrb.org.

368 658.3 DEU ISSN 0014-0279
DIE ERSATZKASSE. Text in German. 1916. m. EUR 25.77 (effective 2006). adv. bk.rev. illus.; stat. **Document type:** *Bulletin.*
Indexed: WBSS.
—GNLM.
Published by: Verband der Angestellten-Krankenkassen e.V., Frankfurter Str 84, Siegburg, 53721, Germany. TEL 49-2241-1080, FAX 49-2241-108248, kontakt@vdak-aev.de. Circ: 6,544.

368 DEU ISSN 0170-2793
ERSATZKASSEN-REPORT. Text in German. 1978. irreg. free. **Document type:** *Bulletin.*
Published by: Verband der Angestellten-Krankenkassen e.V., Frankfurter Str 84, Siegburg, 53721, Germany. Ed. Rainer Josten.

362.2 USA ISSN 2155-3483
ESPERANZA; hope to cope with anxiety and depression. Text in English. 2008. q. USD 19.95 domestic; CAD 19.95 in Canada; USD 49.95 elsewhere (effective 2010). adv. illus. **Document type:** *Magazine, Consumer.* **Description:** Contains summaries of news stories, profiles of people coping with depression, articles and short pieces on techniques for coping, and a few book reviews.
Address: US - Editorial & Sales, 374 Delaware Ave, Ste 302, Buffalo, NY 14202. TEL 716-614-4673, 877-575-4673, FAX 716-614-4676. Ed. Nicole Peradotto.

360 ITA ISSN 0014-0678
ESPERIENZA; mensile di attualita, cultura e informazione. Text in Italian. 1951. m. free to members. adv. bk.rev. **Document type:** *Magazine, Consumer.*
Published by: Associazione Nazionale Lavoratori Anziani di Azienda, Via Monte delle Gioie 13, Rome, 00199, Italy. TEL 39-06-86321128, FAX 39-06-86322076, info@anla.it, http://www.anla.it. Circ: 140,000.

362.7 USA ISSN 0251-9119
ESTADO MUNDIAL DE LA INFANCIA. Text in Spanish. 1979. a. **Document type:** *Journal, Trade.*
Related titles: Online - full text ed.: ISSN 1564-9776. 1999. free (effective 2011); ◆ French ed.: La Situation des Enfants dans le Monde. ISSN 1020-2129; ◆ English ed.: The State of the World's Children. ISSN 0251-9100.
Published by: United Nations Children's Fund/Fonds des Nations Unies pour l'Enfance, 3 United Nations Plz, New York, NY 10017. TEL 212-326-7000, FAX 212-887-7465.

ESTUDIOS DE LA FUNDACION ONCE SOBRE EL ESTADO DE BIENESTAR. *see* HANDICAPPED

ETHICAL HUMAN PSYCHOLOGY AND PSYCHIATRY; an international journal of critical inquiry. *see* MEDICAL SCIENCES—Psychiatry And Neurology

361 GBR ISSN 1749-6535
➤ **ETHICS AND SOCIAL WELFARE.** Text in English. 2007. 3/yr. GBP 274 combined subscription in United Kingdom to institutions (print & online eds.); EUR 396, USD 498 combined subscription to institutions (print & online eds.) (effective 2012). adv. back issues avail.; reprint service avail. from PSC. **Document type:** *Journal, Academic/Scholarly.* **Description:** Publishes articles of a critical and reflective nature concerned with the ethical issues surrounding social welfare practice and policy.
Related titles: Online - full text ed.: ISSN 1749-6543. GBP 246 in United Kingdom to institutions; EUR 357, USD 448 to institutions (effective 2012).
Indexed: A22, CA, E01, P48, P53, P54, PAIS, PQC, PhilInd, PsycInfo, S02, S03, SSA, T02.
—IE. **CCC.**
Published by: Routledge (Subsidiary of: Taylor & Francis Group), 4 Park Sq, Milton Park, Abingdon, Oxon OX14 4RN, United Kingdom. TEL 44-20-70176000, FAX 44-20-70176336, subscriptions@tandf.co.uk, http://www.routledge.com. Eds. Derek Clifford, Sarah Banks. Adv. contact Linda Hann TEL 44-1344-779945. **Subscr. to:** Taylor & Francis Ltd., Journals Customer Service, Sheepen Pl, Colchester, Essex CO3 3LP, United Kingdom. TEL 44-20-70175544, FAX 44-20-70175198.

362.84 NZL ISSN 1177-2530
ETHNIC LINKS; refugee and migrant directory of services. Text in English. 2005. a. **Document type:** *Directory.*
Published by: North Shore Community Health Network Inc. - Raeburn House, PO Box 36-336, Northcote, Auckland, New Zealand. TEL 64-9-4418989.

360 GBR ISSN 1757-0980
➤ **ETHNICITY AND INEQUALITIES IN HEALTH AND SOCIAL CARE.** Text in English. 2008. q. EUR 689 combined subscription in Europe (print & online eds.); USD 889 combined subscription in the Americas (print & online eds.); GBP 529 combined subscription in the UK & elsewhere (print & online eds.); AUD 999 combined subscription in Australasia (print & online eds.) (effective 2012). adv. back issues avail. **Document type:** *Journal, Academic/Scholarly.*
Related titles: Online - full text ed.: ISSN 2042-8367.
Indexed: CA, H05, PsycInfo, S02, S03, T02.
—IE. **CCC.**
Published by: Pier Professional Ltd. (Subsidiary of: Emerald Group Publishing Ltd.), Ste N4, The Old Market, Upper Market St, Hove, BN3 1AS, United Kingdom. TEL 44-1273-783720, FAX 44-1273-783723, info@pierprofessional.com. Ed. David Sallah. Adv. contact Paul Somerville TEL 44-1273-783724. B&W page GBP 350; 160 x 245.

➤ **EUROPEAN COMMUNITY HUMANITARIAN OFFICE. ANNUAL REPORT.** *see* BUSINESS AND ECONOMICS—International Development And Assistance

360 GBR ISSN 1369-1457
HV236
➤ **EUROPEAN JOURNAL OF SOCIAL WORK**; the forum for the social work professional. Text in English. 1998. q. GBP 523 combined subscription in United Kingdom to institutions (print & online eds.); EUR 690, USD 867 combined subscription to institutions (print & online eds.) (effective 2012). adv. bk.rev. illus. back issues avail.; reprint service avail. from PSC. **Document type:** *Journal, Academic/Scholarly.* **Description:** Provides a forum for academic debate in the social professions, analyses, and promotes European and international developments in social policy, social service institutions and strategies of social change by publishing key issues.
Incorporates (1994-2004): Social Work in Europe (1353-1670)
Related titles: Online - full text ed.: ISSN 1468-2664. GBP 470 in United Kingdom to institutions; EUR 621, USD 781 to institutions (effective 2012) (from IngentaConnect).
Indexed: A10, A22, B04, B21, BRD, C06, C07, C08, CA, CINAHL, CurCont, E01, E17, ESPM, IBSS, P34, P42, PAIS, S02, S03, SCOPUS, SSA, SSAI, SSAb, SSCI, SSI, SWR&A, SociolAb, T02, V03, W01, W02, W03, W07.
—IE, Infotrieve, Ingenta. **CCC.**
Published by: Routledge (Subsidiary of: Taylor & Francis Group), 4 Park Sq, Milton Park, Abingdon, Oxon OX14 4RN, United Kingdom. TEL 44-20-70176000, FAX 44-20-70176336, subscriptions@tandf.co.uk, http://www.routledge.com. Ed. Suzy Braye. Adv. contact Linda Hann TEL 44-1344-779945. Circ: 550. **Subscr. in N. America to:** Taylor & Francis Inc., Customer Services Dept, 325 Chestnut St, 8th Fl, Philadelphia, PA 19106. TEL 215-625-8900, 800-354-1420, FAX 215-625-2940, customerservice@taylorandfrancis.com; **Subscr. to:** Taylor & Francis Ltd., Journals Customer Service, Sheepen Pl, Colchester, Essex CO3 3LP, United Kingdom. TEL 44-20-70175544, FAX 44-20-70175198, tf.enquiries@tfinforma.com.

361 IRL ISSN 1029-8630
EUROPEAN SOCIAL FUND. EVALUATION UNIT. IMPACT OF EVALUATIONS (YEAR). Text in English. 1995. a. **Document type:** *Corporate.*
Published by: European Social Fund, Evaluation Unit, Davitt House, 65A Adelaide Rd., Dublin, 2, Ireland. TEL 353-1-6614444, FAX 353-1-6611272.

353.5 AUT ISSN 0258-6193
EUROSOCIAL REPORTS. Text in German, English, French. 1974. irreg. (3-5/yr.). **Document type:** *Monographic series, Academic/Scholarly.*
—BLDSC (3830.429500), IE, Ingenta.
Published by: European Centre for Social Welfare Policy and Research, Berggasse 17, Vienna, W 1090, Austria. TEL 43-1-3194505-27, FAX 43-1-3194505-19, stamatiou@euro.centre.org, http://www.euro.centre.org. Ed. Bernd Marin. R&P Willem Stamatiou.

361.73 USA ISSN 1082-3441
EVENTS; ideas & resources for fundraising events. Text in English. 1993. bi-m. USD 45 (effective 2001). bk.rev. index. back issues avail. **Document type:** *Newsletter, Trade.*
Address: PO Box 3206, University City, MO 63130-0606. TEL 513-541-4564. Ed., Pub. Michael Donovan.

361 SWE ISSN 1654-8825
EVIDENS; branschtidning foer behandlingshem i Sverige. Text in Swedish. 2007. q. **Document type:** *Magazine, Trade.*
Related titles: Online - full text ed.
Published by: Queen Media Group AB, Nygatan 57, Skelleftea, 93130, Sweden. TEL 46-910-39585, info@queenmedia.se, http://www.queenmedia.se. Ed. Anci Malmen.

361.73 USA
EXCHANGE (NEW YORK). Text in English. 1985. 3/yr. back issues avail. **Description:** Covers organizational activities, social exchange issues, philanthropy, and donors.
Formerly: Donor Update
Published by: Funding Exchange, 666 Broadway, Ste 500, New York, NY 10012. TEL 212-529-5300. Ed. Nan Robin. Circ: 4,000.

361 USA
EYE ON L S S I. (Lutheran Social Services of Illinois) Text in English. 1988. 3/yr. free. illus. **Document type:** *Newsletter.* **Description:** Introduces programs and achievements of the organization.
Published by: Lutheran Social Services of Illinois, 1001 E Touhy Ave, Des Plaines, IL 60018. TEL 708-635-4600. Ed. Sherie L Beirne. Circ: 82,000.

360 AUS ISSN 1833-8372
F R R R COMMUNITY REPORT. Text in English. 2005. triennial. **Description:** Features articles about some of the projects FRRR and its partners supported in the every three years.
Related titles: Online - full text ed.: ISSN 1833-8380. free (effective 2009).
Published by: Foundation for Rural & Regional Renewal, PO Box 41, Bendigo, VIC 3552, Australia. TEL 61-3-54302399, 800-170-020, FAX 61-3-54438900, info@frrr.org.au.

360 AUS ISSN 1833-7996
F R R R NEWSLETTER. Text in English. 2002. 3/yr. back issues avail. **Description:** Features news and informative articles on rural and regional development programs in Australia.
Related titles: Online - full text ed.: ISSN 1833-8003. free (effective 2009).
Published by: Foundation for Rural & Regional Renewal, PO Box 41, Bendigo, VIC 3552, Australia. TEL 61-3-54302399, 800-170-020, FAX 61-3-54438900, info@frrr.org.au.

362.7 ARG
F U N D A M I N D REVISTA. (Fundacion Asistencia Materno-Infantil de Ayuda a Ninos Carenciados y Discapacitados) Text in Spanish. 1997. q. **Description:** Includes news and short articles on children's welfare and assistance.
Media: Online - full text.
Published by: F U N D A M I N D, 24 de Noviembre 140, Buenos Aires, 1170, Argentina. TEL 54-11-4957-7333, FAX 54-11-4957-7111, gmitre@fundamind.org.ar, http://www.fundamind.org.ar/. Ed. Gerardo Isaac Mitre.

360 AUS ISSN 1833-4407
FA C S I A RESEARCH NEWS. Text in English. 1999. q. free (effective 2008). **Document type:** *Newsletter, Government.* **Description:** Contains brief summaries of completed research, project updates, contact details, forthcoming events and coverage of important research events, plus details of recently released departmental publications.
Formerly (until 2006): Fa C S Research News (1442-7524)
Related titles: Online - full text ed.
Published by: Australia. Department of Families, Community Services and Indigenous Affairs, GPO Box 7788, Canberra Mail Centre, ACT 2610, Australia. TEL 61-2-62445458, 300-653-227, FAX 61-2-62446589, enquiries@fahcsia.gov.au.

FACTFILE; facts and figures about children in the UK. *see* CHILDREN AND YOUTH—About

FACTFILE (SCOTLAND); facts and figures about Scotland's children. *see* CHILDREN AND YOUTH—About

362.82 NOR ISSN 1503-8750
FAMILIA (ONLINE). Text in Norwegian. 1998. q. free. back issues avail. **Document type:** *Magazine, Government.*
Formerly (until 2004): Familia (Print) (1500-3507); Which was formed by the merger of (1978-1997): Likestilling (0803-4311); (1992-1997): Ta Barn paa Alvor (0807-3236)
Published by: Barne- og Familiedepartementet/The Ministry of Children and Family Affairs, Akersgate 59, PO Box 8036, Oslo, 0030, Norway. TEL 47-22-249090, http://www.bfd.dep.no.

FAMILIA Y SOCIEDAD. *see* SOCIOLOGY

362.82 NZL ISSN 1177-8172
FAMILIES COMMISSION. INNOVATIVE PRACTICE REPORT. Text in English. 2006. irreg. **Document type:** *Monographic series.*
Related titles: Online - full text ed.: ISSN 1177-8180.
Published by: Families Commission, Level 6, Public Trust Bldg, 117-125 Lambton Quay, PO Box 2839, Wellington, New Zealand. TEL 64-4-9177040, FAX 64-4-9177059, enquiries@nzfamilies.org.nz, http://www.nzfamilies.org.nz.

361.3 USA ISSN 1044-3894
HV1 CODEN: FASOEN
➤ **FAMILIES IN SOCIETY**; the journal of contemporary social services. Abbreviated title: F I S. Text in English. 1920. q. USD 228 domestic to institutions; USD 258 in Canada to institutions; USD 288 elsewhere to institutions; USD 67 combined subscription domestic to individuals (print & online eds.); USD 97 combined subscription in Canada to individuals (print & online eds.); USD 127 combined subscription elsewhere to individuals (print & online eds.); USD 315 combined subscription domestic to institutions (print & online eds.); USD 345 combined subscription in Canada to institutions (print & online eds.); USD 375 combined subscription elsewhere to institutions (print & online eds.); free to members (effective 2009). adv. bk.rev. illus. index. back issues avail.; reprints avail. **Document type:** *Journal, Academic/Scholarly.* **Description:** Provides informative articles that deal with the theory, practice, and management of family, individual and group counseling and therapy for human service professionals.
Former titles (until Jan.1990): Social Casework (0037-7678); (until 1950): Journal of Social Casework (8755-4879); (until 1946): The Family (0887-400X)
Related titles: Microform ed.: (from PQC); Online - full text ed.: ISSN 1945-1350. USD 52 domestic to individuals; USD 286 to institutions (effective 2009).
Indexed: A01, A02, A03, A08, A20, A21, A22, A25, A26, AC&P, AHCMS, ASCA, ASG, Acal, B04, B14, BRD, BRI, BehAb, CA, CBRI, CMM, CPLI, CPerI, Chicano, CommAb, CurCont, DIP, E-psyche, E08, ECER, ERA, F09, FamI, G05, G06, G07, G08, G10, H09, H10, HRA, HospLI, I05, IBR, IBZ, M06, M12, MEA&I, P02, P03, P06, P10, P13, P25, P27, P30, P34, P46, P48, P53, P54, PCI, PQC, PSI, PsycInfo, PsycholAb, RI-1, RI-2, S02, S03, S05, S08, S09, S11, S20, S21, SCOPUS, SFSA, SOPODA, SSA, SSAI, SSAb, SSCI, SSI, SWR&A, SociolAb, T02, V&AA, W03, W07, W09.
—BLDSC (3865.553973), IE, Infotrieve, Ingenta.
Published by: Alliance for Children and Families, 11700 W Lake Park Dr, Milwaukee, WI 53224. TEL 414-359-6521, FAX 414-359-1074, http://www.alliance1.org/. Ed. Dr. William E Powell. Pub. Mr. Peter B Goldberg. adv.: B&W page USD 800; bleed 8.625 x 11.125. Circ: 2,100 (paid).

362.7 346.01 SWE ISSN 1102-2353
FAMILJEFOERENINGEN FOER INTERNATIONELL ADOPTION. Text in Swedish. 1980. 3/yr. SEK 290 to members (effective 1999). **Document type:** *Bulletin.*
Former titles (until vol.2, 1988): Familjenytt; (until vol.1, 1982): Information fraan Familjefoereningen foer Adoption
Published by: Familjefoereningen foer Internationell Adoption (FFIA), Fack 12027, Goeteborg, 40241, Sweden.

362.82 USA ISSN 1941-7462
HV6626.2
FAMILY & INTIMATE PARTNER VIOLENCE QUARTERLY; the journal of advocacy, programming, research, and law. Abbreviated title: F I P V. Text in English. 2008. q. USD 139.95 to individuals; USD 239.95 to institutions (effective 2010). back issues avail. **Document type:** *Journal, Academic/Scholarly.* **Description:** Summarizes important research on violence, abuse, and maltreatment with a focus on specific strategies for bringing healing and justice to the lives of victims.
Related titles: Online - full text ed.: ISSN 2157-0078.
Indexed: CJA, T02.
—CCC.
Published by: Civic Research Insitute, PO Box 585, Kingston, NJ 08528. TEL 609-683-4450, FAX 609-683-7291, order@civicresearchinstitute.com. Ed. Kathleen A Kendall-Tackett TEL 212-686-5690.

FAMILY HISTORY NETLETTER. *see* SOCIOLOGY

FAMILY MATTERS. *see* SOCIOLOGY

346 362.82 GBR ISSN 1350-9756
FAMILY MEDIATION. Text in English. 1991. 3/yr. GBP 10. adv. bk.rev. **Document type:** *Bulletin.* **Description:** Provides information and commentary on the work of National Family Meditation, its affiliated services in the UK, and similar agencies elsewhere.
Formerly (until 1994): Family Conciliation
—Infotrieve.
Published by: National Family Mediation, 9 Tavistock Pl, London, W11 1AT, United Kingdom. TEL 44-171-383-5993, FAX 44-171-383-5994. Ed., Adv. contact Arthur Robinson. Circ: 700.

FAMILY PLANNING ASSOCIATION OF NEPAL. ANNUAL REPORT. *see* BIRTH CONTROL

362.82 USA ISSN 1085-0430
HV697
FAMILY PRESERVATION JOURNAL. Text in English. 1995. a. USD 40 per issue to individuals; USD 80 per issue to institutions (effective 2010). back issues avail. **Document type:** *Journal, Academic/ Scholarly.* **Description:** Devoted to presenting theoretical, research and practice articles on family preservation and support, thereby assisting professionals to develop and implement the best possible programs.
Indexed: S02, S03, SCOPUS, SWR&A, T02.
Published by: (New Mexico State University, Family Preservation Institute), Eddie Bowers Publishing, PO Box 130, Peosta, IA 52068. TEL 800-747-2411, FAX 563-876-3206, eddiebowerspub@aol.com. Ed. Marianne Berry.

FAMILY RELATIONS - STATE CAPITALS. *see* LAW—Family And Matrimonial Law

FAMILY SUPPORT BULLETIN. *see* HANDICAPPED—Physically Impaired

FAMILY THERAPY MAGAZINE. *see* PSYCHOLOGY

362.82 364 USA ISSN 1067-7283
HV6626.2 CODEN: FVSBET
FAMILY VIOLENCE & SEXUAL ASSAULT BULLETIN. Short title: F V S A B. Text in English. 1985. q. USD 45 domestic to individuals; USD 80 domestic to institutions; USD 60 in Canada & Mexico; USD 75 elsewhere (effective 2007). adv. video rev.; Website rev.; bk.rev. 60 p./no. 2 cols./p.; back issues avail. **Document type:** *Bulletin, Consumer.* **Description:** Focuses exclusively on family violence and addresses issues of family violence, sexual assault, and child and teen maltreatment.
Formerly (until 1991): Family Violence Bulletin (1055-7938)
Indexed: F09, S02, S03, SCOPUS, SFSA, SOPODA, T02, V&AA.
Published by: Institute on Violence, Abuse and Trauma, 6160 Cornerstone Court E, San Diego, CA 92121. TEL 858-623-2777, FAX 858-646-0761, ivat@alliant.edu, http://www.ivatcenters.org. adv.: page USD 550. Circ: 1,000.

362.82 USA ISSN 1556-4827
RC569.5.F3
➤ **FAMILY VIOLENCE PREVENTION & HEALTH PRACTICE.** Text in English. 2005 (Jan.). s-a. free (effective 2010). **Document type:** *Journal, Academic/Scholarly.* **Description:** Aims to improve the health, safety, and quality of care for survivors of family violence.
Media: Online - full text.
Indexed: S02, S03, T02.
Published by: Family Violence Prevention Fund, 383 Rhode Island St, Ste 304, San Francisco, CA 94103. TEL 415-252-8900, 800-595-4889, FAX 415-252-8991, info@endabuse.org, http://www.endabuse.org. Ed. Linda Chamberlain.

362.82 NZL ISSN 1177-1011
FAMILY VOICE. Text in English. 2005. 3/yr. free (effective 2006). **Document type:** *Newsletter.*
Published by: Families Commission, Level 6, Public Trust Bldg, 117-125 Lambton Quay, PO Box 2839, Wellington, New Zealand. TEL 64-4-9177040, FAX 64-4-9177059, enquiries@nzfamilies.org.nz, http://www.nzfamilies.org.nz.

THE FAR EAST; mission magazine of the Columban fathers. *see* RELIGIONS AND THEOLOGY—Roman Catholic

FAST FACTS & FIGURES ABOUT SOCIAL SECURITY (YEAR). *see* INSURANCE

FAZHI YU SHEHUI FAZHAN. *see* LAW

FEDERAL BENEFITS FOR VETERANS AND DEPENDENTS. *see* MILITARY

336 361.73 USA ISSN 1949-3177
FEDERAL GRANTS & CONTRACTS. Text in English. bi-w. GBP 2,777 in United Kingdom to institutions; EUR 3,255 in Europe to institutions; USD 4,415 in United States to institutions; USD 4,511 in Canada & Mexico to institutions; USD 4,547 elsewhere to institutions; GBP 3,195 combined subscription in United Kingdom to institutions (print & online eds.); EUR 3,745 combined subscription in Europe to institutions (print & online eds.); USD 5,079 combined subscription in United States to institutions (print & online eds.); USD 5,175 combined subscription in Canada & Mexico to institutions (print & online eds.); USD 5,211 combined subscription elsewhere to institutions (print & online eds.) (effective 2012). **Document type:** *Newsletter, Trade.* **Description:** Comprehensive round-up of education, health research and social service funding opportunities across all federal agencies.
Related titles: Online - full text ed.: ISSN 1949-3185. GBP 2,696 in United Kingdom to institutions; EUR 3,160 in Europe to institutions; USD 4,415 elsewhere to institutions (effective 2012).
Indexed: B01, N06, T02.
—CCC.
Published by: Jossey-Bass Inc., Publishers (Subsidiary of: John Wiley & Sons, Inc.), 111 River St, Hoboken, NJ 07030. TEL 201-748-6000, FAX 201-748-6088, jbsubs@jbp.com, http://www.josseybass.com/ WileyCDA/. Pub. Sue Lewis.

FEE-HELP INFORMATION. *see* EDUCATION

361 ISL ISSN 1670-5513
FELAGSTHJONUSTAN I REYKJAVIK. ARSSKYRSLA. Text in Icelandic. 1971. a. charts; stat. back issues avail. **Document type:** *Yearbook.*
Formerly (until 1998): Felagsmalastofnun Reykjavikurborgar. Arsskyrsla (1670-5521)
Related titles: Online - full text ed.
Published by: Felagsthjonustan i Reykjavik/Reykjavik Social Services, Tryggvagoetur 17, Reykjavik, 101, Iceland. TEL 354-411-9000.

360 FRA ISSN 0248-3165
FEUILLE DE ROUTE QUART MONDE. Text in French. 1969. m. EUR 8 (effective 2009). back issues avail. **Document type:** *Newsletter.* **Description:** Discusses the struggles of families around the world living in poverty.
Formerly (until 1976): Quart Monde (0248-322X)
Published by: (Mouvement International A T D Quart Monde/International Movement A T D Fourth World), Editions Quart Monde, 107 Av. du General Leclerc, Pierrelaye, 95480, France. TEL 33-01-34083140, FAX 33-01-34304636, editions@atd-quartmonde.org, http://www.atd-quartmonde.org. Ed. Louis Join Lambert. Circ: 100,000.

FIAPAS. *see* HANDICAPPED—Hearing Impaired

360 FIN ISSN 1795-6897
FINLAND. SOSIAALI- JA TERVEYSALAN TUTKIMUS- JA KEHITTAMISKESKUS. DISCUSSION PAPERS. Text in English. 1992. irreg. **Document type:** *Monographic series, Government.*
Formerly (until 2005): Finland. Sosiaali- ja Terveysalan Tutkimus- ja Kehittamiskeskus. Themes (1235-4775)
Related titles: Online - full text ed.: ISSN 1795-8202.
Published by: Sosiaali- ja Terveysalan Tutkimus- ja Kehittamiskeskus/ National Research and Development Centre for Welfare and Health, PO Box 220, Helsinki, 00531, Finland. TEL 358-9-39671, FAX 358-9-396761307, infolib@stakes.fi.

360 FIN ISSN 0788-6098
HA1448
FINLAND. SOSIAALI- JA TERVEYSHALLITUS. KOTIPALVELU/ FINLAND. NATIONAL AGENCY FOR WELFARE AND HEALTH. HOME HELP/FINLAND. SOCIAL- OG HAELSOSTYRELSEN. HEMSERVICE. Text in English, Finnish, Swedish. 1939. biennial. **Document type:** *Government.*
Supersedes in part (in 1990): Finland. Suomen Virallen Tilasto. 21 A, Huoltoapu (0355-4759); Which was formerly (1890-1938): Finland. Suomen Virallen Tilasto. 21 A, Koyhainhoitoliasto
Related titles: ◆ Series of: Sosiaaliturva. ISSN 0785-4625.
Published by: Sosiaalihallitus, Siltasaarenkatu 18 C, Helsinki, 00530, Finland. Ed. Kyllikki Korpi. **Dist. by:** Government Printing Centre, PL 516, Helsinki 00100, Finland.

360 FIN ISSN 1236-2050
FINLAND. SOSIAALI- JA TERVEYSMINISTERIO. JULKAISUJA/ FINLAND. MINISTRY OF SOCIAL AFFAIRS AND HEALTH. PUBLICATIONS/FINLAND. SOCIAL- OCH HAELSOVAARDSMINISTERIET. PUBLIKATIONER. Text in English, Finnish, Swedish. 1989. irreg. back issues avail. **Document type:** *Government.*
Formerly (until 1993): S T M:n Julkaisuja (0786-9320)
Related titles: Online - full text ed.; ◆ Series: Tyottomyyspaivarahat. ISSN 1238-2620.
Published by: Sosiaali- ja Terveysministerio/Ministry of Social Affairs and Health, Meritullinkatu 8, PO Box 33, Helsinki, 00171, Finland. TEL 358-9-1601, FAX 358-9-1602590, kirjaamo.stm@stm.fi.

360 305.897 CAN ISSN 1910-7080
FIRST NATIONS AND INUIT HOME AND COMMUNITY CARE PROGRAM. UPDATE. Text in English. 2004. q. **Document type:** *Newsletter, Trade.*
Formerly (until 2005): National Evaluation Update (1710-3878)
Published by: Health Canada/Sante Canada, Address Locator 0900C2, Ottawa, ON K1A OK9, Canada. TEL 613-957-2991, 866-225-0709, FAX 613-941-5366, info@www.hc-sc.gc.ca, http://www.hc-sc.gc.ca.

FIT!; D A K Magazin. *see* PUBLIC HEALTH AND SAFETY

353.9 USA
FLORIDA. DEPARTMENT OF CORRECTIONS. ANNUAL REPORT. Text in English. 1973. a. free. stat. **Document type:** *Government.*
Formerly: Florida. Division of Corrections. Financial Report (0094-6435)
Related titles: Microfiche ed.: (from CIS).
Indexed: SRI.
Published by: Department of Corrections, 2601 Blair Stone Rd, Tallahassee, FL 32399-2500. TEL 850-488-1801, FAX 850-922-2685. Circ: 5,000.

360 USA ISSN 1931-3454
FLYER (LOGAN). Text in English. 2006. q. **Document type:** *Newsletter, Trade.*
Related titles: Online - full text ed.: ISSN 1931-3462.
Published by: Utah State University, National Clearinghouse of Rehabilitation Training Materials, 6524 Old Main Hill, Logan, UT 84322-6524. TEL 866-821-5355, FAX 435-797-7537, ncrtm@cc.usu.edu, http://ncrtm.org.

360 GBR
FOCUS (BELFAST). Text in English. 1889. q. **Document type:** *Newsletter.* **Description:** Contains mission news and prayer topics.
Formerly (until 2004): Forward
Published by: Sandes Soldiers' & Airmen's Centres, Unit 7, 30 Island St, Belfast, BT4 1DH, United Kingdom. info@sandes.org.uk, http:// www.sandes.org.uk/. Ed., R&P, Adv. contact Hazel Knox. Circ: 3,000.

362.5 USA
FOCUS (MADISON) (ONLINE). Text in English. 2007. q. free (effective 2011). back issues avail. **Document type:** *Newsletter, Trade.* **Description:** Provides information on poverty-related research, events, and issues, and to acquaint a large audience with the work of the Institute for Research on Poverty by means of short essays on selected pieces of research.
Media: Online - full text.
Published by: University of Wisconsin at Madison, Institute for Research on Poverty, 3412 Social Science Bldg, 1180 Observatory Dr, Madison, WI 53706. TEL 608-262-6358, FAX 608-265-3119, irppubs@ssc.wisc.edu, http://www.ssc.wisc.edu/irp/. Ed. Emma Caspar TEL 608-265-4168.

362.2 649 SWE ISSN 1653-9109
FOERAELDRAKRAFT. Text in Swedish. 2006. 8/yr. SEK 349 domestic; SEK 490 In Nordic countries; SEK 545 in the European Union; SEK 645 elsewhere (effective 2007). adv. **Document type:** *Magazine, Consumer.* **Description:** For parents with children with special needs.
Related titles: Online - full text ed.
Published by: FaktaPress AB, Backebogatan 3, Haegersten, 12940, Sweden. TEL 46-709-560852, http://www.faktapress.se. Ed. Sara Bengtsson TEL 46-738-130436. Pub. Valter Bengtsson. adv.: page SEK 19,900. Circ: 20,000.

FOKUS PAA FAMILIEN; tidsskrift for familiebehandling. *see* MEDICAL SCIENCES—Psychiatry And Neurology

362.7 FRA ISSN 2106-5438
FOND'ACTION. Text in French. 2003. 3/yr. **Document type:** *Newsletter, Consumer.*
Published by: Fondation d'Auteuil, 40 Rue Jean de La Fontaine, Paris, 75016, France. TEL 33-1-44147575, http://www.fondation-auteuil.org.

362.5 280.4 FRA ISSN 1636-1377
FONDATION DE L'ARMEE DU SALUT. LE MAGAZINE. Text in French. 1993. q. EUR 6.10 (effective 2008). **Document type:** *Magazine, Consumer.*
Formerly (until 2001): Soupes de Nuit (1247-4223)
Published by: Armee du Salut, 60 rue des Freres Flavien, Paris, Cedex 20 75976, France. TEL 1-33-43622500.

361 NLD ISSN 1877-8992
FONDS 1818 MAGAZINE. Text in Dutch. 200?. q. free (effective 2011).
Published by: Fonds 1818, Postbus 895, The Hague, 2501 CW, Netherlands. TEL 31-70-3641141, FAX 31-70-3641891, info@fonds1818.nl, http://www.fonds1818.nl.

360 USA
FOOD & POVERTY NOTES. Text in English. 1976. bi-m. USD 10 (effective 1999). **Document type:** *Newsletter.* **Description:** Covers various issues dealing with food assistance, advocacy and the hunger problem nationwide.
Published by: Maryland Food Committee, 2521 N Charles St, Baltimore, MD 21218. TEL 410-366-0600, FAX 410-366-3963. Ed., R&P Lindsay Stroh. Circ: 37,000.

362.1 USA
FOOD EQUALS LOVE. Text in English. 1993 (vol.5). q. **Document type:** *Newsletter.* **Description:** News of the organization, which sends meals to homebound people with AIDS in the NYC area.
Formerly (until Sep. 1996): Good News Letter (New York)
Published by: God's Love We Deliver, 166 Ave of the Americas, New York, NY 10013-1207. TEL 212-294-8100, FAX 212-294-8101. Ed., R&P Carlos Sousa TEL 212-294-8134.

FOOTPRINTS; the supporters' magazine for spurgeons. *see* CHILDREN AND YOUTH—About

363.8 GBR ISSN 0962-2861
FOOTSTEPS. Text in English. 1989. q. **Document type:** *Newsletter, Trade.* **Description:** Aims to share information, ideas, contacts and experience in a Christian context at grassroots level.
Related titles: Online - full text ed.: free (effective 2009); Spanish ed.: Paso a Paso. ISSN 0969-3858. 1990; Portuguese ed.: Passo a Passo. ISSN 1353-9868. 1994; French ed.: Pas a Pas. ISSN 1350-1399. 1990.
—CCC.
Published by: T E A R Fund, 100 Church Rd, Teddington, TW11 8QE, United Kingdom. TEL 44-845-3558355, enquiry@tearfund.org, http://www.tearfund.org. Ed. Rebecca Dennis TEL 44-20-89779144.

362.4 NLD ISSN 2210-5255
▼ **FOPPE.** Text in Dutch. 2010. a. EUR 10 (effective 2010). adv.
Published by: (Stichting Het Foppe Fonds), Sucks Media & Design bv, Zuidvliet 22, Leeuwarden, 8921 BL, Netherlands. TEL 31-58-2881202, FAX 31-58-2880508, info@sucksmedia.nl, http:// www.sucksmedia.nl. Eds. Ben Wagenaar, Marieke Vinckers. Adv. contact Els Breuker. color page EUR 1,450; 230 x 275.

361 NOR ISSN 1503-9803
FOR VELFERDSSTATEN. SKRIFTSERIE. Text in Norwegian. 2003. irreg., latest vol.5, 2005. free. back issues avail. **Document type:** *Monographic series.*
Published by: For Velferdsstaten/Broad Alliance for the Welfare State, Storgate 23 C, Oslo, 0184, Norway. FAX 47-22-427510, aksjon@velferdsstaten.no.

360 GBR
FORCED MIGRATION REVIEW (ARABIC EDITION). Text in Arabic. 1997. 3/yr. free (effective 2005). **Document type:** *Magazine.* **Description:** It provides the humanitarian community with a practice-oriented forum for debate on issues facing refugees and internally displaced people in order to improve policy and practice.
Related titles: Online - full text ed.: free (effective 2007); ◆ English ed.: Forced Migration Review (English Edition). ISSN 1460-9819; ◆ Spanish ed.: Forced Migration Review (Spanish Edition); Ed.: Forced Migration Review (French Edition). 2005.
Published by: Refugee Studies Centre, Department of International Development, University of Oxford, 3 Mansfield Rd, Oxford, OX1 3TB, United Kingdom. TEL 44-1865-280700, FAX 44-1865-270721, fmr@qeh.ox.ac.uk.

360 GBR ISSN 1460-9819
HV640
FORCED MIGRATION REVIEW (ENGLISH EDITION). Abbreviated title: F M R. Text in English. 1987. 3/yr. free (effective 2009). back issues avail. **Document type:** *Magazine, Consumer.* **Description:** Provides a forum for debate on issues facing refugees and internally displaced people in order to improve policy and practice.
Formerly (until 1998): Refugee Participation Network (0965-7460)
Related titles: Online - full text ed.: free (effective 2007); ◆ Arabic ed.: Forced Migration Review (Arabic Edition); ◆ Spanish ed.: Forced Migration Review (Spanish Edition); Ed.: Forced Migration Review (French Edition). 2005.
Indexed: A01, A36, C25, CA, CABA, E12, GH, I02, I11, M10, P02, P10, P30, P34, P42, P45, P46, P48, P53, P54, PAIS, PQC, PSA, R12, S02, S03, S11, S13, S16, SCOPUS, SociolAb, T02, T05, TAR, W11.

S

Published by: Refugee Studies Centre, Department of International Development, University of Oxford, 3 Mansfield Rd, Oxford, OX1 3TB, United Kingdom. TEL 44-1865-281700, FAX 44-1865-281730. Eds. Marion Couldrey, Maurice Herson.

360 GBR
FORCED MIGRATION REVIEW (SPANISH EDITION)/MIGRACIONES FORZADAS. Text in Spanish. 1997. 3/yr. free (effective 2005). **Document type:** *Magazine.* **Description:** It provides the humanitarian community with a practice-oriented forum for debate on issues facing refugees and internally displaced people in order to improve policy and practice.
Related titles: Online - full text ed.: 1998. free (effective 2007); ◆ English ed.: Forced Migration Review (English Edition). ISSN 1460-9819; ◆ Arabic ed.: Forced Migration Review (Arabic Edition); Ed.: Forced Migration Review (French Edition). 2005.
Published by: Refugee Studies Centre, Department of International Development, University of Oxford, 3 Mansfield Rd, Oxford, OX1 3TB, United Kingdom. TEL 44-1865-280700, FAX 44-1865-270721, fmr@qeh.ox.ac.uk.

FORENINGEN AF DANSKE DOEVBLINDE. MEDLEMSNYT. *see* HANDICAPPED—Visually Impaired

360 DEU ISSN 0071-7835
FORTBILDUNG UND PRAXIS. Text in German. 1949. irreg., latest vol.133, 2006. price varies. **Document type:** *Monographic series, Academic/Scholarly.*
Related titles: ◆ Supplement(s): Wege zur Sozialversicherung. ISSN 0043-2059.
Published by: Asgard-Verlag Dr. Werner Hippe GmbH, Einsteinstr 10, St. Augustin, 53757, Germany. TEL 49-2241-31640, FAX 49-2241-316436, service@asgard.de, http://www.asgard.de.

FORTUNE NEWS. *see* CRIMINOLOGY AND LAW ENFORCEMENT

362.7 FRA ISSN 2105-6196
FORUM DE LA CONVENTION NATIONALE DES ASSOCIATIONS DE PROTECTION DE L'ENFANT. Text in French. 1998. q.
Former titles (until 2009): Forum du Conseil National des Associations de Protection de l'Enfant (2101-471X); (until 2008): Forum des Sauvegardes (1289-8961)
Published by: Conseil National des Associations de Protection de l'Enfant, 118, Rue du Chateau des Rentiers, Paris, 75013, France. TEL 33-1-45835060, FAX 33-1-45868036, contact@unasea.org, http://www.cnape.fr/fr/home.html.

360 DEU ISSN 0947-8957
➤ **FORUM ERZIEHUNGSHILFEN.** Text in German. 1972. 5/yr. EUR 37; EUR 31 to students; EUR 8.50 newsstand/cover (effective 2011). adv. index. back issues avail. **Document type:** *Journal, Academic/Scholarly.*
Formerly (until 1994): Materialen zur Heimerziehung (0723-2047)
Indexed: IBR, IBZ.
Published by: (Internationale Gesellschaft fuer erzieherische Hilfen), Juventa Verlag GmbH, Ehretstr 3, Weinheim, 69469, Germany. TEL 49-6201-90200, FAX 49-6201-902013, juventa@juventa.de, http://www.juventa.de. Ed. Josef Koch. Adv. contact Thekla Steinmetz. Circ: 3,000 (paid and controlled).

362.7 364 DEU ISSN 0171-7669
FORUM JUGENDHILFE. Text in German. 1950. q. EUR 15; EUR 5 newsstand/cover (effective 2008). adv. bk.rev. **Document type:** *Magazine, Trade.*
Former titles (until 1976): A G J Mitteilungen (0171-7685); (until 1973): Arbeitsgemeinschaft fuer Jugendhilfe. Mitteilungen (0171-7677); (until 1972): Arbeitsgemeinschaft fuer Jugendpflege und Jugendfuersorge. Mitteilungen (0003-7710)
Indexed: DIP, IBR, IBZ.
Published by: Arbeitsgemeinschaft fuer Kinder- und Jugendhilfe, Muehlendamm 3, Berlin, 10178, Germany. TEL 49-30-40040200, FAX 49-30-40040232, agj@agj.de. Ed. Matthias Hoener. R&P Peter Klausch. Circ: 1,300.

360 DEU ISSN 1433-3945
FORUM SOZIAL. Text in German. 1994. 4/yr. EUR 40; EUR 10 newsstand/cover (effective 2011). adv. **Document type:** *Magazine, Trade.*
Formerly (until 1995): D B S H - Deutscher Berufsverband der Sozialarbeiter/Sozialarbeiterinnen, Sozialpaedagogen/Sozialpaedagoginnen, Heilpaedagogen/Heilpaedagoginnen (1433-3937); Which was formed by the merger of (1970-1994): Sozial (1433-3929); (1960-1994): Die Berufliche Sozialarbeit (0935-1930); Which was formerly (until 1988): Der Sozialarbeiter (0724-3340)
Indexed: DIP, IBR, IBZ.
Published by: Deutscher Berufsverband fuer Soziale Arbeit e.V., Friedrich-Ebert-Str 30, Essen, 45127, Germany. TEL 49-201-820780, FAX 49-201-8207840, info@dbsh.de. Ed. Wilfried Nodes. Adv. contact Joern Rabeneck. Circ: 8,000 (controlled).

362.14 DEU ISSN 0171-1490
FORUM SOZIALSTATION; Das Magazin fuer ambulante Pflege. Text in German. 1977. bi-m. EUR 52 domestic; EUR 55.50 foreign; EUR 10.40 newsstand/cover (effective 2007). adv. **Document type:** *Magazine, Trade.*
Published by: Tintenfass Verlag, Luisenstr 56, Bonn, 53129, Germany. TEL 49-228-264628, FAX 49-228-264629. Ed. Uschi Grieshaber. adv.: B&W page EUR 908, color page EUR 1,452.80. Circ: 5,500 (paid and controlled).

FOSTER CARE. *see* CHILDREN AND YOUTH—About

362 USA ISSN 1531-409X
HV881
FOSTERING FAMILIES TODAY. Abbreviated title: F F T. Text in English. 2001. bi-m. USD 24 domestic; USD 29.50 in Canada; USD 5.95 per issue in US & Canada; USD 7.75 per issue elsewhere (effective 2010). back issues avail. **Document type:** *Magazine, Consumer.* **Description:** Focuses on the parents, children and the professionals of foster care and domestic adoption.
Related titles: Online - full text ed.: USD 12 (effective 2010).
Published by: Louis & Company Publishing, 541 E Garden Dr, Unit N, Windsor, CO 80550-3150. TEL 970-686-7412, 888-924-6736, FAX 970-686-7412. Ed., Pub. Richard Fischer.

362.82 155.4 AUS ISSN 1833-0622
FOSTERING OUR FUTURE; newsletter for foster carers. Text in English. 2005. q. free (effective 2009). back issues avail. **Document type:** *Newsletter, Consumer.*
Related titles: Online - full text ed.
Published by: New South Wales, Department of Community Services, Locked Bag 4028, Ashfield, NSW 2131, Australia. fostercarers@community.nsw.gov.au, http://www.community.nsw.gov.au.

361 SWE ISSN 1652-5477
FOU-RAPPORT. (Forskning och Utveckling) Text in Swedish. 2004. irreg. price varies. back issues avail. **Document type:** *Monographic series, Academic/Scholarly.*
Published by: Forskning och Utveckling Nordost, Svaerdvaegen 11D, Danderyd, 18233, Sweden. FAX 46-8-7554721, kgf@lidingo.se, http://www.fouvalfard.org/nordost/Om%20FoU%20Nordost.htm.

361.12 USA ISSN 1081-2792
FOUNDATION & CORPORATE FUNDING ADVANTAGE. Abbreviated title: F F A. Text in English. 1995. m. USD 240 (effective 2008). **Document type:** *Newsletter, Trade.* **Description:** Brings out national and regional grant opportunities and provides busy nonprofit fundraisers with inside information for getting foundation and corporate grants.
Published by: Progressive Business Publications, 370 Technology Dr, Malvern, PA 19355. TEL 610-695-8600, 800-220-5000, FAX 610-647-8089, customer_service@pbp.com. Ed. Susan Wade Elnicki. R&P Curt Brown. Circ: 4,110 (paid).

361.73 USA ISSN 1549-716X
AS911.A2
THE FOUNDATION DIRECTORY PART 2; a guide to grant programs fifty thousand dollars to two hundred thousand dollars. Text in English. 1992. a. **Document type:** *Directory, Trade.* **Description:** Provides current information on over 10,000 foundations that maintain mid-sized grant programs. Also features over 34,000 grant descriptions.
Formerly (until 1996): Foundation Directory Part 2: A Guide to Grant Programs Twenty Five Thousand Dollars to One Hundred Thousand Dollars (1058-6210)
Published by: Foundation Center, 79 Fifth Ave, 16th St, New York, NY 10003. TEL 212-620-4230, 800-634-2953, FAX 212-807-3677, customerservice@foundationcenter.org.

361 TZA ISSN 1821-5335
JQ3519.A15
THE FOUNDATION NEWS. Text in Swahili. 2006. q.
Published by: The Foundation for Civil Society, Haidery Plaza, 5th Flr, Upanga/Kisutu St, PO Box 7192, Dar es Salaam, Tanzania. TEL 255-22-2138530, FAX 255-22-2138533, information@thefoundation-tz.org, http://www.thefoundation-tz.org. Ed. Joseph Mzinga.

360 USA ISSN 1055-4998
HV97.A3
FOUNDATION REPORTER; comprehensive profiles & giving analysis of America's major private foundations. Text in English. 1971. a., latest . USD 599 (effective 2011). **Document type:** *Directory, Trade.* **Description:** Contains important contact, financial and grant information and covers the top 1,000 private foundations in the U. S.
Former titles (until 1990): Taft Foundation Reporter (0730-6237); Which superseded in part (in 19??): Taft Foundation Reporter. Regional Edition. New England, Region 1 (0273-3897); Taft Foundation Reporter. Regional Edition. Region 2: New York; Taft Foundation Reporter. Regional Edition. Region 3: New Jersey/Pennsylvania; (in 197?): Taft Foundation Reporter. Regional Edition. Region 4, Mid-Atlantic (0273-3889); (in 197?): Taft Foundation Reporter. Regional Edition. Region 5, Southeast (0273-3870); (in 197?): Taft Foundation Reporter. Regional Edition. Region 6, Michigan/Ohio (0273-3862); (in 197?): Taft Foundation Reporter. Regional Edition. Region 7, North Central (0273-3900); (in 197?): Taft Foundation Reporter. Regional Edition. Region 8, South West/Rocky Mountain (0273-3854); Taft Foundation Reporter. Regional Edition. Region 9: Western; (until 197?): Taft Foundation Reporter. National Edition (0197-0240); Foundation Reporter
Published by: Information Today, Inc., 143 Old Marlton Pike, Medford, NJ 08055. TEL 609-654-6266, 800-300-9868, FAX 609-654-4309, custserv@infotoday.com, http://www.infotoday.com. Ed. Owen O'Donnell.

361 USA ISSN 1944-5660
HV40
▼ ➤ **THE FOUNDATION REVIEW**; journal of philanthropy. Text in English. 2009. q. USD 495 combined subscription domestic to institutions (print & online eds.); USD 530 combined subscription foreign to institutions (print & online eds.); USD 649 combined subscription domestic to libraries (print & online eds.); USD 684 combined subscription foreign to libraries (print & online eds.) (effective 2010). adv. **Document type:** *Journal, Academic/Scholarly.* **Description:** Includes reports about all aspects of philanthropy.
Related titles: Online - full text ed.: ISSN 1944-5679. USD 446 to institutions; USD 584 to libraries (effective 2010) (from IngentaConnect).
Published by: Grand Valley State University, Johnson Center for Philanthropy and Nonprofit Leadership, Bicycle Factory, Ste 200, 201 Front Ave SW, Grand Rapids, MI 49504. TEL 616-331-7585, FAX 616-331-7592, http://www.gvsu.edu/jcp/. Ed. Teri Behrens. Adv. contact Robert Shalett TEL 202-365-0273. page USD 2,025; 6 x 9. Circ: 10,000. **Subscr. to:** PO Box 7065, Lawrence, KS 66044. TEL 800-627-0326, FAX 785-843-6153.

➤ **FOUNDATIONS (RUSHOLME)**; making connections for Christian social action. *see* RELIGIONS AND THEOLOGY

➤ **FOURTH WORLD JOURNAL.** *see* POLITICAL SCIENCE—Civil Rights

361 FRA ISSN 2106-6582
FOYER DEPARTEMENTAL DE L'ENFANCE ET DE LA FAMILLE DE LA LOIRE. LA FEUILLE. Text in French. 200?. m. **Document type:** *Newsletter, Consumer.*
Published by: Foyer Departemental de l'Enfance et de la Famille de la Loire, 20, Rue Charles de Gaulle, Saint-Etienne, 42000, France. TEL 33-4-77479334, FAX 33-4-77479402, fdef-loire@fdef42.fr.

362.8 FRA ISSN 2101-8081
FRANCE. CAISSE NATIONALE DES ALLOCATIONS FAMILIALES. POLITIQUES SOCIALES ET FAMILIALES. Text in French. 1985. q. free (effective 2011). **Document type:** *Journal, Government.*
Formerly (until 2009): France. Caisse Nationale des Allocations Familiales. Recherches et Previsions (1149-1590)
Related titles: Online - full text ed.: ISSN 2107-0210.
Indexed: FR, IBSS.
—INIST.
Published by: Caisse Nationale des Allocations Familiales, 32 Av. de la Sibelle, Paris, Cedex 14 75685, France. TEL 33-1-45655252, publications-stats@cnaf.fr, http://www.caf.fr/.

FRANCE. INSTITUT NATIONAL DE LA STATISTIQUE ET DES ETUDES ECONOMIQUES. RECUEIL D'ETUDES SOCIALES. *see* BUSINESS AND ECONOMICS—Economic Systems And Theories, Economic History

362.7 GBR
FUEL RIGHTS HANDBOOK. Text in English. 1993. irreg., latest 2008, 14th ed. GBP 17 per issue to non-members; free to members (effective 2009). **Document type:** *Handbook/Manual/Guide, Trade.* **Description:** Offers child welfare rights advisers and counselors the guidance they need to help clients scope with their fuel bills, debt, and related problems with household fuel supply.
Published by: Child Poverty Action Group, 94 White Lion St, London, N1 9PF, United Kingdom. TEL 44-20-78377979, FAX 44-20-78376414, info@cpag.org.uk. Ed. Alan Murdie.

360 DEU ISSN 0945-3253
FUERSORGERECHTLICHE ENTSCHEIDUNGEN DER VERWALTUNGS- UND SOZIALGERICHTE. Abbreviated title: F E V S. Text in German. 1951. m. EUR 104 (effective 2010). adv. **Document type:** *Bulletin, Trade.*
Formerly: Fuersorgerechtliche Entscheidungen
Published by: Richard Boorberg Verlag GmbH und Co. KG, Scharrstr 2, Stuttgart, 70563, Germany. TEL 49-711-73850, FAX 49-711-7385100, mail@boorberg.de. Ed. J Basse. Circ: 1,550 (paid).

361.8 NZL ISSN 1176-9599
FUNDING HAMILTON & WAIKATO REGION. Text in English. 1999. a. **Document type:** *Government.*
Formerly (until 2005): Funding Hamilton (1174-9334)
Published by: Hamilton City Council, Funding Information Service, Private Bag 3010, Hamilton, 2020, New Zealand. TEL 64-7-8386623, info@hcc.govt.nz.

361.73 GBR ISSN 2046-2506
THE FUNDRAISER. Text in English. 2001. m. GBP 166 (effective 2011). **Document type:** *Magazine, Trade.* **Description:** Provides information and assistance on applying for grants and other charitable donations.
Formerly (until 2010): Charity Funding Report (1752-8747)
—CCC.
Published by: Wilmington Publishing & Information Ltd., 6-14 Underwood St, London, N1 7JQ, United Kingdom. TEL 44-20-75498708, FAX 44-20-74908238.

361.73 USA ISSN 1530-5813
FUND$RAISER CYBERZINE. Text in English. 199?. m. adv. **Document type:** *Magazine, Trade.* **Description:** Publishes news and ideas about fundraising.
Media: Online - full content. **Related titles:** E-mail ed.: Fundraising Providers and Suppliers Newsletter. ISSN 1530-6143. 2000; Fundraising for Small Groups Newsletter. ISSN 1530-6127. 2000.
Published by: Fund$Raiser Group, 12101 7 Mile Rd NE, Belding, MI 48809-9617 . TEL 616-691-7574, FAX 616-691-8079, brengled@fundsraiser.com, http://www.fundsraiser.com. Ed. Deane R. Brengle III.

361.73 ZAF
FUNDRAISING JOURNAL. Text in English. 1998. base vol. plus irreg. updates. ZAR 46.50. **Document type:** *Journal, Trade.* **Description:** Offers tips on raising funds effectively and ethically.
Published by: Southern Africa Institute of Fundraising, PO Box 1360, Sanlamhof, 7532, South Africa. TEL 27-21-946-4110. Ed. Carl Swart. Pub. Madeleine Swart.

FUNDRAISING SUCCESS. *see* BUSINESS AND ECONOMICS—Management

361.73 658.15 USA ISSN 1930-9236
FUNDRAISING SUCCESS ADVISOR. Text in English. 2004. w. free (effective 2008). adv. back issues avail. **Document type:** *Newsletter, Trade.* **Description:** Contains useful tips and how-to articles from fundraising experts that will help development professionals.
Media: E-mail.
Published by: North American Publishing Co., 1500 Spring Garden St., 12th Fl, Philadelphia, PA 19130. TEL 215-238-5300, FAX 215-238-5213, magazinecs@napco.com, http://www.napco.com. Pub. Kevin Landers TEL 973-956-8585.

361.7 FRA ISSN 1952-7284
FUNDRAIZINE. Text in French. 2006. q. EUR 35 to individuals (effective 2008). **Document type:** *Magazine, Trade.*
Formerly (until 2006): Trait d'Union pour la Generosite (1771-7760)
Published by: Association Francaise des Fundraisers, 6 Rue de Londres, Paris, 75009, France. TEL 33-1-43733465, FAX 33-1-43496877, info@fundraisers.fr.

360 JPN ISSN 1341-6383
FUREAI KEA. Text in Japanese. 1995. m. JPY 12,240. **Description:** Provides a journal for careworkers of homes for the aged and homehelpers, with information and case studies.
Published by: Zenkoku Shakai Fukushi Kyogikai/National Council of Social Welfare, 3-3-2 Kasumigaseki, Chiyoda-ku, Tokyo, 100-0013, Japan. Circ: 17,000.

THE FUTURE OF CHILDREN. *see* CHILDREN AND YOUTH—About

THE FUTURE OF THE PUBLIC SECTOR; a series on the long-term forces affecting U.S. social policy. *see* PUBLIC ADMINISTRATION

361.6 TUR ISSN 1301-5745
G A P DERGISI. (Guneydogu Anadolu Projesi) Text in English, Turkish. 1993. q. **Document type:** *Journal, Academic/Scholarly.*
Indexed: MLA-IB.
Published by: T.C. Basbakanlik, Guneydogu Anadolu Projesi, Bolge Kalkinma Idaresi Baskanligi/Republic of Turkey Prime Ministry, Southeastern Anatolia Project, Regional Development Administration, Willy Brandt Sok No. 5, Ankara, 06680, Turkey. TEL 90-312-4422324, FAX 90-312-4401384.

360 DEU
G E K K O. Text in German. 1992. 4/yr. adv. **Document type:** *Magazine, Consumer.*

Published by: (Gmuender ErsatzKasse), S V Corporate Media GmbH (Subsidiary of: Sueddeutscher Verlag GmbH), Emmy-Noether-Str 2, Munich, 80992, Germany. TEL 49-89-5485201, FAX 49-89-54852192, info@sv-medien-service.de, http://www.sv-medien-service.de/svcm/. Ed. Katrin Lange. Adv. contact Lutz Boden. B&W page EUR 3,500, color page EUR 5,000; trim 185 x 250. Circ: 189,208 (controlled).

G L C S INK. (Gay and Lesbian Counselling Service) *see* HOMOSEXUALITY

362.7 PRT ISSN 0016-3910
GAIATO; obra de rapazes, para rapazes, pelos rapazes. Text in Portuguese. 1944. s-m. adv. **Document type:** *Newspaper.*
Related titles: Microform ed.
Published by: Casa do Gaiato, Paco de Sousa, 4560, Portugal. TEL 351-255-752285, FAX 351-255-753799, casadogaiato.no.sapo.pt. Ed. Carlos Galamba. Adv. contact Julio Mendes. Circ: 70,000.

360 330 AUS ISSN 1833-5977
GAWLER COMMUNITY INFORMATION & BUSINESS DIRECTORY. Text in English. 1981. a. free (effective 2009). adv. **Document type:** *Directory, Trade.* **Description:** Provides listings of nonprofit clubs and associations, as well as agencies which are involved with the physical, mental, emotional and spiritual well-being of the community.
Former titles (until 2006): Gawler Business & Information Directory; (until 1990): Community Information Directory
Published by: Town of Gawler, 89 Murray St, PO Box 130, Gawler, SA 5118, Australia. TEL 61-8-85229211, FAX 61-8-85229212, council@gawler.sa.gov.au.

362.4 NLD ISSN 1875-2187
GAZET (TILBURG). Text in Dutch. 2007. q. free (effective 2010).
Formed by the merger of (1982-2007): P O G Magazine (1567-360X); Which was formerly (until 1999): P O G-Info (0927-2542); (1982-1990): Provinciaal Overleg Gehandikaptenbeleid Noord-Brabant. Informatiebulletin (0927-2534); (2004-2007): PrismaScoop (1573-3122); Which was formerly (until 2004): Scoop (1381-1347); (until 1993): Prisma-Scoop (1384-5403); (1990-1992): Provinciaal Instituut Samenlevingsopbouw en Maatschappelijke Aktivering. Vlugschrift (1381-1681)
Published by: Stichting Zet, Postbus 271, Tilburg, 5000 AG, Netherlands. TEL 31-13-5441440, FAX 31-13-5440605, info@zet-brabant.nl.

362 FRA ISSN 1769-0552
LA GAZETTE SANTE SOCIAL. Text in French. 2004. m. EUR 67.58 combined subscription to individuals print & online eds.; EUR 89 to institutions print & online eds. (effective 2010). **Document type:** *Magazine, Trade.*
Related titles: Online - full text ed.
Published by: Groupe Moniteur, 17 rue d'Uzes, Paris, 75108, France. TEL 33-1-40133030, FAX 33-1-40135021, groupemoniteur@groupemoniteur.fr, http://editionsdumoniteur.com.

360 JPN ISSN 1341-6669
GEKKAN FUKUSHI. Text in Japanese. 1909. m. JPY 12,240. **Document type:** *Trade.* **Description:** Deals with the spectrum of social welfare and services, including social policy, social security system, social service practice, and volunteering.
Published by: Zenkoku Shakai Fukushi Kyogikai/National Council of Social Welfare, 3-3-2 Kasumigaseki, Chiyoda-ku, Tokyo, 100-0013, Japan. Ed. Hisashi Kawagoe. Circ: 17,000.

GENERATION NEXT. *see* BUSINESS AND ECONOMICS—International Development And Assistance

361 338.91 FRA ISSN 2106-6590
GENRE EN ACTION. Text in French. 2003. irreg. **Document type:** *Newsletter, Consumer.*
Related titles: Online - full text ed.: Reseau Genre en Action. Bulletin. ISSN 2107-044X. 200?.
Published by: Reseau Genre en Action, CEAN/IEP, 11, Allee Ausone, Pessac Cedex, 33607, France. coordination@genreenaction.net, http://www.genreenaction.net.

362.5 USA ISSN 1524-3974
K7
GEORGETOWN JOURNAL ON POVERTY LAW AND POLICY. Text in English. 1993. s-a. USD 30 domestic; USD 35 foreign; USD 15 per issue (effective 2009). back issues avail.; reprint service avail. from WSH. **Document type:** *Journal, Academic/Scholarly.* **Description:** Publishes articles from distinguished law professors and practitioners in poverty-related fields. In addition, the Journal features student research, works from scholars in poverty-related disciplines, and the "voices" of persons living in poverty nation's.
Formerly (until 1999): Georgetown Journal on Fighting Poverty (1075-0827)
Related titles: Microfiche ed.: (from WSH); Microform ed.: (from WSH); Online - full text ed.: ISSN 1930-6946.
Indexed: A01, A03, A08, A26, B01, B06, B07, B09, CA, CJA, FamI, G08, I02, L03, LRI, P34, R02, S02, S03, SWR&A, T02.
—BLDSC (4158.269950), CIS, Ingenta.
Published by: Georgetown University Law Center, 600 New Jersey Ave, NW, Washington, DC 20001. TEL 202-662-9000. Ed. Christina L Schoppert.

GERIATRIC CARE. *see* GERONTOLOGY AND GERIATRICS

GERON; tijdschrift voor ouder worden en maatschappij. *see* GERONTOLOGY AND GERIATRICS

360 DEU ISSN 1869-8794
▼ **GESCHLOSSENE HAEUSER**; historische Studien zu Institutionen und Orten der Separierung, Verwahrung und Bestrafung. Text in German. 2010. irreg., latest vol.3, 2010. price varies. **Document type:** *Monographic series, Academic/Scholarly.*
Published by: Leipziger Universitaetsverlag GmbH, Oststr 41, Leipzig, 04317, Germany. TEL 49-341-9900440, FAX 49-341-9900440, info@univerlag-leipzig.de.

GESETZLICHE UNFALLVERSICHERUNG. *see* INSURANCE

368.4 CRI ISSN 1409-1259
GESTION; revista de ciencias administrativas y financieras de la seguridad social. Variant title: Revista de Ciencias Administrativas y Financieras de la Seguridad Social. Text in Spanish. 1993. bi-m. back issues avail. **Document type:** *Journal, Academic/Scholarly.*
Related titles: Online - full text ed.: free (effective 2006).
Published by: Caja Costarricense del Seguro Social, Centro de Desarrollo Estrategico e Informacion en Salud y Seguridad Social, Apdo de Correos 10105, San Jose, 1000, Costa Rica. TEL 506-2568187. Ed. Jorge Valverde Castillo.

GESUNDHEIT IM BRENNPUNKT. *see* PUBLIC HEALTH AND SAFETY

360 AUT
GESUNDHEIT - MENSCH - GESELLSCHAFT. Text in German. 1994. irreg., latest vol.17, 2007. price varies. **Document type:** *Monographic series, Academic/Scholarly.*
Published by: Trauner Verlag und Buchservice GmbH, Koeglstr 14, Linz, 4020, Austria. TEL 43-732-778241212, FAX 43-732-778241400, office@trauner.at, http://www.trauner.at.

362.4 CAN ISSN 1719-833X
GET CONNECTED. Text in English. 2005. s-a. **Document type:** *Newsletter, Consumer.*
Published by: Canadian Hearing Society/Societe Canadienne de l'Ouie, 271 Spadina Rd, Toronto, ON M5R 2V3, Canada. TEL 416-928-2500, FAX 416-928-2523, http://www.chs.ca.

360 GBR ISSN 0956-3229
GINGER. Text in English. 1973. q. GBP 12 to individuals; GBP 15 to institutions (effective 2000). adv. bk.rev. illus. **Document type:** *Newspaper.* **Description:** Contains self-help information for single-parent families in England and Wales.
Published by: Gingerbread Association for One Parent Families, 16-17 Clerkenwell Close, London, EC1R 0AN, United Kingdom. TEL 44-20-7336-8183, FAX 44-20-7336-8155. Ed., R&P Kirsten Denker. Circ: 10,000.

361.73 USA
▼ **GIVE MAGAZINE**; lifestyles of success & charity. Text in English. 2009 (Mar.). bi-m. adv. **Document type:** *Magazine, Consumer.* **Description:** Focuses on charities, charity events and the lifestyile of people involved with charities.
Published by: Give Worldwide LLC, 1615 Wilcox Ave, #4125, Hollywood, CA 90078-4125. TEL 310-795-6757. Pub. Robert Dean. Adv. contact Mike Walker TEL 213-896-9210. color page USD 8,746; trim 8.375 x 10.875.

361.74 ITA ISSN 1972-8530
GIVING; una rivista per la filantropia. Text in Multiple languages. 2007. s-a. **Document type:** *Journal, Academic/Scholarly.*
Published by: Universita degli Studi di Bologna, Bononia University Press, Via Zamboni 33, Bologna, 40126, Italy. http://www.buponline.com.

360 USA ISSN 2161-1084
▼ **GIVING BACK.** Abbreviated title: G B. Text in English. 2010. m. USD 38; USD 3.95 per issue (effective 2011). adv. back issues avail. **Document type:** *Magazine, Consumer.*
Related titles: Online - full text ed.: free (effective 2011).
Published by: Daesvi, Llc., 4809 Clairemont Dr, Ste 347, San Diego, CA 92117. TEL 619-260-8353. Ed. Esteban Villanueva.

361.73 USA
HV89
GIVING U S A (ONLINE); the annual report on philanthropy. Text in English. 1956. a. free (effective 2010). **Document type:** *Journal, Academic/Scholarly.*
Former titles (until 2010): Giving U S A (Print) (0436-0257); (until 19??): Giving U S A Annual Report
Media: Online - full text. **Related titles:** Microfiche ed.: (from CIS).
Indexed: SRI.
Published by: (Giving Institute), Giving USA Foundation, 4700 W Lake Ave, Glenview, IL 60025. TEL 847-375-4709, 800-462-2372, FAX 888-374-7258, info@givinginstitute.org, http://www.aafrc.org. Circ: 9,000. **Subscr. to:** PO Box 3781, Oak Brook, IL 60522.

361.73 USA
HV41
GIVING U S A QUARTERLY. Text in English. 1955. q. bk.rev. **Document type:** *Newsletter, Trade.*
Former titles (until 2004): Giving U S A Update (0899-3793); (until 1988): Fund-Raising Review (0735-8873); (until 1982): Giving U S A Bulletin (0731-5678); (until 1973): American Association of Fund-Raising Counsel. Bulletin (0002-743X)
Published by: (Giving Institute), Giving USA Foundation, 4700 W Lake Ave, Glenview, IL 60025. TEL 847-375-4709, 800-462-2372, FAX 888-374-7258, info@givinginstitute.org, http://www.aafrc.org.

361 GBR ISSN 0143-7429
GLASGOW DIRECTORY OF VOLUNTARY ORGANIZATIONS. Text in English. 1980. biennial. GBP 5. adv. illus. **Document type:** *Directory.*
Published by: Glasgow Council for Voluntary Service, 11 Queen's Cres, Glasgow, G4 9AS, United Kingdom. TEL 041-332-2444, FAX 041-332-0175. Circ: 2,000.

THE GLEANER (MADISON). *see* HOMOSEXUALITY

361.7 USA ISSN 2157-264X
GLOBAL GIVING MATTERS. Text in English. 2001. q. free (effective 2010). back issues avail. **Document type:** *Newsletter, Trade.*
Media: Online - full text.
Indexed: N06.
Published by: Synergos Institute, 51 Madison Ave, 21st Fl, New York, NY 10010. TEL 212-447-8111, FAX 212-447-8119, synergos@synergos.org.

361 USA ISSN 2157-1252
▼ **GLOBAL MAJORITY E-JOURNAL.** Text in English. 2010. s-a. free (effective 2010). **Document type:** *Journal, Academic/Scholarly.* **Description:** Discusses topics about poverty, population growth, access to safe water, climate change, agricultural development, etc.
Media: Online - full text.
Published by: American University, Department of Economics, 4400 Massachusetts Ave, NW, Washington, DC 20016. TEL 202-885-3770, FAX 202-885-3790, econ@american.edu, http://www.american.edu/cas/economics/index.cfm. Ed. Bernhard G Gunter.

360 GBR ISSN 1468-0181
HN1
➤ **GLOBAL SOCIAL POLICY**; an interdisciplinary journal of public policy and social development. Abbreviated title: G S P. Text in English. 2001 (Apr.). 3/yr. USD 606, GBP 328 combined subscription to institutions (print & online eds.); USD 594, GBP 321 to institutions (effective 2011). adv. back issues avail.; reprint service avail. from PSC. **Document type:** *Journal, Academic/Scholarly.* **Description:** Aims to advance the understanding of the impact of globalization upon social policy and social development. Analyzes the contribution of a range of international actors to global social policy discourse and practice and encourages discussion of the implications for social welfare of the dynamics of the global economy.
Related titles: Online - full text ed.: ISSN 1741-2803. USD 545, GBP 295 to institutions (effective 2011).
Indexed: A01, A03, A08, A22, C06, C07, C08, CA, CINAHL, E01, ERA, ESPM, EconLit, FamI, GEOBASE, I13, I14, IBSS, JEL, LeftInd, P30, P34, P42, PAIS, PSA, S02, S03, S19, S21, SCOPUS, SSciA, SociolAb, T02.
—BLDSC (4195.479290), IE, Ingenta. **CCC.**
Published by: Sage Publications Ltd. (Subsidiary of: Sage Publications, Inc.), 1 Oliver's Yard, 55 City Rd, London, EC1Y 1SP, United Kingdom. TEL 44-20-73248500, FAX 44-20-73248600, info@sagepub.co.uk, http://www.uk.sagepub.com/home.nav. adv.: B&W page GBP 350; 130 x 205. **Subscr. in the Americas to:** Sage Publications, Inc., 2455 Teller Rd, Thousand Oaks, CA 91320. TEL 805-499-9774, FAX 805-499-0871, journals@sagepub.com.

361.73 NLD ISSN 1388-5596
GOEDE DOELEN GIDS. Text in Dutch. 1998. a. EUR 12.50 (effective 2010).
Published by: (Vereniging van Fondsenwervende Instellingen), Lenthe Publishers, De Pastorie, Dorpsstraat 34, Amstelveen, 1182 JE, Netherlands. TEL 31-20-3479090, FAX 31-20-3479099, info@lenthe.nl, http://www.lenthe.nl.

360 614 GBR
GOOD PRACTICE IN HEALTH, SOCIAL CARE AND CRIMINAL JUSTICE. Text in English. 1993. irreg., latest 2009. price varies. back issues avail. **Document type:** *Monographic series, Academic/Scholarly.* **Description:** Explores current topics of concern to professionals working in social work, health care and the probation service.
Formerly (until 2006): Good Practice Series (1369-4030)
—BLDSC (4201.351600). **CCC.**
Published by: Jessica Kingsley Publishers, 116 Pentonville Rd, London, N1 9JB, United Kingdom. TEL 44-20-78332307, FAX 44-20-78372917, post@jkp.com. Ed. Jacki Pritchard.

GOVERNMENT ASSISTANCE ALMANAC. *see* PUBLIC ADMINISTRATION—Municipal Government

052 GBR
THE GOVERNMENT FUNDING GUIDE. Text in English. 1990. irreg. GBP 35 per issue (effective 2009). **Document type:** *Directory, Trade.* **Description:** Provides overview of funding from local, regional and national government as well as European sources.
Formerly (until 2009): The Central Government Grants Guide (1362-9506)
—CCC.
Published by: Directory of Social Change, 24 Stephenson Way, London, NW1 2DP, United Kingdom. TEL 44-20-73914800, FAX 44-20-73914808, publications@dsc.org.uk.

354 AUS
GOVERNMENT OF WESTERN AUSTRALIA. DEPARTMENT FOR CHILD PROTECTION. ANNUAL REPORT. Text in English. 1973. a. free (effective 2009). stat. back issues avail. **Document type:** *Government.* **Description:** Reports on the activities and performance of the department as well as the future directions and financial statements.
Former titles (until 2007): Western Australia. Department for Community Development. Annual Report (1320-0666); (until 2002): Western Australia. Family and Children's Services. Annual Report; (until 1992): Western Australia. Department for Community Services. Annual Report (0817-1327); (until 1985): Western Australia. Department for Community Welfare. Annual Report
Related titles: Online - full text ed.: free (effective 2009).
Published by: Government of Western Australia, Department for Child Protection, PO Box 6334, East Perth, W.A. 6892, Australia. TEL 61-8-93251232, 800-622-258, FAX 61-8-92222776, corporate.communications@dcp.wa.gov.au.

360 JAM
GRACE, KENNEDY FOUNDATION. ANNUAL REPORT. Text in English. 1984. a. free. back issues avail. **Document type:** *Corporate.*
Published by: Grace, Kennedy Foundation, 64 Harbour St., P.O. Box 86, Kingston, Jamaica. TEL 809-922-3440, FAX 809-922-7567, TELEX 2290. Ed. Marjorie Humphreys. Circ: 500. **Subscr. to:** One St. Lucia Cres., Kingston 5, Jamaica.

GRANTS AND FUNDING FOR HIGHER EDUCATION. *see* EDUCATION—Higher Education

GRANTS, FELLOWSHIPS, AND PRIZES OF INTEREST TO HISTORIANS (YEAR). *see* HISTORY

GRANTS FOR LIBRARIES HOTLINE. *see* LIBRARY AND INFORMATION SCIENCES

360 USA
GRANTSMANSHIP CENTER MAGAZINE; a compendium of resources for nonprofit organizations. Text in English. 1984. irreg. free to qualified personnel. adv. bk.rev. **Document type:** *Newspaper.*
Formerly: Whole Nonprofit Catalog
Published by: Grantsmanship Center, PO Box 17220, Los Angeles, CA 90017. TEL 213-482-9860, FAX 213-482-9863. Ed., R&P, Adv. contact Marc Green. Pub. Norton J Kiritz. Circ: 175,000.

361.8 USA ISSN 0740-4832
GRASSROOTS FUNDRAISING JOURNAL. Text in English. 1982. bi-m. USD 39 domestic to non-profit organizations; USD 46 foreign to non-profit organizations (effective 2005). adv. bk.rev. back issues avail. **Document type:** *Magazine, Consumer.* **Description:** Provides information for small to medium sized nonprofits on how to raise money from individuals. Articles include case studies, profiles of major donors, tax laws affecting nonprofits, and the historical background of grassroots fundraising.
Indexed: AltPI.

S

—Ingenta.
Published by: Grassroots Fundraising, Inc., 3781 Broadway, Oakland, CA 94611. TEL 510-596-8160, FAX 510-596-8822. Ed., R&P Stephanie Roth. Pub. Kim Klein. Adv. contact Jennifer Boyden TEL 510-596-8160. Circ: 2,500 (paid).

GREAT BRITAIN. CONTRIBUTIONS AGENCY. FRAMEWORK DOCUMENT (YEAR). *see* INSURANCE

362 GBR
GREAT BRITAIN. DEPARTMENT FOR WORK AND PENSIONS. WORKING PAPER. Text in English. 2001. irreg., latest vol.72, 2009. back issues avail. **Document type:** *Monographic series, Trade.*
Related titles: Online - full text ed.: free (effective 2009).
Published by: Great Britain. Department for Work and Pensions, Social Research Branch, Analytical Services Division, 4th Fl, The Adelphi, 1-11 John Adam Street, London, WC2N 6HT, United Kingdom. TEL 44-20-79628192.

GREAT BRITAIN. DEPARTMENT OF HEALTH. HEALTH BUILDING NOTES. *see* HEALTH FACILITIES AND ADMINISTRATION

362.7 GBR
GREAT BRITAIN. DEPARTMENTS OF HEALTH AND SOCIAL SECURITY. N H S DAY CARE FACILITIES. Text in English. biennial. GBP 5.50 per issue. **Document type:** *Government.*
Published by: Departments of Health and Social Security, Library Departmental Publications Information Unit, Rm G17C, Skipton House, 80 London Rd, London, SE1 6LH, United Kingdom. TEL 44-171-972-5945.

361.6 IRL
GREAT BRITAIN. SOCIAL SERVICES INSPECTORATE. REGISTRATION AND INSPECTION UNITS IN NORTHERN IRELAND. Text in English. biennial.
Published by: Social Services Inspectorate, Castle Buildings, Room C3.28, Stormont, BT4 3RA, Ireland. TEL 44-028-90520732, FAX 44-028-90528159, maire.mcmahon@dhsspsni.gov.uk.

362.82 USA
GREATER NORTHERN NEWS. Text in English. 1990. q. **Document type:** *Newsletter.* **Description:** Informs donors and others interested in the family-planning services this organization provides; urges readers to take action on specific issues.
Published by: Planned Parenthood of Greater Northern New Jersey, Inc., 196 Speedwell Ave, Morristown, NJ 07960. TEL 973-539-9580. Ed. Marci Berger.

360 GBR ISSN 0951-824X
GROUPWORK. Text in English. 1988. 3/yr. GBP 35 in Europe to individuals; USD 60 in North America to individuals; GBP 40 elsewhere to individuals; GBP 75 in Europe to institutions; USD 125 in North America to institutions; GBP 80 elsewhere to institutions; GBP 165 combined subscription in Europe to libraries (print & online eds.); USD 250 combined subscription in North America to libraries (print & online eds.); GBP 170 combined subscription elsewhere to libraries (print & online eds.) (effective 2009). index. back issues avail. **Document type:** *Journal, Academic/Scholarly.* **Description:** Covers groupwork of all types.
Related titles: Online - full text ed.: ISSN 1746-6091 (from IngentaConnect).
Indexed: A22, ASSIA, CA, CJA, DIP, E-psyche, FR, IBR, IBSS, IBZ, P03, PsycInfo, PsycholAb, S02, S03, S21, SCOPUS, SOPODA, SSA, SWR&A, SociolAb, T02.
—BLDSC (4220.460000), IE, Ingenta, INIST. **CCC.**
Published by: Whiting & Birch Ltd., 90 Dartmouth Rd, London, SE23 3NZ, United Kingdom. TEL 44-20-82442421, FAX 44-20-82442448, enquiries@whitingbirch.net. Eds. Mark Doel, Pamela Trevithick.

360 338.91 327 KOR ISSN 1975-017X
GUGJE SAHOE BOJANG DONGHYANG/INTERNATIONAL SOCIAL SECURITY TODAY. Text in Korean. 2006. q. membership. **Document type:** *Journal, Academic/Scholarly.*
Published by: Korea Institute for Health and Social Affairs/Hangug Bogeon Sahoe Yeonguweon, San 42-14 Bulgwang-Dong, Eunpyung-Ku, Seoul, 122-705, Korea, S. TEL 82-2-3808000, FAX 82-2-3529129, library@kihusa.re.kr, http://www.kihusa.re.kr.

360 ESP ISSN 1577-7928
GUIA PRACTICA DE SEGURIDAD SOCIAL. Text in Spanish. 1998. a. **Document type:** *Bulletin, Government.*
Published by: Asociacion de Cajas de Ahorros para Relaciones Laborales, C/ Principe 5-4o, Madrid, 28012, Spain. TEL 34-91-4296596, FAX 34-91-4291026, http://www.acarl.es.

362.7 346.017 FRA ISSN 1624-6179
LE GUIDE DE LA PROTECTION DE L'ENFANCE. Text in French. 2001. base vol. plus q. updates. looseleaf. EUR 119 base vol(s).; EUR 125 (effective 2009).
Published by: E S F Editeur (Subsidiary of: Reed Business Information France), 2 rue Maurice Hartmann, Issy-les-Moulineaux, 92133 Cedex, France. TEL 33-1-46294629, FAX 33-1-46294633, info@esf-editeur.fr.

360 FRA ISSN 1291-2484
LE GUIDE DE L'INTERVENTION SOCIALE. Text in French. 1999. base vol. plus bi-m. updates. EUR 119 base vol(s).; EUR 109 updates (effective 2009).
Published by: E S F Editeur (Subsidiary of: Reed Business Information France), 2 rue Maurice Hartmann, Issy-les-Moulineaux, 92133 Cedex, France. TEL 33-1-46294629, FAX 33-1-46294633, info@esf-editeur.fr.

360 368 FRA ISSN 1243-5082
LE GUIDE DES ASSURANCES SOCIALES. Text in French. 1993. base vol. plus q. updates. EUR 125 base vol(s).; EUR 135 updates (effective 2009).
Published by: E S F Editeur (Subsidiary of: Reed Business Information France), 2 rue Maurice Hartmann, Issy-les-Moulineaux, 92133 Cedex, France. TEL 33-1-46294629, FAX 33-1-46294633, info@esf-editeur.fr.

361.73 CAN ISSN 0849-0104
GUIDE DES DONATEURS CANADIENS FAISANT ETAT DES ORGANISMES DE SOUSCRIPTION DE FONDS. Text in French. 1989. a.
Related titles: English ed.: Canadian Donor's Guide to Fund Raising Organizations in Canada. ISSN 0831-0386.
Published by: Canadian Centre for Philanthropy, 425 University Ave, Ste 700, Toronto, ON M5G 1T6, Canada. TEL 416-597-2293, 800-263-1178, FAX 416-597-2294, info@ccp.ca, http://www.ccp.ca.

360 CAN ISSN 1719-7279
GUIDE DES PROGRAMMES D'APPUI FINANCIER DU PATRIMOINE CANADIEN (EN LIGNE). Text in French. 2006. a., latest 2006. **Document type:** *Handbook/Manual/Guide, Consumer.*
Media: Online - full text. **Related titles:** ◆ English ed.: Guide to Canadian Heritage Financial Support Programs. ISSN 1704-8125.
Published by: Canadian Heritage/Patrimoine Canadien, 15 Eddy St, Gatineau, PQ K1A 0M5, Canada. TEL 819-997-0055, 866-811-0055, pch-qc@pch.gc.ca.

GUIDE TO ARKANSAS FUNDING SOURCES. *see* BUSINESS AND ECONOMICS—Management

360 CAN ISSN 1704-8125
CA1CH4-56
GUIDE TO CANADIAN HERITAGE FINANCIAL SUPPORT PROGRAMS. Text in English. 2002. a. **Document type:** *Handbook/Manual/Guide, Trade.*
Related titles: Online - full text ed.: ISSN 1719-7260. 2002; ◆ French ed.: Guide des Programmes d'Appui Financier du Patrimoine Canadien (En Ligne). ISSN 1719-7279.
Published by: Canadian Heritage/Patrimoine Canadien, 15 Eddy St, Gatineau, PQ K1A 0M5, Canada. TEL 819-997-0055, 866-811-0055, pch-qc@pch.gc.ca.

052 GBR
A GUIDE TO GRANTS FOR INDIVIDUALS IN NEED (YEAR). Text in English. 1987. irreg., latest 2009, 11th ed. GBP 50 per issue (effective 2009). **Document type:** *Directory, Consumer.* **Description:** Contains details of over 2,100 charities concerned with individual poverty, together giving a yearly total of #120 million.
Related titles: Online - full text ed.: free (effective 2009).
Published by: Directory of Social Change, 24 Stephenson Way, London, NW1 2DP, United Kingdom. TEL 44-20-73914800, FAX 44-20-73914808, publications@dsc.org.uk.

363.582 GBR ISSN 1476-2323
GUIDE TO HOUSING BENEFIT AND COUNCIL TAX BENEFIT. Text in English. 1985. a. GBP 25 (effective 2010). **Document type:** *Journal, Trade.*
Former titles (until 1993): Guide to Housing Benefit and Community Charge Benefit (0960-4251); (until 1990): Guide to Housing Benefit (0957-5731)
—BLDSC (4229.259800). **CCC.**
Published by: Shelter, 88 Old St, London, EC1V 9HU, United Kingdom. TEL 44-844-5152000, FAX 44-844-5152956, info@shelter.org.uk.

052 GBR ISSN 1368-0145
A GUIDE TO MAJOR TRUSTS (YEAR). Text in English. 1986. biennial. GBP 45 per issue (effective 2009). back issues avail. **Document type:** *Directory, Consumer.* **Description:** Provides information on grant-making trusts.
Formerly (until 1988): Guide to the Major Grant Making Trusts
—BLDSC (4229.570950). **CCC.**
Published by: Directory of Social Change, 24 Stephenson Way, London, NW1 2DP, United Kingdom. TEL 44-20-73914800, FAX 44-20-73914808, publications@dsc.org.uk.

362 GBR ISSN 0072-8756
GUIDE TO THE SOCIAL SERVICES. Text in English. 1882. a. GBP 32.50 per issue (effective 2009). **Document type:** *Directory.* **Description:** Reference book on the structure and organization of the public social services in the UK.
—CCC.
Published by: (Family Welfare Association), Waterlow Professional Publishing, 6-14 Underwood St, London, N1 7JQ, United Kingdom. TEL 44-20-74900049, FAX 44-20-72531308, legalweb@waterlow.com, http://www.waterlow.com/.

052 GBR
THE GUIDE TO U K COMPANY GIVING (YEAR). Text in English. 1984. biennial. GBP 50 per issue (effective 2009). **Document type:** *Directory, Trade.* **Description:** Covers the charitable donations and community distributions, totalling over #200 million, of 1,400 companies. Each entry shows contact details, financial statistics, what the company will and will not support, typical grants range, and whether it prefers local or national causes.
Formerly (until 1998): The Guide to Company Giving (Year) (0957-5723)
Related titles: Online - full text ed.: free (effective 2009).
—CCC.
Published by: Directory of Social Change, 24 Stephenson Way, London, NW1 2DP, United Kingdom. TEL 44-20-73914800, FAX 44-20-73914808, publications@dsc.org.uk.

A GUIDE TO WINNIPEG FOR ABORIGINAL NEWCOMERS. *see* OCCUPATIONS AND CAREERS

362.41 USA
GUILD BRIEFS. Text in English. m. free (effective 2009). **Document type:** *Newsletter, Consumer.* **Description:** Announces Guild programs and reprints information from local and national publications pertaining to blindness. "Guild Briefs" is also available via Phonotes.
Media: Large Type (22 pt.). **Related titles:** Audio cassette/tape ed.; Braille ed.; E-mail ed.
Published by: Guild for the Blind, 180 North Michigan Ave, Ste 1700, Chicago, IL 60601-7463. TEL 312-236-8569, FAX 312-236-8128, info@guildfortheblind.org. R&P Kerry Obrist.

GUOWAI YIXUE (SHEHUI YIXUE FENCE)/FOREIGN MEDICAL SCIENCES (SOCIAL MEDICINE). *see* MEDICAL SCIENCES

THE H C C A - A I S MEDICAID COMPLIANCE NEWS. (Health Care Compliance Association - Atlantic Information Services) *see* INSURANCE

H MAGAZINE. *see* RELIGIONS AND THEOLOGY

331.105 HRV ISSN 1332-1684
H U S. Text in Croatian. 1994. bi-m. **Document type:** *Magazine, Trade.*
Formerly (until 1994): Dok (1332-1692)
Published by: Hrvatska Udruga Sindikata, Put Supavia 19, Split, 21000, Croatia.

HA-LOHEM. *see* MILITARY

HABITAT WORLD. *see* HOUSING AND URBAN PLANNING

361.3 SWE ISSN 1653-1558
HAELSOHOEGSKOLAN I JOENKOEPING. RAPPORTSERIE. Text in Swedish. 2005. irreg. **Document type:** *Monographic series, Academic/Scholarly.*
Published by: Haelsahoegskolan i Joenkoeping/University of Joenkoeping. School of Health Sciences, PO Box 1026, Joenkoeping, 55111, Sweden. TEL 46-36-101000, FAX 46-36-101180, info@hhj.hj.se, http://www.hhj.hj.se.

362.7 NLD ISSN 1874-4923
HAND IN HAND. Text in Dutch. 1995. s-a.
Formerly (until 2006): Open Huis (1385-6618)
Published by: Ronald McDonald Kinderfonds, Postbus 25, De Bilt, 3730 AA, Netherlands. TEL 31-30-2219000, FAX 31-30-2219001, info@kinderfonds.nl. Circ: 77,000.

360 NLD ISSN 1574-0110
HANDBOOK OF SOCIAL CHOICE AND WELFARE. Text in English. 2002. irreg. **Document type:** *Monographic series, Academic/Scholarly.*
Related titles: Online - full text ed.: ISSN 1875-581X.
Indexed: SCOPUS.
—CCC.
Published by: Elsevier BV, North-Holland (Subsidiary of: Elsevier Science & Technology), Sara Burgerhartstraat 25, Amsterdam, 1055 KV, Netherlands. TEL 31-20-4853911, FAX 31-20-4852457, JournalsCustomerServiceEMEA@elsevier.com, http://www.elsevier.com.

HANDBOOK ON THE ECONOMICS OF GIVING, RECIPROCITY AND ALTRUISM. *see* BUSINESS AND ECONOMICS

362.4 362.6 DNK
HANDICAPPEDE, SINDSLIDENDE, AELDRE (ONLINE). Text in Danish. irreg. **Document type:** *Consumer.* **Description:** Covers social services for the elderly and the handicapped in Denmark.
Media: Online - full text.
Published by: Jurainformation, Vesterbrogade 10, Copenhagen V, 1620, Denmark. TEL 45-70-230102, FAX 45-70-230103, post@jurainformation.dk, http://www.jurainformation.dk. Ed. Erik Voelund Mortensen.

HANDISCOOP. *see* HANDICAPPED

362.6 371.33 SWE ISSN 1403-3070
HANDLEDARSKAP I AELDRE OCH HANDIKAPPOMSORG. Variant title: Handledarskap: Tidningen Aeldreomsorg. Text in Swedish. bi-m. SEK 373; SEK 75 per issue (effective 2006). back issues avail. **Document type:** *Trade.*
Related titles: ◆ Issued with: Tidningen Aeldreomsorg. ISSN 1403-7025.
Published by: Fortbildningsfoerlaget, PO Box 34, Solna, 17111, Sweden. TEL 46-8-54545330, FAX 46-8-54545349, info@fortbild.se, http://www.fortbild.se.

HANDLING CHILD CUSTODY, ABUSE, AND ADOPTION CASES. *see* LAW—Family And Matrimonial Law

360 USA
HAPPENINGS. Text in English. m. free to members. 8 p./no. 2 cols./p.; **Document type:** *Newsletter.* **Description:** Relates the events and interests of those involved in Rescue Mission and other Rescue ministries.
Published by: Association of Gospel Rescue Missions, 1045 Swift Ave, Kansas City, MO 64116-4127. TEL 816-471-8020, iugm@iugm.org. R&P Stephen E Burger TEL 816-471-8020. Circ: 1,500.

HARVARD JOURNAL OF AFRICAN AMERICAN PUBLIC POLICY. *see* PUBLIC ADMINISTRATION

361.8 USA ISSN 1932-426X
HD2769.15
HAUSER CENTER FOR NONPROFIT ORGANIZATIONS. WORKING PAPER. Text in English. 2000. irreg., latest vol.43, 2008. free (effective 2010). back issues avail. **Document type:** *Monographic series, Academic/Scholarly.*
Media: Online - full text.
Published by: Harvard University, John F. Kennedy School of Government, Hauser Center for Nonprofit Organizations, The Belfer Bldg, 79 John F. Kennedy St, Cambridge, MA 02138. TEL 617-496-5675, FAX 617-495-0996, hauser_center@harvard.edu.

360 DEU ISSN 0935-2074
HAUSHALTSRECHT DER SOZIALVERSICHERUNG. Text in German. 1978. base vol. plus updates 3/yr. looseleaf. EUR 86 base vol(s).; EUR 28.90 updates per issue (effective 2009). **Document type:** *Monographic series, Trade.*
Published by: Erich Schmidt Verlag GmbH & Co. (Berlin), Genthiner Str 30 G, Berlin, 10785, Germany. TEL 49-30-2500850, FAX 49-30-250085305, vertrieb@esvmedien.de, http://www.erich-schmidt-verlag.de.

360 USA ISSN 1938-2197
HV85
➤ **HAWAII PACIFIC JOURNAL OF SOCIAL WORK PRACTICE.** Text in English. 2008. s-a. free (effective 2009). **Document type:** *Journal, Academic/Scholarly.* **Description:** Focuses on publication of HPU MSW professional papers and other contributions related to social work practice especially in emerging and multi-cultural fields.
Media: Online - full content.
Published by: Hawai'i Pacific University, 1188 Fort St, Ste 201B, Honolulu, HI 96813. TEL 808-544-0200, FAX 808-543-8014, businessoffice@hpu.edu, http://www.hpu.edu. Ed. Mary S Sheridan TEL 808-566-2489.

325 USA
HEADLINES & HIGHLIGHTS. Text in English. 1983. bi-m. free. bk.rev. illus. **Document type:** *Newsletter, Trade.*
Former titles (until 1992): H I A S Reporter; H I A S Bulletin (0097-0263); U H S Bulletin (0041-509X)
Published by: H I A S Inc., 333 Seventh Ave, 16th Fl, New York, NY 10001-5004. TEL 212-967-4100, FAX 212-629-0921, info@hias.org, http://www.hias.org. Ed. Rita Zilberman. Circ: 10,000.

HEALING HAND. *see* RELIGIONS AND THEOLOGY

360 USA
HEALTH & HUMAN SERVICES DIRECTORY; health and social agencies in Greater Cleveland. Text in English. 1946. a. USD 40 newsstand/cover (effective 2001). **Document type:** *Directory.* **Description:** Deals with health and human issues.
Former titles: Human Services Directory; Health and Welfare Directory
Published by: The Center for Community Solutions, 1226 Huron Rd, Ste 300, Cleveland, OH 44115. TEL 216-781-2944, FAX 216-781-2988, sbanks@CommunitySolutions.com, http://www.CommunitySolutions.com. Ed., R&P Sheryl McLean. Circ: 2,000.

HEALTH AND SOCIAL SERVICE WORKFORCE IN ALBERTA. *see* PUBLIC HEALTH AND SAFETY

360 USA ISSN 0360-7283
HV687.5.U5 CODEN: HSWODK

➤ **HEALTH & SOCIAL WORK.** Text in English. 1976. q. EUR 118 in Europe to institutions; USD 149 in US & Canada to institutions; GBP 78 to institutions in the UK & elsewhere; EUR 128 combined subscription in Europe to institutions (print & online eds.); USD 163 combined subscription in US & Canada to institutions (print & online eds.); GBP 85 combined subscription to institutions in the UK & elsewhere; (print & online eds.) (effective 2012). adv. bk.rev. illus. index. back issues avail.; reprints avail. **Document type:** *Journal, Academic/Scholarly.* **Description:** Examines health-related social problems and issues dealing with the client and the community.
Related titles: Microfiche ed.: (from PQC); Online - full text ed.: ISSN 1545-6854. EUR 107 in Europe to institutions; USD 135 in US & Canada to institutions; GBP 71 to institutions in the UK & elsewhere (effective 2012) (from IngentaConnect).
Indexed: A01, A02, A03, A08, A20, A22, A25, A26, AC&P, AHCMS, AMHA, ASCA, ASG, AbAn, AgeL, BRD, C06, C07, C08, C11, C12, CA, CINAHL, ChPerl, Chicano, CurCont, DSHAb, DentInd, E-psyche, E02, E03, E07, E08, E15, E16, ECER, EMBASE, ERA, ERI, ERIC, EdA, Edl, ExcerpMed, F09, Faml, G05, G06, G07, G08, H01, H02, H04, H05, H12, H13, HRA, I05, I07, IBSS, INI, IndMed, M01, M02, MEDLINE, P02, P03, P10, P13, P18, P19, P20, P22, P24, P25, P27, P30, P34, P43, P46, P48, P50, P53, P54, PCI, PQC, PsycInfo, PsycholAb, R10, Reac, RehabLit, S02, S03, S08, S09, S11, S19, S20, S21, S23, SCOPUS, SOPODA, SSA, SSAI, SSAb, SSCI, SSI, SWR&A, SociolAb, T02, V05, W01, W02, W03, W07, W09, WBSS.
—BLDSC (4274.884000), GNLM, IE, Infotrieve, Ingenta. **CCC.**
Published by: (National Association of Social Workers), Oxford University Press (Subsidiary of: Oxford University Press), 2001 Evans Rd, Cary, NC 27513. TEL 919-677-0977, 800-445-9714, FAX 919-677-1303, jnlorders@oup-usa.org, http://www.oxfordjournals.org. Ed. Stephen Gorin. adv.: page USD 525. Circ: 6,500 (paid).

362.8292 CAN ISSN 1482-2121
HEALTH CANADA. TRANSITION HOUSES AND SHELTERS FOR ABUSED WOMEN IN CANADA. Text in English, French. 1987. irreg., latest 2002.
Formerly (until 1996): National Clearing House on Family Violence. Transition Houses and Shelters for Battered Women in Canada (1207-1633)
Related titles: Online - full text ed.: ISSN 1497-3979.
Published by: (National Clearinghouse on Family Violence), Health Canada/Sante Canada, Address Locator 0900C2, Ottawa, ON K1A OK9, Canada. TEL 613-957-2991, FAX 613-941-5366, info@www.hc-sc.gc.ca, http://www.hc-sc.gc.ca.

HEALTH CARE FINANCING REVIEW. MEDICARE AND MEDICAID STATISTICAL SUPPLEMENT. *see* PUBLIC HEALTH AND SAFETY

361 610 USA ISSN 0268-1153
RA440.A1 CODEN: HRTPE2

➤ **HEALTH EDUCATION RESEARCH.** Abbreviated title: H E R. Text in English. 1986. bi-m. GBP 593 in United Kingdom to institutions; EUR 890 in Europe to institutions; USD 1,184 in US & Canada to institutions; GBP 593 elsewhere to institutions; GBP 647 combined subscription in United Kingdom to institutions (print & online eds.); EUR 971 combined subscription in Europe to institutions (print & online eds.); USD 1,291 combined subscription in US & Canada to institutions (print & online eds.); GBP 647 combined subscription elsewhere to institutions (print & online eds.) (effective 2012). bk.rev. Index. back issues avail.; reprint service avail. from PSC. **Document type:** *Journal, Academic/Scholarly.* **Description:** Promotes understanding of the processes, rationale and philosophy underlying the work of practicing health educators in an international forum.
Related titles: Online - full text ed.: ISSN 1465-3648. 1999. GBP 523 in United Kingdom to institutions; EUR 785 in Europe to institutions; USD 1,044 in US & Canada to institutions; GBP 523 elsewhere to institutions (effective 2012) (from IngentaConnect).
Indexed: A20, A22, A34, A36, ASCA, ASSIA, AbAn, B21, B28, B29, BRD, C06, C07, C08, CA, CABA, CINAHL, CPE, CTD, ChPerl, CommAb, CurCont, D01, E-psyche, E01, E02, E03, E12, EMBASE, ERI, ESPM, EdA, Edl, ExcerpMed, F09, FR, FS&TA, Faml, GH, H&SSA, H17, HRIS, IndMed, IndVet, LT, MEDLINE, N02, N03, P03, P20, P21, P22, P24, P25, P30, P32, P33, P34, P37, P40, P48, P50, P54, PCI, PEI, PQC, PsycInfo, PsycholAb, R08, R10, R12, RM&VM, RRTA, Reac, RiskAb, SCOPUS, SSCI, T02, T05, THA, VS, W03, W05, W07, W11.
—BLDSC (4275.011440), GNLM, IE, Infotrieve, Ingenta, INIST. **CCC.**
Published by: (International Union for Health Promotion and Education FRA), Oxford University Press (Subsidiary of: Oxford University Press), 2001 Evans Rd, Cary, NC 27513. TEL 919-677-0977, FAX 919-677-1303, http://www.oxfordjournals.org. Ed. Dr. Michael Eriksen.

➤ **HEALTH PROFESSIONS COUNCIL OF SOUTH AFRICA. REGISTER OF SUPPLEMENTARY HEALTH SERVICES PROFESSIONS.** *see* MEDICAL SCIENCES

➤ **THE HEALTH SERVICE JOURNAL**; for people involved in NHS management. *see* HEALTH FACILITIES AND ADMINISTRATION

306.461 AUS ISSN 1446-1242
RA418

➤ **HEALTH SOCIOLOGY REVIEW.** Text in English. 1991. q. AUD 225 in Australia & New Zealand to individuals includes China, South & South-East Asia, Pacific, South America and Africa; USD 225 elsewhere to individuals; AUD 660 combined subscription in Australia & New Zealand to institutions includes China, South & South-East Asia, Pacific, South America and Africa; USD 660 combined subscription elsewhere to institutions (effective 2008). adv. back issues avail. **Document type:** *Journal, Academic/Scholarly.* **Description:** Explores the contribution of sociology and sociological research methods to the understanding of health and illness; to health policy, promotion and practice; and to equity, social justice, social policy, and social work.
Formerly (until 2001): Annual Review of Health Social Sciences (1036-6733)
Related titles: Online - full text ed.
Indexed: A01, A02, A03, A08, A26, A36, AusPAIS, C06, C07, C08, CA, CABA, CINAHL, D01, ESPM, GH, H05, H12, I05, IBSS, N02, N03, P03, P24, P27, P30, P46, P48, P50, P54, PQC, PsycInfo, R12, RiskAb, S02, S03, SCOPUS, SSCI, SociolAb, T02, T05, W07, W11.
—BLDSC (4275.135500), IE, Ingenta. **CCC.**
Published by: eContent Management Pty Ltd, PO Box 1027, Maleny, QLD 4552, Australia. TEL 61-7-54352900, FAX 61-7-54352911, info@e-contentmanagement.com, http://www.e-contentmanagement.com. Eds. Jane Edwards, Peter Gale, Fran Collyer. Circ: 350 (controlled). **Co-publisher:** The Australian Sociological Association.

➤ **HEALTH WORKFORCE IN ALBERTA. ANNUAL REPORT.** *see* PUBLIC HEALTH AND SAFETY

➤ **HEALTHCARE TRENDS REPORT**; the monthly digest of business and public policy news. *see* MEDICAL SCIENCES

➤ **HEALTHMATTERS (ONLINE).** *see* PUBLIC HEALTH AND SAFETY

360 330.9 USA
THE HEARTLANDER. Text in English. q. free to members (effective 2010). adv. back issues avail. **Document type:** *Newsletter, Academic/Scholarly.*
Formerly (until 1991): Heartland Insider
Related titles: Online - full text ed.: free (effective 2010).
Published by: Heartland Institute, 19 S LaSalle St, Ste 903, Chicago, IL 60603. TEL 312-377-4000, FAX 312-377-5000, publications@heartland.org. Ed. Diane Carol Bast. Pub. Joseph L Bast.

360 AUT
HELFT UNS HELFEN. Text in German. 6/yr. **Document type:** *Newspaper.*
Published by: Wiener Hilfswerk, Falkestr 3, Vienna, W 1010, Austria. TEL 43-1-5123661, FAX 43-1-512366133, wrhi@wiener.hilfswerk.at, http://www.wiener.hilfswerk.at. Ed. Johanna Czech. Adv. contact Gerlinde Burger. Circ: 5,000.

362 NOR ISSN 1503-1780
HELSE. Text in Norwegian. 2002. bi-m. free. back issues avail. **Document type:** *Magazine, Consumer.* **Description:** About health and health care delivery in Central Norway.
Related titles: Online - full text ed.
Published by: Helse Midt-Norge RHF/Central Norway Regional Health Authority, PO Box 464, Stjoerdal, 7501, Norway. TEL 47-74-839900, FAX 47-74-839901, postmottak@helse-midt.no. Ed. Synnoeve Farstad. Circ: 16,000.

362.1094846 NOR ISSN 1890-1581
HELSE FINNMARK. NYTHETSBREV. Text in Norwegian. 2002. bi-m. back issues avail. **Document type:** *Newsletter, Consumer.*
Former titles (until 2004): Egenmeldingen (1503-5433); (until 2003): Foretaksnytt (1503-5425)
Related titles: Online - full text ed.: ISSN 1890-1646. 2004.
Published by: Helse Finnmark, Sykehusveien 35, Hammerfest, 9613, Norway. TEL 47-78-421100, FAX 47-78-421107, postmottak@helse-finnmark.no. Ed. Marit Kvorum TEL 47-78-421138. Circ: 1,000.

362.1 NOR ISSN 1504-3703
HELSE I VEST. Text in Norwegian. 2002. bi-m. free. back issues avail. **Document type:** *Magazine, Consumer.*
Related titles: Online - full text ed.: ISSN 1504-3711.
Published by: Helse Vest RHF/Western Norway Regional Health Authority, PO Box303, Forus, Stavanger, 4066, Norway. TEL 47-51-963800, helse@helse-vest.no. Circ: 15,000.

HEM OCH SAMHAELLE. *see* HOME ECONOMICS

HEMPELS STRASSENMAGAZIN. *see* GENERAL INTEREST PERIODICALS—Germany

361.7634 SWE
HENRY; roeda korsets tidning. Text in Swedish. 1978. 4/yr. SEK 150 to members (effective 2007). adv. bk.rev. abstr.; illus. **Document type:** *Magazine, Consumer.*
Former titles (until 2007): Roeda Korsets Tidning (1103-4904); (until 1992): Roeda Korset (1101-413X); (until 1990): Apropaa Roeda Korset (0348-4947); Which was formed by the merger of (1968-1978): Reflex (0345-987X); (1974-1978): Socialt Apropaa (0347-0474)
Related titles: Audio cassette/tape ed.
Published by: Roeda Korset/Swedish Red Cross, PO Box 17563, Stockholm, 11891, Sweden. TEL 46-8-4524600, FAX 46-8-4524791, info@redcross.se. Ed. Anna-Carin Heden. Circ: 350,000.

HERE'S HELP. *see* GERONTOLOGY AND GERIATRICS

HEROIN ADDICTION AND RELATED CLINICAL PROBLEMS. *see* DRUG ABUSE AND ALCOHOLISM

HINZ & KUNZT; das Hamburger Strassenmagazin. *see* GENERAL INTEREST PERIODICALS—Germany

LA HISTORIA NO CONTADA. *see* WOMEN'S INTERESTS

362.1 NOR ISSN 1504-3762
HOEGSKOLAN I SOER-TROENDELAG. AVDELING FOR HELSE- OG SOSIALFAG OG AVDELING FOR SYKEPLEIE. HIST-A H S/A S P. Variant title: HIST-AHS/ASP-Notat. Text in Norwegian. 1999. irreg. **Document type:** *Monographic series, Academic/Scholarly.*
Formerly (until 2004): Hoegskolan i Soer-Troendelag. Avdeling for Helse- og Sosialfag. Hist/A H S (1500-7146)
Published by: (Hoegskolen i Soer-Troendelag, Avdeling for Sykepleie/ University College of Soer-Troendelag, Faculty of Nursing), Hoegskolen i Soer-Troendelag, Avdeling Helse- og Sosialfag/ University College of Soer-Troendelag. Faculty of Education and Social Work, Ranheimsveien 10, Trondheim, 7004, Norway. TEL 47-73-559150, FAX 47-73-559151, postmottag@ahs.hist.no, http://www.ahs.hist.no. **Co-publisher:** Hoegskolen i Soer-Troendelag, Avdeling for Sykepleie/University College of Soer-Troendelag, Faculty of Nursing.

362.42 SWE ISSN 1652-8387
HOERSELSKADADES RIKSFOERBUND. AARSBOK. Text in Swedish. 2002. a. back issues avail. **Document type:** *Consumer.*
Related titles: Online - full text ed.
Published by: Hoerselskadades Riksfoerbund (HRF)/Swedish Association of Hard of Hearing People, Gaevlegatan 18A, PO Box 6605, Stockholm, 11384, Sweden. TEL 46-8-4575501, FAX 46-8-4575503, hrf@hrf.se.

362.29 DEU ISSN 1435-7798
HOHENRODTER STUDIEN. Text in German. 1998. irreg. price varies. **Document type:** *Monographic series, Academic/Scholarly.*
Published by: V W B - Verlag fuer Wissenschaft und Bildung, Postfach 110368, Berlin, 10833, Germany. TEL 49-30-2510415, FAX 49-30-2511136, info@vwb-verlag.com.

360 649 JPN ISSN 0018-327X
HOIKU NO TOMO. Text in Japanese. 1952. m. JPY 7,320 (effective 1999). adv. bk.rev. **Description:** Covers childcare services and programs at day nurseries.
Published by: Zenkoku Shakai Fukushi Kyogikai/National Council of Social Welfare, 3-3-2 Kasumigaseki, Chiyoda-ku, Tokyo, 100-0013, Japan. Ed. Hisashi Kawagoe. Circ: 35,000.

360 AUS ISSN 1832-7796
HOME AND COMMUNITY CARE SOUTH AUSTRALIA. Text in English. 2005. a. free (effective 2009). **Document type:** *Journal, Trade.* **Description:** Covers home and comunity information of Australia.
Related titles: Online - full text ed.
Published by: South Australia, Department for Families and Communities, Office for the Ageing, GPO Box 292, Adelaide, NSW 5001, Australia. TEL 61-8-82070522, FAX 61-8-82070555, OFTA@dfc.sa.gov.au, http://www.dfc.sa.gov.au/pub/default.aspx?tabid=481.com.

362.76 618.92 USA
HOME CARE FAMILY NEWSLETTER. Text in English. 1991. bi-m. free. **Document type:** *Newsletter, Consumer.* **Description:** Informs parents of the Children's Hospital Home Care support group for parents of children with chronic illness. Alerts parents of special-needs children of services and other resources in the greater Philadelphia area.
Published by: Children's Hospital of Philadelphia, Home Care Department, Driscoll Bldg, 34th and Civic Center Blvd, Philadelphia, PA 19104-4399. TEL 215-590-3272. Ed., R&P Peggy MacGregor. Circ: 1,300.

361.6 HND
HONDURAS. SECRETARIA DE TRABAJO Y PREVISION SOCIAL. BOLETIN DE ESTADISTICAS LABORALES. Text in Spanish. 1973. a. free. **Document type:** *Government.* **Description:** Provides labor statistics.
Published by: Ministerio de Trabajo y Prevision Social, Planificacion Sectorial y Estadistica Laboreal, Tegucigalpa DC, Honduras. TEL 22-15-58, FAX 22-32-20. Circ: 500.

360 SGP ISSN 0219-2462
CODEN: HKJWEQ

➤ **HONG KONG JOURNAL OF SOCIAL WORK/HONG KONG SHEHUI GONGZUO XUEBAO.** Abbreviated title: H K J S W. Text in Chinese, English. 1998. s-a. SGD 229, USD 140, EUR 118 combined subscription to institutions (print & online eds.) (effective 2012). adv. back issues avail. **Document type:** *Journal, Academic/Scholarly.* **Description:** Brings out symposia, research, theoretical papers, review articles, notes and discussions on social work theory and practice, and new developments in social work.
Related titles: Online - full text ed.: SGD 208, USD 127, EUR 107 to institutions (effective 2012).
Indexed: A10, CA, IBSS, S02, S03, SCOPUS, SSA, SociolAb, T02, V03.
—BLDSC (4326.386000). **CCC.**
Published by: (Hong Kong Social Workers Association HKG), World Scientific Publishing Co. Pte. Ltd., 5 Toh Tuck Link, Singapore, 596224, Singapore. TEL 65-6466-5775, FAX 65-6467-7667, wspc@wspc.com.sg, http://www.worldscientific.com. Ed. Chiu Yu-lung Marcus. **Dist. by:** World Scientific Publishing Co., Inc., 27 Warren St, Ste 401-402, Hackensack, NJ 07601. TEL 201-487-9655, 800-227-7562, FAX 201-487-9656, 888-977-2665, wspc@wspc.com; World Scientific Publishing Ltd., 57 Shelton St, London WC2H 9HE, United Kingdom. TEL 44-207-8360888, FAX 44-207-8362020, sales@wspc.co.uk.

362.2 NLD ISSN 1877-5055
DE HOOP NIEUWS. Text in Dutch. 197?. bi-m. free (effective 2011).
Formerly (until 2009): De Hoop Magazine (1384-9204)
Published by: De Hoop ggz, Provincialeweg 122, Dordrecht, 3329 KP, Netherlands. FAX 31-78-6111110, info@dehoop.org.

360 USA ISSN 0275-3065
HOOSHARAR - MIOUTUNE. Text in Armenian. 1914. m. (except Jul. & Aug.). USD 10 to non-members (effective 1998). adv.
Published by: Armenian General Benevolent Union, 55 E 59th St, New York, NY 10022-1112. TEL 212-319-6383, FAX 212-319-6508. Ed. Antranig Basmajian. Adv. contact Helen Misk. Circ: 2,000.

360 CAN
HORIZONS NEWSLETTER. Text in English. s-a. **Document type:** *Newsletter.* **Description:** Provides news of this international development agency, committed to addressing causes of poverty and injustice in Mesoamerica.
Published by: Horizons of Friendship, 50 Covert St, P O Box 402, Cobourg, ON K9A 4L1, Canada. TEL 905-372-5483, FAX 905-372-7095.

HOSPICE MANAGEMENT ADVISOR. *see* HEALTH FACILITIES AND ADMINISTRATION

362 USA
HOSPICE TODAY. Text in English. 1981. q. free. bk.rev. **Document type:** *Newsletter.* **Description:** Informs friends, volunteers, and financial supporters about the activities and programs of the agency, its services to the community, and its role as a resource and an advocate on issues related to death, grief and terminal illness.
Formerly (until 1987): Hospice Care Newsletter
Published by: Hospice of the Florida Suncoast, 5771 Roosevelt Blvd, Clearwater, FL 33760. TEL 727-586-4432, http://www.thehospice.com/. Ed. Kimberly Walter. Circ: 65,000 (controlled).

THE HOUSING ADVOCATE. *see* HOUSING AND URBAN PLANNING

363.585094105 GBR ISSN 1460-8790
HOUSING, CARE AND SUPPORT; a journal on policy, research and practice. Text in English. 1998. q. EUR 689 combined subscription in Europe (print & online eds.); USD 889 combined subscription in the Americas (print & online eds.); GBP 529 combined subscription in the UK & elsewhere (print & online eds.); AUD 999 combined subscription in Australasia (print & online eds.) (effective 2012). adv. back issues avail. **Document type:** *Journal, Academic/Scholarly.* **Description:** Offers a whole range of information including policy updates and developments, perspectives and experiences across housing, health and social care and is committed to keeping professionals up to date with all aspects of supported housing.
Related titles: Online - full text ed.: ISSN 2042-8375.
Indexed: C06, C07, C08, CA, CINAHL, E-psyche, P02, P10, P16, P19, P24, P48, P53, P54, PQC, S02, S03, S11, SCOPUS, SWR&A, T02.
—BLDSC (4335.097100), IE, Ingenta. **CCC.**

S

Published by: Pier Professional Ltd. (Subsidiary of: Emerald Group Publishing Ltd.), Ste N4, The Old Market, Upper Market St, Hove, BN3 1AS, United Kingdom. TEL 44-1273-783720, FAX 44-1273-783723, info@pierprofessional.com. Eds. Gary Lashko, Lynn Vickery. Adv. contact Paul Somerville TEL 44-1273-783724. B&W page GBP 350; 160 x 245.

HOUSING FOR SENIORS REPORT. *see* HOUSING AND URBAN PLANNING

361 CHN ISSN 1674-1838
HUANQIU CISHAN/GLOBAL CHARITY. Text in Chinese. 1992. m. **Document type:** *Magazine, Consumer.*
Supersedes in part (in 2008): Zhonghua Shaonian (1004-2377)
Published by: Song Qingling Jijinhui/China Soong Ching Ling Foundation, 154, Guolou Xi Dajie, Beijing, 100009, China. TEL 86-10-64079706, FAX 86-10-84020786, http://www.sclf.org/.

HULP MAGAZINE. *see* POLITICAL SCIENCE—Civil Rights

361.26 FRA ISSN 1774-5012
HUMACOOP INFOS; la lettre d'information. Text in French. 2005. s-a. **Document type:** *Bulletin, Consumer.*
Published by: Humacoop, 8 rue Chenoise, Grenoble, 38000, France. info@humacoop.com, http://humacoop.com.

323.4 USA
➤ **HUMAN RIGHTS.** Abbreviated title: H R. Text in English. 1972. q. USD 20 to members; USD 6.50 per issue (effective 2009). adv. back issues avail.; reprints avail. **Document type:** *Newsletter, Trade.* **Description:** Aims to promote legal recognition of, and protection for, human rights and advise the lawyers and citizens of Illinois about the nature of individual rights.
Former titles (until 2004): Constitutional Law and Liberty; (until 1983): Individual Liberty; (until 1980): Individual Rights and Responsibilities Newsletter (0090-2608)
Related titles: Online - full text ed.: free to members (effective 2008).
Published by: (Illinois State Bar Association, Human Rights Law Section), Illinois State Bar Association, Illinois Bar Center, 424 S Second St, Springfield, IL 62701. TEL 217-525-1760, 800-252-8908, FAX 217-525-9063, jfenski@isba.org, http://www.isba.org. Adv. contact Nancy Vonnahmen TEL 217-747-1437. page USD 400; 7 x 9.625. Circ: 867.

➤ **HUMAN RIGHTS & GLOBALIZATION LAW REVIEW.** *see* LAW

323.4 USA
HUMAN SERVE CAMPAIGN NEWSLETTER. Text in English. irreg. (3-4/yr.). free.
Published by: Human Serve Campaign, c/o Columbia University, 622 W 113th St, Rm 410, New York, NY 10025. TEL 212-854-4053.

361.007 USA ISSN 0890-5428
HV88
➤ **HUMAN SERVICE EDUCATION.** Abbreviated title: H S E. Text in English. 1982. a. USD 40 per issue to non-members; free to members (effective 2011). bk.rev. illus. back issues avail.; reprints avail. **Document type:** *Journal, Academic/Scholarly.* **Description:** Aimed at individuals working with college students majoring in mental health and human services.
Formerly (until 1987): National Organization Human Service Educators. Journal (0195-3826)
Indexed: CA, E03, ERI, S02, S03, T02.
Published by: National Organization for Human Service Education, 5341 Old Hwy 5, Ste 206, 214, Woodstock, GA 30188. TEL 770-924-8899.

361 USA
HUMAN SERVICE YELLOW PAGES OF MASSACHUSETTS RHODE ISLAND (YEAR). Text in English. 1988. a. USD 24.95 (effective 1999). adv. back issues avail. **Document type:** *Directory.*
Media: Diskette.
Published by: George D. Hall Company, Inc., 45 Portland Rd., Ste. 7-23, Kennebunk, ME 04043-6660. TEL 617-439-3255, FAX 617-951-3993.

301.4 USA ISSN 0164-6079
HUMAN SERVICES REPORTER. Text in English. 1978. 6/yr. free.
Incorporates (in 1978): Family
Published by: Department of Human Services, CN 700, Trenton, NJ 08625. TEL 609-292-3703, FAX 609-393-4846. Eds. Ed Rogan, Margaret Bergmann. Circ: 33,500.

361 USA
THE HUMANITARIAN. Text in English. 2001. q. **Document type:** *Magazine, Consumer.* **Description:** Provides readers with information they can use to improve their own lives and inspires them to get involved in helping the Red Cross enhance and save the lives of others.
Published by: American Red Cross, 2025 E St, NW, Washington, DC 20006. TEL 202-303-4498, info@usa.redcross.org. Ed. Holly Hall.

361.77 AUS ISSN 1833-8666
THE HUMANITARIAN. Text in English. 199?. 3/yr. free to members (effective 2008). back issues avail. **Document type:** *Magazine, Consumer.* **Description:** Contains information about Australian Red Cross.
Formerly (until 2006): Action Abroad (1324-5139)
Related titles: Online - full text ed.: free (effective 2008).
Published by: Australian Red Cross, 155 Pelham St, PO Box 196, Carlton, VIC 3053, Australia. TEL 61-3-93451800, FAX 61-3-93482513, natinfo@redcross.org.au. Ed. Kelly Chandler.

383.8 USA ISSN 2154-8056
HUNGER (YEAR). Variant title: Hunger Report. Text in English. 1990. a. USD 20 per issue (effective 2010). charts; maps; stat. 150 p./no. 2 cols./p.; back issues avail. **Document type:** *Report, Academic/Scholarly.* **Description:** Reports on the state of world hunger. Includes statistics on over 160 countries.
Related titles: Online - full text ed.: free (effective 2010); German ed.
Published by: Bread for the World Institute, 50 F St, NW, Ste 500, Washington, DC 20001. TEL 202-639-9400, FAX 202-639-9401, bread@bread.org.

338.1 360 USA
BV639.P6
HUNGER NEWS & HOPE. Text in English. 1977. q. adv. bk.rev. **Document type:** *Magazine, Consumer.* **Description:** Offers analysis and information to understand U.S. and world hunger and poverty issues.
Formerly (until 1999): Seeds (0194-4495)
Related titles: Online - full text ed.
Indexed: CWI.
Published by: Seeds of Hope, Inc., 602 James Ave, Waco, TX 76706-1476. TEL 254-755-7745, FAX 254-753-1909, seedshope@aol.com. Ed. L Katherine Cook. Circ: 1,500.

363.8 USA
HD9000.6
HUNGER NOTES (ONLINE). Text in English. 1976. q. free (effective 2011). bk.rev. illus. **Document type:** *Newsletter, Trade.* **Description:** Presents facts and insights on hunger, poverty, grassroots self-help, and socioeconomic development for policy-makers, educators and activists. Acts as a guide to organizations and print resources on the specific focus of each issue.
Former titles (until 19??): Hunger Notes (Print) (0740-1116); (until 1977): Hunger Workshop Notes
Media: Online - full text.
Indexed: HRIR, PAIS.
Published by: World Hunger Education Service, PO Box 29056, Washington, DC 20017. TEL 202-269-6322.

360 USA ISSN 1040-3604
HD9000.1
HUNGER REPORT. Text in English. 1988. a.
Published by: Alan Shawn Feinstein World Hunger Program, Box 1831, Brown University, Providence, RI 02912.

HYGEIA; an online journal for pregnancy and neonatal loss. *see* PSYCHOLOGY

361 HKG
HV6
I A S S W DIRECTORY. Text in English. 19??. biennial. free to members (effective 2009). **Document type:** *Directory, Trade.* **Description:** Contains a database of schools of social work throughout the world.
Former titles (until 19??): I A S S W Directory: Member Schools and Associations (0098-8278); International Association of Schools of Social Work. Directory of Members and Constitution
Related titles: CD-ROM ed.
Published by: International Association of Schools of Social Work, c/o Shirley Fisher, Asst to President, The Hong Kong Polytechnic University, Department of Applied Social Sciences (Rm HJ412), Hung Hom, Kowloon, Hong Kong. ssfisher@inet.polyu.edu.hk.

362.7 IND
I C C W JOURNAL. Text in English. 1954. q. bibl.; charts; illus. **Document type:** *Journal, Academic/Scholarly.* **Description:** Covers nutrition, education, labor, health and allied disciplines relevant to the welfare of children.
Formerly (until 1993): I C C W News Bulletin (0018-8867)
Published by: Indian Council for Child Welfare, 4 Deen Dayal Upadhayaya Marg, New Delhi, 110 002, India. TEL 91-11-23239539, iccw@bol.net.in. **Dist. by:** H P C Publishers Distributors Pvt. Ltd. TEL 91-11-325-4401, FAX 91-11-686-3511.

360 USA ISSN 1065-1675
I F C O NEWS. Text in English. 1970. irreg. (2-4/yr.). USD 25 to institutions; USD 30 to libraries (effective 1999). adv. bk.rev. bibl.; illus. back issues avail. **Document type:** *Newsletter.* **Description:** Focuses on local, national and international community organizing efforts.
Published by: Interreligious Foundation for Community Organization, 402 W 145th St, New York, NY 10031. TEL 212-926-5757, FAX 212-926-5842. Ed., R&P, Adv. contact Gail Walker. Circ: 13,000.

338.91 363.8 USA ISSN 1933-8910
I F P R I FORUM. Text in English. 2003. q. **Document type:** *Newspaper, Trade.* **Description:** Focuses on global social issues as they relate to food production, nutrition and economics.
Formed by the 2003 merger of: I F P R I Perspectives; 2020 News and Views
Related titles: Online - full text ed.: ISSN 1933-8813. free (effective 2010).
Indexed: A35, AgBio, AgrForAb, C25, CABA, E12, F08, F12, GH, I11, N02, P32, P40, PGegResA, R11, R12, S13, S16, T05, TAR, W11.
Published by: International Food Policy Research Institute, 2033 K St, NW, Washington, DC 20006. TEL 202-862-5600, FAX 202-467-4439, ifpri@cgiar.org.

362 USA ISSN 1063-4398
I H S PRIMARY CARE PROVIDER. (Indian Health Service) Text in English. 1976. m. free (effective 2005). back issues avail.
Related titles: Online - full text ed.: ISSN 1941-3602.
Indexed: P30.
—Ingenta.
Published by: U.S. Department of Health and Human Services, Indian Health Service, Clinical Support Center, 801 Thompson Ave Ste 400, Rockville, MD 20852-1627. TEL 301-443-1083, http://www.ihs.gov/AboutIHS/index.asp. Ed. John F Saari. Circ: 6,000.

362.5 PHL
I P C POVERTY RESEARCH SERIES. Text in English. irreg. **Document type:** *Monographic series.*
Published by: Ateneo de Manila University, Institute of Philippine Culture, PO Box 154, Manila, Philippines. TEL 632-426-6068, http://www.ipc-ateneo.org/. R&P Germelino M Bautista TEL 632-426-6067.

360 325 USA
THE I R C AT WORK. Text in English. 3/yr. free. 6 p./no. 3 cols./p.; **Description:** Studies refugee issues.
Formerly (until 1997): International Rescue Committee. Field Reports
Published by: International Rescue Committee, Attn: Edward P Bligh, 122 E 42nd St, 12th Fl, New York, NY 10168-1289. TEL 212-551-3000, FAX 212-551-3183, ebligh@intrescom.org, http://www.intrescom.org. Circ: 65,000.

360 SGP ISSN 0218-8961
I S E A S WORKING PAPERS SERIES: SOCIAL AND CULTURAL ISSUES. Text in English. irreg. **Document type:** *Monographic series, Academic/Scholarly.*
Published by: Institute of Southeast Asian Studies, 30 Heng Mui Keng Terrace, Pasir Panjang, Singapore, 119614, Singapore. FAX 65-67756259, pubsunit@iseas.edu.sg, http://www.iseas.edu.sg/.

362.4 615.82 FIN ISSN 0356-7249
I T - INVALIDITYOE. Text in Finnish, Swedish. 1941. m. EUR 46 domestic; EUR 50 foreign (effective 2005). adv. bk.rev. illus. **Document type:** *Magazine, Consumer.* **Description:** Covers disability, social welfare, and rehabilitation.
Formerly: Suomen Invalidi (0049-2566)
Related titles: Audio cassette/tape ed.: Invalidityoe. 1980; Online - full text ed.
Published by: Invalidiliitto r.y./Finnish Association of People with Mobility Disabilities, Kumpulantie 1 A, Helsinki, 00520, Finland. TEL 358-9-613191, FAX 358-9-1461443, http://www.invalidiliitto.fi. Eds. Sirkkt Kivi, Voitto Korhonen. adv.: B&W page EUR 1,100, color page EUR 2,310; 210 x 297. Circ: 60,162.

354.2 JAM ISSN 0799-1401
BF108.C27
IDEAZ. Text in English. 2002. a. **Document type:** *Monographic series, Academic/Scholarly.*
Indexed: CA, P42, PSA, S02, S03, SCOPUS, SociolAb, T02.
Published by: Arawak Publications, 17 Kensington Cres Unit 5, Kingston, 5, Jamaica. TEL 876-960-7538, FAX 876-960-8219, arawakpubl@cwjamaica.com.

360 CHE
IDEELLE. Text in German. 1912. 10/yr. adv. **Document type:** *Bulletin, Trade.*
Formerly: Zentral Blatt
Published by: Schweizerischer Gemeinnuetziger Frauenverein, Haegiweidstr 6, Rifferswil, 8911, Switzerland. TEL 41-1-7641138, FAX 41-1-7643138, m.lienhard@bluewin.ch. Ed. Margrit Lienhard. Circ: 6,000.

IKAGAKU OYO KENKYU ZAIDAN KENKYU HOKOKU/SUZUKEN MEMORIAL FOUNDATION. RESEARCH PAPERS. *see* PUBLIC HEALTH AND SAFETY

ILCO-PRAXIS. *see* MEDICAL SCIENCES—Oncology

362.7 USA ISSN 1934-3612
HV742.I3
ILLINOIS CHILD WELFARE. Text in English. 2004. a. USD 10 per issue (effective 2010). adv. back issues avail. **Document type:** *Journal, Academic/Scholarly.* **Description:** Designed for practitioners, program managers, and policy-makers in the field of child welfare who are looking for knowledge that helps improve services to children and families.
Related titles: Online - full text ed.: ISSN 1934-3620.
Published by: Loyola University Chicago, School of Social Work, 820 N Michigan Ave, Chicago, IL 60611. TEL 312-915-8900, socialwork@luc.edu, http://www.luc.edu/socialwork/. Ed. Katherine Tyson McCrea TEL 312-915-7028.

361 GBR ISSN 2046-312X
IMPACT. Text in English. 1975. q. back issues avail. **Document type:** *Newsletter, Trade.*
Former titles (until 2010): In Focus (1466-1195); (until 1998): Buckinghamshire Council for Voluntary Service. Newsletter (0309-0922)
Related titles: Online - full text ed.: free (effective 2011).
Published by: Community Impact Bucks, Unit B The Firs, Aylesbury Rd, Bierton, Bucks HP22 5DX, United Kingdom. TEL 44-845-3890389, FAX 44-1296-331464, info@communityimpactbucks.org.uk.

360 AUS ISSN 0706-5914
IMPACT (MELBOURNE). Text in English. 1979. q. back issues avail. **Description:** Report on Melbourne City mission's services for families, children, homeless, young people and adults, aged persons, the terminally ill and the intellectually disabled.
Former titles (until 19??): Hospice Program Newsletter (0706-5922); (until Jun.1981): Melbourne City Mission Hospice. Newsletter (0727-8438)
Published by: Melbourne Citymission, Law Courts PO, PO Box 13210, Melbourne, VIC 8010, Australia. TEL 61-3-86254444, FAX 61-3-86254410, info@mcm.org.au, http://www.melbournecitymission.org.au.

IMPACT! (SEATTLE). *see* BUSINESS AND ECONOMICS—International Development And Assistance

360 AUS ISSN 1032-4321
IMPACT (STRAWBERRY HILLS). Text in English. 1971. q. AUD 59 to non-members; free to members (effective 2008). adv. bk.rev. back issues avail. **Document type:** *Magazine, Trade.* **Description:** Provides news, information and articles that are of interest to people interested in social services.
Former titles (until 1988): Australian Social Welfare: Impact (0157-3373); (until 1978): Australian Social Welfare (0310-6713)
Related titles: E-mail ed.: AUD 43 (effective 2004); Online - full text ed.: AUD 44 (effective 2008).
Indexed: A26, AusPAIS, I05, P02, P10, P14, P21, P27, P48, P50, P53, P54, PQC, S11, WBSS.
—Ingenta.
Published by: Australian Council of Social Service, Locked Bag 4777, Strawberry Hills, NSW 2012, Australia. TEL 61-2-93106200, FAX 61-2-93104822, acoss@acoss.org.au. Ed. Jason Donohoe. Adv. contact Al Parmeter TEL 61-2-93104844. page AUD 500; 170 x 255. Circ: 1,100.

361.77 DEU
IMPULS. Text in German. q. adv. **Document type:** *Magazine, Trade.*
Published by: (Bayerisches Rotes Kreuz), S V Corporate Media GmbH (Subsidiary of: Sueddeutscher Verlag GmbH), Emmy-Noether-Str 2, Munich, 80992, Germany. TEL 49-89-5485201, FAX 49-89-54852192, info@sv-medien-service.de, http://www.sv-medien-service.de/svcm/. adv.: B&W page EUR 4,500, color page EUR 6,000. Circ: 230,000 (controlled).

IMPULSE (HAMBURG, 1996). *see* HANDICAPPED

361.77 DEU
IMPULSE (WIESBADEN). Text in German. 1952. 4/yr. adv. **Document type:** *Magazine, Trade.*
Former titles (until 1987): Rotes Kreuz in Hessen; (until 1974): Deutsches Rotes Kreuz. Landesverband Hessen. Mitteilungsblatt
Published by: Deutsches Rotes Kreuz, Landesverband Hessen, Abraham-Lincoln-Str 7, Wiesbaden, 65189, Germany. TEL 49-611-79090, FAX 49-611-701099, nicole.tappe@drk-hessen.de, http://www.drk-hessen.de. Ed. Gisela Prellwitz. Circ: 14,000 (controlled).

360 AUS ISSN 0728-6503
IN UNITY (ONLINE). Text in English. 1949. irreg., latest 2006. free (effective 2009). bk.rev. back issues avail. **Document type:** *Newspaper, Trade.*
Formerly (until 2004): In Unity (Print) (0442-3844); Which incorporated (in Jan.1978): Christian Action News
Media: Online - full text.

Published by: National Council of Churches in Australia, Locked Bag 199, Sydney, NSW 1230, Australia. TEL 61-2-92992215, 800-025-101, FAX 61-2-92624514, actforpeace@ncca.org.au.

360 ITA ISSN 0046-8819
INCHIESTA. Text in Italian. 1971. q. EUR 40 domestic; EUR 80 foreign (effective 2009). adv. charts. back issues avail. **Document type:** *Magazine, Consumer.* **Description:** Includes research on social issues in Italy. For students, researchers, social and political workers.
Indexed: CA, IBR, IBZ, P34, P42, PAIS, PSA, RASB, S02, S03, SCOPUS, SOPODA, SSA, SociolAb, T02.
—BLDSC (4374.960000), INIST.
Published by: Edizioni Dedalo, Viale Luigi Jacobini 5, Bari, BA 70123, Italy. TEL 39-080-5311413, FAX 39-080-5311414, info@edizionidedalo.it, http://www.edizionidedalo.it. Ed. Vittorio Capecchi. Circ: 12,000.

363.3 NLD ISSN 1877-4903
INCIDENT. Text in Dutch. 2001. 10/yr. EUR 81.50 combined subscription (print & online eds.) (effective 2010). adv. **Document type:** *Magazine, Trade.*
Related titles: Online - full text ed.: EUR 65.20 (effective 2010).
Published by: Sdu Uitgevers bv, Postbus 20025, The Hague, 2500 EA, Netherlands. TEL 31-70-3789911, FAX 31-70-3854321, sdu@sdu.nl, http://www.sdu.nl/. Ed. M Debets. Pub. Roel Roos. adv.: B&W page EUR 1,327, color page EUR 1,847; trim 210 x 297. Circ: 4,700.

362.4 NLD ISSN 2210-8122
INCLUSIEF. Key Title: Incl. Text in Dutch. 1994. q. EUR 20 (effective 2010).
Former titles (until 2010): C G-Raad Nieuws (1569-0474); (until 2001): Gehandicaptenraad Nieuws (1386-5617)
Published by: Chronisch Zieken en Gehandicapten Raad Nederland, Postbus 169, Utrecht, 3500 AD, Netherlands. TEL 31-30-2916600, FAX 31-30-2970404, secretariaat@cg-raad.nl.

362.6 USA ISSN 1073-1393
HQ1064.U5
INCOME OF THE AGED CHARTBOOK. Text in English. 1990. biennial. charts; stat. **Document type:** *Government.* **Description:** Highlights selected data from the biennial report, Income of the Population 55 or Older. Focuses on the receipt and shares of income from Social Security, pensions, assets, earnings, and public assistance using data from the U.S. Bureau of the Census.
Related titles: Online - full text ed.: free (effective 2011).
Published by: U.S. Social Security Administration, Office of Research, Evaluation and Statistics, Office of Public Inquiries, Windsor Park Bldg, 6401 Security Blvd, Baltimore, MD 21235. TEL 800-772-1213, ores.publications@ssa.gov, http://www.ssa.gov/policy/about/ORES.html.

INCOME OF THE POPULATION 55 OR OLDER. *see* INSURANCE

360 USA ISSN 0743-1236
HV97.I47
INDEPENDENT SECTOR. ANNUAL REPORT. Text in English. 1980. a. free. **Document type:** *Corporate.* **Description:** Overview of the independent sector's activities: communications, research, government relations.
Published by: Independent Sector, 1200 Eighteenth St, N W, Ste 200, Washington, DC 20036. TEL 202-467-6100, FAX 202-467-6101, info@indepsec.org, http://www.independentsector.org. Circ: 10,000.

362 CAN ISSN 1704-4286
INDIAN AND NORTHERN AFFAIRS CANADA. UPDATE. Text in English. 2002. q. **Document type:** *Newsletter.*
Related titles: Online - full text ed.: ISSN 1704-7315.
Published by: Indian and Northern Affairs Canada/Affaires Indiennes et du Nord Canada, Terrasses de la Chaudiere, 10 Wellington St, N Tower, Rm 1210, Gatineau, PQ K1A 0H4, Canada. TEL 800-567-9604, infopubs@ainc-inac.gc.ca.

360 IND ISSN 0019-5634
HV1 CODEN: IJSWA3
➤ **INDIAN JOURNAL OF SOCIAL WORK.** Text in English. 1940. q. INR 600 domestic to individuals; USD 40 to individuals in South Asia; USD 70 to individuals in South-East Asia, The Middle East, Africa And South America; USD 120 to individuals in North America, Europe, Australia and New Zealand; INR 250 domestic to institutions; USD 25 to institutions in South Asia; USD 55 to institutions in South-East Asia, The Middle East, Africa And South America; USD 65 to institutions in North America, Europe, Australia and New Zealand (effective 2011). bk.rev.; video rev. charts. index. back issues avail.; reprints avail. **Document type:** *Journal, Academic/Scholarly.* **Description:** Takes an interdisciplinary approach to the study of social work and the social sciences; devoted to the scientific interpretation of social problems.
Related titles: Microfilm ed.: (from PQC).
Indexed: A20, A22, AMHA, ASCA, ASD, BAS, BibInd, CA, CurCont, F09, FamI, IBSS, IPsyAb, P06, P30, P34, PAA&I, PsycholAb, RASB, REE&TA, RehabLit, S02, S03, SCOPUS, SOPODA, SSA, SSCI, SWR&A, SociolAb, T02, W07, W09.
—BLDSC (4421.200000), IE, Infotrieve, Ingenta.
Published by: Tata Institute of Social Sciences, Deonar, PO Box 8313, Mumbai, 400 088, India. TEL 91-22-25525000, FAX 91-22-25525050. Ed. S Parasuraman.

➤ **INFANCIA E JUVENTUDE.** *see* LAW—Family And Matrimonial Law

360 DEU ISSN 1862-0469
INFO ALSO. Text in German. 1983. bi-m. EUR 48; EUR 30 to students (effective 2011). adv. reprint service avail. from SCH. **Document type:** *Magazine, Consumer.*
Formerly (until 2005): Informationen zum Arbeitslosenrecht und Sozialhilferecht (0179-8863)
Indexed: IBR, IBZ.
Published by: Nomos Verlagsgesellschaft mbH und Co. KG, Waldseestr 3-5, Baden-Baden, 76530, Germany. TEL 49-7221-21040, FAX 49-7221-210427, nomos@nomos.de, marketing@nomos.de, http://www.nomos.de. Adv. contact Bettina Roos. Circ: 3,600 (controlled).

360 362.1 CAN ISSN 1718-1704
INFO.CA DE L'AGENCE. Text in French. 2005. m. **Document type:** *Bulletin, Government.*
Published by: Quebec, Agence de Developpement de Reseaux Locaux de Services de Sante et de Services Sociaux de Montreal, 3725, rue Saint-Denis, Montreal, PQ H2X 3L9, Canada. TEL 514-286-6500.

INFO WET MAATSCHAPPELIJKE ONDERSTEUNING. *see* PUBLIC ADMINISTRATION

361 ESP ISSN 1988-7604
INFOPORTALSOCIAL.NET. Text in Catalan. 2003. w.
Media: Online - full text.
Published by: Generalitat de Catalunya, Departament de Accio Social i Ciutadania, Placa Pau Vila, 1, Barcelona, 08039, Spain. TEL 34-93-4831000, FAX 34-93-4831011, biblioteca.benestar@gencat.net, http://www.gencat.net/benestar/.

INFORMATION JUIVE. *see* RELIGIONS AND THEOLOGY—Judaic

INFORMATION PLUS REFERENCE SERIES. HEALTH AND WELLNESS; illness among Americans. *see* PUBLIC HEALTH AND SAFETY

INFORMATION PLUS REFERENCE SERIES. IMMIGRATION AND ILLEGAL ALIENS; burden or blessing?. *see* POLITICAL SCIENCE—International Relations

362.5 USA ISSN 1930-3300
HC79.P6
INFORMATION PLUS REFERENCE SERIES. WORLD POVERTY. Text in English. 2006 (Nov.). biennial. USD 49 per issue (effective 2008). back issues avail. **Document type:** *Monographic series, Academic/Scholarly.*
Related titles: Online - full text ed.; ◆ Series: Information Plus Reference Series.
Published by: Gale (Subsidiary of: Cengage Learning), 27500 Drake Rd, Farmington Hills, MI 48331. TEL 248-699-4253, 800-877-4253, FAX 877-363-4253, gale.galeord@cengage.com.

360 FRA ISSN 0046-9459
HN421
INFORMATIONS SOCIALES. Text in French. 6/yr. EUR 33 (effective 2009). adv. bk.rev. back issues avail. **Document type:** *Journal, Trade.*
Related titles: Microfiche ed.: (from BHP).
Indexed: FR, IBSS, PAIS, WBSS.
—INIST.
Published by: Caisse Nationale des Allocations Familiales, 32 Av. de la Sibelle, Paris, Cedex 14 75685, France. TEL 33-1-45655432, FAX 33-1-45655377, http://www.caf.fr/. Ed. Daniel Bequignon. Circ: 12,000.

INFORMATIONSDIENST ALTERSFRAGEN. *see* GERONTOLOGY AND GERIATRICS

360 CHE
INFORMATIONSZEITSCHRIFT FUER A H V UND KRANKENKASSEN. Text in French, German. m.
Address: Via Dufour 4, Case Postale 3365, Lugano, 6901, Switzerland. TEL 091-227518, FAX 091-238171. Ed. G Santoro. Circ: 30,000.

INFORME ESTADISTICO DE LA SEGURIDAD SOCIAL. ADMINISTRACION PUBLICA. *see* PUBLIC ADMINISTRATION

351 ARG ISSN 1852-835X
▼ **INFORME ESTADISTICO DE LA SEGURIDAD SOCIAL. AUTORIDADES DEL PODER EJECUTIVO Y LEGISLATIVO Y LEGISLADORES.** Text in Spanish. 2010. m. back issues avail. **Document type:** *Bulletin, Consumer.*
Media: Online - full text.
Published by: Caja de Jubilaciones, Pensiones y Retiros de Cordoba, Gral. Alvear 15, Centro, Cordoba, X5000ILA, Argentina.

361.6 ARG ISSN 1852-8597
INFORME ESTADISTICO DE LA SEGURIDAD SOCIAL. BANCARIOS. Text in Spanish. 2008. m. back issues avail. **Document type:** *Bulletin, Consumer.*
Media: Online - full text.
Published by: Caja de Jubilaciones, Pensiones y Retiros de Cordoba, Gral. Alvear 15, Centro, Cordoba, X5000ILA, Argentina.

361.6 ARG ISSN 1852-8589
INFORME ESTADISTICO DE LA SEGURIDAD SOCIAL. DOCENTES. Text in Spanish. 2008. m. **Document type:** *Bulletin, Consumer.*
Media: Online - full text.
Published by: Caja de Jubilaciones, Pensiones y Retiros de Cordoba, Gral. Alvear 15, Centro, Cordoba, X5000ILA, Argentina.

361.6 ARG ISSN 1852-8627
INFORME ESTADISTICO DE LA SEGURIDAD SOCIAL. E.P.E.C. (Informe Estadistico de la Seguridad Social. Empresa Provincial de Energia Electrica) Text in Spanish. 2008. m. back issues avail. **Document type:** *Bulletin, Consumer.*
Media: Online - full text.
Published by: Caja de Jubilaciones, Pensiones y Retiros de Cordoba, Gral. Alvear 15, Centro, Cordoba, X5000ILA, Argentina.

352 ARG ISSN 1852-8635
INFORME ESTADISTICO DE LA SEGURIDAD SOCIAL. MUNICIPALIDAD CIUDAD CORDOBA. Text in Spanish. 2008. m. back issues avail. **Document type:** *Bulletin, Consumer.*
Media: Online - full text.
Published by: Caja de Jubilaciones, Pensiones y Retiros de Cordoba, Gral. Alvear 15, Centro, Cordoba, X5000ILA, Argentina.

INFORME ESTADISTICO DE LA SEGURIDAD SOCIAL, POLICIA Y SERVICIO PENITENCIARIO DE LA PROVINCIA. *see* CRIMINOLOGY AND LAW ENFORCEMENT

300 ECU
INFORME SOCIAL. BOLIVIA. Text in Spanish. 1994. irreg.
Published by: Instituto Latinoamericano de Investigaciones Sociales, Casilla 17-03-367, CALAMA, 354, Quito, Pichincha, Ecuador. TEL 593-2-562103, FAX 593-2-504337. **Co-sponsor:** Centro de Estudios para el Desarrollo Laboral y Agrario.

300 ECU
INFORME SOCIAL. ECUADOR. Text in Spanish. 1993. irreg.
Published by: Instituto Latinoamericano de Investigaciones Sociales, Casilla 17-03-367, CALAMA, 354, Quito, Pichincha, Ecuador. TEL 593-2-562103, FAX 593-2-504337.

360 CHE ISSN 1022-4432
INFORUM. Text in German. 1942. q. **Document type:** *Magazine, Consumer.*
Formerly (until 1994): Pro Infirmis (1022-4424)
Related titles: French ed.: ISSN 1022-4440.
Published by: Pro Infirmis, Feldeggstr 71, Postfach 1332, Zuerich, 8032, Switzerland. TEL 41-1-3882626, FAX 41-1-3882600, contact@proinfirmis.ch, http://www.proinfirmis.ch. Circ: 3,000.

360 CHE ISSN 1660-7236
INFOSANTESUISSE (FRENCH EDITION). Text in French. 1986. 10/yr. CHF 54 (effective 2001). adv. illus.; stat. **Document type:** *Magazine, Consumer.*
Former titles (until 2001): C A M S Actuel (1423-4416); (until 1994): C C M S Actuel (1423-4424); (until 1994): Journal des Caisses Maladie Suisses (1423-4432)
Published by: Santesuisse, Roemerstr 20, Solothurn, 4500, Switzerland. TEL 41-32-6254274, FAX 41-32-6254270, info@santesuisse.ch, http://www.santesuisse.ch. Ed. N. Bulliard. Circ: 850 (paid and controlled).

361.1 CHE ISSN 1660-7228
INFOSANTESUISSE (GERMAN EDITION). Text in German. 1925. 24/yr.
Former titles (until 2001): K S K Aktuell (1423-4440); (until 1994): S K Z (0253-0414); (until 1952): Schweizerische Krankenkassen Zeitung (0253-0422)
Indexed: P30.
Published by: Santesuisse, Roemerstr 20, Solothurn, 4500, Switzerland. TEL 41-32-6254141, info@santesuisse.ch, http://www.santesuisse.ch. Circ: 11,000.

360 DEU
INNENSICHTEN. Text in German. 2000. irreg., latest vol.2, 2002. price varies. **Document type:** *Monographic series, Academic/Scholarly.*
Published by: V W B - Verlag fuer Wissenschaft und Bildung, Postfach 110368, Berlin, 10833, Germany. TEL 49-30-2510415, FAX 49-30-2511136, info@vwb-verlag.com.

361 CAN ISSN 0319-0323
INSIDE OXFAM. Text in English. 1965. irreg. **Document type:** *Bulletin, Trade.*
Formerly (until 1971): Oxfam Canada News (0319-0331)
—CCC.
Published by: Oxfam Canada, 250 City Centre Ave, Ste 400, Ottawa, ON K1R 6K7, Canada. TEL 613-237-5236, FAX 613-237-0524, info@oxfam.ca, http://www.oxfam.ca.

360 USA
INSIGHTS (BOSTON). Text in English. 1995 (vol.9). 3/yr. free. **Document type:** *Newsletter.* **Description:** Reports on human rights and developments issues in Haiti, Mexico, Eritrea, Brazil and Palestine.
Published by: Grassroots International, 179 Boylston St, 4th Fl, Boston, MA 02130-4520. TEL 617-524-1400, FAX 617-524-5525. Circ: 3,000.

362 AUS
INSPIRE (ADELAIDE). Text in English. 1958. q. adv. bk.rev.
Formerly: Caring (0312-3502)
Published by: Service to Youth Council Inc., 72 Currie St, Adelaide, SA 5000, Australia. TEL 61-8-82216477, FAX 61-8-82122180, http://www.syc.net.au.

361.37 177.7 USA ISSN 1557-2382
HV85
INSPIRE YOUR WORLD; celebrating the people, companies and causes that inspire is to give back. Text in English. 2004 (Apr./May). bi-m. USD 21.50 domestic; USD 6 newsstand/cover domestic; USD 8 newsstand/cover in Canada (effective 2007). adv. **Document type:** *Magazine, Consumer.* **Description:** Features a wide range of stories to reach its broad audience, reporting on issues and trends in volunteerism and philanthropy from a human-interest perspective.
Related titles: Online - full text ed.: ISSN 1557-2420.
Published by: BizExUSA. Llc., 825 Carlton Ave, North Plainfield, NJ 07060-2644. Ed. Eric Feil. Pub. Gary F Schneider. adv.: color page USD 11,500; trim 8.75 x 11.75. Circ: 120,000.

361.73 GBR ISSN 2046-3480
▼ **INSPIRED!.** Text in English. 2010. 3/yr. back issues avail. **Document type:** *Magazine, Consumer.* **Description:** Contains national news, events and fund raising activities of Cystic Fibrosis Trust supporters across the UK.
Formed by the merger of (2000-2010): Focus on Fundraising. Northern Region (1477-5506); (2000-2010): Focus on Fundraising. Southern Region (1477-5514); (2000-2010): Focus on Fundraising. Central Region (1477-5522)
Related titles: Online - full text ed.: ISSN 2046-3499. free (effective 2011).
Published by: Cystic Fibrosis Trust, 11 London Rd, Bromley, Kent BR1 1BY, United Kingdom. TEL 44-20-84647211, FAX 44-20-83130472, enquiries@cftrust.org.uk. Ed. Jacqueline Ali.

INSTITUTO MEXICANO DEL SEGURO SOCIAL. REVISTA MEDICA. *see* MEDICAL SCIENCES

INTEGRA. *see* HANDICAPPED

INTEGRATION. *see* HANDICAPPED

360 CAN ISSN 1719-8542
L'INTER-ACTION. Text in French. 2005. irreg. **Document type:** *Monographic series, Consumer.*
Supersedes: Le Contact (1702-2509)
Published by: Le Centre de Sante et de Service Sociaux de Gatineau, Hopital de Gatineau, 909, boul. La Verendrye Ouest, Gatineau, PQ J8P 7H2, Canada. TEL 819-561-8100, FAX 819-561-8306, chvo@ssss.gouv.qc.ca, http://www.chvo.qc.ca/CHVO/chvo_interne_ete/index_f.aspx?ArticleID=153.

360 BRA
INTERCAMBIO; revista quadrimestral de informacao e cultura. Text in Portuguese. 1965-1976; N.S. 1980; N.S. 1988. 3/yr. free. bibl.
Formerly (until 1987): Brazil. Servico Social do Comercio. Boletim de Intercambio
Published by: (Brazil. Assessoria de Divulgacao e Promocao Institucional), Servico Social do Comercio, Rua Voluntarios da Patria, 169 Andar 11, Rio De Janeiro, RJ 22270-000, Brazil. Circ: 2,500.

300 AUT ISSN 0020-5362
INTERESSE; soziale Information. Text in German. 1963. q. per issue contribution. bk.rev. **Document type:** *Bulletin, Consumer.*
Published by: Pastoralamt der Dioezese Linz, Sozialreferat, Kapuzinerstrasse 84, Linz, O 4020, Austria. TEL 43-732-76103251, FAX 43-732-76103779, sozialreferat@dioezese-linz.at. Ed. Alfred Koller. Circ: 4,900.

INTERIGHTS BULLETIN. *see* POLITICAL SCIENCE—Civil Rights

362.7 NLD ISSN 1572-0489
INTERNATIONAL CHILD HEALTH STUDIES. Text in English. 2003. irreg., latest 2006. price varies. **Document type:** *Monographic series, Academic/Scholarly.*

S

Published by: Rozenberg Publishers, Lindengracht 302 D&E, Amsterdam, 1015 KM, Netherlands. TEL 31-20-6255429, FAX 31-20-6203395, info@rozenbergps.com.

361.77 CHE
INTERNATIONAL COMMITTEE OF THE RED CROSS. ANNUAL REPORT/COMITE INTERNATIONAL DE LA CROIX ROUGE. RAPPORT ANNUEL. Text in English, French. 1949. a. CHF 12 (effective 2003). back issues avail. **Document type:** *Yearbook, Corporate.* **Description:** Comprises multiple chapters, each dealing with a specific field of ICRC activity. summarizing work in the field, and reviewing legal matters, administrative affairs, dissemination of information, and ICRC finances and accounts for the year.
Related titles: Online - full text ed.
Published by: International Committee of the Red Cross/Comite International de la Croix Rouge, 19 ave de la Paix, Geneva, 1202, Switzerland. TEL 41-22-734-6001, FAX 41-22-733-2057, webmaster.gva@icrc.org, http://www.icrc.org.

361.77 325.21 CHE
INTERNATIONAL COMMITTEE OF THE RED CROSS. FORUM. Text in English. 1998. a. CHF 20 (effective 2000). illus.; maps. **Document type:** *Journal, Academic/Scholarly.* **Description:** Fosters reflection and debate on issues of serious international humanitarian concern.
Published by: International Committee of the Red Cross/Comite International de la Croix Rouge, 19 ave de la Paix, Geneva, 1202, Switzerland. TEL 41-22-734-6001, FAX 41-22-733-2057.

361.77 CHE
INTERNATIONAL COMMITTEE OF THE RED CROSS. PANORAMA. Text in English. biennial. CHF 3 (effective 2000). illus. **Document type:** *Corporate.* **Description:** Contains a summary of the ICRC's activities during the year, including its field operations to protect and assist civilian and military victims of armed conflicts and internal disturbances; its work in the area of principles and law, and the activities of its administrative support staff and Central Tracing Agency at headquarters.
Formerly: International Committee of the Red Cross. Reference Report
Related titles: Arabic ed.; French ed.; Spanish ed.; Japanese ed.; Russian ed.; German ed.
Published by: International Committee of the Red Cross/Comite International de la Croix Rouge, 19 ave de la Paix, Geneva, 1202, Switzerland. TEL 41-22-734-6001, FAX 41-22-734-8280.

361 CAN ISSN 0074-2961
INTERNATIONAL CONFERENCE ON SOCIAL WELFARE. CONFERENCE PROCEEDINGS. Text in English. 1928. biennial. price varies. **Document type:** *Proceedings.*
Indexed: SpeleolAb.
Published by: International Council on Social Welfare/Conseil International de l'Action Sociale, c/o Stephen King, Exe Dir, 380 St Antoine St W, Ste 3200, Montreal, PQ H2Y 3X7, Canada. TEL 514-287-3280, FAX 514-287-9702.

INTERNATIONAL ENCYCLOPAEDIA OF LAWS. SOCIAL SECURITY LAW. *see* INSURANCE

INTERNATIONAL JOURNAL OF DEVELOPMENTAL DISABILITIES. *see* EDUCATION—Special Education And Rehabilitation

362.6 AUS ISSN 1834-2663
➤ **INTERNATIONAL JOURNAL OF HEALTH AND AGEING MANAGEMENT.** Text in English. 2006. s-a. **Document type:** *Journal, Academic/Scholarly.*
Media: Online - full text.
Published by: Academic Global Publications TEL 61-4-1298-6730, exec_ed@academicglobalpublications.com.

360 GBR ISSN 0749-6753
RA394.9 CODEN: IJHMEO
➤ **INTERNATIONAL JOURNAL OF HEALTH PLANNING AND MANAGEMENT.** Text in English. 1986. q. GBP 1,272 in United Kingdom to institutions; EUR 1,609 in Europe to institutions; USD 2,494 elsewhere to institutions; GBP 1,463 combined subscription in United Kingdom to institutions (print & online eds.); EUR 1,850 combined subscription in Europe to institutions (print & online eds.); USD 2,868 combined subscription elsewhere to institutions (print & online eds.) (effective 2012). adv. back issues avail.; reprint service avail. from PSC. **Document type:** *Journal, Academic/Scholarly.* **Description:** Discusses major issues in health planning, management systems, and practices; maintains a balance between practice and theory from a variety of schools of thought.
Related titles: Online - full text ed.: ISSN 1099-1751. GBP 1,272 in United Kingdom to institutions; EUR 1,609 in Europe to institutions; USD 2,494 elsewhere to institutions (effective 2012).
Indexed: A22, A36, AHCMS, ASCA, ASSIA, B21, C06, C07, CABA, CurCont, EMBASE, ESPM, ExcerpMed, FR, Faml, GEOBASE, GH, H&SSA, H17, LT, MEDLINE, N02, N03, P02, P10, P30, P33, P39, P48, P50, P52, P53, P54, P56, PAIS, PQC, R10, R12, Reac, S11, SCOPUS, SOPODA, SSCI, SociolAb, T05, TAR, W07, W11.
—GNLM, IE, Infotrieve, Ingenta. **CCC.**
Published by: John Wiley & Sons Ltd. (Subsidiary of: John Wiley & Sons, Inc.), 1-7 Oldlands Way, PO Box 808, Bognor Regis, West Sussex PO21 9FF, United Kingdom. TEL 44-1865-778315, FAX 44-1243-843232, cs-journals@wiley.com, http://eu.wiley.com/WileyCDA/. Ed. Calum Paton. **Subscr. in the Americas to:** John Wiley & Sons, Inc., 111 River St, Hoboken, NJ 07030. TEL 201-748-6645, subinfo@wiley.com; **Subscr. to:** 1-7 Oldlands Way, PO Box 809, Bognor Regis, West Sussex PO21 9FG, United Kingdom. TEL 44-1865-778054, cs-agency@wiley.com.

➤ **INTERNATIONAL JOURNAL OF INTEGRATED CARE.** *see* HEALTH FACILITIES AND ADMINISTRATION

➤ **INTERNATIONAL JOURNAL OF MENTAL HEALTH.** *see* PSYCHOLOGY

362.87 GBR ISSN 1747-9894
INTERNATIONAL JOURNAL OF MIGRATION, HEALTH AND SOCIAL CARE. Text in English. 2005. q. EUR 689 combined subscription in Europe (print & online eds.); USD 889 combined subscription in the Americas (print & online eds.); GBP 529 combined subscription in the UK & elsewhere (print & online eds.); AUD 999 combined subscription in Australasia (print & online eds.) (effective 2012). adv. back issues avail. **Document type:** *Journal, Academic/Scholarly.* **Description:** Focuses on international migration covering legal migration, asylum seekers, refugees, and undocumented migrants, with an emphasis on health and social care and mental health issues.
Related titles: Online - full text ed.: ISSN 2042-8650.
Indexed: B28, CA, H05, S02, S03, SCOPUS, T02.
—BLDSC (4542.359000), IE. **CCC.**
Published by: Pier Professional Ltd. (Subsidiary of: Emerald Group Publishing Ltd.), Ste N4, The Old Market, Upper Market St, Hove, BN3 1AS, United Kingdom. TEL 44-1273-783720, FAX 44-1273-783723, info@pierprofessional.com. Ed. Dr. Charles Watters. Adv. contact Paul Somerville TEL 44-1273-783724. B&W page GBP 350; 160 x 245.

INTERNATIONAL JOURNAL OF NARRATIVE THERAPY AND COMMUNITY WORK. *see* PSYCHOLOGY

INTERNATIONAL JOURNAL OF NONPROFIT AND VOLUNTARY SECTOR MARKETING. *see* BUSINESS AND ECONOMICS—Marketing And Purchasing

360 GBR ISSN 1369-6866
HV316
➤ **INTERNATIONAL JOURNAL OF SOCIAL WELFARE.** Text in English. 1992. q. GBP 506 in United Kingdom to institutions; EUR 643 in Europe to institutions; USD 847 in the Americas to institutions; USD 991 elsewhere to institutions; GBP 582 combined subscription in United Kingdom to institutions (print & online eds.); EUR 739 combined subscription in Europe to institutions (print & online eds.); USD 975 combined subscription in the Americas to institutions (print & online eds.); USD 1,140 combined subscription elsewhere to institutions (print & online eds.) (effective 2012). adv. bk.rev. illus. back issues avail.; reprint service avail. from PSC. **Document type:** *Journal, Academic/Scholarly.* **Description:** Aims to encourage debate about the global implications of the most pressing social welfare issues of the day.
Formerly (until 1999): Scandinavian Journal of Social Welfare (0907-2055)
Related titles: Online - full text ed.: ISSN 1468-2397. 1999. GBP 506 in United Kingdom to institutions; EUR 643 in Europe to institutions; USD 847 in the Americas to institutions; USD 991 elsewhere to institutions (effective 2012) (from IngentaConnect).
Indexed: A01, A03, A08, A20, A22, A26, ASCA, ASG, AgeL, CA, CJPI, CurCont, E01, ESPM, Faml, IBSS, P02, P03, P27, P30, P34, P42, P48, P54, PQC, PSA, PsycInfo, PsycholAb, RiskAb, S02, S03, SCOPUS, SSA, SSCI, SociolAb, T02, W07.
—BLDSC (4542.566000), IE, Infotrieve, Ingenta. **CCC.**
Published by: Wiley-Blackwell Publishing Ltd. (Subsidiary of: John Wiley & Sons, Inc.), 9600 Garsington Rd, Oxford, OX4 2DQ, United Kingdom. TEL 44-1865-776868, FAX 44-1865-714591, customerservices@blackwellpublishing.com. Ed. Sven Hessle TEL 46-8-164221. adv.: B&W page GBP 445, B&W page USD 823; 140 x 210. Circ: 595.

➤ **INTERNATIONAL JOURNAL OF SOCIOLOGY AND SOCIAL POLICY.** *see* SOCIOLOGY

360 USA ISSN 1942-728X
CODEN: JVAIF5
➤ **THE INTERNATIONAL JOURNAL OF VOLUNTEER ADMINISTRATION.** Text in English; Text occasionally in French, Spanish. 1967. 3/yr. USD 40 to individuals; USD 300 to libraries (effective 2009). bk.rev. abstr.; bibl.; charts; illus. cum.index: 1982-1992. back issues avail.; reprints avail. **Document type:** *Journal, Academic/Scholarly.* **Description:** Aims to provide an exchange of ideas and a sharing of knowledge and insights about volunteerism and volunteer management and administration.
Former titles (until 2006): Journal of Volunteer Administration (0733-6535); (until 1982): Volunteer Administration (0362-773X)
Media: Online - full content.
Indexed: A22, ASG, BPIA, E03, ERI, P30, PAIS, SCOPUS, SOPODA.
—BLDSC (5072.517500), IE, Infotrieve, Ingenta.
Published by: North Carolina State University, Department of 4-H Youth Development and Family & Consumer Sciences, Campus Box 7606, Raleigh, NC 27695-7606. TEL 919-513-0306, FAX 919-515-7812, 4h_pubs@ncsu.edu, http://www.nc4h.org. Ed. Dale Safrit.

360 NGA ISSN 1993-8225
JZ4841
➤ **INTERNATIONAL N G O JOURNAL.** (Non Governmental Organizations) Text in English. 2006 (June). m. free (effective 2011). **Document type:** *Journal, Academic/Scholarly.* **Description:** Publishes proposals, appraisals and reports of NGO projects. The aim is to have a centralized information for NGO activities where stakeholders including beneficiaries of NGO services can find useful information about ongoing projects and where to obtain particular assistance.
Media: Online - full content.
Indexed: A34, A35, A36, AgBio, AgrForAb, B21, BA, C25, CABA, E12, ESPM, F08, F11, F12, FCA, GH, H16, IIBP, LT, N02, N03, P32, P37, P40, PHN&I, R07, R12, RRTA, S12, S13, S16, SSciA, T05, TAR, VS, W11.
Published by: Academic Journals, PO Box 73023, Victoria Island, Lagos, Nigeria. service@academicjournals.org. Ed. Dr. Philomena Imonivwerha.

361 USA ISSN 0538-9461
INTERNATIONAL RESCUE COMMITTEE. ANNUAL REPORT. Text in English. a. free.
Published by: International Rescue Committee, Attn: Edward P Bligh, 122 E 42nd St, 12th Fl, New York, NY 10168-1289. TEL 212-551-3000.

INTERNATIONAL REVIEW OF THE RED CROSS. *see* LAW—International Law

INTERNATIONAL REVIEW OF VICTIMOLOGY. *see* CRIMINOLOGY AND LAW ENFORCEMENT

360 NLD ISSN 0924-4859
➤ **INTERNATIONAL SERIES IN SOCIAL WELFARE.** Text in English. 1982. irreg., latest vol.7, 1985. price varies. **Document type:** *Monographic series, Academic/Scholarly.*
Published by: Springer Netherlands (Subsidiary of: Springer Science+Business Media), Van Godewijckstraat 30, Dordrecht, 3311 GX, Netherlands. TEL 31-78-6576050, FAX 31-78-6576474.

➤ **INTERNATIONAL SOCIAL SECURITY SERIES.** *see* INSURANCE

360 GBR ISSN 0020-8728
HV1
➤ **INTERNATIONAL SOCIAL WORK.** Abbreviated title: I S W. Text in English. 1959. bi-m. GBP 708, USD 1,310 to institutions; GBP 722, USD 1,337 combined subscription to institutions (print & online eds.) (effective 2012). bk.rev. illus. index, cum.index: 1958-1977. back issues avail.; reprint service avail. from PSC. **Document type:** *Journal, Academic/Scholarly.* **Description:** Designed to promote communication and extend knowledge in the fields of social development, social welfare and human services.
Formerly (until 1958): Social Welfare in South-East-Asia
Related titles: Microform ed.: (from PQC); Online - full text ed.: ISSN 1461-7234. GBP 650, USD 1,203 to institutions (effective 2012).
Indexed: A01, A02, A03, A08, A10, A20, A22, A25, A26, ASCA, B04, B07, BRD, C06, C07, C08, CA, CINAHL, CurCont, DIP, E-psyche, E01, E08, ESPM, Faml, G08, H04, H12, HRA, I05, I14, IBR, IBSS, IBZ, IPsyAb, MEA&I, P02, P03, P06, P10, P25, P27, P30, P34, P48, P53, P54, PQC, PSI, PsycInfo, PsycholAb, S02, S03, S08, S09, S11, SCOPUS, SOPODA, SSA, SSAI, SSAb, SSCI, SSI, SSciA, SWR&A, SociolAb, T02, V02, V03, W03, W05, W07, W09, WBSS.
—BLDSC (4549.500000), IE, Infotrieve, Ingenta. **CCC.**
Published by: (International Council on Social Welfare NLD), Sage Publications Ltd. (Subsidiary of: Sage Publications, Inc.), 1 Oliver's Yard, 55 City Rd, London, EC1Y 1SP, United Kingdom. TEL 44-20-73248500, FAX 44-20-73248600, info@sagepub.co.uk, http://www.uk.sagepub.com/home.nav. Eds. Lena Dominelli, Simon Hackett. **Subscr. in the Americas to:** Sage Publications, Inc., 2455 Teller Rd, Thousand Oaks, CA 91320. TEL 805-499-9774, FAX 805-499-0871, journals@sagepub.com. **Co-sponsors:** International Association of Schools of Social Work; International Federation of Social Workers.

360 USA ISSN 1930-6865
INTERNATIONAL UPDATE. Text in English. 2003. m. free (effective 2009). **Document type:** *Newsletter, Consumer.*
Media: Online - full text.
Published by: U.S. Social Security Administration, Office of Policy, Division of Information Resources, 500 E St, SW, 8th Fl, Washington, DC 20254. TEL 202-358-6274, FAX 202-358-6192, op.publications@ssa.gov, http://www.ssa.gov/policy/index.html.

INTERNATIONAL WORKCAMP LISTING (YEAR). *see* BUSINESS AND ECONOMICS—International Development And Assistance

360 DEU ISSN 1864-5577
INTERNATIONALE SOZIALARBEIT. Text in German. 2007. irreg., latest vol.3, 2009. price varies. **Document type:** *Monographic series, Academic/Scholarly.*
Published by: Paulo Freire Verlag, Unterm Berg 65a, Oldenburg, 26123, Germany. TEL 49-441-381674, FAX 49-441-9330056, pfv@freire.de, http://www.paulo-freire-verlag.de.

361 CAN ISSN 0047-1321
HV2I57
INTERVENTION. Text in English, French. 1969. 3/yr. CAD 30 domestic to individuals; CAD 35 foreign to individuals; CAD 40 domestic to institutions; CAD 45 foreign to institutions. adv. bk.rev. bibl. **Description:** Provides opportunities for members of the corporation to publish and share the results of their research and professional experience. Stimulates new ideas and serves as a source of information and continuing education.
Related titles: Audio cassette/tape ed.
Indexed: PdeR.
Published by: Ordre Professionnelle des Travailleurs Sociaux du Quebec/Professional Order of Social Workers of Quebec, 255 boul Cremazie Est, Bureau 520, Montreal, PQ H2M 1M2, Canada. TEL 514-731-3925, FAX 514-731-6785. Ed. Josee Louise Jette. Circ: 2,000.

362 GBR ISSN 1571-8883
HV689
➤ **INTERVENTION**; international journal of mental health, psychosocial work and counselling in areas of armed conflict. Text in English. 2003. 3/yr. USD 137 domestic to institutions; USD 170 foreign to institutions (effective 2011). adv. back issues avail.; reprints avail. **Document type:** *Journal, Academic/Scholarly.* **Description:** Covers significant articles on mental health, psychosocial work and counseling in areas of armed conflict.
Related titles: Online - full text ed.: ISSN 1872-1001.
Indexed: A01, CA, P03, P30, PsycInfo, PsycholAb, T02.
—BLDSC (4557.471640), IE, Ingenta. **CCC.**
Published by: (War Trauma Foundation NLD), Lippincott Williams & Wilkins, Ltd., 250 Waterloo Rd, London, SE1 8RD, United Kingdom. TEL 44-20-79810600, FAX 44-20-79810601, customerservice@lww.com, http://www.lww.com. Ed. Peter Ventevogel. Pub. Phil Daly.

352.73 CAN ISSN 1489-761X
CA2PQABAI56
INVENTAIRE DES PROGRAMMES D'AIDE FINANCIERE AUX INDIVIDUS, ENTREPRISES ET ORGANISMES. Text in French. 1997. a. **Document type:** *Journal, Trade.*
Related titles: English ed.: List of Financial Aid Programs for Individuals, Firms and Organizations. ISSN 1489-7628.
—CCC.
Published by: Quebec. Secretariat aux Affaires Autochtones, 905 avenue Honore-Mercier, Etage 1, Quebec, PQ G1R 5M6, Canada. TEL 418-643-3166, FAX 418-646-4918, http://www.saa.gouv.qc.ca.

INVENTORY OF HEALTH WORKFORCE IN ALBERTA. *see* PUBLIC HEALTH AND SAFETY

360 DEU ISSN 1865-455X
IPUNKT; Mitteilungsblatt der Unfallkasse Sachsen. Text in German. 1992. 2/yr. EUR 19; EUR 6 newsstand/cover (effective 2004). **Document type:** *Magazine, Trade.*
Formerly (until 2004): Aktuell Informiert (1435-8034)
Published by: (Unfallkasse Sachsen), Satztechnik Meissen GmbH, Am Sand 1c, Nieschuetz, 01665, Germany. TEL 49-3525-71860, FAX 49-3525-718612, info@satztechnik-meissen.de, http://www.satztechnik-meissen.de. Ed. Karsten Janz. Circ: 6,100 (paid).

362.509417 IRL ISSN 1649-6388
IRELAND. CENTRAL STATISTICS OFFICE. EUROPEAN UNION SURVEY ON INCOME AND LIVING CONDITIONS. Text in English. 2003. a.

Published by: Ireland. Central Statistics Office/Eire, An Phriomh-Oifig Staidrimh, Skehard Rd, Cork, Ireland. TEL 353-21-4535000, FAX 353-21-4535555, information@cso.ie.

360 IRL
IRELAND. DEPARTMENT OF SOCIAL WELFARE. STATISTICAL INFORMATION ON SOCIAL WELFARE SERVICES. Text in English. 1983. a. **Document type:** *Government.*
Published by: Department of Social Welfare, Statistics Unit, Store St., 4th Fl., Dublin, 1, Ireland. TEL 353-1-7043000. Circ: 1,300 (controlled).

IRYO TO FUKUSHI/JAPANESE JOURNAL OF MEDICAL SOCIAL WORK. *see* MEDICAL SCIENCES

ISSUES IN CHILD ABUSE ACCUSATIONS (ONLINE). *see* CHILDREN AND YOUTH—About

J A C S VOLUNTEER. *see* OCCUPATIONS AND CAREERS

360 JPN
J A N P O R A NEWSLETTER. (Japan Nonprofit Organization Research Association) Text in Japanese. 1999. q. **Document type:** *Newsletter, Academic/Scholarly.*
Published by: Nihon N P O Gakkai/Japan Nonprofit Organization Research Association, c/o Secretariat: Osaka School of International Public Policy, Osaka University1-31, Machikaneyama-cho, Toyonaka-City, Osaka 560-0043, Japan. janpora@ml.osipp.osaka-u.ac.jp, http://www.osipp.osaka-u.ac.jp/janpora/.

361 DEU
J O. (Junge Ortskrankenkasse) Text in German. 1974. bi-m. adv. **Document type:** *Magazine, Consumer.*
Published by: (AOK-Bundesverband), W D V Gesellschaft fuer Medien & Kommunikation mbH & Co. OHG, Siemensstr 6, Bad Homburg, 61352, Germany. TEL 49-6172-6700, FAX 49-6172-670144, info@wdv.de, http://www.wdv.de. adv.: page EUR 16,000; trim 190 x 260. Circ: 1,219,737 (controlled).

360 DEU ISSN 1615-7737
KK3270.5.A63
JAHRBUCH DES SOZIALRECHTS; Gesetzgebung - Verwaltung - Rechtsprechung - Literatur. Text in German. 1963. a. EUR 149 (effective 2011). back issues avail.; reprints avail. **Document type:** *Journal, Academic/Scholarly.*
Former titles (until 1999): Jahrbuch des Sozialrechts der Gegenwart (0173-6515); (until 1979): Sozialordnung der Gegenwart (0561-290X)
Published by: Erich Schmidt Verlag GmbH & Co. (Berlin), Genthiner Str 30 G, Berlin, 10785, Germany. TEL 49-30-2500850, FAX 49-30-250085305, esv@esvmedien.de, http://www.esv.info.

JAHRBUCH KRITISCHE MEDIZIN. *see* MEDICAL SCIENCES

JANUS. *see* BUSINESS AND ECONOMICS—Labor And Industrial Relations

362.5 AUS
JESUIT SOCIAL SERVICES NEWS. Text in English. 1995. q. free (effective 2009). back issues avail. **Document type:** *Newsletter, Consumer.* **Description:** Contains news about programs and services supporting the marginalized in local society.
Formerly (until 2007): Jesuit Social Services Newsletter
Related titles: Online - full text ed.
Published by: Jesuit Social Services Ltd., 371 Church St, PO Box 271, Richmond, VIC 3121, Australia. TEL 61-3-94277388, FAX 61-3-94271819, jss@jss.org.au.

JEUGD EN CO KENNIS. *see* CHILDREN AND YOUTH—About

360 DEU ISSN 1435-2230
DIE JOHANNITER. Text in German. 1987. 4/yr. adv. 32 p./no.; **Document type:** *Journal, Consumer.*
Published by: Johanniter-Unfall-Hilfe e.V., Luetzowstr 94, Berlin, 10785, Germany. TEL 49-30-269970, FAX 49-30-26997444, info@juh.de. Ed. Bernhard Schneidewind. adv.: B&W page EUR 12,500, color page EUR 14,000. Circ: 1,342,589 (controlled).

JONQUIL. *see* CLUBS

JORNAL BRASILEIRO DE PREVENCAO E TRATAMENTO DAS OFENSAS SEXUAIS. *see* LAW—Family And Matrimonial Law

JOURNAL DE LA SANTE AUTOCHTONE. *see* NATIVE AMERICAN STUDIES

361 FRA ISSN 1272-5137
JOURNAL DES ORPHELINS DE GUERRE. Text in French. 1930. bi-m.
Formerly (until 1944): Le Fils des Tues (1272-5129)
Related titles: Online - full text ed.
Published by: Federation Nationale des Fils et Filles des Morts pour la France, 27 Rue de l'Arcade, Paris, 75008, France. TEL 33-1-42653583, FAX 33-1-47423096, fed.filsdestues@wanadoo.fr, http://www.orphelins-de-guerre.fr.

JOURNAL OF ABORIGINAL HEALTH. *see* NATIVE AMERICAN STUDIES

JOURNAL OF ADDICTIONS & OFFENDER COUNSELING. *see* PSYCHOLOGY

THE JOURNAL OF ADULT PROTECTION; evidence-based practice in relation to safeguarding adults. *see* LAW

362.4 USA ISSN 0047-2220
HD7255 CODEN: JRCOD3
JOURNAL OF APPLIED REHABILITATION COUNSELING. Abbreviated title: J A R C. Text in English. 1970. q. USD 100 domestic to non-members; USD 125 foreign to non-members; USD 20 per issue to non-members; free to members (effective 2011). bk.rev. reprints avail. **Document type:** *Journal, Academic/Scholarly.* **Description:** Covers opinion and research in professional rehabilitation counseling and addresses the needs of individuals employed in a wide variety of work settings and with wide-ranging professional interests.
Related titles: Microfilm ed.: (from PQC); Online - full text ed.
Indexed: A22, AMED, CJPI, Chicano, E-psyche, ECER, P03, P24, P25, P27, P46, P48, P50, P54, PQC, PsycInfo, PsycholAb, RehabLit, S02, S03.
—BLDSC (4947.030000), GNLM, IE, Ingenta.
Published by: National Rehabilitation Counseling Association, PO Box 4480, Manassas, VA 20108. TEL 703-361-2077, FAX 703-361-2489, info@nrca-net.org. Ed. Jamie Satcher.

370 USA ISSN 1098-1608
LC143
JOURNAL OF AT-RISK ISSUES. Text in English. 1994. q. USD 25; USD 15 per issue (effective 2005). **Document type:** *Journal, Consumer.*
Indexed: BRD, CA, E02, E03, ERI, EdA, EdI, T02, W03, W05.
—BLDSC (4947.600000).
Published by: National Dropout Prevention Network, Clemson University, 209 Martin St, Clemson, SC 29631-1555. TEL 864-656-2599, FAX 864-656-0136, ndpc@clemson.edu. Eds. Connie Rhul-Smith, James Smith.

360 USA ISSN 1084-7219
HV11
➤ **JOURNAL OF BACCALAUREATE SOCIAL WORK.** Abbreviated title: J B S W. Text in English. 1995. s-a. USD 90 domestic institution, libraries; USD 105 foreign institution, libraries (effective 2009). adv. back issues avail. **Document type:** *Journal, Academic/Scholarly.* **Description:** Emphasizes the contributions of the baccalaureate community in promoting the continuing development and excellence of baccalaureate social work education and practice.
Related titles: Online - full text ed.
Indexed: BRD, CA, FamI, P03, PsycInfo, S02, S03, SCOPUS, SSAI, SSAb, SSI, SWR&A, T02, W03, W05.
—BLDSC (4950.700000), Ingenta. **CCC.**
Published by: (Association of Baccalaureate Social Work Program Directors), Lyceum Books, Inc., 341 N Charlotte St, Lombard, IL 60148. TEL 630-620-7132, FAX 630-620-7522, lyceum@lyceumbooks.com, http://www.lyceumbooks.com. Ed. Needha Boutte-Queen. Pub. David C Follmer TEL 773-643-1902. adv.: page USD 500; 4.5 x 7.

➤ **JOURNAL OF BEHAVIORAL HEALTH SERVICES AND RESEARCH.** *see* PUBLIC HEALTH AND SAFETY

➤ **JOURNAL OF CHILD AND YOUTH CARE WORK.** *see* CHILDREN AND YOUTH—About

➤ **JOURNAL OF CHILD CUSTODY**; research, issues & practices. *see* CHILDREN AND YOUTH—About

362.76 USA ISSN 1053-8712
HV6570 CODEN: JCABEK
➤ **JOURNAL OF CHILD SEXUAL ABUSE**; research, treatment & program innovations for victims, survivors & offenders. Abbreviated title: J C S A. Text in English. 1992. bi-m. GBP 516 combined subscription in United Kingdom to institutions (print & online eds.); EUR 668, USD 678 combined subscription to institutions (print & online eds.) (effective 2012). adv. bk.rev. 120 p./no. 1 cols./p.; back issues avail.; reprint service avail. from PSC. **Document type:** *Journal, Academic/Scholarly.* **Description:** Covers research issues, clinical issues, case studies and brief reports on young victims, adult survivors and the offenders.
Related titles: Microfiche ed.: (from PQC); Microform ed.; Online - full text ed.: ISSN 1547-0679. GBP 464 in United Kingdom to institutions; EUR 601, USD 610 to institutions (effective 2012).
Indexed: A01, A02, A03, A08, A22, ASSIA, AbAn, B21, C06, C07, C08, C22, C28, CA, CDA, CINAHL, CJA, CJPI, CPE, CurCont, DIP, DNP, E-psyche, E01, E03, ECER, EMBASE, ERI, ESPM, ExcerpMed, F09, FamI, G10, GSS&RPL, H&SSA, H13, IBR, IBZ, IPARL, M02, MEDLINE, P02, P03, P10, P18, P20, P24, P25, P30, P46, P48, P53, P54, P55, PQC, PRA, PsycInfo, PsycholAb, R10, Reac, RiskAb, S02, S03, SCOPUS, SFSA, SOPODA, SSA, SSCI, SWR&A, SociolAb, T02, V&AA, W07, W09.
—BLDSC (4957.905000), GNLM, IE, Infotrieve, Ingenta. **CCC.**
Published by: Routledge (Subsidiary of: Taylor & Francis Group), 325 Chestnut St, Ste 800, Philadelphia, PA 19106. TEL 215-625-8900, 800-354-1420, FAX 215-625-8914, journals@routledge.com, http://www.routledge.com. Ed. Dr. Robert A Geffner. adv.: B&W page USD 315, color page USD 550; trim 4.375 x 7.125. Circ: 844 (paid).

360 GBR ISSN 1079-6126
HV699
➤ **JOURNAL OF CHILDREN & POVERTY.** Text in English. 1995. s-a. GBP 232 combined subscription in United Kingdom to institutions (print & online eds.); EUR 308, USD 385 combined subscription to institutions (print & online eds.) (effective 2012). adv. back issues avail.; reprint service avail. from PSC. **Document type:** *Journal, Academic/Scholarly.* **Description:** Provides articles on issues concerning children and families in poverty.
Related titles: Online - full text ed.: ISSN 1469-9389. GBP 209 in United Kingdom to institutions; EUR 277, USD 346 to institutions (effective 2012) (from IngentaConnect).
Indexed: A01, A03, A08, A22, CA, E01, ESPM, FamI, IBSS, P34, P42, PAIS, PSA, RiskAb, S02, S03, SCOPUS, SSA, SSciA, SociolAb, T02.
—BLDSC (4957.916000), IE, Infotrieve, Ingenta. **CCC.**
Published by: (Institute for Children and Poverty USA), Routledge (Subsidiary of: Taylor & Francis Group), 4 Park Sq, Milton Park, Abingdon, Oxon OX14 4RN, United Kingdom. TEL 44-20-70176000, FAX 44-20-70176336, subscriptions@tandf.co.uk, http://www.routledge.com. Adv. contact Linda Hann TEL 44-1344-779945. **Subscr. in N. America to:** Taylor & Francis Inc., Customer Services Dept, 325 Chestnut St, 8th Fl, Philadelphia, PA 19106. TEL 215-625-8900, 800-354-1420, FAX 215-625-2940, customerservice@taylorandfrancis.com; **Subscr. to:** Taylor & Francis Ltd., Journals Customer Service, Sheepen Pl, Colchester, Essex CO3 3LP, United Kingdom. TEL 44-20-70175544, FAX 44-20-70175198.

362.705 GBR ISSN 1746-6660
➤ **JOURNAL OF CHILDREN'S SERVICES**; research informing policy and practice. Text in English. 2006. q. EUR 689 combined subscription in Europe (print & online eds.); USD 889 combined subscription in the Americas (print & online eds.); GBP 529 combined subscription in the UK & elsewhere (print & online eds.); AUD 999 combined subscription in Australasia (print & online eds.) (effective 2012). adv. bk.rev. back issues avail. **Document type:** *Journal, Academic/Scholarly.* **Description:** Designed to encourage the development of research-based, outcome-focused services to better safeguard and promote the well-being of vulnerable children and their families.
Related titles: Online - full text ed.: ISSN 2042-8677.
Indexed: B28, CA, S02, S03, T02.
—BLDSC (4957.970000), IE. **CCC.**
Published by: (Dartington Social Research Unit), Pier Professional Ltd. (Subsidiary of: Emerald Group Publishing Ltd.), Ste N4, The Old Market, Upper Market St, Hove, BN3 1AS, United Kingdom. TEL 44-1273-783720, FAX 44-1273-783723, info@pierprofessional.com. Eds. Michael Little, Nick Axford. Adv. contact Paul Somerville TEL 44-1273-783724. B&W page GBP 350; 160 x 245.

360 USA ISSN 1070-5422
HN1 CODEN: JOPREN
➤ **JOURNAL OF COMMUNITY PRACTICE**; organizing, planning, development & change. Text in English. 1994. q. GBP 378 combined subscription in United Kingdom to institutions (print & online eds.); EUR 490, USD 497 combined subscription to institutions (print & online eds.) (effective 2012). adv. back issues avail.; reprint service avail. from PSC. **Document type:** *Journal, Academic/Scholarly.* **Description:** Discusses the development, debate and exchange of ideas on community practice in research, theory development, intervention models, curriculum development, and teaching.
Related titles: Microform ed.: (from PQC); Online - full text ed.: ISSN 1543-3706. GBP 340 in United Kingdom to institutions; EUR 441, USD 447 to institutions (effective 2012).
Indexed: A01, A03, A22, AltPI, C06, C07, C08, CA, CINAHL, DIP, E01, ESPM, FamI, GSS&RPL, I13, IBR, IBZ, IPARL, M02, ORMS, P30, P34, P42, PAIS, S02, S03, SCOPUS, SOPODA, SSA, SSciA, SWR&A, SociolAb, T02, TRA.
—BLDSC (4961.745000), IE, Ingenta. **CCC.**
Published by: (Association for Community Organization and Social Administration), Routledge (Subsidiary of: Taylor & Francis Group), 325 Chestnut St, Ste 800, Philadelphia, PA 19106. TEL 800-354-1420, FAX 215-625-2940, journals@routledge.com, http://www.routledge.com. Eds. Louise Simmons, Tracy M Soska.

361 GBR ISSN 1748-6831
HV1
➤ **JOURNAL OF COMPARATIVE SOCIAL WELFARE.** Text in English. 1984. 3/yr. GBP 268 combined subscription in United Kingdom to institutions (print & online eds.); EUR 352, USD 440 combined subscription to institutions (print & online eds.) (effective 2012). adv. back issues avail.; reprint service avail. from PSC. **Document type:** *Journal, Academic/Scholarly.* **Description:** Seeks to promote interdisciplinary discourse and analysis with emphasis on internationalism as a bioglobal movement of peace, social justice and equality.
Former titles (until 2006): New Global Development (1080-9716); (until 1995): Journal of International and Comparative Social Welfare (0898-5847)
Related titles: Online - full text ed.: ISSN 1748-684X. GBP 241 in United Kingdom to institutions; EUR 316, USD 396 to institutions (effective 2012).
Indexed: A22, CA, E01, IBSS, P34, P42, PSA, S02, S03, SCOPUS, SSA, SWR&A, SociolAb, T02.
—BLDSC (4963.330000), IE, Ingenta. **CCC.**
Published by: Routledge (Subsidiary of: Taylor & Francis Group), 4 Park Sq, Milton Park, Abingdon, Oxon OX14 4RN, United Kingdom. TEL 44-20-70176000, FAX 44-20-70176336, subscriptions@tandf.co.uk, http://www.routledge.com. Eds. Mark Drakeford, Brij Mohan. Adv. contact Linda Hann TEL 44-1344-779945. **Subscr. to:** Taylor & Francis Ltd., Journals Customer Service, Sheepen Pl, Colchester, Essex CO3 3LP, United Kingdom. TEL 44-20-70175544, FAX 44-20-70175198.

360 GBR ISSN 1471-7646
CODEN: CNGEEP
➤ **JOURNAL OF CRITICAL PSYCHOLOGY, COUNSELLING, AND PSYCHOTHERAPY.** Abbreviated title: J C P C P. Text in English. 19??. q. GBP 35 domestic to individuals; GBP 40 in Europe to individuals; GBP 45 elsewhere to individuals; GBP 135 domestic to institutions; GBP 145 in Europe to institutions; GBP 150 elsewhere to institutions (effective 2009); 30. bk.rev. back issues avail.; reprints avail. **Document type:** *Journal, Academic/Scholarly.* **Description:** Provides a forum for ideas, experiences, and views of people working in psychology, nursing, education, medicine, and social work.
Former titles (until 2001): Psychology and Psychotherapy Association. Changes (0263-8371); (until 1982): Psychology and Psychotherapy Association. New Forum (0143-4942); (until 1978): Psychology and Psychotherapy Association. Forum
Indexed: A22, ASSIA, P30, PhilInd.
—BLDSC (4965.641000), GNLM, IE, Infotrieve, Ingenta. **CCC.**
Published by: (Psychology and Psychotherapy Association), P C C S Books Ltd., 2 Cropper Row, Alton Rd, Ross-on-Wye, HR9 5LA, United Kingdom. TEL 44-1989-763900, FAX 44-1989-763901, contact@pccs-books.co.uk. Ed. Craig Newnes.

621 623.26 USA ISSN 2154-1469
JOURNAL OF E R W AND MINE ACTION. Text in English. 1999. 3/yr. free (effective 2005). **Document type:** *Journal, Academic/Scholarly.* **Description:** Covers landmine-related issues and topics.
Formerly (until 2010): Journal of Mine Action (1533-9440)
Related titles: Online - full content ed.: ISSN 2154-1485.
Published by: James Mason University, Mine Action Information Center, MSC 8504, Harrisonburg, VA 22807. TEL 540-568-2756, FAX 540-568-8176. Ed. Lois Carter Fay.

361.61 AUS ISSN 1325-2224
➤ **JOURNAL OF ECONOMIC & SOCIAL POLICY.** Abbreviated title: J E S P. Text in English. 1995. s-a. AUD 44 to institutions (effective 2009). adv. bk.rev. **Document type:** *Journal, Academic/Scholarly.* **Description:** provides a forum for debate on matters of public policy with articles written in a style that will cater to a diverse readership.
Related titles: Online - full text ed.: free (effective 2011).
Indexed: A11, AusPAIS, EconLit, JEL.
—BLDSC (4972.609000).
Published by: (Coffs Harbour School of Business), Southern Cross University, Centre for Policy Research, PO Box 157, Lismore, NSW 2480, Australia. TEL 61-2-66203000, FAX 61-2-66221300. Eds. Alex Millmow, Jeremy Buultjens, Malcolm Cook. Circ: 130 (controlled).

361.3 USA ISSN 1531-3204
HV3176 CODEN: JMSWE5
➤ **JOURNAL OF ETHNIC & CULTURAL DIVERSITY IN SOCIAL WORK**; innovations in theory, research & practice. Abbreviated title: E C D S W. Text in English. 1991. q. GBP 427 combined subscription in United Kingdom to institutions (print & online eds.); EUR 554, USD 562 combined subscription to institutions (print & online eds.) (effective 2012). adv. bk.rev. illus. 120 p./no. 1 cols./p.; back issues avail.; reprint service avail. from PSC. **Document type:** *Journal, Academic/Scholarly.* **Description:** Develops knowledge and promotes understanding of the impact of culture, ethnicity, race, and class on the individual, group, organization, and community on the delivery of human services.
Formerly (until 2000): Journal of Multicultural Social Work (1042-8224)

S

Related titles: Microform ed.: (from PQC); Online - full text ed.: ISSN 1531-3212. GBP 385 in United Kingdom to institutions; EUR 499, USD 505 to institutions (effective 2012).
Indexed: A01, A02, A03, A08, A10, A22, A26, B04, B21, BRD, BRI, C06, C07, C08, CA, CBRI, CINAHL, CJPI, CMM, ChPerl, Chicano, DIP, E01, E02, E03, E07, E08, E17, ERI, ERIC, ESPM, EdA, EdI, FamI, G08, H12, I05, IBR, IBZ, IIBP, IPARL, L01, L02, M02, P03, P30, PQC, PerIslam, PsycInfo, PsycholAb, RefZh, S02, S03, S09, S21, SCOPUS, SOPODA, SSA, SSAI, SSAb, SSI, SSciA, SWR&A, SociolAb, T02, V03, W03.
—BLDSC (4979.600500), IE, Ingenta. **CCC.**
Published by: Routledge (Subsidiary of: Taylor & Francis Group), 325 Chestnut St, Ste 800, Philadelphia, PA 19106. TEL 215-625-8900, 800-354-1420, FAX 215-625-8914, journals@routledge.com, http://www.routledge.com. Ed. Dr. Mo Yee Lee. adv.: B&W page USD 315, color page USD 550; trim 4.375 x 7.125. Circ: 563 (paid).

360 USA ISSN 1543-3714
HV40
➤ **JOURNAL OF EVIDENCE-BASED SOCIAL WORK**; advances in practice, programming, research, and policy. Text in English. 2004 (Spr.). q. GBP 600 combined subscription in United Kingdom to institutions (print & online eds.); EUR 778, USD 784 combined subscription to institutions (print & online eds.) (effective 2012). reprint service avail. from PSC. **Document type:** *Journal, Academic/Scholarly.* **Description:** Examines the use of evidence-based practice in everyday care, identifying and evaluating cutting-edge theory, techniques, and strategies.
Related titles: Online - full text ed.: ISSN 1543-3722. 2004 (Spr.). GBP 540 in United Kingdom to institutions; EUR 700, USD 706 to institutions (effective 2012).
Indexed: A01, A03, A10, A22, C06, C07, C08, CA, CINAHL, CJA, E01, E03, EMBASE, ERI, ExcerpMed, FamI, IBR, IBZ, MEDLINE, P30, P34, S02, S03, S21, SCOPUS, SSA, SWR&A, SociolAb, T02, V03.
—BLDSC (4979.641450), IE, Ingenta. **CCC.**
Published by: Routledge (Subsidiary of: Taylor & Francis Group), 325 Chestnut St, Ste 800, Philadelphia, PA 19106. TEL 215-625-8900, 800-354-1420, FAX 215-625-8914, journals@routledge.com, http://www.routledge.com. Eds. Dr. John S Wodarski, Dr. Marvin D Feit.

361.3 USA ISSN 1052-2158
HV697 CODEN: JFSWEO
➤ **JOURNAL OF FAMILY SOCIAL WORK.** Abbreviated title: J F S W. Text in English. 1981. q. GBP 294 combined subscription in United Kingdom to institutions (print & online eds.); EUR 384, USD 394 combined subscription to institutions (print & online eds.) (effective 2012). adv. bk.rev. 120 p./no. 1 cols./p.; back issues avail.; reprint service avail. from PSC. **Document type:** *Journal, Academic/Scholarly.* **Description:** Serves as a forum for family practitioners, scholars and educators in social work concerning sexual and marital counseling.
Formerly (until 1995): Journal of Social Work and Human Sexuality (0276-3850)
Related titles: Microfiche ed.: (from PQC); Microform ed.; Online - full text ed.: ISSN 1540-4072. 2002. GBP 265 in United Kingdom to institutions; EUR 345, USD 355 to institutions (effective 2012).
Indexed: A01, A03, A10, A22, AC&P, ASSIA, AbAn, BehAb, C06, C07, C08, CA, CDA, CINAHL, CPLI, DIP, E01, E03, ERI, ESPM, FamI, IBR, IBZ, IPARL, M02, P30, PC&CA, PerIslam, PsycholAb, RefZh, RiskAb, S02, S03, SCOPUS, SFSA, SOPODA, SSA, SWR&A, SociolAb, T02, V&AA, V03.
—BLDSC (4983.737000), GNLM, IE, Infotrieve, Ingenta, INIST. **CCC.**
Published by: Routledge (Subsidiary of: Taylor & Francis Group), 325 Chestnut St, Ste 800, Philadelphia, PA 19106. TEL 215-625-8900, 800-354-1420, FAX 215-625-8914, journals@routledge.com, http://www.routledge.com. Ed. Pat Conway. adv.: B&W page USD 300, color page USD 525; trim 4.375 x 7.125. Circ: 408 (paid).

➤ **JOURNAL OF GAY & LESBIAN MENTAL HEALTH.** *see* PSYCHOLOGY

306.766 USA ISSN 1053-8720
HV1449 CODEN: JGLSEI
➤ **JOURNAL OF GAY & LESBIAN SOCIAL SERVICES**; the quarterly journal of community & clinical practice. Abbreviated title: J G L S S. Text in English. 1994. q. (in 1 vol.). GBP 218 combined subscription in United Kingdom to institutions (print & online eds.); EUR 283, USD 301 combined subscription to institutions (print & online eds.) (effective 2012). adv. illus. 120 p./no.; back issues avail.; reprint service avail. from PSC. **Document type:** *Journal, Academic/Scholarly.* **Description:** Focuses on policy, program and practice issues aiming to promote the well-being of homosexuals and bisexuals in contemporary society.
Related titles: Microform ed.: (from PQC); Online - full text ed.: ISSN 1540-4056. GBP 197 in United Kingdom to institutions; EUR 255, USD 270 to institutions (effective 2012).
Indexed: A01, A03, A22, AgeL, CA, CJA, CWI, DIP, DNP, E01, E03, ERI, FamI, GW, IBR, IBZ, IPARL, L01, L02, P03, P30, P34, P48, PAIS, PQC, PsycInfo, PsycholAb, S02, S03, SCOPUS, SOPODA, SSA, SWR&A, SociolAb, T02, V&AA.
—BLDSC (4987.643000), IE, Ingenta. **CCC.**
Published by: Routledge (Subsidiary of: Taylor & Francis Group), 325 Chestnut St, Ste 800, Philadelphia, PA 19106. TEL 215-625-8900, 800-354-1420, FAX 215-625-8914, journals@routledge.com, http://www.routledge.com. Ed. Dr. Michael Sullivan. adv.: B&W page USD 315, color page USD 550; trim 4.375 x 7.125. Circ: 280 (paid).

361.73 USA ISSN 1096-5297
HV41.9.U6
THE JOURNAL OF GIFT PLANNING. Text in English. 1997. q. USD 45 to individuals; free to members (effective 2005). adv. **Document type:** *Magazine, Consumer.*
Related titles: Online - full text ed.: ISSN 1556-0783 (from IngentaConnect).
—Ingenta.
Published by: National Committee on Planned Giving, 233 McCrea St Ste 400, Indianapolis, IN 46225. TEL 317-269-6274, FAX 317-269-6276, ncpg@ncpg.org, http://www.ncpg.org/. Adv. contact Gloria Kermeen.

361.3 USA ISSN 1944-6039
HV1
➤ **JOURNAL OF GLOBAL SOCIAL WORK PRACTICE.** Variant title: J G S W P. Text in English. 2008. s-a. free (effective 2011). **Document type:** *Journal, Academic/Scholarly.* **Description:** Dedicated to all aspects of developing international social work practice, including practice methods, skills building, theoretical framework development and professional tactics and techniques.
Media: Online - full text.
Published by: Dominican University, Graduate School of Social Work, 7200 W Division St, River Forest, IL 60305. TEL 708-366-3463, FAX 708-366-3446, msw@dom.edu, http://www.dom.edu/academics/gssw/index.html. Ed. Jan A Rodgers.

➤ **JOURNAL OF HEALTH CARE FOR THE POOR AND UNDERSERVED.** *see* MEDICAL SCIENCES

362.1 USA ISSN 1538-1501
RA643.75
➤ **JOURNAL OF HIV - AIDS & SOCIAL SERVICES.** Text in English. 2002. q. GBP 373 combined subscription in United Kingdom to institutions (print & online eds.); EUR 485, USD 491 combined subscription to institutions (print & online eds.) (effective 2012). adv. reprint service avail. from PSC. **Document type:** *Journal, Academic/Scholarly.* **Description:** Provides a forum in which social workers and other professionals in the field of HIV/AIDS work can access the latest research and techniques in order to provide effective social, educational, and clinical services to all individuals affected by HIV/AIDS.
Related titles: Online - full text ed.: ISSN 1538-151X. GBP 336 in United Kingdom to institutions; EUR 436, USD 442 to institutions (effective 2012).
Indexed: A01, A03, A22, A36, AMED, B21, BiolDig, C06, C07, C08, CA, CABA, CINAHL, DIP, E-psyche, E01, E03, E12, ERI, ESPM, FamI, GEOBASE, GH, H&SSA, H05, IBR, IBZ, L01, L02, P03, P30, P34, PAIS, PsycInfo, R12, RefZh, S02, S03, SCOPUS, SSA, SWR&A, T02, T05, VirolAbstr, W11.
—BLDSC (5002.430000), IE, Ingenta. **CCC.**
Published by: (National Social Work AIDS Network), Routledge (Subsidiary of: Taylor & Francis Group), 325 Chestnut St, Ste 800, Philadelphia, PA 19106. TEL 215-625-8900, 800-354-1420, FAX 215-625-8914, journals@routledge.com, http://www.routledge.com. Eds. Dr. Dorie J Gilbert, Dr. Nathan L Linsk. adv.: B&W page USD 375, color page USD 650; trim 4.375 x 7.125. Circ: 56 (paid).

360 USA ISSN 1091-1359
HM251 CODEN: JHBEF2
➤ **JOURNAL OF HUMAN BEHAVIOR IN THE SOCIAL ENVIRONMENT.** Text in English. 1998. 8/yr. GBP 569 combined subscription in United Kingdom to institutions (print & online eds.); EUR 737, USD 753 combined subscription to institutions (print & online eds.) (effective 2012). adv. back issues avail.; reprint service avail. from PSC. **Document type:** *Journal, Academic/Scholarly.* **Description:** Helps social workers grasp developing issues in human behavior.
Related titles: Microform ed.; Online - full text ed.: ISSN 1540-3556. 2002 (June). GBP 512 in United Kingdom to institutions; EUR 664, USD 678 to institutions (effective 2012).
Indexed: A01, A03, A22, AmHI, B21, C06, C07, C08, CA, CINAHL, CJA, CJPI, DIP, E-psyche, E01, E03, ERI, ESPM, FR, FamI, H&SSA, H07, HPNRM, IBR, IBZ, L01, L02, P03, P30, P34, PQC, PsycInfo, PsycholAb, RefZh, RiskAb, S02, S03, SCOPUS, SOPODA, SSA, SSciA, SWR&A, SociolAb, T02.
—BLDSC (5003.413400), IE, Infotrieve, Ingenta, INIST. **CCC.**
Published by: Routledge (Subsidiary of: Taylor & Francis Group), 270 Madison Ave, New York, NY 10016. TEL 212-216-7800, FAX 212-244-1563, journals@routledge.com, http://www.routledge.com. Eds. Dr. John S Wodarski, Dr. Marvin D Feit.

363.3 GBR ISSN 2042-6747
▼ ➤ **JOURNAL OF HUMANITARIAN LOGISTICS AND SUPPLY CHAIN MANAGEMENT.** Text in English. forthcoming 2011 (May). 2/yr. EUR 369 combined subscription in Europe (print & online eds.); USD 539 combined subscription in the Americas (print & online eds.); GBP 319 combined subscription in the UK & elsewhere (print & online eds.); AUD 579 combined subscription in Australasia (print & online eds.) (effective 2012). **Document type:** *Journal, Academic/Scholarly.* **Description:** Contains research on all aspects of humanitarian logistics and supply chain management.
—**CCC.**
Published by: Emerald Group Publishing Ltd., Howard House, Wagon Ln, Bingley, W Yorks BD16 1WA, United Kingdom. TEL 44-1274-777700, FAX 44-1274-785201, information@emeraldinsight.com. Eds. Gyongyi Kovacs, Karen Spens.

➤ **JOURNAL OF HUNGER AND ENVIRONMENTAL NUTRITION.** *see* NUTRITION AND DIETETICS

➤ **JOURNAL OF IMMIGRANT & REFUGEE STUDIES.** *see* POLITICAL SCIENCE—International Relations

360 305.897 USA ISSN 2150-2684
▼ ➤ **JOURNAL OF INDIGENOUS VOICES IN SOCIAL WORK.** Text in English. 2010 (Jan.). a. free (effective 2010). **Document type:** *Journal, Academic/Scholarly.* **Description:** Features scholarly work on social services and indigenous communities.
Media: Online - full content.
Published by: University of Hawaii, Myron B. Thompson School of Social Work, Henke Hall, 1800 East West Rd, Honolulu, HI 96822. TEL 808-956-6242, mturney@hawaii.edu, http://www.hawaii.edu/sswork/index.html.

364.4 610 IRN ISSN 2008-2053
➤ **JOURNAL OF INJURY AND VIOLENCE RESEARCH.** Text in English. 2008. q. **Document type:** *Journal, Academic/Scholarly.*
Related titles: Online - full text ed.: ISSN 2008-4072. free (effective 2011).
Indexed: P02, P10, P30, P48, P53, P54, PQC, S02, S03.
Published by: Kermanshah University of Medical Sciences/Danishgah-i Ulum-i Pizishki-i Kirmanshah, Shahid Beheshti Blvd., Kirmanshah, 67144, Iran. http://www.kums.ac.ir/home-en.html. Ed. Mahmoudreza Moradi.

360 GBR ISSN 1476-9018
JOURNAL OF INTEGRATED CARE; practical evidence for service development. Text in English. 1993. bi-m. EUR 689 combined subscription in Europe (print & online eds.); USD 889 combined subscription in the Americas (print & online eds.); GBP 529 combined subscription in the UK & elsewhere (print & online eds.); AUD 999 combined subscription in Australasia (print & online eds.) (effective 2012). adv. back issues avail. **Document type:** *Journal, Academic/Scholarly.* **Description:** Aims to keep all managers and practitioners up-to-date with developments in community care.
Former titles (until 2003): M C C (1477-5190); (until 2002): Managing Community Care (1461-5436); (until 1998): Community Care Management and Planning (0968-9249)
Related titles: Online - full text ed.: ISSN 2042-8685.
Indexed: AMED, B28, C06, C07, C08, CINAHL, E-psyche, P19, P24, P48, PQC, S02, S03, SWR&A.
—BLDSC (5007.538280), IE, Ingenta. **CCC.**
Published by: (Research in Practice for Adults), Pier Professional Ltd. (Subsidiary of: Emerald Group Publishing Ltd.), Ste N4, The Old Market, Upper Market St, Hove, BN3 1AS, United Kingdom. TEL 44-1273-783720, FAX 44-1273-783723, info@pierprofessional.com. Ed. Peter Thistlethwaite. Adv. contact Paul Somerville TEL 44-1273-783724. B&W page GBP 350; 160 x 245.

JOURNAL OF INTELLECTUAL DISABILITY RESEARCH. *see* MEDICAL SCIENCES—Psychiatry And Neurology

JOURNAL OF MARITAL AND FAMILY THERAPY. *see* PSYCHOLOGY

JOURNAL OF NEPHROLOGY SOCIAL WORK. *see* MEDICAL SCIENCES—Urology And Nephrology

JOURNAL OF OFFENDER REHABILITATION; a multidisciplinary journal of innovation in research, services, and programs in corrections and criminal justice. *see* CRIMINOLOGY AND LAW ENFORCEMENT

JOURNAL OF OPIOID MANAGEMENT; a medical journal of proper and adequate use. *see* MEDICAL SCIENCES

361 USA ISSN 1558-8742
HN1
➤ **JOURNAL OF POLICY PRACTICE**; frontiers of social policy as contemporary social work intervention. Text in English. 2002 (Spr.). q. GBP 362 combined subscription in United Kingdom to institutions (print & online eds.); EUR 472, USD 478 combined subscription to institutions (print & online eds.) (effective 2012). adv. reprint service avail. from PSC. **Document type:** *Journal, Academic/Scholarly.* **Description:** Covers social policy research and thought, policy practice, administration and history, teaching of social policy and so on.
Formerly (until 2006): Social Policy Journal (1533-2942)
Related titles: Online - full text ed.: ISSN 1558-8750. 2002. GBP 326 in United Kingdom to institutions; EUR 425, USD 431 to institutions (effective 2012).
Indexed: A01, A03, A22, B21, C06, C07, C08, CA, CINAHL, DIP, E-psyche, E01, E17, ESPM, FamI, IBR, IBZ, M02, P34, P42, PAIS, PRA, PSA, S02, S03, SCOPUS, SSA, SociolAb, T02.
—BLDSC (5040.843500), IE, Ingenta. **CCC.**
Published by: Routledge (Subsidiary of: Taylor & Francis Group), 325 Chestnut St, Ste 800, Philadelphia, PA 19106. TEL 215-625-8900, 800-354-1420, FAX 215-625-8914, journals@routledge.com, http://www.routledge.com. Ed. Richard Hoefer. adv.: B&W page USD 315, color page USD 550; trim 4.375 x 7.125. Circ: 26 (paid).

362.5 USA ISSN 1087-5549
HC110.P6 CODEN: JPOVF4
➤ **JOURNAL OF POVERTY**; innovations on social, political & economic inequalities. Abbreviated title: J Pov. Text in English. 1997. q. GBP 269 combined subscription in United Kingdom to institutions (print & online eds.); EUR 350, USD 357 combined subscription to institutions (print & online eds.) (effective 2012). adv. illus. 120 p./no. 1 cols./p.; back issues avail.; reprint service avail. from PSC. **Document type:** *Journal, Academic/Scholarly.* **Description:** Deals with the study and eradication of poverty.
Related titles: Microform ed.: (from PQC); Online - full text ed.: ISSN 1540-7608. GBP 242 in United Kingdom to institutions; EUR 315, USD 321 to institutions (effective 2012).
Indexed: A01, A03, A22, AmHI, CA, CDA, DIP, E01, E03, ERI, ESPM, FR, FamI, GSS&RPL, H07, IBR, IBZ, IPARL, M02, P30, P34, P42, PAIS, PC&CA, PSA, RefZh, RiskAb, S02, S03, SCOPUS, SOPODA, SSA, SSciA, SWR&A, SociolAb, T02.
—BLDSC (5041.175000), IE, Ingenta, INIST. **CCC.**
Published by: Routledge (Subsidiary of: Taylor & Francis Group), 325 Chestnut St, Ste 800, Philadelphia, PA 19106. TEL 215-625-8900, 800-354-1420, FAX 215-625-8914, journals@routledge.com, http://www.routledge.com. Eds. Alfred L Joseph Jr., Maria Vidal de Haymes. adv.: B&W page USD 315, color page USD 550; trim 4.375 x 7.125. Circ: 193 (paid).

360 338.91 KOR ISSN 2233-6192
▼ ➤ **JOURNAL OF POVERTY ALLEVIATION AND INTERNATIONAL DEVELOPMENT.** Text in English. 2010. s-a. KRW 20,000 domestic to individuals; USD 20 foreign to individuals; USD 50,000 domestic to institutions; USD 50 foreign to institutions (effective 2011). back issues avail. **Document type:** *Journal, Academic/Scholarly.*
Published by: Yonsei University, Institute for Poverty Alleviation and International Development, Wonju Campus, 316 Jeongui Hall, 1 Yonseidae-gil, Wonju, Gangwon-do 220-710, Korea, S. TEL 82-33-760-2534, FAX 82-33-760-2572. R&P, Adv. contact Christal Phillips TEL 82-33-760-2538.

361.60941 GBR ISSN 1759-8273
➤ **THE JOURNAL OF POVERTY AND SOCIAL JUSTICE.** Text in English. 1988. 3/yr. GBP 212, EUR 279 combined subscription in Europe to institutions (print & online eds.); USD 411 combined subscription in the Americas to institutions (print & online eds.); GBP 239 combined subscription elsewhere to institutions (print & online eds.) (effective 2012). adv. **Document type:** *Journal, Academic/Scholarly.* **Description:** Provides a summary of current social security issues and events.
Former titles (until 2010): Benefits (0962-7898); (until 1991): Benefits Research (0954-7355)
Related titles: Online - full text ed.: ISSN 1759-8281. EUR 251 in Europe to institutions; USD 349 in the Americas to institutions; GBP 180 to institutions in the UK & elsewhere (effective 2011) (from IngentaConnect).
Indexed: A01, A03, A08, CA, I02, IBSS, P05, P34, P42, PAIS, PSA, R02, S02, S03, SSA, SociolAb, T02.

—BLDSC (5041.175500), IE, Infotrieve, Ingenta. **CCC.**
Published by: The Policy Press, University of Bristol, 4th Fl, Beacon House, Queen's Rd, Bristol, BS8 1QU, United Kingdom. TEL 44-117-3314054, FAX 44-117-3314093, tpp-info@bristol.ac.uk, http://www.policypress.org.uk. Eds. Caroline Paskell, Fran Bennett. adv.: page GBP 120; 190 x 277. Circ: 300 (paid and controlled). **Subscr. to:** Portland Customer Services, Commerce Way, Colchester CO2 8HP, United Kingdom. TEL 44-1206-796351, FAX 44-1206-799331, sales@portland-services.com, http://www.portland-services.com.

360 610.73 GBR ISSN 1460-6690
➤ **JOURNAL OF PRACTICE TEACHING IN HEALTH & SOCIAL WORK.** Abbreviated title: J P T H S W. Text in English. 1998. 3/yr. GBP 35 in Europe to individuals; USD 60 in North America to individuals; GBP 40 elsewhere to individuals; GBP 75 in Europe to institutions; USD 125 in North America to institutions; GBP 80 elsewhere to institutions; GBP 165 combined subscription in Europe to libraries (print & online eds.); USD 250 combined subscription in North America to libraries (print & online eds.); GBP 170 combined subscription elsewhere to libraries (print & online eds.) (effective 2009). bk.rev. bibl. back issues avail. **Document type:** *Journal, Academic/Scholarly.* **Description:** Covers field education, workplace learning & training in social work, health education, etc.
Related titles: Online - full text ed.: ISSN 1746-6113. 2004 (from IngentaConnect).
Indexed: CA, CPE, DIP, FR, IBR, IBZ, S02, S03, S21, SCOPUS, SSA, SWR&A, SociolAb, T02.
—IE, Ingenta, INIST. **CCC.**
Published by: Whiting & Birch Ltd., 90 Dartmouth Rd, London, SE23 3NZ, United Kingdom. TEL 44-20-82442421, FAX 44-20-82442448, enquiries@whitingbirch.net. Ed. Jonathan Parker.

360 USA ISSN 1042-8232
HV85 CODEN: JPHSER
➤ **JOURNAL OF PROGRESSIVE HUMAN SERVICES;** successor to catalyst: a socialist journal of the social services. Abbreviated title: J Pro. Text in English. 1978. q. GBP 441 combined subscription in United Kingdom to institutions (print & online eds.); EUR 573, USD 579 combined subscription to institutions (print & online eds.) (effective 2012). adv. bk.rev.; film rev. 120 p./no. 1 cols./p.; back issues avail.; reprint service avail. from PSC. **Document type:** *Journal, Academic/Scholarly.* **Description:** Deals with social problems and human services from the progressive perspective.
Formerly (until 1990): Catalyst (New York, 1978) (0191-040X)
Related titles: Microfiche ed.: (from PQC); Microform ed.; Online - full text ed.: ISSN 1540-7616. GBP 397 in United Kingdom to institutions; EUR 515, USD 521 to institutions (effective 2012).
Indexed: A01, A03, A22, AltPI, B21, CA, CJA, DIP, E01, E03, E17, ERI, ESPM, FamI, IBR, IBZ, L01, L02, LeftInd, P03, P34, PAIS, PRA, PsycInfo, PsycholAb, RefZh, S02, S03, SCOPUS, SOPODA, SSA, SWR&A, SociolAb, T02.
—BLDSC (5042.745000), IE, Ingenta. **CCC.**
Published by: (Institute for Social Services Alternatives, Inc.), Routledge (Subsidiary of: Taylor & Francis Group), 325 Chestnut St, Ste 800, Philadelphia, PA 19106. TEL 215-625-8900, 800-354-1420, FAX 215-625-8914, journals@routledge.com, http://www.routledge.com. adv.: B&W page USD 315, color page USD 550; trim 4.375 x 7.125. Circ: 452 (paid).

➤ **JOURNAL OF PSYCHOSOCIAL NURSING AND MENTAL HEALTH SERVICES.** *see* MEDICAL SCIENCES—Nurses And Nursing

362.7 USA ISSN 1554-8732
HV741
➤ **JOURNAL OF PUBLIC CHILD WELFARE.** Text in English. 2007 (Spr.). q. GBP 245 combined subscription in United Kingdom to institutions (print & online eds.); EUR 319, USD 330 combined subscription to institutions (print & online eds.) (effective 2012). adv. back issues avail.; reprint service avail. from PSC. **Document type:** *Journal, Academic/Scholarly.* **Description:** Provides a broad forum for theory-based and applied research in child welfare.
Related titles: Online - full text ed.: ISSN 1554-8740. 2007 (Spr.). GBP 221 in United Kingdom to institutions; EUR 287, USD 297 to institutions (effective 2012).
Indexed: A01, A03, A22, B21, C06, C07, CA, E01, E03, ERI, ESPM, FamI, H&SSA, M02, P30, P34, P48, P50, P54, PQC, RiskAb, S02, S03, SCOPUS, SSA, SociolAb, T02.
—BLDSC (5043.491500), IE, Ingenta. **CCC.**
Published by: Routledge (Subsidiary of: Taylor & Francis Group), 270 Madison Ave, New York, NY 10016. TEL 212-216-7800, FAX 212-244-1563, journals@routledge.com, http://www.routledge.com. Eds. Alberta J Ellett, Rowena G Wilson.

➤ **JOURNAL OF PUBLIC MENTAL HEALTH;** the art, science and politics of creating a mentally healthy society. *see* PUBLIC HEALTH AND SAFETY

➤ **JOURNAL OF REHABILITATION.** *see* MEDICAL SCIENCES—Physical Medicine And Rehabilitation

➤ **JOURNAL OF REHABILITATION ADMINISTRATION.** *see* MEDICAL SCIENCES—Physical Medicine And Rehabilitation

362.4 IND ISSN 0973-2497
JOURNAL OF REHABILITATION COUNCIL OF INDIA. Variant title: J R C I. Text in English. 2005. a. INR 400 per issue to individuals; INR 450 per issue to institutions (effective 2011). back issues avail. **Document type:** *Journal, Academic/Scholarly.*
Published by: Rehabilitation Council of India, B-22, Qutab Institutional Area, New Delhi, 110 016, India. TEL 91-11-26532816, FAX 91-11-26534291, rehabstd@nde.vsnl.net.in, http://www.rehabcouncil.nic.in.

362.1786 617.03 SWE ISSN 1650-1977
RM695 CODEN: JRMOAG
➤ **JOURNAL OF REHABILITATION MEDICINE.** Text in English. 1969. 8/yr. EUR 160 combined subscription to individuals print & online eds.; EUR 370 combined subscription to institutions print & online eds. (effective 2007). adv. bk.rev. charts; illus. reprint service avail. from PSC. **Document type:** *Journal, Academic/Scholarly.* **Description:** Publishes articles concerned with medical, psychological, social, economic and technological aspects of rehabilitation.
Formerly (until 2001): Scandinavian Journal of Rehabilitation Medicine (0036-5505)
Related titles: Online - full text ed.: ISSN 1651-2081. EUR 130 to individuals; EUR 300 to institutions (effective 2007) (from IngentaConnect).
Indexed: A01, A02, A03, A08, A20, A22, AMED, ASSIA, B21, B25, BDM&CN, BIOSIS Prev, C06, C07, C08, C11, CA, CINAHL, CTA, CurCont, E01, ECER, EMBASE, ESPM, ErgAb, ExcerpMed, FoSS&M, H&SSA, H04, IBR, IBZ, INI, IndMed, Inpharma, MEDLINE, MycolAb, P30, P43, PEI, PsycholAb, R09, R10, Reac, SCI, SCOPUS, SD, SportS, T02, W07.
—BLDSC (5048.954000), GNLM, IE, Infotrieve, Ingenta, INIST. **CCC.**
Published by: (European Academy of Rehabilitation Medicine/Academie Europeenne de Medicine de Readaptation BEL, International Society of Physical and Rehabilitation Medicine BEL), Stiftelsen Rehabiliteringsinformation/Information on Rehabilitation Foundation, Tradgardsgatan 14, Uppsala, 753 09, Sweden. TEL 46-18-6115095, FAX 46-18-557332. Ed. Gunnar Grimby. Circ: 1,200.

361 200 USA ISSN 1542-6432
HN30
➤ **JOURNAL OF RELIGION AND SPIRITUALITY IN SOCIAL WORK;** social thought. Text in English. 1974. q. GBP 318 combined subscription in United Kingdom to institutions (print & online eds.); EUR 415, USD 420 combined subscription to institutions (print & online eds.) (effective 2012). adv. bk.rev. charts; illus. index. back issues avail.; reprint service avail. from PSC. **Document type:** *Journal, Academic/Scholarly.* **Description:** Focuses on topics pertaining to institutional and noninstitutional religion, as well as sectarian and nonsectarian approaches to spirituality as it relates to social work and the other helping professions. Initially published by Catholic Charities.
Formerly (until 2003): Social Thought (0099-183X)
Related titles: Microform ed.: (from PQC); Online - full text ed.: ISSN 1542-6440. GBP 286 in United Kingdom to institutions; EUR 373, USD 379 to institutions (effective 2012).
Indexed: A01, A03, A22, AMHA, B21, C06, C07, C08, CA, CERDIC, CINAHL, CPL, DIP, E01, E17, ESPM, FR, FamI, GSS&RPL, IBR, IBZ, M02, P03, P06, P30, PC&CA, PRA, PsycInfo, S02, S03, SCOPUS, SOPODA, SSA, SWR&A, SociolAb, T02.
—BLDSC (5049.352070), IE, Ingenta, INIST. **CCC.**
Published by: Routledge (Subsidiary of: Taylor & Francis Group), 325 Chestnut St, Ste 800, Philadelphia, PA 19106. TEL 215-625-8900, 800-354-1420, FAX 215-625-8914, journals@routledge.com, http://www.routledge.com. Ed. Frederick L Ahearn Jr. adv.: B&W page USD 315, color page USD 550; trim 4.375 x 7.125. Circ: 370 (paid).

360 BGD
JOURNAL OF SOCIAL DEVELOPMENT. Text in Bengali, English. 1966-1969; resumed 1984. s-a. BDT 25, USD 3 per issue. bk.rev.
Formerly (until 1984): Social Horizon (0037-7759)
Published by: (Institute of Social Welfare and Research), University of Dhaka, Ramna, Dhaka, 1000, Bangladesh. Circ: 200.

360 ZWE ISSN 1012-1080
HN780.Z9
➤ **JOURNAL OF SOCIAL DEVELOPMENT IN AFRICA.** Text in English. 1986. s-a. ZWD 300 domestic; USD 35 in developing nations; USD 65 rest of world (effective 2007). adv. bk.rev. index bi-annual - complete TOC available on request. 150 p./no.; back issues avail. **Document type:** *Journal, Academic/Scholarly.* **Description:** Publishes analyses of social development issues as they affect the poor and marginalized.
Related titles: Online - full text ed.: ISSN 1726-3700.
Indexed: A22, ARDT, ASD, ASSIA, ATA, CA, FamI, GEOBASE, IBR, IBSS, IBZ, IIBP, P30, P42, PCI, PQC, PSA, PerIslam, S02, S03, SCOPUS, SOPODA, SSA, SWR&A, SociolAb, T02.
—BLDSC (5064.752700), IE, Infotrieve, Ingenta.
Published by: School of Social Work, Kopje, Private Bag 66022, Harare, Zimbabwe. TEL 263-4-751815, FAX 263-4-751903, ssw@esanet.zw. Ed. Rodreck Mupedziswa. Circ: 70 (paid); 120.

361.61 GBR ISSN 0047-2794
HV1
➤ **JOURNAL OF SOCIAL POLICY.** Text in English. 1972. q. GBP 288, USD 485 to institutions; GBP 299, USD 520 combined subscription to institutions (print & online eds.) (effective 2009). adv. bk.rev. index. back issues avail.; reprint service avail. from PSC. **Document type:** *Journal, Academic/Scholarly.* **Description:** Provides a theoretical, historical analysis of social policy worldwide, and investigation of processes and obstacles to enacting social policy at local and national levels.
Related titles: Microform ed.: (from PQC); Online - full text ed.: ISSN 1469-7823. GBP 262, USD 447 to institutions (effective 2009).
Indexed: A01, A02, A03, A08, A12, A20, A22, A26, ABCPolSci, ABIn, ASCA, ASG, ASSIA, B04, B28, BRD, C28, CA, CurCont, DIP, E01, E08, ERA, ESPM, FamI, G08, G10, GEOBASE, H09, HRA, I05, IBR, IBSS, IBZ, ILD, MCR, MEA&I, P02, P06, P10, P24, P27, P30, P34, P42, P45, P46, P48, P51, P53, P54, PAA&I, PAIS, PCI, PQC, PSA, PSI, PsycholAb, RASB, S02, S03, S05, S09, S11, S19, S20, S21, SCOPUS, SOPODA, SPAA, SSA, SSAI, SSAb, SSCI, SSI, SSciA, SociolAb, T02, THA, W03, W07, W09, WBSS.
—BLDSC (5064.780000), IE, Infotrieve, Ingenta. **CCC.**
Published by: (Social Policy Association), Cambridge University Press, The Edinburgh Bldg, Shaftesbury Rd, Cambridge, CB2 8RU, United Kingdom. TEL 44-1223-312393, FAX 44-1223-315052, journals@cambridge.org, http://www.cambridge.org/uk. Eds. Hartley Dean, Tania Burchardt. R&P Linda Nicol TEL 44-1223-325702. adv.: page GBP 520, page USD 985. Circ: 2,000. **Subscr. to:** Cambridge University Press, 100 Brook Hill Dr, W Nyack, NY 10994. TEL 845-353-7500, 800-872-7423, FAX 845-353-4141, journals_subscriptions@cup.org.

➤ **JOURNAL OF SOCIAL SECURITY LAW.** *see* LAW

360 USA ISSN 0148-8376
HV1 CODEN: JSSRDV
➤ **JOURNAL OF SOCIAL SERVICE RESEARCH.** Abbreviated title: J S S R. Text in English. 1977. q. GBP 707 combined subscription in United Kingdom to institutions (print & online eds.); EUR 918, USD 925 combined subscription to institutions (print & online eds.) (effective 2012). adv. bk.rev. illus. 120 p./no. 1 cols./p.; back issues avail.; reprint service avail. from PSC. **Document type:** *Journal, Academic/Scholarly.* **Description:** Deals with empirical research and its application to the design, delivery, and management of social services.
Related titles: Microfiche ed.: (from PQC); Microform ed.; Online - full text ed.: ISSN 1540-7314. GBP 636 in United Kingdom to institutions; EUR 827, USD 832 to institutions (effective 2012).
Indexed: A01, A03, A20, A22, AC&P, AMHA, ASCA, ASG, BehAb, CA, CPLI, CurCont, DIP, E-psyche, E01, FR, FamI, IBR, IBZ, LeftInd, P02, P03, P10, P30, P34, P48, P53, P54, PC&CA, PQC, PsycInfo, PsycholAb, RILM, S02, S03, S11, SCOPUS, SFSA, SOPODA, SSA, SSCI, SWR&A, SociolAb, T02, W07.
—BLDSC (5064.913000), IE, Infotrieve, Ingenta, INIST. **CCC.**
Published by: Routledge (Subsidiary of: Taylor & Francis Group), 325 Chestnut St, Ste 800, Philadelphia, PA 19106. TEL 215-625-8900, 800-354-1420, FAX 215-625-8914, journals@routledge.com, http://www.routledge.com. Ed. Sophia F Dziegielewski. adv.: B&W page USD 315, color page USD 550; trim 4.375 x 7.125. Circ: 435 (paid).

➤ **THE JOURNAL OF SOCIAL WELFARE AND FAMILY LAW.** *see* LAW—Family And Matrimonial Law

360 GBR ISSN 1468-0173
HV1
➤ **JOURNAL OF SOCIAL WORK.** Abbreviated title: J S W. Text in English. 2001 (Apr.). q. USD 718, GBP 388 combined subscription to institutions (print & online eds.); USD 704, GBP 380 to institutions (effective 2011). adv. back issues avail.; reprint service avail. from PSC. **Document type:** *Journal, Academic/Scholarly.* **Description:** Dedicated to advancing theoretical understanding, shaping policy and informing practice by creating a forum for the publication, dissemination and debate of key ideas in social work. It encourages the publication and development of key aspects of social work, while also publishing material at the interface of the human service professions.
Related titles: Online - full text ed.: ISSN 1741-296X. USD 646, GBP 349 to institutions (effective 2011).
Indexed: A01, A03, A08, A22, C06, C07, C08, CA, CINAHL, CurCont, DIP, E-psyche, E01, ESPM, FamI, IBR, IBSS, IBZ, P03, P34, PsycInfo, PsycholAb, RiskAb, S02, S03, SCOPUS, SSA, SSCI, SociolAb, T02, W07.
—BLDSC (5064.918600), IE, Ingenta. **CCC.**
Published by: Sage Publications Ltd. (Subsidiary of: Sage Publications, Inc.), 1 Oliver's Yard, 55 City Rd, London, EC1Y 1SP, United Kingdom. TEL 44-20-73248500, FAX 44-20-73248600, info@sagepub.co.uk, http://www.uk.sagepub.com/home.nav. Ed. Steven M Shardlow. adv.: B&W page GBP 350; 130 x 205. **Subscr. in the Americas to:** Sage Publications, Inc., 2455 Teller Rd, Thousand Oaks, CA 91320. TEL 805-499-9774, FAX 805-499-0871, journals@sagepub.com.

360 ISR ISSN 0334-9977
HV378.5
JOURNAL OF SOCIAL WORK AND POLICY IN ISRAEL; theory, research and practice. Text in English; Summaries in Hebrew. irreg., latest no.10, 1997. USD 17 per issue (effective 2008); price varies. 185 p./no.; back issues avail. **Document type:** *Journal, Academic/Scholarly.*
Published by: (Bar-Ilan University), Bar-Ilan University Press (Subsidiary of: Bar-Ilan University), Journals, Ramat-Gan, 52900, Israel. TEL 972-3-5318401, FAX 972-3-5353446, press@mail.biu.ac.il, http://www.biu.ac.il/Press. Eds. F M Loewenberg, M H Spero.

361 USA ISSN 1043-7797
HV11
➤ **JOURNAL OF SOCIAL WORK EDUCATION.** Text in English. 1964. 3/yr. USD 300 domestic to institutions; USD 310 in Canada & Mexico to institutions; USD 320 in Central America to institutions includes Caribbean & South America; USD 336 in the Middle East to institutions includes Western Europe & Africa; USD 346 in Australia & New Zealand to institutions includes Asia & Philippines; free to members (effective 2009). adv. bk.rev. charts. cum.index. back issues avail.; reprints avail. **Document type:** *Journal, Academic/Scholarly.* **Description:** Contains research articles on education in the fields of social work knowledge and social welfare, focusing on developments, innovations, and problems pertaining to social work education at the undergraduate, master's, and postgraduate levels.
Formerly (until 1985): Journal of Education for Social Work (0022-0612)
Related titles: Online - full text ed.
Indexed: A01, A02, A03, A08, A10, A20, A22, A25, A26, ASCA, ASSIA, B04, BRD, C06, C07, C12, CA, CPE, CurCont, DIP, E-psyche, E02, E03, E06, E07, E08, ERI, EdA, EdI, FamI, G08, I05, IBR, IBZ, M01, M02, MEA&I, P03, P04, P07, P18, P24, P25, P30, P43, P46, P48, P53, P54, PQC, PsycInfo, PsycholAb, S02, S03, S08, S09, S21, SCOPUS, SOPODA, SSA, SSCI, SWR&A, SociolAb, T02, V03, W03, W05, W07.
—BLDSC (5064.918950), IE, Infotrieve, Ingenta. **CCC.**
Published by: Council on Social Work Education, 1725 Duke St, Ste 500, Alexandria, VA 22314. TEL 703-683-8080, FAX 703-683-8099, info@cswe.org. Ed. Colleen Balambos. adv.: page USD 780; 5.5 x 8.5. Circ: 4,100. **Subscr. to:** EBSCO Information Services, PO Box 361, Birmingham, AL 35201. TEL 205-995-1567, 800-633-4931, FAX 205-995-1588, cswe@ebsco.com, http://www2.ebsco.com.

362.4 USA ISSN 1536-710X
HV1553
JOURNAL OF SOCIAL WORK IN DISABILITY & REHABILITATION. Text in English. 2002 (Spr.). q. GBP 408 combined subscription in United Kingdom to institutions (print & online eds.); EUR 529, USD 535 combined subscription to institutions (print & online eds.) (effective 2012). adv. back issues avail.; reprint service avail. from PSC. **Document type:** *Journal, Academic/Scholarly.* **Description:** Covers issues related to disabilities and social policy, practice, research and theory.
Related titles: Online - full text ed.: ISSN 1536-7118. GBP 367 in United Kingdom to institutions; EUR 476, USD 482 to institutions (effective 2012).
Indexed: A01, A03, A22, AMED, C06, C07, C08, CA, CINAHL, CPE, DIP, E01, EMBASE, ExcerpMed, FamI, IBR, IBZ, MEDLINE, P30, S02, S03, SCOPUS, SSA, SWR&A, SociolAb, T02.
—BLDSC (5064.918940), IE, Ingenta. **CCC.**
Published by: Routledge (Subsidiary of: Taylor & Francis Group), 325 Chestnut St, Ste 800, Philadelphia, PA 19106. TEL 215-625-8900, FAX 215-625-8914, journals@routledge.com, http://www.routledge.com. Ed. Francis K O Yuen.

S

360 369.4 GBR ISSN 0265-0533
HV1 CODEN: JSWPEC
➤ **JOURNAL OF SOCIAL WORK PRACTICE.** Text in English. 1983. q. GBP 701 combined subscription in United Kingdom to institutions (print & online eds.); EUR 932, USD 1,164 combined subscription to institutions (print & online eds.) (effective 2012). adv. bk.rev. index. back issues avail.; reprint service avail. from PSC. **Document type:** *Journal, Academic/Scholarly.* **Description:** Publishes articles devoted to the exploration and analysis of practice in social welfare and allied health professions from psychodynamic and systemic perspectives, including counselling, social care planning, education and training, research, institutional life, management and organisation or policy-making.
Related titles: Microfiche ed.; Online - full text ed.: ISSN 1465-3885. GBP 631 in United Kingdom to institutions; EUR 838, USD 1,047 to institutions (effective 2012) (from IngentaConnect).
Indexed: A01, A03, A08, A20, A22, ASCA, ASSIA, B28, C06, C07, C08, C28, CA, CINAHL, CurCont, E01, FamI, IBSS, P03, P34, P43, P48, PCI, PQC, PsycInfo, PsycholAb, S02, S03, SCOPUS, SOPODA, SSA, SSCI, SWR&A, SociolAb, T02, V&AA, W07.
—IE, Infotrieve, Ingenta. **CCC.**
Published by: Routledge (Subsidiary of: Taylor & Francis Group), 4 Park Sq, Milton Park, Abingdon, Oxon OX14 4RN, United Kingdom. TEL 44-20-70176000, FAX 44-20-70176336, subscriptions@tandf.co.uk, http://www.routledge.com. Eds. Lynn Froggett, Martin Smith, Stephen Briggs. **Subscr. to:** Taylor & Francis Ltd., Journals Customer Service, Sheepen Pl, Colchester, Essex CO3 3LP, United Kingdom. TEL 44-20-70175544, FAX 44-20-70175198.

361.3 616.86 USA ISSN 1533-256X
HV5800
JOURNAL OF SOCIAL WORK PRACTICE IN THE ADDICTIONS. Text in English. 2001. q. GBP 275 combined subscription in United Kingdom to institutions (print & online eds.); EUR 356, USD 363 combined subscription to institutions (print & online eds.) (effective 2012). adv. back issues avail.; reprint service avail. from PSC. **Document type:** *Journal, Academic/Scholarly.* **Description:** Features articles on innovative individual, family, group work, and community practice models for treating and preventing substance abuse and other addictions in diverse populations.
Related titles: Online - full text ed.: ISSN 1533-2578. GBP 248 in United Kingdom to institutions; EUR 320, USD 327 to institutions (effective 2012).
Indexed: A01, A03, A22, B21, C06, C07, C08, CA, CINAHL, CJA, DIP, E-psyche, E01, E17, ESPM, FamI, IBR, IBZ, P03, P30, PRA, PsycInfo, PsycholAb, S02, S03, SCOPUS, SSA, SWR&A, SociolAb, T02, V&AA.
—BLDSC (5064.919500), IE, Ingenta. **CCC.**
Published by: Routledge (Subsidiary of: Taylor & Francis Group), 270 Madison Ave, New York, NY 10016. TEL 212-216-7800, FAX 212-244-1563, journals@routledge.com, http://www.routledge.com. Ed. Shulamith Lala Ashenberg Straussner.

361.3 USA ISSN 1553-6947
JOURNAL OF SOCIAL WORK VALUES & ETHICS. Abbreviated title: J S W V E. Text in English. 2004 (Fall). q. free (effective 2011). **Document type:** *Journal, Academic/Scholarly.* **Description:** Examines the ethical and values issues that impact and are interwoven with social work practice, research and theory development.
Media: Online - full text.
Indexed: A01, A39, C27, C29, CA, D03, D04, E13, P30, R14, S02, S03, S14, S15, S18, SSA, T02.
Published by: White Hat Communications, PO Box 5390, Harrisburg, PA 17110. TEL 717-238-3787, FAX 717-238-2090, http://www.whitehatcommunications.com/. Ed. Jerry Finn.

JOURNAL OF SOCIOLOGY AND SOCIAL WELFARE. *see* SOCIOLOGY

360 USA
JOURNAL OF STUDENT SOCIAL WORK. Text in English. 2003. a., latest 2006. **Document type:** *Journal, Academic/Scholarly.*
Related titles: Online - full text ed.
Indexed: CA, S02, S03.
Published by: Columbia University, School of Social Work, 1255 Amsterdam Ave, New York, NY 10027. TEL 212-851-2300, socialwork@columbia.edu, http://www.columbia.edu/cu/ssw/.

JOURNAL OF TEACHING IN SOCIAL WORK; innovations in instruction, training & educational practice. *see* EDUCATION—Teaching Methods And Curriculum

362.7 DEU ISSN 0022-5940
JUGENDHILFE. Text in German. 1963. 6/yr. EUR 69; EUR 45 to students; EUR 16 newsstand/cover (effective 2011). adv. charts; illus.; stat. index. **Document type:** *Journal, Trade.*
Related titles: ◆ Online - full text ed.: jugendhilfe-netz.
Indexed: DIP, IBR, IBZ, RASB.
Published by: Hermann Luchterhand Verlag GmbH (Subsidiary of: Wolters Kluwer Deutschland GmbH), Heddesdorfer Str 31, Neuwied, 56564, Germany. TEL 49-2631-8012222, FAX 49-2631-8012223, info@luchterhand.de, http://www.luchterhand.de. Ed. Christiane Jaeger. Adv. contact Marcus Kipp. Circ: 2,250 (paid and controlled).

362.7 DEU ISSN 1614-3027
➤ **JUGENDHILFE AKTUELL.** Text in German. 1969. q. bk.rev.; film rev.; software rev. 100 p./no. 1 cols./p.; back issues avail. **Document type:** *Academic/Scholarly.* **Description:** Contains information on social, educational and vocational matters involving young persons and youth organizations.
Formed by the 2004 merger of: Landschaftsverband Westfalen-Lippe. Mitteilungen des Landesjugendamtes (0937-7123); Jugendhilfe-Info (1614-3019)
Published by: Landschaftsverband Westfalen-Lippe, Landesjugendamt, Freiherr-vom-Stein-Platz 1, Muenster, 48133, Germany. TEL 49-251-5913457, FAX 49-251-591275, lja@lwl.org, http://www.lwl.org. Eds. Andreas Gleis, Veronika Spogis. Circ: 3,800.

362.7 DEU
JUGENDHILFE-NETZ. Text in German. m.
Media: Online - full text. **Related titles:** ◆ Print ed.: Jugendhilfe. ISSN 0022-5940.
Published by: Hermann Luchterhand Verlag GmbH (Subsidiary of: Wolters Kluwer Deutschland GmbH), Heddesdorfer Str 31, Neuwied, 56564, Germany. http://www.luchterhand.de.

362.7 DEU
JUGENDHILFE REPORT. Text in German. 1990. 4/yr. free (effective 2007). adv. **Document type:** *Magazine, Trade.*
Published by: Landschaftsverband Rheinland, Kennedyufer 2, Cologne, 50663, Germany. TEL 49-221-8090, FAX 49-221-8092200, presse@lvr.de. adv.: B&W page EUR 1,200. Circ: 6,500 (controlled).

JURISPRUDENTIE WET WERK EN BIJSTAND (ONLINE). *see* INSURANCE

362.5 NZL ISSN 1176-8185
JUST CHANGE. Text in English. 2002. every 4 mos. free (effective 2009). back issues avail. **Document type:** *Magazine, Consumer.* **Description:** For those concerned with sustainable development, social justice, and human rights.
Formerly (until 2004): Dev-zine (1175-7663)
Published by: (Development Resource Centre), Dev-Zone, Floor 2, James Smith Bldg., 49-55 Cuba St., PO Box 12440, Wellington, New Zealand. TEL 64-4-4729549, FAX 64-4-4969599, info@dev-zone.org.

350 AUS ISSN 1323-2266
➤ **JUST POLICY**; a journal of Australian social policy. Text in English. 19??. q. AUD 60 to individuals; AUD 108 to institutions; free to members (effective 2009). adv. bk.rev. back issues avail. **Document type:** *Journal, Academic/Scholarly.* **Description:** Aims to promote critical, well-informed debate about major issues in social policy.
Former titles (until 1994): Policy Issues Forum (0810-4085); (until 1981): Policy Newsletter
Indexed: AusPAIS, CA, P34, T02.
—Ingenta.
Published by: Victorian Council of Social Service, Level 8, 128 Exhibition St, Melbourne, VIC 3000, Australia. TEL 61-3-96545050, 800-133-340, FAX 61-3-96545749, vcoss@vcoss.org.au. Ed. Priscilla Blake. adv.: B&W page AUD 197, color page AUD 260; 184.6 x 220.

360 364 CAN ISSN 0225-4115
JUSTICE - DIRECTORY OF SERVICES/JUSTICE - REPERTOIRE DES SERVICES. Text in English, French. 1980. a. CAD 20 per issue to members; CAD 25 per issue to non-members (effective 2005). **Document type:** *Directory, Trade.* **Description:** Addresses, phone numbers and names of persons responsible for criminal justice and related services in Canada.
Formerly: Directory of Correctional Services in Canada - Repertoire des Services de Correction du Canada (0070-5381)
Published by: Canadian Criminal Justice Association/Association Canadienne de Justice Penale, 320 Parkdale Ave, Ste 301, Ottawa, ON K1Y 4X9, Canada. TEL 613-725-3715, FAX 613-725-3720, ccja@bellnet.ca. Circ: 700.

JUSTICE REPORT/ACTUALITES JUSTICE. *see* CRIMINOLOGY AND LAW ENFORCEMENT

JUSTICE RESEARCH NOTES. *see* CRIMINOLOGY AND LAW ENFORCEMENT

360 USA ISSN 2161-315X
▼ **JUSTSOUTH QUARTERLY.** Text in English. 2009. q. free (effective 2011). back issues avail. **Document type:** *Journal, Academic/Scholarly.*
Related titles: Online - full text ed.: ISSN 2161-3168.
Published by: Jesuit Social Research Institute, 6363 St. Charles Ave, PO Box 94, New Orleans, LA 70118. TEL 504-864-7746, jsri@loyno.edu.

610 363.5 SWE ISSN 1652-6775
K A M E D O - REPORT. (Katastorfmedicinska Organisationskommitten-Rapport) Text in Swedish; Summaries in English. 1965. irreg. back issues avail. **Document type:** *Government.*
Former titles (until 2003): K A M E D O (1104-7739); (until 1989): Foersvarets Forskningsanstalt, Huvudavdeling 5. Rapport (0281-2223); (until 1976): Foersvarsmedicinska Forskningsdelegationen och dess.Rapport (0348-3495)
Related titles: Online - full text ed.
Published by: Socialstyrelsen/National Board of Health and Welfare, Raalambsvaegen 3, Stockholm, 10630, Sweden. TEL 46-8-55553000, FAX 46-8-55553252, socialstyrelssen@socialstyrelsen.se.

362.7 DEU
K J R BURG INFO; Jugendpolitik und Jugendarbeit im Landkreis Muenchen. Text in German. 1972. m. bk.rev. **Document type:** *Newsletter.*
Formerly (until 1992): Informationen ueber Jugendarbeit und Jugendpolitik in Landkreis Muenchen
Published by: Kreisjugendring Muenchen-Land, Burg Schwaneck, Pullach, 82049, Germany. TEL 089-7441400, FAX 089-74414033. Eds. Christoph Poschenrieder, Marlis Kuepper. Circ: 2,000.

360 DEU ISSN 0942-6485
K S A - KINDERSCHUTZ AKTUELL. Text in German. 1958. q. EUR 12 (effective 2003). adv. bk.rev. back issues avail. **Document type:** *Magazine, Consumer.*
Former titles (until 1991): Kinderschutz Aktuell (0930-0775); (until 1974): Schutz dem Kinde (0930-0996)
Indexed: DIP, IBR, IBZ.
Published by: Deutscher Kinderschutzbund e.V., Bundesgeschaeftsstelle, Schiffgraben 29, Hannover, 30159, Germany. TEL 49-511-30485-0, FAX 49-511-3048549, infodat@dksb.de, http://www.dksb.de. adv.: page EUR 3,070; trim 183 x 254. Circ: 48,750 (controlled).

KANUKOKA. NUTAARSIASSAT. (Kalaallit Nunaanni Kommuneqarfiit Kattuffiat) *see* PUBLIC ADMINISTRATION

362.2 NZL ISSN 1177-5386
KEEP WELL. Text in English. 2007. s-a. free. **Document type:** *Newsletter, Consumer.* **Description:** Outlines key achievements, news and activities over the past six months in Australia and New Zealand.
Related titles: Online - full text ed.: ISSN 1177-5394.
Published by: Keepwell (NZ) Ltd, PO Box 10 771, The Terrace, Welllington, New Zealand. FAX 64-4-3841233, keepwellnz@gmail.com.

360 FIN ISSN 1797-0466
KEHITYSVAMMALIITTO. TUTKIMUKSIA/FINNISH ASSOCIATION ON INTELLECTUAL AND DEVELOPMENTAL DISABILITIES. STUDIES. Text in Finnish. 1980. irreg. **Document type:** *Monographic series, Academic/Scholarly.*
Former titles (until 2007): Kotu-Tutkimuksia (1795-1909); (until 2004): Valtakunnallisen Tutkimus- ja Kokeiluyksikon. Julkaisuja (0358-0474)
Published by: Kehitysvammaliitto Ry/Finnish Association on Intellectual and Developmental Disabilities, Viljatie 4 A, Helsinki, 00700, Finland. TEL 358-9-348090, FAX 358-9-3853398, kvl@kvl.fi, http://www.kehitysvammaliitto.fi.

362.7 USA
KENTUCKY. DEPARTMENT OF HUMAN RESOURCES. ANNUAL REPORT. Text in English. a. **Document type:** *Government.*
Incorporates: Kentucky. Department of Child Welfare. Annual Report
Published by: Department for Human Resources, Frankfort, KY 40601. TEL 502-564-2336.

360 304.6 KEN
KENYA. CENTRAL BUREAU OF STATISTICS. POPULATIONS AND HOUSING CENSUS (YEAR); population distribution by administrative areas and urban centres. Text in English. 1948. irreg., latest vol.2, 1999. KES 2,000 per issue (effective 2001). stat. **Document type:** *Government.*
Published by: Ministry of Finance and Planning, Central Bureau of Statistics, PO Box 30266, Nairobi, Kenya. TEL 254-2-317011, 254-2-333970, FAX 254-2-333030, http://www.treasury.go.ke.cbs.

360 KEN
KENYA. CENTRAL BUREAU OF STATISTICS. SECOND REPORT ON POVERTY IN KENYA. Text in English. 1998. irreg., latest vol.3, 2000. KES 600 per issue (effective 2001). stat.; maps. **Document type:** *Government.*
Published by: Ministry of Finance and Planning, Central Bureau of Statistics, PO Box 30266, Nairobi, Kenya. TEL 254-2-333970, 254-2-317011, FAX 254-2-333030, http://www.treasury.go.ke.cbs.

KENYA. MINISTRY OF COOPERATIVES AND SOCIAL SERVICES. SESSIONAL PAPERS. *see* PUBLIC ADMINISTRATION

353.5 KEN ISSN 0075-594X
KENYA. PUBLIC SERVICE COMMISSION. ANNUAL REPORT. Text in English. a. **Document type:** *Government.*
Published by: (Kenya. Public Service Commission), Government Printing and Stationery Department, PO Box 30128, Nairobi, Kenya.

KENYA SOCIETY FOR THE BLIND. ANNUAL REPORT AND ACCOUNTS. *see* HANDICAPPED—Visually Impaired

616.89 DEU ISSN 0724-5165
DIE KERBE; Forum fuer Sozialpsychiatrie. Text in German. 1983. 4/yr. EUR 22.80; EUR 6 per issue (effective 2011). adv. **Document type:** *Journal, Academic/Scholarly.*
Published by: (Bundesverband Evangelische Behindertenhilfe e.V.), Evangelische Gemeindepresse GmbH, Augustenstr 124, Stuttgart, 70197, Germany. TEL 49-711-6010040, kontakt@elk-wue.de. Ed. Juergen Armbruster. adv.: B&W page EUR 804. Circ: 1,358 (paid and controlled).

362 NLD ISSN 1871-5354
KERNGEGEVENS MAATSCHAPPELIJKE ZORG. Text in Dutch. 1999. biennial.
Supersedes in part (in 2005): Patientenpanel Chronisch Zieken. Kerngegevens (1871-5338)
Published by: (Patientenpanel Chronisch Zieken), Nederlands Instituut voor Onderzoek van de Gezondheidszorg, Postbus 1568, Utrecht, 3500 BN, Netherlands. TEL 31-30-2729700, FAX 31-30-2729729, nivel@nivel.nl, http://www.nivel.nl.

362 NLD ISSN 1871-5346
KERNGEGEVENS ZORG. Text in Dutch. 1999. biennial.
Supersedes in part (in 2004): Patientenpanel Chronisch Zieken. Kerngegevens (1871-5338)
Published by: (Patientenpanel Chronisch Zieken), Nederlands Instituut voor Onderzoek van de Gezondheidszorg, Postbus 1568, Utrecht, 3500 BN, Netherlands. TEL 31-30-2729700, FAX 31-30-2729729, nivel@nivel.nl, http://www.nivel.nl.

362.3 FIN ISSN 0355-2918
➤ **KETJU.** Text in Finnish. 1964. bi-m. EUR 21 (effective 2007). adv. bk.rev. back issues avail. **Document type:** *Magazine, Academic/Scholarly.* **Description:** Professional periodical on intellectual disability covering social services and the handicapped.
Published by: Kehitysvammaliitto Ry/Finnish Association on Intellectual and Developmental Disabilities, Viljatie 4 A, Helsinki, 00700, Finland. TEL 358-9-348090, FAX 358-9-3853398, kvl@kvl.fi. Ed. Veli-Pekka Sinervuo TEL 358-9-34809214. Adv. contact Anneli Puhakka TEL 358-9-34809217. B&W page EUR 864, color page EUR 1,792; 210 x 279. Circ: 4,000 (paid).

361.73 338 GBR
KEY NOTE MARKET ASSESSMENT. CHARITY FUNDING. Text in English. 19??. irreg., latest 2005. GBP 799 per issue (effective 2010). **Document type:** *Report, Trade.* **Description:** Provides an in-depth strategic analysis across a broad range of industries and contains an examination on the scope, dynamics and shape of key UK markets in the consumer, financial, lifestyle and business to business sectors.
Incorporates: Key Note Market Report: Charities (1461-3425); Which was formerly (1991-1997): Key Note Report: Charities (0963-4436)
Published by: Key Note Ltd. (Subsidiary of: Bonnier Business Information), Harlequin House, 5th Fl, 7 High St, Teddington, Richmond upon Thames, TW11 8EE, United Kingdom. TEL 44-845-5040452, FAX 44-845-5040453, sales@keynote.co.uk.

KEY NOTE MARKET ASSESSMENT. CHILDCARE. *see* CHILDREN AND YOUTH—About

KIDS COUNT DATA BOOK. *see* CHILDREN AND YOUTH—About

362.6 NLD ISSN 1877-0762
KIJK OP K B O LIMBURG. (Katholieke Bond van Ouderen) Text in Dutch. 2007. q. adv. **Document type:** *Newspaper, Consumer.*
Published by: K B O Limburg, Wilhelminasingel 25, Roermond, 6041 CH, Netherlands. TEL 31-475-381740, info@kbolimburg.nl. Ed. Cees Versteden. Circ: 37,500.

KINDEROPVANG. *see* CHILDREN AND YOUTH—About

KING OF PENSION FUNDS CD-ROM. *see* BUSINESS AND ECONOMICS—Labor And Industrial Relations

360 266 USA ISSN 0023-1703
BV2155
KINSHIP. Text in English. 1961. q. USD 7 (effective 2001). illus. **Document type:** *Newsletter.*

Published by: Glenmary Home Mission Sisters of America, 405 W Parrish Ave, Box 22264, Owensboro, KY 42304-2264. TEL 270-686-8401, FAX 270-686-8759, development@glenmarysisters.org, http://www.glenmarysisters.org/. Ed. Sr Christine Beckett. R&P Kristin Foulke. Circ: 11,000.

361.7 NOR ISSN 1503-9862
KIRKENS NOEDHJELP MAGASINET. Text in Norwegian. 1962. 5/yr. free. back issues avail. **Document type:** *Magazine, Consumer.*
Former titles (until 2004): Medmenneske (0803-902X); (until 1992): K N - Nytt (0803-9054); (until 1984): Kirkens Noedhjelp Nytt (0803-9062); (until 1967): Abakaliki-Nytt (0805-9616)
Related titles: Online - full text ed.: ISSN 0809-8964. 2000.
Published by: Kirkens Noedhjelp/Norwegian Church Aid, PO Box 7100, Oslo, 0130, Norway. TEL 47-22-092700, FAX 47-22-092720, nca-oslo@nca.no, http://www.nca.no.

362.7 362.82 NLD ISSN 2210-8009
▼ **DE KLEINE GIDS CENTRUM VOOR JEUGD EN GEZIN.** Text in Dutch. 2010. a. EUR 13.95 (effective 2010).
Published by: Kluwer B.V. (Subsidiary of: Wolters Kluwer N.V.), Postbus 23, Deventer, 7400 GA, Netherlands. TEL 31-570-673449, FAX 31-570-691555, info@kluwer.nl, http://www.kluwer.nl.

362.82 NLD ISSN 2211-9221
▼ **DE KLEINE GIDS EIGEN KRACHT-CONFERENTIE.** Text in Dutch. 2011. a. EUR 15.75 (effective 2011).
Published by: Kluwer B.V. (Subsidiary of: Wolters Kluwer N.V.), Postbus 23, Deventer, 7400 GA, Netherlands. TEL 31-570-673449, FAX 31-570-691555, info@kluwer.nl, http://www.kluwer.nl.

▼ **DE KLEINE GIDS MENSEN MET EEN LICHT VERSTANDELIJKE BEPERKING.** *see* HANDICAPPED

362.7 NLD ISSN 2211-6982
▼ **DE KLEINE GIDS OMGAAN MET PRIVACY EN BEROEPSGEHEIM IN DE JEUGDZORG.** Text in Dutch. 2011. a. EUR 13.95 (effective 2011).
Published by: Kluwer B.V. (Subsidiary of: Wolters Kluwer N.V.), Postbus 23, Deventer, 7400 GA, Netherlands. TEL 31-570-673449, FAX 31-570-691555, info@kluwer.nl, http://www.kluwer.nl.

362.4 NLD ISSN 2211-2162
▼ **DE KLEINE GIDS VOOR DE ZIEKE EN ARBEIDSONGESCHIKTE AMBTENAAR.** Text in Dutch. 2010. a. EUR 15.75 (effective 2011).
Published by: Kluwer B.V. (Subsidiary of: Wolters Kluwer N.V.), Postbus 23, Deventer, 7400 GA, Netherlands. TEL 31-570-673449, FAX 31-570-691555, info@kluwer.nl, http://www.kluwer.nl.

362 NLD ISSN 1879-9124
▼ **DE KLEINE GIDS ZORG- EN ADVIESTEAMS.** Text in Dutch. 2010. a. EUR 13.95 (effective 2010).
Published by: Kluwer B.V. (Subsidiary of: Wolters Kluwer N.V.), Postbus 23, Deventer, 7400 GA, Netherlands. TEL 31-570-673449, FAX 31-570-691555, info@kluwer.nl, http://www.kluwer.nl.

362.4 NLD ISSN 0166-5782
KLIK; maandblad voor de verstandelijk gehandicaptenzorg. Text in Dutch. 1973. m. (11/yr.). EUR 62.50 domestic to individuals; EUR 69.90 in Belgium to individuals; EUR 77.85 in Europe to individuals; EUR 104.95 domestic to institutions; EUR 108.95 in Belgium to institutions; EUR 119.95 in Europe to institutions; EUR 37.50 to students (effective 2010). adv.
Related titles: Online - full text ed.: EUR 44.96 (effective 2010).
—IE.
Published by: Stichting Maandblad Klik, Postbus 8632, Rotterdam, 3009, Netherlands. TEL 31-10-2894019, FAX 31-10-2894076. Eds. Annemarie de Graaff TEL 31-10-2894015, Marieke van den Ende. adv.: B&W page EUR 940, color page EUR 1,675; trim 220 x 280. Circ: 4,038.

362.7 DEU
KLINGE. Text in German. 1954. q. bk.rev. bibl.; illus. **Description:** Focuses on child welfare.
Formerly: Jugenddorf-Zeitung (0022-5924)
Published by: Kinder- und Jugenddorf Klinge e.V., Klingestr 30, Seckach, 74743, Germany. TEL 49-6292-780, FAX 49-6292-78200, info@klinge-seckach.de. Ed. Peter Schmackeit. Circ: 9,000.

KOINONIA PARTNERS. NEWSLETTER. *see* RELIGIONS AND THEOLOGY—Other Denominations And Sects

362.4 353.538 ISR ISSN 0793-646X
KOL N'KHE MILHAMA. Text in Hebrew. 1963. s-a. **Document type:** *Bulletin.*
Published by: Irgun N'khe Ha-Milhama 8 Ha-Arba'a St., Tel Aviv, 64739, Israel. TEL 972-3-5614411, FAX 972-3-5613187, selfhelp@selfhelp.org.il, http://www.selfhelp.org.il/detail-org.php?id=372&idtop=18.

301.4 DEU ISSN 0023-2947
KOLPINGBLATT. Text in German. 1900. m. adv. bk.rev.; film rev. abstr.; illus.; stat. **Document type:** *Newsletter, Trade.*
Published by: Kolpingwerk Deutschland, Kolpingplatz 5-11, Cologne, 50667, Germany. TEL 49-221-207010, FAX 49-221-2070138, info@kolping.de. Ed. Heinrich Wullhorst. adv.: B&W page EUR 9,034, color page EUR 13,099. Circ: 184,711 (controlled).

361.8 DEU
KOMBA RUNDSCHAU. Text in German. bi-m. **Document type:** *Bulletin.*
Published by: Komba Gewerkschaft Schleswig-Holstein, Lerchenstr 17, Kiel, 24103, Germany. TEL 49-431-673318, FAX 49-431-673000. Ed. Horst Bendixen.

KOMBATANT. *see* MILITARY

360 DEU
KOMMUNALES ECHO RHEINLAND-PFALZ. Text in German. 1966. m. adv. **Document type:** *Magazine, Trade.*
Published by: (Komba Gewerkschaft Rheinland-Pfalz), Vereinigte Verlagsanstalten GmbH, Hoeherweg 278, Duesseldorf, 40231, Germany. TEL 49-211-73570, FAX 49-211-7357123, info@vva.de, http://www.vva.de. Adv. contact Panagiotis Chrissovergis. B&W page EUR 480, color page EUR 650. Circ: 5,200 (controlled).

362.7 DEU ISSN 2191-7701
▼ **KOMPETENZ IN DER JUGENDHILFE.** Text in German. 2011. 4/yr. EUR 12; EUR 5 newsstand/cover (effective 2011). **Document type:** *Journal, Trade.*
Published by: Institut fuer Vollzeitpflege- und Adoption (IVA) e.V., Heinrich-Hoffmann-Str 3, Frankfurt a.M., 60528, Germany. TEL 49-69-6706286, FAX 49-69-6706288, info@iva-institut.de.

KONTENRAHMEN FUER DIE TRAEGER DER GESETZLICHEN KRANKENVERSICHERUNG, KONTENRAHMEN FUER DIE TRAEGER DER SOZIALEN PFLEGEVERSICHERUNG UND DEN AUSGLEICHSFONDS. *see* PUBLIC HEALTH AND SAFETY

KOSEI NO SHIHYO/JOURNAL OF HEALTH AND WELFARE STATISTICS. *see* PUBLIC HEALTH AND SAFETY

360 DEU ISSN 1617-6804
KOSTENERSTATTUNGSRECHTLICHE ENTSCHEIDUNGEN DER SCHIEDS- UND VERWALTUNGSGERICHTE. Text in German. 1947. m. EUR 94.80; EUR 11.30 newsstand/cover (effective 2010). **Document type:** *Journal, Trade.*
Formerly (until 1999): Entscheidungen der Spruchstellen fuer Fuersorgestreitigkeiten (0343-656X)
—CCC.
Published by: W. Kohlhammer GmbH, Hessbruehlstr 69, Stuttgart, 70565, Germany. TEL 49-711-78630, FAX 49-711-78638204, kohlhammerkontakt@kohlhammer.de, http://www.kohlhammer.de. Circ: 970.

362 GHA
KPODOGA. Text in Ewe; Summaries in English. 1976. m. (Ewe; 3/yr., English). bk.rev.; play rev. illus. 8 p./no. 4 cols./p.; **Document type:** *Newspaper.* **Description:** Rural community paper promoting literacy and rural development.
Published by: Institute of Adult Education, University of Ghana, PO Box 31, Legon, Ghana. TEL 233-31-918259. Ed. Yao Aduamah. Circ: 2,000 (paid). **Co-sponsor:** United Nations Fund for Population Activities.

KRANKENDIENST; Zeitschrift fuer kath. Krankenhaeuser, Sozialstationen und Pflegeberufe. *see* HEALTH FACILITIES AND ADMINISTRATION

KRASNYI KREST ROSSII. *see* LAW—International Law

KUULOVIESTI/HEARING NEWS/HOERSELTTIDNINGEN. *see* HANDICAPPED—Hearing Impaired

KYREX. *see* GERONTOLOGY AND GERIATRICS

L A S NEWS. (London Ambulance Service) *see* MEDICAL SCIENCES—Orthopedics And Traumatology

360 GBR ISSN 2044-4672
L C V S MAGAZINE. Text in English. 1966. q. free to members (effective 2010). bk.rev. **Document type:** *Magazine, Trade.*
Formerly (until 2009): Liverpool Link (0266-8750); Which superseded (in 1984): Castle Street Circular (0045-592X); Which was formerly (until 1966): Liverpool Council of Social Service. Bulletin
Related titles: Online - full text ed.: free (effective 2010).
Published by: Liverpool Council for Voluntary Service, 151 Dale St, Liverpool, L2 2AH, United Kingdom. TEL 44-151-2275177, FAX 44-151-2373998. Ed. Minna Alanko.

362.5 USA ISSN 2151-8939
L I H E A P E-BULLETIN. (Low-Income Home Energy Assistance Program) Text in English. 2008. q. free (effective 2009). back issues avail. **Document type:** *Bulletin, Trade.* **Description:** Covers information compiled by the LIHEAP Clearinghouse.
Media: Online - full content.
Published by: National Center for Appropriate Technology, LIHEAP Clearinghouse, 3040 Continental Dr, Butte, MT 59702. TEL 406-494-8662, FAX 406-494-2905.

L L E G O. LA GUIA. *see* HOMOSEXUALITY

360 POL ISSN 1425-994X
L O S; czasopismo samopomocy spolecznej. (Lubelski Osrodek Samopomocy) Text in Polish. 1996. q. 44 p./no.
Published by: Stowarzyszenie Lubelski Osrodek Samopomocy, ul Zielona 3, Lublin, 20082, Poland. TEL 48-81-5328875. Ed. Anna Maciag. Circ: 500.

360 DEU
L S V AKTUELL; Praevention - Gesundheit - Aktuelles. Text in German. 1963. q. free (effective 2007). adv. back issues avail. **Document type:** *Magazine, Trade.*
Formerly: Sicher Schaffen - Laenger Leben
Published by: Land- und Forstwirtschaftliche Sozialversicherung, Niederbayern-Oberpfalz und Schwaben, Dr-Georg-Heim-Allee 1, Landshut, 84036, Germany. TEL 49-871-696226, FAX 49-871-696488, Direktion@landshut.lsv.de, http://www.lsv.de. Ed. Norbert Gradl. Adv. contact Irmhild Kemser. page EUR 2,780. Circ: 475,000 (controlled).

360 DEU
L W V INFO; Bericht Nachricht. Text in German. 1989. q. free. **Document type:** *Newsletter.*
Formerly: L W V-Nachrichten
Published by: Landeswohlfahrtsverband Hessen, Staendeplatz 6-10, Kassel, 34117, Germany. TEL 49-561-1004-0. Circ: 8,800.

362.7 FRA ISSN 1959-2302
L'ACCUEIL DU JEUNE ENFANT EN (YEAR). Text in French. 2007. a.
Published by: Caisse Nationale des Allocations Familiales, 32 Av. de la Sibelle, Paris, Cedex 14 75685, France. TEL 33-1-45655432, FAX 33-1-45655377, publications-stats@cnaf.fr, http://www.caf.fr/.

LANDELIJKE CLIENTENRAAD. NIEUWSBRIEF. *see* BUSINESS AND ECONOMICS—Labor And Industrial Relations

LANDTECHNISCHE SCHRIFTENREIHE. *see* AGRICULTURE

360 FIN ISSN 0789-8525
LAPSEN ELATUS JA HUOLTO/CHILD MAINTENANCE AND CUSTODY/UNDERHAALL OCH VAARDNAD AV BARN. Text in Finnish, Swedish, English. 1990. a. **Document type:** *Government.*
Formerly (until 1991): Elatustuki (0788-611X)
Related titles: Online - full text ed.; ◆ Series of: Sosiaaliturva. ISSN 0785-4625.
Published by: Sosiaali- ja Terveysalan Tutkimus- ja Kehittamiskeskus/National Research and Development Centre for Welfare and Health, PO Box 220, Helsinki, 00531, Finland. TEL 358-9-39671, FAX 358-9-396761307, infolib@stakes.fi, http://www.stakes.fi.

362.7 FIN ISSN 0786-0188
LAPSEN MAAILMA/CHILD'S WORLD. Text in Finnish. 1938. m. adv. bk.rev. bibl.; illus. index. **Document type:** *Magazine, Consumer.*
Former titles (until 1989): Lapset Ja Yhteiskunta (0355-3736); (until 1973): Lapsi Ja Nuoriso (0047-407X)
Related titles: ◆ Supplement(s): Children in Finland. ISSN 0783-6244.
Published by: Lastensuojelun Keskusliitto/Central Union for Child Welfare in Finland, Kauppakeskus Columbus, Vuotie 45, Helsinki, 00980, Finland. TEL 358-45-6361222, info@lapsenmaailma.fi. Circ: 30,000.

360 FIN ISSN 0788-6101
LASTENSUOJELU/BARNSKYDDET/CHILD WELFARE. Text in English, Finnish, Swedish. 1993. irreg. stat. back issues avail. **Document type:** *Government.*
Related titles: ◆ Series of: Sosiaaliturva. ISSN 0785-4625; ◆ Series of: Aiheita. ISSN 1236-9845.
Published by: Sosiaali- ja Terveysalan Tutkimus- ja Kehittamiskeskus/National Research and Development Centre for Welfare and Health, PO Box 220, Helsinki, 00531, Finland. TEL 358-9-39671, FAX 358-9-396761307, infolib@stakes.fi, http://www.stakes.fi.

636.0832 USA ISSN 0740-5820
LATHAM LETTER. Text in English. 1980. q. USD 15 domestic; USD 20 in Canada & Mexico; USD 27 elsewhere; USD 5 per issue (effective 2010). bk.rev. 24 p./no.; back issues avail. **Document type:** *Magazine, Consumer.* **Description:** Provides information on humane issues and activities and links between child and animal abuse and domestic violence.
Indexed: IAB, WildRev.
Published by: Latham Foundation, Latham Plaza Bldg, 1826 Clement Ave, Alameda, CA 94501. TEL 510-521-0920, FAX 510-521-9861, info@latham.org. Ed., Pub. Hugh H Tebault III.

300 BRA
LATINIDAD; revista de integracao do cone sul. Text in Portuguese. 1994. q.?. BRL 3 newsstand/cover.
Published by: I R R A Editora, Rua Dr Abel Capela, 346, Coqueiros, Florianopolis, SC 88080-250, Brazil. TEL 55-48-2242370. Ed. Rogerio Mosimann.

IL LAVORATORE ELETTRICO. *see* ENERGY

360 ITA ISSN 1721-4149
LAVORO SOCIALE. Text in Italian. 2001. 3/yr. EUR 32.50 to individuals; EUR 43.50 domestic to institutions; EUR 55 foreign to institutions (effective 2008). **Document type:** *Journal, Trade.*
Published by: Edizioni Erickson, Via Praga 5, Settore E, Gardolo, TN 38100, Italy. TEL 39-0461-950690, FAX 39-0461-950698, info@erickson.it. Ed. Fabio Folgheraiter.

LAW OF ASSOCIATIONS: AN OPERATING LEGAL MANUAL FOR EXECUTIVES AND COUNSEL. *see* LAW

361.6 CAN ISSN 1496-8622
LEARNING WHAT WORKS. Text in English, French. 2001. s-a. back issues avail. **Document type:** *Newsletter, Trade.*
Related titles: Online - full text ed.: ISSN 1496-8630; French ed.: Decouvrir Les Approches Efficaces. ISSN 1496-8649.
Published by: Social Research and Demonstration Corporation, 55 Murray St, Ste 400, Ottawa, ON K1N 5M3, Canada. TEL 613-237-4311, FAX 613-237-5045, info@srdc.org.

360 DEU ISSN 0724-3820
LEBEN UND WEG; Magazin fuer Koerperbehinderte. Text in German. 1960. bi-m. EUR 22 membership (effective 2005). adv. **Document type:** *Magazine, Consumer.*
Published by: Bundesverband Selbsthilfe Koerperbehinderter e.V., Altkrautheimerstr 17, Krautheim, 74238, Germany. TEL 49-6294-42810, FAX 49-6294-428179, zentrale@bsk-ev.de, http://www.bsk-ev.de. Ed. Ulrich Mannsbart. Adv. contact Peter Reichert TEL 49-6294-68225. B&W page EUR 1,575; trim 210 x 297. Circ: 10,000.

362.7 369.4 SWE ISSN 0345-7060
LEDARTIPS; Oe M Us tidskrift foer foeraeldrar, barn- och ungdomsledare. Text in Swedish. 1956. bi-m. SEK 50 (effective 1991).
Published by: Oerebromissionens Ungdom, Fack 1623, Orebro, 70116, Sweden.

LEDERFORUM. *see* LABOR UNIONS

362.582 CAN ISSN 1201-0278
LEGAL AID IN CANADA: DESCRIPTION OF OPERATIONS. Text in English, French. 1985. a. **Description:** Describes the administration and structure of provincial and territorial legal aid services in Canada.
Formerly (until 1994): Legal Aid in Canada (0831-2281)
Related titles: Online - full content ed.: ISSN 1481-1626. CAD 30.
Published by: (Statistics Canada, Canadian Centre for Justice Statistics), Statistics Canada/Statistique Canada, Publications Sales and Services, Ottawa, ON K1A 0T6, Canada. TEL 613-951-8116, infostats@statcan.ca, http://www.statcan.gc.ca.

361.8 790.019 FRA ISSN 1954-944X
LEO. Variant title: Leo Mag. Text in French. 2004. q. free. back issues avail. **Document type:** *Magazine, Consumer.*
Related titles: Online - full text ed.: ISSN 1960-6168.
Published by: Federation Nationale Leo Lagrange, 153 Av. Jean Lolive, Pantin, Cedex 93695, France. TEL 33-1-48106565, FAX 33-1-48106566, espace.ressources@leolagrange.org.

362.82 CAN
LET'S TALK FAMILIES!. Text in English. 1984. 3/yr. CAD 45, USD 44. adv. back issues avail. **Document type:** *Newsletter.* **Description:** Publicizes activities of FSC, addresses issues affecting families in Canada, major issues faced by organizations providing services to families and provides a forum for information exchange on resources and national events related to family life.
Related titles: French ed.
Published by: Family Service Canada/Services a la Famille-Canada, 404 383 Parkdale Ave, Ottawa, ON K1Y 4R4, Canada. TEL 613-722-9006, FAX 613-722-8610. Ed. Margaret Fietz. Adv. contact Kim Tytler. Circ: 3,000 (controlled).

362.5 FRA
LETTRE AUX AMIS DU MONDE. Text in French, English, Spanish. 1981. 3/yr. EUR 8 (effective 2009). index. back issues avail. **Description:** Acts as a voice to all who act to fight against poverty around the world.
Related titles: Spanish ed.; English ed.: Letter to Friends Around the World.
Published by: (Mouvement International A T D Quart Monde/International Movement A T D Fourth World), Editions Quart Monde, 107 Av. du General Leclerc, Pierrelaye, 95480, France. TEL 33-01-34304636, editions@atd-quartmonde.org. Ed. Alwine de Vos van Steenwijk. Circ: 3,500.

▼ **LA LETTRE DES PARTENAIRES.** *see* HOUSING AND URBAN PLANNING

S

363.3 USA ISSN 1527-7208
HV553
LIAISON FOR CIVIL-MILITARY HUMANITARIAN RELIEF COLLABORATIONS. Text in English. 1999. s-a.
Published by: Center of Excellence in Disaster Management & Humanitarian Assistance, Tripler Army Medical Center, 1 Jarrett White Rd (MCPA-DM), Tripler AMC, HI 96859-5000. TEL 808-433-7035, FAX 808-433-1757, education@coe-dmha.org, http://coe-dmha.org/index.htm. Ed. Robin Hyden.

361 FRA ISSN 2106-8860
LIAISON LES AILES BRISEES. BULLETIN. Text in French. 1925. 3/yr. **Document type:** *Newsletter, Consumer.*
Formerly (until 2009): Les Ailes Brisees (1269-441X)
Published by: Association d'Entraide aux Aviateurs Blesses en Service Aerien, Veuves, Orphelins et Ascendants, 5 Rue Christophe Colomb, Paris, France. TEL 33-1-40738240, FAX 33-1-40738248, ailes.brisees@ailesbrisees.asso.fr, http://www.ailesbrisees.asso.fr.

331 361 FRA ISSN 1621-2282
LIAISONS SOCIALES EUROPE. Text in French. 2000. s-m. EUR 680 combined subscription print & online eds. (effective 2009). **Document type:** *Newsletter.*
Related titles: Online - full text ed.
Published by: Groupe Liaisons (Subsidiary of: Wolters Kluwer France), 1 Rue Eugene et Armand Peugeot, Rueil Malmaison, 92500, France. TEL 33-1-41297751, FAX 33-1-41297754. Ed. Frederic Turlan TEL 33-6-29870300.

LIAISONS SOCIALES QUOTIDIEN. *see* BUSINESS AND ECONOMICS—Labor And Industrial Relations

616.834 DEU ISSN 1614-7863
LIDWINA. Text in German. 2004. 4/yr. **Document type:** *Magazine, Consumer.*
Published by: Gieseking Verlag GmbH, Deckertstr 30, Bielefeld, 33617, Germany. TEL 49-521-14674, FAX 49-521-143715, kontakt@gieseking-verlag.de, http://www.gieseking-verlag.de.

360 FRA ISSN 0994-1819
LIEN SOCIAL (TOULOUSE). Text in French. 1988. w. EUR 96 domestic to individual members; EUR 96 DOM-TOM to individual members; EUR 124 in Switzerland to individual members; EUR 60 domestic to students (effective 2010). **Document type:** *Magazine, Trade.* **Description:** Offer a setting for the exchange of information on social work. Created by and for social workers.
Related titles: Online - full text ed.: ISSN 1950-6058.
Indexed: FR.
Published by: Lien Social, rue Garrance, B P 47310, Labege, 31673 Cedex, France. TEL 33-5-62733440, FAX 33-5-62730029. Ed. Monique Castro. Adv. contact Annick Esteve TEL 33-5-62733444.

361.61 CAN ISSN 1204-3206
HN1 CODEN: LSPRF6
LIEN SOCIAL ET POLITIQUES - R I A C. Text in French; Abstracts in English, French, Spanish. 1954. s-a. CAD 31.92 domestic to individuals; CAD 40 foreign to individuals; CAD 45.60 domestic to institutions; CAD 48 foreign to institutions. adv. bk.rev. abstr.; charts; stat. cum.index every 2 yrs. back issues avail. **Document type:** *Abstract/Index.* **Description:** Critical debate on new trends in social policy: studies relationships in the social sector.
Former titles (until 1994): Revue Internationale d'Action Communautaire (0707-9699); (until 1978): International Review of Community Development (0020-854X)
Indexed: A22, DIP, EIP, FR, I13, IBR, IBZ, P06, PCI, PdeR, S02, S03, SCOPUS, SOPODA, SociolAb, T02.
—BLDSC (5208.522400), IE, Infotrieve, Ingenta, INIST.
Published by: Forum International d'Action Communautaire, INRS Culture et Societe, 306 place d Youville, bur B 10, Montreal, PQ H2Y 2B6, Canada. TEL 514-841-4035, FAX 514-841-4015. Ed. Frederic Lesemann. R&P Frederic Leseman TEL 514-841-4025. Circ: 1,500. **Subscr. to:** L S P Periodica, C P 444, Outremont, PQ H2V 4R6, Canada.

613.04244 CAN
LIFE GUARDIAN. Text in English. 1971. bi-m. CAD 10. adv. back issues avail. **Document type:** *Newsletter.* **Description:** Articles on counselling, human interest, information on running a crisis pregnancy center.
Published by: Birthright, 777 Coxwell Ave, Toronto, ON M4C 3C6, Canada. TEL 416-469-4789, FAX 416-469-1772. Ed., R&P, Adv. contact Mary Berney. Circ: 1,600.

LIFETIME FOR WOMEN CONSIDERING ADOPTION. *see* CHILDREN AND YOUTH—About

LIGHT (WHEATON). *see* HANDICAPPED—Visually Impaired

362.41 USA
LIGHTHOUSE INTERNATIONAL ANNUAL REPORT. Text in English. a. free (effective 2004). back issues avail. **Document type:** *Corporate.* **Description:** Reviews Lighthouse programs and services, as well as providing financial statements for the most recent fiscal year.
Formerly (until 1998): Lighthouse, Inc. Annual Report
Related titles: Audio cassette/tape ed.; Braille ed.
Published by: Lighthouse International, 111 E 59th St, New York, NY 10022. TEL 212-821-9200, 800-829-0500, FAX 212-821-9713, info@lighthouse.org, http://www.lighthouse.org. Ed. Laurie Siversweig TEL 212-821-9564.

362.2 613 NLD ISSN 2211-9795
▼ **LINK+.** Text in Dutch. 2011. 3/yr. **Document type:** *Magazine, Trade.*
Published by: G G Z Oost Brabant, :Postbus 3, Boekel, 5427 ZG, Netherlands. TEL 31-492-846000, communicatie@ggzoostbrabant.nl. Ed. Vivianne Viguurs.

LIVING. *see* MEDICAL SCIENCES—Endocrinology

LIVSGLEDE. *see* HANDICAPPED—Physically Impaired

360 GBR
LOCAL AUTHORITY SOCIAL WORK EXPENDITURE. Text in English. 1994. irreg. **Document type:** *Bulletin, Government.*
Published by: Social Work Services Group, Statistics Branch, Rm 52, James Craig Walk, Edinburgh, EH1 3BA, United Kingdom. TEL 44-131-244-5431, FAX 44-131-244-5315. **Dist. by:** Her Majesty's Stationery Office Bookshop, 71 Lothian Rd, EH3 9AZ, Edinburgh, Midlothian EH3 9AZ, United Kingdom. TEL 44-131-244-5315.

LOCAL/STATE FUNDING REPORT. *see* BUSINESS AND ECONOMICS—Public Finance, Taxation

361.73 060 GBR ISSN 1749-0901
THE LONDON & U K DATEBOOK. Variant title: The London & United Kingdom Datebook. Text in English. 1994 (Sep.). q. GBP 25 (effective 2009). adv. **Document type:** *Magazine, Consumer.* **Description:** Provides a comprehensive listing of the major charitable events throughout the UK including articles, useful information, pictures from charity events and information about venues for all kinds of functions.
Published by: The London & U K Datebook, Production Office, Finchingfield, PO Box 935, Braintree, Essex, United Kingdom. TEL 44-1371-810999, FAX 44-1371-810520. Ed. Mary Kay Eyerman TEL 44-1371-851870. Adv. contact Bob Williams TEL 44-1400-283566.

LONDON DISABILITY NEWS. *see* HANDICAPPED

360 GBR ISSN 1460-9770
LONDON SCHOOL OF ECONOMICS AND POLITICAL SCIENCE. C A S E BRIEFS. (Centre for Analysis of Social Exclusion) Text in English. 1997. irreg., latest no.27, 2004. back issues avail. **Document type:** *Monographic series, Academic/Scholarly.*
Related titles: Online - full text ed.: free (effective 2010).
—CCC.
Published by: London School of Economics and Political Science, Centre for Analysis of Social Exclusion, Houghton St, London, WC2A 2AE, United Kingdom. TEL 44-20-79556679, FAX 44-20-79556951.

360 GBR ISSN 1460-5023
LONDON SCHOOL OF ECONOMICS AND POLITICAL SCIENCE. C A S E PAPERS. (Centre for Analysis of Social Exclusion) Text in English. 1985. irreg., latest no.139, 2009. back issues avail. **Document type:** *Monographic series, Academic/Scholarly.*
Formerly (until 1997): Welfare State Programme Discussion Paper Series (0969-4463)
Related titles: Online - full text ed.: free (effective 2010).
—CCC.
Published by: London School of Economics and Political Science, Centre for Analysis of Social Exclusion, Houghton St, London, WC2A 2AE, United Kingdom. TEL 44-20-79556679, FAX 44-20-79556951.

305 GBR ISSN 1465-3001
LONDON SCHOOL OF ECONOMICS AND POLITICAL SCIENCE. C A S E REPORTS. (Centre for Analysis of Social Exclusion) Text in English. 1998. irreg., latest no.60, 2010. back issues avail. **Document type:** *Monographic series, Academic/Scholarly.*
Related titles: Online - full text ed.: free (effective 2010).
Published by: London School of Economics and Political Science, Centre for Analysis of Social Exclusion, Houghton St, London, WC2A 2AE, United Kingdom. TEL 44-20-79556679, FAX 44-20-79556951.

LONG TERM CARE. *see* GERONTOLOGY AND GERIATRICS

362.82 361.73 200 USA ISSN 0024-6425
BV2660
LOOKOUT (NEW YORK). Text in English. 1909. 3/yr. USD 5 (effective 1999). bk.rev. illus. **Document type:** *Newsletter.* **Description:** Informs and educates the public about the institute's activities on behalf of merchant seafarers and the maritime issues that affect them and the institute's work. Also includes personal profiles, maritime art, articles on maritime history, and fundraising reports.
Indexed: L09.
Published by: Seamen's Church Institute of New York and New Jersey, 241 Water St, New York, NY 10038. TEL 212-349-9090, FAX 212-349-8342. Ed. Bev Jatek. Circ: 11,000 (controlled).

362.1 612 616.5 USA
LOOSE CONNECTIONS. Text in English. 1986. q. USD 25 domestic membership; USD 30 in Canada & Mexico membership; USD 35 elsewhere membership. adv. bk.rev. **Document type:** *Newsletter, Consumer.* **Description:** Provides emotional support and information to persons who suffer from Ehlers Danlos syndrome and serves as communication link with the medical community.
Published by: Ehlers-Danlos National Foundation, 6399 Wilshire Blvd., Ste. 203, Los Angeles, CA 90048-5705. Ed. Maggie Buckley. Pub. Keith Clarke. R&P, Adv. contact Linda Neuman-Potash. Circ: 2,000.

361.73 900 910.2 USA ISSN 0891-7310
LOS ANGELES MASTERPLANNER. Text in English. 1986 (Aug.). m. USD 180 (effective 2002). **Document type:** *Directory, Consumer.* **Description:** Lists complete information about thousands of major fundraisers, openings and special events planned for the coming year. Also contains advice on planning and attending social, fund-raising and business events.
Published by: Masterplanner Media, Inc., 8899 Beverly Blvd, Ste. 408, Los Angeles, CA 90048. TEL 310-888-8566, FAX 310-888-1866, http://www.masterplanneronline.com. Ed. Janice Mall. Pub. Elisabeth Familian. Adv. contact Cindi Richardson.

360 ARG ISSN 1852-7299
▼ **LOS TRABAJOS Y LOS DIAS.** Text in Spanish. 2009. bi-m. back issues avail. **Document type:** *Journal, Academic/Scholarly.*
Published by: Universidad Nacional de la Plata, Facultad de Trabajo Social, Calle # 9 Esq 63, La Plata, 1900, Argentina. TEL 54-221-4525317, tsocial@isis.unlp.edu.ar, http://www.trabajosocial.unlp.edu.ar.

360 610 CAN
M A P NEWS. Text in English. 1989. q. free. bk.rev. illus. **Document type:** *Newsletter.* **Description:** Reports on the events and medical conditions in the Occupied Territories.
Related titles: French ed.: Info A M P.
Published by: Medical Aid for Palestine/Aide Medicale pour la Palestine, 356 Sherbrooke E, Montreal, PQ H2X 1E6, Canada. TEL 514-843-7875, FAX 514-843-3061. Circ: 2,000.

M C C ANNUAL REPORT. *see* RELIGIONS AND THEOLOGY—Other Denominations And Sects

360 289.7 USA
M C C RESOURCE UPDATE. Text in English. s-a. free (effective 2010). **Document type:** *Newsletter, Consumer.* **Description:** Provides information about new MCC audiovisual and printed materials.
Published by: Mennonite Central Committee, 21 S 12th St, PO Box 500, Akron, PA 17501. TEL 717-859-1151, 888-563-4676, sam@mcc.org.

360 AUS ISSN 1837-588X
▼ **M D 201 N2 LIONS NEWSLETTER.** (Multiple District) Text in English. 2009. q. **Document type:** *Newsletter, Trade.* **Description:** Encompasses South-east New South Wales and the Australian Capital Territory, comprising 65 Lions Clubs, 7 Leo Clubs, and 6 Lioness Clubs serving their communities in South-west suburbs of Sydney, Southern Highlands etc.
Related titles: Online - full text ed.: ISSN 1837-5898. free (effective 2011).
Published by: Lions District M D 201 N2, 6 Hoskings Cres, Kiama Downs, NSW 2533, Australia. TEL 61-2-42375523, http://201n2.lions.org.au. Ed. David Robson.

361.6 780 CAN ISSN 1910-9512
M E P. ANNUAL REPORT. (Music Entrepreneur Program) Text in English. 2004. a. **Document type:** *Report, Trade.*
Published by: (Canadian Heritage, Canada Music Fund/Fonds de la Musique du Canada), Canadian Heritage/Patrimoine Canadien, 15 Eddy St, Gatineau, PQ K1A 0M5, Canada. TEL 819-997-0055, 866-811-0055, pch-qc@pch.gc.ca, http://www.pch.gc.ca.

360 CAN ISSN 0315-9655
M I C MISSION NEWS. Text in English. 1973. q. CAD 3.
Published by: Missionary Sisters of the Immaculate Conception, 120 Pl. Juge-Desnoyers, Laval, PQ H7G 1A4, Canada. TEL 450-663-6460, FAX 450-972-1512. Ed. Sr Anthea Raso. Circ: 3,500.

360 USA
M M I BULLETIN. Text in English. m. USD 90 to non-members; USD 80 to members (effective 2001). bk.rev. **Document type:** *Bulletin.* **Description:** Contains timely updates neatly packaged for state medical staff and persons with similar interests. Includes federal register highlights, court cases, legislation introduced in Congress, medical waivers, reports and conferences.
Formerly: M I A P Bulletin
Published by: Medicaid Management Institute, c/o American Public Welfare Association, 810 First St, N E, Ste 500, Washington, DC 20002-4267. TEL 202-682-0100, FAX 202-289-6555. Ed. Lee Partridge.

360 PHL
M S D D DIGEST. Text in English. 1978. q.
Published by: Department of Social Welfare and Development, Public Information Division, 389 San Rafael St, Manila, Philippines. Ed. Susan Argel.

361 NLD ISSN 1567-6587
MAATWERK. Text in Dutch. 1972. bi-m. EUR 86, USD 129 combined subscription to institutions (print & online eds.) (effective 2009). adv. bk.rev. **Document type:** *Journal, Trade.*
Former titles (until 1998): Maatschappelijk Werk Magazine (1382-3329); (until 1994): L V M W Nieuws (0926-0161); (until 1989): N O W Nieuws (0166-6037); (until 1978): N V M W Nieuws (0049-0725)
Related titles: Online - full text ed.: ISSN 1876-6021.
Indexed: A22, E01.
Published by: (Nederlandse Vereniging voor Maatschappelijk Werkers), Bohn Stafleu van Loghum B.V. (Subsidiary of: Springer Science+Business Media), Postbus 246, Houten, 3990 GA, Netherlands. TEL 31-30-6383830, FAX 31-30-6383999, boekhandels@bsl.nl, http://www.bsl.nl. Ed. Margot Scholte. adv.: page EUR 751; trim 210 x 297. Circ: 4,900.

MA'DANG: JOURNAL OF CONTEXTUAL THEOLOGY IN EAST ASIA. *see* RELIGIONS AND THEOLOGY

360 SWE ISSN 1651-0224
MAENNISKORS VAERDE, HAELSA OCH VITALISERANDE PROCESSER. Text in Swedish. 2001. irreg., latest 2003. back issues avail. **Document type:** *Proceedings, Academic/Scholarly.*
Published by: Oerebro Universitet, Universitetsbiblioteket/University of Oerebro. University Library, Fakultetsgatan 1, Oerebro, 70182, Sweden. TEL 46-19-303240, FAX 46-19-331217, biblioteket@ub.oru.se. Ed. Joanna Jansdotter.

360 AUT
MAGAZIN MOBIL. Text in German. m.
Published by: Verein Aktion Mobil, Laxenburgerstrasse 90a-10, Vienna, A-1100, Austria. TEL 01-626393. Ed. Peter Schumann. Circ: 25,000.

360 CAN ISSN 1719-4482
MAGAZINE DU NOUVEL ARRIVANT AU CANADA. Text in French. 2004. q. **Document type:** *Magazine, Consumer.*
Published by: Ontario Council of Agencies Serving Immigrants, 110 Eglinton Ave West, Ste 200, Toronto, ON M4R 1A3, Canada. TEL 416-322-4950, FAX 416-322-8084, generalmail@ocasi.org, http://www.ocasi.org/index.php.

362 363.5 NLD ISSN 2210-7509
▼ **MAGAZINE W M O EN WONEN.** Text in Dutch. 2010. s-a. free (effective 2010). **Document type:** *Magazine, Consumer.*
Published by: Kenniscentrum WMO en Wonen, Postbus 106, Purmerend, 1440 AC, Netherlands. TEL 31-299-418700, wmowonen@primo-nh.nl. Ed. Minja Holzhaus. Circ: 18,000.

361.77 DEU
MAHLZEIT!, Kundenmagazin im Naturkostfachhandel. Text in German. 1982. m. free (effective 2010). adv. **Document type:** *Magazine, Consumer.*
Published by: Fegers Druck und Verlag GmbH, Rosental 51-53, Nettetal-Lobberich, 41334, Germany. TEL 49-2153-91680, FAX 49-2153-916827, verlag@fegers.de. Ed. Marita Offermanns. Adv. contact Michael Duss. Circ: 50,000 (controlled).

361 USA ISSN 1064-2587
HC107.M2
MAINE POLICY REVIEW. Text in English. 1991. 3/yr. Donation (effective 2007). **Document type:** *Magazine, Consumer.* **Description:** Publishes independent analyses of public policy issues relevant to Maine by providing accurate information and thoughtful commentary. Issues range from snowmobiling to housing. Majority of articles written by Maine citizens, many of whom are readers of the journal.
Published by: Margaret Chase Smith Center for Public Policy, University of Maine, 5784 York Complex, Bldg 4, Orono, ME 04469-5784. mcsc@umit.maine.edu, http://www.umaine.edu/mcsc/mpr.htm. Ed. Ann Acheson.

361.8 051 305.4 USA ISSN 2151-0431
MAKE IT BETTER; north shore: family, community and you. Text in English. m. free (effective 2009). **Document type:** *Magazine, Consumer.* **Description:** Contains articles and features for women from the North Shore area of Chicago interested in community and philanthropy.
Published by: Make It Better, LLC, 1150 Wilmette Ave, Ste J, Wilmette, IL 60091. TEL 847-256-4642, larry@makeitbetter.net.

MAKING HOMECOMINGS POSSIBLE. *see* CHILDREN AND YOUTH—About

330.9 338.9 CAN ISSN 1192-2427
HC117
MAKING WAVES; Canada's community economic development magazine. Text in English. 1989. q. CAD 36 domestic to individuals; CAD 44 in United States to individuals; CAD 54 elsewhere to individuals; CAD 48 domestic to institutions; CAD 56 in United States to institutions; CAD 66 elsewhere to institutions (effective 2006). adv. bk.rev. illus. back issues avail. **Document type:** *Magazine, Academic/Scholarly.* **Description:** Examines the principles and practice of economic development that help rebuild the power and prosperity of impoverished communities.
Related titles: Online - full text ed.
Indexed: APW, AltPI, PQC.
Published by: Centre for Community Enterprise, 1601, 25th Ave, Vernon, BC V1T 1M8, Canada. TEL 888-255-6779, mcnair@cedworks.com, http://www.cedworks.com. Ed. Michael Lewis. R&P, Adv. contact Donald McNair TEL 250-542-7057. B&W page CAD 575; trim 8.75 x 7. Circ: 650.

MALAY; dyornal ng humanidades at agham panlipunan - journal of humanities and social sciences. *see* HUMANITIES: COMPREHENSIVE WORKS

360 DEU ISSN 1436-641X
MALTESER-MAGAZIN. Text in German. 1985. q. adv. **Document type:** *Magazine, Consumer.*
Formerly (until 1998): Malteser-Mitteilungen (0939-348X)
Published by: Deutsche Malteser gGmbH, Kalker Hauptstr 22-24, Cologne, 51103, Germany. TEL 49-221-982201, FAX 49-221-9822399, malteser@maltanet.de. adv.: B&W page EUR 6,490, color page EUR 6,490; trim 210 x 297. Circ: 96,150 (controlled).

MALTRATTAMENTO E ABUSO ALL'INFANZIA. *see* CHILDREN AND YOUTH—About

MAMA LIANYIHUI JIANXUN. *see* CHILDREN AND YOUTH—About

MANAGEMENT ISSUES IN SOCIAL CARE. *see* PUBLIC HEALTH AND SAFETY

MANAGEMENT KINDEROPVANG. *see* CHILDREN AND YOUTH—About

658.048 321.3 GBR ISSN 0968-6630
MANAGEMENT OF VOLUNTARY ORGANISATIONS. Variant title: Croner's Management of Voluntary Organisations. Text in English. 1993. base vol. plus updates 3/yr. looseleaf. GBP 487 base vol(s). (effective 2010). **Document type:** *Journal, Trade.* **Description:** Provides practical advice on legal issues and good working practices.
Published by: Croner C C H Group Ltd. (Subsidiary of: Wolters Kluwer UK Ltd.), 145 London Rd, Kingston upon Thames, Surrey KT2 6SR, United Kingdom. TEL 44-20-85473333, FAX 44-20-85472638, info@croner.co.uk.

362.5 304.6 301 ITA ISSN 1594-7920
MANITESE. Text in Italian. 1964. m. EUR 20 (effective 2008). **Document type:** *Magazine, Consumer.*
Published by: Manitese, Piazza Gambara 7-9, Milan, 20146, Italy. TEL 39-02-4075165, FAX 39-02-4046890, manitese@manitese.it, http://www.manitese.it.

361.73 361.8 ESP ISSN 0214-5979
MANOS UNIDAS. Text in Spanish. 1967. q. bk.rev. charts; illus.; bibl. Supplement avail. **Document type:** *Bulletin, Consumer.*
Formerly (until 19??): Campana Contra el Hambre en el Mundo. Boletin (0214-5960)
Published by: Campana Contra el Hambre en el Mundo, Barquillo 38, 3o, Madrid, 28004, Spain. TEL 34-91-3082020, FAX 34-91-2400707, info@manosunidas.org, http://www.manosunidas.org. Ed. Ana de Felipe. Pub. Javier Marmol.

360 DEU
MARKT UND CHANCE - BEWERBERPROFILE. Text in German. 1955. 2/w. looseleaf. free. **Document type:** *Trade.*
Formerly (until 2001): Zentraler Bewerberanzeiger Markt und Chance (0177-3836)
Published by: Bundesagentur fuer Arbeit, Regensburger Str 104, Nuernberg, 90478, Germany. TEL 49-911-1790, FAX 49-911-1792123, zentrale@arbeitsagentur.de, http://www.arbeitsagentur.de.

MATERIA SOCIO MEDICA. *see* MEDICAL SCIENCES

368.4 MUS
MAURITIUS. MINISTRY OF SOCIAL SECURITY. NATIONAL SOLIDARITY AND REFORM INSTITUTIONS. Text in English. 1962. a. MUR 25. **Document type:** *Government.* **Description:** Information on various branches of the ministry.
Former titles: Mauritius. Ministry for Employment and of Social Security and National Solidarite; (until 1982): Mauritius. Ministry of Social Security. Annual Report (0076-5538)
Published by: Ministry of Social Security National Solidarity and Reform Institution, Astor Court, Lislet Geoffroy St., Port Louis, Mauritius. Circ: 300. **Orders to:** Government Printing Office, Elizabeth II Ave, Port Louis, Mauritius.

360 USA ISSN 1931-5457
LC220.5
MCMASTER SCHOOL FOR ADVANCING HUMANITY. JOURNAL. Text in English. 2006. a. back issues avail. **Document type:** *Journal, Academic/Scholarly.* **Description:** Serve as a focal point for teaching, service, scholarship, and action to improve the human condition worldwide.
Related titles: Online - full text ed.: free (effective 2010).
Published by: Defiance College, McMaster School for Advancing Humanity, 701 N Clinton St, Defiance, OH 43512. TEL 419-783-2552, 800-520-4632, admissions@defiance.edu, http://www.defiance.edu/mcmaster_school.html. Ed. Laurie Worrall.

360 SAU ISSN 1658-5151
▼ **MEDAD JOURNAL**; a semi-annual journal for charitable work studies. Text in Arabic; Summaries in Arabic, English. 2010 (Jun). s-a. SAR 50 domestic to individuals; SAR 100 domestic to institutions; USD 25 foreign to individuals; USD 60 foreign to institutions; free to qualified personnel (effective 2010). **Document type:** *Journal, Academic/Scholarly.* **Description:** Charitable work in the Arab Gulf region: beginnings and development, challenges facing Islamic charitable work in Africa: a strategic perspective, charitable work conferences and seminars held in the member states of the Gulf Cooperation Council (GCC) in the period 2000-2008: a descriptive and analytical study, opinion polls and their use in charitable work and fund raising.
Published by: al Markaz al-Duwali lil-'abhathi wa'al-Dirasati (M E D A D)/International Center for Research and Studies (M E D A D), PO Box 120500, Jeddah, 21322, Saudi Arabia. TEL 966-2-6285454, FAX 966-2-6285030, info@medadcenter.com, http://www.medadcenter.com. Ed. D Khalid Bin Abdullah Al-Serihi. Circ: 2,000 (paid and controlled).

MEDIATEUR ACTUALITES. *see* PUBLIC ADMINISTRATION

361 GBR ISSN 1476-699X
MEDIATION MATTERS. Text in English. 1984. q. GBP 41 to individual members; GBP 250 to institutional members; GBP 17.50 to students (effective 2005). back issues avail. **Document type:** *Magazine, Consumer.* **Description:** Addresses individuals and organizations seeking alternatives to legal action to resolve conflicts.
Formerly (until 2002): Mediation (0960-5894)
Published by: Mediation U K, Alexander House, Telephone Ave, Bristol, Avon BS1 4BS, United Kingdom. TEL 44-117-9046661, FAX 44-117-9043331, enquiry@mediationuk.org.uk, http://www.mediationuk.org.uk/. Ed., R&P Tara Barker.

360 USA
MEDICAID DIRECTORS' NETWORK. Text in English. m.
Published by: State Medicaid Directors' Association, c/o American Public Welfare Association, 810 First St, N E, Ste 500, Washington, DC 20002-4205. TEL 202-682-0100, FAX 202-289-6555.

MEDICARE AND MEDICAID FRAUD AND ABUSE. *see* CRIMINOLOGY AND LAW ENFORCEMENT

MEDICARE & MEDICAID RESEARCH REVIEW. *see* MEDICAL SCIENCES

361.6 347.30423 USA ISSN 0733-4672
KF3608.A4
MEDICARE EXPLAINED. Text in English. a. USD 47 (effective 2006).
Supersedes in part (in 1979): Social Security and Medicare Explained (0162-6361); Which was formerly (until 1971): Medicare and Social Security Explained
Published by: C C H Inc. (Subsidiary of: Wolters Kluwer N.V.), 2700 Lake Cook Rd, Riverwoods, IL 60015. TEL 847-267-7000, cust_serv@cch.com, http://www.cch.com.

MEDICARE PART D NEWS. *see* INSURANCE

EL MEDICO. ANUARIO DE LA SANIDAD Y DEL MEDICAMENTO EN ESPANA. *see* PUBLIC HEALTH AND SAFETY

MEDIZINSOZIOLOGIE UND GESUNDHEITSWISSENSCHAFTEN. *see* PUBLIC HEALTH AND SAFETY

362.4 NLD ISSN 1876-7818
MEE MAGAZINE. Text in Dutch. 1996. q.
Former titles (until 2008): Stuifmeel (1574-7832); (until 2004): De Spin (1387-4705)
Published by: MEE Zuid-Limburg, Frankenlaan 7, Heerlen, 6419 BT, Netherlands. TEL 31-45-5718577, FAX 31-45-5740090. Eds. Jantsje Hoogeveen, Lex van Wijk. Circ: 2,500.

MEE MAGAZINE (LEIDSCHENDAM). *see* HANDICAPPED

362.4 NLD ISSN 2210-3546
▼ **MEE MAGAZINE (UTRECHT).** Text in Dutch. 2009. q. **Document type:** *Magazine, Consumer.*
Published by: MEE Utrecht, Gooi en Vecht, Postbus 9168, Utrecht, 3506 GD, Netherlands. TEL 31-900-6336363, FAX 31-30-2642201, info@mee-ugv.nl, http://www.mee-ugv.nl. Circ: 15,000.

362.4 NLD ISSN 2210-8610
MEE MAGAZINE (WEST-BRABANT). Text in Dutch. 2008. q. free (effective 2010). **Document type:** *Magazine, Consumer.*
Published by: MEE West-Brabant, Postbus 3207, Breda, 4800 DE, Netherlands. TEL 31-76-5223090, FAX 31-76-5149010, info@meewestbrabant.nl, http://www.meewestbrabant.nl. Circ: 7,000.

362.4 NLD ISSN 1573-4145
MEEDELEN (MIDDELBURG). Text in Dutch. 2004. 3/yr. free (effective 2009).
Published by: MEE Zeeland, Postbus 174, Middelburg, 4330 AD, Netherlands. TEL 31-118-432000, FAX 31-118-432010, meezeeland@meezeeland.nl.

MEGAPHON. *see* GENERAL INTEREST PERIODICALS—Austria

360 AUS ISSN 0728-1897
MELBOURNE CITYMISSION. ANNUAL REPORT. Text in English. 1855. a. back issues avail. **Document type:** *Corporate.* **Description:** Highlights the activities of the Melbourne Citymission in achieving the goal of providing a fair and just community, where people have equal access to opportunities and resources.
Former titles (until 1979): Community Welfare Foundation. Annual Report (0728-1889); (until 1970): Melbourne City Mission. Annual Report of the Melbourne City Mission
Related titles: Online - full text ed.: free (effective 2009).
Published by: Melbourne Citymission, Law Courts PO, PO Box 13210, Melbourne, VIC 8010, Australia. TEL 61-3-86254444, FAX 61-3-86254410, info@mcm.org.au.

MEMO W W B INKOMEN. (Wet Werk en Bijstand) *see* BUSINESS AND ECONOMICS—Labor And Industrial Relations

362.82 331.11 NLD ISSN 1573-2231
MEMO W W B REINTEGRATIE. Key Title: Wet Werk en Bijstand. Cover title: W W B Reintegratie Memo. Text in Dutch. 2004. a. EUR 47.70 (effective 2009).
Published by: Kluwer B.V. (Subsidiary of: Wolters Kluwer N.V.), Postbus 23, Deventer, 7400 GA, Netherlands. TEL 31-570-673555, FAX 31-570-691555, info@kluwer.nl, http://www.kluwer.nl.

360 AUT ISSN 1023-8220
MENSCHEN BRAUCHEN MENSCHEN..UND INFORMATIONEN. Text in German. 1963. q. looseleaf. EUR 4 (effective 2002). adv. bk.rev. illus.; stat. **Document type:** *Newsletter, Consumer.*
Formerly (until 1998): Lebenshilfe
Related titles: Diskette ed.; E-mail ed.; Fax ed.; Online - full text ed.
Published by: Lebenshilfe Oesterreich, Foerstergasse 6, Vienna, 1020, Austria. TEL 43-1-812-26-42, FAX 43-1-812-26-42-85, kommunikation@lebenshilfe.at, http://www.lebenshilfe.at. Ed., R&P Birgit Primig. Adv. contact Andrea Pescha. Circ: 14,500.

360 DEU
MENSCHEN IM BLICKPUNKT. Text in German. 1989. q. adv. **Document type:** *Magazine, Trade.*
Published by: Bayerisches Rotes Kreuz, Seitzstr 8, Munich, 80538, Germany. TEL 49-89-23730, FAX 49-89-237344222, info@brk.de. adv.: color page EUR 5,090. Circ: 72,500 (controlled).

MENSEN IN NOOD NIEUWS. *see* BUSINESS AND ECONOMICS—International Development And Assistance

362.2 GBR ISSN 1463-9610
MENTAL HEALTH ACT COMMISSION. BIENNIAL REPORT. Text in English. 1985. biennial. GBP 25 per issue (effective 2009). back issues avail.
—BLDSC (2041.950000).
Published by: Care Quality Commission, Mental Health Act Commission, National Correspondence, Citygate, Gallowgate, Newcastle upon Tyne, NE1 4PA, United Kingdom. TEL 44-3000-616161, enquiries@cqc.org.uk.

360 150 GBR ISSN 2042-8308
MENTAL HEALTH AND SOCIAL INCLUSION. Text in English. 1997. q. EUR 689 combined subscription in Europe (print & online eds.); USD 889 combined subscription in the Americas (print & online eds.); GBP 529 combined subscription in the UK & elsewhere (print & online eds.); AUD 999 combined subscription in Australasia (print & online eds.) (effective 2012). adv. **Document type:** *Journal, Academic/Scholarly.* **Description:** Focuses on social inclusion issues for people who have mental health problems.
Formerly (until 2010): A Life in the Day (1366-6282)
Related titles: Online - full text ed.: ISSN 2042-8316.
Indexed: B28, C06, C07, C08, CINAHL, E-psyche, P19, P24, P25, P48, PQC, SCOPUS.
—CCC.
Published by: Pier Professional Ltd. (Subsidiary of: Emerald Group Publishing Ltd.), Ste N4, The Old Market, Upper Market St, Hove, BN3 1AS, United Kingdom. TEL 44-1273-783720, FAX 44-1273-783723, info@pierprofessional.com. Ed. Adam Pozner.

THE MENTAL HEALTH REVIEW JOURNAL. *see* MEDICAL SCIENCES—Psychiatry And Neurology

362.2 USA ISSN 0892-0664
RA790.6
MENTAL HEALTH: UNITED STATES. Text in English. 1983. biennial. **Document type:** *Government.*
Published by: U.S. Department of Health and Human Services, National Mental Health Information Center, 5600 Fishers Ln, Rockville, MD 20857. TEL 301-443-1805, 800-789-2647, FAX 301-984-8796, http://www.mentalhealth.samhsa.gov.

353.5 USA
MICHIGAN. DEPARTMENT OF SOCIAL SERVICES. ASSISTANCE PAYMENTS STATISTICS. Text in English. m. **Document type:** *Government.*
Related titles: Microfiche ed.: (from CIS).
Indexed: SRI.
Published by: Department of Social Services, 300 S Capitol Ave, PO Box 30037, Lansing, MI 48909. TEL 517-373-2005.

MIETERZEITUNG. *see* HOUSING AND URBAN PLANNING

MISSION ACTION. *see* RELIGIONS AND THEOLOGY—Protestant

360 AUS ISSN 1834-2523
MISSION AUSTRALIA. ANNUAL REVIEW. Text in English. 2006. a. **Document type:** *Journal, Trade.*
Related titles: Online - full text ed.: ISSN 1834-2531.
Published by: Mission Australia, GPO Box 3515, Sydney, NSW 2001, Australia. TEL 61-2-9219-2000, http://www.mission.com.au.

360 SWE ISSN 1403-1248
MISSION I STOCKHOLM. Text in Swedish. 1998. q. free (effective 2004).
Related titles: Online - full text ed.
Published by: Stadsmissionen/Stockholm's City Mission, Stortorget 3, PO Box 2266, Stockholm, 10317, Sweden. TEL 46-8-7878600, FAX 46-8-7878634, info@stadsmissionen.se.

353.9 USA
MISSOURI. DIVISION OF YOUTH SERVICES. ANNUAL REPORT. Text in English. 1949. a. illus.; stat. **Document type:** *Government.*
Formerly: Missouri. State Board of Training Schools. Annual Report (0098-0110)
Published by: Department of Social Services, Division of Youth Services, Broadway State Office Bldg, Box 447, Jefferson City, MO 65101. TEL 314-751-3324. Ed. Mark Steward. Circ: 500.

MITEINANDER (WUERZBURG). *see* MEDICAL SCIENCES

364 NLD ISSN 0929-2187
MO/SAMENLEVINGSOPBOUW. Text in Dutch. 1982. q. EUR 49; EUR 12.50 newsstand/cover (effective 2009). adv.
Formerly (until 1993): Mededelingen Opbouwwerk (0168-065X)
Published by: Movisie, Postbus 19129, Utrecht, 3501 DC, Netherlands. TEL 31-30-7892000, FAX 31-30-7892111, info@movisie.nl. Ed. Fenny Gerrits.

362.7 NLD ISSN 0929-9254
MOBIEL; tijdschrift voor pleegzorg. Text in Dutch. 194?. bi-m. EUR 28.65 domestic; EUR 30.10 in Belgium; EUR 5 newsstand/cover (effective 2009). adv. **Document type:** *Bulletin.* **Description:** Provides information on foster care.
Formerly (until 1973): Poort (0166-6819)
Related titles: E-mail ed.; Fax ed.; Online - full text ed.
Address: Postbus 753, Zwolle, 8000 AT, Netherlands. TEL 31-33-4767297, FAX 31-38-4226898, uitgever@mobiel-pleegzorg.nl, http://www.mobiel-pleegzorg.nl. Ed. Jolanda Stellingwerff. adv.: B&W page EUR 940; trim 210 x 297. Circ: 8,800.

MOBILISE. *see* HANDICAPPED

361 338.91 USA ISSN 1043-8157
MONDAY DEVELOPMENTS. Text in English. 1983. 22/yr. USD 65 to individuals; USD 275 to institutions. adv. bk.rev. **Document type:** *Newsletter.* **Description:** Contains news and commenatry on international humanitarian activities, including crisis situations abroad, sustainable development work, policy changes, newly available resources, coming events and employment opportunities.
Indexed: P30.
Published by: (InterAction: American Council for Voluntary International Action), InterAction, 1717 Massachusetts Ave, N W, 8th Fl, Washington, DC 20036. TEL 202-667-8227, FAX 202-667-8236. Ed. Michael Kernan. Circ: 2,500.

MONITOR ARBEIDSGEHANDICAPTEN. *see* HANDICAPPED

S

362 368.382 NLD ISSN 1871-9678
MONITOR BEHEERSKOSTEN AWBZ ZORGKANTOREN. Text in Dutch. 200?. a. free (effective 2008).
Published by: College voor Zorgverzekeringen, Postbus 320, Diemen, 1110 AH, Netherlands. TEL 31-20-7978555, FAX 31-20-7978500, info@cvz.nl, http://www.cvz.nl.

MONITOR GESUBSIDIEERDE RECHTSBIJSTAND. *see* LAW—Legal Aid

362.7 USA
MOUNTAIN SPIRIT. Text in English. 1982. q. cum.index: 1982-1992. back issues avail. **Document type:** *Magazine, Consumer.* **Description:** Describes the problems of people who live in Appalachia and how CAP attempts to resolve the issues in question.
Published by: Christian Appalachian Project, P.O. Box 511, Lancaster, KY 40444-0511. TEL 859-792-3051, FAX 859-792-6560, 866-270-4227, capinfo@chrisapp.org, http://www.chrisapp.org. Ed. Margaret Gabriel. Circ: 30,000.

362.4 CAN ISSN 1484-2246
MOVING AHEAD. Variant title: On va de l'Avant. Text in English, French. 1997. irreg. **Document type:** *Newsletter.*
Related titles: Online - full content ed.: ISSN 1495-8678.
Published by: (Canadian Transportation Agency, Accessible Transportation Directorate), Canadian Transportation Agency/Office des Transports du Canada, 15 Eddy St, Ottawa, ON K1A 0N9, Canada. TEL 819-953-8353, 888-222-2592, FAX 819-953-5686, cta.comment@cta-otc.gc.ca.

300 FRA ISSN 1765-0917
MUTUALISTES. Text in French. 1972. bi-m. adv. film rev. illus. **Document type:** *Newspaper.*
Formerly (until 2003): Objectif et Action Mutualistes (0154-8530)
Published by: Cooperative d'Information et d'Edition Mutualiste (C.I.E.M.), 67 rue Blomet, Paris, 75015, France. TEL 33-1-44496100, FAX 33-1-44496104. Ed. Philippe Marchal.

362 305.896 NLD ISSN 1872-5597
MZINE. Text in Dutch. 2002. bi-m. EUR 39.95; EUR 4.75 newsstand/cover (effective 2010). adv. **Document type:** *Magazine, Consumer.*
Published by: Stichting Diversity Affairs, Postbus 463, Waalwijk, 5140 AL, Netherlands. TEL 31-73-7040138, FAX 31-73-7040333. adv.: color page EUR 4,565; trim 210 x 285. Circ: 10,000.

N A A C P ANNUAL REPORT. *see* ETHNIC INTERESTS

N A C R O ANNUAL REVIEW. *see* CRIMINOLOGY AND LAW ENFORCEMENT

368.4 USA
N A D E ADVOCATE. Text in English. 1978. bi-m. USD 40. adv. stat.; tr.lit. back issues avail.
Published by: National Association of Disability Examiners, c/o Donna Hilton, Ed, 1117 Sunshine Dr, Aurora, MO 65605. TEL 417-888-4152, FAX 417-888-4069, drhilton@sofnet.com. Circ: 2,500.

N A D MAG. (National Association of the Deaf) *see* HANDICAPPED—Hearing Impaired

361.7 USA
N A E I R ADVANTAGE. Text in English. 1982. bi-m. free. **Document type:** *Newsletter.* **Description:** Discusses corporate donations of excess inventory for use by schools and charities, and the subsequent tax benefits for the donors.
Formerly: N A E I R News
Published by: National Association for the Exchange of Industrial Resources, 560 McClure St, Box 8076, Galesburg, IL 61402. TEL 309-343-0704, 800-562-0955, FAX 309-343-0862, jez@naeir.org, http://www.naeir.org. Ed., R&P Jack Zavada. Pub. Gary C Smith. Circ: 30,000 (controlled).

N A H R O AGENCY AWARDS OF MERIT IN HOUSING AND COMMUNITY DEVELOPMENT. *see* HOUSING AND URBAN PLANNING

360 USA
N A P C W A NETWORK. Text in English. 1983. q. USD 75 membership (effective 2000). bk.rev. **Document type:** *Newsletter.*
Published by: National Association of Public Child Welfare Administrators, c/o American Public Welfare Association, 810 First St, N E, Ste 500, Washington, DC 20002-4205. TEL 202-682-0100, FAX 202-289-6555. Ed. Gretchen Test. Circ: 700.

360 CAN ISSN 1196-6564
N A P O NEWS/ECHO DE L'O N A P. Text in English, French. 1983. q. membership. bk.rev. back issues avail. **Document type:** *Newspaper.* **Description:** News on poverty, anti-poverty organizations and issues of importance to low-income Canadians.
Former titles (until 1993): Anti-Poverty News (1196-6572); (until 1992): N A P O News (0820-7364); (until 1983): N A P O Info News (0225-7130); (until 1978?): N A P O Info (0380-1012)
Published by: National Anti-Poverty Organization, 325 Dalhousie St Ste 440, Ottawa, ON K1N 7G2, Canada. TEL 613-789-0096, FAX 613-789-0141. Circ: 3,000.

361.8 USA
N A S C O GUIDE TO CAMPUS CO-OPS. Text in English. 1974. triennial. USD 3. adv. **Document type:** *Directory.* **Description:** Lists the publications that NCBA and other cooperative organizations publish on various types of retail, housing, and service cooperatives.
Former titles: N A S C O Campus Co-Op Directory; Cooperatives in Campus Areas of North America
Related titles: Online - full text ed.
Published by: North American Students of Cooperation, PO Box 7715, Ann Arbor, MI 48107. TEL 313-663-0889. Circ: 2,000.

360 USA ISSN 0027-6022
N A S W NEWS. Text in English. 1955. m. (except Aug. & Dec.). USD 34 domestic libraries/institutions; USD 53 foreign libraries/institutions (effective 2010). adv. illus. reprints avail. **Document type:** *Newspaper, Trade.* **Description:** Serves as a primary information vehicle for practitioners, administrators, researchers, faculty, and students.
Formerly: Personnel Information; Incorporates: American Association of Psychiatric Services for Children. Newsletter (0093-0237); Which was formerly: American Association of Psychiatric Clinics for Children. Newsletter (0569-2733)
Related titles: Microform ed.: (from PQC).
Indexed: A22.
—CCC.
Published by: (National Association of Social Workers), N A S W Press, 750 First St NE, Ste 700, Washington, DC 20002-4241. TEL 202-408-8600, 800-227-3590, FAX 202-336-8312, press@naswdc.org, http://www.naswpress.org. adv.: B&W page USD 6,595. Circ: 127,000 (paid).

360 USA ISSN 0277-0695
HV89
N A S W REGISTER OF CLINICAL SOCIAL WORKERS. (National Association of Social Workers) Text in English. 1976. biennial. USD 60 per issue (effective 2004). **Document type:** *Directory.*
Published by: National Association of Social Workers, 750 First St., NE, Ste. 700, Washington, DC 20002-4241. TEL 202-408-8600, FAX 202-336-8312, http://www.socialworkers.org.

N C D BULLETIN. (National Council on Disability) *see* HANDICAPPED

361 CAN ISSN 1718-9675
N C I L NEWS. (Niagara Centre for Independent Living) Text in English. 2006. q. **Document type:** *Newsletter, Consumer.*
Published by: The Niagara Centre for Independent Living, The Normandy Resource Centre, 111 Church St, St. Catharines, ON L2R 3C9, Canada. TEL 905-684-7111, FAX 905-684-1199, reception@abilityforlife.ca, http://www.abilityforlife.ca/index.html.

362.4 363.5 GBR
N H A BENEFITS GUIDE. Text in English. 1980. a. GBP 10.45 per vol. (effective 2000). **Document type:** *Handbook/Manual/Guide, Trade.* **Description:** Provides an authoritative reference source for advisers and counselors working with single homeless persons.
Formerly: C H A R Benefits Guide
Published by: National Homeless Alliance, 5-15 Cromer St, London, WC1H 8LS, United Kingdom. TEL 44-20-7833-2071, FAX 44-20-7278-6685.

N H O NEWSLINE. *see* ALTERNATIVE MEDICINE

346.01 SWE
N I A INFORMERAR. (Naemnd foer Internationella Adoptionsfraagor) Text in Swedish. 2001. quadrennial. free.
Media: Online - full content.
Published by: Statens Naemnd foer Internationella Adoptionsfraagor/ Swedish National Board for Intercountry Adoptions, PO Box 22086, Stockholm, 10422, Sweden. TEL 46-8-54555680, FAX 46-8-6504110, adoption@nia.se. Ed., R&P, Adv. contact Gunilla Bodin.

N I D A NOTES. (National Institute on Drug Abuse) *see* DRUG ABUSE AND ALCOHOLISM

360 IND ISSN 0253-6757
N I H F W TECHNICAL REPORTS. Text in English. 1978. irreg. **Document type:** *Report, Academic/Scholarly.*
Published by: National Institute of Health and Family Welfare, Baba Gang Nath Marg, Munirka, New Delhi, 110 067, India. TEL 91-11-26165959, 91-11-26101623, info.nihfw@nic.in.

336.185 346.02 USA ISSN 1551-8965
N I H GUIDE FOR GRANTS AND CONTRACTS (ONLINE). Text in English. 19??. irreg. back issues avail. **Document type:** *Government.*
Formerly (until 1997): N I H Guide for Grants and Contracts (Print) (1050-9364)
Media: Online - full text.
Indexed: EMBASE, ExcerpMed, MEDLINE, P30, SCOPUS.
—Infotrieve.
Published by: National Institutes of Health (Subsidiary of: U.S. Department of Health and Human Services), 9000 Rockville Pike, Bethesda, MD 20892. TEL 301-496-2125, 301-496-4000, nihinfo@od.nih.gov, http://www.nih.gov.

362 NOR ISSN 1890-6435
N O V A. NOTAT. (Norsk Institutt for Forskning om Opvekst, Velferd og Aldring) Text mainly in Norwegian; Text occasionally in English. 1997. irreg., latest 2010. price varies. back issues avail. **Document type:** *Monographic series, Academic/Scholarly.*
Formerly (until 2008): N O V A. Skriftserie (0808-9183)
Related titles: Online - full text ed.
Published by: Norsk Institutt for Forskning om Opvekst, Velferd og Aldring/Norwegian Social Research, PO Box 3223, Elisenberg, Oslo, 0208, Norway. TEL 47-22-541200, FAX 47-22-541201, nova@nova.no.

362 NOR ISSN 0808-5013
N O V A. RAPPORT. (Norsk Institutt for Forskning om Opvekst, Velferd og Aldring) Text in Norwegian. 1997. irreg., latest 2011. price varies. back issues avail. **Document type:** *Monographic series, Academic/Scholarly.*
Incorporates (1991-1997): U N Gforsk. Rapport (0803-446X); (1989-1997): Barnevernets Utviklingssenter. Rapportserie (0802-4278); (1973-1997): Norsk Gerontologisk Institutt. Rapport (0332-9593); Which was formerly (1971-1972): Norsk Gerontologisk Institutt. Nasjonalforeningen for Folkehelse. Rapport (0332-964X); (1970-1997): I N A S. Rapport (0800-5753); Which was formerly (1968-1970): Rapport fra I N A S (0801-292X)
Related titles: Online - full text ed.
Published by: Norsk Institutt for Forskning om Opvekst, Velferd og Aldring/Norwegian Social Research, PO Box 3223, Elisenberg, Oslo, 0208, Norway. TEL 47-22-541200, FAX 47-22-541201, nova@nova.no.

361.73 AUT
N P O - FORUM. (Non Profit Organisation) Text in German. m. **Document type:** *Journal, Trade.* **Description:** Provides information on issues and trends involving non-profit organizations.
Published by: Austria Presse Agentur, Gunoldstr 14, Vienna, W 1190, Austria. TEL 43-1-360600, FAX 43-1-360603099, kundenservice@apa.at, http://www.apa.at. Ed. Walter Eisenwort.

N'AMERIND FRIENDSHIP CENTRE. NEWSLETTER. *see* ETHNIC INTERESTS

NAMIBIA DEVELOPMENT BRIEFING; the voice of the Namibian non-governmental forum. *see* BUSINESS AND ECONOMICS—International Development And Assistance

362.7 USA ISSN 1046-5103
NATIONAL ADOPTION REPORT. Text in English. 1979. m. free. **Document type:** *Newsletter, Consumer.* **Description:** Examines and explains the many issues in adoption.
Incorporates: Unmarried Parents Today; National Council for Adoption. Legal Notes; Which was formerly: National Committee for Adoption. Legal Notes
Related titles: Online - full text ed.
Published by: National Council for Adoption, Inc., 225 N Washington St, Alexandria, VA 22314-2561. FAX 703-299-6004, ncfa@adoptioncouncil.org. Ed. Lee Allen.

362.7 USA
NATIONAL ADVOCATE. Text in English. 1981. q. USD 35 (effective 2007). bk.rev. back issues avail. **Document type:** *Magazine, Consumer.* **Description:** Practical resource for foster and adoptive parents, child and family advocates and child welfare agencies, highlighting current issues and topics of interest to care givers, listing supportive resources available, and providing opportunities for involvement in the organization as well as in the child welfare community.
Published by: National Foster Parent Association, Inc., 7512 Stanich Ave. #6, Gig Harbor, WA 98335. TEL 253-853-4000, 800-557-5238, FAX 253-853-4001, info@NFPAinc.org. Circ: 3,500.

360 USA
NATIONAL CERTIFIED COUNSELOR. Text in English. 3/yr. **Document type:** *Newsletter.*
Formerly (until 2000): N B C C News Notes (0886-7089)
Published by: National Board for Certified Counselors, Inc., PO Box 7387, Greensboro, NC 37417-0387. TEL 336-547-0607, FAX 336-547-0017, nbcc@nbcc.org, http://www.nbcc.org. Ed. Pam Leary.

362.7 344.0327 CAN ISSN 1498-9220
NATIONAL CHILD BENEFIT PROGRESS REPORT. Text in English. 1999. a.
Related titles: Online - full text ed.: ISSN 1498-4237.
Published by: National Child Benefit, Box 307, Ottawa, ON K1A 0J9, Canada. mcssinfo@govonca2.gov.on.ca.

362.7 IRL ISSN 1649-4245
NATIONAL CHILDREN'S OFFICE. ANNUAL REPORT. Text in English. 2002. a.
Incorporates (in 2003): Oifig Naisiunta Leanai. Tuarascail Bhliantuil (1649-623X)
Published by: National Children's Office, St Martin's House, 1st Fl, Waterloo Rd, Dublin, 4, Ireland. TEL 353-1-2420000, nco@health.gov.ie.

361.763 USA ISSN 1556-150X
NATIONAL COMMITTEE ON PLANNED GIVING. CONFERENCE PROCEEDINGS. Text in English. 2000 (Oct.). a. free membership (effective 2006). **Document type:** *Proceedings.*
Related titles: Online - full text ed.: (from IngentaConnect).
—Ingenta.
Published by: National Council on Planned Giving, 233 McCrea St, Ste 400, Indianapolis, IN 46225. TEL 317-269-6274, FAX 317-269-6276, ncpg@ncpg.org, http://www.ncpg.org/.

361.6 USA
NATIONAL CONFERENCE OF STATE SOCIAL SECURITY ADMINISTRATORS. PROCEEDINGS. Text in English. 1952. a. membership only. **Document type:** *Proceedings, Government.*
Published by: National Conference of State Social Security Administrators, c/o Jim Larche, Deputy Dir, Social Security Div, Employee Retirement System of Georgia, Two Northside 75, Ste 300, Atlanta, GA 30318. TEL 404-352-6400. Circ: (controlled).

360 CAN
NATIONAL COUCIL OF WELFARE. THE COST OF POVERTY. Text in English. irreg.
Published by: National Council of Welfare, 112 Kent St, 9th Fl., Place de Ville, Tower B, Ottawa, ON K1A 0J9, Canada. TEL 613-957-2961, FAX 613-957-0680, ncw@maqi.com.

362.7 USA
NATIONAL COUNCIL FOR ADOPTION. MEMO. Text in English. bi-w. USD 500 to members. **Document type:** *Newsletter.* **Description:** Covers fast-breaking news on adoption and related topics.
Formerly: National Committee for Adoption. Memo (1046-509X)
Published by: National Council for Adoption, Inc., 225 N Washington St, Alexandria, VA 22314-2561. ncfa@adoptioncouncil.org.

360 GBR
NATIONAL COUNCIL FOR VOLUNTARY ORGANIZATIONS. ANNUAL REPORT. Text in English. 19??. a. free to members (effective 2009). back issues avail. **Document type:** *Report, Trade.*
Formerly: National Council of Social Service. Annual Report (0077-409X)
Related titles: Online - full text ed.: free (effective 2009).
Published by: National Council for Voluntary Organisations, Regent's Wharf, 8 All Saints St, London, N1 9RL, United Kingdom. TEL 44-20-77136161, FAX 44-20-77136300, ncvo@ncvo-vol.org.uk, http://www.ncvo-vol.org.uk.

NATIONAL COUNCIL NEWS. *see* MEDICAL SCIENCES—Psychiatry And Neurology

305.42 296.67 USA ISSN 1946-5041
NATIONAL COUNCIL OF JEWISH WOMEN. NEW YORK SECTION. BULLETIN. Text in English. 19??. q. free to members (effective 2009). **Document type:** *Bulletin.*
Published by: National Council of Jewish Women, New York Section, 820 2nd Ave, New York, NY 10017. TEL 212-687-5030, FAX 212-687-5032, info@ncjwny.org, http://www.ncjwny.org.

360 CAN
NATIONAL COUNCIL OF WELFARE. CHILD POVERTY PROFILE. Text in English. a.
Published by: National Council of Welfare, 112 Kent St, 9th Fl., Place de Ville, Tower B, Ottawa, ON K1A 0J9, Canada. TEL 613-957-2961, FAX 613-957-0680, ncw@maqi.com.

360 CAN
NATIONAL COUNCIL OF WELFARE. JUSTICE AND THE POOR. Text in English. irreg.
Published by: National Council of Welfare, 112 Kent St, 9th Fl., Place de Ville, Tower B, Ottawa, ON K1A 0J9, Canada. TEL 613-957-2961, FAX 613-957-0680, ncw@maqi.com.

360 CAN ISSN 1204-2390
HC120.P6
NATIONAL COUNCIL OF WELFARE. POVERTY PROFILE. Text in English. a.
—CCC.
Published by: National Council of Welfare, 112 Kent St, 9th Fl., Place de Ville, Tower B, Ottawa, ON K1A 0J9, Canada. TEL 613-957-2961, FAX 613-957-0680, ncw@maqi.com.

360 CAN ISSN 1193-5243
HV101
NATIONAL COUNCIL OF WELFARE. WELFARE INCOMES REPORT (YEAR). Text in English. a.
Related titles: Online - full text ed.: ISSN 1494-5045.
Published by: National Council of Welfare, 112 Kent St, 9th Fl., Place de Ville, Tower B, Ottawa, ON K1A 0J9, Canada. TEL 613-957-2961, FAX 613-957-0680, ncw@maqi.com.

360 CAN
NATIONAL COUNCIL OF WELFARE. WELFARE-TO-WORK ROUNDTABLE. Text in English. irreg.
Published by: National Council of Welfare, 112 Kent St, 9th Fl., Place de Ville, Tower B, Ottawa, ON K1A 0J9, Canada. TEL 613-957-2961, FAX 613-957-0680, ncw@maqi.com.

NATIONAL COUNCIL ON AGEING AND OLDER PEOPLE. REPORT. *see* GERONTOLOGY AND GERIATRICS

360 USA ISSN 1559-1344
HV89
THE NATIONAL DIRECTORY OF ADULT & SENIOR SERVICES. Text in English. 2006. a. USD 199 per issue (effective 2010). **Document type:** *Directory, Trade.* **Description:** Designed for professionals who serves adults and seniors. Provides comprehensive data about the people and organizations to do the job for constituents.
Related titles: Online - full text ed.: ISSN 1559-1352.
Published by: Dorland Health, 4 Choke Cherry Rd, 2nd Fl, Rockville, MD 20850. TEL 301-354-2000, 888-707-5814, FAX 301-309-3847, kimluna@dorlandhealth.com.

NATIONAL DIRECTORY OF CHILDREN, YOUTH & FAMILIES SERVICES. *see* CHILDREN AND YOUTH—About

060 USA ISSN 1048-8154
AS29.5
NATIONAL DIRECTORY OF NONPROFIT ORGANIZATIONS; a comprehensive guide providing profiles and procedures for nonprofit organizations. Text in English. 1987. a. (in 3 vols.), latest 2009, 23rd ed. USD 390 (effective 2009). back issues avail. **Document type:** *Directory, Trade.* **Description:** Provides guidance to the nonprofit world, covering many nonprofit organizations required to file 990 returns with the internal revenue service.
Formerly (until 1990): Taft Directory of Nonprofit Organizations
Related titles: Online - full text ed.
Published by: Gale (Subsidiary of: Cengage Learning), 27500 Drake Rd, Farmington Hills, MI 48331. TEL 248-699-4253, 800-877-4253, FAX 877-363-4253, gale.customerservice@cengage.com, http://gale.cengage.com.

360 711.4 GBR ISSN 1462-8546
NATIONAL HOUSING FEDERATION DIRECTORY OF MEMBERS. Key Title: N H F Directory of Members. Text in English. 1982. a. GBP 125 combined subscription per issue to non-members; GBP 50 per issue to members (effective 2009). adv. **Document type:** *Directory, Trade.* **Description:** Provides up-to-date information on the federation's member organisations.
Formerly (until 1997): Housing Associations. Directory and Yearbook (1747-3098)
Related titles: Online - full text ed.: free to members (effective 2009).
—BLDSC (6109.460500). **CCC.**
Published by: National Housing Federation, Lion Ct, 25 Procter St, London, WC1V 6NY, United Kingdom. TEL 44-20-70671010, FAX 44-20-70671011, info@housing.org.uk, http://www.housing.org.uk/. Adv. contact Gareth Macfarlane TEL 44-845-2260477. page GBP 1,495; bleed 130 x 215.

NATIONAL INSTITUTE OF HEALTH SCIENCES. RESEARCH BULLETIN. *see* MEDICAL SCIENCES

NATIONAL INSURANCE INSTITUTE, JERUSALEM. ANNUAL SURVEY/S'QIRA SH'NATIT. *see* INSURANCE

361 USA
NATIONAL LEAGUE OF FAMILIES OF AMERICAN PRISONERS AND MISSING IN ACTION IN SOUTHEAST ASIA NEWSLETTER. Text in English. 1974. bi-m. looseleaf. USD 25 (effective 2001). adv. stat. back issues avail.; reprints avail. **Document type:** *Newsletter, Consumer.* **Description:** Purpose is the return of all prisoners, the fullest possible accounting for the missing and the repatriation of remains of those who died while serving in Southeast Asia.
Related titles: E-mail ed.; Online - full content ed.
Published by: National League of Families of American Prisoners and Missing in Action in Southeast Asia, 1005 N. Glebe Rd., Ste. 160, Arlington, VA 22201-5758. TEL 202-223-6846, FAX 202-785-9410, powmiafam@aol.comrve.com. Ed. Ann Mills Griffiths. Adv. contact Karen McManus. Circ: 2,000.

360 USA
NATIONAL ORGANIZATION FOR VICTIM ASSISTANCE NEWSLETTER. Text in English. 1977. a. looseleaf. USD 30 membership; USD 50 foreign membership; USD 100 to institutions. bk.rev. back issues avail. **Document type:** *Newsletter.* **Description:** Covers victim rights and services in the U.S. and abroad.
Published by: National Organization for Victim Assistance, 510 King St., Ste. 424, Alexandria, VA 22314-3132. TEL 202-232-6682, FAX 202-462-2255. Ed., R&P John H Stein. Circ: 3,500.

360 USA ISSN 0164-7415
HQ767.15
NATIONAL RIGHT TO LIFE NEWS. Text in English. 1973. s-m. USD 16 domestic; USD 28 foreign (effective 2000). adv. bk.rev.; film rev.; play rev. charts; illus.; pat.; stat. index. back issues avail. **Document type:** *Newspaper.* **Description:** Covers issues of abortion, infanticide, and euthanasia from medical, ethical, social and public policy perspectives.
Related titles: Online - full text ed.
Indexed: A01, A26, G05, G06, G07, G08, I05, M02, P34, T02.
Published by: National Right to Life Committee, Inc., 419 Seventh St, N W, Ste 500, Washington, DC 20004. TEL 202-626-8824, FAX 202-347-4754. Ed., R&P, Adv. contact Dave Andrusko. Pub. Wanda Franz. Circ: 390,000.

362.6 AUS ISSN 1834-2108
NATIONAL SENIORS PRODUCTIVE AGEING CENTRE. RESEARCH BULLETIN. Text in English. 2005. irreg. **Document type:** *Bulletin, Consumer.*
Media: Online - full text. **Related titles:** Print ed.: ISSN 1834-2094.
Published by: National Seniors Productive Ageing Centre, GPO Box 1450, Brisbane, QLD 4001, Australia. TEL 61-7-3211-9611, FAX 61-7-3211-9339, general@nationalseniors.com.au, http://www.nationalseniors.com.au/Default.htm.

362.7 USA
NATIONAL SERVICE NEWS. Text in English. 1966. bi-w. USD 10; (contribution). bk.rev. **Document type:** *Newsletter.* **Description:** Contains current news about national service.
Formerly: National Service Newsletter (1059-4922)
Published by: Corporation for National and Community Service, 1201 New York Ave. NW, Washington, DC 20525. TEL 202-606-5000, FAX 202-606-3472, info@cns.gov, http://www.nationalservice.org/Default.asp. Ed. Donald J Eberly. Circ: 1,900.

362.7 GBR
NATIONAL SOCIETY FOR THE PREVENTION OF CRUELTY TO CHILDREN. ANNUAL REPORT (ONLINE). Text in English. 1885. a. free (effective 2009). **Document type:** *Corporate.*
Formerly: National Society for the Prevention of Cruelty to Children. Annual Report (Print) (0077-5754)
Media: Online - full text.
Published by: National Society for the Prevention of Cruelty to Children, Weston House, 42 Curtain Rd, London, EC2A 3NH, United Kingdom. TEL 44-20-78252500, FAX 44-20-78252525, help@nspcc.org.uk, http://www.nspcc.org.uk.

NATIONAL YOUTH AFFAIRS RESEARCH SCHEME REPORTS. *see* CHILDREN AND YOUTH—About

300.720489 DNK
H62.5.D4
DET NATIONALE FORSKNINGSCENTER FOR VELFAERD. AARSBERETNING. Text in Danish. 1960. a. free. **Document type:** *Government.*
Former titles (until 2008): Denmark. Socialforskningsinstituttet. Aarsberetning (1397-6125); (until 1995): Denmark. Socialforskningsinstituttet. Aarsberetning (Year) (0907-6514); (until 1992): Denmark. Socialforskningsinstituttet. Beretning om Socialforskningsinstituttets Virksomhed (0107-4377)
Related titles: Online - full text ed.; English ed.
Indexed: RASB.
Published by: Det Nationale Forskningscenter for Velfaerd/The Danish National Centre for Social Research, Herluf Trolles Gade 11, Copenhagen K, 1052, Denmark. TEL 45-33-480800, FAX 45-33-480833, sfi@sfi.dk. Circ: 500.

NATIONS IN TRANSIT (YEAR). *see* SOCIOLOGY

361.3 CAN ISSN 1206-5323
E78.C2
NATIVE SOCIAL WORK JOURNAL. Text in English. 1997. a. CAD 15 to individuals; CAD 20 to institutions. **Document type:** *Journal, Academic/Scholarly.*
Indexed: BNNA, C05.
—**CCC.**
Published by: Laurentian University, Native Human Services Programme, University of Sudbury, Rm 256, Ramsey Lake Rd, Sudbury, ON P3E 2C6, Canada. TEL 705-675-1151, FAX 705-675-4817.

NATURAL HAZARDS CENTER. QUICK RESPONSE REPORTS. *see* SOCIAL SCIENCES: COMPREHENSIVE WORKS

NATURAL HAZARDS CENTER. SPECIAL PUBLICATIONS (ONLINE). *see* SOCIAL SCIENCES: COMPREHENSIVE WORKS

NATURAL HAZARDS RESEARCH WORKING PAPERS. *see* SOCIAL SCIENCES: COMPREHENSIVE WORKS

360 USA
NEBRASKA. DEPARTMENT OF SOCIAL SERVICES. ANNUAL REPORT. Text in English. 1974 (no.38). a. charts; stat. **Document type:** *Government.*
Formerly: Nebraska. Department of Public Welfare. Annual Report
Related titles: Microfiche ed.: (from CIS).
Indexed: SRI.
Published by: Department of Social Services, Research and Finance Division, 301 Centennial Mall So, PO Box 95026, Lincoln, NE 68509. FAX 402-471-9455. Ed. Marvin E Kanne. Circ: 500 (controlled).

360 USA ISSN 1934-5593
NEED. Text in English. 2006 (Winter). q. USD 27 domestic; USD 40 foreign; USD 9 newsstand/cover (effective 2007). adv. **Document type:** *Magazine, Consumer.* **Description:** Covers humanitarian efforts at home and abroad, including stories about the process, survivors, workers, funders, and heroes.
Published by: NEED Communications, 2303 Kennedy St NE, Ste 502, Minneapolis, MN 55413. TEL 612-379-4025, FAX 612-379-4033. Ed. Stephanie Kinnunen. Pub. Kelly Kinnunen. Adv. contact Scott Mattiuz. color page USD 5,750; trim 9 x 10.875. Circ: 6,000 (controlled).

361.8 USA
NEIGHBORLINE. Text in English. 1974. q. USD 15. adv. bk.rev. **Document type:** *Newsletter.* **Description:** Examines community and neighborhood development, as well as housing.
Formerly: R & D for Justice Sake
Published by: University of Dayton, 300 College Park, Dayton, OH 45469. TEL 513-229-4639. Ed., Pub. Jeff Brogan. R&P Larry Lane TEL 937-229-2742. Adv. contact Mike Herrmann. Circ: 900 (controlled).

362.4 CAN ISSN 1912-2764
NEIL SQUIRE SOCIETY ANNUAL REPORT. Text in English. 1987. a.
Former titles (until 2005): Neil Squire Foundation Annual Report (1717-2640); (until 2003): Squire Annual (1717-2632); (until 200?): Neil Squire Foundation. Report (1208-5138); (until 1996): Neil Squire Foundation. Newsletter (1195-387X)
Published by: Neil Squire Society, 2250 Boundary Rd, Suite 220, Burnaby, BC V5M 3Z3, Canada. TEL 604-473-9363, FAX 604-473-9364, info@neilsquire.ca, http://www.neilsquire.ca.

362.2 NOR ISSN 1503-9463
NERVEN; deltakeravis. Text in Norwegian. 199?. s-a. **Document type:** *Newsletter, Consumer.*
Published by: Angstringen Norge, Morellsvei 9, Oslo, 0487, Norway. TEL 47-22-223530, FAX 47-22-226588, angstringen@angstringen.no.

362.82 362.7 NZL ISSN 1177-9543
NETWORK NEWS. Text in English. s-a. free (effective 2008).
Media: Online - full text.
Published by: Family Education Network, PO Box 54 098, Bucklands Beach, Auckland, New Zealand. TEL 64-9-5334281, FAX 64-9-5370930, fen@wait.co.nz.

360 USA
NETWORK NEWS (MADISON). Text in English. 3/yr. free.
Published by: Easter Seals Wisconsin, 101 Nob Hill Rd., Madison, WI 53713. TEL 608-277-8288, FAX 608-277-8333. Ed., Pub. Frances Kliscz.

360 CAN ISSN 1488-1004
NETWORK NEWS (MONTREAL). Text in English. 1999. q. **Document type:** *Newsletter, Consumer.*
Media: Online - full text. **Related titles:** French ed.: Nouvelles du Reseau. ISSN 1488-1012.
Published by: Canadian HIV - AIDS Legal Network/Reseau Juridique Canadien VIH - SIDA, 417, Rue Saint-Pierre, Montreal, PQ H2Y 2M4, Canada. TEL 514-397-6828, FAX 514-397-8570, info@aidslaw.ca, http://www.aidslaw.ca.

361.7 GBR ISSN 0265-783X
NETWORK WALES/RHWYDWAITH CYMRU. Text in English, Welsh. 1982. s-m. free to members (effective 2009). bk.rev. back issues avail. **Document type:** *Newsletter.* **Description:** Discusses volunteer opportunities in Wales and other issues of interest to members.
Related titles: Online - full text ed.: free (effective 2009).
Published by: Wales Council for Voluntary Action/Cyngor Gweithredu Gwirfoddol Cymru, Morfa Hall, Bath St, Rhyl, Denbighshire LL18 3EB, United Kingdom. TEL 44-1745-357540, FAX 44-1745-357541, enquiries@wcva.org.uk. Ed. Lynne Reynolds. Circ: 1,100.

NETWORKS. *see* CRIMINOLOGY AND LAW ENFORCEMENT

360 DEU ISSN 1619-6570
NETZ. Text in German. 1979. q. EUR 20 (effective 2005). bk.rev. back issues avail. **Document type:** *Newsletter.*
Published by: (Partnerschaft fuer Entwicklung und Gerechtigkeit e.V.), Netz, Moritz-Hensoldt-Str 20, Wetzlar, 35576, Germany. TEL 49-6441-26585, FAX 49-6441-26257, info@bangladesch.org.

360 DEU ISSN 1438-7832
HV25
NEUE CARITAS; Politik, Praxis, Forschung. Text in German. 1999. m. EUR 79.69; EUR 53.13 to students (effective 2010). adv. bk.rev. bibl.; charts. index. **Document type:** *Magazine, Consumer.*
Formed by the merger of (1896-1999): Caritas (0008-6614); (1945-1999): Caritas-Korrespondenz (0008-6622); (1920-1999): Jugendwohl (0022-5975)
Indexed: A20, CERDIC, DIP, IBR, IBZ.
—GNLM.
Published by: (Deutscher Caritasverband e.V.), Zweiplus Medienagentur, Pallaswiesenstr. 109, Darmstadt, 64293, Germany. TEL 49-6151-81270, FAX 49-6151-893098, info@zweiplus.de, http://www.zweiplus.de. Ed. Gertrud Rogg. adv.: B&W page EUR 1,500. Circ: 7,200 (paid and controlled).

361 DEU
NEUE CARITAS JAHRBUCH. Text in German. 1927. a. EUR 11.50 (effective 2009). **Document type:** *Journal, Corporate.*
Former titles (until 200?): Caritas (0069-0570); (until 1968): Jahrbuch der Caritaswissenschaft (0447-2535)
Published by: Deutscher Caritasverband e.V., Karlstr 40, Freiburg Im Breisgau, 79104, Germany. TEL 49-761-200229, FAX 49-761-200541, presse@caritas.de, http://www.caritas.de.

360 DEU ISSN 0342-9857
HV275
➤ **NEUE PRAXIS**; Zeitschrift fuer Sozialarbeit, Sozialpaedagogik und Sozialpolitik. Text in German. 1970. bi-m. EUR 78; EUR 63 to students; EUR 19 newsstand/cover (effective 2011). adv. reprint service avail. from SCH. **Document type:** *Journal, Academic/Scholarly.*
Indexed: AC&P, DIP, IBR, IBZ.
—**CCC.**
Published by: Verlag Neue Praxis GmbH, Lahnecktstr 10, Lahnstein, 56112, Germany. TEL 49-2621-187159, FAX 49-2621-187176, http://www.verlag-neue-praxis.de. Ed. Hans-Uwe Otto. Adv. contact Ute Renda-Becker. B&W page EUR 520, color page EUR 1,510; trim 140 x 197. Circ: 1,700 (paid).

301 USA
NEW AMERICAN FAMILY. Text in English. 1978. q. looseleaf. USD 20. adv. bk.rev. back issues avail. **Document type:** *Newsletter.* **Description:** Provides educational information about structuring the household, as well as making other relationships.
Formerly: Stepnews - Stepfamily Foundation Newsletter
Published by: Stepfamily Foundation, Inc., 333 West End Ave, New York, NY 10023. TEL 212-877-3244, FAX 212-362-7030. Ed., Pub. Jeannette Lofas. Adv. contact Heather Prieto. Circ: 2,750.

NEW CENTURY HOUSING. *see* HOUSING AND URBAN PLANNING

362 NZL ISSN 1178-3753
NEW DIALOGUE. Text in English. 1978. q. NZD 25; NZD 40 in Australasia; NZD 45 elsewhere. adv. bk.rev. abstr.; bibl.; charts; illus. index. back issues avail. **Document type:** *Newsletter, Consumer.* **Description:** Covers voluntary sector issues in New Zealand including health, welfare, research, law, biculturalism, funding.
Former titles (until 2007): New Dialogue Mini (1177-0821); (until 2005): New Dialogue (2002) (1175-8228); (until 2002): Social Perspectives (1175-1533); (until 1999): Dialogue (0110-8417)
Related titles: Online - full text ed.: ISSN 1177-0813. 2002. free (effective 2008).
Indexed: INZP.
Published by: New Zealand Federation of Voluntary Welfare Organisations Inc., PO Box 9517, Wellington, New Zealand. TEL 64-4-3850981, FAX 64-4-3853248, comms@nzfvwo.org.nz, http://www.nzfvwo.org.nz. adv.: page NZD 400. Circ: 1,000.

360 USA ISSN 1947-1300
HV98.N4
NEW HAMPSHIRE DIRECTORY OF FOUNDATIONS. Text in English. 2001. a. USD 55 per issue (effective 2009). **Document type:** *Directory, Trade.* **Description:** Lists all foundations incorporated in New Hampshire.
Published by: C P G Enterprises, PO Box 199, Shaftsbury, VT 05262. TEL 802-447-0256. Ed., Pub. Christine Graham.

S

353.9 USA ISSN 0090-077X
RJ506.M4
NEW JERSEY DEVELOPMENTAL DISABILITIES COUNCIL. ANNUAL REPORT. Text in English. 1971. a. free. **Document type:** *Government.*
Supersedes: New Jersey Mental Retardation Planning Board. Annual Report
Related titles: Online - full content ed.
Published by: New Jersey Developmental Disabilities Council, PO Box 700, Trenton, NJ 08625-0700. TEL 609-292-3745, FAX 609-292-7114, norman.reim@njddc.org. Ed. Greg Mizanin. Circ: 3,000.

NEW JERSEY LIBRARY FOR THE BLIND AND HANDICAPPED NEWSLETTER. *see* LIBRARY AND INFORMATION SCIENCES

353.9 USA
HV8691.U5
NEW JERSEY. VICTIMS OF CRIMES COMPENSATION BOARD. ANNUAL REPORT. Key Title: Annual Report of the Violent Crimes Compensation Board (Newark). Text in English. 1971. a.
Formerly: New Jersey. Violent Crimes Compensation Board. Annual Report (0092-3079)
Published by: Victims of Crimes Compensation Board, 50 Park Pl, Newark, NJ 07102. TEL 973-648-2107, http://www.statenj.us/victims.

NEW MEXICO. VETERANS' SERVICE COMMISSION. REPORT. *see* MILITARY

360 AUS ISSN 1447-4565
NEW SOUTH WALES. DEPARTMENT OF AGEING, DISABILITY AND HOME CARE. ANNUAL REPORT. Variant title: D A D H C Annual Report. Text in English. 1993. a. free (effective 2009). back issues avail. **Document type:** *Government.* **Description:** Explains our priorities for improvement and reform in the current period as well as for the future, and provides a sound basis for measuring our performance in the reporting period.
Former titles (until 2002): N S W Government. Ageing and Disability Department. Annual Report (1324-9924); (until 1995): New South Wales. Social Policy Directorate. Annual Report
Related titles: Online - full text ed.
Published by: New South Wales, Department of Ageing, Disability and Home Care, Level 5, 83 Clarence St, Sydney, NSW 2000, Australia. TEL 61-2-82702000, FAX 61-2-82702430, info@dadhc.nsw.gov.au.

NEW STUDIES IN SOCIAL POLICY. *see* POLITICAL SCIENCE

361 USA
NEW YORK (STATE). ASSEMBLY. STANDING COMMITTEE ON CHILDREN AND FAMILIES. ANNUAL REPORT. Text in English. a. **Document type:** *Government.* **Description:** Highlights the year's legislation concerning foster care and adoption, youth services, child care and other related human services areas.
Published by: State Assembly, Standing Committee on Children and Families, Legislative Office Bldg Rm 422, Albany, NY 12248. TEL 518-455-5474, FAX 518-455-5857, webmaster@assembly.state.ny.us, http://assembly.state.ny.us/.

NEW YORK (STATE) ASSEMBLY. STANDING COMMITTEE ON VETERANS' AFFAIRS. ANNUAL REPORT. *see* MILITARY

NEW YORK (STATE). COMMISSION ON QUALITY OF CARE FOR THE MENTALLY DISABLED. ANNUAL REPORT. *see* HEALTH FACILITIES AND ADMINISTRATION

NEW YORK (STATE). OFFICE OF ADVOCATE FOR PERSONS WITH DISABILITIES. ANNUAL REPORT. *see* HANDICAPPED

361 USA
HV98.N7
NEW YORK (STATE). OFFICE OF TEMPORARY AND DISABILITY ASSISTANCE. ANNUAL REPORT. Text in English. 1974. a. free (effective 2011). back issues avail. **Document type:** *Report, Government.*
Former titles: New York (State). Department of Social Services. Annual Report (0363-9835); New York (State). Board of Social Welfare. Annual Report (0363-9843)
Related titles: Online - full text ed.
Indexed: SRI.
Published by: Office of Temporary and Disability Assistance, 40 N Pearl St, Albany, NY 12243. TEL 518-473-1090, nyspio@otda.state.ny.us.

361.73 900 910.2 USA ISSN 1526-4831
NEW YORK MASTERPLANNER. Text in English. m. USD 180 (effective 2002). adv. **Document type:** *Directory, Consumer.* **Description:** Lists complete information about thousands of major fundraisers, openings and special events planned for the coming year. Also contains advice on planning and attending social, fund-raising and business events.
Published by: Masterplanner Media, Inc., 8899 Beverly Blvd, Ste. 408, Los Angeles, CA 90048. TEL 310-888-8566, FAX 310-888-1866, http://www.masterplanneronline.com. Ed. Alex Page. Pub. Elisabeth Familian. Adv. contact Stephanie Gerstein.

362.82 NZL ISSN 1177-147X
NEW ZEALAND FAMILY VIOLENCE CLEARINGHOUSE. NEWSLETTER. Text in English. 2005. q. **Document type:** *Newsletter.*
Related titles: Online - full text ed.: ISSN 1178-4652. free.
Published by: New Zealand Family Violence Clearinghouse, Private Bag 4800, Christchurch, New Zealand. TEL 64-3-3642296, FAX 64-3-3642744, info@nzfvc.org.nz.

361.6 NZL ISSN 1176-3388
HN930.5
NEW ZEALAND. MINISTRY OF SOCIAL DEVELOPMENT. STATISTICAL REPORT. Text in English. 1992. a. stat. **Document type:** *Government.* **Description:** Contains statistical information about how people interact with the service lines of the Ministry of Social Development.
Former titles (until 2002): Social Services Sector Statistical Report (1176-4015); (until 2000): New Zealand. Ministry of Social Policy. Statistics Report (1175-4168); (until 1999): New Zealand. Department of Social Welfare. Statistics Report (1174-0329); (until 1996): New Zealand. Department of Social Welfare. Statistical Information Report (1172-0999)
Related titles: Online - full text ed.: ISSN 1178-3206.
Published by: Ministry of Social Development, PO Box 1556, Wellington, New Zealand. TEL 64-4-9163300, FAX 64-4-9180099, information@msd.govt.nz.

NEW ZEALAND POSITIVE AGEING STRATEGY. ANNUAL REPORT AND ACTION PLAN. *see* PUBLIC ADMINISTRATION

NEW ZEALAND POSITIVE AGEING STRATEGY. HIGHLIGHTS. *see* PUBLIC ADMINISTRATION

361 CAN ISSN 0226-420X
HV109.N4
NEWFOUNDLAND. DEPARTMENT OF SOCIAL SERVICES. ANNUAL REPORT. Text in English. 1950. a. free. **Document type:** *Government.*
Supersedes in part (in 1974): Newfoundland. Department of Social Services and Rehabilitation. Annual Report (0078-0294); Which was formerly (until 1971): Newfoundland. Department of Public Welfare. Annual Report (0549-0855)
Published by: Department of Social Services, Confederation Bldg., W. Block, P O Box 8700, St. John's, NF A1B 4J6, Canada. TEL 709-576-3607, FAX 709-576-6996, TELEX 016-4197. Circ: 500.

NEWS ABOUT TALKING BOOK SERVICES. *see* HANDICAPPED

362.5 USA ISSN 1064-6493
HV701
NEWS AND ISSUES. Variant title: Child Poverty News and Issues. Text in English. 1991. 3/yr. back issues avail. **Document type:** *Newsletter.* **Description:** Promotes strategies that prevent child poverty in the United States and that improve the lives of low income children and their families.
Published by: National Center for Children in Poverty, 215 W. 125th St, 3rd Fl, New York, NY 10027. TEL 646-284-9600, FAX 646-284-9623, info@nccp.org, http://www.nccp.org.

361.73 USA ISSN 1533-6832
NEWS AND PROFESSIONAL POSTINGS. Text in English. 1963. m. free to members. adv. bk.rev. back issues avail. **Document type:** *Newsletter.* **Description:** Current events in the nonprofit fund-raising field.
Former titles (until 2001): N S F R E News and Professional Postings (1525-478X); (until 19??): N S F R E News (National Society of Fund Raising Executives) (0890-2828)
Published by: Association of Fundraising Professionals, 4300 Wilson Blvd, Ste 300, Arlington, VA 22203. TEL 703-684-0410, FAX 703-684-0540, http://www.afpnet.org. Ed. Allison Bohn. Circ: 16,000.

360 AUS ISSN 1038-5509
NEWSBEAT AUSTRALIA. Text in English. 1899. q. back issues avail. **Document type:** *Newsletter.* **Description:** Examines poverty and programs to deal with it: welfare, youth work programs and employment training.
Former titles (until 1991): Newsbeat (1030-794X); (until 1985): Mission Beat (0157-8057); (until 1977): Sydney City Mission Herald
Published by: Mission Australia, Level 7, 580 George St, Sydney, NSW 2000, Australia. TEL 61-2-92192000, FAX 800-777-755, http://www.missionaustralia.com.au.

361.73 NZL ISSN 1179-9722
NEWZ VIEWZ. Text in English. 19??. q. USD 25 to non-members; USD 6.95 per issue to non-members; free to members (effective 2010). adv. **Document type:** *Magazine, Trade.* **Description:** Contains information about the charity and articles on issues such as direct mail, bequests, capital campaigns and technology.
Formerly (until 2010): F I N Z on Fundraising (1176-0354)
Related titles: Online - full text ed.
Published by: Fundraising Institute of New Zealand, Manners St, PO Box 11203, Wellington, 6142, New Zealand. TEL 64-4-4996223, FAX 64-4-4996224, info@finz.org.nz.

362 DEU ISSN 0720-6968
NICHT-MARKT-OEKONOMIK. Text in German. 1973. irreg., latest vol.5, 1985. price varies. **Document type:** *Monographic series, Academic/Scholarly.*
Published by: Duncker und Humblot GmbH, Carl-Heinrich-Becker-Weg 9, Berlin, 12165, Germany. TEL 49-30-7900060, FAX 49-30-79000631, info@duncker-humblot.de.

360 DEU
NIEDERSAECHSISCHE RUNDSCHAU. Text in German. 1958. 10/yr. adv. **Document type:** *Magazine, Trade.*
Published by: (Komba Gewerkschaft Niedersachsen), Vereinigte Verlagsanstalten GmbH, Hoeherweg 278, Duesseldorf, 40231, Germany. TEL 49-211-73570, FAX 49-211-7357123, info@vva.de, http://www.vva.de. Adv. contact Panagiotis Chrissovergis. B&W page EUR 670, color page EUR 1,340. Circ: 5,000 (controlled).

360 NLD ISSN 1572-4964
NIEUWSBRIEF GEMEENTELIJKE ACTIVERING. Text in Dutch. 1997. 20/yr. price varies.
Formerly (until 2004): Nieuwsbrief West Sociale Werkvoorziening/Wet Inschakeling Werkzoekenden (1386-8314)
Published by: Kluwer B.V. (Subsidiary of: Wolters Kluwer N.V.), Postbus 4, Alphen aan den Rijn, 2400 MA, Netherlands. TEL 31-172-466633, info@kluwer.nl, http://www.kluwer.nl.

NIHON SANFUJINKAI KAIHOU/J A O G NEWS. *see* MEDICAL SCIENCES—Obstetrics And Gynecology

361 JPN ISSN 0916-765X
HV4
NIHON SHAKAI JIGYO DAIGAKU KENKYU KIYO/JAPAN COLLEGE OF SOCIAL WORK. STUDY REPORT. Text in Japanese. 1953. a. bk.rev. **Document type:** *Academic/Scholarly.*
Formerly (until 1988): Shakai Jigyo no Shomondai - Issues in Social Work (0546-1324)
Published by: Nihon Shakai Jigyo Daigaku, 3-1-30 Takeoka, Kiyose-shi, Tokyo-to 204-0023, Japan. Ed. Yasuo Hagiwara.

NO. *see* WOMEN'S INTERESTS

THE NONPROFIT ALMANAC. *see* BUSINESS AND ECONOMICS—Management

361.73 USA ISSN 0899-7640
HV1 CODEN: NVSQEQ
➤ **NONPROFIT AND VOLUNTARY SECTOR QUARTERLY.** Text in English. 1972. bi-m. USD 752, GBP 442 combined subscription to institutions (print & online eds.); USD 737, GBP 433 to institutions (effective 2011). adv. bk.rev. illus. Index. back issues avail.; reprint service avail. from PSC. **Document type:** *Journal, Academic/Scholarly.* **Description:** Explores the unique dynamics, needs, and concerns of today's nonprofit and voluntary organizations. Provides cutting-edge research. discussion and analysis of the field and leads its readers to understanding the impact the non-profit sector has on society.
Formerly (until 1988): Journal of Voluntary Action Research (0094-0607)
Related titles: CD-ROM ed.; Microfilm ed.: (from PQC); Online - full text ed.: ISSN 1552-7395. USD 677, GBP 398 to institutions (effective 2011).
Indexed: A01, A03, A08, A12, A13, A17, A20, A22, A28, ABIn, APA, ASCA, ASSIA, BRD, BrCerAb, C&ISA, CA, CA/WCA, CIA, CerAb, CivEngAb, CorrAb, CurCont, DIP, E&CAJ, E01, E02, E03, E11, EEA, EMA, ERI, ESPM, EconLit, EdA, EdI, EnvEAb, FR, FamI, H15, HRA, IBR, IBZ, JEL, M&TEA, M09, MBF, METADEX, N06, P10, P27, P30, P34, P42, P48, P51, P53, P54, PAIS, PQC, PRA, PSA, RiskAb, S02, S03, S11, SCOPUS, SOPODA, SPAA, SSA, SSAI, SSAb, SSCI, SSI, SociolAb, SolStAb, T02, T04, W01, W02, W03, W07, WAA.
—BLDSC (6117.340100), IE, Infotrieve, Ingenta, INIST, Linda Hall. **CCC.**
Published by: (Association for Research on Nonprofit Organizations and Voluntary Action), Sage Publications, Inc., 2455 Teller Rd, Thousand Oaks, CA 91320. TEL 805-499-9774, FAX 805-499-0871, info@sagepub.com, http://www.sagepub.com. Eds. Dwight Burlingame, Wolfgang Bielefeld. Circ: 800. **Subscr. outside the Americas to:** Sage Publications Ltd., 1 Oliver's Yard, 55 City Rd, London EC1Y 1SP, United Kingdom. TEL 44-20-73248701, FAX 44-20-73248733, subscription@sagepub.co.uk.

361.763 USA
THE NONPROFIT CONNECTION; bridging research & practice. Text in English. q. **Document type:** *Newsletter.*
Published by: Seton Hall University, Nonprofit Sector Resource Institute, Jubilee Hall, 400 South Orange Ave, South Orange, NJ 07079. TEL 973-761-9734, FAX 973-313-6162, nsri@shu.edu. Ed. Barkley Calkins.

361.7 USA ISSN 1545-1437
NONPROFIT ONLINE NEWS; news of the online nonprofit community. Text in English. 1997. w. free (effective 2010). back issues avail. **Document type:** *Newsletter, Trade.* **Description:** Discusses ways in which nonprofit organizations can use the Internet to maximize their outreach.
Media: Online - full text. **Related titles:** E-mail ed.
Published by: Gilbert Center, PO Box 46067, Seattle, WA 98146. TEL 206-201-1726, info@gilbert.org, http://www.gilbert.org.

THE NONPROFIT QUARTERLY. *see* BUSINESS AND ECONOMICS—Management

360 JPN
NONPROFIT RESEARCH ANNALS. Text in Japanese. 2000. a. **Document type:** *Academic/Scholarly.*
Published by: Nihon N P O Gakkai/Japan Nonprofit Organization Research Association, c/o Secretariat: Osaka School of International Public Policy, Osaka University1-31, Machikaneyama-cho, Toyonaka-City, Osaka 560-0043, Japan. janpora@ml.osipp.osaka-u.ac.jp, http://www.osipp.osaka-u.ac.jp/janpora/.

361.73 USA ISSN 1553-4855
HD62.6
NONPROFIT WORLD. Text in English. 1983. bi-m. free to members (effective 2010). adv. bk.rev. back issues avail. **Document type:** *Journal, Academic/Scholarly.* **Description:** Focuses on all aspects of running an effective nonprofit organization, including fundraising, income generation, and legal advice.
Formerly (until 1986): Nonprofit World Report (8755-7614)
Related titles: Online - full text ed.
Indexed: A12, A13, A17, A22, ABIn, B01, B06, B07, B09, N06, P48, P51, P53, P54, PQC, PSI, T02.
—BLDSC (6117.340200), IE, Ingenta. **CCC.**
Published by: Society for Nonprofit Organizations, PO Box 510354, Livonia, MI 48151. TEL 734-451-3582, FAX 734-451-5935, info@snpo.org.

360 JPN ISSN 1346-4116
➤ **NONPUROFITTO REBYU/NONPROFIT REVIEW.** Text in English, Japanese. 2001 (Jun.). s-a. **Document type:** *Journal, Academic/Scholarly.*
Related titles: Online - full content ed.: free (effective 2011); Online - full text ed.
Published by: Nihon N P O Gakkai/Japan Nonprofit Organization Research Association, c/o Secretariat: Osaka School of International Public Policy, Osaka University1-31, Machikaneyama-cho, Toyonaka-City, Osaka 560-0043, Japan. janpora@ml.osipp.osaka-u.ac.jp, http://www.osipp.osaka-u.ac.jp/janpora/. Ed. Naoto Yamauchi.

➤ **NORCAL CENTER ON DEAFNESS NEWSLINE.** *see* HANDICAPPED—Hearing Impaired

362.948 DNK ISSN 1395-7562
NORDISK SOCIALSTATISTISK KOMITE. Text in Multiple languages. 1995. irreg. price varies. back issues avail. **Document type:** *Monographic series, Government.*
Related titles: ◆ Series: Social Protection in the Nordic Countries. ISSN 1397-6893; ◆ Social Tryghed i de Nordiske Lande. ISSN 1395-7546.
Address: Islands Brygge 67, Copenhagen S, 2300, Denmark. TEL 45-72-227625, FAX 45-32-955470, mail@nom-nos.dk, http://www.nom-nos.dk.

362.4 371.911 371.912 DNK
NORDISK VELFAERDSCENTER. UDDANNELSE FOR DOEVBLINDEPERSONALE. ARBEJDSTEKST/NORDISK UDDANNELSESCENTER FOR DOEVBLINDEPERSONLE. ARBETSTEXT/NORDISK UDDANNELSESCENTER FOR DOEVBLINDEPERSONLE. PUBLICATION. Text in Multiple languages. 1987. irreg., latest vol.50, 2009. back issues avail. **Document type:** *Monographic series, Government.*
Formerly (until 2009): Nordisk Uddannelsescenter for Doevblindepersonle. Arbejdstekst (1398-3237)
Related titles: Online - full text ed.; Finnish ed.: Pohjoismainen Kuurosokeiden Henkiloestoen Koulutuskeskus. Tyoeteksti. ISSN 1398-3245.

Published by: Nordisk Velfaerdscenter, Uddannelse for Doevblindepersonale/Nordic Centre for Welfare and Social Issues,Training Center for Deafblind Services (Subsidiary of: Nordisk Ministerraad/Nordic Council of Ministers), Slotsgade 8, Dronninglund, 9330, Denmark. TEL 45-96-471600, FAX 45-96-471616, nvcdk@nordicwelfare.org, http://www.nordisktvalfardscenter.org.

362.4 371.911 371.912 DNK ISSN 1903-7899
NORDISK VELFAERDSCENTER. UDDANNELSE FOR DOEVBLINDEPERSONALE. NYHEDSBREVET. Text in Multiple languages. 1981. s-a. back issues avail. **Document type:** *Newsletter, Government.*
Formerly (until 2009): Nordisk Uddannelsescenter for Doevblindepersonale. Nyhedsbrev (0902-7890)
Related titles: Online - full text ed.: ISSN 1903-7902; ♦ Finnish ed.: Pohjoismainen Hyvinvointikeskus. Kuurosokeiden Henkiloston Koulutus. Uutislehti. ISSN 1903-7910.
Published by: Nordisk Velfaerdscenter, Uddannelse for Doevblindepersonale/Nordic Centre for Welfare and Social Issues,Training Center for Deafblind Services (Subsidiary of: Nordisk Ministerraad/Nordic Council of Ministers), Slotsgade 8, Dronninglund, 9330, Denmark. TEL 45-96-471600, FAX 45-96-471616, nvcdk@nordicwelfare.org, http://www.nordisktvalfardscenter.org.

362.4 NOR ISSN 0809-6457
NORGES HANDIKAPFORBUND. OSLOFJORD VEST. REGIONSNYTT. Text in Norwegian. 2004. q. **Document type:** *Newsletter, Consumer.*
Formerly (until 2005): Norges Handikapforbund. Oslofjord Vest.Medlemsnytt (1504-3223); Which was formed by the merger of (1994-2004): Telemark Handikap Info (0805-0686); (1995-2004): Norges Handikapforbund. Buskerud. Medlemsnytt (0806-9859); Which was formerly (1989-1995): Norges Handikapforbund. Buskerud. Fylkesnytt (0806-9840)
Published by: Norges Handikapforbund, Oslofjord Vest/Norwegian Association of the Disabled. Oslofjord West, Tollbugt 115, Drammen, 3041, Norway. TEL 47-32-882929, FAX 47-32-882920, nhf.oslofjordvest@nhf.no. Ed. Arnt-Einar Litsheim TEL 47-32-882921.

361 NOR ISSN 1504-1840
NORGES TEKNISK-NATURVITENSKAPELIGE UNIVERSITET. INSTITUTT FOR SOCIALT ARBEID OG HELSEVITENSKAP. RAPPORTSERIE. Variant title: Rapportserie for Sosialt Arbeid og Helsevitenskap. Text in Norwegian. 1990. irreg., latest vol.62, 200?. price varies. back issues avail. **Document type:** *Monographic series, Academic/Scholarly.*
Formerly (until 2002): Norges Teknisk-Naturvitenskapelige Universitet. Institutt for Socialt Arbeid og Helsevitenskap. Socialt Arbeids Rapportserie (0802-8974)
Published by: Norges Teknisk-Naturvitenskapelige Universitet, Institutt for Socialt Arbeid og Helsevitenskap/Norwegian University of Science and Technology, Department of Social Work and Health Science, Bygg 11, Nivaa 5, Trondheim, 7491, Norway. TEL 47-73-591930, FAX 47-73-591885, ish@svt.ntnu.no, http://www.ntnu.no/ish.

362 NOR ISSN 1503-1403
NORWAY. NASJONALT FOLKEHELSEINSTITUTT. RAPPORT. Text in English, Norwegian. 1999. irreg. back issues avail. **Document type:** *Monographic series, Government.*
Formerly (until 2002): Norway. Statens Institutt for Folkehelse. Rapport (1501-9845)
Related titles: Online - full text ed.: ISSN 1503-6154; ♦ Series: Skadedyr. ISSN 1504-4971.
Published by: Nasjonalt Folkehelseinstitutt/Norwegian Institute of Public Health, PO Box 4404, Nydalen, Oslo, 0403, Norway. TEL 47-21-077000, FAX 47-22-353605, folkehelseinstituttet@fhi.no.

NOTICIAS DE LA ECONOMIA PUBLICA, SOCIAL Y COOPERATIVA. *see* BUSINESS AND ECONOMICS—Economic Situation And Conditions

360 CHE
NOUS, SAMARITAINS. Text in French. 16/yr. CHF 33 (effective 2008). adv. **Document type:** *Magazine, Trade.*
Published by: Schweizerischer Samariterbund/Alliance Suisse des Samaritains, Martin-Disteli-Str 27, Olten, 4601, Switzerland. TEL 41-62-2860200, FAX 41-62-2860202, office@samariter.ch, http://www.samariter.ch. Ed. Chantal Lienert. adv.: B&W page CHF 720, color page CHF 795. Circ: 3,200 (controlled).

301 306.2 CAN ISSN 0843-4468
CODEN: NPSOFD
➤ **NOUVELLES PRATIQUES SOCIALES.** Text in French. 1988. s-a. CAD 32 domestic to individuals; CAD 48 domestic to institutions; CAD 50 foreign; CAD 24 domestic to students (effective 2005). back issues avail. **Document type:** *Journal, Academic/Scholarly.* **Description:** Contains research and reflections on social intervention based on pluralism and the renewal of social practices, from government and non-government agencies. Examines social problems pertinent to all social fields.
Indexed: CA, FR, IBSS, P34, P42, PSA, PdeR, S02, S03, SCOPUS, SOPODA, SSA, SociolAb, T02.
—INIST.
Published by: Presses de l'Universite du Quebec, Le Delta I, 2875 boul. Laurier, bureau 450, Ste Foy, PQ G1V 2M2, Canada. TEL 418-657-4075, FAX 418-657-2096, revues@puq.ca, puq@puq.uquebec.ca, http://www.puq.ca. Ed. Lucie Frechette.

361.6 CAN ISSN 0844-7535
NOVA SCOTIA DEPARTMENT OF COMMUNITY SERVICES (YEAR). Text in English. 1964. a. free. stat. **Document type:** *Government.*
Former titles (until 1988): Social Services for Nova Scotians (0833-3491); (until 1982): Social Services in Nova Scotia (0317-4336); (until 1973): Welfare Services in Nova Scotia (0550-8665); Which incorporates (in 1975): Nova Scotia. Department of Social Services. Annual Report (0383-4808); Which was formerly (until 1974): Nova Scotia. Department of Public Welfare. Annual Report (0550-1776)
Published by: Department of Community Services, P O Box 696, Halifax, NS B3J 2T7, Canada. TEL 902-424-7902, FAX 902-424-0502. Ed. Harry Chapman. Circ: 500.

NURSE AIDE - V I P; published especially for those very important people who care for the elderly. *see* GERONTOLOGY AND GERIATRICS

NURSERY TODAY. *see* CHILDREN AND YOUTH—About

362 DNK
NYHEDSBREVET JOB UDEN VOLD. Text in Danish. 1995. 7/yr. **Document type:** *Newsletter, Consumer.*
Former titles (until 2009): Job uden Vold (1902-3294); (until 2007): Vold som Udtryksform (1396-027X)
Related titles: Online - full text ed.: 2007.
Published by: Vold som Udtryksform/Violence as a Form of Expression, c/o Socialt Udviklingscenter, Nr. Farimagsgade 13, Copenhagen, 1364, Denmark. TEL 45-33-934450, FAX 45-33-935450, sus@sus.dk. Ed. Bjarne Moeller. Circ: 2,000.

360 DNK ISSN 0907-9300
NYT FRA ANKESTYRELSEN. Text in Danish. 1992. q. back issues avail. **Document type:** *Newsletter, Government.* **Description:** News from the Danish National Social Appeals Board.
Related titles: Online - full text ed.: ISSN 1600-5031.
Published by: Den Sociale Ankestyrelse/National Social Appeals Board, Amaliegade 25, PO Box 9080, Copenhagen K, 1022, Denmark. TEL 45-33-411200, FAX 45-33-411400, ast@ast.dk, http://www.cms.ast.dk. Ed. Karin Rasch. Circ: 2,000.

360 SWE ISSN 1401-7172
NYTT FRAAN SOCIALSTYRELSEN. Text in Swedish. 1996. w. free (effective 2005). back issues avail. **Document type:** *Newsletter.*
Related titles: Online - full text ed.
Published by: Socialstyrelsen/National Board of Health and Welfare, Raalambsvaegen 3, Stockholm, 10630, Sweden. TEL 46-8-55553000, FAX 46-8-55553252, socialstyrelssen@socialstyrelsen.se. Ed. Leif-Rune Strandell.

O A S D I BENEFICIARIES BY STATE AND COUNTY. (Old Age, Survivors, Disability Insurance) *see* INSURANCE

O C H A NEWS. (Office for the Coordination of Humanitarian Affairs) *see* LAW—International Law

331.11 FRA
O E C D SOCIAL, EMPLOYMENT AND MIGRATION WORKING PAPERS. (Organisation for Economic Cooperation and Development) Text in English, French. 1990. irreg., latest no.86, 2009. free (effective 2009).
Supersedes in part (in 2002): Labour Market and Social Policy Occasional Papers (1025-899X)
Related titles: Online - full content ed.: ISSN 1815-199X. 2005.
Indexed: IIS.
—IE, Ingenta.
Published by: (Directorate for Education, Employment, Labour and Social Affairs), Organisation for Economic Cooperation and Development (O E C D)/Organisation de Cooperation et de Developpement Economiques (O C D E), 2 Rue Andre Pascal, Paris, 75775 Cedex 16, France. TEL 33-1-45248200, FAX 33-1-45248500.

362.7 AUS ISSN 1034-7232
O O S H UPDATE; a quarterly newsletter for outside school hours services. (Outside of School Hours) Text in English. 200?. q. adv. **Document type:** *Newsletter, Trade.*
Published by: Network of Community Activities, 66 Albion St, Surry Hills, NSW 2010, Australia. TEL 61-2-92123244, FAX 61-2-92819645, network@netoosh.org.au. Eds. Cassandra McBurnie, Pauline O'Kane. Circ: 500 (controlled).

O P C INFOS. (Organisation pour la Prevention de la Cecite) *see* HANDICAPPED—Visually Impaired

362.1 GBR ISSN 1748-8311
O P I ISSUES NOTES. Text in English. 2000. irreg., latest no.4, 2003, Feb. free (effective 2009). back issues avail. **Document type:** *Monographic series, Academic/Scholarly.*
Media: Online - full text.
Published by: Oxford Policy Institute, 3 Mansfield Rd, Oxford, OX1 3TB, United Kingdom. TEL 44-1865-250233, admin@opi.org.uk. Ed. Jesmond Blumenfeld.

362.1 GBR ISSN 1748-8303
O P I POLICY BRIEFS. Text in English. 2000. irreg., latest no.4, 2003, Feb. free (effective 2009). back issues avail. **Document type:** *Monographic series, Academic/Scholarly.*
Media: Online - full text.
Published by: Oxford Policy Institute, 3 Mansfield Rd, Oxford, OX1 3TB, United Kingdom. TEL 44-1865-250233, admin@opi.org.uk. Ed. Jesmond Blumenfeld.

360 351 USA
O R E S WORKING PAPER SERIES. (Office of Research, Evaluation and Statistics) Text in English. 19??. irreg., latest 2008. free (effective 2011). stat. back issues avail. **Document type:** *Monographic series, Government.* **Description:** Consists of papers from the Office, which aims to provide ongoing statistical data and research analyses of the old-age, survivors, and disablity insurance (OASDI) and Supplemental Security Income (SSI) programs.
Related titles: Online - full text ed.
Published by: U.S. Social Security Administration, Office of Research, Evaluation and Statistics, Office of Public Inquiries, Windsor Park Bldg, 6401 Security Blvd, Baltimore, MD 21235. TEL 800-772-1213, ores.publications@ssa.gov, http://www.ssa.gov/policy/about/ORES.html.

OBEROENDE. *see* DRUG ABUSE AND ALCOHOLISM

618.97 362.6 FRA ISSN 1954-9954
OBSERVATOIRE DES DISPOSITIFS DE PRISE EN CHARGE ET D'ACCOMPAGNEMENT DE LA MALADIE D'ALZHEIMER. LA LETTRE. Text in French. 2006. q. back issues avail. **Document type:** *Newsletter.*
Related titles: Online - full text ed.: ISSN 1954-3611. free.
Published by: Fondation Mederic Alzheimer, 30 Rue de Prony, Paris, 75017, France.

OCCUPATIONAL THERAPY IN MENTAL HEALTH; a journal of psychosocial practice and research. *see* MEDICAL SCIENCES—Psychiatry And Neurology

361 SWE ISSN 1651-145X
OEREBRO STUDIES IN SOCIAL WORK. Text in Swedish; Summaries in English. 1999. irreg., latest vol.7, 2006. SEK 180 per issue (effective 2006). back issues avail. **Document type:** *Monographic series, Academic/Scholarly.*
Published by: Oerebro Universitet, Universitetsbiblioteket/University of Oerebro. University Library, Fakultetsgatan 1, Oerebro, 70182, Sweden. TEL 46-19-303240, FAX 46-19-331217, biblioteket@ub.oru.se. Ed. Joanna Jansdotter.

614 AUT ISSN 0029-9901
OESTERREICHISCHES JUGENDROTKREUZ. ARBEITSBLAETTER. Text in German. 1947. q. free (effective 2007). adv. bk.rev. illus. index. **Document type:** *Newsletter, Consumer.* **Description:** News and information of the Austrian Youth Red Cross.
Published by: Oesterreichisches Jugendrotkreuz, Wiedner Hauptstr 32, Vienna, W 1040, Austria. TEL 43-1-58900173, FAX 43-1-58900179, jugendweb@roteskreuz.at. Ed. Karl Zarhuber. Circ: 10,000 (controlled).

362.6 AUS ISSN 1832-1550
OFFICE FOR THE AGEING. ANNUAL REPORT. Text in English. 1996. a. **Document type:** *Government.*
Formerly (until 1995): Commissioner for the Ageing. Annual Report
Published by: South Australia, Department for Families and Communities, Office for the Ageing, GPO Box 292, Adelaide, NSW 5001, Australia. TEL 61-8-82070522, FAX 61-8-82070555, OFTA@dfc.sa.gov.au, http://www.dfc.sa.gov.au/pub/default.aspx?tabid=481.com.

361.6 AUS ISSN 1832-1666
OFFICIAL COMMUNITY VISITORS. ANNUAL REPORT. Text in English. 2003. a. free (effective 2009). **Document type:** *Government.*
Related titles: Online - full text ed.
Published by: N S W Ombudsman's Office, Visitors Team, Level 24, 580 George St, Sydney, NSW 2000, Australia. TEL 61-2-92861000, 800-451-524, FAX 61-2-92832911, nswombo@ombo.nsw.gov.au.

362.1 NOR ISSN 1504-7822
OG BEDRE SKAL DET BLI!. Text in Norwegian. 2006. irreg. **Document type:** *Trade.* **Description:** The Norwegian National Strategy for Quality Improvement in Health and Social services, 2005-2015. For leaders and providers.
Related titles: Online - full text ed.; Ed.: And It's Going to Get Better!.
Published by: Helsedirektoratet/Norwegian Directorate of Health, PO Box 7000, St Olavs Plass, Oslo, 0130, Norway. TEL 47-810-20050, FAX 47-24-163001, postmottak@helsedirektoratet.no.

OKEE-KRANT; de duidelijkste krant voor jou. *see* MEDICAL SCIENCES—Psychiatry And Neurology

360 USA ISSN 0277-8289
OKLAHOMA. DEPARTMENT OF HUMAN SERVICES. ANNUAL REPORT. Text in English. 1936. a. charts; stat. **Document type:** *Government.*
Formerly (until 1979): Oklahoma. Department of Institutions, Social and Rehabilitative Services. Annual Report (0078-4362)
Related titles: Microfiche ed.: (from CIS).
Indexed: SRI.
Published by: Department of Human Services, Planning and Research Unit, PO Box 25352, Oklahoma City, OK 73125. TEL 405-521-2908, FAX 405-521-2073. Ed. Charles Taylor.

360 CAN ISSN 1200-5533
OLD AGE SECURITY, CHILD TAX BENEFIT, CHILDREN'S SPECIAL ALLOWANCES AND CANADA PENSION PLAN. REPORT. Text in English, French. 1985. a. **Document type:** *Report, Trade.*
Formerly (until 1994): Family Allowances, Old Age Security, Canada Pension Plan, Report for the Year Ending (0837-2454); Which was formed by the merger of (1966-1985): Canada Pension Plan Report (0704-1640); Which was formerly (until 1968): Canada Pension Plan. Annual Report (0576-128X); (1976-1985): Family Allowances (0226-6903); Which was formed by the merger of (19??-1976): Report on the Administration of the Family Allowances Act (0226-692X); Which was formerly (until 1964): Expenditures and Administration in Connection with the Family Allowances Act. Annual Report; (19??-1976): l' Administration de la Loi sur les Allocations Familiales. Rapport (0226-6938); Which was formerly (until 1976): Rapport sur l'Application de la Loi Sur les Allocations Familiales (0226-6946); (until 1972): Rapport Touchant l'Administration de la Loi sur les Allocations Familiales (0825-5946); (until 1970): Rapport sur l'Application de la Loi sur les Allocations Familiales (0825-5938); (1977-1985): Old Age Security (0706-4683); Which was formed by the merger of (19??-1977): Rapport sur l'Administration de la Loi sur la Securite de la Vieillesse (0706-4896); (19??-1977): Report of the Administration of the Old Age Security Act (0706-4691)
Published by: Human Resources and Social Development Canada, Public Enquiries Centre, 140 Promenade du Portage, Phase IV, Level 0, Gatineau, PQ K1A 0J9, Canada. FAX 819-953-7260, youth@canada.gc.ca.

306.38 USA ISSN 0146-3640
OLDER AMERICANS REPORT. Text in English. 1976. bi-m. looseleaf. USD 499 domestic; USD 513.40 in Canada; USD 518.20 elsewhere (effective 2008). back issues avail.; reprints avail. **Document type:** *Newsletter, Consumer.* **Description:** Covers the budget changes, new regulations and important legislation and a report of the state and local legislation, regulations and policies that affect America's older citizens.
Incorporates (1978-2002): Aging Research & Training News (0888-6830); Which was formerly (until 198?): Aging News (0197-4017); (1992-1997): Managing Senior Care (1063-035X); Which was formerly (until 198?): Aging Service News (0197-4025)
Related titles: E-mail ed.: USD 431 (effective 2008); Online - full text ed.: ISSN 1545-4916. USD 347 (effective 2005).
Indexed: A26, G05, G06, G07, G08, H11, H12, I05.
—**CCC.**
Published by: Business Publishers, Inc. (Subsidiary of: Eli Research, Inc.), PO Box 17592, Baltimore, MD 21297. TEL 800-274-6737, custserv@bpinews.com. Eds. Robert W Mitchell, Ami Dodson. Pub. Adam P Goldstein.

362.7 NLD ISSN 2210-8432
OMARMEN. Text in Dutch. 2005. q. **Document type:** *Magazine.*
Published by: Stichting Red een Kind, Postbus 40169, Zwolle, 8004 DD, Netherlands. TEL 31-38-4604648, FAX 31-38-4604508, info@redeenkind.nl. Eds. Lineke Karssenberg, Leo Visser.

362.19 610.7361 NOR ISSN 0800-7489
OMSORG; nordisk tidsskrift for palliativ medicin. Text in Norwegian. 1984. q. NOK 345 to individuals; NOK 485 to institutions; NOK 135 per issue (effective 2011). adv. **Document type:** *Magazine, Trade.*
Formerly (until 1989): Omsorg for Alvorlig Syge og Doeende
Published by: Fagbokforlaget, Kanalveien 51, PO Box 6050, Postterminalen, Bergen, 5892, Norway. TEL 47-55-388800, FAX 47-55-388801, fagbokforlaget@fagbokforlaget.no, http://www.fagbokforlaget.no. Ed. Stein Huseboe. Adv. contact Janne-Beate Duke. Circ: 4,000.

ONE FAMILY MATTERS. *see* SOCIOLOGY

ONE IN SEVEN. *see* HANDICAPPED—Hearing Impaired

362.6 AUS ISSN 1838-224X
ONEC O T A. Text in English. 2002. bi-m. free (effective 2011). **Document type:** *Magazine, Trade.* **Description:** Dedicated to provide information to COTA members about previous and upcoming events, programs, workshops and information sessions, the results of member's surveys and research etc.
Former titles (until 2010): MyCOTA (1833-4938); (until 2006): 50 Something Extra
Published by: Council on the Ageing, GPO Box 1583, Adelaide, SA 5001, Australia. TEL 61-8-82320422, 800-182-324, FAX 61-8-82320433, cota@cotaaustralia.org.au, http://www.cota.org.au.

ONTARIO ADVISORY COUNCIL ON SENIOR CITIZENS. ANNUAL REPORT. *see* PUBLIC ADMINISTRATION

362.7 CAN ISSN 0030-283X
ONTARIO ASSOCIATION OF CHILDREN'S AID SOCIETIES. JOURNAL. Text in English. 1952. 4/yr. CAD 26.50 (effective 1999). adv. bk.rev. back issues avail. **Document type:** *Newsletter.* **Description:** Tackles child welfare issues.
Published by: Ontario Association of Children's Aid Societies, 75 Front St E, 2nd Fl, Toronto, ON M5E 1V9, Canada. TEL 416-366-8115, FAX 416-366-8317. Ed. Diane Cresswell. Adv. contact Melanie Persaud. Circ: 5,500.

360 CAN ISSN 1203-3421
ONTARIO ASSOCIATION OF SOCIAL WORKERS. NEWSMAGAZINE. Text in English. 1995. bi-m. USD 25 to individuals; USD 35 to institutions (effective 2008). **Document type:** *Magazine, Trade.*
Former titles (until 1995): Ontario Association of Professional Social Workers. Newsmagazine (1196-2704); (until 1989): O A P S W Newsmagazine (0704-3244); (until 1977): O A P S W. Ontario Association of Professional Social Workers (0319-6119)
Published by: Ontario Association of Social Workers/L'Association des Travailleuses et Travailleurs Sociaux de l'Ontario, 410 Jarvis St, Toronto, ON M4Y 2G6, Canada. TEL 416-923-4848, FAX 416-923-5279, info@oasw.org, http://www.oasw.org/.

362.2 CAN ISSN 0833-0492
ONTARIO MENTAL HEALTH FOUNDATION. ANNUAL REPORT. Text in English. 1983. a.
Formerly (until 1986): Ontario Mental Health Foundation. Annual Report, Research and Major Equipment Grants, Individual Awards (0823-4469)
Published by: Ontario Mental Health Foundation, 489 College St, Suite 508, Toronto, ON M6G 1A5, Canada. TEL 416-920-7721, FAX 416-920-0026, http://www.omhf.on.ca/.

362 CAN
ONTARIO. MINISTRY OF COMMUNITY AND SOCIAL SERVICES. SOCIAL ASSISTANCE REVIEW BOARD. ANNUAL REPORT OF THE BOARD. Text in English. a. **Document type:** *Government.*
Formerly: Ontario. Ministry of Community and Social Services. Social Assistance Review Board. Annual Report of the Chairman
Published by: Ministry of Community and Social Services, Social Assistance Review Board, 119 King St W, Ste 600, Hamilton, ON L8P 4Y7, Canada. TEL 416-326-5104, FAX 416-326-5135. **Subscr. to:** Social Assistance Review Board, 1075 Bay St, 7th Fl, Toronto, ON M5S 2B1, Canada.

OPEN ADOPTION BIRTHPARENT. *see* CHILDREN AND YOUTH—About

OPENMIND; the mental health magazine. *see* MEDICAL SCIENCES—Psychiatry And Neurology

361 NLD ISSN 1872-1818
ORANJE FONDS BERICHT. Text in Dutch. 2002. 3/yr.
Published by: Oranje Fonds, Postbus 90, Utrecht, 3500 AB, Netherlands. TEL 31-30-6564524, FAX 31-30-6562204, info@oranjefonds.nl.

361 CAN ISSN 1716-3706
ORDRE PROFESSIONNEL DES TRAVAILLEURS SOCIAUX DU QUEBEC. BULLETIN. Text in French. 1974. q. **Document type:** *Bulletin.*
Former titles (until 2004): Ordre Professionnel des Travailleurs Sociaux du Quebec. Bulletin de Nouvelles (1200-8710); (until 1994): Corporation Professionnelle des Travailleurs Sociaux du Quebec. Bulletin de Nouvelles (0713-4290); (until 1982): Corporation Professionnelle des Travailleurs Sociaux du Quebec. Bulletin (0318-9627); (until 1975): Elan (0318-9619)
Indexed: FR, SCOPUS, SSA, SocioIAb.
Published by: Ordre Professionnelle des Travailleurs Sociaux du Quebec/Professional Order of Social Workers of Quebec, 255 boul Cremazie Est, Bureau 520, Montreal, PQ H2M 1M2, Canada. TEL 514-731-3925, FAX 514-731-6785, general@optsq.org.

362.1974 NOR ISSN 0804-1253
ORGANET. Text in Norwegian. 1991. 3/yr. NOK 400 (effective 2011). **Document type:** *Magazine, Consumer.*
Related titles: Online - full text ed.: 2006.
Published by: Foreningen for Hjerte-Lunge Transplanterte/Norwegian Association of Heart and Lung Patients, PO Box 4375, Nydalen, Oslo, 0402, Norway. TEL 47-22-799300, FAX 47-22-225037, post@lhl.no, http://www.lhl.no. Ed. Marit Skatvedt. Circ: 800.

061.4 971.4 CAN ISSN 1481-4447
ORGANISMES COMMUNAUTAIRES DU QUEBEC (YEAR). Text in French. 1999. biennial. CAD 59.95 (effective 2001). **Document type:** *Directory.* **Description:** Lists some 2300 non-profit agencies in Quebec within the community.
Published by: Quebec dans le Monde, C P 8503, Sainte Foy, PQ G1V 4N5, Canada. TEL 418-659-5540, FAX 418-659-4143. Ed. Denis Turcotte.

360 CAN ISSN 1719-427X
ORIENTATION MANUAL FOR BOARD MEMBERS/MANUEL D'ORIENTATION POUR LES MEMBRES DU BUREAU. Text in French, English. a. **Document type:** *Internal.*
Published by: Canadian Council on Social Development, 190 O'Connor St, 1st Flr, Ottawa, ON K2P 2R3, Canada. TEL 613-236-8977, FAX 613-236-2750, council@ccsd.ca, http://www.ccsd.ca.

362.7 USA ISSN 1932-3840
ORPHANS INTERNATIONAL WORLDWIDE INTERNEWS. Text in English. 2004. m.
Related titles: Online - full text ed.: ISSN 1932-3859.
Published by: Orphans International Worldwide, 540 Main St. #418, New York, NY 10044. TEL 212-755-7285, FAX 212-755-7302, info@oiww.org, http://www.oiww.org/index.html.

OTTAWA'S VITAL SIGNS. *see* SOCIOLOGY

▼ **DE OUD-HAGENAAR.** *see* GERONTOLOGY AND GERIATRICS

362.7 CAN ISSN 1924-4169
OUR OPPORTUNITIES ARE HERE!. Text in English. 2003. irreg. **Document type:** *Government.* **Description:** Designed for young Manitobans to access information on jobs, education and training, student aid, housing and rental options, and more.
Formerly (until 2008): M B 4 Youth (1915-5522)
Published by: Manitoba Education, Citizenship and Youth, 156 Legislative Bldg, 450 Broadway, Winnipeg, MB R3C 0V8, Canada. TEL 204-945-3720, FAX 204-945-1291, minedu@leg.gov.mb.ca, http://www.edu.gov.mb.ca/index.html.

OUTLOOK (AUCKLAND). *see* HANDICAPPED—Visually Impaired

362.5 CAN ISSN 1494-0825
OXFAM CANADA. ANNUAL REPORT. Text in English. 19??. a. **Document type:** *Journal, Trade.*
Former titles (until 1996): Oxfam Canada. Annual Review (1483-0949); (until 19??): Oxfam of Canada. Annual Report (1199-9845)
—CCC.
Published by: Oxfam Canada, 250 City Centre Ave, Ste 400, Ottawa, ON K1R 6K7, Canada. TEL 613-237-5236, FAX 613-237-0524, info@oxfam.ca, http://www.oxfam.ca.

OXFAM INTERNATIONAL. POLICY PAPERS. *see* BUSINESS AND ECONOMICS—International Development And Assistance

361 NZL ISSN 1179-9013
OXFAM UPDATE. Text in English. 1992. s-a. free (effective 2010). back issues avail. **Document type:** *Newsletter, Consumer.* **Description:** Focuses on Oxfam's latest program and campaign, that is, to create lasting, positive change for the world's poorest people. Oxfam works directly with communities at the grassroots level but also campaigns at the national and global levels against the root causes of poverty and injustice.
Formerly (until 2010): Oxfam News (1171-4808)
Media: Online - full text.
Published by: Oxfam New Zealand, PO Box 68357, Newton, Auckland, 1145, New Zealand. TEL 800-400-666, FAX 64-9-3556505, oxfam@oxfam.org.nz.

362.4 AUS ISSN 1446-9154
P D C N LIVE!. Text in English. 1995. q. free (effective 2009). adv. back issues avail. **Document type:** *Newsletter, Trade.* **Description:** Provides information about physical disability in Australia.
Former titles (until 2009): P D C N Advocate; (until 2000): P D C N News; (until 1997): Physical Disability Council of N S W. Newsletter
Related titles: Online - full text ed.: 2000.
Published by: Physical Disability Council of New South Wales, St Helens Community Centre, 184 Glebe Point Rd, Glebe, NSW 2037, Australia. TEL 61-2-95521606, 800-688-831, FAX 61-2-95524644, admin@pdcnsw.org.au. Adv. contact Ruth Robinson TEL 61-2-95521606.

362.82 NZL ISSN 1178-1971
P P D V P NEWS. Text in English. 2006. irreg. free (effective 2011). back issues avail. **Document type:** *Newsletter, Trade.*
Media: Online - full text.
Published by: Pacific Prevention of Domestic Violence Programme, 180 Molesworth St, Wellington, New Zealand. TEL 64-4-4707373, ppdvp@police.govt.nz.

362.1 CAN ISSN 1706-8053
P R H A COMMUNITY LINKS. (Parkland Regional Health Authority) Text in English. 1999. q.
Formerly (until 2001): Community Links (1493-6054)
Published by: Parkland Regional Health Authority, Room 112-27 2nd Ave SW, Dauphin, MB R7N 3E5, Canada. TEL 204-622-6222, FAX 204-622-6232, prha@prha.mb.ca, http://www.prha.mb.ca.

360 USA
P.S. GRANTS; sponsored programs administration newsletter. Text in English. irreg. back issues avail. **Document type:** *Newsletter.* **Description:** Designed for research administrators who are responsible for administering sponsored programs, grants or contracts from federal agencies.
Media: Online - full text.
Published by: Pennsylvania State University, Office of Sponsored Programs, 110 Technology Center, University Park, PA 16802. Ed. Robert Killoren.

360 GBR ISSN 1350-4703
P S S R U BULLETIN. Text in English. 1975. a., latest no.18, 2008. GBP 39 per issue (effective 2010). back issues avail. **Document type:** *Bulletin, Trade.* **Description:** Covers policy research and analysis on equity and efficiency, and so of resources, needs and outcomes in community and long-term care and related areas. The researchers are from a wide range of disciplines and backrounds, including the caring profession.
Formerly (until 1986): P S S R U Newsletter (1351-9468)
Related titles: Online - full text ed.: free (effective 2010).
—BLDSC (6945.964000). **CCC.**
Published by: Personal Social Services Research Unit, University of Kent at Canterbury, Cornwallis Bldg, George Allen Wing, Canterbury, Kent CT2 7NF, United Kingdom. TEL 44-1227-827672, FAX 44-1227-827038, pssru@kent.ac.uk.

P T U NYT. (Polio-, Trafik- of Ulykkesskadede) *see* MEDICAL SCIENCES—Psychiatry And Neurology

PAA FLUKT - WEB. *see* POLITICAL SCIENCE—International Relations

325.21 AUT ISSN 0031-0336
HV640.5.A6
PALESTINE REFUGEES TODAY. Text in German. 1960. s-a. free. bk.rev. charts; illus.; stat. **Document type:** *Bulletin.*
Related titles: Arabic ed.: ISSN 0250-8931. 1960.
Indexed: PerIslam, RefugAb.
Published by: United Nations Relief and Works Agency, Information Office, PO Box 700, Vienna, W 1400, Austria. TEL 43-1-213454531, FAX 43-1-213455877, TELEX 135310 UNRA A. Ed., R&P Sandro Tucci. Circ: 12,500.

362 CHL ISSN 0718-4697
PANORAMA DE SEGURIDAD SOCIAL. Text in Spanish. 2007. q.
Related titles: Ed.: Social Security Panorama. ISSN 0718-4905. 2007.
Published by: Corporacion de Investigacion, Desarrollo y Estudio de la Seguridad Social, San Ignacio No. 50, Santiago, Chile. TEL 56-2-6725881, FAX 56-2-6995436, http://www.ciedess.cl/website/home.asp.

360 DEU ISSN 1866-1718
DER PARITAETISCHE. Text in German. 1950. bi-m. bk.rev. index. **Document type:** *Magazine, Consumer.*
Former titles (until 2007): Nachrichten - Paritaet (0937-7425); (until 1990): D P W V - Nachrichten (0011-510X)
—GNLM.
Published by: Deutscher Paritaetischer Wohlfahrtsverband e.V., Oranienburger Str 13-14, Berlin, 10178, Germany. TEL 49-30-246360, FAX 49-30-24636110, info@paritaet.org, http://www.paritaet.org. Ed. Martin Wisskirchen. Circ: 18,500.

362.1 CAN
PARKLAND REGIONAL HEALTH AUTHORITY. ANNUAL REPORT. Text in English. a. **Document type:** *Yearbook, Government.*
Published by: Parkland Regional Health Authority, Room 112-27 2nd Ave SW, Dauphin, MB R7N 3E5, Canada. TEL 204-622-6222, FAX 204-622-6232, prha@prha.mb.ca.

LE PARTENAIRE. *see* PUBLIC HEALTH AND SAFETY

361 FRA ISSN 1957-4215
LE PARTENAIRE HUMANITAIRE. Text in French. 199?. q. free. back issues avail. **Document type:** *Newsletter, Consumer.*
Formerly (until 2006): Le Partenaire (1283-7687)
Related titles: Online - full text ed.
Published by: Secours Islamique France, 58 Bd. Ornano, Saint-Denis, Cedex 93285, France. TEL 33-1-60141414, FAX 33-1-49171717, info@secours-islamique.org.

362.4 NZL ISSN 1177-2859
PARTICIPATE. Text in English. 200?. irreg. **Document type:** *Newsletter.*
Related titles: Online - full text ed.: ISSN 1177-9608.
Published by: New Zealand. Office of the Honorable Ruth Dyson, Parliament Bldgs, Molesworth St, Wellington, 6160, New Zealand. TEL 64-4-4706570, FAX 64-4-4706784, rdyson@ministers.govt.nz, http://www.beehive.govt.nz/Minister.aspx?MinisterID=41.

▼ **PARTNER ABUSE.** *see* PSYCHOLOGY

362.4 636.7 USA
PARTNERS (SYLMAR). Text in English. q. free.
Former titles: I G E News; International Guiding Eyes. Newsletter
Published by: International Guiding Eyes, 13445 Glenoaks Blvd, Sylmar, CA 91342.

360 305.897 AUS ISSN 1832-2565
PARTNERSHIP FOR ABORIGINAL CARE. ANNUAL REPORT. Text in English. 2006. a. **Document type:** *Report, Trade.*
Published by: Partnership for Aboriginal Care, PO Box 2067, Port Macquarie, NSW 2444, Australia. TEL 61-2-6588-1400, FAX 61-2-6584-7102, info@mncacct.org.au, http://www.pac.org.au.

362.733 DEU ISSN 0176-2982
PATEN. Text in German. 1984. q. EUR 15 (effective 2008). back issues avail. **Document type:** *Magazine, Trade.* **Description:** Provides reports and information for the parents of adopted and fostercare children and professionals in related fields.
Published by: Pflege- und Adoptivfamilien Nordrhein-Westfalen e.V., Heimgart 8, Ratingen, 40883, Germany. TEL 49-2102-67218, FAX 49-2102-67245, info@pan-ev.de. Circ: 700.

PATIENT'S DIGEST. *see* PHARMACY AND PHARMACOLOGY

360 362.4 371.91 RUS
PATRIOT ORENBURZH'YA. Text in Russian. 1990. w. **Description:** Targets the handicapped, veterans, and pensioners.
Published by: Orenburgskoe Oblastnoe Pravlenie, Per Svobodina 4, k 706, Orenburg, 460000, Russian Federation. TEL 7-3532-776198. Ed. L A Shorokhov. Circ: 3,000. **Co-publisher:** Vserossiiskoe Obshchestvo Invalidov.

362 NLD ISSN 1871-1324
PAUL CREMERSLEZING. Text in Dutch. 2003. a.
Published by: (Nederlands Instituut voor Zorg en Welzijn), Stichting Paul Cremerslezing, Postbus 1255, Rijswijk, 2280 CG, Netherlands. TEL 31-70-4142700, pcl@leeuwendaal.nl.

362.3 CAN ISSN 1911-3811
PAVILLON DU PARC. BULLETIN D'INFORMATION. Text in French, English. 1996. irreg. **Document type:** *Bulletin, Consumer.*
Former titles (until 2002): Pavillon du Parc. Bulletin d'Information Trimestriel (1912-1105); (until 2001): Reseau de Services en Deficience Intellectuelle. Bulletin d'Information Trimestriel (1206-6591)
Published by: Pavillon du Parc Foundation, 768 boul. Saint-Joseph, Ste 200, Gatineau, PQ J8Y 4B8, Canada. TEL 819-770-1022, FAX 819-770-1023, info@pavillonduparc.qc.ca.

PAX CONNECTION. *see* BUSINESS AND ECONOMICS—Investments

PEACE NEWSLETTER; central New York's voice for peace and social justice. *see* POLITICAL SCIENCE—International Relations

360 CAN ISSN 1924-5580
THE PEARL. Text in English. 2001. irreg. free (effective 2011). back issues avail. **Document type:** *Bulletin, Trade.* **Description:** Designed for people who affected by mental illness to fulfill their needs and expectations.
Former titles (until 2009): Mental Illness Foundation. Bulletin (1712-803X); (until 2003): Quebec Mental Illness Foundation. Bulletin (1910-3298)
Media: Online - full text. **Related titles:** ◆ French ed.: Fondation des Maladies Mentales. Bulletin. ISSN 1712-8021.
Published by: Mental Illness Foundation/Fondation des Maladies Mentales, 401-2120 Sherbrooke St E, Montreal, PQ H2K 1C3, Canada. TEL 514-529-5354, 888-529-5354, FAX 514-529-9877, info@mentalillnessfoundation.org, http://www.mentalillnessfoundation.org. Ed. Lola Noel.

360 150 371.3 CAN ISSN 1488-6774
THE PEER BULLETIN. Text in English. m. CAD 53.50 domestic to individual members; USD 53.50 foreign to individual members; CAD 107 domestic to institutional members; USD 107 foreign to institutional members; CAD 21.40 domestic to students; USD 21.40 foreign to students (effective 2003). **Description:** Contains short issue articles, training announcements, how-to articles, book reviews.
Media: Online - full text.

Published by: Peer Resources, 1052 Davie St, Victoria, BC V8S 4E3, Canada. TEL 250-595-3503, FAX 250-595-3504, info@peer.ca. Ed., R&P Dr. Rey A Carr.

PENSION AND BENEFITS UPDATE. *see* BUSINESS AND ECONOMICS—Public Finance, Taxation

PENSION FUNDS & THEIR ADVISERS. *see* INSURANCE

368.43 362.6 SWE ISSN 0345-9225
PENSIONAEREN /PRO. Variant title: P R O Pensionaeren. Text in Swedish. 1942. 10/yr. price varies with membership. adv. bk.rev. illus. **Document type:** *Newspaper, Consumer.*
Formerly (until 1972): Folkpensionaeren
Related titles: Audio cassette/tape ed.
Published by: Pensionaerarnas Riksorganisation/Pensioners' National Organization, Adolf Fredriks Kyrkogate 12, PO Box 3274, Stockholm, 10365, Sweden. TEL 46-8-7016700, FAX 46-8-106640, info@pro.se. Ed., Pub. Agneta Berg-Wahlstedt. adv.: B&W page SEK 34,400, color page SEK 41,900; trim 189 x 248. Circ: 296,500.

THE PENSIONER. *see* GERONTOLOGY AND GERIATRICS

360 ESP ISSN 1134-9883
LAS PENSIONES DE LA SEGURIDAD SOCIAL, EN LA C A V. Text in Spanish; Summaries in Spanish. 1985. a. **Document type:** *Magazine, Government.*
Published by: Eusko Jaurlaritzaren Argitalpen-Zerbitzu Nagusia/Servicio Central de Publicaciones del Gobierno Vasco, Donostia-San Sebastian, 1, Vitoria-gasteiz, Alava 01010, Spain. TEL 34-945-018561, FAX 34-945-189709, hac-sabd@ej-gv.es, http://www.ej-gv.net/publicaciones.

305 340 RUS
PENSIONNOE OBESPECHENIE. Text in Russian. m.
Address: Bersenevskaya nab 20/2, Moscow, 109072, Russian Federation.

PENSIONS AGE. *see* INSURANCE

PENSIONS WORLD. *see* INSURANCE

PEOPLE'S MEDICAL SOCIETY NEWSLETTER. *see* CONSUMER EDUCATION AND PROTECTION

360 CAN ISSN 0704-5263
HV1
PERCEPTION. Text in English. 1977. q. free to members; CAD 24 domestic; CAD 34 in United States; CAD 40 elsewhere (effective 2005). adv. bk.rev. illus. reprints avail. **Description:** Journal of social comment.
Formerly: Canadian Welfare (0008-5332)
Related titles: Microfiche ed.: (from MML); Microfilm ed.: (from MML); Microform ed.: (from MIM, MML, PQC).
Indexed: A22, A26, C03, CBCARef, CBPI, CMCI, CPerI, E08, ErgAb, G08, H11, H12, HRA, P06, P30, P48, PAIS, PQC, S09, SWR&A, WBSS.
—BLDSC (6423.160000), Infotrieve. **CCC.**
Published by: Canadian Council on Social Development, 309 Cooper St, 5th Fl, Ottawa, ON K2P 0G5, Canada. TEL 613-236-8977, FAX 613-236-2750, council@ccsd.ca. Circ: 4,500.

360 MYS ISSN 0552-6426
PERSATUAN PURE LIFE. ANNUAL REPORT. Text in English. 1953. a. membership. **Document type:** *Corporate.* **Description:** Aims to establish spiritual and educational institutions, orphanages, workshops and dispensaries.
Published by: Pure Life Society/Persatuan, Batu 6 Jalan Puchong, Jalan Kelang Lama Post Office, Kuala Lumpur, 58200, Malaysia. TEL 03-792-9391, FAX 03-792-8303. Circ: 2,000.

361 USA ISSN 1559-243X
PERSPECTIVES IN PEER PROGRAMS. Abbreviated title: P P P. Text in English. 198?. s-a. USD 10 to non-members; free to members (effective 2011). bk.rev. **Document type:** *Journal, Academic/Scholarly.*
Formerly (until 2005): Peer Facilitator Quarterly (Print) (0741-2282)
Media: Online - full text.
Indexed: A26, CA, E03, E07, ERI, I05, T02.
Published by: National Association of Peer Program Professionals, PO Box 28564, Gladstone, MO 64188. TEL 888-691-1088, FAX 888-691-1088, napp@peerprogramprofessionals.org, http://www.peerhelping.org. Ed. Kimberly Hall.

360 613 GBR ISSN 1757-9139
RA21
➤ **PERSPECTIVES IN PUBLIC HEALTH.** Text in English. 1910. bi-m. USD 519, GBP 281 combined subscription to institutions (print & online eds.); USD 509, GBP 275 to institutions (effective 2011). adv. bk.rev. charts; illus. index. back issues avail.; reprint service avail. from PSC. **Document type:** *Journal, Academic/Scholarly.* **Description:** Concerns all aspects of health and health-related issues; disciplines include medical, social services, environment, health and safety, sanitation, nutrition, construction, pharmaceuticals and health education.
Former titles (until 2009): Royal Society for the Promotion of Health. Journal (1466-4240); Which incorporated (1999-2003): Hygeia (1740-4819); (until 1998): Royal Society of Health. Journal (0264-0325); (until 1983): Royal Society of Health. Journal (0035-9130); (until 1960): Royal Society for the Promotion of Health. Journal (0370-7318); (1894-1955): Royal Sanitary Institute. Journal (0370-7334)
Related titles: Microform ed.: (from PQC); Online - full text ed.: ISSN 1757-9147. USD 467, GBP 253 to institutions (effective 2011).
Indexed: A20, A22, A28, A34, A36, A37, A38, APA, API, ASCA, ASSIA, B21, B28, BrCerAb, BrTechI, C&ISA, C06, C07, C08, CA, CA/WCA, CABA, CIA, CINAHL, CMCI, CerAb, ChemAb, CivEngAb, CorrAb, CurCont, D01, DentInd, E&CAJ, E01, E11, E12, EEA, EMA, EMBASE, ESPM, EnvEAb, ExcerpMed, F09, FS&TA, FamI, GH, H&SSA, H&TI, H06, H13, H15, HRIS, INI, IndMed, LT, M&TEA, M09, MBF, MEDLINE, METADEX, MycolAb, N02, NRN, P10, P20, P21, P24, P27, P30, P33, P34, P48, P50, P52, P53, P54, P56, PAIS, PCI, PEI, PQC, R08, R10, R12, RRTA, Reac, S13, S16, SCOPUS, SD, SOPODA, SSCI, SWR&A, SociolAb, SolStAb, T02, T04, T05, THA, VS, W07, W11, WAA.
—BLDSC (6428.161375), GNLM, IE, Infotrieve, Ingenta, INIST, Linda Hall. **CCC.**
Published by: (The Royal Society for Public Health), Sage Publications Ltd. (Subsidiary of: Sage Publications, Inc.), 1 Oliver's Yard, 55 City Rd, London, EC1Y 1SP, United Kingdom. TEL 44-20-73248500, FAX 44-20-73248600, info@sagepub.co.uk, http://www.uk.sagepub.com/home.nav. **Subscr. to:** Sage Publications, Inc., 2455 Teller Rd, Thousand Oaks, CA 91320. TEL 805-499-9774, FAX 805-499-0871, journals@sagepub.com.

360 282 DEU ISSN 2192-2500
▼ **PFLEGE LEBEN;** Pflege - Werte - Zukunft. Text in German. 2011. q. **Document type:** *Journal, Trade.*
Formed by the merger of (1997-2011): P E P - Pflegekompetenz, Ethik, Persoenlichkeit (1436-8013); (1994-2011): Caritas und Pflege (0948-003X)
Published by: Katholischer Berufsverband fuer Pflegeberufe e.V., Adolf-Schmetzer-Str 2-4, Regensburg, 93055, Germany. TEL 49-941-6048770, FAX 49-941-6048779, info@kathpflegeverband.de, http://www.kathpflegeverband.de.

300 DEU ISSN 1435-4217
PFLEGEFREUND. Text in German. 1998. s-a. adv. **Document type:** *Magazine, Trade.*
Published by: Pflegeverbund Deutschland, Hindenburgstr 41, Bad Liebenzell, 75378, Germany. TEL 49-7052-2025, FAX 49-7052-4415. Ed. Harald Spies. adv.: page EUR 4,800; trim 190 x 267. Circ: 300,000 (controlled).

362.1 DEU ISSN 1438-3144
PFLEGEIMPULS; Zeitschrift fuer Recht und Praxis im Pflegemanagement. Text in German. 1999. m. EUR 89 (effective 2003). reprint service avail. from SCH. **Document type:** *Magazine, Trade.*
Published by: Nomos Verlagsgesellschaft mbH und Co. KG, Waldseestr 3-5, Baden-Baden, 76530, Germany. TEL 49-7221-21040, FAX 49-7221-210427, nomos@nomos.de, http://www.nomos.de. Ed. Johannes Kemser.

360 610 DEU
PFLEGEWISSENSCHAFT UND PFLEGEBILDUNG. Text in German. 2008. irreg., latest vol.3, 2008. price varies. **Document type:** *Monographic series, Academic/Scholarly.*
Published by: V & R Unipress GmbH (Subsidiary of: Vandenhoeck und Ruprecht), Robert-Bosch-Breite 6, Goettingen, 37079, Germany. TEL 49-551-5084303, FAX 49-551-5084333, info@vr-unipress.de, http://www.v-r.de/en/publisher/unipress.

PHILADELPHIA SUPPORT. *see* HANDICAPPED

362 NLD ISSN 1877-5268
PHILANTHROPIC STUDIES. WORKING PAPER SERIES. Text in Dutch, English. 2007. irreg., latest vol.17, 2010. free (effective 2011). **Document type:** *Monographic series, Academic/Scholarly.*
Media: Online - full text.
Published by: (Vrije Universiteit Amsterdam, Werkgroep Filantropische Studies), Geven in Nederland, De Boelelaan 1081, Amsterdam, 1081 HV, Netherlands. gin.fsw@vu.nl.

361.73 USA ISSN 2154-8900
AS911.A2
PHILANTHROPY ANNUAL. Text in English. 2007. a. USD 19.95 per issue (effective 2010). **Document type:** *Directory, Consumer.* **Description:** Includes articles, information and listings for philanthropic organizations.
Published by: Foundation Center, 79 Fifth Ave, 16th St, New York, NY 10003. TEL 212-620-4230, FAX 212-807-3677, orders@fdncenter.org, http://www.foundationcenter.org.

361.74 ITA ISSN 1828-2091
PHILANTHROPY REVIEW. Text in Italian. 2006. s-a. **Document type:** *Magazine, Consumer.*
Related titles: Online - full text ed.: ISSN 1828-2083.
Published by: Edizioni Philanthropy, Philanthropy Centro Studi, Universita di Bologna, Facolta di Economia di Forli, Piazzale della Vittoria 15, Forli, 47100, Italy. TEL 39-0543-374677, FAX 39-0543-374677, http://www.edizioni.philanthropy.it.

360 USA ISSN 1932-2313
PHILANTHROPY WORLD. Text in English. 2003. bi-m. USD 62 (effective 2007). **Document type:** *Magazine, Consumer.*
Formerly (until 2004): Philanthropy (1932-2305)
Published by: Philanthrophy World, 3878 Oak Lawn Ave., Se 200, Dallas, TX 75219. TEL 214-468-8770, FAX 214-468-0885, http://www.philanthropymagazine.com. Pub. Bob Hopkins.

306.85 USA ISSN 1093-5681
HQ728
PHILIPS GRADUATE INSTITUTE. PROGRESS. Text in English. 1992. a.
Indexed: FamI, S02, S03.
Published by: Philips Graduate Institute, 5445 Balboa Blvd, Encino, CA 91316. TEL 818-386-5660, http://www.pgi.edu.

PINE TREE LEGAL ASSISTANCE, INC. ANNUAL REPORT. *see* LAW—Legal Aid

361.73 USA ISSN 1052-4770
PLANNED GIVING TODAY. Abbreviated title: P G T. Text in English. 1990. m. USD 243 domestic to institutions; USD 298 foreign to institutions; USD 283 combined subscription domestic to institutions (print & online eds.); USD 347 combined subscription foreign to institutions (print & online eds.) (effective 2012). adv. **Document type:** *Newsletter, Academic/Scholarly.*
Formerly: Planned Giving Today Newsletter
Related titles: Online - full text ed.: ISSN 1937-4860. USD 439 to institutions (effective 2012).
Indexed: A22, A26, E01, E07, H12, I05.
—IE, Ingenta. **CCC.**
Published by: Mary Ann Liebert, Inc. Publishers, 140 Huguenot St, 3rd Fl, New Rochelle, NY 10801. TEL 914-740-2100, FAX 914-740-2101, 800-654-3237, info@liebertpub.com. Ed. Tom W Cullinan.

361.8 USA ISSN 1095-2160
HN80.C6
PLANNING & ACTION JOURNAL. Text in English. 1948. 8/yr. free (effective 2004). illus. 20 p./no.; **Document type:** *Journal, Consumer.* **Description:** Health, public policy and social issues affecting people in Northeast Ohio.
Former titles: Planning and Action Newsletter; Federation Forum (0300-6999); Welfare Talks
Related titles: Online - full text ed.: 2000. free (effective 2001).
Published by: The Center for Community Solutions, 1226 Huron Rd, Ste 300, Cleveland, OH 44115. TEL 216-781-2944, FAX 216-781-2988, sbanks@CommunitySolutions.com, http://www.CommunitySolutions.com. Ed. Sheryl Banks. Circ: 2,300 (free).

PLAY & PARENTING (ONLINE). *see* CHILDREN AND YOUTH—About

362.6 CAN ISSN 1920-7158
PLURALAGES. Text in English. 1994. 3/yr. back issues avail. **Document type:** *Magazine, Trade.*
Supersedes in part (in 2010): Bien Vieillir (1201-2351)
Related titles: Online - full text ed.: free (effective 2010); French ed.: PluriAGES. ISSN 1920-7166.
Published by: Centre de Recherche et d' Expertise en Gerontologie Sociale, 5800 Blvd Cavendish, 6th Fl, Cote-Saint-Luc, PQ H4W 2T5, Canada. TEL 514-484-7878, ext 1463, FAX 514-485-2978, creges.cvd@ssss.gouv.qc.ca.

362.4 371.911 371.912 DNK ISSN 1903-7910
POHJOISMAINEN HYVINVOINTIKESKUS. KUUROSOKEIDEN HENKILOSTON KOULUTUS. UUTISLEHTI. Text in Finnish. 200?. s-a. free. **Document type:** *Newsletter, Government.*
Formerly (until 2009): Pohjoismainen Kuurosokeiden Henkiloestoen Koulutuskeskus. Uutislehti (1398-3180)
Related titles: Online - full text ed.: ISSN 1903-7929. 200?; ♦ Multiple languages ed.: Nordisk Velfaerdscenter. Uddannelse for Doevblindepersonale. Nyhedsbrevet. ISSN 1903-7899.
Published by: Nordisk Velfaerdscenter, Uddannelse for Doevblindepersonale/Nordic Centre for Welfare and Social Issues,Training Center for Deafblind Services (Subsidiary of: Nordisk Ministerraad/Nordic Council of Ministers), Slotsgade 8, Dronninglund, 9330, Denmark. TEL 45-96-471600, FAX 45-96-471616, nvcdk@nordicwelfare.org, http://www.nordisktvalfardscenter.org.

POLEMIC; an independent journal of law and society. *see* LAW

360 USA ISSN 1942-6828
HV1
POLICY & PRACTICE. Text in English. 1932. bi-m. USD 180 domestic; USD 199 foreign; USD 30 per issue domestic; USD 35 per issue foreign (effective 2009). adv. bk.rev. abstr.; charts; illus. index. back issues avail.; reprint service avail. from PSC. **Document type:** *Magazine, Trade.* **Description:** Contains articles ranging from commentary by national leaders to practical features by administrators and direct service practitioners.
Former titles (until 2003): Policy & Practice of Public Human Services (1520-801X); (until 1998): Public Welfare (0033-3816); (until 1943): Public Welfare News
Related titles: Microform ed.: (from PQC); Online - full text ed.
Indexed: A01, A02, A03, A08, A10, A20, A22, A25, A26, AMHA, ASCA, AmH&L, B04, BRD, C12, CA, CLFP, E08, FamI, G06, G07, G08, H01, H05, H09, HRA, I05, I07, M01, M02, MCR, P02, P05, P06, P10, P21, P27, P30, P34, P48, P53, P54, PQC, S02, S03, S05, S08, S09, S23, SCOPUS, SOPODA, SPAA, SSAI, SSAb, SSI, SWR&A, SociolAb, T02, V03, W03, W05.
—IE, Infotrieve, Ingenta. **CCC.**
Published by: American Public Human Services Association, 1133 19th St, NW, Ste 400, Washington, DC 20036. TEL 202-682-0100, FAX 202-289-6555, MemberServicesHelpDesk@aphsa.org. adv.: B&W page USD 2,000, color page USD 2,500; trim 8.25 x 10.875.

POLICY AND PRACTICE IN HEALTH AND SOCIAL CARE. *see* MEDICAL SCIENCES

POLICY BITES. *see* PUBLIC ADMINISTRATION

361.6105 GBR ISSN 1745-6320
POLICY WORLD. Text in English. 1995. 3/yr. free to members (effective 2009). back issues avail. **Document type:** *Newsletter, Trade.*
Formerly (until 2005): S P A News (1476-4520)
Published by: (Social Policy Association), The Lavenham Press Ltd., 47 Water St, Lavenham, Suffolk CO10 9RN, United Kingdom. TEL 44-1787-247436, FAX 44-1787-248267, http://www.lavenhampress.com/. Ed. Kate Merriam.

POLITFOCUS SOZIALPOLITIK. *see* POLITICAL SCIENCE

360 ITA ISSN 1128-546X
HV286
POLITICHE SOCIALI E SERVIZI. Text in Italian. 1999. s-a. EUR 35 domestic to institutions; EUR 45 foreign to institutions (effective 2009). **Document type:** *Journal, Academic/Scholarly.*
Related titles: Online - full text ed.
Indexed: IBSS.
Published by: Vita e Pensiero (Subsidiary of: Universita Cattolica del Sacro Cuore), Largo Gemelli 1, Milan, 20123, Italy. TEL 39-02-72342335, FAX 39-02-72342260, redazione.vp@mi.unicatt.it. Ed. Giovanna Rossi. Circ: 2,000.

S

361 POL ISSN 0137-4729
HN536
POLITYKA SPOLECZNA. Text in Polish. 1974. m. EUR 49 foreign (effective 2005). **Document type:** *Journal, Academic/Scholarly.*
Indexed: AgrLib, SociolAb.
Published by: Instytut Pracy i Spraw Socjalnych, ul Bellottiego 3B, Wasrsaw, 01022, Poland. TEL 48-22-6361320, instprac@ipiss.com.pl, http://www.ipiss.com.pl. **Dist. by:** Ars Polona, Obroncow 25, Warsaw 03933, Poland. TEL 48-22-5098609, FAX 48-22-5098610, arspolona@arspolona.com.pl, http://www.arspolona.com.pl.

363.470971 CAN ISSN 0840-1136
HQ471
PORNOGRAPHY. Text in English. 1984. irreg. CAD 16.50 per issue (effective 2006).
Related titles: Online - full text ed.: ISSN 1495-3730.
Published by: Library of Parliament, Parliamentary Research Branch, Information Service, Ottawa, ON K1A 0A9, Canada. TEL 613-992-4793, 866-599-4999, info@parl.gc.ca, http://www.parl.gc.ca.

361 CAN ISSN 1923-8525
▼ **LE PORTE-PAROLE.** Text in French. 2010. q. **Document type:** *Trade.*
Published by: Agence de la Sante et des Services Sociaux de la Monteregie, 1255, rue Beauregard, Longueuil, PQ J4K 2M3, Canada. TEL 450-928-6777, FAX 450-679-6443, agencemonteregie@ssss.gouv.qc.ca, http://www.rrsss16.gouv.qc.ca/index.html.

361.021 PRT ISSN 0377-2365
PORTUGAL. INSTITUTO NACIONAL DE ESTATISTICA. INQUERITO AS RECEITAS E DESPESAS FAMILIARES. Text in Portuguese. 1970. 10/yr.
Published by: Instituto Nacional de Estatistica, Av Antonio Jose de Almeida 2, Lisbon, 1000-043, Portugal. TEL 351-21-8426100, FAX 351-21-8426380, http://www.ine.pt.

361.3 ESP ISSN 1578-0236
HV4
PORTULARIA; revista de trabajo social. Text in Spanish. 2001. a. **Document type:** *Journal, Academic/Scholarly.*
Indexed: F04, S02, S03, SCOPUS, SSA, SWR&A, SociolAb, T02.
—INIST.
Published by: Universidad de Huelva, Servicio de Publicaciones, Campus el Carmen, Avenida de las Fuerzas Armadas s/n, Huelva, Andalucia 21071, Spain. TEL 34-95-9018000, publica@uhu.es, http://www.uhu.es/publicaciones/index.html.

360 USA ISSN 2155-1170
AP2
▼ **POSITIVE IMPACT MAGAZINE.** Text in English. 2010 (July). q. USD 13.95 (effective 2011). **Document type:** *Magazine, Consumer.* **Description:** Inspires and encourages the creative ideas that result in long-lasting positive impact on the world.
Related titles: Online - full text ed.
Published by: Charity Beck, Ed. & Pub., 909 Woodbridge, Safety Harbor, FL 34695. TEL 727-743-9557, charity@positiveimpactmagazine.com.

362.7 GBR ISSN 0032-5856
HC260.P63
POVERTY. Text in English. 1966. 3/yr. GBP 3.95 per issue to non-members; free to members (effective 2009). adv. bk.rev. back issues avail. **Document type:** *Magazine, Trade.* **Description:** Provides latest facts and figures and keeps you up-to-date on the people and policies in the fight against poverty.
Related titles: Online - full text ed.: free (effective 2009).
Indexed: ASSIA, WBSS.
—BLDSC (6571.450000), IE, Ingenta. **CCC.**
Published by: Child Poverty Action Group, 94 White Lion St, London, N1 9PF, United Kingdom. TEL 44-20-78377979, FAX 44-20-78376414, info@cpag.org.uk.

362.5 USA ISSN 1944-2858
▼ **POVERTY & PUBLIC POLICY**; a global journal of social security, income, aid, and welfare. Text in English. 2009. q. USD 300 to institutions; USD 900 to corporations (effective 2011). back issues avail. **Document type:** *Journal, Academic/Scholarly.* **Description:** Features most relevant policy research on poverty, income distribution, and welfare programs, across the spectrum of disciplines, academic perspectives, and approaches.
Media: Online - full text.
Indexed: EconLit, SSA, SociolAb.
—**CCC.**
Published by: Berkeley Electronic Press, 2809 Telegraph Ave, Ste 202, Berkeley, CA 94705. TEL 510-665-1200, FAX 510-665-1201, info@bepress.com, http://www.bepress.com/. Ed. Max J Skidmore.

361.68 CZE
PRACE & SOCIALNI POLITIKA. Text in Czech. 1950. m. CZK 120 (effective 2009). bk.rev. charts; illus.; stat. **Document type:** *Magazine, Government.* **Description:** Covers social policy, social development, employment and human resources development, social research, labor law, social security, and information on international developments. Targets both professionals working in related fields and the general public.
Former titles (until 2004): Socialni Politika (0049-0962); (until 1969): Socialni Zabezpeceni
Related titles: Online - full text ed.
Indexed: RASB.
Published by: (Czech Republic. Ministersto Prace a Socialnich Veci/Ministry of Labor and Social Affairs), Press Publishing Group, s. r. o., Nekazanka 11, Prague 3, 11000, Czech Republic. TEL 420-2-24012830, FAX 420-2-24012831, info@pressgroup.cz. Ed. Tomas Rezek. Circ: 6,000.

PRACTICAL THEOLOGY. *see* RELIGIONS AND THEOLOGY

360 GBR ISSN 0950-3153
➤ **PRACTICE (ABINGDON).** Text in English. 1987. q. GBP 263 combined subscription in United Kingdom to institutions (print & online eds.); EUR 340, USD 425 combined subscription to institutions (print & online eds.) (effective 2012). adv. bk.rev. index. back issues avail.; reprint service avail. from PSC. **Document type:** *Journal, Academic/Scholarly.* **Description:** Aims to be relevant to the professional needs and interests of all practitioners, managers, educators, students and policymakers.
Related titles: Online - full text ed.: ISSN 1742-4909. GBP 237 in United Kingdom to institutions; EUR 306, USD 383 to institutions (effective 2012) (from IngentaConnect).
Indexed: A22, ASSIA, B28, C06, C07, C08, CA, CINAHL, DIP, E01, FR, IBR, IBSS, IBZ, P03, PsycInfo, S02, S03, SCOPUS, SOPODA, SSA, SWR&A, SociolAb, T02.
—IE, Ingenta, INIST. **CCC.**
Published by: (British Association of Social Workers), Routledge (Subsidiary of: Taylor & Francis Group), 4 Park Sq, Milton Park, Abingdon, Oxon OX14 4RN, United Kingdom. TEL 44-20-70176000, FAX 44-20-70176336, subscriptions@tandf.co.uk, http://www.routledge.com. Ed. Anne Quinney. Adv. contact Linda Hann TEL 44-1344-779945. **Subscr. to:** Taylor & Francis Ltd., Journals Customer Service, Sheepen Pl, Colchester, Essex CO3 3LP, United Kingdom. TEL 44-20-70175544, FAX 44-20-70175198.

362.7 AUS ISSN 1834-5484
PRACTICE BRIEF. Text in English. 2006. irreg. free (effective 2008). **Document type:** *Monographic series, Trade.* **Description:** Provides practitioners with an update on the latest thinking on specific practice issues.
Media: Online - full text.
Published by: Australian Institute of Family Studies, National Child Protection Clearing House, Level 20, 485 La Trobe St, Melbourne, VIC 3000, Australia. TEL 61-3-92147888, FAX 61-3-92147839, library@aifs.gov.au, http://www.aifs.gov.au/nch/index.html.

361.7 USA ISSN 1545-6781
HG177
PRACTICE MATTERS (NEW YORK); the improving philanthropy project. Text in English. 2003 (Sept.). irreg., latest vol.10, 2006. free (effective 2011). back issues avail. **Document type:** *Monographic series, Academic/Scholarly.*
Media: Online - full text.
Published by: Foundation Center, 79 Fifth Ave, 16th St, New York, NY 10003. TEL 212-620-4230, FAX 212-807-3677, customerservice@foundationcenter.org. Eds. Abby Spector, Kay Sherwood, Patricia Patrizi.

361 AUS ISSN 1834-3635
➤ **PRACTICE REFLEXIONS.** Text in English. 1971. s-a. free (effective 2011). **Document type:** *Journal, Academic/Scholarly.*
Formerly (until 2006): Welfare in Australia (Print) (0310-4869)
Media: Online - full text.
Published by: Australian Institute of Welfare and Community Workers practice.reflexions@arts.monash.edu.au, http://www.aiwcw.org.au/practicereflexions/currentjournal.html.

361 GBR
PRACTITIONER'S GUIDE SERIES. Text in English. irreg. GBP 9.95. **Document type:** *Handbook/Manual/Guide, Trade.* **Description:** Covers a wide range of social welfare issues. Of interest to social workers, care managers, practitioner researchers, and health care professionals. Contains practical guides, as well as commentaries on policy and practice.
Published by: (British Association of Social Workers), Venture Press, 16 Kent St, Birmingham, Warks B5 6RD, United Kingdom. TEL 44-121-622-3911, FAX 44-121-622-4860.

360 CAN ISSN 1922-1800
PRAIRIE INSIGHTS. Text in English. 1971. q. looseleaf. free to members (effective 2010). adv. bk.rev. back issues avail. **Document type:** *Newsletter, Trade.*
Formerly (until 2009): Manitoba Social Worker (0715-3481)
Published by: (Manitoba Institute of Registered Social Workers), Manitoba Association of Social Workers, 103 2033 Portage Ave, Winnipeg, MB R3J 0K6, Canada. TEL 204-888-9477, FAX 204-831-6359.

361 USA ISSN 1546-7325
HV85
PRAXIS (CHICAGO); where reflection & practice meet. Text in English. 2001. a. USD 12 per issue (effective 2010). **Document type:** *Journal, Trade.* **Description:** Brings out scholarly work of school of social work students and alumni to provide a forum in which they can express their diverse viewpoints, as well as learn from and be inspired by one another's ideas.
Published by: Loyola University Chicago, School of Social Work, 820 N Michigan Ave, Chicago, IL 60611. TEL 312-915-8900, socialwork@luc.edu. Ed. Allison Tan TEL 312-915-7005.

360 DEU ISSN 0935-6754
PRAXIS AKTUELL. AUSGABE BADEN-WUERTTEMBERG. Text in German. 1981. q. **Document type:** *Magazine, Trade.*
Published by: (A O K - Bundesverband), C W Haarfeld GmbH (Subsidiary of: Wolters Kluwer Deutschland GmbH), Annastr 32-36, Essen, 45130, Germany. TEL 49-201-720950, FAX 49-201-7209533, online@cw-haarfeld.de, http://www.cw-haarfeld.de.

360 DEU ISSN 1437-9147
PRAXIS AKTUELL. AUSGABE BAYERN. Text in German. 1999. q. **Document type:** *Magazine, Trade.*
Published by: (A O K - Bundesverband), C W Haarfeld GmbH (Subsidiary of: Wolters Kluwer Deutschland GmbH), Annastr 32-36, Essen, 45130, Germany. TEL 49-201-720950, FAX 49-201-7209533, online@cw-haarfeld.de, http://www.cw-haarfeld.de.

360 DEU ISSN 1437-9155
PRAXIS AKTUELL. AUSGABE BERLIN. Text in German. 19??. q. **Document type:** *Magazine, Trade.*
Published by: (A O K - Bundesverband), C W Haarfeld GmbH (Subsidiary of: Wolters Kluwer Deutschland GmbH), Annastr 32-36, Essen, 45130, Germany. TEL 49-201-720950, FAX 49-201-7209533, online@cw-haarfeld.de, http://www.cw-haarfeld.de.

360 DEU ISSN 0940-0060
PRAXIS AKTUELL. AUSGABE BRANDENBURG, MECKLENBURG-VORPOMMERN, OST-BERLIN, SACHSEN-ANHALT, SACHSEN UND THUERINGEN. Text in German. 1990. q. **Document type:** *Magazine, Trade.*
Published by: (A O K - Bundesverband), C W Haarfeld GmbH (Subsidiary of: Wolters Kluwer Deutschland GmbH), Annastr 32-36, Essen, 45130, Germany. TEL 49-201-720950, FAX 49-201-7209533, online@cw-haarfeld.de, http://www.cw-haarfeld.de.

360 DEU ISSN 1437-9171
PRAXIS AKTUELL. AUSGABE BREMEN UND BREMERHAVEN. Text in German. 19??. q. **Document type:** *Magazine, Trade.*
Published by: (A O K - Bundesverband), C W Haarfeld GmbH (Subsidiary of: Wolters Kluwer Deutschland GmbH), Annastr 32-36, Essen, 45130, Germany. TEL 49-201-720950, FAX 49-201-7209533, online@cw-haarfeld.de, http://www.cw-haarfeld.de.

360 DEU ISSN 0935-672X
PRAXIS AKTUELL. AUSGABE HAMBURG. Text in German. 1983. q. **Document type:** *Magazine, Trade.*
Published by: (A O K - Bundesverband), C W Haarfeld GmbH (Subsidiary of: Wolters Kluwer Deutschland GmbH), Annastr 32-36, Essen, 45130, Germany. TEL 49-201-720950, FAX 49-201-7209533, online@cw-haarfeld.de, http://www.cw-haarfeld.de.

360 DEU ISSN 1437-918X
PRAXIS AKTUELL. AUSGABE HESSEN. Text in German. 1997. q. **Document type:** *Magazine, Trade.*
Published by: (A O K - Bundesverband), C W Haarfeld GmbH (Subsidiary of: Wolters Kluwer Deutschland GmbH), Annastr 32-36, Essen, 45130, Germany. TEL 49-201-720950, FAX 49-201-7209533, online@cw-haarfeld.de, http://www.cw-haarfeld.de.

360 DEU ISSN 0935-6738
PRAXIS AKTUELL. AUSGABE MUENCHEN. Text in German. 1980. q. **Document type:** *Magazine, Trade.*
Published by: (A O K - Bundesverband), C W Haarfeld GmbH (Subsidiary of: Wolters Kluwer Deutschland GmbH), Annastr 32-36, Essen, 45130, Germany. TEL 49-201-720950, FAX 49-201-7209533, online@cw-haarfeld.de, http://www.cw-haarfeld.de.

360 DEU ISSN 1437-9279
PRAXIS AKTUELL. AUSGABE RHEINLAND. Text in German. 1976. q. **Document type:** *Magazine, Trade.*
Published by: (A O K - Bundesverband), C W Haarfeld GmbH (Subsidiary of: Wolters Kluwer Deutschland GmbH), Annastr 32-36, Essen, 45130, Germany. TEL 49-201-720950, FAX 49-201-7209533, online@cw-haarfeld.de, http://www.cw-haarfeld.de.

360 DEU ISSN 1437-9287
PRAXIS AKTUELL. AUSGABE RHEINLAND-PFALZ. Text in German. 19??. q. **Document type:** *Magazine, Trade.*
Published by: (A O K - Bundesverband), C W Haarfeld GmbH (Subsidiary of: Wolters Kluwer Deutschland GmbH), Annastr 32-36, Essen, 45130, Germany. TEL 49-201-720950, FAX 49-201-7209533, online@cw-haarfeld.de, http://www.cw-haarfeld.de.

360 DEU ISSN 0935-6746
PRAXIS AKTUELL. AUSGABE SAARLAND. Text in German. 1979. q. **Document type:** *Magazine, Trade.*
Published by: (A O K - Bundesverband), C W Haarfeld GmbH (Subsidiary of: Wolters Kluwer Deutschland GmbH), Annastr 32-36, Essen, 45130, Germany. TEL 49-201-720950, FAX 49-201-7209533, online@cw-haarfeld.de, http://www.cw-haarfeld.de.

360 DEU ISSN 1437-9228
PRAXIS AKTUELL. AUSGABE SCHLESWIG-HOLSTEIN. Text in German. 19??. q. **Document type:** *Magazine, Trade.*
Published by: (A O K - Bundesverband), C W Haarfeld GmbH (Subsidiary of: Wolters Kluwer Deutschland GmbH), Annastr 32-36, Essen, 45130, Germany. TEL 49-201-720950, FAX 49-201-7209533, online@cw-haarfeld.de, http://www.cw-haarfeld.de.

360 DEU ISSN 1437-9244
PRAXIS AKTUELL. AUSGABE WESTFALEN-LIPPE. Text in German. 19??. q. **Document type:** *Magazine, Trade.*
Published by: (A O K - Bundesverband), C W Haarfeld GmbH (Subsidiary of: Wolters Kluwer Deutschland GmbH), Annastr 32-36, Essen, 45130, Germany. TEL 49-201-720950, FAX 49-201-7209533, online@cw-haarfeld.de, http://www.cw-haarfeld.de.

360 DEU ISSN 1614-144X
PRAXIS, FORSCHUNG UND ENTWICKLUNG IN DER SOZIALEN ARBEIT. Text in German. 2004. irreg., latest vol.3, 2006. price varies. **Document type:** *Monographic series, Academic/Scholarly.*
Published by: Shaker Verlag GmbH, Kaiserstr 100, Herzogenrath, 52134, Germany. TEL 49-2407-95960, FAX 49-2407-95969, info@shaker.de.

649.8 362.4 FRA ISSN 1772-8789
PRENDRE SOIN DOMICILE; Le magazine du maintien de l'autonomie a domicile. Text in French. 2005. bi-m. EUR 30 to individuals; EUR 48 to institutions (effective 2009). **Document type:** *Magazine, Trade.*
Published by: Agence Presse Pro, B P 10336, Paris, cedex 05 75229, France. TEL 33-1-43265788, FAX 33-1-43260416, contact@prendresoin.fr.

360 CAN ISSN 1719-7155
PRESENCE (TORONTO). Text in English. 1991. 3/yr. **Document type:** *Newsletter, Consumer.*
Former titles (until 2005): Peace Brigades International (1719-7147); (until 2001): Peace Brigades International. Newsletter (1026-5260)
Published by: Peace Brigades International Canada, 238 Queen St W., Lower Level, Toronto, ON M5V 1Z7, Canada. TEL 416-324-9737, FAX 416-324-9757, info@pbicanada.org, http://www.web.ca/~pbican/index.htm.

PRESS COMPLAINTS COMMISSION. COMPLAINTS REPORT. *see* BUSINESS AND ECONOMICS—Labor And Industrial Relations

361 CAN ISSN 1924-6129
LA PRESSE DU D R M G. (Departement Regional de Medecine Generale) Text in French. 1998. irreg. **Document type:** *Bulletin, Trade.*
Former titles (until 2009): La Presse de l'Agence (1710-6230); (until 2004): Relais (1481-5524); Which was formed by the merger of (1979-1998): Concertaction (0226-5729); (1993-1998): Express Regie (1195-0609); Which was formerly (1981-1993): Informaction (0713-5912)
Published by: Agence de la Sante et des Services Sociaux de la Monteregie, 1255, rue Beauregard, Longueuil, PQ J4K 2M3, Canada. TEL 450-928-6777, FAX 450-679-6443, agencemonteregie@ssss.gouv.qc.ca, http://www.rrsss16.gouv.qc.ca/index.html.

PREVENTING FAMILY VIOLENCE; a catalogue of Canadian videos on family violence for the general public and for professionals working in the field. *see* CRIMINOLOGY AND LAW ENFORCEMENT

PREVENTING SEXUAL VIOLENCE; an educational toolkit for health care professionals. *see* MEDICAL SCIENCES—Pediatrics

362 155.5 USA ISSN 1086-4385
RA790.A1 CODEN: PRREFE
➤ **THE PREVENTION RESEARCHER.** Text in English. 1994. q. USD 42 (effective 2011). adv. **Document type:** *Journal, Academic/Scholarly.* **Description:** Presents the most current research and developments in adolescent behavioral research.
Indexed: A26, ASSIA, BRD, C06, C07, C08, C28, CA, CINAHL, E02, E03, ERI, ERIC, EdA, EdI, H12, I05, P30, S04, SociolAb, T02, W03, W05.
—BLDSC (6612.774380). **CCC.**
Published by: Integrated Research Services, Inc., 66 Club Rd, Ste 370, Eugene, OR 97401. TEL 541-683-9278, 800-929-2955, FAX 541-683-2621. Ed. Dr. Steven Ungerleider. Circ: 40,000 (paid and controlled).

360 GBR ISSN 0264-5033
RA427.9
PRIMARY HEALTH CARE. Text in English. 1982. 10/yr. GBP 83.38 in Europe to non-members; GBP 121 elsewhere to non-members; GBP 70.40 in Europe to members; GBP 103.40 elsewhere to members; GBP 160 combined subscription in Europe to institutions (print & online eds.); GBP 185 combined subscription elsewhere to institutions (print & online eds.); GBP 162.58 combined subscription in Europe to non-members (print & online eds.); GBP 200.20 combined subscription elsewhere to non-members (print & online eds.); GBP 137.28 combined subscription in Europe to members (print & online eds.); GBP 170.28 combined subscription elsewhere to members (print & online eds.) (effective 2009). adv. **Document type:** *Journal, Academic/Scholarly.* **Description:** Focuses on members of staff in health centers, health clinics, and major group practices in the United Kingdom.
Related titles: Online - full text ed.: GBP 79.20 to non-members; GBP 66.88 to members (effective 2009).
Indexed: A01, A03, A08, A22, A26, B28, C06, C07, C08, CA, CINAHL, E08, G08, H11, H12, I05, P20, P24, P27, P34, P48, P50, P54, PQC, S09, T02.
—BLDSC (6612.908900), IE, Ingenta. **CCC.**
Published by: R C N Publishing Co. (Subsidiary of: B M J Group), The Heights, 59-65 Lowlands Rd, Harrow, Middx HA1 3AW, United Kingdom. TEL 44-20-84231066, FAX 44-20-84239196, advertising@rcnpublishing.co.uk, http://www.rcnpublishing.co.uk. Eds. Julie Sylvester, Jean Gray. Adv. contact Neil Hobson TEL 44-20-88723123. page GBP 2,299; trim 216 x 279. Circ: 7,444.

PRIME TIME NEWS & OBSERVER. *see* GERONTOLOGY AND GERIATRICS

PRIME TIMES (OAK BROOK). *see* GERONTOLOGY AND GERIATRICS

361.73 USA ISSN 1930-109X
PRIVATE GRANTS ALERT; your monthly roundup of the latest funding from foundations, corporations and individuals. Abbreviated title: P G A. Text in English. 2006 (Jan.). m. USD 307 combined subscription (print & online eds.) (effective 2008). back issues avail. **Document type:** *Newsletter, Trade.* **Description:** Features information on the new grant opportunities available and contains essential details that allows to prepare letters of intent and applications quickly.
Related titles: Online - full text ed.: ISSN 1930-1162. USD 277 (effective 2008).
Published by: C D Publications, Inc., 8204 Fenton St, Silver Spring, MD 20910. TEL 301-588-6380, 800-666-6380, FAX 301-588-6385, info@cdpublications.com. Ed. Frank Klimko. Pub. Mike Gerecht.

360 USA ISSN 1097-4911
HV11
➤ **PROFESSIONAL DEVELOPMENT**; the international journal of continuing social work education. Text in English. 1981. s-a. USD 110 domestic; USD 165 foreign (effective 2010). 40 p./no. 2 cols./p.; back issues avail. **Document type:** *Journal, Academic/Scholarly.* **Description:** Aims to advance the science of professional development and continuing social work education, to foster understanding among educators, practitioners, and researchers, and to promote discussion that represents a broad spectrum of interests in the field.
Formerly (until 1998): Journal of Continuing Social Work Education (0276-0878)
Related titles: Online - full text ed.
Indexed: CA, S02, S03, SCOPUS, SSA, SWR&A, T02.
—BLDSC (6857.627000), IE, Ingenta.
Published by: Temple University, Center for Social Policy and Community Development, The University of Texas at Austin SSW, 1 University Sta D3500, Austin, TX 78712. TEL 512-471-9831, cspcd@temple.edu, http://www.temple.edu/cspcd/. Eds. Michael J Kelly, Michael L Lauderdale.

361.8 GBR ISSN 0961-5679
PROFESSIONAL FUNDRAISING. Abbreviated title: P F. Text in English. 1990. m. (11/yr.). GBP 120 (effective 2009). adv. back issues avail. **Document type:** *Magazine, Trade.* **Description:** Offers professional development features to help you progress in your career and promotes best practice.
Related titles: Supplement(s): PF Plus. ISSN 1466-4666.
Published by: Civil Society Media Ltd., 15 Prescott Pl, London, SW4 6BS, United Kingdom. TEL 44-20-78191200, FAX 44-20-78191201, info@civilsociety.co.uk, http://www.civilsociety.co.uk/. Ed. Lucy Harvey TEL 44-20-78191206. Pub. Daniel Phelan. Adv. contact Gordon Palmer TEL 44-20-78191228.

360 GBR ISSN 1352-3112
PROFESSIONAL SOCIAL WORK. Text in English. 1994. m. GBP 39.50 domestic; GBP 58.50 foreign; free to members (effective 2011). adv. bk.rev. **Document type:** *Magazine, Trade.* **Description:** Provides news, features and opinion pieces on topical issues, as well as areas relevant to improving social work practice.
Related titles: Online - full text ed.
Indexed: S02, S03.
—BLDSC (6864.220350), IE, Ingenta. **CCC.**
Published by: British Association of Social Workers, 16 Kent St, Birmingham, B5 6RD, United Kingdom. TEL 44-121-6223911, FAX 44-121-6224860, info@basw.co.uk. Ed. Joseph Devo TEL 44-121-6228404. Adv. contact Christine Sedgwick. Circ: 10,000 (paid).

360 ITA ISSN 1122-6307
HV286
LA PROFESSIONE SOCIALE; rivista di studio analisi e ricerca. Text in Italian. 1991. s-a. **Document type:** *Monographic series, Academic/Scholarly.*
Related titles: Online - full text ed.: ISSN 1826-7165.
Indexed: IBR, IBZ.
Published by: (Centro Studi di Servizio Sociale), Casa Editrice C L U E B, Via Marsala 31, Bologna, BO 40126, Italy. TEL 39-051-220736, FAX 39-051-237758, clueb@clueb.com, http://www.clueb.eu/home.html. Ed. Edda Samory.

360 MAR
PROGRAMME DE PRIORITES SOCIALES; indicateurs de suivi. Text in French. 1998. a. MAD 22 foreign (effective 2000). stat.
Published by: Morocco. Direction de la Statistique, B P 178, Rabat, Morocco. TEL 212-7-77-36-06, FAX 212-7-773042.

360 614 ITA ISSN 0393-9510
PROSPETTIVE SOCIALI E SANITARIE. Text in Italian. 1970. bi-w. (22/yr.). bk.rev. abstr.; bibl.; charts; stat. 22 p./no. 3 cols./p.; back issues avail. **Document type:** *Monographic series, Academic/Scholarly.*
Indexed: IBR, IBZ.
Published by: (Istituto per la Ricerca Sociale (I R S)), Franco Angeli Edizioni, Viale Monza 106, Milan, 20127, Italy. TEL 39-02-2837141, FAX 39-02-26144793, redazioni@francoangeli.it, http://www.francoangeli.it. Ed. Emanuele Ranci Ortigosa.

362.7 364 USA ISSN 0893-4231
PROTECTING CHILDREN. Text in English. 1984. q. price varies. adv. index. **Document type:** *Journal, Trade.* **Description:** Focuses on child abuse, child neglect; child protection and child welfare systems; research; training and education for child welfare professionals; advocacy and public information; and association membership information.
Formerly (until 1984): National Child Protective Services Newsletter
Indexed: AMHA, C28, CA, CJA, F09, S02, S03, SWR&A, T02.
Published by: American Humane Association, Children's Service, 63 Inverness Dr E, Englewood, CO 80112-5117. TEL 303-792-9900, FAX 303-792-5333, amyj@americanhumane.org. Ed., R&P, Adv. contact Amy Jacober. Circ: 1,500.

362.7609425 GBR ISSN 1741-6086
PROTECTING CHILDREN UPDATE. Text in English. 2003. m. (10/yr). GBP 89 combined subscription domestic to individuals (print & online eds.); GBP 161 combined subscription domestic to institutions (print & online eds.); GBP 202 combined subscription foreign to institutions (print & online eds.) (effective 2009). **Document type:** *Newsletter, Trade.* **Description:** Brings up to date with the ongoing changes in this area and how they will affect you in your role.
Related titles: Online - full text ed.
—CCC.
Published by: Optimus Publishing, 33-41 Dallington St, London, EC1V 0BB, United Kingdom. TEL 44-20-79543445, FAX 44-20-72519050, info@teachingexpertise.com. Ed. Chris Robertson.

362.7 FRA ISSN 1957-6285
PROTECTION DE L'ENFANCE ET DE L'ADOLESCENCE. Text in French. 2006. base vol. plus updates 3/yr. looseleaf. EUR 99 base vol(s).; EUR 26 updates per month (effective 2009). **Document type:** *Trade.*
Published by: Editions Weka, 249 Rue de Crimee, Paris, 75935 Cedex 19, France. TEL 33-1-53351717, FAX 33-1-53351701, http://www.weka.fr.

360 FRA ISSN 1243-4477
PROTECTION SOCIALE INFORMATIONS. Text in French. 1993. w. EUR 1,169 combined subscription (print & online eds.) (effective 2009). **Document type:** *Newsletter, Trade.*
Related titles: Online - full text ed.
Indexed: FR.
Published by: Groupe Liaisons (Subsidiary of: Wolters Kluwer France), 1 Rue Eugene et Armand Peugeot, Rueil Malmaison, 92500, France. TEL 33-1-41297751, FAX 33-1-41297754.

PSYCHIATRIC REHABILITATION JOURNAL. *see* MEDICAL SCIENCES—Psychiatry And Neurology

360 616.89 USA ISSN 1522-8878
HV40
➤ **PSYCHOANALYTIC SOCIAL WORK.** Abbreviated title: P S W. Text in English. 1987. s-a. GBP 438 combined subscription in United Kingdom to institutions (print & online eds.); EUR 569, USD 573 combined subscription to institutions (print & online eds.) (effective 2012). adv. bk.rev. illus. 120 p./no. 1 cols./p.; back issues avail.; reprint service avail. from PSC. **Document type:** *Journal, Academic/Scholarly.* **Description:** Provides social work clinicians and clinical educators with highly informative and stimulating articles relevant to the practice of psychoanalytic social work with the individual client.
Former titles (until 1999): Journal of Analytic Social Work (1052-9950); (until 1992): Journal of Independent Social Work (0883-7562)
Related titles: Microfiche ed.: (from PQC); Microform ed.; Online - full text ed.: ISSN 1522-9033. GBP 394 in United Kingdom to institutions; EUR 512, USD 516 to institutions (effective 2012).
Indexed: A01, A03, A22, AbAn, B21, CA, DIP, E-psyche, E01, E17, ESPM, FamI, IBR, IBZ, P03, PerIslam, PsycInfo, PsycholAb, RefZh, S02, S03, S21, SCOPUS, SOPODA, SSA, SWR&A, SociolAb, T02, V&AA.
—BLDSC (6946.274200), IE, Ingenta. **CCC.**
Published by: Routledge (Subsidiary of: Taylor & Francis Group), 325 Chestnut St, Ste 800, Philadelphia, PA 19106. TEL 215-625-8900, 800-354-1420, FAX 215-625-8914, journals@routledge.com, http://www.routledge.com. Ed. Jerrold R Brandell. adv.: B&W page USD 315, color page USD 550; trim 4.375 x 7.125. Circ: 164 (paid).

➤ **PSYCHOSOZIALE UMSCHAU.** *see* MEDICAL SCIENCES—Psychiatry And Neurology

➤ **PSYCHOTHERAPY NETWORKER**; the magazine for today's helping professional. *see* PSYCHOLOGY

362.2 NOR ISSN 0809-8352
PSYKISK. Text in Norwegian. 2006. s-a. (2-3/yr). free. back issues avail. **Document type:** *Magazine, Consumer.*
Related titles: Online - full text ed.: ISSN 1890-2995.
Published by: Helsedirektoratet/Norwegian Directorate of Health, PO Box 7000, St Olavs Plass, Oslo, 0130, Norway. TEL 47-810-20050, FAX 47-24-163001, postmottak@helsedirektoratet.no. Ed. Jon Hilmar Iversen.

PUBLIC ASSISTANCE & WELFARE TRENDS - STATE CAPITALS. *see* LAW

360 USA ISSN 1521-1320
HV89
PUBLIC HUMAN SERVICES DIRECTORY (YEAR). Text in English. 1940. a. USD 199 combined subscription per issue domestic to non-members (print & online eds.); USD 240 combined subscription per issue foreign to non-members (print & online eds.); USD 159 combined subscription per issue to members (print & online eds.) (effective 2009). **Document type:** *Directory, Government.* **Description:** Describes welfare programs and agencies in the US and Canada.
Formerly (until 1999): Public Welfare Directory (0163-8297)
Related titles: Online - full text ed.
Published by: American Public Human Services Association, 1133 19th St, NW, Ste 400, Washington, DC 20036. TEL 202-682-0100, FAX 202-289-6555.

PUBLIC POLICY AND SOCIAL WELFARE. *see* POLITICAL SCIENCE

360 PRI
PUERTO RICO. DEPARTMENT OF HEALTH. BOLETIN ESTADISTICO. Text in Spanish. 1979. irreg. price varies. **Document type:** *Government.*
Incorporates (in 2000): Puerto Rico. Department of Health. Informe de Recursos Humanos de la Salud; Which was formerly (until 1979): Puerto Rico. Department of Health. Informe del Registro de Profesionales de la Salud
Published by: (Puerto Rico. Division of Statistics USA), Department of Health, Auxiliary Secretariat for Planning, Evaluation, Statistics and Information Systems, P O Box 70184, San Juan, 00936, Puerto Rico. TEL 787-274-7875, FAX 787-274-7877. Circ: 500.

PUERTO RICO. DEPARTMENT OF HEALTH. INFORME ESTADISTICO DE FACILIDADES DE SALUD. *see* HEALTH FACILITIES AND ADMINISTRATION

361.8 USA
PUGET SOUND CO-OP FEDERATION NEWSLETTER. Text in English. q. USD 30. adv. **Document type:** *Newsletter.* **Description:** For and about the cooperative community in the Pacific Northwest.
Published by: Puget Sound Co-op Federation, 4201 Roosevelt Way, N E, Seattle, WA 98105-6092. TEL 206-632-4559, FAX 206-545-7131. Ed., R&P, Adv. contact Audrey Malan.

▼ **PURPOSE DRIVEN CONNECTION (ONLINE).** *see* RELIGIONS AND THEOLOGY—Protestant

360 USA
Q C REVIEW. (Quality Control) Text in English. q. membership.
Published by: National Association of Human Service Quality Control Directors, c/o American Public Welfare Association, 810 First St N E, Ste 500, Washington, DC 20002-4205. TEL 202-682-0100, FAX 202-289-6555.

360 ITA ISSN 1970-8939
QUADERNI EUROPEI SUL NUOVO WELFARE. Text in Italian. 2005. s-a. **Document type:** *Journal, Academic/Scholarly.*
Related titles: Online - full text ed.: ISSN 1972-4543. free (effective 2011); English ed.: European Papers on the New Welfare. ISSN 1970-8947.
Indexed: S02, S03.
Published by: The Risk Institute/L' Istituto del Rischio, Via della Torretta 10, Trieste, 34121, Italy. Ed. Orio Giarini.

361 ESP ISSN 1888-4636
QUADERNS D'ACCIO SOCIAL I CIUTADANIA. Text in Catalan, Spanish. 2008. q.
Published by: Generalitat de Catalunya, Departament de Accio Social i Ciutadania, Placa Pau Vila, 1, Barcelona, 08039, Spain. TEL 34-93-4831000, FAX 34-93-4831011, biblioteca.benestar@gencat.net, http://www.gencat.net/benestar/.

360 GBR ISSN 1473-3250
HV40
QUALITATIVE SOCIAL WORK; research and practice. Text in English. 2002 (Mar.). q. USD 749, GBP 405 combined subscription to institutions (print & online eds.); USD 734, GBP 397 to institutions (effective 2011). adv. back issues avail.; reprint service avail. from PSC. **Document type:** *Journal, Academic/Scholarly.* **Description:** Provides a forum for those interested in qualitative research and evaluation in qualitative approaches to practice. It facilitates interactive dialogue and integration between those interested in qualitative research and methodology and those involved in the world of practice.
Related titles: Online - full text ed.: ISSN 1741-3117. USD 674, GBP 365 to institutions (effective 2011).
Indexed: A01, A03, A08, A22, C06, C07, C08, CA, CINAHL, CJA, DIP, E-psyche, E01, FamI, IBR, IBZ, P03, P34, PsycInfo, PsycholAb, S02, S03, SCOPUS, SSA, SWR&A, SociolAb, T02.
—BLDSC (7168.124470), IE, Ingenta. **CCC.**
Published by: Sage Publications Ltd. (Subsidiary of: Sage Publications, Inc.), 1 Oliver's Yard, 55 City Rd, London, EC1Y 1SP, United Kingdom. TEL 44-20-73248500, FAX 44-20-73248600, info@sagepub.co.uk, http://www.uk.sagepub.com/home.nav. Eds. Ian F Shaw, Roy Ruckdeschel. adv.: B&W page GBP 350; 130 x 205. **Subscr. in the Americas to:** Sage Publications, Inc., 2455 Teller Rd, Thousand Oaks, CA 91320. TEL 805-499-9774, FAX 805-499-0871, journals@sagepub.com.

QUALITY LIFE/LEEFTYD; for your total wellbeing. *see* GERONTOLOGY AND GERIATRICS

360 CAN ISSN 1718-0392
QUEBEC PROVINCE. MINISTERE DE LA FAMILLE, DES AINES ET DE LA CONDITION FEMININE. RAPPORT ANNUEL DE GESTION. Text in French. 2003. a. **Document type:** *Government.*
Supersedes in part (in 2004): Quebec Province. Ministere de l'Emploi, de la Solidarite Sociale et de la Famille. Rapport Annuel de Gestion (1912-0826); Which was formed by the merger of (2002-2003): Quebec Province. Ministere de la Famille et de l'Enfance. Rapport Annuel de Gestion (1706-8827); Which was formerly (until 2001): Quebec. Ministere de la Famille et de l'Enfance. Rapport Annuel (1481-837X); (until 1997): Quebec. Office des Services de Garde a l'Enfance. Rapport Annuel (0838-097X); (until 1986): Office des Services de Garde a l'Enfance. Rapport d'Activite (0837-5992); (1981-1983): Office des Services de Garde a l'Enfance. Rapport Annuel (0229-9488); (2002-2003): Quebec Province. Ministere de l'Emploi et de la Solidarite Sociale. Rapport Annuel de Gestion (1706-9580); Which was formerly (until 2001): Quebec. Ministere de l'Emploi et de la Solidarite Sociale. Rapport Annuel (1701-2074); (until 2000): Quebec. Ministere de la Solidarite Sociale. Rapport Annuel (1495-0499); (1998-1999): Quebec. Ministere de l'Emploi et de la Solidarite. Rapport Annuel (1490-294X)
Published by: Quebec, Ministere de la Famille, des Aines et de la Condition Feminine, 425, rue Saint-Amable, RC, Quebec, PQ G1R 4Z1, Canada. http://www.mfacf.gouv.qc.ca/index.asp.

361 AUS ISSN 1837-3313
▼ **QUEENSLAND GOVERNMENT. DEPARTMENT OF COMMUNITY SAFETY. ANNUAL REPORT.** Text in English. 2009. a. free (effective 2010). back issues avail. **Document type:** *Report, Government.*
Media: Online - full text.

S

Published by: Queensland Government, Department of Community Safety, GPO Box 1425, Brisbane, QLD 4001, Australia. TEL 61-7-32478604, 300-369-003, FAX 61-7-32478535.

QUINNEHTUKQUT LEGAL NEWS. *see* LAW—Legal Aid

360 AUS ISSN 1832-519X
R A PLINK NEWSLETTER. (Regional Action Partnership) Text in English. 2001. m. free (effective 2009). back issues avail. **Document type:** *Newsletter, Consumer.*
Media: Online - full text.
Published by: RAPlink Inc., PO Box 670, Mawson, ACT 2607, Australia. TEL 61-4-28866722, FAX 61-2-62902364. Ed. Elizabeth Murphy.

R E C I I S. REVISTA ELETRONICA DE COMUNICACAO, INFORMACAO & INOVACAO EM SAUDE. *see* MEDICAL SCIENCES

362.7 NLD ISSN 2212-0157
R M U JONGERENSPECIAL. Text in Dutch. a.
Published by: Reformatorisch Maatschappelijke Unie, Postbus 900, Veenendaal, 3900 AX, Netherlands. TEL 31-318-543030, FAX 31-318-542522, info@rmu.org, http://www.rmu.org.

353.538 NZL
R S A REVIEW. (Returned Services Association) Variant title: Official R S A Journal. Text in English. 1921. bi-m. NZD 10 to members; NZD 15 domestic to non-members; NZD 20 foreign to non-members (effective 2009). adv. back issues avail. **Document type:** *Journal, Trade.*
Description: Covers military issues and pension and welfare matters.
Formerly (until 1943): New Zealand R S A Review
Published by: Royal New Zealand Returned and Services' Association, 181-183 Willis St, PO Box 27248, Wellington, 6141, New Zealand. TEL 64-4-3847994, FAX 64-4-3853325, enquiries@rnzrsa.org.nz. adv.: page NZD 1,350. Circ: 106,000 (controlled).

364 ESP ISSN 0212-7210
R T S. (Revista de Trabajo Social) Text in Spanish, Catalan. 1968. q. **Document type:** *Magazine, Academic/Scholarly.*
Formerly (until 1969): Revista de Servicio Social (1138-4522)
Indexed: CA, S02, S03, SWR&A, T02.
Published by: Col.legi Oficial de Diplomats en Treball Social i Assitents Social/Asociacion de Asistentes Sociales para el estudio y Especulacion del Trabajo Social, C Portaferrissa 18, 1r. 1a, Barcelona, 08002, Spain. TEL 34-93-3185593, FAX 34-93-4122408. Ed. Montserrat Bacardi i Busquet.

361.7 NZL ISSN 1177-2581
RAMPANT. Text in English. 2005. s-a. **Document type:** *Magazine, Consumer.*
Published by: World Vision New Zealand, Private Bag 92078, Auckland, New Zealand. TEL 64-9-5807700, FAX 64-9-5807799, nzcommunications@worldvision.org.nz.

362.7 GBR ISSN 1462-8007
RAPPORT. Text in English. 1938. bi-m. GBP 15 domestic to non-members; GBP 20 foreign to non-members; free to members (effective 2009). adv. bk.rev. back issues avail. **Document type:** *Journal, Trade.* **Description:** Designed for the members of the Community and Youth Worker's Union.
Related titles: Online - full text ed.: free (effective 2009).
Published by: Community and Youth Workers' Union, Transport House, 211 Broad St, Birmingham, B15 1AY, United Kingdom. TEL 44-121-6436221, FAX 44-121-6330184, cywu@compuserve.com. Ed. Kev Henman. Adv. contact Kerry Jenkins. page GBP 450.

360 SWE
RAPPORTSERIE I SOCIALT ARBETE. Text in Swedish. 2004. irreg. back issues avail. **Document type:** *Monographic series, Academic/ Scholarly.*
Formerly (until 2010): Vaexjoe Universitet. Institutionen foer Vaardvetenskap och Socialt Arbete. Rapportserie i Socialt Arbete (1652-8573)
Published by: Linneuniversitetet, Institutionen foer Socialt Arbete/ Linnaeus University. School Social Work, Georg Lueckligs Vaeg 8, Vaexjoe, 35195, Sweden. TEL 46-470-708000, FAX 46-470-36310, http://lnu.se/institutioner/institutionen-for-socialt-arbete.

360 ITA ISSN 0033-9601
RASSEGNA DI SERVIZIO SOCIALE. Text in Italian. 1962. q. EUR 40 (effective 2008). adv. bk.rev. abstr.; charts; stat. index. **Document type:** *Magazine, Consumer.*
Published by: Ente Italiano di Servizio Sociale (E I S S), Viale Ferdinando Baldelli 41, Rome, 00146, Italy. TEL 39-06-5410603, FAX 39-06-5402762, info@eiss.it, http://www.eiss.it.

REACH NEWSLETTER. *see* EDUCATION—Special Education And Rehabilitation

REAL PATRONATO SOBRE DISCAPACIDAD. BOLETIN. *see* HANDICAPPED

360 FRA ISSN 0220-9926
REALITES FAMILIALES. Text in French. 1946. 3/yr. EUR 22 domestic; EUR 25 foreign (effective 2009). adv. bk.rev.; film rev. illus. index.
Formerly (until 1979): U N A F. Bulletin de Liaison (0041-5219)
Indexed: FR.
Published by: Union Nationale des Associations Familiales, 28 place Saint Georges, Paris, 75009, France. TEL 33-1-49953600, FAX 33-1-49953667, fheil@unaf.fr. Ed. Francoise Heil. Circ: 7,000.

RECHERCHE COMMUNAUTAIRE AUTOCHTONE SUR LE VIH/SIDA. REVUE CANADIENNE. *see* ETHNIC INTERESTS

360 DEU ISSN 0944-0216
RECHT DER GEMEINNUETZIGEN ORGANISATIONEN UND EINRICHTUNGEN; Ergaenzbares Handbuch der Rechtsvorschriften und Materialien. Text in German. 1975. base vol. plus a. updates. looseleaf. EUR 96 base vol(s).; EUR 34.80 updates per issue (effective 2009). **Document type:** *Monographic series, Trade.*
Published by: Erich Schmidt Verlag GmbH & Co. (Berlin), Genthiner Str 30 G, Berlin, 10785, Germany. TEL 49-30-2500850, FAX 49-30-25008305, vertrieb@esvmedien.de, http://www.erich-schmidt-verlag.de.

360 DEU ISSN 0944-5579
RECHTSDIENST DER LEBENSHILFE. Text in German. 1993. q. EUR 35 to non-members; EUR 25 to members (effective 2009). adv. **Document type:** *Magazine, Consumer.* **Description:** Contains articles about social policy and legislation concerning people with mental disabilities and their families in Germany.
Published by: Bundesvereinigung Lebenshilfe fuer Menschen mit Geistiger Behinderung e.V., Raiffeisenstr 18, Marburg, 35043, Germany. TEL 49-6421-4910, FAX 49-6421-491167, bundesvereinigung@lebenshilfe.de. Ed. Klaus Lachwitz. Circ: 5,150 (paid).

RECHTSPRAAK ZORGVERZEKERING. *see* INSURANCE

362.6 351 USA
HQ1064.U5
RECOGNITION OF EXCELLENCE IN AGING RESEARCH, COMMITTEE REPORT, REPORT OF THE SPECIAL COMMITTEE ON AGING, UNITED STATES SENATE. Text in English. 19??. a. back issues avail. **Document type:** *Report, Government.*
Formerly: Developments in Aging (0734-3213)
Published by: U.S. Government Printing Office, 732 N Capitol St, NW, Washington, DC 20401. TEL 202-512-1800, 866-512-1800, FAX 202-512-2104, ContactCenter@gpo.gov, http://www.gpo.gov.

360 USA ISSN 0360-4608
HV86
RECORD (NASHVILLE). Text in English. 1938. s-a. free. illus. **Document type:** *Government.*
Formerly (until 1975): Tennessee Public Welfare Record (0040-3377)
Indexed: P06, P30.
Published by: Department of Human Services, 400 Deaderick St, Citizens Plaza, Nashville, TN 37219. FAX 615-741-3241. Ed. Patricia Harris Moorehead. Circ: 9,800.

360 CAN ISSN 1208-0608
HV110.V3
RED BOOK. Text in English. 1958. a. looseleaf. CAD 70 (effective 2006).
Former titles (until 1996): Directory of Services for the Lower Mainland (1208-0594); (until 1992): Information Services Vancouver. Directory of Services (1184-1753); (until 1986): Directory of Services for Greater Vancouver (0319-0242); (until 1974): Directory of Services - Health Welfare Recreation in the Lower Mainland (0319-0250); (until 1970): Directory of Services - Health Welfare Recreation in Metropolitan Vancouver (0319-0285)
Published by: Information Services Vancouver, 202-3102 Main St, Vancouver, BC V5T 3G7, Canada. TEL 604-875-6431, FAX 604-660-9415, inform@communityinfo.bc.ca. Circ: 3,000.

361.7 CHE ISSN 1019-9349
RED CROSS, RED CRESCENT. Text in English. 1985. q. free. bk.rev. **Document type:** *Bulletin.* **Description:** Reviews the activities of the Red Cross and Red Crescent societies, adressing a wide variety of issues of humanitarian concern.
Related titles: Spanish ed.: Cruz Roja, Media Luna Roja. ISSN 1019-9357; French ed.: Croix-Rouge, Croissant-Rouge. ISSN 1019-9330.
Indexed: PAIS, PerIslam.
Published by: International Federation of Red Cross and Red Crescent Societies, PO Box 372, Geneva 19, 1211, Switzerland. TEL 41-22-7304222, FAX 41-22-7530395, TELEX 412133-FRC-CH. Eds. Jean Milligan TEL 41-22-7304373, Jean Francois Berger. R&P Jean Milligan TEL 41-22-7304373. Circ: 60,000. **Co-sponsor:** International Committee of the Red Cross/Comite International de la Croix Rouge.

364 BOL
RED DE INVESTIGACION Y ACCION PARA EL DESARROLLO LOCAL. BOLETIN. Variant title: Boletin RADIAL. Text in Spanish. bi-w.
Related titles: E-mail ed.
Published by: Centro Boliviano de Estudios Multidisciplinarios, Ave. Ecuador no. 2330, esq. C. Rosendo Gutierrez, La Paz, Bolivia. TEL 591-2-2415324, FAX 591-2-2414726, cebem@cebem.com, http://www.cebem.com/.

360 GBR
REFERRALS OF CHILDREN TO REPORTERS AND CHILDREN'S HEARINGS (YEAR). Text in English. 1979. a. GBP 2. **Document type:** *Bulletin, Government.*
Published by: Social Work Services Group, Statistics Branch, Rm 52, James Craig Walk, Edinburgh, EH1 3BA, United Kingdom. TEL 44-131-244-5431, FAX 44-131-244-5315. **Dist. by:** Her Majesty's Stationery Office Bookshop, 71 Lothian Rd, EH3 9AZ, Edinburgh, Midlothian EH3 9AZ, United Kingdom. TEL 44-131-228-4181.

REFLECTIONS (LONG BEACH); narratives of professional helping. *see* EDUCATION—Special Education And Rehabilitation

362 610 USA ISSN 1095-483X
RA448.5.I5
REGIONAL DIFFERENCES IN INDIAN HEALTH. Text in English. 1990. a.
Published by: U.S. Department of Health and Human Services, Indian Health Service, Clinical Support Center, 801 Thompson Ave Ste 400, Rockville, MD 20852-1627. TEL 301-443-1083.

362.4 NOR ISSN 1504-2707
REGIONSNYTT (SKI). Text in Norwegian. 2004. s-a. **Document type:** *Newsletter, Consumer.*
Formed by the merger of (1983-2004): Fylkesnytt (Greaaker) (1504-2715); (1988-2004): Norges Handikapforbund. Akershus. Fylkesnytt (1500-3566)
Published by: Norges Handikapforbund, Oest/Norwegian Association of the Disabled. East, Holteveien 5, Ski, 1400, Norway. TEL 47-64-878844, FAX 47-64-878849, nhfoest@nhf.no. Eds. Sverre Bergenholdt, Johan Sundby.

360 GBR
REGISTERED HOMES AND SERVICES. Text in English. 1996. m. GBP 96 (effective until Apr. 2001). bk.rev. **Document type:** *Newsletter.* **Description:** Politically neutral journal covering legal, professional, political and market developments concerning long-term care in registered homes and regulated care services in the UK.
Formerly (until 1998): Registered Homes (1363-5492)
Published by: Rideau Douglas Ltd., 30 Byne Rd, London, SE26 5JE, United Kingdom. TEL 44-20-8325-6743, FAX 44-20-8325-6743. Ed., Pub., R&P, Adv. contact Paul Remes.

362.6 CAN ISSN 1718-4789
REGISTRE DES RESIDENCES PRIVEES POUR PERSONNES AGEES AVEC SERVICES. Text in French. 2000. irreg. **Document type:** *Monographic series, Consumer.*
Formerly (until 2003): Ressources d'Habitation Privees de la Region de Montreal-Centre (1497-1283)
Related titles: English ed.: Private Residences for Autonomous Seniors in the Montreal-Centre. ISSN 1497-1291. 2000.
Published by: Quebec, Agence de Developpement de Reseaux Locaux de Services de Sante et de Services Sociaux de Montreal, 3725, rue Saint-Denis, Montreal, PQ H2X 3L9, Canada. TEL 514-286-6500, http://www.santemontreal.qc.ca.

360 DEU ISSN 1614-4759
REIHE QUALITAET UND QUALITAETSSICHERUNG IN DER SOZIALEN ARBEIT. Text in German. 2003. irreg., latest vol.8, 2006. price varies. **Document type:** *Monographic series, Academic/ Scholarly.*
Published by: Ibidem Verlag, Melchiorstr 15, Stuttgart, 70439, Germany. TEL 49-711-9807954, FAX 49-711-9807952, ibidem@ibidem-verlag.de, http://www.ibidem-verlag.de.

360 GBR ISSN 0954-3406
RELATE NEWS. Text in English. m. GBP 6 (effective 2000). adv. bk.rev. back issues avail. **Document type:** *Newspaper.*
—CCC.
Published by: Relate Marriage Guidance, Herbert Gray College, Little Church St, Rugby, Warks CV21 3AP, United Kingdom. TEL 44-1788-573241, FAX 44-1788-535007. Ed., R&P, Adv. contact Suzy Powling TEL 44-1788-563811. B&W page GBP 1,400; trim 273 x 393. Circ: 5,500.

RELATIONAL CHILD & YOUTH CARE PRACTICE. *see* CHILDREN AND YOUTH—About

361 CAN ISSN 0034-3781
BX802
RELATIONS. Text in French. 1941. 8/yr. CAD 30 domestic; USD 35 foreign (effective 2001). adv. bk.rev. bibl. index. back issues avail.; reprints avail. **Document type:** *Journal, Academic/Scholarly.*
Description: Concerned with social welfare and economic justice for the poor.
Related titles: CD-ROM ed.; Microform ed.: (from PQC).
Indexed: A01, C03, CBCARef, CBPI, CERDIC, CPL, CPerI, I05, MLA-IB, PCI, PQC, PdeR.
Published by: (Peres de la Compagnie de Jesus), Revue Relations, 25 Jarry Guest, Montreal, PQ H2P 1S6, Canada. TEL 514-387-2541, FAX 514-387-0206. Ed. Jean Pichette. R&P Anne Marie Aitken. adv.: B&W page USD 350. Circ: 4,000.

361.77 338.91 CHE
RELIEFWEB; a global information system to support the delivery of humanitarian assistance. Text in English. 1996. irreg. free.
Description: Provides a central information system on the Internet to disseminate information about humanitarian emergencies resulting from warfare and natural disasters, with the aim of strengthening the ability of the international community to respond accordingly.
Published by: United Nations, Office for the Coordination of Humanitarian Affairs, Palais des Nations, 8-14 ave. de la Paix, Geneva, 1211, Switzerland. TEL 41-22-9171234, FAX 41-22-9170023. Ed. Madelaine Moulin Acevedo.

361.73 USA
RELIGIOUS FUNDING RESOURCE GUIDE. Text in English. 1994 (11th ed.). a. USD 75 to individuals; USD 90 to institutions. **Document type:** *Directory.* **Description:** Provides information about religious funders who support national and local organizations working for change in their communities.
Formerly: Church Funding Resource Guide
Published by: ResourceWomen, 4527 S Dakota Ave, N E, Washington, DC 20017. TEL 202-832-8071. Ed. Jennifer E Griffith. R&P Eileen Paul.

REMEMBERING YESTERDAY; recalling those happy memories from the golden age of our past. *see* GERONTOLOGY AND GERIATRICS

RENALINK. *see* MEDICAL SCIENCES—Urology And Nephrology

REPERE SOCIAL; revue d'information sociale. *see* SOCIAL SCIENCES: COMPREHENSIVE WORKS

362 304.64 AUS
REPORT OF REVIEWABLE DEATHS. Text in English. 2004. a. AUD 22 per issue (effective 2009). back issues avail. **Document type:** *Government.*
Formerly (until 2005): Reviewable Deaths Annual Report (1832-1674)
Related titles: Online - full text ed.: free (effective 2009).
Published by: New South Wales Ombudsman, Level 24, 580 George St, Sydney, NSW 2000, Australia. TEL 61-2-92861000, 800-451-524, FAX 61-2-92832911, nswombo@ombo.nsw.gov.au.

REPORT ON EMOTIONAL & BEHAVIORAL DISORDERS IN YOUTH. *see* PSYCHOLOGY

266 USA ISSN 1049-586X
RESCUE (KANSAS CITY). Text in English. 1985. bi-m. free. adv. bk.rev. 20 p./no.; **Document type:** *Newsletter.* **Description:** For ministries and individuals ministering to the homeless, addicted and urban poor in inner cities of North America and the world.
Formerly: Horizons
Published by: Association of Gospel Rescue Missions, 1045 Swift Ave, Kansas City, MO 64116-4127. TEL 816-471-8020, FAX 816-471-3718, agrm@agrm.org, http://rescuemissions.org. Ed. Stephen E Burger TEL 816-471-8020. R&P, Adv. contact Phil Rydman. page USD 720; trim 8.5 x 11. Circ: 3,500.

360 GBR ISSN 0955-7970
RESEARCH HIGHLIGHTS IN SOCIAL WORK. Text in English. 1981. irreg., latest 2009. price varies. back issues avail. **Document type:** *Monographic series, Academic/Scholarly.* **Description:** Examines areas of interest to persons in community work and related fields. Highlights relevant research and draws out implications for policy and practice.
Formerly (until 1982): Research Highlights (0261-5568)
—BLDSC (7741.304500), IE, Ingenta. **CCC.**
Published by: Jessica Kingsley Publishers, 116 Pentonville Rd, London, N1 9JB, United Kingdom. TEL 44-20-78332307, FAX 44-20-78372917, post@jkp.com. Ed. Joyce Lishman.

RESEARCH ON SOCIAL WORK PRACTICE. *see* SOCIOLOGY

360 GBR ISSN 0264-519X
HV241
RESEARCH, POLICY AND PLANNING. Text in English. 1977. 3/yr. GBP 45 domestic; GBP 55 foreign (effective 2009). adv. bk.rev. back issues avail. **Document type:** *Journal, Academic/Scholarly.* **Description:** Publishes research of relevance to policy-makers, planners, practitioners and other researchers in the caring services.
Formerly (until 1983): Social Services Research Group. Journal (0144-0640)

Related titles: Online - full text ed.: free to members (effective 2009).
Indexed: A22.
—IE, Ingenta. **CCC.**
Published by: Social Services Research Group, c/o Jackie Watson, Wolvercott, The Street, Swannington, Norfolk NR9 5NW, United Kingdom. TEL 44-1603-261951, FAX 44-1603-261951, jackie@wolvercott.co.uk.

362.6 AUS ISSN 1834-318X
RESIDENTIAL AGED CARE CORONIAL COMMUNIQUE. Text in English. 2006. q. **Document type:** *Newsletter, Trade.*
Media: Online - full text.
Published by: Victorian Institute of Forensic Medicine, 57-83 Kavanagh St, Southbank, VIC 3006, Australia. TEL 61-3-96844444, FAX 61-3-96827353, assist@vifm.org, http://www.vifm.org.

361.73 USA ISSN 1065-0008
HV16
RESPONSIVE PHILANTHROPY. Text in English. 1979. q. USD 25; free to members (effective 2005). adv. bk.rev. back issues avail. **Document type:** *Newsletter.* **Description:** Covers changes and trends in philanthropy and fund raising, with emphasis on "social justice" and non-profit organizations.
Published by: National Committee for Responsive Philanthropy, 2001 S St, N W, Ste 620, Washington, DC 20009. TEL 202-387-9177, FAX 202-332-5084, info@ncrp.org, http://www.ncrp.org/index.asp. Ed., R&P Michael May. Pub. Robert O Bothwell. Adv. contact Kate Conover. Circ: 6,000 (paid).

361.609172 NOR ISSN 1891-1374
RESULTATRAPPORT. Text in Norwegian. 2005. a. **Document type:** *Report, Consumer.*
Related titles: Online - full text ed.; ◆ English ed.: Results Report. ISSN 1891-4047.
Published by: Direktoratet for Utviklingssamarbeid/Norwegian Agency for Development Cooperation, PO Box 8034, Dep, Oslo, 0030, Norway. TEL 47-22-242030, FAX 47-22-242031, postmottag@norad.no.

361.609172 NOR ISSN 1891-4047
RESULTS REPORT. Text in English. 2005. a. **Document type:** *Report, Consumer.*
Related titles: Online - full text ed.; ◆ Norwegian ed.: Resultatrapport. ISSN 1891-1374.
Published by: Direktoratet for Utviklingssamarbeid/Norwegian Agency for Development Cooperation, PO Box 8034, Dep, Oslo, 0030, Norway. TEL 47-22-242030, FAX 47-22-242031, postmottag@norad.no.

362.4 617.06 NLD ISSN 1877-0827
REVALIDATIE BRANCHERAPPORT. Text in Dutch. 200?. a. **Document type:** *Report, Trade.*
Published by: Revalidatie Nederland, Postbus 9696, Utrecht, 3506 GRg, Netherlands. TEL 31-30-2739384, FAX 31-30-2739406, info@revalidatie.nl, http://www.revalidatie.nl.

REVEILLE; the voice of New South Wales serving and ex-service men and women. *see* MILITARY

REVERENCE. *see* PHILOSOPHY

THE REVIEW OF DISABILITY STUDIES. *see* HANDICAPPED

360 HRV ISSN 1330-2965
➤ **REVIJA ZA SOCIJALNU POLITIKU.** Text in Croatian, English. 1994. q. **Document type:** *Journal, Academic/Scholarly.* **Description:** Addresses labor issues, unemployment, poverty, the welfare system and other social problems and current social processes.
Related titles: Online - full text ed.: ISSN 1845-6014. free (effective 2011).
Indexed: A01, A02, A03, A08, A26, CA, FR, GEOBASE, I05, IBR, IBSS, IBZ, P34, P42, PSA, S02, S03, SCOPUS, SSA, SSCI, SWR&A, SociolAb, T02, W07.
—INIST.
Published by: Sveuciliste u Zagrebu, Pravni Fakultet/University of Zagreb, Faculty of Law, Trg Marsala Tita 14, Zagreb, Croatia. TEL 385-1-4564-332, FAX 385-1-4564-030, dekanat@pravo.hr, http://www.pravo.hr. Ed. Sinisa Zrinscak.

360 COL ISSN 0121-2818
REVISTA COLOMBIANA DE TRABAJO SOCIAL. Text in Spanish. 1989. a. **Document type:** *Magazine, Trade.*
Published by: Federacion Colombiana de Trabajadores Sociales (F E C T S), Carrera 4 D, No 37-48, Barrio Magisterio, Ibaque, Colombia. TEL 57-2648031, FAX 57-2668089.

360 ESP ISSN 0211-4364
HQ799.S7
REVISTA DE ESTUDIOS DE JUVENTUD. Text in Spanish. 1980. q. bk.rev. cum.index: 1980-1986. back issues avail. **Document type:** *Magazine, Consumer.*
Formerly: De Juventud: Revista de Estudios e Investigaciones
Indexed: PsycholAb, RASB, S02, S03.
Published by: Ministerio de Trabajo y Asuntos Sociales, Instituto de la Juventud, Jose Ortega y Gasset, 71, Madrid, 28006, Spain. TEL 34-91-3477690, FAX 34-91-4022194, http://www.injuve.mtas.es. Circ: 3,000.

362 ESP ISSN 0213-9731
REVISTA DE SORIA. Text in Spanish. 1967. bi-m. **Document type:** *Magazine, Government.*
Related titles: Online - full text ed.
Published by: Diputacion Provincial de Soria, C. Caballeros, 17, Soria, 42003, Spain. TEL 34-975-101000, FAX 34-975-101091, http://www.dipsoria.com/.

REVISTA EKOSOL; como vamos ciudadanos?. *see* EDUCATION

REVISTA JURIDICA DE ECONOMIA PUBLICA, SOCIAL Y COOPERATIVA. *see* LAW

360 BRA ISSN 1414-4980
HV194.S26
REVISTA KATALYSIS. Text in Portuguese, Spanish. 1997. s-a. **Document type:** *Journal, Academic/Scholarly.*
Related titles: Online - full text ed.: free (effective 2011).
Published by: Universidade Federal de Santa Catarina, Programa de Pos-Graduacao em Servico Social, Campus Universitario Reitor Joao David Ferreira Lima, Florianopolis, Santa Catarina 88010-970, Brazil. TEL 55-48-37216524, FAX 55-48-37216514.

360 CHL ISSN 0716-2642
HV4
REVISTA TRABAJO SOCIAL. Text in Spanish. 1970. s-a. CLP 6,000; USD 37 foreign (effective 1999). bk.rev. **Document type:** *Academic/Scholarly.* **Description:** Dedicated to providing information on poverty, social problems, social politics, and social work.
Formerly: Trabajo Social
Indexed: C01, IBR, IBZ.
Published by: Pontificia Universidad Catolica de Chile, Escuela de Trabajo Social, Casilla 306, Correo 22, Vicuna Mackena, 4860, Santiago, Chile. TEL 56-2-686-4606, FAX 56-2-686-4667. Ed. Teresita Matus Sepulveda. Pub. Margarita Quezada Venegas. Circ: 700.

REVUE BELGE DE SECURITE SOCIALE/BELGIAN SOCIAL SECURITY JOURNAL. *see* PUBLIC ADMINISTRATION

REVUE DE L'INFIRMIERE. *see* MEDICAL SCIENCES—Nurses And Nursing

REVUE DU TRAVAIL. *see* BUSINESS AND ECONOMICS—Labor And Industrial Relations

360 FRA ISSN 0297-0376
BX1751.2
REVUE FRANCAISE DE SERVICE SOCIAL. Text in French. 1945. q. EUR 46 domestic to individuals; EUR 52 foreign to individuals; EUR 25 to students (effective 2009). adv. bk.rev. illus. **Description:** Covers the training, methhods and practices of social workers.
Formerly (until 1971): Feuillets de l'A N A S (0004-5586)
—IE.
Published by: Association Nationale des Assistants de Service Social, 15 rue de Bruxelles, Paris, 75009, France. TEL 33-1-45263379, FAX 33-1-42800703, http://anas.travail-social.com/. Ed. Francoise Vanbelle. Circ: 2,700 (controlled).

362 GBR ISSN 0379-0312
REVUE INTERNATIONALE DE SECURITE SOCIALE. Text in French. 1967. q. **Document type:** *Journal, Academic/Scholarly.*
Formerly (until 1966): l' Association internationale de la Securite Sociale. Bulletin (1011-1565)
Related titles: Online - full text ed.: ISSN 1752-1718. GBP 158 in United Kingdom to institutions; EUR 201 in Europe to institutions; USD 265 in the Americas to institutions; USD 310 elsewhere to institutions (effective 2010) (from IngentaConnect); ◆ English ed.: International Social Security Review. ISSN 0020-871X; ◆ German ed.: Internationale Revue fuer Soziale Sicherheit. ISSN 0379-0282; ◆ Spanish ed.: Revista Internacional de Seguridad Social. ISSN 0250-605X.
Indexed: A22, B01, B07, CA, E01, FR, IBSS, RASB, T02, V01.
—IE, Infotrieve. **CCC.**
Published by: (International Social Security Association (I S S A)/Association Internationale de la Securite Sociale CHE), Wiley-Blackwell Publishing Ltd. (Subsidiary of: John Wiley & Sons, Inc.), 9600 Garsington Rd, Oxford, OX4 2DQ, United Kingdom. TEL 44-1865-776868, FAX 44-1865-714591, customerservices@blackwellpublishing.com, http://www.wiley.com/WileyCDA/. Ed. Roddy McKinnon.

360 FRA ISSN 0980-7764
REVUE QUART MONDE; vaincre l'exclusion. Text in French. 1986. q. EUR 26 (effective 2009). illus. back issues avail. **Document type:** *Journal.*
Former titles (until 1986): Igloos (0766-3811); (until 1984): Quart Monde Igloos (0290-6686); (until 1976): Igloos le 4e Monde (0290-6678); (until 1969): Igloos (0290-666X)
Indexed: IBSS.
Published by: (Mouvement International A T D Quart Monde/International Movement A T D Fourth World), Editions Quart Monde, 107 Av. du General Leclerc, Pierrelaye, 95480, France. TEL 33-01-34083140, FAX 33-01-34304636, editions@atd-quartmonde.org, http://www.atd-quartmonde.org. Ed. Jean Tonglet. Circ: 3,000.

360 SVK ISSN 1338-1075
▼ **REVUE SOCIALNYCH SLUZIEB.** Text in Slovak. 2009. 2/yr. EUR 4.90 (effective 2011).
Published by: Vydavatel'stvo OLIVA, Botanicka 7, Trnava, 91708, Slovakia. oliva60@ttonline.sk, http://oliva.tso.sk. Ed. Dr. Jana Levicka.

362.7 NLD ISSN 2210-7746
RIGHT!; tijdschrift voor de rechten van het kind. Text in Dutch. 1984. q. EUR 35 (effective 2010). **Document type:** *Magazine, Trade.*
Former titles (until 2010): Tijdschrift voor de Rechten van het Kind (0927-1333); (until 1991): D C I Info (0169-6599)
—IE.
Published by: Defence for Children-ECPAT Nederland, Postbus 11103, Leiden, 2301 EC, Netherlands. TEL 31-71-5160980, FAX 31-71-5160989, info@ecpat.nl, http://www.ecpat.nl.

360 USA
RIGHT-TO-KNOW PLANNING GUIDE (SERIES). Text in English. 1987 (Oct.). bi-w. looseleaf. USD 833 (effective 2009). Index. back issues avail. **Document type:** *Newsletter, Trade.* **Description:** Reference service providing information on both the new right-to-know community and emergency-response program community.
Related titles: Online - full text ed.: USD 545 (effective 2009); ◆ Series: Right-to-Know Planning Guide Report. ISSN 1074-8652.
Published by: The Bureau of National Affairs, Inc., 1801 S Bell St, Arlington, VA 22202. TEL 703-341-3000, FAX 703-341-4634, bnaplus@bna.com, http://www.bna.com. Pub. Gregory C McCaffery.

353.5 AUS ISSN 1442-4134
RIGHTS REVIEW. Text in English. 1983. q. AUD 33 (effective 2009). back issues avail. **Document type:** *Newsletter, Trade.* **Description:** Contains information, news, and opinion about Social Security law and administration from a client's rights perspective.
Formerly (until 1994): Welfare Rights Centre Newsletter
Related titles: E-mail ed.: AUD 22 (effective 2009).
Published by: Welfare Rights Centre, 102/55 Holt St, Surry Hills, NSW 2010, Australia. TEL 61-2-92115389, FAX 61-2-92115268, welfarerights@welfarerights.org.au. Ed. Michael Raper. R&P Danny Shaw.

362.4 JPN ISSN 0035-5305
RIHABIRITESHON/REHABILITATION (TOKYO, 1953). Text in Japanese. 1953. 10/yr. JPY 260 per issue. adv. bk.rev. charts; illus.
Published by: Handicapped Persons Association of Japan Railways/Tetsudo Shinshosha Kyokai, 5-1 Koji-Machi, Chiyoda-ku, Tokyo, 102-0083, Japan. Ed. Takeo Oshida. Circ: 8,000.

360 ITA ISSN 1970-5212
LA RIVISTA DELLE FONDAZIONI. Text in Italian. 2003. bi-m. **Document type:** *Magazine, Trade.*
Published by: Fondazione Allegra, Viale Parioli 53, Rome, 00197, Italy. TEL 39-06-8084053, FAX 39-06-80669157, http://www.fondazioneallegra.it.

360 ITA ISSN 0035-6522
RIVISTA DI SERVIZIO SOCIALE. Text in Italian. 1961. q. EUR 40 domestic; EUR 55 in Europe; EUR 62 elsewhere (effective 2009). adv. bk.rev. abstr.; bibl.; tr.lit. index. **Document type:** *Journal, Academic/Scholarly.*
Indexed: PAIS.
Published by: Istituto per gli Studi sui Servizi Sociali (I S T I S S), Viale di Villa Pamphili 84, Rome, 00152, Italy. TEL 39-06-5897179, info@istiss.it, http://www.istiss.it.

ROA GIFU. *see* HANDICAPPED—Hearing Impaired

361.7 USA ISSN 1052-8881
HV97.R6
ROCKEFELLER FOUNDATION. ANNUAL REPORT. Text in English. 1914. a. **Document type:** *Corporate.*
Former titles (until 1986): Rockefeller Foundation. President's Review and Annual Report (0557-885X); Which was formed by the 1966 merger of: Rockefeller Foundation. President's Review from the Annual Report (0145-0808); Rockefeller Foundation. Annual Report (0080-3391)
Related titles: Microfiche ed.: (from BHP).
—GNLM, Linda Hall.
Published by: Rockefeller Foundation, 420 Fifth Ave, New York, NY 10018. TEL 212-869-8500, FAX 212-764-3468. R&P Denise Gray Felder. Circ: 18,000 (controlled).

360 RUS ISSN 0869-7698
Q4
ROSSIISKAYA AKADEMIYA NAUK. DAL'NEVOSTOCHNOE OTDELENIE. VESTNIK/RUSSIAN ACADEMY OF SCIENCES. FAR EASTERN BRANCH. BULLETIN. Text in Russian; Contents page in English. 1990. bi-m. USD 141 (effective 1998). adv. bk.rev. **Document type:** *Bulletin, Academic/Scholarly.* **Description:** Contains research papers and reviews of recent developments in all areas of science.
Formerly: Akademiya Nauk S.S.S.R. Dal'nevostochnoe Otdelenie. Vestnik (0235-8611)
Indexed: GeoRef, RASB, RefZh, SpeleolAb, Z01.
—East View, Linda Hall.
Published by: Rossiiskya Akademiya Nauk, Dal'nevostochnoe Otdelenie/Russian Academy of Sciences, Far Eastern Branch, Ul Svetlanskaya 50, Vladivostok, 690600, Russian Federation. Ed. Alexey V Zhirmunsky. Circ: 1,000. **Dist. by:** M K - Periodica, ul Gilyarovskogo 39, Moscow 129110, Russian Federation. TEL 7-095-2845008, FAX 7-095-2813798, info@periodicals.ru, http://www.mkniga.ru.

ROSTER OF AFRICA SOCIAL SCIENTISTS. *see* BUSINESS AND ECONOMICS—International Development And Assistance

360 AUT
DAS ROTE KREUZ. Text in German. 1929. q. bk.rev. illus. **Document type:** *Newsletter, Consumer.*
Published by: Oesterreichisches Rotes Kreuz, Wiedner Hauptstr 32, Vienna, 1041, Austria. TEL 43-1-58900153, FAX 43-1-58900159, ferdinand.urbach@roteskreuz.at, http://www.roteskreuz.at. Ed. Thomas Aistleitner. R&P Ursula Fraisl. Adv. contact Michael Opriesnig. Circ: 810,000.

361.77 DEU ISSN 0938-9687
ROTES KREUZ. Text in German. 1953. bi-m. adv. bk.rev. index. **Document type:** *Magazine, Trade.*
Formed by the 1991 merger of: Rotkreuz-Zeitung (0722-3897); Rotkreuz (0863-5455); Which was formerly (until 1990): Deutsches Rotes Kreuz der Deutschen Demokratischen Republik (0323-567X); (until 1964): D K R in der Deutschen Demokratischen Republik (0323-729X); Rotkreuz-Zeitung was formerly (until 1982): Deutsches Rotes Kreuz (0415-746X)
—GNLM.
Published by: (Deutsches Rotes Kreuz/German Red Cross), S V Corporate Media GmbH (Subsidiary of: Sueddeutscher Verlag GmbH), Emmy-Noether-Str 2, Munich, 80992, Germany. TEL 49-89-5485201, FAX 49-89-54852192, 49-89-54852192, info@sv-medien-service.de, http://www.sv-medien-service.de/svcm/. Adv. contact Lutz Boden. B&W page EUR 2,200, color page EUR 3,700; trim 185 x 250. Circ: 15,000 (controlled).

361.77 DEU
ROTKREUZ MAGAZIN. Text in German. 4/yr. adv. **Document type:** *Magazine, Trade.*
Published by: D R K - Kreisverband Karlsruhe e.V., Am Mantel 3, Bruchsal, 76646, Germany. TEL 49-7251-922201, redaktion@drk-karlsuhe.de. adv.: B&W page EUR 2,200, color page EUR 3,700. Circ: 15,000 (controlled).

361.77 DEU
DIE ROTKREUZ-SCHWESTER. Text in German. 1989. q. membership. adv. **Document type:** *Magazine, Trade.*
Published by: (Verband der Schwesternschaften vom Deutschen Roten Kreuz e.V.), Verlag W. Waechter GmbH, Elsasser Str 41, Bremen, 28211, Germany. TEL 49-421-348420, FAX 49-421-3476766, info@waechter.de, http://www.waechter.de. adv.: B&W page EUR 2,641, color page EUR 4,620; trim 180 x 250. Circ: 22,000 (controlled).

361.77 DEU
ROTKREUZMAGAZIN. Text in German. 1955. q. free to members (effective 2008). adv. illus. **Document type:** *Magazine, Consumer.*
Former titles (until 2008): Helfen und Retten; (until 2005): Das Magazin fuer Rotkreuzmitglieder (1610-3203); (until 2001): Die Gute Tat (0017-5803)
Published by: Deutsches Rotes Kreuz/German Red Cross, Carstennstr 58, Berlin, 12205, Germany. TEL 49-30-854040, FAX 49-30-85404450, drk@drk.de, http://www.drk.de. adv.: B&W page EUR 9,000, color page EUR 10,500; trim 185 x 250. Circ: 698,403 (controlled).

S

362.7 USA
THE ROUNDTABLE (SOUTHFIELD, ONLINE). Text in English. 1986. s-a. free. bk.rev. back issues avail. **Document type:** *Newsletter, Consumer.* **Description:** Informs adoption practitioners, administrators and advocates of the center's activities and of new developments in the field of special needs adoption. Shares ideas, problems and successes.
Formerly: The Roundtable (Southfield, Print)
Media: Online - full text.
Published by: Spaulding for Children, National Child Welfare Resource Center for Adoption, 16250 Northland Dr, Ste 120, Southfield, MI 48075-4325. TEL 248-443-0306, FAX 248-443-7099, nrc@nrcadoption.org. Ed. Barbara Mucha. Circ: 12,000.

179.3 GBR
ROYAL HUMANE SOCIETY. ANNUAL REPORT. Text in English. 1774. a. GBP 5 per issue (effective 2010). **Document type:** *Corporate.* **Description:** Reports on activities; revelant articles; annual accounts.
Related titles: Online - full text ed.
Published by: Royal Humane Society, Brettenham House, Lancaster Pl, London, WC2E 7EP, United Kingdom. TEL 44-20-78368155, info@royalhumanesociety.org.uk. Ed. C Tyler. Circ: 800.

362.41 GBR
ROYAL NATIONAL INSTITUTE FOR THE BLIND. CAMPAIGN NEWS. Text in English. bi-m. **Document type:** *Newsletter.* **Description:** Gives an overview of current campaigns being undertaken at RNIB.
Related titles: Online - full text ed.
Published by: Royal National Institute of Blind People, 105 Judd St, London, WC1H 9NE, United Kingdom. TEL 44-20-73881266, FAX 44-20-73882034, helpline@rnib.org.uk.

362 CHL ISSN 0718-4182
RUMBOS TS; un espacio critico para la reflexion en trabajo social. (Trabajo Social) Text in Spanish. 2006. a.
Published by: Universidad Central de Chile, Facultad de Ciencias Sociales, Campus La Reina, Carlos Silva Vidosola, 9783, La Reina, Santiago, Chile. TEL 56-2-5826505, FAX 56-2-5826502, sdecano@ucentral.cl, http://www.fcscentral.cl/. Ed. Carlos Silva Vidosola.

RURAL POLICY BRIEF. see PUBLIC HEALTH AND SAFETY

362 AUS ISSN 1833-3060
➤ **RURAL SOCIAL WORK AND COMMUNITY PRACTICE.** Text in English. 1993. s-a. **Document type:** *Journal, Academic/Scholarly.* **Description:** Covers issues of welfare practice and service delivery in rural and remote areas.
Formerly (until 2006): Rural Social Work (1321-6627)
Indexed: A10, C06, C07, C08, CA, CINAHL, P03, PsycholAb, S02, S03, SCOPUS, SSA, SociolAb, T02, V03.
—BLDSC (8052.620050), IE.
Published by: (University of South Australia, Department of Social Work and Social Policy), La Trobe University, School of Social Work and Social Policy, Level 2, Health Sciences 2, Bundoora, VIC 3086, Australia. TEL 61-3-94792570, FAX 61-3-94793590, http://www.latrobe.edu.ac/socialwork/. **Co-publisher:** University of South Australia, Department of Social Work and Social Policy.

➤ **RURAL WOMEN NEW ZEALAND.** see AGRICULTURE

➤ **RURITAN.** see CLUBS

362.6 CAN ISSN 1912-0087
S A G E LINK. Text in English. 19??. irreg. **Document type:** *Monographic series, Trade.*
Former titles (until 2006): Society News (1498-4636); (until 1998): News for Seniors (1484-8287); (until 1996): Today's Choices (1198-3949); (until 1995): Today's Maturity (1204-170X); (until 1994): News for Seniors (0710-958X)
Published by: Seniors Association of Greater Edmonton, 15 Sir Winston Churchill Sq., Edmonton, AB T5J 2E5, Canada. http://www.mysage.ca/index.cfm.

S C I PSYCHOSOCIAL PROCESS. (Spinal Cord Injury) see PSYCHOLOGY

S D A D NEWS. see HANDICAPPED—Hearing Impaired

S E T FREE; the newsletter against television. see COMMUNICATIONS—Television And Cable

360 FRA ISSN 0766-4133
S O S AMITIE. (Save Our Souls) Text in French. 1961. q. adv. bk.rev. **Document type:** *Magazine, Consumer.*
Former titles (until 1984): S O S Amitie France (0397-1856); (until 1975): S O S Amitie France. Bulletin (0397-2984); S O S Amitie France. Bulletin National (0003-1887)
Published by: S.O.S. Amitie France, 11 rue des Immeubles Industriels, Paris, 75011, France. TEL 33-1-40091522, FAX 33-1-40097435, admin@sos-amitie.org. Ed. Marie Fernande Cabannes. Circ: 2,000.

362.7 AUT
S O S KINDERDORF INTERNATIONAL. Text in English, German. 1962. q. illus. **Document type:** *Newsletter.*
Formerly: S O S Messenger (0036-178X)
Published by: S O S Kinderdorf Oesterreich, Stafflerstr 10a, Innsbruck, T 6020, Austria. TEL 43-5918-308.

362.7 AUT ISSN 0023-1509
S O S KINDERDORFBOTE. Text in German. 1950. q. free. illus. **Document type:** *Magazine, Consumer.*
Published by: S O S Kinderdorf Oesterreich, Stafflerstr 10a, Innsbruck, T 6020, Austria. TEL 43-512-5918, FAX 43-512-5918320, info@sos-kd.org, https://www.sos-kinderdorf.at. Circ: 1,000,000.

360 AUS
S P R C NEWSLETTER. Text in English. 1980. q. free (effective 2008). bk.rev. stat.; tr.lit. back issues avail. **Document type:** *Newsletter, Trade.* **Description:** Provides a regular summary of the research activities of the centre, notices of upcoming conferences and seminars, and book reviews.
Formerly (until 1989): S W R C Newsletter (0159-9615)
Related titles: Online - full text ed.
Published by: Social Policy Research Centre, c/o University of New South Wales, Sydney, NSW 2052, Australia. TEL 61-2-93857800, FAX 61-2-93857838, sprc@unsw.edu.au.

360 AUS ISSN 1446-4179
S P R C REPORT. Text in English. 1980. irreg. free (effective 2008). stat. back issues avail. **Document type:** *Monographic series, Academic/Scholarly.* **Description:** Contains reports of commissioned research.
Former titles (until 2000): S P R C Reports and Proceedings (1036-2835); (until 1989): S W R C Reports and Proceedings (0159-9607)
Related titles: Online - full text ed.
—Ingenta.
Published by: Social Policy Research Centre, c/o University of New South Wales, Sydney, NSW 2052, Australia. TEL 61-2-93857800, FAX 61-2-93857838, sprc@unsw.edu.au. Ed. Diana Encel. R&P Sharon Hancock.

361.3 USA
S S A MAGAZINE. (Social Service Administration) Text in English. 1993. s-a. free (effective 2010). back issues avail. **Document type:** *Magazine, Academic/Scholarly.* **Description:** Serves a primary vehicle for communicating news and information about the school and the fields of social work and social welfare with a broad audience.
Media: Online - full text.
Published by: University of Chicago, School of Social Service Administration, 969 E 60th St, Chicago, IL 60637. TEL 773-702-1250, FAX 773-702-0874, info@ssa.uchicago.edu. Ed. Carl Vogel.

S S I RECIPIENTS BY STATE AND COUNTY (YEAR). (Social Security Insurance) see INSURANCE

360 NLD ISSN 1871-2495
S Z BULLETIN. (Sociale Zekerheid) Text in Dutch. 1990. m. price varies.
Formerly (until 2005): S Z W Nieuws (1381-8732)
—Infotrieve.
Published by: Sdu Uitgevers bv, Postbus 20025, The Hague, 2500 EA, Netherlands. TEL 31-70-3789911, FAX 31-70-3854321, sdu@sdu.nl, http://www.sdu.nl/.

363.5 USA
SAFETY NETWORK. Text in English. 1982. 6/yr. adv. bk.rev. **Document type:** *Newsletter.*
Published by: National Coalition for the Homeless, 2201 P St NW, Washington, DC 20037-1033. TEL 202-737-6444, FAX 202-737-6445. Ed., R&P, Adv. contact Jill Lee. Circ: 10,000 (paid).

361 USA ISSN 1048-1621
SAGE SOURCEBOOKS FOR THE HUMAN SERVICES SERIES. Text in English. 1977. irreg., latest 2008. price varies. back issues avail.; reprints avail. **Document type:** *Monographic series, Academic/Scholarly.*
Formerly (until 1987): Sourcebooks for Improving Human Services (1048-1613)
Indexed: A22.
—BLDSC (8069.271100). **CCC.**
Published by: Sage Publications, Inc., Books (Subsidiary of: Sage Publications, Inc.), 2455 Teller Rd, Thousand Oaks, CA 91320. TEL 800-818-7243, FAX 800-583-2665, books.claim@sagepub.com. Pub. Sara Miller McCune.

361.8 USA
ST. PAUL URBAN LEAGUE. ANNUAL REPORT. Text in English. 1924. a. free. **Document type:** *Corporate.*
Published by: St. Paul Urban League, 401 Selby Ave., St. Paul, MN 55102-1724. TEL 612-224-5771. Ed. Willie Mae Wilson. Circ: 3,000.

SALUD & DESARROLLO SOCIAL; revista de educacion para la salud y el desarrollo social. see PUBLIC HEALTH AND SAFETY

362.82 CAN ISSN 1499-495X
SALUTE!; proudly serving Canada's veteran community. Text in English. 2001. q. free to qualified personnel (effective 2011). back issues avail. **Document type:** *Newsletter, Consumer.* **Description:** Provide veterans and their families with information on departmental policies, programs and services that affect them.
Related titles: Online - full text ed.: free (effective 2011).
Published by: Veterans Affairs Canada/Anciens Combattants Canada, PO Box 7700, Charlottetown, PE C1A 8M9, Canada. TEL 866-522-2122, information@vac-acc.gc.ca.

360 ITA ISSN 0392-4505
SALUTE E TERRITORIO. Text in Italian. 1978. bi-m. EUR 41.32 domestic; EUR 46.48 foreign (effective 2011). **Document type:** *Journal, Academic/Scholarly.*
Indexed: IBR, IBZ.
Published by: Edizioni E T S, Piazza Carrara 16-19, Pisa, Italy. TEL 39-050-29544, FAX 39-050-20158, info@edizioniets.it, http://www.edizioniets.it.

360 CUB
SALVACION. Text in Spanish. s-m.
Published by: Ejercito de Salvacion, 96 No. 5513rd, 55 y 57 Marianao 14, Havana, Cuba.

SAMARITAN. see RELIGIONS AND THEOLOGY

362.4 NLD ISSN 1877-640X
▼ **SAMEN.** Text in Dutch. 2009. 3/yr. EUR 17.50 membership (effective 2011). **Document type:** *Magazine, Consumer.*
Published by: Vereniging Helpende Handen, Postbus 404, Woerden, 3440 AK, Netherlands. TEL 31-348-489970, FAX 31-348-483305, info@helpendehanden.nl, http://www.helpendehanden.nl. Eds. Siegbert Beukens, Rene Hubregtse.

349.2 DEU ISSN 0342-2003
SAMMLUNG VON ENTSCHEIDUNGEN AUS DEM SOZIALRECHT. Variant title: Breithaupt. Text in German. 1954. m. EUR 194.40 (effective 2010). adv. **Document type:** *Magazine, Trade.*
Formerly (until 1977): Sammlung von Entscheidungen der Sozialversicherung, Versorgung und Arbeitslosenversicherung (0342-2011)
—**CCC.**
Published by: Richard Boorberg Verlag GmbH und Co. KG, Scharrstr 2, Stuttgart, 70563, Germany. TEL 49-711-73850, FAX 49-711-7385100, mail@boorberg.de. Ed. Hans Peter Spiegl.

SAMSPRAAK. see LINGUISTICS

361.73 900 910.2 USA ISSN 1542-4782
SAN DIEGO MASTERPLANNER. Text in English. 2002 (Nov.). m. USD 180 (effective 2002). adv. **Document type:** *Directory, Consumer.* **Description:** Lists complete information about thousands of major fundraisers, openings and special events planned for the coming year. Also contains advice on planning and attending social, fund-raising and business events.
Published by: Masterplanner Media, Inc., 8899 Beverly Blvd, Ste. 408, Los Angeles, CA 90048. TEL 310-888-8566, FAX 310-888-1866, http://www.masterplanneronline.com. Ed. Paula Skinner. Pub. Elisabeth Familian. Adv. contact Susan Wilson.

360 ITA
SAN SEBASTIANO. Text in Italian. 1949. q. free. **Document type:** *Magazine, Consumer.* **Description:** Treats history, art, culture, and voluntary social and public health work.
Published by: Venerabile Arciconfraternita della Misericordia di Firenze, Piazza del Duomo 19-20, Florence, 50122, Italy. TEL 39-55-239393, http://www.misericordia.firenze.it.

SANS FRONTIERES. see MEDICAL SCIENCES

SANTA CRUZ ACTION NETWORK. NEWSLETTER. see HOUSING AND URBAN PLANNING

SANTE DE L'HOMME (ONLINE). see MEDICAL SCIENCES

362.4 IND ISSN 0036-4835
SARVODAYA. Text in English. 1951. m. bk.rev. illus. index. **Description:** Presents Gandhi's ideal of social service.
Published by: Tamilnadu Sarvodaya Sangh, No 18, T P K Rd, Madurai, 625001, India. TEL 91-452-2339758.

360 CAN
SASKATCHEWAN. DEPARTMENT OF SOCIAL SERVICES. ANNUAL REPORT. Text in English. 1915. a. free. illus. **Document type:** *Corporate.*
Formerly: Saskatchewan. Department of Social Welfare. Annual Report (0708-3882)
Published by: Department of Social Services, 1920 Broad St, Regina, SK S4P 3V6, Canada. TEL 306-787-3494.

362.7 USA
SAVE THE CHILDREN. ANNUAL REPORT. Text in English. a. free. **Document type:** *Corporate.* **Description:** Informs donors and other interested persons about how this organization allocates its financial resources, along with an analysis of sources of funds. Outlines some of the programs Save the Children sponsors.
Published by: Save the Children, Public Affairs and Communications Department, 54 Wilton Rd, Westport, CT 06881. TEL 203-341-6528, 800-728-3843, twebster@savechildren.org, http://www.savethechildren.org. Ed. Renee Wessels.

SCANDINAVIAN JOURNAL OF PUBLIC HEALTH. see MEDICAL SCIENCES

SCANDINAVIAN JOURNAL OF PUBLIC HEALTH. SUPPLEMENT. see MEDICAL SCIENCES

361.3 USA ISSN 0161-5653
LB3013.4
➤ **SCHOOL SOCIAL WORK JOURNAL.** Text in English. 1976. s-a. USD 30 domestic to individuals; USD 45 foreign to individuals; USD 60 domestic institution, libraries; USD 75 foreign institution, libraries (effective 2009). bk.rev. back issues avail.; reprints avail. **Document type:** *Journal, Academic/Scholarly.* **Description:** Contains articles relevant to the practice of school social work, including areas of education, special education, individual, group and family therapy, and the interface of community issues as related to school social work.
Related titles: Microform ed.: (from PQC); Online - full text ed.
Indexed: A22, AMHA, BRD, C28, CA, P03, PsycInfo, PsycholAb, S02, S03, SCOPUS, SSA, SSAI, SSAb, SSI, SWR&A, SociolAb, T02, W03, W05.
—BLDSC (8093.508000), IE, Ingenta. **CCC.**
Published by: (Illinois Association of School Social Workers), Lyceum Books, Inc., 5758 S Blackstone Ave, Chicago, IL 60637. lyceum@lyceumbooks.com. Ed. Carol Massat. Pub. David C Follmer TEL 773-643-1902.

➤ **SCHRIFTEN ZUM SOZIAL- UND ARBEITSRECHT.** see LAW

360 DEU ISSN 0720-6739
SCHRIFTENREIHE FUER INTERNATIONALES UND VERGLEICHENDES SOZIALRECHT. Text in German. 1977. irreg., latest vol.18, 2001. price varies. **Document type:** *Monographic series, Academic/Scholarly.*
Published by: Duncker und Humblot GmbH, Carl-Heinrich-Becker-Weg 9, Berlin, 12165, Germany. TEL 49-30-7900060, FAX 49-30-79000631, info@duncker-humblot.de.

301.3 DEU ISSN 0080-7133
SCHRIFTENREIHE FUER LAENDLICHE SOZIALFRAGEN. Text in German. 1951. irreg., latest vol.148, 2007. price varies. index. **Document type:** *Monographic series, Academic/Scholarly.*
Published by: Agrarsoziale Gesellschaft e.V., Kurze Geismarstr 33, Goettingen, 37073, Germany. TEL 49-551-497090, FAX 49-551-4970916, info@asg-goe.de, http://www.asg-goe.de.

360 CHE
SCHWEIZER HEIMWESEN. Text in German. m.
Address: Seegartenstr 2, Zuerich, 8008, Switzerland. TEL 41-1-7103560, FAX 41-1-7104073. Ed. Erika Ritter. Circ: 4,050.

360 CHE ISSN 0255-9072
K23
SCHWEIZERISCHE ZEITSCHRIFT FUER SOZIALVERSICHERUNG UND BERUFLICHE VORSORGE/REVUE SUISSE DES ASSURANCES SOCIALES ET DE LA PREVOYANCE PROFESSIONNELLE. Text in French, German. 1957. bi-m. CHF 220.30 combined subscription domestic (print & online eds.); CHF 237 combined subscription foreign (print & online eds.) (effective 2011). adv. bk.rev. bibl.; charts. index. **Document type:** *Journal, Trade.*
Formerly: Schweizerische Zeitschrift fuer Sozialversicherung (0036-7877)
Related titles: Online - full text ed.: CHF 173 (effective 2011).
Indexed: ASCA, DIP, IBR, IBZ, PAIS, WBSS.
—IE. **CCC.**
Published by: Staempfli Verlag AG (Subsidiary of: LexisNexis Europe and Africa), Woelflistr 1, Bern, 3001, Switzerland. TEL 41-31-3006666, FAX 41-31-3006688, verlag@staempfli.com, http://www.staempfli.com.

SCOTTISH SOCIAL WORK LEGISLATION. see LAW

362.6 GBR ISSN 0958-3467
SEARCH (YORK). Text in English. 1989. irreg. (2-3/yr.). bk.rev. back issues avail. **Document type:** *Magazine, Trade.* **Description:** Contains reviews of the findings of economic analyses and public consultations about where we are now - and how we want to move forward as a society.
Related titles: Online - full text ed.: free (effective 2010).
—BLDSC (8214.370000), IE, Ingenta. **CCC.**

Published by: Joseph Rowntree Foundation, The Homestead, 40 Water End, York, YO30 6WP, United Kingdom. TEL 44-1904-629241, FAX 44-1904-620072, publications@jrf.org.uk, http://www.jrf.org.uk. Ed. Sharon Telfer.

SECTION 504 COMPLIANCE ADVISOR. *see* EDUCATION—Special Education And Rehabilitation

SECTION 504 COMPLIANCE HANDBOOK. *see* HANDICAPPED

SECTOR- EN BEDRIJFSINFORMATIE SOCIALE WERKGELEGENHEID EN ARBEIDSINTEGRATIE. *see* BUSINESS AND ECONOMICS—Labor And Industrial Relations

360 CHE ISSN 1424-8786
SECURITE SOCIALE. Text in French. 2001. irreg., latest vol.6, 2004. price varies. **Document type:** *Monographic series, Academic/ Scholarly.*
Related titles: German ed.: Soziale Sicherheit. ISSN 1424-8778. 2001.
Published by: Peter Lang AG (Subsidiary of: Peter Lang Publishing Group), Hochfeldstr 32, Postfach 746, Bern 9, 3000, Switzerland. TEL 41-31-3061717, FAX 41-31-3061727, info@peterlang.com.

THE SEEING EYE ANNUAL REPORT. *see* HANDICAPPED—Visually Impaired

THE SEEING EYE GUIDE. *see* HANDICAPPED—Visually Impaired

360 614.8 MEX ISSN 0379-0304
SEGURIDAD SOCIAL. Text in Spanish, English. 1958. bi-m. MXN 500, USD 65 (effective 2003). film rev. charts; illus.; stat. 50 p./no.; Supplement avail.; back issues avail. **Document type:** *Journal, Academic/Scholarly.*
Indexed: C01, WBSS.
Published by: (Instituto Mexicano del Seguro Social), Conferencia Interamericana de Seguridad Social/Inter-American Conference on Social Security, Calle San Ramon sn, Unidad Independencia, Mexico City, DF 10100, Mexico. TEL 52-55-55950011, FAX 52-55-56838524. Ed., R&P Eduardo Rodriguez-Oreggia. Circ: 700.

360 614.8 ARG ISSN 1852-5873
▼ **LA SEGURIDAD SOCIAL ES NUESTRO DERECHO.** Text in Spanish. 2009. bi-m. **Document type:** *Journal, Trade.*
Published by: Central de Trabajadores de la Argentina, Piedras 1065, Buenos Aires, 1070, Argentina. TEL 54-11-43073829, FAX 54-11-43001015, sitio@cta.org.ar, http://www.cta.org.ar/base.

360 JPN ISSN 1341-6677
SEIKATSU TO FUKUSHI. Text in Japanese. 1956. m. JPY 4,860.
Description: A journal for caseworkers in social welfare office, with emphasis on public assistance programs.
Published by: Zenkoku Shakai Fukushi Kyogikai/National Council of Social Welfare, 3-3-2 Kasumigaseki, Chiyoda-ku, Tokyo, 100-0013, Japan. Ed. Hisashi Kawagoe. Circ: 8,000.

360 DEU ISSN 0724-5572
SELBSTHILFE. Text in German. 1926. 4/yr. bk.rev. illus. **Document type:** *Magazine, Trade.*
Formerly (until 1983): Bundesarbeitsgemeinschaft Hilfe fuer Behinderte. Rundbrief-Dienst (0720-5821)
—CCC.
Published by: Bundesarbeitsgemeinschaft Selbsthilfe e.V., Kirchfeldstr 149, Duesseldorf, 40215, Germany. TEL 49-211-310060, FAX 49-211-3100648, info@bag-selbsthilfe.de. Ed. Dr. Rolf Bieker.

360 340 DEU ISSN 0943-9196
SELBSTVERWALTUNGSRECHT DER SOZIALVERSICHERUNG. Text in German. 1976. base vol. plus a. updates. looseleaf. EUR 49.80 base vol(s).; EUR 56.80 updates per issue (effective 2009). **Document type:** *Monographic series, Trade.*
Published by: Erich Schmidt Verlag GmbH & Co. (Berlin), Genthiner Str 30 G, Berlin, 10785, Germany. TEL 49-30-2500850, FAX 49-30-250085305, vertrieb@esvmedien.de, http://www.esv.info.

SELF-HELP 2000. *see* PSYCHOLOGY

361.8 614.58 USA
SELF-HELP MAGAZINE. Text in English. 1994. d. free. adv. bk.rev. **Document type:** *Newsletter, Consumer.*
Formerly: Self-Help and Psychology Magazine
Media: Online - full text.
Indexed: E-psyche.
Published by: Pioneer Development Resources, Inc. TEL 858-277-2772. Ed., Pub., R&P, Adv. contact Dr. Marlene Maheu. Circ: 184,000.

361.8 614.58 USA ISSN 8756-1425
HV547
THE SELF-HELP SOURCEBOOK; your guide to community and online support group. Text in English. 1986. biennial. **Description:** Lists national, international and model groups, toll-free helplines and clearinghouses around the world for persons working in the health, mental health, and social service fields. Also contains a how-to section for starting up groups and accessing them via personal computer.
Former titles (until 1986): Self-Help Group Directory (0740-7548); Self-Help Group Sourcebook
Indexed: E-psyche.
Published by: American Self-Help Clearinghouse, 100 E Hanover Ave, Ste 202, Cedar Knolls, NJ 07297. TEL 973-326-6789, FAX 973-326-9467, http://www.njgroups.org. Ed. E Madara. R&P Ed Madara TEL 201-625-9565. Circ: 4,000.

362.86 CAN ISSN 0848-5038
SENATE OF CANADA. SUBCOMMITTEE ON VETERANS AFFAIRS. PROCEEDINGS/DELIBERATIONS DU SOUS-COMITE DES AFFAIRES DES ANCIENS COMBATTANTS. Text in English, French. 1985. irreg.
Former titles (until 1990): Senate of Canada. Subcommittee on Veterans Affairs and Senior Citizens. Proceedings (0839-9409); (until 1988): Senate of Canada. Sub-Committee on Veterans Affairs. Proceedings (0837-9947)
Published by: Senate of Canada, Subcommittee on Veterans Affairs, Parliament of Canada, Ottawa, ON K1A 0A9, Canada. TEL 613-992-4793, 866-599-4999, info@parl.gc.ca, http://www.parl.gc.ca.

SENIOR BULLETIN. *see* GERONTOLOGY AND GERIATRICS

SENIOREN TANZEN. *see* DANCE

SENIOREN ZEITSCHRIFT. *see* PUBLIC ADMINISTRATION

362.6 NOR ISSN 1503-9404
SENIORPOLITIKK.NO. Text in Norwegian. 1992. bi-m. free. **Document type:** *Newsletter, Consumer.*
Former titles (until 2004): 45+ (1500-2837); (until 1997): Arbeid Plan Pensjon (0806-1300)
Related titles: Online - full text ed.: ISSN 1503-9412.
Published by: Senter for Seniorpolitikk, St. Olavs Plass 3, Oslo, 0165, Norway. TEL 47-23-156550, FAX 47-23-156551, ssp@seniorpolitikk.no. Ed. Per Halvorsen.

362.6 CAN ISSN 1912-6999
SENIORS ADVISORY COUNCIL FOR ALBERTA. UPDATE NEWSLETTER. Text in English. 1996. q. **Document type:** *Newsletter, Consumer.*
Formerly (until 2004): Seniors Advisory Council for Alberta. Update (1209-8345)
Published by: Seniors Advisory Council for Alberta, c/o Alberta Seniors and Community Supports, 600 Standard Life Centre, 10405 Jasper Ave, Edmonton, AB T5J 4R7, Canada. TEL 780-422-2321, FAX 780-422-8762, saca@gov.ab.ca, http://www.seniors.gov.ab.ca/index.asp.

362.6 CAN ISSN 1719-4075
SENIORS' NEWS. Text in English. 1981. q. **Document type:** *Newsletter, Consumer.*
Former titles (until 2005): Senior Citizens Secretariat (1196-1023); (until 1986): Senior Citizens Secretariat. Newsletter (0825-4346)
Published by: Seniors' Secretariat, PO Box 2065, Halifax, NS B3J 2Z1, Canada. TEL 902-424-0065, 800-670-0065, FAX 902-424-0561, scs@gov.ns.ca, http://www.gov.ns.ca/scs.

362.6 CAN ISSN 1912-3299
SENIORS' ORGANIZATIONS IN ALBERTA. DIRECTORY. Text in English. 200?. irreg. **Document type:** *Directory, Consumer.*
Published by: Alberta Seniors and Community Supports, Box 3100, Edmonton, AB T5J 4W3, Canada. TEL 800-642-3853, FAX 780-422-8762, http://www.seniors.gov.ab.ca.

361.7 ITA ISSN 2038-6893
SENZA FRONTIERE. Text in Italian. 2001. q. **Document type:** *Magazine, Consumer.*
Address: Via S Apollonio 6, Castel Goffredo, MN 46042, Italy. http://www.senzafrontiere.com.

360 AFG
SERAMIASHT. Text in English, Persian, Modern, Pushto. 1977. q.
Published by: Afghan Red Crescent Society, Pul-i Hartan, P O Box 3066, Kabul, Afghanistan. TEL 30969, TELEX 318 ARC AF.

361.5 CAN ISSN 0227-034X
SERVICE. Text in English, French. 1940. q. free.
Formerly (until 1977): Despatch (0046-0087)
Published by: Canadian Red Cross Society, National Headquarters, 5700 Cancross Court, Mississauga, ON L5R 3E9, Canada. TEL 416-890-1000. Circ: 60,000.

361.5 USA
SERVICE ILLUSTRATED. Text in English. 1947. s-a. free. bk.rev. charts; illus. **Document type:** *Newsletter, Consumer.* **Description:** Reports on the many activities of the Church World Service to help the poor help themselves, with special emphasis on the CWS Blanket and Tools of Hope Program.
Supersedes in part: Harvest News (1034-5183); Which was formerly (until 1983): Service News (Elkhart) (0037-2617)
Published by: Church World Service, 28606 Phillips St, Elkhart, IN 46515. TEL 800-297-1516, FAX 219-269-0966. Eds. Ron Kaser, Ronda Hughes. R&P Ron Kaser. Circ: 110,000.

360 362.7 GBR
SERVICES FOR CHILDREN. Text in English. 1991. a. GBP 2. **Document type:** *Government.*
Published by: Social Work Services Group, Statistics Branch, Rm 52, James Craig Walk, Edinburgh, EH1 3BA, United Kingdom. TEL 44-131-244-5431, FAX 44-131-244-5315. **Subscr. to:** Her Majesty's Stationery Office Bookshop.

362.6 USA ISSN 1540-1022
LOS SERVICIOS SOCIALES PARA LAS PERSONAS MAYORES EN IBEROAMERICA; estructura, avatares y necesidades. Text in Spanish. 2002. a. USD 12 newsstand/cover (effective 2002).
Published by: National Hispanic Council on Aging, 1341 Connecticut Ave NW, # 4A, Washington, DC 20036-1801. TEL 202-265-1888, FAX 202-745-2522, nhcoa@worldnet.att.net, http://www.nhcoa.org.

361 BRA ISSN 0101-6628
HV193
SERVICO SOCIALE E SOCIEDADE. Text in Portuguese. 1979. 3/yr. USD 80 (effective 1999). **Document type:** *Academic/Scholarly.*
Description: Provides professionals in social service and related areas with the latest news regarding themes dealing with social reality. Introduces theoretical and practical proposals within the new concept of citizenship for all people.
Indexed: IBR, IBZ, PAIS.
Published by: Cortez Editora, Rua Bartira, 387, Perdizes, Sao Paulo, SP 05009-000, Brazil. TEL 55-11-8640111, FAX 55-11-8644290. Ed. Elizabete Borgiani. Pub., R&P Jose Xavier Cortez.

360 GBR ISSN 2043-7714
▼ **SERVING IN MISSION.** Abbreviated title: S I M. Text in English. 2010. 3/yr. free to qualified personnel (effective 2010). **Document type:** *Magazine, Consumer.*
Published by: S I M - UK/Europe, Wetheringsett Manor, Wetheringsett, Stowmarket, Suffolk IP14 5QX, United Kingdom. TEL 44-1449-766464, FAX 44-1449-767148, info@sim.co.uk.

360 ITA ISSN 1825-1633
SERVIZI SOCIALI OGGI; cultura e gestione del sociale. Text in Italian. 1995. bi-m. EUR 60 to individuals; EUR 100 to institutions (effective 2008). **Document type:** *Magazine, Trade.* **Description:** Informs those who work in the social assistance sector of changes and reforms in public administration.
Formerly (until 2003): I P A B Oggi (1123-9689)
Published by: (Istituti Previdenziali di Assistenza e Beneficenza), Maggioli Editore, Via del Carpino 8/10, Santarcangelo di Romagna, RN 47822, Italy. Circ: 5,000.

360 ITA
SERVIZIO SOCIALE. Text in Italian. 1994. irreg., latest vol.11, 1999. price varies. **Document type:** *Monographic series, Academic/Scholarly.*
Published by: Liguori Editore, Via Posillipo 394, Naples, 80123, Italy. TEL 39-081-7206111, FAX 39-081-7206244, liguori@liguori.it, http://www.liguori.it. Ed. Lia Sanicola.

SETTLEMENTS INFORMATION NETWORK AFRICA NEWSLETTER. *see* HOUSING AND URBAN PLANNING

362 USA
THE SHADOW; information is strength - knowledge is power. Text in English. 1988. 10/yr. USD 10; USD 0.50 newsstand/cover. adv. bk.rev. illus. 24 p./no. 4 cols./p.; back issues avail. **Document type:** *Newspaper, Consumer.* **Description:** Covers housing, homelessness, police brutality, political lying and other issues.
Published by: Shadow Press, PO Box 20298, New York, NY 10009. TEL 212-631-1181. Eds. A Kronstadt, Chris Flash. Circ: 5,000.

360 JPN
SHAKAI FUKUSHI NO DOKO. Text in Japanese. 1957. a. JPY 2,200 (effective 1996). **Description:** Provides an overview of social welfare-service systems and programs in Japan.
Published by: Chuo Hoki Shuppan, 2-27-4 Yoyogi, Shibuya-ku, Tokyo, 151-0053, Japan. Ed. Hisashi Kawagoe. Circ: 9,000.

360 CHN ISSN 1007-0613
SHEHUI BAOZHANG ZHIDU/SOCIAL SECURITY SYSTEM. Text in Chinese. m. USD 63.80 (effective 2009). 48 p./no.; **Document type:** *Journal, Academic/Scholarly.* **Description:** Contains articles on policies of Chinese social security system, including social welfare, medical insurance, employment and unemployment benefit.
Related titles: Alternate Frequency ed(s).: a. USD 34.20 newsstand/ cover (effective 2002).
Published by: Zhongguo Renmin Daxue Shubao Ziliao Zhongxin/Renmin University of China, Information Center for Social Sciences, Dongcheng-qu, 3, Zhangzizhong Lu, Beijing, 100007, China. TEL 86-10-64039458, FAX 86-10-64015080, center@zlzx.org, http://www.zlzx.org/. **Dist. in US by:** China Publications Service, PO Box 49614, Chicago, IL 60649. TEL 312-288-3291, FAX 312-288-8570; **Dist. by:** China International Book Trading Corp, 35 Chegongzhuang Xilu, Haidian District, PO Box 399, Beijing 100044, China. TEL 86-10-68412045, FAX 86-10-68412023, cibtc@mail.cibtc.com.cn, http://www.cibtc.com.cn.

360 CHN ISSN 1674-9758
▼ **SHEHUI YU GONGYI/SOCIETY AND PUBLIC WELFARE.** Text in Chinese. 2010. m. **Document type:** *Journal, Academic/Scholarly.*
Published by: Zhongguo Shehui Gongzuo Xiehui/China Association of Social Workers, No.6(A), Baijiazhuang Rd., Chaoyang District, Beijing, 100020, China. TEL 86-10-65931572, FAX 86-10-65931572, http://www.cncasw.org/.

360 CHN ISSN 1674-1323
SHETUAN GUANLI YANJIU/RESEARCH OF ADMINISTRATION OF N P OS. Text in Chinese. 2007. m. **Document type:** *Journal, Government.*
Related titles: Online - full text ed.
Published by: Guojia Minjian Zuzhi Guangliju, 55, Donganmen Dajie, Dongcheng-qu, Beijing, 100721, China. TEL 86-10-85203114, cnpo@mca.gov.cn.

331.105 HRV ISSN 1330-1640
HD6788
SINDIKALNA AKCIJA. Text in Croatian. 1991. fortn. **Document type:** *Magazine, Trade.*
Published by: Savez Samostalnih Sindikata Hrvatske, Kresimirov Trg. 2, Zagreb, 10000, Croatia. TEL 385-1-4655111, FAX 385-1-4655052. Ed. Hasim Bahtijari.

361 SWE ISSN 1654-6040
SIS I FOKUS; aktuellt om forskning och behandling fraan statens institutionsstyrelse. (Statens Institutionsstyrelse) Text in Swedish. 1995. q. free (effective 2007). **Document type:** *Newsletter, Government.*
Formerly (until 2007): S I Stone (1400-2876)
Related titles: Online - full text ed.
Published by: Statens Institutionsstyrelse/The National Board of Institutional Care, PO Box 16363, Stockholm, 10326, Sweden. TEL 46-8-4534000, FAX 46-8-4534050, registrator@stat-inst.se. Ed. Birgitta Hedman-Lindgren.

362.7 USA ISSN 1020-2129
LA SITUATION DES ENFANTS DANS LE MONDE. Text in French. 1979. a. **Document type:** *Report, Trade.*
Formerly (until 199?): L' Etat des Enfants dans le Monde (0251-9097)
Related titles: Online - full text ed.: ISSN 1564-9768. 1996. free (effective 2011); ♦ Spanish ed.: Estado Mundial de la Infancia. ISSN 0251-9119; ♦ English ed.: The State of the World's Children. ISSN 0251-9100.
Published by: United Nations Children's Fund/Fonds des Nations Unies pour l'Enfance, 3 United Nations Plz, New York, NY 10017. TEL 212-326-7000, FAX 212-887-7465.

SJOMANNADAGSBLADID. *see* TRANSPORTATION—Ships And Shipping

SMALL TOWN. *see* HOUSING AND URBAN PLANNING

360 USA ISSN 0037-7317
HV1 CODEN: SMSWAW
➤ **SMITH COLLEGE STUDIES IN SOCIAL WORK.** Text in English. 1930. q. GBP 176 combined subscription in United Kingdom to institutions (print & online eds.); EUR 229, USD 237 combined subscription to institutions (print & online eds.) (effective 2012). bk.rev. abstr. index. 150 p./no.; back issues avail.; reprint service avail. from PSC. **Document type:** *Journal, Academic/Scholarly.* **Description:** Covers various clinical and research topics in social work.
Related titles: Online - full text ed.: ISSN 1553-0426. GBP 158 in United Kingdom to institutions; EUR 206, USD 213 to institutions (effective 2012).
Indexed: A01, A03, A20, A22, ASCA, BibInd, C06, C07, C08, C28, CA, CINAHL, CurCont, E-psyche, E01, F09, FamI, IBR, IBZ, MEA&I, P03, P06, P25, P27, P30, P46, P48, P54, PAIS, PCI, PQC, PsycInfo, PsycholAb, S02, S03, SCOPUS, SOPODA, SSA, SSCI, SWR&A, SociolAb, T02, W07, W09.
—BLDSC (8311.200000), IE, Infotrieve, Ingenta. **CCC.**
Published by: (Smith College, School for Social Work), Routledge (Subsidiary of: Taylor & Francis Group), 325 Chestnut St, Ste 800, Philadelphia, PA 19106. TEL 215-625-8900, 800-354-1420, FAX 215-625-8914, journals@routledge.com, http://www.routledge.com. Ed. Kathryn Basham. Circ: 2,000 (paid).

360 DEU
SO V D ZEITUNG. Text in German. m. **Document type:** *Newspaper, Consumer.*

S

Published by: Sozialverband Deutschland e.V., Kurfuerstenstr. 131, Berlin, 10785, Germany. TEL 49-30-2639103, FAX 49-30-26391055, contact@sozialverband.de, http://www.sovd.de.

360 NLD ISSN 0921-5344
SOCIAAL BESTEK; tijdschrift voor werk, inkomen en zorg. Text in Dutch. 1938. 11/yr. EUR 175.85 (effective 2009). adv. **Document type:** *Magazine, Trade.* **Description:** Covers issues relating to the provision of social services, including social security, care of the elderly, unemployment assistance, and related topics, with emphasis on the local level.
Former titles (until 1986): Sociaal Bestek en Lektuurkeuze Welzijnsterrein (0921-5352); (until 1982): Sociaal Bestek (0165-8344); (until 1969): Sociale Zorg
Related titles: Talking Book ed.
—IE, Infotrieve.
Published by: Reed Business bv (Subsidiary of: Reed Business), Postbus 152, Amsterdam, 1000 AD, Netherlands. TEL 31-20-5159222, info@reedbusiness.nl, http://www.reedbusiness.nl. Ed. Y Bommelje. adv.: B&W page EUR 1,743, color page EUR 3,242; trim 210 x 297. Circ: 1,161.

SOCIAAL COMPENDIUM SOCIALE-ZEKERHEIDSRECHT. *see* INSURANCE

SOCIAAL PRAKTIJKBOEK. *see* LAW—Civil Law

360 331.8 FRA ISSN 0758-0959
SOCIAL ACTUALITE; mensuel des administrateurs de la protection sociale. Text in French. 1984. 10/yr. adv. bk.rev. index. back issues avail.
Published by: Confederation Francaise Democratique du Travail, 4 bd. de la Villette, Paris, Cedex 19 75955, France. TEL 33-1-42038140, FAX 33-1-42038148, gestionpresse@cfdt.fr, http://www.cfdt.org. Ed. Verollet Yves. Circ: 3,600.

303.3 USA ISSN 1948-3023
HM671
➤ **SOCIAL ADVOCACY AND SYSTEMS CHANGE.** Abbreviated title: S A S C. Text in English. 2008. s-a. free (effective 2009). back issues avail. **Document type:** *Journal, Academic/Scholarly.* **Description:** Addresses issues related to social justice, via the systemic transformation of socially constructed systems.
Media: Online - full content.
Indexed: S02, S03, T02.
Published by: State University of New York College at Cortland, PO Box 2000, Cortland, NY 13045. TEL 607-753-2011, http://www.cortland.edu. Ed. Judy K. C Bentley.

360 GBR ISSN 2042-0919
▼ **SOCIAL CARE AND NEURODISABILITY.** Text in English. 2010. q. EUR 689 combined subscription in Europe (print & online eds.); USD 889 combined subscription in the Americas (print & online eds.); GBP 529 combined subscription in the UK & elsewhere (print & online eds.); AUD 999 combined subscription in Australasia (print & online eds.) (effective 2012). **Document type:** *Journal, Academic/Scholarly.* **Description:** Provides information on good practice and advances in the rehabilitation, treatment and care of people who have neurological conditions. Audience includes people involved in social work, case management, social care and all others interested in neurodisability and neuroscience.
Related titles: Online - full text ed.: ISSN 2042-874X.
Indexed: T02.
—CCC.
Published by: Pier Professional Ltd. (Subsidiary of: Emerald Group Publishing Ltd.), Ste N4, The Old Market, Upper Market St, Hove, BN3 1AS, United Kingdom. TEL 44-1273-783720, FAX 44-1273-783723, info@pierprofessional.com. Eds. Andy Mantell, Patti Simonson.

360 DEU ISSN 0176-1714
➤ **SOCIAL CHOICE AND WELFARE.** Text in English. 1984. bi-m. EUR 1,058, USD 1,294 combined subscription to institutions (print & online eds.) (effective 2012). adv. back issues avail.; reprint service avail. from PSC. **Document type:** *Journal, Academic/Scholarly.* **Description:** Covers the ethical and positive aspects of welfare economics and collective theory, with topics including social choice and voting theory, as well as all aspects of welfare theory.
Related titles: Online - full text ed.: ISSN 1432-217X (from IngentaConnect).
Indexed: A01, A03, A08, A12, A17, A20, A22, A26, ABIn, ASCA, ASG, B01, B06, B07, B09, CA, CCMJ, CurCont, E01, ESPM, EconLit, FamI, H01, IBSS, JEL, MSN, MathR, P02, P10, P20, P21, P27, P30, P34, P42, P45, P48, P50, P51, P53, P54, PAIS, PQC, PSA, PhilInd, RASB, S02, S03, S11, SCOPUS, SOPODA, SSA, SSCI, SSciA, SociolAb, T02, W07, Z02.
—BLDSC (8318.072000), IE, Infotrieve, Ingenta. **CCC.**
Published by: Springer (Subsidiary of: Springer Science+Business Media), Tiergartenstr 17, Heidelberg, 69121, Germany. TEL 49-6221-4870, FAX 49-6221-345229. Ed. Maurice Salles. **Subscr. in the Americas to:** Springer New York LLC, Journal Fulfillment, PO Box 2485, Secaucus, NJ 07096. TEL 800-777-4643, 201-348-4033, FAX 201-348-4505, journals-ny@springer.com, http://www.springer.com; **Subscr. to:** Springer Distribution Center, Kundenservice Zeitschriften, Haberstr 7, Heidelberg 69126, Germany. TEL 49-6221-3454303, FAX 49-6221-3454229, subscriptions@springer.com.

360 USA ISSN 0147-1473
HV1
➤ **SOCIAL DEVELOPMENT ISSUES.** Abbreviated title: S D I. Text in English. 1968. 3/yr. USD 90 domestic to libraries; USD 112.50 foreign to libraries; free to members (effective 2011). bk.rev. bibl. **Document type:** *Journal, Academic/Scholarly.* **Description:** Designed to serves as a forum for achieving linkages between multiple disciplines, nations, and cultures.
Supersedes (in 1977): Iowa Journal of Social Work (0021-0536)
Related titles: Online - full text ed.
Indexed: A22, BRD, CA, FamI, IBSS, P03, P30, P34, PAIS, PsycInfo, S02, S03, SCOPUS, SOPODA, SSA, SSAI, SSAb, SSI, SWR&A, SociolAb, T02, W01, W02, W03, W05.
—BLDSC (8318.079400), IE, Infotrieve, Ingenta. **CCC.**
Published by: (Inter - University Consortium for International Social Development), Lyceum Books, Inc., 5758 S Blackstone Ave, Chicago, IL 60637. TEL 773-643-1902, FAX 773-643-1903, lyceum@lyceumbooks.com, http://www.lyceumbooks.com. Ed. Joe Leung. Pub. David C Follmer TEL 773-643-1902.

361 CAN ISSN 1026-3950
SOCIAL DEVELOPMENT REVIEW. Text in English. 1996. q. USD 20; USD 10 in developing nations. adv. **Document type:** *Journal, Trade.* **Description:** Focuses on social and economic development issues, giving news, reporting on policies and providing analysis.
Published by: International Council on Social Welfare/Conseil International de l'Action Sociale, c/o Stephen King, Exe Dir, 380 St Antoine St W, Ste 3200, Montreal, PQ H2Y 3X7, Canada. TEL 514-287-3280, FAX 514-287-9702. Adv. contact Lilian Chatterjee.

360 FRA ISSN 1957-9403
SOCIAL EN PRATIQUES. Text in French. 2007. irreg. **Document type:** *Monographic series, Academic/Scholarly.*
Published by: Editions Vuibert, 5 Allee de la 2e DB, Paris, 75015, France. TEL 33-1-42794400, FAX 33-1-42794680, http://www.vuibert.com.

362.7 DNK ISSN 1903-7406
SOCIAL FOKUS, BOERN & UNGE. Text in Danish. 2003. s-a. free. back issues avail. **Document type:** *Magazine, Government.*
Supersedes in part (in 2009): Social Fokus (1902-8571); Which was formerly (until vol. 4, 2007): Styrelsen for Specialraadgivning og Social Service (1902-150X); (until 2007): Social Service (1603-5607)
Related titles: Online - full text ed.: ISSN 1903-7414. 2003.
Published by: Servicestyrelsen/National Board of Social Services, Edisonsvej 18, Odense C, 5000, Denmark. TEL 45-72-423700, FAX 45-72-423709, servicestyrelsen@servicestyrelsen.dk. Circ: 8,000.

362.4 DNK ISSN 1903-6221
SOCIAL FOKUS, HANDICAP. Text in Danish. 2003. s-a. free. **Document type:** *Magazine, Government.*
Supersedes in part (in 2009): Social Fokus (1902-8571); Which was formerly (until vol. 4, 2007): Styrelsen for Specialraadgivning og Social Service (1902-150X); (untl 2007): Social Service (1603-5607)
Related titles: Online - full text ed.: ISSN 1903-6426.
Published by: Servicestyrelsen/National Board of Social Services, Edisonsvej 18, Odense C, 5000, Denmark. TEL 45-72-423700, FAX 45-72-423709, servicestyrelsen@servicestyrelsen.dk.

361 DNK ISSN 1903-8933
SOCIAL FOKUS, UDSAT. Text in Danish. 2004. s-a. free. **Document type:** *Magazine, Government.*
Formerly (until 2009): Udsat (1603-8606)
Related titles: Online - full text ed.: ISSN 1903-8941.
Published by: Servicestyrelsen/National Board of Social Services, Edisonsvej 18, Odense C, 5000, Denmark. TEL 45-72-423700, FAX 45-72-423709, servicestyrelsen@servicestyrelsen.dk.

948.9057 DNK ISSN 0903-7535
HN541
SOCIAL FORSKNING. Text in Danish. 1977. 4/yr. free. back issues avail. **Document type:** *Magazine, Government.*
Formerly (until 1988): S F I Nyt (0105-6093)
Related titles: Online - full text ed.; ◆ Special ed(s).: Social Forskning. Tema-Nummer. ISSN 0908-0031.
Published by: Det Nationale Forskningscenter for Velfaerd/The Danish National Centre for Social Research, Herluf Trolles Gade 11, Copenhagen K, 1052, Denmark. TEL 45-33-480800, FAX 45-33-480833, sfi@sfi.dk. Eds. Carsten Wulff, Ulla Haahr. Circ: 4,800.

362.5 GBR
THE SOCIAL FUND: LAW AND PRACTICE. Text in English. 1995. irreg., latest 2009, 3rd ed. GBP 89 per issue (effective 2009). **Document type:** *Handbook/Manual/Guide, Trade.* **Description:** Includes the latest information on recent and forthcoming changes to the UK discretionary social fund.
Published by: (Child Poverty Action Group), Sweet & Maxwell Ltd. (Subsidiary of: Thomson Reuters Corp.), 100 Avenue Rd, London, NW3 3PF, United Kingdom. TEL 44-20-73937000, FAX 44-20-74491144, sweetandmaxwell.customer.services@thomson.com, http://www.sweetandmaxwell.co.uk. Ed. Trevor Buck. **Subscr. outside the UK to:** PO Box 1000, Andover SP10 9AF, United Kingdom. TEL 44-20-73938051, sweetandmaxwell.international.queries@thomson.com.

SOCIAL ISSUES AND POLICY REVIEW. *see* SOCIOLOGY

360 DNK ISSN 1600-0293
SOCIAL- & SUNDHEDSSEKTORENS HAANDBOG. Variant title: Social- & Sundhedssektorens Hvem, Hvad, Hvor. Text in Danish. 1985. a. DKK 1,395 per vol. (effective 2010). adv. **Document type:** *Directory, Trade.*
Former titles (until 2000): Haandbog for Social- og Sundhedssektor (0908-6226); (until 1993): Haandbog for Social-, Sygehus- og Sundhedssektor (0907-4562); (until 1992): Haandbog for Social- og Sundhedssektor (0901-2389); Which was formed by the merger of (1982-1985): Plejehjemshaandbogen (0108-0857); (1983-1985): Bistandshaandbogen (0108-8351)
Related titles: Print ed.
Published by: Stockmann-Gruppen A-S, c/o Retail Institut Scandinavia, Hoeve Straede 1, Asnaes, 4550, Denmark. TEL 45-70-233010, FAX 45-59-365056, info@retailinstitutscandinavia.dk, http://www.stockmann.dk.

362.4 362.6 SWE ISSN 0280-848X
SOCIAL OMSORG. Text in Swedish. 1950. s-m. SEK 140 (effective 2004). adv. 16 p./no. 3 cols./p.; **Document type:** *Trade.*
Former titles (until 1982): Aaldringsvaard (0346-5098); (until 1971): Medlemsblad foer Foereningen Sveriges Aalderdomshemsfoerestandare
Published by: Foereningen Social Omsorg, PO Box 391, Umeaa, 90108, Sweden. Eds. Hanna Jonsson TEL 46-4-9210048, Katarina Nilsson TEL 46-570-711155. adv.: B&W page SEK 3,600, color page SEK 6,600; trim 270 x 186. Circ: 3,300.

SOCIAL POLICY; organizing for social and economic justice. *see* SOCIAL SCIENCES: COMPREHENSIVE WORKS

361.61 GBR ISSN 0144-5596
H1
➤ **SOCIAL POLICY AND ADMINISTRATION**; an international journal of policy and research. Text in English. 1967. 7/yr. GBP 749 in United Kingdom to institutions; EUR 951 in Europe to institutions; USD 1,523 in the Americas to institutions; USD 1,776 elsewhere to institutions; GBP 861 combined subscription in United Kingdom to institutions (print & online eds.); EUR 1,094 combined subscription in Europe to institutions (print & online eds.); USD 1,752 combined subscription in the Americas to institutions (print & online eds.); USD 2,043 combined subscription elsewhere to institutions (print & online eds.) (effective 2012). adv. bk.rev. bibl.; charts; illus.; stat. index. back issues avail.; reprint service avail. from PSC. **Document type:** *Journal, Academic/Scholarly.* **Description:** Covers politics of policy-making to the sociology of a wide range of social issues including poverty/income protection, health, crime, education, housing, social control and social care.
Formerly (until 1979): Social and Economic Administration (0037-7643)
Related titles: Online - full text ed.: ISSN 1467-9515. GBP 749 in United Kingdom to institutions; EUR 951 in Europe to institutions; USD 1,523 in the Americas to institutions; USD 1,776 elsewhere to institutions (effective 2012) (from IngentaConnect).
Indexed: A01, A03, A08, A20, A22, A26, AC&P, AMHA, APEL, ASCA, B01, B06, B07, B09, CA, CurCont, E01, ESPM, FR, FamI, GEOBASE, IBSS, MCR, P02, P06, P27, P30, P34, P42, P48, P54, PAIS, PCI, PQC, PSA, RASB, RiskAb, S02, S03, SCOPUS, SOPODA, SSA, SSCI, SociolAb, T02, W07, WBA, WBSS.
—BLDSC (8318.130400), IE, Infotrieve, Ingenta. **CCC.**
Published by: Wiley-Blackwell Publishing Ltd. (Subsidiary of: John Wiley & Sons, Inc.), 9600 Garsington Rd, Oxford, OX4 2DQ, United Kingdom. TEL 44-1865-776868, FAX 44-1865-714591, customerservices@blackwellpublishing.com. Eds. Bent Greve TEL 45-4-6742585, Martin Powell TEL 44-1214-144462. Adv. contact Craig Pickett TEL 44-1865-476267.

➤ **SOCIAL POLICY JOURNAL OF NEW ZEALAND**; te puna whakaaro. *see* POLITICAL SCIENCE

361.6 AUS ISSN 1832-4339
SOCIAL POLICY WORKING PAPERS. Text in English. 2004. irreg., latest vol.8, 2007. free (effective 2008). back issues avail. **Document type:** *Monographic series, Academic/Scholarly.*
Media: Online - full text.
Published by: (University of Melbourne, Centre for Public Policy), Brotherhood of St. Laurence, 67 Brunswick St, Fitzroy, VIC 3065, Australia. TEL 61-3-94831183, FAX 61-3-94172691, info@bsl.org.au.

362.948 DNK ISSN 1397-6893
HD7198
SOCIAL PROTECTION IN THE NORDIC COUNTRIES; scope, expenditure and financing. Text in English. 1965. a. price varies. stat. back issues avail. **Document type:** *Government.*
Formerly (until 1997): Social Security in the Nordic Countries (1395-7554)
Related titles: Online - full text ed.; ◆ Danish ed.: Social Tryghed i de Nordiske Lande. ISSN 1395-7546; ◆ Series of: Nordisk Socialstatistisk Komite. ISSN 1395-7562.
Published by: Nordisk Socialstatistisk Komite/Nordic Social-Statistical Committee, Islands Brygge 67, Copenhagen S, 2300, Denmark. TEL 45-72-227625, FAX 45-32-955470, mail@nom-nos.dk. Ed. Johannes Nielsen.

SOCIAL SECURITY/BITAHON SOTZIYALI; journal of welfare and social security studies. *see* INSURANCE

SOCIAL SECURITY BULLETIN. *see* INSURANCE

361.6 347.30423 USA ISSN 0277-0539
KF3649
SOCIAL SECURITY EXPLAINED. Text in English. a. USD 46.50 (effective 2006).
Supersedes in part (in 197?): Social Security and Medicare Explained (0162-6361); Which was formerly (until 1971): Medicare and Social Security Explained
Published by: C C H Inc. (Subsidiary of: Wolters Kluwer N.V.), 2700 Lake Cook Rd, Riverwoods, IL 60015. TEL 847-267-7000, cust_serv@cch.com, http://www.cch.com.

SOCIAL SECURITY LAW AND PRACTICE. *see* INSURANCE

362.5 GBR
SOCIAL SECURITY LEGISLATION (YEAR). Text in English. 2000. 4 base vols. plus a. updates. GBP 89 base vol(s). (effective 2009). **Document type:** *Handbook/Manual/Guide, Trade.* **Description:** Covers the primary non-means-tested benefits for persons receiving public assistance in the UK. Updates readers on changes in legislation, case law, decision-making, and appeals.
Formed by the 2000 merger of: Non Means Tested Benefits (1367-112X); C P A G S Income Related Benefits; Great Britain Medical and Disability Appeal Tribunals
—IE.
Published by: (Child Poverty Action Group), Sweet & Maxwell Ltd. (Subsidiary of: Thomson Reuters Corp.), 100 Avenue Rd, London, NW3 3PF, United Kingdom. TEL 44-20-73937000, FAX 44-20-74491144, sweetandmaxwell.customer.services@thomson.com, http://www.sweetandmaxwell.co.uk. Eds. D Bonner, I Hooker, R White. **Subscr. outside the UK to:** PO Box 1000, Andover SP10 9AF, United Kingdom. TEL 44-20-73938051, sweetandmaxwell.international.queries@thomson.com.

SOCIAL SECURITY PRACTICE ADVISORY. *see* INSURANCE

SOCIAL SECURITY PRACTICE GUIDE. *see* INSURANCE

368.4 USA ISSN 1936-6477
HD7237
SOCIAL SECURITY PROGRAMS THROUGHOUT THE WORLD. AFRICA. Text in English. 2003. biennial. free (effective 2011). **Document type:** *Government.*
Supersedes in part (in 2003): Social Security Programs Throughout the World
Related titles: Online - full text ed.
Published by: U.S. Social Security Administration, Office of Research, Evaluation and Statistics, Office of Public Inquiries, Windsor Park Bldg, 6401 Security Blvd, Baltimore, MD 21235. TEL 800-772-1213, ores.publications@ssa.gov, http://www.ssa.gov/policy/about/ORES.html.

368.4 USA ISSN 1939-8972
SOCIAL SECURITY PROGRAMS THROUGHOUT THE WORLD. ASIA AND THE PACIFIC. Text in English. 2002. biennial. free (effective 2011). back issues avail. **Document type:** *Government.*
Supersedes in part (in 2002): Social Security Programs Throughout the World (0566-0351)
Related titles: Online - full text ed.: ISSN 1936-8755.
Published by: U.S. Social Security Administration, Office of Research, Evaluation and Statistics, Office of Public Inquiries, Windsor Park Bldg, 6401 Security Blvd, Baltimore, MD 21235. TEL 800-772-1213, ores.publications@ssa.gov, http://www.ssa.gov/policy/about/ORES.html.

368.4 USA
HD7164
SOCIAL SECURITY PROGRAMS THROUGHOUT THE WORLD. EUROPE. Text in English. 2002. biennial. free (effective 2011). back issues avail. **Document type:** *Government.*
Related titles: Online - full text ed.
Published by: U.S. Social Security Administration, Office of Research, Evaluation and Statistics, Office of Public Inquiries, Windsor Park Bldg, 6401 Security Blvd, Baltimore, MD 21235. TEL 800-772-1213, ores.publications@ssa.gov, http://www.ssa.gov/policy/about/ORES.html.

368.4 USA ISSN 1936-8712
HD7091
SOCIAL SECURITY PROGRAMS THROUGHOUT THE WORLD: THE AMERICAS. Text in English. 2003. biennial. free (effective 2011). back issues avail. **Document type:** *Government.*
Supersedes in part (in 2003): Social Security Programs Throughout the World
Related titles: Online - full text ed.: ISSN 1936-8720.
Published by: U.S. Social Security Administration, Office of Research, Evaluation and Statistics, Office of Public Inquiries, Windsor Park Bldg, 6401 Security Blvd, Baltimore, MD 21235. TEL 202-358-6263, 800-772-1213, ores.publications@ssa.gov, http://www.ssa.gov/policy/about/ORES.html.

368.4021 CAN ISSN 1189-5594
SOCIAL SECURITY STATISTICS, CANADA AND PROVINCES. Text in English. 1983. biennial.
Related titles: Online - full text ed.: ISSN 1497-0538. 1995.
Published by: Human Resources and Social Development Canada, Public Enquiries Centre, 140 Promenade du Portage, Phase IV, Level 0, Gatineau, PQ K1A 0J9, Canada. FAX 819-953-7260, youth@canada.gc.ca.

360 340 USA
SOCIAL SERVICE AND RELATED LAWS OF NORTH CAROLINA. Text in English. irreg., latest 2006. USD 136 per issue (effective 2008). **Document type:** *Monographic series, Trade.* **Description:** Contains selected provisions governing laws relating to social services.
Published by: LexisNexis (Subsidiary of: LexisNexis North America), 701 E Water St, PO Box 7587, Charlottesville, VA 22906. TEL 434-972-7600, 800-446-3410, FAX 800-643-1280, customer.support@lexisnexis.com, http://www.lexisnexis.com/. Ed. George Harley.

SOCIAL SERVICE JOBS. *see* OCCUPATIONS AND CAREERS

360 USA ISSN 0037-7961
CODEN: SSRVA
➤ **SOCIAL SERVICE REVIEW.** Abbreviated title: S S R. Text in English. 1927. q. USD 240 combined subscription to institutions (print & online eds.) (effective 2012). adv. bk.rev. bibl.; illus.; abstr. Index. 176 p./no.; back issues avail.; reprint service avail. from PSC. **Document type:** *Journal, Academic/Scholarly.* **Description:** Examines social welfare practice and evaluates its effects. Covers such topics as poverty, ethnicity, income distribution, family conflict, social welfare policy, mental health services, community development, and deviancy.
Related titles: Microform ed.: (from MIM, PMC, PQC); Online - full text ed.: ISSN 1537-5404. USD 204 to institutions (effective 2012).
Indexed: A01, A02, A03, A08, A20, A21, A22, A26, AC&P, AMHA, ASCA, ASG, ASSIA, AmH&L, B01, B04, B06, B07, B09, B14, BRD, BRI, C28, CA, CBRI, Chicano, CurCont, E06, E07, E08, ERA, EconLit, F09, FamI, G08, H09, H10, HRA, HistAb, I05, IBR, IBSS, IBZ, JEL, MCR, MEA&I, P02, P03, P06, P07, P10, P25, P27, P30, P34, P42, P46, P48, P53, P54, PAIS, PCI, PQC, PSA, PSI, PsycInfo, PsycholAb, RASB, RI-1, RI-2, S02, S03, S05, S09, S11, S20, S21, SCOPUS, SFSA, SOPODA, SPAA, SSA, SSAI, SSAb, SSCI, SSI, SWR&A, SociolAb, T02, W03, W07, W09.
—BLDSC (8318.203000), IE, Infotrieve, Ingenta. **CCC.**
Published by: (University of Chicago, University of Chicago, School of Social Service Administration), University of Chicago Press, 1427 E 60th St, Chicago, IL 60637. TEL 773-702-7600, FAX 773-702-0694, subscriptions@press.uchicago.edu. Ed. Michael R Sosin. Adv. contact Cheryl Jones TEL 773-702-7361. **Subscr. to:** PO Box 370050, Chicago, IL 60637. TEL 773-753-3347, 877-705-1878, FAX 773-753-0811, 877-705-1879.

361.6 USA
SOCIAL SERVICES BULLETIN. Text in English. 19??. irreg. **Document type:** *Bulletin, Academic/Scholarly.* **Description:** Addresses social services issues of interest to local and state government employees and officials.
Related titles: Online - full text ed.: free.
Published by: University of North Carolina at Chapel Hill, School of Government, Knapp-Sanders Bldg, Campus Box 3330, Chapel Hill, NC 27599. TEL 919-966-5381, FAX 919-962-0654, sales@sog.unc.edu, http://sog.unc.edu.

360 GBR ISSN 1351-5586
SOCIAL SERVICES RESEARCH. Text in English. 198?. irreg. **Document type:** *Monographic series, Academic/Scholarly.*
—CCC.
Published by: Social Services Research Group, c/o Jackie Watson, Wolvercott, The Street, Swannington, Norfolk NR9 5NW, United Kingdom. TEL 44-1603-261951, webmaster@ssrg.org.uk, http://www.ssrg.org.uk/.

360 GBR ISSN 0307-093X
HV245
SOCIAL SERVICES YEARBOOK. Text in English. 1972. a. GBP 135 per issue (effective 2009). **Document type:** *Directory, Trade.* **Description:** Provides contact details of all statutory and non-statutory social services related organizations in the UK.
—BLDSC (8318.206000).
Published by: Pearson Education Limited (Subsidiary of: Pearson plc), Edinburgh Gate, Harlow, Essex CM20 2JE, United Kingdom. TEL 44-1279-623623, FAX 44-870-8505255, enq.orders@pearson.com.

362.948 DNK ISSN 1395-7546
HD7198
SOCIAL TRYGHED I DE NORDISKE LANDE/SOCIAL TRYGGHET I DE NORDISKA LAENDERNA/SOSIAL TRYGGHET I DE NORDISKE LAND; omfang, udgifter og finansiering. Text in Danish, Norwegian, Swedish. 1965. a. price varies. stat. back issues avail. **Document type:** *Government.*
Related titles: Online - full text ed.; ◆ English ed.: Social Protection in the Nordic Countries. ISSN 1397-6893; ◆ Series of: Nordisk Socialstatistisk Komite. ISSN 1395-7562.
Published by: Nordisk Socialstatistisk Komite/Nordic Social-Statistical Committee, Islands Brygge 67, Copenhagen S, 2300, Denmark. TEL 45-72-227625, FAX 45-32-955470, mail@nom-nos.dk, http://www.nom-nos.dk. Ed. Johannes Nielsen.

360 IND ISSN 0037-8038
HV1
SOCIAL WELFARE. Text in English, Hindi. 1954. m. INR 100 domestic; INR 400, USD 14 SAARC; INR 1,200, USD 40 elsewhere; INR 10 newsstand/cover (effective 2011). bk.rev. bibl.; charts; illus. **Document type:** *Magazine, Consumer.* **Description:** Contains articles on women and child development, welfare services, sociology and anthropology.
Indexed: BAS, F09, G10, P30, PAA&I, RASB, W09, WBSS.
—BLDSC (8318.219800), IE, Infotrieve, Ingenta.
Published by: Central Social Welfare Board, B-12, Qutub Institutional Area, Durgabai Deshmukh Samaj Kalyan Bhawan, New Delhi, Delhi 110016, India. cswb_1@yahoo.co.in. **Subscr. to:** I N S I O Scientific Books & Periodicals.

360 USA ISSN 1937-3295
HV85
SOCIAL WELFARE: FIGHTING POVERTY AND HOMELESSNESS. Text in English. 2007. biennial, latest 2009. USD 55 per issue (effective 2010). back issues avail. **Document type:** *Directory, Academic/Scholarly.* **Description:** Provides statistical data on 32 of today's controversial and studied social issues.
Formed by the merger of (1984-2007): Social Welfare. Help or Hindrance (1532-1177); (1989-2007): Homeless in America, How Could it Happen Here (1536-5204)
Published by: Gale (Subsidiary of: Cengage Learning), 27500 Drake Rd, Farmington Hills, MI 48331. TEL 248-699-4253, 800-877-4253, FAX 877-363-4253, gale.customerservice@cengage.com.

360 ZAF ISSN 0037-8054
➤ **SOCIAL WORK/MAATSKAPLIKE WERK**; a professional journal for the social worker. Text in Afrikaans, English; Summaries in English. 1965. q. ZAR 120 domestic to individuals; USD 250 foreign to individuals; ZAR 300 domestic to institutions; USD 300 foreign to institutions (effective 2003). adv. bk.rev. abstr.; bibl. index. 100 p./no.; back issues avail. **Document type:** *Journal, Academic/Scholarly.* **Description:** A professional journal for social workers.
Related titles: Online - full text ed.
Indexed: CA, ChPerI, GEOBASE, ISAP, S02, S03, SCOPUS, SOPODA, SSA, SociolAb, T02.
—BLDSC (8318.223100), IE, Ingenta.
Published by: Universiteit Stellenbosch, Department of Social Work/Stellenbosch University, PO Box 223, Stellenbosch, 7599, South Africa. TEL 27-21-8082070, FAX 27-21-8083765. Ed., R&P Sulina Green. Adv. contact Hester Uys. page ZAR 750. Circ: 2,000.

360 USA ISSN 0037-8046
HV1 CODEN: SOWOA
➤ **SOCIAL WORK.** Text in English. 1956. q. EUR 133 in Europe to institutions; USD 169 in US & Canada to institutions; GBP 89 to institutions in the UK & elsewhere; EUR 141 combined subscription in Europe to institutions (print & online eds.); USD 178 combined subscription in US & Canada to institutions (print & online eds.); GBP 93 combined subscription to institutions in the UK & elsewhere; (print & online eds.) (effective 2012). adv. bk.rev. illus. index. back issues avail.; reprints avail. **Document type:** *Journal, Academic/Scholarly.* **Description:** Includes scholarly research, critical analyses of the profession and current information on social issues.
Related titles: Microform ed.: (from PQC); Online - full text ed.: ISSN 1545-6846. EUR 110 in Europe to institutions; USD 139 in US & Canada to institutions; GBP 73 to institutions in the UK & elsewhere (effective 2012) (from IngentaConnect).
Indexed: A01, A02, A03, A08, A20, A22, A25, A26, AHCMS, ASCA, ASG, AbAn, AcaI, AgeL, AmH&L, B04, BRD, C06, C07, C08, C11, C12, C28, CA, CBRI, CINAHL, CJA, CMM, CPE, Chicano, CurCont, E-psyche, E02, E03, E07, E08, ECER, EMBASE, ERA, ERI, ERIC, EdA, EdI, ExcerpMed, F09, FamI, G05, G06, G07, G08, H01, H02, H04, H09, H11, H12, HRA, HospLI, I05, I07, IndMed, M01, M02, MASUSE, MEA&I, MEDLINE, P02, P03, P06, P07, P10, P13, P18, P19, P20, P22, P24, P25, P27, P30, P34, P43, P46, P48, P50, P53, P54, PAA&I, PAIS, PCI, PQC, PSI, PsycInfo, PsycholAb, RASB, RehabLit, S02, S03, S05, S08, S09, S11, S21, S23, SCOPUS, SFSA, SOPODA, SSA, SSAI, SSAb, SSCI, SSI, SWR&A, SociolAb, T02, V&AA, W01, W02, W03, W07, W09, WBSS.
—BLDSC (8318.221100), GNLM, IE, Infotrieve, Ingenta. **CCC.**
Published by: (National Association of Social Workers), Oxford University Press (Subsidiary of: Oxford University Press), 2001 Evans Rd, Cary, NC 27513. TEL 919-677-0977, FAX 919-677-1303, jnlorders@oup-usa.org, http://www.oxfordjournals.org. Ed. Elizabeth Pomeroy. adv.: B&W page USD 1,465. Circ: 151,000 (paid and free).

➤ **SOCIAL WORK AND CHRISTIANITY.** *see* RELIGIONS AND THEOLOGY

360 GBR ISSN 0953-5225
HV1 CODEN: SWSREN
➤ **SOCIAL WORK AND SOCIAL SCIENCES REVIEW**; an internal journal of applied research. Text in English. 1989. 3/yr. GBP 35 in Europe to individuals; USD 60 in North America to individuals; GBP 40 elsewhere to individuals; GBP 75 in Europe to institutions; USD 125 in North Africa to institutions; GBP 80 elsewhere to institutions; GBP 165 combined subscription in Europe to libraries (print & online eds.); USD 250 combined subscription in North America to libraries (print & online eds.); GBP 170 combined subscription elsewhere to libraries (print & online eds.) (effective 2009). adv. bk.rev. back issues avail. **Document type:** *Journal, Academic/Scholarly.* **Description:** Sets out to reinforce and expand the links between social work practice and the various disciplines which inform it. It is aimed at fully committed professionals whether practising in the agencies themselves or in teaching or research in universities and colleges.
Related titles: Online - full text ed.: ISSN 1746-6105 (from IngentaConnect).
Indexed: A22, ASCA, ASSIA, B28, CA, CJA, DIP, E-psyche, FamI, IBR, IBSS, IBZ, P03, PsycInfo, PsycholAb, S02, S03, SCOPUS, SOPODA, SSA, SWR&A, SociolAb, T02.
—BLDSC (8318.223400), IE, Ingenta, INIST. **CCC.**
Published by: Whiting & Birch Ltd., 90 Dartmouth Rd, London, SE23 3NZ, United Kingdom. TEL 44-20-82442421, FAX 44-20-82442448, enquiries@whitingbirch.net. Ed. Carol Lewis.

360 DEU ISSN 1613-8953
HV10.5
➤ **SOCIAL WORK AND SOCIETY.** Text in English, German. 2003. 3/yr. free (effective 2011). **Document type:** *Journal, Academic/Scholarly.* **Description:** Dedicated to critical analysis of the relationship between social work, social policy, the state and economic forces.
Media: Online - full text.
Indexed: SCOPUS, SSA, SociolAb.
—CCC.
Published by: Di P P - N R W, Juelicher Str 6, Cologne, 50674, Germany. TEL 49-221-400750, FAX 49-221-40075180, dipp@hbz-nrw.de, http://www.dipp.nrw.de.

360 GBR ISSN 0261-5479
➤ **SOCIAL WORK EDUCATION**; a journal for education and training in local authority. Text in English. 1980. 8/yr. GBP 957 combined subscription in United Kingdom to institutions (print & online eds.); EUR 1,276, USD 1,602 combined subscription to institutions (print & online eds.) (effective 2012). adv. index. back issues avail.; reprint service avail. from PSC. **Document type:** *Journal, Academic/Scholarly.* **Description:** Covers social work education and training.
Incorporates (1981-1999): Issues in Social Work Education (0261-4154)
Related titles: Online - full text ed.: ISSN 1470-1227. GBP 861 in United Kingdom to institutions; EUR 1,148, USD 1,442 to institutions (effective 2012) (from IngentaConnect).
Indexed: A01, A02, A03, A08, A10, A22, ASSIA, B21, B29, CA, CJA, CPE, DIP, E01, E03, E17, ERI, ESPM, FR, IBR, IBZ, P03, P04, P34, PsycInfo, S02, S03, SCOPUS, SOPODA, SSA, SWR&A, SociolAb, T02, V03.
—IE, Infotrieve, Ingenta, INIST. **CCC.**
Published by: Routledge (Subsidiary of: Taylor & Francis Group), 4 Park Sq, Milton Park, Abingdon, Oxon OX14 4RN, United Kingdom. TEL 44-20-70176000, FAX 44-20-70176336, subscriptions@tandf.co.uk, http://www.routledge.com. Eds. Richard Perry, Viviene Cree. Adv. contact Linda Hann TEL 44-1344-779945. **Subscr. to:** Taylor & Francis Ltd., Journals Customer Service, Sheepen Pl, Colchester, Essex CO3 3LP, United Kingdom. TEL 44-20-70175544, FAX 44-20-70175198; **Subscr. to:** Taylor & Francis Inc., Customer Services Dept, 325 Chestnut St, 8th Fl, Philadelphia, PA 19106. TEL 215-625-8900, 800-354-1420, FAX 215-625-2940, customerservice@taylorandfrancis.com.

360 296 USA ISSN 1536-691X
HV3190 CODEN: DSYYAD
➤ **SOCIAL WORK FORUM.** Text in English. 1963. a., latest vol.35. free (effective 2011). adv. bk.rev. charts. back issues avail. **Document type:** *Journal, Academic/Scholarly.* **Description:** Deals with social work issues.
Formerly (until 1999): The Jewish Social Work Forum (0021-6712)
Related titles: Online - full text ed.
Indexed: A10, CA, MEA&I, PAIS, S02, S03, SCOPUS, SOPODA, SSA, SWR&A, SociolAb, T02, V03.
Published by: Yeshiva University, Wurzweiler School of Social Work, 2495 Amsterdam Ave, New York, NY 10033. TEL 212-960-0800, wssw@yu.edu. Eds. Daniel Pollack TEL 212-960-0836, Eric Levine TEL 212-463-0400 ext 5195.

S

361 GBR
SOCIAL WORK IN A CHANGING WORLD. Text in English. irreg. GBP 12.95 per issue. **Description:** Investigates social work in a post-modern, post-industrial and post-communist world. Contributors emphasize the positive contribution of social work to society and provide a critical assessment of its activities. Written by educators, researchers and practitioners from ten countries.
Published by: (British Association of Social Workers), Venture Press, 16 Kent St, Birmingham, Warks B5 6RD, United Kingdom. TEL 44-121-622-3911, FAX 44-121-622-4860. Ed. Shulamit Ramon.

360 362 USA ISSN 0098-1389
HV687.A2 CODEN: SWHCDO
➤ **SOCIAL WORK IN HEALTH CARE.** Abbreviated title: S W H C. Text in English. 1975. 8/yr. GBP 1,055 combined subscription in United Kingdom to institutions (print & online eds.); EUR 1,372, USD 1,386 combined subscription to institutions (print & online eds.) (effective 2012). adv. bk.rev. abstr.; charts; illus. 120 p./no.; back issues avail.; reprint service avail. from PSC. **Document type:** *Journal, Academic/Scholarly.* **Description:** Deals with social work, theory, practice, and administration in a wide variety of health care settings.
Related titles: Microfiche ed.: (from PQC); Microform ed.; Online - full text ed.: ISSN 1541-034X. GBP 950 in United Kingdom to institutions; EUR 1,234, USD 1,248 to institutions (effective 2012).
Indexed: A01, A02, A03, A08, A20, A22, AHCMS, AMHA, ASCA, ASG, ASSIA, AgeL, BehAb, C06, C07, C08, CA, CINAHL, CMM, CPLI, Chicano, CurCont, DIP, E-psyche, E01, EMBASE, ExcerpMed, F09, FamI, H05, HRA, HospAb, IBR, IBZ, INI, IndMed, M01, M02, MCR, MEDLINE, P02, P03, P10, P30, P34, P48, P53, P54, PQC, PSI, PsycInfo, PsycholAb, R10, Reac, RefZh, RehabLit, S02, S03, S11, SCOPUS, SFSA, SOPODA, SSA, SSCI, SWR&A, SociolAb, T02, W07, W09.

—BLDSC (8318.225600), GNLM, IE, Infotrieve, Ingenta. **CCC.**
Published by: Routledge (Subsidiary of: Taylor & Francis Group), 325 Chestnut St, Ste 800, Philadelphia, PA 19106. TEL 215-625-8900, FAX 215-625-8914, journals@routledge.com, http://www.routledge.com. Ed. Gary Rosenberg.

362.2 USA ISSN 1533-2985
HV689
➤ **SOCIAL WORK IN MENTAL HEALTH**; the journal of behavioral and psychiatric social work. Text in English. 2002. bi-m. GBP 454 combined subscription in United Kingdom to institutions (print & online eds.); EUR 592, USD 600 combined subscription to institutions (print & online eds.) (effective 2012). adv. back issues avail.; reprint service avail. from PSC. **Document type:** *Journal, Academic/Scholarly.* **Description:** Provides quality articles on clinical practice, education, research, collaborative relationships, mental health policy, and the delivery of mental health care services.
Related titles: Online - full text ed.: ISSN 1533-2993. 2002. GBP 409 in United Kingdom to institutions; EUR 532, USD 540 to institutions (effective 2012).
Indexed: A01, A03, A22, AgeL, C06, C07, C08, CA, CINAHL, DIP, E01, Faml, IBR, IBZ, M02, P03, P30, PsycInfo, S02, S03, SCOPUS, SSA, SWR&A, SociolAb, T02.
—BLDSC (8318.225980), IE, Ingenta, INIST. **CCC.**
Published by: Routledge (Subsidiary of: Taylor & Francis Group), 270 Madison Ave, New York, NY 10016. TEL 212-216-7800, FAX 212-244-1563, journals@routledge.com, http://www.routledge.com. Eds. Andrew Weissman, Gary Rosenberg.

360 614.8 USA ISSN 1937-1918
RA418
➤ **SOCIAL WORK IN PUBLIC HEALTH.** Abbreviated title: J H S P. Text in English. 1989. bi-m. GBP 710 combined subscription in United Kingdom to institutions (print & online eds.); EUR 924, USD 928 combined subscription to institutions (print & online eds.) (effective 2012). adv. bk.rev. illus. 120 p./no. 1 cols./p.; back issues avail.; reprint service avail. from PSC. **Document type:** *Journal, Academic/Scholarly.* **Description:** Addresses health and social policy issues, concerns, and questions.
Formerly (until 2008): Journal of Health & Social Policy (0897-7186)
Related titles: Microfiche ed.: (from PQC); Microform ed.; Online - full text ed.: ISSN 1937-190X. GBP 640 in United Kingdom to institutions; EUR 831, USD 835 to institutions (effective 2012).
Indexed: A01, A03, A08, A10, A22, A34, A35, A36, AbAn, AgeL, C06, C07, CA, CABA, DIP, E-psyche, E01, E03, E12, EMBASE, ERI, ExcerpMed, F09, Faml, GEOBASE, GH, H05, I13, IBR, IBZ, INI, L01, L02, M02, MEDLINE, N02, N03, P30, P34, P42, PAIS, PEI, PsycholAb, R12, S02, S03, SCOPUS, SOPODA, SPAA, SSA, SWR&A, SociolAb, T02, T05, THA, V03, W11.
—BLDSC (8318.225930), GNLM, IE, Infotrieve, Ingenta. **CCC.**
Published by: Routledge (Subsidiary of: Taylor & Francis Group), 325 Chestnut St, Ste 800, Philadelphia, PA 19106. TEL 215-625-8900, 800-354-1420, FAX 215-625-8914, journals@routledge.com, http://www.routledge.com. Eds. Dr. Marvin D Feit, Stanley F Battle. adv.: B&W page USD 315, color page USD 550; trim 4.375 x 7.125. Circ: 172 (paid).

360 GBR ISSN 1363-0059
SOCIAL WORK MONOGRAPHS. Text in English. 1982. irreg. **Document type:** *Monographic series.*
—IE, Ingenta. **CCC.**
Published by: University of East Anglia, School of Economic and Social Studies, School of Economics, Norwich, NR4 7TJ, United Kingdom. TEL 44-1603-456161, FAX 44-1603-458553, g.neff@uea.ac.uk, http://www.uea.ac.uk/menu/acad_depts/soc/.

362.70993 NZL ISSN 1173-4906
HV802.5
SOCIAL WORK NOW; the practice journal of child, youth and family. Text in English. 1995. 3/yr. free (effective 2011). **Document type:** *Journal, Trade.* **Description:** Focuses on social work practice and theory as it relates to children, young people and families.
Related titles: Online - full text ed.: ISSN 1177-7192.
Indexed: S02, S03.
—CCC.
Published by: Child, Youth and Family, PO Box 2620, Wellington, New Zealand. TEL 64-4-9189100. Ed. Bronwyn Bannister.

649 360 GBR ISSN 2044-9577
▼ **SOCIAL WORK NOW.** Text in English. 2010. m. (10/yr.). free (effective 2010); included subscr. with Children & Young People Now. adv. **Document type:** *Magazine, Consumer.* **Description:** Contains insight on practice, career development, a news round-up and expert comment and advice.
Published by: Haymarket Publishing Ltd. (Subsidiary of: Haymarket Media Group), West Coast Labs, Unit 9 Oak Tree Ct, Mulberry Dr, Cardiff Gate Business Park, Cardiff, CF23 8RS, United Kingdom. TEL 44-29-20548400, sales@westcoast.com. Ed. Jo Stephenson.

360 ZAF
SOCIAL WORK PRACTICE. Text and summaries in English. 1983. 3/yr. free. bk.rev. cum.index: 1983-1994. **Document type:** *Government.* **Description:** Devoted to enhancing the professionalism of social workers.
Indexed: ISAP.
Published by: Department of Welfare/Departement van Welsyn, Private Bag X901, Pretoria, 0001, South Africa. TEL 27-12-3127648, FAX 27-12-3242647, TELEX 321366. Ed. Marisa Manley. Circ: 4,500.

361.3 USA ISSN 8756-5013
SOCIAL WORK PRACTICE MONOGRAPH SERIES. Key Title: Practice Monograph Series. Text in English. 1985. irreg., latest vol.3, 1987. price varies. back issues avail. **Document type:** *Monographic series, Academic/Scholarly.*
Formerly: North American Association of Christians in Social Work. Practice Monograph Series
Published by: North American Association of Christians in Social Work, PO Box 121, Botsford, CT 06404. TEL 888-426-4712, FAX 888-426-4712, info@nacsw.org.

360 USA ISSN 1070-5309
HV1
➤ **SOCIAL WORK RESEARCH.** Text in English. 1977. q. EUR 118 in Europe to institutions; USD 149 in US & Canada to institutions; GBP 78 to institutions in the UK & elsewhere; EUR 128 combined subscription in Europe to institutions (print & online eds.); USD 163 combined subscription in US & Canada to institutions (print & online eds.); GBP 85 combined subscription to institutions in the UK & elsewhere; (print & online eds.) (effective 2012). adv. illus. index. back issues avail.; reprints avail. **Document type:** *Journal, Academic/Scholarly.* **Description:** Covers new technology, strategies and methods, and results of research and evaluation.
Supersedes in part (in 1994): Social Work Research and Abstracts (0148-0847); Which was formerly (until 1977): Abstracts for Social Workers (0001-3412)
Related titles: Microform ed.: (from PQC); Online - full text ed.: ISSN 1545-6838. EUR 107 in Europe to institutions; USD 135 in US & Canada to institutions; GBP 71 to institutions in the UK & elsewhere (effective 2012) (from IngentaConnect).
Indexed: A01, A02, A03, A08, A20, A22, A26, ASCA, ASG, AbAn, B04, BRD, C06, C07, C08, C11, C12, CA, CINAHL, CJA, CurCont, E-psyche, E02, E03, E07, E08, ERA, ERI, ERIC, EdA, EdI, Faml, G08, H01, H02, H04, H12, I05, M01, M02, P03, P10, P18, P19, P24, P25, P27, P30, P34, P43, P46, P48, P50, P53, P54, PQC, PsycInfo, PsycholAb, S02, S03, S09, S11, SCOPUS, SSA, SSAI, SSAb, SSCI, SSI, SWR&A, SociolAb, T02, V&AA, W03, W07.
—BLDSC (8318.229800), IE, Infotrieve, Ingenta. **CCC.**
Published by: (National Association of Social Workers), Oxford University Press (Subsidiary of: Oxford University Press), 2001 Evans Rd, Cary, NC 27513. TEL 919-677-0977, FAX 919-677-1303, jnlorders@oup-usa.org, http://www.oxfordjournals.org. Ed. Matthew Howard. adv.: B&W page USD 465. Circ: 3,000 (paid).

360 GBR
SOCIAL WORK RESEARCH CENTRE. RESEARCH REPORTS. Text in English. irreg., latest vol.33, 1994. GBP 3 (effective 2000). **Document type:** *Monographic series.*
Published by: University of Stirling, Social Work Research Centre, University Of Stirling, Stirling, FK9 4LA, United Kingdom. TEL 44-1786-67724, FAX 44-1786-466319, g.c.mcivor@stir.ac.uk.

360 GBR
SOCIAL WORK RESEARCH CENTRE. WORKING PAPERS. Text in English. 1986. irreg., latest vol.21, 1990. GBP 2 (effective 2000). **Document type:** *Monographic series.*
Published by: University of Stirling, Social Work Research Centre, University Of Stirling, Stirling, FK9 4LA, United Kingdom. TEL 44-1786-67724, FAX 44-1786-466319, g.c.mcivor@stir.ac.uk.

360 GBR
SOCIAL WORK SERVICES GROUP. COMMUNITY SERVICE. Text in English. 1981. a. GBP 2. **Document type:** *Bulletin, Government.*
Published by: Social Work Services Group, Statistics Branch, Rm 52, James Craig Walk, Edinburgh, EH1 3BA, United Kingdom. TEL 44-131-244-5431, FAX 44-131-244-5315. **Dist. by:** Her Majesty's Stationery Office Bookshop, 71 Lothian Rd, EH3 9AZ, Edinburgh, Midlothian EH3 9AZ, United Kingdom. TEL 44-131-228-4181.

360 USA ISSN 1540-420X
SOCIAL WORK TODAY. Abbreviated title: S W T. Text in English. 2001 (Aug.). bi-m. USD 14.99 domestic; USD 30 in Canada; USD 47 elsewhere (effective 2011). adv. back issues avail.; reprints avail. **Document type:** *Magazine, Trade.* **Description:** Provides features, departments, and columns on clinical issues, healthcare trends, and professional practices that will both interest and educate readers.
Related titles: Online - full text ed.: free (effective 2010).
Indexed: A10, V03.
Published by: Great Valley Publishing Company, Inc., 3801 Schuylkill Rd, Spring City, PA 19475. TEL 610-948-9500, 800-278-4400, FAX 610-948-4202, Sales@gvpub.com, http://www.gvpub.com. Ed. Marianne Mallon. Pub., Adv. contact Mara E Honicker. Circ: 30,000.

362.8 USA ISSN 0160-9513
HV45 CODEN: SWGRDU
➤ **SOCIAL WORK WITH GROUPS**; a journal of community and clinical practice. Abbreviated title: S W G. Text in English. 1978. q. GBP 621 combined subscription in United Kingdom to institutions (print & online eds.); EUR 805, USD 810 combined subscription to institutions (print & online eds.) (effective 2012). adv. bk.rev. bibl.; illus. back issues avail.; reprint service avail. from PSC. **Document type:** *Journal, Academic/Scholarly.* **Description:** Covers the areas of groupwork in psychiatric, rehabilitative, and multipurpose social work and social services agencies.
Related titles: Microfiche ed.: (from PQC); Microform ed.; Online - full text ed.: ISSN 1540-9481. GBP 558 in United Kingdom to institutions; EUR 725, USD 729 to institutions (effective 2012); Supplement(s): Journal of Social Work with Groups. Monographic Supplement. ISSN 0897-8441.
Indexed: A01, A02, A03, A08, A10, A20, A22, A25, A26, AMHA, ASCA, ASSIA, B04, B21, BRD, C06, C07, C08, C28, CA, CINAHL, ChPerl, DIP, E-psyche, E01, E08, E17, ESPM, F09, Faml, G08, GSS&RPL, H12, I05, IBR, IBZ, P02, P03, P10, P24, P27, P30, P48, P53, P54, PQC, PsycInfo, PsycholAb, S02, S03, S08, S09, S11, S21, SCOPUS, SOPODA, SSA, SSAI, SSAb, SSI, SWR&A, SociolAb, T02, V03, W03, W09.
—BLDSC (8318.225000), IE, Infotrieve, Ingenta, INIST. **CCC.**
Published by: Routledge (Subsidiary of: Taylor & Francis Group), 270 Madison Ave, New York, NY 10016. TEL 212-216-7800, FAX 212-244-1563, journals@routledge.com, http://www.routledge.com. Ed. Andrew Malekoff.

362.6 NLD ISSN 1879-9493
▼ **SOCIALE KAART OUDERENZORG.** Text in Dutch. 2009. a. EUR 57.50 (effective 2010).
Published by: Bohn Stafleu van Loghum B.V. (Subsidiary of: Springer Science+Business Media), Postbus 246, Houten, 3990 GA, Netherlands. TEL 31-30-6383736, FAX 31-30-6383999, boekhandels@bsl.nl, http://www.bsl.nl.

362 NLD ISSN 1570-3606
DE SOCIALE STAAT VAN NEDERLAND. Text in Dutch. 1985. biennial. price varies.
Formerly (until 2001): Sociale en Culturele Verkenningen (0927-0736)
Related titles: Online - full text ed.: ISSN 1569-4720.
Published by: Sociaal en Cultureel Planbureau/Social and Cultural Planning Office, Postbus 16164, The Hague, 2500 BD, Netherlands. TEL 31-70-3407000, FAX 31-70-3407044, info@scp.nl.

360 SWE ISSN 0037-8100
SOCIALFOERFATTNINGAR. Text in Swedish. 1957. 20/yr. SEK 1,550. adv. charts. index. **Document type:** *Newsletter.*
Published by: Foerlagshuset Gothia AB, Goetgatan 22 A, PO Box15169, Stockholm, 10465, Sweden. info.gothia@verbum.se, http://www.gothia.verbum.se. Ed. Karl Aake Claesson. R&P Olle Sundlinj. Circ: 1,300.

SOCIALISM AND HEALTH. *see* PUBLIC HEALTH AND SAFETY

SOCIALMEDICINSK TIDSKRIFT. *see* MEDICAL SCIENCES

364 SVK ISSN 1336-8915
SOCIALNA A CHARITATIVNA SLUZBA. Text in Slovak. 2006. s-a. **Document type:** *Journal, Academic/Scholarly.*
Published by: Presovska Univerzita, Pravoslavna Bohoslovecka Fakulta, Ul Masarykova c 15, Presov, 080 01, Slovakia. TEL 421-51-7724729, http://www.unipo.sk/pbf/index.php.

364 SVK ISSN 1336-9679
SOCIALNA PREVENCIA. Text in Slovak. 2006. q. **Document type:** *Magazine, Consumer.*
Published by: Narodne Osvetove Centrum, Nam. SNP 12, Bratislava, 81234, Slovakia. TEL 421-918-716018, FAX 421-2-52922875, nocka@nocka.sk. Ed. Ingrid Hupkova.

360 305.4 301 SVN ISSN 0352-7956
➤ **SOCIALNO DELO/SOCIAL WORK.** Text in Slovenian, English. 1961. bi-m. EUR 36.22 to individuals; EUR 63.39 to institutions (effective 2007). bk.rev. charts; illus.; abstr.; stat.; tr.lit. 70 p./no. 2 cols./p.; back issues avail. **Document type:** *Journal, Academic/Scholarly.* **Description:** Serves professionals, researchers and policy-makers in social work and related services.
Indexed: CA, DIP, IBR, IBSS, IBZ, S02, S03, S21, SCOPUS, SSA, SWR&A, SociolAb, T02.
—BLDSC (8318.426500).
Published by: (Republic of Slovenia, Ministry of Science and Technology USA), Univerza v Ljubljani, Fakulteta za Socialno Delo/University of Ljubljana, Department of Social Work, Topniska 31, Ljubljana, 1000, Slovenia. TEL 386-1-2809260, FAX 386-1-2809270. Ed. Bogdan Lesnik. Pub. Vito Flaker. Circ: 750.

360 372.21 DNK ISSN 0105-5399
SOCIALPAEDAGOGEN. Text in Danish. 1944 (vol.24). fortn. DKK 843 membership; DKK 37 per issue (effective 2009). adv. 4 cols./p.; **Document type:** *Magazine, Trade.*
Former titles (until 1967): Boernesagspaedagogen (0901-4667); (until 1961): Boernesagsarbejderen (0901-4659); Incorporates (1979-1980): Socialpaedagogen Aap-Bladet (0106-9195); Incorporates (1976-1980): Aap-Bladet (0105-9092)
Related titles: Online - full text ed.
Published by: Socialpaedagogernes Landsforbund/National Federation of Social Educators, Brolaeggerstraede 9, Copenhagen K, 1211, Denmark. TEL 45-72-486000, sl@sl.dk, http://www.sl.dk. Ed. Lone Marie Pedersen TEL 45-33-962926. adv.: page DKK 10,624; 198 x 271.

320.1 SWE ISSN 1104-6376
SOCIALPOLITIK. Text in Swedish. 1994. 4/yr. SEK 390 domestic; SEK 559 foreign; SEK 189 to students; SEK 79 per issue (effective 2011). adv. bk.rev. **Document type:** *Magazine, Consumer.*
Related titles: Online - full text ed.
Published by: Foereningen Socialpolitisk Debatt, c/o Maria Wallin, Eriksberg 137, Udevalla, 45196, Sweden. TEL 46-70-2072222. Ed. Maria Wallin. Adv. contact Efva Bengtsson Ahlstroem TEL 46-8-103920.

361 DNK ISSN 0108-6103
SOCIALRAADGIVEREN. Text in Danish. 1938. 21/yr. DKK 600 (effective 2009). adv. bk.rev. **Document type:** *Magazine, Trade.*
Incorporates (1970-1980): Socialraadgiveren, A, Meddelelser fra Dansk Socialraadgiverforening (0108-8742)
Related titles: ◆ Includes: Uden for Nummer. ISSN 1600-888X.
Published by: Dansk Socialraadgiverforening/Danish Association of Social Workers, Toldbodgade 19 A, PO Box 69, Copenhagen K, 1003, Denmark. TEL 45-70-101099, FAX 45-33-913069, ds@sovialrdg.dk. Ed. Mette Ellegaard. Circ: 13,382.

360 SWE ISSN 1104-1420
➤ **SOCIALVETENSKAPLIG TIDSKRIFT.** Text in Swedish; Summaries in English. 1994. q. SEK 175 domestic to individuals; SEK 210 in Scandinavia to individuals; SEK 220 elsewhere to individuals; SEK 375 domestic to institutions; SEK 410 in Scandinavia to institutions; SEK 420 elsewhere to institutions; SEK 110 per issue (effective 2010). adv. back issues avail. **Document type:** *Journal, Academic/Scholarly.*
Published by: Foerbundet foer Forskning i Socialt Arbete/Swedish Association for Social Work Research, Vingavaegen 3H, Vaexjoe, 35263, Sweden. http://www.forsa.nu. Eds. Stefan Sjoestroem TEL 46-90-7867797, Stina Johansson TEL 46-90-7865425. adv.: page SEK 4,000. Circ: 1,400.

360 ITA
SOCIETA ECONOMICA DI CHIAVARI. ATTI. Text in Italian. 1791. biennial. back issues avail. **Document type:** *Bulletin, Corporate.* **Description:** Presents information on the society's activities, news of the library, museum, gallery, demonstrations, scholarships and prizes.
Published by: Societa Economica di Chiavari http://www.societaeconomica.it. Circ: (controlled).

▼ **SOCIETY AND MENTAL HEALTH.** *see* MEDICAL SCIENCES—Psychiatry And Neurology

360 ISR ISSN 0334-4029
SOCIETY AND WELFARE/HEVRA U-REVAHA; quarterly for social work. Text in Hebrew, English. 1978. irreg. ILS 20, USD 15. bk.rev.
Related titles: Online - full text ed.
Indexed: IBSS, IHP.
Published by: Ministry of Labour and Social Affairs, P O Box 1260, Jerusalem, 91000, Israel. TEL 972-2-6719081. Ed. Dr. Shimon Spiro.

360 USA ISSN 1948-822X
HV11
▼ ➤ **SOCIETY FOR SOCIAL WORK AND RESEARCH. JOURNAL.** Text in English. 2009. irreg. free (effective 2011). **Document type:** *Journal, Academic/Scholarly.* **Description:** Features research related to social problems and the effectiveness of social programs and policies.
Media: Online - full text.

Published by: Society for Social Work and Research, 11240 Waples Mill Rd, Ste 200, Fairfax, VA 22030. TEL 703-352-7797, FAX 703-359-7562, info@sswr.org, http://www.sswr.org/.

➤ **SOCIOECONOMIC REPORT.** *see* BUSINESS AND ECONOMICS—Economic Situation And Conditions

361 FRA ISSN 1297-6628
LE SOCIOGRAPHE. Text in French. 1999. 3/yr.
Related titles: Online - full text ed.: ISSN 2107-0636. 200?; Supplement(s): Le Sociographe. Hors-serie. ISSN 1779-3629. 2004; Le Sociographe. Congres & Colloques. ISSN 2101-2121. 2007.
Published by: Institut Regional du Travail Social, 1011 Rue du Pont de Laverune, Montpellier Cedex 3, 70022, France. TEL 33-4-67070230, FAX 33-4-67472846, contactmontpellier@irts-lr.fr, http://www.irts-lr.fr.

301 DEU ISSN 0038-0164
HM1.A1
SOCIOLOGIA INTERNATIONALIS; internationale Zeitschrift fuer Soziologie, Kommunikations- und Kulturforschung. Text in English, French, German, Spanish; Summaries in English. 1963. s-a. EUR 104 combined subscription to individuals (print & online eds.); EUR 188 combined subscription to institutions (print & online eds.); EUR 68 newsstand/cover (effective 2012). adv. bk.rev. **Document type:** *Journal, Academic/Scholarly.*
Related titles: Online - full text ed.: ISSN 1865-5580. 2008.
Indexed: A22, BAS, CA, DIP, IBR, IBSS, IBZ, P06, P42, PAIS, PCI, PSA, RASB, RILM, S02, S03, SCOPUS, SOPODA, SSA, SociolAb, T02.
—BLDSC (8319.605000), IE, Infotrieve, Ingenta, INIST. **CCC.**
Published by: Duncker und Humblot GmbH, Carl-Heinrich-Becker-Weg 9, Berlin, 12165, Germany. TEL 49-30-7900060, FAX 49-30-79000631, info@duncker-humblot.de. Ed. Clemens Albrecht. Circ: 200 (paid and controlled).

331.105 SWE ISSN 0283-1929
➤ **SOCIONOMEN.** Text in Swedish. 1958. 8/yr. SEK 270 domestic to individuals; SEK 290 in Scandinavia to individuals; SEK 750 to institutions (effective 2010). adv. back issues avail. **Document type:** *Magazine, Trade.*
Supersedes in part (in 1987): S S R Tidningen Socionomen (0282-1001); Which was formerly (until 1984): Socionomen (0038-044X)
Published by: Akademikerfoerbundet SSR, Mariedalsvaegen 4, PO Box 12800, Stockholm, 11296, Sweden. TEL 46-8-6174400, FAX 46-8-6174401, kansli@akademssr.se, http://www.akademssr.se. Ed. Lena Engelmark TEL 46-8-6174437. Adv. contact Robin Zackrisson TEL 46-8-103920. B&W page SEK 17,000, color page SEK 19,700; trim 185 x 249. Circ: 10,500 (paid and controlled).

360 FIN ISSN 1238-0814
SOCIUS/SOCIAL REVIEW. Text in Finnish; Summaries in English, Swedish. 1918. 6/yr. **Document type:** *Government.* **Description:** Problems of public health, social welfare, social security and occupational health.
Formerly (until 1995): Sosiaalinen Aikakauskirja (0038-1594)
Related titles: Online - full text ed.; ◆ English ed.: Socius Finland. ISSN 1238-4569.
Published by: Sosiaali- ja Terveysministerio/Ministry of Social Affairs and Health, Meritullinkatu 8, PO Box 33, Helsinki, 00171, Finland. TEL 358-9-1601, FAX 358-9-1602590, kirjaamo.stm@stm.fi, http://www.stm.fi. Ed. Helena Puro. Circ: 3,993.

360 FIN ISSN 1238-4569
SOCIUS FINLAND; international edition. Text in English. 1995. s-a.
Related titles: Online - full text ed.; ◆ Finnish ed.: Socius. ISSN 1238-0814.
Published by: Sosiaali- ja Terveysministerio/Ministry of Social Affairs and Health, Meritullinkatu 8, PO Box 33, Helsinki, 00171, Finland. TEL 358-9-1601, FAX 358-9-1602590, kirjaamo.stm@stm.fi. Ed. Helena Puro.

305.42 FRA ISSN 0338-1757
SOLIDAIRES (PARIS). Text in French. 1956. q. adv. bk.rev. illus. back issues avail. **Document type:** *Newspaper.*
Formerly: Survivre
Published by: (Federation des Associations de Conjoints Survivants), Favec, 28 place Saint Georges, Paris, 75009, France. TEL 33-1-42851830, FAX 33-1-45960106, http://www.favec.asso.fr. Ed. Herve Nicole. Circ: 58,000.

360 TWN ISSN 1026-4493
HV426
SOOCHOW JOURNAL OF SOCIAL WORK. Text in Chinese, English. 1995. a. USD 21. **Document type:** *Journal, Academic/Scholarly.*
Published by: Soochow University, Wai Shuang Hsi, Shih Lin, Taipei, Taiwan. FAX 886-2-8831340.

362.7 NLD ISSN 2210-710X
SOS KINDERDORPEN. Text in Dutch. 1969. 3/yr. **Document type:** *Newspaper, Consumer.*
Former titles (until 2010): SOS Bulletin (1570-4424); (until 1999): SOS Kinderdorpen (1380-5088); (until 1994): 't Kinderdorpkrantje (1380-507X)
Address: Postbus 9104, Amsterdam, 1006 AC, Netherlands. TEL 31-20-4080190, FAX 31-20-6696452, info@soskinderdorpen.nl, http://www.soskinderdorpen.nl.

362.4 FIN ISSN 0049-1349
SOTAINVALIDI. Text in Finnish, Swedish. 1940. 6/yr. EUR 42.50 to members (effective 2005). adv. bk.rev. **Document type:** *Newspaper, Consumer.* **Description:** News for disabled war veterans.
Related titles: Audio cassette/tape ed.: ISSN 1238-6715.
Indexed: RASB.
Published by: Sotainvalidien Veljesliitto/Disabled War Veterans Association of Finland, Kasarmikatu 34 A, Helsinki, 00130, Finland. TEL 358-9-478500, FAX 358-9-47850100. Ed. Juhani Saari. Circ: 37,000 (controlled).

SOTSIALNO OSIGURIAVANE. *see* INSURANCE

361.6 AUS ISSN 1832-8938
SOUTH AUSTRALIA. DEPARTMENT FOR FAMILIES AND COMMUNITIES. ANNUAL REPORT. Text in English. 2002. a. **Document type:** *Government.*
Supersedes in part (in 2005): South Australia. Department of Human Services. Annual Report (Online Edition) (1448-8728)
Media: Online - full text.
Published by: South Australia, Department for Families and Communities, GPO Box 292, Adelaide, SA 5001, Australia. TEL 61-8-82268800, FAX 61-8-84139003, http://www.dfc.sa.gov.au/.

362.7 AUS ISSN 1833-9484
SOUTH AUSTRALIA. OFFICE OF THE GUARDIAN FOR CHILDREN AND YOUNG PEOPLE. ANNUAL REPORT. Text in English. 2005. a. free (effective 2009). back issues avail. **Document type:** *Government.* **Description:** Contains the summary of the activities and achievements of the organisation for the financial year.
Related titles: Online - full text ed.: ISSN 1833-9492.
Published by: South Australia, Office of the Guardian for Children and Young People, GPO Box 2281, Adelaide, SA 5001, Australia. TEL 61-8-82268570, FAX 61-8-82268577, gcyp@saugov.sa.gov.au.

360 AUS ISSN 1033-3177
SOUTH AUSTRALIAN VOLUNTEERING. Text in English. 19??. bi-m. bk.rev. **Document type:** *Newsletter.* **Description:** Focuses on information sharing and raising volunteering issues, policy and practice matters for managing volunteer programs.
Former titles (until 1987): South Australia Volunteering (0816-9594); (until 1984): Volunteer Centre of S A. Newsletter
Published by: Volunteering Australia, 4th Fl, 247-251 Flinders Ln, Melbourne, VIC 3000, Australia. volaus@volunteeringaustralia.org, http://www.volunteeringaustralia.org.

SOUTHEAST ASIAN AFFAIRS. *see* POLITICAL SCIENCE

SOUTHEASTERN VIRGINIA JEWISH NEWS. *see* RELIGIONS AND THEOLOGY—Judaic

300 DEU ISSN 1861-1281
SOZIAL; Magazin fuer Politik, Kirche und Gesellschaft in Baden-Wuerttemberg. Text in German. 2003. q. free (effective 2009). **Document type:** *Magazine, Consumer.*
Formed by the merger of (1998-2003): Haus am Berg Nachrichten (1862-5940); (1998-2003): Bruderhaus Journal (1437-1901); Which was formerly (1949-1998): Das Bruderhaus (0172-0996)
Published by: BruderhausDiakonie, Gustav-Werner-Str 24, Reutlingen, 72762, Germany. TEL 49-7121-278225, FAX 49-7121-278955, info@bruderhausdiakonie.de. Ed. Klara Kohlstadt. Circ: 20,000.

360 AUT ISSN 1019-7729
SOZIALARBEIT IN OESTERREICH. Text in German. 1965. 4/yr. EUR 65.41; EUR 36.34 to students (effective 2005). adv. bk.rev. index. **Document type:** *Magazine, Government.*
Published by: Oesterreichischer Berufsverband Diplomierter SozialarbeiterInnen, Mariahilferstr 81-1-14, Vienna, W 1060, Austria. TEL 43-1-5874656, FAX 43-1-587465610, oesterreich@sozialarbeit.at, http://www.sozialarbeit.at. Ed. Michael Reiter. Adv. contact Christina Kocer. Circ: 3,000.

300 DEU ISSN 1435-8220
SOZIALARBEITERBRIEF. Text in German. 1998. 3/yr. adv. **Document type:** *Journal, Trade.*
Published by: Pflegeverbund Deutschland, Hindenburgstr 41, Bad Liebenzell, 75378, Germany. TEL 49-7052-2025, FAX 49-7052-4415. Ed. Harald Spies. adv.: page EUR 1,100; trim 188 x 256. Circ: 15,000 (controlled).

360 DEU ISSN 1613-8538
SOZIALCOURAGE. Text in German. 1935. q. EUR 12.78 (effective 2009). adv. back issues avail. **Document type:** *Magazine, Consumer.*
Former titles (until 1996): Caritas Aktuell; (until 1972): Die 7 Werke; (until 1963): Caritasruf
Published by: Deutscher Caritasverband e.V., Karlstr 40, Freiburg Im Breisgau, 79104, Germany. TEL 49-761-200229, FAX 49-761-200541, presse@caritas.de, http://www.caritas.de. adv.: B&W page EUR 3,900, color page EUR 6,070. Circ: 169,000 (paid and controlled).

360 DEU ISSN 0490-1606
HV3
SOZIALE ARBEIT; Zeitschrift fuer soziale und sozialverwandte Gebiete. Text in German. 1951. 11/yr. EUR 61.50; EUR 46.50 to students; EUR 6.50 newsstand/cover (effective 2008). adv. bk.rev. abstr.; bibl. 40 p./no.; **Document type:** *Magazine, Trade.*
Indexed: DIP, IBR, IBZ, PCI.
Published by: Deutsches Zentralinstitut fuer soziale Fragen, Bernadottestr 94, Berlin, 14195, Germany. TEL 49-30-8390010, FAX 49-30-8314750, sozialinfo@dzi.de. adv.: B&W page EUR 310. Circ: 750 (paid and controlled).

360 DEU ISSN 1866-931X
SOZIALE ARBEIT (BERLIN). Text in German. 2008. irreg., latest vol.3, 2009. price varies. **Document type:** *Monographic series, Academic/Scholarly.*
Published by: (S R H Hochschule Heidelberg), Logos Verlag Berlin, Comeniushof, Gubener Str 47, Berlin, 10243, Germany. TEL 49-30-42851090, FAX 49-30-42851092, redaktion@logos-verlag.de.

361.6 DEU ISSN 0932-416X
SOZIALE PRAXIS. Text in German. 1981. irreg., latest 2010. price varies. **Document type:** *Monographic series, Academic/Scholarly.*
Formerly (until 1986): I S A Schriftenreihe (0721-9857)
Published by: (Institut fuer Soziale Arbeit e.V.), Waxmann Verlag GmbH, Steinfurter Str 555, Muenster, 48159, Germany. TEL 49-251-265040, FAX 49-251-2650426, info@waxmann.com.

361 DEU ISSN 0490-1630
SOZIALE SICHERHEIT; Zeitschrift fuer Arbeit und Soziales. Text in German. 1952. m. EUR 102; EUR 52.80 to students; EUR 9.50 newsstand/cover (effective 2009). adv. **Document type:** *Journal, Trade.*
Indexed: A22, DIP, IBR, IBZ.
—IE, Infotrieve. **CCC.**
Published by: Bund-Verlag GmbH, Heddernheimer Landstr 144, Frankfurt Am Main, 60439, Germany. TEL 49-69-79501020, FAX 49-69-79501010, kontakt@bund-verlag.de, http://www.bund-verlag.de. Eds. Hans Nakielski, Rolf Winkel. Adv. contact Hartmut Griesbach. page EUR 1,075; trim 180 x 260. Circ: 3,700 (paid and controlled).

SOZIALGESETZBUCH: KINDER- UND JUGENDHILFE. *see* LAW—Civil Law

SOZIALGESETZBUCH: SOZIALHILFE. *see* LAW—Civil Law

SOZIALHILFE- UND ASYLBEWERBERLEISTUNGSRECHT; Aktueller Rechtsprechungs- und Informationsdienst. *see* LAW—International Law

360 DEU ISSN 0340-8469
SOZIALMAGAZIN; die Zeitschrift fuer soziale Arbeit. Text in German. 1976. 11/yr. EUR 58; EUR 46 to students; EUR 6 newsstand/cover (effective 2011). adv. bk.rev. index. 64 p./no.; **Document type:** *Magazine, Trade.*
Indexed: DIP, IBR, IBZ.
—CCC.
Published by: Juventa Verlag GmbH, Ehretstr 3, Weinheim, 69469, Germany. TEL 49-6201-90200, FAX 49-6201-902013, juventa@juventa.de, http://www.juventa.de. Ed. Ria Puhl. Adv. contact Karola Weiss. Circ: 4,000 (paid and controlled).

360 AUT ISSN 1990-732X
SOZIALPOLITISCHE MONOGRAFIEN. Text in German. 1991. irreg., latest vol.35, 2008. price varies. **Document type:** *Monographic series, Academic/Scholarly.*
Published by: Trauner Verlag und Buchservice GmbH, Koeglstr 14, Linz, 4020, Austria. TEL 43-732-778241212, FAX 43-732-778241400, office@trauner.at, http://www.trauner.at.

SOZIALPSYCHIATRISCHE INFORMATIONEN. *see* PSYCHOLOGY

362 DEU ISSN 1434-7261
SOZIALRECHT AKTUELL; Zeitschrift fuer Sozialberatung. Text in German. 1992. 6/yr. EUR 82 (effective 2011). adv. reprint service avail. from SCH. **Document type:** *Magazine, Trade.*
Published by: (Caritas Verband fuer die Dioezese Muenster e.V.), Nomos Verlagsgesellschaft mbH und Co. KG, Waldseestr 3-5, Baden-Baden, 76530, Germany. TEL 49-7221-21040, FAX 49-7221-210427, nomos@nomos.de, http://www.nomos.de. Ed. Peter Frings. Adv. contact Bettina Roos. Circ: 1,400 (controlled).

362 DEU ISSN 0939-401X
SOZIALRECHT & PRAXIS; Fachzeitschrift des VdK Deutschland fuer Vertrauensleute der Behinderten und fuer Sozialpolitiker. Text in German. 1950. m. EUR 25 (effective 2003). 68 p./no. 2 cols./p.; **Document type:** *Bulletin, Consumer.* **Description:** Covers social politics, social law, laws covering pensions, health and accident insurance and other aspects of international social welfare laws.
Former titles: V D K - Mitteilungen Sozialpolitische Fachzeitschrift; V D K - Mitteilungen (0042-1774)
—IE.
Published by: Sozialverband V d K Deutschland, Wurzerstr 4A, Bonn, 53175, Germany. TEL 49-228-82093-0, FAX 49-228-8209343, kontakt@vdk.de, http://www.vdk.de. Ed. Sabine Kohls. R&P Ulrich Laschet. Circ: 6,000.

360 AUT
SOZIALVERSICHERUNG AKTUELL. Text in German. 4/yr. adv. **Document type:** *Magazine, Trade.*
Published by: Oesterreichischer Wirtschaftsverlag GmbH (Subsidiary of: Sueddeutscher Verlag GmbH), Wiedner Hauptstr 120-124, Vienna, W 1051, Austria. TEL 43-1-546640, FAX 43-1-54664406, office@wirtschaftsverlag.at, http://www.wirtschaftsverlag.at. Ed. Gerhard Schumlits. Adv. contact Erhard Witty. color page EUR 8,000; trim 210 x 280. Circ: 450,000 (controlled).

360 DEU ISSN 1613-0707
SOZIALWIRTSCHAFT; Zeitschrift fuer Sozialmanagement. Text in German. 1991. bi-m. EUR 109 (effective 2011). adv. reprint service avail. from SCH. **Document type:** *Magazine, Trade.*
Formerly: Socialmanagement (0939-7027)
Indexed: DIP, IBR, IBZ.
Published by: Nomos Verlagsgesellschaft mbH und Co. KG, Waldseestr 3-5, Baden-Baden, 76530, Germany. TEL 49-7221-21040, FAX 49-7221-210427, marketing@nomos.de, nomos@nomos.de, http://www.nomos.de. Ed. Gerhard Pfannendoerfer. Adv. contact Bettina Roos. Circ: 1,700 (paid and controlled).

360 DEU ISSN 1619-2427
SOZIALWIRTSCHAFT AKTUELL. Text in German. 2002. 22/yr. EUR 124 (effective 2011). adv. reprint service avail. from SCH. **Document type:** *Journal, Academic/Scholarly.*
Published by: Nomos Verlagsgesellschaft mbH und Co. KG, Waldseestr 3-5, Baden-Baden, 76530, Germany. TEL 49-7221-21040, FAX 49-7221-210427, nomos@nomos.de, http://www.nomos.de. Ed. Gerhard Pfannendoerfer. Adv. contact Bettina Roos. Circ: 1,100 (paid).

SOZIALWISSENSCHAFTEN UND BERUFSPRAXIS. *see* SOCIAL SCIENCES: COMPREHENSIVE WORKS

SOZIALWISSENSCHAFTLICHE LITERATURRUNDSCHAU; Sozialarbeit - Sozialpaedagogik - Sozialpolitik - Gesellschaftspolitik. *see* SOCIAL SCIENCES: COMPREHENSIVE WORKS

362 NLD ISSN 1872-0072
SOZIO; vakblad voor sociale en pedagogische beroepen. Text in Dutch. 1994. bi-m. EUR 37 to individuals; EUR 56 to institutions; EUR 29 to students (effective 2008). adv. bk.rev. index. back issues avail.
Formerly (until 2006): S P H (1381-5296); Which incorporated (in 1995): Periodiek over Sociotherapie (0925-6334); Which was formerly (1986-1989): Socio (0920-7856); S P H was formed by the 1994 merger of: Extract Extra (1381-0677); (1993-1994): Extract (0929-5739); Which was formerly (until 1993): Tijdschrift K en O voor Jeugdwelzijnswerk (0929-5771); (until 1980): Tijdschrift voor Kinderverzorging en Opvoeding (0040-7534); (1958-1972): K en O. Tijdschrift voor Kinderverzorging en Oudervoorlichting (0022-9970)
Published by: Uitgeverij S W P, Postbus 257, Amsterdam, 1000 AG, Netherlands. TEL 31-20-3307200, FAX 31-20-3308040, swp@swpbook.com, http://www.swpbook.com. Ed. Olaf Stomp. Pub. Paul Roosenstein. adv.: page EUR 745; 170 x 246. Circ: 5,000.

360 GBR ISSN 2046-3030
SPECTRUM (ONLINE); Scotland's magazine for volunteer development. Text in English. 19??. q. free (effective 2011). back issues avail. **Document type:** *Magazine, Trade.*
Former titles (until 2010): Spectrum (Print) (1479-7518); (until 2003): Volunteering Matters in Scotland (1362-0568); (until 1996): Volunteering Matters (0953-7740); (until 1988): V D S Members' Bulletin
Media: Online - full text.
Published by: Volunteer Development Scotland, Jubilee House, Forthside Way, Stirling, FK8 1QZ, United Kingdom. TEL 44-1786-479593, FAX 44-1786-849767, vds@vds.org.uk. Ed. Shirley Bwye.

S

360 USA
SPIRIT (METAIRIE). Text in English. 1993. 3/yr. free. bk.rev. back issues avail. **Document type:** *Magazine, Consumer.* **Description:** Describes the mission and work of Volunteers of America across the nation.
Formerly: Volunteer's Gazette
Published by: Volunteers of America, 1660 Duke St, Alexandria, VA 22314-3427. TEL 800-899-0089, http://www.voa.org. Ed. DeQuendre Neeley-Bertrand. Circ: 23,000 (controlled).

360 CHE
SPITAELER ALTERS PFLEGEHEIME. Text in German. q.
Address: Masanserstr 124, Postfach 92, Chur 5, 7005, Switzerland. TEL 081-225252, FAX 081-274939. Ed. Giovanni Viecelli. Circ: 8,600.

659 361.8 CAN ISSN 1201-5326
THE SPONSORSHIP REPORT. Text in English. 1986. m. CAD 219.35 to non-profit organizations; CAD 256.80 to corporations (effective 2004). **Document type:** *Newsletter, Trade.* **Description:** Publishes information about sponsorships between Canadian corporations and arts groups, sports organizations, charities, government initiatives, events, and festivals.
Formerly (until 1988): Sponsorship and Events Marketing Report (1189-2781)
Published by: Database Publishing, Station Main, PO Box 378, Campbellford, ON K0L 1L0, Canada. TEL 705-653-1112, FAX 705-653-1113, dbp@redden.on.ca, http://server.redden.on.ca/~dbp/. Ed. Mark Sabourin.

362 NLD ISSN 1875-6069
***SPRANK.** Text in Dutch. 2007. 10/yr. EUR 84 (effective 2010). adv. **Document type:** *Magazine, Trade.*
Published by: Verenigingsbureau Divosa, Postbus 407, Utrecht, 3500 AK, Netherlands. TEL 31-30-2332337, FAX 31-30-2333726, cb@divosa.nl, http://www.divosa.nl. Circ: 2,000.

360 CAN ISSN 1911-1983
SPRINGTIDE RESOURCES. NEWSLETTER. Text in English. 1987. irreg. **Document type:** *Newsletter, Consumer.*
Formerly (until 2006): Education Wife Assault. Newsletter (0841-6435)
Published by: Springtide Resources, 215 Spadina Ave, Ste 220, Toronto, ON M5T 2C7, Canada. TEL 416-968-3422, FAX 416-968-2026, info@womanabuseprevention.com, http://www.springtideresources.org.

361.8 GBR
STAFF OF SCOTTISH LOCAL AUTHORITY SOCIAL WORK SERVICES. Text in English. 1979. a. back issues avail. **Document type:** *Government.* **Description:** Features statistics relevant to staffing in the Scottish local authority social work services.
Former titles (until 2000): Staff of Scottish Local Authority Social Work Departments; (until 1998): Staff of Scottish Social Work Departments (0260-5457); Which superseded in part (in 1979): Scottish Social Work Statistics (0307-9597)
Related titles: Online - full text ed.: free (effective 2010).
Published by: Social Work Services Group, Statistics Branch, Scottish Government, Education Directorate, Mail Point 1, 1-B (S), Victoria Quay, Edinburgh, EH6 6QQ, United Kingdom. TEL 44-131-2440313, FAX 44-131-2440354, info@statistics.gov.uk.

362.2 USA ISSN 1542-2232
RA790.6
STANDARDS FOR BEHAVIORAL HEALTH CARE. Abbreviated title: S B H C. Text in English. 1998. biennial. USD 110 per issue (effective 2009). reprints avail. **Document type:** *Handbook/Manual/Guide, Trade.*
—CCC.
Published by: Joint Commission on Accreditation of Healthcare Organizations, 1 Renaissance Blvd, Oakbrook Terrace, IL 60181. TEL 630-792-5000, FAX 630-792-5005, customerservice@jointcommission.org, http://www.jointcommission.org/. Ed. Audrie Bretl TEL 630-792-5439.

362 USA ISSN 1096-0546
RA997
STANDARDS FOR LONG TERM CARE SUBACUTE PROGRAMS, AND DEMENTIA SPECIAL CARE UNITS. Text in English. 1998. biennial. USD 110 per issue (effective 2007). **Document type:** *Handbook/Manual/Guide, Trade.* **Description:** Contains information for long-term care facilities seeking accreditation under Medicare and Medicaid.
Published by: Joint Commission on Accreditation of Healthcare Organizations, 1 Renaissance Blvd, Oakbrook Terrace, IL 60181. TEL 630-792-5000, FAX 630-792-5005, customerservice@jointcommission.org, http://www.jointcommission.org/.

START!. *see* PUBLIC HEALTH AND SAFETY

362.7 USA ISSN 1084-3191
HV741
STATE OF AMERICA'S CHILDREN YEARBOOK (YEAR); an analysis of our nation's investment in children. Text in English. 1981. a. charts; stat. **Document type:** *Journal, Trade.* **Description:** Presents an analysis of federal programs affecting children and families. Includes recommendations for positive investments in children.
Former titles (until 1992): State of America's Children (1055-9213); (until 1991): Vision for America's Future; (until 1989): Children's Defense Budget (0736-6701)
Indexed: SRI.
Published by: (National Association for the Education of Young Children), Children's Defense Fund, 25 E St, N W, Washington, DC 20001. TEL 202-628-8787, cdfinfo@childrensdefense.org. Circ: 18,000.

362.7 USA ISSN 0251-9100
HQ792.2
THE STATE OF THE WORLD'S CHILDREN. Text in English, French, Spanish. 1979. a. USD 25 per issue (effective 2011). **Document type:** *Magazine, Trade.* **Description:** Discusses development issues related to children.
Related titles: Diskette ed.; Online - full text ed.: ISSN 1564-975X. 1996; ◆ French ed.: La Situation des Enfants dans le Monde. ISSN 1020-2129; ◆ Spanish ed.: Estado Mundial de la Infancia. ISSN 0251-9119.
Indexed: HRIR, IIS.
—CCC.
Published by: United Nations Children's Fund/Fonds des Nations Unies pour l'Enfance, 3 United Nations Plz, New York, NY 10017. TEL 212-326-7000, FAX 212-887-7465.

361.6 153.1 USA ISSN 0743-5916
HV3006.P4
STATE PLAN FOR DEVELOPMENTAL DISABILITIES. Text in English. 1977. a. **Document type:** *Government.*
Formerly: Pennsylvania. Development Disabilities Planning Council. Pennsylvania State Plan (0193-1423)
Indexed: E-psyche.
Published by: Developmental Disabilities Planning Council, Health & Welfare Bldg, Harrisburg, PA 17120. Circ: 2,000.

360 SWE ISSN 1404-2584
STATENS INSTITUTIONSSTYRELSE. ALLMAEN SIS-RAPPORT. Text in Swedish. 1994. irreg. back issues avail. **Document type:** *Monographic series, Government.*
Supersedes in part (in 2000): Statens Institutionsstyrelse. Rapport (1104-6155)
Related titles: Online - full text ed.
Published by: Statens Institutionsstyrelse/The National Board of Institutional Care, PO Box 16363, Stockholm, 10326, Sweden. TEL 46-8-4534000, FAX 46-8-4534050, registrator@stat-inst.se.

360 SWE ISSN 1404-2576
STATENS INSTITUTIONSSTYRELSE. FORSKNINGSRAPPORT. Text in Swedish. 1994. irreg., latest 2007. price varies. back issues avail. **Document type:** *Monographic series, Government.*
Supersedes in part i (in 1999): Statens Institutionsstyrelse. Rapport (1104-6155)
Related titles: Online - full text ed.
Published by: Statens Institutionsstyrelse/The National Board of Institutional Care, PO Box 16363, Stockholm, 10326, Sweden. TEL 46-8-4534000, FAX 46-8-4534050, registrator@stat-inst.se.

STATISTICS ON SOCIAL WORK EDUCATION IN THE UNITED STATES. *see* SOCIAL SERVICES AND WELFARE—Abstracting, Bibliographies, Statistics

362.7 AUT
STATISTIK AUSTRIA. STATISTIK DER JUGENDWOHLFAHRT. Text in German. 1965. a. EUR 18.17. **Document type:** *Government.* **Description:** Activity of tribunals and administrative authorities, with information on education assistance and child welfare work.
Former titles: Austria. Statistisches Zentralamt. Statistik der Jugendwohlfahrt; Austria. Statistisches Zentralamt. Jugendwohlfahrtspflege
Related titles: ◆ Series of: Beitraege zur Oesterreichischen Statistik. ISSN 0067-2319.
Published by: Statistik Austria, Guglgasse 13, Vienna, W 1110, Austria. TEL 43-1-711280, FAX 43-1-711287728, info@statistik.gv.at, http://www.statistik.at.

DE STEM VAN DE OUDERS. *see* HANDICAPPED

362.4 NLD ISSN 2211-1182
STERK. Text in Dutch. 200?. q. **Document type:** *Magazine, Consumer.*
Published by: R B O, Damsport 1, Postbus 351, Groningen, 9700 AJ, Netherlands. TEL 31-50-5262900, info@rbo.nl, http://www.rbo.nl. Circ: 10,000.

362.7 NLD ISSN 1878-4771
STICHTING WEESKINDEREN IN RWANDA. NIEUWSBRIEF. Text in Dutch. 2001. a. **Document type:** *Newsletter, Consumer.*
Published by: Stichting Weeskinderen in Rwanda, Willibrorduslaan 34, Eersel, 5521 KC, Netherlands. TEL 31-497-515394, FAX 31-497-513539, info@weeskindereninrwanda.nl, http://www.weeskindereninrwanda.nl.

361.73 DEU ISSN 1438-0617
STIFTUNG & SPONSORING; das Magazin fuer Non-Profit-Management und -Marketing. Text in German. 1998. bi-m. EUR 126.80 (effective 2011). adv. **Document type:** *Magazine, Trade.*
Published by: Stiftung & Sponsoring Verlag GmbH, Moewenweg 20, Verl, 33415, Germany. TEL 49-5246-921912, FAX 49-5246-921999, verlag@stiftung-sponsoring.de. Ed. Christoph Mecking.

360 SWE ISSN 0281-2851
STOCKHOLM STUDIES IN SOCIAL WORK. Text in English. 1983. irreg., latest 2010. price varies. back issues avail. **Document type:** *Monographic series, Academic/Scholarly.*
Related titles: Online - full text ed.: 2000.
—BLDSC (8465.741000).
Published by: Stockholms Universitet, Institutionen foer Socialt Arbete/Stockholm University, School of Social Work, Sveavaegen 160, Stockholm, 10691, Sweden. TEL 46-8-162000, FAX 46-8-6747555, info@socarb.su.se. Ed. Hans Berglind. Circ: 500.

STRATEGIC AGEING. *see* GERONTOLOGY AND GERIATRICS

STRATHCLYDE PAPERS ON SOCIOLOGY AND SOCIAL POLICY. *see* SOCIOLOGY

362.5 USA ISSN 1069-5478
STREET BEAT QUARTERLY; first-hand perspectives on homelessness and poverty. Text in English. 1990. q. USD 10; USD 2.50 newsstand/cover (effective 1999). adv. illus. back issues avail. **Description:** Includes poetry, fiction, opinions, and stories.
Published by: Community Human Services Corp., Wood Street Commons, 301 Third Ave, Pittsburgh, PA 15222. TEL 412-765-3302. Ed., Pub., R&P, Adv. contact Sharon Thorp. page USD 250. Circ: 2,000.

361 AUS ISSN 1834-4496
STREET RIGHTS N S W. (New South Wales) Text in English. 2004. irreg. **Document type:** *Newsletter, Trade.*
Related titles: Online - full text ed.: ISSN 1834-450X.
Published by: Public Interest Advocacy Centre, Homeless Persons' Legal Service, Level 9, 299 Elizabeth St, Sydney, NSW 2000, Australia. TEL 61-2-8898-6500, FAX 61-2-8898-6555, piac@piac.asn.au, http://piac.asn.au.

362 USA ISSN 1064-4504
STREET SHEET; the newsletter of the coalition on homelessness. Text in English. 1989. m. USD 20; USD 30 foreign. **Document type:** *Newsletter.* **Description:** Provides a forum of public opinion on homelessness as well as an outlet for expression by homeless people.
Published by: Coalition on Homelessness, 468 Turk St, San Francisco, CA 94102. TEL 415-346-3740, FAX 415-775-5639. Ed. Lydia Ely. Circ: 36,000.

360 796.334 USA
STREET TALK. Text in English. s-a. **Document type:** *Newsletter.*
Published by: Soccer in the Streets, Inc., 2323 Perimeter Park Drive NE, Atlanta, GA 30341. TEL 678-993-2113, FAX 770-452-1946, sits@sits.org.

STRIJDKREET. *see* RELIGIONS AND THEOLOGY—Protestant

361.6 NZL ISSN 1177-2018
STRONGER TOGETHER. Text in English. 2006. q. **Document type:** *Newsletter, Consumer.*
Published by: (Housing New Zealand Corporation), Ministry of Social Development, PO Box 1556, Wellington, New Zealand. TEL 64-4-9163300, FAX 64-4-9180099, information@msd.govt.nz.

THE STUDENT ADVOCATE. *see* EDUCATION—Special Education And Rehabilitation

STUDIENSTIFTUNG. JAHRESBERICHT. *see* EDUCATION—Special Education And Rehabilitation

360 NLD ISSN 1568-2536
STUDIES IN EMPLOYMENT AND SOCIAL POLICY. Text in English. 1997. irreg. price varies. **Document type:** *Monographic series, Academic/Scholarly.*
Formerly (until 1999): Studies in Social Policy (1387-5221)
Published by: Kluwer Law International (Subsidiary of: Aspen Publishers, Inc.), PO Box 316, Alphen aan den Rijn, 2400 AH, Netherlands. TEL 31-172-641562, FAX 31-172-641555, sales@kluwerlaw.com, http://www.kluwerlaw.com. Eds. Alan C Neal, Manfred Weiss.

STUDIES IN HEALTH AND HUMAN SERVICES. *see* PUBLIC HEALTH AND SAFETY

STUDIES IN INCOME DISTRIBUTION SERIES. *see* BUSINESS AND ECONOMICS—Economic Situation And Conditions

360 USA ISSN 1934-4848
HV4997
SUBSTANCE ABUSE FUNDING NEWS. Text in English. 1992. 48/yr. USD 269 (effective 2007). 18 p./no. 2 cols./p.; back issues avail.; reprints avail. **Document type:** *Newsletter.* **Description:** Provides public and private grant announcements of alcohol, tobacco, and drug abuse programs, and teen-age homelessness. It offers advice on grant seeking and proposal writing.
Former titles (until 2006): Substance Abuse Funding Week (1551-7888); (until 2004): Substance Abuse Funding News (1067-0165)
Related titles: Online - full text ed.: ISSN 1934-4856.
—CCC.
Published by: C D Publications, Inc., 8204 Fenton St, Silver Spring, MD 20910. TEL 301-588-6380, 800-666-6380, FAX 301-588-6385, subscriptions@cdpublications.com, http://www.cdpublications.com. Eds. J J Smith, John Reistrup. Pub. Mike Gerecht.

361.73 USA ISSN 1070-9061
SUCCESSFUL FUND RAISING. Text in English. 1993. m. USD 120; USD 130 foreign (effective 2000). adv. bk.rev.; software rev. back issues avail. **Document type:** *Newsletter.* **Description:** Provides a monthly report of successful fund-raising ideas, strategies and management issues.
Published by: Stevenson, Inc., PO Box 4528, Sioux City, IA 51104. TEL 712-239-3010, FAX 712-239-2166. Ed., Pub., R&P, Adv. contact Scott C Stevenson.

361.73 USA ISSN 1944-5938
▼ **SUCCESSFUL FUND RAISING (SCHOOLS EDITION).** Text in English. 2009. m. (except Jun. & Jul.). USD 99 (effective 2009). adv. **Document type:** *Newsletter, Trade.* **Description:** Provides schools with information on how to raise funds for endowment, athletics, music, drama, capital improvements, teacher development and much more.
Media: Online - full content.
Published by: Stevenson, Inc., PO Box 4528, Sioux City, IA 51104. TEL 712-239-3010, FAX 712-239-2166, inquiry@stevensoninc.com.

SUIZIDPROPHYLAXE. *see* MEDICAL SCIENCES—Psychiatry And Neurology

360 DEU ISSN 1434-2901
SUMMA SUMMARUM. Text in German. 1997. bi-m. **Document type:** *Magazine, Trade.*
Published by: C W Haarfeld GmbH (Subsidiary of: Wolters Kluwer Deutschland GmbH), Annastr 32-36, Essen, 45130, Germany. TEL 49-201-720950, FAX 49-201-7209533, online@cw-haarfeld.de.

362.4 USA ISSN 1047-952X
SUPPORTED EMPLOYMENT INFOLINES. Text in English. 1990. m. USD 99 in North America; USD 139 elsewhere (effective 2000). adv. bk.rev. back issues avail. **Document type:** *Newsletter.* **Description:** Contains news, trends, hands-on tips and strategies, and research for professionals who support people with all types of disabilities in jobs in the community. Provides career and vocational guidance.
Published by: Training Resource Network, Inc., PO Box 439, St. Augustine, FL 32085-0439. TEL 904-823-9800, FAX 904-823-3554. Ed., R&P, Adv. contact Dawn Langton TEL 904-824-7121. Pub. Dale Dileo. Circ: 5,000.

SURVEY. *see* BUSINESS AND ECONOMICS—Management

SVENSK FAMILJETERAPI. *see* MEDICAL SCIENCES—Psychiatry And Neurology

362.4 SWE ISSN 0346-2129
SVENSK HANDIKAPPTIDSKRIFT. Text in Swedish. 1923. 8/yr. SEK 225 (effective 2007). adv. **Document type:** *Magazine, Consumer.*
Formerly (until 1966): Svensk Vanfoeretidskrift
Published by: Handikappades Riksfoerbund, PO Box 47305, Stockholm, 10074, Sweden. TEL 46-8-6858070, FAX 46-8-6456541, info@dhr.se. Ed. Elisabet Geite. Adv. contact Lars-Goeran Andersson TEL 46-8-57163422. B&W page SEK 14,700, color page SEK 18,700; trim 270 x 190. Circ: 19,000.

360 SWE ISSN 0346-6019
SWEDEN. SOCIALSTYRELSEN. FOERFATTNINGSSAMLING: SOCIAL. Variant title: S O S F S (S). Text in Swedish. 1883. irreg. (approx. 4/yr.). looseleaf. SEK 193 (effective 2005). index. **Document type:** *Directory.* **Description:** Directory and general advice in the field of social welfare.
Supersedes in part (in 1976): Sweden. Medicinalvaesendet. Foerfattningssamling (0346-5837)
Related titles: Online - full text ed.
Published by: Socialstyrelsen/National Board of Health and Welfare, Raalambsvaegen 3, Stockholm, 10630, Sweden. TEL 46-8-55553000, FAX 46-8-55553252, socialstyrelssen@socialstyrelsen.se, http://www.socialstyrelsen.se.

360 DEU
▼ **SYSTEMISCHE IMPULSE FUER DIE SOZIALE ARBEIT.** Text in German. 2010. irreg. price varies. **Document type:** *Monographic series, Academic/Scholarly.*
Published by: Ibidem Verlag, Melchiorstr 15, Stuttgart, 70439, Germany. TEL 49-711-9807954, FAX 49-711-9807952, ibidem@ibidem-verlag.de, http://www.ibidem-verlag.de.

360 344.03258 USA ISSN 2153-7992
KFM2749
T A F D C AND E A ADVOCACY GUIDE; an advocate's guide to the Massachusetts welfare rules for families. (Transitional Aid to Families with Dependent Children and Emergency Assistance) Text in English. 1996. irreg. **Document type:** *Guide, Consumer.* **Description:** Explains the rules of the TAFDC (Transitional Aid to Families with Dependent Children, or "Welfare") for people who are applying for the program.
Formerly (until 2008): T A F D C Advocacy Guide (1529-0336)
Related titles: Online - full text ed.
Published by: Massachusetts Law Reform Institute, 99 Chauncey St, Ste 500, Boston, MA 02111-1703. TEL 617-357-0700, FAX 617-357-0777, aduke@mlri.org, http://www.mlri.org.

362.5 GBR ISSN 0955-2324
T E A R TIMES. (The Evangelical Alliance Relief) Text in English. 197?. q. free (effective 2009). **Document type:** *Magazine, Trade.* **Description:** Features about Tearfund's work worldwide.
Related titles: Audio CD ed.; Braille ed.
—CCC.
Published by: T E A R Fund, 100 Church Rd, Teddington, TW11 8QE, United Kingdom. TEL 44-845-3558355, FAX 44-20-89433594, enquiry@tearfund.org, http://www.tearfund.org.

361 323 FRA ISSN 1962-932X
T G H INFO. (Triangle Generation Humanitaire) Text in French. 1995. a., latest 2008. back issues avail. **Document type:** *Journal, Trade.*
Formerly (until 2007): Info Generation Humanitaire (1622-9789)
Published by: Association Triangle Generation Humanitaire, 1 Rue Montribloud, B P 9014, Lyon, Cedex 09 69265, France. TEL 33-4-72205010, FAX 33-4-72205011, info@trianglegh.org. Circ: 6,000.

360 FRA
T S A MENSUEL. (Travail Social Actualites) Text in French. 1983. m. adv.
Former titles: T S A Hebdo (1967-0192); (until 1993): Travail Social Actualites (0753-9711)
Related titles: Online - full text ed.
Indexed: FR.
Published by: Editions Legislatives, 80 Av. de la Marne, Montrouge, Cedex 92546, France. TEL 33-1-40923636. Circ: 13,000.

658.152 USA
TAFT MONTHLY PORTFOLIO. Text in English. 1962. m. USD 75 (effective 2000). adv. bk.rev. index. **Document type:** *Newsletter.* **Description:** Contains articles on sources for and examples of philanthropic fund-raising ideas and techniques. For individuals and nonprofit organizations.
Former titles: Taft Group; F R I Monthly Portfolio (0014-6137)
Published by: Taft Group, 27500 Drake Rd, Farmington Hills, MI 48331-3535. TEL 800-877-4253. Adv. contact Laurie Fundukian. Circ: 500.

TAGESSATZ. *see* GENERAL INTEREST PERIODICALS—Germany

362.4 GBR
TALKING SENSE. Text in English. 1956. 4/yr. GBP 10. adv. bk.rev. bibl. **Document type:** *Newsletter.* **Description:** Covers the entire spectrum of topics relevant to deafblind people, their families and professionals in the field.
Former titles: National Association for Deaf - Blind and Rubella Handicapped. Newsletter; National Association for Deaf - Blind and Rubella Children. Newsletter
Media: Duplicated (not offset).
Published by: Sense - National Deaf-Blind and Rubella Association, 11-13 Clifton Terr, London, N4 3SR, United Kingdom. TEL 44-171-272-7774, FAX 44-171-272-6012. Circ: 4,000.

361.77 NOR ISSN 0804-9807
TANKEKORS. Text in Norwegian. 1921. 6/yr. adv. bk.rev. illus. **Document type:** *Bulletin, Consumer.*
Former titles (until 1992): Roede Kors (0333-2985); (until 1981): Over Alle Graenser (0030-7335); (until 1955): Norges Roede Kors (0332-5326)
—CCC.
Published by: Norges Roede Kors/Norwegian Red Cross, Postboks 1, Groenland, Oslo, 0133, Norway. TEL 47-22-05-40-00, FAX 47-22-05-40-40, TELEX 76011 NORCR N. Ed. Liv Ronglan. R&P Gro Flataboe. adv.: B&W page NOK 15,000, color page NOK 30,000; trim 210 x 285. Circ: 300,000 (controlled).

TAPPING TECHNOLOGY. *see* HANDICAPPED—Physically Impaired

360 340 DEU ISSN 0934-3059
TASCHENLEXIKON SOZIALVERSICHERUNGSRECHTLICHER ENTSCHEIDUNGEN. Text in German. 1959. irreg. price varies. **Document type:** *Monographic series, Trade.*
Published by: Erich Schmidt Verlag GmbH & Co. (Berlin), Genthiner Str 30 G, Berlin, 10785, Germany. TEL 49-30-2500850, FAX 49-30-250085305, esv@esvmedien.de, http://www.esv.info.

TAVANBAKHSHI-I NUVIN/MODERN REHABILITATION. *see* MEDICAL SCIENCES—Physical Medicine And Rehabilitation

362.82 NZL ISSN 1177-7826
TE RITO NEWS. Text in English. 2005. irreg. **Document type:** *Newsletter, Consumer.*
Related titles: Online - full text ed.: ISSN 1177-7834.
Published by: Ministry of Social Development, Family & Community Services, PO Box 1556, Wellington, New Zealand. TEL 64-4-9136601, FAX 64-4-9172080, information@familyservices.govt.nz.

361.73 600 USA ISSN 1534-5785
T173.8
TECHNOLOGY GRANT NEWS. Text in English. 1999. q. USD 125 to institutions; USD 85 to non-profit organizations (effective 2003). 16 p./no.; **Description:** Presents grant announcements for technology and other initiatives by tech funders, government and trade associations — for nonprofits, social service providers, towns & cities and schools & universities.
Published by: Partnerships for Community Inc., 561 Hudson St., No. 23, New York, NY 10014. TEL 212-741-8101, FAX 212-645-7495.

TEILHABE; Die Fachzeitschrift der Lebenshilfe. *see* EDUCATION—Special Education And Rehabilitation

TEKNOLOGI & HANDICAP. *see* EDUCATION—Special Education And Rehabilitation

361.6 CRI ISSN 0492-6471
TEMAS SOCIALES. Text in Spanish. 1954. q.
Published by: Ministerio de Trabajo y Prevision Social, Apartado 2041, San Jose, Costa Rica.

362 USA
TEXAS. DEPARTMENT ON AGING. ANNUAL REPORT. Text in English. 1982. a. free. **Document type:** *Government.*
Former titles: Texas Department on Aging. Biennial Report; Texas. Department on Aging. Annual Report; Texas. Governor's Committee on Aging. Biennial Report (0082-3058)
Published by: Department on Aging, PO Box 12786, Capitol Sta, Austin, TX 78711. TEL 512-444-2727. Ed. James Grabbs.

360 BRA ISSN 1679-2041
F2510
TEXTOS & CONTEXTOS. Text in Portuguese, Spanish. 2003. 3/yr. **Document type:** *Journal, Academic/Scholarly.*
Related titles: Online - full text ed.: ISSN 1677-9509. free (effective 2011).
Published by: Editora da P U C R S, Avenida Ipiranga 6681, Predio 33, Porto Alegre, RS 90619-900, Brazil. http://www.pucrs.br/edipucrs/.

360 CHE
THEMA. Text in German. 1903. q. CHF 36.80 (effective 1999). adv. bk.rev. **Document type:** *Bulletin.*
Former titles: Pro Juventute (1012-7895); (until 1920): Jugendwohlfahrt (1422-0768); (until 1916): Schweizerische Blaetter fuer Schulgesundheitspflege und Kinderschutz (1422-0741)
Indexed: DIP, IBR, IBZ.
Published by: Verlag Pro Juventute, Seehofstr 15, Zuerich, 8022, Switzerland. TEL 41-1-2520719, FAX 41-1-2522824. Ed., Adv. contact Christian Urech. Circ: 3,300.

360 DEU ISSN 0342-2275
➤ **THEORIE UND PRAXIS DER SOZIALEN ARBEIT.** Text in German. 1947. bi-m. EUR 38; EUR 32 to students; EUR 9 newsstand/cover (effective 2011). adv. bk.rev. **Document type:** *Journal, Academic/Scholarly.* **Description:** News about social work and social politics.
Formerly (until 1972): Neues Beginnen (0028-3592)
Indexed: DIP, IBR, IBZ.
Published by: (Arbeiterwohlfahrt Bundesverband e.V.), Juventa Verlag GmbH, Ehretstr 3, Weinheim, 69469, Germany. TEL 49-6201-90200, FAX 49-6201-902013, juventa@juventa.de, http://www.juventa.de. Ed. Wolfgang Bodenbender. Adv. contact Thekla Steinmetz. Circ: 3,000 (paid and controlled).

362.6 USA ISSN 1934-435X
HQ1064.U5
THESTREET.COM RATINGS' CONSUMER GUIDE TO ELDER CARE CHOICES. Text in English. 2002. a. USD 63.95 (effective 2008). **Document type:** *Guide, Consumer.*
Former titles (until 2006): Weiss Ratings Consumer Guide to Elder Care Choices; (until 2003): Consumer Guide to Elder Care Choices (1546-7856)
Published by: TheStreet.com Ratings, Inc. (Subsidiary of: TheStreet.com), 15430 Endeavour Dr, Jupiter, FL 33478. TEL 561-354-4400, 800-289-9222, FAX 561-354-4497, http://www.thestreet.com.

360 GBR ISSN 0969-9406
THIRD FORCE NEWS. Text in English. 1985. w. free membership; GBP 110 to non-members (effective 2010). adv. bk.rev. back issues avail.; reprints avail. **Document type:** *Magazine, Trade.* **Description:** Provides news and information for voluntary and community organizations in Scotland.
Formerly (until 1992): Third Sector (0267-3053)
—CCC.
Published by: Scottish Council for Voluntary Organisations, Mansfield Traquair Ctr, 15 Mansfield Pl, Edinburgh, EH3 6BB, United Kingdom. TEL 44-131-5563882, enquiries@scvo.org.uk.

362 GBR ISSN 1355-6371
THIRD SECTOR; the news magazine for the charities world. Text in English. 1992. w. GBP 116; GBP 85 to qualified personnel (effective 2009). adv. bk.rev. back issues avail. **Document type:** *Magazine, Trade.* **Description:** Provides professionals involved in charitable organizations with news, analysis, opinion, and job information.
Related titles: Online - full text ed.
Indexed: A10, A15, ABIn, B01, B07, N06, P34, P48, P51, PQC, V03.
—CCC.
Published by: Haymarket Publishing Ltd. (Subsidiary of: Haymarket Media Group), 174 Hammersmith Rd, London, W6 7JP, United Kingdom. TEL 44-20-82675000, FAX 44-20-82674987, info@haymarket.com, http://www.haymarket.com. Ed. Stephen Cook TEL 44-20-82674858. Adv. contact Natasha Lumsden TEL 44-20-82674813. Circ: 13,354 (paid). **Subscr. to:** 12-13 Cranleigh Gardens Industrial Estate, Southall UB1 2DB, United Kingdom. TEL 44-84-51557355, FAX 44-8451-948840, http://www.haymarketbusinesssubs.com.

649.8 GBR ISSN 0268-4047
THIS CARING BUSINESS. Text in English. 1985. 10/yr. GBP 50 domestic; GBP 75 in Europe; GBP 80 elsewhere (effective 2001). adv. bk.rev. charts; stat.; tr.lit. back issues avail. **Document type:** *Journal, Trade.* **Description:** Covers commercially oriented matters relating to long-stay health and residential care.
Published by: Careworld Publishing House Ltd., 1 St Thomass Rd, Hastings, E Sussex TN34 3LG, United Kingdom. TEL 44-1424-718406, FAX 44-1424-718460. Ed. Michael Monk. R&P, Adv. contact Jonathan Heyes TEL 44-1422-375317. Circ: 18,366.

362.6 SWE ISSN 1403-7025
TIDNINGEN AELDREOMSORG. Text in Swedish. 1983. bi-m. SEK 373; SEK 373.01 per issue (effective 2006). **Document type:** *Trade.*
Former titles (until 2003): Aeldreomsorg (1104-6546); (until 1994): Vi i Hemtjaenst och Primaervaard (0282-5864); (until 1985): Vi i Hemtjaensten (0280-9036)
Related titles: ◆ Includes: Handledarskap i Aeldre och Handikappomsorg. ISSN 1403-3070.
Published by: Fortbildningsfoerlaget, PO Box 34, Solna, 17111, Sweden. TEL 46-8-54545330, FAX 46-8-54545349, info@fortbild.se, http://www.fortbild.se. Ed. Elisabet Spjurth TEL 46-8-54545331. Adv. contact Anders Tensjoe TEL 46-8-54545332.

TIDSSKRIFT FOR ARBEJDSLIV. *see* BUSINESS AND ECONOMICS—Labor And Industrial Relations

361 NOR ISSN 0809-2052
➤ **TIDSSKRIFT FOR VELFERDSFORSKNING.** Text in Norwegian; Summaries in English. 1998. q. NOK 445 to individuals; NOK 610 to institutions; NOK 265 to students; NOK 145 per issue (effective 2011). adv. bk.rev. **Document type:** *Journal, Academic/Scholarly.* **Description:** Journal on welfare research.
Related titles: Online - full text ed.
Published by: Fagbokforlaget, Kanalveien 51, PO Box 6050, Postterminalen, Bergen, 5892, Norway. TEL 47-55-388800, FAX 47-55-388801, fagbokforlaget@fagbokforlaget.no, http://www.fagbokforlaget.no. Ed. Nanna Kildahl. Adv. contact Janne-Beate Duke.

362.76 364 NLD ISSN 1876-2433
TIJDSCHRIFT KINDERMISHANDELING. Cover title: T K M. Text in Dutch. 2008. q. **Document type:** *Journal, Trade.* **Description:** For practitioners, policymakers and researchers involved in dealing with and care about abused children, their parents and perpetrators of child abuse.
Published by: Augeo Foundation, Postbus 592, Zeist, 3700 AN, Netherlands. TEL 31-343-536040, info@augeo-foundation.nl, http://www.augeo-foundation.nl. Ed. Marielle Dekker.

TIJDSCHRIFT VOOR BEDRIJFS- EN VERZEKERINGSGENEESKUNDE. *see* MEDICAL SCIENCES

HET TIJDSCHRIFT VOOR VERZORGENDEN. *see* MEDICAL SCIENCES—Nurses And Nursing

360 305.8924 CAN ISSN 1719-3834
TIKUN OLAM. Text in English, French. 2004. m. **Document type:** *Newsletter, Consumer.*
Published by: Federation C J A, 5151 Cote St Catherine Rd, Montreal, PQ H3W 1M6, Canada. TEL 514-345-2600, FAX 514-735-8972, http://www.federationcja.org/splash.php.

362.7 374 NLD ISSN 2211-7075
TIMON THUIS. Text in Dutch. 2001. q.
Formerly (until 2010): TImon Magazine (1569-6634)
Published by: Timon, Postbus 462, Zeist, 3700 AL, Netherlands. TEL 31-30-6940070, FAX 31-30-6940080, info@timon.nl, http://www.timon.nl.

TINNITUS TODAY. *see* MEDICAL SCIENCES—Otorhinolaryngology

THE TIZARD LEARNING DISABILITY REVIEW. *see* MEDICAL SCIENCES—Psychiatry And Neurology

361.7 USA
TOLSTOY FOUNDATION NEWS. Text in English, Russian. 1978. s-a. free. **Document type:** *Newsletter.*
Published by: Tolstoy Foundation, Inc., 104 Lake Rd, Valley Cottage, NY 10989-2459. TEL 212-677-7770, FAX 914-268-6937. Ed. Xenia Woyevodsky. Circ: 10,000 (controlled).

361.932505 NZL ISSN 1177-5688
TOMORROW'S MANUKAU. Text in English. 2007. a. **Document type:** *Newsletter, Consumer.* **Description:** Provides guidance and inspiration for agencies, organizations and communities to work together towards a progressive city of proud and prosperous people.
Published by: Manukau City Council, Private Bag 76917, Manukau City, 2104, New Zealand. TEL 64-9-2628900, FAX 64-9-2625737, 64-9-2625151, http://www.manukau.govt.nz.

362 CAN ISSN 1911-0987
TOMORROW'S NEWS. Text in English. 2001. s-a. **Document type:** *Newsletter, Consumer.*
Published by: Alberta Cancer Board, The Tomorrow Project (Subsidiary of: Alberta Cancer Board), c/o Tom Baker Cancer Centre, 1331 - 29 Street N.W., Calgary, AB T2N 4N2, Canada. TEL 403-521-3122, 877-919-9292, tomorrow@cancerboard.ab.ca, http://www.thetomorrowproject.org.

360 GBR ISSN 1468-957X
TOP 1000 CHARITIES IN SCOTLAND (YEAR). Text in English. 1998. a. GBP 84 per issue charities; GBP 168 per issue non-charities (effective 2009). **Document type:** *Directory, Trade.* **Description:** Provides the accurate and up-to-date information, giving you a comprehensive overview of the Scottish charity sector.
Formerly (until 1999): Top Charities in Scotland
Published by: CaritasData Ltd., 6-14 Underwood St, London, N1 7JQ, United Kingdom. TEL 44-20-73242362, FAX 44-20-75498677, enquiries@caritasdata.co.uk.

362 GBR ISSN 1470-7845
TOP 3000 CHARITIES (YEAR). Text in English. 1993. a. GBP 135 per issue charities; GBP 270 per issue non-charities (effective 2010). **Document type:** *Directory, Trade.* **Description:** Features comprehensive financial analysis of the UK's top 3000 charities. includes the latest financial accounts of the top charities, league tables, charity sector statistics, grantmaking charities and corporate donors.
Former titles (until 2000): Baring Asset Management Top 3000 Charities (Year) (1463-5992); (until 1997): Henderson Top 2000 Charities (Year) (1357-1478); (until 1994): Henderson Top 1000 Charities (Year) (0967-8352)
Related titles: Online - full text ed.
—BLDSC (3623.423500). **CCC.**
Published by: CaritasData Ltd., 6-14 Underwood St, London, N1 7JQ, United Kingdom. TEL 44-20-73242362, FAX 44-20-75498677, enquiries@caritasdata.co.uk.

300 MEX ISSN 0187-7542
F1234
TOPODRILO; sociedad, ciencia y arte. Text in Spanish. 1988. bi-m. USD 45. **Description:** Presents the new cultural, political, artistic, scientific and social trends in Mexico. Reflects Mexico's current problems and worries.
Related titles: Online - full text ed.: ISSN 1605-573X.
Published by: Universidad Autonoma Metropolitana - Iztapalapa, Division de Ciencias Sociales y Humanidades. Departamento de Antropologia, Ave San Rafael Atlixco # 186, Col Vicentina, Del Iztapalapa, Mexico City, 09340, Mexico. TEL 52-55-7724-4760. Ed. Antulio Sanchez Garcia.

S

051 USA ISSN 1545-9071
TOWN HALL JOURNAL. Text in English. 193?. s-m. **Document type:** *Journal, Trade.*
Former titles (until 2000): Town Hall Los Angeles (1529-8132); (until 1994): Town Hall Journal (0732-4049); (until 1968): Town Hall of California (0732-4057); (until 1967): Town Hall (0732-4030)
Indexed: P30.
Published by: Town Hall Los Angeles, 515 S. Flower St., Ste. 1650, Los Angeles, CA 90071-2253. townhall-la@townhall-la.org, http://www.townhall-la.org.

361.3 MEX ISSN 0188-1396
HV111
TRABAJO SOCIAL. Text in Spanish. 1974. q. MXN 50, USD 25 (effective 2000). **Description:** Covers social welfare, social development and casework. Features interviews of well-known social workers.
Indexed: C01.
Published by: Universidad Nacional Autonoma de Mexico, Instituto de Investigaciones Juridicas, Circuito Mario de la Cueva S/N, Ciudad Universitaria, Mexico City, 04510, Mexico. TEL 52-5-6228757, FAX 52-5-6228771, rodvil@servidor.unam.mx. Ed. Maria Himelda Ramirez.

362.2 PER ISSN 2218-2896
TRABAJO SOCIAL. Text in Spanish. 2005. a. **Document type:** *Monographic series, Academic/Scholarly.*
Published by: Universidad Nacional de San Agustin, Facultad de Ciencias Historico Sociales, Ave. Venezuela, s-n, Pab. Sociales 2o. Piso, Arquipa, Peru. fchs@unsa.edu.pe, http://www.unsa.edu.pe/. Ed. Jeannette Bengoa Lazarte.

360 COL ISSN 0123-4986
HV201
TRABAJO SOCIAL (COLOMBIA). Text in Spanish. 1999. a.
Published by: Universidad Nacional de Colombia, Facultad de Ciencias Humanas, Biblioteca Central, Division de Canje, Apartado Aereo 14490, Bogota, Colombia. TEL 57-4-3165000, FAX 57-4-2225285. Ed. Maria Himelda Ramirez.

362.2 ESP ISSN 1134-0991
TRABAJO SOCIAL HOY. Text in Spanish. 1984. q.
Formerly (until 1993): Eslabon (1133-3081)
Related titles: Online - full text ed.
Published by: Colegio Oficial de Diplomados en Trabajo Social y Asistentes Sociales de Madrid, Ave Reina Victoria No. 37 2o. C, Madrid, 28003, Spain. TEL 34-91-5415776, FAX 34-91-5353377, madrid@cgtrabajosocial.es, http://www.cgtrabajosocial.es/.

360 ESP ISSN 1130-2976
TRABAJO SOCIAL Y SALUD. Text in Multiple languages. 1987. 3/yr. EUR 210 to members; EUR 240 to non-members; EUR 180 to students (effective 2008). **Document type:** *Magazine, Trade.*
Published by: Asociacion Espanola de Trabajo Social y Salud, Universidad de Zaragoza, C/ Carmen 26, Zaragoza, 50005, Spain. reproimsa@kobo.es, http://www.unizar.es/atss/.

TRADE WINDS. *see* CLOTHING TRADE

361 USA ISSN 1941-2193
HV40.8.U6
TRAINING AND DEVELOPMENT IN HUMAN SERVICES. Text in English. 2007. a. USD 25 per issue (effective 2008). **Document type:** *Journal, Trade.*
Published by: National Staff Development and Training Association, 810 1st St NE, Ste 500, Washington, DC 20002. TEL 202-682-0100, FAX 202-289-6555, http://nsdta.aphsa.org.

360 DEU
▼ **TRANSPOSITION**; Ostschweizer Beitraege zu Lehre, Forschung und Entwicklung in der Sozialen Arbeit. Text in German. 2010. irreg. price varies. **Document type:** *Monographic series, Academic/Scholarly.*
Published by: Frank und Timme GmbH, Wittelsbacherstr 27a, Berlin, 10707, Germany. TEL 49-30-88667911, FAX 49-30-86398731, info@frank-timme.de.

360 CAN ISSN 1205-5395
TRAVAILLEUR SOCIAL. Text in French. 1995. q. **Document type:** *Journal, Academic/Scholarly.*
Incorporates in part: Social Worker (0037-8089)
—IE, Ingenta.
Published by: Myropen Publications Ltd., 383 Parkdale Ave, Ste 402, Ottawa, ON K1Y 4R4, Canada. TEL 613-729-6668, FAX 613-729-9608, casw@casw-acts.ca, http://www.casw-acts.ca.

TREFFPUNKT BOULEVARD; aktiv - positiv - initiativ. *see* GENERAL INTEREST PERIODICALS—Switzerland

TRENDS IN SOCIAL SECURITY. *see* INSURANCE

300 DEU ISSN 0939-2564
TRIGON; Kunst, Wissenschaft und Glaube im Dialog. Text in German. 1990. irreg., latest vol.8, 2009. **Document type:** *Journal, Academic/Scholarly.*
Published by: Guardini Stiftung e.V., Askanischer Platz 4, Berlin, 10963, Germany. TEL 49-30-2173580, FAX 49-30-21735899, info@guardini.de.

TUSIAH-I RUSTAYI/JOURNAL OF RURAL DEVELOPMENT. *see* AGRICULTURE

360 ITA ISSN 0393-7798
TUTELA. Text in Italian. 1985. q. **Document type:** *Magazine, Consumer.*
Published by: Istituto Nazionale di Assistenza Sociale (I N A S), Viale Aventino 45, Rome, 00153, Italy. http://www.inas.it.

360 FIN ISSN 1238-2620
TYOTTOMYYSPAIVARAHAT. Text in Finnish. 1989. a. **Document type:** *Government.*
Related titles: ◆ Series of: Finland. Sosiaali- ja Terveysministerio. Julkaisuja. ISSN 1236-2050; ◆ Series of: Sosiaaliturva. ISSN 0785-4625.
Published by: Sosiaali- ja Terveysministerio/Ministry of Social Affairs and Health, Meritullinkatu 8, PO Box 33, Helsinki, 00171, Finland. TEL 358-9-1601, FAX 358-9-1602590, kirjaamo.stm@stm.fi, http://www.stm.fi.

U C S F MAGAZINE. (University of California at San Francisco) *see* MEDICAL SCIENCES

361 362.7 NLD ISSN 2211-7571
U M. (UNICEF Magazine) Text in Dutch. 1966. s-a. **Document type:** *Magazine, Consumer.*
Former titles (until 2010): U N I C E F Magazine (1878-9196); (until 2009): Kinderen Eerst! (1389-904X); (until 1999): U N I C E F Nieuws (0925-9139)
Published by: Nederlands Comite U N I C E F, Postbus 67, Voorburg, 2270 AB, Netherlands. TEL 31-70-3339300, FAX 31-70-3824774, info@unicef.nl, http://www.unicef.nl.

362 USA ISSN 0161-2417
HV91.N25b
U.S. NATIONAL CENTER FOR SOCIAL STATISTICS. HEARINGS IN PUBLIC ASSISTANCE. Text in English. 1970. s-a. free. stat.
Formerly (until 1976): U.S. National Center for Social Statistics. Fair Hearings in Public Assistance (0145-9422)
Published by: U.S. National Center for Social Statistics, U S Department of Health, Education and Welfare, 330 Independence Ave, S W, Washington, DC 20201. TEL 301-436-7900.

360 USA ISSN 0082-8556
U S O ANNUAL REPORT. (United Service Organizations) Text in English. a. free. **Document type:** *Corporate.*
Published by: United Service Organizations, Inc., U S O World Headquarters, Washington Navy Yard, 901 M St, S E, Bldg 198, Washington, DC 20374-5096. TEL 202-610-5700, FAX 202-610-5701. Ed. Miguel Monteverde. Circ: 5,000.

361 USA ISSN 1946-3634
U.S. OFFICE OF PRIVATE SECTOR INITIATIVES. PEACE CORPS. PARTNERSHIP. Text in English. 2007. q. free (effective 2009). back issues avail. **Document type:** *Newsletter, Trade.*
Media: Online - full content.
Published by: Peace Corps, Office of Private Sector Initiatives, 1111 20th St, NW, Washington, DC 20526. TEL 202-692-2170, 800-424-8580, FAX 202-692-2171, pcpp@peacecorps.gov, http://www.peacecorps.gov.

360 NLD
UBUNTU (DUTCH EDITION, ONLINE). Text in Dutch. 2003. q. free (effective 2010). **Document type:** *Newsletter.*
Formerly (until 2003): Ubuntu (Dutch Edition, Print) (1572-428X)
Media: Online - full text. **Related titles:** ◆ English ed.: Ubuntu (English Edition, Online).
Published by: South Africa Foundation/Stichting Projecten Zuid-Afrika, Zandstroom A6, Blijham, 9697 NW, Netherlands. TEL 31-182-582035, FAX 31-84-7352214, info@spza.org, http://www.spza.org/. Eds. Martje Nooij, Hilde von Michaelis.

360 NLD
UBUNTU (ENGLISH EDITION, ONLINE). Text in English. 2002. q. free (effective 2010). **Document type:** *Newsletter.*
Formerly (until 2003): Ubuntu (English Edition, Print) (1572-4298)
Media: Online - full text. **Related titles:** ◆ Dutch ed.: Ubuntu (Dutch Edition, Online).
Published by: South Africa Foundation/Stichting Projecten Zuid-Afrika, Zandstroom A6, Blijham, 9697 NW, Netherlands. TEL 31-182-582035, FAX 31-84-7352214, info@spza.org, http://www.spza.org/. Eds. Martje Nooij, Hilde von Michaelis.

360 DNK ISSN 1600-888X
UDEN FOR NUMMER; tidsskrift for social forskning. Text in Danish. 2000. s-a. **Document type:** *Magazine, Trade.*
Related titles: Online - full text ed.: ISSN 1604-844X; ◆ Issued with: Socialraadgiveren. ISSN 0108-6103.
Published by: Dansk Socialraadgiverforening/Danish Association of Social Workers, Toldbodgade 19 A, PO Box 69, Copenhagen K, 1003, Denmark. TEL 45-70-101099, FAX 45-33-913069, ds@socialrdg.dk. Ed. Lise Faerch.

UNDERSTANDING CHILDREN'S SOCIAL CARE. *see* CHILDREN AND YOUTH—About

360 FRA ISSN 0041-7041
HV2
UNION SOCIALE. Text in French. 1947. m. adv. illus. index. **Document type:** *Magazine, Trade.*
Formerly (until 1957): Union Sociale des Oeuvres Privees (0991-9236)
Indexed: FR.
Published by: Union Nationale Interfederale des Oeuvres et Organismes Prives Sanitaires et Sociaux (U N I O P S S), 15 Rue Albert, Paris, Cedex 13 75214, France. Ed. Jean Vellard. Circ: 8,000.

UNIONIST (NEW YORK). *see* LABOR UNIONS

360 FRA ISSN 2106-6566
UNIS-CITE. LA LETTRE. Text in French. 200?. 3/yr. **Document type:** *Newsletter, Consumer.*
Published by: Unis-Cite, 16, Place des Abbesses, Paris, 75018, France. TEL 33-1-53418143, FAX 33-1-53418144, http://www.uniscite.fr/qui-sommes-nous-organisation.php.

360 GBR ISSN 1368-230X
UNIT COSTS OF HEALTH & SOCIAL CARE. Text in English. 1993. a. GBP 42 per issue (effective 2010). charts; stat. back issues avail. **Document type:** *Bulletin, Trade.*
Formerly (until 1996): Unit Costs of Community Care (0969-4226)
—CCC.
Published by: Personal Social Services Research Unit, University of Kent at Canterbury, Cornwallis Bldg, George Allen Wing, Canterbury, Kent CT2 7NF, United Kingdom. TEL 44-1227-827773, 44-1227-827672, FAX 44-1227-827038, pssru@kent.ac.uk, http://www.pssru.ac.uk/.

361 362.7 USA ISSN 0254-2447
UNITED NATIONS CHILDREN'S FUND. ANNUAL REPORT. Cover title: UNICEF Annual Report. Text in English, French, Spanish. 1977. a. free. back issues avail. **Document type:** *Proceedings, Corporate.* **Description:** Discusses the work that UNICEF has done over the past year to improve the condition of children worldwide.
Related titles: Online - full content ed.
Indexed: IIS.
Published by: United Nations Children's Fund, Division of Communication, 3 United Nations Plaza, New York, NY 10017. pubdoc@unicef.org. Circ: 66,650 (controlled).

361 362.7 USA ISSN 1013-3178
HV713
UNITED NATIONS CHILDREN'S FUND. PROGRAMME DIVISION. STAFF WORKING PAPERS SERIES. Text in English. 1988. irreg. (2-4/yr). price varies. **Document type:** *Monographic series, Academic/Scholarly.*
Related titles: Microform ed.
Published by: (Programme Division), United Nations Children's Fund/Fonds des Nations Unies pour l'Enfance, 3 United Nations Plz, New York, NY 10017. TEL 212-326-7000, FAX 212-887-7465, http://www.unicef.org/.

325.21 USA ISSN 0082-8386
JX1977
UNITED NATIONS RELIEF AND WORKS AGENCY FOR PALESTINE REFUGEES IN THE NEAR EAST. REPORT OF THE COMMISSIONER-GENERAL. Text in English. 1963. a. USD 7 (effective 2008). **Document type:** *Journal, Trade.*
Related titles: Spanish ed.: ISSN 0250-8958; Arabic ed.: ISSN 0250-8966; Chinese ed.: ISSN 0251-7973; Russian ed.: ISSN 0251-7965; French ed.: ISSN 0250-8974.
—CCC.
Published by: (United Nations Relief and Works Agency, Information Office AUT), United Nations Publications, 2 United Nations Plaza, Rm DC2-853, New York, NY 10017. TEL 212-963-8302, 800-253-9646, FAX 212-963-3489, publications@un.org.

361.8 USA ISSN 0190-9630
HV89
UNITED WAY OF AMERICA. ANNUAL REPORT. Text in English. a.
Published by: United Way of America, 701 N Fairfax, Alexandria, VA 22314. TEL 703-836-7112, http://unitedway.org.

360 AUS ISSN 1832-1925
UNITINGCARE WESLEY NEWS. Text in English. 2003. s-a. back issues avail. **Document type:** *Newsletter, Consumer.* **Description:** Features short news stories that summarise the work undertaken by the individual organisations as well as collaborative activities.
Formed by the merger of (1976-2003): Port Report; (1973-198?): Transmission; Which was formerly: Trans Mission
Related titles: Online - full text ed.: free (effective 2009).
Published by: UnitingCare Wesley Adelaide Inc., 10 Pitt St, Adelaide, SA 5000, Australia. TEL 61-8-82025111, enquiries@ucwesleyadelaide.org.au, http://www.ucwesleyadelaide.org.au/default.htm. Eds. Diane Harris, Mark Henley TEL 61-8-82025135.

360 COL ISSN 0121-1722
UNIVERSIDAD PONTIFICIA BOLIVARIANA. FACULTAD DE TRABAJO SOCIAL. REVISTA. Text in Spanish. 1985. a. **Document type:** *Journal, Academic/Scholarly.*
Published by: Universidad Pontificia Bolivariana, Biblioteca, Apartado Aereo 56006, Medellin, Colombia. TEL 57-4-159075, FAX 57-4-118513.

361 NOR ISSN 1501-9071
UNIVERSITETET I OSLO. HELSEOEKONOMISK FORSKNINGSPROGRAM. WORKING PAPER. Text in English. 1999. irreg. back issues avail. **Document type:** *Monographic series, Academic/Scholarly.*
Related titles: Online - full text ed.: ISSN 1890-1735.
Published by: Universitetet i Oslo, Helseoekonomisk Forskningsprogram/University of Oslo, Health Economics Research Programme, PO Box 1089, Oslo, 0317, Norway. TEL 47-22-845048, FAX 47-22-845091, hero@hero.uio.no.

360 GBR
UNIVERSITY OF BIRMINGHAM. DEPARTMENT OF SOCIAL POLICY AND SOCIAL WORK. WORKING WITH POVERTY SERIES. Text in English. irreg. GBP 4. **Document type:** *Monographic series.*
Published by: University of Birmingham, Department of Social Policy and Social Work, University Of Birmingham, Edgbaston, Birmingham, Worcs B15 2TT, United Kingdom. TEL 44-121-414-5719, FAX 44-121-414-5726.

333.338 GBR ISSN 1468-6147
UNIVERSITY OF YORK. INDEX OF PRIVATE RENTS AND YIELDS. Text in English. 1996. q. **Document type:** *Report, Trade.*
Formerly (until 1999): Joseph Rowntree Foundation Index of Private Rents and Yields (1366-6274)
—CCC.
Published by: University of York, Centre for Housing Policy, Heslington, York, YO10 5DD, United Kingdom. TEL 44-1904-321480, FAX 44-1904-321481, chp@york.ac.uk, http://www.york.ac.uk/inst/chp/.

361.61094105 GBR ISSN 1749-3854
UNIVERSITY OF YORK. SOCIAL POLICY RESEARCH UNIT. RESEARCH WORKS. Text in English. 2000. irreg., latest 2009. **Document type:** *Monographic series, Academic/Scholarly.* **Description:** The series summarises findings from projects undertaken by the Unit.
Related titles: Online - full text ed.: ISSN 1749-3862. free (effective 2009).
Published by: University of York, Social Policy Research Unit, Heslington, York, YO10 5DD, United Kingdom. TEL 44-1904-321950, FAX 44-1904-321953, spruinfo@york.ac.uk, http://www.york.ac.uk/inst/spru/index.html.

331.252 AUT
UNSERE GENERATION. Text in German. 1950. m. EUR 20 membership (effective 2007). adv. **Document type:** *Magazine, Consumer.*
Former titles (until 1992): Rentner und Pensionist (0034-4540); (until 1959): Der Arbeiterrentner
Published by: Pensionistenverband Oesterreichs, Gentzgasse 129, Vienna, W 1180, Austria. FAX 43-1-3137212, office@pvoe.at, http://www.pvoe.at. Ed. Erwin Liebeg. Circ: 350,000.

362.5 USA
UPDATE (CHICAGO). Text in English. q. **Document type:** *Newsletter.* **Description:** Describes the work Second Harvest is doing with some 200 local food banks nationwide to provide adequate nutrition to America's poorest citizens, 42 percent of whom are children.
Published by: Second Harvest, 116 S Michigan Ave, Ste 4, Chicago, IL 60603-6001. TEL 312-263-2303, FAX 312-263-5626. Ed. Mary Chase.

UPDATE (WASHINGTON). *see* LIBRARY AND INFORMATION SCIENCES

307.1 USA ISSN 0042-0832
HT101
URBAN AND SOCIAL CHANGE REVIEW. Text in English. 1967. s-a. USD 8. adv. bk.rev.; film rev. reprints avail.
Formerly: Institute of Human Sciences. Review
Related titles: Microform ed.: (from PQC).
Indexed: ABCPolSci, AIAP, AMHA, AmH&L, KES, MCR, P30, PMA, S02, S03, SWR&A, TRA.

Published by: Boston College, Graduate School of Social Work, McGuinn Hall, Rm 109, Chestnut Hill, MA 02167. TEL 617-552-4038. Ed. Robert M Moroney. Circ: 2,500.

URBAN DIRECTIONS. *see* HOUSING AND URBAN PLANNING

362.1 NOR ISSN 1890-1468
UTVIKLINGSTREKK I HELSE- OG SOCIALSEKTOREN. Variant title: Sosial- og Helsedirektoratet. Rapport. Text in Norwegian. 2006. a. **Document type:** *Yearbook, Consumer.*
Related titles: Online - full text ed.
Published by: Helsedirektoratet/Norwegian Directorate of Health, PO Box 7000, St Olavs Plass, Oslo, 0130, Norway. TEL 47-810-20050, FAX 47-24-163001, postmottak@helsedirektoratet.no.

V A C R O REPORTER. *see* CRIMINOLOGY AND LAW ENFORCEMENT

355 DEU
V D K ZEITUNG. (Verband der Kriegsbeschaedigten, Kriegshinterbliebenen und Sozialrentner Deutschlands) Text in German. 1946. 10/yr. EUR 4.50 per month membership (effective 2008). adv. 24 p./no.; **Document type:** *Newspaper, Consumer.*
Description: Covers social politics, social law, laws covering pensions, health and accident insurance and other aspects of international social welfare laws.
Formerly: Fackel (0014-6447)
Related titles: Regional ed(s).: V d K Zeitung. Ausgabe Hessen. ISSN 0943-2655. 1947; V d K Zeitung. Ausgabe Westfalen-Lippe. ISSN 0943-271X. 1947; V d K Zeitung. Ausgabe Mittelfranken. ISSN 0943-2612. 1993; V d K Zeitung. Ausgabe Niederbayern. ISSN 0943-2574. 1993; V d K Zeitung. Ausgabe Niederrhein. ISSN 0943-2698. 1983; V d K Zeitung. Ausgabe Nordbaden. ISSN 0943-2531. 1955; V d K Zeitung. Ausgabe Nordwuerttemberg. ISSN 0943-2515. 1955; V d K Zeitung. Ausgabe Oberbayern. ISSN 0943-2566. 1993; V d K Zeitung. Ausgabe Oberfranken. ISSN 0943-2604. 1993; V d K Zeitung. Ausgabe Oberpfalz. ISSN 0943-2582. 1993; V d K Zeitung. Ausgabe Rheinland. ISSN 0943-268X. 1947; V d K Zeitung. Ausgabe Rheinland-Pfalz. ISSN 0943-2728. 1947; V d K Zeitung. Ausgabe Saarland. ISSN 0943-2736. 19??; V d K Zeitung. Ausgabe Schwaben. ISSN 0943-2590. 1993; V d K Zeitung. Ausgabe Suedbaden. ISSN 0943-254X. 1955; V d K Zeitung. Ausgabe Unterfranken. ISSN 0943-2620. 1993; V d K Zeitung. Ausgabe Westfalen. ISSN 0943-2701. 1983; V d K Zeitung. Ausgabe Hamburg - Schleswig-Holstein. ISSN 0943-2647. 1993.
Published by: Sozialverband V d K Deutschland, Wurzerstr 4A, Bonn, 53175, Germany. TEL 49-228-820930, FAX 49-228-8209343, kontakt@vdk.de, http://www.vdk.de. Ed. Sabine Kohls. R&P Ulrich Laschet. adv.: B&W page EUR 30,751, color page EUR 35,606; trim 280 x 428. Circ: 1,282,338 (paid and controlled).

362.82 USA
V M C VOICE; volunteer - opportunity - information - community - education. Text in English. 1997. q. free. illus. **Document type:** *Newsletter.* **Description:** Reports on VMC's efforts to coordinate volunteers for social services in the Morris County, NJ, area.
Published by: Volunteers for Morris County, 280 West Hanover Ave, Morristown, NJ 07960. TEL 973-538-7200, FAX 973-984-7658. Eds. Ellen Konwiser, Nancy Hess.

VADE MECUM: BEGROTING VAN DE SOCIALE BESCHERMING (YEAR)/SOCIAL PROTECTION BUDGET. *see* PUBLIC ADMINISTRATION

VADE MECUM: BEGROTINGSCONTROLE (YEAR)/BUDGET CONTROL. *see* PUBLIC ADMINISTRATION

362 NLD ISSN 2210-4607
VAKBLAD VOOR CONTEXTUELE HULPVERLENING. Text in Dutch. 1995. q. EUR 40; EUR 12.50 newsstand/cover (effective 2010). adv. **Document type:** *Magazine, Trade.*
Published by: Vereniging van Contextueel Werkers, Postbus 2834, Utrecht, 3500 GV, Netherlands. TEL 31-6-24571048, info@contextueelwerkers.eu, http://www.contextueelwerkers.nl. Ed. Rene Knip.

VANDALISME, CRIMINALITEIT EN VOLKSHUISVESTING. *see* HOUSING AND URBAN PLANNING

711.4 USA ISSN 0892-6433
VANGUARD (MILWAUKEE, 1970). Text in English. 1970. q. USD 85 domestic (effective 2001); USD 95 foreign; includes the Journal. adv. reprints avail. **Document type:** *Newsletter.*
Related titles: Online - full text ed.: ISSN 1931-7026.
—Infotrieve.
Published by: Community Development Society, 17 S High St, Ste 200, Columbus, OH 43215. TEL 614-221-1900 ext 217, FAX 614-221-1989, kate@assnoffices.com, http://www.comm-dev.org. adv.: 1/2 page USD 100.

361.6 VEN ISSN 0798-9474
VENEZUELA. MINISTERIO DE SANIDAD Y ASISTENCIA SOCIAL. MEMORIA Y CUENTA. Text in Spanish. 1936. a. **Document type:** *Government.*
Published by: Ministerio de Sanidad y Asistencia Social, c/o Oficina de Publicaciones Biblioteca y Archivo,, Centro Simon Bolivar, Torre Sur 5o, Caracas, DF 1010, Venezuela. Ed. Manuel Boet. Circ: 3,000.

368 AUT
VERBAND DER VERSICHERUNGSUNTERNEHMEN OESTERREICHS. JAHRESBERICHT. Text in German. 1956. a. **Document type:** *Yearbook, Corporate.*
Former titles: Verband der Versicherungsunternehmen Oesterreichs. Geschaeftsbericht; Verband der Versicherungsunternehmungen Oesterreichs. Bericht ueber das Geschaeftsjahr (0083-5501)
Published by: Verband der Versicherungsunternehmen Oesterreichs, Schwarzenbergplatz 7, Vienna, W 1030, Austria. TEL 43-1-711560, FAX 43-1-71156270, sari@vvo.at, http://www.vvo.at. Ed., R&P Gregor Kozak. Circ: 1,000.

VERDANDISTEN; spraakroer foer socialpolitik och medmaenskiighet. *see* DRUG ABUSE AND ALCOHOLISM

360 DEU ISSN 0935-1558
DIE VERSORGUNGSVERWALTUNG. Text in German. 1949. bi-m. EUR 54 (effective 2005). adv. **Document type:** *Magazine, Trade.*
Formerly (until 1989): Versorgungsbeamte (0340-3289)
—CCC.
Published by: (Gewerkschaft der Versorgungsverwaltung), SZ Offsetdruck-Verlag, Martin-Luther-Str 2-6, Sankt Augustin, 53757, Germany. TEL 49-2241-91330, FAX 49-2241-913333, office@sz-druck.de. adv.: B&W page EUR 824. Circ: 5,025 (controlled).

360 RUS
VESTNIK PSIKHOSOTSYAL'NOI I KORREKTSIONNO-REABILITATSIONNOI RABOTY. Text in Russian. 1994. q. USD 99.95 in United States. 96 p./no.; **Document type:** *Bulletin.*
Description: Covers psycho-social support of children and families from group of risk as well as correctional and rehabilittion techniques.
Indexed: RASB.
Published by: Sotsyal'noe Zdorov'e Rossii, Rublevskoe shosse 87, korp 2, Moscow, 121467, Russian Federation. TEL 7-095-1415086, FAX 7-095-1415086. Ed. S. A. Belicheva. Circ: 25,000 (paid); 3,000 (controlled). **Dist. by:** East View Information Services, 10601 Wayzata Blvd, Minneapolis, MN 55305. TEL 952-252-1201, 800-477-1005, FAX 952-252-1202, info@eastview.com, http://www.eastview.com.

361 SWE ISSN 1653-2562
VETERANEN. Text in Swedish. 1977. 9/yr. SEK 270 to non-members (effective 2011). **Document type:** *Magazine, Consumer.*
Former titles (until 2004): Veteranposten (1102-8610); (until 1991): Pensionaerstidningen Veteranposten (0282-1788); (until 1983): Sveriges Folkpensionaerers Riksfoerbunds Tidning Veteranposten (0346-0673); Which was formed by the 1977 merger of: Veteran-Posten; (1962-1977): Sveriges Folkpensionaerers Riksfoerbunds Tidning
Related titles: Online - full text ed.
Published by: Sveriges Paensionaers Foerbund, PO Box 22574, Stockholm, 10422, Sweden. TEL 46-8-6923250, FAX 46-8-6510929, info@spfpension.se, http://www.spfpension.se. Ed. Ylva Bergman. Adv. contact Katarina Lindstroem.

VICTIMIZATION OF THE ELDERLY AND DISABLED; preventing abuse, mistreatment and neglect. *see* CRIMINOLOGY AND LAW ENFORCEMENT

360 AUS
VICTORIA. DEPARTMENT OF HUMAN SERVICES. COMMUNITY CARE DIVISION. RESEARCH MATTERS. Text in English. 1999 (Aug., vol.1, no.3). irreg. back issues avail. **Document type:** *Newsletter, Government.* **Description:** Provides an overview of research projects and planning being undertaken by Youth and Family Services, Department of Human Services.
Media: Online - full content.
Published by: Victoria, Department Of Human Services, Community Care Division (Subsidiary of: Victoria, Department of Human Services), 50 Lonsdale St, Melbourne, VIC 3000, Australia. TEL 61-3-90960000, 300-650-172, http://www.dhs.vic.gov.au.

VICTORIA. OFFICE OF THE CHILD SAFETY COMMISSIONER. VICTORIAN CHILD DEATH REVIEW COMMITTEE. ANNUAL REPORT OF INQUIRIES INTO THE DEATHS OF CHILDREN KNOWN TO CHILD PROTECTION (YEAR). *see* CHILDREN AND YOUTH—About

360 VNM
VIETNAM'S URGENT ISSUES. Text in English. 2000. bi-m. USD 15.70 domestic; USD 30.30 in Asia; USD 31.32 in Europe; USD 32.52 in Africa; USD 33 in United States (effective 2002). **Document type:** *Journal, Academic/Scholarly.* **Description:** Contains a collection of press articles on various topics: population, labour and employment, education and training, ethnicity and religion, hunger eradications and poverty reduction, eco-environment, etc. This also includes overviews, reports, statistical data from various branches and industries, and legal documents relevant to foreign residents in Vietnam. The series gives the readers insights into the realities of Vietnam and how this country deals with arising questions.
Published by: Gioi Publishers/Foreign Languages Publishing House, 46 Tran Hung Dao, Hanoi, Viet Nam. TEL 84-4-8253841, FAX 84-4-8269578, thegioi@hn.vnn.vn.

VIEWPOINT (LONDON, 1995). *see* MEDICAL SCIENCES—Psychiatry And Neurology

VIGO! JOBFIT BLEIBGESUND. *see* OCCUPATIONS AND CAREERS

VIGO! UNILIFE BLEIBGESUND. *see* PUBLIC HEALTH AND SAFETY

362.7 NLD ISSN 1872-5422
VILLA PARDOES MAGAZINE. Text in Dutch. 2000. s-a.
Formerly (until 2005): Villa Pardoes Nieuws (1571-635X)
Published by: Villa Pardoes, Postbus 133, Kaatsheuvel, 5170 AC, Netherlands. TEL 31-416-387222, FAX 31-416-387220, info@villapardoes.nl, http://www.villapardoes.nl.

362.6 333.33 AUS ISSN 1833-4857
VILLAGE COMMUNITIES OF AUSTRALIA. Text in English. 2006. s-a. AUD 9.95 (effective 2007). **Document type:** *Directory, Consumer.* **Description:** Written for people 55+ in consideration of their retirement options.
Published by: Villages Publishing, Dockside 8, 37 Nicholson St, East Balmain, NSW 2041, Australia. TEL 61-2-9810-5555, FAX 61-2-9810-5577, info@villages.com.au, http://www.villages.com.au.

362.7 ZAF
VILLAGE NEWS. Text in English. 1993. a. illus. **Document type:** *Newsletter.*
Published by: S O S Children's Village Association of South Africa, PO Box 22, Randburg, Gauteng 2125, South Africa. TEL 27-11-7929324, FAX 27-11-7929329. Ed. Phil MacKenzie. Circ: 90,000.

VIOLENCE AND VICTIMS. *see* SOCIOLOGY

362.4 CAN ISSN 1718-4274
VISION - ERE. Text in French. 2000. 3/yr. **Document type:** *Magazine, Consumer.*
Published by: Regroupement des Personnes Handicapees Visuelles, 503, rue du Prince Edouard, bureau 100, Quebec, PQ G1K 2M8, Canada. TEL 418-649-0333, rphv@rphv0312.org.

361.7 NZL ISSN 1176-9904
VISTA. Running title: V S A Magazine. Text in English. s-a. NZD 30 to individual members; NZD 100 to institutional members (effective 2008). back issues avail. **Document type:** *Magazine, Trade.*
Former titles (until 2005): Manu Rere (1171-0187); (until 1991): V S A Broadsheet
Published by: Te Tuao Tawahi Volunteer Service Abroad, Freepost 100017, PO Box 12-246, Wellington, New Zealand. TEL 64-4-4725759, FAX 64-4-4725052, vsa@vsa.org.nz.

VISUAL DIAGNOSIS OF CHILD ABUSE ON CD-ROM. *see* MEDICAL SCIENCES—Pediatrics

VIVRE ENSEMBLE. *see* EDUCATION—Special Education And Rehabilitation

362.7 CAN
VOCALPOINT. Text in English. 1996. 3/yr. CAD 10 to individuals; CAD 25 to institutions (effective 2006). **Document type:** *Journal, Academic/Scholarly.*
Formerly (until 2004): Focus on Children and Youth (1208-8110); Which was formed by the merger of (198?-1995): Society for Children and Youth of B.C. Newsletter (1200-8230); (1984-1995): Child Abuse Newsletter (0843-3275); Which was formerly (until 1988): Child Sexual Abuse Newsletter (0831-9634)
Published by: The Society for Children and Youth of B.C., 802-207 W Hastings St, Vancouver, BC V6B 1H7, Canada. TEL 604-433-4180, FAX 604-669-7054, info@scyofbc.org. Ed. Lynne Melcombe.

325.73 ITA ISSN 0394-8153
VOCE DELL'EMIGRANTE; periodico sulle problematiche dell'emigrazione ed immigrazione. Text in Italian. 1974. m. EUR 12 domestic; EUR 14 in Europe; EUR 18 in the Americas; EUR 21 in Australia (effective 2008). adv. bk.rev. bibl.; charts; illus.; stat.; tr.lit. back issues avail. **Document type:** *Newspaper, Consumer.*
Description: Focuses on immigration and emigration issues.
Related titles: E-mail ed.; Online - full text ed.; Supplement(s): Italiamondo. 1953. USD 20.
Published by: Comitato Regionale Emigranti Abruzzesi, Vico Sportello, 10, Casella Postale 7, Pratola Peligna, AQ 67035, Italy. TEL 39-0864-53147, FAX 39-0864-53147, http://utenti.tripod.it/emigrante. Ed. Angelo De Bartolomeis. Circ: 12,000.

360 640.73 AUS
THE VOICE. Text in English. 1956. 11/yr. AUD 12 (effective 2008). adv. bk.rev.; film rev.; play rev. stat. **Description:** Covers social services and welfare, consumer education and protection and taxation information, social security entitlements.
Formerly: Pensioners Voice (1035-3615)
Published by: Combined Pensioners and Superannuants Association of N.S.W. Inc., Level 9, 28 Foveaux St, Surry Hills, NSW 2010, Australia. TEL 61-2-9281-3588, 1800-451-488, FAX 61-2-9281-9716, cpsa@cpsa.org.au, http://www.cpsa.org.au/MAIN/Home.php. Circ: 15,000.

THE VOICE (AUSTIN, 1923)). *see* CHILDREN AND YOUTH—About

360 IND ISSN 0974-3545
VOICE OF DALIT. Text in English. 2008. s-a. INR 750 domestic (print or online ed.); USD 75 foreign (print or online ed.); INR 1,250, USD 125 combined subscription domestic (print & online eds.) (effective 2010). **Document type:** *Journal, Academic/Scholarly.* **Description:** Provide information on the oppression, marginalization and socio-economic exclusion of the Indian "dalits," covering issues such as Illiteracy, malnutrition, unemployment and under-employment, displacement and violence.
Related titles: Online - full text ed.
Indexed: P10, P48, P53, P54, PQC.
Published by: M D Publications Pvt Ltd, 11 Darya Ganj, New Delhi, 110 002, India. TEL 91-11-41563325, FAX 91-11-23275542, contact@mdppl.com. Ed. Debi Chatterjee.

614 362 USA ISSN 1530-7867
R726
VOICES (WASHINGTON). Text in English. 1975. q. bk.rev. illus. **Document type:** *Newsletter.*
Former titles (until 2000): Choices (Washington) (1079-2953); (until 1994): Choice in Dying News; Concern for Dying - Society for the Right to Die Newsletter; (until 1985): Concern for Dying Newsletter (0192-1096); (until 1978): Euthanasia News (0164-1581)
Related titles: Online - full text ed.
Indexed: A04, P30.
Published by: Partnership for Caring, 1620 Eye Street NW, Ste 202, Washington, DC 20006. TEL 202-296-8071, 800-989-9455, FAX 202-296-8352, pfc@partnershipforcaring.org, http://www.partnershipforcaring.org. Ed., R&P Karen Kaplan. Circ: 80,000.

VOICES OF THAI WOMEN. *see* WOMEN'S INTERESTS

360 FRA ISSN 1272-968X
LA VOIX DE FRANCE. Text in French. 1928. m. EUR 17 domestic; EUR 22 foreign; EUR 3 per issue (effective 2010). adv. illus. **Document type:** *Magazine, Consumer.*
Former titles (until 1949): Union des Francais de l'Etranger. Circulaire (1272-9671); (until 1944): La Voix de France, l'Appel Francais (1272-9663); Which was formed by the 1932 merger of: La Voix de France (1272-9647); L' Appel Francais (1272-9655)
Published by: Union des Francais de l'Etranger, 28, rue de Chateaudun, Paris, 75009, France. TEL 33-01-53251550, FAX 33-01-53251014, http://www.ufe.asso.fr. Ed. Bruno de Leusse.

LA VOIX DES PARENTS. *see* HANDICAPPED

360 FRA ISSN 2104-9416
LA VOIX DU COMBATTANT. Text in French. 1976. m. EUR 14 domestic to individuals; EUR 23.50 foreign to individuals (effective 2011). **Document type:** *Consumer.*
Formerly (until 1992): La Voix du Combattant, La Voix du Djebel, Flamme (0182-5593)
Published by: Union Nationale des Combattants, 18 Rue Vezelay, Paris, 75008, France. TEL 33-1-53890413, 33-1-53890404, uncnationale@unc.fr, http://www.unc.fr/index.php.

VOKSNE (ONLINE). *see* PUBLIC HEALTH AND SAFETY

360 AUT ISSN 0504-6998
VOLKSHILFE. Text in German. 1954. q. free. back issues avail. **Document type:** *Magazine, Trade.*
Published by: Volkshilfe Oesterreich, Auerspergstr 4, Vienna, 1010, Austria. TEL 43-1-4026209, office@volkshilfe.at, http://www.volkshilfe.at.

VOLKSHUISVESTINGSBELEID EN WONINGMARKT. *see* HOUSING AND URBAN PLANNING

360 CHL ISSN 0717-6481
VOLUNTARIOS. Text in Spanish. 2001. bi-m. **Document type:** *Magazine, Trade.*
Published by: Asociacion Chilena de Voluntarios, Serrano 14, Of 901, Santiago, Chile. TEL 56-2-6642710, FAX 56-2-6323306, achv@entelchile.net.

S

360 GBR ISSN 0951-4481
VOLUNTARY AGENCIES DIRECTORY. Text in English. 1928. a. GBP 60 per issue to non-members; GBP 35 per issue to members (effective 2009). back issues avail. **Document type:** *Directory, Trade.* **Description:** Lists over 2,500 leading national agencies, ranging from small, specialized self-help groups to long-established charities.
Former titles (until 1986): Voluntary Organisations (0263-3922); (until 1980): Voluntary Social Services (0083-6907)
—BLDSC (9254.573300). **CCC.**
Published by: National Council for Voluntary Organisations, Regent's Wharf, 8 All Saints St, London, N1 9RL, United Kingdom. TEL 44-20-77136161, FAX 44-20-77136300, ncvo@ncvo-vol.org.uk, http://www.ncvo-vol.org.uk.

361.37 USA ISSN 0957-8765
HD62.6 CODEN: VOLUE8
➤ **VOLUNTAS**; international journal of voluntary and non-profit organizations. Text in English; Abstracts in French, German, Spanish. 1990. q. EUR 564, USD 593 combined subscription to institutions (print & online eds.) (effective 2012). adv. bk.rev. back issues avail.; reprint service avail. from PSC. **Document type:** *Journal, Academic/Scholarly.* **Description:** Provides a forum for worldwide research in the area between the state, market, and household sectors.
Related titles: Online - full text ed.: ISSN 1573-7888 (from IngentaConnect).
Indexed: A01, A03, A08, A12, A22, A26, ABIn, BibInd, BibLing, CA, CurCont, E01, GEOBASE, IBSS, N06, P10, P27, P34, P42, P48, P51, P53, P54, PAIS, PQC, PSA, S02, S03, SCOPUS, SOPODA, SSA, SSCI, SWR&A, SociolAb, T02, W07.
—BLDSC (9254.577800), IE, Infotrieve, Ingenta. **CCC.**
Published by: (Internal Society for Third Sector Research), Springer New York LLC (Subsidiary of: Springer Science+Business Media), 233 Spring St, New York, NY 10013. TEL 212-460-1500, FAX 212-460-1575, service-ny@springer.com, http://www.springer.com/. Ed. Bernard Enjolras.

360 USA
HV89
VOLUNTEER! (NEW YORK, 1944); the comprehensive guide to voluntary service in the US and abroad. Text in English. 1944. s-a. adv. **Document type:** *Directory, Trade.* **Description:** Directory of voluntary service and work camp opportunities in the US and abroad for all ages.
Formerly (until 1985): Invest Yourself (0148-6802)
Published by: Council on International Educational Exchange, 633 3rd Ave., New York, NY 10017-6706. TEL 212-661-1414. Ed. Richard Christiano. Adv. contact Stephanie Orange. Circ: 8,000.

VOLUNTEER AND VISTORS' GUIDE. *see* GERONTOLOGY AND GERIATRICS

360 USA ISSN 1527-411X
HV91
VOLUNTEER LEADERSHIP. Text in English. 1996. q. USD 25. adv. bk.rev. **Document type:** *Newsletter.*
Formerly: Leadership (Washington, 1992); Supersedes (in 1992): Voluntary Action Leadership (0149-6492); Incorporates (1970-1976): Voluntary Action News (0300-6638)
Indexed: P30.
—Ingenta.
Published by: Points of Light Foundation, 1737 H St, N W, Washington, DC 20006. TEL 202-223-9186. Ed. Jane Harvey. R&P Cathy Soffin TEL 202-223-9186 ext.146. Adv. contact Patty Dugan. Circ: 5,000.

360 USA ISSN 1091-3777
HN90.V64
THE VOLUNTEER MANAGEMENT REPORT. Text in English. 1996. m. USD 119; USD 129 foreign (effective 2000). bk.rev.; software rev. back issues avail. **Document type:** *Newsletter.* **Description:** Provides ideas for those who manage volunteers.
Published by: Stevenson, Inc., PO Box 4528, Sioux City, IA 51104. TEL 712-239-3010, FAX 712-239-2166. Ed., Pub. Scott C Stevenson. R&P Jodi Spencer.

361.8 GBR
VOLUNTEERING (ONLINE). Text in English. 1978. 10/yr. free to members (effective 2009). bk.rev. illus. index. back issues avail. **Document type:** *Magazine, Trade.* **Description:** Deals with all issues relevant to volunteering.
Former titles (until 2004): Volunteering (Print) (1355-266X); (until 1994): Volunteers (0961-5075); (until 1990): Involve (0143-0831); Which incorporated (in 1978): Involve (Health Services Edition)
Media: Online - full text.
Published by: National Centre for Volunteering, Regents Wharf, 8 All Saints St, London, N1 9RL, United Kingdom. TEL 44-845-3056979, FAX 44-20-75208910, volunteering@volunteeringengland.org.

361.8 USA ISSN 0890-1090
VOLUNTEERING VIRGINIA. Text in English. q.
Published by: Virginia Office of Volunteerism, 730 E Brad St, Richmond, VA 2321-1849. TEL 804-692-1950, FAX 804-692-1999, vol2@ema1.dss.state.va.us.

360 ESP ISSN 1138-2171
VOLVER A SER. Text in Spanish. 1993. q. free (effective 2008). **Document type:** *Bulletin, Consumer.*
Published by: Caritas Espanola, San Bernardo, 99 bis 7a, Madrid, 28015, Spain. TEL 34-91-4441000, FAX 34-91-5934882, publicaciones@caritas-espa.org, http://www.caritas.es.

VOTE AND SURVEY; magazine of political, social and economic issues. *see* POLITICAL SCIENCE

360 CHE
VOTRE CROIX ROUGE. Text in French. 1974. q. CHF 20; CHF 7 newsstand/cover (effective 2008). **Document type:** *Journal, Trade.*
Published by: Croix-Rouge Suisse, Section Genevoise, 9 route des Acacias, Geneva 24, 1211, Switzerland. TEL 41-22-3040404, FAX 41-22-3003183, info@croix-rouge-ge.ch, http://www.croixrougegenevoise.ch. Circ: 500.

VOYAGER INTERNATIONAL. *see* SOCIOLOGY

361.6 331 NLD ISSN 2211-9914
▼ **VRIJWILLIGE INZET.** Text in Dutch. 2010. 3/yr. free (effective 2011). **Document type:** *Magazine, Trade.*
Published by: ZonMW, Postbus 93 245, The Hague, 2509 AE, Netherlands. TEL 31-70-3495111, FAX 31-70-3495100, info@zonmw.nl, http://www.zonmw.nl.

VULNERABLE CHILDREN AND YOUTH STUDIES; an international interdisciplinary journal for research, policy and care. *see* CHILDREN AND YOUTH—About

W M O MAGAZINE. (Wet Maatschappelijke Ondersteuning) *see* HANDICAPPED

WABANAKI LEGAL NEWS. *see* LAW—Legal Aid

360 GBR
WALES COUNCIL FOR VOLUNTARY ACTION. BRIEFING PAPER/ CYNGOR GWEITHREDU GWIRFODDOL CYMRU. PAPARAU CRYNHOI. Text in English. 19??. irreg., latest 2009, Nov. free (effective 2009). back issues avail. **Document type:** *Monographic series, Academic/Scholarly.* **Description:** Discusses various aspects of managing voluntary organizations.
Related titles: Online - full text ed.
Published by: Wales Council for Voluntary Action/Cyngor Gweithredu Gwirfoddol Cymru, Morfa Hall, Bath St, Rhyl, Denbighshire LL18 3EB, United Kingdom. TEL 44-1745-357540, FAX 44-1745-357541, enquiries@wcva.org.uk.

WASHINGTON COUNSELETTER. *see* OCCUPATIONS AND CAREERS

361.7 USA
HV98.W3
WASHINGTON STATE CHARITABLE TRUST DIRECTORY. Text in English. 1967. biennial. USD 20 (effective 1999). **Document type:** *Directory, Government.* **Description:** Consists of charitable trusts registered with the Office of the Secretary of State.
Former titles (until 1993): Washington (State). Attorney General's Office. Charitable Trust Directory (0148-3188); (until 1975): Washington (State). Attorney General's Office. Directory of Charitable Organizations and Trusts Registered with the Office of Attorney General (0093-6693)
Published by: Office of the Secretary of State, Charitable Trust Division, PO Box 40234, Olympia, WA 98504-0234. TEL 360-664-0742, FAX 360-664-4250. Ed. Frances Sant. Circ: 1,000.

WASHINGTON WINDOW. *see* RELIGIONS AND THEOLOGY—Protestant

WASHINGTON WIRE. *see* HOUSING AND URBAN PLANNING

360 CAN ISSN 1718-2336
A WEALTH OF RESOURCES; the ultimate guide to programs, services, and affordability in Kamloops. Text in English. 2006. a. **Document type:** *Directory, Consumer.*
Published by: One Hill Productions, 867 Battle St, Kamloops, BC V2C 2M7, Canada. support@onehill.ca.

360 DEU ISSN 0043-2059
WEGE ZUR SOZIALVERSICHERUNG; Zeitschrift fuer die Sozialversicherungs-Praxis. Text in German. 1947. m. EUR 67.20; EUR 7.50 newsstand/cover (effective 2012). adv. bk.rev. abstr.; bibl. **Document type:** *Journal, Academic/Scholarly.*
Related titles: Online - full text ed.: ISSN 2191-7345. EUR 67.20 (effective 2012); ◆ Supplement to: Fortbildung und Praxis. ISSN 0071-7835.
Indexed: DIP, IBR, IBZ, PAIS, WBSS.
Published by: Erich Schmidt Verlag GmbH & Co. (Berlin), Genthiner Str 30 G, Berlin, 10785, Germany. TEL 49-30-2500850, FAX 49-30-250085305, esv@esvmedien.de, http://www.esv.info.

362.7 GBR
WELFARE BENEFITS AND TAX CREDITS HANDBOOK. Text and summaries in English. 1999. a. (2 nos./vol.). GBP 37 per issue to non-members; free to members (effective 2010). back issues avail. **Document type:** *Directory, Trade.* **Description:** Provides a comprehensive coverage of all welfare benefits and tax credits.
Formerly (until 2003): Welfare Benefits Handbook (1467-2081); Which was formed by the merger of (199?-1999): Jobseeker's Allowance Handbook; (1972-1999): National Welfare Benefits Handbook (0308-5996); (1990-1999): Rights Guide to Non-Means-Tested Benefits (1365-5795); Which was formerly (until 1990): Rights Guide to Non-Means-Tested Social Security Benefits; (until 1980): Guide to Contributory Benefits and Child Benefit
Related titles: CD-ROM ed.
—CCC.
Published by: Child Poverty Action Group, 94 White Lion St, London, N1 9PF, United Kingdom. TEL 44-20-78377979, FAX 44-20-78376414, info@cpag.org.uk.

WELFARE BENEFITS GUIDE; health plans and other employer sponsored benefits. *see* BUSINESS AND ECONOMICS—Labor And Industrial Relations

WELFARE LAW. *see* LAW

360 USA
WELFARE NEWS. Text in English. bi-m. USD 40; USD 60 to libraries; includes Welfare Bulletin. back issues avail. **Document type:** *Newsletter.* **Description:** Reports on national policy developments and state developments that effect cash assistance for needy families and individuals. Includes a focus on low-income group activities.
Published by: Center on Social Welfare Policy and Law, 275 Seventh Ave, Ste 1205, New York, NY 10001-6708. TEL 212-633-6967, FAX 212-633-6371. Circ: 900.

362.7 GBR ISSN 0263-2098
WELFARE RIGHTS BULLETIN. Text in English. 1974. bi-m. GBP 32 to non-members; free to members (effective 2009). back issues avail. **Document type:** *Bulletin, Trade.* **Description:** Covers information about the rights information, practice, law, news, and reviews for the UK welfare adviser.
Indexed: ELJI, LJI.
—IE. **CCC.**
Published by: Child Poverty Action Group, 94 White Lion St, London, N1 9PF, United Kingdom. TEL 44-20-78377979, FAX 44-20-78376414, info@cpag.org.uk.

331.259 USA ISSN 1060-5622
HV85
WELFARE TO WORK; a review of developments in the welfare job training and placement field. Text in English. 1992. bi-w. USD 297 (effective 2004). bk.rev. charts; maps; stat. back issues avail. **Document type:** *Newsletter.* **Description:** Targets transitioning aid recipients to self-sustaining jobs.
Indexed: CWI.
Published by: M I I Publications, Inc., 773 15th St NW Ste 900, Washington, DC 20005-2112. TEL 202-347-4822, FAX 202-347-4893, service@miipublications.com, http://www.miipublications.com. Eds. Ryan Hess, Cecilio J Morales. Pub. Cecilio J Morales. R&P David Barrows TEL 202-347-4822 ext 101.

360 616.89 GBR ISSN 1365-9820
WELFARE WORLD. Text in English. 19??. q. free to members (effective 2009). adv. bk.rev. illus. back issues avail. **Document type:** *Newspaper, Trade.* **Description:** Contains news and information about the work of the Institute of Welfare and a wide range of other welfare-related topics.
Former titles (until 1996): Welfare (0269-879X); (until 1985): Welfare and Social Services Journal (0261-4049); (until 1980): Welfare Officer (0043-2350)
Related titles: Online - full text ed.: free (effective 2009).
Indexed: E-psyche.
—BLDSC (9294.157300).
Published by: Institute of Welfare Officers, 2nd, Fl, Newland House, 137-139 Hagley Rd, Edgbaston, Birmingham, B16 8UA, United Kingdom. TEL 44-121-4548883, FAX 44-121-4547873, info@instituteofwelfare.co.uk. Ed. Sally Bundock TEL 44-20-83925241. adv.: page GBP 150.

WELLCOME HISTORY. *see* MEDICAL SCIENCES

WELLCOME NEWS. *see* MEDICAL SCIENCES

WELLCOME TRUST ANNUAL REVIEW. *see* MEDICAL SCIENCES

362.7 NLD ISSN 1871-9570
WERELDDELEN. Text in Dutch. 1922. q. free (effective 2010).
Formerly (until 2006): Woord en Daad (0167-2924)
Published by: Stichting Woord en Daad, Postbus 560, Gorinchem, 4200 AN, Netherlands. TEL 31-183-611800, FAX 31-183-611808, info@woordendaad.nl, http://www.woordendaad.nl. Eds. Joke Martens-Bevelander, Rina Molenaar. Circ: 76,000.

WERELDOUDERS. NIEUWSBRIEF. *see* LAW—International Law

WETBOEK SOCIAAL ZEKERHEIDSRECHT. *see* LAW—Civil Law

360 USA ISSN 1067-4896
HN90.V64
WHAT YOU CAN DO FOR YOUR COUNTRY. Text in English. 1993. a.
Published by: Serve DC, 441 4th St NW, Ste 1040S, Washington, DC 20001. TEL 202-727-7925, FAX 202-727-9198, serve@dc.gov, http://serve.dc.gov.

360 GBR ISSN 0141-7126
WHO MINDS?. Text in English. 1977. bi-m. free to members (effective 2009). adv. **Document type:** *Magazine, Trade.* **Description:** Provides news and information on home-based childcare, views and opinions, inspiring creative ideas, important business issues and real-life stories.
—CCC.
Published by: National Childminding Association, Royal Court, 81 Tweedy Rd, Bromley, Kent BR1 1TG, United Kingdom. TEL 44-845-8800044, info@ncma.org.uk. Ed. Liz Duffey. Adv. contact Maria Pollard TEL 44-1765-607570. page GBP 2,750; 210 x 297. Circ: 48,000.

361.7632092241 GBR ISSN 1468-1609
WHO'S WHO IN CHARITIES; essential information on individuals within the charity sector. Text in English. 1999. a. GBP 129 per issue charities; GBP 257 per issue non-charities (effective 2010). back issues avail. **Document type:** *Directory, Trade.* **Description:** Provides a guide for those looking to expand their networking knowledge within the charity sector.
—CCC.
Published by: CaritasData Ltd., 6-14 Underwood St, London, N1 7JQ, United Kingdom. TEL 44-20-73242362, FAX 44-20-75498677, enquiries@caritasdata.co.uk.

360 DEU ISSN 0721-8834
WIDERSPRUECHE. Text in German. 1981. 4/yr. EUR 36; EUR 23.50 to students (effective 2006). **Document type:** *Bulletin.*
Formed by the merger of (1972-1981): Informationsdienst Sozialarbeit (0170-2688); (1974-1981): Informationsdienst Gesundheitswesen (0344-1040); (1976-1981): Informationsdienst Arbeitsfeld Schule (0170-267X)
Indexed: DIP, IBR, IBZ.
—GNLM.
Published by: (Sozialistisches Buero), Kleine Verlag GmbH, Postfach 101668, Bielefeld, 33516, Germany. TEL 49-521-14610, FAX 49-521-140043, kv@kleine-verlag.de, http://www.kleine-verlag.de. Circ: 4,500.

361.7 GBR
WILL TO CHARITY GROUP: CHARITIES' STORY BOOK. Text in English. 1971. a. free. adv. illus. Index. **Document type:** *Handbook/ Manual/Guide, Consumer.*
Formerly: Will to Charity: Charities' Story Book
Published by: Will to Charity Ltd., 8 Hamble House, Meadrow, Godalming, Surrey, United Kingdom. TEL 44-1483-429800, FAX 44-1483-429500, willtocharity@btconnect.com, http://www.willtocharity.co.uk/. Ed. Anne Frazer Simpson. Circ: 20,000.

361.7 GBR
WILL TO CHARITY GROUP. THE REGIONAL CHARITY FINDER. Variant title: U K's Regional Charity Finder. Text in English. 1978. a. free. **Document type:** *Directory, Consumer.*
Formerly (until 1999): Will to Charity Group: Charities by Counties and Regions
Published by: Will to Charity Ltd., 8 Hamble House, Meadrow, Godalming, Surrey, United Kingdom. TEL 44-1483-429800, FAX 44-1483-429500, willtocharity@btconnect.com, http://www.willtocharity.co.uk/.

360 GBR
WILLIAM TEMPLE FOUNDATION. OCCASIONAL PAPER. Text in English. 199?. irreg., latest vol.32. free (effective 2009). **Document type:** *Monographic series.* **Description:** Features the role of the church within debates about localism as a response to forces of globalisation.
Related titles: Online - full text ed.
Published by: William Temple Foundation, Luther King House, Brighton Grove, Rusholme, Manc M14 5JP, United Kingdom. TEL 44-161-2492502, FAX 44-161-2561142, temple@wtf.org.uk.

360 IRL ISSN 1649-9743
WILLIAM THOMPSON WORKING PAPERS. Text in English. 2007. irreg., latest vol.7, 2007. **Document type:** *Monographic series.*
Media: Online - full text.
Published by: (University College Cork, College of Arts, Celtic Studies and Social Sciences), European Social Organisational and Science Consultancy, Jasnaja Poljana, Clonmoyle, Aghabullogue, Co. Cork, Ireland. TEL 353-21-7334833, esosc@esosc.org, http://www.esosc.org.

360 DEU ISSN 1862-7889
WISSENSCHAFTLICHE BEITRAEGE ZUR SOZIALEN ARBEIT. Text in German. 2006. irreg., latest vol.4, 2009. price varies. **Document type:** *Monographic series, Academic/Scholarly.*
Published by: Shaker Verlag GmbH, Kaiserstr 100, Herzogenrath, 52134, Germany. TEL 49-2407-95960, FAX 49-2407-95969, info@shaker.de.

362.8 DEU ISSN 0948-7441
WOHNUNGSLOS; Aktuelles aus Theorie und Praxis. Text in German. 1959. q. EUR 24; EUR 6 newsstand/cover (effective 2009). adv. bk.rev. index. **Document type:** *Journal, Trade.* **Description:** Covers the topic of homelessness of single persons in Germany.
Former titles (until 1995): Gefaehrdetenhilfe (0016-5794); (until 1969): Der Wanderer (0507-8628)
Indexed: DIP, IBR, IBZ.
Published by: Bundesarbeitsgemeinschaft Wohnungslosenhilfe e.V., Postfach 130148, Bielefeld, 33544, Germany. TEL 49-521-143960, FAX 49-521-1439619, info@bagw.de, http://www.bag-wohnungslosenhilfe.de. Ed. Heinrich Holtmannspoetter. Circ: 2,000.

360 305.4 AUS ISSN 1834-4941
➤ **WOMEN IN WELFARE EDUCATION (ONLINE).** Text in English. 1994. biennial. **Document type:** *Journal, Academic/Scholarly.* **Description:** Encourages and publishes women's writing on research, theory, and practice in social work and welfare education.
Formerly (until 2005): Women in Welfare Education (Print) (1320-3584)
Media: Online - full text.
Indexed: A26, CA, E03, E07, I05, S02, S03, T02.
Published by: Women in Welfare Education Group, c/o Karen Heycox, Convenor WIWE Editorial Board, UNSW School of Social Work, Sydney, NSW 2052, Australia. k.heycox@unsw.edu.au.

➤ **WOMEN'S DIARY (YEAR).** *see* WOMEN'S INTERESTS

305.42 USA ISSN 1522-144X
WOMEN'S PHILANTHROPY INSTITUTE NEWS. Text in English. 1997. q. USD 50 domestic; USD 55 foreign (effective 2000). bk.rev. back issues avail. **Document type:** *Newsletter.* **Description:** Highlights topics such as African-American woman's giving, challenging myths about women's volunteer leadership, and women as stewards of private wealth.
Published by: Women's Philanthropy Institute, 550 W. North St., Ste. 301, Indianapolis, IN 46202-3491. TEL 608-270-5205, FAX 608-270-5207. Ed. Lynn Entine. Circ: 1,000; 600 (paid).

361 USA
WOODEN BELL. Text in English. 5/yr. **Description:** Informs donors of what's happening in the world of CRS. Highlights various development programs and disaster relief efforts in different countries.
Formerly: Spectrum (New York)
Published by: Catholic Relief Services, 209 W Fayette St, Baltimore, MD 21201-3443. TEL 410-625-2220, FAX 410-234-2983. Ed. Margaret Guellich.

WORD FROM WASHINGTON (WASHINGTON, D.C.). *see* HANDICAPPED

WORK AND FAMILY LIFE. *see* EDUCATION

WORKING TOGETHER (SEATTLE); to prevent sexual and domestic violence. *see* CRIMINOLOGY AND LAW ENFORCEMENT

WORKING TOGETHER FOR CHILDREN IN NEED. CONFERENCE REPORT. *see* CHILDREN AND YOUTH—About

362.6 GBR ISSN 1366-3666
WORKING WITH OLDER PEOPLE; practical approaches to work, leisure, lifestyle and learning. Text in English. 1997. q. EUR 689 combined subscription in Europe (print & online eds.); USD 889 combined subscription in the Americas (print & online eds.); GBP 529 combined subscription in the UK & elsewhere (print & online eds.); AUD 999 combined subscription in Australasia (print & online eds.) (effective 2012). adv. back issues avail. **Document type:** *Journal, Academic/Scholarly.* **Description:** Supports all staff in social services, health and housing - whether voluntary or independent sector - to meet the demands of caring for the increasing population of older people.
Related titles: Online - full text ed.: ISSN 2042-8790.
Indexed: B28, C06, C07, C08, CA, CINAHL, E-psyche, H13, P02, P10, P16, P19, P20, P21, P24, P48, P53, P54, PQC, S02, S03, SCOPUS, SWR&A, T02.
—IE. **CCC.**
Published by: Pier Professional Ltd. (Subsidiary of: Emerald Group Publishing Ltd.), Ste N4, The Old Market, Upper Market St, Hove, BN3 1AS, United Kingdom. TEL 44-1273-783720, FAX 44-1273-783723, info@pierprofessional.com. Ed. Deborah Klee. Adv. contact Paul Somerville TEL 44-1273-783724. B&W page GBP 350; 160 x 245.

361 USA
WORLD ARK; ending hunger, saving the earth. Text in English. 1996. q. bk.rev. back issues avail. **Document type:** *Newsletter, Trade.* **Description:** Informs persons concerned about global economics, development, hunger, women's issues and the environment.
Published by: Heifer Project International, 1015 Louisiana St, Little Rock, AR 72202. TEL 501-907-2644, FAX 800-422-0474, http://www.heifer.org. Ed. Ray White. Pub. Michael Matchett. R&P Anna H Bedford. Circ: 80,000.

369.4 NZL
WORLD COUNCIL OF SERVICE CLUBS. MINUTES OF THE GENERAL MEETING. Text in English. 1962. a. free. **Document type:** *Proceedings.*
Formerly: World Council of Young Men's Service Clubs. Minutes of the General Meeting (0052-2678)
Media: Duplicated (not offset).
Published by: World Council of Service Clubs, PO Box 9324, Christchurch, New Zealand. TEL 64-3-3431989, FAX 64-3-3436165, graeme.bickley@amcom.co.nz, http://www.wocotours.co.nz/. Circ: 500.

WORLD DISASTERS REPORT. *see* PUBLIC HEALTH AND SAFETY

361.7 USA ISSN 0818-4984
WORLD GOODWILL NEWSLETTER. Text in English. 1955. q. free. bk.rev. **Document type:** *Newsletter, Consumer.* **Description:** Provides current information on constructive current action in world affairs as well as details on the work and program of World Goodwill.
Related titles: Danish ed.; Dutch ed.; French ed.; German ed.; Greek ed.; Spanish ed.; Icelandic ed.; Italian ed.; Portuguese ed.; Russian ed.; Hungarian ed.
Published by: Lucis Publishing Co., 120 Wall St, Fl 24, New York, NY 10005-4001. TEL 212-292-0707, FAX 212-292-0808. Ed. Dominic Dibble. Pub. Sarah McKechnie. **In the UK:** Lucis Press Ltd., 3 Whitehall Ct, London SW1A 2DD, United Kingdom.

362.7 CHE ISSN 1020-0010
HD7801 CODEN: WOWFN
WORLD OF WORK; the magazine of the ILO. Text in English, French, Spanish. 1965. 3/yr. free (effective 2011). bk.rev. illus. back issues avail.; reprints avail. **Document type:** *Bulletin, Academic/Scholarly.* **Description:** Explores the conditions of work and labour worldwide, particularly in developing nations.
Formerly (until 1992): I L O Information (0379-1734)
Related titles: Online - full text ed.: ISSN 1564-460X. 1996; ♦ French ed.: Travail. ISSN 1020-0002; Czech ed.; Danish ed.; Finnish ed.; Hungarian ed.; Japanese ed.; Norwegian ed.; Russian ed.: ISSN 1564-5673; Spanish ed.: ISSN 1020-0037; Swedish ed.; Chinese ed.; Arabic ed.; German ed.
Indexed: A22, BRI, CBRI, ErgAb, F&EA, HRIR, LeftInd, P30, PAIS, RASB, SCOPUS, SOPODA, SociolAb, T02, W09, WorkRelAb.
—BLDSC (9360.418000), IE, Infotrieve, Ingenta. **CCC.**
Published by: I L O, 4 Route des Morillons, Geneva, 1211, Switzerland. TEL 41-22-7996111, FAX 41-22-7988655, ilo@ilo.org. Ed. Hans von Rohland.

WORLD VISION MAGAZINE. *see* RELIGIONS AND THEOLOGY—Protestant

WORLD YOUTH REPORT. *see* CHILDREN AND YOUTH—About

WORLD'S WOMAN'S CHRISTIAN TEMPERANCE UNION. TRIENNIAL REPORT. *see* DRUG ABUSE AND ALCOHOLISM

360 USA ISSN 1069-2266
HV699.3.W8
WYOMING. DEPARTMENT OF FAMILY SERVICES. ANNUAL STATISTICAL BULLETIN. Text in English. 1960. q. USD 25. charts; stat. **Document type:** *Bulletin, Government.*
Formerly: Wyoming. Division of Public Assistance and Social Services. Quarterly Statistical Bulletin
Published by: Department of Family Services, Information Services Division, Hathaway Bldg, 3rd Fl, 2300 Capitol Ave, Cheyenne, WY 82002. TEL 307-777-5357, FAX 307-777-7747. Ed. Bruce Twine. Circ: 100.

360 CHN ISSN 1674-8956
▼ **XIWANG GONGCHENG/PROJECT HOPE.** Text in Chinese. 2010. m. **Document type:** *Magazine, Consumer.*
Published by: Zhongguo Qingshaonian Fazhan Jijinhui/China Youth Development Foundation, 51, Wangjing Xi Lu, Chaoyang-qu, Beijing, 100102, China. TEL 86-10-647906852, FAX 86-10-64790622, http://www.cydf.org.cn.

267.3 USA ISSN 0084-4292
Y M C A DIRECTORY. (Young Men's Christian Association) Text in English. 1877. a. adv. **Document type:** *Directory.*
Formerly: Y M C A Yearbook and Official Roster
Published by: Y M C A of the U S A, 101 N Wacker Dr, Chicago, IL 60606-1718. TEL 312-977-0031, FAX 312-977-9063. Circ: 2,000.

360 AUS ISSN 1837-8374
YARNIN UP!. Text in English. 200?. s-a. back issues avail. **Document type:** *Newsletter, Trade.*
Related titles: Online - full text ed.: ISSN 1837-8382. free (effective 2010).
Published by: Aboriginal and Torres Strait Islander Early Childhood Sector Advisory Group, PO Box 276, Enmore, NSW 2042, Australia. TEL 61-2-95164473, FAX 61-2-95165495, admin@aecssu.org.au.

YEDI'ON. *see* HUMANITIES: COMPREHENSIVE WORKS

YIXUE YU SHEHUI/MEDICAL SCIENCES AND SOCIETY. *see* MEDICAL SCIENCES

YOUNG; Nordic journal of youth research. *see* CHILDREN AND YOUTH—About

360 DEU ISSN 1439-7943
YOUNG LOOK; Tipps, Trends und News fuer die Friseurprofis von morgen. Text in German. 1996. q. film rev. back issues avail. **Document type:** *Magazine, Trade.*
Formerly: Locke (0724-1429)
Published by: Berufsgenossenschaft fuer Gesundheitsdienst und Wohlfahrtspflege, Pappelallee 35-37, Hamburg, 22089, Germany. TEL 49-40-202070, FAX 49-40-202072495, webmaster@bgw-online.de. Circ: 70,000.

YOUTH AND POLICY; the journal of critical analysis. *see* CHILDREN AND YOUTH—About

YOUTH LAW NEWS. *see* LAW

362 DEU ISSN 1434-5668
KK3431.3
Z F S H - S G B SOZIALRECHT IN DEUTSCHLAND UND EUROPA. (Zeitschrift fuer Sozialhilfe - Sozialgesetzbuch) Text in German. 1962. m. EUR 208; EUR 23.50 newsstand/cover (effective 2011). adv. **Document type:** *Magazine, Trade.*
Former titles (until 1997): Zeitschrift fuer Sozialhilfe und Sozialgesetzbuch (0724-4711); (until 1983): Zeitschrift fuer Sozialhilfe (0514-2768)
Indexed: A22, DIP, IBR, IBZ.
—IE, Infotrieve.
Published by: Hermann Luchterhand Verlag GmbH (Subsidiary of: Wolters Kluwer Deutschland GmbH), Heddesdorfer Str 31, Neuwied, 56564, Germany. TEL 49-2631-8012222, FAX 49-2631-8012223, info@luchterhand.de, http://www.luchterhand.de. Adv. contact Marcus Kipp. Circ: 1,150 (paid).

360 CHE
Z O K U INFO. Text in German. q.
Published by: Schweizerische Kranken und Unfallkasse Z O K U, Schwamendingerstr 44, Zuerich, 8050, Switzerland. TEL 01-3118081, FAX 01-3111803. Ed. H U Regius. Circ: 45,000.

361.1 FRA ISSN 1296-8366
ZAAMA. Text in French. 1999. q.
Indexed: FR.
—INIST.
Published by: Centre Regional d'Etudes et d'Observation des Politiques et Pratiques Sociales, Rue des Heures Claires, Manosque, 04100, France. TEL 33-4-92710412, FAX 33-4-92710413, creops@wanadoo.fr.

ZAGADNIENIA WYCHOWAWCZE A ZDROWIE PSYCHICZNE. *see* MEDICAL SCIENCES—Psychiatry And Neurology

ZAIHAIXUE/JOURNAL OF CATASTROPHOLOGY. *see* CIVIL DEFENSE

360 ZMB
ZAMBIA. DEPARTMENT OF SOCIAL DEVELOPMENT. REPORT. Text in English. 1964. irreg. (approx. a.). **Document type:** *Government.*
Formed by the merger of: Zambia. Department of Social Welfare. Report (0084-4667); Zambia. Department of Community Development. Report (0084-4608)
Published by: (Zambia. Department of Social Development), Government Printing Department, PO Box 30136, Lusaka, Zambia.

360 ZMB ISSN 0084-5035
ZAMBIA. PUBLIC SERVICE COMMISSION. REPORT. Text in English. 1964. a. **Document type:** *Government.*
Published by: (Zambia. Public Service Commission MUS), Government Printing Department, PO Box 30136, Lusaka, Zambia.

362.4 DEU
ZEITSCHRIFT: BEHINDERTE IM BERUF. Variant title: Z B. Text in German. 1967. q. looseleaf. free. bk.rev. **Document type:** *Bulletin, Trade.*
Formerly (until 1993): Gute Wille
Published by: (Arbeitsgemeinschaft der Deutschen Hauptfuersorgestellen), Universum Verlagsanstalt GmbH KG, Taunusstr 54, Wiesbaden, 65183, Germany. TEL 49-611-9030-0, FAX 49-611-9030382, info@universum.de, http://www.universum.de. Ed., R&P Sabine Wolf. Circ: 300,000.

360 DEU ISSN 0342-3379
ZEITSCHRIFT FUER DAS FUERSORGEWESEN. Text in German. 1948. m. EUR 88.80 (effective 2010). adv. **Document type:** *Magazine, Trade.*
Published by: (Hannover. Stadt Hannover, Hannover. Sozialamt), Richard Boorberg Verlag GmbH und Co. KG, Kestnerstr 44, Hannover, 30159, Germany. TEL 49-511-810592, FAX 49-511-810575, mail@boorberg.de. Ed. Ulrich Harmening.

360 DEU ISSN 1432-6000
➤ **ZEITSCHRIFT FUER MIGRATION UND SOZIALE ARBEIT.** Variant title: Migration und Soziale Arbeit. Text in German. 1979. 4/yr. EUR 48; EUR 14 newsstand/cover (effective 2011). adv. bk.rev.; film rev. abstr.; bibl. back issues avail. **Document type:** *Journal, Academic/Scholarly.*
Formerly (until 1995): Informationsdienst zur Auslaenderarbeit (0172-746X)
Indexed: DIP, IBR, IBZ.
Published by: (Institut fuer Sozialarbeit und Sozialpaedagogik e.V.), Juventa Verlag GmbH, Ehretstr 3, Weinheim, 69469, Germany. TEL 49-6201-90200, FAX 49-6201-902013, juventa@juventa.de, http://www.juventa.de. Ed. Sibylle Muench. Adv. contact Thekla Steinmetz. Circ: 1,500 (paid and controlled).

360 CHE
ZEITSCHRIFT FUER SOZIALHILFE; Monatsschrift fuer oeffentliche Fuersorge und Jugendhilfe. Text in German. m. CHF 79 domestic; CHF 104 foreign (effective 2001). **Document type:** *Journal, Trade.*
Former titles (until 1997): Zeitschrift fuer Oeffentliche Fuersorge (0044-3204); Armenpfleger
Indexed: IBR, IBZ.
Published by: (Schweizerische Konferenz fuer Sozialhilfe), Schulthess Juristische Medien AG, Zwinglipatz 2, Zuerich, 8022, Switzerland. TEL 41-1-2519336, FAX 41-1-2616394, zs.verlag@schulthess.com, http://www.schulthess.com. Circ: 1,950 (paid and controlled).

ZEITSCHRIFT FUER SOZIALREFORM. *see* POLITICAL SCIENCE

360 ESP ISSN 1134-7147
ZERBITZUAN; revista de servicios sociales. Text in Spanish, Basque; Summaries in Spanish, Basque. 1986. irreg. price varies. **Document type:** *Magazine, Government.*
Published by: Eusko Jaurlaritzaren Argitalpen-Zerbitzu Nagusia/Servicio Central de Publicaciones del Gobierno Vasco, Donostia-San Sebastian, 1, Vitoria-gasteiz, Alava 01010, Spain. TEL 34-945-018561, FAX 34-945-189709, hac-sabd@ej-gv.es, http://www.ej-gv.net/publicaciones.

ZERO TO THREE. *see* CHILDREN AND YOUTH—About

360 CHN
ZHONGGUO HONGSHIZI BAO. Text in Chinese. 1986. s-w. (Tue & Fri).
Related titles: Online - full text ed.
Published by: (Zhongguo Hongshizihui/Chinese Red Cross), Zhongguo Hongshizihui Zonghui Baokanshe, 43, Ganmian Hutong, Beijing, 100010, China. TEL 86-10-65254766, faxing@cnrcpress.com, http://www.redcrossol.com/index.asp.

360 CHN
ZHONGGUO HONGSHIZI NIANJIAN. Text in Chinese. 2005. a. **Document type:** *Yearbook, Corporate.*
Related titles: Online - full text ed.
Published by: (Zhongguo Hongshizihui/Chinese Red Cross), Zhongguo Hongshizihui Zonghui Baokanshe, 43, Ganmian Hutong, Beijing, 100010, China. TEL 86-10-85114419, FAX 86-10-65238052, faxing@cnrcpress.com, http://www.redcrossol.com/index.asp.

362 NLD ISSN 1871-0727
ZOA MAGAZINE. Text in Dutch. 1977. s-a.
Formerly (until 2005): ZOA Nieuws (0165-9308)
Published by: ZOA Vluchtelingenzorg, Sleutelbloemstraat 8, Postbus 4130, Apeldoorn, 7320 AC, Netherlands. TEL 31-55-3663339, FAX 31-55-3668799, info@zoa.nl, http://www.zoa.nl.

360 NLD ISSN 1381-4664
ZORG & WELZIJN; opiniemagazine voor de sector zorg en welzijn. Text in Dutch. 1976. m. EUR 95 to individuals; EUR 199.50 to institutions (effective 2009). adv. bk.rev. index. **Document type:** *Journal, Academic/Scholarly.* **Description:** Examines issues of interest to caregivers and nurses.
Formerly (until 1994): Welzijnsweekblad (0169-0639); Which superseded in part (in 1980): T M W Welzijnsweekblad (0165-117X); Which was formerly (until 1978): Welzijnsweekblad (0169-3697); And incorporates part (1981-1981): Welzijnsmaandblad (0169-3190); Which was formerly (1979-1981): T M W Welzijnsmaanblad (0165-1277); (1972-1979): Tijdschrift voor Maatschappijvraagstukken en Welzijnwerk (0169-3247); (1946-1972): Tijdschrift voor Mens en Welzijn
—Infotrieve.
Published by: Elsevier Overheid (Subsidiary of: Reed Business bv), Postbus 152, Amsterdam, 1000 AD, Netherlands. TEL 31-20-5159222, FAX 31-20-5159145, http://www.elsevieroverheid.nl. Ed. Martin Zuithof. Pub. Ludo de Boo. **Subscr. to:** Elsevier Den Haag, Postbus 16500, The Hague 2500 BM, Netherlands. TEL 31-70-381-9900, FAX 31-70-333-8399.

362 NLD ISSN 1878-8300
ZORG EN ZEGGENSCHAP NIEUWS. Text in Dutch. 200?. 10/yr. **Document type:** *Newsletter, Trade.*
Published by: Landelijke Organisatie Clientenraden, Postbus 700, Utrecht, 3500 AS, Netherlands. TEL 31-30-2843200, FAX 31-30-2843201, loc@loc.nl.

ZORGBELANG. *see* HANDICAPPED

362.4 NLD ISSN 1879-9485
▼ **ZORGEN VOOR EEN ANDER.** Text in Dutch. 2009. a. EUR 11.50 (effective 2010).
Published by: Bohn Stafleu van Loghum B.V. (Subsidiary of: Springer Science+Business Media), Postbus 246, Houten, 3990 GA, Netherlands. TEL 31-30-6383736, boekhandels@bsl.nl, http://www.bsl.nl.

362.1 NLD ISSN 1568-6116
ZORGMONITOR. Text in Dutch. 1975. a.
Former titles (until 2000): Vektis. Jaarboek (1568-6108); (until 1994): Stichting K L O Z Informatiesysteem Gezondheidszorg. Jaarboek (0922-7598)
Related titles: Online - full text ed.: ISSN 1875-0818.
Published by: Vektis BV, Postbus 703, Zeist, 3700 AS, Netherlands. TEL 31-30-6988323, FAX 31-30-6988216, info@vektis.nl, http://www.vektis.nl. Eds. Hazel Hull, Niels Hoeksema, Robert de Bie.

360 DEU
ZUKUNFT JETZT. Text in German. 1954. q. free to members (effective 2008). adv. **Document type:** *Magazine, Consumer.*
Formerly (until 2006): Gesichertes Leben (0016-9153)
Published by: (Deutsche Rentenversicherung Bund), W D V Gesellschaft fuer Medien & Kommunikation mbH & Co. OHG, Siemensstr 6, Bad Homburg, 61352, Germany. TEL 49-6172-6700, FAX 49-6172-670144, info@wdv.de, http://www.wdv.de. Ed. Dirk von der Heide. Adv. contact Walter Piezonka. B&W page EUR 22,800, color page EUR 22,800; trim 182 x 236. Circ: 2,400,000 (controlled).

360 ESP ISSN 1132-2012
60 Y MAS. Text in Spanish. 1984. m. **Document type:** *Magazine, Consumer.*
Indexed: FR.
Published by: Ministerio de Trabajo y Asuntos Sociales, Centro de Publicaciones, Agustin de Bethencourt 11, Madrid, 28003, Spain. http://www.mtas.es.

360 USA
111 MAGAZINE; truth, beauty & charity on the California desert. Text in English. 2003. 7/yr. adv. **Document type:** *Magazine, Consumer.*
Published by: 111, LLC, PO Box 536, Palm Desert, CA 92261-0536. TEL 760-770-5033, FAX 760-770-3705. Adv. contact Steve Tolin TEL 760-321-1200. color page USD 2,875; trim 9 x 11.75. Circ: 12,600.

361.73 USA ISSN 0897-5736
501 (C) (3) MONTHLY LETTER. Text in English. 1980. m. USD 46; USD 50 foreign. adv. bk.rev. charts; stat. **Document type:** *Newsletter.* **Description:** For nonprofit organizations. Emphasizes fundraising, communication and management.
Published by: Great Oaks Communication Services, 400 Chestnut St, Box 192, Atlantic, IA 50322. TEL 712-243-5257. Ed., R&P Marilyn Miller. Adv. contact James Kenney. Circ: 5,000 (paid).

SOCIAL SERVICES AND WELFARE—Abstracting, Bibliographies, Statistics

016.362 USA
A R N O V A ABSTRACTS. Text in English. q. **Document type:** *Abstract/Index.* **Description:** Provides abstracts dealing with all facets of voluntary action, nonprofits, and philanthropic activity.
Formerly: Citizen Participation and Voluntary Action Abstracts
Published by: Association for Research on Nonprofit Organizations and Voluntary Action, c/o Katherine M Finley, Exec Dir, 340 W. Michigan St., Canal Level, Ste. A, Indianapolis, IN 46202. TEL 317-684-2120, FAX 317-684-2128, exarnova@iupui.edu. Ed. Roger Lohmann.

360 USA ISSN 1553-0949
HD7123
ANNUAL STATISTICAL SUPPLEMENT TO THE SOCIAL SECURITY BULLETIN. Text in English. 19??. a. free (effective 2011). stat. **Document type:** *Bulletin, Government.*
Former titles (until 1992): Social Security Bulletin. Annual Statistical Supplement (0098-6259); (until 1955): Social Security Yearbook
Related titles: Online - full text ed.: ISSN 1553-0663; ◆ Supplement to: Social Security Bulletin. ISSN 0037-7910.
Indexed: EMBASE, ExcerpMed, IndMed, MEDLINE, P30, SCOPUS.
Published by: U.S. Social Security Administration, Office of Research, Evaluation and Statistics, Office of Public Inquiries, Windsor Park Bldg, 6401 Security Blvd, Baltimore, MD 21235. TEL 800-772-1213, ores.publications@ssa.gov, http://www.ssa.gov/policy/about/ORES.html.

302.021 ESP ISSN 2172-0401
ANUARIO DE ESTADISTICAS CULTURALES. Text in Spanish. a. back issues avail. **Document type:** *Yearbook, Consumer.*
Related titles: Online - full text ed.: ISSN 2172-0398.
Published by: Ministerio de Cultura, Plaza del Rey, No. 1, Madrid, 28004, Spain. TEL 34-91-7017000, FAX 34-91-7017352.

362.2021 AUS
AUSTRALIA. BUREAU OF STATISTICS. AUSTRALIA'S CHILDREN: THEIR HEALTH AND WELLBEING. Text in English. 1998. biennial. **Document type:** *Government.* **Description:** Provides comprehensive information on the current and long-term status of children's health, and on the risk and protective factors influencing their health and wellbeing.
Published by: Australian Bureau of Statistics, Locked Bag 10, Belconnen, ACT 2616, Australia. TEL 61-2-92684909, 61-2-62527037, 300-135-070, FAX 61-2-62528103, client.services@abs.gov.au.

362.2021 AUS
AUSTRALIA. BUREAU OF STATISTICS. AUSTRALIA'S YOUNG PEOPLE: THEIR HEALTH AND WELLBEING. Text in English. 1999. biennial. **Document type:** *Government.* **Description:** Provides comprehensive information from currently available data sources, and is the first in a series of biennial reports on youth health.
Published by: Australian Bureau of Statistics, Locked Bag 10, Belconnen, ACT 2616, Australia. TEL 61-2-92684909, 61-2-62527037, 300-135-070, FAX 61-2-62528103, client.services@abs.gov.au.

362.2021 AUS
AUSTRALIA. BUREAU OF STATISTICS. CARING IN THE COMMUNITY, AUSTRALIA (ONLINE). Text in English. 1998. irreg., latest 1998. free (effective 2009). **Document type:** *Government.* **Description:** Provides information on informal carers from the 1998 survey of disability, ageing and carers.
Formerly: Australia. Bureau of Statistics. Caring in the Community, Australia (Print)
Media: Online - full text.
Published by: Australian Bureau of Statistics, Locked Bag 10, Belconnen, ACT 2616, Australia. TEL 61-2-92684909, 61-2-62527037, 300-135-070, FAX 61-2-62528103, client.services@abs.gov.au.

362.5021 AUS
AUSTRALIA. BUREAU OF STATISTICS. CENSUS OF POPULATION AND HOUSING: OCCASIONAL PAPER - COUNTING THE HOMELESS (ONLINE). Text in English. 1996. irreg., latest 1996. free (effective 2009). **Document type:** *Government.* **Description:** Features reports on a research project to analyse information on the homeless population in Australia using 1996 census data and administrative data.
Formerly: Australia. Bureau of Statistics. Census of Population and Housing: Occasional Paper - Counting the Homeless (Print)
Media: Online - full text.
Published by: Australian Bureau of Statistics, Locked Bag 10, Belconnen, ACT 2616, Australia. TEL 61-2-92684909, 300-135-070, FAX 61-2-92684654, client.services@abs.gov.au.

AUSTRALIA. BUREAU OF STATISTICS. CHILD CARE, AUSTRALIA (ONLINE). *see* CHILDREN AND YOUTH—Abstracting, Bibliographies, Statistics

360.021 AUS
AUSTRALIA. BUREAU OF STATISTICS. COMMUNITY SERVICES, AUSTRALIA (ONLINE). Text in English. 1996. irreg., latest 2000. free (effective 2009). back issues avail. **Document type:** *Government.* **Description:** Presents results, in respect of the financial year, from an Australian Bureau of Statistics (ABS) survey of employing businesses and other public and private sector organisations involved in the provision of community services.
Formerly: Australia. Bureau of Statistics. Community Services, Australia (Print)
Media: Online - full text.
Published by: Australian Bureau of Statistics, Locked Bag 10, Belconnen, ACT 2616, Australia. TEL 61-2-92684909, 61-2-62527037, 300-135-070, FAX 61-2-62528103, client.services@abs.gov.au.

360.021 AUS
AUSTRALIA. BUREAU OF STATISTICS. COMMUNITY SERVICES, AUSTRALIA, PRELIMINARY (ONLINE). Text in English. 1996. irreg., latest 1996. free (effective 2009). **Document type:** *Government.* **Description:** Contains preliminary summary data on expenditure on community service activity by the government and private sectors.
Formerly: Australia. Bureau of Statistics. Community Services, Australia, Preliminary (Print)
Media: Online - full text.
Published by: Australian Bureau of Statistics, Locked Bag 10, Belconnen, ACT 2616, Australia. TEL 61-2-92684909, 61-2-62527037, 300-135-070, FAX 61-2-62528103, client.services@abs.gov.au.

362.6021 AUS
AUSTRALIA. BUREAU OF STATISTICS. DISABILITY, AGEING AND CARERS, AUSTRALIA: DISABILITY AND LONG-TERM HEALTH CONDITIONS (ONLINE). Text in English. 2003. irreg., latest 2003. free (effective 2009). **Document type:** *Government.*
Formerly: Australia. Bureau of Statistics. Disability, Ageing and Carers, Australia: Disability and Long-term Health Conditions (Print)
Media: Online - full text.
Published by: Australian Bureau of Statistics, Locked Bag 10, Belconnen, ACT 2616, Australia. TEL 61-2-92684909, 61-2-62527037, 300-135-070, FAX 61-2-62528103, client.services@abs.gov.au.

362.6021 AUS
AUSTRALIA. BUREAU OF STATISTICS. DISABILITY, AGEING AND CARERS, AUSTRALIA: HEARING IMPAIRMENT (ONLINE). Text in English. 1993. irreg., latest 1993. free (effective 2009). **Document type:** *Government.* **Description:** Contains national statistics on hearing impairment, disability and handicap status, need for and receipt of help, and aids used and needed.
Formerly: Australia. Bureau of Statistics. Disability, Ageing and Carers, Australia: Hearing Impairment (Print)
Media: Online - full text.
Published by: Australian Bureau of Statistics, Locked Bag 10, Belconnen, ACT 2616, Australia. TEL 61-2-92684909, 61-2-62527037, 300-135-070, FAX 61-2-62528103, client.services@abs.gov.au.

362.6021 AUS
AUSTRALIA. BUREAU OF STATISTICS. DISABILITY, AGEING AND CARERS, AUSTRALIA: SUMMARY OF FINDINGS (ONLINE). Text in English. 1993. quinquennial. free (effective 2009). back issues avail. **Document type:** *Government.* **Description:** Presents a summary of results from the survey of disability, ageing and carers conducted by the ABS throughout Australia from june to november 2003.
Formerly: Australia. Bureau of Statistics. Disability, Ageing and Carers, Australia: Summary of Findings (Print)
Media: Online - full text.
Published by: Australian Bureau of Statistics, Locked Bag 10, Belconnen, ACT 2616, Australia. TEL 61-2-92684909, 61-2-62527037, 300-135-070, FAX 61-2-62528103, client.services@abs.gov.au.

362.6021 AUS
AUSTRALIA. BUREAU OF STATISTICS. DISABILITY, AGEING AND CARERS, AUSTRALIA: VISUAL IMPAIRMENT (ONLINE). Text in English. 1993. irreg., latest 1993. free (effective 2009). **Document type:** *Government.* **Description:** Contains national statistics on visual impairment, disability and handicap status, need for and receipt of help, and aids used and needed.
Formerly: Australia. Bureau of Statistics. Disability, Ageing and Carers, Australia: Visual Impairment (Print)
Media: Online - full text. **Related titles:** Diskette ed.
Published by: Australian Bureau of Statistics, Locked Bag 10, Belconnen, ACT 2616, Australia. TEL 61-2-92684909, 61-2-62527037, 300-135-070, FAX 61-2-62528103, client.services@abs.gov.au.

362.2021 AUS
AUSTRALIA. BUREAU OF STATISTICS. DISABILITY, AGEING AND CARERS, SUMMARY TABLES, AUSTRALIAN CAPITAL TERRITORY (ONLINE). Text in English. 1998. quinquennial, latest 1998. free (effective 2009). **Document type:** *Catalog, Government.* **Description:** Contains a tables for The Australian Territory from the 1998 survey of disability, ageing and carers with data on people with disabilities, their carers and people aged 65 years and over.
Formerly: Australia. Bureau of Statistics. Disability, Ageing and Carers, Summary Tables, Australian Capital Territory (Print)
Media: Online - full text.
Published by: Australian Bureau of Statistics, Northern Territory Office, GPO BOX 3796, Darwin, N.T. 0801, Australia. TEL 61-2-92684909, 300-135-070.

362.6021 AUS
AUSTRALIA. BUREAU OF STATISTICS. DISABILITY, AGEING AND CARERS: USER GUIDE, AUSTRALIA (ONLINE). Text in English. 1993. quinquennial, latest 1998. **Document type:** *Government.* **Description:** Describes the background, nature and content of the survey, sampling and estimation, collection and processing, and issues relating to quality.
Formerly: Australia. Bureau of Statistics. Disability, Ageing and Carers: User Guide, Australia (Print)
Media: Online - full text. **Related titles:** Diskette ed.
Published by: Australian Bureau of Statistics, Locked Bag 10, Belconnen, ACT 2616, Australia. TEL 61-2-92684909, 61-2-62527037, 300-135-070, FAX 61-2-62528103, client.services@abs.gov.au.

362.6021 AUS
AUSTRALIA. BUREAU OF STATISTICS. DISABILITY AND DISABLING CONDITIONS (ONLINE). Text in English. 1993. irreg., latest 1998. free (effective 2009). back issues avail. **Document type:** *Government.*
Former titles: Australia. Bureau of Statistics. Disability and Disabling Conditions (Print); (until 1998): Australia. Bureau of Statistics. Disability, Ageing and Carers, Australia: Disability and Disabling Conditions
Media: Online - full text.
Published by: Australian Bureau of Statistics, Locked Bag 10, Belconnen, ACT 2616, Australia. TEL 61-2-92684909, 61-2-62527037, 300-135-070, FAX 61-2-62528103, client.services@abs.gov.au.

362.82021 AUS
AUSTRALIA. BUREAU OF STATISTICS. FAMILY CHARACTERISTICS AND TRANSITIONS, AUSTRALIA (ONLINE). Text in English. 1998. irreg., latest 2007. free (effective 2009). back issues avail. **Document type:** *Government.* **Description:** Presents results for the year Family Characteristics and Transitions Survey (FCTS) and compares them to results from the 2003 and 1997 Family Characteristics Surveys (FCS), providing information about changing patterns of family and household composition in contemporary Australia.
Former titles: Australia. Bureau of Statistics. Family Characteristics and Transitions, Australia (Print); (until 2007): Australia. Bureau of Statistics. Family Characteristics, Australia
Media: Online - full text.
Published by: Australian Bureau of Statistics, Locked Bag 10, Belconnen, ACT 2616, Australia. TEL 61-2-62527037, 61-2-92684909, 300-135-070, FAX 61-2-62528103, client.services@abs.gov.au.

362.6021 AUS
AUSTRALIA. BUREAU OF STATISTICS. FOCUS ON FAMILIES - A STATISTICAL SERIES: CARING IN FAMILIES: SUPPORT FOR PERSONS WHO ARE OLDER OR HAVE DISABILITIES (ONLINE). Text in English. 1993. irreg., latest 1995. free (effective 2009). **Document type:** *Government.* **Description:** Includes care needs, types of care provided, and effects of caring role on the caregiver's lifestyle.
Former titles: Australia. Bureau of Statistics. Focus on Families - A Statistical Series: Caring in Families: Support for Persons Who Are Older or Have Disabilities (Print); (until 1995): Australia. Bureau of Statistics. Focus on Families: Caring in Families: Support for Persons Who Are Older or Have Disabilities
Media: Online - full text.
Published by: Australian Bureau of Statistics, Locked Bag 10, Belconnen, ACT 2616, Australia. TEL 61-2-92684909, 61-2-62527037, 300-135-070, FAX 61-2-62528103, client.services@abs.gov.au.

362.2021 AUS
AUSTRALIA. BUREAU OF STATISTICS. HEALTH IN RURAL AND REMOTE AUSTRALIA. Text in English. 1998. irreg. **Document type:** *Government.* **Description:** Provides information on the comparision of the health of those living in rural and remote zones with that of those living in the metropolitan zone by analysing a wide range of national health data sources.
Published by: Australian Bureau of Statistics, Locked Bag 10, Belconnen, ACT 2616, Australia. TEL 61-2-92684909, 61-2-62527037, 300-135-070, FAX 61-2-62528103, client.services@abs.gov.au.

362.2021 AUS
AUSTRALIA. BUREAU OF STATISTICS. INFORMATION PAPER: MENTAL HEALTH AND WELLBEING OF ADULTS, AUSTRALIA, CONFIDENTIALISED UNIT RECORD FILE (ONLINE). Text in English. 1997. irreg., latest 2007. free (effective 2009). **Description:** Provides information about the data content of the 1997 National Survey of Mental Health and Wellbeing of Adults, Confidentialised Unit Record sample file, along with conditions of issue and how to order the file.
Formerly: Australia. Bureau of Statistics. Information Paper: Mental Health and Wellbeing of Adults, Australia, Confidentialised Unit Record File (Print)
Media: Online - full text.
Published by: Australian Bureau of Statistics, Locked Bag 10, Belconnen, ACT 2616, Australia. TEL 61-2-92684909, FAX 61-2-92684654, subscriptions@abs.gov.au.

362.2021 AUS
AUSTRALIA. BUREAU OF STATISTICS. INTERNATIONAL HEALTH - HOW AUSTRALIA COMPARES. Text in English. 1999. irreg., latest 1999. **Document type:** *Government.* **Description:** Brings out data from annual reports to the WHO and the United Nations, complemented by data from AIHW, ABS, the OECD and other national and international organisations.
Published by: Australian Bureau of Statistics, Locked Bag 10, Belconnen, ACT 2616, Australia. TEL 61-2-92684909, 61-2-62527037, 300-135-070, FAX 61-2-62528103, client.services@abs.gov.au.

362.2021 AUS
AUSTRALIA. BUREAU OF STATISTICS. MENTAL HEALTH AND WELLBEING: PROFILE OF ADULTS, AUSTRALIA (ONLINE). Text in English. 1997. decennial, latest 2007. free (effective 2009). back issues avail. **Description:** Contains comprehensive Australian data on key mental health issues including the prevalence of mental disorders, the associated disability, and the use of services.
Formerly: Australia. Bureau of Statistics. Mental Health and Wellbeing: Profile of Adults, Australia (Print)
Media: Online - full text.
Published by: Australian Bureau of Statistics, Locked Bag 10, Belconnen, ACT 2616, Australia. TEL 61-2-92684909, 300-135-070, FAX 61-2-92684654, client.services@abs.gov.au.

362.2021 AUS
AUSTRALIA. BUREAU OF STATISTICS. NATIONAL SURVEY OF MENTAL HEALTH AND WELLBEING: USER'S GUIDE (ONLINE). Text in English. 1997. decennial, latest 2007. free (effective 2009). back issues avail.
Former titles: Australia. Bureau of Statistics. National Survey of Mental Health and Wellbeing of Adults: User's Guide (Print)
Media: Online - full text.
Published by: Australian Bureau of Statistics, Locked Bag 10, Belconnen, ACT 2616, Australia. TEL 61-2-92684909, FAX 61-2-62528103, subscriptions@abs.gov.au.

362.7021 AUS
AUSTRALIA. BUREAU OF STATISTICS. NEW SOUTH WALES OFFICE. CHILD CARE, NEW SOUTH WALES, DATA REPORT (ONLINE). Text in English. 1999. triennial. free (effective 2009). **Document type:** *Government.* **Description:** Contains results for New South Wales from the Child Care Survey conducted throughout Australia.
Formerly: Australia. Bureau of Statistics. New South Wales Office. Child Care, New South Wales, Data Report Hardcopy
Media: Online - full text.
Published by: Australian Bureau of Statistics, New South Wales Office, GPO Box 796, Sydney, NSW 2001, Australia. TEL 61-2-92684909, 300-135-070, client.services@abs.gov.au.

362.2021 AUS
AUSTRALIA. BUREAU OF STATISTICS. NEW SOUTH WALES OFFICE. DISABILITY, AGEING AND CARERS, SUMMARY TABLES, NEW SOUTH WALES (ONLINE). Text in English. 1998. quinquennial. free (effective 2009). **Document type:** *Government.* **Description:** Contains information on the age, sex, living arrangements and educational and labour force experience of people with disabilities and people aged 65 and over.
Forrmerly: Australia. Bureau of Statistics. New South Wales Office. Disability, Ageing and Carers, Summary Tables, New South Wales (Print)
Media: Online - full text.
Published by: Australian Bureau of Statistics, New South Wales Office, GPO Box 796, Sydney, NSW 2001, Australia. TEL 61-2-92684909, 300-135-070, client.services@abs.gov.au.

362.2021 AUS
AUSTRALIA. BUREAU OF STATISTICS. NEW SOUTH WALES OFFICE. DISABILITY, NEW SOUTH WALES (ONLINE). Text in English. 2001. irreg., latest 2001. free (effective 2009). **Document type:** *Catalog, Government.* **Description:** Discusses issues concerned with defining, classifying and measuring disability.
Formerly: Australia. Bureau of Statistics. New South Wales Office. Disability, New South Wales (Print)
Media: Online - full text.
Published by: Australian Bureau of Statistics, New South Wales Office, GPO Box 796, Sydney, NSW 2001, Australia. TEL 61-2-92684909, 300-135-070.

362.2021 AUS
AUSTRALIA. BUREAU OF STATISTICS. NEW SOUTH WALES OFFICE. MENTAL HEALTH AND WELLBEING: PROFILE OF ADULTS, NEW SOUTH WALES, DATA REPORT. Text in English. 1997. irreg., latest 1997. **Document type:** *Government.* **Description:** Contains the first comprehensive data on key mental health issues including the prevalence of mental disorders, the associated disability, and the use of services.
Related titles: Online - full text ed.
Published by: Australian Bureau of Statistics, New South Wales Office, GPO Box 796, Sydney, NSW 2001, Australia. TEL 61-2-92684909, 300-135-070.

362.6021 AUS
AUSTRALIA. BUREAU OF STATISTICS. NEW SOUTH WALES OFFICE. OLDER PEOPLE, NEW SOUTH WALES (ONLINE). Text in English. 1995. irreg., latest 2004. free (effective 2009). **Document type:** *Government.* **Description:** Provides a rich source of information on key issues relating to community participation, health and wellbeing, living arrangements, financial security, and mobility.
Former titles (until 200?): Australia. Bureau of Statistics. New South Wales Office. Older People, New South Wales (Print); (until 2000): Australia. Bureau of Statistics. New South Wales Office. Older People in New South Wales: A Profile
Media: Online - full text.
Published by: Australian Bureau of Statistics, New South Wales Office, GPO Box 796, Sydney, NSW 2001, Australia. TEL 61-2-92684909, 300-135-070, client.services@abs.gov.au.

362.2021 AUS
AUSTRALIA. BUREAU OF STATISTICS. NORTHERN TERRITORY OFFICE. DISABILITY, AGEING AND CARERS, SUMMARY TABLES, NORTHERN TERRITORY (ONLINE). Text in English. 1998. irreg., latest 1998. free (effective 2009). **Document type:** *Catalog, Government.* **Description:** Contains a tables for the Northern Territory from the 1998 survey of disability, ageing and carers with data on people with disabilities, their carers and people aged 65 years and over.
Formerly: Australia. Bureau of Statistics. Northern Territory Office. Disability, Ageing and Carers, Summary Tables, Northern Territory (Print)
Media: Online - full text.
Published by: Australian Bureau of Statistics, Northern Territory Office, GPO BOX 3796, Darwin, N.T. 0801, Australia. TEL 61-2-92684909, 300-135-070.

362.6021 AUS
AUSTRALIA. BUREAU OF STATISTICS. OLDER PEOPLE, AUSTRALIA: A SOCIAL REPORT (ONLINE). Text in English. 1999. irreg., latest 1999. free (effective 2009). **Description:** Provides information about people aged 65 and over living in Australia.
Former titles: Australia. Bureau of Statistics. Older People, Australia: A Social Report (Print); Australia's Aged Population
Media: Online - full text.
Published by: Australian Bureau of Statistics, Locked Bag 10, Belconnen, ACT 2616, Australia. TEL 61-2-92684909, 300-135-070, FAX 61-2-92684654, client.services@abs.gov.au.

362.2021 310 AUS
AUSTRALIA. BUREAU OF STATISTICS. QUEENSLAND OFFICE. DISABILITY, AGEING AND CARERS, SUMMARY TABLES, QUEENSLAND (ONLINE). Text in English. 1998. irreg. free (effective 2009). **Document type:** *Government.* **Description:** Includes information on the age, sex, living arrangements and educational and labour force experience of people with disabilities and people aged 65 and over.
Formerly: Australia. Bureau of Statistics. Queensland Office. Disability, Ageing and Carers, Summary Tables, Queensland (Print)
Media: Online - full text.
Published by: Australian Bureau of Statistics, Queensland Office, GPO Box 9817, Brisbane, QLD 4001, Australia. TEL 61-2-92684909, 300-135-070, client.services@abs.gov.au.

362.2021 310 AUS
AUSTRALIA. BUREAU OF STATISTICS. QUEENSLAND OFFICE. MENTAL HEALTH AND WELLBEING: PROFILE OF ADULTS, QUEENSLAND, DATA REPORT (ONLINE). Text in English. 1997. irreg. free (effective 2009). **Document type:** *Government.* **Description:** Presents an overview for Queensland of the main topics covered in the National Survey of Mental Health and Wellbeing.
Formerly: Australia. Bureau of Statistics. Queensland Office. Mental Health and Wellbeing: Profile of Adults, Queensland, Data Report (Print)
Media: Online - full text.
Published by: Australian Bureau of Statistics, Queensland Office, GPO Box 9817, Brisbane, QLD 4001, Australia. TEL 61-2-92684909, 300-135-070, client.services@abs.gov.au.

362.6021 310 AUS
AUSTRALIA. BUREAU OF STATISTICS. QUEENSLAND OFFICE. PERSONS AGED FIFTY YEARS AND OVER, QUEENSLAND (ONLINE). Text in English. 1998. irreg. free (effective 2009). **Document type:** *Government.* **Description:** Provides the estimation of aged fifty years and over live in Queensland.
Formerly: Australia. Bureau of Statistics. Queensland Office. Persons Aged Fifty Years and Over, Queensland (Print)
Media: Online - full text.
Published by: Australian Bureau of Statistics, Queensland Office, GPO Box 9817, Brisbane, QLD 4001, Australia. TEL 61-2-92684909, 300-135-070, client.services@abs.gov.au.

362.2021 AUS
AUSTRALIA. BUREAU OF STATISTICS. SOUTH AUSTRALIAN OFFICE. DISABILITY, AGEING AND CARERS, SUMMARY TABLES, SOUTH AUSTRALIA (ONLINE). Text in English. 1998. quinquennial, latest 1998. free (effective 2009). **Document type:** *Government.* **Description:** Contains tables for South Australia from Survey of Disability, Ageing and Carers with data on people with disabilities, their carers and people aged 65 years and over.
Formerly: Australia. Bureau of Statistics. South Australian Office. Disability, Ageing and Carers, Summary Tables, South Australia (Print)
Media: Online - full text.
Published by: Australian Bureau of Statistics, South Australian Office, GPO Box 2272, Adelaide, SA 5001, Australia. TEL 61-2-92684909, 300-135-070, client.services@abs.gov.au.

362.2021 AUS
AUSTRALIA. BUREAU OF STATISTICS. SOUTH AUSTRALIAN OFFICE. MENTAL HEALTH AND WELLBEING: PROFILE OF ADULTS, SOUTH AUSTRALIA, DATA REPORT (ONLINE). Text in English. 1997. quinquennial, latest 1997. **Document type:** *Government.* **Description:** Presents an overview for South Australia of the main topics covered in National Survey of Mental Health and Wellbeing.
Formerly: Australia. Bureau of Statistics. South Australian Office. Mental Health and Wellbeing: Profile of Adults, South Australia, Data Report (Print)
Media: Online - full text.
Published by: Australian Bureau of Statistics, South Australian Office, GPO Box 2272, Adelaide, SA 5001, Australia. TEL 61-2-92684909, 300-135-070, client.services@abs.gov.au.

362.2021 AUS
AUSTRALIA. BUREAU OF STATISTICS. TASMANIAN OFFICE. DISABILITY, AGEING AND CARERS, SUMMARY TABLES, TASMANIA (ONLINE). Text in English. 1998. quinquennial, latest 2003. free (effective 2009). **Document type:** *Government.* **Description:** Presents a summary of results from the Survey of Disability, Ageing and Carers (SDAC) conducted by the Australian Bureau of Statistics (ABS) throughout Australia, from June to November 2003.
Formerly (until 199?): Australia. Bureau of Statistics. Tasmanian Office. Disability, Ageing and Carers, Summary Tables, Tasmania (Print)
Media: Online - full text.
Published by: Australian Bureau of Statistics, Tasmanian Office, GPO Box 66A, Hobart, TAS 7001, Australia. TEL 61-2-92684909, 300-135-070, client.services@abs.gov.au.

362.2021 AUS
AUSTRALIA. BUREAU OF STATISTICS. VICTORIAN OFFICE. DISABILITY, AGEING AND CARERS, SUMMARY TABLES, VICTORIA. Text in English. 1998. quinquennial. **Document type:** *Government.* **Description:** Contains tables for Victoria from the survey of disability, ageing and carers with data on people with disabilities, their carers and people aged 65 years and over.
Published by: Australian Bureau of Statistics, Victorian Office, GPO Box 2796Y, Melbourne, VIC 3001, Australia. TEL 61-2-62524909, 300-135-070, client.services@abs.gov.au.

362.2021 AUS
AUSTRALIA. BUREAU OF STATISTICS. VICTORIAN OFFICE. MENTAL HEALTH AND WELLBEING: PROFILE OF ADULTS, VICTORIA, DATA REPORT (ONLINE). Text in English. 1997. irreg., latest 1997. free (effective 2009). **Document type:** *Government.* **Description:** Contains the first comprehensive data on key mental health issues including the prevalence of mental disorders, the associated disability, and the use of services. The focus is on anxiety, affective and substance use disorders.
Formerly: Australia. Bureau of Statistics. Victorian Office. Mental Health and Wellbeing: Profile of Adults, Victoria, Data Report (Print)
Media: Online - full text.
Published by: Australian Bureau of Statistics, Victorian Office, GPO Box 2796Y, Melbourne, VIC 3001, Australia. TEL 61-2-62524909, 300-135-070, client.services@abs.gov.au.

361.8021 AUS
AUSTRALIA. BUREAU OF STATISTICS. VOLUNTARY WORK, AUSTRALIA (ONLINE). Text in English. 1995. irreg., latest 2006. free (effective 2009). back issues avail. **Document type:** *Government.* **Description:** Contains results from the national Voluntary Work Survey conducted throughout Australia for the year as part of the General Social Survey (GSS).
Formerly: Australia. Bureau of Statistics. Voluntary Work, Australia (Print)
Media: Online - full text.
Published by: Australian Bureau of Statistics, Locked Bag 10, Belconnen, ACT 2616, Australia. TEL 61-2-62527037, 61-2-92684909, 300-135-070, FAX 61-2-62528103, client.services@abs.gov.au.

361.8021 AUS
AUSTRALIA. BUREAU OF STATISTICS. VOLUNTARY WORK, AUSTRALIA, PRELIMINARY (ONLINE). Text in English. 1995. irreg. free (effective 2009). **Document type:** *Government.* **Description:** Contains preliminary national and state data on the number of persons who carry out voluntary work and the amount of time spent.
Formerly: Australia. Bureau of Statistics. Voluntary Work, Australia, Preliminary (Print)
Media: Online - full text.
Published by: Australian Bureau of Statistics, Locked Bag 10, Belconnen, ACT 2616, Australia. TEL 61-2-62527037, 61-2-92684909, 300-135-070, FAX 61-2-62528103, client.services@abs.gov.au.

362.2021 AUS
AUSTRALIA. BUREAU OF STATISTICS. WESTERN AUSTRALIAN OFFICE. MENTAL HEALTH AND WELLBEING OF ADULTS, WESTERN AUSTRALIA: CONFIDENTIALISED UNIT RECORD FILE ON CD-ROM. Text in English. 1997. irreg., latest 1997. **Document type:** *Government.* **Description:** Contains the first comprehensive Western Australian data on key mental health issues including the prevalence of mental disorders, the associated disability, and the use of services.
Media: CD-ROM.
Published by: Australian Bureau of Statistics, Western Australian Office, GPO Box K881, Perth, W.A. 6842, Australia. TEL 61-2-62524909, 300-135-070, client.services@abs.gov.au.

360 DEU ISSN 1430-3264
BAYERISCHES LANDESAMT FUER STATISTIK UND DATENVERARBEITUNG. STATISTISCHE BERICHTE K: OEFFENTLICHE SOZIALLEISTUNGEN. Text in German. 1969. irreg. **Document type:** *Government.*
Formerly (until 1982): Bayerisches Statistisches Landesamt. Statistische Berichte K (1430-3094)
Related titles: Abridged ed.: Wohngeld in Bayern. ISSN 0934-7798. 1970. EUR 13.20 (effective 2011).
Published by: Bayerisches Landesamt fuer Statistik und Datenverarbeitung, Neuhauser Str 8, Munich, 80331, Germany. TEL 49-89-2119205, FAX 49-89-2119410, poststelle@statistik.bayern.de, http://www.statistik.bayern.de.

S

BELGIUM. FEDERAAL MINISTERIE VAN SOCIALE ZAKEN, VOLKSGEZONDHEID EN LEEFMILIEU. STATISTISCH JAARBOEK VAN DE SOCIALE ZEKERHEID/STATISTICS SOCIAL SECURITY YEARBOOK. *see* INSURANCE—Abstracting, Bibliographies, Statistics

361.0021 BEL ISSN 0067-5563
BELGIUM. INSTITUT NATIONAL DE STATISTIQUE. STATISTIQUES SOCIALES. Key Title: Statistiques Sociales (Brussels). Text in French. 1970. irreg. (approx 3/yr). charts. back issues avail. **Document type:** *Government.* **Description:** Provides a statistical overview of social conditions and trends in Belgium.
Related titles: ◆ Dutch ed.: Belgium. Nationaal Instituut voor de Statistiek. Sociale Statistieken. ISSN 0771-7881.
Indexed: PAIS, RASB.
Published by: Institut National de Statistique/Nationaal Instituut voor de Statistiek (Subsidiary of: Ministere des Affaires Economiques), Rue de Louvain 44, Brussels, 1000, Belgium. TEL 32-2-548-6211, FAX 32-2-548-6367.

BELGIUM. MINISTERE FEDERAL DES AFFAIRES SOCIALES DE LA SANTE PUBLIQUE ET DE L'ENVIRONNEMENT. ANNUAIRE STATISTIQUE DE SECURITE SOCIALE/STATISTICS SOCIAL SECURITY YEARBOOK. *see* INSURANCE—Abstracting, Bibliographies, Statistics

361.0021 BEL ISSN 0771-7881
BELGIUM. NATIONAAL INSTITUUT VOOR DE STATISTIEK. SOCIALE STATISTIEKEN. Key Title: Sociale Statistieken - Nationaal Instituut voor de Statistiek. Text in Dutch. 1970. irreg. (approx 3/yr). charts. back issues avail. **Document type:** *Government.* **Description:** Provides a statistical overview of social conditions and trends in Belgium.
Related titles: ◆ French ed.: Belgium. Institut National de Statistique. Statistiques Sociales. ISSN 0067-5563.
Published by: Institut National de Statistique/Nationaal Instituut voor de Statistiek (Subsidiary of: Ministere des Affaires Economiques), Rue de Louvain 44, Brussels, 1000, Belgium. TEL 32-2-548-6211, FAX 32-2-548-6367.

362.7 DEU
BERLIN. SENATSVERWALTUNG FUER FRAUEN, JUGEND UND FAMILIE. STATISTISCHER DIENST. Text in German. 1980. s-a. free. back issues avail. **Description:** Annotated statistics on children's and youth services and welfare, and the situation of women in West Berlin.
Published by: Senatsverwaltung fuer Frauen Jugend und Familie, Am Karlsbad 8, Berlin, 10785, Germany. TEL 030-26041, FAX 030-2628864. Circ: 400.

360 016 BRA
BRAZIL. DEPARTAMENTO NACIONAL DO SERVICO SOCIAL DO COMERCIO. BOLETIM BIBLIOGRAFICO. Text in Portuguese. 1969. s-a. free. charts; stat. **Document type:** *Bibliography.* **Description:** Social services bibliography.
Published by: Departamento Nacional do Servico Social do Comercio, Divisao Administrativo, Rua Voluntarios da Patria, 169, Rio De Janeiro, RJ 22270-000, Brazil. TEL 286-5152, FAX 286-2638, TELEX 021-22782.

362.82021 CAN ISSN 1480-784X
CANADA. STATISTICS CANADA. FAMILY VIOLENCE IN CANADA, A STATISTICAL PROFILE. Text in English. 1998. a.
Related titles: Online - full text ed.: ISSN 1480-7165. 1998; French ed.: Violence Familiale au Canada, Un Profil Statistique. ISSN 1480-7858. 1998.
Published by: Statistics Canada, Canadian Centre for Justice Statistics (Subsidiary of: Statistics Canada/Statistique Canada), Rm 1500 Main Bldg, Holland Ave, Ottawa, ON K1A OT6, Canada. TEL 613-951-8116, infostats@statcan.ca.

CARING CANADIANS, INVOLVED CANADIANS; highlights from the Canada survey of giving, volunteering and participating. *see* SOCIAL SERVICES AND WELFARE

A CHILD'S DAY: (YEAR) (SELECTED INDICATORS OF CHILD WELL-BEING) (ONLINE). *see* CHILDREN AND YOUTH—Abstracting, Bibliographies, Statistics

360 LBN ISSN 1012-7801
HA4666
COMPENDIUM OF SOCIAL STATISTICS AND INDICATORS. Text in Multiple languages. 1988. irreg., latest vol.5, 2001. USD 45 (effective 2004).
Published by: United Nations, Economic and Social Commission for Western Asia, PO Box 11-8575, Beirut, Lebanon. TEL 961-1-981301, FAX 961-1-981510, http://www.escwa.org.lb/.

361.3016 ESP ISSN 1133-1828
COMUNIDAD DE MADRID. CONSEJERIA DE FAMILIA Y ASUNTOS SOCIALES. BOLETIN DE NOVEDADES. Text in Spanish. 1993. q. **Document type:** *Bulletin, Consumer.*
Related titles: Online - full text ed.: ISSN 2171-732X. 2010.
Published by: Comunidad de Madrid, Consejeria de Familia y Asuntos Sociales, C Alcala, 63, Salamanca, Madrid, 28001, Spain. TEL 34-900-444555, FAX 34-91-4208697.

361.9489 349.489 DNK ISSN 1601-0973
DENMARK. DANMARKS STATISTIK. SOCIALE FORHOLD, SUNDHED OG RETSVAESEN (ONLINE). Text in Danish. 200?. irreg. **Document type:** *Government.*
Former titles (until 2007): Denmark. Danmarks Statistik. Sociale Forhold, Sundhed og Retsvaesen (Print) (1399-0659); (until 1999): Denmark. Danmarks Statistik. Social Sikring og Retsvaesen (0108-5441); Which superseded in part (in 1983): Statistiske Efterretninger A (0105-306X); (in 1983): Statistiske Efterretninger B (0105-3078); Both of which superseded in part (1909-1976): Statistiske Efterretninger (0039-0674)
Media: Online - full content. **Related titles:** ◆ Series of: Denmark. Danmarks Statistik. Statistiske Efterretninger. Indhold (Online).
Published by: Danmarks Statistik/Statistics Denmark, Sejroegade 11, Copenhagen OE, 2100, Denmark. TEL 45-39-173917, FAX 45-39-173939, dst@dst.dk.

360 GBR
DIMENSIONS. Text in English. 1978. a. GBP 20 per issue (effective 2005). **Document type:** *Bulletin.* **Description:** Report and analysis on the income and expenditure of the UK voluntary sector.
Former titles (until 1998): Dimensions of the Voluntary Sector (1359-0758); (until 1993): Charity Trends (0969-1707); (until 1992): Charity Statistics (0142-0216)
Related titles: Online - full text ed.
Published by: Charities Aid Foundation, Charities Aid Foundation, Kings Hill Avenue, Kings Hill, West Malling, Kent ME19 4TA, United Kingdom. TEL 44-1732-520000, FAX 44-1732-520001, research@cafonline.org. Ed. Cathy Pharoah. Circ: 2,000.

361.6 318 DOM
DOMINICAN REPUBLIC. SECRETARIA DE SANIDAD Y ASISTENCIA PUBLICA. CUADROS ESTADISTICOS. Text in Spanish. irreg.
Published by: Secretaria de Sanidad y Asistencia Publica, Ciudad Trujillo, Dominican Republic.

360.0021 FRA ISSN 1958-587X
RA407.5.F7
DOSSIERS SOLIDARITE ET SANTE (ONLINE). Text in French. 1972. q. free. **Document type:** *Government.*
Former titles (until 2007): Dossiers Solidarite et Sante (Print) (1296-2120); (until 1998): Solidarite Sante. Etudes Statistiques (0764-4493); (until 1983): Sante Securite Sociale (0338-3423); (until 1975): Bulletin de Statistiques de Sante et de Securite Sociale (0338-3415); Which superseded in part (in 1972): Bulletin Mensuel de Statistiques Sociales. Supplement C (0766-7949)
Media: Online - full text. **Related titles:** Microfiche ed.
Indexed: A22, FR, IBSS.
—IE, Infotrieve, INIST.
Published by: (France. Ministere du Travail, des Relations Sociales, de la Famille, de la Solidarite et de la Ville), Documentation Francaise, 29-31 Quai Voltaire, Paris, Cedex 7 75344, France. FAX 33-1-40157230, http://www.ladocumentationfrancaise.fr. Ed. M Vandamme.

EKONOMICHESKOE I SOTSIAL'NOE RAZVITIE KORENNYKH MALOCHISLENNYKH NARODOV SEVERA/ECONOMIC AND SOCIAL DEVELOPMENT OF INDIGENOUS SMALL NATIONALITIES OF THE FAR NORTH. *see* BUSINESS AND ECONOMICS—Abstracting, Bibliographies, Statistics

360 GRC ISSN 0256-3630
HD7181
ENQUETE ANNUELLE SUR L'ACTIVITE DES ORGANISMES DE SECURITE SOCIALE. Text in Greek; Summaries in French. 1968. a., latest 1993. back issues avail. **Document type:** *Government.*
Published by: National Statistical Service of Greece, Statistical Information and Publications Division/Ethniki Statistiki Yperesia tes Ellados, 14-16 Lykourgou St, Athens, 101 66, Greece. TEL 30-1-3244-748, FAX 30-1-3241-102, http://www.statistics.gr, http://www.statistics.gr/Main_eng.asp.

360 PAN ISSN 1023-330X
HN172.7
ESTADISTICA PANAMENA. INDICADORES SOCIALES. SECCION 012. Text in Spanish. 1985. biennial. PAB 1 domestic (effective 2000). **Document type:** *Bulletin, Government.* **Description:** Presents data on population, housing, education, health, services, social security, justice, and public safety.
Supersedes in part (in 1994): Estadistica Panamena. Indicadores Economicos y Sociales. Seccion 011 (0378-4940)
Published by: Direccion de Estadistica y Censo, Contraloria General, Apdo. 5213, Panama City, 5, Panama. FAX 507-210-4801. Circ: 800.

318 PAN
ESTADISTICA PANAMENA. SITUACION SOCIAL. SECCION 431. SERVICIOS DE SALUD. Text in Spanish. 1957. a. PAB 1 domestic (effective 2000). **Document type:** *Bulletin, Government.* **Description:** Presents numerical information on health institutions, beds, doctors, dentists, nurses, pharmacists, laboratory technicians, x-ray technicians, and auxiliary health personnel.
Formerly: Estadistica Panamena. Situacion Social. Seccion 431. Asistencia Social (0378-262X)
Published by: Direccion de Estadistica y Censo, Contraloria General, Apdo. 5213, Panama City, 5, Panama. FAX 507-210-4801. Circ: 800.

360 LUX ISSN 1681-9365
HJ7757
EUROPEAN SOCIAL STATISTICS. SOCIAL PROTECTION. EXPENDITURE AND RECEIPTS. Text in English. 1998. a. **Document type:** *Bulletin, Trade.*
Supersedes in part (in 2000): EUROSTAT. Ausgaben und Einnahmen des Sozialschutzes (1562-8868)
Related titles: Ed.: Europaeische Sozialistik. Sozialschutz. Ausgaben und Einnahmen. ISSN 1681-9357; Ed.: Statistiques Sociales Europeennes. Protection Sociale. Depenses et Recettes. ISSN 1681-9373.
Published by: (European Commission, Statistical Office of the European Communities (E U R O S T A T)), European Commission, Office for Official Publications of the European Union, 2 Rue Mercier, Luxembourg, L-2985, Luxembourg. TEL 352-29291, FAX 352-29291, info@publications.europa.eu, http://publications.europa.eu.

EXCERPTA MEDICA. SECTION 20: GERONTOLOGY AND GERIATRICS. *see* GERONTOLOGY AND GERIATRICS—Abstracting, Bibliographies, Statistics

EXCERPTA MEDICA. SECTION 40: DRUG DEPENDENCE, ALCOHOL ABUSE AND ALCOHOLISM. *see* DRUG ABUSE AND ALCOHOLISM—Abstracting, Bibliographies, Statistics

361.0021 FIN ISSN 1455-7460
FINLAND. SOSIAALI- JA TERVEYSALAN TUTKIMUS- JA KEHITTAMISKESKUS. TILASTORAPORTTI/FINLAND. FORSKNINGS- OCH UTVECKLINGSCENTRALKEN FOER SOCIAL- OCH HAELSOVAERDEN. STATISTIKRAPPORT/ FINLAND. NATIONAL RESEARCH AND DEVELOPMENT CENTRE FOR WELFARE AND HEALTH. STATISTICAL REPORT. Text in English, Finnish, Swedish. 1994. irreg. back issues avail. **Document type:** *Government.*
Formerly (until 1998): Finland. Sosiaali- ja Terveysalan Tutkimus- ja Kehittamiskeskus. Tilastotiedote (1237-251X)
Published by: Sosiaali- ja Terveysalan Tutkimus- ja Kehittamiskeskus/ National Research and Development Centre for Welfare and Health, PO Box 220, Helsinki, 00531, Finland. TEL 358-9-39671, FAX 358-9-396761307, infolib@stakes.fi, http://www.stakes.fi.

360 FIN ISSN 1796-7848
FINLAND. SOSIAALI- JA TERVEYSALAN TUTKIMUS- JA KEHITTAMISKESKUS. YKSITYINEN PALVELUTUOTANTO SOSIAALI- JA TERVEYDENHUOLLOSSA/FINLAND. FORSKNINGS- OCH UTVECLINGSCENTRALEN FOER SOCIAL- OCH HAELSOEVAARDEN. PRIVAT SERVICEPRODUKTION INOM SOCIALVAARDEN OCH HAELSO- OCH SJUKVAARDEN/ FINLAND. NATIONAL RESEARCH AND DEVELOPMENT CENTRE FOR WELFARE AND HEALTH. PRIVATE SERVICE PROVISION IN SOCIAL AND HEALTH CARE. Text in English, Finnish, Swedish. 2007. biennial. EUR 29 (effective 2008). **Document type:** *Government.*
Related titles: ◆ Series of: Finland. Tilastokeskus. Suomen Virallinen Tilasto. ISSN 1795-5165.
Published by: Sosiaali- ja Terveysalan Tutkimus- ja Kehittamiskeskus/ National Research and Development Centre for Welfare and Health, PO Box 220, Helsinki, 00531, Finland. TEL 358-9-39671, FAX 358-9-396761307, infolib@stakes.fi, http://www.stakes.fi.

360.021 FIN ISSN 1456-3096
HQ1075.F5
FINLAND. TILASTOKESKUS. TASA-ARVOBAROMETRI. Text in Finnish. 1998. biennial. **Document type:** *Government.*
Published by: Tilastokeskus/Statistics Finland, Tyopajakatu 13, Statistics Finland, Helsinki, 00022, Finland. TEL 358-9-17341, FAX 358-9-17342279, http://www.stat.fi.

010 060 USA ISSN 0190-3357
Z733
FOUNDATION CENTER. ANNUAL REPORT. Text in English. 1956. a. adv. back issues avail. **Document type:** *Report, Corporate.* **Description:** Describes how network of cooperating libraries works to provide free, convenient access to accurate information on private funding sources to nonprofit groups and other interested individuals and organizations throughout the country.
Formerly (until 1968): Foundation Center. Report (0548-7269)
Related titles: Online - full text ed.: free (effective 2011).
Published by: Foundation Center, 79 Fifth Ave, 16th St, New York, NY 10003. TEL 212-620-4230, 800-634-2953, FAX 212-807-3677, customerservice@foundationcenter.org, http://www.foundationcenter.org.

010 060 USA ISSN 0071-8092
AS911.A2
THE FOUNDATION DIRECTORY. Text in English. 1960. a. USD 215 per issue (effective 2011). charts; stat. index. Supplement avail. **Document type:** *Directory, Trade.* **Description:** Contains current information on the nation's largest grantmakers.
Supersedes: American Foundation and Their Fields
Related titles: CD-ROM ed.: ISSN 1548-5544; Online - full text ed.
—BLDSC (4024.923000).
Published by: Foundation Center, 79 Fifth Ave, 16th St, New York, NY 10003. TEL 212-620-4230, customerservice@foundationcenter.org.

361.73 USA ISSN 1536-7657
FOUNDATION GIVING TRENDS; update on funding priorities. Text in English. 1981. a. USD 45 per issue (effective 2011). **Document type:** *Report, Trade.* **Description:** Provides a comprehensive overview of the latest trends in foundation grant-making. Explores changes in giving interests by subject focus, recipient type, type of support, population group served, and geographic focus.
Supersedes in part (until 2000): Foundation Giving (Year) (1066-0445); Which was formerly (until 1991): Foundations Today
Indexed: SRI.
Published by: Foundation Center, 79 Fifth Ave, 16th St, New York, NY 10003. TEL 212-620-4230, 800-634-2953, FAX 212-807-3677, customerservice@foundationcenter.org, http://www.foundationcenter.org.

361.73 USA
LB2336
FOUNDATION GRANTS TO INDIVIDUALS. Text in English. 1977. biennial. USD 75 per issue (effective 2011). **Document type:** *Directory, Consumer.* **Description:** Profiles more than 5,400 foundation programs that make grants to individuals for education, arts and culture, general welfare, etc.
Related titles: CD-ROM ed.: ISSN 1550-5839; Online - full text ed.: USD 99.95 per issue (effective 2011).
Published by: Foundation Center, 79 Fifth Ave, 16th St, New York, NY 10003. TEL 212-620-4230, 800-634-2953, FAX 212-807-3677, customerservice@foundationcenter.org.

360.021 GRC ISSN 0253-9454
RA407.5.G73
GREECE. NATIONAL STATISTICAL SERVICE. SOCIAL WELFARE AND HEALTH STATISTICS. Text in English, Greek. 1967. a., latest 1995. back issues avail. **Document type:** *Government.*
Formerly (until 1976): Greece. National Statistical Service. Bulletin of Social Welfare and Health Statistics
Published by: National Statistical Service of Greece, Statistical Information and Publications Division/Ethniki Statistiki Yperesia tes Ellados, 14-16 Lykourgou St, Athens, 101 66, Greece. TEL 30-1-3289-397, FAX 30-1-3241-102, http://www.statistics.gr/Main_eng.asp, http://www.statistics.gr.

HONG KONG SPECIAL ADMINISTRATIVE REGION OF CHINA. CENSUS AND STATISTICS DEPARTMENT. SOCIAL DATA COLLECTED VIA THE GENERAL HOUSEHOLD SURVEY: SPECIAL TOPICS REPORT. *see* POPULATION STUDIES—Abstracting, Bibliographies, Statistics

330 360 FIN ISSN 0788-4141
HYVINVOINTIKATSAUS. Text in Finnish. 1990. q. EUR 47 (effective 2008). back issues avail. **Document type:** *Magazine, Government.* **Description:** The Finnish citizens' standard of living is analysed from prosperity's point of view. Each issue has a theme which is related to citizens' well-being.
Related titles: Online - full text ed.
Published by: Tilastokeskus/Statistics Finland, Tyopajakatu 13, Statistics Finland, Helsinki, 00022, Finland. TEL 358-9-17341, FAX 358-9-17342279. Ed. Riitta Harala.

362.021 USA
ILLINOIS. DEPARTMENT OF HUMAN SERVICES. DIVISION OF DISABILITY AND BEHAVIORAL HEALTH SERVICES. ILLINOIS STATISTICS. Text in English. 1930. a. free. **Document type:** *Government.*

Former titles: Mental Health Statistics for Illinois (0076-6453); Illinois. Department of Mental Health. Administrator's Data Manual
Indexed: SRI.
Published by: Department of Human Services, Division of Disability and Behavioral Health Services, 100 Sount Grand Ave E, Lowest level, Springfield, IL 62762. TEL 217-785-9404. Ed. Jim Kane. Circ: 950.

KOUSEIROUDOUSHOU. KOSEI TOKEI YORAN/JAPAN. MINISTRY OF HEALTH, LABOUR AND WELFARE. HANDBOOK OF HEALTH AND WELFARE STATISTICS. *see* PUBLIC HEALTH AND SAFETY—Abstracting, Bibliographies, Statistics

362 315 JPN ISSN 0448-4002
KOUSEIROUDOUSHOU. SEIKATSU HOGO DOTAI CHOSA HOKOKU/ JAPAN. MINISTRY OF HEALTH, LABOUR AND WELFARE. REPORT ON SURVEY OF PUBLIC ASSISTANCE. Text in Japanese. 1960. a. JPY 6,830 (effective 1998). **Document type:** *Government.*
Published by: Kouseiroudoushou/Ministry of Health, Labour and Welfare, 1-2-2 Kasumigaseki Chiyoda-ku, Tokyo, 100-8916, Japan. TEL 81-3-52531111, http://www.mhlw.go.jp/. R&P Yoke Kanegae.

362 315 JPN ISSN 0448-4010
HV411
KOUSEIROUDOUSHOU. SHAKAI FUKUSHI GYOSEI GYOMU HOKOKU/JAPAN. MINISTRY OF HEALTH, LABOUR AND WELFARE. STATISTICAL REPORT ON SOCIAL WELFARE ADMINISTRATION AND SERVICES. Text in Japanese. 1960. a. JPY 7,875 (effective 1998). **Document type:** *Government.*
Published by: Kouseiroudoushou/Ministry of Health, Labour and Welfare, 1-2-2 Kasumigaseki Chiyoda-ku, Tokyo, 100-8916, Japan. TEL 81-3-52531111, http://www.mhlw.go.jp/. R&P Yoke Kanegae.

362 315 JPN ISSN 0448-4029
KOUSEIROUDOUSHOU. SHAKAI FUKUSHI SHISETSU TOU CHOSA HOKOKU/JAPAN. MINISTRY OF HEALTH, LABOUR AND WELFARE. REPORT ON SURVEY OF SOCIAL WELFARE INSTITUTIONS. Text in Japanese. 1960. a. JPY 11,340 (effective 1998). **Document type:** *Government.*
Published by: Kouseiroudoushou/Ministry of Health, Labour and Welfare, 1-2-2 Kasumigaseki Chiyoda-ku, Tokyo, 100-8916, Japan. TEL 81-3-52531111, http://www.mhlw.go.jp/. R&P Yoke Kanegae.

360 KWT
KUWAIT. CENTRAL STATISTICAL OFFICE. SOCIAL STATISTICS BULLETIN/KUWAIT. AL-IDARAH AL-MARKAZIYYAH LIL-IHSA'. NASHRAT AL-IHSA'AT AL-IJTIMA'IYYAH. Text in Arabic, English. 1972. a., latest covers 1995. **Document type:** *Government.*
Description: Provides statistical data on public health, education, security and justice, cultural, social and religious services.
Supersedes in part (in 1981): Kuwait. Al-Idarah al-Markaziyyah lil-Ihsa'. Nashrah Sanawiyyah li-Ihsa'at al-Khadamat al-Aamah
Published by: Central Statistical Office/Al-Idarah al-Markaziyyah lil-Ihsa', P O Box 26188, Safat, 13122, Kuwait. TEL 965-2428200, FAX 965-2430464.

MALAWI. NATIONAL STATISTICAL OFFICE. SURVEY OF HANDICAPPED PERSONS. *see* HANDICAPPED—Abstracting, Bibliographies, Statistics

315.951 MYS ISSN 0127-4686
HN700.6
MALAYSIA. DEPARTMENT OF STATISTICS. SOCIAL STATISTICS BULLETIN, MALAYSIA/MALAYSIA. JABATAN PERANGKAAN. BULETIN PERANGKAAN SOSIAL, MALAYSIA. Text in English, Malay. **Document type:** *Government.*
Published by: Malaysia. Department of Statistics/Jabatan Perangkaan, Jalan Cenderasari, Kuala Lumpur, 50514, Malaysia. TEL 60-3-294-4264, FAX 60-3-291-4535.

361 USA ISSN 0093-7835
HV86
MICHIGAN. DEPARTMENT OF SOCIAL SERVICES. PROGRAM STATISTICS. Key Title: Program Statistics - Michigan Department of Social Services. Text in English. a. **Document type:** *Government.*
Supersedes: Michigan. Department of Social Services. Public Assistance Statistics (0093-6774)
Published by: Department of Social Services, 300 S Capitol Ave, PO Box 30037, Lansing, MI 48909. TEL 517-373-2005.

360 317 USA ISSN 0091-1143
HV86
MONTANA. DEPARTMENT OF SOCIAL AND REHABILITATION SERVICES. STATISTICAL REPORT. Text in English. 1974 (vol.36). m. free. charts; stat. **Document type:** *Government.*
Related titles: Microfiche ed.: (from CIS).
Indexed: SRI.
Published by: Department of Social and Rehabilitation Services, 111 Sanders St, Helena, MT 59601. TEL 406-449-3860. Circ: 400.

362.1021 USA ISSN 2152-2901
MONTHLY STATISTICAL SNAPSHOT. Text in English. 19??. m. free (effective 2010). back issues avail. **Document type:** *Report, Trade.*
Media: Online - full text.
Published by: U.S. Social Security Administration, Office of Retirement and Disability Policy, 2100 M St, NW, Washington, DC 20037. TEL 800-772-1213, op.publications@ssa.gov, http://www.ssa.gov/policy/about.html.

016.3628292 CAN ISSN 1494-1791
NATIONAL CLEARINGHOUSE ON FAMILY VIOLENCE. PUBLICATIONS. Variant title: Centre National d'Information sur la Violence dans la Famile, Sante Canada. Liste des Publications. Text in English, French. 1994. a.
Related titles: Online - full text ed.: ISSN 1700-9758.
Published by: National Clearinghouse on Family Violence, Jeanne Mance Bldg, 1907D1, Tunney's Pasture, Ottawa, ON K1A 1B4, Canada. TEL 613-957-2938, 800-267-1291, FAX 613-941-8930, ncfv-cnivf@hc-sc.gc.ca, http://www.hc-sc.gc.ca/nc-cn.

361.73 USA ISSN 1050-9852
HV89
NATIONAL DIRECTORY OF CORPORATE GIVING. Text in English. 1989. a. USD 195 per issue (effective 2011). back issues avail. **Document type:** *Directory, Trade.* **Description:** Features essential information on on 3,600 corporate grantmakers: application guidelines, key personnel, types of support awarded, giving limitations,and financial data including assets, annual giving, and the average size of grants.
Published by: Foundation Center, 79 Fifth Ave, 16th St, New York, NY 10003. TEL 212-620-4230, FAX 212-807-3677, customerservice@foundationcenter.org.

360.0021 314.921 NLD ISSN 1573-2215
HC321
NETHERLANDS. CENTRAAL BUREAU VOOR DE STATISTIEK. SOCIAAL-ECONOMISCHE TRENDS. Key Title: Sociaal-Economische Trends. Text in Dutch. 1953. q. EUR 50.35; EUR 13.80 newsstand/cover (effective 2008). charts. **Document type:** *Government.* **Description:** Offers statistics and data on social and economic situations and conditions in the Netherlands.
Former titles (until 2004): Netherlands. Centraal Bureau voor de Statistiek. Sociaal-Economische Maandstatistiek (0168-549X); (until 1984): Netherlands. Centraal Bureau voor de Statistiek. Sociale Maandstatistiek (0470-6978)
Published by: Centraal Bureau voor de Statistiek, Henri Faasdreef 312, The Hague, 2492 JP, Netherlands. TEL 31-70-3373800, infoserv@cbs.nl.

NEW LITERATURE ON SIGHT PROBLEMS. *see* HANDICAPPED—Abstracting, Bibliographies, Statistics

360 USA
NEW YORK (STATE). OFFICE OF TEMPORARY AND DISABILITY ASSISTANCE. TEMPORARY AND DISABILITY ASSISTANCE STATISTICS (ONLINE). Text in English. 19??. m. free (effective 2011). back issues avail. **Document type:** *Report, Government.* **Description:** Contains statistical data relating to NY state social services programs, including public assistance, Medicaid and food stamps.
Former titles (until 2001): New York (State). Office of Temporary and Disability Assistance. Temporary and Disability Assistance Statistics (Print); (until 1998): New York (State). Office of Temporary and Disability Assistance. Social Statistics; New York (State). Department of Social Services. Social Statistics
Media: Online - full text.
Published by: Office of Temporary and Disability Assistance, 40 N Pearl St, Albany, NY 12243. TEL 518-473-1090, nyspio@otda.state.ny.us.

360 NOR ISSN 1891-3598
NOEKKELTALL FOR HELSESEKTOREN. Text in Norwegian. 2007. a. stat. **Document type:** *Consumer.*
Formerly (until 2009): Hundre Noekkeltal for Helse- og Sosialsektoren (1504-8462)
Related titles: Online - full text ed.
Published by: Helsedirektoratet/Norwegian Directorate of Health, PO Box 7000, St Olavs Plass, Oslo, 0130, Norway. TEL 47-810-20050, FAX 47-24-163001, postmottak@helsedirektoratet.no.

016.36 USA
▼ **NONPROFIT ORGANIZATION REFERENCE CENTER.** Text in English. 2009. base vol. plus w. updates. **Document type:** *Database, Abstract/Index.* **Description:** Focuses on supporting the ongoing functional and information needs of the nonprofit sector.
Media: Online - full text.
Published by: EBSCO Publishing (Subsidiary of: EBSCO Industries, Inc.), 10 Estes St, PO Box 682, Ipswich, MA 01938. TEL 800-653-2726, FAX 978-356-6565, information@ebscohost.com.

362.7 USA
OHIO. DEPARTMENT OF HUMAN SERVICES. CHILD WELFARE STATISTICS. Text in English. q. looseleaf. free. back issues avail. **Document type:** *Government.*
Published by: Department of Human Services, 30 E Broad St, 30th Fl, Columbus, OH 43215. TEL 614-466-0292, FAX 614-466-3863. Ed. Florence C Odita. Circ: 500.

016 ITA
POLLICINO; banca dati su emarginazione disagio giovanile professioni e politiche sociali. Variant title: Il Centro Studi Documentazione e Ricerche. Text in Italian. base vol. plus irreg. updates. **Document type:** *Bibliography.* **Description:** Contains bibliographic data on such social issues as addiction, problems of youth and adolescents, crime and encarceration, homosexuality, prostitution, AIDS, and immigration problems, as well as conflict resolution.
Media: Online - full text. **Related titles:** CD-ROM ed.
Published by: Edizioni Gruppo Abele, Corso Trapani 95, Turin, TO 10141, Italy. TEL 39-011-3841011, FAX 39-011-3841031, segreteria@gruppoabele.org, http://www.gruppoabele.org.

PORTUGAL. INSTITUTO NACIONAL DE ESTATISTICA. INQUERITO AS RECEITAS E DESPESAS FAMILIARES. *see* SOCIAL SERVICES AND WELFARE

REFUGEE SURVEY QUARTERLY. *see* POPULATION STUDIES—Abstracting, Bibliographies, Statistics

649.8021 GBR
RESIDENTIAL CARE HOMES SCOTLAND. STATISTICAL INFORMATION NOTE. Text in English. a.
Former titles: Residential Community Care Scotland. Statistical Information Note; (until 1997): Community Care, Scotland
Published by: Community Care Statistics, Room 52, James Craig Walk, Edinburgh, EH1 3BA, United Kingdom. TEL 44-131-2443777. Ed. Steven Gillespie.

362.021 USA ISSN 1940-0411
RURAL POVERTY AT A GLANCE. Text in English. 19??. a. **Document type:** *Report, Government.*
Media: Online - full text.
Published by: U.S. Department of Agriculture, Economic Research Service, 1800 M St NW, Washington, DC 20036. TEL 202-694-5050, ersinfo@ers.usda.gov.

360 SEN
SENEGAL. MINISTERE DE L'ECONOMIE, DES FINANCES ET DU PLAN. ENQUETE DEMOGRAPHIQUE ET SANTE II (YEAR). Text in French. irreg. XOF 10,000; XOF 15,000 foreign (effective 1998). **Document type:** *Government.*
Published by: Ministere de l'Economie des Finances et du Plan, Direction de la Prevision et de la Statistique, BP 116, Dakar, Senegal. TEL 221-21-03-01. Pub. Ibrahima Sarr.

360 SEN
SENEGAL. MINISTERE DE L'ECONOMIE, DES FINANCES ET DU PLAN. ENQUETE EMPLOI, SOUS EMPLOI ET CHOMAGE. Text in French. irreg. XOF 5,000; XOF 7,000 foreign (effective 1998). **Document type:** *Government.*
Published by: Ministere de l'Economie des Finances et du Plan, Direction de la Prevision et de la Statistique, BP 116, Dakar, Senegal. TEL 221-21-03-01. Pub. Ibrahima Sarr.

360 SEN
SENEGAL. MINISTERE DE L'ECONOMIE, DES FINANCES ET DU PLAN. ENQUETE SUR LES PRIORITES: DIMENSIONS SOCIALES DE L'AJUSTEMENT (YEAR). Text in French. 1992. irreg. XOF 5,000; XOF 7,000 foreign (effective 1998). **Document type:** *Government.*
Published by: Ministere de l'Economie des Finances et du Plan, Direction de la Prevision et de la Statistique, BP 116, Dakar, Senegal. TEL 221-21-03-01. Pub. Ibrahima Sarr.

304.6 SEN
SENEGAL. MINISTERE DE L'ECONOMIE, DES FINANCES ET DU PLAN. POPULATION DU SENEGAL. Text in French. 1994. irreg. XOF 10,000; XOF 15,000 foreign (effective 1998). **Document type:** *Government.*
Published by: Ministere de l'Economie des Finances et du Plan, Direction de la Prevision et de la Statistique, BP 116, Dakar, Senegal. TEL 221-21-03-01. Pub. Ibrahima Sarr.

360 SEN
SENEGAL. MINISTERE DE L'ECONOMIE, DES FINANCES ET DU PLAN. TABLEAU DE BORD DE LA SITUATION SOCIALE. Text in French. irreg. XOF 7,000; XOF 10,000 foreign (effective 1998). **Document type:** *Government.*
Published by: Ministere de l'Economie des Finances et du Plan, Direction de la Prevision et de la Statistique, BP 116, Dakar, Senegal. TEL 221-21-03-01. Pub. Ibrahima Sarr.

360 315 JPN ISSN 0289-1360
SHAKAI SEIKATSU TOKEI SHIHYO/SOCIAL INDICATORS BY PREFECTURE (YEAR). Text in Japanese. 1989. a. stat. back issues avail. **Document type:** *Report, Government.*
Related titles: CD-ROM ed.: JPY 43,050 (effective 2000); Magnetic Tape ed.: JPY 43,050 for cartridge magnetic tape; JPY 44,625 for open-reel magnetic tape (effective 2000).
Published by: Japan. Ministry of Internal Affairs and Communications. Statistics Bureau/Somucho. Tokeikyoko, 19-1 Wakamatsu-cho, Shinjyuku-ku, Tokyo, 162-8668, Japan. TEL 81-3-5273-2020. R&P Akihiko Ito.

360 315 TWN
SOCIAL AFFAIRS STATISTICS OF TAIWAN/CHUNG HUA MIN KUO T'AI-WAN SHENG SHE HUI SHIH YEH T'UNG CHI. Text in Chinese, English. a. stat.
Published by: Department of Social Affairs, Nantou Hsien, Taiwan.

360.021 CAN ISSN 1912-9858
HC120.I5
SOCIAL ASSISTANCE STATISTICAL REPORT. Text in English. 200?. a. **Document type:** *Government.*
Related titles: Online - full text ed.: ISSN 1912-9505. 2004; French ed.: L' Aide Sociale. Rapport Statistique. ISSN 1912-9866.
Published by: Human Resources and Social Development Canada, Public Enquiries Centre, 140 Promenade du Portage, Phase IV, Level 0, Gatineau, PQ K1A 0J9, Canada. TEL 800-935-5555, FAX 819-953-7260, http://www.hrsdc.gc.ca.

310 360 GBR ISSN 2044-9178
HV245
SOCIAL CARE STATISTICS. ACTUALS (ONLINE). Text in English. 1973. a. back issues avail. **Document type:** *Report, Trade.*
Former titles (until 2008): Chartered Institute of Public Finance and Accountancy. Social Care Statistics. Actuals (Print) (1758-1168); (until 2007): Chartered Institute of Public Finance and Accountancy. Personal Social Services Statistics. Actuals (0309-653X); Which superseded in part (in 1976): Chartered Institute of Public Finance and Accountancy. Local Health and Social Services. Statistics (0307-0506); Which was formed by the merger of (19??-1973): Chartered Institute of Public Finance and Accountancy. Children's Services Statistics (0443-3750); (19??-1973): Chartered Institute of Public Finance and Accountancy. Welfare Services Statistics; (1951-1973): Institute of Municipal Treasurers and Accountants. Society of County Treasurers. Local Health Services Statistics (0443-3785)
—CCC.
Published by: Chartered Institute of Public Finance and Accountancy, 3 Robert St, London, WC2N 6RL, United Kingdom. TEL 44-20-75435600, FAX 44-20-75435700, info@cipfa.org.uk, http://www.cipfa.org.uk.

360 GBR ISSN 1743-2642
SOCIAL POLICY, HOUSING & HEALTH BULLETIN (ONLINE). Text in English. 1992. fortn. **Document type:** *Abstract/Index.* **Description:** Covers the social services and health.
Formerly (until 200?): Social Policy, Housing & Health Bulletin (Print) (1477-5972); Which was formed by the merger of (1992-2002): Social Services Bulletin (0964-9891); (1987-2002): Housing Abstracts (0952-8156)
Media: Online - full text.
Published by: London Research Centre, Research Library, Greater London Authority, City Hall, The Queen's Walk, More London, London, SE1 2AA, United Kingdom. TEL 44-20-79834000, http://www.london.gov.uk.

016.36 USA
SOCIAL SERVICES ABSTRACTS. Text in English. 1979. base vol. plus m. updates. **Document type:** *Database, Abstract/Index.*
Description: Provides bibliographic coverage of current research focused on social work, human services, and related areas, including social welfare, social policy, and community development.
Media: Online - full text.
Published by: ProQuest LLC (Bethesda) (Subsidiary of: Cambridge Information Group), 789 E Eisenhower Pky, Ann Arbor, MI 48103. TEL 734-761-4700, FAX 734-997-4222, info@proquest.com.

361.6 GBR
SOCIAL SERVICES STATISTICS FOR WALES. Variant title: Social Services Statistics Wales. Text in English. 1998. irreg., latest 2009. free (effective 2009). **Document type:** *Government.* **Description:** Features statistics on social services provided or funded by local authorities.

S

Formerly (until 1998): Personal Social Services Statistics for Wales (1362-3591); Which was formed by the merger of (1982-1998): Activities of Social Services Department in Wales (0262-5261); (1980-1998): Staff of Social Services Departments in Wales (0262-5172); (1993-1998): Children Looked After by Local Authorities in Wales (0968-4050); Which was formerly (1982-1993): Children in Care or Under Supervision Orders in Wales (0263-2667); (1995-1998): Residential Care Homes and Nursing Homes in Wales (1352-8076); Which was formerly (1980-1995): Residential Accomodation for Elderly People and People with Physical or Visual Disabilities (0965-2248)
Published by: Local Government of Welsh, Data Unit, Local Government House, Drake Walk, Cardiff, CF10 4LG, United Kingdom. TEL 44-29-20468600, housing@dataunitwales.gov.uk.

016.362 USA ISSN 1070-5317
HV1
➤ **SOCIAL WORK ABSTRACTS.** Text in English. 1965. q. USD 133 domestic libraries/institutions; USD 159 foreign libraries/institutions (effective 2010). adv. illus. index. back issues avail.; reprints avail. **Document type:** *Journal, Academic/Scholarly.* **Description:** Provides abstracts of articles appearing in major social work and human services journals.
Supersedes in part (in 1994): Social Work Research and Abstracts (0148-0847); Which was formerly (until 1977): Abstracts for Social Workers (0001-3412)
Related titles: Microform ed.: (from PQC); Online - full text ed.
Indexed: P27, P48, P50, P54, PQC.
—Ingenta. **CCC.**
Published by: (National Association of Social Workers), N A S W Press, 750 First St NE, Ste 700, Washington, DC 20002-4241. TEL 800-227-3590, FAX 202-336-8312, press@naswdc.org. Circ: 2,500.

361.0021 FIN ISSN 1458-1671
HV315.5
SOSIAALI- JA TERVEYDENHUOLLON TILASTOLLINEN VUOSIKIRJA/ STATISTICAL YEARBOOK ON SOCIAL WELFARE AND HEALTH CARE/STATISTISK AARSBOK FOER SOCIAL- OCH HAELSOVAERDEN. Text in English, Finnish, Swedish. 2001. a. EUR 35 per issue (effective 2006).
Related titles: ◆ Series of: Sosiaaliturva. ISSN 0785-4625.
Published by: Sosiaali- ja Terveysalan Tutkimus- ja Kehittamiskeskus/ National Research and Development Centre for Welfare and Health, PO Box 220, Helsinki, 00531, Finland. TEL 358-9-39671, FAX 358-9-396761307, infolib@stakes.fi.

360 FIN ISSN 1458-5286
SOSIAALI- JA TERVEYSMENOT. Text in Finnish. 1993. a.
Formerly (until 2001): Sosiaalyurva Suomessa (1236-3650)
Related titles: Online - full text ed.; English ed.: Social Welfare and Health Care Expenditure. ISSN 1237-5004; ◆ Series of: Sosiaaliturva. ISSN 0785-4625.
Published by: Sosiaali- ja Terveysalan Tutkimus- ja Kehittamiskeskus/ National Research and Development Centre for Welfare and Health, PO Box 220, Helsinki, 00531, Finland. TEL 358-9-39671, FAX 358-9-396761307, infolib@stakes.fi, http://www.stakes.fi.

360 FIN ISSN 0785-4625
HD7197.3
SOSIAALITURVA. Text in English, Finnish. 1988. irreg. back issues avail. **Document type:** *Government.*
Related titles: ◆ Series: Finland. Sosiaali- ja Terveyshallitus. Kotipalvelu. ISSN 0788-6098; ◆ Sosiaali- ja Terveydenhuollon Tilastollinen Vuosikirja. ISSN 1458-1671; ◆ Sosiaali- ja Terveysmenot. ISSN 1458-5286; ◆ Lapsen Elatus ja Huolto. ISSN 0789-8525; ◆ Tyottomyyspaivarahat. ISSN 1238-2620; ◆ Paihdetilastollinen Vuosikirja. ISSN 1455-7444; ◆ Lastensuojelu. ISSN 0788-6101; ◆ Tyolakemenotilasto Alueittain. ISSN 0785-4633; Toimeentulotuki. ISSN 1455-1756.
Published by: (Sosiaali- ja Terveysalan Tutkimus- ja Kehittamiskeskus/ National Research and Development Centre for Welfare and Health), Elaketurvakeskus/Finnish Centre for Pensions, Kirjurinkatu 3, Helsinki, 00065, Finland. TEL 358-10-7511, FAX 358-9-1481172, tutkimus@etk.fi, http://www.etk.fi.

360 316.8 ZAF ISSN 0258-7777
SOUTH AFRICA. STATISTICS SOUTH AFRICA. CENSUS OF SOCIAL, RECREATIONAL AND PERSONAL SERVICES - WELFARE ORGANISATIONS. Key Title: Sensus van Welsynsorganisasies. Text in Afrikaans, English. irreg., latest 1990. **Document type:** *Government.*
Formerly (until Aug.1998): South Africa. Central Statistical Service. Census of Social, Recreational and Personal Services - Welfare Organisations
Published by: Statistics South Africa/Statistieke Suid-Afrika, Private Bag X44, Pretoria, 0001, South Africa. TEL 27-12-3108911, FAX 27-12-3108500, info@statssa.gov.za, http://www.statssa.gov.za.

360 316.8 ZAF
SOUTH AFRICA. STATISTICS SOUTH AFRICA. STATISTICAL RELEASE. CENSUS OF SOCIAL, RECREATIONAL AND PERSONAL SERVICES (YEAR). Text in English. irreg., latest 1988. **Document type:** *Government.*
Formerly (until Aug. 1998): South Africa. Central Statistical Service. Statistical Release. Census of Social, Recreational and Personal Services (Year)
Published by: Statistics South Africa/Statistieke Suid-Afrika, Private Bag X44, Pretoria, 0001, South Africa. TEL 27-12-3108911, FAX 27-12-3108500, info@statssa.gov.za, http://www.statssa.gov.za.

360 310 USA
SOUTH DAKOTA. STATE DEPARTMENT OF SOCIAL SERVICES. ANNUAL STATISTICAL REPORT. Text in English. 1971. a. adv. stat. **Document type:** *Government.*
Formerly: South Dakota. State Department of Public Welfare. Research and Statistical Annual Report (0099-2305)
Indexed: SRI.
Published by: State Department of Social Services, Office of Management Information, Richard F Kneip Bldg, 700 Governors Dr, Pierre, SD 57501. TEL 605-773-3348, FAX 605-773-4855. Ed., Pub., R&P, Adv. contact Richard Jensen. Circ: 320.

362.721 CAN ISSN 1912-743X
SOUTIEN AUX ENFANTS. STATISTIQUES. Text in French. 1967. a. **Document type:** *Report, Trade.*
Former titles (until 2005): Prestations Familiales. Statistiques (1488-5999); (until 1997): Allocations d'Aide aux familles. Statistiques (1192-2559); (until 1991): Regie des Rentes du Quebec. Statistiques (0836-9275); (until 1986): Perspectives Statistiques (0712-8223); Which superseded in part (in 1979): Regime de Rentes du Quebec. Bulletin Statistique (0225-4514); Which was formerly (until 1972): Regie des Rentes du Quebec. Bulletin Statistique (0701-600X); Which incorporates (1967-1970): Quebec Pension Board. Statistical Bulletin (0701-6018)
Published by: Regie des Rentes du Quebec, C P 5200, Quebec, PQ G1K 7S9, Canada. FAX 418-528-1909, http://www.rrq.gouv.qc.ca/fr.

361.307021 USA ISSN 0163-1403
HV11
STATISTICS ON SOCIAL WORK EDUCATION IN THE UNITED STATES. Text in English. 19??. a. price varies. back issues avail. **Document type:** *Abstract/Index.*
Former titles (until 1974): Statistics on Graduate Social Work Education in the United States (0091-7192); (until 1972): Statistics on Social Work Education (0589-9931)
Related titles: Online - full text ed.
Indexed: SRI.
Published by: Council on Social Work Education, 1725 Duke St, Ste 500, Alexandria, VA 22314. TEL 703-683-8080, FAX 703-683-8099, info@cswe.org, http://www.cswe.org. Circ: 1,400.

360 DEU ISSN 1433-2523
STATISTISCHE BERICHTE - BADEN-WUERTTEMBERG. K: SOZIALLEISTUNGEN. Text in German. 1956. irreg. **Document type:** *Government.*
Formerly (until 1992): Statistisches Landesamt Baden-Wuerttemberg. Statistische Berichte K (1433-2345)
Published by: Statistisches Landesamt Baden-Wuerttemberg, Boeblinger Str 68, Stuttgart, 70199, Germany. TEL 49-711-6410, FAX 49-711-6412440, poststelle@stala.bwl.de.

360 DEU ISSN 1430-5143
STATISTISCHE BERICHTE - RHEINLAND-PFALZ. K: SOZIALLEISTUNGEN. Text in German. 1951. irreg. **Document type:** *Government.*
Formerly (until 1976): Statistisches Landesamt Rheinland-Pfalz. Statistische Berichte K (1430-4996); Which superseded in part (in 1956): Statistisches Landesamt Rheinland-Pfalz. Mitteilungen (0482-8887)
Published by: Statistisches Landesamt Rheinland-Pfalz, Mainzerstr 14-16, Bad Ems, 56130, Germany. TEL 49-2603-713240, FAX 49-2603-71193240, pressestelle@statistik.rlp.de.

SUPPLEMENTAL SECURITY INCOME MONTHLY STATISTICS. *see* INSURANCE—Abstracting, Bibliographies, Statistics

360 314 SWE ISSN 0283-8605
SWEDEN. STATISTISKA CENTRALBYRAAN. STATISTISKA MEDDELANDEN. SERIE S, SOCIALTJAENST OCH SOCIALFOERSAEKRING. Text in Swedish; Summaries in English. 1963. irreg. SEK 1,000.
Former titles (until vol.26, 1982): Sweden. Statistiska Centralbyraan. Statistiska Meddelanden. Serie S, Socialtjaenst och Socialfoersaekring; (until 1977): Sweden. Statistiska Centralbyraan. Statistiska Meddelanden. Serie S, Socialvaard, Haelso- och Sjukvaard; (until 1976): Sweden. Statistiska Centralbyraan. Statistiska Meddelanden, S; (until 1969): Sweden. Statistiska Centralbyraan. Statistiska Meddelanden. Serie S, Social-, Haelso- och Sjukvaard
Published by: Statistiska Centralbyraan/Statistics Sweden, Publishing Unit, Orebro, 70189, Sweden. Circ: 1,300.

361.0021 FIN ISSN 0785-4633
TYOLAKEMENOTILASTO ALUEITTAIN. Text in Finnish. 1988. a.
Related titles: ◆ Series of: Sosiaaliturva. ISSN 0785-4625.
Published by: Tilastokeskus/Statistics Finland, PO Box 4V, Helsinki, 00022, Finland. http://www.stat.fi.

300.711 FRA ISSN 1630-0165
UNIVERSITES. STATISTIQUES SCIENCES HUMAINES. Text in French. 2001. irreg. back issues avail. **Document type:** *Monographic series, Academic/Scholarly.*
Related titles: ◆ Series of: Universites. ISSN 1258-195X.
Published by: Editions Ellipses, 8-10 Rue de La Quintinie, Paris, 75740 Cedex 15, France. TEL 33-1-56566410, FAX 33-1-45310767, edito@editions-ellipses.fr.

360 DEU ISSN 0934-1935
VERZEICHNIS BERATUNGSSTELLEN DER OEFFENTLICHEN UND FREIEN WOHLFAHRTSPFLEGE IN BAYERN. Text in German. 1987. irreg. EUR 15.50 per issue (effective 2011). **Document type:** *Government.*
Published by: Bayerisches Landesamt fuer Statistik und Datenverarbeitung, Neuhauser Str 8, Munich, 80331, Germany. TEL 49-89-2119205, FAX 49-89-2119410, poststelle@statistik.bayern.de, http://www.statistik.bayern.de.

WELFARE BULLETIN. *see* LAW—Abstracting, Bibliographies, Statistics

SOCIOLOGY

see also FOLKLORE ; POPULATION STUDIES ; SOCIAL SCIENCES: COMPREHENSIVE WORKS ; SOCIAL SERVICES AND WELFARE

301 USA
A A P O R NEWS. Text in English. q. membership. **Document type:** *Newsletter.*
Published by: American Association for Public Opinion Research, PO Box 1248, Ann Arbor, MI 48106. Ed. Lydia Saad. Circ: 1,579.

A B Q CORRESPONDENT. *see* TECHNOLOGY: COMPREHENSIVE WORKS

306.85 AUS ISSN 1834-2434
A F R C BRIEFING. (Australian Family Relationships Clearinghouse) Text in English. 2006. bi-m. **Document type:** *Newsletter, Trade.*
Media: Online - full text.
Published by: Australian Family Relationships Clearinghouse (Subsidiary of: Australian Institute of Family Studies), 300 Queen St, Melbourne, VIC 3000, Australia. TEL 61-3-9214-7888, FAX 61-3-9214-7839, afrc@aifs.gov.au.

A F T A MONOGRAPH SERIES. *see* PSYCHOLOGY

659.3 DEU ISSN 0939-8074
A K M - STUDIEN. Text in German. 1974. irreg., latest vol.41, 2006. price varies. **Document type:** *Monographic series, Academic/Scholarly.*
Formerly (until 1985): A f k Studien (0721-1651)
Published by: (Arbeitsgruppe Kommunikationsforschung Muenchen), U V K Verlagsgesellschaft mbH, Schuetzenstr 24, Konstanz, 78462, Germany. TEL 49-7531-90530, FAX 49-7531-905398, nadine.ley@uvk.de, http://www.uvk.de.

305 USA ISSN 2156-3748
A M P S INDY. (African-aMerican People Succeeding) Variant title: A M P S Magazine. Text in English. 2005. bi-m. USD 20 (effective 2010). adv. back issues avail. **Document type:** *Magazine, Trade.*
Related titles: Online - full text ed.: ISSN 2156-3756. free (effective 2010).
Published by: One WRIGHT Company, LLC, PO Box 858, Fishers, IN 46037. TEL 317-828-8544, FAX 866-591-5657. Ed. Akilah Webster. adv.: page USD 500.

A N S S CURRENTS. (Anthropology and Sociology Section) *see* LIBRARY AND INFORMATION SCIENCES

301 USA ISSN 0749-6931
HM1
A S A FOOTNOTES. Text in English. 1973. 9/yr. USD 40 in US & Canada to non-members; USD 55 elsewhere to non-members; USD 3 per issue; free to members (effective 2009). adv. back issues avail. **Document type:** *Newsletter, Trade.* **Description:** Contains departmental news, activities of the ASA and the executive office; developments on the Washington scene; and the ASA official reports and proceedings.
Related titles: Online - full text ed.
Published by: American Sociological Association, 1430 K St, NW, Ste 600, Washington, DC 20005. TEL 202-383-9005, FAX 202-638-0882, infoservice@asanet.org. Ed. Sally T Hillsman. adv.: page USD 3,235; 10 x 14. Circ: 14,500.

307 DEU ISSN 0176-8433
A S A - STUDIEN. (Arbeits- und Studienaufenthalte) Text in German. 1984. irreg., latest vol.35, 2001. price varies. **Document type:** *Monographic series, Academic/Scholarly.*
Indexed: IBR, IBZ.
Published by: Lit Verlag, Grevener Str/Fresnostr 2, Muenster, 48159, Germany. TEL 49-251-235091, FAX 49-251-231972, lit@lit-verlag.de, http://www.lit-verlag.de.

A S B B S E-JOURNAL. *see* BUSINESS AND ECONOMICS

306.09 NZL ISSN 1176-9882
A U P STUDIES IN CULTURAL AND SOCIAL HISTORY. Variant title: Studies in Cultural and Social History. Text in English. 2005. s-a. NZD 34.99 per issue (effective 2006). **Document type:** *Monographic series, Academic/Scholarly.*
Published by: Auckland University Press, Private Bag 92019, Auckland, New Zealand. TEL 64-9-3737528, FAX 64-9-3737465, aup@auckland.ac.nz, http://www.auckland.ac.nz/uoa/aup/.

307.14 DEU ISSN 0946-0195
AACHENER BEITRAEGE ZUR AFRIKA- UND ENTWICKLUNGSLAENDERFORSCHUNG. Text in German. 1995. irreg., latest vol.3, 1997. price varies. **Document type:** *Monographic series, Academic/Scholarly.*
Indexed: IBR, IBZ.
Published by: Verlag fuer Entwicklungspolitik Saarbruecken GmbH, Auf der Adt 14, Saarbruecken, 66130, Germany. TEL 49-6893-986094, FAX 49-6893-986095, vfe@verlag-entwicklungspolitik.de.

951 DEU ISSN 0178-1332
AACHENER BEITRAEGE ZUR VERGLEICHENDEN SOZIOLOGIE UND ZUR CHINA-FORSCHUNG. Text in German. 1986. irreg., latest vol.13, 1999. price varies. **Document type:** *Monographic series, Academic/Scholarly.*
Published by: Peter Lang GmbH (Subsidiary of: Peter Lang Publishing Group), Eschborner Landstr 42-50, Frankfurt Am Main, 60489, Germany. TEL 49-69-7807050, FAX 49-69-78070550, zentrale.frankfurt@peterlang.com.

301 400 DNK ISSN 0903-8892
AALBORG UNIVERSITET. INSTITUT FOR SPROG OG INTERNATIONALE KULTURSTUDIER. PUBLIKATIONER. Variant title: Aalborg University. Department of Languages and Intercultural Studies. Publication. Universitaet Aalborg. Institut fuer Sprache und Interkulturelle Studien. Publikation. Text in Danish, English, German. 1987. irreg., latest vol.42, 2004. price varies. back issues avail. **Document type:** *Monographic series, Academic/Scholarly.*
Related titles: ◆ Multiple languages ed.: Aalborg University. Department of Language and Culture. Research News. ISSN 1902-9543; German ed.: Universitaet Aalborg. Arbeitspapiere des Instituts fuer Sprache und Interkulturelle Studien.
Published by: Aalborg Universitet, Institut for Sprog og Kultur/Aalborg University. Department of Language and Culture, Kroghstraede 3, Aalborg OE, 9220, Denmark. TEL 45-99-409130, FAX 45-98-157887, http://www.sprog.auc.dk.

301 DNK ISSN 0904-4760
HN541
AARHUS UNIVERSITET. CENTER FOR KULTURFORSKNING. ARBEJDSPAPIRER, GROEN SERIES. Text in Multiple languages. 1993. irreg. back issues avail. **Document type:** *Monographic series, Academic/Scholarly.*
Related titles: Online - full text ed.: ISSN 1398-7526.
Published by: Aarhus Universitet, Center for Kulturforskning/University of Aarhus. Centre for Cultural Research, Jens Chr. Skous Vej 3, Aarhus C, 8000, Denmark. TEL 45-89-426900, FAX 45-89-426919, cfk@au.dk.

ACADEMIA; Zeitschrift fuer Politik und Kultur. *see* LITERARY AND POLITICAL REVIEWS

ACADEMIA DE STIINTE A REPUBLICII MOLDOVA. BULETINUL. ECONOMIE SI SOCIOLOGIE/AKADEMIYA NAUK RESPUBLIKI MOLDOVA. IZVESTIYA. EKONOMIKA I SOTSIOLOGIYA. *see* BUSINESS AND ECONOMICS—Economic Situation And Conditions

303 USA ISSN 1092-6534
HM1281
➤ **THE ACORN.** Text in English. 1986. s-a. USD 15 (effective 2010). adv. back issues avail. **Document type:** *Journal, Academic/Scholarly.* **Description:** Examines the theory and practice of nonviolence, especially as it relates to the philosophies of M. K. Gandhi and Martin Luther King, Jr.

Related titles: Online - full text ed.: ISSN 2153-8263. USD 45 to individuals; USD 65 to institutions (effective 2010).
Indexed: PhilInd.
Published by: (Gandhi-King Society), Philosophy Documentation Center, PO Box 7147, Charlottesville, VA 22906. TEL 434-220-3300, FAX 434-220-3301, order@pdcnet.org, http://www.pdcnet.org. Ed. Barry L Gan TEL 716-375-2275. Adv. contact Greg Swope.

301 GBR ISSN 0001-6993
HM1.A1
➤ **ACTA SOCIOLOGICA.** Text in English. 1955. q. GBP 271, USD 503 to institutions; GBP 277, USD 513 combined subscription to institutions (print & online eds.) (effective 2012). adv. bk.rev. charts; illus. index. back issues avail.; reprint service avail. from PSC. **Document type:** *Journal, Academic/Scholarly.* **Description:** Publishes innovative sociological research written from different theoretical and methodological starting points written by both Scandinavian and non-Scandinavian sociologists, presenting alternative ways of understanding and conceptualizing social life.
Related titles: Microform ed.: (from PQC, SWZ); Online - full text ed.: ISSN 1502-3869. GBP 249, USD 462 to institutions (effective 2012) (from IngentaConnect).
Indexed: A01, A02, A03, A08, A20, A22, A26, ABCPolSci, AMHA, ASCA, AbAn, B01, B04, B06, B07, B09, BRD, CA, CurCont, DIP, E01, E08, EI, ERA, ESPM, FR, FamI, G08, H09, HistAb, I05, I13, I14, IBR, IBSS, IBZ, MEA&I, MLA-IB, P02, P03, P06, P10, P27, P30, P42, P48, P53, P54, PAIS, PCI, PQC, PSA, PsycInfo, PsycholAb, RASB, RILM, RiskAb, S02, S03, S05, S09, S11, S19, S21, SCOPUS, SOPODA, SSA, SSAI, SSAb, SSCI, SSI, SSciA, SociolAb, T02, W01, W02, W03, W07, W09.
—BLDSC (0663.350000), IE, Infotrieve, Ingenta, INIST. **CCC.**
Published by: (Nordic Sociological Association NOR), Sage Publications Ltd. (Subsidiary of: Sage Publications, Inc.), 1 Oliver's Yard, 55 City Rd, London, EC1Y 1SP, United Kingdom. TEL 44-20-73248500, FAX 44-20-73248600, info@sagepub.co.uk, http://www.uk.sagepub.com/home.nav. Eds. Arne Mastekaasa, Lise Kjolsrod.

301 MEX ISSN 0186-6028
HM409 CODEN: ACSOFH
ACTA SOCIOLOGICA. Text in Spanish; Abstracts in English, Spanish. 1969. 3/yr. MXN 300 domestic; USD 110 foreign (effective 2004). bibl.; illus. **Document type:** *Academic/Scholarly.* **Description:** Discusses various sociological and political science topics.
Indexed: AbAn, C01, CA, DIP, FR, I13, IBR, IBZ, P09, P42, PAIS, PCI, PSA, S02, S03, SOPODA, SSA, SociolAb, T02.
—INIST.
Published by: Universidad Nacional Autonoma de Mexico, Facultad de Ciencias Politicas y Sociales, Circuito Cultural Mario de la Cueva, Ciudad Universitaria, Edif. C, 2o piso, Mexico City, DF 04510, Mexico. TEL 52-5-6229414 52-5-6229414, FAX 52-5-6668334, http://socilan.politicas.unam.mx/. Ed. Adriana Murguia Lores. Circ: 1,000.

306.43 POL ISSN 0208-600X
HM7
ACTA UNIVERSITATIS LODZIENSIS: FOLIA SOCIOLOGICA. Text in Polish; Summaries in Multiple languages. 1975. irreg., latest vol.34, 2009. price varies. **Document type:** *Monographic series, Academic/Scholarly.* **Description:** Covers studies on culture, sociology of art, industry and occupations, basic theory of interactions and methodology.
Supersedes in part (in 1980): Uniwersytet Lodzki. Zeszyty Naukowe. Seria 3: Nauki Ekonomiczne i Socjologiczne (0076-0374)
Indexed: RASB, SociolAb.
Published by: Wydawnictwo Uniwersytetu Lodzkiego/Lodz University Press, ul Lindleya 8, Lodz, 90-131, Poland. TEL 48-42-6655861, FAX 48-42-6655861, wdwul@uni.lodz.pl, http://www.wydawnictwo.uni.lodz.pl.

301 POL
ACTA UNIVERSITATIS WRATISLAVIENSIS. SOCJOLOGIA. Text in Polish; Summaries in English, German. 1992. irreg., latest vol.49, 2010. price varies. **Document type:** *Monographic series, Academic/Scholarly.*
Published by: (Uniwersytet Wroclawski), Wydawnictwo Uniwersytetu Wroclawskiego Sp. z o.o., pl Uniwersytecki 15, Wroclaw, 50137, Poland. TEL 48-71-3752809, FAX 48-71-3752735, marketing@wuwr.com.pl, http://www.wuwr.com.pl. Ed. Jan Maciejewski.

ACTA WASAENSIA. *see* BUSINESS AND ECONOMICS—Economic Systems And Theories, Economic History

301 FRA ISSN 1950-0610
ACTEURS DE LA SOCIETE. Text in French. 2006. irreg. **Document type:** *Monographic series.*
Published by: Editions Autrement, 77 Rue du Faubourg St Antoine, Paris, 75011, France. TEL 33-1-44738000, FAX 33-1-44730012, contact@autrement.com.

ACTIVITES. *see* PSYCHOLOGY

AD MARGINEM; Randbemerkungen zur Musikalischen Volkskunde. *see* MUSIC

AL ADA AL-IQTISADI WA-AL-IJTIMA'I AL-MUQARAN LI-MISR MA' BA'AD DUWAL AL-ALAM/ECONOMIC AND SOCIAL PERFORMANCE OF EGYPT COMPARED TO SOME WORLD COUNTRIES. *see* BUSINESS AND ECONOMICS

ADMINISTRATIVE SCIENCE QUARTERLY. *see* PUBLIC ADMINISTRATION

301 ITA
ADULTITA. Text in Italian. 1995. s-a. EUR 36 domestic; EUR 46 foreign (effective 2008). **Document type:** *Journal, Academic/Scholarly.*
Published by: (Universita degli Studi di Milano, Universita degli Studi di Trieste, Istituto di Pedagogia), Edizioni Angelo Guerini e Associati SpA, Viale Angelo Filippetti 28, Milan, MI 20122, Italy. TEL 39-02-582980, FAX 39-02-58298030, info@guerini.it, http://www.guerini.it. Ed. Duccio Demetrio.

ADVANCED DEVELOPMENT. *see* PSYCHOLOGY

▼ **ADVANCED STUDIES IN BEHAVIOUR INFORMATICS.** *see* COMPUTERS—Information Science And Information Theory

301 700 GBR ISSN 1742-9412
NX1
ADVANCES IN ART & URBAN FUTURES. Text in English. 2000. irreg., latest 2005. price varies. back issues avail. **Document type:** *Monographic series, Academic/Scholarly.*
Related titles: Online - full text ed.
Indexed: A01, A02, A03, A08, A30, A31, CA, T02.
—**CCC.**
Published by: Intellect Ltd., The Mill, Parnall Rd, Fishponds, Bristol, BS16 3JG, United Kingdom. TEL 44-117-9589910, FAX 44-117-9589911, info@intellectbooks.com. Pub. Masoud Yazdani.

ADVANCES IN ENVIRONMENT, BEHAVIOR AND DESIGN. *see* ENVIRONMENTAL STUDIES

302 USA ISSN 0065-2601
HM251.A35 CODEN: AXSPAQ
➤ **ADVANCES IN EXPERIMENTAL SOCIAL PSYCHOLOGY.** Text in English. 1964. irreg., latest vol.43, 2010. USD 109 per vol. (effective 2010). index. back issues avail.; reprints avail. **Document type:** *Monographic series, Academic/Scholarly.* **Description:** Contains contributions of major empirical and theoretical interest. It represents the new research, theory, and practice in social psychology.
Related titles: Online - full text ed.: ISSN 1557-8410.
Indexed: A20, A22, ASCA, E-psyche, P30, PCI, RASB, SCOPUS, SSCI, W07.
—BLDSC (0706.100000), IE, Ingenta, INIST. **CCC.**
Published by: Academic Press (Subsidiary of: Elsevier Science & Technology), 3251 Riverport Ln, Maryland Heights, MO 63043. TEL 314-447-8010, FAX 314-447-8030, JournalCustomerService-usa@elsevier.com, http://www.elsevierdirect.com/imprint.jsp?iid=5. Ed. Zanna Mark.

302.3 658 NLD ISSN 1871-935X
ADVANCES IN GROUP DECISION AND NEGOTIATION. Cover title: A G D N. Text in English. 2003. irreg., latest vol.3, 2008. price varies. **Document type:** *Monographic series, Academic/Scholarly.* **Description:** Aims to unify approaches to group decision and negotiation processes.
Published by: Springer Netherlands (Subsidiary of: Springer Science+Business Media), Van Godewijckstraat 30, Dordrecht, 3311 GX, Netherlands. TEL 31-78-6576050, FAX 31-78-6576474. Ed. Melvin F Shakun.

305 GBR ISSN 0882-6145
HM131
ADVANCES IN GROUP PROCESSES. Text in English. 1984. a. price varies. back issues avail. **Document type:** *Monographic series, Academic/Scholarly.* **Description:** Publishes theoretical, review, and empirically-based papers on group phenomena.
Related titles: Online - full text ed.
Indexed: CA, S02, S03, SCOPUS, SSA, SociolAb, T02.
—BLDSC (0709.007500), Ingenta. **CCC.**
Published by: Emerald Group Publishing Ltd., Howard House, Wagon Ln, Bingley, W Yorks BD16 1WA, United Kingdom. TEL 44-1274-777700, FAX 44-1274-785201, emerald@emeraldinsight.com. Eds. Edward Lawler, Shane R Thye. **Dist. by:** Turpin Distribution Services Ltd., Pegasus Dr, Stratton Business Park, Biggleswade, Bedfordshire SG18 8QB, United Kingdom. TEL 44-1767-604951, FAX 44-1767-601640, custserv@turpin-distribution.com, http://www.turpin-distribution.com/.

302.3 NLD ISSN 1879-873X
▼ **ADVANCES IN INTERACTION STUDIES.** Text in English. 2011. irreg. price varies. **Document type:** *Monographic series, Academic/Scholarly.* **Description:** Provides a forum for research relevant to the advancement of knowledge in the field of interaction studies.
Published by: John Benjamins Publishing Co., PO Box 36224, Amsterdam, 1020 ME, Netherlands. TEL 31-20-6304747, FAX 31-20-6739773, customer.services@benjamins.nl. Eds. Angelo Cangelosi, Kerstin Dautenhahn.

301 GBR ISSN 1057-6290
RA418 CODEN: AMSOEI
ADVANCES IN MEDICAL SOCIOLOGY. Text in English. 1990. irreg., latest vol.10, 2008. price varies. back issues avail. **Document type:** *Monographic series, Academic/Scholarly.* **Description:** Provides current trends in medical sociology.
Related titles: Online - full text ed.: ISSN 1875-8053.
Indexed: A22, CA, HPNRM, P30, S02, S03, SCOPUS, SOPODA, SSA, SSciA, SociolAb, T02.
—BLDSC (0709.376200), GNLM, IE, Infotrieve, Ingenta. **CCC.**
Published by: Emerald Group Publishing Ltd., Howard House, Wagon Ln, Bingley, W Yorks BD16 1WA, United Kingdom. TEL 44-1274-777700, FAX 44-1274-785201, books@emeraldinsight.com, http://www.emeraldinsight.com. Ed. Barbara Katz Rothman.

ADVANCES IN SUICIDOLOGY. *see* SOCIAL SERVICES AND WELFARE

301 ITA ISSN 0390-1181
H7
AFFARI SOCIALI INTERNAZIONALI. Text in Italian. 1972. q. EUR 79 combined subscription domestic to institutions (print & online eds.); EUR 127 combined subscription foreign to institutions (print & online eds.) (effective 2009). bk.rev. bibl. **Document type:** *Journal, Academic/Scholarly.*
Related titles: Online - full text ed.: ISSN 1971-8497.
Indexed: A22, DIP, ELLIS, IBR, IBZ, ILD, P30, PAIS.
—BLDSC (0731.400000), IE, Infotrieve, Ingenta.
Published by: Franco Angeli Edizioni, Viale Monza 106, Milan, 20127, Italy. TEL 39-02-2837141, FAX 39-02-26144793, redazioni@francoangeli.it, http://www.francoangeli.it. Circ: 5,000.

AFRICA. *see* HISTORY—History Of Africa

AFRICA MEDIA MONOGRAPH SERIES. *see* JOURNALISM

302.2 KEN ISSN 0258-4913
➤ **AFRICA MEDIA REVIEW/REVUE AFRICAINE DES MEDIAS.** Abbreviated title: A M R. Text in English, French. 1987. 3/yr. USD 45 in Africa; USD 60 elsewhere. back issues avail. **Document type:** *Journal, Academic/Scholarly.* **Description:** Provides a forum for the study of communication theory, practice, and policy in African countries.
Indexed: AbAn, CMM, IIBP, P30, PAIS, PLESA, RASB, SCOPUS.
—BLDSC (0732.160950), Infotrieve.
Published by: African Council for Communication Education/Conseil Africain pour l'Enseignement de la Communication, PO Box 47495, Nairobi, Kenya. TEL 254-2-227043, FAX 254-2-216135, acce@wananchi.com. Circ: 700.

➤ **AFRICA POLICY JOURNAL.** *see* BUSINESS AND ECONOMICS

305.896 USA ISSN 1948-0946
AFRICAN AMERICAN PERSPECTIVES. Text in English. 2006. q. **Document type:** *Magazine, Trade.* **Description:** Committed to uplifting and promoting the African American spirit by providing relevant information for the soul, body, and mind. It aims to connect African Americans with each other and the larger community by serving as a conduit for continuous dialogue, information sharing, and the transfer of knowledge.
Published by: Diversified Publishing Co. LLC., PO BOX 687, Jonesboro, AR 72401. TEL 870-926-8962.

305.896 USA
AFRICAN AMERICAN RESEARCH PERSPECTIVES. Text in English. 1994. irreg., latest vol.8, 2002.
Published by: University of Michigan, Institute for Social Research, PO Box 1248, Ann Arbor, MI 48106-1248. TEL 734-763-0045, FAX 734-763-0044, prba@isr.umich.edu.

306 NLD ISSN 1569-2094
DT1 CODEN: SENMER
➤ **AFRICAN AND ASIAN STUDIES.** Text in English. 2002. q. EUR 301, USD 422 to institutions; EUR 329, USD 461 combined subscription to institutions (print & online eds.) (effective 2012). bk.rev. reprint service avail. from PSC. **Document type:** *Journal, Academic/Scholarly.* **Description:** Provides a scholarly account of studies of individuals and societies in Africa and Asia.
Supersedes in part: Journal of Asian and African Studies (0021-9096)
Related titles: Microform ed.: (from SWZ); Online - full text ed.: ISSN 1569-2108. EUR 274, USD 384 to institutions (effective 2012) (from IngentaConnect).
Indexed: A01, A02, A03, A08, A22, ABCPolSci, AICP, APEL, ASCA, ASD, ASSIA, AbAn, AmHI, AnthLit, B04, BAS, BRD, BibLing, CA, CCA, DIP, E01, EI, FamI, GEOBASE, H07, HistAb, I02, I08, I13, IBR, IBSS, IBZ, IIBP, IZBG, MEA&I, P02, P10, P27, P34, P42, P48, P53, P54, PAIS, PQC, PSA, R02, RASB, REE&TA, RI-1, RI-2, S02, S03, SCOPUS, SOPODA, SSA, SSAI, SSAb, SSCI, SSI, SociolAb, T02, W01, W02, W03, W07.
—IE, Ingenta. **CCC.**
Published by: Brill, PO Box 9000, Leiden, 2300 PA, Netherlands. TEL 31-71-5353500, FAX 31-71-5317532, cs@brill.nl. Ed. Tukumbi Lumumba-Kasongo. **Dist. by:** Turpin Distribution Services Ltd., Pegasus Dr, Stratton Business Park, Biggleswade, Bedfordshire SG18 8QB, United Kingdom. TEL 44-1767-604954, FAX 44-1767-601640, custserv@turpin-distribution.com, http://www.turpin-distribution.com/.

308 ZAF ISSN 1992-1284
AFRICAN CENTURY PUBLICATIONS SERIES. Text in English. 2000. irreg., latest vol.19, 2004. **Document type:** *Monographic series.*
Published by: Africa Institute of South Africa, PO Box 630, Pretoria, 0001, South Africa. TEL 27-12-3286970, FAX 27-12-3238153, ai@ai.org.za, http://www.ai.org.za.

AFRICAN JOURNAL FOR THE PSYCHOLOGICAL STUDY OF SOCIAL ISSUES. *see* PSYCHOLOGY

301 KEN ISSN 1010-4127
HM22.A4
AFRICAN JOURNAL OF SOCIOLOGY. Text in English. 1981. s-a.
Indexed: ASD, MLA-IB, P30.
Published by: University of Nairobi, Department of Sociology, PO Box 30022, Nairobi, Kenya.

303 960.3 NLD ISSN 1568-1203
AFRICAN SOCIAL STUDIES SERIES. Text in English. 2000. irreg., latest vol.27, 2011. price varies. **Document type:** *Monographic series, Academic/Scholarly.*
Indexed: IZBG.
—BLDSC (0733.775000).
Published by: Brill, PO Box 9000, Leiden, 2300 PA, Netherlands. TEL 31-71-5353500, FAX 31-71-5317532, cs@brill.nl.

301 SEN ISSN 1027-4332
HN771
➤ **AFRICAN SOCIOLOGICAL REVIEW/REVUE AFRICAINE DE SOCIOLOGIE.** Text and summaries in English, French. 1973-1995 (vol.7, no.2); resumed 1997. s-a. ZAR 40 domestic to individuals; USD 40 foreign to individuals; ZAR 70 domestic to institutions; USD 70 foreign to institutions (effective 2002). adv. bk.rev. bibl.; charts; illus.; maps. back issues avail. **Document type:** *Journal, Academic/Scholarly.* **Description:** Aims at sociologists and social scientists, both generalist and Southern Africa area specific.
Incorporates (in 1995): South African Sociological Review (1015-1370); Which was formerly (until 1988): A S S A Proceedings (Association for Sociology in South Africa)
Related titles: Microfiche ed.; Online - full text ed.
Indexed: ASD, CA, IBSS, IIBP, ISAP, P42, PSA, S02, S03, SCOPUS, SOPODA, SSA, SociolAb, T02.
—BLDSC (0733.850000), IE, Ingenta.
Published by: Council for the Development of Social Science Research in Africa, Avenue Cheikh, Anta Diop x Canal IV, BP 3304, Dakar, Senegal. TEL 221-825-9823, FAX 221-824-1289, codesria@ssonatel.senet.net, seth@warthog.ru.ac.za. Ed., R&P, Adv. contact Fred Hendricks TEL 221-825-9814. Circ: 600. **Subscr. to:** Rhodes University, Department of Sociology, Grahamstown, East Cape 6140, South Africa. TEL 27-46-622-5570.

301 609 PRT ISSN 1645-9970
AFRICANOLOGIA; revista lusofona de estudos africanos. Text in Portuguese. 2008. s-a. **Document type:** *Journal, Academic/Scholarly.*
Published by: Universidade Lusofona de Humanidades e Tecnologia, Edicoes Universitarias, Campo Grande 376, Lisbon, 1749-024, Portugal. TEL 351-217-515500, FAX 351-217-577006, http://ulusofona.pt.

AFRIKA JAHRBUCH. *see* POLITICAL SCIENCE

AFRIKA SPECTRUM; Zeitschrift fuer gegenwartsbezogene Afrikaforschung. *see* POLITICAL SCIENCE

AFTERLOSS; the monthly newsletter to comfort and care for those who mourn. *see* MEDICAL SCIENCES—Psychiatry And Neurology

S

301 COL ISSN 2011-3439
AGENDA FE Y ALEGRIA DE COLOMBIA. Text in Spanish. 2008. a.
Published by: Fe y Alegria de Colombia, Diagonal 34 No. 4-94, Teusaquillo, Bogota, Colombia. TEL 57-1-3237775, recepcion.bogota@feyalegria.org.co, http://www.feyalegria.org/colombia.

301 649 FRA ISSN 1268-5666
AGORA; debats - jeunesse. Text in French. 1995. q. EUR 52 (effective 2008). **Document type:** *Journal, Trade.*
Indexed: FR, IBSS.
—INIST.
Published by: L' Harmattan, 5 Rue de l'Ecole Polytechnique, Paris, 75005, France. TEL 33-1-43257651, FAX 33-1-43258203.

301 ESP ISSN 1139-2134
AGORA; revista de ciencias sociales. Text in Spanish. 1996. s-a. EUR 20 domestic; EUR 26 in Europe; EUR 30 elsewhere (effective 2008). back issues avail. **Document type:** *Journal, Academic/Scholarly.*
Published by: Centre d'Estudis Politics i Socials, Carniceros, 8 Bajo-izq., Valencia, 46001, Spain. TEL 34-963-926342, FAX 34-963-918771, ceps@ceps.es, http://www.ceps.es/.

EL AGORA U S B. (Universidad de San Buenaventura) *see* PHILOSOPHY

301 DEU ISSN 0944-4165
AGRARSOZIALE GESELLSCHAFT. ARBEITSBERICHT. Text in German. 1950. biennial. free. **Document type:** *Monographic series, Academic/Scholarly.*
Former titles: Agrarsoziale Gesellschaft. Geschaefts- und Arbeitsbericht (0065-437X); (until 1968): Agrarsoziale Gesellschaft. Arbeitsbericht
Published by: Agrarsoziale Gesellschaft e.V., Kurze Geismarstr 33, Goettingen, 37073, Germany. TEL 49-551-497090, FAX 49-551-4970916, info@asg-goe.de, http://www.asg-goe.de.

301 DEU ISSN 0170-7671
AGRARSOZIALE GESELLSCHAFT. KLEINE REIHE. Text in German. 1970. irreg., latest vol.63, 2001. price varies. **Document type:** *Monographic series, Academic/Scholarly.*
Published by: Agrarsoziale Gesellschaft e.V., Kurze Geismarstr 33, Goettingen, 37073, Germany. TEL 49-551-497090, FAX 49-551-4970916, info@asg-goe.de, http://www.asg-goe.de.

301 DEU ISSN 0344-5712
AGRARSOZIALE GESELLSCHAFT. MATERIALSAMMLUNG. Text in German. 1953. irreg., latest vol.202, 2000. price varies. **Document type:** *Monographic series, Academic/Scholarly.*
Published by: Agrarsoziale Gesellschaft e.V., Kurze Geismarstr 33, Goettingen, 37073, Germany. TEL 49-551-497090, FAX 49-551-4970916, info@asg-goe.de, http://www.asg-goe.de.

AGRICULTURE AND HUMAN VALUES. *see* AGRICULTURE

AGRO SUR. *see* AGRICULTURE

301 613.2 VEN ISSN 1316-0354
TX360.V4
AGROALIMENTARIA. Text in Spanish. 1995. s-a. VEB 70 domestic; USD 35 in Latin America; USD 40 elsewhere (effective 2009). **Document type:** *Journal, Academic/Scholarly.* **Description:** Covers the area of social science related to studies on feeding.
Related titles: Online - full text ed.: free (effective 2011).
Indexed: A26, ASFA, B21, C01, ESPM, EconLit, H21, I04, I05, P08, SCOPUS, SSciA.
Published by: Universidad de Los Andes, Centro de Investigacion Agroalimentaria, Merida, Venezuela. TEL 58-74401031, FAX 58-74401031, ciaalgut@faces.ula.ve. Ed. Rafael Cartay.

AGROEKONOMIKA. *see* AGRICULTURE—Agricultural Economics

AGROTROPICA. *see* AGRICULTURE

301 JPN ISSN 1881-0373
AICHI SHUKUTOKU DAIGAKU GENDAI SHAKAI KENKYUUKA KENKYUU HOUKOKU/RESEARCH ON CONTEMPORARY SOCIETY. Text in Japanese. 2006. a. **Document type:** *Academic/Scholarly.*
Published by: Aichi Shukutoku Daigaku, Gendai Shakai Kenkyuuka/Aichi Shukutoku University, Department of Studies on Comporary Society, 9 Katahira Nagakute, Nagakute-cho, Aichi-gun, Aichi-ken 480-1197, Japan. http://www2.aasa.ac.jp/faculty/focs/index.html.

AKTUELLT OM MIGRATION; tidskrift foer forskning och debatt. *see* POPULATION STUDIES

307 USA ISSN 1059-3632
ALABAMA COOPERATIVE EXTENSION SERVICE. CIRCULAR C R D. Text in English. 1979. irreg., latest vol.83, 2007. back issues avail. **Document type:** *Monographic series, Trade.*
Related titles: Online - full text ed.
Indexed: Agr.
Published by: Alabama Cooperative Extension Service, 109-D Duncan Hall, Auburn University, AL 36849. TEL 334-844-4444.

301 DEU ISSN 0175-9191
ALLENSBACHER JAHRBUCH DER DEMOSKOPIE. Text in German. 1947. irreg., latest vol.11, 2002. price varies. adv. bk.rev. **Document type:** *Monographic series, Academic/Scholarly.*
Formerly (until 1977): Jahrbuch der Oeffentlichen Meinung (0075-2347)
Published by: (Institut fuer Demoskopie, Allensbach), De Gruyter Saur (Subsidiary of: Walter de Gruyter GmbH & Co. KG), Mies-van-der-Rohe-Str 1, Munich, 80807, Germany. TEL 49-89-769020, FAX 49-89-76902150, wdg-info@degruyter.com. Circ: 3,000.

303.4 FRA ISSN 1770-3670
ALLIANCE POUR UNE EUROPE DES CONSCIENCES. Text in French. 2004. bi-m. EUR 40 for 2 yrs. domestic; EUR 48 for 2 yrs. in the European Union; EUR 55 for 2 yrs. in Africa; EUR 6 per issue domestic; EUR 7 per issue foreign (effective 2010). back issues avail. **Document type:** *Magazine, Consumer.*
Published by: (Institut Gandhi-Europe des Consciences), Terre du Ciel, Domaine de Chardenoux, Bruailles, 71500, France. TEL 33-3-85604033, FAX 33-3-85604031, infos@terre-du-ciel.fr.

302.23 DEU ISSN 1864-4058
ALLTAG, MEDIEN UND KULTUR. Text in German. 2007. irreg., latest vol.7, 2010. price varies. **Document type:** *Monographic series, Academic/Scholarly.*
Published by: U V K Verlagsgesellschaft mbH, Schuetzenstr 24, Konstanz, 78462, Germany. TEL 49-7531-90530, FAX 49-7531-905398, nadine.ley@uvk.de, http://www.uvk.de. Ed. Lothar Mikos.

317.3 USA ISSN 0887-0519
HA203
ALMANAC OF THE 50 STATES. Text in English. 1985. a. price varies.
Published by: Information Publications, Incorporated, 2995 Woodside Rd, Suite 400-182, Woodside, CA 94062. TEL 650-851-4250, 877-544-4636, FAX 650-529-9980, 877-544-4635, info@informationpublications.com. Ed. Manthi Nguyen.

301 USA
ALTAR MAGAZINE. Text in English. 2005. q. USD 4 newsstand/cover (effective 2005). **Document type:** *Magazine, Consumer.* **Description:** Covers socially progressive issues.
Address: 955 Metropolitan Ave., Ste. 4R, Brooklyn, NY 11211. Ed., Pub. Mandy Van Deven.

ALTERNATIVE RESEARCH NEWSLETTER. *see* LITERARY AND POLITICAL REVIEWS

301 FRA ISSN 1159-8549
ALTERNATIVES SOCIALES. Text in French. 1990. irreg., latest 2010, May. **Document type:** *Monographic series.*
Formed by the merger of (1988-1990): Alternatives Sociales. Serie Synthese (0993-6793); (1988-1990): Alternatives Sociales. Serie Analyse (1140-0439)
Published by: Editions La Decouverte, 9 bis, Rue Abel-Hovelacque, Paris, 75013, France. TEL 33-1-44088401, FAX 33-1-44088439, ladecouverte@editionsladecouverte.com, http://www.editionsladecouverte.fr. R&P Delphine Ribouchon.

306 AUS ISSN 1444-1160
➤ **ALTITUDE**; an e-journal of emerging humanities work. Text in English. 2000. irreg. free (effective 2011). back issues avail. **Document type:** *Journal, Academic/Scholarly.* **Description:** Focuses on textual and cultural studies.
Media: Online - full text.
Published by: A P I Network, c/o Australia Research Institute, Division of Humanities, Curtin University of Technology, GPO Box U1987, Perth, W.A. 6845, Australia. TEL 61-8-92664788, FAX 61-8-92663836, contact@api-network.com. Eds. Clifton Evers, Emily Potter.

➤ **AM ZUEGEL DER EVOLUTION.** *see* MEDICAL SCIENCES

302.23 ESP ISSN 1139-1979
AMBITOS. REVISTA ANDALUZA DE COMUNICACION. Text in Spanish. 1998. a. back issues avail. **Document type:** *Journal, Academic/Scholarly.*
Related titles: Online - full text ed.
Published by: Universidad de Sevilla, Facultad de Ciencias de la Informacion, C Gonzalo Bilbao, 7-9, Sevilla, 41003, Spain. TEL 34-95-4486062, FAX 34-95-4486085, mjruiz@pop.cica.es, http://www.ull.es/publicaciones/latina/ambitos/ambitos.htm. Ed. Ramon Reig.

973.0495 USA ISSN 0044-7471
E184.O6 CODEN: AMEJEZ
➤ **AMERASIA JOURNAL**; the national interdisciplinary journal of scholarship, criticism, and literature on Asian and Pacific American. Text in English. 1971. 3/yr. USD 99.99 domestic to individuals; USD 124.99 foreign to individuals; USD 445 domestic to institutions; USD 470 foreign to institutions (effective 2010). adv. bk.rev. bibl.; charts; illus. Index. back issues avail.; reprints avail. **Document type:** *Journal, Academic/Scholarly.* **Description:** Contains information about Asian-American history and life including bibliography of Asian-American studies.
Related titles: Microform ed.: (from PQC); Online - full text ed.
Indexed: A01, A02, A03, A08, A20, A22, A25, A26, ASCA, AmH&L, AmHI, ArtHuCI, B04, B14, BAS, BRD, BRI, CA, CBRI, CurCont, DIP, E03, E07, E08, G05, G06, G07, G08, G10, H07, H08, HAb, HistAb, HumInd, I05, IBR, IBZ, M01, M02, M08, MLA-IB, MagInd, P02, P10, P13, P30, P34, P42, P48, P53, P54, PCI, PQC, RI-1, RI-2, RILM, S02, S03, S08, S09, SCOPUS, SOPODA, SRRA, SociolAb, T02, W03, W07, W09.
—BLDSC (0809.655000), IE, Infotrieve, Ingenta.
Published by: University of California, Los Angeles, Asian American Studies Center, 3230 Campbell Hall, PO Box 951546, Los Angeles, CA 90095. TEL 310-825-2974, FAX 310-206-9844, aascpress@aasc.ucla.edu. Ed. Russell C Leong. adv.: page USD 300; 4.7 x 7.5.

301 PER ISSN 1019-4460
AMERICA PROBLEMA. Text in Spanish. 1968. irreg., latest vol.16, 1993. price varies. back issues avail. **Document type:** *Monographic series, Academic/Scholarly.*
Published by: (Instituto de Estudios Peruanos), I E P Ediciones (Subsidiary of: Instituto de Estudios Peruanos), Horacio Urteaga 694, Jesus Maria, Lima, 11, Peru. TEL 51-14-3326194, FAX 51-14-3326173, libreria@iep.org.pe, http://iep.perucultural.org.pe.

AMERICAN CATHOLIC STUDIES. *see* RELIGIONS AND THEOLOGY—Roman Catholic

302.23 USA ISSN 1532-5865
P87
➤ **AMERICAN COMMUNICATION JOURNAL.** Text in English. 1996. 3/yr. **Document type:** *Journal, Academic/Scholarly.* **Description:** Provides conscientious analysis and criticism of significant communicative artifacts.
Media: Online - full text.
Indexed: A39, C27, C29, CA, CMM, CommAb, D03, D04, E13, R14, S14, S15, S18, SCOPUS, T02.
Published by: American Communication Association, c/o Dale Cyphert, College of Business Administration, The University of Northern Iowa, 1227 W 27th St, Cedar Falls, IA 50614. TEL 319-273-6150, acjournal@email.com, http://www.americancomm.org/.

302 USA ISSN 0091-0562
RA790.A1 CODEN: AJCPCK
➤ **AMERICAN JOURNAL OF COMMUNITY PSYCHOLOGY.** Text in English. 1973. q. EUR 1,435, USD 1,498 combined subscription to institutions (print & online eds.) (effective 2012). adv. illus. Index. back issues avail.; reprint service avail. from PSC. **Document type:** *Journal, Academic/Scholarly.* **Description:** Features quantitative and qualitative research on community psychological interventions at the social, neighborhood, organizational, group, and individual levels.
Related titles: Microfilm ed.: (from PQC); Online - full text ed.: ISSN 1573-2770 (from IngentaConnect).
Indexed: A01, A02, A03, A08, A20, A22, A26, AC&P, AIDS Ab, AMHA, ASCA, B04, B21, BRD, BibLing, C06, C07, C08, CA, CINAHL, ChPerI, Chicano, CurCont, DIP, E-psyche, E01, E08, ECER, EMBASE, ESPM, ExcerpMed, F09, FR, FamI, G08, G10, H&SSA, H12, I05, IBR, IBZ, IndMed, MEA&I, MEDLINE, P02, P03, P10, P12, P13, P20, P21, P22, P24, P25, P26, P27, P30, P34, P46, P48, P50, P53, P54, PCI, PQC, PSI, PsycInfo, PsycholAb, R10, RASB, Reac, RefZh, RiskAb, S02, S03, S09, S23, SCOPUS, SFSA, SOPODA, SSA, SSAI, SSAb, SSCI, SSI, SUSA, SWR&A, SociolAb, T02, THA, W03, W05, W07, W09.
—BLDSC (0824.070000), GNLM, IE, Infotrieve, Ingenta, INIST. **CCC.**
Published by: (American Psychological Association), Springer New York LLC (Subsidiary of: Springer Science+Business Media), 233 Spring St, New York, NY 10013. TEL 212-460-1500, FAX 212-460-1575, service-ny@springer.com. Ed. Jacob Kraemer Tebes.

➤ **AMERICAN JOURNAL OF FAMILY THERAPY.** *see* PSYCHOLOGY

301 USA ISSN 0002-9602
HM1
➤ **AMERICAN JOURNAL OF SOCIOLOGY.** Abbreviated title: A J S. Text in English. 1895. bi-m. USD 424 combined subscription to institutions (print & online eds.) (effective 2012). adv. bk.rev. abstr.; bibl.; charts; illus. cum.index: vols.1-70 (1895-1965), vols.71-75 (1965-1970), vols.76-80 (1971-1980). 300 p./no.; back issues avail.; reprint service avail. from PSC. **Document type:** *Journal, Academic/Scholarly.* **Description:** Publishes articles and review essays on the theory, methods, and practice of sociology.
Related titles: Microform ed.: (from PQC); Online - full text ed.: ISSN 1537-5390. USD 360 to institutions (effective 2012).
Indexed: A01, A02, A03, A08, A12, A20, A21, A22, A25, A26, ABCPolSci, ABIn, ABS&EES, AC&P, AICP, APEL, ASCA, AbAn, AcaI, AmH&L, B01, B04, B05, B06, B07, B09, B14, BAS, BRD, BRI, C28, CA, CBRI, CIS, CJPI, CMM, CPM, ChPerI, Chicano, CommAb, CurCont, DIP, E-psyche, E02, E03, E06, E07, E08, EAA, EMBASE, ERA, ERI, EdA, EdI, ExcerpMed, F01, F02, F09, FR, FamI, G05, G06, G07, G08, G10, GSS&RPL, H09, H10, HRA, HistAb, I05, I07, I13, I14, IBR, IBSS, IBZ, ILD, IPARL, L09, M06, MEDLINE, MLA-IB, MResA, P02, P03, P06, P10, P18, P21, P25, P26, P27, P28, P30, P34, P42, P46, P48, P51, P53, P54, PAIS, PCI, PQC, PRA, PSA, PopulInd, PsycInfo, PsycholAb, R04, R05, RASB, REE&TA, RI-1, RI-2, RILM, S02, S03, S05, S08, S09, S11, S19, S21, S23, SCOPUS, SFSA, SOPODA, SRRA, SSA, SSAI, SSAb, SSCI, SSI, SUSA, SWR&A, SociolAb, T02, W03, W07, W09.
—BLDSC (0838.300000), IE, Infotrieve, Ingenta, INIST. **CCC.**
Published by: (University of Chicago), University of Chicago Press, 1427 E 60th St, Chicago, IL 60637. TEL 773-702-7600, FAX 773-702-0694, subscriptions@press.uchicago.edu. Ed. Andrew Abbott TEL 773-702-8580. Adv. contact Cheryl Jones TEL 773-702-7361. **Subscr. to:** PO Box 370050, Chicago, IL 60637. TEL 773-753-3347, 877-705-1878, FAX 773-753-0811, 877-705-1879.

➤ **AMERICAN RENAISSANCE.** *see* ETHNIC INTERESTS

301 USA
AMERICAN SEXUALITY. Text in English. 2003. 7/yr. free (effective 2011). **Document type:** *Magazine, Trade.* **Description:** Contains interviews, critical essays, and easy-to-read articles on state-of-the-art sex research.
Media: Online - full text.
Published by: National Sexuality Resource Center, 835 Market St, Ste 517, San Francisco, CA 94110. TEL 415-817-4525, FAX 415-817-4540, nsrcinfo@sfsu.edu.

320 303.48 USA ISSN 1939-1226
AMERICAN SOCIAL AND POLITICAL MOVEMENTS. Text in English. 2007 (Dec.). irreg. USD 44.95, GBP 31.95 per issue (effective 2010). **Document type:** *Monographic series, Academic/Scholarly.* **Description:** Covers analysis on labor's inability to move forward and proposes strategies and tactics to turn things around.
Related titles: Online - full text ed.
Published by: Praeger Publishers (Subsidiary of: Greenwood Publishing Group Inc.), 88 Post Rd W, Westport, CT 06881. TEL 800-368-6868, tech.support@greenwood.com, http://www.greenwood.com. Ed. Martha Burk.

301 USA ISSN 1052-7184
HM9
AMERICAN SOCIOLOGICAL ASSOCIATION. BIOGRAPHICAL DIRECTORY OF MEMBERS. Text in English. 1970. biennial. price varies. **Document type:** *Directory, Trade.*
Formerly (until 1990): American Sociological Association. Directory of Members (0093-898X)
Published by: American Sociological Association, 1430 K St, NW, Ste 600, Washington, DC 20005. TEL 202-383-9005, FAX 202-638-0882, publications@asanet.org, http://www.asanet.org.

301 USA ISSN 0003-1224
CODEN: ASRRB
➤ **AMERICAN SOCIOLOGICAL REVIEW.** Abbreviated title: A S R. Text in English. 1936. bi-m. USD 329, GBP 194 to institutions; USD 336, GBP 198 combined subscription to institutions (print & online eds.) (effective 2012). adv. charts; illus. Index. back issues avail.; reprint service avail. from PSC. **Document type:** *Journal, Academic/Scholarly.* **Description:** Publishes work of interest to the discipline in general: new theoretical developments, results of research advancing understanding of fundamental social processes, and methodological innovations.
Related titles: Microform ed.: (from MIM, PQC); Online - full text ed.: ISSN 1939-8271. USD 302, GBP 178 to institutions (effective 2012).
Indexed: A01, A02, A03, A08, A12, A20, A21, A22, A25, A26, A34, A36, ABCPolSci, ABIn, ABS&EES, AC&P, AMHA, ASCA, ASG, AbAn, AcaI, AmH&L, B01, B02, B04, B06, B07, B09, B15, B17, B18, BAS, BEL&L, BRD, C28, CA, CABA, CBRI, CIS, CPM, ChPerI, Chicano, CommAb, CurCont, D01, DIP, E-psyche, E01, E02, E03, E07, E08, E12, EAA, EI, ERA, ERI, EdA, EdI, F09, FR, FamI, G04, G08, GEOBASE, GH, GSS&RPL, H01, H09, H10, HRA, HistAb, I05, I13, IBR, IBSS, IBZ, ILD, IPARL, LT, M06, MEA&I, MLA-IB, N02, N03, P02, P03, P06, P10, P13, P21, P24, P25, P26, P27, P30, P34, P42, P46, P48, P50, P51, P53, P54, PAIS, PCI, PQC, PRA, PSA, PopulInd, PsycInfo, PsycholAb, R12, RASB, RI-1, RI-2, RILM, RRTA, S02, S03, S05, S08, S09, S11, S21, SCIMP, SCOPUS, SFSA, SOPODA, SRRA, SSA, SSAI, SSAb, SSCI, SSI, SUSA, SWR&A, SociolAb, T02, T05, W03, W07, W09, W11.
—BLDSC (0857.500000), IE, Infotrieve, Ingenta, INIST. **CCC.**

Published by: (American Sociological Association), Sage Publications, Inc., 2455 Teller Rd, Thousand Oaks, CA 91320. TEL 800-818-7243, FAX 800-583-2665, info@sagepub.com, http://www.sagepub.com/.

301 USA ISSN 0003-1232
HM9

➤ **THE AMERICAN SOCIOLOGIST.** Text in English. 1965. 3/yr. EUR 351, USD 479 combined subscription to institutions (print & online eds.) (effective 2012). bk.rev. illus. back issues avail.; reprint service avail. from PSC. **Document type:** *Journal, Academic/Scholarly.* **Description:** Features papers, comments, and other writings on topics of professional and disciplinary concern to sociologists.
Related titles: Microform ed.: (from PQC); Online - full text ed.: ISSN 1936-4784 (from IngentaConnect).
Indexed: A01, A02, A03, A08, A22, A26, B07, CA, Chicano, DIP, E01, E03, E07, E08, EI, ERI, FR, G06, G07, G08, G10, H09, I05, I13, IBR, IBSS, IBZ, MEA&I, P30, P34, P42, PAIS, PCI, PSA, RASB, S02, S03, S05, S09, SCOPUS, SOPODA, SSA, SociolAb, T02, V&AA, W09.
—BLDSC (0857.503000), IE, Infotrieve, Ingenta, INIST. **CCC.**
Published by: (American Sociological Association), Springer New York LLC (Subsidiary of: Springer Science+Business Media), 233 Spring St, New York, NY 10013. TEL 212-460-1500, FAX 212-460-1575, journals@springer-ny.com. Ed. Lawrence T Nichols.

302.23 DEU ISSN 1610-6814
AMERICAN STUDIES AND MEDIA. Text in English. 2007. irreg. price varies. **Document type:** *Monographic series, Academic/Scholarly.*
Published by: Peter Lang GmbH (Subsidiary of: Peter Lang Publishing Group), Eschborner Landstr 42-50, Frankfurt Am Main, 60489, Germany. TEL 49-69-7807050, FAX 49-69-78070550, zentrale.frankfurt@peterlang.com. Eds. Elzbieta Oleksy, Wieslaw Oleksy.

306.4 USA ISSN 1559-2375
AMERICAN SUBCULTURES. Text in English. 2006. irreg., latest 2007. USD 39.95, GBP 27.95 per issue (effective 2010). back issues avail. **Document type:** *Monographic series.* **Description:** Provides Knitting related information.
Published by: Praeger Publishers (Subsidiary of: Greenwood Publishing Group Inc.), 88 Post Rd W, Westport, CT 06881. TEL 800-368-6868, tech.support@greenwood.com, http://www.greenwood.com. Ed. Bruce Jackson.

THE AMERICAN UNIVERSITY JOURNAL OF GENDER, SOCIAL POLICY & THE LAW. *see* LAW

301 USA ISSN 1553-8931
E169.1

➤ **AMERICANA (HOLLYWOOD).** Text in English. 2003 (Spring). s-a. free (effective 2011). **Document type:** *Journal, Academic/Scholarly.* **Description:** Dedicated to the art of semiotic analysis, or the analysis of the signs of popular culture.
Media: Online - full text.
Indexed: A39, C27, C29, CA, D03, D04, E13, MLA-IB, R14, S02, S03, S14, S15, S18, T02.
Published by: Institute for the Study of American Popular Culture, 7095-1240 Hollywood Blvd, Hollywood, CA 90028. Ed. Leslie Kreiner Wilson.

➤ **AMERICANS FOR THE ARTS. MONOGRAPHS.** *see* ART

306 FRA ISSN 2107-0806
▼ **AMERIKA.** Text in French, Spanish. 2010. s-a. **Document type:** *Academic/Scholarly.*
Media: Online - full text.
Published by: Universite Rennes II Haute Bretagne, L I R A - E R I M I T, Place du Recteur Henri Le Moal, CS 24307, Rennes, 35043, France. TEL 33-2-99141667, amerika@revues.org, http://amerika.revues.org.

AMNESIA VIVACE. *see* ART

302.23 COL ISSN 1692-2522
P92.C7
ANAGRAMAS; rumbos y sentidos de la comunicacion. Variant title: Rumbos y Sentidos de la Comunicacion. Text in Spanish. 2002. s-a. COP 12,000 domestic; USD 20 foreign. **Document type:** *Journal, Academic/Scholarly.*
Indexed: A26, C01, F04, I04, I05, S02, S03, T02.
Published by: Universidad de Medellin, Facultad de Comunicacion y Relaciones Corporativas, Cra 87 No.30-65 Ofic 11-102, Los Alpes, Medellin, Colombia. TEL 57-94-3405422, FAX 57-94-3405216, lcorrea@udem.edu.co, http://www.udem.edu.co/. Ed. Lorenza Correa Restrepo.

301 PRT ISSN 0003-2573
HM7
ANALISE SOCIAL. Text in Portuguese; Summaries in English, French. 1963. 4/yr. bk.rev. charts. back issues avail. **Document type:** *Journal, Academic/Scholarly.*
Related titles: Online - full text ed.: free (effective 2011).
Indexed: A01, CA, F03, F04, FR, HistAb, I13, IBR, IBSS, IBZ, P30, P34, P42, PSA, S02, S03, SCOPUS, SOPODA, SSA, SociolAb, T02.
—INIST.
Published by: Universidade de Lisboa, Instituto de Ciencias Sociais, Ave Prof Anibal de Bettencourt, 9, Lisbon, 1600-189, Portugal. TEL 351-21-7804700, FAX 351-21-7940274, http://www.ics.ul.pt/.

303.33 USA ISSN 1529-7489
➤ **ANALYSES OF SOCIAL ISSUES AND PUBLIC POLICY.** Abbreviated title: A S A P. Text in English. 2001. a., latest vol.5, 2005. USD 840 combined subscription in the Americas to institutions (print & online eds.); GBP 647 combined subscription in United Kingdom to institutions (print & online eds.); EUR 822 combined subscription in Europe to institutions (print & online eds.); USD 1,267 combined subscription elsewhere to institutions (print & online eds.); USD 764 in the Americas to institutions (print or online ed.); GBP 587 in United Kingdom to institutions (print or online ed.); EUR 746 in Europe to institutions (print or online ed.); USD 1,151 elsewhere to institutions (print or online ed.) (effective 2010). adv. **Document type:** *Journal, Academic/Scholarly.* **Description:** Designed to be an outlet for timely and innovative social science scholarship with implications for social action and policy.
Related titles: Online - full text ed.: ISSN 1530-2415 (from IngentaConnect).
Indexed: A01, A03, A08, A22, A26, C06, C07, C08, CA, CINAHL, E01, GEOBASE, H12, P03, P10, P34, P42, P48, P53, P54, PAIS, PQC, PSA, PsycInfo, PsycholAb, S02, S03, S11, SCOPUS, SSA, SociolAb, T02.
—BLDSC (0892.077450), IE, Ingenta, INIST. **CCC.**
Published by: (Society for the Psychological Study of Social Issues), Wiley-Blackwell Publishing, Inc. (Subsidiary of: Wiley-Blackwell Publishing Ltd.), Commerce Pl, 350 Main St, Malden, MA 02148. TEL 781-388-8206, FAX 781-388-8232, info@wiley.com, http://www.wiley.com/WileyCDA/. Ed. Geoffrey Maruyama. adv.: B&W page USD 400; trim 6 x 9. Circ: 2,999 (paid).

306.482 USA ISSN 1942-6453
➤ **ANALYSIS OF GAMBLING BEHAVIOR.** Abbreviated title: A G B. Text in English. 2007. s-a. USD 40 (effective 2011). back issues avail. **Document type:** *Journal, Academic/Scholarly.* **Description:** Contains original general interest and discipline specific articles related to the scientific study of gambling.
Related titles: Online - full content ed.
Indexed: A01, A26, CA, H12, I05, P05.
Address: c/o Jeffrey N Weatherly, Department of Psychology, University of North Dakota, Grand Forks, ND 58202. TEL 701-777-3470, FAX 701-777-3454. Ed. Mark R Dixon.

➤ **ANARCHIST STUDIES.** *see* POLITICAL SCIENCE

➤ **ANCIENT GREEK CITIES REPORT.** *see* HOUSING AND URBAN PLANNING

305.3 DEU ISSN 1861-1915
ANGEWANDTE GENDERFORSCHUNG/GENDER RESEARCH APPLIED. Text in German. 2005. irreg., latest vol.4, 2008. price varies. **Document type:** *Monographic series, Academic/Scholarly.*
Published by: Peter Lang GmbH (Subsidiary of: Peter Lang Publishing Group), Eschborner Landstr 42-50, Frankfurt Am Main, 60489, Germany. TEL 49-69-7807050, FAX 49-69-78070550, zentrale.frankfurt@peterlang.com. Ed. Ingelore Welpe.

301 AUT ISSN 0587-5234
ANGEWANDTE SOZIALFORSCHUNG. Text in German. 1972. q. adv. bk.rev. **Document type:** *Journal, Academic/Scholarly.*
Indexed: CA, DIP, FR, IBR, IBZ, P42, S02, S03, SOPODA, SociolAb, T02.
Published by: Institut fuer Angewandte Soziologie, Lerchenfelder Str 36, Vienna, W 1080, Austria. henrik.kreutz@univie.ac.at. Ed. Henrik Kreutz.

ANGLO-RUSSIAN AFFINITIES. *see* POLITICAL SCIENCE—International Relations

301 ITA ISSN 0392-5870
ANIMAZIONE SOCIALE; mensile per gli operatori sociali. Text in Italian. 1971. m. (10/yr.). EUR 42 domestic to individuals; EUR 57 domestic to institutions; EUR 67 foreign (effective 2009). **Document type:** *Magazine, Trade.* **Description:** Deals with social issues, as they relate to political and cultural institutions.
Indexed: IBR, IBZ.
Published by: Edizioni Gruppo Abele, Corso Trapani 95, Turin, TO 10141, Italy. TEL 39-011-3841011, FAX 39-011-3841031, segreteria@gruppoabele.org, http://www.gruppoabele.org. Ed. Franco Floris.

ANIMER; le Magazine rural. *see* BUSINESS AND ECONOMICS—Economic Situation And Conditions

301 FRA ISSN 0395-2649
AP20
➤ **ANNALES (PARIS)**; histoire, sciences sociales. Text in French. 1929. bi-m. EUR 81 domestic to individuals; EUR 104 foreign to individuals; EUR 109 domestic to institutions; EUR 139 foreign to institutions; EUR 62 domestic to students (effective 2008). adv. bk.rev. illus. reprint service avail. from PSC,SCH. **Document type:** *Journal, Academic/Scholarly.* **Description:** Aims to contribute to a better understanding of present times through interdisciplinary studies of history and the social sciences.
Former titles (until 1946): Annales d'Histoire Sociale (1243-258X); (until 1945): Melanges d'Histoire Sociale (1243-2571); (until 1942): Annales d'Histoire Sociale (1243-2563); (until 1939): Annales d'Histoire Economique et Sociale (0003-441X)
Related titles: Microform ed.: 1929 (from PQC).
Indexed: A20, A22, B24, BrArAb, CA, CISA, DIP, FR, HistAb, I13, I14, IBR, IBSS, IBZ, NumL, P30, P42, PCI, PSA, PopulInd, RASB, RILM, S02, S03, SCOPUS, SOPODA, SSA, SociolAb, T02.
—BLDSC (0979.770000), IE, Infotrieve, Ingenta, INIST. **CCC.**
Published by: Armand Colin, 21 Rue du Montparnasse, Paris, 75283 Cedex 06, France. TEL 33-1-44395447, FAX 33-1-44394343, infos@armand-colin.fr, http://www.armand-colin.com. Circ: 5,000.

➤ **ANNALES UNIVERSITATIS MARIAE CURIE-SKLODOWSKA. SECTIO I. PHILOSOPHIA - SOCIOLOGIA.** *see* PHILOSOPHY

301 DEU ISSN 0394-2120
ANNALI DI SOCIOLOGIA/SOZIOLOGISCHES JAHRBUCH. Text in German, Italian. 1964. irreg. EUR 46 combined subscription per issue (print & online eds.) (effective 2011). adv. bk.rev. **Document type:** *Journal, Academic/Scholarly.*
Formerly (until 1985): Annali di Sociologia (Milan) (0066-2275)
Related titles: Online - full text ed.: 2008.
Indexed: DIP, IBR, IBZ, RILM, SOPODA, SociolAb.
—INIST.
Published by: Duncker und Humblot GmbH, Carl-Heinrich-Becker-Weg 9, Berlin, 12165, Germany. TEL 49-30-7900060, FAX 49-30-79000631, info@duncker-humblot.de.

301 FRA ISSN 0066-2399
HM3
➤ **L'ANNEE SOCIOLOGIQUE.** Text in French; Abstracts in French, English. 1898. s-a. EUR 83 foreign to institutions (effective 2012). reprint service avail. from PSC,SCH. **Document type:** *Journal, Academic/Scholarly.* **Description:** Covers general, political, and theoretical sociology, methodology, social and cultural anthropology, religious, demographic and family sociology, criminology.
Formed by the merger of (1896-1949): Annales Sociologiques. Serie A, Sociologie Generale (0245-906X); Annales Sociologiques. Serie B, Sociologie Religieuse (0245-9078); Annales Sociologiques. Serie C, Sociologie Juridique et Morale (0245-9086); Annales Sociologiques. Serie D, Sociologie Economique (0245-9094); Annales Sociologiques. Serie E, Morphologie Sociale, Langage, Technologie, Esthetique (0245-9108); All of which superseded in part (in 1925): L' Annee Sociologique (0245-9051)
Related titles: Online - full text ed.: ISSN 1969-6760.
Indexed: AICP, CA, CERDIC, DIP, FR, I13, IBR, IBSS, IBZ, P30, P42, PCI, PSA, RASB, S02, S03, SCOPUS, SOPODA, SSA, SociolAb, T02.
—INIST. **CCC.**
Published by: Presses Universitaires de France, 6 Avenue Reille, Paris, 75685, France. TEL 33-1-58103161, FAX 33-1-45897530, revues@puf.com, http://www.puf.com. Ed. Bernard Valade.

306.89 CAN ISSN 1189-8119
KE564.57
ANNOTATED DIVORCE ACT. Text in English. 1991. a. CAD 88 per issue domestic; USD 74.58 per issue foreign (effective 2005).
Published by: Carswell (Subsidiary of: Thomson Reuters Corp.), One Corporate Plz, 2075 Kennedy Rd, Toronto, ON M1T 3V4, Canada. TEL 416-609-8000, FAX 416-298-5094, carswell.customerrelations@thomson.com, http://www.carswell.com.

ANNUAL EDITIONS: DRUGS, SOCIETY & BEHAVIOR. *see* DRUG ABUSE AND ALCOHOLISM

ANNUAL EDITIONS: DYING, DEATH, AND BEREAVEMENT. *see* PSYCHOLOGY

ANNUAL EDITIONS: HUMAN SEXUALITIES. *see* PSYCHOLOGY

302.23 USA ISSN 1092-0439
P92.U5
ANNUAL EDITIONS: MASS MEDIA. Text in English. 1993. a. USD 22.25 per issue (effective 2010). illus. back issues avail. **Document type:** *Journal, Academic/Scholarly.* **Description:** Contains a compilation of carefully selected articles from the public press. Articles come from such sources as Newsweek, The Washington Post Magazine, and American Journalism Review. Covers such topics as: Feminist Media Criticism and Feminist Media Practices, The Contest of Television Violence and Media Culpas.
Related titles: Online - full text ed.
Published by: McGraw-Hill, Contemporary Learning Series (Subsidiary of: McGraw-Hill Companies, Inc.), 1221 Ave of the Americas, New York, NY 10020. TEL 212-904-2000, FAX 212-512-2000, customer.service@mcgraw-hill.com, http://www.mhhe.com/cls/.

ANNUAL EDITIONS: SOCIAL PSYCHOLOGY. *see* PSYCHOLOGY

301 USA ISSN 0277-9315
HM1
➤ **ANNUAL EDITIONS: SOCIOLOGY.** Text in English. 1972. a. USD 22.25 per issue (effective 2010). illus. index. back issues avail. **Document type:** *Journal, Academic/Scholarly.* **Description:** Covers such topics as tribal cultures; socialization and social control; social inequalities; and social changes.
Formerly (until 19??): Annual Editions: Readings in Sociology (0090-4236)
Related titles: Online - full text ed.
Published by: McGraw-Hill, Contemporary Learning Series (Subsidiary of: McGraw-Hill Companies, Inc.), 1221 Ave of the Americas, New York, NY 10020. TEL 212-904-2000, FAX 212-512-2000, customer.service@mcgraw-hill.com, http://www.mhhe.com/cls/.

➤ **ANNUAL EDITIONS: THE FAMILY.** *see* MATRIMONY

307.1416 USA ISSN 0735-2425
HT101
➤ **ANNUAL EDITIONS: URBAN SOCIETY.** Text in English. 1978. a. USD 22.25 per issue (effective 2010). illus. index. back issues avail. **Document type:** *Journal, Academic/Scholarly.*
Formerly (until 1982): Focus: Urban Society (0160-9815)
Related titles: Online - full text ed.
Published by: McGraw-Hill, Contemporary Learning Series (Subsidiary of: McGraw-Hill Companies, Inc.), 1221 Ave of the Americas, New York, NY 10020. TEL 212-904-2000, FAX 212-512-2000, customer.service@mcgraw-hill.com, http://www.mhhe.com/cls/.

301 USA ISSN 0360-0572
HM1 CODEN: ARVSDB
➤ **ANNUAL REVIEW OF SOCIOLOGY.** Text in English. 1975. a. USD 251 combined subscription per issue to institutions (print & online eds.); USD 209 per issue to institutions (print or online ed.) (effective 2012). bibl.; charts; abstr. cum.index. back issues avail.; reprint service avail. from PSC. **Document type:** *Journal, Academic/Scholarly.* **Description:** Synthesizes and filters primary research to identify the principal contributions in the field of sociology.
Related titles: Microfilm ed.: (from PQC); Online - full text ed.: ISSN 1545-2115.
Indexed: A01, A02, A03, A08, A12, A20, A22, A26, ABIn, ABS&EES, ASCA, B01, B02, B04, B06, B07, B09, B15, B17, B18, BRD, CA, CJPI, CommAb, CurCont, DIP, E-psyche, E08, ERA, F09, FR, G04, G06, G07, G08, H09, I05, I13, IBR, IBSS, IBZ, LeftInd, P02, P03, P10, P25, P26, P27, P30, P42, P43, P46, P48, P51, P53, P54, PAIS, PCI, PQC, PSA, PSI, PopulInd, PsycInfo, PsycholAb, RASB, S02, S03, S05, S09, S11, S21, SCOPUS, SOPODA, SSA, SSAI, SSAb, SSCI, SSI, SociolAb, T02, W03, W05, W07, W09.
—BLDSC (1529.100000), IE, Infotrieve, Ingenta, INIST. **CCC.**
Published by: Annual Reviews, PO Box 10139, Palo Alto, CA 94303. TEL 650-493-4400, FAX 650-424-0910, 800-523-8635, service@annualreviews.org. Eds. Douglas S Massey TEL 609-258-4949, Karen S Cook TEL 650-723-1194, Samuel Gubins.

201.6 NLD ISSN 1877-5233
▼ **ANNUAL REVIEW OF THE SOCIOLOGY OF RELIGION.** Text in English. 2010. a. EUR 121, USD 166 (effective 2012). **Document type:** *Journal, Academic/Scholarly.* **Description:** Aims to describe and interpret the complexity of religious phenomena within different geopolitical situations, highlighting similarities and discontinuities.
Published by: Brill, PO Box 9000, Leiden, 2300 PA, Netherlands. TEL 31-71-5353500, FAX 31-71-5317532, cs@brill.nl. Eds. Enzo Pace, Giuseppe Giordan, Luigi Berzano.

301 DEU ISSN 0937-7476
ANSTOESSE ZUR FRIEDENSARBEIT. Text in German. 1990. irreg., latest vol.12, 1995. price varies. **Document type:** *Monographic series, Academic/Scholarly.*
Published by: Georg Olms Verlag, Hagentorwall 7, Hildesheim, 31134, Germany. TEL 49-5121-15010, FAX 49-5121-150150, info@olms.de, http://www.olms.de.

301 ARG ISSN 1515-8438
JC571
ANTIGONA. Text in Spanish. 1999. s-a. **Document type:** *Journal, Academic/Scholarly.*
Published by: Universidad Nacional de Rio Cuarto, Facultad de Ciencias Humanas, Ruta Nac 36 Km 601, Cordoba, 5804, Argentina. TEL 54-358-4676297, FAX 54-358-4680280, http://www.unrc.edu.ar. Ed. Lilian Fernandez del Moral. Circ: 250.

S

305 NOR ISSN 1501-6048
ANTIRASISTEN. Text in Norwegian. 1995. 5/yr. NOK 50 membership (effective 2006). adv. back issues avail. **Document type:** *Magazine, Consumer.*
Formerly (until 1996): S O S Rapport (1502-9131)
Related titles: Online - full text ed.: ISSN 1500-6883.
Published by: S O S Rasisme, PO Box 9427, Groenland, Oslo, 9427, Norway. TEL 47-23-002900, FAX 47-23-002901, au@sos-rasisme.no, http://www.sos-rasisme.no. Ed. Trond Thorbjoernsen. adv.: page NOK 4,000.

ANUARIO FILOSOFIA, PSICOLOGIA Y SOCIOLOGIA. *see* PHILOSOPHY

301 VEN ISSN 0798-2992
P87
ANUARIO ININCO. Text in Spanish. 1989. a. back issues avail. **Document type:** *Journal, Academic/Scholarly.*
Related titles: Online - full text ed.
Published by: Universidad Central de Venezuela, Instituto de Investigaciones de la Comunicacion, Ave Neveri, Centro Comerciasl Los Chaguaramos, Piso 3, Caracas, 1040, Venezuela. TEL 58-2-6930077, ininco@camelot.rect.ucv.ve. Ed. Oscar Lucien. Circ: 1,000.

ANVESAK. *see* BUSINESS AND ECONOMICS

ANYTHING THAT MOVES; the bisexual magazine. *see* HOMOSEXUALITY

APPLIED DEVELOPMENTAL SCIENCE. *see* PSYCHOLOGY

301 PRY ISSN 0044-8524
AQUI. Text in Spanish. 1971. w. USD 50. **Description:** Treats themes in the political and judicial atmospheres and covers social and economic issues.
Published by: Editorial Emegebe S.A., ALBERDI, 1393, Asuncion, Paraguay. TEL 448-688-443-536, FAX 448-271-495-901.

301 330.9 USA ISSN 1992-7622
ARAB HUMAN DEVELOPMENT REPORT (YEAR); towards freedom in the Arab world. Text in English. 2002-2005; N.S. 2008. a. free. **Document type:** *Government.*
Related titles: Online - full text ed.
Published by: (United Nations Development Programme, Arab Fund for Economic and Social Development/Al-Sandouq al-Arabi lil-Enma' al-Eqtissadi wa al-Ejtima'i KWT, Arab Gulf Programme for United Nations Development Organizations), United Nations Publications, 2 United Nations Plaza, Rm DC2-853, New York, NY 10017. TEL 212-963-8302, 800-253-9646, FAX 212-963-3489, publications@un.org, https://unp.un.org.

301 DEU ISSN 1617-0407
ARBEIT UND LEBEN IM UMBRUCH. Text in German. 2001. irreg., latest vol.20, 2010. price varies. **Document type:** *Monographic series, Academic/Scholarly.*
Published by: Rainer Hampp Verlag, Marktplatz 5, Mering, 86415, Germany. TEL 49-8233-4783, FAX 49-8233-30755, info@rhverlag.de, http://www.rhverlag.de.

306 DEU ISSN 0940-3744
ARBEITSKREISE ZUR LANDENTWICKLUNG IN HESSEN. DORFENTWICKLUNG. Text in German. 1988. irreg., latest vol.3, 1990. price varies. **Document type:** *Monographic series, Academic/Scholarly.*
Published by: Agrarsoziale Gesellschaft e.V., Kurze Geismarstr 33, Goettingen, 37073, Germany. TEL 49-551-497090, FAX 49-551-4970916, info@asg-goe.de, http://www.asg-goe.de.

306 DEU ISSN 0940-3752
ARBEITSKREISE ZUR LANDENTWICKLUNG IN HESSEN. LANDNUTZUNG. Text in German. 19??. irreg., latest vol.11, 1991. price varies. **Document type:** *Monographic series, Academic/Scholarly.*
Published by: Agrarsoziale Gesellschaft e.V., Kurze Geismarstr 33, Goettingen, 37073, Germany. TEL 49-551-497090, FAX 49-551-4970916, info@asg-goe.de, http://www.asg-goe.de.

306 DEU ISSN 0940-3760
ARBEITSKREISE ZUR LANDENTWICKLUNG IN HESSEN. STALLBAU UND TECHNIK. Text in German. 1986. irreg., latest vol.4, 1988. price varies. **Document type:** *Monographic series, Academic/Scholarly.*
Published by: Agrarsoziale Gesellschaft e.V., Kurze Geismarstr 33, Goettingen, 37073, Germany. TEL 49-551-497090, FAX 49-551-4970916, info@asg-goe.de, http://www.asg-goe.de.

306 DEU ISSN 0940-3779
ARBEITSKREISE ZUR LANDENTWICKLUNG IN HESSEN. WOHNEN UND WOHNUMWELT. Text in German. 1984. irreg., latest vol.12, 1996. price varies. **Document type:** *Monographic series, Academic/Scholarly.*
Published by: Agrarsoziale Gesellschaft e.V., Kurze Geismarstr 33, Goettingen, 37073, Germany. TEL 49-551-497090, FAX 49-551-4970916, info@asg-goe.de, http://www.asg-goe.de.

305.5 DNK ISSN 1901-7847
➤ **ARBEJDERMUSEET OG ARBEJDERBEVAEGELSENS BIBLIOTEK OG ARKIV. AARBOG.** Text in Danish. 2006. a. **Document type:** *Consumer.*
Published by: Arbejdermuseet og Arbejderbevaegelsens Bibliotek og Arkiv/Workers' Museum & the Labour Movement's Library and Archives, Roemersgade 22, Copenhagen K, 1362, Denmark. TEL 45-33-932575, FAX 45-33-145258, am@arbejdermuseet.dk, http://www.aba.dk.

960 306 FRA ISSN 1956-7812
L'ARBRE A PALABRES; culture et developpement. Text in French. 200?. s-a. EUR 30 domestic to individuals; EUR 36 in the European Union to individuals; EUR 39 elsewhere to individuals; EUR 77 domestic to institutions; EUR 80 in the European Union to institutions; EUR 85 elsewhere to institutions (effective 2009). back issues avail. **Document type:** *Magazine, Consumer.*
Indexed: MLA-IB.
Published by: Dunia Cultures et Developpement, 4-6 Rue Bellefond, Paris, 75009, France. TEL 33-1-42855796.

301 GBR ISSN 0003-9756
HM1.A1
➤ **ARCHIVES EUROPEENNES DE SOCIOLOGIE/EUROPAEISCHES ARCHIV FUER SOZIOLOGIE/EUROPEAN JOURNAL OF SOCIOLOGY.** Text in English, French, German. 1960. 3/yr. GBP 152, EUR 210, USD 252 to institutions; GBP 160, EUR 225, USD 265 combined subscription to institutions (print & online eds.) (effective 2012). adv. bk.rev. bibl.; charts; illus.; stat. index, cum.index. back issues avail.; reprint service avail. from PSC. **Document type:** *Journal, Academic/Scholarly.* **Description:** Encourages comparative studies of societies worldwide, paying special attention to the processes of change in Eastern Europe, as well as to the various expressions of ethnicity and nationalism.
Related titles: Microform ed.: (from PQC); Online - full text ed.: ISSN 1474-0583. 2001. GBP 142, EUR 200, USD 232 to institutions (effective 2012).
Indexed: A12, A20, A22, ABIn, AC&P, ASCA, BAS, CA, CurCont, DIP, E01, FR, GEOBASE, H09, HistAb, I08, I13, IBR, IBSS, IBZ, P06, P10, P30, P34, P42, P46, P48, P51, P53, P54, PAA&I, PAIS, PCI, PQC, PSA, RASB, RI-1, RI-2, S02, S03, S05, S11, SCOPUS, SOPODA, SSA, SSCI, SociolAb, T02, W07.
—BLDSC (1634.278000), IE, Infotrieve, Ingenta, INIST. **CCC.**
Published by: (France. Centre National de la Recherche Scientifique FRA), Cambridge University Press, The Edinburgh Bldg, Shaftesbury Rd, Cambridge, CB2 8RU, United Kingdom. TEL 44-1223-312393, FAX 44-1223-315052, journals@cambridge.org, http://www.cambridge.org/uk. Eds. Christopher Hann, Claus Offe, Hans Joas, Jaques Lautman, Steven Lukes. R&P Linda Nicol TEL 44-1223-325702. adv.: page GBP 460, page USD 875. Circ: 950. **Subscr. to:** Cambridge University Press, 32 Ave of the Americas, New York, NY 10013. TEL 212-337-5000, FAX 212-691-3239, journals_subscriptions@cup.org

➤ **ARCHIVOS HISPANOAMERICANOS DE SEXOLOGIA.** *see* PSYCHOLOGY

301 MEX ISSN 0187-5795
ARGUMENTOS; estudios criticos de la sociedad. Text in Spanish. 1987. q. MXN 300 domestic; USD 80 foreign (effective 2011). back issues avail. **Document type:** *Journal, Academic/Scholarly.*
Related titles: Online - full text ed.: free (effective 2011) (from SciELO).
Indexed: C01, RASB.
Published by: Universidad Autonoma Metropolitana - Xochimilco, Division de Ciencias Sociales y Humanidades, Calz del Hueso 1100, Col Villa Quietud, Mexico City, DF 04960, Mexico. TEL 52-5-7245060, FAX 52-5-7235415, argument@cueyatl.uam.mx, http://cueyatl.uam.mx/~dpyc/arg/index.htm.

301 ARG ISSN 1666-8979
ARGUMENTOS; revista electronica de critica social. Text in Spanish. 2002. irreg. back issues avail. **Document type:** *Journal, Academic/Scholarly.*
Media: Online - full text.
Published by: Universidad de Buenos Aires, Instituto de Investigaciones Gino Germani, Uriburu 950 Piso 6, Buenos Aires, 1114, Argentina. TEL 54-11-45083822, FAX 54-11-45083815, argument@mail.fsoc.uba.ar. Ed. Pedro Krotsch.

ARISTAS. *see* HISTORY

305.868 306 USA ISSN 1096-2492
F1408.3
➤ **ARIZONA JOURNAL OF HISPANIC CULTURAL STUDIES.** Variant title: H C S. Text in English. 1997. a. **Document type:** *Journal, Academic/Scholarly.*
Related titles: Online - full text ed.: ISSN 1934-9009.
Indexed: A22, E01, H21, MLA-IB, P08.
—IE.
Published by: University of Arizona, Department of Spanish and Portuguese, Modern Languages 545, PO Box 210067, Tucson, AZ 85721. TEL 520-621-3730, FAX 520-621-6104, chuffee@email.arizona.edu, http://www.coh.arizona.edu.

301 325.2 GBR ISSN 1472-3824
ARKLETON RESEARCH PAPERS. Text in English. 2000. irreg., latest vol.6. back issues avail. **Document type:** *Monographic series.*
Related titles: Online - full text ed.: free (effective 2009).
—BLDSC (1682.075500).
Published by: University of Aberdeen, The Arkleton Centre, St. Mary's, King's College, Aberdeen, AB24 3UF, United Kingdom. TEL 44-1224-273901, FAX 44-1224-273902, ark@abdn.ac.uk, http://www.abdn.ac.uk/arkleton.

▼ **ARKTIKA: OBSHCHESTVO I EKONOMIKA/ARCTIC: SOCIETY & ECONOMICS**; nauchnyi zhurnal. *see* BUSINESS AND ECONOMICS

ARMED FORCES AND SOCIETY; an interdisciplinary journal on military institutions, civil-military relations, arms control and peacekeeping, and conflict management. *see* MILITARY

307.72 USA
AROUND THE SOUTH (ONLINE EDITION). Text in English. q. free. **Document type:** *Newsletter.* **Description:** Offers a synopsis of key information/resources being published by our Center and other entities that address issues of critical importance to the South.
Former titles (until 2004): Southern Perspectives (Print Edition); (until 1997): Capsules
Media: Online - full content.
Published by: Southern Rural Development Center, 410 Bost Extension Bldg, PO Box 9656, Mississippi State, MS 39762. TEL 662-325-3207, FAX 662-325-8915. Ed. Emily E Shaw.

301 ITA ISSN 1973-8285
ARTE & LAVORO. Text in Italian. 2004. irreg. **Document type:** *Monographic series, Consumer.*
Published by: Ediesse srl, Via dei Frentani 4A, Rome, 00185, Italy. TEL 39-06-44870283, FAX 39-06-44870335, ediesse@cgil.it, http://www.ediesseonline.it.

301 ESP ISSN 1137-7038
HM409
➤ **ARXIUS DE SOCIOLOGIA.** Text in Catalan, Spanish; Summaries in English. 1997. a. EUR 24 domestic to individuals; EUR 29 foreign to individuals; EUR 29 domestic to institutions; EUR 35 foreign to institutions (effective 2009). back issues avail. **Document type:** *Magazine, Academic/Scholarly.* **Description:** Challenges that sociology has raised at the present historical moment: multiculturalism, postmaterialism, ecological sustainability, and urban planning.
Published by: Editorial Afers S.L., La Llibertat, 12, Apartat de Correus 267, Catarroja, Valencia 46470, Spain. TEL 34-961-268654, FAX 34-961-272582, afers@provicom.com, http://www.editorialafers.cat/. Ed. Antonio Arino. Pub. Vicent Olmos. R&P Carme Pastor. Circ: 1,500.

➤ **ASIA INFO.** *see* ASIAN STUDIES

307.14 THA
ASIAN INSTITUTE OF TECHNOLOGY. H S D CONFERENCE - SEMINAR PROCEEDINGS. Text in English. 1980. irreg. price varies. **Document type:** *Proceedings, Academic/Scholarly.*
Published by: (Human Settlements Development Program), Asian Institute of Technology, School of Environment, Resources and Development, Klong Luang, PO Box 4, Pathum Thani, 12120, Thailand. TEL 66-2-524-5610, FAX 66-2-524-6132.

307.14 THA
ASIAN INSTITUTE OF TECHNOLOGY. H S D MONOGRAPHS. Text in Thai. 1981. irreg. price varies. **Document type:** *Monographic series, Academic/Scholarly.*
Published by: (Human Settlements Development Program), Asian Institute of Technology, School of Environment, Resources and Development, Klong Luang, PO Box 4, Pathum Thani, 12120, Thailand. TEL 66-2-524-5610, FAX 66-2-524-6132.

302.2 SGP ISSN 0129-2056
ASIAN MASS COMMUNICATIONS BULLETIN. Text in English. 1971. bi-m. free to members. bk.rev. bibl. **Document type:** *Bulletin, Academic/Scholarly.*
Indexed: RASB.
Published by: Asian Media Information and Communication Centre, Publications Unit, PO Box 360, Jurong Point, 916412, Singapore. TEL 65-7927570, FAX 65-7927129, enquiries@amic.org.sg, http://www.amic.org.sg. Ed. Vijay Menon. R&P, Adv. contact Gordon Hogan. Circ: 1,500.

301.07 ESP ISSN 1988-7302
ASOCIACION DE SOCIOLOGIA DE LA EDUCACION. REVISTA. Short title: RASE. Text in Spanish. 2008. 3/yr.
Media: Online - full text.
Published by: Asociacion de Sociologia de la Educacion, UCM - FCPS, Campus de Somasaguas, Madrid, 28223, Spain. rase@ual.es, http://www.rase.es/.

ASPARKIA; investigacio feminista. *see* WOMEN'S STUDIES

303.4 307.14 FRA ISSN 1950-6929
GN1
ASSOCIATION EURO-AFRICAINE POUR L'ANTHROPOLOGIE DU CHANGEMENT SOCIAL ET DU DEVELOPPEMENT. BULLETIN (ONLINE). Variant title: Bulletin de l' A P A D (Online). Text in French, English. 2006. s-a. **Document type:** *Bulletin.*
Media: Online - full text. **Related titles:** ◆ Print ed.: Association Euro-Africaine pour l'Anthropologie du Changement Social et du Developpement. Bulletin (Print).
Published by: Association Euro-Africaine pour l'Anthropologie du Changement Social et du Developpement (A P A D), Centre de la Vieille Charite, 2 Rue de la Charite, Marseilles, 13002, France. TEL 33-4-91140777, FAX 33-4-91913401, apad@ehess.cnrs-mrs.fr.

306 941 GBR
TD169
ASSOCIATION FOR HERITAGE INTERPRETATION. INTERPRETATION JOURNAL. Text in English. 1995. 3/yr. free to members (effective 2009). adv. bk.rev. back issues avail. **Document type:** *Journal, Academic/Scholarly.* **Description:** Covers innovative work, cutting-edge issues, case studies and research results.
Formerly (until 2000): Interpretation (1357-9401); Which was formed by the merger of (1986-1995): Environmental Interpretation (0950-0995); (19??-1995): Interpretation Journal; Which was formerly (until 19??): Heritage Interpretation (0265-3664); (until 1983): Interpretation (0306-8897)
Related titles: Online - full text ed.
Indexed: A01, CA, GSS&RPL, H&TI, T02.
—BLDSC (4557.346000), IE, Ingenta.
Published by: (Society for the Interpretation of Britain's Heritage), Association for Heritage Interpretation, 131 Trafalgar St, Gillingham, Kent, ME7 4RP, United Kingdom. TEL 44-560-2747737, mail@ahi.org.uk, http://www.ahi.org.uk/.

306.874 CAN ISSN 1488-0989
HQ759
➤ **ASSOCIATION FOR RESEARCH ON MOTHERING. JOURNAL.** Text in English. 1999. s-a. CAD 90 combined subscription domestic to institutions (print & online eds.); USD 90 combined subscription foreign to institutions (print & online eds.) (effective 2009). bk.rev. illus. back issues avail. **Document type:** *Journal, Academic/Scholarly.* **Description:** Publishes scholarship on mothering-motherhood. Considers motherhood in an international context and from a multitude of perspectives including differences of class, race, sexuality, age, ethnicity, ability and nationality.
Related titles: Online - full content ed.
Indexed: CA, F09, FemPer, MLA-IB, P42, PAIS, S02, S03, SCOPUS, SociolAb, T02, W09.
—BLDSC (4705.232000). **CCC.**
Published by: Association for Research on Mothering, 726 Atkinson, York University, 4700 Keele St, Toronto, ON M3J 1P3, Canada. TEL 416-736-2100 ext 60366, FAX 416-736-5766, arm@yorku.ca.

301 USA
ASSOCIATION FOR THE SOCIOLOGY OF RELIGION. NEWS AND ANNOUNCEMENTS. Text in English. 1965. q. membership only. back issues avail. **Document type:** *Newsletter, Trade.* **Description:** Social analysis on religion.
Related titles: E-mail ed.
Published by: Association for the Sociology of Religion, c o William H. Swatos, 618 SW 2nd Ave, Galva, IL 61434. TEL 309-932-2727, FAX 309-932-2282, swatos@microd.com, http://www.sociologyofreligion.com.

ASSOCIATION INTERNATIONALE D'ETUDES DU SUD-EST EUROPEEN. BULLETIN. *see* HISTORY—History Of Europe

305.3 GBR ISSN 2042-387X
▼ ➤ **ASSUMING GENDER.** Text in English. 2010. s-a. free (effective 2010). **Document type:** *Journal, Academic/Scholarly.* **Description:** Features research from a diverse range of methodologies and approaches to gender studies, and include work in feminist theories, queer theories, critical and cultural theory, literature, film studies, sociology and other relevant fields.
Media: Online - full text.
Published by: Cardiff University, School of English, Communication and Philosophy, Humanities Bldg, Colum Dr, Cardiff, CF10 3EU, United Kingdom. TEL 44-29-20876049, FAX 44-2920874502, encap@cardiff.ac.uk, http://www.cardiff.ac.uk/encap.

301 FRA ISSN 0587-3746
ASSURE SOCIAL. Text in French. 1964. bi-m. adv. bk.rev.
Published by: (Union Nationale pour l'Avenir de la Medecine), B.C. Savy, 18 av. de la Marne, Asnieres-sur-Seine, 92600, France. Circ: 15,000.

301 ARG ISSN 1668-7515
ASTROLABIO. Text in Spanish. 2004. s-a. **Document type:** *Journal, Academic/Scholarly.*
Media: Online - full text.
Published by: Universidad Nacional de Cordoba, Centro de Estudios Avanzados, Ave. Velez Sarsfield, 153, Cordoba, 5000, Argentina. TEL 54-351-4332086, FAX 54-351-4332087, centro@cea.unc.edu.ar. Ed. Marceono Casarin.

302.2 VEN
ASUNTO. Text in Spanish. 1975. irreg.
Published by: Universidad del Zulia, Escuela de Comunicacion Social, Maracaibo, Venezuela.

301 CAN
@ PHILIA. Text in English. 2002. m. **Document type:** *Magazine, Consumer.*
Formerly (until Aug. 2004): The Philia Ezine (1912-1458)
Media: Online - full text.
Published by: Philia Dialogue on Caring Citizenship, #260 - 3665 Kingsway, Vancouver, BC V5R 5W2, Canada. TEL 604-439-9566, FAX 604-439-7001, haveyoursay@philia.ca, http://www.philia.ca/cms%5Fen/index.cfm?group_id=1000.

306.4 FRA ISSN 1958-3532
ATELIER DE SOCIOLINGUISTIQUE. CARNETS. Variant title: Carnets d'Atelier de Sociolinguistiques. Text in French. 2007. irreg. back issues avail. **Document type:** *Journal, Academic/Scholarly.*
Published by: L' Harmattan, 5 Rue de l'Ecole Polytechnique, Paris, 75005, France. TEL 33-1-43257651, FAX 33-1-43258203.

302.2 USA ISSN 1545-6870
P87
➤ **ATLANTIC JOURNAL OF COMMUNICATION.** Abbreviated title: A J C. Text in English. 1993. 5/yr. GBP 187 combined subscription in United Kingdom to institutions (print & online eds.); EUR 249, USD 313 combined subscription to institutions (print & online eds.) (effective 2012). adv. bk.rev. charts; illus. back issues avail.; reprint service avail. from PSC. **Document type:** *Journal, Academic/Scholarly.* **Description:** Concerned with the study of communication theory, practice, and policy.
Formerly (until 2004): New Jersey Journal of Communication (1067-9154)
Related titles: Online - full text ed.: ISSN 1545-6889. GBP 168 in United Kingdom to institutions; EUR 224, USD 282 to institutions (effective 2012) (from IngentaConnect).
Indexed: A01, A22, AmHI, CA, CMM, CommAb, E01, FamI, H07, T02.
—BLDSC (1765.910000), CIS, IE, Ingenta. **CCC.**
Published by: (New Jersey Communications Association, New York Communications Association), Routledge (Subsidiary of: Taylor & Francis Group), 325 Chestnut St, Ste 800, Philadelphia, PA 19106. TEL 215-625-8900, 800-354-1420, FAX 215-625-2940, journals@routledge.com, http://www.routledge.com. Ed. Gary P Radford. Adv. contact Linda Hann TEL 44-1344-779945.

➤ **ATMA JAYA RESEARCH CENTRE. SOCIO-MEDICAL RESEARCH REPORT/PUSAT PENELITIAN ATMA JAYA. PENELITIAN TENTANG KEBUTUHAN KESEHATAN MASYARAKAT DAN SISTEM PELEYANAN KESEHATAN DI KECAMATAN PENJARINGAN.** *see* MEDICAL SCIENCES

➤ **ATMA JAYA RESEARCH CENTRE. SOCIO-RELIGIOUS RESEARCH REPORT/PUSAT PENELITIAN ATMA JAYA. LAPORAN PENELITIAN KEAGAMAAN.** *see* RELIGIONS AND THEOLOGY

301 FRA ISSN 2108-5463
▼ **AU CARREFOUR DU SOCIAL.** Text in French. 2009. irreg. **Document type:** *Monographic series, Academic/Scholarly.*
Published by: L' Harmattan, 5 Rue de l'Ecole Polytechnique, Paris, 75005, France. TEL 33-1-43257651, FAX 33-1-43258203, diffusion.harmattan@wanadoo.fr.

AUFHEBEN; revolutionary perspectives. *see* POLITICAL SCIENCE

301 DEU
AUSGEWAEHLTE VORTRAEGE GRUENE SEITEN. Text in German. 1990. irreg., latest vol.77, 2008. price varies. **Document type:** *Monographic series, Academic/Scholarly.*
Published by: Bund Katholischer Unternehmer e.V., Georgstr 18, Cologne, 50676, Germany. TEL 49-221-272370, FAX 49-221-2723727, service@bku.de. Ed. Peter Unterberg.

AUSTRALASIAN CANADIAN STUDIES; a multidisciplinary journal for the humanities and social sciences. *see* ANTHROPOLOGY

AUSTRALASIAN JOURNAL OF BUSINESS AND SOCIAL INQUIRY. *see* BUSINESS AND ECONOMICS

306.85 AUS ISSN 0814-723X
HQ10 CODEN: ANZTE7
➤ **AUSTRALIAN AND NEW ZEALAND JOURNAL OF FAMILY THERAPY;** innovative and contextual approaches to human problems. Abbreviated title: A N Z J F T. Text in English. 1979. q. AUD 237 combined subscription domestic to institutions (print & online eds.); AUD 250 combined subscription in New Zealand to institutions (print & online eds.); AUD 260 combined subscription elsewhere to institutions (print & online eds.) (effective 2011). adv. bk.rev.; video rev. a. cum.index. 60 p./no.; back issues avail. **Document type:** *Journal, Academic/Scholarly.* **Description:** Promotes theory and practice of family therapy.
Formerly (until 1985): Australian Journal of Family Therapy (0156-8779)
Related titles: Online - full text ed.: ISSN 1467-8438.
Indexed: A01, A03, A08, A11, A22, A26, AEI, C06, C07, CA, E-psyche, E01, F09, FamI, P03, P43, PsycInfo, PsycholAb, S02, S03, SCOPUS, SFSA, SOPODA, SSA, SSCI, SWR&A, SociolAb, T02, W07.
—BLDSC (1796.886500), IE, Infotrieve, Ingenta. **CCC.**
Published by: Australian Academic Press Pty. Ltd., 55 Archdeacon Rd, Nedlands, W.A. 6009, Australia. TEL 61-8-63891165, aap@australianacademicpress.com.au, http://www.australianacademicpress.com.au. Eds. Alistar Campbell, Glenn Larner. Circ: 1,100.

➤ **AUSTRALIAN FOLKLORE;** a yearly journal of folklore studies. *see* FOLKLORE

➤ **AUSTRIAN STUDIES IN SOCIAL ANTHROPOLOGY.** *see* ANTHROPOLOGY

301 GBR ISSN 1467-4653
AUXOLOGY: ADVANCES IN THE STUDY OF HUMAN GROWTH AND DEVELOPMENT. Text in English. 1999. a., latest vol.6. GBP 25 per issue (effective 2010). **Document type:** *Monographic series, Academic/Scholarly.*
—BLDSC (1835.720000).
Published by: Smith-Gordon and Co. Ltd., Media House, Burrel Rd, St Ives, Cambridgeshire PE27 3LE, United Kingdom. TEL 44-1480-465233, FAX 44-1480-466053, publishing@smith-gordon-publishing.com.

301 GBR
B A A S PAPERBACKS. (British Association for American Studies) Text in English. irreg. price varies. back issues avail. **Document type:** *Monographic series, Academic/Scholarly.* **Description:** Covers American studies with a specific topic for each volume.
Published by: (British Association for American Studies), Edinburgh University Press, 22 George Sq, Edinburgh, Scotland EH8 9LF, United Kingdom. TEL 44-131-6504218, FAX 44-131-6503286, journals@eup.ed.ac.uk. Eds. Carol Smith, Simon Newman.

305.5 GBR ISSN 2041-7667
▼ **B BEYOND.** Text in English. 2010. q. GBP 200; GBP 50 per issue (effective 2011). back issues avail. **Document type:** *Magazine, Trade.* **Description:** Focuses on and profiling the global Ultra High Net Worth market and community.
Related titles: Online - full text ed.: free (effective 2011).
Published by: B B Publications, 40 Craven St Charing Cross, Ste 7, London, WC2N 5NG, United Kingdom. info@bbpublications.org.

305 USA ISSN 1946-1410
B D P A TODAY. (Black Data Processing Associates) Text in English. 2007. m. free to members (effective 2009). adv. back issues avail.; reprints avail. **Document type:** *Newsletter, Trade.*
Related titles: Online - full text ed.: ISSN 1946-1429.
Published by: B D P A, D.C. Chapter, 611 Pennsylvania Ave, SE 213, Washington, DC 20003. TEL 202-659-5367, 800-727-2372, FAX 301-576-5456, washingtondc@bdpa.org, http://www.bdpa-dc.org. adv.: page USD 2,500; trim 8.125 x 10.875.

301 IRL ISSN 1017-4877
HD5164.5
B E S T. (Best European Studies on Time) Text in English. 2/yr. free. **Document type:** *Bulletin.*
Related titles: German ed.: Bulletin fuer Europaeische Zeitstudien; French ed.: Bulletin Europeen d'Etudes Europeennes sur le Temps.
Published by: European Foundation for the Improvement of Living and Working Conditions/Fondation Europeenne pour l'Amelioration des Conditions de Vie et de Travail, Wyattville Rd, Loughlinstown, Co. Dublin 18, Ireland. TEL 353-1-2043100, FAX 353-1-2826456, information@eurofound.europa.eu, http://www.eurofound.europa.eu.

301 BGD
B I D S MONOGRAPH. Text in Bengali. 1949. irreg., latest vol.9. price varies. **Document type:** *Monographic series.*
Published by: Bangladesh Unnayan Gobeshona Protishthan/ Bangladesh Institute of Development Studies, E-17 Agargaon, Sher-e-Banglanagar, GPO Box 3854, Dhaka, 1207, Bangladesh. TEL 325041.

B I D S NEWSLETTER. *see* BUSINESS AND ECONOMICS—International Development And Assistance

301 BGD
B I D S RESEARCH REPORTS. Text in English. irreg., latest vol.72.
Published by: Bangladesh Unnayan Gobeshona Protishthan/ Bangladesh Institute of Development Studies, E-17 Agargaon, Sher-e-Banglanagar, GPO Box 3854, Dhaka, 1207, Bangladesh. TEL 325041.

301 BGD
B I D S WORKING PAPER. Text in Bengali. irreg., latest vol.4, 1987. price varies.
Published by: Bangladesh Unnayan Gobeshona Protishthan/ Bangladesh Institute of Development Studies, E-17 Agargaon, Sher-e-Banglanagar, GPO Box 3854, Dhaka, 1207, Bangladesh. TEL 325041.

306.7 ISL ISSN 1670-5971
B OG B. Text in Icelandic. 1989. m. ISK 899 newsstand/cover (effective 2005). adv. **Document type:** *Magazine, Consumer.* **Description:** Focuses on issues and events related to sex and the relationship between the sexes. Contributors are chiefly physicians, psychologists, sex therapists, nurses and other members of the medical and health professions.
Formerly (until 2004): Bleikt og Blatt (1021-7150)
Indexed: E-psyche.
Published by: Frodi Ltd., Hoefdabakka 9, Reykjavik, 110, Iceland. TEL 354-515-5500, FAX 354-515-5599, frodi@frodi.is. Ed. David Thor Jonsson. Adv. contact Sigrun Thorvardardottir. color page ISK 187,983.

306.85 362.85 649 IRL ISSN 1649-9859
B.OPEN; supporting one parent families in Ireland. Text in English. 2007. 3/yr. free (effective 2007). **Document type:** *Magazine, Consumer.*
Related titles: Online - full text ed.
Published by: O P E N, National Centre, 7 Red Cow Ln, Smithfield, Dublin, 7, Ireland. TEL 353-1-8148860, FAX 353-1-8148890, enquiries@oneparent.ie. Ed. Jane Beatty.

302.23 DEU ISSN 1865-553X
▼ **BABELSBERGER SCHRIFTEN ZU MEDIENDRAMATURGIE UND -AESTHETIK.** Text in German. 2009. irreg. price varies. **Document type:** *Monographic series, Academic/Scholarly.*
Published by: Peter Lang GmbH (Subsidiary of: Peter Lang Publishing Group), Eschborner Landstr 42-50, Frankfurt Am Main, 60489, Germany. TEL 49-69-7807050, FAX 49-69-78070550, zentrale.frankfurt@peterlang.com. Ed. Kerstin Stutterheim.

306 USA ISSN 1059-8235
BAD SEED. Text in English. 1983. q. USD 15 (effective 2007). bk.rev.; film rev. back issues avail. **Document type:** *Magazine, Consumer.* **Description:** Contains studies, discussions, and research on juvenile delinquency in popular culture: film, literature, media.
Published by: Norton Records, PO Box 646, Cooper Sta, New York, NY 10276-0646. TEL 718-789-4438, FAX 718-398-9215, http://www.nortonrecords.com. Ed., Pub., R&P Miriam Linna. Circ: 2,000.

301 SWE ISSN 1691-001X
BALTIC 21 NEWSLETTER. Variant title: Baltic Twenty One Newsletter. Text in English. 1999. s-a. free. back issues avail. **Document type:** *Newsletter, Consumer.*
Related titles: Online - full text ed.
Published by: Baltic 21, PO Box 2010, Stockholm, 10311, Sweden. TEL 46-8-4401920, FAX 46-8-4401944, secretariat@baltic21.org.

301 SWE ISSN 1029-7790
BALTIC 21 SERIES. Variant title: Baltic Twenty One Series. Text in Multiple languages. 1998. irreg., latest 2006. free. back issues avail. **Document type:** *Monographic series, Academic/Scholarly.* **Description:** Focus on economic and environmental developments in the Baltic region.
Related titles: Online - full text ed.
Published by: Baltic 21, PO Box 2010, Stockholm, 10311, Sweden. TEL 46-8-4401920, FAX 46-8-4401944, secretariat@baltic21.org.

301 BGD ISSN 1819-8465
➤ **BANGLADESH E-JOURNAL OF SOCIOLOGY.** Text in English. 2004. s-a. Index. **Document type:** *Journal, Academic/Scholarly.* **Description:** Covers all major areas of sociology.
Media: Online - full text.
Indexed: A34, CA, CABA, GH, H16, IBSS, LT, R12, RRTA, S02, S03, T02, T05, TAR, W11.
Published by: Bangladesh Sociological Society, Arts Faculty Bldg, Rm 1054, University of Dhaka, Dhaka, 1000, Bangladesh. Ed. Nazrul Islam.

301 ARG ISSN 1575-0825
HN590.C363
BARATARIA. Text in Spanish. 1998. a. back issues avail. **Document type:** *Journal, Academic/Scholarly.*
Related titles: Online - full text ed.: ISSN 2172-3184. 1998.
Published by: Asociacion Civil Medicina y Sociedad, Sarmiento 1889 1o B, Buenos Aires, Argentina. TEL 54-11-43724019, FAX 54-11-43724042, info@medyscoc.org.ar, http://www.medicinaysociedad.org.ar/. Ed. Alberto Cesar Manterola.

301 IRN ISSN 2008-8973
➤ **BARRISI-I MASAIL-I IJTIMAI-I IRAN/IRANIAN JOURNAL OF SOCIAL PROBLEMS.** Text in Persian, Modern. 1968. q. IRR 1,500 domestic; USD 8 foreign to individuals; USD 7 foreign to institutions (effective 2011). abstr.; bibl.; charts; stat. back issues avail. **Document type:** *Journal, Academic/Scholarly.*
Supersedes in part (in 2010): Namah-i Ulum-i Ijtimai/Journal of Social Sciences (1010-2809)
Published by: Danishgah-i Tihran, Danishkadah-i Ulum-i Ijtimai/ University of Tehran, Faculty of Social Sciences, Tehran, Iran. TEL 98-21-88025997, FAX 98-21-88012111, http://social.ut.ac.ir/. Ed. Rahmat Sedigh Sarvestani. Pub. Gholamreza Jamshidiha.

▼ ➤ **BASISTEXTE ZUR WIRTSCHAFTS- UND SOZIALGESCHICHTE.** *see* HISTORY—History Of Europe

➤ **BAYREUTH AFRICAN STUDIES SERIES.** *see* ETHNIC INTERESTS

▼ ➤ **BECAUSE;** women's lives are worth saving. *see* POLITICAL SCIENCE—Civil Rights

➤ **BEHAVIOR AND SOCIAL ISSUES.** *see* PSYCHOLOGY

➤ **BEIRAT FUER WIRTSCHAFTS UND SOZIALFRAGEN. PUBLIKATIONEN.** *see* BUSINESS AND ECONOMICS

➤ **BEITRAEGE ZUR ALTERNS- UND LEBENSLAUFFORSCHUNG.** *see* GERONTOLOGY AND GERIATRICS

300 DEU ISSN 0949-1120
BEITRAEGE ZUR DISSIDENZ. Text in German. 1996. irreg., latest vol.24, 2010. price varies. **Document type:** *Monographic series, Academic/Scholarly.*
Published by: Peter Lang GmbH (Subsidiary of: Peter Lang Publishing Group), Eschborner Landstr 42-50, Frankfurt Am Main, 60489, Germany. TEL 49-69-7807050, FAX 49-69-78070550, zentrale.frankfurt@peterlang.com. Ed. Claudia von Werlhof.

BEITRAEGE ZUR ETHNOMEDIZIN. *see* MEDICAL SCIENCES

329 DEU
BEITRAEGE ZUR GESCHICHTE DES NATIONALSOZIALISMUS. Text in German. 1985. irreg., latest vol.25, 2009. price varies. bk.rev. back issues avail. **Document type:** *Monographic series, Academic/Scholarly.*
Formerly: Beitraege zur Nationalsozialistischen Gesundheits- und Sozialpolitik
Published by: Wallstein Verlag GmbH, Geiststr 11, Goettingen, 37073, Germany. TEL 49-551-548980, FAX 49-551-5489833, info@wallstein-verlag.de, http://www.wallstein-verlag.de. Ed. Sven Reichardt. Circ: 2,500.

300 DEU ISSN 0175-8098
BEITRAEGE ZUR GESELLSCHAFTSFORSCHUNG. Text in German. 1975. irreg., latest vol.21, 2004. price varies. **Document type:** *Monographic series, Academic/Scholarly.*
Formerly (until 1984): Gesellschaftsforschung und Gesellschaftspolitik (0172-1267)
Published by: Peter Lang GmbH (Subsidiary of: Peter Lang Publishing Group), Eschborner Landstr 42-50, Frankfurt Am Main, 60489, Germany. TEL 49-69-7807050, FAX 49-69-78070550, zentrale.frankfurt@peterlang.com. Eds. Guenter Bueschges, Werner Raub.

201.6 DEU ISSN 0175-5137
BEITRAEGE ZUR GESELLSCHAFTSPOLITIK. Text in German. 1968. irreg., latest vol.37, 2006. price varies. **Document type:** *Monographic series, Academic/Scholarly.*

S

Published by: Bund Katholischer Unternehmer e.V., Georgstr 18, Cologne, 50676, Germany. TEL 49-221-272370, FAX 49-221-2723727, service@bku.de.

BEITRAEGE ZUR PLANUNGS- UND ARCHITEKTURSOZIOLOGIE. *see* ARCHITECTURE

BEITRAEGE ZUR PSYCHOLOGIE UND SOZIOLOGIE DES KRANKEN MENSCHEN. *see* PSYCHOLOGY

306 GBR ISSN 1354-3601
➤ **BERG EUROPEAN STUDIES SERIES.** Text in English. 1992. irreg., latest 1994. price varies. **Document type:** *Monographic series, Academic/Scholarly.* **Description:** Aims to provide a multi-angled perspective on the culture of modern and contemporary Europe.
Published by: Berg Publishers (Subsidiary of: Oxford International Publishers Ltd.), 1st Fl Angel Ct, 81 St Clements St, Oxford, Berks OX4 1AW, United Kingdom. TEL 44-1865-245104, FAX 44-1865-791165, enquiry@bergpublishers.com. Eds. Brian Nelson, Geraldine Billingham.

301 SWE ISSN 1653-4492
BERGSLAGSFORSKNING. Text in Swedish. 2006. irreg., latest vol.1, 2006. SEK 180 per issue (effective 2006). **Document type:** *Monographic series, Academic/Scholarly.*
Published by: Oerebro Universitet, Universitetsbiblioteket/University of Oerebro. University Library, Fakultetsgatan 1, Oerebro, 70182, Sweden. TEL 46-19-303240, FAX 46-19-331217, biblioteket@ub.oru.se, http://www.ub.oru.se. Ed. Joanna Jansdotter.

BERITA I D S DEVELOPMENT REVIEW. *see* BUSINESS AND ECONOMICS

301 USA ISSN 0067-5830
HM1
BERKELEY JOURNAL OF SOCIOLOGY. Text in English. 1955. a. bk.rev. index. back issues avail. **Document type:** *Journal, Academic/Scholarly.* **Description:** Publishes papers published by students and untenured faculty, and has in recent years also featured a contribution of some kind by a leading member of the discipline - Craig Calhoun and Arthur Stinchcombe, among others, and this year Juliet Schor.
Formerly (until 1959): Berkeley Publications in Society and Institutions. (1073-0060)
Indexed: A22, ABS&EES, AltPI, BAS, CA, Chicano, DIP, FR, FamI, I13, IBR, IBSS, IBZ, LeftInd, MEA&I, MLA-IB, P30, P34, P42, PAIS, PCI, PSA, RILM, S02, S03, S21, SOPODA, SSA, SociolAb, T02.
—BLDSC (1940.350000), IE, Infotrieve, Ingenta, INIST.
Published by: University of California, Berkeley, Sociology Department, 410 Barrows Hall, Berkeley, CA 94720-. TEL 510-642-4766, FAX 510-642-0659.

BERKELEY LA RAZA LAW JOURNAL. *see* LAW

BERLINER BEITRAEGE ZUR ETHNOLOGIE. *see* ANTHROPOLOGY

302.23 DEU ISSN 1612-4464
BERLINER BEITRAEGE ZUR MEDIENGESCHICHTE. Text in German. 2003. irreg., latest vol.2, 2006. price varies. **Document type:** *Monographic series, Academic/Scholarly.*
Published by: Weissensee Verlag e.K., Simplonstr 59, Berlin, 10245, Germany. TEL 49-30-29049192, FAX 49-30-27574315, mail@weissensee-verlag.de.

301 DEU ISSN 0863-1808
HM5 CODEN: BJSOE8
➤ **BERLINER JOURNAL FUER SOZIOLOGIE.** Text in German. 1991. 4/yr. EUR 260.75, USD 321 combined subscription to institutions (print & online eds.) (effective 2012). adv. bk.rev. reprint service avail. from PSC. **Document type:** *Journal, Academic/Scholarly.*
Related titles: Online - full text ed.: ISSN 1862-2593.
Indexed: A20, A22, A26, ASCA, CA, CurCont, DIP, E01, FR, IBR, IBSS, IBZ, P10, P30, P42, P46, P48, PCI, PQC, PSA, S02, S03, SCOPUS, SOPODA, SSA, SSCI, SociolAb, T02, W07.
—IE, Infotrieve, Ingenta. **CCC.**
Published by: (Institut fuer Soziologie), V S - Verlag fuer Sozialwissenschaften (Subsidiary of: Springer Fachmedien Wiesbaden GmbH), Abraham-Lincoln-Str 46, Wiesbaden, 65189, Germany. TEL 49-611-78780, FAX 49-611-7878400, springerfachmedien-wiesbaden@springer.com, http://www.vs-verlag.de.

302.23 DEU ISSN 1869-0041
▼ **BERLINER SCHRIFTEN ZUR MEDIENWISSENSCHAFT.** Text in German. 2009. irreg., latest vol.9, 2009. price varies. **Document type:** *Monographic series, Academic/Scholarly.*
Related titles: Online - full text ed.: ISSN 1869-005X. 2009.
Published by: Technische Universitaet Berlin, Universitaetsbibliothek, Fasanenstr 88, Berlin, 10623, Germany. TEL 49-30-31476131, FAX 49-30-31476133, publikationen@ub.tu-berlin.de. Ed. Jakob Dittmar.

BETA ONLINE; technology - culture. *see* TECHNOLOGY: COMPREHENSIVE WORKS

302.23 ESP ISSN 2172-2781
BIBLIOTECA DE CIENCIAS DE LA COMUNICACION. Text in Spanish. 2004. a. **Document type:** *Monographic series, Academic/Scholarly.*
Published by: Editorial Fragua, C Andres Mellado, 64, Madrid, 28015, Spain. TEL 34-91-5491806, FAX 34-91-5431794, pedidos@editorialfragua.com, http://www.editorialfragua.com/.

306 ITA ISSN 1972-0246
BIBLIOTECA. LE MAPPE; cultura e societa. Text in Italian. 1982. irreg., latest vol.8, 1995. price varies. adv. **Document type:** *Monographic series, Academic/Scholarly.*
Published by: Liguori Editore, Via Posillipo 394, Naples, 80123, Italy. TEL 39-081-7206111, FAX 39-081-7206244, liguori@liguori.it, http://www.liguori.it. Eds. G Bechelloni, G Pagliano. Pub. Guido Liguori. Adv. contact Maria Liguori.

302.23 ITA ISSN 1972-0297
BIBLIOTECA. SOCIOLOGIA DEI MEDIA. Text in Italian. 1988. irreg., latest vol.12, 1999. price varies. adv. **Document type:** *Monographic series, Academic/Scholarly.*
Published by: Liguori Editore, Via Posillipo 394, Naples, 80123, Italy. TEL 39-081-7206111, FAX 39-081-7206244, liguori@liguori.it, http://www.liguori.it. Eds. Giovanni Bechelloni, Milly Buonanno. Pub. Guido Liguori. Adv. contact Maria Liguori.

301 DEU ISSN 1866-5055
BIBLIOTHECA ACADEMICA. REIHE SOZIOLOGIE. Text in German. 2000. irreg., latest vol.7, 2009. price varies. **Document type:** *Monographic series, Academic/Scholarly.*
Published by: Ergon Verlag, Keesburgstr 11, Wuerzburg, 97074, Germany. TEL 49-931-280084, FAX 49-931-282872, service@ergon-verlag.de, http://www.ergon-verlag.de.

307 DEU ISSN 0171-7537
BIELEFELDER STUDIEN ZUR ENTWICKLUNGSSOZIOLOGIE. Text in German. 1978. irreg., latest vol.65, 1997. price varies. **Document type:** *Monographic series, Academic/Scholarly.*
Indexed: IBR, IBZ.
Published by: Verlag fuer Entwicklungspolitik Saarbruecken GmbH, Auf der Adt 14, Saarbruecken, 66130, Germany. TEL 49-6893-986094, FAX 49-6893-986095, vfe@verlag-entwicklungspolitik.de.

305 CAN ISSN 1718-7346
BIEN GRANDIR. Text in French. 2001. m. **Document type:** *Magazine, Consumer.*
Former titles (until 2005): Jasette (1709-9315); (until 2003): Jasette Officielle (1499-0008)
Published by: Fondation Lucie et Andre Chagnon, 2001 McGill College Ave., Ste. 1000, Montreal, PQ H3A 1G1, Canada. TEL 514-380-2001, FAX 514-380-8434, info@fondationchagnon.org, http://www.fondationchagnon.org.

301 CHL ISSN 0718-1132
HT101
➤ **BIFURCACIONES.** Text in Spanish. 2004. q. free (effective 2011). **Document type:** *Journal, Academic/Scholarly.*
Media: Online - full text.
Indexed: C01. Ed. Ricardo F Greene.

305.569 AUS ISSN 1326-639X
THE BIG ISSUE. Text in English. 1996. fortn. AUD 155; AUD 5 newsstand/cover (effective 2008). adv. back issues avail. **Document type:** *Magazine, Consumer.* **Description:** Committed to all forms of social justice, it features articles and images on a range of subjects including arts and entertainment, current affairs, street culture and lifestyle.
Related titles: ◆ Regional ed(s).: Big Issue. ISSN 0967-5000; ◆ Big Issue Cape Town. ISSN 1608-0378; ◆ Big Issue Namibia. ISSN 1684-2642.
Published by: The Big Issue Australia, 148 Lonsdale St, GPO Box 4911VV, Melbourne, VIC 3001, Australia. TEL 61-3-96634533, FAX 61-3-96634252, bigissue@bigissue.org.au. Ed. Alan Attwood. Adv. contact John Currey. page AUD 2,200; trim 190 x 250. Circ: 29,000.

306.43 DEU ISSN 1619-9561
BILDUNG IN UMBRUCHSGESELLSCHAFTEN. Text in German. 2002. irreg., latest vol.8, 2009. price varies. **Document type:** *Monographic series, Academic/Scholarly.*
Published by: Waxmann Verlag GmbH, Steinfurter Str 555, Muenster, 48159, Germany. TEL 49-251-265040, FAX 49-251-2650426, info@waxmann.com, http://www.waxmann.com. Eds. Ursula Neumann, Wolfram Weisse.

BIOETICA & SOCIETA. *see* BIOLOGY

BIOSECURITY BULLETIN. *see* PUBLIC HEALTH AND SAFETY

156 GBR
BIOSOCIAL SOCIETY SYMPOSIUM SERIES. Text in English. 1988. irreg., latest vol.15, 2003. price varies. back issues avail.; reprints avail. **Document type:** *Monographic series, Academic/Scholarly.* **Description:** Examines topics and issues of biological and social importance and promotes studies of biosocial matters.
Formerly (until 199?): Biosocial Society Series (0958-6539)
—**CCC.**
Published by: Cambridge University Press, The Edinburgh Bldg, Shaftesbury Rd, Cambridge, CB2 8RU, United Kingdom. TEL 44-1223-312393, FAX 44-1223-315052, journals@cambridge.org, http://www.cambridge.org/uk. Ed. Catherine Panter-Brick.

BISEXUAL RESOURCE GUIDE. *see* HOMOSEXUALITY

306 363.7 USA ISSN 1548-9620
BISHOP MUSEUM BULLETINS IN CULTURAL AND ENVIRONMENTAL STUDIES. Text in English. 2004. irreg., latest vol.4, 2009. price varies. back issues avail. **Document type:** *Monographic series, Academic/Scholarly.*
Related titles: Online - full text ed.: free (effective 2010).
Indexed: Z01.
Published by: (Bernice Pauahi Bishop Museum), Bishop Museum Press, 1525 Bernice St, Honolulu, HI 96817. TEL 808-847-3511, FAX 808-841-8968, press@bishopmuseum.org, http://www.bishopmuseum.org.

306 058.7 SWE ISSN 1654-5370
BIZ&ART; ett magasin om kultur och affaersliv i Uppsala. Text in Swedish. 2007. q. adv. **Document type:** *Magazine, Consumer.* **Description:** Covers current cultural life in Uppsala.
Address: Oevre Slottsgatan 6, Stockholm, 75310, Sweden. TEL 46-18-262600, FAX 46-18-262606, kontakt@bizart.se, http://www.bizart.se. Eds. Lillemor Berg, Stewen Quigley.

302.23 AUS ISSN 1443-4342
THE BLACK BOOK DIRECTORY. Variant title: Indigenous Arts & Media Directory. Text in English. 2000. a. free (effective 2008). **Document type:** *Directory, Trade.* **Description:** Lists more than 2,700 indigenous people and organizations working in the arts, media and cultural industries.
Related titles: Online - full text ed.
Published by: Blackfella Films, PO Box 1714, Strawberry Hills, NSW 2012, Australia. TEL 61-2-93804000, FAX 61-2-93195030.

302.23 384.558 NLD ISSN 1877-5802
BLIK. Text in Dutch. 2006. 3/yr. EUR 14.95 to individuals; EUR 24.95 to institutions; EUR 9.95 to students; EUR 4.95 newsstand/cover (effective 2011). **Document type:** *Magazine, Academic/Scholarly.*
Published by: (Universiteit Utrecht, Departement Media- en Cultuurwetenschappen), Stichting BLIK, Muntstraat 2A, Utrecht, 3512 EV, Netherlands. Ed. Rob van Grinsven.

BLINK. *see* BUSINESS AND ECONOMICS—Marketing And Purchasing

301 AUS ISSN 1832-2107
BOB WHITE MEMORIAL LECTURE. Text in English. 2003. a., latest 2006. free (effective 2009). back issues avail. **Document type:** *Monographic series, Academic/Scholarly.*
Related titles: Online - full text ed.
Published by: University of Tasmania, School of Sociology and Social Work, Private Bag 17, Hobart, TAS 7001, Australia. TEL 61-3-62262186, FAX 61-3-62262279, Secretary@sociol.utas.edu.au, http://fcms.its.utas.edu.au/arts/sociology.

303.4 USA
BODY, COMMODITY, TEXT. Text in English. 1996. irreg. price varies. back issues avail.; reprints avail. **Document type:** *Monographic series, Academic/Scholarly.*
Published by: Duke University Press, 905 W Main St, Ste 18 B, Durham, NC 27701. TEL 888-651-0122, FAX 888-651-0124, subscriptions@dukeupress.edu.

301 ESP ISSN 2172-9190
▼ **BOLETIN ANELIER.** Text in Spanish. 2010. a. **Document type:** *Bulletin, Consumer.*
Published by: Asociacion Cultural Anelier, C Monasterio de Vadolvengo, 4 1o. D, Pamplona, 31008, Spain. TEL 34-675-639423, asociacion.anelier@gmail.com.

BOLETIN REFORME. *see* PUBLIC ADMINISTRATION

301 URY ISSN 0006-6508
BOLETIN URUGUAYO DE SOCIOLOGIA. Text in Spanish; Summaries in English, French, Portuguese, Spanish. 1961. q. USD 6. adv. bk.rev. abstr.; bibl.; charts; stat. index.
Published by: Mario Bon Espasandin, Ed. & Pub., Calle Juncal 1395, Piso 2, Escritorio 5, Montevideo, Uruguay. Circ: 1,500.

302.23 DEU ISSN 1617-8432
BONNER BEITRAEGE ZUR MEDIENWISSENSCHAFT. Text in German. 2002. irreg., latest vol.9, 2009. price varies. **Document type:** *Monographic series, Academic/Scholarly.*
Published by: Peter Lang GmbH (Subsidiary of: Peter Lang Publishing Group), Eschborner Landstr 42-50, Frankfurt Am Main, 60489, Germany. TEL 49-69-7807050, FAX 49-69-78070550, zentrale.frankfurt@peterlang.com. Ed. Caja Thimm.

307.14 DEU ISSN 0721-815X
BONNER STUDIEN ZUR LAENDLICHEN ENTWICKLUNG IN DER DRITTEN WELT. Text in German. 1982. irreg., latest vol.17, 1992. price varies. **Document type:** *Monographic series, Academic/Scholarly.*
Published by: Verlag fuer Entwicklungspolitik Saarbruecken GmbH, Auf der Adt 14, Saarbruecken, 66130, Germany. TEL 49-6893-986094, FAX 49-6893-986095, vfe@verlag-entwicklungspolitik.de.

301 GBR ISSN 0007-1315
HM1
➤ **BRITISH JOURNAL OF SOCIOLOGY.** Abbreviated title: B J S. Text in English. 1950. q. GBP 342 in United Kingdom to institutions; EUR 436 in Europe to institutions; USD 623 in the Americas to institutions; USD 670 elsewhere to institutions; GBP 375 combined subscription in United Kingdom to institutions (print & online eds.); EUR 480 combined subscription in Europe to institutions (print & online eds.); USD 683 combined subscription in the Americas to institutions (print & online eds.); USD 736 combined subscription elsewhere to institutions (print & online eds.) (effective 2012). adv. bk.rev. illus. index, cum.index every 10 yrs. back issues avail.; reprint service avail. from PSC. **Document type:** *Journal, Academic/Scholarly.* **Description:** Covers the entire span of sociological thought and research.
Related titles: Microfilm ed.: (from WMP); Online - full text ed.: ISSN 1468-4446. GBP 326 in United Kingdom to institutions; EUR 415 in Europe to institutions; USD 591 in the Americas to institutions; USD 636 elsewhere to institutions (effective 2012) (from IngentaConnect).
Indexed: A01, A02, A03, A08, A12, A17, A20, A21, A22, A26, ABIn, AC&P, AEI, AICP, AMHA, ASCA, AbAn, AmH&L, B02, B04, B05, B15, B17, B18, BAS, BRD, C28, CA, CJPI, CMM, CPM, CommAb, CurCont, DIP, E-psyche, E01, E08, EI, EMBASE, ESPM, ExcerpMed, F09, FR, FamI, G04, G08, H09, H10, HECAB, HistAb, I05, I13, IBR, IBSS, IBZ, ILD, IndMed, MEA&I, MEDLINE, MLA-IB, MResA, P02, P03, P06, P10, P27, P30, P34, P42, P48, P51, P53, P54, PCI, PQC, PRA, PSA, PsycInfo, PsycholAb, R05, R10, RASB, RI-1, RI-2, RILM, Reac, RiskAb, S02, S03, S05, S09, S11, SCIMP, SCOPUS, SOPODA, SSA, SSAI, SSAb, SSCI, SSI, SociolAb, T02, W03, W07, W09.
—BLDSC (2324.800000), IE, Infotrieve, Ingenta, INIST. **CCC.**
Published by: (London School of Economics and Political Science), Wiley-Blackwell Publishing Ltd. (Subsidiary of: John Wiley & Sons, Inc.), 9600 Garsington Rd, Oxford, OX4 2DQ, United Kingdom. TEL 44-1865-776868, FAX 44-1865-714591, customerservices@blackwellpublishing.com. Eds. Fran Tonkiss, Richard Wright. Adv. contact Craig Pickett TEL 44-1865-476267. page GBP 225; trim 190 x 115. Circ: 2,700.

➤ **BRITISH JOURNAL OF SOCIOLOGY OF EDUCATION.** *see* EDUCATION

307.76 USA ISSN 1528-7084
HT101
BROOKINGS-WHARTON PAPERS ON URBAN AFFAIRS (YEAR). Text in English. 2000. a. USD 36 per issue (effective 2010). 250 p./no.; back issues avail. **Document type:** *Monographic series, Academic/Scholarly.* **Description:** Serves as a forum for research on urban areas and issues such as urban sprawl, crime, taxes, education, poverty.
Related titles: Online - full content ed.: ISSN 1533-4449. 2000.
Indexed: A01, A03, A08, A12, A17, A22, ABIn, B01, B06, B07, B09, CA, E01, EconLit, JEL, P05, P10, P27, P46, P48, P51, P53, P54, PQC, S02, S03, SCOPUS, SSAI, SSAb, SSI, T02, W03, W05.
—**CCC.**
Published by: Brookings Institution Press, 1775 Massachusetts Ave, NW, Washington, DC 20036. TEL 202-797-6000, 800-275-1447, FAX 202-536-3623, communications@brookings.edu.

306 USA ISSN 1946-1437
BROWNBAG. Text in English. 2006. q. free (effective 2009). back issues avail. **Document type:** *Magazine, Consumer.* **Description:** Provides news and opinion on the arts, culture and society in the New York area and beyond.
Media: Online - full content.
Published by: Brownscape Productions, PO Box 2161, New York, NY 10101. info@brownscapeprod.com. Ed. Noel Agnew.

302.23 DEU
BUCKOWER MEDIENGESPRAECHE. Text in German. 2001. irreg., latest vol.14, 2011. price varies. **Document type:** *Monographic series, Academic/Scholarly.*
Published by: KoPaed Verlag, Pfaelzer-Wald-Str 64, Munich, 81539, Germany. TEL 49-89-68890098, FAX 49-89-6891912, info@kopaed.de, http://www.kopaed.de.

301 CAN ISSN 1923-7871
THE BULLET. Text in English. 2005. d. free (effective 2011). back issues avail. **Document type:** *Bulletin, Trade.* **Description:** To encourage principled debate amongst the left and the working class to advance a viable socialist movement in Canada.
Media: Online - full text.
Published by: Socialist Project, PO Box 85, Sta E, Toronto, ON M6H 4E1, Canada. info@socialistproject.ca.

THE BULLETIN; news and reports from the Social Issues Team. *see* RELIGIONS AND THEOLOGY—Protestant

301 GBR ISSN 0759-1063
HM585
➤ **BULLETIN DE METHODOLOGIE SOCIOLOGIQUE/BULLETIN OF SOCIOLOGICAL METHODOLOGY.** Variant title: B M S. Text in French. 1983. s-a. USD 378, GBP 205 combined subscription to institutions (print & online eds.); USD 370, GBP 201 to institutions (effective 2011). reprint service avail. from PSC. **Document type:** *Journal, Academic/Scholarly.*
Related titles: Online - full text ed.: ISSN 2070-2779. USD 340, GBP 185 to institutions (effective 2011).
Indexed: A22, CA, E01, FR, P30, P42, PSA, S02, S03, SCOPUS, SSA, SociolAb, T02.
—BLDSC (2879.600000), IE, Ingenta, INIST. **CCC.**
Published by: (Association Internationale de Methodologie Sociologique FRA), Sage Publications Ltd. (Subsidiary of: Sage Publications, Inc.), 1 Oliver's Yard, 55 City Rd, London, EC1Y 1SP, United Kingdom. TEL 44-20-73248500, FAX 44-20-73248733, info@sagepub.co.uk, http://www.uk.sagepub.com/home.nav. Ed. Karl Van Meter.

➤ **BUMMMEI/CIVILIZATIONS.** *see* ANTHROPOLOGY

➤ **BUSINESS, CULTURE AND CHANGE.** *see* BUSINESS AND ECONOMICS

➤ **C**; magazine over communicatie. *see* BUSINESS AND ECONOMICS—Management

➤ **C A P SULE (LEVITTOWN).** (Children of Aging Parents) *see* GERONTOLOGY AND GERIATRICS

301 DNK ISSN 0905-7218
C A S A NYT; alternativ samfundsanalyse. (Center for Alternativ Samfundsanalyse) Text in Danish. 1990. irreg. free (effective 2004). back issues avail. **Document type:** *Bulletin, Consumer.*
Related titles: Online - full text ed.: ISSN 1902-1194.
Published by: Center for Alternativ Samfunds-Analyse/Centre for Alternative Social Analysis, Linnesgade 25, Copenhagen K, 1361, Denmark. TEL 45-33-320555, FAX 45-33-330554, casa@casa-analyse.dk. Ed. Karl Vogt-Nielsen.

301 BRA ISSN 0102-9711
HN281
C E A S CADERNOS. (Centro de Estudos e Acao Social) Text in Portuguese. 1969. bi-m. BRL 25; USD 50 foreign. adv. bk.rev. bibl.; charts; stat. **Document type:** *Academic/Scholarly.*
Indexed: C01, HRIR, IBR, IBZ, ILD, RASB.
Published by: Centro de Estudos e Acao Social (C E A S), Rua Professor Aristides Novis, 101, Federacao, Salvador, BA 40210-630, Brazil. TEL 55-71-2471232, FAX 55-71-3320680. Eds. Alfredo Sousa Dorea, Paulo Sergio Vaillant. Adv. contact Armando Brazlim. Circ: 1,500.

C E D E S CADERNOS. *see* EDUCATION

301 ESP ISSN 1695-6494
HM621
➤ **C E I C. PAPELES.** (Centro de Estudios sobre la Identidad Colectiva) Text in Spanish, English, French. 2001. 5/yr. free (effective 2011). **Document type:** *Journal, Academic/Scholarly.*
Media: Online - full text.
Indexed: F04, P46, SociolAb.
Published by: Universidad del Pais Vasco, Centro de Estudios sobre la Identidad Colectiva, Departamento de Sociologia 2, Campus de Leioa s/n, Leioa, Vizcaya 48940, Spain. TEL 34-94-6015093, FAX 34-94-4648299, cjxsceic@lg.ehu.es.

301 ITA ISSN 1128-9163
C E N S I S NOTE E COMMENTI. Text in Italian. 1965. m. EUR 44 domestic; EUR 90 foreign (effective 2008). stat. index. **Document type:** *Journal, Academic/Scholarly.* **Description:** Investigates and interprets the most significant events in the Italian socio-economic and cultural phenomenology and in the sectors of social policy.
Formerly: C E N S I S Quindicinale di Note e Commenti (0007-8271)
Published by: Centro Studi Investimenti Sociali, Piazza di Novella 2, Rome, 00199, Italy. TEL 39-06-860911, FAX 39-06-86211367, http://www.censis.it. Circ: 4,500.

305.8 GBR ISSN 1753-1381
C F S R. Variant title: Journal of the Centre for Study and Research. Text in English. 2006. a. GBP 50 domestic; GBP 90 foreign (effective 2009). **Document type:** *Journal, Academic/Scholarly.*
—BLDSC (3128.522900).
Published by: Centre for Study and Research, Stewarts House, Kingsway East, Dundee, Scotland DD4 7RE, United Kingdom. info@cfsr-uk.com, http://www.cfsr.org.uk. Ed. Iqbal M Mostafa.

305.8 NZL ISSN 1176-9971
C I G A D BRIEFING NOTES. (Centre for Indigenous Governance and Development) Text in English. 2005. irreg. **Document type:** *Monographic series, Academic/Scholarly.*
Media: Online - full text.
Published by: Massey University, Centre for Indigenous Governance and Development, Private Bag 11 222, Palmerston North, New Zealand. TEL 64-6-3569099 ext. 2869, FAX 64-6-3505737, http://cigad.massey.ac.nz.

305.8 NZL ISSN 1176-9025
C I G A D WORKING PAPER SERIES. (Centre for Indigenous Governance and Development) Text in English. 2005. irreg., latest 2006. **Document type:** *Monographic series, Academic/Scholarly.*
Media: Online - full text.
Published by: Massey University, Centre for Indigenous Governance and Development, Private Bag 11 222, Palmerston North, New Zealand. TEL 64-6-3569099 ext. 2869, FAX 64-6-3505737, http://cigad.massey.ac.nz.

307.14 DEU ISSN 0722-9232
C I M - ARBEITSMATERIALIEN. Text in German. 1982. irreg., latest vol.7, 1987. price varies. **Document type:** *Monographic series, Academic/Scholarly.*
Published by: (Centrum fuer Internationale Migration und Entwicklung), Verlag fuer Entwicklungspolitik Saarbruecken GmbH, Auf der Adt 14, Saarbruecken, 66130, Germany. TEL 49-6893-986094, FAX 49-6893-986095, vfe@verlag-entwicklungspolitik.de.

C I R E S CAHIERS. *see* BUSINESS AND ECONOMICS

306.941 GBR ISSN 1749-7108
C L S BRIEFINGS. (Centre for Longitudinal Studies) Text in English. 2005. q. free (effective 2006). **Document type:** *Journal, Academic/Scholarly.* **Description:** Provide examples of findings from the three cohort studies.
Related titles: Online - full text ed.: ISSN 1749-7116.
Published by: (Bedford Group for Lifecourse & Statistical Studies), Institute of Education, Centre for Longitudinal Studies, 20 Bedford Way, London, WC1H 0AL, United Kingdom. TEL 44-20-76126860, FAX 44-20-76126880, clsfeedback@ioe.ac.uk.

301 FRA ISSN 1242-8671
C N R S SOCIOLOGIE. (Centre Nationale de la Recherche Scientifique) Text in French. 1993. irreg. price varies. **Document type:** *Monographic series, Academic/Scholarly.*
Published by: Centre National de la Recherche Scientifique, Campus Gerard-Megie, 3 Rue Michel-Ange, Paris, 75794, France. TEL 33-1-44964000, FAX 33-1-44965390, http://www.cnrseditions.fr.

301 CAN ISSN 1484-8619
C R C C F. (Centre de Recherche en Civilisation Canadienne-Francaise) Text in French. 1997. m. **Document type:** *Bulletin, Academic/Scholarly.*
Related titles: Online - full text ed.: ISSN 1719-8119.
Published by: University of Ottawa, Centre de Recherche en Civilisation Canadienne-Francaise, Universite d'Ottawa, Pavillon Lamoureux, piece 271, 145, rue Jean-Jacques-Lussier, Ottawa, ON K1N 6N5, Canada. TEL 613-562-5877, FAX 613-562-5143, crccf@uottawa.ca, http://www.uottawa.ca/academic/crccf.

301 GBR ISSN 2042-2075
▼ **C R R S BRIEFING PAPER SERIES.** (Centre for Remote and Rural Studies) Text in English. 2009. irreg., latest 2010. free (effective 2010). back issues avail. **Document type:** *Monographic series, Trade.* **Description:** Provides accessible summaries of research on a particular topic, evaluate and recommend particular policy options in relation to a topic or summarise a particular research project and extract policy messages.
Related titles: Online - full text ed.: ISSN 2042-2083.
Published by: U H I Centre for Remote and Rural Studies, Academy Lodge, Crown Ave, Inverness, IV2 3NG, United Kingdom. TEL 44-1463-273563, FAX 44-1463-273569, crrs@uhi.ac.uk.

301 GBR ISSN 0969-8914
C R S P ANNUAL REPORT. Text in English. 1991. a. free. **Document type:** *Corporate.*
Published by: (Loughborough University, Department of Social Sciences), Centre for Research in Social Policy (Subsidiary of: Loughborough University, Department of Social Sciences), Department of Social Sciences, Loughborough University, Loughborough, Leics LE11 3TU, United Kingdom. TEL 44-1509-223372, FAX 44-1509-213409, crsp@lboro.ac.uk. Ed. Laura Adelman.

THE C S I HANDBOOK. (Corporate Social Investment) *see* BUSINESS AND ECONOMICS—Investments

C THEORY. *see* POLITICAL SCIENCE

301 USA ISSN 0749-8799
C U B COMMUNICATOR. Text in English. 1976. m. USD 50; USD 65 foreign. adv. bk.rev. **Document type:** *Newspaper.*
Published by: Concerned United Birthparents, Inc., 503475, San Diego, CA 92150-3475. TEL 800-822-2777. Ed. Marylee MacDonald. Circ: 2,500.

302.23 USA
C U B COMMUNICATOR. ADOPTION NEWSLETTER. Text in English. 1978. m. USD 50 membership. **Document type:** *Newsletter.* **Description:** Contains news and articles about adoption and letters and articles by or about birthparents.
Published by: Concerned United Birthparents, Inc., 503475, San Diego, CA 92150-3475. TEL 800-822-2777. Ed. Marylee MacDonald.

301 BRA ISSN 1809-1814
CADERNOS DE SOCIOLOGIA E POLITICA. Text in Portuguese. 1995. a. back issues avail. **Document type:** *Journal, Academic/Scholarly.*
Published by: Instituto Universitario de Pesquisas do Rio de Janeiro, Rua da Matriz, 82, Botafogo, Rio De Janeiro, RJ 22260-100, Brazil. TEL 55-21-25378020, FAX 55-21-22867146, http://www.iuperj.br/index.php.

CADERNOS DE SOCIOMUSEOLOGIA. *see* MUSEUMS AND ART GALLERIES

301 BRA ISSN 0104-8333
HQ1541
CADERNOS PAGU. Text in Portuguese, Spanish. 1993. s-a. back issues avail. **Document type:** *Journal, Academic/Scholarly.* **Description:** Aims to enlarge and consolidate the gender studies field in Brazil.
Related titles: Online - full text ed.: ISSN 1809-4449. 2004. free (effective 2011).
Indexed: C01, CA, DIP, H21, IBR, IBZ, MLA-IB, P08, P42, PSA, S02, S03, SCOPUS, SSA, SociolAb, T02, W09.
Published by: Universidade Estadual de Campinas, Nucleo de Estudos de Genero-Pagu, Campinas, SP 13083-970, Brazil. TEL 55-19-37887873, FAX 55-19-37881704, pagu@unicamp.br, http://www.unicamp.br/pagu/.

301 BRA ISSN 0102-6518
CADERNOS RIOARTE. Text in Portuguese. 1985. 2/yr.
Published by: Instituto Municipal de Arte e Cultura, Rua Rumania, 20, Laranjeiras, Rio De Janeiro, RJ 22240-140, Brazil.

CAG UNIVERSITY JOURNAL OF SOCIAL SCIENCES. *see* BUSINESS AND ECONOMICS

CAHIERS CRITIQUES DE THERAPIE FAMILIALE ET DE PRATIQUES DE RESEAUX. *see* PSYCHOLOGY

301 FRA ISSN 1292-6930
LES CAHIERS DE LA MEDIATION. Text in French. 1999. q. **Document type:** *Magazine, Trade.*
Published by: Centre National de la Mediation, 127 Rue Notre Dame des Champs, Paris, 75006, France. TEL 33-1-40460001.

CAHIERS DE PRAXEMATIQUE. *see* LINGUISTICS

301 CAN ISSN 0831-1048
HM3C32 CODEN: CARSEV
CAHIERS DE RECHERCHE SOCIOLOGIQUE. Text in English. 1983. s-a.
Indexed: CA, FR, P30, P42, PAIS, PSA, PdeR, RILM, S02, S03, SOPODA, SSA, SociolAb, T02.
—INIST.
Published by: Universite du Quebec a Montreal, C.P. 8888, Succ. A, Montreal, PQ H3C 3P8, Canada. TEL 514-987-4380. Ed. Jean-Guy Lacroix.

306.4 FRA ISSN 0761-9871
GN502
CAHIERS DE SOCIOLOGIE ECONOMIQUE ET CULTURELLE. Text in French. 1984. s-a. EUR 35 domestic; EUR 38 foreign (effective 2009). back issues avail.; reprints avail. **Document type:** *Journal, Academic/Scholarly.*
Formed by the merger of (1959-1982): Cahiers de Sociologie Economique (0007-9987); (1946-1982): Ethnopsychologie (0046-2608); Which was formerly (until 1970): Revue de Psychologie des Peuples (0035-1717)
Related titles: Microform ed.: (from SWZ).
Indexed: ASD, BAS, CA, DIP, FR, IBR, IBSS, IBZ, MLA-IB, P42, PAIS, PCI, PSA, PsycholAb, RILM, S02, S03, SCOPUS, SOPODA, SSA, SociolAb, T02.
—INIST. **CCC.**
Published by: Institut Havrais de Sociologie Economique et Culturelle, 56 rue Anatole France, Le Havre, 76600, France. TEL 33-2-35424755, FAX 33-2-35424755, albert.gueissaz@sfr.fr. Ed. Jean-Pierre Castelain.

303.4 FRA ISSN 1955-9798
LES CAHIERS DE SOL ET CIVILISATION. Text in French. 2007. a.
Published by: Sol et Civilisation, 5 Rue Joseph et Marie Hackin, Paris, 75016, France. TEL 33-1-44311661, FAX 33-1-44311674, soletcivilisation@soletcivilisation.fr.

301 FRA ISSN 0989-5191
CAHIERS DU BRESIL CONTEMPORAIN. Text in French. 1987. q. **Document type:** *Academic/Scholarly.*
Related titles: Online - full text ed.: ISSN 2105-1240. 200?.
Indexed: FR.
Published by: Ecole des Hautes Etudes en Sciences Sociales, Centre de Recherches sur le Bresil Contemporain (Subsidiary of: Ecole des Hautes Etudes en Sciences Sociales), 190-198 Av de France, Salles 419 a 422, Paris, 75013, France. TEL 33-1-49542085, http://www.ehess.fr/crbc.

301 FRA ISSN 1298-6046
CAHIERS DU GENRE. Text in French. 1991. q. EUR 45 domestic; EUR 50 foreign (effective 2008). **Document type:** *Journal, Academic/Scholarly.*
Formerly (until 1999): G E D I S S T. Cahiers (1165-3558)
Indexed: FR, IBSS, SD.
Published by: L' Harmattan, 5 Rue de l'Ecole Polytechnique, Paris, 75005, France. TEL 33-1-43257651, FAX 33-1-43258203, http://www.editions-harmattan.fr.

305.3 FRA ISSN 1633-5708
CAHIERS GENRE ET DEVELOPPEMENT. Text in French. 2000. a. **Document type:** *Journal, Academic/Scholarly.*
Published by: L' Harmattan, 5 Rue de l'Ecole Polytechnique, Paris, 75005, France. TEL 33-1-43257651, FAX 33-1-43258203.

CAHIERS LENDEMAINS. *see* LITERARY AND POLITICAL REVIEWS

CAHIERS LILLOIS D'ECONOMIE ET DE SOCIOLOGIE. *see* BUSINESS AND ECONOMICS—Economic Situation And Conditions

306 ROM ISSN 1582-960X
DR201
CAIETELE ECHINOX. Text in multiple languages. 2001. s-a. **Document type:** *Journal, Academic/Scholarly.*
Indexed: AmHI, CA, H07, MLA-IB, T02.
Published by: (Fundatia Culturala Echinox), Universitatea "Babes-Bolyai", Centrul de Cercetare a Imaginarului, Mihail Kogalniceanu 1, Cluj-Napoca, 40082, Romania. TEL 40-264-405300, FAX 40-264-591906, staff@staff.ubbcluj.ro, http://www.ubbcluj.ro.

CALIFORNIA FAMILY LAW: PRACTICE AND PROCEDURE. *see* LAW—Family And Matrimonial Law

301 USA
CALIFORNIA STUDIES IN CRITICAL HUMAN GEOGRAPHY. Text in English. 1997. irreg., latest vol.9, 2004. price varies. back issues avail. **Document type:** *Monographic series, Academic/Scholarly.*
Related titles: Online - full text ed.
Published by: University of California Press, Book Series, 2120 Berkeley Way, Berkeley, CA 94704. TEL 510-642-4247, FAX 510-643-7127, foundation@ucpress.edu. **Subscr. to:** California - Princeton Fulfillment Services, Inc., 1445 Lower Ferry Rd, Ewing, NJ 08618. TEL 609-883-1759, 800-777-4726, FAX 800-999-1958, orders@cpfsinc.com.

301 ROM ISSN 1018-0389
CALITATEA VIETII. Text in Romanian. 1990. 4/yr.
Related titles: Online - full text ed.
Indexed: PAIS, RASB, SociolAb.
Published by: (Academia Romana/Romanian Academy, Institutul de Cercetarea Calitatii Vietii), Editura Academiei Romane/Publishing House of the Romanian Academy, Calea 13 Septembrie 13, Sector 5, Bucharest, 050711, Romania. TEL 40-21-3188146, FAX 40-21-3182444, edacad@ear.ro. Ed. Catalin Zamfir. **Dist. by:** Rodipet S.A., Piata Presei Libere 1, sector 1, PO Box 33-57, Bucharest 3, Romania. TEL 40-21-2226407, 40-21-2224126, rodipet@rodipet.ro.

301 ITA
CAMBIAMENTO SOCIALE IN EUROPA. Text in Italian. 1995. irreg., latest vol.4, 1999. price varies. adv. **Document type:** *Monographic series, Academic/Scholarly.*
Published by: Liguori Editore, Via Posillipo 394, Naples, 80123, Italy. TEL 39-081-7206111, FAX 39-081-7206244, liguori@liguori.it, http://www.liguori.it. Pub. Guido Liguori. Adv. contact Maria Liguori.

CAMBRIDGE JOURNAL OF REGIONS, ECONOMY AND SOCIETY. *see* POLITICAL SCIENCE

S

301 GBR ISSN 1754-9876
CAMBRIDGE STUDIES IN SOCIETY AND THE LIFE SCIENCES. Text in English. 2004. irreg., latest 2007. price varies. adv. back issues avail.; reprints avail. **Document type:** *Monographic series, Academic/Scholarly.* **Description:** Promotes interdisciplinary works in the social sciences that focus on the social shaping, social meaning and social implications of recent developments in the life sciences.
Published by: Cambridge University Press, The Edinburgh Bldg, Shaftesbury Rd, Cambridge, CB2 8RU, United Kingdom. TEL 44-1223-312393, FAX 44-1223-315052, journals@cambridge.org, http://www.cambridge.org/uk. Eds. Michael Morange, Patrick Bateson, Paul Billinge.

302.23 GBR
CAMBRIDGE STUDIES IN THE HISTORY OF MASS COMMUNICATION. Text in English. 1996. irreg., latest 2009. price varies. adv. back issues avail.; reprints avail. **Document type:** *Monographic series, Academic/Scholarly.* **Description:** Examines communications processes and systems within social, cultural, and political contexts.
Published by: Cambridge University Press, The Edinburgh Bldg, Shaftesbury Rd, Cambridge, CB2 8RU, United Kingdom. TEL 44-1223-312393, FAX 44-1223-315052, journals@cambridge.org, http://www.cambridge.org/uk. Eds. David Culbert, Garth Jowett, Kenneth Short.

CAMPUS REVIEW. *see* LITERARY AND POLITICAL REVIEWS

305.26 CAN ISSN 1706-3086
HQ1064.C2
CANADIAN INSTITUTES OF HEALTH RESEARCH. INSTITUTE OF AGING. ANNUAL REPORT OF ACTIVITIES. Variant title: Instituts de Recherche en Sante du Canada. Institut du Viellissement. Rapport Annuel des Activites. Text in English, French. 2002. a.
Related titles: ◆ Online - full text ed.: Canadian Institutes of Health Research. Institute of Aging. Biennial Report. ISSN 1910-1163.
Published by: (Canadian Institutes of Health Research (C I H R)/Instituts de Recherche en Sante au Canada (I R S C)), Canadian Institutes of Health Research, Institute of Aging/Instituts de Recherche en Sante du Canada, Institut du Viellissement, University of British Columbia, 2080 West Mall, Vancouver, BC V6T 1Z2, Canada. TEL 604-822-0905, FAX 604-822-8656, aging@interchange.ubc.ca, http://www.cihr-irsc.gc.ca/e/8671.html.

305.26 CAN ISSN 1910-1163
CANADIAN INSTITUTES OF HEALTH RESEARCH. INSTITUTE OF AGING. BIENNIAL REPORT. Text in English. 2002. biennial. **Document type:** *Report, Trade.*
Formerly (until 2005): Institute of Aging. Annual Report of Activities (1709-3147)
Media: Online - full text. **Related titles:** ◆ Print ed.: Canadian Institutes of Health Research. Institute of Aging. Annual Report of Activities. ISSN 1706-3086; French ed.: Instituts de Recherche en Sante du Canada, Institut du Vieillissement. Rapport Biennal. ISSN 1910-1171.
Published by: Canadian Institutes of Health Research, Institute of Aging/Instituts de Recherche en Sante du Canada, Institut du Viellissement, University of British Columbia, 2080 West Mall, Vancouver, BC V6T 1Z2, Canada. TEL 604-822-0905, FAX 604-822-8656, aging@interchange.ubc.ca, http://www.cihr-irsc.gc.ca/e/8671.html.

301 305.897 CAN ISSN 1912-0958
➤ **CANADIAN JOURNAL OF ABORIGINAL COMMUNITY-BASED HIV/AIDS RESEARCH.** Short title: C J A C B R. Text in English. 2006 (Summer). a. **Document type:** *Journal, Academic/Scholarly.*
Related titles: Online - full text ed.
Published by: Canadian Aboriginal AIDS Network, 602-251 Bank St, Ottawa, ON K2P 1X3, Canada. TEL 613-567-1817, 888-285-2226, info@caan.ca, http://www.caan.ca. Ed. Randy Jackson.

➤ **CANADIAN JOURNAL OF BEHAVIOURAL SCIENCE/REVUE CANADIENNE DES SCIENCES DU COMPORTEMENT.** *see* PSYCHOLOGY

302.23 CAN ISSN 0705-3657
P92.C3
➤ **CANADIAN JOURNAL OF COMMUNICATION.** Text in English, French; Summaries in English, French. 1974. q. CAD 50 domestic to individuals member; CAD 60 domestic to individuals non-member; USD 60 foreign to individuals; CAD 100 domestic to institutions member; CAD 100 domestic to institutions non-member; USD 100 foreign to institutions; CAD 30 domestic to students member; CAD 35 domestic to students non-member; USD 35 foreign to students; CAD 23 per issue domestic; USD 23 per issue foreign (effective 2004). adv. bk.rev. charts; stat. index. back issues avail. **Document type:** *Journal, Academic/Scholarly.* **Description:** Covers the entire field of communication and journalism studies as practiced in Canada or with relevance to Canada.
Formerly (until 1977): Media Probe (0384-1618)
Related titles: Microfiche ed.: (from MML); Microform ed.: (from MML); Online - full text ed.: ISSN 1499-6642. free (effective 2005).
Indexed: A01, A03, A12, A22, A26, ABIn, C03, CA, CBCARef, CBPI, CMM, CPerI, CWPI, CommAb, ERA, F01, F02, G08, Inspec, P27, P46, P48, P51, P52, P53, P54, PQC, PRA, RILM, S02, S03, S21, T02.
—BLDSC (3031.045000), AskIEEE, CIS, IE, Infotrieve, Ingenta. **CCC.**
Address: c/o Canadian Centre for Studies in Publishing, 515 W Hastings St, Vancouver, BC V6B 5K3, Canada. TEL 604-291-5240, FAX 604-291-5239, subscriptions@cjc-online.ca. Ed. David Mitchell. Pub. Rowland Lorimer. R&P, Adv. contact Marilyn Bittman. B&W page CAD 200. Circ: 460 (paid and controlled).

➤ **CANADIAN JOURNAL OF LAW AND SOCIETY.** *see* LAW

301 CAN ISSN 1710-1123
➤ **CANADIAN JOURNAL OF SOCIOLOGY (ONLINE).** Text in English. irreg. plus q. updates. free (effective 2011). bk.rev. **Document type:** *Journal, Academic/Scholarly.* **Description:** Publishes research articles and innovative theoretical essays by social scientists from around the world, providing insight into the issues facing Canadian society as well as social and cultural systems in other countries.
Media: Online - full content.
Published by: University of Toronto Press, Journals Division, 5201 Dufferin St, Toronto, ON M3H 5T8, Canada. TEL 416-667-7810, FAX 416-667-7881, journals@utpress.utoronto.ca, http://www.utpress.utoronto.ca. Ed. Kevin D Haggerty.

302.234 CAN ISSN 0829-1888
P92.C3
CANADIAN MEDIA DIRECTORS' COUNCIL. MEDIA DIGEST. Text in English. 197?. a. CAD 25 domestic; USD 40 foreign (effective 2004).
Published by: Canadian Media Directors' Council, c/o Marketing Magazine, 777 Bay St, Toronto, ON M5W 1A7, Canada. TEL 416-596-5160, FAX 416-596-3482. Ed. Jim McElgunn.

301 USA ISSN 1755-6171
➤ **CANADIAN REVIEW OF SOCIOLOGY/REVUE CANADIENNE DE SOCIOLOGIE.** Text in English, French. 1964. q. GBP 146 combined subscription in United Kingdom to institutions (print & online eds.); EUR 197 combined subscription in Europe to institutions (print & online eds.); USD 291 combined subscription in the Americas to institutions (print & online eds.); USD 304 combined subscription elsewhere to institutions (print & online eds.) (effective 2012). adv. bk.rev. charts; illus. index, cum.index 1964-1984. 1 cols./p.; back issues avail.; reprint service avail. from PSC. **Document type:** *Journal, Academic/Scholarly.* **Description:** Carries articles, commentaries and book reviews on key research findings and the current theoretical debates in the social sciences.
Formerly (until 2008): The Canadian Review of Sociology and Anthropology (0008-4948)
Related titles: Microform ed.: (from MIM, PQC); Online - full text ed.: ISSN 1755-618X. GBP 133 in United Kingdom to institutions; EUR 168 in Europe to institutions; USD 265 in the Americas to institutions; USD 258 elsewhere to institutions (effective 2012).
Indexed: A01, A02, A03, A08, A20, A21, A22, A26, ABS&EES, AICP, ASCA, AbAn, AmH&L, B04, BNNA, BRD, C03, C05, C12, CA, CBCARef, CBPI, CPerI, CurCont, DIP, E-psyche, E01, E08, EMBASE, ESPM, ExcerpMed, F09, FR, FamI, G08, G10, H09, HPNRM, HistAb, I05, I13, IBR, IBSS, IBZ, M01, M02, MEA&I, MEDLINE, MLA-IB, P02, P03, P10, P25, P26, P27, P30, P42, P43, P45, P46, P48, P53, P54, PCI, PQC, PSA, PsycInfo, PsycholAb, R05, RASB, RI-1, RI-2, S02, S03, S05, S09, S11, SCOPUS, SOPODA, SRRA, SSA, SSAI, SSAb, SSCI, SSI, SSciA, SociolAb, T02, W03, W05, W07, W09.
—BLDSC (3044.649000), IE, Infotrieve, Ingenta, INIST. **CCC.**
Published by: (Canadian Sociological Association/Societe Canadienne de Sociologie CAN), Wiley-Blackwell Publishing, Inc. (Subsidiary of: Wiley-Blackwell Publishing Ltd.), 111 River St, Hoboken, NJ 07030. TEL 201-748-6000, FAX 201-748-6088, info@wiley.com. Ed. Reza Nakhaie. Adv. contact Kristin McCarthy TEL 201-748-7683.

306.09 620 USA ISSN 0892-3515
➤ **CANAL HISTORY AND TECHNOLOGY PROCEEDINGS.** Text in English. 1982. a. **Document type:** *Journal, Academic/Scholarly.* **Description:** Deals social and political history and engineering of canals, gravity railroads, anthracite coal, anthracite iron, and early railroads.
Indexed: AmH&L.
Published by: Canal History and Technology Press, National Canal Museum, 30 Centre Sq, Easton, PA 18042.

301 FRA ISSN 2105-0708
LES CARNETS DU L A H I C. (Laboratoire d'Anthropologie et d'Histoire de l'Institution de la Culture) Text in French. 2006. irreg. **Document type:** *Monographic series.*
Media: Online - full text.
Published by: Laboratoire d'Anthropologie et d'Histoire de l'Institution de la Culture, 11, Rue du Seminaire de Conflans, Charenton-le-Pont, 94220, France. TEL 33-1-40157620, FAX 33-1-40157675, nadine.boillon@culture.fr, http://www.iiac.cnrs.fr/lahic/spip.php?rubrique1.

THE CATALYST (TORONTO). *see* POLITICAL SCIENCE—Civil Rights

CATHOLIC FAMILY PERSPECTIVES. *see* RELIGIONS AND THEOLOGY—Roman Catholic

302.2 ARG
CAUSAS Y AZARES; los lenguajes de la comunicacion y la cultura en (la) crisis. Text in Spanish. 1994. q. ARS 7 per issue.
Published by: Ediciones El Cielo por Asalto, Lambare 873, Buenos Aires, 1185, Argentina. TEL 54-114-8657554, FAX 54-114-3432999.

301 360 334 VEN ISSN 1317-5734
HM548
➤ **CAYAPA**; revista venezolana de economia social. Text in Spanish; Summaries in English, French. 2001. s-a. free (effective 2011). abstr. Index. back issues avail. **Document type:** *Journal, Academic/Scholarly.* **Description:** Publishes information and analysis about cooperatives and other third world organizations.
Media: Online - full text.
Indexed: A26, C01, CA, I04, I05, IBSS, P42, S02, S03, SociolAb, T02.
Published by: (C I R I E C - Venezuela), Universidad de los Andes, Av 4 entre Calles 18 y 19, Edif General Masini, Piso 3, Of A-3, Merida, 5101, Venezuela. TEL 58-274-2524192, info@saber.ula.ve, http://www.ula.ve. Circ: 150 (controlled); 350 (paid).

301 GBR ISSN 1939-2397
BJ1470.5
▼ **CELEBRITY STUDIES.** Text in English. 2009 (Apr.). 3/yr. GBP 239 combined subscription in United Kingdom to institutions (print & online eds.); EUR 300, USD 478 combined subscription to institutions (print & online eds.) (effective 2012). adv. reprints avail. **Document type:** *Journal, Academic/Scholarly.* **Description:** Focuses on the critical exploration of celebrity, stardom and fame.
Related titles: Online - full text ed.: ISSN 1939-2400. GBP 215 in United Kingdom to institutions; EUR 269, USD 431 to institutions (effective 2012).
Indexed: T02.
—CCC.
Published by: Routledge (Subsidiary of: Taylor & Francis Group), 4 Park Sq, Milton Park, Abingdon, Oxon OX14 4RN, United Kingdom. TEL 44-20-70176000, FAX 44-20-70176336, subscriptions@tandf.co.uk, http://www.routledge.com. Ed. Sean Redmond. Adv. contact Linda Hann TEL 44-1344-779945. **Subscr. to:** Taylor & Francis Ltd., Journals Customer Service, Sheepen Pl, Colchester, Essex CO3 3LP, United Kingdom. TEL 44-20-70175544, FAX 44-20-70175198, tf.enquiries@tfinforma.com.

CENSORED ALERT. *see* COMMUNICATIONS

302.3 USA ISSN 0889-0765
HN31
CENTER FOCUS. Text in English. 1971. q. USD 25 domestic; USD 25 foreign (effective 2000). adv. bk.rev. back issues avail. **Document type:** *Newsletter.* **Description:** Publishes articles on current global issues from a theological and ethical point of view. Topics includes globalization, development, global poverty, women's issues, trade issues, the World Bank, IMF, and more.
Indexed: CCR, CERDIC, HRIR.
Published by: Center of Concern, 1225 Otis Street NE, Washington, DC 20017. TEL 202-635-2757, FAX 202-832-9494. Ed. Jane Deren. Circ: 10,000 (paid and controlled).

▼ **CENTER OF STUDIES ON POLITICS AND SOCIETY. WORKING PAPERS SERIES.** *see* POLITICAL SCIENCE

301 330 JPN
CENTRAL RESEARCH INSTITUTE OF ELECTRIC POWER INDUSTRY. SOCIO-ECONOMIC RESEARCH CENTER. TECHNICAL REPORTS (ENGLISH EDITION). Text in English. irreg.
Related titles: Online - full content ed.; Japanese ed.
Published by: Central Research Institute of Electric Power Industry, Socio-Economic Research Center, 1-6-1 Ohte-machi, Chiyoda-ku, Tokyo, 100-8126, Japan. TEL 81-3-3201-6601, FAX 81-3-3287-2863, http://criepi.denken.or.jp/jpn/serc/index.html.

449 306 FRA ISSN 1961-9340
CENTRE DE RECHERCHE ET D'ETUDES CATALANES. REVUE. Key Title: R E C E R C. Text in French, Catalan. 2008. s-a. **Document type:** *Journal, Academic/Scholarly.*
Media: Online - full text.
Published by: Centre de Recherche et d'Etudes Catalanes, Chemin de la Passio Vella, Perpignan, 66100, France. TEL 33-4-68662209, crec@univ-perp.fr.

301 331 GBR ISSN 1742-9757
CENTRE FOR CIVIL SOCIETY. INTERNATIONAL WORKING PAPER. Text in English. 1998. irreg., latest vol.14, 2003. back issues avail. **Document type:** *Monographic series, Trade.* **Description:** For policy makers, NGO practitioners and researchers. Aims to increase an understanding of the third sector outside the UK and analyzes issues in the management of non-governmental organizations working in the development field.
Formerly (until 1999): Centre for Voluntary Organisation. International Working Paper (1462-9445)
Related titles: Online - full text ed.: free (effective 2009).
Published by: London School of Economics and Political Science, Centre for Civil Society, London School of Economics, Houghton St, London, WC2A 2AE, United Kingdom. TEL 44-20-79557205, FAX 44-20-79556039, ccs@lse.ac.uk. Ed. David Lewis.

301 ZAF
CENTRE FOR CONFLICT RESOLUTION. ANNUAL REPORT. Text in English. 1968. a. free. bibl. **Document type:** *Corporate.* **Description:** Reports on the centre's activities in promoting constructive, creative and cooperative approaches to the resolution of conflict and the reduction of violence in South Africa.
Former titles (until 1994): Centre for Intergroup Studies. Annual Report; Abe Bailey Institute of Inter-Racial Studies. Annual Report
Published by: Centre for Conflict Resolution, c/o University of Cape Town, Rhodes Gift Post Office, Rondebosch, Cape Town 7707, South Africa. TEL 27-21-4222512, FAX 27-21-4222622, http://www.ccrweb.ccr.uct.ac.za. Ed. Laurie Nathan. Circ: 2,200 (controlled).

301 GBR ISSN 1350-9101
CENTRE FOR RESEARCH IN SOCIAL POLICY. WORKING PAPERS SERIES. Text in English. 1990. irreg., latest vol.554, 2006. price varies. back issues avail. **Document type:** *Monographic series, Academic/Scholarly.* **Description:** Publishes research in all areas of sociology and society.
Published by: (Loughborough University, Department of Social Sciences), Centre for Research in Social Policy (Subsidiary of: Loughborough University, Department of Social Sciences), Department of Social Sciences, Loughborough University, Loughborough, Leics LE11 3TU, United Kingdom. TEL 44-1509-223372, FAX 44-1509-213409, crsp@lboro.ac.uk, http://www.crsp.ac.uk.

CENTRE FOR URBAN AND COMMUNITY STUDIES. BIBLIOGRAPHIC SERIES. *see* HOUSING AND URBAN PLANNING

CENTRE FOR URBAN AND COMMUNITY STUDIES. MAJOR REPORT SERIES. *see* HOUSING AND URBAN PLANNING

CENTRE FOR URBAN AND COMMUNITY STUDIES. RESEARCH PAPERS. *see* HOUSING AND URBAN PLANNING

307.76 ARG ISSN 0326-8470
CENTRO DE ESTUDIOS URBANOS Y REGIONALES. BOLETIN. Text in Spanish. 1986. 2/yr. USD 4. **Description:** Articles and research news on urban and regional development.
Published by: Centro de Estudios Urbanos y Regionales, Av Corrientes 2835, A 7o Piso, Buenos Aires, 1193, Argentina. Circ: 500.

307.76 ARG ISSN 0326-1417
HT395.A7
CENTRO DE ESTUDIOS URBANOS Y REGIONALES. CUADERNOS. Text in Spanish. 1982. irreg. **Description:** Monographs and short research reports on urban and regional social problems.
Published by: Centro de Estudios Urbanos y Regionales, Av Corrientes 2835, A 7o Piso, Buenos Aires, 1193, Argentina. Circ: 500.

307.76 ARG
CENTRO DE ESTUDIOS URBANOS Y REGIONALES. INFORMES DE INVESTIGACION. Text in Spanish. 1985. irreg. **Description:** Research reports on Argentine and Latin American development process on urban and regional problems.
Published by: Centro de Estudios Urbanos y Regionales, Av Corrientes 2835, A 7o Piso, Buenos Aires, 1193, Argentina. Circ: 500.

CENTRO DE INVESTIGACIONES SOCIO HISTORICAS. CUADERNOS. *see* HISTORY

CENTRO NEWS. *see* ETHNIC INTERESTS

CETERIS PARIBUS; revista de economia de Puerto Rico. *see* BUSINESS AND ECONOMICS

307.14094194 IRL ISSN 1649-5985
CHANGING IRELAND. Text in English. 2001. q. free (effective 2006). **Document type:** *Magazine, Consumer.* **Description:** Highlights efforts to fight the causes and effects of poverty and exclusion in Ireland.
Published by: C D N Moyross, Unit 3, Sarsfield Business Centre, Moyross, Limerick, Ireland. TEL 353-61-458011, FAX 353-61-325300. Ed. Allen Meagher.

301 CHN ISSN 1673-1395
H8.C47
CHANGJIANG DAXUE XUEBAO (SHEHUI KEXUEBAN)/YANGTZE UNIVERSITY. JOURNAL (SOCIAL SCIENCES). Text in Chinese. 1978. bi-m. **Document type:** *Journal, Academic/Scholarly.*
Formerly (until 2003): Jianghan Shiyou Xueyuan Xuebao (Shekeban)/ Jianghan Petroleum Institute. Journal (Social Science Edition) (1009-0010)
Related titles: Online - full text ed.
Published by: Changjiang Daxue/Yangtze University, 1, Nanhuan Lu, Jingzhou, 434023, China. TEL 86-716-8060802. **Dist. by:** China International Book Trading Corp, 35 Chegongzhuang Xilu, Haidian District, PO Box 399, Beijing 100044, China. TEL 86-10-68412045, FAX 86-10-68412023, cibtc@mail.cibtc.com.cn, http://www.cibtc.com.cn.

301 384 ECU ISSN 0254-2129
CHASQUI; revista latinoamericana de comunicacion. Text in Spanish. 1983. q. **Document type:** *Journal, Academic/Scholarly.*
Related titles: Online - full text ed.: ISSN 1390-1079. 2002. free (effective 2011).
—IE.
Published by: Centro Internacional de Estudios Superiores de Comunicacion para America Latina, Avenida Diego de Almagro N32-133 y Andrade Marin, Quito, Ecuador. TEL 593-2-2548011, FAX 593-2-2502487, info@ciespal.net, http://www.ciespal.net.

CHEMNITZER BEITRAEGE ZUR SOZIALPAEDAGOGIK. *see* EDUCATION

CHICAGO JOURNAL OF INTERNATIONAL LAW. *see* LAW—International Law

301 USA ISSN 0300-6921
F548.9.N3
CHICAGO REPORTER. Text in English. 1972. bi-m. USD 12 (effective 2007). adv. bk.rev. illus. index. **Document type:** *Magazine, Consumer.* **Description:** Reports and comments on the social, economic and political issues of metropolitan Chicago, with a special focus on race and poverty.
Related titles: Online - full text ed.
Indexed: APW, AltPI, ENW, G06, G07, G08, I05, P27, P46, P48, P54, PQC.
Published by: Community Renewal Society, 332 S Michigan Ave, Ste 500, Chicago, IL 60604-4301. TEL 312-427-4830, FAX 312-427-6130. Ed., Pub. Alysia Tate. Adv. contact Brian Foster. Circ: 3,100.

302 USA ISSN 0738-0151
HV701 CODEN: CASWDD
➤ **CHILD AND ADOLESCENT SOCIAL WORK JOURNAL.** Text in English. 1970. bi-m. EUR 970, USD 1,004 combined subscription to institutions (print & online eds.) (effective 2012). adv. bk.rev. bibl.; illus. back issues avail.; reprint service avail. from PSC. **Document type:** *Journal, Academic/Scholarly.* **Description:** Focuses on clinical social work practice with children, adolescents and their families.
Former titles (until 1982): Family and Child Mental Health Journal (0190-230X); (until 1980): Issues in Child Mental Health (0362-403X); (until vol.5, 1977): Psychosocial Process (0556-431X)
Related titles: Online - full text ed.: ISSN 1573-2797 (from IngentaConnect).
Indexed: A01, A02, A03, A08, A22, A26, AMHA, ASSIA, Agr, BRD, BibLing, C06, C07, C22, C28, CA, CDA, CMM, E-psyche, E01, E02, E03, E07, E08, ERI, ESPM, EdA, EdI, F09, FamI, G08, I05, IBR, IBZ, P02, P03, P10, P18, P20, P24, P25, P27, P30, P46, P48, P50, P53, P54, PQC, PsycInfo, PsycholAb, RiskAb, S02, S03, S09, S11, SCOPUS, SOPODA, SSA, SSAI, SSAb, SSI, SWR&A, SociolAb, T02, W03, W05, W09.
—BLDSC (3172.914000), GNLM, IE, Infotrieve, Ingenta. **CCC.**
Published by: Springer New York LLC (Subsidiary of: Springer Science+Business Media), 233 Spring St, New York, NY 10013. TEL 212-460-1500, FAX 212-460-1575, service-ny@springer.com. Ed. Thomas K Kenemore.

301 USA ISSN 1546-6752
CHILDREN AND YOUTH; history and culture. Text in English. 2004. irreg., latest 2007. price varies. back issues avail. **Document type:** *Monographic series, Academic/Scholarly.* **Description:** Provides a narrative history of key topics in the contexts of the lives of children and youth in the U.S. and around the world.
Published by: Greenwood Publishing Group Inc. (Subsidiary of: A B C - C L I O), 88 Post Rd W, PO Box 5007, Westport, CT 06881. TEL 203-226-3571, 800-225-5800, FAX 877-231-6980, sales@greenwood.com. Ed. Miriam Forman-Brunnel.

302.23 CHN
CHINA ENTERTAINMENT. Text in English. m. **Document type:** *Newsletter, Trade.* **Description:** Provides news and analysis in China's fast-growing sectors of film, television, music and multimedia.
Published by: Clear Thinking Corp., 2-F Profit Tower, 17 Chaoyangmenwai Ave, Beijing, 100020, China. TEL 86-1-65991631, 86-1-65991634, FAX 86-1-65991639, marketing@clearthinking.com.

306 GBR ISSN 2043-0345
CHINA ETHOS. Text in English. 2007. q. GBP 15 domestic; GBP 55 in Europe; GBP 85 elsewhere (effective 2010). adv. **Document type:** *Magazine, Consumer.* **Description:** Promotes closer cultural and business exchange between China and United Kingdom.
Formerly (until 2009): S L Magazine (1756-1965)
Published by: China Media Ltd., London House, 271-273 King St, London, W6 9LZ, United Kingdom. TEL 44-20-82332888, FAX 44-20-82332866.

CHINA HERITAGE QUARTERLY. *see* ASIAN STUDIES

THE CHINA SOCIETY YEARBOOK. *see* ASIAN STUDIES

301 USA ISSN 0009-4625
HM1
➤ **CHINESE SOCIOLOGY AND ANTHROPOLOGY.** Abbreviated title: C S A. Text in English. 1968. q. USD 990 combined subscription domestic to institutions (print & online eds.); USD 1,074 combined subscription foreign to institutions (print & online eds.) (effective 2011). adv. illus. index. back issues avail.; reprint service avail. from PSC. **Document type:** *Journal, Academic/Scholarly.* **Description:** Features articles focusing on the People's Republic of China, Hong Kong and Taiwan, covering themes such as social classes and stratification, social movements, popular culture, newly emerging subcultures and social mores, marriage patterns and family structure, and ethnic minorities.
Related titles: Online - full text ed.: ISSN 1558-1004. 2004 (Sep.). USD 901 to institutions (effective 2011).
Indexed: A01, A03, A08, A20, A22, A26, AICP, APEL, B04, BAS, BRD, CA, E-psyche, E01, E08, G08, G10, I05, IBR, IBSS, IBZ, MLA-IB, P30, P34, PCI, RASB, S02, S03, S09, SCOPUS, SSAI, SSAb, SSCI, SSI, SociolAb, T02, W03, W05, W07, W09.
—BLDSC (3181.100000), IE, Infotrieve, Ingenta. **CCC.**
Published by: M.E. Sharpe, Inc., 80 Business Park Dr, Armonk, NY 10504. TEL 914-273-1800, 800-541-6563, FAX 914-273-2106, custserv@mesharpe.com. Eds. Gregory Guldin, Zhou Daming. Adv. contact Barbara Ladd TEL 914-273-1800.

201.6 261.8 FRA ISSN 1257-127X
CHRETIENS ET SOCIETES XVIE-XXE SIECLES. Text in French. 1979. a. **Document type:** *Bulletin.*
Formerly (until 1994): Centre Regional Interuniversitaire d'Histoire Religieuse. Bulletin (0223-8152)
Related titles: Online - full text ed.
Indexed: FR.
—INIST.
Published by: (Centre Regional Interuniversitaire d'Histoire Religieuse), Institut d'Histoire du Christianisme, Universite Jean Moulin-Lyon 3, 18 rue Chevreul, Lyon, Cedex 07 69362, France. TEL 33-4-78787165, FAX 33-4-78787426, ihc@univ-lyon3.fr, http://resea-ihc.univ-lyon3.fr/publicat/publicat.html.

201.6 USA ISSN 1040-8622
CHRISTIAN IRELAND TODAY. Text in English. 1987. m. free. back issues avail. **Document type:** *Newsletter.* **Description:** Deals with issues of reconciliation, violence and non-violence, and cross-cultural cooperation.
Published by: Christian Ireland Ministries Inc., PO Box 11057, Albany, NY 12211. TEL 518-329-3003. Ed. Rev. Francis G McCloskey. Circ: 763.

CHRONIC POVERTY RESEARCH CENTRE. WORKING PAPERS. *see* SOCIAL SERVICES AND WELFARE

CIENCIAS DA RELIGIAO. *see* RELIGIONS AND THEOLOGY

306.874 USA
CIRCLES OF PEACE - CIRCLES OF JUSTICE NEWSLETTER. Text in English. 1981. bi-m. free to members. bk.rev.; film rev.; video rev. bibl. back issues avail. **Document type:** *Newsletter, Consumer.* **Description:** Offers families, schools, faith communities, and local organizations practical ways of living and sharing the Pledge of Nonviolence and/or responding to some aspect of violence challenging our communities, nation, and world.
Formerly: Parenting for Peace & Justice Network Newsletter (0890-3859)
Published by: Parenting for Peace & Justice Network, Institute for Peace & Justice, 475 E Lockwood Ave, St. Louis, MO 63119. ppjn@aol.com, http://members.aol.com/ppjn/index.html. Ed. Nanette Ford. Circ: 2,500.

301 GBR ISSN 1877-9166
HT101
▼ **CITY, CULTURE AND SOCIETY.** Text in English. 2010. q. EUR 416 in Europe to institutions; JPY 54,100 in Japan to institutions; USD 553 elsewhere to institutions (effective 2012). **Document type:** *Journal, Academic/Scholarly.* **Description:** Promotes pioneering research on cities and to foster the sort of urban administration that has the vision and authority to reinvent cities adapted to the challenges of the 21st century.
Related titles: Online - full text ed.: ISSN 1877-9174 (from ScienceDirect).
Indexed: SCOPUS.
—**CCC.**
Published by: Elsevier Ltd (Subsidiary of: Elsevier Science & Technology), The Blvd, Langford Ln, Kidlington, Oxford, OX5 1GB, United Kingdom. TEL 44-1865-843434, FAX 44-1865-843970, journalscustomerserviceemea@elsevier.com. Ed. M Sasaki.

CIVILIAN CONGRESS; includes a directory of persons holding executive branch-military office in Congress contrary to constitutional prohibition (Art.1, Sec.6, Cl.2) of concurrent office-holding. *see* LAW

303.4 BEL ISSN 0009-8140
AP1
CIVILISATIONS; revue international de sciences humaines et des civilisation differentes. Text in English, French. 1951. s-a. bk.rev. bibl. index. reprints avail. **Document type:** *Academic/Scholarly.*
Indexed: ABCPolSci, AICP, ASD, BAS, BibInd, CA, EI, FR, HistAb, IBR, IBSS, IBZ, MEA&I, MLA-IB, P06, P30, PAIS, PCI, RASB, RILM, S02, S03, SociolAb, T02.
—Ingenta, INIST.
Published by: (Universite Libre de Bruxelles, Universite Libre de Bruxelles, Institut de Sociologie), Revue Civilisations, Av Jeanne 44, Brussels, 1050, Belgium. TEL 32-2-650-3359, FAX 32-2-650-3521, TELEX 23069 UNILIB B. Ed. Jacqueline Gilissen. Circ: 1,000.

CLON: CYBERZINE DE ARTE Y CULTURA. *see* ART

302 SVK ISSN 1335-3608
H8
CLOVEK A SPOLOCNOST. Text in Slovak. 1998. q. free (effective 2011). **Document type:** *Journal, Academic/Scholarly.*
Media: Online - full text.
Published by: Slovenska Akademia Vied, Spolocenskovedny Ustav, Karpatska 5, Kosice, 04001, Slovakia. TEL 421-55-6251986, FAX 421-55-6255856, http://www.saske.sk/SVU.

COGNITION AND CULTURE BOOK SERIES. *see* PSYCHOLOGY

307 GBR ISSN 2045-1814
▼ **COHESION & SOCIETY.** Text in English. 2010. 3/yr. free to members (effective 2010). **Document type:** *Journal, Trade.*
Media: Online - full text.
Published by: Institute of Community Cohesion, Futures Institute, 10 Innovation Village, Coventry Technology Park, Cheetah Way, Coventry CV1 2TL, United Kingdom. TEL 44-24-76795757, cohesion@coventry.ac.uk.

306.85 ESP ISSN 2172-2986
COLECCION ACCION FAMILIAR. Text in Spanish. 2005. a. **Document type:** *Monographic series, Academic/Scholarly.*
Published by: Ediciones Cinca, General Ibanez Ibero, 5 A, Esq 1, 1o. A, Madrid, 28003, Spain. TEL 34-91-5532272, FAX 34-91-5543790, http://www.edicionescinca.com/.

301 ESP ISSN 1698-9864
COLECCION RAZON Y SOCIEDAD. Text in Spanish. 1998. irreg. price varies. back issues avail. **Document type:** *Monographic series, Academic/Scholarly.*
Published by: Editorial Biblioteca Nueva, C. Almagro 38, Madrid, 28010, Spain. TEL 34-91-3100436, FAX 34-91-2198235, editorial@bibliotecanueva.es, http://www.bibliotecanueva.es/.

COLLANA DI STORIA ECONOMICA E SOCIALE. *see* BUSINESS AND ECONOMICS—Economic Situation And Conditions

301 CAN ISSN 1912-5755
COLLECTION COMMUNICATION. GROUPES ET ORGANISATIONS. Text in French. 2003. irreg. CAD 32 per issue (effective 2007). **Document type:** *Monographic series, Trade.*
Published by: Presses de l'Universite du Quebec, Le Delta I, 2875 boul. Laurier, bureau 450, Ste Foy, PQ G1V 2M2, Canada. TEL 418-657-4075, FAX 418-657-2096, puq@puq.uquebec.ca.

300 FRA ISSN 1243-0935
COLLECTION CURSUS. SOCIOLOGIE. Variant title: Cursus. Sociologie. Text in French. 1993. irreg. price varies. **Document type:** *Monographic series, Academic/Scholarly.*
Published by: Armand Colin, 21 Rue du Montparnasse, Paris, 75283 Cedex 06, France. TEL 33-1-44395447, FAX 33-1-44394343, infos@armand-colin.fr.

307.76 FRA ISSN 1769-6518
COLLECTION VILLES EN MOUVEMENT. Variant title: Villes en Mouvement. Text in French. 2004. irreg. **Document type:** *Monographic series, Consumer.* **Description:** Presents a unique way to explore the cities of the world through the eyes of a writer and photographer who follow innovative artists and social workers as they go about their lives.
Published by: Editions Autrement, 77 Rue du Faubourg St Antoine, Paris, 75011, France. TEL 33-1-44738000, FAX 33-1-44730012, contact@autrement.com.

COLOMBIA INTERNACIONAL. *see* POLITICAL SCIENCE

COLUMBIA JOURNAL OF LAW AND SOCIAL PROBLEMS. *see* LAW

COLUMBIANA; bioregional journal for the Intermountain Northwest. *see* CONSERVATION

COMMON GROUND. *see* RELIGIONS AND THEOLOGY

302.23 NLD ISSN 1572-5227
COMMUNICATIE MEMO. Text in Dutch. 1996. irreg., latest vol.47, 2008. EUR 15.41 per vol. (effective 2009). **Document type:** *Monographic series.*
Published by: Kluwer B.V. (Subsidiary of: Wolters Kluwer N.V.), Postbus 23, Deventer, 7400 GA, Netherlands. TEL 31-570-673555, FAX 31-570-691555, info@kluwer.nl, http://www.kluwer.nl.

302.2 ZAF ISSN 0250-0167
➤ **COMMUNICATIO**; South African journal for communication theory and research. Text in Afrikaans, English. 1974. 3/yr. GBP 258 combined subscription in United Kingdom to institutions (print & online eds.); EUR 404, USD 506 combined subscription to institutions (print & online eds.) (effective 2012). bk.rev. back issues avail.; reprint service avail. from PSC. **Document type:** *Journal, Academic/Scholarly.* **Description:** Publishes articles reflecting communications research in Africa.
Related titles: Online - full text ed.: ISSN 1753-5379. GBP 232 in United Kingdom to institutions; EUR 363, USD 456 to institutions (effective 2012).
Indexed: A22, AmHI, CA, CMM, CommAb, E01, H07, IIBP, ISAP, P27, P46, P48, P54, PQC, RILM, T02.
—BLDSC (3341.390000), IE. **CCC.**
Published by: (University of South Africa), UniSA Press, PO Box 392, Pretoria, 0003, South Africa. TEL 27-12-4292953, FAX 27-12-4293449, unisa-press@unisa.ac.za, http://www.unisa.ac.za/press. Ed. Pieter J Fourie. Circ: 4,360 (controlled). **Subscr. outside Africa to:** Routledge, Customer Services Dept, Rankine Rd, Basingstoke, Hants RG24 8PR, United Kingdom. TEL 44-1256-813000, FAX 44-1256-330245, tf.enquiries@tfinforma.com, http://www.tandf.co.uk/journals, http://www.routledge.com/journals/.

302.2 BEL ISSN 0378-0880
P87
➤ **COMMUNICATION & COGNITION.** Text in English. 1968. q. EUR 24.50 to individuals; EUR 27.30 to institutions (effective 2005). adv. bk.rev. bibl. 100 p./no.; back issues avail.; reprints avail. **Document type:** *Journal, Academic/Scholarly.*
Indexed: A20, A22, A28, APA, BibLing, BrCerAb, C&ISA, CA/WCA, CIA, CerAb, CivEngAb, CommAb, CorrAb, DIP, E&CAJ, E-psyche, E11, EEA, EMA, ESPM, EnvEAb, FR, H15, IBR, IBZ, IPB, L&LBA, M&TEA, M09, MBF, METADEX, MLA-IB, MathR, P03, PhilInd, PsycInfo, PsycholAb, SCOPUS, SOPODA, SociolAb, SolStAb, T04, WAA.
—BLDSC (3359.260000), IE, Infotrieve, Ingenta, INIST, Linda Hall. **CCC.**
Published by: (Rijksuniversiteit te Gent), Communication and Cognition, Blandijnberg 2, Ghent, 9000, Belgium. TEL 32-9-2643952, FAX 32-9-2644197, fernand.vandamme@2ug.ac.be. Ed., R&P, Adv. contact Fernand Vandamme. B&W page EUR 250; 230 x 160. Circ: 550.

302.2 USA ISSN 1936-6221
P87
➤ **COMMUNICATION AND SOCIAL CHANGE.** Text in English. 2007 (May). a. back issues avail. **Document type:** *Journal, Academic/Scholarly.*
Related titles: Online - full text ed.: free (effective 2010).
Published by: Clark Atlanta University, Center for Excellence in Communication Arts, 223 James P Brawley Dr, SW, Atlanta, GA 30314. TEL 404-880-8290, FAX 404-880-6226, http://www.cau.edu. Ed. Cheryl Renee Gooch.

S

302 USA ISSN 1936-623X
P87
➤ **COMMUNICATION ARTS FORUM.** Text in English. 2007 (May). a. **Document type:** *Journal, Academic/Scholarly.*
Related titles: Online - full text ed.: free (effective 2010).
Published by: Clark Atlanta University, Center for Excellence in Communication Arts, 223 James P Brawley Dr, SW, Atlanta, GA 30314. TEL 404-880-8290, FAX 404-880-6226, http://www.cau.edu. Ed. Cheryl Renee Gooch.

302.2 GBR ISSN 1753-9129
COMMUNICATION, CULTURE & CRITIQUE. Text in English. 2008. q. EUR 107 combined subscription in Europe to individuals; USD 100 combined subscription in the Americas to individuals; GBP 71 combined subscription elsewhere to individuals includes UK, Europe (non Euro zone); GBP 694 combined subscription domestic to institutions; EUR 881 combined subscription in Europe to institutions; USD 1,138 combined subscription in the Americas to institutions; USD 1,359 combined subscription elsewhere to institutions; free to members (effective 2010); combined subscr. includes: Communication Theory and Human Communication Research & Journal of Communication and Journal of Computer-Mediated Communication. reprint service avail. from PSC. **Document type:** *Journal, Academic/Scholarly.* **Description:** Provides an international forum for critical, interpretive, and qualitative research examining the role of communication and cultural criticism in today's world.
Related titles: Online - full text ed.: ISSN 1753-9137. 2008. GBP 631 domestic to institutions; EUR 801 in Europe to institutions; USD 1,034 in the Americas to institutions; USD 1,235 elsewhere to institutions (effective 2010) (from IngentaConnect).
Indexed: A22, CA, CMM, CommAb, E01, IBR, IBZ, T02.
—IE. **CCC.**
Published by: (International Communication Association USA), Wiley-Blackwell Publishing Ltd. (Subsidiary of: John Wiley & Sons, Inc.), 9600 Garsington Rd, Oxford, OX4 2DQ, United Kingdom. TEL 44-1865-776868, FAX 44-1865-714591, customer@wiley.co.uk. Ed. Karen Ross.

302.2 USA ISSN 1555-8711
HN49.C6
COMMUNICATION FOR DEVELOPMENT AND SOCIAL CHANGE. Text in English. 2006 (Sum.). q. **Document type:** *Journal, Academic/ Scholarly.*
Indexed: CA, CMM, CommAb, T02.
Published by: Hampton Press, Inc., 23 Broadway, Cresskill, NJ 07626. TEL 201-894-1686, hamptonpr1@aol.com. Ed. Jan Servaes.

302.23 384 AUS ISSN 1836-0645
PR1
➤ **COMMUNICATION, POLITICS & CULTURE.** Short title: C P C. Text in English. 1963. 2/yr. AUD 101.20 per issue domestic to institutions; AUD 116 per issue foreign to institutions (effective 2008). bk.rev. Index. back issues avail. **Document type:** *Journal, Academic/ Scholarly.* **Description:** Publishes scholarly articles that connect communication and cultural technologies to areas of legislative or parliamentary politics, to governance of social organizations and the institutions they constitute, or to broader negotiations of power.
Formerly (until 2008): Southern Review (0038-4526)
Related titles: Online - full text ed.
Indexed: A20, A22, AES, AusPAIS, MLA, MLA-IB, PCI, RASB.
—BLDSC (3362.650000), IE, Ingenta.
Published by: R M I T, School of Media & Communication, Bldg. 6, Level 3, RMIT University, GPO Box 2476V, Melbourne, VIC 3001, Australia. http://www.rmit.edu.au/browse/Our%20Organisation/Faculties/Art,%20Design%20%26%20Communication/Schools/Applied%20Communication/. Ed. Cathy Greenfield. Circ: 400 (paid).

302.2 USA ISSN 0146-3373
PN4071 CODEN: SCAUE6
➤ **COMMUNICATION QUARTERLY.** Text in English. 1953. q. USD 278, GBP 169, EUR 221 combined subscription to institutions (print & online eds.) (effective 2010); Subscr. includes Communication Research Reports (RCRR) and Qualitative Research Reports in Communication (RQRR). adv. bk.rev. bibl.; illus. index. reprint service avail. from PSC. **Document type:** *Journal, Academic/Scholarly.* **Description:** Features research reports, critical studies, state of the art reviews, reports of topical interest, supported opinion papers, and other essays related to the interest groups of ECA and its affiliate organizations.
Formerly (until 1976): Today's Speech (0040-8573)
Related titles: Microform ed.: (from PQC); Online - full text ed.: ISSN 1746-4102. USD 265 to institutions (effective 2010) (from IngentaConnect).
Indexed: A01, A02, A03, A08, A21, A22, A25, A26, AmHI, B04, BRD, CA, CMM, CPE, CommAb, E01, E02, E03, E06, E07, E08, ERI, EdA, EdI, F01, F02, G05, G06, G07, G08, G10, H07, H08, H09, H10, H14, HAb, HumInd, I05, IJCS, M06, MEA&I, MLA-IB, P02, P10, P13, P18, P21, P27, P47, P48, P52, P53, P54, PCI, PQC, RI-1, RI-2, RILM, S02, S03, S04, S08, S09, S23, SCOPUS, SOPODA, SSAI, SSAb, SSI, SociolAb, T02, V&AA, W03, W05.
—BLDSC (3363.020000), IE, Infotrieve, Ingenta. **CCC.**
Published by: (Eastern Communication Association), Routledge (Subsidiary of: Taylor & Francis Group), 325 Chestnut St, Ste 800, Philadelphia, PA 19106. TEL 215-625-8900, 800-354-1420, FAX 215-625-2940, orders@taylorandfrancis.com. Ed. Trevor Parry-Giles.

302.2 USA ISSN 0093-6502
P91 CODEN: CRESDG
➤ **COMMUNICATION RESEARCH.** Text in English. 1974. bi-m. USD 1,007, GBP 593 combined subscription to institutions (print & online eds.); USD 987, GBP 581 to institutions (effective 2011). adv. bk.rev. illus.; bibl. index. back issues avail.; reprint service avail. from PSC. **Document type:** *Journal, Academic/Scholarly.* **Description:** Provides an interdisciplinary forum for scholars and professionals to present new research in communication.
Related titles: Online - full text ed.: ISSN 1552-3810. USD 906, GBP 534 to institutions (effective 2011).
Indexed: A01, A02, A03, A08, A12, A20, A22, A26, ABIn, APC, ASCA, AbAn, AmHI, B01, B02, B06, B07, B08, B09, B15, B17, B18, BRD, CA, CMM, CommAb, CurCont, E-psyche, E01, E02, E03, E07, E08, ERA, ERI, EdA, EdI, F01, F02, FamI, G04, G08, H07, H08, H14, HAb, HRA, HumInd, I05, IJCS, L&LBA, MLA-IB, P02, P03, P06, P07, P10, P13, P18, P25, P27, P30, P34, P42, P48, P51, P53, P54, PAIS, PQC, PRA, PSA, PsycInfo, PsycholAb, RASB, RILM, S02, S03, S09, S21, SCOPUS, SFSA, SOPODA, SPAA, SSA, SSAI, SSAb, SSCI, SSI, SociolAb, T02, V&AA, W01, W02, W03, W07.
—BLDSC (3363.120000), IE, Infotrieve, Ingenta. **CCC.**
Published by: Sage Publications, Inc., 2455 Teller Rd, Thousand Oaks, CA 91320. TEL 805-499-9774, 800-818-7243, FAX 805-499-0871, 800-583-2665, info@sagepub.com. Eds. Michael E Roloff, Pamela Shoemaker. Circ: 800 (paid). **Subscr. outside the Americas to:** Sage Publications Ltd., 1 Oliver's Yard, 55 City Rd, London EC1Y 1SP, United Kingdom. TEL 44-20-73248701, FAX 44-20-73248733, subscription@sagepub.co.uk.

302.2 USA ISSN 0882-4096
P87
➤ **COMMUNICATION RESEARCH REPORTS.** Text in English. 1984. q. USD 278, GBP 169, EUR 221 combined subscription to institutions (print & online eds.) (effective 2010); subscr. includes Communication Quarterly; Qualitative Research Reports in Communication. adv. illus. index. back issues avail.; reprint service avail. from PSC. **Document type:** *Journal, Academic/Scholarly.* **Description:** Contains articles on research relevant to human communication.
Related titles: Microfilm ed.: (from PQC); Online - full text ed.: ISSN 1746-4099. USD 265 to institutions (effective 2010).
Indexed: A22, CA, CMM, CommAb, E-psyche, E01, E03, ERI, IJCS, P30, P42, PsycholAb, S02, S03, SCOPUS, SOPODA, SociolAb, T02.
—BLDSC (3363.133000), IE, Infotrieve, Ingenta. **CCC.**
Published by: (Eastern Communication Association), Routledge (Subsidiary of: Taylor & Francis Group), 325 Chestnut St, Ste 800, Philadelphia, PA 19106. TEL 215-625-8900, 800-354-1420, FAX 215-625-2940, orders@taylorandfrancis.com. Ed. Wendy Samter.

302.23 USA ISSN 0144-4646
P91.3
➤ **COMMUNICATION RESEARCH TRENDS.** Text in English. 1980. q. USD 50 (effective 2010). adv. bk.rev. bibl. back issues avail. **Document type:** *Monographic series, Academic/Scholarly.* **Description:** Each issue is a monographic review of the state-of-the-art in a sub-field of communications research.
Formerly (until 1980): Centre for the Study of Communication and Culture. Newsletter
Related titles: Online - full text ed.
Indexed: A22, A26, CA, CMM, CommAb, E08, G08, I05, S09, T02.
—BLDSC (3363.135000), IE, Infotrieve, Ingenta.
Published by: Centre for the Study of Communication and Culture, c/o Communication Department, Santa Clara University, 500 El Camino Real, Santa Clara, CA 95053. TEL 408-554-5498, FAX 408-554-4913, cscc@slu.edu, http://cscc.scu.edu/CSCC.

302.23 GBR ISSN 1051-0974
PN4001 CODEN: CSTDEK
➤ **COMMUNICATION STUDIES.** Text in English. 1949. 5/yr. GBP 209 combined subscription in United Kingdom to institutions (print & online eds.); EUR 277, USD 345 combined subscription to institutions (print & online eds.) (effective 2012). adv. bk.rev. bibl.; charts; stat.; tr.lit.; illus. index. back issues avail.; reprint service avail. from PSC. **Document type:** *Journal, Academic/Scholarly.* **Description:** Publishes essays and reports of studies should make important and noteworthy contributions to the advancement of human communication scholarship.
Formerly (until 1989): Central States Speech Journal (0008-9575)
Related titles: Microform ed.; Online - full text ed.: ISSN 1745-1035. GBP 188 in United Kingdom to institutions; EUR 249, USD 311 to institutions (effective 2012) (from IngentaConnect).
Indexed: A01, A02, A03, A08, A20, A22, A26, CA, CMM, CommAb, E01, E03, E07, E08, ERI, G08, H14, I05, IJCS, M06, MEA&I, MLA-IB, P02, P10, P18, P25, P30, P34, P48, P53, P54, PCI, PQC, PsycholAb, RILM, S02, S03, S09, SCOPUS, SOPODA, SociolAb, T02.
—IE, Ingenta. **CCC.**
Published by: (Central States Communication Association USA), Routledge (Subsidiary of: Taylor & Francis Group), 4 Park Sq, Milton Park, Abingdon, Oxon OX14 4RN, United Kingdom. TEL 44-20-70176000, FAX 44-20-70176336, subscriptions@tandf.co.uk, http://www.routledge.com. Eds. Jim L Query Jr., William Benoit. Adv. contact Linda Hann TEL 44-1344-779945. Circ: 2,700. **Subscr. to:** Taylor & Francis Ltd., Journals Customer Service, Sheepen Pl, Colchester, Essex CO3 3LP, United Kingdom. TEL 44-20-70175544, FAX 44-20-70175198.

302.23 SVK ISSN 1338-130X
▼ ➤ **COMMUNICATION TODAY**; scientific journal on mass media and marketing communications. Text in English, Slovak, Czech, Polish, German; Summaries in English. 2010. 2/yr. bk.rev. abstr.; bibl.; charts; illus. back issues avail. **Document type:** *Journal, Academic/ Scholarly.* **Description:** Presents theoretical and empirical studies on mass media and marketing communications.
Published by: Univerzita sv. Cyrila a Metoda v Trnave, Fakulta Masmedialnej Komunikacie/University of Ss. Cyril and Methodius in Trnava, Faculty of Mass Media Communication, Namestie Jozefa Herdu 2, Trnava, 917 01, Slovakia. TEL 421-33-5565424, FAX 421-33-5503236. Ed., Pub. Slavomir Magal. R&P Martin Solik.

302.23 FRA ISSN 0588-8018
P87
COMMUNICATIONS. Text in French. 1961. s-a. EUR 16 per issue (effective 2004). bk.rev. bibl. **Document type:** *Magazine, Consumer.* **Description:** Contains sociological and semiological studies of mass media.
Indexed: A22, DIP, FR, IBR, IBSS, IBZ, IIFP, IITV, RASB, SCOPUS, SOPODA, SociolAb.
—BLDSC (3343.750000), IE, Infotrieve, Ingenta, INIST. **CCC.**
Published by: (Ecole Pratique des Hautes Etudes, Centre d'Etudes des Communications de Masse), Editions du Seuil, 27 Rue Jacob, Paris, 75006, France. TEL 33-1-40465050, FAX 33-1-40464300, contact@seuil.com, http://www.seuil.com. Eds. Edgar Morin, Nicole Lapierre.

COMMUNITIES DIRECTORY. *see* LIFESTYLE

307 USA ISSN 2153-5523
▼ **COMMUNITY CONNECT**; the journal of civic voices. Text in English. 2009. s-a. free to qualified personnel (effective 2010). **Document type:** *Journal, Consumer.* **Description:** Features a conversation by several communities on housing issues and projects, as well as profiles of the community of Larimore and the Western Wellness Foundation & Best Friends Mentoring Program in Dickinson.
Related titles: Online - full text ed.: ISSN 2153-554X.
Published by: University of North Dakota, Center for Community Engagement, 317 Cambridge St - Stop 8254, Grand Forks, ND 58202. TEL 701-777-0675, cce@und.edu, http://learn.aero.und.edu/pages.asp?PageID=134554. Ed. Gregory Gagnon.

301 AUS ISSN 1832-7974
COMMUNITY DIRECTORY. Text in English. 2005. irreg., latest 2006. **Document type:** *Directory, Consumer.*
Published by: Baulkham Hills Holroyd Parramatta Migrant Resource Centre Inc., PO Box 1081, Parramatta, NSW 2124, Australia. TEL 61-2-96879901, FAX 61-2-96879990, enquiries@bhhpmrc.org.au, http://www.bhhpmrc.org.au. Ed. Aung Thu.

307 USA
COMMUNITY JOURNAL. Text in English. 1943. q. USD 25 domestic; USD 30 foreign (effective 2000). bk.rev. back issues avail. **Document type:** *Journal, Academic/Scholarly.* **Description:** Contains essays, commentary, and announcements pertaining to the growth of small communities as a basic social institution that encompasses units of economic, social, and spiritual developme nt.
Former titles (until 1998): Community Service Newsletter (0277-6189); Community Comments (0010-3780)
Indexed: NPI.
Published by: Community Service, Inc., 243, Yellow Spgs, OH 45387-0243. TEL 937-767-2161, FAX 937-767-2826. Ed., R&P Don Wallis. Circ: 1,500 (paid); 350 (controlled).

302.23 USA ISSN 1074-9004
HE8700
COMMUNITY MEDIA REVIEW. Short title: C M R. Text in English. 1977. q. USD 35 to non-members; free membership (effective 2005). adv. illus. index. back issues avail.; reprints avail. **Document type:** *Magazine, Trade.* **Description:** Devoted to media issues affecting community media workers and the empowerment of citizens through access to media.
Formerly: Community Television Review
Indexed: AltPI.
Published by: Alliance for Community Media, 666 11th St, NW, Ste 740, Washington, DC 20001-4542. TEL 202-393-2650, FAX 202-393-2653, government@alliancececm.org. R&P Maggie Juliano. Adv. contact Frank Ashea. B&W page USD 500, color page USD 1,504. Circ: 8,500 (controlled).

301 GBR ISSN 0195-6310
HM1
COMPARATIVE SOCIAL RESEARCH. Text in English. 1978. a. price varies. back issues avail. **Document type:** *Monographic series, Academic/Scholarly.* **Description:** Aims at furthering the international orientation in the social sciences.
Formerly (until 1979): Comparative Studies in Sociology (0164-1247)
Related titles: Online - full text ed.; Supplement(s): ISSN 1052-3650. 1990.
Indexed: A22, AmH&L, CA, HistAb, IBSS, P30, P42, PSA, S02, S03, SCOPUS, SOPODA, SSA, SociolAb, T02.
—BLDSC (3363.820000), IE, Infotrieve, Ingenta. **CCC.**
Published by: Emerald Group Publishing Ltd., Howard House, Wagon Ln, Bingley, W Yorks BD16 1WA, United Kingdom. TEL 44-1274-777700, FAX 44-1274-785201, emerald@emeraldinsight.com. Ed. Fredrik Engelstad. **Dist. by:** Turpin Distribution Services Ltd., Pegasus Dr, Stratton Business Park, Biggleswade, Bedfordshire SG18 8QB, United Kingdom. TEL 44-1767-604951, FAX 44-1767-601640, custserv@turpin-distribution.com, http://www.turpin-distribution.com/.

301 NLD ISSN 1569-1322
HM403 CODEN: CSOOBP
COMPARATIVE SOCIOLOGY. Text in English. 1960. 6/yr. EUR 562, USD 787 to institutions; EUR 613, USD 858 combined subscription to institutions (print & online eds.) (effective 2012). bk.rev. reprint service avail. from PSC. **Document type:** *Journal, Academic/Scholarly.* **Description:** Presents a detailed account of studies made in different cultures on a comparative basis.
Supersedes in part (in 2002): International Journal of Comparative Sociology (0020-7152)
Related titles: Online - full text ed.: ISSN 1569-1330. EUR 511, USD 715 to institutions (effective 2012) (from IngentaConnect).
Indexed: A01, A02, A03, A08, A20, A22, AICP, B04, BRD, CA, DIP, E01, GEOBASE, I13, I14, IBR, IBSS, IBZ, IZBG, LeftInd, P02, P10, P27, P34, P42, P48, P53, P54, PAIS, PQC, PSA, S02, S03, S11, SCOPUS, SSA, SSAI, SSAb, SSI, SociolAb, T02, W01, W02, W03.
—BLDSC (3363.825200), IE, Ingenta. **CCC.**
Published by: Brill, PO Box 9000, Leiden, 2300 PA, Netherlands. TEL 31-71-5353500, FAX 31-71-5317532, cs@brill.nl. Ed. David Sciulli. **Dist. by:** Turpin Distribution Services Ltd., Pegasus Dr, Stratton Business Park, Biggleswade, Bedfordshire SG18 8QB, United Kingdom.

301.09 GBR ISSN 0010-4175
H1
➤ **COMPARATIVE STUDIES IN SOCIETY AND HISTORY**; an international quarterly. Abbreviated title: C S S H. Text in English. 1959. q. GBP 140, USD 220 to institutions; GBP 150, USD 235 combined subscription to institutions (print & online eds.) (effective 2012). adv. bk.rev. bibl.; charts; illus. index. back issues avail.; reprint service avail. from PSC. **Document type:** *Journal, Academic/ Scholarly.* **Description:** Compares change and stability in societies all over the world and in all eras: topics such as slavery, colonialism, revolution, religious movements and women's roles.
Related titles: Microform ed.: (from PQC); Online - full text ed.: ISSN 1475-2999. GBP 128, USD 200 to institutions (effective 2012).

Indexed: A01, A02, A03, A08, A12, A20, A21, A22, A25, A26, ABCPolSci, ABIn, ABS&EES, AICP, APEL, ASCA, AcaI, AgrForAb, AmH&L, AmHI, ArtHuCI, B04, BAS, BRD, CA, CABA, CurCont, DIP, E01, E08, EI, F08, F12, FR, FamI, G08, GEOBASE, GH, H07, H08, H09, H10, H14, H16, HAb, HistAb, HumInd, I05, I13, I14, IBR, IBSS, IBZ, LT, MEA&I, MLA-IB, N02, P02, P06, P10, P13, P27, P30, P34, P42, P45, P46, P47, P48, P51, P53, P54, PCI, PQC, PRA, PSA, PerIslam, R12, RASB, RI-1, RI-2, RILM, RRTA, S02, S03, S05, S08, S09, SCOPUS, SOPODA, SRRA, SSA, SSCI, SociolAb, T02, T05, TAR, W03, W07, W09, W11.
—BLDSC (3363.850000), IE, Infotrieve, Ingenta, INIST. **CCC.**
Published by: (Society for the Comparative Study of Society and History USA), Cambridge University Press, The Edinburgh Bldg, Shaftesbury Rd, Cambridge, CB2 8RU, United Kingdom. TEL 44-1223-312393, FAX 44-1223-315052, journals@cambridge.org, http://www.cambridge.org/uk. Ed. Andrew Shryock. Adv. contact Rebecca Roberts TEL 44-1223-325083. **Subscr. to:** Cambridge University Press, 32 Ave of the Americas, New York, NY 10013. TEL 212-337-5000, FAX 212-691-3239, journals_subscriptions@cup.org.

➤ **COMPARATIVE STUDIES OF SOUTH ASIA, AFRICA AND THE MIDDLE EAST.** *see* HISTORY—History Of Asia

➤ **COMPARATIVE URBAN AND COMMUNITY RESEARCH.** *see* HOUSING AND URBAN PLANNING

301 USA
COMPLEXITY AND EMERGENCE IN ORGANIZATIONS. Text in English. 200?. irreg. **Document type:** *Monographic series, Academic/Scholarly.* **Description:** Presents research on theories of human organization, including ethics from the fields of complexity sciences, psychology and sociology.
Related titles: Online - full text ed.: ISSN 2154-9621.
Published by: C R C Press, LLC (Subsidiary of: Taylor & Francis Group), 6000 Broken Sound Pky, NW, Ste 300, Boca Raton, FL 33487. TEL 561-994-0555, FAX 561-989-9732, journals@crcpress.com, http://www.crcpress.com.

303 384 PRT ISSN 1646-4877
COMUNICACAO & CULTURA. Text in Portuguese. 2006. s-a. **Document type:** *Journal, Academic/Scholarly.*
Published by: Universidade Catolica Portuguesa, Faculdade de Ciencias Humanas, Palma de Cima, Lisbon, 1649-023, Portugal. TEL 351-21-424000, FAX 351-21-7270256, info@reitoria.ucp.pt, http://www.ucp.pt.

302.23 VEN ISSN 0251-3153
HM258
COMUNICACION. Text in Spanish. 1975. irreg. bk.rev.
Indexed: C01.
Published by: Centro de Comunicacion "Jesus M. Pellin.", Apdo 4 838, Carmeliatas, Caracas, DF 1010, Venezuela. Ed. Jose I Rey. Circ: 2,500.

302.23 MEX ISSN 0188-252X
P92.M45
➤ **COMUNICACION Y SOCIEDAD.** Variant title: Comunicacion y Sociedad. Cuadernos del CEIC. Text in Spanish. 1987. s-a. MXN 160 domestic; USD 25 in Latin America; USD 35 elsewhere (effective 2011). back issues avail. **Document type:** *Journal, Academic/Scholarly.*
Related titles: Online - full text ed.: 2004. free (effective 2011) (from SciELO).
Indexed: A01, A26, C01, CA, CMM, CommAb, F03, F04, H21, I04, I05, P08, T02.
—IE.
Published by: Universidad de Guadalajara, Departamento de Estudios de la Comunicacion Social, Paseo Poniente 2093, Jardines del Country, Guadalajara, JAL 44210, Mexico. TEL 52-3-8237505, FAX 52-3-8237631, http://fuentes.csh.udg.mx/coysoc/comysoc.htm.

302.2 ITA
P92.I8
COMUNICAZIONI SOCIALI. Text in Italian. 1973. 3/yr. EUR 50 domestic; EUR 70 foreign (effective 2009). adv. bk.rev. **Document type:** *Journal, Academic/Scholarly.* **Description:** Forum publishes scientific works elaborated from a secondary school setting. Focus is given to communication; cinema, television, radio, journalism, theater and advertising are analyzed through a theoretical and historical point of view.
Related titles: Online - full text ed.: Comunicazioni Sociali On-line. ISSN 2037-0415. 2009.
Indexed: DIP, IBSS, RILM.
Published by: (Universita Cattolica del Sacro Cuore), Vita e Pensiero (Subsidiary of: Universita Cattolica del Sacro Cuore), Largo Gemelli 1, Milan, 20123, Italy. TEL 39-02-72342335, FAX 39-02-72342260, redazione.vp@mi.unicatt.it. Ed. Gianfranco Bettetini. Circ: 550.

301 ARG ISSN 0327-7860
CONCEPTOS BOLETIN. Text in Spanish. 1912. bi-m. free. bk.rev. abstr.; bibl. **Description:** Includes articles about law, politics, economy, and sociology.
Formerly (until 1987): Museo Social Argentino. Boletin (0045-3331)
Indexed: SCOPUS, SOPODA, SociolAb.
Published by: Museo Social Argentino, Corrientes, 1723, Buenos Aires, 1042, Argentina.

302 DEU
➤ **CONFLICT & COMMUNICATION ONLINE.** Text in English, German. 2002. s-a. free. **Document type:** *Journal, Academic/Scholarly.* **Description:** Aims to promote discussion and exchange among researchers of different nationalities and disciplines, and by creatively employing the special possibilities offered by the Internet to set new quality standards.
Media: Online - full content.
Published by: Universitaet Konstanz, Fachbereich Psychologie, c/o Verlag Irena Regener, Ostseestrasse 109, Berlin, D-78457, Germany. Ed. Wilhelm Kempf.

301 USA ISSN 0899-9910
CONFLICT AND CONSCIOUSNESS; studies in war, peace and social thought. Text in English. 1989. irreg., latest vol.10, 2001. price varies. **Document type:** *Monographic series, Academic/Scholarly.* **Description:** Discusses topics on individual consciousness, personal and collective belief systems, and social practices involving coercion and violence.
—BLDSC (3410.651080).

Published by: Peter Lang Publishing, Inc. (Subsidiary of: Peter Lang Publishing Group), 29 Broadway, New York, NY 10006. TEL 212-647-7700, 212-647-7706, 800-770-5264, FAX 212-647-7707, customerservice@plang.com. Ed. Charles P Webel.

CONFRONTATION - CHANGE REVIEW. *see* BUSINESS AND ECONOMICS

CONGRESSO BRASILEIRO DE ECONOMIA E SOCIOLOGIA RURAL. ANAIS. *see* AGRICULTURE—Agricultural Economics

CONNEXIONS. *see* PSYCHOLOGY

302.23 USA
CONSOLE-ING PASSIONS. Text in English. 1995. irreg., latest 2009. price varies. back issues avail.; reprints avail. **Document type:** *Monographic series, Academic/Scholarly.*
Published by: Duke University Press, 905 W Main St, Ste 18 B, Durham, NC 27701. TEL 888-651-0122, FAX 888-651-0124, subscriptions@dukeupress.edu.

303.482 FRA ISSN 1953-762X
CONTACTS SANS FRONTIERE. Text in French. 2000. q. free. **Document type:** *Newsletter.* **Description:** Encourages cultural exchanges and experience through long-term stays in the homes of families all over the world. For young adults.
Published by: A F S Vivre Sans Frontiere, 46 Rue du commandant Jean Duhail, Fontenay sous Bois, 94120, France. info-france@afs.org.

301.6 USA ISSN 1075-7201
BL65.V55
CONTAGION; journal of violence, mimesis, and culture. Text in English. 1994. a. USD 42 (effective 2011). reprint service avail. from PSC. **Document type:** *Journal, Academic/Scholarly.* **Description:** Explores the relationship between violence and religion in the genesis and maintenance of culture.
Related titles: Online - full text ed.: ISSN 1930-1200.
Indexed: A22, AmHI, CA, E01, H07, I02, MLA-IB, P10, P27, P28, P46, P48, P53, P54, PQC, S11, SCOPUS, T02.
—IE. **CCC.**
Published by: (Colloquium on Violence and Religion), Michigan State University Press, 1405 S Harrison Rd, Manly Miles Bldg, Ste 25, East Lansing, MI 48823. TEL 517-355-9543, FAX 517-432-2611, msupress@msu.edu, http://www.msupress.msu.edu. Ed. William A Johnsen.

CONTEMPORARY FAMILY THERAPY; an international journal. *see* PSYCHOLOGY

301 GBR ISSN 0069-942X
CONTEMPORARY ISSUES SERIES. Text in English. 1969. a.
Published by: Peter Owen Ltd., 73 Kenway Rd, London, SW5 0RE, United Kingdom. TEL 071-373-5628, FAX 071-373-6760. **Dist. in U.S. by:** Dufour Editions Inc., PO Box 449, Chester, PA 19425. TEL 215-458-5005.

CONTEMPORARY PSYCHOANALYTIC STUDIES. *see* PSYCHOLOGY

CONTEMPORARY SEXUALITY; the international resource for educators, researchers and therapists. *see* PSYCHOLOGY

301 USA ISSN 0094-3061
HM1
➤ **CONTEMPORARY SOCIOLOGY.** Text in English. 1972. bi-m. USD 298, GBP 175 combined subscription to institutions (print & online eds.); USD 292, GBP 172 to institutions (effective 2011). adv. bk.rev. illus. Index. reprint service avail. from PSC. **Document type:** *Journal, Academic/Scholarly.* **Description:** Publishes reviews and critical discussions of recent works in sociology and in related disciplines which merit the attention of sociologists.
Related titles: Microform ed.: (from PQC); Online - full text ed.: ISSN 1939-8638. USD 268, GBP 158 to institutions (effective 2011).
Indexed: A01, A02, A03, A08, A20, A21, A22, A25, A26, ABS&EES, AMHA, ASCA, AcaI, B04, B05, B14, BRD, BRI, C28, CA, CBRI, CMM, ChPerI, Chicano, CurCont, DIP, E01, E08, EI, F09, FamI, G08, G10, I05, IBR, IBZ, MEA&I, P02, P06, P10, P13, P27, P30, P34, P42, P46, P48, P53, P54, PCI, PQC, PSA, RASB, RI-1, RI-2, RefSour, S02, S03, S08, S09, S11, SCOPUS, SOPODA, SRRA, SSA, SSAI, SSAb, SSCI, SSI, SociolAb, T02, W01, W02, W03, W07, W09.
—BLDSC (3425.305000), IE, Infotrieve, Ingenta. **CCC.**
Published by: (American Sociological Association), Sage Publications, Inc., 2455 Teller Rd, Thousand Oaks, CA 91320. TEL 805-499-9774, FAX 805-499-0871, info@sagepub.com, http://www.sagepub.com/. Ed. Alan Sica. adv.: page USD 640. Circ: 5,000.

301 GBR
CONTEMPORARY STUDIES IN SOCIOLOGY. Text in English. 1983. irreg., latest vol.19, 2000. price varies. back issues avail. **Document type:** *Monographic series, Academic/Scholarly.*
Published by: Emerald Group Publishing Ltd., Howard House, Wagon Ln, Bingley, W Yorks BD16 1WA, United Kingdom. TEL 44-1274-777700, FAX 44-1274-785201, emerald@emeraldinsight.com, http://www.emeraldinsight.com. **Dist. by:** Turpin Distribution Services Ltd., Pegasus Dr, Stratton Business Park, Biggleswade, Bedfordshire SG18 8QB, United Kingdom. TEL 44-1767-604951, FAX 44-1767-601640, custserv@turpin-distribution.com, http://www.turpin-distribution.com/.

CONTEXTES. *see* LITERATURE

301 300 USA ISSN 1536-5042
H62.A1
CONTEXTS; understanding people in their social worlds. Text in English. 2002 (Feb). q. USD 205 combined subscription to institutions (print & online eds.) (effective 2010). adv. bk.rev. 72 p./no.; back issues avail.; reprint service avail. from PSC. **Document type:** *Journal, Academic/Scholarly.* **Description:** Provides information for diverse readers & sociologist who wish to be current about social science knowledge, emerging trends, and their relevance.
Related titles: Online - full text ed.: ISSN 1537-6052. USD 171 to institutions (effective 2010) (from IngentaConnect).
Indexed: A22, ABS&EES, ASIP, CA, E01, ENW, FamI, LeftInd, P10, P19, P46, P48, P53, P54, PAIS, PQC, S02, S03, S11, SCOPUS, SociolAb, T02.
—BLDSC (3425.440000), IE, Ingenta. **CCC.**
Published by: (American Sociological Association), University of California Press, Journals Division, 2000 Ctr St, Ste 303, Berkeley, CA 94704. TEL 510-643-7154, FAX 510-642-9917, customerservice@ucpressjournals.com, http://www.ucpressjournals.com. adv.: B&W page USD 395, color page USD 585; 6.75 x 9.

303.4 NLD ISSN 1875-4007
CONTEXTUALS. Text in English. irreg., latest vol.9, 2009. **Document type:** *Monographic series, Trade.*
Media: Online - full text.
Published by: Context, International Cooperation, Cornelis Houtmanstraat 15, Utrecht, 3572 LT, Netherlands. TEL 31-30-2737500, FAX 31-30-2737509, info@developmenttraining.org, http://www.developmenttraining.org.

CONTINUITY AND CHANGE; a journal of social structure, law and demography in past societies. *see* POPULATION STUDIES

304 USA
CONTRADICTIONS OF MODERNITY SERIES. Variant title: Contradictions Series. Text in English. 1995. irreg., latest vol.24, 2009. price varies. back issues avail. **Document type:** *Monographic series, Academic/Scholarly.* **Description:** Explores the problems of theorizing the many and sometimes contradictory concepts of modernity and examines the specific locations of theory within the modern.
Published by: University of Minnesota Press, Ste 290, 111 Third Ave S, Minneapolis, MN 55401. TEL 612-627-1970, FAX 612-627-1980, ump@umn.edu. Ed. Craig Calhoun. **Dist. by:** c/o Chicago Distribution Center, 11030 S Langley Ave, Chicago, IL 60628; Plymbridge Distributors Ltd, Estover Rd, Plymouth, Devon PL6 7PY, United Kingdom. TEL 44-1752-202-301, FAX 44-1752-202-331.

301 IND ISSN 0069-9659
➤ **CONTRIBUTIONS TO INDIAN SOCIOLOGY - NEW SERIES.** Text in English. N.S. 1957. 3/yr. USD 374, GBP 202 combined subscription to institutions (print & online eds.); USD 367, GBP 198 to institutions (effective 2011). adv. bk.rev. index. reprint service avail. from PSC. **Document type:** *Journal, Academic/Scholarly.* **Description:** Presents a diversity of theoretical approaches to the study of society in India. It provides a forum for divergent views on Indian society, believing that differences of approach are born of genuine scholarly concerns. Regular features include research articles, review articles, a 'discussion' section, book reviews and notes.
Formerly: Contributions to Indian Sociology (0069-9667)
Related titles: Microfiche ed.: N.S. (from PQC); Online - full text ed.: ISSN 0973-0648. USD 337, GBP 182 to institutions (effective 2011).
Indexed: A20, A22, AICP, ASCA, AnthLit, B07, BAS, CA, CurCont, DIP, E01, F09, FR, FamI, GEOBASE, I13, I14, IBR, IBSS, IBZ, M10, P30, P42, PAA&I, PCI, PSA, RASB, S02, S03, SCOPUS, SOPODA, SSA, SSCI, SociolAb, T02, W07, W09.
—BLDSC (3458.650000), IE, Infotrieve, Ingenta, INIST. **CCC.**
Published by: (Institute of Economic Growth), Sage Publications India Pvt. Ltd. (Subsidiary of: Sage Publications, Inc.), M-32 Market, Greater Kailash-I, PO Box 4215, New Delhi, 110 048, India. TEL 91-11-6444958, FAX 91-11-6472426, journalsubs@sagepub.in, http://www.indiasage.com/. Eds. Dipankar Gupta, Patricia Uberoi. Adv. contact Sunanda Ghosh. page USD 75. Circ: 900. **Subscr. in Europe, Middle East, Africa & Australasia to:** Sage Publications Ltd., 1 Oliver's Yard, 55 City Rd, London EC1Y 1SP, United Kingdom. TEL 44-207-3248701, FAX 44-207-3248733, subscription@sagepub.co.uk; **Subscr. in the Americas to:** Sage Publications, Inc., 2455 Teller Rd, Thousand Oaks, CA 91320. TEL 805-499-9774, FAX 805-499-0871, journals@sagepub.com.

306.44 DEU ISSN 1861-0676
P41
➤ **CONTRIBUTIONS TO THE SOCIOLOGY OF LANGUAGE.** Text in German. 1972. irreg., latest vol.100, 2011. price varies. back issues avail. **Document type:** *Monographic series, Academic/Scholarly.* **Description:** Presents research on sociolinguistic theory, methods, findings and applications.
Indexed: BibLing.
—BLDSC (3461.450000), IE, Ingenta. **CCC.**
Published by: De Gruyter Mouton (Subsidiary of: Walter de Gruyter GmbH & Co. KG), Genthiner Str 13, Berlin, 10785, Germany. TEL 49-30-260050, FAX 49-30-26005251, mouton@degruyter.de. Ed. Joshua Fishman.

➤ **CONTRIBUTIONS TO THE STUDY OF POPULAR CULTURE.** *see* ANTHROPOLOGY

301 ITA ISSN 1125-4661
CONTROTEMPO; forme dell'esperienza nella modernita. Text in Italian. 1996. a. EUR 21 for 2 yrs. domestic; EUR 50 for 2 yrs. foreign (effective 2009). **Document type:** *Magazine, Consumer.* **Description:** Confronts the issues created by modernity.
Published by: Moretti e Vitali Editori, Via Sergentini 6a, Bergamo, BG 24128, Italy. TEL 39-035-251300, FAX 39-035-4329409, http://www.morettievitali.it.

CONVERGING EVIDENCE IN LANGUAGE AND COMMUNICATION RESEARCH. *see* LINGUISTICS

327.17 USA ISSN 0259-3882
T49.5
COOPERATION SOUTH. Text in English. 1979. s-a.
Formerly (until 1986): Technical Cooperation Among Developing Countries. News (0252-6433)
Related titles: Spanish ed.: Cooperacion Sur. ISSN 1014-0298; French ed.: Cooperation Sud. ISSN 1010-4437.
Published by: United Nations Development Programme, Technical Cooperation Among Developing Countries, One United Nations Plaza, New York, NY 10017. FAX 212-906-5364.

334 JPN
COOPERATIVE LIFE/GEKKAN KYODOTAI. Text in Japanese. 1963. m. JPY 1,000, USD 5. adv. bk.rev. abstr.; charts; stat. index.
Formerly: Gekkan Kibbutz (0016-5956)
Published by: Japanese Commune Movement, 2083 Sakae-cho, Imaichi-shi, Tochigi-ken 321-1200, Japan. Ed. Hisao Okumura. Circ: 1,000.

LE COQ HERON. *see* MEDICAL SCIENCES—Psychiatry And Neurology

303.4 AUS ISSN 1837-5391
▼ ➤ **COSMOPOLITAN CIVIL SOCIETIES;** an interdisciplinary journal. Text in English. 2009. irreg., latest vol.2, no.1, 2010. free (effective 2010). back issues avail. **Document type:** *Journal, Academic/Scholarly.* **Description:** Aims to provide a forum for investigation of cosmopolitan engagement through collective action and learning; strengthening civil societies; migration, cultural diversity and racism; human rights and social justice.
Media: Online - full text.
Indexed: A01.

Published by: Cosmopolitan Civil Societies Research Centre, Level 3, MaryAnn House, 645 Harris St, PO Box 123, Broadway, NSW 2007, Australia. TEL 61-2-95149647, FAX 61-2-95149651, ccs@uts.edu.au, http://www.ccs.uts.edu.au.

301.6 USA
COURAGE IN THE STRUGGLE FOR JUSTICE AND PEACE. Text in English. 1986. 10/yr. free. bk.rev. back issues avail. **Description:** Covers social justice issues.
Published by: United Church of Christ, Office for Church Society, 110 Maryland Ave, N E, Washington, DC 20002. TEL 202-543-1517. Circ: 16,000.

303.842 FRA ISSN 1957-5130
COVE-ATAKPAME. Text in French. 1986. bi-m. EUR 20 (effective 2008). **Document type:** *Magazine, Consumer.*
Formerly (until 2007): Atakpame (0768-8008)
Published by: Association Niortaise de Jumelage et de Cooperation avec Atakpame, 12 Rue J. Cugnot, NIORT, 79000, France. TEL 33-5-49090712, anjca@free.fr.

CREDO; det kristne studentermagasinet. *see* RELIGIONS AND THEOLOGY—Protestant

301 ITA ISSN 0011-1546
HM7
LA CRITICA SOCIOLOGICA. Text in Italian; Summaries in English. 1967. q. EUR 245 combined subscription domestic to institutions (print & online eds.); EUR 345 combined subscription foreign to institutions (print & online eds.) (effective 2009). bk.rev. bibl.; illus. reprints avail.
Related titles: Online - full text ed.: ISSN 1972-5914 (from PQC).
Indexed: A22, CA, DIP, FR, I13, IBR, IBSS, IBZ, MLA-IB, P30, P42, PCI, PSA, RASB, RILM, S02, S03, SCOPUS, SOPODA, SSA, SociolAb, T02.
—BLDSC (3487.410000), IE, Infotrieve, Ingenta, INIST.
Published by: Fabrizio Serra Editore (Subsidiary of: Accademia Editoriale), c/o Accademia Editoriale, Via Santa Bibbiana 28, Pisa, 56127, Italy. TEL 39-050-542332, FAX 39-050-574888, accademiaeditoriale@accademiaeditoriale.it, http://www.libraweb.net.

301 GBR ISSN 1752-3079
CRITICAL APPROACHES TO DISCOURSE ANALYSIS ACROSS DISCIPLINES. Text in English. 2007. s-a. free (effective 2011). **Document type:** *Journal, Academic/Scholarly.*
Media: Online - full text.
Indexed: L&LBA.
Published by: Critical Approaches to Discourse Analysis Across Disciplines (C A D A A D), c/o Christopher Hart, School of Humanities, University of Hertfordshire, Hatfield, Hertfordshire AL10 9AB, United Kingdom. Ed. Christopher Hart.

302.2 ZAF ISSN 0256-0046
P92.S58
➤ **CRITICAL ARTS**; a south-north journal of cultural and media studies. Text in English. 1980. s-a. GBP 304 combined subscription in United Kingdom to institutions (print & online eds.); EUR 474, USD 592 combined subscription to institutions (print & online eds.) (effective 2012). adv. bk.rev. back issues avail.; reprint service avail. from PSC. **Document type:** *Journal, Academic/Scholarly.* **Description:** Examines the relationship between texts and contexts of media in the Third World, cultural formations and popular forms of expression.
Related titles: Online - full text ed.: ISSN 1992-6049. GBP 275 in United Kingdom to institutions; EUR 426, USD 533 to institutions (effective 2012).
Indexed: A01, A02, A03, A08, A22, A26, A30, A31, ASD, AltPI, AmHI, ArtHuCI, BEL&L, CA, CurCont, DIP, E01, E08, G08, H07, HRIR, I05, IBR, IBT&D, IBZ, IIBP, ISAP, L&LBA, L05, L06, M01, M02, MLA, MLA-IB, PCI, RILM, S02, S03, S09, SOPODA, SSCI, SociolAb, T02, W07.
—IE. **CCC.**
Published by: (Critical Arts Projects), University of KwaZulu-Natal, Graduate Programme in Cultural and Media Studies, King George V Ave, Durban, 4041, South Africa. TEL 27-31-2602505, FAX 27-31-2601519, govends@nu.ac.za. Ed., R&P Keyan G Tomaselli. Adv. contact Susan Govender. Circ: 400. **Subscr. outside of Africa to:** Routledge, Customer Services Dept, Rankine Rd, Basingstoke, Hants RG24 8PR, United Kingdom. TEL 44-1256-813000, FAX 44-1256-330245, tf.enquiries@tfinforma.com.

301 USA ISSN 1528-6118
CRITICAL CULTURAL COMMUNICATIONS STUDIES. Text in English. 2002. irreg., latest vol.12, 2008. price varies. **Document type:** *Monographic series, Academic/Scholarly.* **Description:** Interrogates (from a critical perspective) the role of communication in intercultural contact, in both domestic and international contexts.
Published by: Peter Lang Publishing, Inc. (Subsidiary of: Peter Lang Publishing Group), 29 Broadway, New York, NY 10006. TEL 212-647-7700, 800-770-5264, FAX 212-647-7707, customerservice@plang.com, http://www.peterlangusa.com. Ed. Thomas K Nakayama.

303 144 GBR ISSN 1440-9917
B809.3.A1
➤ **CRITICAL HORIZONS.** Text in English. 2000. 3/yr. USD 300 combined subscription in North America to institutions (print & online eds.); GBP 185 combined subscription elsewhere to institutions (print & online eds.) (effective 2012). adv. bk.rev. back issues avail.; reprints avail. **Document type:** *Journal, Academic/Scholarly.* **Description:** Brings out articles from critical theorists working in social and political philosophy, aesthetics, spatial and urban theory, anthropology, history of ideas, film and art theory, gender studies, comparative literature, social, and critical theory.
Related titles: Online - full text ed.: ISSN 1568-5160. USD 240 in North America to institutions; GBP 148 elsewhere to institutions (effective 2012) (from IngentaConnect).
Indexed: A01, A03, A08, A22, CA, E01, IZBG, LeftInd, P42, PSA, PhilInd, S02, S03, SCOPUS, SSA, SociolAb.
—BLDSC (3487.452600), IE, Ingenta. **CCC.**
Published by: Equinox Publishing Ltd., Unit S3, Kelham House, 3 Lancaster St, Sheffield, S6 3AF, United Kingdom. TEL 44-114-2725957, FAX 44-560-3459046, journals@equinoxpub.com, http://www.equinoxpub.com/. Adv. contact Val Hall.

302.23 USA ISSN 1947-6264
▼ **A CRITICAL INTRODUCTION TO MEDIA AND COMMUNICATION THEORY.** Text in English. forthcoming 2011. irreg. price varies. **Document type:** *Monographic series, Academic/Scholarly.* **Description:** Book series featuring theories and theorists in media and communications.
Published by: Peter Lang Publishing, Inc. (Subsidiary of: Peter Lang Publishing Group), 29 Broadway, New York, NY 10006. TEL 212-647-7700, FAX 212-647-7707, customerservice@plang.com, http://www.peterlang.com.

303 GBR ISSN 1753-0873
LC196
CRITICAL LITERACY; theories and practices. Text in English. 2007. s-a. free (effective 2011). **Document type:** *Journal, Academic/Scholarly.*
Media: Online - full text.
Indexed: E03.
Published by: University of Nottingham, Centre for the Study of Social and Global Justice, Law and Social Sciences Bldg, University Park, Nottingham, NG7 2RD, United Kingdom. TEL 44-0115-9868135, FAX 44-0115-9514859, http://www.nottingham.ac.uk/CSSGJ/Contact.aspx. Eds. Lynn Mario T M de Souza, Vanessa Andreotti.

302.23 DEU
▼ **CRITICAL MEDIA STUDIES.** Text in German. 2009. irreg., latest vol.5, 2011. price varies. **Document type:** *Monographic series, Academic/Scholarly.*
Published by: Transcript, Muehlenstr 47, Bielefeld, 33607, Germany. TEL 49-521-63454, FAX 49-521-61040, live@transcript-verlag.de.

306 USA ISSN 1933-0979
CRITICAL PERSPECTIVES ON MODERN CULTURE. Text in English. 199?. irreg., latest 2003. price varies. **Document type:** *Monographic series, Academic/Scholarly.* **Description:** Aims to make available to a general readership original, well-written works of cultural history and contemporary criticism that cut across established disciplinary boundaries.
Published by: University of Massachusetts Press, PO Box 429, Amherst, MA 01004. TEL 413-545-2217, FAX 413-545-1226, info@umpress.umass.edu. Ed. David Gross. **Dist. by:** Hopkins Fulfillment Services, PO Box 50370, Baltimore, MD 21211. TEL 800-537-5487, FAX 410-516-6998, hfscustserv@mail.press.jhu.edu.

301 AUS ISSN 1838-8310
CRITICAL RACE AND WHITENESS STUDIES. Text in English. 2005. irreg. free (effective 2011). **Document type:** *Journal, Academic/Scholarly.*
Formerly (until 2011): Australian Critical Race and Whiteness Studies (1832-3898)
Media: Online - full text.
Published by: Australian Critical Race and Whiteness Studies Association (A C R A W S A) Ed. Holly Randell-Moon.

CRITICAL REVIEW OF INTERNATIONAL SOCIAL AND POLITICAL PHILOSOPHY. *see* POLITICAL SCIENCE—International Relations

301.5 GBR ISSN 0268-1803
HM1
CRITICAL SOCIAL RESEARCH. Text in English. 1984. s-a. **Document type:** *Journal, Academic/Scholarly.*
Indexed: P30.
—BLDSC (3487.485700).
Published by: British Sociological Association, Bailey Suite, Palatine House, Belmont Business Park, Belmont, Durham DH1 1TW, United Kingdom. TEL 44-191-3830839, FAX 44-191-3830782, enquiries@britsoc.org.uk, http://www.britsoc.co.uk/.

CRITICAL SOCIOLOGY. *see* LITERARY AND POLITICAL REVIEWS

CRITICAL STUDIES IN EDUCATION AND CULTURE. *see* EDUCATION

302.23 USA ISSN 1529-5036
P87
➤ **CRITICAL STUDIES IN MEDIA COMMUNICATION.** Text in English. 1984. 5/yr. GBP 229 combined subscription in United Kingdom to institutions (print & online eds.); EUR 297, USD 372 combined subscription to institutions (print & online eds.) (effective 2012). adv. bk.rev. illus. cum.index. reprint service avail. from PSC. **Document type:** *Journal, Academic/Scholarly.* **Description:** Features cross-disciplinary works that enrich debates among various disciplines, critical traditions, methodological and analytical approaches, and theoretical standpoints.
Formerly (unti 2000): Critical Studies in Mass Communication (0739-3180)
Related titles: Online - full text ed.: ISSN 1479-5809. GBP 208 in United Kingdom to institutions; EUR 269, USD 338 to institutions (effective 2012) (from IngentaConnect).
Indexed: A01, A02, A03, A08, A20, A22, A26, ABS&EES, ASCA, AmH&L, AmHI, B04, BRD, CA, CMCI, CMM, CommAb, CurCont, DIP, E01, E02, E03, E07, E08, ERI, EdA, EdI, F01, F02, FamI, G08, H07, H08, H14, HAb, HumInd, I05, IBR, IBSS, IBZ, IJCS, MLA-IB, P02, P10, P13, P18, P27, P30, P42, P48, P53, P54, PAIS, PQC, PSA, RI-1, RI-2, RILM, S02, S03, S09, SCOPUS, SOPODA, SSA, SSAI, SSAb, SSCI, SSI, SociolAb, T02, W03, W07.
—IE, Infotrieve, Ingenta. **CCC.**
Published by: (National Communication Association), Routledge (Subsidiary of: Taylor & Francis Group), 325 Chestnut St, Ste 800, Philadelphia, PA 19106. TEL 215-625-8900, 800-354-1420, FAX 215-625-2940, orders@taylorandfrancis.com. Ed. Eric King Watts.

301 USA ISSN 1948-5832
▼ **CRITICAL THEORY & SOCIAL JUSTICE JOURNAL OF UNDERGRADUATE RESEARCH.** Abbreviated title: C T S J. Text in English. 2009. s-a. free (effective 2010). **Document type:** *Journal, Academic/Scholarly.* **Description:** Features undergraduate students' critical research and writing on the intersections of race, sexuality, and nationality as related to problems of social justice.
Media: Online - full text.
Published by: Occidental College, 1600 Campus Rd, Los Angeles, CA 90041. TEL 323-349-0635, http://www.oxy.edu.

CRITIQUE OF ANTHROPOLOGY. *see* ANTHROPOLOGY

CROIRE AUJOURD'HUI. *see* RELIGIONS AND THEOLOGY

303 CAN ISSN 1712-8358
CROSS - CULTURAL COMMUNICATION/COMMUNICATION CROIX - CULTURELLE. Text in English, Chinese, Russian. 2005. q. back issues avail. **Document type:** *Journal, Academic/Scholarly.*
Related titles: Online - full text ed.: ISSN 1923-6700. free (effective 2011).
Indexed: A01, A03, A12, A17, A26, ABIn, C03, C05, CA, CBCABus, CPerI, E08, I05, P10, P48, P51, P52, P53, P54, PQC, S02, S03, S09, T02.
Published by: Canadian Academy of Oriental and Occidental Culture (C A O O C), 3-265 Melrose, Montreal, PQ H4H 1T2, Canada. caooc@hotmail.com. Ed. Jenny Ding.

CROSS-CULTURAL COMMUNICATION. *see* LINGUISTICS

301 USA ISSN 1075-1300
E184.O6
CROSS CURRENTS (LOS ANGELES). Text in English. 1977. s-a. Included with subscr. to Amerasia Journal and AAPI Nexus Journal. back issues avail. **Document type:** *Newsletter, Consumer.*
Related titles: Online - full text ed.: free (effective 2010).
Indexed: PerIslam, RILM.
—BLDSC (3488.954950).
Published by: University of California, Los Angeles, Asian American Studies Center, 3230 Campbell Hall, PO Box 951546, Los Angeles, CA 90095. TEL 310-825-2974, FAX 310-206-9844, aascpress@aasc.ucla.edu. Ed. Christina Aujean Lee.

303.842 DNK ISSN 1563-2857
CROSSING BORDERS. Text in English. 1999. bi-m. **Document type:** *Magazine, Consumer.*
Published by: (Palestinian Youth Association for Leadership And Rights Activation ISR), Crossing Borders, Krogerupvej 9, Humlebaek, DK 3050, Denmark. TEL 45-49213371, cb@crossingborder.org.

306 GBR ISSN 2040-4344
▼ ➤ **CROSSINGS**; journal of migration and culture. Text in English. 2010. a. GBP 36, USD 68 per issue to individuals; GBP 132, USD 185 per issue to institutions (effective 2012). adv. back issues avail. **Document type:** *Journal, Academic/Scholarly.* **Description:** Aims to advance the study of the plethora of cultural texts on migration produced by an increasing number of cultural practitioners across the globe who face questions of culture in the context of migration.
Related titles: Online - full text ed.: ISSN 2040-4352. GBP 99, USD 140 per issue (effective 2012).
Indexed: S02, S03, T02.
Published by: Intellect Ltd., The Mill, Parnall Rd, Fishponds, Bristol, BS16 3JG, United Kingdom. TEL 44-117-9589910, FAX 44-117-9589911, info@intellectbooks.com. Pub. Masoud Yazdani. **Dist. by:** Turpin Distribution Services Ltd., Pegasus Dr, Stratton Business Park, Biggleswade, Bedfordshire SG18 8QB, United Kingdom. TEL 44-1767-604951, FAX 44-1767-601640, custserv@turpin-distribution.com, http://www.turpin-distribution.com/.

306 USA ISSN 1096-3782
HN39.U6
CRUSADE MAGAZINE. Text in English. 1979. bi-m. USD 30 domestic; USD 42 foreign (effective 2000 - 2001). **Document type:** *Magazine, Consumer.*
Former titles (until 1996): Tradition, Family and Property; (until 1993): T F P Newsletter
Published by: American Society for the Defense of Tradition, Family and Property, PO Box 1868, York, PA 17405-1868. TEL 717-225-5199, FAX 717-225-1675. Ed. C Preston Noell III. R&P Antonio Fragelli. Circ: 3,500 (paid).

306 ESP ISSN 1699-3853
CUADERNO CULTURAL PRIMULA. Text in Spanish. 2004. s-a.
Related titles: Online - full text ed.: ISSN 1699-387X. 2004.
Published by: Hospital Cabuenes, Apartado 205, Gijon, Asturias 33394, Spain. ccprimula@yahoo.es. Ed. Maria Aurora Rodriguez-Alonso.

301 ARG ISSN 1851-9970
CUADERNOS DE INVESTIGACION ETNOGRAFICAS. Text in Spanish. 2008. q. **Document type:** *Journal, Academic/Scholarly.*
Published by: Universidad Nacional de San Martin, Centro de Investigaciones Etnograficas, Ave 25 de Mayo y Francias, San Martin, Buenos Aires, Argentina. TEL 54-11-45807302, cietno@unsam.edu.ar, http://www.unsam.edu.ar/.

301 CHL ISSN 0718-0586
CUADERNOS INTERCULTURALES. Text in Spanish. 2003. s-a. **Document type:** *Journal, Academic/Scholarly.*
Related titles: Online - full text ed.: free (effective 2011).
Indexed: H21, P08.
Published by: Universidad de Valparaiso, Errazuriz 2190, Valparaiso, Chile. http://www.uv.cl. Ed. Luis Castro Castro.

306 MEX
CUADERNOS POLITECNICAS; ciencia y cultura. Text in Spanish. 1973. bi-m. MXN 60, USD 5.
Published by: Instituto Politecnico Nacional, Comision de Operacion y Fomento de Actividades Academicas, Unidad Profesional Zacatenco, Col Lindavista, Mexico City, DF 07738, Mexico. Circ: 6,000.

301 ESP ISSN 1889-1489
CUENTA Y RAZON. Text in Spanish. 1981. bi-m. back issues avail. **Document type:** *Journal, Academic/Scholarly.*
Former titles (until 2008): Cuenta y Razon del Pensamiento Actual (1136-811X); (until 1991): Cuenta y Razon (0211-1381)
Related titles: Online - full text ed.: ISSN 1989-2705.
Indexed: P09, PCI, RILM.
Published by: FUNDES, Serrano, 17, Piso 2, Der., Madrid, 28001, Spain. TEL 34-91-4323345, FAX 34-91-5782716, fundes@fundes.es, http://www.fundes.es/.

301 ARG ISSN 1668-1584
CUESTIONES DE SOCIOLOGIA. Text in Spanish. 2003. a. **Document type:** *Journal, Academic/Scholarly.*
Published by: Universidad Nacional de la Plata, Facultad de Humanidades y Ciencias de la Educacion, Calle 48 entre 6 y 7, 1er Subsuelo, La Plata, Buenos Aires 1900, Argentina. TEL 54-221-4230125, ceciroz@.fahce.unlp.edu.ar, http://www.publicaciones.fahce.unlp.edu.ar.

306 CAN ISSN 1918-5480
➤ **CUIZINE**; the journal of Canadian food cultures/revue des cultures culinaires au Canada. Text in English, French. 2008. free (effective 2011). **Document type:** *Journal, Academic/Scholarly.*
Media: Online - full text.
Published by: McGill University Library, McLennan Library Bldg, 3459 McTavish St, Montreal, PQ H3A 1Y1, Canada. http://www.mcgill.ca/library/.

▼ ➤ **CULTIVATE.** *see* ART

➤ **CULTURA Y EDUCACION**; revista de teoria, investigacion y practica. *see* EDUCATION

306 GBR ISSN 1478-0038
HN1
➤ **CULTURAL & SOCIAL HISTORY.** Text in English. 2004. q. USD 365 combined subscription in US & Canada to institutions (print & online eds.); GBP 187 combined subscription elsewhere to institutions (print & online eds.) (effective 2011). adv. bk.rev. bibl.; charts; illus. back issues avail.; reprints avail. **Document type:** *Journal, Academic/Scholarly.* **Description:** Committed to dialogue between social and cultural historians that will reinvigorate the discipline of history in the wake of epistemological challenges that have brought into question many of the foundational assumptions of historians.
Related titles: Online - full text ed.: ISSN 1478-0046. USD 310 in US & Canada to institutions; GBP 159 elsewhere to institutions (effective 2011) (from IngentaConnect).
Indexed: A20, A22, A26, AmH&L, ArtHuCI, BrHumI, CA, E01, H05, HistAb, I05, IBR, IBZ, LeftInd, P10, P42, P48, P53, P54, PQC, PSA, S02, S03, S11, SCOPUS, SociolAb, T02, W07.
—BLDSC (3491.660855), IE, Ingenta. **CCC.**
Published by: (Social History Society), Berg Publishers (Subsidiary of: Oxford International Publishers Ltd.), 1st Fl Angel Ct, 81 St Clements St, Oxford, Berks OX4 1AW, United Kingdom. TEL 44-1865-245104, FAX 44-1865-791165, enquiry@bergpublishers.com. Eds. David Hopkin, Padma Anagol. Pub. Ms. Kathryn Earle. **Dist. by:** Turpin Distribution Services Ltd., Pegasus Dr, Stratton Business Park, Biggleswade, Bedfordshire SG18 8QB, United Kingdom. TEL 44-1767-604800, FAX 44-1767-601640, custserv@turpin-distribution.com, http://www.turpin-distribution.com/.

➤ **CULTURAL CRITIQUE (MINNEAPOLIS, 1985)**; an international journal of cultural studies. *see* ANTHROPOLOGY

306 USA ISSN 1099-9809
RC455.4.E8 CODEN: CDEPFD
➤ **CULTURAL DIVERSITY & ETHNIC MINORITY PSYCHOLOGY.** Text in English. 1995. q. USD 110 domestic to individuals; USD 137 foreign to individuals; USD 398 domestic to institutions; USD 443 foreign to institutions (effective 2011). adv. back issues avail.; reprint service avail. from PSC. **Document type:** *Journal, Academic/Scholarly.* **Description:** Seeks to publish theoretical, conceptual, research, and case study articles that promote the development of knowledge and understanding, application of psychological principles, and scholarly analysis of social-political forces affecting racial and ethnic minorities.
Formerly (until 1999): Cultural Diversity and Mental Health (1077-341X)
Related titles: Microform ed.: (from PQC); Online - full text ed.: ISSN 1939-0106 (from ScienceDirect).
Indexed: A20, A22, B04, BRD, C06, C07, CA, CurCont, E-psyche, E02, E03, EMBASE, ERI, EdA, EdI, ExcerpMed, HEA, IndMed, MEDLINE, P03, P30, PRA, PsycInfo, PsycholAb, R10, Reac, S02, S03, S21, SCOPUS, SSA, SSCI, SWR&A, SociolAb, T02, V&AA, W03, W07.
—BLDSC (3491.662416), GNLM, IE, Infotrieve, Ingenta. **CCC.**
Published by: (The Society for the Psychology Study of Ethnic Minority Issues - Division 45), American Psychological Association, 750 First St, NE, Washington, DC 20002. TEL 202-336-5500, 800-374-2721, journals@apa.org. Ed. Michael A Zarate. Adv. contact Doug Constant TEL 202-336-5574. Circ: 1,500 (controlled).

300 DEU ISSN 1868-1395
▼ **CULTURAL ENCOUNTERS AND THE DISCOURSES OF SCHOLARSHIP.** Text in English. 2009. irreg., latest vol.2, 2010. price varies. **Document type:** *Monographic series, Academic/Scholarly.*
Published by: Waxmann Verlag GmbH, Steinfurter Str 555, Muenster, 48159, Germany. TEL 49-251-265040, FAX 49-251-2650426, info@waxmann.com. Ed. Gesa Mackenthun.

306 AUS ISSN 1838-1340
▼ **CULTURAL FIELDS.** Text in English. 2010. q. free (effective 2011). back issues avail. **Document type:** *Newsletter, Consumer.* **Description:** Covers a wide range of topics that are a part of what is going on in cultural sociology in Australia.
Media: Online - full text.
Published by: Cultural Sociology Thematic Group, c/o Luke Howie, Department of Behavioural Studies, Faculty of Arts, Monash University, PO Box 197, Caulfield East, VIC 3145, Australia. TEL 61-3-99034465, Luke.Howie@arts.monash.edu.au, http://www.culturalsociology.org. Eds. Catherine Strong TEL 61-2-69332780, Nicholas Osbaldiston TEL 61-3-83440624.

CULTURAL MEMORY IN THE PRESENT. *see* ANTHROPOLOGY

306 GBR ISSN 1749-9755
HM 621
CULTURAL SOCIOLOGY. Text in English. 2007. 3/yr. USD 636, GBP 344 combined subscription to institutions (print & online eds.); USD 623, GBP 337 to institutions (effective 2011). adv. back issues avail.; reprint service avail. from PSC. **Document type:** *Journal, Academic/Scholarly.* **Description:** Publishes original research and review articles concerning the sociological analysis of culture.
Related titles: Online - full text ed.: ISSN 1749-9763. USD 572, GBP 310 to institutions (effective 2011).
Indexed: A20, A22, CA, CurCont, E01, IBSS, MLA-IB, S02, S03, SCOPUS, SSCI, SociolAb, T02, W07.
—BLDSC (3491.668395), IE. **CCC.**
Published by: (British Sociological Association), Sage Publications Ltd. (Subsidiary of: Sage Publications, Inc.), 1 Oliver's Yard, 55 City Rd, London, EC1Y 1SP, United Kingdom. TEL 44-20-73248500, FAX 44-20-73248600, info@sagepub.co.uk, http://www.uk.sagepub.com/home.nav. Eds. Andrew Blaikie, David Inglis.

306 GBR ISSN 0950-2386
HM101 CODEN: CUSTE9
➤ **CULTURAL STUDIES.** Text in English. 1983. bi-m. GBP 573 combined subscription in United Kingdom to institutions (print & online eds.); EUR 759, USD 954 combined subscription to institutions (print & online eds.) (effective 2012). adv. bk.rev. illus. back issues avail.; reprint service avail. from PSC. **Document type:** *Journal, Academic/Scholarly.* **Description:** Provides a forum where academics, researchers, students and practitioners can consider and review patterns of power and meaning in contemporary culture, and focus for work in the interlocking areas of media, communication and cultural studies.
Formerly (until 1987): Australian Journal of Cultural Studies (0810-9648)
Related titles: Online - full text ed.: ISSN 1466-4348. GBP 516 in United Kingdom to institutions; EUR 683, USD 858 to institutions (effective 2012) (from IngentaConnect).
Indexed: A01, A03, A08, A20, A22, A25, A26, A36, ASCA, AltPI, AmHI, ArtHuCI, AusPAIS, B04, BRD, BrHumI, CA, CABA, CMM, Chicano, CommAb, CurCont, E01, E08, ERA, FR, G08, GH, H07, H08, HAb, HumInd, I05, IBSS, LT, MLA-IB, N02, P32, P34, P42, PCI, PRA, PSA, R05, R12, RI-1, RI-2, RILM, RRTA, S02, S03, S08, S09, S21, SCOPUS, SOPODA, SSA, SSCI, SociolAb, T02, TAR, W03, W07, W09, W11.
—IE, Infotrieve, Ingenta, INIST. **CCC.**
Published by: Routledge (Subsidiary of: Taylor & Francis Group), 4 Park Square, Milton Park, Abingdon, Oxon OX14 4RN, United Kingdom. subscriptions@tandf.co.uk, http://www.routledge.com. Eds. Della Pollock, Lawrence Grossberg. Adv. contact Linda Hann TEL 44-1344-779945. page GBP 175; trim 190 x 115. Circ: 1,650. **Subscr. to:** Taylor & Francis Ltd., Journals Customer Service, Sheepen Pl, Colchester, Essex CO3 3LP, United Kingdom. TEL 44-20-70175544, FAX 44-20-70175198, tf.enquiries@tfinforma.com.

306 400 DNK ISSN 1901-1911
PN9
CULTURAL TEXT STUDIES. Variant title: C T S. Text in English. 2006. irreg., latest vol.2, 2006. price varies. **Document type:** *Monographic series, Academic/Scholarly.* **Description:** Cultural Text Studies is a series of themed monographs, edited by researchers at the Department of Languages and Intercultural Studies at Aalborg University and associates and friends of the Department. The purpose of the series is to be a forum for the publication of results of research in the broadly defined area of cultural text. .
Published by: Aalborg Universitetsforlag/Aalborg University Press, Niels Jernes Vej 6 B, Aalborg OE, 9220, Denmark. TEL 45-96-357140, FAX 45-96-350075, aauf@forlag.aau.dk, http://www.forlag.aau.dk.

301 MEX ISSN 1870-1191
HM621
CULTURALES. Text in Spanish. 2005. s-a. MXN 60 (effective 2006). **Document type:** *Monographic series, Academic/Scholarly.*
Indexed: C01.
Published by: Universidad Autonoma de Baja California, Centro de Estudios Culturales-Museo, Ave Reforma y Calle L, Col. Nueva, Mexicali, Baja California, 21100, Mexico. TEL 52-686-5541977, FAX 52-686-5525715, http://www.cicmuseo.com/web/home.jsp. Ed. Fernando Vizcarra. Circ: 1,000.

306 USA ISSN 1941-1812
HM621
CULTURE (CHARLOTTESVILLE). Text in English. 2007. s-a. free (effective 2009). **Document type:** *Magazine, Consumer.* **Description:** Aims to serve as a forum to fulfill the mission of the institute to ""understand contemporary cultural change and its individual and social consequences."".
Related titles: Online - full text ed.: ISSN 1941-1820.
Published by: Institute for Advanced Studies in Culture, University of Virginia, PO Box 400816, Charlottesville, VA 22904-4816. FAX 434-243-5590, 434-924-7713, iasc@virginia.edu. Ed. Joseph Davis.

306.44 NLD ISSN 1879-5838
▼ **CULTURE AND LANGUAGE USE**; studies in anthropological linguistics. Text in English. 2010. irreg., latest vol.5, 2011. price varies. **Document type:** *Monographic series, Academic/Scholarly.*
Published by: John Benjamins Publishing Co., PO Box 36224, Amsterdam, 1020 ME, Netherlands. TEL 31-20-6304747, FAX 31-20-6739773, customer.services@benjamins.nl. Ed. Gunter Senft.

CULTURE & PSYCHOLOGY. *see* PSYCHOLOGY

302.23 791.43 USA
CULTURE & THE MOVING IMAGE. Text in English. 1991. irreg., latest 2002. price varies. **Document type:** *Monographic series.*
Published by: Temple University Press, 1601 N Broad St, 306 USB, Philadelphia, PA 19122. Ed. Robert Sklar. **Subscr. to:** University of Chicago, 11030 S Langley, Chicago, IL 60628. TEL 773-568-1550, 800-621-2736, FAX 773-660-2235, 800-621-8476.

306.7 GBR ISSN 1369-1058
HQ21 CODEN: CHSUBK
➤ **CULTURE, HEALTH AND SEXUALITY.** Text in English. 1999. 8/yr. GBP 838 combined subscription in United Kingdom to institutions (print & online eds.); EUR 1,104, USD 1,386 combined subscription to institutions (print & online eds.) (effective 2012). adv. back issues avail.; reprint service avail. from PSC. **Document type:** *Journal, Academic/Scholarly.* **Description:** Publishes scholarly papers in the fields of culture, health, human reproduction and sexuality.
Related titles: Online - full text ed.: ISSN 1464-5351. GBP 754 in United Kingdom to institutions; EUR 994, USD 1,248 to institutions (effective 2012) (from IngentaConnect).
Indexed: A01, A03, A08, A20, A22, A36, AICP, AnthLit, C06, C07, C08, CA, CABA, CINAHL, CurCont, E01, E12, EMBASE, ExcerpMed, FR, G10, GH, H05, HPNRM, IBSS, L01, L02, LT, MEDLINE, N02, P03, P30, P34, P48, P50, P54, PQC, PsycInfo, PsycholAb, R10, R12, RA&MP, RRTA, Reac, S02, S03, SCOPUS, SSA, SSCI, SSciA, SociolAb, T02, T05, W07, W09, W11.
—IE, Infotrieve, Ingenta, INIST. **CCC.**
Published by: (International Association for Study of Sexuality, Culture and Society), Routledge (Subsidiary of: Taylor & Francis Group), 4 Park Sq, Milton Park, Abingdon, Oxon OX14 4RN, United Kingdom. TEL 44-20-70176000, FAX 44-20-70176336, subscriptions@tandf.co.uk, http://www.routledge.com. Ed. Peter Aggleton. Adv. contact Linda Hann TEL 44-1344-779945. **Subscr. in N. America to:** Taylor & Francis Inc., Customer Services Dept, 325 Chestnut St, 8th Fl, Philadelphia, PA 19106. TEL 215-625-8900, 800-354-1420, FAX 215-625-2940; **Subscr. to:** Taylor & Francis Ltd., Journals Customer Service, Sheepen Pl, Colchester, Essex CO3 3LP, United Kingdom. TEL 44-20-70175544, FAX 44-20-70175198, tf.enquiries@tfinforma.com.

306 GBR ISSN 1743-6176
➤ **CULTURE MACHINE**; generating research in culture and theory. Text in English. 2005 (Aug.). irreg., latest 2008. price varies. back issues avail. **Document type:** *Monographic series, Academic/Scholarly.* **Description:** Aims to both reposition cultural theory and reaffirm its continuing intellectual and political importance.
Published by: Berg Publishers (Subsidiary of: Oxford International Publishers Ltd.), 1st Fl Angel Ct, 81 St Clements St, Oxford, Berks OX4 1AW, United Kingdom. TEL 44-1865-245104, FAX 44-1865-791165, enquiry@bergpublishers.com. Eds. Dave Boothroyd, Gary Hall, Joanna Zylinska.

306 GBR ISSN 1465-4121
HB1
➤ **CULTURE MACHINE (COVENTRY).** Text in English. 1999. a. free (effective 2011). back issues avail. **Document type:** *Journal, Academic/Scholarly.* **Description:** Aims to promote the most provocative of new work, and analyses of that work, in culture and theory from a diverse range of international authors.
Media: Online - full text.
Indexed: A39, C27, C29, CA, D04, E13, LeftInd, MLA-IB, S18, T02.
Published by: Culture Machine, c o Gary Hall, Coventry University, School of Art and Design, Priory St, Coventry, CV1 5FB, United Kingdom. gary@garyhall.info. Eds. Dave Boothroyd, Gary Hall, Joanna Zylinska.

300 DEU ISSN 1662-7067
CULTURE - SCHWEIZER BEITRAEGE ZUR KULTURWISSENSCHAFT. Text in German. 2008. irreg., latest vol.5, 2011. price varies. **Document type:** *Monographic series, Academic/Scholarly.*
Published by: Waxmann Verlag GmbH, Steinfurter Str 555, Muenster, 48159, Germany. TEL 49-251-265040, FAX 49-251-2650426, info@waxmann.com.

301 FRA ISSN 0765-0213
CULTURES ET SOCIETES DE L'EST. Text in French. 1985. irreg., latest vol.38, 2003. price varies. **Document type:** *Academic/Scholarly.*
Related titles: ◆ Series: Cahiers de l'Emigration Russe. ISSN 1248-5691.
Published by: Institut d'Etudes Slaves, 9 rue Michelet, Paris, 75006, France. TEL 33-1-43267918, FAX 33-1-43261623, institut.etudes.slaves@wanadoo.fr, http://www.institut-slave.msh-paris.fr. **Co-sponsor:** Centre d'Etudes Slaves.

301 GBR ISSN 1744-5876
➤ **CULTURES OF CONSUMPTION SERIES.** Text in English. 2005 (Nov.). irreg., latest 2009. price varies. back issues avail. **Document type:** *Monographic series, Academic/Scholarly.* **Description:** Explores the changing nature of consumption in a global context. It investigates the different forms, development and consequences of consumption, past and present. Topics covered include consumption in the domestic sphere, the ethical consumer, alternative and sustainable forms of consumption, citizenship and consumption, and the shifting local, metropolitan and transnational boundaries of cultures of consumption.
Published by: Berg Publishers (Subsidiary of: Oxford International Publishers Ltd.), 1st Fl Angel Ct, 81 St Clements St, Oxford, Berks OX4 1AW, United Kingdom. TEL 44-1865-245104, FAX 44-1865-791165, enquiry@bergpublishers.com. Ed. Gary Hall.

306.43 NLD ISSN 1879-8837
CULTUUR + EDUCATIE. Variant title: Cultuur en Netwerk. Text in Dutch. 2001. 3/yr. EUR 37.50; EUR 16.50 per vol. (effective 2010). **Document type:** *Monographic series, Academic/Scholarly.*
Published by: Cultuurnetwerk Nederland, Postbus 61, Utrecht, 3500 AB, Netherlands. TEL 31-30-2361200, info@cultuurnetwerk.nl. Ed. Marjo van Hoorn.

CULTUURKAART MAGAZINE. *see* EDUCATION

307.72 CAN ISSN 1923-7413
▼ **CURB MAGAZINE.** Text in English. 2010. s-a. back issues avail. **Document type:** *Magazine, Trade.* **Description:** Features articles in four main substantive areas such as public spaces, sustainability, infrastructure and governance.
Related titles: Online - full text ed.: free (effective 2011).
Published by: University of Alberta, City-Region Studies Centre, Faculty of Extension - Enterprise Sq, 2-184, 10230 Jasper Ave, Edmonton, AB T5J 4P6, Canada. TEL 780-492-9957, FAX 780-492-0627, crsc@ualberta.ca.

301 GBR ISSN 0278-1204
HM1
CURRENT PERSPECTIVES IN SOCIAL THEORY. Text in English. 1980. irreg., latest vol.26, 2009. price varies. back issues avail. **Document type:** *Monographic series, Academic/Scholarly.* **Description:** Presents essays on major issues in contemporary theoretical sociology.
Related titles: Online - full text ed.
Indexed: A22, CA, RILM, S02, S03, SCOPUS, SOPODA, SSA, SSCI, SociolAb, T02, W07.
—BLDSC (3501.280440), IE, Ingenta. **CCC.**
Published by: Emerald Group Publishing Ltd., Howard House, Wagon Ln, Bingley, W Yorks BD16 1WA, United Kingdom. TEL 44-1274-777700, FAX 44-1274-785201, emerald@emeraldinsight.com. Ed. Harry Dahms. **Dist. by:** Turpin Distribution Services Ltd., Pegasus Dr, Stratton Business Park, Biggleswade, Bedfordshire SG18 8QB, United Kingdom. TEL 44-1767-604951, FAX 44-1767-601640, custserv@turpin-distribution.com, http://www.turpin-distribution.com/.

301 GBR ISSN 0011-3921
Z7161
➤ **CURRENT SOCIOLOGY/SOCIOLOGIE CONTEMPORAINE.** Text in English, French. 1952. bi-m. USD 1,261, GBP 682 combined subscription to institutions (print & online eds.); USD 1,236, GBP 668 to institutions (effective 2011). adv. illus. back issues avail.; reprint service avail. from PSC. **Document type:** *Journal, Academic/Scholarly.* **Description:** Focuses on the theory, research and methodology of contemporary international sociology. Each issue is devoted to a substantial Trend Report on a particular sociological topic.
Related titles: Online - full text ed.: ISSN 1461-7064. USD 1,135, GBP 614 to institutions (effective 2011).
Indexed: A01, A02, A03, A08, A20, A22, A25, A26, AC&P, Acal, B04, B07, BRD, CA, CurCont, DIP, E01, E08, EI, ESPM, FamI, G08, H04, H09, I05, I13, I14, IBR, IBSS, IBZ, IBibSS, ILD, KES, LeftInd, MEA&I, P02, P06, P10, P27, P30, P34, P42, P48, P53, P54, PAA&I, PAIS, PCI, PQC, PSA, PsycholAb, RASB, RILM, RiskAb, S02, S03, S05, S08, S09, S11, S21, SCOPUS, SOPODA, SSA, SSAI, SSAb, SSCI, SSI, SSciA, SociolAb, SportS, T02, V02, W01, W02, W03, W07, W09.
—BLDSC (3504.033000), IE, Infotrieve, Ingenta, INIST. **CCC.**

Published by: (International Sociological Association ESP), Sage Publications Ltd. (Subsidiary of: Sage Publications, Inc.), 1 Oliver's Yard, 55 City Rd, London, EC1Y 1SP, United Kingdom. TEL 44-20-73248500, FAX 44-20-73248600, info@sagepub.co.uk, http://www.uk.sagepub.com/home.nav. Ed. Dennis Smith. **Subscr. in the Americas to:** Sage Publications, Inc., 2455 Teller Rd, Thousand Oaks, CA 91320. TEL 805-499-9774, FAX 805-499-0871, journals@sagepub.com.

➤ **CYBERPSYCHOLOGY**; journal of psychosocial research in cyberspace. *see* PSYCHOLOGY

➤ **CYBERPSYCHOLOGY, BEHAVIOR AND SOCIAL NETWORKING.** *see* COMPUTERS—Internet

301 DNK ISSN 1902-1542
D D A INFO. Text in Danish. 2005. 3/yr. free. **Document type:** *Newsletter, Consumer.*
Related titles: Online - full text ed.: ISSN 1902-1550.
Published by: Statens Arkiver, Dansk Data Arkiv/Danish National Archives. Danish Data Archives, Islandsgade 10, Odense, 5000, Denmark. TEL 45-46-113010, FAX 45-46-113060, mailbox@dda.sa.dk, http://www.sa.dk/dda. Ed. Anne Sofie Fink.

D E P DEPORTATE ESULI PROFUGHE; rivista telematica di studi sulla memoria femminile. *see* WOMEN'S STUDIES

301 DNK ISSN 0106-696X
D U F, DANSK UNGDOMS FAELLESRAAD. AARSBERETNING. Text in Danish. 1973. a. back issues avail. **Document type:** *Consumer.*
Related titles: Online - full text ed.
Published by: Dansk Ungdoms Faellesraad/Danish Youth Council, Scherfigsvej 5, Copenhagen OE, 2100, Denmark. TEL 45-39-298888, FAX 45-39-298882, duf@duf.dk.

305 DNK ISSN 1902-5807
D U F FOKUS. (Dansk Ungdoms Faellesraad) Text in Danish; Text occasionally in English. 2007. free. back issues avail. **Document type:** *Magazine, Consumer.*
Published by: Dansk Ungdoms Faellesraad/Danish Youth Council, Scherfigsvej 5, Copenhagen OE, 2100, Denmark. TEL 45-39-298888, FAX 45-39-298882, duf@duf.dk.

D W D NEWSLETTER. *see* GERONTOLOGY AND GERIATRICS

301 USA
DAD ETIPS. Text in English. 2/w. **Document type:** *Newsletter, Consumer.*
Supersedes in part: Smart Dads; Which was formerly: Dads Only
Media: E-mail.
Published by: Smart Families, Inc., PO Box 500050, San Diego, CA 92150-0050. TEL 858-513-7150, FAX 858-513-7142, plewis@familyuniversity.com. Ed., Pub. Paul Lewis.

301 330 800 ITA ISSN 1970-2175
DAEDALUS (ONLINE). Text in Italian. 1988. a. **Document type:** *Magazine, Consumer.*
Formerly (until 2006): Daedalus (Print) (1122-5734)
Media: Online - full text.
Published by: (Laboratorio di Storia Daedalus), Universita degli Studi della Calabria, Dipartimento di Sociologia e di Scienza Politica, Campus di Arcavacata, Arcavacata di Rende, CS, Italy. http://www.unical.it.

DANSALAN QUARTERLY. *see* RELIGIONS AND THEOLOGY—Islamic

301 DNK ISSN 0905-5908
HN541 CODEN: DSOCE3
➤ **DANSK SOCIOLOGI.** Text in Danish; Summaries in English. 1990. q. DKK 400 to individuals; DKK 600 to institutions; DKK 300 to students; DKK 100 per issue (effective 2009). adv. bk.rev. back issues avail. **Document type:** *Journal, Academic/Scholarly.*
Indexed: CA, P42, PCI, PSA, S02, S03, SCOPUS, SOPODA, SSA, SociolAb, T02.
Published by: Dansk Sociologforening/Danish Sociological Association, Oester Farimagsgade 5, Copenhagen K, 1014, Denmark. TEL 45-35-323502, FAX 45-35-323940, mail@sociologi.dk, http://www.sociologi.dk. Eds. Lene El Mongy, Rasmus Antoft, Thomas Boje. Adv. contact Lene El Mongy.

301 GBR ISSN 2041-3254
HT1561
DARKMATTER. Text in English. 2007. s-a. free (effective 2011). **Document type:** *Journal, Academic/Scholarly.*
Media: Online - full text.
Published by: Darkmatter Journal Eds. Ash Sharma, Sanjay Sharma.

DE L'ALLEMAGNE. *see* ANTHROPOLOGY

DEATH STUDIES; counseling - research - education - care - ethics. *see* PSYCHOLOGY

301 ARG ISSN 1514-0814
DEBATE ABIERTO. Text in Spanish. 1992. q. back issues avail. **Document type:** *Bulletin, Government.*
Published by: Fundacion de Estudios Municipales y Sociales, Ave Mitre, 1601, Avellanada, Buenos Aires, 1870, Argentina. Ed. Siro Fabian. Circ: 5,000.

301 PER ISSN 0254-9220
F3401
➤ **DEBATES EN SOCIOLOGIA.** Text in Spanish. 1977. a. USD 30 (effective 2003). bk.rev. charts; illus. **Document type:** *Academic/Scholarly.*
Supersedes: Revista de Debates: Debates de Sociologia
Indexed: A01, C01, CA, F03, F04, FR, RASB, S02, S03, T02.
Published by: (Pontificia Universidad Catolica del Peru, Departamento de Ciencias Sociales), Pontificia Universidad Catolica del Peru, Avenuda Universitaria, Cdra 18 s/n, san Miguel, Lima, 32, Peru. TEL 51-14-626390, FAX 51-14-611785. Ed. Denis Sulmont.

➤ **LA DECROISSANCE.** *see* POLITICAL SCIENCE

➤ **DELEUZE CONNECTIONS.** *see* PHILOSOPHY

➤ **DEMOKRATIE UND GESCHICHTE.** *see* HISTORY—History Of Europe

306.7 USA ISSN 2158-6047
▼ **DENOVO.** Text in English. 2010. q. USD 21 per issue (effective 2011). adv. back issues avail. **Document type:** *Magazine, Consumer.*
Related titles: Online - full text ed.: USD 6 per issue (effective 2011).
Published by: Robert Anthony, Ed. & Pub., 329 Clinton St, Ste 3, Brooklyn, NY 11231.

DESARROLLO DE BASE. *see* BUSINESS AND ECONOMICS—International Development And Assistance

302.23 DEU ISSN 1433-7665
DEUTSCHE GESELLSCHAFT FUER PUBLIZISTIK- UND KOMMUNIKATIONSWISSENSCHAFT. SCHRIFTENREIHE. Text in German. 1978. irreg., latest vol.38, 2011. price varies. **Document type:** *Monographic series, Academic/Scholarly.*
Published by: U V K Verlagsgesellschaft mbH, Schuetzenstr 24, Konstanz, 78462, Germany. TEL 49-7531-90530, FAX 49-7531-905398, nadine.ley@uvk.de, http://www.uvk.de.

DEUTSCHE JUGEND; Zeitschrift fuer die Jugendarbeit. *see* CHILDREN AND YOUTH—About

DEVELOPING ECONOMIES. *see* BUSINESS AND ECONOMICS—International Development And Assistance

DEVELOPMENT AND SOCIETY. *see* POPULATION STUDIES

303 378 NLD ISSN 1566-4821
DEVELOPMENT ISSUES. Variant title: DevISSues. Text in English. 1990. s-a.
Formerly (until 1999): I S S Alumni Magazine (0924-1132)
Published by: Institute of Social Studies, The Hague, PO Box 29776, The Hague, 2502 LT, Netherlands. TEL 31-70-4260460, FAX 31-70-4260799, information@iss.nl. Ed. Jane Pocock. Circ: 6,500.

301 CHE ISSN 0378-7931
HM291
DEVIANCE ET SOCIETE. Text in French; Abstracts in English, German. 1977. q. CHF 107 to individuals; CHF 185 to institutions (effective 2007). **Document type:** *Journal, Academic/Scholarly.*
Related titles: Online - full text ed.
Indexed: AC&P, CA, CJA, E-psyche, FR, IBSS, P03, P42, PSA, PsycInfo, PsycholAb, S02, S03, SCOPUS, SSA, SSCI, SociolAb, T02, W07.
—BLDSC (3579.099700), INIST. **CCC.**
Published by: (Universite Catholique de Louvain, Departement de Criminologie et Droit Penal BEL), Editions Medecine et Hygiene, Chemin de la Mousse 46, CP 475, Chene-Bourg 4, 1225, Switzerland. TEL 41-22-7029311, FAX 41-22-7029355, abonnements@medhyg.ch, http://www.medhyg.ch. Ed. Philippe Robert.

301 USA ISSN 0163-9625
HM1 CODEN: DEBEDF
➤ **DEVIANT BEHAVIOR**; an interdisciplinary journal. Text in English. 1979. 8/yr. GBP 762 combined subscription in United Kingdom to institutions (print & online eds.); EUR 1,003, USD 1,260 combined subscription to institutions (print & online eds.) (effective 2012). adv. bk.rev. bibl.; charts; illus. index. back issues avail.; reprint service avail. from PSC. **Document type:** *Journal, Academic/Scholarly.* **Description:** Presents scientific findings on cultural norm violations from a wide variety of perspectives.
Related titles: Microfiche ed.: (from PQC); Online - full text ed.: ISSN 1521-0456. GBP 686 in United Kingdom to institutions; EUR 903, USD 1,134 to institutions (effective 2012) (from IngentaConnect).
Indexed: A01, A03, A08, A20, A22, AC&P, ASCA, AbAn, C28, CA, CJA, CJPI, ChPerI, CurCont, E-psyche, E01, ESPM, FR, FamI, G10, I02, L03, P03, P30, PAIS, PQC, PsycInfo, PsycholAb, RASB, RILM, RiskAb, S02, S03, SCOPUS, SFSA, SOPODA, SSA, SSCI, SUSA, SociolAb, T02, V&AA, W07, W09.
—IE, Infotrieve, Ingenta, INIST. **CCC.**
Published by: Taylor & Francis Inc. (Subsidiary of: Taylor & Francis Group), 325 Chestnut St, Ste 800, Philadelphia, PA 19106. TEL 215-625-8900, 800-354-1420, FAX 215-625-8914, orders@taylorandfrancis.com, http://www.taylorandfrancis.com. Eds. C Eddie Palmer, Clifton D Bryant, Dr. Craig J Forsyth. **Subscr. outside N. America to:** Taylor & Francis Ltd., Journals Customer Service, Sheepen Pl, Colchester, Essex CO3 3LP, United Kingdom. TEL 44-20-70175544, FAX 44-20-70175198, subscriptions@tandf.co.uk.

➤ **DHARAM NARAIN MEMORIAL LECTURE SERIES.** *see* BUSINESS AND ECONOMICS

301 NPL ISSN 1994-2664
HM477.N35
➤ **DHAULAGIRI JOURNAL OF SOCIOLOGY AND ANTHROPOLOGY.** Text in English. 2005. a. **Document type:** *Journal, Academic/Scholarly.* **Description:** It is a compilation of articles, original research reports, review articles, book reviews, dissertation abstracts, professional announcements and other information of interest in the areas of sociology and anthropology of Nepal and other regions.
Related titles: Online - full text ed.: ISSN 1994-2672. free (effective 2011).
Indexed: CA, S02, S03, T02.
Published by: Tribhuvan University, Department of Sociology and Anthropology, c/o Mr. Man Bahadur Khattri, EIC, Mahendra Multiple Campus, Baglung, Nepal. khattrimanbahadur@yahoo.com. Ed. Man Bahadur Khattri.

➤ **DIA-LOGOS**; Schriften zu Philosophie und Sozialwissenschaften. *see* PHILOSOPHY

305.868 USA ISSN 1090-4972
E184.S75
DIALOGO. Text in English. 1996. s-a. USD 15 newsstand/cover (effective 2005).
Published by: DePaul University, Center for Latino Research, 2320 N Kenmore Ave Ste 5A-H, Chicago, IL 60614-3298. TEL 773-325-7316, FAX 773-325-7166, http://condor.depaul.edu/~dialogo/center_for_latino_research.htm.

301 PAN ISSN 0046-0206
HN1
DIALOGO SOCIAL. Text in Spanish. 1967. m. (except Jan.). PAB 15; USD 35 in US & Canada; USD 35 in Europe; USD 40 in Africa; USD 40 in Asia. adv. bk.rev.; film rev. bibl.; illus.; stat. index, cum.index: 1967-1977.
Indexed: C01, RASB.
Published by: Centro de Capacitacion Social, Calle 71 Este Bis, Panama, Panama. TEL 507-229-1542, FAX 507-261-0215, ccspanama@cwpanama.net, http://www.hri.ca/partners/ccs/. Circ: 7,800 (controlled).

306.85 FRA ISSN 0242-8962
➤ **DIALOGUE**; recherches cliniques et sociologiques sur le couple et la famille. Text in French. 1961. q. EUR 60 domestic to individuals; EUR 72 foreign to individuals; EUR 70 domestic to institutions (effective 2011). back issues avail. **Document type:** *Journal, Academic/Scholarly.* **Description:** Discusses family therapy.
Related titles: Online - full text ed.: ISSN 1961-8662.
Indexed: FR.
—INIST.
Published by: (Association Francaise des Centres de Consultation Conjugale), Editions Eres, 33 Av. Marcel Dassault, Toulouse, 31500, France. TEL 33-5-61751576, FAX 33-5-61735289, eres@edition-eres.com. Ed. Jean Lemaire. Circ: 2,000.

303.6 327.172 USA ISSN 1936-1289
DIALOGUE (MONTEREY). Text in English. 2007. s-a. back issues avail. **Document type:** *Journal, Academic/Scholarly.* **Description:** Devoted to topics in non-violent resolution to global conflicts. Each issue focuses on a particular region of the globe and includes articles, art and field reports from specific countries.
Related titles: CD-ROM ed.: ISSN 1936-1297; Online - full text ed.: ISSN 1936-1300.
Published by: Global Majority, 411 Pacific St, Ste 318, Monterey, CA 93940. TEL 831-372-5518, FAX 831-372-5519, info@globalmajority.ne, http://globalmajority.org.

306.44 NLD ISSN 1875-1792
➤ **DIALOGUE STUDIES.** Text in English. 2007. irreg., latest vol.11, 2011. **Document type:** *Monographic series, Academic/Scholarly.* **Description:** Addresses the complex phenomenon of dialogic language use.
Published by: John Benjamins Publishing Co., PO Box 36224, Amsterdam, 1020 ME, Netherlands. TEL 31-20-6304747, FAX 31-20-6739773, customer.services@benjamins.nl. Ed. Edda Weigand.

301 330 CAN ISSN 1712-8986
DIALOGUES (CALGARY). Text in English. 2005. q. **Document type:** *Magazine, Consumer.*
Related titles: Online - full text ed.: ISSN 1712-8994.
Published by: Canada West Foundation, Ste 900, 1202 Centre St S, Calgary, AB T2G 5A5, Canada. TEL 403-264-9535, 888-825-5293, FAX 403-269-4776, cwf@cwf.ca. Ed. Robert Roach.

303 FRA ISSN 1276-4248
DIASPORIQUES; cultures en mouvement. Text in French. 1968. q. EUR 10 for 6 mos. domestic; EUR 12.50 for 6 mos. in Europe; EUR 15 for 6 mos. elsewhere (effective 2010). back issues avail. **Document type:** *Journal, Academic/Scholarly.* **Description:** Studies the increasing complexity of cultures living together in one society and the related social injustices.
Formerly (until 1997): Cahiers du Cercle Gaston Cremieux (0399-788X)
Published by: Ligue Francaise de l'Enseignement et de l'Education Permanente, 3 rue Recamier, Paris, Cedex 7 75341, France. TEL 33-1-43589793, FAX 33-1-43589696, info-ligue@ligue.cie.fr, http://www.laligue.cie.fr.

302.23 DEU
DIETER BAACKE PREIS HANDBUCH. Text in German. 2006. irreg., latest vol.5, 2010. price varies. **Document type:** *Monographic series, Academic/Scholarly.*
Published by: (Gesellschaft fuer Medienpaedagogik und Kommunikationskultur), KoPaed Verlag, Pfaelzer-Wald-Str 64, Munich, 81539, Germany. TEL 49-89-68890098, FAX 49-89-6891912, info@kopaed.de, http://www.kopaed.de.

DIFFERENCES; a journal of feminist cultural studies. *see* WOMEN'S STUDIES

303 004 AUS ISSN 1836-8301
L11
▼ **DIGITAL CULTURE & EDUCATION.** Text in English. 2009. bi-m. free (effective 2011). **Document type:** *Journal, Academic/Scholarly.*
Media: Online - full text. Eds. Christopher Walsh, Thomas Apperley.

302.23 GBR ISSN 2043-7633
DIGITAL ICONS; studies in Russian, Eurasian and Central European new media. Abbreviated title: D I. Text in English, German, Russian. 2008. s-a. free (effective 2010). back issues avail. **Document type:** *Journal, Academic/Scholarly.*
Formerly (until 2009): The Russian Cyberspace Journal (2040-462X)
Media: Online - full text.
Published by: School of Modern Languages and Cultures, University of Leeds, Woodhouse lane, Leeds, LS2 9JT, United Kingdom. TEL 44-113-3431779, FAX 44-113-3433287, http://www.leeds.ac.uk/smlc/. Ed. Vlad Strukov TEL 44-113-3433294.

301 BRA ISSN 1983-5922
HM1121
DILEMAS; revista de estudos de conflito e controle social. Text in Portuguese. 2008. q. **Document type:** *Journal, Academic/Scholarly.*
Related titles: Online - full text ed.: ISSN 2178-2792. free (effective 2011).
Published by: Universidade Federal do Rio de Janeiro, Instituto de Filosofia e Ciencias Sociais, Largo de Sao Francisco de Paula 1, Sala 320 B, Centro, Rio De Janeiro, RJ 20051-071, Brazil. TEL 55-21-2210034, FAX 55-21-22211470, http://www.ifcs.ufrj.br/, direcao@ifcs.ufrj.br. Eds. Alexandre Werneck, Michel Misse.

302.2 USA ISSN 0730-1081
P87
DISCOURSE (DETROIT); journal for theoretical studies in media and culture. Text in English. 1979. 3/yr. USD 44 to individuals; USD 125 to institutions (effective 2010). back issues avail. **Document type:** *Journal, Academic/Scholarly.* **Description:** Explores a variety of topics in contemporary cultural studies, theories of media and literature, and the politics of sexuality, including questions of language and psychoanalysis.
Related titles: Microfilm ed.: 1978; Online - full text ed.: ISSN 1536-1810.
Indexed: A22, B04, DIP, IBR, IBZ, IIPA, L&LBA, MLA-IB, RASB, RILM, SOPODA, SSAI, SSAb, SSI, SociolAb, W03, W05.
—BLDSC (3595.740000), IE, Ingenta.
Published by: Wayne State University Press, The Leonard N Simons Bldg, 4809 Woodward Ave, Detroit, MI 48201. TEL 313-577-6120, 800-978-7323, FAX 313-577-6131, bookorders@wayne.edu. Eds. Akira Mizuta Lippit, Carl Good, Rolando J Romero.

302.23 DEU ISSN 1528-5162
▼ **DISCOURSE ANALYSIS.** Text in English. forthcoming 2011. irreg. price varies. **Document type:** *Monographic series, Academic/Scholarly.* **Description:** Devoted to the critical and cultural study of discourse.
Published by: Peter Lang GmbH (Subsidiary of: Peter Lang Publishing Group), Eschborner Landstr 42-50, Frankfurt Am Main, 60489, Germany. TEL 49-69-7807050, FAX 49-69-78070550, zentrale.frankfurt@peterlang.com. Ed. Rita Kirk Whillock.

DISCOURSE & SOCIETY; an international journal for the study of discourse and communication in their social, political and cultural contexts. *see* PSYCHOLOGY

DISCOURSE APPROACHES TO POLITICS, SOCIETY AND CULTURE. *see* POLITICAL SCIENCE

301 GBR
▼ **DISCUSSION PAPERS IN CITIZENSHIP, GLOBALIZATION AND GOVERNANCE.** Text in English. 2010. s-a. GBP 50 to institutions (effective 2010). back issues avail. **Document type:** *Report, Consumer.*
Related titles: Online - full text ed.: ISSN 2045-1490. free (effective 2010).
Published by: University of Southampton, Centre for Citizenship, Globalization and Governance, c/o School of Social Sciences, University of Southampton, Highfield, Southampton SO17 1BJ, United Kingdom. TEL 44-23-80597340, g.stoker@soton.ac.uk.

DISCUSSION PAPERS IN ECONOMIC AND SOCIAL HISTORY. *see* BUSINESS AND ECONOMICS

301 DEU
DISKUSSIONSBEITRAEGE. Text in German. 1983. irreg., latest vol.34, 2008. price varies. **Document type:** *Monographic series, Academic/Scholarly.*
Published by: Bund Katholischer Unternehmer e.V., Georgstr 18, Cologne, 50676, Germany. TEL 49-221-272370, FAX 49-221-2723727, service@bku.de.

DISTINKTION; tidsskrift for samfundsteori. *see* POLITICAL SCIENCE

301 ROM ISSN 2067-0931
DIVERSITE ET IDENTITE CULTURELLE EN EUROPE/DIVERSITATE SI IDENTITATE CULTURALA IN EUROPA. Abbreviated title: D I C E. Text in English, French. 2008. irreg. free (effective 2011). **Document type:** *Journal, Academic/Scholarly.*
Media: Online - full text.
Published by: Muzeul National al Literaturii Romane, Bulevardul Dacia 12, Bucharest, 010402, Romania.

306 FRA ISSN 2079-6595
DIVERSITIES. Text in German, English, French. 1998. irreg. free (effective 2011). **Document type:** *Journal, Academic/Scholarly.* **Description:** Includes theoretical perspectives on cultural diversity in modern societies.
Former titles (until 2009): International Journal on Multicultural Societies (1817-4574); (until 2002): M O S T Journal on Multicultural Societies (1564-4901)
Media: Online - full text.
Indexed: CA, IBSS, P42, PAIS, PSA, S02, S03, SCOPUS, SSciA, SociolAb, T02.
Published by: UNESCO Publishing, 7 place de Fontenoy, Paris, 75352, France. http://www.unesco.org/publishing.

306.89 USA
DIVORCENET. Text in English. 1995. m.
Media: Online - full content.
Published by: LawTek, 321 Walnut St, Ste 440, Newton, MA 02160.

LES DIX PLUS GROS MENSONGES. *see* MEDICAL SCIENCES

DOCTOR - PATIENT STUDIES. *see* MEDICAL SCIENCES

301 FRA ISSN 0183-701X
DOCUMENT DE TRAVAIL. Text in French. 1976. irreg. **Document type:** *Monographic series, Trade.*
Indexed: GeoRef.
—IE.
Published by: Futuribles International, 47 Rue de Babylone, Paris, 75007, France. TEL 33-1-53633770, FAX 33-1-42226554, forum@futuribles.com, http://www.futuribles.com.

306 BOL
DOCUMENTOS INSTITUCIONALES OFICIALES. Text in Spanish. 1972. irreg., latest vol.25, 1985. price varies. **Document type:** *Monographic series, Academic/Scholarly.*
Published by: Centro de Investigaciones Sociales, Casilla 6931 - C.C., La Paz, Bolivia. TEL 591-2-352931. Ed. Antonio Cisneros.

DOMESTIC VIOLENCE SOURCEBOOK. *see* CRIMINOLOGY AND LAW ENFORCEMENT

301 ITA ISSN 1972-0785
DOMINI. SOCIO - LOGIE. Text in Italian. 1996. irreg., latest vol.3, 1996. price varies. **Document type:** *Monographic series, Academic/Scholarly.*
Published by: Liguori Editore, Via Posillipo 394, Naples, 80123, Italy. TEL 39-081-7206111, FAX 39-081-7206244, liguori@liguori.it, http://www.liguori.it.

301 ITA ISSN 1972-0807
DOMINI. STUDI SULL'IDENTITA. Text in Italian. 2000. irreg. **Document type:** *Monographic series, Academic/Scholarly.*
Published by: Liguori Editore, Via Posillipo 394, Naples, 80123, Italy. TEL 39-081-7206111, FAX 39-081-7206244, liguori@liguori.it, http://www.liguori.it.

302.23 ESP ISSN 1696-019X
DOXA COMUNICACION; revista interdisciplinar de estudios de comunicacion y ciencias sociales. Text in Spanish. 2003. a. **Document type:** *Monographic series, Academic/Scholarly.*
Published by: Universidad San Pablo, Facultad de Humanidades y Ciencias de la Comunicacion, Paseo de Juan XXIII 6, Boadilla del Monte, 28040, Spain. TEL 34-91-4564200, FAX 34-91-5543757, sechumsh@ceu.es, http://www.uspceu.com/CNTBNR/humanidades_portal.html.

DREAM WHIP. *see* LITERATURE

305 USA ISSN 1948-2787
THE DRUM. Text in English. 2008. bi-m. USD 25 (effective 2009). adv. **Document type:** *Magazine, Consumer.* **Description:** Serves as a vehicle of information and communication for the community of Africans and Americans who have an interest in the African continent, its peoples and cultures.
Related titles: Online - full text ed.: ISSN 1948-2795.
Published by: Altru Books Publishers, 8449 W Bellfort Ave, 250, Houston, TX 77071. TEL 713-272-9911, FAX 713-272-9011. Eds. Charles Nwankwo, Emeaba Onuma Emeaba.

302.23 USA
THE DRUM BEAT; communication and change news and issues. Text in English. 1998. bi-m. back issues avail. **Document type:** *Magazine, Trade.* **Description:** Presents information, ideas, linkages and dialogue on communication, development and change.
Media: Online - full text.
Published by: Communication Initiative TEL 250-658-6372, FAX 250-658-1728. Ed. Warren Feek.

301 SVN ISSN 0352-3608
HM578.Y8 CODEN: DBRPF7
DRUZBOSLOVNE RAZPRAVE/SOCIAL SCIENCES DEBATES. Text in Slovenian. 1984. s-a. **Document type:** *Journal, Academic/Scholarly.*
Related titles: Online - full text ed.
Indexed: CA, P42, PSA, S02, S03, SCOPUS, SSA, SociolAb, T02.
Published by: Univerza v Ljubljani, Fakulteta za Druzbene Vede/University of Ljubljana, Faculty of Social Sciences, Kerdeljeva Poscad 5, Ljubljana, 1000, Slovenia. TEL 386-1-5805100, FAX 386-1-5805101, fdv.faculty@fdv.uni-lj.si, http://www.fdv.uni-lj.si.

DUISBURGER STUDIEN; Geistes- und Gesellschaftswissenschaften. *see* PHILOSOPHY

301 GBR ISSN 1362-024X
➤ **DURKHEIMIAN STUDIES.** Text in English, French. 1977. a. GBP 37 combined subscription domestic to institutions (print & online eds.); EUR 50 combined subscription in Europe to institutions (print & online eds.); USD 63 combined subscription elsewhere to institutions (print & online eds.) (effective 2011). adv. bk.rev. 1 cols./p.; back issues avail.; reprint service avail. from PSC. **Document type:** *Journal, Academic/Scholarly.* **Description:** Features articles concerned with all matters relating to Durkheim and his circle.
Formerly (until 1995): Etudes Durkheimiennes (0154-9413)
Related titles: Online - full text ed.: ISSN 1752-2307. GBP 33 domestic to institutions; EUR 45 in Europe to institutions; USD 57 elsewhere to institutions (effective 2011) (from IngentaConnect).
Indexed: B04, CA, FR, P10, P27, P42, P46, P48, P54, PQC, PSA, S02, S03, SCOPUS, SSA, SSAI, SSAb, SSI, SociolAb, T02, W03, W05.
—BLDSC (3632.620000). **CCC.**
Published by: (British Centre for Durkheimian Studies, Institute of Social and Cultural Anthropology), Berghahn Books Ltd, 3 Newtec Pl, Magdalen Rd, Oxford, OX4 1RE, United Kingdom. TEL 44-1865-250011, FAX 44-1865-250056, journals@berghahnbooks.com, http://www.berghahnbooks.com. Ed. W Watts Miller. **Dist. in Europe by:** Turpin Distribution Services Ltd., Pegasus Dr, Stratton Business Park, Biggleswade, Bedfordshire SG18 8QB, United Kingdom. TEL 44-1767-604951, FAX 44-1767-601640, berghahnjournalsuk@turpin-distribution.com, http://www.turpin-distribution.com/; **Dist. outside of Europe by:** Turpin Distribution Services Ltd. berghahnjournalsus@turpin-distribution.com.

➤ **E-BERATUNGSJOURNAL.NET.** *see* COMMUNICATIONS

302.23 DEU ISSN 1439-4820
E C M C WORKING PAPER. (European Centre for Media Competence) Text in German. 1999. irreg., latest vol.6, 2004. price varies. **Document type:** *Monographic series, Academic/Scholarly.*
Published by: KoPaed Verlag, Pfaelzer-Wald-Str 64, Munich, 81539, Germany. TEL 49-89-68890098, FAX 49-89-6891912, info@kopaed.de.

302.23 DEU
E-CULTURE. Text in German. 2005. irreg., latest vol.15, 2010. price varies. **Document type:** *Monographic series, Academic/Scholarly.*
Published by: Trafo Verlag, Finkenstr 8, Berlin, 12621, Germany. TEL 49-30-61299418, FAX 49-30-61299421, info@trafoberlin.de.

E & Z. (Entwicklung und Zusammenarbeit) *see* POLITICAL SCIENCE—International Relations

306 GBR ISSN 1746-0654
TR848
➤ **EARLY POPULAR VISUAL CULTURE.** Abbreviated title: E P V C. Text in English. 2001. 3/yr. GBP 302 combined subscription in United Kingdom to institutions (print & online eds.); EUR 402, USD 506 combined subscription to institutions (print & online eds.) (effective 2012). adv. back issues avail.; reprint service avail. from PSC. **Document type:** *Journal, Academic/Scholarly.* **Description:** Dedicated to stimulating research and interdisciplinary studies in relation to all forms of popular visual culture before 1930.
Formerly (unitl 2003): Living Pictures (1467-0577)
Related titles: Online - full text ed.: ISSN 1746-0662. GBP 271 in United Kingdom to institutions; EUR 362, USD 456 to institutions (effective 2012).
Indexed: A20, A22, AmHI, ArtHuCI, BrHumI, CA, E01, F01, F02, H07, IBR, IBZ, IIFP, T02, W07.
—IE. **CCC.**
Published by: Routledge (Subsidiary of: Taylor & Francis Group), 4 Park Sq, Milton Park, Abingdon, Oxon OX14 4RN, United Kingdom. TEL 44-20-70176000, FAX 44-20-70176336, subscriptions@tandf.co.uk, http://www.routledge.com. Eds. Simon Popple, Vanessa Toulmin. Adv. contact Linda Hann TEL 44-1344-779945. **Subscr. to:** Taylor & Francis Ltd., Journals Customer Service, Sheepen Pl, Colchester, Essex CO3 3LP, United Kingdom. TEL 44-20-70175544, FAX 44-20-70175198.

301 330 USA ISSN 1937-5379
HF1456.5.A64
EAST-WEST DIALOGUE. Text in English. 2007 (Sep.). irreg., latest vol.5, 2010. free (effective 2010). back issues avail. **Document type:** *Monographic series, Academic/Scholarly.* **Description:** Promotes discussion and debate of key issues in Asia-U.S. economic relations.
Related titles: Online - full text ed.: ISSN 1937-5417. free (effective 2010).
Indexed: A01.
Published by: East-West Center, 1601 EW Rd, Honolulu, HI 96848. TEL 808-944-7111, FAX 808-944-7376, ewcbooks@eastwestcenter.org.

EASTERN EUROPE, RUSSIA AND CENTRAL ASIA (YEAR). *see* POLITICAL SCIENCE

306 POL ISSN 1232-8855
HN380.7
EASTERN EUROPEAN COUNTRYSIDE. Text in English. 1995. irreg., latest vol.8, 2005. EUR 27 per vol. (effective 2006). **Document type:** *Monographic series, Academic/Scholarly.*
Indexed: CA, P42, PSA, S02, S03, SCOPUS, SSA, SSCI, SociolAb, T02, W07.
Published by: (Uniwersytet Mikolaja Kopernika/Nicolaus Copernicus University), Wydawnictwo Naukowe Uniwersytetu Mikolaja Kopernika/Nicolaus Copernicus University Press, ul Gagarina 39, Torun, 87100, Poland. TEL 48-56-6114295, FAX 48-56-6114705, dwyd@uni.torun.pl, http://www.wydawnictwo.umk.pl. **Dist. by:** Ars Polona, Obroncow 25, Warsaw 03933, Poland. TEL 48-22-5098609, FAX 48-22-5098610, arspolona@arspolona.com.pl, http://www.arspolona.com.pl.

301 ESP ISSN 1696-2672
DP269
EBRE 38; revista internacional de la Guerra Civil 1936-1939. Text in Multiple languages. 2003. irreg. **Document type:** *Journal, Academic/Scholarly.* **Description:** International review about the Spanish Civil War 1936-1939.
Related titles: Online - full text ed.: ISSN 1885-2580.
Published by: Universitat de Barcelona, Servei de Publicacions, Gran Via Corts Catalanes 585, Barcelona, 08007, Spain. TEL 34-93-4021100, http://www.publicacions.ub.es.

301 ESP ISSN 1577-6395
EL EBRO; revista aragonesista de pensamiento. Text in Spanish. 1999. a., latest 2006. **Document type:** *Monographic series, Academic/Scholarly.*
Published by: Fundacion Gaspar Torrente para la Investigacion y Desarrollo del Aragonesismo, C Moncasi No. 4 Entresuelo Izda., Zaragoza, Aragon 50006, Spain. TEL 34-976-372208, http://www.gaspartorrente.org/. Ed. Antonio Peiro Arroyo.

302.2 BRA
ECO. Text in Portuguese. 1992. s-a. **Document type:** *Academic/Scholarly.*
Published by: (Universidade Federal do Rio de Janeiro, Escola de Comunicacao), Imago Editorial Ltda., Rua Santos Rodrigues, 201-A, Estacio, Rio De Janeiro, RJ 20250-430, Brazil. TEL 293-1092.

THE ECOLOGIST (ONLINE). *see* ENVIRONMENTAL STUDIES

ECONOMIA E SOCIOLOGIA. *see* BUSINESS AND ECONOMICS—Economic Situation And Conditions

ECONOMIC DEVELOPMENT AND CULTURAL CHANGE. *see* BUSINESS AND ECONOMICS—International Development And Assistance

301 330 DEU ISSN 1871-3351
ECONOMIC SOCIOLOGY. Text in English. 1999. q. free (effective 2011). **Document type:** *Journal, Academic/Scholarly.*
Media: Online - full content.
Published by: Max-Planck-Institut fuer Gesellschaftsforschung/Max Planck Institut for the Study of Societies, Paulstr 3, Cologne, 50676, Germany. TEL 49-221-2767176, FAX 49-221-2767555, econsoc@mpifg.de, http://www.mpifg.de. Ed. Patrik Aspers.

ECONOMICHESKIE I SOTSIAL'NYE PEREMENY/ECONOMICAL AND SOCIAL CHANGES: FACTS, TRENDS, FORECAST.; fakty, tendentsii, prognoz. *see* BUSINESS AND ECONOMICS

303.4 NZL ISSN 1179-9625
ED NEWS. Variant title: Education News. Text in English. 200?. q. free (effective 2010). back issues avail. **Document type:** *Newsletter, Trade.* **Description:** Helps people to understand their lives in the context of contemporary global issues and develop the skills and knowledge to become effective.
Formerly (until 2009): G E C News
Media: Online - full text.
Published by: Global Focus Aotearoa, PO Box 12440, Wellington, New Zealand. TEL 64-4-4729549, FAX 64-4-4969599, info@globalfocus.org.nz.

301 AUS ISSN 1832-0090
EDDIE KOIKI MABO LECTURE. Text in English. 2004. a. **Document type:** *Journal, Academic/Scholarly.*
Media: Online - full text.
Published by: James Cook University, PO Box 6811, Cairns, QLD 4870, Australia. TEL 61-7-40421000, 800-246-446, FAX 61-7-40421128, EnquiriesCairns@jcu.edu.au, http://www.jcu.edu.au.

306 GBR
EDINBURGH STUDIES IN CULTURE AND SOCIETY. Text in English. 1989. irreg., latest 1998. price varies. back issues avail. **Document type:** *Monographic series.*
Formerly: Edinburgh Studies in Sociology
Published by: Palgrave Macmillan Ltd. (Subsidiary of: Macmillan Publishers Ltd.), Houndmills, Basingstoke, Hants RG21 6XS, United Kingdom. TEL 44-1256-329242, FAX 44-1256-810526, bookenquiries@palgrave.com, http://www.palgrave.com.

302.23 DEU ISSN 1434-5307
EDITION SAGE & SCHREIBE. Text in German. 1997. irreg., latest vol.3, 2001. price varies. **Document type:** *Monographic series, Academic/Scholarly.*
Published by: U V K Verlagsgesellschaft mbH, Schuetzenstr 24, Konstanz, 78462, Germany. TEL 49-7531-90530, FAX 49-7531-905398, nadine.ley@uvk.de, http://www.uvk.de.

302.23 DEU
EDITION TELEVIZION. Text in German. 1995. irreg., latest vol.8, 2007. price varies. **Document type:** *Monographic series, Academic/Scholarly.*
Published by: KoPaed Verlag, Pfaelzer-Wald-Str 64, Munich, 81539, Germany. TEL 49-89-68890098, FAX 49-89-6891912, info@kopaed.de, http://www.kopaed.de.

EDUCATION AND SOCIETY. *see* EDUCATION

EDUCATION AND URBAN SOCIETY; an independent quarterly journal of social research. *see* EDUCATION

EDUCATION AS CHANGE. *see* EDUCATION

EDUCATION, BUSINESS AND SOCIETY; contemporary Middle Eastern issues. *see* EDUCATION

EDUCATION ET SOCIETES; revue internationale de sociologie de l'education. *see* EDUCATION

L'EDUCAZIONE SENTIMENTALE. *see* PHILOSOPHY

S

305.4 USA ISSN 1529-5966
HQ1150
➤ **EIGHTEENTH-CENTURY WOMEN**; studies in their lives, work, and culture. Text in English. 2001. a. USD 124.50 per issue (effective 2009). bk.rev. illus.; bibl. Index. 400 p./no.; back issues avail.; reprints avail. **Document type:** *Journal, Academic/Scholarly.* **Description:** Provides articles and book reviews in the fields of literary, biographical, bibliographical, social, and cultural history.
Indexed: FemPer, MLA-IB.
—BLDSC (3665.251500).
Published by: A M S Press, Inc., Brooklyn Navy Yard, 63 Flushing Ave, Bldg 292, Unit #221, Brooklyn, NY 11205. FAX 718-875-3800, queries@amspressinc.com, editorial@amspressinc.com. Ed. Linda V. Troost.

➤ **EKONOMICHESKAYA SOTSIOLOGIYA.** *see* BUSINESS AND ECONOMICS

➤ **EKONOMICHESKIE I SOTSIAL'NYE PROBLEMY ROSSII.** *see* BUSINESS AND ECONOMICS

➤ **ELECTRONIC INTERNATIONAL JOURNAL OF TIME USE RESEARCH.** *see* BUSINESS AND ECONOMICS

301 CAN ISSN 1198-3655
HM401
➤ **ELECTRONIC JOURNAL OF SOCIOLOGY.** Text in English. 1994. irreg. free (effective 2011). back issues avail. **Document type:** *Journal, Academic/Scholarly.* **Description:** Covers general sociology for practitioners.
Media: Online - full text.
Indexed: A39, C03, C27, C29, CA, CBCARef, D03, D04, E13, P48, PQC, R14, S02, S03, S14, S15, S18, SCOPUS, SociolAb, T02.
Address: Athabasca University, 6 Pembina Place, St Albert, AB T8N 4P7, Canada. Eds. Andreas Schneider, Mike Sosteric.

303 004 USA ISSN 1866-6124
GV1469.15
ELUDAMOS; journal for computer game culture. Text in English. 2007. s-a. free (effective 2011). **Document type:** *Journal, Academic/ Scholarly.*
Media: Online - full text.
Indexed: CABA, LT.
Published by: Singapore - MIT GAMBIT Game Lab, 5 Cambridge Center, Cambridge, MA 02139.

EMIGRE. *see* ART

301 NLD ISSN 1572-2236
EMMAUSKRANT. Text in Dutch. 1958. q. EUR 7 (effective 2010). **Description:** Articles about the Emmaus movement in the Netherlands and worldwide.
Formerly (until 2001): Honger en Dorst (1383-3847)
Published by: Stichting Emmaus Nederland, Kloosterlaan 6, Langeweg, 4772 RA, Netherlands. TEL 31-168-336381, secretariaat@emmaus.nl. Eds. Marc Roos, Riet Huneker. Circ: 2,000.

301 ESP ISSN 1139-5737
H61
EMPIRIA. Text in Spanish. 1998. a. back issues avail. **Document type:** *Journal, Academic/Scholarly.*
Related titles: Online - full text ed.: ISSN 2174-0682. 1998.
Indexed: A01, CA, F03, F04, S02, S03, SCOPUS, SociolAb, T02.
—INIST.
Published by: Universidad Nacional de Educacion a Distancia, Facultad de Ciencias Politicas y Sociologia, Obispo Trejo, 2, Madrid, 28040, Spain. TEL 34-91-3987074, FAX 34-91-3989068, http://portal.uned.es/portal/page?_pageid=93,158386&_dad=portal&_schema=PORTAL. Ed. Jose Maria Arriba Macho.

201.6 NLD ISSN 1389-1189
EMPIRICAL STUDIES IN THEOLOGY. Cover title: E S T. Text in English. 1998. irreg., latest vol.20, 2011. price varies. **Document type:** *Monographic series, Academic/Scholarly.* **Description:** Focuses on religion and all of its aspects within secularized and multicultural societies.
Indexed: IZBG.
Published by: Brill, PO Box 9000, Leiden, 2300 PA, Netherlands. TEL 31-71-5353500, FAX 31-71-5317532, cs@brill.nl.

301 USA ISSN 1525-3120
HM686
ENCULTURATION. Text in English. 1997. s-a. free (effective 2011).
Media: Online - full content.
Indexed: A39, C27, C29, D03, D04, E13, MLA-IB, R14, S14, S15, S18.
Published by: George Mason University, Department of English, 4400 University Dr, Fairfax, VA 22030-4444. TEL 703-993-1000, http://www.gmu.edu. Ed. Byron Hawk.

301 306.4 SWE ISSN 1651-6540
ENDANGERED LANGUAGES AND CULTURES. Text in English, Swedish. 2003. irreg., latest vol.2, 2006. back issues avail. **Document type:** *Monographic series, Academic/Scholarly.*
Published by: Uppsala Universitet, Centrum foer Multietnisk Forskning/ Center for Multiethnic Research, Gamla Torget 3, PO Box 514, Uppsala, 75120, Sweden. TEL 46-18-4712359, FAX 46-18-4712363, multietn@multietn.uu.se. Eds. Lena Huus, Satu Groendahl.

301 150 CAN ISSN 1708-6310
HQ1
ENFANCES, FAMILLES, GENERATIONS. Text in French. 2004. s-a. free (effective 2011). **Document type:** *Journal, Academic/Scholarly.*
Media: Online - full text.
Indexed: A39, C27, C29, D03, D04, E13, R14, S02, S03, S14, S15, S18.
Published by: Universite de Quebec, Institut National de la Recherche Scientifique, 490 de la Couronne, Quebec, PQ G1K 9A9, Canada. TEL 418-654-2524, FAX 418-654-2600, info@inrs.ca, http://www.inrs.uquebec.ca. Eds. Eric Gagnon, Helene Bellelau.

301 BRA ISSN 1678-1813
ENFOQUES. Text in Portuguese. 2002. 3/yr. back issues avail. **Document type:** *Journal, Academic/Scholarly.*
Media: Online - full text.
Published by: Universidade Federal do Rio de Janeiro, Instituto de Filosofia e Ciencias Sociais, Largo de Sao Francisco de Paula 1, Sala 320 B, Centro, Rio De Janeiro, RJ 20051-071, Brazil. TEL 55-21-2210034, FAX 55-21-22211470, http://www.ifcs.ufrj.br/, direcao@ifcs.ufrj.br.

301 BRA ISSN 1415-7314
ENGEVISTA. Text in Portuguese. 1995. s-a. **Document type:** *Journal, Academic/Scholarly.*
Related titles: Online - full text ed.: free (effective 2011).
Published by: Universidade Federal Fluminense, Escola de Engenharia, Rua Passo da Patria 156, Sao Domingos, Niteroi, RJ 24210-240, Brazil. TEL 55-021-26295391, FAX 55-021-27174446. Eds. Fabiana Rodrigues Leta, Joao Carlos Soares de Mello.

303.3 CAN ISSN 1719-6027
AN ENGLISH SPEAKER'S GUIDE TO LIFE IN THE EASTERN TOWNSHIPS. Text in English. 2005. a. **Document type:** *Handbook/ Manual/Guide, Consumer.*
Published by: Townshippers' Association, 257 Queen St, Ste 100, Lennoxville, PQ J1M 1Z7, Canada. TEL 819-566-5717, 866-566-5717, FAX 819-566-0271, ta@townshippers.qc.ca.

302.23 MEX ISSN 1605-4210
ENLACE. Text in Spanish. 1996. m. back issues avail.
Media: Online - full text.
Published by: Universidad Regiomontana, Padre Mier Pte. 471, Monterrey, Nuevo Leon, Mexico. TEL 52-8343-1290, FAX 52-8343-3172.

ENQUETE - ECOLE DES HAUTES ETUDES EN SCIENCES SOCIALES. *see* ANTHROPOLOGY

301 FRA ISSN 1951-5219
ENTRETIENS (LA COURNEUVE). Text in French. 2006. irreg. back issues avail. **Document type:** *Monographic series, Consumer.*
Published by: Aux Lieux d'Etre, 51 rue de Geneve, La Courneuve, 93120, France. TEL 33-1-48548181, FAX 33-1-48366224.

307.14 DEU ISSN 0942-4466
ENTWICKLUNGSETHNOLOGIE. Text in German. 1992. 2/yr. EUR 30 (effective 2009). **Document type:** *Journal, Academic/Scholarly.*
Indexed: IBR, IBZ.
Published by: Verlag fuer Entwicklungspolitik Saarbruecken GmbH, Auf der Adt 14, Saarbruecken, 66130, Germany. TEL 49-6893-986094, FAX 49-6893-986095, vfe@verlag-entwicklungspolitik.de.

155.91 USA ISSN 0013-9165
HM206 CODEN: EVBHAF
➤ **ENVIRONMENT AND BEHAVIOR.** Text in English. 1969. bi-m. USD 1,070, GBP 630 combined subscription to institutions (print & online eds.); USD 1,049, GBP 617 to institutions (effective 2011). adv. bk.rev. abstr.; charts; illus. index. back issues avail.; reprint service avail. from PSC. **Document type:** *Journal, Academic/Scholarly.* **Description:** Discusses the interaction of the physical environment and human behavioral systems and covers the study, design, and control of the physical environment. Analyses and records the influence of environment on individuals, groups and institutions.
Related titles: Microfilm ed.: (from PQC); Online - full text ed.: ISSN 1552-390X. USD 963, GBP 567 to institutions (effective 2011).
Indexed: A01, A02, A03, A08, A20, A22, A26, A28, A30, A31, A33, ABS&EES, AIAP, APA, ASCA, ASFA, ASSIA, Agr, B04, B07, B21, BRD, BrCerAb, C&ISA, CA, CA/WCA, CCME, CIA, CIS, CJA, CerAb, CivEngAb, CorrAb, CurCont, DIP, E&CAJ, E-psyche, E01, E02, E03, E04, E05, E07, E08, E11, EEA, EI, EMA, ERI, ERIC, ESPM, EdA, EdI, EnerRev, EnvAb, EnvEAb, EnvInd, FamI, G02, G08, GEOBASE, GardL, GeoRef, H04, H09, H11, H12, H15, HPNRM, HRIS, I05, I14, IBR, IBSS, IBZ, M&TEA, M09, MAB, MBF, METADEX, MagInd, NSA, P02, P03, P04, P10, P12, P13, P25, P27, P30, P34, P42, P48, P52, P53, P54, P56, PAIS, PCI, PQC, PRA, PSA, PsycInfo, PsycholAb, S02, S03, S05, S09, SCOPUS, SOPODA, SSA, SSAI, SSAb, SSCI, SSI, SSciA, SUSA, SWRA, SociolAb, SolStAb, SpeleolAb, T02, T04, V02, W03, W07, WAA, WildRev.
—BLDSC (3791.097000), IE, Infotrieve, Ingenta, INIST, Linda Hall. **CCC.**
Published by: (Environmental Design Research Association), Sage Publications, Inc., 2455 Teller Rd, Thousand Oaks, CA 91320. TEL 805-499-9774, 800-818-7243, FAX 805-499-0871, 800-583-2665, info@sagepub.com. Ed. Robert B Bechtel. adv.: color page USD 775, B&W page USD 385; 4.5 x 7.5. Circ: 1,000 (paid). **Subscr. overseas to:** Sage Publications Ltd., 1 Oliver's Yard, 55 City Rd, London EC1Y 1SP, United Kingdom. TEL 44-207-3248701, FAX 44-207-3248733, subscription@sagepub.co.uk.

➤ **ENVIRONMENT AND PLANNING D: SOCIETY AND SPACE.** *see* HOUSING AND URBAN PLANNING

301 340 CAN ISSN 1719-7295
EQUALITY RIGHTS. ANNUAL REPORT. Text in English. a. **Document type:** *Government.*
Related titles: French ed.: Droits a l'Egalite. Rapport Annuel. ISSN 1719-7309.
Published by: Canadian Council on Social Development, 190 O'Connor St, 1st Flr, Ottawa, ON K2P 2R3, Canada. TEL 613-236-8977, FAX 613-236-2750, council@ccsd.ca, http://www.ccsd.ca.

306 MEX
EQUIS X; cultura y sociedad. Text in Spanish. 1998. m. MXN 300, USD 50 (effective 1999). adv. back issues avail. **Description:** Covers Latin American culture and society with an emphasis on Mexico.
Related titles: Online - full text ed.
Published by: Ulises Ediciones S.A. de C.V., INSURGENTES SUR 470-303, Col Roma Sur, Mexico City, DF 06760, Mexico. TEL 52-5-5646536. Ed. Braulio Peralta.

301 HUN ISSN 0014-0120
ERGONOMIA; munkaelettan, munkalelektan, munkaszociologia. Text in Hungarian. 1967. bi-m. USD 34.50. adv. bk.rev. **Document type:** *Academic/Scholarly.* **Description:** Covers job psychology, human politics, work hygiene and recreation.
Indexed: CISA, ErgAb.
Published by: Ergotop Ltd., PO Box 66, Budapest, 1507, Hungary. TEL 361-13-25-987. Ed. Gyorgy Garamvolgyi. Pub. Laszlo Galsa. Circ: 2,500. **Subscr. to:** Kultura, PO Box 149, Budapest 1389, Hungary.

306.09 DEU
ERINNERUNGEN. Text in German. 2000. irreg., latest vol.9, 2010. price varies. **Document type:** *Monographic series, Academic/Scholarly.* **Description:** Presents recollections and memories from various individuals and social groups.
Published by: Waxmann Verlag GmbH, Steinfurter Str 555, Muenster, 48159, Germany. TEL 49-251-265040, FAX 49-251-2650426, info@waxmann.com.

301 DNK ISSN 1601-9385
ESKIMOLOGIS SKRIFTER. Text mainly in Danish; Text occasionally in English, Eskimo. 1973. irreg., latest vol.19, 2005. price varies. back issues avail. **Document type:** *Monographic series, Academic/ Scholarly.*
Formerly (until 1991): Koebenhavns Universitet. Institut for Eskimologi. Publikation
Published by: Koebenhavns Universitet, Afdeling for Eskimologi og Arktiske Studier/University of Copenhagen, Eskimology and Arctic Studies, c/o Institut for Traerkulturelle og Regionale Studier, Strandgade 102 Bld. H, Copenhagen K, 1401, Denmark. TEL 45-35-329671, FAX 45-35-329661, eskimologi@hum.ku.dk, http://www.eskimologi.ku.dk.

301 VEN ISSN 1315-0006
H53.V4 CODEN: ESABFA
➤ **ESPACIO ABIERTO**; cuaderno venezolano de sociologia. Text in Spanish; Abstracts in English, Spanish. 1992. q. VEB 50 domestic to institutions (effective 2011). bk.rev. illus. **Document type:** *Journal, Academic/Scholarly.* **Description:** Promotes the discussion of sociological matters such as: methodology of social sciences, sociology of education, sociology of health, sociology of gender and family, and sociology of work.
Related titles: Online - full text ed.: free (effective 2011).
Indexed: A01, A26, C01, CA, F03, F04, I04, I05, IBSS, P42, PSA, S02, S03, SCOPUS, SOPODA, SSA, SociolAb, T02.
—IE.
Published by: Universidad del Zulia, Consejo de Desarrollo Cientifico y Humanistico, Av. Universidad (Calle 60) 25-266, Sector Grano de Oro, Maracaibo, Venezuela. TEL 58-61-511400, FAX 58-61-528934. Eds. Alexis Romero Salazar, Maria Cristina Parra-Sandoval. **Co-sponsors:** International Sociological Association; Asociacion Venezolana de Sociologia.

➤ **ESPERANTO-DOKUMENTOJ.** *see* LINGUISTICS

➤ **ESPIRAL**; estudios sobre estado y sociedad. *see* POLITICAL SCIENCE

301 300 CAN
ESPRIT CRITIQUE; revue internationale de sociologie et des sciences sociales. Text in French. 1999. m.
Media: Online - full content. Ed. Orazio Maria Valastro.

306 FRA ISSN 2106-492X
▼ **ESPRIT DE BABEL.** Text in French. 2010. 3/yr. **Document type:** *Consumer.*
Published by: Les Bancs Publics, 3, Rue Bonhomme, Marseille, 13003, France.

ESTADISTICAS DEL MOVIMIENTO MIGRATORIO DE LA COMUNIDAD DE MADRID. *see* POPULATION STUDIES

ESTUDIOS DE HISTORIA SOCIAL Y ECONOMICA DE AMERICA. *see* BUSINESS AND ECONOMICS—Economic Situation And Conditions

306.85 BOL
ESTUDIOS DE SOCIOLOGIA FAMILIAR. Text in Spanish. 1975. irreg., latest vol.7, 1985. **Document type:** *Monographic series, Academic/ Scholarly.*
Published by: Centro de Investigaciones Sociales, Casilla 6931 - C.C., La Paz, Bolivia. TEL 591-2-352931. Ed. Antonio Cisneros.

307.14 VEN ISSN 1013-4069
ESTUDIOS DEL DESARROLLO/DEVELOPMENT STUDIES JOURNAL. Text in English, Spanish. 1990. a. adv. bk.rev. **Description:** Promotes discussion and thought on the present and future problems of development from an interdisciplinary perspective.
Published by: Universidad Central de Venezuela, Centro de Estudios del Desarrollo, Apartado Postal 6622, Caracas, DF 1010-A, Venezuela. TEL 7523266, FAX 7512691. Ed. Nelson Prato Barbosa. Circ: 1,000. **U.S. subscr. addr:** Poba International, 151, Box 02 5255, Miami, FL 33102-5255.

ESTUDIOS MICHOACANOS. *see* HISTORY—History Of North And South America

ESTUDIOS SOBRE LAS CULTURAS CONTEMPORANEAS; revista de investigacion y analisis de la cultura. *see* HUMANITIES: COMPREHENSIVE WORKS

301 DOM ISSN 1017-0596
HN216
ESTUDIOS SOCIALES. Text in Spanish. 1968. q. USD 30. bk.rev. charts; stat. **Document type:** *Academic/Scholarly.*
Indexed: H21, HistAb, P08, P30.
Published by: Centro de Estudios Sociales P. Juan Montalvo, Apdo. 1004, Santo Domingo, Dominican Republic. TEL 809-682-4448, FAX 809-685-0120. Ed., R&P Jesus Zaglul. Circ: 1,000. **Dist. by:** Editora Taller, Apdo. 2190, Santo Domingo, Dominican Republic. TEL 809-682-9369, FAX 809-689-7259.

301 MEX ISSN 0185-4186
CODEN: ESSOE2
ESTUDIOS SOCIOLOGICOS. Text in Spanish. 1983. 3/yr. MXN 225 domestic; USD 60 foreign; MXN 75 newsstand/cover domestic; USD 25 newsstand/cover foreign (effective 2002). adv. back issues avail.
Indexed: C01, CA, FR, H21, IBR, IBSS, IBZ, P08, P09, P30, P42, PCI, PSA, S02, S03, SCOPUS, SOPODA, SSA, SociolAb, T02.
—INIST.
Published by: Colegio de Mexico, A.C., Departamento de Publicaciones, Camino al Ajusco 20, Col. Pedregal Santa Teresa, Mexico City, DF 10740, Mexico. TEL 52-5-4493077, FAX 52-5-4493083, emunos@colmex.mx, http://www.colmex.mx. Ed., R&P Francisco Gomez Rulz TEL 525-449-3080. Adv. contact Maria Cruz Mora. Circ: 2,500.

307.76 BOL
ESTUDIOS URBANOS. Text in Spanish. 1973. irreg., latest vol.6, 1979. price varies. **Document type:** *Monographic series, Academic/ Scholarly.*
Published by: Centro de Investigaciones Sociales, Casilla 6931 - C.C., La Paz, Bolivia. TEL 591-2-352931. Ed. Antonio Cisneros.

301 BRA ISSN 1414-0144
H53.B7
ESTUDOS DE SOCIOLOGIA. Text in Portuguese. 1996. s-a. **Document type:** *Journal, Academic/Scholarly.*
Related titles: Online - full text ed.: ISSN 1982-4718. free (effective 2011).
Indexed: C01, CA, DIP, I13, IBR, IBZ, P42, PSA, S02, S03, SCOPUS, SociolAb, T02.

Published by: Universidade de Sao Paulo, Departamento de Sociologia, Faculdade de Ciencias e Letras, Rodovia Araraquara-Jau km 1, Araraquara, SP 14800-901, Brazil. TEL 55-16-33016275, laboratorioeditorial@fclar.unesp.br, http://www.fclar.unesp.br. Ed. Maria Ribeiro do Valle.

ESTUDOS POLITICOS E SOCIAIS. see POLITICAL SCIENCE

170 GBR ISSN 1744-9642
➤ **ETHICS AND EDUCATION.** Text in English. 2006 (Mar.). s-a. GBP 197 combined subscription in United Kingdom to institutions (print & online eds.); EUR 253, USD 318 combined subscription to institutions (print & online eds.) (effective 2012). adv. back issues avail.; reprint service avail. from PSC. **Document type:** *Journal, Academic/Scholarly.* **Description:** Aims to stimulate discussion and debate around the ethical dimensions of education.
Related titles: Online - full text ed.: ISSN 1744-9650. GBP 177 in United Kingdom to institutions; EUR 228, USD 286 to institutions (effective 2012).
Indexed: A22, B29, CA, CPE, E01, E03, ERI, ERIC, P03, P46, P48, P53, P54, PQC, PhilInd, PsycInfo, T02.
—IE, Ingenta. **CCC.**
Published by: Routledge (Subsidiary of: Taylor & Francis Group), 4 Park Sq, Milton Park, Abingdon, Oxon OX14 4RN, United Kingdom. TEL 44-20-70176000, FAX 44-20-70176336, subscriptions@tandf.co.uk, http://www.routledge.com. Ed. Richard D Smith. Adv. contact Linda Hann TEL 44-1344-779945. **Subscr. to:** Taylor & Francis Ltd., Journals Customer Service, Sheepen Pl, Colchester, Essex CO3 3LP, United Kingdom. TEL 44-20-70175544, FAX 44-20-70175198.

➤ **ETHICS AND JUSTICE**; an interdisciplinary public affairs journal. see LAW

178 USA ISSN 1065-0113
ETHICS & POLICY. Text in English. 1974. q. free to members (effective 2001). bk.rev. back issues avail. **Document type:** *Newsletter.* **Description:** Emphasizes ethics in social policy and business ethics; provides members and others with current information on the work of the center.
Indexed: RI-1, RI-2.
Published by: Graduate Theological Union, Center for Ethics & Social Policy, 2400 Ridge Rd, Berkeley, CA 94709. TEL 510-649-2560, FAX 510-649-2565, cesp@gtu.edu, http://www.gtu.edu. Ed. Lynne Jerome. Circ: 6,000.

ETHNIC STUDIES REVIEW. see ETHNIC INTERESTS

301 GBR ISSN 1758-8685
▼ **ETHNICITY AND RACE IN A CHANGING WORLD**; a review journal. Text in English. 2009 (Jan.). s-a. free (effective 2011). bk.rev. **Document type:** *Journal, Academic/Scholarly.*
Media: Online - full text.
Indexed: IIBP.
Published by: Manchester University Press, Oxford Rd, Manchester, Lancs M13 9NR, United Kingdom. TEL 44-161-2752310, FAX 44-161-2743346, mup@manchester.ac.uk. Eds. Emma Britain, Julie Devonald.

ETHNIEN - REGIONEN - KONFLIKTE; Soziologische und politologische Untersuchungen. see POLITICAL SCIENCE—International Relations

306 HUN ISSN 1787-9396
DB920.5
ETHNO-LORE. Text in Hungarian; Summaries in German. 1968. irreg., latest vol.23, 2007. price varies. abstr.; bibl.; illus. back issues avail. **Document type:** *Monographic series, Academic/Scholarly.*
Formerly (until 2003): Nepi Kultura - Nepi Tarsadalom (0541-9522)
Indexed: MLA-IB, RILM.
Published by: (Neprajzi Kutato Csoport), Akademiai Kiado Rt. (Subsidiary of: Wolters Kluwer N.V.), Prielle Kornelia u 19/D, Budapest, 1117, Hungary. TEL 36-1-4648222, FAX 36-1-4648221, info@akkrt.hu, http://www.akademiai.com.

ETHNOGRAPHY. see ANTHROPOLOGY

ETHNOGRAPHY AND EDUCATION. see EDUCATION

ETHNOPSYCHOANALYSE. see PSYCHOLOGY

306 ITA ISSN 1826-8803
GN301
ETHNOREMA; lingue, popoli e culture. Text in Italian, English. 2005. a. free (effective 2011). **Document type:** *Journal, Academic/Scholarly.*
Media: Online - full text.
Published by: Associazione Ethnorema, Via Bellini 19, Castelnuovo Scrivia, AL 15053, Italy.

ETHOS (MALDEN). see ANTHROPOLOGY

301 658 SWE
ETHOS (ONLINE EDITION). Text in Swedish. 2000. irreg. back issues avail. **Document type:** *Academic/Scholarly.*
Media: Online - full content.
Published by: Etikakademin, Erstagatan 31, Stockholm, 11636, Sweden. TEL 46-8-7149340, FAX 46-8-7149330, info@etikakademin.se, http://www.etikakademin.se. Ed. Gunhild Wallin TEL 46-8-7206344.

301 ITA ISSN 1973-3194
ETNOGRAFIA E RICERCA QUALITATIVA. Text in Italian. 2008. 3/yr. EUR 78 combined subscription domestic; EUR 103.50 combined subscription foreign (effective 2009). **Document type:** *Journal, Academic/Scholarly.*
Related titles: Online - full text ed.
Indexed: IBSS, SociolAb.
Published by: Societa Editrice Il Mulino, Strada Maggiore 37, Bologna, 40125, Italy. TEL 39-051-256011, FAX 39-051-256034, riviste@mulino.it. Ed. Pier Paolo Giglioli.

301 ARG ISSN 1669-2632
ETNOGRAFIAS CONTEMPORANEAS. Text in Spanish. 2005. s-a. back issues avail. **Document type:** *Journal, Academic/Scholarly.*
Published by: Universidad Nacional de San Martin, Centro de Investigaciones Etnograficas, Ave 25 de Mayo y Francias, San Martin, Buenos Aires, Argentina. TEL 54-11-45807302, cietno@unsam.edu.ar, http://www.unsam.edu.ar/.

305 ITA ISSN 1973-9788
ETNOGRAFIE. Text in Italian. 2007. irreg. Price varies. **Document type:** *Monographic series, Academic/Scholarly.*
Published by: Edizioni di Pagina, Via dei Mille 205, Bari, 70126, Italy. info@paginasc.it, http://www.paginasc.it.

ETNOLOSKA TRIBINA. see ANTHROPOLOGY

ETUDES DAHOMEENNES. see HISTORY—History Of Africa

303 FRA ISSN 1962-3364
ETUDES INTERCULTURELLES. Text in French. 2008. a. **Document type:** *Journal, Academic/Scholarly.*
Published by: Universite Catholique de Lyon, Chaire Unesco, 23 Place Carnot, Lyon, Cedex 02 69288, France. TEL 33-4-72325132, communication@univ-catholyon.fr.

307.14 FRA ISSN 0014-2182
HN1
ETUDES RURALES; revue trimestrielle d'histoire, geographie, sociologie et economie des campagnes. Text in French. 1961. q. EUR 46 in the European Union to individuals; EUR 47 elsewhere to individuals; EUR 70 domestic to institutions; EUR 81 in the European Union to institutions; EUR 82 elsewhere to institutions (effective 2009). adv. bk.rev. abstr.; bibl.; charts; illus. index. **Document type:** *Journal, Academic/Scholarly.*
Formerly: Cahiers des Etudes Rurales (0071-2175)
Indexed: A20, A22, AICP, BAS, CA, DIP, FR, HistAb, IBR, IBSS, IBZ, ILD, P30, P42, PAIS, PCI, PSA, RILM, S02, S03, SCOPUS, SOPODA, SSA, SociolAb, T02.
—IE, Infotrieve, INIST.
Published by: College de France, Ecole des Hautes Etudes en Sciences Sociales (E H E S S), 96 Boulevard Raspail, Paris, 75006, France. TEL 33-1-53635658, FAX 33-1-49542428, http://www.ehess.fr. Circ: 800. **Dist. by:** Centre Interinstitutionnel pour la Diffusion de Publications en Sciences Humaines, 131 bd. Saint-Michel, Paris 75005, France. TEL 33-1-43544715, FAX 33-1-43548073.

301 DEU ISSN 0721-3379
EUROPAEISCHE HOCHSCHULSCHRIFTEN. REIHE 22: SOZIOLOGIE. Text in German. 1970. irreg., latest vol.437, 2010. price varies. **Document type:** *Monographic series, Academic/Scholarly.*
Published by: Peter Lang GmbH (Subsidiary of: Peter Lang Publishing Group), Eschborner Landstr 42-50, Frankfurt Am Main, 60489, Germany. TEL 49-69-7807050, FAX 49-69-78070550, zentrale.frankfurt@peterlang.com, http://www.peterlang.com.

796.008 DEU ISSN 0721-362X
EUROPAEISCHE HOCHSCHULSCHRIFTEN. REIHE 35: SPORT UND KULTUR. Text in German. 1978. irreg., latest vol.18, 1999. price varies. **Document type:** *Monographic series, Academic/Scholarly.*
Published by: Peter Lang GmbH (Subsidiary of: Peter Lang Publishing Group), Eschborner Landstr 42-50, Frankfurt Am Main, 60489, Germany. TEL 49-69-7807050, FAX 49-69-78070550, zentrale.frankfurt@peterlang.com, http://www.peterlang.com.

305 NOR ISSN 1500-0303
EUROPAVEGEN. Text in Norwegian. 1996. a. back issues avail. **Document type:** *Consumer.*
Related titles: Online - full text ed.: ISSN 1890-1069. 2000.
Published by: Senter for Internasjonalisering av Hoejere Utdanning/ Norwegian Centre for International Cooperation in Higher Education, PO Box 7800, Bergen, 5020, Norway. TEL 47-55-308800, FAX 47-55-308801, siu@siu.no, http://www.siu.no. Ed. Hanne Alver Krum. Circ: 42,000.

EUROPE - ASIA STUDIES. see BUSINESS AND ECONOMICS

EUROPE INFORMATION SOCIAL (ENGLISH EDITION). see POLITICAL SCIENCE—International Relations

EUROPE INFORMATION SOCIAL (FRENCH EDITION). see POLITICAL SCIENCE—International Relations

303 NZL ISSN 1177-8229
EUROPE - NEW ZEALAND RESEARCH SERIES. Text in English. 2007. irreg. **Document type:** *Monographic series.*
Published by: (Massey University), University of Auckland, Europe Institute, Private Bag 92019, Auckland, 1142, New Zealand. TEL 64-9-3737599, Europe-enquiries@auckland.ac.nz, http://www.europe.auckland.ac.nz.

301 FRA ISSN 0531-2663
EUROPEAN ASPECTS, SOCIAL STUDIES SERIES; a collection of studies relating to European integration. Text in French. 1959. irreg.
Published by: Council of Europe/Conseil de l'Europe, Avenue de l'Europe, Strasbourg, 67075, France. TEL 33-3-88412581, FAX 33-3-88413910, publishing@coe.int, http://www.coe.int. **Dist. in U.S. by:** Manhattan Publishing Co., 468 Albany Post Rd, Croton On Hudson, NY 10520.

302.2 GBR ISSN 0267-3231
P91.3 CODEN: EJCOET
➤ **EUROPEAN JOURNAL OF COMMUNICATION.** Abbreviated title: E J C. Text in English; Summaries in English, French, German. 1986. q. USD 1,001, GBP 541 combined subscription to institutions (print & online eds.); USD 981, GBP 530 to institutions (effective 2011). adv. bk.rev. charts. back issues avail.; reprint service avail. from PSC. **Document type:** *Journal, Academic/Scholarly.* **Description:** Represents the best of communication theory and research in Europe in all its diversity. Promotes interchange among European scholars of different intellectual traditions and national backgrounds.
Related titles: Online - full text ed.: ISSN 1460-3705. USD 901, GBP 487 to institutions (effective 2011).
Indexed: A01, A02, A03, A08, A12, A20, A22, ABIn, ASCA, B01, B06, B07, B08, B09, CA, CMM, CommAb, CurCont, DIP, E01, F01, F02, FamI, I08, I13, IBR, IBSS, IBZ, IIFP, IITV, L&LBA, L04, L13, LISTA, MLA-IB, P03, P10, P34, P42, P48, P51, P53, P54, PAIS, PCI, PQC, PRA, PSA, PsycInfo, PsycholAb, RILM, S02, S03, SCOPUS, SOPODA, SSA, SSCI, SociolAb, T02, W07.
—BLDSC (3829.728220), IE, Infotrieve, Ingenta. **CCC.**
Published by: Sage Publications Ltd. (Subsidiary of: Sage Publications, Inc.), 1 Oliver's Yard, 55 City Rd, London, EC1Y 1SP, United Kingdom. TEL 44-20-73248500, FAX 44-20-73248600, info@sagepub.co.uk, http://www.uk.sagepub.com/home.nav. Eds. Denis McQuail, Liesbet van Zoonen, Peter Golding. adv.: B&W page GBP 400; 130 x 205. **Subscr. in the Americas to:** Sage Publications, Inc., 2455 Teller Rd, Thousand Oaks, CA 91320. TEL 805-499-9774, FAX 805-499-0871, journals@sagepub.com.

306 GBR ISSN 1367-5494
GN357
➤ **EUROPEAN JOURNAL OF CULTURAL STUDIES.** Text in English. 1998. q. USD 968, GBP 523 combined subscription to institutions (print & online eds.); USD 949, GBP 513 to institutions (effective 2011). adv. back issues avail.; reprint service avail. from PSC. **Document type:** *Journal, Academic/Scholarly.* **Description:** Promotes a broad-ranging view of cultural studies bringing together articles from a textual, philosophical and social scientific background, as well as from cultural studies.
Related titles: Online - full text ed.: ISSN 1460-3551. USD 871, GBP 471 to institutions (effective 2011).
Indexed: A01, A02, A03, A08, A20, A22, AICP, AmHI, ArtHuCI, B07, CA, CMM, CommAb, CurCont, DIP, E01, F01, F02, FR, H04, H07, I14, IBR, IBSS, IBZ, IBibSS, LeftInd, MLA, MLA-IB, P42, PSA, S02, S03, SCOPUS, SSA, SSCI, SociolAb, T02, V02, W07.
—BLDSC (3829.728245), IE, Infotrieve, Ingenta, INIST. **CCC.**
Published by: Sage Publications Ltd. (Subsidiary of: Sage Publications, Inc.), 1 Oliver's Yard, 55 City Rd, London, EC1Y 1SP, United Kingdom. TEL 44-20-73248500, FAX 44-20-73248600, info@sagepub.co.uk, http://www.uk.sagepub.com/home.nav. adv.: B&W page GBP 400; 140 x 210. **Subscr. in the Americas to:** Sage Publications, Inc., 2455 Teller Rd, Thousand Oaks, CA 91320. TEL 805-499-9774, FAX 805-499-0871, journals@sagepub.com.

➤ **EUROPEAN JOURNAL OF SOCIAL PSYCHOLOGY.** see PSYCHOLOGY

301 GBR ISSN 1368-4310
H61
➤ **EUROPEAN JOURNAL OF SOCIAL THEORY.** Text in English. 1998. q. USD 987, GBP 533 combined subscription to institutions (print & online eds.); USD 967, GBP 522 to institutions (effective 2011). adv. bk.rev. illus. Index. back issues avail.; reprint service avail. from PSC. **Document type:** *Journal, Academic/Scholarly.* **Description:** Provides a world-wide forum for contemporary social thought, such as critical theory; the approaches of Habermas. Bourdieu, Touraine, Luhmann; neofunctionalism; postmodernism; critical realism; the sociology of knowledge; rational choice; constructivism; and feminist social theory.
Related titles: Online - full text ed.: ISSN 1461-7137. USD 888, GBP 480 to institutions (effective 2011).
Indexed: A01, A02, A03, A08, A20, A22, B01, B06, B07, B09, CA, CurCont, DIP, E01, FR, FamI, H04, I13, IBR, IBSS, IBZ, LeftInd, P34, P42, PAIS, PSA, S02, S03, S21, SCOPUS, SSA, SSCI, SociolAb, T02, V02, W07.
—BLDSC (3829.739600), IE, Infotrieve, Ingenta, INIST. **CCC.**
Published by: Sage Publications Ltd. (Subsidiary of: Sage Publications, Inc.), 1 Oliver's Yard, 55 City Rd, London, EC1Y 1SP, United Kingdom. TEL 44-20-73248500, FAX 44-20-73248600, info@sagepub.co.uk, http://www.uk.sagepub.com/home.nav. Ed. Gerard Delanty. adv.: B&W page GBP 400; 130 x 205. **Subscr. in the Americas to:** Sage Publications, Inc., 2455 Teller Rd, Thousand Oaks, CA 91320. TEL 805-499-9774, FAX 805-499-0871, journals@sagepub.com.

➤ **EUROPEAN PERSPECTIVES**; a series in social thought and cultural criticism. see ANTHROPOLOGY

➤ **EUROPEAN RACE BULLETIN**; a digest on the rise of racism and fascism in Europe. see ETHNIC INTERESTS

307 GBR ISSN 1461-6696
HM22.E9
➤ **EUROPEAN SOCIETIES.** Text in English. 1999. 5/yr. GBP 616 combined subscription in United Kingdom to institutions (print & online eds.); EUR 814, USD 1,022 combined subscription to institutions (print & online eds.) (effective 2012). adv. bk.rev. back issues avail.; reprint service avail. from PSC. **Document type:** *Journal, Academic/Scholarly.* **Description:** Publishes research and debate on the sociological effects of the political, economic and cultural transformations under way in Europe, including studies of immigration in Western Europe and social upheavals in the post-communist nations of Eastern Europe.
Related titles: Online - full text ed.: ISSN 1469-8307. GBP 554 in United Kingdom to institutions; EUR 733, USD 920 to institutions (effective 2012) (from IngentaConnect).
Indexed: A01, A02, A03, A08, A20, A22, CA, CurCont, E01, ESPM, I13, IBSS, P34, P42, PSA, S02, S03, SCOPUS, SSCI, SSciA, SociolAb, T02, W07.
—IE, Infotrieve, Ingenta. **CCC.**
Published by: (European Sociological Association FRA), Routledge (Subsidiary of: Taylor & Francis Group), 4 Park Sq, Milton Park, Abingdon, Oxon OX14 4RN, United Kingdom. TEL 44-20-70176000, FAX 44-20-70176336, http://www.routledge.com. Ed. John Scott. Adv. contact Linda Hann TEL 44-1344-779945. **Subscr. to:** Taylor & Francis Ltd., Journals Customer Service, Sheepen Pl, Colchester, Essex CO3 3LP, United Kingdom. TEL 44-20-70175544, FAX 44-20-70175198, subscriptions@tandf.co.uk.

301 GBR ISSN 0266-7215
HM1
➤ **EUROPEAN SOCIOLOGICAL REVIEW.** Abbreviated title: E S R. Text in English. 1985. 6/yr. GBP 365 in United Kingdom to institutions; EUR 548 in Europe to institutions; USD 730 in US & Canada to institutions; GBP 365 elsewhere to institutions; GBP 398 combined subscription in United Kingdom to institutions (print & online eds.); EUR 598 combined subscription in Europe to institutions (print & online eds.); USD 797 combined subscription in US & Canada to institutions (print & online eds.); GBP 398 combined subscription elsewhere to institutions (print & online eds.) (effective 2012). adv. bk.rev. illus. back issues avail.; reprint serv. avail. from PSC. **Document type:** *Journal, Academic/Scholarly.* **Description:** Aims to present papers in which research expertise is combined with substantive and theoretical significance.
Related titles: Online - full text ed.: ISSN 1468-2672. 2000. GBP 332 in United Kingdom to institutions; EUR 498 in Europe to institutions; USD 664 in US & Canada to institutions; GBP 332 elsewhere to institutions (effective 2012) (from IngentaConnect).
Indexed: A20, A22, ASCA, BRD, CA, CurCont, DIP, E01, ESPM, FR, FamI, I13, IBR, IBSS, IBZ, P10, P30, P42, P46, P48, P53, P54, PCI, PQC, PSA, RiskAb, S02, S03, S11, SCOPUS, SOPODA, SSA, SSAI, SSAb, SSCI, SSI, SSciA, SociolAb, T02, W03, W05, W07, W09.
—BLDSC (3830.108000), IE, Infotrieve, Ingenta, INIST. **CCC.**

S

Published by: (European Consortium for Sociological Research), Oxford University Press, Great Clarendon St, Oxford, OX2 6DP, United Kingdom. TEL 44-1865-556767, FAX 44-1865-556646, enquiry@oup.co.uk, http://www.oxfordjournals.org. Ed. Hans-Peter Blossfeld TEL 49-951-8632595. Pub. Martin Green. Adv. contact Linda Hann TEL 44-1344-779945.

302 POL ISSN 1734-6878
EUROPEAN STUDIES ON INEQUALITIES AND SOCIAL COHESION. Text in English. 2005. q. **Document type:** *Journal, Academic/Scholarly.*
Indexed: SociolAb.
Published by: Wydawnictwo Uniwersytetu Lodzkiego/Lodz University Press, ul Lindleya 8, Lodz, 90-131, Poland. TEL 48-42-6655861, FAX 48-42-6655861, wdwul@uni.lodz.pl, http://www.wydawnictwo.uni.lodz.pl. Ed. Wielislawa Warzywoda-Kruszynska.

302.2 ESP ISSN 1139-3629
EUSKONEWS & MEDIA. Text in Basque. 1998. w. **Document type:** *Newsletter, Consumer.*
Media: Online - full text.
Published by: Eusko Ikaskuntza/Sociedad de Estudios Vascos, Palacio Miramar, Miraconcha 48, Donostia, San Sebastian 20007, Spain. TEL 34-943-310855, FAX 34-943-213956, ei-sev@sc.ehu.es, http://www.eusko-ikaskuntza.org/.

EVALUATION DE LA RECHERCHE EN S H S. (Sciences Humaines et Sociales) *see* SCIENCES: COMPREHENSIVE WORKS

301 GBR ISSN 1743-954X
THE EVALUATOR (LONDON). Text in English. 2004. 3/yr. free to members (effective 2009). **Document type:** *Magazine, Consumer.* **Description:** Features articles on research, on evaluation theory, methods and practice.
Published by: United Kingdom Evaluation Society, 37 Star St, Ware, Herts SG12 7AA, United Kingdom. TEL 44-1920-462411, FAX 44-1920-462730, ukes@profbriefings.co.uk. Eds. Jean Ellis, Richard Thurston.

EVANGELICAL REVIEW OF SOCIETY AND POLITICS. *see* RELIGIONS AND THEOLOGY—Other Denominations And Sects

301 GBR ISSN 2044-4095
▼ ➤ **EXCURSIONS.** Text in English. 2010. irreg. free (effective 2011). **Document type:** *Journal, Academic/Scholarly.*
Media: Online - full text.
Published by: University of Sussex, School of English, Sussex House, Brighton, BN1 9RH, United Kingdom. TEL 44-01273-606755, FAX 44-01273-678335, information@sussex.ac.uk, http://www.sussex.ac.uk.

301 DEU ISSN 0175-3347
HV640
EXILFORSCHUNG; ein internationales Jahrbuch. Text in German. 1983. a. EUR 32 (effective 2009). adv. **Document type:** *Academic/Scholarly.*
Indexed: DIP, IBR, IBZ, MLA-IB, PCI, RILM.
Published by: (Gesellschaft fuer Exilforschung), Edition Text und Kritik in Richard Boorberg Verlag GmbH & Co. KG (Subsidiary of: Richard Boorberg Verlag GmbH und Co. KG), Levelingstr 6A, Munich, 81673, Germany. TEL 49-89-43600012, FAX 49-89-43600019, info@etk-muenchen.de, http://www.etk-muenchen.de. adv.: page EUR 600.

EXPLORING SOCIAL ISSUES THROUGH LITERATURE. *see* LITERATURE

306 USA ISSN 2159-4414
▼ **EYE SEE MEDIA**; social justice - environment - culture. Text in English. 2010. q. USD 21 in North America; USD 25 in Europe; USD 30 elsewhere (effective 2011). **Document type:** *Magazine, Trade.*
Published by: Eye See Media Llc., 2420 Denby Way, Colorado Springs, CO 80919. darcie@eyeseeonline.com.

303.842 FRA ISSN 1957-6668
F A L MAG. (France Amerique Latine) Text in French. 2007. q. EUR 27 to non-members; EUR 15 to members (effective 2009). **Document type:** *Magazine, Consumer.*
Formerly (until 2007): France Amerique Latine Magazine (0988-6230)
Indexed: FR.
Published by: France Amerique Latine, 37 Bd Saint Jacques, Paris, 75014, France. TEL 33-1-45882274, FAX 33-1-45652087, falnationale@franceameriquelatine.fr.

F A O ECONOMIC AND SOCIAL DEVELOPMENT PAPER. (Food and Agriculture Organization) *see* BUSINESS AND ECONOMICS

302.2 ARG ISSN 1669-4015
F I S E C. ESTRATEGIAS. Variant title: Revista Academica del Foro Iberoamericano sobre Estrategias de Comunicacion. Text in Spanish. 2005. a. **Document type:** *Monographic series, Academic/Scholarly.*
Media: Online - full text.
Published by: Foro Iberoamericano sobre Estrategias de Comunicacion, Camino de Cintura y Juan 23, Lomas de Zaragoza, Buenos Aires, 1832, Argentina. TEL 54-11-42825050, FAX 54-11-42832609, editor@fisec-estrategias.com.ar.

F L S - AKTUELLT. *see* EDUCATION

FACE; revista de semiotica e comunicacao. *see* LINGUISTICS

FACTA UNIVERSITATIS. SERIES PHILOSOPHY, SOCIOLOGY AND PSYCHOLOGY. *see* PHILOSOPHY

301 ESP ISSN 1130-8893
FAMILIA; revista de ciencias y orientacion familiar. Text in Spanish. 1990. s-a. **Document type:** *Journal, Academic/Scholarly.*
Formerly (until 1990): Boletin sobre la Familia (1130-8885)
Indexed: DIP, IBR, IBZ.
Published by: Universidad Pontificia de Salamanca, Instituto Superior de Ciencias de la Familia, Compania, 5, Salamanca, 37008, Spain. TEL 34-923-277141, FAX 34-923-277101, cc.familia@upsa.es, http://www.upsa.es/.

231 BRA ISSN 0014-7125
FAMILIA CRISTA; revista da paz e do amor - revista mensal para a familia. Text in Portuguese. 1934. m. BRL 160. adv. bk.rev. charts; illus. **Description:** General interest magazine for family living.
Published by: Pia Sociedade Filhas de Sao Paulo, Rua Domingos de Morais, 678, VI Mariana, Sao Paulo, SP 04010-100, Brazil. Ed. Luzia Rodriguez. Circ: 160,000.

▼ **FAMILIA Y PERSONA.** *see* PSYCHOLOGY

306.85 360 COL ISSN 0120-3215
FAMILIA Y SOCIEDAD. Text in Spanish. 1976. bi-m. USD 28 in Latin America; USD 30 elsewhere. adv. bk.rev. **Document type:** *Academic/Scholarly.*
Published by: Centro de Pastoral Familiar para America Latina, Ave. 28, 37-21, Apartado Aereo 54569, Bogota, CUND, Colombia. TEL 57-1-368-0311, FAX 57-1-368-0540. Ed. Fr Gilberto Gomez. R&P Claudia Duque. Adv. contact Pilar Monroy. Circ: 4,000.

▼ **FAMILIAS SIGLO XXI.** *see* PSYCHOLOGY

302.3 DEU ISSN 1863-9127
FAMILIE UND GESELLSCHAFT. Text in German. 1999. irreg., latest vol.23, 2008. price varies. **Document type:** *Monographic series, Academic/Scholarly.*
Published by: Ergon Verlag, Keesburgstr 11, Wuerzburg, 97074, Germany. TEL 49-931-280084, FAX 49-931-282872, service@ergon-verlag.de, http://www.ergon-verlag.de.

FAMILIENDYNAMIK; Interdisziplinaere Zeitschrift fuer systemorientierte Praxis und Forschung. *see* PSYCHOLOGY

306.85 USA ISSN 1079-0144
FAMILIES IN FOCUS SERIES. Text in English. 1995. irreg. back issues avail. **Document type:** *Monographic series, Academic/Scholarly.*
—**CCC.**
Published by: (Boston College, Sloan Work and Family Research Network), National Council on Family Relations, 1201 W River Pky, Ste 200, Minneapolis, MN 55454. TEL 763-781-9331, FAX 763-781-9348, info@ncfr.org, http://www.ncfr.org/.

306.85 CHL ISSN 0717-4861
FAMILIES Y PROCESOS. Text in Spanish. 1999. s-a. **Document type:** *Journal, Academic/Scholarly.*
Media: Online - full text.
Published by: Universidad de Concepcion, Departamento de Servicio Social, Casilla 1047, Concepcion, Chile. TEL 56-41-204006, FAX 54-41-231984, familias@udec.cl.

306.85 FRA ISSN 0751-6169
FAMILLES DE FRANCE; jeunes familles. Text in French. 1969. q. **Description:** Discusses issues facing young families.
Published by: Federation des Familles de France, 28 Place Saint Georges, Paris, 75009, France. TEL 33-1-44534590, FAX 33-1-45960788, http://www.familles-de-france.org. Ed. Renee Ghislaine. Pub. Jacques Bichot.

LES FAMILLES ET LES ENFANTS AU QUEBEC; principales statistiques. *see* SOCIOLOGY—Abstracting, Bibliographies, Statistics

306.85 CAN ISSN 1195-9428
FAMILY CONNECTIONS. Text in English. 1977. 3/yr. adv.
Formerly (until 1994): British Columbia Council for the Family. Newsletter (0706-9022)
Published by: British Columbia Council for Families, 204-2590 Granville St, Vancouver, BC V6H 3H1, Canada. TEL 604-660-0675, 800-663-5638, FAX 604-732-4813, bccf@bccf.bc.ca. adv.: page CAD 400; 7.25 x 9.5. Circ: 1,000.

FAMILY FOCUS (COLORADO SPRINGS). *see* CHILDREN AND YOUTH—About

306.85 AUS ISSN 1328-2174
FAMILY HISTORY NETLETTER. Text in English. 1997. m. **Document type:** *Newsletter.*
Media: Online - full text.
Published by: White Room Electronic Publishing Pty. Ltd., 3/26 Vautier St, PO Box 305, Elwood, VIC 3184, Australia. tdenniso@bigpond.net.au, http://www.whiteroom.com.au.

306.85 USA ISSN 0892-2691
HQ536
THE FAMILY IN AMERICA; a journal of public policy. Text in English. 1978. q. USD 35 domestic; USD 45 foreign (effective 2010). illus. back issues avail. **Document type:** *Journal, Consumer.* **Description:** Reports on social problems facing the traditional family.
Formerly (until 1987): Persuasion at Work (0163-5387)
Related titles: Online - full text ed.: free (effective 2010); Supplement(s): New Research.
Indexed: CCR.
—**CCC.**
Published by: The Howard Center, The Howard Center for Family, Religion & Society, 934 N Main St, Rockford, IL 61103. TEL 815-964-5819. Ed. Robert W Patterson. Pub. Allan C Carlson.

306.85 900 USA ISSN 1558-6286
FAMILY LIFE THROUGH HISTORY. Text in English. 2005. irreg., latest 2007. price varies. back issues avail. **Document type:** *Monographic series, Consumer.*
Related titles: Online - full text ed.
Published by: Greenwood Publishing Group Inc. (Subsidiary of: A B C - C L I O), 88 Post Rd W, PO Box 5007, Westport, CT 06881. TEL 203-226-3571, 800-225-5800, FAX 877-231-6980, sales@greenwood.com.

306.85 AUS ISSN 1030-2646
HQ706 CODEN: FAMMEL
FAMILY MATTERS. Text in English. 1980. 3/yr. AUD 66 domestic to individuals; AUD 99 domestic to institutions; AUD 120 foreign (effective 2008). bk.rev. back issues avail. **Document type:** *Journal, Academic/Scholarly.* **Description:** Publishes research from the institute and other Australian and international researchers on social, psychological, and legal issues involving families of all types.
Former titles (until 1987): Australian Institute of Family Studies. Newsletter (0818-0229); (until 1986): Institute of Family Studies. Newsletter (0159-9143)
Related titles: Online - full text ed.
Indexed: A01, A03, A08, A11, A26, AEI, CA, CWI, E03, E07, E08, ERI, G05, G06, G07, G08, I05, I06, I07, M01, M02, MASUSE, P30, P34, PAIS, S02, S03, S09, S23, SCOPUS, SOPODA, SSA, SWR&A, SociolAb, T02, WBA, WMB.
—Ingenta. **CCC.**
Published by: Australian Institute of Family Studies, Level 20, 485 La Trobe St, Melbourne, VIC 3000, Australia. TEL 61-3-92147888, FAX 61-3-92147839, afrc@aifs.gov.au, http://www.aifs.org.au. Eds. Lan Wang TEL 61-3-92147838, Meredith Michie. Circ: 4,000.

306.85 USA ISSN 1543-3676
HQ536
FAMILY POLICY REVIEW. Text in English. 2003 (Spr.). s-a. USD 30 to individuals; USD 50 to institutions; USD 15 to students (effective 2003).
Published by: Family Research Council, 801 G St. NW, Washington, DC 2001. TEL 202-393-2100, FAX 202-393-2134, http://www.frc.org. Ed. Alan R. Crippen II.

FAMILY PROCESS. *see* PSYCHOLOGY

FAMILY RELATIONS; interdisciplinary journal of applied family studies. *see* EDUCATION

306.85 AUS ISSN 1833-9077
FAMILY RELATIONSHIPS QUARTERLY. Text in English. 2006. q. free to members (effective 2008). **Document type:** *Newsletter, Consumer.*
Media: Online - full text.
Published by: (Australian Family Relationships Clearinghouse), Australian Institute of Family Studies, Level 20, 485 La Trobe St, Melbourne, VIC 3000, Australia. TEL 61-3-92147888, FAX 61-3-92147839, afrc@aifs.gov.au, http://www.aifs.org.au. Ed. Elly Robinson.

306.85 GBR ISSN 1942-4620
▼ **FAMILY SCIENCE**; global perspectives on research, policy and practice. Text in English. 2010 (Jan.). q. GBP 281 combined subscription in United Kingdom to institutions (print & online eds.); EUR 405, USD 505 combined subscription to institutions (print & online eds.) (effective 2012). **Document type:** *Journal, Academic/Scholarly.* **Description:** Promote the development of family science within Europe and around the globe, by publishing original research, theoretical, methodological and review papers that address issues pertinent to the family.
Related titles: Online - full text ed.: ISSN 1942-4639. GBP 253 in United Kingdom to institutions; EUR 364, USD 454 to institutions (effective 2012).
Indexed: T02.
—**CCC.**
Published by: (European Society on Family Relations NLD), Taylor & Francis Ltd. (Subsidiary of: Taylor & Francis Group), 4 Park Sq, Milton Park, Abingdon, Oxfordshire OX14 4RN, United Kingdom. TEL 44-20-70176000, FAX 44-20-70176336, subscriptions@tandf.co.uk. Ed. Judith Semon Dubas.

301 USA
FAMILY SMART E-TIPS. Text in English. 1978. 2/m. bk.rev. **Document type:** *Newsletter, Consumer.* **Description:** Contains information and advice on fathering, mothering, child development, single parenting, step parenting, grand parenting and marriage.
Supersedes in part: Smart Dads; Which was formerly: Dads Only
Media: E-mail.
Published by: Smart Families, Inc., PO Box 500050, San Diego, CA 92150-0050. TEL 858-513-7150, FAX 858-513-7142, plewis@familyuniversity.com. Ed., Pub. Paul Lewis. Circ: 9,000 (paid).

FAMILY THERAPY MAGAZINE. *see* PSYCHOLOGY

306.85 USA ISSN 1537-6680
HQ756
➤ **FATHERING**; a journal of theory and research about men as parents. Text in English. 2003. 3/yr. USD 220 domestic to institutions; USD 240 foreign to institutions; USD 250 combined subscription to institutions (print & online eds.) (effective 2010). **Document type:** *Journal, Academic/Scholarly.* **Description:** Publishes original empirical and theoretical papers addressing all aspects of fathering.
Related titles: Online - full text ed.: ISSN 1933-026X. USD 210 (effective 2010).
Indexed: A01, A03, A08, A26, C06, C07, CA, E-psyche, E08, Faml, G08, GW, I05, I07, P03, P18, P19, P27, P30, P48, P50, P53, P54, PQC, PsycInfo, PsycholAb, S02, S03, S09, S23, SSA, SociolAb, T02.
—BLDSC (3897.366500), IE, Ingenta. **CCC.**
Published by: Men's Studies Press, PO Box 32, Harriman, TN 37748. TEL 423-369-2375, FAX 423-369-1126, publisher@mensstudies.com. Ed. Dr. Joseph H Pleck.

307.14 AUS ISSN 1839-2016
▼ **FEATURE MAGAZINE.** Text in English. 2011. s-a. free (effective 2011). **Document type:** *Magazine, Government.*
Related titles: Online - full text ed.: ISSN 1839-2024. free (effective 2011).
Published by: Government of South Australia, Department for Families and Communities, GPO Box 292, Adelaide, SA 5001, Australia. TEL 61-8-82268800, FAX 61-8-84139003, enquiries@dfc.sa.gov.a.

301 VEN ISSN 0798-3069
HM22.V4
➤ **FERMENTUM.** Text in English, Portuguese. 1991. 3/yr. **Document type:** *Journal, Academic/Scholarly.* **Description:** Promotes the popularization of sociological and anthropological knowledge in the human sciences.
Indexed: CA, P42, PSA, S02, S03, SCOPUS, SSA, SociolAb, T02.
—INIST.
Published by: Universidad de los Andes, Facultad de Humanidades y Educacion, GISAC-FERMENTUM, Av Universidad, Res Los Caciques, Edf Terepaima, Merida, 5101, Venezuela.

302.23 DEU ISSN 1865-3332
FIKTION UND FIKTIONALISIERUNG. Text in German. 1998. irreg., latest vol.9, 2006. price varies. **Document type:** *Monographic series, Academic/Scholarly.*
Published by: Herbert von Halem Verlag, Lindenstr 19, Cologne, 50674, Germany. TEL 49-221-9258290, FAX 49-221-92582929, info@halem-verlag.de, http://www.halem-verlag.de.

FILM- UND MEDIENWISSENSCHAFT. *see* MOTION PICTURES

FILOSOFIJA, SOCIOLOGIJA. *see* PHILOSOPHY

301 FIN ISSN 0783-005X
FINNISH SOCIETY FOR LABOUR HISTORY AND CULTURAL TRADITIONS. PAPERS ON LABOUR HISTORY. Text in English, German, Swedish. 1986. irreg., latest vol.6, 2002. price varies. back issues avail. **Document type:** *Monographic series, Academic/Scholarly.*
Published by: Tyovaen Historian ja Perinteen Tutkimuksen Seura/Finnish Society for Labour History and Cultural Traditions, c/o Hanna Snelling, Kultuurien Tutkimuksen Laitos Kansatriede, PO Box 59, Helsinki, 00014, Finland. TEL 358-9-19122622, hanna.snelling@helsinki.fi. Ed. Pirjo Markkola.

302.23 DEU ISSN 0931-7945
➤ **FLASCHENPOST**; das authentische Massenmedium. Text in German. 1987. irreg. EUR 2 per issue (effective 2002). adv. bk.rev.; film rev.; music rev. back issues avail. **Document type:** *Journal, Academic/Scholarly.* **Description:** Examines all aspects of mass media.
Address: Lotharstr 65, Duisburg, 47048, Germany. TEL 49-203-3792397, FAX 49-203-3793333. Ed., Adv. contact Ulrich Schmitz. Circ: 1,000 (controlled).

301 PRT ISSN 1647-6123
▼ ➤ **FLUXOS E RISCOS**; revista de estudos sociais. Text in Portuguese. 2010. s-a. free. **Document type:** *Journal, Academic/Scholarly.*
Related titles: Online - full text ed.: ISSN 1647-6131.
Published by: (Universidade Lusofona de Humanidades e Tecnologia, Centro de Pesquisa e Estudos Sociais), Universidade Lusofona de Humanidades e Tecnologia, Edicoes Universitarias, Campo Grande 376, Lisbon, 1749-024, Portugal. TEL 351-217-515500, FAX 351-217-577006, http://ulusofona.pt.

➤ **FOCUS AFRIKA**; I A K Diskussionsbeitraege. *see* POLITICAL SCIENCE

306 ITA ISSN 1972-781X
FOCUS FAMILY. Text in Italian. 2008. q. **Document type:** *Magazine, Consumer.*
Published by: Gruner + Jahr (G + J) Mondadori SpA (Subsidiary of: Arnoldo Mondadori Editore SpA), Corso Monforte 54, Milan, 20122, Italy. TEL 39-02-76210206, FAX 39-02-76013439, info@gujm.it, http://www.mondadori.it.

302.23 COL ISSN 0123-1022
FOLIOS; periodismo para leer. Text in Spanish. s-a. **Document type:** *Journal, Academic/Scholarly.*
Published by: Universidad de Antioquia, Facultad de Comunicaciones, Apartado Postal 1226, Medellin, Colombia. TEL 57-4-210-5920, FAX 57-4-233-4724, jhoyos@venus.intepla.net.co.

303 SWE ISSN 1652-2664
FOLKE BERNADOTTE ACADEMY. CONFERENCE PROCEEDINGS. Text in English. irreg. **Document type:** *Proceedings.*
Published by: Folke Bernadotteakademin/Folke Bernadotte Academy, Sandoevaegen 1, Sandoeverken, 87264, Sweden. TEL 46-612-82200, FAX 46-612-82021, info@folkebernadotteacademy.se, http://www.folkebernadotteacademy.se.

303 SWE ISSN 1652-9456
FOLKE BERNADOTTE ACADEMY. HANDBOOK. Text in English. 2003. irreg.
Published by: Folke Bernadotteakademin/Folke Bernadotte Academy, Sandoevaegen 1, Sandoeverken, 87264, Sweden. TEL 46-612-82200, FAX 46-612-82021, info@folkebernadotteacademy.se, http://www.folkebernadotteacademy.se.

FOOD, CULTURE, AND SOCIETY; an international journal of multidisciplinary research. *see* HOME ECONOMICS

301 DNK ISSN 1603-3493
➤ **FORBINDELSER**; kultur, integration og mangfoldighed. Text in Multiple languages. 2003. irreg. bk.rev. **Document type:** *Magazine, Academic/Scholarly.*
Media: Online - full content.
Published by: Danmarks Biblioteksskole, Institut for Biblioteksudvikling/Royal School of Library & Information Science. Institute of Library and Information Management, Birketinget 6, Copenhagen S, 2300, Denmark. TEL 45-32-586066, cgj@db.dk, http://www.db.dk/instbib. Ed. Hans Elbeshausen.

302 USA ISSN 2159-905X
▼ **FORMATIONS (NEW YORK).** Text in English. 2010. s-a. free (effective 2011). **Document type:** *Journal, Trade.*
Related titles: Online - full text ed.: ISSN 2159-9068.
Published by: Sociology Students Association, The Graduate Center of the City University of New York, The Doctoral Program in Sociology, 365 Fifth Ave, New York, NY 10016. http://opencuny.org/gcsoc/.

▼ **FORMECOS.** (Formation Economique et Sociale) *see* BUSINESS AND ECONOMICS

306.461 SWE ISSN 1654-0131
FORSKNINGSTEMAT MAENNISKA, HAELSA, SAMHAELLE. Text in Swedish. 2006. irreg. **Document type:** *Monographic series, Academic/Scholarly.* **Description:** Main focus on work-related public health research.
Published by: Hoegskolan i Kristianstad, Institutionen foer Haelsovetenskaper/Kristianstad University, Department of Health Sciences, Elmetorpsvaegen 15, Kristianstad, 29188, Sweden. TEL 46-44-204080, FAX 46-44-204043, hv@hkr.se, http://www.hkr.se/hv.

306 BLR ISSN 1029-6816
FORUM; infarmacyjna-kulturny byuleten. Text in Belorussian. 1995. q. **Document type:** *Journal, Academic/Scholarly.* **Description:** Publishes international research in cultural issues, especially those concerning dialogs among cultural and ethnic majority and minority groups.
Published by: Euroforum, Centre for European Studies and Cultural Initiatives, PO Box 31, Minsk, 220036, Belarus. TEL 375-172-563613, FAX 375-172-563613.

FORUM (LORENTON). *see* LITERARY AND POLITICAL REVIEWS

300 USA ISSN 1540-5273
HQ1
➤ **THE FORUM FOR FAMILY AND CONSUMER ISSUES.** Abbreviated title: F F C I. Text in English. 1996. 3/yr. free (effective 2010). back issues avail. **Document type:** *Journal, Academic/Scholarly.* **Description:** Designed to enhance knowledge about matters of current interest to professionals in the fields of family and consumer sciences and 4-H youth development.
Media: Online - full text.
Published by: North Carolina State University, North Carolina Cooperative Extension Service, PO Box 7605, Raleigh, NC 27695. TEL 919-515-9145, FAX 919-513-0159, cbowen@psu.edu, http://www.ces.ncsu.edu. Ed. Jacquelyn W McClelland.

302.23 DEU ISSN 1868-9574
▼ **FORUM KOMPARATIVE KASUISTIK.** Text in German. 2009. irreg., latest vol.9, 2010. price varies. **Document type:** *Monographic series, Academic/Scholarly.*
Media: Online - full content.
Published by: Technische Universitaet Berlin, Universitaetsbibliothek, Fasanenstr 88, Berlin, 10623, Germany. TEL 49-30-31476131, FAX 49-30-31476133, publikationen@ub.tu-berlin.de.

306 NLD ISSN 1873-5819
FORUM MAGAZINE (UTRECHT). Text in Dutch. 2006. q.
Published by: Forum, Instituut voor Multiculturele Vraagstukken, Postbus 201, Utrecht, 3500 AE, Netherlands. TEL 31-20-2974321, FAX 31-20-2960050, informatie@forum.nl, http://www.forum.nl/index.html. Ed. Frans van der Heijden.

302.23 DEU
FORUM NEUE MEDIEN. Text in German. 1997. irreg., latest vol.3, 2005. price varies. **Document type:** *Monographic series, Academic/Scholarly.*
Published by: Herbert von Halem Verlag, Lindenstr 19, Cologne, 50674, Germany. TEL 49-221-9258290, FAX 49-221-92582929, info@halem-verlag.de, http://www.halem-verlag.de.

305.3 UGA ISSN 1992-125X
FOUNTAIN SERIES IN GENDER STUDIES. Text in English. 200?. irreg. price varies. **Document type:** *Monographic series.*
Published by: Fountain Publishers Ltd., PO Box 488, Kampala, Uganda. TEL 256-41-259163, FAX 256-41-251160, fountain@starcom.co.ug, http://www.fountainpublishers.co.ug/.

306 USA ISSN 2160-5114
➤ **FRAME**; a journal of visual and material culture. Text in English. 1997. s-a. free (effective 2011). back issues avail. **Document type:** *Journal, Academic/Scholarly.*
Formerly (until 2011): P A R T (2160-5106)
Media: Online - full text.
Published by: Doctoral Students' Council, The Graduate School and University Center, The City University of New York, 365 Fifth Ave, New York, NY 10016. TEL 212-817-7888, FAX 212-817-2789, dsc@cunydsc.org, http://www.cunydsc.org. Eds. Annie Dell'Aria, Kristin Margelot, Shawn Rice.

➤ **FRAME WORK PRESS**; art books and catalogues. *see* PHOTOGRAPHY

➤ **FRAMING FILM**; the history and art of cinema. *see* MOTION PICTURES

301 SWE ISSN 0281-0492
FRAMTIDER. Text in Swedish. 1982. q. **Document type:** *Academic/Scholarly.*
Related titles: English ed.: Framtider International. ISSN 1400-0199.
Published by: Institutet foer Framtidsstudier (IF)/Institute for Future Studies, Fack 591, Stockholm, 10131, Sweden. TEL 46-8-402-12-00, FAX 46-8-24-50-14. Ed. Ingemar Karlsson. Circ: 19,500.

303 BEL ISSN 1375-4599
FRANCAIS ET SOCIETE. Text in French. 1990. s-a. EUR 17 (effective 2002). bibl. 56 p./no.; back issues avail. **Document type:** *Monographic series.*
Published by: De Boeck Universite (Subsidiary of: Editis), Fond Jean-Paques 4, Louvain-la-Neuve, 1348, Belgium. TEL 32-10-482511, FAX 32-10-482519, info@superieur.deboeck.com, http://superieur.deboeck.com.

301 FRA ISSN 1773-9209
PC2002
FRANCOPHONIE DANS LE MONDE. Text in French. irreg., latest 2001. **Description:** Collection of information on French language, teaching, culture, communication, science and technology in the francophone communities.
Formerly (until 2004): Etat de la Francophonie dans le Monde (1294-2103)
—CCC.
Published by: (Haut Conseil de la Francophonie), Editions Nathan, 25 Av. Pierre de Coubertin, Paris, Cedex 13 75211, France. FAX 33-1-45872662, http://www.nathan.fr.

FRANCOPOLYPHONIES. *see* LITERATURE

306 FRA ISSN 1956-7332
FRANCOSCOPIE (YEAR). Text in French. 1985. biennial. EUR 32 newsstand/cover (effective 2007). **Document type:** *Consumer.* **Description:** Describes and analyzes France and its people. Looks at attitudes, behavior, opinions and values in everyday life.
—CCC.
Published by: Editions Larousse, 21 rue du Montparnasse, Paris, 75283 Cedex 06, France. TEL 33-1-44394400, FAX 33-1-44394343, http://www.editions-larousse.fr.

FRANKFURTER SCHRIFTEN ZUM MEDIENRECHT. *see* LAW

301 USA ISSN 0736-9182
HM1
➤ **FREE INQUIRY IN CREATIVE SOCIOLOGY.** Text in English. 1972. s-a. USD 15 domestic to individuals; USD 20 foreign to individuals; USD 25 domestic to institutions; USD 30 foreign to institutions (effective 2011). adv. back issues avail.; reprints avail. **Document type:** *Journal, Academic/Scholarly.* **Description:** Publishes articles of interest to a non-specialist audience.
Formerly (until Jan.1979): Free Inquiry (0886-1749)
Related titles: Microform ed.: (from PQC).
Indexed: A22, CA, G10, P30, S02, S03, SOPODA, SSA, SociolAb, T02, W09.
—BLDSC (4033.322000), IE, Infotrieve, Ingenta.
Published by: Oklahoma State University, Sociology Department, 006 Classroom Bldg, Stillwater, OK 74078. TEL 405-744-6105, FAX 405-744-5780, sociology@okstate.edu. Ed. Alberto G Mata Jr. TEL 405-325-2339.

302.2 USA
FREEDOM FORUM MEDIA STUDIES CENTER. OCCASIONAL PAPER. Text in English. irreg., latest vol.8, 1991.
Formerly: Gannett Foundation. Occasional Paper
Published by: Colombia University, Freedom Forum Media Studies Center, 2950 Broadway, New York, NY 10027-7004. TEL 212-280-8392, FAX 212-678-6661. Ed. Martha Fitzsimon.

300 DEU ISSN 0947-3076
FREIBURGER BEITRAEGE ZUR SOZIOLOGIE. Text in German. 1994. irreg. price varies. **Document type:** *Monographic series, Academic/Scholarly.*
Published by: Centaurus Verlag & Media KG, Kaiser-Joseph-Str 267, Freiburg, 79098, Germany. TEL 49-761-1525861, FAX 49-761-1525868, info@centaurus-verlag.de.

FREIE UNIVERSITAET BERLIN. OSTEUROPA-INSTITUT. ARBEITSPAPIERE. BEREICH POLITIK UND GESELLSCHAFT. *see* POLITICAL SCIENCE

FREIE UNIVERSITAET BERLIN. OSTEUROPA-INSTITUT. INTERDISZIPLINAERE ARBEITSPAPIERE. *see* POLITICAL SCIENCE

FREIE UNIVERSITAET BERLIN. OSTEUROPA-INSTITUT. PHILOSOPHISCHE UND SOZIOLOGISCHE VEROEFFENTLICHUNGEN. *see* PHILOSOPHY

FRENCH POLITICS, CULTURE & SOCIETY. *see* POLITICAL SCIENCE

301 FRA ISSN 1627-430X
FRONTIERES. Text in French. 2001. irreg. back issues avail. **Document type:** *Monographic series, Consumer.*
Published by: Editions Autrement, 77 Rue du Faubourg St Antoine, Paris, 75011, France. TEL 33-1-44738000, FAX 33-1-44730012, contact@autrement.com.

FUJIAN LUNTAN (SHE-KE JIAOYU BAN)/FUJIAN TRIBUNE (A ECONOMICS & SOCIOLOGY MONTHLY). *see* BUSINESS AND ECONOMICS

301 BRA
FUNDACAO CENTRO DE PESQUISAS ECONOMICAS E SOCIAIS DO PIAUI. RELATORIO DE ATIVIDADES. Cover title: Fundacao Centro de Pesquisas Economicas e Sociais do Piaui. Atividades C E P R O. Text in Portuguese. irreg.
Published by: Fundacao Centro de Pesquisas Economicas e Sociais do Piaui, Av. Miguel Rosa 3190-S, Caixa Postal 429, Teresina, Piaui 6400, Brazil.

301 BRA
FUNDACAO JOAQUIM NABUCO. SERIE ABOLICAO. Text in Portuguese. 1988. irreg., latest vol.22, 1994.
Published by: (Fundacao Joaquim Nabuco), Editora Massangana, Rua Dois Irmaos, 15, Apipucos, Recife, PE 52071-440, Brazil. TEL 081-268-4611, FAX 081-268-9600.

301 BRA
FUNDACAO JOAQUIM NABUCO. SERIE CURSOS E CONFERENCIAS. Text in Portuguese. 1974. irreg., latest vol.51, 1993.
Formerly: Instituto Joaquim Nabuco de Pesquisas Sociais. Serie Cursos e Conferencias
Published by: (Fundacao Joaquim Nabuco), Editora Massangana, Rua Dois Irmaos, 15, Apipucos, Recife, PE 52071-440, Brazil. TEL 81-4415900, FAX 81-441-5458.

301 BRA
FUNDACAO JOAQUIM NABUCO. SERIE DESCOBRIMENTOS. Text in Portuguese. 1992. irreg., latest vol.7, 1996. price varies.
Published by: (Fundacao Joaquim Nabuco), Editora Massangana, Rua Dois Irmaos, 15, Apipucos, Recife, PE 52071-440, Brazil. TEL 081-268-4611, FAX 081-268-4611.

301 BRA
FUNDACAO JOAQUIM NABUCO. SERIE DOCUMENTOS. Text in Portuguese. 1975. irreg., latest vol.40, 1993.
Formerly: Instituto Joaquim Nabuco de Pesquisas Sociais. Serie Documentos
Published by: (Fundacao Joaquim Nabuco), Editora Massangana, Rua Dois Irmaos, 15, Apipucos, Recife, PE 52071-440, Brazil. TEL 081-268-4611, FAX 081-268-9600.

301 BRA
FUNDACAO JOAQUIM NABUCO. SERIE ESTUDOS E PESQUISAS. Text in Portuguese. 1974. irreg., latest vol.79, 1990.
Formerly: Instituto Joaquim Nabuco de Pesquisas Sociais. Serie Estudos e Pesquisas
Published by: (Fundacao Joaquim Nabuco), Editora Massangana, Rua Dois Irmaos, 15, Apipucos, Recife, PE 52071-440, Brazil. TEL 81-4415900, FAX 81-441-5458.

301 BRA
FUNDACAO JOAQUIM NABUCO. SERIE OBRAS DE CONSULTA. Text in Portuguese. 1981. irreg., latest vol.12, 1991. price varies.
Published by: (Fundacao Joaquim Nabuco), Editora Massangana, Rua Dois Irmaos, 15, Apipucos, Recife, PE 52071-440, Brazil. TEL 081-268-4611, FAX 081-268-9600.

302 ITA
FUORIMARGINE. Text in Italian. 1989. irreg., latest vol.10, 1995. price varies. adv. **Document type:** *Monographic series, Consumer.*
Published by: Liguori Editore, Via Posillipo 394, Naples, 80123, Italy. TEL 39-081-7206111, FAX 39-081-7206244, liguori@liguori.it, http://www.liguori.it. Ed. Alberto Abruzzese.

303.4 NZL ISSN 0112-0328
FUTURE TIMES. Text in English. 1982. q. NZD 50 membership (effective 2009). bk.rev. **Document type:** *Journal, Academic/Scholarly.*
Related titles: Online - full text ed.: ISSN 1178-3885.
Indexed: A11, T02.
Published by: New Zealand Futures Trust, PO Box 12-008, Wellington, New Zealand. TEL 64-4-3835080, info@futurestrust.org.nz.

FUTURES; the journal of policy, planning and futures studies. *see* BUSINESS AND ECONOMICS—Economic Situation And Conditions

301 ITA ISSN 1971-0720
CB161
FUTURIBILI. Text in Italian. 1994. 3/yr. EUR 71 combined subscription domestic to institutions; EUR 89.50 combined subscription foreign to institutions (effective 2009). **Document type:** *Journal, Academic/Scholarly.*
Related titles: Online - full text ed.: ISSN 1972-5191. 2004.
Published by: (Istituto di Sociologia Internazionale di Gorizia), Franco Angeli Edizioni, Viale Monza 106, Milan, 20127, Italy. TEL 39-02-2837141, FAX 39-02-26144793, redazioni@francoangeli.it, http://www.francoangeli.it.

301 FRA ISSN 0337-307X
H3
➤ **FUTURIBLES**; analyse et prospective. Text in French; Summaries in English, French. 1975. m. (11/YR.). EUR 115 domestic; EUR 120 foreign (effective 2009). adv. bk.rev. charts; abstr. cum.index: 1975-1998. 96 p./no.; **Document type:** *Journal, Academic/Scholarly.* **Description:** Features analysis, forecasting and prospectives on main contemporary problems with a multidisciplinary approach and in a middle and long-term perspective.

S

Formed by the merger of (1966-1974): Analyse et Prevision (0003-262X); (1973-1975): Prospectives (0033-1503)
Related titles: Microform ed.: (from PQC); Online - full text ed.: ISSN 1958-5764.
Indexed: A20, A22, ABCPolSci, CA, DIP, ELLIS, FR, I13, IBR, IBSS, IBZ, ILD, JEL, KES, P30, P34, P42, PAIS, PCI, PSA, RASB, S02, S03, SCOPUS, SOPODA, SSA, SociolAb, T02.
—BLDSC (4060.689000), IE, Infotrieve, Ingenta, INIST. **CCC.**
Published by: (Futuribles International), E D P Sciences, 17 Ave du Hoggar, Parc d'Activites de Courtaboeuf, BP 112, Cedex A, Les Ulis, F-91944, France. TEL 33-1-69187575, FAX 33-1-69860678, http://www.edpsciences.org. Ed., Pub. Hugues de Jouvenel. R&P, Adv. contact Corinne Roels. B&W page EUR 700; trim 120 x 190. Circ: 5,000.

➤ **FUTUROS.** *see* POLITICAL SCIENCE

306.7 305.90664 NZL ISSN 1177-8474
G A P S S/RANGAHAU TANE AI TANE. (Gay Auckland Periodic Sex Surveys) Text in English. 2002. biennial. **Document type:** *Report, Consumer.*
Related titles: Online - full text ed.: ISSN 1177-8482.
Published by: New Zealand AIDS Foundation, PO Box 6663, Wellesley St, Auckland, New Zealand. TEL 64-9-3033124, FAX 64-9-3093149, contact@nzaf.org.nz.

307.14 DEU ISSN 0721-8141
G F E - DOKUMENTATION. Text in German. 1981. irreg., latest vol.4, 1985. price varies. **Document type:** *Monographic series, Academic/Scholarly.*
Published by: (Gesellschaft fuer Forschung und Entwicklungsprojektierung), Verlag fuer Entwicklungspolitik Saarbruecken GmbH, Auf der Adt 14, Saarbruecken, 66130, Germany. TEL 49-6893-986094, FAX 49-6893-986095, vfe@verlag-entwicklungspolitik.de, http://www.verlag-entwicklungspolitik.de.

G L C S INK. (Gay and Lesbian Counselling Service) *see* HOMOSEXUALITY

G N I F BRAIN BLOGGER; topics from multidimensional biopsychosocial perspectives. (Global Neuroscience Initiative Foundation) *see* BIOLOGY

301 330 USA ISSN 1935-3251
G T I PAPER SERIES; frontiers of a great transition. (Great Transition Initiative) Text in English. 200?. irreg. free (effective 2010). back issues avail. **Document type:** *Monographic series, Academic/Scholarly.* **Description:** Examines key aspects of an alternative global vision and a path forward. Elaborates visions and pathways for a future of enriched lives, human solidarity and a healthy planet.
Formerly (until 2002): Great Transition: the Promise and Lure of Times Ahead
Media: Online - full text.
Published by: Tellus Institute, Inc, 11 Arlington St, Boston, MA 02116. TEL 617-266-5400, FAX 617-266-8303, gti@tellus.org. Eds. Orion Kriegman, Paul Raskin.

GACETA SINDICAL. *see* BUSINESS AND ECONOMICS—Labor And Industrial Relations

GALAXIA. *see* LINGUISTICS

301 CAN ISSN 1197-4303
GALLUP POLL. Text in English. 1941. s-w. CAD 140. back issues avail.
Former titles (until 1993): Gallup Report (1184-891X); (until 1990): Gallup (0834-9061); (until 1987): Gallup Report (0576-5455)
Indexed: A26, CPerI, E08, G08, I05, RASB, S09.
—CCC.
Published by: Gallup Canada, Inc., 55 University Ave., Ste 1805, Toronto, ON M5J 2H7, Canada. TEL 416-586-0808, FAX 416-586-9606, http://www.gallup.com. Ed. Clara Hatton. Circ: 165.

306.482 CAN ISSN 1911-8716
GAMBLING RESEARCH REVEALS. Text in English. 2001. bi-m. free (effective 2011). back issues avail. **Document type:** *Newsletter, Consumer.* **Description:** Promotes research into gaming and gambling in the province.
Formerly (until 2006): Research Reveals (1499-2639)
Related titles: Online - full text ed.: ISSN 1911-8724.
Published by: Alberta Gaming Research Institute, HUB Mall, University of Alberta, 8909S - 112 St, Edmonton, AB T6G 2C5, Canada. TEL 780-492-2856, 780-492-2817, FAX 780-492-6125, abgaming@ualberta.ca. Eds. Garry Smith, Vickii Williams.

303.66 SWE
GANDHI IDAG/GANDHI TODAY. Text in Swedish. 199?. q. SEK 85 (effective 1999). **Description:** A meeting-place between East and West; non-violence as a political and spiritual power.
Published by: Jan Vicklund, Ed. & Pub., Nyborg Spakbacken, Knivsta, 741294, Sweden. TEL 46-18-38-71-87.

178 NLD ISSN 1877-4717
GEDRAAG JE!. Text in Dutch. 200?. a. EUR 8.95 (effective 2011).
Published by: Uitgeverij Van de Berg, Dukdalfweg 15b, Almere, 1332 BH, Netherlands. TEL 31-53-4312773, info@streekboeken.nl, http://www.uitgeverijvandeberg.nl.

306.43 DEU ISSN 0948-7999
GEGENBILDER. Text in German. 1995. irreg., latest vol.7, 2011. price varies. **Document type:** *Monographic series, Academic/Scholarly.*
Published by: (Ethnologie in Schule und Erwachsenenbildung e.V.), Waxmann Verlag GmbH, Steinfurter Str 555, Muenster, 48159, Germany. TEL 49-251-265040, FAX 49-251-2650426, info@waxmann.com. Eds. Lydia Raesfeld, Ursula Bertels.

301 DEU ISSN 1619-4470
GEISTESKULTUR INDIENS. Text in German. 2002. irreg., latest vol.13, 2009. price varies. **Document type:** *Monographic series, Academic/Scholarly.*
Published by: Shaker Verlag GmbH, Kaiserstr 100, Herzogenrath, 52134, Germany. TEL 49-2407-95960, FAX 49-2407-95969, info@shaker.de.

305.3 USA
GENDER AND CULTURE SERIES. Text in English. 1989. irreg., latest 2009. price varies. back issues avail. **Document type:** *Monographic series, Academic/Scholarly.*
Published by: Columbia University Press, 61 W 62nd St, New York, NY 10023. TEL 212-459-0600, FAX 212-459-3678, orderentry@perseusbooks.com. Eds. Nancy K Miller, Victoria Rosner, Jennifer Crewe.

305.3 GBR ISSN 1750-6425
GENDER AND DEVELOPMENT IN BRIEF. Text in English. 1995. s-a. free (effective 2009). back issues avail. **Document type:** *Bulletin, Academic/Scholarly.* **Description:** Focuses on topical gender themes and is targeted at busy policymakers and practitioners.
Formerly (until 2002): Development and Gender in Brief (1358-0612)
Related titles: Online - full text ed.: free (effective 2006).
Indexed: P30.
—CCC.
Published by: University of Sussex, Institute of Development Studies, Brighton, Sussex BN1 9RE, United Kingdom. TEL 44-1273-606261, FAX 44-1273-621202, ids@ids.ac.uk, http://www.ids.ac.uk/.

305.3 USA ISSN 0891-2432
HQ1075
➤ **GENDER & SOCIETY.** Text in English. 1987. bi-m. USD 797, GBP 469 combined subscription to institutions (print & online eds.); USD 781, GBP 460 to institutions (effective 2011). adv. bk.rev. illus. back issues avail.; reprint service avail. from PSC. **Document type:** *Journal, Academic/Scholarly.* **Description:** Focuses on the social and structural study of gender as a basic principal of the social order and as a primary social category, with emphasis on theory and research from micro and macrostructural perspectives.
Related titles: Online - full text ed.: ISSN 1552-3977. USD 717, GBP 422 to institutions (effective 2011).
Indexed: A20, A22, A25, A26, ABS&EES, ASCA, AmH&L, B04, BRD, CA, CMM, CPE, ChPerI, Chicano, CommAb, CurCont, DIP, E-psyche, E01, E08, E15, E16, ERA, ESPM, F09, FR, FamI, FemPer, G08, G10, HPNRM, I05, I14, IBR, IBSS, IBZ, IPsyAb, LeftInd, M12, P02, P03, P10, P13, P25, P27, P30, P34, P42, P48, P53, P54, PCI, PQC, PSA, PerIslam, PsycInfo, PsycholAb, RASB, RI-1, RI-2, RiskAb, S02, S03, S08, S09, S19, S20, S21, SCOPUS, SFSA, SOPODA, SRRA, SSA, SSAI, SSAb, SSCI, SSI, SSciA, SociolAb, T02, V&AA, V05, W03, W06, W07, W09, WSA, WSI.
—BLDSC (4096.401500), IE, Infotrieve, Ingenta, INIST. **CCC.**
Published by: (Sociologists for Women in Society), Sage Publications, Inc., 2455 Teller Rd, Thousand Oaks, CA 91320. TEL 805-499-9774, 800-818-7243, FAX 805-499-0871, 800-583-2665, info@sagepub.com. Ed. Dane M Britton. Circ: 1,800 (paid). **Subscr. outside the Americas to:** Sage Publications Ltd., 1 Oliver's Yard, 55 City Rd, London EC1Y 1SP, United Kingdom. TEL 44-20-73248701, FAX 44-20-73248733, subscription@sagepub.co.uk.

305.3 306.766 DEU ISSN 2191-2548
▼ **GENDER - QUEER - IDENTITY**; Warschauer Beitraege zur Differenzforschung. Text in German. forthcoming 2011. irreg. price varies. **Document type:** *Monographic series, Academic/Scholarly.*
Published by: Peter Lang GmbH (Subsidiary of: Peter Lang Publishing Group), Eschborner Landstr 42-50, Frankfurt Am Main, 60489, Germany. TEL 49-69-7807050, FAX 49-69-78070550, zentrale.frankfurt@peterlang.com. Eds. Bozena Choluj, Ulrich Raether.

305.3 305.4 323 NLD ISSN 2210-8106
GENDER REPORT CARD. Text in English. 2005. a.
Published by: Women's Initiatives for Gender Justice, Anna Palownastraat 103, The Hague, 2518 BC, Netherlands. TEL 31-70-3029911, FAX 31-70-3925270, info@iccwomen.org.

305.3 CZE ISSN 1213-0028
HQ1610.3
GENDER, ROVNE PRILEZITOSTI, VYZKUM. Text in Czech. 2000. s-a. free. **Document type:** *Journal, Academic/Scholarly.*
Related titles: Online - full text ed.: free (effective 2011).
Indexed: A01, CA, S02, S03, T02.
Published by: Akademie Ved Ceske Republiky, Sociologicky Ustav, Jilska 1, Prague 1, 110 00, Czech Republic. TEL 420-222-220924, FAX 420-222-220143, socmail@soc.cas.cz, http://www.soc.cas.cz. Ed. Zuzana Uhde. Circ: 350.

305.3 DEU ISSN 1612-5142
GENDER STUDIES; Interdisziplinaere Schriftenreihe zur Geschlechterforschung. Text in German. 2003. irreg., latest vol.16, 2010. price varies. **Document type:** *Monographic series, Academic/Scholarly.*
Published by: Verlag Dr. Kovac, Leverkusenstr 13, Hamburg, 22761, Germany. TEL 49-40-3988800, FAX 49-40-39888055, info@verlagdrkovac.de.

307.1416 FRA ISSN 1952-0298
GENERATION URBAINE. Text in French. 2006. irreg. back issues avail. **Document type:** *Monographic series, Consumer.*
Published by: Gulf Stream Editeur, Impasse du Forgeron, CP 910, Saint-Herblain, 44806, France. TEL 33-2-40480668, FAX 33-2-40487469, contact@gulfstream.fr.

GENES, BRAIN AND BEHAVIOR. *see* BIOLOGY—Genetics

GENGO BUNKA RONKYU. *see* LINGUISTICS

GENOCIDE STUDIES AND PREVENTION. *see* ANTHROPOLOGY

305.3 306.7 FRA ISSN 2104-3736
HQ21
▼ **GENRE, SEXUALITE & SOCIETE.** Text in French. 2009. s-a. free (effective 2011). **Document type:** *Journal, Academic/Scholarly.*
Media: Online - full text.
Published by: College de France, Ecole des Hautes Etudes en Sciences Sociales (E H E S S), 96 Boulevard Raspail, Paris, 75006, France. TEL 33-1-53635658, FAX 33-1-49542428, editions@ehess.fr, http://www.ehess.fr. Ed. Massimo Prearo.

301 ITA ISSN 1828-8243
GENTI E PROVINCIE D'ITALIA. Text in Italian. 1999. irreg. price varies. **Document type:** *Monographic series, Academic/Scholarly.*
Published by: L' Erma di Bretschneider, Via Cassiodoro 19, Rome, 00193, Italy. TEL 39-06-6874127, FAX 39-06-6874129, lerma@lerma.it, http://www.lerma.it.

305.3 NLD ISSN 1568-1602
GENUS: GENDER IN MODERN CULTURE. Text in English. 2000. irreg., latest vol.9, 2007. price varies. **Document type:** *Monographic series, Academic/Scholarly.* **Description:** Provides a forum for exploring cultural articulations of gender relations in modern society.
Indexed: A01, GW, P27, P46, P48, P54, PQC, T02.
Published by: Editions Rodopi B.V., Tijnmuiden 7, Amsterdam, 1046 AK, Netherlands. TEL 31-20-6114821, FAX 31-20-4472979, info@rodopi.nl. Eds. Frank Lay, Jennifer Yee, Russell West-Pavlov.

305.3 SWE ISSN 1654-7640
GENUS I NORRSKEN. Text in Swedish. 1993-2005; resumed 2008. q. free. back issues avail. **Document type:** *Journal, Academic/Scholarly.*
Former titles (until 2005): Kvinnoforskningsnytt (1401-5390); (until 1996): Centrumnytt (1104-859X)
Related titles: Online - full text ed.
Published by: Luleaa Tekniska Universitet, Avdelingen foer Genus och Teknik/Luleaa University of Technology, Division of Gender and Technology, c/o Institutionen foer Arbetsvetenskap, Luleaa, 97187, Sweden. TEL 46-920-491000, FAX 46-920-491030, http://www.ltu.se/arb/d1691/d22679?l=en. Ed. Petra Jonvallen.

305.3 SWE ISSN 1654-5753
GENUSSTUDIER VID MITTUNIVERSITETET. Text in Swedish. 2007. irreg. **Document type:** *Monographic series, Academic/Scholarly.*
Related titles: Online - full text ed.
Published by: Mittuniversitetet, Forum foer Genusvetenskap/Mid Sweden University, Forum for Gender Science, Campus Oestersund, Oestersund, 83125, Sweden. TEL 46-771-975000, FAX 46-771-975001, siv.fahlgren@miun.se.

GERMAN STUDIES SERIES. *see* BUSINESS AND ECONOMICS

305.83 NZL ISSN 1176-8606
GERMANICA PACIFICA STUDIES. Text in English. 2005. a. price varies. **Document type:** *Monographic series, Academic/Scholarly.*
Published by: University of Auckland, Research Centre for Germanic Connections with New Zealand and the Pacific, Faculty of Arts, Department of Germanic Languages and Literature, Auckland, New Zealand. TEL 64-9-3737599 ext 87672, http://www.arts.auckland.ac.nz/research/index.cfm?S=R_RESGERMNNZ. Ed. James Bade.

GERONTOLOGIE ET SOCIETE. *see* GERONTOLOGY AND GERIATRICS

▼ **GERONTOLOGIE UND GESELLSCHAFT.** *see* GERONTOLOGY AND GERIATRICS

DIE GESCHICHTE UNSERER HEIMAT. *see* HISTORY—History Of Europe

GESCHLECHTERDIFFERENZ UND LITERATUR. *see* LITERATURE

302.23 DEU
▼ **GESELLSCHAFT - ALTERN - MEDIEN.** Text in German. 2011. irreg., latest vol.2, 2011. price varies. **Document type:** *Monographic series, Academic/Scholarly.*
Published by: KoPaed Verlag, Pfaelzer-Wald-Str 64, Munich, 81539, Germany. TEL 49-89-68890098, FAX 49-89-6891912, info@kopaed.de, http://www.kopaed.de.

302.23 DEU ISSN 1619-960X
GESELLSCHAFT FUER MEDIENWISSENSCHAFT. SCHRIFTENREIHE. Text in German. 1987. irreg., latest vol.13, 2005. price varies. **Document type:** *Monographic series, Academic/Scholarly.*
Formerly (until 2002): Gesellschaft fuer Film- und Fernsehwissenschaft. Schriftenreihe (1437-8949)
Published by: (Gesellschaft fuer Medienwissenschaft), Schueren Verlag GmbH, Universitaetsstr 55, Marburg, 35037, Germany. TEL 49-6421-63084, FAX 49-6421-681190, info@schueren-verlag.de, http://www.schueren-verlag.de.

GESELLSCHAFT UND POLITIK; Zeitschrift fuer soziales und wirtschaftliches Engagement. *see* POLITICAL SCIENCE

302.222 306.44 NLD ISSN 1568-1475
BF637.N66
GESTURE. Text in English. 2001. 3/yr. EUR 342 combined subscription (print & online eds.) (effective 2012). 300 p./no.; back issues avail. **Document type:** *Journal, Academic/Scholarly.*
Related titles: Online - full text ed.: ISSN 1569-9773. EUR 332 (effective 2012) (from IngentaConnect).
Indexed: A20, AmHI, ArtHuCI, CA, CMM, CommAb, CurCont, H07, IBR, IBZ, L&LBA, L11, MLA-IB, P03, PsycInfo, PsycholAb, SCOPUS, SSCI, T02, W07.
—BLDSC (4163.812500), IE, Ingenta, INIST. **CCC.**
Published by: John Benjamins Publishing Co., PO Box 36224, Amsterdam, 1020 ME, Netherlands. TEL 31-20-6304747, FAX 31-20-6739773, subscription@benjamins.nl, http://www.benjamins.com. Ed. Adam Kendon.

302.222 306.44 NLD ISSN 1874-6829
➤ **GESTURE STUDIES.** Text in English. 2007. irreg., latest vol.5, 2011. price varies. **Document type:** *Monographic series, Academic/Scholarly.*
Published by: John Benjamins Publishing Co., PO Box 36224, Amsterdam, 1020 ME, Netherlands. TEL 31-20-6304747, FAX 31-20-6739773, customer.services@benjamins.nl. Ed. Adam Kendon.

301 CAN ISSN 1202-6298
GET A LIFE!. Text in English. 1993. a.
Published by: Get a Life Publishing House, 2255 B Queen St E Ste 127, Toronto, ON M4E 1G3, Canada. TEL 416-699-6070, FAX 888-326-5444.

301 GHA ISSN 0435-9380
GHANA JOURNAL OF SOCIOLOGY. Text in English. 1965. s-a. USD 5.
Indexed: MLA-IB, P30.
Published by: Ghana Sociological Association, c/o Department of Sociology, University of Ghana, Legon, Ghana.

GHANA STUDIES. *see* LITERATURE

305.23082 USA ISSN 1938-8209
HQ798
➤ **GIRLHOOD STUDIES**; an interdisciplinary journal. Text in English. 2008 (Mar.). s-a. GBP 107 combined subscription in United Kingdom to institutions (print & online eds.); EUR 154 combined subscription in Europe to institutions (print & online eds.); USD 191 combined subscription elsewhere to institutions (print & online eds.) (effective 2011). adv. reprint service avail. from PSC. **Document type:** *Journal, Academic/Scholarly.* **Description:** Provides a forum for the critical discussion of girlhood from a variety of disciplinary perspectives, and for the dissemination of current research and reflections on girls' lives to a broad, cross-disciplinary audience of scholars, researchers, practitioners in the fields of education, social service and health care and policy makers.

Related titles: Online - full text ed.: ISSN 1938-8322. GBP 96 in United Kingdom to institutions; EUR 139 in Europe to institutions; USD 172 elsewhere to institutions (effective 2011) (from IngentaConnect).
Indexed: B04, SSAI, SSAb, SSI, W03, W05.
—CCC.
Published by: Berghahn Books Inc., 150 Broadway, Ste 812, New York, NY 10038. TEL 212-222-6007, FAX 212-222-6004, journals@berghahnbooks.com, http://www.berghahnbooks.com. Eds. Claudia Mitchell, Jacqueline Reid-Walsh. **Dist. in Europe by:** Turpin Distribution Services Ltd., Pegasus Dr, Stratton Business Park, Biggleswade, Bedfordshire SG18 8QB, United Kingdom. TEL 44-1767-604951, FAX 44-1767-601640, berghahnjournalsuk@turpin-distribution.com, http://www.turpin-distribution.com/; **Dist. outside of Europe by:** Turpin Distribution Services Ltd., The Bleachery, 143 W St, New Milford, CT 06776. TEL 860-350-0041, FAX 860-350-0039, berghahnjournalsus@turpin-distribution.com.

700 301 USA ISSN 1945-3906
GLIMPSE; the art + science of seeing. Text in English. 2008 (Dec.). q. USD 40 to individuals; USD 60 to institutions (effective 2011). **Document type:** *Journal, Academic/Scholarly.* **Description:** Examines the functions, processes, and effects of vision and its implications for being, knowing, and constructing our world(s).
Media: Online - full text. **Related titles:** Print ed.: USD 140 combined subscription domestic to individuals (print & online eds.); USD 146 in Canada to individuals (print & online eds.); USD 195 elsewhere to individuals (print & online eds.); USD 210 domestic to institutions (print & online eds.); USD 216 in Canada to institutions (print & online eds.); USD 265 elsewhere to institutions (print & online eds.) (effective 2011).
Published by: Mho Media, PO Box 382178, Cambridge, MA 02238.

GLOBAL CHANGE, PEACE & SECURITY (ONLINE). see POLITICAL SCIENCE—International Relations

GLOBAL CHANGE, PEACE & SECURITY (PRINT). see POLITICAL SCIENCE—International Relations

GLOBAL DIRECTORY OF PEACE STUDIES & CONFLICT RESOLUTION PROGRAMS. see POLITICAL SCIENCE—International Relations

GLOBAL ENVIRONMENTAL POLITICS. see ENVIRONMENTAL STUDIES

GLOBAL JUSTICE REPORT. see POLITICAL SCIENCE—International Relations

302.23 USA ISSN 1524-7783
P90
GLOBAL MEDIA NEWS. Text in English. 1999 (Summer). q.
Related titles: Online - full text ed.
Published by: Center for Global Media Studies, 3107 E. 62nd Ave., Spokane, WA 99223. gmn@cgms.org. Ed. David Demers.

301 USA ISSN 1470-2266
JZ1318
➤ **GLOBAL NETWORKS (OXFORD)**; a journal of transnational affairs. Text in English. 2001. q. GBP 374 in United Kingdom to institutions; EUR 475 in Europe to institutions; USD 627 in the Americas to institutions; USD 731 elsewhere to institutions; GBP 430 combined subscription in United Kingdom to institutions (print & online eds.); EUR 547 combined subscription in Europe to institutions (print & online eds.); USD 721 combined subscription in the Americas to institutions (print & online eds.); USD 841 combined subscription elsewhere to institutions (print & online eds.) (effective 2012). adv. back issues avail.; reprint service avail. from PSC. **Document type:** *Journal, Academic/Scholarly.* **Description:** Provides a forum for discussion, debate and the refinement of key ideas in this emerging field.
Related titles: Online - full text ed.: ISSN 1471-0374. GBP 374 in United Kingdom to institutions; EUR 475 in Europe to institutions; USD 627 in the Americas to institutions; USD 731 elsewhere to institutions (effective 2012) (from IngentaConnect).
Indexed: A01, A03, A08, A20, A22, A26, CA, CPEI, CurCont, E01, ESPM, EconLit, EngInd, GEOBASE, I13, IBSS, JEL, M10, P34, P42, PAIS, PRA, PSA, RiskAb, S02, S03, SCOPUS, SPAA, SSA, SSCI, SSciA, SociolAb, T02, W07.
—BLDSC (4195.471000), IE, Infotrieve, Ingenta. **CCC.**
Published by: (Great Britain. Economic and Social Research Council GBR), Wiley-Blackwell Publishing, Inc. (Subsidiary of: Wiley-Blackwell Publishing Ltd.), Commerce Pl, 350 Main St, Malden, MA 02148. TEL 781-388-8206, FAX 781-388-8232, info@wiley.com, http://www.wiley.com/WileyCDA/. Ed. Dr. Alisdair Rogers TEL 44-1865-272713. Adv. contact Craig Pickett TEL 44-1865-476267. **Subscr. to:** Wiley-Blackwell Publishing Ltd., 9600 Garsington Rd, Oxford OX4 2DQ, United Kingdom. TEL 44-1865-776868, FAX 44-1865-714591, customerservices@blackwellpublishing.com, http://www.wiley.com/.

303.4 NZL ISSN 1179-5093
GLOBAL PERSPECTIVES. Text in English. 2003. 3/yr. free (effective 2010). back issues avail. **Document type:** *Handbook/Manual/Guide, Consumer.* **Description:** Provides information and ideas for exploring global issues and their impact on youth and the community.
Formerly (until 2010): Global Bits (1176-9467)
Related titles: Online - full text ed.: ISSN 1179-5107. free (effective 2010).
Published by: Global Education Centre, Level 2, James Smith Bldg, Corner of Cuba and Manners St, PO Box 12440, Wellington, Aotearoa, New Zealand. TEL 64-4-4729549, FAX 64-4-4969599, community@globaled.org.nz, http://www.globaled.org.nz.

GLOBAL SPORT CULTURES. see SPORTS AND GAMES

GLOBALER LOKALER ISLAM. see RELIGIONS AND THEOLOGY—Islamic

301 USA
GLOBALIZATION AND COMMUNITY. Text in English. 1998. irreg., latest vol.16, 2010. price varies. back issues avail. **Document type:** *Monographic series, Academic/Scholarly.* **Description:** Provides social science perspective on the economic, social, cultural, and spatial impacts of globalization processes on urban communities.
Published by: University of Minnesota Press, Ste 290, 111 Third Ave S, Minneapolis, MN 55401. TEL 612-627-1970, FAX 612-627-1980, ump@umn.edu. Ed. Susan E Clarke. **Dist. by:** c/o Chicago Distribution Center, 11030 S Langley Ave, Chicago, IL 60628. TEL 800-621-2736; Plymbridge Distributors Ltd, Estover Rd, Plymouth, Devon PL6 7PY, United Kingdom. TEL 44-1752-202-301, FAX 44-1752-202-331.

302.2 SWE ISSN 1654-7985
GLOCAL TIMES. Text in English. 2005. irreg. (3-4/yr). back issues avail. **Document type:** *Magazine, Academic/Scholarly.*
Media: Online - full content.
Published by: Malmoe Hoegskola, Konst, Kultur och Kommunikation/ University of Malmoe, School of Art and Communication, Beijerskajen 8, Malmoe, 20506, Sweden. TEL 46-40-6657000, FAX 46-40-6657305, info@mah.se/k3, http://www.mah.se. Ed. Florencia Enghel.

GOD'S SPECIAL TIME; kairos of Colorado. see RELIGIONS AND THEOLOGY

320 DEU ISSN 1862-507X
GOERLITZER BEITRAEGE ZU REGIONALEN TRANSFORMATIONSPROZESSEN. Text in German. 2007. irreg., latest vol.5, 2010. price varies. **Document type:** *Monographic series, Academic/Scholarly.*
Published by: Peter Lang GmbH (Subsidiary of: Peter Lang Publishing Group), Eschborner Landstr 42-50, Frankfurt Am Main, 60489, Germany. TEL 49-69-7807050, FAX 49-69-78070550, zentrale.frankfurt@peterlang.com.

300 DEU
▼ **GOETTINGER STUDIEN ZUR GENERATIONSFORSCHUNG.** Text in German. 2009. irreg., latest vol.3, 2010. price varies. **Document type:** *Monographic series, Academic/Scholarly.*
Published by: Wallstein Verlag GmbH, Geiststr 11, Goettingen, 37073, Germany. TEL 49-551-548980, FAX 49-551-5489833, info@wallstein-verlag.de, http://www.wallstein-verlag.de.

301 POL ISSN 0072-5013
GORNOSLASKIE STUDIA SOCJOLOGICZNE. Text in Polish. 1963. irreg.
Indexed: RASB.
Published by: Slaski Instytut Naukowy, Ul Graniczna 32, Katowice, 40956, Poland. **Dist. by:** Ars Polona, Obroncow 25, Warsaw 03933, Poland.

305 ESP ISSN 2171-794X
▼ **GRADO-GRAU, VILLA Y ALFOZ.** Text in Spanish. 2009. a. **Document type:** *Monographic series, Academic/Scholarly.*
Published by: Ayuntamiento de Grado, Museo Etnografico de Grado, La Cardose, s-n, Grado, 33820, Spain. TEL 34-985-753073, FAX 34-985-752610, http://www.ayto-grado.es/servicios/cultural/museo.php.

306.85 NZL ISSN 1178-0819
GRANDPARENTS RAISING GRANDCHILDREN TRUST. NATIONAL OFFICE NEWSLETTER. Text in English. 2002. m. back issues avail. **Document type:** *Newsletter, Trade.* **Description:** Aims to provide support and assistance to grandparents who are primary caregivers to their grandchildren in difficult circumstances.
Related titles: Online - full text ed.: ISSN 1178-0827. free (effective 2011).
Published by: Grandparents Raising Grandchildren Trust NZ, Birkenhead, PO Box 34-892, Auckland, 0742, New Zealand. TEL 64-9-4806530, 800-472-637, office@grg.org.nz.

307.14 AUS ISSN 0310-2890
GRASS ROOTS; craft and self-sufficiency for down to earth people. Text in English. 1973. bi-m. AUD 29.50; AUD 36.50 foreign. adv. bk.rev. back issues avail.
Indexed: Gdlns, Pinpoint.
Published by: Night Owl Publishers Pty. Ltd., PO Box 117, Seymour, VIC 3660, Australia. Ed. Megg Miller. Circ: 40,000.

GRASSROOTS DEVELOPMENT. see BUSINESS AND ECONOMICS—International Development And Assistance

305 DEU ISSN 0945-5868
GRAZER BEITRAEGE ZUR EUROPAEISCHEN ETHNOLOGIE. Text in German. 1988. irreg., latest vol.14, 2009. price varies. **Document type:** *Monographic series, Academic/Scholarly.*
Published by: Peter Lang GmbH (Subsidiary of: Peter Lang Publishing Group), Eschborner Landstr 42-50, Frankfurt Am Main, 60489, Germany. TEL 49-69-7807050, FAX 49-69-78070550, zentrale.frankfurt@peterlang.com.

GRAZER LINGUISTISCHE STUDIEN. see LINGUISTICS

301 USA ISSN 0896-0054
CODEN: GPSOF4
THE GREAT PLAINS SOCIOLOGIST. Text in English. 1988. a.
Indexed: CA, P46, P48, PQC, S02, S03, SCOPUS, SociolAb, T02.
Published by: Great Plains Sociological Association, c/o Pat Joffer GPSA, Department of Sociology, SDSU, Box 504 Scobey Hall, Brookings, SD 57007-1296. http://sociology.sdstate.edu/gpsa/gpsa.htm.

GREEN REVOLUTION; a voice for decentralization and balanced living. see PHILOSOPHY

301 USA ISSN 1556-1542
H62.A1
➤ **THE GROUNDED THEORY REVIEW.** Text in English. 1999. 3/yr. USD 60 to individuals; USD 90 to institutions (effective 2009). **Document type:** *Journal, Academic/Scholarly.* **Description:** Contains papers featuring substantive theories developed using classic grounded theory methodology as well as papers with a focus on methodological perspectives.
Related titles: Online - full text ed.: ISSN 1556-1550.
Indexed: B01, B07, CA, S02, S03, T02.
—BLDSC (4220.143803), IE.
Published by: Sociology Press, PO Box 400, Mill Valley, CA 94942. TEL 415-388-8431, FAX 415-381-2254, order@sociologypress.com, http://www.sociologypress.com. Ed. Dr. Judith A Holton. Pub. Dr. Barney G Glaser.

302 GBR ISSN 1368-4302
HM131
➤ **GROUP PROCESSES & INTERGROUP RELATIONS.** Abbreviated title: G P I R. Text in English. 1998. bi-m. USD 1,077, GBP 582 combined subscription to institutions (print & online eds.); USD 1,055, GBP 570 to institutions (effective 2011). adv. bk.rev. back issues avail.; reprint service avail. from PSC. **Document type:** *Journal, Academic/Scholarly.* **Description:** Focuses on basic and applied aspects of group and intergroup phenomena, ranging from small interactive groups to large scale social categories.
Related titles: Online - full text ed.: ISSN 1461-7188. USD 969, GBP 524 to institutions (effective 2011).
Indexed: A01, A03, A08, A12, A17, A20, A22, ABIn, B01, B06, B07, B09, CA, CJA, CMM, CommAb, CurCont, E-psyche, E01, FR, FamI, H04, IBSS, P03, P30, P48, P51, P53, P54, PQC, PsycInfo, PsycholAb, S02, S03, SCOPUS, SSA, SSCI, SWR&A, SociolAb, T02, V02, W07.
—BLDSC (4220.183500), IE, Infotrieve, Ingenta, INIST. **CCC.**
Published by: Sage Publications Ltd. (Subsidiary of: Sage Publications, Inc.), 1 Oliver's Yard, 55 City Rd, London, EC1Y 1SP, United Kingdom. TEL 44-20-73248500, FAX 44-20-73248600, info@sagepub.co.uk, http://www.uk.sagepub.com/home.nav. Eds. Dominic Abrams, Michael Hogg. adv.: B&W page GBP 400; 140 x 210. **Subscr. in the Americas to:** Sage Publications, Inc., 2455 Teller Rd, Thousand Oaks, CA 91320. TEL 805-499-9774, FAX 805-499-0871, journals@sagepub.com.

305.232 USA ISSN 1938-6095
GROWING UP; history of children and youth. Text in English. 2007 (May). irreg., latest 2007. USD 39.95, GBP 27.95 per issue (effective 2010). back issues avail. **Document type:** *Monographic series, Academic/Scholarly.*
Published by: Praeger Publishers (Subsidiary of: Greenwood Publishing Group Inc.), 88 Post Rd W, Westport, CT 06881. TEL 800-368-6868, tech.support@greenwood.com, http://www.greenwood.com. Ed. Priscilla Clement.

GRUPPENDYNAMIK UND ORGANISATIONSBERATUNG; Zeitschrift fuer angewandte Sozialpsychologie. see PSYCHOLOGY

301.0711 CAN
GUIDE TO DEPARTMENTS OF SOCIOLOGY, ANTHROPOLOGY AND ARCHAEOLOGY IN UNIVERSITIES AND MUSEUMS IN CANADA/ ANNUAIRE DES DEPARTEMENTS DE SOCIOLOGIE, D'ANTHROPOLOGIE ET D'ARCHEOLOGIE DES UNIVERSITES ET DES MUSEES DU CANADA. Text in English. 1974. irreg. CAD 17. **Document type:** *Handbook/Manual/Guide, Academic/Scholarly.*
Formerly: Guide to Departments of Sociology and Anthropology in Canadian Universities (0315-0895)
Published by: Canadian Sociological Association/Societe Canadienne de Sociologie, Concordia University, 1455 de Maisonneuve W/Ouest, Montreal, PQ H3G 1M8, Canada. Ed. Daegen Reimer.

301.0711 USA ISSN 0091-7052
HM47.U6
GUIDE TO GRADUATE DEPARTMENTS OF SOCIOLOGY. Text in English. 1965. a. USD 50 to non-members; USD 30 to members; USD 20 to students (effective 2009). back issues avail.; reprints avail. **Document type:** *Directory, Trade.* **Description:** Provides comprehensive information for academic administrators, advisors, faculty, students, and a host of others seeking information on social science departments in the US, Canada, and abroad.
Published by: American Sociological Association, 1430 K St, NW, Ste 600, Washington, DC 20005. TEL 202-383-9005, FAX 202-638-0882, infoservice@asanet.org, http://www.asanet.org.

301 IND ISSN 0970-0242
GURU NANAK JOURNAL OF SOCIOLOGY. Text in English. 1980. s-a. INR 150 to individuals; INR 300 to institutions (effective 2011). **Document type:** *Journal, Academic/Scholarly.* **Description:** Covers an indepth study in the field of sociology.
Indexed: BAS, CA, FR, P30, P42, PSA, RILM, S02, S03, SOPODA, SSA, SociolAb, T02.
—BLDSC (4232.171100), IE, Infotrieve, Ingenta, INIST.
Published by: Guru Nanak Dev University Press, c/o Ajaib Singh Brar, Amritsar, 143 005, India. TEL 91-183-2258802, FAX 91-183-2258819, vc@gndu.ac.in, http://www.gndu.ac.in/.

HABBANAE. see AGRICULTURE

306.85 ARG ISSN 1851-3786
HACER FAMILIA. Text in Spanish. 2004. bi-m. **Document type:** *Newsletter, Consumer.*
Media: Online - full text.
Published by: Sembrar Valores, A.C., Ituzaingo, 329 20 Cuerpo, 1o. B. San Isidro, Buenos Aires, Argentina. TEL 54-11-45134039, subscripciones@hacerfamilia.com.ar, http://hacerfamilia.com.ar/.

301 255.53 KEN ISSN 1995-6339
HM671
HAKIMANI; Jesuit journal of social justice in Eastern Africa. Text in English. 2007. q.
Related titles: Online - full text ed.: ISSN 1996-7268.
Published by: Jesuit Hakimani Centre, Nairobi, Kenya. TEL 254-20-3870617, jesuithakimani@yahoo.com, http://jesuithakimani.org.

▼ **HAMBURG STUDIES ON LINGUISTIC DIVERSITY.** see LINGUISTICS

307.14 NZL ISSN 1176-1709
HAMILTON DIRECTORY FOR NEW SETTLERS. Text in English. 1996. a. **Document type:** *Directory, Consumer.*
Published by: Hamilton City Council, Community Development Unit, Private Bag 3010, Hamilton, New Zealand. TEL 64-7-8386765, FAX 64-7-8386751, info@hcc.govt.nz, http://www.hamilton.co.nz.

302.23 DEU
HANDBUECHER UND STUDIEN ZUR MEDIENKULTURWISSENSCHAFT. Text in German. 2008. irreg., latest vol.3, 2009. price varies. **Document type:** *Monographic series, Academic/Scholarly.*
Published by: Wissenschaftlicher Verlag Trier, Bergstr 27, Trier, 54295, Germany. TEL 49-651-41503, FAX 49-651-41504, wvt@wvttrier.de, http://www.wvttrier.de.

301 KOR ISSN 1225-0120
HM7 CODEN: HASAF4
➤ **HANGUK SAHOEHAK/KOREAN JOURNAL OF SOCIOLOGY.** Text in Korean. 1964. 8/yr. (bi-m. until 2008). membership. adv. bk.rev. **Document type:** *Journal, Academic/Scholarly.*
Indexed: SCOPUS, SOPODA, SociolAb.

S

Published by: Han'gug Sahoe Haghoe/Korean Sociological Association, 304-28 Sajik-dong, Jongno-gu, Seoul, 110-054, Korea, S. TEL 82-2-7228747, FAX 82-2-7228746, admin@ksa.re.kr, http://www.ksa.re.kr/. Circ: 1,000.

301 649 SWE ISSN 1650-5085
HARO!; en tidning om barn och foeraeldrar. Text in Swedish. 1981. q. SEK 175 (effective 2005). **Document type:** *Journal, Consumer.*
Formerly (until 2000): Haro-Bulletinen (1100-0600)
Published by: Haro, PO Box 113, Oedaakra, 26035, Sweden. haro@haro.se.

HASTINGS RACE AND POVERTY LAW JOURNAL. *see* LAW—Constitutional Law

HEARD HERITAGE; Heard County, Georgia - a history of its people. *see* GENEALOGY AND HERALDRY

306.85 USA
THE HEART THREAD RESOURCE PAGE ON MARRIAGE, PARENTING, FAMILY & SOCIETY. Text in English. 1996. m.
Media: Online - full content.
Published by: FutureRealm Productions, Box 4131, Virginia Beach, VA 23454.

301 USA ISSN 1932-6726
HERMIT KINGDOM STUDIES IN IDENTITY AND SOCIETY. Text in English. 2006. irreg. **Document type:** *Monographic series, Consumer.*
Published by: Hermit Kingdom Press, 12325 Imperial Hwy, Ste 156, Norwalk, CA 90650. info@TheHermitKingdomPress.com, http://www.thehermitkingdompress.com/index.htm.

HESSISCHE STIFTUNG FRIEDENS- UND KONFLIKTFORSCHUNG. JAHRESBERICHT; Bericht ueber Organisation und laufende Forschung. *see* POLITICAL SCIENCE—International Relations

301 JPN ISSN 0912-2087
HM621
HIKAKU BUNMEI/COMPARATIVE CIVILIZATION. Text in Japanese. 1985. a.
Published by: Japan Society for Comparative Study of Civilizations, c/o Kyorisu College of Pharmacy, 1-5-30 Shibakoen, Minato-ku, Tokyo, 105-0011, Japan. TEL 03-261-6190.

303.842 DEU ISSN 1868-372X
▼ **HILDESHEIMER SCHRIFTEN ZUR INTERKULTURELLEN KOMMUNIKATION.** Text in German. 2009. irreg., latest vol.2, 2010. price varies. **Document type:** *Monographic series, Academic/Scholarly.*
Published by: Peter Lang GmbH (Subsidiary of: Peter Lang Publishing Group), Eschborner Landstr 42-50, Frankfurt Am Main, 60489, Germany. TEL 49-69-7807050, FAX 49-69-78070550, zentrale.frankfurt@peterlang.com. Eds. Friedrich Lenz, Stephan Schlickau.

306.4 NPL
➤ **HIMALAYAN JOURNAL OF SOCIOLOGY AND ANTHROPOLOGY.** Text in English. a. **Document type:** *Journal, Academic/Scholarly.* **Description:** Provides a forum for the publication of research articles, research papers, notes and book reviews on topics of interest to provide relevant readings for the students of Sociology/Anthropology.
Related titles: Online - full text ed.
Indexed: S02, S03.
Published by: Tribhuvan University, Department of Sociology and Anthropology, Prithvi Narayan Campus, P O Box 77, Pokhara, Nepal. pncsa@fewanet.com.np. Ed. Biswo Kallyan Parajuli.

➤ **HISTOIRE & SOCIETES**; revue europeenne d'histoire sociale. *see* HISTORY—History Of Europe

306.09 CAN ISSN 0018-2257
HN1
➤ **HISTOIRE SOCIALE/SOCIAL HISTORY**; social history. Abbreviated title: H S S H. Text in English, French. 1968. s-a. USD 55 in North America to institutions; USD 65 elsewhere to institutions (effective 2011). bk.rev. abstr.; bibl. 192 p./no.; back issues avail. **Document type:** *Journal, Academic/Scholarly.* **Description:** Publishes studies pertaining to various types of social phenomena, whether cultural, political, economic or demographic, without methodological, temporal or geographic restrictions.
Related titles: Online - full text ed.
Indexed: A20, A22, ABS&EES, ASCA, AmH&L, ArtHuCI, BAS, BibInd, C03, CA, CBCARef, CurCont, DIP, E01, G10, HistAb, IBR, IBZ, MEA&I, P30, P42, P48, PCI, PQC, PSA, PdeR, S02, S03, S21, SCOPUS, SSA, SociolAb, T02, W07.
—BLDSC (8318.094900), IE, Infotrieve, Ingenta. **CCC.**
Published by: University of Toronto Press, Journals Division, 5201 Dufferin St, Toronto, ON M3H 5T8, Canada. TEL 416-667-7810, FAX 416-667-7881, journals@utpress.utoronto.ca. Ed. Bettina Bradbury TEL 613-562-5983. Adv. contact Audrey Greenwood TEL 416-667-7777 ext 7766. Circ: 376.

➤ **HISTORIA CRITICA.** *see* HISTORY—History Of North And South America

➤ **HISTORIA Y SOCIEDAD.** *see* HISTORY

301 USA ISSN 1541-0021
HISTORICAL GUIDES TO CONTROVERSIAL ISSUES IN AMERICA. Text in English. 2003. irreg. price varies. back issues avail. **Document type:** *Monographic series, Academic/Scholarly.* **Description:** Contains volumes that trace the historical roots and key aspects of questions that Americans have found of compelling importance in shaping our way of life.
Related titles: Online - full text ed.
Published by: Greenwood Publishing Group Inc. (Subsidiary of: A B C - C L I O), 88 Post Rd W, PO Box 5007, Westport, CT 06881. TEL 203-226-3571, 800-225-5800, FAX 877-231-6980, sales@greenwood.com.

HISTORICAL SOCIAL RESEARCH/HISTORISCHE SOZIALFORSCHUNG. *see* HISTORY—History Of Europe

HISTORICAL SOCIOLINGUISTICS AND SOCIOHISTORICAL LINGUISTICS. *see* LINGUISTICS

HISTORISCHE SOZIALKUNDE. *see* HISTORY—History Of Europe

HISTORY OF INTELLECTUAL CULTURE. *see* HISTORY

HOG RIVER JOURNAL. *see* HISTORY—History Of North And South America

HOKOUK NEWSLETTER. *see* ETHNIC INTERESTS

302 NLD ISSN 1871-9899
THE HOLLAND HANDBOOK. Text in English. 2000. a. EUR 29.90 (effective 2010).
Published by: (Nuffic), X-Pat Media, Van Boetzelaerlaan 153, The Hague, 2581 AR, Netherlands. TEL 31-70-3063310, FAX 31-70-3063311, info@xpat.nl. Ed. Stephanie Dijkstra. Pubs. Bert van Essen, Gerjan de Waard.

THE HOLY CROSS JOURNAL OF LAW & PUBLIC POLICY. *see* LAW—Constitutional Law

301 ECU ISSN 1021-044X
F2230
HOMBRE Y AMBIENTE; el punto de vista indigena. Text in Spanish. 1987. q. **Document type:** *Monographic series, Academic/Scholarly.*
Indexed: AICP, IBR, IBZ.
Published by: Ediciones Abya - Yala, Avenida 12 de Octubre 1430 y Wilson, Quito, Ecuador. TEL 593-2-2506251, FAX 593-2-2506267, http://www.abyayala.org. Ed. Jose E Juncosa.

301 FRA ISSN 0018-4306
HM3
L'HOMME ET LA SOCIETE (PARIS, 1966). Text in French. 1966. q. EUR 47.30 domestic; EUR 53.40 foreign (effective 2009). reprint service avail. from SCH. **Document type:** *Journal, Academic/Scholarly.*
Indexed: A22, DIP, FR, I13, IBR, IBSS, IBZ, MLA-IB, PCI, SCOPUS.
—IE, Infotrieve, INIST.
Published by: (Universite de Paris VII (Denis Diderot), Unite de Recherches Migrations et Societe), L' Harmattan, 5 Rue de l'Ecole Polytechnique, Paris, 75005, France. TEL 33-1-43257651, FAX 33-1-43258203.

301 FRA ISSN 1242-9945
L'HOMME ET LA SOCIETE (PARIS, 1993). Text in French. 1993. q. EUR 60 domestic; EUR 65 foreign (effective 2008). **Document type:** *Journal, Academic/Scholarly.*
Published by: L' Harmattan, 5 Rue de l'Ecole Polytechnique, Paris, 75005, France. TEL 33-1-43257651, FAX 33-1-43258203.

HONG KONG JOURNAL; the quarterly online journal about issues relating to Hong Kong and China. *see* POLITICAL SCIENCE

301 HKG ISSN 1606-8610
HN751
HONG KONG JOURNAL OF SOCIOLOGY. Text in Chinese, English. 2000. a. HKD 90, USD 12 to individuals; HKD 155, USD 20 to institutions (effective 2001). adv. bk.rev. 140 p./no.; **Document type:** *Journal, Academic/Scholarly.*
Published by: Zhongwen Daxue Chubanshe/Chinese University Press, The Chinese University of Hong Kong, Shatin, New Territories, Hong Kong. TEL 852-2609-6508, FAX 852-2603-7355, cup@cuhk.edu.hk, http://www.chineseupress.com/. Ed., R&P Siu-kai Lav. Adv. contact Angelina Wong TEL 852-26096500. page HKD 1,500; trim 120 x 210.

HONG KONG SOCIAL AND ECONOMIC TRENDS. *see* BUSINESS AND ECONOMICS—Economic Situation And Conditions

HOPEDANCE; radical solutions inspiring hope. *see* ENVIRONMENTAL STUDIES

306.85 ISR ISSN 0792-1926
HORIM VILADIM. Text in Hebrew. 1987. m. ILS 150. adv. bk.rev. **Document type:** *Magazine, Consumer.*
Related titles: Online - full text ed.: ILS 222 (effective 2008).
Published by: S B C Group, 8 Shefa Tal St., Tel Aviv, 67013, Israel. TEL 972-3-565-2100, FAX 972-3-562-6476, sherut@sbc.co.il, http://www.sbc.co.il/Index.asp.

HOUSTON HISTORY. *see* HISTORY—History Of North And South America

302 USA ISSN 1540-5699
➤ **HUMAN ARCHITECTURE**; journal of the sociology of self-knowledge. Text in English. 2002. q. USD 60 to individuals; USD 120 to institutions; USD 15 per issue to individuals; USD 30 per issue to institutions (effective 2010). back issues avail. **Document type:** *Journal, Academic/Scholarly.*
Related titles: Online - full text ed.: free (effective 2010).
Indexed: A26, CA, E08, I05, P27, P46, P48, P54, PQC, S02, S03, SCOPUS, SociolAb, T02.
Published by: Okcir Press, PO Box 393, Belmont, MA 02478. TEL 617-932-1170, FAX 617-932-1170, info@okcir.com. Ed. Mohammad Tamdgidi.

301 330.9 SVN ISSN 1580-1381
HUMAN DEVELOPMENT REPORT. Text in English. 1998. a. **Description:** Aims to present a number of (macro)economic implications for the quality of living in Slovenia. Intended for policy-makers as well as everyone interested in these issues.
Related titles: ◆ Translation of: Porocilo o Clovekovem Razvoju. ISSN 1580-1373.
Published by: Urad RS za Makroekonomske Analize in Razvoj/Institute of Macroeconomic Analysis and Development, Gregorciceva 27, Ljubljana, 1000, Slovenia. TEL 386-1-4781012, FAX 386-1-4781070, publicistika.umar@gov.si, http://www.umar.gov.si/apublic/ajiidt.php.

577 USA ISSN 1074-4827
GF1 CODEN: HEREF5
➤ **HUMAN ECOLOGY REVIEW.** Abbreviated title: H E R. Text in English. 1994. s-a. free to members (effective 2009). bk.rev. back issues avail. **Document type:** *Journal, Academic/Scholarly.* **Description:** Presents the ideas of the professienal society, which promotes the use of an ecological perspective in both researoh and application.
Indexed: A20, B21, BIOBASE, CA, CurCont, E04, E05, E17, ESPM, EnvAb, EnvInd, HPNRM, IABS, LeftInd, P42, PAIS, PSA, S02, S03, SCOPUS, SSA, SSCI, SSciA, SociolAb, T02, W07.
—BLDSC (4336.064000), IE, Ingenta. **CCC.**
Published by: Society for Human Ecology, 105 Eden Street, College of the Atlantic, Bar Harbor, ME 04609. TEL 207-288-5015, FAX 207-288-3780, mpcote@ecology.coa.edu, http://www.societyforhumanecology.org/. Ed. Susan Clayton.

301 USA ISSN 1942-7786
GF1
➤ **HUMAN GEOGRAPHY**; a new radical journal. Text in English. 2008. s-a. USD 40 to individuals; USD 175 to libraries (effective 2011). back issues avail. **Document type:** *Journal, Academic/Scholarly.* **Description:** Covers topics ranging from geopolitics, through cultural and economic issues, to political ecology.
Published by: Institute for Human Geography, PO Box 307, Bolton, MA 01740. insthugeog@gmail.com. Ed. Richard Peet.

➤ **HUMAN KINDNESS FOUNDATION NEWSLETTER**; a little good news. *see* RELIGIONS AND THEOLOGY

304.667 340 USA ISSN 0097-9783
HQ767
THE HUMAN LIFE REVIEW. Text in English. 1975. q. USD 25 domestic; USD 35 foreign (effective 2010). back issues avail.; reprints avail. **Document type:** *Journal, Academic/Scholarly.* **Description:** Covers abortion and related issues.
Related titles: Microfiche ed.: (from PQC); Online - full text ed.
Indexed: A01, A02, A03, A08, A22, A26, CA, CLFP, CLI, CPL, E08, G06, G07, G08, H01, HPNRM, I05, M01, M02, P02, P05, P10, P19, P21, P26, P27, P30, P34, P46, P48, P53, P54, PAIS, PCI, PQC, R10, Reac, S09, S11, SCOPUS, T02.
—Ingenta.
Published by: Human Life Foundation, Inc., 353 Lexington Ave, Ste 802, New York, NY 10016.

HUMAN NATURE; an interdisciplinary biosocial perspective. *see* SOCIAL SCIENCES: COMPREHENSIVE WORKS

HUMAN RIGHTS & GLOBALIZATION LAW REVIEW. *see* LAW

301 ZAF ISSN 1726-9709
HUMAN SCIENCES RESEARCH COUNCIL REVIEW. Variant title: H S R C Review. Text in English. 2003. 3/yr.
Published by: Human Sciences Research Council/Raad vir Geesteswetenskaplike Navorsing. Sentrum vir Wetenskapontwikkeling, Private Bag X41, Pretoria, 0001, South Africa. TEL 27-12-3022000, FAX 27-12-3022001. Ed. Ina van der Linde.

HUMAN STRESS: CURRENT SELECTED RESEARCH. *see* PSYCHOLOGY

HUMAN STUDIES; a journal for philosophy and the social sciences. *see* PHILOSOPHY

301 USA
THE HUMANIST SOCIOLOGIST. Text in English. 19??. q. free to members (effective 2010). back issues avail. **Document type:** *Newsletter, Trade.* **Description:** Contains information about the organization and its activities.
Related titles: Online - full text ed.: free (effective 2010).
Published by: Association for Humanist Sociology, PO Box 8611, Wichita, KS 67208. http://uhaweb.hartford.edu/doane/ahsweb1.htm. Ed. Jim Wolfe.

301 USA ISSN 0160-5976
HM1
➤ **HUMANITY & SOCIETY.** Text in English. 1977. q. USD 150 domestic to institutions; USD 165 foreign to institutions; free to members (effective 2010). bk.rev. abstr. index. **Document type:** *Journal, Academic/Scholarly.* **Description:** Brings out articles on a wide variety of topics such as studies of inequality (class, race, and/or gender), war, peace, and international relations, aging and gerontology, family, gender and sexuality, health and mental health etc.
Related titles: Microfiche ed.
Indexed: A22, B04, CA, FR, FamI, G10, HPNRM, MLA-IB, P05, P30, P34, P42, PQC, PSA, RASB, RILM, S02, S03, SOPODA, SSA, SSAI, SSAb, SSI, SSciA, SociolAb, T02, W03, W05, W09.
—BLDSC (4336.581200), IE, Infotrieve, Ingenta, INIST.
Published by: Association for Humanist Sociology, PO Box 8611, Wichita, KS 67208. http://uhaweb.hartford.edu/doane/ahsweb1.htm. Ed. Kathy Tiemann.

306.481 DEU ISSN 0933-1719
PN6149.P5 CODEN: HUMRES
➤ **HUMOR**; international journal of humor research. Text in English. 1988. q. EUR 228, USD 342 to institutions; EUR 263, USD 395 combined subscription to institutions (print & online eds.) (effective 2012). adv. bk.rev. illus.; abstr.; bibl. Index. back issues avail.; reprint service avail. from PSC. **Document type:** *Journal, Academic/Scholarly.* **Description:** Scholarly journal for the publication of research papers on humor as an important and universal human faculty.
Former titles: World Humor and Irony Movement Serials Yearbook; World Humor and Irony Membership Serial Yearbook; Western Humor and Irony Membership Serial Yearbook (0737-0342)
Related titles: Online - full text ed.: ISSN 1613-3722. EUR 228, USD 342 to institutions (effective 2012).
Indexed: A01, A02, A03, A08, A20, A22, A26, AmHI, ArtHuCI, BRI, BibInd, BibLing, CA, CBRI, CommAb, CurCont, DIP, E-psyche, E01, FR, H07, I05, IBR, IBSS, IBZ, L&LBA, L06, MLA-IB, P03, P43, PsycInfo, PsycholAb, SCOPUS, SOPODA, SSCI, SociolAb, T02, W07.
—BLDSC (4336.730500), IE, Infotrieve, Ingenta. **CCC.**
Published by: De Gruyter Mouton (Subsidiary of: Walter de Gruyter GmbH & Co. KG), Genthiner Str 13, Berlin, 10785, Germany. TEL 49-30-260050, FAX 49-30-26005251, mouton@degruyter.de. Ed. Salvatore Attardo. Adv. contact Dietlind Makswitat. page EUR 600; trim 110 x 185.

305.8 DEU
HYBRIDE WELTEN. Text in German. 2000. irreg., latest vol.5, 2011. price varies. **Document type:** *Monographic series, Academic/Scholarly.*
Published by: Waxmann Verlag GmbH, Steinfurter Str 555, Muenster, 48159, Germany. TEL 49-251-265040, FAX 49-251-2650426, info@waxmann.com. Ed. Elka Tschernokoshewa.

HYGIEA INTERNATIONALIS; an interdisciplinary journal for the history of public health. *see* PUBLIC HEALTH AND SAFETY

302.2 USA ISSN 1385-4038
I A M H I S T NEWSLETTER. Text in English. 1976. q. membership. adv. bk.rev. **Document type:** *Newsletter, Trade.*
Former titles (until 1991): International Association for Audio-Visual Media in Historical Research and Education. Newsletter (0106-0007); (until 1978): International Association for the Study of History and the Audiovisual Media. Newsletter (0105-3809)
Published by: International Association for Media and History, c/o Cynthia Miller, 484 Bolivar St, Canton, MA 02021. info-contact@iamhist.org, http://www.iamhist.org. Circ: 400 (paid).
Co-sponsor: Stichting Film Wetenschap, NL.

302.2 USA
P87
I C A NEWSLETTER (ONLINE). Text in English. 1973 (vol.22). 10/yr. USD 30 to non-members; free to members (effective 2010). **Document type:** *Newsletter, Trade.* **Description:** Covers latest information about International Communication Association.

Former titles (until 1975): I C A Newsletter (Print) (0018-876X); (until 19??): N S S C Newsletter
Media: Online - full text.
Published by: International Communication Association, 1500 21st St, NW, Washington, DC 20036. TEL 202-955-1444, FAX 202-955-1448, icahdq@icahdq.org. Ed. Michael J West.

I D E OCCASIONAL PAPERS SERIES. *see* BUSINESS AND ECONOMICS

I D E SYMPOSIUM PROCEEDINGS. *see* BUSINESS AND ECONOMICS

I D S BULLETIN. (Institute of Development Studies) *see* BUSINESS AND ECONOMICS—International Development And Assistance

I D S DISCUSSION PAPER. *see* BUSINESS AND ECONOMICS—International Development And Assistance

I D S IN FOCUS POLICY BRIEFING. (Institute of Development Studies) *see* BUSINESS AND ECONOMICS—International Development And Assistance

I D S RESEARCH REPORTS. *see* BUSINESS AND ECONOMICS—International Development And Assistance

I D S WORKING PAPER. *see* BUSINESS AND ECONOMICS—International Development And Assistance

301 AUT ISSN 1433-2760
➤ **I F F TEXTE.** Text in German. 1997. irreg., latest vol.7, 2000. price varies. **Document type:** *Monographic series, Academic/Scholarly.*
Published by: (Institut fuer Interdisziplinaere Forschung und Fortbildung), Springer Wien (Subsidiary of: Springer Science+Business Media), Sachsenplatz 4-6, Vienna, W 1201, Austria. TEL 43-1-3302415-0, FAX 43-1-330242665, books@springer.at, http://www.springer.at. Ed. R Grossmann. R&P Angela Foessl TEL 43-1-3302415517. **Subscr. in N. America to:** Springer New York LLC, 233 Spring St, New York, NY 10013. TEL 800-777-4643, FAX 201-348-4505.

➤ **I F R A DOCUMENTS IN SOCIAL SCIENCES AND HUMANITIES.** *see* POLITICAL SCIENCE—International Relations

➤ **I F R A OCCASIONAL PUBLICATIONS.** *see* POLITICAL SCIENCE—International Relations

➤ **I M F C REVIEW.** (Institute of Marriage and Family Canada) *see* MATRIMONY

301 PHL ISSN 0073-9537
I P C MONOGRAPHS. Text in English. irreg. price varies. **Document type:** *Monographic series.*
Published by: Ateneo de Manila University, Institute of Philippine Culture, PO Box 154, Manila, Philippines. TEL 632-426-6068, http://www.ipc-ateneo.org/. Ed. Alfonso De Guzman II. R&P Germelino M Bautista TEL 632-426-6067.

301 PHL ISSN 0073-9545
I P C PAPERS. Text in English. irreg., latest vol.15. price varies. **Document type:** *Monographic series.*
Published by: Ateneo de Manila University, Institute of Philippine Culture, PO Box 154, Manila, Philippines. TEL 632-426-6068, http://www.ipc-ateneo.org/. R&P Germelino M Bautista TEL 632-426-6067.

303 PHL
I P C REPORTS. Text in English. 1980. irreg., latest 1997.
Published by: Ateneo de Manila University, Institute of Philippine Culture, PO Box 154, Manila, Philippines. TEL 632-426-6068, http://www.ipc-ateneo.org/. R&P Germelino M Bautista TEL 632-426-6067.

301 PHL
I P C REPRINTS. Text in English. irreg., latest vol.23.
Published by: Ateneo de Manila University, Institute of Philippine Culture, PO Box 154, Manila, Philippines. TEL 632-426-6068, http://www.ipc-ateneo.org/.

301 USA
I R S A ITEMS. Text in English; Abstracts occasionally in Spanish. 1977. a. membership. bk.rev.
Published by: International Rural Sociology Association, c/o Dept of Sociology, Michigan State University, East Lansing, MI 48824. Ed. Harry K Schwarzweller. Circ: 1,700.

301 USA
I S A G A NEWSLETTER. Text in English. 1974. q. membership. bk.rev. **Description:** Provides a forum for the exchange of ideas and knowledge on the design, applications, and use of games and simulation throughout the world.
Published by: International Simulation and Gaming Association, c/o Dr S Underwood, 4110 EECS Bldg, University of Michigan, Ann Arbor, MI 48109-2122. TEL 313-936-2999, FAX 313-763-1674. Circ: 1,000.

301 CAN
I S E R CONFERENCE PAPER. Text in English. 1986. irreg., latest vol.5, 1997. price varies. back issues avail. **Document type:** *Proceedings.*
Published by: Memorial University of Newfoundland, Institute of Social and Economic Research, Arts and Administration Bldg, St. John's, NF A1C 5S7, Canada. TEL 709-737-8156, FAX 709-737-2041.

301 CAN ISSN 0828-6868
HC117.N4
I S E R RESEARCH AND POLICY PAPERS. (Institute of Social and Economic Research) Text in English. 1985. irreg., latest no.23. price varies. adv. bk.rev. back issues avail. **Document type:** *Monographic series, Academic/Scholarly.* **Description:** Features article length papers. These papers vary from basic social scientific research to various forms of applied research, to policy analysis and recommendations. Draws mainly on research conducted under the auspices and focuses on Newfoundland and North Atlantic studies.
Published by: Memorial University of Newfoundland, Institute of Social and Economic Research, Arts and Administration Bldg, St. John's, NF A1C 5S7, Canada. TEL 709-737-8156, FAX 709-737-2041. Adv. contact Alvin Potter. Circ: 250.

301 ITA ISSN 1826-3003
I S I G TRIMESTRALE DI SOCIOLOGIA INTERNAZIONALE. (Istituto di Sociologia Internazionale di Gorizia) Text in Multiple languages. 1970. q. **Document type:** *Journal, Academic/Scholarly.*
Former titles (until 2002): I S I G Magazine (1826-3011); (until 1996): I S I G (1826-302X); (until 1982): I S I G Informazioni (1826-3038)
Related titles: Online - full text ed.: ISSN 1826-3046.
Published by: Istituto di Sociologia Internazionale di Gorizia, Via Giuseppe Mazzini 13, Gorizia, 34170, Italy. TEL 39-0481-532094, http://www.isig.it.

THE I U P JOURNAL OF ORGANIZATIONAL BEHAVIOR. *see* BUSINESS AND ECONOMICS—Personnel Management

IDEAS. *see* LINGUISTICS

303.3 DEU ISSN 1863-9232
IDENTITAETEN UND ALTERITAETEN. Text in German. 1999. irreg., latest vol.26, 2007. price varies. **Document type:** *Monographic series, Academic/Scholarly.*
Published by: Ergon Verlag, Keesburgstr 11, Wuerzburg, 97074, Germany. TEL 49-931-280084, FAX 49-931-282872, service@ergon-verlag.de, http://www.ergon-verlag.de.

IDENTITIES; global studies in culture and power. *see* ETHNIC INTERESTS

303 305.8 USA ISSN 1528-3488
BF697
➤ **IDENTITY (PHILADELPHIA)**; an international journal of theory and research. Text in English. 2001. q. GBP 298 combined subscription in United Kingdom to institutions (print & online eds.); EUR 396, USD 498 combined subscription to institutions (print & online eds.) (effective 2012). adv. back issues avail.; reprint service avail. from PSC. **Document type:** *Journal, Academic/Scholarly.* **Description:** Provides a forum for identity theorists and researchers around the globe to share their ideas and findings regarding the problems and prospects of human self-definition.
Related titles: Online - full text ed.: ISSN 1532-706X. 2001. GBP 268 in United Kingdom to institutions; EUR 357, USD 448 to institutions (effective 2012).
Indexed: A01, A03, A08, A22, C32, CA, E01, FamI, P03, P27, P30, P42, P48, P54, PQC, PSA, PsycInfo, PsycholAb, S02, S03, S21, SCOPUS, SSA, SociolAb, T02.
—BLDSC (4362.450050), IE, Infotrieve, Ingenta. **CCC.**
Published by: (Society for Research on Identity Formation), Psychology Press (Subsidiary of: Taylor & Francis Inc.), 325 Chestnut St, Ste 800, Philadelphia, PA 19106. TEL 800-354-1420, FAX 215-625-2940, orders@taylorandfrancis.com, http://www.psypress.com. Ed. Alan S Waterman. Adv. contact Linda Hann TEL 44-1344-779945.

306 320 SEN ISSN 0851-2914
PJ7501
➤ **IDENTITY, CULTURE AND POLITICS/IDENTITE, CULTURE ET POLITIQUE**; an Afro-Asian dialogue. Text in English, French. biennial. USD 8 in Africa; USD 8 South Asia; USD 25 elsewhere (effective 2002). adv. bk.rev. back issues avail. **Document type:** *Journal, Academic/Scholarly.* **Description:** Covers exchanges of ideas and projections amongst African and Asian scholars and activists.
Indexed: CA, IIBP, P42, PSA, S02, S03, SociolAb, T02.
Published by: (International Centre for Ethnic Studies LKA), Council for the Development of Social Science Research in Africa, Avenue Cheikh, Anta Diop x Canal IV, BP 3304, Dakar, Senegal. TEL 221-825-9822, FAX 221-824-1289, codesria@sentoo.sn. Eds. Ahmed Imtiaz, Ousmane Kane. R&P Felicia Oyekanmi. Circ: 600.

306.89 CAN ISSN 1492-2045
ILLINOIS' DIVORCE MAGAZINE. Text in English. 1996. q. USD 12.80.
Formerly (until 2000): Chicago's Divorce Magazine (1481-9163)
Published by: Segue Esprit Inc., 2255B Queen St, E, Ste #1179, Toronto, ON M4E 1G3, Canada. TEL 416-368-8853, FAX 416-368-4978, editors@divorcemag.com, http://www.divorcemag.com.

301 USA ISSN 1054-1373
R726.8
➤ **ILLNESS, CRISIS, AND LOSS.** Abbreviated title: I C L. Text in English. 1991. q. USD 111 combined subscription to individuals (print & online eds.); USD 705 combined subscription to institutions (print & online eds.) (effective 2011). adv. bk.rev. illus. back issues avail.; reprints avail. **Document type:** *Journal, Academic/Scholarly.* **Description:** Covers the fields of life-threatening illness and thanatology will be advanced by bringing together the expertise of professionals in sociology, social work, nursing, and counseling.
Related titles: Online - full text ed.: ISSN 1552-6968. USD 105 to individuals; USD 669 to institutions (effective 2011).
Indexed: A01, A02, A03, A08, A22, ASSIA, B07, C06, C07, C08, CA, CINAHL, CPE, DIP, E-psyche, E01, FamI, H04, IBR, IBZ, P03, PsycInfo, PsycholAb, S02, S03, S21, SCOPUS, SFSA, SSA, SociolAb, T02, V02.
—BLDSC (4365.910000), IE, Infotrieve, Ingenta. **CCC.**
Published by: (University of Wisconsin at La Crosse, Center for Death Education & Bioethics), Baywood Publishing Co., Inc., 26 Austin Ave, PO Box 337, Amityville, NY 11701. TEL 631-691-1270, 800-638-7819, FAX 631-691-1770, Baywood@baywood.com. Ed. Neil Thompson.

➤ **L'IMMAGINE RIFLESSA**; rivista di sociologia della letteratura. *see* LITERATURE

➤ **IMPACT**; studies in language and society. *see* LINGUISTICS

301 USA
IN MOTION MAGAZINE; a multicultural US publication about democracy. Text in English. 1996. d. adv. back issues avail. **Document type:** *Magazine, Academic/Scholarly.* **Description:** Promotes grassroots organizing and art for social change among communities of color and working people.
Media: Online - full text.
Published by: N P C Productions, PO Box 927482, San Diego, CA 92192. Ed., Pub. Nic Paget-Clarke.

307 USA ISSN 1934-8193
IN THE RING. Text in English. 2007. q. USD 100 to members (effective 2007). **Document type:** *Newsletter, Consumer.* **Description:** Examines policies and practices that encourage the development of Michigan-area suburban communities.
Related titles: Online - full text ed.: ISSN 1934-8207.
Published by: Michigan Suburbs Alliance, 300 E Nine Mile Rd, Ferndale, MI 48220. TEL 248-546-2380, FAX 248-546-2369.

IN VISIBLE CULTURE; an electronic journal for visual culture. *see* ART

305 IRL ISSN 1649-8119
INCLUSION THROUGH LOCAL DEVELOPMENT. Variant title: Local Development Social Inclusion Programme. Newsletter. Text in English. 2005. 3/yr. **Description:** Focuses on the program and the work of the area-based partnerships, community partnerships and employment pacts that it funds.
Published by: (Pobal, Local Development Social Inclusion Programme), Pobal, Holbrook House, Holles St, Dublin, 2, Ireland. TEL 353-1-2400700, FAX 353-1-6610411, enquiries@pobal.ie. Ed. Toby Wolfe TEL 353-1-4484817.

INDAGINI E PROSPETTIVE. *see* POLITICAL SCIENCE

302.23 IND
INDIAN INSTITUTE OF MASS COMMUNICATION. ANNUAL REPORT. Text in English. 19??. a. **Document type:** *Report, Consumer.*
Published by: Indian Institute of Mass Communication, JNU New Campus, Aruna Asif Ali Rd, New Delhi, 110 067, India. TEL 91-11-26742920, FAX 91-11-26742462, jaideepbhatnagar@hotmail.com.

INDIAN JOURNAL OF SECULARISM. *see* HISTORY—History Of Asia

303 IND ISSN 0972-3692
HN49.C6
INDIAN JOURNAL OF SOCIAL DEVELOPMENT. Abbreviated title: I J S D. Text in English. 2001. s-a. INR 3,000 domestic to institutions; USD 125 foreign to institutions (effective 2011). **Document type:** *Journal, Academic/Scholarly.*
Indexed: EconLit, JEL.
Published by: Scientific Publishers, 5-A, New Pali Rd, PO Box 91, Jodhpur, Rajasthan 342 001, India. TEL 91-291-2433323, FAX 91-291-2624154, journals@scientificpub.com, http://www.scientificpub.com.

INFILTRATION. *see* LITERARY AND POLITICAL REVIEWS

INFORMACAO & SOCIEDADE; estudos. *see* LIBRARY AND INFORMATION SCIENCES

364.25 306.482 USA ISSN 1543-4915
HV6715
INFORMATION PLUS REFERENCE SERIES. GAMBLING; what's at stake. Text in English. 1978. biennial, latest 2007. USD 49 per issue (effective 2008). **Document type:** *Monographic series, Academic/Scholarly.* **Description:** Provides a compilation of current and historical statistics, with analysis, on aspects of one contemporary social issue.
Formerly (until 2000): Information Series on Current Topics. Gambling, Crime or Recreation
Related titles: Online - full text ed.; ◆ Series of: Information Plus Reference Series.
Published by: Gale (Subsidiary of: Cengage Learning), 27500 Drake Rd, Farmington Hills, MI 48331. TEL 248-699-4253, 800-877-4253, FAX 877-363-4253, gale.customerservice@cengage.com, http://gale.cengage.com.

305.13 USA ISSN 1534-1631
HQ792.U5
INFORMATION PLUS REFERENCE SERIES. GROWING UP IN AMERICA. Text in English. 1987. biennial, latest 2007. USD 49 per issue (effective 2008). **Document type:** *Monographic series, Academic/Scholarly.* **Description:** Provides a compilation of current and historical statistics, with analysis, on aspects of one contemporary social issue.
Related titles: Online - full content ed.; ◆ Series of: Information Plus Reference Series.
Published by: Gale (Subsidiary of: Cengage Learning), 27500 Drake Rd, Farmington Hills, MI 48331. TEL 248-699-4253, 800-877-4253, FAX 877-363-4253, gale.customerservice@cengage.com, http://gale.cengage.com.

INFORMATION PLUS REFERENCE SERIES. GUN CONTROL; restricting rights or protecting people?. *see* CRIMINOLOGY AND LAW ENFORCEMENT

INFORMATION PLUS REFERENCE SERIES. THE ENVIRONMENT; a revolution in attitudes. *see* ENVIRONMENTAL STUDIES

INFORMATION PLUS REFERENCE SERIES. WEIGHT IN AMERICA; obesity, eating disorders, and other health risks. *see* PHYSICAL FITNESS AND HYGIENE

301 AUS ISSN 1033-6273
➤ **INFORMATION, THEORY AND SOCIETY.** Text in English. 2000. s-a. AUD 429 domestic to institutions; AUD 390 in New Zealand to institutions; GBP 135 in Europe to institutions; USD 198 elsewhere to institutions (effective 2003). adv. bk.rev. index. **Document type:** *Journal, Academic/Scholarly.* **Description:** Covers major and current issues in information research, focusing on contemporary cultural studies and problems pertaining to the information age, post-industrialism, individualism, commodities and postmodernity.
Indexed: AEI, CPE.
Published by: James Nicholas Publishers, Pty. Ltd., PO Box 5179, South Melbourne, VIC 3205, Australia. TEL 61-3-96905955, FAX 61-3-96992040, custservice@jnponline.com, http://www.jamesnicholaspublishers.com.au. Ed. Joseph Zajda. Pub. Rea Zajda. R&P Mary Berchmans. Adv. contact Irene Schevchenko.

301 DEU ISSN 0938-0124
INFORMATIONEN FUER EINELTERNFAMILIEN. Text in German. 1990. 9/yr. bk.rev. **Document type:** *Newsletter.*
Published by: Verband Alleinerziehender Muetter und Vaeter e.V., Beethovenallee 7, Bonn, 53173, Germany. TEL 49-228-352995, FAX 49-228-358350. Ed. Peggi Liebisch. Circ: 1,500.

▼ **INFORMES SOCIOECONOMICOS.** *see* LABOR UNIONS

301 ITA ISSN 2039-1838
▼ **INGENERE**; donne e uomini per la societa che cambia. Text in Italian. 2009. s-m. **Document type:** *Newsletter, Consumer.*
Media: Online - full text.
Published by: Fondazione Giacomo Brodolini, Via A Depretis 65, Rome, 00184, Italy. TEL 39-06-4746552, FAX 39-06-4745345.

INICIACOM; revista brasileira de iniciacao cientifica em comunicacao social. *see* COMMUNICATIONS

303 ITA ISSN 1970-9021
INNOVAZIONE E CULTURA. Text in Italian. 2006. m. **Document type:** *Magazine, Consumer.*
Published by: Il Sole 24 Ore Business Media, Via Monte Rosa 91, Milan, 20149, Italy. TEL 39-02-30221, FAX 39-02-312055, info@ilsole24ore.com, http://www.gruppo24ore.com.

306 USA ISSN 1939-313X
INQUIRY (PROVO); the journal of student cross-cultural research. Text in English. 2006. a. free (effective 2010). back issues avail. **Document type:** *Journal, Academic/Scholarly.*
Related titles: Online - full text ed.: ISSN 1939-3148.

S

Published by: Brigham Young University, David M. Kennedy Center for International Studies, 237 HRCB, Provo, UT 84602. TEL 801-422-3377, FAX 801-422-0382, kennedy@byu.edu. Eds. Adam Harris, Nephi Jay Henry.

301 ITA ISSN 1973-1159
INQUISIZIONE E SOCIETA. FONTI. Text in Italian. 1998. irreg. **Document type:** *Journal, Academic/Scholarly.*
Published by: Universita degli Studi di Trieste, Edizioni Universita di Trieste (E U T), Piazzale Europa 1, Trieste, 34127, Italy. TEL 39-040-5587111, http://www.eut.units.it.

INSAKA. *see* RELIGIONS AND THEOLOGY—Protestant

INSTITUT FUER AFRIKA-KUNDE. ARBEITEN. *see* POLITICAL SCIENCE

307.14 DEU ISSN 0721-8125
INSTITUT FUER ENTWICKLUNGSFORSCHUNG, WIRTSCHAFTS- UND SOZIALPLANUNG. SCHRIFTEN. Variant title: Isoplan-Schriften. Text in German. 1981. irreg., latest vol.3, 1989. price varies. **Document type:** *Monographic series, Academic/Scholarly.*
Published by: (Institut fuer Entwicklungsforschung, Wirtschafts- und Sozialplanung), Verlag fuer Entwicklungspolitik Saarbruecken GmbH, Auf der Adt 14, Saarbruecken, 66130, Germany. TEL 49-6893-986094, FAX 49-6893-986095, vfe@verlag-entwicklungspolitik.de, http://www.verlag-entwicklungspolitik.de.

307.14 DEU ISSN 0720-5899
INSTITUT FUER INTERNATIONALE BEGEGNUNGEN. SCHRIFTEN. Text in German. 1979. irreg., latest vol.11, 1988. price varies. **Document type:** *Monographic series, Academic/Scholarly.*
Published by: (Institut fuer Internationale Begegnungen), Verlag fuer Entwicklungspolitik Saarbruecken GmbH, Auf der Adt 14, Saarbruecken, 66130, Germany. TEL 49-6893-986094, FAX 49-6893-986095, vfe@verlag-entwicklungspolitik.de, http://www.verlag-entwicklungspolitik.de.

304.663 USA ISSN 1078-1706
INSTITUTE FOR THE STUDY OF GENOCIDE NEWSLETTER. Text in English. 1988. s-a. USD 30 to members; USD 35 foreign to members. bk.rev. **Document type:** *Newsletter.* **Description:** Analysis of current events pertaining to genocide in the world.
Published by: Institute for the Study of Genocide, 899 Tenth Ave, Rm 325, New York, NY 10019. TEL 617-354-2785, FAX 617-491-8076. Ed., R&P Helen Fein. Circ: 1,000.

951.9 IND ISSN 0970-2814
DS1
INSTITUTE OF ASIAN STUDIES. JOURNAL. Text in English. 1983. s-a. adv. bk.rev. bibl.; illus.; stat. **Document type:** *Journal, Academic/Scholarly.* **Description:** Devoted to comparative studies of literature, languages, philosophy, sociology, archaeology, theology and other disciplines of Asian cultural and literary sensibility.
Formerly (until 1986): Journal of Asian Studies (0970-2806)
Related titles: Online - full text ed.
Indexed: AICP, BAS, DIP, IBR, IBZ.
—INIST.
Published by: Institute of Asian Studies, Chemmancherry, Sholinganallur Post, Chennai, Tamil Nadu 600 019, India. TEL 91-44-24502212, ias@xlweb.com, http://xlweb.com/heritage/asian/index.html.

INSTITUTE OF DEVELOPMENT STUDIES. ANNUAL REPORT. *see* BUSINESS AND ECONOMICS—International Development And Assistance

306 USA ISSN 0738-7105
NX556.A1
INSTITUTE OF MODERN RUSSIAN CULTURE NEWSLETTER. Text in English. 1979. s-a. USD 25 (effective 2000). **Document type:** *Bulletin.* **Description:** Propagates literary and artistic achievements of modern Russian culture.
Published by: Institute of Modern Russian Culture, PO Box 4353, Los Angeles, CA 90089. TEL 213-740-2735, FAX 213-740-8550, TELEX 674803UNIVSOCALLSA. Ed. John E Bowlt. Circ: 1,000 (controlled).

301 PER ISSN 1022-0429
INSTITUTO DE ESTUDIOS PERUANOS. DOCUMENTOS DE TRABAJO. SERIE SOCIOLOGIA, POLITICA. Key Title: Serie Sociologia, Politica. Variant title: Documentos de Trabajo. Serie Sociologia, Politica. Text in Spanish. 1985. irreg., latest vol.98, 1998. price varies. back issues avail. **Document type:** *Monographic series, Academic/Scholarly.* **Description:** Publishes new research into the sociology and politics of Peru.
Related titles: ◆ Series of: Instituto de Estudios Peruanos. Documentos de Trabajo. ISSN 1022-0356.
Published by: (Instituto de Estudios Peruanos), I E P Ediciones (Subsidiary of: Instituto de Estudios Peruanos), Horacio Urteaga 694, Jesus Maria, Lima, 11, Peru. TEL 51-14-3326194, FAX 51-14-3326173, libreria@iep.org.pe, http://iep.perucultural.org.pe.

307.72 PER ISSN 1019-4517
INSTITUTO DE ESTUDIOS PERUANOS. ESTUDIOS DE LA SOCIEDAD RURAL. Text in Spanish. 1967. irreg., latest vol.16, 1996. price varies. back issues avail. **Document type:** *Monographic series, Academic/Scholarly.*
Published by: (Instituto de Estudios Peruanos), I E P Ediciones (Subsidiary of: Instituto de Estudios Peruanos), Horacio Urteaga 694, Jesus Maria, Lima, 11, Peru. TEL 51-14-3326194, FAX 51-14-3326173, libreria@iep.org.pe, http://iep.perucultural.org.pe.

301 NOR ISSN 0801-8863
INSTITUTT FOR SAMFUNNSFORSKNING. AARSMELDING. Text in Norwegian. 199?. a. **Document type:** *Report, Consumer.*
Related titles: Online - full text ed.; English ed.: Institute for Social Research. Annual Report. 2005; ◆ Series of: Institutt for Samfunnsforskning. Rapport. ISSN 0333-3671; ◆ Special ed. of: Institutt for Samfunnsforskning. Rapport. ISSN 0333-3671.
Published by: Institutt for Samfunnsforskning/Institute for Social Research, Munthes Gate 31, PO Box 3233, Elisenberg, Oslo, 0208, Norway. TEL 47-23-086100, FAX 47-23-086101, isf@samfunnsforskning.no.

301 NOR ISSN 0333-3671
INSTITUTT FOR SAMFUNNSFORSKNING. RAPPORT/INSTITUTE FOR SOCIAL RESEARCH. REPORT. Variant title: I S F Rapport. Text mainly in Norwegian; Text occasionally in English. 1948. irreg. back issues avail. **Document type:** *Monographic series, Academic/Scholarly.*
Formerly (until 1982): Institutt for Samfunnsforskning. Serie A (0333-4694); Incorporates (1961-1982): Institutt for Samfunnsforskning. Publications (0801-7409)
Related titles: Online - full text ed.; ◆ Series: Institutt for Samfunnsforskning. Aarsmelding. ISSN 0801-8863; ◆ Special ed(s).: Institutt for Samfunnsforskning. Aarsmelding. ISSN 0801-8863.
Published by: Institutt for Samfunnsforskning/Institute for Social Research, Munthes Gate 31, PO Box 3233, Elisenberg, Oslo, 0208, Norway. TEL 47-23-086100, FAX 47-23-086101, isf@samfunnsforskning.no.

INSTITUUT VOOR PUBLIEK EN POLITIEK. NIEUWSBRIEF. *see* POLITICAL SCIENCE

INSULA; international journal of island affairs. *see* SOCIAL SCIENCES: COMPREHENSIVE WORKS

305.868 USA
THE INTER - AMERICA SERIES. Text in English. 2000. irreg. price varies. illus. back issues avail. **Document type:** *Monographic series, Academic/Scholarly.* **Description:** Explores issues relating to the geopolitical borders of Latin America, especially as they relate to the US, all from a sociological perspective.
Published by: (University of Texas at Austin, Center for Mexican American Studies), University of Texas Press, Books Division, PO Box 7819, Austin, TX 78713. TEL 512-471-4034, 800-252-3206, FAX 512-232-7178, 800-687-6046, cs@utpress.utexas.edu. Eds. Duncan Earle, Howard Campbell, John Peterson.

302.23 306 GBR ISSN 1757-2681
▼ **INTERACTIONS (BRISTOL);** studies in communication & culture. Text in English. 2009. 3/yr. GBP 180 domestic to institutions; GBP 189 in the European Union to institutions; USD 290 in US & Canada to institutions; GBP 192 elsewhere to institutions (effective 2010). adv. back issues avail. **Document type:** *Journal, Academic/Scholarly.* **Description:** Aims to encourage the development of the wide scholarly community both in terms of geographical location and intellectual scope in the fields of media, communication and cultural studies.
Related titles: Online - full text ed.: ISSN 1757-269X. USD 220 in US & Canada to institutions; GBP 147 elsewhere to institutions (effective 2010).
Indexed: CA, CMM, CommAb, T02.
Published by: Intellect Ltd., The Mill, Parnall Rd, Fishponds, Bristol, BS16 3JG, United Kingdom. TEL 44-117-9589910, FAX 44-117-9589911, info@intellectbooks.com. Ed. Anthony McNicholas. Pub. Masoud Yazdani. adv.: color page GBP 250. **Subscr. to:** Turpin Distribution Services Ltd., Pegasus Dr, Stratton Business Park, Biggleswade, Bedfordshire SG18 8QB, United Kingdom. TEL 44-1767-604951, FAX 44-1767-601640, custserv@turpin-distribution.com, http://www.turpin-distribution.com/.

300 DEU ISSN 0175-8101
INTERAKTION UND LEBENSLAUF. Text in German. 1985. irreg., latest vol.13, 1997. price varies. **Document type:** *Monographic series, Academic/Scholarly.*
Published by: Deutscher Studien Verlag (Subsidiary of: Julius Beltz GmbH & Co. KG), Postfach 100154, Weinheim, 69441, Germany. TEL 49-6201-60070, FAX 49-6201-6007310, info@beltz.de, http://www.beltz.de.

303.842 USA ISSN 1057-7769
P94.6
➤ **INTERCULTURAL COMMUNICATION STUDIES.** Abbreviated title: I C S. Text in English. 1991. q. bk.rev. Supplement avail.; back issues avail. **Document type:** *Journal, Academic/Scholarly.* **Description:** Offers a multidisciplinary approach to the study of culture - language problems across cultures, whether major cultural groups or ethnic - socioeconomic subgroups within a larger group.
Indexed: MLA-IB.
—BLDSC (4533.356033), IE, Ingenta.
Published by: International Association for Intercultural Communication Studies, c/o Yinjiao Ye, Department of Communication Studies, University of Rhode Isl, 10 Lippitt Rd, 310 Davis Hall, Kingston, RI 02881. yinjiao_ye@mail.uri.edu.

303.842 GBR ISSN 1467-5986
HN1
➤ **INTERCULTURAL EDUCATION.** Text in English. 1990. bi-m. GBP 731 combined subscription in United Kingdom to institutions (print & online eds.); EUR 968, USD 1,218 combined subscription to institutions (print & online eds.) (effective 2012). adv. index. back issues avail.; reprint service avail. from PSC. **Document type:** *Journal, Academic/Scholarly.* **Description:** Focuses on issues of intercultural education and the relationship between education, the state, and social and cultural diversity.
Formerly (until 2000): European Journal of Intercultural Studies (0952-391X)
Related titles: Online - full text ed.: ISSN 1469-8439. GBP 658 in United Kingdom to institutions; EUR 872, USD 1,096 to institutions (effective 2012) (from IngentaConnect).
Indexed: A01, A02, A03, A08, A22, AEI, ASSIA, B21, B29, CA, CPE, DIP, DRIE, E01, E03, E17, ERI, ERIC, ESPM, IBR, IBZ, L&LBA, MLA-IB, P34, PerIslam, S02, S03, SCOPUS, SD, SOPODA, SRRA, SociolAb, T02.
—IE, Ingenta. **CCC.**
Published by: (International Association for Intercultural Education USA), Routledge (Subsidiary of: Taylor & Francis Group), 4 Park Sq, Milton Park, Abingdon, Oxon OX14 4RN, United Kingdom. TEL 44-20-70176000, FAX 44-20-70176336, subscriptions@tandf.co.uk, http://www.routledge.com. Ed. Barry van Driel. Adv. contact Linda Hann TEL 44-1344-779945. Circ: 1,500. **Subscr. in N America to:** Taylor & Francis Inc., Customer Services Dept, 325 Chestnut St, 8th Fl, Philadelphia, PA 19106. TEL 215-625-8900, 800-354-1420, FAX 215-625-2940, customerservice@taylorandfrancis.com; **Subscr. to:** Taylor & Francis Ltd., Journals Customer Service, Sheepen Pl, Colchester, Essex CO3 3LP, United Kingdom. TEL 44-20-70175544, FAX 44-20-70175198.

➤ **INTERCULTURAL THEOLOGY AND STUDY OF RELIGIONS/ THEOLOGIE INTERKULTURELL UND STUDIUM DER RELIGIONEN.** *see* RELIGIONS AND THEOLOGY

201.6 CAN ISSN 0828-797X
BL3
INTERCULTURE. Text in English. 1968. 2/yr. CAD 19 domestic to individuals; CAD 23 foreign to individuals; CAD 30.84 domestic to institutions; CAD 37 foreign to institutions; CAD 9.81 newsstand/cover (effective 2000). back issues avail. **Document type:** *Journal, Academic/Scholarly.* **Description:** Explores issues raised by the plurality of cultures and their interactions.
Former titles (until July 1981): Revue Monchanin Journal (0712-158X); (until 1976): Monchanin (0383-0977); (until 1972): Monchanin Information (0383-0969)
Related titles: Microfilm ed.: (from WMP); Italian ed.: ISSN 1825-7518. 2005; French ed.: ISSN 0712-1571. 1977.
Indexed: A21, PdeR, R&TA, RI-1, RI-2.
—BLDSC (4533.356070), IE, Ingenta.
Published by: Intercultural Institute of Montreal/Institut Interculturel de Montreal, 4917 St Urbain, Montreal, PQ H2T 2W1, Canada. TEL 514-288-7229, FAX 514-844-6800, info@iim.qc.ca, http://www.iim.qc.ca. Ed., Pub. Robert Vachon. R&P Andre Giguere. Circ: 1,000.

301 ITA ISSN 2038-095X
▼ **INTERDIPENDENZE;** rivista di teoria e ricerca sociale, studi ecologici, etnoscienze. Text in Multiple languages. 2010. s-a. free (effective 2011). **Document type:** *Magazine, Consumer.*
Media: Online - full text.
Published by: Societa di Etnosociologia e Ricerca Sociale (S E R I S), Via Marco Polo 35, Naples, 80124, Italy.

302.23 DEU
INTERDISZIPLINAERE DISKURSE. Text in German. 2006. irreg., latest vol.5, 2010. price varies. **Document type:** *Monographic series, Academic/Scholarly.*
Published by: KoPaed Verlag, Pfaelzer-Wald-Str 64, Munich, 81539, Germany. TEL 49-89-68890098, FAX 49-89-6891912, info@kopaed.de, http://www.kopaed.de.

306.43 DEU ISSN 1432-8186
➤ **INTERKULTURELLE BILDUNGSFORSCHUNG.** Text in German. 1997. irreg., latest vol.17, 2011. price varies. **Document type:** *Monographic series, Academic/Scholarly.*
Published by: Waxmann Verlag GmbH, Steinfurter Str 555, Muenster, 48159, Germany. TEL 49-251-265040, FAX 49-251-2650426, info@waxmann.com. Eds. Ingrid Gogolin, Marianne Krueger-Potratz.

300 DEU ISSN 1866-752X
▼ **INTERKULTURELLER DIALOG.** Text in German. 2010. irreg. price varies. **Document type:** *Monographic series, Academic/Scholarly.*
Published by: Peter Lang GmbH (Subsidiary of: Peter Lang Publishing Group), Eschborner Landstr 42-50, Frankfurt Am Main, 60489, Germany. TEL 49-69-7807050, FAX 49-69-78070550, zentrale.frankfurt@peterlang.com. Ed. Annemarie Profanter.

INTERNATIONAL AND COMPARATIVE SOCIAL HISTORY. *see* HISTORY

302.23 USA ISSN 0270-6075
HM258
INTERNATIONAL AND INTERCULTURAL COMMUNICATION ANNUAL. Abbreviated title: I I C A. Short title: I I C Annual. Text in English. 1974. a., latest 2007. adv. 292 p./no.; back issues avail. **Document type:** *Journal, Academic/Scholarly.* **Description:** A thematic compilation of research, from a variety of perspectives, on international and intercultural communication issues.
Related titles: Online - full text ed.
Indexed: CA, CMM, PCI.
—**CCC.**
Published by: National Communication Association, 1765 N St, NW, Washington, DC 20036. TEL 202-464-4622, FAX 202-464-4600, memberservice@natcom.org.

301 971 305.81 CAN ISSN 1489-713X
➤ **INTERNATIONAL CANADIAN STUDIES SERIES.** Text in English, French. 1998. s-a. price varies. adv. back issues avail. **Document type:** *Monographic series, Academic/Scholarly.*
Published by: University of Ottawa Press/Presses de l'Universite d'Ottawa, 542 King Edward, Ottawa, ON K1N 6N5, Canada. TEL 613-562-5246, FAX 613-562-5247. Ed. Vicki Bennett. R&P Martine Beauchesne. Adv. contact Elizabeth Thebaud. Circ: 500.

302.23 SWE ISSN 1651-6028
HQ784.M3
INTERNATIONAL CLEARINGHOUSE ON CHILDREN, YOUTH AND MEDIA. YEARBOOK. Text in English. 1998. a. price varies. back issues avail. **Document type:** *Monographic series, Academic/Scholarly.* **Description:** The yearbooks contain articles centering on current themes and are written by qualified scholars from different regions of the world.
Formerly (until 2002): Children and Media Violence (1403-4700)
Published by: International Clearinghouse on Children, Youth and Media, c/o Nordicom, University of Goeteborg, PO Box 713, Goeteborg, 40530, Sweden. clearinghouse@nordicom.gu.se, http://www.nordicom.gu.se/clearinghouse.

INTERNATIONAL COMMUNICATION RESEARCH JOURNAL. *see* JOURNALISM

301 016.331 331 CHE ISSN 1014-8620
INTERNATIONAL INSTITUTE FOR LABOUR STUDIES. BIBLIOGRAPHY SERIES. Text in English. 1979. irreg., latest vol.19, 1999. price varies. back issues avail. **Document type:** *Bibliography.* **Description:** Contains bibliographic references and analyses of the literature covering recent and emerging labour and social questions.
Indexed: SociolAb.
Published by: International Institute for Labour Studies, PO Box 6, Geneva 22, 1211, Switzerland. TEL 41-22-799-6114, FAX 41-22-799-8542. Ed. Maryse Gaudier.

301 NLD ISSN 1568-1548
INTERNATIONAL INSTITUTE OF SOCIOLOGY. ANNALS (NEW SERIES). Text in Japanese. 1895; N.S. 2000. irreg., latest vol.11, 2009. price varies. **Document type:** *Monographic series, Academic/Scholarly.*
Formerly (until 2000): International Institute of Sociology. Annals
Indexed: IZBG.
Published by: (International Institute of Sociology JPN), Brill, PO Box 9000, Leiden, 2300 PA, Netherlands. TEL 31-71-5353500, FAX 31-71-5317532, cs@brill.nl.

301 USA ISSN 1556-1720
BF697

➤ **INTERNATIONAL JOURNAL FOR DIALOGICAL SCIENCE.** Abbreviated title: I J D S. Text in English. 2006. s-a. free (effective 2009). back issues avail. **Document type:** *Journal, Academic/Scholarly.* **Description:** Acts as a forum for theorists, researchers, and practitioners around the globe to share their ideas and findings.
Media: Online - full content.
Published by: International Society for Dialogical Science, c/o Vincent W Hevern, Psychology Department, Le Moyne College, 1419 Salt Springs Rd, Syracuse, NY 13214. hevern@lemoyne.edu, http://web.lemoyne.edu/~hevern/ISDS/index.html. Ed. Hubert J M Hermans.

➤ **INTERNATIONAL JOURNAL OF AFRICANA STUDIES.** *see* ETHNIC INTERESTS

➤ **INTERNATIONAL JOURNAL OF ARAB CULTURE, MANAGEMENT AND SUSTAINABLE DEVELOPMENT.** *see* ETHNIC INTERESTS

➤ **INTERNATIONAL JOURNAL OF BEHAVIORAL MEDICINE.** *see* PSYCHOLOGY

➤ **INTERNATIONAL JOURNAL OF BILINGUALISM.** *see* LINGUISTICS

301 CAN ISSN 1180-3991

➤ **INTERNATIONAL JOURNAL OF CANADIAN STUDIES/REVUE INTERNATIONALE D'ETUDES CANADIENNES.** Text in English, French. 1990. s-a. adv. back issues avail. **Document type:** *Journal, Academic/Scholarly.* **Description:** Multidisciplinary and international in scope, dedicated to the analysis of key issues of Canadian society in the social sciences and the arts as well as other disciplines.
Related titles: CD-ROM ed.; Online - full text ed.
Indexed: A26, AmH&L, C03, CA, CBCARef, CBPI, CPerI, E08, G08, HistAb, I05, I13, MLA-IB, P42, P48, PAIS, PQC, PSA, PdeR, RILM, S02, S03, S09, SCOPUS, SociolAb, T02.
Published by: International Council for Canadian Studies/Conseil International d'Etudes Canadiennes, 250 City Centre Ave, Suite 303, Ottawa, ON K1R 6K7, Canada. TEL 613-789-7834, FAX 613-789-7830.

306.85 BEL ISSN 1378-286X

➤ **INTERNATIONAL JOURNAL OF CHILD & FAMILY WELFARE (LEUVEN).** Text in English. 1996. q. EUR 85 to individuals; EUR 130 to institutions (effective 2005). bk.rev. **Document type:** *Journal, Academic/Scholarly.* **Description:** Publishes papers dealing with child and family welfare, as well as youth care. Topics include children in need, child maltreatment, homeless youth, child protection services, family preservation programs, prevention of juvenile delinquency, drug and alcohol abuse, outcomes of out-of-home placement, among others.
Formerly (until 2002): International Journal of Child & Family Welfare (Utrecht) (1383-4134)
Indexed: SCOPUS, SSA, SociolAb.
—BLDSC (4542.165250), IE, Ingenta.
Published by: Uitgeverij Acco, Brusselsestraat 153, Leuven, 3000, Belgium. TEL 32-16-628000, FAX 32-16-628001, uitgeverij@acco.be, http://www.acco.be. Ed. Hans Grietens.

301 CAN ISSN 1920-7298

▼ ➤ **INTERNATIONAL JOURNAL OF CHILD, YOUTH AND FAMILY STUDIES.** Abbreviated title: I J C Y F S. Text in English. 2010. irreg. free (effective 2011). **Document type:** *Journal, Academic/Scholarly.*
Media: Online - full text.
Published by: University of Victoria, School of Child and Youth Care, PO Box 1700, Victoria, BC V8W 2Y2, Canada. Ed. Sibylle Artz.

306.951 330 GBR ISSN 1752-1270

➤ **INTERNATIONAL JOURNAL OF CHINESE CULTURE AND MANAGEMENT.** Text in English. 2007 (Dec.). 4/yr. EUR 494 to institutions (print or online ed.); EUR 672 combined subscription to institutions (print & online eds.) (effective 2012). abstr.; bibl.; charts; stat.; illus. **Document type:** *Journal, Academic/Scholarly.* **Description:** Proposes and fosters discussion on Chinese culture, business, management and related topics. It presents timely and in-depth analyses on these topics, offering the reader a wealth of valuable material on theories and practices which underpin successful business in China.
Related titles: Online - full text ed.: ISSN 1752-1289 (from IngentaConnect).
Indexed: A26, A28, APA, BrCerAb, C&ISA, CA/WCA, CABA, CIA, CerAb, CivEngAb, CorrAb, E&CAJ, E08, E11, EEA, EMA, ESPM, EnvEAb, GH, H15, LT, M&TEA, M09, MBF, METADEX, N02, RiskAb, SSciA, SolStAb, T04, T05, TAR, W11, WAA.
—BLDSC (4542.165560), IE. **CCC.**
Published by: Inderscience Publishers, PO Box 735, Olney, Bucks MK46 5WB, United Kingdom. TEL 44-1234-240519, FAX 44-1234-240515, editorial@inderscience.com. Ed. Dr. Patricia Ordonez de Pablos. **Subscr. to:** World Trade Centre Bldg, 29 Rte de Pre-Bois, Case Postale 856, Geneva 15 1215, Switzerland. FAX 41-22-7910885, subs@inderscience.com.

302 USA ISSN 1932-8036
P87

➤ **INTERNATIONAL JOURNAL OF COMMUNICATION.** Text in English. 2007. irreg. free (effective 2011). bk.rev. **Document type:** *Journal, Academic/Scholarly.* **Description:** An interdisciplinary journal focusing on communication issues from around the world.
Media: Online - full text.
Indexed: A39, B04, BRD, C27, C29, CA, CMM, CommAb, D03, D04, E13, R14, S02, S03, S14, S15, S18, SSAI, SSAb, SSI, T02, W03, W05.
Published by: University of Southern California, Annenberg Center for Communication, Annenberg Press, Kerckhoff Hall, 734 W Adams Blvd, MC7725, Los Angeles, CA 90089. TEL 213-743-2520, FAX 213-747-4981, info@ijoc.org. Eds. Larry Gross, Manuel Castells.

301 GBR ISSN 0020-7152

➤ **INTERNATIONAL JOURNAL OF COMPARATIVE SOCIOLOGY.** Text in English. 1960. bi-m. USD 837, GBP 453 combined subscription to institutions (print & online eds.); USD 820, GBP 444 to institutions (effective 2011). adv. bk.rev. charts; illus. reprint service avail. from PSC. **Document type:** *Journal, Academic/Scholarly.* **Description:** Comprises studies in various cultures on a comparative basis with view to reach a common level of abstraction.
Related titles: Microform ed.: (from SWZ); Online - full text ed.: ISSN 1745-2554. 2002. USD 753, GBP 408 to institutions (effective 2011) (from IngentaConnect).
Indexed: A01, A02, A03, A08, A20, A21, A22, A26, ABCPolSci, AICP, ASCA, BAS, BRD, CA, Chicano, CommAb, CurCont, DIP, E01, E08, ESPM, F09, FR, FamI, G08, GEOBASE, H09, I05, I14, IBR, IBSS, IBZ, M10, MEA&I, P02, P10, P27, P30, P42, P48, P53, P54, PCI, PQC, PSA, R05, RASB, RI-1, RI-2, S02, S03, S05, S09, S11, S21, SCOPUS, SOPODA, SSAI, SSAb, SSCI, SSI, SSciA, SociolAb, T02, W03, W07, W09.
—BLDSC (4542.173000), IE, Ingenta, INIST. **CCC.**
Published by: (York University CAN, Department of Sociology CAN), Sage Publications Ltd. (Subsidiary of: Sage Publications, Inc.), 1 Oliver's Yard, 55 City Rd, London, EC1Y 1SP, United Kingdom. TEL 44-20-73248500, FAX 44-20-73248600, info@sagepub.co.uk, http://www.uk.sagepub.com/home.nav. Ed. Jeffrey Kentor. adv.: B&W page GBP 350; 140 x 210. **Subscr. in the Americas to:** Sage Publications, Inc., 2455 Teller Rd, Thousand Oaks, CA 91320. TEL 805-499-9774, FAX 805-499-0871, journals@sagepub.com.

301 FIN ISSN 0019-6398
HM1

➤ **INTERNATIONAL JOURNAL OF CONTEMPORARY SOCIOLOGY**; a discussion journal of contemporary ideas and research. Text in English. 1963. biennial. USD 35 to individuals; USD 60 to institutions; USD 25 to students; USD 35 per issue (effective 2003). adv. bk.rev. charts; illus. cum.index. back issues avail.; reprints avail. **Document type:** *Journal, Academic/Scholarly.* **Description:** Discussion of contemporary ideas and research in sociology.
Formerly (until 1971): Indian Sociological Bulletin (0537-2550)
Related titles: Microfilm ed.: (from PQC).
Indexed: A22, ASSIA, CA, DIP, FR, HistAb, I13, IBR, IBZ, MLA-IB, P06, P30, P42, PCI, PSA, PerIslam, RASB, S02, S03, SOPODA, SSA, SociolAb, T02, W09.
—BLDSC (4542.176000), IE, Infotrieve, Ingenta, INIST.
Published by: Joensuu University Press, c/o Professor M'hammed Sabour, Dept of Sociology, University of Joensuu, PL 111, Joensuu, 80101, Finland. TEL 358-13-2512332, FAX 358-13-2512714, mhammed.sabour@joensuu.fi. Ed. Raj P Mohan. Pub., Adv. contact M'hammed Sabour. Circ: 200 (paid); 20 (controlled and free).

201.6 USA ISSN 2154-7270

➤ **INTERNATIONAL JOURNAL OF CULTIC STUDIES.** Text in English. 2002. a. **Document type:** *Journal, Academic/Scholarly.* **Description:** Publishes scholarly research on cultic phenomena across a range of disciplines and professions.
Formerly (until 2010): Cultic Studies Review (1539-0152); Which was formed by the merger of (2001-2002): Cults and Society; (1979-2002): Cultic Observer (0892-340X); Which was formerly (1979-1984): The Advisor (0740-1167); (1984-2002): Cultic Studies Journal (0748-6499); Which was formerly (until 1984): Cultic Studies Newsletter
Related titles: Online - full text ed.: ISSN 2154-7289.
Indexed: A21, CA, P03, PsycInfo, RI-1, S02, S03, T02.
—BLDSC (3491.616800), IE, Ingenta.
Published by: International Cultic Studies Association, PO Box 2265, Bonita Springs, FL 34133. TEL 239-514-3081, FAX 305-393-8193, mail@icsamail.com, http://www.icsahome.com.

306 GBR ISSN 1367-8779
HM101

➤ **INTERNATIONAL JOURNAL OF CULTURAL STUDIES.** Abbreviated title: I J C S. Text in English. 1998. bi-m. USD 1,100, GBP 595 combined subscription to institutions (print & online eds.); USD 1,078, GBP 583 to institutions (effective 2011). adv. bk.rev. illus. back issues avail.; reprint service avail. from PSC. **Document type:** *Journal, Academic/Scholarly.* **Description:** Promotes investigation of issues of culture and media in a global context and from a postdisciplinary perspective.
Related titles: Online - full text ed.: ISSN 1460-356X. USD 990, GBP 536 to institutions (effective 2011).
Indexed: A01, A02, A03, A08, A22, AICP, AmHI, ArtHuCI, B07, CA, CMM, CommAb, CurCont, DIP, E01, ESPM, FR, H04, H07, I14, IBR, IBSS, IBZ, MLA-IB, P34, P42, PSA, RiskAb, S02, S03, S21, SCOPUS, SSA, SSCI, SociolAb, T02, V02, W07.
—BLDSC (4542.181250), IE, Infotrieve, Ingenta, INIST. **CCC.**
Published by: Sage Publications Ltd. (Subsidiary of: Sage Publications, Inc.), 1 Oliver's Yard, 55 City Rd, London, EC1Y 1SP, United Kingdom. TEL 44-20-73248500, FAX 44-20-73248600, info@sagepub.co.uk, http://www.uk.sagepub.com/home.nav. Ed. John Hartley. adv.: B&W page GBP 400; 130 x 205. **Subscr. in the Americas to:** Sage Publications, Inc., 2455 Teller Rd, Thousand Oaks, CA 91320. TEL 805-499-9774, FAX 805-499-0871, journals@sagepub.com.

➤ **INTERNATIONAL JOURNAL OF CULTURE, TOURISM AND HOSPITALITY RESEARCH.** *see* TRAVEL AND TOURISM

➤ **INTERNATIONAL JOURNAL OF DIGITAL CULTURE AND ELECTRONIC TOURISM.** *see* COMPUTERS

➤ **THE INTERNATIONAL JOURNAL OF ENVIRONMENTAL, CULTURAL, ECONOMIC AND SOCIAL SUSTAINABILITY.** *see* ENVIRONMENTAL STUDIES

▼ ➤ **INTERNATIONAL JOURNAL OF GENDER AND ENTREPRENEURSHIP.** *see* BUSINESS AND ECONOMICS

305.3 500 600 GBR ISSN 2040-0748
Q130

▼ **INTERNATIONAL JOURNAL OF GENDER, SCIENCE AND TECHNOLOGY.** Text in English. 2009. 3/yr. free (effective 2011). **Document type:** *Journal, Academic/Scholarly.*
Media: Online - full text.
Published by: Open University, Walton Hall, Milton Keynes, Bucks MK7 6AA, United Kingdom. TEL 44-1908-274066, http://www.open.ac.uk. Ed. Clem Herman.

▼ **INTERNATIONAL JOURNAL OF INFORMATION SYSTEMS AND SOCIAL CHANGE.** *see* COMPUTERS—Computer Systems

303.482 GBR ISSN 0147-1767
GN496

➤ **INTERNATIONAL JOURNAL OF INTERCULTURAL RELATIONS.** Abbreviated title: I J I R. Text in English. 1977. 6/yr. EUR 1,127 in Europe to institutions; JPY 149,500 in Japan to institutions; USD 1,260 elsewhere to institutions (effective 2012). adv. bk.rev. back issues avail.; reprints avail. **Document type:** *Journal, Academic/Scholarly.* **Description:** Features advancing knowledge and understanding of theory, practice and research in intergroup relations.
Related titles: Microfilm ed.: (from PQC); Online - full text ed.: ISSN 1873-7552 (from IngentaConnect, ScienceDirect).
Indexed: A12, A17, A20, A22, A26, ABIn, ABS&EES, AMHA, ASCA, ASSIA, BAS, CA, CJPI, CMM, ChPerI, Chicano, CommAb, CurCont, DRIE, E-psyche, ESPM, FamI, I05, IPsyAb, L&LBA, MLA-IB, P03, P27, P30, P34, P42, P53, P54, PCI, PQC, PSA, PsycInfo, PsycholAb, RASB, S02, S03, SCOPUS, SOPODA, SRRA, SSA, SSCI, SSciA, SociolAb, T02, W07.
—BLDSC (4542.311000), IE, Infotrieve, Ingenta, INIST. **CCC.**
Published by: (International Academy for Intercultural Research USA), Pergamon (Subsidiary of: Elsevier Science & Technology), The Blvd, Langford Ln, East Park, Kidlington, Oxford OX5 1GB, United Kingdom. TEL 44-1865-843000, FAX 44-1865-843010, JournalsCustomerServiceEMEA@elsevier.com. **Subscr. to:** Elsevier BV, Radarweg 29, PO Box 211, Amsterdam 1000 AE, Netherlands. TEL 31-20-4853757, FAX 31-20-4853432, http://www.elsevier.nl.

301 AUS ISSN 0918-7545
HM22.J3 CODEN: IJJSEI

➤ **INTERNATIONAL JOURNAL OF JAPANESE SOCIOLOGY.** Abbreviated title: I J J S. Text in English. 1992. a., latest vol.17, 2008. GBP 92 in United Kingdom to institutions; EUR 117 in Europe to institutions; USD 145 in the Americas to institutions; USD 179 elsewhere to institutions; GBP 105 combined subscription in United Kingdom to institutions (print & online eds.); EUR 135 combined subscription in Europe to institutions (print & online eds.); USD 167 combined subscription in the Americas to institutions (print & online eds.); USD 206 combined subscription elsewhere to institutions (print & online eds.) (effective 2012). adv. back issues avail.; reprint service avail. from PSC. **Document type:** *Journal, Academic/Scholarly.* **Description:** Covers sociological research in Japan.
Related titles: Online - full text ed.: ISSN 1475-6781. GBP 92 in United Kingdom to institutions; EUR 117 in Europe to institutions; USD 145 in the Americas to institutions; USD 179 elsewhere to institutions (effective 2012) (from IngentaConnect).
Indexed: A01, A02, A03, A08, A22, A26, CA, E01, S02, S03, SCOPUS, SSA, SociolAb, T02.
—BLDSC (4542.311750), IE, Infotrieve, Ingenta. **CCC.**
Published by: (The Japan Sociological Society/Nippon Shakai Gakkai JPN), Wiley-Blackwell Publishing Asia (Subsidiary of: Wiley-Blackwell Publishing Ltd.), 155 Cremorne St, Richmond, VIC 3121, Australia. TEL 61-3-92743100, FAX 61-3-92743101, melbourne@wiley.com, http://www.wiley.com/WileyCDA/. Ed. Hideki Watanabe. Adv. contact Amanda Munce TEL 61-3-83591071.

301 GBR ISSN 2040-4468

▼ ➤ **INTERNATIONAL JOURNAL OF KNOWLEDGE-BASED DEVELOPMENT.** Text in English. 2010. 4/yr. EUR 494 to institutions (print or online ed.); EUR 672 combined subscription to institutions (print & online eds.) (effective 2012). abstr.; bibl.; illus.; charts; stat. **Document type:** *Journal, Academic/Scholarly.* **Description:** Provides a forum for academicians, scientists, practitioners, managers and industry professionals to integrate diversity and fragments of knowledge-based development.
Related titles: Online - full text ed.: ISSN 2040-4476 (from IngentaConnect).
—**CCC.**
Published by: Inderscience Publishers, PO Box 735, Olney, Bucks MK46 5WB, United Kingdom. TEL 44-1234-240519, FAX 44-1234-240515, editorial@inderscience.com. Ed. Tan Yigitcanlar. **Subscr. to:** World Trade Centre Bldg, 29 Rte de Pre-Bois, Case Postale 856, Geneva 15 1215, Switzerland. FAX 41-22-7910885, subs@inderscience.com.

➤ **INTERNATIONAL JOURNAL OF LAW CRIME AND JUSTICE.** *see* LAW

303.33 USA ISSN 1554-3145
HD57.7

➤ **INTERNATIONAL JOURNAL OF LEADERSHIP STUDIES.** Abbreviated title: I J L S. Text in English. s-a. free (effective 2011). back issues avail. **Document type:** *Journal, Academic/Scholarly.*
Formerly (until 2005): Journal of Organizational Leadership
Media: Online - full text.
Published by: Regent University, School of Global Leadership & Entrepreneurship, 1333 Regent University Dr, Virginia Beach, VA 23464. TEL 757-352-4550, FAX 757-352-4823. Ed. Dr. Dail Fields.

302.23 370 USA ISSN 1943-6068
P96

▼ **INTERNATIONAL JOURNAL OF LEARNING AND MEDIA.** Abbreviated title: I J L M. Text in English. 2009 (Jan.). q. USD 125 in US & Canada to institutions (effective 2012). back issues avail.; reprints avail. **Document type:** *Journal, Academic/Scholarly.* **Description:** Provides an international and intercultural forum for scholars, researchers and practitioners to examine the changing relationships between learning and media across a wide range of forms and settings.
Media: Online - full text.
Published by: M I T Press, 55 Hayward St, Cambridge, MA 02142. TEL 617-253-2889, FAX 617-577-1545, journals-cs@mit.edu, http://mitpress.mit.edu. Eds. David Buckingham, Katie Salen, Tara McPherson.

INTERNATIONAL JOURNAL OF MEDIA AND CULTURAL POLITICS. *see* COMMUNICATIONS

INTERNATIONAL JOURNAL OF MOTORCYCLE STUDIES. *see* SPORTS AND GAMES—Bicycles And Motorcycles

301 USA ISSN 1069-2541
HM278

INTERNATIONAL JOURNAL OF NONVIOLENCE. Text in English; Summaries in Arabic, Chinese, Dutch, English, French, German, Hebrew, Russian, Spanish. 1993. a. USD 8. adv. bk.rev. back issues avail. **Document type:** *Journal, Consumer.* **Description:** Nonviolence for academics, activists, practitioners, and theorists in the "trade" of nonviolence.
Related titles: Diskette ed.
Published by: Nonviolence International, 4530 Cathedral Ave, N W, PO Box 39127, Friendship Sta N W, Washington, DC 20016. TEL 202-244-0951, FAX 202-244-6396. Ed. Paul Hubers. adv.: page USD 100. Circ: 500.

INTERNATIONAL JOURNAL OF PSYCHOSOCIAL REHABILITATION. *see* PSYCHOLOGY

S

201.6 USA ISSN 1935-2409
INTERNATIONAL JOURNAL OF RELIGION AND SOCIETY. Text in English. 2007. q. USD 245 to institutions; USD 367 combined subscription to institutions (print & online eds.) (effective 2012). **Document type:** *Journal, Academic/Scholarly.* **Description:** Presents research from around the globe in the form of expert commentaries, short communications, research studies, abstracts, and book citations.
Related titles: Online - full text ed.: USD 245 to institutions (effective 2012).
Published by: Nova Science Publishers, Inc., 400 Oser Ave, Ste 1600, Hauppauge, NY 11788. TEL 631-231-7269, FAX 631-231-8175, main@novapublishers.com.

INTERNATIONAL JOURNAL OF ROLE-PLAYING. *see* SPORTS AND GAMES

307 IND ISSN 1023-2001
➤ **INTERNATIONAL JOURNAL OF RURAL STUDIES.** Abbreviated title: I J R S. Text in English. 1994. s-a. INR 50 domestic; GBP 20 foreign (effective 2011). bk.rev. 32 p./no. 2 cols./p.; back issues avail. **Document type:** *Journal, Academic/Scholarly.* **Description:** Aims to highlight and encourage socially useful and relevant research in various fields of rural studies. The journal reaches out to rural development workers, activists, students, researchers and academies of rural studies.
Related titles: Online - full text ed.: free (effective 2011).
Indexed: BA, C25, CABA, D01, E12, FCA, GH, H16, LT, MaizeAb, N02, N03, O01, OR, P32, P38, P40, PHN&I, R11, R12, RA&MP, RRTA, SoyAb, T05, TAR, W11.
—BLDSC (4542.542600), IE, Ingenta.
Published by: International Task Force for the Rural Poor, Amarpurkashi Rural Polytechnic, Via Bilari, Bilari, Uttar Pradesh 202 411, India. TEL 91-5921-270567, apk_gram@yahoo.co.uk, http://www.vri-online.org.uk/intaf/. Ed. Mukat Singh TEL 44-208-8644740. **Co-sponsor:** India Volunteers for Community Service, Gramodaya Mahavidalaya Evam Shodh Sansthan.

301 004 USA ISSN 2155-6334
▼ ➤ **INTERNATIONAL JOURNAL OF SOCIAL AND ORGANIZATIONAL DYNAMICS IN I T.** Text in English. 2010. q. USD 210 to individuals; USD 595 to institutions; USD 275 combined subscription to individuals (print & online eds.); USD 860 combined subscription to institutions (print & online eds.) (effective 2012). **Document type:** *Journal, Academic/Scholarly.* **Description:** Presents research on cultural issues, diversity, ethical issues and human interaction within the field of information technology.
Related titles: Online - full text ed.: ISSN 2155-6342. 2010. USD 140 to individuals; USD 595 to institutions (effective 2012).
Published by: I G I Global, 701 E Chocolate Ave, Ste 200, Hershey, PA 17033. TEL 717-533-8845 ext 100, FAX 717-533-8661, cust@igi-global.com, http://www.igi-pub.com.

➤ **INTERNATIONAL JOURNAL OF SOCIAL ECONOMICS.** *see* BUSINESS AND ECONOMICS

301 USA ISSN 0020-7659
HM1
➤ **INTERNATIONAL JOURNAL OF SOCIOLOGY.** Abbreviated title: I J S. Text in English. 1971. q. USD 1,189 combined subscription domestic to institutions (print & online eds.); USD 1,309 combined subscription foreign to institutions (print & online eds.) (effective 2012). adv. illus. back issues avail.; reprint service avail. from PSC. **Document type:** *Journal, Academic/Scholarly.* **Description:** Provides English translations from international sources.
Supersedes (in 1971): Eastern European Studies in Sociology and Anthropology
Related titles: Online - full text ed.: ISSN 1557-9336. 2004 (Apr.). USD 1,077 to institutions (effective 2012).
Indexed: A01, A03, A08, A22, A26, B07, BAS, BRD, CA, CMM, DIP, E-psyche, E01, E08, FR, FamI, G08, I05, IBR, IBZ, MEA&I, P34, P42, PAIS, PCI, PSA, RASB, S02, S03, S09, SCOPUS, SOPODA, SSA, SSAI, SSAb, SSI, SociolAb, T02, W03, W05.
—BLDSC (4542.570000), IE, Infotrieve, Ingenta, INIST. **CCC.**
Published by: M.E. Sharpe, Inc., 80 Business Park Dr, Armonk, NY 10504. TEL 914-273-1800, 800-541-6563, FAX 914-273-2106, custserv@mesharpe.com. Ed. Tadeusz Krauze Jr. Adv. contact Barbara Ladd TEL 914-273-1800.

▼ ➤ **INTERNATIONAL JOURNAL OF SOCIOLOGY AND ANTHROPOLOGY.** *see* ANTHROPOLOGY

301 GBR ISSN 0144-333X
HM1
➤ **INTERNATIONAL JOURNAL OF SOCIOLOGY AND SOCIAL POLICY.** Abbreviated title: I J S S P. Text in English. 1976. m. EUR 5,599 combined subscription in Europe (print & online eds.); USD 6,469 combined subscription in the Americas (print & online eds.); GBP 3,999 combined subscription in the UK & elsewhere (print & online eds.); AUD 5,469 combined subscription in Australasia (print & online eds.) (effective 2012). bk.rev. back issues avail.; reprint service avail. from PSC. **Document type:** *Journal, Academic/Scholarly.* **Description:** Seeks to provide research and promote the exchange of ideas and new concepts in sociology and social policy, as well as evaluating the effects of the implementation of past approaches and strategies.
Formerly (until 1981): Scottish Journal of Sociology (0309-4006)
Related titles: Online - full text ed.: ISSN 1758-6720.
Indexed: A12, A13, A17, A20, A22, ABIn, CA, CJPI, DIP, E01, ESPM, EmerIntel, FR, IBR, IBZ, P10, P27, P30, P34, P42, P45, P46, P48, P51, P53, P54, PAIS, PCI, PQC, PSA, RASB, S02, S03, SOPODA, SSA, SSciA, SociolAb, T02, W09.
—BLDSC (4542.571000), IE, Infotrieve, Ingenta, INIST. **CCC.**
Published by: Emerald Group Publishing Ltd., Howard House, Wagon Ln, Bingley, W Yorks BD16 1WA, United Kingdom. TEL 44-1274-777700, FAX 44-1274-785201, information@emeraldinsight.com. Ed. Colin C Williams. Pub. Andrew Smith. Circ: 200. **Subscr. to:** Emerald Group Publishing Limited, One Mifflin Pl, Ste 400, Harvard Sq, Cambridge, MA 02138. TEL 617-576-5782, 888-309-7810, FAX 617-576-5883.

301 JPN ISSN 0798-1759
CODEN: IJSFEO
➤ **INTERNATIONAL JOURNAL OF SOCIOLOGY OF AGRICULTURE AND FOOD/REVISTA INTERNACIONAL DE SOCIOLOGIA SOBRE AGRICULTURA Y ALIMENTOS.** Text in English, Spanish. 1991. a. adv. back issues avail. **Document type:** *Journal, Academic/Scholarly.* **Description:** Publishes theoretical and empirical articles in the general area of the sociology of agriculture and food.
Related titles: Online - full text ed.: free (effective 2011).
Indexed: A10, A34, A35, A38, AgBio, CA, CABA, D01, E12, F08, F12, GH, H16, IndVet, LT, N02, N04, OR, P32, P37, P40, PHN&I, PN&I, R12, S02, S03, S12, SCOPUS, SOPODA, SSA, SociolAb, T02, TAR, V03, VS, W11.
—CCC.
Published by: The Research Committee on Food and Agriculture, c/o Masashi Tachikawa, Policy Research Institute, MAFF, 2-2-1, Nishigahara, Kita-ku, Tokyo, 114-0024, Japan. TEL 81-3-39103946, tachi@affrc.go.jp, http://homepage2.nifty.com/isaRC40/rc40index.html. Eds. Farshad Araghi, Dr. Mara Miele, Dr. Vaughan Higgins. Circ: 500.

301 600 USA ISSN 1941-6253
HD30.2
▼ ➤ **INTERNATIONAL JOURNAL OF SOCIOTECHNOLOGY AND KNOWLEDGE DEVELOPMENT.** Text in English. 2009. q. USD 210 to individuals; USD 595 to institutions; USD 275 combined subscription to individuals (print & online eds.); USD 860 combined subscription to institutions (print & online eds.) (effective 2012). **Document type:** *Journal, Abstract/Index.*
Related titles: Online - full text ed.: ISSN 1941-6261. 2009. USD 140 to individuals; USD 595 to institutions (effective 2012).
—BLDSC (4542.581000), IE.
Published by: (Information Resources Management Association), I G I Global, 701 E Chocolate Ave, Ste 200, Hershey, PA 17033. TEL 717-533-8845 ext 100, 866-342-6657, FAX 717-533-8661, cust@igi-global.com. Ed. Elayne Coakes.

▼ ➤ **INTERNATIONAL JOURNAL OF SPORT AND SOCIETY.** *see* SPORTS AND GAMES

301 GBR ISSN 1756-2538
➤ **INTERNATIONAL JOURNAL OF SUSTAINABLE SOCIETY.** Text in English. 2008 (Sep.). 4/yr. EUR 494 to institutions (print or online ed.); EUR 672 combined subscription to institutions (print & online eds.) (effective 2012). bk.rev. abstr.; bibl.; charts. **Document type:** *Journal, Academic/Scholarly.*
Related titles: Online - full text ed.: ISSN 1756-2546 (from IngentaConnect).
Indexed: A26, A28, A35, APA, AgBio, BrCerAb, C&ISA, CA/WCA, CABA, CIA, CerAb, CivEngAb, CorrAb, E&CAJ, E08, E11, E12, EEA, EMA, ESPM, EnvEAb, F08, F12, H15, M&TEA, M09, MBF, METADEX, N02, P32, PGegResA, R12, S13, S16, SSciA, SolStAb, T04, TAR, W10, W11, WAA.
—BLDSC (4542.685870), IE. **CCC.**
Published by: Inderscience Publishers, PO Box 735, Olney, Bucks MK46 5WB, United Kingdom. TEL 44-1234-240519, FAX 44-1234-240515, editorial@inderscience.com. Ed. John Wang. **Subscr. to:** World Trade Centre Bldg, 29 Rte de Pre-Bois, Case Postale 856, Geneva 15 1215, Switzerland. FAX 41-22-7910885, subs@inderscience.com.

➤ **INTERNATIONAL JOURNAL OF TECHNOLOGY AND HUMAN INTERACTION.** *see* TECHNOLOGY: COMPREHENSIVE WORKS

➤ **INTERNATIONAL JOURNAL OF TECHNOLOGY, KNOWLEDGE AND SOCIETY.** *see* LIBRARY AND INFORMATION SCIENCES

➤ **INTERNATIONAL JOURNAL OF THE SOCIOLOGY OF LANGUAGE.** *see* LINGUISTICS

➤ **INTERNATIONAL JOURNAL OF TOURISM RESEARCH.** *see* TRAVEL AND TOURISM

306 GBR ISSN 1751-8229
B4870.Z594 A1
➤ **INTERNATIONAL JOURNAL OF ZIZEK STUDIES.** Text in English. 2007 (Jan.). irreg. free (effective 2011). **Document type:** *Journal, Academic/Scholarly.* **Description:** Devoted to investigating, elaborating, and critiquing the work of Slavoj Zizek.
Media: Online - full content.
Indexed: A39, AmHI, C27, C29, D03, D04, E13, H07, R14, S14, S15, S18, T02.
—CCC.
Published by: University of Leeds, Institute of Communications Studies http://ics.leeds.ac.uk/. Eds. David J Gunkel, Paul A Taylor.

303.3 658 USA ISSN 1944-7426
HD57.7
➤ **INTERNATIONAL LEADERSHIP JOURNAL.** Abbreviated title: I L J. Text in English. 2008. q. free (effective 2009). back issues avail. **Document type:** *Journal, Academic/Scholarly.* **Description:** Covers all aspects of leadership, including theory and research, education and development, practice and application, and to all organizational phenomena that may affect or be affected by leadership.
Media: Online - full content.
Published by: Thomas Edison State College, School of Business and Management, 101 W State St, Trenton, NJ 08608. TEL 888-442-8372, info@tesc.edu. Ed. Joseph C Santora TEL 609-984-1130 ext 3200.

301 GBR ISSN 0956-2583
➤ **INTERNATIONAL PERSPECTIVES ON EUROPE.** Text in English. 1989. a., latest 1994. price varies. **Document type:** *Monographic series, Academic/Scholarly.* **Description:** Provides a forum for both critical and mainstream scholarship on selected topics concerning Europe, East and West.
Published by: Berg Publishers (Subsidiary of: Oxford International Publishers Ltd.), 1st Fl Angel Ct, 81 St Clements St, Oxford, Berks OX4 1AW, United Kingdom. TEL 44-1865-245104, FAX 44-1865-791165, enquiry@bergpublishers.com. Ed. John Trumpbour.

301 320 GBR ISSN 1749-5679
JA76
➤ **INTERNATIONAL POLITICAL SOCIOLOGY.** Abbreviated title: I P S. Text in English. 2007 (Mar.). q. includes with subscr. to International Studies Quarterly. adv. back issues avail.; reprints avail. **Document type:** *Journal, Academic/Scholarly.* **Description:** Aims to respond to the need for more productive collaboration among political sociologists, international relations specialists and sociopolitical theorists.
Related titles: Online - full text ed.: ISSN 1749-5687 (from IngentaConnect).
Indexed: A22, CA, CurCont, E01, ESPM, P42, PSA, RiskAb, S02, S03, SCOPUS, SSCI, SociolAb, T02, W07.
—BLDSC (4544.965220), IE. **CCC.**
Published by: (International Studies Association USA), Wiley-Blackwell Publishing Ltd. (Subsidiary of: John Wiley & Sons, Inc.), 9600 Garsington Rd, Oxford, OX4 2DQ, United Kingdom. TEL 44-1865-776868, FAX 44-1865-714591, customerservices@blackwellpublishing.com. Eds. Didier Bigo, R B J Walker.

301 GBR ISSN 1012-6902
GV706
➤ **INTERNATIONAL REVIEW FOR THE SOCIOLOGY OF SPORT.** Abbreviated title: I R S S. Text in English. 1966. bi-m. GBP 572, USD 1,058 to institutions; GBP 584, USD 1,080 combined subscription to institutions (print & online eds.) (effective 2012). bk.rev. abstr.; bibl.; illus. back issues avail.; reprint service avail. from PSC. **Document type:** *Journal, Academic/Scholarly.* **Description:** Disseminates research and scholarship on sport throughout the international academic community.
Formerly (until 1984): International Review of Sport Sociology (0074-7769)
Related titles: Online - full text ed.: ISSN 1461-7218. GBP 526, USD 972 to institutions (effective 2012).
Indexed: A01, A03, A08, A20, A22, A34, A36, B07, BAS, CA, CABA, CurCont, DIP, E01, E12, G10, GH, H04, I14, IBR, IBZ, IndVet, LT, N02, P03, P30, PEI, PsycInfo, R12, RASB, RRTA, S02, S03, S13, SCOPUS, SD, SOPODA, SSA, SSCI, SociolAb, SportS, T02, T05, V02, VS, W07, W09, W11.
—BLDSC (4547.744000), IE, Infotrieve, Ingenta, INIST. **CCC.**
Published by: (The International Sociology of Sport Association), Sage Publications Ltd. (Subsidiary of: Sage Publications, Inc.), 1 Oliver's Yard, 55 City Rd, London, EC1Y 1SP, United Kingdom. TEL 44-20-73248500, FAX 44-20-73248600, info@sagepub.co.uk, http://www.uk.sagepub.com/home.nav. Ed. John Sugden TEL 44-1273-643729. **Subscr. in the Americas to:** Sage Publications, Inc., 2455 Teller Rd, Thousand Oaks, CA 91320. TEL 805-499-9774, FAX 805-499-0871, journals@sagepub.com.

301 ROM ISSN 2069-8267
➤ **INTERNATIONAL REVIEW OF SOCIAL RESEARCH.** Text in English, Romanian; Summaries in English. 3/yr. EUR 60 (effective 2011). back issues avail. **Document type:** *Journal, Academic/Scholarly.* **Description:** Publishes original research articles on sociology and social/cultural anthropology. Also includes occasional special issues, debates and commentaries that focus on the study of human society, social structures, social change, human behavior as it is shaped by social forces, as well as on any aspects of the scientific study of human beings and culture.
Related titles: Online - full text ed.: ISSN 2069-8534.
Published by: (Universitatea din Bucuresti, Facultatea de Sociologie si Asistenta Sociala/University of Bucharest, Department of Sociology and Social Work), Polirom Publishing Ltd., Bulevardul Carol I nr.4, etaj 4, CP 15-728, OP 53, Bucharest, 700506, Romania. TEL 40-23-2214111, FAX 40-23-2214111, office.bucuresti@polirom.ro, http://www.polirom.ro. Ed., R&P, Adv. contact Liviu Chelcea. Pub. Adrian Serban.

301 GBR ISSN 0390-6701
HM3 CODEN: RISOD6
➤ **INTERNATIONAL REVIEW OF SOCIOLOGY.** Key Title: Revue Internationale de Sociologie. Text in English. 1893; N.S. 1990. 3/yr. GBP 425 combined subscription in United Kingdom to institutions (print & online eds.); EUR 563, USD 707 combined subscription to institutions (print & online eds.) (effective 2012). adv. bk.rev. back issues avail.; reprint service avail. from PSC. **Document type:** *Journal, Academic/Scholarly.* **Description:** provides a medium through which up-to-date results of interdisciplinary research can be spread across disciplines as well as across continents and cultures.
Related titles: Online - full text ed.: ISSN 1469-9273. GBP 383 in United Kingdom to institutions; EUR 506, USD 636 to institutions (effective 2012) (from IngentaConnect).
Indexed: A01, A02, A03, A08, A22, B07, CA, E01, I13, IBSS, P34, P42, PCI, PSA, RASB, RILM, S02, S03, SCOPUS, SOPODA, SSA, SociolAb, T02, W09.
—IE, Infotrieve, Ingenta. **CCC.**
Published by: (Universita degli Studi di Roma "La Sapienza" ITA), Routledge (Subsidiary of: Taylor & Francis Group), 4 Park Sq, Milton Park, Abingdon, Oxon OX14 4RN, United Kingdom. TEL 44-20-70176000, FAX 44-20-70176336, subscriptions@tandf.co.uk, http://www.routledge.com. Ed. Marisa Ferrari Occhionero. Adv. contact Linda Hann TEL 44-1344-779945. Circ: 450. **Subscr. to:** Taylor & Francis Ltd., Journals Customer Service, Sheepen Pl, Colchester, Essex CO3 3LP, United Kingdom. TEL 44-20-70175544, FAX 44-20-70175198.

➤ **INTERNATIONAL SOCIETY FOR THE SOCIOLOGY OF RELIGION. DIRECTORY.** *see* RELIGIONS AND THEOLOGY

➤ **INTERNATIONAL SOCIETY FOR THE SOCIOLOGY OF RELIGION. NEWSLETTER - BULLETIN.** *see* RELIGIONS AND THEOLOGY

301 GBR ISSN 0268-5809
HM1
➤ **INTERNATIONAL SOCIOLOGY.** Text in English. 1986. bi-m. GBP 567, USD 1,050 to institutions; GBP 579, USD 1,071 combined subscription to institutions (print & online eds.) (effective 2012). illus. Index. back issues avail.; reprint service avail. from PSC. **Document type:** *Journal, Academic/Scholarly.* **Description:** Draws together work of cross-cultural relevance from the international community of sociologists, focusing on fundamental issues of theory and method and on new directions in empirical research.
Related titles: Online - full text ed.: ISSN 1461-7242. GBP 521, USD 964 to institutions (effective 2012).
Indexed: A01, A03, A08, A20, A22, ABS&EES, ASCA, B01, B06, B07, B09, BAS, CA, CMM, CurCont, DIP, E01, ERA, ESPM, FR, FamI, H04, I13, I14, IBR, IBSS, IBZ, M12, P02, P10, P30, P34, P42, P48, P53, P54, PAIS, PCI, PQC, PSA, RASB, RILM, RiskAb, S02, S03, S11, S19, S21, SCOPUS, SOPODA, SSA, SSCI, SSciA, SociolAb, T02, V02, V05, W07, W09.
—BLDSC (4549.574200), IE, Infotrieve, Ingenta, INIST. **CCC.**

Published by: (International Sociological Association ESP), Sage Publications Ltd. (Subsidiary of: Sage Publications, Inc.), 1 Oliver's Yard, 55 City Rd, London, EC1Y 1SP, United Kingdom. TEL 44-20-73248500, FAX 44-20-73248600, info@sagepub.co.uk, http://www.uk.sagepub.com/home.nav. Ed. Christine Inglis. **Subscr. in the Americas to:** Sage Publications, Inc., 2455 Teller Rd, Thousand Oaks, CA 91320. TEL 805-499-9774, FAX 805-499-0871, journals@sagepub.com.

201.6 NLD ISSN 1573-4293
INTERNATIONAL STUDIES IN RELIGION AND SOCIETY. Text in English. 2004. irreg., latest vol.8, 2008. price varies. **Document type:** *Monographic series, Academic/Scholarly.* **Description:** Covers societal themes and their relation to religion from a social scientific point-of-view.
Indexed: IZBG.
Published by: Brill, PO Box 9000, Leiden, 2300 PA, Netherlands. TEL 31-71-5353500, FAX 31-71-5317532, cs@brill.nl. Eds. Lori G Beaman, Peter Beyer.

301 NLD ISSN 0074-8684
➤ **INTERNATIONAL STUDIES IN SOCIOLOGY AND SOCIAL ANTHROPOLOGY.** Text in Dutch. 1963. irreg., latest vol.109, 2008. price varies. **Document type:** *Monographic series, Academic/Scholarly.* **Description:** Discusses anthropological and sociological aspects of development, political change, and related issues.
Incorporates (1972-1989): Monographs and Theoretical Studies in Sociology and Anthropology in Honour of Nels Anderson (0169-9202)
Indexed: IZBG, SociolAb.
—BLDSC (4549.820000), IE, Ingenta. **CCC.**
Published by: Brill, PO Box 9000, Leiden, 2300 PA, Netherlands. TEL 31-71-5353500, FAX 31-71-5317532, cs@brill.nl. Ed. David Sciulli. R&P Elizabeth Venekamp. **Dist. by:** Turpin Distribution Services Ltd., Pegasus Dr, Stratton Business Park, Biggleswade, Bedfordshire SG18 8QB, United Kingdom. TEL 44-1767-604954, FAX 44-1767-601640, custserv@turpin-distribution.com, http://www.turpin-distribution.com/.

➤ **INTERNATIONAL STUDIES IN SOCIOLOGY OF EDUCATION.** *see* EDUCATION—Teaching Methods And Curriculum

302.23 DEU ISSN 1437-3904
INTERNET COMMUNICATION. Text in English, German. 1999. irreg., latest vol.6, 2005. price varies. **Document type:** *Monographic series, Academic/Scholarly.*
Published by: Peter Lang GmbH (Subsidiary of: Peter Lang Publishing Group), Eschborner Landstr 42-50, Frankfurt Am Main, 60489, Germany. TEL 49-69-7807050, FAX 49-69-78070550, zentrale.frankfurt@peterlang.com. Eds. Thomas Koehler, Wolfgang Frindte.

302.23 NZL ISSN 1176-421X
INTERSECTION; journal of contemporary screen. Text in English. 2004. bi-m. **Document type:** *Journal, Academic/Scholarly.* **Description:** Investigates contemporary questions that illuminate the understanding of film, games, television, and other media.
Media: Online - full text.
Published by: University of Waikato, Screen & Media Department, Private Bag 3105, Hamilton, New Zealand. Ed. Mark McGeady.

301 302.23 USA ISSN 1528-610X
INTERSECTIONS IN COMMUNICATIONS AND CULTURE; global approaches and transdisciplinary perspectives. Text in English. 2001. irreg., latest vol.25, 2009. price varies. **Document type:** *Monographic series, Academic/Scholarly.* **Description:** Aims to publish as wide a range of new critical scholarship as is possible that seeks to engage and transcend the disciplinary isolationism and genre confinement that now characterize so much of contemporary research in communication studies and related fields.
Published by: Peter Lang Publishing, Inc. (Subsidiary of: Peter Lang Publishing Group), 29 Broadway, New York, NY 10006. TEL 212-647-7700, 800-770-5264, FAX 212-647-7707, customerservice@plang.com, http://www.peterlangusa.com. Eds. Angharad N Valdiva, Cameron McCarthy.

301 ESP ISSN 1887-3898
HM409
INTERSTICIOS; revista sociologica de pensamiento critico. Text in Spanish, English, Italian. 2007. s-a. free (effective 2011).
Media: Online - full text.
Published by: Universidad de Murcia, Facultad de Economia y Empresa, Campus de Espinardo s/n, Murcia, 30100, Spain. Ed. Miguel A V Ferreira.

301 ARG ISSN 0020-9961
INVESTIGACIONES EN SOCIOLOGIA. Text in Spanish. 1962. a. USD 6. bk.rev. abstr.; charts; illus.; tr.lit. index. **Document type:** *Academic/Scholarly.*
Published by: Universidad Nacional de Cuyo, Instituto de Sociologia, Casilla de Correos 345, Mendoza, 5500, Argentina. TEL 61-253010, FAX 61-380457.

307 USA ISSN 1059-2504
IOWA STATE UNIVERSITY. CENTER FOR AGRICULTURAL AND RURAL DEVELOPMENT. STAFF REPORT. Text in English. 1986. irreg. **Document type:** *Monographic series, Trade.* **Description:** Provides information about agricultural and rural development.
Indexed: Agr.
Published by: Iowa State University, Center for Agricultural and Rural Development, 578 Heady Hall, Ames, IA 5001. TEL 515-294-1183, FAX 515-294-6336, babcock@iastate.edu, http://www.card.iastate.edu.

305.412 DEU
IPHIS - GENDER STUDIES IN DEN ALTERTUMSWISSENSCHAFTEN; Beitraege zur altertumswissenschaftlichen Genderforschung. Text in German. 2002. irreg., latest vol.3, 2005. price varies. **Document type:** *Monographic series, Academic/Scholarly.*
Published by: Wissenschaftlicher Verlag Trier, Bergstr 27, Trier, 54295, Germany. TEL 49-651-41503, FAX 49-651-41504, wvt@wvttrier.de, http://www.wvttrier.de.

302.3 USA ISSN 1540-7497
JV8790
➤ **IRINKERINDO**; a journal of African migration. Text in English. 2002. irreg., latest no.3, 2004. free (effective 2011). **Document type:** *Journal, Academic/Scholarly.* **Description:** Devoted to the study of African migration and immigration to other parts of the world.
Media: Online - full text.
Indexed: CA, IBSS, IIBP, S02, S03, SociolAb, T02.
Published by: Brooklyn College, Deptartment of Political Science, 3413 James Hall, Brooklyn, NY 11210. TEL 718-951-5306, FAX 718-951-4833, sallyb@brooklyn.cuny.edu, http://www.brooklyn.cuny.edu.

301 GBR ISSN 0791-6035
HM22.I73 CODEN: IJSOEH
➤ **IRISH JOURNAL OF SOCIOLOGY.** Text in English, Irish. 1991. s-a. GBP 130, EUR 169, USD 169 to institutions (effective 2010). bk.rev. back issues avail. **Document type:** *Journal, Academic/Scholarly.*
Related titles: Online - full text ed.: (from IngentaConnect).
Indexed: A01, A03, A08, C23, CA, IBSS, P34, S02, S03, SCOPUS, SOPODA, SSA, SociolAb, T02.
—BLDSC (4572.400000), IE, Ingenta.
Published by: (Sociological Association of Ireland IRL), Manchester University Press, Oxford Rd, Manchester, Lancs M13 9NR, United Kingdom. TEL 44-161-2752310, FAX 44-161-2743346, mup@manchester.ac.uk. Eds. Kathy Glavanis-Grantham, Tracey Skillington.

303.4833 GBR ISSN 2042-5678
➤ **ISCHANNEL**; the information systems student journal. Variant title: Information Systems Channel. Text in English. 2006. a. free (effective 2010). back issues avail. **Document type:** *Journal, Academic/Scholarly.* **Description:** Deals with the development, applications and impact of information technology in organizations and society at large.
Related titles: Online - full text ed.: ISSN 2042-5686. free (effective 2010).
Published by: Information Systems and Innovation Group, Department of Management, London School of Economics, Houghton St, London, WC2A 2AE, United Kingdom. TEL 44-20-74057686, management@lse.ac.uk. Ed. Gabe Chomic.

306.7 610 570 PRT ISSN 1647-4147
▼ **ISEX**; cadernos de sexologia. Text in Portuguese. 2009. s-a. **Document type:** *Journal, Academic/Scholarly.*
Related titles: Online - full text ed.: ISSN 1647-4155.
Published by: Universidade Lusofona de Humanidades e Tecnologia, Edicoes Universitarias, Campo Grande 376, Lisbon, 1749-024, Portugal. TEL 351-217-515500, FAX 351-217-577006, http://ulusofona.pt.

303.6 GBR
ISLAND PAMPHLETS. Text in English. irreg. EUR 1.50 for each title (effective 2001). 32 p./no.
Published by: Island Publications, 132 Serpentine Road, Newtownabbey, Co Antrim BT36 7JQ, United Kingdom. TEL 28-90778771. Ed. Michael Hall.

L'ITALIA COOPERATIVA. *see* BUSINESS AND ECONOMICS—Cooperatives

301 ARG ISSN 1851-3719
ITINERARIOS. Text in Spanish. 2007. a.
Published by: (Universidad Nacional de Rosario, Facultad de Ciencias Politicas y Relaciones Internacionales), Universidad Nacional de Rosario, Editorial, Urquiza 2050, Rosario, 2000, Argentina. TEL 54-341-4470053, FAX 54-341-4802687, editora@sede.unr.edu.ar, http://www.unreditora.unr.edu.ar/.

ITINERARIUM; rivista multidisciplinare dell'Istituto Teologico "S. Tommaso" Messina. *see* RELIGIONS AND THEOLOGY

JAARBOEK SOCIALE PSYCHOLOGIE. *see* PSYCHOLOGY

302.23 384.5532 DEU ISSN 0949-9997
JAHRBUCH FERNSEHEN. Text in German. 1992. a. EUR 34.90 per issue (effective 2011). **Document type:** *Journal, Academic/Scholarly.*
Published by: Adolf Grimme Institut GmbH, Eduard-Weitsch-Weg 25, Marl, 45768, Germany. TEL 49-2365-91890, FAX 49-2365-918989, info@grimme-institut.de.

201.6 DEU ISSN 0075-2584
HN30
JAHRBUCH FUER CHRISTLICHE SOZIALWISSENSCHAFTEN. Text in German. 1960. a. price varies. **Document type:** *Academic/Scholarly.*
Indexed: A21, CERDIC, DIP, FR, IBR, IBSS, IBZ, PCI, RI-1, RI-2.
—INIST.
Published by: (Westfaelische Wilhelms-Universitaet Muenster, Institut fuer Christliche Sozialwissenschaften), Regensberg Druck und Verlags GmbH, Postfach 6667, Muenster, 48035, Germany. TEL 49-251-74980-0, FAX 49-251-7498040.

301 DEU ISSN 0177-4093
JAHRBUCH FUER VERGLEICHENDE SOZIALFORSCHUNG. Text in German. 1984. a. **Document type:** *Journal, Academic/Scholarly.* **Description:** Covers ethnic relations, social comparative research, migration and refugees.
Formerly: Jahrbuch zur Geschichte und Gesellschaft des Vorderen und Mittleren Orients
Indexed: IBR, IBZ.
Published by: (Berliner Institut fuer Vergleichende Sozialforschung), Edition Parabolis, Schliemannstr 23, Berlin, 10437, Germany. TEL 49-30-44651065, FAX 49-30-4441085, info@emz-berlin.de, http://www.emz-berlin.de. Ed. Jutta Aumueller. R&P Jochen Blaschke.

JAKIN/SABER. *see* PHILOSOPHY

301 JPN ISSN 0021-5414
HM415
JAPANESE SOCIOLOGICAL REVIEW/SHAKAIGAKU HYORON. Text in Japanese; Contents page in English. 1950. q. adv. index.
Indexed: CA, FR, RASB, S02, S03, SCOPUS, SOPODA, SSA, SociolAb, T02.
—Ingenta.
Published by: (The Japan Sociological Society/Nippon Shakai Gakkai), Yuhikaku Publishing Co. Ltd., 2-17, Kanda Jimbo-cho, Chiyoda-ku, Tokyo, 101-0051, Japan. Circ: 1,200.

302 AUS ISSN 1037-1397
DS801
➤ **JAPANESE STUDIES.** Text in English. 1991. 3/yr. GBP 318 combined subscription in United Kingdom to institutions (print & online eds.); EUR 420, AUD 467, USD 528 combined subscription to institutions (print & online eds.) (effective 2012). bk.rev.; film rev. illus. Index. reprint service avail. from PSC. **Document type:** *Journal, Academic/Scholarly.* **Description:** Publishes scholarly articles on various aspects of Japan. Includes general editions and guest-edited thematic issues on such themes as postwar politics, environmental issues, popular culture, and literature.
Related titles: Online - full text ed.: ISSN 1469-9338. GBP 286 in United Kingdom to institutions; EUR 379, AUD 420, USD 475 to institutions (effective 2012) (from IngentaConnect).
Indexed: A01, A03, A08, A22, AmH&L, AmHI, B21, BAS, CA, DIP, E01, E17, ESPM, H07, HistAb, I02, IBR, IBZ, L&LBA, MLA-IB, P34, P42, PAIS, PSA, R02, S02, S03, SCOPUS, SociolAb, T02.
—IE, Infotrieve, Ingenta. **CCC.**
Published by: Routledge (Subsidiary of: Taylor & Francis Group), Level 2, 11 Queens Rd, Melbourne, VIC 3004, Australia. TEL 61-03-90098134, FAX 61-03-98668822, http://www.informaworld.com. Ed. Judith Snodgrass. **Subscr. in N. America to:** Taylor & Francis Inc., Customer Services Dept, 325 Chestnut St, 8th Fl, Philadelphia, PA 19106. TEL 215-625-8900, 800-354-1420, FAX 215-625-2940, orders@taylorandfrancis.com; **Subscr. to:** Taylor & Francis Ltd., Journals Customer Service, Sheepen Pl, Colchester, Essex CO3 3LP, United Kingdom. TEL 44-20-70175544, FAX 44-20-70175198.

➤ **JARLIBRO.** *see* LINGUISTICS

➤ **JASZKUNSAG**; social and artistic journal. *see* LITERATURE

306 LUX
LE JEUDI; hebdomadaire Luxembourgeois en francais. Text in French. 1997. w. EUR 72 domestic; EUR 98 foreign (effective 2005). adv. 36 p./no. 6 cols./p.; back issues avail. **Document type:** *Consumer.* **Description:** Describes social, political and cultural conditions in Luxembourg.
Related titles: Online - full text ed.
Published by: Editpress Luxembourg SA, 44 rue du Canal, Esch-sur-Alzette, L-4050, Luxembourg. TEL 352-220550, FAX 352-220544. Adv. contact Yves Gordet.

307.14 305.23 NLD ISSN 1879-5641
JEUGD IN GELDERLAND. Text in Dutch. 1995. 5/yr.
Former titles (until 2009): Spectrum Nieuwsbrief Jeugdzorg (1572-5650); (until 2003): Samenwerkingsverband Jeugdhulpverlening Gelderland. Nieuwsbrief (1385-6421)
Published by: Spectrum C M O Gelderland, Postbus 8007, Velp, 6880 CA, Netherlands. TEL 31-26-3846200, FAX 31-26-3846300, info@spectrum-gelderland.nl, http://www.spectrum-gelderland.nl. Ed. Marcia Veenhuis. Circ: 1,300.

303.4 FRA ISSN 1960-2472
JEUNESSE ET NON-VIOLENCE; education a la non-violence. Text in French. 2007. q. EUR 10 (effective 2007). **Document type:** *Magazine, Consumer.*
Published by: Association Jeunesse et Non-Violence, La Borie Noble, Roqueredonde, 34650, France. TEL 33-6-65485261, FAX 33-4-67572020, j.n.v@hotmail.fr.

JIKKEN SHAKAI SHINRIGAKU KENKYU/JAPANESE JOURNAL OF EXPERIMENTAL SOCIAL PSYCHOLOGY. *see* PSYCHOLOGY

301 FIN ISSN 1455-0377
JOENSUUN YLIOPISTO. SOSIOLOGIAN LAITOS. SOSIOLOGIAN TURKIMUKSIA/UNIVERSITY OF JOENSUU. DEPARTMENT OF SOCIOLOGY. STUDIES IN SOCIOLOGY. Text in English, Finnish. 1997. irreg. **Document type:** *Monographic series, Academic/Scholarly.*
Published by: Joensuun Yliopisto, Sosiologian Laitos/University of Joensuu. Department of Sociology, PO Box 111, Helsinki, 80101, Finland. TEL 358-13-251111, FAX 358-13-2512050, intnl@joensuun.fi, http://www.joensuun.fi.

JORDENS FOLK; etnografisk revy. *see* ANTHROPOLOGY

303.842 338.91 FRA ISSN 1560-9790
LE JOURNAL DE L'AGENCE INTERGOUVERNEMENTALE DE LA FRANCOPHONIE. Text in French. 1990. q. **Document type:** *Journal.* **Description:** Covers the various activities of the Agency in the fields of education, culture and communications, technical cooperation and economic development, judicial cooperation in Francophone countries.
Former titles (until 1998): Journal de l'Agence de la Francophonie (1560-3903); (until 1998): Lettre de la Francophonie (1019-1518)
Published by: Agence de Cooperation Culturelle et Technique, 13 quai Andre Citroen, Paris, 75015, France. TEL 33-1-44-37-33-00. Ed. Jean Louis Roy.

JOURNAL FOR CRIME, CONFLICT AND MEDIA CULTURE. *see* LAW

THE JOURNAL FOR CULTURAL AND RELIGIOUS THEORY. *see* RELIGIONS AND THEOLOGY

303.482 USA
JOURNAL FOR INTERCULTURAL HISTORY. Text in English. 1999. irreg. **Description:** Dedicated to documenting and preserving our intercultural history.
Published by: Society for Intercultural History, 29 Ball Dr, Athens, OH 45701.

306.85 USA
JOURNAL FOR LIVING; a quarterly for empowering families. Abbreviated title: J F L. Text in English. 1994. q. USD 22 domestic; USD 30 in Canada & Mexico; USD 38 elsewhere (effective 2003). adv. bk.rev. illus. 68 p./no.; back issues avail.; reprints avail. **Document type:** *Magazine, Consumer.* **Description:** Specializes in in-depth interviews and articles with cultural and spiritual leaders, experiential essays and stories by a wide range of contributors.
Formerly (until 2000): Journal of Family Life (1078-4667)
Indexed: Faml.
Published by: Free School Press, 22 Elm St, Albany, NY 12202-1703. TEL 518-465-0582, FAX 518-462-6836. R&P Frank Houde. Adv. contact Chris Mercogliano TEL 518-449-5759. page USD 300; 7 x 9. Circ: 4,000 (controlled).

303 ZAF ISSN 1817-4434
THE JOURNAL FOR TRANSDISCIPLINARY RESEARCH IN SOUTHERN AFRICA. Text in English. 2005. s-a.
Published by: North-West University/Yunibesiti ya Bokone-Bophirima Noordwes-Universiteit, PO Box 1174, Vanderbijlpark, 1900, South Africa. TEL 27-16-9503451.

JOURNAL HUMAN PERFORMANCE IN EXTREME ENVIRONMENTS. *see* PSYCHOLOGY

JOURNAL OF ACADEMIC ETHICS. *see* EDUCATION—Higher Education

S

302 301 IND ISSN 0976-4704

▼ ➤ **JOURNAL OF ADVANCES IN DEVELOPMENTAL RESEARCH.** Text in English. 2010. s-a. INR 3,000 domestic to institutions; USD 200 foreign to institutions; USD 5,000 domestic to corporations; USD 400 foreign to corporations (effective 2010). **Document type:** *Journal, Academic/Scholarly.* **Description:** Publishes research articles, general articles, research communications, review article and abstracts of theses from the fields of science, social sciences, sports science, humanities, medical, education, engineering, technology, biotechnology, home science, computer, history, arts and other fields which participates in overall development of society. Aimed to rapidly disseminate the outcomes of research in the fields related with overall development of society. It provides platform to discuss current and future trends of research and their role in development of society.

Related titles: Online - full text ed.: ISSN 0976-4844. free (effective 2011).

Published by: Gujarat Vidyapeeth University, Biogas Research and Extension Centre, Sadra Post, Gandhinagar, Gujarat 380 014, India. TEL 91-79-27540746, FAX 91-79-27542547, pshilpkar@yahoo.com, http://www.gujaratvidyapith.ac.in. Eds. Mayur Shah, Prateek Shilpkar, Sunil Dadhich.

303 200 KEN

JOURNAL OF AFRICAN CULTURES AND RELIGION. Text in English. 2004. s-a.

Formerly: African Cultures and Religion (1818-5401)

Published by: Maryknoll Institute of African Studies, PO Box 15199, Lang'ata, 00509, Kenya. TEL 254-20-890765, FAX 254-20-891145, miasmu@tangaza.org.

302.23 GBR ISSN 2040-199X

▼ ➤ **JOURNAL OF AFRICAN MEDIA STUDIES.** Abbreviated title: J A M S. Text in English. 2009. 3/yr. GBP 180 domestic to institutions; GBP 189 in the European Union to institutions; USD 290 in US & Canada to institutions; GBP 192 elsewhere to institutions (effective 2011). adv. bk.rev.; film rev. back issues avail. **Document type:** *Journal, Academic/Scholarly.* **Description:** Provides a forum for debate on the historical and contemporary aspects of media and communication in Africa.

Related titles: Online - full text ed.: ISSN 1751-7974. USD 220 in US & Canada to institutions; GBP 147 elsewhere to institutions (effective 2011).

Indexed: ArtHuCI, CA, CMM, CommAb, CurCont, SSCI, T02, W07.

Published by: Intellect Ltd., The Mill, Parnall Rd, Fishponds, Bristol, BS16 3JG, United Kingdom. TEL 44-117-9589910, FAX 44-117-9589911, info@intellectbooks.com. Pub. Masoud Yazdani. **Subscr. to:** Turpin Distribution Services Ltd., Pegasus Dr, Stratton Business Park, Biggleswade, Bedfordshire SG18 8QB, United Kingdom. TEL 44-1767-604951, FAX 44-1767-601640, custserv@turpin-distribution.com, http://www.turpin-distribution.com/.

➤ **JOURNAL OF AGING & SOCIAL POLICY**; a journal devoted to aging & social policy. *see* GERONTOLOGY AND GERIATRICS

➤ **THE JOURNAL OF APPLIED BEHAVIORAL SCIENCE.** *see* PSYCHOLOGY

301 USA ISSN 1936-7244
HM403

➤ **JOURNAL OF APPLIED SOCIAL SCIENCE.** Text in English. 1984. s-a. USD 187 combined subscription in US & Canada to institutions (print & online eds.); USD 207 combined subscription elsewhere to institutions (print & online eds.) (effective 2011). bk.rev. **Document type:** *Journal, Academic/Scholarly.* **Description:** Publishes original research articles, essays, research reports, teaching notes, and book reviews on a wide range of topics of interest to the sociological practitioner.

Formerly (until 2007): Journal of Applied Sociology (0749-0232)

Related titles: Online - full text ed.: ISSN 1937-0245.

Indexed: ASSIA, CA, FamI, S02, S03, SCOPUS, SociolAb, T02.

Published by: (Association for Applied and Clinical Sociology), Paradigm Publishers, 2845 Wilderness Pl, Ste 200, Boulder, CO 80301. TEL 303-245-9054, FAX 303-265-9051, journals@paradigmpublishers.com. Ed. Jammie Price.

302.23 GBR ISSN 1751-9411

JOURNAL OF ARAB & MUSLIM MEDIA RESEARCH. Abbreviated title: J A M M R. Text in English. 2008. 3/yr. GBP 210 domestic to institutions; GBP 219 in the European Union to institutions; USD 330 in US & Canada to institutions; GBP 222 elsewhere to institutions (effective 2011). adv. back issues avail. **Document type:** *Journal, Academic/Scholarly.* **Description:** Aims to lead the debate about emerging rapid changes in media and society in Arab and Muslim parts of the world.

Related titles: Online - full text ed.: ISSN 1751-942X. USD 265 in US & Canada to institutions; GBP 177 elsewhere to institutions (effective 2011).

Indexed: CA, CMM, CommAb, T02.

—BLDSC (4947.163050). **CCC.**

Published by: Intellect Ltd., The Mill, Parnall Rd, Fishponds, Bristol, BS16 3JG, United Kingdom. TEL 44-117-9589910, FAX 44-117-9589911, info@intellectbooks.com. Ed. Noureddine Miladi. Pub. Masoud Yazdani. **Subscr. to:** Turpin Distribution Services Ltd., Pegasus Dr, Stratton Business Park, Biggleswade, Bedfordshire SG18 8QB, United Kingdom. TEL 44-1767-604951, FAX 44-1767-601640, custserv@turpin-distribution.com, http://www.turpin-distribution.com/.

302.23 658.45 NLD ISSN 2211-4742

▼ **JOURNAL OF ARGUMENTATION IN CONTEXT.** Text in English. 2012. 3/yr. EUR 280 combined subscription (print & online eds.) (effective 2012). **Document type:** *Journal, Academic/Scholarly.* **Description:** Covers the role of argumentation in political, legal, medical, financial, commercial, academic, educational, problem-solving and interpersonal communications.

Related titles: Online - full text ed.: ISSN 2211-4750. EUR 272 (effective 2012).

Published by: John Benjamins Publishing Co., PO Box 36224, Amsterdam, 1020 ME, Netherlands. TEL 31-20-6304747, FAX 31-20-6739773, subscription@benjamins.nl, http://www.benjamins.com. Eds. Bart Garssen, Frans H van Eemeren.

301 GBR ISSN 1460-7425
H61.3

JOURNAL OF ARTIFICIAL SOCIETIES AND SOCIAL SIMULATION; an inter-disciplinary journal for the exploration and understanding of social processes by means of computer simulation. Abbreviated title: J A S S. Text in English. 1998. q. **Document type:** *Journal, Academic/Scholarly.*

Related titles: Online - full text ed.: free (effective 2011).

Indexed: A20, A39, C27, C29, CA, CurCont, D03, D04, E13, IBSS, R14, S02, S03, S14, S15, S18, SCOPUS, SSA, SSCI, SociolAb, T02, W07.

—CCC.

Published by: University of Surrey, Department of Sociology, Faculty of Arts & Human Sciences, Guildford, GU2 7XH, United Kingdom. TEL 44-1483-259365, FAX 44-1483-259551, information@surrey.ac.uk, http://www.soc.surrey.ac.uk/. Ed. Nigel Gilbert.

973.0495 USA ISSN 1097-2129
E184.O6

➤ **JOURNAL OF ASIAN AMERICAN STUDIES.** Abbreviated title: J A A S. Text in English. 1998. 3/yr. USD 120 to institutions; USD 168 combined subscription to institutions (print & online eds.); USD 48 per issue to institutions (effective 2012). adv. bk.rev. illus. 110 p./no.; back issues avail.; reprint service avail. from PSC. **Document type:** *Journal, Academic/Scholarly.* **Description:** Explores all aspects of Asian American experiences. Brings out works of scholarly interest to the field, including new theoretical developments, research results etc.

Related titles: Online - full text ed.: ISSN 1096-8598. 1998. USD 125 to institutions (effective 2012).

Indexed: A22, AmH&L, BAS, CA, DIP, E01, HistAb, IBR, IBZ, M08, MLA-IB, P02, P10, P48, P53, P54, PQC, S02, S03, SociolAb, T02.

—IE, Infotrieve. **CCC.**

Published by: (Association for Asian American Studies), The Johns Hopkins University Press, 2715 N Charles St, Baltimore, MD 21218. TEL 410-516-6900, FAX 410-516-6968, bjs@press.jhu.edu. Ed. Huping Ling. Pub. William M Breichner. **Subscr. to:** PO Box 19966, Baltimore, MD 21211. TEL 410-516-6987, 800-548-1784, FAX 410-516-3866, jrnlcirc@press.jhu.edu.

306 GBR ISSN 0021-9096
DT1

➤ **JOURNAL OF ASIAN AND AFRICAN STUDIES.** Abbreviated title: J A A S. Text in English. 1965. bi-m. USD 877, GBP 474 combined subscription to institutions (print & online eds.); USD 859, GBP 465 to institutions (effective 2011). adv. back issues avail.; reprints avail. **Document type:** *Journal, Academic/Scholarly.* **Description:** Offers a scholarly account of studies of individuals, societies and cultures in the nations of Asia and Africa. Continued in part by African and Asian Studies, published by Brill Academic Publishers.

Related titles: Online - full text ed.: ISSN 1745-2538. USD 789, GBP 427 to institutions (effective 2011) (from IngentaConnect).

Indexed: A01, A02, A03, A08, A20, A21, A22, A25, A26, AICP, AmH&L, AnthLit, B04, BAS, BRD, CA, DIP, E01, E08, ESPM, FR, FamI, G08, GEOBASE, H09, HistAb, I02, I05, I08, I14, IBR, IBSS, IBZ, IIBP, LeftInd, M10, MLA-IB, P02, P10, P27, P30, P34, P42, P48, P53, P54, PCI, PQC, PRA, PSA, R02, R05, RI-1, RILM, RefZh, RiskAb, S02, S03, S05, S08, S09, S23, SCOPUS, SSAI, SSAb, SSI, SSciA, SociolAb, T02, W03, W09.

—BLDSC (4947.230000), Infotrieve, Ingenta, INIST. **CCC.**

Published by: Sage Publications Ltd. (Subsidiary of: Sage Publications, Inc.), 1 Oliver's Yard, 55 City Rd, London, EC1Y 1SP, United Kingdom. TEL 44-20-73248500, FAX 44-20-73248600, info@sagepub.co.uk, http://www.uk.sagepub.com/home.nav. Ed. Nigel C Gibson. adv.: B&W page GBP 450; 140 x 210. **Subscr. in the Americas to:** Sage Publications, Inc., 2455 Teller Rd, Thousand Oaks, CA 91320. TEL 805-499-9774, FAX 805-499-0871, journals@sagepub.com.

156 GBR ISSN 0021-9320
HQ750.A1 CODEN: JBSLAR

➤ **JOURNAL OF BIOSOCIAL SCIENCE.** Abbreviated title: J B S. Text in English. 1909. bi-m. GBP 350, USD 580 to institutions; GBP 355, USD 600 combined subscription to institutions (print & online eds.) (effective 2012). adv. bk.rev. index, cum.index: 1969-1978. back issues avail.; reprint service avail. from PSC. **Document type:** *Journal, Academic/Scholarly.* **Description:** Contains material dealing with the common ground between biology and sociology, including reproduction and its control, gerontology, ecology, genetics, applied psychology, sociology, education, criminology, demography, health and epidemiology.

Supersedes in part (in 1969): Eugenics Review (0374-7573)

Related titles: Online - full text ed.: ISSN 1469-7599. GBP 295, USD 500 to institutions (effective 2012); Supplement(s): ISSN 0300-9645. 1969.

Indexed: A20, A22, A36, AICP, AMHA, ASCA, AbAn, B25, B28, BAS, BIOSIS Prev, C06, C07, CA, CABA, CLFP, CurCont, D01, DentInd, E-psyche, E01, EMBASE, ESPM, ExcerpMed, F09, FR, FamI, G10, GH, H17, HPNRM, IBR, IBSS, IBZ, ISR, IndMed, LT, M10, MEA&I, MEDLINE, MycolAb, N02, N03, P02, P03, P10, P20, P22, P24, P25, P27, P30, P33, P39, P48, P50, P52, P53, P54, P56, PCI, PQC, PopulInd, PsycInfo, PsycholAb, R08, R10, R12, RRTA, Reac, S02, S03, S11, S21, SCOPUS, SOPODA, SSA, SSCI, SSciA, SociolAb, T02, T05, TAR, THA, W07, W09, W11.

—BLDSC (4954.100000), GNLM, IE, Infotrieve, Ingenta, INIST. **CCC.**

Published by: Cambridge University Press, The Edinburgh Bldg, Shaftesbury Rd, Cambridge, CB2 8RU, United Kingdom. TEL 44-1223-312393, FAX 44-1223-315052, journals@cambridge.org, http://www.cambridge.org/uk. Ed. C G N Mascie Taylor. R&P Linda Nicol TEL 44-1223-325702. Adv. contact Rebecca Roberts TEL 44-1223-325083. **Subscr. to:** Cambridge University Press, 32 Ave of the Americas, New York, NY 10013. TEL 212-337-5000, FAX 212-691-3239, journals_subscriptions@cup.org.

➤ **JOURNAL OF BUSINESS & SOCIAL STUDIES.** *see* BUSINESS AND ECONOMICS

302.23 649 GBR ISSN 1748-2798

➤ **JOURNAL OF CHILDREN AND MEDIA.** Text in English. 2007. q. GBP 304 combined subscription in United Kingdom to institutions (print & online eds.); EUR 404, USD 503 combined subscription to institutions (print & online eds.) (effective 2012). adv. back issues avail.; reprint service avail. from PSC. **Document type:** *Journal, Academic/Scholarly.* **Description:** Provides a space for discussion by scholars and professionals from around the world and across theoretical and empirical traditions who are engaged in the study of media in the lives of children.

Related titles: Online - full text ed.: ISSN 1748-2801. GBP 274 in United Kingdom to institutions; EUR 363, USD 453 to institutions (effective 2012).

Indexed: A22, BrHumI, CA, CMM, CommAb, E01, P50, T02.

—IE. **CCC.**

Published by: Routledge (Subsidiary of: Taylor & Francis Group), 4 Park Sq, Milton Park, Abingdon, Oxon OX14 4RN, United Kingdom. TEL 44-20-70176000, FAX 44-20-70176336, subscriptions@tandf.co.uk, http://www.routledge.com. Ed. Dafna Lemish TEL 972-3-6407407. Adv. contact Linda Hann TEL 44-1344-779945. **Subscr. to:** Taylor & Francis Ltd., Journals Customer Service, Sheepen Pl, Colchester, Essex CO3 3LP, United Kingdom. TEL 44-20-70175544, FAX 44-20-70175198.

➤ **JOURNAL OF CIVIL SOCIETY.** *see* POLITICAL SCIENCE

300 GBR ISSN 1468-795X
HM447

➤ **JOURNAL OF CLASSICAL SOCIOLOGY.** Abbreviated title: J C S. Text in English. 2001 (Mar.). q. USD 947, GBP 512 combined subscription to institutions (print & online eds.); USD 928, GBP 502 to institutions (effective 2011). adv. back issues avail.; reprint service avail. from PSC. **Document type:** *Journal, Academic/Scholarly.* **Description:** Focuses on international contributions to the classical tradition. It will elucidate the origins of sociology and also demonstrate how the classical tradition renews the sociological imagination in the present day. It will be a critical but constructive reflection on the roots and formation of sociology from the enlightment to the twenty first century.

Related titles: Online - full text ed.: ISSN 1741-2897. USD 852, GBP 461 to institutions (effective 2011).

Indexed: A01, A03, A08, A22, B07, CA, DIP, E01, ERA, FR, FamI, I13, IBR, IBSS, IBZ, P03, P42, PSA, PsycInfo, PsycholAb, S02, S03, S21, SCOPUS, SociolAb, T02.

—BLDSC (4958.369470), IE, Ingenta, INIST. **CCC.**

Published by: Sage Publications Ltd. (Subsidiary of: Sage Publications, Inc.), 1 Oliver's Yard, 55 City Rd, London, EC1Y 1SP, United Kingdom. TEL 44-20-73248500, FAX 44-20-73248600, info@sagepub.co.uk, http://www.uk.sagepub.com/home.nav. Eds. Bryan S Turner, John O'Neill, Simon Susen. adv.: B&W page GBP 350; 130 x 205. **Subscr. in the Americas to:** Sage Publications, Inc., 2455 Teller Rd, Thousand Oaks, CA 91320. TEL 805-499-9774, FAX 805-499-0871, journals@sagepub.com.

302.2 USA ISSN 0021-9916
P87

➤ **JOURNAL OF COMMUNICATION.** Text in English. 1951. q. USD 1,072 combined subscription in the Americas to institutions print & online eds.; GBP 654 combined subscription elsewhere to institutions print & online eds. (effective 2008). adv. bk.rev. charts; illus.; stat. index. back issues avail.; reprint service avail. from PSC. **Document type:** *Journal, Academic/Scholarly.* **Description:** Concerned with the study of communication research, theory, history and policy.

Related titles: Microform ed.: (from PQC); Online - full text ed.: ISSN 1460-2466. GBP 556 to institutions; USD 911 in the Americas to institutions (effective 2008) (from IngentaConnect).

Indexed: A01, A02, A03, A08, A12, A13, A17, A18, A20, A22, A25, A26, A36, ABIn, ABS&EES, APEL, ASCA, AcaI, AmH&L, AmHI, B01, B04, B06, B07, B08, B09, B14, BAS, BRD, BRI, CA, CABA, CADCAM, CBRI, CMM, ChLitAb, CommAb, CurCont, DIP, E-psyche, E01, E02, E03, E06, E07, E08, ERA, ERI, EdA, EdI, F01, F02, FR, FamI, FutSurv, G08, G10, GEOBASE, GH, H07, H08, H09, H14, HAb, HistAb, HumInd, I05, I13, IBR, IBSS, IBZ, IIFP, IITV, IJCS, IPARL, IndMed, Inspec, L&LBA, L04, L13, LISTA, LT, M06, MEA&I, MLA, MLA-IB, N02, N03, P02, P03, P07, P10, P13, P18, P20, P21, P25, P27, P30, P34, P42, P47, P48, P51, P53, P54, PAA&I, PCI, PQC, PRA, PSA, PsycInfo, PsycholAb, R12, RASB, RILM, S02, S03, S05, S08, S09, S21, SCOPUS, SOPODA, SPAA, SSA, SSAI, SSAb, SSCI, SSI, SociolAb, T02, T05, TelAb, V&AA, W03, W07, W09.

—BLDSC (4961.500000), GNLM, IE, Infotrieve, Ingenta, INIST. **CCC.**

Published by: (International Communication Association), Wiley-Blackwell Publishing, Inc. (Subsidiary of: Wiley-Blackwell Publishing Ltd.), Commerce Pl, 350 Main St, Malden, MA 02148. TEL 781-388-8206, 800-835-6770, FAX 781-388-8232, info@wiley.com, http://www.wiley.com/WileyCDA/. Ed. Michael Pfau. adv.: B&W page GBP 220, B&W page USD 365. Circ: 6,150 (paid).

302.23 USA ISSN 0196-8599
P87

➤ **JOURNAL OF COMMUNICATION INQUIRY.** Text in English. 1974. q. USD 385, GBP 226 combined subscription to institutions (print & online eds.); USD 377, GBP 221 to institutions (effective 2011). adv. bk.rev. illus. back issues avail.; reprint service avail. from PSC. **Document type:** *Journal, Academic/Scholarly.* **Description:** Emphasizes interdisciplinary inquiry into communication and mass communication phenomena within cultural and historical perspectives.

Related titles: Online - full text ed.: ISSN 1552-4612. USD 347, GBP 203 to institutions (effective 2011).

Indexed: A01, A02, A03, A08, A22, A26, AmH&L, AmHI, B01, B04, B06, B07, B09, BRD, CA, CMM, CommAb, DIP, E-psyche, E01, E08, FamI, G08, H07, H08, H14, HAb, HistAb, HumInd, I05, IBR, IBZ, MLA-IB, P02, P10, P27, P30, P42, P48, P53, P54, PAIS, PQC, PRA, PSA, RILM, S02, S03, S09, S21, SCOPUS, SOPODA, SPAA, SSA, SSAI, SSAb, SSI, SociolAb, T02, V&AA, W01, W02, W03.

—BLDSC (4961.620000), IE, Infotrieve, Ingenta. **CCC.**

Published by: Sage Publications, Inc., 2455 Teller Rd, Thousand Oaks, CA 91320. TEL 805-499-9774, FAX 805-499-0871, info@sagepub.com. Ed. Robin Johnson. Circ: 1,000 (paid). **Subscr. to:** Sage Publications Ltd., 1 Oliver's Yard, 55 City Rd, London EC1Y 1SP, United Kingdom. TEL 44-207-3248701, FAX 44-207-3248733, subscription@sagepub.co.uk.

302.23 USA ISSN 1940-9338
➤ **JOURNAL OF COMMUNICATION STUDIES.** Text in English. 2008 (Feb.). irreg. USD 99.95 soft cover; USD 149 hard cover (effective 2010). bk.rev. **Document type:** *Journal, Academic/Scholarly.* **Description:** Publishes theoretical and empirical papers and essays that advance an understanding of interpersonal, intercultural or organizational communication processes and effects.
Related titles: Online - full content ed.: ISSN 1940-9346. free.
Published by: Marquette Books LLC, 3107 E 62nd Ave, Spokane, WA 99223. TEL 509-443-7057, FAX 509-448-2191, journals@marquettejournals.org, http://www.marquettebooks.com. Ed. Cary W Horvath.

302 USA ISSN 1935-3537
P87
JOURNAL OF COMMUNICATIONS RESEARCH. Text in English. 2007. q. USD 195 to institutions (effective 2012). **Document type:** *Journal, Academic/Scholarly.* **Description:** Includes language and social interaction, nonverbal communication, interpersonal communication, organizational communication and new technologies, mass communication, health communication, intercultural communication, and developmental issues in communication.
Related titles: Online - full text ed.
Indexed: CA, CMM, CommAb, RefZh, T02.
Published by: Nova Science Publishers, Inc., 400 Oser Ave, Ste 1600, Hauppauge, NY 11788. TEL 631-231-7269, FAX 631-231-8175, main@novapublishers.com.

JOURNAL OF COMMUNITY & APPLIED SOCIAL PSYCHOLOGY. *see* PSYCHOLOGY

▼ **JOURNAL OF COMMUNITY ENGAGEMENT AND HIGHER EDUCATION.** *see* EDUCATION—Higher Education

JOURNAL OF COMMUNITY PSYCHOLOGY. *see* PSYCHOLOGY

307.14 GBR ISSN 1475-9047
THE JOURNAL OF COMMUNITY WORK & DEVELOPMENT. Text in English. 1996. s-a. GBP 20 to individuals; GBP 35 to institutions (effective 2002). adv. **Document type:** *Journal, Academic/Scholarly.* **Description:** Provides a focus for material relating to community development and community work research, theory, policy and practice across a range of disciplines within which these approaches are pursued.
Formerly (until 2000): The Scottish Journal of Community Work & Development (1469-0799)
—BLDSC (4961.775000).
Published by: Community Learning Scotland, Rosebury House, 9 Haymarket Ter, Edinburgh, EH12 5EZ, United Kingdom. TEL 44-131-313-2488, FAX 44-131-313-6800, info@cls.dircon.co.uk. Ed. Alan Barr. **Co-publisher:** Scottish Community Development Centre.

306.85 CAN ISSN 0047-2328
HQ1 CODEN: JCFSAO
➤ **JOURNAL OF COMPARATIVE FAMILY STUDIES.** Abbreviated title: J C F S. Text in English; Summaries in English, French, Spanish. 1970. q. USD 200 to individuals; USD 450 to institutions (effective 2010). adv. bk.rev. abstr.; charts; stat.; illus. cum.index. back issues avail.; reprints avail. **Document type:** *Journal, Academic/Scholarly.* **Description:** Features articles specialized in cross-cultural perspectives of the study of the family.
Related titles: CD-ROM ed.; Microfiche ed.: (from MML); Microform ed.: (from MIM, MML, PQC); Online - full text ed.
Indexed: A01, A02, A03, A08, A20, A22, A25, A26, AEI, APC, ASCA, AnthLit, B04, BAS, BRD, C03, C05, CA, CBCARef, CJA, CLFP, CPE, CPerl, Chicano, CurCont, DIP, E-psyche, E07, E08, EI, ERA, F09, FamI, G05, G06, G07, G08, HPNRM, I05, I07, IBR, IBSS, IBZ, IPsyAb, M12, MEA&I, P02, P03, P10, P12, P13, P21, P25, P27, P30, P46, P48, P53, P54, PCI, PQC, PerIslam, PopulInd, PsycInfo, PsycholAb, R10, RILM, Reac, S02, S03, S08, S09, S21, S23, SCOPUS, SFSA, SOPODA, SRRA, SSA, SSAI, SSAb, SSCI, SSI, SSciA, SociolAb, T02, W03, W05, W07, W09.
—BLDSC (4961.930000), IE, Infotrieve, Ingenta. **CCC.**
Published by: University of Calgary, Department of Sociology, 2500 University Dr N W, Calgary, AB T2N 1N4, Canada. TEL 403-220-7317, FAX 403-282-9298. Ed. James White. adv.: B&W page CAD 300; 5 x 8.

305.8 USA ISSN 0891-2416
HT101
➤ **JOURNAL OF CONTEMPORARY ETHNOGRAPHY**; a journal of ethnographic research. Text in English. 1972. bi-m. USD 848, GBP 499 combined subscription to institutions (print & online eds.); USD 831, GBP 489 to institutions (effective 2011). adv. bk.rev. charts; illus. index. back issues avail.; reprint service avail. from PSC. **Document type:** *Journal, Academic/Scholarly.* **Description:** Takes an interdisciplinary approach to ethnography and qualitative research. Features articles by distinguished scholars and professionals from a variety of disciplines concerned with the study of human nature, behavior, organization and culture.
Former titles: Urban Life (0098-3039); (until vol.15): Urban Life and Culture (0049-5662)
Related titles: Microfilm ed.: (from PQC); Online - full text ed.: ISSN 1552-5414. USD 763, GBP 449 to institutions (effective 2011).
Indexed: A01, A02, A03, A08, A20, A22, A26, AICP, APC, ASCA, AbAn, AnthLit, B04, B07, BRD, CA, CJPI, CMM, CommAb, CurCont, DIP, E-psyche, E01, E08, EI, FR, FamI, G08, H04, H09, I05, I14, IBR, IBSS, IBZ, MEA&I, P02, P03, P06, P10, P13, P25, P27, P30, P48, P53, P54, PCI, PQC, PsycInfo, PsycholAb, RASB, RILM, S02, S03, S05, S09, S11, S21, SCOPUS, SOPODA, SSA, SSAI, SSAb, SSCI, SSI, SUSA, SociolAb, T02, V02, W01, W02, W03, W07, W09.
—BLDSC (4965.228000), IE, Ingenta, INIST. **CCC.**
Published by: Sage Publications, Inc., 2455 Teller Rd, Thousand Oaks, CA 91320. TEL 805-499-9774, 800-818-7243, FAX 805-499-0871, 800-583-2665, info@sagepub.com. Eds. Keny Sandstrom, Marybeth Stalp. Circ: 700 (paid). **Subscr. overseas to:** Sage Publications Ltd., 1 Oliver's Yard, 55 City Rd, London EC1Y 1SP, United Kingdom. TEL 44-207-3248701, FAX 44-207-3248733, subscription@sagepub.co.uk.

➤ **JOURNAL OF CRIMINAL JUSTICE AND POPULAR CULTURE.** *see* CRIMINOLOGY AND LAW ENFORCEMENT

➤ **JOURNAL OF CROSS-CULTURAL PSYCHOLOGY.** *see* PSYCHOLOGY

➤ **JOURNAL OF CULTURAL DIVERSITY**; an interdisciplinary journal. *see* MEDICAL SCIENCES—Nurses And Nursing

307.14 MYS ISSN 0128-3863
P92.2
THE JOURNAL OF DEVELOPMENT COMMUNICATION. Text in English. 1991. s-a. USD 42; USD 23 in developing nations (effective 2005). adv. **Description:** Covers communication research, environment, sustainable development, women's development, and youth and population.
Indexed: A26, CA, CMM, CommAb, E08, I05, P30, S02, S03, S09, SCOPUS, T02.
—Ingenta.
Published by: Asian Institute for Development Communication, Level 1, Block B, Kompleks Pejabat Damansara, Jalan Dungan, Damansara Heights, Kuala Lumpur, 50490, Malaysia. TEL 60-3-20938211, FAX 60-3-20938567, aidcom@streamyx.com.

THE JOURNAL OF DEVELOPMENT STUDIES. *see* BUSINESS AND ECONOMICS—International Development And Assistance

301 150 USA ISSN 1947-301X
▼ **JOURNAL OF DISASTER SOCIOLOGY AND PSYCHOLOGY.** Text in English. forthcoming 2011. q. USD 250 per issue (effective 2009). **Document type:** *Journal, Academic/Scholarly.* **Description:** Features research in sociology and psychology related to disasters.
Related titles: Online - full text ed.: ISSN 1947-3028. forthcoming 2009 (Oct.).
Published by: Weston Medical Publishing, LLC, 470 Boston Post Rd, Weston, MA 02493. TEL 781-899-2702, FAX 781-899-4900, brenda_devito@pnpco.com, http://www.pnpco.com.

JOURNAL OF DIVORCE & REMARRIAGE; research and clinical studies in family theory, family law, family mediation and family therapy. *see* MATRIMONY

THE JOURNAL OF EARLY ADOLESCENCE. *see* CHILDREN AND YOUTH—About

▼ **JOURNAL OF EDUCATION AND SOCIOLOGY.** *see* EDUCATION

JOURNAL OF EDUCATIONAL PRACTICE FOR SOCIAL CHANGE. *see* EDUCATION

170 USA ISSN 1556-2646
➤ **JOURNAL OF EMPIRICAL RESEARCH ON HUMAN RESEARCH ETHICS.** Abbreviated title: J E R H R E. Text in English. 2006 (Apr.). q. USD 440 combined subscription to institutions (print & online eds.) (effective 2012). adv. back issues avail.; reprint service avail. from PSC. **Document type:** *Journal, Academic/Scholarly.* **Description:** Aims to improve ethical problem solving in human research and provide an ongoing basis for the establishment of best practice guidelines.
Related titles: Online - full text ed.: ISSN 1556-2654. USD 341 to institutions (effective 2012).
Indexed: A01, A03, A08, A22, CA, CurCont, E01, EMBASE, ExcerpMed, MEDLINE, P03, P20, P25, P27, P28, P30, P45, P46, P48, P50, P53, P54, PQC, PsycInfo, SCI, SCOPUS, SSCI, W07.
—BLDSC (4977.647500), IE. **CCC.**
Published by: University of California Press, Journals Division, 2000 Ctr St, Ste 303, Berkeley, CA 94704. TEL 510-643-7154, 877-262-4226, FAX 510-642-9917, customerservice@ucpressjournals.com. Ed. Joan E. Sieber. Adv. contact Jennifer Rogers TEL 510-642-6188. Circ: 254. **Subscr. to:** 149 5th Ave, 8th Fl, New York, NY 10010. participation@jstor.org.

➤ **JOURNAL OF ETHICS & SOCIAL PHILOSOPHY**; online peer-reviewed journal of moral, political and legal philosophy. *see* PHILOSOPHY

303.3 USA ISSN 1933-1185
JOURNAL OF ETHICS IN LEADERSHIP. Text in English. 2005. q. USD 15 to individuals; USD 50 to institutions (effective 2010). **Document type:** *Journal, Academic/Scholarly.*
Formerly (until 2005): Crossroads (1553-2003)
Indexed: MLA-IB.
Published by: Kennesaw State University, 1000 Chastain Rd, English Bldg. #27/Ste 220, Kennesaw, GA 30144. TEL 678-797-2169, FAX 678-797-2215, ksupress@kennesaw.edu.

JOURNAL OF EXPERIMENTAL SOCIAL PSYCHOLOGY. *see* PSYCHOLOGY

306.85 USA ISSN 1526-7431
HQ535
➤ **JOURNAL OF FAMILY COMMUNICATION.** Abbreviated title: J F C. Text in English. 2001. q. GBP 294 combined subscription in United Kingdom to institutions (print & online eds.); EUR 392, USD 493 combined subscription to institutions (print & online eds.) (effective 2012). adv. back issues avail.; reprint service avail. from PSC. **Document type:** *Journal, Academic/Scholarly.* **Description:** Publishes articles on all aspects of communication in families.
Related titles: Online - full text ed.: ISSN 1532-7698. 2001. GBP 265 in United Kingdom to institutions; EUR 353, USD 444 to institutions (effective 2012).
Indexed: A01, A03, A08, A22, C06, C07, C08, CA, CINAHL, CMM, CommAb, E-psyche, E01, F09, FamI, L&LBA, P03, P48, P50, PAIS, PQC, PsycInfo, S02, S03, SociolAb, T02.
—BLDSC (4983.667000), IE, Infotrieve, Ingenta. **CCC.**
Published by: Routledge (Subsidiary of: Taylor & Francis Group), 325 Chestnut St, Ste 800, Philadelphia, PA 19106. TEL 800-354-1420, FAX 215-625-2940, http://www.tandf.co.uk/journals, http://www.routledge.com. Ed. Caryn E Medved. Adv. contact Linda Hann TEL 44-1344-779945.

306.85 USA ISSN 0363-1990
HQ503
➤ **JOURNAL OF FAMILY HISTORY**; studies in family, kinship and demography. Text in English. 1976. q. USD 759, GBP 446 combined subscription to institutions (print & online eds.); USD 744, GBP 437 to institutions (effective 2011). adv. bk.rev. charts; illus. Index. back issues avail.; reprint service avail. from PSC. **Document type:** *Journal, Academic/Scholarly.* **Description:** Focuses on historically based studies on families, kinship, and demography. Publishes scholarly research from an international perspective concerning the family as an historical social form, with contributions from the disciplines of history, demography, anthropology, sociology, liberal arts and the humanities.
Supersedes: Family in Historical Perspective (0360-3598)
Related titles: Online - full text ed.: ISSN 1552-5473. USD 683, GBP 401 to institutions (effective 2011).
Indexed: A01, A02, A03, A08, A20, A22, A26, ABS&EES, ASCA, AmH&L, AmHI, B04, B07, BRD, CA, CDA, CurCont, DIP, E-psyche, E01, E02, E03, E07, E08, EI, ERI, EdA, EdI, F09, FR, FamI, G08, G10, H04, H07, H08, H09, H10, HAb, HistAb, HumInd, I05, I14, IBR, IBSS, IBZ, MEA&I, P02, P03, P04, P10, P12, P27, P30, P48, P53, P54, PCI, PQC, PopulInd, PsycInfo, PsycholAb, R10, RASB, Reac, S02, S03, S09, S21, SCOPUS, SFSA, SOPODA, SSA, SSAI, SSAb, SSCI, SSI, SWR&A, SociolAb, T02, V02, W03, W05, W07, W09.
—BLDSC (4983.680000), IE, Infotrieve, Ingenta. **CCC.**
Published by: (National Council on Family Relations), Sage Publications, Inc., 2455 Teller Rd, Thousand Oaks, CA 91320. TEL 805-499-9774, FAX 805-499-0871, info@sagepub.com. Ed. Roderick Phillips. Circ: 1,400. **Subscr. outside the Americas to:** Sage Publications Ltd., 1 Oliver's Yard, 55 City Rd, London EC1Y 1SP, United Kingdom. TEL 44-20-73248701, FAX 44-20-73248733, subscription@sagepub.co.uk.

306.85 USA ISSN 0192-513X
HQ1
➤ **JOURNAL OF FAMILY ISSUES.** Text in English. 1980. 8/yr. USD 1,384, GBP 814 combined subscription to institutions (print & online eds.); USD 1,356, GBP 798 to institutions (effective 2011). adv. illus. Index. back issues avail.; reprint service avail. from PSC. **Document type:** *Journal, Academic/Scholarly.* **Description:** Covers contemporary social issues and problems of marriage and family life and to theoretical and professional issues of current interest to those who work with and study families.
Related titles: Microfiche ed.: (from WSH); Microfilm ed.: (from PMC, WSH); Online - full text ed.: ISSN 1552-5481. USD 1,246, GBP 733 to institutions (effective 2011).
Indexed: A01, A02, A03, A08, A20, A22, A25, A26, ASCA, ASG, Agr, B07, BRD, BibAg, C06, C07, C08, CA, CDA, CINAHL, CLFP, Chicano, CurCont, E-psyche, E01, E02, E03, E07, E08, ERI, ERIC, ESPM, EdA, EdI, F09, FamI, G08, G10, H04, H12, HEA, HPNRM, I05, P02, P03, P04, P07, P10, P12, P13, P18, P25, P27, P30, P34, P48, P53, P54, PCI, PQC, PsycInfo, PsycholAb, RASB, RiskAb, S02, S03, S08, S09, S21, SCOPUS, SFSA, SOPODA, SRRA, SSA, SSAI, SSAb, SSCI, SSI, SSciA, SWR&A, SociolAb, T02, V&AA, V02, W03, W07, W09.
—BLDSC (4983.690000), IE, Infotrieve, Ingenta, Linda Hall. **CCC.**
Published by: (National Council on Family Relations), Sage Publications, Inc., 2455 Teller Rd, Thousand Oaks, CA 91320. TEL 805-499-9774, 800-818-7243, FAX 805-499-0871, 800-583-2665, info@sagepub.com. Ed. Constance Shehan. Circ: 1,500 (paid). **Subscr. outside the Americas to:** Sage Publications Ltd., 1 Oliver's Yard, 55 City Rd, London EC1Y 1SP, United Kingdom. TEL 44-20-73248701, FAX 44-20-73248733, subscription@sagepub.co.uk.

306.85 USA ISSN 1943-8338
▼ ➤ **JOURNAL OF FAMILY LIFE.** Text in English. 2009 (Feb.). q. free (effective 2010). **Document type:** *Journal, Academic/Scholarly.* **Description:** Offers general-interest articles and creative works dealing with how modern families (with an emphasis on the American family) make and transmit meaning in their lives as families through story, myth, ritual and celebration.
Media: Online - full content.
Published by: Emory Center for Myth and Ritual in American Life, Emory University, Emory West Ste 413E, 1256 Briarcliff Rd, Atlanta, GA 30306. TEL 404-727-3440, FAX 404-712-9520, marial@learnlink.emory.edu, http://www.marial.emory.edu. Ed. Marshall Duke.

306.85 USA ISSN 1756-2570
HQ1
▼ **JOURNAL OF FAMILY THEORY & REVIEW.** Text in English. 2009. q. **Document type:** *Journal, Academic/Scholarly.*
Related titles: Online - full text ed.: ISSN 1756-2589 (from IngentaConnect).
Indexed: A22, E01, P30, S02, S03, T02.
—BLDSC (4983.738500), IE. **CCC.**
Published by: (National Council on Family Relations), John Wiley & Sons, Inc., 111 River St, Hoboken, NJ 07030. TEL 201-748-6000, FAX 201-748-5915, info@wiley.com, http://www.wiley.com/WileyCDA/. Ed. Robert Milardo.

JOURNAL OF FAMILY THERAPY. *see* MEDICAL SCIENCES—Psychiatry And Neurology

JOURNAL OF FAMILY VIOLENCE. *see* CRIMINOLOGY AND LAW ENFORCEMENT

JOURNAL OF FLUENCY DISORDERS. *see* PSYCHOLOGY

JOURNAL OF FORECASTING. *see* BUSINESS AND ECONOMICS—Management

THE JOURNAL OF GENDER, RACE & JUSTICE. *see* ETHNIC INTERESTS

JOURNAL OF GENOCIDE RESEARCH. *see* POLITICAL SCIENCE

303 RUS ISSN 2075-8103
▼ ➤ **JOURNAL OF GLOBALIZATION STUDIES.** Text in English. 2010. s-a. RUR 500 domestic to individuals; RUR 600 domestic to institutions (effective 2011). bk.rev. bibl. back issues avail. **Document type:** *Journal, Academic/Scholarly.* **Description:** Provides for a broadly international and multicultural forum on issues associated with globalization, and the influence of globalization on particular cultural-geographic regions.
Related titles: Online - full text ed.
Published by: Izdatel'skii Dom Uchitel', ul Kirova 143, Volgograd, 400079, Russian Federation. TEL 7-8442-420408, FAX 7-8442-421771, redaktor@uchitel-izd.ru, http://www.uchitel-izd.ru. Ed. Andrey Korotayev. Pub. Leonid Grinin. Circ: 200 (paid); 300 (controlled).

➤ **JOURNAL OF HAPPINESS STUDIES**; an interdisciplinary forum on subjective well-being. *see* PSYCHOLOGY

302.23 610 USA ISSN 1940-9354
➤ **JOURNAL OF HEALTH & MASS COMMUNICATION.** Abbreviated title: J H M C. Text in English. 2008. irreg. (2-4/yr). USD 149 (effective 2010). bk.rev. reprints avail. **Document type:** *Journal, Academic/Scholarly.* **Description:** Publishes theoretical and empirical papers and essays that advance an understanding of mass media effects or processes with respect to health-related issues or topics.
Related titles: Online - full text ed.: ISSN 1940-9362. free (effective 2010).
Indexed: P30.

S

Published by: Marquette Books LLC, 3107 E 62nd Ave, Spokane, WA 99223. TEL 509-443-7057, FAX 509-448-2191, journals@marquettejournals.org, http://www.marquettebooks.com. Ed. Fiona Chew.

302 USA ISSN 0022-1465
R11 CODEN: JHSBA5

➤ **JOURNAL OF HEALTH AND SOCIAL BEHAVIOR.** Text in English. 1960. q. USD 255, GBP 150 combined subscription to institutions (print & online eds.); USD 250, GBP 147 to institutions (effective 2011). adv. bk.rev. charts; illus. index. back issues avail.; reprint service avail. from PSC. **Document type:** *Journal, Academic/Scholarly.* **Description:** Publishes reports of empirical studies, theoretical analyses, and synthesizing reviews that employ a sociological perspective to clarify aspects of social life bearing on human health and illness, both physical and mental.
Formerly (until 1967): Journal of Health and Human Behavior (0095-9006)
Related titles: Microform ed.: (from MIM, PQC); Online - full text ed.: ISSN 2150-6000. USD 229, GBP 135 to institutions (effective 2011).
Indexed: A01, A02, A03, A08, A20, A22, A25, A26, ASCA, AbAn, AddicA, B28, BRD, C06, C07, C08, CA, CINAHL, Chicano, CurCont, DIP, E-psyche, E01, E08, EMBASE, ERA, ERIC, ExcerpMed, F09, FR, Faml, G08, G10, H09, H11, H12, H13, I05, IBR, IBZ, INI, IndMed, MEDLINE, P02, P03, P10, P13, P19, P20, P21, P22, P24, P25, P27, P30, P34, P46, P48, P50, P52, P53, P54, P56, PCI, PEI, PQC, PsycInfo, PsycholAb, R10, RASB, Reac, S02, S03, S05, S08, S09, S11, SCOPUS, SFSA, SOPODA, SSA, SSAI, SSAb, SSCI, SSI, SWR&A, SociolAb, T02, W03, W07, W09.
—BLDSC (4996.730000), GNLM, IE, Infotrieve, Ingenta, INIST. **CCC.**
Published by: (American Sociological Association), Sage Publications, Inc., 2455 Teller Rd, Thousand Oaks, CA 91320. TEL 805-499-9774, 800-818-7243, FAX 805-499-0871, 800-583-2665, info@sagepub.com, http://www.sagepub.com. Ed. Eliza K Pavalko. Circ: 3,500 (paid).

306.09 GBR ISSN 0952-1909
HM104

➤ **JOURNAL OF HISTORICAL SOCIOLOGY.** Text in English. 1988. q. GBP 455 in United Kingdom to institutions; EUR 578 in Europe to institutions; USD 913 in the Americas to institutions; USD 1,064 elsewhere to institutions; GBP 524 combined subscription in United Kingdom to institutions (print & online eds.); EUR 665 combined subscription in Europe to institutions (print & online eds.); USD 1,051 combined subscription in the Americas to institutions (print & online eds.); USD 1,224 combined subscription elsewhere to institutions (print & online eds.) (effective 2012). adv. back issues avail.; reprint service avail. from PSC. **Document type:** *Journal, Academic/Scholarly.* **Description:** Provides an international forum for historically informed reflection on human society.
Related titles: Online - full text ed.: ISSN 1467-6443. GBP 455 in United Kingdom to institutions; EUR 578 in Europe to institutions; USD 913 in the Americas to institutions; USD 1,064 elsewhere to institutions (effective 2012) (from IngentaConnect).
Indexed: A01, A02, A03, A08, A20, A22, A26, AICP, ASCA, AmH&L, AmHI, BibInd, BrHumI, CA, CurCont, DIP, E01, E08, ERA, Faml, G08, H05, H07, H14, HistAb, I05, IBR, IBSS, IBZ, LeftInd, M12, P03, P10, P30, P34, P42, P48, P53, P54, PCI, PQC, PSA, PsycInfo, PsycholAb, RASB, S02, S03, S09, S11, S19, S20, S21, SCOPUS, SOPODA, SSA, SSCI, SociolAb, T02, W07.
—BLDSC (5000.493000), IE, Infotrieve, Ingenta. **CCC.**
Published by: Wiley-Blackwell Publishing Ltd. (Subsidiary of: John Wiley & Sons, Inc.), 9600 Garsington Rd, Oxford, OX4 2DQ, United Kingdom. TEL 44-1865-776868, FAX 44-1865-714591, customerservices@blackwellpublishing.com. Adv. contact Craig Pickett TEL 44-1865-476267.

➤ **JOURNAL OF HOMOSEXUALITY.** *see* HOMOSEXUALITY

➤ **JOURNAL OF HUMAN SECURITY.** *see* POLITICAL SCIENCE

➤ **JOURNAL OF HUMAN VALUES.** *see* BUSINESS AND ECONOMICS—Management

302.23 170 GBR ISSN 1477-996X

➤ **JOURNAL OF INFORMATION, COMMUNICATION & ETHICS IN SOCIETY.** Abbreviated title: J I C E S. Text in English. 2003. q. EUR 479 combined subscription in Europe (print & online eds.); USD 589 combined subscription in the Americas (print & online eds.); GBP 339 combined subscription in the UK & elsewhere (print & online eds.); AUD 729 combined subscription in Australasia (print & online eds.) (effective 2012). back issues avail.; reprint service avail. from PSC. **Document type:** *Journal, Academic/Scholarly.* **Description:** Provides an interdisciplinary perspective on the impacts of new media and information and communication technologies on society, organizations, the environment and individuals.
Related titles: Online - full text ed.: ISSN 1758-8871 (from IngentaConnect).
Indexed: L13.
—BLDSC (5006.745500), IE, Ingenta. **CCC.**
Published by: Emerald Group Publishing Ltd., Howard House, Wagon Ln, Bingley, W Yorks BD16 1WA, United Kingdom. TEL 44-1274-777700, FAX 44-1274-785201, information@emeraldinsight.com. Eds. N Ben Fairweather, Simon Rogerson. Pub. Lizzie Scott.

303.4 004 USA ISSN 1938-3436

➤ **THE JOURNAL OF INFORMATION TECHNOLOGY IN SOCIAL CHANGE.** Abbreviated title: J I T S C. Text in English. 2007. q. back issues avail. **Document type:** *Journal, Academic/Scholarly.*
Media: Online - full text.
Published by: Gilbert Center, PO Box 46067, Seattle, WA 98146. TEL 206-201-1726, info@gilbert.org.

301 363.7 GBR ISSN 1943-815X
GE1

➤ **JOURNAL OF INTEGRATIVE ENVIRONMENTAL SCIENCES.** Abbreviated title: J I E S. Text in Dutch, English. 1986. q. GBP 274 combined subscription in United Kingdom to institutions (print & online eds.); EUR 361, USD 453 combined subscription to institutions (print & online eds.) (effective 2012). adv. bk.rev. abstr. 80 p./no.; back issues avail.; reprint service avail. from PSC. **Document type:** *Journal, Academic/Scholarly.* **Description:** Publishes original material including theoretical developments, new empirical data, innovative methods and policy analysis on environmental sciences.
Former titles (until 2009): Environmental Sciences (1569-3430); (until 2004): Milieu (0920-2234)
Related titles: Online - full text ed.: ISSN 1943-8168. GBP 246 in United Kingdom to institutions; EUR 324, USD 408 to institutions (effective 2012) (from IngentaConnect).
Indexed: A22, ASFA, CA, E01, E04, E05, E11, ESPM, PollutAb, SWRA, T02, T04.
—BLDSC (3791.622200), IE, Ingenta. **CCC.**
Published by: (European Federation of Associations of Environmental Professionals BEL, Vereniging van Milieuprofessionals NLD), Taylor & Francis Ltd. (Subsidiary of: Taylor & Francis Group), 4 Park Sq, Milton Park, Abingdon, Oxfordshire OX14 4RN, United Kingdom. TEL 44-20-70176000, FAX 44-20-70176336, subscriptions@tandf.co.uk, http://www.taylorandfrancis.com. Eds. Adrian Martin, Andrew Blowers, Jan J Boersema. **Subscr. to:** Journals Customer Service, Sheepen Pl, Colchester, Essex CO3 3LP, United Kingdom. TEL 44-20-70175544, FAX 44-20-70175198, tf.enquiries@tfinforma.com.

303.482 SWE ISSN 1404-1634
P94.6

➤ **JOURNAL OF INTERCULTURAL COMMUNICATION.** Key Title: Intercultural Communication. Text in English. 1999. q. free (effective 2011). back issues avail. **Document type:** *Journal, Academic/Scholarly.* **Description:** Promotes research in the area of intercultural communication.
Media: Online - full text.
Indexed: A39, C27, C29, CA, CMM, CommAb, D03, D04, E03, E13, ERI, IBSS, R14, S02, S03, S14, S15, S18, SociolAb, T02.
Published by: (Goteborgs Universitet, Institutionen foer Lingvistik/ University of Goeteborg, Department of Linguistics), Immigrant Institutet, Katrinedalsgatan 43, Boraas, 50451, Sweden. TEL 46-33-136070, FAX 46-33-136075, migrant@immi.se. Eds. Jens Allwood TEL 46-31-7731876, Miguel Benito.

➤ **JOURNAL OF INTERCULTURAL STUDIES.** *see* ETHNIC INTERESTS

305 USA ISSN 1535-0770
HM726

➤ **JOURNAL OF INTERGENERATIONAL RELATIONSHIPS.** (Announced as: Intergenerational Programming Quarterly) Text in English. 2003. q. GBP 230 combined subscription in United Kingdom to institutions (print & online eds.); EUR 298, USD 306 combined subscription to institutions (print & online eds.) (effective 2012). adv. reprint service avail. from PSC. **Document type:** *Journal, Academic/Scholarly.* **Description:** Informs gerontologists, educators, medical professionals and urban studies researchers about current practice methods and public policy initiatives.
Related titles: Online - full text ed.: ISSN 1535-0932. GBP 207 in United Kingdom to institutions; EUR 268, USD 276 to institutions (effective 2012).
Indexed: A01, A03, A22, A36, ASG, AgeL, AmHI, C06, C07, CA, CABA, E01, E03, ERI, Faml, GH, H07, IBSS, L01, L02, LT, M02, N02, N03, P03, P30, PsycInfo, R12, RRTA, S02, S03, SCOPUS, SFSA, SSA, SWR&A, SociolAb, T02, W11.
—BLDSC (5007.548400), IE, Ingenta. **CCC.**
Published by: Routledge (Subsidiary of: Taylor & Francis Group), 325 Chestnut St, Ste 800, Philadelphia, PA 19106. TEL 215-625-8900, FAX 215-625-8914, journals@routledge.com, http://www.routledge.com. Ed. Sally Newman. adv.: B&W page USD 315, color page USD 550; trim 6 x 8.5.

➤ **JOURNAL OF INTERGROUP RELATIONS.** *see* POLITICAL SCIENCE—Civil Rights

302.23 USA ISSN 1751-3057

JOURNAL OF INTERNATIONAL AND INTERCULTURAL COMMUNICATION. Text in English. 2008 (Feb.). q. GBP 150 combined subscription in United Kingdom to institutions (print & online eds.); EUR 194, USD 293 combined subscription to institutions (print & online eds.) (effective 2012). reprint service avail. from PSC. **Document type:** *Journal, Academic/Scholarly.* **Description:** Features articles on intercultural communication from a range of theoretical, conceptual and methodological perspectives.
Related titles: Online - full text ed.: ISSN 1751-3065. GBP 136 in United Kingdom to institutions; EUR 177, USD 265 to institutions (effective 2012).
Indexed: A22, CA, CMM, CommAb, E01, PQC, T02.
—IE. **CCC.**
Published by: (National Communication Association), Routledge (Subsidiary of: Taylor & Francis Group), 325 Chestnut St, Ste 800, Philadelphia, PA 19106. TEL 215-625-8900, 800-354-1420, FAX 215-625-2940, orders@taylorandfrancis.com. Ed. Thomas Nakayama.

JOURNAL OF INTERNATIONAL BUSINESS AND CULTURAL STUDIES. *see* BUSINESS AND ECONOMICS

302.23 AUS ISSN 1321-6597
P96.I5

➤ **JOURNAL OF INTERNATIONAL COMMUNICATION.** Abbreviated title: J I C. Text in English. 1994. s-a. GBP 148 combined subscription in United Kingdom to institutions (print & online eds.); EUR 178, AUD 288, USD 239 combined subscription to institutions (print & online eds.) (effective 2012). bk.rev. bibl. cum.index: vol.7, no.2 (2001); vol.4, no.2 (1997). back issues avail.; reprint service avail. from PSC. **Document type:** *Journal, Academic/Scholarly.* **Description:** Provides a forum for discussion for the various geoacademic approaches to the study of global communication, including international communication, international relations, international development, international political economy, global sociology, media anthropology, media and cultural studies and post-colonial studies.
Related titles: Online - full text ed.: GBP 134 in United Kingdom to institutions; EUR 160, AUD 260, USD 215 to institutions (effective 2012).
Indexed: A22, CA, CMM, CommAb, T02.
—BLDSC (5007.619000), IE, Infotrieve, Ingenta. **CCC.**
Published by: Macquarie University, Centre for International Communication, Media & Communication Studies Department, Sydney, NSW 2019, Australia. TEL 61-2-98507931, FAX 61-2-98509689, nchitty@ocs1.ocs.mq.edu.au, http://www.mucic.mq.edu.au/. Ed. Naren Chitty TEL 61-2-98508725.

➤ **JOURNAL OF INTERNATIONAL CRIMINAL JUSTICE.** *see* CRIMINOLOGY AND LAW ENFORCEMENT

➤ **JOURNAL OF INTERPERSONAL VIOLENCE;** concerned with the study and treatment of victims and perpetrators of physical and sexual violence. *see* CRIMINOLOGY AND LAW ENFORCEMENT

➤ **JOURNAL OF IRISH URBAN STUDIES.** *see* LITERATURE

306.44 NLD ISSN 2211-3770

▼ **JOURNAL OF LANGUAGE AND SEXUALITY.** Text in English. 2012. s-a. EUR 145 combined subscription (print & online eds.) (effective 2012). **Document type:** *Journal, Academic/Scholarly.* **Description:** Presents research on the discursive formations of sexuality, including sexual desire, sexual identities, sexual politics and sexuality in diaspora.
Related titles: Online - full text ed.: ISSN 2211-3789. EUR 141 (effective 2012).
Published by: John Benjamins Publishing Co., PO Box 36224, Amsterdam, 1020 ME, Netherlands. TEL 31-20-6304747, FAX 31-20-6739773, subscription@benjamins.nl, http://www.benjamins.com. Eds. Heiko Motschenbacher, William L Leap.

JOURNAL OF LANGUAGE AND SOCIAL PSYCHOLOGY. *see* PSYCHOLOGY

JOURNAL OF LAW & SOCIAL CHALLENGES. *see* LAW

THE JOURNAL OF LAW IN SOCIETY. *see* LAW

JOURNAL OF LIFE CARE PLANNING. *see* MEDICAL SCIENCES—Physical Medicine And Rehabilitation

JOURNAL OF MARITAL AND FAMILY THERAPY. *see* PSYCHOLOGY

306.85 USA ISSN 0022-2445
HQ1 CODEN: JMFAA6

➤ **JOURNAL OF MARRIAGE AND FAMILY.** Text in English. 1939. 5/yr. (plus supp.). USD 1,043 combined subscription in the Americas to institutions (print & online eds.); GBP 796 combined subscription in United Kingdom to institutions (print & online eds.); EUR 1,010 combined subscription in Europe to institutions (print & online eds.); USD 1,558 combined subscription elsewhere to institutions (print & online eds.) (effective 2010); subscr. includes Family Relations and Journal of Family Theory & Review. adv. bk.rev. charts; illus. index. 284 p./no.; back issues avail.; reprint service avail. from PSC. **Document type:** *Journal, Academic/Scholarly.* **Description:** Provides a forum covering theory, research interpretation and critical discussion on subjects related to marriage and the family.
Former titles (until 1964): Marriage and Family Living (0885-7059); (until 1941): Living (1538-1420)
Related titles: CD-ROM ed.; Microform ed.: (from PQC); Online - full text ed.: ISSN 1741-3737 (from IngentaConnect).
Indexed: A01, A02, A03, A08, A20, A21, A22, A25, A26, A36, ABS&EES, AC&P, AMHA, ASCA, ASG, AcaI, AddicA, AgeL, Agr, B04, B05, B14, BRD, BibAg, CA, CABA, CBRI, CDA, CERDIC, CLFP, CMM, ChPerI, Chicano, CurCont, D01, E-psyche, E01, E02, E03, E07, E08, ECER, ERI, ERIC, ESPM, EdA, EdI, F09, FAMLI, FR, Faml, G08, G10, GH, GSS&RPL, H09, H10, HPNRM, HRA, I05, IBSS, L01, L02, MEA&I, MLA-IB, MagInd, N02, N03, P02, P03, P06, P10, P12, P13, P18, P19, P25, P27, P28, P30, P46, P48, P53, P54, PC&CA, PCI, PQC, PopulInd, PsycInfo, PsycholAb, R05, R12, RASB, RI-1, RI-2, RefZh, RehabLit, RiskAb, S02, S03, S05, S08, S09, S21, SCOPUS, SFSA, SRRA, SSA, SSAI, SSAb, SSCI, SSI, SSciA, SWR&A, SociolAb, T02, T05, TAR, V&AA, W03, W07, W09, W11, WSI.
—BLDSC (5012.175000), IE, Infotrieve, Ingenta, INIST. **CCC.**
Published by: (National Council on Family Relations), Wiley-Blackwell Publishing, Inc. (Subsidiary of: Wiley-Blackwell Publishing Ltd.), 111 River St, Hoboken, NJ 07030. TEL 201-748-6000, FAX 201-748-6088, info@wiley.com, http://www.wiley.com/WileyCDA/. Ed. David H Demo. Adv. contact Kristin McCarthy TEL 201-748-7683. B&W page USD 875; trim 6.75 x 10. Circ: 4,365 (paid).

302.2 USA ISSN 1936-3648
P87

JOURNAL OF MASS COMMUNICATION AT FRANCIS MARION UNIVERSITY. Variant title: J M C. Text in English. 2007 (Spr.). 3/yr. free (effective 2011). back issues avail. **Document type:** *Journal, Academic/Scholarly.*
Media: Online - full text.
Published by: Francis Marion University, Department of Mass Communication, PO Box 100547, Florence, SC 29502. TEL 800-368-7551, dstewart@fmarion.edu, http://www.fmarion.edu/academics/masscommunication. Ed. William F Loewenstein. Pub. Donald W Stewart.

302.2 USA ISSN 0890-0523
P94

➤ **JOURNAL OF MASS MEDIA ETHICS;** exploring questions of media morality. Abbreviated title: J M M E. Text in English. 1985. q. GBP 416 combined subscription in United Kingdom to institutions (print & online eds.); EUR 556, USD 699 combined subscription to institutions (print & online eds.) (effective 2012). adv. bk.rev. illus. back issues avail.; reprint service avail. from PSC. **Document type:** *Journal, Academic/Scholarly.* **Description:** Stimulates mutually beneficial discussions about mass media ethics and morality among academic and professional groups in the various branches and subdisciplines of communication and ethics.
Related titles: Microform ed.: (from PQC); Online - full text ed.: ISSN 1532-7728. GBP 375 in United Kingdom to institutions; EUR 500, USD 629 to institutions (effective 2012).
Indexed: A01, A02, A03, A08, A22, A25, A26, AmHI, B01, B04, B06, B07, B09, BRD, CA, CMM, CommAb, CurCont, E-psyche, E01, E08, F01, F02, G08, H07, H08, H14, HAb, HumInd, I05, P02, P10, P27, P34, P42, P48, P53, P54, PAIS, PQC, PSA, RI-1, RI-2, S02, S03, S08, S09, SSAI, SSAb, SSCI, SSI, SociolAb, T02, W03, W07.
—BLDSC (5012.179000), CIS, IE, Infotrieve, Ingenta. **CCC.**
Published by: Routledge (Subsidiary of: Taylor & Francis Group), 325 Chestnut St, Ste 800, Philadelphia, PA 19106. TEL 800-354-1420, FAX 215-625-2940, journals@routledge.com, http://www.routledge.com. Ed. Lee Wilkins. Adv. contact Linda Hann TEL 44-1344-779945.

306 GBR ISSN 1359-1835
GN406

➤ **JOURNAL OF MATERIAL CULTURE.** Text in English. 1996. q. USD 881, GBP 476 combined subscription to institutions (print & online eds.); USD 863, GBP 466 to institutions (effective 2011). adv. bk.rev. illus. back issues avail.; reprint service avail. from PSC. **Document type:** *Journal, Academic/Scholarly.* **Description:** Explores the relationship between artifacts and social relations. Aims to promote and develop a general comparative and international perspective, publishing papers on theory and methodology, interpretative strategies and substantive studies of key themes and issues.
Related titles: Online - full text ed.: ISSN 1460-3586. USD 793, GBP 428 to institutions (effective 2011).

Indexed: A01, A03, A08, A20, A22, A30, A31, ABCT, ABM, AICP, AmHI, AnthLit, ArtHuCI, B01, B06, B07, B09, B24, BibInd, BrArAb, BrHumI, CA, CurCont, DIP, E01, GEOBASE, H04, H07, I14, IBR, IBSS, IBZ, IBibSS, MLA-IB, NumL, P02, P03, P10, P42, P48, P53, P54, PQC, PSA, PerIslam, PsycInfo, PsycholAb, S01, S02, S03, S11, SCOPUS, SSA, SSCI, SociolAb, T02, V02, W07.
—BLDSC (5012.195000), IE, Infotrieve, Ingenta. **CCC.**
Published by: Sage Publications Ltd. (Subsidiary of: Sage Publications, Inc.), 1 Oliver's Yard, 55 City Rd, London, EC1Y 1SP, United Kingdom. TEL 44-20-73248500, FAX 44-20-73248600, info@sagepub.co.uk, http://www.uk.sagepub.com/home.nav. adv.: B&W page GBP 450; 130 x 205. **Subscr. in the Americas to:** Sage Publications, Inc., 2455 Teller Rd, Thousand Oaks, CA 91320. TEL 805-499-9774, FAX 805-499-0871, journals@sagepub.com.

302.23 384 NGA ISSN 2141-2545
➤ **JOURNAL OF MEDIA AND COMMUNICATION STUDIES.** Text in English. m. free (effective 2010). adv. **Document type:** *Journal, Academic/Scholarly.*
Media: Online - full text.
Published by: Academic Journals, PO Box 73023, Victoria Island, Lagos, Nigeria. service@academicjournals.org. Eds. Dr. Balakrishnan Parasuraman, Dr. I Arul Aram, Dr. Mohammaad S Ullah.

302.23 SWE ISSN 1652-2354
P96.B87
➤ **JOURNAL OF MEDIA BUSINESS STUDIES.** Text in English. 2004. biennial. SEK 400, EUR 45, USD 55 to individuals; SEK 1,300, EUR 145, USD 170 to institutions (effective 2005). **Document type:** *Journal, Academic/Scholarly.*
Indexed: B01, T02.
—IE.
Published by: Hoegskolan i Joenkoeping, Internationella Handelshoegskolan. Media Management and Transformation Centre/University of Joenkoeping. International Business School. Media Management and Transformation Centre, c/o Joenkoeping Universitet, PO Box 1026, Joenkoeping, 51111, Sweden. TEL 46-36-157700, mmtc@jibs.hj.se, http://www.mmtcentre.se. Ed. Robert G Picard.

➤ **JOURNAL OF MEDIA LAW & ETHICS.** *see* LAW

302.23 USA ISSN 1944-4982
THE JOURNAL OF MEDIA LITERACY; a publication of the National Telemedia Council. Text in English. 1953. 3/yr. USD 35 domestic to individual members; USD 50 domestic to institutional members (effective 2009). bk.rev.; film rev.; Website rev. bibl.; illus. back issues avail.; reprints avail. **Document type:** *Journal, Trade.* **Description:** Brings together the thinking and experiences of the major pioneers, the current practitioners, and the future thinkers in media literacy.
Former titles (until 2006): Telemedium (1541-468X); (until 1984): Better Broadcasts News (0006-0054); Better Broadcasts Newsletter
Published by: National Telemedia Council, Inc., 1922 University Ave, Madison, WI 53705. TEL 608-218-1182, FAX 608-218-1183, ntelemedia@aol.com. Ed., R&P Marieli Rowe. Circ: 600.

JOURNAL OF MEDIA PSYCHOLOGY; theories, methods and applications. *see* PSYCHOLOGY

JOURNAL OF MEDIA PSYCHOLOGY. *see* COMMUNICATIONS

302.23 USA ISSN 1940-9397
➤ **JOURNAL OF MEDIA SOCIOLOGY.** Text in English. 2008 (Feb.). irreg. (2-4/yr). USD 149 (effective 2010). reprints avail. **Document type:** *Journal, Academic/Scholarly.* **Description:** Publishes theoretical and empirical papers and essays and book reviews that advance an understanding of the role and function of mass media and mass communication in society or the world.
Related titles: Online - full text ed.: ISSN 1940-9400. free (effective 2010).
Indexed: SociolAb.
Published by: Marquette Books LLC, 3107 E 62nd Ave, Spokane, WA 99223. TEL 509-443-7057, FAX 509-448-2191, journals@marquettejournals.org, http://www.marquettebooks.com. Ed. Michael Cheney.

➤ **JOURNAL OF MULTICULTURAL DISCOURSES.** *see* LINGUISTICS

305.3 USA ISSN 1948-5751
HM1271
JOURNAL OF MULTICULTURAL, GENDER AND MINORITY STUDIES. Text in English. 2007. s-a. free (effective 2009). **Document type:** *Journal, Academic/Scholarly.*
Media: Online - full content.
Published by: Scientific Journals International (Subsidiary of: Global Commerce & Communication, Inc), 1407 33rd St S, Saint Cloud, MN 56301. TEL 320-217-6019, info@scientificjournals.org.

301 USA ISSN 1556-8180
AZ191
➤ **JOURNAL OF MULTIDISCIPLINARY EVALUATION.** Text in English. 2004. 3/yr. free (effective 2011). **Document type:** *Journal, Academic/Scholarly.*
Media: Online - full text.
Indexed: A39, C29, D03, D04, E13, ERIC, R14, S14, S15, S18.
Published by: Western Michigan University, The Evaluation Center, 4405 Ellsworth Hall, Kalamazoo, MI 49008. http://www.wmich.edu/evalctr/. Eds. Jane Davidson, Michael Scriven.

301 USA ISSN 1938-3444
➤ **THE JOURNAL OF NETWORKS AND CIVIL SOCIETY.** Text in English. 2008. q. back issues avail. **Document type:** *Journal, Academic/Scholarly.*
Media: Online - full text.
Published by: Gilbert Center, PO Box 46067, Seattle, WA 98146. TEL 206-201-1726, info@gilbert.org.

302.23 USA ISSN 1945-8967
P96.T42
➤ **JOURNAL OF NEW COMMUNICATIONS RESEARCH.** Abbreviated title: J N C R. Text in English. 2006. s-a. back issues avail. **Document type:** *Journal, Academic/Scholarly.*
Indexed: CA, CMM, CommAb, T02.
Published by: Society for New Communications Research, 266 Hillsdale Ave, San Jose, CA 95136. TEL 408-266-9658, info@sncr.org.

301 NZL
➤ **JOURNAL OF NEW ZEALAND STUDIES.** Text in English. 1984. q. NZD 25 domestic to non-members; NZD 35 foreign to non-members; NZD 20 to members (effective 2009). **Document type:** *Journal, Academic/Scholarly.*
Former titles (until 1999): New Zealand Studies (1173-6348); (until 1995): Stout Centre Review (1170-4616); (until 1990): Stout Research Centre. Newsletter
Indexed: RILM.
Published by: Victoria University of Wellington, Stout Research Centre, PO Box 600, Wellington, 6015, New Zealand.

➤ **THE JOURNAL OF NORTH AFRICAN STUDIES.** *see* HISTORY—History Of Africa

305 SWE ISSN 1654-5915
DL1
➤ **JOURNAL OF NORTHERN STUDIES.** Text in English, French, German. 2007. s-a. SEK 500 (effective 2011). **Document type:** *Journal, Academic/Scholarly.* **Description:** Specific focus on human activities in northern spaces. Articles concentrate on people as cultural beings, people in society and the interaction between people and the northern environment.
Related titles: Series: Northern Studies. Monographs. ISSN 2000-0405. 2009; Nordliga Studier. ISSN 2000-0391. 2008.
Indexed: A01, T02.
Published by: Umeaa Universitet, Universitetsomraadet, Umea, 90187, Sweden. TEL 46-90-7865000, FAX 46-90-7869995, umea.universitet.umu.se, http://www.umu.se. Eds. Heidi Hansson, Lars-Erik Edlund.

150 USA
➤ **JOURNAL OF ONLINE BEHAVIOR**; dedicated to the empirical study of human behavior online. Abbreviated title: J O B. Text in English. 200?. irreg. **Document type:** *Journal, Academic/Scholarly.* **Description:** Concerned with the empirical study of human behavior in the online environment, and with the impact of evolving communication and information technology upon individuals, groups, organizations, and society.
Related titles: Online - full content ed.
Indexed: PsycholAb.
Published by: Rensselaer Polytechnic Institute, Department of Language, Literature, and Communication, 110 Eighth St, Troy, NY 12180. TEL 518-276-6000, FAX 518 276-4092, colmak@rpi.edu, http://www.llc.rpi.edu/. Ed. Joseph B Walther.

303.4 GBR ISSN 1477-9633
➤ **JOURNAL OF ORGANISATIONAL TRANSFORMATION AND SOCIAL CHANGE.** Abbreviated title: J O T S C. Text in English. 2004. 3/yr. GBP 210 domestic to institutions; GBP 219 in the European Union to institutions; USD 330 in US & Canada to institutions; GBP 222 elsewhere to institutions (effective 2011). adv. back issues avail. **Document type:** *Journal, Academic/Scholarly.* **Description:** Covers the ways in which management science has been influenced by the ever-burgeoning social sciences, and aims to uncover new systems of knowledge generated by this fusion of disciplines.
Related titles: Online - full text ed.: ISSN 2040-056X. USD 265 in US & Canada to institutions; GBP 177 elsewhere to institutions (effective 2011).
Indexed: A12, A17, A22, ABIn, B01, B06, B07, B08, B09, CA, E01, P48, P51, P53, P54, PQC, S02, S03, SociolAb, T02.
—BLDSC (5027.095500), IE, Ingenta. **CCC.**
Published by: Intellect Ltd., The Mill, Parnall Rd, Fishponds, Bristol, BS16 3JG, United Kingdom. TEL 44-117-9589910, FAX 44-117-9589911, info@intellectbooks.com. Eds. Maurice Yolles, Paul Iles. Pub. Masoud Yazdani. **Subscr. to:** Turpin Distribution Services Ltd., Pegasus Dr, Stratton Business Park, Biggleswade, Bedfordshire SG18 8QB, United Kingdom. TEL 44-1767-604951, FAX 44-1767-601640, custserv@turpin-distribution.com, http://www.turpin-distribution.com/.

➤ **JOURNAL OF ORGANIZATIONAL BEHAVIOR.** *see* PSYCHOLOGY

302.3 GBR ISSN 1649-7627
JOURNAL OF ORGANIZATIONAL BEHAVIOR EDUCATION. Abbreviated title: J O B E. Text in English. 2005. a. GBP 105, EUR 155, USD 175 combined subscription per issue to individuals (print & online eds.); GBP 230, EUR 340, USD 395 combined subscription per issue to institutions (print & online eds.); GBP 220, EUR 330, USD 390 per issue to institutions (effective 2010). back issues avail. **Document type:** *Journal, Academic/Scholarly.* **Description:** Aims to enhance organizational behavior education worldwide through the publication of refereed organizational behavior teaching materials.
Related titles: Online - full text ed.: GBP 100, EUR 145, USD 160 per issue to individuals; GBP 210, EUR 320, USD 375 per issue to institutions (effective 2010).
Indexed: P10, P18, P27, P46, P48, P51, P53, P54, PQC.
Published by: NeilsonJournals Publishing, 151 Whitehouse Loan, Edinburgh, EH9 2EY, United Kingdom. TEL 44-131-4473300, FAX 44-131-4640300, pneilson@neilsonjournals.com. Eds. Judith Clair, Lynn Isabella.

JOURNAL OF PACIFIC RIM PSYCHOLOGY. *see* PSYCHOLOGY

306 USA ISSN 1942-6569
DT1
➤ **JOURNAL OF PAN AFRICAN STUDIES (ONLINE).** Text in English. q. free (effective 2011). **Document type:** *Journal, Academic/Scholarly.*
Media: Online - full text.
Indexed: IIBP.
Published by: Journal of Pan African Studies, PO Box 20151, Phoenix, AZ 85036-0151.

303.4 GBR ISSN 0306-6150
HD1513.A3
➤ **THE JOURNAL OF PEASANT STUDIES.** Abbreviated title: J P S. Text in English. 1973. q. GBP 498 combined subscription in United Kingdom to institutions (print & online eds.); EUR 657, USD 825 combined subscription to institutions (print & online eds.) (effective 2012). adv. bk.rev. illus. index. back issues avail.; reprint service avail. from PSC. **Document type:** *Journal, Academic/Scholarly.* **Description:** Focuses on considering peasants within the broader systems and historical situations in which they exist, while examining the role of peasants in political, economic, and social change worldwide.
Related titles: Microfilm ed.: (from PQC); Online - full text ed.: ISSN 1743-9361. GBP 448 in United Kingdom to institutions; EUR 592, USD 743 to institutions (effective 2012) (from IngentaConnect).
Indexed: A20, A22, A34, A35, A38, AICP, APEL, ASCA, ASD, AbAn, AgBio, AgrForAb, AmH&L, AmHI, AnthLit, BAS, BrHumI, C25, CA, CABA, CTFA, CurCont, D01, DIP, E01, E12, EI, ESPM, F08, F12, FCA, FamI, GEOBASE, GH, H07, H16, HistAb, I13, I14, IBR, IBSS, IBZ, ILD, LeftInd, MEA&I, MaizeAb, N02, OR, P02, P06, P10, P30, P32, P40, P42, P48, P53, P54, PAA&I, PAIS, PCI, PGegResA, PHN&I, PQC, PSA, R11, R12, RASB, S02, S03, S11, S13, S16, S17, S21, SCOPUS, SOPODA, SSA, SSCI, SSciA, SociolAb, SoyAb, T02, T05, TAR, TriticAb, VS, W07, W11.
—IE, Infotrieve, Ingenta. **CCC.**
Published by: Routledge (Subsidiary of: Taylor & Francis Group), 4 Park Sq, Milton Park, Abingdon, Oxon OX14 4RN, United Kingdom. TEL 44-20-70176000, FAX 44-20-70176336, subscriptions@tandf.co.uk, http://www.routledge.com. Ed. Saturnino Borras Jr. Adv. contact Linda Hann TEL 44-1344-779945. **Subscr. to:** Taylor & Francis Ltd., Journals Customer Service, Sheepen Pl, Colchester, Essex CO3 3LP, United Kingdom. TEL 44-20-70175544, FAX 44-20-70175198.

➤ **JOURNAL OF PSYCHOSOCIAL RESEARCH.** *see* PSYCHOLOGY

301 USA ISSN 2154-8935
HM786
JOURNAL OF PUBLIC AND PROFESSIONAL SOCIOLOGY. Text in English. 2005. irreg. free (effective 2011). **Document type:** *Journal, Academic/Scholarly.* **Description:** Promotes scientific advances in sociological knowledge on both the pure and applied level.
Media: Online - full text.
Published by: Kennesaw State University, 1000 Chastain Rd, English Bldg. #27/Ste 220, Kennesaw, GA 30144. TEL 770-423-6000, http://www.kennesaw.edu/.

JOURNAL OF RELIGION AND POPULAR CULTURE. *see* RELIGIONS AND THEOLOGY

JOURNAL OF RELIGION AND SOCIETY. *see* RELIGIONS AND THEOLOGY

302 USA
RA790.A1
➤ **JOURNAL OF RURAL COMMUNITY PSYCHOLOGY (ONLINE).** Text in English. 1980. s-a. free (effective 2011). adv. bk.rev. bibl. back issues avail.; reprints avail. **Document type:** *Journal, Academic/Scholarly.* **Description:** Devoted to the dissemination of information related to the sociological, psychological and mental health issues in rural and small community settings.
Formerly: Journal of Rural Community Psychology (Print) (0276-2285)
Media: Online - full text.
Indexed: Agr, PsycholAb.
—Ingenta.
Published by: Journal of Rural Community Psychology, c/o Department of Psychology, Marshall University, One John Marshall Dr, Huntington, WV 25755. jrcp@marshall.edu. Eds. Okey J Napier Jr., Pamela Mulder.

307.1412 IND ISSN 0970-3357
HN690.Z9
➤ **JOURNAL OF RURAL DEVELOPMENT.** Abbreviated title: J R D. Text in English. 1982. q. INR 200 domestic to individuals; INR 500 domestic to institutions; USD 50 foreign (effective 2011). bk.rev. charts; illus. back issues avail. **Document type:** *Journal, Academic/Scholarly.* **Description:** Studies research in rural development with emphasis on social science aspects.
Formed by the merger of (1978-1982): Rural Development Digest; Which was formerly (until 1978): Community Development and Panchayati Raj Digest; (1978-1982): Behavioural Sciences and Rural Development (0379-797X); Which was formerly (until 1978): Behavioural Sciences and Community Development (0005-7843)
Related titles: Online - full text ed.: free (effective 2011).
Indexed: A20, A34, A35, A37, A38, ASCA, Agr, AgrForAb, ApicAb, BAS, C25, CABA, D01, E12, EIA, EnerInd, F08, F12, GEOBASE, GH, H16, I11, IPsyAb, LT, N02, N04, OR, P30, P32, R07, R12, REE&TA, S13, S16, SCOPUS, T05, VS, W11.
—BLDSC (5052.127400), IE, Infotrieve, Ingenta.
Published by: Ministry of Rural Development, National Institute of Rural Development, Rajendranagar, Hyderabad, Andhra Pradesh 500 030, India. TEL 91-40-24008526, FAX 91-40-24016500, cit@nird.gov.in. **Subscr. to:** I N S I O Scientific Books & Periodicals.

333.72 GBR ISSN 0743-0167
HT401 CODEN: JRSTFW
➤ **JOURNAL OF RURAL STUDIES.** Text in English. 1985. 4/yr. EUR 876 in Europe to institutions; JPY 118,400 in Japan to institutions; USD 986 elsewhere to institutions (effective 2012). adv. bk.rev. illus. Index. back issues avail.; reprints avail. **Document type:** *Journal, Academic/Scholarly.* **Description:** Provides a forum for research in the broad spectrum of rural issues, including society, demography, housing, employment, transport, land-use, recreation, agriculture and conservation.
Related titles: Microfilm ed.: (from PQC); Online - full text ed.: ISSN 1873-1392 (from IngentaConnect, ScienceDirect).
Indexed: A20, A22, A26, A34, A35, A37, A38, APEL, ASCA, AgBio, Agr, AgrForAb, BA, BRD, BibAg, C25, CA, CABA, CTFA, CurCont, D01, E02, E03, E04, E05, E08, E12, ERI, ERIC, ESPM, EdA, EdI, EnvAb, F08, F11, F12, FamI, G08, G11, GEOBASE, GH, H16, HPNRM, I05, I11, IBSS, IndVet, LT, N02, OR, P30, P32, P34, P40, P42, PAIS, PCI, PGegResA, PHN&I, PN&I, PSA, R12, RASB, RRTA, RiskAb, S02, S03, S09, S13, S16, SCOPUS, SOPODA, SSA, SSAI, SSAb, SSCI, SSI, SSciA, SociolAb, T02, TAR, VS, W03, W07, W09, W11.
—BLDSC (5052.128900), IE, Infotrieve, Ingenta. **CCC.**
Published by: Pergamon (Subsidiary of: Elsevier Science & Technology), The Blvd, Langford Ln, East Park, Kidlington, Oxford OX5 1GB, United Kingdom. TEL 44-1865-843000, FAX 44-1865-843010, JournalsCustomerServiceEMEA@elsevier.com. Ed. Paul Cloke. **Subscr. to:** Elsevier BV, Radarweg 29, PO Box 211, Amsterdam 1000 AE, Netherlands. TEL 31-20-4853757, FAX 31-20-4853432, http://www.elsevier.nl.

➤ **JOURNAL OF SEX RESEARCH.** *see* PSYCHOLOGY

➤ **JOURNAL OF SOCIAL AND ECONOMIC POLICY.** *see* POLITICAL SCIENCE

306.09 USA ISSN 0022-4529
HN1
➤ **JOURNAL OF SOCIAL HISTORY.** Text in English. 1967. q. GBP 72 in United Kingdom to institutions; EUR 109 in Europe to institutions; USD 138 in US & Canada to institutions; GBP 72 elsewhere to institutions; GBP 79 combined subscription in United Kingdom to institutions (print & online eds.); EUR 118 combined subscription in Europe to institutions (print & online eds.); USD 150 combined subscription in US & Canada to institutions (print & online eds.); GBP 79 combined subscription elsewhere to institutions (print & online eds.) (effective 2012). adv. bk.rev. charts; stat.; illus. index Summer issue. 250 p./no. 1 cols./p.; back issues avail.; reprint service avail. from PSC. **Document type:** *Journal, Academic/Scholarly.*
Description: Contains articles pertinent to historical research in United States.
Related titles: Microform ed.: (from MIM, PQC); Online - full text ed.: ISSN 1527-1897. 1999. GBP 66 in United Kingdom to institutions; EUR 99 in Europe to institutions; USD 125 in US & Canada to institutions; GBP 66 elsewhere to institutions (effective 2012).
Indexed: A01, A02, A03, A08, A20, A21, A22, A25, A26, ABS&EES, ASCA, AmH&L, AmHI, ArtHuCI, B04, B14, BAS, BRD, BRI, C28, CA, CBRI, CurCont, DIP, E01, E08, FamI, G05, G06, G07, G08, H05, H07, H08, H09, H14, HAb, HistAb, HumInd, I05, I07, IBR, IBSS, IBZ, M01, M02, MEA&I, P02, P10, P13, P27, P30, P34, P42, P46, P48, P53, P54, PCI, PQC, PSA, PerIslam, R05, RASB, RI-1, RI-2, RILM, S02, S03, S05, S08, S09, S23, SCOPUS, SOPODA, SRRA, SSA, SSAI, SSAb, SSCI, SSI, SociolAb, T02, W01, W02, W03, W05, W07, W09, WBA, WMB.
—BLDSC (5064.754000), IE, Infotrieve, Ingenta. **CCC.**
Published by: Oxford University Press (Subsidiary of: Oxford University Press), 2001 Evans Rd, Cary, NC 27513. TEL 919-677-0977, 800-445-9714, FAX 919-677-1303, custserv.us@oup.com. Ed. Peter Stearns. adv.: page USD 250; 4.75 x 8. Circ: 1,000.

301 AUS ISSN 1836-8808
▼ ➤ **JOURNAL OF SOCIAL INCLUSION.** Text in English. 2009. s-a. free (effective 2011). **Document type:** *Journal, Academic/Scholarly.*
Media: Online - full text.
Published by: Griffith University, School of Human Services and Social Work, University Drive, Meadowbrook, QLD 4131, Australia. Eds. Donna McAuliffe, Fiona Kumari Campbell, Jayne Clapton.

301 NLD ISSN 1876-8830
HM409
▼ **JOURNAL OF SOCIAL INTERVENTION: THEORY AND PRACTICE.** Text in English. 2009. irreg. free (effective 2011). **Document type:** *Journal, Academic/Scholarly.* **Description:** Publishes academic research and reflections on practice in social intervention, with emphasis on the interface between policy, the development of methodology and professional practice.
Media: Online - full text.
Published by: Igitur, Utrecht Publishing & Archiving Services, Postbus 80124, Utrecht, 3508 TC, Netherlands. TEL 31-30-2536635, FAX 31-30-2536959, info@igitur.uu.nl, http://www.igitur.uu.nl. Ed. Andries Baart.

JOURNAL OF SOCIAL ISSUES. see PSYCHOLOGY

301 USA ISSN 1948-5468
HM403
▼ ➤ **JOURNAL OF SOCIOLOGICAL RESEARCH.** Text in English. 2009. a. free (effective 2009). **Document type:** *Journal, Academic/Scholarly.* **Description:** Provides research on many topics within sociology and social welfare.
Media: Online - full content.
Indexed: A26, E08, I05, P02, P54, S02, S03, T02.
Published by: Macrothink Institute, Inc., 5348 Vegas Dr, Ste 825, Las Vegas, NV 89108. TEL 702-953-1852, FAX 702-387-2666, info@macrothink.org.

301 GBR ISSN 1440-7833
HM1
➤ **JOURNAL OF SOCIOLOGY.** Abbreviated title: J O S. Text in English. 1965. q. USD 581, GBP 314 combined subscription to institutions (print & online eds.); USD 569, GBP 308 to institutions (effective 2011). adv. bk.rev. abstr. cum.index every 2 yrs. back issues avail.; reprint service avail. from PSC. **Document type:** *Journal, Academic/Scholarly.* **Description:** Containes peer refereed articles of sociological research and theory on issues of interest to Austrialian sociology and aims to promote dialogue and exchange between Australian sociologists and the international community of sociology.
Formerly (until 1998): Australian and New Zealand Journal of Sociology (0004-8690)
Related titles: Microfilm ed.: (from PQC); Online - full text ed.: ISSN 1741-2978. USD 523, GBP 283 to institutions (effective 2011).
Indexed: A01, A03, A08, A20, A22, A26, AEI, AESIS, AICP, ASCA, AmH&L, AusPAIS, BibInd, CA, CJPI, CurCont, E01, E08, ESPM, FR, FamI, G08, GeoRef, HistAb, I05, I13, IBSS, INZP, MEA&I, P02, P03, P06, P10, P30, P34, P42, P48, P53, P54, PCI, PQC, PSA, PsycInfo, PsycholAb, RASB, RILM, RiskAb, S02, S03, S09, S11, SCOPUS, SOPODA, SPPI, SSA, SSCI, SSciA, SociolAb, T02, W07, W09.
—BLDSC (5064.930900), IE, Infotrieve, Ingenta, INIST. **CCC.**
Published by: (The Australian Sociological Association AUS), Sage Publications Ltd. (Subsidiary of: Sage Publications, Inc.), 1 Oliver's Yard, 55 City Rd, London, EC1Y 1SP, United Kingdom. TEL 44-20-73248500, FAX 44-20-73248600, info@sagepub.co.uk, http://www.uk.sagepub.com/home.nav. Ed. Andrew Bennett. adv.: B&W page GBP 350; 130 x 205. **Subscr. in the Americas to:** Sage Publications, Inc., 2455 Teller Rd, Thousand Oaks, CA 91320. TEL 805-499-9774, FAX 805-499-0871, journals@sagepub.com.

306 IND ISSN 0976-6634
▼ **JOURNAL OF SOCIOLOGY AND SOCIAL ANTHROPOLOGY.** Text in English. 2010. s-a. USD 75 (effective 2012). back issues avail. **Document type:** *Journal, Academic/Scholarly.* **Description:** Publishes original papers on current research and practical programmes, short notes, news items, book reviews, reports of meetings and professional announcements on all aspects of sociology and social anthropology. It covers but not limited to, anthropology, sociology, environmental studies, home science, public health, demography, cultural studies, ethnography and sociolinguistics, along with their interfaces.
Related titles: Online - full text ed.: free (effective 2012).
Published by: Kamla-Raj Enterprises, 2273 Gali Bari Paharwali, Chawri Bazar, New Delhi, 110 006, India. TEL 91-11-23284126, kre@airtelmail.in.

301 USA ISSN 0191-5096
HN1
➤ **JOURNAL OF SOCIOLOGY AND SOCIAL WELFARE.** Abbreviated title: J S S W. Text in English. 1973. q. USD 40 domestic to individuals; USD 45 foreign to individuals; USD 80 domestic to institutions; USD 90 foreign to institutions (effective 2009). bk.rev. illus. index, cum.index. back issues avail.; reprints avail. **Document type:** *Journal, Academic/Scholarly.* **Description:** Presents articles on social change, gender, race, homelessness, social welfare history, cultural diversity, international social welfare, and the social dimensions of health and mental health.
Related titles: Microform ed.: (from PQC); Online - full text ed.: ISSN 1949-7652.
Indexed: A01, A02, A03, A08, A20, A22, A26, AMHA, ASCA, B04, BRD, C28, CA, CWI, E-psyche, E08, F09, FR, FamI, G08, I05, MEA&I, P03, P30, P34, P43, PAIS, PSI, PsycInfo, PsycholAb, S02, S03, S09, SCOPUS, SOPODA, SSA, SSAI, SSAb, SSI, SWR&A, SociolAb, T02, V&AA, W03, W05, W09.
—BLDSC (5064.935000), IE, Infotrieve, Ingenta, INIST. **CCC.**
Published by: Western Michigan University, School of Social Work, 1903 W Michigan Ave, Kalamazoo, MI 49008. TEL 269-387-3205, FAX 269-387-3217, swrk-jssw@wmich.edu, http://www.wmich.edu/hhs/sw/. Ed. Robert D Leighninger.

➤ **JOURNAL OF SPORT AND SOCIAL ISSUES.** see SPORTS AND GAMES

➤ **JOURNAL OF SPORTS LAW & CONTEMPORARY PROBLEMS.** see LAW

➤ **JOURNAL OF SPORTS MEDIA.** see SPORTS AND GAMES

➤ **JOURNAL OF THE HISTORY OF CHILDHOOD AND YOUTH.** see CHILDREN AND YOUTH—About

306.7 USA ISSN 1043-4070
HQ12 CODEN: JHSEEI
➤ **JOURNAL OF THE HISTORY OF SEXUALITY.** Abbreviated title: J H S. Text in English. 1990. q. USD 228 domestic to institutions; USD 241 in Canada to institutions; USD 250 elsewhere to institutions (effective 2011). adv. bk.rev. illus. back issues avail.; reprints avail. **Document type:** *Journal, Academic/Scholarly.* **Description:** Expresses the history of sexuality in all its expressions, recognizing various differences of class, culture, gender, race, and sexual orientation.
Related titles: Online - full text ed.: ISSN 1535-3605. 2001.
Indexed: A01, A02, A03, A08, A20, A21, A22, A26, ABS&EES, ASCA, AmH&L, AmHI, ArtHuCI, B04, BRD, CA, CurCont, DIP, E-psyche, E01, E03, E07, E08, ERI, FR, FamI, G08, G10, GW, H07, H08, H13, HAb, HistAb, HumInd, I05, I13, IBR, IBSS, IBZ, L01, L02, L06, MLA-IB, P04, P07, P10, P13, P27, P30, P48, P53, P54, PCI, PQC, RASB, RI-1, RI-2, S02, S03, S09, S11, S21, SCOPUS, SOPODA, SSCI, SociolAb, T02, W03, W05, W07, W09.
—BLDSC (5002.050000), GNLM, IE, Infotrieve, Ingenta, INIST. **CCC.**
Published by: University of Texas Press, Journals Division, PO Box 7819, Austin, TX 78713. TEL 512-471-7233 ext 2, FAX 512-232-7178, journals@uts.cc.utexas.edu, http://www.utexas.edu/utpress/journals/journals.html. Ed. Mathew Kuefler. Adv. contact Leah Dixon TEL 512-232-7618.

➤ **JOURNAL OF TOURISM & CULTURAL CHANGE.** see TRAVEL AND TOURISM

▼ ➤ **JOURNAL OF TRANSFORMATIVE STUDIES.** see PSYCHOLOGY

▼ ➤ **JOURNAL OF TRUST RESEARCH.** see PSYCHOLOGY

➤ **JOURNAL OF URBAN AFFAIRS.** see HOUSING AND URBAN PLANNING

301 USA ISSN 1948-0733
➤ **THE JOURNAL OF VALUES BASED LEADERSHIP.** Abbreviated title: J V B L. Text in English. 2008. s-a. free (effective 2010). back issues avail.; reprints avail. **Document type:** *Journal, Academic/Scholarly.* **Description:** Contains articles that provide knowledge that is intellectually well-developed and useful in practice.
Media: Online - full text. **Related titles:** Print ed.: ISSN 2153-019X. USD 20 per issue (effective 2010).
Published by: Valparaiso University, College of Business Administration, 1700 Chapel Dr, Valparaiso, IN 46383. TEL 219-464-5000, http://www.valpo.edu/cba/. Ed. Elizabeth Reiner Gingerich TEL 219-464-5035.

355.02306 GBR ISSN 1752-6272
JOURNAL OF WAR AND CULTURE STUDIES. Abbreviated title: J W C S. Text in English. 2008. 3/yr. GBP 225 domestic to institutions; GBP 234 in the European Union to institutions; USD 350 in US & Canada to institutions; GBP 237 elsewhere to institutions (effective 2011). adv. back issues avail. **Document type:** *Journal, Academic/Scholarly.* **Description:** Analyses the relationship between war and culture in the twentieth century, and onwards into the twenty-first.
Related titles: Online - full text ed.: ISSN 1752-6280. USD 290 in US & Canada to institutions; GBP 192 elsewhere to institutions (effective 2011).
Indexed: AmHI, CA, H07, MLA-IB, T02.
—BLDSC (5072.521250), IE.
Published by: Intellect Ltd., The Mill, Parnall Rd, Fishponds, Bristol, BS16 3JG, United Kingdom. TEL 44-117-9589910, FAX 44-117-9589911, info@intellectbooks.com. Eds. Debra Kelly, Martin Hurcombe, Nicola Cooper. **Subscr. to:** Turpin Distribution Services Ltd., Pegasus Dr, Stratton Business Park, Biggleswade, Bedfordshire SG18 8QB, United Kingdom. TEL 44-1767-604951, FAX 44-1767-601640, custserv@turpin-distribution.com, http://www.turpin-distribution.com/.

JOURNAL OF YOUTH STUDIES. see CHILDREN AND YOUTH—About

JOURNALISM AND MASS COMMUNICATION QUARTERLY. see JOURNALISM

JUNGE KIRCHE; Unterwegs fuer Gerechtigkeit, Frieden und Bewahrung der Schoepfung. see RELIGIONS AND THEOLOGY

306 AUT ISSN 1025-3858
PT2639.093
JURA SOYFER; Internationale Zeitschrift fuer Kulturwissenschaft. Text in German. 1992. q. EUR 8.72; EUR 2.18 newsstand/cover (effective 2006). **Document type:** *Journal, Academic/Scholarly.*
Related titles: Online - full text ed.: ISSN 1607-0135. 2000.
Indexed: MLA-IB.
Published by: Jura Soyfer Gesellschaft, Altes Rathaus, Wipplingerstr 8, Vienna, 1010, Austria. TEL 43-1-748163315, FAX 43-1-748163311, arlt@adis.at. Ed. Herbert Arlt.

306.85 FIN ISSN 1796-105X
JYVASKYLAN YLIOPISTO. PERHETUTKIMUSKESKUS. JULKAISU. Text in Finnish. 1991. irreg. price varies. back issues avail. **Document type:** *Monographic series, Academic/Scholarly.*
Formerly (until 2005): Jyvaskylan Yliopiston. Perhetutkimusyksikon. Julkaisuja (0788-639X)
Published by: Jyvaskylan Yliopisto, Perhetutkimuskeskus/University of Jyvaskyla. Family Research Centre, PO Box 35, Jyvaskyla, 40014, Finland. TEL 358-14-2604551, FAX 358-14-2602811, http://www.jyu.fi/ytk/laitokset/perhetutkimus.

301 USA
K I T NEWSLETTER. Text in English. 1989. m. USD 25; USD 30 foreign (effective 1999). **Document type:** *Newsletter.* **Description:** Contains letters and life stories of graduates and survivors of the Bruderhof community.
Related titles: Online - full text ed.
Published by: K I T Information Service, PO Box 460141, San Francisco, CA 94146-0141. TEL 415-821-2090, FAX 415-282-2369, http://www.perefound.org. Ed., R&P Ramon Sender.

302.23 DEU ISSN 1869-0599
▼ **K J M - SCHRIFTENREIHE.** Text in German. 2009. irreg., latest vol.2, 2010. price varies. **Document type:** *Monographic series, Academic/Scholarly.*
Published by: (Kommission fuer Jugendmedienschutz der Landesmedienanstalten), Vistas Verlag GmbH, Goltzstr 11, Berlin, 10781, Germany. TEL 49-30-32707446, FAX 49-30-32707455, medienverlag@vistas.de.

306 800 DNK ISSN 0905-6998
K & K; kultur og klasse, kritik og kulturanalyse. (Kultur og Klasse) Variant title: K og K. Text in Danish. 1967. s-a. DKK 315 to individuals; DKK 200 to students; DKK 190 per issue (effective 2009). back issues avail. **Document type:** *Journal, Academic/Scholarly.*
Former titles (until 1989): Kultur og Klasse (0105-7367); (until 1977): Poetik (0556-0500)
Indexed: FR, MLA-IB, RILM.
Published by: Forlaget Medusa, PO Box 1, Holte, 2840, Denmark. TEL 45-45-424000, FAX 45-45-424106, medusa@medusa.dk. Eds. Henrik Skov Nielsen, Jacob Boeggild, Mikkel Bolt.

K S A - KINDERSCHUTZ AKTUELL. see SOCIAL SERVICES AND WELFARE

KAILASH; an interdisciplinary journal of Himalayan studies. see HISTORY—History Of Asia

300.720595 950 MYS ISSN 0127-4082
DS591
➤ **KAJIAN MALAYSIA**; journal of Malaysian studies. Text in Multiple languages. 1983. s-a. **Document type:** *Journal, Academic/Scholarly.* **Description:** Focuses on Malaysian studies.
Related titles: Online - full text ed.: free (effective 2011).
Indexed: A01, CA, HistAb, IBSS, RILM, T02.
—Ingenta.
Published by: Universiti Sains Malaysia, Pusat Pengajian Sains Kemasyarakatan, Pulau Pinang, 11800, Malaysia. TEL 60-4-8603361, 60-4-6577888, 60-4-8603876.

306.43 USA ISSN 2151-4712
HT1501
▼ **KALFOU**; a journal of comparative and relational ethnic studies. Text in English. 2010. s-a. USD 20 per issue (effective 2010). **Document type:** *Journal, Academic/Scholarly.* **Description:** Focuses on social movements, social institutions, and social relations.
Published by: University of California, Santa Barbara, Center for Black Studies Research, 4603 S Hall, Santa Barbara, CA 93106. TEL 805-893-3914, FAX 805-893-7243, ctr4blst@cbs.ucsb.edu.

KAN ANDERS. see POLITICAL SCIENCE—International Relations

301 NGA ISSN 0567-4840
AP9
KANO STUDIES/DIRASAT KANU; journal of Saharan and Sudanic research. Text in English. 1973. a. adv. bk.rev. **Document type:** *Academic/Scholarly.* **Description:** Examines Saharan and Sudanic research.
Indexed: ASD, MLA, MLA-IB.
—**CCC.**
Published by: Bayero University, Kano, Nigeria. TELEX 31121 OXONIA NG. Ed. Ibrahim Yaro Yahaya.

TE KARAKA. see POLITICAL SCIENCE

306 USA ISSN 1097-4156
KEEP ON TRUCKIN' RE-VISITED. Text in English. 1997. m. back issues avail.
Media: Online - full text.
Published by: V I P Graphics, PO Box 147, La Junta, CA 81050-0147. TEL 719-384-5837, FAX 719-3845837. Ed., Pub. Vincent Gearhart.

301 USA ISSN 1085-0082
KEN BLANCHARD'S PROFILES OF SUCCESS. Text in English. 1995. m.
Related titles: Online - full text ed.
Indexed: B01, B06, B07, B08, B09, C12, M01, M02.
—**CCC.**
Published by: Select Press, P O Box 37, Corte Madera, CA 94976-0037. TEL 415-435-4461, 800-676-1756, FAX 415-435-4841, selectpr@aol.com.

▼ **KENTUCKY JOURNAL OF ANTHROPOLOGY AND SOCIOLOGY.** see ANTHROPOLOGY

KERNCIJFERS ONDERWIJS CULTUUR EN WETENSCHAPPEN. see EDUCATION

KEY FIGURES EDUCATION, CULTURE AND SCIENCE. see EDUCATION

301 GBR ISSN 1478-1301
KEY NOTE MARKET ASSESSMENT. THE ABC1 CONSUMER. Variant title: ABC1 Consumer Market Assessment. Text in English. 1999. irreg., latest 2008, Sep. GBP 899 per issue (effective 2010). **Document type:** *Report, Trade.* **Description:** Provides an in-depth strategic analysis across a broad range of industries and contains an examination on the scope, dynamics and shape of key UK markets in the consumer, financial, lifestyle and business to business sectors.

Published by: Key Note Ltd. (Subsidiary of: Bonnier Business Information), Harlequin House, 5th Fl, 7 High St, Teddington, Richmond upon Thames, TW11 8EE, United Kingdom. TEL 44-845-5040452, FAX 44-845-5040453, info@keynote.co.uk.

306 DEU ISSN 1616-8208
KIELER STUDIEN ZUR VOLKSKUNDE UND KULTURGESCHICHTE. Text in German. 2001. irreg., latest vol.7, 2009. price varies. **Document type:** *Monographic series, Academic/Scholarly.*
Published by: (Christian-Albrechts-Universitaet zu Kiel, Seminar fuer Europaeische Ethnologie/Volkskunde), Waxmann Verlag GmbH, Steinfurter Str 555, Muenster, 48159, Germany. TEL 49-251-265040, FAX 49-251-2650426, info@waxmann.com.

▼ **KIES KLEUR IN GROEN MAGAZINE.** *see* CONSERVATION

302.23 BOL
KIPUS. Text in Spanish. 1993. m.?. BOB 5 per issue.
Published by: Universidad Mayor de San Andres, Facultad de Ciencias Sociales, Carrera de Comunicacion Social, Casilla 4787, La Paz, Bolivia. Ed. Mamani A Constancio.

303.3 NLD ISSN 2210-8386
▼ **KLEUR (AMERSFOORT).** Text in Dutch. 2009. q. EUR 313 (effective 2010). **Document type:** *Magazine, Trade.*
Published by: Kwintessens Uitgevers, Van Hogendorplaan 10, Postbus 1492, Amersfoort, 3800 BL, Netherlands. TEL 31-33-4606011, FAX 31-33-4606020, http://www.kwintessens.nl.

301 GBR ISSN 0278-1557
BD175 CODEN: KSCPDO
KNOWLEDGE AND SOCIETY. Text in English. 1978. irreg., latest vol.13, 2002. price varies. back issues avail. **Document type:** *Monographic series, Academic/Scholarly.* **Description:** Examins in depth crucial and current issues in the critique of science and engineering as fields of study.
Formerly (until 1981): Research in Sociology of Knowledge, Science and Art (0163-0180)
Indexed: CA, S02, S03, SCOPUS, SOPODA, SociolAb, T02.
—Ingenta. **CCC.**
Published by: Emerald Group Publishing Ltd., Howard House, Wagon Ln, Bingley, W Yorks BD16 1WA, United Kingdom. TEL 44-1274-777700, FAX 44-1274-785201, books@emeraldinsight.com, http://www.emeraldinsight.com. Ed. M de Laet.

306 NLD ISSN 1873-3980
KODEX BULLETIN. Text in English, Hungarian. 2007. 4/yr. EUR 11.50 domestic; EUR 15 in Europe; EUR 18 elsewhere (effective 2009). adv.
Related titles: Online - full text ed.: ISSN 1873-4014.
Published by: Kodex Advisory & Consulting, Sfinxdreef 22, Utrecht, 3564 CN, Netherlands. TEL 31-646-208173, FAX 31-84-7583085, info@kodexconsulting.com. Eds. Kronauer Eva Lilla, Tordai Csilla.

302.2 DEU ISSN 0171-0834
P99
KODIKAS - CODE - ARS SEMEIOTICA; an international journal of semiotics. Text in English, French, German. 1975; N.S. 1979. 2/yr. EUR 78 to individuals; EUR 118 to institutions; EUR 154 combined subscription to institutions (print & online eds.); EUR 62 newsstand/cover (effective 2011). adv. bk.rev. illus. **Document type:** *Journal, Academic/Scholarly.* **Description:** Focuses on the research and discussion of semiotical subjects related to the constitution of signs.
Formed by the 1982 merger of: Kodikas - Code; Ars Semeiotica (0147-5045)
Related titles: Online - full text ed.; ◆ Supplement(s): Kodikas - Code Supplement. ISSN 0941-0139.
Indexed: A20, A22, BibInd, BibLing, CRCL, DIP, FR, IBR, IBZ, L&LBA, MLA-IB, PhilInd, RASB, RILM, SCOPUS, SOPODA.
—IE, Ingenta, INIST. **CCC.**
Published by: Gunter Narr Verlag, Postfach 2567, Tuebingen, 72015, Germany. TEL 49-7071-97970, FAX 49-7071-75288, info@narr.de, http://www.narr.de. Ed. Achim Eschbach. Circ: 500 (paid).

302.2 DEU ISSN 0941-0139
KODIKAS - CODE SUPPLEMENT. Text in German. 1980. irreg., latest vol.30, 2009. price varies. **Document type:** *Monographic series, Academic/Scholarly.*
Related titles: ◆ Supplement to: Kodikas - Code - Ars Semeiotica. ISSN 0171-0834.
Published by: Gunter Narr Verlag, Postfach 2567, Tuebingen, 72015, Germany. TEL 49-7071-97970, FAX 49-7071-75288, info@narr.de, http://www.narr.de.

302 DEU ISSN 0023-2653
➤ **KOELNER ZEITSCHRIFT FUER SOZIOLOGIE UND SOZIALPSYCHOLOGIE.** Text in German. 1927. 4/yr. EUR 297.20, USD 365 combined subscription to institutions (print & online eds.) (effective 2012). adv. bk.rev. charts; illus. index, cum.index. reprint service avail. from PSC. **Document type:** *Journal, Academic/Scholarly.*
Former titles: Koelner Vierteljahreshefte fuer Soziologie; Koelner Vierteljahreshefte fuer Sozialwissenschaften
Related titles: Online - full text ed.: ISSN 1861-891X.
Indexed: A20, A22, A26, AC&P, BibInd, CA, CIS, CurCont, DIP, E-psyche, E01, GJP, I13, IBR, IBSS, IBZ, P03, P10, P30, P42, P46, P48, PAIS, PCI, PQC, PSA, PhilInd, PsycInfo, PsycholAb, RASB, RILM, S02, S03, SCOPUS, SOPODA, SSA, SSCI, SociolAb, T02, W07, W09.
—BLDSC (5104.500000), IE, Infotrieve, Ingenta, INIST. **CCC.**
Published by: V S - Verlag fuer Sozialwissenschaften (Subsidiary of: Springer Fachmedien Wiesbaden GmbH), Abraham-Lincoln-Str 46, Wiesbaden, 65189, Germany. TEL 49-611-78780, FAX 49-611-7878400, springerfachmedien-wiesbaden@springer.com, http://www.vs-verlag.de. Circ: 1,410 (paid).

301 JPN ISSN 0919-3413
KOKUSAI SHAKAIGAKU KENKYUJO KENKYU KIYO/INSTITUTE OF INTERNATIONAL SOCIOLOGY. JOURNAL. Text in English, Japanese. 1993. a.
Published by: Kokusai Shakaigaku Kenkyujo, Kake Kokusai Gakujutsu Koryu Senta/Institute of International Sociology, Kake International Center for Academic Exchange, c/o Bureau of Sociological Research, Hyogo Kyoiku University, Kato-gun, Yashiro-cho, Hyogo-ken 673-14, Japan.

302.23 DEU ISSN 1617-9056
KOMMUNIKATION EXTRA. Text in German. 2001. irreg., latest vol.4, 2006. price varies. **Document type:** *Monographic series, Academic/Scholarly.*
Published by: Bochumer Universitaetsverlag GmbH, Querenburger Hoehe 281, Bochum, 44801, Germany. TEL 49-234-9719780, FAX 49-234-9719786, bou@bou.de, http://bou.de.

302.23 DEU ISSN 1615-9713
KOMMUNIKATIONSFORSCHUNG AKTUELL. Text in German. 2002. irreg., latest vol.13, 2008. price varies. **Document type:** *Monographic series, Academic/Scholarly.*
Published by: Bochumer Universitaetsverlag GmbH, Querenburger Hoehe 281, Bochum, 44801, Germany. TEL 49-234-9719780, FAX 49-234-9719786, bou@bou.de, http://bou.de.

300 DEU ISSN 0933-1190
KONSTANZER BEITRAEGE ZUR SOZIALWISSENSCHAFTLICHEN FORSCHUNG. Text in German. 1985. irreg., latest vol.11, 2003. price varies. **Document type:** *Monographic series, Academic/Scholarly.*
Published by: U V K Verlagsgesellschaft mbH, Schuetzenstr 24, Konstanz, 78462, Germany. TEL 49-7531-90530, FAX 49-7531-905398, nadine.ley@uvk.de, http://www.uvk.de.

305 325 DNK ISSN 1602-3595
KONTUR (ONLINE); tidsskrift for kulturstudier. Text mainly in Danish; Text occasionally in English. 2000. s-a. bk.rev. back issues avail. **Document type:** *Monographic series, Academic/Scholarly.*
Formerly (until 2000): Kontur (Print) (1600-4140); Which was formed by the merger of (1990-2000): Cekvinanyt (0905-7757); (1984-2000): Cekvinaterne (0905-9822); Which was formerly (until 1990): Nyhedsbrev (0905-1546)
Media: Online - full content.
—**CCC.**
Published by: Aarhus Universitet, Institut for Historie og Omraadestudier/Aarhus University, Institute of History and Area Studies, Nordre Ringgade 1410, Aarhus Universitet, Aarhus C, 8000, Denmark. TEL 45-89-421111, FAX 45-89-422047, iho@au.dk, http://www.iho.au.dk. Ed. Kirsten Gomard.

300 DEU ISSN 0948-390X
KONZEPTE DER GESELLSCHAFTSTHEORIE. Text in German. 1995. irreg., latest vol.16, 2010. price varies. **Document type:** *Monographic series, Academic/Scholarly.*
Published by: Mohr Siebeck GmbH & Co. KG, Wilhelmstr 18, Tuebingen, 72074, Germany. TEL 49-7071-9230, FAX 49-7071-51104, info@mohr.de.

344.035 SWE ISSN 1654-871X
KRIMINALVAARDEN. AARSBOK. Text in Swedish. 2008. a. charts; stat. **Document type:** *Government.*
Related titles: Online - full text ed.
Published by: Kriminalvaarden/Swedish Prison and Probation Service, Slottsgatan 78, Norrkoeping, 60180, Sweden. TEL 46-11-4963000, FAX 46-11-4963640, hk@kvv.se, http://www.kvv.se.

KRIMINOLOGIE UND KRIMINALSOZIOLOGIE. *see* CRIMINOLOGY AND LAW ENFORCEMENT

301 DEU
KRITISCHE THEORIE UND KULTURFORSCHUNG. Text in German. irreg., latest vol.10, 2007. price varies. **Document type:** *Monographic series, Academic/Scholarly.* **Description:** Contains theoretical research and studies on all aspects of culture and society.
Published by: Verlag Westfaelisches Dampfboot, Hafenweg 26a, Muenster, 48155, Germany. TEL 49-251-3900480, FAX 49-251-39004850, info@dampfboot-verlag.de.

301 NOR ISSN 1504-6591
KULTMAG; Norges kulturmagasin. Text in Multiple languages. 1979. 10/yr. NOK 693; NOK 346 to students (effective 2011). adv. bk.rev.; dance rev.; film rev.; music rev.; play rev. bibl.; tr.lit. 256 p./no.; back issues avail. **Document type:** *Magazine, Consumer.* **Description:** Covers public cultural activities all over Norway.
Incorporates (2007-2007): Kulturforbundet. Medlemsnyt (1504-792X); Former titles (until 2007): Kulturliv (1502-5578); (until 2001): Kulturnytt (0332-7558)
Published by: Ad Fontes Medier AS, PO Box 1180, Sentrum, Oslo, 0107, Norway. TEL 47-22-310210, FAX 47-22-404101, http://www.adfontesmedier.no. Ed. Esben Hoff. Adv. contact Arnt-Ove Drageset. Circ: 18,000.

303 DEU ISSN 1863-9097
KULTUR, GESCHICHTE, THEORIE; Studien zur Kultursoziologie. Text in German. 2004. irreg., latest vol.3, 2006. price varies. **Document type:** *Monographic series, Academic/Scholarly.*
Published by: Ergon Verlag, Keesburgstr 11, Wuerzburg, 97074, Germany. TEL 49-931-280084, FAX 49-931-282872, service@ergon-verlag.de, http://www.ergon-verlag.de.

306 TUR ISSN 1301-7241
➤ **KULTUR VE ILETISIM/CULTURE & COMMUNICATION.** Text in English, Turkish. 1998. s-a. **Document type:** *Journal, Academic/Scholarly.* **Description:** Publishes works in the fields of communication, cultural criticism, and social thought.
Related titles: Online - full text ed.
Indexed: MLA-IB.
Published by: Ankara Universitesi, Iletisim Fakultesi, Cebeci, Ankara, 06590, Turkey. TEL 90-312-3197714, FAX 90-312-3622717, http://ifel.ankara.edu.tr. Ed. Nur Betul Celik.

303 POL ISSN 0023-5172
AS261
KULTURA I SPOLECZENSTWO. Text in Polish; Contents page in English. 1957. q. EUR 58 foreign (effective 2006). bk.rev. index. **Document type:** *Journal, Academic/Scholarly.*
Indexed: AgrLib, FR, HistAb, IBSS, MLA-IB, P30, RASB.
—INIST.
Published by: Polska Akademia Nauk, Instytut Studiow Politycznych/Polish Academy of Sciences, Institute of Political Studies, ul Polna 18-20, Warsaw, 00625, Poland. TEL 48-22-8255221ext 17, FAX 48-22-8252146, politic@isppan.waw.pl, http://www.isppan.waw.pl. Ed. Antonina Kloskowska. Circ: 2,060. **Dist. by:** Ars Polona, Obroncow 25, Warsaw 03933, Poland. TEL 48-22-5098609, FAX 48-22-5098610, arspolona@arspolona.com.pl, http://www.arspolona.com.pl.

301 LTU ISSN 2029-4573
▼ ➤ **KULTURA IR VISUOMENE/CULTURE AND SOCIETY.** Text in English, Lithuanian. 2010. s-a. **Document type:** *Journal, Academic/Scholarly.*
Related titles: Online - full text ed.: free (effective 2011).
Published by: Vytauto Didziojo Universitetas, Sociologijos Katedra, K. Donelaicio str. 52-309, Kaunas, 44244, Lithuania. Ed. Arturas Tereskinas.

303 DEU
KULTURELLE BILDUNG. Text in German. 2006. irreg., latest vol.23, 2011. price varies. **Document type:** *Monographic series, Academic/Scholarly.*
Published by: (Bundesvereinigung Kulturelle Kinder- und Jugendbildung e.V.), KoPaed Verlag, Pfaelzer-Wald-Str 64, Munich, 81539, Germany. TEL 49-89-68890098, FAX 49-89-6891912, info@kopaed.de.

303.842 RUS ISSN 2073-5588
CB425
KUL'TUROLOGIYA: DAIDZHEST; problemno-tematicheskii sbornik. Text in Russian. 1997. q. **Document type:** *Academic/Scholarly.* **Description:** Contains articles, translations, excerpts from original work by Russian and foreign authors about culture and religion, culture of Russians living abroad, sociological and philosophical ideas in science and culture.
Formerly (until 2002): Kul'turologiya 20-veka
Published by: Rossiiskaya Akademiya Nauk, Institut Nauchnoi Informatsii po Obshchestvennym Naukam, Nakhimovskii pr-t 51/21, Moscow, 117997, Russian Federation. TEL 7-095-1288930, FAX 7-095-4202261, info@inion.ru, http://www.inion.ru.

306 DEU ISSN 0941-343X
KULTURSOZIOLOGIE; Aspekte, Analysen, Argumente. Text in German. 1992. s-a. **Document type:** *Journal, Academic/Scholarly.* **Description:** Contains articles on the cultural and social aspects of changes in the former East Germany as well as Eastern Europe.
Indexed: CA, DIP, IBR, IBZ, RILM, S02, S03, SCOPUS, SSA, SociolAb, T02.
Published by: (Gesellschaft fuer Kultursoziologie e.V.), Karl Dietz Verlag Berlin GmbH, Weydingerstr 14-16, Berlin, 10178, Germany. TEL 49-30-24009290, FAX 49-30-24009590, k-dietzverlag@t-online.de, http://www.dietzverlag.de.

302.23 DEU ISSN 1610-8434
KULTURWISSENSCHAFTLICHE MEDIENFORSCHUNG. Text in German. 2003. irreg., latest vol.2, 2004. price varies. **Document type:** *Monographic series, Academic/Scholarly.*
Published by: Peter Lang GmbH (Subsidiary of: Peter Lang Publishing Group), Eschborner Landstr 42-50, Frankfurt Am Main, 60489, Germany. TEL 49-69-7807050, FAX 49-69-78070550, zentrale.frankfurt@peterlang.com. Ed. Hartmut Schroeder.

302.23 DEU ISSN 1436-5952
KULTURWISSENSCHAFTLICHE WERBEFORSCHUNG. Text in German. 1999. irreg., latest vol.6, 2006. price varies. **Document type:** *Monographic series, Academic/Scholarly.*
Published by: Peter Lang GmbH (Subsidiary of: Peter Lang Publishing Group), Eschborner Landstr 42-50, Frankfurt Am Main, 60489, Germany. TEL 49-69-7807050, FAX 49-69-78070550, zentrale.frankfurt@peterlang.com. Ed. Hartmut Schroeder.

306 EST ISSN 0134-5605
KULTUUR JA ELU/CULTURE AND LIFE. Text in Estonian. 1958. m. USD 48 (effective 1993). back issues avail.
Indexed: RASB.
Published by: Kirjastus Perioodika, Voorimehe 9, Tallinn, 10146, Estonia. TEL 372-627-6421, FAX 372-627-6420. Ed. Sirje Endre. Circ: 3,000.
Subscr. to: Narva mnt 5, PO Box 51, Tallinn 0090, Estonia.

301 BEL ISSN 0023-5288
KULTUURLEVEN. Text in Flemish. 1930. EUR 35.94 domestic; EUR 38.57 in Netherlands; EUR 48.22 elsewhere (effective 2003).
Formerly (until 1933): Thomistisch Tijdschrift voor Katholiek Kultuurleven (0773-3348)
Indexed: MLA-IB.
—IE, Infotrieve.
Address: Ravenstraat 98, Leuven, 3000, Belgium. TEL 32-16-240157, FAX 32-16-240197, kultuurleven@chello.be. Ed. B J De Clercq.

301 ITA ISSN 1724-9163
KUMA; creolizzare l'Europa. Text in Italian. 2001. irreg. **Document type:** *Magazine, Consumer.*
Media: Online - full text.
Published by: Universita degli Studi di Roma "La Sapienza", Facolta di Lettere e Filosofia, Dipartimento di Italianistica e Spettacolo, Piazzale Aldo Moro 5, Rome, 00185, Italy. TEL 39-06-49913786, FAX 39-06-49913684, disp@uniroma1.it. Eds. Flavia Caporuscio, Rosa Rafaele.

300 UKR ISSN 1728-2322
➤ **KYIVS'KYI NATSIONAL'NYI UNIVERSYTET IMENI TARASA SHEVCHENKA. VISNYK. SOTSIOLOHIYA, PSYKHOLOHIYA, PEDAHOHIKA.** Text in Ukrainian. 1995. a. **Document type:** *Journal, Academic/Scholarly.* **Description:** Designed for scientists, teachers, social workers, psychologists-practitioners and students. Deals with the results of theoretical, empirical and scientific-experimental researches in the actual problems of sociology, psychology, pedagogic and social work.
Related titles: ◆ Series: Kyivs'kyi Natsional'nyi Universytet imeni Tarasa Shevchenka. Visnyk. ISSN 1728-3817; ◆ Kyivs'kyi Natsional'nyi Universytet imeni Tarasa Shevchenka. Visnyk. Mizhnarodni Vidnosyny. ISSN 1728-2292; ◆ Kyivs'kyi Natsional'nyi Universytet imeni Tarasa Shevchenka. Visnyk. Yurydychni Nauky. ISSN 1728-2195; ◆ Kyivs'kyi Natsional'nyi Universytet imeni Tarasa Shevchenka. Visnyk. Khimiya. ISSN 1728-2209; ◆ Kyivs'kyi Natsional'nyi Universytet imeni Tarasa Shevchenka. Visnyk. Fizyka. ISSN 1728-2411; ◆ Kyivs'kyi Natsional'nyi Universytet imeni Tarasa Shevchenka. Visnyk. Biolohiya. ISSN 1728-2748; ◆ Kyivs'kyi Natsional'nyi Universytet imeni Tarasa Shevchenka. Visnyk. Ekonomika. ISSN 1728-2667; ◆ Kyivs'kyi Natsional'nyi Universytet imeni Tarasa Shevchenka. Visnyk. Istoriya. ISSN 1728-2640; ◆ Kyivs'kyi Natsional'nyi Universytet imeni Tarasa Shevchenka. Visnyk. Kibernetyka. ISSN 1728-2276; ◆ Kyivs'kyi Natsional'nyi Universytet imeni Tarasa Shevchenka. Visnyk. Problemy Rehulyatsii Fiziolohichnyh Funktsii. ISSN 1728-2624; ◆ Kyivs'kyi Natsional'nyi Universytet imeni Tarasa Shevchenka. Visnyk. Radiofizyka ta Elektronika. ISSN 1728-2306; ◆ Kyivs'kyi Natsional'nyi Universytet

S

imeni Tarasa Shevchenka. Visnyk. Filosofiya, Politolohiya. ISSN 1728-2632; ◆ Kyivs'kyi Natsional'nyi Universytet imeni Tarasa Shevchenka. Visnyk. Introduktsiya ta Zberezhennya Roslynnogo Riznomanittya. ISSN 1728-2284; ◆ Kyivs'kyi Natsional'nyi Universytet imeni Tarasa Shevchenka. Visnyk. Ukrainoznavstvo. ISSN 1728-2330; ◆ Kyivs'kyi Natsional'nyi Universytet imeni Tarasa Shevchenka. Visnyk. Literaturoznavstvo, Movoznavstvo, Fol'klorystyka. ISSN 1728-2659; ◆ Kyivs'kyi Natsional'nyi Universytet imeni Tarasa Shevchenka. Visnyk. Astronomiya. ISSN 1728-273X; ◆ Kyivs'kyi Natsional'nyi Universytet imeni Tarasa Shevchenka. Visnyk. Seriya: Fizyko-Matematychni Nauky. ISSN 1812-5409; ◆ Kyivs'kyi Natsional'nyi Universytet imeni Tarasa Shevchenka. Visnyk. Heohrafiya. ISSN 1728-2721; ◆ Kyivs'kyi Natsional'nyi Universytet imeni Tarasa Shevchenka. Visnyk. Heolohiya. ISSN 1728-2713; ◆ Kyivs'kyi Natsional'nyi Universytet imeni Tarasa Shevchenka. Visnyk. Zhurnalistyka. ISSN 1728-2705; ◆ Kyivs'kyi Natsional'nyi Universytet imeni Tarasa Shevchenka. Visnyk. Inozemna Filolohiya. ISSN 1728-2683; ◆ Kyivs'kyi Natsional'nyi Universytet imeni Tarasa Shevchenka. Visnyk. Shidni Movy ta Literatury. ISSN 1728-242X; ◆ Kyivs'kyi Natsional'nyi Universytet imeni Tarasa Shevchenka. Visnyk. Matematyka ta Mekhanika. ISSN 1684-1565.

Published by: (Kyivs'kyi Natsional'nyi Universytet imeni Tarasa Shevchenka/National Taras Shevchenko University of Kyiv), Vydavnycho-Poligrafichnyi Tsentr Kyivs'kyi Universytet, bul'var Tarasa Shevchenko, 14, ofis 43, Kyiv, 01601, Ukraine. TEL 380-44-2393172, FAX 380-44-2393128. Ed. Volodymyr Evtuh.

301 330.9 GBR ISSN 0023-5962
H1
➤ **KYKLOS**; international review for social sciences. Variant title: International Review for Social Sciences. Internationale Zeitschrift fur Sozialwissenschaften. Revue International des Sciences Sociales. Text in English. 1947. q. GBP 449 in United Kingdom to institutions; EUR 570 in Europe to institutions; USD 752 in the Americas to institutions; USD 878 elsewhere to institutions; GBP 517 combined subscription in United Kingdom to institutions (print & online eds.); EUR 656 combined subscription in Europe to institutions (print & online eds.); USD 865 combined subscription in the Americas to institutions (print & online eds.); USD 1,011 combined subscription elsewhere to institutions (print & online eds.) (effective 2012). adv. bk.rev. abstr.; bibl.; charts; illus. index. back issues avail.; reprint service avail. from PSC. **Document type:** *Journal, Academic/Scholarly.* **Description:** Provides information on political economy worldwide, containing contributions from scholars of international status.
Related titles: Microform ed.: (from PQC); Online - full text ed.: ISSN 1467-6435. GBP 449 in United Kingdom to institutions; EUR 570 in Europe to institutions; USD 752 in the Americas to institutions; USD 878 elsewhere to institutions (effective 2012) (from IngentaConnect).
Indexed: A01, A02, A03, A08, A12, A20, A22, A26, ABIn, ASCA, B01, B02, B04, B06, B07, B09, B15, B16, B17, B18, BAS, BRD, CA, CREJ, CurCont, DIP, E01, E08, EconLit, G04, G08, GEOBASE, H09, HistAb, I05, I13, IBR, IBSS, IBZ, ILD, JEL, KES, MEA&I, P02, P06, P10, P13, P27, P34, P42, P48, P51, P53, P54, PAIS, PCI, PQC, PRA, RASB, S02, S03, S05, S09, SCIMP, SCOPUS, SSAI, SSAb, SSCI, SSI, SociolAb, T02, W03, W05, W07, WBA.
—BLDSC (5134.858000), GNLM, IE, Infotrieve, Ingenta. **CCC.**
Published by: Wiley-Blackwell Publishing Ltd. (Subsidiary of: John Wiley & Sons, Inc.), 9600 Garsington Rd, Oxford, OX4 2DQ, United Kingdom. TEL 44-1865-776868, FAX 44-1865-714591, customerservices@blackwellpublishing.com. Ed. Rene L Frey. Adv. contact Craig Pickett TEL 44-1865-476267.

➤ **LABOUR & INDUSTRY**; a journal of the social and economic relations of work. *see* BUSINESS AND ECONOMICS—Labor And Industrial Relations

301 ITA ISSN 2035-5548
THE LAB'S QUARTERLY/TRIMESTRALE DEL LABORATORIO. Text in English, Italian. 1999. q.
Published by: Universita degli Studi di Pisa, Dipartimento di Scienze Politiche e Sociali, Via Serafini 3 A, Pisa, 56126, Italy. TEL 39-050-2212472, FAX 39-050-2212400.

LABYRINTH; international journal for philosophy, feminist theory and cultural hermeneutics. *see* PHILOSOPHY

301 DEU ISSN 0179-7603
LAENDLICHER RAUM. Text in German. 1950. bi-m. EUR 36 (effective 2008). index. **Document type:** *Journal, Academic/Scholarly.*
Formerly (until 1986): Agrarsoziale Gesellschaft. Rundbriefe (0170-9313)
—Ingenta.
Published by: Agrarsoziale Gesellschaft e.V., Kurze Geismarstr 33, Goettingen, 37073, Germany. TEL 49-551-497090, FAX 49-551-4970916, info@asg-goe.de, http://www.asg-goe.de.

LAMBDA NORDICA; tidskrift foer homosexualitetsforskning. *see* HOMOSEXUALITY

LAND REFORM, LAND SETTLEMENT AND COOPERATIVES. *see* AGRICULTURE—Agricultural Economics

302.23 DEU ISSN 1862-1090
LANDESANSTALT FUER MEDIEN NORDRHEIN-WESTFALEN. SCHRIFTENREIHE MEDIENFORSCHUNG. Text in German. 1991. irreg., latest vol.62, 2009. price varies. **Document type:** *Monographic series, Academic/Scholarly.*
Formerly (until 2002): Landesanstalt fuer Rundfunk Nordrhein-Westfalen. Schriftenreihe Medienforschung
Published by: (Landesanstalt fuer Medien Nordrhein-Westfalen), Vistas Verlag GmbH, Goltzstr 11, Berlin, 10781, Germany. TEL 49-30-32707446, FAX 49-30-32707455, medienverlag@vistas.de, http://www.vistas.de.

307 DNK ISSN 0907-4791
LANDSBYNYT. Text in Danish. 1985. 6/yr. DKK 175 (effective 2009). back issues avail. **Document type:** *Magazine, Consumer.*
Former titles (until 1991): Landsbyen (0903-7667); (until (1987): Landsforeningen af Landsbysamfund. Medlemsblad (0903-8078)
Related titles: Online - full text ed.: 2005.
Published by: Landsforeningen af Landsbysamfund/Danish Village Association, c/o Ole Olesen, Bildsoevej 165, Naesby Strand, Slagelse, 4200, Denmark. TEL 45-58-541050, ole@lal.dk.

LANGAGE & SOCIETE. *see* LINGUISTICS

LANGUAGE & COMMUNICATION; an interdisciplinary journal. *see* LINGUISTICS

300 400 DEU ISSN 2192-2128
▼ **LANGUAGE AND SOCIAL PROCESSES.** Text in English. 2011. irreg., latest vol.2, 2011. price varies. **Document type:** *Monographic series, Academic/Scholarly.* **Description:** Contains research on the sociolinguistic, sociohistorical and linguistic anthropological study of social issues.
Related titles: Online - full text ed.: ISSN 2192-2136. 2011.
Published by: Walter de Gruyter GmbH & Co. KG, Genthiner Str 13, Berlin, 10785, Germany. TEL 49-30-260050, FAX 49-30-26005251, info@degruyter.com, http://www.degruyter.de. Eds. David Britain, Richard Watts.

LANGUAGE AS SOCIAL ACTION. *see* LINGUISTICS

LANGUAGE, CULTURE AND CURRICULUM. *see* LINGUISTICS

LANGUAGE IN SOCIAL LIFE. *see* LINGUISTICS

306.44 DEU ISSN 1861-4175
LANGUAGE, POWER AND SOCIAL PROCESS. Text in English. 1999. irreg., latest vol.28, 2010. price varies. **Document type:** *Monographic series, Academic/Scholarly.* **Description:** Presents new approaches in the sociolinguistic and linguistic anthropological study of social issues and social problems.
—BLDSC (5155.710650), IE.
Published by: De Gruyter Mouton (Subsidiary of: Walter de Gruyter GmbH & Co. KG), Genthiner Str 13, Berlin, 10785, Germany. TEL 49-30-260050, FAX 49-30-26005251, mouton@degruyter.de. Ed. Richard J. Watts.

301 NLD ISSN 1871-3920
LATIN AMERICAN RESEARCH SERIES. Text in English. 1994. irreg., latest 2008. price varies. **Document type:** *Monographic series.*
Formerly (until 2004): Thela Latin America Series (1871-3912)
Published by: Rozenberg Publishers, Lindengracht 302 D&E, Amsterdam, 1015 KM, Netherlands. TEL 31-20-6255429, FAX 31-20-6203395, info@rozenbergps.com, http://www.rozenbergps.com.

301 305.868 GBR ISSN 1476-3435
E184.S75
➤ **LATINO STUDIES.** Text in English. 2003 (Mar.). q. USD 654 in North America to institutions; GBP 352 elsewhere to institutions (effective 2011). adv. illus. Index. back issues avail.; reprint service avail. from PSC. **Document type:** *Journal, Academic/Scholarly.* **Description:** Aims to advance interdisciplinary scholarship about the lived experience and struggles of Latinas and Latinos for equity, representation, and social justice.
Related titles: Online - full text ed.: ISSN 1476-3443 (from IngentaConnect).
Indexed: A13, A22, CA, E01, ENW, H21, I08, IBR, IBSS, IBZ, L&LBA, M08, MLA-IB, P02, P08, P10, P42, P45, P48, P51, P53, P54, PQC, PSA, S02, S03, S11, SCOPUS, SociolAb, T02.
—IE, Ingenta. **CCC.**
Published by: Palgrave Macmillan Ltd. (Subsidiary of: Macmillan Publishers Ltd.), Houndmills, Basingstoke, Hants RG21 6XS, United Kingdom. TEL 44-1256-329242, FAX 44-1256-479476, orders@palgrave.com, http://www.palgrave.com. Ed. Suzanne Oboler. Pub. David Bull TEL 44-1256-329242. Circ: 350. **Subscr. to:** Subscription Department, Brunel Rd, Houndmills, Basingstoke, Hants RG21 2XS, United Kingdom. TEL 44-1256-357893, FAX 44-1256-328339, subscriptions@palgrave.com.

➤ **LAW & SOCIETY REVIEW.** *see* LAW

➤ **LAW, CULTURE & THE HUMANITIES.** *see* LAW

303.3 NZL ISSN 1177-3294
LEADERSHIP AND MANAGEMENT STUDIES IN SUB-SAHARA AFRICA. CONFERENCE PROCEEDINGS. Text in English. 2006. a. **Document type:** *Proceedings, Academic/Scholarly.*
Media: CD-ROM.
Published by: Leadership and Management Studies in Sub-Sahara Africa Conference, c/o Romie Littrell, Auckland University of Technology, Faculty of Business, Private Bag 92006, Auckland, 1142, New Zealand.

THE LEADERSHIP QUARTERLY. *see* BUSINESS AND ECONOMICS—Management

303.33 AUS ISSN 1834-4933
LEADING MINDS. Text in English. 2006. m. **Document type:** *Newsletter, Trade.*
Media: Online - full text.
Published by: Kelly Strategic Influence Pty Ltd, Level 28, 303 Collins St, Melbourne, VIC 3150, Australia. TEL 61-3-9678-9218, FAX 61-2-9878-9009, gkelly@kellystrategicinfluence.com.au.

LEARNING COMMUNITIES; international journal of learning in social contexts. *see* EDUCATION

334 USA ISSN 0023-9836
HX656.T9
LEAVES OF TWIN OAKS. Text in English. 1967. 3/yr. USD 10 to individuals; USD 15 to institutions. illus. reprints avail. **Document type:** *Newsletter.*
Related titles: Microform ed.: (from PQC).
Published by: Twin Oaks Community, 138 Twin Oaks Rd, Louisa, VA 23093-6337. TEL 540-894-5126. Ed. Stevek Kretzmann. R&P Steve Kretzmann. Circ: 800.

LEGACIES SHARED SERIES. *see* ETHNIC INTERESTS

301 GHA ISSN 0855-6261
➤ **LEGON JOURNAL OF SOCIOLOGY.** Text in English. 2004. s-a. GHC 10 domestic; USD 50 foreign (effective 2008). **Document type:** *Journal, Academic/Scholarly.*
Published by: University of Ghana, Department of Sociology, Research and Publication Unit, Legon, PO Box 65, Accra, Ghana. TEL 233-21-775381.

➤ **LEIPZIGER ARBEITEN ZUR SPRACH- UND KOMMUNIKATIONSGESCHICHTE.** *see* LINGUISTICS

301 DEU ISSN 1437-2886
LEIPZIGER SOZIOLOGISCHE STUDIEN. Text in German. 1998. irreg., latest vol.3, 2003. price varies. **Document type:** *Monographic series, Academic/Scholarly.*
Published by: Leipziger Universitaetsverlag GmbH, Oststr 41, Leipzig, 04317, Germany. TEL 49-341-9900440, FAX 49-341-9900440, info@univerlag-leipzig.de.

306.4 GBR ISSN 1468-571X
➤ **LEISURE, CONSUMPTION AND CULTURE.** Text in English. 2000. irreg., latest 2006. price varies. back issues avail. **Document type:** *Monographic series, Academic/Scholarly.*
Published by: Berg Publishers (Subsidiary of: Oxford International Publishers Ltd.), 1st Fl Angel Ct, 81 St Clements St, Oxford, Berks OX4 1AW, United Kingdom. TEL 44-1865-245104, FAX 44-1865-791165, enquiry@bergpublishers.com. Ed. Rudy Koshar.

➤ **LENDEMAINS**; etudes comparees sur la France - vergleichende Frankreichforschung. *see* LITERARY AND POLITICAL REVIEWS

303 ITA ISSN 1592-2898
LETTERA INTERNAZIONALE. Text in Italian. 1984. q. EUR 37 domestic to individuals; EUR 46 domestic to institutions; EUR 74.40 foreign (effective 2008). index. back issues avail. **Document type:** *Journal, Academic/Scholarly.*
Related titles: Online - full text ed.: ISSN 1971-8225. 2006; ◆ Spanish ed.: Letra Internacional. ISSN 0213-4721; ◆ Danish ed.: Lettre Internationale. ISSN 1603-4406; ◆ Hungarian ed.: Magyar Lettre Internationale. ISSN 0866-692X; ◆ Romanian ed.: Lettre Internationale (Romanian Edition). ISSN 1220-5958.
Published by: (Associazione Lettera Internazionale), Fondazione Lelio e Lisli Basso Issoco, Via della Dogana Vecchia 5, Rome, 00186, Italy. TEL 39-06-6879953, FAX 39-06-68307516, basso@fondazionebasso.it, http://www.fondazionebasso.it. Ed. Federico Coen. Circ: 5,000.

302.23 ITA ISSN 0024-144X
AS221
LETTURE; mensile di informazione culturale, letteratura e spettacolo. Text in Italian. 1946. 10/yr. EUR 31 (effective 2008). adv. bk.rev.; film rev.; music rev.; play rev. bibl.; illus. index, cum.index. **Document type:** *Magazine, Consumer.* **Description:** Contains articles on cultural events and trends, reviews and essays on film directors, writers and poets.
Indexed: BibInd, FR, MLA-IB, RASB.
Published by: Edizioni San Paolo, Piazza Soncino 5, Cinisello Balsamo, MI 20092, Italy. TEL 39-02-660751, FAX 39-02-66075211, sanpaoloedizioni@stpauls.it, http://www.edizionisanpaolo.it. Ed. Antonio Frizzolo. Pub. Giuseppe Proietti. R&P Mauro Broggi TEL 39-2-48008838. Adv. contact Giuliano Censi. Circ: 8,000.

301 FRA ISSN 1776-3150
LIANES. Text in English, French. 2005. q. free (effective 2011). **Document type:** *Journal, Academic/Scholarly.*
Media: Online - full text. Ed. Priscilla R Appama.

302.2 PAN
LIBERTAD DE EXPRESION. Text in Spanish. 1988. m.
Published by: Universidad de Panama, Facultad de Comunicacion Social, Estafeta Universitaria, Panama City, Panama.

301 GBR ISSN 0267-7113
LIBERTARIAN ALLIANCE. SOCIOLOGICAL NOTES. Text in English. 1985. irreg., latest 2003. back issues avail. **Document type:** *Monographic series, Trade.*
Related titles: Online - full text ed.: ISSN 2042-2806. free (effective 2009).
Published by: Libertarian Alliance, 2 Lansdowne Row, Ste 35, London, W1J 6HL, United Kingdom. TEL 44-7956-472199. Ed. Nigel Meek.

301 BRA ISSN 1518-9325
LIBERTAS. Text in Portuguese. 2000. s-a. **Document type:** *Journal, Academic/Scholarly.*
Related titles: Online - full text ed.: ISSN 1980-8518. free (effective 2011).
Published by: Universidade Federal de Juiz de Fora, Editora, Rua Jose Lourenco Kelmer s/n, Campus Universitario, Juiz de Fora, MG, Brazil. TEL 55-32-21023800, http://www.ufjf.br.

301 GBR ISSN 1462-219X
➤ **LIBRARY OF PEASANT STUDIES.** Text in English. 1975. irreg. USD 118 to individuals; USD 581 combined subscription to institutions (print & online eds.) (effective 2009). bibl. index. back issues avail.; reprints avail. **Document type:** *Monographic series, Academic/Scholarly.*
Related titles: Online - full text ed.: USD 552 (effective 2009).
Published by: Routledge (Subsidiary of: Taylor & Francis Group), 2 Park Sq, Milton Park, Abingdon, Oxon OX14 4RN, United Kingdom. TEL 44-20-70176000, FAX 44-20-70176699, info@routledge.co.uk, http://www.tandf.co.uk/books. Ed. Tom Brass.

301 ITA ISSN 1590-0002
I LIBRI DEL FONDO SOCIALE EUROPEO. Text in Italian. 1997. irreg. **Document type:** *Monographic series, Academic/Scholarly.*
Published by: Istituto per lo Sviluppo della Formazione Professionale dei Lavoratori (I S F O L), Corso d'Italia 33, Rome, 00198, Italy. TEL 39-06-854471, http://www.isfol.it.

301 FRA ISSN 1285-3097
LE LIEN SOCIAL. Text in French. 1997. irreg. back issues avail. **Document type:** *Monographic series, Academic/Scholarly.*
Published by: Presses Universitaires de France, 6 Avenue Reille, Paris, 75685, France. TEL 33-1-58103161, FAX 33-1-45897530.

306.85 ISR
LIHYOT MISHPAHA/ETRE PARENTS. Text in Hebrew. 1997. m. ILS 444 (effective 2008). **Document type:** *Magazine, Consumer.*
Related titles: Online - full text ed.: ILS 194.40 (effective 2008).
Published by: S B C Group, 8 Shefa Tal St., Tel Aviv, 67013, Israel. TEL 972-3-565-2100, FAX 972-3-562-6476, sherut@sbc.co.il, http://www.sbc.co.il/Index.asp.

LIMES. *see* PHILOSOPHY

201.6 USA ISSN 0024-4414
AP2
LISTENING; journal of religion and culture. Text in English. 1966. 3/yr. USD 10 in US & Canada to individuals; USD 12 elsewhere to individuals; USD 13 in US & Canada to institutions; USD 15 elsewhere to institutions (effective 2004). back issues avail. **Document type:** *Journal, Academic/Scholarly.* **Description:** Explores issues in culture and religion.
Indexed: A22, CPL, MLA-IB, OTA, P30, PhilInd, R&TA, RILM.
—BLDSC (5275.800000), IE, Ingenta.
Published by: Listening, Inc., Lewis University, One University Parkway, Unit 1108, Romeoville, IL 60446-2298. http://www.listeningjournal.org/. Ed. Mark McVann.

307.14 USA ISSN 1936-0134
LIVABLE COMMUNITIES@ WORK. Text in English. 2002. irreg.
Document type: *Newsletter, Consumer.*
Published by: Funders' Network for Smart Growth and Livable Communities, 1500 San Remo Ave, Ste 249, Coral Gables, FL 33146. TEL 305-667-6350, FAX 305-667-6355, info@fundersnetwork.org, www.fundersnetwork.org.

307.14 AUS ISSN 1837-0721
▼ **LIVEABLE COMMUNITIES.** Text in English. 2009. q. free (effective 2011). back issues avail. **Document type:** *Newsletter, Government.* **Description:** Highlights the diverse work of Department of Planning and Community Development (DPCD), all of which is done with valued partners across government, business, not-for-profit groups and with communities.
Related titles: Online - full text ed.: ISSN 1837-0853.
Published by: State Government of Victoria, Department of Planning and Community Development, GPO Box 2392, Melbourne, VIC 3001, Australia. TEL 61-3-92083333, 300-366-356.

306.85 USA
LIVING (GROTTOES); for the whole family. (Avail. in 3 editions: Harrisonburg, VA; Souderton, PA: Lancaster, PA) Text in English. 1991. q. free. adv. 36 p./no. 6 cols./p.; back issues avail. **Document type:** *Newspaper, Consumer.* **Description:** Offers hope and encouragement for healthy and positive relationships at home, in the workplace, and in the community.
Published by: Shalom Foundation, Inc., 1251 Virginia Avenue, Harrisonburg, VA 24441. TEL 540-249-3177, FAX 540-249-3177. Ed. Melodie Davis. Pub. Richard Benner TEL 888-833-3333. Circ: 142,000 (controlled).

301 FRA ISSN 2108-6303
▼ **LIVRE ET SOCIETE.** Text in French. 2010. irreg. **Document type:** *Monographic series, Academic/Scholarly.*
Published by: Presses Universitaires de Paris Ouest, 200 Av de la Republique, Bat A bureau 320, Nanterre Cedex, 92001, France.

301 PRT ISSN 1647-1431
LOCUS SOCI@L. Text in Portuguese. 2008. **Document type:** *Journal, Academic/Scholarly.*
Published by: Universidade Catolica Portuguesa, Faculdade de Ciencias Humanas, Palma de Cima, Lisbon, 1649-023, Portugal. TEL 351-21-424000, FAX 351-21-7270256, info@reitoria.ucp.pt, http://www.ucp.pt.

306.85 FRA ISSN 0753-1419
LOGEMENT ET FAMILLE; le reveil des locataires. Text in French. m. (10/yr). **Document type:** *Magazine.*
Related titles: Online - full text ed.: free.
Published by: Confederation Nationale du Logement, 8 rue Meriel, B.P.119, Montreuil, Cedex 93104, France. Ed. Jean Pierre Giacono.

301 FRA ISSN 0295-7736
LOGIQUES SOCIALES. Text in French. 1984. irreg. **Document type:** *Monographic series.*
Related titles: ◆ Series: Logiques Sociales. Serie Litteratures et Societe. ISSN 1778-4808; ◆ Logiques Sociales. Serie Sociologie des Arts. ISSN 1779-7225; ◆ Logiques Sociales. Serie Sociologies Europeennes. ISSN 1779-7217; ◆ Logiques Sociales. Serie Theories Sociologiques. ISSN 1258-0104; ◆ Logiques Sociales. Serie Etudes Culturelles. ISSN 1952-0697; ◆ Logiques Sociales. Serie Sociologie de la Modernite. ISSN 1629-4793; ◆ Logiques Sociales. Serie Sociologie de la Connaissance. ISSN 1635-0146; ◆ Logiques Sociales. Serie Sociologie de la Gestion. ISSN 1762-1917; ◆ Logiques Sociales. Serie Sociologie Politique. ISSN 1777-5027; ◆ Logiques Sociales. Serie Musiques et Champ Social. ISSN 1275-5842.
Published by: L' Harmattan, 5 Rue de l'Ecole Polytechnique, Paris, 75005, France. TEL 33-1-43257651, FAX 33-1-43258203, http://www.editions-harmattan.fr.

301 FRA ISSN 2108-565X
▼ **LOGIQUES SOCIALES. SERIE ANAMNESE.** Text in French. 2009. irreg. **Document type:** *Monographic series, Academic/Scholarly.*
Published by: L' Harmattan, 5 Rue de l'Ecole Polytechnique, Paris, 75005, France. TEL 33-1-43257651, FAX 33-1-43258203, diffusion.harmattan@wanadoo.fr.

306 FRA ISSN 1952-0697
LOGIQUES SOCIALES. SERIE ETUDES CULTURELLES. Text in French. 2006. irreg. back issues avail. **Document type:** *Monographic series.*
Related titles: ◆ Series of: Logiques Sociales. ISSN 0295-7736.
Published by: L' Harmattan, 5 Rue de l'Ecole Polytechnique, Paris, 75005, France. TEL 33-1-43257651, FAX 33-1-43258203, http://www.editions-harmattan.fr.

301 780 FRA ISSN 1275-5842
LOGIQUES SOCIALES. SERIE MUSIQUES ET CHAMP SOCIAL. Text in French. 1997. irreg. back issues avail. **Document type:** *Monographic series.*
Related titles: ◆ Series of: Logiques Sociales. ISSN 0295-7736.
Published by: L' Harmattan, 5 Rue de l'Ecole Polytechnique, Paris, 75005, France. TEL 33-1-43257651, FAX 33-1-43258203, http://www.editions-harmattan.fr.

301 100 FRA ISSN 1635-0146
LOGIQUES SOCIALES. SERIE SOCIOLOGIE DE LA CONNAISSANCE. Text in French. 2002. irreg. back issues avail. **Document type:** *Monographic series.*
Related titles: ◆ Series of: Logiques Sociales. ISSN 0295-7736.
Published by: L' Harmattan, 5 Rue de l'Ecole Polytechnique, Paris, 75005, France. TEL 33-1-43257651, FAX 33-1-43258203, http://www.editions-harmattan.fr.

301 658 FRA ISSN 1762-1917
LOGIQUES SOCIALES. SERIE SOCIOLOGIE DE LA GESTION. Text in French. 2003. irreg. back issues avail. **Document type:** *Monographic series.*
Related titles: ◆ Series of: Logiques Sociales. ISSN 0295-7736.
Published by: L' Harmattan, 5 Rue de l'Ecole Polytechnique, Paris, 75005, France. TEL 33-1-43257651, FAX 33-1-43258203, http://www.editions-harmattan.fr.

301 FRA ISSN 1629-4793
LOGIQUES SOCIALES. SERIE SOCIOLOGIE DE LA MODERNITE. Text in French. 2001. irreg. back issues avail. **Document type:** *Monographic series.*
Related titles: ◆ Series of: Logiques Sociales. ISSN 0295-7736.
Published by: L' Harmattan, 5 Rue de l'Ecole Polytechnique, Paris, 75005, France. TEL 33-1-43257651, FAX 33-1-43258203, http://www.editions-harmattan.fr.

306.47 FRA ISSN 1779-7225
LOGIQUES SOCIALES. SERIE SOCIOLOGIE DES ARTS. Text in French. 2005. irreg. **Document type:** *Monographic series.*
Related titles: ◆ Series of: Logiques Sociales. ISSN 0295-7736.
Published by: L' Harmattan, 5 Rue de l'Ecole Polytechnique, Paris, 75005, France. TEL 33-1-43257651, FAX 33-1-43258203, http://www.editions-harmattan.fr.

301 320 FRA ISSN 1777-5027
LOGIQUES SOCIALES. SERIE SOCIOLOGIE POLITIQUE. Text in French. 2005. irreg. back issues avail. **Document type:** *Monographic series.*
Related titles: ◆ Series of: Logiques Sociales. ISSN 0295-7736.
Published by: L' Harmattan, 5 Rue de l'Ecole Polytechnique, Paris, 75005, France. TEL 33-1-43257651, FAX 33-1-43258203, http://www.editions-harmattan.fr.

301 FRA ISSN 1779-7217
LOGIQUES SOCIALES. SERIE SOCIOLOGIES EUROPEENNES. Text in French. 2005. irreg. back issues avail. **Document type:** *Monographic series.*
Related titles: ◆ Series of: Logiques Sociales. ISSN 0295-7736.
Published by: L' Harmattan, 5 Rue de l'Ecole Polytechnique, Paris, 75005, France. TEL 33-1-43257651, FAX 33-1-43258203, http://www.editions-harmattan.fr.

301 FRA ISSN 1258-0104
LOGIQUES SOCIALES. SERIE THEORIES SOCIOLOGIQUES. Text in French. 1994. irreg. back issues avail. **Document type:** *Monographic series.*
Related titles: ◆ Series of: Logiques Sociales. ISSN 0295-7736.
Published by: L' Harmattan, 5 Rue de l'Ecole Polytechnique, Paris, 75005, France. TEL 33-1-43257651, FAX 33-1-43258203, http://www.editions-harmattan.fr.

301 USA ISSN 1543-0820
LOGOS (MIDLAND PARK). Text in English. 2002. q. bk.rev. back issues avail. **Description:** Publishes essays and reviews in the social sciences, politics, humanities, and the arts.
Media: Online - full text.
Address: 261 Eire Ave., Midland Park, NJ 07432. http://www.logosjournal.com/. Ed. Michael J Thompson.

LOGOS (ST. PAUL); a journal of Catholic thought and culture. *see* RELIGIONS AND THEOLOGY—Roman Catholic

LOISIR ET SOCIETE/SOCIETY AND LEISURE. *see* LEISURE AND RECREATION

LONDON JOURNAL; a review of metropolitan society past and present. *see* HISTORY—History Of Europe

305 GBR ISSN 1757-9597
▼ ➤ **LONGITUDINAL AND LIFE COURSE STUDIES.** Abbreviated title: L L C S. Text in English. 2009. q. free (effective 2011). back issues avail. **Document type:** *Journal, Academic/Scholarly.* **Description:** Brings together the broad range of specialist fields undertaking and using longitudinal and life course research.
Media: Online - full text.
Indexed: P30.
Published by: Society for Longitudinal and Life Course Studies, 20 Bedford Way, London, WC1H 0AL, United Kingdom. TEL 44-20-74826893, http://www.longstudies.longviewuk.com/.

➤ **LUA NOVA**; cultura e politica. *see* POLITICAL SCIENCE

301 MNE ISSN 0352-4973
B6
LUCA; casopis za filozofiju i sociologiju. Text in Serbo-Croatian. 1984. 2/yr. **Document type:** *Journal, Academic/Scholarly.*
Indexed: MLA-IB.
Published by: Drustvo Sociologa Crne Gore/Association of Sociologists of Montenegro, D Bojovica bb, Niksic. Circ: 1,000.

301 POL ISSN 0076-1435
GR1
LUD. Text in Polish; Summaries in English, German. 1895. a. price varies. bk.rev. index.
Indexed: AICP, AnthLit, FR, MLA-IB.
Published by: Polskie Towarzystwo Ludoznawcze, ul Szewska 36, Wroclaw, 50139, Poland. TEL 48-71-444613. Ed. Zbigniew Jasiewicz. Circ: 800. **Dist. by:** Ars Polona, Obroncow 25, Warsaw 03933, Poland. TEL 48-22-8261201, FAX 48-22-8265334.

302.23 DEU ISSN 2190-4790
LUDWIGSBURGER BEITRAEGE ZUR MEDIENPAEDAGOGIK. Text in German. 2001. irreg., latest vol.13, 2010. **Document type:** *Monographic series, Academic/Scholarly.*
Media: Online - full text.
Published by: Paedagogische Hochschule Ludwigsburg, Interdisziplinaere Zentrum fuer Medienpaedagogik und Medienforschung, Reuteallee 46, Ludwigsburg, 71634, Germany. TEL 49-7141-1400, FAX 49-7141-140434, imort@ph-ludwigsburg.de, http://www.ph-ludwigsburg.de/64.html. Ed. Petra Reinhard-Hauck.

301 SWE ISSN 1102-4712
LUND DISSERTATIONS IN SOCIOLOGY. Text in English, Swedish. 1992. irreg., latest vol.24. price varies. **Document type:** *Monographic series, Academic/Scholarly.*
Published by: Sociologiska Institutionen, Box 114, Lund, 22100, Sweden. FAX 46-46-2224100.

302.23 USA
M A I N. (Media Arts Information Network) Text in English. 1991. q. membership only. bk.rev. **Document type:** *Newsletter.*
Published by: National Alliance for Media Arts and Culture, 346 Ninth St, San Francisco, CA 94103-3809. TEL 415-431-1391, FAX 415-432-1392. Ed., R&P Helen Demichiel.

302.23 384 AUS ISSN 1441-2616
➤ **M / C JOURNAL.** (Media and Culture) Text in English. 1998. bi-m. free (effective 2011). back issues avail. **Document type:** *Journal, Academic/Scholarly.* **Description:** Contains feature articles with a focus on politics and culture.
Media: Online - full text. **Related titles:** Print ed.
Indexed: A39, C27, C29, CA, CMM, D03, D04, E13, R14, S14, S15, S18, T02.
—CCC.
Published by: Queensland University of Technology, Creative Industries Faculty, c/o Dr. Axel Bruns, Z1-515, Creative Industries Precinct, Musk Ave, Kelvin Grove, QLD 4059, Australia. TEL 61-7-31385548.

➤ **M S A LINK.** (Muslim Students' Association) *see* RELIGIONS AND THEOLOGY—Islamic

301 USA ISSN 1941-3742
JZ1320.4
MACALESTER CIVIC FORUM. Text in English. 2008 (Feb.). a. back issues avail. **Document type:** *Journal, Academic/Scholarly.*
Published by: Macalester College, Institute for Global Citizenship, 1600 Grand Ave, St Paul, MN 55105. TEL 651-696-6000, beegle@macalester.edu, http://www.macalester.edu/globalcitizenship/index.html. Ed. Ahmed I Samatar.

306 USA ISSN 1553-8923
E169.1
MAGAZINE AMERICANA. Text in English. 2001. m. free (effective 2010). **Document type:** *Magazine, Consumer.*
Media: Online - full text.
Published by: Institute for the Study of American Popular Culture, 7095-1240 Hollywood Blvd, Hollywood, CA 90028. Ed. Leslie Kreiner Wilson.

305.899442 NZL ISSN 1177-5904
GN380
➤ **MAI REVIEW.** Text in English. 2006. 3/yr. free (effective 2011). **Document type:** *Journal, Academic/Scholarly.* **Description:** Aims to contribute to the body of knowledge about Maori and indigenous development.
Media: Online - full text.
Indexed: S02, S03, T02.
Published by: Nga Pae o te Maramatanga/National Institute of Research Excellence for Maori Development and Advancement, Waipapa Marae Complex, Rehutai Bldg, 16 Wynyard St, University of Auckland, Private Bag 92019, Auckland, 1142, New Zealand. TEL 64-9-3737599 ext 84220, FAX 64-9-3737928, info@maramatanga.ac.nz, http://www.maramatanga.co.nz/. Ed. Les R Tumoana Williams.

300 DEU ISSN 1864-6387
MAINZER BEITRAEGE ZUR KULTURANTHROPOLOGIE. VOLKSKUNDE. Text in German. 1990. irreg., latest vol.3, 2009. price varies. **Document type:** *Monographic series, Academic/Scholarly.*
Formerly (until 2007): Mainzer Kleine Schriften zur Volkskultur
Published by: Waxmann Verlag GmbH, Steinfurter Str 555, Muenster, 48159, Germany. TEL 49-251-265040, FAX 49-251-2650426, info@waxmann.com.

303.4833 SWE ISSN 1653-6606
MALMOE HOEGSKOLA. KONST, KULTUR OCH KOMMUNIKATION. DISSERTATIONS IN ARTS AND COMMUNICATION. Text in English. 2006. irreg. **Document type:** *Monographic series, Academic/Scholarly.*
Media: Online - full content.
Published by: Malmoe Hoegskola, Konst, Kultur och Kommunikation/University of Malmoe, School of Art and Communication, Beijerskajen 8, Malmoe, 20506, Sweden. TEL 46-40-6657000, FAX 46-40-6657305, info@mah.se/k3.

303.4833 SWE ISSN 1652-0343
MALMOE HOEGSKOLA. KONST, KULTUR OCH KOMMUNIKATION. STUDIES IN ARTS AND COMMUNICATIONS. Text in English, Swedish. 2003. irreg. SEK 129 per issue (effective 2006). back issues avail. **Document type:** *Monographic series, Academic/Scholarly.*
Published by: Malmoe Hoegskola, Konst, Kultur och Kommunikation/University of Malmoe, School of Art and Communication, Beijerskajen 8, Malmoe, 20506, Sweden. TEL 46-40-6657000, FAX 46-40-6657305, info@mah.se/k3. Ed. Pelle Ehn.

306.85 POL ISSN 1643-7489
MALZENSTWO I RODZINA; niezalezny kwartalnik naukowy. Text in Polish. 2002. q. PLZ 15 per issue (effective 2002).
Address: Ul Schillera 4 m.35, Warszawa, 00248, Poland. TEL 48-22-8319310. Ed., Pub. Zofia Dabrowska.

301 GBR ISSN 1366-2554
➤ **MANCHESTER SOCIOLOGY OCCASIONAL PAPERS.** Text in English. 1978. irreg., latest vol.51, 1998. GBP 2.50 (effective 1999). **Document type:** *Monographic series, Academic/Scholarly.*
Formerly (until 1996): University of Manchester. Department of Sociology. Occasional Paper (1362-6418)
Published by: (Department of Sociology), University of Manchester, Department of Sociology, School of Social Sciences, Roscoe Building, Manchester, M13 9PL, United Kingdom. http://www.socialsciences.manchester.ac.uk/sociology/. R&P Peter Halfpenny TEL 44-161-2752493.

➤ **MANDE STUDIES.** *see* LITERATURE

➤ **MANITESE.** *see* SOCIAL SERVICES AND WELFARE

➤ **MANNHEIMER STUDIEN ZUR LITERATUR- UND KULTURWISSENSCHAFT.** *see* LITERATURE

301 NLD ISSN 1871-9309
➤ **MANSHOLT PUBLICATION SERIES.** Text in English. 2006. irreg., latest vol.11, 2011. price varies. **Document type:** *Monographic series, Academic/Scholarly.*
Published by: (Mansholt Graduate School of Social Sciences), Wageningen Academic Publishers, PO Box 220, Wageningen, 6700 AE, Netherlands. TEL 31-317-476515, FAX 31-317-453417, info@wageningenacademic.com, http://www.wageningenacademic.com. Eds. Arjen Wals, Wim Heijman.

➤ **MANSHOLT WORKING PAPERS.** *see* BUSINESS AND ECONOMICS

➤ **MANUSIA DAN MASYARAKAT/MAN AND SOCIETY.** *see* ANTHROPOLOGY

➤ **MARGARET GEE'S AUSTRALIAN MEDIA GUIDE.** *see* BUSINESS AND ECONOMICS—Trade And Industrial Directories

➤ **MARRIAGE & FAMILY: A CHRISTIAN JOURNAL.** *see* RELIGIONS AND THEOLOGY—Roman Catholic

S

306.85 USA ISSN 0149-4929
HQ536 CODEN: MFARDJ
➤ **MARRIAGE & FAMILY REVIEW.** Abbreviated title: M F R. Text in English. 1978. 8/yr. GBP 1,350 combined subscription in United Kingdom to institutions (print & online eds.); EUR 1,753, USD 1,759 combined subscription to institutions (print & online eds.) (effective 2012). adv. bk.rev. abstr. index. 120 p./no. 1 cols./p.; back issues avail.; reprint service avail. from PSC. **Document type:** *Journal, Academic/Scholarly.* **Description:** Covers marriage, family planning, and crisis counseling.
Related titles: Microfiche ed.: (from PQC); Microform ed.; Online - full text ed.: ISSN 1540-9635. GBP 1,215 in United Kingdom to institutions; EUR 1,578, USD 1,583 to institutions (effective 2012).
Indexed: A01, A02, A03, A08, A20, A22, A25, A26, AMHA, ASCA, ASSIA, AgeL, Agr, AmHI, B21, BRD, CA, CPLI, CWI, DIP, E-psyche, E01, E02, E03, E08, E17, ERI, ESPM, EdA, EdI, F09, FR, FamI, G08, GSS&RPL, GW, H07, I05, IBR, IBZ, M01, M02, P02, P03, P10, P12, P13, P25, P27, P30, P34, P46, P48, P53, P54, PC&CA, PCI, PQC, PSI, PsycInfo, PsycholAb, S02, S03, S08, S09, SCOPUS, SFSA, SOPODA, SSA, SSAI, SSAb, SSI, SWR&A, SociolAb, T02, W03, W09.
—BLDSC (5382.860000), IE, Infotrieve, Ingenta, INIST. **CCC.**
Published by: Routledge (Subsidiary of: Taylor & Francis Group), 325 Chestnut St, Ste 800, Philadelphia, PA 19106. TEL 215-625-8900, 800-354-1420, FAX 215-625-8914, journals@routledge.com, http://www.routledge.com. Ed. Suzanne K Steinmetz. adv.: B&W page USD 315, color page USD 550; trim 4.375 x 7.125. Circ: 413 (paid).

301 USA ISSN 2153-2761
▼ **MASS COMMUNICATION AND JOURNALISM.** Text in English. forthcoming 2011 (Jan.). irreg. **Document type:** *Monographic series, Academic/Scholarly.*
Published by: Peter Lang Publishing, Inc. (Subsidiary of: Peter Lang Publishing Group), 29 Broadway, New York, NY 10006. TEL 212-647-7700, FAX 212-647-7707, customerservice@plang.com, http://www.peterlang.com.

302.23 USA ISSN 1520-5436
P95.54
➤ **MASS COMMUNICATION AND SOCIETY.** Abbreviated title: M C & S. Text in English. 1973. 5/yr. GBP 494 combined subscription in United Kingdom to institutions (print & online eds.); EUR 660, USD 829 combined subscription to institutions (print & online eds.) (effective 2012). adv. bk.rev. illus. back issues avail.; reprint service avail. from PSC. **Document type:** *Journal, Academic/Scholarly.* **Description:** Examines mass communication theory from a multitude of approaches and perspectives.
Formerly (until 1998): Mass Communications Review (0193-7707)
Related titles: Online - full text ed.: ISSN 1532-7825. GBP 445 in United Kingdom to institutions; EUR 594, USD 747 to institutions (effective 2012).
Indexed: A01, A02, A03, A08, A20, A22, A26, AmHI, BRD, CA, CMM, CommAb, CurCont, E-psyche, E01, E08, FamI, G08, H07, I05, LeftInd, P03, P27, P34, P42, P48, P54, PAIS, PQC, PSA, PsycInfo, PsycholAb, S02, S03, S09, SCOPUS, SSA, SSAI, SSAb, SSCI, SSI, SociolAb, T02, W03, W07.
—BLDSC (5387.905000), IE, Infotrieve, Ingenta. **CCC.**
Published by: Routledge (Subsidiary of: Taylor & Francis Group), 325 Chestnut St, Ste 800, Philadelphia, PA 19106. TEL 800-354-1420, FAX 215-625-2940, journals@routledge.com, http://www.routledge.com. Ed. Stephen D Perry. Adv. contact Linda Hann TEL 44-1344-779945.

302.23 IND
MASS MEDIA IN INDIA. Text in English. 1978. a. INR 400 per issue (effective 2011). back issues avail. **Document type:** *Government.*
Indexed: BAS.
Published by: Ministry of Information & Broadcasting, Publications Division, Soochna Bhawan, C.G.O Complex, Lodi Rd, New Delhi, 110 003, India. http://publicationsdivision.nic.in/.

MASSACHUSETTS STUDIES IN EARLY MODERN CULTURE. *see* HISTORY—History Of Europe

302.23 SWE ISSN 0280-2147
P88.8
MASSMEDIA; handbok foer journalister, informatoerer och andra som foeljar press, radio och TV. Text in Swedish. 1981-2000; resumed 2003. a., latest 2003. price varies. **Document type:** *Yearbook, Trade.*
Related titles: CD-ROM ed.
Published by: Svenska Journalistfoerbundet/Swedish Association of Journalists, Vasagatan 50, PO Box 1116, Stockholm, 11181, Sweden. TEL 46-8-6137500, FAX 46-8-4115835, kansliet@sjf.se, http://www.sjf.se.

MATERIALIEN AUS DER BILDUNGSFORSCHUNG. *see* EDUCATION

302.23 DEU
MATERIALIEN ZUR MEDIENPAEDAGOGIK. Text in German. 1994. irreg., latest vol.9, 2010. price varies. **Document type:** *Monographic series, Academic/Scholarly.*
Published by: KoPaed Verlag, Pfaelzer-Wald-Str 64, Munich, 81539, Germany. TEL 49-89-68890098, FAX 49-89-6891912, info@kopaed.de.

306 GBR ISSN 1460-3349
➤ **MATERIALIZING CULTURE.** Text in English. 1998. irreg., latest 2010. price varies. **Document type:** *Monographic series, Academic/Scholarly.* **Description:** Concerns itself with the social relations involved in material practices.
Published by: Berg Publishers (Subsidiary of: Oxford International Publishers Ltd.), 1st Fl Angel Ct, 81 St Clements St, Oxford, Berks OX4 1AW, United Kingdom. TEL 44-1865-245104, FAX 44-1865-791165, enquiry@bergpublishers.com. Eds. Daniel Miller, Michael Herzfeld, Paul Gilroy.

301 ITA
MECCANISMI SOCIALI. Text in Italian. 1994. irreg., latest vol.3, 1998. price varies. **Document type:** *Monographic series, Academic/Scholarly.*
Published by: Liguori Editore, Via Posillipo 394, Naples, 80123, Italy. TEL 39-081-7206111, FAX 39-081-7206244, liguori@liguori.it, http://www.liguori.it. Ed. Arnaldo Bagnasco. Pub. Guido Liguori. Adv. contact Maria Liguori.

MECHADEMIA; an annual forum for anime, manga and the fan arts. *see* ART

302.23 USA ISSN 0890-7161
MEDIA AND SOCIETY SERIES. Text in English. 1986. irreg., latest vol.6, 1994. price varies. back issues avail. **Document type:** *Monographic series, Academic/Scholarly.* **Description:** Examines issues in the media and how they affect society at large.
Published by: University of Minnesota Press, Ste 290, 111 Third Ave S, Minneapolis, MN 55401. TEL 612-627-1970, FAX 612-627-1980, ump@umn.edu. Ed. Richard Bolton. **Dist. by:** c/o Chicago Distribution Center, 11030 S Langley Ave, Chicago, IL 60628. TEL 800-621-2736; Plymbridge Distributors Ltd, Estover Rd, Plymouth, Devon PL6 7PY, United Kingdom. TEL 44-1752-202-301, FAX 44-1752-202-331.

302.23 MEX
MEDIA COMUNICACION. Text in Spanish. irreg.
Related titles: Online - full text ed.
Published by: Inter Planeta Editorial, SERAFIN OLARTE 54, Xol Independencia, Mexico City, DF 03630, Mexico. TEL 52-5-5394142.

302.23 GBR ISSN 0163-4437
HM258
➤ **MEDIA, CULTURE & SOCIETY.** Abbreviated title: M C S. Text in English. 1979. bi-m. USD 1,702, GBP 920 combined subscription to institutions (print & online eds.); USD 1,668, GBP 902 to institutions (effective 2011). adv. bk.rev. illus. index. back issues avail.; reprint service avail. from PSC. **Document type:** *Journal, Academic/Scholarly.* **Description:** Provides a major international forum for the presentation of research and discussion concerning the media, including the newer information and communication technologies, within their political, economic, cultural and historical contexts.
Related titles: Online - full text ed.: ISSN 1460-3675. USD 1,532, GBP 828 to institutions (effective 2011).
Indexed: A01, A02, A03, A08, A20, A22, A25, A26, ASCA, B04, B07, BRD, BrHumI, CA, CMM, CommAb, CurCont, DIP, E-psyche, E01, E07, E08, F01, F02, FR, FamI, G08, H14, I05, I13, IBR, IBSS, IBT&D, IBZ, IIFP, IITV, L04, LISTA, MLA-IB, P02, P07, P10, P27, P34, P42, P48, P53, P54, PAIS, PCI, PEI, PQC, PRA, PSA, RASB, S02, S03, S08, S09, SCOPUS, SOPODA, SSA, SSAI, SSAb, SSCI, SSI, SociolAb, T02, W03, W07.
—BLDSC (5525.255500), IE, Infotrieve, Ingenta, INIST. **CCC.**
Published by: Sage Publications Ltd. (Subsidiary of: Sage Publications, Inc.), 1 Oliver's Yard, 55 City Rd, London, EC1Y 1SP, United Kingdom. TEL 44-20-73248500, FAX 44-20-73248600, info@sagepub.co.uk, http://www.uk.sagepub.com/home.nav. adv.: B&W page GBP 450; 130 x 205. **Subscr. in the Americas to:** Sage Publications, Inc., 2455 Teller Rd, Thousand Oaks, CA 91320. TEL 805-499-9774, FAX 805-499-0871, journals@sagepub.com.

302.23 USA ISSN 1072-3552
P92.U5
MEDIA CULTURE REVIEW. Text in English. 4/yr. USD 16 to individuals; USD 36 to institutions. **Document type:** *Newsletter.*
Published by: Institute for Alternative Journalism, 77 Federal St, San Francisco, CA 94107. TEL 415-284-1420, FAX 415-284-1414. Ed., R&P Don Hazen.

MEDIA ETHICS. *see* JOURNALISM

302.23 GBR ISSN 1368-8804
P87
➤ **MEDIA HISTORY.** Text in English. 1984 (vol.4). q. GBP 416 combined subscription in United Kingdom to institutions (print & online eds.); EUR 555, USD 693 combined subscription to institutions (print & online eds.) (effective 2012). adv. back issues avail.; reprint service avail. from PSC. **Document type:** *Journal, Academic/Scholarly.* **Description:** Serves as an interdisciplinary journal that addresses media and society from the fifteenth century to the present.
Former titles (until 1998): Studies in Newspaper and Periodical History (1075-0673); (until 1993): Journal of Newspaper and Periodical History (0265-5942)
Related titles: Online - full text ed.: ISSN 1469-9729. GBP 374 in United Kingdom to institutions; EUR 500, USD 623 to institutions (effective 2012) (from IngentaConnect).
Indexed: A01, A03, A08, A22, AmH&L, CA, CMM, CommAb, E01, F01, F02, HistAb, IBSS, MLA-IB, P30, P42, PCI, PSA, RILM, S02, S03, S21, SociolAb, T02.
—IE, Infotrieve, Ingenta. **CCC.**
Published by: Routledge (Subsidiary of: Taylor & Francis Group), 4 Park Sq, Milton Park, Abingdon, Oxon OX14 4RN, United Kingdom. TEL 44-20-70176000, FAX 44-20-70176336, subscriptions@tandf.co.uk, http://www.routledge.com. Adv. contact Linda Hann TEL 44-1344-779945. **Subscr. to:** Taylor & Francis Ltd., Journals Customer Service, Sheepen Pl, Colchester, Essex CO3 3LP, United Kingdom. TEL 44-20-70175544, FAX 44-20-70175198.

302.23 USA ISSN 1550-1043
MEDIA INDUSTRIES. Text in English. 2006. irreg., latest vol.6, 2010. price varies. **Document type:** *Monographic series, Academic/Scholarly.*
Published by: Peter Lang Publishing, Inc. (Subsidiary of: Peter Lang Publishing Group), 29 Broadway, New York, NY 10006. TEL 212-647-7700, 800-770-5264, FAX 212-647-7707, customerservice@plang.com. Ed. David Summner.

302.23 AUS ISSN 1329-878X
➤ **MEDIA INTERNATIONAL AUSTRALIA INCORPORATING CULTURE AND POLICY**; quarterly journal of media research and resources. Abbreviated title: M I A C P(Media International Australia Incorporating Culture and Policy). Text in English. 1976. q. AUD 125 domestic to individuals; AUD 175 foreign to individuals; AUD 250 domestic to institutions; AUD 300 foreign to institutions; AUD 100 domestic to students; AUD 115 foreign to students; AUD 40 per issue (effective 2009). bk.rev. charts; stat. index. 200 p./no.; back issues avail. **Document type:** *Journal, Academic/Scholarly.* **Description:** Features scholarly and applied research on the media, telecommunications, and the cultural industries, and the policy regimes within which they operate.
Former titles (until Nov.1997): Media International Australia (1324-5325); (until Sep.1995): Media Information Australia (0312-9616); (until 1976): Australian Media Notes (0312-9241)
Related titles: Online - full text ed.
Indexed: A26, AEI, AusPAIS, CA, CMM, CommAb, E08, F01, F02, G06, G07, G08, I05, IBSS, IIFP, IITV, MLA-IB, S09, SSCI, T02, W07.
—BLDSC (5525.258185), Ingenta. **CCC.**
Published by: (University of Queensland, Media and Cultural Studies Centre), University of Queensland, School of English, Media Studies & Art History, Fourth Fl, Michie Bldg, St Lucia, QLD 4072, Australia. TEL 61-7-33653102, FAX 61-7-33652799, admin@emsah.uq.edu.au. Ed. Gerard Goggin.

302.2 USA
MEDIA MONITOR (WASHINGTON). Text in English. 1987. 6/yr. USD 50. **Document type:** *Newsletter.* **Description:** Analyzes how news and entertainment media treat social and political issues, relying on content analysis.
Indexed: SRI.
Published by: Center for Media and Public Affairs, 2100 L St, N W, Ste 300, Washington, DC 20037. TEL 202-223-2942, FAX 202-872-4014. Eds. Linda S Lichter, S Robert Lichter. R&P Michelle Fernandez.

302.23 TWN
MEDIA NEWS. Text in Chinese. 1982. 2/w. (Tue. & Fri.). TWD 600, USD 20. adv. bk.rev.; film rev. illus. **Document type:** *Newspaper, Trade.* **Description:** Covers trends and important issues of the media industry in Taiwan for professionals and mass communications scholars and students.
Published by: Ming Chuan University, No 250 Chung Shan N. Rd, Sec 5, Taipei, Taiwan. TEL 886-2-2881-10742, FAX 886-2-2881-8675. Ed. Charles Chih Hung Yang. Pub. Chuan Lee. R&P Charles Chi Hung Yang. Adv. contact Hsiao Hsu Liu. Circ: 4,000 (paid); 6,000 (controlled).

MEDIA PSYCHOLOGY. *see* PSYCHOLOGY

305.42 070.48374 USA ISSN 0145-9651
HQ1402
MEDIA REPORT TO WOMEN. Text in English. 1972. q. USD 40 domestic to individuals; USD 50 foreign to individuals; USD 70 domestic to institutions; USD 80 foreign to institutions (effective 2010). bk.rev. illus. 16 p./no.; back issues avail.; reprints avail. **Document type:** *Newsletter, Trade.* **Description:** Contains reports on the relationship between women and media, particularly the portrayal of women in news, entertainment, and advertising.
Related titles: Online - full text ed.
Indexed: A01, A02, A03, A08, A22, A26, CA, CMM, ChPerI, E08, F01, F02, FemPer, G08, G10, GW, HRIR, I05, P02, P10, P19, P48, P53, P54, PQC, S09, T02, W06, W09, WSA, WSI.
—Ingenta. **CCC.**
Published by: Communication Research Associates, Inc., 11988 Tramway Dr, Cincinnati, OH 45241. TEL 513-733-9229, FAX 513-733-8775, http://www.commres.com. Ed. Sheila Gibbons. Pub. Ray Hiebert. **Subscr. to:** 38091 Beach Rd, PO Box 180, Colton's Point, MD 20626. TEL 301-769-3899, FAX 301-769-3558.

302.32 DEU ISSN 1433-6480
MEDIA-STUDIEN. Text in German. 1997. irreg., latest vol.13, 2008. price varies. **Document type:** *Monographic series, Academic/Scholarly.*
Published by: Leipziger Universitaetsverlag GmbH, Oststr 41, Leipzig, 04317, Germany. TEL 49-341-9900440, FAX 49-341-9900440, info@univerlag-leipzig.de.

301 ESP ISSN 1989-0494
MEDIACIONES SOCIALES. Text in Spanish. 2007. s-a. free (effective 2011). **Document type:** *Journal, Academic/Scholarly.*
Media: Online - full text.
Published by: (Universidad Complutense de Madrid, Grupo de Investigacion "Identidades Sociales y Comunicacion"), Universidad Complutense de Madrid, Servicio de Publicaciones, C/ Obispo Trejo 2, Ciudad Universitaria, Madrid, 28040, Spain. TEL 34-91-3941127, FAX 34-91-3941126, servicio.publicaciones@rect.ucm.es, http://www.ucm.es/publicaciones.

302.23 AUT
MEDIACULT NEWS. Text in English, French, German. 1972. 2/yr. free. bk.rev. **Document type:** *Newsletter, Consumer.* **Description:** Informs about current projects, events and activities involving research about the impact of new communication technologies on culture.
Formerly: Mediacult Newsletter
Published by: Mediacult - Internationales Forschungsinstitut fuer Medien Kommunikation und Kulturelle Entwicklung/International Research Institute for Media, Communication and Cultural Development, Anton-von-Webern-Platz 1, Vienna, W 1030, Austria. TEL 43-1-711558800, FAX 43-1-711558809. Ed. Robert Harauer. Circ: 1,200.

302.23 USA ISSN 1558-478X
PN1993
➤ **MEDIASCAPE.** Text in English. 2005. s-a. free (effective 2011). bk.rev.; film rev.; rec.rev.; music rev.; software rev.; tel.rev.; video rev. illus. cum.index: 2005-2008. back issues avail. **Document type:** *Journal, Academic/Scholarly.* **Description:** Covers interdisciplinary visual cultural studies, focusing on the moving image and all its manifestations. Contents endorse a non-exclusive treatment of visual culture which are from cross-disciplinary, cross-technological, and cross-cultural perspectives.
Media: Online - full text.
Published by: University of California, Los Angeles, School of Theater, Film and Television, 102 East Melnitz Hall, Box 951622, Los Angeles, CA 90095-1622. Eds. Jennifer Porst, Maya Smukler. Pub. Stacey Meeker. **Co-sponsor:** University of California, Los Angeles, Graduate Students Association.

302.2 ESP ISSN 1137-4462
P92.S7
MEDIATIKA. Text in Spanish. 1984. irreg. **Document type:** *Monographic series, Academic/Scholarly.*
Formerly (until 1997): Sociedad de Estudios Vascos. Cuadernos de Seccion. Medios de Comunicacion (0213-0289)
Indexed: MLA-IB.
Published by: Eusko Ikaskuntza/Sociedad de Estudios Vascos, Palacio Miramar, Miraconcha 48, Donostia, San Sebastian 20007, Spain. TEL 34-943-310855, FAX 34-943-213956, ei-sev@sc.ehu.es, http://www.eusko-ikaskuntza.org/.

302.23 NOR ISSN 1891-7771
▼ **MEDIEAARET**; medieutvikling i Norge: fakta og trender. Text in Norwegian. 2010. a. charts; stat. **Document type:** *Report, Consumer.*
Related titles: Online - full text ed.
Published by: Medienorge, c/o Institutt for Informasjons- og Medievetenskap, Fosswinckelsgate 6, Bergen, 5007, Norway. TEL 47-55-589126, FAX 47-55-589121, medienorge@uib.no, http://www.medienorge.no.

302.23 DEU
MEDIEN - KULTUR - ANALYSE. Text in German. 2005. irreg., latest vol.6, 2009. price varies. **Document type:** *Monographic series, Academic/Scholarly.*
Published by: Transcript, Muehlenstr 47, Bielefeld, 33607, Germany. TEL 49-521-63454, FAX 49-521-61040, live@transcript-verlag.de.

MEDIEN UND FIKTIONEN. *see* COMMUNICATIONS

MEDIEN UND MAERKTE. *see* JOURNALISM

302.23 DEU
MEDIEN WELTEN. Text in German. 2005. irreg., latest vol.5, 2011. price varies. **Document type:** *Monographic series, Academic/Scholarly.*
Published by: Transcript, Muehlenstr 47, Bielefeld, 33607, Germany. TEL 49-521-63454, FAX 49-521-61040, live@transcript-verlag.de.

302.23 DEU
MEDIENANALYSEN. Text in German. 2008. irreg., latest vol.10, 2011. price varies. **Document type:** *Monographic series, Academic/Scholarly.*
Published by: Transcript, Muehlenstr 47, Bielefeld, 33607, Germany. TEL 49-521-63454, FAX 49-521-61040, live@transcript-verlag.de.

384.5 DEU ISSN 0948-7654
MEDIENANSTALT BERLIN - BRANDENBURG. SCHRIFTENREIHE. Variant title: Schriftenreihe der MABB. Text in German. 1995. irreg., latest vol.26, 2010. price varies. **Document type:** *Monographic series, Academic/Scholarly.*
Published by: (Medienanstalt Berlin - Brandenburg), Vistas Verlag GmbH, Goltzstr 11, Berlin, 10781, Germany. TEL 49-30-32707446, FAX 49-30-32707455, medienverlag@vistas.de.

384.5 DEU ISSN 1865-4169
MEDIENANSTALT HAMBURG. SCHRIFTENREIHE. Variant title: Schriftenreihe der H A M. Text in German. 1989. irreg., latest vol.3, 2010. price varies. **Document type:** *Monographic series, Academic/Scholarly.*
Formerly (until 2007): Hamburgische Anstalt fuer Neue Medien. Schriftenreihe (0947-4528)
Published by: (Medienanstalt Hamburg - Schleswig-Holstein), Vistas Verlag GmbH, Goltzstr 11, Berlin, 10781, Germany. TEL 49-30-32707446, FAX 49-30-32707455, medienverlag@vistas.de.

384.5 DEU ISSN 1438-7476
MEDIENANSTALT SACHSEN-ANHALT. SCHRIFTENREIHE. Variant title: Schriftenreihe der M S A. Text in German. 1999. irreg., latest vol.8, 2008. price varies. **Document type:** *Monographic series, Academic/Scholarly.*
Published by: (Medienanstalt Sachsen-Anhalt), Vistas Verlag GmbH, Goltzstr 11, Berlin, 10781, Germany. TEL 49-30-32707446, FAX 49-30-32707455, medienverlag@vistas.de.

302.23 DEU
▼ **MEDIENKONVERGENZ/MEDIA CONVERGENCE.** Text in English, German. 2011. irreg., latest vol.2, 2012. price varies. **Document type:** *Monographic series, Academic/Scholarly.*
Published by: Walter de Gruyter GmbH & Co. KG, Genthiner Str 13, Berlin, 10785, Germany. TEL 49-30-260050, FAX 49-30-26005251, info@degruyter.com, http://www.degruyter.de. Ed. Stephan Fuessel.

302.23 659 SWE ISSN 1101-4539
P87
MEDIENOTISER FRAAN NORDICOM-SVERIGE. (Nordic Information Centre for Media and Communication Research) Text in Swedish. 1990. q. price varies. stat. back issues avail. **Document type:** *Trade.*
Published by: N O R D I C O M-Sverige A/B/Nordic Information Centre for Media and Communication Research, PO Box 70396, tockholm, 10724, Sweden. TEL 46-8-50894250, FAX 46-8-217131, info@nordicomsverige.se, http://www.nordicomsverige.s.

302.23 DEU
MEDIENPAEDAGOGIK INTERDISZIPLINAER. Text in German. 2003. irreg., latest vol.8, 2010. **Document type:** *Monographic series, Academic/Scholarly.*
Published by: (Paedagogische Hochschule Ludwigsburg, Interdisziplinaere Zentrum fuer Medienpaedagogik und Medienforschung), KoPaed Verlag, Pfaelzer-Wald-Str 64, Munich, 81539, Germany. TEL 49-89-68890098, FAX 49-89-6891912, info@kopaed.de, http://www.kopaed.de.

302.23 DEU
MEDIENUMBRUECHE. Text in German. 2004. irreg., latest vol.44, 2010. price varies. **Document type:** *Monographic series, Academic/Scholarly.*
Published by: Transcript, Muehlenstr 47, Bielefeld, 33607, Germany. TEL 49-521-63454, FAX 49-521-61040, live@transcript-verlag.de.

302.23 DEU
MEDIENWISSENSCHAFT IN THEORIE UND PRAXIS. Text in German. 2005. irreg., latest vol.6, 2010. price varies. **Document type:** *Monographic series, Academic/Scholarly.*
Published by: KoPaed Verlag, Pfaelzer-Wald-Str 64, Munich, 81539, Germany. TEL 49-89-68890098, FAX 49-89-6891912, info@kopaed.de.

302.23 SWE ISSN 1399-3666
MEDIER I NORDEN. Text in Danish, Finnish, Norwegian, Swedish. 1999. 5/yr. free. back issues avail. **Document type:** *Newsletter, Academic/Scholarly.*
Formed by the merger of (1994-1999): Nordisk Medie Nyt (Online) (1396-9331); (1994-1999): Nordic Media News (1396-934X)
Media: Online - full text. **Related titles:** English ed.: Nordic Media Policy.
Published by: N O R D I C O M A/S/Nordic Information Centre for Media and Communication Research, c/o University of Goeteborg, PO Box 713, Goeteborg, SE 40530, Sweden. TEL 46-31-7731000, FAX 46-31-7734655, info@nordicom.gu.se. Ed. Terje FLisen.

306.09 DEU ISSN 1438-4760
MEDIEVAL TO EARLY MODERN CULTURE/KULTURELLER WANDEL VOM MITTELALTER ZUR FRUEHEN NEUZEIT. Text in German, English. 2001. irreg., latest vol.12, 2009. price varies. **Document type:** *Monographic series, Academic/Scholarly.*
Published by: Peter Lang GmbH (Subsidiary of: Peter Lang Publishing Group), Eschborner Landstr 42-50, Frankfurt Am Main, 60489, Germany. TEL 49-69-7807050, FAX 49-69-78070550, zentrale.frankfurt@peterlang.com, http://www.peterlang.com. Eds. Martin Gosman, Volker Honemann.

301 FRA ISSN 1263-8935
MEDITERRANEES. Text in French. 1994. s-a. EUR 48.80 domestic; EUR 54.90 foreign (effective 2004). **Document type:** *Monographic series, Academic/Scholarly.*
Published by: L' Harmattan, 5 Rue de l'Ecole Polytechnique, Paris, 75005, France. TEL 33-1-43257651, FAX 33-1-43258203.

MEDVIND; medborgarskolan - daer intresse blir kunskap. *see* EDUCATION

307.14 AUS ISSN 1833-5373
MELBOURNE 2030. IMPLEMENTATION BULLETIN. Text in English. 2004. s-a. free (effective 2008). **Document type:** *Bulletin, Government.*
Related titles: Online - full text ed.
Published by: Victoria. Department of Sustainability and Environment, 8 Nicholson St, East Melbourne, VIC 3002, Australia. TEL 61-3-53325000, customer.service@dse.vic.gov.au, http://www.dse.vic.gov.au/dse/index.htm.

MELBOURNE INSTITUTE REPORT. *see* BUSINESS AND ECONOMICS

305.3 USA
MEN ARE FROM MARS & WOMEN ARE FROM VENUS. Text in English. 1998. bi-m.
Published by: News America Incorporated, Four Radnor Corporate Center, 100 Matsonford Rd., Box 400, Radnor, PA 19088-0925. Ed. Janice Kaplan.

301 NLD ISSN 0025-9454
H8
➤ **MENS EN MAATSCHAPPIJ**; tijdschrift voor sociale wetenschappen. Text in Dutch; Summaries in English. 1925. q. (plus special issue). EUR 84 to individuals; EUR 166 to institutions; EUR 49 to students; EUR 106 combined subscription to individuals (print & online eds.); EUR 212 combined subscription to institutions (print & online eds.); EUR 62 combined subscription to students (print & online eds.) (effective 2008). adv. bk.rev. bibl.; illus. index. back issues avail. **Document type:** *Journal, Academic/Scholarly.* **Description:** Examines issues and research in all areas of sociology.
Related titles: Online - full text ed.
Indexed: A22, AICP, BAS, CA, CIS, EI, IBSS, KES, P42, PSA, RASB, S02, S03, SCOPUS, SOPODA, SSA, SociolAb, T02.
—IE, Infotrieve.
Published by: (Stichting Mens en Maatschappij), Amsterdam University Press, Herengracht 221, Amsterdam, 1016 BG, Netherlands. TEL 31-20-4200050, FAX 31-20-4203214, info@aup.nl, http://www.aup.nl.

303 DEU ISSN 0543-4726
DER MENSCH ALS SOZIALES UND PERSONALES WESEN. Text in German. 1963. irreg., latest vol.23, 2010. price varies. adv. reprint service avail. from IRC. **Document type:** *Monographic series, Academic/Scholarly.*
Published by: Lucius und Lucius Verlagsgesellschaft mbH, Gerokstr 51, Stuttgart, 70184, Germany. TEL 49-711-242060, FAX 49-711-242088, lucius@luciusverlag.com.

301 DEU ISSN 1615-732X
MENSCH - TAETIGKEIT - ENTWICKLUNG. Text in German. 2000. irreg. price varies. **Document type:** *Monographic series, Academic/Scholarly.*
Published by: Verlag Dr. Kovac, Leverkusenstr 13, Hamburg, 22761, Germany. TEL 49-40-3988800, FAX 49-40-39888055, info@verlagdrkovac.de. Eds. Georg Rueckriem, Joachim Lompscher.

MENTAL HEALTH, RELIGION & CULTURE. *see* PSYCHOLOGY

303 302 303.842 FRA ISSN 1770-6025
MES TISSAGES. Text in French. 2004. s-a. **Document type:** *Journal.*
Published by: Association A M I, 10 Rue de la Benauge, Bordeaux, 33000, France. TEL 33-5-56869170, FAX 33-5-56869692, AMI.Bordeaux@wanadoo.fr.

302.23 DEU
METABASIS; Transkriptionen zwischen Literaturen, Kuensten und Medien. Text in German. 2008. irreg., latest vol.7, 2011. price varies. **Document type:** *Monographic series, Academic/Scholarly.*
Published by: Transcript, Muehlenstr 47, Bielefeld, 33607, Germany. TEL 49-521-63454, FAX 49-521-61040, live@transcript-verlag.de.

▼ **METAPHOR AND THE SOCIAL WORLD.** *see* LINGUISTICS

302.23 400 NLD ISSN 2210-4836
▼ **METAPHOR IN LANGUAGE, COGNITION AND COMMUNICATION.** Text in English. forthcoming 2012. irreg. **Description:** Aims to present theoretical and empirical research on the effective use of metaphor in language and other modalities for general or specific cognitive and communicative purposes.
Published by: John Benjamins Publishing Co., PO Box 36224, Amsterdam, 1020 ME, Netherlands. TEL 31-20-6304747, FAX 31-20-6739773, customer.services@benjamins.nl. Ed. Gerard J Steen.

302.23 DEU
METHODEN UND FORSCHUNGSLOGIK DER KOMMUNIKATIONSWISSENSCHAFT. Text in German. 2004. irreg., latest vol.5, 2010. price varies. **Document type:** *Monographic series, Academic/Scholarly.*
Formerly (until 2006): Forschungslogik und -design in der Kommunikationswissenschaft (1863-4966)
Published by: Herbert von Halem Verlag, Lindenstr 19, Cologne, 50674, Germany. TEL 49-221-9258290, FAX 49-221-92582929, info@halem-verlag.de, http://www.halem-verlag.de.

301 378.007 GBR ISSN 2043-698X
▼ ➤ **METHODOLOGY**; innovative approaches to research. Text in English. 2010. irreg. **Document type:** *Journal, Academic/Scholarly.* **Description:** Guides for those new to research and others who would appreciate a introduction to a range of methods and approaches to research in the social sciences.
Related titles: Online - full text ed.: free (effective 2010).
Published by: Leeds Metropolitan University, Civic Quarter, Leeds, LS1 3HE, United Kingdom. TEL 44-113-8120000. Eds. Karen Horwood, Katie Hill, Sally Jones.

301 DNK ISSN 1902-1534
METODE & DATA; d d a nyt. Text in Danish; Summaries in English. 1976. a. charts; illus.; stat. back issues avail. **Document type:** *Academic/Scholarly.*
Formerly (until 1999): D D A Nyt (0105-3272)
Related titles: Online - full text ed.: ISSN 1902-1569. 2005.
Published by: Statens Arkiver, Dansk Data Arkiv/Danish National Archives. Danish Data Archives, Islandsgade 10, Odense, 5000, Denmark. TEL 45-46-113010, FAX 45-46-113060, mailbox@dda.sa.dk, http://www.sa.dk/dda. Ed. Anne Sofie Fink. Circ: 1,200.

306.85 USA ISSN 1558-7258
HQ535
➤ **MICHIGAN FAMILY REVIEW (ONLINE).** Text in English. 2004. a. free (effective 2011). back issues avail.; reprints avail. **Document type:** *Journal, Academic/Scholarly.* **Description:** Publishes articles and reviews about critical contemporary problems confronting families and those who provide service to them.
Media: Online - full text.
Published by: (Michigan Council on Family Relations (MiCFR)), University of Michigan, Scholarly Publishing Office, 300 Hatcher N, 920 N University Ave, Ann Arbor, MI 48109. TEL 734-763-7485, FAX 734-763-6850, lib.spo@umich.edu, http://www.lib.umich.edu/spo. Ed. Brad van Eeden-Moorefield TEL 989-774-6436.

301 USA ISSN 1934-7111
HM403 CODEN: MSOREB
MICHIGAN SOCIOLOGICAL REVIEW. Text in English. 1978. a. free to members (effective 2011). **Document type:** *Journal, Academic/Scholarly.* **Description:** Publishes research and pedagogical comments, reviews of books, films, videos, educational software, and keynote speeches of the annual meetings of the MSA.
Indexed: CA, P27, P46, P48, P54, PQC, S02, S03, SSA, SociolAb, T02.
Published by: Michigan Sociological Association, c/o Allen Hill, Sociology Department, Delta College, University Center, MI 48710. aghill@delta.edu, http://members.tm.net/aghill/msa/msa.html.

306 USA ISSN 1063-1763
E169.3
THE MID-ATLANTIC ALMANACK. Text in English. 1992. a. free to members (effective 2011). back issues avail. **Document type:** *Journal, Academic/Scholarly.*
Indexed: MLA-IB.
Published by: Mid-Atlantic Popular/American Culture Association, c/o Gary Earl Ross, State University of New York at Buffalo, Educational Opportunity Ctr, 465 Washington St, Buffalo, NY 14203. geross@buffalo.edu, http://www.mapaca.net/mapaca/mapacaHome.html.

MIDDLE EAST JOURNAL OF CULTURE AND COMMUNICATION. *see* ASIAN STUDIES

301 ESP ISSN 0210-8259
MIENTRAS TANTO. Text in Spanish. 1979. q. EUR 25 domestic; USD 35 in Europe; USD 40 elsewhere (effective 2009). 144 p./no.; **Document type:** *Journal, Academic/Scholarly.* **Description:** Includes general subjects of social sciences, and specific articles and notes around global economic, ecology and political affairs as well as education.
Published by: Icaria Editorial, Arc de Sant Cristofol, 11-23, Barcelona, 08003, Spain. TEL 34-93-3011723, FAX 34-93-2954916, icaria@icariaeditorial.com, http://www.icariaeditorial.com. **Dist. by:** Asociacion de Revistas Culturales de Espana, C Covarruvias 9 2o. Derecha, Madrid 28010, Spain. TEL 34-91-3086066, FAX 34-91-3199267, info@arce.es, http://www.arce.es/.

301 ISR ISSN 0793-0089
MIFNEH. Text in Hebrew. 1993. q. **Document type:** *Journal, Academic/Scholarly.*
Formed by the merger of (1923-1993): Mibbifnim (0046-5178); (1989-1993): Ya'ad (0792-2337); Which was formerly (1971-1988): Ma'asef (0334-3952)
Published by: United Kibbutz Movement, Yad Tabenkin, Hayasmin St. 1, Ramat Efal, 52960, Israel. TEL 972-3-534-4458, FAX 972-3-534-6376, yadtabmaz@bezeqint.net, http://www.yadtabenkin.org.il. Eds. Eli Avrahami, Eli Tzur.

301 572 304.6 HRV ISSN 1333-2546
JV6006 CODEN: MIGTE9
➤ **MIGRACIJSKE I ETNICKE TEME/MIGRATION AND ETHNIC THEMES.** Text in Croatian, English, French, Russian. 1985. q. adv. bk.rev. 150 p./no.; back issues avail. **Document type:** *Journal, Academic/Scholarly.* **Description:** Covers wide range of problems concerning migration, ethnicity and identity.
Formerly (until Jan 2001): Migracijske Teme (0352-5600)
Related titles: Online - full text ed.: free (effective 2011).
Indexed: CA, IBSS, L&LBA, P30, P42, PSA, RASB, S02, S03, SOPODA, SSA, SociolAb, T02.
Published by: Institut za Migracije i Narodnosti/Institute for Migration and Ethnic Studies, Trg Stjepana Radica 3, pp 294, Zagreb, 10000, Croatia. TEL 385-1-6111564, FAX 385-1-6119680. Ed. Mrs. Laura Sakaja. R&P, Adv. contact Mrs. Jasna Blazevic. Circ: 500.

302 303 FRA ISSN 1954-3433
MIGRATIONS ET CITOYENNETE EN EUROPE. Text in French. 2007. irreg. **Document type:** *Monographic series, Academic/Scholarly.*
Related titles: German ed.
Published by: Institut Francais des Relations Internationales, 27 rue de la Procession, Paris, Cedex 15 75740, France. TEL 33-1-40616000, FAX 33-1-40616060, http://www.ifri.org.

307.76 USA ISSN 1549-6945
HT101
MILANO REVIEW. Text in English. 2001. a. USD 12 per issue (effective 2004).
Published by: New School University, Robert J. Milano Graduate School of Management and Urban Policy, 72 Fifth Ave, New York, NY 10011. TEL 212-229-5311, FAX 212-229-5354.

MILLER-MCCUNE; turning research into solutions. *see* POLITICAL SCIENCE

MINDERHEITEN UND MINDERHEITENPOLITIK IN EUROPA. *see* POLITICAL SCIENCE

302.23 370 USA ISSN 2151-2949
▼ **MINDING THE MEDIA**; critical issues for learning and teaching. Text in English. 2010. irreg., latest vol.2, 2010. price varies. **Document type:** *Monographic series, Academic/Scholarly.* **Description:** Book series on teaching mass media issues.
Published by: Peter Lang Publishing, Inc. (Subsidiary of: Peter Lang Publishing Group), 29 Broadway, New York, NY 10006. TEL 212-647-7700, FAX 212-647-7707, customerservice@plang.com.

MINERVA; laboratorio di cultura e politica. *see* POLITICAL SCIENCE

S

305.3 DNK
MINISTER FOR LIGESTILLING. ANNUAL REPORT; perspective and action plan. Text in English. 2007. a. **Document type:** *Government.*
Related titles: Online - full text ed.: ISSN 1902-4444; ◆ Danish ed.: Perspektiv- og Handlingsplan. ISSN 1602-172X.
Published by: Minister for Ligestilling, Ligestillingsafdelingen/Minister for Gender Equality. Department of Equality, Holmens Kanal 20, PO Box 2150, Copenhagen K, 1061, Denmark. TEL 45-72-269780, FAX 45-72-269781, lige@lige.dk, http://www.lige.dk.

MINORITY RIGHTS GROUP INTERNATIONAL. REPORT. *see* POLITICAL SCIENCE—Civil Rights

MINZU WENTI YANJIU/STUDIES OF ETHNIC PROBLEMS. *see* ASIAN STUDIES

307 PRT ISSN 1646-6365
MISERICORDIA DE BRAGA. BOLETIM. Text in Portuguese. 2006. s-a. **Document type:** *Bulletin, Consumer.*
Published by: Santa Casa da Misericordia de Braga, Edificio Nevarte Gulbenkian, Braga, 4700-352, Portugal. TEL 351-253-205100, FAX 351-253-205101, http://scmbraga.no.sapo.pt.

306.85 ISR
MISHPAHA TOVA. Text in Hebrew. 1999. m. ILS 336 (effective 2008). **Document type:** *Magazine, Consumer.* **Description:** Written for religious families.
Related titles: Online - full text ed.: ILS 132 (effective 2008).
Published by: S B C Group, 8 Shefa Tal St., Tel Aviv, 67013, Israel. TEL 972-3-565-2100, FAX 972-3-562-6476, sherut@sbc.co.il, http://www.sbc.co.il/Index.asp.

301 USA
MISSISSIPPI STATE UNIVERSITY. SOCIAL RESEARCH REPORT SERIES. Text in English. 1983. irreg. USD 20 (effective 2000). **Document type:** *Bulletin.*
Formerly: Mississippi State University. Sociology Research Report Series
Indexed: SOPODA.
Published by: Mississippi State University, Social Science Research Center, PO Box 5287, Mississippi State, MS 39762. TEL 601-325-7127, FAX 601-325-7966. Ed. J Gipson Wells. Circ: 700.

302.23 SWE ISSN 1653-2082
MITTUNIVERSITETET. AVDELINGEN FOER MEDIE- OCH KOMMUNIKATIONSVETENSKAP. COMMUNIQUE. Text in Swedish. 2005. a. **Document type:** *Proceedings, Academic/Scholarly.*
Published by: Mittuniversitetet, Avdelingen foer Medie- och Kommunikationsvetenskap/Mid Sweden University. Department of Information Technology and Media, Holmgatan 10, Sundsvall, 851 70, Sweden. TEL 46-60-148801, FAX 46-60-148830, http://www.miun.se.

302.3 USA ISSN 1086-671X
HM281 CODEN: MOBLF3
➤ **MOBILIZATION**; an international journal. Text in English. 1996. q. USD 49.50 domestic; USD 59.50 foreign (effective 2011). adv. bk.rev. back issues avail.; reprints avail. **Document type:** *Journal, Academic/Scholarly.* **Description:** Presents research and theory specializing in social movements, protests, insurgencies, revolutions, and other forms of contentious politics.
Related titles: Online - full text ed.: ISSN 1938-1514.
Indexed: A20, A22, ABS&EES, CA, CurCont, ESPM, IBSS, IBibSS, P34, P42, PSA, S02, S03, SCOPUS, SOPODA, SSA, SSCI, SSciA, SociolAb, T02, W07.
—BLDSC (5879.956050), IE, Ingenta. **CCC.**
Published by: San Diego State University, Department of Sociology, San Diego, CA 92182. TEL 619-594-2835, http://www.sdsu.edu/. Ed. Rory McVeigh. Pub. Hank Johnston.

➤ **MODERN CHURCHPEOPLE'S UNION. OCCASIONAL PAPERS.** *see* RELIGIONS AND THEOLOGY

320 USA
MODERN GERMAN STUDIES. Text in English. 1995. irreg., latest vol.6, 2000. price varies. adv. back issues avail. **Document type:** *Monographic series, Academic/Scholarly.* **Description:** Provides a books on modern and contemporary Germany, concentrating on themes in history, political science, literature and German culture.
Published by: (German Studies Association), Berghahn Books Inc., 150 Broadway, Ste 812, New York, NY 10038. TEL 212-233-6004, FAX 212-233-6007, journals@berghahnbooks.com. Pub. Marion Berghahn. **Dist. in Europe by:** Turpin Distribution Services Ltd.; **Dist. in the Americas by:** Turpin Distribution Services Ltd.

306 GBR ISSN 2041-1022
MODERNIST CULTURES. Text in English. 2005. s-a. GBP 60 domestic to institutions; USD 120 in North America to institutions; GBP 65 elsewhere to institutions; GBP 75 combined subscription domestic to institutions (print & online eds.); USD 150 combined subscription in North America to institutions (print & online eds.); GBP 81 combined subscription elsewhere to institutions (print & online eds.) (effective 2012). adv. back issues avail.; reprints avail. **Document type:** *Journal, Academic/Scholarly.* **Description:** Provides a forum for explorations of the most interesting contemporary debates in modernist studies.
Related titles: Online - full text ed.: ISSN 1753-8629. USD 100 in North America to institutions; GBP 54 elsewhere to institutions (effective 2011).
—CCC.
Published by: Edinburgh University Press, 22 George Sq, Edinburgh, Scotland EH8 9LF, United Kingdom. TEL 44-131-6504218, FAX 44-131-6620053, journals@eup.ed.ac.uk. Eds. Andrzej Gasiorek, Michael Valdez Moses. Adv. contact Ruth Allison TEL 44-131-6504220.

301 ITA ISSN 1972-4888
MONDO MIGRANTI. Text in Multiple languages. 2007. 3/yr. **Document type:** *Newspaper, Consumer.*
Related titles: Online - full text ed.: ISSN 1972-4896.
Published by: Franco Angeli Edizioni, Viale Monza 106, Milan, 20127, Italy. TEL 39-02-2837141, FAX 39-02-26144793, redazioni@francoangeli.it, http://www.francoangeli.it.

306.85 BOL
MONOGRAFIAS DE SOCIOLOGIA FAMILIAR. Text in Spanish. 1974. irreg., latest vol.9, 1984. price varies. **Document type:** *Monographic series, Academic/Scholarly.*
Published by: Centro de Investigaciones Sociales, Casilla 6931 - C.C., La Paz, Bolivia. TEL 591-2-352931. Ed. Antonio Cisneros.

301 ARG ISSN 0328-8773
HQ1104
MORA. Text in Spanish. 1995. a. ARS 16 domestic; USD 20 in the Americas; USD 25 elsewhere (effective 2010). **Document type:** *Journal, Academic/Scholarly.*
Related titles: Online - full text ed.: ISSN 1853-001X. free (effective 2011) (from SciELO).
Published by: Universidad de Buenos Aires, Facultad de Filosofia y Letras, Puan 480, Buenos Aires, 1406, Argentina. TEL 54-11-44320606, FAX 54-11-44320121, info@filo.uba.ar, http://www.filo.uba.ar. Circ: 700.

MORALITY IN MEDIA NEWSLETTER. *see* LAW—Criminal Law

306 USA
MORFOGEN ASSOCIATES NEWS; international culture news. Text in English. 1987. q. USD 100 domestic; USD 120 foreign (effective 2002). back issues avail. **Document type:** *Newsletter.*
Published by: Morfogen Associates, Elm Rd, Box 324, Mt Lakes, NJ 07046. TEL 973-334-0675, FAX 973-334-7458. Ed. Marilyn M Morfogen. Pub. Zachary P Morfogen.

301 RUS ISSN 1029-3736
➤ **MOSKOVSKII GOSUDARSTVENNYI UNIVERSITET. VESTNIK. SERIYA 18: SOTSIOLOGIYA I POLITOLOGIYA.** Text in Russian. 1946. q. USD 122 in North America; USD 177 combined subscription in North America (print & online eds.) (effective 2011). **Document type:** *Journal, Academic/Scholarly.*
Related titles: Online - full text ed.
Indexed: RASB.
Published by: (Moskovskii Gosudarstvennyi Universitet im. M.V. Lomonosova, Sotsiologicheskii Fakul'tet), Izdatel'stvo Moskovskogo Gosudarstvennogo Universiteta im. M. V. Lomonosova/Publishing House of Moscow State University, B Nikitskaya 5/7, Moscow, 103009, Russian Federation. TEL 7-095-2295091, FAX 7-095-2036671, kd_mgu@rambler.ru, http://www.msu.ru/depts/MSUPubl. Ed. V I Dobren'kov. **Dist. by:** East View Information Services, 10601 Wayzata Blvd, Minneapolis, MN 55305. TEL 952-252-1201, 800-477-1005, FAX 952-252-1202, info@eastview.com, http://www.eastview.com.

➤ **MOUTON SERIES IN PRAGMATICS.** *see* LINGUISTICS

301 FRA ISSN 1247-4819
H61
MOUVEMENT ANTI-UTILITARISTE DANS LES SCIENCE SOCIALES. REVUE SEMESTRIELLE. Key Title: Revue du M A U S S Semestrielle. Text in French. 1982. s-a. EUR 50 domestic to individuals; EUR 54 in Europe to individuals; EUR 54 in Africa to individuals; EUR 65 in Asia to individuals; EUR 65 in North America to individuals; EUR 59 domestic to institutions; EUR 63 in Europe to institutions; EUR 63 in Africa to institutions; EUR 71 in Asia to institutions; EUR 71 in North America to institutions (effective 2009). **Document type:** *Journal, Academic/Scholarly.*
Former titles (until 1993): Revue du M A U S S (0990-5642); (until 1988): Bulletin du M A U S S (0294-4278)
Indexed: CA, FR, IBSS, P42, PSA, S02, S03, SCOPUS, SOPODA, SSA, SociolAb, T02.
—INIST. **CCC.**
Published by: (Mouvement Anti-Utilitariste dans les Sciences Sociales (M A U S S)), Editions La Decouverte, 9 bis rue Abel Hovelacque, Paris, 75013, France. TEL 33-1-44088401, FAX 33-1-44088417, ladecouverte@editionsladecouverte.com, http://www.editionsladecouverte.fr.

305.8 DEU ISSN 0177-3429
MUENCHNER BEITRAEGE ZUR VOLKSKUNDE. Text in German. 1983. irreg., latest vol.39, 2009. price varies. **Document type:** *Monographic series, Academic/Scholarly.*
Published by: (Universitaet Muenchen, Institut fuer Deutsche und Vergleichende Volkskunde), Waxmann Verlag GmbH, Steinfurter Str 555, Muenster, 48159, Germany. TEL 49-251-265040, FAX 49-251-2650426, info@waxmann.com.

303 DEU ISSN 1611-3853
MUENDLICHE KOMMUNIKATION. Text in German. 2003. irreg., latest vol.6, 2009. price varies. **Document type:** *Monographic series, Academic/Scholarly.*
Published by: Logos Verlag Berlin, Comeniushof, Gubener Str 47, Berlin, 10243, Germany. TEL 49-30-42851090, FAX 49-30-42851092, redaktion@logos-verlag.de. Ed. Walter Sendlmeier.

MULTILINGUA; journal of cross-cultural and interlanguage communication. *see* LINGUISTICS

301 ITA ISSN 2036-4482
MULTILINGUISMO E SOCIETA. Text in Multiple languages. 2008. a. **Document type:** *Journal, Academic/Scholarly.*
Indexed: MLA-IB.
Published by: Edistudio, Via Massa Fiscaglia 1 A, Rome, 00127, Italy. TEL 39-6-52370333, 39-06-52370333, FAX 39-06-52371824, http://www.edistudio.org.

MUNDO ESLAVO. *see* HISTORY

MUSIK UND GESELLSCHAFT. *see* MUSIC

MUSIKSOZIOLOGIE. *see* MUSIC

301 ITA
MUTAMENTO SOCIALE. Text in Italian. 1997. irreg., latest vol.1, 1997. price varies. adv. **Document type:** *Monographic series, Academic/Scholarly.*
Published by: Liguori Editore, Via Posillipo 394, Naples, 80123, Italy. TEL 39-081-7206111, FAX 39-081-7206244, liguori@liguori.it, http://www.liguori.it.

N A C L A REPORT ON THE AMERICAS. *see* POLITICAL SCIENCE—International Relations

N A T O SCIENCE FOR PEACE AND SECURITY SERIES. E: HUMAN AND SOCIETAL DYNAMICS. (North Atlantic Treaty Organization) *see* POLITICAL SCIENCE—International Relations

306.85 GBR ISSN 2044-2246
N C D S W NEWS. (National Council for Divorced, Separated and Widowed) Text in English. 1976. 3/yr. free (effective 2010). back issues avail. **Document type:** *Newsletter, Trade.*
Former titles (until 2009): N C D S News (0267-1417); (until 1982): National Council for the Divorced and Separated. News Bulletin
Related titles: Online - full text ed.
Published by: National Council for Divorced, Separated and Widowed, 68 Parkes Hall Rd, Woodsetton, Dudley, DY1 3SR, United Kingdom. TEL 44-7041-478120, info@ncds.org.uk.

305 USA ISSN 2152-8195
N C E A E-NEWS. Text in English. 19??. m. free (effective 2010). back issues avail. **Document type:** *Newsletter, Government.*
Formerly (until 2007): National Center on Elder Abuse. Newsletter
Media: Online - full text.
Published by: (National Center on Elder Abuse), Clearinghouse on Abuse and Neglect of the Elderly, Alison Hall W Rm 211, Newark, DE 19716. TEL 302-831-3525, FAX 302-831-6081, CANE-UD@udel.edu, http://www.cane.udel.edu/.

N C O P F ANNUAL REPORT. *see* CHILDREN AND YOUTH—About

305.3 305.31 305.4 NOR ISSN 1502-1521
HQ1181
N I K K MAGASIN. (Nordisk Institutt for Kundskap om Koenn) Text in Danish, Norwegian, Swedish. 1991. 3/yr. free. back issues avail. **Document type:** *Journal, Academic/Scholarly.* **Description:** An interdisciplinary publication presenting Nordic perspectives from various fields in gender research.
Formerly (until 2000): Nytt fra N I K K (0807-3805); Which superseded in part (in 1996): Nordisk Kvinnoforskning (1238-5417)
Related titles: Online - full text ed.: ISSN 1502-5195; English ed.: News from N I K K. ISSN 0807-5239. 1996.
Indexed: FemPer.
Published by: Nordisk Institutt for Kundskap om Koenn/Nordic Gender Institute, c/o Universitetet i Oslo, PO Box 1156, Blindern, Oslo, 0318, Norway. TEL 47-22-858921, FAX 47-22-858950, nikk@nikk.no, http://www.nikk.uio.no. Ed. Solveig Bergman. Circ: 9,000.

305.3 305.31 305.4 NOR ISSN 1891-3172
▼ **N I K K. PUBLIKATIONER.** Text in Danish, Norwegian, Swedish. 2009. irreg., latest vol.1, 2009. **Document type:** *Monographic series, Academic/Scholarly.*
Published by: Nordisk Institutt for Kundskap om Koenn/Nordic Gender Institute, c/o Universitetet i Oslo, PO Box 1156, Blindern, Oslo, 0318, Norway. TEL 47-22-858921, FAX 47-22-858950, nikk@nikk.no, http://www.nikk.uio.no.

302.23 659 SWE ISSN 0349-5949
P91.5.S3
N O R D I C O M - INFORMATION; om masskommunikationsforskning i Norden. (Nordic Information Centre for Media and Communication Research) Text in Danish, Norwegian, Swedish. 1980. q. SEK 250; SEK 200 to students (effective 2007). bk.rev. back issues avail. **Document type:** *Journal, Academic/Scholarly.* **Description:** Articles on Nordic mass communication research; ongoing research projects; critical reviews; lists of new literature.
Related titles: Online - full content ed.
Indexed: RASB.
—CCC.
Published by: N O R D I C O M A/S/Nordic Information Centre for Media and Communication Research, c/o University of Goeteborg, PO Box 713, Goeteborg, SE 40530, Sweden. TEL 46-31-7731000, FAX 46-31-7734655, info@nordicom.gu.se. Ed. Ulla Carlsson TEL 46-31-7731219. Circ: 2,500.

659 302.23 SWE ISSN 1403-1108
P91.5.S3
➤ **N O R D I C O M REVIEW**; Nordic research on media & communication. (Nordic Information Centre for Media and Communication Research) Text in English. 1981. s-a. free (effective 2003). bk.rev. bibl. 150 p./no. 2 cols./p.; back issues avail. **Document type:** *Journal, Academic/Scholarly.* **Description:** Contains articles about Nordic mass communication research, reviews of the essential literature, surveys of literature, surveys of projects.
Formerly (until 1994): Nordicom Review of Nordic Mass Communication Research (0349-6244)
Related titles: Online - full content ed.: free (effective 2011).
Indexed: A39, C27, C29, CA, CMM, CommAb, D03, D04, E13, IBSS, PAIS, R14, RASB, S02, S03, S14, S15, S18, SCOPUS, SOPODA, SociolAb, T02.
—BLDSC (6117.936350). **CCC.**
Published by: N O R D I C O M A/S/Nordic Information Centre for Media and Communication Research, c/o University of Goeteborg, PO Box 713, Goeteborg, SE 40530, Sweden. TEL 46-31-7731000, FAX 46-31-7734655, info@nordicom.gu.se. Ed. Ulla Carlsson TEL 46-31-7731219. Circ: 1,400.

305 NOR ISSN 1890-6710
N O V A-NYTT. (Norsk Institutt for Forskning om Opvekst, Velferd og Aldring) Text in Norwegian. 1997. q. free. **Document type:** *Newsletter, Consumer.*
Formerly (until 2008): Info-N O V A (1502-1041)
Related titles: Online - full text ed.: ISSN 1890-7040. 2003.
Published by: Norsk Institutt for Forskning om Opvekst, Velferd og Aldring/Norwegian Social Research, PO Box 3223, Elisenberg, Oslo, 0208, Norway. TEL 47-22-541200, FAX 47-22-541201, nova@nova.no. Ed. Magnus Rindal.

303.4 NOR ISSN 1890-2022
N T N U SAMFUNNSFORSKNING AS. STUDIO APERTURA. WORK REPORT. (Norges Teknisk-Naturvitenskapelige Universitet) Text in Norwegian. 2005. irreg., latest 2009. **Document type:** *Monographic series, Academic/Scholarly.*
Related titles: Online - full text ed.
Published by: Norges Teknisk-Naturvitenskapelige Universitet, Samfunnsforskning AS. Studio Apertura., NTNU Dragvoll, Trondheim, 7491, Norway. TEL 45-73-596328, FAX 45-73-596330, info@apertura.ntnu.no, http://www.ntnusamfunnsforskning.no.

NASHRAT AL-MU'ASHIRAT AL-IQTISADIYYAT WA-AL-IJTIMA'IYYAT LI-JUMHURIYYAT MISR AL-'ARABIYYAT/ECONOMIC AND SOCIAL INDICATORS BULLETIN OF THE ARAB REPUBLIC OF EGYPT. *see* BUSINESS AND ECONOMICS—Economic Situation And Conditions

306.85 USA ISSN 0278-6168
HQ1
NATIONAL COUNCIL ON FAMILY RELATIONS. REPORT. Text in English. 1955. q. free to members (effective 2010). adv. **Document type:** *Newsletter, Trade.* **Description:** Features updates on national, international and NCFR Association of councils affairs, broad family field news and current issues in marriage and family life.
Formerly (until 198?): National Council on Family Relations. Newsletter (0466-2032)

—CCC.
Published by: National Council on Family Relations, 1201 W River Pky, Ste 200, Minneapolis, MN 55454. TEL 763-781-9331, FAX 763-781-9348, info@ncfr.org, http://www.ncfr.org/. Ed., Adv. contact Nancy Gonzalez TEL 763-231-2887. Circ: 3,500.

NATIONAL IDENTITIES. *see* POLITICAL SCIENCE

301 USA ISSN 0892-4287
NATIONAL JOURNAL OF SOCIOLOGY. Text in English. 1987. s-a. **Document type:** *Journal, Academic/Scholarly.*
Indexed: CA, S02, S03, SCOPUS, SociolAb.
Published by: University of Texas at Austin, Main Bldg 2300, Austin, TX 78712. Ed. John S Butler.

301 TWN ISSN 0077-5851
NATIONAL TAIWAN UNIVERSITY JOURNAL OF SOCIOLOGY. Key Title: Guoli Taiwan Daxue Shehui Xuekan. Text in Chinese, English. 1963. a. USD 5. bk.rev. **Document type:** *Journal, Academic/ Scholarly.*
Indexed: BAS, CIN, ChemAb, ChemTitl, SCOPUS, SOPODA, SociolAb.
Published by: National Taiwan University, Department of Sociology, 21 Hsuchow Rd, Taipei, 10020, Taiwan. TEL 02-351-4239. Ed. Cheng Han Chang. Circ: 500.

301 SGP
NATIONAL UNIVERSITY OF SINGAPORE. DEPARTMENT OF SOCIOLOGY. WORKING PAPER SERIES. Text in English. 1972. irreg. price varies. back issues avail. **Document type:** *Journal, Academic/Scholarly.* **Description:** Provides a forum for staff members, graduate students and visitors to the department to circulate their work in progress.
Published by: National University of Singapore, Department of Sociology, 11 Arts Link AS1 #03-10, Singapore, 117570, Singapore. TEL 65-874-3822, FAX 65-777-9579, socmerb@nus.edu.sg, http://www.fas.nus.edu.sg/soc/. **Dist. by:** Chopsons Private Ltd., Siglap PO Box 264, Singapore 914503, Singapore. TEL 65-4483634, FAX 65-4481071, chopsons@singnet.com.sg; Select Books, 19 Tanglin Rd #03-15, Tanglin Shopping Centre, Singapore 247909, Singapore. TEL 65-732-1515, FAX 65-736-0855, selectbk@cyberway.com.sg.

301 SGP ISSN 0129-8186
NATIONAL UNIVERSITY OF SINGAPORE. DEPARTMENT OF SOCIOLOGY. WORKING PAPERS. Text in English. 1972. irreg., latest no.190, 2009. price varies. back issues avail. **Document type:** *Monographic series, Academic/Scholarly.*
Former titles (until 1985): Sociology Working Papers; (until 1976): University of Singapore. Department of Sociology. Working Papers
Related titles: Online - full text ed.
Published by: National University of Singapore, Department of Sociology, 11 Arts Link, Singapore, 117570, Singapore. FAX 65-6777-9579, http://www.fas.nus.edu.sg/soc/. Circ: 500.

331 301 USA ISSN 1538-6309
JN96.A58
NATIONS IN TRANSIT (YEAR). Text in English. 1995. a. USD 74.95, GBP 44.95, EUR 51.95 per issue (effective 2010). back issues avail.; reprints avail. **Document type:** *Monographic series, Academic/ Scholarly.*
Published by: (Freedom House), Rowman & Littlefield Publishers, Inc., 4501 Forbes Blvd, Ste 200, Lanham, MD 20706. TEL 301-459-3366, 800-462-6420, FAX 301-429-5748, 800-338-4550, custserv@rowman.com.

NATURE AND CULTURE. *see* BIOLOGY

301 GBR ISSN 1750-4708
HD42
NEGOTIATION AND CONFLICT MANAGEMENT RESEARCH. Text in English. 2008. q. GBP 231 in United Kingdom to institutions; EUR 292 in Europe to institutions; USD 412 in the Americas to institutions; USD 451 elsewhere to institutions; GBP 265 combined subscription in United Kingdom to institutions (print & online eds.); EUR 339 combined subscription in Europe to institutions (print & online eds.); USD 473 combined subscription in the Americas to institutions (print & online eds.); USD 520 combined subscription elsewhere to institutions (print & online eds.) (effective 2012). reprint service avail. from PSC. **Document type:** *Journal, Academic/Scholarly.* **Description:** Publishes research that focuses on theory and research on conflict and conflict management across levels, including organizational conflict, interpersonal conflict and inter-group conflict.
Related titles: Online - full text ed.: ISSN 1750-4716. GBP 231 in United Kingdom to institutions; EUR 292 in Europe to institutions; USD 412 in the Americas to institutions; USD 451 elsewhere to institutions (effective 2012) (from IngentaConnect).
Indexed: A22, CA, E01, P03, PsycInfo, S02, S03, T02.
—IE. **CCC.**
Published by: (International Association for Conflict Management USA), Wiley-Blackwell Publishing Ltd. (Subsidiary of: John Wiley & Sons, Inc.), 9600 Garsington Rd, Oxford, OX4 2DQ, United Kingdom. TEL 44-1865-776868, FAX 44-1865-714591, customer@wiley.co.uk, http://www.wiley.com/WileyCDA/. Eds. Karen Jehn, Mara Olekalns. Adv. contact Kristin McCarthy.

302.23 USA
NETCOMTALK. Text in English. irreg. **Document type:** *Newsletter.*
Media: Online - full text.
Published by: Boston University, College of Communication, 640 Commonwealth Ave, Boston, MA 02215. TEL 617-353-3450. Ed. William Lord.

303.482 NLD ISSN 0922-8772
HN511
NETHERLANDS. SOCIAAL EN CULTUREEL PLANBUREAU. SOCIAAL EN CULTUREEL RAPPORT. Key Title: Sociaal en Cultureel Rapport. Text in Dutch, English. 1975. biennial. price varies. charts; stat. back issues avail. **Document type:** *Monographic series, Academic/Scholarly.* **Description:** Reports on social and cultural trends in the Netherlands.
Related titles: Online - full text ed.: ISSN 1569-4763.
Published by: Sociaal en Cultureel Planbureau/Social and Cultural Planning Office, Postbus 16164, The Hague, 2500 BD, Netherlands. TEL 31-70-3407000, FAX 31-70-3407044, info@scp.nl, http://www.scp.nl.

NETHRA. *see* POLITICAL SCIENCE

306.09 DEU ISSN 0932-7665
DIE NEUE ORDNUNG. Text in German. 1946. 6/yr. EUR 25; EUR 5 newsstand/cover (effective 2005). adv. bk.rev. index. back issues avail. **Document type:** *Journal, Academic/Scholarly.* **Description:** Discussion of current history, social issues and changes in society.
Formerly (until 1983): Die Neue Ordnung in Kirche, Staat, Gesellschaft, Kultur (0028-3304)
Indexed: DIP, IBR, IBZ, PAIS.
Published by: Institut fuer Gesellschaftswissenschaften Walberberg e.V., Simrockstr 19, Bonn, 53113, Germany. TEL 49-228-216852, FAX 49-228-220244. Ed. Wolfgang Ockenfels. Circ: 2,400.

302.23 DEU ISSN 1865-2638
NEUE SCHRIFTEN ZUR ONLINE-FORSCHUNG. Text in German. 2007. irreg., latest vol.8, 2010. price varies. **Document type:** *Monographic series, Academic/Scholarly.*
Published by: Herbert von Halem Verlag, Lindenstr 19, Cologne, 50674, Germany. TEL 49-221-9258290, FAX 49-221-9258292, info@halem-verlag.de, http://www.halem-verlag.de.

NEW AMERICANISTS. *see* LITERATURE

THE NEW ATLANTIS; a journal of technology & society. *see* POLITICAL SCIENCE

301 USA ISSN 1545-0384
NEW CULTURAL STUDIES. Text in English. 1990. irreg. price varies. back issues avail. **Document type:** *Monographic series, Academic/ Scholarly.* **Description:** Provides a forum for works exploring the issues of cultural constructions, including the body, gender, and sexuality.
Published by: University of Pennsylvania Press, 3905 Spruce St, Philadelphia, PA 19104. TEL 215-898-6261, FAX 215-898-0404, custserv@pobox.upenn.edu, http://www.pennpress.org.

302.23 USA ISSN 1939-2494
NEW DIRECTIONS IN MEDIA. Text in English. 2008. irreg., latest 2010. price varies. back issues avail. **Document type:** *Monographic series, Academic/Scholarly.*
Published by: Praeger Publishers (Subsidiary of: Greenwood Publishing Group Inc.), 88 Post Rd W, Westport, CT 06881. TEL 800-368-6868, tech.support@greenwood.com, http://www.greenwood.com. Ed. Robin Andersen.

NEW DOCTOR. *see* MEDICAL SCIENCES

NEW ENVIRONMENT BULLETIN. *see* NEW AGE PUBLICATIONS

NEW FORUM BOOKS. *see* POLITICAL SCIENCE

NEW GERMAN-AMERICAN STUDIES/NEUE DEUTSCHE-AMERIKANISCHE STUDIEN. *see* HUMANITIES: COMPREHENSIVE WORKS

303 USA ISSN 1940-0004
NEW GLOBAL STUDIES. Text in English. 2007 (Nov.). irreg. (3-4/yrs). USD 225 to institutions; USD 675 to corporations (effective 2011). back issues avail. **Document type:** *Journal, Academic/Scholarly.* **Description:** Provides the patterns and local effects of economic globalization, global media networks, preservation of the global environment, transnational manifestations of culture, and the methodology of global studies.
Media: Online - full text.
Indexed: ESPM, SSciA, SociolAb.
—CCC.
Published by: Berkeley Electronic Press, 2809 Telegraph Ave, Ste 202, Berkeley, CA 94705. TEL 510-665-1200, FAX 510-665-1201, info@bepress.com.

335.005 GBR ISSN 1464-6757
NEW INTERVENTIONS. Text in English. 1990. q. GBP 9.50 domestic to individuals; GBP 13 foreign to individuals; GBP 13 to institutions (effective 2009). **Document type:** *Magazine, Consumer.* **Description:** Aimed at those who are interested in the future of socialism and provides a forum for discussion unfettered by any orthodoxy of 'party line'.
Indexed: AltPI.
Address: PO Box 485, Coventry, CV5 6ZP, United Kingdom.

302.23 GBR ISSN 1461-4448
QA76.9.C66
➤ **NEW MEDIA & SOCIETY.** Text in English. 1999. 8/yr. USD 1,655, GBP 895 combined subscription to institutions (print & online eds.); USD 1,622, GBP 877 to institutions (effective 2011). adv. bk.rev. back issues avail.; reprint service avail. from PSC. **Document type:** *Journal, Academic/Scholarly.* **Description:** Provides an interdisciplinary forum for the examination of the social dynamics of media and information change.
Related titles: Online - full text ed.: ISSN 1461-7315. USD 1,490, GBP 806 to institutions (effective 2011).
Indexed: A01, A03, A08, A20, A22, B07, BibInd, CA, CMM, CommAb, CurCont, DIP, E01, ESPM, F01, F02, I13, IBR, IBSS, IBZ, MLA-IB, P03, P34, P42, PSA, PsycInfo, PsycholAb, RiskAb, S02, S03, SCOPUS, SSCI, SociolAb, T02, W07.
—BLDSC (6084.477650), IE, Infotrieve, Ingenta. **CCC.**
Published by: Sage Publications Ltd. (Subsidiary of: Sage Publications, Inc.), 1 Oliver's Yard, 55 City Rd, London, EC1Y 1SP, United Kingdom. TEL 44-20-73248500, FAX 44-20-73248600, info@sagepub.co.uk, http://www.uk.sagepub.com/home.nav. Eds. Nicholas Jankowski, Steve Jones. adv.: B&W page GBP 400; 130 x 205. **Subscr. in the Americas to:** Sage Publications, Inc., 2455 Teller Rd, Thousand Oaks, CA 91320. TEL 805-499-9774, FAX 805-499-0871, journals@sagepub.com.

➤ **NEW METRO NEWS.** *see* ETHNIC INTERESTS

➤ **NEW SOCIALIST**; ideas for radical change. *see* POLITICAL SCIENCE

➤ **NEW SOUTH AFRICAN OUTLOOK**; an ecumencial magazine for thinkers and decision makers. *see* RELIGIONS AND THEOLOGY

301.14 GBR ISSN 1465-573X
NEW START (LONDON). Text in English. 1999. w. GBP 125 domestic; GBP 145 in Europe; GBP 165 elsewhere (effective 2009). adv. back issues avail. **Document type:** *Magazine, Trade.* **Description:** Provides significant information for the regeneration practitioners.
Related titles: Online - full text ed.: GBP 95 (effective 2009); Supplement(s): New Start News.
—CCC.
Published by: New Start Publishing, Unit 414, The Workstation, Paternoster Row, Sheffield, S1 2BX, United Kingdom. Eds. Austin Macauley TEL 44-114-2816133, Julian Dobson TEL 44-114-2295726. Adv. contact Chloe Gray TEL 44-114-2816130.

NEW STUDIES IN SOCIAL POLICY. *see* POLITICAL SCIENCE

301 USA ISSN 1935-9357
➤ **THE NEW YORK JOURNAL OF SOCIOLOGY.** Abbreviated title: T N Y J S. Text in English. 2008. a. free (effective 2011). back issues avail. **Document type:** *Journal, Academic/Scholarly.* **Description:** Dedicated to the classical, contemporary and critical traditions of sociological theory and research.
Media: Online - full text.
Published by: State University of New York at Cortland, Department of Sociology and Anthropology, PO Box 2000, Cortland, NY 13045. TEL 607-753-2011, amanda.halliwell@cortland.edu, http://www2.cortland.edu/departments/sociology/. Ed. Mark P Worrell.

306.85 NZL ISSN 1177-3545
NEW ZEALAND. FAMILIES COMMISSION. RESEARCH REPORT. Text in English. 2005. irreg. free (effective 2007). **Document type:** *Monographic series.*
Related titles: Online - full text ed.: ISSN 1178-1289.
Published by: Families Commission, Level 6, Public Trust Bldg, 117-125 Lambton Quay, PO Box 2839, Wellington, New Zealand. TEL 64-4-9177040, FAX 64-4-9177059, enquiries@nzfamilies.org.nz.

302.23 NZL ISSN 1178-9638
➤ **NEW ZEALAND JOURNAL OF MEDIA STUDIES (ONLINE).** Text in English. 1994. s-a. **Document type:** *Journal, Academic/Scholarly.* **Description:** A forum for the scholarly discussion of media research and literacy with regard to theoretical and representational questions and topics, history and policy at both local and global levels.
Formerly (until 2008): New Zealand Journal of Media Studies (Print) (1173-0811)
Media: Online - full text.
Indexed: RILM.
Published by: Massey University, School of English & Media Studies, Private Bag 11 222, Palmerston North, New Zealand. TEL 64-6-356-9099 ext 7311, FAX 64-6-350-5672, http://www.massey.ac.nz. Ed. Tony Schirato.

301 NZL ISSN 0112-921X
HM1
➤ **NEW ZEALAND SOCIOLOGY.** Text in English. 1986. s-a. **Document type:** *Journal, Academic/Scholarly.* **Description:** Disseminates and promotes research and thought that has, as its objective, the clarification and development of theoretically informed research in sociology and related disciplines with a predominant, though not exclusive, concern with New Zealand.
Related titles: Online - full text ed.: ISSN 1173-1036.
Indexed: A11, A26, CA, E08, G08, I05, IBSS, P27, P48, P54, PQC, RILM, S02, S03, S09, SCOPUS, SociolAb, T02.
—BLDSC (6097.243000), IE, Ingenta.
Published by: Sociological Association of Aotearoa New Zealand, University of Waikato, Dept. of Sociology & Social Policy, Faculty of Arts & Social Sciences, Private Bag 3105, Hamilton, New Zealand. http://saanz.science.org.nz/.

362.88 SWE
NEWS ON CHILDREN, YOUTH AND MEDIA IN THE WORLD. Text in English. 1997. 2/yr. free (effective 2007). bk.rev. abstr.; bibl.; stat. back issues avail. **Document type:** *Newsletter, Academic/Scholarly.* **Description:** Publishes articles on children and violence in the media.
Former titles (until 2005): News from I C C V O S (Print Edition); (until 1999): News on Children and Violence on the Screens
Media: Online - full content. **Related titles:** Online - full text ed.
Published by: (International Clearinghouse on Children, Youth and Media), N O R D I C O M A/S/Nordic Information Centre for Media and Communication Research, c/o University of Goeteborg, PO Box 713, Goeteborg, SE 40530, Sweden. TEL 46-31-7731000, FAX 46-31-7734655, info@nordicom.gu.se. Ed. Catharina Bucht.

301 ITA ISSN 2037-5247
NEWSLETTER NUOVI LAVORI. Text in Italian. 2008. s-m. **Document type:** *Newsletter, Consumer.*
Media: Online - full text.
Published by: Associazione Nuovi Lavori, Via Sardegna 55, Rome, Italy. http://www.nuovi-lavori.it.

NICHIBUNKEN JAPAN REVIEW. *see* ASIAN STUDIES

384.5 DEU ISSN 0949-7382
NIEDERSAECHSISCHE LANDESMEDIENANSTALT. SCHRIFTENREIHE. Text in German. 1995. irreg., latest vol.27, 2010. price varies. **Document type:** *Monographic series, Academic/ Scholarly.*
Published by: (Niedersaechsische Landesmedienanstalt), Vistas Verlag GmbH, Goltzstr 11, Berlin, 10781, Germany. TEL 49-30-32707446, FAX 49-30-32707455, medienverlag@vistas.de.

306.85 392.3 NLD ISSN 1877-5616
NIEUW GEZIN. Text in Dutch. 199?. q. EUR 22.50; EUR 6.95 newsstand/ cover (effective 2011). **Document type:** *Magazine, Consumer.*
Formerly (until 2008): Stiefband (1384-9018)
Published by: Stichting Stiefgezinnen Nederland, Sporkehout 58, Huizen, 1273 TG, Netherlands. TEL 31-35-5267658, nieuwgezin@live.nl. Ed. Corrie Haverkort TEL 31-575-511670.

306 NLD ISSN 2210-3341
NIEUWSBRIEF ERFGOEDINSTELLINGEN. Text in Dutch. 2001. q.
Supersedes in part (in 2009): Cultureel Erfgoed Noord-Holland. Nieuwsbrief (2210-3317); Which was formerly (until 2007): Museaal en Historisch Perspectief Noord-Holland. Nieuws (1874-5059); (until 2003): Musea Noord-Holland. Nieuwsbrief (1569-092X)
Published by: Cultureel Erfgoed Noord-Holland, Postbus 205, Haarlem, 2000 AE, Netherlands. TEL 31-23-5531498, FAX 31-23-5318436, info@cultureelerfgoednh.nl, http://www.cultureelerfgoednh.nl.

NIGERIAN JOURNAL OF ECONOMIC & SOCIAL STUDIES. *see* BUSINESS AND ECONOMICS

300 DEU ISSN 0935-7173
NIJMEGEN STUDIES IN DEVELOPMENT AND CULTURAL CHANGE. Text in English. 1989. irreg., latest vol.47, 2009. price varies. **Document type:** *Monographic series, Academic/Scholarly.*
Indexed: IBR, IBZ.
—IE.
Published by: (Nijmeegs Instituut voor Comparatieve Cultuur- en Ontwikkelingsstudies/Nijmegen Interdisciplinary Centre for Development and Cultural Change NLD), Lit Verlag, Grevener Str/Fresnostr 2, Muenster, 48159, Germany. TEL 49-251-235091, FAX 49-251-231972, lit@lit-verlag.de.

S

NINE; a journal of baseball history & culture. *see* SPORTS AND GAMES—Ball Games

302.23 USA ISSN 1542-0280
NMEDIAC; the journal of new media & culture. Text in English. 2002 (Winter). irreg.
Address: 129 Windsor Circle, Chapel Hill, NC 27516. TEL 919-960-7901.

300 COL ISSN 0121-7550
LA565
NOMADAS. Text in Spanish. 1993. s-a. COP 38,000 domestic; USD 80 in the Americas; USD 90 elsewhere (effective 2010). **Document type:** *Journal, Academic/Scholarly.*
Related titles: Online - full text ed.: (from SciELO).
Indexed: C01, CA, H21, P08, P42, PSA, S02, S03, SociolAb, T02.
Published by: Fundacion Universidad Central, Carrera 5, No. 21-38, Bogota, Colombia. TEL 57-1-3239868, 57-1-3266820, http://www.ucentral.edu.co/.

301 340 ESP ISSN 1578-6730
K487.S6
NOMADAS. Text in Spanish. 1985. s-a. free (effective 2011). **Document type:** *Journal, Academic/Scholarly.*
Media: Online - full text.
Indexed: A39, C27, C29, D03, D04, E13, H21, I04, I05, P08, P46, P48, PQC, R14, S14, S15, S18.
—IE. **CCC.**
Published by: (Universidad Complutense de Madrid, Facultad de Ciencias Politicas y Sociologia), Universidad Complutense de Madrid, Servicio de Publicaciones, C/ Obispo Trejo 2, Ciudad Universitaria, Madrid, 28040, Spain. TEL 34-91-3941127, FAX 34-91-3941126, servicio.publicaciones@rect.ucm.es, http://www.ucm.es/publicaciones.

301 USA
NONPROFIT MAILERS FEDERATION. NEWS UPDATE. Text in English. 1982. m. membership. **Document type:** *Newsletter.* **Description:** Promotes non-profit groups and monitors relevant legislation.
Published by: National Federation of Nonprofits, 1111 19th St NW, Ste. 1180, Washington, DC 20036-3637. TEL 202-628-4380, FAX 202-628-4383. R&P Lee M Cassidy.

NORD NU. *see* GENERAL INTEREST PERIODICALS—Scandinavia

NORDEN. *see* GENERAL INTEREST PERIODICALS—Scandinavia

302.23 659 070 SWE ISSN 1401-0410
NORDIC MEDIA TRENDS. Text in English. 1995. a., latest vol.9, 2006. SEK 300, EUR 32 per issue (effective 2007). stat. back issues avail. **Document type:** *Monographic series, Trade.* **Description:** Media Trends in Denmark, Finland, Iceland, Norway and Sweden. Commentaries examine developments country by country. Comparative Nordic statistics shows media structure, ownership, economy, penetration/reach and consumption. The publication includes analyses and overviews of media regulation.
Published by: N O R D I C O M A/S/Nordic Information Centre for Media and Communication Research, c/o University of Goeteborg, PO Box 713, Goeteborg, SE 40530, Sweden. TEL 46-31-7731000, FAX 46-31-7734655, info@nordicom.gu.se. Ed. Eva Harrie.

068.48072 NOR ISSN 1501-8237
➤ **NORDISKE ORGANISASJONSSTUDIER.** Variant title: N O S. Text in Multiple languages. 1999. q. NOK 428 to individuals; NOK 748 to institutions; NOK 186 per issue (effective 2011). adv. **Document type:** *Journal, Academic/Scholarly.* **Description:** Launched as a tool for dialog across disciplines in the exchange of knowledge and understanding of organizations.
Related titles: Online - full text ed.
—BLDSC (6125.385000).
Published by: (Handelshoeyskolen B I/Norwegian Business School, Institute for Business Economics), Fagbokforlaget, Kanalveien 51, PO Box 6050, Postterminalen, Bergen, 5892, Norway. TEL 47-55-388800, FAX 47-55-388801, fagbokforlaget@fagbokforlaget.no, http://www.fagbokforlaget.no. Ed. Paul R Roness. Adv. contact Janne-Beate Duke. Circ: 500.

301 DNK ISSN 1396-3953
➤ **NORDISKE UDKAST**; tidsskrift for kritisk samfundsforskning. Text in Danish, Norwegian, Swedish. 1973-2009; resumed 2011. s-a. DKK 205 to individuals; DKK 360 combined subscription to institutions; DKK 154 to students; DKK 120 per issue (effective 2011). index. back issues avail. **Document type:** *Journal, Academic/Scholarly.* **Description:** Focus on critical social and psychological studies, action research, sociology, and methodology of research.
Formerly (until 1995): Udkast (0105-2691)
Indexed: PsycholAb.
Published by: (Koebenhavns Universitet, Institut for Psykologi/University of Copenhagen, Department of Psychology), Syddansk Universitetsforlag/University Press of Southern Denmark, Campusvej 55, Odense M, 5230, Denmark. TEL 45-66-157999, FAX 45-66-158126, press@forlag.sdu.dk. Eds. Charlotte Hoejhelt, Torben Bechman. Circ: 500.

➤ **NORM UND STRUKTUR**; Studien zum sozialen Wandel in Mittelalter und frueher Neuzeit. *see* HISTORY—History Of Europe

305.31 NOR ISSN 1890-2138
HQ1088
➤ **NORMA**; nordisk tidsskrift for maskulinitetsstudier. Text in Danish, English, Norwegian, Swedish. 2006. s-a. NOK 300 to individuals; NOK 575 to institutions; NOK 220 to students (effective 2010). **Document type:** *Journal, Academic/Scholarly.* **Description:** Aims to facilitate the theoretical development, recognition, promotion and coordination of research concerning multiple forms of masculinities in a Nordic context and beyond.
Related titles: Online - full text ed.: ISSN 1890-2146. NOK 675 (effective 2010).
Published by: (Nordisk Institutt for Kundskap om Koenn/Nordic Gender Institute), Universitetsforlaget AS/Scandinavian University Press (Subsidiary of: Aschehoug & Co.), Sehesteds Gate 3, P O Box 508, Sentrum, Oslo, 0105, Norway. TEL 47-24-147500, FAX 47-24-147501, post@universitetsforlaget.no. Ed. Ulf Mellstroem TEL 47-920-491000.

302.23 NOR ISSN 0804-8452
P92.N8
➤ **NORSK MEDIETIDSSKRIFT.** Text in Norwegian. 1994. q. NOK 510 to individuals; NOK 820 to institutions; NOK 280 to students (effective 2010). **Document type:** *Journal, Academic/Scholarly.* **Description:** Publishes articles on Norwegian, Nordic and international media research.
Related titles: Online - full text ed.: ISSN 0805-9535. NOK 920 (effective 2010).
Published by: (Norsk Medieforskerlag), Universitetsforlaget AS/Scandinavian University Press (Subsidiary of: Aschehoug & Co.), Sehesteds Gate 3, P O Box 508, Sentrum, Oslo, 0105, Norway. TEL 47-24-147500, FAX 47-24-147501, post@universitetsforlaget.no, http://www.universitetsforlaget.no. Ed. Lars Nyre. Circ: 500.

302 DEU ISSN 1868-6206
▼ **NORTE**; ein stereothematisches Studentenmagazin der Fakultaet Gestaltung der Hochschule Wismar. Text in German. 2009. irreg. **Document type:** *Monographic series, Academic/Scholarly.*
Published by: Callidus Verlag, Alter Holzhafen 19, Wismar, 23966, Germany. TEL 49-3841-7582760, FAX 49-3841-229985, callidus@callidusverlag.de, http://www.callidusverlag.de.

NORTH AMERICAN JOURNAL OF PSYCHOLOGY. *see* PSYCHOLOGY

301 NOR ISSN 1890-5226
NORUT TROMSOE. RAPPORT. Text in English, Norwegian. 2008. irreg., latest 2007. back issues avail. **Document type:** *Monographic series, Academic/Scholarly.*
Formed by the merger of (2005-2008): Norut I T. I T-Rapport (1503-1705); (19??-2008): Norut Samfunn. Rapport (0804-6069)
Related titles: Online - full text ed.
Published by: Norut Tromsoe AS, Forskningsparken, PO Box 6434, Tromsoe, 9294, Norway. TEL 47-77-629400, FAX 47-77-629401, post@norut.no, http://www.norut.no.

306 NOR ISSN 1502-2528
NORWAY. NORAD. RAPPORT/NORWAY. NORAD. REPORT. Text mainly in English. 1999. irreg. free. back issues avail. **Document type:** *Monographic series, Government.*
Related titles: Online - full text ed.
Published by: Direktoratet for Utviklingssamarbeid/Norwegian Agency for Development Cooperation, PO Box 8034, Dep, Oslo, 0030, Norway. TEL 47-22-242030, FAX 47-22-242031, postmottag@norad.no.

306 NOR ISSN 1504-4610
NORWAY. NORAD. STUDY. Text in English. 2005. irreg. **Document type:** *Monographic series, Government.*
Published by: Direktoratet for Utviklingssamarbeid/Norwegian Agency for Development Cooperation, PO Box 8034, Dep, Oslo, 0030, Norway. TEL 47-22-242030, FAX 47-22-242031, postmottag@norad.no, http://www.norad.no.

325 USA ISSN 0078-1983
E184.S2
NORWEGIAN-AMERICAN STUDIES. Text in English. 1926. irreg., latest vol.35. price varies. reprints avail. **Document type:** *Monographic series, Academic/Scholarly.*
Former titles (until 1962): Norwegian-American Studies and Records (0885-5900); (until 1931): Studies and Records
Indexed: AmH&L, BibInd, CA, DIP, HistAb, IBR, IBZ, MLA, MLA-IB, PCI.
Published by: Norwegian-American Historical Association, St. Olaf College, Northfield, MN 55057. naha@stolaf.edu. Ed. Todd S Nichol. Circ: 1,900.

307.1416 CAN ISSN 1712-1671
NOS DIVERSES CITES. Text in French. 2004. a., latest 2005. **Document type:** *Journal, Consumer.*
Related titles: Online - full text ed.: ISSN 1712-168X; English ed.: Our Diverse Cities. ISSN 1712-1655.
Published by: Metropolis Project, 219 Laurier Ave West, Ottawa, ON K1A 1L1, Canada. FAX 613-957-5968, canada@metropolis.net, http://www.metropolis.net.

NOTES AFRICAINES. *see* POLITICAL SCIENCE

302.2 ESP ISSN 1130-8842
NOTICIAS DE LA COMUNICACION. Text in Spanish. 1991. 11/yr. EUR 370 domestic; EUR 555 in Europe; EUR 585 in the Americas (effective 2010). adv. **Document type:** *Magazine, Trade.* **Description:** Covers the communications industry, press, magazines, radio, TV and the media in general.
Published by: Noticias de la Comunicacion S.A., Hermosilla, 77, Madrid, 28001, Spain. TEL 34-91-4316624, FAX 34-91-5766724, noticias@noticom.es.

302 FRA ISSN 1951-9532
NOUVELLE REVUE DE PSYCHOSOCIOLOGIE. Text in French. 2006. s-a. EUR 46 domestic to individuals; EUR 52 foreign to individuals; EUR 55 domestic to institutions; EUR 23 domestic to students; EUR 30 foreign to students (effective 2011). back issues avail. **Document type:** *Journal, Academic/Scholarly.*
Related titles: Online - full text ed.: ISSN 1961-8697.
Indexed: P03, PsycInfo.
Published by: Editions Eres, 33 Av. Marcel Dassault, Toulouse, 31500, France. TEL 33-5-61751576, FAX 33-5-61735289, eres@edition-eres.com. Eds. Gilles Amado, Jacqueline Barus-Michel.

NOUVELLES PRATIQUES SOCIALES. *see* SOCIAL SERVICES AND WELFARE

306.43 DEU ISSN 1612-2194
NOVEMBERAKADEMIE. Text in German. 2001. irreg., latest vol.3, 2003. price varies. **Document type:** *Monographic series, Academic/Scholarly.*
Published by: Waxmann Verlag GmbH, Steinfurter Str 555, Muenster, 48159, Germany. TEL 49-251-265040, FAX 49-251-2650426, info@waxmann.com.

305 SWE ISSN 0347-5395
NY LIVSSTIL; foer en raettvis foerdelning av vaerldens resurser. Text in Swedish. 1977. a. SEK 90 to members (effective 2004).
Published by: Framtiden i Vaara Haender, Porkalagatan 7, Kista, 16476, Sweden. TEL 46-8-7506350, FAX 46-70-7952987, gitta_t@yahoo.com. Pub. Gitta Tornerhjelm.

O P T: ONE PARENT TIMES. *see* CHILDREN AND YOUTH—About

301 980 ARG ISSN 1515-3282
F1414.2
OBSERVATORIO SOCIAL DE AMERICA LATINA. Text in Portuguese, Spanish. 2000. q. **Document type:** *Journal, Academic/Scholarly.*
Related titles: Online - full text ed.
Indexed: H21, P08.
Published by: Consejo Latinoamericano de Ciencias Sociales, Avda Callao 875, Piso 3, Buenos Aires, 1023, Argentina. TEL 54-11-48142301, erol@clacso.edu.ar, http://www.clacso.org.

OBSHCHESTVO I PRAVO/SOCIETY AND LAW. *see* LAW

301 150 370 RUS ISSN 2221-2795
▼ ➤ **OBSHCHESTVO: SOTSIOLOGIYA, PSIKHOLOGIYA, PEDAGOGIKA/SOCIETY: SOCIOLOGY, PSYCHOLOGY, PEDAGOGICS.** Text in Russian; Summaries in Russian, English. 2011. q. free. bk.rev. back issues avail. **Document type:** *Journal, Academic/Scholarly.*
Related titles: Online - full text ed.: ISSN 2223-6430.
Published by: Izdatel'skii Dom HORS, ul Yankovskogo 156, Krasnodar, Russian Federation. TEL 7-861-2901335, dom-hors@mail.ru. Eds. Valerii Kas'yanov, Victoria L Kharseeva.

306 NPL ISSN 2091-0312
➤ **OCCASIONAL PAPERS IN SOCIOLOGY AND ANTHROPOLOGY.** Text in English. a. **Document type:** *Journal, Academic/Scholarly.* **Description:** Publishes articles, original research reports, review articles, book reviews, dissertation abstracts, professional announcements, and other information of interest in the areas of the sociology and anthropology of Nepal and other Himalayan regions.
Related titles: Online - full text ed.
Indexed: S03.
Published by: Tribhuvan University, Department of Sociology and Anthropology, c/o Om Gurung, Ed., University Campus, Kirtipur, Kathmandu, Nepal. TEL 977-1-4331852, cdtusoan@enet.com.np. Ed. Om Gurung.

302 SWE ISSN 1651-4785
OEREBRO STUDIES IN MEDIA AND COMMUNICATION. Text in Swedish. 2002. irreg., latest vol.4, 2006. SEK 180 per issue (effective 2006). back issues avail. **Document type:** *Monographic series, Academic/Scholarly.*
Published by: Oerebro Universitet, Universitetsbiblioteket/University of Oerebro. University Library, Fakultetsgatan 1, Oerebro, 70182, Sweden. TEL 46-19-303240, FAX 46-19-331217, biblioteket@ub.oru.se. Ed. Joanna Jansdotter.

301 SWE ISSN 1650-2531
OEREBRO STUDIES IN SOCIOLOGY. Text in English, Swedish. 2000. irreg., latest vol.7, 2004. SEK 180 per issue (effective 2006). back issues avail. **Document type:** *Monographic series, Academic/Scholarly.*
Published by: Oerebro Universitet, Universitetsbiblioteket/University of Oerebro. University Library, Fakultetsgatan 1, Oerebro, 70182, Sweden. TEL 46-19-303240, FAX 46-19-331217, biblioteket@ub.oru.se. Ed. Joanna Jansdotter.

OEREBRO UNIVERSITET. CENTRUM FOER FEMINISTIKA SAMHAELLSSTUDIER. ARBETSRAPPORT/UNIVERSITY OF OEREBRO. CENTER FOR FEMINIST SOCIAL STUDIES. WORKING PAPERS. *see* WOMEN'S STUDIES

OEREBRO UNIVERSITET. CENTRUM FOER FEMINISTISKA SAMHAELLSSTUDIER. SKRIFTSERIE. *see* WOMEN'S STUDIES

301 DEU ISSN 1011-0070
HM5
OESTERREICHISCHE ZEITSCHRIFT FUER SOZIOLOGIE. Text in German. 1976. q. EUR 179.44, USD 221 combined subscription to institutions (print & online eds.) (effective 2012). adv. reprint service avail. from PSC. **Document type:** *Journal, Academic/Scholarly.*
Related titles: Online - full text ed.: ISSN 1862-2585.
Indexed: A22, A26, CA, DIP, E01, I13, IBR, IBSS, IBZ, P10, P34, P42, P46, P48, PQC, PSA, RASB, S02, S03, SCOPUS, SOPODA, SSA, SociolAb, T02, W09.
—BLDSC (6309.750000), IE, Ingenta, INIST. **CCC.**
Published by: (Verwaltungsakademie des Bundes AUT), V S - Verlag fuer Sozialwissenschaften (Subsidiary of: Springer Fachmedien Wiesbaden GmbH), Abraham-Lincoln-Str 46, Wiesbaden, 65189, Germany. TEL 49-611-78780, FAX 49-611-7878400, springerfachmedien-wiesbaden@springer.com, http://www.vs-verlag.de. Circ: 820 (paid and controlled).

301 GBR ISSN 2043-9857
▼ **OH COMELY**; keep your curiosity sacred. Text in English. 2010. bi-m. GBP 18; GBP 4 per issue (effective 2011). back issues avail. **Document type:** *Magazine, Consumer.* **Description:** Contains information about people, their quirks and their creativity.
Published by: Adeline Media, Ltd., 116 High Holborn, Third Fl, London, WC1V 6RD, United Kingdom. TEL 44-20-86162464.

306.13 USA ISSN 1521-7329
DU624.65
OIWI; a native Hawaiian journal. Text in English. 1998. a. USD 18 (effective 2006). **Document type:** *Magazine, Consumer.* **Description:** Dedicated to the mana'o (thoughts) and hana no'eau (works) of Hawaiians, a historical landmark in the revival of the rich and ancient literary heritage of na oiwi o Hawaii nei - the native people of Hawaii.
Indexed: AmHI, CA, H07, T02.
Address: P O Box 61218, Honolulu, HI 96839-1218. TEL 808-956-3031, oiwi@hawaii.edu.

302 320 RUS ISSN 1998-6785
➤ **OJKUMENA**; regional researches. Text in Russian; Summaries in Russian, English. 2006. q. RUR 1,188; RUR 297 per issue (effective 2011). bk.rev. abstr.; bibl.; charts; illus.; maps; stat. back issues avail. **Document type:** *Journal, Academic/Scholarly.* **Description:** Targets university teachers, students and employees of the academic institutions of the Far East and other regions of Russia. Aims to assist in development of methodology of interdisciplinary synthesis in studying of regional systems, both planning and programming on its basis of the further regional researches.
Related titles: Online - full text ed.
Published by: Vladivostokskii Gosudarstvennyi Universitet Ekonomiki i Servisa/Vladivostok State University of Economics and Service, ul Gogolya 41, Vladivostok, 692600, Russian Federation. TEL 7-4232-450853, FAX 7-4232-450853, http://www.vvsu.ru. Ed. Tatiana Rimskaya. Circ: 200 (paid).

➤ **OMEGA: JOURNAL OF DEATH AND DYING.** *see* PSYCHOLOGY

306.09 NLD ISSN 1574-2156
ON THE WATERFRONT. Text in English. 2001. s-a. **Document type:** *Newsletter.*

Published by: (Friends of the International Institute of Social History), Internationaal Instituut voor Sociale Geschiedenis/Netherlands Institute of Social History, PO Box 2169, Amsterdam, 1000 CD, Netherlands. TEL 31-20-6685866, FAX 31-20-6654181, info@iisg.nl. Eds. Jan Lucassen, Mieke Ijzermans.

306.85 362.82 IRL ISSN 1649-4857
ONE FAMILY MATTERS. Text in English. 1974. s-a. **Document type:** *Newsletter.*
Formerly (until 2004): Cherish News (1649-3710)
Published by: One Family, Cherish House, 2 Lower Pembroke St, Dublin, 2, Ireland. TEL 353-1-6629212, FAX 353-1-6629096, info@onefamily.ie, http://www.onefamily.ie.

307.72 USA ISSN 1936-0487
HN90.C6
➤ **ONLINE JOURNAL OF RURAL RESEARCH AND POLICY.** Text in English. 2006. q. free (effective 2011). **Document type:** *Journal, Academic/Scholarly.* **Description:** Presents policy issues, research and commentary about issues affecting the lives of people living in rural areas in the Great Plains Region.
Media: Online - full text.
Indexed: A01, T02.
Published by: North Central Regional Planning Commission, 109 N Mill, Beloit, KS 67420. TEL 785-738-2218, http://www.ncrpc.org. Ed. Thomas Gould. Pub. John Cyr.

301 NLD ISSN 1874-9224
HQ1
➤ **THE OPEN FAMILY STUDIES JOURNAL.** Text in English. 2008. irreg. free (effective 2011). **Document type:** *Journal, Academic/Scholarly.*
Media: Online - full text.
Indexed: A39, C27, C29, D03, D04, E13, ESPM, R14, RiskAb, S02, S03, S14, S15, S18.
Published by: Bentham Open (Subsidiary of: Bentham Science Publishers Ltd.), PO Box 294, Bussum, AG 1400, Netherlands. TEL 31-35-6923800, FAX 31-35-6980150, subscriptions@bentham.org. Ed. Augustine J Kposowa.

➤ **THE OPEN SOCIETY**; serving New Zealand's non-religious community since 1927. *see* PHILOSOPHY

301 NLD ISSN 1874-9461
HM1
➤ **THE OPEN SOCIOLOGY JOURNAL.** Text in English. 2008. irreg. free (effective 2011). **Document type:** *Journal, Academic/Scholarly.*
Media: Online - full text.
Indexed: ESPM, RiskAb, SSciA.
Published by: Bentham Open (Subsidiary of: Bentham Science Publishers Ltd.), PO Box 294, Bussum, AG 1400, Netherlands. TEL 31-35-6923800, FAX 31-35-6980150, subscriptions@bentham.org.

301 USA
OPPORTUNITY IN AMERICA; a series on economic and social mobility. Text in English. 1996. irreg., latest 1997. back issues avail. **Document type:** *Monographic series, Academic/Scholarly.* **Description:** Includes articles on the public philosophy in the US, with its emphasis on equality of opportunity for individuals, and the relationship between expectations and actual social and economic conditions.
Related titles: Online - full text ed.: free (effective 2010).
Published by: Urban Institute, 2100 M St, NW, Washington, DC 20037. TEL 202-833-7200, FAX 202-467-5775, paffairs@ui.urban.org.

301 DEU ISSN 1435-6562
ORBIS; Wissenschaftliche Schriften zur Landeskunde. Text in German. 1993. irreg., latest vol.15, 2009. price varies. **Document type:** *Monographic series, Academic/Scholarly.*
Published by: Verlag Dr. Kovac, Leverkusenstr 13, Hamburg, 22761, Germany. TEL 49-40-3988800, FAX 49-40-39888055, info@verlagdrkovac.de.

ORGANISATIONAL AND SOCIAL DYNAMICS; an international journal for the integration of psychoanalytic, systemic and group behavior perspectives. *see* PSYCHOLOGY

301 PRT ISSN 0871-4835
HD6957.P8 CODEN: ORTRFI
ORGANIZACOES E TRABALHO. Text in Portuguese. 1989. 3/yr. **Document type:** *Magazine, Trade.* **Description:** Its objective is to promote the scientific and technical knowledge of industrial sociology in organizations and work.
Indexed: SociolAb.
Published by: Associacao Portuguesa de Professionais em Sociologia Industrial das Organizacoes e do Trabalho, Rua de Xabregas 20, 3o Andar, Sala 14, Lisbon, 1900-440, Portugal. TEL 351-21-8687941, apsiot@mail.telepac.pt, http://www.apsiot.pt/.

301 USA ISSN 1094-2254
CB151
OTHER VOICES (PHILADELPHIA); the (e)journal of cultural criticism. Text in English. 1997. irreg. free (effective 2011). bk.rev.
Media: Online - full content. **Related titles:** Online - full text ed.
Indexed: A39, AmHI, C27, C29, CA, D03, D04, E13, H07, MLA-IB, R14, S14, S15, S18, T02.
Address: Box 31907, Philadelphia, PA 19104. Ed. Vance Bell.

306.7 SWE ISSN 1650-8017
OTTAR (STOCKHOLM, 2001); tidskrift om sexualitet & samhaella fraan RFSU. Text in Swedish. 1991. q. **Document type:** *Journal, Academic/Scholarly.*
Formerly (until 2001): R F S U Bulletinen (1400-6286)
Published by: Riksfoerbundet foer Sexuell Upplysning (RFSU)/Swedish Organization for Sexual Education, PO Box 12128, Stockholm, 10224, Sweden. TEL 46-8-6920700, http://www.rfsu.se. Ed. Silvia Sjoedahl TEL 46-8-6920728.

307 361 CAN ISSN 1912-6050
OTTAWA'S VITAL SIGNS. Variant title: Ottawa's Vital Signs Report. Vital Signs. Text in English. 2006. a. **Document type:** *Journal, Consumer.*
Related titles: French ed.: Signes V itaux d'Ottawa. ISSN 1912-595X.
Published by: Community Foundation of Ottawa/Fondation Communautaire d'Ottawa, 75 Albert St, Ste 301, Ottawa, ON K1P 5E7, Canada. TEL 613-236-1616, FAX 613-236-1621, info@cfo-fco.ca.

301 DNK ISSN 1904-0210
➤ **OUTLINES**; critical practice studies. Text in English. 1999. free (effective 2011). back issues avail. **Document type:** *Journal, Academic/Scholarly.*
Media: Online - full text.
Indexed: P25, P27, P46, P48, P54, PQC.
Published by: (Foreningen Udkast/The Outlines Association), Koebenhavns Universitet, Institut for Psykologi/University of Copenhagen, Department of Psychology, Oester Farimagsgade 2 A, Copenhagen K, 1353, Denmark. TEL 45-35-324800, FAX 45-35-324802, psykologi@psy.ku.dk, http://www.psy.ku.dk. Ed. Morten Nissen.

➤ **OUTUBRO.** *see* POLITICAL SCIENCE

306.44 USA
OXFORD STUDIES IN SOCIOLINGUISTICS. Text in English. 1992. irreg., latest 2009. price varies. back issues avail. **Document type:** *Monographic series, Academic/Scholarly.*
Published by: Oxford University Press (Subsidiary of: Oxford University Press), 2001 Evans Rd, Cary, NC 27513. TEL 919-677-0977, FAX 919-677-1303, orders.us@oup.com, http://www.us.oup.com.

LE P I A F. (Pour une Information Alternative, Forcement!) *see* POLITICAL SCIENCE

301 352 FRA ISSN 1258-0147
P I R VILLE. CAHIERS. (Programme Interdisciplinaire de Recherche) Variant title: Cahiers - Programme Interdisciplinaire de Recherche sur la Ville. Text in French. 1994. irreg. price varies. **Document type:** *Monographic series, Government.*
Published by: Centre National de la Recherche Scientifique, Campus Gerard-Megie, 3 Rue Michel-Ange, Paris, 75794, France. TEL 33-1-44964000, FAX 33-1-44965390, http://www.cnrseditions.fr.

428 GBR
P L A C E RESEARCH CENTRE. OCCASIONAL PAPERS. (Place, Landscape & Cultural Environment) Text in English. 1997. irreg. **Document type:** *Monographic series.*
Published by: P L A C E Research Centre, Heworth Croft Campus, York St John College, Lord Mayor's Walk, YORK, YO31 7EX, United Kingdom. TEL 44-1904-716753, place@yorksj.ac.uk, http://www.place.uk.com/.

P. PORTUGUESE CULTURAL STUDIES. *see* ANTHROPOLOGY

305 NZL ISSN 1176-5917
PA HARAKEKE. Text in English, Maori. 2004. biennial.
Published by: Te Wananga-o-Raukawa, PO Box 119, Otaki, New Zealand. TEL 64-6-3647820, FAX 64-6-3647822, http://www.twor.ac.nz.

306.089 USA ISSN 1537-0992
E184.P25
PACIFIC VOICES TALK STORY; conversations of american experience. Text in English. 2001. a., latest 2007. USD 22 per issue (effective 2010). **Document type:** *Journal, Academic/Scholarly.* **Description:** Provides information about tribalism and village mentalities.
Published by: Tui Communications, 607 Elmira Rd, PMB 259, Vacaville, CA 95687. TEL 707-451-8788, tuicom@att.net. Ed., Pub. Margo King-Lenson.

303.3 DEU ISSN 1866-4881
PAEDAGOGIK UND ETHIK. Text in German. 2008. irreg., latest vol.3, 2010. price varies. **Document type:** *Monographic series, Academic/Scholarly.*
Published by: Ergon Verlag, Keesburgstr 11, Wuerzburg, 97074, Germany. TEL 49-931-280084, FAX 49-931-282872, service@ergon-verlag.de.

PAEDAGOGIK UND SOZIALWISSENSCHAFTEN. *see* EDUCATION

301 ITA ISSN 1974-1936
PAESI E POPOLI DEL MEDITERRANEO. Text in Italian. 2007. s-a. **Document type:** *Journal, Consumer.*
Published by: Rubbettino Editore, Viale Rosario Rubbettino 10, Soveria Mannelli, CZ 88049, Italy. TEL 39-0968-662034, FAX 39-0968-662055, segreteria@rubbettino.it, http://www.rubbettino.it.

301 ESP ISSN 1132-8886
PAGINA ABIERTA. Text in Spanish. 1991. m. **Document type:** *Magazine, Consumer.*
Address: Hileras, 8, Madrid, 28013, Spain. TEL 34-91-5426700, FAX 34-91-5426299, paginabi@bitmailer.net.

301 ESP ISSN 0210-2862
HM7
PAPERS (BARCELONA, 1973); revista de sociologia. Text in Spanish, Catalan. 1973. q. EUR 12 per issue (effective 2011). **Document type:** *Journal, Academic/Scholarly.* **Description:** Covers various regional and national social issues with the research by UAB staff and students.
Related titles: Online - full text ed.: free (effective 2011).
Indexed: CA, IBSS, P09, PCI, S02, S03, SCOPUS, SSA, SociolAb, T02.
Published by: (Universitat Autonoma de Barcelona, Departament de Sociologia), Universitat Autonoma de Barcelona, Servei de Publicacions, Edifici A, Bellaterra, Cardanyola del Valles, Barcelona, 08193, Spain. TEL 34-93-5811022, FAX 34-93-5813239, sp@uab.es, http://www.uab.es/publicacions/.

306.85 305.23 USA ISSN 1529-5192
HQ755.8
➤ **PARENTING, SCIENCE AND PRACTICE.** Text in English. 2001. q. GBP 279 combined subscription in United Kingdom to institutions (print & online eds.); EUR 371, USD 467 combined subscription to institutions (print & online eds.) (effective 2012). adv. back issues avail.; reprint service avail. from PSC. **Document type:** *Journal, Academic/Scholarly.* **Description:** Promotes the exchange of empirical findings, theoretical perspectives, and methodological approaches from all disciplines that help to define and advance theory, research, and practice in parenting, caregiving, and childrearing broadly construed.
Related titles: Online - full text ed.: ISSN 1532-7922. 2001. GBP 251 in United Kingdom to institutions; EUR 334, USD 420 to institutions (effective 2012).
Indexed: A01, A03, A08, A22, C06, C07, C08, CA, CINAHL, CurCont, E01, Faml, P03, P24, P27, P30, P46, P48, P50, P54, PQC, PsycInfo, PsycholAb, SCOPUS, SSCI, T02, W07.
—BLDSC (6406.205814), IE, Infotrieve, Ingenta. **CCC.**
Published by: Psychology Press (Subsidiary of: Taylor & Francis Inc.), 325 Chestnut St, Ste 800, Philadelphia, PA 19106. TEL 800-354-1420, FAX 215-625-2940, orders@taylorandfrancis.com, http://www.psypress.com. adv.: page USD 350; trim 5 x 8.

306.85 FIN ISSN 1796-850X
PARI & PERHE. Text in Finnish. 2007. q. EUR 30 (effective 2007). **Document type:** *Magazine, Consumer.*
Related titles: Online - full text ed.
Published by: Vaestoliitto/Family Federation of Finland, PO Box 849, Helsinki, 00101, Finland. TEL 358-9-228050, FAX 358-9-6121211. Ed. Helena Hiila. Circ: 5,000.

302.23 DEU ISSN 1867-044X
▼ **PARTICIPATION IN BROADBAND SOCIETY.** Text in German. 2010. irreg., latest vol.2, 2010. price varies. **Document type:** *Monographic series, Academic/Scholarly.*
Published by: Peter Lang GmbH (Subsidiary of: Peter Lang Publishing Group), Eschborner Landstr 42-50, Frankfurt Am Main, 60489, Germany. TEL 49-69-7807050, FAX 49-69-78070550, zentrale.frankfurt@peterlang.com.

301 GBR ISSN 1749-8716
PARTICIP@TIONS; journal of audience & reception studies. Text in English. 2003. s-a. free (effective 2011). back issues avail. **Document type:** *Journal, Academic/Scholarly.* **Description:** Covers all aspects audiences for cultural and media products and practices studies.
Media: Online - full content.
Published by: University of Wales, Department of Theatre, Film and Television Studies, c/o Milly Williamson, Senior Lecturer in Film & Television Studies, School of Arts, Brunel University, Uxbridge Campus, Middlesex, UB8 3PH, United Kingdom. TEL 44-1895-266715, http://www.wales.ac.uk. Eds. Martin Barker, Sue Turnbull.

PASSAGEN & TRANSZENDENZEN; Studien zur materialen Religions- und Kultursoziologie. *see* RELIGIONS AND THEOLOGY

301 DEU ISSN 0941-6676
PASSAUER PAPIERE ZUR SOZIALWISSENSCHAFT. Text in German. 1988. irreg., latest vol.25, 2000. **Document type:** *Monographic series, Academic/Scholarly.*
Published by: Universitaet Passau, Lehrstuhl fuer Soziologie, Innstr 39, Passau, 94032, Germany. TEL 49-851-5092681, FAX 49-851-5092682, Roswitha.Nagelmueller@uni-passau.de, http://www.phil.uni-passau.de/soziologie/.

PEACE & CHANGE; a journal of peace research. *see* POLITICAL SCIENCE—International Relations

PEDAGOGIA SOCIAL; revista interuniversitaria. *see* EDUCATION

PEGASUS OOST-EUROPESE STUDIES. *see* HISTORY—History Of Europe

301 BEL ISSN 1376-0963
PENSEE PLURIELLE. Text in French. 1999. 3/yr. EUR 50 (effective 2011). back issues avail. **Document type:** *Journal, Academic/Scholarly.*
Related titles: Online - full text ed.: ISSN 1782-1479.
Indexed: SCOPUS.
Published by: De Boeck Universite (Subsidiary of: Editis), Fond Jean-Paques 4, Louvain-la-Neuve, 1348, Belgium. TEL 32-10-482511, FAX 32-10-482519, info@superieur.deboeck.com.

IL PENSIERO POLITICO (FLORENCE); rivista di storia delle idee politiche e sociali. *see* POLITICAL SCIENCE

IL PENSIERO POLITICO. BIBLIOTECA. *see* POLITICAL SCIENCE

301.05 AUS ISSN 1039-4788
➤ **PEOPLE AND PLACE.** Text in English. 1993. q. AUD 55 domestic; AUD 65 foreign (effective 2009). back issues avail. **Document type:** *Journal, Academic/Scholarly.* **Description:** Covers trends in demography, labor, urban growth, the environment and other topics.
Related titles: Online - full text ed.: free (effective 2009).
Indexed: A26, AEI, AusPAIS, DRIE, E08, ERO, G08, GEOBASE, I05, IBSS, P30, S02, S03, S09, SCOPUS.
—BLDSC (6422.874800), IE, Ingenta.
Published by: Monash University, Centre for Population and Urban Research, PO Box 11A, Clayton, VIC 3800, Australia. TEL 61-3-99052965, FAX 61-3-99052993, Bronwen.Perry@arts.monash.edu.au. Eds. Katherine Betts, Robert Birrell.

307 GBR ISSN 1753-8041
➤ **PEOPLE, PLACE AND POLICY ONLINE.** Text in English. 2007 (Jul.). 3/yr. free (effective 2010). back issues avail. **Document type:** *Journal, Academic/Scholarly.* **Description:** Provides a forum for debate about the situations and experiences of people and places struggling to negotiate a satisfactory accommodation with the various opportunities, constraints and risks within contemporary society.
Media: Online - full text.
Published by: Sheffield Hallam University, Centre for Regional Economic and Social Research, Howard St, Sheffield, S1 1WB, United Kingdom. TEL 44-114-2253073, http://www.shu.ac.uk/cresr/. Eds. David Robinson, Richard Crisp.

➤ **PERIPHERIE**; Zeitschrift fuer Politik und Oekonomie in der dritten Welt. *see* BUSINESS AND ECONOMICS—International Development And Assistance

306.43 USA ISSN 1078-6287
BF637.S4
PERSONAL EXCELLENCE. Text in English. 1994. m. USD 99 (effective 2005). **Document type:** *Magazine, Consumer.* **Description:** Presents powerful insights, ideas, and strategies on personal improvement and professional development.
Related titles: Online - full text ed.
Indexed: B01, B07, T02.
—CCC.
Published by: Executive Excellence Publishing, 1366 East 1120 South, Provo, UT 84606. TEL 800-304-9782, FAX 801-377-5960, info@eep.com.

301 PRY ISSN 1024-770X
PERSPECTIVA INTERNACIONAL PARAGUAYA. Text in Spanish. 1989. s-a.
Published by: Centro Paraguayo de Estudios Sociologicos, ELIGIO AYALA, 973, Asuncion, Paraguay. TEL 595-21-443-734, FAX 595-21-447-128.

301 ESP ISSN 0210-0436
HN1
PERSPECTIVA SOCIAL. Text in Catalan, Spanish. 1973. bi-m. adv. bk.rev. bibl.; charts; illus. back issues avail. **Document type:** *Bulletin, Academic/Scholarly.*
Indexed: CERDIC.
Published by: Institut Catolic d'Estudis Socials de Barcelona, Enric Granados, 2, Barcelona, 08007, Spain. TEL 93-4532800, FAX 93-4549655. Ed. Maria Martinell I Taxonera. Circ: 500.

S

303.842 FRA ISSN 1769-8863
PERSPECTIVE FRANCE VIETNAM. Text in French. 1961. q. EUR 10 to members (effective 2007). **Document type:** *Bulletin.*
Former titles (until 2003): Association d'Amitie Franco-Vietnamienne. Bulletin d'Information et de Documentation (1142-8988); (until 1972): Association d'Amitie Franco-Vietnamienne. Bulletin Interieur (1142-897X)
Published by: Association d'Amitie Franco-Vietnamienne, 44 Rue Alexis Lepere, Montreuil, 93100, France. TEL 33-1-42874434, FAX 33-1-48584688.

303.6 USA ISSN 1096-5955
E184.A1
PERSPECTIVES (BALTIMORE, 1999); the newsletter of prejudice, ethnoviolence and social policy. Text in English. 1999. bi-m. looseleaf. USD 35 (effective 2002). bk.rev. charts; illus.; stat. back issues avail. **Document type:** *Newsletter.* **Description:** Publishes articles relating to prejudice, social violence and social policy.
Related titles: Online - full text ed.
Indexed: APW, ENW.
Published by: Prejudice Institute, 2743 Maryland Ave, Baltimore, MD 21218. TEL 410-366-9654. Ed. H J Ehrlich.

301 FRA ISSN 1951-5545
PERSPECTIVES SOCIALES. Text in French. 2006. irreg. back issues avail. **Document type:** *Monographic series.*
Published by: Editions Vuibert, 5 Allee de la 2e DB, Paris, 75015, France. TEL 33-1-42794400, FAX 33-1-42794680, http://www.vuibert.com.

301 NOR ISSN 1502-4156
PERSPEKTIV: A5. Variant title: Perspektiv: AFem. Text in Norwegian. 2000. irreg. price varies. back issues avail. **Document type:** *Monographic series, Academic/Scholarly.*
Published by: Unipub Forlag AS, Kristan Ottosens Hus, PO Box 33, Blindern, Oslo, 0313, Norway. TEL 47-22-853300, FAX 47-22-853039, post@unipub.no.

305.3 DNK ISSN 1602-172X
PERSPEKTIV- OG HANDLINGSPLAN; redegoerelse. Text in Danish. 2002. a. **Document type:** *Government.*
Related titles: Online - full text ed.: ISSN 1602-1738; ◆ English ed.: Minister for Ligestilling. Annual Report.
Published by: Minister for Ligestilling, Ligestillingsafdelingen/Minister for Gender Equality. Department of Equality, Holmens Kanal 20, PO Box 2150, Copenhagen K, 1061, Denmark. TEL 45-72-269780, FAX 45-72-269781, lige@lige.dk.

PERSPEKTIVEN D S; Zeitschrift fuer Gesellschaftsanalyse und Reformpolitik. (Demokratischen Sozialismus) *see* POLITICAL SCIENCE

301 PER ISSN 0079-1075
PERU PROBLEMA. Text in Spanish. 1969. irreg., latest vol.26, 1999. price varies. bk.rev. back issues avail. **Document type:** *Monographic series, Academic/Scholarly.*
Published by: (Instituto de Estudios Peruanos), I E P Ediciones (Subsidiary of: Instituto de Estudios Peruanos), Horacio Urteaga 694, Jesus Maria, Lima, 11, Peru. TEL 51-14-3326194, FAX 51-14-3326173, libreria@iep.org.pe, http://iep.perucultural.org.pe.

301 PHL ISSN 0031-7810
HM1
PHILIPPINE SOCIOLOGICAL REVIEW. Text in English. 1953. q. PHP 120, USD 20. adv. bk.rev. bibl.; charts; stat. index, cum.index: 1953-1987.
Related titles: Microfiche ed.; Microfilm ed.
Indexed: AICP, AbAn, BAS, CA, IPP, MLA, MLA-IB, P30, S02, S03, SOPODA, SociolAb, T02.
—INIST.
Published by: Philippine Sociological Society, U.P. Post Office, Diliman, PO Box 205, Quezon City Mm, 1128, Philippines. TEL 02-632-9229621, FAX 02-632-924-4170, TELEX PHILSOSCI, MANILA. Ed. Virgina A Miralao. Circ: 500 (paid).

PHILOSOPHIE UND TRANSKULTURALITAET. *see* PHILOSOPHY

PHILOSOPHISCHE GRENZGAENGE. *see* PHILOSOPHY

PHILOSOPHY OF HISTORY AND CULTURE. *see* PHILOSOPHY

302.23 USA ISSN 2160-4010
▼ **PHOENIX MAGAZINE (VINTON).** Text in English. 2011. m. USD 28 (effective 2011). adv. **Document type:** *Magazine, Consumer.*
Published by: Phoenix Communications VA, 304 W Virginia Ave, Ste D, Vinton, VA 24179. TEL 540-309-8699, vance@phoenixcommunicationsva.com.

PHYSICS AND SOCIETY. *see* PHYSICS

PITTSBURGH STUDIES IN THEATRE AND CULTURE. *see* THEATER

▼ **PLATFORM**; journal of media and communication. *see* COMMUNICATIONS

PLENUM SERIES ON HUMAN EXCEPTIONALITY. *see* PSYCHOLOGY

301 BRA
PLURAL; revista do programa de pos-graduacao em sociologia. Text in Portuguese. a. per issue exchange basis.
Published by: Universidade de Sao Paulo, Faculdade de Filosofia, Letras e Ciencias Humanas, Av Professor Luciano Gualberto 315, Butanta, Sao Paulo, SP 05508-010, Brazil. http://www.fflch.usp.br. Circ: 600.

POCKETTIDNINGEN R. *see* DRUG ABUSE AND ALCOHOLISM

POHJOLA-NORDEN. *see* GENERAL INTEREST PERIODICALS—Scandinavia

302 COL ISSN 1692-0945
POIESIS. Text in Spanish. 2002. s-a. **Document type:** *Journal, Academic/Scholarly.*
Related titles: Online - full text ed.
Published by: Fundacion Universitaria Luis Amigo, Transversal 51 A, Medellin, 67B 90, Colombia. TEL 57-4-4487666, FAX 57-4-3849797, http://www.funlam.edu.com. Ed. Hernando Alberto Bernal.

POLE SUD; revue de science politique de l'Europe Meridionale. *see* POLITICAL SCIENCE

POLEMOS; casopis za interdisciplinama istrazivanja rata i mira. *see* POLITICAL SCIENCE

POLICY SCIENCES; an international journal devoted to the improvement of policy making. *see* POLITICAL SCIENCE

POLIS; ricerche e studi su societa e politica in Italia. *see* POLITICAL SCIENCE

POLISH HISTORICAL LIBRARY. ANTHOLOGIES. MONOGRAPHS. OPERA MINORA. *see* HISTORY—History Of Europe

301 POL ISSN 1231-1413
HM1 CODEN: PSREFL
➤ **POLISH SOCIOLOGICAL REVIEW.** Text in English. 1961. q. EUR 67 foreign (effective 2011). adv. bk.rev. index. 140 p./no.; back issues avail. **Document type:** *Journal, Academic/Scholarly.* **Description:** Publishes papers and reports on various aspects of sociological research and its practical application. Focuses on social theory and post-communist society.
Formerly (until 1993): Polish Sociological Bulletin (0032-2997)
Indexed: A20, A22, BibInd, CA, EIP, IBR, IBZ, P42, PCI, PSA, RASB, S02, S03, SCOPUS, SOPODA, SSA, SSCI, SociolAb, T02, W07.
—BLDSC (6543.782000), IE, INIST.
Published by: Polskie Towarzystwo Socjologiczne/Polish Sociological Association, ul Nowy Swiat 72, pok 216, Warsaw, 00330, Poland. pts@ifispan.waw.pl. Ed. Joanna Kurczewska. Circ: 250. **Dist. by:** Ars Polona, Obroncow 25, Warsaw 03933, Poland. TEL 48-22-5098609, FAX 48-22-5098610, arspolona@arspolona.com.pl, http://www.arspolona.com.pl.

301 BRA ISSN 1677-4140
JA76
POLITICA E SOCIEDADE. Text in Portuguese. 2002. s-a. **Document type:** *Journal, Academic/Scholarly.*
Related titles: Online - full text ed.: free (effective 2011).
Indexed: C01, CA, IBSS, P42, PSA, S02, S03, SociolAb, T02.
Published by: Universidade Federal de Santa Catarina, Programa de Pos-Graduacao em Sociologia Politica, Bairro Trindade, Florianopolis, SC 88040-970, Brazil. TEL 55-48-37219000, FAX 55-48-32344069. Ed. Ricardo Silva.

POLITICA Y CULTURA. *see* POLITICAL SCIENCE

301 USA
➤ **POLITICAL AND MILITARY SOCIOLOGY: AN ANNUAL REVIEW.** Text in English. 1973. a. bk.rev. illus. cum.index. 180 p./no.; back issues avail.; reprints avail. **Document type:** *Journal, Academic/Scholarly.* **Description:** Combines two fields of political sociology and sociology of the military explores issues of political and military nature.
Formerly (until 2011): Journal of Political and Military Sociology (0047-2697)
Related titles: Microform ed.: (from PQC); Online - full text ed.
Indexed: A01, A03, A08, A20, A22, ABCPolSci, ABS&EES, AMB, ASCA, AUNI, AmH&L, BAS, CA, DIP, FR, FamI, HistAb, I02, I13, IBR, IBZ, LID&ISL, M05, M07, MEA&I, MLA-IB, P02, P06, P10, P34, P42, P45, P46, P47, P48, P53, P54, PAIS, PCI, PQC, PRA, PSA, RASB, RI-1, RI-2, RILM, S02, S03, S11, SCOPUS, SOPODA, SPAA, SSA, SociolAb, T02.
—BLDSC (5040.845000), IE, Infotrieve, Ingenta, INIST. **CCC.**
Published by: Transaction Publishers, 390 Campus Dr, Somerset, NJ 07830. TEL 732-445-1245, FAX 732-748-9801, trans@transactionpub.com, http://www.transactionpub.com. Eds. Jonathan Swarts, Neovi M Karakatsanis.

➤ **POLITICAL POWER AND SOCIAL THEORY.** *see* POLITICAL SCIENCE

➤ **POLITICS AND SOCIETY.** *see* POLITICAL SCIENCE

➤ **POLITICS AND SOCIETY IN TWENTIETH CENTURY AMERICA.** *see* POLITICAL SCIENCE

302.23 302.2343 302.3 USA ISSN 1094-6225
POLITICS, MEDIA, AND POPULAR CULTURE. Text in English. 2000. irreg., latest vol.12, 2007. price varies. **Document type:** *Monographic series, Academic/Scholarly.* **Description:** Devoted to both scholarly and teaching materials that examine the ways politics, the media, and popular culture interact and influence social and political behavior.
Published by: Peter Lang Publishing, Inc. (Subsidiary of: Peter Lang Publishing Group), 29 Broadway, New York, NY 10006. TEL 212-647-7700, 800-770-5264, FAX 212-647-7707, customerservice@plang.com, http://www.peterlangusa.com. Ed. David Schultz.

POLITIQUE DU CINEMA. *see* MOTION PICTURES

POLITIQUE ECONOMIQUE ET SOCIALE. *see* POLITICAL SCIENCE

301 POL ISSN 1640-873X
CB161
POLSKA 2000 PLUS. Text in Polish. 1970. s-a. EUR 20 foreign (effective 2005).
Formerly (until 2000): Polska 2000 (0079-3620)
Indexed: RASB.
Published by: Polska Akademia Nauk, Komitet Badan i Prognoz "Polska 2000 Plus", pl Defilad 1, Palac Kultury i Nauki, p XXIII, pok 2320, Warsaw, 00901, Poland. Circ: 2,000. **Dist. by:** Ars Polona, Obroncow 25, Warsaw 03933, Poland. TEL 48-22-5098609, FAX 48-22-5098610, arspolona@arspolona.com.pl, http://www.arspolona.com.pl.

301 FRA ISSN 0182-6220
POMME D'API; c'est bon d'etre un enfant. Text in French. 1966. m. EUR 58.80 domestic; EUR 73.80 DOM-TOM; EUR 73.80 in the European Union; EUR 78.80 elsewhere (effective 2009 & 2010). adv. **Document type:** *Magazine, Consumer.* **Description:** Helps children from 3 to 7 years old become aware of their surroundings.
Published by: Bayard Presse, 3-5 rue Bayard, Paris, 75393 Cedex 08, France. TEL 33-1-44356060, FAX 33-1-44356161, redactions@bayard-presse.com, http://www.bayardpresse.com. Ed. Marie Agnes Gaudrat. Circ: 133,929.

301 410 ESP ISSN 1139-6652
PONTENORGA; revista de estudios sociolinguisticos. Text in Spanish. 1998. a., latest 2004. back issues avail. **Document type:** *Monographic series, Academic/Scholarly.*
Published by: Diputacion Provincial de Pontevedra, Ave. de Monte Rios, s-n, Pontevedra, 36071, Spain. TEL 34-986-804100, FAX 34-986-804124, editorial.revistas@depo.es, http://www.depontevedra.es/.

301 ITA ISSN 1824-8683
POPOLAZIONE E COMPORTAMENTI SOCIALI. Text in Italian. 2004. irreg. **Document type:** *Monographic series, Academic/Scholarly.*
Related titles: Online - full text ed.: ISSN 1824-8675.
Published by: Comune di Verona, Piazza Bra 1, Verina, 37121, Italy. TEL 39-045-8077111, FAX 39-045-8077500, urp@comune.verona.it, http://portale.comune.verona.it.

306.09 GBR ISSN 2040-1035
▼ **POPSAMITI.** Text in English. 2009. a. back issues avail. **Document type:** *Journal, Trade.* **Description:** Designed for artists and writers to explore themes in art and culture with the aim to forge new narratives for the 21st century.
Related titles: Online - full text ed.: ISSN 2040-1043. free (effective 2010).
Published by: Tajender Sagoo, Pub., Old Limehouse Town Hall, 646 Commercial Rd, London, E14 7HA, United Kingdom. Pub. Tajender Sagoo.

300 DEU
▼ **POPULAERE KULTUR UND MUSIK.** Text in German. 2010. irreg., latest vol.2, 2011. price varies. **Document type:** *Monographic series, Academic/Scholarly.*
Published by: Waxmann Verlag GmbH, Steinfurter Str 555, Muenster, 48159, Germany. TEL 49-251-265040, FAX 49-251-2650426, info@waxmann.com. Eds. Michael Fischer, Nils Grosch.

301 306 USA ISSN 1529-2428
POPULAR CULTURE AND EVERYDAY LIFE. Text in English. 2001. irreg., latest vol.19, 2008. price varies. back issues avail. **Document type:** *Monographic series, Academic/Scholarly.* **Description:** Innovates by stressing multiple theoretical, political, and methodological approaches to commodity culture and lived experience, borrowing from sociological, anthropological, and textual disciplines.
Published by: Peter Lang Publishing, Inc. (Subsidiary of: Peter Lang Publishing Group), 29 Broadway, New York, NY 10006. TEL 212-647-7700, 800-770-5264, FAX 212-647-7707, customerservice@plang.com, http://www.peterlangusa.com. Ed. Toby Miller.

301 USA ISSN 0735-8741
POPULAR CULTURE ASSOCIATION. NEWSLETTER AND POPULAR CULTURE METHODS. Text in English. 1971. irreg. membership. adv. reprints avail. **Document type:** *Newsletter.*
Incorporates: Popular Culture Association Newsletter (0048-4822)
Related titles: Microform ed.: (from PQC).
Indexed: MLA-IB.
Published by: (Popular Culture Association), Popular Press, Bowling Green State University, Jerome Library Room 100, Bowling Green, OH 43403. TEL 419-372-7865. Eds. Michael T Marsden, Ray Browne. Circ: 2,500.

301 USA ISSN 1060-8125
AP2
POPULAR CULTURE REVIEW. Text in English. 1989. s-a. USD 15 to individuals; USD 25 to institutions (effective 2004). **Document type:** *Journal, Consumer.*
Indexed: MLA-IB, RILM.
—BLDSC (6550.337000), IE, Ingenta.
Published by: (Far West American Culture Association), Far West Popular Culture Association, c/o Felicia Campbell, Department of English, University of Nevada, 4505 Maryland Parkway, Box 455057, Las Vegas, NV 89154-5057. http://www.unlv.edu/Colleges/Liberal_Arts/English/popcul/. Ed. Felicia F Campbell.

POPULAR MUSIC & SOCIETY. *see* MUSIC

POPULATION RESEARCH LABORATORY. RESEARCH DISCUSSION PAPER SERIES. *see* POPULATION STUDIES

301 330.9 SVN ISSN 1580-1373
HC406.A1
POROCILO O CLOVEKOVEM RAZVOJU. Text in Slovenian. 1998. a.
Related titles: ◆ English Translation: Human Development Report. ISSN 1580-1381.
Published by: Urad RS za Makroekonomske Analize in Razvoj/Institute of Macroeconomic Analysis and Development, Gregorciceva 27, Ljubljana, 1000, Slovenia. TEL 386-1-4781012, FAX 386-1-4781070, publicistika.umar@gov.si, http://www.umar.gov.si/apublic/ajiidt.php. Eds. Jana Javornik, Valerija Korosec. Circ: 1,500.

301 363.7 USA
➤ **POSSIBILITIES (HOUSTON).** Text in English. 1997. irreg. **Document type:** *Monographic series, Academic/Scholarly.*
Media: Online - full content.
Published by: Institute for Advanced Interdisciplinary Research, Box 591351, Houston, TX 77259-1351. Ed. Thomas D Nicodemus.

▼ ➤ **POSTMEDIEVAL**; a journal of medieval cultural studies. *see* LITERATURE

➤ **POSTMODERN CULTURE**; an electronic journal of interdisciplinary criticism. *see* HISTORY

305.8 362.5 USA ISSN 1075-3591
E184.A1
POVERTY & RACE. Text in English. 1992. bi-m. looseleaf. USD 25 domestic; USD 35 foreign (effective 2004). index, cum.index. back issues avail. **Document type:** *Newsletter, Consumer.* **Description:** Contains articles and symposia on issues related to both race and poverty, as well as reports on social science research PRRAC supports and advocacy work that the research assists. Also includes an extensive resource section which comprises reports, conferences, and jobs. Aimed at researchers, activists, and those involved in public policy.
Related titles: Online - full text ed.
Indexed: APW, AltPI, IIBP, P05, P27, P46, P48, P54, PQC.
Published by: Poverty & Race Research Action Council, 1015 15th St NW, Ste. 400, Washington, DC 20005-2605. TEL 202-387-9887, FAX 202-387-0764. Ed. Chester Hartman.

302 NLD ISSN 1879-7105
▼ **THE POWER OF CIVIL SOCIETY.** Text in English. 2010. irreg., latest vol.7, 2010. **Document type:** *Monographic series, Academic/Scholarly.*
Media: Online - full text.
Published by: (Humanistisch Instituut voor Ontwikkelingssamenwerking/Humanist Institute for Development Cooperation), Institute of Social Studies, The Hague, PO Box 29776, The Hague, 2502 LT, Netherlands. TEL 31-70-4260460, FAX 31-70-4260799, information@iss.nl, http://www.iss.nl.

301 POL ISSN 1230-2198
POZNANSKIE TOWARZYSTWO PRZYJACIOL NAUK. KOMISJA SOCJOLOGICZNA. PRACE. Text in Polish, English. 1992. irreg., latest vol.2, 2003. price varies. **Document type:** *Monographic series, Academic/Scholarly.*
Published by: (Poznanskie Towarzystwo Przyjaciol Nauk, Komisja Socjologiczna), Poznanskie Towarzystwo Przyjaciol Nauk/Poznan Society for the Advancement of the Arts and Sciences, ul Sew Mielzynskiego 27-29, Poznan, 61725, Poland. TEL 48-61-8527441, FAX 48-61-8522205, sekretariat@ptpn.poznan.pl, wydawnictwo@ptpn.poznan.pl, http://www.ptpn.poznan.pl.

302.23 USA ISSN 1549-2257
THE PRAEGER TELEVISION COLLECTION. Text in English. 2004. irreg., latest 2010. prices varies. back issues avail. **Document type:** *Monographic series, Academic/Scholarly.*
Published by: Praeger Publishers (Subsidiary of: Greenwood Publishing Group Inc.), 88 Post Rd W, Westport, CT 06881. TEL 800-368-6868, tech.support@greenwood.com, http://www.greenwood.com. Ed. David Bianculli.

▼ **PRAGUE PAPERS ON LANGUAGE, SOCIETY AND INTERACTION/ PRAGER ARBEITEN ZUR SPRACHE, GESELLSCHAFT UND INTERAKTION.** *see* LINGUISTICS

PRAXIS KULTUR- UND SOZIALGEOGRAPHIE. *see* GEOGRAPHY

301 ESP ISSN 1575-0817
HN581
PRAXIS SOCIOLOGICA. Text in Spanish. 1993. s-a. **Document type:** *Journal, Academic/Scholarly.*
Published by: Universidad de Castilla-La Mancha, Facultad de Ciencias Juridicas y Sociales, Cobertizo de San Pedro Martir, s-n, Toledo, 45071, Spain. TEL 34-925-268800, FAX 34-925-268801, juridicossociales.to@uclm.es, http://www.uclm.es/. Ed. Felipe Centelles Bolos.

PREPODAVANIE ISTORII I OBSHCHESTVOZNANIYA V SHKOLE. *see* HISTORY

301 FRA ISSN 1259-2242
PRETENTAINE. Text in French. 1994. a. price varies. back issues avail. **Document type:** *Monographic series.* **Description:** Deals with sociological and anthropological research. Questions the main sociological theories and presents new themes and issues.
Published by: Editions Beauchesne, 7 cite Cardinal Lemoine, Paris, 75005, France. TEL 33-1-53100818, FAX 33-1-53108519, contact@editions-beauchesne.com.

301 PRT ISSN 0874-9698
PRETEXTOS. Text in Portuguese. 2000. bi-m. **Document type:** *Magazine, Trade.*
Published by: Instituto para o Desenvolvimento Social, Rua Carlos Testa 1, Lisbon, 1050-046, Portugal. TEL 351-21-7902170, FAX 351-21-7902175, http://www.fasl.pt.

PRINCETON STUDIES IN AMERICAN POLITICS; historical, international, and comparative perspectives. *see* POLITICAL SCIENCE

301 USA
➤ **PRINCETON STUDIES IN CULTURAL SOCIOLOGY.** Text in English. 2000. irreg., latest 2009. price varies. charts; illus. back issues avail. **Document type:** *Monographic series, Academic/Scholarly.* **Description:** Presents for a broad audience a select number of works by the most prominent and the most promising scholars in cultural sociology.
Published by: Princeton University Press, 41 William St, Princeton, NJ 08540. TEL 609-258-4900, 800-777-4726, FAX 609-258-6305, cpriday@pupress.co.uk. **Subscr. addr. in US:** California - Princeton Fulfillment Services, Inc., 1445 Lower Ferry Rd, Ewing, NJ 08618. TEL 609-883-1759, 800-777-4726, FAX 609-883-7413, 800-999-1958, orders@cpfsinc.com. **Dist. addr. in Canada:** University Press Group.; **Dist. addr. in UK:** John Wiley & Sons Ltd.

➤ **PRO FAMILIA MAGAZIN**; die Zeitschrift fuer Sexualpaedagogik, Sexualberatung und Familienplanung. *see* PSYCHOLOGY

302.2 USA ISSN 0886-6104
PRO MOTION; a quarterly newsletter for the Media Escort Network. Text in English. 1985. q. USD 12 (effective 1999). bk.rev. back issues avail. **Document type:** *Newsletter, Trade.* **Description:** Features news of the publishing and public relations media tours.
Published by: Beyond the Byte, c/o Emily Laisy, Ed, 2501 Laurel Brook Rd, Box 388, Fallston, MD 21047-0388. TEL 410-877-3524, 800-861-1235, FAX 410-877-7064. Ed., Pub. Emily Laisy. Circ: 300 (controlled).

PROBLEME DE PEDAGOGIE CONTEMPORANA. *see* EDUCATION

301 COD ISSN 0379-3729
PROBLEMES SOCIAUX ZAIROIS. Text in French. 1946. q. bk.rev. abstr.; charts; illus.
Formerly: Problemes Sociaux Congolais (0032-9312)
Indexed: MLA-IB, PLESA.
Published by: Centre d'Execution de Programmes Communautaires, 208 av. Kasa-Vubu, BP 1873, Lubumbashi, Congo, Dem. Republic.

301 ITA ISSN 0390-5195
P92.I8
PROBLEMI DELL'INFORMAZIONE; trimestriale di media e comunicazione. Text in Italian. 1976. q. EUR 86.50 combined subscription domestic to institutions (print & online eds.); EUR 132.50 combined subscription foreign to institutions (print & online eds.) (effective 2009). adv. index. back issues avail. **Document type:** *Journal, Academic/Scholarly.*
Related titles: Online - full text ed.: ISSN 1973-817X.
Indexed: DoGi, ELLIS, IBR, IBZ, PAIS, RASB.
Published by: Societa Editrice Il Mulino, Strada Maggiore 37, Bologna, 40125, Italy. TEL 39-051-256011, FAX 39-051-256034, riviste@mulino.it. Ed. Angelo Agostini. Circ: 1,500.

306.85 POL ISSN 0552-2234
PROBLEMY RODZINY. Text in Polish; Summaries in English. 1961. bi-m. PLZ 60; PLZ 10 newsstand/cover (effective 2000). adv. bk.rev. abstr.; bibl.; stat. **Document type:** *Academic/Scholarly.* **Description:** Provides reports on scientific studies on marriages and family conducted in Poland or abroad. The marital and family problems are studied in the aspects of demography, health, economy, social policy, sociology, psychology, law, history, culture, religion, customs and medicine mainly sexology, contraception, obstetrics, pediatrics.
Indexed: P30, RASB.
Published by: Towarzystwo Rozwoju Rodziny, Zarzad Glowny, c/o Problemy Rodziny, Redakcja, Ul Schillera 4-35, Warszawa, 00248, Poland. TEL 48-22-8319310. Ed. Zofia Dabrowska Caban. Circ: 1,200 (controlled).

305.5 UKR ISSN 2078-7812
PROBLEMY TA PERSPEKTYVY FORMUVANNYA NATSIONAL'NOI HUMANITARNO-TEKHNICHNOI ELITY. Text in Ukrainian. 2003. q. **Document type:** *Journal, Academic/Scholarly.*
Published by: Natsional'nyi Tekhnicheskii Universitet "Kharkovskii Politekhnicheskii Institut"/National Technical University "Kharkiv Polytechnical Institute", vul Frunze 21, Kharkiv, 310002, Ukraine. TEL 380-572-7076212, FAX 380-572-7076601, omsroot@kpi.kharkov.ua, http://www.kpi.kharkov.ua. Ed. Aleksandr Romanovskiy.

PROFILES OF ETHNIC COMMUNITIES IN CANADA. *see* ETHNIC INTERESTS

301 ITA ISSN 1972-0386
PROFILI. METROPOLIS. Text in Italian. 1995. irreg., latest vol.12, 1999. price varies. **Document type:** *Monographic series, Academic/ Scholarly.*
Published by: Liguori Editore, Via Posillipo 394, Naples, 80123, Italy. TEL 39-081-7206111, FAX 39-081-7206244, liguori@liguori.it, http://www.liguori.it.

301 ITA ISSN 1973-1523
PROFILI. SOCIETA, TERRITORIO E AMBIENTE. Text in Italian. 1991. irreg. **Document type:** *Monographic series, Academic/Scholarly.*
Former titles (until 1995): Biblioteca. Societa e Ambiente (1973-1531); (until 1991): Ambiente e Societa (1973-154X)
Published by: Liguori Editore, Via Posillipo 394, Naples, 80123, Italy. TEL 39-081-7206111, FAX 39-081-7206244, liguori@liguori.it, http://www.liguori.it.

363.7 USA ISSN 0737-5425
PROGRAM ON ENVIRONMENT AND BEHAVIOR MONOGRAPH SERIES. Text in English. 197?. irreg., latest vol.61, 2003. USD 20 per issue (effective 2010). back issues avail.; reprints avail. **Document type:** *Monographic series, Academic/Scholarly.* **Description:** Presents research findings dealing with social response to extreme environmental events.
Formerly (until 1982): Program on Technology, Environment, and Man (0145-9961)
Indexed: B21, ESPM, GeoRef, H&SSA.
Published by: University of Colorado, Institute of Behavioral Science, Program on Environment and Behavior, Natural Hazards Center, 482 UCB, Boulder, CO 80309. TEL 303-492-6818, FAX 303-492-2151, hazctr@colorado.edu.

303 GLP ISSN 1141-3565
PROGRES SOCIAL. Text in French. 1957. w.
Related titles: Microfilm ed.: (from PQC).
Address: Rue Toussaint l'Ouverture, Basse-Terre, 97100, Guadeloupe. TEL 81-1041. Ed. Henri Rodes. Circ: 5,000.

301 USA ISSN 1557-0541
➤ **PROGRESS IN COMMUNITY HEALTH PARTNERSHIPS**; research, education, and action. Abbreviated title: P C H P. Variant title: Community Based Participatory Research. Text in English. 2006 (Apr.). q. USD 200 to institutions (print or online ed.); USD 280 combined subscription to institutions (print & online eds.); USD 60 per issue to institutions (effective 2011). adv. back issues avail.; reprints avail. **Document type:** *Journal, Academic/Scholarly.* **Description:** Covers the process that involves community members or recipients of interventions in all phases of the research process, including identifying the health issues of concern to the community, developing assessment tools, collecting and interpreting data, determining how that data can be used to improve community health.
Related titles: Online - full text ed.: ISSN 1557-055X. 2006.
Indexed: A22, A36, CABA, E01, E12, EMBASE, GH, LT, MEDLINE, N02, N03, P10, P20, P22, P30, P33, P48, P50, P53, P54, PQC, R08, S13, SCOPUS, T05.
—BLDSC (6867.816000), IE. **CCC.**
Published by: The Johns Hopkins University Press, 2715 N Charles St, Baltimore, MD 21218. TEL 410-516-6900, FAX 410-516-6968, bjs@press.jhu.edu. Ed. Eric B Bass TEL 410-955-9871. Pub. William M Breichner. Circ: 115. **Subscr. to:** PO Box 19966, Baltimore, MD 21211. TEL 410-516-6987, 800-548-1784, FAX 410-516-3866, jrnlcirc@press.jhu.edu.

301 IND ISSN 1464-9934
➤ **PROGRESS IN DEVELOPMENT STUDIES.** Text in English. 2001. q. USD 572, GBP 310 combined subscription to institutions (print & online eds.); USD 561, GBP 304 to institutions (effective 2011). adv. back issues avail.; reprint service avail. from PSC. **Document type:** *Journal, Academic/Scholarly.* **Description:** An essential research tool for academics and students of development studies in departments of geography, sociology, anthropology, economics and international relations and development studies itself, as well as for professionals in national governmental organizations.
Related titles: Online - full text ed.: ISSN 1477-027X. 2001. USD 515, GBP 279 to institutions (effective 2011).
Indexed: A01, A03, A08, A12, A22, A34, A35, A36, ABIn, B01, B06, B07, B09, B21, CA, CABA, CurCont, DIP, E01, E04, E05, E12, ESPM, F08, F11, F12, GEOBASE, GH, IBR, IBSS, IBZ, LT, N02, P10, P27, P32, P34, P42, P46, P48, P51, P53, P54, PAIS, PGegResA, PQC, R07, R12, RRTA, S02, S03, S13, S16, SCOPUS, SSCI, SSciA, SociolAb, T02, TAR, VirolAbstr, W07, W11.
—BLDSC (6868.115000), IE, Infotrieve, Ingenta. **CCC.**
Published by: Sage Publications India Pvt. Ltd. (Subsidiary of: Sage Publications, Inc.), M-32 Market, Greater Kailash-I, PO Box 4215, New Delhi, 110 048, India. TEL 91-11-6444958, FAX 91-11-6472426, sage@vsnl.com, http://www.indiasage.com/. Ed. Robert Potter. adv.: B&W page GBP 370; trim 189 x 246. Circ: 400.

301 DEU ISSN 0342-8176
HB97.5
➤ **PROKLA**; Zeitschrift fuer kritische Sozialwissenschaft. Text in German. 1971. 4/yr. EUR 38; EUR 9.50 per issue (effective 2011). adv. index. back issues avail. **Document type:** *Journal, Academic/Scholarly.*
Formerly (until 1976): Probleme des Klassenkampfs (0342-8168)
Indexed: A22, CA, DIP, IBR, IBSS, IBZ, P42, PAIS, PSA, RASB, S02, S03, SCOPUS, SociolAb, T02.
—IE, Infotrieve.
Published by: (Vereinigung zur Kritik der Politischen Oekonomie e.V.), Verlag Westfaelisches Dampfboot, Hafenweg 26a, Muenster, 48155, Germany. TEL 49-251-3900480, FAX 49-251-39004850, info@dampfboot-verlag.de, http://www.dampfboot-verlag.de. Ed. Michael Heinrich. Circ: 1,500.

▼ ➤ **PROSPEKT-ONLINE.** *see* HISTORY—History Of Europe

➤ **PROTOCULTURE ADDICTS.** *see* ART

➤ **PROTOSOCIOLOGY (ONLINE)**; an international journal of interdisciplinary research. *see* PHILOSOPHY

301 AUS ISSN 1836-7038
HN740.Z9
▼ ➤ **PROVINCIAL CHINA.** Text in English, Chinese. 2009. a. free (effective 2011). **Document type:** *Journal, Academic/Scholarly.* **Description:** The particular perspective of this journal is to focus less on the major centers in the People's Republic of China and more on regional and local developments and diversification.
Media: Online - full text.
Indexed: A01, P30, T02.
Published by: University of Technology, Sydney, ePress, PO Box 123, Broadway, NSW 2007, Australia. Ed. Yingjie Guo.

301 POL ISSN 0033-2356
HM7
PRZEGLAD SOCJOLOGICZNY. Text in Polish; Summaries in English. 1930. 2/yr. PLZ 30 per issue (effective 2011). bk.rev. bibl.; charts. index. **Document type:** *Journal, Academic/Scholarly.* **Description:** Methodological aspects of Polish modern sociology and related sciences.
Indexed: AgrLib, CA, FR, HistAb, IBR, IBSS, IBZ, MLA-IB, P42, PSA, RASB, S02, S03, SCOPUS, SOPODA, SSA, SociolAb, T02.
Published by: Lodzkie Towarzystwo Naukowe/Lodz Scientific Society, ul. M. Sklodowskiej-Curie 11, Lodz, 90-505, Poland. TEL 48-42-6655459, FAX 48-42-6655464, biuro@ltn.lodz.pl. Ed. Jolanta Kulpinska.

PSICHIATRIA DI COMUNITA. *see* PSYCHOLOGY

302 ITA ISSN 1827-5249
PSICOLOGIA DI COMUNITA; gruppi, ricerca-azione e modelli formativi. Text in Italian. 2005. s-a. EUR 51 combined subscription domestic to institutions (print & online eds.); EUR 78 combined subscription foreign to institutions (print & online eds.) (effective 2009). **Document type:** *Journal, Academic/Scholarly.*
Related titles: Online - full text ed.: ISSN 1971-842X. 2005.
Published by: Franco Angeli Edizioni, Viale Monza 106, Milan, 20127, Italy. TEL 39-02-2837141, FAX 39-02-26144793, redazioni@francoangeli.it, http://www.francoangeli.it.

PSYCHOLOGY AND SOCIOLOGY OF SPORT: CURRENT SELECTED RESEARCH. *see* PSYCHOLOGY

302.23 AUS ISSN 1837-0667
▼ ➤ **PUBLIC COMMUNICATION REVIEW.** Abbreviated title: P C R. Text in English. 2009. s-a. free (effective 2011). back issues avail. **Document type:** *Journal, Academic/Scholarly.* **Description:** Dedicated to publish scholarly articles concerned with the field of public communication.
Media: Online - full text.
Published by: University of Technology, Sydney, ePress, PO Box 123, Broadway, NSW 2007, Australia. TEL 61-2-95142000, international@uts.edu.au, http://utsescholarship.lib.uts.edu.au/ epress/. Eds. Jim Macnamara, Robert Crawford TEL 61-2-95142708.

➤ **PUBLIC PULSE.** *see* BUSINESS AND ECONOMICS—Marketing And Purchasing

➤ **PUBLIK-FORUM**; Zeitung kritischer Christen. *see* RELIGIONS AND THEOLOGY

305.8 NZL ISSN 1179-7126
TE PUWANANGA. Text in English. 2003. q. free (effective 2010). back issues avail. **Document type:** *Newsletter, Academic/Scholarly.*
Former titles (until 2010): Te Kairangahau (1178-3028); (until 2007): Nga Pae o te Maramatanga. Newsletter (1177-6358)
Related titles: Online - full text ed.: ISSN 1179-7134. free (effective 2010).
Published by: Nga Pae o te Maramatanga/National Institute of Research Excellence for Maori Development and Advancement, Waipapa Marae Complex, Rehutai Bldg, 16 Wynyard St, University of Auckland, Private Bag 92019, Auckland, 1142, New Zealand. TEL 64-9-3737599, FAX 64-9-3737428, info@maramatanga.ac.nz. Ed. Dr. J S Te Rito.

Q J I. (Quarterly Journal of Ideology) *see* POLITICAL SCIENCE

301 EGY ISSN 1687-6539
QADAYA MUSTAQBALIYYAT/FUTURE CASES SERIES. Text in Arabic. 2006. q. **Document type:** *Government.*
Related titles: Online - full text ed.: ISSN 1687-8930.
Published by: Egypt, The Cabinet. Information and Decision Support Center (I D S C), 1 Magless El Sha'ab St, Cairo, Egypt. TEL 202-2792-9292, FAX 202-2792-9222, info@idsc.net.eg, http:// www.idsc.gov.eg/default.aspx, http://www.eip.gov.eg/Default.aspx.

301 ITA ISSN 1973-5197
I QUADERNI DI ALVEARE; progetto per una democrazia responsabile. Text in Italian. 2007. 3/yr. EUR 25 domestic; EUR 35 foreign (effective 2011).
Published by: G.B. Palumbo & C. Editore SpA, Via Ricasoli 59, Palermo, 90139, Italy. TEL 39-091-588850, FAX 39-091-6111848, http:// www.palumboeditore.it. Ed. Giovanni Notari.

301 ITA ISSN 0033-4952
HM7
QUADERNI DI SOCIOLOGIA. Text in Italian. 1951. 3/yr. EUR 72 in the European Union; EUR 100 elsewhere (effective 2009). bk.rev. bibl. index. reprints avail. **Document type:** *Journal, Academic/Scholarly.*
Indexed: A20, CA, CJA, FR, IBSS, P34, P42, PAIS, PCI, PSA, RASB, S02, S03, SCOPUS, SOPODA, SSA, SociolAb, T02.
—INIST.
Published by: Rosenberg & Sellier, Via Andrea Doria 14, Turin, 10123, Italy. TEL 39-011-8127808, FAX 39-011-8127820, info@rosenbergesellier.it, http://www.rosenbergesellier.it. Ed. Luciano Gallino.

QUADERNI DI TEORIA SOCIALE. *see* SOCIAL SCIENCES: COMPREHENSIVE WORKS

QUADERNI STORICI. *see* HISTORY

S

301 ITA ISSN 0391-8521
QUALITA DELLA VITA. Text in Italian. 1978. irreg., latest vol.21. price varies. **Document type:** *Monographic series, Academic/Scholarly.*
Published by: Edizioni Studium, Via Cassiodoro 14, Rome, 00193, Italy. TEL 39-06-6865846, FAX 39-06-6875456, info@edizionistudium.it, http://www.edizionistudium.it.

301 USA ISSN 0162-0436
HM1
➤ **QUALITATIVE SOCIOLOGY.** Text in English. 1978. q. EUR 1,139, USD 1,175 combined subscription to institutions (print & online eds.) (effective 2012). adv. bk.rev. illus. Index. back issues avail.; reprint service avail. from PSC. **Document type:** *Journal, Academic/Scholarly.* **Description:** Covers research based on the qualitative interpretation of social life, including theory, fieldwork and ethnography, historical and comparative analyses, and photographic studies.
Related titles: Microform ed.: (from PQC); Online - full text ed.: ISSN 1573-7837 (from IngentaConnect).
Indexed: A01, A03, A08, A20, A22, A26, AMHA, AbAn, B01, B06, B07, B09, BibLing, CA, CurCont, DIP, E01, ERA, FR, FamI, G10, IBR, IBSS, IBZ, P10, P30, P34, P42, P46, P48, PQC, PSA, PsycholAb, RASB, RILM, S02, S03, SCOPUS, SOPODA, SSA, SSCI, SWR&A, SociolAb, T02, W07, W09.
—BLDSC (7168.124500), IE, Infotrieve, Ingenta, INIST. **CCC.**
Published by: Springer New York LLC (Subsidiary of: Springer Science+Business Media), 233 Spring St, New York, NY 10013. TEL 212-460-1500, FAX 212-460-1575, service-ny@springer.com. Ed. Javier Auyero.

301 POL ISSN 1733-8077
HM403
QUALITATIVE SOCIOLOGY REVIEW. Text in English. 2005. 3/yr. free (effective 2011). **Document type:** *Journal, Academic/Scholarly.* **Description:** Publishes empirical, theoretical and methodological articles applicable to all fields within sociology.
Media: Online - full text.
Indexed: CA, IBSS, S02, S03, SCOPUS, SociolAb, T02.
Published by: Uniwersytet Lodzki, Wydzial Ekonomiczno-Socjologiczny, Instytut Socjologii/Lodz University, Faculty of Economics and Sociology, Institute of Sociology, Katedra Socjologii Organizacji i Zarzadzania, Rewolucji 1905 Nr 41-43, Lodz, 90-214, Poland. TEL 48-42-6355263. Ed. Krzysztof Tomasz Konecki.

301 DEU ISSN 1617-0164
QUALITATIVE SOZIOLOGIE. Text in German. 2001. irreg., latest vol.12, 2010. price varies. **Document type:** *Monographic series, Academic/Scholarly.*
Published by: Lucius und Lucius Verlagsgesellschaft mbH, Gerokstr 51, Stuttgart, 70184, Germany. TEL 49-711-242060, FAX 49-711-242088, lucius@luciusverlag.com, http://www.luciusverlag.com.

305.4 DEU
QUERELLES; Jahrbuch fuer Frauen- und Geschlechterforschung. Text in German. 1996. a. **Document type:** *Journal, Academic/Scholarly.*
Published by: Freie Universitaet Berlin, Zentraleinrichtung zur Foerderung von Frauen- und Geschlechterforschung, Habelschwerdter Allee 45, Berlin, 14195, Germany. TEL 49-30-83853378, FAX 49-30-83856183, zefrauen@zedat.fu-berlin.de. Ed. Anita Runge.

305.3 DEU ISSN 1862-054X
HQ1103
QUERELLES - NET. Text in German. 2000. 3/yr. free (effective 2011). **Document type:** *Journal, Academic/Scholarly.*
Media: Online - full text.
Indexed: A39, C27, C29, D03, D04, E13, R14, S14, S15, S18.
Published by: Freie Universitaet Berlin, Zentraleinrichtung zur Foerderung von Frauen- und Geschlechterforschung, Habelschwerdter Allee 45, Berlin, 14195, Germany. TEL 49-30-83853378, FAX 49-30-83856183, zefrauen@zedat.fu-berlin.de, http://www.zefg.fu-berlin.de.

301 FRA ISSN 1286-8698
QUESTIONS CONTEMPORAINES. Text in French. 1998. back issues avail. **Document type:** *Monographic series.*
Related titles: ◆ Series: Questions Contemporaines. Serie Globalisation et Sciences Sociales. ISSN 1778-3429.
Published by: L' Harmattan, 5 Rue de l'Ecole Polytechnique, Paris, 75005, France. TEL 33-1-43257651, FAX 33-1-43258203.

301 ITA ISSN 2038-5048
▼ **R A;** la rivista dell' A I S. (Rivista Associazione Italiana di Sociologia) Text in Italian. 2010. irreg. **Document type:** *Magazine, Trade.*
Media: Online - full text.
Published by: Associazione Italiana di Sociologia, c/o Universita degli Studi di Roma "La Sapienza", Via Salaria 113, Rome, 00198, Italy. info@ais-sociologia.it.

301 USA ISSN 0033-6742
R A P. Text in English. 1969. m. USD 10 (effective 2000). bk.rev. **Document type:** *Newsletter.*
Formerly: Vista R A P
Related titles: Microfilm ed.
Published by: Radicals Against Poverty, 42 Melrose Pl, Montclair, NJ 07042. Ed. Arnie Korotkin. Circ: 1,500.

301 370 384 ITA ISSN 2037-0830
▼ **R E M.** (Ricerche su Edicazione e Media) Text in Italian. 2009. s-a. EUR 37 domestic to institutions; EUR 56 foreign to institutions (effective 2011). **Document type:** *Journal, Academic/Scholarly.*
Related titles: Online - full text ed.: ISSN 2037-0849.
Published by: (Societa Italiana di Ricerca sull'Educazione Mediale), Edizioni Erickson, Via Praga 5, Settore E, Gardolo, TN 38100, Italy. TEL 39-0461-950690, FAX 39-0461-950698, info@erickson.it. Ed. Pier Cesare Rivoltella.

301 GBR ISSN 1745-6681
R I H S C. WORKING PAPERS ON COMMUNITY ENGAGEMENT. (Research Institute for Health and Social Change) Text in English. 2005. irreg. **Document type:** *Monographic series, Academic/Scholarly.*
Related titles: Online - full text ed.: ISSN 1745-669X. free (effective 2009).
Published by: Manchester Metropolitan University, Research Institute for Health and Social Change, c o David Brown, Rm E53d, Elizabeth Gaskell Campus, Manchester Metropolitan University, Hathersage Rd, Manchester, M13 0JA, United Kingdom. TEL 44-161-2472563, FAX 44-161-2476842, c.kagan@mmu.ac.uk, http://www.rihsc.mmu.ac.uk/.

R I P S. REVISTA DE INVESTIGACIONES POLITICAS Y SOCIOLOGICAS. *see* POLITICAL SCIENCE

301 IND ISSN 0033-7625
THE RADICAL HUMANIST. Abbreviated title: R H. Text in English. 1937. m. INR 20 per issue (effective 2011). adv. bk.rev. back issues avail.; reprints avail. **Document type:** *Journal, Consumer.* **Description:** Forum for the scientific study of current sociological, philosophical and cultural issues and problems in the spirit of humanism.
Related titles: Microform ed.: 1937 (from PQC); Online - full text ed.: free (effective 2011).
Indexed: BAS, MLA-IB.
Published by: Radical Humanist, D-26 Jangpura B, New Delhi, 110 014, India. Ed. Rekha Saraswat. Pub. N D Pancholi. **Subscr. to:** I N S I O Scientific Books & Periodicals.

RADICAL PEDAGOGY. *see* EDUCATION—Teaching Methods And Curriculum

RADIX. *see* RELIGIONS AND THEOLOGY

301 IND ISSN 0973-3086
RAJAGIRI JOURNAL OF SOCIAL DEVELOPMENT. Text in English. 2005. s-a. INR 150 domestic to individuals; USD 30 foreign to individuals; INR 250 domestic to institutions; USD 30 foreign to institutions (effective 2011). back issues avail. **Document type:** *Journal, Academic/Scholarly.*
Indexed: CA, S02, S03, T02.
Published by: Rajagiri College of Social Sciences, Kalamassery, Kochi, Kerala 683 104, India. TEL 91-484-2555564, FAX 91-484-2532862, admin@rajagiri.edu, http://www.rajagiri.edu.

305.8994 NZL ISSN 1177-5068
RANGIKAINGA. Text in English. 2002. irreg. free (effective 2008). adv. back issues avail. **Document type:** *Newsletter, Consumer.*
Media: Online - full text.
Published by: Indigenous Media Network Ltd., Wellington, New Zealand. TEL 64-27-2954690, panui@tangatawhenua.com. Ed. Potaua Biasiny-Tule. Adv. contact Nikolasa Biasiny-Tule.

RAPA NUI JOURNAL. *see* ANTHROPOLOGY

301 ITA ISSN 0486-0349
HM7 CODEN: RITSBL
RASSEGNA ITALIANA DI SOCIOLOGIA. Text in Italian. 1960. q. EUR 120.50 combined subscription domestic to institutions (print & online eds.); EUR 150.50 combined subscription foreign to institutions (print & online eds.) (effective 2009). index. back issues avail. **Document type:** *Journal, Academic/Scholarly.*
Related titles: Online - full text ed.
Indexed: A22, BibInd, CA, CIS, FR, HistAb, I13, IBR, IBSS, IBZ, MLA-IB, P30, P42, PAIS, PCI, PSA, PsycholAb, RASB, S02, S03, SOPODA, SSA, SociolAb, T02.
—IE, Infotrieve, INIST. **CCC.**
Published by: Societa Editrice Il Mulino, Strada Maggiore 37, Bologna, 40125, Italy. TEL 39-051-256011, FAX 39-051-256034, riviste@mulino.it. Ed. Loredana Sciolla. Circ: 1,800.

302.23 MEX ISSN 1605-4806
P87
RAZON Y PALABRA; revista electronica en America Latina especializada en topicos de comunicacion. Text in Spanish. 1996. q. free (effective 2011). back issues avail. **Document type:** *Journal, Academic/Scholarly.*
Media: Online - full content.
Indexed: MLA-IB.
Published by: Instituto Technologico de Estudios Superiores de Monterrey. Campus Estado de Mexico, Carr. Lago de Guadalupe Km 3.5, Atizapan de Zaragoza, Estado de Mexico, 52926, Mexico. TEL 52-5-8645613, FAX 52-5-8645613, http://www.cem.itesm.mx/. Ed. Alejandro Ocampo Almazan.

302.3 CAN ISSN 1715-9075
LA RECHERCHE SUR L'OPINION PUBLIQUE AU GOUVERNEMENT DU CANADA. RAPPORT ANNUEL. Text in French. 2002. a. **Document type:** *Report, Trade.*
Media: Online - full text.
Published by: (Communication Canada), Public Works and Government Services Canada/Travaux Publics et Services Gouvernementaux Canada, Place du Portage, Phase III, 11 Laurier St, Gatineau, PQ K1A 0S5, Canada. TEL 800-622-6232, Questions@pwgsc.gc.ca, http://www.pwgsc.gc.ca/text/home-e.html.

301 FRA ISSN 1279-8649
DT1
RECHERCHES AFRICAINES. Text in French. 1997. q. **Document type:** *Journal, Academic/Scholarly.*
Published by: L' Harmattan, 5 Rue de l'Ecole Polytechnique, Paris, 75005, France. TEL 33-1-43257651, FAX 33-1-43258203, http://www.editions-harmattan.fr.

301 CAN ISSN 0034-1282
➤ **RECHERCHES SOCIOGRAPHIQUES.** Text in French. 1960. 3/yr. CAD 70 to corporations (effective 2004). adv. bk.rev. abstr.; bibl.; charts; stat. index, cum.index: 1960-1964. **Document type:** *Journal, Academic/Scholarly.* **Description:** Provides an interdisciplinary study of the society of Quebec and French Canada.
Related titles: Microform ed.: (from BNQ, PQC).
Indexed: AmH&L, CA, FR, I13, IBR, IBSS, IBZ, MLA-IB, P30, P42, PAIS, PSA, PdeR, S02, S03, SOPODA, SSA, SociolAb, T02.
—INIST. **CCC.**
Published by: Universite Laval, Departement de Sociologie, Faculte des Sciences Sociales, Sainte-Foy, PQ G1K 7P4, Canada. TEL 418-656-3889, FAX 418-656-7390, jacqueline.arguin@soc.ulaval.ca, http://www.soc.ulaval.ca. Ed. Andree Fortin. Pub. Simon Langlois. Adv. contact Jacqueline Arguin. Circ: 1,500.

301.07 BEL ISSN 1782-1592
RECHERCHES SOCIOLOGIQUES ET ANTHROPOLOGIQUES. Text in French; Summaries in English. 1970. s-a. EUR 35 domestic (effective 2006). bk.rev. back issues avail.; reprints avail. **Document type:** *Journal, Academic/Scholarly.* **Description:** Sociological analysis of social, methodological and theoretical problems.
Formerly (until 2005): Recherches Sociologiques (0771-677X)
Indexed: CA, DIP, FR, IBR, IBSS, IBZ, P42, PAIS, PSA, S02, S03, SCOPUS, SOPODA, SSA, SociolAb, T02.
—BLDSC (7309.255500), IE, Ingenta, INIST.
Published by: Universite Catholique de Louvain, Recherches Sociologiques, Pl Montesquieu 1/10, Louvain-la-Neuve, 1348, Belgium. TEL 32-10-474204, FAX 32-10-474267, http://recsoc.anso.ucl.ac.be/recsoc. Ed., R&P Cecile Wery. Circ: 500.

▼ **RED FEATHER JOURNAL;** an international journal of children's visual culture. *see* CHILDREN AND YOUTH—About

300 150 DEU
REFLEXIVE SOZIALPSYCHOLOGIE. Text in German. 2007. irreg., latest vol.6, 2010. price varies. **Document type:** *Monographic series, Academic/Scholarly.*
Published by: Transcript, Muehlenstr 47, Bielefeld, 33607, Germany. TEL 49-521-63454, FAX 49-521-61040, live@transcript-verlag.de.

301 FRA ISSN 1764-9587
LE REGARD SOCIOLOGIQUE. Text in French. 2003. irreg., latest 2009. price varies. back issues avail. **Document type:** *Monographic series, Academic/Scholarly.*
Published by: Presses Universitaires du Septentrion, Rue du Barreau, BP 30199, Villeneuve d'Ascq, Cedex 59654, France. TEL 33-3-20416680, FAX 33-3-20416690, septentrion@septentrion.com.

301 FRA ISSN 1164-0871
REGARDS SOCIOLOGIQUES. Text in French. 1991. s-a. **Document type:** *Academic/Scholarly.*
Related titles: Online - full text ed.: ISSN 2105-2840. 200?.
Published by: Association Regards Sociologiques, 122 Grand' Rue, Strasbourg, 67000, France. TEL 33-6-82216729, asso_regarsoc@yahoo.fr.

305.3 DEU
REGENSBURGER BEITRAEGE ZUR GENDER-FORSCHUNG. Text in German. 2007. irreg., latest vol.3, 2008. price varies. **Document type:** *Monographic series, Academic/Scholarly.*
Published by: Universitaetsverlag Winter GmbH, Dossenheimer Landstr 13, Heidelberg, 69121, Germany. TEL 49-6221-770260, FAX 49-6221-770269, info@winter-verlag-hd.de, http://www.winter-verlag-hd.de.

300 DEU ISSN 1863-5083
REGENSBURGER SCHRIFTEN ZUR VOLKSKUNDE. VERGLEICHENDEN KULTURWISSENSCHAFT. Text in German. 1984. irreg., latest vol.21, 2010. price varies. **Document type:** *Monographic series, Academic/Scholarly.*
Formerly (until 2006): Regensburger Schriften zur Volkskunde
Published by: Waxmann Verlag GmbH, Steinfurter Str 555, Muenster, 48159, Germany. TEL 49-251-265040, FAX 49-251-2650426, info@waxmann.com.

301 300 MEX ISSN 1870-3925
AS63.A1
➤ **REGION Y SOCIEDAD.** Text in Spanish. 1989. 3/yr. adv. bk.rev. abstr.; bibl.; charts; illus.; maps; stat. back issues avail. **Document type:** *Journal, Academic/Scholarly.* **Description:** Disseminates the results and advances of regional research in the social sciences: history, economics, political science, and health, culture and society. Expands the horizon of regional analysis to locate phenomena within the framework of a reflection about Northern Mexico and its role in national history, economy, society and culture. Introduces a theoretical reflection on the region.
Formerly (until 1997): Colegio de Sonora. Revista (0188-7408)
Related titles: Online - full text ed.: 2000. free (effective 2011).
Indexed: C01, H21, P08, PAIS.
Published by: El Colegio de Sonora, Ave. Obregon 54, Centro, Hermosillo, SON 83000, Mexico. TEL 52-662-2126551, FAX 52-662-2125021, region@colson.edu.mx, http://www.colson.edu.mx. Ed., R&P Ines Martinez de Castro. Pub. Oscar Contreras Montellano.

302.23 DEU
REIHE MEDIENPAEDAGOGIK. Text in German. 1991. irreg., latest vol.17, 2010. price varies. **Document type:** *Monographic series, Academic/Scholarly.*
Published by: KoPaed Verlag, Pfaelzer-Wald-Str 64, Munich, 81539, Germany. TEL 49-89-68890098, FAX 49-89-6891912, info@kopaed.de.

302.23 DEU
REIHE MULTIMEDIA. Text in German. 1997. irreg., latest vol.12, 2009. price varies. **Document type:** *Monographic series, Academic/Scholarly.*
Published by: KoPaed Verlag, Pfaelzer-Wald-Str 64, Munich, 81539, Germany. TEL 49-89-68890098, FAX 49-89-6891912, info@kopaed.de.

302.23 DEU ISSN 1433-7657
REIHE UNI-PAPERS. Text in German. 1978. irreg., latest vol.13, 2000. price varies. **Document type:** *Monographic series, Academic/Scholarly.*
Published by: U V K Verlagsgesellschaft mbH, Schuetzenstr 24, Konstanz, 78462, Germany. TEL 49-7531-90530, FAX 49-7531-905398, nadine.ley@uvk.de, http://www.uvk.de.

RELACIONES; revista al tema del hombre. *see* PSYCHOLOGY

302 MEX ISSN 0188-2643
H8.S7
RELACIONES (MEXICO CITY); publicacion de analisis sociologico. Text in Spanish. 1989. s-a. back issues avail. **Document type:** *Academic/Scholarly.*
Related titles: Online - full text ed.
Indexed: C01, P09, PCI.
Published by: (Departamento de Relaciones Sociales), Universidad Autonoma Metropolitana - Xochimilco, Division de Ciencias Sociales y Humanidades, Calz del Hueso 1100, Col Villa Quietud, Mexico City, DF 04960, Mexico. TEL 52-5-7245090, FAX 52-5-5943966.

RELACIONES (ZAMORA); estudios de historia y sociedad. *see* HISTORY—History Of North And South America

306.85 AUS ISSN 1327-7553
RELATEWELL. Text in English. 1996. q. AUD 28.50 (effective 2009). **Document type:** *Journal, Consumer.* **Description:** Aims to promote the quality of marriages, domestic relationships and family life in all their diversity.
Published by: Family Relationships Institute Incorporated, 21 Bell St, Coubury, VIC 3058, Australia. TEL 61-3-93548854, FAX 61-3-93548860, http://www.relatewell.com.au/.

302.23 AUT ISSN 1025-2339
P87
RELATION; Beitraege zur vergleichenden Kommunikationsforschung. Text in German. 1995. s-a. EUR 23.60 (effective 2010). **Document type:** *Journal, Academic/Scholarly.* **Description:** Provides a forum for all engaged in studying the relations between media, society and history.
Related titles: Online - full text ed.
Indexed: MLA-IB.
—IE.
Published by: Verlag der Oesterreichischen Akademie der Wissenschaften, Postfach 471, Vienna, W 1011, Austria. verlag@oeaw.ac.at, http://verlag.oeaw.ac.at. Ed. Herbert Matis.

RELIGION AND AMERICAN CULTURE; a journal of interpretation. *see* RELIGIONS AND THEOLOGY

201.6 NLD ISSN 1878-5417
▼ ➤ **RELIGION AND GENDER.** Text in English. 2011. s-a. free (effective 2011). bk.rev. **Document type:** *Journal, Academic/Scholarly.* **Description:** Explores the relation, confrontation and intersection of gender and religion, taking into account the multiple and changing manifestations of religion in diverse social and cultural contexts.
Media: Online - full text.
Published by: IWFT Vrouwennetwerk Theologie, Universiteit Utrecht, Faculteit Godgeleerdheid, Heidelberglaan 2, kamer 1206, Utrecht, 3584 CS, Netherlands. TEL 31-30-2531839, FAX 31-30-2533241, iwft@uu.nl, http://www.iwft.nl.

➤ **RELIGION AND SOCIETY IN CENTRAL AND EASTERN EUROPE.** *see* RELIGIONS AND THEOLOGY

➤ **RELIGION AND SOCIETY IN TRANSITION.** *see* RELIGIONS AND THEOLOGY

▼ ➤ **RELIGION IN CHINESE SOCIETIES.** *see* RELIGIONS AND THEOLOGY

➤ **RELIGION IN DER GESELLSCHAFT.** *see* RELIGIONS AND THEOLOGY

➤ **RELIGIONEN IN KULTUR UND GESELLSCHAFT.** *see* RELIGIONS AND THEOLOGY

➤ **RELIGIONI E SOCIETA**; rivista di scienze sociali della religione. *see* RELIGIONS AND THEOLOGY

▼ ➤ **RELIGIOUS HISTORY AND CULTURE SERIES.** *see* RELIGIONS AND THEOLOGY

301 USA ISSN 0082-8068
HN17.5
REPORT ON THE WORLD SOCIAL SITUATION (YEAR). Text in English. 1952. irreg., latest 2003.
Related titles: French ed.: Rapport sur la Situation Sociale dans le Monde. ISSN 0251-6608; Spanish ed.: Informe Sobre la Situacion Social en el Mundo. ISSN 0251-6594.
Published by: United Nations, Division for Social Policy and Development, Department of Economic and Social Affairs, 2 UN Plaza, Room DC2-1320, New York, NY 10017. Ed. Sergei Zelenev TEL 212-963-4732.

RES HUMANAE; Arbeiten fuer die Paedagogik. *see* EDUCATION

301 364 GBR
RESEARCH DEVELOPMENT AND STATISTICS DIRECTORATE. OCCASIONAL PAPERS. Text in English. 19??. irreg., latest no.87. free (effective 2009). stat. back issues avail. **Document type:** *Monographic series, Trade.* **Description:** Provides information that helps ministers and policy makers take evidence-based decisions, and also help the police, probation service, the courts and immigration officials to do their jobs as effectively as possible.
Related titles: Online - full text ed.
Published by: Research Development and Statistics Directorate, Direct Communications Unit, 2 Marsham St, London, SW1P 4DF, United Kingdom. TEL 44-20-70354848, publications.rds@homeoffice.gsi.gov.uk, http://www.homeoffice.gov.uk/rds/index.html.

RESEARCH ETHICS REVIEW. *see* MEDICAL SCIENCES

RESEARCH IN ETHICAL ISSUES IN ORGANIZATIONS. *see* BUSINESS AND ECONOMICS—Management

301 320 GBR ISSN 0895-9935
JA76
RESEARCH IN POLITICAL SOCIOLOGY. Abbreviated title: R P S. Text in English. 1985. irreg., latest vol.17, 2008. price varies. **Document type:** *Monographic series, Academic/Scholarly.* **Description:** Publishes original scholarly manuscripts that increase our understanding and knowledge of political sociology and that can directly aid political sociologists in strengthening and developing the unique perspectives and skills they bring to the profession.
Indexed: A22, ABS&EES, CA, P42, PSA, S02, S03, SCOPUS, SSA, SociolAb, T02.
—BLDSC (7755.077350), Ingenta. **CCC.**
Published by: (American Sociological Association, Section on Political Sociology USA), Emerald Group Publishing Ltd., Howard House, Wagon Ln, Bingley, W Yorks BD16 1WA, United Kingdom. TEL 44-1274-777700, FAX 44-1274-785201, emerald@emeraldinsight.com. Ed. Barbara Wejnert. **Dist. by:** Turpin Distribution Services Ltd., Pegasus Dr, Stratton Business Park, Biggleswade, Bedfordshire SG18 8QB, United Kingdom. TEL 44-1767-604951, FAX 44-1767-601640, custserv@turpin-distribution.com, http://www.turpin-distribution.com/.

RESEARCH IN POLITICS AND SOCIETY. *see* POLITICAL SCIENCE

301 GBR ISSN 1057-1922
HT401
RESEARCH IN RURAL SOCIOLOGY AND DEVELOPMENT. Text in English. 1984. irreg., latest vol.15, 2010. price varies. back issues avail. **Document type:** *Monographic series, Academic/Scholarly.* **Description:** Addresses issues relating to rural social change and its impacts on families and communities, the globalization and restructuring of agriculture and the food industry and the dynamics of development in agrarian societies.
Related titles: Online - full text ed.
Indexed: A22, Agr, CA, P30, S02, S03, SCOPUS, SOPODA, SSA, SociolAb, T02.
—BLDSC (7769.691000), IE, Infotrieve, Ingenta. **CCC.**
Published by: Emerald Group Publishing Ltd., Howard House, Wagon Ln, Bingley, W Yorks BD16 1WA, United Kingdom. TEL 44-1274-777700, FAX 44-1274-785201, emerald@emeraldinsight.com. Ed. Terry Marsden. **Dist. by:** Turpin Distribution Services Ltd., Pegasus Dr, Stratton Business Park, Biggleswade, Bedfordshire SG18 8QB, United Kingdom. TEL 44-1767-604951, FAX 44-1767-601640, custserv@turpin-distribution.com, http://www.turpin-distribution.com/.

303.4 GBR ISSN 0163-786X
HN1
RESEARCH IN SOCIAL MOVEMENTS, CONFLICTS AND CHANGE. Text in English. 1978. a., latest vol.28, 2008. price varies. back issues avail. **Document type:** *Monographic series, Academic/Scholarly.* **Description:** Contains articles on empirical and theoretical research.
Related titles: Online - full text ed.: ISSN 1875-7871; Supplement(s): International Social Movement Research. ISSN 1043-1365. 1988.
Indexed: ABS&EES, CA, ESPM, HPNRM, IBSS, P42, PSA, S02, S03, SCOPUS, SOPODA, SSA, SSciA, SociolAb, T02.
—BLDSC (7770.570000). **CCC.**
Published by: Emerald Group Publishing Ltd., Howard House, Wagon Ln, Bingley, W Yorks BD16 1WA, United Kingdom. TEL 44-1274-777700, FAX 44-1274-785201, books@emeraldinsight.com, http://www.emeraldinsight.com. Ed. Patrick G Coy.

320.6 GBR ISSN 0196-1152
HM1
RESEARCH IN SOCIAL PROBLEMS AND PUBLIC POLICY. Text in English. 1979. irreg., latest vol.16, 2008. price varies. back issues avail. **Document type:** *Monographic series, Academic/Scholarly.* **Description:** Features articles devoted to the sharpening and reshaping of scientific discourse in the area of inquiry implied by its title, involving the intersection of social problems and public policy.
Related titles: Online - full text ed.: ISSN 1875-7928.
Indexed: CA, CJPI, P34, P42, PQC, PSA, PsycholAb, S02, S03, SCOPUS, SOPODA, SSA, SociolAb, T02.
—BLDSC (7770.580000). **CCC.**
Published by: Emerald Group Publishing Ltd., Howard House, Wagon Ln, Bingley, W Yorks BD16 1WA, United Kingdom. TEL 44-1274-777700, FAX 44-1274-785201, books@emeraldinsight.com, http://www.emeraldinsight.com. Eds. Bill Freudenburg, Ted Youn.

305.5 USA ISSN 0276-5624
HT601
RESEARCH IN SOCIAL STRATIFICATION AND MOBILITY. Text in English. 1981. q. EUR 229 in Europe to institutions; JPY 30,600 in Japan to institutions; USD 276 elsewhere to institutions (effective 2012). back issues avail. **Document type:** *Journal, Academic/Scholarly.* **Description:** Publishes research on issues of social inequality from a broad diversity of theoretical and methodological perspectives.
Related titles: Online - full text ed.: ISSN 1878-5654 (from ScienceDirect).
Indexed: A22, A26, CA, ESPM, I05, IBSS, P30, P42, PSA, S02, S03, SCOPUS, SOPODA, SSA, SSciA, SociolAb, T02.
—IE, Ingenta. **CCC.**
Published by: J A I Press Inc. (Subsidiary of: Elsevier Science & Technology), 360 Park Ave S, New York, NY 10010. TEL 212-989-5800, FAX 212-633-3990, usinfo-f@elsevier.com. Ed. M Yaish.

RESEARCH IN SOCIOLOGY OF EDUCATION. *see* EDUCATION

RESEARCH IN THE SOCIOLOGY OF HEALTH CARE. *see* MEDICAL SCIENCES

306 GBR ISSN 0733-558X
HM131
RESEARCH IN THE SOCIOLOGY OF ORGANIZATIONS. Text in English. 1982. irreg., latest vol.28, 2010. price varies. back issues avail. **Document type:** *Monographic series, Academic/Scholarly.* **Description:** Contains cutting edge theoretical, methodological and research issues that are relevant to organizational sociology.
Related titles: Online - full text ed.
Indexed: A22, CA, S02, S03, SCOPUS, SOPODA, SSA, SociolAb, T02.
—BLDSC (7770.733000), Ingenta. **CCC.**
Published by: Emerald Group Publishing Ltd., Howard House, Wagon Ln, Bingley, W Yorks BD16 1WA, United Kingdom. TEL 44-1274-777700, FAX 44-1274-785201, emerald@emeraldinsight.com. Ed. Michael Lounsbury. **Dist. by:** Turpin Distribution Services Ltd., Pegasus Dr, Stratton Business Park, Biggleswade, Bedfordshire SG18 8QB, United Kingdom. TEL 44-1767-604951, FAX 44-1767-601640, custserv@turpin-distribution.com, http://www.turpin-distribution.com/.

301.072 GBR ISSN 0277-2833
HD6951
RESEARCH IN THE SOCIOLOGY OF WORK. Text in English. 1981. irreg., latest vol.19, 2009. price varies. back issues avail. **Document type:** *Monographic series, Academic/Scholarly.* **Description:** Addresses issues of current importance in the study of the workplace, workers, technology, economic organization, and worklife.
Related titles: Online - full text ed.: ISSN 1875-7944.
Indexed: A22, CA, IBSS, P30, S02, S03, SCOPUS, SOPODA, SSA, SociolAb, T02.
—BLDSC (7770.740000), IE, Ingenta. **CCC.**
Published by: Emerald Group Publishing Ltd., Howard House, Wagon Ln, Bingley, W Yorks BD16 1WA, United Kingdom. TEL 44-1274-777700, FAX 44-1274-785201, books@emeraldinsight.com, http://www.emeraldinsight.com. Ed. Lisa A Keister.

301 GBR ISSN 1047-0042
HT101 CODEN: RUSOEN
RESEARCH IN URBAN SOCIOLOGY. Text in English. 1989. irreg., latest vol.9, 2008. price varies. back issues avail. **Document type:** *Monographic series, Academic/Scholarly.* **Description:** Addresses the major subject areas of urban sociology, ethnic and minority groups within the city, social network of urban residents, location of retail and industrial activities within the metropolitan complex, decline of the central cities and emergence of suburban lifestyles, and the core question of community integration itself.
Related titles: Online - full text ed.: ISSN 1875-8029.
Indexed: CA, P42, PSA, S02, S03, SCOPUS, SOPODA, SSA, SociolAb, T02.
—BLDSC (7774.045000). **CCC.**
Published by: Emerald Group Publishing Ltd., Howard House, Wagon Ln, Bingley, W Yorks BD16 1WA, United Kingdom. TEL 44-1274-777700, FAX 44-1274-785201, books@emeraldinsight.com, http://www.emeraldinsight.com. Ed. Ray Hutchinson.

RESEARCH ON LANGUAGE AND SOCIAL INTERACTION. *see* LINGUISTICS

361.3 USA ISSN 1049-7315
HV1 CODEN: RSWPEW
➤ **RESEARCH ON SOCIAL WORK PRACTICE.** Text in English. 1990. bi-m. USD 838, GBP 493 combined subscription to institutions (print & online eds.); USD 821, GBP 483 to institutions (effective 2011). bk.rev. abstr.; illus. Index. back issues avail.; reprint service avail. from PSC. **Document type:** *Journal, Academic/Scholarly.* **Description:** Devoted to the publication of empirical research concerning the methods and outcomes of social work practice. It carries regular features that include new methods of assessment, scholarly reviews, invited essays and book reviews.
Related titles: Online - full text ed.: ISSN 1552-7581. USD 754, GBP 444 to institutions (effective 2011).
Indexed: A01, A02, A03, A08, A10, A20, A22, A26, ASCA, B04, B07, B28, BRD, C06, C07, C08, C28, CA, CINAHL, CurCont, E-psyche, E01, E02, E03, E07, E08, ERI, ERIC, ESPM, EdA, EdI, FamI, G08, H04, H12, HRA, I05, P02, P03, P04, P10, P13, P24, P25, P27, P30, P34, P48, P53, P54, PQC, PsycInfo, PsycholAb, RiskAb, S02, S03, S09, S11, SCOPUS, SFSA, SOPODA, SSA, SSAI, SSAb, SSCI, SSI, SWR&A, SociolAb, T02, V&AA, V02, V03, W03, W07.
—BLDSC (7770.680000), IE, Infotrieve, Ingenta. **CCC.**
Published by: Sage Publications, Inc., 2455 Teller Rd, Thousand Oaks, CA 91320. TEL 805-499-9774, 800-818-7243, FAX 805-499-0871, 800-583-2665, info@sagepub.com. Ed. Bruce A Thyer. Circ: 1,200. **Subscr. outside the Americas to:** Sage Publications Ltd., 1 Oliver's Yard, 55 City Rd, London EC1Y 1SP, United Kingdom. TEL 44-20-73248701, FAX 44-20-73248733, subscription@sagepub.co.uk.

302.23 FRA ISSN 0751-7971
RESEAUX; communication technologie societe. Text in French. 1983. bi-m. **Document type:** *Journal, Academic/Scholarly.*
Related titles: Online - full text ed.
Indexed: CA, FR, IBSS, P26, P27, P42, P46, P48, P54, PQC, PSA, S02, S03, SCOPUS, SociolAb, T02.
—INIST. **CCC.**
Published by: (France. France Telecom, Recherche et Developpement), Lavoisier, 14 rue de Provigny, Cachan, 94236, France. TEL 33-1-47406700, FAX 33-1-47406702, info@lavoisier.fr, http://www.lavoisier.fr.

303.4 016.301 CAN ISSN 1492-4234
HN17.5
RESOURCES FOR RADICALS. Text in English. 1998. a. CAD 20 domestic; USD 24 in United States; USD 30 elsewhere (effective 2005).
Published by: Toronto Action for Social Change, PO Box 73620, Toronto, ON M6C 1C0, Canada. TEL 416-651-5800, tasc@web.ca. Ed. Brian Burch.

RETHINKING MARXISM; a journal of economics, culture and society. *see* POLITICAL SCIENCE

RETIREMENT POLICY AND RESEARCH CENTRE WORKING PAPER. *see* GERONTOLOGY AND GERIATRICS

REVIEW AMERICANA; a literary journal. *see* LITERATURE

301 ITA ISSN 2038-1379
HB1
➤ **REVIEW OF ECONOMICS AND INSTITUTIONS**; economia, societa e istituzioni. Text in English. 1989. 3/yr. free (effective 2011). **Document type:** *Journal, Academic/Scholarly.*
Formerly (until 2009): Economia, Societa e Istituzioni (1593-9456)
Media: Online - full text.
Published by: Universita degli Studi di Perugia, Dipartimento di Economia, Finanza e Statistica, Via A Pascoli 20, Perugia, Italy. TEL 39-075-5855421, FAX 39-075-5855299, http://www.ec.unipg.it/DEFS/. Ed. Carlo Andrea Bollino.

➤ **REVIEW OF SOCIAL ECONOMY.** *see* BUSINESS AND ECONOMICS

301 GBR ISSN 0261-0272
HM1
REVIEWING SOCIOLOGY. Text in English. 1979. 3/yr. bk.rev. cum.index. back issues avail. **Document type:** *Journal, Academic/Scholarly.* **Description:** Book review journal in the social sciences.
Media: Online - full content.
Indexed: SCOPUS, SOPODA, SociolAb.
Published by: University of Central England, Department of Sociology and Applied Social Studies, c o Peter Cook, Plymouth Business School, Drake Circus, Plymouth, PL4 8AA, United Kingdom. TEL 44-1752-232847, FAX 44-1752-232859, peter.cook@pbs.plym.ac.uk, http://www.bcu.ac.uk.

S

301 HRV ISSN 0350-154X
HM7
REVIJA ZA SOCIOLOGIJU/SOCIOLOGICAL REVIEW. Text in Serbo-Croatian; Summaries in English. 1971. s-a. HRK 100; USD 20 foreign. adv. bk.rev. bibl. **Description:** Covers all aspects of sociology.
Indexed: CA, I13, IBSS, P30, P42, PQC, PSA, RASB, S02, S03, SOPODA, SSA, SociolAb, T02.
Published by: Sociolosko Drustvo Hrvatske/Croatian Sociological Association, c/o Filozofski fakultet, I Lucica 3, Zagreb, 10000, Croatia. TEL 385-1-6120007, FAX 385-1-513834. Ed. Vjekoslav Afric. Circ: 1,000.

301 ARG ISSN 1667-9261
REVISTA ARGENTINA DE SOCIOLOGIA. Text in Spanish. 2003. s-a. **Document type:** *Journal, Academic/Scholarly.*
Related titles: Online - full text ed.: ISSN 1669-3248. free (effective 2011) (from SciELO).
Indexed: A01, C01, CA, F03, F04, S02, S03, SCOPUS, SociolAb, T02.
Published by: Consejo de Profesionales en Sociologia (C P S), Avenida Corrientes 2835, Cuerpo B, Piso 7o, Buenos Aires, C1193AAA, Argentina. Circ: 1,000.

301 ESP ISSN 1136-8527
DP302.C616
REVISTA CATALANA DE SOCIOLOGIA. Text in Spanish. 1995. s-a. **Document type:** *Journal, Academic/Scholarly.*
Related titles: Online - full text ed.: ISSN 2013-5149.
Published by: (Associacio Catalana de Sociologia), Institut d'Estudis Catalans, Carrer del Carme 47, Barcelona, 08001, Spain. TEL 34-932-701620, FAX 34-932-701180, informacio@iecat.net, http://www2.iecat.net.

301 CHL ISSN 0717-2087
REVISTA CHILENA DE TEMAS SOCIOLOGICOS. Text in Spanish. 1995. s-a. **Document type:** *Journal, Academic/Scholarly.*
Published by: Universidad Catolica Silva Henriquez, General Jofre 462, Santiago, Chile. TEL 56-2-4601100, FAX 56-2-6354192.

301 COL ISSN 0120-159X
HM7
REVISTA COLOMBIANA DE SOCIOLOGIA. Text in Spanish. 1979. s-a. USD 57 domestic; USD 60 in the Americas; USD 110 elsewhere (effective 2011). bk.rev. abstr.; charts. **Document type:** *Journal, Academic/Scholarly.*
Indexed: IBR, IBZ, RASB, SociolAb.
Published by: Universidad Nacional de Colombia, Departamento de Sociologia, Ciudad Universitaria, Bogota, Colombia. TEL 57-1-3165000, FAX 57-1-3165634, tecs@bacata.usc.unal.edu.co. Ed. Fernando Cubides Cipagauta.

302.2 BRA ISSN 0102-0897
P87
REVISTA COMUNICACOES E ARTES. Key Title: Comunicacoes e Artes. Text in Portuguese. 1970. 3/yr. per issue exchange basis.
Formerly: Universidade de Sao Paulo. Escola de Comunicacoes Culturais. Revista
Published by: Universidade de Sao Paulo, Escola de Comunicacoes e Artes, Av. Prof. Lucio Martins Rodrigues 443, Butanta, SP 05508-900, Brazil. TEL 55-11-30914033, comunica@eca.usp.br, http://www.eca.usp.br/.

301 BRA ISSN 1806-0498
REVISTA CONTEMPORANEA. Text in Portuguese. 2003. 3/yr. free (effective 2011). **Document type:** *Journal, Academic/Scholarly.*
Media: Online - full text.
Published by: Universidade do Estado do Rio de Janeiro, Faculdade de Comunicacao Social, Rua Sao Francisco Xavier 524, Maracana, Rio de Janeiro, 20559-900, Brazil. http://www.uerj.br. Ed. Fernando do Nascimento Goncalves.

301 ROM ISSN 1583-3410
REVISTA DE CERCETARE SI INTERVENTIE SOCIALA/REVIEW OF RESEARCH AND SOCIAL INTERVENTION. Text in English, Spanish, French. 2000. q. **Document type:** *Journal, Academic/Scholarly.*
Related titles: Online - full text ed.: ISSN 1584-5397. free (effective 2011).
Indexed: SSA, SSCI, SociolAb, W07.
Published by: (Universitatea "Alexandru Ioan Cuza" din Iasi/"Alexandru Ioan Cuza" University of Iasi), Editura Lumen/Lumen Publishing House, Tepes Voda, No2, Iasi, Iasi, Romania. TEL 40-332-450133, FAX 40-332-811551, edituralumen@gmail.com, http://edituralumen.ro/. Ed. Stefan Cojocaru.

469 PRT ISSN 0870-7081
REVISTA DE COMUNICACAO E LINGUAGENS. Text in Portuguese. 1985. irreg., latest vol.13, 1990. **Document type:** *Magazine, Consumer.*
Indexed: CA, MLA-IB, S02, S03, SociolAb, T02.
Published by: Relogio d'Agua Editores Lda., Rua Sylvio Rebelo 15, Lisbon, 1000-282, Portugal. TEL 351-218-474450, FAX 351-218-470775, relogiodagua@relogiodagua.pt, http://www.relogiodagua.pt.

REVISTA DE ECONOMIA E SOCIOLOGIA RURAL. *see* AGRICULTURE—Agricultural Economics

REVISTA DE ESTUDIOS ORTEGUIANOS. *see* PHILOSOPHY

301 ESP ISSN 0015-6043
HN1
REVISTA DE FOMENTO SOCIAL; ciencias sociales. Text in Spanish. 1946. q. EUR 36 domestic; EUR 75 in Europe; EUR 85 elsewhere (effective 2008). adv. bk.rev. abstr. index. **Document type:** *Journal, Academic/Scholarly.*
Formerly (1946-1963): Fomento Social (0210-4113)
Indexed: CA, F04, FR, IBR, IBSS, IBZ, P30, P42, PSA, RASB, S02, S03, SociolAb, T02.
Published by: ETEA - Institucion Universitaria de la Compania de Jesus, Calle Escritor Castilla Aguayo 4, Cordoba, 14004, Spain. TEL 34-957-222100, FAX 34-957-222182, comunica@etea.com, http://www.etea.com.

301 600 610 ARG ISSN 1852-4680
▼ **REVISTA DE HUMANIDADES MEDICAS & ESTUDIOS SOCIALES DE LA CIENCIA Y LA TECNOLOGIA/JOURNAL OF MEDICAL HUMANITIES & SOCIAL STUDIES OF SCIENCE AND TECHNOLOGY.** Key Title: ea. Text in English, Portuguese, Spanish. 2009. 3/yr. free (effective 2011). **Document type:** *Journal, Academic/Scholarly.*
Published by: Research Center on Health, Society, Science and Technology info@iso-cyte.org, www.iso-cyte.org. Ed. Gabriela Mijal Bortz.

REVISTA DE LA ECONOMIA SOCIAL Y DE LA EMPRESA. *see* BUSINESS AND ECONOMICS

302 ESP ISSN 1131-6225
REVISTA DE PSICOLOGIA SOCIAL APLICADA. Text in Spanish. 1991. 3/yr. **Document type:** *Journal, Academic/Scholarly.*
Indexed: P03, PsycInfo, PsycholAb, S02, S03.
Published by: Universitat de Valencia, Departamento de Psicobiologia y Psicologia Social, Ave. Blasco Ibanez, 21, Valencia, 4610, Spain. TEL 34-96-3864420, FAX 34-96-3864470, http://www.cazorla.uv.es/.

301 ESP ISSN 1130-7633
REVISTA DE SERVICIOS SOCIALES Y POLITICA SOCIAL. Text in Spanish. 1984. q. back issues avail. **Document type:** *Magazine, Consumer.*
Published by: Consejo General de Colegios Oficiales de Diplomados en Trabajo Social y Asistentes Sociales, Ave Reina Vicoria No. 37 2o. C, Madrid, 28003, Spain. TEL 34-91-5415776, FAX 34-91-5353377, administracion@cgtrabajosocial.es, http://www.cgtrabajosocial.es/. Ed. Maria Luisa Fuertes Cervantes.

301 COL ISSN 0120-1212
REVISTA DE SOCIOLOGIA. Text in Spanish. 1968. s-a. bk.rev. charts; bibl.; stat. **Document type:** *Journal, Academic/Scholarly.*
Indexed: C01, RILM.
Published by: (Universidad Pontificia Bolivariana, Facultad de Sociologia), Universidad Pontificia Bolivariana, Biblioteca, Apartado Aereo 56006, Medellin, Colombia. TEL 57-4-159075, FAX 57-4-118513.

301 BRA ISSN 0104-4478
JA76
➤ **REVISTA DE SOCIOLOGIA E POLITICA.** Text in Portuguese; Summaries in English, French; Abstracts in English, French. 1993. s-a. BRL 30 domestic; USD 20 foreign (effective 2008). adv. bk.rev. abstr.; bibl. cum.index. back issues avail. **Document type:** *Journal, Academic/Scholarly.* **Description:** Publishes current researches and original articles in the social sciences. Contains four distinct sections: a dossier concerning relevent themes in the social sciences, a section with translations to Portuguese of relevant articles, a section of diverse essays and articles, and a section devoted to book reviews.
Related titles: Online - full text ed.: ISSN 1678-9873. free (effective 2011).
Indexed: C01, CA, F04, H21, I13, IBSS, P08, P42, PSA, S02, S03, SCOPUS, SSA, SociolAb, T02.
Published by: Universidade Federal do Parana, Departamento de Ciencias Sociais, Rua General Carneiro, 460, Sala 904, Curitiba, PR 80060-150, Brazil. TEL 55-02141-33605093, FAX 55-02141-32642791, editoriarsp@ufpr.br, http://www.scielo.br/rsocp. Eds. Adriano Nervo Codato, Gustavo Biscaia de Lacerda, Paulo Roberto Neves Costa, Renato Monseff Perissinotto.

301 ESP ISSN 0210-5233
HM7
➤ **REVISTA ESPANOLA DE INVESTIGACIONES SOCIOLOGICAS (SPANISH EDITION).** Text in Spanish. 1965. q. EUR 40 domestic to individuals; EUR 70 foreign to individuals; EUR 50 domestic to institutions; EUR 80 foreign to institutions; EUR 50 combined subscription domestic to individuals print & online eds.; EUR 80 combined subscription foreign to individuals print & online eds.; EUR 180 combined subscription domestic to institutions print & online eds.; EUR 210 combined subscription foreign to institutions print & online eds. (effective 2008). adv. bk.rev. cum.index. back issues avail. **Document type:** *Journal, Academic/Scholarly.* **Description:** Covers topics on sociology and political sciences in general.
Formerly (in 1977): Revista Espanola de la Opinion Publica (0034-9429)
Related titles: Online - full text ed.: ISSN 1988-5903. EUR 40 to individuals; EUR 160 to institutions (effective 2008); English ed.: ISSN 1577-3272. 1996.
Indexed: A01, A22, BibInd, CA, CIS, F03, F04, FR, HistAb, I13, P09, P30, P42, PCI, PSA, PhilInd, PsycholAb, RASB, S02, S03, SCIMP, SCOPUS, SOPODA, SSA, SSCI, SociolAb, T02, W07.
—BLDSC (7854.005000), IE, Infotrieve, Ingenta, INIST. **CCC.**
Published by: Centro de Investigaciones Sociologicas, Montalban, 8, Madrid, 28014, Spain. TEL 34-91-5807600, FAX 34-91-5807619, cis@cis.es, http://www.cis.es. Ed. Belen Barreiro Perez-Prado. Circ: 3,000.

301.4 ESP ISSN 1136-548X
LA REVISTA ESPANOLA DE SEXOLOGIA. Text in Spanish. 1979. bi-m. EUR 66 domestic; USD 62 foreign (effective 2009). back issues avail. **Document type:** *Journal, Academic/Scholarly.*
Formerly (until 1996): Revista de Sexologia (0214-0551)
Published by: Instituto de Sexologia In.Ci.Sex., C. Vinaroz, 16, Madrid, 28002, Spain. incisex@incisex.com.

301 ESP ISSN 1578-2824
REVISTA ESPANOLA DE SOCIOLOGIA. Text in Spanish. 2001. s-a. free to members (effective 2006). back issues avail. **Document type:** *Journal, Academic/Scholarly.*
Indexed: F04, SociolAb, T02.
Published by: Federacion Espanola de Sociologia, Calle Alfonso XII 18, 5o, Madrid, 28014, Spain. TEL 34-91-5232741, info@fes-web.org. Ed. Emilio Camo de Espinoza.

302 PRT ISSN 1646-4419
REVISTA EUROPEIA DE INSERCAO SOCIAL/REVUE EUROPEENNE D'INSERTION SOCIALE. Text in French. 2006. a.
Published by: Instituto Superior de Psicologia Aplicada, Rua Jardim do Tabaco 34, Lisbon, 1149-041, Portugal. TEL 351-21-8811700, FAX 351-21-8860954, info@ispa.pt, http://www.ispa.pt.

302 ESP ISSN 1575-0663
REVISTA IBEROAMERICANA DE DISCURSO Y SOCIEDAD. Text in Spanish. 1999. q.
Published by: Editorial Gedisa, Paseo Bonanova 9, 1o, Barcelona, 08022, Spain. TEL 34-93-2530904, FAX 34-93-2530905, informacion@gedisa.com, http://www.gedisa.com. Ed. Maria Luisa Pardo.

301 MEX ISSN 0187-8468
REVISTA INTERAMERICANA DE SOCIOLOGIA. Text in Spanish. 1966. 3/yr. USD 1.60 per issue. bk.rev.
Indexed: C01.
Published by: Instituto Mexicano de Cultura, PROVIDENCIA 330, Col Del Valle, Mexico City, DF 03100, Mexico. Ed. Lucio Mendieta Y Nunez.

302 ESP ISSN 1135-9692
REVISTA INTERNACIONAL DE PROTOCOLO. Text in Spanish. 1995. q. EUR 60 (effective 2009). back issues avail. **Document type:** *Magazine, Consumer.*
Published by: Ediciones Protocolo, Avenida de Colon 8, 4o B, Oviedo, 33013, Spain. TEL 34-985-241670, FAX 34-902-181107, ediciones@protocolo.com, http://www.edicionesprotocolo.com.

301 ESP ISSN 0034-9712
H8
REVISTA INTERNACIONAL DE SOCIOLOGIA. Text in Spanish. 1941. q. EUR 43.38 domestic; EUR 67 foreign (effective 2009). back issues avail.; reprints avail. **Document type:** *Journal, Academic/Scholarly.* **Description:** Covers sociology, demographics, population problems and social thought.
Related titles: Online - full text ed.: ISSN 1988-429X. free (effective 2011).
Indexed: A22, BibInd, CA, DIP, FR, I13, I14, IBR, IBZ, P09, P30, P42, PAIS, PCI, PSA, RASB, RILM, S02, S03, SCOPUS, SOPODA, SSA, SSCI, SociolAb, T02, W07.
—BLDSC (7861.800000), IE, Infotrieve, Ingenta, INIST.
Published by: (Consejo Superior de Investigaciones Cientificas (C S I C), Instituto de Estudios Sociales Avanzados), Consejo Superior de Investigaciones Cientificas (C S I C), Departamento de Publicaciones, Vitruvio 8, Madrid, 28006, Spain. publ@csic.es, http://www.publicaciones.csic.es. Ed. Eduardo Moyano.

301 ARG ISSN 1852-8759
▼ ➤ **REVISTA LATINOAMERICANA DE ESTUDIOS SOBRE CUERPOS, EMOCIONES Y SOCIEDAD.** Text in Spanish, Portuguese. 2009. 3/yr. free (effective 2011). **Document type:** *Journal, Academic/Scholarly.*
Media: Online - full text.
Indexed: F04, T02.
Published by: Consejo Nacional de Investigaciones Cientificas y Tecnicas, Centro de Estudios Avancados, Av General Paz 154, 2o Piso, Cordoba, 5000, Argentina. TEL 54-351-4341124, FAX 54-351-4332087. Ed. Adrian Scribano.

301 MEX ISSN 0188-2503
H8
➤ **REVISTA MEXICANA DE SOCIOLOGIA.** Text in Spanish; Abstracts in English, Spanish. 1939. q. MXN 250; MXN 60 newsstand/cover (effective 2010). bk.rev. abstr.; bibl.; charts. index, cum.index. reprints avail. **Document type:** *Journal, Academic/Scholarly.* **Description:** Presents the works of the institute's researchers; contributions to social theory, essays on the main trends in sociopolitical thought as well as discussions on the most acute problems of Latin America.
Related titles: Microform ed.: (from PQC); Online - full text ed.: free (effective 2011).
Indexed: A22, BibInd, C01, CA, DIP, FR, H21, I13, IBR, IBZ, ILD, MLA-IB, P08, P09, P30, P34, P42, PAIS, PCI, PSA, PsycholAb, RASB, S02, S03, SCOPUS, SOPODA, SSA, SociolAb, T02.
—BLDSC (7866.410000), IE, Infotrieve, Ingenta, INIST.
Published by: Universidad Nacional Autonoma de Mexico, Instituto de Investigaciones Sociales, Circuito Mario de la Cueva s-n, 2o Nivel H-06, Ciudad de la Investigacion en Humanidades, Zona Cultural, Mexico City, DF 04510, Mexico. TEL 52-5-6227400, FAX 52-5-6652443, iis@servidor.unam.mx, http://www.unam.mx/iisunam/. Ed. Natividad Gutierrez Chong. Circ: 1,000.

301 PAN ISSN 1560-6163
REVISTA PANAMENA DE SOCIOLOGIA. Text in Spanish. 1986. q. **Document type:** *Journal, Academic/Scholarly.*
Indexed: C01.
Published by: Universidad de Panama, Facultad de Humanidades, Ciudad Universitaria Octavio Mendez Pereira, Panama City, Panama. http://201.224.62.65:8084/webup/.

301 PRY ISSN 0035-0354
HM7
REVISTA PARAGUAYA DE SOCIOLOGIA. Text in Spanish. 1964. 3/yr. USD 40. bk.rev. bibl.; charts; stat. reprints avail.
Related titles: Microform ed.: (from PQC).
Indexed: A22, C01, CA, H21, IBR, IBSS, IBZ, ILD, P08, P42, PAIS, RASB, S02, S03, SOPODA, SociolAb, T02.
—BLDSC (7869.520000), IE, INIST.
Published by: Centro Paraguayo de Estudios Sociologicos, ELIGIO AYALA, 973, Asuncion, Paraguay. TEL 595-21-443-734, FAX 595-21-447-128. Ed. Graziella Corvalan. Circ: 1,000.

303.4 004 MEX ISSN 1870-4115
REVISTA PUEBLOS Y FRONTERA DIGITAL. Text in Spanish, English. 2006. irreg. free (effective 2011). **Document type:** *Journal, Academic/Scholarly.*
Media: Online - full text.
Published by: Universidad Nacional Autonoma de Mexico, Ciudad Universitaria, Mexico City, DF 04510, Mexico. TEL 52-55-56221280, FAX 52-55-56160030, http://www.unam.mx.

301 ROM ISSN 1224-9262
HN641
REVISTA ROMANA DE SOCIOLOGIE. Text in English, Romanian. 1972. 3/yr. (3 double issues). bk.rev. bibl.; abstr. back issues avail. **Document type:** *Journal, Academic/Scholarly.* **Description:** Publishes theoretical studies and field research in various branches of sociology and social sciences.
Supersedes in part (in 1997): Sociologie Romaneasca (1220-5389); Which was formerly (until 1990): Viitorul Social (0379-3745)
Related titles: Online - full text ed.; ◆ English ed.: Romanian Journal of Sociology. ISSN 1220-3688.
Indexed: CA, DIP, IBR, IBZ, P30, P46, P48, P54, PQC, RASB, S02, S03, SCOPUS, SOPODA, SSA, SociolAb, T02.
Published by: (Academia Romana, Institutul de Sociologie), Editura Academiei Romane/Romanian Academy's Publishing House, Calea 13 Septembrie nr.13, sector 5, PO BOX 050711, Bucharest, Romania. TEL 40-21-3188146, FAX 40-21-3182444, edacad@ear.ro, http://www.ear.ro/. Ed. Sorin M. Radulescu. Circ: 325. **Dist. by:** S.C. Manpres Distribution S.R.L., Piata Presei Libere, nr.1, Corp B, Etaj 3, Cam.301-302, sector 1, Bucuresti, Romania. TEL 40-21-3146339, FAX 40-21-3146339, office@manpres.ro, http://www.manpres.ro/.

302.23 PRI ISSN 1549-2230
REVISTA TEKNOKULTURA. Variant title: Teknokultura Revista en Linea. Text in Spanish. 2001. a. free (effective 2004). **Document type:** *Journal, Academic/Scholarly.*
Media: Online - full content.
Published by: Universidad de Puerto Rico, Facultad de Ciencias Sociales/University of Puerto Rico, Social Sciences Faculty, P O Box 23345, San Juan, 00931-3345, Puerto Rico. TEL 787-764-0000. Ed. Heidi J Figueroa.

301 BRA ISSN 0104-9259
H8.P8
REVISTA UNIVERSIDADE RURAL. SERIE CIENCIAS HUMANAS. Text in Portuguese. 1971. s-a. BRL 16 to individuals; BRL 12 to students (effective 2004).
Supersedes in part (in 1994): Universidade Federal Rural do Rio de Janeiro. Arquivos (0100-2481)
Indexed: CABA, FR, I11, S13, S16.
—INIST.
Published by: Universidade Federal Rural do Rio de Janeiro, Antiga Rodovia Rio, km 47, Sala 102-P1, Seropedica, RJ 23890-000, Brazil. TEL 55-21-6821210, FAX 55-21-6821201, edur@ufrrj.br, http://www.ufrrj.br/.

REVUE DROIT ET SOCIETE. *see* LAW

REVUE ECONOMIQUE ET SOCIALE. *see* BUSINESS AND ECONOMICS

301 FRA ISSN 0248-9015
DA589.4 CODEN: SGNWD2
REVUE FRANCAISE DE CIVILISATION BRITANNIQUE. Text in French. 1980. s-a.
Indexed: AmH&L, CA, FR, HistAb, IBSS, T02.

—BLDSC (7902.740000), INIST.
Published by: Centre de Recherches et d'Etudes en Civilisation Britannique, Masison des Sciences de l'Homme et de la Societe, Universite de Poitiers, 99 Av du Recteur Pineau, Poitiers, 86022, France.

301 FRA ISSN 0035-2969
HM3
➤ **REVUE FRANCAISE DE SOCIOLOGIE.** Text in French; Summaries in English, German, Spanish. 1960. q. EUR 80 domestic to individuals; EUR 90 domestic to institutions; EUR 60 domestic to students; EUR 100 foreign (incl. English language Suppl.) (effective 2008). adv. bk.rev. bibl.; charts. 200 p./no.; **Document type:** *Journal, Academic/Scholarly.* **Description:** Includes theoretical and methodological articles recording fundamental research, trends and developments, discussions of new developments in the field of sociology, and identifying new areas for sociological research.
Related titles: E-mail ed.; Online - full text ed.: ISSN 1958-5691; Supplement(s):.
Indexed: A20, A22, ASCA, BAS, BibInd, CA, CurCont, DIP, EI, EIP, FR, I13, IBR, IBSS, IBZ, ILD, MLA-IB, P02, P10, P30, P34, P42, P48, P53, P54, PAIS, PCI, PQC, PSA, PdeR, RASB, RILM, S02, S03, S11, SCOPUS, SOPODA, SSA, SSCI, SociolAb, T02, W07.
—BLDSC (7904.430000), IE, Infotrieve, Ingenta, INIST. **CCC.**
Published by: (France. Centre National de la Recherche Scientifique), Ophrys, 25 Rue Ginoux, Paris, 75737, France. TEL 33-1-45783390, FAX 33-1-45753711, editions.ophrys@ophrys.fr, http://www.ophrys.fr. Circ: 3,000.

301 FRA ISSN 0035-2985
HD4807
REVUE FRANCAISE DES AFFAIRES SOCIALES. Text in French. 1946. q. EUR 69.50 in the European Union; EUR 83.40 foreign (effective 2009). adv. bibl.; charts; stat. index. reprint service avail. from SCH. **Document type:** *Journal, Government.*
Formerly (until 1967): Revue Francaise du Travail
Related titles: Microfiche ed.
Indexed: A22, CISA, I13, IBR, IBSS, IBZ, ILD, P30, PAIS, PCI, RASB.
—BLDSC (7902.250000), IE, Infotrieve, Ingenta.
Published by: (France. Ministere du Travail, des Relations Sociales, de la Famille, de la Solidarite et de la Ville), Documentation Francaise, 29-31 Quai Voltaire, Paris, Cedex 7 75344, France. FAX 33-1-40157230. Circ: 3,800.

301 FRA ISSN 0397-7870
E169.1
➤ **REVUE FRANCAISE D'ETUDES AMERICAINES.** Variant title: R F E A. Text in English, French. 1976. 4/yr. bk.rev. bibl. back issues avail. **Document type:** *Journal, Academic/Scholarly.* **Description:** Reference journal for American studies in France.
Related titles: Online - full text ed.: ISSN 1776-3061.
Indexed: A20, ASCA, AmH&L, ArtHuCI, CA, Chicano, CurCont, FR, IBSS, MLA, MLA-IB, P30, PAIS, RILM, SCOPUS, T02, W07.
—INIST.
Published by: (Association Francaise d'Etudes Americaines), Editions Belin, 8 Rue Ferou, Paris, 75278, France. TEL 33-1-55428400, FAX 33-1-43251829, http://www.editions-belin.com. Ed. Catherine Collomp. Circ: 1,000.

302 FRA ISSN 1260-1705
REVUE INTERNATIONALE DE PSYCHOSOCIOLOGIE. Text in French. 1994. s-a. EUR 58 (effective 2009). **Document type:** *Journal, Academic/Scholarly.* **Description:** Seeks to show how this discipline is at the core of reality and change, as well as social life.
Indexed: E-psyche, FR, P25, PQC, SD.
—IE, INIST.
Published by: Editions ESKA, 12 Rue du Quatre-Septembre, Paris, 75002, France. TEL 33-1-40942222, FAX 33-1-40942232, eska@eska.fr.

LA REVUE L I S A. (Litterature, Histoire des Idees, Images, Societes du Monde Anglophone) *see* PHILOSOPHY

201.6 ITA ISSN 0392-1581
BL60
RICERCHE DI STORIA SOCIALE E RELIGIOSA. Text in Italian. 1972. s-a. price varies. bk.rev. illus. **Document type:** *Journal, Academic/Scholarly.*
Indexed: CERDIC, FR, IBR, IBZ.
—INIST.
Published by: (Centro Studi per le Fonti della Storia della Chiesa nel Veneto), Edizioni di Storia e Letteratura, Via delle Fornaci 24, Rome, 00165, Italy. TEL 39-06-670307, FAX 39-06-671250, info@storiaeletteratura.it, http://www.storiaeletteratura.it. **Co-sponsor:** Centro Studi di Storia Sociale e Religiosa nel Mezzogiorno.

301 JPN ISSN 0913-1442
HM7 CODEN: RIHOEC
➤ **RIRON TO HOHO/SOCIOLOGICAL THEORY AND METHODS.** Text in Japanese; Summaries in English. 1986. s-a. JPY 2,800; JPY 1,400 newsstand/cover (effective 1999). adv. bk.rev. back issues avail. **Document type:** *Academic/Scholarly.* **Description:** Covers the theoretical and methodological development in mathematical sociology, quantitative sociology, and related disciplines.
Indexed: A20, ASCA, CA, CurCont, IBSS, S02, S03, SCOPUS, SOPODA, SSA, SSCI, SociolAb, T02, W07.
—BLDSC (8319.650170).
Published by: Japanese Association for Mathematical Sociology, c/o Gaku Doba, 2-12-1 O Okayama, Meguro-ku, Tokyo, 152-0033, Japan. FAX 81-6-5734-3192. Ed., R&P, Adv. contact Gaku Doba TEL 81-3-5734-3192. page JPY 10,000. Circ: 800 (paid). **Subscr. to:** Harvest Sha, 2-11-5 Mukodai-cho, Tanashi-shi, Tokyo-to 188-0013, Japan. TEL 81-424-67-6441, FAX 81-424-67-8661.

➤ **RIVISTA AMBIENTE E LAVORO.** *see* OCCUPATIONAL HEALTH AND SAFETY

306.85 ITA ISSN 1972-7380
RIVISTA DI STUDI FAMILIARI. Text in Italian. 1996. s-a. **Document type:** *Journal, Academic/Scholarly.*
Formerly (until 2006): Famiglia Interdisciplinarita Ricerca (1127-3135)
Related titles: Online - full text ed.: ISSN 1972-5736.
Published by: Franco Angeli Edizioni, Viale Monza 106, Milan, 20127, Italy. TEL 39-02-2837141, FAX 39-02-26144793, redazioni@francoangeli.it, http://www.francoangeli.it.

305 551.46 POL ISSN 0860-6552
HD8039.S4
ROCZNIKI SOCJOLOGII MORSKIEJ. Text in Polish; Summaries in English. 1986. a. price varies. bk.rev. **Document type:** *Monographic series, Academic/Scholarly.* **Description:** Studies and monographs on sociological phenomena occurring in the social groups connected, through their professional activity, with the sea.
Formerly (until 1987): Socjologia Morska (0239-5568)
Indexed: IBR, IBZ.
Published by: (Polska Akademia Nauk, Oddzial w Gdansku, Komisja Prawa Morskiego/Polish Academy of Sciences, Branch in Gdansk, Marine Technology Committee), Polska Akademia Nauk, Oddzial w Gdansku/Polish Academy of Sciences, Section in Gdansk, ul Jaskowa Dolina 31, Gdansk, 80286, Poland. o1pan@ibwpan.gda.pl. Circ: 550. **Dist. by:** Ars Polona, Obroncow 25, Warsaw 03933, Poland. TEL 48-22-5098609, FAX 48-22-5098610, arspolona@arspolona.com.pl, http://www.arspolona.com.pl.

ROMANIAN JOURNAL OF SOCIETY AND POLITICS. *see* POLITICAL SCIENCE

ROMPAN FILAS; familia, escuela y sociedad. *see* EDUCATION

ROOILIJN; tijdschrift voor wetenschap en beleid in de ruimtelijke ordening. *see* GEOGRAPHY

306.89 DEU
ROSENKRIEG; Magazin fuer Trennung, Scheidung und Neuanfang. Text in German. 2005. bi-m. EUR 29.40; EUR 3.90 newsstand/cover (effective 2011). adv. **Document type:** *Magazine, Consumer.* **Description:** Contains articles and features on negotiating all aspects of divorce and separation.
Published by: Verlag Lutz von Gratkowski, Josef-Schoberstr 7, Landsberg am Lech, 89890, Germany. TEL 49-8191-973737, FAX 49-8191-966740. adv.: B&W page EUR 3,560, color page EUR 4,750. Circ: 3,500 (paid and controlled).

302 025.04 USA ISSN 1937-6154
TK5105.888
THE ROUGH GUIDE TO MYSPACE AND ONLINE COMMUNITIES. Text in English. 2006. irreg., latest 2006, 1st ed. USD 10.99 domestic 1st ed.; USD 15.99 in Canada 1st ed.; GBP 6.99 in United Kingdom 1st ed. (effective 2008). back issues avail. **Document type:** *Guide, Consumer.*
Related titles: Online - full text ed.
Published by: Rough Guides, 375 Hudson St, 9th Fl, New York, NY 10014. TEL 212-414-3635, http://www.roughguides.com/default.aspx.

305.567 GBR
ROUTLEDGE STUDIES IN SLAVE AND POST-SLAVE SOCIETIES AND CULTURES. Text in English. 1993. irreg., latest 2007. **Document type:** *Monographic series, Academic/Scholarly.* **Description:** This series is devoted to studying the slave and post-slave societies, from the ancient period to the present. It is also concerned with the dismantling of slave systems and with the after math of emancipation. It is history, sociology and literature.
Former titles (until 2005): Studies in Slave and Post-Slave Societies and Cultures (1462-1770); Slave and Post-Slave Societies and Cultures
—BLDSC (8026.519885).
Published by: Routledge (Subsidiary of: Taylor & Francis Group), 2 Park Sq, Milton Park, Abingdon, Oxon OX14 4RN, United Kingdom. TEL 44-20-70176000, FAX 44-20-70176699, info@routledge.co.uk.

307.72 USA ISSN 1556-9217
➤ **RURAL REALITIES.** Text in English. 2006. q. free (effective 2009). back issues avail. **Document type:** *Journal, Academic/Scholarly.* **Description:** Provides valuable insights on the current and emerging issues impacting people and places in rural America.
Media: Online - full content.
Published by: Rural Sociological Society, 104 Gentry Hall, University of Missouri, Columbia, MO 65211. TEL 573-882-9065, FAX 573-882-1473, ruralsoc@missouri.edu. Ed. Lionel Beaulieu TEL 662-325-3207.

307.72 AUS ISSN 1037-1656
HN841
➤ **RURAL SOCIETY**; the journal of research into rural and regional social issues in Australia. Text in English. 1989. 3/yr. AUD 99 to individuals; USD 440 combined subscription to institutions (print & online eds.) (effective 2008). bk.rev. back issues avail. **Document type:** *Journal, Academic/Scholarly.* **Description:** Disseminates research and other information in the field of rural social issues, embracing topics such as rural health and welfare, social policy, service delivery and rural social conditions.
Formerly (until 1991): Rural Welfare Research Bulletin
Related titles: Online - full text ed.
Indexed: A26, A34, A35, A36, AEI, AgBio, AusPAIS, CA, CABA, D01, E08, E12, ERIC, ESPM, F08, F12, G08, GH, H01, H12, I05, I11, IndVet, LT, N02, OR, P10, P21, P42, P46, P48, PQC, PSA, R07, R12, R13, RRTA, RiskAb, S02, S03, S09, S13, S16, SCOPUS, SSA, SociolAb, T02, T05, TAR, VS, W11.
—Ingenta.
Published by: (Charles Sturt University, Centre for Rural Social Research), eContent Management Pty Ltd, PO Box 1027, Maleny, QLD 4552, Australia. info@e-contentmanagement.com, http://www.e-contentmanagement.com. Ed. Marion Bannister. Circ: 350 (paid); 50 (controlled).

301 USA ISSN 0279-5957
HT401
THE RURAL SOCIOLOGIST. Text in English. 1981. q. USD 25 to non-members; free to members (effective 2009). adv. index. back issues avail. **Document type:** *Journal, Academic/Scholarly.* **Description:** Publishes announcements, articles, commentary and letters that are relevant to concerns of the society.
Indexed: A35, A36, AgBio, Agr, CABA, E12, GH, IBR, IBZ, LT, N02, R12, RRTA, S13, S16, SCOPUS, TAR, W11.
—BLDSC (8052.629000), Ingenta.
Published by: Rural Sociological Society, 104 Gentry Hall, University of Missouri, Columbia, MO 65211. TEL 573-882-9065, FAX 573-882-1473, ruralsoc@missouri.edu.

307.72 USA ISSN 0036-0112
CODEN: RUSCA
➤ **RURAL SOCIOLOGY**; devoted to scientific study of rural and community life. Text in English. 1937. q. GBP 204 in United Kingdom to institutions; EUR 239 in Europe to institutions; USD 333 in the Americas to institutions; USD 374 elsewhere to institutions; GBP 235 combined subscription in United Kingdom to institutions (print & online eds.); EUR 275 combined subscription in Europe to institutions (print & online eds.); USD 384 combined subscription in the Americas to institutions (print & online eds.); USD 430 combined subscription elsewhere to institutions (print & online eds.) (effective 2012). adv. bk.rev. abstr.; bibl.; charts; stat.; illus. index, cum.index: vols.1-20, 21-30, 31-40. back issues avail.; reprint service avail. from PSC. **Document type:** *Journal, Academic/Scholarly.* **Description:** It promotes the development of rural sociology through research, teaching and extension work.
Related titles: Microform ed.: (from PQC); Online - full text ed.: ISSN 1549-0831. GBP 204 in United Kingdom to institutions; EUR 239 in Europe to institutions; USD 333 in the Americas to institutions; USD 374 elsewhere to institutions (effective 2012).
Indexed: A01, A02, A03, A08, A20, A22, A26, A34, A35, A36, A37, A38, ABS&EES, AHCMS, APEL, ARDT, ASCA, AbAn, AgBio, Agr, AgrForAb, AmH&L, B04, BRD, BibAg, C25, C28, CA, CABA, Chicano, CurCont, D01, DIP, E01, E02, E03, E07, E08, E12, EI, EIA, ERI, ERIC, EdA, EdI, EnerInd, F08, F11, F12, FR, FamI, G08, GEOBASE, GH, H09, H16, HPNRM, HRA, HistAb, I05, I13, IBR, IBSS, IBZ, ILD, IndVet, LT, LeftInd, M01, M02, M10, MEA&I, MLA-IB, MaizeAb, N02, N03, OR, P02, P04, P06, P07, P10, P11, P15, P18, P26, P27, P30, P32, P34, P37, P40, P42, P43, P46, P48, P52, P53, P54, P56, PAA&I, PAIS, PCI, PGegResA, PN&I, PQC, PSA, PopulInd, PsycholAb, R12, RASB, RI-1, RI-2, RRTA, S02, S03, S05, S09, S11, S13, S16, S21, SCOPUS, SFSA, SOPODA, SRRA, SSA, SSAI, SSAb, SSCI, SSI, SUSA, SWR&A, SociolAb, T02, T05, TAR, VS, W01, W02, W03, W07, W09, W10, W11.
—BLDSC (8052.630000), IE, Infotrieve, Ingenta, INIST. **CCC.**
Published by: Rural Sociological Society, 104 Gentry Hall, University of Missouri, Columbia, MO 65211. TEL 573-882-9065, FAX 573-882-1473. Ed. Michael D Schulman. adv.: page USD 200; 4.375 x 7.625. **Subscr. to:** John Wiley & Sons, Inc., 111 River St, Hoboken, NJ 07030. TEL 201-748-6645, subinfo@wiley.com.

➤ **RURAL THEOLOGY**; international, ecumenical and interdisciplinary perspectives. *see* RELIGIONS AND THEOLOGY

➤ **RUSSIAN JOURNAL OF COMMUNICATION.** *see* POLITICAL SCIENCE—International Relations

➤ **RUSSIAN POLITICS AND SOCIETY**; international review of Russian studies. *see* POLITICAL SCIENCE—International Relations

301 NLD ISSN 1568-1262
S C P - PUBLICATIE. Text mainly in Dutch; Text occasionally in English. 2000. irreg. price varies. charts; illus.; stat. back issues avail. **Document type:** *Monographic series, Academic/Scholarly.* **Description:** Reports on various social and cultural issues.
Formed by the merger of (1975-2000): Netherlands. Sociaal en Cultureel Planbureau. Cahiers (0927-0833); (1981-2000): Netherlands. Sociaal en Cultureel Planbureau. Sociale en Culturele Studies (1568-1270)
Published by: Sociaal en Cultureel Planbureau/Social and Cultural Planning Office, Postbus 16164, The Hague, 2500 BD, Netherlands. TEL 31-70-3407000, FAX 31-70-3407044, info@scp.nl, http://www.scp.nl.

301 CHE
S G G REVUE. Text in French, German. 1862. bi-m. CHF 30. adv. bk.rev. bibl.; charts; illus. index. **Document type:** *Bulletin.*
Formerly (until 1990): Schweizerische Zeitschrift fuer Gemeinnuetzigkeit (0036-7826)
Published by: Schweizerische Gemeinnuetzige Gesellschaft, Schaffhauserstr 7, Zuerich 6, 8042, Switzerland. TEL 41-1-3634460. Ed. Willy Niederer. Circ: 6,000.

306.43 BRA ISSN 1808-0405
LC191.8.B6
S O C E D BOLETIM. (Sociologia da Educacao) Text in Portuguese. 2005. s-a. **Document type:** *Journal, Academic/Scholarly.*
Media: Online - full text.
Published by: Pontificia Universidade Catolica do Rio de Janeiro, Rua Marques de Sao Vicente, 225,, 22 453, ZC-20, Rio De Janeiro, RJ 22451041, Brazil.

S P R C NEWSLETTER. *see* SOCIAL SERVICES AND WELFARE

S P R C REPORT. *see* SOCIAL SERVICES AND WELFARE

S P W. (Sozialistische Politik und Wirtschaft) *see* POLITICAL SCIENCE

305 FIN ISSN 1796-5551
HQ75
➤ **S Q S/JOURNAL OF QUEER STUDIES IN FINLAND/TIDSKRIFT FOER QUEERFORSKNING I FINLAND**; Suomen queer-tutkimuksen seuran lehti. (Suomen Queer-Tutkimuksen Seura) Text in English, Finnish, Swedish. 2006. s-a. free (effective 2011). back issues avail. **Document type:** *Journal, Academic/Scholarly.*
Media: Online - full content.
Indexed: A39, C27, C29, D03, D04, E13, R14, S14, S15, S18.
Published by: Suomen Queer-Tutkimuksen Seura/Society of Queer Studies in Finland, c/o Annamari Vanska, Teidehistorian Laitos, University of Helsinki, Helsinki, 00014, Finland. Eds. Annamari Vanska, Jenny Kangasvuo.

302 USA ISSN 1932-6963
HV1568
THE S R V JOURNAL. (Social Role Valorization) Text in English. 2006. s-a. USD 150 for 2 yrs. in North America to institutions; USD 170 for 2 yrs. elsewhere to institutions; USD 180 combined subscription for 2 yrs. in North America to institutions (print & online eds.); USD 200 combined subscription for 2 yrs. elsewhere to institutions (print & online eds.) (effective 2010). back issues avail. **Document type:** *Journal, Academic/Scholarly.* **Description:** Aims to disseminate information about Social Role Valorization (SRV) and to assist socially devalued and other vulnerable individuals in society.
Related titles: Online - full text ed.: USD 125 for 2 yrs. to institutions (effective 2010).
Published by: Social Role Valorization Implementation Project, 74 Elm St, Worcester, MA 01609. TEL 508-752-3670, FAX 508-752-4279, info@srvip.org. Ed. Marc Tumeinski.

S

300 DEU ISSN 0724-3901
S S I P - BULLETIN. (Sozialwissenschaftlicher Studienkreis fuer Internationale Probleme) Text in German. 19??. irreg., latest vol.65, 1993. price varies. **Document type:** *Monographic series, Academic/ Scholarly.*
Published by: (Sozialwissenschaftlicher Studienkreis fuer Internationale Probleme e.V.), Verlag fuer Entwicklungspolitik Saarbruecken GmbH, Auf der Adt 14, Saarbruecken, 66130, Germany. TEL 49-6893-986094, FAX 49-6893-986095, vfe@verlag-entwicklungspolitik.de, http://www.verlag-entwicklungspolitik.de.

302 USA
S S S I NOTES. Text in English. irreg., latest vol.30, no.1, 2003. **Document type:** *Newsletter.*
Indexed: E-psyche.
Published by: Society for the Study of Symbolic Interaction, c/o Norman Denzin, Institute of Communications Research, 229 Gregory Hall, 810 S Wright St, Urbana, IL 61801. TEL 217-333-0795, FAX 217-244-9580, http://www.espach.salford.ac.uk/sssi/index.php. Ed. Norman K. Denzin.

305.42 USA ISSN 2160-5564
S W S NETWORK NEWS. Text in English. 1971. q. free (effective 2011). bk.rev. bibl. **Document type:** *Newsletter, Trade.*
Former titles (until 1984): S W S Network (Print) (0734-399X); (until 1979): Sociologists for Women in Society. Newsletter
Media: Online - full text.
—CCC.
Published by: Sociologists for Women in Society, 10 Chafee Rd, Kingston, RI 02881. TEL 401-874-9510, FAX 401-874-2945, swseo@socwomen.org.

S W S - RUNDSCHAU. *see* SOCIAL SCIENCES: COMPREHENSIVE WORKS

384.5 DEU
SAECHSISCHE LANDESANSTALT FUER PRIVATEN RUNDFUNK UND NEUE MEDIEN. SCHRIFTENREIHE. Variant title: Schriftenreihe der S L M. Text in German. 1995. irreg., latest vol.20, 2010. price varies. **Document type:** *Monographic series, Academic/Scholarly.*
Published by: (Saechsische Landesanstalt fuer Privaten Rundfunk und Neue Medien), Vistas Verlag GmbH, Goltzstr 11, Berlin, 10781, Germany. TEL 49-30-32707446, FAX 49-30-32707455, medienverlag@vistas.de.

302.2 USA
SAGE SERIES IN INTERPERSONAL COMMUNICATION. Text in English. 1983. irreg., latest vol.14, 1993. price varies. back issues avail.; reprints avail. **Document type:** *Monographic series, Academic/ Scholarly.*
Published by: Sage Publications, Inc., Books (Subsidiary of: Sage Publications, Inc.), 2455 Teller Rd, Thousand Oaks, CA 91320. TEL 800-818-7243, FAX 800-583-2665, books.claim@sagepub.com. Pub. Sara Miller McCune.

301 USA
SAGE STUDIES IN INTERNATIONAL SOCIOLOGY. Text in English. 1976. irreg., latest 2009. price varies. bibl.; charts; stat. back issues avail.; reprints avail. **Document type:** *Monographic series, Academic/ Scholarly.*
Published by: (International Sociological Association ESP), Sage Publications, Inc., Books (Subsidiary of: Sage Publications, Inc.), 2455 Teller Rd, Thousand Oaks, CA 91320. TEL 800-818-7243, FAX 800-583-2665, books.claim@sagepub.com. Pub. Sara Miller McCune. **Subscr. in Asia to:** Sage Publications India Pvt. Ltd.; **Subscr. in Europe to:** Sage Publications Ltd.

301 USA ISSN 0093-2582
AS30
SAINT CROIX REVIEW. Text in English. 1968. bi-m. USD 35 (effective 2010). bk.rev. charts; illus. back issues avail.; reprints avail. **Document type:** *Journal, Academic/Scholarly.* **Description:** Social criticism of controversial subjects, from a traditional point of view.
Formerly (until 1974): Religion and Society (0034-396X)
Related titles: Microform ed.: (from PQC); Online - full text ed.: USD 25 (effective 2010).
Indexed: A21, A22, CERDIC, RASB, RI-1, RI-2, SCOPUS.
—Ingenta.
Published by: Religion and Society Inc., PO Box 244, Stillwater, MN 55082. TEL 651-439-7190, 800-537-1750, FAX 651-439-7017.

301 RUS
➤ **SAMARSKII GOSUDARSTVENNYI UNIVERSITET. VESTNIK. GUMANITARNAYA SERIYA. SOTSIOLOGIYA I SOTSIAL'NAYA RABOTA.** Text in Russian. 1996. bi-m. **Document type:** *Journal, Academic/Scholarly.*
Published by: (Samarskii Gosudarstvennyi Universitet), Izdatel'stvo Samarskii Universitet/Publishing House of Samara State University, ul Akademika Pavlova 1, k 209, Samara, 443011, Russian Federation. TEL 7-846-3345406, FAX 7-846-3345406, university-press@ssu.samara.ru, http://publisher.samsu.ru. Ed. G P Yarovoi.

305.89455 NOR ISSN 0809-6090
SAMI INSTITUHTTA. UTREDNING. Text in Norwegian, Swedish. 2005. irreg., latest 2007. price varies. **Document type:** *Monographic series, Academic/Scholarly.*
Published by: Sami Allaskuvla/Saami University College, Hannoluohkka 45, Guovdageaidnu, 9520, Norway. TEL 47-78-448400, FAX 47-78-448402, postmottak@samiskhs.no.

SAMISKE SAMLINGER. *see* ANTHROPOLOGY

SANKT-PETERBURGSKII UNIVERSITET. VESTNIK. SERIYA 12. PSIKHOLOGIYA, SOTSIOLOGIYA, PEDAGOGIKA. *see* PSYCHOLOGY

302.23 LKA
SANNIVEDANA. Text in English, Singhalese. a. LKR 3.50.
Published by: University of Sri Lanka, Vidyalankara Campus, Department of Mass Communications, Kelaniya, Sri Lanka.

▼ **SAUDE & TRANSFORMACAO SOCIAL.** *see* PUBLIC HEALTH AND SAFETY

LE SAUVEUR. *see* RELIGIONS AND THEOLOGY

302.23 700 AUS ISSN 1449-1818
N72.S6
➤ **SCAN (SYDNEY)**; journal of media arts culture. Text in English. 2004. 3/yr. free (effective 2011). back issues avail. **Document type:** *Journal, Academic/Scholarly.* **Description:** Provides informaion on media studies, cultural studies, media law, information and technology studies, fine arts and philosophy.
Media: Online - full text.
Indexed: A39, C27, C29, D03, D04, E13, R14, S14, S15, S18.
Published by: Macquarie University, Media Department, 8th Fl, W6A, Sydney, NSW 2109, Australia. TEL 61-2-98508786, FAX 61-2-98506776, media@scmp.mq.edu.au, http://www.media.mq.edu.au.

➤ **SCANDINAVIAN JOURNAL OF DISABILITY RESEARCH.** *see* HANDICAPPED

301 DNK ISSN 1904-4631
SCENARIO (DANISH). Text in Danish. 1974. bi-m. DKK 1,995, EUR 270 (effective 2010). back issues avail. **Document type:** *Monographic series, Academic/Scholarly.*
Former titles (until 2010): Fremtidsorientering (0901-7488); (until 1986): Orientering om Fremtidsforskning (0105-2012); (until 1975): Instituttet for Fremtidsforskning. Orientering (0105-2004)
Related titles: ◆ English ed.: Scenario (English). ISSN 1904-4658.
Published by: Instituttet for Fremtidsforskning/Copenhagen Institute for Futures Studies, Noerre Farimagsgade 65, Copenhagen K, 1364, Denmark. TEL 45-33-117176, FAX 45-33-327766, iff@iff.dk, http://www.cifs.dk. Ed. Morten Groenborg.

301 DNK ISSN 1904-4658
SCENARIO (ENGLISH). Text in English. 2005. bi-m. back issues avail. **Document type:** *Magazine, Academic/Scholarly.*
Formerly (until 2010): F O/Futureorientation (1901-452X)
Related titles: Online - full text ed.: ISSN 1904-464X; ◆ Danish ed.: Scenario (Danish). ISSN 1904-4631.
Published by: Instituttet for Fremtidsforskning/Copenhagen Institute for Futures Studies, Noerre Farimagsgade 65, Copenhagen K, 1364, Denmark. TEL 45-33-117176, FAX 45-33-327766, iff@iff.dk, http://www.cifs.dk, http://www.iff.dk. Ed. Morten Groenborg.

SCHMOLLERS JAHRBUCH; Zeitschrift fuer Wirtschafts- und Sozialwissenschaften. *see* BUSINESS AND ECONOMICS

302.23 DEU ISSN 0941-3723
SCHRIFTEN ZUR MEDIENPAEDAGOGIK. Text in German. 1990. irreg., latest vol.44, 2011. price varies. **Document type:** *Monographic series, Academic/Scholarly.*
Published by: (Gesellschaft fuer Medienpaedagogik und Kommunikationskultur), KoPaed Verlag, Pfaelzer-Wald-Str 64, Munich, 81539, Germany. TEL 49-89-68890098, FAX 49-89-6891912, info@kopaed.de.

302.23 DEU ISSN 1616-9336
SCHRIFTEN ZUR MEDIENWISSENSCHAFT. Text in German. 2001. irreg., latest vol.22, 2009. price varies. **Document type:** *Monographic series, Academic/Scholarly.*
Published by: Verlag Dr. Kovac, Leverkusenstr 13, Hamburg, 22761, Germany. TEL 49-40-3988800, FAX 49-40-39888055, info@verlagdrkovac.de.

301 DEU ISSN 0170-592X
SCHRIFTEN ZUR MITTELSTANDSFORSCHUNG. Text in German. 1962; N.S. 1984. irreg., latest vol.107, 2005. price varies. **Document type:** *Monographic series, Academic/Scholarly.*
Formerly (until 1971): Abhandlungen zur Mittelstandsforschung (0567-5014)
Published by: Institut fuer Mittelstandsforschung, Maximilianstr 20, Bonn, 53111, Germany. TEL 49-228-729970, FAX 49-228-7299734, post@ifm-bonn.org, http://www.ifm-bonn.org.

303.3 DEU ISSN 1613-1479
SCHRIFTEN ZUR SOZIALISATIONSFORSCHUNG. Text in German. 2004. irreg., latest vol.5, 2009. price varies. **Document type:** *Monographic series, Academic/Scholarly.*
Published by: Verlag Dr. Kovac, Leverkusenstr 13, Hamburg, 22761, Germany. TEL 49-40-3988800, FAX 49-40-39888055, info@verlagdrkovac.de.

302.23 DEU ISSN 1612-6734
SCHRIFTENREIHE DER A M L. Text in German. 2002. irreg., latest vol.2, 2003. price varies. **Document type:** *Monographic series, Academic/ Scholarly.*
Published by: (Arbeitsgemeinschaft der Mitteldeutschen Landesmedienanstalten), Vistas Verlag GmbH, Goltzstr 11, Berlin, 10781, Germany. TEL 49-30-32707446, FAX 49-30-32707455, medienverlag@vistas.de.

384.5 DEU ISSN 0947-4536
SCHRIFTENREIHE DER LANDESMEDIENANSTALTEN. Text in German. 1990. irreg., latest vol.45, 2010. price varies. **Document type:** *Monographic series, Academic/Scholarly.*
Published by: (Arbeitsgemeinschaft der Landesmedienanstalten), Vistas Verlag GmbH, Goltzstr 11, Berlin, 10781, Germany. TEL 49-30-32707446, FAX 49-30-32707455, medienverlag@vistas.de.

301 CHE ISSN 0379-3664
HM5
SCHWEIZERISCHE ZEITSCHRIFT FUER SOZIOLOGIE/REVUE SUISSE DE SOCIOLOGIE/SWISS JOURNAL OF SOCIOLOGY. Text and summaries in English, French, German. 1975. 3/yr. CHF 105, EUR 70 to individuals; CHF 125, EUR 84 to institutions (effective 2005). adv. bk.rev. charts; bibl. Index. **Document type:** *Journal, Academic/Scholarly.*
Indexed: A22, CA, CIS, DIP, FR, I13, IBR, IBSS, IBZ, P30, P42, PSA, RASB, S02, S03, SOPODA, SSA, SociolAb, T02, W09.
—BLDSC (7953.394000), IE, Infotrieve, Ingenta, INIST.
Published by: (Swiss Sociological Association), Seismo Verlag, Zaehringerstr 26, Zuerich, 8001, Switzerland. TEL 41-1-2611094, FAX 41-1-2511194. Ed. Beat Fux. Adv. contact Peter Rusterholz. Circ: 900.

302.2 USA ISSN 1075-5470
Q223 CODEN: SCICEQ
➤ **SCIENCE COMMUNICATION.** Text in English. 1979. q. USD 836, GBP 492 combined subscription to institutions (print & online eds.); USD 819, GBP 482 to institutions (effective 2011). adv. bk.rev. abstr. back issues avail.; reprint service avail. from PSC. **Document type:** *Journal, Academic/Scholarly.* **Description:** Provides an interdisciplinary forum for critical and analytical articles addressing communication issues among scientists, scientific content in the mass media, and ethical issues related to the communication of science.
Formerly (until 1994): Knowledge (0164-0259)
Related titles: Online - full text ed.: ISSN 1552-8545. USD 752, GBP 443 to institutions (effective 2011).
Indexed: A01, A03, A08, A20, A22, A34, A35, A36, ASCA, AgBio, B07, BibInd, CA, CABA, CMCI, CMM, CommAb, CurCont, E01, E03, E12, ERI, EnvAb, F08, F12, FR, FamI, FutSurv, GH, H04, H14, H16, IndVet, LT, N02, N03, P02, P04, P10, P26, P30, P32, P34, P37, P40, P42, P48, P53, P54, PAIS, PQC, PSA, PerIslam, R12, RRTA, S02, S03, S13, S16, SCOPUS, SOPODA, SPAA, SSA, SSCI, SociolAb, T02, TAR, V02, VS, W07, W11.
—BLDSC (8141.807000), IE, Infotrieve, Ingenta. **CCC.**
Published by: Sage Publications, Inc., 2455 Teller Rd, Thousand Oaks, CA 91320. TEL 805-499-9774, 800-818-7243, FAX 805-499-0871, 800-583-2665, info@sagepub.com. Ed. Susanna Hornig Priest. Circ: 300 (paid). **Subscr. outside the Americas to:** Sage Publications Ltd., 1 Oliver's Yard, 55 City Rd, London EC1Y 1SP, United Kingdom. TEL 44-20-73248701, FAX 44-20-73248733, subscription@sagepub.co.uk.

➤ **SCIENCE IN SOCIETY SERIES.** *see* SCIENCES: COMPREHENSIVE WORKS

302 ITA ISSN 1826-4662
SCIENZE DEL PENSIERO E DEL COMPORTAMENTO. Text in Italian. 2003. 3/yr. **Document type:** *Newsletter, Trade.*
Formerly (until 2005): Newsletteravios (1824-3509)
Media: Online - full text.
Published by: Agenzia per la Valorizzazione dell'Individuo nelle Organizzazioni di Servizio (A V I O S), Via Ennio Gragnani 6, Ciampino, Rome 00043, Italy.

SCREEN DECADES. *see* MOTION PICTURES

301 GBR
HM1001
SELF, AGENCY AND SOCIETY; a journal of applied sociology. Text in English. 1996. s-a. GBP 25 to individuals; GBP 40 to institutions. **Document type:** *Journal, Academic/Scholarly.*
Formerly (until 1997): Self and Agency (1355-2619)
Indexed: SWR&A, SociolAb.
—Ingenta. **CCC.**
Published by: University of Derby, Kedleton Rd, Derby, DE22 1GB, United Kingdom. TEL 44-1332-622222, FAX 44-1332-294861. Eds. David Chalcraft, Stephen Webb.

306 RUS
SEM'YA. Text in Russian. w. USD 145 in United States.
Related titles: Microfiche ed.: (from EVP).
Address: Ul Lesnaya 43, Moscow, 101508, Russian Federation. TEL 7-095-9785847. Ed. S A Abramov. Circ: 93,000. **Dist. by:** East View Information Services, 10601 Wayzata Blvd, Minneapolis, MN 55305. TEL 952-252-1201, 800-477-1005, FAX 952-252-1202, info@eastview.com, http://www.eastview.com.

305.4 NOR ISSN 1504-324X
SENIOR. Text in Norwegian. 2004. bi-m. NOK 290 membership (effective 2006). **Document type:** *Magazine, Consumer.*
Supersedes in part (2003-2004): Seniormagasinet (1503-6529)
Related titles: Online - full text ed.
Published by: Seniorsaken, Holbergsgate 19, Oslo, 0166, Norway. TEL 47-22-364300, info@seniorsaken.no.

305.260993 NZL ISSN 1177-4711
SENIOR STYLE. Text in English. 2006. m. **Document type:** *Magazine, Consumer.* **Description:** Focuses on lifestyle news, views and information for the over 50's.
Published by: Sun Media Ltd., 428 Devonport Rd, Tauranga, New Zealand. TEL 64-7-5780030, FAX 64-7-5711116.

302 FRA ISSN 2108-5722
▼ **LE SENS DU SPORT.** Text in French. 2010. irreg. **Document type:** *Magazine, Consumer.*
Published by: (Agence pour l'Education par le Sport), Actes Sud Junior, 18, Rue Seguier, Paris, 75006, France. TEL 33-1-55426312, FAX 33-1-55420219, http://www.actes-sud-junior.fr/index.php.

301 BOL
SERIE INVESTIGACIONES SOCIALES. Text in Spanish. 1998. irreg., latest vol.3, 2000. **Document type:** *Monographic series.*
Published by: Neftali Lorenzo E Caraspas, Calle 28 B No 52, Cota Cota, Casiilla 1367, La Paz, Bolivia. TEL 591-2-792642, salflo@mail.megalink.com. Adv. contact Salvador Romero.

301 ESP ISSN 2172-3338
SERIE REVERSOS DEL LEVIATAN. Text in Spanish. 2006. irreg. **Document type:** *Monographic series, Academic/Scholarly.*
Published by: Libros de la Catarata, Fuencarral, 70, Madrid, 28004, Spain. TEL 34-91-5320504, FAX 34-91-5324334, http://www.catarata.org/.

307 USA ISSN 0744-2807
SERTOMAN. Text in English. bi-m. illus. **Document type:** *Bulletin.*
Address: 1912 E Meyer Blvd, Kansas City, MO 64132-1174. Ed. Arthur Bisson. Circ: 28,000.

301 320 AUS ISSN 1838-0743
▼ ➤ **SETTLER COLONIAL STUDIES.** Text in English. 2011. a. free (effective 2011). bk.rev. Index. back issues avail. **Document type:** *Journal, Academic/Scholarly.* **Description:** Publishes original articles, review articles, and proposals for thematic issues on historically-oriented research and analyses covering contemporary issues. Aims to present multidisciplinary and interdisciplinary research, involving areas like history, law, genocide studies, indigenous, colonial and postcolonial studies, anthropology, historical geography, economics, politics, sociology, international relations, political science, literary criticism, cultural and gender studies and philosophy.
Media: Online - full text.

Published by: Swinburne University of Technology, Institute for Social Research, H53 PO Box 218, Hawthorn, VIC 3122, Australia. http://www.sisr.net/. Eds., R&Ps Edward Cavanagh, Lorenzo Veracini.

➤ SEX ROLES; a journal of research. see PSYCHOLOGY

301.4 ESP ISSN 1698-5540
SEXOLOGIA INTEGRAL. Text in Spanish. 2004. q. back issues avail. **Document type:** *Journal, Academic/Scholarly.*
Published by: Spanish Publishers Associates, Edif. Vertice C Antonio Lopez, 249 1o-4o, Madrid, 28041, Spain. TEL 34-91-5002077, FAX 34-91-5002075.

301.4 CUB ISSN 1025-6512
SEXOLOGIA Y SOCIEDAD. Text in Spanish. 1994. q. back issues avail.
Related titles: Online - full text ed.: ISSN 1682-0045. 1999.
Published by: Centro Nacional de Educacion Sexual, Calle 10 No. 460 Esq. 21, Vedado Plaza, Havana, Cuba. TEL 53-78-552528, FAX 53-78-553868, cenesex@infomed.sld.cu. Ed. Aloyma Ravelo Garcia. Circ: 6,000.

301.4 ESP ISSN 0214-042X
SEXPOL; revista de informacion sexologica. Text in Spanish. 1982. bi-m. back issues avail. **Document type:** *Magazine, Consumer.*
Related titles: Online - full text ed.
Published by: Sociedad Sexologica de Madrid, C. Fuencarral, 18 3a. izq., Madrid, 28004, Spain. TEL 34-91-5313459, sexpol@ctv.es.

301 COL ISSN 1909-4337
SEXTANTE; testimonios de ciudad. Text in Spanish. 2006. a. **Document type:** *Magazine, Consumer.*
Published by: Fundacion Universitaria Luis Amigo, Transversal 51 A, Medellin, 67B 90, Colombia. TEL 57-4-4487666, FAX 57-4-3849797, http://www.funlam.edu.com. Eds. Ana Maria Cadavid, Ana Milena Giraldo.

SEXUAL ABUSE; a journal of research and treatment. see PSYCHOLOGY

305.3 USA
SEXUAL CULTURES. Text in English. 1999. irreg., latest 2009. price varies. back issues avail. **Document type:** *Monographic series, Academic/Scholarly.* **Description:** Promotes scholarship about the lived experiences of sexual minorities. Covers manuscripts from a variety of academic disciplines on a wide range of academic and nonacademic subjects.
Published by: New York University Press, 838 Broadway, 3rd Fl, New York, NY 10003. TEL 212-998-2575, 800-996-6987, FAX 212-995-3833, information@nyupress.org. Eds. Ann Pellegrini, Jose Esteban Munoz.

SEXUAL HEALTH RESEARCH REVIEW. see MEDICAL SCIENCES

306.7 USA
SEXUAL SCIENCE (ONLINE). Text in English. q. free. **Document type:** *Newsletter, Academic/Scholarly.* **Description:** Includes information concerning conferences, meetings, programs, training opportunities, job announcements, fellowships, research assistantships, etc.
Media: Online - full text.
Published by: Society for the Scientific Study of Sexuality, PO Box 416, Allentown, PA 18105. TEL 610-530-2483, FAX 610-530-2485, thesociety@sexscience.org. Ed. Robin C Milhausen.

306.7 306.85 PRT ISSN 0872-7023
SEXUALIDADE E PLANEAMENTO FAMILIAR. Text in Portuguese. 1994. irreg. **Document type:** *Magazine, Consumer.*
Indexed: P30, SCOPUS.
Published by: Associacao para o Planeamento da Familia (A P F), Rua da Artilharia Um 38, 2o Dto, Lisbon, 1200-040, Portugal. TEL 351-21-3853993, FAX 351-21-3887379, http://www.apf.pt.

SEXUALITIES; studies in culture and society. see PSYCHOLOGY

306.7 USA ISSN 1095-5143
HQ32
SEXUALITY & CULTURE. Text in English. 1997. q. EUR 361, USD 496 combined subscription to institutions (print & online eds.) (effective 2012). adv. bk.rev. back issues avail.; reprint service avail. from PSC. **Document type:** *Journal, Academic/Scholarly.* **Description:** Provides a forum for the analysis of ethical, cultural, psychological, social, and political issues related to sexual relationships and sexual behavior.
Related titles: Online - full text ed.: ISSN 1936-4822 (from IngentaConnect).
Indexed: A01, A03, A08, A22, A26, AmHI, CA, E-psyche, E01, E08, FamI, G06, G07, G08, GW, H07, H12, I05, L01, L02, P03, P30, P46, P48, PQC, PsycInfo, PsycholAb, S02, S03, S09, SCOPUS, SSA, SociolAb, T02, W09.
—BLDSC (8254.485180), IE, Ingenta. **CCC.**
Published by: Springer New York LLC (Subsidiary of: Springer Science+Business Media), 233 Spring St, New York, NY 10013. TEL 212-460-1500, FAX 212-460-1575, service-ny@springer.com, http://www.springer.com. Ed. Roberto Refinetti.

SEXUALITY AND LITERATURE. see LITERATURE

SEXUALITY RESEARCH AND SOCIAL POLICY. see MEDICAL SCIENCES

301 JPN ISSN 0288-7126
SHAKAIGAKU NENSHI. Text in Japanese. 1956. a. illus.
Published by: Waseda Daigaku, Shakai Gakkai, c/o Waseda Daigaku Bungakubu, 42 Toyama-cho, Shinjuku-ku, Tokyo, Japan.

301 JPN ISSN 0582-933X
SHAKAIGAKU RONSO/JOURNAL OF SOCIOLOGY. Text in Japanese. 1953. irreg. **Document type:** *Journal, Academic/Scholarly.*
Indexed: ERA, SociolAb.
Published by: Nihon Daigaku, Shakaigakkai, c/o College of Humanities and Sciences, 3-25-40 Sakura-jousui, Setagaya-ku, Tokyo, 156-8550, Japan.

SHAREDEBATE INTERNATIONAL; a ShareWare diskette magazine. see SOCIAL SCIENCES: COMPREHENSIVE WORKS

301 USA
SHARING TIMES. Text in English. m. free. back issues avail. **Description:** Stories about changed lives of men and women in prison.
Published by: Christ Truth Ministries, PO Box 610, Upland, CA 91785. TEL 909-981-2838, FAX 909-981-2839. Ed. Carl F Davis Jr. Circ: 3,500 (controlled).

301 SGP ISSN 1099-4882
HM413
➤ **SHEHUI LILUN XUEBAO/JOURNAL OF SOCIAL THEORY.** Abbreviated title: J S T. Text in Chinese. 1998. s-a. SGD 101, USD 63, EUR 53 to institutions (effective 2012). adv. back issues avail. **Document type:** *Journal, Academic/Scholarly.* **Description:** Discusses social theories, research, philosophies, and promotes international scholarly communications and the advancement of Chinese social theories.
—CCC.
Published by: World Scientific Publishing Co. Pte. Ltd., 5 Toh Tuck Link, Singapore, 596224, Singapore. TEL 65-6466-5775, FAX 65-6467-7667, wspc@wspc.com.sg, http://www.worldscientific.com. Ed. Xie Lizhong. **Dist. by:** World Scientific Publishing Co., Inc., 27 Warren St, Ste 401-402, Hackensack, NJ 07601. TEL 201-487-9655, 800-227-7562, FAX 201-487-9656, 888-977-2665, wspc@wspc.com; World Scientific Publishing Ltd., 57 Shelton St, London WC2H 9HE, United Kingdom. TEL 44-207-8360888, FAX 44-207-8362020, sales@wspc.co.uk. **Co-publisher:** Hong Kong Polytechnic University.

301 CHN ISSN 1001-344X
HM413
SHEHUIXUE/SOCIOLOGY. Text in Chinese. 1980. m. USD 79 (effective 2009). 200 p./no.; **Document type:** *Journal, Academic/Scholarly.* **Description:** Contains reprints of articles on sociology and its branches.
Published by: Zhongguo Renmin Daxue Shubao Ziliao Zhongxin/Renmin University of China, Information Center for Social Sciences, Dongcheng-qu, 3, Zhangzizhong Lu, Beijing, 100007, China. TEL 86-10-64039458, FAX 86-10-64015080, center@zlzx.org, http://www.zlzx.org/. **Dist. in US by:** China Publications Service, PO Box 49614, Chicago, IL 60649. TEL 312-371-1761, FAX 312-288-8570.

301 CHN ISSN 1002-5936
HM7
SHEHUIXUE YANJIU/SOCIOLOGICAL STUDIES. Text in Chinese. 1986. bi-m. USD 40.20 (effective 2009). **Document type:** *Journal, Academic/Scholarly.*
Related titles: Online - full text ed.
Published by: Zhongguo Shehui Kexueyuan, Shehuixue Yanjiusuo/Chinese Academy of Social Sciences, Institute of Sociology, 5, Jianguomennei Dajie, Beijing, 100732, China. TEL 86-10-85195564, FAX 86-10-65133870. **Dist. by:** China International Book Trading Corp, 35 Chegongzhuang Xilu, Haidian District, PO Box 399, Beijing 100044, China. TEL 86-10-68412045, FAX 86-10-68412023, cibtc@mail.cibtc.com.cn, http://www.cibtc.com.cn.

301 DEU
SIEGENER BEITRAEGE ZUR SOZIOLOGIE. Text in German, English. 1998. irreg., latest vol.10, 2010. price varies. **Document type:** *Monographic series, Academic/Scholarly.*
Media: Large Type.
Published by: Ruediger Koeppe Verlag, Wendelinstr 73-75, Cologne, 50933, Germany. TEL 49-221-4911236, FAX 49-221-4994336, info@koeppe.de. Eds. Rainer Geissler, Trutz von Trotha.

302.23 DEU ISSN 1435-795X
SIGNIFIKATION; Beitraege zur Kommunikationswissenschaft. Text in German. 1998. irreg., latest vol.7, 2010. price varies. **Document type:** *Monographic series, Academic/Scholarly.*
Published by: Nodus Publikationen - Klaus D Dutz Wissenschaftlicher Verlag, Lingener Str 7, Muenster, 48155, Germany. TEL 49-251-65514, FAX 49-251-661692, dutz.nodus@t-online.de, http://elverdissen.dyndns.org/~nodus/nodus.htm#adr.

SIGNS OF THE TIMES. see RELIGIONS AND THEOLOGY

301 DEU ISSN 1616-2552
SIMMEL STUDIES. Text in German, English. 1991. 2/yr. EUR 26 to individuals; EUR 36 to institutions (effective 2009). **Document type:** *Journal, Academic/Scholarly.*
Formerly (until 1999): Simmel Newsletter (0939-2327)
Indexed: CA, S02, S03, SCOPUS, SSA, SociolAb, T02.
Published by: Georg-Simmel-Gesellschaft e.V., Fakultaet fuer Soziologie, Postfach 100131, Bielefeld, 33501, Germany. TEL 49-521-1064608, FAX 49-522-2029, info@simmel-gesellschaft.de.

306 MEX ISSN 1562-384X
AP63
➤ **SINCRONIA**; revista electronica de estudios culturales. Text in Spanish. 1996. q. **Document type:** *Academic/Scholarly.*
Media: Online - full text.
Indexed: AmHI, MLA-IB.
Published by: Universidad de Guadalajara, Centro Universitario de Ciencias Sociales y Humanidades, Depto de Letras, Centro Universitario de Ciencias Sociales y Humanidades, Universidad de Guadalajara, Jalisco, JAL 44210, Mexico. TEL 52-3-8237631, FAX 52-3-8237631, sgilbert@udgserv.cencar.udg.mx, http://fuentes.csh.udg.mx/CUCSH/Sincronia/index.html. Ed. Stephen W Gilbert.

➤ **SLAVERY AND ABOLITION**; a journal of slave and post-slave studies. see HISTORY

301 CZE ISSN 0037-6833
DD491.S4
➤ **SLEZSKY SBORNIK/ACTA SILESIACA**; ctvertletnik pro vedy o spolecnosti. Text in Czech; Text occasionally in German, Polish; Summaries in English, German. 1878. q. EUR 112 in Europe; USD 135 elsewhere (effective 2009). bk.rev. illus.; maps. cum.index: 1878-1952, 1953-1962. **Document type:** *Journal, Academic/Scholarly.* **Description:** Devoted to social science research in the Czech Republic and Silesia, Czech-Polish relations, and the nationality problem in the Czech Republic.
Formerly (until 1935): Matice Opavska. Vestnik
Indexed: BibLing, CA, HistAb, P30, RASB, SociolAb, T02.
Published by: Slezske Zemske Muzeum, Slezsky Ustav, Nadrazni okruh 31, Opava, 74648, Czech Republic. TEL 42-553-625576, FAX 42-553-622999, machacova@szmo.cz. Ed., R&P Rudolf Zacek TEL 42-653-625344. Circ: 1,050. **Dist. in Western countries by:** Kubon & Sagner Buchexport - Import GmbH, Hessstr 39-41, Munich 80798, Germany. TEL 49-89-542180, FAX 49-89-54218218, postmaster@kubon-sagner.de, http://www.kubon-sagner.de.

➤ **SLOVANSKE STUDIE.** see HISTORY—History Of Europe

➤ **SLOVANSKY PREHLED/SLAVIC SURVEY.** see POLITICAL SCIENCE

➤ **SMALL GROUP RESEARCH**; an international journal of theory, investigation and application. see PSYCHOLOGY

➤ **SOCCER AND SOCIETY.** see SPORTS AND GAMES—Ball Games

301 IRL ISSN 2009-3144
▼ **SOCHEOLAS**; Limerick student journal of sociology. Text in English. 2009. s-a. back issues avail. **Document type:** *Journal, Academic/Scholarly.* **Description:** Topics include the ongoing relevance of Marxist theory; critical evaluations of the welfare state; institutional racism in Irish society.
Related titles: Online - full text ed.
Published by: University of Limerick, Department of Sociology, c/o Anne McCarthy, National Technological Park, Limerick, Ireland. TEL 353-61-202445, anne.mccarthy@ul.ie. Ed. Cliona Barnes.

SOCIAAL - ECONOMISCH BELEID. see POLITICAL SCIENCE

301 AUS ISSN 0155-0306
HN841
➤ **SOCIAL ALTERNATIVES.** Text in English. 1977. q. AUD 40 domestic to individuals; AUD 80 foreign to individuals; AUD 60 domestic to institutions; AUD 100 foreign to institutions (effective 2009). adv. bk.rev.; film rev. back issues avail. **Document type:** *Journal, Academic/Scholarly.* **Description:** Covers a range of concerns relating to social, political, economic and cultural issues.
Related titles: Online - full text ed.
Indexed: A01, A02, A03, A08, A20, AEI, APW, ASCA, AltPI, AusPAIS, CA, G10, HRIR, IBT&D, L01, L02, M01, M02, MLA-IB, P10, P27, P34, P42, P46, P48, P54, PCI, PQC, PSA, PerIslam, RASB, S02, S03, SCOPUS, SOPODA, SSA, SociolAb, T02, W09, WBA, WMB.
—BLDSC (8318.041300), IE, Ingenta. **CCC.**
Address: c/o School of Education, University Of Queensland, Brisbane, QLD 4072, Australia. barbara@socialalternatives.com. Circ: 1,000 (paid).

➤ **SOCIAL ANALYSIS**; international journal of social and cultural practice. see ANTHROPOLOGY

340.115 GBR ISSN 0964-6639
K23 CODEN: SLSTEK
➤ **SOCIAL & LEGAL STUDIES**; an international journal. Text in English. 1992. q. USD 923, GBP 499 combined subscription to institutions (print & online eds.); USD 905, GBP 489 to institutions (effective 2011). adv. bk.rev. back issues avail.; reprint service avail. from PSC. **Document type:** *Journal, Academic/Scholarly.* **Description:** Leading international forum for the latest research in critical legal studies from a variety of perspectives within social theory.
Related titles: Online - full text ed.: ISSN 1461-7390. USD 831, GBP 449 to institutions (effective 2011).
Indexed: A01, A03, A08, A20, A22, A26, AC&P, ASCA, B07, CA, CJA, CJPI, CLI, CurCont, DIP, E01, ELJI, ERA, ESPM, FamI, G08, H04, I05, IBR, IBSS, IBZ, L10, LJI, LRI, M12, P02, P10, P30, P34, P42, P48, P53, P54, PAIS, PQC, PSA, RiskAb, S02, S03, S11, S20, S21, SCOPUS, SOPODA, SPAA, SSA, SSCI, SociolAb, T02, V&AA, V02, W07, W09.
—BLDSC (8318.053530), IE, Infotrieve, Ingenta. **CCC.**
Published by: Sage Publications Ltd. (Subsidiary of: Sage Publications, Inc.), 1 Oliver's Yard, 55 City Rd, London, EC1Y 1SP, United Kingdom. TEL 44-20-73248500, FAX 44-20-73248600, info@sagepub.co.uk, http://www.uk.sagepub.com/home.nav. adv.: B&W page GBP 400; 130 x 205. **Subscr. in the Americas to:** Sage Publications, Inc., 2455 Teller Rd, Thousand Oaks, CA 91320. TEL 805-499-9774, FAX 805-499-0871, journals@sagepub.com.

301 330 MYS ISSN 1675-7017
SOCIAL AND MANAGEMENT RESEARCH JOURNAL. Text in English. 2003. s-a. **Document type:** *Journal, Academic/Scholarly.*
Related titles: Online - full text ed.
Published by: M A R A University of Technology, Research Management Institute/Universiti Teknologi M A R A, Institut Pengurusan Penyelidikan, Shah Alam, Selangor 40450, Malaysia. TEL 60-3-55442095, FAX 60-3-55442096.

SOCIAL BEHAVIOR AND PERSONALITY; an international journal. see PSYCHOLOGY

303.4 IND ISSN 0049-0857
HN681
➤ **SOCIAL CHANGE.** Text in English. 1971. q. USD 295, GBP 159 combined subscription to institutions (print & online eds.); USD 289, GBP 156 to institutions (effective 2011). adv. bk.rev. bibl.; stat.; abstr.; charts. 150 p./no. 1 cols./p.; back issues avail.; reprint service avail. from PSC. **Document type:** *Journal, Academic/Scholarly.* **Description:** Promotes the studies and undertaking of social development, including national and regional policies, planning processes, social and economic interaction in national growth, studies, research and survey techniques.
Related titles: Online - full text ed.: ISSN 0976-3538. USD 266, GBP 143 to institutions (effective 2011).
Indexed: A22, BAS, E01, F09, P30, PAA&I, PSA, SociolAb.
—BLDSC (8318.070500), Ingenta.
Published by: (Council for Social Development/Sangha Rachana), Sage Publications India Pvt. Ltd. (Subsidiary of: Sage Publications, Inc.), M-32 Market, Greater Kailash-I, PO Box 4215, New Delhi, 110 048, India. TEL 91-11-6444958, FAX 91-11-6472426, sage@vsnl.com, http://www.indiasage.com/. Eds. Prashant Kumar Trivedi, Manoranjan Mohanty. adv.: page INR 1,000; 18 x 11. Circ: 1,200 (paid). **Subscr. to:** I N S I O Scientific Books & Periodicals.

201.6 GBR ISSN 0037-7686
BL60
➤ **SOCIAL COMPASS**; international review of sociology of religion. (Includes: Proceedings of the International Society for the Sociology of Religion) Text in English, French. 1953. q. USD 614, GBP 332 combined subscription to institutions (print & online eds.); USD 602, GBP 325 to institutions (effective 2011). adv. bk.rev. bibl.; charts; stat.; illus. index, cum.index: 1953-1973. back issues avail.; reprint service avail. from PSC. **Document type:** *Journal, Academic/Scholarly.* **Description:** Forum for all scholars in sociology, anthropology, religious studies and theology concerned with the sociology of religion. Individual issues focus on a particular topic in current social scientific research on religion in society.
Related titles: Online - full text ed.: ISSN 1461-7404. USD 553, GBP 299 to institutions (effective 2011).

S

Indexed: A01, A03, A08, A20, A21, A22, ASCA, ArtHuCI, B07, BAS, BibInd, CA, CERDIC, CJA, CJPI, CMM, CommAb, CurCont, DIP, E01, EI, FR, FamI, H04, I13, I14, IBR, IBSS, IBZ, IBibSS, L10, MEA&I, MLA-IB, P02, P10, P34, P42, P48, P53, P54, PCI, PQC, PSA, PerIslam, R&TA, RASB, RI-1, RI-2, S02, S03, S11, SCOPUS, SOPODA, SSA, SSCI, SociolAb, T02, V02, W07.
—BLDSC (8318.075000), IE, Infotrieve, Ingenta, INIST. **CCC.**
Published by: Sage Publications Ltd. (Subsidiary of: Sage Publications, Inc.), 1 Oliver's Yard, 55 City Rd, London, EC1Y 1SP, United Kingdom. TEL 44-20-73248500, FAX 44-20-73248600, info@sagepub.co.uk, http://www.uk.sagepub.com/home.nav. Ed. Celine Polain. adv.: B&W page GBP 400; 130 x 205. **Subscr. in the Americas to:** Sage Publications, Inc., 2455 Teller Rd, Thousand Oaks, CA 91320. TEL 805-499-9774, FAX 805-499-0871, journals@sagepub.com.

301 USA ISSN 1055-145X
JC336
THE SOCIAL CONTRACT. Abbreviated title: T S C. Text in English. 1990. q. USD 7.50 per issue (effective 2010). back issues avail. **Document type:** *Journal, Consumer.* **Description:** Covers issues in immigration, preservation and promotion of a shared American language and culture, and other related issues.
Related titles: Online - full text ed.: free (effective 2010).
Published by: Social Contract Press, 445 E Mitchell St, Petoskey, MI 49770. TEL 231-347-1171, 800-352-4843, FAX 231-347-1185. Ed. Wayne Lutton. Pub. Dr. John H Tanton.

301 GBR ISSN 0961-205X
HQ767.8
➤ **SOCIAL DEVELOPMENT.** Text in English. 1992. q. GBP 709 in United Kingdom to institutions; EUR 899 in Europe to institutions; USD 1,066 in the Americas to institutions; USD 1,497 elsewhere to institutions; GBP 816 combined subscription in United Kingdom to institutions (print & online eds.); EUR 1,035 combined subscription in Europe to institutions (print & online eds.); USD 1,226 combined subscription in the Americas to institutions (print & online eds.); USD 1,722 combined subscription elsewhere to institutions (print & online eds.) (effective 2012). adv. bk.rev. back issues avail.; reprint service avail. from PSC. **Document type:** *Journal, Academic/Scholarly.* **Description:** Publishes reports, debates, and commentary on theoretical and empirical issues in social development, emphasizing psychological processes in human development to adulthood.
Related titles: Online - full text ed.: ISSN 1467-9507. GBP 709 in United Kingdom to institutions; EUR 899 in Europe to institutions; USD 1,066 in the Americas to institutions; USD 1,497 elsewhere to institutions (effective 2012) (from IngentaConnect).
Indexed: A01, A03, A08, A20, A22, A26, ASCA, ASSIA, C28, CA, CDA, CMM, CurCont, E-psyche, E01, ERIC, ESPM, FamI, L&LBA, P03, P10, P27, P30, P43, P48, P53, P54, PQC, PsycInfo, PsycholAb, RiskAb, S02, S03, S11, SCOPUS, SSA, SSCI, SociolAb, T02, V&AA, W07.
—BLDSC (8318.079100), IE, Infotrieve, Ingenta. **CCC.**
Published by: Wiley-Blackwell Publishing Ltd. (Subsidiary of: John Wiley & Sons, Inc.), 9600 Garsington Rd, Oxford, OX4 2DQ, United Kingdom. TEL 44-1865-776868, FAX 44-1865-714591, customerservices@blackwellpublishing.com. Eds. Christine Howe, Elizabeth A Lemerise, Robert Coplan. Adv. contact Craig Pickett TEL 44-1865-476267. B&W page GBP 445, B&W page USD 823; 140 x 220. Circ: 365.

301 AUT ISSN 0251-6845
SOCIAL DEVELOPMENT NEWSLETTER. Text in English. 1971. s-a. free. **Document type:** *Newsletter.*
Related titles: Spanish ed.: Boletin Informativo sobre Desarrollo Social. ISSN 1014-8183; French ed.: Bulletin du Developpement Social. ISSN 0255-948X.
Indexed: HRIR.
Published by: United Nations Centre for Social Development and Humanitarian Affairs, Social Development Division, Vienna International Centre, Vienna, W 1400, Austria. TEL 26 310. Circ: 6,000.

SOCIAL ENTERPRISE. *see* BUSINESS AND ECONOMICS

361.765 GBR ISSN 1750-8614
SOCIAL ENTERPRISE JOURNAL. Abbreviated title: S E J. Text in English. 2005. 3/yr. EUR 349 combined subscription in Europe (print & online eds.); USD 509 combined subscription in the Americas (print & online eds.); GBP 259 combined subscription in the UK & elsewhere (print & online eds.); AUD 669 combined subscription in Australasia (print & online eds.) (effective 2012). back issues avail.; reprint service avail. from PSC. **Document type:** *Journal, Academic/Scholarly.* **Description:** Covers both rigorous research papers and shorter case study submissions that address key aspects. Issues of importance, which can be addressed at a global, national and/or individual social enterprise level.
Related titles: Online - full text ed.: ISSN 1750-8533 (from IngentaConnect); Supplement(s): Trail Blazers.
Indexed: A12, A17, ABIn, P27, P41, P46, P48, P51, P53, P54, PQC.
—BLDSC (8318.087430), IE. **CCC.**
Published by: (Social Enterprise Research Group), Emerald Group Publishing Ltd., Howard House, Wagon Ln, Bingley, W Yorks BD16 1WA, United Kingdom. TEL 44-1274-777700, FAX 44-1274-785201, information@emeraldinsight.com, http://www.emeraldinsight.com. Ed. Bob Doherty. Pub. Andrew Smith.

306.09 RUS ISSN 1681-4363
HM626
➤ **SOCIAL EVOLUTION & HISTORY.** Text in English. 2002. s-a. RUR 500 domestic to individuals; RUR 600 domestic to institutions; USD 30 foreign to individuals; USD 40 foreign to institutions (effective 2011). adv. bk.rev. abstr.; bibl.; charts. back issues avail. **Document type:** *Journal, Academic/Scholarly.* **Description:** Devoted to the study of many aspects of the evolutionary changes in human history. Aims to meet the needs of those social scientists who study the development of human societies and to contribute to the integration of anthropology, history and sociology.
Related titles: Online - full content ed.
Indexed: AnthLit.
—East View, IE.
Published by: Izdatel'skii Dom Uchitel', ul Kirova 143, Volgograd, 400079, Russian Federation. TEL 7-8442-420408, FAX 7-8442-421771, redaktor@uchitel-izd.ru, http://www.uchitel-izd.ru. Ed. Dmitrii Bondarenko. Pub. Leonid Grinin. adv.: B&W page USD 100. Circ: 100 (paid); 400 (controlled).

305.26 DNK ISSN 1903-7759
SOCIAL FOKUS, AELDRE. Text in Danish. 2003. s-a. free. **Document type:** *Magazine, Government.*
Supersedes in part (in 2009): Social Fokus (1902-8571); Which was formerly (until vol.4 2007): Styrelsen for Specialraadgivning og Social Service (1902-150X); (until 2007): Social Service (1603-5607)
Related titles: Online - full text ed.: ISSN 1903-7767.
Published by: Servicestyrelsen/National Board of Social Services, Edisonsvej 18, Odense C, 5000, Denmark. TEL 45-72-423700, FAX 45-72-423709, servicestyrelsen@servicestyrelsen.dk.

301 USA ISSN 0037-7732
CODEN: SOFOAP
➤ **SOCIAL FORCES.** Text in English. 1922. q. USD 79.50 domestic to individuals includes OCED Countries; USD 53 foreign to individuals includes Non-OCED countries; USD 318 domestic to institutions; USD 388 foreign to institutions includes Non-OCED countries; USD 265 to institutions includes Non-OECD countries (effective 2009). bk.rev. bibl.; illus.; abstr. cum.index: 1922-1972. back issues avail.; reprint service avail. from PSC,WSH. **Document type:** *Journal, Academic/Scholarly.* **Description:** Content highlights sociological inquiry, but also explores social psychology, anthropology, political science, history, and economics.
Formerly (until 1925): The Journal of Social Forces (1532-1282)
Related titles: Microform ed.: (from MIM, PMC, PQC); Online - full text ed.: ISSN 1534-7605. free (effective 2009).
Indexed: A01, A02, A03, A08, A20, A21, A22, A25, A26, ABCPolSci, ABS&EES, AC&P, AMHA, ASCA, ASG, AbAn, AcaI, AmH&L, B01, B04, B06, B07, B09, B14, BAS, BRD, BRI, C28, CA, CBRI, CIS, CJA, CLFP, ChPerI, Chicano, CommAb, CurCont, DIP, E-psyche, E01, E02, E03, E06, E07, E08, E15, EAA, EI, ERA, ERI, ERIC, EdA, EdI, F09, FR, FamI, G05, G06, G07, G08, H09, H10, HPNRM, HRA, HistAb, I05, I07, I13, IBR, IBSS, IBZ, L01, L02, L09, M01, M05, M06, M10, M12, MEA&I, MLA-IB, P02, P03, P06, P07, P10, P13, P18, P25, P27, P30, P34, P42, P43, P45, P46, P47, P48, P53, P54, PCI, PQC, PRA, PSA, PopulInd, PsycholAb, R05, RASB, RI-1, RI-2, RILM, S02, S03, S05, S08, S09, S11, S19, S20, S21, S23, SCOPUS, SFSA, SOPODA, SPAA, SRRA, SSA, SSAI, SSAb, SSCI, SSI, SSciA, SUSA, SWR&A, SociolAb, T02, V&AA, W03, W05, W07, W09.
—BLDSC (8318.089000), IE, Infotrieve, Ingenta, INIST. **CCC.**
Published by: (The Citadel, Department of Sociology), University of North Carolina Press, Hamilton Hall CB 3210, Department of Socilogy, Chapel Hill, NC 27599. uncpress@unc.edu, http://www.uncpress.unc.edu. Ed. Francois Nielson. Circ: 3,000 (paid and controlled). **Co-sponsor:** Southern Sociological Society.

301 DNK ISSN 0908-0031
H62.5.D4
SOCIAL FORSKNING. TEMA-NUMMER. Text in Danish. 1991. a. price varies. **Document type:** *Monographic series, Government.*
Related titles: Online - full text ed.; ◆ Special ed. of: Social Forskning. ISSN 0903-7535.
Published by: Det Nationale Forskningscenter for Velfaerd/The Danish National Centre for Social Research, Herluf Trolles Gade 11, Copenhagen K, 1052, Denmark. TEL 45-33-480800, FAX 45-33-480833, sfi@sfi.dk. Ed. Ove Karlsson. Circ: 1,000.

SOCIAL HISTORY OF AFRICA SERIES. *see* HISTORY—History Of Africa

THE SOCIAL HISTORY OF ALCOHOL AND DRUGS. *see* DRUG ABUSE AND ALCOHOLISM

301 USA
SOCIAL INDICATORS. Text in English. 1977. bi-m. looseleaf. USD 5. adv. bk.rev.
Indexed: E-psyche.
Published by: American Institutes for Research, Social Indicators Research Program, 1791 Arastradero Rd, Box 1113, Palo Alto, CA 94302. TEL 415-493-3550. Eds. Kevin J Gilmartin, Robert J Rossi. Circ: 300.

361.6105 GBR ISSN 1751-2395
HN28
SOCIAL ISSUES AND POLICY REVIEW. Text in English. 2007 (Dec.). a. USD 764 in the Americas to institutions (print or online ed.); GBP 587 in United Kingdom to institutions (print or online ed.); EUR 746 in Europe to institutions (print or online ed.); USD 1,151 elsewhere to institutions (print or online ed.); USD 840 combined subscription in the Americas to institutions (print & online eds.); GBP 647 combined subscription in United Kingdom to institutions (print & online eds.); EUR 822 combined subscription in Europe to institutions (print & online eds.); USD 1,267 combined subscription elsewhere to institutions (print & online eds.) (effective 2010). adv. reprint service avail. from PSC. **Document type:** *Journal, Academic/Scholarly.* **Description:** Provides state of the art and timely theoretical and empirical reviews of topics and programs of research that are directly relevant to understanding and addressing social issues and public policy.
Related titles: Online - full text ed.: ISSN 1751-2409.
Indexed: A22, E01, H05, P30, S02, S03, SCOPUS, SSA, SociolAb, T02.
—BLDSC (8318.116990), IE. **CCC.**
Published by: Wiley-Blackwell Publishing Ltd. (Subsidiary of: John Wiley & Sons, Inc.), 9600 Garsington Rd, Oxford, OX4 2DQ, United Kingdom. TEL 44-1865-776868, FAX 44-1865-714591, customer@wiley.co.uk, http://www.wiley.com/WileyCDA/. Eds. John Dovidio, Victoria Esses. Adv. contact Kristin McCarthy. B&W page USD 400; trim 6 x 9.

301 SGP
SOCIAL ISSUES IN SOUTHEAST ASIA. Text in English. 1985. irreg., latest vol.26, 2003. price varies. back issues avail. **Document type:** *Monographic series, Academic/Scholarly.* **Description:** Publishes studies on the nature and dynamics of ethnicity, religions, urbanism, and population change in Southeast Asia.
Related titles: Online - full content ed.
Published by: Institute of Southeast Asian Studies, 30 Heng Mui Keng Terrace, Pasir Panjang, Singapore, 119614, Singapore. TEL 65-6870-2447, FAX 65-6775-6259, pubsunit@iseas.edu.sg, http://www.iseas.edu.sg/. Ed., R&P Mrs. Triena Ong TEL 65-6870-2449.

301 USA ISSN 1558-8912
HM671
SOCIAL JUSTICE IN CONTEXT. Text in English. 2005. a., latest 2007. back issues avail. **Document type:** *Journal, Academic/Scholarly.*
Related titles: Online - full text ed.: free (effective 2011).
Indexed: A39, C27, C29, D03, D04, E13, R14, S14, S15, S18.
Published by: East Carolina University, College of Human Ecology. Carolyn Freeze Baynes Institute for Social Justice, E Fifth St, Greenville, NC 27858. TEL 252-328-6131, http://www.ecu.edu/cs-acad/ugcat0708/HumanEcology2.cfm.

301 USA ISSN 0885-7466
JC578 CODEN: SJREEO
➤ **SOCIAL JUSTICE RESEARCH.** Text in English. 1986. q. EUR 881, USD 926 combined subscription to institutions (print & online eds.) (effective 2012). adv. bk.rev. illus. Index. back issues avail.; reprint service avail. from PSC. **Document type:** *Journal, Academic/Scholarly.* **Description:** Features original papers that have broad implications for social scientists investigating the origins, structures, and consequences of justice in human affairs.
Related titles: Microfilm ed.: (from PQC); Online - full text ed.: ISSN 1573-6725 (from IngentaConnect).
Indexed: A01, A03, A08, A20, A22, A26, B04, BAS, BRD, BibLing, CA, CJA, CJPI, CurCont, DIP, E-psyche, E01, FamI, IBR, IBSS, IBZ, P03, P10, P30, P34, P42, P46, P48, PQC, PSA, PsycInfo, PsycholAb, S02, S03, SCOPUS, SOPODA, SSA, SSAI, SSAb, SSCI, SSI, SociolAb, T02, W03, W05, W07.
—BLDSC (8318.121500), IE, Infotrieve, Ingenta. **CCC.**
Published by: (International Society for Justice Research), Springer New York LLC (Subsidiary of: Springer Science+Business Media), 233 Spring St, New York, NY 10013. TEL 212-460-1500, FAX 212-460-1575, service-ny@springer.com. Ed. Curtis D Hardin.

➤ **SOCIAL JUSTICE REVIEW**; pioneer American journal of Catholic social action. *see* RELIGIONS AND THEOLOGY—Roman Catholic

➤ **SOCIAL MEDICINE.** *see* MEDICAL SCIENCES

➤ **SOCIAL NEUROSCIENCE.** *see* MEDICAL SCIENCES—Psychiatry And Neurology

303.4 KEN
SOCIAL PERSPECTIVES. Text in English. irreg. charts; stat. **Document type:** *Government.*
Published by: Ministry of Finance and Planning, Central Bureau of Statistics, PO Box 30266, Nairobi, Kenya.

100 NLD
SOCIAL PHILOSOPHY. Text in English. irreg. price varies. **Document type:** *Monographic series, Academic/Scholarly.* **Description:** Explores theoretical and applied issues in contemporary social philosophy.
Related titles: ◆ Series of: Value Inquiry Book Series. ISSN 0929-8436.
Published by: Editions Rodopi B.V., Tijnmuiden 7, Amsterdam, 1046 AK, Netherlands. TEL 31-20-6114821, FAX 31-20-4472979, info@rodopi.nl. Ed. Andrew Fitz-Gibbon. **Dist. by:** Rodopi - USA, 606 Newark Ave, 2nd fl, Kenilworth, NJ 07033. TEL 908-497-9031, FAX 908-497-9035.

301 GBR ISSN 1474-7464
HN1
➤ **SOCIAL POLICY AND SOCIETY.** Text in English. 2002. q. GBP 288, USD 485 to institutions; GBP 299, USD 520 combined subscription to institutions (print & online eds.) (effective 2009). adv. back issues avail.; reprint service avail. from PSC. **Document type:** *Journal, Academic/Scholarly.* **Description:** Offers discussion of contemporary social policy issues to a wider audience and provides a valuable teaching and research resource to the worldwide social and public policy community.
Related titles: Online - full text ed.: ISSN 1475-3073. GBP 262, USD 447 to institutions (effective 2009).
Indexed: A22, ASSIA, E01, ESPM, I13, IBSS, P27, P46, P48, P54, PQC, SSciA, SociolAb.
—BLDSC (8318.132140), IE, Infotrieve, Ingenta. **CCC.**
Published by: (Social Policy Association), Cambridge University Press, The Edinburgh Bldg, Shaftesbury Rd, Cambridge, CB2 8RU, United Kingdom. TEL 44-1223-312393, FAX 44-1223-315052, journals@cambridge.org, http://www.cambridge.org/uk. Eds. Peter Dwyer, Sharon Wright. Adv. contact Rebecca Roberts TEL 44-1223-325083. B&W page GBP 425, B&W page USD 805, color page GBP 925, color page USD 1,755. Circ: 1,000. **Subscr. to:** Cambridge University Press, 32 Ave of the Americas, New York, NY 10013. TEL 212-337-5000, FAX 212-691-3239, journals_subscriptions@cup.org.

➤ **SOCIAL POLICY JOURNAL OF NEW ZEALAND**; te puna whakaaro. *see* POLITICAL SCIENCE

301 AUS ISSN 1833-4369
➤ **SOCIAL POLICY RESEARCH PAPER.** Text in English. irreg. free (effective 2008). **Document type:** *Monographic series, Academic/Scholarly.* **Description:** Aims to disseminate information, data and analysis that stem from major research projects and evaluations related to social policy.
Former titles (until 2006): Australia. Department of Family and Community Services. Policy Research Paper (1442-7532); (until 1999): Australia. Department of Social Security. Social Policy Division. Policy Research Paper; Policy Discussion Series; Technical Series
Published by: Australia. Department of Families, Community Services and Indigenous Affairs, GPO Box 7788, Canberra Mail Centre, ACT 2610, Australia. TEL 61-2-62445458, 300-653-227, FAX 61-2-62446589, enquiries@fahcsia.gov.au, http://www.facs.gov.au/internet/facsinternet.nsf.

➤ **SOCIAL, POLITICAL & LEGAL PHILOSOPHY.** *see* PHILOSOPHY

➤ **SOCIAL POLITICS**; international studies in gender, state, and society. *see* WOMEN'S STUDIES

301 USA ISSN 0037-7791
HN1 CODEN: SOPRAG
➤ **SOCIAL PROBLEMS.** Abbreviated title: S P. Text in English. 1953. q. USD 256 combined subscription to institutions (print & online eds.) (effective 2012). adv. bk.rev. bibl.; charts; illus. cum.index: vols.1-17, 1952-1970; vols.18-28, 1970-1981. 160 p./no.; back issues avail.; reprint service avail. from PSC,WSH. **Document type:** *Journal, Academic/Scholarly.* **Description:** Covers areas such as conflict, social action, and change, crime and juvenile delinquency, drinking and drugs, mental health etc.
Related titles: Microform ed.: (from PQC); Online - full text ed.: ISSN 1533-8533. USD 216 to institutions (effective 2012).

Indexed: A01, A02, A03, A08, A12, A20, A22, A25, A26, ABIn, ABS&EES, AC&P, APC, ASCA, Acal, AddicA, AmH&L, B04, BAS, BRD, C28, CA, CJA, CJPI, CMM, ChPerI, Chicano, CommAb, CurCont, DIP, E-psyche, E01, E07, E08, F09, FR, FamI, FutSurv, G05, G06, G07, G08, G10, H09, H10, H11, H12, HRA, HistAb, I05, I13, IBR, IBSS, IBZ, IPARL, M01, M02, MEA&I, P02, P03, P06, P07, P10, P13, P19, P25, P27, P30, P34, P42, P45, P46, P48, P50, P51, P53, P54, PAA&I, PAIS, PCI, PQC, PRA, PSA, PsycInfo, PsycholAb, R05, RASB, RI-1, RI-2, S02, S03, S05, S08, S09, S11, S21, SCOPUS, SFSA, SOPODA, SRRA, SSA, SSAI, SSAb, SSCI, SSI, SUSA, SWR&A, SociolAb, T02, W03, W07, W09.
—BLDSC (8318.136000), IE, Infotrieve, Ingenta, INIST. **CCC.**
Published by: (Society for the Study of Social Problems, Inc.), University of California Press, Journals Division, 2000 Ctr St, Ste 303, Berkeley, CA 94704. TEL 510-643-7154, 877-262-4226, FAX 510-642-9917, customerservice@ucpressjournals.com. Ed. Ted Chiricos. Adv. contact Jennifer Rogers TEL 510-642-6188. Circ: 3,046. **Subscr. to:** 149 5th Ave, 8th Fl, New York, NY 10010. participation@jstor.org.

301 USA ISSN 0737-6871
HN933 CODEN: SPHAF5
SOCIAL PROCESS IN HAWAII. Text in English. 1935. irreg., latest vol.41, 2002. price varies. bk.rev. back issues avail. **Document type:** *Monographic series, Academic/Scholarly.* **Description:** Disseminates to scholars, students, and the community, the results of social science research on the people and institutions of Hawaii.
Formerly (until 1979): Social Process
Related titles: Online - full text ed.
Indexed: CA, MLA-IB, P42, PSA, S02, S03, SCOPUS, SOPODA, SociolAb, T02.
Published by: University of Hawaii Press, 2840 Kolowalu St, Honolulu, HI 96822. TEL 808-956-8255, 888-UHPRESS, FAX 808-988-6052, 800-650-7811, uhpbooks@hawaii.edu, http://www.uhpress.hawaii.edu.

SOCIAL PSYCHOLOGICAL APPLICATIONS TO SOCIAL ISSUES. *see* PSYCHOLOGY

SOCIAL PSYCHOLOGY. *see* PSYCHOLOGY

302 USA ISSN 0190-2725
HM1
➤ **SOCIAL PSYCHOLOGY QUARTERLY.** Text in English. 1937. q. USD 255, GBP 150 combined subscription to institutions (print & online eds.); USD 250, GBP 147 to institutions (effective 2011). adv. bibl.; illus. index. back issues avail.; reprint service avail. from PSC. **Document type:** *Journal, Academic/Scholarly.* **Description:** Publishes papers pertaining to the processes and products of social interaction. Includes the study of the primary relations of individuals to one another or to groups, collectives, or institutions, and the study of intra-individual processes insofar as they substantially influence, or are influenced by, social forces.
Former titles (until 1979): Social Psychology (0147-829X); (until 1978): Sociometry (0038-0431)
Related titles: Microform ed.: (from MIM, PQC); Online - full text ed.: ISSN 1939-8999. USD 229, GBP 135 to institutions (effective 2011).
Indexed: A01, A02, A03, A08, A20, A22, A26, ABS&EES, AMHA, ASCA, ASSIA, B04, BRD, CA, CIS, CMM, Chicano, CommAb, CurCont, DIP, E-psyche, E01, E07, E08, EAA, ESPM, FR, FamI, G08, H09, H10, I05, I13, IBR, IBSS, IBZ, M01, M02, MEA&I, MLA, MLA-IB, P02, P03, P06, P07, P10, P13, P24, P25, P26, P27, P30, P42, P46, P48, P53, P54, PCI, PQC, PRA, PSA, PsycInfo, PsycholAb, RASB, RiskAb, S02, S03, S05, S09, S11, S21, SCOPUS, SOPODA, SSA, SSAI, SSAb, SSCI, SSI, SociolAb, T02, W03, W07, W09.
—BLDSC (8318.146300), IE, Infotrieve, Ingenta, INIST. **CCC.**
Published by: (American Sociological Association), Sage Publications, Inc., 2455 Teller Rd, Thousand Oaks, CA 91320. TEL 805-499-9774, FAX 805-499-0871, info@sagepub.com, http://www.sagepub.com/. Ed. Gary Alan Fine TEL 847-491-3495. adv.: page USD 350. Circ: 2,300.

➤ **SOCIAL QUESTIONS BULLETIN.** *see* RELIGIONS AND THEOLOGY—Protestant

306.0993 NZL ISSN 1175-9917
HN930.5.A85
SOCIAL REPORT/PURONGO ORANGA TANGATA. Text in English. 2001. a. **Document type:** *Government.*
Related titles: Online - full text ed.: ISSN 1177-8695.
Published by: Ministry of Social Development, PO Box 1556, Wellington, New Zealand. TEL 64-4-9163300, FAX 64-4-9180099, information@msd.govt.nz, http://www.msd.govt.nz.

306.0993 NZL ISSN 1177-1615
SOCIAL REPORT. REGIONAL INDICATORS. Text in English. 2005. a. **Document type:** *Government.* **Description:** Provide a picture of wellbeing and the quality of life in New Zealand. The regional indicators report is published in conjunction with the social report, and uses similar data at a regional and local level to show how outcomes vary across the country. It is intended to support regional and local councils with decision making.
Published by: Ministry of Social Development, PO Box 1556, Wellington, New Zealand. TEL 64-4-9163300, FAX 64-4-9180099, information@msd.govt.nz, http://www.msd.govt.nz.

301 GBR ISSN 1747-1117
➤ **SOCIAL RESPONSIBILITY JOURNAL.** Text in English. 2004. q. EUR 379 combined subscription in Europe (print & online eds.); USD 539 combined subscription in the Americas (print & online eds.); GBP 269 combined subscription in the UK & elsewhere (print & online eds.); AUD 599 combined subscription in Australasia (print & online eds.) (effective 2012). reprint service avail. from PSC. **Document type:** *Journal, Academic/Scholarly.* **Description:** Publishes theoretical and empirical papers, speculative essays and review articles.
Related titles: Online - full text ed.: (from IngentaConnect).
Indexed: IBSS, PAIS.
—BLDSC (8318.152050), IE. **CCC.**
Published by: (Social Resonsibility Research Network), Emerald Group Publishing Ltd., Howard House, Wagon Ln, Bingley, W Yorks BD16 1WA, United Kingdom. TEL 44-1274-777700, FAX 44-1274-785201, information@emeraldinsight.com. Ed. David Crowther. Pub. Adam Smith.

301 IND ISSN 0975-9751
▼ **SOCIAL SCANNER.** Text in English. 2009. a. **Document type:** *Magazine, Consumer.*
Published by: Akansha Publishing House, 4649-B-21, Ansari Rd, Darya Ganj, New Delhi, 110 002, India. TEL 91-9435116718, 91-11-23263193, ektabooks@yahoo.com, http://www.akanshapublishinghouse.com.

SOCIAL SCIENCE INFORMATION/INFORMATION SUR LES SCIENCES SOCIALES; information sur les sciences sociales. *see* SOCIAL SCIENCES: COMPREHENSIVE WORKS

306 LUX ISSN 1681-1658
HN380.5
THE SOCIAL SITUATION IN THE EUROPEAN UNION. Text in English. 1999. a. **Document type:** *Trade.* **Description:** Covers the quality of life of people living in Europe and provides a view of the population and its social conditions as a background to social policy development.
Related titles: German ed.: Beschreibung der Sozialen Lage in Europa. ISSN 1681-164X; French ed.: La Situation Sociale dans l'Union Europeenne. ISSN 1681-1666.
—BLDSC (8318.206530).
Published by: (European Commission, Statistical Office of the European Communities (E U R O S T A T), European Commission, Employment and Social Affairs BEL), European Commission, Office for Official Publications of the European Union, 2 Rue Mercier, Luxembourg, L-2985, Luxembourg. TEL 352-29291, FAX 352-29291, info@publications.europa.eu, http://publications.europa.eu.

302 CHE ISSN 1424-0467
➤ **SOCIAL STRATEGIES;** monographs on sociology and social policy - Monographien zur Soziologie und Gesellschaftspolitik. Text in English, French, German. 1975. irreg., latest vol.45, 2010. price varies. adv. bk.rev. **Document type:** *Monographic series, Academic/Scholarly.* **Description:** Deals with fundamental sociological questions and socio-political problems closely related to social reality.
Published by: Peter Lang AG (Subsidiary of: Peter Lang Publishing Group), Hochfeldstr 32, Postfach 746, Bern 9, 3000, Switzerland. TEL 41-31-3061717, FAX 41-31-3061727, info@peterlang.com, http://www.peterlang.com. Eds. Hector Schmassmann, Uli Maeder. Circ: 2,000.

➤ **SOCIAL STUDIES OF SCIENCE;** an international review of research in the social dimensions of science and technology. *see* SCIENCES: COMPREHENSIVE WORKS

301 USA ISSN 1933-5415
H62.A1
➤ **SOCIAL SUDIES RESEARCH AND PRACTICE.** Text in English. 2006. 3/yr. free (effective 2011). back issues avail. **Document type:** *Journal, Academic/Scholarly.* **Description:** Covers social studies research and practice manuscripts, lesson plans, reviews, and issues related to higher-level learning outcomes.
Media: Online - full text.
Indexed: A39, C27, C29, CA, D03, D04, E03, E13, R14, S14, S15, S18, T02.
Published by: University of Alabama, PO Box 870342, Tuscaloosa, AL 35487. TEL 205-348-7467, 877-925-2323, FAX 205-348-7473, hrsvctr@ua.edu, http://www.ua.edu. Ed. Janet Smith Strickland.

301 USA ISSN 0164-2472
HN1
SOCIAL TEXT. Text in English. 1979. q. USD 33 to individuals; USD 234 to institutions; USD 246 combined subscription to institutions (print & online eds.); USD 59 per issue to institutions (effective 2012). adv. illus. back issues avail.; reprint service avail. from PSC. **Document type:** *Journal, Academic/Scholarly.* **Description:** Covers a spectrum of social and cultural phenomena, applying the interpretive methods to the world at large. Focuses attention on questions of gender, sexuality, race, and the environment, publishing key works by the influential social and cultural theorists.
Related titles: Online - full text ed.: ISSN 1527-1951. 2000. USD 205 to institutions (effective 2012).
Indexed: A01, A02, A03, A08, A22, ABS&EES, AltPI, AmHI, B04, BRD, CA, E01, FR, G10, H07, H08, HAb, HumInd, L06, LeftInd, MLA-IB, P34, P42, PCI, PSA, RI-1, RI-2, RILM, S02, S03, SCOPUS, SOPODA, SSA, SociolAb, T02, W03.
—BLDSC (8318.217700), IE, Infotrieve, Ingenta, INIST. **CCC.**
Published by: (Center for Cultural Analysis), Duke University Press, 905 W Main St, Ste 18 B, Durham, NC 27701. TEL 919-688-5134, 888-651-0122, FAX 919-688-2615, 888-651-0124, subscriptions@dukeupress.edu, http://www.dukeupress.edu. Eds. Anna McCarthy, Brent Edwards.

362 GBR ISSN 1477-8211
RA441
➤ **SOCIAL THEORY & HEALTH.** Abbreviated title: S T H. Text in English. 2003. q. USD 895 in North America to institutions; GBP 481 elsewhere to institutions (effective 2011). adv. back issues avail.; reprint service avail. from PSC. **Document type:** *Journal, Academic/Scholarly.* **Description:** Aims to develop the theoretical underpinnings of health research and service delivery.
Related titles: Online - full text ed.: ISSN 1477-822X (from IngentaConnect).
Indexed: A22, CA, CurCont, E01, H05, H13, IBR, IBSS, IBZ, P02, P03, P10, P20, P21, P46, P48, P50, P52, P53, P54, P56, PAIS, PQC, PsycInfo, PsycholAb, S02, S03, S11, S21, SCOPUS, SSCI, SociolAb, T02, W07.
—BLDSC (8318.217790), IE, Ingenta. **CCC.**
Published by: Palgrave Macmillan Ltd. (Subsidiary of: Macmillan Publishers Ltd.), Houndmills, Basingstoke, Hants RG21 6XS, United Kingdom. TEL 44-1256-329242, FAX 44-1256-479476, orders@palgrave.com, http://www.palgrave.com. Pub. Neil Henderson TEL 44-1256-302959 ext 3116. Circ: 250. **Subscr. to:** Subscription Department, Brunel Rd, Houndmills, Basingstoke, Hants RG21 2XS, United Kingdom. TEL 44-1256-357893, FAX 44-1256-328339, subscriptions@palgrave.com.

301.07 USA ISSN 1094-5830
HM1
➤ **SOCIAL THOUGHT AND RESEARCH.** Text in English. 1964. s-a. USD 30 to individuals; USD 50 to institutions (effective 2010). bk.rev. illus. reprints avail. **Document type:** *Journal, Academic/Scholarly.* **Description:** Covers socialogical thought and research related information.
Former titles (until 1997): Mid-American Review of Sociology (0732-913X); (until 1976): The Kansas Journal of Sociology (0022-8648)
Related titles: Microform ed.: (from PQC).
Indexed: A20, A22, CA, FR, L&LBA, P27, P30, P46, P48, P54, PQC, PsycholAb, S02, S03, SCOPUS, SOPODA, SSA, SociolAb, T02.
—BLDSC (8318.218500), IE, Ingenta, INIST.
Published by: University of Kansas, Department of Sociology, Fraser Hall, 1415 Jayhawk Blvd, Rm 716, Lawrence, KS 66045. TEL 785-864-9410, FAX 785-864-5280, starjrnl@raven.cc.ku.edu, http://www.sociology.ku.edu/.

301 NLD ISSN 1871-2673
HN751
SOCIAL TRANSFORMATIONS IN CHINESE SOCIETIES. Text in English. 2006. a. price varies. **Document type:** *Monographic series, Academic/Scholarly.* **Description:** Covers the theoretical, methodological, or substantive issues of sociological significance about or related to social transformations in Chinese societies.
Indexed: IZBG.
—BLDSC (8318.219000).
Published by: (Hong Kong Sociological Association HKG), Brill, PO Box 9000, Leiden, 2300 PA, Netherlands. TEL 31-71-5353500, FAX 31-71-5317532, cs@brill.nl. Eds. Kwok-bun Chan, Tak-sing Cheung, Agnes S Ku.

301 IRL
SOCIALARBEIT IN EUROPA/EUROPEAN INTERESTS. Text in English, German. irreg.
Media: Online - full text.
Published by: European Social Organisational and Science Consultancy, Jasnaja Poljana, Clonmoyle, Aghabullogue, Co. Cork, Ireland. TEL 353-21-7334833, FAX 353-21-7334826, esosc@esosc.org, http://www.esosc.org. Eds. Christoph Kusche, Peter Herrmann.

303 NLD ISSN 1872-5252
SOCIALE COHESIE IN NEDERLAND. Variant title: N W O Reeks Sociale Cohesie. Text in Dutch. 2002. irreg. price varies.
Published by: (Nederlandse Organisatie voor Wetenschappelijk Onderzoek/Netherlands Organization for Scientific Research), Uitgeverij Aksant, Cruquiusweg 31, Amsterdam, Netherlands. TEL 31-20-8500150, FAX 31-20-6656411, info@aksant.nl, http://www.aksant.nl. Ed. Karien Stronks.

301 NLD ISSN 0926-3977
HV4
SOCIALE INTERVENTIE. Text in Dutch. 1972. q. **Document type:** *Academic/Scholarly.*
Former titles (until 1992): T V A (0921-5271); (until 1986): Tijdschrift voor Agologie (0168-8626)
Related titles: Online - full text ed.: ISSN 1875-7251.
Indexed: A22.
—IE, Infotrieve.
Published by: Boom Lemma Uitgeverij, Postbus 85576, The Hague, 2508 CG, Netherlands. TEL 31-70-3307033, FAX 31-70-3307030, infodesk@lemma.nl, http://www.lemma.nl. Ed. Sabrina Keinemans. Circ: 1,200.

301 DEU ISSN 1435-6651
SOCIALIA; Studienreihe Soziologische Forschungsergebnisse. Text in German. 1997. irreg., latest vol.105, 2009. price varies. **Document type:** *Monographic series, Academic/Scholarly.*
Published by: Verlag Dr. Kovac, Leverkusenstr 13, Hamburg, 22761, Germany. TEL 49-40-3988800, FAX 49-40-39888055, info@verlagdrkovac.de.

306.43 SVN ISSN 1408-2942
SOCIALNA PEDAGOGIKA. Text in Multiple languages. 1997. q.
Indexed: SCOPUS, SSA, SociolAb.
Published by: Zdruzenje za Socialno Pedagogiko/Association for Social Pedagogy, Kardeljeva pl. 16, Ljubljana, 1000, Slovenia. FAX 386-1-1892233, zssp@uni-lj.si. Eds. Alenka Kobolt, Bojan Dekleva.

301 CZE ISSN 1214-813X
➤ **SOCIALNI STUDIA.** Text in Czech; Summaries in Multiple languages. 1957. q. CZK 250; CZK 75 per issue (effective 2009). adv. bk.rev. **Document type:** *Journal, Academic/Scholarly.* **Description:** Contains articles about sociology and social work.
Former titles (until 2004): Brnenskw Univerzity. Sbornik Praci Fakulty Socialnich Studii. Socialni Studia (1212-365X); (until 1998): Masarykova Univerzita. Filozoficka Fakulta. Sbornik Praci. G: Rada Socialnevedna. Socialni Studia (1211-6815); (until 1996): Univerzita J.E. Purkyne. Filozoficka Fakulta. Sbornik Praci. G: Rada Socialnevedna (0231-5122)
Indexed: CA, RASB, S02, S03, SCOPUS, SOPODA, SSA, SociolAb, T02.
Published by: Masarykova Univerzita, Fakulta Socialnich Studii, Jostova 10, Brno, 602 00, Czech Republic. TEL 420-549-491911, FAX 420-549-491920, info@fss.muni.cz, http://www.fss.muni.cz. adv.: page USD 500.

344.03 DNK ISSN 1398-4403
SOCIALREFORMEN. Text in Danish. 1998. a. DKK 898 per issue (effective 2009). **Document type:** *Trade.*
Formed by the merger of (1993-1998): Bistandsloven og alle dens Regler (0909-5837); (1993-1998): Bistandsloven og alle dens Regler. Supplementsbind (1395-1483)
Related titles: Supplement(s): Socialreformen 1-2 og Aktivlovene. Supplementsbind. ISSN 1901-6700. 2006. DKK 260 per issue (effective 2009).
Published by: Dafolo A/S, Suderbovej 24, Frederikshavn, 9900, Denmark. TEL 45-96-206666, FAX 45-98-429711, mi@dafolo.dk, http://www.dafolo-online.dk.

301 USA ISSN 1542-6300
H62.A1
➤ **SOCIATION TODAY.** Text in English. 2003. irreg., latest vol.7, no.2, 2009. free (effective 2011). **Document type:** *Journal, Academic/Scholarly.*
Media: Online - full text.
Indexed: A39, C27, C29, CA, D03, D04, E13, R14, S02, S03, S14, S15, S18, SociolAb, T02.
Published by: North Carolina Sociological Association, c/o Cathy Zimmer, CB 3355, 22 Manning Hall, University of North Carolina-Chapel Hill, Chapel Hill, NC 27599. ncsa@list.appstate.edu. Ed. George H Conklin.

301 CHL ISSN 0717-3512
SOCIEDAD HOY. Text in Spanish. 1997. s-a. **Document type:** *Journal, Academic/Scholarly.*

S

Published by: Universidad de Concepcion, Departamento de Sociologia y Antropologia, Ciudad Universitaria s-n, Concepcion, 1047, Chile. TEL 56-41-2204760, FAX 56-41-2215860. Ed. Manuel Antonio Baeza.

301 URY ISSN 0081-0649
SOCIEDAD URUGUAYA. Text in Spanish. irreg.
Published by: Editorial Arca, Colonia, 1263, Montevideo, 11107, Uruguay.

330 301 CHL ISSN 0717-991X
SOCIEDAD & CONOCIMIENTO. Text in Spanish. 1991. 3/yr. **Document type:** *Journal, Academic/Scholarly.*
Formerly (until 2002): Universidad y Sociedad (0716-9213)
Published by: Universidad Central de Chile, Toesca 1783, Santiago, Chile. TEL 56-2-5826000, http://www.ucentral.cl.

301 ESP ISSN 1133-6706
SOCIEDAD Y UTOPIA; revista de ciencias politicas y sociales. Text in Spanish. 1993. s-a. **Document type:** *Journal, Academic/Scholarly.*
Published by: Universidad Pontificia de Salamanca, Facultad de Ciencias Politicas y Sociologia "Leon XIII" Fundacion Pablo VI, Paseo Juan XXIII, 3, Madrid, 28040, Spain. TEL 34-91-5141707, FAX 34-91-5535249.

301 BRA ISSN 0102-6992
HN281 CODEN: SOESE2
SOCIEDADE E ESTADO. Text in Portuguese. 1986. s-a. **Document type:** *Journal, Academic/Scholarly.*
Related titles: Online - full text ed.: free (effective 2011).
Indexed: A35, AgBio, C01, CA, CABA, E12, F08, F11, F12, FR, G11, GH, LT, N02, P42, PSA, R12, RRTA, S02, S03, S13, S16, SCOPUS, SOPODA, SSA, SociolAb, T02, T05, TAR, W11.
—INIST.
Published by: Editora Universidade de Brasilia, SCS, Quadra 2, Bloco C, No 78Edificio OK, Brasilia, DF 70302-907, Brazil. contato@editora.unb.br, http://www.editora.unb.br. Ed. Lourdes Maria Bandeira.

301 PRT ISSN 0873-6308
SOCIEDADE E TERRITORIO. Text in Portuguese. 1984. irreg., latest 2004. price varies.
Indexed: AIAP.
Published by: Edicoes Afrontamento, Lda., Rua de Costa Cabral, 859, Porto, 4200-225, Portugal. TEL 351-22-5074220, FAX 351-22-5074229, editorial@edicoesafrontamento.pt, http://www.edicoesafrontamento.pt. Ed. Antonio Fonseca Ferreira.

301 ITA ISSN 1591-2094
LE SOCIETA. Text in Italian. 1981. m. EUR 215 combined subscription (effective 2008). adv. **Document type:** *Magazine, Consumer.*
Related titles: CD-ROM ed.: ISSN 1591-2108. 1987; Online - full text ed.
Indexed: DoGi.
Published by: IPSOA Editore (Subsidiary of: Wolters Kluwer Italia Srl), Strada 1, Palazzo F6, Milanofiori, Assago, MI 20090, Italy. TEL 39-02-82476888, FAX 39-02-82476436, http://www.ipsoa.it. Ed. Francesco Zuzic. Adv. contact Luciano Alcaro Menichini. Circ: 17,840.

301 ITA
SOCIETA, TERRITORIO, AMBIENTE. Text in Italian. 1991. irreg., latest vol.10, 1999. price varies. adv. **Document type:** *Monographic series, Academic/Scholarly.*
Formerly: Societa e Ambiente
Published by: Liguori Editore, Via Posillipo 394, Naples, 80123, Italy. TEL 39-081-7206111, FAX 39-081-7206244, liguori@liguori.it, http://www.liguori.it. Ed. Franco Martinelli.

301 ITA ISSN 2038-3150
▼ **SOCIETAMUTAMENTOPOLITICA.** Text in Multiple languages. 2010. s-a. free (effective 2011). **Document type:** *Journal, Academic/Scholarly.*
Media: Online - full text.
Published by: Firenze University Press, Borgo Albizi 28, Florence, 50122, Italy. TEL 39-055-2743051, FAX 39-055-2743058, info@fupress.com, www.fupress.com/index.asp. Ed. Gianfranco Bettin Lattes.

301 CAN ISSN 0537-6211
SOCIETE SAINT-JEAN-BAPTISTE DE MONTREAL. INFORMATION NATIONALE. Text in English. 1962. m. CAD 5. adv. bk.rev. illus.
Formerly: Societe Saint-Jean-Baptiste de Montreal Bulletin
Published by: Societe de Publication l'Information Nationale Inc., 82 rue Sherbrooke W, Montreal, PQ H2X 1X3, Canada. TEL 514-843-8851. Ed. Pierre Lussier. Circ: 15,000.

301 BEL ISSN 0765-3697
H3
➤ **SOCIETES**; revue des sciences humaines et sociales. Text in French. 1984. q. EUR 120 to individuals; EUR 90 to students (effective 2011). bk.rev. abstr. 128 p./no.; back issues avail. **Document type:** *Journal, Academic/Scholarly.* **Description:** Brings all the necessary information about research, about the different activities published in sociology, and the ways of integrating specialized knowledge in a large reflection.
Related titles: Online - full text ed.: ISSN 1782-155X.
Indexed: A20, ArtHuCI, CA, CurCont, DIP, FR, IBR, IBSS, IBZ, P42, PSA, RILM, S02, S03, SCOPUS, SOPODA, SSA, SociolAb, T02, W07.
—BLDSC (8319.181500), INIST. **CCC.**
Published by: De Boeck Universite (Subsidiary of: Editis), Fond Jean-Paques 4, Louvain-la-Neuve, 1348, Belgium. TEL 32-10-482511, FAX 32-10-482519, info@superieur.deboeck.com.

301 FRA ISSN 1275-4099
SOCIETES AFRICAINES ET DIASPORA. Variant title: Collection Societes Africaines et Diaspora. Text in French. 1996. q. **Document type:** *Journal, Academic/Scholarly.*
Incorporates (1996-2001): Societes Africaines et Diaspora (Paris, 1996) (1271-2418)
Published by: L' Harmattan, 5 Rue de l'Ecole Polytechnique, Paris, 75005, France. TEL 33-1-43257651, FAX 33-1-43258203, http://www.editions-harmattan.fr.

301 FRA ISSN 1150-1944
HM3 CODEN: SOCCEC
SOCIETES CONTEMPORAINES. Text in French. 1990. q. EUR 46 domestic to individuals; EUR 52 foreign to individuals; EUR 50 domestic to institutions; EUR 56 foreign to institutions (effective 2008). **Document type:** *Journal, Academic/Scholarly.*
Related titles: Online - full text ed.: ISSN 1950-6899.
Indexed: CA, FR, IBR, IBSS, IBZ, P42, PSA, S02, S03, SCOPUS, SOPODA, SSA, SociolAb, T02.
—INIST. **CCC.**
Published by: (Institut de Recherche sur les Societes Contemporaines), Presses de Sciences Po, 117 Boulevard Saint Germain, Paris, 75006, France. TEL 33-1-45498331, FAX 33-1-45498334, info@presses.sciences-po.fr, http://www.sciences-po.fr.

301 FRA ISSN 1773-5440
SOCIETES EN CHANGEMENT. Text in French. 2005. irreg. back issues avail. **Document type:** *Monographic series, Consumer.*
Published by: Editions Eres, 33 Av. Marcel Dassault, Toulouse, 31500, France. TEL 33-5-61751576, FAX 33-5-61735289, eres@edition-eres.com, http://www.edition-eres.com.

301 FRA ISSN 1148-5833
SOCIETES EN MOUVEMENT. Text in French. 1989. irreg. price varies. **Document type:** *Monographic series, Academic/Scholarly.*
Published by: Centre National de la Recherche Scientifique, Campus Gerard-Megie, 3 Rue Michel-Ange, Paris, 75794, France. TEL 33-1-44964000, FAX 33-1-44965390, http://www.cnrseditions.fr.

301 FRA ISSN 1953-8375
SOCIETES ET JEUNESSES EN DIFFICULTE. Text in French, English, 2006. s-a. free (effective 2011). **Document type:** *Journal, Academic/Scholarly.*
Media: Online - full text.
Published by: Centre National de Formation et d'Etudes de la Protection Judiciaire de la Jeunesse, 54 Rue de Garches, Vaucresson, 92420, France. TEL 33-1-47959827, FAX 33-1-47959867. Ed. Dominique Youf.

301 CAN ISSN 0381-1794
SOCIETY/SOCIETE. Text in English, French. 1977. 3/yr. CAD 36 domestic to institutional members; USD 36 foreign to institutional members (effective 2005). reprints avail. **Document type:** *Newsletter.* **Description:** Internal publication of official documents of the Society.
Related titles: Online - full text ed.
Indexed: ABS&EES, AnthLit, GSS&RPL, SWR&A.
Published by: Canadian Sociological Association/Societe Canadienne de Sociologie, Concordia University, 1455 de Maisonneuve W/Ouest, Montreal, PQ H3G 1M8, Canada. TEL 514-848-8780, FAX 514-848-4514, info@csaa.ca, http://www.csaa.ca. Ed. Richard Apostle. Circ: 1,600.

178 330 GBR ISSN 1746-5680
➤ **SOCIETY AND BUSINESS REVIEW.** Abbreviated title: S B R. Text in English. 2006. 3/yr. EUR 459 combined subscription in Europe (print & online eds.); USD 619 combined subscription in the Americas (print & online eds.); GBP 319 combined subscription in the UK & elsewhere (print & online eds.); AUD 829 combined subscription in Australasia (print & online eds.) (effective 2012). back issues avail.; reprint service avail. from PSC. **Document type:** *Journal, Academic/Scholarly.* **Description:** Aims to cultivate and share knowledge and ideas in order to assist businesses to enhance their commitment in societies. Seeks to provide a platform for diverse academic and practitioner communities to debate a broad spectrum of social issues and disciplinary perspectives, globally.
Related titles: Online - full text ed.: ISSN 1746-5699 (from IngentaConnect).
Indexed: A12, A17, A22, ABIn, E01, ESPM, P27, P46, P48, P51, P53, P54, PQC, RiskAb.
—BLDSC (8319.187505), IE, Ingenta. **CCC.**
Published by: Emerald Group Publishing Ltd., Howard House, Wagon Ln, Bingley, W Yorks BD16 1WA, United Kingdom. TEL 44-1274-777700, FAX 44-1274-785201, information@emeraldinsight.com. Ed. Dr. Yvon Pesqueux. Pub. Andrew Smith.

960 301 320 USA ISSN 1083-3323
SOCIETY AND POLITICS IN AFRICA. Text in English. 1997. irreg., latest vol.20, 2009. price varies. back issues avail. **Document type:** *Monographic series, Academic/Scholarly.* **Description:** Provides innovative approaches to the study and appreciation of contemporary African society.
Published by: Peter Lang Publishing, Inc. (Subsidiary of: Peter Lang Publishing Group), 29 Broadway, New York, NY 10006. TEL 212-647-7700, 800-770-5264, FAX 212-647-7707, customerservice@plang.com, http://www.peterlangusa.com. Ed. Yakubu Saaka.

301 330 NPL ISSN 1999-3536
➤ **SOCIO-ECONOMIC DEVELOPMENT PANORAMA.** Text in English. 2007. s-a. **Document type:** *Journal, Academic/Scholarly.* **Description:** Examines the trends and issues on social and economic aspects of Nepal.
Related titles: Online - full text ed.
Published by: (Human Action for Rapid Development), Promotional Consultancy Service Pvt. Ltd., c/o Rishav Sigdel, Tebahal, New Rd, G P O Box 23870, Kathmandu, Nepal. TEL 997-1-4233415, mail@procon.com.np. Ed. Bamadev Sigdel.

➤ **SOCIO-ECONOMIC PLANNING SCIENCES.** *see* PUBLIC ADMINISTRATION

➤ **SOCIO-ECONOMIC REVIEW.** *see* BUSINESS AND ECONOMICS—Economic Situation And Conditions

340 IND ISSN 0973-5216
K23
SOCIO-LEGAL REVIEW. Text in English. 2005. a. INR 150 per issue to individuals; INR 75 per issue to students (effective 2011). **Document type:** *Journal, Academic/Scholarly.* **Description:** Explores the relationship between law and society.
Related titles: Online - full text ed.: free (effective 2011).
Published by: National Law School of India University, Law and Society Committee, Nagarbhavi, PO Box 7201, Bangalore, 560 072, India. TEL 91-80-23213160, FAX 91-80-23160534, registrar@nls.ac.in, http://www.nls.ac.in.

301 FRA ISSN 1159-9170
SOCIO-LOGIQUES. Text in French. 1992. irreg., latest vol.8, 1998. price varies. **Document type:** *Monographic series.* **Description:** Highlights the complex methods of the construction of social being.
Published by: Presses Universitaires du Mirail, Universite de Toulouse II (Le Mirail), 5, Allee Antonio Machado, Toulouse, 31058, France. TEL 33-05-61503810, FAX 33-05-61503800, pum@univ-tlse2.fr, http://www.univ-tlse2.fr.

301 FRA ISSN 1950-6724
HM405
SOCIO - LOGOS. Text in French. 2006. s-a. free (effective 2011). **Document type:** *Journal, Academic/Scholarly.*
Media: Online - full text.
Indexed: A39, C27, C29, D03, D04, E13, R14, S14, S15, S18, SociolAb.
Published by: Association Francaise de Sociologie, AFS/IRESCO, 59-61 Rue Pouchet, Paris, 75017, France. TEL 33-1-40251075, afs@iresco.

SOCIOCRITICISM: LITERATURE, SOCIETY, AND HISTORY. *see* LITERATURE

301 USA
SOCIOECONOMIC NEWSLETTER. Text in English. 1976. 6/yr. free. charts; illus. reprints avail.
Related titles: Microfiche ed.: (from PMC, WSH).
Published by: Institute for Socioeconomic Studies, Airport Rd, White Plains, NY 10604. TEL 914-428-7400. Ed. B A Rittersporn Jr. Circ: 17,500 (controlled).

301 SVK ISSN 0049-1225
HM7
➤ **SOCIOLOGIA/SOCIOLOGY.** Text in Slovak, English; Summaries in English. 1969. bi-m. EUR 137.10 in Eastern Europe; EUR 150 elsewhere (effective 2011). bk.rev. **Document type:** *Journal, Academic/Scholarly.* **Description:** Publishes original contributions from the theory, history and methodology of sociology.
Related titles: Online - full text ed.: ISSN 1336-8613; Ed.: Slovak Sociological Review.
Indexed: A20, CA, CurCont, IBSS, P42, PSA, RASB, S02, S03, SCOPUS, SOPODA, SSA, SSCI, SociolAb, T02, W07.
Published by: (Slovenska Akademia Vied, Sociologicky Ustav/Slovak Academy of Sciences, Institute of Sociology), Slovak Academic Press Ltd., Nam Slobody 6, PO Box 57, Bratislava, 81005, Slovakia. TEL 421-2-55421729, FAX 421-2-55565862, sap@sappress.sk, http://www.sappress.sk. Ed. Monika Cambalikova. **Dist. by:** Slovart G.T.G. s.r.o., Krupinska 4, PO Box 152, Bratislava 85299, Slovakia. TEL 421-2-63839472, FAX 421-2-63839485, info@slovart-gtg.sk, http://www.slovart-gtg.sk.

301 PRT ISSN 0873-6529
HN491
SOCIOLOGIA. Text in Portuguese. 1986. s-a.
Indexed: CA, F04, P42, PSA, S02, S03, SCOPUS, SSA, SociolAb, T02.
Published by: Instituto Superior de Ciencias do Trabalho e da Empresa, Ave das Forcas Armadas, Lisboa, 1649-026, Portugal. TEL 351-217-903000, iscte@iscte.pt, http://www.iscte.pt.

306.09 ITA ISSN 0038-0156
HM7
SOCIOLOGIA (ROME); rivista di scienze storiche e sociali. Text in Italian. 1956. 3/yr. EUR 30 domestic; EUR 60 foreign (effective 2009). adv. bibl. **Document type:** *Monographic series, Academic/Scholarly.*
Indexed: CA, FR, IBSS, P42, PCI, PSA, RASB, S02, S03, SCOPUS, SOPODA, SSA, SociolAb, T02.
—INIST.
Published by: (Istituto Luigi Sturzo), Gangemi Editore, Piazza San Pantaleo 4, Rome, Italy. TEL 39-06-6872774, FAX 39-06-68806189, info@gangemieditore.it, http://www.gangemi.com. Ed. Gabriele De Rosa.

331 ESP ISSN 0210-8364
HD6957.S7 CODEN: SOTRE6
SOCIOLOGIA DEL TRABAJO. Text in Spanish. 1979. q. **Document type:** *Journal, Academic/Scholarly.*
Indexed: CA, P42, PSA, S02, S03, SCOPUS, SSA, SociolAb, T02.
Published by: Siglo XXI Editores, Menendez Pidal 3 bis, Madrid, 28036, Spain. TEL 34-91-5617748, FAX 34-91-5615819, sigloxxi@sigloxxieditores.com. Ed. Juan Jose Castillo.

302.2 ITA ISSN 1121-1733
HM258
SOCIOLOGIA DELLA COMUNICAZIONE. Text in Italian. 1982. s-a. EUR 49.50 combined subscription domestic to institutions (print & online eds.); EUR 70 combined subscription foreign to institutions (print & online eds.) (effective 2009). **Document type:** *Journal, Academic/Scholarly.*
Related titles: Online - full text ed.: ISSN 1972-4926.
Indexed: DIP, IBR, IBZ, RASB.
—INIST.
Published by: Franco Angeli Edizioni, Viale Monza 106, Milan, 20127, Italy. TEL 39-02-2837141, FAX 39-02-26144793, redazioni@francoangeli.it, http://www.francoangeli.it.

301 ITA ISSN 0390-4229
HM131
SOCIOLOGIA DELL'ORGANIZZAZIONE. Text in Italian. 1973. s-a. **Document type:** *Journal, Academic/Scholarly.*
Published by: Universita degli Studi di Padova, Facolta di Lettere e Filosofia, Via Beato Pellegrino 1, Padua, 35137, Italy. TEL 39-049-8274906, FAX 39-049-8274919, http://www.unipd.it.

301 ITA ISSN 1591-2027
HN1
SOCIOLOGIA E POLITICHE SOCIALI. Text in Italian. 1998. 3/yr. EUR 59 combined subscription domestic to institutions (print & online eds.); EUR 83.50 combined subscription foreign to institutions (print & online eds.) (effective 2009). **Document type:** *Journal, Academic/Scholarly.*
Related titles: Online - full text ed.: ISSN 1972-5116.
Indexed: CA, P42, PAIS, PSA, S02, S03, SCOPUS, SSA, SociolAb, T02.
Published by: (Universita degli Studi di Bologna, Dipartimento di Sociologia), Franco Angeli Edizioni, Viale Monza 106, Milan, 20127, Italy. TEL 39-02-2837141, FAX 39-02-26144793, redazioni@francoangeli.it, http://www.francoangeli.it.

301 ITA ISSN 1121-1148
SOCIOLOGIA E RICERCA SOCIALE. Text in Italian. 1980. 3/yr. EUR 80 combined subscription domestic to institutions (print & online eds.); EUR 107.50 combined subscription foreign to institutions (print & online eds.) (effective 2009). adv. bk.rev. **Document type:** *Journal, Academic/Scholarly.*
Related titles: Online - full text ed.: ISSN 1971-8446. 1986.
Indexed: CA, FR, IBR, IBZ, P42, PSA, S02, S03, SCOPUS, SSA, SociolAb, T02.
—INIST.

Published by: Franco Angeli Edizioni, Viale Monza 106, Milan, 20127, Italy. TEL 39-02-2837141, FAX 39-02-26144793, redazioni@francoangeli.it, http://www.francoangeli.it.

301 GBR ISSN 0038-0199
HT401
➤ **SOCIOLOGIA RURALIS.** Text in English, French, German. 1960. q. GBP 337 in United Kingdom to institutions; EUR 428 in Europe to institutions; USD 567 in the Americas to institutions; USD 661 elsewhere to institutions; GBP 387 combined subscription in United Kingdom to institutions (print & online eds.); EUR 492 combined subscription in Europe to institutions (print & online eds.); USD 652 combined subscription in the Americas to institutions (print & online eds.); USD 761 combined subscription elsewhere to institutions (print & online eds.) (effective 2012). adv. bk.rev. abstr.; bibl. index. back issues avail.; reprint service avail. from PSC. **Document type:** *Journal, Academic/Scholarly.* **Description:** Serves as an international forum for social scientists engaged in a wide variety of disciplines focusing on social, political, and cultural aspects of rural development.
Related titles: Online - full text ed.: ISSN 1467-9523. GBP 337 in United Kingdom to institutions; EUR 428 in Europe to institutions; USD 567 in the Americas to institutions; USD 661 elsewhere to institutions (effective 2012) (from IngentaConnect).
Indexed: A01, A03, A08, A20, A22, A26, A34, A35, A36, A38, ARDT, ASCA, AgBio, BA, BAS, BibInd, C25, CA, CABA, CurCont, D01, E01, E12, EI, ESPM, EnvAb, F08, FR, G10, GEOBASE, GH, H16, I11, I13, IBR, IBSS, IBZ, ILD, IndVet, LT, MEA&I, MaizeAb, N02, N03, N04, OR, P06, P11, P27, P30, P32, P34, P37, P38, P40, P42, P48, P52, P54, P56, PAIS, PCI, PGegResA, PHN&I, PQC, PSA, R12, RASB, RRTA, S02, S03, S12, S13, S16, S17, SCOPUS, SOPODA, SSA, SSCI, SSciA, SociolAb, SoyAb, T02, TAR, VS, W07, W09, W10, W11.
—BLDSC (8319.620000), IE, Infotrieve, Ingenta, INIST. **CCC.**
Published by: (European Society for Rural Sociology FIN), Wiley-Blackwell Publishing Ltd. (Subsidiary of: John Wiley & Sons, Inc.), 9600 Garsington Rd, Oxford, OX4 2DQ, United Kingdom. TEL 44-1865-776868, FAX 44-1865-714591, customerservices@blackwellpublishing.com. Ed. Henry Buller TEL 44-1392-263836. Adv. contact Craig Pickett TEL 44-1865-476267.

301 ITA ISSN 0392-4939
HM7
SOCIOLOGIA URBANA E RURALE. Text in Italian. 1979. 3/yr. EUR 59 combined subscription domestic to institutions (print & online eds.); EUR 97 combined subscription foreign to institutions (print & online eds.) (effective 2009). **Document type:** *Journal, Academic/Scholarly.*
Related titles: Online - full text ed.: ISSN 1971-8403.
Indexed: DIP, FR, IBR, IBZ, PAIS, RASB.
—INIST.
Published by: Franco Angeli Edizioni, Viale Monza 106, Milan, 20127, Italy. TEL 39-02-2837141, FAX 39-02-26144793, redazioni@francoangeli.it, http://www.francoangeli.it.

301 BRA ISSN 1517-4522
HM417.P7
SOCIOLOGIAS. Text in Portuguese. 1989. s-a. BRL 30 domestic; BRL 60 foreign (effective 2004).
Formerly (until 1999): Cadernos de Sociologia (0103-894X)
Related titles: Online - full text ed.: free (effective 2011).
Indexed: A34, A35, AgBio, C01, C25, CA, CABA, E12, GH, H16, LT, N02, P32, P33, P39, P40, P42, PSA, R12, RRTA, S02, S03, S12, S13, S16, SCOPUS, SociolAb, T02, T05, TAR, VS, W11.
Published by: (Universidade Federal do Rio Grande do Sul, Instituto de Filosofia e Ciencias Humanas), Universidade Federal do Rio Grande do Sul, Programa de Pos-Graduacao em Sociologia, Av Bento Goncalves, 9500 Predio 43111 sala 103, Porto Alegre, RS 91509-900, Brazil. TEL 55-51-33166635, FAX 55-51-33166646. Eds. Jose Vicente Tavares dos Santos, Maira Baumgarten Correa.

301 ITA ISSN 1971-8853
SOCIOLOGICA. Text in Multiple languages. 2007. 3/yr. **Document type:** *Journal, Academic/Scholarly.*
Media: Online - full text.
Indexed: IBSS, SociolAb.
Published by: Societa Editrice Il Mulino, Strada Maggiore 37, Bologna, 40125, Italy. TEL 39-051-256011, FAX 39-051-256034, riviste@mulino.it, http://www.mulino.it. Ed. F Barbera.

301 MEX ISSN 0187-0173
HM7
➤ **SOCIOLOGICA.** Text in Spanish. 1986. 3/yr. MXN 150 domestic; USD 40 in Latin America to institutions; USD 65 elsewhere to institutions (effective 2010). adv. bk.rev. abstr.; charts; maps. **Document type:** *Journal, Academic/Scholarly.* **Description:** Presents research on theoretical and empirical sociology.
Related titles: CD-ROM ed.; Online - full text ed.
Indexed: A01, C01, CA, F03, F04, P42, PSA, S02, S03, SCOPUS, SOPODA, SSA, SociolAb, T02.
—INIST.
Published by: Universidad Autonoma Metropolitana - Azcapotzalco, Departamento de Sociologia, Ave. San PABLO 180, Edif. H Piso 3, Azcapotzalco, Mexico City, DF 02200, Mexico. TEL 52-5-3189502, FAX 52-5-3948093, revisoci@correo.azc.uam.mx, http://www.nostromo.uam.mx/sociologica. Ed. Maria Garcia Castro.

301 AUT ISSN 1814-5647
SOCIOLOGICA. Text in German. 1987. irreg., latest vol.14, 2010. price varies. **Document type:** *Monographic series, Academic/Scholarly.*
Published by: Wilhelm Braumueller Universitaets-Verlagsbuchhandlung GmbH, Servitengasse 5, Vienna, 1090, Austria. TEL 43-1-3191159, FAX 43-1-3102805, office@braumueller.at. Ed. Hilde Weiss.

301 IND ISSN 0038-0229
HN681
SOCIOLOGICAL BULLETIN. Text in English. 1952. s-a. INR 1,000, USD 100 (effective 2011). bk.rev. bibl.; stat. index, cum.index. back issues avail. **Document type:** *Bulletin, Academic/Scholarly.* **Description:** Contains papers all over the world to provide comparative analysis of social structures, social processes and cultures.
Related titles: Diskette ed.; Microform ed.
Indexed: BAS, CA, FR, G10, IBSS, P30, PAA&I, PCI, S02, S03, SCOPUS, SOPODA, SSA, SociolAb, T02, W09.
—Ingenta, INIST.
Published by: Indian Sociological Society, Institute of Social Sciences, 8 Nelson Mandela Rd, Vasant Kunj, New Delhi, 110 070, India. TEL 91-11-43158800, FAX 91-11-43158823, issnd@vsnl.com.

301 USA ISSN 0038-0237
HM1
➤ **SOCIOLOGICAL FOCUS.** Text in English. 1927. q. GBP 230 combined subscription in United Kingdom to institutions (print & online eds.); EUR 276, USD 345 combined subscription to institutions (print & online eds.) (effective 2012). adv. bk.rev. bibl.; charts. back issues avail.; reprints avail. **Document type:** *Journal, Academic/Scholarly.* **Description:** Publishes work representing all aspects of sociology and its subdisciplines, including theory, empirical studies, qualitative and quantitative research and applied work with policy implications.
Former titles (until 1967): Ohio Valley Sociologist; (until 1938): Ohio Sociologist
Related titles: Microform ed.: (from PMC, PQC, WSH); Online - full text ed.: ISSN 2162-1128. GBP 207 in United Kingdom to institutions; EUR 248, USD 310 to institutions (effective 2012).
Indexed: A20, A22, ASCA, BAS, CA, CLI, CommAb, FR, FamI, G10, IBR, IBZ, MEA&I, P10, P27, P30, P42, P46, P48, P54, PCI, PQC, PSA, S02, S03, SCOPUS, SOPODA, SRRA, SSA, SociolAb, T02, W09.
—BLDSC (8319.624500), IE, Infotrieve, Ingenta, INIST. **CCC.**
Published by: (North Central Sociological Association), Paradigm Publishers, 2845 Wilderness Pl, Ste 200, Boulder, CO 80301. TEL 303-245-9054, FAX 303-265-9051, journals@paradigmpublishers.com, http://www.paradigmpublishers.com. Eds. Eline Zehavi, Gustavo S Mesch TEL 972-4-8240993. **Co-publisher:** University of Cincinnati, Department of Sociology.

301 USA ISSN 0884-8971
HM1
➤ **SOCIOLOGICAL FORUM;** official journal of the Eastern Sociological Society. Text in English. 1986. q. GBP 456 combined subscription in United Kingdom to institutions (print & online eds.); EUR 558 combined subscription in Europe to institutions (print & online eds.); USD 765 combined subscription in the Americas to institutions (print & online eds.); USD 860 combined subscription elsewhere to institutions (print & online eds.) (effective 2012). adv. bk.rev. illus. Index. reprint service avail. from PSC. **Document type:** *Journal, Academic/Scholarly.* **Description:** Examines and presents the central interests of sociology in social organization and change as generic phenomena.
Related titles: Microfilm ed.: (from PQC); Online - full text ed.: ISSN 1573-7861. GBP 415 in United Kingdom to institutions; EUR 527 in Europe to institutions; USD 696 in the Americas to institutions; USD 811 elsewhere to institutions (effective 2012) (from IngentaConnect).
Indexed: A01, A03, A08, A20, A22, A26, ASCA, BibLing, CA, ChPerI, CommAb, CurCont, DIP, E-psyche, E01, FR, FamI, G10, IBR, IBSS, IBZ, MLA-IB, P03, P30, P34, P42, PSA, PsycInfo, PsycholAb, RILM, S02, S03, SCOPUS, SOPODA, SSA, SSCI, SociolAb, T02, W07, W09.
—BLDSC (8319.624600), IE, Infotrieve, Ingenta, INIST. **CCC.**
Published by: (Eastern Sociological Society), Wiley-Blackwell Publishing, Inc. (Subsidiary of: Wiley-Blackwell Publishing Ltd.), 111 River St, Hoboken, NJ 07030. TEL 201-748-6000, FAX 201-748-6088, info@wiley.com, http://www.wiley.com/WileyCDA/. Ed. Karen A Cerulo. Adv. contact Kristin McCarthy TEL 201-748-7683.

301 USA ISSN 1077-5048
HM1 CODEN: SIMAEE
➤ **SOCIOLOGICAL IMAGINATION.** Text in English. 1960. q. bk.rev.; video rev. back issues avail. **Document type:** *Journal, Academic/Scholarly.* **Description:** Covers issues pertaining to all areas of sociological inquiry and practice, including basic and applied research, teaching and curriculum matters, and clinical practice.
Formerly (until 1994): The Wisconsin Sociologist (0043-6666)
Indexed: CA, CJA, FR, P30, S02, S03, SCOPUS, SOPODA, SociolAb, T02.
—BLDSC (8319.624900), INIST.
Published by: Wisconsin Sociological Association, 410 S 3rd Street, River Falls, WI 54022. TEL 715-425-3911, sociology@uwrf.edu, http://www.uwrf.edu/SOCI/WSAWelcome.cfm.

301 USA ISSN 0038-0245
HM1
➤ **SOCIOLOGICAL INQUIRY.** Text in English. 1930. q. GBP 165 in United Kingdom to institutions; EUR 209 in Europe to institutions; USD 215 in the Americas to institutions; USD 323 elsewhere to institutions; GBP 190 combined subscription in United Kingdom to institutions (print & online eds.); EUR 241 combined subscription in Europe to institutions (print & online eds.); USD 247 combined subscription in the Americas to institutions (print & online eds.); USD 371 combined subscription elsewhere to institutions (print & online eds.) (effective 2012). adv. bk.rev. abstr.; illus. index. reprint service avail. from PSC. **Document type:** *Journal, Academic/Scholarly.* **Description:** Publishes the work of researchers and theorists in sociology.
Related titles: Microform ed.: (from PQC); Online - full text ed.: ISSN 1475-682X. GBP 165 in United Kingdom to institutions; EUR 209 in Europe to institutions; USD 215 in the Americas to institutions; USD 323 elsewhere to institutions (effective 2012) (from IngentaConnect).
Indexed: A01, A02, A03, A08, A20, A21, A22, A26, ABCPolSci, AMHA, ASCA, AbAn, AmH&L, B04, BRD, CA, CJPI, CommAb, CurCont, DIP, E01, E08, EAA, ESPM, FR, FamI, G08, G10, H09, HistAb, I05, I13, IBR, IBZ, MEA&I, P02, P03, P10, P27, P30, P34, P42, P48, P53, P54, PAIS, PQC, PRA, PSA, PsycInfo, PsycholAb, RI-1, RI-2, RILM, RiskAb, S02, S03, S05, S09, S11, S21, SCOPUS, SOPODA, SSA, SSAI, SSAb, SSCI, SSI, SociolAb, T02, W03, W07, W09.
—BLDSC (8319.625000), IE, Infotrieve, Ingenta, INIST. **CCC.**
Published by: (Alpha Kappa Delta - International Sociology Honor Society), Wiley-Blackwell Publishing, Inc. (Subsidiary of: Wiley-Blackwell Publishing Ltd.), 111 River St, Hoboken, NJ 07030. TEL 201-748-6000, FAX 201-748-6088, info@wiley.com, http://www.wiley.com/WileyCDA/. Ed. Sampson Lee Blair. Adv. contact Kristin McCarthy TEL 201-748-7683.

301.01 USA ISSN 0081-1750
HM24
➤ **SOCIOLOGICAL METHODOLOGY.** Text in English. 1969. a. GBP 242 in United Kingdom to institutions; EUR 308 in Europe to institutions; USD 306 in the Americas to institutions; USD 447 elsewhere to institutions; GBP 260 combined subscription in United Kingdom to institutions (print & online eds.); EUR 330 combined subscription in Europe to institutions (print & online eds.); USD 329 combined subscription in the Americas to institutions (print & online eds.); USD 481 combined subscription elsewhere to institutions (print & online eds.) (effective 2011). adv. back issues avail.; reprint service avail. from PSC. **Document type:** *Journal, Academic/Scholarly.* **Description:** Publishes the best work on current issues in methodology for social research.
Related titles: Microform ed.: (from PQC); Online - full text ed.: ISSN 1467-9531. GBP 242 in United Kingdom to institutions; EUR 308 in Europe to institutions; USD 306 in the Americas to institutions; USD 447 elsewhere to institutions (effective 2011) (from IngentaConnect).
Indexed: A01, A03, A08, A22, A26, ASCA, CA, CIS, E01, IBSS, P02, P10, P26, P30, P42, P46, P48, P54, PCI, PQC, PSA, RASB, S02, S03, SCOPUS, SOPODA, SSA, SSCI, SociolAb, T02, W07.
—BLDSC (8319.629000), IE, Infotrieve, Ingenta. **CCC.**
Published by: (American Sociological Association), Wiley-Blackwell Publishing, Inc. (Subsidiary of: Wiley-Blackwell Publishing Ltd.), 111 River St, Hoboken, NJ 07030. TEL 201-748-6000, FAX 201-748-6088, info@wiley.com, http://www.wiley.com/WileyCDA/. Ed. Tim Liao.

301.07 USA ISSN 0049-1241
HM1
➤ **SOCIOLOGICAL METHODS & RESEARCH.** Abbreviated title: S M R. Text in English. 1972. q. USD 874, GBP 514 combined subscription to institutions (print & online eds.); USD 857, GBP 504 to institutions (effective 2011). bk.rev. charts; illus.; abstr. index. back issues avail.; reprint service avail. from PSC. **Document type:** *Magazine, Academic/Scholarly.* **Description:** Disseminates quantitative research and methodology in the social sciences. It brings empirically-based articles from a variety of perspectives, exploring research methods that are applicable to a wide range of fields, including anthropology, economics, political science, criminology, education, psychology, demography, management and sociology.
Related titles: Microform ed.: (from PQC); Online - full text ed.: ISSN 1552-8294. USD 787, GBP 463 to institutions (effective 2011).
Indexed: A01, A02, A03, A08, A20, A22, A36, ASCA, B07, BAS, BibInd, CA, CABA, CCMJ, CIS, CJPI, CMM, CommAb, CurCont, DIP, E-psyche, E01, E03, ERI, FR, FamI, GH, H04, IBR, IBSS, IBZ, JCQM, MEA&I, MSN, MathR, N02, N03, P02, P03, P04, P06, P10, P25, P26, P30, P34, P48, P53, P54, PAIS, PCI, PQC, PersLit, PsycInfo, PsycholAb, RASB, S02, S03, S11, SCOPUS, SOPODA, SSA, SSCI, SWR&A, SociolAb, T02, V02, W07.
—BLDSC (8319.629500), IE, Infotrieve, Ingenta, INIST. **CCC.**
Published by: Sage Publications, Inc., 2455 Teller Rd, Thousand Oaks, CA 91320. TEL 805-499-9774, FAX 805-499-0871, info@sagepub.com. Ed. Christopher Winship. Circ: 750. **Subscr. in Asia to:** Sage Publications India Pvt. Ltd., M-32 Market, Greater Kailash-I, PO Box 4215, New Delhi 110 048, India. FAX 91-11-647-2426, journalsubs@sagepub.in; **Subscr. in Europe to:** Sage Publications Ltd., 1 Oliver's Yard, 55 City Rd, London EC1Y 1SP, United Kingdom. TEL 44-207-3248701, FAX 44-207-3248733, subscription@sagepub.co.uk.

301 USA ISSN 0149-4872
SOCIOLOGICAL OBSERVATIONS. Text in English. 1977. irreg., latest 2000. price varies. back issues avail.; reprints avail. **Document type:** *Monographic series, Academic/Scholarly.*
Related titles: Online - full text ed.
—**CCC.**
Published by: Sage Publications, Inc., Books (Subsidiary of: Sage Publications, Inc.), 2455 Teller Rd, Thousand Oaks, CA 91320. TEL 800-818-7243, books.claim@sagepub.com. Pub. Sara Miller McCune. **Subscr. to:** Sage Publications India Pvt. Ltd.; Sage Publications Ltd.

306 ISR ISSN 0793-1069
HM1.A1 CODEN: SOPAE3
➤ **SOCIOLOGICAL PAPERS.** Text in English. 1992. 4/yr. free (effective 2009). **Document type:** *Journal, Academic/Scholarly.* **Description:** Presents individual research and theoretical articles concerning new developments in social life, including community life, ethnic relations, problems and developments in the fields of religion, education, the family, social stratification and mobility.
Indexed: PSA, SCOPUS, SOPODA, SSA, SociolAb.
—BLDSC (8319.629830).
Published by: (Leon Tamman Foundation for Research into Jewish Communities), Sociological Institute for Community Studies, Bar-Ilan University, Ramat Gon, 52900, Israel. TEL 972-3-534-4449, FAX 972-3-635-0422. Eds. Ernest Krausz, Gitta Tulea. Circ: 400.

301 USA ISSN 0731-1214
HM1
➤ **SOCIOLOGICAL PERSPECTIVES.** Abbreviated title: S P. Text in English. 1957. q. USD 436 combined subscription to institutions (print & online eds.) (effective 2012). adv. charts; stat.; illus. cum.index every 5 yrs. back issues avail.; reprint service avail. from PSC. **Document type:** *Journal, Academic/Scholarly.* **Description:** Provides 170 pages of pertinent articles within the field of sociology.
Formerly (until 1983): Pacific Sociological Review (0030-8919)
Related titles: Microfilm ed.: (from PQC); Online - full text ed.: ISSN 1533-8673. USD 353 to institutions (effective 2012).
Indexed: A01, A02, A03, A08, A20, A22, A26, ABCPolSci, AC&P, ASCA, AbAn, AmH&L, B01, B04, B06, B07, B09, BAS, BRD, CA, CERDIC, CIS, CMM, Chicano, CommAb, CurCont, E-psyche, E01, E07, E08, FR, FamI, G08, I05, IBR, IBSS, IBZ, IPsyAb, M01, M02, MEA&I, P02, P03, P06, P07, P10, P25, P27, P30, P34, P42, P45, P46, P48, P53, P54, PCI, PQC, PSA, PsycInfo, PsycholAb, RASB, RILM, S02, S03, S09, S11, S21, SCOPUS, SOPODA, SRRA, SSA, SSAI, SSAb, SSCI, SSI, SWR&A, SociolAb, T02, W03, W07, W09.
—BLDSC (8319.629860), IE, Infotrieve, Ingenta, INIST. **CCC.**
Published by: (Pacific Sociological Association), University of California Press, Journals Division, 2000 Ctr St, Ste 303, Berkeley, CA 94704. TEL 510-643-7154, 877-262-4226, FAX 510-642-9917, customerservice@ucpressjournals.com. Eds. Charles Powers, Marilyn Fernandez. Circ: 1,770. **Subscr. to:** 149 5th Ave, 8th Fl, New York, NY 10010. participation@jstor.org.

S

301 USA ISSN 0038-0253
HM1 CODEN: SOLQAR

➤ **THE SOCIOLOGICAL QUARTERLY.** Text in English. 1960. q. GBP 269 in United Kingdom to institutions; EUR 341 in Europe to institutions; USD 448 in the Americas to institutions; USD 524 elsewhere to institutions; GBP 309 combined subscription in United Kingdom to institutions (print & online eds.); EUR 393 combined subscription in Europe to institutions (print & online eds.); USD 516 combined subscription in the Americas to institutions (print & online eds.); USD 604 combined subscription elsewhere to institutions (print & online eds.) (effective 2012). bk.rev. charts; illus. cum.index: 1953-1973, 1974-1983. 102 p./no.; back issues avail.; reprint service avail. from PSC. **Document type:** *Journal, Academic/Scholarly.* **Description:** Devoted to publishing cutting-edge research and theory in all areas of sociological inquiry.

Formerly (until 1960): Midwest Sociologist (1948-1586)

Related titles: Microfilm ed.: (from WSH); Online - full text ed.: ISSN 1533-8525. GBP 269 in United Kingdom to institutions; EUR 341 in Europe to institutions; USD 448 in the Americas to institutions; USD 524 elsewhere to institutions (effective 2012) (from IngentaConnect).

Indexed: A01, A02, A03, A08, A20, A21, A22, A26, ABCPolSci, ABS&EES, AC&P, AMHA, ASCA, AbAn, AmH&L, B01, B04, B06, B07, B09, BAS, BRD, CA, CERDIC, CJPI, CPM, Chicano, CommAb, CurCont, DIP, E-psyche, E01, E07, E08, EI, ESPM, FR, FamI, G08, H09, H10, HistAb, I05, I13, IBR, IBSS, IBZ, M01, M02, MEA&I, MLA-IB, P02, P03, P07, P10, P25, P27, P30, P34, P42, P45, P46, P48, P53, P54, PAIS, PCI, PQC, PRA, PSA, PSI, PhilInd, PsycInfo, PsycholAb, R05, RASB, RI-1, RI-2, RILM, RiskAb, S02, S03, S05, S09, S11, SCOPUS, SD, SOPODA, SRRA, SSA, SSAI, SSAb, SSCI, SSI, SWR&A, SociolAb, T02, W03, W07, W09.

—BLDSC (8319.630000), IE, Infotrieve, Ingenta, INIST. **CCC.**

Published by: (Midwest Sociological Society), Wiley-Blackwell Publishing, Inc. (Subsidiary of: Wiley-Blackwell Publishing Ltd.), 111 River St, Hoboken, NJ 07030. TEL 201-748-6000, FAX 201-748-6088, info@wiley.com, http://www.wiley.com/WileyCDA/. Eds. Brian L Donovan, William G Staples.

301.07 USA ISSN 1061-0154
HX542

➤ **SOCIOLOGICAL RESEARCH.** Abbreviated title: S O R. Text in English. 1962. bi-m. USD 1,380 combined subscription domestic to institutions (print & online eds.); USD 1,488 combined subscription foreign to institutions (print & online eds.) (effective 2012). adv. illus. index. back issues avail.; reprint service avail. from PSC. **Document type:** *Journal, Academic/Scholarly.* **Description:** Contains translations of articles that have been selected to reflect trends in the sociological literature and to be of value to researchers interested in the region and the study of societies in transition.

Formerly (until 1992): Soviet Sociology (0038-5824)

Related titles: Online - full text ed.: 2004 (Feb.). USD 1,275 to institutions (effective 2012).

Indexed: A01, A03, A08, A20, A22, A26, ABS&EES, AMHA, B01, B06, B07, B09, BRD, CA, E-psyche, E01, E08, FR, FamI, G08, I05, IBR, IBZ, P06, P30, P34, P42, PAIS, PCI, PSA, PopulInd, S02, S03, S09, SCOPUS, SSAI, SSAb, SSI, SociolAb, T02, W03, W05.

—IE, Infotrieve, Ingenta, INIST. **CCC.**

Published by: M.E. Sharpe, Inc., 80 Business Park Dr, Armonk, NY 10504. TEL 914-273-1800, 800-541-6563, FAX 914-273-2106, custserv@mesharpe.com. Ed. Anthony Jones. Adv. contact Barbara Ladd TEL 914-273-1800.

301 GBR ISSN 1360-7804
HM1

➤ **SOCIOLOGICAL RESEARCH ONLINE**; an electronic journal. Text in English. 1996. q. GBP 180 (effective 2010). bk.rev.; software rev. illus. back issues avail.; reprints avail. **Document type:** *Journal, Academic/Scholarly.* **Description:** Covers theoretical and empirical studies in sociology and on issues relevant to the current political and cultural debates.

Media: Online - full text. **Related titles:** Print ed.

Indexed: A20, B07, CA, CurCont, G10, IBSS, IBibSS, PAIS, S02, S03, SCOPUS, SSA, SSCI, SociolAb, T02, W07, W09.

—CCC.

Published by: Sage Publications Ltd. (Subsidiary of: Sage Publications, Inc.), 1 Oliver's Yard, 55 City Rd, London, EC1Y 1SP, United Kingdom. TEL 44-20-73248500, FAX 44-20-73248600, info@sagepub.co.uk, http://www.uk.sagepub.com/home.nav. Eds. Rosaline Barbour, Susan Eley.

301 GBR ISSN 0038-0261
HM1

➤ **THE SOCIOLOGICAL REVIEW.** Text in English. 1908; N.S. 1953. q. GBP 319 combined subscription in United Kingdom to institutions (print & online eds.); EUR 404 combined subscription in Europe to institutions (print & online eds.); USD 620 combined subscription in the Americas to institutions (print & online eds.); USD 722 combined subscription elsewhere to institutions (print & online eds.) (effective 2012). adv. bk.rev. charts; bibl.; illus. index, cum.index. back issues avail.; reprint service avail. from PSC. **Document type:** *Journal, Academic/Scholarly.* **Description:** Discusses subjects related to sociology, with topical essays on health and work, job training, equal opportunities and skills, social attitudes to family relationships, and more.

Related titles: Microform ed.: N.S. (from PQC); Online - full text ed.: ISSN 1467-954X. 1997. GBP 289 in United Kingdom to institutions; EUR 367 in Europe to institutions; USD 563 in the Americas to institutions; USD 655 elsewhere to institutions (effective 2012) (from IngentaConnect).

Indexed: A01, A02, A03, A08, A20, A22, A25, A26, A34, A35, A36, AICP, AMHA, ASCA, AgBio, B04, B07, BRD, C25, C28, CA, CABA, CBRI, CJPI, CPM, CommAb, CurCont, DIP, E01, E08, E12, ERA, ESPM, F09, FR, FamI, G08, G10, GH, H09, H10, HistAb, I05, I13, IBR, IBSS, IBZ, LT, M06, MEA&I, MLA-IB, MaizeAb, N02, P02, P03, P06, P10, P27, P30, P32, P34, P40, P42, P48, P53, P54, PAA&I, PAIS, PCI, PQC, PRA, PSA, PsycInfo, PsycholAb, R12, RASB, RRTA, RiskAb, S02, S03, S05, S08, S09, S11, S13, S16, S19, S21, SCOPUS, SOPODA, SSA, SSAI, SSAb, SSCI, SSI, SociolAb, T02, TAR, VS, W03, W07, W09, W11.

—BLDSC (8319.640000), IE, Infotrieve, Ingenta, INIST. **CCC.**

Published by: (University of Keele), Wiley-Blackwell Publishing Ltd. (Subsidiary of: John Wiley & Sons, Inc.), 9600 Garsington Rd, Oxford, OX4 2DQ, United Kingdom. TEL 44-1865-776868, FAX 44-1865-714591, customerservices@blackwellpublishing.com.

301 GBR ISSN 0081-1769
HM15

SOCIOLOGICAL REVIEW. MONOGRAPH. Text in English. 1958. a., latest 2005. price varies. back issues avail.; reprints avail. **Document type:** *Monographic series, Academic/Scholarly.* **Description:** Contains previously unpublished scholarly articles on a topic of general sociological interest that is intended to appeal to a broad sociology public.

Related titles: Online - full text ed.

Indexed: ASCA, CA, FR, IndMed, P30, RASB, RILM, S02, S03, SOPODA, SociolAb, T02, W09.

—IE, Infotrieve, INIST. **CCC.**

Published by: (University of Keele), Wiley-Blackwell Publishing Ltd. (Subsidiary of: John Wiley & Sons, Inc.), 9600 Garsington Rd, Oxford, OX4 2DQ, United Kingdom. TEL 44-1865-776868, FAX 44-1865-714591, customerservices@blackwellpublishing.com.

301 USA ISSN 0273-2173
HM1 CODEN: SOSPDS

➤ **SOCIOLOGICAL SPECTRUM**; official journal of the Mid-South Sociological Association . Text in English. 1981. bi-m. GBP 498 combined subscription in United Kingdom to institutions (print & online eds.); EUR 659, USD 829 combined subscription to institutions (print & online eds.) (effective 2012). adv. bk.rev. abstr.; bibl.; illus.; stat. index. back issues avail.; reprint service avail. from PSC. **Document type:** *Journal, Academic/Scholarly.* **Description:** Discusses current thoughts in theoretical and applied psychology, education, social psychology, political science, and anthropology.

Formed by the merger of (1968-1980): Sociological Symposium (0038-027X); (1978-1980): Sociological Forum (0160-3469)

Related titles: Online - full text ed.: ISSN 1521-0707. GBP 448 in United Kingdom to institutions; EUR 594, USD 746 to institutions (effective 2012) (from IngentaConnect).

Indexed: A01, A02, A03, A08, A20, A22, ABS&EES, ASCA, B07, CA, CJPI, CMM, CommAb, CurCont, E-psyche, E01, ESPM, FR, FamI, G10, MEA&I, P03, P06, P30, P34, P42, PQC, PSA, PsycInfo, PsycholAb, RILM, RiskAb, S02, S03, SCOPUS, SOPODA, SSA, SSCI, SSciA, SociolAb, T02, W07, W09.

—IE, Infotrieve, Ingenta, INIST. **CCC.**

Published by: (Mid-South Sociological Association), Taylor & Francis Inc. (Subsidiary of: Taylor & Francis Group), 325 Chestnut St, Ste 800, Philadelphia, PA 19106. TEL 215-625-8900, 800-354-1420, FAX 215-625-8914, orders@taylorandfrancis.com, http://www.taylorandfrancis.com. Ed. John Lynxwiler. **Subscr. in Europe to:** Taylor & Francis Ltd., Journals Customer Service, Sheepen Pl, Colchester, Essex CO3 3LP, United Kingdom. TEL 44-20-70175544, FAX 44-20-70175198, subscriptions@tandf.co.uk.

➤ **SOCIOLOGICAL STUDIES.** *see* POLITICAL SCIENCE—International Relations

301 USA ISSN 0735-2751
HM24

➤ **SOCIOLOGICAL THEORY.** Text in English. q. GBP 252 in United Kingdom to institutions; EUR 318 in Europe to institutions; USD 313 in the Americas to institutions; USD 464 elsewhere to institutions; GBP 271 combined subscription in United Kingdom to institutions (print & online eds.); EUR 343 combined subscription in Europe to institutions (print & online eds.); USD 337 combined subscription in the Americas to institutions (print & online eds.); USD 499 combined subscription elsewhere to institutions (print & online eds.) (effective 2011). reprint service avail. from PSC. **Document type:** *Journal, Academic/Scholarly.* **Description:** Covers sociological theory, new substantive theories, history of theory, metatheory, and formal theory construction.

Related titles: Online - full text ed.: ISSN 1467-9558. GBP 252 in United Kingdom to institutions; EUR 318 in Europe to institutions; USD 313 in the Americas to institutions; USD 464 elsewhere to institutions (effective 2011) (from IngentaConnect).

Indexed: A01, A03, A08, A20, A22, A26, ASCA, CA, CurCont, DIP, E-psyche, E01, FR, FamI, IBR, IBSS, IBZ, P02, P26, P46, P48, P54, PQC, RASB, S02, S03, SCOPUS, SOPODA, SSA, SSCI, SociolAb, T02, W07.

—BLDSC (8319.650150), IE, Infotrieve, Ingenta, INIST. **CCC.**

Published by: (American Sociological Association), Wiley-Blackwell Publishing, Inc. (Subsidiary of: Wiley-Blackwell Publishing Ltd.), 111 River St, Hoboken, NJ 07030. TEL 201-748-6000, FAX 201-748-6088, info@wiley.com, http://www.wiley.com/WileyCDA/. Ed. Neil Gross. Adv. contact Kristin McCarthy TEL 201-748-7683.

301 USA ISSN 1060-0876
HM1 CODEN: SOCVEZ

➤ **SOCIOLOGICAL VIEWPOINTS.** Text in English. 1984. a. free to members (effective 2011). bk.rev. bibl. back issues avail. **Document type:** *Journal, Academic/Scholarly.* **Description:** Publishes articles and critical essays on topics in sociology, including original empirical research, methodological and theoretical issues, and critiques of social events.

Related titles: Online - full text ed.: ISSN 2161-7775. free (effective 2011).

Indexed: A01, A02, A03, A08, CA, P27, P46, P48, P54, PQC, S02, S03, SCOPUS, SOPODA, SSA, SociolAb, T02.

Published by: Pennsylvania Sociological Society, 13 Matthew Dr, Coatesville, PA 19320. Carla.Messikomer@verizon.net.

301 CZE ISSN 0038-0288
CODEN: SLCSB2

➤ **SOCIOLOGICKY CASOPIS/CZECH SOCIOLOGICAL REVIEW.** Text in Czech, English. 1965. bi-m. (4 issues in Czech, 2 issues in English). CZK 450; CZK 75, USD 4, EUR 4 per issue (effective 2008). adv. bk.rev. abstr.; bibl. **Document type:** *Journal, Academic/Scholarly.* **Description:** Covers studies devoted to general sociology and methodology, and to specialized sociological fields in Czech Republic and abroad.

Incorporates (1993-2001): Czech Sociological Review (1210-3861)

Indexed: A20, AC&P, ASCA, BibLing, CA, CurCont, IBSS, P30, P42, PCI, PSA, PsycholAb, RASB, RILM, S02, S03, SCOPUS, SOPODA, SSA, SSCI, SociolAb, T02, W07.

—BLDSC (8319.650).

Published by: Akademie Ved Ceske Republiky, Sociologicky Ustav, Jilska 1, Prague 1, 110 00, Czech Republic. TEL 420-222-220924, FAX 420-222-220143, socmail@soc.cas.cz, http://www.soc.cas.cz. Eds. Jiri Vecernik, Marek Skovajsa. **Dist. by:** Kubon & Sagner Buchexport - Import GmbH, Hessstr 39-41, Munich 80798, Germany. TEL 49-89-542180, FAX 49-89-54218218, postmaster@kubon-sagner.de, http://www.kubon-sagner.de.

301 NLD ISSN 1574-3314
HM417.D8

➤ **SOCIOLOGIE.** Text in Dutch, English, French, German; Summaries in English. 2005. q. EUR 79.50 combined subscription domestic to individuals (print & online eds.); EUR 99.50 combined subscription foreign to individuals (print & online eds.); EUR 224 combined subscription domestic to institutions (print & online eds.); EUR 282 combined subscription foreign to institutions (print & online eds.); EUR 53.50 combined subscription to students (print & online eds.) (effective 2008). adv. bk.rev. index. **Document type:** *Journal, Academic/Scholarly.*

Formed by the merger of (1953-2005): Sociologische Gids (0038-0334); (1988-2005): Amsterdams Sociologisch Tijdschrift (0921-4933); Which was formerly (1982-1988): Sociologisch Tijdschrift (0168-731X); (1974-1982): Amsterdams Sociologisch Tijdschrift (0165-0297)

Related titles: Online - full text ed.: ISSN 1875-7138. EUR 64 domestic to individuals; EUR 80 foreign to individuals; EUR 42.50 to students (effective 2008).

Indexed: AC&P, BAS, CA, EI, FR, IBR, IBZ, P30, P42, PCI, PSA, RILM, S02, S03, SCOPUS, SOPODA, SSA, SociolAb, T02.

—BLDSC (8319.653000), IE, Infotrieve, Ingenta, INIST.

Published by: Boom Uitgevers Amsterdam, Prinsengracht 747-751, Amsterdam, 1017 JX, Netherlands. TEL 31-20-6226107, FAX 31-20-6253327, info@uitgeverijboom.nl, http://www.uitgeverijboom.nl. Adv. contact Michiel Klaasen TEL 31-20-5200122. page EUR 425; trim 110 x 210. Circ: 550.

301 FRA ISSN 2108-8845

▼ ➤ **SOCIOLOGIE.** Text in French; Abstracts in French, English. 2010. q. EUR 90 foreign to institutions (effective 2012). **Document type:** *Journal, Academic/Scholarly.*

Related titles: Online - full text ed.: ISSN 2108-6915.

Published by: Presses Universitaires de France, 6 Avenue Reille, Paris, 75685, France. TEL 33-1-58103161, FAX 33-1-45897530, revues@puf.com, http://www.puf.com. Ed. Serge Paugam.

➤ **SOCIOLOGIE DE L'ART.** *see* ART

➤ **SOCIOLOGIE DU TRAVAIL.** *see* BUSINESS AND ECONOMICS—Labor And Industrial Relations

301 CAN ISSN 0038-030X
HM3

SOCIOLOGIE ET SOCIETES. Text in French; Summaries in English, French, Spanish. 1969. 2/yr. bibl.; charts; stat. reprints avail. **Document type:** *Journal, Academic/Scholarly.*

Related titles: Microform ed.; Online - full text ed.: ISSN 1492-1375.

Indexed: A22, CA, CWPI, DIP, FR, I13, IBR, IBSS, IBZ, ILD, P30, P34, P42, PAIS, PSA, PdeR, PsycholAb, S02, S03, SCOPUS, SOPODA, SSA, SociolAb, T02.

—BLDSC (8319.650800), IE, Infotrieve, Ingenta, INIST. **CCC.**

Published by: Presses de l'Universite de Montreal, 3535, chemin Queen-Mary, Bureau 206, Montreal, PQ H3V 1H8, Canada. TEL 514-343-6933, pum@umontreal.ca, http://www.pum.umontreal.ca. Ed. Pierre Hamel.

301 NLD ISSN 1877-8216

SOCIOLOGIE MAGAZINE. Text in Dutch. 1993. q. **Document type:** *Magazine, Trade.*

Formerly (until 2009): Facta (0928-5350); Which was formed by the merger of (1976-1993): Sociodrome (0165-1676); (1972-1993): Berichten over Onderzoek (0166-8951)

—IE, Infotrieve.

Published by: (Nederlandse Sociologische Vereniging), Virtumedia, Postbus 595, Zeist, 3700 AN, Netherlands. TEL 31-30-6920677, FAX 31-30-6913312, info@virtumedia.nl, http://www.virtumedia.nl.

301 FRA ISSN 0220-777X

SOCIOLOGIE PERMANENTE. Text in French. 1978. irreg. **Document type:** *Journal, Academic/Scholarly.*

Published by: Editions du Seuil, 27 Rue Jacob, Paris, 75006, France. TEL 33-1-40465050, FAX 33-1-40464300, contact@seuil.com, http://www.seuil.com. Ed. Alain Touraine.

301 FRA ISSN 1992-2655
HM405

➤ **SOCIOLOGIES.** Text in French. 2006. a. free (effective 2011). **Document type:** *Journal, Academic/Scholarly.*

Media: Online - full text.

Indexed: A39, C27, C29, D03, D04, E13, R14, S14, S15, S18.

Published by: Association Internationale des Sociologues de Langue Francaise (A I S L F), Universite de Toulouse Le Mirail, Batiment de l'Arche, Bureau AR 104 bis, 5 Allee Antonio Machado, Toulouse, 31058, France. sociologies@revues.org. Ed. Marc-Henry Soulet.

301 FRA ISSN 1295-9278

SOCIOLOGIES PRATIQUES. Text in French. 1999. s-a. EUR 43 domestic to individuals; EUR 50.64 foreign to individuals; EUR 47, EUR 55.92 domestic to institutions (effective 2009). **Document type:** *Journal, Academic/Scholarly.*

Indexed: FR, IBSS.

—INIST.

Published by: (Association des Professionnels en Sociologie), Presses Universitaires de France, 6 Avenue Reille, Paris, 75685, France. TEL 33-1-58103161, FAX 33-1-45897530, revues@puf.com, http://www.puf.com. Ed. Isabelle Berrebi-Hoffman.

301 SRB ISSN 0038-0318

SOCIOLOGIJA; casopis za sociologiju, socijalnu psihologiju i socijalnu antropologiju. Text in Serbo-Croatian. 1959. q. adv. bk.rev. **Document type:** *Journal, Academic/Scholarly.*

Related titles: Online - full text ed.: free (effective 2011).

Indexed: BibInd, CA, FR, IBSS, RASB, S02, S03, SCOPUS, SOPODA, SSA, SociolAb, T02.

Published by: (Univerzitet u Beogradu, Filozofski Fakultet/University of Belgrade, Faculty of Philosophy), Sociolosko Udruzenje Srbije/Sociological Association of Serbia, Studentski trg 15, Belgrade, 11000.

630 307.72 HRV ISSN 1846-5226
HT401
SOCIOLOGIJA I PROSTOR; casopis za istrazivanje prostornoga i sociokulturnog razvoja/quaterly for spatial and sociocultural development studies. Text in Croatian; Contents page in English, Russian, German, French. 1962. q. HRK 250 domestic to institutions; EUR 35 foreign to institutions (effective 2010). bk.rev. cum.index. **Document type:** *Journal, Academic/Scholarly.* **Description:** Publishes articles, research papers on rural sociology, rural economics, history and demography.
Supersedes in part (in 2007): Sociologija Sela (0038-0326)
Related titles: Online - full text ed.
Indexed: A26, CA, CABA, F08, F12, I13, N02, P30, P42, PSA, RASB, RILM, S02, S03, S13, SCOPUS, SOPODA, SSA, SSCI, SociolAb, T02, W07, W11.
Published by: Sveuciliste u Zagrebu, Institut za Drustvena Istrazivanja/University of Zagreb, Institute for Social Research, Amruseva 8/III, PO Box 280, Zagreb, 10001, Croatia. TEL 385-1-4922925, FAX 385-1-4810263, sip@idi.hr, http://www.idi.hr. Ed. Ankica Marinovic-Bobinac. Circ: 600.

301 BEL
SOCIOLOGISCHE VERKENNINGEN. Text in Dutch. 1972 (no.2). irreg., latest vol.10, 1986. price varies. **Document type:** *Academic/Scholarly.* **Description:** Disseminates research into topics of sociological inquiry.
Published by: Leuven University Press, Blijde Inkomststraat 5, Leuven, 3000, Belgium. TEL 32-16-325345, FAX 32-16-325352, university.press@upers.kuleuven.ac.be, http://www.kuleuven.ac.be/upers.

301 SWE ISSN 0038-0342
HM7 CODEN: NDGEA4
➤ **SOCIOLOGISK FORSKNING.** Text in Swedish. 1964. q. SEK 500 domestic; SEK 575 foreign (effective 2009). adv. bk.rev. cum.index: 1964-74. **Document type:** *Journal, Academic/Scholarly.*
Indexed: A20, A22, ASCA, CA, IBR, IBZ, PCI, S02, S03, SCOPUS, SOPODA, SSA, SSCI, SociolAb, T02, W07.
—BLDSC (8319.654000), IE, Ingenta.
Published by: Sveriges Sociologfoerbund/Swedish Sociological Association, c/o Samhaellsvetenskapelige Institutionen, Vaexjoe Universitet, Vaexjoe, 35195, Sweden. Ed. Hedvig Ekerwald. Circ: 750.

301 DNK ISSN 1603-4058
➤ **SOCIOLOGISK TIDENDE.** Variant title: Dialektisk Dialog. Text in Danish. 2001. irreg. bk.rev. back issues avail. **Document type:** *Journal, Academic/Scholarly.*
Related titles: Online - full text ed.
Published by: Aalborg Universitet, Institut for Sociologi, Socialt Arbejde og Organisation/Aalborg University. Department of Sociology, Social Work and Organization, Kroghstraede 5, Aalborg, 9220, Denmark. TEL 45-96-358080, FAX 45-98-157575. Ed. Kristian Molbo Jacobsen.

155.82 DEU ISSN 0038-0377
HM3
SOCIOLOGUS; Zeitschrift fuer empirische Ethnosoziologie und Ethnopsychologie. Text in English, German. 1951. s-a. EUR 96 combined subscription to individuals (print & online eds.); EUR 178 combined subscription to institutions (print & online eds.); EUR 62 newsstand/cover (effective 2012). adv. bk.rev. abstr.; illus. index. reprints avail. **Document type:** *Journal, Academic/Scholarly.*
Related titles: Online - full text ed.: ISSN 1865-5106. 2008.
Indexed: A22, AICP, AnthLit, BAS, BibLing, CA, CTFA, DIP, EI, FR, IBR, IBSS, IBZ, MLA-IB, P06, P30, P42, PAIS, PCI, PSA, RASB, S02, S03, SCOPUS, SSCI, SociolAb, T02, W07.
—BLDSC (8319.660000), IE, Infotrieve, Ingenta, INIST. **CCC.**
Published by: Duncker und Humblot GmbH, Carl-Heinrich-Becker-Weg 9, Berlin, 12165, Germany. TEL 49-30-7900060, FAX 49-30-79000631, info@duncker-humblot.de. Circ: 300 (paid and controlled).

301 GBR ISSN 0038-0385
HM1
➤ **SOCIOLOGY.** Text in English. 1967. bi-m. USD 787, GBP 425 combined subscription to institutions (print & online eds.); USD 771, GBP 417 to institutions (effective 2011). adv. bk.rev. charts; illus. index. back issues avail.; reprint service avail. from PSC. **Document type:** *Journal, Academic/Scholarly.* **Description:** Publishes outstanding and original articles which advance the theoretical understanding of, and promote and report empirical research about, the widest range of sociological topics. The journal encourages and welcomes, submission of papers which report findings using both quantitative and qualitative research methods; articles challenging conventional concepts and proposing new conceptual approaches; and accounts of methodological innovation and the research process.
Related titles: Microform ed.: (from PQC); Online - full text ed.: ISSN 1469-8684. USD 708, GBP 383 to institutions (effective 2011).
Indexed: A01, A02, A03, A08, A12, A17, A20, A22, A25, A26, A36, ABIn, AC&P, ASCA, ASG, B01, B04, B06, B07, B08, B09, BAS, BRD, C28, CA, CABA, CMM, CPM, CurCont, DIP, E01, E07, E08, FR, FamI, G05, G06, G07, G08, GH, H09, HECAB, HistAb, I05, I13, I14, IBR, IBSS, IBZ, LT, MEA&I, N02, N03, P02, P03, P07, P10, P13, P27, P30, P34, P42, P48, P51, P53, P54, PCI, PQC, PSA, PsycInfo, PsycholAb, R12, RASB, RRTA, S02, S03, S05, S08, S09, S11, S23, SCIMP, SCOPUS, SOPODA, SSA, SSAI, SSAb, SSCI, SSI, SociolAb, T02, W03, W07, W09, W11, WBA, WMB.
—BLDSC (8319.670000), IE, Infotrieve, Ingenta, INIST. **CCC.**
Published by: (British Sociological Association), Sage Publications Ltd. (Subsidiary of: Sage Publications, Inc.), 1 Oliver's Yard, 55 City Rd, London, EC1Y 1SP, United Kingdom. TEL 44-20-73248500, FAX 44-20-73248600, info@sagepub.co.uk, http://www.uk.sagepub.com/home.nav. adv.: B&W page GBP 350; 130 x 205. **Subscr. in the Americas to:** Sage Publications, Inc., 2455 Teller Rd, Thousand Oaks, CA 91320. TEL 805-499-9774, FAX 805-499-0871, journals@sagepub.com.

301 USA ISSN 1062-4120
SOCIOLOGY AND SOCIAL HISTORY OF MUSIC. Text in English. 1983. irreg. price varies. back issues avail. **Document type:** *Monographic series, Trade.*
Published by: Pendragon Press, PO Box 190, Hillsdale, NY 12529. TEL 518-325-6100, FAX 518-325-6102, orders@pendragonpress.com. Ed. Ardal Powell.

301 AUS ISSN 1838-5214
▼ ➤ **SOCIOLOGY AT WORK. WORKING NOTES.** Text in English. 2010. s-a. free (effective 2011). back issues avail. **Document type:** *Bulletin, Academic/Scholarly.* **Description:** Promotes the use of sociology by practitioners who work outside academia.
Media: Online - full text.
Published by: Sociology at Work http://sociologyatwork.org. Eds. Anthony Hogan, Dina Bowman.

301 GBR ISSN 1751-9020
HM403
➤ **SOCIOLOGY COMPASS.** Text in English. 2008 (Jan.). bi-m. GBP 660 in United Kingdom to institutions; EUR 838 in Europe to institutions; USD 522 in the Americas to institutions; USD 1,292 elsewhere to institutions (effective 2012). back issues avail. **Document type:** *Journal, Academic/Scholarly.* **Description:** Aimed at senior undergraduates, postgraduates and academics. Provides a reference tool for researching essays, preparing lectures, writing a research proposal and keeping up with new developments in a specific area of interest.
Media: Online - full text.
Indexed: PAIS, SociolAb.
—BLDSC (8319.677050), IE.
Published by: Wiley-Blackwell Publishing Ltd. (Subsidiary of: John Wiley & Sons, Inc.), 9600 Garsington Rd, Oxford, OX4 2DQ, United Kingdom. TEL 44-1865-776868, FAX 44-1865-714591, customerservices@blackwellpublishing.com, http://www.wiley.com/. Ed. Joel Best.

301 USA ISSN 2160-083X
▼ ➤ **SOCIOLOGY MIND.** Abbreviated title: S M. Text in English. 2011. q. USD 156 (effective 2011). **Document type:** *Journal, Academic/Scholarly.* **Description:** Aims to synergize sociological imagination in the 21st century toward a critical understanding of new social and cultural forces that call for scientific interpretation and analysis of facts and values.
Related titles: Online - full text ed.: ISSN 2160-0848. free (effective 2011).
Published by: Scientific Research Publishing, Inc., PO Box 54821, Irvine, CA 92619. service@scirp.org. Ed. Asafa Jalata.

➤ **SOCIOLOGY OF CRIME, LAW AND DEVIANCE.** *see* CRIMINOLOGY AND LAW ENFORCEMENT

➤ **SOCIOLOGY OF EDUCATION.** *see* EDUCATION

301 GBR ISSN 0141-9889
RA418
➤ **SOCIOLOGY OF HEALTH AND ILLNESS**; a journal of medical sociology. Text in English. 1979. bi-m. (plus special issue). GBP 540 in United Kingdom to institutions; EUR 685 in Europe to institutions; USD 1,216 in the Americas to institutions; USD 1,418 elsewhere to institutions; GBP 621 combined subscription in United Kingdom to institutions (print & online eds.); EUR 788 combined subscription in Europe to institutions (print & online eds.); USD 1,399 combined subscription in the Americas to institutions (print & online eds.); USD 1,631 combined subscription elsewhere to institutions (print & online eds.) (effective 2012). adv. bk.rev. illus. index. back issues avail.; reprint service avail. from PSC. **Document type:** *Journal, Academic/Scholarly.* **Description:** An international journal which publishes sociological articles on all aspects of health, illness and medicine, focusing on empirical research of a qualitative kind. Provides a sociological perspective on the theory of medical knowledge, the practice of medical work, and the experience of receiving or giving medical care.
Incorporates (1995-1999): Sociology of Health and Illness Monograph Series
Related titles: Microform ed.; Online - full text ed.: ISSN 1467-9566. GBP 540 in United Kingdom to institutions; EUR 685 in Europe to institutions; USD 1,216 in the Americas to institutions; USD 1,418 elsewhere to institutions (effective 2012) (from IngentaConnect).
Indexed: A01, A02, A03, A08, A20, A22, A26, A36, AHCMS, ASCA, ASG, B04, B28, BRD, C06, C07, C08, C11, CA, CABA, CINAHL, CurCont, D01, E-psyche, E01, E08, E12, EMBASE, ESPM, ExcerpMed, FR, FamI, G08, GH, H04, H05, H11, H12, H13, I05, IBSS, LT, MCR, MEA&I, MEDLINE, N02, N03, P02, P03, P10, P20, P30, P34, P37, P42, P48, P53, P54, PCI, PQC, PSA, PsycInfo, PsycholAb, R12, RASB, RRTA, RiskAb, S02, S03, S09, S11, SCOPUS, SOPODA, SSA, SSAI, SSAb, SSCI, SSI, SociolAb, T02, T05, VS, W01, W02, W03, W07, W09, W11.
—BLDSC (8319.692000), GNLM, IE, Infotrieve, Ingenta, INIST. **CCC.**
Published by: (Foundation for the Sociology of Health and Illness), Wiley-Blackwell Publishing Ltd. (Subsidiary of: John Wiley & Sons, Inc.), 9600 Garsington Rd, Oxford, OX4 2DQ, United Kingdom. TEL 44-1865-776868, FAX 44-1865-714591, customerservices@blackwellpublishing.com, http://www.wiley.com/. Adv. contact Craig Pickett TEL 44-1865-476267.

201.6 USA ISSN 1069-4404
HN51
➤ **SOCIOLOGY OF RELIGION**; a quarterly review. Text in English. 1940. q. GBP 84 in United Kingdom to institutions; EUR 120 in Europe to institutions; USD 126 in US & Canada to institutions; GBP 84 elsewhere to institutions; GBP 91 combined subscription in United Kingdom to institutions (print & online eds.); EUR 131 combined subscription in Europe to institutions (print & online eds.); USD 138 combined subscription in US & Canada to institutions (print & online eds.); GBP 91 combined subscription elsewhere to institutions (print & online eds.) (effective 2012). adv. bk.rev. charts; stat.; illus. index, cum.index: vols.1-50. 140 p./no. 1 cols./p.; back issues avail.; reprint service avail. from PSC. **Document type:** *Journal, Academic/Scholarly.* **Description:** Aims to advance the scholarship in sociological study of religion.
Former titles (until 1993): S A. Sociological Analysis; (until 1973): Sociological Analysis (0038-0210); (until 1964): The American Catholic Sociological Review (0362-515X)
Related titles: Microform ed.: (from PQC); Online - full text ed.: ISSN 1759-8818. GBP 76 in United Kingdom to institutions; EUR 109 in Europe to institutions; USD 114 in US & Canada to institutions; GBP 76 elsewhere to institutions (effective 2012) (from IngentaConnect).
Indexed: A01, A02, A03, A08, A20, A21, A22, A25, A26, ABS&EES, ASCA, AmH&L, ArtHuCI, B04, BRD, CA, CLFP, CPL, Chicano, CurCont, E08, FR, FamI, G05, G06, G07, G08, G10, GSS&RPL, HEA, HistAb, I05, I07, I13, IBSS, M01, M02, P02, P10, P13, P27, P28, P30, P42, P46, P48, P53, P54, PCI, PQC, PSA, R&TA, R05, RASB, RI-1, RI-2, S02, S03, S08, S09, S11, S23, SCOPUS, SOPODA, SSA, SSAI, SSAb, SSCI, SSI, SociolAb, T02, W03, W05, W07, W09.
—BLDSC (8319.695500), IE, Infotrieve, Ingenta, INIST. **CCC.**
Published by: (Association for the Sociology of Religion), Oxford University Press (Subsidiary of: Oxford University Press), 2001 Evans Rd, Cary, NC 27513. TEL 919-677-0977, FAX 919-677-1303, http://www.oxfordjournals.org. Ed. David Yamane TEL 336-758-3260. Circ: 1,595.

790 USA ISSN 0741-1235
➤ **SOCIOLOGY OF SPORT JOURNAL.** Short title: S S J. Text in English. 1984. q. USD 368 domestic to institutions; USD 378 foreign to institutions; USD 426 combined subscription domestic to institutions (print & online eds.); USD 436 combined subscription foreign to institutions (print & online eds.) (effective 2012). adv. bk.rev. bibl.; charts; stat.; illus. Index. back issues avail.; reprint service avail. from PSC. **Document type:** *Journal, Academic/Scholarly.* **Description:** Focuses on the relationship between sport, society, and social institutions from the perspectives of social psychology, sociology and anthropology.
Related titles: Online - full text ed.: ISSN 1543-2785. USD 368 to institutions (effective 2012).
Indexed: A01, A03, A08, A20, A22, A26, ASCA, B04, B14, BRD, BRI, C03, C25, CA, CABA, CBCARef, CPerl, CommAb, CurCont, DIP, E02, E03, E07, E08, E12, ERI, ESPM, EdA, EdI, FoSS&M, G08, G10, GH, I05, IBR, IBZ, LT, N02, N03, P03, P30, P48, PEI, PQC, PsycInfo, PsycholAb, R12, RILM, RRTA, RiskAb, S02, S03, S09, SCI, SCOPUS, SD, SOPODA, SSA, SSAI, SSAb, SSCI, SSI, SociolAb, SportS, T02, W03, W07, W09, W11.
—BLDSC (8319.696830), IE, Infotrieve, Ingenta. **CCC.**
Published by: (North American Society for the Sociology of Sport), Human Kinetics, 1607 N Market St, Champaign, IL 61820. TEL 800-747-4457, FAX 217-351-2674, info@hkusa.com, http://www.humankinetics.com. Ed. Pirkko Markula. Pub. Rainer Martens. R&P Martha Gullo TEL 217-403-7534. Adv. contact Amy Bleich TEL 217-403-7803.

301 NLD ISSN 1388-428X
➤ **SOCIOLOGY OF THE SCIENCES LIBRARY.** Text in English. 1982; N.S. 1998. irreg., latest vol.1, 1998. price varies. **Document type:** *Monographic series, Academic/Scholarly.*
Formerly: Sociology of the Sciences Monographs (1388-4298)
Published by: Springer Netherlands (Subsidiary of: Springer Science+Business Media), Van Godewijckstraat 30, Dordrecht, 3311 GX, Netherlands. TEL 31-78-6576050, FAX 31-78-6576474.

➤ **SOCIOLOGY OF THE SCIENCES. YEARBOOK.** *see* SCIENCES: COMPREHENSIVE WORKS

301 AUS ISSN 0155-0632
SOCIOLOGY RESEARCH MONOGRAPHS. Text in English. 1978. irreg. back issues avail. **Document type:** *Monographic series, Academic/Scholarly.*
Published by: (Discipline of Social Science), University of New England, School of Social Science, Armidale, NSW 2351, Australia.

301 GBR ISSN 0959-8499
SOCIOLOGY REVIEW. Text in English. 1985. 4/yr. (Sept.-Apr.). GBP 26.95 domestic; GBP 33 in Europe; GBP 38 elsewhere (effective 2010). adv. **Document type:** *Magazine, Academic/Scholarly.*
Supersedes in part (in 1991): Social Studies Review (0267-0712)
Related titles: Online - full text ed.: free to qualified personnel (effective 2010).
Indexed: G05, G06, G07, G08, I05, I06, I07, SCOPUS, SociolAb.
—BLDSC (8319.699600), IE, Ingenta. **CCC.**
Published by: Philip Allan Updates, Market Pl, Deddington, Banbury, Oxon OX15 0SE, United Kingdom. TEL 44-1869-338652, FAX 44-1869-337590, sales@philipallan.co.uk. **Subscr. to:** Turpin Distribution, Pegasus Dr, Stratton Business Park, Biggleswade, Bedfordshire SG18 8TQ, United Kingdom. TEL 44-1767-604974, FAX 44-845-0095840, custserv@turpin-distribution.com.

301 USA ISSN 2159-5526
▼ **SOCIOLOGY STUDY.** Text in English. 2011. m. **Document type:** *Journal, Academic/Scholarly.*
Related titles: Online - full text ed.: ISSN 2159-5534.
Published by: David Publishing Co., Inc., 1840 Industrial Dr, Ste 160, Libertyville, IL 60048. TEL 847-281-9822, FAX 847-281-9855, order@davidpublishing.com, http://www.davidpublishing.com.

301 BEL
SOCIOLOGY TODAY. Text in Dutch, English. 1998. irreg. price varies. **Document type:** *Monographic series, Academic/Scholarly.*
Published by: Leuven University Press, Blijde Inkomststraat 5, Leuven, 3000, Belgium. TEL 32-16-325345, FAX 32-16-325352, university.press@upers.kuleuven.ac.be, http://www.kuleuven.ac.be/upers.

301 SRB ISSN 0085-6320
HM7
SOCIOLOSKI PREGLED/SOCIOLOGICAL REVIEW. Text in Serbo-Croatian; Summaries in English, French. 1961. 4/yr. EUR 50 foreign (effective 2009). adv. **Document type:** *Journal, Academic/Scholarly.*
Indexed: RASB, SOPODA, SociolAb.
Published by: Sociolosko Drustvo Srbije/Sociological Society of Serbia, Narodnog Fronta 45, Belgrade, 11000. TEL 381-11-3613158. Ed. Zsolt Lazar.

301 UKR ISSN 2218-2470
▼ ➤ **SOCIOPROSTIR.** Text in Ukrainian. 2010. irreg. (1-3/yr.). free (effective 2011). **Document type:** *Journal, Academic/Scholarly.* **Description:** Dedicated to critical analysis of different social problems from different perspectives, searching for their causes and ways of solution. The main aspect is analysis through contemporary social changes and their impacts on individual and society, and finding relationships between theory, research, education and practice.
Media: Online - full text.

S

Published by: (Kharkivs'kyi Natsional'nyi Universytet im. V.N. Karazina, Sotsiolohichnyi Fakul'tet, Kafedra Sotsiolohii Upravlinnya ta Sotsial'noi Roboty/V.N. Karazin Kharkiv National University, School of Sociology, Department of Sociology of Management and Social Work), Kharkivs'kyi Natsional'nyi Universytet im. V.N. Karazina/V.N. Karazin Kharkiv National University, Maidan Svobody 4, Kharkiv, 61077, Ukraine. TEL 380-572-436196, FAX 380-572-437044, postmaster@univer.kharkov.ua, http://www-ukr.univer.kharkov.ua. Ed. Valerii Nikolayevskii.

➤ **SOCIOVISION C O F R E M C A. LA LETTRE.** *see* BUSINESS AND ECONOMICS—Marketing And Purchasing

307.1 JPN ISSN 0386-3506
SOGO TOSHI KENKYU/COMPREHENSIVE URBAN STUDIES. Text in Japanese; Abstracts in English. 1977. 3/yr. free. **Document type:** *Academic/Scholarly.*
Indexed: IBSS.
Published by: Tokyo Metropolitan University, Center for Urban Studies, 1-1 Minami-Osawa, Hachioji-shi, Tokyo-to 192-0364, Japan. TEL 0426-77-2351, FAX 0426-77-2352. Ed. Yuetsu Takahashi.

301 SGP ISSN 0217-9520
HN690.8
➤ **SOJOURN**; journal of social issues in Southeast Asia. Text in English. 1986. s-a. (Apr. & Oct.). SGD 42 to individuals in Singapore, Malaysia & Brunei; USD 33 to individuals in Asia, Australia, New Zealand & Japan; USD 45 elsewhere to individuals; SGD 75 to institutions in Spingapore, Malaysia & Brunei; USD 62 to institutions in Asia, Australia, New Zealand & Japan; USD 84 elsewhere to institutions (effective 2010 & 2011). adv. bk.rev. abstr.; bibl. Index. back issues avail.; reprint service avail. from SCH. **Document type:** *Journal, Academic/Scholarly.* **Description:** Deals with issues of ethnicity, religion, urbanism, and population change. Includes articles, research notes, and occasional English translations of pivotal research first published in Southeast Asian languages.
Related titles: Microform ed.: (from PQC); Online - full text ed.: free to subscribers of print ed.; non-subscribers S$7(US $50) per article.
Indexed: A01, A03, A08, A11, A22, A26, APEL, B01, B06, B07, B08, B09, BAS, C12, C25, CA, CABA, DIP, E01, E08, G08, GH, HistAb, I05, IBR, IBSS, IBZ, LT, M05, M06, N02, P30, P34, P42, PAIS, PCI, PSA, PerIslam, R12, RASB, RRTA, S02, S03, S09, S13, S16, SCOPUS, SOPODA, SSA, SociolAb, T02, TAR, W11, WBA, WMB.
—BLDSC (8327.118750), IE, Infotrieve, Ingenta.
Published by: Institute of Southeast Asian Studies, 30 Heng Mui Keng Terrace, Pasir Panjang, Singapore, 119614, Singapore. FAX 65-67756259, pubsunit@iseas.edu.sg, http://www.iseas.edu.sg/. Eds. Hock Guan Lee, Kee Beng Ooi, Terence Chong, Theresa Devasahayam, Yew-Foong Hui.

306 ITA ISSN 1826-3801
IL SOLE 24 ORE CULTURA. Text in Italian. 2005. m. **Document type:** *Magazine, Consumer.*
Published by: Il Sole 24 Ore Business Media, Via Monte Rosa 91, Milan, 20149, Italy. TEL 39-02-30221, FAX 39-02-312055, info@ilsole24ore.com, http://www.gruppo24ore.com.

303 170 NLD ISSN 1389-6717
SOLIDARITY AND IDENTITY/SOLIDARITEIT EN IDENTITEIT. Text in Dutch. 1999. irreg. price varies. **Document type:** *Monographic series.*
Published by: Amsterdam University Press, Herengracht 221, Amsterdam, 1016 BG, Netherlands. TEL 31-20-4200050, FAX 31-20-4203214, info@aup.nl, http://www.aup.nl.

302 FRA ISSN 0489-7293
SONDAGES. Variant title: Revue Francaise de l'Opinion Publique. Text in French. 1939. q. **Document type:** *Magazine, Trade.*
Published by: Institut Francais d'Opinion Publique, 6-8 Rue Eugene Oudine, Paris, 75013, France. TEL 33-1-45841444, FAX 33-1-45855939, http://www.ifop.com.

301 JPN ISSN 0584-1380
HM7
SOSHIOROJI. Text in Japanese. 1952. 3/yr. back issues avail. **Document type:** *Journal, Academic/Scholarly.*
Indexed: CA, P42, PSA, S02, S03, SCOPUS, SSA, SociolAb, T02.
—BLDSC (8328.758000).
Published by: Shakaigaku Kenkyukai, Kyoto University, Department of Sociology, oshida Honmachi, Sakyo-ku, Kyoto, 606-8501, Japan. TEL 81-75-7532751 ext 2758, FAX 81-75-7532836.

301 NOR ISSN 0801-3845
SOSIALE OG OEKNOMISKE STUDIER. Text in English, Norwegian; Summaries in English. 1986. irreg. price varies. **Document type:** *Monographic series, Government.*
Formed by the merger of (1954-1986): Norway. Statistisk Sentralbyraa. Samfunnsoekonomiske Studier (0085-4344); (1957-1986): Norway. Statistisk Sentralbyraa. Artikler (0085-431X); (1972-1986): Norway. Statistisk Sentralbyraa. Statistiske Analyser (0333-0621)
Published by: Statistisk Sentralbyraa/Statistics Norway, Kongensgate 6, P O Box 8131, Dep, Oslo, 0033, Norway. TEL 47-21-090000, FAX 47-21-094973, ssb@ssb.no. Circ: 3,000.

301 NOR ISSN 0333-3205
SOSIOLOG-NYTT. Text in Norwegian. 1975. q. bk.rev. back issues avail. **Document type:** *Magazine, Trade.*
Related titles: Online - full text ed.: ISSN 1503-6669. 2002.
Published by: Norsk Sosiologforening/Norwegian Sociological Association, c/o Institutt for Samfunnsforskning, PO Box 3233, Elisenberg, Oslo, 0208, Norway. TEL 47-23-086100, FAX 47-23-086101, nsf@samfunnsforskning.no. Ed. Jon Rogstad. Circ: 800.

301 NOR ISSN 0332-6330
HM7
➤ **SOSIOLOGI I DAG.** Text in Norwegian. 1971. q. NOK 300 to individuals; NOK 500 to institutions (effective 2011). bk.rev. back issues avail. **Document type:** *Journal, Academic/Scholarly.*
Published by: Novus Forlag AS, Herman Foss Gate 19, Oslo, 0171, Norway. TEL 47-22-717450, FAX 47-22-718107, novus@novus.no. Ed. Lars Klemsdal. Circ: 400.

301 FIN ISSN 0038-1640
HM7
SOSIOLOGIA. Text in Finnish. 1964. q. EUR 42 domestic; EUR 58 foreign; EUR 9.50 per issue (effective 2005). adv. bk.rev. abstr. **Document type:** *Academic/Scholarly.*
Indexed: CA, P30, P42, PSA, S02, S03, SOPODA, SSA, SociolAb, T02.
—INIST.
Published by: Westermarck-Seura/Westermarck Society. The Finnish Sociological Association, c/o Harri Melin, PO Box 124, Turku, 20521, Finland. TEL 358-2-3336322, FAX 358-2-3335080, westermarck@utu.fi, http://org.utu.fi/yhd/westermarck/. Ed. Kimmo Jokinen.

301 NOR ISSN 0808-288X
➤ **SOSIOLOGISK AARBOK. NY SERIE.** Text in Multiple languages. 1993. 3/yr. NOK 300 to individuals; NOK 450 to institutions; NOK 200 to students (effective 2011). back issues avail. **Document type:** *Journal, Academic/Scholarly.*
Supersedes in part (in 1996): Sosiologisk Tidsskrift (0804-0486); Which incorporated (1985-1992): Sosiologisk Aarbok (0800-7497)
Published by: Novus Forlag AS, Herman Foss Gate 19, Oslo, 0171, Norway. TEL 47-22-717450, FAX 47-22-718107, novus@novus.no, http://www.novus.no. Ed. Per Otnes.

301 NOR ISSN 0804-0486
HM7
SOSIOLOGISK TIDSSKRIFT/JOURNAL OF SOCIOLOGY. Text in Danish, English, Norwegian, Swedish. 1993. q. NOK 500 to individuals; NOK 780 to institutions; NOK 270 to students (effective 2010). **Document type:** *Journal, Academic/Scholarly.* **Description:** Presents articles on sociological research results in Norway.
Incorporates (1985-1992): Sosiologisk Aarbok (0800-7497)
Related titles: Online - full text ed.: ISSN 1504-2928. 2004. NOK 880 (effective 2010).
Indexed: CA, DIP, IBR, IBZ, P42, PSA, S02, S03, SCOPUS, SSA, SociolAb, T02.
Published by: (Norsk Sosiologforening/Norwegian Sociological Association), Universitetsforlaget AS/Scandinavian University Press (Subsidiary of: Aschehoug & Co.), Sehesteds Gate 3, P O Box 508, Sentrum, Oslo, 0105, Norway. TEL 47-24-147500, FAX 47-24-147501, post@universitetsforlaget.no, http://www.universitetsforlaget.no. Eds. Aksel Tjora, Johan Fredrik Rye. Circ: 1,200.

SOSYOEKONOMI. *see* BUSINESS AND ECONOMICS

301 BGR ISSN 0324-1572
SOTSIOLOGICHESKI PROBLEMI. Abstracts in English, Bulgarian; Text in Bulgarian. 1969. q. BGL 6 domestic; BGL 2 newsstand/cover (effective 2002). bk.rev. reprint service avail. from IRC. **Document type:** *Journal.* **Description:** Publishes articles by Bulgarian and foreign authors dealing with all aspects of sociological knowledge including both purely theoretical considerations on key question of sociology and interpretations of empirical data from different spheres of contemporary social reality.
Indexed: RASB.
Published by: (Bulgarska Akademiya na Naukite/Bulgarian Academy of Sciences, Institut po Sotsiologiia), Sofiiski Universitet Sv. Kliment Ohridski, Universitetsko Izdatelstvo/Sofia University St. Kliment Ohridski University Press, Akad G Bonchev 6, Sofia, 1113, Bulgaria. Ed. Kolyo Koev. Circ: 470. **Dist. by:** Hemus, 6 Rouski Blvd., Sofia 1000, Bulgaria. **Co-sponsor:** Bulgarska Sotsiologicheska Asotsiatsiia.

301 RUS ISSN 0132-1625
HM7
➤ **SOTSIOLOGICHESKIE ISSLEDOVANIYA.** Text in Russian. m. RUR 250 for 6 mos. domestic; USD 300 in United States (effective 2004). **Document type:** *Journal, Academic/Scholarly.*
Related titles: Microfilm ed.: (from EVP); Online - full text ed.
Indexed: A20, CA, CurCont, IBSS, P30, P42, PSA, PopulInd, RASB, RILM, RefZh, S02, S03, SCOPUS, SOPODA, SSA, SSCI, SociolAb, T02, W07.
—East View. **CCC.**
Published by: Izdatel'stvo Nauka, Profsoyuznaya ul 90, Moscow, 117864, Russian Federation. TEL 7-095-3347151, FAX 7-095-4202220, secret@naukaran.ru, http://www.naukaran.ru. **Dist. by:** East View Information Services, 10601 Wayzata Blvd, Minneapolis, MN 55305. TEL 952-252-1201, 800-477-1005, FAX 952-252-1202, info@eastview.com, http://www.eastview.com.

301 RUS
SOTSIOLOGICHESKII FORUM/RUSSIAN SOCIOLOGICAL FORUM. Text in Russian, English. 1998. q. free. bk.rev. **Document type:** *Journal, Academic/Scholarly.* **Description:** Publishes academic-level articles in all areas on sociology and related social sciences.
Media: Online - full text.
Published by: (Mezhdunarodnyi Tsentr Sotsiologicheskogo Obrazovaniya/International Center for Sociological Education), Rossiiskaya Akademiya Nauk, Institut Sotsiologii/Russian Academy of Sciences, Institute of Sociology, Ul. Krzhizhanovskogo 24/35, stroenie 5, Moscow, 117218, Russian Federation. TEL 7-095-1288257, FAX 7-095-1289161. Ed. Inna F Deviatko.

301 RUS ISSN 1562-2495
HM7
SOTSIOLOGICHESKII ZHURNAL. Text in Russian. 1994. q. USD 168 foreign (effective 2003). 192 p./no.; **Document type:** *Journal, Academic/Scholarly.*
Related titles: Online - full text ed.: ISSN 1684-1581. 1997.
Indexed: CA, P42, PSA, RASB, S02, S03, SCOPUS, SSA, SociolAb, T02.
—East View.
Published by: Rossiiskaya Akademiya Nauk, Institut Sotsiologii/Russian Academy of Sciences, Institute of Sociology, Ul. Krzhizhanovskogo 24/35, stroenie 5, Moscow, 117218, Russian Federation. TEL 7-095-1288257, FAX 7-095-1289161. **Dist. by:** East View Information Services, 10601 Wayzata Blvd, Minneapolis, MN 55305. TEL 952-252-1201, 800-477-1005, FAX 952-252-1202, info@eastview.com, http://www.eastview.com.

301 BLR
➤ **SOTSIOLOGIYA.** Text in Russian. 1997. q. USD 206 foreign (effective 2006). **Document type:** *Journal, Academic/Scholarly.* **Description:** Presents articles on sociologic studies, the theories and practice of researches.
Published by: Belorusskii Gosudarstvennyi Universitet/Belorussian State University, Vul Babruiskaya 5a, Minsk, Belarus. http://www.bsu.by. **Dist. by:** East View Information Services, 10601 Wayzata Blvd, Minneapolis, MN 55305. TEL 952-252-1201, 800-477-1005, FAX 952-252-1202, info@eastview.com, http://www.eastview.com.

307.76 RUS ISSN 1994-3520
➤ **SOTSIOLOGIYA GORODA.** Text in Russian; Summaries in Russian, English. 2007. q. RUR 1,774 (effective 2010). abstr.; bibl.; charts; illus. reprints avail. **Document type:** *Journal, Academic/Scholarly.* **Description:** Contains results of the scientific research from Volgogradskii Gosudarstvennyi Arkhitekturno-Stroitel'nyi Universitet and other scientific organizations and universities in the sphere of sociology, philosophy, cultural sciences and other humanities.
Related titles: Online - full text ed.: ISSN 2077-9402. free (effective 2011).
Published by: Volgogradskii Gosudarstvennyi Arkhitekturno-Stroitel'nyi Universitet, ul Akademicheskaya 1, Volgograd, 400074, Russian Federation. TEL 7-442-974872, FAX 7-442-974933, info@vgasu.ru. Ed. B A Navrotskiy. Pub. S Yu Kalashnikov. Circ: 500 (paid).

301 UKR
SOTSIOLOHIYA: TEORIYA, METODY, MARKETINH. Text in Ukrainian. bi-m. USD 90 in United States. **Document type:** *Academic/Scholarly.*
Published by: Instytut Sotsiolohii, Ul Shelkovichnaya 12, Kiev, Ukraine. TEL 380-44-291-5107. **Dist. by:** East View Information Services, 10601 Wayzata Blvd, Minneapolis, MN 55305. TEL 952-252-1201, 800-477-1005, FAX 952-252-1202, info@eastview.com, http://www.eastview.com.

302 300 UKR ISSN 1680-4325
SOTSIONIKA, MENTOLOGIYA I PSIKHOLOGIYA LICHNOSTI. Text in Russian; Summaries in English. 1995. bi-m. USD 48 domestic; USD 132 foreign; USD 22 newsstand/cover (effective 2002). index. back issues avail. **Document type:** *Journal, Academic/Scholarly.* **Description:** Covers questions of selection of the personnel management, skill conduct business negotiation, definition of human compatibility in family and at work, education and training of children.
Related titles: Online - full text ed.; English ed.: Socionics, Mentology and Personality Psychology. ISSN 1680-8185. 2002.
Published by: Mezhdunarodnyi Institut Sotsioniki/International Socionics Institute, a/s 23, Kiev, 02206, Ukraine. TEL 380-44-5580935, admin@socionics.ibc.com.ua, socionic@ukrpack.net, http://www.socionics.ibc.com.ua/esocint.html. Eds. A. V. Dr. Bukalov, E. A. Dr. Donchenko, Yu. I. Prof. Saenko. Circ: 600 (paid). **Dist. by:** East View Information Services, 10601 Wayzata Blvd, Minneapolis, MN 55305. TEL 952-252-1201, 800-477-1005, FAX 952-252-1202, info@eastview.com, http://www.eastview.com.

301 RUS ISSN 2078-7081
▼ **SOTSIOSFERA.** Text in Russian. 2010. q. **Document type:** *Journal, Academic/Scholarly.*
Related titles: Online - full text ed.: free (effective 2011).
Published by: Nauchno-Izdatel'skii Tsentr Sotsiosfera, ul Mira, dom 74, komn 14, Penza, 440046, Russian Federation. TEL 7-412-686845. Ed. Boris Doroshin.

307 RUS ISSN 0868-4960
HN530.2
SOTSYAL'NAYA ZASHCHITA. Text in Russian. m. USD 129.95 in United States.
Indexed: RASB.
—East View.
Address: Pl Birzhevaya 1, Moscow, 103012, Russian Federation. TEL 7-095-2038323, FAX 7-095-2038958. Ed. N I Polezhaeva. **Dist. by:** East View Information Services, 10601 Wayzata Blvd, Minneapolis, MN 55305. TEL 952-252-1201, 800-477-1005, FAX 952-252-1202, info@eastview.com, http://www.eastview.com.

301 RUS
SOTSYAL'NAYA ZASHCHITA NASELENIYA. SERIYA. ORGANIZATSIYA SOTSYAL'NOGO OBESPECHENIYA PENSIONEROV. Text in Russian. q. USD 85 in United States.
Indexed: RASB.
Published by: Ministerstvo Sotsyal'noi Zashchity Naseleniya, Shabolovka 14, str 2, Moscow, 117049, Russian Federation. TEL 7-095-2364625. **Dist. by:** East View Information Services, 10601 Wayzata Blvd, Minneapolis, MN 55305. TEL 952-252-1201, 800-477-1005, FAX 952-252-1202, info@eastview.com, http://www.eastview.com.

301 RUS
SOTSYAL'NAYA ZASHCHITA NASELENIYA. SERIYA. PROTEZIROVANIE I PROTEZOSTROENIE. Text in Russian. 5/yr. USD 85 in United States.
Published by: Ministerstvo Sotsyal'noi Zashchity Naseleniya, Shabolovka 14, str 2, Moscow, 117049, Russian Federation. TEL 7-095-2364625. **Dist. by:** East View Information Services, 10601 Wayzata Blvd, Minneapolis, MN 55305. TEL 952-252-1201, 800-477-1005, FAX 952-252-1202, info@eastview.com, http://www.eastview.com.

301 RUS
SOTSYAL'NAYA ZASHCHITA NASELENIYA. SERIYA. SOTSYAL'NAYA POMOSHCH' SEM'E I DETYAM. Text in Russian. 5/yr. USD 85 in United States.
Indexed: RASB.
Published by: Ministerstvo Sotsyal'noi Zashchity Naseleniya, Shabolovka 14, str 2, Moscow, 117049, Russian Federation. TEL 7-095-2364625. **Dist. by:** East View Information Services, 10601 Wayzata Blvd, Minneapolis, MN 55305. TEL 952-252-1201, 800-477-1005, FAX 952-252-1202, info@eastview.com, http://www.eastview.com.

302.3 RUS
SOTSYAL'NAYA ZASHCHITA NASELENIYA. SERIYA. SOTSYAL'NO BYTOVOE OBSLUZHIVANIE PENSIONEROV I INVALIDOV. Text in Russian. 10/yr. USD 125 in United States.
Indexed: RASB.
Published by: Ministerstvo Sotsyal'noi Zashchity Naseleniya, Shabolovka 14, str 2, Moscow, 117049, Russian Federation. TEL 7-095-2364625. **Dist. by:** East View Information Services, 10601 Wayzata Blvd, Minneapolis, MN 55305. TEL 952-252-1201, 800-477-1005, FAX 952-252-1202, info@eastview.com, http://www.eastview.com.

301 RUS
SOTSYAL'NAYA ZASHCHITA NASELENIYA. SERIYA. VRACHEBNO-TRUDOVAYA EKSPERTIZA. SOTSYAL'NO-TRUDOVAYA REABELITATSIYA INVALIDOV. Text in Russian. q. USD 85 in United States.
Indexed: RASB.

Published by: Ministerstvo Sotsyal'noi Zashchity Naseleniya, Shabolovka 14, str 2, Moscow, 117049, Russian Federation. TEL 7-095-2364625. **Dist. by:** East View Information Services, 10601 Wayzata Blvd, Minneapolis, MN 55305. TEL 952-252-1201, 800-477-1005, FAX 952-252-1202, info@eastview.com, http://www.eastview.com.

305.896 USA ISSN 1099-9949
E185.5
SOULS; a critical journal of Black politics, culture, and society. Text in English. 1999. q. GBP 165 combined subscription in United Kingdom to institutions (print & online eds.); EUR 222, USD 279 combined subscription to institutions (print & online eds.) (effective 2012). back issues avail.; reprint service avail. from PSC. **Document type:** *Journal, Academic/Scholarly.* **Description:** Covers the intellectual contours of the contemporary Black experience: the various ideological debates, politics, culture, and recent history of African American people.
Related titles: Online - full text ed.: ISSN 1548-3843. GBP 149 in United Kingdom to institutions; EUR 200, USD 251 to institutions (effective 2012) (from IngentaConnect).
Indexed: A22, AltPI, AmH&L, B21, CA, E01, E17, ESPM, HistAb, IIBP, LeftInd, P42, PAIS, PSA, S02, S03, SRRA, SociolAb, T02.
—IE, Ingenta. **CCC.**
Published by: Taylor & Francis Inc. (Subsidiary of: Taylor & Francis Group), 325 Chestnut St, Ste 800, Philadelphia, PA 19106. TEL 215-625-8900, 800-354-1420, FAX 215-625-8914, orders@taylorandfrancis.com, http://www.taylorandfrancis.com. Ed. Dr. Manning Marable. **Subscr. to:** Taylor & Francis Ltd., Journals Customer Service, Sheepen Pl, Colchester, Essex CO3 3LP, United Kingdom. TEL 44-20-70175544, FAX 44-20-70175198, subscriptions@tandf.co.uk.

SOURCE (SEATTLE). *see* RELIGIONS AND THEOLOGY

303.4 GBR ISSN 2152-8586
HM1
➤ **SOUTH AFRICAN REVIEW OF SOCIOLOGY.** Text in English. 1970. s-a. GBP 222 combined subscription in United Kingdom to institutions (print & online eds.); EUR 293, USD 365 combined subscription to institutions (print & online eds.) (effective 2012). reprint service avail. from PSC. **Document type:** *Journal, Academic/Scholarly.* **Description:** Examines South Africa's transition to a democratic society, along with the social dynamics of an emerging unity.
Former titles (until 2005): Society in Transition (1028-9852); (until 1998): Suid Afrikaanse Tydskrif vir Sosiologie - South African Journal of Sociology (0258-0144)
Related titles: Online - full text ed.: ISSN 2072-1951. GBP 200 in United Kingdom to institutions; EUR 264, USD 329 to institutions (effective 2012).
Indexed: A01, A02, A03, A08, AICP, AnthLit, CA, DIP, IBR, IBSS, IBZ, ISAP, M01, M02, MLA-IB, P30, P42, PSA, RILM, S02, S03, S21, SCOPUS, SOPODA, SSA, SSCI, SociolAb, T02, W07.
—BLDSC (8345.175500), IE, Ingenta. **CCC.**
Published by: (South African Sociological Association ZAF), Routledge (Subsidiary of: Taylor & Francis Group), 4 Park Sq, Milton Park, Abingdon, Oxon OX14 4RN, United Kingdom. TEL 44-20-70176000, FAX 44-20-70176336, journals@routledge.com, http://www.routledge.com. Circ: 250. **Co-publisher:** UniSA Press.

➤ **SOUTH ASIA**; journal of South Asian studies. *see* HISTORY—History Of Asia

301 GBR
SOUTH BANK UNIVERSITY. FACULTY OF HUMANITIES AND SOCIAL SCIENCE. SOCIAL SCIENCE RESEARCH PAPERS. Text in English. irreg. **Document type:** *Report, Academic/Scholarly.*
Formerly: South Bank University. School of Education, Politics and Social Science. Social Science Research Papers
Published by: South Bank University, Faculty of Humanites and Social Science, 103 Borough Rd, London, SE1 0AA, United Kingdom. TEL 44-20-7928-8989, FAX 44-20-7815-8155.

SOUTH EUROPEAN SOCIETY & POLITICS. *see* POLITICAL SCIENCE—International Relations

346.71 CAN ISSN 1481-9155
SOUTHERN CALIFORNIA'S DIVORCE MAGAZINE. Text in English. 1997. q. USD 13.95 (effective 2005).
Published by: Segue Esprit Inc., 2255B Queen St, E, Ste #1179, Toronto, ON M4E 1G3, Canada. TEL 416-368-8853, FAX 416-368-4978, editors@divorcemag.com. Ed., Pub. Dan Couvrette.

SOUTHERN CHRISTIAN FAMILY; keeping the family together through Christian values. *see* RELIGIONS AND THEOLOGY

301.092 USA ISSN 0038-4577
HM1
SOUTHERN SOCIOLOGIST. Text in English. 1968. 3/yr. USD 15 to non-members. adv. reprints avail. **Document type:** *Newsletter.*
Related titles: Microform ed.: (from PQC).
Published by: Southern Sociological Society, Department of Sociology and Anthropology, Mississippi State, MS 39762. TEL 601-325-7869, FAX 601-325-4564, jones@soc.msstate.edu, rent@grad.msstate.edu. Eds. George S Rent, James D Jones. Adv. contact James D Jones. Circ: 2,000 (paid).

SOUTHWESTERN & MEXICAN PHOTOGRAPHY. *see* PHOTOGRAPHY

SOZIAL- UND WIRTSCHAFTSPOLITIK. *see* POLITICAL SCIENCE

300 DEU ISSN 0945-8484
SOZIALE PROBLEME; Studien und Materialien. Text in German. 1995. irreg., latest vol.4, 2007. price varies. **Document type:** *Monographic series, Academic/Scholarly.*
Published by: Centaurus Verlag & Media KG, Kaiser-Joseph-Str 267, Freiburg, 79098, Germany. TEL 49-761-1525861, FAX 49-761-1525868, info@centaurus-verlag.de.

301 DEU ISSN 0948-423X
HM407
➤ **SOZIALE SYSTEME**; Zeitschrift fuer Soziologische Theorie. Text in German. 1995. 2/yr. EUR 52 to individuals; EUR 68 to institutions; EUR 36 to students; EUR 38 newsstand/cover (effective 2011). adv. 160 p./no.; back issues avail.; reprint service avail. from SCH. **Document type:** *Journal, Academic/Scholarly.*
Indexed: CA, DIP, IBR, IBSS, IBZ, P42, PSA, S02, S03, SCOPUS, SOPODA, SSA, SociolAb, T02.
—BLDSC (8361.066000), IE.
Published by: Lucius und Lucius Verlagsgesellschaft mbH, Gerokstr 51, Stuttgart, 70184, Germany. TEL 49-711-242060, FAX 49-711-242088, lucius@luciusverlag.com, http://www.luciusverlag.com. Ed. Dirk Baecker. Pub. Wulf von Lucius. Circ: 500 (paid). **Dist. by:** Brockhaus Commission, Kreidlerstr 9, Kornwestheim 70806, Germany. TEL 49-7154-13270, FAX 49-7154-132713, info@brocom.de.

301 DEU ISSN 0038-6073
H5
➤ **SOZIALE WELT**; Zeitschrift fuer sozialwissenschaftliche Forschung und Praxis. Text in German. 1949. q. EUR 99 (effective 2011). adv. bk.rev. charts. index. reprint service avail. from SCH. **Document type:** *Journal, Academic/Scholarly.*
Indexed: A20, A22, ASCA, BibInd, CA, CurCont, DIP, FR, IBR, IBSS, IBZ, PAIS, PCI, PRA, PhilInd, RASB, RILM, S02, S03, SCOPUS, SOPODA, SSCI, SociolAb, T02, W07, WBSS.
—BLDSC (8361.070000), IE, Infotrieve, Ingenta, INIST. **CCC.**
Published by: (Arbeitsgemeinschaft Sozialwissenschaftlicher Institute e.V.), Nomos Verlagsgesellschaft mbH und Co. KG, Waldseestr 3-5, Baden-Baden, 76530, Germany. TEL 49-7221-21040, FAX 49-7221-210427, marketing@nomos.de, nomos@nomos.de, http://www.nomos.de. Ed. Irmhild Saake. Adv. contact Bettina Roos. Circ: 1,200 (paid and controlled).

303 DEU ISSN 1439-9326
SOZIALER SINN; Zeitschrift fuer hermeneutische Sozialforschung. Text in German. 2000. 2/yr. EUR 66 to individuals; EUR 82 to institutions; EUR 49.50 to students; EUR 46 newsstand/cover (effective 2011). adv. **Document type:** *Journal, Academic/Scholarly.* **Description:** Provides a forum for the study of various social and cultural issues.
Indexed: CA, DIP, IBR, IBSS, IBZ, P42, PSA, S02, S03, SociolAb, T02.
—CCC.
Published by: Lucius und Lucius Verlagsgesellschaft mbH, Gerokstr 51, Stuttgart, 70184, Germany. TEL 49-711-242060, FAX 49-711-242088, lucius@luciusverlag.com.

▼ **SOZIALPHILOSOPHISCHE STUDIEN.** *see* PHILOSOPHY

316 AUT ISSN 1990-3553
SOZIALPHYSIK. Text in German. 2006. m. **Document type:** *Journal, Academic/Scholarly.*
Media: Online - full content.
Address: Gaertnerstr 16-9, Linz, 4020, Austria. Ed. Gudrun Tischler. Pub. Klemens Auinger.

SOZIOLINGUISTIK UND SPRACHKONTAKT. *see* LINGUISTICS

301 ESP ISSN 1575-7005
SOZIOLOGIAZKO EUSKAL KOADERMOAK/CUADERNOS SOCIOLOGICOS VASCOS. Text in Spanish; Summaries in Spanish. 1999. irreg. **Document type:** *Magazine.*
Published by: Eusko Jaurlaritzaren Argitalpen-Zerbitzu Nagusia/Servicio Central de Publicaciones del Gobierno Vasco, Donostia-San Sebastian, 1, Vitoria-gasteiz, Alava 01010, Spain. TEL 34-945-018561, FAX 34-945-189709, hac-sabd@ej-gv.es, http://www.ej-gv.net/publicaciones.

301 DEU ISSN 0340-918X
HM5
➤ **SOZIOLOGIE**; Forum der Deutschen Gesellschaft fuer Soziologie. Text in German. 1973. q. EUR 70 to individuals; EUR 110 to institutions; EUR 19 newsstand/cover (effective 2008). adv. reprint service avail. from IRC. **Document type:** *Journal, Academic/Scholarly.*
Related titles: Online - full text ed.: ISSN 1862-2550.
Indexed: A22, A26, CA, DIP, E01, FR, IBR, IBSS, IBZ, RASB, S02, S03, SCOPUS, SOPODA, SociolAb, T02.
—IE, Ingenta, INIST. **CCC.**
Published by: (Deutsche Gesellschaft fuer Soziologie), Campus Verlag GmbH, Kurfuerstenstr 49, Frankfurt Am Main, 60486, Germany. TEL 49-69-9765160, FAX 49-69-97651678, info@campus.de, http://www.campus.de. Ed. Georg Vobruba. adv.: page EUR 735. Circ: 2,000 (paid).

301 DEU ISSN 0721-4073
SOZIOLOGIE UND ANTHROPOLOGIE. Text in German. 1981. irreg., latest vol.11, 2000. price varies. **Document type:** *Monographic series, Academic/Scholarly.*
Published by: Peter Lang GmbH (Subsidiary of: Peter Lang Publishing Group), Eschborner Landstr 42-50, Frankfurt Am Main, 60489, Germany. TEL 49-69-7807050, FAX 49-69-78070550, zentrale.frankfurt@peterlang.com. Ed. Christian Sigrist.

301 DEU ISSN 0584-6048
SOZIOLOGISCHE ABHANDLUNGEN. Text in German. 1961. irreg., latest vol.13, 1971. price varies. **Document type:** *Monographic series, Academic/Scholarly.*
Published by: Duncker und Humblot GmbH, Carl-Heinrich-Becker-Weg 9, Berlin, 12165, Germany. TEL 49-30-7900060, FAX 49-30-79000631, info@duncker-humblot.de.

301 DEU ISSN 0343-4109
HM5
➤ **SOZIOLOGISCHE REVUE**; Besprechungen neuer Literatur. Text in German. 1978. q. EUR 218; EUR 59.80 to students; EUR 64.80 newsstand/cover (effective 2011). adv. bk.rev. index. back issues avail.; reprint service avail. from SCH. **Document type:** *Journal, Academic/Scholarly.* **Description:** Contains critical reviews of newly published books in all fields of sociology, and the sociological aspects of law, politics, medicine, and religion.
Related titles: Online - full text ed.: EUR 218; EUR 59.80 to students (effective 2011).
Indexed: A22, CA, DIP, IBR, IBSS, IBZ, P42, PSA, RASB, S02, S03, SCOPUS, SOPODA, SSA, SociolAb, T02, W09.
—BLDSC (8361.217500), IE, Infotrieve, Ingenta. **CCC.**
Published by: Oldenbourg Wissenschaftsverlag GmbH, Rosenheimer Str 145, Munich, 81671, Germany. TEL 49-89-450510, FAX 49-89-45051204, orders@oldenbourg.de, http://www.oldenbourg.de. Circ: 2,400 (paid and controlled).

301 DEU ISSN 0584-6064
SOZIOLOGISCHE SCHRIFTEN. Text in German. 1964. irreg., latest vol.81, 2008. price varies. **Document type:** *Monographic series, Academic/Scholarly.*
Published by: Duncker und Humblot GmbH, Carl-Heinrich-Becker-Weg 9, Berlin, 12165, Germany. TEL 49-30-7900060, FAX 49-30-79000631, info@duncker-humblot.de.

301 CHE ISSN 1660-3346
SOZ:MAG. Text in German. 2002. irreg. **Document type:** *Journal, Academic/Scholarly.*
Related titles: Online - full text ed.: ISSN 1660-3354. free (effective 2011).
Published by: Verein Virtuelle Soziologinnen, Andreasstr 15, Zurich, 8055, Switzerland. TEL 41-44-2415179, info@soziologie.ch, http://www.soziologie.ch.

SPACES FOR DIFFERENCE. *see* SOCIAL SCIENCES: COMPREHENSIVE WORKS

SPATIAL PRACTICES; an interdisciplinary series in cultural history, geography and literature. *see* HISTORY

301 ITA ISSN 2036-9824
SPAZIO OLTRE. Text in Italian. 2008. q. **Document type:** *Newspaper, Consumer.*
Published by: Associazione "La Nuvola e il Delfino", Via Ostiense 2236, Ostia Antica, RM 00119, Italy. http://www.nuvolaedelfino.com.

307.14 DEU ISSN 0176-277X
SPEKTRUM (MUENSTER). Text in German. 1984. irreg., latest vol.104, 2010. price varies. **Document type:** *Monographic series, Academic/Scholarly.*
Indexed: IBR, IBZ.
Published by: Lit Verlag, Grevener Str/Fresnostr 2, Muenster, 48159, Germany. TEL 49-251-235091, FAX 49-251-231972, lit@lit-verlag.de.

301 FRA ISSN 2107-2698
▼ **SPORT, MEMOIRE ET SOCIETE.** Text in French. 2010. irreg. **Document type:** *Monographic series.*
Published by: Atlantica, BP 90041, Biarritz Cedex, 64201, France. TEL 33-5-59528400, FAX 33-5-59528401, http://www.atlantica.fr.

301 DEU ISSN 1610-3181
SPORT UND GESELLSCHAFT/SPORTS AND SOCIETY. Text in German. 2004 (Feb.). 3/yr. EUR 58; EUR 39 to students; EUR 24 per issue (effective 2011). adv. **Document type:** *Journal, Academic/Scholarly.*
Indexed: SD.
Published by: Lucius und Lucius Verlagsgesellschaft mbH, Gerokstr 51, Stuttgart, 70184, Germany. TEL 49-711-242060, FAX 49-711-242088, lucius@luciusverlag.com, http://www.luciusverlag.com. **Dist. by:** Brockhaus Commission, Kreidlerstr 9, Kornwestheim 70806, Germany. TEL 49-7154-13270, FAX 49-7154-132713, info@brocom.de.

301 796 DEU ISSN 1865-777X
SPORT UND GESELLSCHAFTLICHE PERSPEKTIVEN. Text in German. 2008. irreg. price varies. **Document type:** *Monographic series, Academic/Scholarly.*
Published by: Peter Lang GmbH (Subsidiary of: Peter Lang Publishing Group), Eschborner Landstr 42-50, Frankfurt Am Main, 60489, Germany. TEL 49-69-7807050, FAX 49-69-78070550, zentrale.frankfurt@peterlang.com. Ed. Martin Schweer.

302.23 DEU ISSN 1863-7833
SPORTKOMMUNIKATION. Text in German. 2004. irreg., latest vol.6, 2010. price varies. **Document type:** *Monographic series, Academic/Scholarly.*
Published by: Herbert von Halem Verlag, Lindenstr 19, Cologne, 50674, Germany. TEL 49-221-9258290, FAX 49-221-92582929, info@halem-verlag.de, http://www.halem-verlag.de.

301 ITA ISSN 1973-9141
LO SQUADERNO. Text in Italian, English. 2006. q. free (effective 2011). **Document type:** *Journal, Academic/Scholarly.*
Media: Online - full text.
Published by: Professionaldreamers losquaderno@professionaldreamers.net, http://www.losquaderno.professionaldreamers.net. Ed. Andrea Mubi Brighenti.

301 USA
STANDARDS; the international journal of multicultural studies. Text in English. 1992-2002; resumed. a. illus.
Media: Online - full content.
Published by: University of Colorado, Campus Box 226, Boulder, CO 80309. TEL 303-442-7631, FAX 303-492-7272.

STATE, LAW AND SOCIETY. *see* POLITICAL SCIENCE

306.85 283 AUS ISSN 1832-5564
STATE OF THE FAMILY. Text in English. 2000. a., latest 2005. **Document type:** *Journal, Consumer.*
Related titles: Online - full text ed.: ISSN 1833-931X.
Published by: Anglicare Australia, GPO 1307, Canberra, ACT 2601, Australia. TEL 61-2-62301775, FAX 61-2-62301704, anglicare@anglicare.asn.au. Ed. Sean Regan.

STATO E MERCATO. *see* POLITICAL SCIENCE

301 SWE ISSN 1653-851X
STOCKHOLM STUDIES IN ETHNOLOGY. Text in English. 2006. irreg., latest vol.4, 2010. **Document type:** *Monographic series, Academic/Scholarly.*
Related titles: ◆ Series of: Acta Universitatis Stockholmiensis. ISSN 0346-6418.
Published by: (Stockholms Universitet, Institutionen foer Etnologi, Religionshistoria och Genusstudier/Stockholm University, Department of Ethnology, History of Religion and Gender Studies), Stockholms Universitet, Acta Universitatis Stockholmiensis, c/o Stockholms Universitetsbibliotek, Universitetsvaegen 10, Stockholm, 10691, Sweden. TEL 46-8-162800, FAX 46-8-157776, http://www.sub.su.se. Ed. Margaretha Fathli. **Dist. by:** Eddy.se AB, Norra Kyrkogatan 3, Visby 62155, Sweden. TEL 46-498-253900, FAX 46-498-249789, info@eddy.se, order@eddy.se, http://www.eddy.se, http://acta.bokorder.se.

301 SWE ISSN 0491-0885
STOCKHOLM STUDIES IN SOCIOLOGY. Text in Multiple languages. 1956. irreg., latest vol.47, 2010. price varies. back issues avail. **Document type:** *Monographic series, Academic/Scholarly.*
Related titles: ◆ Series of: Acta Universitatis Stockholmiensis. ISSN 0346-6418.

S

Published by: (Stockholms Universitet, Sociologiska Institutionen/ Stockholm University, Department of Sociologi), Stockholms Universitet, Acta Universitatis Stockholmiensis, c/o Stockholms Universitetsbibliotek, Universitetsvaegen 10, Stockholm, 10691, Sweden. TEL 46-8-162800, FAX 46-8-157776, http://www.sub.su.se. Ed. Margaretha Fathli. **Dist. by:** Eddy.se AB, Norra Kyrkogatan 3, Visby 62155, Sweden. TEL 46-498-253900, FAX 46-498-249789, info@eddy.se, order@eddy.se, http://www.eddy.se, http://acta.bokorder.se.

301 SWE ISSN 1654-1189
STOCKHOLM UNIVERSITY. LINNAEUS CENTER FOR INTEGRATION STUDIES. WORKING PAPERS. Text in English. 2007. irreg., latest 2010. **Document type:** *Monographic series, Academic/Scholarly.*
Related titles: Online - full text ed.
Published by: Stockholms Universitet, Linnecentum foer Integrationsstudier/Stockholm University, Linnaeus Center for Integration Studies, c/o Institut foer Social Forskning, Stockholms Universitet, Stockholm, 10691, Sweden. eskil.wadensjo@sofi.su.se, http://www.su.se/pub/jsp/polopoly.jsp?d=3486.

301 ITA ISSN 2036-9476
STORIA E SOCIOLOGIA DELLA MODERNITA. Text in Italian. 2002. irreg. **Document type:** *Monographic series, Academic/Scholarly.*
Published by: Edizioni Plus - Universita di Pisa (Pisa University Press), Lungarno Pacinotti 43, Pisa, Italy. TEL 39-050-2212056, FAX 39-050-2212945, http://www.edizioniplus.it.

301 USA
STRAND THREE. Text in English. 1995. s-a. **Description:** Contains articles with information necessary in fostering a futurist society.
Media: Online - full text.
Address: c/o Speakeasy Cafe, 2304 Second Ave, Seattle, WA 98121. TEL 206-441-2504. Ed. Max Chandler.

301 GBR ISSN 1356-0522
STRATHCLYDE PAPERS ON SOCIOLOGY AND SOCIAL POLICY. Text in English. 1994. irreg. **Document type:** *Monographic series.*
Published by: University of Strathclyde, Department of Government, McCance Bldg, 16 Richmond St, Glasgow, G1 1XQ, United Kingdom. Ed. Isobel Lindsay.

301 USA ISSN 0884-870X
STRESS IN MODERN SOCIETY. Text in English. 1984. irreg., latest vol.19, 1989. index. back issues avail. **Document type:** *Monographic series.* **Description:** Monographs covering a broad range of topics from specific causes of stress to intervention methods.
Published by: A M S Press, Inc., Brooklyn Navy Yard, 63 Flushing Ave, Bldg 292, Unit #221, Brooklyn, NY 11205. TEL 718-875-8100, FAX 718-875-3800, editorial@amspressinc.com, queries@amspressinc.com, http://www.amspressinc.com.

STREVEN; cultureel maatschappelijk maandblad. *see* GENERAL INTEREST PERIODICALS—Belgium

STRUCTURAL EQUATION MODELING; a multidisciplinary journal. *see* PSYCHOLOGY

301 370 ITA ISSN 1825-1625
STRUMENTI (MILAN). Text in Italian. 199?. 3/yr. free. **Document type:** *Magazine, Consumer.*
Published by: Manitese, Piazza Gambara 7-9, Milan, 20146, Italy. TEL 39-02-4075165, FAX 39-02-4046890, manitese@manitese.it.

301 331 ITA ISSN 2038-6370
▼ **STRUMENTI PER.** Text in Italian. 2010. irreg. **Document type:** *Monographic series, Academic/Scholarly.*
Published by: Istituto per lo Sviluppo della Formazione Professionale dei Lavoratori (I S F O L), Corso d'Italia 33, Rome, 00198, Italy. TEL 39-06-854471, http://www.isfol.it.

301 ITA ISSN 0039-291X
HM7
STUDI DI SOCIOLOGIA. Text in English, French, Italian. 1963. q. EUR 60 domestic; EUR 100 foreign (effective 2009). adv. bk.rev. bibl.; charts. index. **Document type:** *Journal, Academic/Scholarly.* **Description:** Covers current issues in sociology.
Related titles: Online - full text ed.
Indexed: CA, DIP, FR, IBR, IBSS, IBZ, P30, P42, PCI, PSA, RASB, S02, S03, SOPODA, SSA, SociolAb, T02.
—INIST.
Published by: (Universita Cattolica del Sacro Cuore, Universita degli Studi di Urbino, Istituto di Sociologia), Vita e Pensiero (Subsidiary of: Universita Cattolica del Sacro Cuore), Largo Gemelli 1, Milan, 20123, Italy. TEL 39-02-72342335, FAX 39-02-72342260, redazione.vp@mi.unicatt.it, http://www.vitaepensiero.it. Ed. Vincenzo Cesareo. Circ: 700.

STUDI EMIGRAZIONE/EMIGRATION STUDIES. *see* POPULATION STUDIES

306.85 ITA ISSN 1827-5397
STUDI INTERDISCIPLINARI SULLA FAMIGLIA. Text in Italian. 1983. irreg. price varies. **Document type:** *Monographic series, Academic/ Scholarly.*
Published by: (Universita Cattolica del Sacro Cuore, Centro Sudi e Ricerche sulla Famiglia), Vita e Pensiero (Subsidiary of: Universita Cattolica del Sacro Cuore), Largo Gemelli 1, Milan, 20123, Italy. TEL 39-02-72342335, FAX 39-02-72342260, redazione.vp@mi.unicatt.it, http://www.vitaepensiero.it.

STUDIA ANTHROPONYMICA SCANDINAVICA; tidskrift foer nordisk personnamnsforskning. *see* LINGUISTICS

STUDIA AUGUSTANA; Augsburger Forschungen zur europaeischen Kulturgeschichte. *see* HISTORY—History Of Europe

301 ESP ISSN 1138-6355
K23
STUDIA CARANDE. Text in Spanish. 1998. s-a. **Document type:** *Journal, Academic/Scholarly.*
Published by: Universidad Rey Juan Carlos, Centro de Estudios Superiores Ramon Carande, C. Tulipan, s-n, Madrid, 28933, Spain. TEL 34-91-6655060, FAX 34-91-6147120.

STUDIA NAD RODZINA. *see* RELIGIONS AND THEOLOGY—Roman Catholic

301 CZE
STUDIA SOCIOLOGICA. Variant title: Acta Universitatis Carolinae: Philosophica et Historica. Studia Sociologica. Text in Czech; Summaries in English, German, Russian. a. USD 28.60 (effective 1999). **Document type:** *Academic/Scholarly.*
Published by: (Univerzita Karlova v Praze, Filozoficka Fakulta/Charles University in Prague, Faculty of Philosophy), Nakladatelstvi Karolinum, Ovocny trh 3/5, Prague 1, 11636, Czech Republic. TEL 420-224491275, FAX 420-224212041, cupress@cuni.cz, http://cupress.cuni.cz. Ed. Ivan Hlavacek. Circ: 400.

301 SWE ISSN 0585-5551
STUDIA SOCIOLOGICA UPSALIENSIA. Text in Multiple languages. 1962. irreg., latest vol.49, 2003. price varies. back issues avail. **Document type:** *Monographic series, Academic/Scholarly.*
Related titles: ◆ Series of: Acta Universitatis Upsaliensis. ISSN 0346-5462.
Indexed: P30.
Published by: Uppsala Universitet, Acta Universitatis Upsaliensis/ University Publications from Uppsala, PO Box 256, Uppsala, 75105, Sweden. TEL 46-18-4716804, FAX 46-18-4716804, acta@ub.uu.se, http://www.ub.uu.se/upu/auu/index.html. Ed. Bengt Landgren. **Dist. by:** Almqvist & Wiksell International, PO Box 614, Soedertaelje 15127, Sweden. TEL 46-8-5509497, FAX 46-8-55016710.

301 POL ISSN 0039-3371
H8 CODEN: STSOCP
STUDIA SOCJOLOGICZNE. Text in Polish. q. USD 68 foreign (effective 2002). bk.rev. bibl.; charts. index. **Document type:** *Academic/ Scholarly.* **Description:** Treatises on theoretical and methodological aspects of sociology.
Indexed: CA, DIP, IBR, IBSS, IBZ, MLA-IB, P42, PSA, PsycholAb, RASB, S02, S03, SCOPUS, SOPODA, SSA, SSCI, SociolAb, T02, W07.
Published by: Polska Akademia Nauk, Instytut Filozofii i Socjologii, Nowy Swiat 72, Warsaw, 00330, Poland. secretar@ifispan.waw.pl. Ed. Janusz Slucha. **Dist. by:** Ars Polona, Obroncow 25, Warsaw 03933, Poland. **Co-sponsor:** Polska Akademia Nauk, Komitet Nauk Socjologii.

301 ROM ISSN 1224-8703
➤ **STUDIA UNIVERSITATIS BABES-BOLYAI. SOCIOLOGIA.** Text in English. 1970. s-a. exchange basis. abstr.; bibl.; stat.; charts; illus. **Document type:** *Journal, Academic/Scholarly.*
Supersedes in part (in 1996): Studia Universitatis "Babes-Bolyai". Sociologia - Politica (1221-8197); Which was formerly (until 1990): Studia Universitatis "Babes-Bolyai". Series Sociologica (1221-812X)
Related titles: Online - full text ed.: ISSN 2066-0464.
Indexed: CA, IBSS, PQC, RASB, T02.
Published by: Universitatea "Babes-Bolyai", Studia/Babes-Bolyai University, Studia, 51 Hasdeu Str, Cluj-Napoca, 400371, Romania. TEL 40-264-405352, FAX 40-264-591906, office@studia.ubbcluj.ro. Eds. Cristina Rat, Dan Chiribuca, Mircea Comsa. **Dist by:** "Lucian Blaga" Central University Library, International Exchange Department, Clinicilor st no 2, Cluj-Napoca 400371, Romania. TEL 40-264-597092, FAX 40-264-597633, iancu@bcucluj.ro.

➤ **STUDIEN UND BERICHTE.** *see* EDUCATION

306.85 DEU ISSN 1435-6775
STUDIEN ZUR FAMILIENFORSCHUNG. Text in German. 1996. irreg., latest vol.25, 2009. price varies. **Document type:** *Monographic series, Academic/Scholarly.*
Published by: Verlag Dr. Kovac, Leverkusenstr 13, Hamburg, 22761, Germany. TEL 49-40-3988800, FAX 49-40-39888055, info@verlagdrkovac.de.

307.14 DEU ISSN 1618-3657
STUDIEN ZUR GEOGRAPHISCHEN ENTWICKLUNGSFORSCHUNG. Text in German. 1993. irreg., latest vol.35, 2009. price varies. **Document type:** *Monographic series, Academic/Scholarly.*
Formerly (until 2001): Freiburger Studien zur Geographischen Entwicklungsforschung (0943-7045)
Indexed: IBR, IBZ.
—BLDSC (8483.645970).
Published by: Verlag fuer Entwicklungspolitik Saarbruecken GmbH, Auf der Adt 14, Saarbruecken, 66130, Germany. TEL 49-6893-986094, FAX 49-6893-986095, vfe@verlag-entwicklungspolitik.de.

STUDIEN ZUR KINDHEITS- UND JUGENDFORSCHUNG. *see* CHILDREN AND YOUTH—About

300 DEU ISSN 1619-084X
STUDIEN ZUR SEXUALWISSENSCHAFT UND SEXUALPAEDAGOGIK. Text in German. 1985. irreg., latest vol.18, 2006. price varies. **Document type:** *Monographic series, Academic/ Scholarly.*
Published by: Peter Lang GmbH (Subsidiary of: Peter Lang Publishing Group), Eschborner Landstr 42-50, Frankfurt Am Main, 60489, Germany. TEL 49-69-7807050, FAX 49-69-78070550, zentrale.frankfurt@peterlang.com, http://www.peterlang.com.

302.2 AUT ISSN 1814-5655
STUDIENBUECHER ZUR PUBLIZISTIK- UND KOMMUNIKATIONSWISSENSCHAFT. Text in German. 1986. irreg., latest vol.13, 2011. price varies. **Document type:** *Monographic series, Academic/Scholarly.*
Published by: Wilhelm Braumueller Universitaets-Verlagsbuchhandlung GmbH, Servitengasse 5, Vienna, 1090, Austria. TEL 43-1-3191159, FAX 43-1-3102805, office@braumueller.at. Ed. Wolfgang Langenbucher.

STUDIENREIHE KONFLIKTFORSCHUNG. *see* POLITICAL SCIENCE—International Relations

STUDIES IN AFRICAN AND AFRICAN-AMERICAN CULTURE. *see* HISTORY—History Of Africa

STUDIES IN APPLIED ETHICS. *see* PHILOSOPHY

STUDIES IN BILINGUALISM. *see* LINGUISTICS

302.23 CHE ISSN 1424-4896
➤ **STUDIES IN COMMUNICATION SCIENCES/STUDI DI SCIENZE DELLA COMUNICAZIONE.** Text in English. 2001. s-a. CHF 75, EUR 50, USD 50 to individuals; CHF 100, EUR 75, USD 75 to institutions (effective 2003). bk.rev. 200 p./no.; **Document type:** *Journal, Academic/Scholarly.* **Description:** Publishes original articles of high quality in all areas of communication, including linguistics, semiotics, rhetoric, media, mass communication, corporate and institutional communication, management of communication, information and communication technology, formal models of communication, communication in educational environment, intercultural communication, sociology and psychology of communication.
Related titles: Online - full text ed.
Indexed: CA, CMM, CommAb, DIP, IBR, IBZ, L11, MLA-IB, T02.
—BLDSC (8490.170800).
Published by: Universita della Svizzera Italiana, Facolta di Scienze della Comunicazione, Via Giuseppe Buffi 13, Lugano, 6904, Switzerland. TEL 41-91-9124646, FAX 41-91-9124647, admin@lu.unisi.ch, http://www.lu.unisi.ch/com. Ed. Peter Schulz. Adv. contact Alessandra Filippi.

303.842 NLD ISSN 1879-7350
▼ **STUDIES IN CULTURAL TRANSFER AND TRANSMISSION.** Text in English. 2009. s-a.
Published by: Barkhuis Publishing, Zuurstukken 37, Eelde, 9761 KP, Netherlands. TEL 31-50-3080936, FAX 31-50-3080934, info@barkhuis.nl, http://www.barkhuis.nl. Ed. Petra Broomans.

306 GBR ISSN 2040-6150
▼ **STUDIES IN CULTURE AND INNOVATION.** Abbreviated title: S C I N. Text in English. forthcoming 2011. s-a. GBP 103 domestic to institutions; GBP 112 in the European Union to institutions; USD 115 in US & Canada to institutions; GBP 115 elsewhere to institutions (effective 2011). adv. **Document type:** *Journal, Academic/Scholarly.* **Description:** Explores to highlight research in interdisciplinary exchanges between arts and humanities research and the science and technology sectors.
Related titles: Online - full text ed.: ISSN 2040-6169. forthcoming. USD 85 in US & Canada to institutions; GBP 70 elsewhere to institutions (effective 2011).
Indexed: AmHI, H07, T02.
Published by: Intellect Ltd., The Mill, Parnall Rd, Fishponds, Bristol, BS16 3JG, United Kingdom. TEL 44-117-9589910, FAX 44-117-9589911, info@intellectbooks.com. Eds. Calvin Taylor, Derek Hales. Pub. Masoud Yazdani. **Dist. by:** Turpin Distribution Services Ltd., Pegasus Dr, Stratton Business Park, Biggleswade, Bedfordshire SG18 8QB, United Kingdom. TEL 44-1767-604951, FAX 44-1767-601640, custserv@turpin-distribution.com, http://www.turpin-distribution.com/.

STUDIES IN FAMILY PLANNING. *see* POPULATION STUDIES

305.3 306.7 USA ISSN 1524-0657
HQ60
➤ **STUDIES IN GENDER AND SEXUALITY.** Abbreviated title: S G S. Text in English. 2000. q. GBP 190 combined subscription in United Kingdom to institutions (print & online eds.); EUR 252, USD 316 combined subscription to institutions (print & online eds.) (effective 2012). adv. back issues avail.; reprint service avail. from PSC. **Document type:** *Journal, Academic/Scholarly.* **Description:** Provides a forum for examining gender and sexuality that is both multidisciplinary and interdisciplinary; in this way it seeks to broaden the purview - theoretical, clinical, and cultural - of all its readers and to promote constructive exchanges among them.
Related titles: Online - full text ed.: ISSN 1940-9206. GBP 172 in United Kingdom to institutions; EUR 227, USD 285 to institutions (effective 2012).
Indexed: A01, A03, A08, A22, CA, DIP, E-psyche, E01, FamI, FemPer, G10, GW, IBR, IBZ, L01, L02, MLA-IB, P03, P19, P25, P48, PQC, PsycInfo, PsycholAb, S02, S03, SCOPUS, SociolAb, T02, W09.
—BLDSC (8490.580400), IE, Ingenta. **CCC.**
Published by: Routledge (Subsidiary of: Taylor & Francis Group), 325 Chestnut St, Ste 800, Philadelphia, PA 19106. TEL 800-354-1420, FAX 215-625-2940, journals@routledge.com, http://www.routledge.com. Ed. Muriel Dimen.

306.09 NLD ISSN 1874-6705
➤ **STUDIES IN GLOBAL SOCIAL HISTORY.** Text in English. 2008. irreg., latest vol.1, 2008. price varies. **Document type:** *Monographic series.* **Description:** Aims to demonstrate how the present global society has materialized from uneven and combined developments and from interaction between acts of varied peoples, from rulers, entrepreneurs, politicians and administrators to slaves, peasants, indentured laborers, wage-earners, and housewives.
Indexed: IZBG.
Published by: Brill, PO Box 9000, Leiden, 2300 PA, Netherlands. TEL 31-71-5353500, FAX 31-71-5317532, cs@brill.nl. Ed. Marcel van der Linden.

301 NLD ISSN 0920-6221
CODEN: SUGSEK
➤ **STUDIES IN HUMAN SOCIETY.** Text in Dutch. 1986. irreg., latest vol.11, 1996. price varies. back issues avail. **Document type:** *Monographic series, Academic/Scholarly.*
Indexed: IZBG.
—**CCC.**
Published by: Brill, PO Box 9000, Leiden, 2300 PA, Netherlands. TEL 31-71-5353500, FAX 31-71-5317532, cs@brill.nl, http://www.brill.nl. R&P Elizabeth Venekamp. **Dist. in N. America by:** Brill, PO Box 605, Herndon, VA 20172-0605. TEL 703-661-1585, 800-337-9255, FAX 703-661-1501, cs@brillusa.com; **Dist. by:** Turpin Distribution Services Ltd., Pegasus Dr, Stratton Business Park, Biggleswade, Bedfordshire SG18 8QB, United Kingdom. TEL 44-1767-604954, FAX 44-1767-601640, custserv@turpin-distribution.com, http://www.turpin-distribution.com/.

➤ **STUDIES IN INTERACTIONAL SOCIOLINGUISTICS.** *see* LINGUISTICS

303.842 DEU ISSN 0931-2420
STUDIES IN INTERCULTURAL COMMUNICATION/STUDIEN ZUR INTERKULTURELLEN KOMMUNIKATION. Text in German. 1986. irreg., latest vol.13, 1995. price varies. **Document type:** *Monographic series, Academic/Scholarly.*
Indexed: IBR, IBZ.
—**CCC.**
Published by: Verlag fuer Entwicklungspolitik Saarbruecken GmbH, Auf der Adt 14, Saarbruecken, 66130, Germany. TEL 49-6893-986094, FAX 49-6893-986095, vfe@verlag-entwicklungspolitik.de, http://www.verlag-entwicklungspolitik.de.

STUDIES IN LAW, POLITICS, AND SOCIETY. *see* LAW

306 USA ISSN 0888-5753
E169.1
➤ **STUDIES IN POPULAR CULTURE.** Abbreviated title: S I P C. Text in English. 1977. s-a. free to members (effective 2010). back issues avail. **Document type:** *Journal, Academic/Scholarly.* **Description:** Publishes articles on film, literature, radio, television, music, graphics, the print media, and other aspects of popular culture from a multidisciplinary perspective.
Related titles: Online - full text ed.: free (effective 2010).
Indexed: A22, AmHI, CA, ChLitAb, F01, F02, H07, IBT&D, MLA-IB, RILM, T02.

—Ingenta.
Published by: Popular Culture Association in the South, c/o Diane Calhoun-French, Jefferson Community College-Southwest, Louisville, KY 40272. TEL 502-935-9840 ext 3201, dcf@piglet.jcc.uky.edu, http://www.pcasacas.org. Ed. Rhonda V Wilcox. **Subscr. to:** Diane Calhoun-French.

➤ **STUDIES IN PRAGMATISM AND VALUES.** *see* PHILOSOPHY

301 IND
STUDIES IN SOCIAL CHANGE AND DEVELOPMENT. Text in English. 1971. irreg., latest vol.5, 1989. price varies. **Document type:** *Monographic series.*
Formerly (until no.4, 1980): Studies in Asian Social Development
Published by: Institute of Economic Growth, University of Enclave, New Delhi, 110 007, India. TEL 91-11-27666364, FAX 91-11-27667410, system@iegindia.or.

320 301 100 CAN ISSN 1911-4788
➤ **STUDIES IN SOCIAL JUSTICE.** Text in English. 2007. irreg. free (effective 2011). **Document type:** *Journal, Academic/Scholarly.* **Description:** Covers issues dealing with the social, cultural, economic, political, and philosophical problems associated with the struggle for social justice.
Media: Online - full text.
Indexed: PhilInd, SCOPUS, SociolAb.
Published by: University of Windsor, Centre for Studies in Social Justice, 251-1 Chrysler Hall South, Windsor, ON N9B 3P4, Canada. TEL 519-253-3000, http://www.uwindsor.ca/socialjustice/.

301 DEU ISSN 1618-775X
STUDIES IN SOCIOLOGY. Text in English. 2002. irreg., latest vol.6, 2010. price varies. **Document type:** *Monographic series, Academic/ Scholarly.*
Published by: Peter Lang GmbH (Subsidiary of: Peter Lang Publishing Group), Eschborner Landstr 42-50, Frankfurt Am Main, 60489, Germany. TEL 49-69-7807050, FAX 49-69-78070550, zentrale.frankfurt@peterlang.com, http://www.peterlang.com. Eds. Elzbieta Halas, Risto Heiskala.

301 CAN ISSN 1923-0176
▼ ➤ **STUDIES IN SOCIOLOGY OF SCIENCE.** Text in English. 2010. s-a. **Document type:** *Journal, Academic/Scholarly.*
Related titles: Online - full text ed.: ISSN 1923-0184. free (effective 2011).
Indexed: A26, CPerI, I05, P10, P48, P53, P54, PQC, S02, S03, T02.
Published by: Canadian Research & Development Center of Sciences and Cultures, 3-265 Melrose, Montreal, PQ H4H 1T2, Canada. http://www.cscanada.org. Ed. Jenny Ding.

301 USA ISSN 1058-5621
STUDIES IN SOUTHERN ITALIAN AND ITALIAN-AMERICAN CULTURE/STUDI SULLA CULTURA DELL'ITALIA MERIDIONALE E ITALO-AMERICANA. Text in English. 1992. irreg., latest vol.9, 1997. price varies. **Document type:** *Monographic series, Academic/ Scholarly.* **Description:** Publishes studies of the literature, arts, spoken modes and socio-historical life of Southern Italian society, as well as studies of the culture of Italian-Americans whose ancestry stems from Southern Italy.
Published by: Peter Lang Publishing, Inc. (Subsidiary of: Peter Lang Publishing Group), 29 Broadway, New York, NY 10006. TEL 212-647-7700, 212-647-7706, 800-770-5264, FAX 212-647-7707, customerservice@plang.com. Ed. Giose Rimanelli.

305 GBR ISSN 0163-2396
HM1
STUDIES IN SYMBOLIC INTERACTION. Text in English. 1978. irreg., latest vol.32, 2008. price varies. illus. back issues avail. **Document type:** *Monographic series, Academic/Scholarly.* **Description:** Consists of original research and theory within the general sociological perspective known as symbolic interactionism.
Related titles: Online - full text ed.; Supplement(s): Studies in Symbolic Interaction. Supplement. ISSN 1059-728X.
Indexed: A20, A22, CA, MLA-IB, PsycholAb, RILM, S02, S03, SCOPUS, SOPODA, SSA, SSCI, SociolAb, T02, W07.
—BLDSC (8491.788000), IE, Ingenta. **CCC.**
Published by: Emerald Group Publishing Ltd., Howard House, Wagon Ln, Bingley, W Yorks BD16 1WA, United Kingdom. TEL 44-1274-777700, FAX 44-1274-785201, books@emeraldinsight.com, http://www.emeraldinsight.com. Ed. Norman K Denzin.

307 IND ISSN 0973-7189
➤ **STUDIES ON HOME AND COMMUNITY SCIENCE.** Text in English. 2007. 3/yr. USD 100 (effective 2012). back issues avail. **Document type:** *Journal, Academic/Scholarly.* **Description:** Publishes reports of original research, theoretical articles and timely reviews, and brief communications in the interdisciplinary field of home and community environment.
Related titles: Online - full text ed.: free (effective 2012).
—BLDSC (8490.678700).
Published by: Kamla-Raj Enterprises, 2273 Gali Bari Paharwali, Chawri Bazar, New Delhi, 110 006, India. TEL 91-11-23284126, kre@airtelmail.in.

▼ ➤ **STYLES OF COMMUNICATION.** *see* COMMUNICATIONS

➤ **SUBJECT MATTERS**; a journal of communications and the self. *see* COMMUNICATIONS

301 NOR ISSN 1890-5056
SUDAN WORKING PAPERS. Text in English. 2008. irreg. **Document type:** *Monographic series.*
Published by: Chr. Michelsen Institute, PO Box 6033 Postterminalen, Bergen, 5892, Norway. TEL 47-55-574000, FAX 47-55-574166, cmi@cmi.no.

301 USA ISSN 1520-5681
SUICIDAL BEHAVIOR: A SURVEY OF OREGON HIGH SCHOOL STUDENTS, (YEAR). Text in English. 1997. every 2 yrs. stat. **Description:** Provides narrative, tables, and figures collected from Adolescent Suicide Attempt Reports and Youth Risk Behavior Survey results.
Published by: Department of Human Services Center for Health Statistics, Center for Disease Prevention and Epidemiology, Health Division, 800 N E Oregon St, Portland, OR 97232-2109. TEL 503-731-4354, FAX 503-731-3076.

305.896972 NLD ISSN 1876-228X
THE SURINAM HIGHLIGHTS. Text in Dutch. 2007. m. EUR 16 (effective 2011). adv. **Document type:** *Newspaper, Consumer.*
Related titles: Online - full text ed.: ISSN 1876-2298.
Published by: Oliemex, Postbus 2027, Alphen aan den Rijn, 2400 CA, Netherlands. TEL 31-172-897193, info@oliemex.nl.

301 USA
SURVEY RESEARCH. Text in English. 1969. 3/yr. USD 15 to individuals; USD 60 to institutions (effective 2011). back issues avail. **Document type:** *Newsletter, Trade.* **Description:** Publishes current research, personnel news, new methodological publications, and job openings in survey research. Announces calls for papers in survey-related conferences.
Published by: University of Illinois, Survey Research Laboratory, 505 E Green St, Ste 3, Champaign, IL 61820. TEL 217-333-4273, FAX 217-244-4408, info@srl.uic.edu.

306.8 USA
SURVIVORS OUTREACH SERIES. Text in English. 1980. 8/yr. USD 24 domestic; USD 32 in Canada; USD 36 elsewhere; USD 4.50 per issue (effective 2000). bk.rev. **Document type:** *Monographic series.* **Description:** Helps newly widowed cope with their grief.
Published by: Theos Foundation, 322 Blvd of the Allies, Ste 105, Pittsburgh, PA 15222-1919. TEL 412-471-7779, FAX 412-471-7782. Circ: 25.

301 AUS ISSN 1446-2974
SUSTAINING REGIONS. Text in English. 2001. s-a. AUD 30 (effective 2002). adv. bibl. 60 p./no.; back issues avail. **Document type:** *Journal, Academic/Scholarly.* **Description:** Contains articles and information on the issues affecting all Australian regions: Metropolitan, remote, urban and rural.
Related titles: Online - full text ed.: ISSN 1446-2982. 2001.
Published by: Australian and New Zealand Regional Science Association Inc., c/o School of Economics and Information Systems, University of Wollongong, Northfields Ave, Wollongong, NSW 2522, Australia. TEL 61-2-4221-3666, FAX 61-2-4221-3725, http://www.anzrsai.org/index.pl?page=2. Ed., R&P, Adv. contact Andrew Beer TEL 61-8-8201-3522.

302.23 DEU
T L M - SCHRIFTENREIHE. Text in German. 1997. irreg., latest vol.21, 2010. price varies. **Document type:** *Monographic series, Academic/ Scholarly.*
Published by: (Thueringer Landesmedienanstalt), Vistas Verlag GmbH, Goltzstr 11, Berlin, 10781, Germany. TEL 49-30-32707446, FAX 49-30-32707455, medienverlag@vistas.de, http://www.vistas.de.

TABOO; the journal of culture and education. *see* EDUCATION

301 TWN
TAIWAN SHEHUI XUEKAN/TAIWAN JOURNAL OF SOCIOLOGY. Text in Chinese. 1971. s-a.
Formerly: Zhongguo Shehui Xuekan/Chinese Journal of Sociology (1011-2219)
Indexed: SCOPUS, SociolAb.
Published by: Taiwan Shehuiyuan/Taiwanese Sociological Association, Wenshan district, Section 2, no. 64, Zhinan Road, Room 270848, Taipei, 116, Taiwan. TEL 886-2-29393091 ext 50848, tsa@gate.sinica.edu.tw, http://tsa.sinica.edu.tw/.

TAKING SIDES: CLASHING VIEWS IN ENERGY AND SOCIETY. *see* ENERGY

306.85 USA
TAKING SIDES: CLASHING VIEWS IN FAMILY AND PERSONAL RELATIONSHIPS. Text in English. 1992. biennial. illus. back issues avail. **Document type:** *Catalog, Academic/Scholarly.* **Description:** Presents controversial issues in a debate-style format designed to stimulate student interest and develop critical thinking skills.
Formerly (until 2008): Taking Sides: Clashing Views on Controversial Issues in Family and Personal Relationships
Indexed: E-psyche.
Published by: McGraw-Hill, Contemporary Learning Series (Subsidiary of: McGraw-Hill Companies, Inc.), 1221 Ave of the Americas, New York, NY 10020. TEL 212-904-2000, 800-243-6532, FAX 212-512-2000, customer.service@mcgraw-hill.com, http://www.mhhe.com/cls/.

302.23 USA
HN90.M3
TAKING SIDES: CLASHING VIEWS IN MASS MEDIA AND SOCIETY. Text in English. 1991. irreg., latest 2009, 10th ed. illus. back issues avail. **Document type:** *Catalog, Academic/Scholarly.* **Description:** Presents current controversial issues in a debate-style format designed to stimulate student interest and develop critical thinking skills.
Formerly (until 2007): Taking Sides: Clashing Views on Controversial Issues in Mass Media and Society (1084-4651)
Published by: McGraw-Hill, Contemporary Learning Series (Subsidiary of: McGraw-Hill Companies, Inc.), 1221 Ave of the Americas, New York, NY 10020. TEL 212-904-2000, 800-243-6532, FAX 212-512-2000, customer.service@mcgraw-hill.com, http://www.mhhe.com/cls/.

301 USA
TAKING SIDES: CLASHING VIEWS ON SOCIAL ISSUES. Text in English. 1980. irreg., latest 2010, 15th ed. illus. back issues avail. **Document type:** *Catalog, Academic/Scholarly.* **Description:** Presents current controversial issues in a debate-style format designed to stimulate student interest and develop critical thinking skills.
Formerly (until 2007): Taking Sides: Clashing Views on Controversial Social Issues
Published by: McGraw-Hill, Contemporary Learning Series (Subsidiary of: McGraw-Hill Companies, Inc.), 1221 Ave of the Americas, New York, NY 10020. TEL 212-904-2000, 800-243-6532, FAX 212-512-2000, customer.service@mcgraw-hill.com, http://www.mhhe.com/cls/.

301 302 FIN ISSN 0785-6105
TAMPEREEN YLIOPISTO. SOSIOLOGIAN JA SOSIAALIPSYKOLOGIAN LAITOS. A, TUTKIMUKSIA/ UNIVERSITY OF TAMPERE. DEPARTMENT OF SOCIOLOGY AND SOCIAL PSYCHOLOGY. SERIES A, RESEARCH PAPERS. Text in Finnish. 1973. irreg. back issues avail. **Document type:** *Monographic series, Academic/Scholarly.*
Formerly (until 1986): Tampereen Yliopiston Sosiologian ja Sosiaalipsykologian laitoksen Sarja. A, Tutkimuksia (0359-9434); Which superseded in part (1973-1982): Tampereen Yliopiston Sosiologian ja Sosiaalipsykologian Laitoksen Tutkimuksia (0355-5224)
Published by: Tampereen Yliopisto, Sosiologian ja Sosiaalipsykologian Laitos/University of Tampere. Department of Sociology and Social Psychology, Kalevantie 5, Tampere, 33014, Finland. TEL 358-3-35516586, FAX 358-3-35516080, sosio.laitos@uta.fi.

301 302 FIN ISSN 1235-8908
TAMPEREEN YLIOPISTO. SOSIOLOGIAN JA SOSIAALIPSYKOLOGIAN LAITOS. B, TYORAPORTTEJA/ UNIVERSITY OF TAMPERE. DEPARTMENT OF SOCIOLOGY AND SOCIAL PSYCHOLOGY. B, WORKING PAPERS. Text in Multiple languages. 1983. irreg. back issues avail. **Document type:** *Monographic series, Academic/Scholarly.*
Formerly (until 1991): Tampereen Yliopiston Sosiologian ja Sosiaalipsykologian Laitoksen Sarja. B, Tyoraportteja (0359-8144); Which superseded in part (1973-1982): Tampereen Yliopiston Sosiologian ja Sosiaalipsykologian Laitoksen Tutkimuksia (0355-5224)
Published by: Tampereen Yliopisto, Sosiologian ja Sosiaalipsykologian Laitos/University of Tampere. Department of Sociology and Social Psychology, Kalevantie 5, Tampere, 33014, Finland. TEL 358-3-35516586, FAX 358-3-35516080, sosio.laitos@uta.fi.

301 302 FIN ISSN 1796-7929
TAMPEREEN YLIOPISTO. SOSIOLOGIAN JA SOSIAALIPSYKOLOGIAN LAITOS. VERKKOJULKAISUSARJA A. Text in Finnish. 2007. irreg. **Document type:** *Monographic series, Academic/Scholarly.*
Media: Online - full content.
Published by: Tampereen Yliopisto, Sosiologian ja Sosiaalipsykologian Laitos/University of Tampere. Department of Sociology and Social Psychology, Kalevantie 5, Tampere, 33014, Finland. TEL 358-3-35516586, FAX 358-3-35516080, sosio.laitos@uta.fi.

▼ **TAPESTRIES**; interwoven voices of global identities. *see* ETHNIC INTERESTS

344.03 HUN ISSN 0231-2522
H8
TARSADALOMKUTATAS/SOCIAL SCIENCE RESEARCH. Text in Hungarian. 1983. q. (in 1 vol., 4 nos./vol.). EUR 88, USD 122 combined subscription (print & online eds.) (effective 2011). adv. bk.rev. abstr. 120 p./no.; back issues avail. **Document type:** *Journal, Academic/Scholarly.* **Description:** Covers broad field of studies covered by the Department of Economic Science and Jurisprudence of the Hungarian Academy of Sciences. Includes issues such as European integration or the sociological approaches to the environment.
Formerly: Gazdasag es Jogtudomany (0580-4795)
Related titles: Online - full text ed.: ISSN 1588-2918. EUR 75, USD 105 (effective 2011).
Indexed: CA, IBSS, P42, PSA, RASB, RILM, S02, S03, SCOPUS, SOPODA, SSA, SociolAb, T02.
—Ingenta.
Published by: (Magyar Tudomanyos Akademia/Hungarian Academy of Sciences), Akademiai Kiado Rt. (Subsidiary of: Wolters Kluwer N.V.), Prielle Kornelia u 19/D, Budapest, 1117, Hungary. TEL 36-1-4648222, FAX 36-1-4648221, journals@akkrt.hu. Ed. Kalman Kulcsar.

TE AWATEA REVIEW. *see* CRIMINOLOGY AND LAW ENFORCEMENT

301.071 USA ISSN 0092-055X
HM1
➤ **TEACHING SOCIOLOGY.** Text in English. 1973. q. USD 255, GBP 150 combined subscription to institutions (print & online eds.); USD 250, GBP 147 to institutions (effective 2011). adv. bk.rev. illus. index. back issues avail.; reprint service avail. from PSC. **Document type:** *Journal, Academic/Scholarly.* **Description:** Publishes research articles, teaching tips, and reports on teaching sociology.
Incorporates (1979-1985): Teaching Newsletter; Which was formerly (197?-1979): On Teaching Undergraduate Sociology Newsletter
Related titles: Online - full text ed.: ISSN 1939-862X. USD 229, GBP 135 to institutions (effective 2011).
Indexed: A20, A22, ASCA, ASSIA, B04, BRD, CA, CIS, CPE, CommAb, CurCont, DIP, E01, E02, E03, E06, ERI, EdA, EdI, FR, FamI, G10, HECAB, IBR, IBZ, MEA&I, MLA-IB, P18, P30, P46, P48, P53, P54, PQC, RASB, RILM, S02, S03, S21, SCOPUS, SOPODA, SSA, SSCI, SociolAb, T02, W03, W07, W09.
—BLDSC (8614.340000), IE, Infotrieve, Ingenta, INIST. **CCC.**
Published by: (American Sociological Association), Sage Publications, Inc., 2455 Teller Rd, Thousand Oaks, CA 91320. TEL 805-499-9774, FAX 805-499-0871, info@sagepub.com, http://www.sagepub.com/. Ed. Elizabeth Grauerholz TEL 407-823-2227. adv.: page USD 350. Circ: 2,400.

➤ **TECHNOLOGICAL FORECASTING AND SOCIAL CHANGE.** *see* TECHNOLOGY: COMPREHENSIVE WORKS

301 GBR ISSN 0160-791X
T14.5
➤ **TECHNOLOGY IN SOCIETY.** Text in English. 1979. 4/yr. EUR 1,192 in Europe to institutions; JPY 158,600 in Japan to institutions; USD 1,336 elsewhere to institutions (effective 2012). adv. bk.rev. charts; illus.; stat. index. back issues avail.; reprints avail. **Document type:** *Journal, Academic/Scholarly.* **Description:** Focuses on the role of technology in society, including articles on economic, political and cultural dynamics, the social forces that shape technological decisions, and the choices open to societies with respect to the uses of technology.
Related titles: Microfilm ed.: (from PQC); Online - full text ed.: ISSN 1879-3274 (from IngentaConnect, ScienceDirect).
Indexed: A20, A22, A26, ABS&EES, ASCA, BAS, Biostat, CA, CIS, CLOSS, CMM, CPEI, CommAb, E03, ERI, ESPM, EngInd, EnvAb, FutSurv, GEOBASE, GeoRef, HPNRM, I05, IBSS, IPARL, ORMS, P30, P42, PAIS, PSA, PsycholAb, QC&AS, RASB, S02, S03, SCOPUS, SOPODA, SSA, SSciA, SociolAb, T02.
—BLDSC (8761.023000), IE, Infotrieve, Ingenta, Linda Hall. **CCC.**
Published by: Pergamon (Subsidiary of: Elsevier Science & Technology), The Blvd, Langford Ln, East Park, Kidlington, Oxford OX5 1GB, United Kingdom. TEL 44-1865-843000, FAX 44-1865-843010, JournalsCustomerServiceEMEA@elsevier.com. Eds. A George Schillinger, George Bugliarello. **Subscr. to:** Elsevier BV, Radarweg 29, PO Box 211, Amsterdam 1000 AE, Netherlands. TEL 31-20-4853757, FAX 31-20-4853432.

305.235 USA ISSN 1540-4897
TEEN LIFE AROUND THE WORLD. Text in English. 2003 (May). irreg. price varies. back issues avail. **Document type:** *Monographic series.*
Related titles: Online - full text ed.

S

Published by: Greenwood Publishing Group Inc. (Subsidiary of: A B C - C L I O), 88 Post Rd W, PO Box 5007, Westport, CT 06881. TEL 203-226-3571, 800-225-5800, FAX 877-231-6980, sales@greenwood.com. Ed. Jeffrey Kaplan.

301 ISR ISSN 0792-0601
TEL AVIV - YAFO. CENTER FOR ECONOMIC AND SOCIAL RESEARCH. RESEARCH AND SURVEYS SERIES/TEL AVIV-YAFO. HA-MERKAZ LE-MEHKAR KALKALI VE-HEVRATI. MEHKARIM U-SEQARIM. Text in Hebrew. 1963. irreg. **Document type:** *Government.* **Description:** Contains research reports on various social and urban topics concerning Tel Aviv - Yafo.
Formerly: Tel Aviv - Yafo. Research and Statistical Department. Special Surveys (0082-2639)
Published by: Center for Economic and Social Research, Tel Aviv - Yafo Municipality, Itzhak Rabin Square, Tel Aviv, 64162, Israel. TEL 340-3-5217827, FAX 340-3-5217850. Ed. Menashe Hadad. Circ: 600.

TELEVISION & NEW MEDIA. *see* COMMUNICATIONS—Television And Cable

TEMAS AMERICANISTAS. *see* HISTORY—History Of North And South America

TEMAS DE POLITICA Y SOCIOLOGIA. *see* POLITICAL SCIENCE

301 BOL ISSN 0040-2915
TEMAS SOCIALES. Text in Spanish. 1968. q. USD 8. charts.
Indexed: PAIS.
Published by: Universidad Mayor de San Andres, Facultad de Derecho, Casilla 4787, La Paz, Bolivia. Ed. Mario Diez.

301 SRB ISSN 0353-7919
TEME; casopis za drustvene nauke. Text in Serbo-Croatian; Summaries in English, French, German, Russian. 1977. q. bk.rev. **Document type:** *Journal, Academic/Scholarly.*
Formerly (until June 1990): Marksisticke Teme (0351-1685)
Related titles: Online - full text ed.: ISSN 1820-7804. free (effective 2011).
Indexed: A01.
Published by: Univerzitet u Nisu, Trg Univerzitetski 2, Nis, Serbia 18000. TEL 018 25-868, FAX 18-24488, TELEX 16362 UNIUNI YU. Ed. Dragoljub B Dordevic.

301 ITA ISSN 2037-2965
▼ ➤ **TEMPERANTER.** Text in English, French, Italian. 2010. q. EUR 150; EUR 10 per issue (effective 2010). abstr.; bibl.; charts; stat. Index. back issues avail. **Document type:** *Journal, Academic/Scholarly.* **Description:** Aims to analyze social and cultural topics of national and international interest in a transdisciplinary perspective in order to question cliches, stereotypes and prejudices in societies.
Published by: (Intercultural Studies Initiative - Initiative Etudes Interculturelles (ISI - IEI) FRA), Centro Internazionale per le Ricerche e Studi Interculturali (C I R S I)/International Research Centre for Intercultural Studies, V.le R. Sanzio 17, Trieste, 34128, Italy. TEL 39-334-3994638, cirsi@cirsi.net, http://www.cirsi.net/. Ed. Lorenzo Dugulin. Circ: 1,000.

301 BRA ISSN 0103-2070
HM22.B8
➤ **TEMPO SOCIAL.** Text in Portuguese. 1989. s-a. USD 30. **Document type:** *Journal, Academic/Scholarly.* **Description:** Publishes on all aspects of sociology.
Related titles: Online - full text ed.: free (effective 2011).
Indexed: BibInd, C01, CA, FR, I13, IBSS, P42, PAIS, PSA, RASB, S02, S03, SCOPUS, SSA, SSCI, SociolAb, T02, W07.
—INIST.
Published by: Universidade de Sao Paulo, Faculdade de Filosofia, Letras e Ciencias Humanas, Av Professor Luciano Gualberto 315, Butanta, Sao Paulo, SP 05508-010, Brazil. http://www.fflch.usp.br. Ed. Sergio Miceli Pessoa de Barros.

➤ **TEMPORALITES;** revue des sciences sociales et humaines. *see* HUMANITIES: COMPREHENSIVE WORKS

302.3 ITA ISSN 1970-5476
TEORIA E CRITICA DELLA REGOLAZIONE SOCIALE. Text in Multiple languages. 2006. s-a. **Document type:** *Journal, Academic/Scholarly.*
Media: Online - full text.
Published by: Universita degli Studi di Catania, Facolta di Giurisprudenza, Via Gallo 24, Catania, 95124, Italy. TEL 39-095-230111, FAX 39-095-230456, http://www.lex.unict.it.

301 ITA ISSN 1972-0637
TEORIE E OGGETTI DELLE SCIENZE SOCIALI. Text in Italian. 1995. irreg., latest vol.4, 1999. price varies. adv. **Document type:** *Monographic series, Academic/Scholarly.*
Published by: Liguori Editore, Via Posillipo 394, Naples, 80123, Italy. TEL 39-081-7206111, FAX 39-081-7206244, liguori@liguori.it, http://www.liguori.it.

TEORIYA I PRAKTYKA UPRAVLINNYA SOTSIAL'NYMY SYSTEMAMY/ THEORY AND PRACTICE OF SOCIAL SYSTEMS MANAGEMENT. *see* BUSINESS AND ECONOMICS—Management

301 305.8924 ISR ISSN 0792-7223
➤ **TE'ORIYA UVIQORET/THEORY AND CRITICISM.** Text in Hebrew; Summaries in English, Arabic. 1991. s-a. ILS 118 (effective 2008). back issues avail. **Document type:** *Journal, Academic/Scholarly.* **Description:** A critical examination of Israeli culture and society.
Published by: The Van Leer Jerusalem Institute, PO Box 4070, Jerusalem, 91040, Israel. TEL 972-2-5605222, FAX 972-2-5619293, yonar@vanleer.org.il, http://www.vanleer.org.il/default_e.asp. Ed. Yehouda Shenhav.

➤ **TERRAIN.** *see* ANTHROPOLOGY

➤ **TEXAS PAN AMERICAN SERIES.** *see* ETHNIC INTERESTS

➤ **TEXT & TALK;** an interdisciplinary journal of language, discourse & communication studies. *see* HUMANITIES: COMPREHENSIVE WORKS

305.8 SWE ISSN 1651-453X
TEXTER FRAAN MIGRATIONS- OCH ETNICITETSSEMINARIET. Text in Swedish. 2002. irreg. **Document type:** *Monographic series, Academic/Scholarly.*
Published by: Stockholms Universitet, Pedagogiska Institutionen/ Stockholm University, Department of Education, Stockholm, 10691, Sweden. TEL 46-8-162000, FAX 46-8-158354, info@ped.su.se, http://www.ped.su.se.

301 SWE ISSN 1653-3062
TEXTER OM KONSTRUKTION AV NORMALITET, GENUS OCH ETNICITET. Text in Swedish. 2005. irreg. **Document type:** *Monographic series, Academic/Scholarly.*
Published by: Stockholms Universitet, Pedagogiska Institutionen/ Stockholm University, Department of Education, Stockholm, 10691, Sweden. TEL 46-8-162000, FAX 46-8-158354, info@ped.su.se, http://www.ped.su.se.

301 MEX ISSN 0185-9439
TEXTUAL; analisis del medio rural Latinoamericano. Text in Spanish. 1982. q. **Document type:** *Journal, Academic/Scholarly.*
Indexed: A34, C01, C25, CA, CABA, E12, F04, H16, N02, OR, P38, R12, S13, S16, S17, T02, VS, W11.
Published by: Universidad Autonoma de Chapingo, Km. 38.5 Carretera Mexico-Texcoco, Chapingo, Edo. de Mexico, 56230, Mexico. TEL 52-595-9521500, FAX 52-595-9521569, cori@chapingo.mx. Ed. Liberio Victorino Ramirez.

306 393 FRA ISSN 1955-4621
THANATOLOGIE. Text in French. 2007. irreg. back issues avail. **Document type:** *Monographic series, Academic/Scholarly.*
Published by: (Centre de Recherches Thanatologiques USA), L' Harmattan, 5 Rue de l'Ecole Polytechnique, Paris, 75005, France. TEL 33-1-43257651, FAX 33-1-43258203.

THEOLOGY AND CULTURE NEWSLETTER. *see* RELIGIONS AND THEOLOGY

THEOLOGY AND SEXUALITY. *see* RELIGIONS AND THEOLOGY

THEORETICAL POPULATION BIOLOGY. *see* BIOLOGY

301 DEU
THEORIE UND GESCHICHTE DER BUERGERLICHEN GESELLSCHAFT. Text in German. irreg., latest vol.23, 2008. price varies. **Document type:** *Monographic series, Academic/Scholarly.*
Published by: Verlag Westfaelisches Dampfboot, Hafenweg 26a, Muenster, 48155, Germany. TEL 49-251-3900480, FAX 49-251-39004850, info@dampfboot-verlag.de.

302.23 DEU ISSN 1865-3367
THEORIE UND GESCHICHTE DER KOMMUNIKATIONSWISSENSCHAFT. Text in German. 2004. irreg., latest vol.6, 2010. price varies. **Document type:** *Monographic series, Academic/Scholarly.*
Published by: Herbert von Halem Verlag, Lindenstr 19, Cologne, 50674, Germany. TEL 49-221-9258290, FAX 49-221-92582929, info@halem-verlag.de, http://www.halem-verlag.de.

301 501 CAN ISSN 1527-5558
➤ **THEORY & SCIENCE.** Text in English. 2000. s-a. free (effective 2011). bk.rev. back issues avail. **Document type:** *Journal, Academic/Scholarly.* **Description:** Discusses theory, science, and social change.
Media: Online - full text.
Indexed: A39, C27, C29, CA, D03, D04, E03, E13, ERI, R14, S02, S03, S14, S15, S18, SCOPUS, SociolAb, T02.
Published by: International Consortium for the Advancement of Academic Publication, c/o Jill Calliou, University Research Services, Athabasca University, 1 University Dr, Athabasca, AB T9S 3A3, Canada. TEL 780-675-6102, 800-788-9041 ext 6102, FAX 780-675-6722, icaap@athabascau.ca, http://www.icaap.org.

301 NLD ISSN 0304-2421
➤ **THEORY AND SOCIETY;** renewal and critique in social theory. Text in English. 1974. bi-m. EUR 790, USD 975 combined subscription to institutions (print & online eds.) (effective 2012). adv. bk.rev. illus. index. back issues avail.; reprint service avail. from PSC. **Document type:** *Journal, Academic/Scholarly.* **Description:** Publishes theoretically informed analyses of social processes, including theoretical and methodological issues, discussions of individuals and national societies and cultures from prehistory to contemporary times.
Related titles: Microform ed.: (from PQC); Online - full text ed.: ISSN 1573-7853 (from IngentaConnect).
Indexed: A01, A03, A08, A20, A22, A26, ASCA, AltPI, BAS, BibLing, CA, CommAb, CurCont, DIP, E01, ERA, FR, FamI, I13, IBR, IBSS, IBZ, LeftInd, P10, P30, P34, P42, P46, P48, PAIS, PCI, PQC, PSA, RASB, S02, S03, S21, SCOPUS, SOPODA, SSA, SSCI, SociolAb, T02, W07.
—BLDSC (8814.630000), IE, Infotrieve, Ingenta, INIST. **CCC.**
Published by: Springer Netherlands (Subsidiary of: Springer Science+Business Media), Van Godewijckstraat 30, Dordrecht, 3311 GX, Netherlands. TEL 31-78-6576050, FAX 31-78-6576474, http://www.springer.com.

306 GBR ISSN 0263-2764
H1
➤ **THEORY, CULTURE & SOCIETY;** explorations in critical social science. Text in English. 1982. 8/yr. USD 1,536, GBP 830 combined subscription to institutions (print & online eds.); USD 1,505, GBP 813 to institutions (effective 2011). adv. bk.rev. illus. Index. back issues avail.; reprint service avail. from PSC. **Document type:** *Journal, Academic/Scholarly.* **Description:** Caters for the resurgence of interest in culture within contemporary social science. Features papers by and about modern social and cultural theorists.
Related titles: Online - full text ed.: ISSN 1460-3616. USD 1,382, GBP 747 to institutions (effective 2011); Supplement(s): Theory, Culture & Society. Supplement. ISSN 1759-6017.
Indexed: A01, A02, A03, A08, A12, A13, A17, A20, A22, A26, ABIn, AICP, ASCA, AltPI, ArtHuCI, B07, BibInd, CA, CMM, CommAb, CurCont, DIP, E-psyche, E01, E08, ERA, FR, FamI, G08, G10, H04, I05, I13, I14, IBR, IBSS, IBZ, IBibSS, LeftInd, MLA, MLA-IB, P34, P42, P48, P51, P53, P54, PAIS, PCI, PQC, PSA, PhilInd, RASB, RILM, S02, S03, S09, S21, SCOPUS, SOPODA, SSA, SSCI, SociolAb, T02, V&AA, V02, W07, W09.
—BLDSC (8814.631500), IE, Infotrieve, Ingenta, INIST. **CCC.**
Published by: (Nottingham Trent University, Theory, Culture & Society Centre), Sage Publications Ltd. (Subsidiary of: Sage Publications, Inc.), 1 Oliver's Yard, 55 City Rd, London, EC1Y 1SP, United Kingdom. TEL 44-20-73248500, FAX 44-20-73248600, info@sagepub.co.uk, http://www.uk.sagepub.com/home.nav. Ed. Mike Featherstone. adv.: B&W page GBP 450; 130 x 205. **Subscr. in the Americas to:** Sage Publications, Inc., 2455 Teller Rd, Thousand Oaks, CA 91320. TEL 805-499-9774, FAX 805-499-0871, journals@sagepub.com.

306 IND ISSN 0974-1542
THIRD FRAME; literature, culture and society. Text in English. 2008. q. INR 1,800 domestic; USD 100 foreign (effective 2010). **Document type:** *Journal, Academic/Scholarly.*
Published by: Cambridge University Press India Pvt. Ltd., Cambridge House, 4381/4, Ansari Rd, Daryaganj, New Delhi, 110 002, India. TEL 91-11-43543500, FAX 91-11-23288534, cupdel@cambridge.org, http://www.cambridgeindia.org. Eds. Mushirul Hasan, Rakhshanda Jalil.

306 USA ISSN 1069-6776
HM101
THRESHOLDS; viewing culture. Cover title: Viewing Culture. Text in English. 1991. a.
Related titles: Online - full content ed.: 1997.
Indexed: MLA-IB.
Published by: University of California, Santa Barbara, Graduate Students Association, University Center, Santa Barbara, CA 93106. Ed. William Stern.

TIDSSKRIFT FOR UNGDOMSFORSKNING. *see* CHILDREN AND YOUTH—About

306.09 330.1 NLD ISSN 1572-1701
HN1
TIJDSCHRIFT VOOR SOCIALE EN ECONOMISCHE GESCHIEDENIS. Text in Dutch. 2004. q. EUR 44 to individual members; EUR 65 to institutional members; EUR 27.50 to students (effective 2009). **Document type:** *Journal, Academic/Scholarly.*
Formed by the merger of (1975-2004): Tijdschrift voor Social Geschiedenis (0303-9935); (1987-2004): N E H A Bulletin (0920-9875); (1994-2004): N E H A Jaarboek voor Economische, Bedrijfs- en Techniekgeschiedenis (1380-5517); Which was formed by the merger of (1984-1994): Jaarboek voor de Geschiedenis van Bedrijf en Techniek (0920-7724); (1916-1994): Economisch- en Sociaal-historisch Jaarboek (0167-7942); Which was formerly (until 1971): Economisch-Historisch Jaarboek (0167-7845)
Indexed: A22, CA, HistAb, IBR, IBSS, IBZ, SCOPUS, T02.
—BLDSC (8844.480000), IE, Ingenta.
Published by: (Vereniging het Nederlandsch Economisch-Historisch Archief), Internationaal Instituut voor Sociale Geschiedenis/ Netherlands Institute of Social History, PO Box 2169, Amsterdam, 1000 CD, Netherlands. TEL 31-20-6685866, FAX 31-20-6654181, info@iisg.nl, http://www.iisg.nl.

301 BEL ISSN 0777-883X
➤ **TIJDSCHRIFT VOOR SOCIOLOGIE.** Text in Dutch. 1980. q. EUR 40 to individuals; EUR 85 to institutions; EUR 25 to students (effective 2009). **Document type:** *Journal, Academic/Scholarly.*
Indexed: CA, P42, PSA, S02, S03, SSA, SociolAb, T02.
—IE.
Published by: Uitgeverij Acco, Blijde Inkomststr 22, Leuven, 3000, Belgium. TEL 32-16-628000, FAX 32-16-628001, uitgeverij@acco.be, http://www.acco.be. Ed. Karel Van den Bosch.

➤ **TILT (ONLINE).** *see* EDUCATION

➤ **TIME AND MIND;** the journal of archaeology, consciousness and culture. *see* ARCHAEOLOGY

301 GBR ISSN 0961-463X
HM299 CODEN: TIMSEB
➤ **TIME & SOCIETY.** Text in English. 1992. 3/yr. USD 1,077, GBP 582 combined subscription to institutions (print & online eds.); USD 1,055, GBP 570 to institutions (effective 2011). adv. bk.rev. back issues avail.; reprint service avail. from PSC. **Document type:** *Journal, Academic/Scholarly.* **Description:** Publishes empirical and theoretical analyses on the subject of temporality, relating it to society and culture and to theories of individual and social behavior and action.
Related titles: Online - full text ed.: ISSN 1461-7463. USD 969, GBP 524 to institutions (effective 2011).
Indexed: A01, A03, A08, A20, A22, AICP, ASCA, B07, CA, CurCont, DIP, E-psyche, E01, FamI, H04, I13, IBR, IBSS, IBZ, IBibSS, LeftInd, MLA-IB, P02, P03, P10, P34, P42, P48, P53, P54, PQC, PSA, PsycInfo, PsycholAb, S02, S03, S11, S21, SCOPUS, SOPODA, SSA, SSCI, SociolAb, T02, V02, W07.
—BLDSC (8852.070000), IE, Infotrieve, Ingenta. **CCC.**
Published by: Sage Publications Ltd. (Subsidiary of: Sage Publications, Inc.), 1 Oliver's Yard, 55 City Rd, London, EC1Y 1SP, United Kingdom. TEL 44-20-73248500, FAX 44-20-73248600, info@sagepub.co.uk, http://www.uk.sagepub.com/home.nav. Eds. Hartmut Rosa, Robert Hassan. adv.: B&W page GBP 400; 105 x 185. **Subscr. in the Americas to:** Sage Publications, Inc., 2455 Teller Rd, Thousand Oaks, CA 91320. TEL 805-499-9774, FAX 805-499-0871, journals@sagepub.com.

301 GRC
➤ **TO MATSAKONI.** Text in Greek. 1985. irreg. (approx. 2/yr.). **Document type:** *Academic/Scholarly.*
Related titles: Online - full text ed.
Address: c/o John Giannopoulos, 3 Samara St, Patissia, Athens 111 44, Greece.

302.2 USA ISSN 0040-8263
PN4193.O4
TOASTMASTER. Text in English. 1933. m. free to members (effective 2011). bk.rev. illus. index. back issues avail.; reprints avail. **Document type:** *Magazine, Consumer.* **Description:** Covers public speaking, leadership, language usage, and communications in general.
Formerly: The Toastmasters International
Related titles: Online - full text ed.
Indexed: IMI.
Published by: Toastmasters International, PO Box 9052, Mission Viejo, CA 92690. TEL 949-858-8255, FAX 949-858-1207, letters@toastmasters.org. Ed. Suzanne Frey. Pub. Daniel Rex.

303.3 CAN ISSN 0730-479X
H1
➤ **TOCQUEVILLE REVIEW/REVUE TOCQUEVILLE.** Abbreviated title: T T R. Text in English, French. 1979. s-a. USD 55 in North America; USD 75 elsewhere (effective 2011). adv. bk.rev. **Document type:** *Journal, Academic/Scholarly.* **Description:** Devoted to the comparative study of social change, primarily in Europe and the United States, but also covering major developments in other parts of the world, in the spirit of Alexis de Tocqueville's pioneer investigations.
Related titles: Online - full text ed.

Indexed: A22, AmH&L, C03, CA, CBCARef, E01, HistAb, I13, IBSS, P42, P48, PCI, PQC, PSA, S02, S03, SCOPUS, SOPODA, SSA, SociolAb, T02.
—BLDSC (8859.720660), IE, Ingenta, INIST. **CCC.**
Published by: (Tocqueville Society FRA), University of Toronto Press, Journals Division, 5201 Dufferin St, Toronto, ON M3H 5T8, Canada. TEL 416-667-7810, FAX 416-667-7881, journals@utpress.utoronto.ca. Eds. Cheryl Welch, Francoise Melonio, Laurence Guellec. Circ: 210.

➤ **TOPIA REVISTA**; psicoanalisis, sociedad y cultura. *see* PSYCHOLOGY

301 500 TUR ISSN 1300-9354
H8.T87 CODEN: TOBIF3
TOPLUM VE BILIM. Text in Turkish. 1977. irreg. USD 59.90 (effective 2004). **Document type:** *Consumer.*
Indexed: CA, HistAb, M10, P30, P42, PSA, S02, S03, SCOPUS, SSA, SociolAb, T02.
Published by: Iletisim Yayincilik AS, Klodfarer Cad. Iletisim Han 7/2 Cagaloglu, Istanbul, 34400, Turkey. TEL 90-212-516-22-60, FAX 90-212-516-12-58, iletisim@iletisim.com.tr, http://www.iletisim.com.tr.

TOURISM, CULTURE & COMMUNICATION. *see* TRAVEL AND TOURISM

TRABAJO Y SOCIEDAD. *see* BUSINESS AND ECONOMICS—Labor And Industrial Relations

TRACES (ITHACA); a multilingual series of cultural theory and translation. *see* LINGUISTICS

303.4 ITA ISSN 1970-4410
TRAGUARDI SOCIALI. Text in Italian. 1973. m. **Document type:** *Magazine, Trade.*
Published by: Movimento Cristiano dei Lavoratori (M C L), Via Luigi Luzzatti 13a, Rome, 00185, Italy. TEL 39-06-7005110, FAX 39-06-7005153, info@mcl.it.

301 AUS ISSN 1833-8542
➤ **TRANS/FORMING CULTURES**; eJournal. Text in English. 2006. s-a. free (effective 2011). back issues avail. **Document type:** *Journal, Academic/Scholarly.* **Description:** Investigates transformation in cultural history, cultural interaction and new media, international activism, place and environment, and transnational cultures.
Media: Online - full text.
Indexed: T02.
Published by: (University of Technology, Sydney, Faculty of Humanities and Social Sciences), U T S ePress, PO Box 123, Broadway, NSW 2007, Australia. http://utsescholarship.lib.uts.edu.au/.

302.3 DEU
TRANSFORMATIONEN (WUERZBURG); Gesellschaften im Wandel. Text in German. 2000. irreg., latest vol.6, 2003. price varies. **Document type:** *Monographic series, Academic/Scholarly.*
Published by: Ergon Verlag, Keesburgstr 11, Wuerzburg, 97074, Germany. TEL 49-931-280084, FAX 49-931-282872, service@ergon-verlag.de, http://www.ergon-verlag.de.

301 USA ISSN 1052-5017
CODEN: TANSFT
➤ **TRANSFORMATIONS (WAYNE)**; the journal of inclusive scholarship and pedagogy. Text in English. 1990. s-a. USD 20 to individuals; USD 50 to institutions (effective 2011). adv. bk.rev. back issues avail. **Document type:** *Journal, Academic/Scholarly.* **Description:** Provides a forum for pedagogical scholarship exploring intersections of identities, power, and social justice.
Related titles: Online - full text ed.
Indexed: APW, AltPI, BRD, CA, DYW, E02, E03, ERI, EdA, EdI, FemPer, GW, LeftInd, MLA-IB, P18, P27, P46, P48, P53, P54, PQC, SCOPUS, SOPODA, SociolAb, T02, W03, W05.
—BLDSC (9020.616000), Ingenta.
Published by: New Jersey City University, 2039 Kennedy Blvd, Jersey City, NJ 07305. http://web.njcu.edu. Eds. Edvige Giunta, Jacqueline Ellis.

➤ **TRANSIT.** *see* HISTORY—History Of Europe

306.85 CAN ISSN 0049-4429
HQ559.T7
TRANSITION. Text in English, French. 1970. 4/yr. CAD 30 domestic to individuals; USD 20 foreign to individuals; CAD 65 domestic to institutions (effective 1999). bk.rev.; film rev. bibl.; stat. **Document type:** *Bulletin.* **Description:** Articles on family issues.
Related titles: Online - full text ed.
Indexed: AIAP, BLI, CA, PerIslam, S02, S03, T02.
Published by: Vanier Institute of the Family, 94 Centrepointe Dr, Ottawa, ON K2G 6B1, Canada. TEL 613-228-8500, FAX 613-228-8007, amirabelli@vifamily.ca. Ed., R&P Donna McCloskey. Pub. Alan Mirabelli. Circ: 8,000 (paid).

TRANSNATIONAL ASSOCIATIONS/ASSOCIATIONS TRANSNATIONALES. *see* POLITICAL SCIENCE—International Relations

TRANSPORTATION PLANNING AND TECHNOLOGY. *see* TRANSPORTATION

301 BEL ISSN 1377-4573
CODEN: CRREF7
TRAVAIL EMPLOI FORMATION. Text in French. 1979. q. bk.rev. **Document type:** *Academic/Scholarly.*
Formerly (until 1989): Critique Regionale (0770-0075)
Indexed: CA, FR, PAIS, S02, S03, SOPODA, SociolAb, T02.
—INIST.
Published by: (Universite Libre de Bruxelles), Centre de Sociologie et d'Economie Regionales, Rue de Bruxelles 39, Nivelles, 1400, Belgium. TEL 32-2-6503430, FAX 32-2-6503335. Ed. Mateo Alaluf. R&P Adinda Vanheersynghels. **Co-sponsor:** Comite pour l'Etude des Problemes de l'Emploi et du Chomage.

TRAVAIL, GENRE ET SOCIETES; la revue du M A G E. *see* BUSINESS AND ECONOMICS—Labor And Industrial Relations

LE TRAVAIL HUMAIN. *see* PSYCHOLOGY

304.6 NLD ISSN 2212-0513
TRENDRAPPORT LANDELIJKE JEUGDMONITOR. Text in Dutch. 2008. a. EUR 6.50 (effective 2011).
Formerly (until 2010): Jaarrapport Landelijke Jeugdmonitor (1876-9942)
Published by: (Ministerie van Volksgezondheid, Welzijn en Sport), Centraal Bureau voor de Statistiek, Henri Faasdreef 312, The Hague, 2492 JP, Netherlands. TEL 31-70-3373800, FAX 31-70-3375994, infoserv@cbs.nl, http://www.cbs.nl. Circ: 1,275.

301 RUS ISSN 0234-6192
HV5840.S65
TREZVOST' I KUL'TURA/ABSTINENCE AND CULTURE. Text in Russian. 1986. bi-m. USD 99.95 in United States. **Document type:** *Journal, Consumer.* **Description:** Asserts abstinence as a norm of life; includes anti-alcoholic propagation; distribution of knowledge about drugs and smoking.
Indexed: RASB.
—East View.
Published by: Sovet Mezhdunarodnoi Ligi Trezvosti i Zdorov'ya, Ul Chekhova 18, Moscow, 103006, Russian Federation. TEL 7-095-2992763, FAX 7-095-2991159. Ed. I G Astaf'ev. **Dist. by:** East View Information Services, 10601 Wayzata Blvd, Minneapolis, MN 55305. TEL 952-252-1201, 800-477-1005, FAX 952-252-1202, info@eastview.com, http://www.eastview.com.

301 ESP ISSN 1130-7331
TRIBUNA SOCIAL. Text in Spanish. 1984. m. EUR 374.40 domestic; EUR 375 in Europe; EUR 380 elsewhere (effective 2008). **Document type:** *Magazine, Consumer.*
Formerly (until 1990): Cuadernos Practicos de Seguridad Social y Laboral (1130-7323)
Published by: CISS (Wolters Kluwer Spain) (Subsidiary of: Wolters Kluwer N.V.), Colon 1, 5a, Valencia, 46004, Spain. TEL 34-96-3103080, FAX 34-96-3522538, http://www.ciss.es. Ed. Jose Ignacio Garcia Ninet.

302 ESP ISSN 1138-3305
P87
TRIPODOS. Text in Spanish. 1996. s-a. **Document type:** *Journal, Academic/Scholarly.*
Formerly (until 1996): Tripode (1136-2413)
Related titles: Online - full text ed.: free (effective 2011).
Published by: Universitat Ramon Llull, Facultat de Ciencies de la Comunicacio Blanquerna, C. Valldonzella, 23, Barcelona, 08001, Spain. TEL 34-93-2533096, FAX 34-93-2533099.

301 320 FRA ISSN 1243-549X
TUMULTES. Text in French. 1992. s-a. EUR 34 (effective 2009). **Document type:** *Journal, Academic/Scholarly.*
Indexed: FR, IBSS.
Published by: (Universite de Paris VII, Centre de Sociologie des Pratiques et des Representations Politiques (C S P R P)), Editions Kime, 2 Impasse des Peintres, Paris, 75002, France. TEL 33-1-42213072, FAX 33-1-42213084, kime.editions@wanadoo.fr, http://perso.orange.fr/kime.

TURNING THE TIDE; journal of anti-racist action, research and education. *see* POLITICAL SCIENCE

303.66 SWE ISSN 1653-4573
U C D P PAPERS. (Uppsala Conflict Data Program) Text in English. 2005. irreg., latest vol.1, 2005. **Document type:** *Monographic series, Academic/Scholarly.*
Media: Online - full content.
Published by: Uppsala Universitet, Institutionen foer Freds- och Konfliktforskning/University of Uppsala, Department of Peace and Conflict Research, Gamla Torget 3, PO Box 514, Uppsala, 75120, Sweden. TEL 46-18-4710000, FAX 46-18-695102, info@pcr.uu.se, http://www.pcr.uu.se.

U K ALCOHOL ALERT. *see* DRUG ABUSE AND ALCOHOLISM

U N U - M E R I T WORKING PAPER SERIES. (United Nations University, Maastricht Economic Research Institute on Innovation and Technology) *see* BUSINESS AND ECONOMICS

301 AUS ISSN 1834-2027
➤ **U T S SHOPFRONT MONOGRAPH SERIES.** (University of Technology, Sydney) Text in English. 2005. irreg. **Document type:** *Monographic series, Academic/Scholarly.*
Published by: University of Technology, Sydney, Shopfront, PO Box 123, Broadway, NSW 2007, Australia. TEL 61-2-9514-2900.

300 DEU ISSN 1430-1962
UEBERGAENGE (FREIBURG). Text in German. 1996. irreg., latest vol.3, 2001. price varies. **Document type:** *Monographic series, Academic/Scholarly.*
Published by: Centaurus Verlag & Media KG, Kaiser-Joseph-Str 267, Freiburg, 79098, Germany. TEL 49-761-1525861, FAX 49-761-1525868, info@centaurus-verlag.de, http://www.centaurus-verlag.de.

301 028.5 GBR ISSN 2047-3400
▼ **UGLY DUCK.** Text in English. 2011. q. adv. **Document type:** *Magazine, Consumer.*
Related titles: Online - full text ed.: ISSN 2047-3672. free (effective 2011).
Published by: Wake Up!, The Albany, Douglas Way, London, Deptford SE8 4AG, United Kingdom. TEL 44-20-86924446 ext 272, http://wakeupnow.co.uk/. Ed. Jack Mitchell. Adv. contact David Thomas.

301 UKR
UKRAINS'KA DYASPORA. Text in Ukrainian. s-a. USD 75 in United States.
Published by: Natsional'na Akademiya Nauk Ukrainy, Instytut Sotsiolohii, Ul Shelkovichnaya 12, Kiev, Ukraine. **Dist. by:** East View Information Services, 10601 Wayzata Blvd, Minneapolis, MN 55305. TEL 952-252-1201, 800-477-1005, FAX 952-252-1202, info@eastview.com, http://www.eastview.com.

301 CHL ISSN 0717-4691
HN291
ULTIMA DECADA. Text in Spanish. 1993. s-a. CLP 12,000 domestic; USD 15 foreign (effective 2010). **Document type:** *Journal, Academic/Scholarly.*
Related titles: Online - full text ed.: ISSN 0718-2236. 1993. free (effective 2011) (from SciELO).
—IE.
Published by: Centro de Investigacion y Difusion Poblacional de Achupallas, Luis Vicentini 96, Achupallas, Vina del Mar, Chile. Eds. Oscar Davila Leon, Oscar Romelio Davila. Circ: 1,000.

301 SWE ISSN 1100-3553
UMEAA STUDIES IN SOCIOLOGY. Text in English. 1968. irreg., latest vol.119, 2005. **Document type:** *Monographic series, Academic/Scholarly.*
Formerly (until 1988): University of Umeaa. Department of Sociology. Research Reports (0566-7518)
Indexed: CA, S02, S03, SCOPUS, SociolAb, T02.
Published by: Umeaa Universitet, Sociologiska Institutionen/University of Umeaa. Department of Sociology, Umeaa, 90187, Sweden. TEL 46-90-7865000, FAX 46-90-7866694, http://www.umu.se/soc.

301 USA ISSN 2152-1875
HM671
▼ **UNDERSTANDING AND DISMANTLING PRIVILEGE.** Text in English. forthcoming 2010 (Apr.). s-a. free (effective 2010). **Document type:** *Journal, Academic/Scholarly.* **Description:** Focuses on the intersectional aspects of privilege, bridging academia and practice, highlighting activism, and offering a forum for creative introspection on issues of inequity, power and privilege.
Media: Online - full text.
Published by: (The Matrix Center for the Advancement of Social Equity and Inclusion), Scholarly Exchange, Inc., 320 Dudley St, Brookline, MA 02445. info@scholarlyexchange.org, http://www.scholarlyexchange.org/.

302.2 NGA
UNILAG COMMUNICATION REVIEW; a quarterly review of the communication media. Text in English. 1977. q. NGN 10. adv.
Published by: University of Lagos, Department of Mass Communication, PO Box 12003, Lagos, Nigeria.

UNION SIGNAL. *see* DRUG ABUSE AND ALCOHOLISM

302.2 SEN ISSN 0253-5858
UNIR CINE MEDIA; bulletin de la commission des moyens de communication sociale de la conference episcopale regionale de l'Afrique de l'ouest. Text in French. 1982. s-a. XOF 5,000; includes Unir Cinema. bk.rev.; film rev. index.
Published by: R.P. Jean Vast Ed. & Pub., 1 rue Neuville, BP 160, St Louis, Senegal.

301 VEN ISSN 1012-2508
HC236
UNIVERSIDAD CENTRAL DE VENEZUELA. CENTRO DE ESTUDIOS DEL DESARROLLO. CUADERNOS DEL C E N D E S. Text in Spanish; Abstracts in English. 1983. 3/yr. adv. bk.rev. back issues avail. **Document type:** *Academic/Scholarly.* **Description:** Covers Venezuelan development problems and those of the Third World in general.
Related titles: Online - full text ed.: free (effective 2011).
Indexed: C01, CA, H21, P08, P09, P30, P42, PCI, PSA, S02, S03, SCOPUS, SociolAb, T02.
Published by: Universidad Central de Venezuela, Centro de Estudios del Desarrollo, Apartado Postal 6622, Caracas, DF 1010-A, Venezuela. TEL 7523266, FAX 582-7512691. Ed. Sergio Arauda. Circ: 2,000.
U.S. subscr. addr.: Poba International, 151, Box 02 5255, Miami, FL 33102-5255.

306.36 ARG ISSN 1666-4884
UNIVERSIDAD DE BUENOS AIRES. CENTRO DE ESTUDIOS DE SOCIOLOGIA DEL TRABAJO. DOCUMENTOS DE TRABAJO. Text in Spanish. 1996. q. back issues avail. **Document type:** *Monographic series, Academic/Scholarly.*
Related titles: Online - full text ed.: ISSN 1666-4892. 1996.
Published by: Universidad de Buenos Aires, Centro de Estudios de Sociologia del Trabajo, Ave Cordoba 2122 2o. Piso, Ofic. 211, Buenos Aires, C1120AAQ, Argentina. TEL 54-11-43706161, cesot@econ.uba.ar.

301 PRI
UNIVERSIDAD DE PUERTO RICO. CENTRO DE INVESTIGACIONES SOCIALES. INFORME ANUAL. Text in Spanish. 1974. a. free. bk.rev. bibl. **Document type:** *Academic/Scholarly.*
Published by: Universidad de Puerto Rico, Centro de Investigaciones Sociales, Recinto de Rio Piedras, Apdo 23345, Estacion UPR, San Juan, 00931-3345, Puerto Rico. Ed. Wenceslao Serra Deliz. Circ: 1,000.

301 ESP ISSN 1988-8090
UNIVERSIDAD PABLO DE OLAVIDE. CENTRO DE SOCIOLOGIA Y POLITICAS LOCALES. DOCUMENTOS DE TRABAJO. Text in Spanish. 2008. q.
Media: Online - full text.
Published by: Universidad Pablo de Olavide, Centro de Sociologia y Politicas Locales, Edif. No. 8 Felix de Azara, Ctra, de Utrera Km. 1, Sevilla, 41013, Spain. TEL 34-954-9779622, cps@upo.es, http://www.upo.es/cspl/index.htm.

301 CUB ISSN 2218-3620
▼ ➤ **UNIVERSIDAD Y SOCIEDAD.** Text in Spanish. 2009. 3/yr. free (effective 2011). **Document type:** *Journal, Academic/Scholarly.*
Media: Online - full text.
Published by: Universidad de Cienfuegos, Carretera a Rodas Km 4, Cuatro Caminos, Cienfuegos, Cuba. reducf@ucf.edu.cu. Ed. Liosdany Figuera Marante.

301 BRA ISSN 0104-6713
UNIVERSIDADE DE SAO PAULO. DEPARTAMENTO DE SOCIOLOGIA. SERIE ESCRITOS. Text in Portuguese. irreg. per issue exchange basis.
Published by: Universidade de Sao Paulo, Faculdade de Filosofia, Letras e Ciencias Humanas, Av Professor Luciano Gualberto 315, Butanta, Sao Paulo, SP 05508-010, Brazil. http://www.fflch.usp.br. Circ: 200.

301 PRT ISSN 0872-3419
UNIVERSIDADE DO PORTO. FACULDADE DE LETRAS. SOCIOLOGIA. Text in Portuguese. 1991. a. **Document type:** *Journal, Academic/Scholarly.*
Related titles: Online - full text ed.: free (effective 2011).
Published by: Universidade do Porto, Faculdade de Letras, Praca Gomes Teixeira, Oporto, 4099-002, Portugal. TEL 351-220-408000, FAX 351-220-408186, up@up.pt, http://www.up.pt.

301 ITA ISSN 1828-955X
UNIVERSITA DEGLI STUDI DI TRENTO. DIPARTIMENTO DI SOCIOLOGIA E RICERCA SOCIALE. QUADERNI. Text in Italian. 1983. irreg. **Document type:** *Monographic series, Academic/Scholarly.*
Formerly (until 1994): Universita degli Studi di Trento. Dipartimento di Politica Sociale. Quaderni (1828-9541)
Published by: Universita degli Studi di Trento, Dipartimento di Sociologia e Ricerca Sociale, Piazza Venezia 41, 3o Piano, Trento, 38100, Italy. TEL 39-0461-881433, FAX 39-0461-881348.

S

305.26 DEU ISSN 1869-0009
▼ **UNIVERSITAET VECHTA. ZENTRUM ALTERN UND GESELLSCHAFT. WORKING PAPER.** Text in German. 2009. irreg. **Document type:** *Monographic series, Academic/Scholarly.*
Media: Online - full text.
Published by: Universitaet Vechta, Zentrum Altern und Gesellschaft, Driverstr 22, Vechta, 49377, Germany. TEL 49-4441-15233, FAX 49-4441-15614, christine.hammer@uni-vechta.de.

UNIVERSITE D'ABIDJAN. ANNALES. SERIE F: ETHNOSOCIOLOGIE. *see* ANTHROPOLOGY

301 CAN ISSN 1914-1629
UNIVERSITE LAVAL. LABORATOIRE DE RECHERCHES SOCIOLOGIQUES. COLLECTION RAPPORTS DE RECHERCHE. Text in French. 199?. irreg. **Document type:** *Monographic series, Academic/Scholarly.*
Published by: Universite Laval, Laboratoire de Recherches Sociologiques, Pavillon Charles-De Koninck, Bureau 3469, Quebec, PQ G1K 7P4, Canada. TEL 418-656-2227, FAX 418-656-7390, soc@soc.ulaval.ca, http://www.soc.ulaval.ca.

301 BEL ISSN 0066-2380
HN501
UNIVERSITE LIBRE DE BRUXELLES. INSTITUT DE SOCIOLOGIE. ANNEE SOCIALE. Key Title: Annee Sociale - Institut de Sociologie. Text in French. 1960. a. EUR 25 (effective 2005). bk.rev. **Document type:** *Academic/Scholarly.*
Indexed: CA, IBSS, P30, P42, PAIS, PSA, RASB, S02, S03, SCOPUS, SociolAb, T02.
Published by: Universite Libre de Bruxelles, Institut de Sociologie, Av Jeanne 44, Brussels, 1050, Belgium. TEL 32-2-650-3489, FAX 32-2-650-3521.

301 NOR ISSN 1504-9280
UNIVERSITETET I AGDER. SKRIFTSERIEN. Text in Norwegian. 1995. irreg., latest vol.155, 2011. back issues avail. **Document type:** *Monographic series, Academic/Scholarly.*
Formerly (until 2007): Hoegskolen i Agder. Skriftserien (0806-5942)
Related titles: Online - full text ed.: ISSN 1504-9299.
Published by: Universitetet i Agder/Agder University, PO Box 422, Kristiansand, 4604, Norway. TEL 47-38-141000, FAX 47-38-141001, post@uia.no.

302.23 NOR ISSN 1504-1697
UNIVERSITETET I BERGEN. INSTITUTT FOR INFORMASJONS- OG MEDIEVITENSKAP. RAPPORT. Text mainly in Norwegian; Text occasionally in English. 1986. irreg., latest vol.60, 2005. price varies. back issues avail. **Document type:** *Monographic series, Academic/Scholarly.*
Former titles (until 2004): Universitetet i Bergen. Institutt for Medievitenskap. Publikasjon (1504-0755); (until 2002): Universitetet i Bergen. Institutt for Medievitenskap. I M V Utgivelse (1502-2382); (until 2001): Universitetet i Bergen. Department of Mediastudies. Rapport (1500-8304); (until 1994): Universitetet i Bergen. Institutt for Massekommunikasjon. Rapport (0801-2814)
Published by: Universitetet i Bergen, Institutt for Informasjons- og Medievitenskap, PO Box 7800, Bergen, 5020, Norway. TEL 47-55-589100, FAX 47-55-589149, post@infomedia.no.

330 USA
UNIVERSITY OF ALASKA. INSTITUTE OF SOCIAL AND ECONOMIC RESEARCH. RESEARCH SUMMARY. Text in English. 1980. irreg. free (effective 2011). bk.rev. charts; stat. back issues avail. **Document type:** *Monographic series, Academic/Scholarly.*
Related titles: Online - full text ed.
Published by: University of Alaska, Institute of Social and Economic Research, 3211 Providence Dr, Anchorage, AK 99508t. TEL 907-786-7710, http://www.iser.uaa.alaska.edu/.

▼ **UNIVERSITY OF AMSTERDAM. KNOWLEDGE PROGRAMME CIVIL SOCIETY IN WEST ASIA. WORKING PAPERS.** *see* ANTHROPOLOGY

301 SWE ISSN 1100-3618
UNIVERSITY OF GOTHENBURG. DEPARTMENT OF SOCIOLOGY. MONOGRAPH. Text in Swedish; Summaries in English. 1968. irreg., latest vol.33, 1984. price varies. **Document type:** *Monographic series, Academic/Scholarly.*
Formerly (until 1987): Goeteborgs Universitet. Sociologiska Institutionen. Monografier (0072-5102)
Published by: Goeteborgs Universitet, Sociologiska Institutionen/ University of Gothenburg. Department of Sociology, Spraengkullsgatan 23, PO Box 40530, Goeteborg, 40530, Sweden. TEL 46-31-773 10 00, FAX 46-31-773 47 64.

301 GBR
UNIVERSITY OF HULL. DEPARTMENT OF SOCIOLOGY AND SOCIAL ANTHROPOLOGY. OCCASIONAL PAPERS. Text in English. 1986. irreg., latest vol.15, 1996. price varies. **Document type:** *Monographic series.*
Published by: University of Hull, Department of Sociology and Social Anthropology, University Of Hull, Cottingham Rd, Hull, HU6 7RX, United Kingdom. TEL 44-1482-466213, FAX 44-1482-466366. Ed. Allison James.

UNIVERSITY OF LAGOS. HUMAN RESOURCES RESEARCH UNIT. MONOGRAPH. *see* POPULATION STUDIES

301 GBR
UNIVERSITY OF LEEDS. SCHOOL OF SOCIOLOGY AND SOCIAL POLICY. RESEARCH WORKING PAPER. Text in English. 19??. irreg., latest 2008. free (effective 2009). **Document type:** *Monographic series.* **Description:** Features reserach information about School of Sociology and Social Policy.
Formerly (until 1993): University of Leeds. Department of Social Policy and Sociology. Research Working Paper
Published by: University of Leeds, School of Sociology and Social Policy, Leeds, W Yorks LS2 9JT, United Kingdom. TEL 44-113-3434418, FAX 44-113-3434415, l.j.byrne@leeds.ac.uk, http://www.sociology.leeds.ac.uk/.

302.23 GBR ISSN 1475-7222
➤ **UNIVERSITY OF LEICESTER. DISCUSSION PAPERS IN MASS COMMUNICATIONS (ONLINE).** Text in English. 1992. irreg., latest 2006. free (effective 2009). **Document type:** *Monographic series, Academic/Scholarly.*
Formerly (until 2002): University of Leicester. Discussion Papers in Mass Communications (Print) (1363-7185)
Media: Online - full text.
Published by: University of Leicester, Department of Media and Communication, University Rd, Leicester, LE1 7RH, United Kingdom. TEL 44-116-2523863, FAX 44-116-2525276, mediacom@le.ac.uk, http://www.le.ac.uk/mc/.

➤ **UNIVERSITY OF LOUISVILLE LAW REVIEW.** *see* LAW—Family And Matrimonial Law

➤ **UNIVERSITY OF NOTTINGHAM. INTERNATIONAL CENTRE FOR CORPORATE SOCIAL RESPONSIBILITY. RESEARCH PAPER SERIES.** *see* BUSINESS AND ECONOMICS

301 JAM
UNIVERSITY OF THE WEST INDIES. INSTITUTE OF SOCIAL AND ECONOMIC RESEARCH. WORKING PAPERS. Text in English. 1975 (no.7). irreg., latest vol.35.
Published by: University of the West Indies, Sir Arthur Lewis Institute of Social and Economic Research, Mona Campus, Kingston, 7, Jamaica. TEL 809-927-1020, FAX 809-927-2409.

UNIVERSITY OF VAASA. PROCEEDINGS. DISCUSSION PAPERS. *see* BUSINESS AND ECONOMICS—Economic Systems And Theories, Economic History

306.0993 NZL ISSN 1177-4266
UNIVERSITY OF WAIKATO. DEPARTMENT OF SOCIETIES AND CULTURES. OCCASIONAL PAPER SERIES. Text in English. 2006. irreg., latest vol.3, 2006. **Document type:** *Monographic series, Academic/Scholarly.*
Related titles: Online - full text ed.: ISSN 1177-5246.
Published by: University of Waikato, Department of Societies and Cultures, Private Bag 3105, Hamilton, New Zealand.

UNIVERSITY OF WESTMINSTER. FACULTY OF BUSINESS, MANAGEMENT AND SOCIAL STUDIES. RESEARCH WORKING PAPER SERIES. *see* BUSINESS AND ECONOMICS

307.760711 USA
UNIVERSITY URBAN PROGRAMS. Text in English. 1980. quadrennial.
Published by: Urban Affairs Association, 298 Graham Hall, University of Delaware, Newark, DE 19716.

UNIVERZITET U ZAGREBU. PRAVNI FAKULTET. ZBORNIK. *see* LAW

306.85 POL
UNIWERSYTET OPOLSKI. WYDZIAL TEOLOGICZNY. CZLOWIEK - RODZINA - SPOLECZENSTWO. Text in Polish. 2002. irreg., latest vol.1, 2002. price varies. **Document type:** *Monographic series, Academic/Scholarly.*
Published by: (Uniwersytet Opolski, Wydzial Teologiczny), Wydawnictwo Uniwersytetu Opolskiego, ul Sienkiewicza 33, Opole, 45037, Poland. TEL 48-77-4410878, wydawnictwo@uni.opole.pl.

UNIWERSYTET SLASKI W KATOWICACH. PRACE NAUKOWE. Z PROBLEMATYKI PRAWA PRACY I POLITYKI SOCJALNEJ. *see* LAW

301 USA ISSN 0042-0468
HV553
UNSCHEDULED EVENTS; research committee on disasters newsletter. Text in English. 1967. q. free to members. adv. bk.rev. abstr. back issues avail. **Document type:** *Newsletter.*
Published by: International Research Committee on Disasters, c/o Dr. Brenda D. Phillips, 519 Math Science Bldg, Oklahoma State University, Stillwater, OK 74074. TEL 405-744-5298, FAX 405-744-6534, aguirre@udel.edu, http://www.udel.edu/DRC/IRCD.html. Ed. Henry W Fischer III. Circ: 250.

302.23 DEU ISSN 1862-3069
UNTERHALTUNGSFORSCHUNG. Text in German. 2006. irreg., latest vol.5, 2008. price varies. **Document type:** *Monographic series, Academic/Scholarly.*
Published by: Herbert von Halem Verlag, Lindenstr 19, Cologne, 50674, Germany. TEL 49-221-9258290, FAX 49-221-92582929, info@halem-verlag.de, http://www.halem-verlag.de.

306.9 ITA ISSN 1127-4107
UOMINI & STORIE. Text in Italian. 1998. a. **Document type:** *Magazine, Consumer.*
Published by: Editoriale Giorgio Mondadori SpA (Subsidiary of: Cairo Communication SpA), Via Tucidide 56, Torre 3, Milan, 20134, Italy. TEL 39-02-748111, FAX 39-02-70100102, info@cairocommunication.it, http://www.cairocommunication.it.

302.2 SWE ISSN 1651-4777
➤ **UPPSALA STUDIES IN MEDIA AND COMMUNICATION.** Text in Swedish. 2002. irreg., latest vol.2, 2003. price varies. back issues avail. **Document type:** *Monographic series, Academic/Scholarly.*
Related titles: ◆ Series of: Acta Universitatis Upsaliensis. ISSN 0346-5462.
Published by: Uppsala Universitet, Acta Universitatis Upsaliensis/ University Publications from Uppsala, PO Box 256, Uppsala, 75105, Sweden. TEL 46-18-4716804, FAX 46-18-4716804, acta@ub.uu.se, http://www.ub.uu.se/upu/auu/index.html. Ed. Bengt Landgren.

301 SWE ISSN 0566-8808
UPPSALA UNIVERSITY. DEPARTMENT OF PEACE AND CONFLICT RESEARCH. REPORT. Text in English. 1969. irreg., latest vol.71, 2005. price varies.
Published by: Uppsala Universitet, Institutionen foer Freds- och Konfliktforskning/University of Uppsala, Department of Peace and Conflict Research, Gamla Torget 3, PO Box 514, Uppsala, 75120, Sweden. TEL 46-18-4710000, FAX 46-18-695102, info@pcr.uu.se.

307 NZL ISSN 1177-8970
URBAN. Text in English. 2007. q. NZD 40 (effective 2009). adv. **Document type:** *Magazine, Trade.*
Published by: T P L. Media (Trade Publications), Newmarket, PO Box 9596, Auckland, 1149, New Zealand. TEL 64-9-5293027, FAX 64-9-5293001, info@tplmedia.co.nz, http://www.tplmedia.co.nz/. Ed. Graham Hawkes. Pub. Chauncey Stark. Adv. contact Charles Fairburn.

THE URBAN REVIEW; issues and ideas in public education. *see* EDUCATION—School Organization And Administration

URBAN STUDIES; an international journal for research in urban studies. *see* HOUSING AND URBAN PLANNING

▼ **URBAN STUDIES RESEARCH.** *see* HOUSING AND URBAN PLANNING

307.14 USA ISSN 2151-1896
HT123
URBANA; urban affairs and public policy. Text in English. 199?. irreg. free (effective 2009). back issues avail. **Description:** Contains methodology, teaching, practice and decision making related to urban and regional studies.
Media: Online - full content.
Published by: Texas A & M University, Real Estate Center, College Station, TX 77843. http://www.tamu.edu. Eds. Jesus A Trevinio, Michael A McAdams.

307.1416 GBR ISSN 2042-034X
▼ **URBIS RESEARCH FORUM REVIEW.** Text in English. 2009. bi-m. free (effective 2010). back issues avail. **Document type:** *Journal, Trade.*
Media: Online - full text.
Published by: Urbis, Town Hall, Albert Sq, PO Box 532, Manchester, M60 2LA, United Kingdom. TEL 44-161-6058200, info@urbis.org.uk, http://www.urbis.org.uk. Ed. Mark Rainey.

UTOPIE UND ALTERNATIVE. *see* POLITICAL SCIENCE

VAASAN YLIOPISTO. JULKAISUJA. TUTKIMUKSIA/UNIVERSITY OF VAASA. PROCEEDINGS. RESEARCH PAPERS. *see* BUSINESS AND ECONOMICS—Economic Systems And Theories, Economic History

301 FIN ISSN 0788-6748
VAASAN YLIOPISTO. JULKAISUJA. TUTKIMUKSIA. SOSIOLOGIA. Text in Multiple languages, 1971. irreg. price varies. back issues avail. **Document type:** *Monographic series, Academic/Scholarly.*
Former titles (until 1993): Vaasan Korkeakoulu. Julkaisuja. Tutkimuksia. Sosiologia (0359-3525); (until 1983): Vaasan Kauppakorkeakoulu. Julkaisuja. Tutkimuksia. Sosiologia (0359-3444)
Related titles: ◆ Series of: Vaasan Yliopisto. Julkaisuja. Tutkimuksia. ISSN 0788-6667.
Published by: Vaasan Yliopisto/University of Vaasa, PO Box 700, Vaasa, 65101, Finland. TEL 358-6-3248111, FAX 358-6-3248187.

301 COL ISSN 0123-6180
VADEMECUM DEL GRUPO BITACORA. Text in Spanish. s-a. USD 3 newsstand/cover (effective 2000).
Published by: Universidad de Antioquia, Facultad de Ciencias Sociales y Humanas, Apod. Aereo 1226, Medellin, ANT, Colombia. TEL 57-4-210-5763.

301 FIN ISSN 0782-2332
VAKI VOIMAKAS. Text in Finnish. 1985. irreg., latest vol.18. price varies. back issues avail. **Document type:** *Monographic series, Academic/Scholarly.*
Published by: Tyovaen Historian ja Perinteen Tutkimuksen Seura/ Finnish Society for Labour History and Cultural Traditions, c/o Hanna Snelling, Kultuurien Tutkimuksen Laitos Kansatriede, PO Box 59, Helsinki, 00014, Finland. TEL 358-9-19122622, hanna.snelling@helsinki.fi. Ed. Pirjo Markkola.

301 HUN ISSN 0324-7228
AP82
VALOSAG. Text in Hungarian. 1957. m. USD 159.90 foreign (effective 2008). adv. bk.rev.
Related titles: Online - full content ed.
Indexed: IBSS, MLA-IB, RASB, RILM.
Published by: Tudomanyos Ismeretterjeszto Tarsulat, Pf. 176, Budapest, 1431, Hungary. TEL 36-1-4832540, FAX 36-1-4832549, titlap@telc.hu, http://www.titnet.hu. Circ: 9,000.

301 NOR ISSN 0809-5302
VELFERD; sosial trygd, arbeid og helse. Text in Norwegian. 1997. 8/yr. NOK 395 to individuals; NOK 438 to institutions; NOK 315 to students (effective 2011). adv. bk.rev. abstr.; illus. **Document type:** *Magazine, Trade.*
Formed by the merger of (1996-1998): Velferdsmagasinet Sosial Trygd (0808-050X); Which was formerly (until 1996): Sosial Trygd (0038-1608); Formerly (1912-1937): Sygeforsikringsbladet (0332-9526); (1986-1998): Helse- og Sosial Forum (0801-1842); Which was formerly (until 1986): Sosialt Forum - Sosialt Arbeid (0332-8791); Formed by the merger of (1927-1972): Sosialt Arbeid (0038-1632); (1870-1972): Sosialt Forum (0332-8783); Incorporates (1970-1974): Nemm-Kontakt (0809-5310)
Published by: Stiftelsen Sosial Trygd, Hegdehaugsveien 36 A, Oslo, 0352, Norway. TEL 47-22-850770, FAX 47-22-850771. Ed. Karin Helene Haugen TEL 47-22-850772. Circ: 3,000.

▼ **VERTREKNL.** *see* POPULATION STUDIES

VICTIMS OF VIOLENCE NEWSLETTER. *see* LAW—Criminal Law

301 FRA ISSN 0042-5605
H3
VIE SOCIALE. Text in French. 1964. 4/yr. EUR 52 domestic; EUR 60 foreign (effective 2009). bk.rev. back issues avail. **Document type:** *Monographic series, Academic/Scholarly.* **Description:** A collection of stories, reflections, information and documentation.
Indexed: FR, RASB.
—INIST. **CCC.**
Published by: Centre d'Etudes de Documentation d'Information et d'Action Sociales (CEDIAS), 5 rue Las-Cases, Paris, 75007, France. TEL 33-1-45516610, FAX 33-1-44180181. Circ: 1,750 (controlled).

303.6 USA ISSN 1077-8012
HV6250.4.W65 CODEN: VAWOFG
➤ **VIOLENCE AGAINST WOMEN**; an international and interdisciplinary journal. Text in English. 1995. m. USD 1,141, GBP 671 combined subscription to institutions (print & online eds.); USD 1,118, GBP 658 to institutions (effective 2011). adv. bk.rev. bibl.; illus. back issues avail.; reprint service avail. from PSC. **Document type:** *Journal, Academic/Scholarly.* **Description:** Publishes empirical research, as well as cross-cultural and historical analyses, on all aspects of violence against women and girls.
Related titles: Online - full text ed.: ISSN 1552-8448. USD 1,027, GBP 604 to institutions (effective 2011).
Indexed: A01, A02, A03, A08, A20, A22, A26, B04, B07, B21, BRD, C06, C07, C08, CA, CINAHL, CJA, CJPI, CurCont, E-psyche, E01, E08, EMBASE, ESPM, ExcerpMed, F09, FamI, FemPer, G08, G10, H&SSA, H04, H12, I05, IBSS, IPsyAb, MEDLINE, P02, P03, P10, P24, P25, P27, P30, P34, P48, P50, P53, P54, PQC, PRA, PsycInfo, PsycholAb, RiskAb, S02, S03, S09, S21, SCOPUS, SFSA, SOPODA, SSA, SSAI, SSAb, SSCI, SSI, SUSA, SociolAb, T02, V&AA, V02, W01, W02, W03, W06, W07, W09.
—BLDSC (9237.750800), IE, Infotrieve, Ingenta. **CCC.**

Published by: Sage Publications, Inc., 2455 Teller Rd, Thousand Oaks, CA 91320. TEL 805-499-9774, 800-818-7243, FAX 805-499-0871, 800-583-2665, info@sagepub.com. Ed. Claire M Renzetti. Circ: 700 (paid and free). **Subscr. overseas to:** Sage Publications Ltd., 1 Oliver's Yard, 55 City Rd, London EC1Y 1SP, United Kingdom. TEL 44-207-3248701, FAX 44-207-3248733, subscription@sagepub.co.uk.

303.6 USA ISSN 0886-6708
HV6250
➤ **VIOLENCE AND VICTIMS.** Text in English. 1986. bi-m. USD 125 domestic to individuals; USD 175 foreign to individuals; USD 346 domestic to institutions; USD 406 foreign to institutions; USD 188 combined subscription domestic to individuals (print & online eds.); USD 278 combined subscription foreign to individuals (print & online eds.); USD 519 combined subscription domestic to institutions (print & online eds.); USD 609 combined subscription foreign to institutions (print & online eds.) (effective 2010). adv. bk.rev.; software rev.; video rev.; Website rev. abstr.; bibl. back issues avail.; reprints avail. **Document type:** *Journal, Academic/Scholarly.* **Description:** Provides a forum for the latest developments in theory, research, policy, clinical practice and social services in the areas of interpersonal violence and victimization.
Related titles: Online - full text ed.: ISSN 1945-7073. USD 115 domestic to individuals; USD 175 foreign to individuals; USD 316 domestic to institutions; USD 376 foreign to institutions (effective 2010) (from IngentaConnect).
Indexed: A21, A22, A26, AC&P, BRD, C06, C07, CA, CJA, CJPI, CurCont, E-psyche, E08, EMBASE, ESPM, ExcerpMed, F09, FamI, G08, H12, I05, IndMed, MEDLINE, P03, P10, P12, P19, P20, P22, P25, P27, P30, P42, P46, P48, P53, P54, PQC, PRA, PSA, PsycInfo, PsycholAb, RI-1, RI-2, RiskAb, S02, S03, S09, S11, SCOPUS, SFSA, SOPODA, SSA, SSAI, SSAb, SSCI, SSI, SWR&A, SociolAb, T02, V&AA, W03, W07, W09.
—BLDSC (9237.751000), GNLM, IE, Infotrieve, Ingenta, INIST. **CCC.**
Published by: Springer Publishing Company, 11 W 42nd St, 15th Fl, New York, NY 10036. TEL 212-431-4370, 877-687-7476, FAX 212-941-7842, journals@springerpub.com. Ed. Roland Maiuro. Adv. contact Carrie Neff TEL 212-431-4370 ext 221.

302.23 USA
➤ **VISIBLE EVIDENCE SERIES.** Text in English. 1997. irreg., latest vol.22, 2008. price varies. back issues avail. **Document type:** *Monographic series, Academic/Scholarly.* **Description:** Examines pubic perception of social and cultural issues and trends, as reflected in the public media.
Published by: University of Minnesota Press, Ste 290, 111 Third Ave S, Minneapolis, MN 55401. TEL 612-627-1970, FAX 612-627-1980. Eds. Ginsburg Faye, Jane Gaines, Michael Renov. **Dist. in UK by:** Plymbridge Distributors Ltd, Estover Rd, Plymouth, Devon PL6 7PY, United Kingdom. TEL 44-1752-202-301, FAX 44-1752-202-331; **Dist. by:** c/o Chicago Distribution Center, 11030 S Langley Ave, Chicago, IL 60628. TEL 800-621-2736, ump@umn.edu.

384.5 DEU ISSN 0947-4552
VISTASCRIPT; Forum fuer Medien und Kommunikation. Text in German. 1986. irreg., latest vol.16, 2007. price varies. **Document type:** *Monographic series, Academic/Scholarly.*
Published by: Vistas Verlag GmbH, Goltzstr 11, Berlin, 10781, Germany. TEL 49-30-32707446, FAX 49-30-32707455, medienverlag@vistas.de.

301 GBR ISSN 1472-586X
HM500 CODEN: VISOEH
➤ **VISUAL STUDIES.** Text in English. 1986. 3/yr. GBP 309 combined subscription in United Kingdom to institutions (print & online eds.); EUR 405, USD 508 combined subscription to institutions (print & online eds.) (effective 2012). adv. back issues avail.; reprint service avail. from PSC. **Document type:** *Journal, Academic/Scholarly.* **Description:** Investigates the relationship between society and photographic, film, and video images.
Former titles (until 2002): Visual Sociology (1067-1684); (until 1991): Visual Sociology Review
Related titles: Online - full text ed.: ISSN 1472-5878. GBP 278 in United Kingdom to institutions; EUR 364, USD 457 to institutions (effective 2012) (from IngentaConnect).
Indexed: A01, A03, A08, A20, A22, A30, A31, ABM, AmHI, ArtHuCI, CA, D05, E01, ErgAb, H07, IBSS, MLA-IB, S02, S03, SCOPUS, SOPODA, SociolAb, T02, W07.
—IE, Infotrieve, Ingenta. **CCC.**
Published by: (International Visual Sociology Association USA), Routledge (Subsidiary of: Taylor & Francis Group), 4 Park Sq, Milton Park, Abingdon, Oxon OX14 4RN, United Kingdom. TEL 44-20-70176000, FAX 44-20-70176336, subscriptions@tandf.co.uk, http://www.routledge.com. Ed. Darren Newbury. Adv. contact Linda Hann TEL 44-1344-779945. **Subscr. to:** Taylor & Francis Ltd., Journals Customer Service, Sheepen Pl, Colchester, Essex CO3 3LP, United Kingdom. TEL 44-20-70175544, FAX 44-20-70175198, tf.enquiries@tfinforma.com.

▼➤ **VOICE**; an immigration dialogue. *see* LAW—Civil Law

306.09 900 USA ISSN 1556-942X
VOICES OF TWENTIETH CENTURY CONFLICT. Text in English. 2003. irreg. price varies. back issues avail. **Document type:** *Monographic series, Academic/Scholarly.*
Related titles: Online - full text ed.
Published by: Greenwood Publishing Group Inc. (Subsidiary of: A B C - C L I O), 88 Post Rd W, PO Box 5007, Westport, CT 06881. TEL 203-226-3571, 800-225-5800, FAX 877-231-6980, sales@greenwood.com, http://www.greenwood.com. Ed. Carol Schulz.

307.1412 IND ISSN 0042-8647
JS7008
VOLUNTARY ACTION. Text in English. 1958. bi-m. bk.rev. cum.index vols.1-13. **Document type:** *Journal, Academic/Scholarly.*
Formerly: A V A R D Newsletter
Published by: Association of Voluntary Agencies for Rural Development (A V A R D), 5 (FF),Institutional Area,, Deen Dayal Upadhyay Marg, Kamala Devi Bhavan, New Delhi, 110002, India. TEL 91-11-23234690, FAX 91-11-23232501, avard@bol.net.in, www.avard.in.

VORONEZHSKII GOSUDARSTVENNYI UNIVERSITET. VESTNIK. SERIYA: ISTORIYA, POLITOLOGIYA, SOTSIOLOGIYA. *see* HISTORY

301 360 THA ISSN 1040-8541
VOYAGER INTERNATIONAL. Text in English. 1984. m. USD 58 (effective 2003). adv. bk.rev.; film rev. cum.index: 1987-1991. 32 p./no.; back issues avail. **Document type:** *Newsletter.* **Description:** Evaluates the world for the discerning traveler.
Published by: Argonaut Enterprises, Inc., Chaiyapruk Mansion, 9-8 Sukhumvt, 501 65 Prakanong, Bangkok, 10110, Thailand. Ed. Jason N Fisher. R&P Nigel Ficher. Circ: 20,000.

302.23 NLD
W R R WEBPUBLICATIES. Text in Dutch. irreg. price varies. **Document type:** *Monographic series, Academic/Scholarly.*
Published by: (Wetenschappelijke Raad voor het Regeringsbeleid), Amsterdam University Press, Herengracht 221, Amsterdam, 1016 BG, Netherlands. TEL 31-20-4200050, FAX 31-20-4203214, info@aup.nl, http://www.aup.nl.

WARSAW AGRICULTURAL UNIVERSITY. S G G W. ANNALS. AGRICULTURAL ECONOMICS AND RURAL SOCIOLOGY. *see* AGRICULTURE—Agricultural Economics

▼ **WEATHER, CLIMATE, AND SOCIETY.** *see* METEOROLOGY

WEBACTIVE. *see* GENERAL INTEREST PERIODICALS—United States

WEEKLY PROBES. *see* POLITICAL SCIENCE

320 NGA ISSN 0308-4450
HN820
WEST AFRICAN JOURNAL OF SOCIOLOGY AND POLITICAL SCIENCE. Text in English. q. USD 40. adv. bk.rev. bibl. back issues avail. **Document type:** *Journal, Academic/Scholarly.*
Indexed: CCA, MLA-IB, P42.
Published by: University of Ibadan, Sociology Department, Ibadan, Oyo, Nigeria. Ed. Justin Labinjon. Circ: 1,000.

301 FIN ISSN 0357-1823
WESTERMARCK-SEURA. TRANSACTIONS. Text in Multiple languages. 1947. irreg. price varies. **Document type:** *Monographic series, Academic/Scholarly.*
Related titles: ♦ Series: Bibliography of Finnish Sociology. ISSN 0781-9706.
Indexed: AICP, PCI.
Published by: Westermarck-Seura/Westermarck Society. The Finnish Sociological Association, c/o Harri Melin, PO Box 124, Turku, 20521, Finland. TEL 358-2-3336322, FAX 358-2-3335080, westermarck@utu.fi, http://org.utu.fi/yhd/westermarck/.

WESTERN JOURNAL OF COMMUNICATION. *see* LINGUISTICS

WHAT IS ASIA SERIES/AJIA O MIRUME SERIES. *see* BUSINESS AND ECONOMICS—International Development And Assistance

307 304.6 NZL ISSN 1178-2536
WHERE TO LIVE IN AUCKLAND. Text in English. 2002. biennial. NZD 35.51 per issue (effective 2008). **Document type:** *Handbook/Manual/ Guide, Consumer.*
Published by: Barbican Publishing Ltd, PO Box 91572, Auckland, New Zealand. TEL 64-9-3764849, FAX 64-9-3764879.

THE WHITE DOT - SURVIVAL GUIDE FOR THE T V - FREE. *see* LIFESTYLE

WHITE RIBBON MAGAZINE. *see* DRUG ABUSE AND ALCOHOLISM

303.4 USA ISSN 2161-4768
HM831
WIDE WORLD CHANGING. Text in English. 1978. irreg. USD 2 per issue (effective 2011). **Document type:** *Journal, Trade.*
Published by: Rational Island Publishers, PO Box 2081, Main Office Station, Seattle, WA 98111. TEL 206-284-0311, FAX 206-284-8429, litsales@rc.org, http://www.rationalisland.com.

▼ **WINE STUDIES.** *see* NUTRITION AND DIETETICS

307 USA ISSN 2150-7791
▼ **WINFIELD POST**; enlightening our community. Text in English. 2010. w. USD 35 (effective 2011). **Document type:** *Magazine, Trade.*
Address: PO Box 77, Winfield, IL 60190. TEL 630-682-3890. Pub. Marie Kisiel.

303.4833 GBR ISSN 1758-8332
▼ **WIRED.** Text in English. 2009 (Mar.). m. GBP 24 domestic; GBP 48 (in Europe and USA); GBP 58 elsewhere (effective 2010). adv. back issues avail. **Document type:** *Magazine, Consumer.* **Description:** Covers the people involved with the digital revolution and related changes in computer and communications technologies and life-styles.
Related titles: Online - full text ed.
Published by: Conde Nast Publications Ltd. (Subsidiary of: Advance Publications, Inc.), Vogue House, Hanover Sq, London, W1S 1JU, United Kingdom. TEL 44-20-74999080, FAX 44-20-74951102, newbusiness@condenast.co.uk, http://www.condenast.co.uk. Ed. David Rowan.

303.4833 USA ISSN 1059-1028
TK5105.5 CODEN: WREDEM
WIRED. Text in English. 1993. m. USD 10 domestic; USD 40 in Canada; USD 70 elsewhere (effective 2009). adv. bk.rev. illus. reprints avail. **Document type:** *Magazine, Consumer.* **Description:** Covers the people involved with the digital revolution and related changes in computer and communications technologies and life-styles.
Related titles: Online - full text ed.: ISSN 1078-3148; Regional ed(s).: Wired (UK Edition). ISSN 1357-0978. 1995. USD 79 to individuals (effective 1999); GBP 3.95 newsstand/cover.
Indexed: A21, A22, A28, A33, ABS&EES, APA, ASIP, B04, BRD, BrArAb, BrCerAb, C&ISA, C10, CA/WCA, CCR, CIA, CerAb, CivEngAb, CompD, CorrAb, E&CAJ, E11, EEA, EMA, ESPM, EnvEAb, FutSurv, G05, G06, G07, G08, G09, H15, I05, I07, Inpharma, L04, LISTA, M&TEA, M02, M06, M09, MBF, METADEX, MLA-IB, MicrocompInd, P02, P10, P17, P26, P29, P41, P48, P49, P52, P53, P54, PQC, R03, R06, RGAb, RGPR, RI-1, SD, SoftBase, SolStAb, T02, T04, W03, WAA.
—BLDSC (9323.650000), IE, Infotrieve, Ingenta, Linda Hall. **CCC.**
Published by: Conde Nast Publications Inc., Wired Ventures Ltd., 520 Third St, 3rd Fl, San Francisco, CA 94107. TEL 415-276-5000, FAX 415-276-4970, http://www.condenast.com. Ed. Evan Hansen. Pub. Howard Mittman. adv.: B&W page USD 52,780, color page USD 78,760; trim 8 x 10.875. Circ: 700,000. **Dist. in UK by:** Comag, Tavistock Rd, W Drayton, Middlesex UB7 7QE, United Kingdom. TEL 44-1895-433800, FAX 44-1895-433602.

302.23 DEU ISSN 1861-7530
WISSENSCHAFTLICHE BEITRAEGE AUS DEM TECTUM-VERLAG. REIHE MEDIENWISSENSCHAFTEN. Text in German. 1999. irreg., latest vol.8, 2010. price varies. **Document type:** *Monographic series, Academic/Scholarly.*
Published by: Tectum Wissenschaftsverlag Marburg, Biegenstr 4, Marburg, 35037, Germany. TEL 49-6421-481523, FAX 49-6421-43470, email@tectum-verlag.de.

WISSENSCHAFTLICHE PAPERBACKS. SOZIAL- UND WIRTSCHAFTSGESCHICHTE. *see* BUSINESS AND ECONOMICS—Economic Systems And Theories, Economic History

301 DEU
WISSENSCHAFTLICHE SCHRIFTENREIHE SOZIOLOGIE. Text in German. 1994. irreg., latest vol.5, 2008. price varies. **Document type:** *Monographic series, Academic/Scholarly.*
Published by: Verlag Dr. Koester, Rungestr 22-24, Berlin, 10179, Germany. TEL 49-30-76403224, FAX 49-30-76403227, verlag-koester@t-online.de.

302.23 DEU ISSN 0948-9398
WISSENSCHAFTSFORUM PUBLIZISTIK, KOMMUNIKATIONSWISSENSCHAFT, MEDIEN. Text in German. 1994. irreg., latest vol.9, 2002. price varies. **Document type:** *Monographic series, Academic/Scholarly.*
Published by: U V K Verlagsgesellschaft mbH, Schuetzenstr 24, Konstanz, 78462, Germany. TEL 49-7531-90530, FAX 49-7531-905398, nadine.ley@uvk.de, http://www.uvk.de.

302.23 004 DEU ISSN 1861-1710
WISSENSPROZESSE UND DIGITALE MEDIEN. Text in German. 2005. irreg., latest vol.18, 2010. price varies. **Document type:** *Monographic series, Academic/Scholarly.*
Published by: Logos Verlag Berlin, Comeniushof, Gubener Str 47, Berlin, 10243, Germany. TEL 49-30-42851090, FAX 49-30-42851092, redaktion@logos-verlag.de. Ed. Friedrich Hesse.

001.3 340.115 USA ISSN 2154-6487
▼ **WITNESS (CHESTNUT HILL)**; a journal of social responsibility. Text in English. 2010 (Apr.). a. free (effective 2011). **Document type:** *Journal, Academic/Scholarly.* **Description:** Includes poetry, creative non-fiction, short fiction, criticism, interviews, reviews, photography, paintings, sculptures, videos, and music related to social justice.
Related titles: Online - full text ed.: ISSN 2154-6495. 2010 (Apr.). free (effective 2011).
Published by: Boston College, 140 Comoonwealth Ave, Chestnut Hill, MA 02467. TEL 617-552-4820, 617-552-2441, bcm@bc.edu, http://bcm.bc.edu.

305.4 NLD ISSN 1570-7628
HQ1236.5.M43
WOMEN AND GENDER: THE MIDDLE EAST AND THE ISLAMIC WORLD. Text in English. 2002. irreg., latest vol.7, 2008. price varies. **Document type:** *Monographic series, Academic/Scholarly.*
Indexed: IZBG.
Published by: Brill, PO Box 9000, Leiden, 2300 PA, Netherlands. TEL 31-71-5353500, FAX 31-71-5317532, cs@brill.nl. Eds. Margot Badran, Valentine Moghadam.

WOMEN IN CULTURE AND SOCIETY. *see* WOMEN'S INTERESTS

500 305.4 USA ISSN 1943-1767
WOMEN, MINORITIES, AND PERSONS WITH DISABILITIES IN SCIENCE AND ENGINEERING (ONLINE). Text in English. 1982. biennial. **Document type:** *Report, Academic/Scholarly.* **Description:** Presents trends in the participation of women, minorities, and persons with disabilities in science and engineering fields.
Former titles: Women, Minorities, and Persons with Disabilities in Science and Engineering (Print) (1943-1775); (until 1994): Women and Minorities in Science and Engineering (0739-666X)
Media: Online - full text.
Published by: National Science Foundation, 4201 Wilson Blvd, Arlington, VA 22230. TEL 703-292-5111, 800-877-8339, FAX 703-292-9092, info@nsf.gov.

301 CAN ISSN 1499-0369
RA778.A1
➤ **WOMEN'S HEALTH AND URBAN LIFE.** Text in English. 2002. s-a. CAD 85 domestic to institutions; USD 85 foreign to institutions (effective 2010). **Document type:** *Journal, Academic/Scholarly.* **Description:** The journal addresses a wide range of topics that directly or indirectly affect both the physical and mental health of girls, teenage and adult women living in urban or urbanizing pockets of the world.
Related titles: Online - full text ed.: free (effective 2011).
Indexed: A39, C27, C29, CA, D03, D04, E13, FemPer, G10, R14, S02, S03, S14, S15, S18, T02, W09.
—**CCC.**
Published by: University of Toronto, Department of Sociology, 1265 Military Trail, Scarborough, ON M1C 1A4, Canada. Ed. Aysan Sev'er.

301 USA ISSN 0730-8884
HT675
➤ **WORK AND OCCUPATIONS**; an international sociological journal. Text in English. 1974. q. USD 838, GBP 493 combined subscription to institutions (print & online eds.); USD 821, GBP 483 to institutions (effective 2011). bk.rev. illus. index. back issues avail.; reprint service avail. from PSC. **Document type:** *Journal, Academic/Scholarly.* **Description:** Provides an outlet for sociological research and theory in the substantive areas of work, occupations, and leisure and treats their structures and interrelationships.
Formerly (until 1982): Sociology of Work and Occupations (0093-9285)
Related titles: Microform ed.: (from PQC); Online - full text ed.: ISSN 1552-8464. USD 754, GBP 444 to institutions (effective 2011).
Indexed: A01, A02, A03, A08, A10, A12, A13, A17, A20, A22, A25, A26, A28, ABIn, APA, ASCA, B01, B02, B04, B06, B07, B08, B09, B11, B15, B17, B18, B21, BPI, BPIA, BRD, BrCerAb, C&ISA, C06, C07, C08, CA, CA/WCA, CIA, CINAHL, CPE, CerAb, CivEngAb, CorrAb, CurCont, DIP, E&CAJ, E-psyche, E01, E03, E04, E05, E07, E08, E11, EEA, EMA, ERI, ESPM, Emerald, EnvEAb, ErgAb, FR, FamI, G04, G06, G07, G08, G10, H&SSA, H04, H12, H15, HRA, I05, IBR, IBSS, IBZ, ILD, M&TEA, M09, MBF, MEA&I, METADEX, P02, P03, P04, P06, P10, P13, P16, P18, P25, P30, P48, P51, P53, P54, PQC, PRA, PersLit, PsycInfo, PsycholAb, RASB, S02, S03, S08, S09, S11, S21, SCOPUS, SOPODA, SSA, SSCI, SWR&A, SociolAb, SolStAb, T02, T04, V02, V03, W01, W02, W03, W07, W09, WAA, WorkRelAb.
—BLDSC (9348.075000), IE, Infotrieve, Ingenta, INIST, Linda Hall. **CCC.**

S

Published by: Sage Publications, Inc., 2455 Teller Rd, Thousand Oaks, CA 91320. TEL 805-499-9774, 800-818-7243, FAX 805-499-0871, 800-583-2665, info@sagepub.com. Ed. Daniel B Cornfield. Circ: 750 (paid). **Subscr. outside the Americas to:** Sage Publications Ltd., 1 Oliver's Yard, 55 City Rd, London EC1Y 1SP, United Kingdom. TEL 44-20-73248701, FAX 44-20-73248733, subscription@sagepub.co.uk.

301 GBR ISSN 0950-0170
HD6951
➤ **WORK, EMPLOYMENT & SOCIETY.** Abbreviated title: W E S. Text in English. 1987. q. USD 526, GBP 284 combined subscription to institutions (print & online eds.); USD 515, GBP 278 to institutions (effective 2011). adv. bk.rev. back issues avail.; reprint service avail. from PSC. **Document type:** *Journal, Academic/Scholarly.*
Description: Analyzes all forms of work and their relation to wider social processes and structures, and to quality of life. It embraces the study of the labor process; industrial relations; changes in labor markets; and the gender and domestic divisions of labor.
Related titles: Microform ed.: (from PQC); Online - full text ed.: ISSN 1469-8722. USD 473, GBP 256 to institutions (effective 2011).
Indexed: A12, A13, A14, A17, A20, A22, ABIn, ASCA, ASSIA, B07, B21, BibInd, CA, CPM, ChPerI, CurCont, DIP, E01, ESPM, Emerald, FR, FamI, G10, H&SSA, HRA, IBR, IBSS, IBZ, ILD, P03, P42, P48, P51, P53, P54, PAIS, PCI, PMA, PQC, PRA, PSA, PsycInfo, PsycholAb, RASB, S02, S03, SCOPUS, SOPODA, SSA, SSCI, SociolAb, T02, W07, W09.
—BLDSC (9348.149000), IE, Infotrieve, Ingenta, INIST. **CCC.**
Published by: (British Sociological Association), Sage Publications Ltd. (Subsidiary of: Sage Publications, Inc.), 1 Oliver's Yard, 55 City Rd, London, EC1Y 1SP, United Kingdom. TEL 44-20-73248500, FAX 44-20-73248600, info@sagepub.co.uk, http://www.uk.sagepub.com/home.nav. Eds. Christopher Warhurst, Philip Taylor. adv.: B&W page GBP 350; 130 x 205. **Subscr. in the Americas to:** Sage Publications, Inc., 2455 Teller Rd, Thousand Oaks, CA 91320. TEL 805-499-9774, FAX 805-499-0871, journals@sagepub.com.

306 USA ISSN 1084-1377
HD4904.25
WORK + FAMILY NEWSBRIEF. Text in English. 1990. m. **Description:** Helps employer to create a workplace that is both supportive and effective.
Related titles: Online - full text ed.
Indexed: A26, B01, B02, B07, B15, B17, B18, E08, G04, G06, G07, G08, I05, I07, S09, S22.
Published by: Work & Family Connection, Inc., 5197 Beachside Dr, Minnetonka, MN 55343. TEL 952-936-7898, 800-487-7898, FAX 952-935-0122, info@workfamily.com, http://www.workfamily.com.

306 USA ISSN 2161-6418
WORKING FOR A LIVING. Text in English. 1976. irreg. USD 3 per issue (effective 2011). back issues avail. **Document type:** *Journal, Trade.*
Published by: Rational Island Publishers, PO Box 2081, Main Office Station, Seattle, WA 98111. TEL 206-284-0311, FAX 206-284-8429, litsales@rc.org, http://www.rationalisland.com.

302.23 NZL ISSN 1177-3707
➤ **WORKING PAPERS IN COMMUNICATION RESEARCH.** Variant title: W P C R. Text in English. 2001. irreg. **Document type:** *Journal, Academic/Scholarly.*
Media: Online - full text.
Published by: Auckland University of Technology, Institute of Culture, Discourse & Communication, Private Bag 92006, Auckland, 1142, New Zealand. TEL 64-9-9219683, FAX 64-9-9219460. Eds. Mark Jackson, Philippa Smith.

301 ITA ISSN 2037-5239
WORKING PAPERS NUOVI LAVORI. Text in Italian. 2008. 3/yr. **Document type:** *Monographic series, Academic/Scholarly.*
Media: Online - full text.
Published by: Associazione Nuovi Lavori, Via Sardegna 55, Rome, Italy. http://www.nuovi-lavori.it.

307 TTO
WORKING PAPERS ON CARIBBEAN SOCIETY. SERIES A: NEW PERSPECTIVES IN THEORY AND ANALYSIS. Text in English. 1978. irreg. USD 2.
Published by: University of the West Indies, Department of Sociology, St. Augustine W I, Trinidad & Tobago.

307 TTO
WORKING PAPERS ON CARIBBEAN SOCIETY. SERIES C: RESEARCH FINDINGS. Text in English. irreg.
Published by: University of the West Indies, Department of Sociology, St. Augustine W I, Trinidad & Tobago.

303.4 ITA ISSN 2037-5050
▼ **WORKING PAPERS RES.** Text in Italian. 2009. irreg. **Document type:** *Monographic series, Academic/Scholarly.*
Published by: Fondazione Res, Via Cerda 24, Palermo, 90139, Italy. TEL 39-091-6087434, http://www.resricerche.it.

307.14 ZAF ISSN 1819-8635
WORLD JOURNAL OF COMMUNITY DEVELOPMENT. Text in English. 2006. q. USD 120 in Africa to individuals; USD 180 elsewhere to individuals; USD 350 in Africa to institutions; USD 450 elsewhere to institutions; USD 85 in Africa to students; USD 100 elsewhere to students (effective 2007). **Description:** Covers community organizing, planning, social administration, organizational development, community development, and social change.
Published by: (World Research Organization), Isis Press, PO Box 1919, Cape Town, 8000, South Africa. TEL 27-21-4471574, FAX 27-86-6219999, orders@unwro.org, http://www.unwro.org/isispress.html.

307.72 USA ISSN 1944-6543
▼ **WORLD RURAL OBSERVATIONS.** Text in English. 2009. q. back issues avail. **Document type:** *Journal, Academic/Scholarly.*
Description: Provides a forum for discussing rural problems. Brings out papers, reviews, rapid communications, and any debates and opinions in all the fields of rural area.
Related titles: Online - full text ed.: ISSN 1944-6551. free (effective 2010).
Published by: Marsland Press, PO Box 21126, Lansing, MI 48909. TEL 347-321-7172, sciencepub@gmail.com.

306 200 IND ISSN 0043-9185
WORLD UNION. Text in English. 1961. q. bk.rev. charts; illus. back issues avail. **Description:** Broadly related to the subject socio-cultural, philosophical and spiritual and educational.
Published by: World Union International Centre, Sri Aurobindo Ashram, Pondicherry, Tamil Nadu 605 002, India. TEL 91-413-2223328, FAX 91-413-2223328, mail@sabda.in, http://www.sriaurobindoashram.org/.

303 USA
WORLDMARK ENCYCLOPEDIA OF CULTURES AND DAILY LIFE. Text in English. 1998. irreg., latest 2007. USD 459 per issue (effective 2008). **Document type:** *Monographic series, Academic/Scholarly.*
Description: Covers cultural groups in Asia, Europe, the Americas and Africa.
Related titles: Online - full text ed.
Published by: Gale (Subsidiary of: Cengage Learning), 27500 Drake Rd, Farmington Hills, MI 48331. TEL 248-699-4253, 800-877-4253, FAX 877-363-4253, gale.galeord@cengage.com.

301 CHN
XIANGGANG FENGQING/HONG KONG CUSTOMS. Text in Chinese. bi-m.
Published by: Guangdong Renmin Chubanshe, Qikan Bu/Guangdong People's Publishing House, No 10, 4 Malu, Dashatou, Guangzhou, Guangdong 510102, China. TEL 335210. Ed. Liu Bansheng.

XIBEI MINZU YANJIU/NORTH WEST ETHNO-NATIONAL STUDIES. *see* ASIAN STUDIES

XIN WENHUA SHILIAO/HISTORICAL RECORDS OF THE NEW CULTURE. *see* HISTORY—History Of Asia

302.2 CHN ISSN 1006-4699
YANJIANG YU KOUCAI/SPEECH AND ELOQUENCE. Text in Chinese. 1983. m. USD 43.20 (effective 2009). 48 p./no.; **Document type:** *Journal, Academic/Scholarly.* **Description:** Aims to enhance people's speaking ability.
—East View.
Published by: Yanjiang yu Koucai Zazhishe, Jilin Dajie Sanya Lu 7, Jilin, 132013, China. TEL 86-432-4678170, FAX 86-432-4661708. Circ: 1,050,000. **Dist. overseas by:** China International Book Trading Corp, 35 Chegongzhuang Xilu, Haidian District, PO Box 399, Beijing 100044, China.

301 GBR ISSN 1749-4311
YOUNG FOUNDATION. WORKING PAPERS. Text in English. 2002; N.S. 2005 (Oct.). irreg. **Document type:** *Monographic series, Academic/Scholarly.*
Formerly (until 2005): I C S Working Paper (1477-951X)
Related titles: Online - full text ed.: ISSN 1749-432X. 2004.
Published by: The Young Foundation, 18 Victoria Pk Sq, Bethnal Green, London, E2 9PF, United Kingdom. TEL 44-20-89806263, FAX 44-20-89816719, helen.crumley@youngfoundation.org, http://www.youngfoundation.org.uk.

307.14 GBR ISSN 1750-6700
YOUR E U. (European Union) Text in English. 2006. q. back issues avail. **Document type:** *Magazine, Trade.* **Description:** Provides updates on some of the PEACE and INTERREG funded projects as well as includes all the latest news about the programmes and information on upcoming events.
Related titles: Online - full text ed.: ISSN 1750-6719. free (effective 2009).
Published by: (European Union Special Support Programme for Peace and Reconciliation, INTERREG III), Special E U Programmes Body, EU House, 6 Cromac Pl, Belfast, BT7 2JB, United Kingdom. TEL 44-28-90266660, FAX 44-28-90266661, info@seupb.org.

306.874 USA ISSN 1545-2492
HQ759.92
YOUR STEPFAMILY; embrace the journey. Text in English. 1980. bi-m. USD 21 domestic; USD 33 foreign (effective 2003). bk.rev. illus. cum.index 1980-1995. back issues avail.; reprints avail. **Description:** For the men, women and children of today's stepfamilies. It chronicles the changes and challenges that millions of stepfamily members face and highlights the new practices they can employ to strengthen family members from within.
Former titles (until Aug.2002): S A A Families; (until 2000): Stepfamilies; (until 1989): Stepfamily Bulletin (0195-5969)
Related titles: CD-ROM ed.; Microform ed.: (from PQC); Online - full text ed.
Indexed: M01, M02, MASUSE.
Published by: (Stepfamily Association of America), Y S F, Llc., 2615 Three Oaks Rd., Ste 1B, Cary, IL 60013. TEL 847-639-2200, FAX 847-639-8148. Ed. Sharon Stober. Circ: 1,200.

YOUTH & SOCIETY. *see* CHILDREN AND YOUTH—About

302.23 649 USA ISSN 1945-7316
HQ799.2.M35
YOUTH MEDIA REPORTER; the professional journal of the youth media field. Text in English. 2007. a. **Document type:** *Magazine, Consumer.*
Description: Documents insights and lessons in engaging young people in video, film, television, radio, music, web, art, and print.
Related titles: Online - full text ed.: ISSN 1945-7324.
Indexed: CA, CMM.
Published by: Academy for Educational Development, 680 Fifth Ave, New York, NY 10019. TEL 212-243-1110, FAX 212-627-0407, http://www.aed.org. Ed. Ingrid Hu Dahl.

306 DEU ISSN 1437-2940
➤ **Z F F - ZEITSCHRIFT FUER FAMILIENFORSCHUNG;** Beitraege zu Haushalt, Verwandtschaft und Lebenslauf. Text in German. 1989. 3/yr. EUR 59; EUR 23 per issue (effective 2011). **Document type:** *Journal, Academic/Scholarly.*
Formerly (until 1998): Zeitschrift fuer Familienforschung (0935-4018)
Indexed: CA, DIP, IBR, IBSS, IBZ, S02, S03, SCOPUS, SSCI, T02, W07.
—**CCC.**
Published by: Verlag Barbara Budrich, Stauffenbergstr 7, Leverkusen, 51379, Germany. TEL 49-2171-344594, FAX 49-2171-344693, info@budrich-verlag.de, http://www.budrich-verlag.de. Ed. Kurt P Bierschock.

➤ **ZADOK CENTRE READING GUIDES.** *see* RELIGIONS AND THEOLOGY

➤ **ZADOK PAPERS.** *see* RELIGIONS AND THEOLOGY

➤ **ZADOK PERSPECTIVES.** *see* RELIGIONS AND THEOLOGY

➤ **ZDANIE.** *see* POLITICAL SCIENCE

➤ **ZEITSCHRIFT FUER AGRARGESCHICHTE UND AGRARSOZIOLOGIE.** *see* AGRICULTURE

➤ **ZEITSCHRIFT FUER GANZHEITSFORSCHUNG;** Philosophie - Gesellschaft - Wirtschaft. *see* PHILOSOPHY

302.23 DEU ISSN 1861-2687
ZEITSCHRIFT FUER KOMMUNIKATIONSOEKOLOGIE UND MEDIENETHIK. Text in German. 1999. irreg. **Document type:** *Journal, Academic/Scholarly.*
Formerly (until 2005): Zeitschrift fuer Kommunikationsoekologie (1437-9988)
Published by: Institut fuer Informations- und Kommunikationsoekologie e.V., Am Botanischen Garten 8, Duisburg, 47058, Germany. TEL 49-203-331010, FAX 49-203-332153, schicha@ikoe.de, http://www.ikoe.de.

302.23 DEU ISSN 1869-1366
P91
▼ **ZEITSCHRIFT FUER MEDIEN- UND KULTURFORSCHUNG.** Text in German. 2009. 2/yr. EUR 48; EUR 28 newsstand/cover (effective 2010). **Document type:** *Journal, Academic/Scholarly.*
Related titles: Online - full text ed.: (from IngentaConnect).
Published by: Felix Meiner Verlag GmbH, Richardstr 47, Hamburg, 22081, Germany. TEL 49-40-2987560, FAX 49-40-29875620, info@meiner.de.

302.23 DEU ISSN 1869-1722
▼ **ZEITSCHRIFT FUER MEDIENWISSENSCHAFT.** Text in German. 2009. 2/yr. EUR 69.80 combined subscription; EUR 39.80 newsstand/cover (effective 2011). adv. **Document type:** *Journal, Academic/Scholarly.*
Related titles: Online - full text ed.: 2009. EUR 59.80 (effective 2011).
Published by: Akademie Verlag GmbH (Subsidiary of: Oldenbourg Wissenschaftsverlag GmbH), Markgrafenstr 12-14, Berlin, 10969, Germany. TEL 49-30-4220060, FAX 49-30-42200657, info@akademie-verlag.de. Ed. Ulrike Bergermann.

340.115 DEU ISSN 0174-0202
K202
ZEITSCHRIFT FUER RECHTSSOZIOLOGIE. Text in German. 1979. s-a. EUR 62 to individuals; EUR 82 to libraries; EUR 43 to students; EUR 46 per issue (effective 2011). adv. back issues avail.; reprint service avail. from SCH. **Document type:** *Journal, Academic/Scholarly.*
Indexed: A22, CA, DIP, FLP, FR, IBR, IBZ, MLA-IB, P42, PCI, PSA, S02, S03, SCOPUS, SOPODA, SSA, SociolAb, T02.
—IE, Infotrieve, INIST. **CCC.**
Published by: Lucius und Lucius Verlagsgesellschaft mbH, Gerokstr 51, Stuttgart, 70184, Germany. TEL 49-711-242060, FAX 49-711-242088, lucius@luciusverlag.com. Ed. Wolfgang Ludwig-Mayerhofer. Circ: 400 (paid). **Dist. by:** Brockhaus Commission, Kreidlerstr 9, Kornwestheim 70806, Germany. TEL 49-7154-13270, FAX 49-7154-132713, info@brocom.de.

ZEITSCHRIFT FUER SEMIOTIK. *see* PHILOSOPHY

301 DEU ISSN 0340-1804
HM5
➤ **ZEITSCHRIFT FUER SOZIOLOGIE.** Text in German. 1972. bi-m. EUR 86 to individuals; EUR 122 to institutions; EUR 43 to students; EUR 24 per issue (effective 2011). adv. bibl. back issues avail.; reprint service avail. from IRC. **Document type:** *Journal, Academic/Scholarly.*
Related titles: Online - full text ed.
Indexed: A12, A20, A22, ABIn, ASCA, BibInd, CA, CIS, CommAb, CurCont, DIP, FR, I13, IBR, IBSS, IBZ, P03, P06, P10, P25, P30, P34, P42, P46, P48, P51, P53, P54, PAIS, PCI, PQC, PRA, PSA, PsycInfo, PsycholAb, RASB, S02, S03, S11, SCOPUS, SOPODA, SSA, SSCI, SociolAb, T02, W07.
—BLDSC (9486.393000), IE, Infotrieve, Ingenta, INIST. **CCC.**
Published by: Lucius und Lucius Verlagsgesellschaft mbH, Gerokstr 51, Stuttgart, 70184, Germany. TEL 49-711-242060, FAX 49-711-242088, lucius@luciusverlag.com. Ed. Wolfgang Ludwig-Mayerhofer. Circ: 1,100 (paid and controlled). **Dist. by:** Brockhaus Commission, Kreidlerstr 9, Kornwestheim 70806, Germany. TEL 49-7154-13270, FAX 49-7154-132713, info@brocom.de.

301 DEU ISSN 1436-1957
HQ767.8
ZEITSCHRIFT FUER SOZIOLOGIE DER ERZIEHUNG UND SOZIALISATION/JOURNAL FOR SOCIOLOGY OF EDUCATION AND SOCIALIZATION. Text in English, German. 1980. q. EUR 75; EUR 21.50 newsstand/cover (effective 2011). adv. bk.rev. index. back issues avail.; reprint service avail. from SCH. **Document type:** *Journal, Academic/Scholarly.*
Formerly (until 1997): Zeitschrift fuer Sozialisationsforschung und Erziehungssoziologie (0720-4361)
Indexed: A22, CA, CPE, DIP, E15, ERA, IBR, IBZ, M12, P42, PSA, RILM, S02, S03, S19, S20, S21, SCOPUS, SOPODA, SSA, SSCI, SociolAb, T02, W07.
—BLDSC (9534.826000), IE, Ingenta. **CCC.**
Published by: Juventa Verlag GmbH, Ehretstr 3, Weinheim, 69469, Germany. TEL 49-6201-90200, FAX 49-6201-902013, juventa@juventa.de, http://www.juventa.de. Eds. Ullrich Bauer, Barbara Dippelhofer-Stiem. Adv. contact Annette Hopp. Circ: 650 (paid and controlled).

ZHONGGUO XING KEXUE/CHINESE JOURNAL OF HUMAN SEXUALITY. *see* BIOLOGY—Physiology

ZIXUN SHEHUI YANJIU/JOURNAL OF CYBER CULTURE AND INFORMATION SOCIETY. *see* COMPUTERS—Internet

ZNANSTVENO RAZISKOVALNO SREDISCE REPUBLIKE SLOVENIJE. ANNALES. SERIES HISTORIA ET SOCIOLOGIA. *see* HISTORY

302.23 NLD ISSN 1878-4992
▼ **609 CULTUUR EN MEDIA.** Text in Dutch. 2009. q. free (effective 2010). **Document type:** *Magazine, Consumer.*
Published by: Mediafonds - Stimuleringsfonds Nederlandse Culturele Mediaproducties/Dutch Cultural Media Fund, Herengracht 609, Amsterdam, 1017 CE, Netherlands. TEL 31-20-6233901, FAX 31-20-6257456, info@mediafonds.nl, http://www.mediafonds.nl. Eds. Koen Kleijn, Titia Vuyk.

SOCIOLOGY—Abstracting, Bibliographies, Statistics

301.4021 AUS
AUSTRALIA. BUREAU OF STATISTICS. FAMILY, HOUSEHOLD AND INCOME UNIT VARIABLES. Text in English. 1995. irreg., latest 2005. free (effective 2009). **Document type:** *Government.* **Description:** Provide an accurate statistical picture of the structures of families in society.
Formerly (until 2005): Australia. Bureau of Statistics. Standards for Statistics on the Family (Print)
Media: Online - full text.
Published by: Australian Bureau of Statistics, Locked Bag 10, Belconnen, ACT 2616, Australia. TEL 61-2-62527037, 61-2-92684909, 300-135-070, FAX 61-2-62528103, client.services@abs.gov.au.

306.85021 AUS
AUSTRALIA. BUREAU OF STATISTICS. HOUSEHOLD AND FAMILY PROJECTIONS, AUSTRALIA (ONLINE). Text in English. 1996. quinquennial, latest 2001. free (effective 2009). back issues avail. **Description:** Features the number of households and families in Australia by state and capital city/balance of state for period 2001 to 2026. Describes the method and assumptions used to produce these projections.
Formerly: Australia. Bureau of Statistics. Household and Family Projections, Australia (Print)
Media: Online - full text.
Published by: Australian Bureau of Statistics, Locked Bag 10, Belconnen, ACT 2616, Australia. TEL 61-2-92684909, 300-135-070, FAX 61-2-92684654, client.services@abs.gov.au.

301.021 AUS
AUSTRALIA. BUREAU OF STATISTICS. MEASURING WELLBEING: FRAMEWORKS FOR AUSTRALIAN SOCIAL STATISTICS (ONLINE). Text in English. 1992. irreg., latest 2001. free (effective 2009). stat. **Document type:** *Government.*
Former titles: Australia. Bureau of Statistics. Measuring Wellbeing: Frameworks for Australian Social Statistics (Print); Australia. Bureau of Statistics. Measuring Social Wellbeing; Australia. Bureau of Statistics. A Guide to Australian Social Statistics
Media: Online - full text.
Published by: Australian Bureau of Statistics, Locked Bag 10, Belconnen, ACT 2616, Australia. TEL 61-2-92684909, 300-135-070, FAX 61-2-92684654, client.services@abs.gov.au.

016.30685 AUS
AUSTRALIAN FAMILY AND SOCIETY ABSTRACTS (ONLINE). Text in English. base vol. plus q. updates. **Document type:** *Database, Abstract/Index.*
Media: Online - full content.
Published by: Australian Institute of Family Studies, Level 20, 485 La Trobe St, Melbourne, VIC 3000, Australia. TEL 61-3-92147888, FAX 61-3-92147839, afrc@aifs.gov.au.

016.3053 GBR ISSN 1359-2726
B R I D G E BIBLIOGRAPHY. (Briefings on Development and Gender) Text in English. 199?. irreg., latest no.21, 2008. free (effective 2009). back issues avail. **Document type:** *Magazine, Bibliography.* **Description:** Provides key resources in spanish on gender and development.
Related titles: Online - full text ed.
—CCC.
Published by: University of Sussex, Institute of Development Studies, Brighton, Sussex BN1 9RE, United Kingdom. TEL 44-1273-606261, FAX 44-1273-621202, ids@ids.ac.uk, http://www.ids.ac.uk/.

BELGIUM. INSTITUT NATIONAL DE STATISTIQUE. STATISTIQUES SOCIALES. *see* SOCIAL SERVICES AND WELFARE—Abstracting, Bibliographies, Statistics

BELGIUM. NATIONAAL INSTITUUT VOOR DE STATISTIEK. SOCIALE STATISTIEKEN. *see* SOCIAL SERVICES AND WELFARE—Abstracting, Bibliographies, Statistics

016.301 FIN ISSN 0781-9706
BIBLIOGRAPHY OF FINNISH SOCIOLOGY. Text in Multiple languages. 1966. irreg. **Document type:** *Bibliography.*
Related titles: ◆ Series of: Westermarck-Seura. Transactions. ISSN 0357-1823.
Published by: Westermarck-Seura/Westermarck Society. The Finnish Sociological Association, c/o Harri Melin, PO Box 124, Turku, 20521, Finland. TEL 358-2-3336322, FAX 358-2-3335080, westermarck@utu.fi, http://org.utu.fi/yhd/westermarck/.

307.021 USA ISSN 0891-2718
HA261
CALIFORNIA CITIES, TOWNS AND COUNTIES. Text in English. 1987. a. USD 92 (effective 2004). **Description:** Alphabetically profiles every municipality and county in the state.
Published by: Information Publications, Incorporated, 3790 El Camino Real, Suite 162, Palo Alto, CA 94306. TEL 650-851-4250, 877-544-4636, FAX 650-529-9980, 877-544-4635, info@informationpublications.com. Ed. Manthi Nguyen.

302.23021 CHL
CHILE. INSTITUTO NACIONAL DE ESTADISTICAS. CULTURA Y MEDIOS DE COMUNICACION. Text in Spanish. 1984. a. CLP 1,800; USD 12.50 in United States; USD 14.90 elsewhere.
Published by: Instituto Nacional de Estadisticas, Casilla 498, Correo 3, Ave. Bulnes, 418, Santiago, Chile. TEL 56-2-6991441, FAX 56-2-6712169.

COMMUNICATION & MASS MEDIA COMPLETE. *see* COMMUNICATIONS—Abstracting, Bibliographies, Statistics

016.301 USA ISSN 0887-3569
CONTEMPORARY SOCIAL ISSUES: A BIBLIOGRAPHIC SERIES. Text in English. 1986. q. USD 70 (effective 2000). back issues avail. **Document type:** *Monographic series, Bibliography.* **Description:** Series of bibliographies on current social issues and problems.
Published by: Reference and Research Services, 1446 Filbert St., San Francisco, CA 94109-1633. TEL 831-426-4479. Ed. Joan Nordquist.

302.045195 NLD ISSN 1876-8598
CONTINU ONDERZOEK BURGERPERSPECTIEVEN. Variant title: Kwartaalbericht Continu Onderzoek Burgerperspectieven. Text in Dutch. 2008. q. EUR 9.90 newsstand/cover (effective 2010). **Document type:** *Report, Government.*
Published by: Sociaal en Cultureel Planbureau/Social and Cultural Planning Office, Postbus 16164, The Hague, 2500 BD, Netherlands. TEL 31-70-3407000, FAX 31-70-3407044, info@scp.nl, http://www.scp.nl.

302.045195 NZL ISSN 1177-4428
CULTURAL INDICATORS FOR NEW ZEALAND/TOHU AHUREA MO AOTEAROA. Text in English. 2006. irreg. NZD 40 per issue (effective 2008).
Related titles: Online - full text ed.: ISSN 1177-4533.
Published by: (Ministry for Culture and Heritage), Statistics New Zealand/Te Tari Tatau, Statistics House, The Blvd, Harbour Quays, PO Box 2922, Wellington, 6140, New Zealand. TEL 64-4-9314600, FAX 64 4-9314035, info@stats.govt.nz.

CURRENT LEGAL SOCIOLOGY; a periodical publication of abstracts and bibliography in law and society. *see* LAW—Abstracting, Bibliographies, Statistics

ECONOMIC AND SOCIAL STATISTICS OF SRI LANKA. *see* BUSINESS AND ECONOMICS—Abstracting, Bibliographies, Statistics

302.045195 NLD ISSN 1569-4674
EMANCIPATIEMONITOR. Text in Dutch. 2000. biennial. EUR 23.50 (effective 2011).
Related titles: Online - full text ed.: ISSN 1569-4682.
Published by: (Netherlands. Centraal Bureau voor de Statistiek), Sociaal en Cultureel Planbureau/Social and Cultural Planning Office, Postbus 16164, The Hague, 2500 BD, Netherlands. TEL 31-70-3407000, FAX 31-70-3407044, info@scp.nl, http://www.scp.nl. **Co-publisher:** Centraal Bureau voor de Statistiek.

302.015195 PRT ISSN 0870-4406
HD6490.W38
ESTATISTICAS DE PROTECCAO SOCIAL. ASSOCIACOES SINDICAIS E PATRONAIS. Text in Portuguese. 1938. a. **Document type:** *Government.* **Description:** Describes social welfare and annual activities of employees and employers associations.
Former titles (until 1985): Estatisticas de Seguranca Social, Associacoes Sindicais e Patronais. Continente, Acores e Madeira (0870-6506); (until 1978): Estatisticas des Associacoes Sindicais, Patronais e Previdencia (0377-211X); (until 1974): Estatistica da Organizacao Corporativa e Previdencia Social (0871-0236); (until 1960): Organizacao Corporativa e Previdencia Social (0870-7049); (until 1950): Estatistica da Organizacao Corporativa (0870-7057)
Published by: Instituto Nacional de Estatistica, Av Antonio Jose de Almeida 2, Lisbon, 1000-043, Portugal. TEL 351-21-8426100, FAX 351-21-8426380, ine@ine.pt, http://www.ine.pt.

310 306.85 CAN ISSN 1715-6610
LES FAMILLES ET LES ENFANTS AU QUEBEC; principales statistiques. Text in French. 2001. a. **Document type:** *Journal, Trade.*
Published by: (Quebec, Ministere de l'Emploi et de la Solidarite Sociale), Quebec, Ministere de la Famille, des Aines et de la Condition Feminine, 425, rue Saint-Amable, RC, Quebec, PQ G1R 4Z1, Canada. TEL 418-643-4721, 888-643-4721, famille@mfacf.gouv.qc.ca, http://www.mfacf.gouv.qc.ca/index.asp.

016.306 USA
FAMILY & SOCIETY STUDIES WORLDWIDE. Text in English. base vol. plus w. updates. USD 895 (effective 2000). **Document type:** *Database, Abstract/Index.* **Description:** Covers articles on family social science. Includes research, policy, and practice literature in the fields of Family Science, Human Ecology, Human Development, and Social Welfare.
Media: Online - full text.
Published by: EBSCO Publishing (Subsidiary of: EBSCO Industries, Inc.), 10 Estes St, PO Box 682, Ipswich, MA 01938. TEL 978-356-6500, FAX 978-356-6565, information@ebscohost.com, http://www.ebscohost.com.

016.30685 USA
FAMILY STUDIES ABSTRACTS. Text in English. base vol. plus s-m. updates. **Document type:** *Database, Abstract/Index.*
Media: Online - full text.
Published by: EBSCO Publishing (Subsidiary of: EBSCO Industries, Inc.), 10 Estes St, PO Box 682, Ipswich, MA 01938. TEL 978-356-6500, 800-653-2726, FAX 978-356-6565, information@ebscohost.com.

301 FIN ISSN 0788-1347
FINLAND. TILASTOKESKUS. FINNISH MASS MEDIA. Text in English. 1990. s-a. stat. **Document type:** *Magazine, Government.*
Published by: Tilastokeskus/Statistics Finland, Tyopajakatu 13, Statistics Finland, Helsinki, 00022, Finland. TEL 358-9-17341, FAX 358-9-17342279, http://www.stat.fi.

302.045195 FIN ISSN 1455-9447
FINLAND. TILASTOKESKUS. JOUKKOVIESTIMET/FINLAND. STATISTICS FINLAND. FINNISH MASS MEDIA/FINLAND. STATISTIKCENTRALEN. MASSMEDIER. Text in English, Finnish, Swedish. 1992. biennial. EUR 45 (effective 2008). **Document type:** *Government.*
Formerly (until 1998): Joukkoviestintatilasto (0787-5584)
Related titles: ◆ Series of: Finland. Tilastokeskus. Suomen Virallinen Tilasto. ISSN 1795-5165.
Published by: Tilastokeskus/Statistics Finland, Tyopajakatu 13, Statistics Finland, Helsinki, 00022, Finland. TEL 358-9-17341, FAX 358-9-17342279, http://www.stat.fi.

302.045195 FIN ISSN 1456-825X
DL1017
FINLAND. TILASTOKESKUS. KULTTUURITILASTO/FINLAND. STATISTICS FINLAND. CULTURAL STATISTICS. Text in English, Finnish. 1999. biennial, latest 2005. EUR 45 (effective 2008). **Document type:** *Government.*
Related titles: Online - full text ed.; ◆ Series of: Finland. Tilastokeskus. Suomen Virallinen Tilasto. ISSN 1795-5165.
Published by: Tilastokeskus/Statistics Finland, Tyopajakatu 13, Statistics Finland, Helsinki, 00022, Finland. TEL 358-9-17341, FAX 358-9-17342279, http://www.stat.fi.

302.045195 310 FIN ISSN 1456-2618
FINLAND. TILASTOKESKUS. NAISET JA MIEHET SUOMESSA. Text in Finnish. 1994. irreg. EUR 8 (effective 2008). **Document type:** *Government.*
Related titles: Online - full text ed.; Ed.: Finland. Statistics Finland. Women and Men in Finland. ISSN 1456-808X. 1999; ◆ Series of: Finland. Tilastokeskus. Suomen Virallinen Tilasto. ISSN 1795-5165.
Published by: Tilastokeskus/Statistics Finland, Tyopajakatu 13, Statistics Finland, Helsinki, 00022, Finland. TEL 358-9-17341, FAX 358-9-17342279.

302.045195 310 FIN ISSN 1457-5604
FINLAND. TILASTOKESKUS. SUKUPUOLTEN TASA-ARVO/FINALND. STATISTIKCENTRALEN. JAEMSTAELLDHETEN MELLAN KVINNOR OCH MAEN I FINLAND/FINLAND. STATISTICS FINLAND. GENDER EQUALITY IN FINLAND. Text in English, Finnish, Swedish. 1998. irreg. EUR 8 (effective 2008). **Document type:** *Government.*
Related titles: Online - full text ed.
Published by: Tilastokeskus/Statistics Finland, Tyopajakatu 13, Statistics Finland, Helsinki, 00022, Finland. TEL 358-9-17341, FAX 358-9-17342279.

016.3053 USA
GENDERWATCH (ONLINE). Text in English. 1996. base vol. plus d. updates. back issues avail. **Document type:** *Database, Abstract/Index.* **Description:** Provides over 260 titles, with more than 240 in text, from an array of academic, radical, community and independent presses.
Former titles (until 200?): GenderWatch (CD-ROM) (1520-0655); (until 1998): Women 'R' (1091-5672)
Media: Online - full text.
Published by: ProQuest (Subsidiary of: Cambridge Information Group), 789 E Eisenhower Pky, PO Box 1346, Ann Arbor, MI 48106. TEL 734-761-4700, 800-521-0600, FAX 734-997-4040, 888-241-5612, info@proquest.com.

302.015195 USA ISSN 0161-3340
HN29
GENERAL SOCIAL SURVEYS. Text in English. 1972. 2/yr. USD 36 (effective 2000). **Description:** Presents surveys of representative samples of U.S. population, attitudes and behavior.
Related titles: Microfiche ed.
Indexed: SRI.
Published by: National Opinion Research Center, 1155 E 60th St, Chicago, IL 60637. TEL 773-256-6000, FAX 773-753-7886. Ed., R&P Tom W Smith TEL 773-256-6288.

302.015195 GBR ISSN 0306-7742
GREAT BRITAIN. OFFICE FOR NATIONAL STATISTICS. SOCIAL TRENDS. Text in English. 1970. a. GBP 55 per issue (effective 2010). charts; stat. **Document type:** *Government.* **Description:** Compiles data pertaining to employment and leisure, education, health, transportation, and housing and analyzes trends.
Related titles: Online - full text ed.: ISSN 2040-1620 (from PQC).
Indexed: P06.
—BLDSC (8318.219300).
Published by: (Great Britain. Office for National Statistics), Palgrave Macmillan Ltd. (Subsidiary of: Macmillan Publishers Ltd.), Houndmills, Basingstoke, Hants RG21 6XS, United Kingdom. TEL 44-1256-329242, FAX 44-1256-810526, bookenquiries@palgrave.com, http://www.palgrave.com.

HAN'GUG UI SAHOE JI'PYO/KOREA (REPUBLIC). NATIONAL STATISTICAL OFFICE. SOCIAL INDICATORS IN KOREA. *see* POPULATION STUDIES—Abstracting, Bibliographies, Statistics

016.301 USA ISSN 1946-4525
HARRIS POLL (ONLINE). Text in English. 1963. irreg. looseleaf. free to members (effective 2009). stat.; illus. index. back issues avail.; reprints avail. **Document type:** *Newsletter, Trade.* **Description:** Discusses current political, social, economic and international issues. Contains tables with questions from national cross-section of population.
Former titles (until 2007): Harris Poll (Print) (0895-7983); (until 1988): A B C News - Harris Survey (0273-1037); Which superseded (1963-1978): Harris Survey Column Subscription (0046-6875)
Media: Online - full text.
Indexed: PAIS, RASB.
Published by: Harris Interactive, 135 Corporate Woods, Rochester, NY 14623. TEL 585-272-8400, 800-866-7655, info@harrisinteractive.com, http://www.harrisinteractive.com.

302.015195 USA ISSN 0161-5440
H1
➤ **HISTORICAL METHODS**; a journal of quantitative and interdisciplinary history . Text in English. 1967. q. GBP 167 combined subscription in United Kingdom to institutions (print & online eds.); EUR 222, USD 277 combined subscription to institutions (print & online eds.) (effective 2012). adv. bk.rev. charts; stat.; illus. Index. back issues avail.; reprint service avail. from PSC. **Document type:** *Journal, Academic/Scholarly.* **Description:** Features an international audience of historians and other social scientists concerned with historical problems.
Formerly (until 1978): Historical Methods Newsletter (0018-2494)
Related titles: CD-ROM ed.; Microform ed.; Online - full text ed.: ISSN 1940-1906. GBP 151 in United Kingdom to institutions; EUR 200, USD 249 to institutions (effective 2012).
Indexed: A01, A02, A03, A08, A20, A22, A26, ABS&EES, ASCA, AmH&L, AmHI, ArtHuCI, BAS, BRD, CA, CurCont, DIP, E03, E07, E08, ERI, Faml, G08, GEOBASE, H05, H07, H08, H14, HAb, HistAb, HumInd, I05, I07, IBR, IBZ, M01, M02, MASUSE, P04, P07, P10, P30, P48, P53, P54, PCI, PQC, PopulInd, RASB, S02, S03, S09, S23, SCOPUS, SociolAb, T02, W03, W04, W05, W07.
—BLDSC (4316.490500), IE, Infotrieve, Ingenta. **CCC.**
Published by: (University of Illinois at Chicago Circle, Department of History, University of Pittsburgh), Routledge (Subsidiary of: Taylor & Francis Group), 325 Chestnut St, Ste 800, Philadelphia, PA 19106. TEL 215-625-8900, FAX 215-625-2940, journals@routledge.com, http://www.routledge.com. **Co-sponsor:** Helen Dwight Reid Educational Foundation.

➤ **HONG KONG SPECIAL ADMINISTRATIVE REGION OF CHINA. CENSUS AND STATISTICS DEPARTMENT. CRIME AND ITS VICTIMS IN HONG KONG.** *see* CRIMINOLOGY AND LAW ENFORCEMENT—Abstracting, Bibliographies, Statistics

016.30223 DNK ISSN 1397-5307
INDEX DANMARK/GALLUP. Text in Danish. 1968. a. looseleaf. charts; stat. back issues avail. **Document type:** *Consumer.* **Description:** Measurements and statistics of the use of media by the Danish population.
Formerly (until 1996): Dansk Media Index (0105-4678); Which incorporated (1983-1984): Gallup Marketing Index (0108-7932)
Related titles: CD-ROM ed.: ISSN 1603-3957. 2002.

S

Published by: T N S Gallup A/S, Masnedsoegade 22-26, Copenhagen OE, 2100, Denmark. TEL 45-39-272727, FAX 45-39-275080, gallup@tnsgallup.dk, http://www.tnsgallup.dk.

302.045195 306.089021 CAN ISSN 0846-8737
E78.C2
INDIAN AND NORTHERN AFFAIRS CANADA. BASIC DEPARTMENTAL DATA. Variant title: Affaires Indiennes et du Nord Canada. Donnees Ministerielles de Base. Text in English, French. 1988. a.
Related titles: Online - full text ed.: ISSN 1495-5326.
Published by: Indian & Northern Affairs Canada, Evaluation Directorate, 10 Wellington St, Ottawa, ON K1A 0H4, Canada. TEL 800-567-9604, FAX 819-953-3017, 866-817-3977, infopubs@ainc-inac.gc.ca.

INFORMATSIYA O SOTSIAL'NO-EKONOMICHESKOM POLOZHENII ROSSII/INFORMATION ON SOCIAL AND ECONOMIC SITUATION OF RUSSIA. *see* BUSINESS AND ECONOMICS—Abstracting, Bibliographies, Statistics

016.301 NOR ISSN 0804-6832
INSTITUTT FOR SAMFUNNSFORSKNING. I S F SAMMENDRAG. Variant title: I S F Sammendrag. Text in Norwegian. 1987. s-a. (2-3/yr). free. back issues avail. **Document type:** *Journal, Abstract/ Index.* **Description:** Contains abstracts of recent Institute reports and articles.
Formerly (until 1992): Institutt for Samfunnsforskning. Sammendragsserie (0801-6496)
Related titles: Online - full text ed.: ISSN 1504-7997. 2004.
Published by: Institutt for Samfunnsforskning/Institute for Social Research, Munthes Gate 31, PO Box 3233, Elisenberg, Oslo, 0208, Norway. TEL 47-23-086100, FAX 47-23-086101, isf@samfunnsforskning.no. Ed. Johanne Severinsen.

016.301 GBR ISSN 0085-2066
Z7161
INTERNATIONAL BIBLIOGRAPHY OF THE SOCIAL SCIENCES. SOCIOLOGY/BIBLIOGRAPHIE INTERNATIONALE DE SOCIOLOGIE. Added title page title: International Bibliography of Sociology. Text in English; Prefatory materials in French. 1952. a., latest vol.52, 2002. USD 495 per issue (effective 2009). adv. back issues avail. **Document type:** *Bibliography.* **Description:** Covers with sociological theory, methodology and current sociological studies.
Related titles: ◆ Online - full text ed.: International Bibliography of the Social Sciences; ◆ Print ed.: International Bibliography of the Social Sciences. Anthropology; ◆ International Bibliography of the Social Sciences. Economics. ISSN 0085-204X; ◆ International Bibliography of Political Science. ISSN 0085-2058.
Indexed: AICP, RASB.
—BLDSC (4537.113000).
Published by: (British Library of Political and Economic Science), Routledge (Subsidiary of: Taylor & Francis Group), 4 Park Sq, Milton Park, Abingdon, Oxon OX14 4RN, United Kingdom. TEL 44-20-70176000, FAX 44-20-70176336, subscriptions@tandf.co.uk, http://www.routledge.com.

305.3 302.045195 IRL ISSN 1649-6299
HN400.3.A85
IRELAND. CENTRAL STATISTICS OFFICE. WOMEN AND MEN IN IRELAND. Text in English. 2004. a. EUR 5 (effective 2006).
Published by: Ireland. Central Statistics Office/Eire, An Phriomh-Oifig Staidrimh, Skehard Rd, Cork, Ireland. TEL 353-21-4535000, FAX 353-21-4535555, information@cso.ie.

302.015195 USA ISSN 0022-250X
HM1
➤ **JOURNAL OF MATHEMATICAL SOCIOLOGY.** Text in English. 1971. q. GBP 1,427 combined subscription in United Kingdom to institutions (print & online eds.); EUR 1,452, USD 1,821 combined subscription to institutions (print & online eds.) (effective 2012). illus. index. back issues avail.; reprint service avail. from PSC. **Document type:** *Journal, Academic/Scholarly.* **Description:** Features articles dealing primarily with the use of mathematical models in social science, the logic of measurement, computers and computer programming, applied mathematics, statistics, or quantitative methodology.
Related titles: Microform ed.; Online - full text ed.: ISSN 1545-5874. GBP 1,284 in United Kingdom to institutions; EUR 1,306, USD 1,639 to institutions (effective 2012) (from IngentaConnect).
Indexed: A01, A03, A08, A20, A22, ASCA, B07, CA, CIS, CMCI, CurCont, E01, FR, Inspec, MathR, P17, P26, P30, P49, P53, P54, PQC, PsycholAb, RASB, S01, S02, S03, SCI, SCOPUS, SOPODA, SSA, SSCI, SociolAb, T02, W07, Z02.
—IE, Infotrieve, Ingenta, INIST. **CCC.**
Published by: Taylor & Francis Inc. (Subsidiary of: Taylor & Francis Group), 325 Chestnut St, Ste 800, Philadelphia, PA 19106. TEL 215-625-8900, 800-354-1420, FAX 215-625-8914, orders@taylorandfrancis.com, http://www.taylorandfrancis.com. Ed. Phillip Bonacich. **Subsc. in Europe:** Taylor & Francis Ltd., Journals Customer Service, Sheepen Pl, Colchester, Essex CO3 3LP, United Kingdom. TEL 44-20-70175544, FAX 44-20-70175198, subscriptions@tandf.co.uk.

016.3034 USA
JOURNALS OF DISSENT AND SOCIAL CHANGE; a bibliography of titles in the California State University, Sacramento, library. Text in English. 1969. irreg., latest vol.7, 1993. USD 25 (effective 1999). **Document type:** *Bibliography.* **Description:** Subject-arranged catalog to over 4000 journals in the Dissent and Social Change Collection.
Published by: California State University, Sacramento, Library, 2000 State University Drive E, Sacramento, CA 95819-6039. TEL 916-278-6446. Ed. John Liberty. Circ: (controlled). **Subscr. to:** University Bookstore, California State Univ, Sacramento, 6000 J St, Sacramento, CA 95819.

302.015195 JPN ISSN 0385-5481
➤ **KODO KEIRYOGAKU/JAPANESE JOURNAL OF BEHAVIORMETRICS.** Text in Japanese; Summaries in English. 1974. s-a. JPY 2,100 (effective 2001). **Document type:** *Academic/ Scholarly.*
Related titles: Online - full text ed.
Indexed: CCMJ, CIS, E-psyche, L&LBA, MSN, MathR, P03, PsycInfo, PsycholAb, S02, S03, SCOPUS, SOPODA, ST&MA, SociolAb, Z02.
—BLDSC (4651.013000).
Published by: Nihon Kodo Keiryo Gakkai/Behaviormetric Society of Japan, 6-7 Minami-Azabu 4-chome, Minato-ku, Tokyo, 106-0047, Japan. TEL 81-3-5421-8766, fumih@toyoeiwa.ac.jp. Ed. Fumi Hayashi.

302.015195 MWI
MALAWI. NATIONAL STATISTICAL OFFICE. FAMILY FORMATION SURVEY (YEAR). Text in English. 1984. irreg. MWK 40. **Document type:** *Government.*
Published by: (Malawi. Commissioner for Census and Statistics), National Statistical Office, PO Box 333, Zomba, Malawi. TEL 265-50-522377, FAX 265-50-523130.

016.30223 SGP ISSN 0217-1287
Z5632
MASS COM PERIODICAL LITERATURE INDEX. Text in English. s-a. **Document type:** *Abstract/Index.* **Description:** Provides up-to-date bibliographic information on articles relating to the field of mass communication.
Published by: Asian Media Information and Communication Centre, Publications Unit, PO Box 360, Jurong Point, 916412, Singapore. TEL 65-7927570, FAX 65-7927129, enquiries@amic.org.sg, http://www.amic.org.sg.

302.015195 DEU ISSN 1864-6956
➤ **METHODEN, DATEN, ANALYSEN.** Text in German. 2007. s-a. free (effective 2010). bk.rev. **Document type:** *Journal, Academic/ Scholarly.*
Formed by the merger of (1977-2006): Z A - Information (0723-5607); (1992-2006): Z U M A - Nachrichten (0944-1670); Which was formerly (1977-1992): Zumanachrichten (0721-8516)
Related titles: Online - full text ed.
Indexed: E-psyche.
—**CCC.**
Published by: Gesellschaft Sozialwissenschaftlicher Infrastruktureinrichtungen e.V., Postfach 122155, Mannheim, 68072, Germany. TEL 49-621-12460, FAX 49-621-1246100, gesis@gesis.org. Eds. Christof Wolf, Marek Fuchs. Circ: 4,000.

016.301 016.95 USA
MIDDLE EASTERN & CENTRAL ASIAN STUDIES. Text in English. base vol. plus w. updates. **Document type:** *Database, Abstract/Index.*
Media: Online - full text.
Published by: EBSCO Publishing (Subsidiary of: EBSCO Industries, Inc.), 10 Estes St, PO Box 682, Ipswich, MA 01938.

016.3058 USA
MULTICULTURAL MODULE. Text in English. base vol. plus d. updates. **Document type:** *Database, Abstract/Index.*
Media: Online - full text.
Published by: ProQuest (Subsidiary of: Cambridge Information Group), 789 E Eisenhower Pky, PO Box 1346, Ann Arbor, MI 48106. TEL 734-761-4700, 800-521-0600, FAX 734-997-4040, 888-241-5612, info@proquest.com, http://www.proquest.com.

302.045195 NLD ISSN 1874-9941
DE NEDERLANDSE SAMENLEVING. Text in Dutch. 2007. a. EUR 32.50 (effective 2010).
Published by: Centraal Bureau voor de Statistiek, Henri Faasdreef 312, The Hague, 2492 JP, Netherlands. TEL 31-70-3373800, FAX 31-70-3375994, infoserv@cbs.nl, http://www.cbs.nl.

302.015195 JPN
NIHON KODO KEIRYO GAKKAI TAIKAI HAPPYO RONBUN SHOROKUSHU. Text in Japanese. 1973. a. abstr. **Document type:** *Proceedings.* **Description:** Contains abstracts from the annual meeting of the society.
Indexed: E-psyche.
Published by: Nihon Kodo Keiryo Gakkai/Behaviormetric Society of Japan, 6-7 Minami-Azabu 4-chome, Minato-ku, Tokyo, 106-0047, Japan. TEL 81-3-5421-8766. Ed. Kazouo Shigemasu.

302.015195 NOR ISSN 0800-7233
HA1501
NORWAY. STATISTISK SENTRALBYRAA. LEVEKAARSUNDERSOEKELSEN. Text in Norwegian. 1973. quadrennial. **Document type:** *Government.*
Formerly (until 1980): Norway. Statisk Sentralbyraa. Levekaar (0332-799X)
Related titles: ◆ Series of: Norges Offisielle Statistikk. ISSN 0300-5585.
Published by: Statistisk Sentralbyraa/Statistics Norway, Kongensgate 6, P O Box 8131, Dep, Oslo, 0033, Norway. TEL 47-21-090000, FAX 47-21-094973, ssb@ssb.no.

302.015195 NOR ISSN 1504-2316
HA1501
NORWAY. STATISTISK SENTRALBYRAA. SOSIALHJELP, BARNEVERN OG FAMILIEVERN/STATISTICS NORWAY. SOCIAL ASSISTANCE, CHILD WELFARE STATISTICS AND FAMILY COUNSELING SERVICES. Text in Norwegian. 1978. a. back issues avail. **Document type:** *Government.*
Former titles (until 2003): Norway. Statistisk Sentralbyraa. Sosialhjelp og Barnevern (1501-9993); (until 2001): Norway. Statistisk Sentralbyraa. Sosialstatistikk (0333-2055); Which was formed by the merger of (1963-1978): Barneomsorg (0302-4474); Which was formerly (until 1966): Barnevernstatistikk (1502-3494); (1960-1978): Sosialhjelpstatistikk (1502-3478); Which was formerly (until 1966): Forsorgsstoenad og Kummunal Trygd (1502-346X); (196?-1978): Sosial Hjemmehjelp (1502-3486); Which was formerly (until 1966): Husmorvikarvirksomhet og Hjemmesykepleie (1502-3508)
Related titles: Online - full text ed.: ISSN 1504-2324; ◆ Series of: Norges Offisielle Statistikk. ISSN 0300-5585.
Published by: Statistisk Sentralbyraa/Statistics Norway, Kongensgate 6, P O Box 8131, Dep, Oslo, 0033, Norway. TEL 47-21-090000, FAX 47-21-094973, ssb@ssb.no.

NOVAYA LITERATURA PO SOTSIAL'NYM I GUMANITARNYM NAUKAM. FILOSOFIYA I SOTSIOLOGIYA; bibliograficheskii ukazatel'. *see* PHILOSOPHY—Abstracting, Bibliographies, Statistics

302.015195 USA ISSN 0193-2713
BF698.75
OPERANT SUBJECTIVITY; the international journal of Q methodology. Text in English. 1977. q. free to members (effective 2011). bk.rev. bibl. back issues avail. **Document type:** *Journal, Academic/Scholarly.* **Description:** Aims to understanding of subjectivity through presentation of original research, theoretical and philosophical critique, and methodological clarification.
Indexed: PsycholAb.
—Ingenta.
Published by: (International Society for the Scientific Study of Subjectivity), Kent State University, Department of Political Science, University Campus, Kent, OH 44242. ecrawle1@kent.edu, http://www.kent.edu/polisci/index.cfm. Ed. Amanda M Wolf TEL 64-4-4635712.

302.045195 CAN ISSN 1712-8420
UN PORTRAIT STATISTIQUE DES FAMILLES AU QUEBEC. Text in French. 2005. a. **Document type:** *Handbook/Manual/Guide, Trade.*
Published by: Quebec, Ministere de la Famille, des Aines et de la Condition Feminine, 425, rue Saint-Amable, RC, Quebec, PQ G1R 4Z1, Canada. TEL 418-643-4721, 888-643-4721, http://www.mfacf.gouv.qc.ca/index.asp.

016.301 USA
PROQUEST SOCIOLOGY. Text in English. 2008. base vol. plus updates. **Document type:** *Database, Abstract/Index.* **Description:** Covers the international literature of sociology and social work, including culture and social structure, history and theory of sociology, social psychology, substance abuse and addiction, and more.
Media: Online - full text.
Published by: ProQuest (Subsidiary of: Cambridge Information Group), 789 E Eisenhower Pky, PO Box 1346, Ann Arbor, MI 48106. TEL 734-761-4700, 800-521-0600, FAX 734-997-4040, 888-241-5612, info@proquest.com.

302.015195 NLD ISSN 0033-5177
H61 CODEN: QQEJAV
➤ **QUALITY AND QUANTITY**; international journal of methodology. Text in English. 1967. 6/yr. EUR 1,695, USD 1,145 combined subscription to institutions (print & online eds.) (effective 2012). adv. bk.rev. bibl.; charts; illus. index. back issues avail.; reprint service avail. from PSC. **Document type:** *Journal, Academic/Scholarly.* **Description:** Publishes papers on causal analysis, models of classification, graph theory applications, mathematical models of voting behavior and social mobility, and other topics related to the development of rigorous scientific methodologies for the social sciences.
Related titles: Microform ed.: (from PQC); Online - full text ed.: ISSN 1573-7845 (from IngentaConnect).
Indexed: A01, A03, A08, A12, A20, A22, A26, ABIn, AEI, ASCA, B16, BibLing, CA, CIS, CMCI, CurCont, DIP, E01, FR, FamI, HPNRM, IBR, IBSS, IBZ, IndMed, JCQM, P03, P10, P30, P42, P46, P48, P51, P53, P54, PQC, PSA, PsycInfo, PsycholAb, RASB, RefZh, S02, S03, SCI, SCOPUS, SOPODA, SSA, SSCI, SSciA, ST&MA, SociolAb, T02, W07.
—BLDSC (7168.135000), IE, Infotrieve, Ingenta, INIST. **CCC.**
Published by: Springer Netherlands (Subsidiary of: Springer Science+Business Media), Van Godewijckstraat 30, Dordrecht, 3311 GX, Netherlands. TEL 31-78-6576050, FAX 31-78-6576474, http://www.springer.com. Ed. Vittorio Capecchi.

016.3054 USA
RACE RELATIONS ABSTRACTS. Text in English. 1999. base vol. plus s-m. updates. GBP 516, USD 904 to institutions (effective 2008). **Document type:** *Database, Abstract/Index.*
Formerly (until 2008): Sage Race Relations Abstracts (Online) (1461-7366)
Media: Online - full text.
—**CCC.**
Published by: EBSCO Publishing (Subsidiary of: EBSCO Industries, Inc.), 10 Estes St, PO Box 682, Ipswich, MA 01938. TEL 978-356-6500, 800-653-2726, FAX 978-356-6565, information@ebscohost.com.

REGIONY ROSSII. SOTSIAL'NO-EKONOMICHESKIE POKAZATELI (YEAR). *see* BUSINESS AND ECONOMICS—Abstracting, Bibliographies, Statistics

RESOURCES FOR RADICALS. *see* SOCIOLOGY

ROSSIISKII STATISTICHESKII YEZHEGODNIK/RUSSIAN STATISTICAL YEARBOOK. *see* BUSINESS AND ECONOMICS—Abstracting, Bibliographies, Statistics

ROSSIYA V TSIFRAKH (YEAR); kratkii statisticheskii zbornik. *see* BUSINESS AND ECONOMICS—Abstracting, Bibliographies, Statistics

302.045195 USA ISSN 1940-042X
RURAL AMERICA AT A GLANCE. Text in English. 199?. a. free (effective 2011). back issues avail. **Document type:** *Report, Government.*
Media: Online - full text.
Published by: U.S. Department of Agriculture, Economic Research Service, 1800 M St NW, Washington, DC 20036. TEL 202-694-5050, 800-999-6779, ersinfo@ers.usda.gov.

RUSSIA IN FIGURES (YEAR). *see* BUSINESS AND ECONOMICS—Abstracting, Bibliographies, Statistics

302.015195 USA ISSN 0885-6729
HN25
S I N E T. (Social Indicators Network News) Text in English. 1973. q. bk.rev. bibl. back issues avail. **Document type:** *Journal, Academic/ Scholarly.* **Description:** Brings together information on social indicator and quality of life developments from Asia, the Pacific, Europe, and the Americas.
Formerly (until 1984): Social Indicators Newsletter (0363-3195)
Address: Dept of Sociology, Duke University, PO Box 90088, Durham, NC 27708. TEL 919-660-5615, FAX 919-660-5623. Ed. Kenneth C Land.

SAHOE TONG'GYE JO'SA BO'GO'SEO/KOREA (REPUBLIC). NATIONAL STATISTICAL OFFICE. REPORT ON THE SOCIAL STATISTICS SURVEY. *see* POPULATION STUDIES—Abstracting, Bibliographies, Statistics

302.015195 NOR ISSN 0801-7603
HN561
SAMFUNNSSPEILET. Text in Norwegian. 1987. 6/yr. NOK 220 to individuals; NOK 330 to institutions; NOK 65 per issue (effective 2004). **Document type:** *Magazine, Government.* **Description:** Analysis of research results concerning the economic, demographic, and cultural changes in the Norwegian society.
Related titles: Online - full text ed.: ISSN 0809-4713.
Published by: Statistisk Sentralbyraa/Statistics Norway, Kongensgate 6, P O Box 8131, Dep, Oslo, 0033, Norway. TEL 47-21-090000, FAX 47-21-094973, ssb@ssb.no. Ed. Johan-Kristian Toender. Circ: 12,200.

016.301 CHN ISSN 1009-7414
SHEHUIXUE WENZHAI KA/SOCIOLOGY ABSTRACTS ON CARDS. Text in Chinese. q. CNY 20 (effective 2004). **Document type:** *Abstract/Index.*
Published by: Zhongguo Renmin Daxue Shubao Ziliao Zhongxin/Renmin University of China, Information Center for Social Sciences, Dongcheng-qu, 3, Zhangzizhong Lu, Beijing, 100007, China. TEL 86-10-64039458, FAX 86-10-64015080, center@zlzx.org, http://www.zlzx.org/. **Dist. by:** China Publications Service, PO Box 49614, Chicago, IL 60649. TEL 312-288-3291, FAX 312-288-8570; China International Book Trading Corp, 35 Chegongzhuang Xilu, Haidian District, PO Box 399, Beijing 100044, China. TEL 86-10-68412045, FAX 86-10-68412023, cibtc@mail.cibtc.com.cn, http://www.cibtc.com.cn.

302.01591 NLD ISSN 0303-8300
HN25
➤ **SOCIAL INDICATORS RESEARCH**; an international and interdisciplinary journal for quality-of-life measurement. Text in English. 1974. 15/yr. EUR 2,711, USD 2,818 combined subscription to institutions (print & online eds.) (effective 2012). adv. bk.rev. illus. index. back issues avail.; reprint service avail. from PSC. **Document type:** *Journal, Academic/Scholarly.* **Description:** Publishes results of empirical, philosophical and methodological research studies dealing with problems related to the measurement of all aspects of the quality of life.
Related titles: Microform ed.: (from PQC); Online - full text ed.: ISSN 1573-0921 (from IngentaConnect).
Indexed: A01, A02, A03, A08, A12, A13, A17, A20, A22, A25, A26, A34, A36, ABIn, AEI, ASCA, ASG, Agr, B01, B06, B07, B08, B09, BAS, BibInd, BibLing, C12, CA, CABA, CERDIC, CIS, CMM, CurCont, D01, DIP, E01, E03, E07, E08, E12, EI, ERI, ERIC, ESPM, FR, FamI, FutSurv, G08, GEOBASE, GH, H01, H05, HRA, I05, IBR, IBSS, IBZ, IPsyAb, IndMed, LT, M&MA, M01, M02, MEA&I, N02, N03, OR, P02, P03, P06, P10, P21, P25, P27, P30, P33, P34, P39, P42, P46, P48, P50, P51, P53, P54, PAIS, PCI, PN&I, PQC, PSA, PhilInd, PsycInfo, PsycholAb, R08, R12, RASB, RRTA, RefZh, RiskAb, S02, S03, S08, S09, S11, S13, S16, SCOPUS, SFSA, SOPODA, SPAA, SSA, SSCI, SSciA, SUSA, SWR&A, SociolAb, T02, T05, TAR, W07, W09, W11, WBSS.
—BLDSC (8318.116000), IE, Infotrieve, Ingenta, INIST. **CCC.**
Published by: Springer Netherlands (Subsidiary of: Springer Science+Business Media), Van Godewijckstraat 30, Dordrecht, 3311 GX, Netherlands. TEL 31-78-6576050, FAX 31-78-6576474, http://www.springer.com. Ed. Alex C Michalos.

016.301 USA ISSN 0887-3577
SOCIAL THEORY: A BIBLIOGRAPHIC SERIES. Text in English. 1986. q. USD 70. back issues avail. **Document type:** *Monographic series, Bibliography.* **Description:** Series of bibliographies on and about the work of social theorists.
Published by: Reference and Research Services, 1446 Filbert St., San Francisco, CA 94109-1633. TEL 831-426-4479. Ed. Joan Nordquist.

016.301 USA
SOCINDEX. Text in English. base vol. plus w. updates. **Document type:** *Database, Abstract/Index.*
Media: Online - full text.
Published by: EBSCO Publishing (Subsidiary of: EBSCO Industries, Inc.), 10 Estes St, PO Box 682, Ipswich, MA 01938. TEL 978-356-6500, 800-653-2726, FAX 978-356-6565, information@ebscohost.com.

016.301 USA
SOCINDEX WITH FULL TEXT. Text in English. base vol. plus w. updates. **Document type:** *Database, Abstract/Index.*
Media: Online - full text.
Published by: EBSCO Publishing (Subsidiary of: EBSCO Industries, Inc.), 10 Estes St, PO Box 682, Ipswich, MA 01938. TEL 978-356-6500, 800-653-2726, FAX 978-356-6565, information@ebscohost.com.

016.301 USA
SOCIOLOGICAL ABSTRACTS (ONLINE). Text in English. base vol. plus m. updates. **Document type:** *Database, Abstract/Index.*
Media: Online - full text. **Related titles:** ♦ Print ed.: Sociological Abstracts (Print). ISSN 0038-0202.
Published by: ProQuest LLC (Bethesda) (Subsidiary of: Cambridge Information Group), 7200 Wisconsin Ave, Ste 715, Bethesda, MD 20814. TEL 301-961-6700, FAX 301-961-6720, service@csa.com, http://www.csa.com.

016.301 USA ISSN 0038-0202
HM1 CODEN: SOABA
SOCIOLOGICAL ABSTRACTS (PRINT). Text in English. 1953. bi-m. USD 985; USD 1,155 (includes a. cum. ed. & index in print & on CD-ROM) (effective 2011). adv. illus. cum.index. back issues avail.; reprints avail. **Document type:** *Abstract/Index.*
Related titles: ♦ Online - full text ed.: Sociological Abstracts (Online); Cumulative ed(s).: Sociological Abstracts Annual. USD 325 per vol. (effective 2011).
Indexed: RASB.
—BLDSC (8319.622000).
Published by: ProQuest LLC (Bethesda) (Subsidiary of: Cambridge Information Group), 7200 Wisconsin Ave, Ste 715, Bethesda, MD 20814. TEL 301-961-6798, 800-843-7751, FAX 301-961-6799, journals@csa.com. Eds. Chris Adcock, Sandra Stanton, Sonia V Diaz. Circ: 1,900.

SOCIOLOGY OF EDUCATION ABSTRACTS. *see* EDUCATION—Abstracting, Bibliographies, Statistics

SOSIALE OG OEKNOMISKE STUDIER. *see* SOCIOLOGY

016.301 RUS
SOTSIAL'NYE I GUMANITARNYE NAUKI. OTECHESTVENNAYA I ZARUBEZHNAYA LITERATURA. SOTSIOLOGIYA; referativnyi zhurnal. Text in Russian. 1972. q. USD 165 in United States (effective 2004). **Document type:** *Abstract/Index.* **Description:** Contains abstracts of foreign and Russian books devoted to sociology acquired lately by INION.
Formerly (until 1991): Obshchestvennye Nauki za Rubezhom. Sotsiologiya (0868-4448); Which superseded in part: Obshchestvennye Nauki za Rubezhom. Filosofiya i Sotsiologiya (0132-7356)
Indexed: RASB.
Published by: Rossiiskaya Akademiya Nauk, Institut Nauchnoi Informatsii po Obshchestvennym Naukam, Nakhimovskii pr-t 51/21, Moscow, 117997, Russian Federation. TEL 7-095-1288930, FAX 7-095-4202261, info@inion.ru, http://www.inion.ru. Ed. V I Dobren'kov. **Dist. by:** East View Information Services, 10601 Wayzata Blvd, Minneapolis, MN 55305. TEL 952-252-1201, 800-477-1005, FAX 952-252-1202, info@eastview.com, http://www.eastview.com.

302.045195 GBR ISSN 1746-5982
SURVEY METHODOLOGY BULLETIN. Text in English. 1977. irreg. **Document type:** *Government.* **Description:** Aims to inform staff in the Office for National Statistics and the government statistical service about the work on social survey methodology carried out by social survey division of the Office for National Statistics.
Former titles (until 2003): Social Survey Methodology Bulletin (1475-3987); (until 2001): Survey Methodology Bulletin (0263-158X)
Related titles: Online - full text ed.: free (effective 2010).
Indexed: PCI.
—BLDSC (8318.216550), IE. **CCC.**
Published by: Office for National Statistics, Rm 1.101, Government Bldgs, Cardiff Rd, Newport, S Wales NP10 8XG, United Kingdom. TEL 44-1633-653599, FAX 44-1633-652747, info@statistics.gov.uk, http://www.statistics.gov.uk/default.asp.

016.301 HUN ISSN 0133-2074
SZOCIOLOGIAI INFORMACIO/SOCIOLOGICAL INFORMATION; a magyar nyelvu es magyar vonatkozasu szakirodalom valogatott bibliografiaja. Text in Hungarian. 1972. a. HUF 1,200. adv. bk.rev. index. **Document type:** *Bulletin.* **Description:** Current national bibliography of books and articles on Hungarian sociology written by Hungarian sociologists in the country or abroad, and by foreign sociologists about Hungary and Hungarians.
Related titles: Diskette ed.
Published by: Fovarosi Szabo Ervin Konyvtar, Szociologiai Dokumentacios Osztaly, Szabo Ervin ter 1, Budapest, 1088, Hungary. TEL 36-1-1186799, FAX 36-1-1185-914. Ed. Erika Karbach. Circ: 300. **Co-sponsor:** Budapest Fovaros Onkormanyzata.

016.301 BRA
UNIVERSIDADE DE SAO PAULO. DEPARTAMENTO DE SOCIOLOGIA. SERIE BIBLIOGRAFIA. Text in Portuguese. irreg., latest vol.3. per issue exchange basis. **Document type:** *Bibliography.*
Published by: Universidade de Sao Paulo, Faculdade de Filosofia, Letras e Ciencias Humanas, Av Professor Luciano Gualberto 315, Butanta, Sao Paulo, SP 05508-010, Brazil. http://www.fflch.usp.br. Circ: 400.

016.3054 USA
URBAN STUDIES ABSTRACTS. Text in English. base vol. plus s-m. updates. **Document type:** *Database, Abstract/Index.*
Formerly (until 2008): Sage Urban Studies Abstracts (Online) (1940-2317)
Media: Online - full text.
Published by: EBSCO Publishing (Subsidiary of: EBSCO Industries, Inc.), 10 Estes St, PO Box 682, Ipswich, MA 01938. TEL 978-356-6500, 800-653-2726, FAX 978-356-6565, information@ebscohost.com.

016.3036 USA ISSN 1940-4050
VIOLENCE & ABUSE ABSTRACTS. Text in English. base vol. plus s-m. updates. **Document type:** *Database, Abstract/Index.*
Media: Online - full text.
Published by: EBSCO Publishing (Subsidiary of: EBSCO Industries, Inc.), 10 Estes St, PO Box 682, Ipswich, MA 01938. TEL 978-356-6500, 800-653-2726, FAX 978-356-6565, information@ebscohost.com.

WOMEN'S STUDIES INTERNATIONAL. *see* WOMEN'S STUDIES—Abstracting, Bibliographies, Statistics

SOCIOLOGY—Computer Applications

301 USA ISSN 1094-2629
QA76.9.C66
ANNUAL EDITIONS: COMPUTERS IN SOCIETY. Text in English. 1986. a. USD 22.25 per issue (effective 2010). illus. back issues avail. **Document type:** *Journal, Academic/Scholarly.*
Related titles: Online - full text ed.
Published by: McGraw-Hill, Contemporary Learning Series (Subsidiary of: McGraw-Hill Companies, Inc.), 1221 Ave of the Americas, New York, NY 10020. TEL 212-904-2000, FAX 212-512-2000, customer.service@mcgraw-hill.com, http://www.mhhe.com/cls/.

BEHAVIOUR AND INFORMATION TECHNOLOGY; an international journal on the human aspects of computing. *see* PSYCHOLOGY

COMPUTER BITS. *see* COMPUTERS

651.8 USA
QA76 CODEN: CMSCD3
COMPUTERS & SOCIETY (ONLINE). Text in English. 19??. q. free to members (effective 2010). bk.rev. illus. back issues avail.; reprints avail. **Document type:** *Newsletter, Academic/Scholarly.* **Description:** Features all aspects of the social, ethical and cultural impact of computing.
Former titles (until 2002): Computers & Society (Print) (0095-2737); (until 1969): S I G C A S Newsletter
Media: Online - full text.
Indexed: A22, A28, APA, BrCerAb, C&ISA, CA/WCA, CIA, CerAb, CivEngAb, CompC, CompR, CorrAb, E&CAJ, E11, EEA, EMA, ErgAb, H15, Inspec, M&TEA, M09, MBF, METADEX, SolStAb, T04, WAA.
—AskIEEE, IE, Infotrieve, Ingenta.
Published by: Association for Computing Machinery, Inc., 2 Penn Plz, Ste 701, New York, NY 10121. TEL 212-626-0500, 800-342-6626, FAX 212-944-1318, acmhelp@acm.org, http://www.acm.org.

301 004 GBR ISSN 0747-5632
BF39.5 CODEN: CHBEEQ
➤ **COMPUTERS IN HUMAN BEHAVIOR.** Text in English. 1985. 6/yr. EUR 1,446 in Europe to institutions; JPY 192,300 in Japan to institutions; USD 1,619 elsewhere to institutions (effective 2012). adv. bk.rev. back issues avail.; reprints avail. **Document type:** *Journal, Academic/Scholarly.* **Description:** Examines the use of computers from a psychological perspective.
Related titles: Microfilm ed.; Online - full text ed.: ISSN 1873-7692 (from IngentaConnect, ScienceDirect).
Indexed: A01, A03, A08, A20, A22, A26, A28, AHCI, APA, ASCA, B02, B04, B17, B18, BRD, BrCerAb, C&ISA, C10, CA, CA/WCA, CIA, CMCI, CPEI, CerAb, CivEngAb, CommAb, CompAb, CompLI, CorrAb, CurCont, DIP, E&CAJ, E-psyche, E02, E03, E08, E11, E15, E16, EEA, EMA, ERA, ERI, ESPM, EdA, EdI, EngInd, EnvEAb, ErgAb, FR, G01, G04, G08, H15, HEA, I05, IBR, IBZ, IPsyAb, Inspec, L&LBA, M&TEA, M09, M12, MBF, METADEX, MicrocompInd, P03, P30, PsycInfo, PsycholAb, RASB, S01, S02, S03, S09, S19, S20, S21, SCOPUS, SOPODA, SSA, SSAI, SSAb, SSCI, SSI, SociolAb, SolStAb, T02, T04, V05, W03, W07, WAA.
—BLDSC (3394.921600), AskIEEE, GNLM, IE, Infotrieve, Ingenta, INIST, Linda Hall. **CCC.**
Published by: Pergamon (Subsidiary of: Elsevier Science & Technology), The Blvd, Langford Ln, East Park, Kidlington, Oxford OX5 1GB, United Kingdom. TEL 44-1865-843000, FAX 44-1865-843010, JournalsCustomerServiceEMEA@elsevier.com. Ed. Robert D Tennyson. **Subscr. to:** Elsevier BV, Radarweg 29, PO Box 211, Amsterdam 1000 AE, Netherlands. http://www.elsevier.nl.

310 USA ISSN 1044-7318
QA76.9.H85 CODEN: IJHIEC
➤ **INTERNATIONAL JOURNAL OF HUMAN-COMPUTER INTERACTION.** Text in English. 1989. m. GBP 1,062 combined subscription in United Kingdom to institutions (print & online eds.); EUR 1,416, USD 1,779 combined subscription to institutions (print & online eds.) (effective 2012). adv. index. back issues avail.; reprint service avail. from PSC. **Document type:** *Journal, Academic/Scholarly.* **Description:** Addresses the cognitive, social, health, and ergonomic aspects of interactive computing.
Related titles: Online - full text ed.: ISSN 1532-7590. GBP 955 in United Kingdom to institutions; EUR 1,274, USD 1,601 to institutions (effective 2012).
Indexed: A01, A02, A03, A08, A12, A20, A22, A28, ABIn, AHCI, AIA, APA, ASCA, B01, B06, B07, B09, BrCerAb, C&ISA, C10, C23, CA, CA/WCA, CIA, CMCI, CerAb, CivEngAb, CompLI, CorrAb, CurCont, E&CAJ, E-psyche, E01, E11, EEA, EMA, ErgAb, H15, ISR, Inspec, L&LBA, L13, M&TEA, M09, MBF, METADEX, P02, P03, P10, P17, P26, P30, P43, P48, P49, P51, P53, P54, PQC, PsycInfo, PsycholAb, S01, S11, SCI, SCOPUS, SSCI, SolStAb, T02, T04, W07, WAA.
—BLDSC (4542.288000), AskIEEE, IE, Infotrieve, Ingenta, Linda Hall. **CCC.**
Published by: (International Ergonomics Association SGP), Taylor & Francis Inc. (Subsidiary of: Taylor & Francis Group), 325 Chestnut St, Ste 800, Philadelphia, PA 19106. TEL 215-625-2940, 800-354-1420, orders@taylorandfrancis.com, http://www.taylorandfrancis.com. Eds. Gavriel Salvendy, Julie A Jacko. Adv. contact Linda Hann TEL 44-1344-779945. **Co-sponsor:** Human Factors and Ergonomics Society.

301 330 USA ISSN 1947-8429
T58.5
▼ ➤ **INTERNATIONAL JOURNAL OF KNOWLEDGE SOCIETY RESEARCH.** Text in English. 2010. q. USD 210 to individuals; USD 595 to institutions; USD 275 combined subscription to individuals (print & online eds.); USD 860 combined subscription to institutions (print & online eds.) (effective 2012). **Document type:** *Journal, Academic/Scholarly.* **Description:** Features research on the knowledge society in the areas of health, education, culture, science, and business.
Related titles: Online - full text ed.: ISSN 1947-8437. 2010. USD 140 to individuals; USD 595 to institutions (effective 2012).
Indexed: L13.
Published by: I G I Global, 701 E Chocolate Ave, Ste 200, Hershey, PA 17033. TEL 717-533-8845 ext 100, FAX 717-533-8661, cust@igi-global.com, http://www.igi-pub.com. Ed. Miltiadis Lytras.

301 USA ISSN 1522-8835
HV41 CODEN: JTHSFM
➤ **JOURNAL OF TECHNOLOGY IN HUMAN SERVICES.** Abbreviated title: J T H S. Text in English. 1985. q. GBP 574 combined subscription in United Kingdom to institutions (print & online eds.); EUR 748, USD 753 combined subscription to institutions (print & online eds.) (effective 2012). adv. bk.rev. bibl.; illus. 120 p./no. 1 cols./p.; back issues avail.; reprint service avail. from PSC. **Document type:** *Journal, Academic/Scholarly.* **Description:** Emphasizes the internet and other electronic technologies and their impact on Human Services.
Formerly (until 1999): Computers in Human Services (0740-445X); Incorporates (in 1991): Computer Use in Social Services Network. Newsletter (0889-6194)
Related titles: Microfiche ed.: (from PQC); Microform ed.; Online - full text ed.: ISSN 1522-8991. GBP 517 in United Kingdom to institutions; EUR 673, USD 678 to institutions (effective 2012).
Indexed: A01, A03, A10, A22, A28, AHCI, AHCMS, APA, ASSIA, BrCerAb, C&ISA, C06, C07, C08, C10, CA, CA/WCA, CIA, CINAHL, CerAb, CivEngAb, CompAb, CompLI, CompR, CorrAb, DIP, E&CAJ, E-psyche, E01, E11, EEA, EMA, ESPM, EnvEAb, FamI, H15, HRA, IBR, IBZ, IPsyAb, Inspec, L04, LISTA, M&TEA, M09, MBF, METADEX, MicrocompInd, P03, P30, PerIslam, PsycInfo, PsycholAb, RefZh, S02, S03, S21, SCOPUS, SOPODA, SSA, SWR&A, SociolAb, SolStAb, T02, T04, V03, WAA.
—BLDSC (5068.562500), AskIEEE, IE, Infotrieve, Ingenta, Linda Hall. **CCC.**
Published by: Routledge (Subsidiary of: Taylor & Francis Group), 325 Chestnut St, Ste 800, Philadelphia, PA 19106. TEL 215-625-8900, 800-354-1420, FAX 215-625-8914, journals@routledge.com, http://www.routledge.com. Ed. Dick Schoech. adv.: B&W page USD 315, color page USD 550; trim 4.375 x 7.125. Circ: 250 (paid).

SOFTWARE

see COMPUTERS—Software

SOLAR ENERGY

see ENERGY—Solar Energy

S

SOUND

see PHYSICS—Sound

SOUND RECORDING AND REPRODUCTION

see also MUSIC

621.389 USA ISSN 1549-4950
TK5981 CODEN: ADIOA3
➤ **A E S.** Text in English. 1953. 10/yr. USD 280 to non-members; USD 695 combined subscription to non-members (print & online eds.); free to members (effective 2011). adv. bk.rev. abstr.; bibl.; charts; illus. index. cum.index: 1953-1980. reprints avail. **Document type:** *Journal, Academic/Scholarly.*
Formerly (until 200?): Audio Engineering Society. Journal (0004-7554)
Related titles: Microfilm ed.: (from PQC); Online - full text ed.: USD 525 (effective 2011).
Indexed: A05, A20, A22, A23, A24, AS&TA, AS&TI, ASCA, AcoustA, B04, B10, B13, C&ISA, C10, CA, CPEI, CurCont, E&CAJ, EngInd, FR, ISMEC, ISR, Inspec, MLA-IB, P30, RILM, SCI, SCOPUS, SolStAb, T02, TM, W07.
—BLDSC (4706.000000), AskIEEE, IE, Infotrieve, Ingenta, INIST, Linda Hall. **CCC.**
Published by: Audio Engineering Society, 60 E 42nd St, Ste 2520, New York, NY 10165. TEL 212-661-8528, FAX 212-682-0477, hq@aes.rog. Ed. John Vanderkooy. Adv. contact Christine Carleo.

789.9 USA ISSN 2151-4402
ML1
➤ **A R S C JOURNAL.** Text in English. 1968. s-a. looseleaf. free to members (effective 2010). adv. bk.rev.; rec.rev. bibl.; illus.; stat. cum.index. back issues avail. **Document type:** *Journal, Academic/Scholarly.* **Description:** Devoted to the results of research, technical developments, unusual discoveries, discographies, and articles of general interest in the field.
Incorporates (1968-1988): A R S C Bulletin (0587-1956); Formerly (until 1985): Association for Recorded Sound Collections. Journal (0004-5438)
Related titles: Online - full text ed.
Indexed: A20, A26, B04, BRD, CA, E08, I05, IIMP, IIPA, L04, L07, L08, L13, LISTA, LibLit, M11, MAG, MLA, MusicInd, RILM, S09, T02, W03, W05.
—IE, Ingenta.
Published by: Association for Recorded Sound Collections, Inc., c/o Peter Shambarger, PO Box 543, Annapolis, MD 21404. execdir@arsc-audio.org. Ed. Barry A Ashpole. Pub. Ted P Sheldon. Adv. contact Dan Shiman.

621.389 USA ISSN 0196-9145
ML1
A R S C NEWSLETTER. Text in English. 1977. 3/yr. free to members (effective 2010). adv. back issues avail. **Document type:** *Newsletter, Trade.* **Description:** Provides coverage of ARSC activities, free brief notices of information desired and items offered or wanted.
Related titles: Online - full text ed.: free (effective 2010).
Indexed: A01, M11, MusicInd, RILM, T02.
Published by: Association for Recorded Sound Collections, Inc., c/o Peter Shambarger, PO Box 543, Annapolis, MD 21404. execdir@arsc-audio.org. Ed. Franz Kunst. Adv. contact Dan Shiman.

780 USA ISSN 0097-1138
TK7881.4
THE ABSOLUTE SOUND; the high end journal of audio & music. Short title: T A S. Text in English. 1973. 10/yr. USD 19.95 domestic; USD 35.95 in Canada; USD 54.95 elsewhere (effective 2010). adv. bk.rev.; rec.rev. illus. index. back issues avail.; reprints avail. **Document type:** *Magazine, Consumer.*
Related titles: Microform ed.: (from PQC); Online - full text ed.: USD 14.95; USD 4.99 per issue (effective 2010); ◆ Supplement(s): High End.
Indexed: MAG.
—Ingenta.
Published by: NextScreen, LLC, 4544 S Lamar Blvd, Bldg G300, Austin, TX 78745. TEL 512-892-8682, info@avguide.com, http://www.nextscreen.com/. Ed. Chris Martens. Pub. Jim Hannon. Circ: 33,000.

ANNUAIRE DE LA MUSIQUE, DE L'IMAGE ET DU SON. *see* MUSIC

621.3893 USA
THE ARCHITECT'S MUSE. Text in English. bi-m. free. **Document type:** *Newsletter.* **Description:** Presents information and news on acoustics and sound recording systems.
Published by: Orpheus Acoustics, 925 Virginia Ave, Lancaster, PA 17603. TEL 717-291-9123, FAX 717-291-5453. Ed. Christopher Brooks.

621.389 USA ISSN 0146-4701
TK7881.4
AUDIO CRITIC. Text in English. 1977. q. USD 24 (effective 2000). adv. bk.rev.; rec.rev. **Document type:** *Magazine, Consumer.*
Indexed: RILM.
Address: PO Box 978, Quakertown, PA 18951. TEL 215-536-8884, FAX 215-538-5432. Ed., Pub., R&P, Adv. contact Peter Aczel.

621.3893 GBR ISSN 0960-7471
AUDIO MEDIA; the world's leading professional audio technology magazine. Text in English. 1990. m. GBP 43 domestic; GBP 60 in Europe; GBP 75 elsewhere; free to qualified personnel (effective 2009). adv. back issues avail. **Document type:** *Magazine, Trade.* **Description:** Covers pro audio technology, technique, and business for the post, broadcast, recording, media authoring, sound reinforcement, location, and mastering markets.
Related titles: Online - full text ed.
Published by: I M A S Publishing UK Ltd., 1 Cabot House, Compass Point Business Park, St Ives, Cambridgeshire PE27 5JL, United Kingdom. TEL 44-1480-461555, FAX 44-1480-461550, pr@imaspub.com. Ed. Paul Mac. Pub., Adv. contact Nick Humbert. color page GBP 1,950; trim 210 x 297.

621.389 FRA ISSN 1766-4098
AUDIO VIDEO PRESTIGE. Text in French. 1995. m. adv. **Document type:** *Magazine, Consumer.* **Description:** Features up-to-date information on the newest technology in the world of high fidelity and home cinema.
Formerly (until 2003): Prestige Audio Video (1262-0289)
Published by: Sonovision - Transoceanic, 3 Bd Ney, Paris, 75018, France. info@sonovision.com.

621.389 ITA ISSN 1123-2692
AUDIOCARSTEREO. Abbreviated title: A C S. Text in Italian. 1990. m. (11/yr.). adv. back issues avail. **Document type:** *Magazine, Consumer.*
Related titles: Online - full text ed.
Published by: Technipress Srl, Via Olindo Guerrini 20 D, Rome, 00139, Italy. TEL 39-06-8720331, FAX 39-06-87139141, http://www.technipress.it. Circ: 80,000.

620.2 USA
AUDIOCRAFT; an introduction to the tools and techniques of audio production. Text in English. irreg., latest vol.2, 1989. USD 32 to non-members; USD 22 to members. **Document type:** *Guide, Trade.* **Description:** Offers a practical, results-oriented guide covering topics from the basic concept of sound to the production of full-scale documentaries and concert recordings.
Published by: National Federation of Community Broadcasters, Ft Mason Center, Bldg D, San Francisco, CA 94123. TEL 415-771-1160. Ed. Randy Thom. R&P Sean Simplicio.

621.389 ITA ISSN 1592-3770
AUDIOGUIDA CAR. Text in Italian. 1990. a. adv. back issues avail. **Document type:** *Directory, Consumer.*
Published by: Technipress Srl, Via Olindo Guerrini 20 D, Rome, 00139, Italy. TEL 39-06-8720331, FAX 39-06-87139141, http://www.technipress.it. Circ: 65,000.

621.389 ITA ISSN 1592-3819
AUDIOGUIDA HI-FI. Text in Italian. 1989. a. adv. back issues avail. **Document type:** *Directory, Trade.*
Formerly (until 2000): Audioguida Hi-Fi & Home Theater (1128-4951)
Published by: Technipress Srl, Via Olindo Guerrini 20 D, Rome, 00139, Italy. TEL 39-06-8720331, FAX 39-06-87139141, http://www.technipress.it. Circ: 62,000.

621.389 DEU
AUDIOPHILE. Text in German. 1998-2004; N.S. 2011. 4/yr. EUR 19.80 newsstand/cover (effective 2011). adv. **Document type:** *Magazine, Consumer.*
Published by: W E K A Media Publishing GmbH, Gruberstr 46a, Poing, 85586, Germany. TEL 49-8121-950, FAX 49-8121-951199, online@wekanet.de, http://www.weka-media-publishing.de. Ed. Christine Tantschinez. Adv. contact Michael Hackenberg. Circ: 13,500 (paid and controlled).

621.389 ITA
AUDIOREVIEW. Text in Italian. 1981. m. (11/yr.). adv. back issues avail. **Document type:** *Magazine, Consumer.*
Published by: Technipress Srl, Via Olindo Guerrini 20 D, Rome, 00139, Italy. TEL 39-06-8720331, FAX 39-06-87139141, http://www.technipress.it. Ed. Paolo Nuti. Circ: 85,000.

AUSTRALIA. BUREAU OF STATISTICS. SOUND RECORDING STUDIOS, AUSTRALIA (ONLINE). *see* PHYSICS—Abstracting, Bibliographies, Statistics

620.2 AUS ISSN 1442-1259
AUSTRALIAN HI-FI AND HOME THEATRE TECHNOLOGY. Text in English. 1970. bi-m. AUD 40.60 domestic; AUD 95 foreign (effective 2008). adv. bk.rev. charts; illus. **Document type:** *Magazine, Consumer.* **Description:** Covers hi-fidelity systems and components.
Former titles (until 1997): Australian Hi-Fi (1328-4037); (until 1996): Australian Hi-Fi for Sound Advice (1038-7242); (until 1991): Australian Hi-Fi and Home Entertainment (1037-0633); (until 1991): Australian Hi-Fi and Music Review (1033-7628); (until 1988): Australian Hi-Fi (0159-0030)
Related titles: ◆ Supplement(s): Home Cinema & Hi-Fi Living. ISSN 1442-2824.
Indexed: Pinpoint.
Published by: Wolseley Media Pty Ltd., Level 5, 55 Chandos St, PO Box 5555, St. Leonards, NSW 2065, Australia. TEL 61-2-99016100, FAX 61-2-99016198, contactsubs@wolseleymedia.com.au. Ed. Greg Borrowman TEL 61-2-99016156. Adv. contact Lewis Preece TEL 61-2-99016175. color page AUD 3,250; trim 210 x 297.

621.389 AUS ISSN 1035-8323
AUSTRALIAN INCAR ENTERTAINMENT. Text in English. 1991. bi-m. AUD 39 domestic; AUD 95 foreign; AUD 7.50 newsstand/cover (effective 2008). adv. **Document type:** *Magazine, Consumer.* **Description:** Provides car audio, installations, satellite navigation and car security.
Published by: Wolseley Media Pty Ltd., Level 5, 55 Chandos St, PO Box 5555, St. Leonards, NSW 2065, Australia. TEL 61-2-99016100, FAX 61-2-99016198, contactsubs@wolseleymedia.com.au. Ed. Edgar Kramer TEL 61-2-99016148. Adv. contact Jim Preece TEL 61-2-99016150. color page AUD 2,850; trim 210 x 297.

AUTO HIFI. *see* TRANSPORTATION—Automobiles

621.389 JPN ISSN 1345-613X
AUTO SOUND. Text in Japanese. 1989. q. JPY 8,720 (effective 2008). adv. **Document type:** *Magazine, Consumer.*
Published by: Sutereo Saundo/Stereo Sound Publishing Inc., 3-8-4 Motoazabu, Minato-ku, Tokyo, 106-0046, Japan. Pub. Katsuyoshi Harada. Adv. contact Takazumi Arai.

621.389 USA ISSN 0195-0908
B A S SPEAKER. Text in English. 1972. bi-m. USD 25 (effective 2000). bk.rev. **Document type:** *Newsletter.* **Description:** Hi-fi consumer network.
Published by: Boston Audio Society, PO Box 211, Mattapan, MA 02126-0002. TEL 617-282-8335. Ed. Dave Moran. Circ: 1,500.

BILLBOARD (NEW YORK); the international newsweekly of music, video, and home entertainment. *see* MUSIC

BIOACOUSTICS; the international journal of animal sound and its recording. *see* BIOLOGY—Zoology

621.389 ESP ISSN 1135-7134
C D COMPACT; musica clasica y alta fidelidad. Text in Spanish. 1987. m. EUR 52.80 domestic; EUR 120 foreign (effective 2009). music rev. 76 p./no.; **Document type:** *Magazine, Consumer.* **Description:** Provides information on what is new on the record market. Reviews over 150 CDs and laser discs of classical and jazz.
Related titles: Online - full text ed.
Published by: Hi-Tech S.L., C Roca I Batlle 5, entlo. 1a, Barcelona, 08023, Spain. TEL 34-93-4184724, FAX 34-93-4184312. Ed., Pub. Jaime Rosal. R&P, Adv. contact Birgitta Sandberg. Circ: 20,000. **Dist. by:** Asociacion de Revistas Culturales de Espana, C Covarruvias 9 2o. Derecha, Madrid 28010, Spain. TEL 34-91-3086066, FAX 34-91-3199267, info@arce.es, http://www.arce.es/.

621.389 CAN ISSN 0840-6154
C I R P A NEWSLETTER. Text in English. 1975. 4/yr. CAD 40, USD 40 to non-members. **Document type:** *Newsletter.*
Indexed: CMPI.
Published by: Canadian Independent Record Production Association, 214 King St W Ste 614, Toronto, ON M5H 3S6, Canada. TEL 416-593-1665, FAX 416-593-7563. Ed. Richard Sutherland. Circ: 550.

621.389 AUS ISSN 1448-2010
C X; the news magazine for entertainment technology. Text in English. 1990. bi-m. AUD 33 (effective 2009). back issues avail. **Document type:** *Magazine, Trade.*
Former titles (until 2003): Connections (1320-5595); Which incorporated (in 2000): Presentech magazine (1442-7311); (until 1992): Channels
Published by: Juliusmedia Pty Ltd., Locked Bag 30, Epping, NSW 1710, Australia. TEL 61-2-96385955, 800-635-514. Ed., Pub. Julius Grafton.

621.38 388.3 USA ISSN 0898-3720
CAR AUDIO & ELECTRONICS. Text in English. 1988. m. USD 15 domestic; USD 27 in Canada; USD 39 elsewhere (effective 2007). adv. illus. back issues avail. **Document type:** *Magazine, Consumer.* **Description:** Dedicated to helping people buy, install and enjoy electronics for their cars.
Related titles: Spanish ed.: ISSN 1076-8033.
Indexed: A10, V03.
—**CCC.**
Published by: Source Interlink Companies, 2400 E Katella Ave, 11th Fl, Anaheim, CA 92806. TEL 714-939-2400, FAX 714-978-6390, dheine@sourceinterlink.com, http://www.sourceinterlink.com. Ed. Ben Oh. Pub. Howard Lim. adv.: B&W page USD 8,680, color page USD 12,420; trim 8 x 10.75. Circ: 67,205.

COMPUTER MUSIC JOURNAL. *see* MUSIC—Computer Applications

621.389 USA ISSN 0011-7145
TK7881.4 CODEN: DBSEDB
DB; the sound engineering magazine. Text in English. 1967. bi-m. USD 15. adv. bk.rev. charts; illus.; tr.lit. reprints avail.
Related titles: Microfilm ed.: (from PQC).
Indexed: A05, A20, A22, A23, A24, AS&TA, AS&TI, B04, B13, CompC, Inspec.
—AskIEEE, Ingenta, Linda Hall. **CCC.**
Address: 203 Commack Rd, Ste 1010, Commack, NY 11725. TEL 516-586-6530. Ed. Larry Zide. Circ: 20,000.

621.389 CHN ISSN 1002-8684
DIANSHENG JISHU/AUDIO ENGINEERING. Text in Chinese. m. **Document type:** *Magazine, Trade.*
Indexed: A28, APA, BrCerAb, CA/WCA, CIA, CerAb, CivEngAb, E11, EEA, EMA, ESPM, EnvEAb, H15, M&TEA, M09, MBF, METADEX, T04.
—BLDSC (1787.955500).
Published by: (Dianshi Diansheng Yanjiusuo (Zhongguo Dianzi Keji Jituan Gongsi Di 3 Yanjiusuo)/Research Institute of TV and Electro-Acoustics (C E T C No.3 Reserach Institute)), Beijing Dianshi Diansheng Zazhishe/T V & Audio Engineering Publishing House, PO Box 100015, Beijing, 100015, China. TEL 86-10-64313649 ext 8108, 8005. **Dist. by:** China International Book Trading Corp, 35 Chegongzhuang Xilu, Haidian District, PO Box 399, Beijing 100044, China. TEL 86-10-68412045, FAX 86-10-68412023, cibtc@mail.cibtc.com.cn, http://www.cibtc.com.cn.

DIANYING YISHU/FILM ART. *see* MOTION PICTURES

DIGITAL MUSIC WEEKLY. *see* COMPUTERS—Internet

DIGITAL TESTED. *see* COMMUNICATIONS—Television And Cable

DISC COLLECTOR. *see* MUSIC

253 USA ISSN 0192-334X
DISCOGRAPHIES. Text in English. 1979. irreg., latest 2004. price varies. back issues avail. **Document type:** *Monographic series, Academic/Scholarly.*
—BLDSC (3595.543000), IE, Ingenta.
Published by: Greenwood Publishing Group Inc. (Subsidiary of: A B C - C L I O), 88 Post Rd W, PO Box 5007, Westport, CT 06881. TEL 203-226-3571, 800-225-5800, FAX 877-231-6980, sales@greenwood.com, http://www.greenwood.com. Ed. Michael Gray.

621.389 789 USA ISSN 1050-7868
E Q (NEW YORK). (Equalization) Text in English. 1990. m. USD 15 domestic; USD 30 in Canada; USD 40 elsewhere (effective 2008). adv. back issues avail.; reprints avail. **Document type:** *Magazine, Consumer.* **Description:** Covers projects recording and sound studio techniques for the professional audio market.
Related titles: Online - full text ed.; ◆ Supplement(s): Extreme Groove.
Indexed: B02, B15, B17, B18, G04, G05, G06, G07, G08, I05, M01, M02, M11, P16, P48, P49, P53, P54, PQC, T02.
—CIS. **CCC.**
Published by: NewBay Media, LLC (Subsidiary of: The Wicks Group of Companies, LLC.), 810 Seventh Ave, 27th Fl, New York, NY 10019. TEL 212-378-0400, FAX 212-378-0470, customerservice@nbmedia.com, http://www.nbmedia.com. Ed. Matthew Harper TEL 650-238-0284. adv.: page USD 5,275; trim 8 x 10.5. Circ: 34,734.

ENTERTAINMENT BUSINESS. *see* MUSIC

621.389 POL ISSN 1427-0404
ESTRADA I STUDIO. Text in Polish. 1996. m. PLZ 161.70 domestic; EUR 102 in Europe; EUR 122 elsewhere (effective 2005). **Document type:** *Magazine, Trade.*
Related titles: CD-ROM ed.; Online - full content ed.: ISSN 1689-3573.

Published by: A V T- Korporacja Sp. z o. o., ul Burleska 9, Warsaw, 01939, Poland. TEL 48-22-5689941, FAX 48-22-5689944, redakcja@ep.com.pl, http://www.avt.pl. Ed. Tomasz Wroblewski.

621.389 DEU ISSN 1687-4714
➤ **EURASIP JOURNAL ON AUDIO, SPEECH, AND MUSIC PROCESSING.** Text in English. 2006. **Document type:** *Journal, Academic/Scholarly.* **Description:** Presents research and articles on the theory and applications of the processing of various audio signals, with a specific focus on speech and music.
Related titles: Online - full text ed.: ISSN 1687-4722. free (effective 2011).
Indexed: A26, A28, APA, BrCerAb, C&ISA, C10, CA, CA/WCA, CIA, CerAb, CivEngAb, CorrAb, CurCont, E&CAJ, E08, E11, EEA, EMA, ESPM, EnvEAb, H15, I05, M&TEA, M09, M11, MBF, METADEX, P52, SCI, SCOPUS, SolStAb, T02, T04, W07, WAA.
—IE.
Published by: SpringerOpen (Subsidiary of: Springer Science+Business Media), Tiergartenstr 17, Heidelberg, 69121, Germany. info@springeropen.com, http://www.springeropen.com.

➤ **FEDELTA DEL SUONO.** *see* MUSIC

621.3 GBR
FEDERATION OF BRITISH TAPE RECORDISTS. RECORDING NEWS. Text in English. 1965. q. free to members (effective 2009). adv. bk.rev. **Document type:** *Magazine, Trade.* **Description:** Features reviews, reports and technical features as well as contest results, letters and general news about the association.
Formerly: Federation of British Tape Recordists. News and Views
Published by: British Sound Recording Association, Cardiff and District Recording Club, c/o John Willett, President, 14 Waveney Close, Bicester, Oxfordshire OX26 2GP, United Kingdom. TEL 44-1494-551540, jw@soundhunters.com, http://www.soundhunters.com/fbtrc.

FONOFORUM; Klassik, Jazz und HiFi. *see* MUSIC

FOR THE RECORD (CUPAR). *see* ANTIQUES

FOTO VIDEO AUDIO NEWS (DUTCH EDITION). *see* PHOTOGRAPHY

FOTOMUNDO. *see* PHOTOGRAPHY

FOTOMUNDO. *see* PHOTOGRAPHY

621.389 USA
FRONT OF HOUSE; the news magazine for live sound. Text in English. 2002. m. free to qualified personnel (effective 2003). adv. **Document type:** *Magazine, Trade.* **Description:** Serves the theatrical and live sound industry.
Media: Online - full content. **Related titles:** Print ed.: ISSN 1549-831X.
Published by: Timeless Communications, Inc., 18425 Burbank Blvd, Ste 613, Tarzana, CA 91356. TEL 818-654-2474, FAX 818-654-2485. Pub. Terry Lowe. adv.: B&W page USD 4,695, color page USD 5,995; trim 11 x 14.625. Circ: 20,000.

621.38 JPN
GEKKAN EBUI FURONTO/AUDIO VIDEO FRONT. Text in Japanese. 1973. m. JPY 1,000.
Published by: Kyodo Tsushinsha/Kyodo News Enterprise Ltd., 9-20 Akasaka 1-chome, Minato-ku, Tokyo, 107-0052, Japan.

681 787.87 NLD ISSN 0928-8007
GITARIST. Text in Dutch. 1991. m. EUR 59; EUR 5.90 newsstand/cover (effective 2010). adv. **Document type:** *Magazine, Consumer.*
Published by: Uitgeverij de Inzet, Postbus 11497, Amsterdam, 1001 GL, Netherlands. TEL 31-20-6755308, FAX 31-20-5312019. Circ: 11,500.

GOOD VIBRATIONS. *see* HANDICAPPED—Visually Impaired

620 USA ISSN 1056-165X
ML27.U5
GRAMMY MAGAZINE. Text in English. q. USD 3.95, CAD 5.75 newsstand/cover. adv. **Document type:** *Magazine, Trade.*
Formerly: Grammy Pulse (1056-1668)
Indexed: RILM.
Published by: National Academy of Recording Arts and Sciences, 3402 Pico Blvd, Santa Monica, CA 90405-2118. Ed. David Konjoyan. Adv. contact Brad Burkhart.

GRAMOPHONE; your guide to the best in recorded classical music. *see* MUSIC

THE GRAMOPHONE CLASSICAL MUSIC GUIDE. *see* MUSIC

621.389 780 DEU
HANDBUCH FUER MUSIKER. Text in German. 1982. a. adv. **Document type:** *Trade.* **Description:** Full listing of music equipment.
Formerly (until 1996): Productiv's Handbuch fuer Musiker
Published by: Musik Productiv, Fuggerstr 6, Ibbenbueren, 49479, Germany. TEL 49-5451-909-0, FAX 49-5451-909190. Ed. Harald Hentschel. R&P Heinz Rebellius. Adv. contact Birgit Bovenschulte. Circ: 85,000.

HEAR + SEE. *see* COMMUNICATIONS—Video

621.389 DEU
HEIMKINO LAUTSPRECHER TEST; das Testmagazin fuer Surround-Systeme. Text in German. 2007. a. EUR 2.30 newsstand/cover (effective 2011). adv. **Document type:** *Magazine, Consumer.*
Formerly (until 2010): Heimkino Lautsprecher
Published by: Michael E. Brieden Verlag GmbH, Gartroper Str 42, Duisburg, 47138, Germany. TEL 49-203-42920, FAX 49-203-4292149, info@brieden.de, http://www.brieden.de.

621.389 PRT ISSN 0871-6188
HI-FI. Text in Portuguese. 1988. 12/yr.
Address: Rua D. Estefania 32-1o, Lisbon, 1000, Portugal. TEL 1-544307, FAX 522643, TELEX 64198. Ed. Antonio Panciarelli. Circ: 11,000.

789.9 GBR ISSN 1465-5950
HI-FI +; reproducing the recorded arts. Text in English. 1999. 7/yr. GBP 30 domestic; GBP 40 in Western Europe, USA, & Canada; GBP 54 elsewhere (effective 2009). adv. music rev. back issues avail. **Document type:** *Magazine, Consumer.* **Description:** Contains major features and loads of reviews on stereo equipment and products, music and musicians, new formats and collectable vinyl.
Published by: Absolute Media (UK) Ltd., Cornerways House, School Ln, Ringwood, Hants BH24 1LG, United Kingdom. TEL 44-1425-461155, accounts@hifiplus.com. Ed. Alan Sircom.

621.389 GBR ISSN 0955-1115
HI-FI CHOICE; passion for sound. Abbreviated title: H F C. Text in English. 1975. 13/yr. GBP 44.96 domestic; GBP 58.58 in Europe; GBP 82.47 elsewhere; GBP 3.99 newsstand/cover (effective 2010). adv. back issues avail. **Document type:** *Magazine, Consumer.* **Description:** Guides to audio excellence in the home. It is a no-nonsense guide to the finest products available, from vinyl and valves, to multi-channel digital audio and high-fidelity video.
Related titles: Online - full text ed.: GBP 82.47; GBP 6.70 per issue (effective 2010).
—CCC.
Published by: Future Publishing Ltd., Beauford Ct, 30 Monmouth St, Bath, Avon BA1 2BW, United Kingdom. TEL 44-1225-442244, FAX 44-1225-446019, customerservice@subscription.co.uk, http://www.futureplc.com. Ed. Dan George. **Subscr. to:** Tower House, Sovereign Park, Market Harborough, Leicestershire LE16 9EF, United Kingdom. TEL 44-844-8481602, FAX 44-1858-438795, future@subscription.co.uk.

621.389 GBR ISSN 0961-7663
HI-FI WORLD. Text in English. 1991. m. GBP 41.04 domestic; GBP 50 in Europe; GBP 70 elsewhere (effective 2009). adv. back issues avail. **Document type:** *Magazine, Consumer.* **Description:** Contains informative reviews and radical kit designs for hi-fi enthusiasts and engineers.
Related titles: Online - full text ed.
Published by: Audio Publishing Ltd., Ste G4, Argo House, Park Business Centre, Kilburn Park Rd, London, NW6 5LF, United Kingdom. letters@hi-fiworld.co.uk. Ed. David Price TEL 44-1275-371386. Pub. Noel Keywood. **Subscr. to:** PO Box 464, Berkhamsted, Hertfordshire HP4 2UR, United Kingdom. TEL 44-1442-879097, FAX 44-1442-872279, hifiworld@webscribe.co.uk. **Dist. by:** MarketForce UK Ltd.

621.389 DEU
▼ **HIFI DIGITAL**; Streaming - Netzwerk - iPod. Text in German. 2010. 4/yr. EUR 16.80; EUR 4.90 newsstand/cover (effective 2011). adv. **Document type:** *Magazine, Consumer.*
Published by: Reiner H. Nitschke Verlags GmbH, Eifelring 28, Euskirchen, 53879, Germany. TEL 49-2251-650460, FAX 49-2251-6504699, service@nitschke-verlag.de, http://www.nitschke-verlag.de.

621.389 780 SWE ISSN 0346-0576
HIFI & MUSIK. Text in Swedish. 1970. 10/m. (10/yr.). SEK 49 newsstand/cover (effective 2004). adv. 84 p./no. 4 cols./p.; **Document type:** *Consumer.*
Formerly (until 1977): Stereo-hifi
Related titles: Audio cassette/tape ed.
Indexed: RILM.
Published by: Tidningen HiFi Musik AB, PO Box 23084, Stockholm, 10435, Sweden. TEL 46-8-342970, FAX 46-8-342971. Ed. Lars Erik Frej.

HIFI TEST. *see* ELECTRONICS

789.7 FRA ISSN 2103-3196
ML5
HIFI VIDEO. Text in French. 1969. m. adv. bk.rev. illus. **Document type:** *Magazine, Consumer.* **Description:** Contains buyer's guides, results of trials, and reports on new technologies. Directed to a broad audience.
Former titles (until 2008): Hifi Video Home Cinema (1281-1548); (until 1997): Hifi Video (0988-7091); (until 1991): Hifi Stereo (0337-1891)
Published by: Sonovision - Transoceanic, 3 Bd Ney, Paris, 75018, France. info@sonovision.com. Circ: 17,000 (paid).

621.3 FIN ISSN 1796-6507
HIFIMAAILMA. Text in Finnish. 2007. 8/yr. EUR 39 (effective 2007). adv. back issues avail. **Document type:** *Magazine, Consumer.*
Published by: Performance Magazines Oy, Olarinluoma 15, Espoo, 02200, Finland. TEL 358-10-7786404, FAX 358-9-88152101. Ed. Teppo HirviKunnas. adv.: color page EUR 2,490; 215 x 300.

621.389 DNK ISSN 0108-657X
HIGH FIDELITY (DANISH EDITION); lyd, billede og teknologi. Text in Danish. 1967. 6/yr. DKK 596 (effective 2009). adv. music rev. illus.; tr.lit. index. back issues avail. **Document type:** *Magazine, Consumer.* **Description:** Articles and reviews of the latest in hi-fi.
Incorporates (1980-1998): Hi Fi & Elektronik (0107-0274)
Related titles: ◆ Swedish ed.: High Fidelity (Swedish Edition). ISSN 0905-1740.
Indexed: Acal.
—CCC.
Published by: High Fidelity ApS, A. P. Moellers Alle 9 C, Dragoer, 2791, Denmark. TEL 45-70-237001, FAX 45-70-237002. Ed. Michael Madsen. Adv. contact Bettina Richards. page DKK 15,800; 175 x 246. Circ: 25,000.

621.389 DNK ISSN 0905-1740
HIGH FIDELITY (SWEDISH EDITION); ljud, bild och teknik. Variant title: Nya High Fidelity. Text in Swedish. 1987. 6/yr. DKK 596 (effective 2009). adv. **Document type:** *Magazine, Consumer.*
Related titles: ◆ Danish ed.: High Fidelity (Danish Edition). ISSN 0108-657X.
Published by: High Fidelity ApS, A. P. Moellers Alle 9 C, Dragoer, 2791, Denmark. TEL 45-70-237001, FAX 45-70-237002. Ed. Sven Bilen. Adv. contact Bettina Richards. page DKK 15,800; 175 x 246. Circ: 25,000.

621.389 JPN ISSN 1345-6113
HIVI. Text in Japanese. 1983. m. JPY 14,000 (effective 2008). adv. **Document type:** *Magazine, Consumer.*
Formerly: Sound Boy
Published by: Sutereo Saundo/Stereo Sound Publishing Inc., 3-8-4 Motoazabu, Minato-ku, Tokyo, 106-0046, Japan. Ed. Koji Yamamoto. Pub. Katsuyoshi Harada. Adv. contact Takazumi Arai.

621.389 NOR ISSN 1890-0291
HJEMMEKINO. Text in Norwegian. 2001. 11/yr. NOK 499; NOK 69 newsstand/cover (effective 2009). adv. **Document type:** *Magazine, Consumer.*
Former titles (until 2006): D V D og Hemmekino (1503-4488); (until 2002): Eyefi (1502-8216)
Published by: Hjemmet Mortensen AS, Gullhaugveien 1, Nydalen, Oslo, 0441, Norway. TEL 47-22-585000, FAX 47-22-585959, firmapost@hm-media.no, http://www.hm-media.no.

HOLLYWOOD MUSIC INDUSTRY DIRECTORY. *see* MUSIC

621.389 GBR ISSN 0957-6614
TK7881.4
HOME & STUDIO RECORDING; the magazine for the recording musician. Text in English. 1983. m. GBP 20 domestic; GBP 25 foreign. adv. bk.rev. **Description:** Focuses on recording for the home studio, with reviews of the latest recording equipment used in the home or project studio environment.
Formerly: Home Studio Recording
Published by: Music Maker Publications Ltd., Alexander House, Fore Hill, Ely, Cambs CB7 4AF, United Kingdom. TEL 44-1353-665577, FAX 44-1353-662489. Ed. Paul White. Circ: 20,000.

534 AUS ISSN 1442-2824
HOME CINEMA & HI-FI LIVING. Text in English. 1970. a. AUD 11, AUD 17 per issue (effective 2008). **Document type:** *Magazine, Consumer.* **Description:** Covers hi-fidelity systems and components; technical advice.
Former titles: Australian Hi-Fi Annual (0310-8902); (until 2000): Audio Yearbook (1329-0533)
Related titles: ◆ Supplement to: Australian Hi-Fi and Home Theatre Technology. ISSN 1442-1259.
Indexed: Pinpoint.
Published by: Wolseley Media Pty Ltd., Level 5, 55 Chandos St, PO Box 5555, St. Leonards, NSW 2065, Australia. TEL 61-2-99016100, FAX 61-2-99016198, contactsubs@wolseleymedia.com.au, http://www.wolseleymedia.com.au.

621.38 NLD ISSN 1875-3272
HOME EMOTION. Text in Dutch. 2007. q. EUR 15 domestic; EUR 18 in Belgium (effective 2009). adv. **Document type:** *Magazine, Consumer.*
Published by: Van der Geld Sales & Support b.v., Postbus 6808, Nijmegen, 6503 GH, Netherlands. TEL 31-24-3735881, FAX 31-24-3734148. Ed. Ivo van den Broek. Pub. Rene van der Geld.

621.389 384.558 791.43 JPN ISSN 1346-0390
HOMU SHIATA/HOME THEATER. Text in Japanese. 1999. q. JPY 8,720 (effective 2008). **Document type:** *Magazine, Consumer.*
Published by: Sutereo Saundo/Stereo Sound Publishing Inc., 3-8-4 Motoazabu, Minato-ku, Tokyo, 106-0046, Japan.

HORN SPEAKER; the newspaper for the hobbyist of vintage electronics and sound. *see* ANTIQUES

621.389 ZAF ISSN 1021-562X
ML26
I A S A JOURNAL. Text mainly in English; Text occasionally in German, French. 1971. 2/yr. GBP 100 to institutional members (effective 2002). bk.rev.; rec.rev.; video rev. bibl. **Document type:** *Academic/Scholarly.*
Formerly (until 1992): Phonographic Bulletin (0253-004X)
Indexed: BrHuml, CA, L04, L13, LISTA, RILM, T02.
—BLDSC (4359.540200). **CCC.**
Published by: International Association of Sound and Audiovisual Archives, c/o Ilse Assmann, South African Broadcasting Corporation, PO Box 931, Auckland Park, 2006, South Africa. TEL 44-20-7412-7411, FAX 44-20-7412-7413. Ed. Chris Clark. Circ: 450.

I T M PRAKTIKER - MULTI MEDIA UND ELEKTRONIK; die internationale Zeitschrift fuer Technik und Praxis, Industrie- und Konsumelektronik, Funk, Elektroakustik. *see* ENGINEERING—Electrical Engineering

ICHOS & EIKONA/SOUND & HI FI. *see* MUSIC

IMAGE HIFI. *see* ELECTRONICS

621.3 FIN ISSN 1797-030X
INNERWORLDAUDIO; sound, music, design. Text in English, Finnish. 2007. 5/yr. **Document type:** *Magazine, Consumer.*
Related titles: Online - full text ed.: ISSN 1797-0296.
Published by: Melomane, Harjuviita 22 A 10, Helsinki, 02100, Finland. TEL 358-4-7077721, http://www.melomane.fi. Ed. Kari Nevaleinen.

621.389 GBR ISSN 2046-3774
INSTALLATION EUROPE; audio, video, lighting. Abbreviated title: I E. Text in English. 1997. m. GBP 5, EUR 8 per issue; free to qualified personnel (effective 2011). adv. back issues avail. **Document type:** *Magazine, Trade.* **Description:** Delivers all the latest industry news for audio, video from the installation market across Europe.
Former titles (until 1999): Sound Installation; (until 1998): Sound Reinforcement Europe
Related titles: Online - full text ed.: free (effective 2011).
Published by: U B M Information Ltd. (Subsidiary of: United Business Media Limited), Ludgate House, 245 Blackfriars Rd, London, SE1 9UY, United Kingdom. TEL 44-20-79215000, FAX 44-20-79218060, communications@ubm.com, http://www.ubm.com. Ed. Paddy Baker TEL 44-20-79218317. Adv. contact Cara Turner TEL 44-20-79218363.

621.385 780 NLD ISSN 1383-2255
INTERFACE (AMSTERDAM, 1995). Text in Dutch. 1991. 10/yr. EUR 49.50 (effective 2010). adv. **Document type:** *Magazine, Consumer.*
Formerly (until 1995): Shiva M I D I Bulletin (0926-5465); Incorporates (2002-2008): Keyboard Plus (1570-5269); Which was formed by the merger of (1997-2002): Keyboards & M I D I (1385-9927); Which was formerly (until 1997): Orgel en Keyboard (0923-6937); (until 1989): Orgelwereld en Kyboardnieuws (0923-6929); (1980-1984): Orgelwereld (0923-6910); (1999-2002): Keys & Audio (1567-1879); Which was formerly (19??-1999): Midiklavier (1385-1136); Incorporates (in 1998): M I D I & Recording (1380-7250); Which was formerly (1989-1994): M I D I Magazine (0924-011X)
Published by: Interface Media bv, Postbus 11497, Amsterdam, 1001 GL, Netherlands. TEL 31-20-6755308, FAX 31-20-5312019. Eds. Jean-Louis Gayet, Mark van Schaick. Circ: 11,000.

621.389 GBR ISSN 1742-6758
▼ ➤ **INTERNATIONAL JOURNAL OF PRODUCT SOUND QUALITY.** Text in English. forthcoming 2011. 4/yr. **Document type:** *Journal, Academic/Scholarly.* **Description:** Aims to provide an international authoritative refereed reference in the multi-disciplinary field of product sound quality.
Related titles: Online - full text ed.: ISSN 1742-6766. forthcoming.
—CCC.
Published by: Inderscience Publishers, PO Box 735, Olney, Bucks MK46 5WB, United Kingdom. TEL 44-1234-240519, FAX 44-1234-240515, editorial@inderscience.com. Ed. Dr. M A Dorgham. **Subscr. to:** World Trade Centre Bldg, 29 Rte de Pre-Bois, Case Postale 856, Geneva 15 1215, Switzerland. FAX 41-22-7910885, subs@inderscience.com.

S

621.398 JPN ISSN 0388-158X
J A S JOURNAL. Text in Japanese. 1958. m. JPY 500 per issue.
Published by: Japan Audio Society/Nihon Odio Kyokai, 14-34 Jingu-Mae 1-chome, Shibuya-ku, Tokyo, 150-0001, Japan.

621.389 GBR ISSN 1754-9892
JOURNAL ON THE ART AND RECORD PRODUCTION. Abbreviated title: J A R P. Text in English. 2007 (Feb.). s-a. free to members (effective 2009). back issues avail. **Document type:** *Journal, Academic/Scholarly.*
Media: Online - full text.
Published by: Art of Record Production

621.389 JPN ISSN 1345-6148
KANKYU OKOKU. Text in Japanese. 1995. q. JPY 11,840 (effective 2008). **Document type:** *Magazine, Consumer.*
Published by: Sutereo Saundo/Stereo Sound Publishing Inc., 3-8-4 Motoazabu, Minato-ku, Tokyo, 106-0046, Japan.

621.389 658 GBR
KEY NOTE MARKET ASSESSMENT. IN-CAR ENTERTAINMENT. Variant title: In-Car Entertainment Market Assessment. Text in English. 1995. irreg., latest 2000, Oct. GBP 499 per issue (effective 2010). **Document type:** *Report, Trade.* **Description:** Provides strategic analysis across a broad range of industries and contains an examination on the scope, dynamics and shape of key UK markets in the consumer, financial, lifestyle and business to business sectors.
Formerly (until 2000): Key Note Market Report: In-Car Entertainment
Published by: Key Note Ltd. (Subsidiary of: Bonnier Business Information), Harlequin House, 5th Fl, 7 High St, Teddington, Richmond upon Thames, TW11 8EE, United Kingdom. TEL 44-845-5040452, FAX 44-845-5040453, info@keynote.co.uk.

KEYBOARDS RECORDING. *see* MUSIC

621.389 DEU ISSN 0933-0097
KLANG & TON; Lautsprecher-Selbstbau fuer HiFi, Heimkino und Beschallung. Text in German. 1986. bi-m. EUR 23.10; EUR 4.50 newsstand/cover (effective 2011). adv. **Document type:** *Magazine, Consumer.*
Published by: Michael E. Brieden Verlag GmbH, Gartroper Str 42, Duisburg, 47138, Germany. TEL 49-203-42920, FAX 49-203-4292149, info@brieden.de, http://www.brieden.de. Ed. Holger Barske. Adv. contact Udo Schulz. Circ: 25,000 (paid and controlled).

621.389 643 AUS
THE KOUCH. Text in English. 1996. irreg. **Description:** Covers hi-fi, multi-room hi-fi, home automation, home theatre and more.
Media: Online - full text.
Published by: Jim Tate Stereo, 323 Goodwood Rd, Kings Park, SA 5034, Australia. TEL 61-8-83732323, FAX 61-8-83833176, helpline@jimtatestereo.com.au, http://www.jimtatestereo.com.au.

LANGUAGE LEARNING JOURNAL. *see* LINGUISTICS

621.389 NLD ISSN 2211-9760
▼ **LINEAR AUDIO.** Text in English. 2010. s-a. EUR 21.50 newsstand/cover (effective 2011). bk.rev. **Document type:** *Magazine, Consumer.* **Description:** Provides technical information, developments and the state of the art of audio from a technical perspective.
Published by: Linear Audio Publishing, Opbraakstraat 60, Hoensbroek, 6432 BP, Netherlands. sales@linearaudio.net. Ed., Pub. Jan Didden.

621.389 USA ISSN 1079-0888
TK7881.9
LIVE SOUND! INTERNATIONAL. Text in English. 1992. 8/yr. USD 60 in US, Canada & Mexico; USD 140 elsewhere (effective 2007). adv. bk.rev.; music rev. illus.; tr.lit. back issues avail.; reprints avail. **Document type:** *Magazine, Trade.* **Description:** Dedicated solely to the performance audio disciplines of music, threatre corporate and industrial presentations and sacred gatherings.
Formerly: Live Sound! and Touring Technology (1066-0224)
Related titles: Online - full text ed.
Address: 169 Beulah St, San Francisco, CA 94117. TEL 415-387-4009, FAX 415-752-8144. Ed. Keith Clark. Pub. Mark Herman. Adv. contact Julie Clark. page USD 4,647; trim 10.88 x 8.38. Circ: 27,000.

621.389 JPN ISSN 1345-8817
M J MUSEN TO JIKKEN/AUDIO TECHNOLOGY. Text in Japanese. 1924. m. JPY 13,540 (effective 2008). **Document type:** *Magazine, Consumer.*
Formerly: Musen to Jikken
Published by: Seibundo Shinkosha Inc., 3-3-11 Hongo, Bunkyoku, Tokyo, 164-0013, Japan. TEL 81-3-58005775, FAX 81-3-58005773, http://www.seibundo-shinkosha.net/. Circ: 60,000.

MAGAZYN HI-FI. *see* ELECTRONICS

▼ **MEDIAZINE KOOPGIDS. BEELD EN GELUID.** *see* COMMUNICATIONS—Video

MIX ANNUAL DIRECTORY OF RECORDING INDUSTRY FACILITIES AND SERVICES. *see* BUSINESS AND ECONOMICS—Trade And Industrial Directories

620.2 USA ISSN 0164-9957
ML74.7
MIX MAGAZINE; professional audio & music production. Text in English. 1977. m. USD 35.97 domestic; USD 48 in Canada & Mexico; USD 60 elsewhere; USD 41.97 combined subscription domestic (print & online eds.); USD 54 combined subscription in Canada & Mexico (print & online eds.); USD 66 combined subscription elsewhere (print & online eds.) (effective 2011). adv. bk.rev.; software rev. illus. back issues avail. **Document type:** *Magazine, Consumer.* **Description:** Covers the entire spectrum of audio and music for readers, including professionals involved in studio recording, live sound production, sound for picture, digital audio technology, facility design, broadcast production and education.
Related titles: Online - full text ed.
Indexed: A09, A10, A15, ABIn, B01, B06, B07, B09, BPI, BRD, F01, F02, I05, IBT&D, IIMP, IIPA, M01, M02, M11, MAG, P48, P51, P52, PQC, PROMT, T02, V02, V03, V04, W01, W02, W03, W05.
—CIS, IE, Ingenta. **CCC.**
Published by: Penton Media, Inc., 6400 Hollis St, Ste 12, Emeryville, CA 94608. TEL 510-653-3307, FAX 510-653-5142, information@penton.com, http://www.pentonmedia.com. Circ: 53,671.

621.389 AUS ISSN 1441-1822
MIXDOWN MONTHLY. Text in English. 1994. m. AUD 36 (effective 2008). **Document type:** *Magazine, Consumer.*
Published by: Furst Media Pty Ltd., 3 Newton St, Richmond, VIC 3121, Australia. TEL 61-3-94283600, FAX 61-3-94283611, info@furstmedia.com.au, http://www.furstmedia.com.au.

MIXTAPE. *see* MUSIC

MOBILE BEAT; the DJ magazine. *see* MUSIC

MUSIC AND SOUND RETAILER; the newsmagazine for musical instrument and sound product merchandisers. *see* MUSIC

621.389 NLD ISSN 1872-6399
MUSIC EMOTION. Text in Dutch. 2005. m. (11/yr.). EUR 39.95 domestic; EUR 44.95 in Belgium (effective 2009). adv. **Document type:** *Magazine, Consumer.*
Published by: Van der Geld Sales & Support b.v., Postbus 6808, Nijmegen, 6503 GH, Netherlands. TEL 31-24-3735881, FAX 31-24-3734148. Ed. Ivo van den Broek. Pub. Rene van der Geld.

MUSIK & LJUDTEKNIK. *see* MUSIC

MUSIKINDUSTRIE IN ZAHLEN. *see* MUSIC

621.389 USA ISSN 1051-5097
ML1055
N A R A S JOURNAL. Text in English. 1990. s-a. membership only.
Indexed: MusicInd.
—Ingenta.
Published by: National Academy of Recording Arts and Sciences, 3402 Pico Blvd, Santa Monica, CA 90405-2118.

▼ **THE NEW SOUNDTRACK.** *see* MOTION PICTURES

620.2 GBR
NOSTALGIA. Text in English. 1969. q. GBP 2. adv. bk.rev. charts; illus.
Incorporates: Street Singer
Address: c/o Charlie Wilson, 39 Leicester Rd, New Barnet, Barnet, Herts EN5 5EW, United Kingdom.

621.389 GBR ISSN 0268-8786
ONE TO ONE (LONDON); technology and business for media manufacturers. Text in English. 1985. bi-m. free to qualified personnel (effective 2010). adv. charts; illus.; stat. **Document type:** *Magazine, Trade.* **Description:** Covers the international mastering, vinyl and CD pressing, and tape duplication industries.
Related titles: Online - full text ed.
Indexed: A09, A10, A15, ABIn, B03, B11, P16, P48, P51, P52, P53, P54, PQC, PROMT, V03, V04.
—IE. **CCC.**
Published by: U B M Information Ltd. (Subsidiary of: United Business Media Limited), Ludgate House, 245 Blackfriars Rd, London, SE1 9UY, United Kingdom. TEL 44-20-79215000, FAX 44-20-79218060, http://www.unitedbusinessmedia.com. Ed. Elizabeth Toppin TEL 44-1600-890623. Pub. Joe Hosken TEL 44-20-79218336. adv.: page GBP 3,563, page EUR 4,110, page USD 5,787; trim 245 x 335.

621.389 DEU ISSN 1437-5699
P M A PRODUCTION MANAGEMENT; das Magazin fuer Studio- und Veranstaltungsproduktion. Text in German. 1999. bi-m. EUR 40.80 domestic; EUR 48.60 foreign; EUR 7.60 newsstand/cover (effective 2008). adv. **Document type:** *Magazine, Trade.* **Description:** Provides information and insight on all aspects of music studio production, recording and management.
Related titles: Online - full text ed.
Published by: P P V Medien GmbH, Postfach 57, Bergkirchen, 85230, Germany. TEL 49-8131-56550, FAX 49-8131-565510, ppv@ppvmedien.de, http://www.ppvmedien.de. Ed. Tom Becker. Adv. contact Bianca Klessinger. B&W page EUR 2,000, color page EUR 3,200. Circ: 7,200 (paid and controlled).

PHOTO VIDEO AUDIO NEWS (FRENCH EDITION). *see* PHOTOGRAPHY

621.389 GBR ISSN 0952-2360
PLAYBACK. Text in English. 1956. s-a. free (effective 2010). back issues avail. **Document type:** *Bulletin, Trade.* **Description:** Provides information on the Archive's current and future activities, and news from the world of sound archives and audio preservation.
Former titles (until 1992): Recorded Sound (0034-1630); (until 1961): British Institute of Recorded Sound. Bulletin (0524-6253)
Related titles: Online - full text ed.
Indexed: M11, MLA-IB.
—BLDSC (6539.142000). **CCC.**
Published by: (British Library National Sound Archive), British Library, St Pancras, 96 Euston Rd, London, NW1 2DB, United Kingdom. TEL 44-870-4441500, FAX 44-1937-546860, Customer-Services@bl.uk. Ed. Alan Ward.

621.389 USA
TK7881.4
POSITIVE FEEDBACK (ONLINE). Text in English. 1990. q. USD 20; USD 50 foreign. **Document type:** *Magazine, Consumer.*
Formerly: Positive Feedback (Print) (1082-2178)
Published by: Positive Feedback Online, 9138 SE Hunters Bluff Ave, Portland, OR 97266-9133. TEL 503-771-6200, FAX 503-771-6400, dclark@positive-feedback.com. Ed. David W Robinson.

POST (CLEVELAND); where technology and talent meet. *see* COMMUNICATIONS

PRO AUDIO REVIEW. *see* ELECTRONICS

621.389 338.4 USA ISSN 0164-6338
PRO SOUND NEWS; the international newsmagazine for the professional recording & sound production industry. Text in English. 1978. m. USD 59 domestic; USD 109 in Canada; USD 169 elsewhere; USD 10 newsstand/cover; free to qualified personnel (effective 2008). adv. reprints avail. **Document type:** *Magazine, Consumer.* **Description:** Addresses issues of interest to the pro audio industry such as studio owners, producers, engineers, record artists, manufacturers and top decision makers.
Related titles: Online - full text ed.
Indexed: A09, A10, A15, ABIn, B01, B02, B03, B07, B15, B17, B18, G04, G08, I05, P16, P48, P51, P52, P53, P54, PQC, V03, V04.
—CIS. **CCC.**
Published by: NewBay Media, LLC (Subsidiary of: The Wicks Group of Companies, LLC.), 810 Seventh Ave, 27th Fl, New York, NY 10019. TEL 212-378-0400, FAX 212-378-0470, customerservice@nbmedia.com, http://www.nbmedia.com. Ed. Frank Wells TEL 615-848-1769. Pub. Margaret Sekelsky TEL 516-641-0259. Circ: 25,000.

621.389 GBR ISSN 0269-4735
PRO SOUND NEWS EUROPE. Abbreviated title: P S N E. Text in English. 1986. m. free to qualified personnel (effective 2010). adv. bk.rev. charts; illus. back issues avail. **Document type:** *Magazine, Trade.* **Description:** Provides news items and features on the technological, marketing and operational aspects of the European sound production industry, focusing on tour and studio equipment and production, technical developments by country, and product surveys.
Related titles: Online - full text ed.: free (effective 2010).
Indexed: A15, ABIn, I05, P48, P51, P52, PQC, PROMT.
—CCC.
Published by: U B M Information Ltd. (Subsidiary of: United Business Media Limited), Ludgate House, 245 Blackfriars Rd, London, SE1 9UY, United Kingdom. TEL 44-20-79215000, FAX 44-20-79218060, http://www.unitedbusinessmedia.com. Ed. David Robinson TEL 44-20-79218319. Adv. contact Steve Connolly TEL 44-20-79218316. page GBP 2,635, page EUR 3,625, page USD 5,168; trim 245 x 335. Circ: 8,458.

PRODUCAO PROFISSIONAL. *see* COMMUNICATIONS—Television And Cable

PRODUCAO PROFISSIONAL. *see* COMMUNICATIONS—Television And Cable

PRODUCCION PROFESIONAL. *see* COMMUNICATIONS—Television And Cable

621.389 DEU ISSN 0938-4073
PRODUCTION PARTNER; Das Fachmagazin fuer Beschallung, Licht, Buhne, Event-Technik und Projektion. Text in German. 1990. 10/yr. EUR 61 domestic; EUR 69 foreign; EUR 7.10 newsstand/cover (effective 2011). adv. **Document type:** *Magazine, Trade.*
Incorporates (1990-2002): Audio Professional (0941-5084); (1986-1990): Magazin fuer Studiotechnik (0930-4215)
Indexed: TM.
Published by: Musik - Media Verlag GmbH (Subsidiary of: Ebner Verlag GmbH), Emil-Hoffmann-Str 13, Cologne, 50996, Germany. TEL 49-2236-962170, FAX 49-2236-962175, info@musikmedia.de, http://www.musikmedia.de. Ed. Walter Wehrhan. Adv. contact Angelika Mueller. Circ: 4,783 (paid and controlled).

621.389 780 DEU
PRODUCTIV'S SOLO. Text in German. 1987. bi-m. adv. back issues avail. **Document type:** *Consumer.* **Description:** Tests of music equipment, stories and interviews.
Published by: Musik Productiv, Gildestr 60, Ibbenbueren, 49477, Germany. TEL 49-5451-909200, FAX 49-5451-909207. Ed. Christoph Rocholl. Adv. contact Birgit Bovenschulte. Circ: 45,000.

621.389 DEU
PROFESSIONAL AUDIO; das Magazin fuer Aufnahmetechnik. Text in German. 2006. m. EUR 66; EUR 6.50 newsstand/cover (effective 2011). adv. **Document type:** *Magazine, Trade.*
Former titles (until 2011): Professional Audio Musik und Equipment (1869-1943); (until 2009): Professional Audio-Magazin (1862-5371)
Published by: Sonic Media Verlag GmbH, Hauptstr 31, Bad Honnef, 53604, Germany. TEL 49-2224-988260, FAX 49-2224-9882679, info@sonic-media-verlag.de, http://www.sonic-media-verlag.de. Ed. Hans-Guenther Beer. Adv. contact Claudia Wagner.

621.389 JPN ISSN 1345-6121
PROSOUND. Text in Japanese. 1984. bi-m. JPY 11,880 (effective 2008). adv. **Document type:** *Magazine, Consumer.*
Formerly: Tape Sound
Published by: Sutereo Saundo/Stereo Sound Publishing Inc., 3-8-4 Motoazabu, Minato-ku, Tokyo, 106-0046, Japan. Ed. Susumu Nakamura. Pub. Katsuyoshi Harada. Adv. contact Takazumi Arai.

RECORD EXCHANGER. *see* MUSIC

621.389 USA ISSN 1078-8352
TK7881.4
RECORDING; the magazine for the recording musician. Text in English. 1987. m. USD 19.95 domestic; USD 31.95 in Canada; USD 44.95 elsewhere; USD 3.50 newsstand/cover (effective 2005). adv. bk.rev. back issues avail. **Document type:** *Magazine, Trade.* **Description:** Focuses on recording in the home and studio environment. Features reviews of the latest available recording equipment and articles on techniques and applications.
Formerly (until 1994): Home and Studio Recording (0896-7172); Incorporates (1987-1990): Music Technology (0896-2480); Which was formerly (1986-1987): Music Technology Magazine (0891-7264)
Related titles: Spanish ed.: Recording (Spanish Edition). ISSN 1078-8670. 1993.
—Ingenta.
Published by: Music Maker Publications Inc., 5412 Idylwild Trail, Ste. 100, Boulder, CO 80301-3523. TEL 303-516-9118, FAX 303-516-9119. Eds. Lorenz Rychner, Nicholas Batzdorf. Pubs. Tom Hawley, Tom Hawley. Adv. contacts Jim Donnelly, Brent Heintz. Circ: 42,000.

789.9 FRA ISSN 1298-115X
LA REVUE DU SON & DU HOME CINEMA. Text in French. 1953. m. EUR 45 (effective 2008). adv. bk.rev.; rec.rev. abstr.; bibl.; charts; illus.; tr.lit. index. **Document type:** *Magazine, Consumer.*
Former titles (until 1999): Nouvelle Revue du Son (0397-3190); (until 1976): Revue du Son (0035-2675); Which incorporated (1951-1956): Arts et Techniques Sonores (1153-8376)
Indexed: PdeR, RASB.
—INIST, Linda Hall.
Published by: Mondadori France, 1 Rue du Colonel Pierre-Avia, Paris, Cedex 15 75754, France. TEL 33-1-41335001, contact@mondadori.fr, http://www.mondadori.fr. Circ: 39,000.

ROOTS & RHYTHM NEWSLETTER. *see* MUSIC

621.389 GBR ISSN 2045-5070
▼ **S O S SMART GUIDES (UK EDITION).** (Sound on Sound) Text in English. 2010. irreg. GBP 7.99 per issue (effective 2011). **Document type:** *Handbook/Manual/Guide, Consumer.* **Description:** Designed to accompany the Smart Guides series published by Sound on Sound magazine.
Published by: S O S Publications Group, Media House, Trafalgar Way, Bar Hill, Cambridge, CB23 8SQ, United Kingdom. TEL 44-1954-789888, FAX 44-1954-789895.

621.389 GBR ISSN 2047-0762
▼ **S O S SMART GUIDES (USA EDITION).** (Sound On Sound) Text in English. 2010. q. **Document type:** *Handbook/Manual/Guide, Trade.*

Published by: SOS Publications, Media House, Trafalgar Way, Bar Hill, Cambridge, CB23 8SQ, United Kingdom. TEL 44-1954-789888, FAX 44-1954-789895, news@soundonsound.com, http://www.soundonsound.com/.

789.9 USA ISSN 1525-6138
SONGWRITER'S MONTHLY; the stories behind today's songs. Text in English. 1992. m. **Document type:** *Magazine, Trade.*
Address: 332 Eastwood Ave, Feasterville, PA 19053. TEL 215-953-0952, http://www.lafay.com/sm. Ed. Allen Foster. Circ: 2,500.

621.389 FRA ISSN 0243-4938
SONO MAGAZINE; light-show, orchestres, discotheques. Text in French. 1975. m. (except Aug.). EUR 29.90 (effective 2009).
Former titles (1978): Le Haut-Parleur. Sono (0243-492X); (until 1976): Le Haut-Parleur. Questions & Reponses (0248-7659)
Indexed: CMPI.
Published by: Publications Georges Ventillard, 12 rue de Bellevue, 2A, Paris, 75019, France. TEL 33-1-44848484, FAX 33-1-42418940. Ed. Jean Paul Poincignon. Pub. Jean Pierre Ventillard. Circ: 25,498.

621.382 USA ISSN 0038-1845
QC228.3
SOUND & COMMUNICATIONS. Text in English. 1955. m. USD 25 (effective 2005). adv. bk.rev. **Document type:** *Magazine, Trade.* **Description:** Covers contracting, engineering, design and construction in the sound, video, and communications fields.
Indexed: CMM, S&VD.
Published by: Testa Communications, Inc., 25 Willowdale Ave, Port Washington, NY 11050. TEL 516-767-2500, FAX 516-944-8372, 516-767-9335. Ed. David Silverman. Pub. Vincent P Testa. Circ: 20,300 (paid and controlled).

621.389 DEU ISSN 1862-4863
SOUND & RECORDING; producer, engineer, composer & musician. Text in German. 2006. m. EUR 50.65 domestic; EUR 62.90 foreign; EUR 5.50 newsstand/cover (effective 2011). adv. **Document type:** *Magazine, Trade.*
Published by: Musik - Media Verlag GmbH (Subsidiary of: Ebner Verlag GmbH), Emil-Hoffmann-Str 13, Cologne, 50996, Germany. TEL 49-2236-962170, FAX 49-2236-962175, info@musikmedia.de, http://www.musikmedia.de. Eds. Gerald Dellmann, Walter Wehrhan. Adv. contact Christiane Weyres. Circ: 11,112 (paid and controlled).

621.38833 USA ISSN 0741-1715
SOUND & VIDEO CONTRACTOR. Abbreviated title: S V C. Text in English. 1983. m. USD 33 in US & Canada; USD 67 elsewhere; free to qualified personnel (effective 2011). adv. tr.lit. back issues avail. **Document type:** *Magazine, Trade.* **Description:** Reaches an international readership of contractors, designers, engineers and installers in the areas of sound, video, security, communications, data transmission, home theater and residential electronics systems.
Related titles: Microform ed.: (from PQC); Online - full text ed.: ISSN 2161-959X.
Indexed: A01, A03, A05, A08, A09, A10, A15, A26, ABIn, AS&TA, AS&TI, B04, B07, BRD, C10, CA, E08, G06, G07, G08, I05, P16, P26, P52, P53, P54, PQC, S04, S09, T02, V03, V04, W03, W05.
—CIS. **CCC.**
Published by: Penton Media, Inc., 249 W 17th St, New York, NY 10011. TEL 212-204-4200, FAX 212-206-3622, information@penton.com, http://www.penton.com. Ed. Cynthia Wisehart TEL 818-236-3667. Adv. contact Adam Goldstein.

789.9 USA ISSN 1537-5838
TK7881.3
SOUND & VISION; home theater - audio - video - multimedia - movies - music. Text in English. 1999. 10/yr. USD 12 domestic; USD 22 foreign; USD 4.50 newsstand/cover (effective 2008). adv. bk.rev.; film rev.; music rev.; rec.rev.; video rev. charts; illus. index. Supplement avail.; back issues avail.; reprints avail. **Document type:** *Magazine, Consumer.* **Description:** Offers readers reliable information on all types of entertainment electronics, including home theatre, stereo, video, and multimedia.
Formerly (until 2003): Stereo Review's Sound and Vision (1522-810X); Which was formed by the merger of (1978-1999): Video Magazine (1044-7288); Which was formerly (until 1987): Video (New York) (0147-8907); (1960-1999): Stereo Review (0039-1220); Which was formerly (until 1968): HiFi Stereo Review (1045-3474); Superseded (1959-1989): High Fidelity (0018-1455); Which was formerly (until 1959): High Fidelity & Audiocraft; Which was formed by the merger of (1957-1958): Audiocraft for the Hi-Fi Hobbyist; (1951-1958): High Fidelity (0735-925X)
Related titles: Diskette ed.; Online - full text ed.: Stereo Review's Sound & Vision Online. USD 15 (effective 2008).
Indexed: A01, A02, A03, A08, A09, A10, A11, A22, A25, A26, ARG, Acal, B04, BRD, C05, C10, C12, CBRI, CPerI, ConsI, E08, F01, F02, G05, G06, G07, G08, G09, I05, I07, IIMP, M01, M02, M11, MAG, MASUSE, MagInd, MicrocompInd, MusicInd, P02, P10, P16, P48, P53, P54, PMR, PQC, R03, R04, R06, RASB, RGAb, RGPR, RILM, S08, S09, TOM, V03, V04, W03.
—Ingenta, Linda Hall. **CCC.**
Published by: Hachette Filipacchi Media U.S., Inc. (Subsidiary of: Hachette Filipacchi Medias S.A.), 1633 Broadway, New York, NY 10019. TEL 212-767-6000, FAX 212-767-5600, flyedit@hfmus.com, http://www.hfmus.com. Eds. Rob Medich, Mike Mettler. Pub. Stephen Shepherd TEL 212-767-6203. adv.: B&W page USD 43,860, color page USD 61,400; trim 7.8 x 10.5. Circ: 500,000 (paid). **Dist. by:** Curtis Circulation Co.

338.4 USA ISSN 1537-0798
SOUND & VISION BUYERS' GUIDE. Text in English. 1957. a. USD 5.95 newsstand/cover (effective 2007). adv. **Document type:** *Magazine, Consumer.*
Former titles: Stereo Buyers' Guide (1060-8133); (until 198?): Stereo Review's Stereo Buyers' Guide (0736-6515); Stereo Directory and Buying Guide (0090-6786); Stereo Hi-Fi Directory (0081-5470)
Indexed: A22.
Published by: Hachette Filipacchi Media U.S., Inc. (Subsidiary of: Hachette Filipacchi Medias S.A.), 1633 Broadway, New York, NY 10019. TEL 212-767-6000, FAX 212-767-5600, saleshfmbooks@hfmus.com, http://www.hfmus.com. Circ: 200,000 (paid and controlled).

SOUND CHOICE. *see* MUSIC

SOUND ON SOUND. *see* MUSIC

621.388 GBR ISSN 1755-8387
SOUND VISION INSTALL; the trade's finest home electronics resource. Abbreviated title: S V I. Text in English. 2002. m. GBP 2.95 per issue (effective 2009). adv. **Document type:** *Magazine, Trade.*
Former titles (until 2007): What's New Sound Vision Install (1747-7492); (until 2005): What's New in Sound and Vision (1478-1123)
Related titles: Online - full text ed.: free (effective 2009).
—**CCC.**
Published by: Aceville Publications Ltd., 21-23 Phoenix Ct, Hawkins Rd, Colchester, Essex CO2 8JY, United Kingdom. TEL 44-1206-505962, FAX 44-1206-505915, aceville@servicehelpline.co.uk, http://www.aceville.com. Ed. Jacob Stow. Pub. Matthew Tudor. Adv. contact Bonnie Howard TEL 44-1206-506249. color page GBP 950; trim 210 x 297. **Subscr. to:** 800 Guillat Ave, Kent Science Park, Sittingbourne, Kent ME9 8GU, United Kingdom. TEL 44-844-8440381, FAX 44-845-4567143.

780.7094105 GBR ISSN 1464-6730
SOUNDING BOARD. Text in English. 1990. q. free to members (effective 2009). **Document type:** *Journal, Consumer.* **Description:** Features news, opinions, discussion and debates about community music.
Published by: Sound Sense, 7 Tavern St, Stowmarket, Suffolk IP14 1PJ, United Kingdom. TEL 44-1449-673990, FAX 44-1449-673994, info@soundsense.org.

SOUNDTRACK; the journal for music & media. *see* MUSIC

SPIN. *see* MUSIC

621.389 798.91 JPN ISSN 0289-3622
STEREO. Text in Japanese. 1963. m. JPY 980. adv. **Document type:** *Consumer.* **Description:** Provides information aimed at lovers of record playing and audio techniques.
Published by: Ongaku No Tomo Sha Corp., c/o KakuyukiNabeshima, 6-30 Kagura-Zaka, Shinjuku-ku, Tokyo, 162-0825, Japan. FAX 81-3-3235-2129. Ed. Seizaburo Mogami. Pub. Jun Meguro. R&P Tetsuo Morita TEL 81-3-3235-2111. Adv. contact Takao Oya. B&W page JPY 336,000, color page JPY 624,000; trim 182 x 257. Circ: 150,000.

780.5 DEU ISSN 0340-0778
ML5
STEREO; Magazin fuer HiFi - High End - Musik. Text in German. 1974. m. EUR 54; EUR 5.30 newsstand/cover (effective 2011). adv. illus. **Document type:** *Magazine, Consumer.*
Related titles: Online - full text ed.
Published by: Reiner H. Nitschke Verlags GmbH, Eifelring 28, Euskirchen, 53879, Germany. TEL 49-2251-650460, FAX 49-2251-6504699, service@nitschke-verlag.de. Ed. Michael Lang. Adv. contact Ilhami Duzgun. **Subscr. to:** P M S GmbH & Co. KG, Postfach 104139, Duesseldorf 40032, Germany. TEL 49-211-6907890, FAX 49-211-69078950.

621.389 AUS ISSN 0819-0216
STEREO BUYER'S GUIDE. AUDIO YEARBOOK. Text in English. 1971. a. **Document type:** *Handbook/Manual/Guide, Consumer.* **Description:** Hi-fidelity component product reviews and buying advice.
Former titles (until 1987): Australian Hi-Fi Stereo Buyer's Guide Manual. Audio Yearbook (0816-3227); (until 1986): Australian Hi-Fi Stereo Buyer's Guide. Manual (0312-0058)
Published by: Words Words Words, PO Box 209, Church Point, NSW 2105, Australia. Ed. Greg Borrowman.

621.387 AUS ISSN 0819-0194
STEREO BUYER'S GUIDE. LOUDSPEAKERS, AMPLIFIERS AND TUNERS. Text in English. 1971. a. **Document type:** *Handbook/Manual/Guide, Consumer.* **Description:** Loudspeaker, amplifier and tuner reviews, and buying advice.
Former titles: Stereo Buyer's Guide. Amplifiers, FM Tuners and Receivers (0727-4459); Stereo Buyer's Guide. Amplifiers
Published by: Words Words Words, PO Box 209, Church Point, NSW 2105, Australia. Ed. Greg Borrowman.

621.389 JPN ISSN 1345-6105
STEREO SOUND. Text in Japanese. 1967. q. JPY 10,100 (effective 2008). adv. **Document type:** *Magazine, Consumer.*
Published by: Sutereo Saundo/Stereo Sound Publishing Inc., 3-8-4 Motoazabu, Minato-ku, Tokyo, 106-0046, Japan. Ed. Kaoru Nakamura. Pub. Katsuyoshi Harada. Adv. contact Takazumi Arai.

621.389 USA ISSN 0585-2544
TK7881.8
STEREOPHILE. Text in English. 1962. m. USD 12.97 domestic; USD 24.97 in Canada; USD 36.97 elsewhere (effective 2010). adv. bk.rev.; music rev.; rec.rev. illus. Index. back issues avail.; reprints avail. **Document type:** *Magazine, Consumer.* **Description:** Provides information on music and music reproduction.
Related titles: Online - full text ed.
Indexed: G06, G07, G08, I05, M11, RILM, S23.
—Ingenta. **CCC.**
Published by: Source Interlink Companies, 6420 Wilshire Blvd, 10th Fl, Los Angeles, CA 90048. TEL 323-782-2000, FAX 323-782-2585, dheine@sourceinterlink.com, http://www.sourceinterlinkmedia.com. Ed. John Atkinson. Pub., Adv. contact Keith Pray TEL 212-915-4157. B&W page USD 11,065, color page USD 14,570; trim 7.5 x 10.25. Circ: 74,000 (paid).

621.389 USA ISSN 1528-5391
ML3790
SURROUND PROFESSIONAL. Text in English. 1998. bi-m. USD 30 in US & Canada; USD 60 elsewhere; free to qualified personnel (effective 2006). adv. **Document type:** *Magazine, Trade.*
Related titles: Online - full text ed.
Indexed: B02, B15, B17, B18, CompD, G04, G08, I05, P16, P48, P52, P53, P54, PQC.
Published by: C M P Entertainment Media, Inc. (Subsidiary of: C M P Information Ltd.), 810 Seventh Ave., 27th Fl, New York, NY 10019. TEL 212-378-0400, FAX 212-378-2160, http://www.cmpemedia.com/. adv.: B&W page USD 4,040, color page USD 5,270; trim 8.375 x 10.75. Circ: 21,500 (controlled).

621.389 GBR
TALKING MACHINE REVIEW INTERNATIONAL. Text in English. 1962. q. GBP 12 in Europe; USD 25 in US & Canada; GBP 15 elsewhere. adv. bk.rev.; rec.rev. charts; illus.; pat. index. back issues avail. **Document type:** *Journal, Consumer.* **Description:** Covers the history of sound recordings, discographies, artists, techniques and developments in archival-retrieval systems of disc, cylinder and other pre-CD-digital recordings. Provides histories of people and companies in the recording industry.
Formerly: Talking Machine Review (0039-9191)
Published by: International Talking Machine Review, 105 Sturdee Ave, Gillingham Rd, Gillingham, Kent ME7 4RR, United Kingdom. TEL 44-1634-851823, FAX 44-1634-851823. Ed., Pub., R&P, Adv. contact John W Booth. Circ: 1,000. **Subscr. in US & Canada to:** W. Klinger, 13532 Bass Lake Rd, Chardon, OH 44024. TEL 216-564-9340.

621.389 USA
TAPE OP; the creative music recording magazine. Text in English. 1996. bi-m. USD 12 domestic; USD 37.50 foreign (effective 2001). adv. **Document type:** *Magazine, Trade.* **Description:** Provides insight and information on the creative processes and technologies within recording studios.
Address: PO Box 14517, Portland, OR 97293. TEL 503-239-5389, FAX 503-239-5389, info@tapeop.com, gearads@tapeop.com. Ed. Larry Crane. Adv. contact John Baccigaluppi.

THE TEXAS MUSIC INDUSTRY DIRECTORY. *see* BUSINESS AND ECONOMICS—Trade And Industrial Directories

621.389 DEU ISSN 0948-9185
TON - VIDEO REPORT. Text in German. 1957. bi-m. EUR 2.60 newsstand/cover (effective 2005). adv. bk.rev. **Document type:** *Magazine, Consumer.*
Formerly (until 1993): Ton - Report
Published by: Ring der Tonband- und Videofreunde e.V., Bahnhofstr 71, Waiblingen, 71332, Germany. TEL 49-7151-59394, FAX 49-7151-55122. Ed. Guenter Schassberger. Circ: 4,000.

621.389 DEU
TONMEISTER INFORMATIONEN. Text in German. 1985. bi-m. bk.rev.
Published by: Verband Deutscher Tonmeister, Wallensteinstr 121, Nuernberg, 90431, Germany. TEL 0911-6590-482, FAX 0911-6590-199.

621.389 DEU ISSN 1613-4443
TOOLS 4 MUSIC. Text in German. 2001. bi-m. EUR 18.90 (effective 2005). adv. **Document type:** *Magazine, Consumer.*
Published by: P N P Verlag, Ringstr 33, Neumarkt, 92318, Germany. TEL 49-9181-463730, FAX 49-9181-463732, info@pnp-verlag.de, http://www.pnp-verlag.de. Ed. Christoph Rocholl. Adv. contact Tina Mueller.

621.389 789.49 USA ISSN 1093-3182
TK7881.4
ULTIMATE AUDIO; defining excellence. Text in English. 1997. 4/yr. USD 18.95 domestic; USD 24.95 in Canada; USD 39.95 elsewhere; USD 3.95 newsstand/cover. adv. bk.rev.; music rev.; software rev. illus. back issues avail. **Document type:** *Magazine, Consumer.* **Description:** Features reports on the finest new state-of-the-art home audio electronic components, covering all technological advances. Reviews top CDs and LPs.
Address: 304 Park Ave S, 11th Fl, New York, NY 10010. TEL 718-796-2825, FAX 718-796-6247. Ed. Thomas O'Neil. Pub. Myles B Astor. Adv. contact Beth Kuda. Circ: 10,000. **Dist. by:** Ingram Periodicals Inc., 1240 Heil Quaker Blvd, Box 7000, La Vergne, TN 37086. TEL 800-627-6247.

620.2 GBR
VINTAGE RECORD MART. Text in English. 1970. bi-m. GBP 3.60. adv. charts.
Address: 16 London Hill, Rayleigh, Essex SS6 7HP, United Kingdom. Ed. Frank K Bailey. Circ: 400.

789.9 USA ISSN 0042-8299
VOICESPONDENT. Text in English. 1953. q. USD 5 (effective 2000). adv. **Document type:** *Newsletter.*
Related titles: Audio cassette/tape ed.
Published by: Voicespondence Club, 2373 S York St, Denver, CO 80210-5340. TEL 303-733-1078. Ed., R&P Gail Selfridge. Adv. contact Charles Owen. Circ: 500 (paid).

621.389 004.565 621.388 FRA ISSN 1770-0426
WHAT HI-FI? SON & HOME CINEMA. Text in French. 2003. m. EUR 30 (effective 2008). back issues avail. **Document type:** *Magazine, Consumer.*
Published by: B & B Media, 40 Rue de Paradis, Paris, 75010, France. TEL 33-1-53249970, FAX 33-1-53249979, info@bandbmedia.com.

621.389 GBR ISSN 1474-2764
WHAT HI-FI? SOUND AND VISION. Text in English. 1975 (vol.5). 13/yr. GBP 44.75 (effective 2009). adv. charts; illus.; tr.lit. back issues avail. **Document type:** *Magazine, Consumer.* **Description:** Offers news, insight into the latest issues and a place for buyers to exchange advice and opinions on hot products and technologies.
Former titles (until 2001): What Hi-Fi? (0309-3336); (until 1976): Popular Hi-Fi; Incorporates (2000-2001): D V D (1470-3769)
Related titles: Supplement to: What Hi-Fi? Sound and Vision. Ultimate Guide. ISSN 1740-8660.
Indexed: U01.
—BLDSC (9309.737100). **CCC.**
Published by: Haymarket Publishing Ltd. (Subsidiary of: Haymarket Media Group), Teddington Studios, Broom Rd, Teddington, Middlesex, TW11 9BE, United Kingdom. TEL 44-20-82675050, FAX 44-20-82675844, info@haymarket.com, http://www.haymarket.com. Ed. Clare Newsome. Circ: 55,373. **Subscr. to:** PO Box 568, Haywards Heath RH16 3XQ, United Kingdom. TEL 44-8456-777800, Haymarket.subs@qss-uk.com, http://www.themagazineshop.com.

591.594 GBR ISSN 0963-3251
WILDLIFE SOUND. Text in English. 19??. s-a. free to members (effective 2009). **Document type:** *Journal, Academic/Scholarly.* **Description:** Covers information about Wildlife Sound Recording Society.
Indexed: Z01.
Published by: Wildlife Sound Recording Society, c/o Robert C Boughton, Croftfoot, Ennerdale Cleator, Cumbria CA23 3AU, United Kingdom. enquiries@wildlife-sound.org, http://www.wildlife-sound.org/.

YINGYONG SHENGXUE/APPLIED ACOUSTICS. *see* PHYSICS—Sound

S

SOUND RECORDING AND REPRODUCTION—Abstracting, Bibliographies, Statistics

015 789.91 DEU ISSN 1613-8945
ML156.2
DEUTSCHE NATIONALBIBLIOGRAPHIE. REIHE T: MUSIKTONTRAEGERVERZEICHNIS. Text in German. 1974. m. EUR 460 (effective 2006). bibl. index. **Document type:** *Directory, Bibliography.*
Former titles (until 2004): Deutsche Nationalbibliographie. Reihe T: Musiktontraeger (0939-0642); (until 1991): Deutsche Bibliographie. Musiktontraeger-Verzeichnis (0170-1029); (until 1978): Deutsche Bibliographie. Schallplatten-Verzeichnis (0170-2904)
Media: CD-ROM.
Published by: (Deutsche Bibliothek), M V B - Marketing- und Verlagsservice des Buchhandels GmbH, Postfach 100442, Frankfurt Am Main, 60004, Germany. TEL 49-69-13060, FAX 49-69-1306201, info@mvb-online.de, http://www.mvb-online.de.

011.38 781.7 ISL ISSN 0254-4067
ML156.2
ISLENSK HLJODRITASKRA/BIBLIOGRAPHY OF ICELANDIC SOUND RECORDINGS. Text in Icelandic. 1979. a. ISK 3,000 (effective 2001); includes Islensk Bokaskra.
Related titles: ◆ Supplement(s): Islensk Bokaskra. ISSN 0254-1378.
Published by: Landsbokasafn Islands - Haskolabokasafn/National and University Library of Iceland, Arngrimsgata 3, Reykjavik, 107, Iceland. TEL 354-525-5600, FAX 354-525-5615. Ed. Hildur G. Eythorsdottir.

SOUND RECORDING AND REPRODUCTION—Computer Applications

SYSTEMS CONTRACTOR NEWS; serving the electronic systems industry. *see* ELECTRONICS

▼ **SYSTEMS CONTRACTOR NEWS ASIA.** *see* ELECTRONICS

SPECIAL EDUCATION AND REHABILITATION

see EDUCATION—Special Education And Rehabilitation

SPORTS AND GAMES

see also MEDICAL SCIENCES—Sports Medicine ; SPORTS AND GAMES—Ball Games ; SPORTS AND GAMES—Bicycles And Motorcycles ; SPORTS AND GAMES—Boats And Boating ; SPORTS AND GAMES—Horses And Horsemanship ; SPORTS AND GAMES—Outdoor Life

725.74 DEU ISSN 0932-3872
A.B. - ARCHIV DES BADEWESENS. Text in German. 1948. m. EUR 67; EUR 6.50 newsstand/cover (effective 2009). adv. **Document type:** *Magazine, Trade.*
Formerly (until 1987): Archiv des Badewesens (0340-5540)
Published by: Bundesfachverband Oeffentliche Baeder e.V., Alfredstr 73, Essen, 45130, Germany. TEL 49-201-879690, FAX 49-201-8796920, info@boeb.de, http://www.boeb.de. Ed. Joachim Heuser. Adv. contact Sebastian Friedrich. B&W page EUR 1,220, color page EUR 1,814; trim 177 x 251. Circ: 4,500 (paid and controlled).

796 USA
A C C AREA SPORTS JOURNAL. Text in English. 1977. bi-w. (b-w. Thu.). USD 49; USD 3.50 newsstand/cover (effective 2005). **Document type:** *Newspaper, Consumer.*
Published by: A C C Sports.com, P O Box 4323, Chapel Hill, NC 27515-4323. TEL 800-447-7667. Ed. Dave Glenn. Pub. Dennis Wuycik. Circ: 25,200 (paid).

794.2 790.13 USA ISSN 1045-8034
A C F BULLETIN. Text in English. 1952. bi-m. USD 25 domestic; USD 35 in Canada; USD 40 elsewhere (effective 2008). illus. reprints avail. **Document type:** *Bulletin, Consumer.* **Description:** Covers news of checker events worldwide and includes annotated games of national tournament.
Published by: American Checker Federation, PO Box 365, Petal, MS 39465. TEL 601-582-7090. Ed. Charles C Walker. Circ: 1,000.

796 FRA ISSN 1623-944X
A E F A. ASSOCIATION DES ENTRAINEURS FRANCAIS D'ATHLETISME. Text in French. 1963. q. EUR 45 domestic; EUR 60 foreign (effective 2009). **Document type:** *Magazine, Trade.*
Former titles (until 1996): A E F A. Revue (0755-5075); (until 1980): Amicale des Entraineurs Francais d'Athletisme (0755-687X)
Published by: Association des Entraineurs Francais d'Athletisme (A E F A), 33 Av Pierre de Coubertin, Paris, 75640, France. http://www.aefathle.org.

A F I BUYING DIRECTORY. *see* BUSINESS AND ECONOMICS—Trade And Industrial Directories

A K C GAZETTE; the official journal for the sport of purebred dogs . (American Kennel Club) *see* PETS

A N Z S L A COMMENTATOR. *see* LAW

794.1 USA
A P C T NEWS BULLETIN. Text in English. 1967. 6/yr. USD 18; USD 36 foreign (effective 1998). adv. bk.rev. **Document type:** *Bulletin, Trade.* **Description:** Reports on annotated and non-annotated games. Includes "how-to-improve" articles, computer chess, and theory.
Published by: American Postal Chess Tournaments, PO Box 305, Western Springs, IL 60558-0305. TEL 630-663-0688, FAX 630-663-0689. Ed., R&P Helen Warren. Adv. contact Jim Warren. Circ: 1,000.

A S AVIAZIONE SPORTIVA. *see* AERONAUTICS AND SPACE FLIGHT

797 USA ISSN 0747-6000
A S C A NEWSLETTER. Text in English. 1980. bi-m. **Document type:** *Newsletter, Trade.*
Indexed: SD, T02.
—CCC.
Published by: American Swimming Coaches Association, 5101 NW 21st Ave, Ste 200, Fort Lauderdale, FL 33309. TEL 954-563-4930, 800-356-2722, FAX 954-563-9813, asca@swimmingcoach.org, http://www.swimmingcoach.org.

796 HND
A S DEPORTIVA. Text in Spanish. 1994. 25/yr. HNL 320 domestic (effective 2006). **Document type:** *Magazine, Consumer.*
Published by: Editorial Hablemos Claro, Edificio Torre Libertad, Boulevard Suyapa, Residencial La Hacienda, Tegucigalpa, Honduras. http://www.hablemosclaro.com. Ed. Rodrigo Wong Arevalo.

790.1 617.1 USA
A S M A NEWS. Text in English. a. USD 50 to members. adv. bk.rev. back issues avail. **Document type:** *Newsletter.* **Description:** Covers sports medicine, injury prevention, athletic training, sports medicine certification.
Published by: American Sports Medicine Association, Board of Certification, 660 W Duarte Rd, Arcadia, CA 91007. TEL 818-445-1978, FAX 818-574-1999. Ed. Steve Lewis. Circ: 3,500 (controlled).

900 AUS ISSN 1833-1947
A S S H STUDIES IN SPORTS HISTORY. Text in English. irreg. price varies. **Document type:** *Magazine, Consumer.*
Published by: Australian Society for Sports History, Rob Hess, Sport History Unit, F022, School of Human Movement, Recreation and Performance, Victoria University, PO Box 14428, Melbourne City MC, VIC 8001, Australia. Eds. Ian Warren, Lionel Frost.

796.046 USA
A S X. Text in English. 2005. bi-m. USD 9.95 (effective 2005). adv. **Document type:** *Magazine, Consumer.* **Description:** Covers adventure and extreme sports, including trail running, mountain biking, paddling and rock climbing to mountaineering, snowboarding, skydiving, surfing and scuba diving. Also covers gear, apparel and music.
Related titles: Online - full content ed.: USD 5.95 (effective 2005).
Published by: R F A Media, Inc., 2336 Wisteria Dr., Ste. 350, Snellville, GA 30078. TEL 770-817-9000, FAX 770-817-9001. Ed. Brian Metzler. Pub. Scot Love.

790.1 059.927 SAU ISSN 1319-0881
GV663.S33
AALAM AR-RIYADAH. Key Title: A'lam ar-riyadat. Text in Arabic. 1991. w. adv. **Document type:** *Magazine, Consumer.* **Description:** Covers local and international sporting events for a young Arab audience.
Published by: Saudi Research & Publishing Co., P O Box 478, Riyadh, 11411, Saudi Arabia. TEL 966-1-4419933, FAX 966-1-4429555, editorial@majalla.com, http://www.srpc.com/main. adv.: color page SAR 12,200; trim 220 x 285. Circ: 78,686 (paid).

796.9 SWE ISSN 0282-860X
AARETS ISHOCKEY. Text in Swedish. 1957. a. SEK 799. illus.
Formerly: Ishockey (0347-2221)
Published by: (Svenska Ishockeyfoerbundet), Stroembergs Idrottsboecker, Fack 65, Vallingby, 16211, Sweden.

790.1 USA
THE ACADEMY. Text in English. 1978. q. free. **Document type:** *Newsletter.* **Description:** Provides news about educational programs and activities of the U.S. Sports Academy.
Formerly: U S S A News
Published by: United States Sports Academy, 1 Academy Dr, Daphne, AL 36526. TEL 205-626-3303, FAX 205-626-3874. Ed. Dr. Robert Lyster. Pub. Dr. Thomas P Rosandich. Circ: 10,000 (controlled).

797 NLD ISSN 1574-7565
ACCESS KITEBOARDING MAGAZINE. Variant title: Soul Access Kiteboarding Magazine. Text in Dutch. 5/yr. EUR 29.75 (effective 2010). adv. **Document type:** *Magazine, Consumer.*
Published by: Soul Media, Stetweg 43C, Castricum, 1901 JD, Netherlands. TEL 31-251-674911, FAX 31-251-674378, info@soulonline.nl, http://www.soulonline.nl.

796 NLD ISSN 1875-2349
ACHILLES. Variant title: Sporttijdschrift Achilles. Text in Dutch. 2007. s-a. EUR 12.50 newsstand/cover (effective 2009).
Formerly: Tussenstand (1875-2330)
Published by: L.J. Veen Uitgeversgroep, Herengracht 481, Amsterdam, 1017 BT, Netherlands. TEL 31-20-5249800, FAX 31-20-6276851, info@ljveen.nl, http://www.ljveen.nl. Eds. Ad van Liempt, Jan Luitzen.

790.1 CAN
ACTION CANADA MAGAZINE. Text in English. bi-m. **Document type:** *Magazine, Consumer.*
Published by: Athletes in Action, Canada, Box 300, Vancouver, BC V6C 2X3, Canada. TEL 604-514-2000, FAX 604-514-2124, aia@athletesinaction.com, http://www.athletesinaction.com. Ed. Shannon Hill.

ACTION MARTIAL ARTS. *see* PHYSICAL FITNESS AND HYGIENE

790.1 USA ISSN 0893-9489
ACTION PURSUIT GAMES; world's leading magazine of paintball sports. Text in English. 1987. m. USD 24.95; USD 4.99 per issue (effective 2011). adv. illus. back issues avail.; reprints avail. **Document type:** *Magazine, Consumer.* **Description:** Provides diverse in-depth coverage of the drenaline-filled sport of paintball. Coverage ranges from new, hightech gear to fast-moving pro speedball tournaments and challenging woodsball scenario games.
Published by: Beckett Media Llc, 2400 E Katella Ave, Ste 300, Anaheim, CA 92806. TEL 714-939-9991, customerservice@beckett.com, http://www.beckett.com. Adv. contact Gabe Frimmel TEL 800-332-3330 ext 238.

796 AUS ISSN 1445-2723
ACTIVE STATE. Text in English. 1993. 3/yr. free (effective 2009). **Document type:** *Magazine, Government.* **Description:** Aims to inform the sports and recreation industry of activities and programs.
Related titles: Online - full text ed.: ISSN 1835-6680. free (effective 2009).
Published by: Sport and Recreation Victoria, GPO Box 2392, Melbourne, VIC 3001, Australia. TEL 61-3-92083333, FAX 61-3-92083520, info@sport.vic.gov.au, http://www.sports.vic.gov.au/.

ACTIVITES PHYSIQUES ET SPORTIVES. *see* LAW

796.815 CHL ISSN 0718-5669
ACTUALIDADES Y NOTICIAS DEL AIKIDO. Text in Spanish. 2000. m.
Formerly (until 2006): Akikai Chile (Print) (0717-6007)
Media: Online - full text.
Published by: Federacion Deportiva Chilena de Aikido, Libertad No. 86, Santiago, Chile. TEL 56-2-6817703, informaciones@fedenaa.cl.

790.1 GBR
ADRENALIN (LONDON, 1999); surf. skate. snow. Text in English. q. GBP 14 (effective 2004). **Document type:** *Magazine, Consumer.*
Published by: The Media Cell, 10-16 Tiller Rd, Docklands, London, E14 8PX, United Kingdom. TEL 44-207-3455066, FAX 44-207-3455066, mail@themediacell.com, http://www.themediacell.com. Ed. Michael Fordham.

ADRESSBUCH DES SPORTS (CD-ROM). *see* BUSINESS AND ECONOMICS—Management

ADSUM. *see* MILITARY

796 USA ISSN 1542-5541
ADVENTURE SPORTS MAGAZINE. Text in English. 2003 (Mar.). m. USD 29.70 domestic; USD 39.70 in Canada & Mexico; USD 51.60 elsewhere (effective 2004). **Document type:** *Magazine, Consumer.* **Description:** Covers the fast-growing sport of adventure racing, the disciplines that make up the sport, and other outdoor adventure pursuits. It will focus on races, interesting personalities, training techniques, destinations and the latest and greatest gear.
Published by: R F A Media, Inc., PO Box 926, Grayson, GA 30017. TEL 678-521-8418. Ed. Brian Metzler. Pub. Scot Love.

THE ADVISER. *see* PETS

AETHLON; the journal of sport literature. *see* LITERATURE

799.32 ZAF ISSN 1818-9113
AFRICAN ARCHER & ADVENTURER. Text in English. 2006. bi-m. ZAR 78 domestic; ZAR 168 in Southern Africa; USD 45 elsewhere (effective 2006).
Published by: Africa's Bowhunter Magazine, 759 7th Ave, Wonderbook South, 0084, South Africa. TEL 27-12-3351998, FAX 27-12-3355066.

AFRICAN JOURNAL FOR PHYSICAL, HEALTH EDUCATION, RECREATION AND DANCE. *see* PHYSICAL FITNESS AND HYGIENE

AFRICAN JOURNAL OF CROSS-CULTURAL PSYCHOLOGY AND SPORT FACILITATION. *see* PSYCHOLOGY

796 USA ISSN 1941-2754
▼ **AFRICAN SPORTS NETWORK JOURNAL.** Text in English. 2009. q. USD 4.99 per issue (effective 2009). **Document type:** *Magazine, Consumer.* **Description:** Presents sports news from Africa, America and the rest of the globe.
Published by: Ernest Awasum, Ed. & Pub., PO Box 1579, New York, NY 10027. TEL 646-785-1471, editor@africansportsnetworkjournal.com.

796 ESP ISSN 1578-2174
AGORA PARA LA EDUCACION FISICA Y EL DEPORTE. Text in Spanish, Portuguese, English. 2001. 3/yr. **Document type:** *Journal, Academic/Scholarly.*
Related titles: Online - full text ed.: ISSN 1989-7200. free (effective 2011).
Published by: Foro para la Educacion Fisica, la Actividad Fisica Recreativa y el Deporte de Castilla y Leon, Paseo de Belen 1, Campus Miguel Delibes, Valladolid, 47011, Spain.

AL-AHLY. *see* CLUBS

796.815 JPN ISSN 1340-5624
AIKIDO JOURNAL. Text in English. 1974. q. USD 35 domestic; USD 40 in Canada & Mexico; USD 45 elsewhere. adv. bk.rev. illus. back issues avail. **Document type:** *Journal, Consumer.* **Description:** For serious practitioners of Japanese martial arts. Contains interviews with top instructors, history and philosophy, illustrated technical articles, self-defense, reviews of martial arts publications, and event announcements and reports.
Formerly (until vol.21, no.3, 1994): Aiki News (0915-9517)
Related titles: Online - full text ed.
Indexed: SD, SportS.
Published by: K.K. Aiki News, 14-17-103 Matsugae-cho, Sagamihara-shi, Kanagawa-ken 228-0813, Japan. TEL 81-427-48-2423, FAX 81-427-48-2421. Ed. Stanley Pranin. Circ: 12,000.

796.8154 USA ISSN 1060-9415
GV1114.35
AIKIDO TODAY MAGAZINE; a non-partisan journal of the art of aikido. Text in English. 1987. bi-m. USD 26.50 domestic; USD 31 foreign (effective 2000). **Document type:** *Magazine, Consumer.* **Description:** An international journal of the martial art and spiritual discipline of aikido.
Published by: Arete Press, PO Box 1060, Claremont, CA 91711-1060. TEL 909-624-7770, 800-445-2454, FAX 909-398-1840. Eds. Ronald Rubin, Susan Perry. Adv. contact John Schleis.

799.202 790.1 CAN ISSN 0382-4373
AIM. Text in English, French. 1968. 4/yr. CAD 25, USD 35 domestic; CAD 50 foreign (effective 1999). adv. bk.rev. **Document type:** *Newsletter.*
Indexed: SD, SportS, T02.
Published by: Shooting Federation of Canada/Federation de Tir du Canada, 45 Shirley Blvd, Nepean, ON K2K 2W6, Canada. TEL 613-727-7483, FAX 613-727-7487, sfc@freenet.carleton.ca. Adv. contact Sandra Deeks. Circ: 10,000.

790.1 GBR ISSN 0266-4224
AIR GUNNER. Text in English. 1984. m. GBP 25 domestic; GBP 47.20 foreign; free to members (effective 2010). adv. illus. back issues avail. **Document type:** *Magazine, Consumer.* **Description:** Covers all aspects of air gun shooting.
Related titles: Online - full text ed.: GBP 15 (effective 2010).
—CCC.
Published by: Archant Specialist Ltd. (Subsidiary of: Archant Group), 3 The Courtyard, Denmark St, Wokingham, Berkshire RG40 2AZ, United Kingdom. TEL 44-118-9771677, miller.hogg@archant.co.uk, http://www.archant.co.uk/business_specialist.aspx. Ed. Matt Clark. Adv. contact James Westbrook TEL 44-118-9897244.

AIR SPORTS INTERNATIONAL. *see* AERONAUTICS AND SPACE FLIGHT

797.55099305 NZL ISSN 1170-9928
AIRBORN. Text in English. 1980. bi-m. NZD 36 domestic; NZD 40 foreign (effective 2008). adv. **Document type:** *Magazine, Consumer.* **Description:** Contains safety bulletins, competition results and contact details for local clubs as well as instructional and entertaining photos and articles on flying.

Published by: New Zealand Hang Gliding Association, Richmond, PO Box 3370, Nelson, New Zealand. nzhgpa.admins@clear.net.nz, http://www.nzhgpa.org.nz.

AIRBORNE (TULLAMARINE); comprehensive coverage of radio control modelling sports. *see* HOBBIES

790.1 GBR ISSN 2042-7107

▼ **AIRGUN SPORT.** Text in English. 2010. m. **Document type:** *Magazine, Consumer.*

Published by: Archant Specialist Ltd. (Subsidiary of: Archant Group), 3 The Courtyard, Denmark St, Wokingham, Berkshire RG40 2AZ, United Kingdom. TEL 44-118-9897246, 44-118-9771677, http://www.archant.co.uk/. Ed. Terry Doe. Adv. contact Neil Dyson TEL 44-118-9897264.

799.202 GBR ISSN 0143-8255

AIRGUN WORLD. Text in English. 1977. m. GBP 25 domestic; GBP 47.20 foreign; GBP 3.50 per issue; free to members (effective 2010). adv. illus. back issues avail. **Document type:** *Magazine, Consumer.* **Description:** For airgun enthusiasts and novices alike who enjoy shooting, targeting and hunting.

Related titles: Online - full text ed.: GBP 15 (effective 2010).

—CCC.

Published by: Archant Specialist Ltd. (Subsidiary of: Archant Group), 3 The Courtyard, Denmark St, Wokingham, Berkshire RG40 2AZ, United Kingdom. TEL 44-118-9771677, 44-118-9897246, miller.hogg@archant.co.uk, http://www.archant.co.uk/business_specialist.aspx. Adv. contact James Westbrook TEL 44-118-9897244.

AIRSHOW PROFESSIONAL; the catalog of professional airshow performers & support services. *see* AERONAUTICS AND SPACE FLIGHT

AIRSPORT. *see* AERONAUTICS AND SPACE FLIGHT

794.1 ARG

AJEDREZ DE ESTILO. Text in Spanish. 1982. 24/yr. USD 119. adv. bk.rev. **Description:** Contains almost 2000 annotated national and international games each year, theory and combinations.

Published by: Ajedrez Integral, Casilla de Correo 51, Sucursal 49, Buenos Aires, 1449, Argentina. TEL 54-114-3316988, FAX 54-114-3316988. Ed. Juan Sebastian Morgado. Circ: 2,000.

796.05 FRA ISSN 1774-4873

AKKRO MAGAZINE. Variant title: Akkro Free. Text in French. 2005. irreg. free (effective 2006). **Document type:** *Magazine, Consumer.*

Published by: Akkro Editions, Batiment Athena 1, Site d'Archamps, Archamps, 74160, France.

▼ **AKKRO MAGAZINE KARBONE.** *see* LEISURE AND RECREATION

796 DEU

AKTIV LAUFEN. Text in German. 2002. bi-m. EUR 21; EUR 3.80 newsstand/cover (effective 2011). adv. **Document type:** *Magazine, Consumer.*

Published by: Marken Verlag GmbH, Hansaring 97, Cologne, 50670, Germany. TEL 49-221-9574270, FAX 49-221-95742777, marken-info@markenverlag.de, http://www.markenverlag.de. Adv. contact Frank Krauthaeuser. Circ: 29,599 (paid and controlled).

796 NOR

AKTIV LIVSSTIL (ONLINE EDITION). Text in Norwegian. 1952. 10/yr. **Document type:** *Magazine, Consumer.*

Former titles (until 2005): Aktiv Livsstil (Print Edition) (0807-5077); (until 1996): Bedriftsidrett (0804-0117); (until 1992): B I F - Nytt (0800-4420); (until 1984): Bedrifts-Idrett (0800-4439).

Media: Online - full content.

Published by: Norges Mosjons- og Bedriftsidrettsforbund, Sognsveien 75, PO Box 1, Ullevaal Stadion, Oslo, 0840, Norway. TEL 47-21-029450, FAX 47-21-029451, forbund@bedriftsidrett.no, http://www.bedriftsidrett.no. Ed. Charlotte Svenson.

790.1 DEU

AKTIV SPORTMAGAZIN. Text in German. 1970. 11/yr. adv. **Document type:** *Magazine, Consumer.*

Published by: J. Fink GmbH & Co. KG, Zeppelinstr 29-32, Ostfildern, 73760, Germany. TEL 49-711-4506463, FAX 49-711-4506460, dscheuin@jfink.de, http://www.jfink.de. adv.: B&W page EUR 9,800, color page EUR 13,700. Circ: 216,269 (controlled).

793.7 DEU

DIE AKTUELLE PREISRAETSEL MAGAZIN. Text in German. m. EUR 21.60; EUR 1.65 newsstand/cover (effective 2011). adv. **Document type:** *Magazine, Consumer.*

Published by: Deutscher Raetselverlag GmbH & Co. KG (Subsidiary of: Gong Verlag GmbH & Co. KG), Muenchener Str 101-09, Ismaning, 85737, Germany. TEL 49-89-272708620, FAX 49-89-272707890, info@raetsel.de, http://www.deutscher-raetselverlag.de. Circ: 120,000 (controlled).

306.4 CAN ISSN 1499-7436

ALBERTA GAMING RESEARCH INSTITUTE. ANNUAL REPORT. Text in English. a. **Document type:** *Report, Academic/Scholarly.*

Related titles: Online - full text ed.: ISSN 1499-7444. 2001.

Published by: Alberta Gaming Research Institute, HUB Mall, University of Alberta, 8909S - 112 St, Edmonton, AB T6G 2C5, Canada. TEL 780-492-2817, FAX 780-492-6125, abgaming@ualberta.ca, http://www.abgaminginstitute.ualberta.ca.

790 SVK

ALBUM SLAVNYCH SPORTOVCOV. Text in Slovak. irreg., latest vol.4, 1976. price varies. illus.

Published by: Sport, Vajnorska cesta 100-a, Bratislava, 83258, Slovakia.

797 USA ISSN 1084-2985
GV840.S78

ALERT DIVER. Text in English. 1985. bi-m. USD 25 (effective 2007). adv. bk.rev. 64 p./no.; **Document type:** *Magazine, Consumer.* **Description:** Discusses medical issues and promotes safety in scuba diving.

Published by: Divers Alert Network, 6 W Colony Pl, Durham, NC 27705-5588. TEL 919-684-2948, FAX 919-490-6630, rduncan@dan.duke.edu, http://www.diversalertnetwork.org/. Ed. Renee Duncan Westerfield. R&P L Renee Westerfield. Adv. contact Christine McTaggart. page USD 8,300; trim 7.75 x 10.5. Circ: 155,000 (controlled).

794.1 COL

ALFIL DAMA; revista colombiana de ajedrez. Text in Spanish. 6/yr. USD 25. **Description:** Contains selections of national and international games, "how-to-improve" articles, scholastic chess, and problems.

Published by: Liga de Ajedrez de Antioquia, c/o Juan Gonzalo Arboleda, Exec. Dir., Carrera 50, 59-06, Medellin, ANT, Colombia.

795.41 USA ISSN 1554-7167

ALL IN; the world's leading poker magazine. Text in English. 2005 (Jan./Feb.). bi-m. USD 4.99 newsstand/cover domestic; USD 5.99 newsstand/cover in Canada (effective 2007). adv. **Document type:** *Magazine, Consumer.*

Published by: All in, 45 W 21st St, Ste 403, New York, NY 10010-6864. TEL 212-880-6493. Ed., Pub. Bhu Srinivasan. Circ: 150,000.

790.1 USA

ALL-STATER SPORTS; America's high school sports magazine. Text in English. 1995. bi-m. **Document type:** *Magazine, Consumer.*

Published by: All-Stater Publishing, 1373 Grandview Ave, Ste 206, Columbia, OH 43212. TEL 614-487-1280, FAX 614-487-1283, jvaughn@all-statersports.com, http://www.all-statersports.com. Circ: 100,000 (paid).

796.41 DNK ISSN 1604-8660

ALT OM GYMNASTIK. Text in Danish. 1946. irreg. adv. back issues avail. **Document type:** *Magazine, Corporate.* **Description:** Reports on gymnastics competitions and informs on coming competitions; articles on gymnastics research.

Former titles (until 2005): Gymnastik (Print) (0108-3678); (until 1982): Vidar (0108-366X)

Media: Online - full content.

Published by: Dansk Gymnastik Forbund, Idraettens Hus, Broendby Stadion 20, Broendby, 2605, Denmark. TEL 45-43-262601, FAX 45-43-262610, dgf@dgf.dk.

790.1 USA ISSN 0002-6808
GV741

AMATEUR ATHLETE. Text in English. 1987. 8/yr. USD 15 (effective 1998). adv. **Document type:** *Magazine, Consumer.* **Description:** Lists more than 800 running, bicycling, and triathlon events in the Midwest.

Published by: Eliot Wineberg, Ed. & Pub., 7840 N Lincoln Ave, Skokie, IL 60077. TEL 847-675-0200, FAX 847-675-2903. Adv. contact Jeremy Solomon. Circ: 55,000 (controlled).

796 USA
GV563

AMATEUR ATHLETIC UNION OF THE UNITED STATES. OFFICIAL A A U CODE DIRECTORY. Cover title: A A U Code Directory. Text in English. 1888. a. USD 10 (effective 1998). illus. **Document type:** *Directory.*

Formerly: Amateur Athletic Union of the United States. Official Handbook of the A A U Code (0091-3405)

Published by: Amateur Athletic Union of the United States, 1910 Hotal Plaza Blvd, P O Box 22409, Lake Buena Vista, FL 32830. TEL 407-934-7200, FAX 407-934-7242, anita@aausports.org, http://aausports.org.

796.962 USA

AMATEUR SPEEDSKATING UNION OF THE UNITED STATES. OFFICIAL HANDBOOK. Text in English. 1930. biennial. USD 6 (effective 1999). adv. **Document type:** *Newsletter.*

Formerly: Amateur Skating Union of the United States. Official Handbook (0516-866X)

Published by: Amateur Speedskating Union of the United States, S651 Forest St., Winfield, IL 60190-1541. TEL 630-790-3230. Ed. William Houghton. R&P Shirley Yates. Adv. contact Timothy Affholter. Circ: 3,000.

797.21 GBR

AMATEUR SWIMMING ASSOCIATION HANDBOOK. Text in English. 1905. a. free to members (effective 2009). adv. back issues avail. **Document type:** *Handbook/Manual/Guide, Trade.* **Description:** Contains news of the association administration; champions holding records in swimming, diving, synchronized swimming, and water polo in the UK and abroad; and updates regarding teaching and coaching certificates.

Formerly (until 2006): North Eastern Counties Amateur Swimming Association. Handbook

Related titles: Online - full text ed.

Published by: Amateur Swimming Association, Harold Fern House, Derby Sq, Loughborough, Leics LE11 5AL, United Kingdom. TEL 44-1509-618700, FAX 44-1509-618701, customerservices@swimming.org. Circ: 3,700.

796 USA ISSN 0569-1796

AMATEUR WRESTLING NEWS. Text in English. 1955. 12/yr. (Sep.-July). USD 35; USD 45 combined subscription (print & online eds.) (effective 2010). adv. illus. 64 p./no. 3 cols./p.; back issues avail.; reprints avail. **Document type:** *Magazine, Consumer.* **Description:** Features informative articles on Amateur Wrestling.

Formerly (until 1957): Wrestling News and Reports

Related titles: Online - full text ed.: USD 19 (effective 2010).

Indexed: SD, SPI, SportS.

Address: PO Box 54679, Oklahoma City, OK 73154. TEL 405-521-8750, FAX 405-521-8240. Ed. Ron Good. Pub. John Hoke TEL 800-275-8551.

799.202 USA

AMERICAN AIRGUN FIELD TARGET ASSOCIATION. NEWSLETTER. Text in English. m. membership. **Document type:** *Newsletter, Consumer.* **Description:** Dedicated to promoting the sport of air rifle field target shooting. Includes matches, scores, and club news.

Published by: American Airgun Field Target Association, 180 Mill Creek Rd, Bayville, NJ 08721. TEL 732-269-3303.

AMERICAN BOARD OF SPORT PSYCHOLOGY. JOURNAL. *see* PSYCHOLOGY

769.41 USA ISSN 1079-9885

AMERICAN CHEERLEADER. Text in English. 1995. bi-m. USD 14.95 domestic; USD 25 in Canada; USD 35 elsewhere (effective 2008). adv. bk.rev. illus. back issues avail. **Document type:** *Magazine, Consumer.* **Description:** Provides information on everything from stunts, training and tryouts tips to the coolest fashions and beauty advice for cheer and school.

Incorporates: American Cheerleader Junior (1534-6838)

Related titles: Online - full text ed.; Supplement(s): American Cheerleader All - Star Insider; American Cheerleader Caoch's Handbook.

Indexed: A27, M01, M02, M04, MASUSE, P10, P19, P48, P53, P54, PQC, T02.

Published by: Macfadden Performing Arts Media, LLC., 110 William St, 23rd Fl, New York, NY 10038. TEL 646-459-4800, FAX 646-459-4900, http://dancemedia.com/. Eds. Jenn Smith, Marisa Walker. Pub. Brandy Bean TEL 321-752-6794. adv.: B&W page USD 6,116, color page USD 8,373; bleed 8.25 x 11.125. Circ: 200,000. **Subscr. to:** Kable Fulfillment Services, Inc., Kable Sq, Mount Morris, IL 61054. TEL 800-800-7451, info@kable.com, http://www.kable.com/.

796.86 USA ISSN 0002-8436
U860

AMERICAN FENCING. Text in English. 1949. q. free to members (effective 2010). illus. index. 36 p./no. 2 cols./p.; back issues avail. **Document type:** *Magazine, Trade.* **Description:** Contains articles concerning the Olympic sport of fencing in the United States including articles on training, technique, and maintenance and care of equipment.

Related titles: Microform ed.: (from PQC).

Indexed: A22, SD, SPI, SportS.

—Ingenta.

Published by: United States Fencing Association, Inc., One Olympic Plaza, Colorado Springs, CO 80909. TEL 719-866-4511, FAX 719-632-5737, http://www.usfencing.org.

658.8 338.476 USA ISSN 0164-8136

AMERICAN FIREARMS INDUSTRY. Text in English. 1973. m. free to qualified personnel. adv. bk.rev. charts; illus.; stat.; tr.lit. back issues avail. **Document type:** *Magazine, Trade.* **Description:** Provides business and product information for licensed firearms dealers.

Published by: (National Association of Federally Licensed Firearms Dealers), P G R A Inc., 2400 E Las Olas, Ste 397, Fort Lauderdale, FL 33301. TEL 954-467-9994, FAX 954-463-2501. Ed. Kathleen Molchan. Pub., R&P Andrew Molchan. Circ: 25,000.

793 USA ISSN 0148-0243
GV1459

AMERICAN GO JOURNAL. Text in English. 1948. q. USD 30 (effective 1999). adv. bk.rev. 50 p./no.; back issues avail. **Document type:** *Journal, Trade.* **Description:** Contains news and instructions on the ancient Asian game of Go (Paduk, Weiqi).

Related titles: Supplement(s): American Go Newsletter.

Published by: American Go Association, PO Box 397, Old Chelsea Sta, New York, NY 10113. TEL 917-449-8125, FAX 212-662-5501. Ed., Adv. contact Chris Garlock. Circ: 1,500.

AMERICAN HANDGUNNER. *see* HOBBIES

796 USA

AMERICAN HOCKEY LEAGUE OFFICIAL GUIDE AND RECORD BOOK (YEAR). Text in English. a. USD 12.95 (effective 2008). **Document type:** *Bulletin.* **Description:** History and record book of the American Hockey League; includes current team directories and records.

Formerly (until 1992): American Hockey League Media Guide (Year); Which incorporated (in 1992): A H L Playoff Guide

Published by: American Hockey League, 1 Monarch Place, Ste 2400, Springfield, MA 01144. TEL 413-781-2030, FAX 413-733-4767, info@thenhl.com, http://www.thenhl.com. Circ: 2,000.

796 USA

AMERICAN HOCKEY LEAGUE OFFICIAL RULE BOOK (YEAR). Text in English. a. USD 6.95 (effective 2008). **Document type:** *Bulletin.*

Published by: American Hockey League, 1 Monarch Place, Ste 2400, Springfield, MA 01144. TEL 413-781-2030, FAX 413-733-4767, info@thenhl.com, http://www.thenhl.com.

AMERICAN KENNEL CLUB AWARDS. *see* PETS

636.596 USA ISSN 0003-0686
SF481

AMERICAN RACING PIGEON NEWS. Text in English. 1885. m. (Sep.-July). USD 25. bk.rev. illus. **Description:** Provides "how-to" articles, news and opinions on the sport of pigeon breeding, training, racing and showing on an international basis.

Address: 34 E Franklin St, Bellbrook, OH 45305-2098. TEL 513-848-4972, FAX 513-848-3012. Ed. Michael D Reinke. adv.: B&W page USD 225, color page USD 800; 11 x 8.5. Circ: 5,000.

799.2 USA ISSN 0003-083X

AMERICAN RIFLEMAN. Text in English. 1885. m. free to members; USD 15 to non-members (effective 2009). bk.rev. charts; illus.; pat.; stat. index. reprints avail. **Document type:** *Magazine, Consumer.* **Description:** Provides shooters and firearms enthusiast with information on to rifles, shotguns, handguns, ammunition, reloading, optics and shooting accessories.

Former titles (until 1923): Arms and the Man (0271-6917); (until 1906): Shooting and Fishing (0271-6828); (until 1888): Rifle

Related titles: Microform ed.: (from PQC); Online - full text ed.

Indexed: A22, ConsI, G05, G06, G07, G08, G09, I05, M01, M02, M06, MagInd, P02, P10, P19, P48, P53, P54, PMR, PQC, SPI, SportS.

—Ingenta, Linda Hall.

Published by: (National Rifle Association of America), N R A Publications, 11250 Waples Mill Rd, Fairfax, VA 22030. TEL 800-672-3888, publications@nrahq.org, http://www.nrapublications.org. Ed. Mark A Keefe IV.

290.1 USA

AMERICAN SPORTS HISTORY SERIES. Text in English. 1993. irreg., latest vol.11, 2005. price varies. back issues avail. **Document type:** *Monographic series.*

Published by: Scarecrow Press, Inc. (Subsidiary of: Rowman & Littlefield Publishers, Inc.), 4501 Forbes Blvd, Ste 200, Lanham, MD 20706. TEL 301-459-3366, 800-462-6420, FAX 301-429-5748, 800-338-4550, custserv@rowman.com, http://www.scarecrowpress.com. Ed. David B Biesel. Pub. Mr. Edward Kurdyla TEL 301-459-3366 ext 5604. R&P Clare Cox TEL 212-529-3888 ext 308.

797.2 USA ISSN 0747-5853
GV837.65

AMERICAN SWIMMING COACHES ASSOCIATION WORLD CLINIC YEARBOOK. Text in English. 1974. a. USD 30 per issue (effective 2009). **Document type:** *Yearbook, Trade.*

Indexed: SD.

—CCC.

Published by: American Swimming Coaches Association, 5101 NW 21st Ave, Ste 200, Fort Lauderdale, FL 33309. TEL 954-563-4930, 800-356-2722, FAX 954-563-9813, asca@swimmingcoach.org, http://www.swimmingcoach.org.

S

796.72 USA
AMERICAN THUNDER. Text in English. 2004 (Feb.). m. USD 14.95, USD 24.95, USD 34.95 (effective 2004). adv. **Document type:** *Magazine, Consumer.* **Description:** Provides insider access to NASCAR veterans and new stars as well as articles on the latest cars and trucks, tools to help you in the garage and around the house, technology and games, and step-by-step tips and advice for homeowners.
Published by: American Content, Inc., 303 Sacramento St, 2nd Fl, San Francisco, CA 94111. TEL 888-268-4863.

796.4257 USA
AMERICAN TRI. Text in English. 2002. q. (m. in 2003). USD 22.95; USD 3.99 newsstand/cover (effective 2002). adv. **Document type:** *Magazine, Consumer.* **Description:** Provides information and features on all aspects of training and competing in triathlons.
Address: 1313 5th St SE, Minneapolis, MN 55414. TEL 612-379-5950, info@americantri.com. Ed., Pub. Kyle du Ford. adv.: color page USD 3,467.

AMERICA'S 1ST FREEDOM. *see* LITERARY AND POLITICAL REVIEWS

799.2 USA
HV7431
AMERICA'S FIRST FREEDOM. Text in English. 1997. m. free to members (effective 2009). adv. bk.rev. charts; illus.; pat.; stat. back issues avail. **Document type:** *Magazine, Consumer.* **Description:** Features articles on personal protection and survival, recreational and sport shooting, and Second Amendment issues; reviews all types of firearms.
Formerly (until 2000): American Guardian (1094-7515)
Published by: (National Rifle Association of America), N R A Publications, 11250 Waples Mill Rd, Fairfax, VA 22030. TEL 800-672-3888, publications@nrahq.org. Ed. Mark Chesnut.

796.8 FRA ISSN 1969-8801
▼ **AMPLITUDE.** Text in French. 2009. q. EUR 13.50 (effective 2011). **Document type:** *Magazine, Consumer.*
Published by: Federation Francaise de Lutte, 2, Rue Louis Pergaud, Maisons Alfort, 94706, France. TEL 33-1-41795910, FAX 33-1-43684053, ffl@fflutte.org, http://www.fflutte.com.

790.1 305.4 USA ISSN 1524-8631
AMY LOVE'S REAL SPORTS. Variant title: Real Sports. Text in English. 1998. bi-m. USD 16.83; USD 3.95 newsstand/cover (effective 2000). illus. **Document type:** *Magazine, Consumer.* **Description:** Features girls and women's sports, professional, collegiate and amateur sports, outstanding photo journalism and top sports writers contributions.
Published by: A D L, Inc., PO Box 8204, San Jose, CA 95155. TEL 408-918-9150, FAX 408-918-9155, amy@real-sports.com. Ed. Jill Dorson. Pub. Amy D Love. R&P Holmbeck Laura. Adv. contact Cynthia Atencio. Circ: 150,000 (paid and controlled).

ANALYSIS OF GAMBLING BEHAVIOR. *see* SOCIOLOGY

ANDHRA PRABHA. *see* GENERAL INTEREST PERIODICALS—India

796 CHN ISSN 1008-7761
ANHUI TIYU KEJI/JOURNAL OF ANHUI SPORTS SCIENCE. Text in Chinese. 1980. bi-m. **Document type:** *Journal, Academic/Scholarly.*
Related titles: Online - full text ed.
Published by: Anhui Sheng Tiyu Zhihe Jishu Xueyuan/Anhui Professional & Technical Institute of Athletics, 1, Renmin Dajie, Hefei, 230051, China. TEL 86-551-3686559.

793 DEU ISSN 1434-1352
ANSTOSS; das Billard-Sport Magazin. Text in German. 1997. m. adv. **Document type:** *Magazine, Consumer.*
Formed by the merger of (1991-1997): Anstoss (0942-2048); (1965-1997): Billard-Sport Magazin (0941-8571); Which was formerly (until 1991): Billard-Sport (0936-2665); Which incoporated (1955-1990): Billard (0138-1199); Which was formerly (until 1967): Der Billard-Sport (0232-7252)
Published by: (Deutsche Billard Union e.V.), K und L Verlag, Tilsiter Weg 2, Schwetzingen, 68723, Germany. TEL 49-6202-12121, FAX 49-6202-17876, verlag@anstoss.com, http://www.anstoss.com. Ed. Thomas Lindemann. Circ: 6,000.

793.7 DEU
APOTHEKEN RAETSEL MAGAZIN. Text in German. 1998. m. adv. **Document type:** *Magazine, Consumer.*
Published by: Gebr. Storck GmbH & Co. Verlags-oHG, Duisburger Str 375, Oberhausen, 46049, Germany. TEL 49-208-8480211, FAX 49-208-8480238, kalender@storckverlag.de, http://www.storckverlag.de. adv.: page EUR 3,500. Circ: 87,607 (controlled).

793.7 DEU
APOTHEKEN-RAETSEL SPEZIAL. Text in German. 2000. m. adv. **Document type:** *Magazine, Consumer.*
Published by: Media Dialog Verlag, Am Bahndamm 2, Ortenberg, 63683, Germany. TEL 49-6041-823390, FAX 49-6041-8233920, info@media-dialog.com, http://www.media-dialog.com. Ed. Claudia Sarkady. Pub. Maik Dollar. Adv. contact Steve Stuertz. page EUR 5,011. Circ: 250,000 (controlled).

790.1 USA ISSN 1546-2323
GV201
➤ **APPLIED RESEARCH IN COACHING AND ATHLETICS ANNUAL.** Abbreviated title: A R C A A. Text in English. 1986. a. USD 39 per issue domestic; USD 67 per issue in Canada; USD 77 per issue elsewhere (effective 2010). back issues avail. **Document type:** *Journal, Academic/Scholarly.* **Description:** Aims to fill the void between research in the field of athletics through dissemination of information to those who can utilize it in a practical setting, including coaches, athletic administrators and interested educators.
Formerly (until 1990): The Journal of Applied Research in Coaching and Athletics
Indexed: SD.
—BLDSC (1576.574000), IE. **CCC.**
Published by: American Press, 60 State St, Ste 700, Boston, MA 02109. TEL 617-247-0022, americanpress@flash.net. Ed. Warren K Simpson.

790.1 ESP ISSN 0214-8757
➤ **APUNTS. EDUCACIO FISICA I ESPORTS.** Text in Catalan. 1964. q. EUR 20 domestic; EUR 30 foreign (effective 2011). back issues avail. **Document type:** *Journal, Academic/Scholarly.* **Description:** Publishes original articles on scientific issues related to the science of physical activity and sport, with the professional scopes arising from them and to the promotion, in general, of sports culture. Contents include: Editorial; humanities and social sciences; physical activity and health; physical education; sport pedagogy; physical preparation; sports training; sports management, active leisure and tourism; woman and sport; opinion; and abstracts of doctoral theses.
Supersedes in part (in 1989): Apunts. Educacio Fisica (0213-3466); Which superseded in part (in 1985): Apunts d'Educacio Fisica i Medicina Esportiva (0212-4009); Which was formerly (until 1982): Apuntes de Medicina Deportiva (0211-8459)
Related titles: Online - full text ed.
Published by: Institut Nacional d'Educacio Fisica de Catalunya/Instituto Nacional de Educacion Fisica de Cataluna, Av. de l'Estadi 12-22, Barcelona, 08038, Spain. TEL 34-93-4255445, FAX 34-93-4263617, info@inefc.net, http://www.inefc.net/. Ed. Javier Olivera Betran. Pub. Elena Gil Gonzalez. R&P Jordi Serrano Valdes.

790.1 ESP ISSN 1577-4015
➤ **APUNTS. EDUCACION FISICA Y DEPORTES/APUNTS. PHYSICAL EDUCATION AND SPORTS.** Text in Spanish. 1964. q. EUR 20 domestic; EUR 30 foreign (effective 2011). back issues avail. **Document type:** *Journal, Academic/Scholarly.* **Description:** Publishes original articles on scientific issues related to the science of physical activity and sport, with the professional scopes arising from them and to the promotion, in general, of sports culture. Contents include: Editorial; humanities and social sciences; physical activity and health; physical education; sport pedagogy; physical preparation; sports training; sports management, active leisure and tourism; woman and sport; opinion; and abstracts of doctoral theses.
Formerly (until 1994): Apunts. Educacio Fisica i Esports (Spanish Edition) (1130-250X); Which superseded in part (in 1989): Apunts. Educacio Fisica (0213-3466); Which superseded in part (in 1985): Apunts d'Educacio Fisica i Medicina Esportiva (0212-4009); Which was formerly (until 1982): Apuntes de Medicina Deportiva (0211-8459)
Related titles: Online - full text ed.
Indexed: A01, SD.
Published by: Institut Nacional d'Educacio Fisica de Catalunya/Instituto Nacional de Educacion Fisica de Cataluna, Av. de l'Estadi 12-22, Barcelona, 08038, Spain. TEL 34-93-4255445, FAX 34-93-4263617, info@inefc.net, http://www.inefc.net/. Ed. Javier Olivera Betran. Pub. Elena Gil Gonzalez. R&P Jordi Serrano Valdes. Circ: 6,000.

790.1 ESP ISSN 1886-6581
APUNTS. MEDICINA DE L'ESPORT (ONLINE). Text in Spanish, Catalan. 1964. q. free (effective 2009). **Document type:** *Journal, Academic/Scholarly.*
Formerly (until 2005): Apunts. Medicina de l'Esport (Print) (0213-3717); Which superseded in part (in 1985): Apunts. d'Educacio Fisica i Medicina Esportiva (0212-4009); Which was formerly (until 1982): Apuntes de Medicina Deportiva (0211-8459)
Media: Online - full text (from ScienceDirect).
Indexed: EMBASE, ExcerpMed, SCOPUS, SD.
—**CCC.**
Published by: Institut Nacional d'Educacio Fisica de Catalunya/Instituto Nacional de Educacion Fisica de Cataluna, Av. de l'Estadi 12-22, Barcelona, 08038, Spain. TEL 34-93-4255445, FAX 34-93-4263617, info@inefc.net, http://www.inefc.net/.

797.21 658 USA ISSN 1058-7039
AQUATICS INTERNATIONAL; the source for facility management, products and services. Text in English. 1989. 11/yr. USD 30 domestic; USD 45 in Canada; USD 95 elsewhere; free to qualified personnel (effective 2011). charts; stat.; tr.lit. back issues avail. **Document type:** *Magazine, Trade.* **Description:** Covers various aquatic facilities and recreation with public or semi-public pools; features articles addressing the application of materials and equipment involved in the design, management, maintenance and programming of these aquatic facilities.
Formerly (until 1991): Aquatics (1042-9697); Incorporates (1989-1991): Aquatics Buyers' Guide
Related titles: Online - full text ed.; ◆ Supplement(s): Aquatics International Directory. ISSN 1553-3441.
Indexed: A26, E08, G06, G07, G08, I05, S09, SD.
—Ingenta. **CCC.**
Published by: Hanley Wood, LLC (Subsidiary of: J.P. Morgan Chase & Co.), 6222 Wilshire Blvd, Ste 600, Los Angeles, CA 90048. TEL 323-801-4900, FAX 323-801-4902, fanton@hanleywood.com, http://www.hanleywood.com. Ed. Gary Thill TEL 503-288-4402. Pub. Dick Coleman TEL 323-801-4903. Adv. contact Gary Carr.

797.2 NLD ISSN 1877-5276
AQUAVISION. Text in Dutch. 1985. bi-m. EUR 39 domestic; EUR 49 foreign (effective 2011). adv. **Document type:** *Magazine, Trade.*
Former titles (until 2008): Swim Biz (1871-2819); (until 2005): Het Grootste Zwemblad van Nederland (1570-5455); (until 2003): Zwemblad (0924-7238)
Published by: Body Biz International B.V., Postbus 178, Gennep, 6590 AD, Netherlands. TEL 31-485-513316, FAX 31-485-518461, info@bodybiz.nl. Circ: 2,700.

799.32 FRA ISSN 1148-3652
L'ARCHER. Text in French. 1906. s-a. adv. **Document type:** *Newspaper.*
Published by: (Associations d'Archers du Nord de la France), Independant du Pas-de-Calais, 14 rue des Clouteries, St Omer, 62500, France. TEL 33-3-21122223, FAX 33-3-21397250. Circ: 750.

796.8 USA ISSN 1643-8698
➤ **ARCHIVES OF BUDO.** Text in English. 2005. q. **Document type:** *Journal, Academic/Scholarly.*
Media: Online - full text.
Published by: International Scientific Literature Inc., 361 Forest Lane, Smithtown, NY 11787. TEL 516-874-4341, office@isl-science.com, http://www.isl-science.com. Ed. Roman M Kalina.

796.72 USA ISSN 1041-3251
AREA AUTO RACING NEWS. Text in English. 1963. w. USD 44 domestic; USD 70 in Canada; USD 99 elsewhere (effective 2006). adv. bk.rev. **Document type:** *Magazine, Consumer.* **Description:** Covers all Northeast circle track auto races and all national series.
Published by: Area Auto Racing News, Inc., PO Box 8547, Trenton, NJ 08650-0547. TEL 609-888-3618, FAX 609-888-2538. Ed., Pub. Len Sammons. Adv. contact Joe Pratt. Circ: 72,000 (paid).

790.1 GBR ISSN 1356-1219
ARENA (GLASGOW). Text in English. 1979. irreg., latest 2007. illus. **Document type:** *Magazine, Consumer.*
Formerly (until 1989): Scottish Sports Council. Bulletin (0142-6761)
Related titles: Online - full text ed.: free.
Published by: Scottish Sports Council, Doges, Templeton on the Green, Glasgow, G40 1DA, United Kingdom. TEL 44-141-5346500, FAX 44-141-5346501, sportscotland.enquiries@sportscotland.org.uk.

796 ESP ISSN 1576-4400
ARIAN. Text in Spanish. 2000. 3/yr. **Document type:** *Magazine, Consumer.*
Published by: Comunidad de Madrid, Consejeria de Educacion y Cultura. Direccion General de Deportes, C. Juan Esplandiu, 1, Madrid, 28007, Spain. TEL 34-91-5805200, FAX 34-91-573-0973, http://www.madrid.org/deportes/index.html.

796.962 USA
ARIZONA RUBBER MAGAZINE; from kids to coyotes, the desert's authoritative voice of ice and inline hockey. Text in English. 2006. 10/yr. USD 29.95 (effective 2010). adv. **Document type:** *Magazine, Consumer.*
Published by: Good Sport Media, Inc., PO Box 24024, Edina, MN 55424. TEL 612-929-2171, FAX 612-920-8326, info@goodsportmedia.com, http://www.goodsportmedia.com.

ARMAS. *see* MILITARY

790.1 USA ISSN 1043-3120
THE ARMBENDER. Text in English. 1971. q. USD 25 (effective 2000). adv. back issues avail. **Document type:** *Magazine, Consumer.* **Description:** Promotes arm wrestling as a sport. Includes competition results, tips and tales of arm wrestlers.
Published by: (American Armwrestling Association), Boss Publications, PO Box 79, Scranton, PA 18504-0079. TEL 717-342-4984, FAX 717-342-1368. Eds. Bobbye Kimble, Richard Kimble. Pub. Bob O'Leary. Circ: 1,500. **Co-sponsor:** World Armsport Federation, Bob O'Leary Sports Science.

799.32 GBR ISSN 0144-7424
ARROWHEAD. Text in English. 1958. s-a. GBP 15 to members (effective 2003). bk.rev. **Document type:** *Newsletter.* **Description:** Devoted to archery.
Formerly: Society of Archer-Antiquaries. Newsletter (0049-1187)
Media: Duplicated (not offset).
Indexed: NumL, SD, SportS.
Published by: Society of Archer-Antiquaries, c/o Edward Hart, 36 Myrtledene Rd., Abbey Wood, London, SE2 0EZ, United Kingdom. TEL 44-1262-601604. Ed. Bob Brown.

ARTUS. *see* PHYSICAL FITNESS AND HYGIENE

ASIA-PACIFIC JOURNAL OF HEALTH, PHYSICAL EDUCATION AND RECREATION. *see* EDUCATION

▼ **ASIA-PACIFIC JOURNAL OF HEALTH, SPORT AND PHYSICAL EDUCATION.** *see* PHYSICAL FITNESS AND HYGIENE

▼ **ASIAN JOURNAL OF GAMBLING ISSUES AND PUBLIC HEALTH.** *see* PUBLIC HEALTH AND SAFETY

▼ **ASIAN JOURNAL OF SPORTS MEDICINE.** *see* MEDICAL SCIENCES

ASSER INTERNATIONAL SPORTS LAW SERIES. *see* LAW

ASSOCIATION FOR THE STUDY OF PLAY NEWSLETTER. *see* PSYCHOLOGY

790 ESP ISSN 2171-4096
▼ **ASTURIAS DC.** Text in Spanish. 2009. q. **Document type:** *Magazine, Consumer.*
Published by: Grupo DC, C Navarra 4 y 5 Bajo, Gijon, Asturias, 33207, Spain. TEL 34-985-353745, FAX 34-985-347438, contacto@grupo-dc.com, http://www.grupo-dc.com/.

790.1 USA ISSN 1074-8547
ATHLETES IN ACTION. Text in English. 1988. q. USD 10 domestic; USD 13 foreign (effective 2000). adv. bk.rev. **Document type:** *Magazine, Consumer.* **Description:** Christian sports ministry.
Address: 651 Taylor Dr., Xenia, OH 45385-7246. TEL 513-933-2421, FAX 513-933-2424. Eds. Greg Stoughton, Wendel Deyo. R&P, Adv. contact Greg Stoughton. Circ: 12,373.

790.1 USA ISSN 0747-315X
ATHLETIC BUSINESS; the leading resource for athletic, fitness & recreation professionals. Text in English. 1977. m. USD 55 in US & Canada includes Mexico; USD 130 elsewhere; USD 8 per issue includes Mexico; USD 15 per issue elsewhere (effective 2008). adv. bk.rev. illus. Index. back issues avail.; reprints avail. **Document type:** *Magazine, Trade.* **Description:** For owners and operators of athletic, recreation and fitness facilities.
Formerly (until 1984): Athletic Purchasing and Facilities (0192-5482)
Related titles: Online - full text ed.
Indexed: A22, SD, SportS.
—BLDSC (1765.878750), IE, Ingenta.
Published by: Athletic Business Publications, Inc., 4130 Lien Rd, Madison, WI 53704-3602. TEL 608-249-0186, 800-722-8764, FAX 608-249-1153, http://www.athleticbusiness.com. Ed. Andrew Cohen. Pub. Sue Searls. adv.: B&W page USD 4,285, color page USD 5,410; trim 8.125 x 10.875. Circ: 43,000.

796 AUS ISSN 0300-4600
ATHLETIC ECHO. Text in Greek. 1961. w. bk.rev.
Published by: Petranis Press, 8 Atkin St, North Melbourne, VIC 3051, Australia. Circ: 5,000.

ATHLETIC MANAGEMENT. *see* EDUCATION—School Organization And Administration

ATHLETIC TRAINING EDUCATION JOURNAL. *see* MEDICAL SCIENCES—Sports Medicine

796 CAN ISSN 0229-4966
ATHLETICS; the Canadian track & field running magazine. Text in English. 1976. 9/yr. CAD 19.80 domestic; CAD 22.50 in United States; CAD 42 elsewhere; CAD 3 newsstand/cover (effective 2004). adv. bk.rev. illus. **Document type:** *Magazine, Consumer.* **Description:** Offers coverage of track, field and road racing in Canada. Covers all major competitions around the world, including Canada.

Formerly: Ontario Athletics
Related titles: Microfiche ed.: (from MML); Microform ed.: (from MML).
Indexed: A26, C03, CBCARef, CBPI, CPerI, G08, P48, PQC, SD, SportS, T02.
Published by: Athletics Inc., 1185 Eglinton Ave E, Ste 302, Toronto, ON M3C 3C6, Canada. TEL 416-426-7216, FAX 416-426-7358, ontrack@eol.ca. Ed. John Craig. Adv. contact Bernie Eckler. Circ: 8,000.

796 USA ISSN 0044-9873
GV343.5
ATHLETICS ADMINISTRATION; official publication of the National Association of Collegiate Directors of Athletics. Text in English. 1966. bi-m. USD 15 to non-members. adv. bk.rev. charts; illus.; tr.lit. Index. reprints avail. **Document type:** *Journal, Trade.* **Description:** Publishes features relating to the administration of college athletics programs.
Indexed: SD, SPI, SportS.
—IE, Ingenta.
Published by: (National Association of Collegiate Directors of Athletics), Host Communications, Inc., 546 E Main St, Lexington, KY 40508. info@hostcommunications.com, http://www.hostcommunications.com. Ed., R&P Laurie Garrison. Adv. contact Rob Smith. Circ: 6,500.

ATHLETICS EMPLOYMENT WEEKLY. see OCCUPATIONS AND CAREERS

796.4 NZL ISSN 1177-5262
ATHLETICS IN ACTION (ONLINE). Text in English. bi-m. **Document type:** *Magazine, Consumer.*
Media: Online - full text.
Published by: (Athletics New Zealand), Executive Publishing Network New Zealand Limited, PO Box 741, Wellington, 6140, New Zealand. TEL 64-4-3846021, FAX 64-4-3851758. Ed. Gary Nesbit TEL 64-4-4616635.

796 GBR ISSN 0004-6671
ATHLETICS WEEKLY. Text in English. 1945. w. GBP 72.20; GBP 93.20 foreign (effective 1999). adv. bk.rev. illus. back issues avail. **Document type:** *Magazine, Consumer.*
Incorporates: Modern Athletics; Women's Athletics
Indexed: RASB, SD, SportS.
Published by: Emap Active Ltd. (Bretton House), Bretton Ct, Bretton, Peterborough, Cambs PE3 8DZ, United Kingdom. TEL 44-1733-264666, FAX 44-1733-465498. Ed. Nigel Walsh. Circ: 16,000. **Subscr. to:** CDS Global, Tower House, Sovereign Park, Market Harborough, Leics LE16 9EF, United Kingdom. TEL 44-1858-435339, FAX 44-1858-434958.

ATHLETIKE PSUHOLOGIA. see PSYCHOLOGY

790.1 FRA ISSN 1629-5935
ATHLETISME MAGAZINE. Text in French. m. (10/yr.). EUR 41 domestic; EUR 51 foreign (effective 2009). **Document type:** *Magazine, Consumer.*
Formerly (until 2001): Athletisme (1144-4487)
Published by: Federation Francaise d'Athletisme, 33 Avenue Pierre de Coubertin, Paris, 75640 Cedex 13, France. TEL 33-1-53807000. Ed. Philippe Lamblin.

796 PRT ISSN 1647-368X
▼ **ATHLETISSIMA.** Text in Portuguese. 2009. q. **Document type:** *Magazine, Consumer.*
Published by: Federacao Portuguesa de Atletismo, Largo da Lagoa, Linda-a Velha, 2799-538, Portugal. TEL 351-21-4146020, FAX 351-21-4146021, fpa@fpaatletismo.pt, http://fpatletismo.sapo.pt.

796 USA
ATLANTA SPORTING FAMILY. Text in English. bi-m. free. **Document type:** *Magazine, Consumer.*
Published by: The Publishing Group, Inc., 240 Prospect Pl Bldg E1, Alpharetta, GA 30005. TEL 678-297-7747, FAX 678-534-6841. Ed. Jennifer J Morrell. Pub. Tina D'Aversa-Williams. Adv. contact Whitney Noonan.

790.1 USA
ATLANTA SPORTS AND FITNESS MAGAZINE; Atlanta's guide to a healthy and active lifestyle. Text in English. 1990. m. USD 6; free (effective 2006). adv. bk.rev.; video rev. **Document type:** *Magazine, Consumer.* **Description:** Contains information on sports, health, fitness, and nutrition.
Formerly (until 1993): Atlanta Health and Fitness Magazine
Related titles: ◆ Supplement(s): Georgia Athlete.
Published by: Dickey Publishing, 3535 Piedmont Rd, Bldg 14, 12th Fl, Atlanta, GA 30305. TEL 404-843-2257, FAX 404-843-1339. Ed. Beth Weitzman. Pub. Caroline Oberg. Adv. contact Scott Thompson. B&W page USD 2,600, color page USD 3,000; trim 9.75 x 12. Circ: 75,000.

790.1 CAN
ATLANTIC SNOWMOBILER. Text in English. 1993. q. CAD 9 domestic; CAD 9 foreign; CAD 2.50 newsstand/cover (effective 1999). adv. video rev. tr.lit.; tr.mk. back issues avail. **Document type:** *Magazine, Consumer.* **Description:** Publishes news of the world of snowmobiling, including racing, rumours, industry updates and travels.
Published by: (New Brunswick Federation of Snowmobile Clubs), Atlantic Snowmobiler Publishing Inc., 527 Beaverbrook Court, Ste 510, Fredericton, NB E3B 1X6, Canada. TEL 506-444-6489. Ed. Kent Lester. Pub. Terrence D Kehoe. R&P Raymond Kehoe TEL 905-898-8585. Adv. contact Harold McCann. B&W page CAD 2,785, color page CAD 3,715; trim 10.88 x 8.13. Circ: 20,000. **Subscr. to:** 78 Main St S, Newmarket, ON L3Y 3Y6, Canada.

613.7 ITA ISSN 1825-9944
ATLETICAMENTE. Text in Italian. 2005. m. **Document type:** *Magazine, Consumer.*
Published by: Vannini Editrice, Via Leonardo da Vinci 6, Gussago, BS 25064, Italy. TEL 39-030-313374, FAX 39-030-314078, http://www.vanniniedit rice.it.

796 ITA ISSN 0390-6671
ATLETICASTUDI; ricerca scientifica & tecnica applicata all'atletica leggera. Text in Italian. 1970. 4/yr. **Document type:** *Magazine, Consumer.*
Related titles: CD-ROM ed.
Indexed: SportS.
—IE, INIST.
Published by: Federazione Italiana di Atletica Leggera (F I D A L), Via Flaminia Nuova 830, Rome, 00191, Italy. TEL 39-06-36851, http://www.fidal.it. Circ: 14,000.

796 PRT ISSN 1647-2187
ATLETICO CLUBE DE PORTUGAL. JORNAL. Text in Portuguese. 2008. m. **Document type:** *Newspaper, Consumer.*
Related titles: Online - full text ed.
Published by: Atletico Clube de Portugal, Estadio da Tapadinha, Lisbon, 1300-604, Portugal. TEL 351-21-3637986, FAX 351-21-3621581, http://www.atleticocp.pt.

796 ESP ISSN 1133-8946
ATLETICO DE MADRID. Text in Spanish. 1994. m. **Document type:** *Magazine, Consumer.*
Published by: Club Atletico de Madrid, C. Aranjuez 7, Madrid, 28039, Spain. TEL 34-91-2260403, FAX 34-91-3669811, comunicacion@clubatleticodemadrid.com, http://www.clubatleticodemadrid.com/. Ed. Emilio Gutierrez Boullosa.

796.805 AUS ISSN 1321-7771
AUSTRALASIAN TAEKWONDO MAGAZINE. Text in English. 1992. q. AUD 27 domestic; AUD 67 foreign (effective 2008). adv. back issues avail. **Document type:** *Magazine, Consumer.* **Description:** Features coverage of both the WTF and ITF forms of taekwondo and a variety of other Korean martial arts styles, including hapkido.
Indexed: SD.
Published by: Blitz Publications, PO Box 4075, Mulgrave, VIC 3170, Australia. TEL 61-3-95748460, FAX 61-3-95748899, info@blitzmag.com.au. Ed. Ruth Brown. Adv. contact Keith Rozario.

388.34 629.283042 AUS ISSN 1839-0080
AUSTRALIAN 4 W D ACTION. (Wheel Drive) Text in English. 1999. 17/yr. AUD 127 domestic; AUD 195 in New Zealand; AUD 305 elsewhere (effective 2011). adv. 260 p./no.; **Document type:** *Magazine, Consumer.* **Description:** Contains new vehicle reviews, custom 4WD and special features.
Former titles (until Nov.2007): Australian 4 W D Monthly Action; (until May.2007): Australian 4 W D Monthly; (until May.1999): 4 W D Off-Road Australia; (until Jan.1999): Offroad Action
Related titles: Online - full text ed.
Published by: Express Publications Pty. Ltd., 2-4 Stanley St, Locked Bag 111, Silverwater, NSW 2168, Australia. **Subscr. to:** Magshop, Locked Bag 111, Silverwater, NSW 1811, Australia. subs@magstore.com.au, http://shop.magstore.com.au.

799.202 AUS ISSN 1448-3939
AUSTRALIAN & NEW ZEALAND HANDGUN. Text in English. 2003. a., latest no.7, 2009. AUD 14 per issue domestic; AUD 16 per issue in New Zealand; AUD 20 per issue elsewhere (effective 2009). adv. **Document type:** *Magazine, Consumer.* **Description:** Provides information about handguns for sport shooting competitors and those who use handguns in their profession.
Published by: Sporting Shooters Association of Australia, PO Box 906, St. Marys, NSW 1790, Australia. TEL 61-2-88890400, as@ssaa.org.au. Adv. contact Karoline Minicozzi. B&W page AUD 1,315, color page AUD 1,660; trim 230 x 275.

790.1 AUS
AUSTRALIAN AND NEW ZEALAND SNOWBOARDING. Text in English. 1992. 3/yr. AUD 23.85 domestic; AUD 28.85 in New Zealand; AUD 35.85 elsewhere; AUD 7.95 newsstand/cover (effective 2008). adv. **Document type:** *Magazine, Consumer.* **Description:** Provides informations, interviews, events, travel related to snowboarding.
Formerly (until 2002): Australia Snowboarding (1448-7144)
Related titles: ◆ Supplement to: Tracks. ISSN 1032-3317.
Published by: A C P Magazines Ltd. (Subsidiary of: P B L Media Pty Ltd.), 54-58 Park St, Sydney, NSW 2000, Australia. TEL 61-2-92828000, FAX 61-2-91263769, research@acpaction.com.au. adv.: page AUD 2,840; bleed 245 x 310. Circ: 20,000.

AUSTRALIAN AND NEW ZEALAND SPORTS LAW JOURNAL. see LAW

796.71 AUS ISSN 1320-2073
AUSTRALIAN AUTO ACTION. Text in English. 197?. w. AUD 5.50 newsstand/cover (effective 2008). adv. **Document type:** *Magazine, Consumer.* **Description:** Contains articles and features for motor sport enthusiasts.
Indexed: A11.
Published by: A C P Magazines Ltd. (Subsidiary of: P B L Media Pty Ltd.), 54-58 Park St, Sydney, NSW 2000, Australia. TEL 61-2-92828000, FAX 61-2-91263769. Ed. Andrew McLean. Adv. contact Paul Franks TEL 61-2-82686258. color page AUD 2,550; bleed 307 x 322. Circ: 13,353. **Subscr. to:** Magshop, Reply Paid 4967, Sydney, NSW 2001, Australia. TEL 61-2-136116, subs@magstore.com.au, http://shop.magstore.com.au.

795.415 AUS ISSN 0814-3889
AUSTRALIAN BRIDGE. Text in English. 1970. bi-m. AUD 49 domestic; AUD 64 in Asia including New Zealand; AUD 75 elsewhere; AUD 12 per issue (effective 2008). adv. bk.rev. **Document type:** *Magazine, Consumer.* **Description:** Contains instructive articles and match reports from all the major events related to the game of bridge.
Address: PO Box 1426, Double Bay, NSW 1360, Australia. TEL 61-2-93274599, FAX 61-2-93639326. Circ: 2,200.

794.1 AUS ISSN 1442-7745
AUSTRALIAN CHESS FORUM. Text in English. 1998. m. AUD 44; AUD 4.40 per issue (effective 2008). 48 p./no.; **Document type:** *Magazine, Consumer.* **Description:** Provides news and information on chess.
Address: PO Box 1201, Belconnen, ACT 2616, Australia. Shaun.Press@cs.anu.edu.au. Eds. Paul Dunn, Shaun Press.
Co-sponsor: Australian Chess Federation.

799.2 AUS ISSN 1321-3903
AUSTRALIAN CLAY TARGET SHOOTING NEWS. Text in English. 1947. m. AUD 44 (effective 2008). adv. bk.rev. back issues avail. **Document type:** *Magazine, Consumer.* **Description:** Covers shooting sports and club shooting throughout Australia and internationally.
Related titles: Online - full text ed.
Indexed: SD.
Published by: Australian Clay Target Association Inc., PO Box 466, Wagga Wagga, NSW 2650, Australia. TEL 61-2-69310122, FAX 61-2-69310125, info@claytarget.com.au, http://www.claytarget.com.au. Ed., R&P, Adv. contact Andrew Sanders. B&W page AUD 650; trim 210 x 270. Circ: 12,000.

793 AUS ISSN 0819-7806
AUSTRALIAN CORRESPONDENCE CHESS QUARTERLY. Abbreviated title: A C C Q. Text in English. 1948. q. free to members (effective 2008). bk.rev. **Document type:** *Magazine, Trade.* **Description:** Contains news, games, results of tourneys, notice of up-coming events, articles and an updated ratings list of Correspondence Chess League of Australia.
Formerly (until 1986): C C L A Record (0819-7792)
Published by: Correspondence Chess League of Australia, PO Box 2360, Sydney, NSW 2001, Australia. ccla@alphalink.com.au, http://www.ccla.asn.au. Ed. Shaun Press.

AUSTRALIAN GAMBLING STATISTICS (ONLINE). see SPORTS AND GAMES—Abstracting, Bibliographies, Statistics

AUSTRALIAN INSTITUTE OF SPORT ALUMNI NEWS. see EDUCATION—Higher Education

AUSTRALIAN INTERNATIONAL AIRSHOW. see AERONAUTICS AND SPACE FLIGHT

AUSTRALIAN IRONMAN; bodybuilding and fitness magazine. see PHYSICAL FITNESS AND HYGIENE

796 AUS ISSN 1448-3467
AUSTRALIAN SPORTS FOUNDATION. NEWSLETTER. Text in English. 2002. s-a. free (effective 2008). 8 p./no.; back issues avail. **Document type:** *Newsletter, Consumer.* **Description:** Provides information that meets the needs of a range of ASF stakeholders including Australian organizations that are looking towards fundraising for sport related projects.
Related titles: Online - full text ed.: free (effective 2008).
Published by: Australian Sports Foundation Ltd, PO Box 176, Belconnen, ACT 2616, Australia. TEL 61-2-62147863, FAX 61-2-62147865, info@asf.org.au. Circ: 2,000.

796.426 AUS ISSN 1320-5773
AUSTRALIAN TRIATHLETE. Text in English. 1993. 9/yr. AUD 51 domestic; AUD 90 in New Zealand; AUD 126 elsewhere (effective 2008). adv. **Document type:** *Magazine, Consumer.* **Description:** Covers all aspects of the sport: age group to elite competitors, short course to Ironman distance, training advice to mental preparation, news and previews, etc.
Indexed: SD.
—BLDSC (1823.640000).
Published by: Publicity Press Pty. Ltd., Level One, 1121 High St, PO Box 8019, Armadale, VIC 3143, Australia. TEL 61-3-98044700, FAX 61-3-98044711, sales@publicitypress.com.au, http://www.publicitypress.com.au. Eds. Amy White, Shane Smith. Adv. contact Marcus Altmann. color page AUD 1,355; trim 210 x 297. Circ: 15,000.

AUTO; prvi srpski magazin za automobilizam i auto moto sport. see TRANSPORTATION—Automobiles

796.72 DEU ISSN 1617-4100
AUTO BILD MOTORSPORT. Text in German. 2001. 40/yr. EUR 1.50 newsstand/cover (effective 2011). adv. **Document type:** *Magazine, Consumer.*
Incorporates (1966-2001): Rallye Racing (0033-9148); Which incorporated (1974-1987): Sportfahrer (0176-8808); and (1953-1991): Illustrierter Motorsport (0442-3054); Which was formerly (1951-1953): Motorsport (0323-7095)
Published by: A S Autoverlag GmbH (Subsidiary of: Axel Springer Verlag AG), Axel-Springer-Platz 1, Hamburg, 20350, Germany. TEL 49-40-34725934, FAX 49-40-34727073, dk@autoverlag.de, http://www.autojournal.de. Ed. Olaf Schilling. Circ: 331,265 (paid and controlled).

AUTO HEBDO. see TRANSPORTATION—Automobiles

796.7 ROM ISSN 1224-6891
AUTO MONDIAL. Text in Romanian. 1996. m. ROL 325,000 (effective 2002). adv. **Document type:** *Magazine, Consumer.*
Published by: Auto Press Group, Calea 13 Septembrie, 59-61, OP 5, sector 5, Bucharest, Romania. TEL 40-21-4112301.

AUTO MOTOR & SPORT. see TRANSPORTATION—Automobiles
AUTO MOTOR & SPORT. see TRANSPORTATION—Automobiles
AUTO MOTOR & SPORT. see TRANSPORTATION—Automobiles
AUTO MOTOR I SPORT. see TRANSPORTATION—Automobiles
AUTO MOTOR SI SPORT. see TRANSPORTATION—Automobiles
AUTO MOTOR UND SPORT. see TRANSPORTATION—Automobiles
AUTO MOTOR UND SPORT SPEZIAL GEBRAUCHTWAGEN. see TRANSPORTATION—Automobiles
AUTO MOTOR UND SPORT TESTJAHRBUCH. see TRANSPORTATION—Automobiles

796.72 USA
AUTO RACING DIGEST ANNUAL GUIDE. Text in English. a. **Document type:** *Magazine, Consumer.*
Published by: Century Publishing Inc., E 5710 Seltice Way, Post Falls, ID 83854. TEL 208-765-6300, 800-824-1806, FAX 208-676-8476, privacy@CenturyPublishing.com, http://www.centurypublishing.com.

629.2 GBR ISSN 0067-2432
AUTOCOURSE; the world's leading Grand Prix annual. Text in English. 1951. a. GBP 34 per issue (effective 2010). adv. illus. **Document type:** *Magazine, Consumer.* **Description:** Reviews the events and gives the results for race-by-race coverage of the formula 1 season.
Published by: Icon Publishing Ltd., Regent Lodge, 4 Hanley Rd, Malvern, WR14 4PQ, United Kingdom. TEL 44-1684-564511. Ed. Alan Henry.

379.5 ESP ISSN 1139-8922
AUTODEFINIDOS. Text in Spanish. 1996. m. EUR 1.35 newsstand/cover. adv. **Document type:** *Magazine, Consumer.*
Published by: H. Bauer Ediciones S.L. (Subsidiary of: Bauer Media Group), Calle Pedro Teixeira, 8 - 5o. Planta, Madrid, 28020, Spain. TEL 34-91-5476800, FAX 34-91-5413523, http://www.bauer.es/.

AUTODEFINIDOS BOOM. see HOBBIES
AUTODEFINIDOS EXPRESS. see HOBBIES
AUTODEFINIDOS EXTREME. see HOBBIES
AUTODEFINIDOS FANTASTICOS. see HOBBIES
AUTODEFINIDOS GOLD. see HOBBIES
AUTODEFINIDOS MANIA. see HOBBIES
AUTODEFINIDOS POCKET. see HOBBIES

S

AUTODEFINIDOS POCKET. EXTRA. *see* HOBBIES

AUTODEFINIDOS PREMIER. *see* HOBBIES

AUTODEFINIDOS QUICK. *see* HOBBIES

388.34 FRA ISSN 1778-8129
AUTOMOBILE REVUE. SPECIAL 4 X 4. Cover title: Automobile Revue 4 X 4. Variant title: Automobile Revue. Special Quatre Fois Quatre. Text in French. 2005. q. EUR 44 for 2 yrs. (effective 2010). **Document type:** *Magazine, Consumer.*
Published by: Lafont Presse, 53 Rue du Chemin Vert, Boulogne-Billancourt, 92100, France. TEL 33-1-46102121, http://www.lafontpresse.fr.

796.72 MEX
AUTOMUNDO DEPORTIVO; sports. Text in Spanish. 1969. m. USD 60. adv. illus.
Formerly: Automondo
Published by: Nueva Impresora y Editora, S.A. de C.V., Carr Lago de Guadalupe Km. 15, San Mateo Tecoloapan, Atizapan de Zaragoza, Estado de Mexico, 52920, Mexico. TEL 52-55-30030100, FAX 52-55-30030129. Ed. Romulo O'Farril Jr. Circ: 100,000.

AUTOSPORT. *see* TRANSPORTATION—Automobiles

796.72 DNK ISSN 0908-7648
AUTOSPORT. Text in Danish. 1965. 10/yr. DKK 500 (effective 2008). adv. bk.rev. **Document type:** *Magazine, Consumer.*
Former titles (until 1993): Aktuel Bilsport (0109-6338); (until 1984): Auto Orienting (0105-6468); (until 1974): Auto (0909-590X); (until 1972): K D A K Auto (0909-5988); (until 1966): K D A K Nyt (0909-5896)
Published by: Dansk Automobil Sports Union, Idraettens Hus, Broendby Stadion, Brondby, 2605, Denmark. TEL 45-43-262880, FAX 45-43-262881, dasu@dasu.dk, http://www.dasu.dk. Ed. Jens Faergemann. Adv. contact Michael Eisenberg. Circ: 8,000.

AUTOSPORT. *see* TRANSPORTATION—Automobiles

796.72 HUN ISSN 1785-9484
AUTOSPORT ES FORMULA. Text in Hungarian. 2000. m. **Document type:** *Magazine, Consumer.*
Former titles (until 2004): Formula (1589-6560); (until 2002): Formula 1 (1585-9363)
Published by: Beta Press Kft., Eszterhazy ut 29, Miskolc, 3529, Hungary. TEL 36-46-505490, FAX 36-46-505491.

796.72 ITA ISSN 0005-1748
AUTOSPRINT. Text in Italian. 1961. w. bk.rev. **Document type:** *Magazine, Consumer.* **Description:** Focuses on racing cars.
Published by: Conti Editore SpA, Via del Lavoro 7, San Lazzaro di Savena, BO 40068, Italy. http://www.contieditore.it. Circ: 77,350.

793 USA ISSN 0888-1081
AVALON HILL GENERAL. Text in English. 1964. bi-m. USD 18; USD 36 in Canada & Mexico; USD 48 elsewhere. adv. charts; illus. **Document type:** *Magazine, Consumer.* **Description:** Devoted to the strategy and play of strategy games, with emphasis on military, political and economic history.
Published by: Avalon Hill Game Co. (Subsidiary of: Girls' Life Acquisitions Corp.), 4517 Harford Rd, Baltimore, MD 21214. TEL 410-426-9600, FAX 410-254-0991, AHGeneral@aol.com. Ed. Stuart K Tucker. Circ: 25,000 (paid).

790.1 IRN ISSN 1021-6316
AVARD MAGAZINE. Text in Persian, Modern. 1993. 12/yr. USD 30 (effective 1994). adv. bk.rev.; film rev. **Document type:** *Consumer.* **Description:** Covers boxing and all forms of martial arts. Includes interviews, articles on technique and training, and other news of interest.
Address: Mirza-e Shirazi Ave., 22nd St., No. 25, P O Box 14335-398, Tehran, Iran. TEL 98-21-8801087, FAX 98-21-2577692. Ed. Mohammed Ali Masoud. Adv. contact F Karimi. Circ: 50,000 (paid).

306.4 USA ISSN 1547-2426
AVERY CARDOZA'S PLAYER; the total gambling lifestyle magazine. Text in English. 2003. bi-m. USD 9; USD 4.99 newsstand/cover (effective 2007). **Document type:** *Magazine, Consumer.* **Description:** Covers the gambling lifestyle, including advice on various games, articles on casinos and clubs, and other gambling related stories.
Published by: Cardoza Publishing, Inc., 857 Broadway, 3rd Fl, New York, NY 10003. TEL 212-255-6661, 800-577-9467, FAX 212-255-6671, cardozapub@aol.com, http://www.cardozapub.com/. Ed., Pub. Avery Cardoza. **Subscr. to:** PO Box 3, Cooper Station, New York, NY 10276.

797.5 ESP ISSN 1575-1112
AVIACION GENERAL Y DEPORTIVA. Text in Spanish. 1998. m. EUR 53 domestic (effective 2009). adv. **Document type:** *Magazine, Consumer.*
Formerly (until 1999): Aviacion Deportiva (1139-1448)
Published by: M C Ediciones, Paseo de Sant Gervasi 16-20, Barcelona, 08022, Spain. TEL 34-93-2541250, FAX 34-93-2541262, http://www.mcediciones.net.

799.32 CAN ISSN 0226-7691
B.C. ARCHER. Text in English. bi-m. **Document type:** *Magazine, Consumer.*
Published by: British Columbia Archery Association, c/o Val Canham, RR 3, S 22, C 17, Oliver, BC V0H 1T0, Canada. TEL 604-498-2212, 888-548-2212, FAX 604-498-2271. Ed. Sheri Luckhurst TEL 250-701-0068.

796.077 CAN ISSN 1209-6245
B C COACH'S PERSPECTIVE. Text in English. 1997. q.
Formed by the merger of (1992-1996): Coach's Perspective (1209-6237); (1991-1996): B C Coach (1197-1673)
Indexed: SD.
Published by: Coaches Association of British Columbia, 1367 W Broadway, Suite 345, Vancouver, BC V6H 4A9, Canada. TEL 604-298-3137, FAX 604-738-7175, info@coaches.bc.ca.

B INTERNATIONAL. *see* GENERAL INTEREST PERIODICALS—Hong Kong, Special Administrative Region Of P R C

790 USA
THE B.O.S.S. REPORT; the bicycle, outdoor, and snow-sports trade newsletter. Text in English. w. USD 279 (effective 2009). back issues avail. **Document type:** *Newsletter, Trade.* **Description:** Provides comprehensive coverage, in-depth analysis and unique insight into the the trade news servicing the bicycle, outdoor and snowsports markets.
Media: Online - full content. **Related titles:** E-mail ed.
Published by: SportsOneSource Group, 2151 Hawkins St, Ste 200, Charlotte, NC 28269. TEL 704-987-3450, FAX 704-987-3455, info@sportsonesource.com. Eds. Andy Kerrigan, Tom Ryan.

796.305896 USA
B S T M (ONLINE). Text in English. 2004. m. free (effective 2006). adv. **Document type:** *Magazine, Consumer.* **Description:** Examines the achievements of minority athletes, sports issues of noteworthiness, historical sports' information, HBCU major conferences athletic teams, and other areas of sports impacting the minority community.
Formerly (until Dec.2005): Black Sports the Magazine (Print)
Media: Online - full text.
Published by: B S T M, PO Box 44577, Washington, DC 20040. TEL 202-882-9444. Pub. Melvin Bell. adv.: color page USD 1,500; trim 8.357 x 10.875.

790.1 DEU
B T V SPIEGEL. Text in German. 1960. q. free to members (effective 2008). illus.; stat. **Document type:** *Magazine, Consumer.*
Published by: Bremer Turnvereinigung von 1877 e.V., Hamburger Str 71, Bremen, 28205, Germany. TEL 49-421-442792, FAX 49-421-4309153, info@btv1877.de, http://www.btv1877.de. Circ: 1,400.

796.41 DEU ISSN 0721-2828
BADISCHE TURNZEITUNG. Text in German. 195?. m. EUR 30 (effective 2009). adv. **Document type:** *Magazine, Trade.*
Published by: Badischer Turner-Bund e.V., Postfach 1405, Karlsruhe, 76003, Germany. TEL 49-721-18150, FAX 49-721-26176, zentrale@badischer-turner-bund.de. Ed. Kurt Klumpp. Adv. contact Henning Paul. B&W page EUR 520, color page EUR 900; trim 210 x 297. Circ: 5,800 (controlled).

796.345 GBR ISSN 0262-1940
BADMINTON ASSOCIATION OF ENGLAND. ANNUAL HANDBOOK. Text in English. 1900. a. adv. index. 190 p./no.; **Document type:** *Bulletin, Consumer.* **Description:** Contains contact details for all BADMINTON England staff and representatives, facts and records, rules of the association, tournament rules and regulations and a diary of events.
Formerly: Badminton Association of England. Official Handbook (0067-2882)
Published by: Badminton Association of England Ltd., National Badminton Centre, Bradwell Rd, Loughton Lodge, Milton Keynes, Bucks MK8 9LA, United Kingdom. TEL 44-1908-268400, enquiries@badmintonengland.co.uk. Circ: 8,000.

796.345 AUS
BADMINTON BEAT. Text in English. 1976. q.
Former titles (until 1998): Sidelines; (until 1994): Badminton Sidelines (0813-006X)
Published by: Victorian Badminton Association, PO Box 28, South Melbourne, VIC 3205, Australia. **Subscr. to:** Badminton Sidelines.

796.342 JPN
BADMINTON MAGAZINE. Text in Japanese. 1980. m. JPY 8,640 (effective 2000).
Published by: Baseball Magazine Sha, 3-10-10 Misaki-cho, Chiyoda-ku, Tokyo, 101-0061, Japan. FAX 81-3-3238-0106. Ed. Haruko Ekuni.

796.345 DEU ISSN 0943-6014
BADMINTON SPORT. Text in German. 1953. 10/yr. EUR 30; EUR 3 newsstand/cover (effective 2011). adv. 42 p./no. 3 cols./p.; back issues avail. **Document type:** *Magazine, Consumer.* **Description:** Contains information on and about badminton as it is played in Germany.
Published by: (Deutscher Badminto-Verband e.V.), Meyer & Meyer Verlag, Von-Coels-Str 390, Aachen, 52080, Germany. TEL 49-241-958100, FAX 49-241-9581010, verlag@m-m-sports.com, http://m-m-sports.de. Circ: 15,000 (paid and controlled).

796.345 NLD ISSN 1877-3664
BADMINTONINFO. Text in Dutch. 2006. q. EUR 17.95 (effective 2011). **Document type:** *Magazine, Consumer.*
Published by: (Stichting Bevordering Topbadminton, Nederlandse Badminton Bond), Sport Unlimited, Postbus 140, Elburg, 8080 AC, Netherlands. TEL 31-525-681311, FAX 31-525-683184, info@sportunlimited.nl, http://www.sportunlimited.nl.

797 USA ISSN 0887-6061
BALLOON LIFE; the magazine for hot air ballooning. Text in English. 1986. m. USD 30; USD 33 in Canada & Mexico; USD 66 elsewhere (effective 2000). adv. bk.rev. illus. back issues avail. **Document type:** *Magazine, Consumer.* **Description:** Covers the sport of hot air ballooning - events, issues, and people.
Published by: Balloon Life Magazine, Inc., 10123 Airport Way, Snohomish, WA 98296-8237. TEL 206-935-3649, FAX 206-935-3326. Ed., Pub., R&P, Adv. contact Tom Hamilton. Circ: 4,000.

BALLOONING. *see* AERONAUTICS AND SPACE FLIGHT

797.21 ESP ISSN 1888-2986
BALNEARIO D'HOTELS. Text in Spanish, Catalan. 2006. a.
Published by: Asociacion Valenciana de Estaciones Termales, Baldovi, 2, Valencia, 46002, Spain. TEL 34-96-3530055.

797.21 MEX
BALNEARIOS; donde ir a nadar. Text in Spanish. 1972. 3/yr. adv.
Address: AGUSTIN MELGAR 44-5, Col Condesa, Mexico City, DF 06140, Mexico. Ed. Juan Flores Sedano. Circ: 30,000.

BASEBALL CASE BOOK. *see* SPORTS AND GAMES—Ball Games

BASEBALL RULES BOOK. *see* SPORTS AND GAMES—Ball Games

BASKETBALL OFFICIALS MANUAL. *see* SPORTS AND GAMES—Ball Games

BASKETBALL RULES BOOK. *see* SPORTS AND GAMES—Ball Games

BASKETBALL - SIMPLIFIED & ILLUSTRATED RULES. *see* SPORTS AND GAMES—Ball Games

790.1 GBR
BATTLEFLEET; the journal of the Naval Wargames Society. Text in English. 1966. q. free to members (effective 2009). **Document type:** *Journal, Consumer.* **Description:** Covers all the aspects of naval wargaming / naval history (with a view to wargaming).
Published by: Naval Wargames Society, c/o Peter Colbeck, Down House, 76, Church Rd, Winterbourne Down, Bristol, BS36 1BY, United Kingdom. Ed. Christopher White.

799.202 DEU ISSN 1436-834X
BAYERISCHER SCHUETZENZEITUNG. Text in German. 1950. m. EUR 39 (effective 2009). adv. bk.rev.; video rev. bibl.; illus. back issues avail. **Document type:** *Newsletter, Consumer.* **Description:** Provides news and information to members of shooting clubs in Bavaria.
Published by: Bayerischer Sportschuetzenbund, Olympia Schiessanlage Hochbrueck, Ingolstaedter Landstr 110, Garching, 85748, Germany. TEL 49-89-3169490, FAX 49-89-31694950, gs@bssb.de. Ed. Claus Peter Schlagenhauf. Circ: 7,500 (paid).

790.1 DEU ISSN 0171-9572
BAYERNSPORT. Text in German. 1970. w. adv. bk.rev.; film rev. back issues avail. **Document type:** *Magazine, Consumer.*
Published by: Bayerischer Landes-Sportverband e.V., Georg-Brauchle-Ring 93, Munich, 80992, Germany. TEL 49-89-157020, FAX 49-89-15702299, info@blsv.de. Ed. Werner Schudeleit. Circ: 23,500 (paid and controlled).

790 DEU ISSN 0005-7231
BAYERNTURNER. Text in German. 1953. m. adv. **Document type:** *Magazine, Trade.*
Published by: Bayerischer Turnverband e.V., Georg-Brauchle-Ring 93, Munich, 80992, Germany. TEL 49-89-15702313, FAX 49-89-15702317, mail@turnverband-bayern.de. Ed. Fritz Hausmann. Adv. contact Renate Triukl. B&W page EUR 400, color page EUR 700. Circ: 4,200 (controlled).

796 DEU ISSN 1436-8064
BAYREUTHER BEITRAEGE ZUR SPORTWISSENSCHAFT. Text in German. 1998. irreg. **Document type:** *Monographic series, Academic/Scholarly.*
Published by: Universitaet Bayreuth, Institut fuer Sportwissenschaft, Universitaetsstr 30, Bayreuth, 95440, Germany. TEL 49-921-553461, FAX 49-921-553468, Institut.Sportwissenschaft@uni-bayreuth.de, http://www.sport.uni-bayreuth.de.

793 942 GBR ISSN 1460-7182
BEAUMAINS; the arthurian magazine for gamers. Text in English. 1993. irreg. GBP 2.50 per issue. adv. bk.rev.; film rev.; software rev.; tel.rev.; video rev. illus.; maps. back issues avail. **Document type:** *Magazine, Consumer.* **Description:** Features Arthurian topics of all sorts, including background and adventures for roleplaying games.
Published by: Taupe Games, 3 Stagbrake Close, Holbury, Hamps, United Kingdom. TEL 44-1703-496127. Ed., Adv. contact Gareth Jones. Circ: 500.

BECKETT ALMANAC OF BASEBALL CARDS AND COLLECTIBLES. *see* HOBBIES

BECKETT BASEBALL CARD ALPHABETICAL CHECKLIST. *see* HOBBIES

BECKETT BASKETBALL CARD ALPHABETICAL CHECKLIST. *see* HOBBIES

796 790.13 USA ISSN 1559-9124
BECKETT ELITE. Text in English. 2007. q. USD 9.99 domestic; USD 29.99 foreign (effective 2008). adv. back issues avail. **Document type:** *Magazine, Consumer.* **Description:** Features advice, news, pricing and information about collectibles and memorabilia in sports.
Related titles: Online - full text ed.
Published by: Beckett Media Llc, 4635 McEwen Rd, Dallas, TX 75244. TEL 714-939-9991, FAX 714-456-0146, customerservice@beckett.com. Pub. Claire B. Amano. Adv. contact Ted Barker TEL 972-448-9173. color page USD 3,000; trim 8 x 10.75. Circ: 45,000.

796 USA ISSN 1935-7915
BECKETT ESPORTS. Text in English. 2007 (Mar.). bi-m. USD 4.99 per issue (effective 2008). back issues avail. **Document type:** *Magazine, Consumer.*
Related titles: Online - full text ed.
Published by: Beckett Media Llc, 4635 McEwen Rd, Dallas, TX 75244. TEL 714-939-9991, FAX 714-456-0146, customerservice@beckett.com.

BECKETT FOOTBALL CARD ALPHABETICAL CHECKLIST. *see* HOBBIES

BECKETT GRADED CARD INVESTOR AND PRICE GUIDE. *see* HOBBIES

BECKETT HOCKEY. *see* HOBBIES

790.13 796.962 USA ISSN 1541-7867
BECKETT HOCKEY CARD PLUS. Text in English. 2001 (Nov.). bi-m. USD 4.99 per issue (effective 2008). adv. back issues avail. **Document type:** *Magazine, Consumer.*
Related titles: Online - full text ed.
Published by: Beckett Media Llc, 4635 McEwen Rd, Dallas, TX 75244. TEL 714-939-9991, FAX 714-456-0146, customerservice@beckett.com, http://www.beckett.com. Ed. Al Muir. Pub. James Beckett. adv.: B&W page USD 950, color page USD 2,000; trim 8 x 10.75. Circ: 8,000.

THE BECKETT HOCKEY CARD PRICE GUIDE & ALPHABETICAL CHECKLIST. *see* HOBBIES

BECKETT RACING. *see* HOBBIES

BECKETT RACING COLLECTIBLES PRICE GUIDE AND ALPHABETICAL CHECKLIST. *see* HOBBIES

BECKETT SPORTS COLLECTOR MONTHLY. *see* HOBBIES

796 TUR ISSN 1307-6477
BEDEM EGITIMI VE SPOR BILIMLERI DERGISI/JOURNAL OF PHYSICAL EDUCATION AND SPORTS SCIENCE. Text in Turkish. 2007. irreg. free (effective 2011). **Document type:** *Journal, Academic/Scholarly.*
Media: Online - full text.
Indexed: SD, T02.
Published by: Nigde Universitesi, School of Physical Education and Sports http://dergi.nigde.edu.tr.

796 TUR ISSN 1300-9915
BEDEN EGITIMI VE SPOR BILIM DERGISI/JOURNAL OF PHYSICAL EDUCATION AND SPORT SCIENCE. Text in Turkish, English. 1996. s-a. **Document type:** *Journal, Academic/Scholarly.*
Related titles: Online - full text ed.: ISSN 1309-6567. free (effective 2011).
Indexed: CABA, GH, LT, N02, N03, T05.
Published by: Selcuk Universitesi, Alaadin Keykubat Kampusu, Selcuklu, Konya, Turkey. Ed. Nurtekin Erkmen.

BEGA DISTRICT NEWS. *see* GENERAL INTEREST PERIODICALS—Australia

796.72 BEL ISSN 1784-2999
BELGIAN MOTOR SPORT (DUTCH EDITION). Text in Dutch. 2006. a. **Document type:** *Magazine, Consumer.*
Related titles: ◆ French ed.: Belgian Motor Sport (French Edition). ISSN 1784-2980.
Published by: Transporama Publishing, Mechelsesteenweg 326/4, Edegem, 2650, Belgium. TEL 32-3-4558795, FAX 32-3-4551087, info@ transporama.be, http://www.transporama.be.

796.72 BEL ISSN 1784-2980
BELGIAN MOTOR SPORT (FRENCH EDITION). Text in French. 2006. a. **Document type:** *Magazine, Consumer.*
Related titles: ◆ Dutch ed.: Belgian Motor Sport (Dutch Edition). ISSN 1784-2999.
Published by: Transporama Publishing, Mechelsesteenweg 326/4, Edegem, 2650, Belgium. TEL 32-3-4558795, FAX 32-3-4551087, info@ transporama.be, http://www.transporama.be.

BENDEL STATE. MINISTRY OF INFORMATION, SOCIAL DEVELOPMENT AND SPORTS. ESTIMATE. *see* SOCIAL SERVICES AND WELFARE

790 PRT ISSN 0005-8785
BENFICA. Text in Portuguese. 1941. w. looseleaf.
Published by: Sport Lisboa e Benfica, Rua do Jardim do Regedor, 19-3, Lisbon, 1100, Portugal. benficaonline@hotmail.com. Ed. Bernardo Azevedo. Circ: 20,000.

790.1 USA
BERG'S REVIEW OF GAMES. Text in English. bi-m. USD 19.95 domestic; USD 23 in Canada; USD 26 in Europe; USD 28 in Asia & the Pacific (effective 2001).
Published by: Coalition Web, Inc., 161 Lambertville-HQ Rd, Stockton, NJ 08559. TEL 609-397-4265, FAX 609-397-9433, magweb@magweb.com, http://www.magweb.com. Ed. Richard Berg.

794 DEU ISSN 1430-5224
BERICHTE AUS DER SPORTWISSENSCHAFT. Text in German. 1996. irreg., latest 2008. price varies. **Document type:** *Monographic series, Academic/Scholarly.*
Published by: Shaker Verlag GmbH, Kaiserstr 100, Herzogenrath, 52134, Germany. TEL 49-2407-95960, FAX 49-2407-95969, info@shaker.de.

BERLINER BEITRAEGE ZUM SPORTRECHT. *see* LAW

796.815 AUS ISSN 1833-3834
BEST OF BLITZ. Text in English. 2006. q. **Document type:** *Magazine, Consumer.*
Published by: Blitz Publications, PO Box 4075, Mulgrave, VIC 3170, Australia. stefanie@blitzmag.com.au, http://www.sportzblitz.net.

795 GBR
BETTING BUSINESS; the monthly publication for the betting industry. Text in English. 19??. m. GBP 5.20, EUR 8.30 newsstand/cover (effective 2009). adv. back issues avail. **Document type:** *Magazine, Trade.* **Description:** Represents a media channel for organisations wishing to get their products and services in front of the people that matter at land-based betting offices and throughout the remote gaming sector. It covers news reporting and analysis, expert industry opinion and comprehensive sections dedicated to new products and services.
Related titles: Online - full text ed.: free (effective 2009).
Published by: Gaming Business Media LLP, Bolton Technology Exchange, 33 Queensbrook, Bolton, BL1 4AY, United Kingdom. TEL 44-1204-396397, FAX 44-1204-392748, jsullivan@gbmedia.eu. Ed. Andrew McCarron TEL 44-20-85638425. Adv. contact Neil Judson TEL 44-1204-396397. Circ: 3,000.

306.482 GBR ISSN 1758-2709
BETTING MONTHLY; the monthly magazine for recreational and serious punters. Text in English. 2007. m. GBP 19.99 domestic; GBP 29.99 in Europe; GBP 39.99 elsewhere; GBP 2.95 per issue (effective 2009). adv. back issues avail. **Document type:** *Magazine, Consumer.* **Description:** Features betting and gaming information as well as analysis, stats, views from the experts - including Alan Brazil, Angus Loughran and Charlie McCann.
Formerly (until 2008): Antepost (1754-8233)
Related titles: Online - full text ed.: GBP 12.50 (effective 2009).
Published by: Antepost Magazine, Betrescue Ltd., Chelwood House, Chelwood Dr, Leeds, LS8 2AT, United Kingdom. TEL 44-845-8330909, FAX 44-845-8330910. Ed. Peter Sharkey.

613.7 DEU ISSN 1866-1653
BEWEGUNG, SPIEL, SPORT. Text in German. 2008. irreg., latest vol.7, 2011. price varies. **Document type:** *Monographic series, Academic/Scholarly.*
Published by: Logos Verlag Berlin, Comeniushof, Gubener Str 47, Berlin, 10243, Germany. TEL 49-30-42851090, FAX 49-30-42851092, redaktion@logos-verlag.de. Ed. Herbert Haag.

790.1 USA ISSN 2153-9189
TS532
THE BIG SHOW JOURNAL; your guide to gun & knife shows & auctions nationwide!. Text in English. bi-m. USD 19.95 (effective 2010). adv. **Document type:** *Magazine, Consumer.*
Published by: Big Show Journal, PO Box 10485, Reno, NV 89510-0485. TEL 800-781-5301. Adv. contact Jodean Boersma. **Subscr. to:** N9816 Lund Rd., Iola, WI 54945-9278.

BIL MAGASINET. *see* TRANSPORTATION—Automobiles

796.72 ISL ISSN 1670-5378
BILAR & SPORT. Text in Icelandic. 2005. m. **Document type:** *Magazine, Consumer.*
Published by: Alurt ehf., Duggovogi 21, Reykjavik, 104, Iceland. TEL 354-588-7888, info@bilarogsport, http://www.bilarogsport.is. Ed. Haukur Gudjonsson.

793 DEU
BILD UND FUNK SPEZIAL RAETSEL. Text in German. m. EUR 18; EUR 1.50 newsstand/cover (effective 2011). adv. **Document type:** *Magazine, Consumer.* **Description:** Contains a wide variety of word games and puzzles.
Published by: Deutscher Raetselverlag GmbH & Co. KG (Subsidiary of: Gong Verlag GmbH & Co. KG), Muenchener Str 101-09, Ismaning, 85737, Germany. TEL 49-89-272708620, FAX 49-89-272707890, info@raetsel.de, http://www.deutscher-raetselverlag.de. Circ: 134,000 (controlled).

796.72 SWE ISSN 1651-1301
BILSPORT BOERSEN. Text in Swedish. 2001. m. SEK 249 for 6 mos. (effective 2010). adv. **Document type:** *Magazine, Consumer.*
Published by: Foerlags AB Albinsson & Sjoeberg, PO Box 529, Karlskrona, 37123, Sweden. TEL 46-455-335325, FAX 46-455-311715, fabas@fabas.se, http://www.fabas.se. Ed. Thomas Lindberg. Adv. contact Simon Johansson. page SEK 11,200; trim 190 x 275. Circ: 9,900 (paid).

790.1 USA
BINGO BUGLE; North America's bingo and casino newspaper. (65 eds. across N. America) Text in English. 1980. m. adv. maps. **Document type:** *Newspaper, Consumer.* **Description:** Features interesting articles on Bingo game.
Related titles: Online - full text ed.
Published by: Frontier Publications, Inc., 17205 Vashon Hwy SW, BLD D-1, Vashon, WA 98070. TEL 800-327-6437, FAX 206-463-5630. Adv. contact Dennis Conroy. Circ: 900,000.

051 CAN
BINGO CALLER NEWS. Text in English. bi-m. CAD 50.
Published by: Nielsens' Publications Corporation, 19607 88th Ave, Langley, BC V3A 6Y3, Canada. TEL 604-888-7477, FAX 604-888-7489. Ed. Egon Nielsen. Circ: 10,000.

BIOGRAPHY TODAY SPORTS SERIES; profiles of people of interest to young readers. *see* BIOGRAPHY

BIOLOGY OF EXERCISE. *see* PHYSICAL FITNESS AND HYGIENE

BIOLOGY OF SPORT; a quarterly journal of sport and exercise sciences. *see* MEDICAL SCIENCES—Sports Medicine

799.202 USA
BIRD DOG & RETRIEVER NEWS. Text in English. 1992. bi-m. USD 20 (effective 2007). adv. bk.rev. 64 p./no. 3 cols./p.; **Document type:** *Magazine, Consumer.*
Published by: Dennis Guldan, Pub., 563 17th Ave, NW, New Brighton, MN 55112. TEL 651-636-8045. adv.: page USD 1,500; 7.25 x 9.5. Circ: 18,000.

796.8 USA ISSN 0277-3066
GV1114.3
BLACK BELT MAGAZINE. Variant title: Black Belt. Text in English. 1961. m. USD 29 domestic; USD 39 in Canada; USD 51 elsewhere (effective 2010). adv. back issues avail.; reprints avail. **Document type:** *Magazine, Consumer.* **Description:** Contains significant articles on martial arts.
Former titles (until 2005): Karate - Kung Fu Illustrated (0888-031X); (until 1991): Karate Illustrated (0022-9016)
Indexed: B04, G06, G07, G08, I05, I07, R03, RGAb, RGPR, SD, SportS, W03, W05.
Published by: Black Belt Communications, Inc. (Subsidiary of: Active Interest Media), 24900 Anza Dr, Unit E, Valencia, CA 91355. TEL 661-257-4066, FAX 661-257-3028. Adv. contact Cheryl Angelheart.

796.72 GBR ISSN 2045-7472
BLACK BOOK FORMULA ONE. Text in English. 200?. a. adv. back issues avail. **Document type:** *Directory, Trade.* **Description:** Contains information about the business and strategies behind Formula One and provides readers with a database of the people who make and shape Formula One.
Published by: SportsPro Media Ltd., Henley Media Group, Trans-World House, 100 City Rd, London, EC1Y 2BP, United Kingdom. TEL 44-20-78710123, FAX 44-20-75493255, info@sportspromedia.com, http://www.sportspromedia.com. Circ: 4,500.

799.202 NZL ISSN 1176-9246
BLACK POWDER EXPRESS; a publication dedicated to black powder shooting in New Zealand. Text in English. bi-m. NZD 16 domestic; USD 20 foreign (effective 2008). **Document type:** *Magazine, Consumer.* **Description:** Covers the New Zealand Black Powder scene and contains a number of photographs of club and other activities.
Published by: (New Zealand Black Powder Shooters Federation), B P Express, PO Box 3700, Auckland, New Zealand. TEL 64-21-992290, FAX 64-21-728487.

793 510 USA
BLACKJACK FORUM. Text in English. 1981. q. USD 56 domestic; USD 64 in Canada. adv. bk.rev. charts; stat. back issues avail. **Document type:** *Magazine, Consumer.*
Published by: R G E Publishing, 2565 Chandler Ave., Ste. 8, Las Vegas, NV 89120-4068. TEL 510-465-6452, FAX 510-652-4330. Ed., Pub. Arnold Snyder. Circ: 2,500.

790.1 USA ISSN 1070-390X
BLADES ON ICE. Text in English. 1990. bi-m. USD 29 domestic; USD 39 in Canada; USD 49 in Europe; USD 55 elsewhere; USD 6.95 newsstand/cover (effective 2003). adv. illus. **Document type:** *Magazine, Consumer.* **Description:** Includes current news stories, coverage of the latest amateur and professional competitions, and interviews with skaters.
Indexed: SD.
Published by: Blades on Ice, Inc., 7040 N Mona Lisa Rd, Tucson, AZ 85741-2633. TEL 520-575-1747, 888-525-8605, FAX 520-575-1484, editor@bladesonice.com. Ed., Pub., R&P, Adv. contact Gerri Walbert.

790.1 DEU
BLAU GELB. Text in German. 1975. bi-m. looseleaf.
Published by: Sportgemeinde Weiterstadt 1886 e.V., Am Aulenberg 2, Weiterstadt, 64331, Germany. TEL 06150-3886. Circ: 2,000.

796.962 CAN ISSN 1920-6968
▼ **BLAZE.** Text in English. 2009. m. USD 56; USD 6.99 newsstand/cover (effective 2010). adv. back issues avail. **Document type:** *Magazine, Consumer.* **Description:** Contains player news and interviews, limited edition action photos, hockey stats and trivia, tips from the trainers etc.
Formerly (until 2009): Flames (1922-3862)
Related titles: Online - full text ed.: CAD 36.58 (effective 2010).
Published by: Calgary Flames Hockey Club, Station M, PO Box 1540, Calgary, AB T2P 3B9, Canada. TEL 403-777-4646, customerservice@calgaryflames.com. Ed. Laurie Wheeler. Adv. contact Scott Matheson.

796 DEU ISSN 1861-681X
BLICKPUNKT SPORTMANAGEMENT. Text in German. 2006. irreg., latest vol.2, 2008. price varies. **Document type:** *Monographic series, Academic/Scholarly.*
Published by: Peter Lang GmbH (Subsidiary of: Peter Lang Publishing Group), Eschborner Landstr 42-50, Frankfurt Am Main, 60489, Germany. TEL 49-69-7807050, FAX 49-69-78070550, zentrale.frankfurt@peterlang.com. Ed. Ronald Wadsack.

796.805 AUS ISSN 0818-9595
BLITZ; Australasian martial arts magazine. Text in English. 1987. m. AUD 95 domestic; AUD 135 foreign (effective 2008). adv. back issues avail. **Document type:** *Magazine, Consumer.* **Description:** Features the latest news from the Australian and international martial arts scenes. Also publishes interviews with martial artists of all styles, kickboxing news and movies reviews.
Indexed: SD.
Published by: Blitz Publications, PO Box 4075, Mulgrave, VIC 3170, Australia. TEL 61-3-95748460, FAX 61-3-95748899, info@blitzmag.com.au. Ed. Ben Stone. Adv. contact Keith Rozario.

794.1 USA ISSN 1053-3087
BLITZ CHESS. Text in English. 1988. q. USD 4 newsstand/cover domestic; USD 4.50 newsstand/cover in Canada & Mexico; USD 5 newsstand/cover elsewhere (effective 2001). adv. illus. reprints avail. **Description:** Features blitz (5-minute) games, a quarterly rating list, and a calendar of events, including where to play in the U.S. Discusses the history of chess, chess problems, and the grand masters. Also in-depth coverage of top international events, chess matches, and endgame article by Pal Benko.
Published by: World Blitz Chess Association, 8 Parnassus Rd, Berkeley, CA 94708. TEL 510-549-1169, FAX 510-486-8078. Ed., Pub., R&P, Adv. contact Walter S Browne. page USD 150; 7.5 x 10. Circ: 1,200 (paid). **Dist. by:** Ubiquity Distributors Inc., 607 DeGraw St, Brooklyn, NY 11217.

371.7 USA ISSN 1067-750X
GV351
BLUE BOOK OF COLLEGE ATHLETICS OF SENIOR, JUNIOR AND COMMUNITY COLLEGES. Text in English. 1930. a., latest 2003-04. USD 44.95 per issue (effective 2003). adv. **Document type:** *Directory.*
Formerly: Blue Book of College Athletics; Incorporates (1958-1988): Blue Book of Junior and Community College Athletics
Published by: Athletic Publishing Co., PO Box 931, Montgomery, AL 36101-0931. TEL 334-263-4436, FAX 334-263-4437. Ed. Christine Beazley. Pub., R&P, Adv. contact John Allen Dees. Circ: 10,000.

799.202 USA ISSN 1524-6043
TS532.4
BLUE BOOK OF GUN VALUES. Text in English. 1981. a. USD 49.95 newsstand/cover (effective 2003).
Formerly: Barry Fain's Private Blue Book of Gun Values (0273-2874)
Published by: Blue Book Publications, 8009 34th Ave S, Ste 175, Minneapolis, MN 55425. TEL 952-854-5229, 800-877-4867, FAX 952-853-1486, bluebook@bluebookinc.com, http://www.bluebookinc.com. Ed. S.P. Fjestad. Circ: 17,000.

683.4075 USA ISSN 1529-7349
TS536.6.M8
BLUE BOOK OF MODERN BLACK POWDER VALUES. Text in English. 2000. irreg. **Description:** Contains up-to-date information and prices on most recently manufactured black powder reproductions and replicas.
Published by: Blue Book Publications, 8009 34th Ave S, Ste 175, Minneapolis, MN 55425. TEL 952-854-5229, 800-877-4867, FAX 952-853-1486, bluebook@bluebookinc.com, http://www.bluebookinc.com. Ed. S.P. Fjestad.

796 USA
BLUE RAIDER NATION. Text in English. 2006. m. USD 12 (effective 2005); dist. free in some locations. **Document type:** *Magazine, Consumer.* **Description:** Covers Middle Tennessee Blue Raider athletics.
Address: 2126 Sulphur Springs Rd, Murfreesboro, TN 37129-6405. TEL 615-849-1222. Ed. Kevin Halpern.

796.692 USA ISSN 1063-4924
BLUESHIRT BULLETIN. Text in English. 1992. 10/yr. USD 35 domestic; USD 50 in Canada; USD 65 elsewhere (effective 2010). adv. **Document type:** *Magazine, Consumer.* **Description:** Covers all aspects of the New York Rangers ice hockey team.
Related titles: Online - full text ed.
Address: 31 Grove St, New York, NY 10014. TEL 212-965-1459, FAX 646-356-7026.

795 ZAF ISSN 1997-0552
BLUFF; the thrill of poker. Text in English. 2008. m. ZAR 314.55 (effective 2008). **Document type:** *Magazine, Consumer.*
Published by: Maverick Media cc, PO Box 1669, Hougton, South Africa. TEL 27-11-8375590, FAX 27-11-8372349. Ed. Jon Stephenson. Pub. Tanja Carruthers. Adv. contact Dirk Steenekamp.

795.412 USA
BLUFF; the thrill of poker. Text in English. 2005. m. USD 29.95 domestic; USD 39.95 in Canada; USD 49.95 elsewhere; USD 4.99 newsstand/cover domestic; USD 6.99 newsstand/cover in Canada (effective 2007). **Document type:** *Magazine, Consumer.*
Published by: Bluff Media, 1200 Lake Hearn Dr Ste 450, Atlanta, GA 30319. Ed. Michael Caselli.

790.1 HKG
BO/EVENEMENT SPORTIF. Text in Chinese. 1994. m. adv. **Document type:** *Consumer.*
Published by: Hachette Filipacchi Hong Kong Ltd., 15-F, East Wing, Warwick House, Taikoo Place, 979 King s Rd, Quarry Bay, Hong Kong, Hong Kong. TEL 852-2567-8707, FAX 852-2568-4650. Ed. He Huixian. Adv. contact Tony Lo. color page USD 6,050; trim 214 x 275. Circ: 120,000.

796 CHN ISSN 1005-9024
BO/SPORTS EVENTS. Text in Chinese. m. CNY 120 (effective 2004). **Document type:** *Magazine, Consumer.*
Related titles: Online - full content ed.
Published by: Zhongguo Tiyubao Yezongshe, 8, Tiyuguan Lu, Chongwen-qu, Beijing, 100061, China. TEL 86-10-67137513. **Dist. by:** China International Book Trading Corp, 35 Chegongzhuang Xilu, Haidian District, PO Box 399, Beijing 100044, China. TEL 86-10-68412045, FAX 86-10-68412023, cibtc@mail.cibtc.com.cn, http://www.cibtc.com.cn.

790.1 USA
THE BOARDGAMER. Text in English. 1995. q. USD 13.

S

Published by: The Boardgamer, 177 S Lincoln St, Minster, OH 45865-1240. Ed. Bruce Monnin.

790.1 USA
BOB WATKINS SPORTS 24 MAGAZINE. Text in English. 1989. m. USD 2 per issue. **Description:** Feature articles on people in sports, short features on local, regional and state athletic events, as well as opinion pieces.
Published by: Bob Watkins, Ed. & Pub., PO Box 124, Glendale, KY 42740. TEL 502-737-5585.

796.41 612 ROM ISSN 2066-8007
BODY BUILDING SCIENCE JOURNAL. Text in English. q. free. **Document type:** *Journal, Academic/Scholarly.* **Description:** Publishes original articles on body building, including research activities regarding the programs, equipments, supplements, effects, correlations between programs and results, studies of dynamics and performance evaluation using quantitative methods.
Media: Online - full text.
Published by: Academia de Studii Economice din Bucuresti, Catedra de Informatica Economica/Academy of Economic Studies Bucharest,Computer Science Department, c/o Prof. Ion Ivan, Piata Romana no.6, sector 1, Bucuresti, 2413, Romania. http://cs.ase.ro/ro/index.aspx. Ed. Ion Ivan.

797.3 USA ISSN 1938-6125
BODYBOARDER. Text in English. 2007 (Jul.). q. USD 29.99 (effective 2007). **Document type:** *Magazine, Consumer.*
Published by: Edje Media, 1740 Magnolia Ave, Carlsbad, CA 92008. info@edjemedia.com, http://edjemedia.com.

790.1 RUS ISSN 0135-4973
BOEVOE ISKUSSTVO PLANETY. Text in Russian. 10/yr.
—East View.
Published by: Ozdorovitel'nyi i Nauchno-Informatsionnyi Tsentr Zdorov'e Naroda, Ul Nizhnyaya Pervomaiskaya 45, Moscow, 105203, Russian Federation. TEL 7-095-9654749, FAX 7-095-9652629. Ed. S V Yurkov. **Dist. by:** East View Information Services, 10601 Wayzata Blvd, Minneapolis, MN 55305. TEL 952-252-1201, 800-477-1005, FAX 952-252-1202, info@eastview.com, http://www.eastview.com.

799.32 AUT ISSN 1818-2364
BOGENSPORT JOURNAL. Text in German. 2000. q. EUR 20; EUR 4 newsstand/cover (effective 2006). adv. **Document type:** *Magazine, Consumer.*
Published by: Vorderegger O E G Bogensportverlag, Schillinghofstr 46, Salzburg, 5023, Austria. TEL 43-662-640550, FAX 43-662-648679. Ed. Dietmar Vorderegger. adv.: B&W page EUR 1,585, color page EUR 2,085. Circ: 9,950 (paid and controlled).

799.32 DEU
BOGENSPORT MAGAZIN; das Magazin rund um Pfeil und Bogen. Text in German. 1995. bi-m. EUR 22.80; EUR 4 newsstand/cover (effective 2006). adv. **Document type:** *Magazine, Consumer.* **Description:** Covers all aspects of archery and related sporting events.
Published by: Kuhn Fachverlag GmbH & Co. KG, Bert-Brecht-Str 15-19, Villingen-Schwenningen, 78054, Germany. TEL 49-7720-3940, FAX 49-7720-394175, kataloge@kuhnverlag.de, http://www.kuhn-kataloge.de. Ed. Guenther Baumann. Adv. contact Andre Gegg. B&W page EUR 1,585, color page EUR 2,085. Circ: 9,950 (paid).

796.8 CHN ISSN 1004-5643
GV1112
BOJI/TECHNIQUE OF SELF-DEFENSE. Text in Chinese. 1984. m. USD 49.20 (effective 2009). **Document type:** *Journal, Academic/Scholarly.*
Related titles: Online - full text ed.
—East View.
Published by: Shanxi Sheng Tiyubao Kanshe, 9, Dayingpankouzhuang Beijie, Taiyuan, 030012, China. TEL 86-351-7040060 ext 8277.

790.1 IDN ISSN 0852-6729
GV561
BOLA. Text in Indonesian. w.
Address: Jalan Palmerah Selatan 17, Jakarta, 10270, Indonesia. TEL 021-5483008. Ed. Hikmat Kusumaningrat. Circ: 407,850.

790.1 PRT ISSN 0870-1776
A BOLA. Text in Portuguese. 1945. 4/w. **Document type:** *Newspaper, Consumer.*
Published by: Sociedade Vicra Desportiva Lda., Travessa da Queimada, 23, Lisbon, 1294-113, Portugal. TEL 351-213-232-100, FAX 351-213-432-215. Eds. Joaquim Rita, Vitor Serpa. Circ: 150,000 (paid and controlled).

796.72 USA
BONNEVILLE RACING NEWS. Text in English. 1990. 10/yr. USD 24; USD 50 foreign (effective 2001). adv. **Document type:** *Newspaper.* **Description:** Covers automobile and motorcycle land speed racing at Bonneville, El Mirage and other such attempts worldwide.
Address: PO Box 730, Hemet, CA 92546. TEL 909-926-2277, FAX 909-926-4619. Ed. Wendy Jeffries. Circ: 20,000.

796 ITA ISSN 1828-9282
BORMIO SPORT. Text in Italian. 1987. m. **Document type:** *Magazine, Consumer.*
Published by: Unione Sportiva Bormiese, Centro Sportivo, Via Manzoni, Bormio, Sondrio 23032, Italy. TEL 39-0342-901482, FAX 39-0342-911423, http://www.usbormiese.org.

790.1 USA ISSN 0361-6398
BOSTON BRUINS OFFICIAL YEARBOOK. Text in English. 19??. a. adv. **Document type:** *Yearbook, Consumer.*
Published by: Phoenix Media / Communications Group, 126 Brookline Ave, Boston, MA 02215. TEL 617-859-8201, letters@phx.com, http://www.thephoenix.com. Adv. contact Howard Temkin TEL 617-859-3242.

790 USA
BOSTON MARATHON. Text in English. 1979. a. adv. **Document type:** *Magazine, Consumer.*
Published by: Phoenix Media / Communications Group, 126 Brookline Ave, Boston, MA 02215. TEL 617-859-8201, letters@phx.com, http://www.thephoenix.com. Adv. contact Howard Temkin TEL 617-859-3242.

796 ESP ISSN 2171-5726
▼ **BOUS.** Text in Spanish. 2010. m. **Document type:** *Magazine, Consumer.*
Published by: Valencia Producciones Bous de Carrer, Ave Alfinach, 9 Bajo, Puzol, Valencia, 46530, Spain. TEL 34-96-1424050, revista@bousalcarreer.com, http://www.bausalcarrer.com/.

794 USA ISSN 1095-0435
BOWLERS JOURNAL INTERNATIONAL. Text in English. 1913. m. USD 32 domestic; USD 57 foreign (effective 2011). adv. bk.rev. charts; illus.; stat. back issues avail. **Document type:** *Magazine, Trade.*
Former titles (until 1993): Bowlers Journal (0164-9183); National Bowlers Journal and Billiard Revue (0027-8793); Bowlers Journal and Billiard Revue (0006-8411)
Indexed: PEI, SD, SPI, SportS.
Published by: Luby Publishing, 122 S Michigan Ave, Ste 1506, Chicago, IL 60603. TEL 312-341-1110, FAX 312-341-1469, email@lubypublishing.com, http://www.lubypublishing.com. Ed. Bob Johnson TEL 312-341-1110 ext 224. Pub. Mike Panozzo.

796.355 780 USA ISSN 1089-9685
BOX. Text in English. 1995. bi-m. USD 17; USD 2.99 newsstand/cover (effective 2007). adv. film rev.; music rev.; video rev. back issues avail. **Document type:** *Magazine, Consumer.* **Description:** Focuses on aggresive in-line skating. Includes articles on lifestyle, music, and fitness.
Published by: Source Interlink Companies, 6420 Wilshire Blvd, 10th Fl, Los Angeles, CA 90048. TEL 323-782-2000, FAX 323-782-2585, dheine@sourceinterlink.com, http://www.sourceinterlinkmedia.com. Circ: 30,000.

796.8 MEX ISSN 0006-8470
BOX Y LUCHA; el mundo del ring. Text in Spanish. 1951. w. MXN 832, USD 29.29. illus.
Published by: Periodismo Especializado S.A., PRESIDENTES 187, Portales, Mexico City, DF 03300, Mexico. Ed. Antonio Elizarraras Corona.

796.83 USA
BOXEO LA REVISTA. Text in Spanish, English. 2007. m. USD 24 (effective 2010). **Document type:** *Magazine, Consumer.* **Description:** News about boxing in Mexico, Puerto Rico and the U.S.
Related titles: Online - full text ed.: ISSN 2155-773X. 2010.
Published by: Jimenez Communications, 9668 Milliken Ave, Ste 104-293, Ranch Cucamonga, CA 91730. TEL 909-224-4176, jimenez@jimenezcommunications.com, http://www.jimenezcommunications.com/.

796 USA ISSN 1042-5292
BOXING (YEAR). Text in English. 1999. m. adv. **Document type:** *Magazine, Consumer.*
Published by: London Publishing Co. (Subsidiary of: Kappa Publishing Group, Inc.), 6198 Butler Pike, Ste 200, Blue Bell, PA 19422. TEL 215-643-6385, FAX 315-628-3571, custsrvc@kappapublishing.com, http://www.kappapublishing.com. Adv. contact Sharon Liggio. **Dist. by:** Curtis CIRC Company, 641 Lexington Ave, New York, NY 10022; **Dist. in UK by:** Comag, Tavistock Rd, W Drayton, Middlesex UB7 7QE, United Kingdom.

796.13 USA ISSN 1084-9610
GV1115
BOXING ALMANAC AND BOOK OF FACTS. Text in English. 1996. a.
Published by: London Publishing Co. (Subsidiary of: Kappa Publishing Group, Inc.), 6198 Butler Pike, Ste 200, Blue Bell, PA 19422. TEL 215-643-6385, FAX 315-628-3571, custsrvc@kappapublishing.com, http://www.kappapublishing.com.

796.332 GHA
BOXING AND FOOTBALL ILLUSTRATED. Text in English. 1976. m. **Document type:** *Magazine, Consumer.*
Address: PO Box 8392, Accra, Ghana. Ed. Nana O Ampomah. Circ: 10,000.

796.83 JPN
BOXING MAGAZINE. Text in Japanese. 1956. m. JPY 9,960 (effective 2000).
Published by: Baseball Magazine Sha, 3-10-10 Misaki-cho, Chiyoda-ku, Tokyo, 101-0061, Japan. FAX 81-3-3238-0106. Ed. Junichi Hirata.

796.83 GBR ISSN 0956-098X
BOXING MONTHLY. Text in English. 1989. m. GBP 42 domestic; GBP 50 in Europe; GBP 55 in US & Canada; GBP 75 in Australasia; GBP 3.40 per issue domestic; USD 6.95 per issue in United States (effective 2009). adv. back issues avail. **Document type:** *Magazine, Consumer.* **Description:** Provides analysis of international boxing.
Published by: Top Wave Ltd., 40 Morpeth Rd, London, E9 7LD, United Kingdom. TEL 44-20-89864141, FAX 44-20-89864145, mail@boxing-monthly.demon.co.uk. Ed. Glyn Leach. adv.: B&W page GBP 800, color page GBP 900; trim 210 x 297. **Dist. by:** Magazine Marketing Co., Octagon House, White Hart Meadows, Ripley, Woking, Surrey GU23 6HR, United Kingdom.

796.83 GBR ISSN 0006-8519
BOXING NEWS. Abbreviated title: B N. Text in English. 1909. w. GBP 97.50 domestic; EUR 139 in Europe; USD 209 in US & Canada; GBP 124 elsewhere; GBP 2.70 per issue (effective 2010). adv. bk.rev. back issues avail. **Document type:** *Magazine, Consumer.* **Description:** Provides the sport with unmatched coverage to keep fights fans and industry figures up-to-date with every fight, every punch, every week.
Former titles (until 1940): Boxing; (until 19??): Boxing, Racing and Football; (until 19??): Boxing and Racing; (until 19??): Boxing
Related titles: Supplement(s): Boxing Heroes. ISSN 1749-5237. GBP 5.99 per issue (effective 2010); Boxing News Health & Fitness. ISSN 1755-988X; Brit Power. ISSN 1753-0156.
Indexed: SportS.
Published by: Newsquest Specialist Media Ltd., 30 Cannon St, London, EC4M 6YJ, United Kingdom. TEL 44-20-76183456, info@newsquestspecialistmedia.com, http://www.newsquestspecialistmedia.com. Ed. Claude Abrams TEL 44-20-76183069. Adv. contact Steve Turner TEL 44-20-76183428. Circ: 10,689.

796.83 USA
THE BOXING RECORD BOOK. Text in English. 1996 (13th). a. USD 62; USD 67 foreign (effective 1998). adv.
Published by: Fight Fax, Inc, PO Box 896, Sicklerville, NJ 08081. TEL 609-782-8868. Ed., R&P Phill Marder. Adv. contact Jay Seidman.

796.83 USA
BOXING U S A. Text in English. 1981. q. USD 15 (effective 1998). **Document type:** *Newsletter.*
Published by: United States Amateur Boxing (U S A Boxing), Inc., One Olympic Plaza, Colorado Springs, CO 80909. TEL 719-578-4506, FAX 719-632-3426. R&P Shilpa Bakre. Circ: 35,000.

790.1 DEU ISSN 0948-2520
BOXSPORT. Text in German. 1982. m. EUR 45.60; EUR 3.80 newsstand/cover (effective 2009). adv. **Document type:** *Magazine, Consumer.*
Published by: D S V Deutscher Sportverlag GmbH, Im Mediapark 8, Cologne, 50670, Germany. TEL 49-221-25870, FAX 49-221-2587212, kontakt@dsv-sportverlag.de, http://www.dsv-sportverlag.de. Ed. Hans Reski. Adv. contact Tanja Schmidt-Sennewald. page EUR 3,000; trim 210 x 285. Circ: 15,250 (paid and controlled).

794.1 362.41 GBR ISSN 0006-8756
BRAILLE CHESS MAGAZINE. Text in English. 1934. q. GBP 1.14 per issue (effective 2009). index. **Document type:** *Magazine, Consumer.* **Description:** Covers news of the current trends and competitions in Chess.
Media: Braille. **Related titles:** Diskette ed.
Published by: Royal National Institute of Blind People, 105 Judd St, London, WC1H 9NE, United Kingdom. TEL 44-20-73881266, FAX 44-20-73882034, helpline@rnib.org.uk.

793 USA ISSN 2150-3613
BRAIN GAMES. Text in English. 2007. m. **Document type:** *Magazine, Consumer.* **Description:** Contains puzzles designed to stimulate brain's cognitive functions, keeping it strong and fit.
Published by: Publications International Ltd., 7373 N Cicero Ave, Lincolnwood, IL 60712. TEL 847-676-3470, 800-595-8484, FAX 847-676-3671, customer_service@pubint.com.

790.1 028.5 DEU ISSN 0948-0161
BRAVO SPORT. Text in German. 1994. fortn. EUR 50.70; EUR 1.95 newsstand/cover (effective 2010). adv. **Document type:** *Magazine, Consumer.* **Description:** Covers a wide range of sports and fitness.
Published by: Heinrich Bauer Smaragd KG (Subsidiary of: Bauer Media Group), Charles-de-Gaulle-Str 8, Munich, 81737, Germany. TEL 49-89-67860, FAX 49-89-6702033, kommunikation@hbv.de, http://www.hbv.de. Ed. Fred Wipperfuerth. Adv. contact Arne Sill. page EUR 15,542. Circ: 194,687 (paid).

794 SRB
▼ **BRAVO SPORT.** Text in Serbian. 2010. m. CSD 294; CSD 49 newsstand/cover (effective 2011). adv. **Document type:** *Magazine, Consumer.*
Published by: Color Media International, Temerinska 102, Novi Sad, 21000. TEL 381-21-4897100, FAX 381-21-4897126, milan.sobot@color.rs, http://www.color.rs. Ed. Igor Conic. Adv. contact Goran Radulovic. Circ: 35,000 (paid).

796 POL ISSN 1428-1791
BRAVO SPORT. Text in Polish. 1997. fortn. PLZ 3.50 newsstand/cover (effective 2011). adv. **Document type:** *Magazine, Consumer.*
Published by: Wydawnictwo Bauer Sp. z o.o. (Subsidiary of: Bauer Media Group), ul Motorowa 1, Warsaw, 04-035, Poland. TEL 48-22-5170500, FAX 48-22-5170125, kontakt@bauer.pl, http://www.bauer.pl.

794.1 ISL
BREFSKAKTIDINDI. Text in Icelandic. 1979. irreg. (3-4/yr.). USD 16. adv.
Published by: Icelandic Correspondence Chess Federation, Grettisgata 42 B, Reykjavik, 101, Iceland. Ed. Gunnar Hannesson. Circ: 200.

790.1 DEU ISSN 0932-8823
GV428
BRENNPUNKTE DER SPORTWISSENSCHAFT. Text in German. 1987. irreg., latest vol.29, 2005. price varies. **Document type:** *Monographic series, Academic/Scholarly.* **Description:** Aimed at sports scientists, coaches and students.
Formerly: Jahrbuecher der Deutschen Sporthochschule Koeln
Indexed: IBR, IBZ.
Published by: (Deutsche Sporthochschule Koeln), Academia Verlag GmbH, Bahnstr 7, Sankt Augustin, 53757, Germany. TEL 49-2241-345210, FAX 49-2241-345316, kontakt@academia-verlag.de.

796 FRA ISSN 2116-6226
▼ **BREVES DE SPORTS.** Text in French. 2011. q. **Document type:** *Newsletter, Consumer.*
Published by: Association Sportive Municipale de Chambourcy, 5 Rue du Mur du Parc, Chambourcy, 78240, France. TEL 33-1-39791831, FAX 33-1-30742591, asmc78@sfr.fr, http://asm-chambourcy.com.

795.414 NLD ISSN 0006-9825
BRIDGE. Text in Dutch. 1932. m. (11/yr.). EUR 33.50 domestic; EUR 52 foreign (effective 2009). adv. bk.rev.; software rev.; Website rev. charts; illus. index. 76 p./no. 4 cols./p.; **Document type:** *Bulletin.*
Published by: Nederlandse Bridge Bond, Kennedylaan 9, Utrecht, 3533 KH, Netherlands. TEL 31-30-2759911, FAX 31-30-2759900, nbb@bridge.nl, http://www.bridge.nl. Ed. Marjo Chorus TEL 31-30-2759931. adv.: B&W page EUR 3,055, color page EUR 4,259; trim 210 x 285. Circ: 75,425 (paid).

795.414 SWE ISSN 1652-1943
BRIDGE. Text in Swedish. 1969. 5/yr. SEK 230 (effective 2011). adv. **Document type:** *Magazine, Consumer.*
Former titles (until 2003): Svensk Bridge (0282-4809); (until 1984): Bridge med Ungdomsnyt (0348-6443); (until 1977): Bridge (Stockholm) (0345-1747)
Related titles: Online - full text ed.
Published by: Forbundet Svensk Bridgefoerbund, Hattmakargatan 17, Gaevle, 80311, Sweden. TEL 46-26-656070, FAX 46-26-122500, kansliet@svenskbridge.se.

794.41 NLD ISSN 1877-2021
BRIDGE BETER KALENDER. Text in Dutch. 2008. a. EUR 11.95 (effective 2011).
Published by: Alpha Bridge B.V., Rijndijk 5 a, Hazerswoude Rijndijk, 2394 AA, Netherlands. TEL 31-71-3419005, FAX 31-71-3416168, info@bridgebeter.nl, http://www.bridgebeter.nl.

795.414 USA ISSN 1089-6376
THE BRIDGE BULLETIN. Text in English. 1935. m. free to members (effective 2010). adv. bk.rev.; software rev.; Website rev. charts; illus. 132 p./no.; back issues avail.; reprints avail. **Document type:** *Magazine, Trade.* **Description:** Covers all contract bridge activity in North America, plus reports about foreign tournaments. Includes results, schedules, features and instructional material.
Former titles: American Contract Bridge League. Bulletin (1071-3131); (until 1993): Contract Bridge Bulletin (0010-7840)

Published by: American Contract Bridge League, 2990 Airways Blvd, Memphis, TN 38116. TEL 901-332-5586, FAX 901-398-7754, service@acbl.org. Ed. Brent Manley TEL 901-332-5586 ext 1291. Adv. contact Eva Niknahad TEL 901-332-5586 ext 1292. B&W page USD 2,903.68, color page USD 4,537; trim 8.375 x 10.5. Circ: 150,000 (paid).

795.414 CAN
BRIDGE CANADA. Text in English. 1968. 3/yr. adv.
Former titles (until 1998): Canadian Bridge Digest (0707-9524); (until 1977): Bridge Digest (0317-9281)
Published by: Canadian Bridge Federation, 2719 E Jolly Pl, Regina, SK S4V 0X8, Canada. TEL 306-761-1677, FAX 306-789-4919, can.bridge.fed@sasktel.net. Ed. Jude Goodwin TEL 604-892-4997. adv.: page CAD 500.

795.414 ITA ISSN 0006-985X
BRIDGE D'ITALIA. Abbreviated title: B D I. Text in Italian. 1936. m. free to members. bk.rev. **Document type:** *Magazine, Consumer.*
Related titles: Online - full text ed.
Published by: Federazione Italiana Gioco Bridge, Via Ciro Menotti 11-C, Milan, 20129, Italy. TEL 39-02-70000333, FAX 39-02-70001398, figb@federbridge.it, http://www.federbridge.it. Ed. Niki Di Fabio.

793 DEU
BRIDGE MAGAZIN. Text in German. 1951. m. adv. **Document type:** *Newsletter.*
Formerly: Deutsches Bridge-Verbandsblatt
Published by: (Deutscher Bridge-Verband e.V.), Topp & Moeller GmbH & Co. KG, Postfach 2854, Detmold, 32718, Germany. TEL 49-5231-9199-0, FAX 49-5231-919910. Ed. Stefan Back. Adv. contact Jochen Ehrhardt. Circ: 26,000.

795.414 GBR ISSN 1351-4261
BRIDGE MAGAZINE. Text in English. 1926. m. GBP 44.95 domestic; GBP 54.95 in Europe; GBP 60 in US & Canada; GBP 64.95 elsewhere; GBP 4.50 per issue domestic; GBP 5 per issue in Europe; GBP 5.50 per issue elsewhere (effective 2010). adv. bk.rev. illus. index. **Document type:** *Magazine, Consumer.* **Description:** Contains articles on bidding and play, instruction, competitions, tournament reports and humour.
Incorporates (1980-200?): International Popular Bridge Monthly (0951-1555); Which was formerly (until 1980): Popular Bridge Monthly; Former titles (until 1993): Bridge (Sutton Coldfield) (0958-6768); (until 1989): Bridge International (0267-8799); (until 1984): Bridge Magazine (0006-9868); (until 1930): Auction Bridge Magazine; Bridge Magazine incorporated: British Bridge World (0407-1891)
Related titles: Online - full text ed.
Published by: Chess & Bridge Ltd., 369 Euston Rd, London, NW1 3AR, United Kingdom. TEL 44-207-3882404, FAX 44-207-3882407, info@chess.co.uk, http://www.chess.co.uk. Ed. Mark Horton.

795.414 SWE ISSN 0006-9906
BRIDGE TIDNINGEN. Text in Swedish. 1939. 10/yr. SEK 290 domestic; SEK 270 in Scandinavia; SEK 340 in Europe; SEK 400 elsewhere (effective 2001). adv. bk.rev. 52 p./no.; back issues avail.
Published by: Magnus Lindkvist, Ed. & Pub., Storgatan 7, Hoeoer, 24330, Sweden. TEL 46-8-650-61-61, FAX 46-705-389-896.

795.415 FRA ISSN 0184-8127
BRIDGERAMA; journal des amateurs de bridge. Text in French. 1978. m. EUR 39 domestic; EUR 44 foreign (effective 2010). adv. **Document type:** *Magazine, Consumer.*
Published by: Le Bridgeur, 28 Rue Richelieu, Paris, 75001, France. TEL 33-1-42962550, FAX 33-1-40209234, http://www.lebridgeur.fr. Ed. Robert Berthe. Pub. Jean-Paul Meyer. Adv. contact Jean Paul Meyer. Circ: 7,000 (controlled).

795.414 FRA ISSN 1267-8430
LE BRIDGEUR; revue francaise de bridge. Text in French. 1959. 11/yr. EUR 73 domestic; EUR 88 foreign; EUR 10 per issue (effective 2010). adv. bk.rev. illus. back issues avail. **Document type:** *Magazine, Consumer.*
Formerly (until 1997): Revue Francaise de Bridge, Le Bridgeur. (0241-0206); Which was formed by the merger of (1959-1979): Le Bridgeur (0006-9914); (1958-1979): Revue Francaise de Bridge (0035-2861); Both of which incorporated in part (197?-197?): Revue Francaise de Bridge, Le Bridgeur. Sud (0243-184X); and in part (197?-197?): Revue Francaise de Bridge, Le Bridgeur. Nord (0243-1831)
Published by: (Federation Francaise de Bridge), Le Bridgeur, 28 Rue Richelieu, Paris, 75001, France. TEL 33-1-42962550, FAX 33-1-40209234, http://www.lebridgeur.fr. Ed. Jean-Paul Meyer. Pub. Jean Paul Meyer. Adv. contact Muriel Clement. Circ: 24,000.

794.1 GBR ISSN 0007-0440
GV1313
BRITISH CHESS MAGAZINE. Text in English. 1881. m. GBP 42 domestic; GBP 45 in Europe; GBP 49 elsewhere; GBP 4.05 per issue (effective 2009). adv. bk.rev. illus. index. back issues avail.; reprints avail. **Document type:** *Magazine, Consumer.* **Description:** Contains reports of current tournaments, historical features, problems and studies in correspondence chess and opening theory. Written for players of all strengths and covers the international as well as the British chess scene.
Indexed: RASB.
Published by: British Chess Magazine Ltd., 44 Baker St, London, W1U 7RT, United Kingdom. TEL 44-20-74868222, FAX 44-20-74863355, bcmshop@googlemail.com. Circ: 4,000.

796 CAN ISSN 1187-4910
BRITISH COLUMBIA WINTER GAMES RULES BOOK. GENERAL RULES. Text in English. 1979. a.
Former titles (until 1989): British Columbia Winter Games Rules Book (1187-4929); (until 1983): British Columbia Winter Games. General Rules (0713-0724)
Published by: British Columbia Games Society, 990 Fort St, Suite 200, Victoria, BC V8V 3K2, Canada. TEL 250-387-1375, FAX 250-387-4489, info@bcgames.org.

796 GBR ISSN 0068-1938
GV1049
BRITISH CYCLING FEDERATION. HANDBOOK. Text in English. 1959. a. free to members (effective 2009). adv. **Document type:** *Directory, Trade.* **Description:** Contains rules and technical regulations for BMX, cycle speedway, cyclo-cross, mountain bike, road and track, including details of anti-doping regulations.
Formerly: British Cycling Federation. Racing Handbook
Published by: British Cycling Federation, Stuart St, Manchester, Lancs M11 4DQ, United Kingdom. TEL 44-161-2742000, FAX 44-161-2742001, info@britishcycling.org.uk, http://new.britishcycling.org.uk. Circ: 10,000.

598.2 GBR ISSN 0007-0777
BRITISH HOMING WORLD. Text in English. 1933. w. GBP 54 domestic; GBP 82 in Europe; GBP 104 elsewhere; GBP 0.65 newsstand/cover (effective 2009). adv. bk.rev. **Document type:** *Magazine, Consumer.* **Description:** Features articles devoted to pigeon racing includes race results, letters to the editor, regional show reports and news on the pigeon racing world.
Published by: Royal Pigeon Racing Association, The General Manager, The Reddings, Cheltenham, Glos GL51 6RN, United Kingdom. TEL 44-1452-713529, FAX 44-1452-857119, gm@rpra.org. adv.: page GBP 164.85. Circ: 24,000. **Subscr. to:** British Homing World, Severn Farm Industrial Estate, Severn Rd, Welshpool SY21 7DF, United Kingdom. TEL 44-1938-552360.

799.202 GBR ISSN 1360-0419
THE BRITISH RIFLEMAN. Text in English. 1995. bi-m. GBP 13; GBP 15 in Europe; GBP 17 elsewhere. adv. **Document type:** *Magazine, Consumer.*
Published by: Piedmont Publishing, Ltd., Seychelles House, Brightlingsea, Colchester, Essex CO7 0NN, United Kingdom. TEL 44-1206-305204, FAX 44-1206-304522. Ed. Richard Munday. Adv. contact Tony Smith. B&W page USD 450, color page USD 600. Circ: 14,000 (paid).

BROKEN SPOKE. *see* TRANSPORTATION—Automobiles

790.1 SWE ISSN 0345-1186
BROTTNING. Text in Swedish. 1968. m. (8/yr.). SEK 538 (effective 1999). adv.
Published by: (Svenska Brottningsfoerbundet), Daus Tryck och Media, Daushuset, Bjaesta, 89380, Sweden. TEL 46-660-266100, FAX 46-660-266128, http://www.daus.se. Circ: 6,600.

790.1 USA ISSN 0883-6833
BUCKEYE SPORTS BULLETIN. Text in English. 1981. 30/yr. adv. back issues avail. **Document type:** *Newspaper.* **Description:** Provides complete coverage of Ohio State University sports.
Published by: C S P Publishing Corp., 1350 W Fifth Ave, Ste 30, Columbus, OH 43212. TEL 614-486-2202, FAX 614-486-3650. Ed. Steve Helwagen. Pub., Adv. contact Frank Moskowitz. page USD 365. Circ: 20,000.

796.815 DEU ISSN 1435-4683
BUDO, KARATE. Text in German. 1998. bi-m. EUR 3.90 newsstand/cover (effective 2006). adv. **Document type:** *Magazine, Consumer.*
Formed by the merger of (198?-1998): Budo International (0946-0772); (1976-1998): Karate - Budo Journal (0179-7700); Which was formerly (until 1983): Karate (0179-793X); (until 1979): Karate-Revue (0179-7921); (until 1977): Karate-Journal (0179-7913)
Published by: Satori Verlagsanstalt GmbH, Bergstr 18, Kempen, 47894, Germany. TEL 49-2845-80593, FAX 49-2845-80392, satori@budoworld.net, http://www.budoworld.net. Ed. Norbert Schiffer. Adv. contact Hans Simon. B&W page EUR 3,150, color page EUR 4,280. Circ: 23,800 (paid and controlled).

796 ESP ISSN 0214-9060
EL BUDOKA; revista de artes marciales. Text in Spanish. 1972. 11/yr. EUR 27.50 domestic; EUR 45 in the European Union; EUR 42 elsewhere (effective 2009). adv. bk.rev. back issues avail. **Document type:** *Magazine, Consumer.*
Formerly: Revista de las Artes Marciales (0214-9052)
Published by: Editorial Alas, C. Villarroel 124, Barcelona, 08011, Spain. TEL 34-934-537506, FAX 34-934-537506, info@editorial-alas.com, http://www.editorial-alas.com. Ed. Jose Sala. Circ: 12,000.

796.815 DEU ISSN 0948-4124
DER BUDOKA. Text in German. 1972. 10/yr. EUR 28 (effective 2009). adv. bk.rev. back issues avail. **Document type:** *Magazine, Consumer.*
Published by: Dachverband fuer Budotechniken Nordrhein-Westfalen e.V., Friedrich-Alfred-Str 25, Duisburg, 47055, Germany. TEL 49-203-7381622, FAX 49-203-7381624, info@budo-nrw.de. Ed. Erik Gruhn. Circ: 3,500 (paid).

790.1 CHE
BUENDNER SPORT INFORMATION. Text in German. m.
Address: Kasernanstr 95, Chur, 7007, Switzerland. TEL 081-222843. Ed. Norbert Wasser. Circ: 2,008.

794 CHE ISSN 1661-5158
BULLETIN LEMANIQUE DE GO. Text in French. 2006. 3/yr. CHF 18 (effective 2007). **Document type:** *Magazine, Consumer.*
Address: 13 rue des Pitons, Geneva, 1205, Switzerland. TEL 41-22-7862585. Ed. Bassand Xavier.

790.1 DEU
BUNDESINSTITUT FUER SPORTWISSENSCHAFT. SPORTWISSENSCHAFTLICHE FORSCHUNGSPROJEKTE. Text in German. 1990. a. free (effective 2009). back issues avail. **Document type:** *Directory, Abstract/Index.*
Media: Online - full content.
Published by: Bundesinstitut fuer Sportwissenschaft, Graurheindorfer Str 198, Bonn, 53117, Germany. TEL 49-228-996400, FAX 49-228-996409008, info@bisp.de, http://www.bisp.de. Circ: 400.

790.1 658.8 GBR ISSN 1473-494X
BUSINESS RATIO REPORT. THE BETTING & GAMING INDUSTRY. Text in English. 1987. a., latest no.22, 2008, Feb. GBP 365 per issue (effective 2010). charts; stat. back issues avail. **Document type:** *Report, Trade.* **Description:** Covers companies active in the betting and gaming industry.
Former titles (until 2001): Business Ratio. The Betting and Gaming Industry (1469-8927); (until 2000): Business Ratio Plus: Betting and Gaming Industry (1355-0004); (until 1994): Business Ratio Report. Betting and Gaming (0951-516X)
Published by: Key Note Ltd. (Subsidiary of: Bonnier Business Information), Harlequin House, 5th Fl, 7 High St, Teddington, Richmond upon Thames, TW11 8EE, United Kingdom. TEL 44-845-5040452, FAX 44-845-5040453, sales@keynote.co.uk.

388.76 GBR ISSN 1473-3943
BUSINESS RATIO REPORT. THE SPORTS EQUIPMENT INDUSTRY (YEAR). Text in English. 1979. a., latest no.30, 2008, Nov. GBP 365 per issue (effective 2010). back issues avail. **Document type:** *Report, Trade.* **Description:** Covers companies active in the sports equipment industry.
Former titles (until 2000): Business Ratio. The Sports Equipment Industry (1469-2651); (until 1999): Business Ratio Plus: Sports Equipment Industry (1358-362X); (until 1994): Business Ratio Report. Sports Equipment Industry (1351-4962); (until 1992): Business Ratio Report: Sports Goods Manufacturers and Distributors (0261-9555)
Published by: Key Note Ltd. (Subsidiary of: Bonnier Business Information), Harlequin House, 5th Fl, 7 High St, Teddington, Richmond upon Thames, TW11 8EE, United Kingdom. TEL 44-845-5040452, FAX 44-845-5040453, sales@keynote.co.uk.

793 USA
BUZZ DALY'S PLAYERS GUIDE TO LAS VEGAS SPORTS BOOKS (YEAR) - FOOTBALL EDITION. Text in English. a. USD 6.95 newsstand/cover (effective 2001). adv. **Description:** Includes information on licensed sports books in Las Vegas for those who bet on football.
Published by: Players Guide Publishing, 11000 S Eastern Ave, 1618, Henderson, NV 89052. TEL 702-361-4602, FAX 702-361-4605. Pub. Buzz Daly.

613.7 USA ISSN 0273-6896
C A H P E R D JOURNAL/TIMES. Text in English. 1934. m. (Oct.-May). USD 75 to individual members; USD 95 to institutional members (effective 2005). adv. bk.rev. reprints avail. **Document type:** *Newspaper, Consumer.*
Former titles (until 1980): C A H P E R Journal/Times (0194-8261); Until 1979: C A H P E R Journal (0007-7763)
Related titles: Microfiche ed.: (from MML); Microform ed.: 1934 (from PQC).
Indexed: A22, CA, CBPI, PEI, SD, T02.
Published by: California Association for Health, Physical Education, Recreation and Dance, 1501 El Camino Ave, Ste 3, Sacramento, CA 95815-2748, membership@cahperd.org. Circ: 4,000.

790.1 AUS ISSN 1446-3911
C A M S MAGAZINE. Text in English. 1966. 3/yr. free to members (effective 2008). adv. bk.rev. back issues avail. **Document type:** *Magazine, Consumer.* **Description:** Provides specific news and information on all disciplines of motor sport, including the areas of safety, medical, officiating, licensing, technical and sports development.
Formerly (until 2000): C A M S Report (1033-0518)
Related titles: Online - full text ed.
Published by: Confederation of Australian Motor Sport, 851 Dandenong Rd, Malvern East, VIC 3145, Australia. TEL 61-3-95937777, FAX 61-3-95937700, info@cams.com.au. Adv. contact Janene Champion TEL 61-3-58623090. page AUD 3,586; trim 210 x 275. Circ: 30,000.

790.1 AUS ISSN 1033-0526
C A M S MANUAL OF MOTOR SPORT. Text in English. 1959. a. AUD 22; AUD 11 CAMS Accredited Officials (effective 2008). adv. back issues avail. **Document type:** *Yearbook, Trade.* **Description:** Contains the National Competition Rules (NCRs) to which all CAMS permitted motor sport events in Australia must abide by.
Formerly (until 1972): Manual of Motor Sport in Australia, Including National Competition Rules for
Published by: Confederation of Australian Motor Sport, 851 Dandenong Rd, Malvern East, VIC 3145, Australia. TEL 61-3-95937777, FAX 61-3-95937700, info@cams.com.au. Adv. contact Janene Champion TEL 61-3-58623090.

796 PRT ISSN 1647-3280
▼ **C I D E S D BOLETIM INFORMATIVO DE PERFORMANCE DESPORTIVA.** (Centro de Investigacao em Desporto, Saude e Desenvolvimento Humano) Text in Portuguese. 2009. 3/yr. **Document type:** *Bulletin, Consumer.*
Published by: Universidade de Tras-os-Montes e Alto Douro, Centro de Investigacao em Desporto, Saude e Desenvolvimento Humano/ University of Tras-os-Montes and Alto Douro, Research Centre for Sports Sciences, Health and Human Development, Rua Dr. Manuel Cardona, Vila Real, 5000-558, Portugal. TEL 351-259-330100, FAX 351-259-330169, http://cidesd.org.

796 ESP ISSN 2171-4991
▼ **C O E EXPRESS.** Text in Spanish. 2009. q. **Document type:** *Magazine, Consumer.*
Published by: Comite Olimpico Espanol, C Arequipa, 13, Madrid, 28043, Spain. TEL 34-91-3815500, FAX 34-91-3819639, correo@coe.es, http://www.coe.es/.

796 USA
C O S I D A DIGEST. Text in English. 1957. 11/yr. free to members (effective 2008). adv. bk.rev. **Document type:** *Newsletter, Consumer.* **Description:** Contains ideas, opinions, contest information, information on job openings and articles on the top people in the profession.
Related titles: Online - full text ed.
Published by: College Sports Information Directors of America, c/o Jeff Hodges, University of North Alabama, UNA Box 5038, Florence, AL 35632-0001. TEL 256-765-4595, FAX 256-765-4659, sportsinformation@una.edu. Circ: 700.

790.1 USA
C3I. Text in English. 1992. q. USD 20 per issue (effective 2010). back issues avail. **Document type:** *Magazine, Consumer.*
Related titles: Online - full text ed.
Published by: G M T Games, PO Box 1308, Hanford, CA 93232. TEL 800-523-6111, gmtoffice@gmtgames.com, http://www.gmtgames.com. Pub. Rodger MacGowan.

796 BRA ISSN 1676-2533
CADERNO DE EDUCACAO FISICA. Text in Portuguese. 1999. s-a. **Document type:** *Journal, Academic/Scholarly.*
Related titles: Online - full text ed.: ISSN 1983-8883. free (effective 2011).
Published by: Universidade Estadual do Oeste do Parana, Rua Universitaria 1619, Jardim Universitario, Cascavel, Parana, Brazil. TEL 55-45-32203027, saber@unioeste.br, http://www.unioeste.br. Ed. Mauro Myskiw.

795 USA
CAESARS PLAYER; the luxury lifestyle and gaming magazine of Caesars. Text in English. 2005. 3/w. free in Caesar Entertainment locations (effective 2006). adv. **Document type:** *Magazine, Consumer.* **Description:** Covers luxury lifestyle and gaming, including food, fashion, upscale products, and gambling.

S

Published by: (Caesar Entertainment), Onboard Media, 960 Alton Rd, Miami Beach, FL 33139. TEL 305-673-0400, FAX 305-673-3575, info@onboard.com, http://www.onboard.com. Pub. Robin Rosenbaum TEL 305-938-1225. adv.: page USD 18,687; trim 8.375 x 10.875. Circ: 185,000 (paid and controlled).

794.7 FRA ISSN 1773-4207
LES CAHIERS DE LA PETANQUE; guide de l'educateur. Text in French. 2004. irreg. **Document type:** *Bulletin, Consumer.*
Published by: Federation Francaise de Petanque et de Jeu Provencal, 13 rue Trigance, Marseille, 13002, France.

796.5 GBR ISSN 0068-5267
CAIRNGORM CLUB JOURNAL. Text in English. 1893. biennial. free to members (effective 2009). bk.rev. index. **Document type:** *Journal, Trade.* **Description:** Designed for the members of Cairngorm club.
Published by: Cairngorm Club, c/o Secretary R.C. Shirreffs, 18 Bon-Accord Sq, Aberdeen, Aberdeenshire AB9 1YE, United Kingdom. TEL 44-1569-730989, FAX 44-1330-860333, enquiries@cairngormclub.org.uk.

799.202 DEU ISSN 0933-3738
CALIBER; Das Magazin fuer den modernen Schiesssport. Text in German. 1987. m. EUR 53.10 (effective 2010). adv. bk.rev. back issues avail. **Document type:** *Magazine, Consumer.*
Published by: V S Medien GmbH, Wipsch 1, Bad Ems, 56130, Germany. TEL 49-2603-5060201, FAX 49-2603-5060202, vertrieb@vsmedien.de, http://www.visier.de. Ed. Stefan Perey. adv.: B&W page EUR 2,300, color page EUR 2,900; trim 184 x 250. Circ: 28,000 (paid).

CALIFORNIA CONVERSATIONS. *see* POLITICAL SCIENCE

797.23 USA ISSN 1084-3264
CALIFORNIA DIVING NEWS. Text in English. 1984. m. USD 21 domestic; USD 45 foreign (effective 2001); free newsstand/cover. adv. bk.rev. **Document type:** *Newspaper, Consumer.*
Published by: Saint Brendan Corp., PO Box 11231, Torrance, CA 90510. TEL 310-792-2333, FAX 310-792-2336. Ed. Kim Sheckler. Pub., R&P Dale Sheckler. Adv. contact David Reed. page USD 1,650; trim 13 x 11. Circ: 35,000.

796 USA
CALIFORNIA HOCKEY & SKATING. Text in English. m. adv. **Description:** Covers all forms of skating.
Published by: Spotlight Publishing, 701 DeLong Ave, I, Novato, CA 94945. TEL 415-898-5414, FAX 415-892-6484. Ed. Reggie Winner. Pub. William Schoen.

796.962 USA
CALIFORNIA RUBBER MAGAZINE; california's authoritative voice of ice and inline hockey. Text in English. 2008. 10/yr. USD 29.95; USD 3.95 newsstand/cover (effective 2010). adv. **Document type:** *Magazine, Consumer.*
Published by: Good Sport Media, Inc., PO Box 24024, Edina, MN 55424. TEL 612-929-2171, FAX 612-920-8326, info@goodsportmedia.com, http://www.goodsportmedia.com.

790.1 USA
CALIFORNIA SPORTS PROFILES MAGAZINE. (Los Angeles) Text in English. 1986. bi-m. USD 10 (effective 2000). adv. **Document type:** *Magazine, Consumer.* **Description:** Covers local professional and college sports teams.
Formerly: L A Sports Profiles
Published by: Sports Profiles, 4711 Golf St, Ste 900, Skokie, IL 60076. TEL 847-673-0592, FAX 847-673-0633. Ed. Paula Blaine. Pub. Lisa Levine. Circ: 40,000.

CAMPING-CAR MAGAZINE. *see* TRANSPORTATION

CAMPING & FRITID. *see* LEISURE AND RECREATION

794.1 CAN ISSN 0045-4540
CANADIAN CHESS CHAT. Text in English. 1946. 6/yr. CAD 16. bk.rev. **Description:** Covers national and international games, correspondence chess, endgame studies and opening theory.
Published by: Glenquaich Press Limited, P O Box 553, Sta Q, Toronto, ON M4T 2M5, Canada. Ed. Michael D Sharpe. Circ: 1,000.

796.964 CAN ISSN 1493-9339
CANADIAN CURLING ASSOCIATION. FACT BOOK. Variant title: Season of Champions Fact Book. Text in English. 198?. a.
Formerly (until 199?): Curling Fact Book (1189-7597)
Published by: Canadian Curling Association, 1660 Vimont Court, Cumberland, ON K4A 4J4, Canada. TEL 613-834-2076, 800-550-2875, FAX 613-834-0716, info@curling.ca, http://www.curling.ca.

795 CAN ISSN 1911-2378
CANADIAN GAMING BUSINESS. Text in English. 2006. bi-m. free to qualified personnel. **Document type:** *Magazine, Trade.*
Published by: MediaEdge Communications, Llc, 5255 Yonge St, Ste 1000, Toronto, ON M2N 6P4, Canada. TEL 416-512-8186, 866-216-0860, FAX 416-512-8344, info@mediaedge.ca, http://www.mediaedge.ca. Ed. Lucie Grys.

790.1 CAN ISSN 1496-1539
CANADIAN JOURNAL FOR WOMEN IN COACHING ONLINE. Text in English. 2000. bi-m.
Media: Online - full content.
Indexed: SD.
Published by: Coaching Association of Canada, The Women in Coaching Program, Suite 300, 141 Laurier Ave W, Ottawa, ON K1P 5J3, Canada.

CANADIAN SPORTING GOODS & PLAYTHINGS. DIRECTORY. *see* BUSINESS AND ECONOMICS—Trade And Industrial Directories

CANADIAN SPORTS COLLECTOR. *see* HOBBIES

793 CAN ISSN 0845-518X
CANADIAN WARGAMER'S JOURNAL. Text in English. 1986. q. USD 15.50. adv. illus. illus. **Document type:** *Journal, Consumer.* **Description:** Reviews games and reports on events in Canada and Australia. Lists other wargame magazines from around the world.
Published by: Canadian Wargamer's Group, P O BOX 1725, Sta M, Calgary, AB T2P 2L7, Canada. Ed. Keith Martens.

796.8 CAN ISSN 0829-3767
CANADIAN WRESTLER NEWSLETTER/LUTTEUR CANADIEN. Text in English. 1977. 4/yr. CAD 16 (effective 1998 & 1999). adv. bk.rev. **Document type:** *Newsletter.*
Former titles (until 1982): Canadian Wrestler (0705-176X); (until 1977): Wrestler (0382-4063); (until 1974): Canadian Amateur Wrestler (0381-8101)
Indexed: SportS.
Published by: Canadian Amateur Wrestling Association/Association Canadienne de Lutte Amateur, 1600 James Naismith, Gloucester, ON, Canada. TEL 613-748-5686, FAX 613-748-5756. Ed. Greg Mathieu. Circ: 7,500.

CAR CRAFT; do-it-yourself street performance. *see* TRANSPORTATION—Automobiles

793 USA ISSN 1089-2044
CARD PLAYER. Text in English. 1988. bi-w. USD 39.95; USD 4.95 per issue (effective 2008). adv. bk.rev. illus. back issues avail.; reprints avail. **Document type:** *Magazine, Consumer.* **Description:** Covers casino and sports gambling, poker, and gambling industry news.
Published by: Shulman, Barry and Jeff, 6940 O'Bannon Dr, Las Vegas, NV 89117. adv.: color page USD 9,800; trim 8.125 x 10.75. Circ: 5,000 (paid); 48,000 (controlled).

795 USA
CARD PLAYER COLLEGE. Text in English. 25/yr. USD 39.95; USD 4.95 per issue (effective 2006). adv. **Document type:** *Magazine, Consumer.*
Published by: Card Player Media, LLC, 3140 S Polaris Ave, Las Vegas, NV 89102. TEL 702-871-1720, FAX 702-871-2674, http:/ www.cardplayer.com. Adv. contact Trey Aldridge. color page USD 11,500; trim 8.125 x 10.75.

306.4 USA ISSN 1747-0447
CARD PLAYER EUROPE. Text in English. 2005. 26/yr. USD 25.95 domestic; USD 79.95 in Canada; USD 99.95 elsewhere (effective 2007). **Document type:** *Magazine, Consumer.*
Published by: Card Player Media, LLC, 3140 S Polaris Ave, Las Vegas, NV 89102. TEL 702-871-1720, FAX 702-871-2674, http:/ www.cardplayer.com.

794.42 CZE ISSN 1803-9995
▼ **CARDPLAYER.** Text in Czech. 2009. bi-m. CZK 445 (effective 2010). adv. **Document type:** *Magazine, Consumer.*
Published by: Poker Production s.r.o., Markova 529/12, Prague 5, 158 00, Czech Republic. TEL 420-251-550752, redakce@pokerzive.cz, http://www.pokerzive.cz.

CAREER CONNECTIONS (CHANDLER). *see* OCCUPATIONS AND CAREERS

790.1 USA
CARIBBEAN SPORTS & TRAVEL. Text in English. 1992. q. USD 8. bk.rev. illus. **Description:** Covers diving, cruising, fishing, charters, and golf packages in the Caribbean islands.
Incorporates (1971-1990): Pleasure Boating
Published by: Graphcom Publishing Co., Inc., 1995 N E 150 St, Ste 107, N, Miami, FL 33181. TEL 305-945-7403, FAX 305-947-6410. Ed. V C Hanna. adv.: B&W page USD 1,580, color page USD 2,330; trim 10.75 x 8. Circ: 40,000.

CARMA. *see* TRANSPORTATION—Automobiles

796 USA ISSN 0274-7723
CAROLINA BLUE. Text in English. 1980. 27/yr. (w. mid-Aug.-Apr.). USD 47.95 (effective 2011). adv. **Document type:** *Magazine, Consumer.*
Published by: 247 Sports, PO Box 1498, Shelbyville, KY 40066. TEL 888-474-8669, info@247sports.com, http://247sports.com.

790.1 647.94 USA ISSN 0889-9797
CASINO CHRONICLE; a weekly newsletter focusing on the gaming industry. Text in English. 1983. w. (48/yr.). USD 195 domestic; USD 210 in Canada & Mexico; USD 245 elsewhere (effective 2007). adv. bk.rev.; film rev.; play rev. pat.; stat.; tr.lit.; illus. back issues avail.; reprints avail. **Document type:** *Newsletter, Trade.* **Description:** Focuses on the gaming industry in US.
Address: PO Box 740465, Boynton Beach, FL 33474-0465. Ed., Pub., R&P, Adv. contact Ben A Borowsky. Circ: 1,500 (paid and controlled).

795 USA
CASINO CITY'S CASINO VENDORS GUIDE. Text in English. 2004. a. USD 49.95; USD 174.95 (print or CD-ROM ed.) (effective 2008). adv. **Document type:** *Directory, Trade.* **Description:** Provides a directory of more than 1,000 gaming products and services and 10,000 gaming industry suppliers, plus coverage of casinos in more than 125 countries around the world.
Former titles (until 2006): Casino City's Worldwide Casino Vendors Guide; (until 2005): Casino City's Worldwide Casino Guide (1552-4396)
Related titles: CD-ROM ed.: ISSN 1552-440X. USD 149.95 (effective 2008).
Published by: Casino City Press, 95 Wells Ave, Newton, MA 02459. TEL 617-332-2850, 800-490-1715, FAX 617-964-2280, customerservice@casinocitypress.com. Ed. Steve Bloom.

CASINO CITY'S GAMING BUSINESS DIRECTORY; casinos, card rooms, horse tracks, dog tracks, cruise ships, online casinos, and property owners. *see* BUSINESS AND ECONOMICS—Trade And Industrial Directories

306.482 USA
CASINO CITY'S GAMING REVENUE NEWS. Text in English. 2001. m. USD 149.95 (print or e-mail ed.) (effective 2009). **Document type:** *Newsletter, Trade.* **Description:** Provides up-to-date analysis of the gaming revenue performance of the major jurisdictions in Nevada, Colorado, Mississippi and New Jersey.
Formerly (until 2006): Gaming Revenue Newsletter (1539-5375); Which was formed by the merger of (19??-2001): Nevada Gaming Newsletter; Atlantic City Colorado Mississippi Gaming Newsletter
Related titles: E-mail ed.
Published by: Casino City Press, 95 Wells Ave, Newton, MA 02459. TEL 617-332-2850, 800-490-1715, FAX 617-964-2280, customerservice@casinocitypress.com.

795 USA ISSN 1550-2171
HV6710
CASINO CITY'S GLOBAL GAMING ALMANAC. Text in English. 2004. a. USD 374.95; USD 474.95 combined subscription (print or CD-ROM ed.) (effective 2008). **Document type:** *Handbook/Manual/Guide, Trade.* **Description:** Describes each segment of the gaming industry including casino and card room gaming, lotteries, race and sports wagering, charitable gaming, and online gaming.
Related titles: CD-ROM ed.: ISSN 1550-218X. USD 449.95 (effective 2008).
Published by: Casino City Press, 95 Wells Ave, Newton, MA 02459. TEL 617-332-2850, 800-490-1715, FAX 617-964-2280, customerservice@casinocitypress.com.

795 USA
CASINO CITY'S IGAMING BUSINESS DIRECTORY. Text in English. 2004. a. USD 199.95; USD 399.95 (print or CD-ROM ed.) (effective 2008). **Document type:** *Directory, Trade.* **Description:** Provides guidance on the people, websites, portals, affiliate programs and other industry businesses that are major components of the online gaming industry's explosive growth.
Formerly: Casino City's Online Gaming Business Directory (1550-3968)
Related titles: CD-ROM ed.: ISSN 1550-3976. 2004. USD 374.95 (effective 2008).
Published by: Casino City Press, 95 Wells Ave, Newton, MA 02459. TEL 617-332-2850, 800-490-1715, FAX 617-964-2280, customerservice@casinocitypress.com.

306.4 USA ISSN 1549-7313
E98.G18
CASINO CITY'S INDIAN GAMING INDUSTRY REPORT. Text in English. 2004. a. USD 249.95 (print or CD-ROM ed.); USD 274.95 combined subscription (print & CD-ROM eds.) (effective 2008 - 2009). **Document type:** *Newsletter, Trade.* **Description:** Provides current, unique, cutting-edge research on the Indian gaming industry appropriate for executives in the industry, gaming analysts, regulators, consultants, lawyers, lobbyists, academics, and any individuals interested in the state of Indian gaming.
Formerly: Economic Impact of Indian Gaming
Related titles: CD-ROM ed.
Published by: Casino City Press, 95 Wells Ave, Newton, MA 02459. TEL 617-332-2850, 800-490-1715, FAX 617-964-2280, customerservice@casinocitypress.com.

795 USA ISSN 1553-9032
CASINO CITY'S NEVADA GAMING ALMANAC. Text in English. 1991. a. USD 324.95; USD 424.95 (print or CD-ROM ed.) (effective 2008). **Document type:** *Directory, Trade.* **Description:** Provides five-year revenue statistics for each jurisdiction along with essential ratios like slots per room, slots per game, games per games sq ft, and summary pages with current fiscal year P & L results.
Formerly (until 2004): Nevada Gaming Almanac (1539-4670)
Related titles: CD-ROM ed.: ISSN 1553-9040. USD 399.95 (effective 2008); Online - full text ed.
Published by: Casino City Press, 95 Wells Ave, Newton, MA 02459. TEL 617-332-2850, 800-490-1715, FAX 617-964-2280, customerservice@casinocitypress.com. Ed. Steve Bloom.

795 USA ISSN 1550-2198
GV1301
CASINO CITY'S NORTH AMERICAN GAMING ALMANAC. Text in English. 2004. a. USD 449.95; USD 549.95 combined subscription (print & CD-ROM eds.) (effective 2008). **Document type:** *Newsletter, Trade.* **Description:** Covers casino and card room gaming, lotteries, race and sports wagering, and charitable gaming in every U.S. state and Canadian province.
Related titles: CD-ROM ed.: ISSN 1550-2201. USD 524.95 (effective 2008).
Published by: Casino City Press, 95 Wells Ave, Newton, MA 02459. TEL 617-332-2850, 800-490-1715, FAX 617-964-2280, customerservice@casinocitypress.com.

306.4 USA
CASINO CONNECTION. Text in English. 2004. m. free. **Document type:** *Magazine, Trade.* **Description:** Focuses on the positive contributions of the gaming industry for Atlantic City's casino employees.
Published by: Global Gaming Business LLC, 1600 West Riverside Dr, Atlantic City, NJ 08401 . TEL 609-344-7561, FAX 609-344-6235.

795 ITA ISSN 1827-7527
CASINO DE LA VALLEE. Text in Italian. 2006. s-m. **Document type:** *Magazine, Consumer.*
Published by: De Agostini Editore, Via G da Verrazzano 15, Novara, 28100, Italy. TEL 39-0321-4241, FAX 39-0321-424305, info@deagostini.it, http://www.deagostini.it.

CASINO ENTERPRISE MANAGEMENT. *see* BUSINESS AND ECONOMICS—Management

795 USA
CASINO GAMES MAGAZINE. Text in English. 1994. q. USD 3.95. adv. back issues avail. **Document type:** *Magazine, Consumer.* **Description:** In-flight magazine that provides the consumer with the facts and photo features on casino games.
Published by: Compass International, Inc., 1009 Nawkee Dr, Ste 711, North Las Vegas, NV 89031-1425. TEL 702-399-3998, FAX 702-399-3997. Pub., Adv. contact Sam Micco. B&W page USD 1,550, color page USD 1,900. Circ: 150,000 (controlled).

790 058 GBR ISSN 1467-9175
CASINO INTERNATIONAL. Text in English. 1990. m. GBP 55 domestic; EUR 130 in Europe; USD 165 in Americas and Middle East; USD 195 in Far East; free to qualified personnel (effective 2009). adv. back issues avail. **Document type:** *Magazine, Trade.* **Description:** Contains articles on the world wide casino and gaming business, suppliers, manufacturers and personalities.
Supersedes in part (in 1999): Euroslot (0966-0259); Which incorporated part of (1998-199?): Park World (1462-4796)
Related titles: Online - full text ed.: free to qualified personnel (effective 2009).
Indexed: B07, H&TI, H06, T02.
—CCC.
Published by: Datateam Publishing Ltd, 15a London Rd, Maidstone, Kent ME16 8LY, United Kingdom. TEL 44-1622-687031, FAX 44-1622-757646, info@datateam.co.uk, http://www.datateam.co.uk. Pub. Paul Ryder TEL 44-1622-699105. adv.: color page GBP 2,100; trim 229 x 306.

793 USA ISSN 1535-2110
HV6711
CASINO JOURNAL. Text in English. 1995. m. USD 161 domestic; USD 198 in Canada; USD 211 elsewhere; free to qualified personnel (print or online ed.) (effective 2009). adv. back issues avail.; reprints avail. **Document type:** *Magazine, Trade.* **Description:** Provides real-world solutions to challenges facing North America-based casino resort operators.
Formerly (until 199?): Casino Executive (1523-1674)
Related titles: Online - full text ed.
Indexed: A09, A10, H&TI, H06, T02, V03, V04.
—CCC.

Published by: B N P Media, 505 E Capovilla Ave, Ste 102, Las Vegas, NV 89119. TEL 702-794-0718, FAX 702-794-0799, portfolio@bnpmedia.com, http://www.bnpmedia.com. Ed. Marian Green. Pub. Charles Anderer TEL 718-432-8529. Adv. contact Terry Davis TEL 404-320-0072. B&W page USD 4,120, color page USD 5,345; trim 8 x 10.875. Circ: 9,000.

794 DEU ISSN 1867-0415
CASINO NEWS (DUISBURG EDITION). Text in German. 2002. 4/yr. adv. **Document type:** *Magazine, Consumer.*
Supersedes in part (in 2008): Casino Live (1619-1803)
Related titles: Regional ed(s).: Casino News (Hohensyburg Edition)). ISSN 1867-0350. 2002; Casino News (Bad Oeynhausen Edition). ISSN 1867-0369. 2002; Casino News (Aachen Edition). ISSN 1867-0407. 2002; Casino News (Bremen/Bremerhaven Edition). ISSN 1867-0385. 2002; Casino News (Berlin Edition). ISSN 1867-0393. 2002; Casino News (Erfurt Edition)). ISSN 1867-0377. 2002.
Published by: corps - Corporate Publishing Services GmbH, Kasernenstr 69, Duesseldorf, 40213, Germany. TEL 49-211-54227700, FAX 49-211-54227722, info@corps-verlag.de, http://www.corps-verlag.de.

790 USA ISSN 1087-2647
GV1301
CASINO PLAYER; America's gaming magazine. Text in English. 1988. m. USD 24 combined subscription (print & online eds.); USD 3.95 newsstand/cover (effective 2011). adv. **Document type:** *Magazine, Consumer.* **Description:** For gaming enthusiasts who know that educated gamblers win more.
Formerly (until 1991): The Player (1047-5303)
Related titles: Online - full text ed.: 1988. USD 9.95 (effective 2011).
Published by: Casino Journal Publishing Group, 8025 Black Horse Pike, Ste 470, Atlantic City, NJ 08232. TEL 609-641-8846, FAX 609-645-1661, customerservice@casinocenter.com, http://www.casinocenter.com. Adv. contact Laurie Leaf. Circ: 125,330. **Dist. by:** International Publishers Direct.

794.9 AUT ISSN 1992-8262
DAS CASINO UND POKER MAGAZIN. Text in German. 2006. bi-m. adv. **Document type:** *Magazine, Consumer.*
Published by: Full House Verlagsgesellschaft mbH, Knoellgasse 19-21, Vienna, 1100, Austria. TEL 43-1-3077000, office@fullhouseverlag.at, http://fullhouseverlag.at.

779.202 USA
THE CAST BULLET. Text in English. 1977. bi-m. USD 14 (effective 1998). adv. bk.rev. cum.index: 1977-1988. back issues avail. **Document type:** *Newsletter.* **Description:** Disseminates technology of cast lead bullets for target shooting and hunting.
Formerly (until 1993): Fouling Shot
Published by: Cast Bullet Association, Inc., 4103 Foxcraft Dr, Traverse City, MI 49684. TEL 616-929-0553. Ed., R&P, Adv. contact Ralland J Fortier. Circ: 1,600.

796 ESP ISSN 2173-9404
CATALOGO DE PUBLICACIONES DEL CONSEJO SUPEIOR DE DEPORTES. Text in Spanish. 1995. a. **Document type:** *Catalog, Consumer.*
Media: Online - full text. **Related titles:** Online - full text ed.: ISSN 2174-0119. 2009.
Published by: Consejo Superior de Deportes, Servicio de Documentacion, Av. Martin Fierro s/n, Madrid, 28040, Spain. TEL 34-91-5896938, FAX 34-91-5896614, publicaciones@csd.gob.es.

790.1 ESP ISSN 2171-8989
▼ **CATCH LIVE.** Text in Spanish. 2009. bi-m. **Document type:** *Magazine, Consumer.*
Published by: Cesar Editions, Ave Pastor, s-n, Rosas, Girona, 17480, Spain.

796 USA
THE CAT'S PAUSE. Text in English. 19??. 30/yr. (w. Sep.-Apr.; m.May-Aug.). USD 49.95 (effective 2011). adv. **Document type:** *Magazine, Consumer.* **Description:** Covers Kentucky Wildcats sports.
Published by: 247 Sports, PO Box 1498, Shelbyville, KY 40066. TEL 888-474-8669, info@247sports.com, http://247sports.com.

796 340 DEU ISSN 1660-8399
CAUSA SPORT; Die Sport-Zeitschrift fuer nationales und internationales Recht sowie fuer Wirtschaft. Text in German. 2004. q. EUR 86; EUR 62 to students (effective 2010). adv. **Document type:** *Journal, Academic/Scholarly.*
Published by: Richard Boorberg Verlag GmbH und Co. KG, Scharrstr 2, Stuttgart, 70563, Germany. TEL 49-711-73850, FAX 49-711-7385100, mail@boorberg.de.

796 USA ISSN 2151-660X
GV584.N7
▼ **CENTRAL NEW YORK SPORTS MAGAZINE.** Text in English. 2009. q. USD 19.80 (effective 2010). **Document type:** *Magazine, Consumer.* **Description:** Features news about professional, college and high school sports in the Syracuse area.
Announced as: Central New York Sportslife Magazine
Published by: Herald Co., 1 Clinton Square, PO Box 4915, Syracuse, NY 13221.

CENTRE FOR SPORTS SCIENCE AND HISTORY. SERIAL HOLDINGS. *see* EDUCATION—Abstracting, Bibliographies, Statistics

796 BRA ISSN 2176-963X
▼ **CENTRO DE DOCUMENTACAO E BIBLIOTECA / SECRETARIA MUNICIPAL DE ESPORTES, LAZER E RECREACAO. REVISTA ELETRONICA.** Variant title: Revista Eletronica do C E D O C / S E M E. Text in Portuguese; Summaries in English, Portuguese. 2009. s-a. free. **Document type:** *Magazine, Government.* **Description:** Contains papers on sports and physical education by SEME and outisde contributions.
Formerly: I B I C T
Media: Online - full text.
Published by: Secretaria Municipal de Esportes, Lazer e Recreacao, Centro de Documentacao e Biblioteca, Alameda Irae, 35, Indianopolis, Sao Paulo 04075-000, Brazil. TEL 55-11-33966453, FAX 55-11-33966490, eme.biblioteca@prefeitura.sp.gov.br, http://www.prefeitura.sp.gov.br/cidade/secretarias/esportes/biblioteca/a_biblioteca/index.php?p=6865. R&P Maria Antonia G.M. Botelho. Adv. contact Ana Maria R.C. da C. Monteiro.

CHALLENGE (ROCKVILLE). *see* HANDICAPPED—Physically Impaired

797.2 CAN ISSN 1918-9087
▼ **CHALLENGES.** Text in English. 2009. q. USD 3 per issue (effective 2010). back issues avail. **Document type:** *Magazine, Consumer.*
Related titles: Online - full text ed.: free (effective 2010).
Published by: Wayland Sports Ltd., 10451 Palmberg Rd, Richmond, BC V6W 1C5, Canada. TEL 604-275-2888, FAX 604-275-3888, info@waylandsports.com. Ed. Matthew Zhang.

790.1 SRB ISSN 1464-5890
CHAMPIONS. Variant title: Champions Leauge. Text in English. 1996. m. adv. **Document type:** *Magazine, Consumer.*
Related titles: French ed.; Chinese ed.; Spanish ed.; German ed.
Published by: Alliance International Media Ltd., Kneginje Zorke 11b, Belgrade, 11000. TEL 381-11-3089977, FAX 381-11-3089988, office@allianceinternationalmedia.com.

793 USA
CHANCE (NEW YORK, 1997); the best of gaming. Text in English. 1997. bi-m. USD 21.99 domestic; USD 28.99 in Canada; USD 38.99 per issue elsewhere (effective 2001); USD 4.95 newsstand/cover (effective 1998). adv. bk.rev. illus. back issues avail. **Document type:** *Magazine, Consumer.* **Description:** Includes playing tips for blackjack, baccarat, craps, poker, pai gow and more. Also includes features on casino hotel and resort events and related travel, tournament information, and a section on online casinos.
Related titles: Online - full text ed.
Published by: A R C Publishing LLC, 16 E 41st St, 2nd fl, New York, NY 10017. TEL 212-889-3467, 888-242-6238, FAX 212-889-3630, arcpublish@aol.com. Ed. Anthony Reilly. Pub., R&P Matthew Tolan. adv.: B&W page USD 8,100, color page USD 10,800; trim 10.88 x 8. Circ: 165,000.

363.4 CAN ISSN 1489-8411
HV6722.C23
CHARITABLE GAMING IN ALBERTA (YEAR/YEAR) IN REVIEW. Text in English. 1981. a. free. back issues avail. **Document type:** *Government.* **Description:** Provides information about Alberta's charitable gaming model including: Which groups are eligible for gaming licenses; how charitable gaming funds are used; the amount generated by charities from each gaming activity and how the province maintains the integrity of gaming activities.
Former titles (until 1997): Gaming in Alberta (Year) Review (1208-090X); (until 1990): Alberta Gaming Commission. Annual Review (0821-8633)
Related titles: Online - full text ed.: free.
Published by: Alberta Gaming and Liquor Commission, 50 Corriveau Ave., St. Albert, AB T8N 3T5, Canada. TEL 780-447-8600.

790.1 NZL
CHEAPSKATES. Text in English. 2000. 2/yr. **Document type:** *Magazine, Consumer.* **Description:** Contains news, reviews, info, interviews and giveaways relating to skateboarding.
Address: 243 High St., Level 2, Christchurch, New Zealand. TEL 64-3-365-4841, web@cheapskates.co.nz, http://www.cheapskates.co.nz.

794.1 CAN ISSN 1187-3337
CHECK!. Text in English. 1928. q. CAD 24; CAD 29 in the Americas; CAD 33 elsewhere. adv. bk.rev. index. back issues avail. **Document type:** *Bulletin.* **Description:** Reports on national and international games and news; includes problems and studies, as well as opening articles.
Formerly (until 1968): Canadian Correspondence Chess Association. Bulletin (1191-4521)
Published by: Canadian Correspondence Chess Association, c/o Manny Migicousky, 1669 Front Rd W, Lorignal, ON K0B 1K0, Canada. TEL 416-234-0207. Ed., R&P William Roach. Circ: 600.

791.64 USA ISSN 1553-9431
CHEER BIZ NEWS. Text in English. 2004. bi-m. free to qualified personnel (effective 2008). **Document type:** *Magazine, Trade.* **Description:** Features the latest developments in cheer training and coaches certification and covers cheer industry news, from people on the move to division developments.
Published by: Macfadden Performing Arts Media, LLC., 110 William St, 23rd Fl, New York, NY 10038. TEL 646-459-4800, FAX 646-459-4900, http://dancemedia.com/. Ed. Marisa Walker. Pub. Sheila Noone. Adv. contact Brandy Bean TEL 321-752-6794.

791.64 GBR ISSN 1759-9296
▼ **CHEERLEADER UK.** Text in English. 2009. m. GBP 48 (effective 2010). adv. back issues avail. **Document type:** *Magazine, Consumer.*
Address: The Bofet Bldg, Chumleigh Gardens, Chumleigh St, Burgess Park, London, SE5 0RS, United Kingdom.

306.766 FRA ISSN 2105-7117
CHEMIN DES CIMES. Text in French. 2002. q. **Document type:** *Newsletter, Consumer.*
Address: 38 Rue Azalais d'Altier, Montpellier, 34080, France. TEL 33-6-66531847, http://www.chemindescimes.fr.

790.1 UKR
CHEMPION. Text in Ukrainian. q. USD 90 in United States.
Published by: Sport Press, Ul Vladimirskaya 45, Kiev, Ukraine. TEL 228-5273, FAX 224-5012. **Dist. by:** East View Information Services, 10601 Wayzata Blvd, Minneapolis, MN 55305. TEL 952-252-1201, 800-477-1005, FAX 952-252-1202, info@eastview.com, http://www.eastview.com.

796 CHN ISSN 1001-9154
CHENGDU TIYU XUEYUAN XUEBAO/CHENGDU SPORT UNIVERSITY. JOURNAL. Text in Chinese. 1960. m. **Document type:** *Journal, Academic/Scholarly.*
Former titles (until 1990): Chengdu Ti-Yuan Xuebao; (until 1981): Chengdu Tiyu Xueyuan Xuebao; (until 1960): Chengdu Tiyu Xueyuan Yuankan
Related titles: Online - full text ed.
Indexed: CA, SD, T02.
Published by: Chengdu Tiyu Xueyuan/Chengdu Sport University, 2, Ti-Yuan Lu, Chengdu, 610041, China. TEL 86-28-85095371, FAX 86-28-85095371, http://www.cdsu.edu.cn/.

794.1 GBR ISSN 0964-6221
CHESS. Text in English. 1935. m. GBP 44.95 domestic; GBP 54.95 in Europe; GBP 60 in US & Canada; GBP 64.95 elsewhere (effective 2010). adv. bk.rev. charts; illus.; stat. index. back issues avail. **Document type:** *Magazine, Consumer.* **Description:** Provides reports on international events, features on players, instructional articles, competitions, and humor.
Former titles (until 19??): Pergamon Chess; (until 1988): Chess (0009-3319)
Related titles: Online - full text ed.
Published by: Chess & Bridge Ltd., 369 Euston Rd, London, NW1 3AR, United Kingdom. TEL 44-207-3882404, FAX 44-207-3882407, info@chess.co.uk, http://www.chess.co.uk.

794.1 CAN
CHESS CANADA (OTTAWA). Text in English, French. 1973. q. CAD 14.95 domestic; CAD 25 in United States; CAD 36 elsewhere (effective 2008). adv. bk.rev. illus. reprints avail. **Document type:** *Magazine, Consumer.*
Former titles (until 2001): En Passant (0822-5672); (until 1983): Chess Canada (0225-7351); (until 1979): Chess Federation of Canada. Bulletin (0317-8064)
Published by: Chess Federation of Canada, 2212 Gladwin Cres E 1, Ottawa, ON K1B 5N1, Canada. TEL 613-733-2844, FAX 613-733-5209. Ed. Hal Bond. Circ: 3,000.

794.1 USA ISSN 0009-3327
GV1313
CHESS CORRESPONDENT. Text in English. 1926. bi-m. USD 31 domestic to individuals; USD 27 foreign to individuals; USD 10 domestic to institutions (effective 2008). adv. bk.rev. illus. reprints avail. **Document type:** *Magazine, Consumer.* **Description:** Includes "how-to-improve" articles, theory, rating list, large annotated game section, and international news.
Published by: C C L A, PO Box 257, Galesburg, IL 61402-0257. Circ: 1,000.

794.1 USA ISSN 0147-2569
GV1313
CHESS HORIZONS. Text in English. 1969. q. USD 12 domestic; USD 18 foreign (effective 2005). adv. bk.rev.; software rev. 64 p./no.; back issues avail. **Document type:** *Magazine, Consumer.* **Description:** New England coverage emphasized but offers national and international news, games and theory.
Published by: Massachusetts Chess Association, c/o Bob Messenger, 4 Hamlett Dr., #12, Nashua, NH 03062-4641. Ed. Mark Donlan. R&P, Adv. contact Maryanne Reilly. Circ: 1,200.

794.1 USA ISSN 1044-8888
CHESS IN INDIANA. Text in English. 1988. irreg. USD 12 (effective 2000). adv. charts; illus.; stat. index. back issues avail. **Document type:** *Newsletter.* **Description:** News and history of chess tournaments, champions, and clubs in the state of Indiana.
Published by: Indiana State Chess Association, PO Box 353, Osceola, IN 46561. TEL 219-257-9033, r.blaine@mppl.lib.in.us. Ed. William K Deer. Pub. Michael Turner. Circ: 475.

CHESS JOURNALIST. *see* JOURNALISM

794.1 USA ISSN 0197-260X
GV1313
CHESS LIFE. Text in English. 1969. m. free to members (effective 2010). adv. bk.rev. charts; illus.; stat. Index. back issues avail.; reprints avail. **Document type:** *Magazine, Consumer.* **Description:** Features news of major chess events including tournaments, with an emphasis on exploits of American players.
Formerly (until 1980): Chess Life and Review (0009-3351)
Related titles: Microform ed.: (from PQC); Online - full text ed.
Indexed: A22, MLA-IB.
—Ingenta.
Published by: United States Chess Federation, PO Box 3967, Crossville, TN 38557. TEL 931-787-1234, FAX 931-787-1200, feedback@uschess.org. Ed. Daniel Lucas TEL 931-200-5509. Adv. contact Ray West TEL 931-787-1234 ext 132. page USD 2,690.

794.1 028.5 USA ISSN 1932-5894
CHESS LIFE FOR KIDS. Text in English. 2006. bi-m. free to members (effective 2010). back issues avail. **Document type:** *Magazine, Consumer.* **Description:** Features chess articles relevant to kids.
Published by: United States Chess Federation, PO Box 3967, Crossville, TN 38557. TEL 931-787-1234, 800-388-5464, FAX 931-787-1200, feedback@uschess.org. Ed. Glenn Peterson. Adv. contact Ray West TEL 931-787-1234 ext 132.

794.1 IND ISSN 0970-9142
CHESS MATE; Asia's only chess monthly. Text in English. 1983. m. adv. bk.rev. bibl. **Document type:** *Magazine, Trade.* **Description:** Covers the international chess scene. Includes "how-to-improve" articles, theory, combinations, and interviews.
Address: No. 16, 6 th Main Rd, Kasthuribai Nagar, Adyar, Chennai, Tamil Nadu 600 020, India. TEL 91-44-4918503, FAX 91-44-4918503. Eds. Arvind Aaron, Manuel Aaron. Pub. Anand Aaron.

794.1 DEU ISSN 1432-8992
CHESSBASE MAGAZIN. Text in German. 198?. 6/yr. EUR 19.95 newsstand/cover (effective 2009). adv. **Document type:** *Magazine, Consumer.* **Description:** Covers current games, opening theory, endgame analyses, and includes articles.
Published by: ChessBase GmbH, Mexikoring 35, Hamburg, 22297, Germany. TEL 49-40-6390600, FAX 49-40-631282, info@chessbase.com, http://www.chessbase.com.

794.1 GBR
CHESSMOVES. Text in English. 19??. bi-m. free to members (effective 2009). adv. **Document type:** *Newsletter, Trade.*
Formerly (until 1995): B C F Newsletter
Published by: English Chess Federation, The Watch Oak, Chain Ln, Battle, E Sussex TN33 0YD, United Kingdom. TEL 44-1424-775222, FAX 44-1424-775904, office@englishchess.org.uk, http://www.englishchess.org.uk.

CHESSTAMP REVIEW. *see* PHILATELY

796 KOR ISSN 1598-2920
CHEYUG GWAHAG YEON'GU/KOREAN JOURNAL OF SPORT SCIENCE. Text in Korean. 1990. 3/yr. KRW 30,000; KRW 10,000 per issue (effective 2009). **Document type:** *Journal, Academic/Scholarly.*
Formerly (until 1996): Ceyug Gwahag Noncong/Journal of Sport Science (1225-7648)
Related titles: Online - full text ed.
Published by: Korea Institute of Sport Science/Han'gug Ceyug Gwahag Yeon'guweon, 223-19 gongneung-dong, Nowon-Gu, Seoul, Korea, S. TEL 82-2-9709500, FAX 82-2-9709651, publ@sports.re.kr, http://www.sports.re.kr/. Circ: 800.

S

794.4 USA
CHICAGO PLAYING CARD COLLECTOR. Text in English. q. USD 15. adv. **Document type:** *Bulletin.* **Description:** Covers the study of playing cards.
Published by: Chicago Playing Card Collectors, Inc., 1559 W Pratt Blvd, Chicago, IL 60626. TEL 312-274-0250. Ed., Adv. contact Bernice DeSomer.

790.1 USA
CHICAGO SPORTS PROFILES MAGAZINE. Text in English. 1986. q. USD 10 (effective 2000). adv. **Document type:** *Magazine, Consumer.* **Description:** Covers local professional and college sports teams.
Published by: Sports Profiles, 4711 Golf St, Ste 900, Skokie, IL 60076. TEL 847-673-0592, FAX 847-673-0633. Ed. Paula Blaine. Pub. Lisa Levine. Circ: 40,000.

790.1 CHN ISSN 0577-8948
GV651
CHINA SPORTS/ZHONGGUO TIYU. Text in Chinese, English. 1957. m. USD 80.40 (effective 2009). adv. illus. **Document type:** *Magazine, Consumer.* **Description:** Covers athletic events, sports training, traditional Chinese sports and martial arts.
Formerly (until 1980): China's Sports
Related titles: Online - full content ed.
Indexed: RASB, SD, SportS.
Published by: (State Physical Culture and Sports Commission), China Sports, 90, Jianwei Dajie, Zhaoyang-qu, Beijing, 100022, China. TEL 86-10-85805274. Circ: 50,000. **Dist. by:** China International Book Trading Corp, 35 Chegongzhuang Xilu, Haidian District, PO Box 399, Beijing 100044, China. TEL 86-10-68412045, FAX 86-10-68412023, cibtc@mail.cibtc.com.cn, http://www.cibtc.com.cn.

790.1 USA
CHOKEHOLD. Text in English. 1988. irreg. (2-3/m.). USD 1.50 per issue. adv. **Document type:** *Newsletter.* **Description:** Contains both serious and humorous stories about life in the wrestling world. Includes commentary on pop culture.
Address: 507 W 43rd Pl, Chicago, IL 60609. TEL 312-536-0909. Ed. Lance Levine. Pub. Peter North. Adv. contact Terry Earl Bollea. Circ: 300 (paid).

CHOREGIA. *see* BUSINESS AND ECONOMICS—Management

793.73 POL ISSN 1643-1588
CHWILA NA 100 PANORAMICZNYCH. Text in Polish. 2001. m. PLZ 2.20 newsstand/cover (effective 2011). adv. **Document type:** *Magazine, Consumer.*
Published by: Phoenix Press, Sw Antoniego 7, Wroclaw, 50-073, Poland. TEL 48-71-3449813, FAX 48-71-3460174, phoenix@phoenix.pl, http://phoenix.pl. Adv. contact Adam Michrowski.

CIBLES. *see* HOBBIES

CICLISMO. *see* SPORTS AND GAMES—Bicycles And Motorcycles

CIENCIA Y DEPORTE. *see* SCIENCES: COMPREHENSIVE WORKS

796.72 USA ISSN 1052-9624
TL236
CIRCLE TRACK. Text in English. 1982. m. USD 15 domestic; USD 27 in Canada; USD 39 elsewhere (effective 2008). adv. illus. back issues avail.; reprints avail. **Document type:** *Magazine, Consumer.* **Description:** Emphasizes expert-level car construction, engine building and tuning, safety equipment use, chassis tuning and racing technique.
Formerly (until 1990): Petersen's Circle Track (0734-5437)
Related titles: Online - full text ed.
Indexed: A25, A26, E08, G06, G07, G08, I05, S08, S09, S23.
—CCC.
Published by: Source Interlink Companies, 9036 Brittany Way, Tampa, FL 33619. TEL 813-675-3500, dheine@sourceinterlink.com, http://www.sourceinterlinkmedia.com. Ed. Rob Fisher. Pub. Don Parrish TEL 813-675-3482. adv.: B&W page USD 11,740, color page USD 18,930; trim 10.5 x 7.75. Circ: 81,218 (paid).

613.7 ROM ISSN 1582-8131
CITIUS ALTIUS FORTIUS. Text in Romanian. 2001. q.
Related titles: Online - full text ed.: free (effective 2011).
Indexed: P19, P20, P48, P54, PQC, SD, T02.
Published by: Editura Universitatea din Pitesti, Str Targu din Vale 1, Arges, Pitesti, 110040, Romania. TEL 40-248-218804, FAX 40-248-216448, http://www.upit.ro.

796 USA ISSN 0191-8400
CITY SPORTS MONTHLY. Variant title: CitySports. Text in English. 19??. m. USD 25 (effective 2002). adv. **Document type:** *Magazine, Consumer.* **Description:** Covers triathlon, running, biking, swimming and endurance sports for the Northern California area.
Related titles: Online - full content ed.; Regional ed(s).: City Sports Magazine (Los Angeles Edition). ISSN 0891-4001; City Sports Northwest Magazine. USD 30 (effective 2002); City Sports Magazine (Metro Edition). ISSN 0891-401X.
Published by: Competitor, Inc., 444 S Cedros Ave, 185, Solana Beach, CA 92075. TEL 858-793-2711, FAX 858-793-2710.

790.1 USA
CITYSPORTS. Text in English. 11/yr. **Document type:** *Magazine, Consumer.*
Published by: Bob Babbitt, Pub., 444 South Cedros Ave, No 185, Solana Beach, CA 92075. TEL 858-793-2711, FAX 858-793-2710, hagman2@home.com, http://www.citysportsmag.com.

CIVITAS. REVISTA ESPANOLA DE DERECHO DEPORTIVO. *see* LAW

796.8 USA ISSN 1547-416X
CLASSICAL FIGHTING ARTS. Text in English, Japanese. 1993. q. USD 20 domestic; USD 25 in Canada; USD 39 elsewhere; USD 5.95 newsstand/cover domestic; USD 8.95 newsstand/cover in Canada (effective 2003). adv. bk.rev.; tel.rev.; video rev. illus.; stat. **Document type:** *Newspaper.* **Description:** Covers historical, instructional, and anthropological material on the martial arts of Japan, China, and the Okinawan archipelago. Book, video, and equipment reviews; interviews with noted instructors.
Formerly (until 2003): Dragon Times
Published by: Dragon Associates Inc., PO Box 6039, Thousand Oaks, CA 91359-6039. TEL 818-889-3856, 800-717-6288, FAX 818-879-0681, dragon@dragon-tsunami.org, http://dragon-tsunami.org. Ed. Robert Dohrenwend. Pub. David Chambers. R&P John N Edwards. Adv. contact Paul Moser. page USD 1,200; trim 17 x 11. Circ: 24,000. **Dist. by:** International Periodical Distributors, 674 Vie De La Valle, Ste. 200, Solano Beach, CA 92075. TEL 800-999-1170, FAX 619-481-5848.

799.2 GBR ISSN 0956-814X
CLAY SHOOTING; for the sporting clays, five stand and parcours de chasse shooter. Text in English. 1989. bi-m. GBP 31.95 in United States; GBP 62.95 elsewhere (effective 2010). adv. **Document type:** *Magazine, Consumer.*
Related titles: Online - full text ed.
Published by: Brunton Business Publications Ltd., 1 Salisbury Office Park, London Rd, Salisbury, Wiltshire SP1 3HP, United Kingdom. TEL 44-1722-337038, publications@brunton.co.uk, http://www.brunton.co.uk. Pub. Michael Brunton. Adv. contact John Imboden. page USD 1,650; trim 8.25 x 11.

790.1 USA
CLOSE QUARTER COMBAT. Text in English. 2000. bi-m. USD 39.95 domestic; USD 59.95 in Canada & Mexico; USD 79.95 elsewhere (effective 2001). adv. bk.rev.; film rev.; tel.rev.; video rev. illus.; maps. back issues avail.; reprints avail. **Document type:** *Magazine, Consumer.*
Related titles: E-mail ed.; Online - full text ed.
Published by: Lauric Enterprises, Inc., Box 5372, Fort Oglethorpe, GA 30742. TEL 423-400-9458, FAX 706-866-2657, LauricPres@aol.com. Ed. Jane Eden. Pub. W Hock Hochheim.

790.1 CAN
CO-OPERATIVE GAME CATALOG; family pastimes, co-operative games, puzzles & books. Text in English. 1970. s-a. free. adv. bk.rev. illus. **Document type:** *Catalog, Consumer.*
Published by: Family Pastimes, R R 4, Perth, ON K7H 3C6, Canada. TEL 613-267-4819, FAX 613-264-0696. Ed. Jim Deacove. R&P, Adv. contact James Deacove. Circ: 40,000.

THE COACH. *see* SPORTS AND GAMES—Ball Games

790.1 USA ISSN 2159-6573
GV711
COACH AND ATHLETIC DIRECTOR. Text in English. 1931. m. USD 19.95 domestic; USD 24.95 foreign (effective 2011). adv. bk.rev.; tel.rev. charts; illus.; stat. Index. back issues avail.; reprints avail. **Document type:** *Magazine, Trade.* **Description:** Technical articles for coaches and athletic administrators of team sports.
Former titles (until 2010): Successful Coach and Athletic Director (2159-6565); (until 2009): Coach and Athletic Director (1087-2000); (until 1995): Scholastic Coach and Athletic Director (1077-5625); (until 1994): Scholastic Coach (0036-6382); Which incorporated (1927-1987): Athletic Journal (0004-6655); (1953-1982): Coach & Athlete (0009-9872)
Related titles: Online - full text ed.
Indexed: A01, A02, A03, A08, A22, A25, A26, AcaI, B04, BRD, BRI, CA, E02, E03, E06, E07, E08, E09, ERI, EdA, EdI, G06, G07, G08, I05, I07, M01, M02, P02, P04, P07, P10, P18, P19, P48, P53, P54, P55, PEI, PQC, R06, RASB, S08, S09, S22, SD, SPI, SportS, T02, W03, W05.
—IE, Ingenta.
Published by: Lessiter Publications, PO Box 624, Brookfield, WI 53008. TEL 262-782-1252, 800-645-8455, info@lesspub.com, http://www.lesspub.com/. Pub. Todd Rank. Adv. contact Bob Frantell TEL 800-645-8455, Ext 435. Circ: 39,000 (paid).

796.077 NLD ISSN 1384-4571
COACHEN. Text in Dutch. 1988. 4/yr. EUR 19.95 (effective 2008). adv. **Document type:** *Magazine, Trade.*
Incorporates (1996-2001): Sportwerk (1387-0998)
Published by: Arko Sports Media (Subsidiary of: Arko Uitgeverij BV), Postbus 393, Nieuwegein, 3430 AJ, Netherlands. TEL 31-30-6004780, FAX 31-30-6052618, info@arko.nl, http://www.arko.nl. Ed. Frans Oosterwijk. Pub. Michel van Troost. adv.: B&W page EUR 1,270, color page EUR 1,925; bleed 210 x 297. Circ: 6,755 (paid and controlled).

790.1 CAN ISSN 1198-5720
GV711
COACHES REPORT. Text in English. q. CAD 19.26 domestic; USD 23 in United States; CAD 30 elsewhere.
Formerly (until 1994): S P O R T S
Related titles: French ed.
Indexed: SD.
—CCC.
Published by: Canadian Professional Coaches Association/Association Canadienne des Entraineurs, 1600 James Naismith Dr, Gloucester, ON K1B 5N4, Canada. TEL 613-748-5624, FAX 613-748-5707.

796.077 ITA ISSN 1590-7880
COACHING & SPORT SCIENCE JOURNAL. Text in English. 1996. 3/yr. EUR 56 (effective 2009). **Document type:** *Journal, Trade.* **Description:** Provides articles, reviews and reports related to coaching; with topics ranging from biomechanics, physiology, sports medicine, psychology, motor learning and sociology.
Published by: (Universita degli Studi di Roma "Tor Vergata", Facolta di Medicina e Chirurgia), Societa Stampa Sportiva, Via G. Guinizelli 56, Rome, 00152, Italy. TEL 39-06-5817311, FAX 39-06-5806526. Ed. Antonio Lombardo.

790.1 GBR
COACHING EDGE; the UK's quarterly coaching magazine. Abbreviated title: F H S. Text in English. 1985. q. free to members (effective 2010). adv. back issues avail. **Document type:** *Magazine, Trade.*
Former titles (until Autumn.2005): Faster, Higher, Stronger (1464-4495); (until no.37, 1998): Coaching Focus (0267-4416)
Indexed: SD.
—IE, Ingenta. **CCC.**
Published by: Sports Coach UK, 114 Cardigan Rd, Headingley, Leeds, LS6 3BJ, United Kingdom. TEL 44-113-2744802, FAX 44-113-2755019, coaching@sportscoachuk.org.

796.077 USA
COACHING SCIENCE ABSTRACTS. Text in English. 1995. bi-m. free (effective 2001).
Related titles: Online - full text ed.
Published by: Sports Science Associates, 4225 Orchad Dr, Spring Valley, CA 919977. brushall@mail.sdsu.edu. Ed. Brent S Rushall.

769.41 CAN ISSN 1926-4615
COAST & KAYAK MAGAZINE. Text in English. 1991. q. USD 20; free to qualified personnel (effective 2011). adv. back issues avail. **Document type:** *Magazine, Consumer.*
Formerly (until 2011): Wave-Length (1188-5432)
Related titles: Online - full text ed.: free (effective 2011).
Published by: WaveLength Communications, Inc., #6-10 Commercial St, Nanaimo, BC V9R 5G2, Canada. TEL 250-244-6437, 866-984-6437, FAX 250-244-1937, 866-654-1937. Ed. John Kimantas. Adv. contact Brent Daniel.

790.1 IRL ISSN 1649-3060
COIN-OP NEWS EUROPE; the multilingual European amusement trade journal. Text in Czech, English, German, Greek, Hungarian, Polish, Romanian, Russian. 1992. m. adv. back issues avail. **Document type:** *Journal, Trade.* **Description:** News about the amusement and leisure industries in Central, Easternand Southern Europe and Ireland.
Formerly (until 2000): Coin-Op News; Which incorporated (in 1995): Fair Play
Published by: M D Associates, Enterprise Centre, Melitta Rd., Kildare, Ireland. TEL 353-45-521190, FAX 353-45-521198, mdassociates@eircom.net. Ed., R&P Martin Dempsey. Adv. contact Susan Feery. Circ: 5,000.

COLLEGE ATHLETICS AND THE LAW. *see* EDUCATION—Higher Education

796.8 GBR
COMBAT. Text in English. 1973. m. GBP 44.95 domestic; GBP 75 in Europe; GBP 90 elsewhere; GBP 3.75 newsstand/cover (effective 2010). back issues avail. **Document type:** *Magazine, Consumer.* **Description:** Features news, techniques and interviews on various Martial Arts fighting methods.
Related titles: Online - full text ed.: free (effective 2010).
Published by: Martial Arts Publications, Unit 20, Maybrook Business Park, 20 Maybrook Rd, Minworth, Sutton Coldfield, B76 1BE, United Kingdom. TEL 44-121-3516930, office@combatmag.co.uk, http://www.martialartsinprint.com. Ed., Pub. Paul Clifton. Adv. contact Andrew Reader TEL 44-121-3516930.

799.202 623.4 USA ISSN 1043-7584
HD9744.P58
COMBAT HANDGUNS. Text in English. 1980. 8/yr. USD 23.97 in US & Canada; USD 47.94 elsewhere (effective 2009). adv. back issues avail. **Document type:** *Magazine, Trade.*
Related titles: Online - full text ed.
Published by: Harris Publications, Inc., 1115 Broadway, New York, NY 10010. TEL 212-807-7100, FAX 212-924-2352, subscriptions@harris-pub.com, http://www.harris-pub.com. adv.: B&W page USD 3,715, color page USD 5,020; trim 8 x 10.875.

796.812 USA
COMBAT SPORTS. Text in English. 1978. bi-m. USD 15; USD 24 foreign (effective 1999). adv. **Document type:** *Newsletter, Consumer.* **Description:** Covers wrestling matches and related topics.
Related titles: ◆ Supplement to: New Wave Wrestling. ISSN 1060-5908.
Address: PO BOX 651, GRACIE STA, New York, NY 10028-0006. Ed., Pub., R&P, Adv. contact Michael O'Hara. Circ: 6,600 (paid).

790.1 USA
COMMUNITY SPORTS NEWS; adult recreational sports. Text in English. 1983. m. adv. film rev.; bk.rev. **Document type:** *Newspaper.* **Description:** Covers local sports, with commentary.
Published by: Community Sports News Inc., 123 Barclay Rd, Chapel Hill, NC 27516. TEL 919-968-8741, FAX 919-968-8741. Ed., Pub., Adv. contact Joel S Bulkley. Circ: 5,000 (free).

790.1 GBR
COMPASSSPORT; Britain's national orienteering magazine. Text in English. 1980. bi-m. GBP 25 domestic to non-members; GBP 29 in Europe to non-members; GBP 33 elsewhere to non-members; GBP 24 domestic to members; GBP 28 in Europe to members; GBP 32 elsewhere to members (effective 2009). adv. bk.rev. back issues avail. **Document type:** *Magazine, Consumer.* **Description:** Features crammed with orienteering excitement.
Formerly (until 1997): Compass Sport - Orienteer (0263-6697); Which was formed by the merger of (19??-1982): Compass Sport; (1968-1982): Orienteer (0306-0705)
Indexed: SportS.
Published by: (British Orienteering Federation), Compass Sport Publications, 85 Deacon Rd, Kingston Upon Thames, Surrey KT2 6LS, United Kingdom. Subscriptions@CompassSport.co.uk. Ed., Adv. contact Nick Barrable TEL 44-772-0952241. page GBP 400.

338.6048 GBR ISSN 2046-195X
COMPERS NEWS. Text in English. 2001. m. GBP 44 domestic; GBP 57 foreign; GBP 3.16 per issue (effective 2011). back issues avail. **Document type:** *Newsletter, Trade.* **Description:** Helps to find, enter and win the UK's biggest and best prize competitions. Also contain competition and prize draw listings.
Related titles: Online - full text ed.: ISSN 2046-1968.
Published by: Accolade Publishing Ltd., Tower House, Sovereign Park, Market Harborough, LE16 9EF, United Kingdom. TEL 44-1858-438737, pdw@accoladepublishing.co.uk, http://www.accoladepublishing.co.uk/. Ed. Steve Middleton.

796 USA ISSN 1946-3189
COMPETE; the gay sports magazine. Text in English. 19??. m. USD 17.95 domestic; USD 22.95 in Canada & Mexico; USD 29.95 elsewhere (effective 2009). adv. back issues avail. **Document type:** *Magazine, Consumer.* **Description:** Provides global sports information to, and for, the gay community.
Formerly (until 2009): Sports Out Loud
Related titles: Online - full text ed.: ISSN 1946-3197.
Published by: Media Out Loud, LLC, 4701 S Lakeshore Dr, Ste 1, Tempe, AZ 85282. TEL 480-222-4223. Ed. Buddy Early. Pub. David Riach. Adv. contact Eric Carlyle.

790.1 USA
COMPETITOR. Text in English. 11/yr. **Document type:** *Magazine, Consumer.*
Indexed: IIBP, SD.
Published by: Competitor, Inc., 444 S Cedros Ave, 185, Solana Beach, CA 92075. TEL 858-793-2711, FAX 305-663-2640. Pub. Bob Babbit.

338.6048 GBR
COMPETITORS COMPANION. Text in English. 1981. m. GBP 59.40; GBP 0.95 per issue (effective 2009). **Document type:** *Newsletter, Trade.* **Description:** Lists slogan competitions with advice on how to enter them.
Formerly (until 1989): Competitors Journal
Published by: Accolade Publishing Ltd., Zetland House, 5-25 Scrutton St, London, EC2A 4HJ, United Kingdom. TEL 44-20-76137477, editorial@accoladepublishing.co.uk. **Subscr. to:** 800 Guillat Ave, Kent Science Park, Sittingbourne, Kent ME9 8GU, United Kingdom. TEL 44-844-8150853.

338.6048 GBR
COMPETITORS UPDATE. Text in English. 19??. m. GBP 42; GBP 0.95 per issue (effective 2010). back issues avail. **Document type:** *Newsletter, Trade.*
Published by: Accolade Publishing Ltd., Zetland House, 5-25 Scrutton St, London, EC2A 4HJ, United Kingdom. TEL 44-20-76137477, accolade@servicehelpline.co.uk, editorial@accoladepublishing.co.uk, http://www.accoladepublishing.co.uk/. **Subscr. to:** 800 Guillat Ave, Kent Science Park, Sittingbourne, Kent ME9 8GU, United Kingdom. TEL 44-844-8150853.

COMPUTERSCHAAK. *see* COMPUTERS—Computer Games

796 ESP ISSN 2172-0460
COMUNICACIONES TECNICAS. Text in Spanish. 2005. q. **Document type:** *Magazine, Trade.*
Media: Online - full text.
Published by: Federacion Espanola de Orientacion, Polideportivo Alhondiga Sector III, Carrera Leganes - Getafe Km. 0.8, Madrid, 28905, Spain. TEL 34-91-6952108, FAX 34-91-6968862.

796.22 CAN ISSN 1708-3338
CONCRETE WAVE; one hundred percent skateboarding. Text in English. 2002. 5/yr. USD 15 in US & Canada; USD 30 elsewhere (effective 2003).
Published by: North of La Jolla, 1054 Center St., Ste 293, Thornhill, ON L4J 8E6, Canada. TEL 905-738-0804, FAX 605-761-5295, mbrooke@interlog.com, http://www.concretewavemag.com. Ed., Pub. Michael Brooke.

790.1 USA
CONCUSSION. Text in English. 3/yr. USD 15; USD 3.50 newsstand/cover (effective 2000). adv. **Document type:** *Magazine, Consumer.* **Description:** Covers the worlds of skating, surfing and alternative music.
Published by: Concussion Productions, PO Box 1024, Santa Cruz, CA 96061-1024. TEL 831-471-0501, concussion@concussion.org, http://www.concussion.org. adv.: page USD 250. Circ: 3,500. **Dist. by:** Desert Moon Periodicals, 1226 A Calle de Comercio, Santa Fe, NM 87505. TEL 505-474-6311, FAX 505-474-6317.

790.1 DEU ISSN 0946-3003
CONDITION; Ratgebermagazin fuer Lauf- und Ausdauersport. Text in German. 1969. 10/yr. EUR 38; EUR 3.50 newsstand/cover (effective 2011). adv. 52 p./no. 3 cols./p.; back issues avail. **Document type:** *Magazine, Consumer.* **Description:** Covers distance running and other endurance sports.
Former titles (until 1994): Sport Special - Condition (0940-192X); (until 1991): Condition (0340-2991)
Related titles: Supplement(s): Condition Aktuell.
Published by: (Interessengemeinschaft der Langstreckenlaeufer), Meyer & Meyer Verlag, Von-Coels-Str 390, Aachen, 52080, Germany. TEL 49-241-958100, FAX 49-241-9581010, verlag@m-m-sports.com, http://m-m-sports.de. Circ: 15,000 (paid and controlled).

796 BRA ISSN 1516-4381
CONEXOES. Text in Portuguese, Spanish. 1996. irreg. free (effective 2011). **Document type:** *Journal, Academic/Scholarly.*
Media: Online - full text.
Published by: Universidade Estadual de Campinas, Faculdade de Educacao Fisica, Cidade Universitaria Zeferino Vas, Rua Erico Verissimo 701, Campinas, SP 13081-957, Brazil. Ed. Gustavo Luis Gutierrez.

382 BRA
CONFEDERACAO BRASILEIRA DE FUTEBOL. RELATORIO. Text in Portuguese. a. illus.
Formerly (after 1983): Confederacao Brasileira de Desportos. Relatorio
Published by: Confederacao Brasileira de Desportos, Rua da Alfandega, 70, Centro, Rio De Janeiro, RJ 20070-001, Brazil.

790.1 COD
CONGO SPORTS. Text in French. w. adv.
Address: 99 rue de Tshela Com., Kinshasa, Congo, Dem. Republic.

790.1 USA ISSN 1079-0500
CONNECTICUT CHESS MAGAZINE. Text in English. 1976. s-a. free. adv. bk.rev. **Document type:** *Newsletter.* **Description:** News and information from Connecticut chess clubs, including games played, ratings of players, and minutes of meetings.
Former titles: Waterbury Chess Club Bulletin (0894-0606); Connecticut Backgammon Magazine
Published by: Connecticut State Chess Association, 54 Calumet St, Waterbury, CT 06710. TEL 203-596-1443. Ed., Pub., Adv. contact Rob Roy. Circ: 2,000.

796.3 USA ISSN 1947-4903
▼ **CONNECTICUT STUDENT-ATHLETE MAGAZINE.** Text in English. 2009 (Sep.). bi-m. USD 16; USD 4.95 newsstand/cover (effective 2010). adv. Index. back issues avail. **Document type:** *Magazine, Consumer.* **Description:** Provides coverage of local student-athletes and youth teams across Connecticut. Topics include: Recruiting, college scholarships, nutrition, and training to student-athletes, parents of student-athletes, and coaches.
Published by: iOpening Sports Media (Subsidiary of: iOpening Media, LLC.), 15 Hubbard Rd, #7660, Wilton, CT 06897. TEL 203-482-1587. Ed. Janine Smith. Pub. Shaun Harris. R&P, Adv. contact Jennifer Anda TEL 203-554-8579. B&W page USD 1,850; trim 8.25 x 10.75. Circ: 7,000 (paid); 4,000 (controlled).

790.1 NLD ISSN 0045-8406
CONTRACTSPELER. Text in Dutch. 1961. s-a. adv. bk.rev. tr.lit.
Published by: Vereniging van Contractspelers/Professional Players Union of Holland, Taurusavenue 35, Hoofddorp, 2132 LS, Netherlands. TEL 31-23-5546930, FAX 31-23-5546931, info@vvcs.nl, http://www.vvcs.nl. **Co-sponsors:** Professional Cyclists Union of Holland; Professional Trotter and Jockey Union of Holland.

790.1 362.41 GBR
CONUNDRUM. Text in English. 19??. m. GBP 0.57 per issue (effective 2009). **Document type:** *Magazine, Consumer.* **Description:** Provides persons who are blind or visually impaired with challenging crossword, anagram, logic puzzles, and general-knowledge quizzes.
Media: Braille. **Related titles:** Diskette ed.
Published by: Royal National Institute of Blind People, 105 Judd St, London, WC1H 9NE, United Kingdom. TEL 44-20-73881266, FAX 44-20-73882034. **Subscr. to:** Customer Services, PO Box 173, Peterborough PE2 6WS, United Kingdom. TEL 44-303-1239999, FAX 44-1733-375001.

795.05 GBR ISSN 1747-6747
COOL PLAYER. Text in English. 2005. q. **Document type:** *Magazine, Consumer.* **Description:** Contains news, views and analysis about the world of gaming.
Published by: Gaming World Media Ltd., 145-147 St John St, London, EC1V 4PY, United Kingdom. admin@gamingworldmedia.com, http://www.gamingworldmedia.com/.

796 305.4 GBR ISSN 1746-9171
COOLER. Text in English. 2005. bi-m. GBP 15 in United Kingdom; EUR 28.50 in Europe; USD 37.50 elsewhere (effective 2009). adv. back issues avail. **Document type:** *Magazine, Consumer.*
Related titles: Online - full text ed.
Published by: Factory Media, Studio 153, 355 Byres Rd, Glasgow, G12 8QZ, United Kingdom. TEL 44-141-9455019, FAX 44-141-9455019, http://www.factorymedia.com. Adv. contact Ian Gunner. **Subscr. to:** Dovetail Services UK Ltd, 800 Guillat Ave, Kent Science Park, Sittingbourne, Kent ME9 8GU, United Kingdom. TEL 44-1795-414628, Cooler@servicehelpline.co.uk, http://www.dovetailservices.com/.

796 BRA ISSN 1516-6023
CORPORIS. Text in Portuguese. 1996. s-a. back issues avail. **Document type:** *Journal, Academic/Scholarly.*
Related titles: Online - full text ed.: ISSN 1516-621X.
Published by: Universidade Federal de Pernambuco, Escola Superior de Educacao Fisica, Ave Agamenon Magalhaes, s-n, Santo Amero, Recife, PE 50-100-010, Brazil. TEL 55-81-34164000.

794.1 GBR ISSN 0961-7736
CORRESPONDENCE CHESS. Text in English. 1949. q. free to members (effective 2010). bk.rev. back issues avail. **Document type:** *Magazine, Consumer.* **Description:** Features BCCA news, BCCA best games, letters to editor, crossword and much more.
Formerly (until 1954): B C C A Magazine
Published by: British Correspondence Chess Association, c/o Stan Grayland, Gen. Sec., 61 Swanswell Rd, Solihull, W Midlands B92 7ET, United Kingdom. webmaster@bcca.info. Ed. Neil Limbert. Circ: 600.

CORRICOLARI; el corredor y su mundo. *see* PHYSICAL FITNESS AND HYGIENE

790.1 ITA ISSN 1124-8483
CORRIERE DELLO SPORT. Text in Italian. 1924. d. EUR 207 (effective 2009). **Document type:** *Newspaper, Consumer.*
Address: Piazza dell' Indipendenza 11 B, Rome, RM 00185, Italy. TEL 39-06-4992231, FAX 39-06-4992690.

790.1 075 ITA ISSN 1824-8969
IL CORRIERE LAZIALE. Text in Italian. 1973. 3/w. **Document type:** *Newspaper, Consumer.* **Description:** Covers local events, sports, and tourist info for the central region of Italy.
Related titles: Online - full text ed.
Published by: Il Corriere Laziale, Via Acqua Bullicante 248, Rome, 00177, Italy. TEL 39-06-2456561, FAX 39-06-24565656.

613.7 ITA ISSN 1129-2334
LA CORSA. Text in Italian. 1980. bi-m. EUR 4.50 newsstand/cover (effective 2009). adv. back issues avail. **Document type:** *Magazine, Consumer.* **Description:** Reports news of long-distance races, marathons and adventure.
Former titles (until 1997): Jogging - La Grande Corsa (1129-2350); (until 1992): Jogging (1129-2342)
Published by: Publimaster Srl, Via Winckelmann 2, Milan, 20146, Italy. TEL 39-02-424191, FAX 39-02-47710278, publimaster@publimaster.it. Ed. Elena Bolgiani. Circ: 24,000.

796.7 388 USA ISSN 1544-3183
TL215.C6
CORVETTE ENTHUSIAST. Text in English. 1998 (Sept.). m. USD 19.99 domestic; USD 34.99 in Canada; USD 49.99 elsewhere; USD 5.99 per issue (effective 2011). adv. back issues avail. **Document type:** *Magazine, Consumer.* **Description:** Covers the entire spectrum of Corvette interests from shows to auctions, restoration to racing, and from the first generation dating back to 1953 right up to the C6. It delivers the kind of up-to-date news and information Corvette enthusiasts need, along with technical articles, the hottest new products, lifestyle experiences and powerful photography of Corvettes from the early classics to the latest cruisers.
Formerly (until Jul.2003): Cars & Parts Corvette (1528-1051)
Related titles: Online - full text ed.: free (effective 2011).
Published by: Amos Publishing, Automotive (Subsidiary of: Amos Publishing), 911 Vandemark Rd, PO Box 926, Sidney, OH 45365. cuserv@amospress.com, http://www.amospress.com. Ed. Larry Jewett. Pub. John Nichols TEL 863-937-8097.

COSMOS TOU TENNIS/WORLD OF TENNIS. *see* SPORTS AND GAMES—Ball Games

COST OF DOING BUSINESS FOR RETAIL SPORTING GOODS STORES. *see* BUSINESS AND ECONOMICS—Domestic Commerce

THE COUNTRYMAN'S WEEKLY; Britain's countrysports newspaper. *see* SPORTS AND GAMES—Outdoor Life

THE COURIER (BROCKTON); North America's foremost miniature wargaming magazine. *see* HOBBIES

796 FRA ISSN 1777-943X
COURIR PASSION. Text in French. 2004. s-a. **Document type:** *Bulletin.*
Published by: Confederation Nationale de la Course a Pied, Cafe de la Paix, BP 93, Mende cedex, 48001, France. courir.passion@free.fr.

790.1 CMR
COURRIER SPORTIF DU BENIN. Text in French. w. adv.
Address: BP 17, Douala, Cameroon. Ed. Henri Jong.

796.345 GBR ISSN 2045-3612
COURTSIDE. Text in English. 1982. q. free to members (effective 2010). adv. bk.rev. illus. **Document type:** *Magazine, Consumer.*
Former titles (until 2009): Badminton (1355-5057); (until 1991): Badminton Now; Which superseded: Badminton Gazette (0005-3805)
Indexed: SD, SportS.
Published by: (Badminton Association of England Ltd.), 2b Graphic Design Ltd., 9 The Waits, St Ives, Cambridgeshire PE27 5BY, United Kingdom. FAX 44-1480-465081, peter@2bgraphicdesign.co.uk, http://www.twobdesn.demon.co.uk. Circ: 7,000.

797.2 POL ISSN 1734-4476
CRAZY WINDSURFER. Text in Polish. 2006. bi-m. PLZ 59.90 (effective 2011). **Document type:** *Magazine, Consumer.*
Published by: Twoje Media, ul Saska 9a, Warsaw, 03968, Poland. TEL 48-22-6161604, FAX 48-22-6161524, poczta@twojemedia.pl, http://www.twojemedia.pl.

790.1 USA
CRITICAL HIT. Text in English. 19??. q. illus. back issues avail. **Document type:** *Magazine, Trade.* **Description:** Covers information about players & games.
Address: PO Box 279, Croton Falls, NY 10519. TEL 845-278-9125, FAX 845-278-4822, Ray@Criticalhit.com.

CROSS. *see* HOBBIES

797 GBR
CROSS COUNTRY. Text in English; Summaries in Spanish, Japanese. 1990. bi-m. GBP 36.95 includes UK, USA & Europe; GBP 38.95 elsewhere; GBP 40.95 combined subscription (print & online eds.) (effective 2009). 80 p./no.; back issues avail. **Document type:** *Magazine, Trade.* **Description:** Aims to reflect passion for free flying for over 20 years and is read by pilots in 75 countries throughout the world.
Related titles: Online - full text ed.: GBP 31.95 (effective 2009).
Published by: X C Media, 5 St Georges Place, Brighton, BN1 4GA, United Kingdom. TEL 44-1273-673000, http://www.xcmedia.com/. Ed. Bob Drury. Adv. contact Verity Sowden.

796.428 USA ISSN 0746-083X
CROSS COUNTRY JOURNAL. Text in English. 1983. bi-m. USD 29 domestic; USD 32 in Canada; USD 35 elsewhere (effective 2003). **Document type:** *Magazine, Trade.* **Description:** Covers recruiting, race tactics, motivation, running techniques, injury prevention and new ideas to use in practice.
Published by: I D E A, Inc., PO Box 1004, Austin, MN 55912. FAX 800-828-1231. Ed. Mike Koch. Pub. Knowles Dougherty.

790.1 USA
CROSSFIRE PAINTBALL DIGEST. Text in English. 2000. m. USD 29.95; USD 4.50 newsstand/cover (effective 2001). adv. **Document type:** *Magazine, Consumer.*
Published by: Digest Publications, 29 Fostertown Rd, Medford, NJ 08055. TEL 609-953-4900, FAX 609-953-4905, mail@crossfiremag.com, http://www.crossfiremag.com. Ed., Pub. Missy Sowers.

793.7 ARG ISSN 0328-4328
CRUCIGRAMA. Text in Spanish. 1972. bi-w. adv. **Document type:** *Magazine, Consumer.* **Description:** Contains crosswords and various other types of games and entertainment.
Related titles: Supplement(s): Crucigrama Clasicos. ISSN 0328-8277. 1996; Crucigrama Extra. ISSN 0328-9621. 1997.
Published by: Editorial Perfil S.A., Chacabuco 271, Buenos Aires, Buenos Aires 1069, Argentina. TEL 54-11-4341-9000, FAX 54-11-4341-9090, correo@perfil.com.ar, http://www.perfil.com.ar. Circ: 15,000 (paid).

796 CAN ISSN 1715-9857
CRUX (BOUCHERVILLE); le magazine des sports alternatifs. Text in French. 2006. q. **Document type:** *Magazine, Consumer.*
Published by: Agence Alternative Crux Inc., 550, de Mortagne, Bureau 390, Boucherville, PQ J4B 5E6, Canada. http://www.lecrux.com/fr/sections.php?pksections=700598432. Ed. Mathieu Faucher.

CUADERNOS DE PSICOLOGIA DEL DEPORTE. *see* PSYCHOLOGY

796 613.71 ESP ISSN 1696-5043
CULTURA, CIENCIA Y DEPORTE. Text in Spanish. 2004. s-a. EUR 150 domestic to institutions; EUR 225 foreign to institutions (effective 2009). back issues avail. **Document type:** *Journal, Academic/Scholarly.*
Related titles: Online - full text ed.
Indexed: CA, F04, SCOPUS, SD, T02.
Published by: Universidad Catolica San Antonio, Facultad de Ciencias de la Salud, de la Actividad Fisica y del Deporte, Campus de los Jeronimos s/n, Guadalupe, Murcia 30107, Spain. TEL 34-968-278806. Ed. Eduardo Segara Vicens.

795.42 USA ISSN 1081-2636
CURRENT BLACKJACK NEWS. Text in English. 1979. m. (plus irreg. special issues). looseleaf. USD 79; USD 15 newsstand/cover (effective 2007). **Document type:** *Newsletter.* **Description:** Contains news and updates on the rules and playing conditions for the casino game of blackjack in legal casinos, as well as reports on other casino games that can be beaten.
Formerly (until 1979): Stanford Wong's Blackjack Newsletter (0197-5595)
Related titles: Online - full text ed.: USD 49 (effective 2001).
Published by: Pi Yee Press, 4855 W. Nevso Dr., Las Vegas, NV 89103-3787. TEL 702-579-7711. Eds. Frank Jackson, Stanford Wong. Circ: 800 (paid).

796 FIN ISSN 0788-6012
CURRENT RESEARCH IN PHYSICAL SCIENCES IN FINLAND. Text in English. 1984. biennial. **Document type:** *Monographic series, Academic/Scholarly.*
Formerly (until 1990): Current Research in Physical Culture in Finland (0781-4119)
Related titles: ♦ Series of: Liikuntatieteellisen Seura. Julkaisuja. ISSN 0356-746X.
Published by: Liikuntatieteellinen Seura ry/Finnish Society for Research in Sport and Physical Education, Stadion, Etelakaarre, Helsinki, 00250, Finland. TEL 358-9-4542720, FAX 358-9-45427222, toimisto@lts.fi, http://www.lts.fi.

S

CUSTOM CLASSIC TRUCKS. *see* TRANSPORTATION—Trucks And Trucking

793 ARG ISSN 1851-3859
CYBER AUTODEFINIDOS. Text in Spanish. 2007. m.
Published by: M4 Editora, San Pedro 140, Avellanada, Buenos Aires, 1870, Argentina. m4editora@speedy.com.ar.

796 GBR ISSN 0969-2576
CYCLE SPORT. Text in English. 1993. m. GBP 39.99 domestic; EUR 80.90 in Europe; GBP 61.80 elsewhere; GBP 4.10 newsstand/cover (effective 2009). adv. bk.rev. back issues avail. **Document type:** *Magazine, Consumer.* **Description:** Covers the continental European professional bicycle racing scene.
Published by: I P C Country & Leisure Media Ltd. (Subsidiary of: I P C Media Ltd.), Leon House, 233 High St, Croydon, CR9 1HZ, United Kingdom. TEL 44-20-87268000, http://www.ipcmedia.com. Ed. Robert Garbutt TEL 44-20-87268461. Adv. contact Kevin Attridge TEL 44-20-87268409. color page GBP 1,260. Circ: 17,073. **Subscr. to:** Rockwood House, Perrymount Rd, Haywards Heath RH16 3DH, United Kingdom. TEL 44-845-1231231, IPCsubs@quadrantsubs.com, http://www.magazinesdirect.co.uk. **Dist. by:** MarketForce UK Ltd, The Blue Fin Bldg, 3rd Fl, 110 Southwark St, London SE1 0SU, United Kingdom. TEL 44-20-31483300, FAX 44-20-31488105, salesinnovation@marketforce.co.uk, http://www.marketforce.co.uk/.

790.1 DEU
D J K - DAS MAGAZIN. (Deutsche Jugendkraft) Text in German. 1913. bi-m. EUR 14.50; EUR 2.55 newsstand/cover (effective 2009). adv. back issues avail. **Document type:** *Magazine, Consumer.*
Former titles (until 2006): D J K - Sportmagazin; (until 1989): Deutsche Jugendkraft
Published by: Deutsche Jugendkraft e.V., Carl-Mosterts-Platz 1, Duesseldorf, 40477, Germany. TEL 49-211-948360, FAX 49-211-9483636, info@djk.de, http://www.djk.de.

790.1 DEU
D J K SPORTMAGAZIN. (Deutsche Jugendkraft) Text in German. bi-m. EUR 14.50; EUR 2.55 newsstand/cover (effective 2009). adv. **Document type:** *Magazine, Consumer.*
Published by: D J K Sportverband e.V., Carl-Mosterts-Platz 1, Duesseldorf, 40477, Germany. TEL 49-211-94836-0, FAX 49-211-9483636, info@djk.de. adv.: color page EUR 960. Circ: 4,715 (controlled).

797.21 DEU
D L R G - AKTUELL. (Deutsche Lebens-Rettungs-Gesellschaft) Text in German. 1984. q. **Document type:** *Bulletin, Consumer.*
Published by: D L R G - Kreisverband Kaufbeuren Ostallgaeu, Gewerbestr 83, Kaufbeuren-Neugablonz, 87600, Germany. TEL 49-8341-98298, FAX 49-8341-98299, vorstand@kaufbeuren.dlrg.de, http://www.dlrg.de/Gliederung/Bayern/Schwaben/Kaufbeuren-Ostallgaeu/index.htm. Circ: 600.

796.72 DEU
D M V INSIDE. (Deutscher Motorsport-Verband) Text in German. 4/yr. adv. **Document type:** *Magazine, Trade.*
Former titles (until 2010): M X; (until 2001): Motor-Extra
Published by: D M V - Wirtschaftsdienst GmbH, Otto-Fleck-Schneisse 12, Frankfurt am Main, 60528, Germany. TEL 49-69-6950020, FAX 49-69-69500220, dmv@dmv-motorsport.de. Circ: 20,000 (paid and controlled).

796 ESP ISSN 2171-3758
▼ **D MUJER.** Text in Spanish. 2010. a. back issues avail. **Document type:** *Magazine, Consumer.*
Related titles: Online - full text ed.: ISSN 1989-9734. 2010.
Published by: Consejo Superior de Deportes, Servicio de Documentacion, Av. Martin Fierro s/n, Madrid, 28040, Spain. TEL 34-91-5896938, FAX 34-91-5896614, publicaciones@csd.gob.es.

790.1 DEU
D O S B PRESSE. Text in German. 1990. w. **Document type:** *Newsletter, Trade.*
Formerly (until 200?): D S B Presse (0949-7226)
Published by: Deutscher Olympischer Sportbund, Otto-Fleck-Schneise 12, Frankfurt Am Main, 60528, Germany. TEL 49-69-67000, FAX 49-69-674906, info@dsb.de.

797 DEU ISSN 1431-3707
D S W '12 NACHRICHTEN. (Darmstaedter Schwimm- und Wassersportclub) Text in German. 1955. m. adv. **Document type:** *Newsletter, Consumer.*
Published by: Darmstaedter Schwimm- und Wassersportclub 1912 e.V., Alsfelder Str 31, Darmstadt, 64289, Germany. TEL 49-6151-713077, FAX 49-6151-783043, geschaeftsstelle@dsw-1912.de, http://www.dsw-1912.com. Circ: 1,300 (controlled).

794.2 NLD ISSN 0011-5959
HET DAMSPEL. Text in Dutch. 1911. 5/yr. adv. bk.rev. bibl.; charts. **Document type:** *Magazine, Consumer.*
Published by: Koninklijke Nederlandse Dambond/Royal Dutch Draughts Association, Postbus 100, Rheden, 6990 AC, Netherlands. TEL 31-26-4952309, bondsbureau@kndb.nl, http://www.kndb.nl.

790.1 CHN ISSN 1002-6169
DANGDAI TIYU/MODERN SPORTS. Text in Chinese. 1983. w. USD 213.20 (effective 2009). illus. 52 p./no.; **Document type:** *Consumer.* **Description:** General interest sports magazine.
Related titles: Online - full text ed.; ◆ Supplement(s): Jingwu. ISSN 1002-6177.
—East View.
Published by: (Heilongjiang Sheng Tiyu Yundong Weiyuanhui), Dangdai Tiyu Zazhishe, 99 Xuanxua Jie, Nangang-qu, Harbin, Heilongjiang 150001, China. TEL 86-451-82526535, FAX 86-451-82510474. Ed. Wang Lihei. **Dist. by:** China International Book Trading Corp, 35 Chegongzhuang Xilu, Haidian District, PO Box 399, Beijing 100044, China. TEL 86-10-68412045, FAX 86-10-68412023, cibtc@mail.cibtc.com.cn, http://www.cibtc.com.cn.

795.414 DNK ISSN 0011-6238
DANSK BRIDGE. Text in Danish. 1941. m. DKK 250 domestic; NOK 320 in Norway; SEK 360 in Sweden; DKK 280 other Nordic countries; DKK 350 elsewhere (effective 2008). adv. bk.rev. **Document type:** *Magazine, Consumer.*
Related titles: Online - full text ed.: ISSN 1399-669X. 1999.
Published by: Danmarks Bridgeforbund/Danish Bridge League, Smedevej 1, Asaa, 9340, Denmark. TEL 45-48-475213, FAX 45-48-476213, dansk@bridge.dk, http://www.bridge.dk. Ed., Adv. contact Ib Lundby. page DKK 6,000.

797.21 658 DNK ISSN 0901-9847
DANSK SVOEMMEBADSTEKNISK FORENING. PUBLIKATION. Text in Danish. 1977. irreg. price varies. **Document type:** *Monographic series, Trade.*
Formerly (until 1981): Dansk Svoemmebadsteknisk Forening (0901-9855)
Published by: Dansk Svoemmebadsteknisk Forening, Jens Olsens Vej 9, Aarhus N, 8200, Denmark. TEL 45-43-525353, FAX 45-87-394699, kontakt@svommebad.dk, http://www.svommebad.dk.

790.1 GBR ISSN 0267-2286
DARTS PLAYER. Text in English. 1985. a. GBP 3.50, USD 5. adv. back issues avail. **Document type:** *Magazine, Consumer.*
Published by: World Magazines Ltd., 9 Kelsey Park Rd, Beckenham, Kent BR3 6LH, United Kingdom. Ed. A J Wood. Adv. contact M Vansittart. Circ: 19,450.

799.32 GBR ISSN 0140-6000
DARTS WORLD. Text in English. 1972. m. GBP 32.10 domestic; GBP 39 in Europe; GBP 2.95 newsstand/cover (effective 2009). adv. bk.rev. **Document type:** *Magazine, Consumer.* **Description:** Covers sports information.
Incorporates (1977-19??): Darts News and Double Top; Pub Sports Monthly
Indexed: SportS.
Published by: World Magazines Ltd., M B Graphics, 25 Orlestone View, Hamstreet, Ashford, Kent, United Kingdom. TEL 44-1233-733558.

794.3 NLD ISSN 1878-9501
DARTS6.NL. Text in Dutch. 2008. bi-m. EUR 29.95 domestic; EUR 39.95 in Belgium; EUR 39.95 in Spain (effective 2010). **Document type:** *Magazine, Consumer.*
Formerly (until 2009): Darts International (1876-1828); Which was formed by the merger of (2002-2008): Darts4you (1573-5907); (2004-2008): Grand Slam Darts Magazine (1574-0323)
Published by: Publi Force, Postbus 229, Alblasserdam, 2950 AE, Netherlands. TEL 31-78-6522700, FAX 31-78-6522701, info@publiforce.nl, http://www.publiforce.nl.

796.72 CHN
DAZHONG QICHE (F1 SUBAO)/F1 EXPRESS. Text in Chinese. 2004. m. **Document type:** *Magazine, Consumer.*
Published by: Dazhong Qiche Zazhishe (Subsidiary of: Jilin Chuban Jituan/Jilin Publishing Group), Jike Zhongda Chuanmei Guanggao, 16-17, A225, Chunshuyuan Xiao-qu, Beijing, 100052, China. TEL 86-10-63109491.

790.1 USA
DEAFDIGEST SPORTS. Text in English. 1996. w. free. **Document type:** *Newsletter, Consumer.*
Formerly (until 2007): DeafSportZine
Media: E-mail.
Published by: DeafDigest barry@deafdigest.com, http://www.deafdigest.com. Ed. Barry Strassler.

306.4 USA
THE DEALER'S NEWS. Text in English. m. USD 7.50 for 6 mos. (effective 2001). **Document type:** *Newsletter, Trade.* **Description:** Covers industry news for gaming employees.
Published by: The Dealer's News, No. 37, 1801 E Tropicana Ave, Las Vegas, NV 89119. FAX 702-891-0037, news711@aol.com, http://www.thedealersnews.com.

797 ITA ISSN 1121-3817
DELTA & PARAPENDIO; hang-gliding and para-gliding. Text in Italian. 1991. m. (11/yr.). adv. 96 p./no.; back issues avail. **Document type:** *Magazine, Consumer.* **Description:** Covers every aspect of hang-gliding and paragliding; techniques, tools, events, and contests.
Published by: Gruppo Editoriale Olimpia SpA, Via E Fermi 24, Loc Osmannoro, Sesto Fiorentino, FI 50129, Italy. TEL 39-055-30321, FAX 39-055-3032280, http://www.edolimpia.it. Circ: 25,000. **Dist. by:** Parrini & C, Piazza Colonna 361, Rome, RM 00187, Italy. TEL 39-06-695141.

790.1 CUB ISSN 0138-6611
DEPORTE - DERECHO DEL PUEBLO. Text in Spanish. 1968. bi-m. USD 22 in South America; USD 24 in North America; USD 32 elsewhere. illus. **Document type:** *Government.* **Description:** Presents articles, interviews and photo features on current national and international events, including information on the military, cultural, sports and recreational activities of the Armed Forces.
Published by: (Instituto Nacional de Deportes, Educacion Fisica y Recreacion), Ediciones Cubanas, Obispo 527, Havana, Cuba. Ed. Manuel Vailannt Carpente. Circ: 15,000.

790.1 DOM
DEPORTES. Text in Spanish. 1967. fortn.
Published by: Publicaciones Ahora, Apdo. Postal 1402, Ave San Martin 236, Santo Domingo, Dominican Republic. Ed. L R Cordero. Circ: 5,000.

790.1 VEN
DEPORTES. Text in Spanish. 1978. fortn.
Published by: C.A. Editorial Hipodromo, Torre de la Prensa, Plaza del Panteon, Apdo 2976, Caracas, DF 1010-A, Venezuela. Ed. Raul Hernandez. Circ: 71,927.

796 COL ISSN 2011-3048
DEPORTES QUINDIO. Text in Spanish. 2007. bi-m. **Document type:** *Magazine, Consumer.*
Address: Km. 1 Via el Eden 1er Piso, Quindio, Colombia. TEL 57-96-7476268, presidente@corporaciondeportivaquindio.com, http://www.corporaciondeportesquindio.com.

790.1 CHL
DEPORTIVO. Text in Spanish. irreg.
Published by: Consorcio Periodistico de Chile S.A., Vicuna Mackenna 1870, Santiago, Chile. TEL 56-2-550-7000, FAX 56-2-550-7999, http://www.copesa.cl.

799.32 DEU
DEUTSCHE DARTSPORT ZEITUNG. Abbreviated title: D D Z. Text in German. 10/yr. EUR 45; EUR 4.50 newsstand/cover (effective 2009). adv. **Document type:** *Newspaper, Consumer.* **Description:** Reports on darts competitions, tournaments and leagues in Germany.
Published by: Deutscher Dart Verband e.V., Kreulichweg 116, Essen, 45307, Germany. TEL 49-201-556899, FAX 49-201-556899, sport@ddv-online.com, http://www.ddv-online.com.

DEUTSCHE GEHOERLOSEN-ZEITUNG. *see* HANDICAPPED—Hearing Impaired

796 DEU ISSN 0948-2628
DEUTSCHE HOCKEY ZEITUNG. Text in German. 1947. 42/yr. EUR 112 domestic; EUR 120 foreign (effective 2006). adv. back issues avail. **Document type:** *Magazine, Consumer.*
Former titles (until 1994): Hockey (0942-3486); (until 1992): D H Z. Deutsche Hockey-Zeitung (0936-5176); (until 1989): Deutsche Hockey-Zeitung (0720-0765); (until 1980): Hockey (0342-4413)
Published by: Sportverlag Schmidt und Dreisilker GmbH, Boeblinger Str 68/1, Sindelfingen, 71065, Germany. TEL 49-7031-862800, FAX 49-7031-862801. Ed. Hannes Hasspacher. Adv. contact Dietmar Froeberg-Suberg TEL 49-7031-862851. color page EUR 1,300, B&W page EUR 850. Circ: 2,283 (paid and controlled).

799.3 DEU ISSN 0012-0707
DEUTSCHE SCHUETZENZEITUNG; das Magazin fuer Sport & Tradition. Text in German. 1954. m. EUR 38; EUR 4.50 newsstand/cover (effective 2006). adv. bk.rev. 68 p./no.; back issues avail. **Document type:** *Newspaper, Consumer.*
Published by: (Deutscher Schuetzenbund e.V.), Umschau Zeitschriftenverlag Breidenstein GmbH, Otto-Volger-Str 15, Sulzbach, 65843, Germany. TEL 49-6196-76670, FAX 49-6196-7667269, info@uzv.de, http://www.uzv.de. Ed. Harald Strier. Adv. contact Barbara Goerlach. B&W page EUR 1,510, color page EUR 2,280; trim 210 x 297. Circ: 9,856 (paid and controlled).

794 DEU ISSN 1430-2225
DEUTSCHE VEREINIGUNG FUER SPORTWISSENSCHAFT. SCHRIFTEN. Text in German. 1981. irreg., latest vol.169, 2007. price varies. **Document type:** *Monographic series, Academic/Scholarly.*
Formerly (until 1992): D V S - Protokolle (0938-3239)
Published by: Deutsche Vereinigung fuer Sportwissenschaft e.V., Bei der Neuen Muenze 4a, Hamburg, 22145, Germany. TEL 49-40-67941212, FAX 49-40-67941213, info@sportwissenschaft.de.

796 DEU ISSN 1864-3019
DEUTSCHER LEICHTATHLETIK-VERBAND. JAHRBUCH. Text in German. 1956. a. EUR 19.50 (effective 2009). **Document type:** *Yearbook, Trade.*
Former titles (until 2006): Leichtathletik-Jahrbuch (1613-9631); (until 2002): D L V Jahrbuch (0722-1797); (until 1980): Jahrbuch der Leichtathletik (0341-745X)
Indexed: IBR, IBZ.
Published by: Deutscher Leichtathletik-Verband, Alsfelder Str 27, Darmstadt, 64289, Germany. TEL 49-6151-770840, FAX 49-6151-770811, info@leichtathletik.de, http://www.leichtathletik.de.

796 DEU ISSN 1438-3403
GV204.G4
DEUTSCHER TURNER-BUND. JAHRBUCH. Text in German. 1906. a. EUR 11 (effective 2009). **Document type:** *Journal, Trade.*
Former titles (until 1999): Deutscher Turner-Bund. Amtliches Jahrbuch (1438-339X); (until 1993): Deutscher Turner-Bund (0342-863X); (until 1975): Deutscher Turner-Bund. Jahrbuch der Turnkunst (0075-2401)
Published by: Deutscher Turner-Bund, Otto-Fleck-Schneise 8, Frankfurt Am Main, 60528, Germany. TEL 49-69-678010, FAX 49-69-67801111, hotline@dtb-online.de, http://www.dtb-online.de. Circ: 6,500 (controlled).

790.1 DEU ISSN 0343-5318
DEUTSCHES TURNEN. Text in German. 1856. m. EUR 34; EUR 3.50 newsstand/cover (effective 2011). adv. 36 p./no. 3 cols./p.; back issues avail. **Document type:** *Magazine, Consumer.*
Published by: (Deutscher Turner-Bund), Meyer & Meyer Verlag, Von-Coels-Str 390, Aachen, 52080, Germany. TEL 49-241-958100, FAX 49-241-9581010, verlag@m-m-sports.com, http://m-m-sports.de. Circ: 18,905 (paid and controlled). **Subscr. to:** Deutscher Turner-Bund.

790.1 UAE
AL-DHAID. Text in Arabic. 1985. m. **Description:** Covers local sports and cultural events.
Published by: Nadi al-Dhaid al-Riyadi/Al-Dhaid Sporting Club, P O Box 12532, Al-Dhaid, United Arab Emirates. TEL 0822750, FAX 822631. Ed. Muhammad Bin Salim Al Qasimi. Circ: 1,000.

790.1 ESP
DIA CUATRO QUE FUERA. Text in Spanish. 1970. m. free. **Document type:** *Magazine, Consumer.*
Published by: Junta Central de Fiestas de Moros y Cristianos, Plaza de Santiago 3, Villena, Alicante 03400, Spain.

796.72 USA ISSN 1528-4182
DICK BERGGREN'S SPEEDWAY ILLUSTRATED. Variant title: Speedway Illustrated. Text in English. 2000. m. USD 14.97 domestic; USD 29.97 foreign (effective 2006). adv. **Document type:** *Magazine, Consumer.* **Description:** Covers various aspects of American stock car racing including NASCAR's big leagues and local short track activity.
Published by: Performance Media LLC, 107 Elm St, Salisbury, MA 01952. TEL 978-465-9099, FAX 978-465-9033. Ed. Dick Berggreen. Pub. Robert Fernald. Adv. contact Dave Ferrato.

790.1 340 FRA ISSN 1290-0214
DICTIONNAIRE PERMANENT: DROIT DU SPORT. Text in French. 2 base vols. plus m. updates. looseleaf. EUR 305 base vol(s).; EUR 28 per month (effective 2009).
Related titles: CD-ROM ed.; Online - full text ed.
Published by: Editions Legislatives, 80 ave de la Marne, Montrouge, Cedex 92546, France. TEL 33-1-40923636, FAX 33-1-40923663, infocom@editions-legislatives.fr, http://www.editions-legislatives.fr. Ed. Dominique Remy. Pub. Michel Vaillant.

DIESEL; mensile di cultura, attualita, tecnica che tratta di tutte le motorizzazioni diesel per usi industriali, agricoli, nautici. *see* ENGINEERING—Mechanical Engineering

796.7 USA ISSN 1559-8632
DIESEL WORLD. Text in English. 2006. m. USD 24.95; USD 4.99 per issue (effective 2011). adv. **Document type:** *Magazine, Consumer.* **Description:** Covers everything that relates to Diesel propulsion, including 4x4s, tow rigs, over-the-round trucks and recreational vehicles using diesel power.

Published by: Beckett Media Llc, 4635 McEwen Rd, Dallas, TX 75244. TEL 714-939-9991, 800-764-6278, FAX 714-456-0146, customerservice@beckett.com, http://www.beckett.com. Ed. Kevin Wilson. Adv. contact Eric Gomez TEL 714-939-9991 ext 282. Circ: 150,000.

688.76 ESP
DIFFUSION SPORT. Text in Spanish. 1982. s-a. EUR 75.40 domestic; EUR 100.21 in the Canarias; EUR 115.36 in Europe; EUR 143.17 in the Americas; EUR 164.80 rest of world (effective 2009). adv. back issues avail. **Document type:** *Journal, Trade.* **Description:** Contains news, views, products, interviews and economics related to the sport and leisure sector.
Related titles: Online - full text ed.
Published by: Difusion Ediciones S.L., Rosellon 102, Entlo. 1a, Barcelona, 08029, Spain. TEL 34-93-235702, FAX 34-93-236080. Ed., Pub. Manuel Freixas. Adv. contact Alicia Casals. Circ: 5,500.

DIFFUSION SPORT DIRECTORY. *see* BUSINESS AND ECONOMICS—Trade And Industrial Directories

688.76 ESP
DIFFUSION SPORT GACETA. Text in Spanish. 1985. 20/yr. EUR 45 domestic; EUR 70 in Europe; EUR 85 in the Americas; EUR 100 elsewhere (effective 2009). adv. back issues avail. **Document type:** *Newspaper, Trade.* **Description:** Provides information on sports firms, shows and fairs, retailers, sporting goods and more.
Published by: Difusion Ediciones S.L., Rosellon 102, Entlo. 1a, Barcelona, 08029, Spain. TEL 34-93-235702, FAX 34-93-236080. Ed., Pub. Manuel Freixas. Adv. contact Alicia Casals. Circ: 5,500.

DINAMANI. *see* GENERAL INTEREST PERIODICALS—India

793 USA
DIPLOMACY WORLD. Text in English. 1974. q. USD 400.
Published by: Pandemonium Press, 1273 Crest Dr, Encinitas, CA 92024. Ed. R C Walker. Circ: 400.

790.1 GBR
DIRECTORY OF SPORT IN LONDON. Text in English. 1986. a. **Document type:** *Directory.*
Published by: Sport England, Crystal Palace NSC, Ledrington Rd, PO Box 480, London, SE19 2BB, United Kingdom. TEL 44-181-778-8600, FAX 44-181-676-9812. Ed. Scilla Ashdown. Circ: 4,000.

790.1 GBR
DIRECTORY OF SPORT IN THE SOUTH EAST. Text in English. 1986. a. GBP 5 (effective 1999). **Document type:** *Directory.*
Published by: Sport England, Crystal Palace NSC, Ledrington Rd, PO Box 480, London, SE19 2BB, United Kingdom. TEL 44-181-778-8600, FAX 44-181-676-9812. Ed. Judith Richards. Circ: 4,000.

790.1 USA
DIRT ROCKET. Text in English. 2001 (Jun.). q. USD 8; USD 3.50 newsstand/cover; USD 4.50 newsstand/cover in Canada (effective 2001). adv. **Document type:** *Magazine, Consumer.* **Description:** Devoted to all aspects of the sport of mountainboarding, including competitions, spots to ride, interviews with professionals, and reports on the global scene.
Address: PO Box 558, Cave Creek, AZ 85327.

796 USA ISSN 2160-3626
DISC GOLFER. Abbreviated title: D G. Text in English. 1990. q. USD 20 to non-members; USD 5 per issue to non-members; free to members (effective 2011). adv. back issues avail. **Document type:** *Magazine, Consumer.*
Published by: Professional Disc Golf Association, Wildwood Park, 3828 Dogwood Ln, Appling, GA 30802. TEL 706-261-6342, FAX 706-261-6347, instruction@pdga.com. Ed. Randy Michael Signor TEL 206-306-5231. Adv. contact Brian Graham TEL 706-309-9285.

790.1 USA
DISCGOLFER. Text in English. 1997. irreg. **Document type:** *Magazine, Consumer.* **Description:** Devoted to the sport of disc golf.
Media: Online - full text. Ed., Pub. David Henrickson.

613.7 ROM ISSN 1454-3907
DISCOBOBUL. Text in Romanian. 1996. m. **Document type:** *Magazine, Consumer.*
Published by: Academia Nationale de Educatie Fizica si Sport, Str Constantin Noica 140, Bucharest, 77221, Romania. TEL 40-21-6385315, FAX 40-21-3120400, anefs@kappa.ro.

797.2 910.91 GBR ISSN 1471-6240
DIVE; the magazine diving deserves. Text in English. 1995. m. GBP 35 domestic to non-members; GBP 45 in Europe to non-members; GBP 55 elsewhere to non-members; free to members (effective 2010). adv. bk.rev.; Website rev.; tel.rev. illus.; maps; mkt. index. back issues avail. **Document type:** *Magazine, Consumer.* **Description:** Covers all aspects of the sport of diving.
Formerly (until 1999): Dive International (1360-6913)
Published by: (British Sub-Aqua Club), Dive International Publishing Ltd., One Victoria Villas, Richmond, Surrey TW9 2GW, United Kingdom. TEL 44-20-83328400, FAX 44-20-83329307. Ed. Simon Rogerson TEL 44-20-83328401. Pub. Paul Critcher TEL 44-20-83328409. Adv. contact Ben Bovill TEL 44-20-83328436.

797.21 CAN
DIVE. Text in English, French. q. free.
Formerly: Platformance
Published by: Canadian Amateur Diving Association, 1600 James Naismith Dr, Ste 705, Gloucester, ON K1B 5N4, Canada. TEL 613-748-5631. Ed. Don Adams. Circ: 1,500.

797.23 GBR ISSN 1465-3613
DIVE GIRL. Text in English. 1998. q. free (effective 2009). illus. back issues avail. **Document type:** *Magazine, Consumer.* **Description:** Covers a variety of topics pertaining to underwater scuba diving for women; profiles interesting women divers.
Address: 2a Wallace Rd, London, N1 2PG, United Kingdom. Ed. Louise Trewavas.

797.23 NZL ISSN 1174-5622
DIVE NEW ZEALAND. Text in English. 1990. bi-m. NZD 45.50 domestic; NZD 92 in Australia; NZD 110 in the Pacific; NZD 121 in the US & East Asia; NZD 126.50 in Europe; NZD 137 elsewhere (effective 2008). adv. bk.rev.; Website rev.; video rev. tr.lit.; bibl. Index. 96 p./no.; back issues avail. **Document type:** *Magazine, Consumer.* **Description:** Dedicated to the sport of scuba diving, covering local and international events.
Formerly (until 1998): Dive Log New Zealand (1170-5418)
Published by: (New Zealand Way Ltd.), Sea Tech Ltd., Mission Bay, PO Box 55069, Auckland, New Zealand. TEL 64-9-5210684, FAX 64-9-5213675, graham@DiveNewZealand.co.nz. Ed., R&P Dave Moran. Adv. contact Lee Czerniak. Circ: 18,000.

797.23 NZL
DIVE PACIFIC. Text in English. bi-m. NZD 42; NZD 7 newsstand/cover (effective 2008). Website rev.; video rev.; bk.rev. tr.lit.; bibl. 96 p./no.; back issues avail. **Document type:** *Magazine, Consumer.* **Description:** Dedicated to the sport of scuba diving, covering local and international events.
Published by: (New Zealand Way Ltd.), Sea Tech Ltd., Mission Bay, PO Box 55069, Auckland, New Zealand. TEL 64-9-5210684, FAX 64-9-5213675, graham@DiveNewZealand.co.nz, http://www.divenewzealand.com. Ed. Dave Moran. Adv. contact Lee Czerniak. Circ: 5,000 (paid).

797.21 USA ISSN 1061-3323
DIVE TRAINING. Text in English. 1991. m. USD 24.95 domestic; USD 39.95 foreign (effective 2000). adv. bk.rev. **Document type:** *Magazine, Consumer.* **Description:** Contains how-to information for new divers and their instructors. Offers safety information and promotes the diving experience.
Published by: Dive Training, Ltd., 5215 N W Crooked Rd, Parkville, MO 64152. TEL 816-741-5151, FAX 816-741-6458. Ed. Catherine Castle. Pub., R&P, Adv. contact Mark E Young. Circ: 90,000 (paid and controlled).

799 AUS
DIVELOG AUSTRALASIA. Text in English. 1988. m. AUD 40.50 (effective 2009). adv. back issues avail. **Document type:** *Magazine, Consumer.* **Description:** Covers diving experiences, equipment, competitions, and diver destinations.
Formerly (until 1999): Dive Log Australia
Related titles: Online - full text ed.: free (effective 2009).
Published by: Mountain Ocean & Travel Publications Pty Ltd., PO Box 355, Upper Beaconsfield, VIC 3808, Australia. TEL 61-3-59443774, FAX 61-3-59444024. Ed. Robert Torelli. Pub. Barry Andrewartha. Adv. contact Leanne Wylie. B&W page AUD 1,133, color page AUD 1,978; bleed 280 x 340. Circ: 120,000.

797.21 USA ISSN 0273-8589
DIVER. Text in English. 1980. bi-m. USD 15; USD 20 foreign (effective 1999). adv. bk.rev. illus. **Document type:** *Magazine, Consumer.* **Description:** Covers everything relating to springboard and platform diving.
Indexed: SportS.
—CCC.
Published by: Taylor Publishing, PO Box 28, St. Petersburg, FL 33731. TEL 813-866-9856, FAX 813-866-9740. Ed., Pub. Bob Taylor. Circ: 1,000 (paid).

797.23 GBR ISSN 0141-3465
DIVER; the magazine of sub-aqua diving, undersea exploration and research. Text in English. 1955. m. GBP 42.95 domestic; GBP 41.95 foreign (effective 2009). adv. bk.rev. charts; illus. back issues avail. **Document type:** *Magazine, Consumer.* **Description:** Covers topics in sport sub-aqua diving, including introduction to the sport, training, underwater recreation, travel, technology, equipment, wrecks and salvage, conservation, exploration, marine archaeology, marine biology, and underwater photography.
Formerly (until 1978): Triton (0041-3119)
Indexed: SportS.
Published by: Eaton Publications, 55 High St, Teddington, Middx TW11 8HA, United Kingdom. TEL 44-20-89434288, FAX 44-20-89434312, enquiries@divermag.co.uk. Eds. Steve Weinman, Nigel Eaton. Pub. Bernard Eaton.

797 910 CAN ISSN 0706-5132
DIVER MAGAZINE. Text in English. 1975. 8/yr. CAD 26.50 domestic; USD 35 foreign (effective 2007). adv. bk.rev. illus. back issues avail. **Document type:** *Magazine, Consumer.* **Description:** Covers Canadian and North American regional dive destination articles and travel features.
Former titles (until 1978): Diver and Underwater Adventure (0704-5220); (until 1977): Pacific Diver and Underwater Adventure (0317-6991)
Indexed: SD.
Published by: Seagraphic Publications Ltd., 241 East 1st St, North Vancouver, BC V7L 1B4, Canada. TEL 604-948-9937, 877-974-4333, FAX 604-948-9985. Ed. Virginia Cowell. Pub. Phil Nuytten. R&P Martina Campbell. Adv. contact Sherri Golbeck. B&W page CAD 2,546, color page CAD 3,356; trim 10.88 x 8.25. Circ: 6,000 (paid); 4,000 (controlled).

797.2 ESP
DIVING A FONDO. Text in Spanish. 2000. m. adv. **Document type:** *Magazine, Consumer.* **Description:** Provides stories and articles on diving and other underwater sports.
Published by: Motorpress Iberica (Subsidiary of: Gruner + Jahr AG & Co), Ancora 40, Madrid, 28045, Spain. TEL 34-91-3470100, FAX 34-91-3470152, http://www.motorpress-iberica.es. Ed. Sonia Torres Fernando. Circ: 25,000 (paid and controlled).

796.22 GBR ISSN 1758-5171
DOCUMENT (DORCHESTER). Text in English. 1998. 9/yr. adv. **Document type:** *Magazine, Consumer.*
Former titles (until 2007): Document Skateboard Magazine (1473-2998); (until 2001): Document (1464-200X)
Related titles: Online - full text ed.
Published by: Factory Media, Studio 153, 355 Byres Rd, Glasgow, G12 8QZ, United Kingdom. TEL 44-141-9455019, FAX 44-141-9455019, http://www.factorymedia.com. Adv. contact Ian Gunner. **Subscr. to:** Dovetail Services UK Ltd, 800 Guillat Ave, Kent Science Park, Sittingbourne, Kent ME9 8GU, United Kingdom. TEL 44-1795-414555, contact@dovetailservices.com, http://www.dovetailservices.com/.

DOEVE-IDRAET. *see* HANDICAPPED—Hearing Impaired

DOG SPORTS. *see* PETS

613.714 ESP ISSN 0212-2308
DOJO. Text in Spanish. 1976. m. EUR 21; EUR 2.10 newsstand/cover (effective 2003). adv. bibl.; illus. 46 p./no.; back issues avail. **Document type:** *Magazine, Consumer.* **Description:** Covers martial arts: training, philosophy, nutrition, and masters.
Formerly (until 1981): Budo (0212-2294)
Published by: Ediciones A.M. S.L., Ferraz, 11, Madrid, 28008, Spain. TEL 34-91-5401880, FAX 34-91-5415055. Pub., R&P Mariano Alonso. Adv. contact Hector Alonso. color page EUR 962; 180 x 260. Circ: 25,000.

796.0711 DEU ISSN 0173-0843
DOKUMENTE ZUM HOCHSCHULSPORT. Text in German. 1976. irreg., latest vol.30, 2000. price varies. **Document type:** *Monographic series, Academic/Scholarly.*
Published by: (Freie Universitaet Berlin, Zentraleinrichtung Hochschulsport), Czwalina Verlag, Bei der Neuen Muenze 4a, Hamburg, 22145, Germany. TEL 49-40-6794300, FAX 49-40-67943030, post@feldhaus-verlag, http://www.edition-czwalina.de.

797 USA ISSN 0744-3226
DOLPHIN DIGEST. Text in English. 1974. 26/yr. USD 42.95 domestic; USD 130 foreign (effective 2000). adv. back issues avail. **Document type:** *Newspaper.* **Description:** Football publication devoted to the Miami Dolphins and the NFL.
Published by: Curtis Publishing Co. (Miami), 8033 N W 36th St, Miami, FL 33166. TEL 305-594-0508, FAX 305-594-0518. Ed. Andrew Cohen. Pub. Tom Curtis. Adv. contact Ken Keidel. Circ: 40,000.

790.1 IRN
DONYAYE VARZESH. Text in Persian, Modern. 1970. w. GBP 148 in Iran; GBP 148 in Pakistan; GBP 192 in Europe; GBP 192 in Japan; GBP 256 in North America; GBP 256 in Australia & New Zealand (effective 1999). adv. **Document type:** *Consumer.* **Description:** Covers sports in Iran and at the international level.
Published by: Ettela'at Publications, Mirdamad Blvd., Naft-e Jonubi St., Ettala'at Bldg., Tehran, 1549951199, Iran. TEL 98-21-29993241, FAX 98-21-3111223, TELEX 212336. Ed. Gholamhossein Sha'bani. Circ: 250,000.

793 USA
DOUBLEDOWN; your guide to casino action and entertainment. Text in English. q.
Published by: View & Travel Publishing, Inc, 332 S Michigan Ave, 1144, Chicago, IL 60604. Pub. Reginald Ware TEL 312-913-1450.

796 CIV ISSN 1563-9622
DOUZE. Text in French. d. XOF 150 newsstand/cover.
Media: Online - full text.
Published by: Editions Olympe, Abidjan, Ivory Coast. Circ: 22,000.

796.72 USA ISSN 1096-326X
DRAG NEWS MAGAZINE. Text in English. 1988. m. USD 14 (effective 2005). adv. 112 p./no.; back issues avail. **Document type:** *Magazine, Consumer.* **Description:** Regional publication devoted to coverage of sportsman drag racing.
Formerly: Midwest Drag Racing
Published by: Midwest Motorsport Magazines Inc., 330 W Rocky St, Athens, IL 62613. TEL 217-636-8103, laurie@dragnews.com. Ed. Todd Silvey. Pub., R&P Laurie Silvey. Adv. contact Scott Sparrow.

796.72 USA ISSN 1094-5547
TL236.2
DRAG RACER; your 1 source for America's first extreme sport. Text in English. 1997. bi-m. USD 19.95; USD 5.99 per issue (effective 2011). adv. illus. back issues avail. **Document type:** *Magazine, Consumer.* **Description:** Covers all aspects of drag racing with technical articles, interviews, latest industry news, full coverage of major events, and more.
Related titles: Online - full text ed.
Published by: Beckett Media Llc, 2400 E Katella Ave, Ste 300, Anaheim, CA 92806. TEL 714-939-9991, 800-764-6287, FAX 714-456-0146, customerservice@beckett.com, http://www.beckett.com. Ed. Randy Fish TEL 714-939-9991 ext 213. Adv. contact Eric Gomez TEL 714-939-9991 ext 282. Circ: 130,000.

796.72 USA
DRAG SPORT; the world's largest import performance sport. Text in English. m. USD 29.98 domestic; USD 41.98 in Canada; USD 44.98 elsewhere; USD 4.99 per issue (effective 2003). adv. back issues avail. **Document type:** *Magazine, Consumer.*
Related titles: Online - full text ed.
Published by: Import Drag Racing Circuit, Inc., 21405 Brookhurst St, Huntington Beach, CA 92646. TEL 714-593-0280, FAX 714-593-0281. Pub. Michael Ferrara. Adv. contact Bryan Phan. B&W page USD 2,976, color page USD 4,682; trim 10.5 x 14.5.

796.72 AUS
DRAGS & PRO STREET MAGAZINE. Text in English. 2003. 9/yr. AUD 66; AUD 7.95 newsstand/cover domestic; AUD 8.95 newsstand/cover in New Zealand (effective 2009). back issues avail. **Document type:** *Magazine, Consumer.*
Formerly (until 2007): Drags Magazine (1448-7616)
Published by: Investment Vehicles, Unit 5, Mirra Business Park, 9 Mirra Ct, Bundoora, VIC 3083, Australia. pitcrew@motormania.com.au.

797.2 NLD ISSN 1572-1868
DUIKMAGAZINE. Text in Dutch. 2004. bi-m. EUR 20.50; EUR 4.50 newsstand/cover (effective 2009). adv. **Document type:** *Magazine, Consumer.*
Published by: BCM Publishing, Postbus 1392, Eindhoven, 5602 BJ, Netherlands. TEL 31-40-8447644, FAX 31-40-8447655, bcm@bcm.nl, http://www.bcm.nl. Ed. Marlies Strik. Adv. contact Jeroen van der Linden. Circ: 15,000.

796 ROM
➤ **DUNAREA DE JOS UNIVERSITY OF GALATI. ANNALS. PHYSICAL EDUCATION AND SPORT MANAGEMENT, FASCICLE XV/ UNIVERSITATEA "DUNAREA DE JOS" GALATI. ANALELE. FASCICULA XV, EDUCATIE FIZICA SI MANAGEMENT IN SPORT.** Text in English; Summaries in English, French, Romanian. 2000. s-a. **Document type:** *Journal, Academic/Scholarly.* **Description:** Covers all aspects of physical education and sports management, including specializations such as kineto therapy, sports management, high performance sports, physical education of people with disabilities, sports for all and adaptive sports.
Related titles: Online - full text ed.: free (effective 2011).
Published by: (Universitatea "Dunarea de Jos" din Galati, Facultatea de Educatie Fizica si Sport/"Dunarea de Jos" University of Galati, Physical Education and Sports Faculty), Editura Universitatii Dunarea de Jos/Galati University Press, 47 Domneasca Str., Galati, 800008, Romania. TEL 40-336-130139, FAX 40-236-461353, gup@ugal.ro, http://www.gup.ugal.ro/. Eds. Claudiu Mereuta, Alexandru Pacuraru. Pub. Elena Mereuta.

S

➤ **DUNE BUGGIES & HOT V WS**; the fun car journal. *see* TRANSPORTATION—Automobiles

790.1 USA
DURHAM COMMUNITY SPORTS NEWS. Text in English. 1985. m. adv. bk.rev.; film rev. 8 p./no.; **Document type:** *Newspaper.* **Description:** Covers local sports, with commentary.
Published by: Durham Community Sports News Inc., 123 Barclay Rd, Chapel Hill, NC 27516. Ed., Pub., Adv. contact Joel S Bulkley. Circ: 5,000 (free).

790.1 JOR
AD-DUSTOUR AR-RIYADI; riyadiyyah - usbu'iyyah - mutakhassisah. Text in Arabic. w. adv. bibl. 32 p./no. 8 cols./p.; **Document type:** *Newspaper, Consumer.*
Published by: Jordan Press and Publishing Co., Queen Rania St., P O Box 591, Amman, 11118, Jordan. TEL 962-6-5664153, FAX 962-6-5667170, TELEX 21392 MEDIA JO, dustour@addustour.com.jo, http://www.addustour.com. Adv. contact Mohammed Shanti. Circ: 25,000.

DUSTY TIMES. *see* SPORTS AND GAMES—Bicycles And Motorcycles

796.72 NLD ISSN 2210-8769
DUTCH SUPERCAR CHALLENGE. Text in Dutch. 2005. a. EUR 30 (effective 2010). **Document type:** *Yearbook.*
Published by: V-max Racing Management B.V., Schapendreef 78, Breda, 4824 AM, Netherlands. TEL 31-76-5430200, FAX 31-76-3798219.

796 ESP ISSN 1885-7019
GV1017.H2
E - BALONMANO.COM; revista de ciencias del deporte. Text in Spanish, English, Portuguese. 2005. 3/yr. free (effective 2011). **Document type:** *Journal, Academic/Scholarly.*
Media: Online - full text.
Published by: Federacion Extremena de Balonmano, Calle Platon 1, Merida, 06800, Spain. Ed. Sebastian Feu Molina.

794.1 GBR
THE E C F YEARBOOK. Text in English. 1919. a. free to members (effective 2009). stat. index. **Document type:** *Yearbook, Consumer.* **Description:** Contains past champions, network contacts, results, chess problems, junior activities and a directory of counties, leagues and clubs.
Formerly (until 19??): Year Book of Chess (0305-5132)
Published by: English Chess Federation, The Watch Oak, Chain Ln, Battle, E Sussex TN33 0YD, United Kingdom. TEL 44-1424-775222, FAX 44-1424-775904, office@englishchess.org.uk, http://www.englishchess.org.uk. Circ: 2,500.

796 DEU
E C S S NEWS BULLETIN. Text in English. 2/yr. free to members. **Document type:** *Bulletin.* **Description:** Contains information related to the situation and development of the ECSS.
Published by: European College of Sport Science, c/o Thomas Delaveaux, German Sport University Cologne, Am Sportpark Muengersdorf 6, Koeln, 50933, Germany. TEL 49-221-49827640, FAX 49-221-49827650, king@hrz.dshs-koeln.de, http://www.ecss.de.

796 306.766 NLD ISSN 1876-1763
E G L S F NEWSLETTER. Text in English. 2007. m. free (effective 2011). **Document type:** *Newsletter, Consumer.*
Media: Online - full text.
Published by: European Gay & Lesbian Sport Federation, c/o NCS, Meeuwenlaan 41, Amsterdam, 1021 HS, Netherlands. eglsf@eglsf.info.

794.1 NZL
E P. Text in English. 1979. a. free to members. **Description:** Reports on national and international news, games, and studies on problems.
Formerly (until no.2, 1979): Move It; Incorporates (1933-1979): New Zealand Correspondence Chess Association. Secretary Treasurer's Report
Published by: New Zealand Correspondence Chess Association, c/o J W (Sandy) Maxwell, Sec., PO Box 3278, Wellington, New Zealand. TEL 64-4-2374753, http://www.poisonpawn.co.nz/corrrespondence.htm. Circ: 250 (controlled).

796 MEX ISSN 1933-947X
E S P N DEPORTES; la revista. (Entertainment Sports Programming Network) Text in Spanish. 2005. m. adv. **Document type:** *Magazine, Consumer.* **Description:** Includes interviews with major sports figures, news from major sports leagues, personal profiles of the best athletes and an insider's look at some of the worldzzzzes most famous and coveted sports events.
Published by: Editorial Televisa, Vasco de Quiroga 2000, Edificio E, Colonia Santa Fe, Mexico City, DF 01210, Mexico. TEL 52-55-52612761, FAX 52-55-52612704, info@editorialtelevisa.com, http://www.esmas.com/editorialtelevisa/. Circ: 55,000 (paid).

790.1 USA ISSN 1555-8304
GV741
E S P N SPORTS ALMANAC (YEAR). (Entertainment Sports Programming Network) Text in English. a. USD 12.99 per vol. (effective 2005). adv. stat. **Description:** Provides comprehensive worldwide sports statistics.
Former titles (until 2004): E S P N Information Please Sports Almanac (Year) (1098-4526); (until 1998): Information Please Sports Almanac (Year) (1046-4980)
Related titles: Online - full text ed.
Published by: Hyperion, 77 W 66th St, 11th Fl, New York, NY 10023. http://www.hyperionbooks.com/index.asp.

796 USA ISSN 1097-1998
E S P N THE MAGAZINE. Text in English. 1998. bi-w. USD 26 domestic; USD 49 in Canada; USD 95 elsewhere; USD 4.99 newsstand/cover (effective 2010). adv. illus. reprints avail. **Document type:** *Magazine, Consumer.* **Description:** Covers sports news,focuses on baseball, hockey, basketball and foot ball, but also features articles on sports like in-line skating, bicycling and snowboarding.
Related titles: Online - full text ed.; Chinese Translation: Tiyu Pindao. ISSN 1818-4650.
Indexed: PEI, SD, T02.
—CCC.
Published by: E S P N The Magazine, Inc., 19 E 34th St, New York, NY 10016. TEL 888-267-3684. Ed. Gary Belsky. **Subscr. to:** PO Box 37325, Boone, IA 50037. **Dist. in UK by:** Comag, Tavistock Rd, W Drayton, Middlesex UB7 7QE, United Kingdom.

793.7 FIN ISSN 1795-8938
E T - RISTIKOT. Text in Finnish. 2005. m. EUR 34 (effective 2009). **Document type:** *Magazine, Consumer.*
Published by: Sanoma Magazines Finland Corporation, Lapinmaentie 1, Helsinki, 00350, Finland. TEL 358-9-1201, FAX 358-9-1205171, info@sanomamagazines.fi, http://www.sanomamagazines.fi.

794.1 CAN ISSN 0825-0049
ECHEC PLUS. Text in English. 1978. bi-m. CAD 32 domestic; CAD 37 in United States (effective 2000). adv. bk.rev. index. back issues avail. **Document type:** *Bulletin.* **Description:** News and events: game analysis, problems, combinations.
Published by: (Federation Quebecoise des Echecs), Editions Echec Plus, C P 640, Succ C, Montreal, PQ H2L 4L5, Canada. TEL 514-252-3034, FAX 514-251-8038, TELEX 0582647, http://www.fqchecs.qc.ca. Ed. Jean Hebert. Pub., R&P, Adv. contact Richard Berube. Circ: 2,500 (paid).

794.1 BEL
ECHIQUIER BELGE. Text in Dutch, French. 1942. m. (except July-Aug. combined). USD 55 foreign (effective 1999). adv. bk.rev. **Document type:** *Bulletin.* **Description:** Includes annotated games, combinations, results, and studies on problems.
Address: Rue Van Waeyenberg 12, Brussels, 1140, Belgium. TEL 02-216-47-37. Ed. Henri Muller.

796 SWE ISSN 1653-5014
EDGE MAGAZINE (STOCKHOLM); intense living magazine. Text in Swedish. 2005. bi-m. SEK 199 (effective 2006). adv. **Document type:** *Magazine, Consumer.*
Published by: Ledge Media Produktion, PO Box 1390, Solna, 17127, Sweden. TEL 46-8-56436000, FAX 46-8-56436005. Eds. Irja Berntsen, Patrik Mattson TEL 46-76-2477152. Pub. Christina Wennlund. Adv. contact Jascha Buckholt TEL 46-8-4415683. color page SEK 31,000; 215 x 295.

790.1 DEU ISSN 1437-448X
EDITION GLOBALE - LOKALE SPORTKULTUR. Text in German. 1999. irreg., latest vol.28, 2011. price varies. **Document type:** *Monographic series, Academic/Scholarly.*
Published by: Waxmann Verlag GmbH, Steinfurter Str 555, Muenster, 48159, Germany. TEL 49-251-265040, FAX 49-251-2650426, info@waxmann.com. Ed. Dieter H. Juetting.

790.1 COL ISSN 0120-677X
EDUCACION FISICA Y DEPORTE. Text in Spanish. 1979. s-a. bk.rev. **Document type:** *Journal, Academic/Scholarly.* **Description:** Includes varios articles on physical education, fitness, and sports education.
Related titles: Online - full text ed.: ISSN 2145-5880. 1979. free (effective 2011).
Indexed: A36, CABA, GH, LT, T05.
Published by: Universidad de Antioquia, Instituto Universitario de Educacion Fisica y Deporte, Apartado Aereo 1226, Medellin, ANT, Colombia. TEL 57-4-4259267, FAX 57-4-4259261. Eds. Juan David Gomez Valenzuela, William Moreno. Circ: 1,000.

790.1 FRA ISSN 0245-8977
EDUCATION PHYSIQUE ET SPORTIVE AU 1ER DEGRE. Abbreviated title: E P S 1. Text in French. 1981. 5/yr. adv. **Document type:** *Magazine, Trade.* **Description:** Helps in planning elementary school physical education classes.
Indexed: SD.
—IE. **CCC.**
Published by: (Comite d'Etudes et d'Informations Pedagogiques de l'Education Physique et du Sport), Editions Revue E P S, 11 av. du Tremblay, Paris, 75012, France. TEL 33-1-48083087, FAX 33-1-43983738, http://www.revue-eps.com. Ed. Claudine Leray.

DER EINWURF. *see* HANDICAPPED—Visually Impaired

796.962 DEU
EISHOCKEY NEWS. Text in German. 1993. w. EUR 130 domestic; EUR 182 in Europe; EUR 234 elsewhere; EUR 2.95 newsstand/cover (effective 2009). adv. back issues avail. **Document type:** *Magazine, Consumer.* **Description:** Covers all aspects of ice hockey leagues, players and fans.
Related titles: CD-ROM ed.
Published by: Eishockey News Verlags GmbH und Co. KG, Finkenstr 48, Straubing, 94315, Germany. TEL 49-9421-781630, FAX 49-9421-781640, engl@eishockeynews.de. Ed. Wolfgang Karl. R&P Willi Schuessler. Adv. contact Heinz Wanninger TEL 49-9421-781638. B&W page EUR 3,200, color page EUR 4,200; trim 284 x 425. Circ: 34,000 (controlled). **Dist. by:** MZV - Moderne Zeitschriften Vertrieb GmbH & Co. KG, Breslauerstr 5, Eching 85386, Germany. TEL 49-89-319060, FAX 49-89-31906113, mzv@mzv.de, http://www.mzv.de.

790.1 DEU ISSN 1438-0420
DER EISSTOCKSPORT. Text in German. 1976. s-m. adv. bk.rev. **Document type:** *Magazine, Consumer.*
Formerly (until 1998): Der Eisstockschuetze (0937-0218)
Published by: Deutscher Eisstock Verband e.V., St Martin Str 72, Garmisch-Partenkirchen, 82467, Germany. TEL 49-8821-95100, FAX 49-8821-951015, info@eisstock-verband.de, http://www.eisstock-verband.de. Ed. Hermann Binder. Circ: 1,950 (controlled).

796.83 USA
ELECTRONIC BOXING WEEKLY. Text in English. 1998. d. free. adv. **Document type:** *Magazine, Consumer.* **Description:** Contains a plethora of boxing information that ranges from feature articles to next-day bout coverage and interviews, rankings, and betting guides.
Formerly: Electronic Boxing Monthly
Media: Online - full content.
Published by: Comp-U-Sports, 571 S Gosser Hill Rd, Leechburg, PA 15656. TEL 724-845-9775, FAX 724-639-8514. Ed., Pub., R&P, Adv. contact Jim Trunzo. online banner USD 50.

▼ **EMASF**; revista digital de educacion fisica. *see* PHYSICAL FITNESS AND HYGIENE

EMPLOYEE SERVICES MANAGEMENT; the journal of employee services, recreation, health and education. *see* BUSINESS AND ECONOMICS—Management

796.023 FRA ISSN 1774-7007
EN JEUX SPORT. Variant title: Enjeux Sport. Text in French. 200?. irreg. **Document type:** *Magazine, Consumer.*
Published by: Comite Departementale Olympique et Sportif Seine-Saint-Denis, Espace 22, 5 rue de Rome, Rosny-sous-Bois, 93561, France.

791.8 DOM
EN LA TRABA. Text in Spanish. m. adv. **Document type:** *Magazine, Consumer.* **Description:** Covers all aspects of cock-fighting in the Dominican Republic.
Published by: OK Publicaciones, S.A., Autopista San Isidro, Pradera del Este, Manz 2 No 5, Santo Domingo, Dominican Republic. TEL 809-245-6588, ok.publicaciones@gmail.com.

794.1 USA
EN PASSANT. Text in English. 1946. bi-m. USD 12 (effective 2000). adv. bk.rev. **Document type:** *Bulletin.* **Description:** Presents news and results of the club's events.
Published by: Chess Enterprises, 107 Crosstree Rd, Coraopolis, PA 15108. TEL 412-262-2138, FAX 412-262-2138. Ed. Bobby Dudley. Circ: 400 (paid).

THE ENCYCLOPEDIA OF SPORTS BUSINESS CONTACTS; the sports networking reference guide. *see* BUSINESS AND ECONOMICS—Trade And Industrial Directories

796.8 615.85 FRA ISSN 1777-3806
ENERGIES (PARIS). Text in French. 2005. q. EUR 23.80 (effective 2009). **Document type:** *Magazine, Consumer.*
Published by: Europeenne de Magazines, 44 av. George V, Paris, 75008, France. TEL 33-1-49521415, FAX 33-1-49521444.

797.21 GBR
ENGLISH SCHOOLS SWIMMING ASSOCIATION HANDBOOK. Text in English. 1950. a. adv. back issues avail. **Document type:** *Yearbook, Consumer.* **Description:** Provides latest news and results, together full details of ESSA council and divisional contacts plus forthcoming championships.
Related titles: Online - full text ed.
Published by: English Schools Swimming Association, c/o Richard Thorp, President, Dragon School, Bardwell Rd, Oxford, OX2 6SS, United Kingdom. TEL 44-1865-315456, r.thorp@essa-schoolswimming.com.

790.1 GBR
ENGLISH SPORTS COUNCIL. ANNUAL REPORT (YEAR). Text in English.
Formerly (until 1996): Sports Council. Annual Report (Year)
Published by: English Sports Council, 16-18 Upper Woburn Pl, London, WC1H 0QP, United Kingdom. TEL 44-171-273-1500, FAX 44-171-383-5740.

ENTERTAINMENT AND SPORTS LAW JOURNAL. *see* LAW

ENTERTAINMENT AND SPORTS LAWYER. *see* LAW

790.1 DEU ISSN 0932-7797
ENTWICKLUNGSZUSAMMENARBEIT IM SPORT; Analysen - Dokumentationen - Lehrmaterialen. Text in German. 1988. irreg., latest vol.8, 1990. price varies. **Document type:** *Monographic series, Academic/Scholarly.*
Published by: Czwalina Verlag, Bei der Neuen Muenze 4a, Hamburg, 22145, Germany. TEL 49-40-6794300, FAX 49-40-67943030, post@feldhaus-verlag, http://www.edition-czwalina.de.

796 AUS
EPIC. Text in English. 1995. q. free (effective 2008). back issues avail. **Document type:** *Newsletter, Consumer.*
Media: Online - full text. **Related titles:** E-mail ed.
Published by: Australian National University, Mountaineering Club, Sports Union ANU, Canberra, ACT 0200, Australia. Eds. Bronwen Davies, Sam Keech-Marx, Tiago Pereira.

790.1 FRA ISSN 0153-1069
L'EQUIPE. Text in French. 1946. d. EUR 139.05 for 6 mos. (effective 2008). adv. **Document type:** *Newspaper, Consumer.*
Related titles: Microfilm ed.: (from PQC); Online - full text ed.: ISSN 1951-6967; ◆ Supplement(s): L' Equipe Magazine. ISSN 0245-3312.
Indexed: SportS.
—CCC.
Published by: L' Equipe, 145 Rue Jean-Jacques Rousseau, Issy-les-Moulineaux, Cedex 92138, France. TEL 33-1-41233000, http://www.lequipe.fr. Ed. Gerome Bureau. Pub. Philippe Amaury. Circ: 545,145 (paid).

796 FRA ISSN 0245-3312
L'EQUIPE MAGAZINE. Text in French. 1964. w. **Document type:** *Magazine, Consumer.*
Related titles: ◆ Supplement to: L' Equipe. ISSN 0153-1069.
Published by: L' Equipe, 145 Rue Jean-Jacques Rousseau, Issy-les-Moulineaux, Cedex 92138, France. TEL 33-1-41233000, http://www.lequipe.fr.

ERNIE SAXTON'S MOTORSPORTS SPONSORSHIP - MARKETING NEWS; the latest marketing promotion & sponsorship news in all forms of motorsports. *see* ADVERTISING AND PUBLIC RELATIONS

790.1 SYR
ESBOU AL-RIADI. Text in Arabic. 1955. w. adv.
Address: Firdoisse Ave., Tibi Bldg., Damascus, Syria. Ed. Kamel El Bounni.

796.86 FRA ISSN 0298-3141
ESCRIME MAGAZINE. Text in French. 1977. m. (10/yr). EUR 26 domestic; EUR 33 foreign (effective 2009). **Document type:** *Magazine, Consumer.*
Formerly (until 1985): Escrime (0153-4661)
Published by: Federation Francaise d'Escrime, 14 rue Moncey, Paris, 75009, France. TEL 33-1-44532750, FAX 33-1-40239618, http://www.escrime-ffe.fr. Eds. Brigitte Dumont, Magali Ouradou. Pub. Pierre Abric.

794 ESP ISSN 1888-7732
ESPABOX; guia del boxeo espanol e internacional. Text in Spanish. 1994. a. **Document type:** *Directory.*
Published by: Federacion Espanola Boxeo, Ferraz, 16, Madrid, 28008, Spain. TEL 34-91-5477791, FAX 34-91-5474297, info@feboxeo.com, http://www.feboxeo.com/.

ESPACO; revista de ciencia do desporto dos paises de lingua portuguesa. *see* PHYSICAL FITNESS AND HYGIENE

ESPECIAL AUTODEFINIDOS GOLD. *see* HOBBIES

ESPECIAL AUTODEFINIDOS POCKET. *see* HOBBIES

ESPECIAL EUTODEFINIDOS PREMIER. *see* HOBBIES

796 BRA ISSN 1809-1296
GV561
ESPORTE E SOCIEDADE. Text in Portuguese, English, Spanish. 2005. q. **Document type:** *Journal, Academic/Scholarly.* **Description:** Its objective is to advance sports studies based on a dialogue rooted in the social and human sciences.
Media: Online - full text.
Indexed: A36, CABA, E12, GH, LT, PEI, R12, RRTA, SD, SociolAb, W11.
Published by: Esporte y Sociedade alvitobr@yahoo.com.br. Ed. Antonio Holzmeister Oswaldo.

796 FRA ISSN 1775-0970
LES ESSAIS DU SPORT. Text in French. 2004. irreg. **Document type:** *Monographic series, Trade.*
Published by: Savoir Gagner, 39 bd des Recollets, Toulouse, 31400, France. TEL 33-5-34312481, FAX 33-5-34312482, info@savoirgagner.com, http://www.savoirgagner.com/savgagn.php.

790.1 ECU
ESTADIO. Text in Spanish. 1962. s-m. USD 100 in United States; USD 160 in Europe (effective 2000). adv. **Document type:** *Consumer.*
Published by: Editores Nacionales, Aguirre 730 y Boyaca, Casilla 1239, Guayaquil, Guayas, Ecuador. TEL 593-4-327200, FAX 593-4-320499. Ed. Arcadio Arosemena. R&P Rodrigo Bustamante TEL 593-4-328505. Adv. contact Roberto Camacho. Circ: 30,000 (controlled).

797.21 AUS
ESWIMMER. Text in English. 1994. m. free (effective 2008). **Document type:** *Newsletter, Consumer.* **Description:** Provides scoops, stories and up to date information about swimming.
Former titles (until 2002): The Swimmer (Print) (1445-1174); (until 2000): Australian Swimming and Fitness (1327-6085); (until 1996): Swimmer (1324-8405)
Media: Online - full content. **Related titles:** E-mail ed.: free (effective 2004).
Published by: Australian Swimming, Inc., 12/7 Beissel St, Belconnen, ACT 2617, Australia. TEL 61-2-62195600, FAX 61-2-62195606, admin@swimming.org.au, http://www.swimming.org.au/.

796.332 ITA ISSN 1591-254X
EUROCALCIO. Text in Italian. 2000. m. EUR 2 newsstand/cover (effective 2009). **Document type:** *Magazine, Consumer.*
Published by: Edizioni Mimosa, Piazza E de Angeli 9, Milan, 20146, Italy. TEL 39-02-3650507, FAX 39-02-48110494, segreteria@edizionimimosa.it, http://www.edizionimimosa.it.

790.1 USA
THE EUROPA MAGAZINE (COLORADO SPRINGS). Text in English. irreg.
Published by: G R D Games, 3302 Adobe Court, Colorado Springs, CO 80907-5442.

EUROPAEISCHE HOCHSCHULSCHRIFTEN. REIHE 35: SPORT UND KULTUR. *see* SOCIOLOGY

794.1 FRA ISSN 0014-2794
EUROPE-ECHECS. Text in French. 1956. m. (except Jul.-Aug. combined). EUR 49.95 domestic; EUR 83.75 foreign (effective 2009). adv. bk.rev.; play rev. **Document type:** *Magazine, Consumer.* **Description:** Contains annotated games, national and international news, interviews, combinations, correspondence chess, and computer chess.
Formerly (until 1959): L' Echiquier de France (2020-9576)
Related titles: Online - full text ed.: EUR 49.90 (effective 2009).
Published by: Promotion Jeux de l'Esprit, 4B2, rue Roussillon, Besancon, 25000, France. TEL 33-3-81526722. Circ: 31,000.

796.8 DEU ISSN 1436-1892
EUROPEAN INSTITUTE FOR T'AI CHI STUDIES. JOURNAL. Text in German. 1994. irreg. **Document type:** *Journal, Academic/Scholarly.* **—CCC.**
Published by: European Institute for T'ai Chi Studies e.V., Conventstr 8-10, Haus C, Hamburg, 22089, Germany. TEL 49-40-218454, shayuquan@eurotaichi.de, http://www.shayuquan.de.

790.1 DEU ISSN 1613-8171
EUROPEAN JOURNAL FOR SPORT AND SOCIETY. Text in English. 2004. s-a. EUR 98 (effective 2011). **Document type:** *Journal, Academic/Scholarly.* **Description:** Aims to promote closer co-operation and networking between experts dealing with social issues related to physical activity and sport in Europe.
Indexed: P03, PsycInfo.
—BLDSC (3829.744200).
Published by: (European Association for Sociology of Sport), Waxmann Verlag GmbH, Steinfurter Str 555, Muenster, 48159, Germany. TEL 49-251-265040, FAX 49-251-2650426, info@waxmann.com, http://www.waxmann.com. Ed. Dieter H. Juetting.

796 GBR ISSN 1746-1391
➤ **EUROPEAN JOURNAL OF SPORT SCIENCE.** Abbreviated title: E J S S. Text in English. 2001. bi-m. GBP 451 combined subscription in United Kingdom to institutions (print & online eds.); EUR 539, USD 677 combined subscription to institutions (print & online eds.) (effective 2012). adv. back issues avail.; reprint service avail. from PSC. **Document type:** *Journal, Academic/Scholarly.* **Description:** Covers the biological, behavioral, and social sciences as they pertain to sport and exercise.
Related titles: Online - full text ed.: ISSN 1536-7290. GBP 405 in United Kingdom to institutions; EUR 485, USD 609 to institutions (effective 2012) (from IngentaConnect).
Indexed: A01, A02, A03, A08, A22, C06, C07, CA, E01, FoSS&M, P03, PEI, PsycInfo, PsycholAb, R09, SCI, SCOPUS, SD, T02, W07.
—BLDSC (3829.744400), IE, Ingenta. **CCC.**
Published by: (European College of Sport Science DEU), Taylor & Francis Ltd. (Subsidiary of: Taylor & Francis Group), 4 Park Sq, Milton Park, Abingdon, Oxfordshire OX14 4RN, United Kingdom. TEL 44-20-70176000, FAX 44-20-70176336, subscriptions@tandf.co.uk, http://www.taylorandfrancis.com. Ed. Asker E Jeukendrup. Adv. contact Linda Hann. **Subscr. to:** Journals Customer Service, Sheepen Pl, Colchester, Essex CO3 3LP, United Kingdom. TEL 44-20-70175544, FAX 44-20-70175198, tf.enquiries@tfinforma.com.

➤ **EUROPEAN JOURNAL OF WILDLIFE RESEARCH.** *see* ANIMAL WELFARE

796 GRC ISSN 1791-3837
EUROPEAN PSYCHOMOTRICITY JOURNAL. Text in English, Greek. 2008. 3/yr.
Related titles: Online - full text ed.: free (effective 2011).
Published by: Scientific Psychomotor Association Hellas, Department of Physical Education and Sport Scoence, Democritus University of Thrace Campus, Komotini, 69100, Greece.

790.1 GBR ISSN 1618-4742
GV713
➤ **EUROPEAN SPORT MANAGEMENT QUARTERLY.** Abbreviated title: E S M Q. Text in English. 2001. q. GBP 469 combined subscription in United Kingdom to institutions (print & online eds.); EUR 623, USD 781 combined subscription to institutions (print & online eds.) (effective 2012). adv. back issues avail.; reprint service avail. from PSC. **Document type:** *Journal, Academic/Scholarly.* **Description:** Covers all types of sport organization and examines public, voluntary and commercial sport bodies, both amateur and professional; businesses that produce sport-related commodities; and service organizations in the sport industry.
Related titles: Online - full text ed.: ISSN 1746-031X. GBP 422 in United Kingdom to institutions; EUR 561, USD 703 to institutions (effective 2012) (from IngentaConnect).
Indexed: A22, CA, E01, P03, PEI, PsycInfo, SD, SSCI, SociolAb, T02, W07.
—BLDSC (3830.232240), IE, Ingenta. **CCC.**
Published by: (European Association for Sport Management FIN), Routledge (Subsidiary of: Taylor & Francis Group), 4 Park Sq, Milton Park, Abingdon, Oxon OX14 4RN, United Kingdom. TEL 44-20-70176000, FAX 44-20-70176336, subscriptions@tandf.co.uk, http://www.routledge.com. Ed. Marijke Taks. Adv. contact Linda Hann TEL 44-1344-779945. **Subscr. to:** Taylor & Francis Ltd., Journals Customer Service, Sheepen Pl, Colchester, Essex CO3 3LP, United Kingdom. TEL 44-20-70175544, FAX 44-20-70175198.

▼ ➤ **EUROPEAN SPORTS LAW AND POLICY BULLETIN.** *see* LAW

790.1 ITA
➤ **EUROPEAN STUDIES IN SPORTS HISTORY.** Abbreviated title: E S S H. Variant title: Academic Journal E S S H. Text in English, French, German. 2000. a. adv. bk.rev. **Document type:** *Journal, Academic/Scholarly.* **Description:** Contains scientific papers on European sport history.
Published by: European Committee for Sports History, Via Marucelli 12, Rome, 00135, Italy.

➤ **EUROSLOT.** *see* BUSINESS AND ECONOMICS—Marketing And Purchasing

796.72 DEU
EUROSPORT MOTORMAGAZIN. Text in German. 2005. m. EUR 39.60; EUR 3.80 newsstand/cover (effective 2006). adv. **Document type:** *Magazine, Consumer.*
Published by: Motiv Medien GmbH, Postfach 6106, Wunstorf, 31509, Germany. TEL 49-5031-51830, FAX 49-5031-518311, info@motivmedien.de. Ed. Claudius Lueder. Pub. Frank Sievers. adv.: page EUR 7,140. Circ: 7,367 (paid).

790.1 GBR ISSN 0267-5358
EVENTING; the international magazine for the sport of horse trials. Text in English. 1985. m. GBP 34.99 domestic; USD 64.40 in US & Canada; EUR 70 in Europe; GBP 44.80 elsewhere; GBP 3.95 newsstand/cover (effective 2009). adv. bk.rev. back issues avail. **Document type:** *Magazine, Consumer.* **Description:** Provides an insight into the world of eventing, including news, results, features, opinions and instructional articles.
Published by: I P C Country & Leisure Media Ltd. (Subsidiary of: I P C Media Ltd.), The Blue Fin Bldg, 110 Southwark St, London, SE1 0SU, United Kingdom. TEL 44-20-31485000. Ed. Julie Harding TEL 44-20-31484545. Adv. contact Emma Sharp TEL 44-20-31484226. B&W page GBP 813, color page GBP 1,183; trim 210 x 297. Circ: 12,000. **Subscr. to:** Rockwood House, Perrymount Rd, Haywards Heath RH16 3DH, United Kingdom. TEL 44-845-1231231, IPCsubs@quadrantsubs.com, http://www.magazinesdirect.co.uk. **Dist. by:** MarketForce UK Ltd. salesinnovation@marketforce.co.uk, http://www.marketforce.co.uk/.

796.77 FRA ISSN 1774-5187
EVO. Text in French. 2005. bi-m. EUR 29 (effective 2009). **Document type:** *Magazine, Consumer.*
Published by: Bleucom Editions, 12-14 Rue de l'Eglise, Paris, 75015, France. TEL 33-1-45717500, direction@bleucom.net, http://www.bleucom.net/.

EXPLORE (CALGARY); Canada's outdoor magazine. *see* SPORTS AND GAMES—Outdoor Life

793.7 DEU
EXTRA; Reisen & Raten fuer alle. Text in German. 1987. m. EUR 1.80 newsstand/cover (effective 2011). adv. **Document type:** *Magazine, Consumer.*
Published by: Klambt Verlag GmbH, Im Neudeck 1, Speyer, 67346, Germany. TEL 49-6232-3100, FAX 49-6232-310226, info@klambt.de, http://www.klambt.de. Ed. Matthias Albrecht. Circ: 110,000 (paid).

EXTRA AUTODEFINIDOS EXPRESS. *see* HOBBIES

EXTRA AUTODEFINIDOS GOLD. *see* HOBBIES

EXTRA AUTODEFINIDOS QUICK. *see* HOBBIES

793.7 DEU
EXTRA RAETSEL. Text in German. bi-m. EUR 13.20; EUR 1.80 newsstand/cover (effective 2011). adv. **Document type:** *Magazine, Consumer.*
Published by: Deutscher Raetselverlag GmbH & Co. KG (Subsidiary of: Gong Verlag GmbH & Co. KG), Muenchener Str 101-09, Ismaning, 85737, Germany. TEL 49-89-272708620, FAX 49-89-272707890, info@raetsel.de, http://www.deutscher-raetselverlag.de. Circ: 115,000 (paid and controlled).

796.046 CAN
EXTREME. Text in English. 1993-1998; resumed 2004. bi-m. **Document type:** *Magazine, Consumer.*
Published by: Canadian Association Publishers, PO Box 90510, Scarborough, ON M1J 3N7, Canada. TEL 416-955-1550, FAX 416-955-1391, info@capmagazines.ca, http://www.capmagazines.ca/.

798.8 USA ISSN 1942-972X
EXTREME FIGHTING MAGAZINE. Text in English. 2008. q. USD 3.99 per issue domestic; USD 3.50 per issue in Mexico (effective 2008). **Document type:** *Magazine, Consumer.* **Description:** Features event coverage of mixed martial arts, fight results, profiles of MMA fighters as well as techniques and moves to improve performance.
Published by: U L A LLC, 4356 Gage Ave, Ste 202, Bell, CA 90201. editor@extremefighting.tv. Ed. Roger Grajeda. **Subscr. to:** PO Box 811873, Los Angeles, CA 90081.

796.72 BEL ISSN 1379-5503
F 1 I MAGAZINE/FORMULE UN INTENSE MAGAZINE. Text in French. 2001. 10/yr. adv. **Document type:** *Magazine, Consumer.*
Former titles (until 2003): F 1 Magazine (1624-6837); (until 2001): Grand Prix Special (1375-5358)
Published by: Editions Ventures, Lasne Business Park, 431D Chaussee de Louvain, Lasnes, 1380, Belgium. TEL 32-2-3792990, FAX 32-2-3792999.

796.71 FRA ISSN 1294-4513
F 1 RACING. (Formula 1) Variant title: Formule Un Racing. Text in French. 1999. m. EUR 39 (effective 2008). adv. back issues avail. **Document type:** *Magazine, Consumer.*
Published by: B & B Media, 40 Rue de Paradis, Paris, 75010, France. TEL 33-1-53249970, FAX 33-1-53249979, info@bandbmedia.com. **Subscr. to:** Viapresse, 7 Impasse Marie Blanche, Paris 75018, France. serviceclients@viapresse.com.

796.72 CZE ISSN 1213-0443
F 1 RACING. (Formula 1) Text in Czech. 1996. m. CZK 715 (effective 2009). adv. 48 p./no. 4 cols./p.; **Document type:** *Magazine, Consumer.*
Formerly (until 1999): Formule (1211-9601)
Published by: Stratosfera s.r.o., Drtinova 8, Prague 5, 150 00, Czech Republic. TEL 420-234-109540, FAX 420-234-109264, online@stratosfera.cz, http://www.stratosfera.cz. Adv. contact Martina Palkoskova. page CZK 130,000. Circ: 25,000 (paid). **Subscr. to:** SEND Predplatne s.r.o., PO Box 141, Prague 4 140 21, Czech Republic. TEL 420-225-985225, FAX 420-225-341425, send@send.cz.

796.72 TUR
F 1 RACING. (Formula 1) Text in Turkish. 2000. m. adv. **Document type:** *Magazine, Consumer.*
Published by: Dogus Yayin Group Corporation, Old Buyukdere St, USO Center No.61, Maslak, Istanbul, 80660, Turkey. TEL 90-212-3354820, FAX 90-212-3300323, info@dogusiletisim.com, http://www.dogusiletisim.com.

796.72 SWE ISSN 1651-5099
F 1 RACING. (Formula 1) Text in Swedish. 2002. m. SEK 599; SEK 69 per issue (effective 2006). adv. back issues avail. **Document type:** *Magazine, Consumer.*
Published by: First Publishing Group AB, Deltavaegen 3, PO Box 3187, Vaexjoe, 35043, Sweden. TEL 46-470-762400, FAX 46-470-762425, info@firstpublishing.se, http://www.firstpublishing.se. Ed. Mats Olsson. Adv. contact Magnus Kintzelt TEL 46-90-711528.

796.72 AUS
F 1 RACING. (Formula 1) Text in English. m. AUD 74.95; AUD 8.50 newsstand/cover (effective 2008). **Document type:** *Magazine, Consumer.*
Published by: Derwent Howard Media Pty Ltd., PO Box 1037, Bondi Junction, NSW 1355, Australia. TEL 61-2-83056900, FAX 61-2-83056999, enquiries@derwenthoward.com.au. Ed. Damian Francis. Adv. contact Toby de Pyper TEL 61-2-83056904. **Subscr. to:** Magshop, Reply Paid 4967, Sydney, NSW 2001, Australia. TEL 61-2-136116, subs@magstore.com.au, http://shop.magstore.com.au.

796.72 GBR ISSN 1361-4487
F 1 RACING. (Formula 1) Text in English. 1996. m. GBP 38.70 (effective 2009). adv. back issues avail. **Document type:** *Magazine, Consumer.* **Description:** Covers all aspects of Formula One car racing, including sites, personalities and automobiles.
Related titles: Polish ed.: ISSN 1732-7032.
—CCC.
Published by: Haymarket Publishing Ltd. (Subsidiary of: Haymarket Media Group), Teddington Studios, Broom Rd, Teddington, Middlesex, TW11 9BE, United Kingdom. TEL 44-20-82675630, FAX 44-20-82675759, info@haymarket.com, http://www.haymarket.com. Ed. Hans Seeberg TEL 44-20-82675198. Pub. Rob Aherne TEL 44-20-82675428. adv.: page GBP 5,490; trim 220 x 295. Circ: 58,806. **Subscr. to:** PO Box 568, Haywards Heath RH16 3XQ, United Kingdom. TEL 44-8456-777800, Haymarket.subs@qss-uk.com, http://www.themagazineshop.com.

796.75 FRA
F. F. M. ANNUAIRE - LIGUES, COMITES DEPARTEMENTAUX ET CLUBS. (Federation Francaise de Motocyclisme) Text in French. a. Price varies. adv.
Formerly: F. F. M. Annuaire Officiel (Print) (0071-4186)
Media: Online - full text.
Published by: Federation Francaise de Motocyclisme (F F M), 74 Av. Parmentier, Paris, 75011, France.

796.41 USA ISSN 1939-4837
F X M. Variant title: Great Lakes Fitness Extreme Magazine. Text in English. 2007. bi-m. USD 15 (effective 2007). **Document type:** *Magazine, Consumer.* **Description:** Features advice and techniques for bodybuilders, news about bodybuilding competitions and profiles of notable industry figures.
Published by: Great Lakes Publishing & Consulting, PO Box 320784, Flint, MI 48532. contact@xtrememusclemag.com. Pub. Joseph Janiga.

796 GBR ISSN 1750-6913
F1SHOUTBOX.NET. Variant title: F1shoutbox. Text in English. 2006. d. **Document type:** *Journal, Consumer.*
Media: Online - full text.
Published by: Formula One

796.962 GBR ISSN 1470-9597
FACE-OFF; the inline & ice hockey magazine. Text in English. m. GBP 29.95 domestic; GBP 44.95 in Europe; GBP 54.95 elsewhere (effective 2001). adv. **Document type:** *Magazine, Consumer.* **Description:** Covers all levels of ice hockey and as well as the growing inline hockey market.
Related titles: Online - full text ed.
Published by: Face-Off (UK) Ltd., Revenue Chambers, St Peter's St, Huddersfield, HD1 1DL, United Kingdom. TEL 44-1484-435011, FAX 44-1484-422177. Ed. Dave Hawkins. Adv. contact Moira Spencer. **Dist. by:** M M C Distribution Ltd, Octagon House, White Hart Meadows, Ripley, Woking, Surrey GU23 6HR, United Kingdom. TEL 44-1483-211222.

S

FACTS ON FILE. WORLD NEWS DIGEST YEARBOOK. *see* HISTORY—History Of North And South America

796.93 GBR ISSN 2046-2956
FALL-LINE SKIING & SNOWBOARDING. Text in English. 1991. bi-m. GBP 28.65 domestic; GBP 37.50 in Europe; GBP 44.90 in US & Canada; GBP 48.90 in Japan; GBP 3.95 newsstand/cover (effective 2011). adv. illus. back issues avail. **Document type:** *Magazine, Consumer.* **Description:** Features photos and articles on skiing, avalanches, and ski equipment.
Former titles (until 2010): Fall Line Skiing (1748-2909); (until 2001): Fall Line (0967-6759)
Related titles: Online - full text ed.
Published by: Fall Line Media Ltd., S Wing, Broadway Ct, Broadway, Peterborough, PE1 1RP, United Kingdom. TEL 44-1733-293250, FAX 44-1733-293269. Ed. Nicola Iseard. Pub. Richard Fincher. Adv. contact Sian Curphey.

790.1 TUR
FANATIK. Text in Turkish. 1995. d. adv. **Document type:** *Newspaper, Consumer.*
Published by: Dogan Yayin Holding/Dogan Media Center, Hurriyet Medya Towers, Gunesli, Istanbul, 34212, Turkey. TEL 90-212-6770000, support@dmg.com.tr, http://www.dmg.com.tr.

796 USA
FANTASY SPORTS REPORTER. Text in English. 2005. bi-m. USD 41.70 (effective 2005). **Document type:** *Magazine, Consumer.* **Description:** Covers fantasy football, baseball, basketball, golf, hockey, and NASCAR.
Published by: HumWare Media Corp., 78 Rogers Court, Golden, CO 80401. TEL 303-273-9446, FAX 720-226-0664, Info@humware.com, http://www.humware.com/.

793 028.5 USA
FANZINE PRESENTS: POKEMON GOLD COLLECTOR'S GUIDE. Text in English. 2000. m. **Document type:** *Magazine, Consumer.*
Published by: Fanzine International, Inc., 230 W 41st St, New York, NY 10036.

FAST FACTS. *see* AERONAUTICS AND SPACE FLIGHT

794 ESP
FEBOX-BOXEO. Text in Spanish. 1975 (no.19). m. USD 6.
Published by: Federacion Espanola Boxeo, Ferraz, 16, Madrid, 28008, Spain. TEL 34-91-5477791, FAX 34-91-5474297, info@feboxeo.com, http://www.feboxeo.com/.

796.86 CHE
FECHTEN/ESCRIME/SCHERMA. Text in German. 1978. q. **Document type:** *Trade.*
Indexed: SportS.
Published by: Schweizerischer Fechtverband, Postfach 856, Basel, 4001, Switzerland. TEL 41-61-2633329, FAX 41-61-2698770, info@swiss-fencing.ch, http://www.swiss-fencing.ch. Circ: 7,000.

796.86 DEU ISSN 0720-2229
FECHTSPORT. Text in German. 1980. bi-m. EUR 20; EUR 4 newsstand/cover (effective 2011). adv. bk.rev. 36 p./no.; back issues avail. **Document type:** *Magazine, Consumer.* **Description:** Contains information on all the activities of the German Fencing Federation.
—CCC.
Published by: (Deutscher Fechterbund e.V.), Meyer & Meyer Verlag, Von-Coels-Str 390, Aachen, 52080, Germany. TEL 49-241-958100, FAX 49-241-9581010, verlag@m-m-sports.com, http://m-m-sports.de. Circ: 15,000 (paid and controlled).

796 371.17 CHE ISSN 0428-1659
FEDERATION INTERNATIONALE DE GYMNASTIQUE. BULLETIN. Text in French. 1950. q. CHF 30 (effective 1997). adv. **Document type:** *Bulletin.*
Indexed: SD, SportS.
Published by: Federation Internationale de Gymnastique, Rue des Oeuches 10, Case Postale 359, Moutier, 2740, Switzerland. TEL 41-32-4946410, FAX 41-32-4946419, TELEX 934961-FIG-CH. Ed. Andre Gueisbuhler. Adv. contact Laurent Joliat.

799.3 CAN ISSN 0226-773X
FEDERATION OF CANADIAN ARCHERS. RULES BOOK. Text in English. 1984. irreg. CAD 10. **Document type:** *Bulletin.*
Related titles: French ed.: Livret des Reglements de la Federation Canadienne des Archers. ISSN 0706-3180.
Published by: Federation of Canadian Archers/Federation Canadienne des Archers, 1600 James Naismith Dr, Gloucester, ON K1B 5N4, Canada. TEL 613-748-5604, FAX 613-748-5785.

796.86 USA
FENCERS QUARTERLY MAGAZINE; fencing gear for the brain. Text in English. 1996. q. USD 14 domestic; USD 30 foreign; USD 3.50 newsstand/cover (effective 2001). adv. bk.rev.; film rev.; video rev.; Website rev. illus. 36 p./no.; back issues avail. **Document type:** *Magazine, Consumer.*
Formerly (until Jun. 2000): Veteran Fencers Quarterly
Address: 6751 CR 3850, Peace Valley, MO 65788. TEL 417-256-0432. Ed., R&P, Adv. contact Nick Evangelista. page USD 225. Circ: 5,000 (paid).

793.7 HRV ISSN 1330-8572
FENIKS. Text in Croatian. 1994. fortn. **Document type:** *Magazine, Consumer.*
Published by: Novi List, Zvonimirova 20a, Rijeka, 51000, Croatia. TEL 385-51-650011, FAX 385-51-672114. Ed. Pero Galoza.

796.77 ITA ISSN 1828-8081
LA FERRARI GRANTURISMO. Text in Italian. 2000. w. **Document type:** *Magazine, Consumer.*
Published by: De Agostini Editore, Via G da Verrazzano 15, Novara, 28100, Italy. TEL 39-0321-4241, FAX 39-0321-424305, info@deagostini.it, http://www.deagostini.it.

796.355 USA
GV1017.H7
FIELD HOCKEY RULES BOOK. Text in English. 19??. a. USD 6.95 per issue (effective 2009). adv. **Document type:** *Handbook/Manual/Guide, Trade.* **Description:** Contains the official rules for field hockey and is used by coaches, officials, players and many fans who wish to know more about the rules of the game.
Formerly: Field Hockey Rules. National Federation Edition (0275-5394)
Published by: National Federation of State High School Associations, PO Box 690, Indianapolis, IN 46206. TEL 317-972-6900, 800-776-3462, FAX 317-822-5700, info@nfhs.org, http://www.nfhs.org.

798.8 USA ISSN 1941-3270
FIGHT!; the premier mixed martial arts magazine. Text in English. 2007. m. USD 19.95 (effective 2010). adv. **Document type:** *Magazine, Consumer.*
Published by: Bluff Media, 1200 Lake Hearn Dr Ste 450, Atlanta, GA 30319. TEL 404-250-1798, FAX 404-250-1943, http://www.bluffmagazine.com. Ed. Donovan Craig TEL 404-250-1798 ext 124. adv.: color page USD 10,555; trim 8.375 x 10.875.

796.81 FRA ISSN 1957-1755
FIGHT INSIDE. Text in French. 2006. irreg. **Document type:** *Magazine, Consumer.*
Published by: Antigua, 24 Bd Paul Vaillant Couturier, Ivry sur Seine, 94200, France. TEL 33-8-92231836, FAX 33-1-43901999.

796.8 FRA ISSN 1954-1929
FIGHT TALK; paroles de combattants. Text in French. 2006. bi-m. **Document type:** *Magazine, Consumer.*
Published by: Antigua, 24 Bd Paul Vaillant Couturier, Ivry sur Seine, 94200, France. TEL 33-8-92231836, FAX 33-1-43901999.

796.805 NZL
FIGHT TIMES. Text in English. 2004. bi-m. adv. **Document type:** *Magazine, Consumer.*
Related titles: Online - full text ed.: ISSN 1176-8266.
Address: PO Box 5579, Dunedin, New Zealand. TEL 64-3-4778902, FAX 64-3-4778902, nzcqb@es.co.nz.

798.8 GBR ISSN 2042-8219
▼ **FIGHTING FIT.** Text in English. 2009. bi-m. GBP 19.99 domestic; GBP 32.99 foreign; GBP 4.35 per issue (effective 2010). adv. back issues avail. **Document type:** *Magazine, Trade.*
Published by: Newsquest Specialist Media Ltd., 30 Cannon St, London, EC4M 6YJ, United Kingdom. TEL 44-20-76183456, info@newsquestspecialistmedia.com, http://www.newsquestspecialistmedia.com. Ed. Tris Dixon TEL 44-20-76183072. Adv. contact Steve Turner TEL 44-20-76183428.

796.8 FRA ISSN 1767-4034
FIGHTSPORT. Text in French. 2004. bi-m. **Document type:** *Magazine, Consumer.*
Related titles: Ed.: ISSN 1777-0459. 2005; Supplement(s): Les Cahiers Techniques du M M A. ISSN 1965-1643. 2009.
Published by: Antigua, 24 Bd Paul Vaillant Couturier, Ivry sur Seine, 94200, France. TEL 33-8-92231836, FAX 33-1-43901999.

796.815 USA ISSN 1540-0158
FIGHTSPORT. Text in English. 2002. bi-m. USD 24 domestic; USD 48 in Canada (effective 2002).
Published by: Black Belt Communications, Inc. (Subsidiary of: Active Interest Media), 24900 Anza Dr, Unit E, Valencia, CA 91355. Ed. Stephen Quadros. Pub. Richard Price.

790.1 USA ISSN 0147-0051
FIRE & MOVEMENT; the forum of conflict simulation. Abbreviated title: F & M. Text in English. 1976. q. USD 8 per issue (effective 2010). adv. bk.rev. illus. Index. 48 p./no.; back issues avail.; reprints avail. **Document type:** *Magazine, Consumer.* **Description:** Publishes reviews of historical board games and family games.
Published by: Decision Games, PO Box 21598, Bakersfield, CA 93390. TEL 661-587-9633, FAX 661-587-5031, dgservice@earthlink.net. Ed. Jon Compton. Circ: 2,000.

795.412 SWE ISSN 1653-5642
FIRST POKER. Text in Swedish. 2005. m. SEK 489 (effective 2006). adv. **Document type:** *Magazine, Consumer.*
Published by: First Publishing Group AB, Deltavaegen 3, PO Box 3187, Vaexjoe, 35043, Sweden. TEL 46-470-762400, FAX 46-470-762425, info@firstpublishing.se, http://www.firstpublishing.se. adv.: page SEK 29,000; trim 210 x 297.

FIT FOR FUN. *see* PHYSICAL FITNESS AND HYGIENE

FIT FOR FUN. *see* PHYSICAL FITNESS AND HYGIENE

790.1 USA
FITNESS AMERICA. Text in English. 1984. m. adv. **Document type:** *Magazine, Consumer.* **Description:** Covers recreational fitness and bodybuilding.
Formerly (until 1999): American Sports
Related titles: Online - full text ed.
Published by: American Sports Network Inc., PO Box 6100, Rosemead, CA 91770. TEL 626-280-0000, FAX 626-280-0001.

796.015 613.7 NLD ISSN 1877-8232
FITNESS EXPERT. Text in Dutch. 1994. q. EUR 46.50 (effective 2011). adv. **Document type:** *Magazine, Trade.*
Former titles (until 2009): Fitness Update (1572-7599); (until 2003): Club Business Update (1571-9804); Which was formed by the merger of (2000-2002): Club Business Update. Manager (1568-2021); (2000-2002): Club Business Update. Instructor (1568-203X); Which was superseded in part (in 2001): Club Business Update (1389-2878); Which was formerly (1994-1998): E F A A Update (1568-993X)
Published by: (European Fitness and Aerobics Association), EFAA Health Management, Houtstraat 14, Weert, 6001 SJ, Netherlands. TEL 31-495-533229, FAX 31-495-520791, info@efaa.nl. Ed. Babette Marges. Adv. contact Nicole Timmerman. Circ: 2,500.

796 RUS ISSN 0130-5670
FIZKUL'TURA I SPORT. Text in Russian. 1922. m. USD 164 foreign (effective 2005). bibl.; illus. index. **Document type:** *Magazine, Consumer.*
—East View.
Address: Dolgorukovskaya ul 27, Moscow, 101421, Russian Federation. TEL 7-095-9721732. Ed. Igor Yur'evich Sosnovskii. Circ: 38,000. **Dist. by:** East View Information Services, 10601 Wayzata Blvd, Minneapolis, MN 55305. TEL 952-252-1201, 800-477-1005, FAX 952-252-1202, info@eastview.com, http://www.eastview.com.

796.7 IRL ISSN 1649-6663
FLAT 2 THE MAT. Text in English. 2005. w. EUR 178 (effective 2006).
Published by: Flat2theMat, High Rd, Letterkenny, Co. Donegal, Ireland. TEL 353-74-9126410.

FLIEGER-REVUE; Magazin fuer Luft- und Raumfahrt. *see* AERONAUTICS AND SPACE FLIGHT

FLORAL UNDERAWL & GAZETTE TIMES. *see* HOBBIES

790.1 USA
FLORIDA SPORTS MAGAZINE. Text in English. 1987. m. USD 25 (effective 2002). adv. **Description:** Includes sports such as aerobic dance, bicycling, bodybuilding, golf, martial arts, racquetball, rugby, running, sailing, snow skiing, swimming, tennis, triathlon, and water polo. Features sports and athlete profiles, event coverage, training suggestions, nutrition and sports medicine columns, travel section, multi-sport calendar, and club listings.
Formerly: Florida Sports Review (0891-7949)
Published by: Competitor, Inc., 605 Belvedere Rd, 9, West Palm Beach, FL 33045. TEL 561-838-9060, FAX 561-838-9037. Pubs. Bob Babbit, John Smith, Lois Schwartz. Adv. contact John Smith. Circ: 70,000.

790.1 USA ISSN 1085-5769
SH456.2
FLY FISHING IN SALTWATERS. Text in English. 1994. bi-m. USD 19.97 domestic; USD 25.97 in Canada; USD 31.97 elsewhere; USD 4.99 newsstand/cover (effective 2008). adv. bk.rev.; video rev. back issues avail.; reprints avail. **Document type:** *Magazine, Consumer.* **Description:** Guides the saltwater fly fishermen with healthy doses of techniques and product coverage, along with features of prime saltwater fishing destinations.
Related titles: Online - full text ed.: USD 19.97 (effective 2008).
Indexed: P52, P56.
—CCC.
Published by: World Publications LLC (Subsidiary of: Bonnier Magazine Group), 460 N Orlando Ave, Ste 200, Winter Park, FL 32789. TEL 407-628-4802, FAX 407-628-7061, info@worldpub.net, http://www.bonniercorp.com. Eds. Mike Mazur, Scott Leon. Pubs. Gary Jennings TEL 407-571-4856, Glenn Hughes. Adv. contact Gary Jennings TEL 407-571-4856. B&W page USD 3,375, color page USD 4,515; trim 8.125 x 10.75. Circ: 27,384 (paid). **Dist. in UK by:** Seymour Distribution Ltd, 86 Newman St, London W1T 3EX, United Kingdom.

FLYMAGASINET; medlemsblad for AOPA Norway. *see* AERONAUTICS AND SPACE FLIGHT

FLYV. *see* AERONAUTICS AND SPACE FLIGHT

FOOTBALL HANDBOOK (INDIANAPOLIS). *see* SPORTS AND GAMES—Ball Games

FOOTBALL OFFICIALS HANDBOOK. *see* SPORTS AND GAMES—Ball Games

FOOTBALL OFFICIALS MANUAL. *see* SPORTS AND GAMES—Ball Games

FOOTBALL RULES BOOK. *see* SPORTS AND GAMES—Ball Games

FOOTBALL RULES - SIMPLIFIED AND ILLUSTRATED. *see* SPORTS AND GAMES—Ball Games

796.72 DEU ISSN 1614-662X
FORMEL 1 - F1 RACING. Text in German. 2004. m. EUR 54 domestic; EUR 62.60 foreign (effective 2008). adv. **Document type:** *Magazine, Consumer.*
Formed by the merger of (1996-2004): F1 Racing (1611-5635); (1994-2004): Formel 1 (0948-5333)
Published by: B P A Sportpresse GmbH, Leonhardtstr 2a, Hannover, 30175, Germany. TEL 49-511-1233280, FAX 49-511-12332811, verlag@bpa-sportpresse.de, http://www.bpa-sportpresse.de.

796.72 ITA
FORMULA 1 CHAMPIONSHIP YEARBOOK (ITALIAN EDITION). Text in Italian. a., latest 2001. price varies. **Document type:** *Yearbook, Consumer.*
Related titles: ◆ English ed.: Formula 1 (Year) Championship Yearbook. ISSN 1527-5337.
Published by: S E P Editrice, Via Roma 74, Cassina de Pecchi, MI 20060, Italy. TEL 39-02-9520026, FAX 39-02-9522330, info@sepeditrice.it, http://www.sepeditrice.com.

796.72 USA ISSN 1527-5337
GV1029
FORMULA 1 (YEAR) CHAMPIONSHIP YEARBOOK; the complete record of the Grand Prix season. Text in English. 1999. a., latest 2001. USD 34.95 newsstand/cover (effective 2001). charts; illus.; stat. 202 p./no. 4 cols./p.; back issues avail. **Document type:** *Yearbook, Consumer.* **Description:** Provides an overview of the year's Formula 1 car racing activity.
Related titles: ◆ Italian ed.: Formula 1 Championship Yearbook (Italian Edition); Regional ed(s).: Formula 1 Championship Yearbook (United Kingdom Edition).
Published by: Voyageur Press, Inc., 123 N Second St, Stillwater, MN 55082. TEL 651-430-2210, 800-888-9633, FAX 651-430-2211, books@voyageurpress.com, http://www.voyageurpress.com. Ed., R&P Michael Dregni TEL 651-430-2210 ext 12. Pub. Tom Lebovsky. Adv. contact Dennis Tomfohrde TEL 651-430-2210 ext 18. Circ: 100,000 (paid).

796.72 NLD ISSN 1878-867X
▼ **FORMULE1.NL.** Text in Dutch. 2009. 19/yr. EUR 60; EUR 4.75 newsstand/cover (effective 2011). adv. illus. back issues avail. **Document type:** *Magazine, Consumer.* **Description:** Covers the entire world of Formula 1 auto racing worldwide.
Formed by the merger of (1994-2009): Formule 1 (1386-0887); (2006-2009): Formule 1 Racereport (1878-8661)
Published by: Sanoma Men's Magazines, Haaksbergweg 75, Amsterdam (ZO), 1101 BR, Netherlands. TEL 31-20-7518000, FAX 31-20-7518301, sales@smm.nl, http://www.smm.nl. Ed. Tonie Broekhuijsen. Pub. Eric Ariens.

796.09489 DNK ISSN 1904-2183
GV627
➤ **FORUM FOR IDRAET**; historie og samfund. Text in Danish; Text occasionally in English. 1985. s-a. DKK 198 (effective 2011). back issues avail. **Document type:** *Magazine, Academic/Scholarly.*
Formerly (until 2009): Idraetshistorisk Aarbog (0900-8632)
Published by: (Denmark. Forum for Idraet, Historie og Samfund), Syddansk Universitetsforlag/University Press of Southern Denmark, Campusvej 55, Odense M, 5230, Denmark. TEL 45-66-157999, FAX 45-66-158126, press@forlag.sdu.dk. Eds. Bo Vestergaard Madsen, Linnea Ytting. Circ: 700.

796 371.3 DEU ISSN 1868-8683
▼ **FORUM SPORTPAEDAGOGIK.** Text in German. 2009. irreg. price varies. **Document type:** *Monographic series, Academic/Scholarly.*

Published by: Shaker Verlag GmbH, Kaiserstr 100, Herzogenrath, 52134, Germany. TEL 49-2407-95960, FAX 49-2407-95969, info@shaker.de, http://www.shaker.de.

796 028.5 FRA ISSN 1961-3873
FOU 2 SPORT. Variant title: Fou deux Sport. Text in French. 2008. m. **Document type:** *Magazine, Consumer.*
Published by: F 2 S, Hotel d'Entreprises, Parc des Saules, Val de Reuil, 27100, France. TEL 33-2-32562468, contact@f2s-editions.fr.

796.962 CAN
THE FOURTH PERIOD; hockey lifestyle magazine. Text in English. q. CAD 9; CAD 4.95 newsstand/cover (effective 2010). adv. **Document type:** *Magazine, Consumer.* **Description:** Contains professional ice hockey features, celebrity interviews, behind-the-scenes coverage, player profiles, and in-depth team analysis.
Published by: T F P Media, Inc., 4-2880 Queen St E, Ste 242, Brampton, ON L6S 6H4, Canada. TEL 905-794-7701. Ed. David Pagnotta. Circ: 50,000 (paid and controlled).

796 USA ISSN 1930-4609
FOX SPORTS EN ESPANOL MAGAZINE. Text in Spanish. 2006. m. **Document type:** *Magazine, Consumer.*
Published by: Cuatro Media, Inc., 230 Park Ave, Ste 1512, New York, NY 10169. http://www.cuatro-media.com/.

796.93 051 USA
FREESKIER. Text in English. 1998. 4/yr. USD 9.95 (effective 2004). illus. **Document type:** *Magazine, Consumer.* **Description:** Includes ski features, humor, photography, ski news, product reviews, and more.
Published by: Storm Mountain Publishing Co., 1630 30th St, 272, Boulder, CO 80301. TEL 303-449-2165, FAX 303-449-2427. Ed. Patrick Crawford. Pub. Bradford Fayfield. Circ: 56,000.

793.7 DEU
FREIZEIT REVUE PROFI RAETSEL. Variant title: Profi Raetsel. Text in German. 13/yr. EUR 1.60 newsstand/cover (effective 2010). adv. **Document type:** *Magazine, Consumer.*
Published by: Burda Senator Verlag GmbH (Subsidiary of: Hubert Burda Media Holding GmbH & Co. KG), Am Kestendamm 1, Offenburg, 77652, Germany. TEL 49-781-842264, FAX 49-781-842034, http://www.hubert-burda-media.com. Ed. Gabriele Henkel. Circ: 105,000 (controlled).

793.7 DEU
FREIZEIT REVUE RAETSEL HITPARADE. Variant title: Raetsel Hitparade. Text in German. 6/yr. EUR 1.60 newsstand/cover (effective 2010). adv. **Document type:** *Magazine, Consumer.*
Published by: Burda Senator Verlag GmbH (Subsidiary of: Hubert Burda Media Holding GmbH & Co. KG), Am Kestendamm 1, Offenburg, 77652, Germany. TEL 49-781-842264, FAX 49-781-842034, http://www.hubert-burda-media.com. Ed. Gabriele Henkel. Circ: 93,500 (paid and controlled).

793.7 DEU
FREIZEIT REVUE SENATOR RAETSEL. Variant title: Senator Raetsel. Text in German. m. EUR 1.50 newsstand/cover (effective 2010). adv. **Document type:** *Magazine, Consumer.*
Published by: Burda Senator Verlag GmbH (Subsidiary of: Hubert Burda Media Holding GmbH & Co. KG), Am Kestendamm 1, Offenburg, 77652, Germany. TEL 49-781-842264, FAX 49-781-842034, http://www.hubert-burda-media.com. Ed. Gabriele Henkel. Circ: 124,500 (paid and controlled).

793.7 DEU
FREIZEIT REVUE SPECIAL RAETSEL. Text in German. 13/yr. EUR 1.50 newsstand/cover (effective 2010). adv. **Document type:** *Magazine, Consumer.*
Published by: Burda Senator Verlag GmbH (Subsidiary of: Hubert Burda Media Holding GmbH & Co. KG), Am Kestendamm 1, Offenburg, 77652, Germany. TEL 49-781-842264, FAX 49-781-842034, http://www.hubert-burda-media.com. Ed. Gabriele Henkel. Circ: 167,500 (paid and controlled).

793.7 DEU ISSN 0948-6496
FREIZEIT UND RAETSELMAGAZIN; Raetseln, Raten & Gewinnen. Text in German. 1994. m. EUR 1.60 newsstand/cover (effective 2011). adv. **Document type:** *Magazine, Consumer.* **Description:** Contains puzzles and games of amusement with chances to win prizes and money.
Published by: Klambt Verlag GmbH, Im Neudeck 1, Speyer, 67346, Germany. TEL 49-6232-3100, FAX 49-6232-310226, info@klambt.de, http://www.klambt.de. Ed. Matthias Albrecht. Circ: 125,000 (paid).

790.1 NOR ISSN 0332-9666
FRIIDRETT. Text in Norwegian. 1950. 6/yr. NOK 310 (effective 2006). adv. **Document type:** *Magazine, Consumer.* **Description:** Focuses on athletics in Norway.
Incorporates (1980-1982): Trening, utdanning, friidrett (0333-0354) —CCC.
Published by: (Norges Friidrettsforbund/Norwegian Athletics Association), Sportsmedia AS, Myrveien 3, PO Box A, Askim, 1801, Norway. TEL 47-69-819700, FAX 47-69-889980, http:// www.sportsmedia.no. Ed. Henrik Hasboe. Adv. contact Bjoern Gaaserud TEL 47-90-699488. Circ: 5,000.

FRITID MAGASIN. *see* SPORTS AND GAMES—Bicycles And Motorcycles

340 USA ISSN 1054-1950
KF3989.A15
FROM THE GYM TO THE JURY; State of the Art Risk Management Strategies. Text in English. 1989. 5/yr. USD 69 (effective 2001). index. **Document type:** *Newsletter, Trade.* **Description:** Provides the latest information on legal issues involving sports.
Published by: Center for Sports Law and Risk Management, 8080 North Central Expwy, Ste 400, Dallas, TX 75206. TEL 800-379-7767, FAX 214-739-1749. Ed. Herb Appenzeller TEL 336-643-0701. Pub., R&P Ron Baron.

799.31 ITA ISSN 1825-1056
FUCILI & MITRA. Text in Italian. 2005. s-m. **Document type:** *Magazine, Consumer.*
Published by: R C S Libri (Subsidiary of: R C S Mediagroup), Via Mecenate 91, Milan, 20138, Italy. TEL 39-02-5095-2248, FAX 39-02-5095-2975, http://rcslibri.corriere.it/libri/index.htm.

790.1 617.1 CHN ISSN 1004-8790
FUJIAN TIYU KEJI/FUJIAN SPORTS SCIENCE AND TECHNOLOGY. Text in Chinese. 1982. bi-m. CNY 7 newsstand/cover (effective 2006). **Document type:** *Journal, Academic/Scholarly.* **Description:** Covers sports theory, training, psychology, medicine as well as sports biophysics and biochemistry.
Related titles: Online - full text ed.
Published by: Fujiansheng Tiyu Kexue Yanjiusuo/Fujian Sports Science Institute, 151, Fufei Lu, Fuzhou, 350003, China. TEL 86-591-87712714. Ed. He Fangsheng. **Co-sponsor:** Fujian Tiyu Kexue Xuehui.

FUN FOR KIDZ. *see* CHILDREN AND YOUTH—For

▼ **FUNCTIONAL SPORTS NUTRITION JOURNAL.** *see* NUTRITION AND DIETETICS

796.815 USA ISSN 1083-9631
FURYU; the budo journal. Text in English. 1994. q. USD 36 domestic for 6 nos.; USD 40 in Canada for 6 nos.; USD 50 elsewhere for 6 nos. **Document type:** *Magazine, Consumer.* **Description:** Features about the elegant, classical time-honored and historical aspects of traditional Japanese martial arts.
Related titles: Online - full text ed.: Furyu Online.
Published by: Tengu Press, PO Box 61637, Honolulu, HI 96839. Ed., Pub. Wayne Muromoto. **Dist. by:** Desert Moon Periodicals, 1226 A Calle de Comercio, Santa Fe, NM 87505. TEL 505-474-6311, FAX 505-474-6317.

FUSSBALLTRAINING. *see* SPORTS AND GAMES—Ball Games

G O R P TRAVEL NEWSLETTER. *see* TRAVEL AND TOURISM

795 USA ISSN 1941-9872
G P W A TIMES. Text in English. 2007. q. **Document type:** *Newsletter, Trade.* **Description:** Provides information of interest to the portal webmaster community for gaming and gambling websites.
Related titles: Online - full text ed.: ISSN 1941-9880.
Published by: Gambling Portal Webmasters Association, Casino City, 95 Wells Ave, Newton Centre, MA 02459. TEL 617-332-2850, FAX 617-964-2280.

796 305.4 USA
G W S NEWS. (Girls and Women in Sport) Text in English. 3/yr. **Document type:** *Newsletter.* **Description:** Contains updates on the latest NAGWS happenings, advocacy efforts, publications, research and other information affecting girls and women in sport.
Media: Online - full text.
Indexed: GW.
Published by: National Association for Girls and Women in Sport, 1900 Association Dr, Reston, VA 20191. TEL 703-476-3400, http:// www.aahperd.org/nagws.

790.1 IRL ISSN 0791-1521
GAELIC SPORT. Text in English. 1958. bi-m. bk.rev. **Document type:** *Magazine, Consumer.*
Indexed: SportS.
Published by: Holyrood Publications Ltd., 136 Baldoyle Industrial Estate, Baldoyle, Dublin, 13, Ireland. TEL 353-1-8395060, FAX 353-1-8395062, paul@irishbroker.ie. Ed. Thomas McQuaid. Adv. contact Paul Gibson. Circ: 38,612.

790.1 059.916 IRL ISSN 0332-1274
GAELIC WORLD; iris oifigiuil Cumann Luthchleas Gael. Text in English. 1979. m. adv. bk.rev. illus. **Document type:** *Magazine, Consumer.* **Description:** Covers Gaelic football, hurling and handball.
Published by: Costar Associates, 13 Abbey Lane, Abbey Farm, Celbridge, Co. Kildare, Ireland. TEL 353-1-6279666, FAX 353-1-6279667. Pub., R&P, Adv. contact Michael Wright. color page EUR 2,200; trim 210 x 297. Circ: 26,500.

798.8 ESP
GALGOS. Text in Spanish. 1977 (vol.29). bi-m. adv. **Document type:** *Magazine, Consumer.*
Formerly (until Oct. 1979): Federacion Espanola Galguera. Boletin Mensual Informativo
Published by: Federacion Espanola de Galgos, Barquillo, 38 1o., Madrid, 28004, Spain. TEL 34-91-3198262, FAX 34-91-7024046, info@fedegalgos.com, http://www.fedegalgos.com/. Circ: 2,500.

GALLERIA FERRARI. YEARBOOK. *see* TRANSPORTATION—Automobiles

794.1 ROM ISSN 1222-5754
GAMBIT. Text in Romanian. 1950. bi-m. **Document type:** *Magazine, Consumer.* **Description:** Contains national and international chess news plus games, theory, problems.
Former titles (until 1994): Revista Romana de Sah (1220-5516); (until 1974): Revista de Sah (1220-5575)
Published by: Clubul de Sah Elisabeta Polihroniade/Chess Club Elisabeta Polihroniade http://www.elisabetapolihroniade.ro.

790.1 CAN
THE GAMBLER. Text in English. 2001. m. adv. **Document type:** *Magazine, Consumer.*
Published by: Evermore Publishing, 1600 Steeles Ave W, Unit 18, Concord, ON L4K 4M2, Canada.

795 GBR
GAMBLING.COM. Text in English. 2006. bi-m. free to Platinum Members. adv. **Document type:** *Magazine, Consumer.* **Description:** Covers online gambling, including personalities, strategies, news and general interest articles.
Published by: Newbold Enterprises Ltd., 17 Seaton House, Seaton Pl., St. Helier, Jersey JE2 3QL, United Kingdom. adv.: page GBP 5,000, page USD 8,750; trim 8 x 10.5. Circ: 50,000.

795.38 GBR ISSN 2043-9466
▼ **GAMBLING INSIDER.** Text in English. 2010. 3/yr. **Document type:** *Magazine, Trade.* **Description:** Covers interviews with CEOs and top government officials to market analysis and trends to provide knowledge about gambling industry.
Published by: Players Publishing Ltd., 7 Chapel Pl, Rivington St, London, EC2A 3DQ, United Kingdom. TEL 44-20-77396999, FAX 44-20-77399918, info@playerspublishing.co.uk.

GAMBLING MATTERS. *see* MEDICAL SCIENCES—Psychiatry And Neurology

793 USA ISSN 2150-2587
GV1469.6
▼ **GAME FORCES.** Text in English. 2009. bi-m. USD 9.99 per issue (effective 2009). **Document type:** *Magazine, Consumer.* **Description:** Features information on miniatures for gaming.
Published by: CoolMini Or Not, 4910 Bagley Ter, Alpharetta, GA 30004. TEL 415-671-6250, chernann@coolminiornot.com, http:// www.coolminiornot.com/.

791.8 USA ISSN 0016-4313
GAMECOCK (HARTFORD). Text in English. 1935. m. (Aug.-Sep. combined). USD 25 domestic; USD 40 foreign (effective 2005). adv. **Document type:** *Magazine, Trade.*
Published by: Marburger Publishing Co., Inc., PO Box 158, Hartford, AR 72938-0158. Pub. J C Griffiths. adv.: B&W page USD 250, color page USD 400. Circ: 9,000 (paid).

GAMEPRO; where gamers go first!. *see* COMPUTERS—Computer Games

790.1 USA ISSN 1061-611X
GAMER'S CONNECTION. Text in English. 1992. q. USD 8. adv. bk.rev. back issues avail. **Document type:** *Newspaper, Consumer.* **Description:** Covers role-playing games. Presents product reviews, supplemental rules, gamemaster tips, humor, and game industry news.
Published by: Gold Rush Games, Box 2531, Elk Grove, CA 95759-2531. mark@goldrushgames.com, http://www.goldrushgames.com. Ed., Adv. contact Mark Arsenault. page USD 250; trim 16 x 10.

THE GAMES. *see* BUSINESS AND ECONOMICS—Economic Situation And Conditions

790.1 USA ISSN 0199-9788
GV1199
GAMES; the magazine for creative minds at play. Text in English. 1977-1990; resumed 1991. 10/yr. USD 26.95 domestic; USD 45.45 foreign (effective 2009). adv. bk.rev. illus. back issues avail.; reprints avail. **Document type:** *Magazine, Consumer.* **Description:** Features a wide variety of verbal and visual puzzles, brainteasers, trivia quizzes, contests, as well as reviews of new board games and electronic games.
Indexed: CBRI, JHMA.
Published by: Games Publications, Inc. (Subsidiary of: Kappa Publishing Group, Inc.), PO Box 184, Fort Washington, PA 19034. TEL 215-643-6385, FAX 215-628-3571.

GAMES & BUSINESS; Fachzeitschrift fuer das moderne Muenzspiel. *see* BUSINESS AND ECONOMICS—Management

793.9 794.8 USA ISSN 1555-4120
GV1469.17.S63
➤ **GAMES AND CULTURE**; a journal of interactive media. Text in English. 2006. q. USD 626, GBP 368 combined subscription to institutions (print & online eds.); USD 613, GBP 361 to institutions (effective 2011). adv. reprint service avail. from PSC. **Document type:** *Journal, Academic/Scholarly.* **Description:** Aims to publish innovative theoretical and empirical research about games and culture within the context of interactive media.
Related titles: Online - full text ed.: ISSN 1555-4139. 2006. USD 563, GBP 331 to institutions (effective 2011).
Indexed: A22, ArtHuCI, CurCont, E01, P03, PsycInfo, SCOPUS, SSCI, SociolAb, W07.
—BLDSC (4069.167500), IE. **CCC.**
Published by: Sage Publications, Inc., 2455 Teller Rd, Thousand Oaks, CA 91320. TEL 805-499-9774, 800-818-7243, FAX 805-499-0871, 800-583-2665, info@sagepub.com, http://www.sagepub.com. Ed. Douglas Thomas. **Subscr. to:** Sage Publications Ltd., 1 Oliver's Yard, 55 City Rd, London EC1Y 1SP, United Kingdom. TEL 44-207-3248701, FAX 44-207-3248733, subscription@sagepub.co.uk.

795 ZAF ISSN 1025-210X
GAMING FOR AFRICA. Text in English. 1995. bi-m. ZAR 95 domestic; ZAR 395 foreign (effective 2001). adv. **Document type:** *Magazine, Trade.* **Description:** Covers developments in legislation, new products, marketing and sales, promotions and general casino resort tourism trends in Africa.
Published by: Afrogames (Pty) Ltd., PO Box 2561, North Riding, Johannesburg, 2162, South Africa. TEL 27-11-704-3147, FAX 27-11-704-1616. Ed., Pub. Roy Bannister. Adv. contact Ronel Gauche. color page ZAR 7,150; trim 210 x 297. Circ: 8,000 (paid and controlled).

GAMING LAW REVIEW & ECONOMICS; regulation, compliance, and policy. *see* LAW

GAMING SYSTEMS SOURCE DIRECTORY. *see* BUSINESS AND ECONOMICS—Trade And Industrial Directories

796 USA ISSN 1531-7463
GATOR BAIT MAGAZINE. Text in English. 19??. 30/yr. (w. mid-Aug.-Apr.; m. May-Jul.). adv. **Document type:** *Magazine, Consumer.* **Description:** Covers University of Florida sports.
Formerly: Gator Bait (0744-0995)
Published by: 247 Sports, PO Box 1498, Shelbyville, KY 40066. TEL 888-474-8669, info@247sports.com, http://247sports.com.

794 USA ISSN 2151-8335
GATOR COUNTRY. Text in English. 2006. m. free to members (effective 2010). adv. back issues avail. **Document type:** *Magazine, Consumer.* **Description:** Features stories and information, the latest recruiting news, excellent commentary, and outstanding photographs about University of Florida sports.
Related titles: Online - full text ed.: ISSN 2151-8343.
Published by: Florida Media Inc., 999 Douglas Ave, Ste 3301, Altamonte Springs, FL 32714 . TEL 407-816-9596, sales@floridamagazine.com. Pub. Raymond Hines III. adv.: color page USD 2,274; bleed 7 x 10.

790.1 PRT ISSN 0870-1989
GAZETA DOS DESPORTOS. Text in Portuguese. 1981. 3/w. USD 90. **Document type:** *Newspaper.*
Address: Rua dos Caetanos, 26 1o, Lisbon, 1200, Portugal. TEL 346-05-17, FAX 346-05-44. Ed. Eugenio Queiros.

796 ROM ISSN 1220-8248
GAZETA SPORTURILOR. Text in Romanian. 1967. d. **Document type:** *Newspaper, Consumer.*
Formerly (until 1989): Sportul (1221-1958)
Published by: Jurnalul SA, Piata Presei Libere nr. 1, corp D, et. 8, sector 1, Bucharest, Romania. TEL 40-21-2243866, FAX 40-21-2229082, jurnalul@jurnalul.ro, http://www.jurnalul.ro.

S

790.1 ITA ISSN 1120-5067
LA GAZZETTA DELLO SPORT; lo sport come emozione. Text in Italian. 1897. d. adv. video rev. illus. **Document type:** *Newspaper, Consumer.* **Description:** Reports on sports activities and news in Italy and worldwide. Includes game scores and commentary.
Related titles: CD-ROM ed.; Online - full text ed.; ◆ Supplement(s): La Gazzetta dello Sport. I Quaderni. ISSN 1120-5180.
Published by: R C S Quotidiani (Subsidiary of: R C S Mediagroup), Via San Marco 21, Milan, 20121, Italy. TEL 39-02-25844111, http://www.rcsmediagroup.it. Ed. Candido Cannavo.

790.1 ITA ISSN 1120-5180
LA GAZZETTA DELLO SPORT. I QUADERNI. Text in Italian. 1977. irreg. **Document type:** *Magazine, Consumer.*
Related titles: ◆ Supplement to: La Gazzetta dello Sport. ISSN 1120-5067.
Published by: R C S Quotidiani (Subsidiary of: R C S Mediagroup), Via San Marco 21, Milan, 20121, Italy. TEL 39-02-25844111, http://www.rcsmediagroup.it.

794 NLD ISSN 1879-3681
▼ **GEBRUIK JE HERSENS SCHEURKALENDER.** Text in Dutch. 2009. a. EUR 8.99 (effective 2011).
Published by: Uitgeverij Verba, Birkstraat 143A, Soest, 3768 HE, Netherlands. TEL 31-33-4943909, FAX 31-33-4655174, info@uitgeverijdelantaarn.nl, http://www.ruitenbergboek.nl.

796 USA
GEEZERJOCK. Text in English. 2005. q. free (effective 2006). adv. **Document type:** *Magazine, Consumer.* **Description:** Covers masters, senior athlete for people 40-and-over, sports and fitness.
Published by: GeezerJock Media, LLC, 1 IBM Plaza, Ste 2401, 330 N Wabash, Chicago, IL 60611. Ed. Sean Callahan TEL 312-622-4593. Pub. Brian Reilly TEL 312-203-3246. Adv. contact Bill Ferguson TEL 312-305-2530. B&W page USD 5,630, color page USD 6,620; trim 8.375 x 10.875.

796.86 JPN
GEKKAN KENDO NIPPON/MONTHLY JAPANESE FENCING. Text in Japanese. 1976. m. JPY 9,600 (effective 2008). **Document type:** *Magazine, Consumer.*
Published by: Skui Janaru Kabushiki Kaisha/Ski Journal Publisher Inc., Araki-cho 20-Banchi, Shinjuku-ku, Intech 88 Bldg, Tokyo, 160-0007, Japan. TEL 81-3-33536631, FAX 81-3-33536633, sjsales@skijournal.co.jp.

796.7 USA ISSN 1542-7870
GENERATION SPEED. Text in English. 2003. 4/yr. USD 12.95 domestic; USD 16.95 in Canada (effective 2003).
Published by: Mosaic Publishing Group, Inc., 1127 Grove St. Ste. 200, Clearwater, FL 33755. TEL 727-443-7870, FAX 727-443-7866, info@mosaicpublishing.net. Ed. Natalie K. Wattam. Pub. Joseph J. Wattam.

794.5 ITA ISSN 1592-5013
GENTE ENIGMISTICA. Text in Italian. 2000. m. adv. **Document type:** *Magazine, Consumer.*
Published by: Hachette Rusconi SpA (Subsidiary of: Hachette Filipacchi Medias S.A.), Viale Sarca 235, Milan, 20126, Italy. TEL 39-02-66192629, FAX 39-02-66192469, dirgen@rusconi.it, http://portale.hachettepubblicita.it. Circ: 60,000 (controlled).

790.1 USA
GEORGIA ATHLETE. Text in English. 5/yr. adv. **Document type:** *Magazine, Consumer.* **Description:** Profiles various sports and outdoor activities; reports on events of interest to sports and fitness enthusiasts in the Atlanta area.
Related titles: ◆ Supplement to: Atlanta Sports and Fitness Magazine.
Published by: Dickey Publishing, 3535 Piedmont Rd, Bldg 14, 12th Fl, Atlanta, GA 30305. TEL 404-843-2257, FAX 404-843-1339. Ed. Beth Weitzman. Pubs. Caroline Oberg, Scott Thompson. adv.: B&W page USD 1,145, color page USD 2,095; trim 7.5 x 10. Circ: 35,000.

790.1 DEU
GERMAN AND AMERICAN STUDIES IN SPORT. Text in English. 1991. irreg., latest vol.5, 2004. price varies. **Document type:** *Monographic series, Academic/Scholarly.* **Description:** Focuses on the differences and similarities of German and American national and social developments in physical culture and sport.
Published by: Waxmann Verlag GmbH, Steinfurter Str 555, Muenster, 48159, Germany. TEL 49-251-265040, FAX 49-251-2650426, info@waxmann.com.

794 DEU ISSN 1616-0339
GEWINNEN!; Der Informationsdienst fuer Ihre erfolgreiche Gewinnspielteilnahme. Text in German. 2000. m. EUR 9.80 per issue (effective 2009). **Document type:** *Newsletter, Consumer.*
Published by: F I D Verlag GmbH, Koblenzer Str 99, Bonn, 53177, Germany. TEL 49-228-9550333, FAX 49-228-82055756, info@fid-verlag.de, http://www.fid-verlag.de.

793.7 DEU
GEWINNEN SIE; Jede Menge Gewinn-Raetsel. Variant title: Die Neue Frau - Gewinnen Sie. Text in German. 1999. m. EUR 1.60 newsstand/cover (effective 2010). adv. **Document type:** *Magazine, Consumer.*
Published by: Klambt Verlag GmbH, Im Neudeck 1, Speyer, 67346, Germany. TEL 49-6232-3100, FAX 49-6232-310226, info@klambt.de, http://www.klambt.de. Adv. contact Anita Weiss. page EUR 2,339; trim 215 x 280. Circ: 125,000 (paid).

793.7 DEU
GEWINNRAETSEL; das beliebte Preisraetsel-Magazin. Variant title: Frau mit Herz Gewinnraetsel. Text in German. 1987. m. EUR 1.60 newsstand/cover (effective 2011). adv. **Document type:** *Magazine, Consumer.*
Published by: Klambt Verlag GmbH, Im Neudeck 1, Speyer, 67346, Germany. TEL 49-6232-3100, FAX 49-6232-310226, info@klambt.de, http://www.klambt.de. Ed. Matthias Albrecht. Circ: 125,000 (paid).

793 ARG ISSN 1851-3867
GIGA SOPAS DE LETRAS. Text in Spanish. 2007. m.
Published by: M4 Editora, San Pedro 140, Avellanada, Buenos Aires, 1870, Argentina. m4editora@speedy.com.ar.

796.41 ITA ISSN 1973-8110
IL GINNASTA (ONLINE). Text in Italian. 1895. m. adv. charts; illus. 32 p./no.; Supplement avail. **Document type:** *Magazine, Consumer.* **Description:** Covers gymnastics with special focus on the Italians in international competition, as well as profiles of the athletes and coaches.
Formerly (until 2001): Il Ginnasta (Print) (0017-0046)
Media: Online - full text.
Published by: Federazione Ginnastica d'Italia, Palazzo delle Federazioni Sportive Nazionali, Viale Tiziano 70, Rome, 00196, Italy. TEL 39-06-36858372, FAX 39-06-36858113, info@federginnastica.it.

GIRLJOCK. *see* HOMOSEXUALITY

GIUSTIZIA SPORTIVA.IT; rivista giuridica. *see* LAW

796.8 USA
GLADIATOR MAGAZINE; face fear. conquer fear. be feared. Text in English. 2007. bi-m. USD 32; USD 6.95 newsstand/cover (effective 2008). **Document type:** *Magazine, Consumer.*
Related titles: Online - full text ed.
Published by: Full Circle Press, Inc., 4646 Manhattan Beach Blvd, Ste D, Lawndale, CA 90260. Ed., Pub. Todd Hester.

793 USA ISSN 1555-922X
HV6711
GLOBAL GAMING BUSINESS; the most influential international gaming trade publication. Text in English. 2002. m. USD 99; USD 10 newsstand/cover (effective 2002). adv. **Document type:** *Magazine, Trade.* **Description:** Covers issues of importance to the international casino and gaming industry.
Published by: Global Gaming Business LLC, 6625 S. Valley View Blvd., Ste. 422, Las Vegas, NV 89118-4559. Ed. Roger Gros. Pub. Paul Dworin. R&P James Rutherford. Adv. contact Nikki Phillips-Cote. B&W page USD 2,655, color page USD 3,450. Circ: 15,000 (paid and controlled).

688.76 SGP ISSN 1756-0918
GLOBAL SOURCES. SPORTS & LEISURE. Text in English. 2007. m. USD 75; USD 6.25 per issue (effective 2010). adv. back issues avail. **Document type:** *Magazine, Trade.* **Description:** Features comprehensive reports on new products, market issues and supply trends in Asia's sports and leisure products industry.
Related titles: Online - full text ed.: ISSN 2045-6050. free (effective 2010).
Published by: Global Sources, c/o Media Data Systems Pte Ltd, PO Box 0203, Raffles City, 911707, Singapore. TEL 65-6547-2800, FAX 65-6547-2888, service@globalsources.com, http://www.globalsources.com/.

790.1 GBR ISSN 1472-2909
➤ **GLOBAL SPORT CULTURES.** Text in English. 2001. irreg., latest 2004. price varies. back issues avail. **Document type:** *Monographic series, Academic/Scholarly.* **Description:** Examines and evaluates the role of sport in the contemporary world.
Published by: Berg Publishers (Subsidiary of: Oxford International Publishers Ltd.), 1st Fl Angel Ct, 81 St Clements St, Oxford, Berks OX4 1AW, United Kingdom. TEL 44-1865-245104, FAX 44-1865-791165, enquiry@bergpublishers.com. Eds. David L Andrews, Gary Armstrong, Richard Giulianotti.

▼ ➤ **GLOBAL SPORTS LAW AND TAXATION REPORTS.** *see* LAW

793.7 DEU
GLORIA RAETSEL. Text in German. 1958. w. EUR 80.60; EUR 1.55 newsstand/cover (effective 2010). adv. **Document type:** *Magazine, Consumer.*
Published by: Pabel-Moewig Verlag KG (Subsidiary of: Bauer Media Group), Karlsruherstr 31, Rastatt, 76437, Germany. TEL 49-7222-130, FAX 49-7222-13218, empfang@vpm.de, http://www.vpm-online.de. Adv. contact Rainer Gross. B&W page EUR 614; trim 134 x 200. Circ: 30,500 (paid). **Subscr. to:** G L P International. TEL 201-871-1010, FAX 201-871-0870, info@glpnews.com, http://www.glpnews.com.

793.7 DEU
GLUECKS-BOX; Raetselsonderheft. Variant title: Die Neue Frau Gluecks-Box. Text in German. 2000. a. EUR 1.80 newsstand/cover (effective 2010). adv. **Document type:** *Magazine, Consumer.*
Published by: Klambt Verlag GmbH, Im Neudeck 1, Speyer, 67346, Germany. TEL 49-6232-3100, FAX 49-6232-310226, info@klambt.de, http://www.klambt.de. Adv. contact Brigitte Butz. B&W page EUR 3,985, color page EUR 4,322; trim 215 x 267. Circ: 60,264 (paid).

793.7 DEU
GLUECKS GEWINN RAETSEL. Text in German. 2000. bi-m. EUR 13.20; EUR 1.80 newsstand/cover (effective 2011). adv. **Document type:** *Magazine, Consumer.*
Published by: Deutscher Raetselverlag GmbH & Co. KG (Subsidiary of: Gong Verlag GmbH & Co. KG), Muenchener Str 101-09, Ismaning, 85737, Germany. TEL 49-89-272708620, FAX 49-89-272707890, info@raetsel.de, http://www.deutscher-raetselverlag.de. Circ: 114,000 (paid and controlled).

793.7 DEU
GLUECKS-REVUE SPEZIAL RAETSEL. Variant title: Spezial Raetsel. Text in German. m. adv. **Document type:** *Magazine, Consumer.*
Published by: Burda Senator Verlag GmbH (Subsidiary of: Hubert Burda Media Holding GmbH & Co. KG), Am Kestendamm 1, Offenburg, 77652, Germany. TEL 49-781-842264, FAX 49-781-842034, http://www.hubert-burda-media.com. Ed. Gabriele Henkel. Circ: 142,000 (paid and controlled).

793.7 DEU
GLUECKS-REVUE SPEZIAL RAETSEL BASAR. Text in German. 4/yr. **Document type:** *Magazine, Consumer.*
Published by: Burda Senator Verlag GmbH (Subsidiary of: Hubert Burda Media Holding GmbH & Co. KG), Am Kestendamm 1, Offenburg, 77652, Germany. TEL 49-781-842264, FAX 49-781-842034, http://www.hubert-burda-media.com. Ed. Gabriele Henkel. Circ: 150,000 (paid and controlled).

793.7 DEU
GLUECKSPILZ; Raetsel & Gewinne. Variant title: Woche der Frau GluecksPilz. Text in German. 1998. m. EUR 1.80 newsstand/cover (effective 2011). adv. **Document type:** *Magazine, Consumer.*
Formerly (until 2000): Gluecks-Pilz-Raetsel
Published by: Klambt Verlag GmbH, Im Neudeck 1, Speyer, 67346, Germany. TEL 49-6232-3100, FAX 49-6232-310226, info@klambt.de, http://www.klambt.de. Ed. Matthias Albrecht. Circ: 105,000 (paid).

793.7 DEU
GLUECKSRAETSEL. Text in German. m. EUR 26.40; EUR 1.80 newsstand/cover (effective 2011). adv. **Document type:** *Magazine, Consumer.*
Published by: Deutscher Raetselverlag GmbH & Co. KG (Subsidiary of: Gong Verlag GmbH & Co. KG), Muenchener Str 101-09, Ismaning, 85737, Germany. TEL 49-89-272708620, FAX 49-89-272707890, info@raetsel.de, http://www.deutscher-raetselverlag.de. Circ: 124,000 (paid and controlled).

790.1 JPN ISSN 0286-0376
GV1459
GO WORLD. Text in English. 1977. q. USD 32; USD 50 in Europe (effective 2000). adv. bk.rev. illus. index. reprints avail. **Description:** Covers all the important tournaments of Go in Japan, Korea, and China. Also contains instructional articles.
—Ingenta.
Published by: (Scharak en Godwinkel Het Paard NLD), Kiseido Publishing Company, C.P.O. Box 1140, Tokyo, Japan. FAX 81-467-57-5815, kiseido@yk.rim.or.jp, http://www.kiseido.com. Ed., Adv. contact Richard Bozulich. Circ: 10,500. **Subscr. in US to:** 2255 29th St, Santa Monica, CA 90405. FAX 800-988-6463.

796.962 CAN ISSN 1490-7690
GOALIES' WORLD MAGAZINE. Text in English. 1996. bi-m. CAD 31.75 domestic; USD 29.99 in United States; CAD 49 elsewhere (effective 2007). adv. **Document type:** *Magazine, Consumer.*
Formerly (until 1998): Goalies' World (1203-7230)
Indexed: SD.
Address: 33 Vezina, Quebec, PQ G2B 4B7, Canada. TEL 418-847-0861.

796 USA
GOGIRLGO!. (3 editions Chicago, Atlanta & Boston) Text in English. 1994. m. membership. **Document type:** *Newsletter, Consumer.* **Description:** Includes grant announcements, curriculum ideas, event listings and more.
Formerly: SportsTalk (Print)
Media: E-mail.
Published by: Women's Sports Foundation, Eisenhower Park, East Meadow, NY 11554-1000. TEL 800-227-3988, 516-542-4700, FAX 516-542-4716, info@womenssportsfoundation.org, http://www.womenssportsfoundation.org/. R&P Deana Monahan.

GOL; fodbalovy a hokejovy tydenik. *see* SPORTS AND GAMES—Ball Games

790.1 DEU
GOLF TENNIS POLO; magazine for sports, journeys, pastime, society and fashion. Text in German. 1986. 3/yr. back issues avail.
Published by: Reinhold Sommerfeld GmbH, Kunigundenstr 38, Munich, 80801, Germany. TEL 49-89-3604750, FAX 49-89-369999. Circ: 30,000.

790.1 ESP
GOLFDIGEST. Text in Spanish. 1998. m. **Document type:** *Magazine, Consumer.*
Published by: Unidad Editorial, Ave de San Luis, 25-27, Madrid, 28033, Spain. TEL 34-91-4435000, http://www.unidadeditorial.com.

793.7 DEU
GONG RAETSELKISTE. Variant title: Raetselkiste. Text in German. 13/yr. EUR 21.45; EUR 1.45 newsstand/cover (effective 2011). adv. **Document type:** *Magazine, Consumer.*
Published by: Deutscher Raetselverlag GmbH & Co. KG (Subsidiary of: Gong Verlag GmbH & Co. KG), Muenchener Str 101-09, Ismaning, 85737, Germany. TEL 49-89-272708620, FAX 49-89-272707890, info@raetsel.de, http://www.deutscher-raetselverlag.de. Circ: 79,000 (paid and controlled).

796.72 629.283 USA
GOODGUYS GOODTIMES GAZETTE. Text in English. 1988. m. USD 20. adv. **Document type:** *Magazine, Consumer.* **Description:** Covers motorsports-hobbyist activities. Includes personality profiles.
Published by: Goodguys Enterprises, Inc., PO Box 424, Alamo, CA 94507. TEL 510-838-9876, FAX 510-820-8241. Ed. Steve Anderson. Pub. Tim Holt. Adv. contact Jack Williams. Circ: 28,000.

749 NLD ISSN 2210-3570
GOUD. Variant title: Olympisch Goud. Text in Dutch. 2008. biennial. **Document type:** *Magazine, Consumer.*
Published by: Niehe Media, Brediusweg 55, Bussum, 1401 AC, Netherlands. TEL 31-35-6929080, FAX 31-35-6929089, info@niehemedia.nl, http://www.niehemedia.nl. Eds. Carla Snepvangers, Margriet Zegers.

790 ARG ISSN 0017-291X
EL GRAFICO. Text in Spanish. 1919. w. adv. illus. **Document type:** *Magazine, Consumer.*
Published by: Editorial Atlantida S.A., Azopardo 565, Buenos Aires, 1307, Argentina. TEL 54-11-43460240, FAX 54-11-43431362, info@atlantidadigital.com.ar, http://www.atlantida.com.ar. Ed. Constancio C Vigil. Circ: 127,000.

795 USA
GREAT LAKES GAMING AND POKER MAGAZINE. Text in English. 2007. q. USD 24.95; USD 4.95 newsstand/cover (effective 2007). adv. **Document type:** *Magazine, Consumer.* **Description:** Contains regional casino profiles and poker room reviews, full coverage of local professionals, updates on various poker leagues, strategy tips and more.
Published by: Media Engine, LLC, 1318 W Court St, Flint, MI 48503. TEL 810-233-3000, FAX 810-239-1797. Pub. Matt Zacks TEL 810-210-0372. Adv. contact David Kile TEL 810-955-9546. color page USD 3,000; trim 16.75 x 10.75.

THE GREYHOUND RECORDER. *see* PETS

798.8 USA ISSN 1042-4016
GREYHOUND REVIEW. Text in English. 1911. m. USD 30 domestic; USD 54 foreign (effective 2005). adv. bk.rev. illus.; stat. **Document type:** *Magazine, Consumer.* **Description:** Features greyhound racing news, regional correspondence, pedigree analyses, and records of breeding.
Formerly: Coursing News (0045-8929)
—Ingenta.
Published by: National Greyhound Association, PO Box 543, Abilene, KS 67410. TEL 785-263-4660, FAX 785-263-4689, nga@jc.net, http://nga.jc.net. Circ: 3,700 (paid).

791.8 USA ISSN 0017-4297
GRIT AND STEEL. Text in English. 1899. m. USD 24 domestic; USD 40 foreign (effective 2005). adv. illus. **Document type:** *Magazine, Consumer.* **Description:** Contains articles on game fowl, breeding and health. Reports on club activities and other sport news.

Published by: De Camp Publishing Co., PO Box 280, Gaffney, SC 29342. TEL 800-834-7760, FAX 864-489-3917. Ed. Joe Mac Skinner. Circ: 5,000 (paid).

793 DEU
DIE GROSSE RAETSEL-ZEITUNG; Gut fuer Ihre Augen. Text in German. 1984. m. EUR 25.80; EUR 1.75 newsstand/cover (effective 2011). adv. **Document type:** *Magazine, Consumer.* **Description:** Filled with easy-to-read puzzles and word games.
Published by: Deutscher Raetselverlag GmbH & Co. KG (Subsidiary of: Gong Verlag GmbH & Co. KG), Muenchener Str 101-09, Ismaning, 85737, Germany. TEL 49-89-272708620, FAX 49-89-272707890, info@raetsel.de, http://www.deutscher-raetselverlag.de. Circ: 42,000 (controlled).

795 USA
GUARANTEED WINNING LOTTERY SYSTEMS QUARTERLY. Text in English. 1993. q. **Document type:** *Journal, Consumer.* **Description:** Presents ways and means to enhance and improve lottery playing. Includes do's and don'ts for better potential wins.
Published by: Gibbs Publishing Company, PO Box 97, Sylva, NC 28779. gibbsic@aol.com. Ed. James Calvin Gibbs.

790.1 ITA ISSN 1122-1712
GUERIN SPORTIVO; il settimanale di critica e politica sportiva. Text in Italian. 1912. w. (50/yr.). adv. **Document type:** *Magazine, Consumer.*
Published by: Conti Editore SpA, Via del Lavoro 7, San Lazzaro di Savena, BO 40068, Italy. http://www.contieditore.it. Circ: 42,240.

796.07 ESP ISSN 1988-7795
GUIAS PARA ENSENANZAS MEDIAS. EDUCACION FISICA. Text in Spanish. 2007. m. **Document type:** *Monographic series, Academic/Scholarly.*
Media: Online - full text.
Published by: Wolters Kluwer Espana - Educacion (Subsidiary of: Wolters Kluwer N.V.), C Collado Mediano 9, Las Rozas, Madrid, 28230, Spain. TEL 34-902-250510, FAX 34-902-250515, cleintes@wkeducacion.es, http://www.wkeducacion.es/index.asp. Ed. Joaquin Gairin.

GUN DIGEST. *see* HOBBIES

GUN DIGEST. *see* ANTIQUES

799.202 USA ISSN 1083-8333
GUN GAMES MAGAZINE. Text in English. 1995. bi-m. USD 16.50; USD 3.50 newsstand/cover. adv. back issues avail. **Document type:** *Magazine, Consumer.* **Description:** A shooting sports and recreation magazine. Covers only the fun side of guns, with nothing on self-defense or hunting.
Related titles: Online - full text ed.
Published by: WallyWorld Publishing, 12125 Day St., Ste. F306, Moreno Valley, CA 92557-6727. TEL 909-485-6628, FAX 909-485-6628. Ed. Roni Toldanes. Pub., Adv. contact Wally Arida. Circ: 150,000 (paid).

THE GUN REPORT; dedicated to the interests of gun enthusiasts everywhere. *see* HOBBIES

799.202 USA ISSN 0883-4431
TS532.4
GUN TRADERS GUIDE. Text in English. 1953. a. USD 23.95 (effective 2000). adv. **Document type:** *Directory, Consumer.*
Published by: Stoeger Publishing Co., 17603 Indian Head Hwy., # 200, Accokeek, MD 20607-2501. http://www.stoegerbooks.com/. Ed. John Traister. Pub., Adv. contact David C Perkins.

799.3 USA ISSN 0017-5641
GUN WORLD; for the firearms & hunting enthusiast. Text in English. 1960. m. USD 24.95; USD 4.99 per issue (effective 2011). adv. bk.rev. illus. reprints avail. **Document type:** *Magazine, Consumer.* **Description:** Covers all facets of shooting, with emphasis on new firearms.
Related titles: Microform ed.: 1960 (from PQC).
Indexed: A22.
Published by: Beckett Media Llc, 2400 E Katella Ave, Ste 300, Anaheim, CA 92806. TEL 714-939-9991, 800-764-6287, FAX 714-456-0146, customerservice@beckett.com, http://www.beckett.com. Ed. Steve Quinlan. Circ: 130,000.

GUNMAKER; the journal on custom gunmaking. *see* BUSINESS AND ECONOMICS—Production Of Goods And Services

GUNS & WEAPONS FOR LAW ENFORCEMENT. *see* CRIMINOLOGY AND LAW ENFORCEMENT

799.202 AUS ISSN 0157-1729
GUNS AUSTRALIA; firearms, ammunition & accessories. Text in English. 1978. q. AUD 26.40 domestic; AUD 35 in New Zealand; AUD 45 in Asia; AUD 55 elsewhere; AUD 8.50 newsstand/cover (effective 2008). adv. **Document type:** *Magazine, Consumer.* **Description:** Provides comprehensive reviews for the enjoyment of shooting and collecting guns.
Published by: Yaffa Publishing Group Pty Ltd., 17-21 Bellevue St, Surry Hills, NSW 2010, Australia. TEL 61-2-92812333, FAX 61-2-92812750, info@yaffa.com.au. Ed. John Robinson TEL 61-4-11886884. Adv. contact Michelle Carneiro TEL 61-2-92138219. B&W page AUD 1,700, color page AUD 2,380; trim 210 x 275. Circ: 7,000. **Subscr. to:** GPO Box 606, Sydney, NSW 2001, Australia.

GUNS ILLUSTRATED (YEAR). *see* HOBBIES

799.3 USA ISSN 1044-6257
GUNS MAGAZINE; finest in the firearms field. Text in English. 1955. m. USD 24.95 domestic; USD 44.95 foreign (effective 2008). adv. bk.rev. illus. Supplement avail.; back issues avail. **Document type:** *Magazine, Consumer.* **Description:** Features proper gun use, hunting techniques, collecting, firearms legislation, and new guns and accessories.
Former titles: Guns (0017-5676); Guns Magazine
Related titles: CD-ROM ed.; Online - full text ed.; Supplement(s): Guns Annual. ISSN 0434-9636.
Indexed: G06, G07, G08, I05, M06.
Published by: Publishers Development Corp., F M G Publications, 12345 World Trade Dr, San Diego, CA 92128. TEL 858-605-0202, 800-826-2216, FAX 858-605-0247, http://www.ArtsandActivities.com. Adv. contact Jeff Morey TEL 858-605-0215. B&W page USD 4,291, color page USD 6,887; trim 8 x 11.5. Circ: 160,000 (paid).

799.20283 NZL
GUNSHOT. Text in English. 1950. bi-m. adv. back issues avail. **Document type:** *Magazine, Trade.*
Related titles: Online - full text ed.
Published by: New Zealand Clay Target Association, Inc., Papanui, PO Box 5355, Christchurch, New Zealand. TEL 64-3-3528577, FAX 64-3-3520077, nzcta@xtra.co.nz. Circ: 2,500.

796.41 GBR
THE GYMNAST MAGAZINE. Text in English. 1890. 10/yr. GBP 30 to non-members; free to members (effective 2009). adv. bk.rev. illus.; stat.; tr.lit. **Document type:** *Magazine, Trade.* **Description:** Official journal of the British Amateur Gymnastics Association. Covers European events, gymnastic and acrobatic techniques and club news.
Published by: British Gymnastics, Ford Hall, Lilleshall National Sports Centre, Newport, Shrops TF10 9NB, United Kingdom. TEL 44-845-1297129, FAX 44-845-1249089, information@british-gymnastics.org. Adv. contact George Miller TEL 44-208-9718463.

769.41 FRA ISSN 1242-1316
LE GYMNASTE. Text in French. m. (10/yr). EUR 29 domestic; EUR 48 foreign (effective 2009). **Description:** Covers the world of gymnastics through interviews, in-depth coverage and a schedule of competitions.
Indexed: SD.
Published by: Federation Francaise de Gymnastique, 7 ter cours des Petites-Ecuries, Paris, 75010, France. TEL 33-1-48012448, FAX 33-1-47701607. Ed. Josette Roux. Pub. Jacques Rey.

796.41 SWE ISSN 1401-5269
GYMNASTIK MAGASINET. Text in Swedish. 1942-2000; resumed 2002. 2/yr. bk.rev. illus.; stat. **Document type:** *Consumer.* **Description:** News of events, features, trends, portraits, product news and a forum for debate and discussion.
Former titles (until 1996): Gymnastik (1104-5531); (until 1993): Svensk Gymnastik (0281-5443); (until 1983): Gymnastikledaren (0017-5978)
Published by: Svenska Gymnastikfoerbundet/Swedish Gymnastic Federation, c/o Idrottens Hus, Fiskartorpsvaegen 15A, Stockholm, 11473, Sweden. TEL 46-8-6996000, FAX 46-8-6996495, http://www.gymnastik.se. Circ: 10,000.

796.41 NOR ISSN 0017-596X
GYMNASTIKK OG TURN. Text in Norwegian. 1948. 6/yr. NOK 150 (effective 1997). adv. illus.
—CCC.
Published by: Norges Gymnastikk- og Turnforbund, Hauger Skolevei, 1351 Rud, Norway. Ed. Torill Aas Sundby.

790.1 USA ISSN 0898-6894
TL1
H P V NEWS. (Human Powered Vehicle) Text in English. irreg. (4-6/yr). USD 32 in North America; USD 37 elsewhere (effective 1999). illus. **Document type:** *Newsletter.*
Related titles: Online - full text ed.
Indexed: SD, SportS, T02.
Published by: International Human Powered Vehicle Association, P O Box 1307, San Luis Obispo, CA 93406-1307. TEL 805-466-8010, hpvnews@hpva.org. Ed. Jean Seay.

790 DEU ISSN 1436-4212
H S V LIVE. (Hamburger Sport Verein) Text in German. 1959. s-m. adv. **Document type:** *Magazine, Consumer.*
Former titles (until 1996): H S V - Journal (0944-5293); H S V Sport Illustrierte (0174-2515)
Published by: Hamburger Sport - Verein e.V., Sylvesterallee 7, Hamburg, 22525, Germany. TEL 49-40-415501, FAX 49-40-41551060, Info@hsv.de, http://www.hsv.de. adv.: color page EUR 1,900. Circ: 25,000 (paid and controlled).

797.2 GBR ISSN 2046-2379
▼ **H2OPEN**; open water swimming. Text in English. 2011. bi-m. GBP 20 combined subscription domestic (print & online eds.); GBP 26 combined subscription foreign (print & online eds.) (effective 2011). **Document type:** *Magazine, Consumer.* **Description:** Covers all the aspects of the sport of swimming including training and racing advice, suggestions as well as interviews from famous swimmers.
Related titles: Online - full text ed.: ISSN 2046-2387. GBP 20 in Europe; GBP 16.67 elsewhere (effective 2011).
Published by: ZG Publishing, 20 Burnell Ave, Ham, Richmond, TW10 7YE, United Kingdom. TEL 44-7958-312607, marketing@h2openmagazine.com.

790.1 USA
HALL OF FAME NEWS. Text in English. 1979. q. donation. **Document type:** *Newsletter.* **Description:** Discusses Hall of Fame activities and reports.
Published by: International Tennis Hall of Fame, 100 Park Ave, New York, NY 10017. TEL 212-880-4179. Ed. Mary Lx. Circ: 15,000.

790 DEU ISSN 0017-6982
HAMBURGER SPORT - MITTEILUNGEN. Text in German. 1949. w. adv. bk.rev.
Published by: (Hamburger SportBund e.V.), Sport- und Jugend-Verlag GmbH und Co. KG, Laemmersieth 21, Hamburg, 22305, Germany. Ed. Anne Heitmann. Circ: 5,500.

796.8 USA
HAN WEI WUSHU! NEWSLETTER; a martial arts community newsletter. Text in English. m. **Document type:** *Newsletter.* **Description:** Includes news and articles promoting martial arts.
Media: Online - full text.
Published by: Han Wei Wushu, 3216 Payne Ave, Cleveland, OH 44114. TEL 216-579-9707. Ed. Johnny Oon.

796 AUT
HANDBALL IN OESTERREICH. Text in German. 1992. irreg. **Document type:** *Bulletin, Consumer.*
Formerly (until 1988): Handball und Faustball in Oesterreich (0072-9698)
Published by: Oesterreichischer Handball Bund, Hauslabgasse 24a, Vienna, W 1050, Austria. TEL 43-1-5444379, FAX 43-1-5442712, oehb@oehb.at, http://www.oehb.at. Ed. Martin Hausleitner. R&P Martin Schobert.

799.32 NLD ISSN 1380-6157
HANDBOOGSPORT. Text in Dutch. 1951. 5/yr. adv. **Document type:** *Magazine, Consumer.*
Former titles (until 1992): De Handboogsporter (0921-1942); (until 1987): Handboogschutter (0166-9443)
Published by: Nederlandse Handboog Bond, Postbus 10101, Rosmalen, 5240 GA, Netherlands. TEL 31-72-5210101. adv.: B&W page EUR 995; trim 210 x 297. Circ: 8,500.

799.202 GBR ISSN 0260-8693
HANDGUNNER: BRITAIN'S FOREMOST FIREARMS JOURNAL. Text in English. 1980. 6/yr. GBP 15 domestic; GBP 17 in Europe; GBP 18 elsewhere. adv. bk.rev. illus. back issues avail. **Document type:** *Journal, Consumer.* **Description:** Covers all aspects of modern small arms for a high-level professional readership worldwide.
Indexed: LID&ISL.
Published by: Piedmont Publishing, Ltd., Seychelles House, Brightlingsea, Colchester, Essex CO7 0NN, United Kingdom. TEL 44-1206-305204, FAX 44-1206-304522. Ed. Richard A I Munday. Adv. contact Tony Smith. B&W page GBP 450, color page GBP 600. Circ: 20,000.

HANDGUNS (YEAR). *see* HOBBIES

796.0456 FRA ISSN 0753-521X
HANDISPORT MAGAZINE. Text in French. 1964. q. adv.
Formerly (until 1982): Second Souffle (0048-9972)
Published by: Federation Francaise Handisport, 42 rue Louis Lumiere, Paris, 75020, France. TEL 33-1-40314500, FAX 33-1-40314542. Pub. Charles de Belder.

796 150 KOR ISSN 1226-685X
HAN'GUG SEUPOCEU SIMRI HAGHOEJI/KOREAN JOURNAL OF SPORT PSYCHOLOGY. Text in Korean. 1990. s-a. **Document type:** *Journal, Academic/Scholarly.*
—BLDSC (5113.574710).
Published by: Han'gug Sport Simri Haghoe/Korean Society of Sport Psychology, Korea Chungang University, College of Education, Heukseok-dong Dongjak-gu, Seoul, 156-756, Korea, S. TEL 82-2-8206371, FAX 82-2-8266371, kssp21@hanmail.net, http://ksa.sports.re.kr/.

794 GBR ISSN 1746-1219
HANJIE. Text in English. 2000. m. GBP 2.95 newsstand/cover (effective 2009). **Document type:** *Magazine, Consumer.* **Description:** Contains 45 puzzles ranging in size from 15x15 to 30x30.
Formerly (until 2005): Japanese Puzzles (1470-7527)
—CCC.
Published by: Puzzler Media Limited, PO Box 453, Dovetail, Sittingbourne ME9 8WT, United Kingdom. help@puzzler.com, http://www.puzzlermedia.com/.

790.1 USA ISSN 1090-1116
GV584.5.A75
HARNETT'S SPORTS ARIZONA. Text in English. 1996. bi-m. USD 15 (effective Mar. 2000); USD 2.95 newsstand/cover. adv. back issues avail. **Document type:** *Magazine, Consumer.* **Description:** In-depth coverage of all sports in Arizona.
Published by: SportsSouthwest, 67 E Weldon Ave, Ste 240, Phoenix, AZ 85012. TEL 602-279-7999, FAX 602-277-7857. Ed. Curt Blakeney. Pub. Joel Harnett. Adv. contact Dave Marchese. page USD 3,000. Circ: 35,000 (paid and controlled).

793 USA
HARRAH'S WORLD. Text in English. 2000. q. **Document type:** *Magazine, Consumer.*
Former titles: Harrah's People; (until 1990): Harrah Scope
Published by: Time Inc. (Subsidiary of: Time Warner Inc.), 1271 Ave of the Americas, New York, NY 10020. TEL 212-522-1212, information@timeinc.com, http://www.timeinc.com. Ed. Scott Mowbray. Pub. Tim Hilderbrand.

794.1 GBR ISSN 2044-5393
▼ **HARRY POTTER CHESS MANUAL.** Text in English. 2010. w. **Document type:** *Handbook/Manual/Guide, Trade.*
Published by: De Agostini UK Ltd, Griffin House, 161 Hammersmith Rd, London, W6 8SD, United Kingdom. TEL 44-20-86002000, http://www.deagostini.co.uk.

▼ **HARVARD JOURNAL OF SPORTS & ENTERTAINMENT LAW.** *see* LAW

793 GBR ISSN 2043-9490
▼ **HAYEMAKER SPORTS MAGAZINE.** Variant title: Hayemaker. Text in English. 2010. s-a. GBP 7.99 per issue (effective 2011). adv. back issues avail. **Document type:** *Magazine, Consumer.*
Published by: Hayemaker Boxing Ltd., 57 Jackson Rd, Bromley, Kent, BR2 8NT, United Kingdom.

HEALTH AND FITNESS SPORTS MAGAZINE. *see* PHYSICAL FITNESS AND HYGIENE

HEAVY HITTERS; live large, floss daily. *see* TRANSPORTATION—Automobiles

790.1 USA
HECKLER. Text in English. 1992. m. USD 16 domestic; CAD 20 in Canada; USD 25 elsewhere (effective 2002). adv. music rev.; video rev.; Website rev. illus. 100 p./no.; back issues avail. **Document type:** *Magazine, Consumer.* **Description:** Contains articles, photos and features on all aspects of skateboarding, snowboarding and music.
Address: 5019 Roberts Ave., Mcclellan, CA 95652-2602. Eds. John Buccigaluppi, Sonny Mayugba. Pub., R&P Sam Toll TEL 916-456-2300 Ext 29.

796 NLD ISSN 1878-819X
▼ **HELDEN**; magazine over bloed, zweet & trainen. Text in Dutch. 2009. q. EUR 17.50; EUR 5.95 newsstand/cover (effective 2011). adv. **Document type:** *Magazine, Consumer.*
Published by: Sanoma Uitgevers B.V., Postbus 1900, Hoofddorp, 2130 JH, Netherlands. TEL 31-23-5566770, FAX 31-23-5565376, corporatecommunications@sanomamedia.nl, http://www.sanomamedia.nl.

794 FIN ISSN 1456-1727
HELPOT RISTIKOT. Text in Finnish. 1996. m. EUR 23; EUR 1.95 newsstand/cover (effective 2009). **Document type:** *Magazine, Consumer.*
Published by: Sanoma Magazines Finland Corporation, Lapinmaentie 1, Helsinki, 00350, Finland. TEL 358-9-1201, FAX 358-9-1205171, info@sanomamagazines.fi, http://www.sanomamagazines.fi.

S

796.7 USA ISSN 1550-0691
HEMMINGS MUSCLE MACHINES. Text in English. 2003 (Oct.). m. USD 18.95 domestic; USD 29.48 in Canada; USD 32.95 elsewhere (effective 2009). adv. back issues avail. **Document type:** *Magazine, Consumer.* **Description:** Features in-depth muscle car profiles and road tests, historical and engineering research, and restoration and general-interest technical articles as well as special departments devoted to the latest books and literature, model cars, parts and accessories, auction results, and all the new Detroit performance cars to come.
—CCC.
Published by: Hemmings Publishing (Subsidiary of: American City Business Journals, Inc.), 222 Main St, PO Box 256, Bennington, VT 05201. TEL 802-442-3101, FAX 802-447-1561, hmnmail@hemmings.com, http://www.hemmings.com. adv.: B&W page USD 4,300, color page USD 5,525; trim 8.375 x 10.875.

796.72 796.77 USA ISSN 1555-6867
TL236
HEMMINGS SPORTS & EXOTIC CAR. Text in English. 2005 (Sept.). m. USD 18.95 domestic; USD 29.48 in Canada; USD 32.95 elsewhere (effective 2009). adv. back issues avail. **Document type:** *Magazine, Consumer.* **Description:** Covers the world of Sports and Exotic Cars, from entry-level British roadsters to high-end German sports cars, forgotten sports GTs from Japan, rally-inspired road cars from Sweden and distinctive designs from France.
—CCC.
Published by: Hemmings Publishing (Subsidiary of: American City Business Journals, Inc.), 222 Main St, PO Box 256, Bennington, VT 05201. TEL 802-442-3101, FAX 802-447-1561, hmnmail@hemmings.com, http://www.hemmings.com. adv.: B&W page USD 1,600, color page USD 2,205; bleed 8.5 x 11.25.

796.815 MEX ISSN 2013-2654
HERMANO CERDO; revista de artes marciales y literatura. Text in Spanish. 2006. 3/yr. back issues avail. **Document type:** *Newsletter, Consumer.*
Media: Online - full text.
Address: mauriciosalvador@gmail.com. Ed. Mauricio Salvador.

HIGH PERFORMANCE MAGAZINE. *see* NUTRITION AND DIETETICS

HIGH SCHOOL BASKETBALL HANDBOOK. *see* SPORTS AND GAMES—Ball Games

796.41 USA
GV461
HIGH SCHOOL BOYS GYMNASTICS RULES (CD-ROM). Text in English. 19??. biennial. USD 10 per issue (effective 2009). adv. **Document type:** *Handbook/Manual/Guide, Trade.* **Description:** Contains the official rules for high school gymnastics and is used by coaches, officials, players and many fans who wish to know more about the rules of the game.
Former titles: High School Boys Gymnastics Rules (Print); (until 199?): Boys Gymnastics Rules Book (1072-8554); Official High School Boys Gymnastics Rules (0740-9532); (until 1983): Boys Gymnastics Rule Book. National Federation Edition (0277-8386); Boys Gymnastics Rules. National Federation Edition (0160-3280)
Media: CD-ROM.
Published by: National Federation of State High School Associations, PO Box 690, Indianapolis, IN 46206. TEL 317-972-6900, 800-776-3462, FAX 317-822-5700, info@nfhs.org, http://www.nfhs.org.

HIGH SCHOOL FOOTBALL CASE BOOK. *see* SPORTS AND GAMES—Ball Games

796.41 USA ISSN 1069-6393
GV464
HIGH SCHOOL GIRLS GYMNASTICS RULES AND MANUAL. Text in English. a. **Document type:** *Handbook/Manual/Guide, Trade.* **Description:** Provides in-depth information on the actual play situations for those who wish to enter the field of officiating or to those who are interested in improving their competence in the field of gymnastics.
Former titles (until 1992): Official High School Girls Gymnastics Rules and Manual (0739-9804); (until 1983): Girls Gymnastics Rule Book and Manual (0731-8537); (until 1981): Girls Gymnastics Rules (0270-2029); Incorporates: Girls Gymnastics Judging Manual. National Federation Edition (0197-162X)
Published by: National Federation of State High School Associations, PO Box 690, Indianapolis, IN 46206. TEL 317-972-6900, 800-776-3462, FAX 317-822-5700, info@nfhs.org, http://www.nfhs.org.

795 USA
HIGHROLLER. Text in English. 2005 (May/Jun.). bi-m. USD 29.95 domestic; USD 49.95 foreign (effective 2005). adv. **Document type:** *Magazine, Consumer.* **Description:** Covers gambling lifestyle related topics, including casino, poker, travel, entertainment, dining and toys.
Related titles: Online - full content ed.: USD 14.95 (effective 2005).
Published by: High Roller Life, 11877 Douglas Rd, # 102-300, Alpharetta, GA 30005. TEL 678-990-0285, FAX 678-990-0288, inquiry@highrollerlife.com. Pub. Rick Craven TEL 678-990-0285. Adv. contact Jim Foregger. page USD 9,000; trim 8.125 x 10.75.

790.1 028.5 USA ISSN 1532-0677
HIGHWIRED SPORTS; America's high school sports magazine & almanac. Text in English. 1995. bi-m. USD 14.95; USD 12.95 to students; USD 20.95 in Canada; USD 38.95 elsewhere; USD 2.95 newsstand/cover. adv. **Document type:** *Magazine, Consumer.* **Description:** Dedicated exclusively to high school sports nationwide, including profiles on the nation's top athletes and programs; nutrition, strength and fitness information; recruiting and college search tips; camps and tournaments; products, news and more.
Formerly (until 2000): All-Stater Sports (1096-6900)
Published by: HighWired.com, Inc., 1373 Grandview Ave, Ste 206, Columbus, OH 43212. TEL 800-636-5688, contact@highwired-inc.com, http://www.hws.com. Ed., R&P Nancy Petro. Adv. contact Ben Ledyard. Circ: 100,000 (paid).

790.1 VEN
HIPODROMO. Text in Spanish. m.
Address: Apdo 1192, Caracas, DF 1010-A, Venezuela. Circ: 98,140.

790.1 USA ISSN 0896-1379
GV859
HISTORICAL ROLLER SKATING OVERVIEW. Text in English. 1982. bi-m. USD 35 domestic membership; USD 45 foreign membership (effective 1999). bk.rev. illus.; pat. back issues avail. **Document type:** *Newsletter.* **Description:** Covers the history of roller skating through its collection of artifacts, photographs, archival materials and other skating memorabilia.
Published by: National Museum of Roller Skating, 4730 South St, PO Box 6579, Lincoln, NE 68506-0579. TEL 402-483-7551, FAX 402-483-1465, http://www.usacrs.com/museum.htm. Ed., Pub., R&P Deborah Wallis. Circ: 500 (paid).

793 028.5 USA
HIT SENSATIONS PRESENTS: DIGIMON. Text in English. 2000. m. **Document type:** *Magazine, Consumer.*
Published by: Fanzine International, Inc., 230 W 41st St, New York, NY 10036.

793 028.5 USA
HIT SENSATIONS PRESENTS: DIGIMON VS. POKEMON. Text in English. 2000. m. **Document type:** *Magazine, Consumer.*
Published by: Fanzine International, Inc., 230 W 41st St, New York, NY 10036.

793 USA
HIT SENSATIONS PRESENTS: DRAGONBALL Z. Text in English. 2000. m. **Document type:** *Magazine, Consumer.*
Published by: Fanzine International, Inc., 230 W 41st St, New York, NY 10036.

793 028.5 USA
HIT SENSATIONS PRESENTS: POKEMANIA (YEAR). Text in English. 2000. irreg. **Document type:** *Magazine, Consumer.*
Published by: Fanzine International, Inc., 230 W 41st St, New York, NY 10036.

793 028.5 USA
HIT SENSATIONS PRESENTS: POKEMON BONANZA. Text in English. 2000. m. **Document type:** *Magazine, Consumer.*
Published by: Fanzine International, Inc., 230 W 41st St, New York, NY 10036.

793 028.5 USA
HIT SENSATIONS PRESENTS: THE ULTIMATE BATTLE NEO POKEMON VS. DRAGONBALL Z. Text in English. 2000. m. **Document type:** *Magazine, Consumer.*
Published by: Fanzine International, Inc., 230 W 41st St, New York, NY 10036.

HLAVICKA. *see* CHILDREN AND YOUTH—For

790.1 613.7 378.198 DEU
HOCHSCHULSPORT. Text in German. 1953. s-a. adv. **Document type:** *Journal, Academic/Scholarly.*
Published by: Technische Universitaet Muenchen, Sportzentrum, Connollystr 32, Munich, 80809, Germany. TEL 49-89-289-24667, FAX 49-89-289-24664, zhs-h@lrz.tu-muenchen.de, http://www.mhs.mhn.de. Circ: 70,000.

796 DEU ISSN 1864-189X
HOCHSCHULSPORT: BILDUNG UND WISSENSCHAFT. Text in German. 2007. irreg., latest vol.2, 2009. price varies. **Document type:** *Monographic series, Academic/Scholarly.*
Published by: Universitaetsverlag Goettingen, Platz der Goettinger Sieben 1, Goettingen, 37073, Germany. TEL 49-551-395243, FAX 49-551-3922457, pabst@sub.uni-goettingen.de.

796 DEU
HOCHSCHULSPORT WUERZBURG. Text in German. 1981. s-a. adv. **Document type:** *Journal, Academic/Scholarly.*
Published by: Sportzentrum der Universitaet Wuerzburg, Judenbuehlweg 11, Wuerzburg, 97082, Germany. TEL 49-931-8886502, FAX 49-931-8886505, sportzentrum@mail.uni-wuerzburg.de, http://www.uni-wuerzburg.de/sportzentrum. adv.: page EUR 252. Circ: 7,100 (controlled).

796.962 SWE ISSN 0345-4347
HOCKEY. Text in Swedish. 1965. m. SEK 487 domestic; SEK 687 in Scandinavia; SEK 787 elsewhere (effective 2004). adv. bk.rev.
Incorporates (1970-1974): Svenskt Ishockeymagasin (0049-2698)
Published by: (Svenska Ishockeyfoerbundet), Daus Tryck och Media, Daushuset, Bjaesta, 89380, Sweden. TEL 46-660-266100, FAX 46-660-266128, http://www.daus.se. Ed. Charlie Wedin. Adv. contact Jan Dylicki TEL 46-660-266105. B&W page SEK 13,200, color page SEK 17,200; 185 x 260.

796.962 796.355 CAN ISSN 1081-9754
HOCKEY BUSINESS NEWS; the magazine for the North American hockey industry. Text in English. 1994. 4/yr. CAD 32.05 domestic; USD 29.95 in United States; USD 60 elsewhere; free to qualified personnel (effective 2007). adv. charts; mkt.; stat. back issues avail. **Document type:** *Magazine, Trade.* **Description:** Features regular editorial contributions from hockey industry leaders in the fields of manufacturing, retailing, facility management and team management.
Indexed: C05, SD, T02.
Published by: Transcontinental Media, Inc. (Subsidiary of: Transcontinental, Inc.), 25 Sheppard Ave West, Ste 100, Toronto, ON M2N 6S7, Canada. TEL 416-733-7600, FAX 416-218-3544, info@transcontinental.ca, http://www.medias-transcontinental.com. Ed. Jason Kay. Pub. Caroline Andrews. adv.: color page CAD 4,865; trim 9.625 x 13. Circ: 5,500 (controlled).

796.962 USA
HOCKEY DIGEST ANNUAL GUIDE. Text in English. a. **Document type:** *Magazine, Consumer.*
Published by: Century Publishing Inc., E 5710 Seltice Way, Post Falls, ID 83854. TEL 208-765-6300, 800-824-1806, FAX 208-676-8476, privacy@CenturyPublishing.com, http://www.centurypublishing.com.

796.962 USA
HOCKEY GUIDE AND REGISTER. Variant title: Sporting News Hockey Guide and Register. Text in English. 1991. a. USD 18.95 (effective 2007). **Document type:** *Magazine, Consumer.*
Supersedes in part (in 1997): The Complete Hockey Book (1052-7133); Which was formed by the 1991 merger of: Hockey Register (0090-2292); (1982-1991): Hockey Guide (0278-4955); Which was formerly (until 1982): Pro and Amateur Hockey Guide (0090-0818); Pro and Senior Hockey Guide (0079-550X)
Published by: American City Business Journals, Inc. (Subsidiary of: Advance Publications, Inc.), 120 W Morehead St, Charlotte, NC 28202. TEL 704-973-1000, FAX 704-973-1001, http://www.acbj.com.

796.962 CAN ISSN 1911-2696
HOCKEY, LE MAGAZINE. Text in French. 2007. 9/yr. CAD 39.95 (effective 2008). adv. **Document type:** *Magazine, Consumer.*
Related titles: English ed.: Hockey, the Magazine. ISSN 1911-2688. 2007.
Published by: Editions Gesca, C.P. 9425, Succ. Sainte-Foy, Sainte-Foy, PQ G1V 4B8, Canada. TEL 514-904-5537, 877-997-4653, contact@editionsgesca.ca.

796.962 CAN ISSN 0018-3016
THE HOCKEY NEWS; the international hockey weekly. Text in English. 1947. 34/yr. CAD 52.95 domestic (effective 2011). adv. illus. reprints avail. **Document type:** *Magazine, Consumer.*
Related titles: Microfilm ed.: (from MML); Online - full content ed.
Indexed: A22, A33, C03, C05, CBCARef, CBPI, CPerI, G08, PQC, RASB, SD, SPI, SportS, T02.
Published by: Transcontinental Media, Inc. (Subsidiary of: Transcontinental, Inc.), 25 Sheppard Ave West, Ste 100, Toronto, ON M2N 6S7, Canada. TEL 416-733-7600, FAX 416-218-3544, info@transcontinental.ca, http://www.transcontinental-gtc.com/en/home.html. Circ: 110,000.

796.962 CAN ISSN 1910-2003
HOCKEY NOW. Text in English. 2000. m. **Document type:** *Magazine, Consumer.*
Former titles (until 2006): Alberta Hockey Now (1709-609X); (until 2002): Hockey Now (Alberta Edition) (1709-6081)
Published by: Hockey Now Communications Ltd., #300 - 92 Lonsdale Ave, N. Vancouver, BC V7M 2E6, Canada. TEL 604-990-1432, 877-990-0520, FAX 604-990-1433, sales@hockeynow.ca. Ed. Sarah Simpson. Pub. Don McIntosh. Adv. contact Larry Feist.

796.962 USA
HOCKEY PLAYER MAGAZINE (ONLINE). Text in English. 1991. m. adv. illus. **Document type:** *Magazine, Consumer.* **Description:** Written for and by recreational ice, roller and street hockey players. Each issue includes interviews, columns, departments, product news and playing tips to improve games.
Formerly (until 1998): Hockey Player Magazine (Print)
Media: Online - full text.
Published by: Hockey Player Magazine L.P. Ed. Alex Carswell.

796 USA
GV847.5
HOCKEY PREVIEW. Text in English. 1991. a. illus.; stat. back issues avail. **Document type:** *Magazine, Consumer.*
Supersedes in part (in 1997): The Complete Hockey Book (1052-7133); Which was formed by the merger of (19??-1991): Hockey Register (0090-2292); (19??-1991): Hockey Guide (0278-4955); Which was formerly (until 1982): Pro and Amateur Hockey Guide (0090-0818); Pro and Senior Hockey Guide (0079-550X)
Published by: American City Business Journals, Inc. (Subsidiary of: Advance Publications, Inc.), 120 W Morehead St, Charlotte, NC 28202. TEL 704-973-1000, FAX 704-973-1001, http://www.acbj.com. Circ: 4,000.

796.962 USA ISSN 0746-7451
HOCKEY WEEKLY. Text in English. 1974. 30/yr. USD 32 domestic; USD 45 in Canada; USD 2 newsstand/cover. adv. stat. back issues avail. **Document type:** *Newspaper.* **Description:** Covers amateur hockey in Michigan and surrounding states. Emphasis on mites through midgets, but has features on high school, juniors, college, and NHL. Promotes youth and amateur hockey. Includes articles on hockey schools, tournaments, arenas, leagues, and suppliers.
Formerly (until 1983): Michigan Hockey Weekly (0274-9254)
Related titles: Online - full text ed.
Indexed: P10, P19, P48, P53, P54, PQC.
Published by: Castine Communications, Inc., 33425 Grand River Ave, Ste 101, Farmington, MI 48335-3567. TEL 313-563-9130, FAX 313-563-9538. Ed. Paul Harris. Pub. John Castine. R&P Peggy Castine. Adv. contact Rose Formosa. B&W page USD 500; trim 15 x 11.5.

796.96 SWE ISSN 0347-2663
HOCKEYBOKEN. Text in Swedish. 1944. a. SEK 130 (effective 2004). adv.
Formerly (until 1971): Ishockeyboken
Published by: (Svenska Ishockeyfoerbundet), Daus Tryck och Media, Daushuset, Bjaesta, 89380, Sweden. TEL 46-660-266100, FAX 46-660-266128, http://www.daus.se.

796 GBR ISSN 0073-3164
HOMING WORLD STUD BOOK. Text in English. 1938. a. GBP 5 per issue (effective 2010). adv. **Document type:** *Handbook/Manual/Guide, Consumer.*
Formerly (until 1941): Homing World Diary
Published by: Royal Pigeon Racing Association, The General Manager, The Reddings, Cheltenham, Glos GL51 6RN, United Kingdom. TEL 44-1452-713529, FAX 44-1452-857119, gm@rpra.org, http://www.rpra.org.

796 BIH ISSN 1512-8822
➤ **HOMO SPORTICUS/SCIENTIFIC JOURNAL OF SPORT AND PHYSICAL EDUCATION.** Text in English. 1998. s-a. EUR 10 (effective 2010). **Document type:** *Journal, Academic/Scholarly.* **Description:** Covers all scientific dipsciplines in sport, concerning a wide area of sport (Physical education, training, sport for all, fitness and health-related activities, sociology of sport, philosophy of sport, physical conditioning, pedagogy of sport, research methodology, top-level sport, management of sport, history of sport and the olympic movement, biomechanics, motor control, biology, medicine of sport and exercise, adapted physical activity and sport for the disabled, biochemistry).
Related titles: Online - full text ed.: ISSN 1840-4324.
Indexed: CA, CABA, GH, LT, SD, T02.
Published by: Univerzitet u Sarajevu, Fakultet Sporta i Tjelesnog Odgoja/University of Sarajevo, Bosnia and Herzegovina, Faculty of Sport and Physical Education, Patriotske lige 41, Sarajevo, 71 000, Bosnia Herzegovina. TEL 387-33-668768, FAX 387-33-211537. Ed., Pub. Izet Radjo.

➤ **HONDENSPORT & SPORTHONDEN**; het tijdschrift voor liefhebbers van hondensport en africhting. *see* PETS

796 DEU ISSN 1617-125X
HORIZONT SPORT BUSINESS. Text in German. 2001. bi-m. **Document type:** *Magazine, Trade.*
Related titles: Online - full text ed.
Published by: Deutscher Fachverlag GmbH, Mainzer Landstr 251, Frankfurt Am Main, 60326, Germany. TEL 49-69-75952052, FAX 49-69-75952999, info@dfv.de, http://www.dfv.de. Circ: 6,000 (paid and controlled).

HORIZONTE; revista de educacao fisica e desporto. *see* PHYSICAL FITNESS AND HYGIENE

HOT ROD. *see* TRANSPORTATION—Automobiles

797.23 CAN
HOT WATER. Text in English. 1993. q. **Document type:** *Journal, Consumer.*
Published by: Taylor Publishing Group, 2585 Skymark Ave, Ste 306, Mississauga, ON L4W 4L5, Canada. TEL 905-624-8218, FAX 905-624-6764. Ed. Karen Hill. Circ: 18,000 (paid).

HRVATSKI SPORTSKOMEDICINSKI VJESNIK. *see* MEDICAL SCIENCES

HUANQIU TIYU SHICHANG/GLOBAL SPORT MARKET. *see* BUSINESS AND ECONOMICS

790.1 USA ISSN 0898-6908
TL1
HUMAN POWER. Text in English. irreg. illus. **Document type:** *Magazine, Trade.*
Indexed: SD, SportS, T02.
—BLDSC (4336.363000), IE, Ingenta.
Published by: International Human Powered Vehicle Association, P O Box 1307, San Luis Obispo, CA 93406-1307. TEL 805-466-8010, office@ihpva.org, http://www.ihpva.org. Ed. David Gordon Wilson.

790 ITA ISSN 0018-7933
HURRA JUVENTUS. Text in Italian. 1963. m. EUR 35.90 domestic (effective 2008). adv. illus. **Document type:** *Magazine, Consumer.*
Published by: Cantelli Editore Srl, Via Saliceto 22c, Castelmaggiore, BO 40013, Italy. TEL 39-051-6328811, FAX 39-051-6328815, cantelli.editore@cantelli.net, http://www.cantelli.net. Circ: 184,400.

790.1 USA
HUSKY BLUE & WHITE. Text in English. 14/yr. USD 35 (effective 1998). **Document type:** *Magazine, Consumer.* **Description:** Provides comprehensive coverage of University of Connecticut athletics.
Related titles: Online - full text ed.
Published by: L S I Productions, 45 Laurel Rd, PO Box 1269, Pinehurst, NC 28370-1269. TEL 910-295-5559, FAX 910-295-6566, mechanic@uconnhusky.com, http://www.superhuskies.com. Pub. Nanci Donald.

HVATI; rit Ithrottasambands Fatladra. *see* HANDICAPPED

I A S M H F NEWSLETTER. *see* MUSEUMS AND ART GALLERIES

796 ESP ISSN 2172-2161
I C D. (Consejo Superior de Deportes) Text in Spanish. 1996. m. **Document type:** *Bulletin, Government.*
Published by: Consejo Superior de Deportes, Servicio de Documentacion, Av. Martin Fierro s/n, Madrid, 28040, Spain. TEL 34-91-5896938, FAX 34-91-5896614, publicaciones@csd.gob.es, http://www.csd.gob.es/.

790.1 USA ISSN 1522-4651
I S I EDGE; the professional journal for the ice skating industry. Text in English. 1961. 6/yr. membership. adv. back issues avail. **Document type:** *Journal, Trade.*
Formerly: Ice Skating Institute Newsletter
Published by: Ice Skating Institute, 17120 N Dallas Pkwy, Ste 140, Dallas, TX 75248-1187. TEL 972-735-8800, FAX 972-735-8815, isi@skateisi.org, http://www.skateisi.org. Ed., R&P Lori Fairchild. Adv. contact Carol Jackson. Circ: 5,000 (paid).

799.3 DEU
I S S F NEWS. Text in English, French, German, Spanish. 1961. 6/yr. EUR 25.50 (effective 2009). adv. bk.rev. charts; illus. **Document type:** *Magazine, Consumer.*
Former titles (until 1998): U I T Journal (0721-572X); Shooting Sport (0535-2452)
Related titles: Online - full text ed.
Indexed: SD.
Published by: International Shooting Sport Federation, Bavariaring 21, Munich, 80336, Germany. TEL 49-89-5443550, munich@issf-sports.org. Ed. Wolfgang Schreiber. Circ: 4,000.

796 CHE
I S U CONSTITUTION AND GENERAL REGULATIONS. Text in English. biennial. CHF 20. **Document type:** *Bulletin, Consumer.*
Formed by the merger of: I S U Constitution; I S U Regulations
Published by: International Skating Union, Chemin de Primerose 2, Lausanne, 1007, Switzerland. TEL 41-21-6126666, FAX 41-21-6126677, info@isu.ch, http://www.isu.org.

796.077 GBR ISSN 1812-2302
GV991
I T F COACHING & SPORT SCIENCE REVIEW (ENGLISH EDITION). (International Tennis Federation) Text in English. 1993. 3/yr. **Document type:** *Journal, Academic/Scholarly.*
Related titles: Online - full text ed.: free (effective 2011).
Indexed: SD.
Published by: International Tennis Federation, Bank Lane, Roehampton, London, SW15 5XZ, United Kingdom. TEL 44-20-88786464, FAX 44-20-88787799.

796.962 JPN
ICE HOCKEY MAGAZINE. Text in Japanese. 10/yr. JPY 11,280 (effective 2000).
Published by: Baseball Magazine Sha, 3-10-10 Misaki-cho, Chiyoda-ku, Tokyo, 101-0061, Japan. FAX 81-3-3238-0106. Ed. Naruyoshi Nishida.

796.962 USA
GV847.5
ICE HOCKEY RULES BOOK. Text in English. 19??. a. USD 6.95 per issue (effective 2009). adv. **Document type:** *Handbook/Manual/ Guide, Trade.* **Description:** Contains the official rules for ice hockey and is used by coaches, officials, players and many fans who wish to know more about the rules of the game.
Former titles: Official High School Ice Hockey Rules (0735-651X); (until 1983): National Federation of State High School Associations. Ice Hockey Rule Book (0732-8117); National Federation of State High School Associations. Ice Hockey Rules (0191-7625)
Published by: National Federation of State High School Associations, PO Box 690, Indianapolis, IN 46206. TEL 317-972-6900, 800-776-3462, FAX 317-822-5700, info@nfhs.org, http://www.nfhs.org.

796 DNK ISSN 0109-3835
IDRAETSLIV. Text in Danish. 1949. 11/yr. DKK 250 (effective 2008). adv. back issues avail. **Document type:** *Magazine, Consumer.*
Formerly (until 1952): Dansk Idraetsforbund. Officielle Meddelelser
Related titles: Online - full text ed.
Published by: Danmarks Idraets-Forbund/Sport in Denmark, Idraettens Hus, Broendby Stadion 20, Broendby, 2605, Denmark. TEL 45-43-262626, FAX 45-43-262628, dif@dif.dk. Ed. Jacob Buch Andersen TEL 45-43-262028. Adv. contact Anja Loenbo TEL 45-43-262002. B&W page DKK 11,100, color page DKK 13,900; 182 x 236. Circ: 19,000.

796 NOR ISSN 1503-0628
IDRETT & ANLEGG. Text in Norwegian. 1988. 7/yr. NOK 449 (effective 2007). adv. back issues avail. **Document type:** *Magazine, Trade.*
Formerly (until 2002): Idrettsanlegg (0802-3026)
Published by: (Kulturdepartmentet), Sport Media AS, Vestre Ringvei 5, PO Box A, Askim, 1801, Norway. TEL 47-69-819700, FAX 47-69-889433, sportsmedia@sportsmedia.no, http://www.sportmedia.no. Ed. Erik Unaas TEL 47-69-819703. Adv. contact Irene Paulsen. Circ: 4,300.

796 SWE ISSN 0280-2775
GV631
IDROTT, HISTORIA OCH SAMHAELLE. Text in Swedish. 1981. a. SEK 100 to individual members; SEK 150 to institutional members (effective 2007). back issues avail. **Document type:** *Yearbook, Academic/Scholarly.*
Published by: Svenska Idrottshistoriska Foereningen, c/o Jan Lindroth, Framnaesbacken 26, Solna, 17166, Sweden. TEL 46-8-6531509, jan.lindroth@historia.su.se. Eds. Johan R Norberg, Leif Lyttergren.

796 613.711 SWE
IDROTT & HAELSE; organ foer Svenska idrottslaerarfoereningen. Text in Swedish. 1874. 8/yr. SEK 520 (effective 2005). adv. bk.rev. **Document type:** *Journal, Trade.* **Description:** Covers areas of interest to physical education teachers: Working conditions and environment, empirical and non-empirical research, conferences, methodology in education, health promotion.
Former titles (until 2005): Tidskrift i Gymnastik och Idrott (0281-5338); (until 1984): Tidskrift i Gymnastik (0346-3214)
Published by: Svenska Gymnastiklaerarsaellskapet, c/o Per Nylander, Tegelbruksgatan 17, Sundswall, 85356, Sweden. TEL 46-60-174862, FAX 46-60-679185. Ed., Adv. contact Per Nylander TEL 46-60-174862. color page SEK 2,693; 139 x 200. Circ: 2,700.

790 SWE
IDROTT & KUNSKAP. Text in Swedish. 2004. q. SEK 200 (effective 2005). adv. **Document type:** *Magazine, Consumer.*
Address: Dalenum 118, Lidingoe, 18170, Sweden. TEL 46-8-309905, FAX 46-70-4222530, info@idrottochkunskap.se. Ed. Christian Carlsson. Adv. contact Roger Skoog. page SEK 14,000; 185 x 270.

796.72 SWE ISSN 0345-5106
IDROTTSBLADET; motorsport. Abbreviated title: I B. Text in Swedish. 1910. 25/m. SEK 490 domestic; SEK 855 in Scandinavia (effective 2001). adv. **Document type:** *Newspaper, Consumer.*
Incorporates (1979-1984): Rallysport Fart & Bilar (0282-1486); Which was formerly (until 1983): Rallysport & Rallynytt (0280-0209)
Related titles: ◆ Supplement(s): Idrottsbladet. Special. ISSN 0345-5114.
Published by: (Svenska Bilsportfoerbundet), Idrottsbladet Foerlags AB, Box 1274, Liding, 18124, Sweden. TEL 46-8-550-327-70, FAX 46-8-731-94-79. Ed. Christer Flythstroem TEL 46-8-54481752. Adv. contact Solveig Vaeisaenen. B&W page SEK 22,000, color page SEK 29,000; trim 255 x 370. Circ: 24,000 (paid). **Co-sponsor:** Svenska Racerbaatfoerbundet (SVERA).

796.72 SWE ISSN 0345-5114
IDROTTSBLADET. SPECIAL. Text in Swedish. 1974.
Related titles: ◆ Supplement to: Idrottsbladet. ISSN 0345-5106.
Published by: Idrottsbladet Foerlags AB, Box 1274, Liding, 18124, Sweden. TEL 46-8-550-327-70, FAX 46-8-731-94-79.

796 SWE ISSN 1652-7224
IDROTTSFORUM.ORG; nordic sport science forum. Text in Danish, English, Norwegian, Swedish. 2003. s-m. bk.rev. **Document type:** *Magazine, Academic/Scholarly.* **Description:** The journal covers issues related to the social science and humanistics perspectives on the sport sciences and addresses researchers, teachers and students within sport sciences and sport science research, as well as athletes, sport managers and sport officials within the practical applications of sports.
Media: Online - full content.
Published by: Malmoe Hoegskola, Laerarutbildningen. Idrottvetenskap/ Malmoe University, School of Teacher Education. Department of Sport Sciences, Malmoe, 20506, Sweden. TEL 46-40-6657000, FAX 46-40-6657305, http://www.mah.se/fakulteter-och-omraden/ Lararutbildningen/Enheter/Idrottsvetenskap-IDV. Ed. Kjell Eriksson. Pub. Aage Radmann.

793 JPN ISSN 1345-8809
IGO. Text in Japanese. 1951. m. JPY 10,680 (effective 2008). **Document type:** *Magazine, Consumer.* **Description:** Covers the the sport of Go board game.
Published by: Seibundo Shinkosha Inc., 3-3-11 Hongo, Bunkyoku, Tokyo, 164-0013, Japan. Ed. Yuzaburo Takeda. Circ: 55,000.

797.23 USA
IMMERSED MAGAZINE; the international technical diving magazine. Text in English. 1996. q. **Document type:** *Magazine, Consumer.*
Published by: Immersed LLC, 638, FDR Station, Chester, NY 10918-0638. bsterner@prodigy.net, http://www.immersed.com. Ed., Pub. Bob Sterner. Circ: 25,000.

IMPIANTI SPORT VERDE; ricreazione, piscine, attrezzature, fitness. *see* LEISURE AND RECREATION

793 USA
IMPOSSIBILITY - CHALLENGER. Text in English. 1981. q.
Published by: (Sri Chinmoy Centre), AUM Publications, PO Box 32433, Jamaica, NY 11431. TEL 718-523-1166. Ed. David Burke.

796 NLD ISSN 2211-5005
IN BEWEGING!. Text in Dutch. 200?. s-a.
Published by: Nederlands Instituut voor Sport en Bewegen, Postbus 643, Ede, 6710 BP, Netherlands. TEL 31-318-490900, FAX 31-318-490995, info@nisb.nl, http://www.nisb.nl. Circ: 5,000.

IN MOTO. *see* SPORTS AND GAMES—Bicycles And Motorcycles

796.043 USA
IN THE CLUTCH. Text in English. m. USD 16.95 per issue; USD 4.95 per issue (effective 2004). adv. **Document type:** *Magazine, Consumer.* **Description:** Features college athletes, sports, students and college life. Focuses on uncovered action, humor and truth in various aspects of college sports and the culture of its players and fans.
Published by: Intensity Publishing, 8910 University Center Ln, San Diego, CA 92122. TEL 866-461-0673, FAX 866-374-2137, support@intensitypublishing.com, http:// www.intensitypublishing.com. adv.: B&W page USD 6,120, color page USD 6,800; trim 8.25 x 10.875. Circ: 110,000 (paid).

796 USA ISSN 1945-1458
IN THE GAME; high school sports magazine. Variant title: High School Sports Magazine. Text in English. 2008. m. USD 37.45; free to qualified personnel (effective 2009). adv. back issues avail. **Document type:** *Magazine, Consumer.* **Description:** Provides information about local high school athletic programs.
Published by: Dykes Publishing Group, Inc, 113 E Front St, Sylvester, GA 31791.

790.1 USA ISSN 1097-430X
GV790.6
INDEPENDENT ROWING NEWS; the journal of competitive rowing. Text in English. bi-w. USD 30 domestic; USD 35 in Canada; USD 60 elsewhere (effective 2001). adv. **Description:** Includes news and features on rowing, containing race results and a calendar of rowing events.
Indexed: PEI.
Address: PO Box 831, Hanover, NH 03755. FAX 603-643-0606.

796 USA
INDIAN GAMING; the national information site of the American Indian gaming industry. Text in English. 1990. m. USD 85 domestic; USD 99 in Canada; USD 135 elsewhere (effective 2005). **Document type:** *Magazine, Consumer.* **Description:** Devoted solely to the North American Indian gaming industry.
Indexed: BNNA, H&TI.
Published by: Arrowpoint Media, Inc., 14205 S E 36th St., Ste 100, Bellevue, WA 98006. TEL 425-519-3710, FAX 425-883-7209, info@indiangaming.com.

795 USA ISSN 1948-6952
INDIAN GAMING BUSINESS. Abbreviated title: I G B. Text in English. 1998. bi-m. included with subscr. to International Gaming & Wagering Business. adv. back issues avail.; reprints avail. **Document type:** *Magazine, Trade.* **Description:** Aims to promote the benefits of gaming in strengthening tribal governments and developing economic growth and healthy and safe tribal communities for the next generations.
Related titles: ◆ Supplement to: International Gaming & Wagering Business. ISSN 1066-145X.
Indexed: H&TI.
Published by: B N P Media, 505 E Capovilla Ave, Ste 102, Las Vegas, NV 89119. TEL 702-794-0718, FAX 702-794-0799, portfolio@bnpmedia.com, http://www.bnpmedia.com. Ed. Marian Green. Pub. Charles Anderer TEL 718-432-8529. Adv. contact Roy Taylor TEL 702-794-0718 ext 8703. Circ: 9,000 (controlled).

354 USA ISSN 1076-867X
INDIANA GAMING INSIGHT. Text in English. 1993. 44/yr. USD 375 by email; USD 475 by fax (effective 2005). **Document type:** *Newsletter.* **Description:** Covers riverboat gaming, horse racing, Hoosier Lottery and Bingo, and raffle activity in Indiana.
Published by: INGroup, PO Box 383, Noblesville, IN 46061-0383. TEL 317-817-9997, FAX 317-817-9998.

790.1 USA
INDOOR GYM CLIMBER. Text in English. bi-m. **Description:** Contains tips for beginning climbers, as well as features on climbers, product reviews, and nutritional advice.
Published by: Coyne Publishing, 1313 Paseo Alamos, PO Box 337, San Dimas, CA 91773. TEL 800-351-2738, FAX 909-599-2691. Pub. Charles Coyne.

796 USA ISSN 0279-9863
INFO A A U. Text in English. 1929. bi-m. USD 12. **Document type:** *Newsletter.* **Description:** Highlights events, athletes, individuals and news of the organization.
Formerly (until 198?): A A U News (0199-6991)
Indexed: SPI.
Published by: Amateur Athletic Union of the United States, 1910 Hotal Plaza Blvd, P O Box 22409, Lake Buena Vista, FL 32830. Ed. David Morton.

796 CHL
INFORMA. Text in Spanish. 2000. m. back issues avail. **Document type:** *Newsletter.*
Media: Online - full text.
Published by: Colegio de Kinesiologos de Chile colkine@ctcinternet.cl. Ed. Patricio V Figueroa.

793.8 NLD ISSN 2211-3363
INFORMAGIE. Text in Dutch. 197?. q. EUR 47.50 membership (effective 2011). adv. **Document type:** *Magazine, Consumer.*
Formerly (until 1989): Hocus (2211-534X)
Published by: De Nederlandse Magische Unie, Frankendaal 8, Ede, 6715 JK, Netherlands. secretaris@goochelen-nmu.nl. Eds. Aris Smit, Marcel Ledder TEL 31-6-26020966, Marjolein Etten.

INFORMATION PLUS REFERENCE SERIES. GAMBLING; what's at stake. *see* SOCIOLOGY

790.1 DEU
INFORMATIONEN FUER MITARBEITER UND VEREINE. Variant title: H L V-Informationen. Text in German. 4/yr. EUR 12 (effective 2005).
Published by: Hessischer Leichtathletik-Verband, Otto-Fleck-Schneise 4, Frankfurt Am Main, 60528, Germany. TEL 49-69-6789211, FAX 49-69-679708, info@hlv.de, http://www.hlv.de.

796.355 NZL
INNER CIRCLE. Text in English. 2002. 3/yr. NZD 10 (effective 2008). **Document type:** *Magazine, Consumer.*

S

Former titles (until 2008): New Zealand Hockey Magazine (1177-4118); (until 2006): Hockey (1177-0694); (until 2005): New Zealand Hockey Magazine (1176-0230)
Published by: Hockey New Zealand, PO Box 24-024, Royal Oak, Auckland, 1345, New Zealand. TEL 64-9-6292932, FAX 64-9-6292934, support@hockeynz.co.nz, http://www.hockeynz.co.nz.

793 808.838 USA
INPHOBIA. Text in English. 1986. m. USD 28; USD 38 in Canada; USD 58 elsewhere. **Document type:** *Magazine, Consumer.* **Description:** Reviews and previews fantasy games, large and small.
Formerly: White Wolf Magazine (0897-9391)
Published by: White Wolf, Inc., 780 Park North Rd, Clarkston, GA 30021. TEL 800-454-9653, FAX 404-292-9664.

INQUIRIES IN SPORT & PHYSICAL EDUCATION. *see* PHYSICAL FITNESS AND HYGIENE

794.1 USA
INSIDE CHESS. Text in English. 1988. m. free (effective 2000). adv. bk.rev. index, cum.index. back issues avail. **Document type:** *Magazine, Consumer.* **Description:** Covers amateur to international level player interest in the game of chess.
Formerly (until 2000): Inside Chess (Print) (0896-8195)
Media: Online - full content.
Published by: International Chess Enterprises, Inc., PO Box 19457, Seattle, WA 98109-1457. TEL 206-286-9764, 800-262-4377, FAX 206-283-4363. Ed. Michael Franett. Adv. contact Russell Miller. Circ: 4,000 (paid).

796.44 USA ISSN 1543-110X
INSIDE GYMNASTICS. Text in English. 2002. bi-m. USD 19.95 domestic; USD 36.95 foreign (effective 2003).
Published by: Inside Publications, LLC, P. O. Box 88605, Atlanta, GA 30356. TEL 770-346-8538, FAX 770-234-6733. Ed. Caleb McKay. Pub. Chris Korotky. Adv. contact Karen McGee.

790.1 USA ISSN 0199-8501
INSIDE KUNG FU; the ultimate in martial arts coverage!. Text in English. 1973. m. USD 4.99 per issue (effective 2011). adv. bk.rev. charts; illus. **Document type:** *Magazine, Consumer.* **Description:** It is an oldest and most-influential Chinese-style martial arts magazine. It provides a rare, compelling and always informative look into the history, philosophy and technique that have made the Chinese styles popular for centuries.
Indexed: SportS.
Published by: Beckett Media Llc, 2400 E Katella Ave, Ste 300, Anaheim, CA 92806. TEL 714-939-9991, 800-764-6287, FAX 714-456-0146, customerservice@beckett.com, http://www.beckett.com. Ed. Dave Cater. Adv. contact Gabe Frimmel TEL 800-332-3330 ext 238.

791 USA ISSN 1541-5007
INSIDE LACROSSE. Text in English. 1997 (Mar.). m. USD 32.95 (effective 2002). adv. stat. back issues avail. **Document type:** *Newspaper, Consumer.*
Related titles: Online - full content ed.: Inside Lacrosse.com.
—CCC.
Address: PO Box 5570, Towson, MD 21285. letter@insidelacrosse.com. Eds. John Jiloty, Mike Keegan. Pub. Robert Carpenter.

796.86 AUS ISSN 1837-6258
▼ **INSIDE M M A.** (Mixed Martial Arts) Text in English. 2009. bi-m. AUD 49.95 domestic; AUD 99.50 foreign; AUD 9.50, NZD 10.20 newsstand/cover (effective 2011). adv. **Document type:** *Magazine, Trade.* **Description:** Dedicated to local and international Mixed Martial Arts.
Related titles: Online - full text ed.: free (effective 2011).
Published by: Blitz Publications, PO Box 4075, Mulgrave, VIC 3170, Australia. TEL 61-3-95748460, FAX 61-3-95748899, info@blitzmag.com.au, http://www.sportzblitz.net. Ed. Jarrah Lol. Pub. Silvio Morelli.

796.72 CAN ISSN 1924-7729
INSIDE MOTO X & OFF ROAD. Abbreviated title: I M X. Text in English. 2002. bi-m. CAD 14.99 (effective 2011). back issues avail. **Document type:** *Magazine, Trade.* **Description:** Focuses on the busy Canadian motocross and off road scene.
Formerly (until 2009): Inside Moto X (1704-233X)
Related titles: Online - full text ed.: free (effective 2011).
Published by: Inside Track Communications, Stn A, PO Box 7100, Toronto, ON M5W 1X7, Canada. TEL 416-962-7223, FAX 416-962-7208.

790 GBR ISSN 1756-896X
INSIDE POKER. Text in English. 2004 (Mar.). m. GBP 9.99 domestic; GBP 48.20 in Europe; GBP 78.40 elsewhere; GBP 3 newsstand/cover (effective 2009). adv. **Document type:** *Magazine, Consumer.* **Description:** Provides in-depth strategy and high-value freerolls for poker players.
Formerly (until 2007): Inside Edge (1742-8084)
—CCC.
Published by: Dennis Publishing Ltd., 30 Cleveland St, London, W1T 4JD, United Kingdom. TEL 44-20-79076000, FAX 44-20-79076020, reception@dennis.co.uk, http://www.dennis.co.uk/. Ed. Alun Bowden TEL 44-20-79076491. Pub. Richard Downey. Adv. contact Russell Blackman. page GBP 6,454; trim 210 x 275.

794.7 USA ISSN 1547-3511
INSIDE POOL MAGAZINE. Text in English. 2001 (Dec.). bi-m. USD 19.99 domestic; USD 28 in Canada; USD 39 elsewhere; USD 3.95 per issue domestic; USD 5.95 per issue in Canada (effective 2010). adv. **Document type:** *Magazine, Consumer.*
Related titles: Online - full text ed.: free.
Published by: Spheragon Publishing, PO Box 972, Kittanning, PA 16201. TEL 724-543-3700, 888-428-7665. Ed. Sally P Timko.

795 NZL ISSN 1177-1879
INSIDE RUNNING. Text in English. 2005. m. **Document type:** *Bulletin.* **Description:** Highlights the successes and developments taking place across the New Zealand racing industry.
Published by: New Zealand Racing Board, PO Box 28899, Wellington Mail Centre, Petone, New Zealand. TEL 64-4-5766999, FAX 64-4-5766942.

790.1 AUS ISSN 1037-1648
INSIDE SPORT. Text in English. 1991. m. AUD 79.95 in Australia & New Zealand; AUD 149 elsewhere; AUD 7.95 newsstand/cover (effective 2009). adv. bk.rev.; software rev.; video rev. back issues avail. **Document type:** *Magazine, Consumer.* **Description:** Provides the Australian and New Zealand sports fans with interesting articles on sports supported by extraordinary photography.
Related titles: Online - full text ed.
Indexed: A11, SD, T02, WBA, WMB.
—Ingenta.
Published by: Gemkilt Publishing Pty. Ltd., 55 Chandos St, St Leonards, NSW 2065, Australia. Ed. Graem Sims TEL 61-2-99016382. Pub. Peter Horwitz. Adv. contact Hamish Bayliss TEL 61-2-99016176. color page AUD 4,000; trim 225 x 297. Circ: 23,873. **Subscr. to:** PO Box 3355, St Leonards, NSW 1590, Australia.

796 AUS
INSIDE SPORT (ST.LEONARDS). Text in English. m. AUD 87.95 domestic; AUD 140 in New Zealand; AUD 150 elsewhere; AUD 7.95 newsstand/cover (effective 2008). adv. back issues avail. **Document type:** *Magazine, Consumer.* **Description:** Provides Australian and New Zealand sports fans with core values of award-winning journalism, photography and sporting entertainment.
Published by: Wolseley Media Pty Ltd., Level 5, 55 Chandos St, PO Box 5555, St. Leonards, NSW 2065, Australia. TEL 61-2-99016100, FAX 61-2-99016198, contactsubs@wolseleymedia.com.au, http://www.wolseleymedia.com.au. Ed. Graem Sims TEL 61-2-99016382. Adv. contact Hamish Bayliss TEL 61-2-99016176. color page AUD 4,000; trim 225 x 297. Circ: 23,873.

796 USA ISSN 1552-9975
INSIDE WISCONSIN SPORTS. Text in English. 1988. m. USD 14.97 (effective 2009). adv. back issues avail. **Document type:** *Magazine, Consumer.*
Published by: R B Publishing, Inc., 2901 International Ln, Ste 200, Madison, WI 53704. TEL 608-241-8777, 800-536-1992, FAX 608-241-8666, rbpub@rbpub.com, http://www.rbpub.com. Ed. Allison Lloyd TEL 360-471-3566. Pub. Chad Griepentrog TEL 608-442-5083. **Subscr. to:** PO Box 259098, Madison, WI 53725.

796.812 USA ISSN 1047-9562
INSIDE WRESTLING. Text in English. 1968. m. (plus additional issue in Dec.). adv. charts; illus.; tr.lit. **Document type:** *Magazine, Consumer.*
Published by: London Publishing Co. (Subsidiary of: Kappa Publishing Group, Inc.), 6198 Butler Pike, Ste 200, Blue Bell, PA 19422. TEL 215-643-6385, FAX 315-628-3571, custsrvc@kappapublishing.com, http://www.kappapublishing.com. Ed. David Lenker. Pub. Stuart M Saks. Adv. contact Sharon Liggio. **Dist. by:** Curtis CIRC Company, 641 Lexington Ave, New York, NY 10022; **Dist. in UK by:** Comag, Tavistock Rd, W Drayton, Middlesex UB7 7QE, United Kingdom. TEL 44-1895-444055, FAX 44-1895-433602.

THE INSIDER (PHOENIX). *see* OCCUPATIONS AND CAREERS

795 917.904 USA ISSN 1525-3899
INSIDER VIEWPOINT OF LAS VEGAS. Variant title: Insider Viewpoint Magazine. Text in English. 1994. s-m. USD 30. **Description:** Covers Las Vegas events, entertainment, restaurants, hotels, casinos, gambling, contests, employment, conventions, and travel.
Related titles: E-mail ed.: ISSN 1525-8793; Online - full text ed.
Published by: Insider Viewpoint Magazine of Las Vegas, PO Box 15110, Las Vegas, NV 89114. TEL 702-242-4482, FAX 702-893-0600. Ed., Pub. Richard Reed. Circ: 100,000.

791.45 USA
INSIDERS SPORTSLETTER. Text in English. 1981. bi-m. USD 50; USD 35 to students (effective 2005). adv. bk.rev. back issues avail. **Document type:** *Newsletter, Consumer.*
Published by: American Sportscasters Association Inc., 225 Broadway., Ste 2030, New York, NY 10007-3001. TEL 212-227-8080, FAX 212-571-0556, info@americansportscastersonline.com, http://www.americansportscastersonline.com. Ed., Pub., R&P, Adv. contact Louis O Schwartz. Circ: 2,500.

799.2 USA ISSN 0747-007X
INSIGHTS (FAIRFAX); N R A news for young shooters. Text in English. 1980. m. USD 9.95 to members (effective 2009). adv. 24 p./no.; back issues avail. **Document type:** *Magazine, Consumer.* **Description:** Features informative articles on shooting sports including information on firearm safety, gun care, competition and hunting for readers aged 7-20.
Formerly (until 1982): N R A Junior News
Published by: National Rifle Association of America, 11250 Waples Mill Rd, Fairfax, VA 22030. TEL 800-672-3888, publications@nrahq.org, http://www.nra.org. adv.: B&W page USD 1,065, color page USD 1,745; trim 7.625 x 10.5.

INSTITUT FUER DEUTSCHES UND INTERNATIONALES SPORTRECHT. SCHRIFTENREIHE. *see* LAW

796 DEU ISSN 0947-4501
INSTITUT FUER SPORTPUBLIZISTIK. BEITRAEGE. Text in German. 1993. irreg., latest vol.6, 2000. price varies. **Document type:** *Monographic series, Academic/Scholarly.*
Published by: (Institut fuer Sportpublizistik), Vistas Verlag GmbH, Goltzstr 11, Berlin, 10781, Germany. TEL 49-30-32707446, FAX 49-30-32707455, medienverlag@vistas.de.

797 USA
INSTITUTE OF DIVING. NEWSLETTER. Text in English. 1977. q. USD 25 to members (effective 2001). adv. bk.rev. **Document type:** *Newsletter.*
Published by: Institute of Diving, 17314 Panama City Beach Pkwy, Panama City, FL 32413. TEL 850-235-4101, FAX 850-235-4101. Ed., R&P Gregory Frye. Pub. Howie Doyle. Circ: 500.

797.2 GBR
INSTITUTE OF SPORT AND RECREATION MANAGEMENT. ANNUAL CONFERENCE AND SEMINAR PROCEEDINGS. Text in English. a.
Published by: Institute of Sport and Recreation Management, Giffard House, 36-38 Sherrard St, Melton Mowbray, Leics LE13 1XJ, United Kingdom. TEL 44-1664-565531, FAX 44-1664-501155, ralphriley@isrm.co.uk.

797.21 GBR
INSTITUTE OF SWIMMING TEACHERS & COACHES DIRECTORY OF MEMBERSHIP. Text in English. 1982. biennial. GBP 22.50 to members. adv. bk.rev. **Document type:** *Directory.*
Published by: Institute of Swimming Teachers & Coaches, Dawson House, 63 Forest Rd, Loughborough, Leics LE11 3NW, United Kingdom. TEL 01509-264357, FAX 01509-219349. Ed., Adv. contact D.L. Freeman-Wright. R&P D L Freeman Wright. Circ: 12,000.

796 613.7 GBR ISSN 1754-3371
GV743
INSTITUTION OF MECHANICAL ENGINEERS. PROCEEDINGS. PART P: JOURNAL OF SPORTS, ENGINEERING AND TECHNOLOGY/ JOURNAL OF SPORTS, ENGINEERING AND TECHNOLOGY. Text in English. 2008. q. USD 992 combined subscription in North America to institutions (print & online eds.); GBP 571 combined subscription elsewhere to institutions (print & online eds.) (effective 2011). reprint service avail. from PSC. **Document type:** *Journal, Academic/ Scholarly.* **Description:** Covers the development of novel sports apparel, footwear, and equipment; and the materials, instrumentation, and processes that make advances in sports possible.
Related titles: Online - full text ed.: ISSN 1754-338X. USD 894 in North America to institutions; GBP 514 elsewhere to institutions (effective 2011).
Indexed: A28, APA, BrCerAb, C&ISA, CA/WCA, CIA, CPEI, CerAb, CivEngAb, CorrAb, E&CAJ, E11, EEA, EMA, EMBASE, ESPM, EnvEAb, ExcerpMed, H15, M&TEA, M09, MBF, METADEX, PEI, SCI, SolStAb, T04, W07, WAA.
—BLDSC (6724.907000), IE, Linda Hall. **CCC.**
Published by: (Institution of Mechanical Engineers), Sage Publications Ltd. (Subsidiary of: Sage Publications, Inc.), 1 Oliver's Yard, 55 City Rd, London, EC1Y 1SP, United Kingdom. TEL 44-20-73248500, FAX 44-20-73248600, info@sagepub.co.uk, http://www.uk.sagepub.com/home.nav.

306.4 USA
INTERACTIVE GAMING NEWS. Text in English. d. USD 595; USD 495 government rate (effective 2001). **Document type:** *Magazine, Trade.* **Description:** Covers the latest law, business, marketing, technology and e-commerce developments in the interactive gaming industry.
Media: Online - full content.
Published by: River City Group LLC, 205 S Main St, St Charles, MO 63301. TEL 636-946-0820, FAX 636-946-0566, http://www.rivercitygroup.com. Ed., R&P Mark Balestra. Pub. Sue Schneider.

796 371.3 DEU ISSN 1866-3095
INTERDISZIPLINAERE BEITRAEGE ZUR TRAININGSPAEDAGOGIK. Text in German. 2008. irreg., latest vol.3, 2010. price varies. **Document type:** *Monographic series, Academic/Scholarly.*
Published by: Cuvillier Verlag, Nonnenstieg 8, Goettingen, 37075, Germany. TEL 49-551-547240, FAX 49-551-5472421, info@cuvillier.de.

688.752 GBR ISSN 1356-966X
INTERGAME. Text in English. 1994. m. GBP 100 Europe & Middle East; GBP 120 N. America, S. America & Africa; GBP 130 Asia & Australia (effective 2009). adv. back issues avail. **Document type:** *Magazine, Trade.* **Description:** Provides a comprehensive coverage of coin-operated amusement games for arcades, street locations, FECs, parks and casinos.
Published by: InterGame Ltd., Office Block 1, Southlink Business Park, Hamilton St, Oldham, Lancashire OL4 1DE, United Kingdom. TEL 44-161-6330100, FAX 44-161-6270009. Ed. Helen Fletcher. Pub. Christine Butterworth. Adv. contact Susan Ratcliffe.

688.79 GBR ISSN 2046-3294
INTERGAME .. YEARBOOK. Text in English. 200?. a. GBP 50 per issue in Europe; GBP 60 per issue in North America includes South America, Aisa, Africa, Australia (effective 2011). adv. **Document type:** *Yearbook, Consumer.* **Description:** Covers coin-operated amusements and gaming industry, as well as running industry-related conferences.
Published by: InterGame Ltd., Office Block 1, Southlink Business Park, Hamilton St, Oldham, Lancashire OL4 1DE, United Kingdom. TEL 44-161-6330100, FAX 44-161-6270009, intergame@intergame.ltd.uk.

795 GBR ISSN 1357-7891
INTERGAMING. Text in English. 1995. m. GBP 80 Europe & Middle East; GBP 90 N. America, S. America & Africa; GBP 100 Asia & Australia (effective 2009). adv. back issues avail. **Document type:** *Magazine, Trade.* **Description:** Provides a comprehensive coverage of the international casino industry.
Published by: InterGame Ltd., Office Block 1, Southlink Business Park, Hamilton St, Oldham, Lancashire OL4 1DE, United Kingdom. TEL 44-161-6330100, FAX 44-161-6270009. Ed. Phil Clegg. Pub. Christine Butterworth. Adv. contact Sarah Lawrence TEL 44-1474-747339.

790.1 CAN
INTERNATIONAL ASSOCIATION FOR SPORTS INFORMATION. NEWSLETTER. Text in Dutch. 1977. q. adv. bk.rev. **Document type:** *Bulletin.* **Description:** News bulletin for library and documentation centers in the field of sports and physical education.
Formerly (until 1995): International Bulletin of Sports Information (0378-4037)
Indexed: SportS.
Published by: International Association for Sports Information, c/o Gretchen Ghent, University of Calgary Library, MLB 405A, 2500 University Dr NW, Calgary, AB T2N 1N4, Canada. TEL 403-220-6097. Ed. Gretchen Ghent.

796 371 JPN ISSN 0074-1728
INTERNATIONAL ASSOCIATION OF PHYSICAL EDUCATION AND SPORTS FOR GIRLS AND WOMEN. PROCEEDINGS OF THE INTERNATIONAL CONGRESS. (Proceedings published by host countries) Text in Japanese. irreg., latest 1969, 6th, Tokyo. **Document type:** *Proceedings.*
Published by: (International Association of Physical Education and Sports for Girls and Women), Japan Association of Physical Education for Women and Girls, 6-102 OMYC, 3-1 Jinen-cho Yoyogi, Shibuya-ku, Tokyo, Japan. Circ: (controlled).

796.345 MYS ISSN 0255-4437
INTERNATIONAL BADMINTON FEDERATION. ANNUAL STATUTE BOOK. Text in English. 1935. a., latest 2002. GBP 13 (effective 2000). index. 192 p./no.; **Document type:** *Yearbook.* **Description:** Contains the rules of badminton, competition regulations, and results of IBF events.
Formerly: International Badminton Federation. Annual Handbook (0074-1981)

Published by: International Badminton Federation, Batu 3 1/2 Jalan Cheras, Kuala Lumpur, Glos 56000, Malaysia. TEL 60-3-92837155, FAX 60-3-92847155, ibf@internationalbadminton.org, http://www.internationalbadminton.org. Circ: 2,000.

796.345 GBR ISSN 2042-7603
INTERNATIONAL BADMINTON MAGAZINE. Text in English. 2005. q. GBP 3, EUR 4.50, USD 5.50 per issue; free to qualified personnel (effective 2010). adv. back issues avail. **Document type:** *Magazine, Consumer.* **Description:** Covers information about world's most exciting sports, appealing to a diverse and dynamic audience of enthusiasts and players of all standards from recreational and club players to professionals.
Related titles: Online - full text ed.: free (effective 2010).
Published by: International Sport Group, No 4 The Spinney, Chester Rd, Poynton, Cheshire SK12 1HB, United Kingdom. TEL 44-7973-544719, info@isportgroup.com. Ed. Paul Walters. Adv. contact Dean Finegold TEL 44-7967-362589. page GBP 2,000; trim 210 x 297. Circ: 40,000.

THE INTERNATIONAL DIRECTORY OF SPORTING GOODS AND TOYS IMPORTERS. *see* BUSINESS AND ECONOMICS—Trade And Industrial Directories

THE INTERNATIONAL ELECTRONIC JOURNAL OF HEALTH EDUCATION. *see* PHYSICAL FITNESS AND HYGIENE

INTERNATIONAL ENCYCLOPAEDIA OF LAWS. SPORTS LAW. *see* LAW—International Law

790.1 USA ISSN 1070-9568
INTERNATIONAL FIGURE SKATING. Abbreviated title: I F S. Variant title: Figure Skating. Text in English. 1993. bi-m. USD 28 (effective 2010). adv. film rev.; tel.rev.; video rev. charts; stat.; illus. back issues avail.; reprints avail. **Document type:** *Magazine, Consumer.* **Description:** Provides comprehensive coverage of figure skating.
Related titles: Online - full text ed.: USD 20 (effective 2010).
Indexed: B04, BRD, G09, P10, P53, P54, PQC, R03, RGAb, RGPR, SD, T02, W03, W05.
—Ingenta. **CCC.**
Published by: Madavor Media, Llc., 85 Quincy Ave, Ste B, Quincy, MA 02169. TEL 617-706-9110, FAX 617-536-0102, info@madavor.com, http://www.madavor.com. Ed. Susan Wessling TEL 617-706-9095. Pub. Susan Fitzgerald TEL 617-706-9086. Adv. contact Miene Smith TEL 617-706-9092. B&W page USD 2,415, color page USD 3,675; trim 7.875 x 10.5.

INTERNATIONAL GAMBLING STUDIES. *see* PSYCHOLOGY

790.1 330 USA ISSN 1066-145X
HV6715
INTERNATIONAL GAMING & WAGERING BUSINESS. Text in English. 1980. m. USD 161 domestic; USD 198 in Canada; USD 211 elsewhere; free to qualified personnel (effective 2009). adv. back issues avail.; reprints avail. **Document type:** *Magazine, Trade.* **Description:** Provides unbiased and in-depth information on gaming market trends and developments from around the world.
Former titles (until 1990): Gaming and Wagering Business (8750-8222); (until 1984): Gaming Business (0736-0916); (until 19??): Gaming Business Magazine (0196-2213)
Related titles: Online - full text ed.; ◆ Supplement(s): SlotManager. ISSN 1949-9728; ◆ Indian Gaming Business. ISSN 1948-6952; Directory.
Indexed: A09, A10, B02, B15, B17, B18, G04, H&TI, H06, I05, PROMT, RASB, T02, V03, V04.
—**CCC.**
Published by: B N P Media, 505 E Capovilla Ave, Ste 102, Las Vegas, NV 89119. TEL 702-794-0718, FAX 702-794-0799, portfolio@bnpmedia.com, http://www.bnpmedia.com. Ed. James Rutherford TEL 702-794-0718. Pub. Charles Anderer TEL 718-432-8529. Adv. contact Terry Davis TEL 404-320-0072. color page USD 8,365, B&W page USD 7,300; trim 10.25 x 13.625. Circ: 12,500 (paid).

796.41 USA ISSN 0891-6616
GV461
INTERNATIONAL GYMNAST. Text in English. 1972. 10/yr. USD 30 domestic; USD 40 in Canada; USD 50 elsewhere (effective 2010). adv. bk.rev. bibl.; illus. index. reprints avail. **Document type:** *Magazine, Consumer.* **Description:** Covers gymnastics with in-depth competition reports, personalities and photos.
Former titles (until 1986): International Gymnast Magazine (0890-2437); (until 1982): International Gymnast (0735-7567); (until 1981): International Gymnast Magazine (0276-1041); (until 1979): International Gymnast (0162-9867); (until 1976): Gymnast (0046-6670); Which was formed by the merger of (1966-1971): Mademoiselle Gymnast (0024-9408); (1956-1972): Modern Gymnast (0026-7813); Incorporates (1975-1980): Gymnastics World (0098-8677)
Related titles: Microform ed.: 1956 (from PQC); Online - full text ed.: International Gymnast Magazine Online. USD 24.95 (effective 2010).
Indexed: A22, G09, M01, M02, MEA&I, P02, P10, P19, P48, P53, P54, PQC, RASB, SD, SPI, SportS, T02.
—BLDSC (4540.673000), IE, Infotrieve, Ingenta.
Published by: Paul Ziert & Associates, Inc., 3214 Bart Conner Dr, Norman, OK 73072. TEL 405-447-9988, FAX 405-447-5810, orders@intlgymnast.com. Pub. Paul Ziert. Adv. contact Ben Fox.

795.4 USA ISSN 1078-0807
INTERNATIONAL HOME AND PRIVATE POKER PLAYERS NEWSLETTER. Text in English. 1988. bi-m. looseleaf. USD 7 (effective 2000). back issues avail. **Document type:** *Newsletter.* **Description:** Contains news of members and poker tournament results.
Published by: International Home & Private Poker Players' Association, 220 E Flamingo Rd, Apt 127, Las Vegas, NV 89109. TEL 702-893-9851. Ed. Edwin E Wuehle. Circ: 300.

306.483 KOR ISSN 1598-2939
INTERNATIONAL JOURNAL OF APPLIED SPORTS SCIENCES. Text in English. 1989. s-a. KRW 20,000; KRW 10,000 per issue (effective 2009). **Document type:** *Journal, Academic/Scholarly.*
Formerly (until 2000): Korean Journal of Sport Science (1225-763X)
Indexed: CA, R09, SD, T02.
—BLDSC (4542.100950), IE, Ingenta.
Published by: Korea Institute of Sport Science/Han'gug Ceyug Gwahag Yeon'guweon, 223-19 gongneung-dong, Nowon-Gu, Seoul, Korea, S. TEL 82-2-9709500, FAX 82-2-9709651, publ@sports.re.kr, http://www.sports.re.kr/. Ed. Ju-Ho Chang. Circ: 1,000.

INTERNATIONAL JOURNAL OF AQUATIC RESEARCH AND EDUCATION. *see* PHYSICAL FITNESS AND HYGIENE

796 KOR ISSN 1975-8286
INTERNATIONAL JOURNAL OF COACHING SCIENCE. Text in English. 2007. s-a. USD 30 to individuals; USD 120 to institutions (effective 2008). **Document type:** *Journal, Academic/Scholarly.*
Indexed: CA, SD, T02.
—BLDSC (4542.172193), IE.
Published by: (International Council for Coach Education), Korea Coaching Development Center, 3F Pyeonghwa Bldg, 1451-34 Seocho-dong, Seocho-gu, Seoul, Gyeonggido 137-867, Korea, S. TEL 82-2-34712469, FAX 82-2-34716261, KCDC@paran.com, http://www.ikcdc.net/.

INTERNATIONAL JOURNAL OF EMOTIONAL PSYCHOLOGY AND SPORT ETHICS. *see* PSYCHOLOGY

796 GBR
➤ **INTERNATIONAL JOURNAL OF PERFORMANCE ANALYSIS IN SPORT.** Text in English. 2001 (Jul.). 3/yr. USD 48 to individuals; GBP 99 to institutions; USD 30 per issue (effective 2009). **Document type:** *Journal, Academic/Scholarly.* **Description:** Covers all aspects of athletic performances analysis, including behavior, technology, and biomechancis.
Related titles: Online - full text ed.: ISSN 1474-8185 (from IngentaConnect).
Indexed: SD.
Published by: U W I C Press, Cyncoed Rd, Cyncoed, Cardiff, CF23 6XD, United Kingdom. TEL 44-29-20416515, cgrove@uwic.ac.uk, http://www.uwicpress.co.uk/. Ed. Peter O'Donoghue.

➤ **INTERNATIONAL JOURNAL OF PHYSICAL EDUCATION/ INTERNATIONALE ZEITSCHRIFT FUER SPORTPAEDAGOGIK.** *see* EDUCATION—Teaching Methods And Curriculum

200 796 USA ISSN 2151-0679
GV706.42
▼ ➤ **INTERNATIONAL JOURNAL OF RELIGION AND SPORT.** Abbreviated title: I J R S. Text in English. 2009. s-a. USD 30 per issue (effective 2009). **Document type:** *Journal, Academic/Scholarly.* **Description:** Analyzes the interchanges between world religions, religious practice, spirituality, and global sport.
Published by: Mercer University Press, 1400 Coleman Ave, Macon, GA 31207. TEL 478-301-2880, 866-895-1472, FAX 478-301-2585, mupressorders@mercer.edu, http://www.mupress.org/index.html. Eds. Christopher J Anderson, Gordon Marino.

795 306 700 NLD ISSN 2210-4909
➤ **INTERNATIONAL JOURNAL OF ROLE-PLAYING.** Text in English. 2008. s-a. free (effective 2011). **Document type:** *Journal, Academic/Scholarly.* **Description:** Aims to act as the focal point, for pushing the limits of role-playing knowledge, and to improve sharing of knowledge across the knowledge networks involved with role-playing and related work.
Media: Online - full text.
Published by: Hogeschool voor de Kunsten marinka.copier@kmt.hku.nl, http://marinakacopier.nl/ijrp.

➤ **INTERNATIONAL JOURNAL OF SPORT AND EXERCISE PSYCHOLOGY.** *see* PSYCHOLOGY

➤ **INTERNATIONAL JOURNAL OF SPORT AND HEALTH SCIENCE.** *see* PHYSICAL FITNESS AND HYGIENE

796 301 USA ISSN 2152-7857
▼ ➤ **INTERNATIONAL JOURNAL OF SPORT AND SOCIETY.** Text in English. 2010 (May). q. USD 800; USD 950 combined subscription (print & online eds.) (effective 2011). **Document type:** *Journal, Academic/Scholarly.* **Description:** Provides an interdisciplinary examination of sports, including the history, sociology and psychology of sports, sports medicine and health, physical and health education, and sports administration and management.
Related titles: Online - full text ed.: ISSN 2152-7865. 2010 (May). USD 300 (effective 2011).
Indexed: SD.
Published by: Common Ground Publishing, University of Illinois Research Park, 60 Hazelwood Dr, Ste 226, Champaign, IL 61820. TEL 217-328-0405, kathryn@commongroundpublishing.com, http://www.commongroundpublishing.com. Eds. Bill Cope, Keith Gilbert.

796 USA ISSN 1936-3915
➤ **INTERNATIONAL JOURNAL OF SPORT COMMUNICATION.** Text in English. 2008 (Mar.). q. USD 368 domestic to institutions; USD 378 foreign to institutions; USD 426 combined subscription domestic to institutions (print & online eds.); USD 436 combined subscription foreign to institutions (print & online eds.) (effective 2012). adv. **Document type:** *Journal, Academic/Scholarly.* **Description:** Promotes the understanding and advancement of the relationship between sport and communication.
Related titles: Online - full text ed.: ISSN 1936-3907. USD 368 to institutions (effective 2012).
Indexed: CA, CABA, GH, LT, P32, PEI, PGegResA, R12, RRTA, SD, T02, T05.
—BLDSC (4542.680520), IE. **CCC.**
Published by: Human Kinetics, 1607 N Market St, Champaign, IL 61820. TEL 800-747-4457, FAX 217-351-2674, info@hkusa.com. Ed. Paul M Pedersen TEL 812-855-4066. R&P Martha Gullo TEL 217-403-7534. Adv. contact Amy Bleich TEL 217-403-7803. Circ: 129 (paid).

658 USA ISSN 1558-6235
GV716
➤ **INTERNATIONAL JOURNAL OF SPORT FINANCE.** Abbreviated title: I J S F. Text in English. 2006 (Feb.). q. USD 269 domestic to institutions; USD 277 foreign to institutions; USD 63 combined subscription domestic to individuals (print & online eds.); USD 74 combined subscription foreign to individuals (print & online eds.); USD 317 combined subscription domestic to institutions (print & online eds.); USD 331 combined subscription foreign to institutions (print & online eds.) (effective 2010). adv. back issues avail. **Document type:** *Journal, Academic/Scholarly.* **Description:** Serves as a high-level forum for the dissemination of current research on sport finance topics on a worldwide basis.
Related titles: Online - full text ed.: ISSN 1930-076X. USD 63 to individuals; USD 317 to institutions; USD 45 to students (effective 2010).
Indexed: A12, A15, A17, A26, ABIn, B02, B04, B15, B17, B18, BPI, BRD, CA, CABA, CurCont, E08, EconLit, G04, I05, JEL, LT, N02, O01, P48, P51, P53, P54, PEI, PN&I, PQC, RRTA, S09, SCOPUS, SD, SSCI, T02, W01, W02, W03, W05, W07.
—BLDSC (4542.680575), IE. **CCC.**
Published by: Fitness Information Technology Inc., West Virginia University, 275G Coliseum, WVU-PE, PO Box 6116, Morgantown, WV 26506. TEL 304-293-6888, 800-477-4348, FAX 304-293-6658, fitcustomerservice@mail.wvu.edu. Ed. Robert Simmons.

➤ **INTERNATIONAL JOURNAL OF SPORT MANAGEMENT.** *see* BUSINESS AND ECONOMICS—Management

➤ **INTERNATIONAL JOURNAL OF SPORT MANAGEMENT AND MARKETING.** *see* BUSINESS AND ECONOMICS—Management

➤ **INTERNATIONAL JOURNAL OF SPORT MANAGEMENT, RECREATION AND TOURISM.** *see* BUSINESS AND ECONOMICS—Management

796 320.6 GBR ISSN 1940-6940
GV706.35
▼ **INTERNATIONAL JOURNAL OF SPORT POLICY.** Text in English. 2009. 3/yr. GBP 237 combined subscription in United Kingdom to institutions (print & online eds.); EUR 377, USD 472 combined subscription to institutions (print & online eds.) (effective 2012). **Document type:** *Journal, Academic/Scholarly.* **Description:** Addresses all aspects of sport policy irrespective of academic discipline.
Related titles: Online - full text ed.: ISSN 1940-6959. GBP 213 in United Kingdom to institutions; EUR 340, USD 425 to institutions (effective 2012).
Indexed: B21, CA, ESPM, H&SSA, P10, PEI, PQC, SD, T02.
—**CCC.**
Published by: Routledge (Subsidiary of: Taylor & Francis Group), 4 Park Sq, Milton Park, Abingdon, Oxon OX14 4RN, United Kingdom. TEL 44-20-70176000, FAX 44-20-70176336, info@routledge.co.uk, http://www.routledge.com. Ed. Barrie Houlihan. Adv. contact Linda Hann TEL 44-1344-779945.

▼ **THE INTERNATIONAL JOURNAL OF SPORTS AND ENTERTAINMENT BUSINESS.** *see* BUSINESS AND ECONOMICS—Marketing And Purchasing

790.1 658.8 GBR ISSN 1464-6668
GV716
➤ **INTERNATIONAL JOURNAL OF SPORTS MARKETING & SPONSORSHIP.** Abbreviated title: I J S M S. Text in English. 1998. q. GBP 145, EUR 215, USD 260 to institutions; GBP 495, EUR 730, USD 885 to libraries (effective 2009). back issues avail. **Document type:** *Journal, Academic/Scholarly.* **Description:** Designed to be a dissemination tool as well as a bridge between academic and practitioner.
Related titles: Online - full text ed.
Indexed: A01, A02, A03, A08, A26, B02, B15, B17, B18, CA, CurCont, E08, G04, G06, G07, G08, I05, P03, PsycInfo, S09, SCOPUS, SD, SSCI, T02, W07.
—BLDSC (4542.681250), IE, Ingenta. **CCC.**
Published by: International Marketing Reports Ltd., The Barn, The St, Chilham, Canterbury, Kent, CT4 8BX, United Kingdom. TEL 44-1227-731099, FAX 44-1227-731099, info@im-reports.com. Ed. Michel Desbordes. Pub. Chris Hollins.

796 GBR ISSN 1747-9541
➤ **INTERNATIONAL JOURNAL OF SPORTS SCIENCE & COACHING.** Text in English. 2006. q. GBP 211; GBP 224 combined subscription (print & online eds.) (effective 2012). **Document type:** *Journal, Academic/Scholarly.* **Description:** Aims to integrate theory and practice in sports science, as well as to evaluate commonly accepted beliefs about coaching effectiveness and performance enhancement.
Related titles: Online - full text ed.: 2006. GBP 199 (effective 2012).
Indexed: A28, APA, BrCerAb, C&ISA, CA, CA/WCA, CABA, CIA, CerAb, CivEngAb, CorrAb, CurCont, E&CAJ, E11, EEA, EMA, GH, H15, LT, M&TEA, M09, MBF, METADEX, N02, N03, P03, P30, PsycInfo, R12, SCOPUS, SD, SSCI, SolStAb, T02, T04, W07, WAA.
—BLDSC (4542.681315), IE, Ingenta. **CCC.**
Published by: Multi-Science Publishing Co. Ltd., 5 Wates Way, Brentwood, Essex CM15 9TB, United Kingdom. TEL 44-1277-244632, FAX 44-1277-223453, info@multi-science.co.uk. Ed. Simon Jenkins TEL 44-1225-384328.

➤ **THE INTERNATIONAL JOURNAL OF THE HISTORY OF SPORT.** *see* HISTORY

796.805 AUS
INTERNATIONAL KICKBOXER. Text in English. m. AUD 60 domestic; AUD 123 foreign (effective 2008). adv. back issues avail. **Document type:** *Magazine, Consumer.* **Description:** Features latest news, fitness tips, training techniques, fight strategies, boxing drills, cardio kick boxing, conditioning exercises, combat tactics and sports nutrition advice.
Published by: Blitz Publications, PO Box 4075, Mulgrave, VIC 3170, Australia. TEL 61-3-95748460, FAX 61-3-95748899, info@blitzmag.com.au. Ed. Michael Schiavello. Adv. contact Keith Rozario.

796 GRC ISSN 0074-7181
INTERNATIONAL OLYMPIC ACADEMY. REPORT OF THE SESSIONS. Text in English. 1961. a. USD 20; free to qualified personnel. cum.index: 1961-69. **Document type:** *Proceedings.* **Description:** Covers profiles, results, statistics, training information and news, reports, text and photos.
Related titles: Greek ed.; French ed.
Indexed: SportS.
Published by: (International Olympic Academy), Hellenic Olympic Committee, 4 Kapsali St, Athens, 107 64, Greece. FAX 30-1-724-2150, TELEX 219494. Ed. Fotini Karamanbaki. Circ: 9,000.

790.1 HUN ISSN 2060-9469
▼ ➤ **INTERNATIONAL QUARTERLY OF SPORT SCIENCE.** Text in English. 2009. q. free (effective 2011). abstr. back issues avail. **Document type:** *Journal, Academic/Scholarly.* **Description:** Contains original articles on empirical research, theory, practices and policies in sport science.
Media: Online - full text.
Indexed: CABA, GH, LT, N02, N03.
Published by: Hungarian Society of Sport Science, Istvanmezei ut 1-3, Budapest, 1146, Hungary. TEL 36-1-4606980, FAX 36-1-4606980, http://www.iqss.eu/index.php. Ed. Jozsef Tihanyi.

S

796 CHE ISSN 0535-2479
INTERNATIONAL SKATING UNION. MINUTES OF CONGRESS. Text in English. biennial. CHF 10. **Document type:** *Proceedings, Trade.*
Published by: International Skating Union, Chemin de Primerose 2, Lausanne, 1007, Switzerland. TEL 41-21-6126666, FAX 41-21-6126677, info@isu.ch, http://www.isu.org.

796 CHE
INTERNATIONAL SKATING UNION. SPECIAL REGULATIONS FIGURE SKATING. Text in English. biennial. CHF 20 per issue. **Document type:** *Bulletin, Trade.*
Published by: International Skating Union, Chemin de Primerose 2, Lausanne, 1007, Switzerland. TEL 41-21-6126666, FAX 41-21-6126677, info@isu.ch, http://www.isu.org.

796 CHE
INTERNATIONAL SKATING UNION. SPECIAL REGULATIONS ICE DANCING. Text in English. biennial. CHF 20. **Document type:** *Bulletin, Trade.*
Formerly: International Skating Union. Ice Dancing Regulations (0539-0168)
Published by: International Skating Union, Chemin de Primerose 2, Lausanne, 1007, Switzerland. TEL 41-21-6126666, FAX 41-21-6126677, info@isu.ch, http://www.isu.org.

796 CHE
INTERNATIONAL SKATING UNION. SPECIAL REGULATIONS SPEED SKATING & SHORT TRACK SPEED SKATING. Text in English. biennial. CHF 20 per issue. **Document type:** *Bulletin, Trade.*
Published by: International Skating Union, Chemin de Primerose 2, Lausanne, 1007, Switzerland. TEL 41-21-6126666, FAX 41-21-6126677, info@isu.ch, http://www.isu.org.

796 CHE
INTERNATIONAL SKATING UNION. SPECIAL REGULATIONS SYNCHRONIZED SKATING. Text in English. biennial. CHF 20 per issue. **Document type:** *Bulletin, Trade.*
Published by: International Skating Union, Chemin de Primerose 2, Lausanne, 1007, Switzerland. TEL 41-21-6126666, FAX 41-21-6126677, info@isu.ch, http://www.isu.org.

790.1 USA ISSN 1097-1599
GV561
THE INTERNATIONAL SPORTS DIRECTORY. Text in English. 1997. irreg., latest 3rd ed. USD 45 per issue (effective 2011). **Document type:** *Directory, Consumer.* **Description:** Provides addresses, telephone and fax numbers, and contact persons from all sports worldwide.
Published by: Global Sports Productions Ltd., PO Box 221, Clam Gulch, AK 99568. TEL 310-454-9480, Globalnw@earthlink.net.

344.099 GBR ISSN 1467-6680
INTERNATIONAL SPORTS LAW REVIEW. Text in English. 2000. q. GBP 615, EUR 811, USD 1,057 (effective 2012). **Document type:** *Journal, Academic/Scholarly.* **Description:** Discusses current issues and developments in the practice of law as it affects sports business and sports-related litigation.
Incorporates: Sports Law Reports
Related titles: Online - full text ed.
—BLDSC (8574.850000), IE, Ingenta.
Published by: Sweet & Maxwell Ltd. (Subsidiary of: Thomson Reuters Corp.), 100 Avenue Rd, London, NW3 3PF, United Kingdom. TEL 44-20-73937000, FAX 44-20-74491144, sweetandmaxwell.customer.services@thomson.com. Ed. Michael J Beloff. **Subscr. to:** PO Box 1000, Andover SP10 9AF, United Kingdom. TEL 44-20-73938051, sweetandmaxwell.international.queries@thomson.com.

790.1 DEU ISSN 1443-0770
GV201
➤ **INTERNATIONAL SPORTS STUDIES.** Text in English. 1979. s-a. EUR 37 domestic; EUR 42 foreign (effective 2011). bk.rev.; video rev. back issues avail. **Document type:** *Journal, Academic/Scholarly.* **Description:** Contains research papers, reviews of books, video and other computer-based resources, covering topics of research and scholarship in the social sciences that focuses upon international studies of physical education and sport.
Formerly (until 1999): Journal of Comparative Physical Education and Sport (1010-8262)
Indexed: CA, ESPM, PEI, RiskAb, SD, T02.
—BLDSC (4549.627280), IE.
Published by: (International Society on Comparative Physical Education and Sport (ISCPES) INT), Logos Verlag Berlin, Comeniushof, Gubener Str 47, Berlin, 10243, Germany. TEL 49-30-42851090, FAX 49-30-42851092, redaktion@logos-verlag.de. Ed. Robert Chappell. Pub. Volker Buchholtz. Circ: 1,000 (paid).

793 USA ISSN 1076-7886
GV1218.S8 CODEN: BISAFS
INTERNATIONAL STRING FIGURE ASSOCIATION. BULLETIN. Text in English. 19??. a. USD 15 to libraries; free to members (effective 2010). back issues avail. **Document type:** *Bulletin, Academic/Scholarly.* **Description:** Features original material that advances the understanding and enhances the enjoyment of string figures.
Formerly (until 1994): String Figure Association. Bulletin
Indexed: AICP, MLA-IB.
Published by: International String Figure Association, PO Box 5134, Pasadena, CA 91117. TEL 626-398-1057. Ed. Mark A Sherman.

797.21 USA
INTERNATIONAL SWIMMING HALL OF FAME HEADLINES. Text in English. 1965. q. membership. adv. bk.rev. **Document type:** *Newsletter.* **Description:** Covers events at the Swimming Hall of Fame and current news throughout the world of aquatics.
Formerly: International Swimming Hall of Fame News
Published by: International Swimming Hall of Fame, One Hall of Fame Dr., Ft. Lauderdale, FL 33316. TEL 954-462-6536, FAX 954-525-4031. Ed., R&P Holly Heil. Adv. contact Sharon Carlos. Circ: 2,500.

796.962 617.1 USA ISSN 2156-1036
GV848.35
INTERNATIONAL SYMPOSIUM ON SAFETY IN ICE HOCKEY. PAPERS. Variant title: Safety in Ice Hockey. Text in English. 1987. irreg. USD 99 per issue (effective 2010). **Document type:** *Proceedings, Trade.* **Description:** Focuses on both the injuries incurred in the game of ice hockey and the techniques used to decrease the risk of these injuries.
Related titles: Online - full text ed.: ISSN 2156-1044.
Published by: A S T M International, 100 Barr Harbor Dr, PO Box C700, W Conshohocken, PA 19428. TEL 610-832-9500, 800-262-1373, FAX 610-832-9555, service@astm.org.

799.202 CHE ISSN 1017-5547
INTERNATIONALES WAFFEN-MAGAZIN. Text in German; Contents page in English. 1982. 10/yr. CHF 105 (effective 1997). bk.rev. charts; illus. index. **Document type:** *Consumer.* **Description:** Modern and antique firearms, shooting sports, self-defense.
Formerly (until Dec. 1989): Schweizer Waffen-Magazin (0253-4878)
Indexed: IBR, IBZ.
Published by: Habegger Verlag Zuerich, Morgartenstr 6-10, Postfach 9230, Zuerich, 8036, Switzerland. TEL 41-1-2981204, FAX 41-1-2981277. Ed. Peter Ernst Grimm. Circ: 55,000.

791.068 GBR ISSN 1359-6284
INTERPARK. Text in English. 1995. m. GBP 45 Europe & Middle East; GBP 55 N. America, S. America & Africa; GBP 65 Asia & Australia (effective 2009). adv. back issues avail. **Document type:** *Magazine, Trade.* **Description:** Provides coverage of news and developments in the theme park and family entertainment centers industry.
Published by: InterGame Ltd., 8 Bowden Ln, Chapel-En-Le-Frith, Derbyshire SK23 0JQ, United Kingdom. TEL 44-1298-813148, FAX 44-1298-814344, http://www.intergameonline.com. Ed. Andrew Mellor. Pub. Christine Butterworth. Adv. contact John Fosbrooke.

INTERSCHOLASTIC ATHLETIC ADMINISTRATION. *see* EDUCATION—School Organization And Administration

795 NLD ISSN 1872-0781
INTO THE GAME. Text in Dutch. 2005. bi-m. EUR 95 (effective 2010). adv.
Published by: (VAN Speelautomaten Branch-organisatie), Media Business Press BV, Postbus 8632, Rotterdam, 3009 AP, Netherlands. TEL 31-10-2894075, FAX 31-10-2894076, info@mbp.nl, http://www.mbp.nl/. Ed. Maureen van der Mast. adv.: color page EUR 1,205; trim 210 x 297. Circ: 950.

798.8 IRL ISSN 0332-3536
IRISH GREYHOUND REVIEW. Text in English. 1979. a. adv. **Document type:** *Magazine, Consumer.*
Formerly (until 1980): Irish Greyhound Annual (0332-348X)
Published by: Victory Irish Promotions, PO Box 7992, Dun Laoghaire, Co. Dublin, Ireland. TEL 353-1-2804481, FAX 353-1-2804481. Adv. contact Margaret Walsh. B&W page EUR 1,206, color page EUR 1,651; trim 210 x 297. Circ: 12,000 (paid and controlled).

796.7 IRL ISSN 1649-6035
IRISH MOTORSPORT ANNUAL. Text in English. 1977. a. EUR 9.99 (effective 2006). adv.
Former titles (until 1995): Michael O'Carroll's Irish Motorsport Annual (0791-9166); (until 1987): Irish Motorsport Annual (0791-9174)
Published by: Ashville Media Group, Apollo House, Tara St., Dublin, 2, Ireland. TEL 353-1-4322200, FAX 353-1-6727100, info@ashville.com, http://www.ashville.com. Ed. Michael O'Carroll. Adv. contact Neil Batt. color page EUR 2,700. Circ: 3,500.

796.34 IRL ISSN 0791-2501
IRISH RACQUETS REVIEW. Text in English. 1978. 3/yr. **Document type:** *Magazine, Consumer.*
Former titles (until 1989): Irish Squash Review (0332-3579); (until 1979): Squash Review (0332-3560)
Published by: Victory Irish Promotions, PO Box 7992, Dun Laoghaire, Co. Dublin, Ireland. TEL 353-1-2804481, FAX 353-1-2804481. Adv. contact Margaret Walsh.

796.426 IRL ISSN 0332-2947
IRISH RUNNER. Text in English. 1981. bi-m. adv. **Document type:** *Magazine, Consumer.*
Related titles: Supplement(s): Irish Runner Annual. ISSN 0790-6757. 1982.
Published by: Athletic Publications, PO Box 1227, Dublin, 8, Ireland. TEL 353-1-4563629, FAX 353-1-4563599. Adv. contact Frank Greally. B&W page EUR 950, color page EUR 1,200; trim 210 x 297. Circ: 10,400 (paid and controlled).

IRONMAN. *see* PHYSICAL FITNESS AND HYGIENE

IRONMAN MAGAZINE (MOSCOW). *see* PHYSICAL FITNESS AND HYGIENE

796 USA ISSN 1944-1215
ISLAND SPORTS MEDIA. Text in English. 2008. q. USD 19.99 (effective 2008). adv. **Document type:** *Magazine, Consumer.* **Description:** Dedicated to promoting high school and college athletics of the Hawaiian Islands.
Published by: Island Sports Media LLC, 11014 19th Ave Se, Ste 8, PMB 250, Everett, WA 98208. TEL 888-476-0050. Ed. Steve Kajihiro.

794.1 ITA ISSN 0021-2849
L'ITALIA SCACCHISTICA. Text in Italian. 1911. 8/yr. EUR 45 domestic; EUR 65 foreign (effective 2009). adv. bk.rev. charts; illus. index. 64 p./no.; **Document type:** *Magazine, Consumer.* **Description:** Covers every aspect of the game of chess including national and international news.
Published by: Italia Scacchistica, Via Alfonso Lamarmora 40, Milan, MI 20122, Italy. TEL 39-02-5517615, FAX 39-02-55019079.

796 ITA ISSN 2035-7893
▼ **ITALIA SPORT.** Text in Italian. 2009. w. **Document type:** *Magazine, Consumer.*
Published by: Gruppo Editoriale Mazzetti, Viale delle Mura Aurelie, Rome, 00165, Italy. TEL 39-06-62290860, FAX 39-06-622939023.

790.1 USA
J A Q K. (Jack Ace Queen King) Text in English. 2004. 5/yr. USD 15.99; USD 2.99 per issue (effective 2006). adv. **Document type:** *Magazine, Consumer.* **Description:** Caters to the lifestyles and interests of gamblers and other risk-reward people.
Address: 25 W 13th St, Ste 2JN, New York, NY 10011. TEL 917-570-4008. Eds. Jack Wright, Mike Pesca. Pub., Adv. contact Brett Garfinkel. page USD 28,500. Circ: 300,000.

793.7 EST
JAAPANI MOISTATUSED. Text in Estonian. 2004. q. EUR 1.06 newsstand/cover (effective 2011). adv. **Document type:** *Magazine, Consumer.*
Published by: Kuma Ltd., 57 Parnu St, Paide, 72712, Estonia. TEL 372-38-38800, FAX 372-38-38806, kuma@kuma.ee, http://www.kuma.ee. Ed. Jaanus Laidna. adv.: page EEK 2,000.

796 NLD ISSN 1571-3490
JAARBOEK SPORT. Text in Dutch. 2001. a. EUR 60 (effective 2008).
Published by: Arko Sports Media (Subsidiary of: Arko Uitgeverij BV), Postbus 393, Nieuwegein, 3430 AJ, Netherlands. FAX 31-30-6052618, info@arko.nl, http://www.arko.nl.

DER JAGDSPANIEL. *see* PETS

790.1 DEU ISSN 0448-1445
JAHRBUCH DES SPORTS. Text in German. 1955. biennial. EUR 19 (effective 2005). **Document type:** *Bulletin.*
—GNLM.
Published by: (Germany. Deutscher Olympischer Sportbund), Schors-Verlags-Gesellschaft mbH, Postfach 1280, Niedernhausen, 65522, Germany. TEL 49-6127-8029, FAX 49-6127-8812, schors.verlag@t-online.de. Circ: 32,000.

793.7 DEU
JAHRESZEITEN RAETSEL. Text in German. 1986. bi-m. EUR 1.80 newsstand/cover (effective 2011). adv. **Document type:** *Magazine, Consumer.*
Published by: Deutscher Raetselverlag GmbH & Co. KG (Subsidiary of: Gong Verlag GmbH & Co. KG), Muenchener Str 101-09, Ismaning, 85737, Germany. TEL 49-89-272708620, FAX 49-89-272707890, info@raetsel.de, http://www.deutscher-raetselverlag.de. Circ: 195,000 (paid and controlled).

799 NOR ISSN 0800-3041
JAKT & FISKE. Text in Norwegian. 1871. 11/yr. NOK 370 (effective 1998). adv. **Description:** For the hunter and sportsfisherman.
Formerly (until 1983): Jakt-Fiske-Friluftsliv (0021-4051)
Published by: Norges Jeger- og Fiskerforbund/Norwegian Association of Hunters and Anglers, Boks 94, Nesbru, 1378, Norway. TEL 47-66-79-22-00, FAX 47-66-90-15-87. Ed. Viggo Kristiansen. Adv. contact Hilde Merete Vestad. color page NOK 22,300; 192 x 260. Circ: 77,000.

790.1 790.133 790.13 JPN
JAPAN TOY AND GAME JOURNAL. Variant title: Japan Toy and Game Software Journal. Text in English. m. USD 560 (effective 2003). **Document type:** *Journal, Trade.* **Description:** Brings you the latest information from the toy, game and software industry in Japan. Reports on industry news, company news, regulatory information, market reports, joint venture news, new products and research & development as they relate to this industry.
Indexed: A15, CompD, P49, P51.
Published by: Pacific Research Consulting, 4-18-2, Shikahama, Adachi-ku, Tokyo, 123-0864, Japan. TEL 212-532-8815, 81-3-38999953, FAX 81-3-38999968, prc@abelia.ocn.ne.jp, prcnyrep@hotmail.com.

793.7 LVA
JAPANU MIKLAS. Text in Latvian. 2005. q. LVL 0.49 newsstand/cover (effective 2005). **Document type:** *Magazine, Consumer.*
Published by: SIA Kuma, Rinuzu Iela 22-44, Riga, 1015, Latvia. TEL 371-7342879, FAX 371-7342879, kuma@kuma.lv. Ed. Inara Ratnik. Pub. Aida Luts.

790.1 UAE
AL-JAZIRAH. Text in Arabic. 1980. m. **Description:** Covers club sporting activities.
Published by: Nadi al-Jazirah, Al-Lajna al-Thiqafiyyah/Al-Jazirah Club, Cultural Group, PO Box 2750, Abu Dhabi, United Arab Emirates. TEL 464455. Ed. Saif Ahmad Al Hamili. Circ: 1,000.

JERNBANEFRITID. *see* HOBBIES

790 FRA ISSN 0021-6135
LES JEUNES. Text in French. 1903. bi-m. adv. bk.rev.; film rev.; play rev. illus.; stat. **Document type:** *Newsletter, Consumer.*
Indexed: SportS.
Published by: Federation Sportive et Culturelle de France, 22 rue Oberkampf, Paris, 75011, France. TEL 33-1-43385057, FAX 33-1-43140665. Ed. Jean Marie Jouaret. Adv. contact Clement Schertzinger. Circ: 10,000.

790.01 FRA ISSN 0769-4377
LES JEUX DE NOTRE TEMPS. Variant title: Notre Temps Jeux. Text in French. 1986. m. EUR 29.90 domestic; EUR 41.01 DOM-TOM; EUR 41.01 in the European Union; EUR 51.68 elsewhere (effective 2008 - 2009). 68 p./no.; **Document type:** *Magazine, Consumer.* **Description:** Offers 68 pages of games to play and learn from.
Published by: Bayard Presse, 3-5 rue Bayard, Paris, 75393 Cedex 08, France. TEL 33-1-44356060, FAX 33-1-44356161, redactions@bayard-presse.com, http://www.bayardpresse.com. Ed. Olivier Calon. Circ: 110,779.

790.1 CAN ISSN 0712-2632
JIM RENNIE'S SPORTS LETTER. Text in English. 1977. w. CAD 225, USD 175 domestic; CAD 275 foreign (effective 1999). adv. **Document type:** *Newsletter.* **Description:** Details trends and developments in the sporting goods market.
Related titles: E-mail ed.
Indexed: SportS.
—CCC.
Published by: Rennie Publications Inc., P O Box 1000, Collingwood, ON L9Y 4L4, Canada. TEL 705-445-7161, FAX 705-445-8650. Ed., Pub. Jim Rennie. Circ: 1,800 (paid).

790.1 CHN ISSN 1004-2105
JINGJI YU JIANMEI/ATHLETICS & BODY BUILDING. Text in Chinese. 1985. bi-m. **Document type:** *Consumer.* **Description:** Introduces body-building exercises, and scientific methods for improving health, and maintaining good shape.
Published by: Shanghai Tiyu Xueyuan/Shanghai Institute of Physical Education, 650 Qingyuan Huanlu, Shanghai, 200433, China. TEL 5485546. Ed. Dai Binyian. adv.: page CNY 4,000.

790.1 CHN ISSN 1002-6177
JINGWU/WUSHU FINENESS. Text in Chinese. 1984. bi-m. CNY 4.80 per issue (effective 2009). **Document type:** *Magazine, Consumer.*
Related titles: Online - full text ed.; ◆ Supplement to: Dangdai Tiyu. ISSN 1002-6169.
Published by: Dangdai Tiyu Zazhishe, 99 Xuanxua Jie, Nangang-qu, Harbin, Heilongjiang 150001, China. TEL 86-451-82510474, FAX 86-451-82526535 ext 8003. Ed. Wang Lihei.

796.8 NLD ISSN 2211-2588
JIU JITSU ZELFVERDEDIGING. Text in Dutch, English. 2007. q. **Document type:** *Magazine, Consumer.*

Published by: Nederlandse Academie voor Traditionele Krijgskunsten/ Dutch Academy for Traditional Marital Arts, Hoogvensestraat 106, Tilburg, 5017 CH, Netherlands. TEL 31-6-11220232, info@shintairyu.nl, http://www.bushi.eu.

793.7 ARG ISSN 0328-4344
JOKER. Text in Spanish. 1972. bi-w. adv. **Document type:** *Magazine, Consumer.* **Description:** Contains a wide variety of crosswords, games and other forms of entertainment.
Published by: Editorial Perfil S.A., Chacabuco 271, Buenos Aires, Buenos Aires 1069, Argentina. TEL 54-11-4341-9000, FAX 54-11-4341-9090, correo@perfil.com.ar, http://www.perfil.com.ar. Circ: 15,000 (paid).

793 ITA ISSN 2038-2251
▼ **JOKONLINE.** Text in Italian. 2010. m. **Document type:** *Magazine, Consumer.*
Published by: My Way Media, Via Ludovico d'Aragona 11, Milan, 20132, Italy. TEL 39-02-217681, FAX 39-02-21768550, http://www.mywaymedia.it.

790.1 ESP ISSN 1578-9799
JORNADA DEPORTIVA. Text in Spanish. 1953. d. adv. **Document type:** *Newspaper, Consumer.* **Description:** This is the sports newspaper of El Dia, the principal daily of the Canary Islands.
Related titles: Online - full text ed.
Published by: Editorial Leoncio Rodriguez, Ave Buenos Aires 71, Santa Cruz de Tenerife, 38005, Spain. TEL 34-922-238300, FAX 34-922-214247, http://www.eldia.es.

796 370 USA ISSN 1935-7397
GV351
JOURNAL FOR THE STUDY OF SPORTS AND ATHLETES IN EDUCATION. Text in English. 2007 (Mar.). 3/yr. USD 179 to institutions; USD 259 combined subscription to institutions (print & online eds.) (effective 2010). adv. back issues avail. **Document type:** *Journal, Academic/Scholarly.* **Description:** Provides a forum for the discussion of the "unique characteristics" of sports and athletics participation in education.
Related titles: Online - full text ed.: ISSN 1935-7400. 2007 (Mar.).
—BLDSC (5066.928550).
Published by: Left Coast Press, Inc., 1630 N Main St, Ste 400, Walnut Creek, CA 94596. TEL 925-935-3380, FAX 925 935-2916, Explore@LCoastPress.com. Eds. James W Satterfield TEL 864-656-7656, Robin L Hughes.

JOURNAL OF ASIAN MARTIAL ARTS. *see* ASIAN STUDIES

613.713 AUS
➤ **JOURNAL OF AUSTRALIAN STRENGTH AND CONDITIONING (ONLINE).** Abbreviated title: J A S C. Text in English. 1993. q. free to members (effective 2009). **Document type:** *Journal, Academic/ Scholarly.*
Former titles (until 2008): Journal of Australian Strength and Conditioning (Print) (1835-7644); (until 2007): Strength and Conditioning Coach (1324-8006)
Media: E-mail. **Related titles:** Online - full text ed.
Indexed: SD.
—BLDSC (4949.505000), IE.
Published by: Australian Strength and Conditioning Association, Box 71, Beenleigh, QLD 4207, Australia. TEL 61-7-38077119, FAX 61-7-38077445, info@strengthandconditioning.org, http://www.strengthandconditioning.org/about_us.aspx.

➤ JOURNAL OF CLINICAL SPORT PSYCHOLOGY. *see* PSYCHOLOGY

976.07 370 USA ISSN 1938-7016
➤ **JOURNAL OF COACHING EDUCATION.** Text in English. 2007 (Sep.). 10/yr. USD 40 to non-members; USD 150 to institutions; free to members (effective 2010). **Document type:** *Journal, Academic/ Scholarly.*
Media: Online - full text.
Indexed: PEI.
Published by: National Association for Sport and Physical Education, 1900 Association Dr, Reston, VA 20191. TEL 703-476-3410, 800-213-7193, FAX 703-476-8316, naspe@aahperd.org, http://www.aahperd.org/naspe/template.cfm?template=main.html.

617.1027 613.711 USA ISSN 1554-9933
GV583
JOURNAL OF CONTEMPORARY ATHLETICS. Text in English. 2003. q. USD 295 to institutions; USD 442 combined subscription to institutions (print & online eds.) (effective 2012). **Document type:** *Journal, Academic/Scholarly.* **Description:** Covers sports psychology, sports sociology, parental aggression, coaching, drug use in athletics, teamwork, philosophy, history of athletics, athlete administration, ethics, sports management, nutrition and legal issues.
Related titles: Online - full text ed.: USD 295 to institutions (effective 2012).
Published by: Nova Science Publishers, Inc., 400 Oser Ave, Ste 1600, Hauppauge, NY 11788. TEL 631-231-7269, FAX 631-231-8175, main@novapublishers.com. Ed. James Humphrey TEL 301-935-6766.

797.2 USA ISSN 1946-4770
THE JOURNAL OF DIVING HISTORY. Text in English. 1993. q. free to members (effective 2010). back issues avail. **Document type:** *Journal, Academic/Scholarly.*
Formerly (until 2008): Historical Diver (1094-4516)
Indexed: A01, CA, T02.
Published by: Historical Diving Society USA, PO Box 2837, Santa Maria, CA 93457. TEL 805-934-1660, FAX 805-938-0550.

JOURNAL OF EXERCISE SCIENCE AND FITNESS. *see* MEDICAL SCIENCES—Sports Medicine

JOURNAL OF FACILITIES MANAGEMENT. *see* BUSINESS AND ECONOMICS—Management

THE JOURNAL OF GAMBLING BUSINESS AND ECONOMICS. *see* BUSINESS AND ECONOMICS

JOURNAL OF GAMBLING STUDIES (ONLINE). *see* MEDICAL SCIENCES—Psychiatry And Neurology

794.8 GBR ISSN 1757-191X
▼ ➤ **JOURNAL OF GAMING & VIRTUAL WORLDS.** Abbreviated title: J G V W. Text in English. 2009. 3/yr. GBP 180 domestic to institutions; GBP 189 in the European Union to institutions; USD 290 in US & Canada to institutions; GBP 192 elsewhere to institutions (effective 2011). adv. back issues avail. **Document type:** *Journal, Academic/ Scholarly.* **Description:** Focuses on theoretical and applied, empirical, critical, rhetorical, creative, economic and professional approaches to the study of electronic games across platforms and genres as well as ludic and serious online environments.
Related titles: Online - full text ed.: ISSN 1757-1928. USD 220 in US & Canada to institutions; GBP 147 elsewhere to institutions (effective 2011).
Indexed: C10, CA, P52, T02.
Published by: Intellect Ltd., The Mill, Parnall Rd, Fishponds, Bristol, BS16 3JG, United Kingdom. TEL 44-117-9589910, FAX 44-117-9589911, info@intellectbooks.com. Pub. Masoud Yazdani. **Subscr. to:** Turpin Distribution Services Ltd., Pegasus Dr, Stratton Business Park, Biggleswade, Bedfordshire SG18 8QB, United Kingdom. TEL 44-1767-604951, FAX 44-1767-601640, custserv@turpin-distribution.com, http://www.turpin-distribution.com/.

796 USA ISSN 1941-6342
GV347
➤ **JOURNAL OF INTERCOLLEGIATE SPORT.** Text in English. 2008 (Jun.). s-a. USD 314 domestic to institutions; USD 319 foreign to institutions; USD 372 combined subscription domestic to institutions (print & online eds.); USD 377 combined subscription foreign to institutions (print & online eds.) (effective 2012). adv. **Document type:** *Journal, Academic/Scholarly.* **Description:** Publishes articles from the sciences, social sciences, humanities, and professional fields, providing a complete look at all factors affecting intercollegiate sport.
Related titles: Online - full text ed.: ISSN 1941-417X. USD 314 to institutions (effective 2012).
Indexed: CA, PEI, SD, T02.
—**CCC.**
Published by: Human Kinetics, 1607 N Market St, Champaign, IL 61820. TEL 800-747-4457, FAX 217-351-2674, orders@hkusa.com, http://www.humankinetics.com. Ed. R Scott Kretchmar. R&P Martha Gullo TEL 217-403-7534. Adv. contact Amy Bleich TEL 217-403-7803.

➤ JOURNAL OF LEGAL ASPECTS OF SPORT. *see* LAW

796 300 USA ISSN 1559-0410
JOURNAL OF QUANTITATIVE ANALYSIS IN SPORTS. Abbreviated title: J Q A S. Text in English. 2005. q. USD 485 to institutions; USD 1,455 to corporations (effective 2011). bk.rev. back issues avail. **Document type:** *Journal, Trade.* **Description:** Dedicated to statistical analysis in sports. Includes statistics, operations research, economics, psychology, sports management and business. Also serves as an outlet for professionals in the sports world to raise issues and ask questions as they relate to quantitative sports analysis.
Media: Online - full text.
Indexed: A28, APA, BrCerAb, C&ISA, CA, CA/WCA, CABA, CCMJ, CIA, CerAb, CivEngAb, CorrAb, E&CAJ, E11, EEA, EMA, ESPM, EnvEAb, GH, H15, LT, M&TEA, M09, MBF, METADEX, MSN, MathR, PEI, RRTA, SD, SolStAb, T02, T04, WAA, Z02.
—**CCC.**
Published by: Berkeley Electronic Press, 2809 Telegraph Ave, Ste 202, Berkeley, CA 94705. TEL 510-665-1200, FAX 510-665-1201, info@bepress.com. Ed. Benjamin Alamar.

JOURNAL OF RECREATIONAL MATHEMATICS. *see* MATHEMATICS

796 USA ISSN 2151-5786
▼ **JOURNAL OF SPORT ADMINISTRATION & SUPERVISION;** research that matters. Abbreviated title: J S A S. Text in English. 2009. a. free (effective 2009). **Document type:** *Journal, Academic/ Scholarly.* **Description:** Designed to develop, advance, disseminate, promote, and preserve knowledge within the academic discipline of sport management by providing an outlet that is both grounded in academic theory and driven by the needs of practitioners and the environment of the sport industry.
Media: Online - full content.
Indexed: SD.
Published by: Middle Tennessee State University, Sport Management, PO Box 96, Murfreesboro, TN 37132. TEL 615-898-2909, FAX 615-898-5020, http://frank.mtsu.edu/~jubenvil/sports_management/managementmain.htm. Ed. Benjamin D Goss TEL 417-836-6592. Pub. Colby B Jubenville TEL 615-898-2909.

JOURNAL OF SPORT AND EXERCISE PSYCHOLOGY. *see* PSYCHOLOGY

796 613 ESP ISSN 1989-6239
JOURNAL OF SPORT AND HEALTH RESEARCH. Text in Multiple languages. 2005. 3/yr. free (effective 2011). **Document type:** *Journal, Academic/Scholarly.*
Formerly (until 2009): The International Journal of Medicine and Science in Physical Education and Sport (1989-1245)
Media: Online - full text.
Indexed: A36, CABA, GH, LT, N02, N03, T05.
Published by: Asociacion Didactica Andalucia editor@journalshr.com. Ed. Jose A Perez.

796 AZE ISSN 2078-1075
▼ ➤ **JOURNAL OF SPORT AND PHYSICS.** Text in English, French, Spanish, Russian. forthcoming 2011. q. **Document type:** *Journal, Academic/Scholarly.*
Related titles: Online - full text ed.: forthcoming.
Indexed: SD.
Published by: Progress Press Inc., M.Mushfig 4B, Apt.107, Baku, 1006, Azerbaijan. TEL 994-050-6691364, subijar@gmail.com.

301 USA ISSN 0193-7235
GV561
➤ **JOURNAL OF SPORT AND SOCIAL ISSUES.** Text in English. 1977. q. USD 585, GBP 345 combined subscription to institutions (print & online eds.); USD 573, GBP 338 to institutions (effective 2011). adv. bk.rev. illus. Index. back issues avail.; reprint service avail. from PSC. **Document type:** *Journal, Academic/Scholarly.* **Description:** Publishes the latest research, discussion, and analysis on contemporary sports issues, such as race, the media, gender issues, economics, drugs, recruiting, injuries, and youth sports.
Related titles: Online - full text ed.: ISSN 1552-7638. USD 527, GBP 311 to institutions (effective 2011).
Indexed: A01, A02, A03, A08, A20, A22, A28, A36, ABS&EES, APA, AltPI, B07, B21, BrCerAb, C&ISA, C25, CA, CA/WCA, CABA, CIA, CerAb, ChPerI, CivEngAb, CorrAb, CurCont, E&CAJ, E01, E11, E12, EEA, EMA, ESPM, G10, GH, H&SSA, H04, H15, HEA, LT, M&TEA, M09, MBF, METADEX, N02, N03, O01, P02, P03, P10, P34, P42, P48, P53, P54, PAIS, PEI, PQC, PSA, PsycInfo, R12, RRTA, RiskAb, S02, S03, S11, S13, S16, SCOPUS, SD, SOPODA, SSA, SSCI, SociolAb, SolStAb, SportS, T02, T04, V02, W07, W09, W11, WAA.
—BLDSC (5066.184000), IE, Infotrieve, Ingenta, Linda Hall. **CCC.**
Published by: (Northwestern University, Center for the Study of Sport in Society), Sage Publications, Inc., 2455 Teller Rd, Thousand Oaks, CA 91320. TEL 805-499-9774, 800-818-7243, FAX 805-499-0871, 800-583-2665, info@sagepub.com. Ed. C L Cole. adv.: B&W page USD 385, color page USD 775; 4.5 x 7.5. Circ: 550. **Subscr. outside the Americas to:** Sage Publications Ltd., 1 Oliver's Yard, 55 City Rd, London EC1Y 1SP, United Kingdom. TEL 44-20-73248701, FAX 44-20-73248733, subscription@sagepub.co.uk

790.1 150 USA ISSN 0162-7341
GV561
➤ **JOURNAL OF SPORT BEHAVIOR.** Text in English. 1978. q. USD 38 domestic; USD 58 foreign (effective 2010). illus. Index. back issues avail.; reprints avail. **Document type:** *Journal, Academic/Scholarly.* **Description:** Deals with the sociological, psychological, anthropological and related applications to the science of sport.
Related titles: CD-ROM ed.; Microform ed.: (from PQC); Online - full text ed.
Indexed: A01, A02, A03, A08, A22, A26, A36, C12, CA, CABA, E-psyche, E07, E08, E12, FR, G08, GH, I05, I07, LT, M01, M02, N02, P02, P03, P07, P10, P13, P24, P25, P43, P48, P53, P54, PCI, PEI, PQC, PsycInfo, PsycholAb, R09, R12, RILM, RRTA, S02, S03, S09, S11, S23, SD, SportS, T02.
—BLDSC (5066.186000), IE, Infotrieve, Ingenta. **CCC.**
Published by: University of South Alabama, Department of Psychology, Life Sciences Building, Room 320, Mobile, AL 36688-0002. TEL 251-460-6371. Eds. Cay Welsh, Elise Labbe-Coldsmith TEL 251-460-6321.

790.1 USA ISSN 0094-1700
GV571
➤ **JOURNAL OF SPORT HISTORY.** Abbreviated title: J S H. Text in English. 1974. 3/yr. free to members (effective 2010). adv. bk.rev. illus. back issues avail.; reprints avail. **Document type:** *Journal, Academic/Scholarly.* **Description:** Covers topics relating to the history of sport and physical education.
Related titles: Online - full text ed.: ISSN 2155-8450.
Indexed: A20, A22, ABS&EES, ASCA, AmH&L, CA, ChPerI, E01, HistAb, MLA-IB, P30, PCI, PEI, SCOPUS, SD, SportS, T02.
—BLDSC (5066.188000), IE, Infotrieve, Ingenta.
Published by: North American Society for Sport History, c/o Ronald A Smith, PO Box 1026, Lemont, PA 16851. TEL 814-238-1288, FAX 814-238-1288, secretary-treasurer@nassh.org, http://www.nassh.org. Ed. Wray Vamplew. Adv. contact Alison M Wrynn TEL 562-985-4085. page USD 400. Circ: 950.

790.1 658 USA ISSN 0888-4773
GV713
➤ **JOURNAL OF SPORT MANAGEMENT.** Abbreviated title: J S M. Text in English. 1987. bi-m. USD 468 domestic to institutions; USD 483 foreign to institutions; USD 552 combined subscription domestic to institutions (print & online eds.); USD 567 combined subscription foreign to institutions (print & online eds.) (effective 2012). adv. bk.rev. bibl. Supplement avail.; back issues avail.; reprint service avail. from PSC. **Document type:** *Journal, Academic/Scholarly.* **Description:** Fosters exchange of theory and application of management to sport, exercise, dance, and play.
Related titles: Online - full text ed.: ISSN 1543-270X. USD 468 to institutions (effective 2012).
Indexed: A01, A03, A08, A12, A13, A14, A17, A22, ABIn, ASCA, B01, B07, CA, CABA, CurCont, DIP, E12, ESPM, FoSS&M, GH, IBR, IBZ, LT, O01, P32, P48, P51, P53, P54, PEI, PGegResA, PQC, R12, RRTA, RiskAb, S02, S03, SCI, SCOPUS, SD, SSCI, SportS, T02, W07.
—BLDSC (5066.188300), IE, Infotrieve, Ingenta. **CCC.**
Published by: (North American Society for Sport Management), Human Kinetics, 1607 N Market St, Champaign, IL 61820. TEL 800-747-4457, FAX 217-351-2674, info@hkusa.com, http://www.humankinetics.com. Ed. Richard Wolfe TEL 250-853-3870. Pub. Rainer Martens. R&P Martha Gullo TEL 217-403-7534. Adv. contact Amy Bleich TEL 217-403-7803.

▼ ➤ JOURNAL OF SPORTS AND ENTERTAINMENT MARKETING. *see* BUSINESS AND ECONOMICS—Marketing And Purchasing

796.1 USA ISSN 1948-5735
GV561
JOURNAL OF SPORTS & RECREATION RESEARCH AND EDUCATION. Text in English. 2007. s-a. free (effective 2009). **Document type:** *Journal, Academic/Scholarly.*
Media: Online - full content.
Published by: Scientific Journals International (Subsidiary of: Global Commerce & Communication, Inc), 1407 33rd St S, Saint Cloud, MN 56301. TEL 320-217-6019, info@scientificjournals.org.

JOURNAL OF SPORTS ECONOMICS. *see* BUSINESS AND ECONOMICS

JOURNAL OF SPORTS LAW & CONTEMPORARY PROBLEMS. *see* LAW

796 302.23 USA ISSN 1558-4313
GV742
➤ **JOURNAL OF SPORTS MEDIA.** Text in English. 2006 (Spr.). s-a. USD 50 combined subscription domestic to individuals (print & online eds.); USD 40 combined subscription foreign to individuals (print & online eds.); USD 55 combined subscription domestic to institutions (print & online eds.); USD 75 combined subscription foreign to institutions (print & online eds.); USD 22 per issue to individuals; USD 35 per issue to institutions (effective 2011). adv. back issues avail. **Document type:** *Journal, Academic/Scholarly.* **Description:** Provides a exploration of the field and promotes a understanding of sports media in terms of their practices, value, and effect on the culture as a whole.
Related titles: Online - full text ed.: ISSN 1940-5073. 2008.
Indexed: A22, A34, CABA, E01, LT, SD.
—IE. **CCC.**

S

Published by: (University of Mississippi, Department of Journalism), University of Nebraska Press, 1111 Lincoln Mall, Lincoln, NE 68588. TEL 402-472-3581, FAX 402-472-6214, pressmail@unl.edu. Ed. Brad Schultz TEL 662-915-5161. Adv. contact Joyce Gettman TEL 402-472-8330. Circ: 100. **Subscr. to:** PO Box 84555, Lincoln, NE 68501. TEL 402-472-8536, 800-848-6224, FAX 800-272-6817, journals@unlnotes.unl.edu.

790.1 GBR ISSN 0264-0414
GV561 CODEN: JSSCEL

➤ **JOURNAL OF SPORTS SCIENCES.** Text in English. 1983. 14/yr. GBP 2,501 combined subscription in United Kingdom to institutions (print & online eds.); EUR 3,219, USD 4,042 combined subscription to institutions (print & online eds.) (effective 2012). adv. bk.rev. illus. 96 p./no.; back issues avail.; reprint service avail. from PSC. **Document type:** *Journal, Academic/Scholarly.* **Description:** Provides a contact point among the separate disciplines in sports sciences. Includes contributions from the human sciences: anatomy, anthropology, behavioral sciences, physiology, and psychology. Papers cover technologies such as design of playing equipment and sports facilities, as well as applied research in training, team selection, performance prediction or modification, and stress reduction.
Related titles: Online - full text ed.: ISSN 1466-447X. GBP 2,251 in United Kingdom to institutions; EUR 2,897, USD 3,638 to institutions (effective 2012) (from IngentaConnect).
Indexed: A01, A03, A08, A20, A22, A26, A36, AMED, ASCA, ApMecR, B07, B21, B25, BIOSIS Prev, C06, C07, C08, CA, CABA, CINAHL, DIP, E01, E08, E12, EMBASE, ERA, ESPM, ErgAb, ExcerpMed, F05, F06, F07, FoSS&M, G08, GH, H&SSA, H12, I05, I06, I07, IBR, IBZ, IndMed, Inpharma, LT, M06, MEDLINE, MycolAb, N02, N03, P03, P26, P30, P54, PEI, PQC, PsycInfo, PsycholAb, R10, R12, RRTA, Reac, S09, S23, SCI, SCOPUS, SD, SportS, T02, T05, W07, W11.
—GNLM, IE, Infotrieve, Ingenta, INIST. **CCC.**
Published by: (British Association of Sport and Exercise Sciences (BASES), British Association of Sports Sciences), Routledge (Subsidiary of: Taylor & Francis Group), 4 Park Sq, Milton Park, Abingdon, Oxon OX14 4RN, United Kingdom. TEL 44-20-70176000, FAX 44-20-70176336, subscriptions@tandf.co.uk, http://www.routledge.com. Ed. Alan Nevill TEL 44-1902-322838. Adv. contact Linda Hann TEL 44-1344-779945. **Subscr. in US & Canada to:** Taylor & Francis Inc., Customer Services Dept, 325 Chestnut St, 8th Fl, Philadelphia, PA 19106. TEL 215-625-8900, 800-354-1420, FAX 215-625-2940, customerservice@taylorandfrancis.com; **Subscr. to:** Taylor & Francis Ltd., Journals Customer Service, Sheepen Pl, Colchester, Essex CO3 3LP, United Kingdom. TEL 44-20-70175544, FAX 44-20-70175198, tf.enquiries@tfinforma.com.

797 USA ISSN 0747-5993
GV836.2

➤ **JOURNAL OF SWIMMING RESEARCH.** Abbreviated title: J S R. Text in English. 1984. a. free to members (effective 2010). adv. **Document type:** *Journal, Academic/Scholarly.* **Description:** Features manuscripts dealing with original investigations, comprehensive reviews, or brief reviews on the science of swimming and closely related topics.
Indexed: A22, CA, PEI, SD, SportS, T02.
—BLDSC (5067.820000), IE, Infotrieve, Ingenta. **CCC.**
Published by: American Swimming Coaches Association, 5101 NW 21st Ave, Ste 200, Fort Lauderdale, FL 33309. TEL 954-563-4930, 800-356-2722, FAX 954-563-9813, asca@swimmingcoach.org. **Co-sponsor:** U.S. Swimming Sports Medicine.

➤ **JOURNAL OF TEACHING IN PHYSICAL EDUCATION.** *see* EDUCATION—Teaching Methods And Curriculum

796 USA ISSN 0094-8705
GV706 CODEN: JPSPF6

➤ **JOURNAL OF THE PHILOSOPHY OF SPORT.** Abbreviated title: J P S. Text in English. 1974. s-a. USD 314 domestic to institutions; USD 319 foreign to institutions; USD 372 combined subscription domestic to institutions (print & online eds.); USD 377 combined subscription foreign to institutions (print & online eds.) (effective 2012). adv. bk.rev. bibl.; illus. 20 p./no.; back issues avail.; reprint service avail. from PSC. **Document type:** *Journal, Academic/Scholarly.* **Description:** Presnts articles, critical reviews of work completed, and philosophic discussions about the philosophy of sport.
Related titles: Online - full text ed.: ISSN 1543-2939. USD 314 to institutions (effective 2012).
Indexed: A01, A03, A08, A20, A22, ASCA, AmHI, BRD, C03, CA, CABA, CBCARef, DIP, H07, H08, HAb, HumInd, IBR, IBZ, LT, P48, PCI, PEI, PQC, PhilInd, RRTA, S02, S03, SCOPUS, SD, SOPODA, SSCI, SociolAb, SportS, T02, W03, W07.
—BLDSC (5034.520000), IE, Infotrieve, Ingenta. **CCC.**
Published by: (International Association of Philosophy of Sport GBR), Human Kinetics, 1607 N Market St, Champaign, IL 61820. TEL 800-747-4457, FAX 217-351-2674, info@hkusa.com, http://www.humankinetics.com. Ed. J S Russell. Pub. Rainer Martens. R&P Martha Gullo TEL 217-403-7534. Adv. contact Amy Bleich TEL 217-403-7803.

799.202 USA ISSN 1930-7616
KF3941.A15

JOURNAL ON FIREARMS AND PUBLIC POLICY. Text in English. 1988. irreg.
Related titles: Online - full text ed.: ISSN 1930-7624.
Published by: Second Amendment Foundation, 12500 N E 10th Pl, Bellevue, WA 98005. TEL 425-454-7012, 800-426-4302, FAX 425-451-3959.

796.815 FRA ISSN 1272-5161

JUDO. Text in French. 1950. 8/yr. EUR 22 domestic; EUR 38 foreign (effective 2009). adv. **Document type:** *Magazine, Consumer.*
Indexed: SD, SportS.
Published by: Federation Francaise de Judo, Jujitsu, Kendo et Disciplines Associees, 21-25 Ave de la Porte de Chatillon, Paris, 75680 Cedex 14, France. TEL 33-1-40521649, FAX 33-1-40521640, http://www.ffjda.com. Ed. Michel Vial. R&P Brigitte Deydier. Adv. contact Anne Claire Gourmelon. Circ: 20,000.

796.815 USA ISSN 1066-6257

JUDO JOURNAL. Text in English. 1979. bi-m. USD 20 in United States; USD 27 in Canada; USD 45 elsewhere. adv. **Document type:** *Newspaper.* **Description:** Covers techniques, tournaments, gift items and other subjects related to martial arts.
Indexed: SD, SportS.
Published by: Judo Journal Publications, PO Box 18485, Irvine, CA 92713. TEL 949-645-1674, FAX 949-722-9331. Ed. Michael L Watt. Pub. Nori Bunasawa. Adv. contact Nuri Bunasawa. Circ: 20,000.

796.815 DEU ISSN 0179-3535

JUDO MAGAZIN. Text in German. 1961. 11/yr. EUR 29; EUR 3 newsstand/cover (effective 2011). adv. 52 p./no. 3 cols./p.; back issues avail. **Document type:** *Magazine, Consumer.*
Formerly (until 1986): Judo (0179-3527)
Indexed: SD.
Published by: (Deutscher Judo Bund e.V.), Meyer & Meyer Verlag, Von-Coels-Str 390, Aachen, 52080, Germany. TEL 49-241-958100, FAX 49-241-9581010, verlag@m-m-sports.com, http://m-m-sports.de. Circ: 12,000 (paid and controlled).

796.815 CAN ISSN 1193-7149

JUDO ONTARIO NEWSLETTER. Text in English. q. CAD 16, USD 12 (effective 2000). adv. **Document type:** *Newsletter.*
Former titles (until 1992): Ontario Judo Newsletter (0834-2105); (until 1986): Ontario Judoka (0823-9134); (until 1985): Judo Ontario's Newsletter; (until 1984): Ontario Judoka (0826-0567); (until 1983): Judo Ontario's Newsletter (0823-1087); (until 1982): Newsletter - Judo Ontario (0229-5652)
Indexed: SD.
Published by: Judo Ontario, 1185 Eglinton Ave E, North York, ON M3C 3C6, Canada. TEL 416-426-7006, FAX 416-426-7390. Ed., R&P, Adv. contact Tim Dawkins. Circ: 1,000 (paid and controlled).

JUGGLE. *see* HOBBIES

790.1 DEU

JUMP!; Das Trampolinmagazin. Text in German. 1984. bi-m. EUR 20; EUR 12 to students (effective 2005). adv. **Document type:** *Magazine, Consumer.*
Former titles: Trampolin Intern; (until 1992): Trampolinturnen
Published by: Living Sports Bildagentur und Verlags GbR, Eckernfoerder Str 259, Kronshagen, 24119, Germany. TEL 49-431-5700570, FAX 49-431-5700579, info@living-sports.de, http://livi01.synserver.de. Ed. Sascha Klahn. adv.: color page EUR 350, B&W page EUR 250; trim 210 x 297. Circ: 360; 340 (paid).

JUOKSIJA. *see* PHYSICAL FITNESS AND HYGIENE

790.1 DNK ISSN 0901-3334

K F U M IDRAET. Text in Danish. 1921. 4/yr. adv. **Document type:** *Magazine, Consumer.* **Description:** Contains information on YMCA sports activities in Denmark throughout the year.
Formerly (until 1985): Frisk Glad Idraet (0901-2710)
Related titles: Online - full text ed.
Published by: K F U M Idraetsforbund i Danmark, Peter Tofts Vej 21, Kolding, 6000, Denmark. TEL 45-70-237311, FAX 45-70-237312, kfumid@kfumid.dk, http://www.kfumid.dk. Ed. Evan Johansen.

796.83 USA ISSN 1048-1516

K O. (Knock Out) Text in English. 19??. 13/yr. **Document type:** *Magazine, Consumer.*
Published by: London Publishing Co. (Subsidiary of: Kappa Publishing Group, Inc.), 6198 Butler Pike, Ste 200, Blue Bell, PA 19422. TEL 215-643-6385, FAX 315-628-3571, custsrvc@kappapublishing.com, http://www.kappapublishing.com. Ed. Nigel Collins.

790.1 RUS

K SPORTU. Text in Russian. 1995. m. USD 100 in North America (effective 2000).
Published by: Izdatel'stvo K Sportu, Markhlevskogo 18, Moscow, 101000, Russian Federation. TEL 7-095-9241383, FAX 7-095-2130564. **Dist. by:** East View Information Services, 10601 Wayzata Blvd, Minneapolis, MN 55305. TEL 952-252-1201, 800-477-1005, FAX 952-252-1202, info@eastview.com, http://www.eastview.com.

799.3 SRB ISSN 0354-513X

KALIBAR. Text in Serbian. 1994. m. CSD 600 for 6 mos. (effective 2009). **Document type:** *Magazine, Consumer.*
Published by: Kompanija Novosti, Trg Nikole Pasica 7, Belgrade, 11000. TEL 381-11-3398202, FAX 381-11-3398337, redakcija@novosti.co.yu, http://www.novosti.co.yu. Ed. Vojin Kacuric.

796 HUN ISSN 1218-1498
GV201

KALOKAGATHIA; a testnevelesi es sportudomanyi kar kozlemenyei - review of the Faculty of Physical Education and Sport Sciences. Text in English, Hungarian. 1954. 3/yr. HUF 350 (effective 2004). bk.rev. illus. 120 p./no.; back issues avail. **Document type:** *Journal, Academic/Scholarly.* **Description:** Covers physical education and sport physiology, pedagogy, sociology and history.
Former titles: Magyar Testnevelesi Egyetem Kozlemenyei (0866-2401); (until 1989): Testnevelesi Foiskola Kozlemenyei (0230-3337); (until 1981): Magyar Testnevelesi Foiskola. Tudomanyos Kozlemenyei
Published by: Semmelweis Egyetem, Testnevelesi es Sporttudomanyi Kar, Alkotas utca 44, Budapest, 1123, Hungary. TEL 36-1-4879200 ext 1234, FAX 36-1-3566337, marika@mail.hupe.hu, http://www.hupe.hu. Ed. Ferenc Krasovec. Pub. Mihaly Nyerges. Circ: 300 (controlled).

KANNADA PRABHA. *see* GENERAL INTEREST PERIODICALS—India

796.815 FRA ISSN 1243-3853

KARATE, BUSHIDO. Text in French. 1974. m. EUR 34.50 (effective 2009). adv. bk.rev.; video rev. 124 p./no.; back issues avail. **Document type:** *Magazine, Consumer.*
Formed by the merger of (1974-1988): Karate (0335-2552); (1983-1988): Bushido (0760-0097)
Published by: Europeenne de Magazines, 44 av. George V, Paris, 75008, France. TEL 33-1-49521415, FAX 33-1-49521444. Ed. G Barissat. Adv. contact Corinne Bidet TEL 33-01-49521400. Circ: 117,000.

796.76 AUS

KART MAGAZINE; national karting news. Text in English. 1984. m. AUD 66 domestic; AUD 132 foreign (effective 2008). **Document type:** *Magazine, Consumer.* **Description:** Covers Australian karting stars, races. Includes calendar of events, technical articles, local, world and club news.
Address: PO Box 666, Balcatta, W.A. 6914, Australia.

796.76 629.2 USA ISSN 1070-2059

KART MARKETING INTERNATIONAL; the monthly trade magazine for the karting industry. Text in English. 1993. m. bk.rev. index. back issues avail. **Document type:** *Magazine, Trade.*
Media: Online - full text.
Published by: Kart Marketing Group, Inc., PO Box 101, Wheaton, IL 60189. TEL 630-653-7368, FAX 630-653-2637. Ed., R&P Darrell Sitarz TEL 630-653-7368. Adv. contact James Logan. Circ: 6,000.

769.41 DEU ISSN 1432-9085

KASKADE (BILINGUAL EDITION); european juggling magazine - europaeische Jonglierzeitschrift. Text in German, English. 1997. q. EUR 20 domestic; EUR 24 foreign (effective 2009). bk.rev.; software rev. bibl. back issues avail. **Document type:** *Magazine, Consumer.* **Description:** Serves as a forum where jugglers and physical artists of all kinds, both amateur and professional, can exchange views and experiences.
Formed by the merger of (1984-1997): Kaskade (German Edition) (0939-1363); (1984-1997): Kaskade (English Edition) (0939-1371)
Published by: Keast, Keast GbR, Schoenbergstr 92, Wiesbaden, 65199, Germany. TEL 49-611-9465142, FAX 49-611-9465143. Ed. Gabi Keast. Pub. Paul Keast. Circ: 3,500 (paid).

793.7 CZE

KATKA KRIZOVKY. Variant title: Krizovky. Text in Czech. fortn. CZK 338 (effective 2008). adv. **Document type:** *Magazine, Consumer.*
Published by: Burda Praha spol. s.r.o., Premyslovska 2845/43, Prague 2, 13000, Czech Republic. TEL 420-2-21589111, FAX 420-2-21589368, burda@burda.cz, http://www.burda.cz. adv.: page CZK 75,000; trim 190 x 268. Circ: 150,000 (paid and controlled). **Subscr. to:** SEND Predplatne s.r.o., PO Box 141, Prague 4 140 21, Czech Republic. TEL 420-225-985225, FAX 420-225-341425, send@send.cz, http://www.send.cz.

790.1 IRN ISSN 1024-9842

KAYHAN VARZESHI. Text in Persian, Modern. w. USD 478 in North America. adv. **Document type:** *Consumer.*
Published by: Kayhan Publications, Ferdowsi Ave., P O Box 11365-9631, Tehran, Iran. TEL 98-21-3110251, FAX 98-21-3114228. Circ: 125,000.

797.2 NLD ISSN 1878-7975

KEERPUNT. Text in Dutch. 2005. 8/yr. EUR 35 domestic; EUR 47.50 in Belgium (effective 2011). **Document type:** *Magazine, Consumer.*
Published by: Aquataal Media, Postbus 8016, Ede, 6710 AA, Netherlands. TEL 31-318-693310, FAX 31-318-693320, info@aquataal.nl.

796 HUN ISSN 1589-9284

KEPES SPORT. Text in Hungarian. 1954. q. HUF 9,948 (effective 2006). adv. **Document type:** *Magazine, Consumer.*
Former titles (until 2003): Heti Sport (1585-4833); (until 1993): Kepes Sport (0450-1284)
Published by: Ringier Kiado Kft., Szuglo Utca 83-85, Budapest, 1141, Hungary. TEL 36-1-4602500, FAX 36-1-4602501, kiado@ringier.hu, http://www.ringier.hu.

KEY NOTE MARKET REPORT: BETTING & GAMING. *see* BUSINESS AND ECONOMICS—Production Of Goods And Services

688.76 GBR ISSN 1368-3713

KEY NOTE MARKET REPORT: SPORTS EQUIPMENT. Variant title: Sports Equipment Market Report. Text in English. 19??. irreg., latest 2009, Jun. GBP 460 per issue (effective 2010). **Document type:** *Report, Trade.* **Description:** Provides an overview of a specific UK market segment and includes executive summary, market definition, market size, industry background, competitor analysis, current issues, forecasts, company profiles, and more.
Formerly (until 1997): Key Note Report: Sports Equipment (0267-5005); Incorporates: Key Note Market Report: Health & Fitness Equipment
Related titles: CD-ROM ed.; Online - full text ed.
Published by: Key Note Ltd. (Subsidiary of: Bonnier Business Information), Harlequin House, 5th Fl, 7 High St, Teddington, Richmond upon Thames, TW11 8EE, United Kingdom. TEL 44-845-5040452, FAX 44-845-5040453, info@keynote.co.uk.

798 658 GBR

KEY NOTE MARKET REPORT: SPORTS SPONSORHIP. Variant title: Sports Sponsorhip Market Report. Text in English. 2001. irreg., latest 2009, Sep. GBP 460 per issue (effective 2010). **Description:** Provides an overview of a specific UK market segment and includes executive summary, market definition, market size, industry background, competitor analysis, current issues, forecasts, company profiles, and more.
Published by: Key Note Ltd. (Subsidiary of: Bonnier Business Information), Harlequin House, 5th Fl, 7 High St, Teddington, Richmond upon Thames, TW11 8EE, United Kingdom. TEL 44-845-5040452, FAX 44-845-5040453, info@keynote.co.uk.

796.30223 616.863 GBR ISSN 1745-7890

➤ **KEY TEXTS IN SPORTS STUDIES.** Text in English. 2007 (Jul.). a. price varies. **Document type:** *Monographic series, Academic/Scholarly.* **Description:** Offers students short, introductory guides to the major issues in the field. Covers broad themes ranging form sport and media to drug use in sport and draws on international case material to satisfy the needs of students in the UK, Europe and North America.
Published by: Berg Publishers (Subsidiary of: Oxford International Publishers Ltd.), 1st Fl Angel Ct, 81 St Clements St, Oxford, Berks OX4 1AW, United Kingdom. TEL 44-1865-245104, FAX 44-1865-791165, enquiry@bergpublishers.com, http://www.bergpublishers.com/. Eds. John Bale, Murray Phillips.

➤ **KEYNOTES (OAK BROOK).** *see* BUSINESS AND ECONOMICS—Management

790.1 PAK

KHEL KI DUNYA. Text in Urdu. s-m.
Published by: Jamil Ahmad, 6-13 al-Yusuf Chambers, Hayat Bros., P O Box 340, Karachi, Pakistan.

790.1 IND

KHELA. Text in Bengali. 1982. w. INR 250 (effective 2011). adv. **Document type:** *Newspaper, Trade.*
Published by: AAjkaal Publishers Ltd., B P-7, Sector-5, Bidhannagar, Kolkata, 700091, India. TEL 91-33-30110800, FAX 91-33-23675502, http://www.aajkaal.net/.

796.962 RUS

KHOKKEI. Text in Russian. w. USD 236 in North America (effective 2000).
Published by: Moskovskaya Pravda, ul 1905 Goda 7, Moscow, 123846, Russian Federation. dejurka@mospravda.ru, http://www.mospravda.ru. **Dist. by:** East View Information Services, 10601 Wayzata Blvd, Minneapolis, MN 55305. TEL 952-252-1201, 800-477-1005, FAX 952-252-1202, info@eastview.com, http://www.eastview.com.

796 DEU ISSN 0023-1290
KICKER - SPORTMAGAZIN; aktuell - fachlich - kritisch. Text in German. 1968. 2/w. EUR 189.60; EUR 2.30 newsstand/cover Mon. edition; EUR 1.80 newsstand/cover Thu. edition (effective 2010). adv. bk.rev. abstr.; illus. **Document type:** *Magazine, Consumer.* **Description:** Contains international and national results and inside information for the serious soccer fan.
Formed by the merger of (1951-1968): Kicker (0344-5143); (1953-1968): Sport-Magazin. Ausgabe A (0344-5151); (1953-1968): Sport-Magazin. Ausgabe B (0344-516X); (1953-1968): Sport-Magazin. Ausgabe C (0344-5178); Incorporated (1965-1993): Fuwo. Fussball-Woche (0323-8407)
Related titles: Online - full text ed.; Supplement(s): Kicker - Sportmagazin. Sonderheft Bundesliga. ISSN 0948-7964. 19??.
Indexed: RASB.
—CCC.
Published by: Olympia Verlag GmbH, Badstr 4-6, Nuernberg, 90402, Germany. TEL 49-911-2160, FAX 49-911-2162741, anzeigen@olympia-verlag.de, http://www.olympia-verlag.de. Ed. Klaus Smentek. Adv. contact Axel Nieber. B&W page EUR 22,600, color page EUR 22,600; trim 220 x 305. Circ: 203,780 (paid).

KIDS' STUFF. *see* CHILDREN AND YOUTH—For

796.812 JPN ISSN 0388-208X
KINDAI JUDO. Text in Japanese; Summaries in English, French. 1979. m. JPY 9,120 (effective 2000).
Published by: Baseball Magazine Sha, 3-10-10 Misaki-cho, Chiyoda-ku, Tokyo, 101-0061, Japan. FAX 81-3-3238-0106. Ed. Kunio Kiryuh.

796 CHL ISSN 0716-4173
KINESIOLOGIA; revista oficial del colegio de kinesiologos de Chile. Text in Spanish. 1981. bi-m.
Related titles: Online - full text ed.
Published by: Colegio de Kinesiologos de Chile colkine@ctcinternet.cl, http://www.colkinechile.cl/. Ed. Patricio V Figueroa.

790.1 BGD
KIRAJAGAT. Text in Bengali. 1977. fortn. **Document type:** *Magazine, Consumer.*
Published by: National Sports Control Board, 62-3 Purana Paltan, Dhaka, Bangladesh. FAX 880-2-9563422. Ed. Mahmud Dulal. Circ: 7,000.

794.1 FIN ISSN 0358-1071
KIRJESHAKKI. Text in Finnish. 1961. 6/yr. EUR 42 domestic; EUR 50 foreign (effective 2004). adv. bk.rev.
Published by: Esko Nuutilainen Ed. & Pub., PO Box 61, Jaervenpaeae, 04401, Finland. FAX 358-9-2918336. Circ: 1,300.

797.21 CAN
KITEBOARD. Text in English. 2000. q. USD 3.99 newsstand/cover. adv. **Document type:** *Magazine, Consumer.* **Description:** Contains reviews and articles on kiteboarding events, equipment, personalities, and techniques.
Published by: S B C Media, 2255 B Queen St E, Ste 3266, Toronto, ON M4E 1G3, Canada. TEL 416-698-0138, FAX 416-698-8080, info@sbcmedia.com, http://www.sbcmedia.com. Ed. John Bryja. Pub. Steve Jarrett.

796.694 ZAF ISSN 1751-9624
KITEBOARD PRO WORLD TOUR MAG. Variant title: K P W T Mag. Text in English. 2007. q. EUR 30.50, USD 40; EUR 10, USD 13 newsstand/cover (effective 2007). adv.
Published by: Eventsys Management Ltd., PO Box 481, Melkbosstrand, Cape Town 7437, South Africa. TEL 27-21-5566206, FAX 27-21-5531849. adv.: page ZAR 1,640; 210 x 285.

793.7 DEU
DER KLEINE RAETSELSPASS. Text in German. m. EUR 1 newsstand/cover (effective 2011). adv. **Document type:** *Magazine, Consumer.*
Published by: Deutscher Raetselverlag GmbH & Co. KG (Subsidiary of: Gong Verlag GmbH & Co. KG), Muenchener Str 101-09, Ismaning, 85737, Germany. TEL 49-89-272708620, FAX 49-89-272707890, info@raetsel.de, http://www.deutscher-raetselverlag.de. Circ: 55,000 (controlled).

790.1 DEU
KLUBB NACHRICHTEN. Text in German. 1950. bi-m. membership. back issues avail. **Document type:** *Newsletter, Consumer.*
Published by: Turn-Klubb zu Hannover, Maschstr 16, Hannover, 30169, Germany. TEL 49-511-8093483, FAX 49-511-889941, info@turn-klubb.de, http://www.turn-klubb.de. Ed., Adv. contact Christian Baermann. Circ: 3,500.

790.1 USA ISSN 1554-3277
KNUCKLEBONES. Text in English. 2005. bi-m. USD 27.95 domestic; USD 42.95 foreign; USD 5.99 per issue (effective 2008). adv. back issues avail. **Document type:** *Magazine, Consumer.* **Description:** Includes entertaining reviews, interviews, brain-teasers, games and puzzles. It's about family, friends and good times.
Related titles: Online - full text ed.
Indexed: H20.
Published by: Jones Publishing, Inc., N 7450 Aanstad Rd, PO Box 5000, Iola, WI 54945. TEL 715-445-5000, 800-331-0038, FAX 715-445-4053, jonespub@jonespublishing.com, http://www.jonespublishing.com. Ed. Sarah Gloystein Peterson TEL 715-445-5000 ext 114. Pub. Joe Jones. Adv. contact Teresa Mead TEL 715-445-5000 ext 138. B&W page USD 1,360, color page USD 1,875; trim 8.25 x 10.75. Circ: 21,000.

796.815 USA ISSN 1931-5287
KOKORO. Text in English. 2006. q. **Document type:** *Magazine, Consumer.*
Published by: Kokoro Press, 454 N. Chugach, Palmer, AK 99645. editor@kokoro-press.com, http://www.bjsfingerpaints.com/index.htm.

057.1 UKR ISSN 2075-7115
KOMANDA. Text in Russian. 1995. 156/yr. USD 787 in North America (effective 2010). **Document type:** *Newspaper, Consumer.*
Published by: Redaktsiya Gazety Komanda, vul Marshala Timoshenka, 2L, Kyiv, 04212, Ukraine. TEL 380-44-2054884. Circ: 110,000 (paid and controlled). **Dist. by:** East View Information Services, 10601 Wayzata Blvd, Minneapolis, MN 55305. TEL 952-252-1201, 800-477-1005, FAX 952-252-1202, info@eastview.com, http://www.eastview.com.

793.7 EST
KOOLI RUUDUD. Text in Estonian. 1994. m. EUR 1.08 newsstand/cover (effective 2011). adv. **Document type:** *Magazine, Consumer.*
Published by: Kuma Ltd., 57 Parnu St, Paide, 72712, Estonia. TEL 372-38-38800, FAX 372-38-38806, kuma@kuma.ee, http://www.kuma.ee. Ed. Jaanus Laidna. adv.: page EEK 2,500.

794.1 SWE ISSN 1403-5057
KORRSCHACK. Text in Swedish. 1953. 6/yr. adv. bk.rev. **Document type:** *Consumer.*
Former titles (until 1997): S S K K Bulletinen (0347-5867); (until 1974): Korrespondensschack-bulletinen
Published by: Sveriges Schackfoerbunds Korrespondensschackkommitte, Dag Hammerskjoelds Vaeg 5B, Lund, 22464, Sweden. sskk@schack.se, http://www.schack.se/sskk. Ed. Lars Grahn.

794 FIN ISSN 1796-590X
KOTIRISTIKKO EXTRA. Text in Finnish. 1977. 6/yr. EUR 3.95 newsstand/cover (effective 2009). **Document type:** *Magazine, Consumer.*
Formerly (until 2004): Kotiristikko (0356-1534)
Published by: Sanoma Magazines Finland Corporation, Lapinmaentie 1, Helsinki, 00350, Finland. TEL 358-9-1201, FAX 358-9-1205171, info@sanomamagazines.fi, http://www.sanomamagazines.fi.

794.5 HRV ISSN 1332-6740
KRIZALJKE & REBUSI. Text in Croatian. 2000. m. **Document type:** *Magazine, Consumer.*
Published by: Revije d.d., Slavonska avenija 4, Zagreb, 10000, Croatia. TEL 385-1-6161035, FAX 385-1-6161028, revije@revije.hr, http://www.revije.hr.

KRONOS; la revista cientifica de actividad fisica y deporte. *see* PHYSICAL FITNESS AND HYGIENE

793.7 EST
KROONIKA RISTSONAD. Text in Estonian. m. EUR 10.80; EUR 1.05 newsstand/cover (effective 2011). **Document type:** *Magazine, Consumer.*
Published by: Ajakirjade Kirjastus, Maakri 23A, Tallinn, 10145, Estonia. TEL 372-666-2600, FAX 372-666-2557, sekr@kirjastus.ee, http://www.kirjastus.ee. Ed. Tarmo Tuule.

KROPPSOEVING. *see* EDUCATION

793.7 SWE ISSN 0345-6609
KRYSSDAX. Text in Swedish. 1967. q. SEK 14.50 per issue.
Published by: Acadius Foerlags AB, Fack 45088, Stockholm, 10430, Sweden.

793.7 SWE ISSN 0345-6617
KRYSSET. Text in Swedish. 1957. 13/yr. SEK 222 (effective 1991).
Incorporates (1958-1990): Chansen
Published by: Semic Specialpress, Fack 1074, Sundbyberg, 17222, Sweden. **Subscr. to:** Pressdata AB, Fack 3217, Stockholm 10364, Sweden.

794 FIN ISSN 1459-1626
KULTARISTIKOT EXTRA. Text in Finnish. 1990. m. EUR 32; EUR 2.90 newsstand/cover (effective 2009). **Document type:** *Magazine, Consumer.*
Formerly (until 2003): Elakevaen Ristikot Extra (1239-7911)
Published by: Sanoma Magazines Finland Corporation, Lapinmaentie 1, Helsinki, 00350, Finland. TEL 358-9-1201, FAX 358-9-1205171, info@sanomamagazines.fi, http://www.sanomamagazines.fi.

793.7 EST
KUMA KANGE. Text in Estonian. 2005. m. EUR 1.59 newsstand/cover (effective 2011). adv. **Document type:** *Magazine, Consumer.*
Published by: Kuma Ltd., 57 Parnu St, Paide, 72712, Estonia. TEL 372-38-38800, FAX 372-38-38806, kuma@kuma.ee, http://www.kuma.ee. Ed. Jaanus Laidna. adv.: page EEK 2,500.

793.7 EST
KUMAKE. Text in Estonian. 1993. m. EUR 0.95 newsstand/cover (effective 2011). adv. **Document type:** *Magazine, Consumer.*
Published by: Kuma Ltd., 57 Parnu St, Paide, 72712, Estonia. TEL 372-38-38800, FAX 372-38-38806, kuma@kuma.ee, http://www.kuma.ee. Ed. Jaanus Laidna. adv.: page EEK 2,000.

793.7 LVA
KUMINS. Text in Latvian. 1995. m. LVL 0.49 newsstand/cover (effective 2005). **Document type:** *Magazine, Consumer.*
Published by: SIA Kuma, Rinuzu Iela 22-44, Riga, 1015, Latvia. TEL 371-7342879, FAX 371-7342879, kuma@kuma.lv. Ed. Inara Ratnik. Pub. Aida Luts.

793.7 HRV
KVISKOTEKA. Text in Croatian. w. EUR 2.50 newsstand/cover. **Document type:** *Magazine, Consumer.*
Address: Palmotiaeva 22, Zagreb, 10000, Croatia. TEL 385-1-4922723, FAX 385-1-4922724.

793.7 HRV
KVIZORAMA. Text in Croatian. w. EUR 2.05 newsstand/cover. **Document type:** *Magazine, Consumer.*
Published by: Zrenik d.o.o., Savska 141, Zagreb, 10000, Croatia. TEL 385-1-6190738, FAX 385-1-6190753. Ed. Boris Nazansky.

794.1 USA ISSN 0148-057X
KXE6S VEREIN CHESS SOCIETY. ADVISORY BOARD RECORD. Text in English. 1976. bi-m. adv. bk.rev. abstr.; bibl.; charts; illus.; stat. index, cum.index. back issues avail.
Published by: Kxe6s Verein Chess Society, PO Box 2066, Chapel Hill, NC 27514. Ed. Steven Buntin. Circ: 500.

794.1 USA ISSN 0148-0561
KXE6S VEREIN NEWSLETTER. Text in English. 1975. bi-m. USD 10. adv. bk.rev. bibl.; charts; illus.; stat. index. back issues avail.
Published by: Kxe6s Verein Chess Society, PO Box 2066, Chapel Hill, NC 27514. Eds. Jerry Clark, Steven Buntin.

L S A NEWSLETTER. *see* LEISURE AND RECREATION

796.347 USA ISSN 1069-5893
GV989
LACROSSE MAGAZINE. Text in English. 1978. 8/yr. adv. illus.; stat.; tr.lit. back issues avail. **Document type:** *Magazine, Consumer.* **Description:** Covers men's and women's lacrosse at all levels. Includes action photographs and news on the Lacrosse Foundation.
Formerly: Lacrosse (0194-7893)
Indexed: SD.
—Ingenta.
Published by: Lacrosse Foundation, Inc., 113 W University Parkway, Baltimore, MD 21210. TEL 410-235-6882, FAX 410-366-6735. Ed. Brian Logue. Adv. contact Kira Muller. Circ: 14,000.

796.86 CAN
LAIDO NEWSLETTER. Text in English. 1989. irreg. **Document type:** *Newsletter.* **Description:** Deals with all aspects of the Japanese sword arts.
Related titles: Online - full text ed.
Published by: Sei Do Kai Iaudo, 205 Riviera Dr, Unit 1, Markham, ON L3R 5J8, Canada. TEL 416-445-1481, FAX 416-445-0519. Ed. Kim Taylor.

LAKELAND BOATING; the Great Lakes boating magazine. *see* SPORTS AND GAMES—Boats And Boating

790.1 340 FRA ISSN 1760-5873
LAMY DROIT DU SPORT. Text in French. 2 base vols. plus s-a. updates. looseleaf. EUR 1,068 base vol(s). print & CD-ROM eds. (effective 2010). **Document type:** *Directory, Trade.*
Related titles: CD-ROM ed.: ISSN 1956-8274; Online - full text ed.: EUR 182 (effective 2003).
Published by: Lamy S.A. (Subsidiary of: Wolters Kluwer France), 1 Rue Eugene et Armand Peugeot, Rueil-Malmaison, 92856 Cedex, France. TEL 33-1-76733000, FAX 33-1-76734809, lamy@lamy.fr.

LAS VEGAS ADVISOR. *see* TRAVEL AND TOURISM

LAS VEGAS INSIDER. *see* TRAVEL AND TOURISM

306.4 USA
LAS VEGAS SPORTING NEWS. Text in English. w. USD 97 (effective 2001). adv. **Document type:** *Magazine, Consumer.* **Description:** Covers sports news and analysis for gambling.
Related titles: Online - full content ed.
Address: 850 3rd St, Whitehall, PA 18052. TEL 800-325-8259, reolvsn@aol.com, http://www.lvsn.com/.

306.4 USA
LAS VEGAS SPORTING NEWS FOOTBALL ANNUAL. Text in English. 2001 (Aug.). a. **Document type:** *Magazine, Consumer.* **Description:** Covers college and pro football, including news and analysis focused on gambling odds.
Published by: Las Vegas Sporting News, 850 3rd St, Whitehall, PA 18052. TEL 800-325-8259, reolvsn@aol.com, http://www.lvsn.com/.

LAS VEGAS STYLE. *see* TRAVEL AND TOURISM

796.72 USA ISSN 1057-2643
LATE MODEL DIGEST. Text in English. 1989. fortn. USD 25; USD 35 foreign (effective 1998). adv. **Document type:** *Newspaper, Trade.*
Published by: Back Porch Publications LLC., PO Box 69, Marble, NC 28905-0069. TEL 704-837-9539, FAX 704-837-7718. Ed. Tim Lee. Pub., R&P Bob Appleget. Adv. contact Carolyn McLeod. Circ: 4,000 (paid).

796.7 USA
LATE MODEL ILLUSTRATED. Text in English. 2008. m. USD 30 domestic; USD 50 in Canada (effective 2008). **Document type:** *Magazine, Consumer.*
Published by: McLeod Media LLC, PO Box 340, Murphy, NC 28906. TEL 828-837-1353, FAX 828-837-7718. Ed. Tim Lee. Pubs. Brian McLeod, Carolyn McLeod.

LAW OF PROFESSIONAL AND AMATEUR SPORTS. *see* LAW

796 ARG ISSN 0329-0069
LECTURAS EDUCACION FISICA Y DEPORTES; revista digital. Text in English, Portuguese, Spanish. irreg. back issues avail. **Document type:** *Monographic series, Academic/Scholarly.*
Related titles: Online - full text ed.: ISSN 1514-3465. 1997.
Published by: Centro de Altos Estudios Latinoamericanos, R. Scalabrini Ortiz 427, 7o-26, Buenos Aires, 1414, Argentina. TEL 54-114-8547207. Ed. Julio Guterman.

796.48 NLD ISSN 1872-0110
LEDENTAL N O C, N S F. (Nederlands Olympisch Comite, Nederlandse Sport Federatie) Text in Dutch. 199?. a. EUR 10 (effective 2009).
Published by: Nederlands Olympisch Comite, Nederlandse Sport Federatie, Postbus 302, Arnhem, 6800 AH, Netherlands. TEL 31-26-4834400, FAX 31-26-4821245, info@noc-nsf.nl, http://www.nocnsf.nl.

796.3 USA ISSN 1067-4748
LEGENDS SPORTS MEMORABILIA. Text in English. 1988. bi-m. USD 120 (effective 1999). **Document type:** *Magazine, Trade.* **Description:** Offers articles and price guide relating to sports collectibles; features by sports-beat writers.
Published by: Legends Sports Memorabilia, Inc., 9900 Aspen Knoll Ct., Las Vegas, NV 89117-0956. Ed. Greg Hary. Pub. Joe Kaufenberg. adv.: B&W page USD 2,500. Circ: 90,000.

796 RUS ISSN 0024-4155
GV1060.5
LEGKAYA ATLETIKA. Text in Russian. 1955. m. USD 68 foreign (effective 2003). illus. index.
—East View.
Published by: Vserossiiskaya Federatsiya Legkoi Atletiki, Rozhdestvenskii bulv 10-7, Moscow, 103031, Russian Federation. TEL 7-095-9289672, FAX 7-095-9288272. Ed. A K Shedchenko. Circ: 75,000. **Dist. by:** M K - Periodica, ul Gilyarovskogo 39, Moscow 129110, Russian Federation. TEL 7-095-2845008, FAX 7-095-2813798, info@periodicals.ru, http://www.mkniga.ru; East View Information Services, 10601 Wayzata Blvd, Minneapolis, MN 55305. TEL 952-252-1201, 800-477-1005, FAX 952-252-1202, info@eastview.com, http://www.eastview.com.

793.7 DEU
LEIPZIGER RAETSELHEFT. Text in German. m. EUR 12.60; EUR 1 newsstand/cover (effective 2011). adv. **Document type:** *Magazine, Consumer.*
Published by: Deutscher Raetselverlag GmbH & Co. KG (Subsidiary of: Gong Verlag GmbH & Co. KG), Muenchener Str 101-09, Ismaning, 85737, Germany. TEL 49-89-272708620, FAX 49-89-272707890, info@raetsel.de, http://www.deutscher-raetselverlag.de. Circ: 79,000 (controlled).

613.7 790.1 DEU ISSN 0941-5270
LEIPZIGER SPORTWISSENSCHAFTLICHE BEITRAEGE. Text in German; Summaries in English, French, German, Russian. 1959. 2/yr. EUR 30; EUR 17.50 newsstand/cover (effective 2008). bk.rev. illus. index. **Document type:** *Journal, Academic/Scholarly.*
Formerly: Deutsche Hochschule fuer Koerperkultur. Wissenschaftliche Zeitschrift (0457-3919)
Indexed: DIP, IBR, IBZ, SD.

S

Published by: (Fakultaet fuer Sportwissenschaft, Universitaet Leipzig), Academia Verlag GmbH, Bahnstr 7, Sankt Augustin, 53757, Germany. TEL 49-2241-345210, FAX 49-2241-345316, kontakt@academia-verlag.de. Circ: 400.

790.1 DEU ISSN 0341-7387
LEISTUNGSSPORT. Text in German. 1970. bi-m. EUR 39.60 domestic; EUR 44.40 foreign (effective 2011). adv. back issues avail. **Document type:** *Magazine, Trade.*
Indexed: A22, DIP, IBR, IBZ, RASB, SD, SportS.
—BLDSC (5182.205000), IE, Infotrieve, Ingenta.
Published by: Philippka-Sportverlag Konrad Honig, Rektoratsweg 36, Muenster, 48159, Germany. TEL 49-251-230050, FAX 49-251-2300579, info@philippka.de, http://www.philippka.de. Ed. Peter Tschiene. Adv. contact Peter Moellers TEL 49-251-2300528.

LEISURE INDUSTRY REPORT. *see* LEISURE AND RECREATION

THE LEISURE REVIEW; an independent view of the leisure industry. *see* LEISURE AND RECREATION

LEISURE SCIENCES; an interdisciplinary journal. *see* LEISURE AND RECREATION

LEISURE STUDIES ASSOCIATION. PUBLICATIONS. *see* LEISURE AND RECREATION

790.1 USA
LET'S MAKE IT OFFICIAL. Text in English. a. USD 5 per issue (effective 2009). **Document type:** *Magazine, Consumer.* **Description:** Provides an overview of officiating, pointing out the commitment and responsibilities as well as the rewards and satisfactions.
Published by: National Federation of State High School Associations, PO Box 690, Indianapolis, IN 46206. TEL 317-972-6900, 800-776-3462, FAX 317-822-5700, info@nfhs.org, http://www.nfhs.org.

796 USA ISSN 0889-4795
LET'S PLAY HOCKEY. Text in English. 1972. 29/yr. USD 49 domestic (effective 2005). adv. **Document type:** *Magazine, Consumer.* **Description:** Targets youth and amateur players, parents, coaches and fans.
Related titles: Online - full text ed.
Published by: Let's Play, Inc., 2721 E 42nd St, Minneapolis, MN 55406. TEL 612-729-0023, FAX 612-729-0259. Ed. Steve Carroll. Pub. Doug Johnson. adv.: B&W page USD 1,005, color page USD 1,385; 10.125 x 16. Circ: 13,500 (controlled).

794.1 HUN ISSN 0230-5151
LEVELEZESI SAKKHIRADO. Text in Hungarian. 1967. 6/yr. USD 4. adv. bk.rev. **Description:** Covers national and international chess games and news, tables and results.
Published by: Hungarian Chess Association, Correspondence Committee, Klauzal ter 5 II 30, Budapest, 1072, Hungary. TEL 361-1213-832. Ed. Dezso Solt. Circ: 1,000.

796 USA
LIBERTY SPORTS MAGAZINE. Text in English. 2005. q. free (effective 2005). **Document type:** *Magazine, Consumer.* **Description:** Covers race previews and reviews, advice on training, buying equipment, choosing nutrition.
Address: 2000 Spring Garden St., Philadelphia, PA 19130. TEL 215 564 2047, FAX 215-440-0845. Ed. Christian Wareiks. Pubs. Bob Ingram, Josh Markel. Circ: 60,000 (free).

LICHAMELIJKE OPVOEDING. *see* EDUCATION—Teaching Methods And Curriculum

LIDER. *see* EDUCATION

793.7 LVA
LIELAS RUTIS. Text in Latvian. 2002. m. LVL 0.69 newsstand/cover (effective 2005). **Document type:** *Magazine, Consumer.*
Published by: SIA Kuma, Rinuzu Iela 22-44, Riga, 1015, Latvia. TEL 371-7342879, FAX 371-7342879, kuma@kuma.lv. Ed. Inara Ratnik. Pub. Aida Luts.

790.1 LTU
LIETUVOS SPORTAS. Text in Lithuanian. 1922. 3/w. LTL 300, USD 100 (effective 1998). adv. bk.rev. **Document type:** *Newspaper, Consumer.*
Address: Odminits str 9, Vilnius, 2000, Lithuania. TEL 370-2-616757, FAX 370-2-616757. Ed. Bronius Cekanauskas. Circ: 8,000 (controlled).

796.07 FIN ISSN 0358-7010
LIIKUNTA & TIEDE. Text in Finnish. 1963. bi-m. EUR 36 domestic; EUR 40 foreign; EUR 8 per issue (effective 2005). adv. back issues avail. **Document type:** *Magazine, Consumer.*
Formerly (until 1981): Stadion (0561-7731)
Indexed: SD.
Published by: Liikuntatieteellinen Seura ry/Finnish Society for Research in Sport and Physical Education, Stadion, Etelakaarre, Helsinki, 00250, Finland. TEL 358-9-4542720, FAX 358-9-45427222, toimisto@lts.fi. Eds. Kari L Keskinen, Toiriina Kukkonen-Harjula. adv.: B&W page EUR 650, color page EUR 1,100; 210 x 297. Circ: 4,000.

796.07 FIN ISSN 0356-746X
GV288.F5
LIIKUNTATIETEELLISEN SEURA. JULKAISUJA/FINNISH SOCIETY FOR RESEARCH IN SPORT AND PHYSICAL EDUCATION. PUBLICATION. Text in English, Finnish. 1954. irreg., latest vol.158, 200?. price varies. back issues avail. **Document type:** *Monographic series, Academic/Scholarly.*
Formerly (until 1962): Suomen Urheiluakatemia. Julkaisusarja (0491-5623)
Related titles: ◆ Series: Current Research in Physical Sciences in Finland. ISSN 0788-6012.
—BLDSC (5215.750000).
Published by: Liikuntatieteellinen Seura ry/Finnish Society for Research in Sport and Physical Education, Stadion, Etelakaarre, Helsinki, 00250, Finland. TEL 358-9-4542-720, FAX 358-9-4542-7222, toimisto@lts.fi.

796.07 FIN ISSN 1237-0576
LIIKUNTATIETEELLISEN SEURAN IMPULSSISARJA. Variant title: Impulssi. Text in Finnish. 1994. irreg., latest vol.23, 2003. price varies. back issues avail. **Document type:** *Monographic series.*
—BLDSC (5215.745000).
Published by: Liikuntatieteellinen Seura ry/Finnish Society for Research in Sport and Physical Education, Stadion, Etelakaarre, Helsinki, 00250, Finland. TEL 358-9-4542720, FAX 358-9-45427222, toimisto@lts.fi.

790.1 DEU
LIMITED SKATEBOARDING MAGAZINE. Text in German. bi-m. EUR 15; EUR 3 newsstand/cover (effective 2007). adv. **Document type:** *Magazine, Consumer.*
Published by: Limited Magazine, Hagenauer Str 51, Wiesbaden, 65203, Germany. TEL 49-611-9287827, FAX 49-611-9287833. Eds. Christian Koch, Thomas Gentsch. Pubs. C Seewaldt, J Ludewig. adv.: B&W page EUR 1,400, color page EUR 2,200. Circ: 27,000 (paid and controlled).

790.1 USA
LINDY'S SPORTS ANNUALS; SEC, ACC, Big 10, Big 12, Pac 10, national college, pro basketball, college basketball, national college football. Text in English. 2002. a. USD 9.50 per issue (effective 2008). adv. back issues avail. **Document type:** *Magazine, Consumer.* **Description:** Covers sports news.
Related titles: Online - full text ed.
Published by: D M D Publications, Inc., 2100 Centennial Dr, Ste 100, Birmingham, AL 35216. TEL 205-871-1182, FAX 205-871-1184, lindy@lindyssports.com, http://www.lindyssports.com/. Pub. Lindy Davis. adv.: B&W page USD 29,120, color page USD 36,400; trim 10.5 x 8. Circ: 600,000 (paid).

796 ITA ISSN 1824-4130
L'INFORMATORE SPORTIVO. Text in Italian. 2003. w. **Document type:** *Newspaper, Consumer.*
Published by: L' Unione Sarda, Viale Regina Elena 12, Cagliari, Italy. TEL 39-070-60131, unione@unionesarda.it, http://www.unionesarda.it.

793.7 SRB ISSN 1451-527X
LISA. UKRSTENICE. Key Title: Ukrstenice. Text in Serbian. 2002. m. adv. **Document type:** *Magazine, Consumer.*
Published by: Isdavacka Kuca Burda Beograd, Takovska 45, Belgrade, 11000. TEL 381-11-3290809, FAX 381-11-3290807, pretplata@burda.co.yu, http://www.burda.co.yu. adv.: page USD 700. Circ: 70,000 (paid and controlled).

793.7 RUS ISSN 1606-8769
LIZA. KROSSVORDY. Text in Russian. 2000. m. adv. **Document type:** *Magazine, Consumer.* **Description:** Provides a mix of crossword puzzles for young and old.
Published by: Izdatel'skii Dom Burda, ul Pravdy 8, Moscow, 125040, Russian Federation. TEL 7-095-7979849, FAX 7-095-2571196, vertrieb@burda.ru, http://www.burda.ru. adv.: page USD 1,600. Circ: 250,000 (paid and controlled).

793.732 UKR
LIZA. KROSSVORDY. Text in Russian. s-m. **Document type:** *Magazine, Consumer.*
Published by: Burda Ukraina, Zhyljanskaja ul. 29, Kiev, 01033, Ukraine. TEL 38-044-4908363, FAX 38-044-4908364, zhestkov@burda.ua, http://www.burda.ua.

LOISIR ET SOCIETE/SOCIETY AND LEISURE. *see* LEISURE AND RECREATION

790.1 CAN ISSN 1192-3326
LOISIR ET SPORT AU QUEBEC. Text in English. biennial. CAD 44.95 (effective 2001). **Document type:** *Directory.* **Description:** Contains listings of recreation departments, community centers, and specialized publications in Quebec.
Published by: Quebec dans le Monde, C P 8503, Sainte Foy, PQ G1V 4N5, Canada. TEL 418-659-5540, FAX 418-659-4143.

LOISIRS SANTE. *see* EDUCATION—Teaching Methods And Curriculum

796 649 USA ISSN 2155-7640
▼ **LONG BEACH YOUTH SPORTS CONNECTION.** Text in English. 2010 (Sept.). m. USD 28 (effective 2011). **Document type:** *Magazine, Consumer.* **Description:** News and information on youth sports in Long Beach, California.
Published by: LBYSC - The Magazine, 6285 E Spting St, No 390N, Long Beach, CA 90808. TEL 562-606-8574. Ed., Pub. Neff Sequoia.

790.1 USA ISSN 1082-2461
LONGBOARD MAGAZINE. Text in English. 1993. 7/yr. (m. Summer; bi-m. Winter). USD 40 (effective 2007). adv. **Document type:** *Magazine, Consumer.* **Description:** Covers the surfing lifestyle.
Formerly (until 1995): Longboard Quarterly (1082-2224)
Address: 110 E Avenida Palizada, Ste. 301, San Clemente, CA 92672. TEL 800-284-1864. Pub. Guy Motil.

796.8 NLD ISSN 1876-4843
LOOKING FOR TAI JI. Cover title: Looking for Taiji. Text in Dutch. 2008. s-a. EUR 6.75 newsstand/cover (effective 2011). adv. **Document type:** *Magazine, Consumer.*
Published by: Jing Wu Culture, Surinamestraat 9, Beverwijk, 1944 XG, Netherlands. TEL 31-6-55161760, jingwu_nl@yahoo.com, http://www.jingwu.nl.

LOTTERY, PARIMUTUEL & CASINO REGULATION - STATE CAPITALS. *see* LAW

795 USA ISSN 2154-1078
▼ **LOTTERY POST**; lottery results almanac. Text in English. 2009. a. USD 59.99 per issue (effective 2010). **Description:** Includes winning numbers for every U.S. lottery game.
Published by: Speednet Group, PO Box 302, Martinsville, NJ 08836. TEL 908-722-8406, info@speednet.biz, http://speednet.biz/.

795 USA
LOTTERY WINNING GUIDE. Text in English. 1993. m. **Document type:** *Journal, Consumer.*
Published by: Gibbs Publishing Company, PO Box 97, Sylva, NC 28779. gibbsic@aol.com. Ed. James Calvin Gibbs.

795 ITA ISSN 0024-6662
LOTTOROSCOPO; periodico mensile di previsioni sul lotto. Text in Italian. 1957. m. (13/yr.). EUR 20.50 (effective 2009). **Document type:** *Newspaper, Consumer.*
Address: Via S Nicolo 7, Casella Postale 94, Parma, PR 43100, Italy. TEL 39-0521-206076. Circ: 5,000.

799.2 HRV ISSN 0024-6999
LOVACKI VJESNIK. Text in Croatian. 1892. m. adv. bk.rev. **Document type:** *Magazine, Consumer.*
Published by: Hrvatski Lovacki Savez, Vladimira Nazora 63, Zagreb, 10000, Croatia. TEL 385-1-433310, FAX 385-1-427598. Ed. Danijel Popovic. Circ: 82,000.

LUFTSPORT; das Magazin fuer den Luftsport. *see* AERONAUTICS AND SPACE FLIGHT

796.215 USA ISSN 0898-4786
GV1102.7.T7
M A TRAINING. (Martial Arts) Text in English. 1973. bi-m. USD 12.97 (effective 2000). adv. charts; illus. **Document type:** *Magazine, Consumer.* **Description:** Covers training for the martial artist in all styles and product reviews.
Former titles (until 1988): M A Weapons (0893-2514); (until 1987): Fighting Stars - Ninja (0886-8786); (until 198?): Fighting Stars (0274-5178)
Published by: Black Belt Communications, Inc. (Subsidiary of: Active Interest Media), 24900 Anza Dr, Unit E, Valencia, CA 91355. TEL 661-257-4066, 800-423-2870, FAX 661-257-3028, http://www.blackbeltmag.com. Ed. Robert Young. Pub. Cheryl Angelheart. Adv. contact Danny Caravello. Circ: 45,000. **Subscr. to:** PO Box 421117, Palm Coast, FL 32142.

796.7 USA ISSN 1557-2617
M C 2 (BREMERTON); the independent American magazine for all Mini owners. (Mini Classic Mini Cooper) Variant title: M C 2 Magazine. Text in English. 2005 (Win.). q. USD 24.95 domestic; USD 32 in Canada & Mexico; USD 40 elsewhere (effective 2006). **Document type:** *Magazine, Consumer.*
Published by: Car Graphic, 4640 Chico Way, Bremerton, WA 98312. TEL 360-698-7926. Ed. Gary Anderson. Pub. Barry Brazier.

796.815 USA ISSN 1947-539X
▼ **M M A CAGE.** (Mixed Martial Arts) Text in English. 2009. q. USD 5.99 per issue (effective 2009). **Document type:** *Magazine, Consumer.* **Description:** Articles on mixed martial arts cage fighting.
Published by: Harris Publications, Inc., 1115 Broadway, New York, NY 10010. TEL 212-807-7100, FAX 212-924-2352, subscriptions@harris-pub.com, http://www.harris-pub.com.

796.83 USA ISSN 1937-1071
M M A WORLDWIDE. (Mixed Martial Arts) Text in English. 2007. bi-m. USD 32 (effective 2007). **Document type:** *Magazine, Consumer.*
Published by: S M P Inc., 5252 Orange Ave, Ste 109, Cypress, CA 90630. TEL 714-226-0585, FAX 714-226-0583. Pub. Robert Pittman.

796.77 GBR
M S A COMPETITORS AND OFFICIALS YEARBOOK. Text in English. 1956. a. GBP 25 per issue (effective 2009). adv. back issues avail. **Document type:** *Yearbook, Consumer.* **Description:** Contains rules, regulations and other information on motor sports.
Supersedes (in 200?): Motor Sports Year Book; Which was formerly (until 1980): R A C Motor Sports Year Book
Related titles: Online - full text ed.: free (effective 2009).
Published by: Motor Sports Association, Motor Sports House, Riverside Park, Colnbrook, Slough, Berks SL3 0HG, United Kingdom. TEL 44-1753-765000, FAX 44-1753-682938. Ed. I R Davis.

796.72 FRA ISSN 1285-8374
M X MAGAZINE. (Motocross) Text in French. 1998. m. EUR 51 (effective 2009). adv. **Document type:** *Magazine, Consumer.*
Published by: Editions Lariviere, 6 Rue Olof Palme, Clichy, 92587, France. TEL 33-1-47565400, http://www.editions-lariviere.fr.

793.7 EST
MAAGILISED RUUDUD. Text in Estonian. 1993. m. EUR 0.95 newsstand/cover (effective 2011). adv. **Document type:** *Magazine, Consumer.*
Published by: Kuma Ltd., 57 Parnu St, Paide, 72712, Estonia. TEL 372-38-38800, FAX 372-38-38806, kuma@kuma.ee, http://www.kuma.ee. adv.: page EEK 2,000.

796 POL ISSN 1428-250X
MAGAZYN SPORTOWY. Text in Polish. 1997. w. **Document type:** *Magazine, Consumer.*
Published by: J M G Sport Publishing (Subsidiary of: Marquard Media AG), ul Nowogrodzka 84-86, Warsaw, 02-018, Poland. TEL 48-22-6289116, FAX 48-22-6218697, http://sports.pl.

793.7 SVK ISSN 1336-8834
MAGICKE OBRAZKY. Text in Slovak. 2006. bi-m. **Document type:** *Magazine, Consumer.*
Published by: Sander Media s.r.o., Bakalarska 2, Prievidza, 97101, Slovakia. TEL 421-46-5439184, FAX 421-46-5439186, sander@sander.sk, http://www.sander.sk.

793.7 LVA
MAGISKAS RUTIS. Text in Latvian. 1995. m. LVL 0.49 newsstand/cover (effective 2005). **Document type:** *Magazine, Consumer.*
Published by: SIA Kuma, Rinuzu Iela 22-44, Riga, 1015, Latvia. TEL 371-7342879, FAX 371-7342879, kuma@kuma.lv.

MALAYSIA SPORTS AND FITNESS DIRECTORY. *see* BUSINESS AND ECONOMICS—Trade And Industrial Directories

796 SWE ISSN 1652-3180
MALMOE STUDIES IN SPORT SCIENCES. Text in English, Swedish. 2004. irreg., latest vol.3, 2006. **Document type:** *Monographic series, Academic/Scholarly.*
Published by: Malmoe Hoegskola, Laerarutbildningen. Idrottvetenskap/ Malmoe University, School of Teacher Education. Department of Sport Sciences, Malmoe, 20506, Sweden. TEL 46-40-6657000, FAX 46-40-6657305, http://www.mah.se/fakulteter-och-omraden/Lararutbildningen/Enheter/Idrottsvetenskap-IDV.

MAN MAGNUM; the shooters' magazine. *see* SPORTS AND GAMES—Outdoor Life

354 CAN
MANITOBA LOTTERIES CORPORATION. ANNUAL REPORT. Text in English. 1971. a. free. illus.; stat.
Former titles: Manitoba Lotteries Foundation. Annual Report (0837-6840); (until 1983): Manitoba Lotteries and Gaming Control Commission. Annual Report (0824-8508); (until 1981): Manitoba Lotteries Commission. Annual Report (0703-0827)
Published by: Manitoba Lotteries Corporation, 830 Empress St, Winnipeg, MB R3G 3H3, Canada. TEL 204-957-2663, FAX 204-957-2621. Circ: 2,000.

796.77 FRA ISSN 1630-4969
LE MANS RACING. Text in French. 200?. 8/yr. EUR 40.60 domestic; EUR 60.90 DOM-TOM; EUR 60.90 in Europe; EUR 60.90 in North Africa; EUR 72.90 in North America; EUR 72.90 in the Middle East (effective 2009); EUR 91.40 elsewhere (effective 2007). back issues avail. **Document type:** *Magazine, Consumer.*
Published by: Sports Presse Editons et Developpement, 9 rue du Port, Le Mans, 72000, France.

796.44 ITA ISSN 2037-1918
▼ **MANUALI DI PILATES.** Text in Italian. 2009. m. **Document type:** *Handbook/Manual/Guide, Consumer.*
Published by: CIGRA 2003 Srl, Viale Vittorio Veneto 28, Milan, 20124, Italy. TEL 39-02-43995439, FAX 39-02-29061863, info@cigra.it.

790.1 USA ISSN 1524-2943
MANY HAPPY RETURNS; newsletter of the United States Boomerang Association. Text in English. 1982. q. membership. adv. bk.rev.; software rev. charts; illus.; tr.lit. back issues avail. **Document type:** *Newsletter, Consumer.* **Description:** Presents a forum for the art, sport, and history of boomerangs with information about the craftsmanship, sports results, and various applicable computer programs available.
Formerly: Many Happy Returns Newsletter
Related titles: E-mail ed.; Online - full text ed.
Published by: United States Boomerang Association, c/o Betsylew Miale-Gix, 3351 236th St SW, Brier, WA 98036-8421. TEL 425-485-1672, FAX 425-485-1672, usba-pr@usba.org, http://www.usba.org. adv.: B&W page USD 100, color page USD 200; trim 10.25 x 7.5. Circ: 500 (paid).

796.962 USA ISSN 2150-5365
GV848.T6
▼ **MAPLE STREET PRESS MAPLE LEAFS ANNUAL.** Variant title: Maple Leafs Annual. Text in English. 2009. a. USD 12.99 per issue (effective 2011). back issues avail. **Document type:** *Handbook/Manual/Guide, Consumer.* **Description:** Features analysis, draft, and prospect coverage for the Toronto Maple Leafs hockey team.
Published by: Maple Street Press, 155 Webster St, Ste B, Hanover, MA 02339. TEL 781-347-4730, FAX 781-347-4732, info@maplestreetpress.com. Ed. Alec Brownscombe.

796.4252 USA ISSN 1088-6672
GV1065
MARATHON & BEYOND; run longer, better, smarter. Abbreviated title: M & B. Text in English. 1997. bi-m. USD 36.95 domestic; USD 47.65 in Canada; USD 54 elsewhere; USD 6.95 per issue (effective 2010). adv. back issues avail. **Document type:** *Magazine, Trade.* **Description:** Focuses on specific needs of marathoners and ultramarathoners, providing the depth of information readers need to run farther, faster, safer and smarter.
Indexed: IBR, IBZ, PEI, SD, T02.
—CCC.
Address: 206 N Randolph St, Ste 400, Champaign, IL 61820. TEL 217-359-9345, 877-972-4230, FAX 217-359-4731. Ed. Richard Benyo. Pub., Adv. contact Jan Colarusso Seeley TEL 217-369-8553.

796.42 SWE ISSN 0283-1015
MARATHONLOEPAREN. Text in Swedish. 1968. bi-m. SEK 250 to members (effective 2004). **Document type:** *Consumer.*
Published by: Svenska Marathonsaellskapet, c/o Per-Arne Allensten, Traalargraend 14, Jaerfaella, 17555, Sweden. TEL 46-8-58030614. Ed. Jan Lind.

790.1 ESP
MARCA. Text in Spanish. 1941. d. adv. illus. 40 p./no. 5 cols./p.; **Document type:** *Newspaper.*
Related titles: Online - full content ed.: tiraMillas.net; kalgan.net; Online - full text ed.: marca.com.
Published by: Unidad Editorial, Ave de San Luis, 25-27, Madrid, 28033, Spain. TEL 34-91-4435000, http://www.unidadeditorial.com. Circ: 396,749 (controlled).

790.1 340 USA ISSN 1533-6484
MARQUETTE SPORTS LAW REVIEW. Text in English. 1990. s-a. USD 35 domestic; USD 45 foreign; USD 20 per issue (effective 2009). adv. bk.rev. illus. Index. back issues avail.; reprint service avail. from WSH. **Document type:** *Journal, Academic/Scholarly.* **Description:** Covers sports law, sports business and sports ethics issues confronting amateur and professional sports.
Formerly (until 2000): Marquette Sports Law Journal (Print) (1057-6029)
Media: Online - full content. **Related titles:** Microfiche ed.: (from WSH); Microform ed.: (from WSH).
Indexed: A26, B04, CA, CLI, G08, I01, I05, ILP, LRI, PEI, SD, T02.
—BLDSC (5382.650600), CIS, IE, Ingenta.
Published by: (National Sports Law Institute), Marquette University, Sensenbrenner Hall, 1103 W Wisconsin Ave, Milwaukee, WI 53201. TEL 414-288-7090, FAX 414-288-6403, law.admission@marquette.edu. Ed. Alex Porteshawver.

796.815 GBR ISSN 0955-5447
MARTIAL ARTS ILLUSTRATED. Abbreviated title: M A I. Text in English. 1988. m. GBP 39.95 domestic; GBP 53.50 in Europe; GBP 69.95 elsewhere; GBP 3.75 newsstand/cover (effective 2010). adv. bk.rev.; film rev. back issues avail. **Document type:** *Magazine, Consumer.* **Description:** Covers all aspects of the martial arts, including karate, kung fu, kickboxing, aikido and taekwondo.
Related titles: Online - full text ed.
Published by: M A I Publications, Revenue Chambers, St. Peter's St, Huddersfield, W Yorkshire HD1 1DL, United Kingdom. TEL 44-1484-435011, FAX 44-1484-422177, martialartsltd@btconnect.com, http://www.martialartsltd.co.uk. Ed. Bob Sykes.

796.8 GBR ISSN 1755-0076
THE MARTIAL ARTS JOURNAL; the online magazine uniting martial artists worldwide. Text in English. 2007. m. GBP 10 (effective 2009). adv. back issues avail. **Document type:** *Magazine, Consumer.* **Description:** Aims to provide a useful tool for the martial arts community world wide.
Media: Online - full text.
Published by: The Martial Arts Journal enquiries@themartialartsjournal.com.

796.8 USA ISSN 1933-7183
GV1101
MARTIAL ARTS MASTERS MAGAZINE. Variant title: Masters Magazine. Text in English. 2007. q. USD 19.95 (effective 2008). **Document type:** *Magazine, Consumer.* **Description:** Features interviews and profiles of martial arts champions, as well as training tips and martial arts philosophy.
Related titles: Online - full text ed.: ISSN 1942-3578.
Published by: Empire Media LLC, 11030 Randall St, Sun Valley, CA 91352. TEL 818-769-7900, FAX 818-767-7922, editorial@mastersmag.com. Ed. Jose M Fraguas. Pub. Michael James.

796.815 USA
MARTIAL ARTS TRAINING. Text in English. 1973. bi-m. **Document type:** *Magazine, Consumer.*
Published by: Rainbow Publications Inc., PO Box 918, Santa Clarita, CA 91380-9018. TEL 805-257-4066, FAX 805-257-3028, rainbow@rsabbs.com, http://www.blackbeltmag.com. Circ: 35,000 (paid).

793 ARG ISSN 1851-3891
MASTER CRUCIGRAMAS. Text in Spanish. 2007. m.
Published by: M4 Editora, San Pedro 140, Avellanada, Buenos Aires, 1870, Argentina. m4editora@speedy.com.ar.

793.93 USA
MASTERS OF ROLE PLAYING. Text in English. q. USD 15 domestic for 6 nos.; USD 24 in Canada for 6 nos.; USD 35 elsewhere for 6 nos. (effective 2000). **Document type:** *Magazine, Consumer.* **Description:** Contains reviews and advice for role playing games enthusiasts.
Published by: Chalice Publications, PO Box 114, American Fork, UT 84003. chalice@mastersrpg.com, http://www.mastersrpg.com. Ed. J C Carter. Pubs. Jason Anderson, Sherrie Anderson. Adv. contact Jason Anderson.

796.815 USA
MASTERS OF THE FIGHTING ARTS. Text in English. 2000. m. USD 5.99 newsstand/cover (effective 2001). adv. **Document type:** *Magazine, Consumer.*
Published by: Publishers Creative Systems, Box 461954, Escondido, CA 92046-1954. TEL 800-877-5528. Ed. Todd Hestor. Pub. Curtis F Wong.

796 305.4 NLD ISSN 2211-2294
▼ **MATCH.** Text in Dutch. 2010. bi-m. EUR 24.75; EUR 4.95 newsstand/ cover (effective 2011). adv. **Document type:** *Magazine, Consumer.*
Published by: Sports Media BV, Professor Eijkmanlaan 2, Haarlem, 2035 XB, Netherlands. TEL 31-23-5430000, FAX 31-23-5359627. Ed. Marieke Ottevanger. Pubs. Johan J R Van Dijk, Lodewijk Severein. Circ: 40,000.

794.1 ESP
MATE POSTAL. Text in English. 1974. q. USD 15. **Document type:** *Bulletin, Trade.*
Related titles: Spanish ed.
Published by: Asociacion Espanola de Ajedrez por Correspondencia, Apdo 439, Ciutatdella de Menorca, Balears, 07760, Spain. mercadal@matepostal.com, http://www.matepostal.com./. Ed. Carlos Ros Miro.

796.09357 ESP ISSN 1887-9586
➤ **MATERIALES PARA LA HISTORIA DEL DEPORTE.** Text in Portuguese, Spanish; Summaries in English, Portuguese, Spanish. 2003 (Sep.). s-a. EUR 9 (effective 2010). back issues avail. **Document type:** *Journal, Academic/Scholarly.* **Description:** Covers sports history, sports sociology, sports information, documentation, and bibliography.
Formerly (until 2007): Materiales para la Historia de la actividad Fisica y el Deporte en Andalucia (1888-1297)
Published by: Asociacion Andaluza de Historia del Deporte, A/A Juan Carlos Fernandez Truan, Universidad Pablo de Olavide, Departamento de Deporte, Carretera de Utrera, km. 1, Sevilla, 41013, Spain. TEL 34-954-977517, FAX 34-954-348377, jcfertru@upo.es. Circ: 250; 160 (paid). **Dist. by:** Wanceulen Editorial Deportiva, Cristo del Desamparo y Abandono 56, Seville 41006, Spain. TEL 34-954-656661, FAX 34-954-921059, infoeditorial@wanceleuen.com, http://www.wanceulen.com. **Co-sponsor:** Instituto Andaluz del Deporte.

794.1 NLD ISSN 1873-9210
MATTEN. Text in Dutch. 2007. s-a. EUR 11.95 newsstand/cover (effective 2009).
Published by: Interchess B.V., PO Box 1093, Alkmaar, 1810 KB, Netherlands. TEL 31-72-5127137, FAX 31-72-5158234, nic@newinchess.com, http://www.newinchess.com/.

790.1 SYR
MAUKEF AL-RIADI. Text in Arabic. w. adv.
Published by: Ouehda Organization, Damascus, Syria.

794.1 NLD ISSN 0927-9768
MAX EUWE-CENTRUM. NIEUWSBRIEF. Text in Dutch. 1987. 2/yr. bk.rev. **Document type:** *Newsletter, Consumer.* **Description:** News about chess activities at the Max Euwe-Centrum.
Published by: Stichting Max Euwe Centrum, Max Euweplein 30a, Amsterdam, 1017 MB, Netherlands. TEL 31-20-6257017, FAX 31-20-6392077, euwemec@xs4all.nl, http://www.maxeuwe.nl.

796 ZAF
MEGALIFE; life enhancing. Text in English. 1994. m. ZAR 75. adv. illus. **Document type:** *Magazine, Consumer.*
Published by: Penta Publications, PO Box 781723, Sandton, Transvaal 2146, South Africa. Ed. Andrea Vinassa. R&P Nicholas Leonsins.

629.11 ITA
MEGATUNING. Text in Italian. 2001. m. adv. **Document type:** *Magazine, Consumer.*
Formerly: Maxi Tuning (1592-7806)
Published by: Acacia Edizioni, Via Copernico 3, Binasco, MI 20082, Italy. http://www.acaciaedizioni.com.

796.8 NLD ISSN 1572-5316
MEIBUKAN MAGAZINE. Text in Dutch. 2004. 3/yr. free (effective 2011). **Document type:** *Magazine, Consumer.* **Description:** Aims to spread the knowledge and spirit of the martial arts.
Media: Online - full text.
Address: PO Box 8, Lent, 6663 ZG, Netherlands. Ed. Lex Opdam.

793.7 EST
MEISTRIRISTIK. Text in Estonian. m. EUR 13.29; EUR 1.30 newsstand/ cover (effective 2011). **Document type:** *Magazine, Consumer.*
Published by: Ajakirjade Kirjastus, Maakri 23A, Tallinn, 10145, Estonia. TEL 372-666-2600, FAX 372-666-2557, sekr@kirjastus.ee, http://www.kirjastus.ee. Ed. Tarmo Tuule.

796 616.462 DEU ISSN 0940-0109
MELLITUS LAUF. Text in German. 1991. 4/yr. EUR 8.80; EUR 2.65 newsstand/cover (effective 2003). adv. **Document type:** *Journal, Academic/Scholarly.*
Published by: Verlag Kirchheim und Co. GmbH, Kaiserstr 41, Mainz, 55116, Germany. TEL 49-6131-96070-0, FAX 49-6131-9607070, info@kirchheim-verlag.de, http://www.kirchheim-verlag.de. Ed. Ulrike Thurm. Circ: 3,500 (controlled).

MEN'S EXERCISE; the fitness guide for today's man. *see* PHYSICAL FITNESS AND HYGIENE

796.8 FRA ISSN 1960-8837
MEN'S FIGHT; le magazine des gentlemen fighters. Text in French. 2008. bi-m. EUR 30 (effective 2008). **Document type:** *Magazine, Consumer.*
Published by: Reactiff, 29 Rue du Marechal-de-Lattre-de-Tassigny, Corbeil-Essonnes, France.

THE MENTAL EDGE. *see* PSYCHOLOGY

MERCURY (LOS ANGELES). *see* CLUBS

790.1 VEN
MERIDIANO. Text in Spanish. d. adv. **Document type:** *Newspaper.*
Published by: Meridiario C.A., Bloque DeArmas, Final Av. San Martin,, Esq La Quebradita 34-2,, Edificio Berlioz Piso 2, Apdo 475, Caracas, DF 1020, Venezuela. Circ: 300,000.

790.1 USA
METROSPORTS BOSTON. Text in English. m. USD 25 (effective 2005); free newsstand/cover. adv. **Document type:** *Magazine, Consumer.*
Related titles: ◆ Regional ed(s).: MetroSports New York; ◆ MetroSports Washington.
Published by: Metrosports Publishing LLC, 1450 W. Randolph, Chicago, IL 60607. TEL 312-421-1551, FAX 312-421-1454. Eds. Jeff Banowetz, Jeff Banowetz. Adv. contact Doug Kaplan. page USD 3,600.

790.1 USA
METROSPORTS NEW YORK. (In 5 eds.: New York Tri-State, Greater Boston, Connecticut, Philadelphia, Washington D.C.) Text in English. 1974. 12/yr. free newsstand/cover. adv. bk.rev. back issues avail. **Document type:** *Magazine, Consumer.* **Description:** Covers all aspects of the areas adult recreational sports and fitness.
Related titles: ◆ Regional ed(s).: MetroSports Washington; ◆ MetroSports Boston.
Indexed: SD.
Address: 259 W. 30th St. 3rd Fl, New York, NY 10001. TEL 212-563-7329, FAX 212-563-7573, info-ny@metrosports.com, http:// www.metrosports.com. Ed. Jeff Banowetz. Pubs. Doug Kaplan, Mary Throne. adv.: color page USD 6,400. Circ: 100,000 (controlled). **Subscr. to:** Windy City Publishing Inc., 1450 W Randolph, Chicago, IL 60607.

790.1 USA
METROSPORTS WASHINGTON. Text in English. m. free newsstand/ cover. **Document type:** *Magazine, Consumer.*
Related titles: ◆ Regional ed(s).: MetroSports New York; ◆ MetroSports Boston.
Indexed: SD.
Published by: MetroSports Washington D.C. (Subsidiary of: Windy City Publishing Inc.), 4405 East West Hwy, Ste 206-B, Bethesda, MD 20814. TEL 301-907-7474, FAX 301-907-0971, infodc@metrosports.com, http://www.metrosportsdc.com/. Ed. Jeremy Shweder. Pubs. Doug Kaplan, Mary Thorne. Adv. contact Doug Kaplan. Circ: 55,000 (paid and controlled).

MI MLADI. *see* CHILDREN AND YOUTH—For

794.1 USA
MICHIGAN CHESS. Text in English. 1971. 6/yr. USD 12. adv. bk.rev. **Document type:** *Newsletter.*
Address: 7500 Anthony, Dearborn, MI 48126. Ed. David Moody. Circ: 1,000.

MICHIGAN OUT-OF-DOORS. *see* CONSERVATION

MICROLIGHT FLYING. *see* AERONAUTICS AND SPACE FLIGHT

796 GBR ISSN 2045-1245
MIDDLESEX MATTERS. Text in English. 19??. s-a. GBP 1 newsstand/ cover; free (effective 2011). **Document type:** *Magazine, Consumer.* **Description:** Covers information about Middlesex affiliated and associated clubs. Aims to promote, grow and develop the game within the County through membership and core values.
Formerly (until 2010): Middlesex Informer
Related titles: Online - full text ed.: free (effective 2011).
Published by: Middlesex Rugby, PK1 Twyford Ave Sports Ground, Twyford Ave, Acton, London, W3 9QA, United Kingdom. TEL 44-20-88963400, FAX 44-20-88969264, countyoffice@middlesexrugby.com. Ed. Lonsdale Leggett-Flynn.

790.1 USA ISSN 1071-4081
MIDWEST PLAYERS; the guide to gaming in the Midwest. Text in English. 1991. m. USD 26 domestic; USD 30 in Canada (effective 2005). adv. bk.rev. illus. Index. **Document type:** *Magazine, Consumer.* **Description:** Provides news of casinos, bingo halls and tracks throughout the Midwest, with columns on recreational gambling, information on promotions and entertainment.
Published by: J Fair Publications, 17321 Sandy Ct. S.E., Big Lake, MN 55309. TEL 763-263-5815, FAX 763-263-5817. adv.: B&W page USD 1,265; 9.5 x 14. Circ: 78,000.

796.72 USA ISSN 0047-732X
MIDWEST RACING NEWS. Text in English. 1959. w. (Apr.-Sep.); m. (Oct.-Dec.). USD 23; USD 1.25 newsstand/cover (effective 2005). adv. bk.rev. illus. **Document type:** *Newspaper, Consumer.* **Description:** Discusses regional and national automobile races and drivers.
Published by: Hometown Publications, 10437 Washington Dr, Germantown, PA 53022. TEL 262-238-6397, FAX 262-242-9450, racenews@mrnol.news. Adv. contact Lyn Ryan. Circ: 10,000 (paid and controlled).

MIGHTY MOPARS. *see* TRANSPORTATION—Automobiles

306.4 USA
MILTON; the luxury gambling magazine. Text in English. 1997. q. USD 16.95; USD 4.95 newsstand/cover; CAD 6.95 newsstand/cover in Canada (effective 1997). adv. **Document type:** *Magazine, Consumer.* **Description:** Presents the luxury lifestyle of gambling, cigars and alcohol.
Published by: Berle - Moll Publishing, 1119 Amalfi Dr, Pacific Palisades, CA 90272. TEL 310-454-8440, 800-645-8432, FAX 310-573-9687. Eds., Pubs. Lorna Berle, Susan Moll. Adv. contact Marshall Marder.

S

794.1 USA
MINNESOTA CHESS JOURNAL. Text in English. 1963. 4/yr. USD 15. adv. bk.rev. **Description:** Reports on national events with local participants, and computer programs.
Published by: Minnesota Chess Association, PO Box 11329, St. Paul, MN 55111-0329. Ed. Keith Hayward. Circ: 800.

796.962 USA
MINNESOTA HOCKEY JOURNAL. Abbreviated title: M H J. Text in English. 2000. q. Dist. free in state. adv. 32 p./no.; back issues avail. **Document type:** *Journal, Consumer.* **Description:** Hockey lifestyle magazine covers news, people and hockey events in Minnesota.
Published by: T P G Sports, Inc., 505 N Hwy 169, Ste 465, Minneapolis, MN 55441. TEL 763-595-0808, 800-597-5656, FAX 763-595-0016, info@tpgsports.com, http://www.tpgsports.com. Ed., R&P Greg Anzelc. Pub. Robert Fallen. Adv. contact Dave Jensen. color page USD 3,960; trim 8.25 x 10.875. Circ: 40,000 (paid).

790.1 RUS
MIR SPORTA. Text in Russian. m. USD 129.95 in United States.
Published by: Firma Evia, Olimpiiskii pr-t 16, Moscow, 129090, Russian Federation. TEL 7-095-9560995, FAX 7-095-9560980. **Dist. by:** East View Information Services, 10601 Wayzata Blvd, Minneapolis, MN 55305. TEL 952-252-1201, 800-477-1005, FAX 952-252-1202, info@eastview.com, http://www.eastview.com.

796 SRB ISSN 1451-9836
MIX. Text in Serbian. 2005. w. CSD 20 per issue domestic (effective 2007). **Document type:** *Magazine, Consumer.*
Published by: Politika, Novine i Magazini/Politika Newspapers and Magazines, Makedonska 29, Belgrade, 11000. TEL 381-11-3301442, FAX 381-11-3373346, ilustrovana@politika.co.yu. **Dist. by:** Global Press, Francuska 56, Belgrade 11060. TEL 381-11-2769301, FAX 381-11-2764538, http://www.globalpress.co.yu.

798.8 USA ISSN 1939-5787
MIXED MARTIAL ARTS AUTHORITY MAGAZINE. Variant title: M M A Authority Magazine. Text in English. 2007 (Feb.). bi-m. USD 5.99 newsstand/cover (effective 2007). adv. **Document type:** *Magazine, Consumer.* **Description:** Devoted to the athletes, fight news and business of mixed martial arts.
Published by: M M A Publications, LLC, 26246 US 19, North Clearwater, FL 33761. TEL 866-488-6622, FAX 727-791-7032, info@mmapublications.com. Pub. Lenny Bogdanos. adv.: page USD 1,100.

793.7 EST
MIXI. Text in Estonian. 1992. m. EUR 0.95 newsstand/cover (effective 2011). adv. **Document type:** *Magazine, Consumer.*
Published by: Kuma Ltd., 57 Parnu St, Paide, 72712, Estonia. TEL 372-38-38800, FAX 372-38-38806, kuma@kuma.ee, http://www.kuma.ee. Ed. Jaanus Laidna. adv.: page EEK 2,000.

796.72 GBR ISSN 1757-7691
MLECZKO TYGODNIK POLSKI. Text in English. 2008. w. back issues avail. **Document type:** *Magazine, Trade.*
Related titles: Online - full text ed.: free (effective 2011).
Published by: Baltic Enterprises UK, 1 Bloemfontein Rd, London, W12 7BH, United Kingdom. TEL 44-20-87462012.

796.1 629.133 SWE ISSN 0345-813X
MODELLFLYGNYTT. Text in Swedish. 1963. bi-m. adv. bk.rev.; software rev.; video rev. 64 p./no.; **Document type:** *Magazine, Consumer.*
Former titles (until 1968): Modellnytt; (until 1966): Modellflygnytt
Published by: Sveriges Modellflygfoerbund, PO Box 750, Falkoeping, 52122, Sweden. TEL 46-46-51537155, FAX 46-46-51537158, smff@flygsport.se, http://www.modellflygforbund.se. Ed. Magnus Oestlund. Circ: 7,000 (controlled).

MODERN GUNS; identification and values. *see* ANTIQUES

MODIFIED MAGAZINE. *see* TRANSPORTATION—Automobiles

796.72 USA ISSN 1939-5728
MODULAR POWER MAGAZINE. Text in English. 2006. q. USD 14.95 (effective 2007). **Document type:** *Magazine, Consumer.*
Address: PO Box 10186, Pompano Beach, FL 33061. info@modularpower.com. Pub. Austin Craig.

797.21 ITA ISSN 1125-1786
MONDO DEL NUOTO. Text in Italian. 1978. bi-m. **Document type:** *Magazine, Consumer.*
Related titles: Online - full text ed.
Published by: SwimmingOnline.net TEL 39-045-577399, FAX 39-045-577549. Circ: 15,000.

MONDO SOMMERSO; international ocean magazine. *see* EARTH SCIENCES—Oceanography

796.522 ESP ISSN 1698-2150
MONTANEROS DE ARAGON. BOLETIN. Text in Spanish. 1949. q. free. adv. bibl.; charts; illus. **Document type:** *Magazine, Consumer.*
Formerly (until 1987): Montaneros de Aragon (0027-0032)
Published by: Montaneros de Aragon, Gran Via11Bajos, Zaragoza, 50006, Spain. info@montanerosdearagon.org, http://www.montanerosdearagon.org. Ed. Miguel Angel Garcia Lopez.

MONTEBIANCO. *see* SPORTS AND GAMES—Outdoor Life

MOON OUTDOORS. CALIFORNIA RECREATIONAL LAKES AND RIVERS; the complete guide to boating, fishing, and water sports. *see* TRAVEL AND TOURISM

796.07 FIN ISSN 0788-0332
MOTION; sport in Finland. Text in English. 1990. s-a. EUR 16 (effective 2005). back issues avail. **Document type:** *Magazine, Consumer.*
Related titles: Online - full text ed.
Indexed: CA, SD, T02.
Published by: Liikuntatieteellinen Seura ry/Finnish Society for Research in Sport and Physical Education, Stadion, Etelakaarre, Helsinki, 00250, Finland. TEL 358-9-4542720, FAX 358-9-45427222, toimisto@lts.fi.

797.148 NLD ISSN 1874-3463
MOTION WINDSURFING MAGAZINE. Text in Dutch. 199?. 5/yr. EUR 29.75 (effective 2010). **Document type:** *Magazine, Consumer.*
Formerly (until 2005): Motion Surfing Magazine (1574-7573)
Published by: Soul Media, Stetweg 43C, Castricum, 1901 JD, Netherlands. TEL 31-251-674911, FAX 31-251-674378, info@soulonline.nl, http://www.soulonline.nl. Circ: 17,900.

MOTOR; East Africa's only independent cars and motorsport magazine. *see* TRANSPORTATION—Automobiles

MOTOR (SYDNEY); the power, the prestige, the passion. *see* TRANSPORTATION—Automobiles

796 USA
MOTOR CITY SPORTS. Abbreviated title: M C S. Text in English. 2005 (Oct.4th). 10/yr. USD 19.99 (effective 2005). adv. **Document type:** *Magazine, Consumer.* **Description:** Covers Michigan sports, including the NFL, NBA, NHL, MLB, minor league sports, NCAA, arena football, and high school athletics.
Published by: Haas Rock Publications, 4527 Joliette SW, Wyoming, MI 49519. TEL 866-462-7624. adv.: page USD 2,819; 8.25 x 10.875. Circ: 15,000.

796.72 AUS ISSN 1039-4516
MOTOR RACING AUSTRALIA. Text in English. 1993. bi-m. AUD 41.95 in Australia & New Zealand; AUD 89 elsewhere; AUD 7.95 newsstand/cover (effective 2008). **Document type:** *Magazine, Consumer.* **Description:** Focuses on the people, vehicles, technology and events that are building blocks of motor racing.
Published by: Chevron Publishing Group Pty. Ltd., PO Box 1421, Lane Cove, NSW 1595, Australia. TEL 61-2-94189225, FAX 61-2-94189641, sales@chevron.com.au. **Subscr. to:** my.magazine.com.au, PO Box 3355, St Leonards, NSW 1590, Australia. TEL 61-2-99016111, 800-227-236, FAX 61-2-99016110, subscribe@mymagazines.com.au, https://www.mymagazines.com.au.

796.72 NLD ISSN 1878-8335
▼ **MOTOR SPECIAAL.** Text in Dutch. 2009. q. EUR 7.95 (effective 2010).
Published by: Target Press, Ambachtweg 2, Moordrecht, 2841 LZ, Netherlands. TEL 31-182-356050, FAX 31-182-356059, studio@targetpress.nl, http://www.targetpress.nl. Ed. Wout Meppelink.

MOTOR SPORT. *see* TRANSPORTATION—Automobiles

796.7 ROM ISSN 1453-9608
MOTOR SPORT. Text in Romanian. 1998. m. adv. **Document type:** *Magazine, Consumer.*
Published by: Auto Press Group, Calea 13 Septembrie, 59-61, OP 5, sector 5, Bucharest, Romania. TEL 40-21-4112301.

796.72 CHE
MOTOR SPORT AKTUELL RENNTERMINKALENDER. Text in German. 1986. a. CHF 2.80. adv. **Document type:** *Consumer.*
Published by: M P S Motor-Presse (Schweiz) AG, Bahnstr 240, Schwerzenbach, 8603, Switzerland. TEL 41-1-8065555, FAX 41-1-8065500. Ed. Peter Wyss. Pub. Richard Stolz. Adv. contact August Hug. Circ: 35,000.

796.7 ROM ISSN 1582-8107
MOTOR XTREM. Text in Romanian. 2001. m. adv. **Document type:** *Magazine, Consumer.*
Published by: Media Sport Promotion, Str. Feleacu nr. 23, bl. 13A, sc. 3, ap. 34, sector 1, Bucharest, Romania. TEL 40-21-2330551, FAX 40-21-2330551, office@motorxtrem.ro.

796.72 USA
MOTORSPORT AMERICA. Text in English. 2000. m. adv. **Document type:** *Magazine, Consumer.*
Published by: C L N, Inc., 750 Willoughby Way, Atlanta, GA 30312. TEL 404-688-5623, FAX 404-614-3599. Ed. Bill Ryan. Pub. Douglas C Allan.

796.72 USA ISSN 1057-0691
MOTORSPORTS. Text in English. bi-m. **Document type:** *Magazine, Consumer.*
Published by: J.L. Quinn & Assoc. Inc., PO Box 8389, Fresno, CA 93747-8389. TEL 209-445-8556. Ed., Pub. Jim Quinn. Circ: 5,000.

796.77 GBR
MOTORSPORTS NOW!. Text in English. 1958. q. adv. back issues avail. **Document type:** *Newsletter, Trade.*
Formerly (until 1999): R A C M S A News
Related titles: Online - full text ed.: free (effective 2009).
Published by: Motor Sports Association, Motor Sports House, Riverside Park, Colnbrook, Slough, Berks SL3 0HG, United Kingdom. TEL 44-1753-765000, FAX 44-1753-682938. Eds. Chris Hough TEL 44-1753-765000 ext 283, I R Davis. Pub. Paula Skinner. Circ: 32,000 (controlled).

MOTOSPRINT. *see* SPORTS AND GAMES—Bicycles And Motorcycles

MOTRICIDAD. *see* PHYSICAL FITNESS AND HYGIENE

MOTRICIDAD Y PERSONA. *see* EDUCATION

790 PRT ISSN 1646-107X
➤ **MOTRICIDADE.** Text in English, Portuguese, Spanish; Section in English, Portuguese. 2005. q. BRL 120 in Brazil to individuals; EUR 45 elsewhere to individuals; BRL 750 in Brazil to institutions; EUR 250 elsewhere to institutions (effective 2010). adv. cum.index: vol.1, no.1, 2005-vol.6, no.1, 2010. back issues avail. **Document type:** *Journal, Academic/Scholarly.* **Description:** Publishes articles focused in the areas of sport, health and human development sciences, contributing to the development and dissemination of scientific knowledge of theoretical and empirical character in the context of physical activity and health, and human performance, as well as in scientific fields related to human development, with particular emphasis on psychology. Audience include: Students, academic and professionals in education, sport and health, and human development researchers.
Related titles: Online - full text ed.: free (effective 2011).
Indexed: A01, A36, CA, CABA, E12, F03, F04, GH, LT, N02, N03, PEI, PsycInfo, SD, T02, T05, W11.
Published by: Universidade de Tras-os-Montes e Alto Douro, Centro de Investigacao em Desporto, Saude e Desenvolvimento Humano/University of Tras-os-Montes and Alto Douro, Research Centre for Sports Sciences, Health and Human Development, Rua Dr. Manuel Cardona, Vila Real, 5000-558, Portugal. TEL 351-259-330100, FAX 351-259-330169. Ed., R&P, Adv. contact Jose Vasconcelos Raposo. Circ: 1,000.

796 BRA ISSN 1980-6574
MOTRIZ. REVISTA DE EDUCACAO FISICA. Text in Portuguese. 1995. s-a. back issues avail. **Document type:** *Journal, Academic/Scholarly.*
Media: Online - full text.
Indexed: FoSS&M, SCI, W07.
Published by: Universidade Estadual Paulista "Julio de Mesquita Filho", Departamento de Educacao Fisica, Ave 24-A 1414 Bela Vista, Rio Claro, SP 13506-9000, Brazil. TEL 55-19-35264305, FAX 55-19-35264321, http://cecemca.rc.unesp.br/ojs/index.php/motriz/index. Ed. Benedito Sergio Denadai.

MOUNTAIN BIKE ACTION. *see* SPORTS AND GAMES—Bicycles And Motorcycles

790.1 GBR
MOUNTAIN ONLINE. Text in English. 1996. m.
Media: Online - full content.
Published by: Ikhaya Design, 23 Manor Rd, Bladon, OX20 1RU, United Kingdom.

796.172 028.5 BGR
MOVE. Text in Bulgarian. 1998. BGL 1.60 newsstand/cover (effective 2002). **Document type:** *Magazine, Consumer.* **Description:** Presents events from extreme sports, such as skateboarding, BMX, surfing and the concomitant street culture. The main purpose of the magazine is to develop these kinds of sports as an opposition to drugs and to build creativity among the youth.
Published by: Art Dom 21, Druzhba 318, PO Box 134, Sofia, 1113, Bulgaria. move9@hotmail.com. Ed. Veselin Zografov.

796 BRA ISSN 0104-754X
MOVIMENTO (PORTO ALEGRE). Text in Portuguese. 1994. s-a. back issues avail. **Document type:** *Journal, Academic/Scholarly.*
Related titles: Online - full text ed.: ISSN 1982-8918. free (effective 2011).
Indexed: CABA, GH, LT, N02, N03, SCOPUS, SD, SSCI, T05, W07.
Published by: Universidade Federal do Rio Grande do Sul, Escola de Educacao Fisica, Rua Felizardo, 750, Jardim Botanico, Porto Alegre, Brazil. TEL 55-51-33085882, FAX 55-51-33085811, movimento@esef.ufrgs.br, http://www6.ufrgs.br/esef/. Eds. Alex Branco Fraga, Marco Paulo Stigger.

794 613.7 DEU ISSN 1862-9725
MPULS; Magazin fuers Sportliche. Text in German. 2006. m. adv. **Document type:** *Magazine, Consumer.*
Published by: M W B Medien GmbH (Subsidiary of: Sueddeutscher Verlag GmbH), Elsenheimerstr 59, Munich, 80687, Germany. TEL 49-89-570030, FAX 49-89-57003100, info@mwb-medien.de, http://www.mwb-medien.de. Ed. Burkhard Gruss. Adv. contact Ralf Steinbeck. page EUR 7,500. Circ: 200,000 (controlled).

793.7 USA
MUCHO BUSCAR PALABRAS. Text in Spanish. 2003. m. USD 12; USD 1.99 newsstand/cover (effective 2003). adv. **Document type:** *Magazine, Consumer.*
Published by: Odesos Stars, 10915 Bluffside Dr, Ste 129, Studio City, CA 91604. TEL 818-508-9719, nordost292@aol.com. R&P Ventzislav Velinov. Adv. contact Stefka Velinova.

796 PER ISSN 2078-3574
MUEVETE POR TU SALUD. Text in Spanish. 2008. s-a. **Document type:** *Magazine, Consumer.*
Published by: Movimiento Muevete por tu Salud, Ave. Javier Prado, 6970, Lima, 12, Peru. TEL 51-11-7127200, muevete_portusalud_peru@yahoo.com.

790.01 ESP
EL MUNDO DEPORTIVO. Text in Spanish. 1906. d. adv. illus. **Document type:** *Newspaper, Consumer.* **Description:** Covers soccer, basketball and U.S. sports news.
Related titles: Online - full text ed.
Published by: Grupo Godo, Av Diagonal 477, 5o, Barcelona, 08036, Spain. TEL 34-93-3444100, FAX 34-93-3444250, http://www.grupogodo.com.

790.1 USA
MUNDO DEPORTIVO. Text in Spanish. 10/yr. adv. **Document type:** *Magazine, Consumer.*
Published by: J S A en espanol, 2329 Purdue Ave., Los Angeles, CA 90064-1727. TEL 310-914-3007, FAX 310-914-0607. Pub. Marcelino Miyares Jr.

790.1 CAN ISSN 0317-087X
MUSCLE MAG INTERNATIONAL; the "what's new" magazine of bodybuilding. Text in English. 1974. m. USD 44.97 domestic; USD 29.97 in United States; USD 64.97 elsewhere (effective 2005). adv. bk.rev. charts; illus. **Document type:** *Magazine, Consumer.* **Description:** Focuses on bodybuilding and fitness for both men and women.
Indexed: SportS.
Published by: Canusa Products, 5775 Mclaughlin Rd, Mississauga, ON L5R 3P7, Canada. TEL 905-507-3545, FAX 905-507-9935. Ed. Johnny Fitness. Pub., R&P Robert Kennedy. Adv. contact Terry Frendo. B&W page CAD 4,510, color page CAD 5,750. Circ: 330,000.

790.1 GBR ISSN 0955-906X
MUSCLEMAG INTERNATIONAL; building health - fitness - physique. Text in English. 1988. m. GBP 2.95 newsstand/cover; USD 5.99 newsstand/cover in United States; CAD 6.99 newsstand/cover in Canada. **Document type:** *Magazine, Consumer.* **Description:** Reveals tips, insights, training techniques, star profiles, and other advice by and for competitive bodybuilders.
Published by: Fitness Publications Ltd., 53 Lichfield Rd, Aston, Birmingham B6 5RW, United Kingdom. TEL 44-121-327-7525, FAX 44-121-327-0847. **Dist. by:** M M C Ltd., Octagon House, White Hart Meadows, Ripley, Woking, Surrey GU23 6HR, United Kingdom. TEL 44-1483-211222, FAX 44-1483-224541.

MUSCULAR DEVELOPMENT. *see* PHYSICAL FITNESS AND HYGIENE

MUSCULAR DEVELOPMENT (MOSCOW). *see* PHYSICAL FITNESS AND HYGIENE

796 USA ISSN 0148-8910
GV709
N A G W S RESEARCH REPORTS. Text in English. 1977. irreg.
Formerly: D G W S Research Reports: Women in Sports
Published by: (National Association for Girls and Women in Sport), American Alliance for Health, Physical Education, Recreation, and Dance, 1900 Association Dr, Reston, VA 20191. TEL 703-476-3400, FAX 703-476-9527, info@aahperd.org, http://www.aahperd.org.

796 USA ISSN 0077-3336
N A I A HANDBOOK. Text in English. 1959. biennial. USD 35. reprints avail.
Published by: National Association of Intercollegiate Athletics, P.O. Box 472200, Tulsa, OK 74147-2200. TEL 913-791-0044, FAX 913-791-9555. Ed. Robert Rhoads.

796 USA
N A I A NEWS WEEKLY EDITION. Text in English. 1950. w. USD 30. bk.rev. stat. reprints avail. **Document type:** *Newsletter.*

Former titles (until 1998): N A I A News (Print Monthly Edition) (0740-5995); N A I A News and Coach
Media: Online - full text. **Related titles:** Microform ed.: (from PQC); Alternate Frequency ed(s).: d.
Indexed: SportS.
Published by: National Association of Intercollegiate Athletics, P.O. Box 472200, Tulsa, OK 74147-2200. Ed. Dave Webster. Circ: 8,000.

796 USA
GV741
N A I A OFFICIAL CHAMPIONSHIP SUMMARIES. Text in English. 1958. a. USD 15. index. reprints avail.
Former titles: N A I A Official Records Book and Championship Summaries; N A I A Official Records Book (0077-3344)
Published by: National Association of Intercollegiate Athletics, P.O. Box 472200, Tulsa, OK 74147-2200. TEL 913-791-0044, FAX 913-791-9555. Ed. Doug Mosley. Circ: 2,500.

796.72 USA ISSN 1549-5256
N A S C A R ILLUSTRATED. (National Association for Stock Car Auto Racing) Text in English. 1982. m. USD 45 (effective 2009). adv. back issues avail. **Document type:** *Magazine, Consumer.* **Description:** Provides an in-depth look at the people who make NASCAR's racing series a popular form of racing in US.
Former titles (until 200?): N A S C A R Winston Cup Illustrated (1093-5444); (until 199?): Winston Cup Illustrated (1048-6119); (until 1989): Grand National Illustrated (0744-4869)
—CCC.
Published by: (National Association for Stock Car Auto Racing, Inc.), Street & Smith's Sports Group (Subsidiary of: American City Business Journals, Inc.), 120 W Morehead St, Ste 230, Charlotte, NC 28202. TEL 704-973-1300, 800-380-7404, FAX 704-973-1576, annuals@streetandsmiths.com, http://www.streetandsmiths.com. Adv. contact Michael Schriver TEL 704-973-1352. Circ: 112,054.

796.72 USA ISSN 1549-4829
N A S C A R SCENE. (National Association for Stock Car Auto Racing) Text in English. 1977. w. USD 62.50 (effective 2009). adv. bk.rev. **Document type:** *Newspaper, Consumer.* **Description:** Features information on NASCAR garage and provides complete coverage of the nextel cup, nationwide and craftsman truck series.
Former titles (until 200?): N A S C A R Winston Cup Scene (1093-7110); (until 1997): Winston Cup Scene (1053-461X); (until 198?): Grand National Scene (0274-4910)
Related titles: Online - full text ed.: SceneDaily.
—CCC.
Published by: (National Association for Stock Car Auto Racing, Inc.), Street & Smith's Sports Group (Subsidiary of: American City Business Journals, Inc.), 120 W Morehead St, Ste 230, Charlotte, NC 28202. TEL 704-973-1300, 800-380-7404, FAX 704-973-1576, annuals@streetandsmiths.com, http://www.streetandsmiths.com. Adv. contact Michael Schriver TEL 704-973-1352. Circ: 135,000.

026.796 CAN ISSN 1480-5162
GV568
N A S L I N E. Text in English. s-a. free. back issues avail. **Document type:** *Magazine, Trade.* **Description:** Contains news of North American sport libraries, their collections and services and includes a large bibliography of new electronic and print publications.
Media: Online - full text.
Published by: North American Sport Library Network, c/o University of Calgary Library, 2500 University Dr N W, Calgary, AB T2N 1N4, Canada. TEL 403-220-6097, FAX 403-282-6837, http://www.sportquest.com/naslin. Ed. Gretchen Ghent.

790.1 USA
N A Y S I RESOURCE LIST. Text in English. irreg. free. **Document type:** *Bibliography.* **Description:** Includes books, materials and other resources for persons working with tots, children and teens in fitness, recreation, education, sport and health.
Published by: North American Youth Sport Institute, 4985 Oak Garden Dr, Kernersville, NC 27284-9520. TEL 336-784-4926, 800-767-4916, FAX 336-784-5546, jack@naysi.com. Ed. Jack Hutslar.

796 USA ISSN 1937-9064
GV351
N C A A CHAMPION. Text in English. 2008 (Jan.). q. USD 15 (effective 2009). adv. illus. **Document type:** *Magazine, Consumer.*
Related titles: Online - full text ed.: ISSN 1937-9099.
Published by: National Collegiate Athletic Association, 700 W Washington St, PO Box 6222, Indianapolis, IN 46206. TEL 317-917-6222, FAX 317-917-6888, esummers@ncaa.org, http://www.ncaa.org/. Ed. Gary Brown TEL 317-917-6130. Adv. contact Nancy Adams TEL 317-917-6152.

796 USA
N C A A CONVENTION PROCEEDINGS. Text in English. 1906. a. back issues avail. **Document type:** *Proceedings, Trade.* **Description:** Transcripts of all business sessions at the NCAA convention, and a roster of delegates and visitors.
Formerly (until 1989): National Collegiate Athletic Association. Annual Convention. Proceedings (0077-3808); Which superseded in part (in 1967): National Collegiate Athletic Association. Yearbook; Which was formerly (until 1943): National Collegiate Athletic Association. Convention. Annual Convention. Proceedings; (until 1910): United States. Intercollegiate Athletic Association. Annual Convention. Proceedings; (until 19??): United States. Intercollegiate Athletic Association. Meeting. Annual Meeting. Proceedings
Related titles: Online - full text ed.: free (effective 2011).
Published by: National Collegiate Athletic Association, 700 W Washington St, PO Box 6222, Indianapolis, IN 46206. TEL 317-917-6222, FAX 317-917-6888, esummers@ncaa.org, http://www.ncaa.org/.

790.1 USA ISSN 0162-1467
GV347
N C A A DIRECTORY. Text in English. 1976. a., latest 2006. back issues avail. **Document type:** *Directory, Trade.* **Description:** Contains an alphabetical roster of members with district and division designation as well as listing of NCAA committees and the association's administrative structure.
Related titles: Online - full text ed.
Published by: National Collegiate Athletic Association, 700 W Washington St, PO Box 6222, Indianapolis, IN 46206. TEL 317-917-6222, FAX 317-917-6888, http://www.ncaa.org/.

796 USA ISSN 1093-3174
GV563
N C A A DIVISION I MANUAL. (National Collegiate Athletic Association) Text in English. 1988. a. USD 16.50 per issue (effective 2009). **Description:** Contains all NCAA legislation - constitution, operating bylaws and administrative bylaws-applicable to the respective division.
Formerly (until 1998): NCAA Division I Operating Manual
Published by: National Collegiate Athletic Association, 700 W Washington St, PO Box 6222, Indianapolis, IN 46206. TEL 317-917-6222, FAX 317-917-6888, esummers@ncaa.org, http://www.ncaa.org/.

790.1 616.86 USA
N C A A DRUG TESTING PROGRAM. Text in English. 19??. a. back issues avail. **Document type:** *Handbook/Manual/Guide, Trade.* **Description:** Establishes NCAA procedures and regulations for drug testing of student athletes, and includes a list of banned drugs.
Former titles (until 2000): N C A A Sports Sciences Drug-Testing Programs; (until 1999): N C A A Drug Education and Drug Testing Programs; (until 1996): N C A A Drug Testing/Education Programs
Related titles: Online - full text ed.: free (effective 2011).
Published by: National Collegiate Athletic Association, 700 W Washington St, PO Box 6222, Indianapolis, IN 46206. TEL 317-917-6222, FAX 317-917-6888, http://www.ncaa.org/.

796 USA
GV847
N C A A MEN'S AND WOMEN'S ICE HOCKEY RULES AND INTERPRETATIONS. Text in English. 1940. a. USD 7.80 per issue (effective 2011). illus. back issues avail. **Document type:** *Handbook/Manual/Guide, Trade.* **Description:** Covers official signals, interpretations, and rulings.
Former titles (until 2001): N C A A Men's Ice Hockey Rules and Interpretations (0735-9195); (until 1983): N C A A Ice Hockey (0734-5011); (until 1980): Official National Collegiate Athletic Association Ice Hockey Guide; Official Ice Hockey Rules
Related titles: Online - full text ed.: free (effective 2011).
Published by: National Collegiate Athletic Association, 700 W Washington St, PO Box 6222, Indianapolis, IN 46206. TEL 317-917-6222, FAX 317-917-6888, http://www.ncaa.org/.

796.355 USA ISSN 1555-3531
N C A A MEN'S AND WOMEN'S LACROSSE RECORDS BOOK. OFFICIAL RECORDS. Text in English. 2006. a. **Document type:** *Journal, Consumer.*
Related titles: Online - full text ed.: ISSN 1555-354X.
Published by: National Collegiate Athletic Association, 700 W Washington St, PO Box 6222, Indianapolis, IN 46206. TEL 317-917-6222, FAX 317-917-6888, esummers@ncaa.org, http://www.ncaa.org/.

799.202 USA
N C A A MEN'S AND WOMEN'S RIFLE RULES. Text in English. 1980. a. USD 7.80 per issue (effective 2011). adv. illus. back issues avail. **Document type:** *Handbook/Manual/Guide, Trade.* **Description:** Contains diagrams of playing areas, official signals, and official interpretations and rulings.
Formerly (until 1984): N C A A Rifle Rules (0736-5144)
Related titles: Online - full text ed.: free (effective 2011).
Published by: National Collegiate Athletic Association, 700 W Washington St, PO Box 6222, Indianapolis, IN 46206. TEL 317-917-6222, FAX 317-917-6888, http://www.ncaa.org/. Ed. Leslie Danehy.

797.21 USA
N C A A MEN'S AND WOMEN'S SWIMMING AND DIVING RULES AND INTERPRETATIONS. Text in English. 193?. a., latest 2007. illus. back issues avail. **Document type:** *Handbook/Manual/Guide, Trade.* **Description:** Contains diagrams of playing areas, official signals, and official interpretations and rulings.
Former titles (until 200?): N C A A Men's and Women's Swimming and Diving Rules (0736-5128); N C A A Swimming (0272-8095); (until 1980): Official National Collegiate Athletic Association Swimming Guide; (until 19??): National Collegiate Athletic Association Official Rules for Swimming, Fancy Diving, Water Polo
Related titles: Online - full text ed.
Published by: National Collegiate Athletic Association, 700 W Washington St, PO Box 6222, Indianapolis, IN 46206. TEL 317-917-6222, FAX 317-917-6888, http://www.ncaa.org/.

790.1 USA
GV839
N C A A MEN'S AND WOMEN'S WATER POLO RULES AND INTERPRETATIONS. Text in English. 19??. a. USD 7.80 per issue (effective 2011). illus. back issues avail. **Document type:** *Handbook/Manual/Guide, Trade.* **Description:** Contains diagrams of playing areas, official signals, and official interpretations and rulings.
Former titles (until 200?): N C A A Water Polo Rules (1099-7199); (until 1997): N C A A Men's Water Polo Rules (0734-0508); (until 1982): N C A A Water Polo Rules (0271-860X); (until 1979): Official National Collegiate Athletic Association Water Polo Rules
Related titles: Online - full text ed.: free (effective 2011).
Published by: National Collegiate Athletic Association, 700 W Washington St, PO Box 6222, Indianapolis, IN 46206. TEL 317-917-6222, FAX 317-917-6888, http://www.ncaa.org/.

796 USA ISSN 0027-6170
GV347
THE N C A A NEWS. Text in English. 1964. fortn. adv. bk.rev. illus. reprints avail. **Document type:** *Newspaper, Consumer.* **Description:** Reports on issues in the administration of collegiate-level athletics.
Incorporates: Football Statistics Rankings
Related titles: Online - full text ed.
Indexed: SD, SPI, SportS, T02.
Published by: National Collegiate Athletic Association, 700 W Washington St, PO Box 6222, Indianapolis, IN 46206. TEL 317-917-6222, FAX 317-917-6888, esummers@ncaa.org, http://www.ncaa.org/. Circ: 20,000.

790.1 USA
GV1195
N C A A WRESTLING RULES AND INTERPRETATIONS. Text in English. 192?. a. USD 7.80 per issue (effective 2011). illus. back issues avail. **Document type:** *Handbook/Manual/Guide, Trade.* **Description:** Contains diagrams of playing areas, official signals, and official interpretations and rulings.
Former titles (until 1985): N C A A Wrestling Rules (0736-511X); (until 1983): N C A A Wrestling (0738-1603); (until 1980): Official National Collegiate Athletic Association Wrestling Guide; (until 1942): National Collegiate Athletic Association. Wrestling Rules
Related titles: Online - full text ed.: free (effective 2011).
Published by: National Collegiate Athletic Association, 700 W Washington St, PO Box 6222, Indianapolis, IN 46206. TEL 317-917-6222, FAX 317-917-6888, http://www.ncaa.org/.

796 USA ISSN 1524-4385
N C G A GOLF. Text in English. 1961. q. USD 18 newsstand/cover (effective 2001). adv. **Description:** Provides news, articles, information on tournaments, courses and golfers, including association news.
Former titles: N C G A News (0744-1347); Northern California Golf Association. Blue Book
Indexed: SD.
Published by: Northern California Golf Association, 3200 Lopez Rd, Box NCGA, Pebble Beach, CA 93953. TEL 831-625-4653, FAX 831-625-0150, tblofsky@ncga.org. Ed. Ted Blofsky Jr. adv.: B&W page USD 6,339, color page USD 8,803; trim 8.375 x 10.875. Circ: 190,000 (controlled).

796 USA
N J C A A REVIEW. Text in English. 1948. 9/yr. USD 30 (effective 2010). bk.rev. charts; illus.; stat. back issues avail.; reprints avail. **Document type:** *Magazine, Trade.* **Description:** Covers NJCAA national championship recaps, in-depth articles on former NJCAA student-athletes, features on the roles NJCAA colleges play in the community and great pictures from around the nation.
Formerly: Juco Review (0047-2956)
Related titles: Microform ed.: (from PQC); Online - full text ed.: free (effective 2010).
Indexed: A22, PEI, SD, SPI, SportS, T02.
Published by: National Junior College Athletic Association, 1755 Telstar Dr, Ste 103, Colorado Springs, CO 80920. TEL 719-590-9788, FAX 719-590-7324, lbrizzie@njcaa.org.

794.8 GBR ISSN 1751-4584
N - REVOLUTION. (Nintendo) Variant title: nRevolution. Text in English. 19??. m. adv. back issues avail. **Document type:** *Magazine, Consumer.* **Description:** Features Wii and DS previews and reviews (including WiiWare), plus the latest Nintendo news including new games.
Formerly (until 2006): Revolution
Published by: Imagine Publishing Ltd., Richmond House, 33 Richmond Hill, Bournemouth, Dorset BH2 6EZ, United Kingdom. TEL 44-1202-586200. Ed. Phil King.

796 SVK ISSN 1336-9903
N S C REVUE. Text in Slovak. 2005. s-a. **Document type:** *Magazine, Trade.*
Published by: Narodne Sportove Centrum, Trnavska 39, Bratislava, 831 04, Slovakia. TEL 421-2-49200326, FAX 421-2-44372164, office@sportcenter.sk, http://www.sportcenter.sk.

688.76029 USA
N S G A SPORTING GOODS BUYING GUIDE. (National Sporting Goods Association) Text in English. 1967. a. free to members (effective 2009). adv. **Description:** Lists more than 12,000 sporting good suppliers, with names, addresses, phone and fax numbers.
Formerly (until 2007): National Sporting Goods Association Buying Guide
Related titles: Online - full text ed.
Published by: National Sporting Goods Association, 1601 Feehanville Dr, Ste 300, Mount Prospect, IL 60056. TEL 847-296-6742, 800-815-5422, FAX 847-391-9827, info@nsga.org, http://www.nsga.org. Ed. William H Webb.

790.1 DEU
N T B MAGAZIN. Text in German. 1950. m. EUR 32.40 (effective 2007). adv. back issues avail. **Document type:** *Magazine, Consumer.*
Formerly: Niedersachsenturner (0949-720X)
Published by: Niedersaechsischer Turner-Bund e.V., Maschstr 18, Hannover, 30169, Germany. TEL 49-511-980970, FAX 49-511-9809712, info@ntb-infoline.de. Ed. Sybille Schmidt. adv.: B&W page EUR 720, color page EUR 1,300; trim 185 x 270. Circ: 3,100 (paid and controlled).

790.1 SAU
AN-NADI. Text in Arabic. 1991. w. SAR 250; SAR 450 foreign. adv. **Description:** Covers all sports news locally and internationally.
Published by: Okaz Organization for Press and Publication/Mu'assasat 'Ukaz lis-Sihafah wan-Nashr, P O Box 5576, Jeddah, 21432, Saudi Arabia. TEL 966-2-6722630, FAX 966-2-6724277. Ed. Abdu-Hashim Hashim TEL 966-2-6722630. adv.: page SAR 6,000. Circ: 45,000.

NADI ABU DHABI AL-SIYAHI/ABU DHABI TOURIST CLUB. *see* CLUBS

NADI AL-WASL. *see* CLUBS

797.21 FRA ISSN 1141-1872
NAGER SAUVER. Text in French. 1927. m. adv. **Document type:** *Magazine, Trade.*
Formerly (until 1952): L' Association des Professeurs de Natation de France (1141-1864)
Published by: Federation Francaise des Maitres-Nageurs Sauveteurs, 11 Rue Henri Barbusse, Le Bouscat, 33110, France. TEL 33-5-57191860, FAX 33-5-57191862, contact@fmns.fr, http://www.fmns.fr. Circ: 5,000.

AL-NASR. *see* CLUBS

796 USA ISSN 0738-2758
NATIONAL DIRECTORY OF COLLEGE ATHLETICS (MEN'S EDITION). Text in English. 1968. a. USD 43.95 (effective 2001 - 2002). adv. 500 p./no. 3 cols./p.; **Document type:** *Directory.* **Description:** Lists 2,100 senior and junior colleges and vital information about each athletic department. Covers men's intercollegiate athletics in the U.S. and Canada, NCAA, NAIA and NJCAA and other collegiate information.
Published by: (National Association of Collegiate Directors of Athletics), Collegiate Directories, Inc., PO Box 450640, Cleveland, OH 44145. TEL 440-835-1172, 800-426-2232, FAX 440-835-8835. Ed., Adv. contact Kevin Cleary TEL 440-835-1172. Circ: 19,000.

796 USA ISSN 0739-1226
GV439
NATIONAL DIRECTORY OF COLLEGE ATHLETICS (WOMEN'S EDITION). Text in English. 1973. a. USD 43.95 (effective 2001 - 2002). adv. illus. **Document type:** *Directory.*
Formerly: National Directory of Women's Athletics (0092-5489)

S

Published by: Collegiate Directories, Inc., PO Box 450640, Cleveland, OH 44145. TEL 440-835-1172, 800-426-2232, FAX 440-835-8835. Ed., Adv. contact Kevin Cleary TEL 440-835-1172. Circ: 12,000.

796.07 USA
GV697.A1
NATIONAL DIRECTORY OF HIGH SCHOOL COACHES. Text in English. 1963. a., latest 2003-2004. USD 69.95 per issue (effective 2007). adv. **Document type:** *Directory.*
Published by: Athletic Publishing Co., PO Box 931, Montgomery, AL 36101-0931. TEL 334-263-4436, FAX 334-263-4437. Ed. Christine Beazley. Pub., R&P, Adv. contact John Allen Dees. B&W page USD 942, color page USD 1,470; trim 9 x 6. Circ: 18,000.

790.1 USA ISSN 0737-5204
GV710
NATIONAL FEDERATION HANDBOOK. Variant title: N F H S Handbook. Text in English. 19??. a. USD 9 per issue (effective 2009). **Document type:** *Handbook/Manual/Guide, Trade.* **Description:** Contains the constitution, history, policy, programs, statistics, committees, awards, athletics participation survey and a directory of the NFHS committees and members.
Former titles (until 19??): Official Handbook (0146-8626); National Federation of State High School Athletic Associations. Official Handbook (0147-7560)
Related titles: Microfiche ed.: (from CIS).
Indexed: SRI.
Published by: National Federation of State High School Associations, PO Box 690, Indianapolis, IN 46206. TEL 317-972-6900, 800-776-3462, FAX 317-822-5700, info@nfhs.org, http://www.nfhs.org.

798 USA ISSN 0897-9944
NATIONAL GREYHOUND UPDATE. Text in English. 11/yr.
Published by: Hobson Publishing, 21684 Granada Ave, Cupertino, CA 95014. TEL 408-446-0551. Ed. Hobson.

790.1 USA ISSN 0192-978X
GV346
NATIONAL HIGH SCHOOL SPORTS RECORD BOOK. Text in English. 1979. a. USD 12.95 per issue (effective 2009). 448 p./no.; **Document type:** *Directory, Consumer.* **Description:** Contains a list of all time teams and individual performances in 16 sports for boys and girls.
Related titles: Microfiche ed.: (from CIS).
Indexed: SRI.
Published by: National Federation of State High School Associations, PO Box 690, Indianapolis, IN 46206. TEL 317-972-6900, 800-776-3462, FAX 317-822-5700, info@nfhs.org, http://www.nfhs.org. Ed. John Gillis TEL 317-972-6900.

796.9 CAN ISSN 0316-831X
GV847.5
NATIONAL HOCKEY LEAGUE. OFFICIAL RULE BOOK. Text in English. 1931. a. USD 10. illus. **Document type:** *Handbook/Manual/Guide, Consumer.* **Description:** Official rules governing play in the NHL, featuring referee's signals rink diagram and new rules.
Published by: National Hockey League Publishing, 50 Bay St, 11th Fl, Toronto, ON M5J 2X8, Canada. TEL 416-531-6535. Ed. Dan Diamond.

795 USA ISSN 2151-8947
NATIONAL INDIAN GAMING COMMISSION. NEWSLETTER. Text in English. 2006. irreg. free (effective 2009). back issues avail. **Document type:** *Newsletter, Trade.*
Media: Online - full content.
Published by: National Indian Gaming Commission, 1441 L St, NW, Ste 9100, Washington, DC 20005. TEL 202-632-7003, FAX 202-632-7066, info@nigc.gov.

796.76 USA
NATIONAL KART NEWS. Abbreviated title: N K N. Text in English. 1986. m. adv. illus. back issues avail. **Document type:** *Magazine, Consumer.* **Description:** Covers professional go-kart racing worldwide.
Related titles: Online - full text ed.
Address: 51535 Bitterweed Rd, Granger, IN 46530. TEL 574-277-0033, FAX 574-277-4279. Ed. Mike Burrell. Pub. Curt Paluzzi. Adv. contact Francine Jaworski TEL 574-277-0033.

NATIONAL P A L E-NEWS. (Police Athletic Leagues) *see* CHILDREN AND YOUTH—For

796.72 USA ISSN 0028-0208
NATIONAL SPEED SPORT NEWS. Text in English. 1934. w. USD 45; USD 2 newsstand/cover (effective 2007). adv. bk.rev. charts; illus. 36 p./no. 6 cols./p.; **Document type:** *Magazine, Consumer.* **Description:** Covers automobile racing.
Related titles: Microfiche ed.
Published by: Kay Publishing Co., Inc., 6509 Hudspeth Rd, Harrisburg, NC 28075-1210. TEL 704-455-2531, 866-455-2531, FAX 704-455-2605, news@nationalspeedsportnews.com. Ed. Mike Kerchner. Pub. Corinne Economaki. Circ: 51,000 (paid and controlled).

796.72 USA
NATIONAL SPEEDWAY DIRECTORY. Text in English. 1975. a. USD 9; USD 9 newsstand/cover (effective 2001). adv. stat. 544 p./no.; back issues avail. **Document type:** *Directory.* **Description:** Lists every oval track, dragstrip and road course in the U.S. and Canada.
Formerly: Midwest Auto Racing Guide
Address: PO Box 448, Comstock, MI 49321. TEL 616-785-0340, FAX 616-785-0346, speedways@dnx.net, http://www.speedwaysonline.com. Ed. Nancy L Brown. Pub., R&P, Adv. contact Allan E Brown. B&W page USD 580, color page USD 2,000; trim 7 x 4. Circ: 15,000 (paid).

799.3 SWE ISSN 0282-8057
NATIONELLT PISTOLSKYTTE; med meddelanden fraan svenska pistolskyttefoerbundet. Variant title: N P. Text in Swedish. 1978. 4/yr. **Document type:** *Magazine, Consumer.*
Published by: Svenska Pistolskyttefoerbundet, Oesthammarsgatan 70, PO Box 5435, Stockholm, 11484, Sweden. TEL 46-8-55340160, FAX 46-8-55340169, kansli@pistolskytteforbundet.se. Ed. Ulf Hansson. Circ: 17,000.

793 USA
NAVAL WARGAMING REVIEW. Text in English. 1994. bi-m. USD 20. bk.rev. illus.; charts. index. **Document type:** *Newsletter.* **Description:** Contains in-depth articles on naval battles, especially those of the twentieth century.
Address: 405 Kunkle Ln, Mechanicsburg, PA 17055. Ed., Pub., R&P, Adv. contact Nathan A Forney. Circ: 100.

796 CZE ISSN 1801-383X
NEDELNI SPORT. Text in Czech. 2005. w. CZK 624; CZK 12 newsstand/cover (effective 2010). adv. **Document type:** *Newspaper, Consumer.*
Published by: Ringier CR, Komunardu 1584/42, Prague 7, 170 00, Czech Republic. TEL 420-2-25977616, FAX 420-2-67097718, info@ringier.cz, http://www.ringier.cz. Ed. Lukas Tomek. Circ: 42,685 (paid). **Subscr. to:** Mediaservis s.r.o., Pacericka 2773/1, Prague 9 193 00, Czech Republic. TEL 420-2-71199100, FAX 420-2-72700025, info@mediaservis.cz, http://www.mediaservis.cz.

796 NLD ISSN 1873-9091
NEDERLANDSE SPORTALMANAK. Text in Dutch. 2006. a. EUR 194.30 (effective 2008).
Published by: Bohn Stafleu van Loghum B.V. (Subsidiary of: Springer Science+Business Media), Postbus 246, Houten, 3990 GA, Netherlands. TEL 31-30-6383838, FAX 31-30-6383839, boekhandels@bsl.nl.

790.1 HUN ISSN 0866-2517
NEMZETI SPORT. Text in Hungarian. 1945. d. HUF 28,477 (effective 2006). adv. **Document type:** *Newspaper, Consumer.* **Description:** Covers all aspects of sports.
Former titles (until 1990): Nemzeti Nepsport (0865-7556); (until 1990): Nepsport (0133-1809)
Related titles: ◆ Online - full text ed.: Nemzeti Sport Online. ISSN 1418-1630.
Published by: Ringier Kiado Kft., Szuglo Utca 83-85, Budapest, 1141, Hungary. TEL 36-1-4602500, FAX 36-1-4602501, kiado@ringier.hu, http://www.ringier.hu. Ed. Denes Tamas. adv.: color page HUF 1,250,000; trim 280 x 436. Circ: 90,780 (paid).

790.1 HUN ISSN 1418-1630
NEMZETI SPORT ONLINE. Text in Hungarian. d.
Media: Online - full text. **Related titles:** ◆ Print ed.: Nemzeti Sport. ISSN 0866-2517.
Published by: Ringier Kiado Kft., Szuglo Utca 83-85, Budapest, 1141, Hungary. kiado@ringier.hu, http://www.ringier.hu.

028.5 USA ISSN 1547-514X
NEOPETS; the official magazine. Text in English. 2003. bi-m. USD 9.99 per issue (effective 2008). adv. 88 p./no.; back issues avail. **Document type:** *Magazine, Consumer.*
Related titles: Online - full text ed.
—CCC.
Published by: Beckett Media Llc, 4635 McEwen Rd, Dallas, TX 75244. TEL 714-939-9991, FAX 714-456-0146, customerservice@beckett.com. Ed. Doug Kale. Pub. Claire B. Amano. Adv. contact Brett Robertson. color page USD 3,000; trim 8 x 10.75. Circ: 100,000.

796 600 DEU
▼ **NEUE TECHNOLOGIEN IM SPORT.** Text in German. 2009. irreg. price varies. **Document type:** *Monographic series, Academic/Scholarly.*
Published by: Shaker Verlag GmbH, Kaiserstr 100, Herzogenrath, 52134, Germany. TEL 49-2407-95960, FAX 49-2407-95969, info@shaker.de, http://www.shaker.de.

794 NLD ISSN 1877-2404
NEUROCAMPUS MAGAZINE. Cover title: Braintraining. Text in Dutch. 2008. q. EUR 13.95; EUR 3.95 newsstand/cover (effective 2011). adv. **Document type:** *Magazine, Consumer.*
Published by: LunaNL, Postbus 472, Haarlem, 2000 AL, Netherlands. TEL 31-23-5430708, FAX 31-23-5430730.

796.962 USA
NEW ENGLAND HOCKEY JOURNAL. Text in English. 1996. m. USD 39.99 (effective 2011). adv. **Document type:** *Magazine, Consumer.*
Published by: Seamans Media, 1400 Hancock St, Seventh Fl, Quincy, MA 02169. TEL 617-773-9955, FAX 617-773-6688, michelle@seamansmedia.com, http://www.seamansmedia.com. Ed. Eric Beato. Pub., Adv. contact Eric Seamans.

799.3 USA ISSN 0195-1599
NEW GUN WEEK. Text in English. 1967. 3/m. (1st, 10th, & 20th). USD 35 domestic; USD 65 foreign; USD 3 newsstand/cover (effective 2007). adv. bk.rev. illus. 18 p./no. 4 cols./p.; reprints avail. **Document type:** *Newspaper, Consumer.*
Formerly: Gun Week (0017-5633)
Published by: Second Amendment Foundation, 267 Linwood Ave, Buffalo, NY 14209. TEL 716-885-6408, FAX 716-884-4471, http://www.saf.org. Ed. Joseph P Tartaro. Pub. Alan M Gottlieb. adv.: B&W page USD 750. Circ: 20,000 (paid).

794.1 NLD ISSN 0168-8782
NEW IN CHESS MAGAZINE. Text in English. 1968. 8/yr. EUR 68 in the European Union; GBP 48 in United Kingdom; USD 89 in North America; USD 97 elsewhere (effective 2008). adv. bk.rev. bibl.; charts; illus. index. 96 p./no.; back issues avail. **Document type:** *Magazine, Consumer.* **Description:** Articles on new developments in world chess tournament play.
Supersedes in part (in 1984): Schaakbulletin (Amsterdam) (0036-5823)
Indexed: RASB.
—IE.
Published by: Interchess B.V., PO Box 1093, Alkmaar, 1810 KB, Netherlands. TEL 31-72-5127137, FAX 31-72-5158234, nic@newinchess.com. Eds. Dirk Jan Ten Geuzendam, Jan Timman. **Dist. addr. in N. America:** Turpin Distribution Services Ltd., The Bleachery, 143 W St, New Milford, CT 06776. TEL 860-350-0041, FAX 860-350-0036, turpinna@turpin-distribution.com.

794.1 NLD ISSN 0168-7697
GV1449.5
NEW IN CHESS YEARBOOK; supplement to New in Chess Magazine. Text in English. 1984. q. EUR 119 in Europe hardcover; GBP 103 in United Kingdom hardcover; USD 139 in North America hardcover; EUR 121 elsewhere hardcover; EUR 97 in Europe paperback; GBP 84 in United Kingdom paperback; USD 109 in North America papeback; EUR 99 elsewhere paperback (effective 2009). bk.rev. illus.; stat. cumulation. 240 p./no.; back issues avail. **Document type:** *Yearbook, Consumer.* **Description:** Covers all major developments in chess openings; cites 4,000 selected games annually, with many annotations and theoretical analyses.
Published by: Interchess B.V., PO Box 1093, Alkmaar, 1810 KB, Netherlands. TEL 31-72-5127137, FAX 31-72-5158234, nic@newinchess.com. **Dist. addr. in N America:** Turpin Distribution Services Ltd., The Bleachery, 143 W St, New Milford, CT 06776. TEL 860-350-0041, FAX 860-350-0036, turpinna@turpin-distribution.com.

THE NEW INDIAN EXPRESS. *see* GENERAL INTEREST PERIODICALS—India

790.1 USA
NEW JERSEY. CASINO CONTROL COMMISSION. ANNUAL REPORT. Text in English. 1979. a. **Document type:** *Government.*
Related titles: Microfiche ed.: (from CIS).
Indexed: SRI.
Published by: Casino Control Commission, Attn: Public Information Assistant, Arcade Bldg, Tennessee Ave & The Boardwalk, Atlantic City, NJ 08401. TEL 609-441-3749. Ed. Daniel Heneghan. Circ: 1,500.

796 DEU ISSN 0961-933X
NEW STUDIES IN ATHLETICS. Text in English; Summaries in French. 1986. q. USD 60 (effective 2011). adv. bk.rev. bibl. 112 p./no. 2 cols./p.; back issues avail. **Document type:** *Magazine, Consumer.* **Description:** An essential publication in the coaching world designed with coaches in mind. Aims to illustrate the importance the IAAF attaches to scientific and coaching information.
Indexed: SD, SportS.
—BLDSC (6088.775200), IE, Infotrieve.
Published by: (International Amateur Athletic Federation (IAAF) MCO), Meyer & Meyer Verlag, Von-Coels-Str 390, Aachen, 52080, Germany. TEL 49-241-958100, FAX 49-241-9581010, verlag@m-m-sports.com, http://m-m-sports.de. Circ: 5,000. **Co-sponsors:** Bundesinstitut fuer Sportwissenschaft; Fidal-Centro Studi & Ricerche.

796.812 USA ISSN 1060-5908
NEW WAVE WRESTLING. Text in English. 1992. q. USD 6.99 newsstand/cover domestic; USD 9.99 newsstand/cover in Canada (effective 2003). adv. illus. **Document type:** *Magazine, Consumer.* **Description:** Features interviews with prominent wrestling personalities and reports W.W.F., W.C.W. and independent news.
Related titles: ◆ Supplement(s): Combat Sports.
Address: PO Box 651, Gracie Sta, New York, NY 10028-0006. TEL 915-597-1654. Ed., Pub., R&P, Adv. contact Michael O'Hara.

780 USA
NEW YORK FAMILY SPORTS. Text in English. 2008. m. **Document type:** *Magazine, Consumer.* **Description:** Helps parents to obtain information on how to get their children involved in sports. Provides age-appropriate coverage of and feature stories on kiddie leagues, little leagues/middle schools and teen leagues/high schools.
Published by: Manhattan Media, LLC, 63 W 38th St, Ste 206, New York, NY 10018. TEL 212-268-8600, FAX 212-268-9049, information@manhattanmedia.com.

796.692 USA
▼ **NEW YORK HOCKEY JOURNAL.** Text in English. 2011 (Jan.). m. USD 39.99 (effective 2011). adv. **Document type:** *Magazine, Consumer.*
Published by: Seamans Media, 1400 Hancock St, Seventh Fl, Quincy, MA 02169. TEL 617-773-9955, FAX 617-773-6688, michelle@seamansmedia.com, http://www.seamansmedia.com. Ed. Eric Beato. Pub., Adv. contact Eric Seamans.

796.962 USA
NEW YORK RANGERS YEARBOOK; official guide and records. Text in English. 1926. a. USD 6. adv. illus.; stat.
Formerly: New York Rangers Blue Book
Published by: New York Rangers Hockey Club, Madison Square Garden, 4 Pennsylvania Plaza, New York, NY 10001. TEL 212-563-8000, FAX 212-563-8101. Ed. Barry Watkins.

796.42 USA ISSN 1096-9209
NEW YORK RUNNER. Text in English. 1958. bi-m. free to members (effective 2006). adv. bk.rev. stat. back issues avail. **Document type:** *Magazine, Consumer.* **Description:** Regional sports magazine covering running, racewalking, nutrition and fitness.
Former titles (until 199?): New York Running News (0161-7338); (until 1978): New York Runners Club Newsletter (0160-9726)
Indexed: SPI, SportS.
Published by: New York Road Runners Club, 9 E 89th St, New York, NY 10128. TEL 212-423-2260, FAX 212-860-9754, newyorkrun@nyrrc.org, http://www.nyrcc.org. Ed. Gordon Bakoulis. Pub. Mary Wittenberg. Adv. contact Peter Ciaccia. Circ: 45,000 (controlled).

794.1 NZL
NEW ZEALAND CHESS. Text in English. 1974. bi-m. free to members. adv. bk.rev. **Document type:** *Newsletter.* **Description:** Reports on local, national and international games.
Published by: New Zealand Chess Federation, Shortland St, PO Box 216, Auckland, New Zealand. Circ: 380.

795 351 NZL
NEW ZEALAND GAZETTE. SUPPLEMENT. CASINO CONTROL NOTICES. Text in English. irreg. NZD 216 combined subscription inclds. Gazette, supplements & special eds. (effective 2005). **Document type:** *Government.*
Related titles: ◆ Supplement to: New Zealand Gazette. ISSN 0111-5650.
Published by: Department of Internal Affairs, New Zealand Gazette Office, Level 13, Prime Property Tower, 86-90 Lambton Quay, PO Box 805, Wellington, 6011, New Zealand. TEL 64-4-4702930, FAX 64-4-4702932, gazette@parliament.govt.nz, http://www.gazette.govt.nz/diawebsite.nsf.

351 NZL
NEW ZEALAND GAZETTE. SUPPLEMENT. RACING BOARD NOTICES. Text in English. irreg. USD 261 combined subscription inclds. Gazette, supplements & special eds. (effective 2005). **Document type:** *Government.*
Related titles: ◆ Supplement to: New Zealand Gazette. ISSN 0111-5650.
Published by: Department of Internal Affairs, New Zealand Gazette Office, Level 13, Prime Property Tower, 86-90 Lambton Quay, PO Box 805, Wellington, 6011, New Zealand. TEL 64-4-4702930, FAX 64-4-4702932, gazette@parliament.govt.nz, http://www.gazette.govt.nz/diawebsite.nsf.

NEW ZEALAND PHYSICAL EDUCATOR. *see* EDUCATION—Teaching Methods And Curriculum

796.425705 NZL ISSN 2230-3979
NEW ZEALAND TRIATHLON & MULTISPORT. Text in English. 1997. bi-m. NZD 45 domestic; NZD 120 in Australia; NZD 160 elsewhere (effective 2011). adv. **Document type:** *Magazine, Consumer.* **Description:** Contains feature articles on Cycling, Mountain Biking, Adventure Racing, Ironman, Triathlon, Multisport, and Orienteering. Covering local and international events with heaps of news, reviews and cool stuff about your sport. Entry forms to major races, athlete profiles, training information and more.
Former titles (until 2011): New Zealand Multisport and Triathlete (1177-0732); Which incorporated (2002-2008): Femme (1177-1089); (until 2003): New Zealand Multisport (1174-1937)
Related titles: Online - full text ed.: NZD 25 (effective 2011).
Published by: Media Unlimited, PO Box 98, Albert Town, Wanaka, 9344, New Zealand. TEL 64-3-4436295, FAX 64-3-4436294, team@mediaunlimited.co.nz, http://www.mediaunlimited.co.nz.

687.0688 CHE ISSN 0722-446X
NEWS BULLETIN. Text in German. 1982. irreg. **Document type:** *Newsletter, Trade.*
Published by: World Federation of the Sporting Goods Industry, Maison du Sport International, Bdg C, 3rd Fl, Avenue de Rhodanie 54, Lausanne, 1007, Switzerland. TEL 41-21-6126161, FAX 41-21-6126169, info@wfsgi.org, http://www.wfsgi.org.

790.1 DEU ISSN 0948-2962
NIEDERSACHSEN-TENNIS. Text in German. 198?. m. adv. **Document type:** *Consumer.*
Formerly (until 1995): Niedersachsen Tennis Report (0940-3388)
Published by: (Niedersaechsischen Tennisverbandes e.V.), Paragon Verlagsgesellschaft mbH, Misburger Str 119, Hannover, 30625, Germany. TEL 49-511-56059930, FAX 40-511-56059939, verlag@paragon.de.

796.96 NLD ISSN 1877-136X
NIEUWSBRIEF "DE CURLER". Text in Dutch. 198?. q. **Document type:** *Newsletter, Consumer.*
Published by: Nederlandse Curling Bond, van Boetzelaerlaan 30, Hoogland, 3828 NS, Netherlands. TEL 31-33-4892940, FAX 31-33-4612971, ncb@curling.nl. Ed. Alie Kramer.

NIHON RINSHO SUPOTSU IGAKKAISHI/JAPANESE SOCIETY OF CLINICAL SPORTS MEDICINE. JOURNAL. *see* MEDICAL SCIENCES

NIKEPHOROS; Zeitschrift fuer Sport und Kultur im Altertum. *see* HISTORY

NIKEPHOROS-BEIHEFTE. *see* HISTORY

796 658 NLD ISSN 1871-9813
NLCOACH. Text in Dutch. 2006. 5/yr. EUR 28.60; EUR 7.50 newsstand/cover (effective 2010). adv. **Document type:** *Magazine, Trade.*
Published by: Arko Sports Media (Subsidiary of: Arko Uitgeverij BV), Postbus 393, Nieuwegein, 3430 AJ, Netherlands. TEL 31-30-6004780, FAX 31-30-6052618, info@arko.nl, http://www.arko.nl. adv.: B&W page EUR 1,340, color page EUR 2,025; trim 205 x 276. Circ: 3,500.

796.72 NZL ISSN 1179-6820
▼ **NO LIMITS;** New Zealand's extreme lifestyle magazine. Text in English. 2009. q. **Document type:** *Magazine, Trade.* **Description:** Covers all aspects of sports in New Zealand.
Published by: Parkside Media, Herne Bay, PO Box 46020, Auckland, 1147, New Zealand. TEL 64-9-3601480, FAX 64-9-3601470, http://www.parksidemedia.co.nz.

790.1 DNK ISSN 1602-7574
NORMTAL FOR SPORTSBRANCHEN I DANMARK. Text in Danish. 1983. a. DKK 295 (effective 2008). illus. back issues avail. **Document type:** *Consumer.*
Former titles (until 1998): Normtal for Sportsbranchen (1395-5942); (until 1994): Normtalsundersoegelse for Sportsbranchen (0900-0283)
Published by: Danmarks Sportshandler Forening, Naverland 34, Glostrup, 2600, Denmark. TEL 45-43-434646, FAX 45-43-435532, dsfweb@dsfweb.dk.

794.1 NOR ISSN 0332-9771
NORSK SJAKKBLAD. Text in Norwegian. 1906. 6/yr. NOK 200 domestic; NOK 250 in Nordic countries; NOK 300 elsewhere (effective 2011). adv. bk.rev. **Document type:** *Magazine, Consumer.*
Former titles (until 1975): Norsk Tidsskrift for Sjakk (0048-0614); (until 1970): Norsk Sjakkblad (0332-9917); (until 1932): Norsk Schakblad (0332-9925)
Related titles: Online - full text ed.
Published by: Norges Sjakforbund, Sandakerveien 24 D, Oslo, 0473, Norway. TEL 47-22-101241, sjakkfor@online.no, http://www.sjakk.no. Ed. Silje Bjerke.

799.3 NOR ISSN 0333-4538
NORSK SKYTTERTIDENDE. Text in Norwegian. 1882. 9/yr. NOK 200 (effective 2002). adv.
Related titles: Microfilm ed.
Published by: Frivillige Skyttervesen, Loerenvangen 10, Postboks 298, Oekern, Oslo, 0511, Norway. TEL 47-23-17-21-00, FAX 47-23-27-21-01. Ed. Viktor Storsveen. adv.: color page NOK 5,800. Circ: 10,000.

797.2 NOR ISSN 0333-452X
NORSK SVOEMMING. Text in Norwegian. 1947. 8/yr. NOK 255.
Published by: Norges Svoemmeforbund/Norwegian Swimming Federation, Postboks 153, Hamar, 2301, Norway.

NORTH AMERICAN JOURNAL OF SPORTS PHYSICAL THERAPY (ONLINE). *see* MEDICAL SCIENCES—Physical Medicine And Rehabilitation

790.1 973 USA
NORTH AMERICAN SOCIETY FOR SPORT HISTORY. NEWSLETTER. Text in English. 1973. a. membership membership. bk.rev. bibl. **Document type:** *Newsletter.*
Indexed: SD, SportS.
Published by: North American Society for Sport History, c/o Ronald A Smith, PO Box 1026, Lemont, PA 16851. TEL 814-238-1288. Ed. Ronald A Smith.

796 970 980 USA ISSN 0093-6235
GV571
NORTH AMERICAN SOCIETY FOR SPORT HISTORY. PROCEEDINGS. Text in English. 1973. a., latest 2002. adv. back issues avail. **Document type:** *Proceedings.*
Indexed: A22, PopulInd.
—BLDSC (6837.985000), IE, Ingenta.
Published by: North American Society for Sport History, c/o Ronald A Smith, PO Box 1026, Lemont, PA 16851. TEL 814-238-1288, publications-board@nassh.org, http://www.nassh.org. Circ: 1,000.

790.1 USA
NORTH MISSISSIPPI ALL SPORTS REVIEW. Text in English. 2000. m. USD 36; USD 3.95 newsstand/cover (effective 2001). adv. **Document type:** *Magazine, Consumer.*
Published by: Normiss Publishing, Inc., Box 479, Pontotoc, MS 38863. TEL 662-489-3865, FAX 662-489-3745, allsports@onecalline.com. Ed. Don Rowe. Pub. Gary Andrews.

659.1 630 AUS
NORTH WEST MAGAZINE. Text in English. 1972. w. adv. **Document type:** *Newspaper.*
Former titles (until 1988): North West and Hunter Valley Magazine; (until 1975): North West Magazine
Published by: North West Magazine Group, 287 Conadilly St, Gunnedah, NSW 2380, Australia. namoi@mpx.com.au. Circ: 45,000.

794.1 USA ISSN 0146-6941
NORTHWEST CHESS. Text in English. 1947. m. USD 20. adv. bk.rev.
Address: PO Box 84746, Seattle, WA 98124-6046. TEL 206-935-7186, FAX 206-441-4736. Ed. David Roger. Circ: 800.

796.42 USA ISSN 0883-7945
GV1061.23.N95
NORTHWEST RUNNER. Text in English. 1972. m. USD 19.95 domestic; USD 37 in Canada (effective 2007). adv. bk.rev. 2 cols./p.; **Document type:** *Magazine, Consumer.*
Formerly (until 1985): Nor'wester (8750-6076)
Address: 6310 NE 74th St, Ste 217E, Seattle, WA 98115-8169. TEL 206-527-5301, FAX 206-527-1223. Ed., R&P Martin Rudow. Circ: 7,000 (paid).

794.1 USA
NOSTALGIA (VICTORVILLE, E-MAIL EDITION). Text in English. 1960. q. USD 10 to members; USD 20 domestic membership; USD 25 in Canada membership; USD 30 elsewhere membership (effective 2001). adv. bk.rev. 30 p./no.; **Document type:** *Newsletter, Consumer.* **Description:** Covers topics in the game of chess, including games, results, rating and more.
Formerly: Nost-Algia (Print Edition)
Media: E-mail.
Published by: Knights of the Square Table, c/o Donald Cotten, 13393 Mariposa Rd 248, Victorville, CA 92392-5324. http://www.nostgames.com/. Ed., Pub. Don Cotten. Circ: 350.

793.7 SVK ISSN 1336-7587
NOVY CAS SPECIAL. KRIZOVKY. Text in Slovak. 2005. m. adv. **Document type:** *Magazine, Consumer.*
Published by: Ringier Slovakia a. s., Prievozska 14, PO Box 46, Bratislava 24, 82004, Slovakia. TEL 421-2-58227124, FAX 421-2-58227143, http://www.ringier.sk. Ed. Julia Kovacova.

790.1 JPN ISSN 0287-900X
NUMBER/SPORTS GRAPHIC NUMBER. Text in Japanese. 1980. bi-w. JPY 21,060 (effective 2001). **Document type:** *Consumer.*
Published by: Bungei Shunju Ltd., 3-23 Kioi-cho, Chiyoda-ku, Tokyo, 102-8008, Japan. TEL 81-3-32651211, FAX 81-3-32393699, i-choku@bunshun.co.jp, http://www.bunshun.co.jp. Ed. Yusuke Abe. Circ: 290,000.

790.1 ITA ISSN 1590-0908
NUOVO TOTOGUIDA SPORT. Abbreviated title: TGsport. Text in Italian. 1974. w. adv. **Document type:** *Magazine, Consumer.*
Related titles: Online - full text ed.
Published by: Giroal Srl, Piazza Verdi 8, Rome, 00198, Italy. TEL 39-06-8841611, FAX 39-06-85831141, info@giroal.it, http://www.giroal.it. Circ: 100,000.

796 NLD ISSN 2210-6928
NUSPORT. Text in Dutch. 1998. w. EUR 60 (effective 2010). adv. **Document type:** *Magazine, Consumer.*
Formerly (until 2010): Sportweek (1388-3356)
Published by: Sanoma Uitgevers B.V., Postbus 1900, Hoofddorp, 2130 JH, Netherlands. TEL 31-23-5566770, FAX 31-23-5565376, corporatecommunications@sanomamedia.nl, http://www.sanomamedia.nl. Ed. Jasper Boks. Pub. Jan Paul de Wildt.

796.09485 SWE ISSN 1654-4625
O S MAGASINET. (Olympiska Spelen) Text in Swedish. 1999. s-a. SEK 50 (effective 2007). adv. back issues avail. **Document type:** *Magazine, Consumer.*
Formerly (until 2007): S O K Magasin (1404-7187)
Related titles: Online - full text ed.
Published by: Sveriges Olympiska Kommitte, Olympiadstadion, Stockholm, 11433, Sweden. TEL 46-8-4026800, FAX 46-8-4026818. Ed. Bjoern Folin TEL 46-8-4026805.

796.075 USA
ODDBALL INSIDER. Text in English. irreg. free. adv. **Document type:** *Newsletter, Consumer.* **Description:** Dedicated to sport cards collectionists.
Media: Online - full text.
Address: 1925 Juan Tabo N E, Ste B 288, Albuquerque, NM 87112. FAX 505-299-5603. Ed. Matthew Crowder. Circ: 600.

796.35 USA
OFFICIAL RULES OF THE N H L. (National Hockey League) Text in English. 1995. a. USD 9.95 per issue (effective 2011). back issues avail. **Document type:** *Handbook/Manual/Guide, Consumer.*
Published by: Triumph Books, 542 S Dearborn St, Ste 750, Chicago, IL 60605. TEL 312-939-3330, 800-335-5323, FAX 312-663-3557, S.Wilson@TriumphBooks.com.

794.1 USA ISSN 0885-6583
OHIO CHESS BULLETIN. Text in English. 1946. bi-m. USD 10. adv. bk.rev. charts; illus.; stat. index.
Published by: Ohio Chess Association, 621 Hal Bar Dr, Cambridge, OH 43725. Ed. Parley C Long. Circ: 500. **Subscr. to:** James Pechac, 7722 Lucerne Dr, Apt N 35, Middleburg, OH 44130. TEL 216-826-3054.

790 RUS ISSN 0131-2596
SK1
OKHOTA I OKHOTNICH'E KHOZYAISTVO. Text in Russian. 1955. m. USD 81 (effective 1998). bk.rev. index.
Indexed: RefZh.
—East View.
Address: Sadovaya-Spasskaya 18, Moscow, 107807, Russian Federation. TEL 7-095-2072091, FAX 7-095-2072086. Ed. O K Gusev. **Dist. by:** M K - Periodica, ul Gilyarovskogo 39, Moscow 129110, Russian Federation. TEL 7-095-2845008, FAX 7-095-2813798, info@periodicals.ru, http://www.mkniga.ru; East View Information Services, 10601 Wayzata Blvd, Minneapolis, MN 55305. TEL 952-252-1201, 800-477-1005, FAX 952-252-1202, info@eastview.com, http://www.eastview.com.

796.962 SWE ISSN 1654-8345
OLDTIMER HOCKEY. Text in Swedish. 2007. q. adv. **Document type:** *Magazine, Consumer.*
Published by: Swedish Oldtimer's Hockey Association, Vasagatan 42, Mora, 792 31, Sweden. TEL 46-70-3485505, bjorn.aberg@soha.se, http://www.soha.se. Ed. Olof Wigren. Pub., Adv. contact Bjorn Aberg.

790 ARG ISSN 1514-9676
OLE. Text in Spanish. 1996. d. **Document type:** *Newspaper, Consumer.*
Related titles: Online - full content ed.
Published by: Diario Ole oledigital@diario-ole.com.ar, http://www.diario-ole.com.ar.

790.1 GBR
OLEANDER GAMES AND PASTIMES SERIES. Variant title: Games and Pastimes. Text in English. 19??. a. price varies. **Document type:** *Monographic series, Academic/Scholarly.*
Published by: Oleander Press, 16 Orchard St, Cambridge, CB1 1JT, United Kingdom. TEL 44-1223-350898.

790.1 RUS ISSN 0201-4785
OLIMP. Text in Russian. s-a. USD 65 in United States.
Address: A-ya 1805, Izhevsk, 426000, Russian Federation. TEL 3412-768277, FAX 3412-766277. Ed. V Saltykov. **Dist. by:** East View Information Services, 10601 Wayzata Blvd, Minneapolis, MN 55305. TEL 952-252-1201, 800-477-1005, FAX 952-252-1202, info@eastview.com, http://www.eastview.com.

790.1 RUS ISSN 0204-2177
OLIMPIISKAYA PANORAMA. Text in Russian. 1976-1980; resumed 1981. q. USD 48 (effective 1998). **Description:** Covers international competitions, interviews with championship athletes, forthcoming 1992 Olympic games, new sporting events and more.
Related titles: English ed.: Olympic Panorama. ISSN 0204-2592; Spanish ed.: Panorama Olimpico. ISSN 0204-241X; German ed.: Olympisches Panorama. ISSN 0204-2614; French ed.: Panorama Olympique. ISSN 0204-2606.
Published by: National Olympic Committee of the U.S.S.R., Ul Zhdanova 5-7, Moscow, 103031, Russian Federation. TEL 924 65 23, TELEX 411287. Ed. Viacheslav Gavrilin. **Dist. by:** M K - Periodica, ul Gilyarovskogo 39, Moscow 129110, Russian Federation. TEL 7-095-2845008, FAX 7-095-2813798, info@periodicals.ru, http://www.mkniga.ru.

796 AUT
OLYMPIA AKTUELL. Text in German. 1973. 4/yr. adv. bk.rev. **Document type:** *Magazine, Consumer.*
Former titles: Olympische Sport; Olympische Blaetter
Published by: Oesterreichisches Olympisches Comite, Marxergasse 25/5, Vienna, W 1030, Austria. TEL 43-1-7995511, FAX 43-1-799551120, office@oeoc.at, http://www.oeoc.at. Ed. Heinz Jungwirth. Circ: 750.

613.713 ITA ISSN 1126-0874
OLYMPIAN'S NEWS. Text in Italian. 1991. bi-m. EUR 50 (effective 2009). **Document type:** *Magazine, Consumer.* **Description:** Contains articles on muscle and fitness strategies. For competitive body builders.
Address: Via Fiorentina, 72, Figline Valdarno, FI 50063, Italy. TEL 39-055-959530, FAX 39-055-9156982. **Dist. by:** Italian Press Dist, Stampa, Via Ghisalba, 7, Ospiate di Bollate, MI 20021, Italy. TEL 39-02-38300940.

790.1 CHE ISSN 1025-5737
OLYMPIC MESSAGE. Text in English, French. 1982. 3/yr. **Document type:** *Bulletin.*
Supersedes in part (in 1996): Message Olympique (1011-405X)
Indexed: SportS.
—Ingenta.
Published by: International Olympic Committee, Chateau De Vidy, Lausanne, 1007, Switzerland. TEL 021-6216111, FAX 021-6216216. Ed. Fekrou Kidane. Circ: 13,000.

796.48 CHE ISSN 0377-192X
GV721.5
OLYMPIC REVIEW (YEAR). Text in English. 1967. bi-m. CHF 60 (effective 2000). adv. bk.rev. illus. index. **Document type:** *Bulletin, Consumer.* **Description:** News and information concerning the Olympics and the Olympic Movement. Articles cover future games, sporting life, Olympic host cities and countries, news of National Olympic Committees.
Related titles: Spanish ed.: Revista Olimpica. ISSN 1018-1008; French ed.: Revue Olympique. ISSN 0251-3498.
Indexed: SportS.
—BLDSC (6256.405000).
Published by: International Olympic Committee, Chateau De Vidy, Lausanne, 1007, Switzerland. FAX 41-21-6216354, TELEX 454024-ACIO-CH. Ed. Fekrou Kidane. R&P Sylvia Espagnac TEL 41-21-6216417. Adv. contact Sylvie Espagnac. B&W page CHF 4,000, color page CHF 8,000. Circ: 7,000.

790.06 BEL ISSN 0772-2095
OLYMPICS NEWS. Text in French. 1978. q. illus. **Document type:** *Newsletter.*
Supersedes in part: Olympics
Related titles: Dutch ed.: ISSN 0771-7547.
Published by: Comite Olympique et Interfederal Belge/Belgian Olympic and Interfederal Committee, Av de Bouchout 9, Brussels, 1020, Belgium. TEL 32-2-474-5150, FAX 32-2-479-4656, info@olympic.org, http://www.olympic.be. Ed., R&P Guido de Bondt.

790.1 CAN ISSN 1188-5963
GV721.5
➤ **OLYMPIKA;** the international journal of Olympic studies. Text in English. 1992. a., latest vol.7, 1998. CAD 20 domestic; USD 22 in United States; USD 24 elsewhere (effective 2002). bk.rev. **Document type:** *Journal, Academic/Scholarly.* **Description:** Incorporates sociocultural research studies predominantly related to the historical, philosophical and sociological dimensions of the modern Olympic games and the Olympic movement.

S

Indexed: A26, I05, SD.
—BLDSC (6256.406000), IE, Ingenta. **CCC.**
Published by: International Centre for Olympic Studies, Thames Hall, University of Western Ontario, London, ON N6A 3K7, Canada. TEL 519-661-4113, FAX 519-661-4148, kbwamsley@uwo.ca, http://www.uwo.ca/olympic. Ed. Stephen R Wenn. Pub., R&P Kevin B Wamsley.

790.1 DEU ISSN 0471-5640
OLYMPISCHES FEUER. Text in German. 1951. q. back issues avail. **Document type:** *Journal, Consumer.*
Published by: Deutsche Olympische Gesellschaft e.V., Otto-Fleck-Schneise 12, Frankfurt am Main, 60528, Germany. TEL 49-69-6950160, FAX 49-69-6771826, Office@DOG-bewegt.de, http://www.dog-bewegt.de. Circ: 6,500 (controlled).

796.962 CAN
ON ICE. Text in English. 1989. q. CAD 11.97. adv. bk.rev. **Description:** Aimed at adult recreational hockey players aged 20 plus. Keeps readers informed with tournament listings, health reports and tips for improving their game.
Published by: On Ice Magazine Inc., P O BOX 10, STA F, Toronto, ON M4Y 2L4, Canada. TEL 416-469-4367, FAX 416-360-4348. Ed. Jerry Amernic. Circ: 25,000.

796.345 CAN
ONTARIO BADMINTON TODAY. Text in English. q. **Document type:** *Magazine, Consumer.*
Published by: Ontario Badminton Association, 1185 Eglinton Ave. E., #207-B, North York, ON M3C 3C6, Canada.

796.355 CAN ISSN 1926-1586
ONTARIO LACROSSE MAGAZINE. Text in English. 197?. q. free to members (effective 2011). adv. **Document type:** *Magazine, Trade.* **Description:** Features news and informative articles on the sport of lacrosse in Ontario.
Incorporates (197?-2009): Lacrosse Year in Review (1912-189X)
Related titles: Online - full text ed.: free (effective 2011).
Published by: Ontario Lacrosse Association, 3 Concorde Gate, Ste 306, Toronto, ON M3C 3N7, Canada. TEL 416-426-7068, ron@ontariolacrosse.com, http://www.ontariolacrosse.com/. Ed. Paul Grossinger TEL 905-370-0736.

790.1 CAN ISSN 0702-7842
GV56.O6
ONTARIO. MINISTERE DES AFFAIRES CULTURELLES ET DES LOIS DE L'ONTARIO. RAPPORT ANNUEL. Text in English. 1983. a.
Published by: Ministry of Tourism Culture and Recreation, Hearst Block, 900 Bay St, Toronto, ON M7A 2E1, Canada. TEL 800-668-2746. Circ: 10,000.

793.7 EST
ONU UNO VALITUD RISTSONAD. Text in Estonian. 1994. 6/yr. EUR 1.27 newsstand/cover (effective 2011). adv. **Document type:** *Magazine, Consumer.*
Published by: Kuma Ltd., 57 Parnu St, Paide, 72712, Estonia. TEL 372-38-38800, FAX 372-38-38806, kuma@kuma.ee, http://www.kuma.ee. Ed. Jaanus Laidna. adv.: page EEK 2,500.

OPEN ACCESS JOURNAL OF SPORTS MEDICINE. *see* MEDICAL SCIENCES

OPEN LINE. *see* COMMUNICATIONS—Radio

THE OPEN SPORTS MEDICINE JOURNAL. *see* MEDICAL SCIENCES

THE OPEN SPORTS SCIENCES JOURNAL. *see* SCIENCES: COMPREHENSIVE WORKS

790.1 USA
OPERATIONS. Text in English. 1991. q. USD 16. illus.
Published by: Gamers, 500 W Fourth St, Homer, IL 61849. Ed. Dave Demko. Circ: 2,000.

OPTION 4 X 4; l'essentiel de l'equipement 4 X 4 et de la pratique tout terrain. *see* TRANSPORTATION—Automobiles

796.426 USA
OREGON DISTANCE RUNNER. Text in English. 1978. q. USD 25 to members. adv. bk.rev. **Description:** Covers road and track running and walking, with a calendar of events, news articles and features, awards coverage.
Published by: Oregon Road Runners Club, 4840 SW Western Ave., Ste. 200, Beaverton, OR 97005-3450. TEL 503-646-7867, FAX 503-520-0242. Ed., Pub. Bert van Gorder. R&P, Adv. contact Gordon Lovie. Circ: 3,400.

796.426 DNK ISSN 1901-3825
ORIENTERING.DK. Text in Danish. 1951. 4/yr. DKK 200 (effective 2008). adv. bk.rev. charts; illus.; stat. back issues avail. **Document type:** *Magazine, Consumer.*
Former titles (until 2006): Orienteringsloeb.dk (1603-8282); (until 2004): O - Posten (0107-4202)
Related titles: Online - full text ed.: ISSN 1901-3833.
Published by: Dansk Orienterings-Forbund/Danish Orienteering Federation, Idraettens Hus, Broendby Stadion 20, Broendby, 2605, Denmark. TEL 45-43-457730, FAX 45-43-457790, dof@do-f.dk. Ed. Julie Mathiesen. adv.: color page DKK 9,800. Circ: 4,900.

796 USA ISSN 0747-0991
THE OSCEOLA. Text in English. 1983. 32/yr. USD 49.95 (effective 2011). **Document type:** *Magazine, Consumer.*
Published by: 247 Sports, PO Box 1498, Shelbyville, KY 40066. TEL 888-474-8669, info@247sports.com, http://247sports.com.

796 658.8 USA
OUTDOOR BUSINESS. Text in English. 6/yr. USD 59 domestic; USD 99 in Canada & Mexico; USD 149 elsewhere; free to qualified personnel (effective 2008). **Document type:** *Magazine, Trade.*
Published by: SportsOneSource Group, 2151 Hawkins St, Ste 200, Charlotte, NC 28269. TEL 704-987-3450, FAX 704-987-3455, info@sportsonesource.com, http://www.sportsonesource.com. Circ: 8,000 (controlled).

790.1 CAN
OUTDOOR GUIDE. Text in English. s-a. adv. bk.rev.; video rev.; Website rev. **Document type:** *Magazine, Consumer.*
Former titles (until 2001): Outside Guide; Sunsports
Published by: Solstice Publishing Inc., 47 Soho Square, Toronto, ON M5T 2Z2, Canada. TEL 416-595-1252, FAX 416-595-7255. Ed. Iain MacMillan. Pub., R&P, Adv. contact Paul Green. Circ: 50,000.

OXYGEN; women's fitness. *see* WOMEN'S HEALTH

639.37 GBR ISSN 1467-6915
P A D I MEMBER NEWS. Text in English. 1999. q. **Document type:** *Magazine, Consumer.* **Description:** Provides a forum for members and enables PADI to deliver information and practical advice to all its members.
Published by: (Professional Association of Diving Instructors USA), Origin Publishing Ltd. (Subsidiary of: B B C Worldwide Ltd.), Tower House, Fairfax St, Bristol, BS1 3BN, United Kingdom. TEL 44-117-9279009, FAX 44-117-9349008, info@originpublishing.co.uk, http://www.originpublishing.co.uk.

793 USA
P B A TOUR OFFICIAL PROGRAM (YEAR). Text in English. a. USD 5. adv. illus. **Description:** Presents the highlights of the previous year's PBA tournaments.
Published by: Professional Bowlers Association of America, 719 2nd Ave., Ste. 701, Seattle, WA 98104-1747. TEL 216-836-5568, FAX 216-836-2107. Ed., Adv. contact Christopher C Bame. Circ: 110,000.

P E & SPORT TODAY. (Physical Education) *see* EDUCATION—Teaching Methods And Curriculum

P L Y. *see* COMPUTERS—Computer Games

793 DEU
P.M. INTELLIGENZ-TRAINER; mehr Kreativitaet - mehr Konzentration - mehr Phantasie. Text in German. 1999. bi-m. EUR 15; EUR 1.90 newsstand/cover (effective 2010). adv. **Document type:** *Magazine, Consumer.* **Description:** Contains various games and puzzles designed to increase intelligence and creativity.
Published by: Gruner + Jahr AG & Co, Weihenstephaner Str 7, Munich, 81673, Germany. TEL 49-89-41520, FAX 49-89-4152651, guj-redaktion@guj.de, http://www.guj.de. Adv. contact Christian Liesegang. page EUR 5,300. Circ: 30,000 (paid).

793.7 DEU
P.M. KREATIV-TRAINER. Text in German. 2000. bi-m. EUR 15; EUR 1.90 newsstand/cover (effective 2010). adv. **Document type:** *Magazine, Consumer.* **Description:** Publishes a wide variety of crossword and logic puzzles and quizzes.
Published by: Gruner + Jahr AG & Co, Weihenstephaner Str 7, Munich, 81673, Germany. TEL 49-89-41520, FAX 49-89-4152651, guj-redaktion@guj.de, http://www.guj.de. Adv. contact Christian Liesegang. page EUR 5,300. Circ: 50,000 (paid and controlled).

793 DEU
P.M. LOGIK-TRAINER. Text in German. 1988. m. EUR 30; EUR 1.90 newsstand/cover (effective 2010). adv. **Document type:** *Magazine, Consumer.* **Description:** Contains various logic problems and questions to be analyzed and solved.
Published by: Gruner + Jahr AG & Co, Weihenstephaner Str 7, Munich, 81673, Germany. TEL 49-89-41520, FAX 49-89-4152651, guj-redaktion@guj.de, http://www.guj.de. Adv. contact Christian Liesegang. page EUR 5,300. Circ: 34,630 (paid).

793 DEU
P.M. SUDOKU-TRAINER. Text in German. 2006. bi-m. EUR 15; EUR 1.90 newsstand/cover (effective 2010). adv. **Document type:** *Magazine, Consumer.*
Published by: Gruner + Jahr AG & Co, Weihenstephaner Str 7, Munich, 81673, Germany. TEL 49-89-41520, FAX 49-89-4152651, guj-redaktion@guj.de, http://www.guj.de. Adv. contact Christian Liesegang. page EUR 5,300.

P R C A MEDIA GUIDE. *see* SPORTS AND GAMES—Horses And Horsemanship

790.1 USA
PADDLESPORTS BUSINESS. Text in English. 1986. q. free industry members (effective 2007). 38 p./no. 3 cols./p.; **Document type:** *Newsletter, Trade.*
Formerly: Canoe & Kayak Industry News
Published by: Source Interlink Companies, 10526 NE 68th St, Ste 3, Kirkland, WA 98033. dheine@sourceinterlink.com, http://www.sourceinterlinkmedia.com. Circ: 5,000 (paid).

796.72 CAN ISSN 1911-0049
PADDOCK. Text in French. 2006. bi-m. **Document type:** *Magazine, Trade.*
Published by: Editions Gesca, C.P. 9425, Succ. Sainte-Foy, Sainte-Foy, PQ G1V 4B8, Canada. TEL 514-904-5537, 877-997-4653, contact@editionsgesca.ca, http://www.editionsgesca.ca.

796.72 GBR
THE PADDOCK; motorsport's business and lifestyle magazine. Text in English. 2007. m. GBP 50 domestic; GBP 69 in the European Union; GBP 89 elsewhere (effective 2009). adv. back issues avail. **Document type:** *Magazine, Trade.* **Description:** Provides information on all the latest developments that affect the motorsport industry.
Published by: GrandPrix Media Ltd., Unit 504, 7 Garden Walk, London, EC2A 3EW, United Kingdom. TEL 44-20-77395847, FAX 44-20-77295672. Ed. Quentin Spurring TEL 44-20-77395847. Adv. contact Ed Luckas. color page EUR 8,000; trim 210 x 275. Circ: 12,000 (controlled).

790.1 GBR ISSN 1465-3532
PAINTBALL GAMES INTERNATIONAL. Text in English. 1989. m. adv. **Document type:** *Magazine, Consumer.*
Formerly (until 1991): Paintball Games (0955-6605)
—**CCC.**
Published by: Maze Media Ltd., 21-23 Phoenix Ct, Hawkins Rd, Colchester, Essex CO2 0NH, United Kingdom. TEL 44-1206-505900, FAX 44-1206-505915.

796 USA ISSN 1932-5355
GV1202.S87
PAINTBALL SPORTS. Text in English. 1989. m. USD 29.95; USD 4.99 newsstand/cover (effective 2007). adv. 140 p./no.; **Document type:** *Magazine, Consumer.* **Description:** Covers the paintball sports industry worldwide.
Formerly (until 2004): Paintball Sports International (1073-774X)
Published by: Paintball Publications, Inc., 2090 5th Ave, Ste 2, Ronkonkoma, NY 11779. TEL 631-580-7772, FAX 631-580-3725, http://www.paintballsportsinc.com. Ed. Dawn Allcot. adv.: color page USD 8,950; trim 8.125 x 10.875. **Dist. by:** Curtis CIRC Company, 11 W 42nd St, New York, NY 10022. TEL 212-768-1000.

794.1 PAK
PAKISTAN CHESS MAGAZINE. Text in English. 1987. 4/yr. USD 25. adv. bk.rev. **Description:** Reports on national and international games and news, opening theory, endgame studies, problems studies, interviews, and "how to improve" articles.
Published by: Mohammad Aejaz Ali Tahir Ed. & Pub., P O Box 179, Karachi, 74200, Pakistan. TEL 92-21-445742, FAX 92-21-4538539. Circ: 7,000.

PALAESTRA; forum of sport, physical education and recreation for those with disabilities. *see* EDUCATION—Special Education And Rehabilitation

796 TUR ISSN 1309-0356
▼ **PAMUKKALE JOURNAL OF SPORTS SCIENCES/PAMUKKALE SPOR BILIMERI DERGISI.** Text in English, Turkish. 2010. 3/yr. free (effective 2011). **Document type:** *Journal, Academic/Scholarly.*
Media: Online - full text.
Indexed: CABA, GH, LT, N02, N03.
Published by: Pamukkale Universitesi, School of Sports Sciences and Technology, Denizli, Turkey. Ed. Ridvan Ekmekci.

793 POL ISSN 1731-9994
PANORAMY TELE SWIATA. Text in Polish. 1999. bi-m. PLZ 2.80 newsstand/cover (effective 2011). adv. **Document type:** *Magazine, Consumer.*
Published by: Phoenix Press, Sw Antoniego 7, Wroclaw, 50-073, Poland. TEL 48-71-3449813, FAX 48-71-3460174, phoenix@phoenix.pl, http://phoenix.pl. Adv. contact Adam Michrowski.

PANSTADIA; no. 1 journal for the sport & entertainment facility industry worldwide. *see* BUILDING AND CONSTRUCTION

793 USA
PANZERSCHRECK. Text in English. 19??. irreg., latest no.6. price varies. back issues avail. **Document type:** *Magazine, Consumer.* **Description:** Features war-game articles and variants as well as a complete game.
Published by: Minden Games, PO Box 10667, Glendale, AZ 85318. minden2@hotmail.com, http://www.homestead.com/minden_games/.

793 USA
PAPER WARS. Text in English. 1991. bi-m. USD 39.95 domestic; USD 49.95 in Europe; USD 69.95 elsewhere; USD 8 newsstand/cover (effective 2008). adv. illus. **Document type:** *Newsletter, Consumer.*
Formerly (until 1993): Wargame Collector's Journal
Published by: Omega Games, PO Box 2191, Valrico, FL 33595. TEL 813-661-3804, FAX 813-681-7446, omegagames@aol.com. Ed. John Burtt.

797.56 USA ISSN 0031-1588
GV770
PARACHUTIST. Text in English. 1956. m. USD 28 domestic; USD 40 foreign; USD 4.50 newsstand/cover (effective 2001). adv. bk.rev. charts; illus. **Document type:** *Magazine, Trade.* **Description:** Presents information and photographs on events and safety issues in skydiving.
Indexed: SD, SportS.
—Ingenta.
Published by: United States Parachute Association, 1440 Duke St, Alexandria, VA 22314. TEL 703-836-3495, FAX 703-836-2843, publications@uspa.org, http://www.uspa.org. Ed. Kevin Gibson. Adv. contact Nancy J Koreen. B&W page USD 845, color page USD 1,270. Circ: 34,000 (paid).

797.55 USA ISSN 1540-2185
PARAGLIDER. Text in English. 2002. q. USD 29.95 domestic; USD 35.95 in Canada; USD 39.95 elsewhere (effective 2002).
Published by: Schwartz Gaylord Publishing, 26741 Portola Pkwy. Ste. 1E-479, Foothill Ranch, CA 92610-1743. TEL 919-709-3015, info@paraglidermagazine.com. Ed. Sam Gaylord.

PARKS & RECREATION CANADA/PARCS & LOISIRS. *see* LEISURE AND RECREATION

796.91 FRA ISSN 0982-8125
PATINAGE MAGAZINE. Text in French. 1983. bi-m.
Supersedes in part (in 1986): Danse et Patinage (0769-3737); Which was formerly (until 1985): Danse Sportive Magazine (0752-2371)
Published by: Sport de Glace Edition, 39 bd. de la Marne, Rouen, 76000, France. TEL 33-2-35074729. Ed. Patrick Hourcade. Pub. Vincent Guerrier.

796.962 USA ISSN 1060-2429
PENGUINS REPORT. Text in English. 1991. 20/yr. **Description:** Covers the Pittsburgh Penguins hockey team. Features a color poster of a Penguins player in each issue.
Published by: Gateway Publications, Inc., 610 Beatty Rd, Monroeville, PA 15146-1502. TEL 412-856-7400, FAX 412-856-7954. Ed. Tom McMillan. Circ: 7,000 (paid).

PENNSYLVANIA JOURNAL OF HEALTH, PHYSICAL EDUCATION, RECREATION AND DANCE. *see* EDUCATION—Teaching Methods And Curriculum

796 BRA ISSN 1415-4676
PENSAR A PRATICA. Text in Portuguese. 1998. s-a. back issues avail. **Document type:** *Journal, Academic/Scholarly.*
Related titles: Online - full text ed.: ISSN 1980-6183. free (effective 2011).
Indexed: SD.
Published by: Universidade Federal de Goias, Facultadede de Educacao Fisica, Campus II Caixa Postal 131, Goiania, Goias 74001-970, Brazil. TEL 55-62-35211141, FAX 55-62-35211185, guego@fef.ufg.br, http://www.fef.ufg.br/. Ed. Ari Lazzarotti Filho.

355 GBR
PERFIDIOUS ALBION. Text in English. 1976. triennial. **Description:** Provides wargaming commentary.
Address: 75 Richmond Park Rd, London, SW14 8JY, United Kingdom. Ed. Charles Vasey.

796.77 CAN ISSN 1710-1573
PERFORMANCE AUTO & SOUND. Text in English. 1999. bi-m. **Document type:** *Magazine, Consumer.* **Description:** Features products, test reports and coverage from the tuner scene across North America.
Published by: Performance Publications Inc., 44 Prince Andrew Place, Toronto, ON M6P 3M9, Canada. TEL 416-922-7526, http://www.performancepublicationsinc.com.

PERFORMANCE BUSINESS. *see* TRANSPORTATION—Automobiles

796.72 629.228 USA ISSN 1045-3024
PERFORMANCE RACING INDUSTRY. Text in English. 1985. m. USD 25; USD 40 foreign (effective 1997). adv. back issues avail. **Document type:** *Directory, Trade.* **Description:** Trade and industrial directory of automobiles.
Published by: Laguna Coast Publishing Inc., 31706 South Coast Hwy, South Laguna, CA 92677. TEL 714-499-5413, FAX 714-499-0410. Ed. Virginia Demoss. Pub. Steve Lewis. Adv. contact Jennifer Morales. B&W page USD 2,890; trim 10.88 x 8.38. Circ: 21,450.

796.41 DEU
PFAELZER TURNER; Amtliches Organ des Pfaelzer Turnerbundes. Text in German. m. back issues avail. **Document type:** *Bulletin, Consumer.*
Published by: Pfaelzer Turnerbund e.V., Am Schlagbaum 5, Kaiserslautern, 67655, Germany. TEL 49-631-4149950, FAX 49-631-4149959, pfaelzer_turnerbund@t-online.de, http://www.pfaelzer-turnerbund.de.

▼ **PHENEX JOURNAL/REVUE PHENEPS.** *see* PHYSICAL FITNESS AND HYGIENE

794.8 USA
PHUZE; videogames and culture. Text in English. 2004. q. adv. **Document type:** *Magazine, Consumer.*
Published by: Amalgam Media, Inc., 1388 Haight St, #105, San Francisco, CA 94117. TEL 415-861-7583, FAX 415-861-7584. Pub. Andrew Smith TEL 415-861-7583 ext 11. adv.: color page USD 7,800.

PIA KANSAI EDITION. *see* LEISURE AND RECREATION

796 ITA ISSN 0390-3230
PISCINE OGGI; ambiente, design, giochi d'acqua, minipiscine, sauna. Text in Italian. 1973. 5/yr. EUR 39 domestic; EUR 59 in Europe; EUR 99 elsewhere (effective 2011). adv. bk.rev. **Document type:** *Magazine, Trade.*
Published by: Editrice Il Campo, Via Giovanni Amendola 11, Bologna, BO 40121, Italy. TEL 39-051-255544, FAX 39-051-255360, customer@fitnesstrends.com, http://www.ilcampo.it. Circ: 15,000.

790.1 BRA ISSN 0104-1762
PLACAR. Text in Portuguese. 1970. m. BRL 95.40 domestic; USD 85.82 foreign (effective 2005). adv. charts; illus.; stat. back issues avail. **Document type:** *Magazine, Consumer.* **Description:** Covers soccer, sex and rock 'n' roll.
Related titles: Online - full text ed.
Indexed: A26, I04, I05.
Published by: Editora Abril, S.A., Avenida das Nacoes Unidas 7221, Pinheiros, Sao Paulo, SP 05425-902, Brazil. TEL 55-11-50872112, FAX 55-11-50872100, http://www.abril.com.br. Ed. Leao Serva. adv.: page BRL 10,400. Circ: 37,770.

796.8 USA ISSN 1545-6692
PLANET CAPOEIRA. Text in English. 2003 (May). q. USD 20 domestic; USD 49 foreign (effective 2003). adv.
Published by: PLANET CAPOEIRA MEDIA, 530 Main St. Ste. 702, New Rochelle, NY 10801. TEL 914-420-4914. Ed. Brian Donnelly.

790.1 659.1 GBR ISSN 2045-0168
PLATFORM (LONDON, 2010). Text in English. 1982. m. GBP 199, EUR 240, USD 330 (effective 2010). bk.rev. **Document type:** *Magazine, Consumer.* **Description:** Covers information about insight and intelligence, relating to sponsorship & partnership marketing.
Formerly (until 2010): Sponsorship News (0263-3809)
—CCC.
Published by: The Meeting Room, Unit 301b, The Aberdeen Ctr, 22-24 Highbury Grove, London, N5 2EA, United Kingdom. TEL 44-20-74852111, FAX 44-20-74852555, catherine@themeetingroom.org.uk.

496 USA
PLAY (NEW YORK); the New York Times sports magazine. Text in English. 2006. q. back issues avail. **Document type:** *Magazine, Consumer.* **Description:** Features interesting and informative articles on sports.
Published by: New York Times Company, 620 8th Ave, New York, NY 10018. TEL 212-556-1234, FAX 212-556-7088, letters@nytimes.com. Pub. Arthur Ochs Sulzberger Jr. Adv. contact Denise Warren TEL 212-556-7894.

793 USA ISSN 0162-1343
HD9993.E453
PLAY METER. Text in English. 1974. m. USD 60 domestic; USD 150 foreign; USD 10 newsstand/cover domestic; USD 20 newsstand/cover foreign (effective 2007). adv. charts; illus.; tr.lit. index. **Document type:** *Magazine, Trade.* **Description:** Features information on various types of equipment, tax related issues, new products, technical knowledge, latest news and company profiles. Targeted at family entertainment centers.
Published by: Skybird Publishing Co., Inc., PO Box 337, Metaire, LA 70004-0337. TEL 504-488-7003, FAX 504-488-7083. Ed., R&P Valerie Cognevich. Pub. Carol P Lally. Adv. contact Carol Lebell. Circ: 5,000 (paid).

795 USA
THE PLAYBOOK. Text in English. 2007 (sep.). m. free local. adv. **Document type:** *Magazine, Consumer.* **Description:** Covers the gambler lifestyle, including latest trends in technology, fashion, food, automobiles, vacation destination, and other topics.
Published by: The Playbook Publishing Co., 116 Charlotte Ave, Hicksville, NY 11801. TEL 516-931-1905, FAX 516-931-1906. adv.: page USD 3,500; bleed 5.25 x 8.25.

790.1 USA
PLAYER'S CHOICE MAGAZINE. Text in English. 1995. m. USD 12.95 (effective 1999). adv. **Document type:** *Magazine, Consumer.* **Description:** Nighttime guide to sports and entertainment in the Tampa Bay area, focusing on dart and pool tournaments and leagues.
Related titles: Online - full text ed.
Address: PO Box 51, Riverview, FL 33568-0051. TEL 813-643-2483. Ed. M.J. Wilson. Pub., Adv. contact Steve Miller Sr. R&P M J Wilson.

796 USA ISSN 1937-0997
GV716
PLUNKETT'S SPORTS INDUSTRY ALMANAC; the only comprehensive guide to the sports industry. Variant title: Sports Industry Almanac. Text in English. 2005. a. USD 299.99 combined subscription (print & CD-ROM eds.); USD 399.99 combined subscription (print, online & CD-ROM eds.) (effective 2009). **Document type:** *Directory, Trade.* **Description:** Covers data profiles of 350 leading companies of the sports industry.
Related titles: CD-ROM ed.; Online - full text ed.: USD 299.99 (effective 2009).
Published by: Plunkett Research, Ltd, PO Drawer 541737, Houston, TX 77254. TEL 713-932-0000, FAX 713-932-7080, customersupport@plunkettresearch.com, http://www.plunkettresearch.com. Ed. Jack W Plunkett.

795 FRA ISSN 2106-8356
▼ **POKER 52.** Text in French. 2010. m. EUR 35 (effective 2011). **Document type:** *Magazine, Consumer.*
Related titles: Special ed(s).: Poker 52 (Edition Casino). ISSN 2109-1382. 2010; Supplement(s): Poker 52. Hors-serie. ISSN 2109-5078. 2010.
Published by: Game Prod, 14 Rue de Berri, Paris, 75008, France. TEL 33-9-77217475, info@poker52.fr, http://www.poker52.fr.

790.1 USA
POKER DIGEST. Text in English. bi-w. USD 69 domestic; USD 139 foreign (effective 2001). adv. back issues avail. **Document type:** *Magazine, Consumer.* **Description:** Contains stories covering all aspects of poker, interviews with players, and a complete up-to-date listing of tournaments around the world.
Address: 5240 S. Eastern Ave., # A, Las Vegas, NV 89119-2306. TEL 702-740-2273, FAX 702-740-2257, http://www.pokerdigest.com. Pub. June Field.

795.412 USA ISSN 1556-3812
POKER LIFE; where pros come to play. Text in English. 2005. q. USD 15.99; USD 4.99 newsstand/cover (effective 2007). adv. **Document type:** *Magazine, Consumer.*
Published by: Poker Life Magazine, LLC, 366 Park Ave S., 16th Fl, New York, NY 10016. TEL 212-481-1005, FAX 212-481-1009. Ed. Michael Jacobson. Adv. contact Robert Cole TEL 561-304-0951. color page USD 15,800; trim 8.75 x 10.8125.

795.4 USA
POKER PAGES. Text in English. d. back issues avail. **Document type:** *Newsletter.*
Media: Online - full text.
Published by: Poker Pages Press, 3530 Bee Caves Rd, Ste 110, Austin, TX 78746. TEL 512-306-1355, FAX 512-306-0302.

790.1 USA
POKER PLAYER. Text in English. 1981-198?; resumed 2003 (Jun.). bi-w. USD 3.95 newsstand/cover (effective 2004); dist. free to card rooms. **Document type:** *Magazine, Consumer.* **Description:** Presents news and views about playing poker, including tournament news and strategy.
Incorporates: Pan Player Plus
Related titles: Online - full content ed.
Published by: Gambling Times, Inc., 3883 W. Century Blvd., # 608, Inglewood, CA 90303-1003. TEL 310-674-3365.

795.412 USA ISSN 1555-2896
POKER PRO. Text in English. 2005. m. USD 24.95 (effective 2009). **Document type:** *Magazine, Consumer.*
Published by: Poker Pro Media, PO Box 480416, Delray Beach, FL 33448. FAX 561-470-0761. Ed. John Wenzel. Pub. Dan Jacobs.

795.412 USA ISSN 1078-0793
POKER TIPS. Text in English. 1984. bi-m. looseleaf. USD 10 (effective 2000). adv. bk.rev. back issues avail. **Description:** Aimed at home, private club and casino poker players, with emphasis on pokertournaments.
Published by: International Home & Private Poker Players' Association, 220 E Flamingo Rd, Apt 127, Las Vegas, NV 89109. TEL 702-893-9851. Ed., Pub., R&P, Adv. contact Edwin E Wuehel. Circ: 300.

796 POL ISSN 1899-1998
POLISH JOURNAL OF SPORT AND TOURISM. Text in English. 1995. a. **Document type:** *Journal, Academic/Scholarly.*
Former titles (until 2007): Akademia Wychowania Fizycznego Jozefa Pilsudskiego w Warszawie. Zamiejscowy Wydzial Wychowania Fizycznego w Bialej Podlaskiej. Rocznik Naukowy (2080-8585); (until 2000): Akademia Wychowania Fizycznego Jozefa Pilsudskiego w Warszawie. Instytut Wychowania Fizycznego i Sportu w Bialej Podlaskiej. Rocznik Naukowy (1425-3259)
Related titles: Online - full text ed.: ISSN 2082-8799. free (effective 2011).
Indexed: A36, E12, F08, N03, S13, W11.
Published by: Akademia Wychowania Fizycznego Jozefa Pilsudskiego w Warszawie, ul Marymoncka 34, Warsaw, 00968, Poland. TEL 48-22-8340431, FAX 48-22-8640646, bwz@awf.edu.pl, http://www.awf.edu.pl.

796 NOR ISSN 0032-3357
POLITIIDRETT. Text in Norwegian. 1963. bi-m. adv. **Document type:** *Magazine, Consumer.*
Published by: Norges Politiidrettsforbund/Norwegian Police Athletic and Sports Association, PO Box 711, Hafslundsoey, 1733, Norway. TEL 47-69-149356, FAX 47-69-149907, kontor@politiidrett.no, http://www.politiidrett.no. Ed. Knut Alme TEL 47-22-579768.

790.1 USA
POLO PLAYERS' EDITION. Text in English. 19??. m. USD 45 domestic; USD 61.42 in Canada; USD 78 elsewhere (effective 2010). adv. **Document type:** *Magazine, Consumer.*
Published by: Rizzo Management Corp., 9011 Lake Worth Rd, Ste B, Lake Worth, FL 33467. TEL 561-968-5208, FAX 561-968-5209. Ed., Pub. Gwen Rizzo. adv.: color page USD 1,560, B&W page USD 1,240; trim 8 x 10.75.

POOL & SPA MARKETING. *see* BUSINESS AND ECONOMICS—Marketing And Purchasing

797.2 GBR ISSN 2043-9369
▼ **POOL & SPA SCENE.** Text in English. 2010. bi-m. adv. **Document type:** *Magazine, Trade.*
Published by: Waterland Publishing Ltd., Waterland House, The Warren, Witchford, Ely, Cambridgeshire CB6 2HN, United Kingdom. TEL 44-1353-666663, FAX 44-1353-666664, info@thewaterlandgroup.com, http://www.thewaterlandgroup.com/sites/w/waterland/index.php?section=28&page=380. Ed. Christina Connor. adv.: page GBP 1,050; 216 x 303.

796.2 USA
POOL DUST; the Northwest's skateboarding magazine. Text in English. 1989. a. USD 6; USD 2 newsstand/cover (effective 1999). adv. music rev. **Document type:** *Newspaper, Consumer.* **Description:** Includes travel, skateboarding contests, punk rock music, and bachelor of the month.
Address: PO Box 85664, Seattle, WA 98145-1664. TEL 206-547-4756. Ed., Adv. contact Chris Lundry. page USD 100; trim 10.5 x 8. Circ: 5,000 (controlled).

POOL LIFE. *see* HOW-TO AND DO-IT-YOURSELF

POPULAR HOT RODDING. *see* TRANSPORTATION—Automobiles

PORSCHE PANORAMA. *see* TRANSPORTATION—Automobiles

796 CHL ISSN 0718-4921
PORTAL DEPORTIVO. Text in Spanish. 2007. bi-m.
Media: Online - full text.
Address: info@portaldeportivo.cl. Ed. Felipe Areyuna.

790.1 USA
PORTLAND SPORTS PLANNER. Text in English. q.
Published by: Price Media Inc., 11715 Greenwood Ave N, Seattle, WA 98133. TEL 206-418-0747, FAX 206-418-0746, staff@sportsetc.com, http://www.sportsetc.com.

797.21 AUS
PORTSEA BOOMER. Text in English. 1949. m. adv. illus. back issues avail. **Document type:** *Newsletter, Trade.* **Description:** Articles on surf lifesaving.
Former titles (until 19??): Boomer; (until 1956): Sorrento-Portsea Surf Life Saving Club
Related titles: Microform ed.
Published by: Portsea Surf Life Saving Club Ltd., PO Box 270, Carnegie, VIC 3163, Australia. ian.campbell@portseasurf.com.au, http://www.portseasurf.com.au/. Circ: 1,500.

796 USA
POST (PHOENIX). Text in English. 2005. m. USD 29.50 (effective 2005). adv. **Document type:** *Magazine, Consumer.* **Description:** Covers Phoenix sports celebrities, personalities and the sports lifestyle.
Address: 2415 E. Camelback Rd., Ste. 700, Phoenix, AZ 85016. TEL 602-508-6020, FAX 602-508-6099. Ed. Tom Zenner. Pub. Rich Purscell. adv.: page USD 5,980; bleed 10.125 x 12.25. Circ: 50,000.

794.1 NOR
POSTSJAKK. Text in Norwegian. 1945. 6/yr. NOK 200, USD 30. adv. bk.rev. **Description:** Includes annotated correspondence chess games, theory, national and international correspondence chess news.
Published by: Norges Postsjakkforbund/Norwegian Correspondence Chess Federation, Unni Kvil Nordal, Tangenveien 101, Nesoddtangen, 1450, Norway. Ed. Oeystein Sande.

793 GBR ISSN 0268-2109
POT BLACK MAGAZINE. Text in English. 1987. m. GBP 26.20; GBP 2.20 newsstand/cover (effective 1999). back issues avail. **Document type:** *Magazine, Consumer.*
Formerly: Pot Black Snooker Magazine
Published by: W P B S A (Promotions) Ltd., 27 Oakfield Rd, Clifton, Bristol BS8 2AT, United Kingdom. TEL 44-117-974-4491. Ed. Brian Radford. R&P, Adv. contact Tony Riley. page GBP 845; trim 210 x 297. Circ: 20,000 (paid). **Subscr. to:** Tony Riley, Trafalgar House, Grenville Pl, Mill Hill, London NW73, United Kingdom. TEL 44-181-959-3611, FAX 44-181-959-8492. **Dist. by:** Comag, Tavistock Rd, W Drayton, Middlesex UB7 7QE, United Kingdom. TEL 44-1895-433600, FAX 44-189-543-3606.

796 DEU ISSN 1611-4922
POTSDAMER STUDIEN ZUR GESCHICHTE VON SPORT UND GESUNDHEIT. Text in German. 2003. irreg., latest vol.2, 2005. price varies. **Document type:** *Monographic series, Academic/Scholarly.*
Published by: Universitaetsverlag Potsdam, Am Neuen Palais 10, Potsdam, 14469, Germany. TEL 49-331-9774458, FAX 49-331-9774625, ubpub@uni-potsdam.de, http://info.ub.uni-potsdam.de/verlag.htm.

790.1 USA
POWER HOTLINE. Text in English. 1981. s-m. USD 28 (effective 2000).
Published by: Powerlifting U S A, PO Box 467, Camarillo, CA 93011. TEL 805-482-2378. Ed. M Lambert. Circ: 280.

796.72 SWE ISSN 0348-5900
POWER MAGAZINE. Text in Swedish. 1976. bi-m. SEK 249 (effective 2005). adv. **Document type:** *Magazine, Consumer.*
Formerly (until 1978): Power (0347-688X)
Published by: Hjemmet Mortensen AB (Subsidiary of: Hjemmet-Mortensen AS), Gaevlegatan 22, Stockholm, 11378, Sweden. TEL 46-8-6920100, FAX 46-8-6509705, info@hjemmetmortensen.se, http://www.hjemmetmortensen.se. Ed. Kjell Gustafson TEL 46-40-472939. Adv. contact Erik Stigsson TEL 46-18227773. B&W page SEK 9,200, color page SEK 12,850; 184 x 260. Circ: 31,170.

793 ARG ISSN 1851-3875
POWER SOPA DE LETRAS. Text in Spanish. 2007. m.
Published by: M4 Editora, San Pedro 140, Avellanada, Buenos Aires, 1870, Argentina. m4editora@speedy.com.ar.

790.1 USA ISSN 1044-6559
POWEREDGE MAGAZINE. Text in English. 1988. m. USD 2.95 per issue. **Description:** Features the best in the field of skateboarding.
Published by: Power Edge Group, 4201 W Van Owen Pl, Burbank, CA 91505. TEL 213-769-6777.

790.1 USA ISSN 0199-8536
POWERLIFTING U S A. Text in English. 1977. m. USD 31.95 (effective 2000). adv. bk.rev. illus. reprints avail.
Indexed: SD, SportS.
Address: PO Box 467, Camarillo, CA 93011. TEL 805-482-2378. Ed. Mike Lambert. Circ: 17,600.

796.962 GBR
POWERPLAY. Text in English. 1992. w. GBP 44; GBP 66 in United States. adv. bk.rev. back issues avail. **Document type:** *Magazine, Consumer.*
Published by: Powerplay Publications, PO Box 140, Peterborough, Cambs PE1 2XT, United Kingdom. TEL 44-1733-340196, FAX 44-1733-315326. Ed., R&P, Adv. contact Simon Potter. Circ: 6,000.

PRAIRIE CLUB BULLETIN; organized for the promotion of outdoor recreation in the form of walks, outings, camping and canoeing. *see* CONSERVATION

793.7 LVA
PRATNIEKS. Text in Latvian. 1999. m. LVL 0.49 newsstand/cover (effective 2005). **Document type:** *Magazine, Consumer.*
Published by: SIA Kuma, Rinuzu Iela 22-44, Riga, 1015, Latvia. TEL 371-7342879, FAX 371-7342879, kuma@kuma.lv. Ed. Inara Ratnik. Pub. Aida Luts.

S

▼ **PRAXISWISSEN SPORTVEREIN & MANAGEMENT.** *see* BUSINESS AND ECONOMICS—Management

799 USA ISSN 0048-5144
PRECISION SHOOTING; dealing exclusively with extreme rifle accuracy. Text in English. 1956. m. USD 37; USD 3.95 newsstand/cover (effective 2006). adv. bk.rev. charts; illus.; tr.lit. 116 p./no.; back issues avail.; reprints avail. **Document type:** *Magazine, Consumer.* **Description:** Focuses on the subject of extreme rifle accuracy in the target shooting disciplines.
Indexed: SportS.
Published by: Precision Shooting, Inc., 222 McKee St, Manchester, CT 06040. TEL 860-645-8776, FAX 860-643-8215. Ed., Pub., R&P David D Brennan. Adv. contact Kim Woble. B&W page USD 490, color page USD 1,000; 8.5 x 11. Circ: 18,000 (paid).

795 USA ISSN 0199-0705
THE PREDICAMENT. Text in English. 1970. 10/yr. (Aug.-May). USD 25 (effective 2005). adv. bk.rev. illus.; tr.lit. back issues avail. **Document type:** *Newspaper, Consumer.* **Description:** Covers high school, kids, international and college wresting.
Related titles: Online - full text ed.: USD 20 (effective 2005).
Published by: Predicament, Inc., PO Box 14, Osceola, IA 50213. TEL 641-414-1962, FAX 641-342-2060. Pub., Adv. contact Matt Pfiffner. Circ: 2,600.

688.76 USA
PREP STARS RECRUITER'S HANDBOOK. Text in English. 1991. q. (May, June, Sep., Dec.). USD 30; USD 60.95 combined subscription print & online eds.; USD 7.50 newsstand/cover print & online eds. (effective 2005). **Document type:** *Magazine, Trade.*
Related titles: Online - full text ed.: USD 49.95 (effective 2005).
Published by: A C C Sports.com, P O Box 4323, Chapel Hill, NC 27515-4323. TEL 800-447-7667, FAX 919-967-7667. Ed. Dave Glenn. Pub. Dennis Wuycik. Circ: 8,000 (paid and free).

790.1 CAN
PRESTIGE (PIEDMOND). Text in English. 1992. 2/yr. CAD 5.90; CAD 6.40 foreign. **Document type:** *Journal, Consumer.*
Published by: Nowak Publishing, 291 De La Corniche, C P 451, Piedmont, PQ J0R 1K0, Canada. TEL 514-497-1962, FAX 514-227-3089. adv.: B&W page CAD 3,350, color page CAD 8,350; trim 10.75 x 8.5. Circ: 72,500.

790.1 USA
PRIME TIME SPORTS & FITNESS; fitness and club sports. Text in English. 1974. 10/yr. USD 22; USD 4 newsstand/cover (effective 2007). bk.rev.; dance rev.; film rev.; music rev.; play rev.; rec.rev.; software rev.; tel.rev.; video rev.; Website rev. tr.mk. 80 p./no.; **Document type:** *Magazine, Consumer.* **Description:** Covers club fitness and sports, including tennis, paddleball, racquetball, squash, running, and skiing.
Published by: G N D Prime Time Publishing, Box 6097, Evanston, IL 60204. TEL 847-784-1195, FAX 847-784-1194, http://www.bowldtalk.com. Ed. Dennis A Dorner. Adv. contact Steve Vry TEL 847-784-1194. Circ: 39,400 (paid).

794 ESP
▼ **PRIMER ASALTO.** Text in Spanish. 2009. bi-m. **Document type:** *Magazine, Consumer.*
Published by: Federacion Espanola Boxeo, Ferraz, 16, Madrid, 28008, Spain. TEL 34-91-5477791, FAX 34-91-5474297, info@feboxeo.com, http://www.feboxeo.com/.

799 USA ISSN 1089-4268
PRIMITIVE ARCHER. Text in English. 199?. 5/yr. USD 24 domestic; USD 32 in Canada; USD 34 elsewhere (effective 2005). adv. back issues avail. **Document type:** *Magazine, Consumer.* **Description:** Covers the history of archery, including how to information and hunting with more traditional bows such as the longbow.
Published by: Bigger Than That Productions LLC, PO Box 79306, Houston, TX 77279. Ed. Ed Ingold. Pub. Michael M Moore. Adv. contact Ernie Brown. B&W page USD 1,591; 7.25 x 9.75.

793 USA ISSN 1949-3266
▼ **PRINCES IN THE TOWER.** Text in English. forthcoming 2011 (Mar.). bi-m. free (effective 2011). **Document type:** *Magazine, Consumer.* **Description:** A role-playing zine covering Savage Worlds, Fringeworthy and other campaign designs.
Media: Online - full text.
Published by: Wooden Leg Named Smith Publications, PO Box 515, Woodinville, WA 98072. TEL 206-579-6586, 1001nightsand1night@gmail.com.

791.84 USA ISSN 1098-495X
GV1834.45.B84
PRO BULL RIDER. Abbreviated title: P B R. Text in English. 1995. bi-m. USD 19.95; USD 3.99 newsstand/cover (effective 2005). adv. Supplement avail.; reprints avail. **Document type:** *Magazine, Trade.* **Description:** Provides its readers with entertaining, informative feature stories, departments and columns.
Related titles: Online - full text ed.
Published by: (Professional Bull Riders, Inc.), Grand View Media Group, Inc. (Subsidiary of: EBSCO Industries, Inc.), 200 Croft St, Ste 1, Birmingham, AL 35242. TEL 888-431-2877, FAX 205-408-3797, webmaster@grandviewmedia.com. Ed. Jeff Johnstone. Pub. Derrick Nawrocki TEL 205-408-3732. adv.: color page USD 4,895, B&W page USD 3,920; trim 7.75 x 10.625. Circ: 45,000.

796.962 FIN ISSN 1457-7844
PRO HOCKEY; Euroopan suurin NHL-lehti. Text in Finnish. 1995. 10/yr. adv. **Document type:** *Magazine, Consumer.*
Formerly (until 1998): Inside Hockey (1237-9417)
Published by: Egmont Kustannus Oy, PO Box 317, Tampere, 33101, Finland. TEL 358-201-332222, FAX 358-201-332278, info@egmont-kustannus.fi, http://www.egmont-kustannus.fi. Adv. contact Tommy Tenhunen TEL 358-201-332266. page EUR 800; 210 x 297. Circ: 8,000.

796.966 CZE ISSN 1212-3986
PRO HOCKEY. Text in Czech. 1999. 10/yr. CZK 553 (effective 2011). adv. **Document type:** *Magazine, Consumer.*
Published by: Egmont CR s.r.o., Zirovnicka 3124, Prague 10, 10600, Czech Republic. TEL 420-224-800751, FAX 420-272-770044, egmontcr@egmont.cz. Adv. contact Ratislav Packo. Circ: 19,000 (paid and controlled).

796.966 SWE ISSN 1103-1239
PRO HOCKEY. Text in Swedish. 1993. 10/yr. SEK 489 (effective 2009). adv. **Document type:** *Magazine, Consumer.*
Published by: Egmont Serieforlaget AB, Stora Varvsgatan 19A, Malmo, 20507, Sweden. TEL 46-40-385200, FAX 46-40-385396, tord.joensson@egmont.se, http://www.egmont.se. adv.: color page SEK 20,900; trim 210 x 297. Circ: 40,000 (controlled).

079.948 796 ROM ISSN 1453-3707
PRO SPORT. Text in Romanian. 1997. d. ROL 150,000 per month (effective 2006). adv. **Document type:** *Newspaper, Consumer.*
Related titles: Online - full text ed.
Address: Fabrica de Glucoza nr 5, Sector 2, Bucharest, Romania. TEL 40-21-2093334, FAX 40-21-2093350. Circ: 63,500 (paid and controlled).

796.812 USA ISSN 1043-7576
PRO WRESTLING ILLUSTRATED. Abbreviated title: P W I. Text in English. 1979. m. USD 54.20 domestic; USD 87.20 in Canada & Mexico; USD 144.20 elsewhere; USD 8.95 per issue (effective 2009). adv. illus. back issues avail. **Document type:** *Magazine, Consumer.* **Description:** Designed to set a standard for excellence in wrestling journalism and photography.
Related titles: Online - full text ed.
Published by: Sports & Entertainment Publications, LLC, 6198 Butler Pike, Ste 200, Blue Bell, PA 19422. TEL 215-461-0583, FAX 215-643-3176, custsrvcsep@sepublications.com. Ed. Frank Krewda. Pub. Stu Saks.

790.1 USA
PRO WRESTLING ILLUSTRATED PRESENTS WRESTLING ANNUAL (YEAR). Text in English. 19??. a.
Published by: London Publishing Co. (Subsidiary of: Kappa Publishing Group, Inc.), 6198 Butler Pike, Ste 200, Blue Bell, PA 19422. TEL 215-643-6385, FAX 315-628-3571, custsrvc@kappapublishing.com, http://www.kappapublishing.com. **Dist. by:** Curtis CIRC Company.

794.1 367 790.13 GBR ISSN 0032-9398
THE PROBLEMIST. Text in English. 1926. bi-m. free to members (effective 2009). bk.rev. illus. index, cum.index every 2 yrs. 46 p./no. 2 cols./p.; back issues avail. **Document type:** *Magazine, Academic/Scholarly.* **Description:** Contains original chess problems, composing and solving competitions, end-game studies, and articles by leading problemists.
Published by: British Chess Problem Society, c/o Sally Lewis, 16 Cranford Close, Woodmancote, Cheltenham, Glos GL52 9QA, United Kingdom. TEL 44-1242-672865, cjajones1@yahoo.co.uk, http://www.theproblemist.org. Circ: 700 (paid and controlled).

796.72 GBR ISSN 1748-9296
PROFESSIONAL MOTORSPORT WORLD. Abbreviated title: P M W. Text in English. 2006. q. free (effective 2009). back issues avail. **Document type:** *Magazine, Trade.* **Description:** Covers the full spectrum of motorsport technology, issues, politics and strategies, and the general business of operating in the motorsport arena. It will highlight the latest products and services in transportation and logistics, paddock equipment and tooling, metrology, data capture, communications and testing.
Related titles: Online - full text ed.
Published by: U K I P Media & Events Ltd. (Subsidiary of: AutoIntermediates Ltd.), Abinger House, Church St, Dorking, Surrey RH4 1DF, United Kingdom. TEL 44-1306-743744, FAX 44-1306-887546, info@ukintpress.com, http://www.ukipme.com. Ed. Graham Heeps. Adv. contact Nick Barr.

PROFESSIONAL SPORTS WIVES. *see* WOMEN'S INTERESTS

796.812 JPN
PROFESSIONAL WRESTLING SHU-KAN. Text in Japanese. 1972. w. JPY 22,950 (effective 2000).
Published by: Baseball Magazine Sha, 3-10-10 Misaki-cho, Chiyoda-ku, Tokyo, 101-0061, Japan. FAX 81-3-3238-0106. Ed. Yoshinori Hamabe.

791.8 798.2 USA ISSN 0161-5815
PRORODEO SPORTS NEWS. Abbreviated title: P S N. Text in English. 1952. bi-w. USD 37 domestic; USD 48 foreign (effective 2007). adv. bk.rev. charts; illus.; stat.; tr.lit. Supplement avail. **Document type:** *Magazine, Trade.* **Description:** Current news about professional rodeo for fans and contestants.
Formerly (until vol.26, no.11, Apr. 1978): Rodeo Sports News (0035-7758)
Published by: Professional Rodeo Cowboy Association, 101 Pro Rodeo Dr, Colorado Spings, CO 80919. TEL 719-593-8840, FAX 719-548-4889. Eds. Troy Schwindt, Mike Spencer. Adv. contact Blaine Santos. B&W page USD 1,680, color page USD 2,465. Circ: 30,000 (paid).

790.1 CAN ISSN 1711-7496
PROSPECTS. Text in English. 1983. 4/yr. adv.
Formerly (until 2003): O H L News (1185-037X)
Published by: Ontario Hockey League, 305 Milner Ave, Ste 200, Scarborough, ON M1B 3V4, Canada. TEL 416-299-8700, FAX 416-299-8787, dbranch@chl.ca, http://www.ontariohockeyleague.com. Circ: 40,000.

796 RUS
PROSPORT. Text in Russian. 2003. m. USD 25.70 domestic; USD 119 foreign (effective 2005). adv. **Document type:** *Magazine, Consumer.*
Published by: Independent Media (Moscow), 3 Polkovaya Ul, Bldg 1, Moscow, 127018, Russian Federation. TEL 7-095-2323200, FAX 7-095-2321761, podpiska@imedia.ru, http://www.independent-media.ru. Ed. Stanislaw Gridasov. Circ: 60,000.

790.1 POL ISSN 0137-9267
PRZEGLAD SPORTOWY. Text in Polish. 1921. 5/w. adv. illus. **Document type:** *Newspaper, Consumer.*
Related titles: Online - full text ed.: ISSN 1689-2879.
Published by: J M G Sport Publishing (Subsidiary of: Marquard Media AG), ul Nowogrodzka 84-86, Warsaw, 02-018, Poland. TEL 48-22-6289116, FAX 48-22-6218697, redakcja@przeglad.com.pl. Circ: 95,000.

PRZYSLIJ PRZEPIS! KRZYZOWKI. *see* HOME ECONOMICS

793 USA ISSN 1042-1912
HG6111
PUBLIC GAMING INTERNATIONAL. Text in English. 1974. m. USD 145 domestic; USD 165 in Canada & Mexico; USD 225 elsewhere (effective 2005). adv.
Formerly: Public Gaming Magazine
Published by: Public Gaming Research Institute, 4020 Lake Washington Blvd, Ste. 100, NE Kirkland, WA 98033. Ed. Kathleen Ward. Pub. Sharon Sharp. Adv. contact David Mello. Circ: 15,000.

790.1 USA
PULL. Text in English. 1978. a. USD 5 (effective 1999). adv. **Document type:** *Magazine, Consumer.*
Published by: World Pulling International, Inc., 6155-B Huntley Rd, Worthington, OH 43229. TEL 614-436-1761, FAX 614-436-0964, gregg@ntpapull.com. Ed., R&P Rhdawnda Bliss. Adv. contact Gregs Dion. Circ: 20,000.

790.1 USA ISSN 8750-4219
THE PULLER. Text in English. 1971. m. USD 32.95 (effective 2005). adv. 48 p./no. 3 cols./p.; back issues avail. **Document type:** *Magazine, Consumer.*
Published by: World Pulling International, Inc., 6155-B Huntley Rd, Worthington, OH 43229. TEL 614-436-1761, FAX 614-436-0964. Ed. Greg Randall. Adv. contact Gregs Dion. Circ: 6,000.

PURE POWER; when training + science = peak performance. *see* PHYSICAL FITNESS AND HYGIENE

PUZZLER ANNUAL. *see* HOBBIES

793 USA ISSN 1070-0579
PYRAMID (ONLINE). Text in English. 1993. m. USD 70 (effective 2011). adv. illus. **Document type:** *Magazine, Consumer.* **Description:** Covers all adventure and card games, including wargames.
Formerly (until 2010): Pyramid (Print); Which was formed by the merger of (1983-1993): Autoduel Quarterly (0740-3356); (1986-1993): Roleplayer (1050-3609)
Media: Online - full text.
Published by: Steve Jackson Games, Inc., PO Box 18957, Austin, TX 78760. TEL 512-447-7866, FAX 512-447-1144. Ed. Steven Marsh.

794.18 CHN
QIYI/NORTHERN CHESS. Text in Chinese. 1979. s-m. USD 36 (effective 2009). **Document type:** *Magazine, Consumer.*
Formerly (until 1997): Beifang Qiyi/Northern Chess (1000-7679)
Related titles: Online - full text ed.
—East View.
Published by: Dangdai Tiyu Zazhishe, 99 Xuanxua Jie, Nangang-qu, Harbin, Heilongjiang 150001, China. TEL 86-451-82515914 ext 8007, FAX 86-451-82526535 ext 8003.

796.72 FRA ISSN 1779-0581
QUAD PRATIQUE. Text in French. 200?. bi-m. EUR 25 (effective 2009). **Document type:** *Magazine, Consumer.*
Published by: Editions Lariviere, 6 Rue Olof Palme, Clichy, 92587, France. TEL 33-1-47565400, http://www.editions-lariviere.fr.

796 ESP ISSN 2013-4231
▼ **QUADERNS DEL "CASTELLER".** Text in Catalan. 2009. q. back issues avail. **Document type:** *Bulletin, Consumer.*
Media: Online - full text.
Published by: Casteller jclif@elcasteller.cat.

796 GBR ISSN 1939-8441
GV557
▼ **QUALITATIVE RESEARCH IN SPORT AND EXERCISE.** Text in English. 2009 (Apr.). 3/yr. GBP 315 combined subscription in United Kingdom to institutions (print & online eds.); EUR 503, USD 630 combined subscription to institutions (print & online eds.) (effective 2012). adv. reprints avail. **Document type:** *Journal, Academic/Scholarly.* **Description:** Provides a forum for qualitative researchers within all the social scientific areas of sport and exercise the journal offers researchers, practitioners, and students' access to cutting edge inquiry, scholarly dialogues, and the latest developments in qualitative methodologies and methods.
Related titles: Online - full content ed.: ISSN 1939-845X. GBP 283 in United Kingdom to institutions; EUR 453, USD 567 to institutions (effective 2012).
Indexed: CA, P10, PEI, PQC, SD, T02.
—CCC.
Published by: Routledge (Subsidiary of: Taylor & Francis Group), 4 Park Sq, Milton Park, Abingdon, Oxon OX14 4RN, United Kingdom. TEL 44-20-70176000, FAX 44-20-70176336, subscriptions@tandf.co.uk, http://www.routledge.com. Eds. Brett Smith, David Gilbourne. Adv. contact Linda Hann TEL 44-1344-779945. **Subscr. to:** Taylor & Francis Ltd., Journals Customer Service, Sheepen Pl, Colchester, Essex CO3 3LP, United Kingdom. TEL 44-20-70175544, FAX 44-20-70175198, tf.enquiries@tfinforma.com.

796.8 CHN ISSN 1002-7475
QUANJI YU GEDOU/BOXING AND FIGHT. Text in Chinese. 1987. m. **Document type:** *Magazine, Consumer.*
Published by: Quanji yu Gedou Zazhishe, 1571, Renmin Dajie, Changchun, 130051, China. TEL 86-431-7904033, FAX 86-431-2725021.

796 CHN ISSN 1672-4240
QUANTIYU/ALL SPORTS. Text in Chinese. 2003. s-m. CNY 180; CNY 15 per issue (effective 2010).
Published by: Titan Chuanmei Jituan/Titan Culture - Express Co, ltd, Donghuashi Dajie Bei-li Xi-qu #22, Chongwen-qu, Beijing, 100062, China. TEL 86-10-51005876, http://www.titan24.com/.

799.202 USA
QUICKSHOTS. Text in English. 1994. m. USD 25 membership (effective 2000). adv. illus. **Document type:** *Newsletter.* **Description:** Serves as the official newsletter of the national governing body for Olympic shooting sports in the U.S. Aimed at international shooters, coaches, officials and media who cover Olympic style shooting.
Published by: U S A Shooting, 1 Olympic Plaza, Colorado Springs, CO 80909. TEL 719-578-4670, FAX 719-635-7989, heather.addison@usashooting.org, http://www.usashooting.com. Ed. Robert K Mitchell. R&P, Adv. contact Gayle King TEL 719-578-4880. Circ: 3,700 (controlled).

793 USA
THE QUIZ QUEEN. Text in English. 1999. w. adv. Website rev. back issues avail. **Document type:** *Newsletter.*
Media: Online - full content. **Related titles:** E-mail ed.
Published by: Dawggone Communications, 150 University Blvd., Morehead, KY 40351-1684. Ed., Pub. Deanna Mascle. Circ: 1,700.

QUONDAM MAGAZINE. *see* CLUBS

796 ITA ISSN 1825-7453
QUOTIDIANO SPORTIVO. Abbreviated title: Q S. Text in Italian. 2005. d. **Document type:** *Newspaper, Consumer.*
Published by: Poligrafici Editoriale (Subsidiary of: Monrif Group), Via Enrico Mattei 106, Bologna, BO 40138, Italy. TEL 39-051-6006111, FAX 39-051-6006266.

R & R - A F N CABLE & SATELLITE T V. (Rest & Relaxation) *see* COMMUNICATIONS—Television And Cable

796.154 USA ISSN 1559-7903
R C HELI. (Radio Control) Text in English. 2005. bi-m. USD 24.99 to individuals (effective 2007). adv. **Document type:** *Magazine, Consumer.* **Description:** Features models and equipment information for radio control helicopter enthusiasts.
Related titles: Online - full text ed.
Published by: Think Omnimedia LLC, 2000 S. Grove Ave #111-A, Ontario, CA 91761-4804. TEL 909-947-5626, FAX 909-947-8165. Ed. Mike Velez.

R E D. REVISTA DE ENTRENAMIENTO DEPORTIVO. *see* PHYSICAL FITNESS AND HYGIENE

796 797 798 799 ESP ISSN 1885-3137
GV557
➤ **R I C Y D E - REVISTA INTERNACIONAL DE CIENCIAS DEL DEPORTE/R I C Y D E - INTERNATIONAL JOURNAL OF SPORT SCIENCE.** Text in Spanish, English. 2005. q. free (effective 2011). back issues avail. **Document type:** *Journal, Academic/Scholarly.*
Media: Online - full text.
Indexed: A36, CA, CABA, F04, GH, LT, N02, N03, P03, P30, PsycInfo, R12, RRTA, SD, T02, W11. Ed., Pub. Ramon Canto Alcaraz.

796.72 NLD ISSN 1875-4430
R T L G P MAGAZINE. (Radio Televisie Luxemburg Grand Prix) Text in Dutch. 2007. bi-m. EUR 35; EUR 6.95 newsstand/cover (effective 2009). adv. **Document type:** *Magazine, Consumer.*
Published by: Formula Once Publishing BV, Lijndenweg 25a, Postbus 154, Beverwijk, 1940 AD, Netherlands. TEL 31-25-1212104, FAX 31-25-1212390, info@formula-once.nl, http://www.formula-once.nl. adv.: page EUR 2,500; trim 230 x 297. Circ: 50,000.

793 DEU
R T V RAETSEL. (Radio Television) Text in German. bi-m. EUR 1.80 newsstand/cover (effective 2009). adv. **Document type:** *Magazine, Consumer.*
Published by: RTV Media Group GmbH, Breslauer Str 300, Nuernberg, 90471, Germany. TEL 0911-89201-0, FAX 0911-8920135. Adv. contact Annelore Rupp. Circ: 120,000 (paid and controlled).

R V NEWS (ONLINE); the voice of the R V industry. (Recreational Vehicle) *see* TRANSPORTATION

797 GBR ISSN 2044-172X
R Y A MEMBERS' MAGAZINE. Text in English. 1975. q. free to members (effective 2010). adv. bk.rev. **Document type:** *Magazine, Trade.* **Description:** Covers all aspects of boating spectrum.
Former titles (until 2009): R Y A Magazine (1473-7736); (until 199?): R Y A News (0308-5295)
Indexed: SD, SportS.
Published by: Royal Yachting Association, RYA House, Ensign Way, Hamble, Southampton, Hampshire SO31 4YA, United Kingdom. TEL 44-23-80604100, FAX 44-23-80604299, http://www.rya.org.uk/.

R - ZONE. *see* CHILDREN AND YOUTH—For

796.72 USA ISSN 1066-6060
RACER; racing news from the world over. Text in English. 1992. m. USD 49.95 domestic; USD 74.95 in Canada; USD 99.95 elsewhere (effective 2010). adv. Supplement avail.; back issues avail. **Document type:** *Magazine, Consumer.* **Description:** Covers major league auto racing people, technology and events.
Related titles: Online - full text ed.
Indexed: G06, G07, G08, I05, I07, P48, PQC.
—CCC.
Published by: Haymarket Worldwide Inc. (Subsidiary of: Haymarket Media Inc.), 16842 Von Karman Ave, Ste 125, Irvine, CA 92606. TEL 949-417 6711, http://www.haymarketnetwork.com. Pub. Ian Howard. Adv. contact Rick Nitti TEL 949-417-6734. B&W page GBP 3,150, color page GBP 3,995; trim 8.5 x 10.875.

796.71 BRA ISSN 1413-8913
RACING. Text in Portuguese. 1996. m. BRL 3.90 newsstand/cover (effective 2001). adv. **Document type:** *Magazine, Consumer.*
Published by: MotorPress Brasil (Subsidiary of: Gruner + Jahr AG & Co), Rua Benjamin Mota 86, Sao Paulo, SP 04727-070, Brazil. TEL 55-11-56413454, FAX 55-11-56413858. Ed. Americo Teixera. Pubs. Isabel Reis, Sergio Quintanilha. Adv. contact Dario Castilho. Circ: 9,000 (paid).

796.72 NOR ISSN 1503-8696
RACING; Norges motorsportavis. Text in Norwegian. 1986. 39/yr. NOK 798 (effective 2004). adv. **Document type:** *Newspaper, Consumer.*
Former titles (until 2004): Racingavisa (1503-4917); (until 2003): Racing (0802-7293); Which incorporated (1979-1985): Motorsport (0332-8953)
Related titles: Online - full text ed.
Published by: (Norsk Motor Klubb, Norges Bilsport Forbund), Sportsmedia AS, Myrveien 3, PO Box A, Askim, 1801, Norway. TEL 47-69-819700, FAX 47-69-889980, kontaktoss@motorsport.no, http://www.sportsmedia.no. Eds. Kari Nilsen, Erik Unaas. Adv. contact Terje Lund Olsen TEL 47-69-819706.

796.72 NLD ISSN 1574-8243
RACING ACTUEEL. Text in Dutch. 2004. 6/yr. EUR 38 domestic; EUR 45 foreign (effective 2009). adv.
Address: Klapsterweg 74, Woldendorp, 9946 PK, Netherlands. TEL 31-6-21472185, 31-596-601985.

796 GBR ISSN 0033-7366
RACING & FOOTBALL OUTLOOK. Text in English. 1909. m. GBP 50.93 (effective 2009). adv. bk.rev. **Document type:** *Newsletter, Consumer.* **Description:** Contains winner-finding information pinpointing the best bets for racing, football and other sports.
Related titles: ◆ Supplement(s): Racing & Football Outlook: Racing Annual. ISSN 0955-775X.
Published by: Raceform Ltd. (Subsidiary of: Trinity Mirror Plc.), High St, Compton, Newbury, Berks RG20 6NL, United Kingdom. TEL 44-1635-578080, FAX 44-1635-578101, feedback@raceform.co.uk, http://www.raceform.co.uk. Circ: 57,059.

796 GBR ISSN 1753-3341
RACING & FOOTBALL OUTLOOK FOOTBALL GUIDE (YEARS). Text in English. 1912. a. GBP 6.99 per issue (effective 2009). adv. **Document type:** *Handbook/Manual/Guide, Consumer.* **Description:** Contains useful statistics and information .
Formerly (until 2003): Racing and Football Outlook: Football Annual (0262-4699)
Published by: Raceform Ltd. (Subsidiary of: Trinity Mirror Plc.), High St, Compton, Newbury, Berks RG20 6NL, United Kingdom. TEL 44-1635-578080, FAX 44-1635-578101, feedback@raceform.co.uk, http://www.raceform.co.uk. Eds. Daniel Salt, Paul Charlton. Circ: 50,000.

796 GBR ISSN 0955-775X
RACING & FOOTBALL OUTLOOK: RACING ANNUAL. Text in English. 1909. a. adv. **Document type:** *Report, Consumer.*
Formerly: Racing and Football Racing Annual
Related titles: ◆ Supplement to: Racing & Football Outlook. ISSN 0033-7366.
—BLDSC (7225.993210).
Published by: Raceform Ltd. (Subsidiary of: Trinity Mirror Plc.), High St, Compton, Newbury, Berks RG20 6NL, United Kingdom. TEL 44-1635-578080, FAX 44-1635-578101, feedback@raceform.co.uk, http://www.raceform.co.uk. Circ: 40,000.

790.1 SGP
RACING GUIDE. Text in Chinese, English. 1987. s-w.
Address: 1 New Industrial Rd, Times Centre, Singapore, 536196, Singapore. TEL 2848844, FAX 2881186, TELEX 25713. Eds. Benny Ortega, Kuek Chiew Teong. Circ: 20,000.

RACING MILESTONES; America's race fan magazine. *see* TRANSPORTATION—Automobiles

636.596 GBR ISSN 0033-7390
THE RACING PIGEON; the British pigeon racing weekly. Text in English. 1898. w. GBP 58 domestic; GBP 93 in Europe; GBP 125 elsewhere (effective 2009). adv. bk.rev. **Document type:** *Newspaper, Consumer.* **Description:** Contains news about pigeon racing results and methods.
Related titles: Online - full text ed.: GBP 36.40 (effective 2009).
Published by: Racing Pigeon Publishing Co. Ltd., Unit G5, Seedbed Ctr, Wyncolls Rd., Colchester, Essex CO4 9HT, United Kingdom. TEL 44-1206-843456, FAX 44-1206-843442, racing123@btconnect.com. adv.: page GBP 120.

636.96 USA ISSN 0146-8383
RACING PIGEON BULLETIN. Text in English. w. USD 30. bk.rev. back issues avail. **Description:** Provides "how-to" articles, news, and opinions on the sport of pigeon breeding, training and racing.
Address: 34 E Franklin St, Bellbrook, OH 45305-2098. TEL 513-848-4972, FAX 513-848-3012. Ed. Michael D Reinke. adv.: B&W page USD 225, color page USD 800. Circ: 6,100.

RACING POST. *see* SPORTS AND GAMES—Horses And Horsemanship

790.1 GBR
RACING POST FORM BOOK JUMPS. Text in English. 1986. a. GBP 30 per issue (effective 2009).
Published by: Racing Post, One Canada Sq, Canary Wharf, London, E14 5AP, United Kingdom. TEL 44-1635-898781, shop@racingpost.co.uk, http://www.racingpost.com. Ed. Ashley Rumney.

796.72 USA ISSN 1062-4422
RACING WHEELS. Text in English. 1962. w. (40/yr.). USD 40 domestic; USD 50 in Canada (effective 2005). adv. bk.rev.; film rev.; rec.rev.; software rev.; tel.rev.; video rev. illus.; stat. 28 p./no.; **Document type:** *Newspaper, Consumer.* **Description:** Covers all types of road and track racing.
Published by: Gary's Enterprises, 7502 N E 133rd Ave, Box 1555, Vancouver, WA 98668. TEL 360-892-5590, FAX 360-892-8021. Ed., Adv. contact Dale Redinger. Circ: 11,450 (paid).

793.7 DEU
RAETSEL BLITZ. Text in German. 1997. m. EUR 19.80; EUR 1.40 newsstand/cover (effective 2009). adv. **Document type:** *Magazine, Consumer.*
Published by: Pabel-Moewig Verlag KG (Subsidiary of: Bauer Media Group), Karlsruherstr 31, Rastatt, 76437, Germany. TEL 49-7222-130, FAX 49-7222-13218, empfang@vpm.de, http://www.vpm-online.de. Adv. contact Rainer Gross. B&W page EUR 2,127; trim 196 x 263. Circ: 97,000 (paid).

793.7 DEU
RAETSEL-GROSSBAND. Text in German. bi-m. EUR 3.25 newsstand/cover (effective 2011). adv. **Document type:** *Magazine, Consumer.* **Description:** Filled with a variety of crossword puzzles.
Published by: Deutscher Raetselverlag GmbH & Co. KG (Subsidiary of: Gong Verlag GmbH & Co. KG), Muenchener Str 101-09, Ismaning, 85737, Germany. TEL 49-89-272708620, FAX 49-89-272707890, info@raetsel.de, http://www.deutscher-raetselverlag.de. Circ: 36,000 (controlled).

793.7 DEU
RAETSEL KAISER. Text in German. 13/yr. EUR 1.40 newsstand/cover (effective 2009). **Document type:** *Magazine, Consumer.*
Published by: Burda Senator Verlag GmbH (Subsidiary of: Hubert Burda Media Holding GmbH & Co. KG), Am Kestendamm 1, Offenburg, 77652, Germany. TEL 49-781-842264, FAX 49-781-842034, http://www.hubert-burda-media.com. Ed. Gabriele Henkel. Circ: 143,500 (paid and controlled). **Subscr. to:** Burda Medien Abo-Service, Postfach 1230, Offenburg 77602, Germany. TEL 49-1805-913171, FAX 49-1805-913172, service@burdadirect.de.

793.7 DEU
RAETSEL MIT PFIFF; laedt zum Gewinnen ein!. Text in German. 1999. m. EUR 1.60 newsstand/cover (effective 2011). adv. **Document type:** *Magazine, Consumer.*
Published by: Klambt Verlag GmbH, Im Neudeck 1, Speyer, 67346, Germany. TEL 49-6232-3100, FAX 49-6232-310226, info@klambt.de, http://www.klambt.de. Ed. Matthias Albrecht. Circ: 120,000 (paid).

793.7 DEU
RAETSEL-PAUSE; Exklusiv aus Ihrer Apotheke. Text in German. m. adv. **Document type:** *Magazine, Consumer.*
Published by: Apotheken-Spiegel-Verlagsgesellschaft mbH, Edisonstr 3-5, Frankfurt am Main, 60388, Germany. TEL 49-6109-71200, FAX 49-6109-7120222, inbox@as-verlag.com. adv.: B&W page EUR 7,200, color page EUR 11,520; trim 185 x 250.

793.7 DEU
RAETSEL PRINZ. Text in German. 2005. m. EUR 1.40 newsstand/cover (effective 2011). adv. **Document type:** *Magazine, Consumer.*
Published by: Klambt Verlag GmbH, Im Neudeck 1, Speyer, 67346, Germany. TEL 49-6232-3100, FAX 49-6232-310226, info@klambt.de, http://www.klambt.de. Ed. Matthias Albrecht. Circ: 110,000 (paid).

793.7 DEU
RAETSEL REVUE. Text in German. 1986. bi-m. EUR 1.80 newsstand/cover (effective 2011). adv. **Document type:** *Magazine, Consumer.*
Published by: Deutscher Raetselverlag GmbH & Co. KG (Subsidiary of: Gong Verlag GmbH & Co. KG), Muenchener Str 101-09, Ismaning, 85737, Germany. TEL 49-89-272708620, FAX 49-89-272707890, info@raetsel.de, http://www.deutscher-raetselverlag.de. Circ: 125,000 (controlled).

793.7 DEU
RAETSEL SAISON. Text in German. 1986. bi-m. EUR 1.80 newsstand/cover (effective 2011). adv. **Document type:** *Magazine, Consumer.*
Published by: Deutscher Raetselverlag GmbH & Co. KG (Subsidiary of: Gong Verlag GmbH & Co. KG), Muenchener Str 101-09, Ismaning, 85737, Germany. TEL 49-89-272708620, FAX 49-89-272707890, info@raetsel.de, http://www.deutscher-raetselverlag.de. Circ: 138,000 (controlled).

793.7 DEU
RAETSEL UND FREIZEIT; Raetseln & Gewinnen. Text in German. 1948. m. EUR 1.60 newsstand/cover (effective 2011). adv. **Document type:** *Magazine, Consumer.* **Description:** Provides a wide variety of puzzles and games.
Published by: Klambt Verlag GmbH, Im Neudeck 1, Speyer, 67346, Germany. TEL 49-6232-3100, FAX 49-6232-310226, info@klambt.de, http://www.klambt.de. Ed. Matthias Albrecht. Circ: 150,000 (paid).

793.7 DEU
RAETSEL-ZEITUNG. Text in German. 1958. fortn. EUR 46.80; EUR 1.50 newsstand/cover (effective 2011). adv. **Document type:** *Magazine, Consumer.* **Description:** Provides a weekly dose of word games and puzzles.
Formerly (until 1962): Quiz und Test
Published by: Deutscher Raetselverlag GmbH & Co. KG (Subsidiary of: Gong Verlag GmbH & Co. KG), Muenchener Str 101-09, Ismaning, 85737, Germany. TEL 49-89-272708620, FAX 49-89-272707890, info@raetsel.de, http://www.deutscher-raetselverlag.de. Circ: 37,000 (controlled).

793.7 DEU
RAETSELKOENIG; Werden Sie Raetselkoenig. Variant title: 7 Tage Raetselkoenig. Text in German. 1996. m. EUR 1.60 newsstand/cover (effective 2011). adv. **Document type:** *Magazine, Consumer.*
Published by: Klambt Verlag GmbH, Im Neudeck 1, Speyer, 67346, Germany. TEL 49-6232-3100, FAX 49-6232-310226, info@klambt.de, http://www.klambt.de. Ed. Matthias Albrecht. Circ: 125,000 (paid).

793.7 DEU ISSN 0942-6582
RAETSELMUEHLE; mit den beliebsten Raetselarten. Text in German. 19??. w. EUR 91; EUR 1.50 newsstand/cover (effective 2011). adv. **Document type:** *Magazine, Consumer.* **Description:** Contains a wide variety of puzzles and word games.
Published by: Deutscher Raetselverlag GmbH & Co. KG (Subsidiary of: Gong Verlag GmbH & Co. KG), Muenchener Str 101-09, Ismaning, 85737, Germany. TEL 49-89-272708620, FAX 49-89-272707890, info@raetsel.de, http://www.deutscher-raetselverlag.de. Circ: 55,000 (controlled).

796.72 NLD ISSN 1874-0030
RALLY JAAROVERZICHT. Text in Dutch. 2002. a. EUR 30 (effective 2009).
Published by: Raven Produkties, Schoolstraat 8, Een, 9342 PM, Netherlands. TEL 31-592-656170, info@ravenprodukties.nl, http://www.ravenprodukties.nl. Pub. John Raven.

796.77 796.71 ITA ISSN 1122-7141
RALLY SPRINT. Text in Italian. 1994. m. **Document type:** *Magazine, Consumer.* **Description:** Provides updates on all international rally racing championships. Includes interviews with drivers, a schedule of upcoming events and a section on Italian rally racing events.
Published by: Conti Editore SpA, Via del Lavoro 7, San Lazzaro di Savena, BO 40068, Italy. http://www.contieditore.it.

796.72 FRA ISSN 1254-0331
RALLYES MAGAZINE. Text in French. 1993. m. EUR 44.50 (effective 2009). adv. **Document type:** *Magazine, Consumer.*
Related titles: Supplement(s): Rallyes Magazine. Hors Serie. ISSN 1253-8957.
Address: 65 Bd Cote Blatin, Centre Viaduc, Clermont-Ferrand, 63000, France. http://www.rallyes-magazine.tv.

RASSEGNA DI DIRITTO ED ECONOMIA DELLO SPORT. *see* LAW

793.732 RUS ISSN 1563-4477
RAZGADAI!. Text in Russian. 1998. w. adv. **Document type:** *Magazine, Consumer.*
Published by: Izdatel'skii Dom Burda, ul Pravdy 8, Moscow, 125040, Russian Federation. TEL 7-095-7979849, FAX 7-095-2571196, vertrieb@burda.ru, http://www.burda.ru. adv.: page USD 2,700. Circ: 400,000 (paid and controlled).

793.732 UKR
RAZGADAI!. Text in Russian. w. **Document type:** *Magazine, Consumer.*
Published by: Burda Ukraina, Zhyljanskaja ul. 29, Kiev, 01033, Ukraine. TEL 38-044-4908363, FAX 38-044-4908364, zhestkov@burda.ua, http://www.burda.ua.

795.38 USA
REAL LOTTERY WINNING GUIDE. Text in English. 1989. m. **Document type:** *Magazine, Consumer.*
Published by: Gibbs Publishing Company, PO Box 97, Sylva, NC 28779. gibbsic@aol.com. Ed. James Calvin Gibbs.

790.1 MEX
RECORD; revista deportiva. Text in Spanish. 1955. fortn. MXN 10 per issue. adv.
Published by: Nicolas Sanchez, Ed. & Pub., Avda. Juarez 127-12, Mexico City 1, DF, Mexico. Circ: 15,000.

790.1 PRT ISSN 0870-2179
RECORD; actualidade desportiva. Text in Portuguese. 1949. d. adv. **Document type:** *Newspaper, Consumer.* **Description:** Provides information on every type of sport.
Related titles: Online - full text ed.
Published by: Edisport (Subsidiary of: Cofina Media), Av Joao Crisostomo 72, Lisbon, Portugal. TEL 351-213-307700, FAX 351-213-307799.

S

796 BRA ISSN 1982-8985
GV571
RECORDE; revista de historia do esporte. Text in Multiple languages. 2008. s-a. free (effective 2011). **Document type:** *Journal, Academic/Scholarly.*
Media: Online - full text.
Indexed: CA, H21, P08, S02, S03, SD, SociolAb, T02.
Published by: Universidade Federal do Rio de Janeiro, Instituto de Filosofia e Ciencias Sociais, Largo de Sao Francisco de Paula 1, Sala 320 B, Centro, Rio De Janeiro, RJ 20051-071, Brazil. TEL 55-21-2210034, FAX 55-21-22211470, http://www.ifcs.ufrj.br/. Ed. Victor Andrade de Melo.

797.2 GBR ISSN 0961-2580
RECREATION. Text in English. 1934. 10/yr. free to members (effective 2009). adv. bk.rev. index. **Document type:** *Magazine, Trade.* **Description:** Discusses various aspects of pool equipment, mechanical and electrical services, chemicals and water treatment equipment, lockers, management systems, sports hall and gymnastic equipment.
Former titles (until 1990): Baths Service and Recreation Management (0961-2572); (until 1989): I B R M Journal (0954-3279); (until 1988): Baths Service and Recreation Management (0141-8580); (until 1978): Baths Service (0005-626X); (until 1950): Baths and Bath Engineering (0365-9135)
Related titles: Online - full text ed.: free (effective 2009).
Indexed: SportS.
—BLDSC (7326.831000), IE, Ingenta.
Published by: Institute of Sport and Recreation Management, Sir John Beckwith Centre for Sport, Loughborough University, Loughborough, Leics LE11 3TU, United Kingdom. TEL 44-1509-226474, FAX 44-1509-226475, info@isrm.co.uk. Ed. Mike Sewell TEL 44-1223-477439. Adv. contact James Smyth TEL 44-1223-477428. color page GBP 895; bleed 216 x 303.

RECREATION ADVISOR. *see* LEISURE AND RECREATION

797 AUS ISSN 1449-9118
RECREATIONAL AVIATION AUSTRALIA. Text in English. 1987. m. free to members (effective 2009). back issues avail. **Document type:** *Magazine, Consumer.*
Formerly (until 2004): Australian Ultralights (1320-6389)
Published by: (Recreational Aviation Australia Inc.), Zebra Publishing Inc., PO Box 1265, Fyshwick, ACT 2609, Australia. TEL 61-2-62804700, FAX 61-2-62804775, nsw2@raa.asn.au.

790.1 USA ISSN 0164-4106
RECREATIONAL ICE SKATING; the magazine for recreational ice skating/hockey enthusiasts. Text in English. 1976. q. USD 12; USD 4 newsstand/cover (effective 2007). adv. 48 p./no.; back issues avail. **Document type:** *Magazine, Consumer.*
Published by: Ice Skating Institute, 17120 N Dallas Pkwy, Ste 140, Dallas, TX 75248-1187. TEL 972-735-8800, FAX 972-735-8815, http://www.skateisi.org. Ed., R&P Lori Fairchild. Adv. contacts Carol Jackson, Stuart Sedransky. B&W page USD 1,690, color page USD 2,550. Circ: 50,000 (paid).

RECREATIONAL SPORTS DIRECTORY. *see* EDUCATION—Guides To Schools And Colleges

RECREATIONAL SPORTS JOURNAL. *see* EDUCATION—Guides To Schools And Colleges

796 USA ISSN 0733-1436
GV735
REFEREE (FRANKSVILLE); magazine of sports officiating. Text in English. 1976. m. USD 44.95 (effective 2005). adv. bk.rev. charts; illus. index. **Document type:** *Magazine, Trade.*
Indexed: PEI, SD, SPI, SportS, T02.
—Ingenta.
Published by: Referee Enterprises, Inc., PO Box 161, Franksville, WI 53126. TEL 262-632-8855, FAX 262-632-5460. Ed. Bill Topp. Pub., R&P Barry Mano. Circ: 30,000 (paid).

790.1 DEU
REGENSBURGER RUDER KLUB VON 1890 E.V. KLUBNACHRICHTEN. Text in German. 1925. m. membership. **Document type:** *Newsletter, Consumer.*
Formerly: Klubnachrichten
Published by: Regensburger Ruder Klub von 1890 e.V., Messerschmitt-Str 2, Regensburg, 93049, Germany. TEL 49-941-25514, FAX 49-941-2966817, vorstand@regensburger-ruderklub.de, http://www.regensburger-ruder-klub.de. Ed., Adv. contact Gertrude Deckart.

REKREAVAKKRANT. *see* LEISURE AND RECREATION

796 AUS ISSN 1449-7603
RESEARCH AT THE AUSTRALIAN INSTITUTE OF SPORT. Text in English. 2004. a. free (effective 2006).
Published by: (Australian Institute of Sport), Australian Sports Commission, PO Box 176, Belconnen, ACT 2616, Australia. TEL 61-2-62141111, FAX 61-2-62512680, pubs@ausport.gov.au, http://www.ausport.gov.au.

RESEARCH QUARTERLY FOR EXERCISE AND SPORT. *see* PHYSICAL FITNESS AND HYGIENE

RETAIL FOCUS (MOUNT PROSPECT). *see* BUSINESS AND ECONOMICS—Marketing And Purchasing

796.07 ESP ISSN 1579-1726
RETOS. Text in Spanish. 2002. s-a. back issues avail. **Document type:** *Journal, Academic/Scholarly.*
Related titles: Online - full text ed.: ISSN 1988-2041. 2007. free (effective 2011); Cumulative ed(s).: ISSN 1988-2041. 2007. free (effective 2011).
Indexed: A36, CABA, E12, F08, GH, LT, N02, N03, W11.
Published by: Federacion Espanola de Asociaciones de Docentes de Educacion Fisica (F E A D E F), C. Cabo Vidio 27, San Javier, Murcia, 30730, Spain. TEL 34-968-193695, feadef@feadef.org, http://www.feadef.org/. Ed. Francisco Ruiz Juan.

REVENUES FROM SPORTS VENUES. *see* BUSINESS AND ECONOMICS—Economic Situation And Conditions

796.3 DEU
REVIERSPORT - DONNERSTAG. Text in German. 1988. w. EUR 70 (effective 2010). adv. **Document type:** *Newspaper, Consumer.*
Formerly (until 2009): RevierSport am Donnerstag
Published by: Prokom Medienberatungs- und Verlagsgesellschaft mbH, Hesslerstr 37, Essen, 45329, Germany. TEL 49-201-8620652, FAX 49-201-8620622. Ed. Heiko Buschmann. Adv. contact Werner Kluger. B&W page EUR 1,430, color page EUR 2,195; trim 215 x 315.

796.3 DEU
REVIERSPORT - MONTAG. Text in German. 1988. w. EUR 80 (effective 2010). adv. **Document type:** *Newspaper, Consumer.*
Former titles (until 2010): RevierSport - Sonntag; (until 2009): RevierSport am Sonntag
Published by: Prokom Medienberatungs- und Verlagsgesellschaft mbH, Hesslerstr 37, Essen, 45329, Germany. TEL 49-201-8620652, FAX 49-201-8620622. Ed. Heiko Buschmann. Adv. contact Werner Kluger. B&W page EUR 1,430, color page EUR 2,195.

796 ARG ISSN 1515-6699
REVIJUEGOS. Text in Spanish. 2000. m. **Document type:** *Magazine, Consumer.*
Published by: Ediciones del Tercer Milenio, Gral. Heredia 1225-27, Avellaneda, Buenos Aires, Argentina. TEL 54-11-42654564, FAX 54-11-42038998, http://www.edicionestercermilenio.com/.

790.1 BRA ISSN 0101-3289
REVISTA BRASILEIRA DE CIENCIAS DO ESPORTE. Text in Portuguese. 1979. 3/yr. **Document type:** *Journal, Academic/Scholarly.*
Indexed: SD, SportS.
Published by: Colegio Brasileiro de Ciencias do Esporte, Universidade Federal de Goias, Faculdade de Educacao Fisica, Rodovia Goiana-Necropolis Km 12, Goiana, GO 74011-970, Brazil. TEL 55-62-35211513, cbce@fef.ufg.br, http://www.cbce.org.br. Eds. Alex Fraga, Silvana Goellner.

REVISTA BRASILEIRA DE CINEANTROPOMETRIA & DESEMPENHO HUMANO. *see* PHYSICAL FITNESS AND HYGIENE

794.1 BRA
REVISTA BRASILEIRA DE XADREZ POSTAL. Text in Portuguese. 1970. 6/yr. USD 15 to non-members. adv. **Document type:** *Bulletin.* **Description:** Reports on national and international games and news, crosstables, results, and studies-problems. Includes formal opinions on correspondence chess matters.
Published by: Clube de Xadrez Epistolar Brasileiro, Brooklin Paulista, Caixa Postal 21200, Sao Paulo, SP 04698-970, Brazil. TEL 55-11-535-2938, FAX 55-11-535-2938. Ed. Haroldo Wonsowski. Pub., Adv. contact Pedro Luiz de Oliveira Costa Neto. Circ: 1,200 (controlled).

796.8 ESP ISSN 1885-8643
REVISTA DE ARTES MARCIALES ASIATICAS. Text in Spanish. 2006. q. EUR 28 domestic; EUR 32 foreign (effective 2011). **Document type:** *Journal, Academic/Scholarly.*
Related titles: Online - full text ed.: ISSN 2174-0747. 2006; ◆ English ed.: Journal of Asian Martial Arts. ISSN 1057-8358.
Indexed: A01, CA, F03, F04, R15, SD, T02.
Published by: Universidad de Leon, Secretariado de Publicaciones, Campus de Vegazana, Leon, 24071, Spain. TEL 34-987-291558, FAX 34-987-291558, http://www.unileon.es. Ed. Carlos Gutierrez Gacria.

613.7 CRI ISSN 1409-0724
REVISTA DE CIENCIAS DEL EJERCITO Y LA SALUD. Text in Spanish. 2001. s-a. CRC 200 (effective 2006). **Document type:** *Journal, Academic/Scholarly.* **Description:** Aims to disseminate scientific findings related to health and physical activities, mainly, published articles related to original researches, literature reviews, case studies, and technical articles.
Published by: Universidad de Costa Rica, Escuela de Educacion Fisica y Deportes, Carreterra a Sabanilla, San Jose, Costa Rica. TEL 506-207-3016. Circ: 500.

613.7 ARG ISSN 0034-7884
REVISTA DE DERECHO DEPORTIVO. Text in Spanish. 1964 (vol.3). s-a. adv.
Published by: Agricol de Bianchetti, Paraguay 1307, Buenos Aires, 1057, Argentina.

REVISTA DE EDUCACION FISICA; renovacion de teoria y practica. *see* PHYSICAL FITNESS AND HYGIENE

790.1 370 ARG ISSN 1514-7959
LA REVISTA DE LA EDUCACION FISICA. Text in Spanish. 2000. m. **Document type:** *Magazine, Consumer.*
Published by: Editorial Ediba, Brown, 474, Bahia Blanca, Buenos Aires, 8000, Argentina. TEL 54-11-45549800, http://www.ediba.com/.

796 CHL ISSN 0718-4492
REVISTA DE LAS CIENCIAS DE LA ACTIVIDAD FISICA. Text in Spanish. 2004. a. **Document type:** *Monographic series, Academic/Scholarly.*
Formerly (until 2005): Revista de Ciencias de la Actividad Fisica y Deportes (0718-4522)
Published by: Instituto Nacional de Deportes, Fidel Oteiza, 1956 Piso 3, Providencia, Santiago, Chile. TEL 56-2-7540200, FAX 56-2-3689685, http://www.chiledeportes.cl/index.php.

796 PRT ISSN 1646-5059
REVISTA DE PATINAGEM. Text in Portuguese. 2006. irreg.
Published by: Universidade de Coimbra, Faculdade de Ciencias do Desporto e Educacao Fisica, Estadio Universitario de Coimbra, Pavilhao 3, Coimbra, 3040-156, Portugal. TEL 351-239-802770, http://www.fcdef.uc.pt.

REVISTA DE PSICOLOGIA DEL DEPORTE. *see* PSYCHOLOGY

REVISTA IBEROAMERICANA DE PSICOLOGIA DEL EJERCICIO Y EL DEPORTE. *see* PSYCHOLOGY

REVISTA JURIDICA DEL DEPORTE. *see* LAW

REVISTA MACKENZIE DE EDUCACAO FISICA E ESPORTE. *see* EDUCATION—Teaching Methods And Curriculum

795 ARG ISSN 1852-6330
▼ **REVISTA POKERLOGIA.** Text in Spanish. 2009. bi-m. **Document type:** *Magazine, Consumer.*
Published by: Tecmys, S.A., Avellaneda 841, Buenos Aires, 1602, Argentina. TEL 54-911-1555161413, http://www.tecmys.com.ar/.

796.01 PRT ISSN 1645-0523
REVISTA PORTUGUESA DE CIENCIAS DO DESPORTO/ PORTUGUESE JOURNAL OF SPORTS SCIENCES. Text in Portuguese. 2000. 3/yr. **Document type:** *Journal, Academic/Scholarly.*
Indexed: CA, PEI, SD, T02.
—BLDSC (7869.879500).
Published by: Universidade do Porto, Faculdade de Ciencias do Desporto e de Educacao Fisica, Rua D Manuel II, Oporto, 4050-345, Portugal. TEL 351-22-6073500, FAX 351-22-6098736, up@up.pt, http://www.up.pt. Ed. Antonio Teixeira Marques.

REVUE E P S. (Education Physique et Sport) *see* EDUCATION—Teaching Methods And Curriculum

796 FRA ISSN 1961-912X
REVUE EUROPEENNE DE MANAGEMENT DU SPORT (ONLINE). Text in French. 1999. q. **Document type:** *Journal, Trade.*
Formerly (until 2007): Revue Europeenne de Management du Sport (Print) (1297-8019)
Media: Online - full text.
Indexed: SD.
Published by: Reseau Territorial, BP 215, Voiron, Cedex 38506, France. TEL 33-4-76657136, FAX 33-4-76050163, info@infosport.org.

REVUE JURIDIQUE ET ECONOMIQUE DU SPORT. *see* LAW

794.1 ARG ISSN 0326-0011
EL REY; revista argentina de ajedrez. Text in Spanish. 1980. irreg. ARS 10 newsstand/cover (effective 2002). adv. bk.rev.; play rev. bibl.; charts; illus.; stat. index. back issues avail. **Document type:** *Bulletin.* **Description:** Covers chess strategies and game play.
Related titles: CD-ROM ed.
Published by: Hector Ricardo Liso Ed. & Pub., La Pampa, 2975, Buenos Aires, C1428EBA, Argentina. adv.: page USD 300. Circ: 300.

790.1 SYR
RIADA. Text in Arabic. w. adv.
Address: P O Box 292, Damascus, Syria. Ed. Noureddine Rial.

793.7 DEU
RIESEN RAETSEL REVUE. Text in German. 1968. 15/yr. EUR 24.60; EUR 1.65 newsstand/cover (effective 2010). adv. **Document type:** *Magazine, Consumer.*
Published by: Pabel-Moewig Verlag KG (Subsidiary of: Bauer Media Group), Karlsruherstr 31, Rastatt, 76437, Germany. TEL 49-7222-130, FAX 49-7222-13218, empfang@vpm.de, http://www.vpm-online.de.

799.3 USA
RIFLE SHOOTER. Variant title: Petersen's Rifle Shooter. Text in English. 1997. bi-m. USD 15.97 domestic; USD 28.97 in Canada; USD 30.97 elsewhere (effective 2008). adv. **Document type:** *Magazine, Consumer.* **Description:** Covers all types of rifles and rifle shooting with an emphasis on the pursuit of accuracy.
Published by: Source Interlink Companies, 6420 Wilshire Blvd, 10th Fl, Los Angeles, CA 90048. TEL 323-782-2000, FAX 323-782-2585, dheine@sourceinterlink.com, http://www.sourceinterlinkmedia.com. adv.: B&W page USD 3,050, color page USD 4,890. Circ: 69,962 (paid).

799.3 GBR ISSN 0035-5224
THE RIFLEMAN. Text in English. 1906. q. free to members (effective 2009). adv. bk.rev. charts; illus.; stat. **Document type:** *Magazine, Consumer.*
Indexed: SD, SportS.
Published by: National Small-Bore Rifle Association, Lord Roberts Ctr, Bisley Camp, Brookwood, Woking, Surrey GU24 0NP, United Kingdom. TEL 44-1483-485505, FAX 44-14834-76392.

790.1 JPN
RIKUJO KYOGI. Text in Japanese. 1967. m. **Document type:** *Consumer.* **Description:** Track & field magazine for sports lovers.
Published by: Kodansha Ltd., 2-12-21 Otowa, Bunkyo-ku, Tokyo, 112-8001, Japan. TEL 81-3-3946-6201, FAX 81-3-3944-9915, http://www.kodansha.co.jp, http://www.toppan.co.jp/kodansha. Ed. Yutaka Hirose. Circ: 50,000.

796 JPN
RIKUJO-KYOGI MAGAZINE/ATHLETIC SPORTS MAGAZINE. Text in Japanese. 1951. m. JPY 9,720 (effective 2000).
Published by: Baseball Magazine Sha, 3-10-10 Misaki-cho, Chiyoda-ku, Tokyo, 101-0061, Japan. FAX 81-3-3238-0106. Ed. Yukiya Higuchi.

796.83 USA ISSN 0035-5410
THE RING; the bible of boxing. Text in English. 1922. 13/yr. USD 53.70 domestic; USD 86.70 in Canada & Mexico; USD 143.70 elsewhere; USD 8.95 per issue (effective 2009). adv. bk.rev. bibl.; illus.; stat. back issues avail.; reprints avail. **Document type:** *Magazine, Consumer.* **Description:** Features spectacular award-winning photos, provocative interviews with the leading pros and journeys to the coolest undiscovered boxing matches.
Related titles: Online - full text ed.
Indexed: SD, SPI, SportS.
—Ingenta.
Published by: Sports & Entertainment Publications, LLC, 6198 Butler Pike, Ste 200, Blue Bell, PA 19422. TEL 215-461-0583, FAX 215-643-3176, custsrvcsep@sepublications.com. Ed. Nigel Collins. Circ: 200,000. **U.K. dist. addr.:** Comag, Tavistock Rd, W Drayton, Middlesex UB7 7QE, United Kingdom.

790.1 USA
RING RHETORIC. Text in English. 1971. q. looseleaf. membership. adv. bk.rev. back issues avail. **Document type:** *Newsletter.* **Description:** To educate the public on the improvement of boxing and advancing the sport.
Published by: America Association for the Improvement of Boxing, Inc., 86 Fletcher Ave, Mt, Vernon, NY 10552. TEL 914-664-4571. Ed. Stephen H Acunto. Pub. Shea Haaphiann. Circ: 300.

796 CAN
RINGETTE CANADA. OFFICIAL RULES (YEARS). Text in English, French. 1965. irreg. (every 3/yrs.). CAD 6 (effective 2000). adv.
Formerly: Ontario Ringette Association. Official Rules
Published by: Ringette Canada, 1600 James Naismith Dr, Gloucester, ON K1B 5N4, Canada. TEL 613-748-5655, FAX 613-748-5860. Circ: 25,000.

796.35 CAN
RINGETTE REVIEW. Text in English, French. 1979. a. adv. bk.rev. **Document type:** *Newsletter.*
Indexed: SportS.
Published by: Ringette Canada, 1600 James Naismith Dr, Gloucester, ON K1B 5N4, Canada. TEL 613-748-5655, FAX 613-748-5860. Circ: 30,000.

790.1 USA
RINGSIDE. Text in English. bi-m.
Published by: O'Quinn Studios, Inc., 475 Park Ave S, New York, NY 10016. TEL 212-689-2830.

796.83 GBR ISSN 0037-6310
RINGSPORT. Text in English. 1959. bi-m. USD 10. adv. bk.rev. illus.
Supersedes: Skill
Indexed: SportS.
Published by: Ringsport Publications, 5 Stockland St, Caerphilly, Glam CF83 1GD, United Kingdom. Ed. Evan R Treharne. Circ: 15,000.

796.962 USA ISSN 1531-3042
RINK (AMBLER). Text in English. 19??. 3/yr. **Document type:** *Magazine, Consumer.*
Formerly (until 2000): Hockey Stars Presents (1067-7437)
Published by: London Publishing Co. (Subsidiary of: Kappa Publishing Group, Inc.), 6198 Butler Pike, Ste 200, Blue Bell, PA 19422. TEL 215-643-6385, FAX 315-628-3571, custsrvc@kappapublishing.com, http://www.kappapublishing.com. Ed. David Rosenbaum. Pub. Stuart M Saks.

RINKSIDER; independent voice of the industry!. *see* BUSINESS AND ECONOMICS—Management

RIPSIK. *see* CHILDREN AND YOUTH—For

796 USA
RISE. Text in English. 1997. 8/yr. USD 24.95 domestic; USD 37.75 in Canada (effective 2006). adv. **Document type:** *Magazine, Consumer.* **Description:** Covers high school sports.
Formerly (until 2006, Sep.): SchoolSports
Published by: SchoolSports, Inc., 971 Commonwealth Ave, Ste 33, Boston, MA 02215. TEL 877-776-7894, FAX 617-779-9100. Circ: 400,000.

793.7 EST ISSN 1736-2083
RISTIK. Variant title: Ristsonastik. Text in Estonian. 2003. m. EUR 12.78; EUR 1.25 newsstand/cover (effective 2011). **Document type:** *Magazine, Consumer.*
Published by: Ajakirjade Kirjastus, Maakri 23A, Tallinn, 10145, Estonia. TEL 372-666-2600, FAX 372-666-2557, sekr@kirjastus.ee, http://www.kirjastus.ee. Ed. Tarmo Tuule.

790.1 059.927 UAE
AL-RIYADAH WAL-SHABAB. Text in Arabic. 1981. w. **Description:** Covers sports news and youth activities.
Published by: Mu'assasat al-Bayan lil-Sahafah wal-Tiba'a wal-Nashr, PO Box 8837, Dubai, United Arab Emirates. TEL 444400, FAX 449820, TELEX 47707 PRESS EM. Ed. Khalid Muhammad Ahmad.

794.1 DEU ISSN 0943-4356
ROCHADE EUROPA; die vielseitig-informative Schachzeitung. Text in German. 1966. m. EUR 27.60 domestic; EUR 35 foreign (effective 2005). adv. bk.rev. bibl.; charts; illus. **Document type:** *Newspaper, Consumer.*
Former titles (until 1992): Europa-Rochade (0179-3934); (until 1984): Rochade
Address: Postfach 1154, Soemmerda, 99601, Germany. TEL 49-3634-603850, FAX 49-3634-622213. Circ: 20,000.

796 USA
ROCKY MOUNTAIN SPORTS. Text in English. 1986. m. free (effective 2005). adv. 70 p./no.; back issues avail. **Document type:** *Magazine, Consumer.* **Description:** Covers individual outdoor sports in Colorado, including where-to and how-to information.
Formerly: Rocky Mountain Sports and Fitness
Indexed: SD.
Published by: Rocky Mountain Sports Magazine, 2525 15th St, 1A, Denver, CO 80211-3920. TEL 303-861-9229, FAX 303-861-9209, doug@windycitysports.com. Eds. Rebecca Heaton, Jeff Banowetz. Pubs. Doug Kaplan, Mary Thorne. Adv. contact Doug Kaplan. color page USD 7,110, B&W page USD 6,075. Circ: 90,000 (controlled).

793.7 SVK ISSN 1336-8648
RODINNE KRIZOVKY. Text in Slovak. 2006. m. **Document type:** *Magazine, Consumer.*
Published by: F and F Slovensko, s.r.o., Zelezniciarska 6, Bratislava, 81104, Slovakia.

796.21 AUS ISSN 1832-830X
ROLLA. Text in English. 2005. q. AUD 25 domestic; NZD 32 in New Zealand; USD 22 in United States; CAD 28 in Canada; GBP 17 in United Kingdom; EUR 23 in Europe; JPY 1,500 in Japan (effective 2009). back issues avail. **Document type:** *Magazine, Consumer.* **Description:** Provides information about inline skating of Australia.
Published by: Rolla Magazine, PO Box 1040, Hampton North, VIC 3188, Australia. TEL 61-4-12124334, subscribe@rollamag.com. Ed. Michael Bancroft.

796.21 USA ISSN 1073-4678
ROLLER SKATING BUSINESS. Text in English. 1989. bi-m. USD 45 to non-members (effective 2000). adv. charts; illus.; stat. **Document type:** *Journal, Trade.* **Description:** Discusses new products and other topics of interest to owners and operators of roller-skating rinks, as well as roller skating coaches.
Formerly (until 1994): Rink Digest (1053-5772)
Published by: Roller Skating Association International, 6905 Corporate Dr, Indianapolis, IN 46278. TEL 317-347-2626, FAX 317-347-2636. Ed., Adv. contact Melissa Gibson. Circ: 1,900 (controlled).

795 USA
ROLLING GOOD TIMES ONLINE. Text in English. 1995. d. free. adv. **Description:** Includes gambling news stories, betting strategies, an updated sportsticker, and more.
Media: Online - full text.
Published by: R G T Online Inc., 205 S. Main St., St. Charles, MO 63301-2804. TEL 314-946-0820. Ed. Sue Schneider.

796.41 ROM ISSN 1453-1240
ROMANIAN GYMNASTICS. Text in English. 1998. s-a. USD 26 to individuals; USD 45 to institutions. adv. illus. **Description:** Contains the latest information on Romanian gymnastics.
Published by: Center for Romanian Studies, Oficiul Postal I, PO Box 108, Iasi, 6600, Romania. TEL 40-32-219000, FAX 40-32-219010. Ed. Kurt W Treptow. Adv. contact Mihaela Moscaliuc. Circ: 1,000.
Co-sponsor: Romanian Gymnastics Federation.

793.7 EST
ROOMUUD. Text in Estonian. 1997. q. EUR 1.27 newsstand/cover (effective 2011). adv. **Document type:** *Magazine, Consumer.*
Published by: Kuma Ltd., 57 Parnu St, Paide, 72712, Estonia. TEL 372-38-38800, FAX 372-38-38806, kuma@kuma.ee, http://www.kuma.ee. Ed. Jaanus Laidna. adv.: page EEK 3,000.

790.1 AUT
ROUGE ET NOIR. Text in German. 1988. bi-m. bk.rev. **Document type:** *Bulletin.*
Related titles: CD-ROM ed.
Published by: V I P News Verlag GmbH, Taubstummengasse 13-4, Vienna, W 1040, Austria. TEL 01-5050801-0, FAX 01-505080121. Ed. Elisabeth Strunz.

790.1 DEU ISSN 0945-7259
ROVER BLATT. Text in German. 1975. bi-m. EUR 76 membership (effective 2009). adv. back issues avail. **Document type:** *Newsletter, Consumer.* **Description:** Provides club and collector information on all aspects of the Land Rover.
Published by: Deutscher Land Rover Club e.V., Postfach 101740, Aachen, 52017, Germany. TEL 49-241-9214900, FAX 49-241-9214901, koordinator@dlrc.org, http://dlrc.org. Adv. contact Horst Hanke. Circ: 1,000.

796 GBR
ROYAL CALEDONIAN CURLING CLUB. ANNUAL REPORT AND ACCOUNTS. Variant title: R C C C Yearbook. Text in English. 1838. a. adv. 480 p./no.; **Document type:** *Directory.*
Formerly: Royal Caledonian Curling Club. Annual (0080-4282)
Related titles: Online - full text ed.
Published by: Royal Caledonian Curling Club, Cairnie House, Ingliston Showground, Newbridge, Midlothian EH28 8NB, United Kingdom. TEL 44-131-333-3003, FAX 44-131-333-3323. Ed., Adv. contact W J D Thomson. Circ: 25,000 (controlled).

795.412 DEU
ROYAL FLUSH; das Deutsche Poker Magazin. Text in German. 2007. bi-m. EUR 21.99; EUR 3.99 newsstand/cover (effective 2011). adv. **Document type:** *Magazine, Consumer.*
Published by: W E K A Media Publishing GmbH, Gruberstr 46a, Poing, 85586, Germany. TEL 49-8121-950, FAX 49-8121-951199, online@wekanet.de, http://www.magnus.de. Ed. Michael Ausserbauer. Circ: 50,000 (paid).

796.72 GBR
ROYAL SCOTTISH AUTOMOBILE CLUB OFFICIAL HANDBOOK. Text in English. 1907. a. GBP 12.99. adv. **Document type:** *Directory.* **Description:** Motoring and touring guide.
Published by: Royal Scottish Automobile Club, 11 Blythswood Sq, Glasgow, Lanarkshire G2 4AG, United Kingdom. TEL 041-221-3850, FAX 041-221-3805. Ed. Jonathan Lord. Circ: 5,000.

796.35 BEL
RULES OF HOCKEY (YEAR). Text in English. a. GBP 2 per issue includes 2003 supp. (effective 2003). adv. **Document type:** *Handbook/Manual/Guide, Consumer.*
Former titles: Rules of the Game of Field Hockey; International Field Hockey Rules; Official Field Hockey Rules for School Girls (0362-3270)
Published by: International Hockey Federation, Av des Arts 1, Bte 5, Brussels, 1210, Belgium. TEL 32-2-2194537, http://www.FIHockey.org. R&P Mary Coyle. Adv. contact Mr. Steven Morris.

RUMBA SOPA DE LETRAS. *see* HOBBIES

796 SVK ISSN 1337-8317
RUN. Text in Slovak. 2008. bi-m. EUR 8.17; EUR 1.63 newsstand/cover (effective 2009). **Document type:** *Magazine, Consumer.*
Published by: Sanoma Magazines Slovakia s.r.o., Kutlikova 17, Bratislava, 851 02, Slovakia. TEL 421-2-32150111, FAX 421-2-63830093, info@sanomaslovakia.sk, http://www.sanoma.sk. Ed. Andrej Miklanek. Circ: 10,000.

796 AUS
RUN. Text in English. 1979. bi-m. bk.rev. illus. **Document type:** *Magazine, Consumer.*
Formerly (until 1999): Fun Runner; Incorporates: Australasian Track and Field (0157-5295)
Indexed: SportS.
Published by: J P Publications, PO Box 2805, Taren Point, NSW 2229, Australia. TEL 61-2-95427335, FAX 61-2-95427323, jppublic@ozemail.com.au, http://www.magna.com.au/~iphala. Circ: 17,500.

790.1 GBR
THE RUNNER; runners magazine for the north and midlands. Text in English. 1985. m. GBP 18. adv. bk.rev. charts; illus.; stat. **Document type:** *Magazine, Consumer.*
Published by: Trinity International Holdings, Thomson House, Newcastle upon Tyne, Tyne and Wear, United Kingdom. TEL 44-191-477-5599, FAX 44-191-4900047. Ed. Chris White. Adv. contact Trish Roberts. Circ: 10,000.

796.426 USA ISSN 1058-4889
RUNNER TRIATHLETE NEWS. Text in English. 1985. m. USD 18 (effective 2007). adv. **Document type:** *Magazine, Consumer.* **Description:** Covers road racing, cycling, duathlons and triathlons in Texas, New Mexico, Oklahoma, Arkansas and Louisiana.
Address: 2470 Gray Falls Dr, Ste 110, Houston, TX 77077. TEL 281-759-0555, FAX 281-759-7766. Ed. Lance Phegley. Pub. Loren Sheffer. Circ: 12,000.

796.42 USA ISSN 1092-8316
THE RUNNER'S SCHEDULE. Text in English. 1982. m. USD 17; USD 2.95 newsstand/cover (effective 2001). adv. bk.rev. **Description:** For runners and fitness walkers. Includes a complete up-to-date calendar of running and walking events with editorial, coaching advice, health and nutritions, equipment and apparel reviews, and news.
Former titles (until 1996): California Schedule (1087-4585); Northern California Schedule
Published by: Total Race Systems, Inc., 4286 Redwood Hwy, #325, San Rafael, CA 94903-2610. TEL 415-472-7223, FAX 415-472-7233. Ed., R&P, Adv. contact Dave Stringer. Pub. Kees Tuinzing. B&W page USD 1,379, color page USD 1,667; trim 10.88 x 8.38. Circ: 10,500.

613.7172 ESP
RUNNER'S WORLD. Text in Spanish. m. adv. **Document type:** *Magazine, Consumer.*
Published by: Motorpress Iberica (Subsidiary of: Gruner + Jahr AG & Co), Ancora 40, Madrid, 28045, Spain. TEL 34-91-3470100, FAX 34-91-3470152, http://www.motorpress-iberica.es. Ed. Martin Fiz. Circ: 25,000 (paid).

796.355 AUS ISSN 1440-5229
RUNNER'S WORLD. Text in English. 1998. 10/yr. AUD 69 domestic; AUD 73 in New Zealand; AUD 125 Asia & Oceania; AUD 145 elsewhere (effective 2009). adv. **Document type:** *Magazine, Consumer.* **Description:** Covers information on training, nutrition, health, motivation, race calendar, running hot spots and inspiring reader's stories for the sport they love running.
Supersedes in part (in 1998): Australian Runner and Athlete (1321-6325); Which was formerly (until 1994): Australian Runner (0811-0719)
Indexed: SD.
Published by: The Dingoes Refrain Pty Ltd., 4/11 Sabre Dr Port, Melbourne, VIC 3207, Australia. TEL 61-3-96451333, FAX 61-3-96451345. Ed. Lisa Holmes. Pub. Terry O'Halloran. Adv. contact Jane Steinfort.

796.42 SWE ISSN 1654-7837
RUNNER'S WORLD. Text in Swedish. 1982. 10/yr. SEK 399 (effective 2008). adv. **Document type:** *Magazine, Consumer.*
Former titles (until 2007): Springtime med Runner's World (1404-0050); (until 1998): Springtime med Runner's World (1402-5671); Runner's World (1403-5723); (until 1996): Springtime (0281-5419); Incorporates (1979-1999): Jogging (0349-4047)
Published by: (Svenska Friidrottsfoerbundet), Runner's World, Kungsholmstorg 6, Stockholm, 10422, Sweden. TEL 46-8-54553530, FAX 46-8-54553539. Ed. Nils Lodin. Pub. Hans Lodin. Adv. contact Gunnar Lundqvist TEL 46-8-15621072. page SEK 26,000.

796.42 ITA ISSN 1827-2045
RUNNER'S WORLD. Text in Italian. 2006. m. **Document type:** *Magazine, Consumer.*
Published by: Edisport Editoriale SpA, Via Gradisca 11, Milan, MI 20151, Italy. TEL 39-02-38085, FAX 39-02-38010393, edisport@edisport.it, http://www.edisport.it.

796.42 BRA ISSN 1983-8808
RUNNER'S WORLD. Text in Portuguese. 2008. m. BRL 12 newsstand/cover (effective 2010). adv. **Document type:** *Magazine, Consumer.*
Published by: Editora Abril, S.A., Avenida das Nacoes Unidas 7221, Pinheiros, Sao Paulo, SP 05425-902, Brazil. TEL 55-11-50872112, FAX 55-11-50872100, abrilsac@abril.com.br, http://www.abril.com.br. adv.: page BRL 32,700; trim 202 x 266. Circ: 60,311 (paid).

796.42 DEU ISSN 0945-3938
RUNNER'S WORLD; das groesste Laufmagazin der Welt. Text in German. 1993. m. EUR 49.80; EUR 4.20 newsstand/cover (effective 2011). adv. **Document type:** *Magazine, Consumer.* **Description:** Contains information and advice on all aspects of running.
Related titles: Online - full text ed.; ◆ English ed.: Runner's World. ISSN 0897-1706.
Published by: Rodale Motor Presse GmbH und Co. KG (Subsidiary of: Motor Presse Stuttgart GmbH & Co. KG), Leuschnerstr 1, Stuttgart, 70174, Germany. TEL 49-711-18201, FAX 49-711-1821779, aglaessing@motorpresse.de, http://www.motorpresse.de. Ed. Frank Hofmann. Adv. contact Sascha Groeschel. Circ: 55,173 (paid).

796.42 GBR ISSN 1350-7745
RUNNER'S WORLD. Text in English. 1979. m. GBP 29.99 domestic; GBP 4.20 newsstand/cover (effective 2009). adv. illus. back issues avail. **Document type:** *Magazine, Trade.*
Supersedes (in 1993): Running (0144-8560); Incorporates: Jogging Magazine
Related titles: Online - full text ed.; ◆ Regional ed(s).: Runner's World; ◆ Runner's World. ISSN 0897-1706.
Indexed: SportS.
—BLDSC (8052.384600), IE, Ingenta. **CCC.**
Published by: Natmag - Rodale Ltd., 72 Broadwick St, London, W1F 9EP, United Kingdom. natmags@subscription.co.uk, http://www.natmag-rodale.co.uk/. Ed. Andy Dixon TEL 44-207-3394417. Adv. contact Jason Elson TEL 44-207-3394401. Circ: 94,456.

796.42 USA ISSN 0897-1706
GV1061
RUNNER'S WORLD. Text in English. 197?. m. USD 24 domestic; CAD 31 in Canada; USD 60 elsewhere (effective 2011). adv. illus. Index. back issues avail.; reprints avail. **Document type:** *Magazine, Consumer.* **Description:** Provides runners at any skill level with current training techniques, nutritional breakthroughs, equipment reviews, and race information in the United States and around the world.
Former titles (until 1987): Rodale's Runner's World (0892-3744); Which incorporated (1978-1987): Runner (0149-7316); (until 1985): Runner's World (0035-9939); (until 1970): Distance Running News
Related titles: Microform ed.: (from PQC); Online - full text ed.; ◆ German ed.: Runner's World. ISSN 0945-3938; ◆ Regional ed(s).: Runner's World. ISSN 1350-7745; ◆ Runner's World.
Indexed: A11, A22, A25, A26, AcaI, B04, BRD, C05, C11, C12, CPerI, ConsI, E08, G05, G06, G07, G08, G09, H03, H11, H12, HlthInd, I05, I07, M01, M02, M06, MASUSE, MagInd, P02, P10, P48, P53, P54, PEI, PMR, PQC, R03, R06, RASB, RGAb, RGPR, S08, S09, S23, SD, SPI, SportS, T02, TOM, U01, W03, W05, WBA, WMB.
—BLDSC (8052.384500), IE, Infotrieve, Ingenta. **CCC.**
Published by: Rodale, Inc., 33 E Minor St, Emmaus, PA 18098. TEL 610-967-5171, info@rodale.com, http://www.rodaleinc.com. Ed. David Willey.

796.42 ZAF
RUNNER'S WORLD. Text in English. 1993. m. ZAR 8; ZAR 161 foreign. adv. **Document type:** *Magazine, Consumer.* **Description:** Covers running and athletics, advice from the experts on nutrition and injury prevention, training tips, analysis of running gear, and personal accounts from top local and international runners.
Related titles: ◆ Regional ed(s).: Runner's World. ISSN 1350-7745; ◆ Runner's World. ISSN 0897-1706.
Published by: Touchline Media, PO Box 16368, Vlaeberg, Cape Town 8018, South Africa. TEL 27-21-217810, FAX 27-21-215118, http://www.touchline.co.za. Ed. Mike Green. Pub. Rob Moore. R&P Stuart Lowe. Adv. contact Marc Frampton. Circ: 20,000 (paid).

790.1 USA
RUNNER'S WORLD HIGH SCHOOL RUNNER. Text in English. 1992. s-a. free to qualified personnel (effective 2009). **Document type:** *Magazine, Consumer.* **Description:** Covers training, nutrition and gear for teenage runners.
Published by: Rodale, Inc., 33 E Minor St, Emmaus, PA 18098. TEL 610-967-5171, FAX 610-967-8963, customer_service@rodale.com, http://www.rodaleinc.com. Pub. Andrew Hersam.

S

794 DEU ISSN 1619-5590
RUNNING. Text in German. 2000. m. EUR 39.90; EUR 4 newsstand/cover (effective 2008). adv. **Document type:** *Magazine, Consumer.*
Published by: Sportagentur WAG's, Badenweiler Str 2-4, Freiburg, 79117, Germany. TEL 49-761-211720, FAX 49-761-2117211. Pub. Armin Schirmaier. adv.: B&W page EUR 4,320, color page EUR 9,504; trim 210 x 297. Circ: 39,000 (paid).

RUNNING & FITNEWS. *see* PHYSICAL FITNESS AND HYGIENE

794 DEU
RUNNING-PUR. Text in German. 4/yr. EUR 10.50 (effective 2007). adv. **Document type:** *Magazine, Consumer.*
Address: Lindenplatz 6, Roemerstein, 72587, Germany. TEL 49-7382-936565, FAX 49-7382-936566. Ed., Pub. Felix Fuchs. adv.: B&W page EUR 1,300, color page EUR 1,999. Circ: 10,000 (paid and controlled).

790.1 USA ISSN 0147-2968
GV1061
RUNNING TIMES. Abbreviated title: R T. Text in English. 1977. 10/yr. USD 24.95 domestic; CAD 29.96 in Canada; USD 55 elsewhere (effective 2011). adv. bk.rev. illus.; stat. 84 p./no.; back issues avail.; reprints avail. **Document type:** *Magazine, Consumer.* **Description:** Contains information on training and racing, plus writing by runners for runners.
Indexed: B02, B15, B17, B18, G04, G08, I05, PEI, SD, SPI, SportS, T02.
—CCC.
Published by: Rodale, Inc., 33 E Minor St, Emmaus, PA 18098. TEL 610-967-5171, info@rodale.com, http://www.rodaleinc.com. Ed. Jonathan Beverly. Circ: 124,630.

796.72 ZAF ISSN 1998-0272
S A HOT RODS. (South Africa) Text in English. 2008. q. ZAR 75 (effective 2008). adv. **Document type:** *Magazine, Consumer.*
Published by: Picasso Headline (Pty) Ltd, PO Box 60618, Table View, 7439, South Africa. TEL 27-21-5512009, FAX 27-21-5512999, info@picasso.co.za, http://www.picasso.co.za.

796 ZAF ISSN 0258-641X
S A SPORTS ILLUSTRATED. (South Africa) Text in English. 1986. m. ZAR 242 domestic; ZAR 539 neighboring states; ZAR 673 elsewhere (effective 2007). adv. **Document type:** *Magazine, Consumer.* **Description:** Covers local and international sport, including cricket, rugby, tennis, golf, motor racing and boxing.
Related titles: Ed.: Sports Illustrated (Afrikaanse Edition). ISSN 1991-6809.
Published by: Touchline Media, PO Box 16368, Vlaeberg, Cape Town 8018, South Africa. TEL 27-21-4083800, FAX 27-21-4083811, http://www.touchlinr.co.za. Ed. Steve Smith TEL 27-21-4083812. Pub. Nic Wides. Adv. contact Anthony Evlambiou TEL 27-21-4083813. color page ZAR 33,900; trim 210 x 276. Circ: 39,695 (paid).

S A SPORTS TRADER. (South Africa) *see* BUSINESS AND ECONOMICS—Marketing And Purchasing

S A Z BIKE. (Sport Artikel Zeitung) *see* BUSINESS AND ECONOMICS—Marketing And Purchasing

S A Z SPORT. (Sport Artikel Zeitung) *see* BUSINESS AND ECONOMICS—Marketing And Purchasing

S A Z SPORTSFASHION MAGAZIN. (Sport Artikel Zeitung) *see* CLOTHING TRADE—Fashions

S B/CONSTRUCCION DE INSTALLACIONES DEPORTIVAS Y PISCINAS/EQUIPEMENT SPORTIF ET PISCINES/SPORTS FACILITIES AND SWIMMING POOLS. (Sportstaettenbau und Baederanlagen) *see* BUILDING AND CONSTRUCTION

790.1 CAN ISSN 1488-1071
S B C SKATEBOARD. (Snow Board Canada) Text in English. 1999. q. CAD 22.49 domestic; USD 22.49 in United States; USD 50 elsewhere (effective 2007). adv. **Document type:** *Magazine, Consumer.* **Description:** Focuses on the abundance of Canadian skateboard talent, with coast to coast coverage of the country's vibrant skate scene.
Published by: S B C Media, 2255 B Queen St E, Ste 3266, Toronto, ON M4E 1G3, Canada. TEL 416-406-2400, FAX 416-406-0656, info@sbcmedia.com, http://www.sbcmedia.com. Ed., Pub. Steve Jarrett. **Dist. by:** International Publishers Direct, 27500 Riverview Center Blvd, Bonita Springs, FL 34134. TEL 858-320-4563, FAX 858-677-3220.

658.8 790 USA ISSN 1548-7407
S G B; the national news magazine of the sporting goods industry. (Sports Goods Buyer) Text in English. 1967. 16/yr. adv. bibl.; charts; illus.; tr.lit. **Document type:** *Magazine, Trade.* **Description:** Provides news, features, original research and interviews with sporting goods industry movers and shakers.
Formerly (until 200?): Sporting Goods Business (0146-0889); Incorporates (1969-19??): Sports Trend Magazine (0890-8745); Which was formerly (until 1986): Sports Merchandiser (0049-1985)
Related titles: Online - full text ed.
Indexed: A09, A10, A12, A13, A15, A17, A22, ABIn, B01, B02, B03, B06, B07, B08, B09, B15, B17, B18, BusI, C12, G04, G06, G07, G08, I05, M01, M02, P48, P51, P53, P54, PQC, SD, SportS, T&II, T02, V02, V03, V04.
—BLDSC (8254.541000), CIS, Ingenta. **CCC.**
Published by: SportsOneSource Group, 2151 Hawkins St, Ste 200, Charlotte, NC 28269. TEL 704-987-3450, FAX 704-987-3455, info@sportsonesource.com, http://www.sportsonesource.com. Circ: 23,700 (controlled).

S G I MARKET FACTS ATHLETIC FOOTWEAR & APPAREL. (Sporting Goods Intelligence) *see* BUSINESS AND ECONOMICS

796.375 USA ISSN 1555-4716
S P A R Q MAGAZINE. (Speed Power Agility Reaction Quickness) Text in English. 1986. q. USD 19 domestic; USD 29 foreign (effective 2005). adv. bk.rev. **Document type:** *Magazine, Consumer.* **Description:** Contains profiles and articles of interest to students involved in sports. Deals with all aspects of their lives.
Formerly (until 2005): Student Sports (1059-793X)
Published by: Student Sports, 2780 Skypark Dr, Ste 475, Torrance, CA 90505. TEL 310-539-9100, FAX 310-257-4444, brentt@studentsports.com. Ed. John Tawa. Pub., R&P Andy Bark. Adv. contact Karrie Kozar. Circ: 40,000 (paid).

790.1 712 GBR ISSN 2046-7451
S T R I BULLETIN; for sports surface management. Text in English. 1929. q. free to members (effective 2011). bk.rev.; Website rev. 36 p./no.; back issues avail. **Document type:** *Magazine, Trade.* **Description:** Designed for professionals who manage turf for golf, sports, landscaping, parks and outdoor activities.
Former titles (2010): Turfgrass Bulletin (1362-9255); (until 1996): Sports Turf Bulletin (0490-5474); (until 1951): Notes from the St. Ives Research Station
Related titles: Online - full content ed.
Indexed: A37, B23, C30, CABA, E12, F08, F12, GH, GardL, H16, I11, LT, O01, OR, P32, P40, PGrRegA, R07, R13, RRTA, S13, S16, SD, SportS, T02, W10, W11.
—BLDSC (8474.156000), IE, Ingenta. **CCC.**
Published by: Sports Turf Research Institute, St Ives Estate, Bingley, W Yorks BD16 1AU, United Kingdom. TEL 44-1274-565131, FAX 44-1274-561891, info@stri.co.uk, http://www.stri.co.uk. Adv. contact Kerry Haywood TEL 44-1283-735646. Circ: 5,000 (controlled).

796 797 IRL ISSN 1649-783X
S FOUR W. Variant title: Something for the Weekend. Text in English. 2006. a. adv.
Published by: P & G Publishing Ltd., 17 Donnybrook Court, Dublin, 4, Ireland. adv.: page EUR 3,750; trim 210 x 297.

794.1 HRV ISSN 0350-2570
SAHOVKI GLASNIK; organ Sahovskog saveza Hrvatske. Text in Croatian. 1925. m. USD 20. adv. bk.rev.
Published by: (Sahovki Savez Hrvatske), Sahovska Naklada, Bogoviceva 7, Zagreb, 41000, Croatia. TEL 041 273-692. Ed. Drazen Marovic. Circ: 5,500.

794.1 SRB ISSN 0351-1375
GV1313
SAHOVSKI INFORMATOR/CHESS INFORMANT/SHAHMATNYI INFORMATOR. Text in Serbo-Croatian, English. 1966. 3/yr. GBP 18 (effective 2002). **Description:** Offers a selection of the best games played by the world's greatest chess players.
Related titles: CD-ROM ed.; Online - full text ed.
Address: Francuska 31, P.O. Box 375, Belgrade, 11001. TEL 381-11-630109, FAX 381-11-626583, info@sahovski.co.yu. Ed. Zdenko Krnicatanovic. Circ: 30,000.

790.1 USA
ST. JOHN'S BASKETBALL PREVIEW. Text in English. 1995. a. USD 3.95 (effective 1997). adv. back issues avail. **Description:** Includes player features, previews and historical flashbacks.
Published by: Host Communications, Inc., 546 E Main St, Lexington, KY 40508. TEL 606-226-4510, FAX 606-226-4575. Ed. Craig Baroncelli. Adv. contact Andrea Cuzick. page USD 4,500.

794.1 HUN ISSN 0237-2525
SAKKELET. Text in Hungarian. 1889. 6/yr. HUF 1,584, USD 49 (effective 1995). adv. bk.rev. illus. **Document type:** *Newspaper.* **Description:** Includes annotated games, computer and correspondence chess, studies-problems, and combinations. Covers chess events in Hungary.
Related titles: Diskette ed.
Published by: Nemzeti Sport Kft., c/o Andras Ozsvath, Ed., Falk Miksa utca 10, Budapest, 1005, Hungary. TEL 36-1-1312790, FAX 36-1-1319738. Circ: 8,000. **U.S. subscr. addr.:** Center of Hungarian Books, 114 Parkville Ave, Brooklyn, NY 11230. **Dist. by:** Kultura Kulkereskedelmi Vallalat, PO Box 149, Budapest 1389, Hungary.

796 USA ISSN 1938-906X
SALT LIFE MAGAZINE. Text in English. 2007 (Aug.). bi-m. USD 24.95 (effective 2007). **Document type:** *Magazine, Consumer.* **Description:** Devoted to ocean sports and outdoor pursuits such as fishing, boating, surfing and diving.
Address: 313051 Beach Blvd, Jacksonville, FL 32246. TEL 904-241-7258, customerservice@saltlife.com. Pub. Dana Bussiere.

790.1 BEL ISSN 0775-7883
SAMSOM SPORTSECRETARIS. Variant title: Nieuwsbrief Sportsecretariaat. Text in Flemish. 1987. w. **Description:** Provides advice of administrative and fiscal nature on how to run a sports organization.
Related titles: French ed.: Lettre d'Information Hebdomadaire pour la Gestion d'un Cercle Sportif. ISSN 0776-9121.
Published by: C E D Samsom (Subsidiary of: Wolters Samsom Belgie n.v.), Kouterveld 14, Diegem, 1831, Belgium. TEL 32-2-7231111.

796.962 USA
SAN JOSE SHARKS MAGAZINE. Text in English. 1991. 6/yr. (Oct.-Apr.). illus. cum.index: 1991-1996. back issues avail. **Document type:** *Magazine, Consumer.*
Published by: Woodford Publishing, Inc., PO Box 910, Tiburon, CA 94920. TEL 415-397-1853, FAX 415-399-0942. Ed. Ken Arnold. Pub. Laurence J Hyman. R&P David Lilienstein. Adv. contact Tony Khing.

797.2 CAN
SASKATCHEWAN SYNCHRO NEWS. Text in English. q. CAD 15 to members. adv. **Document type:** *Newsletter.*
Published by: Synchro Saskatchewan, 1870 Lorne St, Regina, SK S4P 2L7, Canada. TEL 306-780-9227, FAX 306-781-6021. Eds. Margot Weiner, Wayne Hellquist. Adv. contact Kenda Richards. Circ: 300.

355 USA
SAVAGE AND SOLDIER. Text in English. irreg. USD 22. **Description:** Devoted to the history and miniatures gaming of the colonial period.
Address: 231 N Third St, Lewisburg, PA 17837-1505. Ed. Joe Boeke.

SCANDINAVIAN JOURNAL OF MEDICINE & SCIENCE IN SPORTS. *see* MEDICAL SCIENCES—Sports Medicine

798.001.3 300 SWE ISSN 2000-088X
▼ ➤ **SCANDINAVIAN SPORT STUDIES FORUM.** Variant title: S S S F. Text in Danish, English, Norwegian, Swedish; Summaries in English. 2010. 18/yr. free (effective 2011). **Document type:** *Journal, Academic/Scholarly.* **Description:** Covers the study of sports in all academic disciplines within the social sciences, humanities, and others.
Media: Online - full text.
Published by: Malmoe Hoegskola, Laerarutbildningen. Idrottvetenskap/ Malmoe University, School of Teacher Education. Department of Sport Sciences, Malmoe, 20506, Sweden. TEL 46-40-6657000, FAX 46-40-6657305, http://www.mah.se/fakulteter-och-omraden/ Lararutbildningen/Enheter/Idrottsvetenskap-IDV. Eds. Bo Carlsson, Kjell Eriksson.

688.76 ITA ISSN 1127-4670
SCARPE E SPORT. Text in Italian. 1998. s-a. EUR 10 (effective 2009). **Document type:** *Magazine, Consumer.*
Published by: Editoriale Sport Italia, Via Masaccio 12, Milan, MI 20149, Italy. TEL 39-02-4815396, FAX 39-02-4690907, http://www.sportivi.it.

794.1 NLD ISSN 1385-8807
SCHAAK MAGAZINE. Text in Dutch. 1893. bi-m. EUR 44.46; EUR 2.95 newsstand/cover (effective 2009). adv. bk.rev. charts; illus. index. **Document type:** *Magazine, Consumer.* **Description:** Covers chess.
Formerly (until 1996): Schakend Nederland (0036-5890)
Published by: Koninklijke Nederlandse Schaakbond/Royal Dutch Chess Federation, Frans Halsplein 5, Haarlem, 2021 DL, Netherlands. TEL 31-23-5254025, FAX 31-23-5254353, bondsbureau@schaakbond.nl, http://www.schaakbond.nl. Ed. Minze bij de Weg. Circ: 18,000.

794.1 NLD
SCHAAKSCHAKERINGEN. Text in Dutch. 1966. 6/yr. bk.rev. **Description:** Includes annotated games, results, theory and articles.
Published by: Bestuur Nederlandse Bond van Correspondentieschakers, c/o C A van Wieringen, Jachthavenweg 8A, Amsterdam, 1076 CZ, Netherlands. cavanwieringen@cs.com, http:// www.correspondentieschaken.nl.

794.1 DEU ISSN 0048-9328
SCHACH. Text in German. 1947. m. adv. bk.rev. **Document type:** *Consumer.*
Formerly (until 1950): Schach-Express (0323-8288); Incorporated (in 1996): Schach-Report, Deutsche Schachzeitung (0948-7670); Which was formerly (until 1995): Deutsche Schachblaetter, Schachreport (0930-8121); Which was formed by the merger of (19??-1986): Schach-Report (0930-8652); (1962-1986): Deutsche Schachblaetter (0012-0650); and incorporated in part (1871-1988): Deutsche Schachzeitung (0012-0669)
Published by: Sport und Gesundheit Verlag GmbH, Lindenstr 76, Berlin, 12683, Germany. TEL 49-30-25913028, FAX 49-30-25913085. Ed., Adv. contact Raj Tischbierek. Circ: 10,000.

794.1 AUT
SCHACH AKTIV. Text in German. 1979. 11/yr. **Document type:** *Newspaper, Consumer.* **Description:** Contains national and international chess news and games, opening theory, correspondence chess, studies and problems.
Published by: Oesterreichischer Schachbund, Sackstr 17, Graz, St 8010, Austria. verband@chess.at, http://www.chess.at. Ed. Kurt Fahrner. Circ: 2,100.

794.1 DEU
SCHACH-ARCHIV. Text in German. 1951. 12/yr. USD 30. adv. bk.rev. **Document type:** *Consumer.* **Description:** Deals with theoretical opening questions.
Published by: Schachzentrale Caissa, Weidenbaumsweg 80, Hamburg, 21035, Germany. TEL 040-7244282, FAX 040-7214647. Ed., Pub. Horst Rattmann. Circ: 3,000.

794.1 DEU
SCHACH IN BADEN. Text in German. 1977. 6/yr. adv. bk.rev. **Document type:** *Magazine, Consumer.* **Description:** Contains information for chessplayers in the Baden-Wuerttemberg region of Germany.
Published by: Badischer Schachverband, c/o Fritz Meyer, Blattmannstr 6, Friesenheim, 77948, Germany. TEL 49-7821-61170, FAX 49-7821-998117, praesident@badischer-schachverband.de, http://www.badischer-schachverband.de.

794.1 DEU
SCHACHMAGAZIN 64 - SCHACH-ECHO. Text in German. 1992. m. EUR 48 domestic; EUR 57.60 foreign; EUR 5 newsstand/cover (effective 2009). adv. 28 p./no. 3 cols./p.; **Document type:** *Magazine, Consumer.* **Description:** Contains articles on chess tournaments, theory and strategy. Includes calendar of events.
Formed by the merger of (1978-1992): Schachmagazin 64 (0721-9539); (1953-1992): Schach-Echo (0036-5831); Which incorporated in part (1871-1988): Deutsche Schachzeitung (0012-0669)
Indexed: RASB.
—CCC.
Published by: Carl Ed. Schuenemann KG, Zweite Schlachpforte 7, Bremen, 28195, Germany. TEL 49-421-369030, FAX 49-421-3690339, kontakt@schuenemann-verlag.de, http:// www.schuenemann-verlag.de. adv.: B&W page EUR 765, color page EUR 1,365; trim 185 x 260. Circ: 9,702 (paid and controlled).

794.1 CHE ISSN 0176-2257
DER SCHACHWOCHE; aktuelle Schachnachrichten aus aller Welt. Text in German. 1982. 50/yr. CHF 145. adv. **Description:** Includes current international tournament information and over 2,400 games per year.
Published by: Schachwoche, Schachagentur Caissa AG, Postfach 76, Sarmenstorf, 5614, Switzerland. TEL 057-272061, FAX 057-273181. Ed. Werner Widmer. Circ: 9,500.

794.1 SWE ISSN 0347-0377
SCHACKKORRESPONDENTEN. Text in Swedish. 1955. bi-m. SEK 360 (effective 1991).
Published by: S J Fritidsfoerbund, Fack 250, Stockholm, 10124, Sweden.

794.1 SWE ISSN 0346-0770
SCHACKNYTT. Text in Swedish. 1970. 10/yr. SEK 450 (effective 2005). adv. bk.rev. **Document type:** *Magazine, Consumer.*
Address: Vegagatan 18, Goeteborg, 41309, Sweden. TEL 46-31-244790, FAX 46-18-555-444. Ed., Pub. Ari Ziegler.

796 NLD ISSN 1877-0401
SCHEIDS!. Text in Dutch. 2008. q. EUR 14.95 (effective 2011). **Document type:** *Magazine, Trade.*
Published by: Arko Sports Media (Subsidiary of: Arko Uitgeverij BV), Postbus 393, Nieuwegein, 3430 AJ, Netherlands. TEL 31-30-7073000, FAX 31-30-6052618, sport@sportsmedia.nl, http:// www.sportsmedia.nl. Eds. Janneke Westermann, Maarten Westermann.

796.86 ITA ISSN 0036-6005
LA SCHERMA. Text in Italian. 1959. m. adv. bk.rev. **Document type:** *Magazine, Consumer.* **Description:** Covers fencing.
Published by: Federazione Italiana Scherma, Viale Tiziano 74, Rome, 00196, Italy. TEL 39-06-3233773, FAX 39-06-36858139, http:// www.federscherma.it.

799 NLD ISSN 0048-9344
SCHIETSPORT. Text in Dutch. 1890. m. adv. bk.rev. **Description:** Covers shooting.

Published by: Koninklijke Nederlandse Schutters Associatie/Royal Dutch Shooting Association, Postbus 303, Leusden, 3830 AJ, Netherlands. TEL 31-33-4622388, FAX 31-33-4650626, info@knsa.nl, http://www.knsa.nl.

794.1 CAN ISSN 0847-1428
SCHOLAR'S MATE. Text in English. 1990. 5/yr. CAD 14; USD 14 in United States; USD 18 elsewhere. adv. bk.rev. stat. back issues avail. **Description:** Chess magazine for youngsters.
Published by: Kiril Publishing, P O Box 702, Sta A, Montreal, PQ H3C 2V2, Canada. TEL 514-845-8352, FAX 514-845-8810. Ed., R&P Jeff Coakley. Circ: 1,000 (paid).

SCHRIFTEN ZUR SPORTPSYCHOLOGIE. *see* PSYCHOLOGY

794 DEU ISSN 1435-6546
SCHRIFTEN ZUR SPORTWISSENSCHAFT. Text in German. 1991. irreg., latest vol.89, 2010. price varies. **Document type:** *Monographic series, Academic/Scholarly.*
Published by: Verlag Dr. Kovac, Leverkusenstr 13, Hamburg, 22761, Germany. TEL 49-40-3988800, FAX 49-40-39888055, info@verlagdrkovac.de.

SCHRIFTENREIHE ZUR GLUECKSSPIELFORSCHUNG. *see* PSYCHOLOGY

799.202 DEU
DER SCHUETZE. Text in German. 1965. q.
Published by: Schuetzengesellschaft Pforzheim 1450 e.V., Kirschenpfad 1, Pforzheim, 75181, Germany. TEL 07231-63310. Ed. Frank Herholz. Circ: 1,000.

799.202 DEU ISSN 1437-3343
SCHUETZENWARTE. Text in German. 1998. bi-m. EUR 2 newsstand/cover (effective 2009). adv. **Document type:** *Magazine, Consumer.*
Published by: (Westfaelischer Schuetzenbund e.V.), Brinkmann Henrich Medien GmbH, Heerstr 5, Meinerzhagen, 58540, Germany. TEL 49-2354-77990, FAX 49-2354-779977, info@bhmg.de, http://www.bhmg.de. Ed. Joerg Jagener. adv.: B&W page EUR 1,120, color page EUR 1,990. Circ: 10,500 (paid and controlled).

794.1 DEU ISSN 0048-9506
DIE SCHWALBE. Text in German. 1924. bi-m. EUR 30 (effective 2006). bk.rev. bibl.; charts; illus.
Published by: Schwalbe Deutsche Vereinigung fuer Problemschach, c/o Achim Schoeneberg, Paul-Hindemith-Str 58, Einbeck, 37574, Germany. TEL 49-5561-4727. Ed. Guenter Buesing.

790.1 CHE ISSN 1420-3685
SCHWEIZER SPORT & MODE. Text in German. m. CHF 98; CHF 125 foreign (effective 1999). **Document type:** *Trade.* **Description:** Trade paper for retailers of sporting goods.
Published by: (Schweizer Sporthaendler Verband), Schweizer Sport & Mode, Raffelstr 11, Zuerich, 8045, Switzerland. TEL 41-1-4515155, FAX 41-1-4515166. Ed. Beat Ladner.

794.1 CHE ISSN 0036-7745
SCHWEIZERISCHE SCHACHZEITUNG; revue Suisse des echecs, revista scacchistica Svizzera. Text in French, German, Italian. 1900. m. CHF 70. adv. bk.rev. charts; illus. **Document type:** *Bulletin, Consumer.* **Description:** Covers the Swiss chess scene.
Published by: Schweizerischer Schachbund, Gartenstr 12, Dulliken, 4657, Switzerland. TEL 41-62-2953365. Ed. Markus Angst. Circ: 8,000.

797.21 DEU
SCHWIMMSPORTVEREIN ESSLINGEN. VEREINSNACHRICHTEN. Text in German. 1956. q. membership. adv. **Document type:** *Newsletter.*
Published by: Schwimmsportverein Esslingen e.V., Hohenackerstr 32, Esslingen Am Neckar, 73733, Germany. TEL 0711-3704474, FAX 0711-3704475. Ed. Carola Waegerle. Adv. contact Manfred Kaltmaier. Circ: 1,200.

DER SCHWIMMTEICH; Fachmagazin fuer Planung, Bau und Betrieb. *see* BUILDING AND CONSTRUCTION

796 613.7 IND ISSN 0974-2964
SCIENTIFIC JOURNAL IN SPORT AND EXERCISE. Text in English. 2005. s-a. INR 200 to individuals; INR 400 to institutions (effective 2010). **Document type:** *Journal, Trade.*
Published by: Laxmibai Sports Education and Welfare Society, RZ-T-94, Shukar Bazar, Uttam Nagar, New Delhi, 110 059, India. TEL 91-11-25336622, lsews@lsews.org.

▼ **SCIENZA & SPORT.** *see* SCIENCES: COMPREHENSIVE WORKS

613.7 ITA ISSN 1970-6642
SCIENZE DELLO SPORT. Text in Multiple languages. 2006. q. **Document type:** *Magazine, Trade.*
Media: Online - full text.
Published by: Associazione Italiana Scienze dello Sport, c/o Made in It, Via Cettigne 13, Cagliari, 09129, Italy. TEL 39-070-4525108, info@scienzedellosport.it, http://www.scienzedellosport.it.

794.1 GBR
SCOTTISH CHESS. Text in English. 1960. bi-m. GBP 20.70 to non-members; GBP 19 to members; GBP 3.45 per issue domestic to non-members; GBP 4.50 per issue in Europe to non-members; GBP 6.90 per issue elsewhere to non-members (effective 2009). adv. bk.rev. **Document type:** *Magazine, Consumer.* **Description:** Covers national and international games, and articles about all aspects of chess.
Published by: Chess Scotland, 39 Morningside Park, Edinburg, EH10 5EZ, United Kingdom. membership@chessscotland.com. Ed. David Oswald.

796.96 GBR ISSN 0036-9160
SCOTTISH CURLER. Text in English. 1954. 8/yr. GBP 19.50 domestic; USD 30 in Europe; USD 31.50 elsewhere (effective 2009). adv. bk.rev. illus. back issues avail. **Document type:** *Magazine, Consumer.* **Description:** Covers news, events and features about ice rinks and curling clubs throughout Scotland.
Indexed: SD, SportS.
Published by: Clyde and Forth Press Ltd. (Subsidiary of: Dunfermline Press), Herald Bldg, Dock Rd, Ardrossan, KA22 8DA, United Kingdom. TEL 44-1294-464321. Ed. Bob Cowan TEL 44-1576-470650.

797.23 GBR ISSN 0308-7379
SCOTTISH DIVER. Text in English. 1960. bi-m. GBP 12.50 to non-members; GBP 2.50 per issue to non-members; free to members (effective 2009). adv. bk.rev. illus. cum.index. back issues avail. **Document type:** *Magazine, Trade.* **Description:** Contains articles on sport-diving practices, dive sites worldwide, history of diving.
Related titles: Online - full text ed.: free (effective 2009).
Indexed: SportS.
Published by: Scottish Sub-Aqua Club, Cockburn Centre, 40 Bogmoor Pl, Glasgow, G51 4TQ, United Kingdom. TEL 44-141-4251021, FAX 44-141-4251021, hq@scotsac.com. Ed. Jack Morrison. Adv. contact Terry Brennan TEL 44-141-332-3933.

790.1 GBR
SCOTTISH SPORTS COUNCIL. ANNUAL REVIEW. Text in English. 1973. a. **Document type:** *Corporate.*
Former title (until 2004): Scottish Sports Council. Annual Report; (until 1978): Scottish Sports Council. Report (0140-444X)
Related titles: Online - full text ed.: free (effective 2010).
Published by: Scottish Sports Council, Doges, Templeton on the Green, Glasgow, G40 1DA, United Kingdom. TEL 44-141-5346500, FAX 44-141-5346501, sportscotland.enquiries@sportscotland.org.uk, http://www.sportscotland.org.uk/.

797 SGP
SCUBA DIVER AUSTRALASIA. Text in English. bi-m. SGD 45 in Asia; AUD 50 in Australia, New Zealand & South Pacific; USD 50 elsewhere; free to members PADI Diving Society (effective 2009). adv. **Document type:** *Magazine, Consumer.* **Description:** Provides comprehensive coverage of the recreational diving field.
Former titles (until 2001): Australian Scuba Diver; (until 1999): Scuba Diver (0729-5529)
Published by: (P A D I Diving Society AUS), Asian Geographic Magazines Pte Ltd, No. 1 Syed Alwi Rd, #06-01 Song Lin Building, Singapore, 207628, Singapore. TEL 65-6298-3241, 1800-219-703, FAX 65-6291-2068, http://www.asiangeographic.org. adv.: B&W page AUD 1,710, color page AUD 2,005; trim 210 x 297. Circ: 4,977.

790.1 USA ISSN 0739-568X
SCUBA TIMES; the active diver's magazine. Text in English. 1979. bi-m. USD 17 domestic; USD 22 foreign; USD 2.99 newsstand/cover. adv. illus.; tr.lit.
Published by: G B P, Inc., 33 Music Sq W, Ste 104, Nashville, TN 37203. TEL 800-950-7282. Ed. Christopher Grant. Pub. Fred D Garth. Adv. contact David Benz. Circ: 50,000.

790.1 ITA ISSN 1125-1891
SCUOLA DELLO SPORT; rivista di cultura sportiva. Abbreviated title: S D S. Text in Italian; Summaries in English, French, Spanish. 1982. q. EUR 20 (effective 2008). **Document type:** *Magazine, Consumer.*
—BLDSC (8213.502600), IE, Ingenta.
Published by: (Comitato Olimpico Nazionale Italiano (C O N I)), Calzetti e Mariucci Editori, Via del Sottopasso 7, Localita Ferriera, Torgiano, PG 06089, Italy. http://www.calzetti-mariucci.it. Circ: 8,000.

796 ARG ISSN 1851-345X
SECRETARIA DE DEPORTE DE LA NACION. BOLETIN DE INVESTIGACION. Text in Spanish. 2005. m.
Media: Online - full text. **Related titles:** E-mail ed.: ISSN 1851-3468. 2005.
Published by: Secretaria de Deporte de la Nacion, Crisologo Larralde 1050, Buenos Aires, 1490, Argentina. TEL 54-11-47071684, FAX 54-11-47071651, prensa@deportes.gov.ar.

790.1 DEU ISSN 0930-3308
➤ **SEITENWECHSEL.** Text in German. 1986. s-a. free. adv. bk.rev. **Document type:** *Magazine, Academic/Scholarly.* **Description:** Covers university sports and pastimes.
Published by: Georg-August-Universitaet Goettingen, Zentrale Einrichtung fuer den Allgemeinen Hochschulsport, Sprangerweg 2, Goettingen, 37075, Germany. ifs@sport.uni-goettingen.de, http://www.sport.uni-goettingen.de/ifs. Ed. Andreas Tyrock. Circ: 7,500.

➤ **SELECTIVE SEARCH MAGAZINE.** *see* COMPUTERS—Computer Games

▼ ➤ **LE SENS DU SPORT.** *see* SOCIOLOGY

796 SRB ISSN 1820-6301
SERBIAN JOURNAL OF SPORTS SCIENCES. Text in English. 2007. irreg.
Related titles: Online - full text ed.: ISSN 1452-8827. free (effective 2011).
Indexed: A36, CABA, GH, LT, N02, N03, SD, T02.
Published by: Sportska Akademija Beograd Ed. Milivoj Dopsay.

796.815 FRA ISSN 1771-2025
SESERAGI. Text in French. 1992. s-a. free. back issues avail. **Document type:** *Magazine, Consumer.*
Published by: Federation Francaise d'Aikido et de Budo, Les Allees, Bras, 83149, France. TEL 33-4-98052228, FAX 33-4-94699776.

796 KOR ISSN 1225-7656
SEUPOCEU GWAHAG. Text in Korean. 1982. q. KRW 2,000; KRW 4,000 per issue (effective 2009). **Document type:** *Journal, Academic/Scholarly.*
Related titles: Online - full text ed.
Published by: Korea Institute of Sport Science/Han'gug Ceyug Gwahag Yeon'guweon, 223-19 gongneung-dong, Nowon-Gu, Seoul, Korea, S. TEL 82-2-9709500, FAX 82-2-9709651, publ@sports.re.kr, http://www.sports.re.kr/. Circ: 1,000.

796 USA ISSN 1937-2558
SE7EN. Text in English. 2007. bi-m. USD 17.77 (effective 2007). adv. illus. **Document type:** *Magazine, Consumer.*
Media: Online - full text.
Published by: Se7en Media, Llc. Ed. Kim Malakowsky.

790.1 781.64 CHE
SEVENTH SKY AND SEVENTH SKY PEOPLE. Text in French, German. 1991. m. CHF 39; CHF 7.50 newsstand/cover (effective 1999). adv. music rev. **Document type:** *Consumer.*
Published by: Seventh Sky, Postfach 95, Villars-Ste-Croix, 1029, Switzerland. TEL 41-21-6344141, FAX 41-21-6344110. Pub. Bernard Tache. Adv. contact Corinne Tache Berthe. B&W page CHF 9,500, color page CHF 10,700. Circ: 30,000 (paid).

793.93 USA
SHADIS. Text in English. m. USD 34 domestic; USD 40 in Canada; USD 60 elsewhere (effective 2000). adv. **Document type:** *Magazine, Consumer.* **Description:** Contains articles and information on a variety of role-playing games and products.
Published by: Alderac Entertainment Group, 4045 Guasti Rd, Ste 212, Ontario, CA 91761. TEL 909-390-5444, FAX 909-390-5446, shadis@aol.com. Adv. contact Marcelo Figueroa. Circ: 5,000 (paid).

794.1 BGR
SHAKHMATNA MISL. Text in Bulgarian. 12/yr. USD 30. **Description:** Contains national and international chess game analyses, theory, combinations, studies and problems.
Address: Ul Rakitin 2, Sofia, 1504, Bulgaria. Ed. P Petkov. **Subscr. to:** British Chess Magazine, 9 Market St, St Leonards-on-Sea, E Sussex TN38 0DQ, United Kingdom.

794.1 RUS
SHAKHMATY V ROSSII. Text in Russian. m. USD 125 in United States.
Published by: Izdatel'skii Dom Shakhmaty, Gogolevskii bulv 14, Moscow, 121019, Russian Federation. TEL 7-095-2918578, FAX 7-095-2919770. **Dist. by:** East View Information Services, 10601 Wayzata Blvd, Minneapolis, MN 55305. TEL 952-252-1201, 800-477-1005, FAX 952-252-1202, info@eastview.com, http://www.eastview.com.

790.1 613.7 CHN ISSN 1003-5176
SHAOLIN YU TAIJI. Text in Chinese. 1984. bi-m. USD 28.80 (effective 2009). **Description:** Covers traditional Chinese martial arts including shadow boxing practiced in the Shaolin Buddhist Temple.
Former titles (until 1989): Shaolin Wushu; Zhongzhou Wushu
—East View.
Published by: Henan Tiyu Baokan She, No 3 Jiankang Lu, Zhengzhou, Henan, 450053, China. TEL 0371-3923289. Ed. Qiu Mingnan. **Dist. overseas by:** China International Book Trading Corp, 35 Chegongzhuang Xilu, Haidian District, PO Box 399, Beijing 100044, China.

SHARING THE VICTORY. *see* RELIGIONS AND THEOLOGY

790.1 RUS ISSN 0236-3496
DK285
SHCHIT I MECH. Text in Russian. 1989. 5/w. USD 165 in United States.
Related titles: Microfilm ed.: (from EVP, PQC); Online - full text ed.
—East View.
Address: Ivanovskaya ul 24, Moscow, 127434, Russian Federation. TEL 7-095-976-6644, 7-095-976-2172, FAX 7-095-977-8719. Ed. Valerii Kulik. Circ: 35,000. **Dist. by:** East View Information Services, 10601 Wayzata Blvd, Minneapolis, MN 55305. TEL 952-252-1201, 800-477-1005, FAX 952-252-1202, info@eastview.com, http://www.eastview.com.

THE SHIELD; research journal of physical education and sports science. *see* PHYSICAL FITNESS AND HYGIENE

796 CHN
SHIJIE TIYU ZHOUBAO/WORLD SPORTS NEWS. Text in Chinese. w. CNY 49.92 (effective 2004). **Document type:** *Consumer.*
Related titles: Online - full content ed.
Published by: Zhongguo Tiyubao Yezongshe, 8, Tiyuguan Lu, Chongwen-qu, Beijing, 100061, China. TEL 86-10-67143708. **Dist. by:** China International Book Trading Corp, 35 Chegongzhuang Xilu, Haidian District, PO Box 399, Beijing 100044, China. TEL 86-10-68412045, FAX 86-10-68412023, cibtc@mail.cibtc.com.cn, http://www.cibtc.com.cn.

794.1 UAE
AL-SHIRAH. Text in Arabic, English. 1983. 3/yr. USD 30. adv. illus. **Description:** National and international coverage of games, and junior chess.
Published by: Dubai Chess and Culture Club, P O Box 11354, Dubai, United Arab Emirates. TEL 281362. Ed. Khalid Ali Bin Zayed. Circ: 2,000.

799.202 USA
SHOOT! MAGAZINE. Text in English. 2000. bi-m. USD 32.95; USD 5.95 newsstand/cover (effective 2001). adv. **Document type:** *Magazine, Consumer.*
Published by: Shoot! Magazine Corporation, 1770 West State St, PMB340, Boise, ID 83702. TEL 208-368-9920, FAX 208-338-8428, info@shootmagazine.com, http://www.shootmagazine.com. Ed. Andy Fink.

S

799.202 USA ISSN 0080-9365
TS535
SHOOTER'S BIBLE. Text in English. 1924. a. USD 24.95 (effective 2007). adv. 576 p./no.; **Document type:** *Magazine, Consumer.*
Published by: Stoeger Publishing Co., 17603 Indian Head Hwy., # 200, Accokeek, MD 20607-2501. TEL 301-283-6300, FAX 301-283-4783, http://www.stoegerbooks.com/. Ed. Harris Andrews. Pub. Jennifer Thomas.

799.3 USA ISSN 0037-4148
HD9743.U5
SHOOTING INDUSTRY. Text in English. 1955. m. USD 25; USD 3 per issue (effective 2009). adv. bk.rev. charts; illus.; pat.; stat.; tr.lit. **Document type:** *Magazine, Trade.* **Description:** Guides the retailers to make everyday business decisions easier by offering information such as; what to stock and how to sell it, plus tips on how to keep customers coming back for more.
Related titles: Online - full text ed.
Indexed: A15, ABIn, B02, B15, B17, B18, BusI, G04, G06, G07, G08, I05, M06, P16, P19, P48, P51, P53, P54, PQC, T&II.
Published by: Publishers Development Corp., F M G Publications, 12345 World Trade Dr, San Diego, CA 92128. TEL 858-605-0202, 800-537-3006, FAX 858-605-0247, http://www.fmgpublications.com. Ed. Russ Thurman TEL 858-605-0244. Pub. Thomas von Rosen. Adv. contact Anita Carson TEL 858-605-0209. B&W page USD 4,228, color page USD 6,177; trim 8 x 10.875. Circ: 24,000 (paid and controlled).

799.202 658.8 USA ISSN 0887-9397
SHOOTING SPORTS RETAILER. Text in English. 1983. bi-m. adv. tr.lit. **Document type:** *Magazine, Trade.*
Address: 255 W 36th St, Ste 1202, New York, NY 10018. TEL 212-840-0660, FAX 212-944-1884. Ed. Bob Rogers. Pub., Adv. contact Glenn Karaban. B&W page USD 3,298, color page USD 4,075; trim 8.125 x 10.875. Circ: 16,575.

799.2 USA ISSN 1069-6822
SHOOTING SPORTS U S A. Text in English. 1988. m. adv. back issues avail. **Document type:** *Magazine, Consumer.* **Description:** Covers matches at the local, regional, national, and international levels including how-to articles and a listing of all NRA-sanctioned matches.
Related titles: Online - full text ed.: free (effective 2009).
Published by: National Rifle Association of America, PO Box 420648, Palm Coast, FL 32142. TEL 703-267-1000, 800-672-3888, membership@nrahq.org, http://www.nra.org. Ed. John Zent TEL 703-267-1332. adv.: B&W page USD 2,204, color page USD 3,225; trim 7.625 x 10.5.

799.2 USA ISSN 0038-8084
SHOOTING TIMES. Text in English. 1960. m. USD 16.98 domestic; USD 29.98 in Canada; USD 31.98 elsewhere (effective 2008). adv. illus. **Document type:** *Magazine, Consumer.* **Description:** Targets today's active shooters and hunters with editorial content on firearms, ammunition, accessories, outerwear, and hunting and camping gear.
Related titles: Online - full text ed.
Indexed: ConsI, SPI, SportS.
Published by: Intermedia Outdoors, Inc., 512 7th Ave, 11th Fl, New York, NY 10018. TEL 800-260-6397, FAX 212-302-4472, customerservice@imoutdoors.com, http://www.imoutdoorsmedia.com. Ed. Mike Nischalke. adv.: B&W page USD 8,458, color page USD 13,311. Circ: 175,526 (paid).

799 GBR ISSN 0037-4164
SHOOTING TIMES AND COUNTRY MAGAZINE. Text in English. 1882 (Sep.). w. GBP 89.99 domestic; USD 168.30 in United States; USD 195.30 in Canada; EUR 155.70 in Europe; GBP 126.50 elsewhere (effective 2009). adv. bk.rev. illus. back issues avail. **Document type:** *Magazine, Consumer.* **Description:** Features articles covering all disciplines in shooting, including game, rough and stalking.
Former titles (until 1950): Shooting Times and British Sportsman; (until 1893): Shooting Times and Kennel News; (until 1888): Illustrated Shooting Times and Kennel News; (until 1886): The Shooting, Sport and Kennel News; (until Sep.1884): The Illustrated Shooting Times, Sport and Kennel News; (until Apr.1884): Wildfowler's Illustrated Shooting Times and Kennel News
Related titles: Online - full text ed.
—BLDSC (8268.280000).
Published by: I P C Country & Leisure Media Ltd. (Subsidiary of: I P C Media Ltd.), The Blue Fin Bldg, 110 Southwark St, London, SE1 0SU, United Kingdom. TEL 44-20-31485000, http://www.ipcmedia.com. Ed. Camilla Clark TEL 44-20-31484741. Pub. Fiona Mercer TEL 44-20-31484311. Adv. contact Toby Drought TEL 44-20-31484212. color page GBP 2,500. Circ: 26,071. **Subscr. to:** PO Box 272, Haywards Heath, W Sussex RH16 3FS, United Kingdom. TEL 44-845-6767778, FAX 44-1444-445599, IPCsubs@quadrantsubs.com, http://www.magazinesdirect.co.uk. **Dist. by:** MarketForce UK Ltd. salesinnovation@marketforce.co.uk, http://www.marketforce.co.uk/.

796.72 USA ISSN 1941-4706
GV1029.9.S74
SHORTTRACK. Text in English. 2004. bi-m. USD 18 domestic; USD 35 in Canada (effective 2008). adv. **Document type:** *Magazine, Consumer.* **Description:** For New England shorttrack racers and fans of shorttrack racing. Features analysis of races, personality and car profiles, and discussion of issues in the New England shorttrack racing scene.
Published by: BullRing Publishing, 403 Sayles Ave, Pascoag, RI 02859. TEL 401-568-6916, 866-667-4878, nopitstops@juno.com. Ed. Thom Ring.

799 USA ISSN 0049-0415
SHOTGUN NEWS. Abbreviated title: S G N. Text in English. 1946. 6/m. USD 31.95 domestic; USD 44.95 in Canada; USD 46.95 elsewhere (effective 2008). adv. illus.; tr.lit. **Document type:** *Magazine, Consumer.* **Description:** Lists guns and accessories in more than 440 classifications.
Related titles: Online - full text ed.
Indexed: G08, I05.
Published by: Intermedia Outdoors, Inc., 512 7th Ave, 11th Fl, New York, NY 10018. TEL 800-260-6397, FAX 212-302-4472, customerservice@imoutdoors.com, http://www.imoutdoorsmedia.com. adv.: B&W page USD 1,649, color page USD 4,299; 10 x 12.25. Circ: 102,734 (paid).

362.4 649 796 JPN ISSN 1348-6055
SHOUGAISHA SUPOTSU KAGAKU/JAPANESE JOURNAL OF ADAPTED SPORT SCIENCE. Text in Japanese. a.
Related titles: Online - full text ed.
—BLDSC (8270.094530).
Published by: Nihon Adaputeddo Taiiku Supotsu Gakkai/Japanese Society for Adapted Physical Education and Exercise, Hiroshima University, Graduate School of Integrated Arts and Sciences, 1-7-1, Kagamiyama, Higashi-Hiroshima, 739-8521, Japan. FAX 81-82-4240759, http://asape.jugem.jp/.

796.345 CAN ISSN 1924-2190
THE SHUTTLER. Text in English. 1977. q. **Document type:** *Trade.*
Former titles (until 2010): Ontario Badminton Today (1209-6210); (until 1996): Badminton Today (0841-6036); (until 1987): Ontario Badminton (0709-8308); (until 1978): First Seed (0705-3134)
Published by: Ontario Badminton Association, 3 Concorde Gate, Ste 209, Toronto, ON M3C 3N7, Canada. TEL 416-426-7195, FAX 416-426-7346, jolande.amoraal@badmintonontario.ca, http://www.ontariobadminton.on.ca.

794.1 ITA ISSN 1970-0407
IL SIGNORE DEGLI ANELLI. SCACCHI DA COLLEZIONE. Text in Italian. 2006. s-a. **Document type:** *Magazine, Consumer.*
Published by: De Agostini Editore, Via G da Verrazzano 15, Novara, 28100, Italy. TEL 39-0321-4241, FAX 39-0321-424305, info@deagostini.it, http://www.deagostini.it.

SIKIDS.COM. *see* CHILDREN AND YOUTH—For

790.5 613.7 USA ISSN 0882-9640
SILENT SPORTS. Text in English. 1984. m. USD 18 (effective 2005). adv. back issues avail. **Document type:** *Magazine, Consumer.* **Description:** Covers recreational fitness activities in the upper Midwest: bicycling, cross country skiing, running, canoeing, backpacking, snowshoeing and in-line skating.
Formerly: Wisconsin Silent Sports
Published by: Waupaca Publishing Co., 717 Tenth St, Waupaca, WI 54981. TEL 715-258-5546, FAX 715-258-8162. Ed. Joel Patenaude. Pub. Scott Turner. Adv. contact Jim Wendt. B&W page USD 750. Circ: 10,000.

797.21 SWE
SIMFRAEMJAREN-LIVRAEDDAREN. Text in Swedish. 1935. q. SEK 50. adv.
Published by: Svenska Livraeddningssaellskapet-Simfraemjandet, Fack 8346, Goeteborg, 40279, Sweden. FAX 31-223234. Ed. Anders Werneten. Circ: 14,000.

793 CAN
SIMULACRUM; a quarterly journal of board wargame collecting & accumulating. Text in English. 1999 (Apr.). q. CAD 25 domestic; USD 25 in United States print & online eds.; USD 30 elsewhere print & online eds. (effective 2005). **Document type:** *Magazine, Consumer.*
Related titles: Online - full content ed.
Address: 794 Fort St, RPO Box 38023, Victoria, BC V8W 3N2, Canada. TEL 250-361-4242. Ed., Pub., R&P, Adv. contact John Kula.

SINGAPORE SPORTS DIRECTORY. *see* BUSINESS AND ECONOMICS—Trade And Industrial Directories

796 USA
SIOUX ILLUSTRATED. Text in English. 2003. bi-m. USD 15 to individuals; USD 10 to students; USD 2.99 newsstand/cover (effective 2003). adv. **Document type:** *Magazine, Consumer.* **Description:** Covers the various University of North Dakota athletics programs.
Related titles: Online - full content ed.
Published by: University of North Dakota, Athletic Department, PO BOX 7053, Grand Forks, ND 58202-9987. TEL 877-917-4789. Circ: 90,000 (controlled).

794.1 ISL ISSN 1022-6958
SKAK. Text in Icelandic. 1947. m. **Document type:** *Magazine, Consumer.*
Published by: Skaksamband Islands, Faxafeni 12, Reykjavik, 108, Iceland. TEL 354-568-9141, FAX 354-568-9116, http://www.skaksamband.is.

794.1 DNK ISSN 0037-6043
SKAKBLADET. Text in Danish. 1904. 8/yr. DKK 200 domestic; DKK 300 foreign (effective 2009). adv. bk.rev. charts; illus. index. **Document type:** *Magazine, Consumer.*
Related titles: Online - full text ed.: 2002.
Published by: Dansk Skak Union, c/o Erik Soebjerg, Kongevejen 6A, Ikast, 7430, Denmark. TEL 45-86-133841, formand@skak.dk. Ed. Thorbjoern Rosenlund TEL 45-44-494210.

793.7 HRV ISSN 1331-4254
SKANDI FENIKS. Text in Croatian. 1998. fortn. **Document type:** *Magazine, Consumer.*
Published by: Novi List, Zvonimirova 20a, Rijeka, 51000, Croatia. TEL 385-51-650011, FAX 385-51-672114.

797.23 SWE ISSN 1104-828X
SKANDINAVISK DYK-GUIDE. Text in Swedish. 1994. a. SEK 125 (effective 1994).
Published by: Pronto Press, Fack 5133, Goeteborg, 40223, Sweden.

790.1 DEU
SKATE-MAGAZIN; events - tests- action - sport. Text in German. 1976. bi-m. EUR 22.80 (effective 2009). adv. **Document type:** *Magazine, Consumer.* **Description:** Contains news about all aspects of inline skating and related events.
Former titles (until 2006): Skate-In; (until 2003): Skate-In-Magazin; (until 2001): Rollsport Life; (until 1995): Rollsport
Published by: Verlag Kleine Fluchten, Hauptstr 45c, Kirchzarten, 79199, Germany. TEL 49-7661-9899639, FAX 49-7661-9899640, info@kleine-fluchten.de. Eds. Dietmar Junginger, Gaby Junginger. Pub. Dietmar Junginger. Adv. contact Gaby Junginger.

796.21094105 GBR ISSN 1754-7342
SKATE MAGAZINE U K. Abbreviated title: S M U K. Text in English. 2007. bi-m. GBP 1.50 per issue (effective 2009). adv. back issues avail. **Document type:** *Magazine, Consumer.* **Description:** Features event reviews, team reviews, player reviews, Hockey League information, new products, product reviews, competitions, prizes, letter of the month, photo of the month, skates and skate equipment for sale and more.
Published by: (British Roller Sports Federation), Bardy Bardy Publications, PO Box 10651, London, W5 3GG, United Kingdom. TEL 44-845-8382515, info@bardybardy.com, http://www.bardybardy.com/. Ed. Matt Bardy.

790.1 DEU
SKATEBOARD; monster skateboard magazine. Variant title: Skateboard M S M. Text in German. 1986. m. EUR 36; EUR 3.40 newsstand/cover (effective 2008). adv. **Document type:** *Magazine, Consumer.* **Description:** Provides an inside look at the people, places and products of the skateboarding culture.
Published by: b&d Media Network GmbH, Osterfeldstr 12-14, Hamburg, 22529, Germany. TEL 49-40-4800070, FAX 49-40-48000799, info@bdverlag.de, http://www.bdverlag.de. Adv. contact Christian Strobl. B&W page EUR 3,390, color page EUR 4,490; trim 230 x 300. Circ: 51,773 (paid and controlled). **Subscr. to:** ASV Vertriebs GmbH, Suederstr 77, Hamburg 20097, Germany. TEL 49-40-34729517, abo@asv.de.

796.22 658 USA ISSN 1553-4936
SKATEBOARD TRADE NEWS. Text in English. 2005 (Jan.). 5/yr. free (effective 2009). adv. **Document type:** *Magazine, Trade.* **Description:** Designed for skateboard retailers, shop owners, industry reps, employees and manufacturers. Includes information about new products, new research, proprietory retailer surveys and industry news.
Published by: Future U S, Inc. (Subsidiary of: Future Publishing Ltd.), 4000 Shoreline Ct, Ste 400, South San Francisco, CA 94080. TEL 650-872-1642, FAX 650-872-1643, http://www.futureus.com. Eds. Adam Sullivan, Rob Campbell. Adv. contact Keith Lenharr. Circ: 11,000 (controlled).

790.1 USA ISSN 1535-2889
GV561
SKATEBOARDER. Text in English. 19??. m. USD 14.97 domestic; USD 27.97 in Canada; USD 29.97 elsewhere (effective 2008). adv. back issues avail. **Document type:** *Magazine, Consumer.* **Description:** Showcases various aspects of skateboarding's past, present and future.
Former titles (until 1982): Action Now (0279-8689); (until 1981): Skateboarder's Action Now (0274-7170); (until 1980): Skateboarder (0164-8942)
Related titles: Online - full text ed.
Indexed: Acal, B04, G06, G07, G08, H20, I05, I07, MagInd, R03, RGAb, RGPR, S23, SD, T&II, W03, W05.
—CCC.
Published by: Source Interlink Companies, 6420 Wilshire Blvd, 10th Fl, Los Angeles, CA 90048. TEL 323-782-2000, FAX 323-782-2585, dheine@sourceinterlink.com, http://www.sourceinterlinkmedia.com. Eds. Brian Peech, Jaime Owens. Pub. Roger Harrell. adv.: B&W page USD 5,778, color page USD 8,256; trim 8 x 10.5. Circ: 92,000.

790.1 USA ISSN 0037-6132
GV849.A1
SKATING. Text in English. 1923. 10/yr. USD 25 domestic; USD 35 in Canada; USD 45 elsewhere (effective 2005). adv. bk.rev. illus. 68 p./no.; back issues avail. **Document type:** *Magazine, Consumer.* **Description:** Communicates information about the sport of skating to the USFSA membership and figure skating fans, promoting USFSA programs, personalities, events and trends that affect the sport.
Indexed: IDP, RASB, SD, SPI, SportS.
—Ingenta.
Published by: United States Figure Skating Association, 20 First St, Colorado Springs, CO 80906. TEL 719-635-5200, FAX 719-635-9548, info@usfigureskating.org, http://www.usfsa.org. adv.: B&W page USD 850, color page USD 1,320. Circ: 45,000 (controlled).

799.313 USA ISSN 0037-6140
GV1181
SKEET SHOOTING REVIEW; covering the sport of skeet shooting world wide. Text in English. 1947. m. USD 20 domestic; USD 60 in Canada & Mexico; USD 92 elsewhere (effective 2006). adv. illus. **Document type:** *Magazine, Consumer.* **Description:** Contains information on new products and techniques.
Indexed: SportS.
Published by: National Skeet Shooting Association, 5931 Roft Rd, San Antonio, TX 78253. TEL 210-688-3371, 800-877-5338, FAX 210-688-3632, nssa@nssa-nsca.com, http://www.nssa-nsca.com. Ed. Susie Fluckiger. Circ: 18,000.

790.1 USA ISSN 0890-6076
SKI PATROL MAGAZINE. Text in English. 1984. q. USD 25 domestic; USD 40 foreign (effective 2005). adv. bk.rev. charts; illus. cum.index. **Document type:** *Magazine, Trade.* **Description:** Discusses avalanche safety and rescue, ski mountaineering, equipment, medical updates, outdoor emergency care, fitness, risk management for ski patrollers. Includes ski area profiles.
Indexed: SD.
—Ingenta.
Published by: National Ski Patrol System, Inc., 133 S Van Gordon St Ste 100, Lakewood, CO 80228-1700. TEL 303-988-1111, FAX 303-988-3005, nsp@nsp.org. Ed. Wendy Schrupp. Adv. contact Mark Dorsey. Circ: 26,000 (controlled); 2,000 (free).

796.93 USA ISSN 0037-6213
SKI RACING. Text in English. 1968. 12/yr. USD 32.98 domestic; USD 47.98 in Canada; USD 72.98 elsewhere (effective 2008). adv. bk.rev. charts; illus.; stat. **Document type:** *Magazine, Consumer.* **Description:** Contains comprehensive race information and coverage. Includes race techniques and conditioning secrets from experts.
Indexed: SD, SPI, SportS.
Published by: Inside Communications Inc., 1830 N 55th St, Boulder, CO 80301. TEL 303-440-0601, FAX 303-444-6788. Circ: 20,000 (paid).

797.25 USA ISSN 1946-8490
SKIP SHOT. Text in English. 1969. bi-m. free to members (effective 2009). adv. charts; illus.; stat. **Document type:** *Magazine, Trade.*
Former titles (until 2008): USA Water Polo Magazine (1550-7580); (until 200?): Water Polo Scoreboard (0043-1311)
Published by: U S A Water Polo, Inc., 2124 Main St, Ste 240, Huntington Beach, CA 92648. TEL 714-500-5445, FAX 714-960-2431, dwillems@usawaterpolo.org, http://www.usawaterpolo.org. Ed., Adv. contact Greg Mescall. B&W page USD 1,575, color page USD 1,890.

688.7 POL ISSN 1505-3563
SKLEP SPORTOWY. Text in Polish. 1998. s-a. adv. **Document type:** *Magazine, Trade.*
Published by: Unit Wydawnictwo Informacje Branzowe Sp. z o.o., ul Kierbedzia 4, Warsaw, 00-728, Poland. TEL 48-22-3201500, FAX 48-22-3201506, info@unit.com.pl, http://www.unit.com.pl. Ed. Anna Wakulak. Adv. contact Dorota Mazurek.

796 NZL ISSN 1177-4924
SKY SPORT. Text in English. 2007. m. NZD 5 newsstand/cover (effective 2008). **Document type:** *Magazine, Consumer.*
Published by: (Sky Network Television), Fairfax Magazines (Subsidiary of: Fairfax Media), PO Box 6341, Auckland, 1036, New Zealand. TEL 64-9-9096800, FAX 64-9-9096802. Ed. Eric Young. **Co-publisher:** Sky Network Television.

799.31 DNK ISSN 0037-6663
SKYTTEBLADET. Text in Danish. 1937. 6/yr. adv. bk.rev. **Document type:** *Magazine, Consumer.*
Related titles: Online - full text ed.: 2004.
Published by: Dansk Skytte Union, Idraettens Hus, Broendby Stadion 20, Broendby, 2605, Denmark. TEL 45-43-262626, info@skytteunion.dk. Ed., Adv. contact Tommy Soerensen TEL 45-43262350.

796.172 DEU
SLACK; surf skate snow culture. Text in German. 8/yr. EUR 3 newsstand/cover (effective 2008). adv. **Document type:** *Magazine, Consumer.*
Published by: Pulse Publishing GmbH, Offakamp 9a, Hamburg, 22529, Germany. TEL 49-40-57002670, FAX 49-40-570026718. adv.: B&W page EUR 3,850, color page EUR 4,950. Circ: 59,903 (controlled).

790.1 028.5 USA
GV859.8
SLAP; i got the answer for your question. Text in English. 1991. m. USD 10 domestic; USD 29 in Canada; USD 35 elsewhere; USD 3.99 newsstand/cover (effective 2005). adv. music rev.; video rev. back issues avail. **Document type:** *Magazine, Consumer.* **Description:** Contains the latest for the new school crew into skateboarding, streetstyle fashion and new sounds.
Formerly (until 2005): Slap Skateboard Magazine (1076-9110)

Published by: High Speed Productions, Inc., 1303 Underwood Ave, San Francisco, CA 94124. TEL 415-822-3083, FAX 415-822-8359. Ed. Mark Whiteley. Pub. Edward Riggins. Adv. contact Eden Sterling. B&W page USD 1,500; trim 10.51 x 8.125. Circ: 78,000 (paid). **Dist. by:** Curtis CIRC Company, 730 River Rd., New Milford, NJ 07646.

795 USA ISSN 1949-9728
SLOTMANAGER; the total slot resource. Text in English. 1997. bi-m. included with subscr. to Casino Journal. adv. back issues avail.; reprints avail. **Document type:** *Magazine, Trade.* **Description:** Focuses on slot gaming trends, technology, marketing and operations worldwide to assist slot executives with proficiency in their professions.
Related titles: ♦ Supplement to: International Gaming & Wagering Business. ISSN 1066-145X.
Indexed: G04, H06, V03.
Published by: B N P Media, 505 E Capovilla Ave, Ste 102, Las Vegas, NV 89119. TEL 702-794-0718, FAX 702-794-0799, portfolio@bnpmedia.com, http://www.bnpmedia.com. Ed. Marian Green. Pub. Charles Anderer TEL 718-432-8529. Adv. contact Terry Davis TEL 404-320-0072. color page USD 6,287; trim 8 x 10.675.

790.1 GBR
SMALL SIDE TEAM GAMES AND POTTED SPORTS. Text in English. 1935. irreg. GBP 1.25 per issue. **Document type:** *Monographic series, Consumer.*
Published by: Ministry of Defense, Army Sport Control Board, Clayton Barracks, Aldershot, United Kingdom. R&P K Hitchcock.

796.345 GBR
SMYTHSON'S BADMINTON SPORTING DIARY. Text in English. 1894. a. GBP 29 (effective 2000). **Document type:** *Directory.* **Description:** Covers sporting information and events listings.
Published by: Frank Smythson Ltd., 40 New Bond St, London, W1Y 0DE, United Kingdom. TEL 44-20-7629-8558, FAX 44-20-7495-6111. Ed. Martin Pickering.

794.735 GBR ISSN 0269-0756
SNOOKER SCENE; the magazine that tells you what's really going on. Text in English. 1972. m. GBP 30 domestic; GBP 35 foreign (effective 2009). adv. bk.rev. back issues avail. **Document type:** *Magazine, Consumer.* **Description:** Contains an information section which includes the current world rankings list, tournament results of the modern era, a coaching series and a list of useful addresses.
Published by: Everton's News Agency, Hayley Green Ct, 130 Hagley Rd, Halesowen, B63 1DY, United Kingdom. TEL 44-121-5859188, FAX 44-121-5857117. Ed. Clive Everton.

790.1 DEU ISSN 1437-7233
SNOW; Surf Spezial. Text in German. 1983. 3/yr. EUR 4.50 newsstand/cover (effective 2009). adv. bk.rev. **Document type:** *Magazine, Consumer.*
Formerly (until 1991): Funboard
Published by: Brinkmann Henrich Medien GmbH, Heerstr 5, Meinerzhagen, 58540, Germany. TEL 49-2354-77990, FAX 49-2354-779977, info@bhmg.de, http://www.bhmg.de. adv.: B&W page EUR 2,987, color page EUR 4,979; trim 240 x 300. Circ: 47,381 (controlled).

796.22 658 USA ISSN 1553-4944
SNOWBOARD TRADE NEWS. Text in English. 2005. q. free (effective 2009). adv. **Document type:** *Magazine, Trade.* **Description:** Carries information on how to sell, stock and prepare for seasonal sales. Includes interviews with retailers, reports and discussions on regional sales and industry news.
Published by: Future U S, Inc. (Subsidiary of: Future Publishing Ltd.), 4000 Shoreline Ct, Ste 400, South San Francisco, CA 94080. TEL 650-872-1642, FAX 650-872-1643, http://www.futureus.com. adv.: B&W page USD 3,399, color page USD 4,532; trim 10.5 x 12.25. Circ: 11,000 (controlled).

SNOWBOUND; the frosty zine. *see* LITERATURE—Science Fiction, Fantasy, Horror

SOARING. *see* AERONAUTICS AND SPACE FLIGHT

797 AUS ISSN 1832-4894
SOARING AUSTRALIA. Text in English. 1998. m. AUD 40 domestic to members; AUD 90 in Asia & the Pacific to members; AUD 112 elsewhere to members (effective 2009). adv. bk.rev. back issues avail. **Document type:** *Magazine, Consumer.*
Formerly (until 2002): Australian Gliding Skysailor; Which was formed by the merger of (1975-1998): Skysailor (0313-363X); Which was formerly (until 1975): Journal of the Australasian Self Soar Association (0311-5186); (1950-1998): Australian Gliding
Indexed: SD.
Published by: (Gliding Federation of Australia), Hang Gliding Federation of Australia, 4a/ 60 Keilor Park Dr, Keilor Park, VIC 3042, Australia. TEL 61-3-93367155, FAX 61-3-93367177, office@hgfa.asn.au, http://www.hgfa.asn.au. adv.: B&W page AUD 275, color page AUD 660;. Circ: 1,800.

SOCCER RULES BOOK. *see* SPORTS AND GAMES—Ball Games

796.44 613.7 PRT ISSN 1646-8775
SOCIEDADE PORTUGUESA DE EDUCACAO FISICA. BOLETIM. Text in Portuguese. 1986. irreg. **Document type:** *Bulletin, Consumer.*
Published by: Sociedade Portuguesa de Educacao Fisica (S P E F), Impasse a Rua C, Bairro da Liberdade, Lisbon, 1070-165, Portugal. TEL 351-213-851052, FAX 351-213-861698, geral@spef.pt, http://www.spef.pt.

796.962 CAN ISSN 1910-1414
SOCIETY FOR INTERNATIONAL HOCKEY RESEARCH. NEWSLETTER. Text in English. 1991. q. **Document type:** *Newsletter, Trade.*
Former titles (until 2005): S I H R Plus Newsletter (1701-2783); (until 1996): Society for International Hockey Research. President's Bulletin (1701-2775); (until 1992): Society for International Hockey Research. Bulletin from the President (1701-2767)
Indexed: SD.
Published by: Society for International Hockey Research, 66 Gerrard St East, Ste 300, Toronto, ON M5B 1G3, Canada. TEL 416-585-9373, FAX 416-585 9376, info@sihrhockey.org, http://www.sihrhockey.org/main.cfm.

790.1 GBR ISSN 0560-6152
GV1183
SOCIETY OF ARCHER-ANTIQUARIES. JOURNAL. Text in English. 1958. a. free to members (effective 2009). bk.rev. charts; illus. back issues avail. **Document type:** *Journal, Academic/Scholarly.* **Description:** Covers the study of the history of the bow and arrow, many varying articles, illustrated and prepared by specialist members.
Indexed: BrArAb, SD.
Published by: Society of Archer-Antiquaries, c/o H D H Soar, Hon Sec. S A A, Yew Corner, 29 Batley Ct, Oldland, S.Glos BS30 8YZ, United Kingdom. TEL 44-117-9323276, bogaman@btinternet.com. Ed. Artur Credland.

SOCIOLOGY OF SPORT JOURNAL. *see* SOCIOLOGY

SOFTBALL RULES BOOK. *see* SPORTS AND GAMES—Ball Games

796.72 ESP
SOLO AUTO 4 X 4. Text in Spanish. 1983. m. adv. back issues avail. **Document type:** *Magazine, Consumer.* **Description:** Dedicated to the world of off-road cars, includes news and review of new models.
Published by: Alesport S.A., Gran Via 8-10, Hospitalet de Llobregat, Barcelona, 08902, Spain. TEL 34-93-4315533, FAX 34-93-2973905, http://www.alesport.com. Ed. Chema Huete.

796.96 ESP
SOLO NIEVE. Text in Spanish. m.?. EUR 36 domestic; EUR 60 in Europe; EUR 90 elsewhere (effective 2009). adv. back issues avail. **Document type:** *Magazine, Consumer.* **Description:** Covers winter sports, especially skiing.
Published by: Alesport S.A., Gran Via 8-10, Hospitalet de Llobregat, Barcelona, 08902, Spain. TEL 34-93-4315533, FAX 34-93-2973905, http://www.alesport.com. Ed. Curro Bulto.

796.812 ESP ISSN 1888-3028
SOLO WRESTLING MAGAZINE. Text in Spanish. 2007. bi-m.
Media: Online - full text.
Published by: Asociacion Espanola de Wrestling magazine@solowrestling.com.

796.41 AUS ISSN 1833-427X
SOMERSAULT GYMNASTICS MAGAZINE. Text in English. 2006. bi-m. **Document type:** *Magazine, Consumer.*
Published by: Flic Flac Publishing, 7 Powerscourt St, Maffra, VIC 3860, Australia.

796 USA ISSN 0279-3288
SOONERS ILLUSTRATED. Text in English. 1980. 17/yr. USD 44.90, USD 2.95 (effective 2001). adv. **Document type:** *Magazine, Consumer.* **Description:** Covers University of Oklahoma sports.
Published by: First Down Publications, 2003 Western Ave., Ste. 700, Seattle, WA 98121-2111. TEL 918-270-1826, 800-467-6532. Pub. Melania Ross. adv.: B&W page USD 800, color page USD 1,200; trim 10.88 x 8.25. Circ: 12,500.

SOPA DE LETRAS FANTASTICAS. *see* HOBBIES

SOPAS POCKET. *see* HOBBIES

SOPAS POCKET. EXTRA. *see* HOBBIES

797.23 USA
SOURCES (TAMPA); the journal of underwater education. Text in English. 1960. bi-m. USD 45 (effective 2000). adv. bk.rev.
Formerly: N A U I News
Indexed: SportS.
Published by: National Association of Underwater Instructors, 9942 Currie Davis Dr, Ste H, Tampa, FL 33619-2667. TEL 813-628-6284, FAX 813-628-8253. Ed. Peter Oliver. Circ: 12,000.

SOUTH AFRICAN AERONEWS. *see* AERONAUTICS AND SPACE FLIGHT

306.4 AUS ISSN 1832-3839
SOUTH AUSTRALIA, INDEPENDENT GAMBLING AUTHORITY. ANNUAL REPORT. Text in English. 1996. a. free (effective 2009). back issues avail. **Document type:** *Government.* **Description:** Highlights the activities of the Independent Gambling Authority for the financial year.
Formerly (until 2002): South Australia, Gaming Supervisory Authority. Annual Report
Related titles: Online - full text ed.
Published by: South Australia, Independent Gambling Authority, Level 4, 45 Grenfell St, P O Box 67, Adelaide, SA 5000, Australia. TEL 61-8-82267233, FAX 61-8-82267247, iga@iga.sa.gov.au.

790.1 USA
SOUTHERN GAMEPLAN. Text in English. 1989. 9/yr. USD 17. adv. **Description:** Features stories on national sports events affecting the southern U.S. and rising high school athletic stars, with emphasis on collegiate sports.
Published by: SportsMedia, Inc., PO Box 3618, Annapolis, MD 21403. TEL 410-280-0707, FAX 410-280-3434, info@e-sportsmedia.com. Ed. Ben Cook. Circ: 100,000.

795 USA
SOUTHERN GAMING. Text in English. 2000. m. USD 15 (effective 2001). adv. **Document type:** *Magazine, Consumer.*
Published by: Southern Gaming Publications, LLC, 1444 Peterman Dr, Alexandria, LA 71301. Ed., Pub. Leesha Faulkner.

796.72 USA ISSN 0049-1616
SOUTHERN MOTORACING. Text in English. 1964. bi-w. USD 15 in United States; USD 20 in Canada; USD 0.75 newsstand/cover (effective 2001). adv. bk.rev. stat. **Document type:** *Magazine, Consumer.* **Description:** Devoted to the motor racing fan with emphasis on news and personality stories and a small and general treatment of technical material. Most of the content is aimed at the motor racing fan of the southeastern United States, with brief coverage of national and international motor racing.
Published by: Universal Services, Inc., PO Box 500, Winston Salem, NC 27102. TEL 336-723-5227, FAX 336-722-3757. Ed., Pub. Hank Schoolfield. Adv. contact Don Wilson. col. inch USD 5. Circ: 10,000 (paid).

796.42 USA ISSN 0744-3439
SOUTHERN RUNNER. Text in English. 1981. bi-m. USD 12 (effective 2001). **Document type:** *Magazine, Consumer.*
Address: PO Box 6524, Metairie, LA 70009-6524. TEL 504-891-9999, FAX 504-891-9996. Ed. Valerie D Andrews. Pub. Mike Andrews. R&P Valerie Andrews TEL 228-255-0600. Circ: 15,000.

790.1 RUS ISSN 0233-4283
SOVETSKII SPORT. Text in Russian. 1924. d. USD 499 foreign (effective 2005). adv. **Document type:** *Newspaper, Consumer.* **Description:** Covers national and international sports, with emphasis on the European sport scene.
Related titles: Microfilm ed.: (from EVP, PQC).
Published by: Izdatel'skii Dom Sovetskii Sport, B Spasoglinishchevskii per 8, Moscow, 101990, Russian Federation. TEL 7-095-9242822. Ed. Igor Kots. adv.: page RUR 24,340. Circ: 450,000. **Dist. by:** East View Information Services, 10601 Wayzata Blvd, Minneapolis, MN 55305. TEL 952-252-1201, 800-477-1005, FAX 952-252-1202, info@eastview.com, http://www.eastview.com.

793 ARG ISSN 1851-3840
SPACE AUTODEFINIDOS. Text in Spanish. 2007. m.
Published by: M4 Editora, San Pedro 140, Avellanada, Buenos Aires, 1870, Argentina. m4editora@speedy.com.ar.

790.1 ITA ISSN 1125-1905
SPAZIOSPORT. Text in Italian. 1982. q. bk.rev. **Document type:** *Magazine, Trade.*
Published by: (Comitato Olimpico Nazionale Italiano (C O N I)), Mancosu Editore, Via Alfredo Fusco 71, Rome, 00136, Italy.

796.72 USA ISSN 0747-5403
SPEEDWAY SCENE; Winston Cup Beat. Text in English. 1971. w. USD 40 domestic; USD 65 foreign (effective 2000). adv. 6 cols./p.; **Document type:** *Newspaper, Trade.* **Description:** Covers circle track racing from Winston Cup to local tracks.
Published by: Hockomock Publishing, 50 Washington St, Box 300, N, Easton, MA 02356. TEL 508-238-7016, FAX 508-230-2381. Ed., Pub., R&P Val LeSieur. Adv. contact Dale Wolbrink TEL 508-238-7016. Circ: 60,000.

796.7 CAN
SPEEDWAY USA MAGAZINE. Text in English. 2000. q. USD 20; USD 3.95 newsstand/cover (effective 2001). adv. **Document type:** *Magazine, Consumer.*
Published by: Howden Communications Inc., 1074 Cherriebell Rd, Mississauga, ON L5E 2R3, Canada. TEL 905-270-0343, FAX 905-271-5435, speedwayusa@hotmail.com, http://www.speedwayusa.com. Ed., Pub. Rob Howden.

796.72 USA ISSN 1551-6083
SPEEDWORLD MAGAZINE. Text in English. 2003 (Fall). q. USD 16 (effective 2004). **Document type:** *Magazine, Consumer.*
Published by: Synergy Sports Media, PO Box 17304, Clearwater, FL 33762-0304. TEL 727-536-1340, FAX 727-230-9741. Ed. Natalie K Gargiulo. Pub. Joseph J Wattam.

793.7 DEU
SPEZIAL-RAETSEL. Text in German. 1986. w. EUR 91; EUR 1.50 newsstand/cover (effective 2011). adv. **Document type:** *Magazine, Consumer.* **Description:** Contains challenging crosswords for the experienced puzzler.
Published by: Deutscher Raetselverlag GmbH & Co. KG (Subsidiary of: Gong Verlag GmbH & Co. KG), Muenchener Str 101-09, Ismaning, 85737, Germany. TEL 49-89-272708620, FAX 49-89-272707890, info@raetsel.de, http://www.deutscher-raetselverlag.de. Circ: 165,000 (controlled).

790.1 DEU ISSN 0721-6777
SPIELBOX; das Magazin zum Spielen. Text in German. 1981. bi-m. EUR 39.90 domestic; EUR 45.50 in Europe; EUR 60.90 elsewhere (effective 2010). adv. **Document type:** *Magazine, Consumer.*
Published by: W. Nostheide Verlag GmbH, Bahnhofstr 22, Memmelsdorf, 96117, Germany. TEL 49-951-40666-0, FAX 49-951-4066649, nostheide@nostheide.de, http://www.nostheide.de. Ed. Matthias Hardel. Pub. Jens R Nostheide. adv.: B&W page EUR 1,850, color page EUR 2,400. Circ: 14,790 (paid and controlled).

793 DEU ISSN 1432-3788
SPIELCASINO; Spielzeitung fuer Schueler, Eltern und Lehrer. Text in German. 1979. s-a. EUR 1.50 newsstand/cover (effective 2008). adv. **Document type:** *Magazine, Trade.*
Published by: Adolf Reichwein Schule, Uchteweg 26, Bielefeld, 33689, Germany. TEL 49-521-515534, FAX 49-521-515544, mail@ars-bielefeld.de. Ed. Dirk Hanneforth. adv.: page EUR 50. Circ: 500.

790.1 DEU
SPIELMAGAZIN. Text in German. w. adv. **Document type:** *Consumer.* **Description:** Contains information and reviews on a wide variety of games for the whole family.
Media: Online - full text.
Published by: Spessartweb Online Verlag, Buettnerstr 15, Triefenstein, 97855, Germany. TEL 49-9395-997914, FAX 49-9395-997915, verlag@spielmagazin.de, info@spessartweb.de, http://www.spessartweb.de. Eds. Claudia Sollinger, Markus Sollinger. Pub. Petra Witzl. Adv. contact Markus Sollinger.

796 GBR ISSN 1758-0390
SPIKES; the new heroes of athletics. Text in English. 2008. 3/yr. free (effective 2010). adv. **Document type:** *Magazine, Consumer.* **Description:** Contains information and videos about athletics.
Published by: (International Association of Athletics Federations MCO), Haymarket Network (Subsidiary of: Haymarket Media Group), Teddington Studios, Broom Rd, Teddington, TW11 9BE, United Kingdom. TEL 44-20-82675013, FAX 44-20-82675194, enquiries@haymarket.com, http://www.haymarketnetwork.com. Ed. Simon Kanter TEL 44-20-82675434.

796.41 DEU ISSN 1432-9468
SPIRIT; cheerleading. Text in German. 1996. bi-m. EUR 24.90 (effective 2010). adv. back issues avail. **Document type:** *Magazine, Consumer.*
Published by: C C A - Agentur fuer Kommunikation GmbH, Adam-Klein-Str 156, Nuernberg, 90431, Germany. TEL 49-911-4779070, FAX 49-911-47790777, mail@cca-agentur.de, http://www.cca-agentur.de.

790.1 613.7 USA ISSN 1099-8306
GV836.2
SPLASH! (COLORADO SPRINGS). Text in English. 1993. bi-m. free to members; USD 15 domestic to non-members; USD 25 foreign to non-members (effective 2000). **Document type:** *Magazine, Consumer.* **Description:** Conceived in the hope of improving communication among clubs, coaches, local swimming committees, USA Swimming staff, and the Board of Directors. Provides information on programs and services of USA Swimming and the people and events of the sport of swimming.
Formed by the merger of (1976-1993): Lanelines; (1944-1993): U S Swimming News (0883-0347)

S

Indexed: AmHI, SD.
Published by: U S A Swimming, One Olympic Plaza, Colorado Springs, CO 80909. TEL 719-578-4578, FAX 719-575-4049. Ed., R&P Charlie Snyder. Pub. Chuck Wielgus. Circ: 185,000.

SPONSORS. *see* ADVERTISING AND PUBLIC RELATIONS

073 CHE
SPORT. Text in German. 1920. w. CHF 145; CHF 202 in Europe; CHF 316 elsewhere. adv. **Document type:** *Newspaper, Consumer.*
Published by: Verlag Sport Wochenzeitung AG (Subsidiary of: Axel Springer Schweiz AG), Foerrlicbuckstr 10, Zuerich, 8021, Switzerland. TEL 41-1-4488383, FAX 41-1-4488888. Ed. Franco Carabelli. Pub. Urs Zeier. Adv. contact Manuel Loureiro.

613.7 790 BEL ISSN 0038-7770
SPORT. Text in French. 1958. 4/yr. adv. bk.rev. **Document type:** *Monographic series, Government.*
Related titles: Dutch ed.: ISSN 0776-3794.
Indexed: Acal, SportS.
Published by: Ministere de la Communaute Francaise, Direction Generale du Sport et du Tourisme, Place Surlet de Chokier, 15-17, Bruxelles, 1000, Belgium. TEL 32-2-221-8811, FAX 32-2-221-8885, http://www.cfwb.be/default2.asp. Ed. G Gypens. R&P, Adv. contact Benjamin Stassen. Circ: 1,500.

790 NOR ISSN 0333-3639
SPORT; bransjeblad for sport og fritid. Text in Norwegian. 1924. 8/yr. NOK 500 domestic; NOK 650 foreign (effective 2002). adv.
Formerly (until 1974): Sportshandleren (0049-1993)
Published by: Norspo AS, Sjoelyst Plass 3, Oslo, 0278, Norway. TEL 47-23-00-15-30, FAX 47-23-00-15-32. Ed. Morten Dahl. Pub. Ole Petter Bratlie. Adv. contact Hedda Sponland. B&W page NOK 9,975, color page NOK 14,700; 245 x 330. Circ: 1,983.

790.1 POL ISSN 0137-9305
SPORT. Text in Polish. 1945. d. EUR 278 foreign (effective 2005). **Document type:** *Newspaper, Consumer.*
Published by: J M G Sport Publishing (Subsidiary of: Marquard Media AG), ul Nowogrodzka 84-86, Warsaw, 02-018, Poland. TEL 48-22-6289116, FAX 48-22-6218697. **Dist. by:** Ars Polona, Obroncow 25, Warsaw 03933, Poland. TEL 48-22-5098609, FAX 48-22-5098610, arspolona@arspolona.com.pl, http://www.arspolona.com.pl.

796 FRA ISSN 1264-6806
LE SPORT. Text in French. 1993. irreg., latest no.5. EUR 4.90 per issue (effective 2009). **Document type:** *Magazine, Consumer.*
Formerly (until 1995): Le Journal du Sport (1258-8784)
Published by: Lafont Presse, 53 Rue du Chemin Vert, Boulogne-Billancourt, 92100, France. TEL 33-1-45774141, FAX 33-1-45792211. Pub. Robert Lafont.

796 GBR
SPORT. Text in English. 2006-2009 (Apr.); N.S. 2009 (Jun.). w. free newsstand/cover (effective 2009). adv. **Document type:** *Magazine, Consumer.* **Description:** Covers sports related information.
Related titles: Online - full text ed.
Published by: U T V Media plc, Ormeau Rd, Belfast, BT7 1EB, United Kingdom. TEL 44-28-90328122, FAX 44-28-90246695, info@u.tv, http://www.utvmedia.com. Ed. Simon Caney TEL 44-20-79597951.

796 CZE ISSN 1210-8383
SPORT. Text in Czech. 1953. d. CZK 4,128; CZK 13 newsstand/cover (effective 2010). adv. **Document type:** *Newspaper, Consumer.*
Formerly (until 1993): Ceskoslovensky Sport (0323-1224)
Published by: Ringier CR, Komunardu 1584/42, Prague 7, 170 00, Czech Republic. TEL 420-2-25977616, FAX 420-2-67097718, info@ringier.cz, http://www.ringier.cz. Ed. Lukas Tomek. Circ: 63,601 (paid). **Subscr. to:** Mediaservis s.r.o., Pacericka 2773/1, Prague 9 193 00, Czech Republic. TEL 420-2-71199100, FAX 420-2-72700025, info@mediaservis.cz, http://www.mediaservis.cz.

790.1 POL ISSN 1506-6398
SPORT (WARSAW). Text in Polish. 1998. w. PLZ 54 per month domestic; EUR 15 per month in Europe; USD 23 per month in North America (effective 2011). **Document type:** *Newspaper, Consumer.*
Related titles: ◆ Supplement to: Gazeta Wyborcza. ISSN 0860-908X.
Published by: Agora S.A., ul Czerska 8/10, Warsaw, 00732, Poland. TEL 48-22-5556000, FAX 48-22-5554850, prenumerata@gazeta.pl, http://www.agora.pl.

796.087 362.4 FRA ISSN 1157-6421
SPORT ADAPTE MAGAZINE. Text in French. 198?. q. EUR 30 (effective 2009). **Description:** Focuses on sports competitions for the disabled.
Formerly (until 1991): Sports Adaptes (1260-4305)
Published by: Federation Francaise du Sport Adapte, 9 Rue Jean Daudin, Paris, 75015, France. TEL 33-1-42739000, FAX 33-1-42739010. Ed. M H Lopez. Pub. George Ray Jabalot.

SPORT ADRESSBUCH. *see* BUSINESS AND ECONOMICS—Trade And Industrial Directories

790.1 COD
SPORT AFRICAIN. Text in French. m.
Address: 13e niveau Tour adm, Cite de la Voix du Zaire, BP 3356, Kinshasa-Gombe, Congo, Dem. Republic. Ed. Tshimpumpu Wa Tshimpumpu.

790.1 CHE
SPORT AKTIV. Text in German. 1988. fortn. CHF 37. adv. **Document type:** *Bulletin.*
Related titles: Italian ed.: Gimnasta; French ed.: Gym et Sport.
Published by: (Schweizerischer Turnverband), Vogt-Schild AG, Zuchwilerstr 21, Solothurn, 4501, Switzerland. TEL 41-32-6247474, FAX 065-247235. Ed. Ursi Gisler. Adv. contact Barbara Staugassinger. B&W page CHF 3,130, color page CHF 4,230; trim 270 x 188. Circ: 37,836.

796 GBR ISSN 2040-5847
➤ **SPORT & E U REVIEW.** (European Union) Text in English. 2006. q. free to members (effective 2009). back issues avail. **Document type:** *Newsletter, Academic/Scholarly.* **Description:** Forum for scholarly exchange and debate.
Formerly (until 2009): Sport & E U Newsletter (1754-1298)
Media: Online - full text.
Published by: Association for the Study of Sport and the European Union, c/o Samuli Miettinen, Lady Hale Bldg, Salford Law School, University of Salford, Greater Manchester, M5 4WT, United Kingdom. TEL 44-161-2956928, webmaster@sportandeu.com. Eds. Dr. Samuli Miettinen, Dr. Simona Kustec-Lipicer.

➤ **SPORT AND EXERCISE PSYCHOLOGY REVIEW.** *see* PSYCHOLOGY

796 SVK ISSN 1337-1827
SPORT & FITNES. Text in Slovak. 2003. m. EUR 15.60 (effective 2009). adv. **Document type:** *Magazine, Consumer.*
Formerly (until 2007): Sport Magazin (1336-2437)
Published by: Media - S T s.r.o., Moyzesova 35, Zilina, 010 01, Slovakia. TEL 421-41-5640370, FAX 421-41-5640371, mediast@mediast.sk, http://www.mediast.sk. adv.: B&W page EUR 1,095, color page EUR 1,925.

SPORT AND RECREATION INFORMATION GROUP BULLETIN. *see* LEISURE AND RECREATION

SPORT AND THE LAW JOURNAL. *see* LAW

790 FRA ISSN 0151-6353
SPORT AUTO, VIRAGE AUTO, CHAMPION. Text in French. 1974. m. EUR 59 (effective 2009). adv. bk.rev.; film rev. illus. **Document type:** *Magazine, Consumer.*
Formed by the merger of (1966-1974): Champion (0009-1324); (1974-1974): Sports Auto, Virage Auto (0150-1941); Which was formed by the merger of (1962-1968): Sports Auto (0038-7827); (1962-1974): Virage Auto (1144-0740)
Related titles: ◆ Supplement(s): Sport-Auto. Hors-Serie. ISSN 0224-7283.
Published by: Mondadori France, 1 Rue du Colonel Pierre-Avia, Paris, Cedex 15 75754, France. TEL 33-1-41335001, contact@mondadori.fr. Ed. Nicolas Berthy. Circ: 100,000.

797.21 DEU ISSN 0344-6492
SPORT- BAEDER- FREIZEITBAUTEN; aquatic, sports and recreations buildings. Text in German; Summaries in English, French, Italian. 1961. 6/yr. EUR 40 domestic; EUR 43 foreign (effective 2006). adv. bk.rev. charts; illus.; tr.lit. **Document type:** *Magazine, Trade.* **Description:** International trade publication for the aquatic sport and recreation building industry. Covers various aspects of the construction and design of swimming pools and other sports facilities.
Formerly (until 1974): Sport- und Baederbauten (0038-7924)
Indexed: SD.
—BLDSC (8419.675000), IE, Ingenta.
Published by: Krammer Verlag Duesseldorf AG, Goethestr 75, Duesseldorf, 40237, Germany. TEL 49-211-91493, FAX 49-211-9149450, krammer@krammerag.de, http://www.krammerag.de. Ed. D Fabian. Adv. contact Birgit Vanino. B&W page EUR 1,020; trim 185 x 257. Circ: 3,773 (paid and controlled).

658.8 NLD ISSN 1389-3130
SPORT BESTUUR & MANAGEMENT; vakblad voor sportbestuurders, sportkader en sportoverheden. Text in Dutch. 1998. bi-m. EUR 92.50 to non-members; EUR 77.50 to members (effective 2008). adv. illus. **Document type:** *Journal, Trade.* **Description:** Reports news and events for sports managers, agents, and owners.
Incorporates (1980-2001): Nationaal Sport Magazine (0169-1945); Which was formerly (until 1985): Sport Intermedium
Published by: Arko Sports Media (Subsidiary of: Arko Uitgeverij BV), Postbus 393, Nieuwegein, 3430 AJ, Netherlands. TEL 31-30-6004780, FAX 31-30-6052618, info@arko.nl, http://www.arko.nl. Ed. Karin Horsting. Pub. Michel van Troost. adv.: B&W page EUR 1,765, color page EUR 2,445; bleed 230 x 300. Circ: 7,723 (paid and controlled).

790.1 DEU ISSN 0934-3369
SPORT BILD. Text in German. 1988. w. (Wed.). EUR 1.50 newsstand/cover (effective 2011). adv. **Document type:** *Magazine, Consumer.*
Related titles: Online - full text ed.
—**CCC.**
Published by: Axel Springer Verlag AG, Axel-Springer-Platz 1, Hamburg, 20350, Germany. TEL 49-40-34700, FAX 49-40-34728460, information@axelspringer.de, http://www.asv.de. Ed. Alexander Steudel. Adv. contact Peter Hoffmann TEL 49-40-34725809. Circ: 419,053 (paid and controlled).

658 GBR ISSN 2042-678X
▼ ➤ **SPORT, BUSINESS AND MANAGEMENT.** Text in English. 2011. 3/yr. EUR 369 combined subscription in Europe (print & online eds.); USD 539 combined subscription in the Americas (print & online eds.); GBP 319 combined subscription in the UK & elsewhere (print & online eds.); AUD 579 combined subscription in Australasia (print & online eds.) (effective 2012). **Document type:** *Journal, Academic/Scholarly.*
Related titles: Online - full text ed.: ISSN 2042-6798.
Indexed: CABA, LT, P10, PQC.
—**CCC.**
Published by: Emerald Group Publishing Ltd., Howard House, Wagon Ln, Bingley, W Yorks BD16 1WA, United Kingdom. TEL 44-1274-777700, FAX 44-1274-785201, information@emeraldinsight.com. Ed. Simon Chadwick.

790.1 GBR ISSN 1741-0916
➤ **SPORT COMMERCE AND CULTURE.** Text in English. 2004. irreg., latest 2005. price varies. back issues avail. **Document type:** *Monographic series, Academic/Scholarly.* **Description:** Examines the sociological significance of the sports industry and the sporting world on contemporary cultures around the world.
Published by: Berg Publishers (Subsidiary of: Oxford International Publishers Ltd.), 1st Fl Angel Ct, 81 St Clements St, Oxford, Berks OX4 1AW, United Kingdom. TEL 44-1865-245104, FAX 44-1865-791165, enquiry@bergpublishers.com. Ed. David L Andrews.

797.23 USA ISSN 1077-985X
SPORT DIVER. Text in English. 1993. m. USD 29 domestic; USD 41 in Canada; USD 62 elsewhere (effective 2011). adv. illus. **Document type:** *Magazine, Consumer.* **Description:** Visits the hottest destinations in the world, gives tips on dive and photography skills, presents updates on cutting-edge technology, and more.
Related titles: Online - full text ed.
Indexed: G08, I05.
—**CCC.**
Published by: (Professional Association of Diving Instructors), Bonnier Corp. (Subsidiary of: Bonnier Group), 460 N Orlando Ave, Ste 200, Orlando, FL 32789. TEL 407-628-4802, FAX 407-628-7061, http://www.bonniercorp.com. Ed. Eric Michael.

790.1 RUS
SPORT DLYA VSEKH. Text in Russian. s-m. USD 145 in United States.
Published by: Tvorchesko-Proizvodstvennoe Ob'edinenie Trim-Sport, Sverchkov per 10, Moscow, 101000, Russian Federation. TEL 7-095-9282106, FAX 7-095-2001217. Ed. B A Bazunov. **Dist. by:** East View Information Services, 10601 Wayzata Blvd, Minneapolis, MN 55305. TEL 952-252-1201, 800-477-1005, FAX 952-252-1202, info@eastview.com, http://www.eastview.com.

SPORT & MEDICINA. *see* MEDICAL SCIENCES—Sports Medicine

796.07 GBR ISSN 1357-3322
GV201
➤ **SPORT, EDUCATION AND SOCIETY.** Text in English. 1996. q. GBP 657 combined subscription in United Kingdom to institutions (print & online eds.); EUR 873, USD 1,093 combined subscription to institutions (print & online eds.) (effective 2012). adv. back issues avail.; reprint service avail. from PSC. **Document type:** *Journal, Academic/Scholarly.* **Description:** Provides a focal point for the publication of research on pedagogy, policy and the wide range of associated social, cultural, political and ethical issues in physical activity and sport.
Related titles: Online - full text ed.: ISSN 1470-1243. GBP 592 in United Kingdom to institutions; EUR 785, USD 984 to institutions (effective 2012) (from IngentaConnect).
Indexed: A01, A02, A03, A08, A20, A22, A36, B29, CA, CABA, CPE, CurCont, E01, E03, E09, ERI, ERIC, FoSS&M, GH, LT, N02, N03, P03, P04, P10, P18, P46, P48, P53, P54, P55, PAIS, PEI, PQC, PsycInfo, R12, RRTA, S02, S03, SCI, SCOPUS, SD, SSA, SSCI, SociolAb, T02, T05, W07, W11.
—IE, Infotrieve, Ingenta. **CCC.**
Published by: Routledge (Subsidiary of: Taylor & Francis Group), 4 Park Sq, Milton Park, Abingdon, Oxon OX14 4RN, United Kingdom. TEL 44-20-70176000, FAX 44-20-70176336, subscriptions@tandf.co.uk, http://www.routledge.com. Ed. John Evans. Adv. contact Linda Hann TEL 44-1344-779945. **Subscr. to:** Taylor & Francis Ltd., Journals Customer Service, Sheepen Pl, Colchester, Essex CO3 3LP, United Kingdom. TEL 44-20-70175544, FAX 44-20-70175198.

790.1 RUS
SPORT-EKSPRESS; ezhednevnaya sportivnaya gazeta. Text in Russian. 1992. 296/yr. USD 948 in United States (effective 2007). Supplement avail. **Document type:** *Newspaper, Consumer.*
Published by: Izdatel'skii Tsentr Sport-Ekspress, ul Krasina 27, str 2, Moscow, 123056, Russian Federation. TEL 7-495-2544787, FAX 7-495-7339308. Ed. Vladimir Kuchmii. **Dist. by:** East View Information Services, 10601 Wayzata Blvd, Minneapolis, MN 55305. TEL 952-252-1201, 800-477-1005, FAX 952-252-1202, info@eastview.com, http://www.eastview.com.

790.1 RUS
SPORT-EKSPRESS. ZHURNAL. Text in Russian. 1997. m. USD 175 in United States (effective 2007). **Document type:** *Magazine, Consumer.*
Published by: Izdatel'skii Tsentr Sport-Ekspress, ul Krasina 27, str 2, Moscow, 123056, Russian Federation. TEL 7-495-2544787, FAX 7-495-7339308, sport@sport-express.ru, http://www.sport-express.ru. **Dist. by:** East View Information Services, 10601 Wayzata Blvd, Minneapolis, MN 55305. TEL 952-252-1201, 800-477-1005, FAX 952-252-1202, info@eastview.com, http://www.eastview.com.

796.077 658.8 NLD ISSN 1875-2357
SPORT EN STRATEGIE. Key Title: Sport & Strategie. Text in Dutch. 2007. bi-m. EUR 75; EUR 37.50 to students (effective 2008). adv.
Published by: Arko Sports Media (Subsidiary of: Arko Uitgeverij BV), Postbus 393, Nieuwegein, 3430 AJ, Netherlands. TEL 31-30-6004780, FAX 31-30-6052618, info@arko.nl. Eds. Friso Schotanus, Frans Oosterwijk. Pubs. Cees Wolzak, Michel van Troost. adv.: color page EUR 2,500; bleed 279 x 432. Circ: 10,000.

796 340 FRA ISSN 1957-6498
SPORT ET RESPONSABILITE. Text in French. 2006. base vol. plus updates 2/yr. looseleaf. EUR 121 base vol(s).; EUR 17 updates per month (effective 2007).
Published by: Editions Weka, 249 Rue de Crimee, Paris, 75935 Cedex 19, France. TEL 33-1-53351717, FAX 33-1-53351701.

790.1 FRA ISSN 1152-9563
SPORT ET VIE. Text in French. bi-m. (plus 2 special issues). EUR 40 (effective 2009). **Document type:** *Magazine, Consumer.*
Indexed: SD.
Published by: Editions Faton S.A., 25 Rue Berbisey, Dijon, 21000, France. TEL 33-1-80404104, http://www.faton.fr.

796.170 GBR ISSN 1751-1321
➤ **SPORT, ETHICS AND PHILOSOPHY.** Text in English. 2007. 3/yr. GBP 360 combined subscription in United Kingdom to institutions (print & online eds.); EUR 537, USD 674 combined subscription to institutions (print & online eds.) (effective 2012). adv. back issues avail.; reprint service avail. from PSC. **Document type:** *Journal, Academic/Scholarly.* **Description:** Publishes high quality articles from a wide variety of philosophical traditions.
Related titles: Online - full text ed.: ISSN 1751-133X. GBP 323 in United Kingdom to institutions; EUR 483, USD 606 to institutions (effective 2012).
Indexed: A22, BrHumI, CA, E01, PhilInd, SD, T02.
—IE. **CCC.**
Published by: (British Philosophy of Sport Association), Routledge (Subsidiary of: Taylor & Francis Group), 4 Park Sq, Milton Park, Abingdon, Oxon OX14 4RN, United Kingdom. TEL 44-20-70176000, FAX 44-20-70176336, subscriptions@tandf.co.uk, http://www.routledge.com. Ed. Mike J McNamee TEL 44-1792-205678. Adv. contact Linda Hann TEL 44-1344-779945. **Subscr. to:** Taylor & Francis Ltd., Journals Customer Service, Sheepen Pl, Colchester, Essex CO3 3LP, United Kingdom. TEL 44-20-70175544, FAX 44-20-70175198.

796 613.7 NLD ISSN 1879-7644
SPORT F M. Variant title: Sport Facilities Magazine. Text in Dutch. 2005. bi-m. EUR 39.50 domestic; EUR 47 in Belgium; EUR 54.50 elsewhere (effective 2010). adv. **Document type:** *Magazine, Trade.*

Incorporates (1997-2008): Anton Sportzaken Magazine (1572-0861); Which was formerly (until 2003): Sportzaken (1388-2961); Formerly (until 2008): Sportfacilities (1871-434X); Which was formed by the merger of (2003 -2005): SportClub (1573-2312); Which was formerly (until 2003): Sportfacilities. Club (1570-4602); (2002-2005): SportComplex (1571-375X); Which was formerly (until 2002): Sportfacilities. Complex (1570-4610); Both Sportfacilities. Club and Sportfacilities. Complex superseded in part (in 2001): Sportfacilities (1386-4173); Which was formerly (until 1997): Sportkantine (0929-5089); Which superseded in part (in 1993): Kantine (0922-890X); Which superseded in part (in 1987): Foodmarkt Extra (0922-8888)
Published by: Sportfacilities & Media BV, Postbus 952, Zeist, 3700 AZ, Netherlands. TEL 31-30-6977710, FAX 31-30-6977720, info@sportfacilities.com, http://www.sportfacilities.com. Ed. Floris Schmitz. adv.: B&W page EUR 1,250; trim 210 x 297. Circ: 5,000.

790.1 GBR
SPORT FIRST. Text in English. 1998. w. GBP 0.50 newsstand/cover. adv. **Document type:** *Newspaper, Consumer.* **Description:** Provides spectators and participants with coverage and expert analysis across the sporting spectrum.
Published by: Sport First Publishing Ltd., 20- 26 BrunswickPl, Flat 20, London, N15 5DD, United Kingdom. TEL 44-171-490-7575, FAX 44-171-490-7666. Adv. contact Shawn Russell. B&W page GBP 3,800, color page GBP 5,000. Circ: 61,523 (paid).

799.1 CAN
SPORT FISHING BC NEWS. (British Columbia) Text in English. irreg. adv. **Description:** Features fishing techniques, maps, lodges and guides, tackle stories, lake fishing, river fishing and reports.
Media: Online - full text.
Published by: Sport Fishing BC.com, 1721 Jefferson Ave, Victoria, BC V8N 2B3, Canada. Ed. Hugh Partridge.

790.1 USA ISSN 1087-1659
GV571
➤ **SPORT HISTORY REVIEW/REVUE DE L'HISTOIRE DES SPORTS.** Text in English, French. 1970. s-a. USD 314 domestic to institutions; USD 319 foreign to institutions; USD 372 combined subscription domestic to institutions (print & online eds.); USD 377 combined subscription foreign to institutions (print & online eds.) (effective 2012). adv. bk.rev. bibl.; illus. back issues avail.; reprint service avail. from PSC. **Document type:** *Journal, Academic/Scholarly.* **Description:** Provides a forum for scholarly work in the broad field of sport history.
Former titles (until 1996): Canadian Journal of History of Sport (0712-9815); (until 1981): Canadian Journal of History of Sport and Physical Education (0008-4115)
Related titles: Online - full text ed.: ISSN 1543-2947. USD 314 to institutions (effective 2012).
Indexed: A01, A03, A08, A20, A22, ABS&EES, AmH&L, ArtHuCI, CA, CWPI, DIP, HistAb, IBR, IBZ, P30, PEI, SD, SportS, T02, W07.
—BLDSC (8419.624000), IE, Infotrieve, Ingenta. **CCC.**
Published by: (University of Western Ontario, Faculty of Kinesiology CAN), Human Kinetics, 1607 N Market St, Champaign, IL 61820. TEL 800-747-4457, FAX 217-351-2674, info@hkusa.com, http://www.humankinetics.com. Ed. Don Morrow TEL 519-661-4128. Pub. Rainer Martens. R&P Martha Gullo TEL 217-403-7534. Adv. contact Amy Bleich TEL 217-403-7803.

796 799 BGR ISSN 1310-3393
SPORT I NAUKA/SPORT AND SCIENCE. Text in Bulgarian. 1956. bi-m. USD 50 foreign (effective 2002).
Formerly (until 1993): Vuprosy na Fizicheskata Kultura (0324-136X)
Published by: (Bulgarski Olimpiiski Komitet/Bulgarian Olympic Committee, Natsionalna Sportna Akademia/Bulgarian National Sport Academy), Bulgarski Suiuz za Fizicheska Kultura i Sport/Bulgarian Union for Physical Culture and Sport, 75, Vassil Levski St., Sofia, 1040, Bulgaria. TEL 359-2-855305, FAX 359-2-875637. **Dist. by:** Sofia Books, ul Silivria 16, Sofia 1404, Bulgaria. TEL 359-2-9586257, info@sofiabooks-bg.com, http://www.sofiabooks-bg.com.

796 DEU ISSN 0931-8240
SPORT IN BERLIN. Text in German. 1974. 10/yr. adv. **Document type:** *Magazine, Consumer.*
Published by: Landessportbund Berlin e.V., Jesse-Owens-Allee 2, Berlin, 14053, Germany. TEL 49-30-30002-0, FAX 49-30-30002107, info@lsb-berlin.org, http://www.lsb-berlin.net. adv.: B&W page EUR 450, color page EUR 900. Circ: 6,500 (controlled).

790.1 DEU ISSN 1616-9352
SPORT IN DER HEUTIGEN ZEIT. Text in German. 2001. irreg., latest vol.6, 2006. price varies. **Document type:** *Monographic series, Academic/Scholarly.*
Published by: Attempto Verlag, Dischingerweg 5, Tuebingen, 72070, Germany. TEL 49-7071-97970, FAX 49-7071-979711, info@attempto-verlag.de, http://www.narr.de.

796 DEU
SPORT IN HESSEN. Text in German. fortn. EUR 43.10 (effective 2002). adv. **Document type:** *Magazine, Consumer.*
Published by: (Landessportbund Hessen e.V.), Pressehaus Bintz Verlag GmbH, Waldstr. 226, Offenbach Am Main, 63071, Germany. TEL 49-69-85008400, FAX 49-69-85008499. adv.: B&W page EUR 913, color page EUR 1,375. Circ: 13,000 (paid and controlled).

790.1 GBR ISSN 1746-0263
➤ **SPORT IN HISTORY.** Text in English. 1982. q. GBP 330 combined subscription in United Kingdom to institutions (print & online eds.); EUR 435, USD 548 combined subscription to institutions (print & online eds.) (effective 2012). adv. bk.rev. abstr.; bibl. back issues avail.; reprint service avail. from PSC. **Document type:** *Journal, Academic/Scholarly.* **Description:** Covers the history of sport, physical education, recreation and leisure, particularly in the UK.
Former titles (until 2003): The Sports Historian (1351-5462); (until 1993): British Society of Sports History. Bulletin (0966-1042)
Related titles: Online - full text ed.: ISSN 1746-0271. GBP 296 in United Kingdom to institutions; EUR 391, USD 493 to institutions (effective 2012).
Indexed: A22, A34, AmH&L, BrHumI, CA, CABA, E01, E12, GH, HistAb, LT, P30, PEI, R12, RRTA, SD, T02, VS.
—IE, Ingenta. **CCC.**
Published by: (British Society of Sports History), Routledge (Subsidiary of: Taylor & Francis Group), 4 Park Sq, Milton Park, Abingdon, Oxon OX14 4RN, United Kingdom. TEL 44-20-70176000, FAX 44-20-70176336, subscriptions@tandf.co.uk, http://www.routledge.com. Ed. Martin Johnes. Adv. contact Linda Hann TEL 44-1344-779945. **Subscr. to:** Taylor & Francis Ltd., Journals Customer Service, Sheepen Pl, Colchester, Essex CO3 3LP, United Kingdom. TEL 44-20-70175544, FAX 44-20-70175198.

790.1 306.483 GBR ISSN 1743-0437
➤ **SPORT IN SOCIETY.** Text in English. 1998. 10/yr. GBP 757 combined subscription in United Kingdom to institutions (print & online eds.); EUR 1,002, USD 1,251 combined subscription to institutions (print & online eds.) (effective 2012). adv. bk.rev. back issues avail.; reprint service avail. from PSC. **Document type:** *Journal, Academic/Scholarly.* **Description:** Provides an interdisciplinary forum for social anthropologists, sociologists, social historians, political scientists and others in the arts and social sciences to consider issues associated with sport in societies, cultures and political systems.
Formerly (until 2004): Culture, Sport, Society (1461-0981)
Related titles: Online - full text ed.: ISSN 1743-0445. GBP 681 in United Kingdom to institutions; EUR 902, USD 1,126 to institutions (effective 2012) (from IngentaConnect).
Indexed: A01, A03, A08, A22, B21, CA, E01, ESPM, H&SSA, P03, P42, PEI, PSA, PsycInfo, RiskAb, S02, S03, SCOPUS, SD, SSA, SociolAb, T02.
—IE, Ingenta. **CCC.**
Published by: Routledge (Subsidiary of: Taylor & Francis Group), 4 Park Sq, Milton Park, Abingdon, Oxon OX14 4RN, United Kingdom. TEL 44-20-70176000, FAX 44-20-70176336, subscriptions@tandf.co.uk, http://www.routledge.com. Adv. contact Linda Hann TEL 44-1344-779945. **Subscr. to:** Taylor & Francis Ltd., Journals Customer Service, Sheepen Pl, Colchester, Essex CO3 3LP, United Kingdom. TEL 44-20-70175544, FAX 44-20-70175198.

790.1 900 GBR ISSN 1368-9789
SPORT IN THE GLOBAL SOCIETY. Text in English. 1997. irreg., latest 2009. price varies. back issues avail. **Document type:** *Monographic series, Academic/Scholarly.* **Description:** Draws together many subjects in the expanding study of sport in the global society providing comprehensiveness and comparison within a single series.
Published by: Routledge (Subsidiary of: Taylor & Francis Group), 4 Park Sq, Milton Park, Abingdon, Oxon OX14 4RN, United Kingdom. TEL 44-20-70176000, FAX 44-20-70176336, subscriptions@tandf.co.uk. Eds. Boria Majumdar, J A Mangan.

790.1 DEU ISSN 1438-3152
SPORT-INFORM. Text in German. 1968. m. EUR 1.95 newsstand/cover (effective 2007). adv. **Document type:** *Magazine, Consumer.*
Former titles (until 1998): Sport-Inform. Ausgabe B (0936-9651); (until 1989): Sport in Rheinland-Pfalz. Ausgabe B (0178-1022)
Published by: Landessportbund Rheinland-Pfalz, Rheinallee 1, Mainz, 55116, Germany. TEL 49-6131-28140, FAX 49-6131-2814120, info@lsb-rlp.de, http://www.lsb-rlp.de. adv.: B&W page EUR 855, color page EUR 1,325. Circ: 16,500 (controlled).

790.1 BEL ISSN 1013-4700
SPORT INTERNATIONAL. Text in Arabic, French, German, Spanish. 1959. q. illus. **Description:** Contains case reports, activities of the executive committee, sports medicine section, and results of sport events fostering good will among nations.
Formerly (until 1962): C I S M Magazine (0409-7149)
Indexed: SportS.
Published by: International Military Sports Council/Conseil International du Sport Militaire, Rue Jacques Jordaens 26, Brussels, 1050, Belgium. TEL 32-2-647-6852, FAX 32-2-647-5387, TELEX 29416 CISM B. Ed. J Wanderstein. Circ: 5,000.

796 USA ISSN 1543-9518
GV558
➤ **THE SPORT JOURNAL.** Text in English. 1998. q. free (effective 2011). back issues avail. **Document type:** *Journal, Academic/Scholarly.* **Description:** Designed to further the knowledge of sport by featuring articles written by prominent professionals in the field.
Media: Online - full text.
Indexed: A26, A36, A37, A39, C06, C07, C08, C27, C29, CA, CABA, CINAHL, D03, D04, E02, E03, E12, E13, EdA, EdI, GH, H12, I05, LT, N02, N03, P33, P39, PEI, R12, R14, RRTA, S14, S15, S18, S23, SD, T02, T05, W03, W05.
Published by: United States Sports Academy, 1 Academy Dr, Daphne, AL 36526. TEL 251-626-3303, FAX 251-625-1035, academy@ussa.edu, http://www.ussa.edu. Ed. Dr. Kelly Flanagan. Pub. Dr. Thomas P Rosandich.

796.8 USA ISSN 1064-6507
SPORT KARATE INTERNATIONAL. Variant title: Boice Lydell's Sport Karate International. Text in English, Spanish. 1986. q. USD 17.50; USD 2.95 newsstand/cover. illus. back issues avail. **Document type:** *Magazine, Consumer.* **Description:** Covers National Blackbelt League and Sport Karate International tournaments. Includes local, regional, national and international coverage of events as well as ratings for Sport Karate players.
Published by: SMASH Publications, 341 E Fairmount Ave, Lakewood, NY 14750. TEL 716-763-1111, FAX 716-763-5555. Ed., Pub. Borce Lydell. adv.: page USD 399; trim 9.75 x 7.25. Circ: 25,000. **Subscr. to:** International Publishers Direct, PO Box 19526, Las Vegas, NV 89132. TEL 619-481-5928, FAX 619-259-7580.

SPORT, KULTUR UND GESELLSCHAFT. *see* HISTORY

796 ESP ISSN 1575-1066
SPORT LIFE. Text in Spanish. 1999. m. adv. **Document type:** *Magazine, Consumer.*
Published by: Motorpress Iberica (Subsidiary of: Gruner + Jahr AG & Co), Ancora 40, Madrid, 28045, Spain. TEL 34-91-3470100, FAX 34-91-3470152, http://www.motorpress-iberica.es. Ed. Juanma Montero. Circ: 58,000 (paid).

SPORT LITERATE; honest reflections on life's leisurely diversions. *see* LITERARY AND POLITICAL REVIEWS

796 351 NLD ISSN 1872-2210
SPORT LOKAAL. Text in Dutch. 1953. bi-m. EUR 66.75 domestic; EUR 73.50 foreign; EUR 13 newsstand/cover (effective 2010). adv. **Document type:** *Magazine, Trade.*
Formerly (until 2006): Landelijke Contactraad voor de Gemeentelijke Bemoelingen met de Lichamelijke Opvoeding en de Sport. Landelijk Contact (0166-4662)
—IE.
Published by: Vereniging Sport en Gemeenten, Postbus 103, Oosterbeek, 6860 AC, Netherlands. TEL 31-26-3396410, FAX 31-26-3396412, info@sportengemeenten.nl, http://www.sportengemeenten.nl. Adv. contact Wim Elbertse. Circ: 1,500.

796 CZE ISSN 1214-3677
SPORT MAGAZIN. Text in Czech. 1997. w. CZK 17 newsstand/cover (effective 2010). adv. **Document type:** *Magazine, Consumer.*
Published by: Ringier CR, Komunardu 1584/42, Prague 7, 170 00, Czech Republic. TEL 420-2-25977616, FAX 420-2-67097718, info@ringier.cz, http://www.ringier.cz. Ed. Lukas Tomek. Circ: 59,321 (paid).

796 ROM ISSN 1221-3349
SPORT MAGAZIN. Text in Romanian. 1992. w. **Document type:** *Magazine, Consumer.*
Published by: Jurnalul SA, Piata Presei Libere nr. 1, corp D, et. 8, sector 1, Bucharest, Romania. TEL 40-21-2243866, FAX 40-21-2229082, jurnalul@jurnalul.ro, http://www.jurnalul.ro.

796 BEL ISSN 1376-9081
SPORT MAGAZINE - FOOT MAGAZINE. Text in French. 2001. w. EUR 120 (effective 2010). adv. **Document type:** *Magazine, Consumer.*
Formed by the merger of (1982-2001): Foot Magazine (0770-321X); (1996-2001): Sport Magazine (1372-1135)
Related titles: Dutch ed.: Sport Magazine - Voetbal Magazine. ISSN 1376-909X.
Published by: Roularta Media Group, Research Park, Zellik, 1731, Belgium. TEL 32-2-4675611, FAX 32-2-4675757, communication@roularta.be, http://www.roularta.be. adv.: page EUR 6,100. Circ: 58,055 (paid and controlled).

796 USA ISSN 1875-9785
SPORT MANAGEMENT. Text in English. 2008. irreg., latest 2009. price varies. **Document type:** *Monographic series, Academic/Scholarly.*
Related titles: Online - full text ed.: ISSN 1875-9793.
Published by: Butterworth - Heinemann (Subsidiary of: Elsevier Science & Technology), 3251 Riverport Ln, Maryland Heights, MO 63043. TEL 314-453-7010, 800-545-2522, FAX 314-453-7095, usbkinfo@elsevier.com, http://www.elsevier.com.

796 658 USA ISSN 1938-6974
GV713
➤ **SPORT MANAGEMENT EDUCATION JOURNAL.** Text in English. 2007. a. free (effective 2010). **Document type:** *Journal, Academic/Scholarly.*
Published by: National Association for Sport and Physical Education, 1900 Association Dr, Reston, VA 20191. TEL 703-476-3410, 800-213-7193, FAX 703-476-8316, naspe@aahperd.org, http://www.aahperd.org/naspe/template.cfm?template=main.html. **Co-publisher:** North American Society for Sport Management.

➤ **SPORT MANAGEMENT REVIEW.** *see* BUSINESS AND ECONOMICS—Management

388 GBR ISSN 1472-0663
SPORT MARKET FORECASTS. Text in English. 2001. a. GBP 250 per issue to corporations; GBP 125 per issue to institutions (effective 2009). **Document type:** *Magazine, Trade.* **Description:** Provides detailed economic information on consumer spending for the whole sports market including sport clothing and footwear, sport TV and video, participation sports and spectator sports.
Published by: Sheffield Hallam University, Sport Industry Research Centre, Collegiate Hall, Collegiate Crescent, Sheffield, S10 2BP, United Kingdom. TEL 44-114-2255919, FAX 44-114-2254341, sirc@shu.ac.uk, http://www.shu.ac.uk/research/sirc/index.html.

796.06 658.8 USA ISSN 1061-6934
GV716
➤ **SPORT MARKETING QUARTERLY;** for professionals in the business of marketing sport. Abbreviated title: S M Q. Text in English. 1992. q. USD 63 combined subscription domestic to individuals (print & online eds.); USD 74 combined subscription foreign to individuals (print & online eds.); USD 317 combined subscription domestic to institutions (print & online eds.); USD 331 combined subscription foreign to institutions (print & online eds.) (effective 2010). adv. software rev.; video rev.; bk.rev. charts; stat.; illus. index. 64 p./no. 3 cols./p.; back issues avail.; reprint service avail. from PSC. **Document type:** *Journal, Academic/Scholarly.* **Description:** Aims to provide a publishing outlet for both practicing professionals and academicians in the sports marketing field.
Related titles: Online - full text ed.: ISSN 1557-2528. USD 63 to individuals; USD 317 to institutions (effective 2010).
Indexed: A12, A13, A17, A22, A26, ABIn, B01, B02, B04, B06, B07, B09, B15, B16, B17, B18, BPI, BRD, CA, CABA, E03, E08, ERI, G04, G08, I05, LT, N02, P10, P32, P48, P51, P53, P54, PEI, PGegResA, PN&I, PQC, R12, RRTA, S09, SD, T02, W01, W02, W03, W05.
—BLDSC (8419.629000), IE, Ingenta. **CCC.**
Published by: Fitness Information Technology Inc., West Virginia University, 275G Coliseum, WVU-PE, PO Box 6116, Morgantown, WV 26506. TEL 304-293-6888, 800-477-4348, FAX 304-293-6658, fitcustomerservice@mail.wvu.edu. Ed. Matthew Shank. adv.: B&W page USD 395, color page USD 890.

613 RUS
SPORT NA MNOGO.RU. Text in Russian. irreg. free (effective 2002). **Description:** Covers a variety of sports for the active consumer.
Published by: Sportsmen.ru

790.1 381 NLD ISSN 1381-9283
SPORT PARTNER; magazine for the sports trade in the Bennelux. Text in Dutch. 1988. 10/yr. EUR 77.50 (effective 2009). adv. charts; illus.; stat. back issues avail. **Document type:** *Magazine, Trade.* **Description:** For sporting goods retailers and distributors in the Netherlands, Belgium, and Luxembourg.
Published by: Maruba b.v., Winthontlaan 200, Utrecht, 3526 KV, Netherlands. TEL 31-30-2891073, FAX 31-30-2887415, maruba@maruba.com, http://www.maruba.nl. Pub. Maas H van Drie. adv.: color page EUR 2,950; trim 240 x 300. Circ: 2,400.

790.1 CAN ISSN 0828-9581
SPORT PLUS. Text in French. 1981. m. USD 20. adv.
Former titles (until 1985): Marathon Plus (0828-5853); (until 1984): Marathon (0823-0870); (until 1982): Marathon Magazine (0712-1784)
Address: 1028 Marie Victorin, Laval, PQ H7E 3C1, Canada. TEL 514-661-5586. Ed. Charles Andre Marchand. Circ: 40,000.

S

790.1 FRA ISSN 0992-7697
SPORT PREMIERE MAGAZINE. Text in French. 1976. 10/yr. EUR 60 domestic; EUR 80 foreign (effective 2009). adv. **Document type:** *Magazine, Consumer.*
Formerly (until 1988): Loisirs Service (0337-9353)
Published by: S P E, 3 rue de Teheran, Paris, 75008, France. TEL 42-89-41-04, FAX 45-61-12-00, TELEX 640 369. Ed. Emmanuel Gravaud. Circ: 8,500.

THE SPORT PSYCHOLOGIST. *see* PSYCHOLOGY

796 340 DEU ISSN 2190-1015
▼ **SPORT - RECHT - GESELLSCHAFT.** Text in German. 2010. irreg. price varies. **Document type:** *Monographic series, Academic/ Scholarly.*
Published by: Mohr Siebeck GmbH & Co. KG, Wilhelmstr 18, Tuebingen, 72074, Germany. TEL 49-7071-9230, FAX 49-7071-51104, info@mohr.de.

796.0835 USA
SPORT SCENE (ONLINE); focus on youth programs. Text in English. 1979. 6/yr. free. adv. bk.rev.; Website rev. stat. **Document type:** *Magazine, Consumer.* **Description:** Provides current information about tots, children and teens in sports. Contains articles to help leaders be more effective, parents become more effective coaches, teachers and leaders, increase participation, decrease drop-outs and injuries, and show how sports can be made more fun for children.
Formerly (until 2001): Sport Scene (Print) (0270-1812)
Media: Online - full text.
Indexed: SD, SportS.
Published by: North American Youth Sport Institute, 4985 Oak Garden Dr, Kernersville, NC 27284-9520. TEL 336-784-4926, 800-767-4916, FAX 336-784-5546, jack@naysi.com. Ed. Jack Hutslar. Circ: 8,000.

796 BIH ISSN 1840-3662
SPORT SCIENCE. Text in English, Croatian. 2008. s-a.
Related titles: Online - full text ed.: ISSN 1840-3670. free (effective 2011).
Indexed: CA, SD, T02.
Published by: Univerzitet u Travniku, Kinezioloski Fakultet/Travnik Universty, Faculty of Education info@sposci.com, http://www.unt.ba. Ed. Dobromir Bonacin.

SPORT SCIENCE & PHYSICAL EDUCATION BULLETIN. *see* PHYSICAL FITNESS AND HYGIENE

790.1 617.1 DEU ISSN 0939-3706
SPORT SCIENCES INTERNATIONAL. Text in English. 1994. irreg., latest vol.4, 2007. price varies. **Document type:** *Monographic series, Academic/Scholarly.*
—BLDSC (8419.646000).
Published by: Peter Lang GmbH (Subsidiary of: Peter Lang Publishing Group), Eschborner Landstr 42-50, Frankfurt Am Main, 60489, Germany. TEL 49-69-7807050, FAX 49-69-78070550, zentrale.frankfurt@peterlang.com, http://www.peterlang.com. Eds. Dieter Hackfort, Herbert Haag.

613.7 BIH ISSN 1840-4413
SPORT SCIENTIFIC AND PRACTICAL ASPECTS; international scientific journal of kinesiology. Text in English. 2004. s-a. **Document type:** *Journal, Academic/Scholarly.*
Related titles: Online - full text ed.: ISSN 1840-4561. free (effective 2011).
Indexed: CA, CABA, GH, LT, N02, N03, SD, T02.
Published by: Univerzitet u Tuzli, Ul Dr Tihomila Markovica 1, Tuzla, 75000, Bosnia Herzegovina. TEL 387-35-300500, http://www.untz.ba. Ed. Branimir Mikic.

796 USA
SPORT SHOP NEWS; national magazine for sporting goods buyers and retailers. Text in English. 1989. m. USD 30 domestic; USD 40 foreign (effective 2000). adv. bk.rev. illus.; tr.lit. **Document type:** *Magazine, Trade.* **Description:** Offers sporting-goods retail industry executives advice on merchandising and purchasing; showcases new products.
Published by: Trade Publishing, PO Box 566, Stratford, CT 06615-1219. TEL 203-279-0149. Ed. James Martone. Pub. John Mortimer. Adv. contact Nick Glowatsky. B&W page USD 4,975; 11 x 8.5. Circ: 23,400.

796 DEU ISSN 0931-8178
SPORT SHOW. Text in German. 1986. 3/yr. **Document type:** *Magazine, Trade.*
Published by: Intersport Deutschland eG, Wannenaeckerstr 50, Heilbronn, 74078, Germany. TEL 49-7131-288-0, FAX 49-7131-21257, info@intersport.de, http://www.intersport.de.

796 SRB ISSN 1820-2802
SPORT SPECIJAL. Text in Serbian. 2003. w. adv. **Document type:** *Newspaper, Consumer.*
Published by: Kompanija Novosti, Trg Nikole Pasica 7, Belgrade, 11000. TEL 381-11-3398202, FAX 381-11-3398337, redakcija@novosti.co.yu, http://www.novosti.co.yu.

796.069 FRA ISSN 1772-7693
SPORT STRATEGIES HEBDO; analyse du sport business. Text in French. 2004. w. EUR 790 (effective 2007). **Document type:** *Newspaper, Consumer.*
Related titles: Online - full text ed.: EUR 590 (effective 2007); Supplement(s): Sport Strategies. Annuaire du Marketing Sportif. ISSN 2106-8690. 2009.
Published by: Sport Strategies, 72 Rue Maurice Thorez, Nanterre, 92000, France. TEL 33-1-41917652, http://www.sportstrategies.com.

SPORT SUMMIT SPORTS BUSINESS DIRECTORY. *see* BUSINESS AND ECONOMICS—Trade And Industrial Directories

796.07 USA
SPORT SUPPLEMENT. Text in English. q. free to qualified personnel. bk.rev. **Document type:** *Magazine, Consumer.* **Description:** Covers issues and problems of interest to high school and athletic administrators and coaches.
Related titles: Online - full text ed.: ISSN 1558-6448.
Published by: United States Sports Academy, 1 Academy Dr, Daphne, AL 36526. TEL 205-626-3303, FAX 205-626-3874. Ed. Ric Esposito. Circ: 85,000.

SPORT TRUCK. *see* TRANSPORTATION—Trucks And Trucking

790.1 DEU ISSN 0176-4136
SPORT UND FITNESS; das Fit Aktiv Magazin - Ernaehrung - Lifestyle. Text in German. bi-m. EUR 26; EUR 4.55 newsstand/cover (effective 2002). adv. **Document type:** *Magazine, Consumer.*
Related titles: Online - full text ed.
Published by: Sport und Fitness Verlag Benno Dahmen, Oppumer Str 71, Krefeld, 47719, Germany. TEL 49-2151-6322-0, FAX 49-2151-632218. Ed., Pub., Adv. contact Benno Dahmen. B&W page EUR 1,959, color page EUR 3,260. Circ: 60,000 (paid and controlled).

SPORT UND GESELLSCHAFT/SPORTS AND SOCIETY. *see* SOCIOLOGY

SPORT UND GESELLSCHAFTLICHE PERSPEKTIVEN. *see* SOCIOLOGY

790.1 DEU ISSN 1616-7783
SPORT UND MEHR. Text in German. 1950. m. adv. illus.; stat. **Document type:** *Bulletin, Consumer.* **Description:** Covers sports matters and affairs in lower Saxony, along with information on sports marketing and sport management.
Former titles (until 1998): Sport in Niedersachsen (1616-7775); (until 1962): Amtliche Mitteilungen fuer alle Facharten (1616-7767)
Published by: Landessportbund Niedersachsen e.V., Ferdinand-Wilhelm-Fricke-Weg 10, Hannover, 30169, Germany. TEL 49-511-1268223, FAX 49-511-1268220, info@lsb-niedersachsen.de, http://www.lsb-niedersachsen.de. adv.: B&W page EUR 863, color page EUR 1,725; 210 x 297. Circ: 15,500.

796.07 DEU
SPORT UND MOBILITAET MIT ROLLSTUHL. Text in German. 1982. m. EUR 20 to non-members (effective 2009). adv. illus. back issues avail. **Document type:** *Magazine, Consumer.*
Formerly (until 2008): Rollstuhlsport (0722-1088)
Published by: Deutscher Rollstuhl Sportverband e.V., Friedrich-Alfred-Str 10, Duisburg, 47055, Germany. TEL 49-203-7174180, FAX 49-203-7174181, info@rollstuhlsport.de. Circ: 6,950 (controlled).

790 658.8 DEU ISSN 0049-1926
SPORT UND MODE. Text in French, German. 1948. 16/yr. EUR 98 domestic; EUR 110 foreign; EUR 7 newsstand/cover (effective 2011). adv. bk.rev. abstr.; charts; illus.; pat.; stat. **Document type:** *Magazine, Trade.*
Published by: (Verband Deutscher Sportgeschaefte e.V.), Verlag Chmielorz GmbH und Co., Marktplatz 13, Wiesbaden, 65183, Germany. TEL 49-611-360980, FAX 49-611-301303, info@chmielorz.de, http://www.chmielorz.de. Ed. Andreas Stowasser. Adv. contact Christian Augsburger. Circ: 8,592 (paid).

790.1 375 DEU ISSN 1617-5646
SPORT UND SPIEL. Variant title: Praxis in Bewegung - Sport und Spiel. Text in German. 1985. 4/yr. EUR 40; EUR 14 newsstand/cover (effective 2011). adv. **Document type:** *Journal, Academic/Scholarly.*
Former titles (until 2001): Lehrbogen fuer Bewegung, Spiel und Sport (0947-7098); (until 1994): Lehrbogen fuer Sport und Spiel (0934-2125)
Published by: Erhard Friedrich Verlag GmbH, Im Brande 17, Seelze, 30926, Germany. TEL 49-511-400040, FAX 49-511-40004170, info@friedrich-verlag.de. Circ: 3,500 (paid and controlled).

796 ITA ISSN 0490-5113
SPORT UNIVERSITARIO. Text in Italian. 1951; N.S. 1969. q. free. adv. bk.rev. **Document type:** *Magazine, Consumer.*
Published by: Centro Universitario Sportivo Italiano, Via Angelo Brofferio, 7, Rome, RM 00195, Italy. TEL 39-6-3722206, FAX 39-6-3724479, office@cusi.it, http://www.cusi.it.

790.1 DEU ISSN 1430-1008
SPORT-WELT; die deutsche Galoppsportzeitung. Text in German. 3/w. EUR 404.40; EUR 2.50 newsstand/cover (effective 2009). adv. **Document type:** *Newspaper, Consumer.*
Published by: D S V Deutscher Sportverlag GmbH, Im Mediapark 8, Cologne, 50670, Germany. TEL 49-221-25870, FAX 49-221-2587212, kontakt@dsv-sportverlag.de, http://www.dsv-sportverlag.de. Ed. Hans Reski. adv.: B&W page EUR 4,000, color page EUR 5,200; trim 285 x 525. Circ: 11,000 (controlled).

796 NLD ISSN 0922-4270
SPORTACCOM; magazine voor realisatie, beheer en onderhoud van sportaccomodaties. Text in Dutch. 1963. bi-m. EUR 72.50 (effective 2008). adv. charts; illus.; stat. **Document type:** *Trade.* **Description:** Covers all sports played indoors in the Netherlands and the maintenance of facilities necessary.
Formed by the merger of (1982-1987): Sportcomplex (0922-419X); (1969-1987): Nederlandse Sport Federatie. Afdeling Sportaccomodatie. Technische Mededelingen (0921-0679); Which was formerly: Nederlandse Sport Federatie. Technische Bulletin (0028-2308)
—IE, Infotrieve.
Published by: (Nederlandse Sport Federatie), Arko Sports Media (Subsidiary of: Arko Uitgeverij BV), Postbus 393, Nieuwegein, 3430 AJ, Netherlands. TEL 31-30-6051090, FAX 31-30-6052618, info@arko.nl, http://www.arko.nl. adv.: B&W page EUR 1,875, color page EUR 2,750; bleed 210 x 297. Circ: 1,484.

790.1 MUS
SPORTAMO; magazine-hebdomadaire tele-sport. Text in French. w. MUR 65.
Published by: Nouvelle Imprimerie Mauricienne, 5 rue Jemmapes, Port Louis, Mauritius.

790.1 USA
SPORTBIL. Text in English. 1978. a. adv. **Description:** Presents opinion papers and data on the business of sport, sport events, and sport facilities.
Published by: International Sport Summit, 6550 Rock Spring Dr, Ste 500, Bethesda, MD 20817-1126. FAX 301-493-0536. Circ: 7,500.

797.23 627.72 GBR ISSN 0958-9007
SPORTDIVER. Text in English. 1989. m. GBP 32 domestic; GBP 49.60 foreign (effective 2009). adv. **Document type:** *Magazine, Consumer.* **Description:** Contains informative and entertaining features on both short- and long-haul dive destinations, articles on UK dives suitable for all levels of experience, comprehensive, unbiased equipment reviews carried out by the sport diver test team, news and views from the diving industry and much more.
—**CCC.**
Published by: Archant Specialist Ltd. (Subsidiary of: Archant Group), Archant House, Oriel Rd, Cheltenham, GL50 1BB, United Kingdom. TEL 44-1242-211080, FAX 44-1242-216094, http://www.archant.co.uk/. Ed. Mark Evans TEL 44-118-9897265. Adv. contact Dave Pritchett TEL 44-118-9897236. **Dist. by:** Seymour Distribution Ltd.

797.21 SWE ISSN 0038-7967
SPORTDYKAREN. Text in Swedish. 1958. 5/yr. SEK 210 to members (effective 2004). adv. bk.rev. **Document type:** *Consumer.*
Formerly (until vol.3, 1959): Sportdyrkarbladet
Published by: Svenska Sportdykarfoerbundet (SSDF), Idrrottshuset, Farsta, 12343, Sweden. TEL 46-8-6058802, FAX 46-8-6058832, http://www.ssdf.se. Ed. Johanna Ekstroem TEL 46-8-6058805.

796 NLD ISSN 1871-9937
SPORTERS IN CIJFERS. Text in Dutch. 1991. irreg., latest vol.3, 2002. EUR 15 per issue (effective 2009).
Published by: Nederlands Olympisch Comite, Nederlandse Sport Federatie, Postbus 302, Arnhem, 6800 AH, Netherlands. TEL 31-26-4834400, FAX 31-26-4821245, info@noc-nsf.nl, http://www.nocnsf.nl.

796 SWE ISSN 1103-4246
SPORTFACK. (Special editions: Golf Business No. 4 and 9. Bike Business No. 3 and 10. Fitness Business No. 11.) Text in Swedish. 1993. 10/yr. SEK 508 (effective 2005). adv. back issues avail. **Document type:** *Magazine, Trade.* **Description:** Trade magazine for sports, golf, and bicycles.
Published by: Hjemmet Mortensen AB (Subsidiary of: Hjemmet-Mortensen AS), Gaevlegatan 22, Stockholm, 11378, Sweden. TEL 46-8-6920100, FAX 46-8-6509705, info@hjemmetmortensen.se, http://www.hjemmetmortensen.se. Eds. Magnus Reither, Martin Willners. Adv. contact Martina Wickham. color page SEK 20,000; 226 x 295.

613.7 NLD ISSN 1571-8654
SPORTGERICHT. Text in Dutch. 1991. bi-m. EUR 51 domestic; EUR 67.50 in Europe; EUR 83.50 elsewhere; EUR 39 to students (effective 2009). adv. bk.rev. abstr.; charts; illus. **Document type:** *Magazine, Trade.* **Description:** Covers training theory, physical education, sport and sports sciences.
Formerly (until 2003): R S G (0926-7638); Which was formed by the merger of (1946-1991): Richting (0035-5135); (1979-1991): Sport - Gericht (0165-2087)
—IE.
Published by: Uitgeverij Sportgericht, Oudezijds Voorburgwal 129-II, Amsterdam, 1012 EP, Netherlands. TEL 31-20-4222285, sportgericht@xs4all.nl. Eds. Hanno van der Loo, Jorrit Rehorst, Wigert Thunnissen, Gerard van der Poel. adv.: B&W page EUR 520; bleed 210 x 297. Circ: 1,400 (paid).

796 DEU
SPORTHILFE.DE. Text in German. 4/yr. adv. **Document type:** *Magazine, Consumer.*
Published by: Stiftung Deutsche Sporthilfe, Burnitzstr 42, Frankfurt am Main, 60596, Germany. TEL 49-69-678030, FAX 49-69-676568, info@sporthilfe.de, http://www.sporthilfe.de. adv.: color page EUR 2,500. Circ: 10,000 (controlled).

796 ALB
SPORTI SHQIPTAR. Text in Albanian. 1935. 3/w. USD 89 foreign (effective 2008). adv. **Document type:** *Newspaper, Consumer.*
Formerly: Sporti Popullor
Related titles: Online - full content ed.
Address: Rr Don Bosko, Vilat e Reja, Tirana, Albania. TEL 355-4-233572, FAX 355-4-233526. Pub. Koco Kokedhima.

799.202 USA ISSN 1061-2424
SPORTING CLAYS; the shotgun hunter's magazine. Text in English. 1988. m. USD 29.95 domestic; USD 34.95 foreign; USD 3.95 newsstand/cover. illus. reprints avail. **Document type:** *Magazine, Consumer.* **Description:** Reports on opportunities for bird hunting and sporting clays target practice.
Published by: (National Sporting Clays Association), Patch Communications, 5211 S Washington Ave, Titusville, FL 32780. TEL 321-268-5010, FAX 321-267-1894. Ed. George Conrad. adv.: B&W page USD 1,340, color page USD 1,735; trim 10.88 x 8.13. Circ: 23,557.

790.1 USA
SPORTING GOODS AGENTS ASSOCIATION. MEMBERSHIP ROSTER. Text in English. m. USD 200 (effective 2000). **Document type:** *Directory.*
Formerly: Sporting Goods Agents Association. Newsletter
Published by: Sporting Goods Agents Association, PO Box 998, Morton, IL 60053. TEL 847-296-3670, FAX 847-827-0196, sgaa998@aol.com, http://www.r-sports.com. Ed. Lois Halinton.

790.1 658 USA ISSN 1060-2550
SPORTING GOODS INTELLIGENCE; news and analysis of the international market. Text in English. 1983. 50/yr. USD 535 domestic; USD 575 foreign; USD 680 combined subscription print & fax editions (effective 2005). adv. **Document type:** *Newsletter, Trade.* **Description:** Provides financial news and analysis of sporting goods manufacturing and retail companies and of the U.S. and international sporting goods market. Covers all major sporting goods segments, including footwear, equipment and apparel.
Related titles: E-mail ed.: USD 535 (effective 2004); Fax ed.: USD 630 (effective 2004); ◆ Regional ed(s).: Sporting Goods Intelligence Asia. ISSN 1098-2485; ◆ Sporting Goods Intelligence Europe. ISSN 1143-2462.
Published by: Sports Management News, Inc., 442 Featherbed Ln, Glen Mills, PA 19342. TEL 610-459-4040, 800-328-6397, FAX 610-459-4010, sginews@sginews.com. Ed. Robert W McGee. Pub. John G Horan. Adv. contact Jonathan Bogert.

790.1 USA
THE SPORTING LIFE. Key Title: T S L. Text in English. 1998. bi-m. **Document type:** *Magazine, Consumer.*
Published by: T S L Publications, 21 E 40th St, New York, NY 10016. TEL 212-696-2484, FAX 212-696-1678, racquet@walrus.com. Ed. Stephen Weiss. Circ: 150,000 (paid).

796 USA ISSN 0038-805X
GV561
THE SPORTING NEWS. Abbreviated title: S N. Text in English. 1886. 24/yr. USD 14.97 (effective 2009). adv. bk.rev. illus. back issues avail.; reprints avail. **Document type:** *Magazine, Consumer.* **Description:** Features news articles on pro football, college football, college basketball, baseball, pro basketball, hockey plus freshman recruiting information.
Related titles: Microfilm ed.: (from BHP, PQC); Online - full text ed.; ◆ Supplement(s): Index to the Sporting News. ISSN 1041-2859.

Indexed: A01, A02, A03, A08, A22, A26, C05, CPerI, E07, G05, G06, G07, G08, G09, HlthInd, I05, I06, I07, M01, M02, M04, MASUSE, MagInd, P02, P07, P10, P19, P34, P48, P53, P54, PQC, S23, SD, SPI, SportS, T02, TOM.
—CIS. **CCC.**
Published by: American City Business Journals, Inc. (Subsidiary of: Advance Publications, Inc.), 120 W Morehead St, Ste 400, Charlotte, NC 28202. FAX 704-973-1001, http://www.acbj.com. Ed. Jeff D'Alessio. Pub. Ed Baker. Adv. contact Paul Severini TEL 212-500-0680. B&W page USD 48,418, color page USD 59,884; trim 10 x 11. Circ: 600,000 (paid).

796.355 USA ISSN 1051-6018
GV848.4.U6
THE SPORTING NEWS HOCKEY YEARBOOK. Text in English. 1982. a. USD 7.99 per issue (effective 2008). adv. back issues avail. **Document type:** *Magazine, Consumer.*
Formerly (until 1990): Sporting News Hockey Directory
Published by: American City Business Journals, Inc. (Subsidiary of: Advance Publications, Inc.), 120 W Morehead St, Charlotte, NC 28202. TEL 704-973-1000, FAX 704-973-1001, info@bizjournals.com, http://www.bizjournals.com.

798.8 IRL ISSN 1393-9521
SPORTING PRESS. Text in English. 1923. w. adv. illus. **Document type:** *Newspaper, Consumer.* **Description:** News about dog racing.
Indexed: SportS.
Published by: (Irish Coursing Club), Greyhound & Sporting Press Ltd., Davis Rd., Clonmel, Co. Tipperary, Ireland. TEL 353-52-21422, FAX 353-52-26446. Ed. J L Desmond. Adv. contact Edmund O'Brien. B&W page EUR 1,260; trim 15 x 21. Circ: 7,500.

790.1 NGA
SPORTING RECORDS. Text in English. 1961. w. NGN 52. adv. **Document type:** *Report, Consumer.* **Description:** Presents sporting reports and forecasts.
Published by: Daily Times of Nigeria Ltd., Publications Division, New Isheri Rd., PMB 21340, Ikeja, Agidingbi, Lagos, Nigeria. TEL 234-64-900850-9, TELEX 234-64-21333. Ed. Cyril Kappo. Circ: 222,975.

799.202 GBR ISSN 1748-8737
SPORTING RIFLE. Text in English. 2005. m. GBP 37 domestic (effective 2010). adv. bk.rev. illus. **Document type:** *Magazine, Consumer.*
Incorporates: Target Sports (1369-5754); Which was formerly (until 1997): Target Gun (0143-8751)
Published by: Blaze Publishing, Lawrence House, Morrell St, Leamington Spa, Warwickshire, CV32 5SZ, United Kingdom. TEL 44-1926-339808, FAX 44-1926-470400, info@blazepublishing.co.uk, http://www.blazepublishing.co.uk/. Circ: 24,500.

790.1 CAN ISSN 0824-9849
SPORTING SCENE. Text in English. 1980. m. CAD 20; CAD 25 in United States. adv.
Address: 22 Maberley Cres., West Hill, ON M1C 3K8, Canada. TEL 416-284-0304, FAX 416-284-1299. Ed. Peter Martens. Circ: 19,800 (controlled).

796 AUS ISSN 0813-2577
➤ **SPORTING TRADITIONS.** Variant title: Australian Society for Sports History. Journal. Text in English. 1984. s-a. AUD 50 to individuals; AUD 75 to institutions (effective 2008). bk.rev. 100 p./no.; back issues avail. **Document type:** *Journal, Academic/Scholarly.* **Description:** Promotes the serious study of sport in society.
Related titles: Online - full text ed.
Indexed: AusPAIS, CA, MLA-IB, SD, T02.
—BLDSC (8419.823850), IE, Ingenta.
Published by: Australian Society for Sports History, Rob Hess, Sport History Unit, F022, School of Human Movement, Recreation and Performance, Victoria University, PO Box 14428, Melbourne City MC, VIC 8001, Australia. Ed. Lionel Frost. Circ: 400.

796 305.4 USA ISSN 1935-1259
SPORTING WOMAN QUARTERLY. Cover title: S W Quarterly. Text in English. 2005 (Spring). q. USD 19; USD 5.95 newsstand/cover (effective 2007). adv. **Document type:** *Magazine, Consumer.* **Description:** Features seasonal sports highlights of women's luxury sporting events including polo and equestrian events, golf, tennis, soccer and international sports.
Related titles: Online - full content ed.: 2002.
Published by: EluxMedia, 5 Concourse Pkwy, Ste 3000, 30th Fl, Atlanta, GA 30328. TEL 404-432-6179. Ed. Kimberly Carr-Cavallo. adv.: B&W page USD 33,533, color page USD 45,315. Circ: 40,000.

SPORTINGKID. *see* CHILDREN AND YOUTH—For

794 DEU ISSN 1430-1067
SPORTIV. Text in German. 1996. bi-m. EUR 2 newsstand/cover (effective 2007). adv. **Document type:** *Magazine, Consumer.*
Published by: F.W. Becker GmbH, Grafenstr. 46, Arnsberg, 59821, Germany. TEL 49-2931-5219-0, FAX 49-2931-521933, info@becker-druck-verlag.de, http://becker-druck-verlag.de. adv.: B&W page EUR 715, color page EUR 894. Circ: 3,070 (paid and controlled).

796 RUS ISSN 0038-8092
SPORTIVNAYA ZHIZN' ROSSII. Text in Russian. 1957. m. USD 109.95. adv. illus. index.
Indexed: RASB.
Address: Armyanskii per 13, Moscow, 101000, Russian Federation. TEL 7-095-9246184, FAX 7-095-9280085. Ed. I B Maslennikov. **Dist. by:** East View Information Services, 10601 Wayzata Blvd, Minneapolis, MN 55305. TEL 952-252-1201, 800-477-1005, FAX 952-252-1202, info@eastview.com, http://www.eastview.com.

796 RUS ISSN 0038-8106
SPORTIVNYE IGRY. Text in Russian. 1955. m. illus. index.
Published by: Fizkul'tura i Sport, Dolgorukovskaya ul 27, Moscow, 101421, Russian Federation. TEL 7-095-9782690. Ed. D L Rishkov. Circ: 15,000.

796 DEU ISSN 0014-6145
DER SPORTJOURNALIST. Text in German. 1950. m. EUR 48; EUR 4.20 newsstand/cover (effective 2011). adv. bk.rev. illus. **Document type:** *Magazine, Trade.*
Published by: (Verband Deutscher Sportjournalisten), Meyer & Meyer Verlag, Von-Coels-Str 390, Aachen, 52080, Germany. TEL 49-241-958100, FAX 49-241-9581010, verlag@m-m-sports.com, http://m-m-sports.de. Circ: 4,000 (paid).

796 NLD ISSN 1874-5806
DE SPORTKALENDER. Text in Dutch. 2006. a. EUR 14.95 (effective 2009).
Published by: Uitgeverij de Arbeiderspers B.V., Postbus 2877, Amsterdam, 1000 CW, Netherlands. TEL 31-20-5247500, info@arbeiderspers.nl, http://www.arbeiderspers.nl.

SPORTKOMMUNIKATION. *see* SOCIOLOGY

796 613.7 BIH ISSN 1986-6089
SPORTLOJA. Text in Serbian. 2005. s-a. **Document type:** *Journal, Academic/Scholarly.*
Formerly (until 2009): Fakultet Fizickog Vaspitanja i Sporta. Glasnik (1840-1031)
Related titles: CD-ROM ed.: ISSN 1986-6097; Online - full text ed.: ISSN 1986-6119. free (effective 2011).
Published by: Univerziteta Banja Luka, Fakultet Fizickog Vaspitanja i Sporta/University of Banja Luka, Faculty of Physical Education and Sports, Bulevar Vojvode Petra Bojovica 1A, Banja Luka, 78 000, Bosnia Herzegovina. ffvis@blic.net, http://www.ffvis.net. Ed. Goran Bosnjak.

790.1 AUT
SPORTMAGAZIN. Text in German. 1987. 12/yr. EUR 35 (effective 2008). adv. **Document type:** *Magazine, Consumer.*
Published by: Sportverlag GmbH & Co. KG (Subsidiary of: Styria Medien AG), Kaiserstr 113-115, Vienna, W 1070, Austria. TEL 43-1-360850, FAX 43-1-36085200, office@vsm.at, http://www.vsm.at. Ed. Adi Kornfeld. Adv. contact Nina Pikisch. color page EUR 9,100; trim 185 x 250. Circ: 57,215 (paid).

796 CHE ISSN 1424-6317
SPORTMAGAZIN. Text in German. 2000. 10/yr. adv. **Document type:** *Magazine, Consumer.*
Published by: Ringier AG, Dufourstr 49, Zuerich, 8008, Switzerland. TEL 41-44-2596262, FAX 41-44-2598665, info@ringier.ch, http://www.ringier.ch. adv.: color page CHF 9,500; trim 180 x 251. Circ: 25,000 (paid and controlled).

796 658 DEU ISSN 2190-216X
▼ **SPORTMANAGEMENT.** Text in German. 2010. irreg., latest vol.2, 2010. price varies. **Document type:** *Monographic series, Academic/Scholarly.*
Published by: Erich Schmidt Verlag GmbH & Co. (Berlin), Genthiner Str 30 G, Berlin, 10785, Germany. TEL 49-30-2500850, FAX 49-30-250085305, vertrieb@esvmedien.de.

794 330 DEU ISSN 1611-6763
SPORTOEKONOMIE IN FORSCHUNG UND PRAXIS. Text in German. 2003. irreg., latest vol.10, 2010. price varies. **Document type:** *Monographic series, Academic/Scholarly.*
Published by: Verlag Dr. Kovac, Leverkusenstr 13, Hamburg, 22761, Germany. TEL 49-40-3988800, FAX 49-40-39888055, info@verlagdrkovac.de.

SPORTPAEDAGOGIK; Zeitschrift fuer Sport-, Spiel- und Bewegungserziehung. *see* EDUCATION—Teaching Methods And Curriculum

613.7 DEU ISSN 0176-5906
SPORTPRAXIS; die Fachzeitschrift fuer Sportlehrer und Uebungsleiter. Text in German. 1959. bi-m. EUR 39.50; EUR 33.60 to students; EUR 8 newsstand/cover (effective 2007). adv. bk.rev. back issues avail. **Document type:** *Journal, Academic/Scholarly.* **Description:** For sport teachers and trainers.
Former titles (until 1984): Sport-Praxis in Schule und Verein (0173-2528); (until 1980): Praxis der Leibesuebungen (0342-8400)
Related titles: ♦ Supplement(s): Der Uebungsleiter. ISSN 0342-8419.
Indexed: DIP, IBR, IBZ.
—**CCC.**
Published by: (Germany. Deutscher Olympischer Sportbund), Limpert Verlag GmbH, Industriepark 3, Wiebelsheim, 56291, Germany. TEL 49-6766-903160, FAX 49-6766-903320. Ed. Ulrich Voessing. adv.: B&W page EUR 790, color page EUR 1,350; 181 x 249. Circ: 8,000 (paid and controlled).

SPORTPSYCHOLOGIE. *see* PSYCHOLOGY

796.72 USA
SPORTRACER.COM. Text in English. bi-m. USD 15.95 (effective 2000). adv. **Document type:** *Magazine, Consumer.* **Description:** Covers import and compact car racing scene with articles on performance, imports and compact cars, interests and life style.
Formerly: Street Racer
Related titles: Online - full text ed.
Published by: Drive! Media, 1300 Galaxy Way, Ste 15, Concord, CA 94520. TEL 925-682-9900, 800-764-6278, FAX 925-682-9907. Ed. Scott Ross. Pub. Jeff Donker. adv.: B&W page USD 1,535, color page USD 1,835; trim 9.63 x 6.75. Circ: 45,000.

SPORTRECHT IN FORSCHUNG UND PRAXIS. *see* LAW

790.1 DEU
SPORTREVUE. Text in German. 1964. m. EUR 47.50 domestic; EUR 51 foreign; EUR 4.55 newsstand/cover (effective 2007). adv. **Document type:** *Magazine, Consumer.*
Published by: Intermedia Werbe- und Verlagsgesellschaft mbH, Toemperweg 1, Wachtendonk-Wankum, 47669, Germany. TEL 49-2836-972950, FAX 49-2836-9729565, info@intermedia-verlag.de. Ed. Albert Busek. Adv. contact Juergen Dierich. B&W page EUR 3,276, color page EUR 3,813. Circ: 20,500 (paid and controlled).

796 SGP ISSN 0217-3123
SPORTS. Text in English. 1972. 10/yr. SGD 9. adv. charts; illus.; stat.
Indexed: SportS.
Published by: Singapore Sports Council, National Stadium, Kallang, Singapore, 1439, Singapore. FAX 3409537, TELEX RG 35467-NASTAD. Ed. Ong Poh Choo. Circ: 17,000.

796 CHE ISSN 2075-4663
▼ ➤ **SPORTS.** Text in English. forthcoming 2011. q. free (effective 2011). **Document type:** *Journal, Academic/Scholarly.*
Media: Online - full text.
Published by: M D P I AG, Postfach, Basel, 4005, Switzerland. TEL 41-61-6837734, FAX 41-61-3028918, http://www.mdpi.org/.

790.1 USA
GV583
THE SPORTS ADDRESS BIBLE & ALMANAC; the comprehensive directory of sports addresses. Text in English. 1980. a. USD 39.95 per issue (effective 2011). bk.rev. **Document type:** *Directory, Consumer.* **Description:** Lists addresses, telephone, fax numbers, Web sites, and e-mail addresses and contact persons from Olympic, international, collegiate, professional, scholastic and amateur sports.
Former titles (until 1998): Sports Address Bible; (until 1989): The Comprehensive Directory of Sports Addresses (0743-4561)
Published by: Global Sports Productions Ltd., PO Box 221, Clam Gulch, AK 99568. TEL 310-454-9480, Globalnw@earthlink.net.

790 USA ISSN 1520-7919
GV704
SPORTS AND RECREATIONAL ACTIVITIES. Text in English. 1953. quadrennial. price varies. **Document type:** *Magazine, Consumer.*
Former titles (until 1991): Sports and Recreational Activities for Men and Women; (until 1975): Basic Skills in Sports for Men and Women
—**CCC.**
Published by: McGraw-Hill Companies, Inc., 1221 Ave of the Americas, 43rd fl, New York, NY 10020. TEL 212-512-2000, FAX 212-426-7087, customer.service@mcgraw-hill.com, http://www.mcgraw-hill.com.

SPORTS AND THE LAW. *see* LAW

790.1 GBR ISSN 1357-390X
GV943
SPORTS ARGUS. Text in English. 1897. w. free (effective 2010). adv. bk.rev. 36 p./no. 8 cols./p.; back issues avail. **Document type:** *Newspaper, Consumer.*
Related titles: Online - full text ed.
—CIS.
Published by: Trinity Mirror Midlands Ltd, Fl 6, Fort Dunlop, Fort Pky, PO Box 18, Birmingham, B24 9FF, United Kingdom. TEL 44-121-2363366, post.letters@birminghampost.net, http://www.trinitymirror-midlands.co.uk. Adv. contact Debbie Ellor TEL 44-121-2345163.

796 GBR ISSN 1476-3141
RC1235
SPORTS BIOMECHANICS. Text in English. 2002. q. GBP 320 combined subscription in United Kingdom to institutions (print & online eds.); EUR 462, USD 579 combined subscription to institutions (print & online eds.) (effective 2012). adv. back issues avail.; reprint service avail. from PSC. **Document type:** *Journal, Academic/Scholarly.* **Description:** Covers sports techniques and sports injuries.
Related titles: Online - full text ed.: ISSN 1752-6116. GBP 288 in United Kingdom to institutions; EUR 416, USD 521 to institutions (effective 2012) (from IngentaConnect).
Indexed: A01, A03, A08, A22, B21, C06, C07, C08, CA, CINAHL, E01, EMBASE, ESPM, ExcerpMed, FoSS&M, H&SSA, MEDLINE, P26, P30, P52, P54, P56, PEI, PQC, R09, R10, Reac, SCI, SCOPUS, SD, T02, W07.
—IE. **CCC.**
Published by: (International Society of Biomechanics in Sports USA), Routledge (Subsidiary of: Taylor & Francis Group), 4 Park Sq, Milton Park, Abingdon, Oxon OX14 4RN, United Kingdom. TEL 44-20-70176000, FAX 44-20-70176336, subscriptions@tandf.co.uk, http://www.routledge.com. Ed. Young-Hoo Kwon. Adv. contact Linda Hann TEL 44-1344-779945. **Subscr. to:** Taylor & Francis Ltd., Journals Customer Service, Sheepen Pl, Colchester, Essex CO3 3LP, United Kingdom. TEL 44-20-70175544, FAX 44-20-70175198.

796.330 USA ISSN 1084-3205
THE SPORTS BUSINESS DAILY. Text in English. 1994. w. USD 1,300 to individual members (effective 2008); price varies per user. adv. back issues avail. **Document type:** *Newspaper, Consumer.* **Description:** Provides today's top decision-makers in sports real-time industry news, allowing them to make more informed business decisions.
Related titles: Online - full text ed.
—**CCC.**
Published by: Street & Smith's Sports Group (Subsidiary of: American City Business Journals, Inc.), 120 W Morehead St, Ste 230, Charlotte, NC 28202. TEL 704-973-1300, FAX 704-973-1576, annuals@streetandsmiths.com, http://www.streetandsmiths.com. Adv. contact Patrick Wood TEL 704-973-1358.

330 USA ISSN 1933-4443
GV567.3
SPORTS BUSINESS RESOURCE GUIDE & FACT BOOK. Variant title: Resource Guide & Fact Book. Text in English. 2006. a., latest 2008. USD 335 per issue (effective 2009). adv. **Document type:** *Yearbook, Consumer.* **Description:** Provides information on the sports industry around the world.
Published by: Street & Smith's Sports Group (Subsidiary of: American City Business Journals, Inc.), 120 W Morehead St, Ste 230, Charlotte, NC 28202. TEL 704-973-1300, FAX 704-973-1576, annuals@streetandsmiths.com, http://www.streetandsmiths.com. Adv. contact Patrick Wood TEL 704-973-1358.

790.1 AUS ISSN 0314-5468
SPORTS COACH; Australian coaching magazine. Text in English. 1976. q. AUD 23.50 domestic; AUD 43 foreign (effective 2004). adv. bk.rev. back issues avail. **Document type:** *Magazine, Trade.* **Description:** Aims to provide coaches, in particular beginning and intermediate level coaches, with interesting, useful and up-to-date coaching information.
Indexed: A11, E03, ERI, M01, M02, P04, SD, SportS, T02, WBA, WMB.
—BLDSC (8419.832000), IE, Ingenta. **CCC.**
Published by: (Australian Coaching Council Inc.), Australian Sports Commission, PO Box 176, Belconnen, ACT 2616, Australia. TEL 61-2-62141111, FAX 61-2-62512680, pubs@ausport.gov.au, http://www.ausport.gov.au. adv.: B&W page AUD 990, color page AUD 1,870; trim 210 x 297. Circ: 4,500.

790 FRA
SPORTS DANS LA CITE. Text in French. 1962. q. EUR 26.25 domestic; EUR 35 DOM-TOM; EUR 35 in the European Union; EUR 42 elsewhere (effective 2008). adv. back issues avail. **Document type:** *Magazine, Consumer.*
Published by: Federation Nationale des Offices Municipaux des Sports (F N O M S), 33 Rue Manin, Paris, 75019, France. TEL 33-1-42411198, FAX 33-1-42411226, fnoms@fnoms.org. Circ: 18,000.

796 IRL ISSN 1649-0525
SPORTS DIGEST. Text in English. 2000. bi-m. adv. **Document type:** *Magazine, Consumer.*

Published by: Lacethorn Ltd., 11 Clare St, Dublin, 2, Ireland. TEL 353-1-6624887, FAX 353-1-6624886.

796 USA ISSN 1941-3564
SPORTS EDITION. Text in English. 2005. m. USD 25 domestic; USD 45 in Canada (effective 2008). adv. **Document type:** *Magazine, Consumer.* **Description:** Covers high school, college and professional sports events and news, as well as recreation, health and fitness.
Related titles: Online - full text ed.: ISSN 1937-8114.
Published by: Sports Edition, Inc, PO Box 95, Friendswood, TX 77549. TEL 281-648-5304, FAX 832-895-0974, info@editionmags.com. Pubs. Jeanie McHugh, Steve McKinney. adv.: page USD 1,200.

688.76 GBR ISSN 1369-7072
GV557
➤ **SPORTS ENGINEERING.** Text in English. 1998. q. EUR 381, USD 510 combined subscription to institutions (print & online eds.) (effective 2012). adv. reprint service avail. from PSC. **Document type:** *Journal, Academic/Scholarly.* **Description:** Publishes original papers on the application of engineering and science to sport.
Related titles: Online - full text ed.: ISSN 1460-2687. 1998.
Indexed: A01, A03, A08, A22, A26, A28, APA, ApMecR, B07, BrCerAb, C&ISA, CA, CA/WCA, CIA, CerAb, CivEngAb, CorrAb, E&CAJ, E01, E11, EEA, EMA, ESPM, EnvEAb, ErgAb, GeoRef, H15, M&TEA, M09, MBF, METADEX, PEI, SCOPUS, SD, SolStAb, T02, T04, WAA.
—BLDSC (8419.834020), IE, Infotrieve, Ingenta, Linda Hall. **CCC.**
Published by: (International Sports Engineering Association), Springer U K (Subsidiary of: Springer Science+Business Media), Ashbourne House, The Guildway, Old Portsmouth Rd, Guildford, Surrey GU3 1LP, United Kingdom. TEL 44-1483-734433, FAX 44-1483-734411, postmaster@svl.co.uk, http://www.springer.com/. Ed. Martin Strangwood.

790 USA
SPORTS EXECUTIVE WEEKLY; news - analysis - insight. Abbreviated title: S E W. Text in English. w. USD 429 (effective 2009). back issues avail. **Document type:** *Newsletter, Trade.* **Description:** Provides comprehensive coverage, in-depth analysis and unique insight into the the trade news servicing the sporting goods, athletic footwear and athletic apparel markets.
Media: Online - full content. **Related titles:** E-mail ed.
Published by: SportsOneSource Group, 2151 Hawkins St, Ste 200, Charlotte, NC 28269. TEL 704-987-3450, FAX 704-987-3455, info@sportsonesource.com. Eds. Andy Kerrigan, Tom Ryan.

790.1 JAM
SPORTS FOCUS; the Jamaican quarterly sports magazine. Text in English. 1990. q. USD 10. adv. **Document type:** *Magazine, Consumer.*
Published by: M R C Services Ltd., 2 Easton Ave, Kingston, 5, Jamaica. TEL 809-97-80650, FAX 908-92-65124. Circ: 10,000.

796.962 CAN
SPORTS FORECASTER; the all-in-one hockey annual magazine. Text in English. a. stat. **Document type:** *Yearbook, Consumer.* **Description:** Includes statistics and features on the NHL and its players.
Published by: Fantasy Sports Services, 195 The West Mall, 1060, Toronto, ON M9C 5K1, Canada. FAX 416-644-5195, mag@fantasysports.ca, http://www.fantasysports.ca. Ed. Mario Prata.

796 USA
SPORTS GEEK MAGAZINE; for people who think about sports. Text in English. 2000. w. free. **Document type:** *Newsletter.* **Description:** Deals with the rarely explored issues of race, gender and the huge role of the media in how we perceive professionals sports.
Media: Online - full text.
Address: 1036 Natoma St, San Francisco, CA 94103-2517. TEL 415-864-6907, info@sportsgeekmagazine.com. Ed. Jamie Berger.

687 TWN
SPORTS GOODS BUYER'S GUIDE. Text in English. 1979. s-a. USD 100 (effective 2005). adv. **Document type:** *Directory, Trade.* **Description:** Covers Taiwan's production of exercise equipment and other sports goods for export.
Former titles (until 1995): Taiwan Sports Goods Buyer's Guide (1024-8994); (until 1979): Taiwan Sporting Goods Buyer's Guide
Related titles: CD-ROM ed.: USD 20 (effective 2000).
Published by: Interface Global Taiwan Co., Ltd., PO Box 173-12, Taipei, 116, Taiwan. TEL 886-2-29180500, FAX 886-2-89119381, service@asiatrademart.com, http://www.asiatrademart.com. Ed. Daniel Foong. Pub. Herbert Chen. R&P Donald Shapiro. Adv. contact Melody Lin TEL 886-2-2351-3180. **Subscr. in U.S. to:** Trade Winds Inc., PO Box 820519, Dallas, TX 75382. TEL 972-699-1188, FAX 972-699-1189, twinds8888@aol.com.

796 USA ISSN 0038-822X
GV561
SPORTS ILLUSTRATED. Text in English. 1954. w. USD 39 domestic; CAD 43.91 in Canada (effective 2009). adv. bk.rev. illus. index. reprints avail. **Document type:** *Magazine, Consumer.* **Description:** Covers major sports events and personalities from around the world.
Related titles: Audio cassette/tape ed.; Diskette ed.; Microform ed.: (from PQC); Online - full text ed.: SI.com; Spanish ed.: ISSN 1137-7518; ◆ Special ed(s).: Sports Illustrated (Swimsuit Edition); Sports Illustrated Presents World Champs. ISSN 1930-1545. 2001.
Indexed: A01, A02, A03, A08, A09, A10, A11, A22, A25, A26, A33, ARG, Acal, B04, B07, BRD, C03, C05, C12, CBCARef, CBPI, CBRI, CPerl, E08, G05, G06, G07, G08, G09, HlthInd, I05, I06, I07, IPARL, JHMA, M01, M02, M04, M06, MASUSE, MagInd, P02, P07, P10, P13, P19, P48, P53, P54, PEI, PMR, PQC, R03, R04, R06, RASB, RGAb, RGPR, RGYP, S08, S09, S23, SD, SPI, SportS, T02, TOM, U01, V02, V03, V04, W03, W05, WBA, WMB.
—CIS, IE, Infotrieve, Ingenta. **CCC.**
Published by: Sports Illustrated Group (Subsidiary of: Time Warner Inc.), 135 W 50th St, 4th Fl, New York, NY 10020. TEL 212-522-1212, FAX 212-522-0392, kisd@sikids.timeinc.com. Ed. John Huey. adv.: B&W page USD 204,100, color page USD 336,000. Circ: 3,150,000 (paid). **Subscr. to:** PO Box 30602, Tampa, FL 33630. TEL 800-528-5000.

SPORTS ILLUSTRATED (SWIMSUIT EDITION). *see* CLOTHING TRADE—Fashions

SPORTS ILLUSTRATED FOR KIDS. *see* CHILDREN AND YOUTH—For

796.043 USA
SPORTS ILLUSTRATED ON CAMPUS (ONLINE). Text in English. 2003 (Sep.). 26/school-academic yr. **Document type:** *Magazine, Consumer.*
Formerly (until 2005): S I on Campus (Print)
Media: Online - full content.
Published by: Sports Illustrated Group (Subsidiary of: Time Warner Inc.), 135 W 50th St, 4th Fl, New York, NY 10020. TEL 212-522-1212, FAX 212-522-0392, http://sportsillustrated.cnn.com/.

391 POL ISSN 1642-4042
SPORTS ILLUSTRATED. SWIMSUIT EDITION. Text in Polish. 2001. s-a. adv. **Document type:** *Magazine, Consumer.*
Published by: Ringier Axel Springer Polska, ul Domaniewska 52, Warsaw, 02672, Poland. TEL 48-22-2321400, FAX 48-22-2325540, asp@axelspringer.com.pl, http://www.ringieraxelspringer.pl.

796 USA
SPORTS INSIGHT; trends, perspective and analysis. Text in English. 2005. bi-m. USD 24 domestic; USD 54 foreign (effective 2011). back issues avail. **Document type:** *Magazine, Trade.* **Description:** Provides trends, perspective and analysis on the sports retail marketplace.
Related titles: Online - full text ed.: free (effective 2011).
Published by: Formula4 Media, LLC, PO Box 231318, Great Neck, NY 11023. TEL 518-305-4710, FAX 518-305-4712, http://www.formula4media.com. Eds. Mike Jacobsen TEL 201-612-6601, Mark Sullivan TEL 646-319-7878. Pub. Jeff Gruenhut TEL 404-467-9980. Circ: 15,000.

796.962 CAN ISSN 1718-116X
SPORTS JUNIORS MAGAZINE. Text in French. 2006. q. CAD 16.95 (effective 2006). **Document type:** *Magazine, Consumer.*
Published by: Editions Sports Juniors, CP 5037, Ste-Anne-des-Plaines, PQ J0N 1H0, Canada. TEL 514-578-7720, http://www.sportsjuniors.com. Ed. Alain Harvey.

344.099 USA
SPORTS LAW PRACTICE. Text in English. 1992. irreg. (in 2 vols.), latest 2nd ed. USD 264 2nd ed. (effective 2008). Supplement avail. **Document type:** *Monographic series, Trade.* **Description:** Covers of sports law with time-saving practice aids, Sports Law Practice is the essential resource for the attorney or agent in the arena of sports law.
Related titles: Online - full text ed.
Published by: Michie Company (Subsidiary of: LexisNexis North America), 701 E Water St, Charlottesville, VA 22902. TEL 434-972-7600, 800-446-3410, FAX 434-972-7677, customer.support@lexisnexis.com, http://www.michie.com. Ed. Martin J Greenberg.

796 AUS
SPORTS LINK. Text in English. 19??. bi-m. adv. back issues avail. **Document type:** *Magazine, Trade.* **Description:** Features news on Australian sports, business, products, sponsorships, marketing, profiles, and games.
Indexed: SD.
Published by: M P C Media - Pileport Pty. Ltd., PO Box 813, Tewantin, QLD 4565, Australia. adv.: page AUD 1,890; trim 210 x 297. Circ: 4,000.

THE SPORTS MARKET. *see* BUSINESS AND ECONOMICS—Production Of Goods And Services

796.029 USA ISSN 1055-8020
HD9992.U5
SPORTS MARKET PLACE. Text in English. 1980. a. USD 183 (effective 2001). adv. index. **Document type:** *Directory.* **Description:** Lists over 12000 sports organization's contact information and company profiles.
Formerly (until 1984): Sportsguide (0277-0296); Which was formed by the merger of (1980): Sportsguide For Individual Sports (0198-9987); (1980): Sportsguide For Team Sports (0198-8190)
Related titles: Diskette ed.; Abridged ed.: USD 479 (effective 2001).
Published by: Franklin Covey Co., Sports Division, 1620 S. Stapley Dr., Ste. 224, Mesa, AZ 85204-6656. TEL 480-539-3800, FAX 480-539-3811. Pub. Tom Tyler. Circ: 4,000.

790.1 658 USA ISSN 1049-5495
SPORTS MARKETING LETTER. Text in English. 1989. m. USD 180; USD 200 in Canada & Mexico.
Address: PO Box 99, Southport, CT 06490. TEL 203-255-1787. Ed. Brian J Murphy. Pub., R&P Brian Murphy.

▼ **SPORTS MEDICINE, ARTHROSCOPY, REHABILITATION, THERAPY AND TECHNOLOGY.** *see* MEDICAL SCIENCES

SPORTS MEMORABILIA AND PRICE GUIDE. *see* HOBBIES

SPORTS 'N SPOKES; the magazine for wheelchair sports and recreation. *see* HANDICAPPED—Physically Impaired

796 USA
THE SPORTS NETWORK. Text in English. irreg. **Document type:** *Magazine, Consumer.*
Media: Online - full content.
Published by: The Sports Network, 2200 Byberry Rd, Ste 200, Hatboro, PA 19040. TEL 215-441-8444, FAX 215-441-5767.

796 USA
SPORTS PAGES. Text in English. 1994. m. (June/July & Dec./Jan./Feb. combined). free (effective 2005). **Document type:** *Newspaper.*
Formerly: Sports News
Published by: Greenwood Lake News, Inc., PO Box 1117, Greenwood Lake, NY 10925. TEL 845-477-2572, FAX 845-477-2577. Ed. Ron Nowak. Pub., Adv. contact Ann Chaimowitz. Circ: 23,000 (free).

SPORTS, PARKS AND RECREATION LAW REPORTER. *see* LAW

152.47 796 USA ISSN 1935-5335
SPORTS RAGE ADVISORY. Text in English. 2007 (May). bi-m. USD 77.50 (effective 2007). **Document type:** *Magazine, Consumer.*
Published by: Elder Forest Publishing Group, PO Box 6368, South Bend, IN 46660-6368. TEL 800-428-0552, http://elderforestpublishing.com/index.html. Pub. Mark Bottita.

796 USA
THE SPORTS REPORT. Text in English. w. free. **Document type:** *Newsletter.* **Description:** Covers sportssuch as football, hockey, baseball, basketball and European soccer. It is intended for every sports fan, who wants to hear sport news.
Media: Online - full text.
Published by: Sports Report Ed. Alex Caporicci.

796.812 USA ISSN 1073-1326
SPORTS REVIEW WRESTLING. Text in English. 19??. m. **Document type:** *Magazine, Consumer.*
Former titles (until 1993): Wrestle America (1069-9244); (until 199?): Sports Review Wrestling (1052-0880)
Published by: London Publishing Co. (Subsidiary of: Kappa Publishing Group, Inc.), 6198 Butler Pike, Ste 200, Blue Bell, PA 19422. TEL 215-643-6385, FAX 315-628-3571, custsrvc@kappapublishing.com, http://www.kappapublishing.com. Ed. Stuart M Saks.

796.3 GBR ISSN 1754-1344
THE SPORTS STATISTICIAN. Text in English. 200?. m. GBP 47 (effective 2007). **Document type:** *Newsletter, Consumer.* **Description:** Comprehensive statistical guide to TV-covered sporting events and provides all the information anyone from novice to expert could need to win money on sport.
Related titles: E-mail ed.
Published by: Oxfordshire Press, 61 Hightown Rd, Branbury, Oxon OX16 9BE, United Kingdom. TEL 44-1295-672980, FAX 44-1295-262146, info@oxonpress.com, http://www.oxonpress.com.

796.07 GBR ISSN 0263-8746
SPORTS TEACHER. Text in English. 1976. 3/yr. GBP 20 (effective 2005). **Document type:** *Magazine, Trade.* **Description:** Contains news, articles and features, regular pages on health and fitness, inclusion and professional development.
Formerly (until 1982): School Sport (0308-6097)
Published by: Sportsteacher, 95 Tenison Rd, Cambridge, CB1 2DL, United Kingdom. TEL 44-1223-728100, FAX 44-1223-728101, info@sportsteacher.co.uk. Circ: 22,000.

688.7 GBR ISSN 1934-6182
GV557
➤ **SPORTS TECHNOLOGY.** Text in English. 2008. 6/yr. GBP 312 combined subscription in United Kingdom to institutions (print & online eds.); EUR 413, USD 516 combined subscription to institutions (print & online eds.) (effective 2012). reprint service avail. from PSC. **Document type:** *Journal, Academic/Scholarly.* **Description:** Contains original research and development articles related to the application of technology in sports.
Related titles: Online - full text ed.: ISSN 1934-6190. GBP 281 in United Kingdom to institutions; EUR 371, USD 464 to institutions (effective 2012).
Indexed: SD, T02.
—**CCC.**
Published by: Routledge (Subsidiary of: Taylor & Francis Group), 4 Park Sq, Milton Park, Abingdon, Oxon OX14 4RN, United Kingdom. TEL 44-20-70176000, FAX 44-20-70176336, journals@routledge.com, http://www.routledge.com. Eds. A Subic, F K Fuss, R Metha.

796.077 617.1 AUS ISSN 1032-5506
SPORTS TRAINERS DIGEST. Text in English. 1987. 3/yr. AUD 15 domestic; AUD 20 foreign (effective 2007). back issues avail. **Document type:** *Newsletter, Trade.* **Description:** Covers topical issues for sports trainers and helps keep trainers up to date on the latest advances in sports medicine.
Indexed: SD.
Published by: Sports Medicine Australia, 3-5 Cheney Pl, PO Box 78, Mitchell, ACT 2911, Australia. TEL 61-2-62419344, FAX 61-2-62411611, smanat@sma.org.au. Circ: 13,000.

796 USA ISSN 1945-7804
SPORTS UNLIMITED. Text in English. 2006. 8/yr. free (effective 2008). adv. **Document type:** *Magazine, Consumer.* **Description:** Covers professional and college sports and outdoor life in the Southeastern United States.
Related titles: Online - full text ed.: ISSN 1945-7820.
Published by: All Points Interactive Media, 568 Peachtree Pkwy, Cumming, GA 30041. TEL 678-648-4605.

796 AUS ISSN 1445-7105
SPORTSCAPE. Text in English. 1980. q. adv. Website rev. 90 p./no.; back issues avail. **Document type:** *Magazine, Trade.* **Description:** Covers issues in sport, political commentary, profiles and reports on events, specialist areas in sport, and business in sport.
Former titles (until 2001): Sport (1326-5253); (until 1999): Sports Australia (1443-394X)
Indexed: SD.
Published by: Sport Industry Australia, PO Box 342, Cortin, ACT 2605, Australia. TEL 61-2-62851887, FAX 61-2-62823440, cas@sportforall.com.au, http://www.sportforall.com.au/. Ed., R&P, Adv. contact Mark Garrity. Circ: 5,000.

796.72 SWE ISSN 0282-5678
SPORTSCAR. Text in Swedish. 1961. m. SEK 105. adv. bk.rev. illus.; stat.
Former titles (until 1985): Motor Sport Trend (0282-0978); (until 1982): Illustrerad Motor Sport (0019-249X)
Related titles: Online - full text ed.
Published by: Lerums Boktryckeri AB, Fack 333, Lerum, 44327, Sweden. Ed. Ulf Karlsson. Circ: 33,000.

790.1 USA ISSN 1174-9210
➤ **SPORTSCIENCE.** Text in English. 1997. irreg. free (effective 2011). back issues avail. **Document type:** *Journal, Academic/Scholarly.*
Formerly (until 1999): Sportscience News (1174-0698)
Media: Online - full text.
Indexed: A26, A39, C27, C29, CA, D03, D04, E13, I05, PEI, R14, S14, S15, S18, SD, T02.
—**CCC.**
Published by: Internet Society for Sport Science Ed. Will G Hopkins TEL 64-9-9219793.

797 DNK ISSN 0901-0505
SPORTSDYKKEREN. Text in Danish. 1966. bi-m. adv. **Document type:** *Magazine, Consumer.* **Description:** Covers the sport of diving.
Published by: Dansk Sportsdykker Forbund, Idraettens Hus, Broendby Stadion 20, Broendby, 2605, Denmark. TEL 45-43-262560, FAX 45-43-262561, dsf@sportsdykning.dk, http://www.sportsdykning.dk. Eds. Henrik Zimmermann, Henrik Pontoppidan. Circ: 9,000.

SPORTSFIELD MANAGEMENT. *see* GARDENING AND HORTICULTURE

796 HRV ISSN 0350-7491
SPORTSKE NOVOSTI. Text in Croatian. 1945. d. **Document type:** *Newspaper, Consumer.*
Former titles (until 1962): Narodni Sport (1330-3171); (until 1945): Ilustrirane Fizkulturne Novine (1330-3163)

Address: Slavonska Avenija 4, Zagreb, 10000, Croatia. TEL 385-1-6166666, FAX 385-1-3641950.

796 SRB ISSN 0353-6912
SPORTSKI ZURNAL. Text in Serbian. 1990. d. **Document type:** *Newspaper, Consumer.*
Published by: Politika, Novine i Magazini/Politika Newspapers and Magazines, Makedonska 29, Belgrade, 11000. TEL 381-11-3301442, FAX 381-11-3373346, ilustrovana@politika.co.yu, http://www.politika.co.yu.

790.1 IND ISSN 0971-359X
SPORTSTAR. Text in English. 1978. w. INR 350 domestic; INR 4,000 foreign; INR 12 newsstand/cover (effective 2011). back issues avail. **Document type:** *Journal, Consumer.*
Related titles: Microfilm ed.; Online - full text ed.: INR 1,200; INR 25 per issue (effective 2011).
Published by: Kasturi & Sons Ltd., 859-860, Kasturi Bldg, Anna Salai, Chennai, Tamil Nadu 600 002, India. TEL 91-44-28589060, FAX 91-44-28545703. **Subscr. to:** I N S I O Scientific Books & Periodicals.

796 USA ISSN 1091-5354
SPORTSTRAVEL; team and participant travel. Text in English. 1997. m. **Document type:** *Magazine, Consumer.*
Indexed: SD.
Published by: Schneider Publishing Company, 11835 W Olympic Blvd, 12th fl, Los Angeles, CA 90064. TEL 310-577-3700, FAX 310-577-3715. Ed. Timothy Schneider.

796 CAN ISSN 1913-0546
SPORTSVISION MAGAZINE; cutting edge training for elite athletic performance. Variant title: Sports Vision Magazine. Text in English. 2007. q. USD 35 (effective 2007). **Document type:** *Magazine, Consumer.*
Indexed: SD.
Address: 1425 Fort St., 2nd Floor, Montreal, PQ H3H 2C2, Canada. TEL 514-939-2800, FAX 514-939-2881, info@sportsvisionmagazine.com, http://www.sportsvisionmagazine.com.

790.1 LCA ISSN 1010-5743
SPORTSWATCH. Text in English. 1985. q. USD 10. adv. **Document type:** *Newspaper.*
—CCC.
Published by: A L K I M Communication Production Company, Box MA 020, Marchand Post Office, Castries, St. Lucia. Ed., Adv. contact Albert Deterville. Circ: 5,000.

790.1 IND ISSN 0971-3654
SPORTSWORLD. Text in English. 1978. w. adv. back issues avail.
Published by: Anand Bazar Patrika Ltd., 6 Prafulla Sarkar St, Kolkata, West Bengal 700 001, India. TEL 033-274880, FAX 033-303240, TELEX 021-5468. adv.: B&W page INR 12,000, color page INR 24,000; 235 x 160. Circ: 32,325.

790.1 GBR
SPORTSZINE U K. Text in English. 1996. d. **Description:** Concentrates mainly on British based sports such as golf, rugby, football and cricket. Also focuses on niche sports such as windsurfing and skydiving.
Media: Online - full text.
Address: United Kingdom. webmaster@sportszineuk.co.uk. Ed. Chris Pilling.

797.21 DEU ISSN 0172-8555
SPORTTAUCHER. Text in German. 1980. m. EUR 20; EUR 2 newsstand/cover (effective 2007). adv. **Document type:** *Magazine, Consumer.*
Incorporates: Delphin (0011-796X)
Indexed: GeoRef, SpeleolAb.
Published by: (Verband Deutscher Sporttaucher e.V.), Olympia Verlag GmbH, Badstr 4-6, Nuernberg, 90402, Germany. TEL 49-911-2160, FAX 49-911-2162741, anzeigen@olympia-verlag.de. adv.: B&W page EUR 2,580, color page EUR 4,440; trim 210 x 297. Circ: 62,089 (paid and controlled).

790.1 ROM ISSN 1220-6571
SPORTUL ILUSTRAT. Text in Romanian. 1947. m. USD 25. adv. bk.rev. illus.
Published by: Editura Sportrom, Str. Vasile Conta 16, Bucharest, Romania. TEL 113288, FAX 113459. Ed. Constantin Macovei. Circ: 50,000.

SPORTVERLETZUNG - SPORTSCHADEN; Grundlagen - Praevention - Rehabilitation. *see* MEDICAL SCIENCES

796 371.7 613 DEU ISSN 0342-2380
GV201
➤ **SPORTWISSENSCHAFT.** Text in German; Summaries in English, French, German. 1971. q. EUR 53, USD 72 combined subscription to institutions (print & online eds.) (effective 2012). bk.rev. index. reprint service avail. from PSC. **Document type:** *Journal, Academic/Scholarly.* **Description:** Contains research involving the science and theory of sports.
Related titles: Online - full text ed.: ISSN 1868-1069.
Indexed: A22, A36, CABA, DIP, E01, GH, IBR, IBZ, LT, MLA-IB, N02, N03, R12, RASB, RRTA, SCOPUS, SD, SportS.
—BLDSC (8419.860800), IE, Infotrieve, Ingenta. **CCC.**
Published by: (Deutsche Vereinigung fuer Sportwissenschaft e.V.), Springer (Subsidiary of: Springer Science+Business Media), Tiergartenstr 17, Heidelberg, 69121, Germany. TEL 49-6221-4870, FAX 49-6221-345229, subscriptions@springer.com. Circ: 1,500.

796 DEU ISSN 0342-457X
SPORTWISSENSCHAFT UND SPORTPRAXIS. Text in German. 1970. irreg., latest vol.153, 2009. price varies. **Document type:** *Monographic series, Academic/Scholarly.*
Formerly (until 1978): Schriftenreihe fuer Sportwissenschaft und Sportpraxis (0080-7141)
Published by: Czwalina Verlag, Bei der Neuen Muenze 4a, Hamburg, 22145, Germany. TEL 49-40-6794300, FAX 49-40-67943030, post@feldhaus-verlag, http://www.edition-czwalina.de.

796 DEU ISSN 0944-9604
SPORTWISSENSCHAFTLICHE DISSERTATIONEN UND HABILITATIONEN. Text in German. 1975. irreg., latest vol.56, 2009. price varies. **Document type:** *Monographic series, Academic/Scholarly.*
Formerly (until 1994): Sportwissenschaftliche Dissertationen (0340-0956)
Published by: Czwalina Verlag, Bei der Neuen Muenze 4a, Hamburg, 22145, Germany. TEL 49-40-6794300, FAX 49-40-67943030, post@feldhaus-verlag, http://www.edition-czwalina.de.

790.1 AUT
SPORTWOCHE. Text in German. 1999. w. EUR 48 (effective 2008). adv. **Document type:** *Magazine, Consumer.*
Published by: Sportverlag GmbH & Co. KG (Subsidiary of: Styria Medien AG), Kaiserstr 113-115, Vienna, W 1070, Austria. TEL 43-1-360850, FAX 43-1-36085200, office@vsm.at, http://www.vsm.at. Ed. Adi Kornfeld. Adv. contact Nina Pikisch. color page EUR 7,500; trim 198 x 268. Circ: 72,000 (paid).

796 UKR ISSN 0038-8300
SPORTYVNA HAZETA. Text in Ukrainian. 1934. 208/yr. USD 435. illus.
Formerly (until 1966): Radjanski Sport
Published by: Komitet po Fizkul'turi i Sportu/State Committee of Physical Culture and Sports, Ul Kostel'naya 13, Kiev, Ukraine. TEL 228-09-63. Ed. Yuri Peresunjko.

790.1 909 DEU
SPORTZEITEN. Text in English, German. 1987. 3/yr. EUR 27.60; EUR 9.70 per issue (effective 2010). bibl.; illus. back issues avail.
Former titles (until 2002): SportZeit (1617-7606); (until 2001): Sozial- und Zeitgeschichte des Sports (0931-7031)
Indexed: DIP, IBR, IBZ.
Published by: Verlag die Werkstatt, Koenigstr 43, Rastede, 26180, Germany. TEL 49-4402-926314, FAX 49-4402-926350, info@werkstatt-verlag.de, http://www.werkstatt-verlag.de. Ed. Lorenz Peiffer.

790.1 AUT
SPORTZEITUNG. Text in German. w. EUR 59.90 domestic; EUR 109 foreign (effective 2005). adv. **Document type:** *Newspaper, Consumer.* **Description:** Covers the wide world of sports at all levels.
Formerly: Sport und Toto
Published by: Sportzeitung Verlagsgesellschaft mbH, Linke Wienzeile 40, Vienna, 1060, Austria. TEL 43-1-58557570, FAX 43-1-5855757411. Eds. Gerhard Weber, Horst Hoetsch. Adv. contact Christoph Nestelberger TEL 43-2742-8011367. page EUR 3,590; trim 195 x 270.

790.1 CAN
SPOTLIGHT ON SKATING. Text in English. 5/yr. CAD 37 domestic; USD 30 in United States; USD 50 in Europe; USD 55 elsewhere; USD 6.95 newsstand/cover (effective 2002). adv. **Document type:** *Magazine, Consumer.* **Description:** Covers a diverse range of figure skating interests for the professional or novice - from the beginnings as a junior enthusiast through to the highly developed Olympic hopeful or the professional.
Published by: Spotlight on Skating Inc., 208 Mohawk Rd., Ancaster, ON L9G 2W9, Canada. TEL 905-304-6372, FAX 905-304-1336.

796 790.019 USA ISSN 0740-0802
SPOTLIGHT ON YOUTH SPORTS. Text in English. 1979. q. looseleaf. free to qualified personnel (effective 2006). bk.rev. charts; illus. back issues avail. **Document type:** *Newsletter, Consumer.*
Indexed: SD, SportS.
—CCC.
Published by: Michigan State University, Institute for the Study of Youth Sports, 213 I M Sports Circle Bldg, East Lansing, MI 48824-1049. TEL 517-353-6689, FAX 517-353-5363, ythsprts@msu.edu, http://ed-web3.educ.msu.edu/ysi/. Ed. Marty Ewing. R&P John Haubenstricker TEL 517-355-4741. Circ: 2,000.

796 ITA ISSN 1825-0920
SPRINT & SPORT IN LOMBARDIA. Text in Italian. 2004. w. **Document type:** *Magazine, Consumer.*
Published by: Edisport Editoriale SpA, Via Gradisca 11, Milan, MI 20151, Italy. TEL 39-02-38085, FAX 39-02-38010393, edisport@edisport.it, http://www.edisport.it.

SPURT; Zeitschrift fuer Sport und Recht. *see* LAW

636.596 GBR ISSN 0952-4541
SQUILLS INTERNATIONAL RACING PIGEON YEAR BOOK. Text in English. 1897. a. GBP 7.50 domestic; GBP 10 in Europe; GBP 12 elsewhere (effective 2009). adv. **Document type:** *Yearbook.*
Formerly (until 1944): Squills Stud Book
Published by: Racing Pigeon Publishing Co. Ltd., Unit G5, Seedbed Ctr, Wyncolls Rd., Colchester, Essex CO4 9HT, United Kingdom. TEL 44-1206-843456, FAX 44-1206-843442, racing123@btconnect.com.

796 USA
STACK (CLEVELAND). Text in English. 2005. 9/yr. USD 26.99 (effective 2006). **Document type:** *Magazine, Consumer.* **Description:** Provides information to high school athletes to improve their performance safely and effectively.
Published by: Stack, LLC, 1422 Euclid Ave, #1550, Cleveland, OH 44115. TEL 216-861-7000, FAX 216-861-7533, letters@stackmag.com, http://www.stackmag.com/. Pub. Carl N Mehlhope.

790.1 COG
STADE. Text in French. 1985. w.
Address: BP 114, Brazzaville, Congo, Republic. TEL 81-47-18, TELEX 5285. Ed. Louis Ngami. Circ: 12,000.

STADIA; sports venue design, operations & technology. *see* ARCHITECTURE

STADIA WORLD. *see* ARCHITECTURE

613.7 DEU ISSN 0172-4029
GV561
STADION; Internationale Zeitschrift fuer Geschichte des Sports. Text in English, French, German. 1975. 2/yr. EUR 45; EUR 26 newsstand/cover (effective 2008). adv. bk.rev. back issues avail. **Document type:** *Journal, Academic/Scholarly.* **Description:** Provides a comprehensive and discerning understanding of sport, games, physical education and body culture.
Incorporated: Arena
Indexed: A22, AmH&L, CA, DIP, HistAb, IBR, IBZ, MLA-IB, P30, SCOPUS, SD, SportS, T02.
—IE, Ingenta, INIST. **CCC.**
Published by: Academia Verlag GmbH, Bahnstr 7, Sankt Augustin, 53757, Germany. TEL 49-2241-345210, FAX 49-2241-345316, kontakt@academia-verlag.de. Ed. Manfred Laemmer. Circ: 400.

790.1 UKR
STADION-OLIMPIC. Text in Ukrainian. bi-m. USD 100 in United States.
Address: Ul Stadionnaya 5, Kiev, Ukraine. TEL 245-42-72, FAX 380-44-228-4502. **Dist. by:** East View Information Services, 10601 Wayzata Blvd, Minneapolis, MN 55305. TEL 952-252-1201, 800-477-1005, FAX 952-252-1202, info@eastview.com, http://www.eastview.com.

796 ITA ISSN 0391-7924
STADIUM; problemi dello sport. Text in Italian. 1906-1927; resumed 1944. m. free. adv. **Document type:** *Magazine, Consumer.*
Related titles: Online - full text ed.
Indexed: MLA-IB.
Published by: Centro Sportivo Italiano, Via della Conciliazione 1, Rome, 00193, Italy. TEL 39-06-68404550, FAX 39-06-68802940, csi@csi-net.it, http://www.csi-net.it. Circ: 60,000.

796.075 USA ISSN 1935-0546
GV875.3
STANDARD CATALOG OF BASEBALL CARDS. Text in English. 1988. a. USD 33.75 per issue (effective 2011). 1848 p./no.; back issues avail. **Document type:** *Catalog, Consumer.* **Description:** Contains comprehensive price guide for 15,000 sets issued between the mid-1800s and 2008 are represented, including tobacco cards, bubblegum cards and specialty issues.
Related titles: CD-ROM ed.: Standard Catalog of Baseball Cards (Vintage Edition). USD 15 per issue (effective 2011); Standard Catalog of Baseball Cards (Modern Edition). USD 10 per issue (effective 2011).
Published by: Krause Publications, Inc. (Subsidiary of: F + W Media Inc.), 700 E State St, Iola, WI 54990. TEL 715-445-2214, 800-258-0929, FAX 715-445-4087, info@krause.com, http://www.krause.com. Ed. Bob Lemke.

796 USA ISSN 2150-6167
STAR CITY SPORTS. Text in English. 1994. m. free (effective 2009). adv. back issues avail. **Document type:** *Magazine, Consumer.*
Related titles: Online - full text ed.
Published by: Lincoln Journal Star (Subsidiary of: Lee Enterprises, Inc.), 926 P St, Lincoln, NE 68508. TEL 402-473-7113, FAX 402-473-7159, http://www.journalstar.com. Ed. Dennis Buckley TEL 402-473-7150. Pub. John Maher TEL 402-473-7410. Adv. contact Cassidy Bohac TEL 402-473-2617.

790.1 USA
STAR FLEET TIMES. Text in English. 10/yr. USD 15 domestic; USD 16 in Canada; USD 22 foreign. illus.
Published by: Amarillo Design Bureau, Agents of Gaming, Box 31571, Dayton, OH 45437-0571.

741.6 USA ISSN 1534-5378
STAR WARS GAMER; the force in star wars gaming. Text in English. 2000. bi-m. USD 16.99; USD 6.99 newsstand/cover; USD 9.99 newsstand/cover in Canada (effective 2001). adv. **Document type:** *Magazine, Consumer.* **Description:** Provides extensive Star Wars accessories and gaming-related content as well as new fiction and electronic games previews.
Published by: Wizards of the Coast, Inc., 1801 Lind Ave, PO Box 707, Renton, WA 98057. TEL 206-204-8000, FAX 206-204-5928. Ed. Chris Perkins.

796 UKR ISSN 0131-890X
START. Text in Ukrainian. 1922. m. USD 135.
Published by: Soyuz Sportivnykh Obshchestv i Organizatsii Ukrainy, Ul Degtyarevskaya 38-44, Kiev, Ukraine. TEL 2110402. Ed. Anatolii Chaly. Circ: 115,000. **Dist. by:** East View Information Services, 10601 Wayzata Blvd, Minneapolis, MN 55305. TEL 952-252-1201, 800-477-1005, FAX 952-252-1202, info@eastview.com, http://www.eastview.com.

796.72 NLD ISSN 1871-2274
START. Text in Dutch. 1984. m. EUR 65 (effective 2009). adv. **Document type:** *Magazine, Consumer.*
Formerly (until 2005): Start '84 (1380-9180)
Published by: (Nederlandse Autorensport Vereniging, KNAC Nederlandse Autosport Federatie), Van Helvoort Media, Postbus 22, Gemert, 5420 AA, Netherlands. TEL 31-492-371137, FAX 31-492-371138. Circ: 10,000.

796.72 GBR
STARTLINE. Variant title: StartLine Magazine. Text in English. 1922. bi-m. GBP 3 newsstand/cover to non-members; free to members (effective 2009). adv. bk.rev. illus. back issues avail. **Document type:** *Newsletter, Trade.*
Formerly (until 1981): B A R C News (0005-2647)
Related titles: Online - full text ed.: free (effective 2009).
Indexed: CRIA.
Published by: British Automobile Racing Club, Thruxton Circuit, Andover, Hampshire SP11 8PN, United Kingdom. TEL 44-1264-882200, FAX 44-1264-882233, info@barc.net. Circ: 6,000.

790.1 USA ISSN 0890-9229
STING. Text in English. 1982. 13/yr. USD 19.95. **Document type:** *Magazine, Consumer.* **Description:** For Georgia Tech University sports fans.
Formerly (until 1985): Gold Line (8750-748X)
Published by: A T Fund, 150 Bobby Dodd Way N W, Atlanta, GA 30332. Ed. Bill Ballew. Circ: 6,500.

796.72 USA ISSN 0734-7340
GV1029.9.S74
STOCK CAR RACING. Text in English. 1964. m. USD 15 domestic; USD 27 in Canada; USD 39 elsewhere (effective 2008). adv. illus. back issues avail. **Document type:** *Magazine, Consumer.* **Description:** Presents readers a larger scope of the total oval track racing industry.
—CCC.
Published by: Source Interlink Companies, 5555 Concord Parkway South, Ste 326, Concord, NC 28027. dheine@sourceinterlink.com, http://www.sourceinterlinkmedia.com. Ed. Larry Cothren. Pub. Don Parrish TEL 813-675-3482. adv.: B&W page USD 7,865, color page USD 12,765; trim 10.5 x 7.88. Circ: 257,296 (paid).

796.72 USA
STOPWATCHER. Text in English. 1965. w. USD 15 (effective 1999). bk.rev. **Document type:** *Newsletter.* **Description:** Contains personal interest articles regarding national motorsport events.
Address: 14704 Lancraft Ct., Germantown, MD 20874-3400. TEL 301-493-8888. Ed. Bob Shenton. adv.: B&W page USD 18,150.

793 USA
STRATEGIST. Text in English. m. USD 15 (effective 2001). **Document type:** *Magazine, Consumer.*

S

Published by: Strategy Gaming Society, 87-6 Park Ave, Worcester, MA 01605. Eds. Tim Watson, Vickie Watson. Pub. George Phillies.

790.1 USA ISSN 1098-5972
GV716
STREET & SMITH'S SPORTSBUSINESS JOURNAL. Variant title: Sports Business Journal. SportsBusiness Journal. Text in English. 1998. w. USD 254 domestic; USD 309 in Canada; USD 419 elsewhere (effective 2010). adv. illus. back issues avail. **Document type:** *Magazine, Trade.* **Description:** Covers the business of sports in depth.
Related titles: Online - full text ed.
Indexed: P34, SD.
—CCC.
Published by: American City Business Journals, Street & Smith, 120 W Morehead St, Ste 310, Charlotte, NC 28202. TEL 704-973-1410, 800-829-9839, FAX 704-973-1401, info.sportsbiz@amcity.com. Pub. Richard Weiss. Circ: 17,000.

788 USA
STREET CUSTOMS. Text in English. bi-m. USD 17 (effective 2002). **Document type:** *Magazine, Consumer.*
Published by: Street Customs Magazine, 15034, Whittier, CA 90605-5034. TEL 562-945-9469, FAX 562-945-6959, editors@streetcustoms.com.

796.72 USA ISSN 0112-1669
STREET RODDER; America's street rodding authority. Text in English. 1972. m. USD 24.95 domestic; USD 36.95 in Canada; USD 48.95 elsewhere (effective 2008). adv. bk.rev. back issues avail. **Document type:** *Magazine, Consumer.* **Description:** Dedicated to the building, modification and nostalgia of automobiles built prior to 1949.
Indexed: G06, G07, G08, I05, S23.
Published by: Source Interlink Companies, 774 S Placentia Ave, Placentia, CA 92870. dheine@sourceinterlink.com, http://www.sourceinterlinkmedia.com. Ed. Brian Brennan. Pubs. Jim Foos, Tim Foss TEL 714-939-2409. adv.: B&W page USD 9,535, color page USD 13,390. Circ: 143,502 (paid).

STREET THUNDER. *see* TRANSPORTATION—Automobiles

799.1 CZE ISSN 0322-7650
STRELECKA REVUE. Text in Czech. 1969. m. CZK 720 (effective 2011). adv. **Document type:** *Magazine, Consumer.*
Incorporates (1999-2005): Strelecky Magazin (1211-4014)
Published by: Prazska Vydavatelska Spolecnost, s.r.o., Olsanska 3, Prague 3, 13000, Czech Republic. TEL 420-222-317812, info@pvsp.cz, http://www.pvsp.cz. Ed. Premysl Liska. Adv. contact Jana Lukasova.

793 USA ISSN 1527-5027
STRICTLY SLOTS; the magazine for slot & video poker players. Text in English. 1998. m. USD 24; USD 2.95 newsstand/cover (effective 2011). adv. back issues avail. **Document type:** *Magazine, Consumer.* **Description:** Identifies, illustrates, analyzes and rates every new slot and video poker machine on the market.
Published by: Casino Journal Publishing Group, 8025 Black Horse Pike, Ste 470, Atlantic City, NJ 08232. TEL 609-641-8846, FAX 609-645-1661, comments@casinocenter.com, http://www.casinocenter.com. Adv. contact Laurie Leaf. Circ: 78,750.

793 USA
GV1218.S8
STRING FIGURE OF THE MONTH. Text in English. 1996. m. free to members (effective 2010). back issues avail. **Document type:** *Magazine, Consumer.* **Description:** Explains the string figure terminology.
Former titles (until 2007): String Figure Magazine (Online); (until 2006): String Figure Magazine (Print) (1087-1527)
Media: Video.
Published by: International String Figure Association, PO Box 5134, Pasadena, CA 91117. TEL 626-398-1057, FAX 626-398-1057, webweavers@isfa.org. Eds. Joseph D'Antoni, Mark A Sherman. Pub., R&P Mark A Sherman.

799.202 POL ISSN 1644-4906
STRZAL. Text in Polish. 2002. bi-m. EUR 93 foreign (effective 2006). **Document type:** *Magazine, Consumer.*
Published by: Wydawnictwo Magnum-X, ul Borowskiego 2, p 307, Warsaw, 03475, Poland. magnum@hbz.com.pl. Circ: 14,500. **Dist. by:** Ars Polona, Obroncow 25, Warsaw 03933, Poland. TEL 48-22-5098609, FAX 48-22-5098610, arspolona@arspolona.com.pl, http://www.arspolona.com.pl.

796 SWE ISSN 0283-3883
STUDENTIDROTT. Text in Swedish. 1986-2002; resumed 2008. 4/yr. **Document type:** *Magazine, Trade.*
Published by: Sveriges Akademiska Idrottsfoerbund/Swedish University Sports Federation, PO Box 2052, Uppsala, 75012, Sweden. TEL 46-10-4765490, FAX 46-18-137206, info@saif.se, http://www.studentidrott.se.

STUDIES IN SPORT, PHYSICAL EDUCATION AND HEALTH. *see* PHYSICAL FITNESS AND HYGIENE

797.215 ZAF ISSN 1819-7558
SUBMERGE. Text in English. 2006. bi-m. adv. **Document type:** *Magazine, Consumer.*
Published by: Submerge Publishers cc, PO Box 11703, Erasmuskloof, 0048, South Africa. FAX 086-513-2480. Ed. Sabrina Moolman. Adv. contact Elne Uys.

799.202 DEU
SUEDWESTDEUTSCHE SCHUETZENZEITUNG. Text in German. 2/m. free to members. adv. **Document type:** *Magazine, Consumer.*
Published by: Wuerttembergischer Schuetzenverband 1850 e.V., Fritz-Walter-Weg 19, Stuttgart, 70372, Germany. TEL 49-711-28077300, FAX 49-711-28077303, info@wsv1850.de, http://www.wsv1850.de. adv.: B&W page EUR 327, color page EUR 425. Circ: 4,400 (controlled).

SUGEI PAZURU. *see* MATHEMATICS

797.23 FIN ISSN 1238-2574
SUKELTAJAN MAAILMA; sukeltajan erikoislehti. Text in Finnish. 1995. bi-m. EUR 35 (effective 2007). adv. **Document type:** *Magazine, Consumer.*
Published by: Karprint Oy, Vanha Turunrie 371, Huhmari, 03150, Finland. TEL 358-9-41397300, FAX 358-9-41397405, http://www.karprint.fi. Ed. Jouko Moisala. Adv. contact Arja Blom. page EUR 1,579. Circ: 11,000.

790.1 JPN
SUMO WORLD. Text and summaries in English. 1973. bi-m. JPY 4,500 domestic; USD 35 foreign (effective 2001). adv. bk.rev. 32 p./no.; back issues avail. **Document type:** *Consumer.* **Description:** Covers professional sumo wrestling in Japan.
Address: c/o Foreign Press Club, 1-7-1 Yuraku-cho, Chiyoda-ku, Tokyo, 100-0006, Japan. cpnew@iac.co.jp, http://www.sumoworld.com. Ed., Pub., R&P, Adv. contact Clyde Newton. Circ: 10,000.

796.812 JPN
SUMO WRESTLING (TOKYO, 1949). Text in Japanese. 1949. m. JPY 9,360 (effective 2000). **Document type:** *Consumer.*
Published by: Baseball Magazine Sha, 3-10-10 Misaki-cho, Chiyoda-ku, Tokyo, 101-0061, Japan. FAX 81-3-3238-0106. Ed. Yoshihisa Shimoie.

796.812 JPN
SUMO WRESTLING (TOKYO, 1954). Text in Japanese. 1954. bi-m. JPY 670. adv. **Document type:** *Consumer.*
Published by: Yomiuri Shimbun, 1-7-1 Ote-Machi, Chiyoda-ku, Tokyo, 100-8056, Japan. TEL 81-3-32421111, FAX 81-3-32168749, http://www.yomiuri.co.jp. Ed. Harunobu Kasai.

794.1 FIN ISSN 0355-8096
SUOMEN SHAKKI. Text in Finnish. 1924. m. EUR 40 (effective 2005). adv. bk.rev. **Document type:** *Magazine, Consumer.* **Description:** Includes national and international games, interviews, "how-to-improve" articles, theory, combinations, and studies-problems.
Published by: Esko Nuutilainen Ed. & Pub., PO Box 61, Jaervenpaeae, 04401, Finland. TEL 358-9-2919319, FAX 358-9-2918336. Circ: 2,100.

794.5 HRV ISSN 1330-8602
SUPER FENIKS. Text in Croatian. 1995. q. **Document type:** *Magazine, Consumer.*
Published by: Novi List, Zvonimirova 20a, Rijeka, 51000, Croatia. TEL 385-51-650011, FAX 385-51-672114.

793.7 DEU
SUPER-RAETSEL. Text in German. bi-m. EUR 1.50 newsstand/cover (effective 2011). adv. **Document type:** *Magazine, Consumer.*
Published by: Deutscher Raetselverlag GmbH & Co. KG (Subsidiary of: Gong Verlag GmbH & Co. KG), Muenchener Str 101-09, Ismaning, 85737, Germany. TEL 49-89-272708620, FAX 49-89-272707890, info@raetsel.de, http://www.deutscher-raetselverlag.de. Circ: 69,000 (paid and controlled).

790 ITA ISSN 0039-5706
SUPERBA. Text in Italian. 1977 (vol.10). m. adv. bk.rev. charts; illus. **Document type:** *Magazine, Consumer.*
Published by: Dopolavoro Ferroviario di Genova, Via A. Doria 13, Genoa, GE 16126, Italy. TEL 39-010-261627, FAX 39-010-261806, dlfgenova@dlf.it, http://www.genova.dlf.it.

793.7 LVA
SUPERKUMA. Text in Latvian. 1997. m. LVL 0.74 newsstand/cover (effective 2005). **Document type:** *Magazine, Consumer.*
Published by: SIA Kuma, Rinuzu Iela 22-44, Riga, 1015, Latvia. TEL 371-7342879, FAX 371-7342879, kuma@kuma.lv. Ed. Inara Ratnik. Pub. Aida Luts.

793.7 EST
SUPERKUMA. Text in Estonian. 1991. m. EUR 1.27 newsstand/cover (effective 2011). adv. **Document type:** *Magazine, Consumer.*
Published by: Kuma Ltd., 57 Parnu St, Paide, 72712, Estonia. TEL 372-38-38800, FAX 372-38-38806, kuma@kuma.ee, http://www.kuma.ee. Ed. Jaanus Laidna. adv.: page EEK 3,000.

790.1 KOR
SUPOCHU DONG-A/SPORTS DONG-A. Text in Korean. 1978. w. KRW 12,000 per month (effective 2008). **Document type:** *Magazine, Consumer.*
Published by: Dong-A Ilbo, 139, Chungjongno 3-Ga Seodaemun-Gu, Seoul, 120-715, Korea, S. TEL 82-2-3600319, http://www.donga.com/. Ed. Kwon O Kie. Circ: 184,902.

796.077 JPN ISSN 1347-1015
SUPOTSU KOCHINGU KENKYU/JAPAN JOURNAL OF SPORT COACHING. Text in Japanese; Abstracts in English. 2002. a. free. abstr. back issues avail. **Document type:** *Journal, Academic/Scholarly.*
Media: Online - full text.
Indexed: PEI.
Published by: Supotsukochingu Kenkyukai/Japan Society of Sport Coaching, Institute of Health and Sport Sciences, University of Tsukuba, 1-1-1 Tennodai, Tsukuba, Ibaraki 305-8574, Japan. http://www.taiiku.tsukuba.ac.jp/sc/index.htm.

790.1 GRC
SURF & SKI. Text and summaries in Greek. 1981. bi-m. back issues avail. **Document type:** *Consumer.*
Published by: Liberis Publications S.A./Ekdoseon Lymperi A.E., Ioannou Metaxa 80, Karelas, Koropi 19400, Greece. TEL 30-210-6688000, info@liberis.gr, http://www.liberis.gr. Circ: 12,000.

797.32 FRA ISSN 0767-7987
SURF SESSION. Text in French. 1986. m. EUR 52 domestic; EUR 78 in the European Union; EUR 103 elsewhere (effective 2010). **Document type:** *Magazine, Consumer.*
Address: 20 rue Maryse Bastie, Anglet, 64600, France. TEL 33-5-59417000, FAX 33-5-59412412, surf@atlantel.fr. Ed. Guillaume Dufau. Pub. Pierre Bernard Gascogne. Adv. contact Vincent Nicolas.

793.7 EST
SUURED RUUDUD. Text in Estonian. 1995. m. EUR 1.27 newsstand/cover (effective 2011). adv. **Document type:** *Magazine, Consumer.*
Published by: Kuma Ltd., 57 Parnu St, Paide, 72712, Estonia. TEL 372-38-38800, FAX 372-38-38806, kuma@kuma.ee, http://www.kuma.ee. Ed. Jaanus Laidna. adv.: page EEK 2,500.

793.7 FIN ISSN 0357-2366
SUURI RISTIKKO. Text in Finnish. 1979. 6/yr. **Document type:** *Magazine, Consumer.*
Published by: Sanoma Magazines Finland Corporation, Lapinmaentie 1, Helsinki, 00350, Finland. TEL 358-9-1201, FAX 358-9-1205171, info@sanomamagazines.fi, http://www.sanomamagazines.fi.

797.56 SWE ISSN 0280-011X
SVENSK FALLSKAERMSSPORT. Text in Swedish. 1972. bi-m. SEK 178 (effective 1993).
Published by: Svenska Fallskaermsfoerbundet, Farsta, 12387, Sweden.

796 SWE ISSN 0049-2663
SVENSK IDROTT. Text in Swedish. 1929. 11/yr. SEK 400 domestic; SEK 425 foreign (effective 2001). adv. bk.rev. **Document type:** *Magazine, Consumer.*
Published by: Riksidrottsfoerbundet RF/Swedish Sports Confederation, Farsta, 12387, Sweden. TEL 46-8-605-60-00, FAX 46-8-94-81-84. Ed., Pub. Marie Louise Bergh. adv.: B&W page SEK 19,000, color page SEK 20,000; trim 185 x 265. Circ: 36,300 (paid and controlled).

796 SWE ISSN 1103-4629
SVENSK IDROTTSFORSKNING. Text in Swedish. 1992. q. SEK 200 (effective 2011). **Document type:** *Journal, Academic/Scholarly.*
Related titles: Online - full text ed.: 2006.
Published by: Centrum foer Idrottsforskning/Swedish National Centre for Research in Sports, PO Box 5626, Stockholm, 11486, Sweden. TEL 46-8-4022200, FAX 46-8-4022280, cif@gih.se, http://www.centrumforidrottsforskning.se. Ed. Christine Dartsch.

796.3 SWE ISSN 0283-2208
SVENSK INNEBANDY. Text in Swedish. 1983. 9/yr. SEK 299 (effective 2004). adv. **Document type:** *Magazine, Consumer.*
Published by: Svenska Innebandyfoerbundet/Swedish Floorball Federation, Box 1047, Solna, 17121, Sweden. TEL 46-8-273250, FAX 46-8-822214, info@innebandy.nu, http://www.innebandy.nu. Ed. Magnus Fredriksson TEL 46-31-405220. Adv. contact Martin Zetterstedt. B&W page SEK 17,500, color page SEK 20,000; trim 210 x 297. Circ: 84,200.

799.3 SWE ISSN 2000-4362
▼ **SVENSK SKYTTESPORT.** Text in Swedish. 2009. m. SEK 350 (effective 2010). adv. **Document type:** *Magazine, Consumer.*
Formed by the merger of (1983-2009): Sportskytten (0281-871X); (1932-2009): Svenskt Skytte (0346-2420); Which was formerly (1924-1932): Sveriges Skyttetidning
Related titles: Online - full text ed.
Address: Oesthammarsgatan 70, PO Box 5435, Stockholm, 11484, Sweden. TEL 46-8-6676011. Ed. Lennart Broman. Adv. contact Leif Dylicki.

796 SWE ISSN 1653-2902
SVENSK STYRKELYFT. Text in Swedish. 1998. 8/yr. adv. **Document type:** *Magazine, Consumer.*
Formerly (until 2005): Power (1404-9465)
Related titles: Online - full text ed.
Published by: Svenska Styrkelyftfoerbundet/Swedish Power Lifting Association, Munktell Arenan, Eskilstuna, 63342, Sweden. TEL 46-16-160900, FAX 46-16-134255, kansli@styrkelyft.se, http://www.styrkelyft.se. adv.: page SEK 3,125; 185 x 260.

797.21 658 DNK ISSN 1901-0710
SVOEMMEBADET. Text in Danish. 2005. q. free. adv. back issues avail. **Document type:** *Magazine, Trade.* **Description:** Planning, construction and managing of large baths and swimming pools.
Published by: Dansk Svoemmebadsteknisk Forening, Jens Olsens Vej 9, Aarhus N, 8200, Denmark. TEL 45-43-525353, FAX 45-87-394699, kontakt@svommebad.dk, http://www.svommebad.dk. Ed. Carsten Larsen. Adv. contact Karin Rye Caspersen.

797.21 CAN ISSN 1209-5966
SWIM NEWS. Text in English. 1974. 10/yr. CAD 35; CAD 45 foreign (effective 1999). **Description:** Publishes information on the sport of swimmming. .
Formerly: Swim Canada (0319-0560)
Indexed: SD, SportS.
Address: 356 Sumach St, Toronto, ON M4X 1V4, Canada. TEL 416-963-5599, FAX 416-963-5545. Ed. N J Thierry. Pub. N.J. Thierry. Circ: 4,500.

797.21 USA
SWIMMING AND DIVING RULES BOOK. Text in English. 19??. a. USD 6.95 per issue (effective 2009), adv. **Document type:** *Handbook/Manual/Guide, Trade.* **Description:** Contains the official rules for swimming and diving, and is used by coaches, officials, players and many fans who wish to know more about the rules of the game.
Former titles (until 1982): Swimming and Diving Water Polo Rule Books. National Federation Edition (0275-5068); Swimming and Diving Rules (0163-2884); Swimming and Diving Case Book (0145-3831); Which superseded: Swimming Rules
Published by: National Federation of State High School Associations, PO Box 690, Indianapolis, IN 46206. TEL 317-972-6900, 800-776-3462, FAX 317-822-5700, info@nfhs.org, http://www.nfhs.org.

797.21 JPN
SWIMMING MAGAZINE. Text in Japanese. 1977. m. JPY 7,920 (effective 2000).
Published by: Baseball Magazine Sha, 3-10-10 Misaki-cho, Chiyoda-ku, Tokyo, 101-0061, Japan. FAX 81-3-3238-0106. Ed. Yuko Kato.

SWIMMING POOL NEWS. *see* BUILDING AND CONSTRUCTION

797.21 GBR ISSN 1750-581X
SWIMMING TIMES. Text in English. 1923. m. GBP 22 in British Isles to individuals; GBP 30 in Europe to individuals; GBP 32 elsewhere to individuals; GBP 2.50 per issue (effective 2009). adv. bk.rev. charts; illus. **Document type:** *Magazine, Trade.*
Former titles (until 2005): Swimming (1475-6307); (until 2001): Swimming Times (0039-7423)
Indexed: SD, SportS.
—CCC.
Published by: (Amateur Swimming Association), Swimming Times Ltd., 41 Granby St, Loughborough, Leics LE11 3DU, United Kingdom. TEL 44-1509-632230, FAX 44-1509-618701. Ed. Peter Hassall. Adv. contact Laura Campbell TEL 44-1509-632231. **Co-sponsor:** Institute of Swimming Teachers and Coaches.

797.21 USA
GV837
SWIMMING WORLD MAGAZINE. Text in English. 2005. m. USD 29.95 (effective 2010). adv. bk.rev.; film rev. charts; illus.; stat. index. reprints avail. **Document type:** *Magazine, Consumer.*
Formed by the merger of (1965-2005): Swimming World and Junior Swimmer (0039-7431); Which was formerly (1961-1965): Junior Swimmer - Swimming World; (1960-1961): Swimming World (0586-2183); (199?-2005): Swim Magazine (1082-8486); Which was formerly (1984-199?): Swim (8755-2027); (1997-2005): Swimming Technique; Which was formerly (1996-1997): Technique; (1964-1996): Swimming Technique (0039-7415)
Related titles: Online - full text ed.

Indexed: A11, A22, C05, C12, M01, M02, M04, MASUSE, P10, P19, P48, P53, P54, PEI, PQC, RASB, SD, SPI, SportS, T02, U01, V02. —IE, Infotrieve, Ingenta.
Published by: Sports Publications, Inc., PO Box 20337, Sedona, AZ 86341. TEL 928-284-4005, FAX 928-284-2477, editorial@swiminfo.com. Pub. Brent Rutemiller. Adv. contact Denton Taylor. B&W page USD 2,155, color page USD 3,150; trim 8 x 10.75.

796.86 GBR
SWORD. Text in English. 1948. q. GBP 5 newsstand/cover to non-members; free to members (effective 2009). adv. bk.rev. illus.; stat. **Document type:** *Magazine, Trade.*
Indexed: SportS.
Published by: British Fencing Association, 1 Baron's Gate, 33-35 Rothschild Rd, London, W4 5HT, United Kingdom. TEL 44-20-87423032, FAX 44-20-87423033, headoffice@britishfencing.com. Ed. Malcolm Fare TEL 44-1684-311197.

797.21 USA ISSN 1069-2290
SYNCHRO SWIMMING U S A. Text in English. 1963. q. USD 20 domestic to non-members; USD 30 foreign to non-members; USD 12 to qualified personnel (effective 2005). adv. **Document type:** *Magazine, Trade.* **Description:** Provides news and articles on technique and competitive synchronized swimming results from around the world.
Former titles (until 1992): Synchro (0746-5726); (until Apr. 1979): Synchro - Info
Indexed: SD, SportS.
Published by: United States Synchronized Swimming, 201 S Capitol Ave, Ste 901, Indianapolis, IN 46225. TEL 317-237-5700, FAX 317-237-5705. Eds. Brian Eaton, Kaylene Riemen. R&P Kaylene Riemen. Adv. contact Brian Eaton. Circ: 5,000.

794.1 POL ISSN 1230-2309
SZACHISTA. Text in Polish. 1991. m. USD 75 (effective 1998). adv. bk.rev. charts; illus. **Description:** Contains chess news, chess history, annotated chess games, theory, combinations, studies and problems.
Published by: Res Publica Press International Ltd., Ul Grazyny 13, Warsaw, 02548, Poland. TEL 48-22-452655, FAX 48-22-454216. Ed. Andrzej Filipowicz.

790.1 DEU
T G M ECHO. Text in German. 1975. q. **Document type:** *Newspaper.*
Published by: Turngemeinde 1861 e.V., Kirchstr 45, Mainz, 55124, Germany. TEL 06131-41106. Ed. Jochen Dietz. Circ: 1,500.

T P. (Telovychovny Pracovnik) *see* PHYSICAL FITNESS AND HYGIENE

796 IRL ISSN 2009-3101
▼ **T R I**; Ireland's first and only triathlon magazine. (Triathlon Racing Ireland) Text in English. 2010. m. EUR 25; EUR 2 per issue (effective 2010). adv. back issues avail. **Document type:** *Magazine, Consumer.*
Published by: IrishFit, 91 Upper Georges St, Dublin, Dun Laoghaire, Ireland. TEL 353-1-2846107, sales@irishfit.eu.

790.1 DEU
T S VGG 1848 STADECKEN - ELSHEIM. VEREINSNACHRICHTEN. Text in German. 1980. 3/yr. adv. bk.rev. back issues avail. **Document type:** *Bulletin.* **Description:** Contains news and information about the local sports club and its members.
Published by: T S Vgg 1848 Stadecken - Elsheim e.V., Talstr 56, Stadecken-Elsheim, 55271, Germany. TEL 49-6136-1584. Ed. Karl Heinz Moerixbauer. Adv. contact Karl-Heinz Moerixbauer. Circ: 1,000.

790.1 DEU ISSN 0179-0153
T U S INFO; Informationen aus dem Vereinsleben. (Turn- und-Sportverein) Text in German. 1985. q. adv. illus. back issues avail.
Published by: T U S Witten-Stockum 1945 e.V., Postfach 7042, Witten, 58454, Germany. TEL 49-234-5304243, http://www.tus-witten-stockum.de. Ed., Pub. Karin Wagener. adv.: B&W page EUR 56.24; 125 x 185. Circ: 1,300.

790.1 DEU
T U S VEREINSNACHRICHTEN. Text in German. 1907. q. EUR 12 membership (effective 2005). **Document type:** *Newsletter, Consumer.*
Published by: Turn- und Sportvereinigung Gaarden von 1875 e.V., Roentgenstr 5, Kiel, 24143, Germany. TEL 49-431-7068618, FAX 49-431-7068619, geschaeftsstelle@tusgaarden.de, http://tusgaarden.de. Ed., Adv. contact Dieter Buenning. Circ: 1,000 (controlled).

796.41 DEU
T V K 1877 ECHO. Text in German. 1984. q. EUR 10 (effective 2005). adv. 44 p./no. 2 cols./p.; back issues avail. **Document type:** *Magazine, Consumer.* **Description:** Magazine for members of the Turnverein.
Published by: Turnverein 1877 e.V. Essen-Kupferdreh, Kampmannbruecke 1, Essen, 45257, Germany. TEL 49-201-8486220, FAX 49-201-488179, info@tvk-essen.de. Ed. Arndt Holtstraeter. R&P, Adv. contact Bodo F. Schmischke TEL 49-2324-947090. B&W page EUR 180; trim 150 x 200. Circ: 2,500 (paid and controlled).

791.45 USA
T V SPORTSFILE. Text in English. 1983. irreg. (approx 6/mo.). USD 295. adv. back issues avail. **Document type:** *Newsletter.* **Description:** Covers breaking news affecting the TV sports business.
Supersedes: Cablesports Newsletter; Former titles: Cable - Television Sports Newsletter; Cablesports Newsletter
Related titles: Online - full text ed.
Published by: Gould Media, PO Box 4159, Anna Maria, FL 34216. TEL 941-778-5960, 800-876-6604, FAX 941-778-2895, gm-info@gouldmedia.com. Ed. Dantia Gould.

790.1 USA
TAC NEWS. Text in English. 1987. bi-m. free to qualified personnel (effective 2010). back issues avail. **Document type:** *Newsletter, Consumer.*
Related titles: Online - full text ed.
Published by: G H Q, 28100 Woodside Rd, Shorewood, MN 55331. TEL 612-374-2693, 800-289-1945, FAX 952-470-4428, customerservice@ghqmodels.com.

796.815 DEU
TAE KWON DO SPIEGEL; Magazin fuer Kampfsport. Text in German. bi-m. EUR 9.90; EUR 2.50 newsstand/cover (effective 2007). adv. **Document type:** *Magazine, Consumer.*
Published by: Q-Bus Visual Arts & Concepts GmbH, Dreilindenstr 78, Essen, 45128, Germany. TEL 49-201-365390, info@q-bus.info. Ed., Adv. contact Bernd Schuerenberg. page EUR 2,350. Circ: 12,500 (controlled).

796.815 USA
TAE KWON DO TIMES; martial arts, fitness & health. Text in English. 1980. 6/yr. USD 16; USD 3.99 newsstand/cover (effective 2004). **Document type:** *Newspaper, Consumer.* **Description:** Features interviews, articles and information about martial arts.
Published by: Tri - Mount Publications, 1423 18th St, Bettendorf, IA 52722. TEL 563-359-7202, FAX 563-355-7299. Eds. Rod Speidel, Greg Ryman. Adv. contact Carol Davis Hart.

790.1 DEU
TAEKWONDO AKTUELL. Text in German. 1977. m. EUR 42 domestic; EUR 48 in Europe; EUR 60 elsewhere (effective 2006). back issues avail. **Description:** Information on all aspects of Tae Kwon Do.
Published by: (Deutsche Taekwondo Union), Soo-Nam Park, Pub., Boeblinger Str 32 a, Stuttgart, 70376, Germany.

790.1 GBR
TAEKWONDO & KOREAN MARTIAL ARTS. Text in English. 1996. m. illus. **Document type:** *Magazine, Consumer.* **Description:** Profiles Tae Kwan Do experts and coaches; discusses other Korean martial arts.
Related titles: Online - full text ed.: free (effective 2010).
Published by: Martial Arts Publications, Unit 20, Maybrook Business Park, 20 Maybrook Rd, Minworth, Sutton Coldfield, B76 1BE, United Kingdom. TEL 44-121-3516930, http://www.martialartsinprint.com.

793 SWE ISSN 1101-1696
TAEVLA OCH VINN. Text in Swedish. 1985. m. SEK 389 (effective 2010). **Document type:** *Magazine, Consumer.*
Formerly (until 1990): Vinn (0282-7875); Which incorporated (1984-1986): Bra Kryss (0281-9295); (1980-1986): Hela Svenska Folkets Krysstidning (0349-6341)
Published by: Bonnier Tidskrifter AB, Sveavaegen 53, Stockholm, 10544, Sweden. TEL 46-8-7365200, FAX 46-8-7363842, info@bt.bonnier.se, http://www.bonniertidskrifter.se. Ed. Magnus Palm.

TAIIKUGAKU KENKYU/JAPAN JOURNAL OF PHYSICAL EDUCATION, HEALTH AND SPORT SCIENCES. *see* EDUCATION

796.8 DEU ISSN 1611-1702
TAIJIQUAN & QIGONG JOURNAL. Text in German. 2000. q. EUR 65.60 for 2 yrs.; EUR 8.50 newsstand/cover (effective 2010). adv. **Document type:** *Magazine, Consumer.*
Published by: T Q J Verlag, Kalleby 10, Quern, 24972, Germany. TEL 49-4632-8761928, FAX 49-4632-8761938. Ed., Pub. Helmut Oberlack. Circ: 3,000 (paid).

TALK SHOW HOST DIRECTORY AND RESOURCE GUIDE. *see* BUSINESS AND ECONOMICS—Trade And Industrial Directories

TANZ UND GYMNASTIK. *see* DANCE

796.83 USA ISSN 1937-108X
TAPOUT MAGAZINE. Text in English. 2005. bi-m. USD 32; USD 5.95 newsstand/cover domestic; USD 7.25 newsstand/cover in Canada (effective 2008). adv. **Document type:** *Magazine, Consumer.* **Description:** Covers mixed martial arts and grappling sports, including techniques and training, interviews and features about fighters and coaches and worldwide MMA events.
Published by: S M P Inc., 5252 Orange Ave, Ste 109, Cypress, CA 90630. TEL 714-226-0585, FAX 714-226-0583. Pub. Robert Pittman. adv.: page USD 1,100;.

796.72 CAN ISSN 1911-2335
TARGA NEWFOUNDLAND. Text in English. 2006. a. **Document type:** *Magazine, Consumer.*
Published by: Wanda Cuff Young, Inc., 842 Conception Bay Hwy, Ste 1, Conception Bay S, NF A1X 7T4, Canada. TEL 709-834-7977, 877-834-7977, FAX 709-834-4650, admin@wandacuffyoung.ca, http://www.wandacuffyoung.ca/Index.asp.

TARZAN. *see* MEN'S INTERESTS

794 FIN ISSN 0356-1577
TASKURISTIKKO. Text in Finnish. 1967. m. EUR 1.50 newsstand/cover (effective 2009). **Document type:** *Magazine, Consumer.*
Published by: Sanoma Magazines Finland Corporation, Lapinmaentie 1, Helsinki, 00350, Finland. TEL 358-9-1201, FAX 358-9-1205171, info@sanomamagazines.fi, http://www.sanomamagazines.fi.

797.23 DEU
TAUCH-BRILLE. Text in German. 1986. m. back issues avail. **Description:** News about diving.
Published by: (Saarlaendischer Tauchsportbund), Kurt Huwig Druckerei, Goethestr 50, Riegelsberg, 66292, Germany. TEL 49-6806-4001, FAX 49-6806-2637, kh@druckerei-huwig.de. Ed. Hannelore Huwig. Circ: 1,200.

790.1 578.77 770 910.09 DEU ISSN 0170-4001
TAUCHEN; Europas grosse Tauchzeitschrift. Text in German. 1978. m. EUR 64.80; EUR 5.50 newsstand/cover (effective 2011). adv. bk.rev. charts; illus. index. back issues avail. **Document type:** *Magazine, Consumer.*
Published by: Jahr Top Special Verlag, Troplowitzstr 5, Hamburg, 22529, Germany. TEL 49-40-389060, FAX 49-40-38906300, info@jahr-tsv.de, http://www.jahr-tsv.de. Ed. Carolyn Martin. Adv. contact Evelyn Diekmann. Circ: 28,411 (paid).

658.8 790 USA ISSN 1949-3703
GV743
TEAM BUSINESS. Abbreviated title: T B. Text in English. 1899. bi-m. USD 59 domestic; USD 99 in Canada & Mexico; USD 149 elsewhere (effective 2009). adv. illus.; mkt.; tr.lit. back issues avail. **Document type:** *Magazine, Trade.* **Description:** Covers industry insiders, new products, and merchandising trends affecting team dealers and retailers who serve schools, colleges, consumers, pro and local team and organizations.
Formerly (until 2009): The Sporting Goods Dealer (0038-8017)
Related titles: Online - full text ed.
Indexed: A09, A10, B01, B02, B07, B15, B17, B18, G04, G06, G07, G08, I05, SD, T02, V03, V04.
—CCC.
Published by: SportsOneSource Group, 2151 Hawkins St, Ste 200, Charlotte, NC 28269. TEL 704-987-3450, FAX 704-987-3455, info@sportsonesource.com. Ed. James Hartford.

688.76 USA
TEAM LINE-UP. Text in English. 1970. q. free to members (effective 2009). **Document type:** *Newsletter.*
Published by: National Sporting Goods Association, 1601 Feehanville Dr, Ste 300, Mount Prospect, IL 60056. TEL 847-296-6742, 800-815-5422, FAX 847-391-9827, info@nsga.org, http://www.nsga.org. Ed. Larry Weindruch TEL 847-296-6742 ext 129.

TEAM MARKETING REPORT. *see* BUSINESS AND ECONOMICS—Marketing And Purchasing

796.41 USA ISSN 0748-5999
GV461
TECHNIQUE (INDIANAPOLIS). Text in English. m. USD 25 domestic; USD 48 in Canada & Mexico; USD 60 elsewhere (effective 2005). **Document type:** *Magazine, Consumer.*
Indexed: PEI, SD, T02.
Published by: U S A Gymnastics, Pan American Plaza, 201 S Capitol Ave, Ste 300, Indianapolis, IN 46225. TEL 317-237-5050, FAX 317-237-5069, lpeszek@usa-gymnastics.org.

688.76 FRA
TECHNO - LOISIRS; guide international annuel de la construction et de l'equipement pour le sport et les loisirs. Text in Multiple languages, Esperanto. 1971. biennial. adv. bk.rev.; play rev. bibl.; illus.; pat.; stat.; tr.lit. index. **Document type:** *Directory.*
Related titles: Magnetic Tape ed.
Published by: Editions Techno-Loisirs, 3 rue Sivel, Paris, 75014, France. TEL 33-45-40-9905, FAX 33-45-40-7893. Ed. Georges E Caille. Circ: 10,000.

796 ITA ISSN 1824-6095
TEKNOSPORT (ONLINE). Text in Italian. 1995. bi-m. EUR 30 (effective 2009). **Document type:** *Magazine, Trade.*
Formerly (until 2001): Teknosport (Print) (1824-6141)
Media: Online - full text.
Published by: Kells Edizioni, Via Maggini 127a, Ancona, 60127, Italy. http://www.kells.it.

794.1 ITA
TELESCACCO 2000. Text in Italian. 1983. 11/yr. USD 22. bk.rev. charts. **Document type:** *Magazine, Consumer.* **Description:** Covers annotated games, "how-to-improve" articles, theory, correspondence tournaments and news.
Fotrmer titles (until 1999): Telescacco 92; (until 1992): Telescacco Nuovo
Published by: Associazione Scacchista Italiana Giocatori per Corrispondenza, c/o Franco Mecucci, Via Vernio, 49, Rome, RM 00138, Italy. TEL 06-880-3316.

796 CZE ISSN 1211-6521
TELESNA KULTURA. Text in Multiple languages. 1956. s-a. **Document type:** *Journal, Academic/Scholarly.*
Formerly (until 1988): Telovychovny Sbornik (0495-0445)
Related titles: Online - full text ed.: ISSN 1803-8360. free (effective 2011).
Indexed: SD, T02.
Published by: Univerzita Palackeho v Olomouci, Fakulta Telesne Kultury/Palacky University Olomouc, Faculty of Physical Culture, tr. Miru 115, Olomouc, 77111, Czech Republic. TEL 420-68-5636357, FAX 420-68-5422532, aupo@ftknw.upol.cz, http://www.upol.cz/fakulty/ftk. Ed. Lucie Spatenkova.

613.7 CZE ISSN 1210-7689
➤ **TELESNA VYCHOVA A SPORT MLADEZE**; odborny casopis pro ucitele, trenery a cvicitele. Text in Czech, Slovak. 1932. 8/yr. CZK 210; CZK 35 newsstand/cover (effective 2010). adv. bk.rev. bibl.; illus. **Document type:** *Journal, Academic/Scholarly.* **Description:** Presents new discoveries in the field of physical education and sport. Includes tips for practice and new projects.
Formerly (until 1994): Telesna Vychova Mladeze (0040-2729)
Indexed: RASB.
Published by: Univerzita Karlova v Praze, Fakulta Telesne Vychovy a Sportu, Jose Martiho 31, Prague 6, 16252, Czech Republic. TEL 420-2-20172190, FAX 420-2-42454708, dobry@ftvs.cuni.cz. Ed. Lubomir Dobry. Circ: 4,500.

796 RUS ISSN 1606-0237
TELESPORT. Text in Russian. 1999. w. **Document type:** *Newspaper, Consumer.*
Published by: S K Press, Marksistkaya 34, str 10, Moscow, 109147, Russian Federation. deliver@skpress.ru, http://www.skpress.ru.

790.1 POL ISSN 0137-933X
TEMPO. Text in Polish. 1948. 5/w. adv. illus. **Document type:** *Newspaper, Consumer.*
Formerly (until 1959): Glos Sportowca (0431-9834)
Published by: J M G Sport Publishing (Subsidiary of: Marquard Media AG), ul Nowogrodzka 84-86, Warsaw, 02-018, Poland. TEL 48-22-6289116, FAX 48-22-6218697, redakcja@przeglad.com.pl. Circ: 75,000.

796 ESP ISSN 1575-1074
TENNIS A FONDO. Text in Spanish. 1999. m. adv. **Document type:** *Magazine, Consumer.*
Published by: Motorpress Iberica (Subsidiary of: Gruner + Jahr AG & Co), Ancora 40, Madrid, 28045, Spain. TEL 34-91-3470100, FAX 34-91-3470152, http://www.motorpress-iberica.es. Circ: 12,000 (paid).

796 USA ISSN 0040-4241
TEXAS COACH. Text in English. 1957. m. (except June, July & Dec.). USD 30 membership; USD 15 to students (effective 2005). adv. bk.rev. illus. **Document type:** *Magazine, Consumer.* **Description:** Assists Texas middle school, high school and college sports coaches in overcoming common coaching problems.
Indexed: PEI, SD, SPI, SportS, T02.
—Ingenta.
Published by: Texas High School Coaches Association, 1228 Hwy 123, San Marcos, TX 78669. TEL 512-392-3741, FAX 512-392-3762, http://www.thsca.com/. Ed., R&P, Adv. contact Sheryl Honeycutt. Circ: 16,700.

TEXAS REVIEW OF ENTERTAINMENT AND SPORTS LAW. *see* LAW

790.1 VNM
THE THAO VAN HOA/SPORTS AND CULTURE. Text in Vietnamese. 1982. w. USD 0.12 per issue.
Published by: The Thao Van Hoa, 5 Ly Thuong Kiet, Hanoi, Viet Nam. TEL 84-4-267043, FAX 84-42-267447, TELEX 267043. Ed. Nauyen Huu Vinh. Circ: 90,000.

790.1 VNM
THE THAO VIET-NAM/VIET-NAM SPORTS. Text in Vietnamese. 1968. w.

S

Published by: The Thao Viet-Nam, 5 Trinh Hoai Duc St, Hanoi, Viet Nam. Ed. Tran Can.

790.1 USA ISSN 0889-0692
THRASHER. Text in English. 1980. m. USD 17.95 domestic; USD 43 in Canada; USD 50 elsewhere; USD 3.99 per issue (effective 2010). bk.rev. back issues avail. **Document type:** *Magazine, Consumer.* **Description:** Covers skateboarding, snowboarding, music, video, and aggressive youth-oriented lifestyle.
Formerly (until 198?): Thrasher Skateboard Magazine (0742-4922)
Related titles: Online - full text ed.
Indexed: G06, G07, G08, I05, I07.
Published by: High Speed Productions, Inc., 1303 Underwood Ave, San Francisco, CA 94124. TEL 415-822-3083, FAX 415-822-8359.

794.3 USA
THROWLINES. Text in English. 2005. 3/yr. USD 15 (effective 2006). adv. **Document type:** *Magazine, Consumer.*
Published by: National Dart Association, 5613 W 74th St, Indianapolis, IN 46278. TEL 317-387-1299, 800-808-9884, FAX 317-387-0999, membership@ndadarts.com, http://www.ndsdarts.com/. adv.: B&W page USD 825; trim 8.375 x 10.875. Circ: 118,138 (paid).

794.1 SWE ISSN 0040-6848
TIDSKRIFT FOER SCHACK. Text in Swedish. 1895. 8/yr. SEK 250 in Scandinavia; EUR 30 elsewhere (effective 2011). adv. bk.rev. index. 64 p./no.; back issues avail. **Document type:** *Magazine, Consumer.*
Related titles: Online - full text ed.
Published by: Sveriges Schackfoerbund/Swedish Chess Federation, Kabelvaegen 19, Norrkoeping, 60210t, Sweden. TEL 46-11-107420, kansliet@schack.se. Ed. Niklas Sidmar TEL 46-11-239453.

TIERWELT. *see* BIOLOGY—Ornithology

TIJDSCHRIFT VOOR LICHAMELIJKE OPVOEDING. *see* EDUCATION—Teaching Methods And Curriculum

340 NLD ISSN 1877-4229
▼ **TIJDSCHRIFT VOOR SPORT EN RECHT.** Text in Dutch. 2009. q. EUR 132.50 (effective 2010). **Document type:** *Journal, Academic/Scholarly.*
Related titles: Online - full text ed.: ISSN 1877-4407.
Published by: Uitgeverij Paris bv, Waterstr 5, Zutphen, 7201 HM, Netherlands. TEL 31-575-514299, FAX 31-575-514509. Ed. S F Jellinghaus.

796 340 BEL ISSN 1372-911X
TIJDSCHRIFT VOOR SPORTRECHT. Text in Dutch. 1997. q. **Document type:** *Journal, Trade.*
Published by: Die Keure NV, Kleine Pathoekeweg 3, Bruges, 8000, Belgium. TEL 32-50-471272, FAX 32-50-335154, juridische.uitgaven@diekeure.be, http://www.diekeure.be.

796.8 FRA ISSN 1951-2988
TIN MU'NG. Text in French. 2006. 3/yr. back issues avail. **Document type:** *Bulletin.*
Published by: Federation de Rassemblement des Arts Martiaux Vietnamiens, 1 Route d'Ennezat, Chappes, 63720, France. administration@framv.fr, http://www.framv.fr.

790.1 DEU ISSN 0948-3578
TIPP MIT. Text in German. 1992. w. (Tue.). EUR 80.60; EUR 1.80 newsstand/cover (effective 2009). adv. **Document type:** *Newspaper, Consumer.*
Published by: D S V Deutscher Sportverlag GmbH, Im Mediapark 8, Cologne, 50670, Germany. TEL 49-221-25870, FAX 49-221-2587212, kontakt@dsv-sportverlag.de, http://www.dsv-sportverlag.de. Ed. Hans Reski. Adv. contact Anja Diekmann. B&W page EUR 5,800, color page EUR 5,800; trim 228 x 322. Circ: 56,000 (paid and controlled).

796 CHN
TITAN ZHOUBAO. Text in Chinese. 1988. w. back issues avail. **Document type:** *Magazine, Consumer.*
Related titles: Online - full text ed.
Published by: Titan Chuanmei Jituan/Titan Culture - Express Co, ltd, 1, Tiyuguan Lu, Changsha, 410005, China. TEL 86-731-4556749, http://www.titan24.com/.

796 CHN ISSN 1001-3253
TIYU/PHYSICAL EDUCATION. Text in Chinese. 1978. m. USD 49.90 (effective 2009). 64 p./no.; **Document type:** *Journal, Academic/Scholarly.*
Published by: Zhongguo Renmin Daxue Shubao Ziliao Zhongxin/Renmin University of China, Information Center for Social Sciences, Dongcheng-qu, 3, Zhangzizhong Lu, Beijing, 100007, China. TEL 86-10-64039458, FAX 86-10-64015080, center@zlzx.org, http://www.zlzx.org/. **Dist. in US by:** China Publications Service, PO Box 49614, Chicago, IL 60649. TEL 312-288-3291, FAX 312-288-8570.

790.1 CHN ISSN 1002-879X
TIYU HUABAO/SPORTS PICTORIAL. Text in Chinese. 1963. m. USD 135.20 (effective 2009). **Document type:** *Journal, Academic/Scholarly.*
Related titles: Online - full content ed.
Published by: Zhongguo Tiyubao Yezongshe, 8, Tiyuguan Lu, Chongwen-qu, Beijing, 100061, China. TEL 86-10-67110066 ext 325. **Dist. by:** China International Book Trading Corp, 35 Chegongzhuang Xilu, Haidian District, PO Box 399, Beijing 100044, China. TEL 86-10-68412045, FAX 86-10-68412023, cibtc@mail.cibtc.com.cn, http://www.cibtc.com.cn.

790.1 CHN ISSN 1000-677X
TIYU KEXUE/SPORTS SCIENCE. Text in Chinese; Abstracts in English. 1981. bi-m. USD 74.40 (effective 2009). **Document type:** *Journal, Academic/Scholarly.*
Indexed: SD, SportS.
—BLDSC (8419.839520), East View, IE, Ingenta.
Published by: Zhongguo Tiyu Kexue Xuehui/China Sports Science Society, 9, Tiyuguang Lu, Chongwen-qu, Beijing, 100061, China. TEL 86-10-87182585, office@csss.cn. Circ: 20,000.

796 CHN ISSN 1004-4590
TIYU YU KEXUE/SPORT & SCIENCE. Text in Chinese. 1978. bi-m. USD 37.20 (effective 2009). **Document type:** *Journal, Academic/Scholarly.*
Related titles: Online - full text ed.
—BLDSC (8859.311980).
Published by: Jiangsu sheng Tiyu Kexue Yanjiusuo/Jiangsu Research Institute of Sports Science, 8-1, Linggusi Rd, Nanjing, 210014, China. TEL 86-25-84755315, FAX 86-25-84431877.

796 CHN
TONFAN TIYU RIBAO/ORIENTAL SPORTS DAILY. Text in Chinese. 2002. d. CNY 360; CNY 1 newsstand/cover (effective 2004). **Document type:** *Magazine, Academic/Scholarly.* **Description:** Provides comprehensive information on physical fitness trends in China and abroad along with special coverage of China's football lottery in its Football Fortune edition. It is the first specialized publication to combine physical fitness, recreation and entertainment coverage, and makes innovative use of cartoon images to enhance its appeal.
Former by the merger of: Xinmin Tiyu Bao/Xinmin Sports; Xinmin Go Game
Published by: Wenhui Xinmin Lianhebao Yejietuan/Wenhui Xinmin United Press Group, 840, Luochuan Zhonglu, 4th Fl, no.1, Shanghai, 200072, China. TEL 86-21-52921234, FAX 86-21-52921574, http://www.news365.com.cn/.

796 613.7 AUT
TOP TIMES; das Sportmagazin. Text in German. 2000. bi-m. EUR 12.90 (effective 2008). adv.
Published by: Top Times Medien GmbH, Belgiergasse 3/I, Graz, 8020, Austria. TEL 43-316-903312786, FAX 43-316-903312764, office@toptimes.at. Adv. contact Bertram Taferner. page EUR 5,900; trim 210 x 278. Circ: 60,000 (controlled).

796.962 GBR
TOTAL HOCKEY. Text in English. m. GBP 35.50 domestic; GBP 42.60 foreign; GBP 2.95 newsstand/cover. **Document type:** *Magazine, Consumer.*
Published by: Planet Publications Ltd., Colourset House, Brook St, Watlington, Oxon OX9 5JH, United Kingdom. TEL 44-1491-614999, FAX 44-1491-614645. Ed. Adam Williams. **Dist. by:** M M C Ltd., Octagon House, White Hart Meadows, Ripley, Woking, Surrey GU23 6HR, United Kingdom. TEL 44-1483-211222, FAX 44-1483-224541.

795 ITA ISSN 1590-0916
TOTOGUIDA SCOMMESSE. Text in Italian. 1998. w. **Document type:** *Magazine, Consumer.*
Published by: Giroal Srl, Piazza Verdi 8, Rome, 00198, Italy. TEL 39-06-8841611, FAX 39-06-85831141, info@giroal.it, http://www.giroal.it.

795 ITA ISSN 1590-0924
TOTOGUIDA SUPER LOTTO. Text in Italian. 1998. w. **Document type:** *Magazine, Consumer.*
Related titles: Alternate Frequency ed(s).: Totoguida Super Lotto Mese. ISSN 1590-1653. 1999. m.
Published by: Giroal Srl, Piazza Verdi 8, Rome, 00198, Italy. TEL 39-06-8841611, FAX 39-06-85831141, info@giroal.it, http://www.giroal.it.

793 940.1 USA ISSN 0732-6645
TOURNAMENTS ILLUMINATED. Text in English. 1967. q. free to members (effective 2010). adv. illus. back issues avail.; reprints avail. **Document type:** *Journal, Academic/Scholarly.* **Description:** Presents information on medieval fairs and jousts in the U.S.
Published by: Society for Creative Anachronism, PO Box 360789, Milpitas, CA 95036. TEL 408-263-9305, 800-789-7486, FAX 408-263-0641, membership@sca.org. Eds. Dori Andrepont, Doria Tecla. Adv. contact Theresa Anderson TEL 800-789-7486 ext 208. page USD 925; trim 8.5 x 11.

TRACK AND FIELD AND CROSS COUNTRY RULES BOOK. *see* SPORTS AND GAMES—Outdoor Life

796.72 GBR ISSN 1742-1934
TRACK & RACE CARS. Text in English. 2004. m. GBP 3.99 per issue domestic; GBP 5.99 per issue in Europe; GBP 7.99 per issue elsewhere (effective 2009). adv. back issues avail. **Document type:** *Magazine, Consumer.* **Description:** Covers track day cars and the latest race machinery, plus monthly updates on the up-to-date track & test days in your area, technical insights and an historic look back at the events and cars that helped mould today's track cars.
Related titles: Online - full text ed.: free (effective 2009).
Published by: P1 Media Ltd., 194a Upper Richmond Rd W, London, SW14 8AN, United Kingdom. TEL 44-20-82965467, FAX 44-20-82408901, http://www.p1-media.com/. Ed. Keith Wood. Adv. contact Tom Saunders TEL 44-20-83952653. page GBP 600; trim 210 x 297.

798.4 AUS
TRACKSIDE. Text in English. 1902. m. AUD 130 (effective 2009). adv. cum.index. **Document type:** *Magazine, Trade.* **Description:** Contains racing information such as schedules, programs, race dates, contact information, editorials from department heads and news on the South Australian racing scene.
Formerly (until 2004): South Australian Racing Calendar (0038-2981)
Published by: South Australian Thoroughbred Racing Authority, GPO BOX 2646, Adelaide, SA 5001, Australia. TEL 61-8-81799800, FAX 61-8-83500064, mlaw@racingsa.com.au. Ed. Jason Hickson. Adv. contact Melissa Ware TEL 61-8-81799812. B&W page AUD 495, color page AUD 880; trim 210 x 297. Circ: 1,500.

796.72 USA ISSN 1050-558X
TRACKSIDE MAGAZINE. Text in English. 1990. m. USD 25 (effective 2001). back issues avail. **Document type:** *Magazine, Consumer.*
Published by: Motorsports Publishing LLC, 335 Mountain Rd, Somers, CT 06071. TEL 860-763-5632, FAX 860-763-5639. Ed. Cindy Hopkins. Adv. contact Steve Pighetti.

799.32 USA ISSN 2158-043X
TRADARCHERS' WORLD. Text in English. 200?. q. USD 19 domestic; USD 26 in Canada; USD 39 elsewhere; USD 7 per issue (effective 2010). back issues avail. **Document type:** *Magazine, Trade.* **Description:** Designed for the bowyer craft, archers and bowhunters who make their own bows and other traditional archery equipment.
Related titles: Online - full text ed.: USD 10 (effective 2010).
Published by: Tom Colstad, Ed. & Pub., PO Box 67, Irma, WI 54442. Ed., Pub. Tom Colstad.

796.8153 GBR
TRADITIONAL KARATE. Text in English. 1987. m. **Document type:** *Magazine, Consumer.* **Description:** Informs and advises the karate enthusiast on tournament reports, courses, features, news and calendar of current events.
Related titles: Online - full text ed.: free (effective 2010).
Published by: Martial Arts Publications, Unit 20, Maybrook Business Park, 20 Maybrook Rd, Minworth, Sutton Coldfield, B76 1BE, United Kingdom. TEL 44-121-3516930, office@combatmag.co.uk, http://www.martialartsinprint.com.

796 GBR ISSN 2044-1037
▼ **TRAIL RUNNING.** Text in English. 2010. q. GBP 4.30 newsstand/cover (effective 2010). **Document type:** *Magazine, Trade.* **Description:** Covers reviews and training advice from experts for all types of running.
—CCC.
Published by: Bauer Consumer Media Ltd., Mappin House, 4 Winsley St, London, W1W 8HF, United Kingdom. TEL 44-20-71828000, http://www.bauermedia.co.uk.

613.7 USA ISSN 1058-3548
TRAINING AND CONDITIONING. Abbreviated title: T & C. Text in English. 1991. 9/yr. USD 26; USD 7 per issue; free to qualified personnel (effective 2011). adv. back issues avail. **Document type:** *Magazine, Consumer.* **Description:** Provides pertinent information on the various training and conditioning techniques, trends, procedures and products to professionals involved in the training and conditioning of competitive athletes.
Indexed: PEI, SD, T02.
Published by: Momentum Media Sports Publishing, 31 Dutch Mill Rd, Ithaca, NY 14850. TEL 607-257-6970, FAX 607-257-7328, info@momentummedia.com, http://momentummedia.com. Ed. Eleanor Frankel. Pub. Mark Goldberg TEL 607-257-6970 ext 11.

790.1 SWE
TRANSITION. Text in Swedish. 2002. 6/yr. SEK 245 (effective 2002). adv. **Description:** News about action- and board sports.
Published by: Funsport Media AB, Gasverksvaegen 2, Stockholm, 11542, Sweden. TEL 46-8-23-40-40, FAX 46-8-440-08-75. Ed. Pelle Jansson. Adv. contact Niklas Forsen TEL 46-8-622-62-00. Circ: 20,000.

TRANSWORLD BUSINESS; the leader in boardsports news and information. *see* BUSINESS AND ECONOMICS

797.2 USA ISSN 1532-9402
TRANSWORLD SURF. Text in English. 1999. m. USD 14.97 domestic; USD 29.97 in Canada; USD 59.97 elsewhere; USD 4.99 newsstand/cover (effective 2009). adv. illus. back issues avail. **Document type:** *Magazine, Consumer.* **Description:** Contains articles covering all aspects of surfing, including interviews, equipments, location, and the latest surf-related news and events.
Related titles: Online - full text ed.
Indexed: G08, I05.
—CCC.
Published by: TransWorld Media (Subsidiary of: Bonnier Magazine Group), 2052 Corte del Nogal Ste B, Carlsbad, CA 92011. TEL 760-722-7777, FAX 760-722-0653, http://www.transworldmatrix.com/twmatrix/. Adv. contact Lauren N Machen TEL 760-722-7777 ext 227. color page USD 11,024; trim 8 x 10.5. Circ: 75,005.

796.42 910 USA ISSN 1933-401X
GV1065.2
THE TRAVELING MARATHONER. Text in English. 200?. irreg. USD 19.95 per issue (effective 2008). **Document type:** *Magazine, Consumer.* **Description:** Features information that can help plan a marathon vacation, at any time of the year and at any part of the country.
Published by: Fodor's Travel Publications, Inc. (Subsidiary of: Random House Inc.), 1745 Broadway, 15th Fl, New York, NY 10019. TEL 212-782-9000, 212-572-2313, editors@fodors.com, http://www.fodors.com.

796 DEU ISSN 1435-9944
TRENDSPORTWISSENSCHAFT; neue Methoden - neue Sportarten - neue Theorien. Text in German. 1998. irreg., latest vol.13, 2009. price varies. back issues avail. **Document type:** *Monographic series, Academic/Scholarly.* **Description:** Presents a book series dealing with trends in sport and sport science.
Published by: Czwalina Verlag, Bei der Neuen Muenze 4a, Hamburg, 22145, Germany. TEL 49-40-6794300, FAX 49-40-67943030, post@feldhaus-verlag, http://www.edition-czwalina.de.

793 NZL ISSN 1176-9483
TRI-ALPHAMETIC PUZZLES. Text in English. 2005. s-a. NZD 9.95 newsstand/cover (effective 2008). **Document type:** *Magazine, Consumer.*
Published by: Medieval Mosaic Ltd., 10 Wilson St, Geraldine, New Zealand. TEL 64-3-6939820, c1066@1066.co.nz. Pub. Michael Linton.

796 USA ISSN 1934-3256
TRI-STATE SPORTSLOOK. Text in English. 2006. m. free (effective 2007). adv. **Document type:** *Magazine, Consumer.* **Description:** Features articles, stories, scores and schedules for youth, high school, college and adult athletics in the Dubuque, Iowa metropolitan area, including volleyball, football and skiing.
Published by: Futurus Communications, 1670 Asbury Rd, Dubuque, IA 52001. TEL 563-773-3119, 888-388-8787, FAX 360-343-2341, information@futurus.biz, http://www.futurus.biz/. Ed. Jay Schiesl TEL 563-773-3125.

790.1 ITA ISSN 1828-4345
TRIATHLETE. Text in Italian. 2004. 8/yr. EUR 30 domestic; EUR 70 foreign (effective 2009). **Document type:** *Magazine, Consumer.*
Formerly (until 2005): Multisport, Triathlete (1828-4337); Which was formed by the merger of (1987-2003): Multisport (1828-4329); (1994-2003): Triathlete (1591-6529); Which was formerly (until 1995): Triathlon & Duathlon Magazine (1591-6537)
Published by: Editoriale Sport Italia, Via Masaccio 12, Milan, MI 20149, Italy. TEL 39-02-4815396, FAX 39-02-4690907, http://www.sportivi.it. Circ: 29,500.

790.1 USA ISSN 0898-3410
GV1060.7
TRIATHLETE. Text in English. 1983. m. USD 34.95 domestic; USD 59.95 combined subscription domestic (print & online eds.) (effective 2010). adv. illus. back issues avail.; reprints avail. **Document type:** *Magazine, Consumer.* **Description:** Contains news and features on triathlons, duathlons, and other multi-sport events.
Formerly (until 1986): Triathlon (0745-5917)
Related titles: Online - full text ed.: USD 29.95 (effective 2010).
Indexed: SD, SPI, SportS.
Published by: Triathlon Group North America, 9401 Waples St, Ste 150, San Diego, CA 92121. TEL 800-311-1255, customerservice@competitorgroup.com. Eds. Susan Grant, T J Murphy.

796 GBR ISSN 0955-1085
TRIATHLETE (LONDON). Text in English. 1987. m. GBP 28; GBP 2.50 newsstand/cover (effective 1999). adv. **Description:** Provides information and news to the triathlete, with product guides and reviews, articles on techniques in various sports, and interviews.
Published by: Triathlete UK Ltd., The Apprentice Shop, Merton, 14 Watermill Way, Wimbeldon, London, SW19 2RD, United Kingdom. TEL 44-181-543-9747, FAX 44-181-540-4817. Ed. Katherine Williams. Adv. contact Vic Bickerson. **Dist. by:** Comag, Tavistock Rd, W Drayton, Middlesex UB7 7QE, United Kingdom. TEL 44-1895-444055, FAX 44-1895-433602.

790.1 DEU ISSN 1619-5604
TRIATHLON. Text in German. 1993. bi-m. EUR 39 domestic; EUR 50 foreign; EUR 3.50 newsstand/cover (effective 2007). adv. **Document type:** *Magazine, Consumer.* **Description:** Contains information, news and results on triathlons and duathlons in Germany.
Formerly (until 2001): Triathlon und Duathlon (1432-606X)
Published by: (Deutsche Triathlon Union e.V.), Spomedis GmbH, Altonaer Poststr 13a, Hamburg, 22767, Germany. TEL 49-40-8519243, FAX 49-40-85192444, info@spomedis.de, http://www.spomedis.de. Adv. contact Marcus Baranski TEL 49-40-76750552. page EUR 4,248; 190 x 277. Circ: 28,478 (paid).

790.1 AUS ISSN 1440-9453
TRIATHLON AND MULTI-SPORT MAGAZINE. Text in English. 1998. 10/yr. AUD 64.95; AUD 7.50 per issue (effective 2008). **Document type:** *Magazine, Consumer.*
Related titles: Online - full text ed.
Indexed: SD.
Published by: Blitz Publications, PO Box 4075, Mulgrave, VIC 3170, Australia. TEL 61-3-95748460, FAX 61-3-95748899, info@blitzmag.com.au. Ed. Jonathan Horn TEL 61-3-95748999. Adv. contact Todd Spencer TEL 61-3-95748999.

790.1 USA ISSN 1930-0824
TRIATHLON LIFE; the official magazine of the national governing body for triathlon and related multi-sport events in the U.S. Variant title: U S A Triathlon Life. Text in English. 1985. q. free to members (effective 2006). adv. **Document type:** *Newsletter.*
Former titles: U S A Triathlon Times; Triathlon Times (1068-8277)
Indexed: SD.
Published by: U S A Triathlon, 1365 Garden of the Gods Rd Ste 250, Colorado Springs, CO 80907-3425. TEL 719-597-9090, FAX 719-597-2121, Info@USATriathlon.org, http://www.usatriathlon.org. Ed. Steve Locke. Pub., R&P Tim Yount. Adv. contact Randy Pelton. Circ: 25,000.

796.41 CAN ISSN 1718-2441
TRIATHLON MAGAZINE CANADA. Text in English. 2006. bi-m. CAD 20.95 domestic; CAD 44.95 foreign (effective 2006). **Document type:** *Magazine, Consumer.*
Published by: Gripped Publishing Inc., 344 Bloor St, Unit 510, Toronto, ON M5S 3A7, Canada. TEL 416-927-8198, FAX 416-927-1491, gripped@gripped.com. Ed. Kevin Mackinnon. Pub. Sam Cohen.

790.1 AUS
TRIATHLON SPORTS MAGAZINE. Text in English. 1984. 8/yr. **Document type:** *Magazine, Consumer.* **Description:** For health-conscious adults and serious athletes who swim, bicycle and run for fitness.
Published by: J P Publications, PO Box 2805, Taren Point, NSW 2229, Australia. TEL 61-2-95427335, FAX 61-2-95427323, jppublic@ozemail.com.au, http://www.magna.com.au/~iphala.

796.4 796.6 NLD ISSN 1573-2037
TRIATLON DUATLON SPORT. Text in Dutch. 1988. m. EUR 31 domestic; EUR 44 foreign (effective 2009). adv.
Formerly (until 2003): Triathlon Sport (0922-1468)
Published by: Nederlandse Triathlon Bond, Postbus 1267, Nieuwegein, 3430 BG, Netherlands. TEL 31-30-7513770, FAX 31-30-7513771, info@nedtriathlonbond.org, http://www.nedtriathlonbond.org.

796 ITA ISSN 2037-9455
LA TRIBUNA DELLO SPORT. Text in Italian. 2008. bi-w. **Document type:** *Newspaper, Consumer.*
Related titles: Online - full text ed.: ISSN 2037-9463.
Published by: Seapress, Largo Plebiscito 23, Civitavecchia, 00053, Italy. TEL 39-076-6581606, info@seapress.com, http://www.seapress.com.

790.1 ROM
TRIBUNA SPORTURILOR. Text in Romanian. 1990. w.
Address: Str. George Cosbuc 38, Sibiu, 2400, Romania. TEL 924-12810, FAX 924-12026. Ed. Mircea Bitu. Circ: 20,000.

790.1 CAN
TROPHY ROOMS AROUND THE WORLD; an idea and source book. Text in English. 1995. a. USD 65 (effective 2008). adv. **Document type:** *Handbook/Manual/Guide, Trade.* **Description:** Editorials on displaying hunting trophies, caring for trophies. Source book for creating and designing a trophy room and finding the right supplier to do the job for you.
Published by: Hines Proguide, 659 Avondale Rd, RR #2, Newport, NS B0N 2A0, Canada. TEL 605-507-0954, FAX 905-507-9978. Ed., Adv. contact Jackie Ranahan. Pub. Sherman Hines. color page USD 950. Circ: 3,000.

790.1 CAN
TRUE NORTH VOLLEYBALL; Canada's volleyball magazine. Text in English. 1992. 6/yr. CAD 14.95; CAD 19.95 in United States. adv. bk.rev.; video rev.; software rev. charts; illus.; mkt.; stat.; tr.lit. back issues avail. **Document type:** *Magazine, Consumer.* **Description:** The source of all Canadian volleyball information including indoor and beach, complete with training tips, results, events listings, profiles, features and more.
Formerly: V Canada (1192-1277)
Published by: True North Volleyball Inc., 47 Harmony Hill Rd, Richmond, ON L4C 8Z4, Canada. TEL 905-508-8134, 800-668-8226, FAX 905-508-8134. Ed. Tony Martins. Pub. Ted Graham. Adv. contact Paul Brownstein. B&W page CAD 990; trim 10.75 x 8.13. Circ: 5,000.

790.1 RUS
TSIGUN I SPORT. Text in Russian. bi-m. USD 99.95 in United States.
Address: Zubovskii bulv 17, Moscow, 119847, Russian Federation. TEL 7-095-2469322. Ed. A P Shilov. **Dist. by:** East View Information Services, 10601 Wayzata Blvd, Minneapolis, MN 55305. TEL 952-252-1201, 800-477-1005, FAX 952-252-1202, info@eastview.com, http://www.eastview.com.

688.76 613.7 ITA ISSN 1121-6913
TSPORT; impianti sportivi e ricreativi, piscine, fitness e arredo urbano. Text in English, Italian. 1976. 6/yr. (plus two extra issues). EUR 53 (effective 2009). adv. back issues avail. **Document type:** *Magazine, Trade.*
Related titles: Online - full text ed.; ◆ Supplement(s): Mappa dei Fornitori. ISSN 1121-7456.
Published by: Editoriale Tsport Srl, Via Antonio Saluzzo 16, Milan, MI 20162, Italy. TEL 39-02-6438282, FAX 39-02-64749554, info@tsport.it, http://www.tsport.it. Circ: 7,500.

796.44 DEU ISSN 1861-1338
TURNEN IN HESSEN. Text in German. m. EUR 3 newsstand/cover (effective 2007). adv. **Document type:** *Newspaper, Consumer.*
Formerly (until 2005): Hessische Turnzeitung
Published by: Hessischer Turnverband e.V., Huizener Str 22-24, Bad Vilbel, 61118, Germany. TEL 49-6101-54610, FAX 49-6101-546120, info@htv-online.de, http://www.htv-online.de. adv.: B&W page EUR 550. Circ: 3,000 (paid and controlled).

790 DEU
TURNEN IN RHEINLAND-PFALZ. Text in German. m. adv. **Document type:** *Magazine, Consumer.*
Published by: T V M Sportmarketing GmbH, Rheinau 10, Koblenz, 56075, Germany. TEL 49-261-135156, FAX 49-261-135159, webmaster@tvm.org. adv.: B&W page EUR 370. Circ: 4,000 (controlled).

790 DEU ISSN 0945-666X
TURNEN UND SPORT; fuer Uebungsleiter/innen, Trainer/innen, Gymnastik und Sportlehrkraefte. Text in German. 1926. m. EUR 34.20 domestic; EUR 49.20 foreign (effective 2006). adv. bk.rev. illus. index. back issues avail. **Document type:** *Journal, Trade.*
Former titles (until 1983): T U S - Turnen und Sport (0344-4023); Which incorporated (1953-1972): Leibesuebungen (0024-0613); (until 1972): T U S - Der Turn- und Sportwart (0344-4031)
Indexed: DIP, IBR, IBZ.
—GNLM.
Published by: Pohl Verlag Celle GmbH, Postfach 3207, Celle, 29232, Germany. TEL 49-5141-98890, FAX 49-5141-988922, verlag@pohl-verlag.com, http://www.pohl-verlag.com. Ed. Rudi Luetgeharm. Adv. contact Peter Moellers TEL 49-251-230050. B&W page EUR 880, color page EUR 1,325. Circ: 11,820 (paid and controlled).

796.812 ITA ISSN 1826-0195
TUTTO WRESTLING MAGAZINE. Text in Italian. 2005. m. **Document type:** *Magazine, Consumer.*
Published by: Conti Editore SpA, Via del Lavoro 7, San Lazzaro di Savena, BO 40068, Italy. http://www.contieditore.it.

790 ITA ISSN 0041-4441
TUTTOSPORT. Text in Italian. 1945. d. EUR 232 (effective 2009). adv. bk.rev. **Document type:** *Newspaper, Consumer.*
Published by: Societa Editrice Sportiva, Corso Svizzera 185, Turin, TO 10149, Italy.

790.1 USA
TWIN CITIES SPORTS. Text in English. 1998. m. free newsstand/cover (effective 2005). adv. **Document type:** *Magazine, Consumer.* **Description:** Promotes participation in grass-roots, amateur sports with emphasis on running, cycling, in-line skating, triathlon, volleyball, hiking, paddling, adventure travel, fitness, skiing, swimming, snowboarding & snowshoeing.
Published by: Windy City Publishing Inc., 1450 W Randolph, Chicago, IL 60607. TEL 312-421-1551, FAX 312-421-1454. Ed. Jeff Banowetz. Pubs. Doug Kaplan, Mary Thorne. adv.: color page USD 2,600; 2.25 x 11. Circ: 40,000 (controlled).

790.1 SWE ISSN 1404-594X
TYNGLYFTAREN. Variant title: Tidskriften Kraftsport. Text in Swedish. 1944. 6/yr. SEK 300, EUR 49, USD 57 (effective 2004). adv.
Former titles (until 2000): Nya Kraftsport (0345-8377); (until 1962): Kraftsport; (until vol.3, 1956): Atletik
Published by: Svenska Tyngdlyftningsfoerbundet/Swedish Weightlifting Federation, PO box 15023, Oerebro, 70015, Sweden. TEL 46-19-175580, FAX 46-19-175572, office@tyngdlyfting.org, http://iof3.idrottonline.se/SvenskaTyngdlyftningsforbundet. Circ: 4,500. **Co-sponsor:** Nordiska Tyngdlyftningsfoerbundet.

796 USA ISSN 2153-9936
▼ **U F C.** (Ultimate Fighting Championship) Text in English. 2010 (Apr.). bi-m. USD 5.99 per issue (effective 2011). **Document type:** *Magazine, Consumer.* **Description:** Features news and articles from the Ultimate Fighting Championship.
Related titles: Online - full text ed.: free (effective 2011).
Published by: American Media Consulting, PO BOX 19737, Portland, OR 97280. TEL 503-922-1751.

796.41 AUS ISSN 1838-7268
▼ **U F C.** (Ultimate Fighting Championship) Text in English. 2010. 10/yr. AUD 75; AUD 6.95 newsstand/cover (effective 2011). adv. **Document type:** *Magazine, Consumer.* **Description:** Highlights the training, fashion, gear, strategies, travelling, nutrition and entertainment choices of the world's most famous UFC fighters.
Published by: A C P Magazines Ltd. (Subsidiary of: P B L Media Pty Ltd.), 54-58 Park St, Sydney, NSW 2000, Australia. TEL 61-2-92828000, FAX 61-2-91263769, research@acpaction.com.au, http://www.acp.com.au. Ed. Matthew Coyte TEL 61-2-8114 9487. Circ: 30,368.

306.4 USA ISSN 1535-7589
K25
U N L V GAMING RESEARCH & REVIEW JOURNAL. (University of Nevada, Las Vegas) Text in English. 1994. s-a. USD 34 in US & Canada to individuals; USD 54 elsewhere to individuals; USD 96 to institutions (effective 2010). **Document type:** *Journal, Academic/Scholarly.*
Formerly (until 2001): Gaming Research & Review Journal (1531-0930)
Related titles: Online - full text ed.
Indexed: A01, A03, A08, A10, A12, A13, A17, A37, ABIn, ATI, B01, B06, B07, B09, BRD, C10, CA, CABA, CompLI, E12, ESPM, GH, H&TI, H06, I01, ILP, Inspec, LT, P03, P48, P51, P53, P54, PAIS, PQC, PsycInfo, PsycholAb, R12, RRTA, RiskAb, SD, SociolAb, T02, V03, W03, W05, W11.
—BLDSC (4069.175793).
Published by: University of Nevada, Las Vegas, International Gaming Institute, 4505 Maryland Pky, PO Box 456037, Las Vegas, NV 89154. TEL 702-895-2008, FAX 702-895-1135, igi@ccmail.nevada.edu, http://igi.unlv.edu/. Pub. Stuart H Mann.

790.1 052 USA
U S A B A AGENDA. Text in English. 1976. 12/yr. free. bk.rev. 18 p./no.; **Document type:** *Newspaper-distributed.*
Former titles: SportsScoop; U S A B A Newsletter
Related titles: Talking Book ed.
Published by: United States Association for Blind Athletes, 33 N Institute, Colorado Springs, CO 80903. TEL 719-630-0422, FAX 719-630-0616. Ed. Mark Lucas. Circ: 4,500.

796 USA
U S A BOXING NEWS. Text in English. m. USD 24 domestic; CAD 30 in Canada; USD 40 elsewhere (effective 2002). stat. back issues avail. **Document type:** *Newspaper, Consumer.*
Address: 1358 Hooper Ave, 273, Toms River, NJ 08753. TEL 732-929-2744, 732-929-2620.

796.72 USA ISSN 0744-4702
U S A C NEWS. Text in English. 1956. fortn. membership. illus.; stat. **Document type:** *Newsletter.* **Description:** Covers auto racing.
Published by: United States Auto Club, 4910 W 16th St, Indianapolis, IN 46224. TEL 317-247-5151. Ed. Dick Jordan. Circ: 7,500.

U S A DEAF SPORTS FEDERATION BULLETIN. *see* HANDICAPPED—Hearing Impaired

796.41 USA ISSN 0748-6006
GV461
U S A GYMNASTICS. Text in English. 1960. 6/yr. USD 25 domestic membership; USD 40 in Canada membership; USD 55 elsewhere membership; USD 3.95 newsstand/cover (effective 2005). adv. back issues avail. **Document type:** *Magazine, Trade.* **Description:** Covers national and international gymnastics leading to and including the Olympics. Covers men's, women's rhythmic gymnastics, and trampoline and tumbling.
Related titles: Online - full text ed.
Indexed: PEI, SD, T02.
Address: Pan American Plaza, 201 S Capitol Ave, Ste 300, Indianapolis, IN 46225. TEL 317-237-5050, FAX 317-237-5069, TELEX 272385-USGYM-IND. Ed., R&P, Adv. contact Luan Peszek TEL 317-237-5050 ext 246. Pub. Bob Colarossi. B&W page USD 1,831, color page USD 2,488; trim 8.38 x 10.88. Circ: 83,000.

796.962 USA
GV847.5
U S A HOCKEY ANNUAL GUIDE. Text in English. 19??. a. free to qualified personnel (effective 2009). **Document type:** *Directory, Trade.* **Description:** Covers organization's administrative structure, programs and philosophy, bylaws, rules and regulations and much more.
Former titles: U S A Hockey; Amateur Hockey Association of the United States. Official Guide (0516-8635)
Related titles: Online - full text ed.: free (effective 2009).
Published by: U S A Hockey, 1775 Bob Johnson Dr, Colorado Springs, CO 80906. TEL 719-576-8724, FAX 719-538-1160, usah@usahockey.org.

796.962 USA ISSN 1551-6741
U S A HOCKEY MAGAZINE. Text in English. 1973. 10/yr. free to members (effective 2009). adv. illus. back issues avail.; reprints avail. **Document type:** *Magazine, Consumer.* **Description:** Covers rules, profiles, referees and rink management in amateur ice and inline hockey.
Former titles (until 200?): American Hockey Magazine (8756-3789); (until 198?): American Hockey and Arena; United States Hockey and Arena Biz (0162-654X); Hockey and Arena Biz; U S Hockey Biz
Indexed: SD, SportS.
Published by: U S A Hockey, 1775 Bob Johnson Dr, Colorado Springs, CO 80906. TEL 719-576-8724, FAX 719-538-1160, usah@usahockey.org, http://www.usahockey.com. Ed. Harry Thompson. Adv. contact David Jensen. Circ: 410,594 (paid and controlled). **Co-publisher:** Touchpoint Sports Inc.

796.962 USA
U S A HOCKEY. PLAYING RULES HANDBOOK. Text in English. 19??. biennial.
Former titles: U S A Hockey. Rule Book; Amateur Hockey Association of the United States. Rule Book
Published by: U S A Hockey, 1775 Bob Johnson Dr, Colorado Springs, CO 80906. TEL 719-576-8724, FAX 719-538-1160, usah@usahockey.org, http://www.usahockey.com.

796.355 796.962 USA
U S A JUNIOR HOCKEY MAGAZINE. Text in English. 1999 (Fall). 20/yr. USD 49.95 domestic; USD 69.95 in Canada (effective 2006). adv. **Document type:** *Magazine, Consumer.* **Description:** Promotes the growth of junior hockey in the United States.
Published by: Hockey Media Group LLP, 145 Temple St, Duxbury, MA 02332. TEL 781-934-5888, FAX 781-934-5878. Ed. Brian McDonough. Pub. Rich De Lisle. adv.: B&W page USD 2,029; trim 10 x 12.

796.21 USA ISSN 1532-8929
U S A ROLLER SPORTS. Text in English. 1991. m. (except Aug.). USD 12 per issue domestic; USD 18 per issue foreign (effective 2001). adv. **Description:** Contains news on American competitive roller skating. Covers events, training tips, sports medicine and clinics.
Formerly (until 2000): U S Roller Skating (1044-0801)
Indexed: SD, SportS.
Address: 4730 South St, Lincoln, NE 68506. TEL 402-483-7551, FAX 402-483-1465. Ed. Bill Wolf. R&P Jeanette Tupe. adv.: B&W page USD 480, color page USD 780; trim 7.25 x 9.75. Circ: 65,000.

796 NLD ISSN 2211-4076
▼ **U S A SPORTS.** Text in Dutch. 2010. bi-m. EUR 37.50; EUR 6.95 newsstand/cover (effective 2011). adv. **Document type:** *Magazine, Consumer.*
Published by: De Bruijn Media Productions B.V., Postbus 97843, 's-Gravenhage, 2509 GE, Netherlands. TEL 31-70-4453817, FAX 31-70-4450778, info@debruijnmedia.nl, http://www.debruijnmedia.nl. Ed. Perry Hendriks.

799.202 USA
U S AIRGUN. Text in English. bi-m. USD 25; USD 45 foreign (effective 1999). **Document type:** *Magazine, Consumer.* **Description:** Dedicated to keeping the airgun enthusiast informed and entertained with articles featuring the latest air rifles and pistols to hunting stories and custom airguns.
Published by: U S Airgun Magazine, PO Box 2021, Benton, AR 72018. TEL 501-316-1777, 800-247-4867, FAX 501-316-8549.

S

799.3 USA ISSN 0738-9949
GV1187
THE U S ARCHER. Text in English. 1982. bi-m. USD 20 domestic; USD 35 foreign (effective 2001). adv. 64 p./no. 3 cols./p.; **Document type:** *Magazine, Consumer.* **Description:** Covers the sport of archery in the U.S. and the world. Provides tournament dates.
Incorporates (in 1993): N A A Newletter
Published by: U S Archer, Inc., 7315 N San Anna Dr, Tucson, AZ 85704. TEL 520-742-5846, FAX 520-742-0027. Ed., Pub., R&P Arlyne Rhode TEL 520-742-1235. Adv. contact R Arlyne Rhode. Circ: 9,000.

790.1 USA
CODEN: DYSLEO
U S F A NATIONAL NEWSLETTER (EMAIL). Text in English. 1993. q. free to members (effective 2007). 8 p./no.; **Document type:** *Newsletter, Trade.* **Description:** Presents association news and events.
Formerly: U S F A National Newsletter (Print) (1074-9314)
Media: E-mail.
Indexed: SD.
Published by: United States Fencing Association, Inc., One Olympic Plaza, Colorado Springs, CO 80909. TEL 719-866-4511, FAX 719-632-5737, info@usfencing.org, http://www.usfencing.org. R&P Chris Cuddy TEL 719-866-3606. Circ: 12,000 (paid).

796.86 USA
U S F A RULE BOOK: U S & INTERNATIONAL RULES. Text in English. irreg. USD 15 per issue (effective 2003). Supplement avail.
Formerly: Fencing Rules for Competitions
Published by: United States Fencing Association, Inc., One Olympic Plaza, Colorado Springs, CO 80909. TEL 719-866-4511, FAX 719-632-5737, info@usfencing.org, http://www.usfencing.org.

799.202 USA ISSN 0746-6625
THE U S HANDGUNNER. Text in English. bi-m. membership. adv. back issues avail. **Document type:** *Magazine, Consumer.* **Description:** Contains information on pistol target shooting and pistol matches.
Formerly (until 195?): U S Revolver Association. Bulletin
Published by: U S Revolver Association, RR#1, Box 548, Scotrun, PA 18355. usra1900@verizon.net, http://www.usra1.org/index.html. Circ: 1,500 (paid).

796.060489 DNK ISSN 1604-0988
UDSPIL; D G I Magasinet. Text in Danish. 2004. 11/yr. adv. bk.rev. back issues avail. **Document type:** *Magazine, Consumer.*
Formed by the merger of (1993-2004): Instruktoermagasinet Krumspring (0908-5580); (1997-2004): Ungdom og Idraet (1397-7970); Which was formerly (until 1997): Dansk Ungdom og Idraet (0908-1011); Which was formed by the merger of (1939-1992): Dansk Idraet (0109-5536); Which incorporated (in 1987): Gymnastik Nyt (0904-2342); (1989-1992): Ungdom og Idraet (0905-2518); Which was formerly (1965-1988): Dansk Ungdom og Idraet (0045-9631)
Related titles: Online - full text ed.
Published by: Danske Gymnastik- og Idraetsforeninger/Danish Gymnastics and Sports Organizations, Vingsted Skovvej 1, PO Box 569, Vejle, 7100, Denmark. TEL 45-79-404040, FAX 45-79-404084, info@dgi.dk. Ed. Kim Vejrup. adv.: color page DKK 18,100; 210 x 297. Circ: 60,000.

UE; Magazin fuer Uebungsleiterinnen und Uebungsleiter. *see* EDUCATION—Teaching Methods And Curriculum

790.1 DEU ISSN 0342-8419
DER UEBUNGSLEITER; Arbeitshilfen fuer Uebungsleiter im Deutschen Sportbund. Text in German. 1968. m. looseleaf. back issues avail. **Document type:** *Journal, Academic/Scholarly.* **Description:** Practical help, tips and exercises for trainers.
Related titles: ◆ Supplement to: Sportpraxis. ISSN 0176-5906.
Published by: Limpert Verlag GmbH, Industriepark 3, Wiebelsheim, 56291, Germany. TEL 49-6766-903160, FAX 49-6766-903320. Ed. Friedhelm Kreiss. Circ: 210,000.

796 BRA ISSN 2178-4515
▼ **ULBRA E MOVIMENTO**; revista de educacao fisica. Text in Portuguese. 2010. q. free (effective 2011). **Document type:** *Journal, Academic/Scholarly.*
Media: Online - full text.
Published by: Centro Universitario Luterano de Ji-Parana, Av Eng Manfredo Barata 762, Jardim Aurelio Bernardi, Ji-Parana, RO 76907-438, Brazil.

796.815 USA ISSN 1541-8170
ULTIMATE ATHLETE; the ultimate magazine for the ultimate sport. Text in English. 2001 (Oct.). m. USD 49 domestic; USD 65 in Canada & Mexico; USD 85 elsewhere; USD 5.95 newsstand/cover (effective 2002). adv. **Document type:** *Magazine, Consumer.* **Description:** Provides complete coverage of combat sports, including the martial arts, boxing, kickboxing, wrestling and grappling.
Address: 114 E. Shaw Ave., Ste. 210, Fresno, CA 93710. TEL 559-221-9322, 877-987-9200, http://www.ultimateathlete.tv.

796.8 613.7 USA ISSN 1944-5709
ULTIMATE M M A. (Mixed Martial Arts) Text in English. 1997. m. USD 24.95; USD 5.99 per issue (effective 2011). adv. back issues avail. **Document type:** *Magazine, Consumer.* **Description:** Features comprehensive event coverage of mixed martial arts, interviews with the fighters, ring girl pictorials and more to attract mixed martial arts fans of all ages.
Former titles (until 2009): Ultimate Grappling (1935-7990); (until 2006): Martial Arts Legends Presents (1092-7972); Bruce Lee Jun Fan Jeet Kune Do (1094-1339)
Published by: Beckett Media Llc, 2400 E Katella Ave, Ste 300, Anaheim, CA 92806. TEL 714-939-9991, 800-764-6287, FAX 714-456-0146, customerservice@beckett.com, http://www.beckett.com. Ed. Doug Jeffrey. Adv. contact Gabe Frimmel TEL 800-332-3330 ext 238.

796 GBR ISSN 2041-2940
▼ **ULTIMATE SKATEBOARDER.** Text in English. 2009. w. back issues avail. **Document type:** *Magazine, Consumer.*
Published by: Hachette Partworks Ltd. (Subsidiary of: Hachette Livre), 4th Fl, Jordan House, 47 Brunswick Pl, London, N1 6EB, United Kingdom. http://www.hachettepartworks.co.uk. **Subscr. to:** PO Box 77, Jarrow NE32 3YJ, United Kingdom. TEL 44-871-4724240, FAX 44-871-4724241, hachettepw@jacklinservice.com.

797 USA ISSN 1095-1555
UNDERCURRENT. Text in English. 1975. m. USD 39 in US & Canada; USD 59 in Mexico; USD 74 elsewhere; USD 59 renewals in US & Canada; USD 79 renewals in Mexico; USD 94 renewals elsewhere (effective 2005). adv. reprints avail. **Document type:** *Newsletter, Consumer.* **Description:** For the sport diver featuring resort and equipment reviews, safety tips and ways to have more fun underwater.
Related titles: Online - full text ed.
Published by: Dodd Smith Dann Layher, Inc, 125 E Sir Francis Drake Blvd, Larkspur, CA 94939. TEL 800-326-1896, FAX 415-461-7953. Ed. John Q Trigger. Pub., R&P Ben Davison. Circ: 13,000.

797.23 USA ISSN 1091-6369
UNDERWATER WORLD RESOURCE DIRECTORY; blue pages. Text in English. 1997. a., latest 2000, 2nd ed. USD 19.95 (effective 2002). **Document type:** *Directory, Trade.* **Description:** Offers a comprehensive guide to organizations providing services, products, and information to the scuba diving industry and related underwater sports, activities, and business.
Related titles: CD-ROM ed.
Published by: Yakstis Communications Group, LLC, PO Box 624, St. Louis, MO 63026. TEL 636-349-6088, 888-924-7483, byakstis@att.net, http://www.ycg.com. Ed., Pub. William Yakstis. Circ: 5,000 (paid).

796.83 USA
UNITED STATES AMATEUR BOXING. ANNUAL GUIDE. Abbreviated title: U S A Boxing. Text in English. 1981. a. USD 8. **Description:** Provides a complete history and current information on Olympic-style boxing.
Formerly: U S A Amateur Boxing Federation. Media Guide
Published by: United States Amateur Boxing (U S A Boxing), Inc., One Olympic Plaza, Colorado Springs, CO 80909. TEL 719-578-4506. Ed. Kurt Steneron. Circ: (controlled).

796.83 USA
UNITED STATES AMATEUR BOXING. OFFICIAL RULES. Abbreviated title: U S A Boxing: Official Rules. Text in English. 1981. s-a. USD 15.
Formerly: U S A Amateur Boxing Federation. Official Rules
Published by: United States Amateur Boxing (U S A Boxing), Inc., One Olympic Plaza, Colorado Springs, CO 80909. TEL 719-578-4506. Ed. Kurt Stenerson. Circ: 10,000.

796.42 USA
UNITED STATES CROSS-COUNTRY COACHES ASSOCIATION. ANNUAL BUSINESS MEETING. MINUTES. Text in English. a. free.
Supersedes: United States Cross-Country Coaches Association. Proceedings; Which was formerly: United States Cross-Country and Distance Running Coaches Association. Proceedings (0082-9706)
Published by: United States Cross-Country Coaches Association, c/o Ken O Brien, Sec, Boyden Gym, University of Massachusetts, Amherst, MA 01003. TEL 413-545-2759.

613.7 ROM ISSN 1224-7359
GV341
UNIVERSITATEA "OVIDIUS" CONSTANTA. ANALELE. SERIE EDUCATIE FIZICA SI SPORT. Text in Romanian. 1996. a. **Document type:** *Journal, Academic/Scholarly.*
Related titles: Online - full text ed.: Ovidius University. Annals. Series Physical Education and Sport. free (effective 2011).
Indexed: A26, A36, CABA, E08, GH, I05, LT, N02, N03, SD, T02, T05, W11.
Published by: Tipografia Universitatii Ovidius/Ovidius University Press, B-dul Mamaia, nr 126, Constanta, 900472, Romania. TEL 40-241-551773, FAX 40-241-543045, http://www.univ-ovidius.ro.

796 ROM ISSN 1583-7912
UNIVERSITATEA POLITEHNICA DIN TIMISOARA. BULETINUL STIINTIFIC. SERIA EDUCATIE FIZICA SI SPORT/POLITEHNICA UNIVERSITY OF TIMISOARA. SCIENTIFIC BULLETIN. TRANSACTIONS ON PHYSICAL EDUCATION AND SPORT. Text in English, French, German; Abstracts in English. 1991. a. **Document type:** *Journal, Academic/Scholarly.*
Formerly (until 2002): Universitatea "Politehnica" din Timisoara. Buletinul Stiintific. Seria Stiinte Socio-Umane. Limbi Moderne. Educatie Fizica, Fascicula Educatie Fizica (1454-8852); Which superseded in part (in 1998): Universitatea "Politehnica" din Timisoara. Buletinul Stiintific. Seria Stiinte Socio-Umane. Limbi Moderne. Educatie Fizica (1224-6085); Which was formerly (until 1995): Universitatea Politehnica din Timisoara. Buletinul Stiintific. Seria Stiinte Socio-Umane si Limbi Moderne; (until 1994): Universitatea Tehnice din Timisoara. Buletinul Stiintific si Tehnic. Seria Stiinte Socio-Umane si Limbi Mode; (until 1992): Universitatea Tehnice din Timisoara. Buletinul Stiintific si Tehnic. Seria Stiinte Socio-Umane (1223-1959)
Related titles: Online - full text ed.
Published by: Universitatea Politehnica din Timisoara/"Politehnica" University of Timisoara, Catedra de Educatie Fizica si Sport, Bulevardul Mihai Viteazul nr.2, Timisoara, Romania.

769.41 AUT
UNSER OE T B TURNEN. Text in German. 1954. 11/yr. EUR 17.85 (effective 2005). back issues avail. **Document type:** *Magazine, Consumer.*
Formerly (until 1994): Bundesturnzeitung
Published by: Oesterreichischer Turnerbund, Linzerstr 80a, Postfach 58, Traun, 4050, Austria. TEL 43-7229-65224, FAX 43-7229-652244, gst@oetb.at. Circ: 15,000 (paid).

790.1 DEU
UNSER WANDERBOTE. Text in German. 1972. q. back issues avail. **Document type:** *Consumer.* **Description:** Covers swimming, bicycles and walking.
Published by: Volkssportverein Wanderfreunde Mainz 1971 e.V., Karl-Geib-Haus, Kapellenstr 44, Mainz, 55124, Germany. webmaster@vsv-wanderfreunde-mainz, http://www.vsv-wanderfreunde-mainz.de. Circ: 1,200.

797.23 DEU ISSN 0947-9155
UNTERWASSER; das Tauchmagazin. Text in German. 1995. m. EUR 54; EUR 4.90 newsstand/cover (effective 2007). adv. **Document type:** *Magazine, Consumer.*
Published by: Olympia Verlag GmbH, Badstr 4-6, Nuernberg, 90402, Germany. TEL 49-911-2160, FAX 49-911-2162741, anzeigen@olympia-verlag.de. Adv. contact Werner Wiedemann. B&W page EUR 2,568, color page EUR 4,236; trim 215 x 280. Circ: 38,281 (paid and controlled).

797.23 DEU
UNTERWASSERWELT; das Tauchmagazin exklusiv im Internet. Text in German. 1999. m. adv. **Document type:** *Magazine, Consumer.* **Description:** Provides a resource forum for all matters related to sport diving.
Media: Online - full text.
Address: Muehlenweg 16a, Tulling, 85643, Germany. TEL 49-8094-1229, FAX 49-8094-8376, redaktion@unterwasserwelt.de, http://www.unterwasserwelt.de. Ed., Pub., R&P Michael Goldschmidt. Adv. contact Ulrike Goldschmidt.

UPDATE (RESTON). *see* PHYSICAL FITNESS AND HYGIENE

796 FIN ISSN 0355-6085
URHEILULEHTI. Text in Finnish. 1898. 51/w. EUR 127.80 domestic; EUR 135 in Europe; EUR 147 elsewhere (effective 2005). adv. **Document type:** *Consumer.*
Published by: A-Lehdet Oy, Risto Rytin tie 33, Helsinki, 00081, Finland. TEL 358-9-75961, FAX 358-9-7598600, a-tilaus@a-lehdet.fi. Ed. Jukka Roenkae. Adv. contact Matti Sahravuo TEL 358-9-7596385. color page EUR 2,500; 204 x 276. Circ: 23,309.

796.72 796.77 AUS ISSN 1444-4003
V 8 BATHURST MAGAZINE. Text in English. 1982. a. AUD 12.70 per issue (effective 2008). adv. **Document type:** *Magazine, Consumer.* **Description:** Features interviews, stories on the legends of the mountain, information of the historic races, and review of the V8 supercar series.
Former titles (until 1998): Great Race (1031-6124); (until 1988): James Hardie 1000 (0811-546X)
Published by: Chevron Publishing Group Pty. Ltd., PO Box 1421, Lane Cove, NSW 1595, Australia. TEL 61-2-94189225, FAX 61-2-94189641, sales@chevron.com.au.

V A H P E R D JOURNAL. *see* PHYSICAL FITNESS AND HYGIENE

799.202 DEU
V D B ZEITUNG; alles fuer die schoenere Freizeit. Text in German. 1982. q. **Document type:** *Newspaper, Consumer.*
Formerly (until 1996): V D B Aktuell (0177-1302)
Published by: Verband Deutscher Buechsenmacher und Waffenfachhaendler, Wilhelmstr 16, Marburg, 35037, Germany. TEL 49-6421-161353, FAX 49-6421-22312, info@vdb-waffen.de, http://www.vdb-waffen.de. Circ: 200,000 (paid).

790.1 793 FRA ISSN 0242-312X
VAE VICTIS; le magazine du jeu d'histoire. Text in French. 1974. bi-m. EUR 31 domestic; EUR 37.20 elsewhere (effective 2009). **Document type:** *Magazine, Consumer.*
Published by: Histoire et Collection, 5 Av. de la Republique, Paris, 75011, France. TEL 33-1-40211820, FAX 33-1-47005111, fredbey@club-internet.fr, http://www.histoireetcollections.com. Ed. Frederic Bey. Circ: 15,000.

793.93 795.4 GBR ISSN 1355-2767
VALKYRIE. Text in English. 1994. m. GBP 3 newsstand/cover. illus. reprints avail. **Document type:** *Magazine, Consumer.* **Description:** Contains articles on fantasy gaming and stories, role playing and card games.
Published by: Partizan Press, 816-818 London Rd, Leigh-on-sea, Southend, Essex SS9 3NH, United Kingdom. TEL 44-1702-73986, FAX 44-1702-73986. Ed. Dave Renton. Pubs. Dave Ryan, Hawk Norton. Circ: 12,000. **Dist. by:** Comag, Tavistock Rd, W Drayton, Middlesex UB7 7QE, United Kingdom. TEL 44-1895-433600, FAX 44-189-543-3606.

THE VANGUARD (MOBILE). *see* COLLEGE AND ALUMNI

794 DEU ISSN 0939-3021
VERA'S GLUECKS RATGEBER; Ihr aktueller Gewinnspielservice. Text in German. 1989. m. EUR 9.80 per issue (effective 2009). **Document type:** *Magazine, Consumer.*
Published by: F I D Verlag GmbH, Koblenzer Str 99, Bonn, 53177, Germany. TEL 49-228-9550333, FAX 49-228-82055756, info@fid-verlag.de, http://www.fid-verlag.de.

796 NLD ISSN 1871-9929
VERENIGINGSMONITOR. Text in Dutch. 2000. a. **Document type:** *Report, Trade.*
Published by: W. J. H. Mulier Instituut, Postbus 188, 's-Hertogenbosch, 5201 AD, Netherlands. TEL 31-73-6126401, FAX 31-73-6126413, info@mulierinstituut.nl. **Co-sponsor:** Ministerie van Volksgezondheid, Welzijn en Sport.

796 USA
VERMONT SPORTS TODAY. Text in English. 1990. m. USD 15 domestic; USD 18 in Canada (effective 2001). adv. **Document type:** *Newspaper.* **Description:** Focuses on "aerobic, lifelong" sports in Vermont and northern New England. Also includes a calendar of activities, interviews, product reviews and information on sports medicine.
Address: PO Box 496, Waterbury, VT 05676-0496. TEL 802-244-5796. Ed. Kathryn Carter. Circ: 10,000.

VI BILAEGARE; sveriges stoerste bil- och fritidstidning. *see* TRANSPORTATION—Automobiles

790.1 AUS
VICTORIAN BOWLS IN FOCUS. Text in English. 1984. m. back issues avail. **Document type:** *Magazine, Consumer.*
Former titles (until 2004): Bowls in Victoria (1324-7549); (until 1984): Bowls; Which was incorporated (1954-1984): Bowls News and Views
Related titles: Online - full text ed.
Indexed: SD.
Published by: Victorian Ladies Bowling Association Inc., PO Box 6080, Hawthorn West, VIC 3122, Australia. TEL 61-3-98180711, FAX 61-3-98182992, vlba@bowlsvic.org.au. Adv. contact Bill Johnson.

796.72 USA ISSN 1052-8067
VINTAGE MOTORSPORT; the journal of motor racing history. Text in English. 1982. bi-m. USD 45 domestic; USD 55 in Canada & Mexico; USD 80 in South America; USD 75 includes Europe & Africa; USD 70 includes Bahamas & Beruda; USD 95 elsewhere (effective 2010). adv. **Document type:** *Magazine, Consumer.* **Description:** Provides information about motorsport racing.
Published by: Vintage Motorsport Inc., PO Box 7200, Lakeland, FL 33807. TEL 800-626-9937. Ed. Randy Riggs. Adv. contact Tammie Boyette.

VIRGINIA GAME, INLAND FISH AND BOAT LAWS. *see* CONSERVATION

VIRGINIA SPORTS AND ENTERTAINMENT LAW JOURNAL. *see* LAW

790.1 658 BEL ISSN 0770-9420
VLAAMS TIJDSCHRIFT VOOR SPORTBEHEER. Text in Dutch. 1974. bi-m. EUR 30 domestic; EUR 45 foreign; EUR 15 to students (effective 2005). adv. bk.rev. illus. **Document type:** *Magazine, Trade.*
Published by: (Ministerie van Nederlandse Cultuur NLD), Vlaams Tijdschrift voor Sportbeheer, Plezantstraat 266, St-Niklaas, 9100, Belgium. TEL 32-3-777-3280, FAX 32-3-766-2501, info@buurtsport.be. Ed., R&P, Adv. contact Edwin Aerts. Pub. Dany Punie.

796.3 BEL
VLAAMSE BEDRIJFSSPORT. Text in Dutch. 1977. q. EUR 4; EUR 1 per issue (effective 2005). bk.rev. illus. 20 p./no.; back issues avail. **Document type:** *Magazine, Consumer.* **Description:** Covers corporate sporting events and activities in Belgium and Europe.
Published by: Vlaamse Liga van Bedrijfssportbonden, Joseph Depauwstraat 55 A-10, St-Pieters-Leeuw, 1600, Belgium. vlb@belgacom.net, sunny.side.up@pandora.be, http://www.vlaamse-bedrijfssport.be. Ed., Pub., R&P Guy de Grauwe. Adv. contact Elke Debaets. Circ: 5,000. **Subscr. to:** Boomgaardstraat 22-15, Berchem 2600, Belgium. TEL 32-2-286-0736, FAX 32-2-286-0742. **Subscr. to:** Geers Offset, Eekhoutdriesstraat 67, Oostakker 9041, Belgium. TEL 32-9-251-0575, FAX 32-9-251-6240.

796.099305 NZL ISSN 1176-8134
VO2 MAX. Text in English. 2005. bi-m. NZD 50 domestic; NZD 80 in Australia; NZD 100 elsewhere (effective 2008). **Document type:** *Magazine, Consumer.*
Published by: O2 Publishing Group Ltd., PO Box 55 200, Mission Bay, Auckland, New Zealand. TEL 64-9-5245947, FAX 64-9-5245987.

797.21 629.5 RUS ISSN 1681-4738
VODOLAZNOE DELO; zhurnal dlya professionalov vodolaznogo dela. Text in Russian. 2001. q. RUR 720 domestic; RUR 1,020 foreign (effective 2002). back issues avail. **Document type:** *Magazine, Trade.*
Related titles: Online - full content ed.: ISSN 1681-4746; English ed.: Commercial Diving. ISSN 1681-4754.
Published by: Rusmarin, A-ya, Moscow, 109544, Russian Federation. TEL 7-095-7970483, FAX 7-095-2746219, rusmarin@dol.ru. Ed. Vadim Sementsov.

790.1 FRA ISSN 0752-2525
LA VOIX DES SPORTS. Text in French. 1947. w. 64 p./no. 5 cols./p.; **Document type:** *Newspaper.*
Published by: La Voix du Nord, 8 Place du General de Gaulle, BP 549, Lille, Cedex 59023, France. TEL 33-3-20784040, FAX 33-3-20784244, TELEX 120 687 F, http://www.lavoixdunord.fr. Ed. J L Prevost. Adv. contact Michel Marin. Circ: 80,000.

VOLLEYBALL RULES BOOK. *see* SPORTS AND GAMES—Ball Games

W A D. (We'ar Different) *see* CHILDREN AND YOUTH—For

795.412 USA ISSN 1749-8473
W P T POKER. (World Poker Tour) Text in English. 2006. 13/yr. USD 29.95 domestic; USD 44.95 in Canada (effective 2010). adv. **Document type:** *Magazine, Consumer.*
—CCC.
Published by: W P T Enterprises, Inc, 5700 Wilshire Blvd, Ste 350, Los Angeles, CA 90036. TEL 323-330-9900, FAX 323-330-9901, http://www.worldpokertour.com.

795.38 GBR ISSN 2040-3224
▼ **W P T POKER (NORTH AMERICAN EDITION).** (World Poker Tour) Text in English. 2009. m. **Document type:** *Magazine, Consumer.*
Published by: Players Publishing Ltd., 7 Chapel Pl, Rivington St, London, EC2A 3DQ, United Kingdom. TEL 44-20-77396999, FAX 44-20-77399918, info@playerspublishing.co.uk.

W W E KIDS MAGAZINE. *see* CHILDREN AND YOUTH—For

790.1 USA ISSN 1933-4524
W W MAGAZINE. Text in English. 2006. m. USD 19.97 domestic; USD 24.97 in Canada; USD 39.97 elsewhere (effective 2007). **Document type:** *Magazine, Consumer.*
Formed by the merger of (2002-2006): W W E Raw (1540-2827); Which was formerly (1996-2002): W W F Raw (1087-0164); (2003-2006): SmackDown! Magazine (1547-5379); Which was formerly (2002-2003): W W E (1540-2819); (198?-2002): W W F Magazine (8756-7792); (1984-198?): Official World Wrestling Federation Magazine (0747-4016); (1983-1984): World Wrestling Federation's Victory (0741-2169)
Published by: World Wrestling Entertainment, Inc., 1241 E Main St, Stamford, CT 06902. TEL 203-352-8600, FAX 203-352-8699, smackdownmag@wwe.com, http://www.wwe.com/.

799.202 DEU ISSN 0177-1221
WAFFENMARKT INTERN; Branchen-Information fuer Buechsenmacher, Waffenhaendler und deren Lieferanten. Text in German. 1979. 13/yr. EUR 50 domestic; EUR 55 in Europe; EUR 65 elsewhere (effective 2011). adv. bk.rev. back issues avail. **Document type:** *Magazine, Trade.* **Description:** Trade publication for gunsmiths, gundealers and suppliers.
Published by: Verlag Karlfranz Perey, Theodor-Heuss-Ring 62, Cologne, 50668, Germany. TEL 49-221-2005412, FAX 49-221-2005423. Ed., Pub. Maggy Spindler. adv.: B&W page EUR 2,000, color page EUR 2,600; trim 184 x 260. Circ: 1,200 (paid).

793.7 DEU
WAHRE GESCHICHTEN RAETSEL. Text in German. bi-m. EUR 1.65 newsstand/cover (effective 2005). **Document type:** *Magazine, Consumer.*
Published by: Pabel-Moewig Verlag KG (Subsidiary of: Bauer Media Group), Karlsruherstr 31, Rastatt, 76437, Germany. TEL 49-7222-130, FAX 49-7222-13218, empfang@vpm.de, http://www.vpm-online.de.

797.21 CAN ISSN 1488-2132
WAKEBOARD CANADA. Text in English. 1999. 2/yr. CAD 9 domestic; USD 12 in United States; USD 40 elsewhere; USD 3.50 newsstand/cover (effective 2001). adv. **Document type:** *Magazine, Consumer.* **Description:** Presents equipment reviews, schedules of events, professional profiles, and advice on improving wakeboarding skills.
Published by: S B C Media, 2255 B Queen St E, Ste 3266, Toronto, ON M4E 1G3, Canada. TEL 416-698-0138, FAX 416-698-8080, info@sbcmedia.com, http://www.sbcmedia.com.

797.21 USA ISSN 1079-0136
WAKEBOARDING. Key Title: Wake Boarding. Text in English. 1993. 9/yr. USD 9.97 domestic; USD 18.97 in Canada; USD 27.97 elsewhere; USD 4.99 per issue (effective 2009). adv. illus. back issues avail.; reprints avail. **Document type:** *Magazine, Consumer.* **Description:** Explores the wake-riding lifestyle by offering a broad range of content that helps wake enthusiasts become better riders.
Related titles: Online - full text ed.
Indexed: G08, I05.
—CCC.
Published by: World Publications LLC (Subsidiary of: Bonnier Magazine Group), 460 N Orlando Ave, Ste 200, Winter Park, FL 32789. TEL 407-628-4802, FAX 407-628-7061, info@worldpub.net, http://www.bonniercorp.com. Eds. Kevin Michael TEL 407-571-4862, Luke Woodling TEL 407-571-4524. Adv. contact Laurel Norman TEL 407-571-4962. B&W page USD 6,270, color page USD 9,405; trim 8.125 x 10.75. Circ: 45,823 (paid).

790.1 USA
WARGAMERS INFORMATION. Text in English. 1975. s-a. USD 3 for 12 issues (effective 2003). **Document type:** *Newsletter, Consumer.*
Published by: Flying Buffalo Inc., PO Box 1467, Scottsdale, AZ 85252. TEL 480-945-6917, FAX 480-994-1170, http://www.flyingbuffalo.com. Ed. Rick Loomis. Circ: 500.

793 GBR ISSN 0957-6444
WARGAMES ILLUSTRATED. Text in English. 1987. m. GBP 32 domestic; GBP 34 foreign; GBP 2.75 newsstand/cover. adv. illus. back issues avail. **Document type:** *Magazine, Consumer.*
Published by: Stratagem Publications Ltd., 18 Lovers Ln, Newark, Notts NG24 1HZ, United Kingdom. Ed. Duncan Macfarlane. **Dist. by:** Comag, Tavistock Rd, W Drayton, Middlesex UB7 7QE, United Kingdom. TEL 44-1895-444055, FAX 44-1895-433602; **Dist. in US by:** Wargames, Rte 40 East, PO Box 278, Triadelphia, WV 26059-0278; Essex Minature Ltd., 18 Lovers Ln., 22 Sydney Rd, Hornsby Heights, NSW 2077, Australia.

795 794.8 355 NLD ISSN 2211-503X
▼ **WARGAMES, SOLDIERS & STRATEGY.** Text in English. 2010. bi-m. EUR 33.50 (effective 2011). adv. **Document type:** *Magazine, Consumer.*
Related titles: Online - full text ed.: ISSN 2211-5064. EUR 17.50 (effective 2011).
Published by: Karwansaray BV, Waterstraat 5, Zutphen, 7201 HM, Netherlands. TEL 31-575-776076, http://www.karwansaraypublishers.com.

WARRINGTON PAPERS IN LEISURE AND SPORT RESEARCH. *see* LEISURE AND RECREATION

790.1 LBN
WATAN AL RIYADI. Text in Arabic. 1979. m. adv.
Address: P O Box 615, Beirut, Lebanon. Ed. Antoine Chouery. Circ: 150,000.

797.25 NLD ISSN 2211-6303
WATERPOLO.NL. Text in Dutch. 1998. 8/yr. EUR 35 domestic; EUR 55 in Belgium (effective 2011). adv. **Document type:** *Magazine, Consumer.*
Formerly (until 2011): ManMeer! (1569-7215)
Address: Postbus 8298, Ede, 6710 AG, Netherlands. TEL 31-318-754148, FAX 31-318-754112, info@waterpolo.nl, http://www.waterpolo.nl.

793 GBR ISSN 2040-1779
▼ **WE LOVE DARTS.COM.** Variant title: We Love Darts. Text in English. 2009. m. GBP 35 domestic; GBP 61.90 in Europe; GBP 80.90 elsewhere (effective 2010). adv. back issues avail. **Document type:** *Magazine, Trade.* **Description:** Features all the news and reviews on the sport, and interviews with figures from the darts world.
Published by: We Love Darts, Ltd., 130 Aztec, Aztec W, Bristol, BS32 4UB, United Kingdom. TEL 44-844-8484501.

WEB BOUND SPECIAL EDITION: TOP 12,000 SPORTS WEBSITES. *see* COMPUTERS—Internet

WEEKLY PIA. *see* LEISURE AND RECREATION

799.2 AUT ISSN 1560-9162
WEIDWERK. Text in German. 1928. m. EUR 54 domestic; EUR 68 foreign; EUR 5 newsstand/cover (effective 2005). adv. bk.rev. **Document type:** *Magazine, Consumer.* **Description:** Covers hunting, fishing, environment and nature conservation. Includes news from Austrian hunting associations.
Related titles: Online - full text ed.: ISSN 1605-1335.
Indexed: KWIWR, W08.
Published by: Oesterreichischer Jagd- und Fischereiverlag der J F B GmbH, Wickenburggasse 3, Vienna, W 1080, Austria. TEL 43-1-40516360, FAX 43-1-405163636. Ed. Hans Friedemann Zedka. adv.: B&W page EUR 2,900, color page EUR 3,770; trim 185 x 248. Circ: 48,000 (paid and controlled).

WEIGHTLIFTING U S A. *see* PHYSICAL FITNESS AND HYGIENE

794.2 CHN ISSN 1002-8706
WEIQI TIANDI/WEIQI WORLD. Text in Chinese. 1985. s-m. USD 124.80 (effective 2009). **Document type:** *Magazine, Consumer.* **Description:** Covers the Chinese board game of weiqi.
Related titles: Online - full content ed.
—East View.
Published by: Zhongguo Tiyubao Yezongshe, 8, Tiyuguan Lu, Chongwen-qu, Beijing, 100061, China. TEL 86-10-67092233.

790.1 GBR ISSN 0265-8712
WHITE DWARF. Text in English. 1977. m. GBP 40 (effective 2010). back issues avail. **Document type:** *Magazine, Consumer.* **Description:** Concerns the games workshops hobby.
Published by: Games Workshop Ltd. (Subsidiary of: Black Library), Willow Rd, Lenton, Notts NG7 2WS, United Kingdom. TEL 44-115-9140000, FAX 44-115-9004890, orders@games-workshop.co.uk.

796.332 ITA ISSN 1127-4689
WIN. Text in Italian. 1998. s-a. **Document type:** *Magazine, Consumer.*
Published by: Editoriale Sport Italia, Via Masaccio 12, Milan, MI 20149, Italy. TEL 39-02-4815396, FAX 39-02-4690907, http://www.sportivi.it.

WINCHESTER COLLECTOR. *see* HOBBIES

790.1 USA
WINDY CITY SPORTS. Text in English. 1987. m. free newsstand/cover. adv. bk.rev. charts; illus.; maps. 80 p./no.; back issues avail. **Document type:** *Magazine, Consumer.* **Description:** Promotes participation in grass-root amateur athletics in Chicago and the Midwest.
Indexed: SD.
Published by: Windy City Publishing Inc., 1450 W Randolph, Chicago, IL 60607. TEL 312-421-1551, FAX 312-421-1454, info@windycitysportsmag.com, http://www.windycitysportsmag.com. Ed., R&P Jeff Banowetz. Pubs. Doug Kaplan, Mary Thorne. Adv. contact Doug Kaplan. B&W page USD 6,750, color page USD 7,900; 9 x 11. Circ: 100,000 (controlled).

THE WINGED FOOT; the magazine of the New York atheletic club. *see* PHYSICAL FITNESS AND HYGIENE

793 USA
WINNING WAYS. Text in English. 1996. w. free. adv. **Document type:** *Newsletter, Consumer.* **Description:** Contains articles, hints and tips, and worksheets on how to enter and win sweepstakes prizes.
Media: E-mail.
Address: 77 Cambridge St., Lawrence, MA 01843. FAX 425-871-9785. Ed. Susan Donahue Erler.

790.1 DEU ISSN 1611-3640
WIR IM SPORT. Text in German. 1948. 10/yr. EUR 1.50 newsstand/cover (effective 2007). adv. **Document type:** *Magazine, Consumer.*
Published by: LandesSportBund Nordrhein-Westfalen e.V., Friedrich-Alfred-Str. 25, Duisburg, 47055, Germany. TEL 49-203-7381826, FAX 49-203-7381615, info@lsb-nrw.de, http://www.lsb-nrw.de. adv.: B&W page EUR 2,625, color page EUR 4,645. Circ: 60,000 (paid and controlled).

790.1 USA ISSN 0273-8945
WOLFPACKER; an independant magazine covering NC state sports. Text in English. 1980. bi-m. USD 39.95 (effective 2011). back issues avail. **Document type:** *Magazine, Trade.* **Description:** For N C State University sports fans.
Related titles: Online - full text ed.
Published by: Coman Publishing Company, Inc.

790.1 USA ISSN 1048-9940
WOLVERINE. Text in English. 1989. m. USD 49.95 combined subscription (print & online eds.); USD 6 per issue (effective 2011). back issues avail. **Document type:** *Magazine, Trade.* **Description:** For University of Michigan sports fans.
Related titles: Online - full text ed.: USD 39.95 (effective 2011).
Published by: Coman Publishing Company, Inc.

795.412 CAN
WOMAN POKER PLAYER. Text in English. 2005. bi-m. USD 13.95 (effective 2005). adv. **Document type:** *Magazine, Consumer.* **Description:** address the art, science and mathematics of playing poker and, include the history of poker, profiles of popular professional and celebrity players, improving skills, and lifestyle items such as fashion and wellness as they relate to poker.
Address: 915 Chestnut St., New Westminster, BC V3L 4N4, Canada. TEL 604-628-2358, FAX 516-977-9409. Ed. Barbara Enright. adv.: page USD 1,500; bleed 8.375 x 11.125.

799.3 USA ISSN 1045-7704
GV1151
WOMEN & GUNS MAGAZINE. Abbreviated title: W & G. Text in English. 1989. bi-m. USD 18 domestic; USD 38 foreign; USD 4 newsstand/cover (effective 2010). adv. bk.rev. illus. 64 p./no. 3 cols./p.; reprints avail. **Document type:** *Magazine, Consumer.* **Description:** Provides female gun owners who want to learn more about pleasure shooting and self-defense with information on legislative issues, competition shooting and differences between types of guns.
Published by: Second Amendment Foundation, 12500 N E 10th Pl, Bellevue, WA 98005. TEL 425-454-7012, FAX 425-451-3959, WAGUNS@aol.com, http://www.saf.org. Pub. Julienne Versnel Gottlieb. Adv. contact Susan Snow. **Subscr. to:** PO Box 35, Buffalo, NY 14205.

WOMEN IN SPORT AND PHYSICAL ACTIVITY JOURNAL (ONLINE). *see* WOMEN'S STUDIES—Abstracting, Bibliographies, Statistics

613.711 USA
WOMEN'S RUNNING. Text in English. 2004. 10/yr. USD 19.95 domestic; USD 29.95 in Canada; USD 59.95 elsewhere (effective 2010). adv. 84 p./no.; **Document type:** *Magazine, Consumer.* **Description:** Covers women's sports and active lifestyles, including the latest trends in the women's active sports market, reviews the newest gear, highlights active vacations, and uncovers the latest research in sports and daily nutrition.
Former titles (until 2009): Her Sports + Fitness; (until 20??): Her Sports (1548-2413)
Published by: Wet Dog Media, Inc., 1499 Beach Dr S E, Suite B, St. Petersburg, FL 33701. TEL 727 502-9202, FAX 727 824-0859, http://www.wetdogadvertising.com/. Ed. Breanne George. Pub. Dawna Stone.

790.1 USA ISSN 1061-1568
WOMEN'S SPORTS EXPERIENCE. Text in English. 1985. bi-m. USD 30 membership (effective 2005). back issues avail. **Document type:** *Newsletter.* **Description:** Covers all areas of women in sports, with emphasis on issues that affect women's participation in or leadership of sports.
Formerly (until 1992): Headway (1044-7377)
Indexed: HRIS, SD.
Published by: Women's Sports Foundation, Eisenhower Park, East Meadow, NY 11554-1000. TEL 516-542-4700, 800-227-3988, FAX 516-542-4716, info@womenssportsfoundation.org. Ed., R&P Deana Monahan.

796.83 CHE
WORLD AMATEUR BOXING MAGAZINE. Text in English. 1976. s-a. **Document type:** *Magazine, Consumer.* **Description:** Contains developments in world amateur boxing including training and competition, decisions of the governing bodies, and related scientific research.
Published by: Association Internationale de Boxe Amateur, Avenue de Rhodanie 54, Lausanne, 1007, Switzerland. TEL 41-21-3212777, FAX 41-21-3212772, info@aiba.org, http://www.aiba.org. Ed. Germiliano Lopez. Circ: 4,000 (paid).

S

737 MYS ISSN 0255-4429
WORLD BADMINTON. Text in English. 1970. q. adv. **Document type:** *Magazine, Consumer.* **Description:** Contains articles on the world of badminton: news and views, international events, tournaments and results.
Media: Online - full text.
Indexed: SportS.
Published by: International Badminton Federation, Batu 3 1/2 Jalan Cheras, Kuala Lumpur, Glos 56000, Malaysia. TEL 60-3-92837155, FAX 60-3-92847155, ibf@internationalbadminton.org, http://www.internationalbadminton.org.

WORLD JOURNAL OF EVENTS AND SPORTS TOURISM. *see* TRAVEL AND TOURISM

796 ZAF ISSN 1991-1351
WORLD JOURNAL OF SPORTS MANAGEMENT. Text in English. 2006. q. USD 120 in Africa to individuals; USD 180 elsewhere to individuals; USD 350 in Africa to institutions; USD 450 elsewhere to institutions; USD 85 in Africa to students; USD 100 elsewhere to students (effective 2007). **Document type:** *Journal, Academic/Scholarly.* **Description:** Focuses on the theoretical and applied aspects of management related to sport, exercise, dance, and play.
Published by: (World Research Organization), Isis Press, PO Box 1919, Cape Town, 8000, South Africa. TEL 27-21-4471574, FAX 27-86-6219999, orders@unwro.org, http://www.unwro.org/isispress.html.

WORLD JOURNAL OF TOURISM, LEISURE AND SPORTS. *see* TRAVEL AND TOURISM

WORLD LEISURE JOURNAL. *see* LEISURE AND RECREATION

798.8 AUS ISSN 1835-8748
WORLD MUAYTHAI MAGAZINE; a combat sports & lifestyle magazine. Abbreviated title: W M M. Text in English. 2008. q. AUD 25 domestic; AUD 30 in New Zealand; AUD 45 in Asia; AUD 55 elsewhere; AUD 8.95 newsstand/cover (effective 2011). adv. **Document type:** *Magazine, Consumer.* **Description:** Designed for MUAYTHAI boxing athletes and professionals to address underlying issues from regulation to sanctioning, industry developments and trends by influencing the decisions of governments etc.
Related titles: Online - full text ed.
Address: PO Box 293, Surfers Paradise, QLD 4217, Australia. Ed., Adv. contact John Tozeland TEL 61-416-922151.

790.1 613.7 USA ISSN 0380-4712
THE WORLD OF A S P. Text in English. 1974. q. looseleaf. membership. bk.rev.; Website rev. **Document type:** *Newsletter, Consumer.* **Description:** Covers self-defense, combative sports, body-mind coordination, wellness, and fitness.
Published by: American Self-Protection Association, 825 Greengate Oval, Sagamore Hills, OH 44067. TEL 330-467-7110, FAX 330-457-1750, http://www.americanselfprotection.org. Eds. Evan S Baltazzi, Nellie D Baltazzi. R&P Evan S Baltazzi. Circ: 71 (paid).

790.1 DEU
WORLD OF SPORT. Text in German. 3/yr. adv. illus.
Formerly (until 1990): Sport und Freizeit
Published by: Strebel Zielgruppen Verlag GmbH, Hoehenstr 17, Fellbach, 70736, Germany. TEL 0711-5206-1, FAX 0711-5281424. Ed. Guenter Bayer.

306.4820285 GBR ISSN 1477-2922
WORLD ONLINE GAMBLING LAW REPORT; the newsletter for the industry. Abbreviated title: W O G L R. Text in English. 2002. m. GBP 520 combined subscription domestic (print & online eds.); GBP 540 combined subscription foreign (print & online eds.) (effective 2009). back issues avail. **Document type:** *Newsletter, Trade.* **Description:** Covers matters as diverse as advertising regulations, content clearance, privacy and data protection, online payments, software licensing, advertising, interactive TV, new derivative products, security, cybercrime, money laundering and more.
Related titles: Online - full text ed.: ISSN 1477-2930.
—CCC.
Published by: Cecile Park Publishing Ltd., 17 the Timber Yard, Drysdale St, London, N1 6ND, United Kingdom. TEL 44-20-70121380, FAX 44-20-77296093. Ed. Lindsey Greig.

796 USA
WORLD SPORTS & ENTERTAINMENT. Text in English. 1983. w. **Document type:** *Newspaper, Academic/Scholarly.*
Published by: Franklin Publishing Company, 2723 Steamboat Cir, Arlington, TX 76006. TEL 817-548-1124, FAX 817-369-2689, http://www.franklinpublishing.net. Pub. Dr. Ludwig Otto.

344.099 GBR ISSN 1742-0040
WORLD SPORTS LAW REPORT; the newsletter for the sports business. Text in English. 2003. m. GBP 520 combined subscription domestic (print & online eds.); GBP 540 combined subscription foreign (print & online eds.) (effective 2009). back issues avail. **Document type:** *Newsletter, Trade.* **Description:** Designed to address the key legal and business issues that face those involved in the sports industry.
Related titles: Online - full text ed.: ISSN 1743-615X.
—CCC.
Published by: Cecile Park Publishing Ltd., 17 the Timber Yard, Drysdale St, London, N1 6ND, United Kingdom. TEL 44-20-70121380, FAX 44-20-77296093. Ed. Lindsey Greig.

797 GRC
WORLD WATERPOLO. Text in Greek. q. USD 40 in Europe; USD 60 elsewhere. **Document type:** *Newsletter.* **Description:** Features complete coverage of happenings in the sport of waterpolo throughout the world.
Formerly: Euro Waterpolo
Address: 16 Themistokleous St, Athens, 106 78, Greece. TEL 30-1-72921947, FAX 30-1-7259086.

793.7 DEU ISSN 0942-6590
WORT-SUCHSPIEL. Text in German. 1981. w. EUR 91; EUR 1.50 newsstand/cover (effective 2011). adv. **Document type:** *Magazine, Consumer.* **Description:** Filled with fun and entertaining word puzzles.
Published by: Deutscher Raetselverlag GmbH & Co. KG (Subsidiary of: Gong Verlag GmbH & Co. KG), Muenchener Str 101-09, Ismaning, 85737, Germany. TEL 49-89-272708620, FAX 49-89-272707890, info@raetsel.de, http://www.deutscher-raetselverlag.de. Circ: 111,000 (controlled).

796.812 USA ISSN 1052-0899
THE WRESTLER. Text in English. 1968. 13/yr. adv. charts; illus.; tr.lit. **Document type:** *Magazine, Consumer.*
Published by: London Publishing Co. (Subsidiary of: Kappa Publishing Group, Inc.), 6198 Butler Pike, Ste 200, Blue Bell, PA 19422. TEL 215-643-6385, FAX 315-628-3571, custsrvc@kappapublishing.com, http://www.kappapublishing.com. Ed. Stuart M Saks.

796.812 USA ISSN 1097-4725
THE WRESTLING ANALYST. Text in English. 1998. 6/yr. **Document type:** *Magazine, Consumer.* **Description:** Features articles about wrestling and the World Championship Wrestling wrestlers.
Published by: London Publishing Co. (Subsidiary of: Kappa Publishing Group, Inc.), 6198 Butler Pike, Ste 200, Blue Bell, PA 19422. TEL 215-643-6385, FAX 315-628-3571, custsrvc@kappapublishing.com, http://www.kappapublishing.com. Ed. David Lenker. Pub. Stuart M Saks. **Dist. in N. America by:** Curtis CIRC Company, 641 Lexington Ave, New York, NY 10022; **Dist. in the UK by:** Comag, Tavistock Rd, W Drayton, Middlesex UB7 7QE, United Kingdom.

796.812 USA
WRESTLING CASE BOOK AND MANUAL. Text in English. 19??. a. USD 6.95 per issue (effective 2009). adv. **Document type:** *Handbook/Manual/Guide, Trade.* **Description:** Provides in-depth information on the actual play situations for those who wish to enter the field of officiating or to those who are interested in improving their competence in the field of wrestling.
Supersedes: Wrestling Officials Manual
Published by: National Federation of State High School Associations, PO Box 690, Indianapolis, IN 46206. TEL 317-972-6900, 800-776-3462, FAX 317-822-5700, info@nfhs.org, http://www.nfhs.org.

790.1 USA
WRESTLING CHATTERBOX. Text in English. 1991. m. USD 25; USD 40 foreign; USD 2.50, USD 4 newsstand/cover (effective 1999). adv. bk.rev. illus. **Document type:** *Newsletter.* **Description:** Covers wrestlers and wrestling match results, editorials and pictures, wrestling nostalgia and most other topics related to wrestling.
Published by: Georgiann Makropoulos, Ed. & Pub., 23-44 30th Dr., Astoria, NY 11102-3252. TEL 718-721-2369, FAX 718-721-5334. Adv. contact Georgiann Makroupolos. Circ: 682.

796.812 USA ISSN 1524-0371
WRESTLING DIGEST. Text in English. 1999. bi-m. 68 p./no. 2 cols./p.; back issues avail. **Document type:** *Magazine, Consumer.* **Description:** Features complete coverage of WWF, WCW and ECW wrestling events.
Related titles: Online - full text ed.
Indexed: G05, G06, G07, G08, I05, I07, PEI.
Published by: Century Publishing Inc., E 5710 Seltice Way, Post Falls, ID 83854. TEL 208-765-6300, 800-824-1806, FAX 208-676-8476, privacy@CenturyPublishing.com, http://www.centurypublishing.com. Ed. William Wagner. Pub. Norman Jacobs.

796.812 USA ISSN 0891-0707
THE WRESTLING NEWS. Text in English. 1972. s-a. USD 12; USD 16 foreign (effective 1998). adv. **Document type:** *Magazine, Consumer.*
Published by: (Pro Wrestling Enterprises), Norman Kietzer, Ed. & Pub., 527 S Front St, Mankato, MN 56001-3718. Circ: 9,000.

796.8 USA ISSN 1083-9593
WRESTLING OBSERVER NEWSLETTER. Text in English. 1982. w. USD 117 domestic; CAD 125 in Canada; USD 156 foreign (effective 2005). **Document type:** *Newsletter, Trade.* **Description:** Examines the business aspects of pro-wrestling.
Published by: Dave Meltzer, Ed. & Pub., 3020 Latrobe Dr, Charlotte, NC 28211. TEL 704-364-7818, FAX 704-364-6183. Ed. Dave Meltzeer. Circ: 7,000 (paid and controlled).

790.1 USA
WRESTLING PERSPECTIVE. Text in English. 1990. m. USD 24; USD 2 newsstand/cover (effective 2001). bk.rev.; video rev. back issues avail. **Document type:** *Newsletter.* **Description:** Contains commentaries on wrestling, covers future developments of wrestling promotional strategies, and includes essays and interviews with classic wrestlers and historical columns.
Address: 3011 Hwy 30 W, Ste 101 197, Huntsville, TX 77340. TEL 936-435-0545, wrestlingperspective@yahoo.com. Ed., Pub., R&P, Adv. contact Paul MacArthur. Circ: 200.

796.812 USA
WRESTLING RULES BOOK. Text in English. 19??. a. USD 6.95 per issue (effective 2009). adv. **Document type:** *Handbook/Manual/Guide, Trade.* **Description:** Contains the official rules for wrestling and is used by coaches, officials, players and many fans who wish to know more about the rules of the game.
Former titles (until 1991): Official High School Wrestling Rules (0735-8946); (until 1983): National Federation of State High School Associations. Wrestling Rule Book (0361-641X)
Published by: National Federation of State High School Associations, PO Box 690, Indianapolis, IN 46206. TEL 317-972-6900, 800-776-3462, FAX 317-822-5700, info@nfhs.org, http://www.nfhs.org.

790.1 USA
WRESTLING - THEN & NOW. Text in English. 1990. m. USD 20; USD 2 newsstand/cover (effective 1999). adv. bk.rev.; tel.rev.; video rev. tr.lit. back issues avail. **Document type:** *Newsletter.* **Description:** Contains anecdotes, clippings, and interviews regarding the old-days wrestling business and stories of new developments.
Published by: Evan Ginzburg, Ed. & Pub., PO BOX 640471, OAKLAND GARDENS STA, Flushing, NY 11364. TEL 718-740-4138. R&P, Adv. contact Evan Ginzburg. B&W page USD 40. Circ: 200 (paid); 75 (controlled).

790.1 USA ISSN 0199-6258
GV1195
WRESTLING U S A (MISSOULA). Text in English. 1964. m. USD 35; USD 49 combined subscription (print & online eds.) (effective 2010). illus. back issues avail.; reprints avail. **Document type:** *Magazine, Trade.* **Description:** Geared to wrestling coaches and amateur wrestlers.
Formerly (until 1980): Scholastic Wrestling News
Related titles: Microform ed.; Online - full text ed.: USD 20 (effective 2010).
Indexed: SD.
—Ingenta.
Published by: Wrestling U.S.A. Magazine, c/o Cody Bryant, 109 Apple House Ln, Missoula, MT 59802. Ed. Lanny Bryant.

796.33 613.7 CHN ISSN 1004-5821
WUDANG. Text in Chinese. 1983. bi-m. USD 39.60 (effective 2009). adv. bk.rev. illus. **Document type:** *Consumer.* **Description:** Discusses how to achieve physical fitness through martial arts and Qigong.
Related titles: Online - full text ed.
—East View.
Published by: (Wudang-Wushu Research Association), Wudang Zazhishe/Wudang Journal Press, Yuanjiang Dadao, Xinwen Chuban Dasha, Danjiangkou City, Hubei 442700, China. TEL 86-719-5223531, FAX 86-719-5227401, http://www.dragonsource.com. Ed. Hongyao Liu. R&P, Adv. contact Ruoyu Xiong. page CNY 3,500. Circ: 50,000 (paid). **Dist. overseas by:** China International Book Trading Corp, 35 Chegongzhuang Xilu, Haidian District, PO Box 399, Beijing 100044, China.

796 DEU
▼ **WUERZBURGER BEITRAEGE ZUR SPORTWISSENSCHAFT.** Text in German. 2009. irreg., latest vol.4, 2010. price varies. **Document type:** *Monographic series, Academic/Scholarly.*
Published by: Cuvillier Verlag, Nonnenstieg 8, Goettingen, 37075, Germany. TEL 49-551-547240, FAX 49-551-5472421, info@cuvillier.de.

796.8 CHN
WUHUN/SOUL OF MARTIAL ARTS. Text in Chinese. 1983. m. CNY 5 newsstand/cover (effective 2005). **Document type:** *Magazine, Consumer.*
Published by: Beijing Wushuyuan, 27, Tiantan Dongli, Beijing, 100061, China. TEL 86-10-67113502. **Dist. by:** China International Book Trading Corp, 35 Chegongzhuang Xilu, Haidian District, PO Box 399, Beijing 100044, China. TEL 86-10-68412045, FAX 86-10-68412023, cibtc@mail.cibtc.com.cn, http://www.cibtc.com.cn.

793.932 GBR ISSN 1752-718X
XBOX WORLD 360. Text in English. 2003. 13/yr. GBP 49.99 domestic; GBP 55.49 in Europe; GBP 65.49 elsewhere (effective 2010). adv. **Document type:** *Magazine, Consumer.*
Formerly (until 200?): Xbox World (1479-4969)
Related titles: Online - full text ed.
—CCC.
Published by: Future Publishing Ltd., 29 Monmouth St, Bath, BA1 2BW, United Kingdom. TEL 44-1225-442244, FAX 44-1225-446019, customerservice@subscription.co.uk, http://www.futureplc.com. Ed. Tim Weaver. Adv. contact Andrew Church. **Subscr. to:** Tower House, Sovereign Park, Market Harborough, Leicestershire LE16 9EF, United Kingdom. TEL 44-844-8481602, FAX 44-1858-438795, future@subscription.co.uk.

XI'AN TIYU XUEYUAN XUEBAO/XI'AN INSTITUTE OF PHYSICAL EDUCATION. JOURNAL. *see* PHYSICAL FITNESS AND HYGIENE

794.18 CHN ISSN 1002-1906
XIANGQI YANJIU/CHINESE CHESS STUDIES. Text in Chinese. 1977. bi-m. USD 14.40 (effective 2009). **Document type:** *Journal, Academic/Scholarly.*
—East View.
Published by: Ha'erbin Shi Tiwei, 11, Tiweibaqu Jie, Ha'erbin, Heilongjiang 150020, China. TEL 86-451-8327911 ext 2150, FAX 86-451-67163263. Ed. Jin Qichang.

796 CHN ISSN 0441-3679
GV201
XINTIYU/NEW SPORTS. Text in Chinese. 1950. m. USD 49.20 (effective 2009). **Document type:** *Magazine, Consumer.*
Related titles: Online - full text ed.
—East View.
Published by: Zhongguo Tiyubao Yezongshe, 8, Tiyuguan Lu, Chongwen-qu, Beijing, 100061, China. TEL 86-10-67118042, FAX 86-10-67171848, http://www.sportsol.com.cn/.

796.815 USA ISSN 2150-7074
▼ **XTREME MARTIAL ARTS MAGAZINE.** Text in English. 2009. q. USD 42 (effective 2009). **Document type:** *Magazine, Consumer.* **Description:** Features articles and information on martial arts for a diverse audience.
Published by: Xtreme Martial Arts, 6955 NW 77th Ave, Ste 404, Miami, FL 33166. TEL 786-344-9972, mchomiack@martialartsmag.com.

796.72 ZAF ISSN 1994-2117
XTREME MOTORING MAGAZINE. Text in English. 2006. m. **Document type:** *Magazine, Consumer.*
Published by: Synergy Video Productions (Pty) Ltd, PO Box 2285, Wingate Park, 0153, South Africa. TEL 27-12-9988295, FAX 27-12-9985797.

Y M C A WEEKLY NEWS. (Young Men's Christian Association) *see* PHYSICAL FITNESS AND HYGIENE

796 CHN
YANGCHENG TIYU. Text in Chinese. 1995. w. CNY 207.96 (effective 2004). **Document type:** *Newspaper, Consumer.*
Related titles: Online - full content ed.
Published by: Yangcheng Wanbao Baoye Jituan/Yangcheng Evening Post Press Group, 733, Dongfeng Donglu, Guangzhou, 510085, China. TEL 86-20-87776211, FAX 86-20-87664985, jyw@ycwb.com.

YANGSHENG YUEKAN/BREATH EXERCISE. *see* PHYSICAL FITNESS AND HYGIENE

796 USA ISSN 1935-1429
YOU NAME IT SPORTS. Text in English. 2003. 10/yr. USD 25 (effective 2007). adv. **Document type:** *Magazine, Consumer.* **Description:** Covers high school sports in the Bloomington, Illinois area, including golf, football, track, volleyball and swimming.
Published by: StarNet Digital Publishing, 1708 Hamilton Rd, Ste B, Bloomington, IL 61704. TEL 309-664-6444, http://www.starnetdp.com. adv.: page USD 1,050.

790.1 USA
YOUTH RUNNER. Text in English. q. USD 9.95; USD 2.95 newsstand/cover (effective 2001). adv. **Description:** Includes instruction for runners 8-18, as well as features on standout track athletes.
Published by: T M B Publishing Inc, PO Box 1156, Lake Oswego, OR 97035. TEL 503-236-2524, FAX 503-620-3800. Ed. Dan Kesterson.

797.21 CHN ISSN 1000-3495
YOUYONG/SWIMMING. Text in Chinese. 1983. bi-m. USD 18 (effective 2009). **Document type:** *Magazine, Consumer.*
Related titles: Online - full text ed.
—East View.
Published by: Zhongguo Youyong Xiehui/China Swimming Association, 2, Tiyuguan Lu, Beijing, 100763, China. TEL 86-10-67170578, FAX 86-10-67170595.

796 CHN ISSN 1006-0855
YUNDONG XIUXIAN/SPORTS AND LEISURE. Text in Chinese. 1993. m. USD 80.40 (effective 2009). **Document type:** *Consumer.*
Related titles: Online - full content ed.
—East View.
Published by: Zhongguo Tiyubao Yezongshe, 8, Tiyuguan Lu, Chongwen-qu, Beijing, 100061, China. TEL 86-10-88091476. **Dist. by:** China International Book Trading Corp, 35 Chegongzhuang Xilu, Haidian District, PO Box 399, Beijing 100044, China. TEL 86-10-68412045, FAX 86-10-68412023, cibtc@mail.cibtc.com.cn, http://www.cibtc.com.cn.

796 TWN ISSN 1992-5530
YUNDONG YU YOUQI YANJIU/JOURNAL OF SPORT AND RECREATION RESEARCH. Text in Chinese. 2006. q.
Published by: Shida Shuyuan Youxian Gongsi, Sec.1, no.147, 11-2/F, Heping East Rd., Taipei, Taiwan. TEL 886-2-23973030, FAX 886-2-23975050, st.book@msa.hinet.net, http://www.shtabook.com.tw/.

ZAJI YU MOSHU/ACROBATICS AND MAGIC. *see* HOBBIES

ZAMBIA. MINISTRY OF YOUTH AND SPORT. DEPARTMENT OF YOUTH DEVELOPMENT. ANNUAL REPORT. *see* CHILDREN AND YOUTH—Abstracting, Bibliographies, Statistics

796 ZMB
ZAMBIA. MINISTRY OF YOUTH AND SPORT. REPORT. Text in English. 1968. a. ZMK 100 (effective 1992). **Document type:** *Government.*
Formerly: Zambia. Sports Directorate. Report (0084-506X)
Published by: (Zambia. Ministry of Youth and Sport), Government Printing Department, PO Box 30136, Lusaka, Zambia.

790.1 RUS
ZDOROVYI OBRAZ ZHIZNI; prilozhenie k gazete sovetskii sport. Text in Russian. 24/yr.
Address: B Spasoglinishchevskii per 18, Moscow, 101913, Russian Federation. TEL 7-095-9238823. **Dist. by:** East View Information Services, 10601 Wayzata Blvd, Minneapolis, MN 55305. TEL 952-252-1201, 800-477-1005, FAX 952-252-1202, info@eastview.com, http://www.eastview.com.

790.1 DEU ISSN 0946-8455
ZEITSCHRIFT FUER ANGEWANDTE TRAININGSWISSENSCHAFTEN. Text in German. 1994. a. EUR 19.90 (effective 2011). back issues avail. **Document type:** *Journal, Academic/Scholarly.*
Published by: Meyer & Meyer Verlag, Von-Coels-Str 390, Aachen, 52080, Germany. TEL 49-241-958100, FAX 49-241-9581010, verlag@m-m-sports.com, http://m-m-sports.de.

ZEITSCHRIFT FUER SPORTPSYCHOLOGIE. *see* PSYCHOLOGY

ZEITSCHRIFT FUER WETT- UND GLUECKSSPIELRECHT. *see* LAW

790.1 CHN
ZHONGGUO GUOJI XIANGQI/INTERNATIONAL CHESS IN CHINA. Text in Chinese. bi-m. CNY 60 (effective 2004). **Document type:** *Magazine, Consumer.*
Published by: (Zhongguo Guoji Xiangqi Xiehui), Shurongqiyi Chubanshe, 72, Erdaoqiao Jie, Chengdu, 610071, China. http://www.chessinchina.net/, gjx@mail.sc.cninfo.net. **Dist. by:** China International Book Trading Corp, 35 Chegongzhuang Xilu, Haidian District, PO Box 399, Beijing 100044, China. TEL 86-10-68412045, FAX 86-10-68412023, cibtc@mail.cibtc.com.cn, http://www.cibtc.com.cn.

790.1 CHN
ZHONGGUO TIYU BAO/CHINESE'S SPORTS NEWS. Text in Chinese. 1958. d. (6/wk). USD 117.60 (effective 2009). back issues avail. **Document type:** *Newspaper, Consumer.*
Published by: Zhongguo Tiyubao Yezongshe, 8, Tiyuguan Lu, Chongwen-qu, Beijing, 100061, China. TEL 86-10-67110066 ext 325, FAX 86-10-67170074, http://www.sportsol.com.cn/. **Dist. by:** China International Book Trading Corp, 35 Chegongzhuang Xilu, Haidian District, PO Box 399, Beijing 100044, China. TEL 86-10-68412045, FAX 86-10-68412023, cibtc@mail.cibtc.com.cn, http://www.cibtc.com.cn.

796.8 CHN ISSN 1000-3525
GV1100.7.A2
ZHONGHUA WUSHU/CHINESE MARTIAL ARTS. Text in Chinese. 1982. m. USD 62.40 (effective 2009). **Document type:** *Magazine, Consumer.*
Related titles: Online - full text ed.
—East View.
Published by: (Zhongguo Wushu Xiehui/China Wushu Association), Zhongguo Tiyubao Yezongshe, 8, Tiyuguan Lu, Chongwen-qu, Beijing, 100061, China. **Dist. by:** China International Book Trading Corp, 35 Chegongzhuang Xilu, Haidian District, PO Box 399, Beijing 100044, China. TEL 86-10-68412045, FAX 86-10-68412023, cibtc@mail.cibtc.com.cn, http://www.cibtc.com.cn.

790.1 CHE
ZUERCHER LEICHTATHLET. Text in German. 6/yr.
Address: Postfach 568, Zuerich, 8039, Switzerland. TEL 01-325370, FAX 01-4621915. Circ: 3,500.

790 SRB ISSN 0354-6101
ZVEZDINA REVIJA. Text in Serbo-Croatian. 1960. m.
Former titles (until 1994): Zvezda (0353-6157); (until 1990): Zvezdina Revija (0044-5533)
Published by: Sportsko Drustvo Crvena Zvezda, Ljutice Bogdana 1a, Belgrade, 11000. TEL 381-11-3670394. Ed. M Stojkovic.

797.21 NLD
ZWEMREKREATIE (ONLINE). Text in Dutch. 1987. m. EUR 32.50 (effective 2010). adv. **Document type:** *Trade.* **Description:** For management personnel who work in swimming centers, sports clubs, salons and saunas, as well as industry suppliers.
Formerly: ZwemRekreatie (Print) (1385-1497)
Media: Online - full text.
Published by: R Z Publishers, Eerste Groenelaan 9, Castricum, 1901 HS, Netherlands. TEL 31-251-658022, FAX 31-251-653528.

4 X 4 MECHANIX. *see* TRANSPORTATION—Trucks And Trucking

796.91 USA
6.0 SKATE MAGAZINE. Text in English. 2001. bi-m. USD 25 domestic; USD 30 elsewhere (effective 2001). **Document type:** *Magazine, Consumer.* **Description:** Covers figure skating, personalities, performances, and other related information.
Address: 161 South Main St, Newton, NH 03858. TEL 603-382-1702, Six0SkateMag@aol.com.

796 FRA ISSN 1965-1813
LE 10 SPORT HEBDO. Text in French. 2008. w. **Document type:** *Newspaper, Consumer.*
Formerly (until 2009): Le 10 Sport.com (1959-5824)
Related titles: Online - full text ed.: ISSN 2100-0786.
Published by: La Societe 10 Medias, 18 Rue de la Pepiniere, Paris, 75008, France. TEL 33-1-71194722, http://www.le10sport.com.

794.1 RUS ISSN 0205-8316
64 - SHAKHMATNOE OBOZRENIE/64 - CHESS REVIEW. Text in Russian. 1980. m. USD 125 in United States. **Document type:** *Magazine, Consumer.* **Description:** Created for those who play chess, love this intellectual game.
—East View.
Published by: Shakhmatnoe Obozrenie, Vozdvizhenka 7-6, Moscow, 121019, Russian Federation. TEL 7-095-9468328, FAX 7-095-9430006. Ed. Aleksandr Roshal'. **Dist. by:** East View Information Services, 10601 Wayzata Blvd, Minneapolis, MN 55305. TEL 952-252-1201, 800-477-1005, FAX 952-252-1202, info@eastview.com, http://www.eastview.com.

796.812 ARG ISSN 1851-3700
100 PORCIENTO LUCH. Key Title: 100% Lucha. Text in Spanish. 2007. m. ARS 6.90 newsstand/cover (effective 2008).
Published by: Producciones Publiexpress, Magallanes 1346, Buenos Aires, C1288ABB, Argentina. TEL 54-11-43031484, FAX 54-11-43031280, rrhh@publiexpress.com.ar, http://www.publiexpress.com.ar/. Circ: 31,000.

796 GBR ISSN 1479-1501
220 TRIATHLON. Variant title: Two Twenty Multi Sports Triathlon and Biathlon. Text in English. 1989. 13/yr. GBP 25.87 domestic; GBP 57 in Europe; GBP 67 elsewhere; GBP 3.99 newsstand/cover (effective 2010). adv. back issues avail. **Document type:** *Magazine, Consumer.* **Description:** Covers all aspects of triathlons and multisports from training and equipment to competitions and results.
Formerly (until 2001): 220 (0958-675X)
Published by: Origin Publishing Ltd. (Subsidiary of: B B C Worldwide Ltd.), Tower House, Fairfax St, Bristol, BS1 3BN, United Kingdom. TEL 44-117-9279009, FAX 44-117-9349008, http://www.originpublishing.co.uk. Ed. James Witts TEL 44-117-9338050. Pub. Andrew Healy TEL 44-117-3148316. Adv. contact Eleanor Godwin TEL 44-117-9338013. Circ: 23,500.

SPORTS AND GAMES—Abstracting, Bibliographies, Statistics

001.3021 AUS
AUSTRALIA. BUREAU OF STATISTICS. AUSTRALIAN CLASSIFICATION FRAMEWORK FOR CULTURE AND LEISURE STATISTICS. Text in English. 2000. irreg.
Published by: Australian Bureau of Statistics, Locked Bag 10, Belconnen, ACT 2616, Australia. TEL 61-2-92684909, 61-2-62527037, 300-135-070, FAX 61-2-62528103, client.services@abs.gov.au, http://www.abs.gov.au.

001.3021 AUS
AUSTRALIA. BUREAU OF STATISTICS. AUSTRALIAN CULTURE AND LEISURE CLASSIFICATIONS (ONLINE). Abbreviated title: Australia. Bureau of Statistics. A C L C. Text in English. 2001. irreg., latest 2008, 2nd ed. free (effective 2009). back issues avail. **Document type:** *Government.* **Description:** Aims to develop national standards for culture and leisure information. They comprise three separate classifications, covering culture and leisure related industries, products and occupations.
Former titles: Australia. Bureau of Statistics. Australian Culture and Leisure Classifications (Print); Australia. Bureau of Statistics. Australian Culture and Leisure Classifications. Draft for Consultation; Australia. Bureau of Statistics. Australian Culture and Leisure Classifications
Media: Online - full text.
Published by: Australian Bureau of Statistics, Locked Bag 10, Belconnen, ACT 2616, Australia. TEL 61-2-92684909, 300-135-070, FAX 61-2-92684654, client.services@abs.gov.au.

793.021 AUS
AUSTRALIA. BUREAU OF STATISTICS. CASINOS, AUSTRALIA (ONLINE). Text in English. 1995. a. free (effective 2009). back issues avail. **Document type:** *Government.* **Description:** Presents results, in respect of the financial year, from an Australian Bureau of Statistics (ABS) census of Australian casino businesses.
Formerly: Australia. Bureau of Statistics. Casinos, Australia (Print) (1327-5275)
Media: Online - full text.
Published by: Australian Bureau of Statistics, Locked Bag 10, Belconnen, ACT 2616, Australia. TEL 61-2-92684909, 61-2-62527037, 300-135-070, FAX 61-2-62528103, client.services@abs.gov.au.

001.3021 AUS
AUSTRALIA. BUREAU OF STATISTICS. DIRECTORY OF CULTURE AND LEISURE STATISTICS - WEB SITE VERSION. Text in English. 2002. irreg., latest 2002. stat. **Document type:** *Government.* **Description:** Provides a reference to sources of culture and leisure data.
Media: Online - full content.
Published by: Australian Bureau of Statistics, Locked Bag 10, Belconnen, ACT 2616, Australia. TEL 61-2-92684909, 61-2-62527037, 300-135-070, FAX 61-2-62528103, client.services@abs.gov.au.

AUSTRALIA. BUREAU OF STATISTICS. EMPLOYMENT IN SELECTED SPORT AND RECREATION OCCUPATIONS, AUSTRALIA (ONLINE). *see* BUSINESS AND ECONOMICS—Abstracting, Bibliographies, Statistics

790.1021 AUS
AUSTRALIA. BUREAU OF STATISTICS. EMPLOYMENT IN SPORT AND RECREATION, AUSTRALIA (ONLINE). Text in English. 2001. quinquennial, latest 2006. free (effective 2009). stat. back issues avail. **Document type:** *Government.* **Description:** Presents summary data on selected sport and physical recreation occupations.
Formerly: Australia. Bureau of Statistics. Employment in Sport and Recreation, Australia (Print)
Media: Online - full text.
Published by: Australian Bureau of Statistics, Locked Bag 10, Belconnen, ACT 2616, Australia. TEL 61-2-92684909, 300-135-070, FAX 61-2-92684654, client.services@abs.gov.au.

793.021 AUS
AUSTRALIA. BUREAU OF STATISTICS. GAMBLING INDUSTRIES, AUSTRALIA, PRELIMINARY (ONLINE). Text in English. 1997. irreg., latest 1998. free (effective 2009). **Document type:** *Government.* **Description:** Contains preliminary information on the income, expenses, employment of organisations involved in gambling industries in Australia.
Formerly: Australia. Bureau of Statistics. Gambling Industries, Australia, Preliminary (Print)
Media: Online - full text.
Published by: Australian Bureau of Statistics, Locked Bag 10, Belconnen, ACT 2616, Australia. TEL 61-2-92684909, 300-135-070, FAX 61-2-92684654, client.services@abs.gov.au.

793.021 AUS
AUSTRALIA. BUREAU OF STATISTICS. GAMBLING SERVICES, AUSTRALIA (ONLINE). Text in English. 1995. irreg., latest 2005. free (effective 2009). back issues avail. **Document type:** *Government.* **Description:** Presents a range of statistics in respect of businesses engaged in the provision of gambling services for the financial year.
Former titles: Australia. Bureau of Statistics. Gambling Services, Australia (Print); (until 2005): Australia. Bureau of Statistics. Gambling Industries, Australia
Media: Online - full text.
Published by: Australian Bureau of Statistics, Locked Bag 10, Belconnen, ACT 2616, Australia. TEL 61-2-92684909, 61-2-62527037, 300-135-070, FAX 61-2-62528103, client.services@abs.gov.au.

AUSTRALIA. BUREAU OF STATISTICS. INVOLVEMENT IN ORGANISED SPORT AND PHYSICAL ACTIVITY, AUSTRALIA (ONLINE). *see* BUSINESS AND ECONOMICS—Abstracting, Bibliographies, Statistics

016.796 AUS
AUSTRALIA. BUREAU OF STATISTICS. INVOLVEMENT IN ORGANIZED SPORT AND PHYSICAL ACTIVITY, AUSTRALIA (ONLINE). Text in English. 2001. triennial, latest 2007. free (effective 2009). back issues avail. **Document type:** *Government.* **Description:** Contains data on the number and characteristics of people involved in organised sport and physical activity, by type of involvement, and whether payment is received.
Former titles: Australia. Bureau of Statistics. Involvement in Organized Sport and Physical Activity, Australia (Print); (until 2001): Australia. Bureau of Statistics. Involvement in Sport, Australia
Media: Online - full text.
Published by: Australian Bureau of Statistics, Locked Bag 10, Belconnen, ACT 2616, Australia. TEL 61-2-92684909, 300-135-070, FAX 61-2-92684654, client.services@abs.gov.au.

796.7021 AUS
AUSTRALIA. BUREAU OF STATISTICS. NEW MOTOR VEHICLE REGISTRATION, AUSTRALIA, MOTORCYCLES DATA ON SUPERTABLE (ONLINE). Abbreviated title: Australia. Bureau of Statistics. N M V R Data on SuperTABLE. Text in English. 2000. irreg., latest 2001. free (effective 2009). **Document type:** *Government.* **Description:** Contains details of new motorcycles registered over the previous months. Each month the first month is dropped and the latest month is added to the cube. The details include State of registration, postcode of motorcycle owner and make (model and submodel) of motorcycle.
Formerly: Australia. Bureau of Statistics. New Motor Vehicle Registration, Australia, Motorcycles Data on SuperTABLE (Print)
Media: Online - full text.
Published by: Australian Bureau of Statistics, Locked Bag 10, Belconnen, ACT 2616, Australia. TEL 61-2-92684909, 300-135-070, FAX 61-2-92684654, client.services@abs.gov.au.

790.1021 AUS
AUSTRALIA. BUREAU OF STATISTICS. SELECTED AMUSEMENT AND LEISURE INDUSTRIES, AUSTRALIA (ONLINE). Text in English. 1995. irreg., latest 2001. free (effective 2009). back issues avail. **Document type:** *Government.* **Description:** Includes amusement or arcade operation, theme parks, circus operation, and railways operated as tourist attractions.
Former titles (until 200?): Australia. Bureau of Statistics. Selected Amusement and Leisure Industries, Australia (Print); (until 2000): Australia. Bureau of Statistics. Recreation Services, Australia
Media: Online - full text.
Published by: Australian Bureau of Statistics, Locked Bag 10, Belconnen, ACT 2616, Australia. TEL 61-2-92684909, 61-2-62527037, 300-135-070, FAX 61-2-62528103, client.services@abs.gov.au.

790.1021 AUS
AUSTRALIA. BUREAU OF STATISTICS. SPORT AND RECREATION FUNDING BY GOVERNMENT, AUSTRALIA (ONLINE). Text in English. 2001. irreg., latest 2001. free (effective 2009). stat. **Document type:** *Government.* **Description:** Contains estimates of australian government funding for sport and recreation activities, facilities and services.
Formerly: Australia. Bureau of Statistics. Sport and Recreation Funding by Government, Australia (Print) (1446-9499)
Media: Online - full text.
Published by: Australian Bureau of Statistics, Locked Bag 10, Belconnen, ACT 2616, Australia. TEL 61-2-92684909, 61-2-62527037, 300-135-070, FAX 61-2-62528103, client.services@abs.gov.au.

793.021 AUS
AUSTRALIA. BUREAU OF STATISTICS. SPORT, RECREATION AND GAMBLING INDUSTRIES, AUSTRALIA, PRELIMINARY (ONLINE). Text in English. 1995. irreg., latest 1995. free (effective 2009). **Document type:** *Government.* **Description:** Data items include number of businesses, total employment by sex, number of volunteers working in the industries, major components of income, major expenses items, and net worth.
Formerly: Australia. Bureau of Statistics. Sport, Recreation and Gambling Industries, Australia, Preliminary (Print)
Media: Online - full text.

S

Published by: Australian Bureau of Statistics, Locked Bag 10, Belconnen, ACT 2616, Australia. TEL 61-2-92684909, 61-2-62527037, 300-135-070, FAX 61-2-62528103, client.services@abs.gov.au.

790.1021 AUS
AUSTRALIA. BUREAU OF STATISTICS. SPORTS AND PHYSICAL RECREATION: A STATISTICAL OVERVIEW, AUSTRALIA. Text in English. 1997. irreg., latest 2008. free (effective 2009). stat. back issues avail. **Document type:** *Government.* **Description:** Presents an overview of the sports and physical recreation sector.
Formerly (until 2007): Australia. Bureau of Statistics. Sport and Recreation: A Statistical Overview, Australia
Media: Online - full text.
Published by: Australian Bureau of Statistics, Locked Bag 10, Belconnen, ACT 2616, Australia. TEL 61-2-92684909, 61-2-62527037, 300-135-070, FAX 61-2-62528103, client.services@abs.gov.au, http://www.abs.gov.au.

790.1021 AUS
AUSTRALIA. BUREAU OF STATISTICS. SPORTS AND PHYSICAL RECREATION SERVICES, AUSTRALIA (ONLINE). Text in English. 1995. irreg., latest 2005. free (effective 2009). back issues avail. **Document type:** *Government.* **Description:** Presents results from an Australian Bureau of Statistics (ABS) survey of businesses/ organisations engaged in sports and physical recreation services.
Former titles: Australia. Bureau of Statistics. Sports and Physical Recreation Services, Australia (Print); (until 2005): Australia. Bureau of Statistics. Sports Industries, Australia
Published by: Australian Bureau of Statistics, Locked Bag 10, Belconnen, ACT 2616, Australia. TEL 61-2-92684909, 61-2-62527037, 300-135-070, FAX 61-2-62528103, client.services@abs.gov.au.

790.1021 AUS
AUSTRALIA. BUREAU OF STATISTICS. SPORTS ATTENDANCE, AUSTRALIA (ONLINE). Text in English. 1995. irreg., latest 2006. free (effective 2009). back issues avail. **Document type:** *Government.* **Description:** Presents results from the Multi-Purpose Household Survey (MPHS) relating to attendance at sports events.
Former titles: Australia. Bureau of Statistics. Sports Attendance, Australia (Print); (until 1999): Australia. Bureau of Statistics. Sports Attendance; Australia. Bureau of Statistics. Attendance at Sports
Media: Online - full text.
Published by: Australian Bureau of Statistics, Locked Bag 10, Belconnen, ACT 2616, Australia. TEL 61-2-92684909, 61-2-62527037, 300-135-070, FAX 61-2-62528103, client.services@abs.gov.au.

793 310 AUS ISSN 1833-6337
AUSTRALIAN GAMBLING STATISTICS (ONLINE). Text in English. 1984. a. free. stat. back issues avail. **Document type:** *Government.* **Description:** Provides tables of statistics in relation to gambling throughout all states and territories in Australia.
Formerly (until 2005): Australian Gambling Statistics (Print)
Media: Online - full text. **Related titles:** CD-ROM ed.: AUD 175 per issue (effective 2009).
Published by: Queensland. Office of Economic and Statistical Research, PO Box 15037, City East, QLD 4002, Australia. TEL 61-7-32245326, FAX 61-7-32277437, oesr@treasury.qld.gov.au. Circ: 220 (paid).

796.95021 310 USA ISSN 0163-7207
GV776.A2
BOATING REGISTRATION STATISTICS. Text in English. a. USD 300 per issue to non-members (effective 2008). stat. **Description:** State-by-state analysis of registered pleasure boats by length, hull material and propulsion system.
Indexed: SRI.
Published by: National Marine Manufacturers Association, 200 E Randolph Dr, Ste 5100, Chicago, IL 60601-6436. TEL 312-946-6200, FAX 312-946-1461, orderdesk@nmma.org, http://www.nmma.org.

796.95 USA
BOATING STATISTICS. Variant title: Recreational Boating Statistics. Text in English. 1960. a. stat. back issues avail. **Document type:** *Government.* **Description:** Brings out annual statistics information of fifty states, five U.S. territories and the District of Columbia's accident report data which are submitted to the U.S. Coast Guard.
Formerly: U.S. Coast Guard Boating Statistics (0565-1530)
Related titles: Online - full text ed.: free (effective 2010).
Published by: (Commandant G-NAB), U.S. Coast Guard, 2100 Second St, SW, Washington, DC 20593. TEL 202-267-1061, FAX 202-267-4402, gchappell@comdt.uscg.mil, http://www.uscg.mil/default.asp.

790.1 DEU ISSN 0941-6633
CD-ROM SPORTWISSENSCHAFT. Text in English, German. 1990. irreg., latest 2001. EUR 100 per vol. (effective 2009). abstr.; bibl. **Document type:** *Bibliography.*
Media: CD-ROM.
Published by: (Germany. Bundesinstitut fuer Sportwissenschaft), Czwalina Verlag, Bei der Neuen Muenze 4a, Hamburg, 22145, Germany. TEL 49-40-6794300, FAX 49-40-67943030, post@feldhaus-verlag, http://www.edition-czwalina.de.

CENTRE FOR SPORTS SCIENCE AND HISTORY. SERIAL HOLDINGS. *see* EDUCATION—Abstracting, Bibliographies, Statistics

790.1 GBR ISSN 2046-8334
CHARTERED INSTITUTE OF PUBLIC FINANCE AND ACCOUNTANCY. CULTURE, SPORT AND RECREATION STATISTICS. ESTIMATES (ONLINE). Text in English. 19??. a. GBP 150 per issue (effective 2011). stat. back issues avail. **Document type:** *Report, Trade.* **Description:** Provides an analysis of estimated expenditure and income on: indoor swimming pools; sports halls and leisure centers; community centres and public halls; outdoor sports facilities; golf courses; urban parks and open spaces and other recreation and leisure activities.
Former titles (until 2009): Chartered Institute of Public Finance and Accountancy. Culture, Sport and Recreation Statistics. Estimates (Print) (1755-5515); (until 2007): Chartered Institute of Public Finance and Accountancy. Leisure and Recreation Statistics. Estimates (0141-187X); (until 1977): Chartered Institute of Public Finance and Accountancy. Leisure Estimate Statistics
Media: Online - full text.
—BLDSC (3491.669147).
Published by: (Statistical Information Service), Chartered Institute of Public Finance and Accountancy, 3 Robert St, London, WC2N 6RL, United Kingdom. TEL 44-20-75435600, FAX 44-20-75435700, info@cipfa.org.uk, http://www.cipfa.org.uk.

796.358 GBR
CRICKET STATISTICIAN. Text in English. 1973. q. free to members (effective 2009). adv. bk.rev. stat. back issues avail. **Document type:** *Journal, Consumer.* **Description:** Features historical research articles and cricket statistical analyses.
Published by: Association of Cricket Statisticians & Historians, 3 Radcliffe Rd, West Bridgford, Nottingham, NG2 5FF, United Kingdom. TEL 44-1602-455407. Ed. Simon Sweetman.

796.357 USA
CURRENT BASEBALL PUBLICATIONS. Abbreviated title: C B P. Text in English. 1993 (vol.8, no.2). q. (plus a. summary). adv. back issues avail. **Document type:** *Directory, Bibliography.* **Description:** Lists new books and periodicals dealing with all facets of baseball.
Related titles: Online - full text ed.
Published by: Society for American Baseball Research, Inc., 812 Huron Rd, Ste 719, Cleveland, OH 44115. TEL 216-575-0500, 800-969-7227, FAX 216-575-0502, info@sabr.org. Ed. Richard Arpi.

796.420684 DNK ISSN 0107-4547
D A F I TAL. Text in Danish. 1971. a., latest 2000. illus. **Document type:** *Magazine, Consumer.* **Description:** Yearbook with text, statistics, and pictures of the previous year's activities in Danish sports.
Formerly (until 1978): Dansk Atletik Forbund. Statistik (0904-6186)
Published by: Dansk Atletik Forbund/Danish Athletic Federation, Idraettens Hus, Broendby Stadion 20, Brondby, 2605, Denmark. TEL 45-43-262626, FAX 45-43-262325, daf@dansk-atletik.dk, http://www.dansk-atletik.dk. Ed. Erik Laursen.

790.1 016 GBR ISSN 1352-3201
DIRECTORY OF EUROPEAN SPORTS ORGANISATIONS. Text in English. 1992. irreg., latest 1992, 1st ed. GBP 48 per issue (effective 2009). **Document type:** *Directory.* **Description:** Contains list of 1,500 national sports organizations based in Europe.
Published by: C.B.D. Research Ltd., Chancery House, 15 Wickham Rd, Beckenham, Kent BR3 5JS, United Kingdom. TEL 44-20-86507745, FAX 44-20-86500768, cbd@cbdresearch.com, http://www.cbdresearch.com. **Dist. in the U.S. by:** Gale Research Co., 935 Penobscot Bldg, Detroit, MI 48226.

790.1 616 CAN ISSN 1192-1420
RC1230.01D78
DRUG FILE UPDATE; a current awareness index to publications on drugs and doping in sport. Text in English. 1992. a. USD 25. **Document type:** *Abstract/Index.* **Description:** Reflects the latest literature and concerns about drugs and doping in sport from around the world. References grouped by individual sport and country.
Published by: Sport Information Resource Centre (SIRC)/Centre de Documentation pour le Sport, 180 Elgin St, Ste 1400, Ottawa, ON K2P 2K3, Canada. TEL 613-231-7472, FAX 613-231-3739. **Co-sponsor:** Canadian Centre for Ethics in Sport/Centre Canadien pour l'Ethique dans Sport.

796.021 AUT ISSN 1991-8089
FREIZEITUNFALLSTATISTIK. Text in German. 1992. a. **Document type:** *Journal, Trade.*
Formerly (until 2006): Unfallstatistik (1027-9377)
Published by: Kuratorium fuer Verkehrssicherheit, Schleiergasse 18, Vienna, 1100, Austria. TEL 43-1-5770770, FAX 43-1-5770771186, kfv@kfv.at, http://www.kfv.at.

796.352 USA ISSN 1092-2881
GOLF EQUIPMENT BUYERS GUIDE. Text in English. 1997. a. USD 9 per issue (effective 2011). **Document type:** *Guide, Consumer.*
Published by: Werner Publishing Corporation, 12121 Wilshire Blvd, 12th Fl, Los Angeles, Los Angeles, CA 90025. TEL 310-820-1500, FAX 310-826-5008, http://www.wernerpublishing.com.

796.42 AUS ISSN 1322-4875
HANDBOOK OF RECORDS AND RESULTS. Text in English. 1958. a., latest 2006. AUD 24.95 per issue (effective 2009). adv. **Document type:** *Handbook/Manual/Guide, Trade.* **Description:** Covers records and results of the previous seasons Track and Field performances in Australia.
Formerly: Annual Almanac of Records and Results
Published by: Athletics Australia, Ste 22, Fawkner Towers, 431 St Kilda Rd, Melbourne, VIC 3004, Australia. TEL 61-3-98203511, FAX 61-3-98203544, info@athletics.org.au, http://www.athletics.com.au/. Circ: 4,000. **Co-sponsor:** O P T U S.

790.1 011 USA ISSN 1041-2859
GV583
INDEX TO THE SPORTING NEWS. Text in English. 1991. irreg., latest vol.2. USD 57.50 per vol. vol.2 (effective 2009). **Document type:** *Abstract/Index.* **Description:** Provides a complete subject index to the newspaper of record covering sports.
Related titles: Online - full text ed.: USD 57.50 (effective 2003); ◆ Supplement to: The Sporting News. ISSN 0038-805X.
Published by: John Gordon Burke Publisher, Inc., PO Box 1492, Evanston, IL 60204-1492. TEL 847-866-8625, FAX 847-866-6639, info@jgburkepub.com, http://jgburkepub.com.

796.5021 NOR ISSN 0550-0400
HA1501
JAKTSTATISTIKK (YEAR)/HUNTING STATISTICS. Text in English, Norwegian. 1965. a. **Document type:** *Government.*
Related titles: Online - full text ed.: ISSN 1504-2189; ◆ Series of: Norges Offisielle Statistikk. ISSN 0300-5585.
Published by: Statistisk Sentralbyraa/Statistics Norway, Kongensgate 6, P O Box 8131, Dep, Oslo, 0033, Norway. TEL 47-21-090000, FAX 47-21-094973, ssb@ssb.no.

796.6021 NLD ISSN 2210-6146
KERNCIJFERS TWEEWIELERS. Text in Dutch. 200?. a.
Published by: (Bond van Garagehouders (BOVAG)), R A I Vereniging, Postbus 74800, Amsterdam, 1070 DM, Netherlands. TEL 31-20-5044949, FAX 31-20-6463857, info@raivereniging.nl, http://www.raivereniging.nl.

KINESIOLOGY ABSTRACTS. *see* PHYSICAL FITNESS AND HYGIENE—Abstracting, Bibliographies, Statistics

N C A A BASKETBALL. OFFICIAL (YEAR) MEN'S BASKETBALL RECORDS BOOK. *see* SPORTS AND GAMES—Ball Games

338 USA
N S S R A COST OF DOING BUSINESS SURVEY. Text in English. 1989. biennial. USD 125 to non-members (effective 2001). stat. **Document type:** *Monographic series, Trade.* **Description:** Provides productivity and profitability ratios, balance sheet and income statement data for ski and snowboard shops.
Formerly: Ski Cost of Doing Business Survey (1046-3585)
Published by: National Ski & Snowboard Retailers Association, 1601 Feehanville Dr, Ste 300, Mt. Prospect, IL 60056-6035. TEL 847-391-9825, FAX 847-391-9827, nsgatdoyle@aol.com, http://www.nssra.com. R&P Thomas B Doyle. Circ: 400 (controlled).

796.9 CAN ISSN 0828-6647
GV847.8.N3
NATIONAL HOCKEY LEAGUE. OFFICIAL GUIDE & RECORD BOOK. Text in English. 1932. a. USD 24. **Document type:** *Handbook/ Manual/Guide, Consumer.* **Description:** Statistics of contemporary and historic achievements in the National Hockey League. Contains a complete register of all professional players and prospects.
Formed by the 1984 merger of: National Hockey League. Official Guide (0826-5038); National Hockey League. Official Record Book (0826-0214); Which was formerly (until 1983): National Hockey League Guide (0316-8174); (until 1965): National Hockey League Press and Radio Guide (0466-2997)
Published by: National Hockey League Publishing, 50 Bay St, 11th Fl, Toronto, ON M5J 2X8, Canada. TEL 416-531-6535. Eds. Dan Diamond, Greg Inglis. **Dist. by:** Total Sports Publications, 45 Birch St., Apt. 5H, Kingston, NY 12401-1053.

OFFICIAL (YEAR) N C A A BASEBALL RECORDS. *see* SPORTS AND GAMES—Ball Games

OFFICIAL (YEAR) N C A A MEN'S FINAL FOUR RECORDS BOOK. (National Collegiate Athletic Association) *see* SPORTS AND GAMES—Ball Games

OFFICIAL N C A A WOMEN'S BASKETBALL RECORDS BOOK (YEAR). *see* SPORTS AND GAMES—Ball Games

796.323 USA
THE OFFICIAL NATIONAL COLLEGIATE ATHLETIC ASSOCIATION (YEAR) BASKETBALL STATISTICIANS' MANUAL. Text in English. 19??. a. stat. back issues avail. **Document type:** *Handbook/Manual/ Guide, Trade.* **Description:** Provides official statistics rules, interpretations, and special rulings.
Related titles: Online - full text ed.: free (effective 2011).
Published by: National Collegiate Athletic Association, 700 W Washington St, PO Box 6222, Indianapolis, IN 46206. TEL 317-917-6222, FAX 317-917-6888.

796.332 USA
THE OFFICIAL NATIONAL COLLEGIATE ATHLETIC ASSOCIATION (YEAR) FOOTBALL STATISTICIAN'S MANUAL. Text in English. 19??. a. stat. back issues avail. **Document type:** *Handbook/Manual/ Guide, Trade.* **Description:** Provides official statistics, rules, interpretations, and special rulings.
Related titles: Online - full text ed.: free (effective 2011).
Published by: National Collegiate Athletic Association, 700 W Washington St, PO Box 6222, Indianapolis, IN 46206. TEL 317-917-6222, FAX 317-917-6888.

OFFICIAL RULES OF BASKETBALL (YEAR). *see* SPORTS AND GAMES—Ball Games

799.1 GBR ISSN 1365-4667
PIKE & PREDATORS. Text in English. 1996. m. GBP 36 domestic; GBP 54 foreign (effective 2009). adv. back issues avail. **Document type:** *Magazine, Consumer.* **Description:** Covers all angles of predator fishing and fishermen.
Published by: Predator Publications Ltd., Newport, Yorks HU15 2QG, United Kingdom. TEL 44-1430-440624, FAX 44-1430-441319. Ed. Neville Fickling. Adv. contact Chris Ball TEL 44-1590-678400. **Dist. by:** Comag, Tavistock Rd, W Drayton, Middlesex UB7 7QE, United Kingdom.

796.5 388.344 USA ISSN 0744-9569
R V BUSINESS. (Recreational Vehicle) Text in English. 1972. m. (plus a. directory). USD 48; free to qualified personnel (effective 2005). adv. charts; stat.; tr.lit. **Document type:** *Magazine, Trade.* **Description:** Provides statistics about the economical and business aspects of the industry.
Incorporates: R V Business. Annual R V Industry Directory (0893-6501); Former titles (until 1983): Recreational Vehicle Dealer (0886-0041); (until 1982): R V Dealer (0190-6747); Which incorporated (in 1980): R V R - Recreational Vehicle Retailer (0090-3841)
Related titles: Microfiche ed.: (from CIS); Online - full text ed.
Indexed: B02, B15, B17, B18, BusI, G04, G06, G07, G08, I05, SRI, T&II.
Published by: T L Enterprises, Inc. (Subsidiary of: Affinity Group Inc.), 2575 Vista Del Mar Dr, Ventura, CA 93001. TEL 805-667-4100, FAX 805-667-4484. Ed. John Sullaway. Pubs. Sherman Goldenberg, Sherman Goldenberg. Adv. contact Paul Gillerlain. B&W page USD 2,890, color page USD 4,165; trim 8 x 10.75. Circ: 14,000 (controlled).

380 796 310 CAN ISSN 0318-9422
SANFORD EVANS GOLD BOOK OF SNOWMOBILE DATA AND USED PRICES. Text in English. 1972. a. CAD 19.50. **Description:** Current model year and previous thirteen model years listed with weight, length, track width and engine statistics. Factory suggested price and current resale values are featured.
Published by: Sanford Evans Research Group A Subsidiary of Sun Media Corporation, 1700 Church Ave, Winnipeg, MB R2X 3A2, Canada. TEL 204-694-2022, FAX 204-632-4250. Ed., Pub., R&P Gary Henry.

790.1 CAN ISSN 0831-6317
GV567
SPORT THESAURUS; the thesaurus of terminology used in the Sport Database. Text in English. irreg. USD 95.
Related titles: Online - full text ed.
Published by: Sport Information Resource Centre (SIRC)/Centre de Documentation pour le Sport, 180 Elgin St, Ste 1400, Ottawa, ON K2P 2K3, Canada. TEL 613-231-7472, FAX 613-231-3739.

016.7901 016.613 016.6171 CAN
SPORTDISCUS WITH FULL TEXT. Text in English. 1975. base vol. plus m. updates. **Document type:** *Database, Abstract/Index.* **Description:** Includes over 700,000 citations covering all aspect of sport, health, fitness and sport medicine.
Media: Online - full text.

Published by: Sport Information Resource Centre (SIRC)/Centre de Documentation pour le Sport, 180 Elgin St, Ste 1400, Ottawa, ON K2P 2K3, Canada. TEL 613-231-7472, 800-665-6413, FAX 613-231-3739.

688.76 USA ISSN 0193-8401
HD9992.U5
SPORTING GOODS MARKET. Text in English. 1973. a. USD 340 per issue to non-members; USD 290 per issue to members (effective 2009); subscr. includes Sporting Goods Market on CD-ROM. back issues avail. **Document type:** *Report, Trade.* **Description:** Reports consumer purchases of sports equipment and footwear, with channels of distribution and demographic information on age, sex, income, education and census region.
Related titles: CD-ROM ed.; Online - full text ed.
Indexed: SRI.
Published by: National Sporting Goods Association, 1601 Feehanville Dr, Ste 300, Mount Prospect, IL 60056. TEL 847-296-6742, 800-815-5422, FAX 847-391-9827, info@nsga.org, http://www.nsga.org. Ed. Thomas B Doyle TEL 847-296-6742 ext 107.

688.76 USA
SPORTS CLOTHING PURCHASES IN (YEAR). Text in English. 19??. a., latest 2007. USD 190 to non-members; USD 140 to members (effective 2009). **Document type:** *Report, Trade.* **Description:** Provides demographic and financial analysis of clothing purchases related to sports participation.
Formerly: Sports Clothing Expenditures in (Year) (1073-080X)
Related titles: Online - full text ed.
Published by: National Sporting Goods Association, 1601 Feehanville Dr, Ste 300, Mount Prospect, IL 60056. TEL 847-296-6742, 800-815-5422, FAX 847-391-9827, info@nsga.org, http://www.nsga.org. Ed. Thomas B Doyle TEL 847-296-6742 ext 107.

796 USA
HD9992 .U5
SPORTS EQUIPMENT PURCHASES IN (YEAR). Text in English. 1993. a., latest 2004. USD 190 to non-members; USD 140 to members (effective 2009). **Document type:** *Report, Trade.* **Description:** Provides total dollar sporting goods equipment expenditures for 18 sports, including total number of households, average dollar expenditures per household, and household demographics.
Formerly: Sports Equipment Expenditures in (Year) (1073-0826)
Related titles: Online - full text ed.
Published by: National Sporting Goods Association, 1601 Feehanville Dr, Ste 300, Mount Prospect, IL 60056. TEL 847-296-6742, 800-815-5422, FAX 847-391-9827, info@nsga.org, http://www.nsga.org. Ed. Thomas B Doyle TEL 847-296-6742 ext 107.

688.76 USA
SPORTS PARTICIPATION IN (YEAR): LIFECYCLE DEMOGRAPHICS. Text in English. 19??. a. USD 340 to non-members; USD 290 to members (effective 2009). **Document type:** *Report, Trade.* **Description:** Analyzes sports participation by economic status of the participants.
Related titles: Online - full text ed.
Published by: National Sporting Goods Association, 1601 Feehanville Dr, Ste 300, Mount Prospect, IL 60056. TEL 847-296-6742, 800-815-5422, FAX 847-391-9827, info@nsga.org, http://www.nsga.org. Ed. Thomas B Doyle TEL 847-296-6742 ext 107.

688.76 USA
GV583
SPORTS PARTICIPATION IN (YEAR): SERIES I. Text in English. 1984. a. USD 340 to non-members; USD 290 to members (effective 2009). **Document type:** *Report, Trade.* **Description:** Publishes results of research studies on participation in 31 of the most popular sports, with frequency distributions, average days of participation and extensive demographic data on participants.
Related titles: Online - full text ed.
Published by: National Sporting Goods Association, 1601 Feehanville Dr, Ste 300, Mount Prospect, IL 60056. TEL 847-296-6742, 800-815-5422, FAX 847-391-9827, info@nsga.org, http://www.nsga.org. Ed. Thomas B Doyle TEL 847-296-6742 ext 107.

688.76 USA
SPORTS PARTICIPATION IN (YEAR): SERIES II. Text in English. a. USD 340 to non-members; USD 290 to members (effective 2009). **Document type:** *Report, Trade.* **Description:** Publishes results of research studies on participation in 25 activities, from archery to working out. Includes frequency levels, average days of participation and demographic data by age, sex, income and region of the country.
Related titles: Online - full text ed.
Published by: National Sporting Goods Association, 1601 Feehanville Dr, Ste 300, Mount Prospect, IL 60056. TEL 847-296-6742, 800-815-5422, FAX 847-391-9827, info@nsga.org, http://www.nsga.org. Ed. Thomas B Doyle TEL 847-296-6742 ext 107.

688.76 USA
SPORTS PARTICIPATION IN (YEAR): STATE BY STATE. Text in English. 19??. a. USD 340 to non-members; USD 290 to members (effective 2009). **Description:** Projects sports participation on a state-by-state basis for 33 sports ranging from aerobics and bowling to skiing, tennis and volleyball.
Related titles: Online - full text ed.
Published by: National Sporting Goods Association, 1601 Feehanville Dr, Ste 300, Mount Prospect, IL 60056. TEL 847-296-6742, 800-815-5422, FAX 847-391-9827, info@nsga.org, http://www.nsga.org. Ed. Thomas B Doyle TEL 847-296-6742 ext 107.

688.76 GBR
SPORTS PARTICIPATION IN SCOTLAND (YEAR). Text in English. 19??. a. **Document type:** *Bulletin.*
Related titles: Online - full text ed.: free (effective 2010).
Published by: Scottish Sports Council, The Scottish Sports Council, Caledonia House, Redheughs Rigg, Edinburgh, EH12 9DQ, United Kingdom. sportscotland.enquiries@sportscotland.org.uk, http://www.sportscotland.org.uk/.

798.4 GBR ISSN 0307-0093
THE STATISTICAL RECORD. Text in English. 1971. a. GBP 52 per issue (effective 2010). stat. **Document type:** *Report, Trade.* **Description:** Features extensive leading lists including leading sires and maternal grandsires of group winners in Europe.
Supersedes in part (in 1971): Statistical Abstract; (in 1971): General Stud book. Weatherbys Statistical Supplement
Published by: Weatherbys Group Limited, Sanders Rd, Wellingborough, Northants NN8 4BX, United Kingdom. TEL 44-1933-440077, FAX 44-1933-440807, ihelp@weatherbys.co.uk, http://www.weatherbys.co.uk.

799 310 USA ISSN 0736-6450
SK41
U.S. FISH AND WILDLIFE SERVICE. NATIONAL SURVEY OF FISHING, HUNTING AND WILDLIFE - ASSOCIATED RECREATION. Text in English. 1955. irreg. charts; illus.; stat. **Document type:** *Government.* **Description:** Provides information on the number of anglers, hunters, and wildlife watchers, how often they participate and how much they spend on their activities in the United States.
Former titles (until 1980): U.S. Fish and Wildlife Service. National Survey of Hunting, Fishing and Wildlife - Associated Recreation (0191-6947); (until 1975): U.S. Fish and Wildlife Service. United States. Bureau of Sport Fisheries and Wildlife. National Survey of Fishing and Hunting
Published by: U.S. Department of the Interior, Fish and Wildlife Service, 2800 Cottage Way, W-2606, Sacramento, CA 95825. TEL 916-414-6464, FAX 916-414-6486, fisheries@fws.gov.

SPORTS AND GAMES—Ball Games

796.352 USA ISSN 1932-703X
A A GOLF MAGAZINE. (Asian American) Text in English. 2006. bi-m. **Document type:** *Magazine, Consumer.*
Published by: A A Golf Magazine, Inc., 559 W. Diversey Pkwy #128, Chicago, IL 60614. TEL 888-458-8889, FAX 866-505-9994, info@aagolfmag.com, http://www.aagolfmag.com/home/index.php.

796.323 USA ISSN 0733-0448
GV882 CODEN: TAHCDH
A C C BASKETBALL HANDBOOK. (Atlantic Coast Conference) Text in English. 1974. a. 160 p./no.; back issues avail. **Document type:** *Handbook/Manual/Guide, Consumer.*
Published by: U M I Publications, Inc., PO Box 30036, Charlotte, NC 28230. TEL 800-747-9287, status@umipub.com, http://www.umipub.com/.

796.332 USA
A F L PREVIEW. (Arena Football League) Text in English. 2005. a. **Document type:** *Magazine, Consumer.* **Description:** Provides information and analysis of the upcoming season, including personalities and fantasy football.
Published by: American Media, Inc., 1000 American Media Way, Boca Raton, FL 33464. TEL 561-989-1227, 800-609-8312, FAX 561-989-1294, http://www.americanmediainc.com. Circ: 500,000.

796.334 AUS ISSN 1444-2973
A F L RECORD. (Australian Football League) Text in English. 1912. w. (Apr.-Sep.). AUD 185 (effective 2009). adv. bk.rev. charts; stat. **Document type:** *Magazine, Consumer.*
Formerly (until 1999): Football Record (1324-8340)
Indexed: SD.
Published by: Slattery Media Group, AFL House, Ground Fl, 140 Harbour Esplanade, Docklands, VIC 3008, Australia. TEL 61-3-96272600, FAX 61-3-96272650, askus@slatterymedia.com, http://www.slatterymedia.com/. Ed. Peter Di Sisto TEL 61-3-96272637. Circ: 100,000.

794.6 USA ISSN 0001-1754
GV909
A L B A BOWLS. Text in English. 1962. q. USD 3. adv. illus. index.
Indexed: SportS.
Published by: American Lawn Bowls Association, 445 Surfview Dr, Pacific Palisades, CA 90272. Ed. Ferrell Burton Jr. Circ: 6,000.

796.342 USA
A T P TOUR ONLINE; international tennis weekly. Text in English. w. adv. back issues avail. **Document type:** *Newsletter.* **Description:** Features news about men's professional tennis.
Media: E-mail. **Related titles:** Online - full text ed.
Published by: A T P Tour, 201 ATP Blvd, Ponte Vedra Beach, FL 32082. TEL 904-285-8000, FAX 904-285-5966. Ed. Steve Franke.

796.332 USA
A T S CONSULTANTS' (YEAR) ULTIMATE COLLEGE FOOTBALL ANNUAL. Text in English. 2000. a. USD 5.95 newsstand/cover (effective 2001). adv. **Document type:** *Magazine, Consumer.*
Published by: A T S Consulants, 1498 M Reistertown Rd., Baltimore, MD 21208. TEL 800-772-1287, sales@atswins.com, http://www.atswins.com. Ed. John Ryan. Pub. Bob Chase.

796.332 USA
A T S CONSULTANTS' (YEAR) ULTIMATE FANTASY FOOTBALL. Text in English. 2000. a. USD 5.95 newsstand/cover (effective 2001). adv. **Document type:** *Magazine, Consumer.*
Published by: A T S Consulants, 1498 M Reistertown Rd., Baltimore, MD 21208. TEL 800-772-1287, sales@atswins.com, http://www.atswins.com. Ed. John Ryan. Pub. Bob Chase.

796.332 USA
A T S CONSULTANTS' (YEAR) ULTIMATE PRO FOOTBALL ANNUAL. Text in English. 2000. a. USD 5.95 newsstand/cover (effective 2001). adv. **Document type:** *Magazine, Consumer.*
Published by: A T S Consulants, 1498 M Reistertown Rd., Baltimore, MD 21208. TEL 800-772-1287, sales@atswins.com, http://www.atswins.com. Ed. John Ryan. Pub. Bob Chase.

796.34205 GBR ISSN 1750-4996
ACE TENNIS. Text in English. 1982. 6/yr. free to members (effective 2009). back issues avail. **Document type:** *Magazine, Consumer.* **Description:** Features interviews with the stars, the stories behind the championships, tournament reports, previews, and the ATP/WTA ranking lists.
Former titles (until 2004): Ace (1363-4674); (until 1996): Serve & Volley (0958-3009)
Indexed: A11, U01.
—CCC.
Published by: Tennis G B (Subsidiary of: L T A), National Tennis Ctr, 100 Priory Ln, Roehampton, London, SW15 5JQ, United Kingdom. TEL 44-20-84877000, FAX 44-20-84877301, Info@LTA.org.uk.

796.342 USA ISSN 0149-4082
GV991
ADDVANTAGE MAGAZINE. Text in English. 1977. m. membership. adv. back issues avail. **Document type:** *Magazine, Trade.* **Description:** Provides tennis-teaching professionals with educational pieces on all aspects of teaching and coaching, as well as information on U S P T A programs and events.
Indexed: SD, SportS.
Published by: United States Professional Tennis Association, 1 USPTA Centre, 3535 Briarpark Dr, Ste 1, Houston, TX 77042. TEL 713-978-7782, FAX 713-978-7780, uspta@uspta.org, http://www.addvantageUSPTA.com. Ed., R&P Shawna Riley. Adv. contact Diane Richbourg. Circ: 12,000.

796.342 AUS
ADIDAS INTERNATIONAL. Text in English. a. **Document type:** *Magazine, Consumer.* **Description:** Provides information about the Adidas International Tennis Tournament.
Published by: Nicholson Media Group Pty. Ltd., PO Box 1206, Hawksburn, VIC 3142, Australia. TEL 61-3-98268448, FAX 61-3-98278808.

796.352 USA
ADVIL WESTERN OPEN (YEAR). Text in English. a. USD 4 (effective 2001). adv. **Document type:** *Magazine, Consumer.* **Description:** Covers Chicago's own golf tournament.
Formerly: Motorola Western Open (Year)
Published by: Western Golf Association, 1 Briar Rd, Golf, IL 60029. TEL 847-724-4600, FAX 847-724-7133. Ed. Gary J Holaway. Adv. contact Jim Moorhead. Circ: 20,000.

796.352 USA
AFFLUENT GOLFER. Text in English. bi-m. **Document type:** *Magazine, Consumer.*
Published by: S H R International, 270 Bristol St, 200, Costa Mesa, CA 92626ge. TEL 714-668-1660, FAX 714-668-1948.

796.352 305.89607 USA ISSN 1541-2741
AFRICAN AMERICAN GOLFER'S DIGEST. Text in English. 2003 (Spr.). q. USD 18 domestic; USD 28 foreign (effective 2003). adv.
Published by: Event Planners Plus!, 139 Fulton St. Ste. 209, New York, NY 10038. TEL 212-571-6559, FAX 212-571-1943. Pub. Debert C. Cook.

796.3 GBR ISSN 0967-5477
AFRICAN SOCCER; the authoritative voice of the African game. Text in English. 1992. m. GBP 30 domestic; GBP 36 foreign (effective 2009). adv. back issues avail. **Document type:** *Magazine, Consumer.* **Description:** Covers soccer throughout Africa, as played by Africans in their own countries and abroad.
Address: Octagon Court - Unit F, 443-449 Holloway Rd, London, N7 8LJ, United Kingdom. TEL 44-020-75610011, FAX 44-020-72812377, subscription@africansoccer.com, eMaradas@africansoccermagazine.com. Ed., Pub., R&P Emmanuel Maradas. Adv. contact Nim Caswell. color page GBP 3,200. Circ: 35,000 (paid).

796.334 ITA
AGENDA DELLO SPORT. Text in Italian. 1975. a. free. adv. bk.rev. **Document type:** *Newsletter, Consumer.*
Published by: Maurizio Longega, Ed. & Pub., Casella Postale 6291, Rome, RM 00195, Italy. TEL 39-06-330734215, FAX 39-06-39722092, mlongega@quipo.it.

796.3 USA ISSN 1932-9105
AGGIELAND ILLUSTRATED MAGAZINE. Text in English. 2006. bi-m. USD 18 domestic; USD 30 in Canada; USD 42 elsewhere (effective 2008). adv. **Document type:** *Magazine, Consumer.*
Address: PO Box 6841, Bryan, TX 77805-6841. TEL 979-229-8046, 866-552-4624, http://www.aggielandillustrated.com/index.html.

796.3 USA ISSN 1066-405X
AGGIES ILLUSTRATED. Text in English. 1992. 17/yr. USD 49.90 (effective 1998). adv. **Document type:** *Magazine, Consumer.* **Description:** Covers Texas A&M University sports.
Published by: College Sports Communications, Inc., PO Box 803029, Dallas, TX 75380. TEL 972-851-1700, FAX 972-851-1753. Ed. Chris Greer. Pub., R&P Bob Bennett TEL 972-851-1754. Adv. contact Mario Talkington. B&W page USD 800, color page USD 1,200; trim 10.88 x 8.25. Circ: 5,750.

796.332 USA
ALL PRO WEEKLY. Text in English. w. USD 49.95 (effective 2001). adv. **Document type:** *Magazine, Consumer.*
Published by: All Pro Publishing, 3226 Wind River Circle, Westlake Village, CA 91326. TEL 805-379-5171, 888-897-9784, FAX 805-379-1576, techsupport@allpropublishing.com, http://www.allpropub.com. Pub. Jack Pullman.

796.3 CHE
ALMANACCO CALCISTICO SVIZZERO. Text in Italian. 1950. a. CHF 20. adv. stat.
Published by: (Giornale del Popolo), Armando Libotte, Casella Postale, Castagnola, 6976, Switzerland. Circ: 2,000.

796.323 ITA ISSN 1973-5006
ALMANACCO DEL BASKETBALL FEMMINILE. Text in Italian. 2007. a. **Document type:** *Directory, Consumer.*
Published by: Melting Pot, Via Montello 31, Viterbo, 01100, Italy. TEL 39-0761-326294, FAX 39-0761-328282, http://www.mp-edizioni.it.

796.352 USA
ALPINEGOLF.COM; travel newsletter. Text in English. m. **Document type:** *Magazine, Consumer.*
Media: Online - full text.
Published by: ActiveLifestyle Travel Network, Box 3485, Charlottesville, VA 22903-0485. TEL 804-295-1200, FAX 804-296-0948, http://www.alpinegolf.com. Ed. Sieg Terrence.

796.357 USA ISSN 0002-6816
AMATEUR BASEBALL NEWS. Text in English. 1958. 7/yr. USD 5. adv. bk.rev.; film rev. illus. **Document type:** *Newspaper.*
Indexed: SportS.
Published by: American Amateur Baseball Congress Inc., 100 W. Broadway., Farmington, NM 87401-6420. TEL 269-781-2002, FAX 269-781-2060. Ed. Joseph P Cooper. Circ: 10,000.

S

796.357 USA
AMATEUR SOFTBALL ASSOCIATION OF AMERICA. RULES OF SOFTBALL. Text in English. 1933. a. free to members (effective 2009). **Document type:** *Handbook/Manual/Guide, Trade.*
Description: Provides the rules for both fast- and slow-pitch softball.
Formerly: Amateur Softball Association of America. Official Guide and Rule Book (0065-6739)
Published by: Amateur Softball Association of America, 2801 N E 50th St, Oklahoma City, OK 73111. info@softball.org, http://www.softball.org. Ed. Brian McCall.

796.352 USA
AMAZING GOLF NEWSLETTER. Text in English. 1999. m.
Media: Online - full text.
Published by: Kleban Technologies Inc, 1733 H St, Blaine, WA 98230. TEL 604-803-7272, FAX 604-984-7922, webmaster@winningoffers.com. Pub. Stewart Kleban.

796.332 USA ISSN 1533-1180
AMERICAN FOOTBALL MONTHLY; the magazine for football coaches. Abbreviated title: A F M. Text in English. 1995. m. USD 39 domestic; USD 80 in Canada; USD 110 elsewhere (effective 2009). adv. Supplement avail.; back issues avail. **Document type:** *Magazine, Trade.* **Description:** Provides Football coaches with information on all aspects of the game of Football.
Formerly (until 2000): American Football Coach (1526-6990); Which superseded (in May.1999): American Football Quarterly (1095-4783)
Related titles: Online - full text ed.
Published by: L C Clark Publishing Inc, PO Box 13079, North Palm Beach, FL 33408. TEL 800-537-4271, FAX 561-627-3447, ksullivan@lcclark.com. Pub. Travis Davis. Adv. contact Janet Converse TEL 561-627-3393 ext 311. color page USD 3,320, B&W page USD 2,640; trim 8.375 x 10.875. Circ: 15,000.

796.323 ITA ISSN 1122-827X
AMERICAN SUPERBASKET. Abbreviated title: A S B. Text in Italian. 1992. bi-w. (and weekly during the NCAA playoffs (April-June)). EUR 67 domestic; EUR 125 foreign (effective 2008). adv. back issues avail. **Document type:** *Magazine, Consumer.*
Published by: Cantelli Editore Srl, Via Saliceto 22c, Castelmaggiore, BO 40013, Italy. TEL 39-051-6328811, FAX 39-051-6328815, cantelli.editore@cantelli.net, http://www.cantelli.net.

796.352 USA ISSN 1938-4149
GV965.5
AMPUTEE GOLFER. Text in English. a. **Document type:** *Magazine, Consumer.* **Description:** Offers physical and mental therapy to amputees through involvement with golf.
Indexed: SD, T02.
Published by: National Amputee Golf Association, 11 Walnut Hill Rd, Amherst, NH 03031. TEL 800-633-6242, b1naga@aol.com. Ed. Bob Wilson. R&P Jim Coombes. Adv. contact Patty Johnson.

796.33 FRA
L'ANNEE DU FOOTBALL. Text in French. 1973. a. price varies. illus.
Published by: Editions Calmann-Levy, 31 Rue de Fleurus, Paris, 75006, France. TEL 33-1-49543600, FAX 33-1-49543640, http://www.editions-calmann-levy.com. Ed. Jacques Thibert.

796.33 FRA ISSN 0990-1760
L'ANNEE DU RUGBY. Text in French. 1973. a. price varies. illus.
Published by: Editions Calmann-Levy, 31 Rue de Fleurus, Paris, 75006, France. TEL 33-1-49543600, FAX 33-1-49543640, http://www.editions-calmann-levy.com. Ed. Christian Montaignac.

796.342 FRA ISSN 0242-4878
L'ANNEE DU TENNIS. Text in French. 1979. a. price varies. illus.
Published by: Editions Calmann-Levy, 31 Rue de Fleurus, Paris, 75006, France. TEL 33-1-49543600, FAX 33-1-49543640, http://www.editions-calmann-levy.com.

796.333 AUS
ANNUAL TOM BROCK LECTURE. Text in English. 2000. a. **Document type:** *Journal, Academic/Scholarly.*
—BLDSC (1536.6351000).
Published by: Australian Society for Sport History. Tom Brock Bequest Committee, c/o Gary Osmond, The University of Queensland, School of Human Movement Studies, St Lucia, QLD, Brisbane 4072, Australia. http://www.sporthistory.org/TomBrock.htm.

796.334 ITA ISSN 1825-7240
ANNUARIO DEL CALCIO. Text in Italian. 2005. a. **Document type:** *Magazine, Consumer.*
Published by: De Agostini Editore, Via G da Verrazzano 15, Novara, 28100, Italy. TEL 39-0321-4241, FAX 39-0321-424305, info@deagostini.it, http://www.deagostini.it.

796.352 CAN ISSN 1911-7647
L'ANNUEL GOLF. Text in French. 2006. a. CAD 9.95 per issue (effective 2008). **Document type:** *Magazine, Consumer.*
Published by: Editions Gesca, C.P. 9425, Succ. Sainte-Foy, Sainte-Foy, PQ G1V 4B8, Canada. TEL 514-904-5537, 877-997-4653, contact@editionsgesca.ca, http://www.editionsgesca.ca.

796.325 BRA
ANUARIO DE VOLEIBOL. Text in Portuguese. 1992. a. BRL 25, USD 16. **Document type:** *Consumer.*
Published by: Casa Editorial Ltda., Rua Sampaio Vidal, 652, Jd Paulistano, Sao Paulo, SP 01443-000, Brazil. TEL 55-11-30613688, FAX 55-11-852-9430. adv.: page USD 16,000. Circ: 30,000.

796.352 USA
ARIZONA; the state of golf. Text in English. 1999. bi-m. USD 2.95 newsstand/cover (effective 2001). adv. illus. 40 p./no.; **Document type:** *Magazine, Consumer.*
Published by: (Arizona Golf Association), T P G Sports, Inc., 6160 Summit Dr, Ste 375, Minneapolis, MN 55430. TEL 763-595-0808, 800-597-5656, FAX 763-595-0016, info@tpgsports.com, http://www.tpgsports.com. Ed. Russ Christ. Pub. Robert Fallen. R&P Joseph Oberle TEL 763-595-0808 ext 114. Adv. contact Kevin Hartzell TEL 763-595-0808 ext 100. Circ: 45,534 (paid).

796.352 USA ISSN 1947-654X
▼ **ARIZONA GOLF JOURNAL.** Text in English. forthcoming 2010. m. USD 9.99 per issue (effective 2009). **Document type:** *Magazine, Consumer.* **Description:** Features articles on golf for Arizona.
Published by: In Publishing, 9769 NW 45 Ln, Miami, FL 33178. TEL 736-314-0456, info@miamigolfjournal.com.

796.352 GBR
THE ARTISAN GOLFER. Text in English. 1947. q. free to members. **Document type:** *Magazine, Consumer.*
Formerly: Artisan Golfer
Published by: Artisan Golfer, c/o David Tingley, Ed., Dala, Ham Ln, Scaynes Hill, Haywards Heath, W Sussex RH17 7PW, United Kingdom. TEL 44-1444-831358, http://www.agagolf.co.uk/. Ed. David Tingley.

796.352 HKG ISSN 1024-4565
ASIAN GOLFER. Text in Chinese, English. m.
Published by: Country Club Publishing, Ltd., Yue King Bldg, 12th fl., flat G, 1 Leighton Rd, Happy Valley, Hong Kong, Hong Kong.

796.334 GBR ISSN 0263-0354
ASSOCIATION OF FOOTBALL STATISTICIANS. ANNUAL. Text in English. 1981. a. GBP 15. adv. bk.rev. **Document type:** *Report, Consumer.* **Description:** Contains results and statistics from the English and Scottish football season.
—BLDSC (1073.662000).
Published by: Association of Football Statisticians, 18 St Philip Square, London, Essex SW8 3RS, United Kingdom. TEL 44-20-77205079, enquiries@11v11.com, http://www.11v11.co.uk. Circ: 1,600.

796.357 USA
ATHLETICS MAGAZINE. Text in English. 1998. 5/yr. adv. **Document type:** *Magazine, Consumer.* **Description:** Contains articles and features on the Oakland Athletics professional baseball team and players.
Indexed: SD.
Published by: Diablo Publications, 2520 Camino Diablo, Walnut Creek, CA 94597. TEL 925-943-1111, FAX 925-943-1045, info@cdpubs.com, http://www.dcpubs.com/.

796.352 USA
ATHLON SPORTS GOLF. Text in English. 1999. a. USD 6.99 per issue (effective 2008). back issues avail. **Document type:** *Magazine, Consumer.* **Description:** Provides insight into the personalities, courses and tournaments on the professional golf circuit.
Published by: Athlon Sports Communications, Inc., 220 25th Ave N, Ste 200, Nashville, TN 37203. TEL 615-327-0747, FAX 615-327-1149, info@athlonsports.com, http://www.athlonsports.com. Ed. Robert T Doster. **Dist. by:** Ingram Periodicals Inc.

796.332 USA ISSN 1056-1757
GV958.5.A75
ATHLON'S ATLANTIC COAST CONFERENCE FOOTBALL. Variant title: Atlantic Coast Football. Text in English. 19??. a. USD 6.99 per issue (effective 2008). adv. back issues avail. **Document type:** *Magazine, Consumer.* **Description:** Contains complete coverage of the ACC plus national schedules, predictions, special features on players, and more.
Published by: Athlon Sports Communications, Inc., 220 25th Ave N, Ste 200, Nashville, TN 37203. TEL 615-327-0747, FAX 615-327-1149, info@athlonsports.com, http://www.athlonsports.com. Ed. Charlie Miller. Adv. contact Scott Garrett.

796.3 USA ISSN 1056-1641
ATHLON'S BASEBALL. Variant title: Baseball. Text in English. 1988. a. USD 6.99 per issue (effective 2008). back issues avail. **Document type:** *Magazine, Consumer.*
Published by: Athlon Sports Communications, Inc., 220 25th Ave N, Ste 200, Nashville, TN 37203. TEL 615-327-0747, FAX 615-327-1149, info@athlonsports.com. Ed. Charlie Miller. Adv. contact Scott Garrett.

796.332 USA ISSN 1056-1625
GV958.5.I55
ATHLON'S BIG TEN FOOTBALL. Variant title: Athlon's Big Ten. Big Ten. Really Big Ten. Text in English. 19??. a. USD 6.99 per issue (effective 2008). adv. back issues avail. **Document type:** *Magazine, Consumer.* **Description:** Contains complete coverage of the Big 10 plus national schedules, predictions, special features on players, and more.
Published by: Athlon Sports Communications, Inc., 220 25th Ave N, Ste 200, Nashville, TN 37203. TEL 615-327-0747, FAX 615-327-1149, info@athlonsports.com, http://www.athlonsports.com. Ed. Charlie Miller. Adv. contact Scott Garrett.

796.332 USA
ATHLON'S BIG TWELVE FOOTBALL. Text in English. a. USD 6.99 per issue (effective 2009). adv. back issues avail. **Document type:** *Magazine, Consumer.* **Description:** Contains complete coverage of the Big 12 plus national schedules, predictions, special features on players, and more.
Published by: Athlon Sports Communications, Inc., 220 25th Ave N, Ste 200, Nashville, TN 37203. TEL 615-327-0747, FAX 615-327-1149, info@athlonsports.com, http://www.athlonsports.com. Adv. contact Scott Garrett.

796.3 USA
ATHLON'S COLLEGE FOOTBALL. Text in English. a. USD 6.99 per issue (effective 2008). back issues avail. **Document type:** *Magazine, Consumer.*
Published by: Athlon Sports Communications, Inc., 220 25th Ave N, Ste 200, Nashville, TN 37203. TEL 615-327-0747, FAX 615-327-1149, info@athlonsports.com. Ed. Charlie Miller. R&P Chuck Allen. Adv. contact Scott Garrett.

796.332 USA ISSN 1056-1749
ATHLON'S EASTERN FOOTBALL. Text in English. 1976. a. USD 6.99 per issue (effective 2009). back issues avail. **Document type:** *Magazine, Consumer.* **Description:** Contains complete coverage of the Big East plus national schedules, predictions, special features on players, and more.
Formerly (until 190?): Eastern Football
Published by: Athlon Sports Communications, Inc., 220 25th Ave N, Ste 200, Nashville, TN 37203. TEL 615-327-0747, FAX 615-327-1149, info@athlonsports.com, http://www.athlonsports.com. Ed. Charlie Miller. Adv. contact Scott Garrett.

796.332 USA ISSN 1056-1633
GV958.5.P33
ATHLON'S PAC TEN FOOTBALL. Text in English. 1978. a. USD 6.99 per issue (effective 2008). adv. back issues avail. **Document type:** *Magazine, Consumer.* **Description:** Contains complete coverage of the Pac-10 conference plus national schedules, predictions, special features on players, and more.
Formerly (until 19??): Pac Ten Football
Published by: Athlon Sports Communications, Inc., 220 25th Ave N, Ste 200, Nashville, TN 37203. TEL 615-327-0747, FAX 615-327-1149, info@athlonsports.com, http://www.athlonsports.com. Ed. Charlie Miller. Adv. contact Scott Garrett.

796.3 USA ISSN 0734-2888
GV937
ATHLON'S PRO FOOTBALL. Variant title: Pro Football. Text in English. 1982. a. CAD 6.99 per issue (effective 2008). back issues avail. **Document type:** *Magazine, Consumer.*
Published by: Athlon Sports Communications, Inc., 220 25th Ave N, Ste 200, Nashville, TN 37203. TEL 615-327-0747, FAX 615-327-1149, info@athlonsports.com, http://www.athlonsports.com. Ed. Charlie Miller. R&P Chuck Allen. Adv. contact Scott Garrett.

796.332 USA ISSN 1056-1617
GV958.5.S59
ATHLON'S SOUTHEASTERN FOOTBALL. Variant title: Southeastern Football. Text in English. 19??. a. USD 6.99 per issue (effective 2008). adv. back issues avail. **Document type:** *Magazine, Consumer.* **Description:** Contains complete coverage of the SEC plus national schedules, predictions, special features on players, and more.
Published by: Athlon Sports Communications, Inc., 220 25th Ave N, Ste 200, Nashville, TN 37203. TEL 615-327-0747, FAX 615-327-1149, info@athlonsports.com, http://www.athlonsports.com. Ed. Charlie Miller. Adv. contact Scott Garrett.

796.332 USA ISSN 1056-1730
GV959.5
ATHLON'S WESTERN FOOTBALL. Variant title: Western Football. Text in English. 19??. a. USD 6.99 per issue (effective 2008). adv. back issues avail. **Document type:** *Magazine, Consumer.* **Description:** Contains complete coverage of the WAC and Mountain West conferences plus national schedules, predictions, special features on players, and more.
Published by: Athlon Sports Communications, Inc., 220 25th Ave N, Ste 200, Nashville, TN 37203. TEL 615-327-0747, FAX 615-327-1149, info@athlonsports.com, http://www.athlonsports.com. Ed. Charlie Miller. Adv. contact Scott Garrett.

796.333 AUS ISSN 1832-5076
AUSTRALIA V NEW ZEALAND. Text in English. 200?. a. **Document type:** *Magazine, Consumer.*
Published by: News Magazines Pty Ltd., Level 3, 2 Holt St, Surry Hills, NSW 2010, Australia.

796 AUS
AUSTRALIAN CRICKET TOUR GUIDE. Text in English. 1970. a., latest 2005. **Document type:** *Guide, Consumer.*
Formerly: Australian Cricket Yearbook (0084-7291)
Published by: Ken Piesse Cricket Books, PO Box 868, Mount Eliza, VIC 3930, Australia. TEL 86-3-97878023, FAX 86-3-97879667, kenpiesse@ozemail.com.au, http://www.cricketbooks.com.au/.

796.334 AUS ISSN 1832-987X
FOURFOURTWO. Text in English. 2005. m. AUD 79.95 (effective 2008). adv. back issues avail. **Document type:** *Magazine, Consumer.*
Indexed: SD.
Published by: Haymarket Media Pty. Ltd., 52 Victoria St, McMahons Point, Sydney, NSW 2060, Australia. TEL 61-2-83993611, FAX 61-2-83993622, subscriptions@haymarketmedia.com.au, http://www.haymarketmedia.com.au. Ed. Paul Hansford TEL 61-2-83997668. Pub. Andy Jackson TEL 61-2-83997638. Adv. contact Mike Hemmingway TEL 61-2-89082221.

796.352 AUS ISSN 1324-7476
AUSTRALIAN GOLF DIGEST. Text in English. 1970. m. AUD 72 domestic; AUD 110 in New Zealand; AUD 170 elsewhere (effective 2008). adv. **Document type:** *Magazine, Consumer.* **Description:** Provides readers with everything they need to know about how to play and where to play golf.
Former titles (until 1985): Australian Golf (0727-8535); (until 1976): Australian Golf Instructional (0311-0400); (until 1972): Australian Golf (0004-9212)
Related titles: Online - full text ed.
Indexed: SD, SportS.
Published by: News Magazines Pty Ltd., Level 3, 2 Holt St, Surry Hills, NSW 2010, Australia. TEL 61-2-92883000, http://www.newsspace.com.au/magazines. Ed. Steve Keipert. Adv. contact Peter Curtin TEL 61-3-59844394. color page AUD 4,080; trim 210 x 276. Circ: 34,283.

796.342 AUS ISSN 1321-4217
AUSTRALIAN OPEN OFFICIAL TOURNAMENT MAGAZINE. Text in English. 1976. a. price varies. **Document type:** *Magazine, Consumer.* **Description:** Guide for the year in tennis with detailed profiles on top ranked international players. Includes pictures, rankings, interviews, quizzes and tournament facts.
Formerly: Australian Open Official Souvenir Program
Published by: News Custom Publishing, Level 4, HWT Tower, 40 City Rd, Southbank, VIC 3006, Australia. TEL 61-3-92921347, ncp@hwt.com.au, http://www.newscustompublishing.com.au.

796.333 AUS ISSN 1326-4303
AUSTRALIAN RUGBY REVIEW. Text in English. 1987. m. **Document type:** *Magazine, Consumer.*
Former titles (until 1995): International Rugby Review (1324-096X); Incorporates (1997-1998): Try Time (1329-945X)
Indexed: SD.
Published by: Rugby Press International (Subsidiary of: Rugby Press International), Ste 306 Edgecliff Centre, 203-233 New South Head Rd, Edgecliff, NSW 2027, Australia.

796.342 AUS ISSN 1321-0262
AUSTRALIAN TENNIS MAGAZINE; Asia and the Pacific. Text in English. 1976. m. AUD 75 domestic; AUD 105 in Asia & the Pacific; AUD 130 elsewhere; AUD 7.50 newsstand/cover domestic; AUD 8.40 newsstand/cover in New Zealand (effective 2008). adv. back issues avail. **Document type:** *Magazine, Consumer.* **Description:** Presents interviews, pictures and posters of the top international players, Grand Slams, ATP and WTA tournament previews and reviews.
Formerly (until 1993): Tennis Australia (0313-4407)
Indexed: P34, SD.
Published by: Nicholson Media Group Pty. Ltd., PO Box 1206, Hawksburn, VIC 3142, Australia. TEL 61-3-98268448, FAX 61-3-98278808. Ed. Vivienne Christie. Pub. Patrick Rafter. Adv. contact Jackie Cunningham. page AUD 4,400; trim 206 x 275. Circ: 24,000.

B B I A MEMBERSHIP AND PRODUCT INFORMATION GUIDE. *see* BUSINESS AND ECONOMICS—Trade And Industrial Directories

794.6 381 USA
B B I A NEWSLINE. Text in English. q. free. stat. **Document type:** *Newsletter.*
Formerly: B B I A Flashes
Published by: Billiard and Bowling Institute of America, 200 Castlewood Dr, North Palm Beach, FL 33408. TEL 407-840-1120. Ed. Sebastian Dicasoli.

794.72 USA
B C A BREAK. Text in English. 1964. bi-m. free to members (effective 2008). adv. bibl.; illus.; stat.; tr.lit. back issues avail. **Document type:** *Newsletter, Trade.* **Description:** Highlights and promotes significant events, products and services within the billiard industry.
Formerly: Billiard Congress of America Bulletin
Related titles: Online - full text ed.
Published by: Billiard Congress of America, 12303 Airport Way, Ste 290, Broomfield, CO 80021. TEL 312-341-1110, 866-852-0999, marketing@bca-pool.com, http://www.bca-pool.com. R&P Jason Akst. adv.: B&W page USD 300, color page USD 400; trim 10.88 x 8.25. Circ: 1,800.

796.3 CAN
B C SCHOOL SPORTS REPORT. Text in English. 1993. q. CAD 15 (effective 2000). adv. **Document type:** *Newsletter.* **Description:** For secondary school coaches.
Published by: S B C Distributions Ltd., 1367 W Broadway, Vancouver, BC V6H 4A9, Canada. TEL 604-737-3066, FAX 604-737-9844. Ed., Adv. contact Marilyn Payne. page CAD 400. Circ: 1,500.

B T V SPIEGEL. *see* SPORTS AND GAMES

796.352 IRL ISSN 1393-9122
BACKSPIN. Text in English. 2000. q. EUR 3.75 newsstand/cover (effective 2004). adv. **Document type:** *Magazine, Consumer.*
Published by: Golf Business, 4 Rathmichael Manor, Loughlinstown, Co. Dublin, Ireland. TEL 353-1-2827269, FAX 353-1-2827483, golfbiz@eircom.net. Adv. contact Declan O'Donoghue. B&W page EUR 2,000; trim 210 x 297. Circ: 7,500 (paid and controlled).

796.352 CAN
BACKSPIN MANITOBA'S GOLF NEWSPAPER. Text in English. 1990. 4/yr. CAD 10 (effective 1998). adv. **Document type:** *Newspaper, Consumer.*
Published by: Canadian Publishers, 1465 St James St, Winnipeg, MB R3H 0W9, Canada. TEL 204-949-6100, FAX 204-949-6122. Ed. Ralph Bagley. Pub., R&P Gerald L Dorge. Adv. contact Scott Kaisaris. B&W page CAD 1,152, color page CAD 1,452; trim 10.5 x 8.25.

796.352 USA
BAD GOLFER. Text in English. irreg.
Media: Online - full text.
Published by: Travel Golf Media, 2224 N Fremont Blvd, Flagstaff, AZ 86001. TEL 928-213-8046.

796.332 USA ISSN 2155-031X
GV958.W57
▼ **BADGER KICKOFF.** Text in English. 2010 (June). a. USD 12.99 per issue (effective 2011). **Document type:** *Consumer.* **Description:** A preview analysis of the University of Wisconsin Badgers football team.
Published by: Maple Street Press, 155 Webster St, Ste B, Hanover, MA 02339. info@maplestreetpress.com.

796.345 CAN ISSN 0711-124X
BADMINTON CANADA. Text in English. 1981-1986; N.S. 1988. 6/yr. CAD 6, USD 8. adv. **Description:** Covers badminton in Canada.
Address: 1600 Prof James Naismith Dr, Gloucester, ON K1B 5N4, Canada. TEL 613-748-5605, FAX 613-748-5695. Ed. Roy Roberts. Circ: 3,000.

796.334 MEX ISSN 0005-4410
BALON; futbol mundial. Text in Spanish. 1963. w. MXN 832, USD 34.84. **Description:** Covers world soccer news.
Published by: Periodismo Especializado S.A., PRESIDENTES 187, Portales, Mexico City, DF 03300, Mexico. Ed. Antonio Elizarraras Corona.

796.357 973 USA ISSN 1934-2802
➤ **BASE BALL**; a journal of the early game. Text in English. 2007 (Spring). s-a. USD 40 combined subscription domestic to individuals (print & online eds.); USD 55 combined subscription foreign to individuals (print & online eds.); USD 120 combined subscription domestic to institutions (print & online eds.); USD 135 combined subscription foreign to institutions (print & online eds.) (effective 2010). back issues avail. **Document type:** *Journal, Academic/Scholarly.* **Description:** Examines the early history of baseball, from its early days until 1920, as well its rise to prominence and importance within American culture.
Related titles: Online - full text ed.: ISSN 1934-3167.
Published by: McFarland & Company, Inc., PO Box 611, Jefferson, NC 28640. TEL 336-246-4460, FAX 336-246-5018, info@mcfarlandpub.com. Ed. John Thorn.

796.357 USA
BASEBALL. Text in English. q. USD 12 domestic; USD 24 in Canada; USD 34 elsewhere; USD 3.50 newsstand/cover domestic; USD 5.50 newsstand/cover foreign (effective 2003). bk.rev. **Document type:** *Newsletter.* **Description:** Contains non-fiction how-to articles, personal experiences, photo essays, interviews, articles on current events, history and regional news; also publishes fiction with adventure, folktales, history, horror, inspirational and mystery. Information targets baseball writers.
Published by: Tellstar Productions, 2660 Petersbourg, Herndon, VA 20171. Ed. Shannon Bridget Murphy. Circ: 10,000.

796.357 FRA ISSN 2109-5620
▼ **BASEBALL A LA FRANCAISE MAGAZINE.** Text in French. 2010. s-a. **Document type:** *Magazine, Consumer.*
Published by: Baseball a la Francaise, Impasse de Sports - Bat A1, Breal sous Montfort, 35310, France. TEL 33-6-71886367, Contact@bafinfos.com, http://www.bafinfos.com.

796.357 USA ISSN 0745-5372
BASEBALL AMERICA. Text in English. 1981. bi-w. USD 92.95 (effective 2010). bk.rev. illus. 64 p./no. 4 cols./p.; reprints avail. **Document type:** *Magazine, Consumer.* **Description:** Covers baseball at every level, with an emphasis on finding the best players in high school, college and the minors and tracking their progress.
Formerly (until 1982): All-America Baseball News (0228-6033)
Related titles: Online - full text ed.: USD 66 (effective 2010).
Published by: Baseball America, Inc., 4319 S Alston Ave, Ste 103, Durham, NC 27713. TEL 800-845-2726. Ed. Will Lingo. Pub. Lee Folger. Adv. contact George Shelton.

796.357 USA ISSN 0270-4218
GV877
BASEBALL CASE BOOK. Text in English. 19??. a. USD 6.95 per issue (effective 2009). adv. **Document type:** *Handbook/Manual/Guide, Trade.* **Description:** Provides the baseball enthusiasts with in-depth information on the actual play situations.
Published by: National Federation of State High School Associations, PO Box 690, Indianapolis, IN 46206. TEL 317-972-6900, 800-776-3462, FAX 317-822-5700, info@nfhs.org, http://www.nfhs.org.

796.357 USA ISSN 1931-2024
GV863.A1
THE BASEBALL CHRONICLE; year-by-year history of major league baseball. Text in English. 2001. a. **Document type:** *Yearbook, Consumer.*
Formerly (until 2001): 20th Century Baseball Chronicle
Published by: Publications International Ltd., 7373 N Cicero Ave, Lincolnwood, IL 60712. TEL 847-676-3470, FAX 847-676-3671, customer_service@pubint.com.

796.357 USA ISSN 0005-609X
GV862
BASEBALL DIGEST. Text in English. 1941. m. USD 23.94 domestic; USD 40 in Canada; USD 50 elsewhere (effective 2009). adv. charts; illus.; stat. back issues avail.; reprints avail. **Document type:** *Magazine, Consumer.* **Description:** Publishes articles and facts for serious baseball fans. Provides statistics and stories behind the sport.
Related titles: Microform ed.: (from PQC); Online - full text ed.
Indexed: A22, C05, CPL, CPerI, G05, G06, G07, G08, I05, I06, I07, M01, M02, M04, M06, MASUSE, PEI, S23, SD, SPI, SportS, T02.
Published by: Century Publishing Inc., PO Box 730, Coeur d'Alene, ID 83816. TEL 208-765-6300, FAX 208-667-2856, bb@centurysports.net, http://www.centurypublishing.com. Pub. Norman Jacobs. adv.: B&W page USD 3,087, color page USD 5,014; trim 5.38 x 10.5. Circ: 225,000 (paid and controlled). **Subscr. to:** PO Box 360, Mt Morris, IL 61054-0360.

796.357 USA
BASEBALL DIGEST ANNUAL GUIDE. Text in English. 19??. a. **Document type:** *Magazine, Consumer.*
Published by: Century Publishing Inc., E 5710 Seltice Way, Post Falls, ID 83854. TEL 208-765-6300, 800-824-1806, FAX 208-676-8476, privacy@CenturyPublishing.com, http://www.centurypublishing.com.

796.357 USA
BASEBALL HANDBOOK. Text in English. 1940. a. adv. **Document type:** *Magazine, Consumer.* **Description:** Lists baseball rosters, schedules, ticket data and season outlook and stats for all professional baseball teams. Directed to consumers.
Published by: National Research Bureau, 320 Valley St, Burlington, IA 52601. TEL 319-752-5415, http://www.nrbonline.com. Ed. Teresa Levinson. Pub. Michael S Darnall.

796.357 USA ISSN 0883-1033
GV863.A1
BASEBALL ILLUSTRATED (YEAR). Text in English. a. adv. charts; illus. **Document type:** *Magazine, Consumer.*
Published by: Dorchester Media, PO Box 6640, Wayne, PA 19087. TEL 212-725-8811, 800-481-9191, customerservice@dorchpub.com, http://www.dorchesterpub.com. Ed. Stephen Ciacciarelli. Pub. John Prebich.

796.31 USA
BASEBALL INSIGHT; inside stats for serious fans. Text in English. 1982. 28/yr. (w. Apr.-Oct.). looseleaf. USD 8 newsstand/cover; USD 159 (effective 2007). bk.rev. charts; stat. back issues avail. **Document type:** *Newsletter, Consumer.*
Related titles: ◆ Supplement(s): Baseball Insight Annual.
Published by: Parrish Publications, PO Box 23205, Portland, OR 97223. TEL 503-244-8975. Ed., Pub., R&P Phil Erwin. Circ: 400 (paid).

796.31 USA
BASEBALL INSIGHT ANNUAL. Text in English. a. USD 29.95 (effective 2000). **Document type:** *Newsletter, Consumer.* **Description:** Compendium of baseball information.
Formed by the merger of: Logbook (Year); Pitcher and Team Report (Year)
Related titles: ◆ Supplement to: Baseball Insight.
Published by: Parrish Publications, PO Box 23205, Portland, OR 97223. TEL 503-244-8975. Ed., Pub. Phillip Erwin.

796.357 USA ISSN 1081-6070
BASEBALL PARENT. Text in English. 1995. bi-m. USD 29.95; USD 39.95 foreign (effective 1999). adv. illus. **Document type:** *Newsletter.* **Description:** Newsletter exclusively for the parents and coaches of youth baseball players.
Related titles: Online - full text ed.
Address: 4437 Kingston Pike, Ste 2204, Knoxville, TN 37919-5526. TEL 423-523-1274, 800-714-5768, FAX 423-673-8926. Ed., R&P Wayne Christensen.

796.357 USA ISSN 0734-6891
GV862
BASEBALL RESEARCH JOURNAL. Abbreviated title: B R J. Text in English. 1972. a. free to members (effective 2010). adv. back issues avail. **Document type:** *Journal, Academic/Scholarly.*
Related titles: Online - full text ed.
Indexed: A26, AmH&L, CA, E08, G06, G07, G08, I05, I06, I07, S09, S23, SD, SportS, T02.
—Ingenta.
Published by: Society for American Baseball Research, Inc., 812 Huron Rd, Ste 719, Cleveland, OH 44115. TEL 216-575-0500, 800-969-7227, FAX 216-575-0502, info@sabr.org.

796.357 USA
GV877
BASEBALL RULES BOOK. Text in English. 19??. a. USD 6.95 per issue (effective 2009). adv. **Document type:** *Handbook/Manual/Guide, Trade.* **Description:** Contains the official rules for baseball and is used by coaches, officials, players and many fans who wish to know more about the rules of the game.
Former titles (until 1998): Official High School Baseball Rules (0736-7821); (until 19??): Baseball Rule Book. National Federation Edition (0270-1537); Baseball Rules
Published by: National Federation of State High School Associations, PO Box 690, Indianapolis, IN 46206. TEL 317-972-6900, 800-776-3462, FAX 317-822-5700, info@nfhs.org, http://www.nfhs.org.

796.357 USA ISSN 1556-6102
BASEBALL THE MAGAZINE. Text in English. 2005. q. USD 20 domestic (effective 2007); USD 50 in Canada; USD 4.95 newsstand/cover (effective 2006). **Document type:** *Magazine, Consumer.*
Published by: Brevard Softball Magazine, 38 Nevins Ct., Merritt Is, FL 32953-4657. Pub. Gene Smith. Adv. contact Bob Grey.

796.357 USA
BASEBALL UMPIRES MANUAL. Text in English. 19??. biennial. USD 6.95 per issue (effective 2009). adv. **Document type:** *Handbook/Manual/Guide, Trade.* **Description:** Designed for those who wish to enter the field of officiating or to those who are interested in improving their competence in the field of baseball.
Published by: National Federation of State High School Associations, PO Box 690, Indianapolis, IN 46206. TEL 317-972-6900, 800-776-3462, FAX 317-822-5700, info@nfhs.org, http://www.nfhs.org.

BASEBALL YOUTH; the nation's baseball magazine for kids. *see* CHILDREN AND YOUTH—For

796.357 USA
BASEBALL'S ACTIVE LEADERS. Text in English. 1990. 4/yr. (Apr.-Sep). USD 15; USD 4 newsstand/cover (effective 1999). stat. back issues avail. **Document type:** *Newsletter.* **Description:** Aimed at baseball fans interested in unique statistics, records and the Hall of Fame.
Address: 1359 Garden Rd, Wynnewood, PA 19091. TEL 610-649-0750. Ed., Pub. Dan Heisman. Circ: 30 (paid); 10 (controlled).

796.323 DEU ISSN 0946-9605
BASKET; Basketball-Magazin. Text in German. 1994. 10/yr. EUR 35 in Germany & Austria; EUR 42 in Switzerland; EUR 49 elsewhere; EUR 3.90 newsstand/cover (effective 2011). adv. **Document type:** *Magazine, Consumer.*
Published by: abcverlag GmbH, Waldhofer Str 19, Heidelberg, 69123, Germany. TEL 49-6221-75704100, FAX 49-6221-75704109, info@abcverlag.de, http://www.abcverlag.de.

796.336 ESP
BASKET LIFE. Text in Spanish. m. EUR 2.95 newsstand/cover (effective 2009). adv. back issues avail. **Document type:** *Magazine, Consumer.*
Published by: Grupo V, C Valportillo Primera, 11, Alcobendas, Madrid, 28108, Spain. TEL 34-91-6622137, FAX 34-91-6622654, secretaria@grupov.es, http://www.grupov.es/. Adv. contact Amador Moreno. page EUR 5,150; 20 x 27. Circ: 45,000.

796.323 FRA ISSN 0755-7337
BASKETBALL. Text in French. 1933. m. **Document type:** *Magazine, Consumer.*
Published by: Federation Francaise de Basketball, 14 rue Froment, BP 49, Paris, Cedex 11 75521, France. secretairegeneral@basketfrance.com. Ed. Julien Guerineau. Pub. Jean Pierre Guesdon.

796.323 USA ISSN 1074-5270
BASKETBALL AMERICA. Text in English. 1993. m. USD 30 (effective 1998). adv. bk.rev. illus. back issues avail.; reprints avail. **Document type:** *Newspaper, Consumer.* **Description:** Carries features, interviews and insight on college and professional basketball.
Published by: Moore Productions, Inc., PO Box 2982, Durham, NC 27715-2982. TEL 919-477-4588. Ed. John Roth. Pub. Johnny Moore. Adv. contact Russ Hamilton.

796.32 USA
GV885.45
BASKETBALL CASE BOOK. Text in English. 19??. a. USD 6.95 per issue (effective 2009). adv. illus. **Document type:** *Handbook/Manual/Guide, Trade.* **Description:** Provides the basketball enthusiasts with in-depth information on the actual play situations.
Formerly (until 197?): National Federation of State High School Athletic Associations. Basketball Case Book (0525-4663)
Published by: National Federation of State High School Associations, PO Box 690, Indianapolis, IN 46206. TEL 317-972-6900, 800-776-3462, FAX 317-822-5700, info@nfhs.org, http://www.nfhs.org.

796.323 USA
BASKETBALL DIGEST ANNUAL GUIDE. Text in English. a. **Document type:** *Magazine, Consumer.*
Published by: Century Publishing Inc., E 5710 Seltice Way, Post Falls, ID 83854. TEL 208-765-6300, 800-824-1806, FAX 208-676-8476, privacy@CenturyPublishing.com, http://www.centurypublishing.com.

796.323 USA
BASKETBALL HALL OF FAME NEWSLETTER. Text in English. 1979. q. charts; illus.; stat. **Document type:** *Newsletter, Consumer.*
Published by: Basketball Hall of Fame, 1000 W. Columbus Ave., Springfield, MA 01105-2518. Ed. Robin Deutsch. Circ: 4,500.

796.323 USA
BASKETBALL HALL OF FAME YEARBOOK. Text in English. 1972. irreg. back issues avail. **Document type:** *Magazine, Consumer.*
Published by: Basketball Hall of Fame, 1000 W. Columbus Ave., Springfield, MA 01105-2518. TEL 413-781-6500, FAX 413-781-1939, info@hoophall.com, http:www.hoophall.com. Ed. Robin Deutsch.

796.323 IRL ISSN 1393-5372
BASKETBALL IRELAND. Text in English. 1980. 3/yr. adv. **Document type:** *Magazine, Consumer.*
Former titles (until 1997): I B A Irish Basketball (1393-6115); (until 1995): I B B A Official Basketball Magazine (1393-6107); (until 1990): Irish Basketball (0790-8067); (until 1986): Basketball Ireland (0332-4966)
Published by: Victory Irish Promotions, PO Box 7992, Dun Laoghaire, Co. Dublin, Ireland. TEL 353-1-2804481, FAX 353-1-2804481. Adv. contact Margaret Walsh. B&W page EUR 1,206, color page EUR 1,651; trim 210 x 297. Circ: 9,000 (paid and controlled).

796.323 USA ISSN 0270-4226
GV885.2
BASKETBALL OFFICIALS MANUAL. Text in English. 19??. biennial. USD 6.95 per issue (effective 2009). adv. **Document type:** *Handbook/Manual/Guide, Trade.* **Description:** Designed for those who wish to enter the field of officiating or to those who are interested in improving their competence in the field of basketball.

S

Published by: National Federation of State High School Associations, PO Box 690, Indianapolis, IN 46206. TEL 317-972-6900, 800-776-3462, FAX 317-822-5700, info@nfhs.org, http://www.nfhs.org.

796.323 USA
GV885.45
BASKETBALL RULES BOOK. Text in English. 19??. a. USD 6.95 per issue (effective 2009). adv. **Document type:** *Handbook/Manual/Guide, Trade.* **Description:** Contains the official rules for basketball and is used by coaches, officials, players and many fans who wish to know more about the rules of the game.
Formerly: Official National Federation Basketball Rule Book (0270-8280)
Published by: National Federation of State High School Associations, PO Box 690, Indianapolis, IN 46206. TEL 317-972-6900, 800-776-3462, FAX 317-822-5700, info@nfhs.org, http://www.nfhs.org.

796.323 USA ISSN 0737-5212
GV885.45
BASKETBALL - SIMPLIFIED & ILLUSTRATED RULES. Key Title: Basketball Rules Simplified and Illustrated for Officials. Text in English. 19??. a. USD 7.95 per issue (effective 2009). adv. **Document type:** *Handbook/Manual/Guide, Trade.* **Description:** Provides explanation of the actual play situations of basketball with comprehensive diagrams.
Published by: National Federation of State High School Associations, PO Box 690, Indianapolis, IN 46206. TEL 317-972-6900, 800-776-3462, FAX 317-822-5700, info@nfhs.org, http://www.nfhs.org.

796.323 USA ISSN 0744-2866
BASKETBALL TIMES. Text in English. 1978. m. USD 40 domestic; USD 65 in Canada; USD 99 elsewhere (effective 2007). **Document type:** *Magazine, Consumer.* **Description:** Fresh insight and thought-provoking views on the game of basketball.
Formerly: College and Pro Basketball Times (0164-3096)
Related titles: Online - full text ed.
Published by: L S I Productions, 45 Laurel Rd, PO Box 1269, Pinehurst, NC 28370-1269. TEL 910-295-5559, FAX 910-295-6566, subscription-services@basketballtimes.com, info@lsi.net. Pub. Nanci Donald.

796.323 USA ISSN 0005-6170
GV882
BASKETBALL WEEKLY. Text in English. 1967. w. (during season). USD 34.95. adv. bk.rev. illus.; stat. **Document type:** *Newspaper.*
Indexed: SPI, SportS.
Published by: Curtis Publishing Co. (Miami), 8033 N W 36th St, Miami, FL 33166. TEL 305-594-0508, FAX 305-594-0518. Ed. Kevin Kaminski. Pub. Thomas Curtis. Adv. contact Ken Keidel. Circ: 55,000 (paid). **Subscr. to:** PO Box 526600, Miami, FL 33152.

796.342 DEU ISSN 0342-8915
BAYERN TENNIS. Text in German. 1977. 10/yr. EUR 2.80 newsstand/cover (effective 2009). adv. **Document type:** *Magazine, Consumer.*
Published by: Bayerischer Tennis-Verband e.V., Georg-Brauchle-Ring 93, Munich, 80992, Germany. TEL 49-89-15702641, FAX 49-89-15703200, btv@btv.de, http://www.btv.de. Ed. Ludwig Rembold. Adv. contact Stefanie Battke. B&W page EUR 1,760, color page EUR 2,970. Circ: 24,000 (controlled).

796.332 USA ISSN 1056-4284
BEAR REPORT. Text in English. 26/yr. (w. during football season). USD 39.95; USD 2 newsstand/cover (effective 2001). adv. **Document type:** *Newspaper.* **Description:** Covers the Chicago Bears and the NFL. Includes game stories, statistics, coaches' comments and player profiles.
Published by: Royle Publications, Inc., 726 Lois Ln, Sun Prairie, WI 53590. TEL 608-837-2200, FAX 608-825-3053. Ed. Larry Mayer. Pub., R&P Jeffrey Royle. Adv. contact Ron Royle. Circ: 18,000.

BECKETT BASEBALL. *see* HOBBIES

BECKETT BASEBALL CARD PLUS. *see* HOBBIES

BECKETT BASEBALL CARD PRICE GUIDE. *see* HOBBIES

796.357 USA ISSN 1559-5331
BECKETT BASEBALL PREVIEW. Text in English. 2006. a. USD 6.99 (effective 2007). back issues avail. **Document type:** *Magazine, Consumer.*
Related titles: Online - full text ed.
Published by: Beckett Media Llc, 4635 McEwen Rd, Dallas, TX 75244. TEL 714-939-9991, 800-764-6278, customerservice@beckett.com.

BECKETT BASKETBALL. *see* HOBBIES

790.13 796.323 USA ISSN 1542-2925
BECKETT BASKETBALL CARD PLUS. Variant title: Basketball Card Plus. Text in English. 2001. bi-m. USD 9.99 per issue (effective 2008). adv. back issues avail. **Document type:** *Magazine, Consumer.*
Related titles: Online - full text ed.
Published by: Beckett Media Llc, 4635 McEwen Rd, Dallas, TX 75244. TEL 714-939-9991, FAX 714-456-0146, customerservice@beckett.com. adv.: B&W page USD 950, color page USD 2,000; trim 8 x 10.75. Circ: 5,000.

THE BECKETT BASKETBALL CARD PRICE GUIDE. *see* HOBBIES

BECKETT FOOTBALL. *see* HOBBIES

BECKETT FOOTBALL CARD PLUS. *see* HOBBIES

THE BECKETT FOOTBALL CARD PRICE GUIDE. *see* HOBBIES

794.6 GBR
BEDFORDSHIRE COUNTY BOWLING ASSOCIATION. HANDBOOK. Text in English. 1914. a. adv. **Document type:** *Bulletin.*
Published by: Bedfordshire County Bowling Association, c/o Mark Curtis, General Secretary, 6 College Rd, Bedford, MK42 9PL, United Kingdom. TEL 44-1234-400986, genrlsec@bedscba.co.uk, http://www.bedscba.co.uk/mc1ndex.htm. Circ: 800 (controlled).

796.352 JPN
BEIJING GOLF CLUB NEWS. Text in Japanese. a.
Published by: Pan Asia Corporation, 17-3 Ueno 1-chome, Taito-ku, Tokyo, 110-0005, Japan. TEL 03-8374140, FAX 03-8374217.

796.342 DEU ISSN 0723-1407
BEITRAEGE ZUR THEORIE UND PRAXIS DES TENNISUNTERRICHTS UND -TRAININGS. Text in German. 1981. irreg., latest vol.22, 1999. price varies. **Document type:** *Monographic series, Academic/Scholarly.*
Published by: (Deutscher Tennis Bund, Ausschuss fuer Sportwissenschaft), Czwalina Verlag, Bei der Neuen Muenze 4a, Hamburg, 22145, Germany. TEL 49-40-6794300, FAX 49-40-67943030, post@feldhaus-verlag, http://www.edition-czwalina.de.

796.352 USA
BELLSOUTH CLASSIC SPECTATOR HANDBOOK. Text in English. a. adv.
Published by: Atlanta Classic Foundation, 6425 Powers Ferry Rd, 175, Atlanta, GA 30339. TEL 770-951-8777, FAX 770-951-8838.

796.352 USA ISSN 1557-2358
GV961
THE BEST OF GOLF TIPS. Text in English. 1998. a. USD 9 per issue (effective 2011). **Document type:** *Magazine, Consumer.*
Former titles (until 2005): Golf Instruction Annual (1545-5505); (until 2002): The Best of Golf Tips (Year) Instruction Annual (1521-4893)
Published by: Werner Publishing Corporation, 12121 Wilshire Blvd, 12th Fl, Los Angeles, Los Angeles, CA 90025. TEL 310-820-1500, FAX 310-826-5008, http://www.wernerpublishing.com.

796.352 USA ISSN 1550-5928
THE BEST OF NORTHEAST GOLF. Text in English. 2005. a. **Document type:** *Magazine, Consumer.*
Published by: Madavor Media, Llc., 85 Quincy Ave, Ste B, Quincy, MA 02169. TEL 617-706-9110, FAX 617-536-0102, info@madavor.com, http://www.madavor.com.

796.352 DEU
DIE BESTEN! GOLFCLUBS UND GOLFRESORTS. Text in German. 2006. a. EUR 10.50 newsstand/cover (effective 2006). adv. **Document type:** *Magazine, Consumer.*
Published by: Kern & Kern Media Verlag OHG, Simrockstr 5, Bonn, 53113, Germany. TEL 49-228-9354800, FAX 49-228-93548020. adv.: color page EUR 4,900; trim 210 x 297. Circ: 50,000 (controlled).

796.333 AUS ISSN 0311-175X
BIG LEAGUE. Text in English. 1920. 31/yr. AUD 180 domestic; USD 275 in New Zealand; USD 335 elsewhere; USD 4.95 newsstand/cover (effective 2008). adv. **Document type:** *Magazine, Consumer.* **Description:** Provides fans with a full match day program to enhance their experience at the game.
Formerly (until 1973): Rugby League News
Published by: (National Rugby League Ltd.), News Magazines Pty Ltd., Level 3, 2 Holt St, Surry Hills, NSW 2010, Australia. TEL 61-2-92883000, http://www.newsspace.com.au/magazines. Ed. Nigel Wall. Adv. contact Mike Bartlett. page AUD 3,000; trim 210 x 255.

796.325 USA
BIG TEN RECORDS BOOK. Text in English. 19??. a. adv. **Document type:** *Directory, Consumer.*
Related titles: Online - full text ed.: free (effective 2011).
Published by: Big Ten Conference, 1500 W Higgins Rd, Park Ridge, IL 60068. TEL 847-696-1010, FAX 847-696-1150.

796.3 USA ISSN 0889-5988
GV511
BIGGER, FASTER, STRONGER. Text in English. q. USD 14.95 domestic; USD 20 in Canada; USD 21 elsewhere (effective 2000). **Description:** Dedicated to helping athletes and coaches reach their potential in mind, body, and spirit. Aimed at coaches and athletes, junior high through professional.
Address: 805 West, 2400 S, Salt Lake City, UT 84119. TEL 801-974-0460, 800-628-9737, FAX 801-975-1159. Ed. Brook Bowen. R&P Dr. Greg Shepard.

794.72 NLD ISSN 1381-3595
BILJART TOTAAL. Text in Dutch. 1940. m. (11/yr.). EUR 22 domestic; EUR 27 in Belgium; EUR 48.95 in Europe; EUR 70.75 elsewhere (effective 2009). adv. back issues avail. **Description:** Contains information on billiards games.
Formerly (until 1995): Biljart (0166-8749)
Published by: (Koninlijke Nederlandse Biljart Bond), Coolegem Media, Beursplein 37, Postbus 30166, Rotterdam, 3001 DD, Netherlands. TEL 31-10-4052233, FAX 31-10-4055026, info@coolegem-media.nl, http://www.coolegem-media.nl.

796.357 USA ISSN 1940-7998
GV877
THE BILL JAMES GOLD MINE. Text in English. 2008 (Feb.). a. USD 23.95 per issue (effective 2011). back issues avail. **Document type:** *Magazine, Consumer.* **Description:** Includes a wealth of statistics, profiles of players and teams, analysis and essays of current baseball.
Published by: A C T A Sports, 4848 N Clark St, Chicago, IL 60640. TEL 800-397-2282, info@actasports.com.

796.357 USA ISSN 1940-8668
GV863.A1
THE BILL JAMES HANDBOOK. Text in English. 1990. a. USD 24.95 per issue (effective 2011). back issues avail. **Document type:** *Handbook/Manual/Guide, Consumer.*
Former titles (until 2003): S T A T S Major League Handbook; (until 2002): Bill James Presents S T A T S (Year) Major League Handbook; (until 1992): S T A T S (Year) Major League Handbook
Published by: A C T A Sports, 4848 N Clark St, Chicago, IL 60640. TEL 800-397-2282, info@actasports.com.

794.6 USA ISSN 0164-761X
BILLIARDS DIGEST. Text in English. 1978. m. USD 48 domestic; USD 80 foreign (effective 2011). adv. illus. back issues avail. **Document type:** *Magazine, Consumer.* **Description:** Dedicated to the fine art of billiards.
Related titles: Online - full text ed.: Billiards Digest Interactive.
Published by: Luby Publishing, 122 S Michigan Ave, Ste 1506, Chicago, IL 60603. TEL 312-341-1110, FAX 312-341-1469, email@lubypublishing.com, http://www.lubypublishing.com. Pub. Mike Panozzo. Adv. contact Carla Bonner.

794.72 USA ISSN 1047-2444
GV891.A1
BILLIARDS: THE (YEAR) OFFICIAL B C A RULES & RECORDS BOOK. Text in English. 1948. a. USD 7.50 (effective 2008). adv. charts; illus.; stat. **Document type:** *Magazine, Consumer.* **Description:** Contains rules for games of billiards, competition records, instruction, Hall of Fame listings, and history.
Published by: Billiard Congress of America, 12303 Airport Way, Ste 290, Broomfield, CO 80021. TEL 312-341-1110, 866-852-0999, marketing@bca-pool.com, http://www.bca-pool.com. Ed., Adv. contact Jason Akst. Circ: 90,000.

796.357 305.896 USA ISSN 1939-8484
GV863.A1
➤ **BLACK BALL**; a journal of the Negro leagues. Text in English. 2008 (Spr.). s-a. USD 40 combined subscription domestic to individuals (print & online eds.); USD 55 combined subscription foreign to individuals (print & online eds.); USD 120 combined subscription domestic to institutions (print & online eds.); USD 135 combined subscription foreign to institutions (print & online eds.) (effective 2010). bk.rev. back issues avail. **Document type:** *Journal, Academic/Scholarly.* **Description:** Offer new, authoritative research on all subjects related to black baseball, including the Negro major and minor leagues, teams, and players; pre-Negro League organization and play; barnstorming; segregation and integration; class, gender, and ethnicity; the business of black baseball; and the arts.
Related titles: Online - full text ed.: ISSN 1939-8379.
Indexed: CABA, LT, RRTA.
Published by: McFarland & Company, Inc., 960 NC Hwy 88 W, Jefferson, NC 28640. info@mcfarlandpub.com. Ed. Leslie Heaphy.

796.342 USA
BLACK TENNIS. Text in English. 1977. m. USD 15. adv. bk.rev. back issues avail. **Document type:** *Magazine, Consumer.*
Published by: Black Tennis Magazine, Inc., PO Box 210767, Dallas, TX 75211. Ed., R&P Marcus A Freeman Jr. Circ: 15,000.

796.332 USA ISSN 1944-7213
GV885.43.D85
BLUE DEVIL TIP-OFF. Text in English. 2008 (Oct.). a. USD 12.99 per issue (effective 2011). back issues avail. **Document type:** *Magazine, Consumer.* **Description:** Provides analysis and coverage of the upcoming Duke basketball season.
Related titles: Online - full text ed.: free (effective 2011).
Published by: Maple Street Press, 155 Webster St, Ste B, Hanover, MA 02339. TEL 781-347-4730, FAX 781-347-4732, info@maplestreetpress.com. Ed. Julian D King.

796.332 USA
BLUE RIBBON: COLLEGE FOOTBALL YEARBOOK. Text in English. 2000. a. USD 19.95 per issue. **Document type:** *Magazine, Consumer.*
Published by: Blue Ribbon Media, Box 427, Madison, TN 37116-0427. TEL 800-828-4667, FAX 615-870-1413, http://www.blribbon.com. Ed., Pub. Chris Dortch.

796 PER ISSN 1605-3001
EL BOCON. Text in Spanish. d.
Related titles: Online - full text ed.: ISSN 1605-0991.
Published by: Empresa Periodistica Nacional, S.A.C., Jorge Salazar Araoz, 171, Santa Catalina La Victoria, Lima, 13, Peru. TEL 51-1-4709696, FAX 51-1-4758780, admin@epensa.com.pe, http://www.epensa.com.pe/.

796.352 GBR
BOGEY; old game, new breed. Text in English. q. USD 6.99 newsstand/cover in United States; CAD 7.99 newsstand/cover in Canada (effective 2002). **Document type:** *Magazine, Consumer.*
Published by: The Media Cell, 10-16 Tiller Rd, Docklands, London, E14 8PX, United Kingdom. TEL 44-207-9876166, mail@themediacell.com, http://www.themediacell.com. Ed. Steve Muncey.

796.352 USA
BOGEYS TO BIRDIES. Text in English. 1999. w. back issues avail. **Document type:** *Newsletter.* **Description:** Includes articles dealing with aspects of the game and insights into the people who play on the tour.
Media: Online - full text.
Published by: USA GolfLink.com, PO Box 481, Celina, OH 45822. TEL 419-586-4151.

796.334 DEU
BOLZEN. Text in German. 2004. 4/yr. EUR 8 (effective 2006). adv. **Document type:** *Magazine, Consumer.*
Published by: Intro GmbH & Co. KG, Herwarthstr 12, Cologne, 50672, Germany. TEL 49-221-5890903, FAX 49-221-5626509, intro@intro.de. Ed. Thorsten Schaar. adv.: color page EUR 7,500. Circ: 200,000 (paid and controlled).

796.357 USA
BOOK OF BASEBALL RECORDS. Text in English. a. USD 17.95.
Published by: Seymour Siwoff, Ed. & Pub., 500 Fifth Ave, New York, NY 10110. TEL 212-869-1530.

796.357 USA ISSN 1075-8542
GV875.B6
BOSTON BASEBALL. Text in English. 1990. m. USD 19.95; USD 1.95 newsstand/cover. adv. **Document type:** *Magazine, Consumer.* **Description:** Gives an overview of the Major and Minor League Boston Red Sox.
Formerly (until 1994): Boston Baseball Underground (1070-5678)
Published by: Pennant Publications, Inc., 54 Martin St, Essex, MA 01929-1256. Ed., Adv. contact M. Rutstein. R&P M Rutstein. B&W page USD 400; 10 x 8. Circ: 40,000 (paid).

796.323 USA ISSN 0361-6894
GV885.52.B67
BOSTON CELTICS OFFICIAL YEARBOOK. Text in English. 19??. a. adv. **Document type:** *Yearbook, Consumer.*
Published by: Phoenix Media / Communications Group, 126 Brookline Ave, Boston, MA 02215. TEL 617-859-8201, letters@phx.com, http://www.thephoenix.com. Adv. contact Howard Temkin TEL 617-859-3242.

796.3 FRA ISSN 1950-943X
BOULISME; petanque et jeu provencal. Text in French. 2006. q. EUR 20 (effective 2009). **Document type:** *Magazine, Consumer.*
Address: 26 Rue Marceau, Issy-les-Moulineaux, 92130, France. TEL 33-1-46292912, FAX 33-1-47362052. Ed. Pierre-Marie Vidal.

794.6 SWE ISSN 1101-3273
BOWLAREN MAGAZINET. Text in Swedish. 1922. 6/yr. SEK 180 (effective 2005). **Document type:** *Magazine, Consumer.*
Formerly (until 1990): Bowlaren (0345-1682)
Published by: (Svenska Bowlingfoerbundet/Swedish Bowling Federation), Tidningen Bowlaren, PO Box 1164, Varberg, 43216, Sweden. TEL 46-340-629230, FAX 46-340-629202. Circ: 23,000.

794.6 NLD ISSN 2210-2485
BOWLEN.NL. Text in Dutch. 1969. bi-m. EUR 20.95 (effective 2010). adv. **Document type:** *Magazine, Consumer.*

Former titles (until 2010): Bowling Sportmagazine (0922-3150); (until 1988): Bowling Revue (0166-9346)
Published by: (Nederlandse Bowling Federatie), Bondsbureau Nederlandse Bowling Federatie, Landjuweel 5, Veenendaal, 3905 PE, Netherlands. TEL 31-318-559343, FAX 31-318-559349, info@bowlingnbf.nl, http://www.bowlingnbf.nl. Ed. Peter Onvlee. adv.: page EUR 1,250; trim 210 x 297. Circ: 25,000.

794.6 GBR ISSN 0962-8096
BOWLERS' WORLD. Text in English. 1977. m. GBP 11.75; GBP 0.70 newsstand/cover. adv. bk.rev. **Document type:** *Magazine, Consumer.* **Description:** Covers all aspects of flat green bowling.
Published by: Pressland Services Ltd., 64-68 Greenfield Rd, Dentons Green, St Helens, Merseyside WA10 6SL, United Kingdom. TEL 44-1744-731314, FAX 44-1744-275586. Ed. Terry Magee. R&P Brian Coaley. Adv. contact Dennis Groves. Circ: 13,000.

BOWLING CENTER MANAGEMENT. *see* BUSINESS AND ECONOMICS—Management

794.6 USA
BOWLING NEWS. Text in English. 1940. w. USD 25. adv. bk.rev. **Document type:** *Magazine, Consumer.* **Description:** Bowling news for and about bowling and bowlers.
Formerly: California Bowling News (0008-0918)
Published by: Bowling News, Inc., 2606 W Burbank Blvd, Burbank, CA 91505. TEL 818-849-4664, FAX 818-845-6321. Ed. Al Sabo. Adv. contact Lillian Oak. Circ: 14,000.

796.3 GBR ISSN 0262-6942
BOWLS INTERNATIONAL; Britains's brightest and best read bowls magazine. Text in English. 1981. m. GBP 24 includes domestic & USA; GBP 36 elsewhere; GBP 3.20 per issue (effective 2010). adv. bk.rev. charts; illus. 64 p./no.; back issues avail. **Document type:** *Magazine, Consumer.* **Description:** Provides bowlers with an ideal blend of interesting, entertaining, informative and instructional articles, supported by the latest news and views from some of the sport's biggest and influential names.
Published by: Key Publishing Ltd., PO Box 300, Stamford, Lincs PE9 1NA, United Kingdom. info@keypublishing.com, http://www.keypublishing.com. Ed. Melvyn Beck. Adv. contact David Thorpe.

796.31 AUS
BOWLS N S W MAGAZINE. Text in English. 1992. 10/yr. adv. bk.rev. **Document type:** *Magazine, Consumer.* **Description:** Covers lawn bowling.
Formerly: Bowls Alive (1038-5401); Which was formed by the merger of: N.S.W. Bowls in N.S.W.; (1936-1991): Bowls News (0006-8454)
Related titles: ◆ Supplement(s): N.S.W. Bowls News.
Indexed: SportS.
Published by: Royal New South Wales Bowling Association Inc., PO Box A 2186, Sydney South, NSW 1235, Australia. TEL 61-2-92834555, FAX 61-2-92834252, mswba@rnswba.org.au, http://www.rnswba.org.au. Adv. contact Beverly Trippas. B&W page AUD 3,030, color page AUD 4,841; trim 190 x 270.

796.3 AUS ISSN 1833-9123
BREAK O' DAY. Text in English. 199?. m. **Document type:** *Newsletter, Consumer.*
Related titles: E-mail ed.: ISSN 1833-9131. 2001.
Published by: Australian Cricket Society Tasmania Inc., 6 Liena Rd, Lindisfarne, TAS 7015, Australia.

796 IRL ISSN 1649-0673
BREAKING BALL. Text in English. 2001. m. adv. **Document type:** *Magazine, Consumer.*
Published by: Setanta Media, Broadcasting House, 3a South Princes St., Dublin, 2, Ireland. TEL 353-1-4748044, FAX 353-1-4748050, feedback@setanta.com. adv.: page EUR 2,286; bleed 216 x 303. Circ: 20,000 (paid and controlled).

796.332 NLD ISSN 1877-2889
BRINVEST VOETBALJAARBOEK. Text in Dutch. 2006. a. EUR 14.95 (effective 2011).
Published by: Uitgeverij De Buitenspelers, Gedempte Zalmhaven 315, Rotterdam, 3011 BT, Netherlands. TEL 31-10-4113750, info@debuitenspelers.nl, http://www.debuitenspelers.nl.

796.334 AUS ISSN 1445-7954
BRITISH FOOTBALL WEEK. Abbreviated title: B F W. Text in English. 1986. w. AUD 175 domestic; AUD 256 in Asia & the Pacific; GBP 106 elsewhere (effective 2009). adv. back issues avail. **Document type:** *Newspaper, Consumer.* **Description:** Provides information of match reports and news of players and clubs in UK, detailed results and league standings published in Australia three days after matches are played.
Formerly (until 2001): British Soccer Week (0817-1203)
Related titles: Online - full text ed.: AUD 62, NZD 72, GBP 25, EUR 38, USD 60, CAD 70 (effective 2009).
Published by: The International Publishing Group, PO BOX 393, Belmont, W.A. 6984, Australia. TEL 61-8-93624134, 800-809-233, FAX 61-8-94703162, wa@ipgonline.cc, http://www.ipgaustralia.com. Adv. contact Anita Barker. Circ: 19,100 (paid).

796.332 USA ISSN 1942-0595
GV958.O35
BUCKEYE BATTLE CRY. Text in English. 2008 (Jul). a. USD 12.99 per issue (effective 2011). back issues avail. **Document type:** *Handbook/Manual/Guide, Consumer.* **Description:** Devotes over 100 pages to the storylines that are most important to Buckeye fans heading into the season.
Published by: Maple Street Press, 155 Webster St, Ste B, Hanover, MA 02339. TEL 781-347-4730, FAX 781-347-4732, info@maplestreetpress.com. Ed. Jason Priestas.

796.352 USA
BUICK OPEN TOURNAMENT PROGRAM. Text in English. a. adv. **Description:** Contains golf-related information for those attending the Buick Open golf tournament.
Published by: Buick Open Marketing, 535 Griswold, 2000, Detroit, MI 48226. TEL 800-878-6736, FAX 313-967-9646.

796.357 USA
BULLPEN. Text in English. q. adv. **Description:** Regulation amateur youth baseball and softball program.
Published by: Babe Ruth League, 1770 Brunswick Ave, Box 5000, Trenton, NJ 09638. TEL 609-695-1434, FAX 609-695-2505. Circ: 32,000 (controlled).

794 DEU ISSN 0949-2194
BUNDESLIGA (YEAR). Text in German. 1998. a. adv. **Document type:** *Magazine, Consumer.*
Published by: Axel Springer Verlag AG, Axel-Springer-Platz 1, Hamburg, 20350, Germany. TEL 49-40-34700, FAX 49-40-34728460, bmertin@asv.de, http://www.asv.de. adv.: color page EUR 20,100. Circ: 500,000 (controlled).

794 CHE
BUNDESLIGA-MAGAZIN. Text in German. 2005. m. adv. **Document type:** *Magazine, Trade.*
Published by: (Deutsche Fussball Liga DEU), Sportverlag Europa Medien AG, Seestr 473, Zurich, 8038, Switzerland. TEL 41-43-3050560, FAX 41-43-3050566, info@sportverlageuropa.com, http://www.sportverlageuropa.com. Circ: 36,000 (controlled).

796.334 658.8 GBR ISSN 1759-9237
BUSINESS RATIO REPORT. FOOTBALL CLUBS. Text in English. 1986. irreg., latest no.12, 2009, Jul. GBP 365 per issue (effective 2010). charts; stat. **Document type:** *Report, Trade.*
Former titles (until 2008): Business Ratio. Association Football League Clubs (1467-4572); (until 1999): Business Ratio Plus. Association Football Clubs (1368-5457); (until 1993): Business Ratio Report. Association Football Clubs (0269-9125)
Published by: Key Note Ltd. (Subsidiary of: Bonnier Business Information), Harlequin House, 5th Fl, 7 High St, Teddington, Richmond upon Thames, TW11 8EE, United Kingdom. TEL 44-845-5040452, FAX 44-845-5040453, sales@keynote.co.uk.

796.323 USA
C B A NEWSLETTER. Text in English. 1978. w. (Nov.-Apr.). USD 40. adv. **Document type:** *Newsletter.*
Former titles: C B A Update; C B A Newsweekly
Published by: Continental Basketball Association, 400 N Fifth St, Phoenix, AZ 85004-3902. TEL 602-254-6677. Eds. Brett Meister, Greg Anderson. Circ: 1,500.

796.334 USA
CAL SOUTH YOUTH SOCCER. Text in English. q. membership. adv. bk.rev.; video rev. illus. **Document type:** *Magazine, Consumer.* **Description:** Brings news of Southern California soccer to a regional audience.
Formerly: Cal-South Youth Soccer News
Address: 1029 S. Placentia Ave., Fullerton, CA 92831. TEL 714-778-2972, 888-429-7276, FAX 714-441-0715, ajohnson@calsouth.com, http://www.calsouth.com/. adv.: B&W page USD 2,000, color page USD 3,200; bleed 8.375 x 11.125.

796.332 GBR
CALCIO ITALIA; complete English guide to Italian football. Text in English. 1996. m. GBP 23.95 (effective 2009). adv. back issues avail. **Document type:** *Magazine, Consumer.* **Description:** Provides coverage of all aspects of the Italian football scene.
Formerly (until Sep.2002): Football Italia (1362-1408)
Related titles: Online - full text ed.: GBP 23.95 (effective 2009).
—CCC.
Published by: Anthem Publishing Ltd., Piccadilly House, Ste 6, London Rd, Bath, BA1 6PL, United Kingdom. TEL 44-1225-489984, FAX 44-1225-489980, enquiries@anthem-publishing.com, http://www.anthem-publishing.com/. Ed. John Taylor. Adv. contact Simona Lewis. Circ: 52,000 (paid).

796.352 USA ISSN 1947-6353
▼ **CALIFORNIA GOLF JOURNAL.** Text in English. forthcoming 2010. m. USD 9.99 per issue (effective 2009). **Document type:** *Magazine, Consumer.* **Description:** Features articles on all aspects of golf in California.
Published by: In Publishing, 9769 NW 45 Ln, Miami, FL 33178. TEL 736-314-0456, info@miamigolfjournal.com.

796.352 USA ISSN 1559-5552
CALLAWAY GOLF. Text in English. 2004 (Feb.). q. free (effective 2006). adv. back issues avail. **Document type:** *Magazine, Consumer.* **Description:** Features stories, interviews, tips, travel, finance, real estate, fashion, style, food and the inside track on the latest Callaway products.
Related titles: Online - full text ed.
Published by: MacDuff Publishing, LLC, 2000 RiverEdge Park, Suite 925, Atlanta, GA 30328. TEL 770-859-9600, FAX 770-859-9686, http://www.macduffpublishing.com. Ed. Nick Wright. Pub. Larry Dorman. adv.: color page USD 45,240. Circ: 724,000.

796.352 CAN ISSN 0316-8131
CANADIAN AND PROVINCIAL GOLF RECORDS. Text in English. 1972. a. **Document type:** *Report, Academic/Scholarly.* **Description:** Complete records for all provincial and national golf tournaments in Canada since the 1880's.
Formerly: Royal Canadian Golf Association. National Tournament Records (0316-8212)
Published by: Royal Canadian Golf Association, Golf House, R R 2, Oakville, ON L6J 4Z3, Canada. TEL 416-844-1800, FAX 416-845-7040. Circ: 1,500.

796.352 CAN ISSN 0084-8565
CANADIAN LADIES' GOLF ASSOCIATION. YEAR BOOK. Text in English, French. 1947. a. CAD 5. adv. bk.rev. illus.; stat. index. **Document type:** *Newsletter.*
Published by: Canadian Ladies' Golf Association, Glen Abbey Golf House, 1333 Dorval Dr, Oakville, ON L6J 4Z3, Canada. TEL 905-849-2542, 800-455-2541. Ed., R&P Janet Lymer. Circ: 10,000.

796.335 CAN ISSN 1185-9792
CANADIAN RULE BOOK FOR TACKLE FOOTBALL. Text in English. 1974. irreg., latest 2004.
Former titles (until 1991): Rule Book for Tackle Football (1184-0331); (until 1989): Canadian Rule Book for Amateur Football (0229-2580)
Published by: Football Canada, Lansdowne Park, Civic Centre, 1015 Bank St, Ottawa, ON K1S 3W7, Canada. TEL 613-564-2675, FAX 613-564-6309, http://www.footballcanada.com.

796.325 CAN ISSN 0834-2946
GV1015.39
CANADIAN VOLLEYBALL ASSOCIATION. RULE BOOK. Text in English. a. CAD 8. adv.
Former titles (until 1987): Canadian Volleyball Association. Rule Book and Annual (0831-8794); Canadian Volleyball Annual and Rule Book (0576-6346)
Related titles: French ed.: Association Canadienne de Volley-ball. Regle de Jeu. ISSN 0834-2938.
Published by: Canadian Volleyball Association, 1600 James Naismith Dr, Ste 709, Gloucester, ON K1B 5N4, Canada. TEL 613-748-5681, FAX 613-748-5727, TELEX 053-3660 SPORTREC. Circ: 12,000.

796 VEN
CANCHA. Text in Spanish. 1971. m. adv.
Published by: Urbanizacion Horizonte, 2da Traversal, Qta. Mabel, Caracas, Venezuela.

CARD TRADE; official trade journal of the sports collectible industry. *see* HOBBIES

796.332 GBR ISSN 0966-3061
CELTIC VIEW; the brightest and best club weekly. Text in English. 1965. w. GBP 160 (effective 2009). bk.rev. back issues avail. **Document type:** *Magazine, Consumer.* **Description:** Provides latest news from the club, including exclusive interviews with the manager and first-team players along with a whole variety of great features, including interviews with former Celts and informative historical articles.
Published by: Celtic Football Club, Celtic Park, Glasgow, G40 3RE, United Kingdom. TEL 44-871-2261888, homematches@celticfc.co.uk.

796.345 FRA ISSN 1955-0103
CENT POUR CENT BADMINTON. Key Title: 100% Badminton. Text in French. 2006. q. EUR 2 to qualified personnel; EUR 4 to individuals (effective 2009). **Document type:** *Magazine, Consumer.*
Formerly (until 2006): Badminton Magazine (0996-5815)
Published by: Federation Francaise de Badminton, 9-11 Av. Michelet, Saint-Ouen, 93583 Cedex, France. TEL 33-1-49450707, FAX 33-1-49451871, ffba@ffba.org.

796.342 NLD ISSN 1574-2148
CENTRE COURT. Text in Dutch. q. EUR 11.90; EUR 3.20 newsstand/cover (effective 2009). adv. **Document type:** *Magazine, Consumer.*
Related titles: Online - full text ed.: ISSN 1876-5017.
Published by: Koninklijke Nederlandse Lawn Tennis Bond, Postbus 1617, Amersfoort, 3800 BP, Netherlands. TEL 31-33-4542600, FAX 31-33-4542645, http://www.knltb.nl. Ed. Debbie Best.

796.334 GBR
CHAMPIONS (LONDON). Text in English. 2003 (Sep.). bi-m. GBP 19 (effective 2009). adv. **Document type:** *Magazine, Consumer.* **Description:** Contains articles and photos covering the UEFA Champions League.
Related titles: French ed.; German ed.
Published by: (Union des Associations Europe'ennes de Football CHE), Haymarket Network (Subsidiary of: Haymarket Media Group), Teddington Studios, Broom Rd, Teddington, TW11 9BE, United Kingdom. TEL 44-20-82675013, FAX 44-20-82675194, enquiries@haymarket.com, http://www.haymarketnetwork.com. Circ: 15,000.

796.334 FRA ISSN 1964-9428
CHAMPIONS FUN. Text in French. 2008. q. **Document type:** *Magazine, Consumer.*
Published by: Paperbox, 24 Av. Pierre-et-Marie-Curie, Le Blanc-Mesnil, 93150, France.

796.334 GBR ISSN 1362-8364
CHELSEA. Text in English. 1996-2002; resumed 2004. m. free to members. adv. **Document type:** *Magazine, Consumer.* **Description:** Covers all aspects of the Chelsea Football Club as it battles its way through the English Premier League and European competition.
—CCC.
Published by: (Chelsea Football Club), Profile Sports Media, Marmaid House, 2 Puddle Dock, London, United Kingdom. TEL 44-20-73322000, FAX 44-20-73322001.

796.352 USA ISSN 2155-3963
▼ **CHICAGO AREA GOLF.** Text in English. 2010 (June). m. (Mar. to Nov.). USD 20 (effective 2011). **Document type:** *Magazine, Consumer.*
Related titles: Online - full text ed.: free (effective 2011).
Published by: Chicagoland Golf Media, PO Box 99, Burlington, IL 60109. TEL 847-683-4770, valruss@aol.com.

196.332 USA
CHICAGO CUBS OFFICIAL YEARBOOK. Text in English. 1985. irreg., latest 1994. illus. **Document type:** *Magazine, Consumer.*
Published by: Woodford Publishing, Inc., PO Box 910, Tiburon, CA 94920. TEL 415-397-1853, FAX 415-399-0942. Ed. Jon Rochmis. Pub. Laurence J Hyman. R&P, Adv. contact David Lilienstein.

796.352 USA ISSN 1087-6502
CHICAGO DISTRICT GOLFER. Text in English. 1990. bi-m. free to members (effective 2008). adv. 52 p./no.; back issues avail. **Document type:** *Journal, Academic/Scholarly.* **Description:** Provides information about chicago golf information.
Formerly: Score Card
Related titles: Special ed(s).: Chicago District Golfer. Annual Directory.
Published by: (Chicago District Golf Association), T P G Sports, Inc., 6160 Summit Dr, Ste 375, Minneapolis, MN 55430. TEL 763-595-0808, 800-597-5656, FAX 763-595-0016, info@tpgsports.com. Ed. Cathy Ralston. Pub. Robert Fallen. R&P Joseph Oberle TEL 763-595-0808 ext 114. Adv. contact Kevin Hartzell TEL 763-595-0808 ext 100. page USD 4,700; 8.25 x 10.875. Circ: 70,000.

796.352 USA
CHICAGOLAND GOLF. Text in English. 1989. 15/yr. USD 20 (effective 2007). adv. bk.rev. **Document type:** *Magazine, Consumer.* **Description:** Provides information, previews, photographs and reporting on the PGA events in the area. Covers area courses, travel, teaching techniques and interviews.
Published by: Chicagoland Golf Publishing Co., PO Box 4116, Wheaton, IL 60189. TEL 630-719-1000, FAX 630-719-1030. Ed., Pub. Phil Kosin. Circ: 55,000.

796.357 781.64 USA
CHINMUSIC!. Text in English. irreg. USD 4. **Document type:** *Magazine, Consumer.* **Description:** For avid baseball fans who happen to like alternative music.
Address: PO Box 225029, San Francisco, CA 94122-5029.

S

796.357 USA ISSN 1555-1547
CHOPTALK; official monthly magazine of the Atlanta Braves. Text in English. 1994-2005 (Jan.); resumed 2005 (Apr.). m. USD 36.50 domestic; USD 54.95 in Canada & Mexico; USD 74.95 elsewhere (effective 2007). adv. 64 p./no.; **Document type:** *Magazine, Consumer.* **Description:** Presents official and insider information on the Atlanta Braves baseball team and personnel.
Published by: Wonderdog Publishing Inc., PO Box 922847, Atlanta, GA 30010-2287. TEL 877-655-2467, FAX 770-813-0782. Ed. Gary Caruso. adv.: page USD 1,350. Circ: 20,000.

796.357 GBR
CLUB CRICKET CONFERENCE OFFICIAL YEARBOOK. Abbreviated title: C C C Yearbook. Text in English. 1915. a. free to members (effective 2009). **Document type:** *Yearbook, Trade.* **Description:** Contains details of all clubs, club officials, and contact numbers, along with reports, features, and details of the previous year's representative and Inter-League matches.
Formerly (until 1996): Club Cricket Conference Official Handbook
Published by: Club Cricket Conference, Top Fl, 24-26 High St, Hampton Hill, Middlesex TW12 1PD, United Kingdom. TEL 44-20-89731612, FAX 44-870-1432824, enquiries@club-cricket.co.uk, http://www.club-cricket.co.uk.

796.325 796.077 USA
THE COACH. Text in English. q. USD 20; USD 40 foreign (effective 1998). **Document type:** *Magazine, Trade.*
Published by: American Volleyball Coaches Association, 2365 Harrodsburg Rd, Ste A325, Lexington, KY 40504. TEL 859-226-4315, 866-544-2822, FAX 859-226-4338, members@avca.org, http://www.avca.org.

796.357 USA ISSN 1047-5206
COACHING DIGEST. Text in English. s-a. USD 30 domestic membership; USD 35 in Canada membership; USD 40 elsewhere membership (effective 2007). adv. **Document type:** *Magazine, Trade.* **Description:** Seeks to assist members by increasing their education and awareness of the sport of baseball.
Published by: American Baseball Coaches Association, 108 S. University Ave, Ste 3, Mt. Pleasant, MI 48858-2327. TEL 989-775-3300, FAX 989-775-3600, abca@abca.org. Eds. Betty Rulong, Craig Rutter. R&P Betty Rulong. Adv. contact Dave Keilitz. Circ: 6,000 (controlled).

796.3 USA
COACHING MANAGEMENT. Text in English. 19??. m. price varies. adv. **Document type:** *Magazine, Trade.* **Description:** Discusses new trends in the sport, coaching strategies, and working with players and assistant coaches. The sports that are covered are basketball, football, baseball, volleyball, and softball and track and field.
Published by: Momentum Media Sports Publishing, 31 Dutch Mill Rd, Ithaca, NY 14850. TEL 607-257-6970, FAX 607-257-7328, CoachesNetwork@MomentumMedia.com, http://www.coachesnetwork.com.

796.3 USA ISSN 0894-4237
GV1015.5.C63
COACHING VOLLEYBALL; the official journal of the American Volleyball Coaches Association. Text in English. 1987-1990; resumed 199?. bi-m. USD 43 domestic; USD 60 foreign (effective 2003); free to members (effective 2005). adv. bk.rev. charts; illus.; stat.; tr.lit. 32 p./no.; back issues avail. **Document type:** *Journal, Trade.* **Description:** Offers articles from today's top experts on technique and stragey sports, psychology, nutrition and the state of the game. Geared towards all coaching levels.
Indexed: E03, ERI, PEI, SD.
—BLDSC (3287.762800).
Published by: American Volleyball Coaches Association, 2365 Harrodsburg Rd, Ste A325, Lexington, KY 40504. TEL 859-226-4315, 866-544-2822, FAX 859-226-4338, members@avca.org, http://www.avca.org. Ed., R&P Bill Kauffman. Adv. contact Brian Peterson. B&W page USD 588, color page USD 1,388. Circ: 3,800.

796.332 USA
THE COFFIN CORNER. Text in English. 1979. bi-m. USD 25 membership (effective 2009). **Document type:** *Newsletter, Consumer.* **Description:** Contains articles on the history of professional football's great players, teams, and games of the past.
Indexed: CA.
Published by: Professional Football Researchers Association, 12870 Rt 30, no 39, N. Huntingdon, PA 15642. Bob_Carroll@profootballresearchers.org.

796.342 USA ISSN 0279-1153
COLLEGE AND JUNIOR TENNIS. Text in English. 1972. q. USD 18 (effective 1997). adv. bk.rev. illus. back issues avail. **Document type:** *Magazine, Consumer.* **Description:** Covers college and junior tennis, coverage, draw sheets, schedules, stories, photos, rankings, and results.
Published by: Junior Tennis, Inc., 100 Harbor Rd, Port Washington, NY 11050. TEL 516-883-6601, FAX 516-883-5241. Ed. Marcia Frost. Pub. Richard A Zausner. Adv. contact Madeline Fischbach. Circ: 5,000.

796.93 USA
COLLEGE FOOTBALL SCOREBOOK. Text in English. a. USD 29.95 per issue (effective 2008). **Document type:** *Magazine, Consumer.* **Description:** Features all American team, projected bowl match-up, preseason top 40, Confernence reviews, freshman recruiting information, over/under section, past game histories and bowl section.
Published by: Northcoast Sports, Inc., PO Box 35126, Cleveland, OH 44135. TEL 216-521-9467, 800-654-3448, CustomerSupport@ncsports.com.

796.323 USA
COLLEGE HOOPS ILLUSTRATED. Text in English. 19??. 3/yr. adv. **Description:** Contains features and profiles of college basketball players, coaches and teams.
Published by: Professional Sports Publications (P S P), 519 8th Ave, Ste 2500, New York, NY 10018. TEL 212-697-1460, FAX 212-286-8154, mlewis@pspsports.com, http://www.pspsports.com.

796.31 USA ISSN 0530-9751
GV862
COLLEGIATE BASEBALL; the voice of amateur baseball. Text in English. 1957. 14/yr. USD 28 domestic; USD 50 foreign (effective 2009). adv. software rev.; bk.rev.; video rev. illus.; stat. 5 cols./p.; back issues avail.; reprints avail. **Document type:** *Newspaper, Trade.* **Description:** For baseball players, coaches, students. Covers the latest baseball products, innovative instructional clinics; provides feature stories on baseball personalities, and national college and high school polls.
Related titles: Microfilm ed.: (from PQC).
Indexed: A22.
Published by: Collegiate Baseball Newspaper Inc., c/o Lou Pavlovich, Jr, Ed, Box 50566, Tucson, AZ 85703. adv.: B&W page USD 1,530. Circ: 7,000.

796.352 917.88 USA ISSN 1548-4335
COLORADO AVID GOLFER. Text in English. 2002. 9/yr. USD 17.95 (effective 2004). adv.
Published by: Baker-Colorado Publishing, LLC, 5300 DTC Prkwy. Ste. 400, Greenwood Village, CO 80111. TEL 720-493-1729, 888-711-6211, FAX 720-482-0784. Ed. Jon Rizzi. Pub. Allen J. Walters. Adv. contact Lisa B. Durica.

796.352 USA ISSN 1099-7776
COLORADO GOLF MAGAZINE. Text in English. 1988. q. USD 19.75; USD 3.95 newsstand/cover (effective 2007). adv. bk.rev. charts; illus.; maps; mkt.; stat. 84 p./no.; **Document type:** *Magazine, Consumer.* **Description:** This is a resource for golf in Colorado.
Published by: Pade Publishing, LLC., 559 E Second Ave, Castle Rock, CO 80104. TEL 800-858-9677, http://www.coloradogolf.com/. Ed., Pub., R&P Timothy Pade. Circ: 50,800 (paid).

796.352 ZAF ISSN 1015-8014
COMPLEAT GOLFER; the home of South African golf. Text in English. 1989. m. ZAR 125; ZAR 195 foreign. adv. illus.; stat.; tr.lit. back issues avail. **Document type:** *Magazine, Consumer.* **Description:** Aims to inform South African golfers and interested parties of current golf events and styles of play in order to assist golfer in improving their game. Includes interviews, tips and advice, equipment, reviews on major tournaments and local golf.
Published by: Ramsay, Son & Parker (Pty) Ltd., PO Box 180, Howard Place, Cape Town 7450, South Africa. TEL 27-21-530-3100, FAX 27-21-531-1552. Ed., Pub., Adv. contact Dennis Bruyns. Circ: 17,947 (paid); 863 (controlled).

796.357 USA ISSN 0885-9183
GV877
THE COMPLETE BASEBALL RECORD BOOK. Variant title: Sporting News Official Baseball Record Book. Text in English. 1949. a. USD 17.95 (effective 2007). **Document type:** *Magazine, Consumer.*
Former titles (until 1985): Official Baseball Record Book (0162-5438); (until 1982): Sporting News Official Baseball Record Book (0882-8237); (until 1973): Sporting News Baseball Record Book (0882-8903); Baseball's One for the Book (0067-429X); Official Baseball Record Book (0078-4605)
Published by: American City Business Journals, Inc. (Subsidiary of: Advance Publications, Inc.), 120 W Morehead St, Charlotte, NC 28202. TEL 704-973-1000, FAX 704-973-1001, http://www.acbj.com. Ed. Craig Carter.

796.33 USA ISSN 0361-2988
GV955
COMPLETE HANDBOOK OF PRO FOOTBALL. Text in English. 1975. a. illus. **Document type:** *Magazine, Consumer.*
Published by: Penguin U S A, New American Library, 375 Hudson St, New York, NY 10014. TEL 212-366-2000. Ed. Zander Hollander.

796.352 USA ISSN 1947-6396
▼ **CONNECTICUT GOLF JOURNAL.** Text in English. forthcoming 2010. m. USD 9.99 per issue (effective 2009). **Document type:** *Magazine, Consumer.* **Description:** Features articles on all aspects of golf in Connecticut.
Published by: In Publishing, 9769 NW 45 Ln, Miami, FL 33178. TEL 736-314-0456, info@miamigolfjournal.com.

796.342 GRC
COSMOS TOU TENNIS/WORLD OF TENNIS. Text in Greek. 1982. bi-m. adv. back issues avail.
Published by: Liberis Publications Ltd., 49 Pericleous St, 154 51 N. Psychiko, Athens, Greece. Ed. Dimitri Kanellopoulos. Circ: 10,000.

796.352 ESP ISSN 1133-7346
COSTAGOLF; Spain's magazine for golf and leisure. Text in English, Spanish. 1975. m. adv. bk.rev. illus.; stat.; tr.lit. back issues avail. **Document type:** *Magazine, Consumer.*
Published by: Golf Total, S.L., Avda Garcia Morato, 8, Malaga, 29004, Spain. TEL 34-95-2171997, FAX 34-95-2172073, http://www.servicios-gi.es/costa/indez.html. Ed. Silvia Gomez. Pub. Jose Gomez Bofill. Adv. contact Jack Nusbaum. Circ: 18,000 (paid and controlled).

796.323 USA
COURT AWARENESS. Text in English. 1995. q. USD 10 domestic; USD 15 foreign (effective 2000). adv. bk.rev. back issues avail. **Document type:** *Newsletter.* **Description:** Covers women's basketball, including reviews, interviews, feature articles and profiles.
Published by: Jan Travers Publishing, 2177 Carol Dr, Harrisburg, PA 17110. TEL 717-545-7429, all4wbb@aol.com, http://hometown.aol.com/all4wbb/index.htm. Ed., Pub., R&P, Adv. contact Jan Travers. B&W page USD 100; trim 11 x 8.5. Circ: 1,000 (paid).

796.323 USA ISSN 1522-9483
COURTSIDE. Text in English. q. adv.
Formerly (until 199?): N A B C Courtside (1076-5824)
Published by: (National Association of Basketball Coaches), Host Communications, Inc., 546 E Main St, Lexington, KY 40508. TEL 606-226-4541. Adv. contact Jim Cooke.

796.358 IRL ISSN 2009-0323
COVER POINT. Text in English. 2007. 6/yr. EUR 23 domestic; GBP 15 in United Kingdom (effective 2007). **Document type:** *Magazine, Consumer.*
Address: 12 The Crescent, Fox Lodge Woods, Ratoath, Co. Meath, Ireland. TEL 353-1-8254357. Ed. Liam Rooney.

796.358 IND
CRICINFO (ONLINE). Text in English. 2001 (Dec.)-2005 (Jul.); resumed 2006 (Jan.). m. free (effective 2011). **Document type:** *Magazine, Consumer.* **Description:** Covers all aspects of cricket. Especially for fans in India, Pakistan, Sri Lanka and Bangladesh.
Former titles (until 2007): Cricinfo (Print); (until 2005): Wisden Asia Cricket
Media: Online - full text.
Published by: Wisden Group, 208 Shalimar Morya Park, Andheri Link Rd, Andheri W, Mumbai, 400018, India. TEL 91-22-56782465.

796.358 USA
CRICKET INTERNATIONAL. Text in English. 1996. w. USD 20 (effective 2001). adv. **Document type:** *Newspaper, Consumer.* **Description:** Covers all aspects of cricket.
Published by: Cricket International, Inc., 1811-07 Jamaica Ave, Hollis, NY 11423. TEL 718-641-1830, FAX 718-641-1846. Ed. Ameer Mohamed.

796.357 GBR ISSN 1758-8200
CRICKET YEAR. Variant title: Jonathan Agnew's Cricket Year. Text in English. 1979. a. GBP 24.99 per issue (effective 2009). **Document type:** *Bulletin, Trade.* **Description:** Reports on England and English domestic cricket, as well as on every other Test-playing country. It provides analysis of the main stories of the year and previews the season to come.
Former titles (until 2007): Cheltenham & Gloucester Cricket Year (1745-3526); (until 2003): Benson and Hedges Cricket Year (0264-3871); (until 1982): Pelham Cricket Year
—CCC.
Published by: A & C Black Publishers Ltd (Subsidiary of: Bloomsbury Publishing plc), 38 Soho Sq, London, W1D 3HB, United Kingdom. TEL 44-20-77580200, customerservices@acblack.com. Ed. Jonathan Agnew.

796.358 PAK
THE CRICKETER. Text in English. 1973. m. PKR 275, USD 11. adv. charts; illus.; stat. **Document type:** *Magazine, Consumer.* **Description:** Covers national and international cricket, with interviews, match reports, scores and current statistics and other features of interest to players and fans.
Indexed: SportS.
Published by: Cricketer, Spencers Bldg., 1St Fl., I.I. Chundrigar Rd., G P O Box 3721, Karachi, Pakistan. TEL 92-21-210355, FAX 92-21-2637185. Ed. Hanif Mohammad. Adv. contact Riaz Ahmed Mansuri. B&W page PKR 3,500, color page PKR 7,000; trim 6.75 x 9.5. Circ: 18,000.

796.358 GBR
CRICNET. Text in English. 2002. q. GBP 12 (effective 2002). **Document type:** *Magazine, Consumer.*
Published by: Professional Cricketers Association, 338 Euston Rd, London, NW1 3BT, United Kingdom. TEL 44-207-544-8672, comments@cricnet.com, http://www.cricnet.com/index.html.

796.332 USA
CRIMSON CONNECTION. Text in English. 2000. 20/yr. USD 29.95; USD 2.25 newsstand/cover (effective 2001). adv. **Document type:** *Magazine, Consumer.*
Address: Box 6507, Mobile, AL 36660. TEL 334-479-7494, FAX 334-479-7043, sales@crimsonconnection.com, http://www.crimsonconnection.com. Ed. Mike Wood. Pub. T. Bruce MacKinnon.

796.352 USA
CRITTENDEN GOLF DAILY. Text in English. d. **Document type:** *Newsletter, Trade.* **Description:** Contains up-to-date information and news on the golf industry, covering development, operations, marketing, sales, turf, golf shop, and management companies.
Media: E-mail.
Published by: Cypress Magazines, Inc, 5715 Kerny Villa Rd, Ste108, San Diego, CA 92123. TEL 800-296-9656, FAX 858-503-7588, info@cypressmagazines.com, http://www.cypressmagazines.com.

796.352 333.7 USA ISSN 1074-9276
CRITTENDEN GOLF INC. Variant title: GolfInc. Text in English. 1991. m. adv. **Document type:** *Magazine, Trade.* **Description:** For owners, developers, investors and architects involved in the building of golf courses and resorts.
Formerly (until 1993): Golf Development Magazine (1068-6711)
Published by: Crittenden Magazines, Inc., PO Box 919035, San Diego, CA 92191. TEL 877-465-3462, FAX 858-503-7588, http://www.crittendenmagazines.com. adv.: B&W page USD 1,695, color page USD 2,295; trim 11 x 8.5. Circ: 15,000.

796.354 AUS ISSN 1328-9128
CROQUET AUSTRALIA; keeps you up to date and helps croquet grow. Text in English. 1951. q. AUD 35 domestic; AUD 65 in New Zealand; AUD 45 in United States; AUD 48 in Canada; AUD 26 in United Kingdom (effective 2008). adv. bk.rev. **Document type:** *Magazine, Consumer.* **Description:** Provides news on Australian croquet; general articles on coaching and history.
Formerly (until 1997): Australian Croquet Gazette (0817-6604)
Indexed: SD, SportS.
Published by: Australian Croquet Association, c/o Judith Evans, PO Box 3353, Mornington, VIC 3931, Australia. Ed. Carolyn Ribone TEL 61-7-32985576. Adv. contact Judith Evans. Circ: 1,200 (paid).

796.354 GBR ISSN 1363-5646
CROQUET GAZETTE. Text in English. 1901. bi-m. free to members (effective 2009). adv. bk.rev. illus. back issues avail. **Document type:** *Magazine, Trade.* **Description:** Contains news and views on the sport of croquet; aimed at tournament, club, and casual players.
Former titles (until 1996): Croquet (0011-1880); (until 19??): Croquet Gazette
Indexed: SportS.
Published by: Croquet Association, Cheltenham Croquet Club, Old Bath Rd, Cheltenham, Glos GL53 7DF, United Kingdom. caoffice@croquet.org.uk. Ed. Gail Curry TEL 44-7752-356880.

796 USA ISSN 1047-3084
CUBS VINE LINE. Text in English. 1986. m. USD 19.95. adv. bk.rev.
Published by: Chicago National League Ball Club, Inc., PO Box 1159, Skokie, IL 60076-8159. FAX 312-404-4129. Ed. Ned Colletti. Circ: 30,000.

796.0915 IRL ISSN 1649-0266
CUL SPORT. Text in English. 2000. bi-m. adv. **Document type:** *Magazine, Consumer.*

Published by: Ashville Media Group, Apollo House, Tara St., Dublin, 2, Ireland. TEL 353-1-4322200, FAX 353-1-6727100, info@ashville.com, http://www.ashville.com. Ed. Mairtin Breathnach. Adv. contact Brian O'Neill. Circ: 15,000 (controlled).

796.3 ZAF ISSN 1991-8127
THE CUP; South Africa's leading sports guide. Text in English. 2002. s-a. adv.
Published by: Tau Sports & Media, CCMA House, 3rd Flr, 78 Darling St, Cape Town, 8000, South Africa. TEL 27-21-4612856, FAX 27-21-4617580, taumedia@telkomsa.net. adv.: color page ZAR 24,000. Circ: 35,000.

CURRENT BASEBALL PUBLICATIONS. *see* SPORTS AND GAMES—Abstracting, Bibliographies, Statistics

796.352 NZL ISSN 1175-0545
THE CUT; N Z's no.1 golf magazine. Text in English. 1999. m. NZD 45 domestic; NZD 65 in Australia; NZD 115 elsewhere (effective 2010). **Document type:** *Magazine, Consumer.*
Formed by the merger of (1992-1999): New Zealand Golfing World (1171-6835); Which was formerly (until 1992): New Zealand Golfing Today (1171-3755); (1989-1999): New Zealand Golf (1170-7488); Which was formerly (until 1989): Golf (0113-3217); (1976-1985): New Zealand Golf Magazine (0113-3187)
Published by: Armada Publishing Ltd., Parnell, PO Box 37745, Auckland, New Zealand. TEL 64-9-3772114, FAX 64-9-3772115.

796.333 FRA ISSN 1954-4758
D F O MAG. (Des Filles en Ovalie) Text in French. 2006. 3/yr. EUR 12 (effective 2007). **Document type:** *Magazine, Consumer.*
Published by: Des Filles en Ovalie, 130 Rue d'Aboukir, Paris, 75002, France. TEL 33-6-88937410, dfo@desfillesenovalie.com.

796.334 USA ISSN 1552-2962
GV943
D K WORLD SOCCER YEARBOOK. (Dorling Kindersley) Text in English. 2003. a. USD 30 (effective 2006). **Document type:** *Yearbook, Consumer.*
Published by: D K Publishing (Subsidiary of: Penguin Books U S A, Inc.), 375 Hudson St, New York, NY 10014. TEL 212-213-4800, 800-631-8571, FAX 212-689-4828, publicity@dk.com, http://us.dk.com.

796.342 NLD
DAGJOURNAAL ORDINA OPEN. Text in Dutch. a. adv.
Published by: EFKA Uitgevers bv, Postbus 155, Weert, 6000 AD, Netherlands. TEL 31-495-450105, FAX 31-495-539485, info@efka-uitgevers.nl, http://www.efka-uitgevers.nl.

796.332 USA
DALLAS COWBOYS OUTLOOK. Text in English. 1967. a. USD 4.21. adv.
Published by: Sports Communications, Inc., P O Box 95, Waco, TX 76703. TEL 817-752-4351. Ed. Dave Campbell. Circ: 55,622.

796.352 DNK ISSN 1399-8706
DANSK GOLF. Text in Danish. 1943. 6/yr. adv. bk.rev. illus. **Document type:** *Magazine, Consumer.*
Formerly (until 1999): Golf (0902-8927)
Indexed: SportS.
—CCC.
Published by: Dansk Golf Union, c/o Idraettens Hus, Broendby Stadion 20, Broendby, 2605, Denmark. TEL 45-43-262700, FAX 45-43-262701, info@dgu.org, http://www.dgu.org. Ed. Thomas Vennekilde TEL 45-43-262688. Adv. contact Peter Kroeyer TEL 45-43-262719. color page DKK 32,900; trim 190 x 271. Circ: 103,302.

796.352 DNK ISSN 1603-2454
DANSKE GOLFBANER. Text in Danish. 1989. a. price varies. adv. **Document type:** *Consumer.* **Description:** For golf players who are members of golf clubs within DGU, members of DGU and visiting foreign golf players in Denmark.
Former titles (until 2003): Bogen med Alle Danske Golfbaner (1396-4089); (until 1996): Dansk Golf Guide (0904-4019)
Published by: Art - Work Administration AS, Hovedgaden 28, Hoersholm, 2970, Denmark. TEL 45-39-183311, FAX 45-39-180232.

794.6 DEU
DELMENHORSTER KEGLER ZEITUNG. Text in German. 1968. q.
Published by: (Sportkegler Vereins Delmenhorst), Fink Druck GmbH, Brandenburger Str 4, Delmenhorst, 27755, Germany. TEL 04221-2768. Circ: 1,300.

796.332 GBR
DELOITTE & TOUCHE SPORT. ANNUAL REVIEW OF FOOTBALL FINANCE. Variant title: Annual Review of Football Finance. Text in English. 199?. a. GBP 600 per issue; GBP 60 per issue to students (effective 2009). back issues avail. **Document type:** *Handbook/Manual/Guide, Trade.* **Description:** Provides the European football finance with not only a track record up to the end of the 2007/08 season, but also includes some pointers as to how the industry has developed in 2008/09 and is likely to change in the future.
Published by: Deloitte & Touche Sport, 2 Hardman St, Manchester, M3 3HF, United Kingdom. TEL 44-161-8323555, FAX 44-161-8293800, https://www.deloitte.com. Ed. Gerry Boon.

796.352 USA ISSN 1522-9777
DESERT GOLF MAGAZINE. Text in English. 1998. q. USD 19.80 (effective 2007). adv. bk.rev. charts; illus.; maps; mkt.; stat. 84 p./no.; back issues avail.; reprints avail. **Document type:** *Magazine, Consumer.*
Published by: Pade Publishing, LLC., 559 E Second Ave, Castle Rock, CO 80104. TEL 303-688-5853, 800-858-9677. Ed., Pub., R&P Timothy Pade. adv.: B&W page USD 4,500, color page USD 5,000. Circ: 100,000 (paid).

796.352 USA
DEUCE. Text in English. 2002. a. USD 18.95; USD 4.95 newsstand/cover (effective 2005). adv. illus. **Document type:** *Magazine, Consumer.*
Published by: (A T P Tour), Skies America International Publishing and Communications, 9655 S W Sunshine Court, Ste 500, Beaverton, OR 97005. TEL 503-520-1955, FAX 503-520-1275, skies@skies.com, http://www.skies.com, http://www.skiesamerica.com. Ed. David Higdon. adv.: color page USD 13,200; trim 9 x 10.78. Circ: 75,000.

796.342 DEU ISSN 0176-0599
DEUTSCHE TENNIS ZEITUNG. Text in German. 1946. m. EUR 55 domestic; EUR 62 foreign (effective 2006). adv. bk.rev. charts; illus. 64 p./no. 4 cols./p.; back issues avail. **Document type:** *Magazine, Consumer.*
Formerly (until 1981): Tennis
Published by: Sportverlag Schmidt und Dreisilker GmbH, Boeblinger Str 68/1, Sindelfingen, 71065, Germany. TEL 49-7031-862800, FAX 49-7031-862801. Ed. Brigitte Schurr. Adv. contact Yvonne Damast TEL 49-7031-862831. B&W page EUR 1,950, color page EUR 2,950. Circ: 19,773 (paid and controlled).

796.334 DEU
DEUTSCHER FUSSBALL-BUND. OFFIZIELLE MITTEILUNGEN. Text in German. 1952. m. **Document type:** *Bulletin, Trade.* **Description:** Covers the official announcements of the German Soccer Association.
Formerly (until 2001): Deutscher Fussball-Bund. Amtliche Mitteilungen
Published by: Deutscher Fussball-Bund/German Soccer Association, Otto-Fleck-Schneise 6, Frankfurt Am Main, 60528, Germany. TEL 49-69-67880, FAX 49-69-6788204, info@dfb.de. Circ: 1,300.

796.323 USA ISSN 1554-7159
DIME; the game, the player, the life. Text in English. 2002. 9/yr. USD 12 domestic; USD 26 in Canada; USD 40 elsewhere; USD 4.99 newsstand/cover domestic; USD 5.99 newsstand/cover in Canada (effective 2007). adv. **Document type:** *Magazine, Consumer.*
Published by: Dime Magazine Publishing Co., Inc., 291 Broadway, Ste 1204, New York, NY 10007. TEL 212-629-5066, FAX 212-564-9219. Ed., Adv. contact Josh Gotthelf. Pubs. Josh Gotthelf, Matt O'Neil. color page USD 6,825. Circ: 115,000.

796 USA
DIRECTV ON SPORTS. Text in English. 11/yr. USD 14; USD 3 newsstand/cover (effective 2001).
Published by: C E Publishing, 30400 Van Dyke Ave, Warren, MI 48093. TEL 810-574-9100, FAX 810-558-5897. Adv. contact Kenneth Ripley.

DISCOVERY Y M C A. (Young Men's Christian Association) *see* SOCIAL SERVICES AND WELFARE

796.357 USA ISSN 1057-9168
DODGERS DUGOUT NEWSMAGAZINE. Text in English. 1986. bi-w. USD 21.95; USD 24 in Canada; USD 40 elsewhere (effective 2000). adv. 32 p./no. 3 cols./p.; back issues avail. **Document type:** *Newspaper, Consumer.* **Description:** Covering the Dodgers, major and minor league, past and present, with features, photos, games reports and statistics.
Published by: Holmes Publishing, 1321 Ave. D, PO Box 11, Gothenburg, NE 69138-0011. TEL 308-537-3335, FAX 308-537-3335, hp72820@autel.net, http://www.dodgersdugout.swnebr.net. Ed., R&P Tot Holmes. Pub., Adv. contact Pearlie Holmes. B&W page USD 80; trim 9.5 x 6. Circ: 3,000 (paid).

796.332 NLD
D'OLLE GRIEZE. Text in Dutch. 1984. 8/yr.
Published by: Supportersvereniging F C Groningen, Postbus 9527, Groningen, 9703 LM, Netherlands. http://www.svfcgroningen.nl.

796.334 ESP ISSN 1137-8247
DON BALON. Text in Spanish. 1975. w. adv. **Document type:** *Magazine, Consumer.*
Address: Avinguda Diagonal, 435 1o 2A, Barcelona, 08036, Spain. TEL 93-2092000, FAX 93-2092611, donbalon@donbalon.es, http://www.donbalon.es. Ed. Juan Pedro Martinez.

796.332 USA ISSN 1054-2191
DON HEINRICH'S COLLEGE FOOTBALL. Text in English. a. USD 4.95. **Document type:** *Magazine, Consumer.*
Published by: Preview Publishing, 2415 2nd Ave, Apt 341, Seattle, WA 98121-1411. TEL 201-944-4471, FAX 201-944-3193.

794.72 NLD ISSN 1569-4984
DRIEBANDENNIEUWS. Text in Dutch. 1986. 20/yr. (during billiards season). EUR 49.50 (effective 2009). adv. back issues avail. **Description:** For players of three cushion billiards.
Published by: Francis Productions B.V., Beursplein 37, Postbus 30166, Rotterdam, 3001 DD, Netherlands. TEL 31-10-4052233, FAX 31-10-4055026, info@francisproductions.nl.

796.3 NLD ISSN 1875-1970
DUCK OUT. Text in Dutch. 2007. q. EUR 13 (effective 2011). adv. **Document type:** *Magazine, Consumer.*
Published by: Sanoma Uitgevers B.V., Postbus 1900, Hoofddorp, 2130 JH, Netherlands. TEL 31-23-5566770, FAX 31-23-5565376, corporatecommunications@sanomamedia.nl, http://www.sanomamedia.nl.

796.323 USA
E S P N SPECIAL: DICK VITALE'S COLLEGE BASKETBALL (YEAR) PREVIEW. Text in English. 2000. a. **Document type:** *Magazine, Consumer.*
Published by: Disney Publishing Worldwide Inc., 114 Fifth Ave, New York, NY 10011. TEL 212-633-4400, FAX 212-633-4817. **Subscr. to:** E S P N The Magazine, Inc., PO Box 37325, Boone, IA 50037.

796.334 DEU
EINTRACHT-AKTUELL. Text in German. 17/yr. EUR 40; EUR 2 newsstand/cover (effective 2009). adv. **Document type:** *Magazine, Consumer.*
Published by: Eintracht Braunschweig Marketing GmbH, Hamburger Str 210, Braunschweig, 38112, Germany. TEL 49-531-232300, FAX 49-531-2323030, eintracht@eintracht.com, http://www.eintracht.com. adv.: B&W page EUR 880, color page EUR 1,390. Circ: 10,000 (controlled).

796.334 DEU
EINTRACHT FRANKFURT; Stadionmagazin. Text in German. 17/yr. adv. **Document type:** *Magazine, Consumer.*
Former titles (until 2008): Unsere Eintracht; StadionMagazin von Eintracht Frankfurt
Published by: Eintracht Frankfurt Fussball AG, Moerfelder Landstr 362, Frankfurt am Main, 60528, Germany. TEL 49-69-955030, FAX 49-69-95503139, info@eintracht.de, http://www.eintracht.de.

796.332 NLD ISSN 1875-0222
ELF VOETBAL. Text in Dutch. 1981. m. (11/yr.). EUR 46.50; EUR 4.75 newsstand/cover (effective 2009). adv.
Formerly (until 2007): Elf (1381-7094)
Published by: Elf BV, Postbus 97843, The Hague, 2516 EH, Netherlands. Eds. Patrick Leemans, Jan-Hermen de Bruijn. Adv. contact Marc van der Steeg. color page EUR 7,850; trim 210 x 297. Circ: 82,938.

796.357 USA ISSN 1526-6346
ELYSIAN FIELDS QUARTERLY; the baseball review. Text in English. 1981. q. USD 22.50 domestic; USD 30 in Canada & Mexico; USD 38 elsewhere surface mail (effective 2005). adv. bk.rev. illus. back issues avail. **Document type:** *Magazine, Consumer.* **Description:** Offers a long-awaited literate and intelligent, quirky, iconoclastic, funny, and opinionated journal for people who enjoy great writing and truly love baseball.
Formerly (until Jan. 1992): Minneapolis Review of Baseball (1049-9555)
Published by: Knothole Publishing, PO Box 14385, St Paul, MN 55114-0385. TEL 651-644-8558, FAX 651-644-8086, efq@citilink.com. Pub., R&P, Adv. contact Tom Goldstein. Circ: 1,100 (paid).

796.3 GBR
ENGLAND HOCKEY. NATIONAL HANDBOOK. Text in English. 1900. a. adv. abstr.; charts; stat. index, cum.index. **Document type:** *Directory.* **Description:** Provides a guide to the organization and relocation of field hockey in England. Contains information on local and national hockey administration, plus a list of contacts.
Supersedes (in 200?): A-Z of English Hockey; Which was formerly: Hockey Association. Official Handbook (0085-1566)
Published by: England Hockey, The National Hockey Stadium, Silbury Blvd, Milton Keynes, MK9 1HA, United Kingdom. TEL 44-1908-544644, FAX 44-1908-241106, info@englandhockey.org, http://www.englandhockey.co.uk/. Ed., R&P Ian Thomas. adv.: B&W page GBP 400, color page GBP 700. Circ: 5,000.

796.352 333.33 USA
ESTATES WEST GOLF LIVING. Text in English. 2006. a. adv. **Document type:** *Magazine, Consumer.* **Description:** Focuses on luxury golf travel, exclusive fairway communities and the lifestyle and spirit of the game of golf.
Published by: Media That Deelivers, Inc., 8132 N 87th Pl, Scottsdale, AZ 85258. TEL 480-460-5203, FAX 480-460-2345, general@mediathatdeelivers.com, http://www.mediathatdeelivers.com. Pub. Michael Dee TEL 480-460-5203 ext 202. adv.: color page USD 8,800, B&W page USD 7,000; trim 9 x 10.75. Circ: 50,000 (controlled).

796.334 ROM
EUROFOTBAL. Text in Romanian. m. **Document type:** *Magazine, Consumer.*
Published by: Krater, Calea Dorobanti nr. 151, sector 1, Bucharest, Romania. TEL 40-21-2316836, FAX 40-21-6796108.

796.3 GBR
EVENING TIMES WEE RED BOOK; the football annual. Text in English. 1920. a. USD 1.30 (effective 2000). adv. **Document type:** *Newspaper.*
Published by: George Outram & Co. Ltd., 195 Albion St, Glasgow, G1 1NY, United Kingdom. TEL 44-141-552-6255, FAX 44-141-553-1355, TELEX 779818. Ed. John D Scott. R&P Rod Ramsay TEL 44-141-552-3241. Adv. contact Steve Montgomery. Circ: 40,000 (paid).

796.352 USA
EXECUTIVE GOLFER. Text in English. 1972. bi-m. USD 9 (effective 2008). adv. bk.rev. illus. **Document type:** *Magazine, Consumer.*
Formerly: Country Club Golfer (0194-2387)
Indexed: SportS.
Published by: Pazdur Publishing, Inc., 2171 Campus Dr, Ste 330, Irvine, CA 92715-1499. TEL 949-752-6474, 800-367-8653. Ed., Pub., R&P Edward F Pazdur. Adv. contact Mark Pazdur. Circ: 104,000 (controlled).

796.332 USA ISSN 1942-2008
GV958.U5862
THE EYES OF TEXAS. Text in English. 2007. a. USD 12.99 per issue (effective 2011). back issues avail. **Document type:** *Handbook/Manual/Guide, Consumer.*
Published by: Maple Street Press, 155 Webster St, Ste B, Hanover, MA 02339. TEL 781-347-4730, FAX 781-347-4732, info@maplestreetpress.com.

796.332 NLD ISSN 1873-6645
F C GRONINGEN PRESENTATIEGIDS. Variant title: Voetbal Club Groningen Presentatiegids. Text in Dutch. 2006. a. free (effective 2009).
Published by: (Supportersvereniging F C Groningen), F C Groningen Media, Postbus 1080, Groningen, 9701 BB, Netherlands. TEL 31-50-5878762, FAX 31-50-3143817, media@fcgroningen.nl, http://www.fcgroningen.nl.

796.334 DEU
F F MAGAZIN. (Frauenfussball) Text in German. 2004. bi-m. EUR 15; EUR 2.50 newsstand/cover (effective 2006). adv. **Document type:** *Magazine, Consumer.*
Published by: R&P Verlag GmbH, Hohemarkstr 20, Oberursel, 61440, Germany. TEL 49-6171-693251, FAX 49-6171-693250. Ed. Monika Koch-Emsermann. Pub. Hansjuergen Ruschke. Adv. contact Cordula Vierkotten. B&W page EUR 2,200, color page EUR 2,600. Circ: 3,500 (paid and controlled).

796.355 USA
F H LIFE. (Field Hockey) Text in English. 1994. q. USD 25 (effective 2011). **Document type:** *Magazine, Trade.* **Description:** Provides information on USFHA programs and US national field hockey teams, umpiring and coaching.
Former titles (until 2011): Field Hockey News (1539-0020); (until 2002): Hockey News (1096-7125)
Published by: United States Field Hockey Association, Inc., USFHA National Office, One Olympic Plaza, Colorado Springs, CO 80909. TEL 719-866-4567, FAX 719-632-0979, information@usafieldhockey.com. Adv. contact Katelyn Nerbonne. Circ: 10,000 (controlled).

796.323 SRB ISSN 1465-7120
F I B A BASKETBALL. Text in English. 1990. m. **Document type:** *Magazine, Consumer.* **Description:** Action-packed coverage of basketball worldwide.
Formerly (until 199?): F I B A Basketball Monthly (0959-888X)
Related titles: French ed.; German ed.; Flemish ed.; Korean ed.; Greek ed.; Italian ed.; Chinese ed.; Spanish ed.
Published by: (Federation Internationale de Basketball Amateur GBR), Alliance International Media Ltd., Kneginje Zorke 11b, Belgrade, 11000. TEL 381-11-3089977, FAX 381-11-3089988, office@allianceinternationalmedia.com.

S

796.334 CHE
F I F A HANDBOOK. Text in French. a. CHF 50 (effective 2001). **Document type:** *Bulletin, Trade.* **Description:** Contains directory of committees and international referees as well as laws, association and competitions regulations plus guides for referees. Focuses on football (soccer).
Published by: Federation Internationale de Football Association, Hitzigweg 11, PO Box 85, Zuerich, 8030, Switzerland. TEL 41-1-3849595, FAX 41-1-3849696, media@fifa.org, http://www.fifa.com.

796.334 CHE
F I F A NEWS. Text in English. 1963. m. CHF 80 (effective 2001). bk.rev. **Document type:** *Newsletter, Trade.*
Superseded: F I F A Official Bulletin (0427-8321)
Related titles: French ed.; Spanish ed.; German ed.
Indexed: SD.
Published by: Federation Internationale de Football Association, Hitzigweg 11, PO Box 85, Zuerich, 8030, Switzerland. TEL 41-1-3849595, FAX 41-1-3849696, TELEX 817240-FIF-CH, media@fifa.org, http://www.fifa.com. Circ: 12,000.

796.334 CHE
F I F A OLYMPIC FOOTBALL TOURNAMENT. Text in English, French, German, Spanish. 1980. quadrennial. CHF 35 per vol. **Document type:** *Bulletin, Trade.*
Related titles: ◆ Series of: F I F A Technical Reports.
Published by: Federation Internationale de Football Association, Hitzigweg 11, PO Box 85, Zuerich, 8030, Switzerland. TEL 41-1-3849595, FAX 41-1-3849696, media@fifa.org, http://www.fifa.com.

764.334 CHE
F I F A TECHNICAL REPORTS. Text in English, French, German, Spanish. irreg. price varies. **Document type:** *Monographic series, Trade.*
Formerly: F I F A Technical Notes
Related titles: ◆ Series: F I F A World Youth Championship; ◆ F I F A Olympic Football Tournament; ◆ F I F A U-17 World Championship.
Published by: Federation Internationale de Football Association, Hitzigweg 11, PO Box 85, Zuerich, 8030, Switzerland. TEL 41-1-3849595, FAX 41-1-3849696, media@fifa.org, http://www.fifa.com.

796.334 CHE
F I F A U-17 WORLD CHAMPIONSHIP. Text in English, French, German, Spanish. 1985. biennial. CHF 30. **Document type:** *Bulletin, Trade.*
Formerly: F I F A U-17 World Tournament
Related titles: ◆ Series of: F I F A Technical Reports.
Published by: Federation Internationale de Football Association, Hitzigweg 11, PO Box 85, Zuerich, 8030, Switzerland. TEL 41-1-3849595, FAX 41-1-3849696, media@fifa.org, http://www.fifa.com.

796.334 CHE
F I F A WORLD CUP. Text in English, French, German, Spanish. 1978. quadrennial. CHF 70 per vol. **Document type:** *Bulletin, Trade.* **Description:** Includes official reports of matches.
Published by: Federation Internationale de Football Association, Hitzigweg 11, PO Box 85, Zuerich, 8030, Switzerland. TEL 41-1-3849595, FAX 41-1-3849696, media@fifa.org, http://www.fifa.com.

796.334 CHE
F I F A WORLD YOUTH CHAMPIONSHIP. Variant title: F I F A - Coca-Cola Cup. Text in English, French, German, Spanish. 1981. biennial. price varies. **Document type:** *Bulletin, Trade.*
Related titles: ◆ Series of: F I F A Technical Reports.
Published by: Federation Internationale de Football Association, Hitzigweg 11, PO Box 85, Zuerich, 8030, Switzerland. TEL 41-1-3849595, FAX 41-1-3849696, media@fifa.org, http://www.fifa.com.

796.334 FRO ISSN 1603-8886
F S F - TIDINDI. (Fotboltssamband Foeroya) Text in Faroese. 2003. back issues avail. **Document type:** *Magazine, Consumer.*
Published by: Fotboltssamband Foeroya, PO Box 3028, Torshavn, 110, Faeroe Islands. TEL 298-351979, FAX 298-319079, fsf@football.fo, http://www.football.fo.

796.323 GBR ISSN 2041-2134
▼ **FADE AWAY**; the UK's biggest & only basketball magazine. Text in English. 2009. q. GBP 2.50 newsstand/cover (effective 2010). adv. **Document type:** *Magazine, Trade.* **Description:** Covers all aspects of the global game.
Related titles: Online - full text ed.
Published by: Big Smoke Projects, Response Studios, 369B High Rd, Leyton, London, E10 5NA, United Kingdom. TEL 44-20-85583501. Ed. Greg Tanner.

796.3 FRA ISSN 1952-9295
FAIRPLAY MAG. Text in French. 2006. bi-m. EUR 24.90 (effective 2007). **Document type:** *Magazine, Consumer.*
Published by: Melting Sport, 12 Rue Ampere, B P 267, Grenoble, 38016 Cedex 1, France. TEL 33-4-76091138, contact@meltingsport.com.

796.352 DEU
FAIRWAYS; Golf-Lifestyle-Magazin. Text in German. 5/yr. EUR 16 domestic; EUR 26 foreign (effective 2010). adv. **Document type:** *Magazine, Consumer.*
Published by: Ziegler Verlags GmbH, Birkenweiherstr 14, Langenselbold, 63505, Germany. TEL 49-6184-923330, FAX 49-6184-923355, info@ziegler-verlag.de. Ed. Alexandra Philipp. Adv. contact Ralf Ziegler. color page EUR 2,607, B&W page EUR 1,431. Circ: 7,980 (paid).

796.352 USA ISSN 1098-4305
FAIRWAYS. Text in English. 19??. q. adv. **Document type:** *Magazine, Consumer.*
Former titles (until 199?): Utah Golf (1059-8421); (until 1990): Utah Golf News Magazine (0896-3029)
Published by: (Utah Golf Association), Fairways Media Inc., 3315 W Mayflower Ave, Ste 2, Lehi, UT 84043. TEL 801-766-5709, mikes@fairwaysmag.com, http://www.fairwaysmag.com/fairwaysmedia.html. Circ: 20,000.

796.352 910.91 USA ISSN 1535-7805
FAIRWAYS & GREENS (NEVADA EDITION). Text in English. 1997. m. USD 19.95; USD 2.95 newsstand/cover (effective 2002). adv. **Description:** Covers golf, travel and lifestyle news for the West with particular attention to California, Nevada, Oregon and Utah. It also includes course reviews, golf real estate, resorts and their ancillary amenities (spas, dining, lodging), instruction, equipment and a specific golf travel region (i.e., Central Oregon or Lake Tahoe). Regular columns focus on personalities, history, humor, the mental game, fitness and money.
Published by: Fairways & Greens Publishing, 1055 Riverside Dr., Reno, NV 89503-5430. info@fairwaysgreens.com, http://www.fairwaysgreens.com. Ed. Vic Williams. adv.: color page USD 2,850; trim 8.375 x 10.875. Circ: 10,000 (paid); 40,000 (free).

796.334 DEU
FAN GEHT VOR. Text in German. 1991. m. EUR 20; EUR 1 newsstand/cover (effective 2010). adv. **Document type:** *Magazine, Consumer.*
Address: Schulze-Delitzsch-Str 20, Idstein, 65510, Germany. FAX 49-1805-23363331899. Ed. Mathias Scheurer. Circ: 1,600 (controlled).

796.357 USA
THE FANTASY BASEBALL GUIDE (PROFESSIONAL EDITION). Text in English. 2000. a. USD 6.99 newsstand/cover (effective 2007). adv. **Document type:** *Magazine, Consumer.*
Formerly: Rotonews Fantasy Baseball Guide (Year)
Published by: R F P, LLC, 330 7th Ave, New York, NY 10001. TEL 212-838-7733, FAX 212-308-7165. Ed. Peter Kreutzer. Pub. Jermey Bucovetsky.

796.357 USA
FANTASY BASEBALL INDEX. Text in English. a. USD 5.99 newsstand/cover; USD 7.99 newsstand/cover in Canada (effective 2001). adv. **Document type:** *Magazine, Consumer.* **Description:** Contains player ratings, rotisserie dollar values, stat projections, depth charts, expanded coverage of minor league prospects, three-year-stats, expert opinions, strategy and team-by-team analysis.
Published by: Fantasy Index, PO Box 15277, Seattle, WA 98115. TEL 206-527-4444, FAX 206-527-4840, staff@fantasyindex.com, http://www.fantasyindex.com. adv.: B&W page USD 1,000, color page USD 1,500; trim 7.25 x 10.

796.332 USA
FANTASY FOOTBALL. Text in English. 1987. a. USD 4.95; USD 5.95 in Canada.
Published by: Preview Publishing, 2415 2nd Ave, Apt 341, Seattle, WA 98121-1411. FAX 206-284-2083.

796.93 USA
FANTASY FOOTBALL GUIDE. Text in English. a. **Document type:** *Magazine, Consumer.* **Description:** Contains football team and player statistics, rules, schedules, and other information for fantasy football leagues.
Published by: Northcoast Sports, Inc., PO Box 35126, Cleveland, OH 44135. TEL 216-521-9467, 800-654-3448, CustomerSupport@ncsports.com, http://www.ncsports.com.

796.332 USA
FANTASY FOOTBALL INDEX. Text in English. a. USD 5.99 newsstand/cover; USD 7.99 newsstand/cover in Canada (effective 2001). adv. **Document type:** *Magazine, Consumer.* **Description:** Contains information on player ratings, team analysis, stat projections, defensive player analysis, unique stat charts, sleeper picks, rule suggestions, offensive line analysis, and more.
Published by: Fantasy Index, PO Box 15277, Seattle, WA 98115. TEL 206-527-4444, FAX 206-527-4840, staff@fantasyindex.com, http://www.fantasyindex.com. adv.: B&W page USD 2,325, color page USD 3,250; trim 7.25 x 10.

796.332 USA
FANTASY FOOTBALL PRO FORECAST. Text in English. a. USD 5.99 newsstand/cover (effective 2001). adv.
Published by: Fantasy Sports Publications, 5305 Arbustos Ct NE, Albuquerque, NM 87111. TEL 505-293-0509, FAX 505-294-2100. Ed., Pub. Emil Kadlec.

796.332 USA
FANTASY GURU MAGAZINE. Variant title: FantasyGuru.com Magazine. Text in English. 2003 (Jul.). a. USD 29.95 newsstand/cover (effective 2007). adv. 164 p./no.; **Document type:** *Magazine, Consumer.*
Published by: (Guru Fantasy Reports, Inc.), Krause Publications, Inc. (Subsidiary of: F + W Media Inc.), 700 E State St, Iola, WI 54990. TEL 800-258-0929, info@krause.com, http://www.krause.com. Pub., Adv. contact John Hansen. B&W page USD 1,295, color page USD 1,895; trim 8 x 10.875. **Subscr. to:** PO Box 420235, Palm Coast, FL 32142. TEL 386-246-3442, 877-300-0256.

FANTASY SPORTS. *see* HOBBIES

796.357 USA ISSN 1940-3771
FASTPITCH FOREVER. Text in English. 2003. q. USD 12.95 (effective 2007). adv. **Document type:** *Magazine, Consumer.* **Description:** Devoted to young female athletes who play fastpitch softball.
Published by: Blitz Publishing, Inc., 3905 Snag Ln, Spring, TX 77388. TEL 713-992-3254. adv.: page USD 100; 8.5 x 11.

796.333 ZAF ISSN 1681-4487
FIFTEEN; the official S A rugby magazine. Text in English. 2001. q. adv. **Document type:** *Magazine, Consumer.*
Published by: Highbury Safika Media, PO Box 8145, Roggebaai, 8012, South Africa. TEL 27-21-4160141, FAX 27-21-4180132, info@hsm.co.za. adv.: color page ZAR 24,950. Circ: 20,000.

796.323 DEU ISSN 1614-9297
FIVE. Text in German. 2003. 10/yr. EUR 3.90 newsstand/cover (effective 2006). adv. **Document type:** *Magazine, Consumer.*
Published by: Piranha Media GmbH, Rolandstr 69, Cologne, 50677, Germany. TEL 49-221-5797800, FAX 49-221-5797879. adv.: page EUR 3,500. Circ: 60,000 (paid and controlled).

796.334 USA
FLAG & TOUCH FOOTBALL RULEBOOK AND OFFICIAL'S MANUAL. Text in English. 1983. biennial. EUR 7.20 per issue in Europe; GBP 6.50 per issue in United Kingdom; CAD 9.95 per issue in Canada; AUD 14 per issue in Australia; NZD 18 per issue in New Zealand; USD 9 per issue elsewhere (effective 2010). **Document type:** *Handbook/Manual/Guide, Consumer.* **Description:** Contains the official rules for flag and touch football.
Formerly (until 1990): National Collegiate Flag & Touch Football Rulebook and Official's Manual
Published by: National Intramural - Recreational Sports Association Foundation, 4185 SW Research Way, Corvallis, OR 97333. TEL 541-766-8211, FAX 541-766-8284, nirsa@nirsa.org, http://www.nirsa.org.

796.332 USA
FLORIDA FOOTBALL. Text in English. a. **Document type:** *Magazine, Consumer.*
Published by: Varsity Sports Media, 3401 Russ Circle, Ste E, Alcoa, TN 37701. TEL 865-379-0625, FAX 865-379-9653.

796.352 USA ISSN 1947-6485
▼ **FLORIDA GOLF JOURNAL.** Text in English. forthcoming 2010. m. USD 9.99 per issue (effective 2009). **Document type:** *Magazine, Consumer.* **Description:** Features articles on golf for Florida.
Published by: In Publishing, 9769 NW 45 Ln, Miami, FL 33178. TEL 736-314-0456, info@miamigolfjournal.com.

796.342 USA
FLORIDA TENNIS. Text in English. 1992. m. USD 17 domestic; USD 35 in Canada; USD 45 elsewhere (effective 2000). adv. bk.rev. back issues avail. **Document type:** *Magazine, Consumer.* **Description:** Covers all aspects of amateur and professional tennis in Florida.
Published by: Martz Productions, 1760 N.W. 107th Ave., Pembroke Pines, FL 33026-2806. TEL 954-431-4069, FAX 954-438-7330. Ed., Pub., R&P, Adv. contact Jim Martz. B&W page USD 1,995; trim 13 x 10.25. Circ: 36,000 (controlled).

796.334 DNK ISSN 0109-9876
FODBOLD, DANSKE KAMPE. Text in Danish. 1968. a. price varies. 80 p./no.; **Document type:** *Yearbook, Consumer.*
Formerly (until 1984): Fodboldaarbogen (0109-9868)
Published by: Lindhardt og Ringhof, Vognmagergade 11, Copenhagen K, 1148, Denmark. TEL 45-33-695000, info@lindhardtogringhof.dk, http://www.lindhardtogringhof.dk.

796.334 DNK ISSN 0905-4006
FODBOLD, INTERNATIONALE KAMPE; aarets bedste fodbold. Text in Danish. 1961. a. price varies. **Document type:** *Yearbook, Consumer.*
Former titles (until 1989): Fodbold, Udenlandske Kampe (0109-9892); (until 1984): Fodbold, Aarets Bedste (0109-9884); (until 1972): Aarets Bedste Foldboldkampe (1396-8688)
Published by: Lindhardt og Ringhof, Vognmagergade 11, Copenhagen K, 1148, Denmark. TEL 45-33-695000, info@lindhardtogringhof.dk, http://www.lindhardtogringhof.dk.

796.334 FRA ISSN 2108-8306
▼ **FOOT 100% CHAMPIONS.** Text in French. 2010. bi-m. **Document type:** *Magazine, Consumer.*
Published by: 2B2M, 145 Rue de Belleville, Paris, 75019, France. TEL 33-1-47750091, FAX 33-9-72130123, info@2b2m.fr, http://www.2b2m.fr.

796.334 FRA ISSN 1772-0958
LE FOOT BRETAGNE. Text in French. 2004. m. EUR 38 (effective 2010). **Document type:** *Magazine, Consumer.*
Published by: Lafont Presse, 53 Rue du Chemin Vert, Boulogne-Billancourt, 92100, France. TEL 33-1-46102121, FAX 33-1-45792211.

796.334 FRA ISSN 2107-3120
LE FOOT HEBDO. Text in French. 1992. w. **Document type:** *Newspaper, Consumer.*
Formerly (until 2010): Le Foot (1244-8397)
Published by: Lafont Presse, 53 Rue du Chemin Vert, Boulogne-Billancourt, 92100, France. TEL 33-1-46102121, redac.entreprendre@wanadoo.fr, http://www.lafontpresse.fr.

796.334 FRA ISSN 1953-5961
LE FOOT LYON MAGAZINE. Text in French. 2006. q. EUR 25 for 2 yrs. (effective 2010). **Document type:** *Magazine, Consumer.*
Published by: Lafont Presse, 53 Rue du Chemin Vert, Boulogne-Billancourt, 92100, France. TEL 33-1-46102121, FAX 33-1-45792211.

796.334 FRA ISSN 1777-9227
LE FOOT MAGAZINE. Text in French. 2005. bi-m. EUR 38 for 2 yrs. (effective 2010). **Document type:** *Magazine, Consumer.* **Description:** Reports on soccer from an international perspective.
Published by: Lafont Presse, 53 Rue du Chemin Vert, Boulogne-Billancourt, 92100, France. TEL 33-1-46102121, FAX 33-1-45792211.

796.334 FRA ISSN 1952-8655
LE FOOT MARSEILLE MAGAZINE. Text in French. 2006. q. EUR 25 for 2 yrs. (effective 2010). **Document type:** *Magazine, Consumer.*
Published by: Lafont Presse, 53 Rue du Chemin Vert, Boulogne-Billancourt, 92100, France. TEL 33-1-46102121, FAX 33-1-45792211.

796.334 FRA ISSN 1957-4584
LE FOOT PARIS MAGAZINE. Text in French. 2007. bi-m. EUR 38 for 2 yrs. (effective 2010). **Document type:** *Magazine, Consumer.*
Published by: Lafont Presse, 53 Rue du Chemin Vert, Boulogne-Billancourt, 92100, France. TEL 33-1-46102121, FAX 33-1-45792211. Ed. Bernard Pace.

796.334 FRA ISSN 1769-1265
LE FOOT SAINT-ETIENNE. Text in French. 2004. m. EUR 38 (effective 2010). **Document type:** *Magazine, Consumer.*
Published by: Lafont Presse, 53 Rue du Chemin Vert, Boulogne-Billancourt, 92100, France. TEL 33-1-46102121, FAX 33-1-45792211.

796.334 FRA ISSN 1955-012X
LE FOOT ST-ETIENNE MAGAZINE. Text in French. 2006. q. EUR 25 for 2 yrs. (effective 2010). **Document type:** *Magazine, Consumer.*
Published by: Lafont Presse, 53 Rue du Chemin Vert, Boulogne-Billancourt, 92100, France. TEL 33-1-46102121, FAX 33-1-45792211.

796.334 USA
FOOTBAG WORLD. Text in English. 1983. s-a. USD 5 newsstand/cover (effective 2000). adv. bk.rev. back issues avail. **Document type:** *Magazine, Consumer.* **Description:** Covers footbag games and its players. Includes a calendar of events, tournament results, stories, coaching advice, health tips, and a footbag product catalog.
Media: Online - full text.
Indexed: SportS.

Published by: World Footbag Association, PO Box 775208, Steamboat Springs, CO 80477-5208. TEL 970-870-9898, 800-878-8797, FAX 970-870-2846. Ed., R&P Bruce Guettich. Adv. contact Randy Nelson. Circ: 5,000. **Dist. by:** 1250 S Lincoln Ave, Sundance Plaza Fl 2, Steamboat Springs, CO 80488.

796.334 AUS ISSN 1832-1461
FOOTBALL BUDGET. Text in English. 1936. w. (during football season). AUD 3 newsstand/cover (effective 2009). adv. back issues avail. **Document type:** *Magazine, Trade.*
Former titles (until 2001): Football W A (1832-1518); (until 1998): Real Footy (1832-150X); (until 1997): The Football Budget (1832-1496)
Related titles: Online - full text ed.
Published by: West Australian Football League, Gate 6 Subiaco Rd, Subiaco, W.A. 6008, Australia. TEL 61-8-93815599, FAX 61-8-93817743, wafl@wafc.com.au, http://www.wafl.com.au. Ed. Brad Elborough.

796.332 USA
FOOTBALL DIGEST ANNUAL GUIDE. Text in English. a. **Document type:** *Magazine, Consumer.*
Published by: Century Publishing Inc., E 5710 Seltice Way, Post Falls, ID 83854. TEL 208-765-6300, 800-824-1806, FAX 208-676-8476, privacy@CenturyPublishing.com, http://www.centurypublishing.com.

796.332 USA
FOOTBALL HANDBOOK (BURLINGTON). Text in English. 1940. a. adv. **Document type:** *Magazine, Consumer.* **Description:** Lists pro and college schedules, rosters and ticket information for all interested in football.
Published by: National Research Bureau, 320 Valley St, Burlington, IA 52601. TEL 319-752-5415. Ed. Teresa Levinson. Pub. Michael S Darnall.

796.332 USA
FOOTBALL HANDBOOK (INDIANAPOLIS). Text in English. 19??. biennial. USD 6.95 per issue (effective 2009). adv. **Document type:** *Handbook/Manual/Guide, Trade.*
Published by: National Federation of State High School Associations, PO Box 690, Indianapolis, IN 46206. TEL 317-972-6900, 800-776-3462, FAX 317-822-5700, info@nfhs.org, http://www.nfhs.org. Ed. Dick Schindler.

796.334 USA
FOOTBALL HEROES. Text in English. 2001. bi-m. USD 11.80; USD 2.95 newsstand/cover; USD 4.25 newsstand/cover in Canada (effective 2001). adv. **Document type:** *Magazine, Consumer.*
Published by: Game Day Media, LLC, 6945 Orion Ave., Van Nuys, CA 91406. http://www.gamedaymedia.com. Ed. Mark Paniccia. Pub. Herb Dogan.

796.334 FRA ISSN 1777-3318
FOOTBALL MAG. Text in French. 2005. bi-m. EUR 25 for 2 yrs. (effective 2010). **Document type:** *Magazine, Consumer.*
Published by: Lafont Presse, 53 Rue du Chemin Vert, Boulogne-Billancourt, 92100, France. TEL 33-1-46102121, FAX 33-1-45792211.

796.332 378.198 USA
FOOTBALL MEDIA GUIDE. Text in English. 19??. a. charts; illus.; stat. back issues avail. **Document type:** *Handbook/Manual/Guide, Consumer.*
Former titles (until 1997): Big Ten Football Guide; (until 1996): Football Media Guide; (until 1994): Big Ten Conference Football
Related titles: Online - full text ed.: free (effective 2011).
Published by: Big Ten Conference, 1500 W Higgins Rd, Park Ridge, IL 60068. TEL 847-696-1010, FAX 847-696-1150.

796.333 GBR ISSN 0266-481X
FOOTBALL MONTHLY. Text in English. 1974. m. GBP 30; GBP 2.50 newsstand/cover. adv. bk.rev. **Document type:** *Magazine, Consumer.*
Formerly (until 1980): Football Magazine (0307-8108); Which was formed by the merger of: Football Pictorial (0015-6787); Charles Buchan's Football Monthly (0009-1758)
Address: Unit 4, Gibbs Reed Farm, Ticehurst, E Sussex TN5 7HE, United Kingdom. TEL 44-1580-200657, FAX 44-1580-200616. Circ: 42,649.

796.332 USA
FOOTBALL OFFICIALS HANDBOOK. Text in English. biennial. **Document type:** *Handbook/Manual/Guide, Trade.* **Description:** Features the brief history of the football game, rules of for flag football and touch football, procedures followed in developing the rules and an emphasis on the philosophy of the rules committees.
Published by: National Federation of State High School Associations, PO Box 690, Indianapolis, IN 46206. TEL 317-972-6900, 800-776-3462, FAX 317-822-5700, info@nfhs.org, http://www.nfhs.org.

796.332 USA ISSN 0163-6219
GV954.35
FOOTBALL OFFICIALS MANUAL. Text in English. 19??. biennial. USD 6.95 per issue (effective 2009). adv. **Document type:** *Handbook/Manual/Guide, Trade.* **Description:** Designed for those who wish to enter the field of officiating or to those who are interested in improving their competence in the field of football.
Published by: National Federation of State High School Associations, PO Box 690, Indianapolis, IN 46206. TEL 317-972-6900, 800-776-3462, FAX 317-822-5700, info@nfhs.org, http://www.nfhs.org.

796.334 GBR
FOOTBALL REFEREE. Text in English. 1974. 8/yr. GBP 0.50 per issue. adv. bk.rev. **Document type:** *Magazine, Trade.* **Description:** Discusses soccer matches and teams, and refereeing matters.
Published by: Referees' Association, 15 Penrith Ave, Whitefield, Manchester, M45 6JJ, United Kingdom. TEL 44-161-773-5917, FAX 44-161-773-5917. Ed. Paul Gresty. Circ: 8,000 (controlled).

796.332 USA
GV956.8
FOOTBALL RULES BOOK. Text in English. 19??. a. USD 6.95 per issue (effective 2009). adv. **Document type:** *Handbook/Manual/Guide, Trade.* **Description:** Contains the official rules for football and is used by coaches, officials, players and many fans who wish to know more about the rules of the game.
Former titles (until 1998): High School Football Rules; (until 1991): High School Rules, Football; (until 1990): Official High School Football Rules (0747-9808); (until 198?): Football Rule Book (0891-3285)
Published by: National Federation of State High School Associations, PO Box 690, Indianapolis, IN 46206. TEL 317-972-6900, 800-776-3462, FAX 317-822-5700, info@nfhs.org, http://www.nfhs.org.

796.332 USA ISSN 0731-9533
GV956.8
FOOTBALL RULES - SIMPLIFIED AND ILLUSTRATED. Text in English. 19??. a. USD 7.95 per issue (effective 2009). adv. illus. **Document type:** *Handbook/Manual/Guide, Trade.* **Description:** Provides explanation of the actual play situations of football with comprehensive diagrams.
Formerly (until 19??): Official High School Football Rules Simplified and Illustrated for Officials, Coaches, Players, Spectators (0163-6472)
Published by: National Federation of State High School Associations, PO Box 690, Indianapolis, IN 46206. TEL 317-972-6900, 800-776-3462, FAX 317-822-5700, info@nfhs.org, http://www.nfhs.org.

796.334 AUS ISSN 1442-3146
➤ **FOOTBALL STUDIES.** Text in English. 1998. s-a. **Document type:** *Journal, Academic/Scholarly.* **Description:** Devoted to the cultural, social, political and economic study of football codes.
Formerly (until 1999): Occasional Papers in Football Studies (1440-2319)
Indexed: CA, SD, T02.
—BLDSC (3984.988060).
Published by: Football Studies Group, University of the Sunshine Coast, Maroochydore, QLD 4558, Australia. TEL 61-7-5431244, magdalinski@usc.edu.au, http://www.footballstudiesgroup.com.

796.332 USA ISSN 1079-1787
FOOTBALL'S FINEST. Text in English. 1993. a. stat. **Document type:** *Magazine, Trade.* **Description:** Provides historical reference with year by year and career statistics of NCAA football greats and top coaches.
Published by: National Collegiate Athletic Association, 700 W Washington St, PO Box 6222, Indianapolis, IN 46206. TEL 317-917-6222, FAX 317-917-6888, esummers@ncaa.org, http://www.ncaa.org/.

796.336 028.5 AUS ISSN 1036-2940
FOOTY STARS. Text in English. 1991. 3/yr. (during football season: May, June, July). adv. back issues avail. **Document type:** *Magazine, Consumer.* **Description:** For children from early to mid-teens about Australian rules football.
Published by: Text Magazine Co., Level 5, 171 La Trobe St, Melbourne, VIC 3000, Australia. TEL 61-3-2724700, FAX 61-3-2724799. Circ: 37,500.

796.352 USA ISSN 0300-8509
FORE. Text in English. 1968. bi-m. free to members. adv. bk.rev. illus. **Document type:** *Magazine, Trade.*
Indexed: SportS.
Published by: Southern California Golf Association, 3740 Cahuenga Blvd, North Hollywood, CA 91604. TEL 818-980-3630, FAX 818-980-1808. Ed., Pub., R&P Robert D Thomas. Adv. contact Thomas Black. Circ: 150,000.

796.334 ITA ISSN 1122-8059
FORZA MILAN!. Text in Italian. 1962. m. EUR 34.99 (effective 2008). adv. **Document type:** *Magazine, Consumer.*
Published by: Arnoldo Mondadori Editore SpA, Via Mondadori 1, Segrate, 20090, Italy. TEL 39-02-66814363, FAX 39-030-3198412, http://www.mondadori.com. Circ: 113,970.

796.334 SWE ISSN 0347-2752
FOTBOLL (STOCKHOLM). Text in Swedish. 1957. a. SEK 880 (effective 1990).
Incorporates (1956-2001): Aarets Fotboll (0567-4565)
Published by: (Svenska Fotbollfoerbundet), Stroemberg - Brunnhage, Fack 65, Vallingby, 16211, Sweden.

796.334 SWE ISSN 0349-8484
FOTBOLLBOKEN; med Svenska Fotbollfoerbundets taevlingskalender. Text in Swedish. 1932. a. price varies. back issues avail. **Document type:** *Yearbook, Consumer.*
Formerly (until 1972): Nya Fotbollboken
Published by: Svenska Fotbollfoerbundet, Box 1216, Solna, 17123, Sweden. TEL 46-8-7350900, FAX 46-8-7350901, svff@svenskfotboll.se, http://www.svenskfotboll.se.

796.334 GBR ISSN 1355-0276
FOUR FOUR TWO. Text in English. 1994. m. GBP 39.36 (effective 2009). adv. back issues avail. **Document type:** *Magazine, Consumer.* **Description:** Provides interviews and a constant flow of news stories.
Incorporates (in 1999): Goal (1359-9763)
Indexed: U01.
—CCC.
Published by: Haymarket Publishing Ltd. (Subsidiary of: Haymarket Media Group), 174 Hammersmith Rd, London, W6 7JP, United Kingdom. TEL 44-20-82674210, info@haymarket.com, http://www.haymarket.com. Eds. Gary Parkinson TEL 44-20-82675337, Hugh Sleight TEL 44-20-82675335. Adv. contact Saed Souissi TEL 44-20-82675609. Circ: 105,531. **Subscr. to:** PO Box 568, Haywards Heath RH16 3XQ, United Kingdom. TEL 44-8456-777800, Haymarket.subs@qss-uk.com, http://www.themagazineshop.com.

796.334 POL
▼ **FOUR FOUR TWO.** Text in Polish. 2010. m. PLZ 4.90 newsstand/cover (effective 2011). **Document type:** *Magazine, Consumer.*
Published by: Ginza Media Group, ul Srodziemnomorska 47, Warsaw, 02-758, Poland. TEL 48-22-2034880, FAX 48-22-6424524, http://www.ginzamediagroup.pl. Ed. Wojciech Szaniawski. Adv. contact Malgorzata Karasiewicz.

796.332 NLD ISSN 2210-8424
▼ **FOURFOURTWO.** Text in Dutch. 2010. q. EUR 4.95 newsstand/cover (effective 2010). adv. **Document type:** *Magazine, Consumer.*
Published by: Vipmedia Publishing en Services, Takkebijsters 57a, Breda, 4817 BL, Netherlands. TEL 31-76-5301717, FAX 31-76-5144531, info@vipmedia.nl, http://www.vipmedia.nl. Ed. Jurgen Gommeren. adv.: color page EUR 3,195; trim 220 x 300. Circ: 40,000.

796.333 FRA ISSN 0015-9557
FRANCE FOOTBALL. Text in French. 1946. bi-w. EUR 86 (effective 2009). adv. illus. **Document type:** *Magazine, Consumer.*
Formerly: Football Magazine
Indexed: RASB, SportS.
Published by: S N C L'Equipe, 145 Rue JJ Rousseau, Issy les Moulineaux, Cedex 92138, France. TEL 33-1-40932020, FAX 33-1-40932405. Ed. Dennis Chaumier. Pub. Jean Pierre Courcol. Circ: 310,000 (paid).

796.334 DEU
FRAUENFUSSBALL MAGAZIN. Variant title: FF Magazin. Text in German. 2004. 10/yr. EUR 38; EUR 4 newsstand/cover (effective 2011). adv. **Document type:** *Magazine, Consumer.*
Published by: Meyer & Meyer Verlag, Von-Coels-Str 390, Aachen, 52080, Germany. TEL 49-241-958100, FAX 49-241-9581010, verlag@m-m-sports.com, http://m-m-sports.de.

796.334 USA
FREEKICK. Text in English. 1996. 5/yr. adv. **Document type:** *Magazine, Consumer.* **Description:** Provides information and features on the players and teams of Major League Soccer.
Published by: (Major League Soccer, LLC), Professional Sports Publications (P S P), 519 8th Ave, Ste 2500, New York, NY 10018. TEL 212-697-1460, FAX 212-286-8154, mlewis@pspsports.com, http://www.pspsports.com. Pub. Kevin Hahn. Adv. contact Chris Greiner.

796.352 USA ISSN 1534-9683
FRINGEGOLF. Text in English. 2001. bi-m. USD 19.95 domestic; USD 27.95 in Canada; USD 34.95 elsewhere; USD 4.95 newsstand/cover; USD 5.95 newsstand/cover in Canada (effective 2001). adv. **Document type:** *Magazine, Consumer.* **Description:** Provides an interactive media platform designed to take modern golfers beyond the trend, enabling them to appreciate the game on their own terms.
Related titles: Online - full text ed.
Published by: Fringe, Inc., PO Box 77505, San Francisco, CA 94107-0505. TEL 415-777-3673, 888-374-6434, FAX 415-777-3296, info@fringegolf.com.

796.323 USA
FULL COURT PRESS; the woman's basketball journal. Text in English. w. USD 19.95. **Document type:** *Magazine, Consumer.* **Description:** Covers high school, college, professional and international women's basketball.
Media: Online - full text.
Address: 900 N. Michigan Ave., Ste. 2100, Chicago, IL 60611. TEL 312-208-2311, FAX 312-280-2322. Ed. Maggi Brown. Pub. Clay Kallam.

796.334 USA
FUNDAMENTAL SOCCER. Variant title: Interactive Youth Soccer. Text in English. irreg. free. **Description:** Created and designed especially for beginning coaches, parents and youth soccer players.
Media: Online - full text.
Published by: FunSoccer Enterprises, 828 E Portland, Fresno, CA 93720. TEL 559-447-1869. Ed. Karl Dewazien.

796 DEU ISSN 0009-9600
FUSSBALL CLUB PFORZHEIM. CLUB-NACHRICHTEN. Text in German. 1952. m. membership. adv.
Published by: (Fussball Club Pforzheim), J. Esslinger Druckerei und Verlag, Poststr 5, Pforzheim, 75172, Germany. Circ: 1,500.

796.33463 DEU
FUSSBALL LIVE. Text in German. 2004. m. EUR 31.80 domestic; EUR 37.80 foreign; EUR 3.50 newsstand/cover (effective 2009). adv. **Document type:** *Magazine, Consumer.*
Former titles (until 2008): FourFourTwo (1863-2211); (until 2006): Top in Sport (1863-0049)
Published by: B P A Sportpresse GmbH, Leonhardtstr 2a, Hannover, 30175, Germany. TEL 49-511-1233280, FAX 49-511-12332811, verlag@bpa-sportpresse.de, http://www.bpa-sportpresse.de. Ed. Oliver Buss. Circ: 180,000 (controlled).

796.72 DEU ISSN 1863-8570
FUSSBALL MAGAZIN BAYERN MUENCHEN. Text in German. 2001. 6/yr. adv. **Document type:** *Magazine, Consumer.*
Formerly (until 2006): Top in Sport Bayern Muenchen (1863-0057)
Published by: B P A Sportpresse GmbH, Leonhardtstr 2a, Hannover, 30175, Germany. TEL 49-511-1233280, FAX 49-511-12332811, verlag@bpa-sportpresse.de, http://www.bpa-sportpresse.de.

796.334 DEU
FUSSBALL-REPORT. Text in German. q. adv. **Document type:** *Magazine, Consumer.*
Published by: Verlagsgesellschaft Tischler GmbH, Kaunstr 34, Berlin, 14163, Germany. TEL 49-30-8011018, FAX 49-30-8016661, media-service@firmengruppe-tischler.de. adv.: B&W page EUR 1,450, color page EUR 2,350. Circ: 10,200 (controlled).

796 DEU
FUSSBALL-WOCHE. Text in German. 1924. w. EUR 1.80 newsstand/cover (effective 2007). adv. **Document type:** *Magazine, Consumer.*
Published by: Olympia Verlag GmbH, Badstr 4-6, Nuernberg, 90402, Germany. TEL 49-911-2160, FAX 49-911-2162741, anzeigen@olympia-verlag.de, http://www.olympia-verlag.de. adv.: B&W page EUR 1,744, color page EUR 2,800. Circ: 12,007 (paid).

796.334 DEU ISSN 1616-4385
FUSSBALLNEWSLETTER. Text in German. 2000. d. **Document type:** *Newsletter, Consumer.*
Media: Online - full content.
Address: Hohe Heide 21, Wennigsen, 30974, Germany. Ed., Pub. Nils Warmboldt.

796.07 DEU ISSN 0016-3228
DER FUSSBALLTRAINER. Text in German. 1950. m. EUR 33.60 (effective 2002). adv. bk.rev. illus. index. 36 p./no. 4 cols./p.; back issues avail. **Document type:** *Magazine, Trade.* **Description:** Devoted to news and information for soccer trainers and coaches. Articles cover various aspects of soccer, tips for training, tactics, personal stories.
Indexed: RASB.
Published by: Sportverlag Schmidt und Dreisilker GmbH, Boeblinger Str 68/1, Sindelfingen, 71065, Germany. TEL 49-7031-862800, FAX 49-7031-862801. Ed. Brigitte Schurr. Adv. contact Dietmar Froeberg-Suberg TEL 49-7031-862851. color page EUR 1,400. Circ: 10,000.

796.334 DEU ISSN 0174-6227
FUSSBALLTRAINING. Text in German. 1983. m. EUR 46.20 domestic; EUR 49.80 foreign (effective 2011). back issues avail. **Document type:** *Magazine, Trade.*
Indexed: RASB.
Published by: (Deutscher Fussball-Bund/German Soccer Association), Philippka-Sportverlag Konrad Honig, Rektoratsweg 36, Muenster, 48159, Germany. TEL 49-251-230050, FAX 49-251-2300579, info@philippka.de, http://www.philippka.de. Adv. contact Peter Moellers TEL 49-251-2300528.

S

796.332 FIN ISSN 0359-4378
FUTARI. Text in Finnish. 1982. 10/yr. EUR 45 domestic; EUR 47 in Europe; EUR 56 elsewhere (effective 2005). adv. **Document type:** *Magazine, Consumer.* **Description:** Provides information about Finnish and international soccer.
Published by: (Football Association of Finland), A-Lehdet Oy, Risto Rytin tie 33, Helsinki, 00081, Finland. TEL 358-9-75961, FAX 358-9-7598600, a-tilaus@a-lehdet.fi. Ed. Juha Kuosa. Adv. contact Matti Sahravuo TEL 358-9-7596385. color page KRW 2,150; 209 x 255. Circ: 82,445 (controlled).

796.334 UKR
FUTBOL. Text in Ukrainian. w. USD 220 in United States. illus. **Document type:** *Consumer.* **Description:** Covers football (soccer).
Published by: Telenedelya Kiev, Pr Obolonskii 16, Kiev, Ukraine. TEL 380-44-418-7426. **Dist. by:** East View Information Services, 10601 Wayzata Blvd, Minneapolis, MN 55305. TEL 952-252-1201, 800-477-1005, FAX 952-252-1202, info@eastview.com, http://www.eastview.com.

796.334 RUS
FUTBOL. Text in Russian. w. USD 199.95 in United States.
Address: Ul Arkhipova 8, Moscow, 101000, Russian Federation. TEL 7-095-9236509, FAX 7-095-9249114. **Dist. by:** East View Information Services, 10601 Wayzata Blvd, Minneapolis, MN 55305. TEL 952-252-1201, 800-477-1005, FAX 952-252-1202, info@eastview.com, http://www.eastview.com.

796.334 ESP ISSN 1135-2817
FUTBOL CUADERNOS TECNICOS. Text in Spanish. 1995. 3/yr. **Document type:** *Magazine, Trade.*
Published by: Wanceulen Editorial Deportiva, Cristo del Desamparo y Abandono 56, Seville, 41006, Spain. TEL 34-95-4921511, FAX 34-95-4921059, infoeditorial@wanceleuen.com.

796.334 UKR
FUTBOL INTER. Text in Ukrainian. m. USD 190 in United States.
Address: Ul Rishel'evskaya 45, Kiev, Ukraine. TEL 21-74-58, FAX 22-32-75. **Dist. by:** East View Information Services, 10601 Wayzata Blvd, Minneapolis, MN 55305. TEL 952-252-1201, 800-477-1005, FAX 952-252-1202, info@eastview.com, http://www.eastview.com.

796.334 RUS
FUTBOL REVIEW. Text in Russian. 48/yr. USD 145 in United States.
Address: Ul Kirovogradskaya 21-a, Moscow, 113519, Russian Federation. TEL 7-095-3385945, FAX 7-095-3886290. Ed. K A Stolbovskii. **Dist. by:** East View Information Services, 10601 Wayzata Blvd, Minneapolis, MN 55305. TEL 952-252-1201, 800-477-1005, FAX 952-252-1202, info@eastview.com, http://www.eastview.com.

796.334 MEX
FUTBOL TOTAL. Text in Spanish. 1998. m. MXN 15, USD 2.95 newsstand/cover (effective 2000).
Published by: Grupo Editorial Total, Eugenio Sue 122, Col Polanco, Mexico, D.F. 11560, Mexico. TEL 52-5-280-2794. Ed. Eduardo Avayou.

796.334 ESP
FUTBOLISTA LIFE. Text in Spanish. m. EUR 2.50 newsstand/cover (effective 2009). adv. back issues avail. **Document type:** *Magazine, Trade.*
Published by: Grupo V, C Valportillo Primera, 11, Alcobendas, Madrid, 28108, Spain. TEL 34-91-6622137, secretaria@grupov.es, http://www.grupov.es/. Adv. contact Amador Moreno. page EUR 4,500; 20 x 27. Circ: 57,558.

796.3 FRA ISSN 1954-3875
FUTSAL SPIRIT. Text in French. 2005. bi-m. EUR 29.90 (effective 2009). back issues avail. **Document type:** *Magazine, Consumer.*
Media: Online - full text.
Published by: Union Nationale des Clubs de Futsal, 27 Rue de Sevres, Boulogne-Billancourt, 92100, France.

796.323 USA
FUTURE STARS. Text in English. m. USD 45 (effective 1998). **Document type:** *Magazine, Consumer.* **Description:** Provides a source for basketball recruiting information and ratings.
Related titles: Online - full text ed.
Published by: L S I Productions, 45 Laurel Rd, PO Box 1269, Pinehurst, NC 28370-1269. TEL 910-295-5559, FAX 910-295-6566, mechanic@futurestars.com. Pub. Nanci Donald.

796.352 USA ISSN 1944-4397
▼ **G**; a magazine for the modern golfer. Text in English. 2009 (May). bi-m. USD 5.95 per issue (effective 2009). **Document type:** *Magazine, Consumer.*
Published by: Concept Media USA, 276 NE 60th St, Miami, FL 33137. TEL 786-206-7269, http://conceptmediausa.com.

796.352 USA ISSN 1944-4389
▼ **G FOR WOMEN.** Text in English. 2009 (Jan.). bi-m. USD 5.95 per issue (effective 2009). **Document type:** *Magazine, Consumer.*
Published by: Concept Media USA, 276 NE 60th St, Miami, FL 33137. TEL 786-206-7269, FAX 305-751-4129, info@conceptmediausa.com, http://conceptmediausa.com.

796.352 DEU
G.O.L.F.-TIME. Text in German. 1998. 8/yr. EUR 32.50; EUR 4.50 newsstand/cover (effective 2010). adv. **Document type:** *Magazine, Consumer.*
Related titles: Online - full text ed.
Published by: (Deutscher Golf Verband e.V.), G.O.L.F.-Time Verlag GmbH, Truderinger Str 302, Munich, 81825, Germany. TEL 49-89-42718181, FAX 49-89-42718171, info@golftime.de. Ed. Oskar Brunnthaler. Circ: 63,147 (paid and controlled).

796.09415 IRL ISSN 0791-119X
GAELIC STARS. Text in English. 1966. irreg. **Document type:** *Magazine, Consumer.*
Former titles (until 1975): Cluichi na Gael (0791-1181); (until 1973): Gaelic Stars (0791-1173)
Published by: Oisin Publications, 4 Iona Dr., Dublin, 9, Ireland. TEL 353-1-8305236, FAX 353-1-8307860, oisinpr@iol.ie.

796.323 USA
GAMEPLAN BASKETBALL ANNUAL. Text in English. a. USD 6.50 newsstand/cover (effective 2001). **Document type:** *Magazine, Consumer.* **Description:** Contains in-depth team writeups and analysis for every professional and major college basketball team, including pointspread results, schedules, trends, and statistics.
Published by: GamePlan Magazines, 113 E Taft Rd, North Syracuse, NY 13212. TEL 315-452-0518, 866-777-0877, FAX 315-452-1504, info@gameplanmagazines.com, http://www.gameplanmagazines.com. **Dist. by:** Rider Circulation Services, 3700 Eagle Rock Blvd, Los Angeles, CA 90065. TEL 323-344-1200.

796.332 USA ISSN 1055-9256
GAMEPLAN COLLEGE FOOTBALL ANNUAL PREVIEW. Text in English. a. USD 6.50 newsstand/cover (effective 2001). **Document type:** *Magazine, Consumer.* **Description:** Contains in-depth team writeups and analysis for every major college football team, including pointspread results, schedules, trends, and statistics.
Published by: GamePlan Magazines, 113 E Taft Rd, North Syracuse, NY 13212. TEL 315-452-0518, 866-777-0877, FAX 315-452-1504, info@gameplanmagazines.com, http://www.gameplanmagazines.com. **Dist. by:** Rider Circulation Services, 3700 Eagle Rock Blvd, Los Angeles, CA 90065. TEL 323-344-1200.

796.332 USA ISSN 1055-9248
GAMEPLAN PRO FOOTBALL ANNUAL PREVIEW. Text in English. a. USD 6.50 newsstand/cover (effective 2001). **Document type:** *Magazine, Consumer.* **Description:** Contains in-depth team writeups and analysis for all of the professional football teams, including pointspread results, schedules, statistics and trends.
Published by: GamePlan Magazines, 113 E Taft Rd, North Syracuse, NY 13212. TEL 315-452-0518, 866-777-0877, FAX 315-452-1504, info@gameplanmagazines.com, http://www.gameplanmagazines.com. **Dist. by:** Rider Circulation Services, 3700 Eagle Rock Blvd, Los Angeles, CA 90065. TEL 323-344-1200.

796.352 CHN ISSN 1009-6698
GAOERFU/GOLF. Text in Chinese. 2000. m. USD 213.60 (effective 2009). **Document type:** *Magazine, Consumer.*
Related titles: Online - full content ed.
—East View.
Published by: Zhongguo Tiyubao Yezongshe, 8, Tiyuguan Lu, Chongwen-qu, Beijing, 100061, China. TEL 86-10-67143708, http://www.sportsol.com.cn/. **Dist. by:** China International Book Trading Corp, 35 Chegongzhuang Xilu, Haidian District, PO Box 399, Beijing 100044, China. TEL 86-10-68412045, FAX 86-10-68412023, cibtc@mail.cibtc.com.cn, http://www.cibtc.com.cn.

796.352 CHN ISSN 1673-3223
GAOERFU DASHI/GOLF DIGEST. Text in Chinese. m. CNY 478.80; CNY 39.90 per issue (effective 2010). back issues avail. **Document type:** *Magazine, Consumer.*
Published by: Titan Chuanmei Jituan/Titan Culture - Express Co, ltd, 1, Tiyuguan Lu, Changsha, 410005, China. TEL 86-731-4556749, http://www.titan24.com/.

796.323 USA
GBALL; for girls who play basketball. Text in English. 1999. fortn. free (effective 2011). back issues avail. **Document type:** *Magazine, Consumer.* **Description:** Contains information and articles on girls' and women basketball.
Media: Online - full text.
Indexed: GW.
Published by: Momentum Media Sports Publishing, 2488 N Triphammer Rd, Ithaca, NY 14850. TEL 607-257-6970, FAX 607-257-7328, info@gballmag.com.

796.332 USA
GEORGIA FOOTBALL. Text in English. a. **Document type:** *Magazine, Consumer.*
Published by: Varsity Sports Media, 3401 Russ Circle, Ste E, Alcoa, TN 37701. TEL 865-379-0625, FAX 865-379-9653.

796.352 USA ISSN 1930-773X
GEORGIA GOLF. Text in English. 1988. bi-m. membership. adv. **Document type:** *Magazine, Consumer.* **Description:** Features news, information and feature articles on people and events related to golf in Georgia and golf in general.
Formerly (Aug. 1993-Feb. 1994): Fairways & Greens
Published by: (Georgia State Golf Association), Level Par Media, Inc., 3660 Hadfield Dr, Marietta, GA 30062. TEL 678-560-7100, FAX 678-560-7400, http://www.levelparmedia.com. Ed. Joanna S Capo. Pub. Shannon Bower. Circ: 74,935.

796.352 USA ISSN 1947-2560
▼ **GEORGIA GOLF JOURNAL.** Text in English. forthcoming 2010. m. USD 9.99 (effective 2009). **Document type:** *Magazine, Consumer.* **Description:** Features articles on golf for Georgia.
Published by: In Publishing, 9769 NW 45 Ln, Miami, FL 33178. TEL 736-314-0456, info@miamigolfjournal.com.

796.323 ESP
GIGANTES DEL BASKET. Text in Spanish. w. adv. **Document type:** *Magazine, Consumer.*
Published by: Editorial America Iberica, C. Miguel Yuste 33bis, Madrid, 28037, Spain. TEL 34-91-3277950, FAX 34-91-3044746, editorial@eai.es, http://www.eai.es/. Ed. Paco Torres. adv.: page EUR 2,700; trim 210 x 285.

796.323 ITA ISSN 1122-1801
GIGANTI DEL BASKET. Variant title: B T & M Giganti del Basket. Text in Italian. 1966. m. EUR 49 domestic (effective 2008). adv. bk.rev. back issues avail. **Document type:** *Magazine, Consumer.* **Description:** Technical newsletter for coaches, players, sports doctors, managers and others associated with basketball.
Published by: Cantelli Editore Srl, Via Saliceto 22c, Castelmaggiore, BO 40013, Italy. TEL 39-051-6328811, FAX 39-051-6328815, cantelli.editore@cantelli.net, http://www.cantelli.net. Circ: 12,500.

796.334 GBR
GLORY GLORY MAN UNITED. Text in English. 1999 (vol.6, no.8). m. GBP 1.75 newsstand/cover (effective 2002). **Document type:** *Magazine, Consumer.* **Description:** Contains articles and features on the Manchester United football club.
Published by: Manchester United PLC, Sir Matt Busby Way, Old Trafford, Manchester, M16 0RA, United Kingdom. TEL 44-161-930-1968, FAX 44-161-876-5502. Eds. Alex Leith, Jim Drewett. **Dist. by:** M M C Ltd., Octagon House, White Hart Meadows, Ripley, Woking, Surrey GU23 6HR, United Kingdom. TEL 44-1483-211222, FAX 44-1483-224541.

796.334 USA ISSN 1947-8348
GO INDOOR. Text in English. 1996. q. USD 15; USD 4.50 per issue (effective 2009). **Document type:** *Magazine, Consumer.* **Description:** For indoor soccer players, fans and facility operators.
Former titles (until 2009): Goal Indoor (1540-5400); (until 2000): Goal International (1091-5109)
Published by: United States Indoor Soccer Association, 1340 N Great Neck Rd, Ste 1272-142, Virginia Beach, VA 23454. TEL 703-310-6151, pr@usindoor.com.

796.33 DNK ISSN 0909-8208
GOAL; international fodbold. Text in Danish. 1994. m. DKK 599 (effective 2009). adv. **Document type:** *Magazine, Consumer.* **Description:** Aimed at teen soccer enthusiasts.
Related titles: Includes: Goal, Dansk Fodbold. ISSN 1903-3370. 2002.
Published by: Egmont Serieforlaget A/S, Vognmagergade 11, Copenhagen, 1148, Denmark. TEL 45-70-205035, FAX 45-33-305760, ida@egmont.com, http://www.serieforlaget.dk. adv.: page DKK 17,500; trim 210 x 297. Circ: 20,000 (paid and controlled).

796.332 TUR
GOAL; football brings the world to your home goal. Text in Turkish. m. TRY 4 newsstand/cover domestic; USD 4 newsstand/cover foreign (effective 2009). **Document type:** *Magazine, Consumer.* **Description:** Features information about world's most famous football team, football news, comment and analysis in terms of visual images.
Published by: Dogan Egmont Yayincilik ve Yapimcilik A.S., 19 Mayis Mahallesi, Golden Plaza No 1, Kat 10, Posta Kodu 34360, Istanbul, Turkey. TEL 90-212-2464646, FAX 90-212-2466666, fguven@de.com.tr, marketing@de.com.tr, http://www.doganegmont.com.tr.

796.332 SWE ISSN 1104-3385
GOAL. Text in Swedish. 1994. 12/yr. SEK 559 (effective 2009). adv. **Document type:** *Magazine, Consumer.*
Published by: Egmont Serieforlaget AB, Stora Varvsgatan 19A, Malmo, 20507, Sweden. TEL 46-40-385200, FAX 46-40-385396, tord.joensson@egmont.se, http://www.egmont.se. adv.: color page SEK 17,200; trim 210 x 297. Circ: 40,000 (controlled).

796.334 NLD ISSN 2210-9633
GOAL!. Text in Dutch. 2007. m. EUR 24.95; EUR 3.10 newsstand/cover (effective 2010). adv. **Document type:** *Magazine, Consumer.*
Published by: Z-Press Junior Media, Postbus 1015, Dordrecht, 3300 BA, Netherlands. TEL 31-78-6397070, FAX 31-78-6397071, mailbox@zpress-magazines.nl, http://www.zpress-magazines.nl. Ed. Maaike Petri. Pub. Robert van Ginhoven.

796.350 GBR ISSN 1356-5699
GOING FOR GOLF. Text in English. 1995. q. GBP 7.50; GBP 2.50 newsstand/cover (effective 1999). illus. **Document type:** *Magazine, Consumer.* **Description:** Features articles on the golf courses of the world.
Published by: Going for Golf Ltd., 71 St Stephens Rd, Canterbury, Kent CT2 7JW, United Kingdom. TEL 44-1227-457948, FAX 44-1227-763384. **Dist. by:** Post Scriptum, Unit 1, Pylon Trading Estate, Cody Rd, London E16 4SP, United Kingdom. TEL 44-171-473-0771, FAX 44-171-473-0772.

796.334 796.962 CZE ISSN 0323-0686
GOL; fodbalovy a hokejovy tydenik. Text in Czech. 1968. w. CZK 1,300 (effective 2009). illus. index. **Document type:** *Magazine, Consumer.* **Description:** Focuses on soccer and hockey.
Published by: AS Press s. r. o., ul Marie Cibulkove 26, Prague 4, 14000, Czech Republic. TEL 420-2-41407018. Ed. Stanislav Hrab. Pub. Jaromir Jarusek. Circ: 55,000.

796.332 USA
GOLDEN STATE WARRIORS OFFICIAL YEARBOOK. Text in English. 1993. irreg., latest 1995. adv. illus. **Document type:** *Magazine, Consumer.*
Published by: Woodford Publishing, Inc., PO Box 910, Tiburon, CA 94920. TEL 415-397-1853, FAX 415-399-0942. Ed. Jon Rochmis. Pub. Laurence J Hyman. R&P, Adv. contact David Lilienstein.

796.352 BEL
GOLF. Text in Dutch, French. 1945. 8/yr. EUR 35; EUR 4.50 per issue (effective 2005). adv. **Document type:** *Magazine, Consumer.*
Published by: (Federation Royale Belge de Golf), Belgame S.A., Av Montjoie 167, Brussels, 1180, Belgium. TEL 32-2-3430845, FAX 32-2-3435772. Ed., R&P, Adv. contact Claire Rolin. B&W page EUR 1,364, color page EUR 2,230; bleed 210 x 297. Circ: 12,000.

796.352 SGP ISSN 0218-4818
GOLF. Text in English. 1990. m. free at golf courses and country clubs. **Document type:** *Magazine, Consumer.*
Published by: Eastern Publishing Pte Ltd (Subsidiary of: Eastern Holdings Ltd), 1100 Lower Delta Rd, #04-01, EPL Bldg, Singapore, 169206, Singapore. TEL 65-6-3792888, FAX 65-6-3792803.

796.352 GBR ISSN 1479-9413
GOLF. Variant title: P G A Yearbook. Text in English. 199?. a. (Mar.). GBP 3.95 per issue (effective 2009). adv. **Document type:** *Yearbook.* **Description:** Features the associations most important events of the past 12 months while also casting a forward glance to the forthcoming attractions on the golfing calendar.
Formerly (until 2003): Professional Golfers' Association. Official Yearbook
Related titles: Online - full text ed.
Published by: (Professional Golfers' Association), V R Associates, PO Box 324, Fleet, Hamps GU51 3ZH, United Kingdom. TEL 44-1252-621513, pga@vrassociates.co.uk. Ed. Adrian Milledge.

796.352 DEU
GOLF AKTUELL. Text in German. 1988. bi-m. EUR 18; EUR 2.80 newsstand/cover (effective 2010). adv. **Document type:** *Magazine, Consumer.*
Published by: v. Bentzel & Partner GmbH, Konrad-Zuse-Platz 10, Munich, 81829, Germany. TEL 49-89-5468540, FAX 49-89-5804439. Circ: 71,120 (controlled).

796.352 PRT ISSN 1646-5865
GOLF ALGARVE. Text in Portuguese. 2006. irreg. **Document type:** *Magazine, Consumer.*
Published by: Golfocus, Lda., Largo de S Francisco, Galeria S Francisco 18, Loule, Algarve 8100-692, Portugal. http://www.golfocus.com.

796.352 SGP
GOLF ANNUAL. Text in English. a. **Document type:** *Magazine, Consumer.*
Published by: Eastern Publishing Pte Ltd (Subsidiary of: Eastern Holdings Ltd), 1100 Lower Delta Rd, #04-01, EPL Bldg, Singapore, 169206, Singapore. TEL 65-6-3792888, FAX 65-6-3792803.

796.352 AUS ISSN 0818-5077
GOLF AUSTRALIA. Text in English. 1987. m. AUD 75 domestic; AUD 100 in New Zealand; AUD 115 elsewhere; AUD 7.50 newsstand/cover (effective 2008). adv. back issues avail. **Document type:** *Magazine, Consumer.* **Description:** Covers all aspects of the sport: players, tournaments, instruction, travel, equipment, features, results, etc.
Indexed: SD.
Published by: Wolseley Media Pty Ltd., Level 5, 55 Chandos St, PO Box 5555, St. Leonards, NSW 2065, Australia. TEL 61-2-99016100, FAX 61-2-99016198, contactsubs@wolseleymedia.com.au, http://www.wolseleymedia.com.au. Ed. Brendan James TEL 61-2-99016142. Adv. contact David Gleeson TEL 61-2-99016131. page AUD 2,650; trim 210 x 297. Circ: 26,000.

796.352 DEU ISSN 1862-3085
GOLF CLUB-MAGAZIN. Text in German. 1972. 10/yr. EUR 3 newsstand/cover (effective 2006). adv. bk.rev. **Document type:** *Magazine, Consumer.*
Former titles (until 2005): Golfclub Magazin (0931-573X); (until 1985): Golf in Schleswig-Holstein (0724-5602)
Published by: Jahr Top Special Verlag, Troplowitzstr 5, Hamburg, 22529, Germany. TEL 49-40-389060, FAX 49-40-38906300, info@jahr-tsv.de, http://www.jahr-tsv.de. adv.: B&W page EUR 3,912, color page EUR 6,840; trim 185 x 248. Circ: 32,278 (paid).

796.352 658 GBR ISSN 0267-1166
GOLF CLUB MANAGEMENT. Text in English. 1933. m. GBP 60 domestic to non-members; GBP 90 in Europe to non-members; GBP 120 elsewhere to non-members; free to members (effective 2009). adv. bk.rev. **Document type:** *Journal, Trade.* **Description:** Contains the latest news and issues discussed from the National Secretary, day to day management issues, information, new initiatives. Round the Regions - update on all activities affecting members on a regional basis. Business Digest - reviews golf news. Club Profiles. Buyers Guide - a must for all those involved with Golf Club management covering the Golf course, Club house, Professional & Office.
Formerly (until 1976): Golf Course and Club House Management
Indexed: SportS.
—CCC.
Published by: Golf Club Managers Association, 7a Beaconsfield Rd, Weston-Super-Mare, Somerset BS23 1YE, United Kingdom. TEL 44-1934-641166, FAX 44-1934-644254, hq@gcma.org.uk.

796.352 USA
GOLF CONNOISSEUR. Text in English. 2005. bi-m. (q. until May/Jun., 2006). USD 29.99 domestic; USD 39.99 in Canada; USD 72.99 elsewhere (effective 2006). adv. **Document type:** *Magazine, Consumer.*
Incoporated (in 2006): Luxury Golf & Travel
Published by: Patience Publishing, 8988-L S Sheridan Rd, Ste 360, Tulsa, OK 74133. TEL 918-492-0660, 866-587-4653, FAX 918-492-0680, 866-587-4653. Pubs. Joe Kelly TEL 214-507-9950, Ken Wallace TEL 914-276-2151. adv.: B&W page USD 22,031, color page USD 29,375; trim 10 x 12.

GOLF COURSE ARCHITECTURE; the quarterly journal of golf course design and modification. *see* ARCHITECTURE

GOLF COURSE BUILDERS ASSOCIATION OF AMERICA. DIRECTORY. *see* BUILDING AND CONSTRUCTION

796.352 USA
GV975.5
GOLF COURSE INDUSTRY. Text in English. 1989. m. USD 33 domestic; USD 42 in Canada & Mexico; USD 88 elsewhere; free to qualified personnel (effective 2009). adv. back issues avail.; reprints avail. **Document type:** *Magazine, Consumer.* **Description:** Provides information on golf course management and maintenance for supervisors, golf directors, architects, developers and builders.
Formerly (until 2007): Golf Course News (1054-0644)
Related titles: Online - full text ed.; International ed.: Golf Course News International.
Indexed: A15, ABIn, P48, P51, PQC.
Published by: G I E Media Inc., 4020 Kinross Lakes Pky, Richfield, OH 44286. TEL 800-456-0707, FAX 330-659-0823, pmorales@gie.net, http://www.giemedia.com/pages/home/default.aspx. Eds. Jonathan Walsh, Marisa Palmieri. Pub. Kevin Gilbride TEL 330-523-5368. adv.: B&W page USD 5,011, color page USD 6,009; trim 9 x 10.875. Circ: 30,570 (controlled).

796.352 USA ISSN 0192-3048
GV975 CODEN: GCMAEA
GOLF COURSE MANAGEMENT. Abbreviated title: G C M. Text in English. 1927. m. USD 60 domestic; USD 110 foreign (effective 2010). adv. illus. 124 p./no. 2 cols./p.; back issues avail. **Document type:** *Magazine, Trade.*
Former titles (until 1979): Golf Superintendent (0017-1840); (until 1966): Golf Course Reporter (0096-2376); (until 1951): Greenskeepers' Reporter (0096-2481); (until 1933): Greenkeepers' Bulletin
Related titles: Online - full text ed.: ISSN 2157-3085. free (effective 2010).
Indexed: SportS.
—Ingenta.
Published by: Golf Course Superintendents Association of America, 1421 Research Park Dr, Lawrence, KS 66049. TEL 785-841-2240, 800-472-7878, FAX 785-832-3643, infobox@gcsaa.org. Eds. Scott Hollister, Ed Hiscock. Adv. contact Mark Bisbing.

796.352 CAN
GOLF COURSE RANKING MAGAZINE. Text in French. 1996. a. adv. **Document type:** *Magazine, Consumer.* **Description:** Ranks public and resort golf courses and publishes golf editorial of general interest.
Published by: Longhurst Golf Corporation, 236 Wynchwood Ave, Tornoto, ON, Canada. TEL 905-764-5409, FAX 905-764-5462. Ed. Bruce Ballentine. Pub. Bruce Longhurst. Circ: 100,000.

658 USA ISSN 0436-1474
GV975
GOLF COURSE SUPERINTENDENTS ASSOCIATION OF AMERICA. MEMBERSHIP DIRECTORY; who's who in golf course management. Spine title: G C S A A Membership Directory. Text in English. 19??. a. free to members (effective 2011). adv. **Document type:** *Directory, Trade.*
Related titles: Online - full text ed.
Published by: Golf Course Superintendents Association of America, 1421 Research Park Dr, Lawrence, KS 66049. TEL 785-841-2240, 800-472-7878, FAX 785-832-3643, infobox@gcsaa.org.

796.352 USA
THE GOLF COURSE TRADES. Text in English. m. adv. **Description:** Provides information about products and services for the golf course industry.
Published by: The Trades Publishing Company, 20 Our Way Dri, Crossville, TN 38555. TEL 931-484-8819, FAX 931-484-8825, sales@thetrades.com, http://www.golfcoursetrades.com. adv.: B&W page USD 1,500, color page USD 2,025.

796.352 USA ISSN 1092-9649
GOLF COURSE TURF & IRRIGATION. Text in English. 6/yr. USD 40; USD 65 foreign (effective 1997). **Description:** Directed to greens committee chairmen, superintendents and architects of golf courses, and foremen of manufacturing, distribution and supplier firms.
Formerly: Golf Course Irrigation Magazine (1090-7556)
Published by: Hunter Publishing Limited Partnership, 2101 S Arlington Heights Rd, Ste 150, Arlington, IL 60005. TEL 847-427-9512, FAX 847-427-9649.

GOLF DAYS. GOLF COURSES IN IRELAND. *see* TRAVEL AND TOURISM

GOLF DESTINATIONS. *see* TRAVEL AND TOURISM

796.352 333.7 USA
GOLF DEVELOPMENTS. Text in English. 2/m. **Document type:** *Newsletter, Trade.* **Description:** Provides the latest information on the major golf course developers, builders, architects, and industry suppliers.
Published by: Cypress Magazines, Inc., 5715 Kerny Villa Rd, Ste108, San Diego, CA 92123. TEL 800-296-9656, FAX 858-503-7588, info@cypressmagazines.com, http://www.cypressmagazines.com.

796.352 CZE ISSN 1214-8814
GOLF DIGEST. Text in Czech. 2003. m. CZK 891; CZK 99 newsstand/cover (effective 2008). adv. **Document type:** *Magazine, Consumer.*
Formerly (until 2004): G D - Oficialni Ceska Verze Golf Digest (1214-2867)
Related titles: Online - full text ed.: ISSN 1801-4364.
Published by: Atemi s.r.o., Velvarska 1626 - 45, Prague 6, 160 00, Czech Republic. TEL 420-233-025501, FAX 420-233-025502, info@atemi.cz, http://www.atemi.cz. Ed. Cenek Lorenc. adv.: page CZK 120,000; trim 203 x 267. Circ: 12,000 (paid and controlled).

796.352 USA ISSN 0017-176X
GV961
GOLF DIGEST. Text in English. 1950. m. USD 12 domestic; USD 21.97 foreign (effective 2009). adv. bk.rev. charts; illus.; tr.lit. back issues avail.; reprints avail. **Document type:** *Magazine, Consumer.* **Description:** Features advice from players and experienced teachers of the Golf sport.
Formerly (until 1950): Arrowhead Golf Digest
Related titles: Microfilm ed.: (from PQC); Online - full text ed.: GolfDigest.com.
Indexed: A11, A22, A25, A26, C05, C11, C12, CPerI, ConsI, E08, G05, G06, G07, G08, G09, H03, I05, I06, I07, M01, M02, M04, MASUSE, P02, P10, P53, P54, PEI, PMR, PQC, R06, S08, S09, S23, SD, SPI, SportS, T02, U01.
—Ingenta. **CCC.**
Published by: The Golf Digest Companies (Subsidiary of: Advance Publications, Inc.), 20 Westport Rd, Wilton, CT 06897. TEL 203-761-5100, 800-438-0491, FAX 203-761-5135, glscustserv@cdsfulfilment.com. Ed. Jerry Tarde. Pub. Thomas J Bair. Adv. contact Jonathan Wall TEL 203-761-5395. B&W page USD 95,800, color page USD 119,760; trim 8 x 10.5.

796.352 SWE ISSN 1103-3762
GOLF DIGEST. Text in Swedish. 1986. 8/yr. adv. **Document type:** *Magazine, Consumer.*
Formerly (until 1992): Golf Digest Sverige (0284-1452)
Published by: T T G Sverige AB (Subsidiary of: De Telegraaf Tijdschriftengroep), PO Box 26206, Stockholm, 10041, Sweden. TEL 46-8-50667800, FAX 46-8-50667859, info@ttg.se, http://www.ttg.se. Ed. Tommy Jeppsson. Adv. contact Johan Kjellberg TEL 46-8-224480. color page SEK 48.50; 217 x 280. Circ: 29,400.

796.352 DEU ISSN 1616-2498
GOLF DIGEST. Text in German. 1988. m. **Document type:** *Magazine, Consumer.* **Description:** Provides tips and techniques for the amateur golfer as well as coverage of the world of professional golf.
Formerly (until 1999): Golf Sport (0934-6368)
Published by: Top Special Verlag GmbH, Nebendahlstr 16, Hamburg, 22041, Germany. TEL 49-40-34724673, FAX 49-40-34725733, abo@tsv.de, http://www.tsv.de. Ed. Dieter Genske. Adv. contact Beate Asmus. Circ: 25,471 (paid).

796.352 SGP
GOLF DIGEST SINGAPORE. Text in English. 2007. m. SGD 78 (effective 2008). **Document type:** *Magazine, Consumer.*
Published by: S P H Magazines Pte Ltd. (Subsidiary of: Singapore Press Holdings Ltd.), 82 Genting Ln Level 7, Media Centre, Singapore, 349567, Singapore. TEL 65-6319-6319, FAX 65-6319-6345, sphmag@sph.com.sg, http://www.sphmagazines.com.sg/.

796.352 ZAF
GOLF DIGEST SOUTH AFRICA. Text in English. 1995. m. ZAR 95 domestic; ZAR 167 foreign. illus. **Document type:** *Magazine, Consumer.* **Description:** Covers international and local golf, including profiles of leading players, technical advice and instruction.
Published by: Touchline Media, PO Box 16368, Vlaeberg, Cape Town 8018, South Africa. TEL 27-21-217810, FAX 27-21-215118, http://www.touchline.co.za. Ed. Stuart McLean. Pub. Rob Moore. R&P Stuart Lowe. Adv. contact Paul Ingpen. Circ: 13,000 (paid).

796.352 USA
GOLF DIGEST WOMAN. Text in English. 2000. 4/yr. **Document type:** *Magazine, Consumer.* **Description:** Contains articles, instruction and advice on golf, health and lifestyles.
Published by: The Golf Digest Companies (Subsidiary of: Advance Publications, Inc.), 20 Westport Rd, Wilton, CT 06897. TEL 203-761-5100, 800-438-0491, FAX 203-761-5129, glscustserv@cdsfulfilment.com.

796.352 FRA ISSN 1775-7924
GOLF DRIVER MAG; le premier magazine d'achat 100% dedie aux golfeurs. Text in French. 2005. bi-m. EUR 30 (effective 2009); EUR 6 per issue (effective 2006). **Document type:** *Magazine, Consumer.*
Published by: New Life, 50-52 route des Fusilles-de-la-Resistance, Nanterre, 92000, France. TEL 33-1-41449830, FAX 33-1-41449831. Ed. Emmanuel Surun.

796.352 ITA ISSN 1828-9258
GOLF E TORNEI. Text in Italian. 2005. m. **Document type:** *Magazine, Consumer.*
Published by: Alfa Print Editore, Via Bellini 24, Busto Arsizio, VA 21052, Italy. TEL 39-0331-620100, FAX 39-0331-321116, mensil@alfaprint.com.

796.352 ITA ISSN 1123-4830
GOLF & TURISMO. Text in Italian. 1994. 9/yr. EUR 45 (effective 2009). adv. 220 p./no.; **Document type:** *Magazine, Consumer.*
Related titles: Online - full text ed.
Published by: Go.Tu. Srl, Via Winckelmann 2, Milan, MI 20146, Italy. TEL 39-02-424191, FAX 39-02-48953252, redazione@golfeturismo.it. Circ: 26,000.

796.352 NLD ISSN 1877-6973
GOLF & LIFESTYLE. Text in Dutch. 2008. q. adv. **Document type:** *Magazine, Consumer.*
Published by: New Publishers, Postbus 5244, Groningen, 9700 GE, Netherlands. TEL 31-50-5496749, FAX 31-50-5493612, info@newpublishers.nl, http://www.newpublishers.nl. Ed. Irene Bentum. Adv. contacts Audrey Hindriks, Henk Krans. page EUR 1,750; trim 220 x 297. Circ: 10,000.

796.352 613.7 NLD ISSN 1878-8998
▼ **GOLF & WELLNESS.** Text mainly in Dutch. 2010. bi-m. EUR 30 (effective 2010). adv. **Document type:** *Magazine, Consumer.*
Related titles: Online - full text ed.: ISSN 1878-9005.
Published by: HP Media, Bachstraat 95, Capelle aan den IJssel, 2901 JZ, Netherlands. TEL 31-10-2021417, FAX 31-84-7565528. Ed. Harry Mulder. adv.: color page EUR 3,500; trim 230 x 297. Circ: 20,000.

796.352 GBR ISSN 1360-9513
GOLF ENTERPRISE EUROPE. Text in English. 1990. bi-m. GBP 45, USD 100. adv. **Document type:** *Magazine, Trade.*
Published by: Golf Business Communications Ltd., 5-7 High St, Dorchester-On-Thames, Oxfords OX10 7HH, United Kingdom. TEL 44-1865-341580, FAX 44-1865-341575. Ed., Pub. Geoffrey Russell. Adv. contact Lynn Miles. B&W page GBP 800, color page GBP 1,100; trim 8.25 x 11.75. Circ: 7,500.

796.352 NLD ISSN 1875-5070
GOLF ESTATE; wonen & reizen. Text in Dutch. 2007. bi-m. adv. **Document type:** *Magazine, Consumer.*
Published by: Pelican Magazines Hearst, Delflandlaan 4, Amsterdam, 1062 EB, Netherlands. TEL 31-20-7581000, FAX 31-20-7581003, info@pelicanmags.nl, http://www.pelicanmags.nl. Pub. Frank Kloppert.

796.352 FRA ISSN 0040-3458
GOLF EUROPEEN. Text in French. 1914. m. EUR 49.90 (effective 2008). adv. bk.rev. illus. **Document type:** *Magazine, Consumer.*
Former titles (until 1970): Tennis et Golf (1142-4605); (until 1951): Plaisir des Sports (1142-4591); (until 1949): Tennis, Golf et Ski (1142-4583); (until 1946): Tennis et Golf (1142-4575)
Indexed: SportS.
Published by: Mondadori France, 1 Rue du Colonel Pierre-Avia, Paris, Cedex 15 75754, France. TEL 33-1-41335001, contact@mondadori.fr, http://www.mondadori.fr. Circ: 30,000.

796.352 USA
GOLF EVENT; the resource for golf outings and events. Text in English. 2006. q. USD 19.95; USD 5 newsstand/cover (effective 2009). adv. back issues avail. **Document type:** *Magazine, Trade.* **Description:** Offers business insight and creative strategies for success, from corporate outings to charitable fundraising.
Related titles: Online - full content ed.: free (effective 2009).
Published by: Symphony Publishing LLC, 26202 Detroit Rd, Ste 300, Westlake, OH 44145. TEL 440-871-1300, FAX 440-835-8306, http://www.symphonypublishing.com. Ed. April Miller TEL 440-871-1300 ext 113. Pub. Brad Seybert TEL 440-871-1300 ext 103. Adv. contact Phil Dietz TEL 770-740-9656.

796.352 613.7 USA
GOLF FITNESS. Text in English. 2007. bi-m. USD 14.50 (effective 2007). **Document type:** *Magazine, Consumer.* **Description:** Covers golf performance, conditioning, and physical training.
Published by: Golf Fitness Magazine, Inc., 2706 Rew Circle, Ocoee, FL 34761. TEL 407-864-5077, FAX 407-574-7016. Pub. Steve Gomen.

796.352 CAN ISSN 1484-2793
GOLF GUIDE (NATIONAL EDITION); national golf course directory. Text in English. 1996. a. CAD 2.95 (effective 1998). adv. illus. back issues avail. **Document type:** *Directory.* **Description:** Lists the golf courses across the country.
Related titles: ◆ Regional ed(s).: Golf Guide (Western Edition). ISSN 1199-3057.
Published by: Golf Guide Inc., 16410 137 Ave, Edmonton, AB T5L 4H8, Canada. TEL 403-447-2128, 800-661-1606, FAX 403-447-1933. Ed., Pub., R&P Paul McCracken. Adv. contact Bruce Fowler.

796.352 CAN ISSN 1199-3057
GV985 .C3 G85
GOLF GUIDE (WESTERN EDITION). Text in English. 1984. a. CAD 4.95. adv. illus. back issues avail. **Document type:** *Directory.* **Description:** Directory of more than 900 golf courses in British Columbia, Alberta and Saskatchewan and Manitoba.
Former titles: Golf Guide. Annual Golf Course Directory: British Columbia, Alberta, Saskatchewan and Manitoba (1184-6291); Golf Courses of Alberta; Alberta Golf Guide (0832-8803); Incorporates: British Columbia Golf Guide (0848-8398)
Related titles: ◆ Regional ed(s).: Golf Guide (National Edition). ISSN 1484-2793.
Published by: Golf Guide Inc., 16410 137 Ave, Edmonton, AB T5L 4H8, Canada. TEL 403-447-2128, 800-661-1606, FAX 403-447-1933. Ed., Pub., R&P Paul McCracken. Adv. contact Bruce Fowler. B&W page CAD 2,075, color page CAD 2,395; trim 8.25 x 10.63. Circ: 40,000.

796.352 GBR ISSN 0263-4066
GOLF GUIDE - WHERE TO PLAY AND WHERE TO STAY. Text in English. 1977. a. GBP 12.99 per issue (effective 2009). adv. stat. index. **Document type:** *Handbook/Manual/Guide, Consumer.* **Description:** Lists over 3000 clubs and courses in Britain and Ireland, and selected holiday courses in Cyprus, France, Portugal, Spain, Thailand and USA.
Formerly (until 1980): Where to Stay and Where to Play

S

Published by: F H G Guides Ltd. (Subsidiary of: F H G Publications Ltd.), Abbey Mill Business Ctr, Seedhill, Paisley, PA1 1TJ, United Kingdom. TEL 44-141-8870428, FAX 44-141-8897204, sales@fhguides.co.uk, http://www.fhguides.co.uk.

796.352 USA ISSN 0160-6808
GV961
GOLF ILLUSTRATED. Text in English. 1973. q. USD 13.99 (effective 2009). bk.rev. illus. back issues avail. **Document type:** *Magazine, Consumer.* **Description:** Covers all aspects of the game of golf, including equipment, instruction, travel, fashion, and fitness.
Related titles: Online - full text ed.
Indexed: SPI.
Published by: NatCom, Inc., 7580 E 151st St, Bixby, OK 74008. TEL 918-366-6191, 800-554-1999, FAX 918-366-6512, cs@natcom-publications.com, http://www.natcom-publications.com. Adv. contact Shannon Land TEL 918-366-6191 ext 139. **Dist. in UK by:** Seymour Distribution Ltd, 86 Newman St, London W1T 3EX, United Kingdom. TEL 44-20-73968000, FAX 44-20-73968002, enquiries@seymour.co.uk, http://www.seymour.co.uk.

796.352 DEU
GOLF IN HAMBURG. Text in German. 1968. bi-m. adv. **Document type:** *Magazine, Consumer.*
Published by: L.A. CH. Schulz Gesellschaft fuer Anzeigen, Werbung und Verlag mbH, Mattentwiete 5, Hamburg, 20457, Germany. TEL 49-40-3698040, FAX 49-40-36980444, info@lachschulz.de, http://www.lachschulz.de. adv.: B&W page EUR 1,980, color page EUR 2,360. Circ: 12,947 (controlled).

796.352 DEU
GOLF IN HAMBURG JAHRBUCH. Text in German. a. adv. **Document type:** *Magazine, Consumer.*
Published by: L.A. CH. Schulz Gesellschaft fuer Anzeigen, Werbung und Verlag mbH, Mattentwiete 5, Hamburg, 20457, Germany. TEL 49-40-3698040, FAX 49-40-36980444, info@lachschulz.de, http://www.lachschulz.de. adv.: B&W page EUR 2,070, color page EUR 2,470. Circ: 13,000 (controlled).

796.352 DEU
GOLF IN NIEDERSACHSEN - BREMEN JAHRBUCH. Text in German. a. adv. **Document type:** *Magazine, Consumer.*
Published by: L.A. CH. Schulz Gesellschaft fuer Anzeigen, Werbung und Verlag mbH, Mattentwiete 5, Hamburg, 20457, Germany. TEL 49-40-3698040, FAX 49-40-36980444, info@lachschulz.de, http://www.lachschulz.de. adv.: B&W page EUR 2,305, color page EUR 2,705. Circ: 13,300 (controlled).

796.352 DEU
GOLF IN SCHLESWIG-HOLSTEIN JAHRBUCH. Text in German. a. adv. **Document type:** *Magazine, Consumer.*
Published by: L.A. CH. Schulz Gesellschaft fuer Anzeigen, Werbung und Verlag mbH, Mattentwiete 5, Hamburg, 20457, Germany. TEL 49-40-3698040, FAX 49-40-36980444, info@lachschulz.de, http://www.lachschulz.de. adv.: B&W page EUR 2,305, color page EUR 2,705. Circ: 13,300 (controlled).

796.352 USA
GV962
GOLF INDEX. Text in English. 1980. s-a. USD 40. adv. **Document type:** *Directory, Trade.*
Formerly (until 1992): International Golf Directory (0272-1775)
Published by: Ingledue Travel Publications, 4466, Glendale, CA 91222-0466. TEL 818-247-5530, FAX 818-247-5535. Ed., Pub. Ronald Ingledue. Circ: 10,000.

796.352 DEU
GOLF INSIDE; Das Business-Magazin. Text in German. 1999. m. adv. **Document type:** *Magazine, Trade.*
Published by: Atlas Verlag GmbH, Brienner Str 41, Munich, 80333, Germany. TEL 49-89-552410, FAX 49-89-55241100, info@atlas-verlag.de, http://www.atlas-verlag.de. Ed. Guenter Reiter. Adv. contact Benedikt Aidelsburger. Circ: 4,000 (controlled).

796.352 GBR ISSN 1368-4027
GOLF INTERNATIONAL; essential reading from the best in the game. Text in English. 1997. bi-m. GBP 32.99 domestic; GBP 39.99 in Europe; GBP 44.99 elsewhere; GBP 4.25 newsstand/cover (effective 2009). adv. illus. back issues avail. **Document type:** *Magazine, Consumer.*
Related titles: Online - full text ed.
Published by: Golf International Services Ltd., 10 Buckingham Pl, London, SW1E 6HX, United Kingdom. TEL 44-20-78283003. Eds. Richard Simmons, Robert Green. Adv. contact Peter Simmons. page GBP 2,640; trim 210 x 297. **Subscr. to:** Alliance Media, Bournehall House, Bournehall Rd, Bushey, Herts WD23 3YG, United Kingdom. TEL 44-20-89557018.

796.352 IRL ISSN 1393-9165
GOLF IRELAND; Ireland's national golf magazine. Text in English. 1997. bi-m. adv. **Document type:** *Magazine, Consumer.*
Address: PO Box 8111, Crumlin, Dublin, 12, Ireland. TEL 353-1-4734100, FAX 353-1-4731056. Ed. Mick Carwood. Adv. contact Greg Francis. page EUR 2,222. Circ: 37,000 (paid and controlled).

796.352 DEU ISSN 0949-8850
GOLF JOURNAL. Text in German. 1982. 12/yr. EUR 52.80; EUR 5 newsstand/cover (effective 2011). adv. bk.rev. charts; illus. **Document type:** *Magazine, Consumer.*
Formed by the merger of (1982-1996): Golf Journal (Ausgabe Nord) (0944-2189); (1982-1996): Golf Journal (Ausgabe Sued) (0944-2197); Both of which superseded in part (in 1988): Golf Journal (0933-8470); Which incorporated (1972-1988): Golf - Contact
Published by: Atlas Verlag GmbH, Brienner Str 41, Munich, 80333, Germany. TEL 49-89-552410, FAX 49-89-55241100, info@atlas-verlag.de, http://www.atlas-verlag.de. Ed. Stefan Engert. Adv. contact Benedikt Aidelsburger. Circ: 39,183 (paid and controlled).

796.352 CHE ISSN 1661-7797
GOLF LEADER; Das Magazin zum Golfspiel. Text in German. 2006. 4/yr. CHF 7 newsstand/cover (effective 2007). adv. **Document type:** *Magazine, Consumer.*
Published by: Image-Consulting, Engelgasse 13, St. Gallen, 9000, Switzerland. TEL 41-71-2233331, FAX 41-86-0796345454. Ed. Adelheid Hess. adv.: page CHF 6,600; trim 195 x 277.

796.352 USA ISSN 1066-6389
GOLF LESSONS. Text in English. 1992. m. **Document type:** *Magazine, Consumer.*
Published by: Harris Publications, Inc., 1115 Broadway, New York, NY 10010. TEL 212-807-7100, FAX 212-924-2352, subscriptions@harris-pub.com, http://www.harris-pub.com. Ed. Sean Sundra. Pub. Stanley R Harris. Adv. contact Arlene Jaffee.

796.352 CHE
GOLF.LIFESTYLE; das Magazin fuer den Golfer. Text in German. q. CHF 39; CHF 13 newsstand/cover (effective 2002). adv. **Document type:** *Magazine, Consumer.*
Published by: Mediax AG, Schneebergstr 7, Sankt Gallen, 9000, Switzerland. TEL 41-71-2264040, FAX 41-71-2264045, info@mediaxag.ch, http://www.mediaxag.ch. Ed. Klaus Braun. adv.: color page CHF 6,600; trim 225 x 300. Circ: 35,000 (paid and controlled).

796.352 USA
GOLF LIVING. Text in English. 2005 (Sep.). q. USD 12.35 (effective 2005). **Document type:** *Magazine, Consumer.* **Description:** Covers the golf enthusiasts' lifestyle, including exclusive destination travel, fine dining and luxurious living.
Published by: Angeles Publications (Subsidiary of: Tribune Los Angeles, Inc.), 8640 Hayden Pl, Culver City, CA 90232.

796.352 910.202 FRA ISSN 0181-2750
GOLF MAGAZINE. Text in French. 1976. m. EUR 49 (effective 2008). adv. illus. **Document type:** *Magazine, Consumer.*
Related titles: Microfiche ed.: (from NBI); Online - full text ed.
Published by: Mondadori France, 1 Rue du Colonel Pierre-Avia, Paris, Cedex 15 75754, France. TEL 33-1-41335001, contact@mondadori.fr, http://www.mondadori.fr. Circ: 25,000.

796.352 USA ISSN 1056-5493
GV961
GOLF MAGAZINE. Text in English. 1959. m. USD 16 domestic; CAD 26 in Canada; USD 3.99 newsstand/cover domestic (effective 2008). adv. illus. reprints avail. **Document type:** *Magazine, Consumer.* **Description:** Offers instruction and profiles of top golf players for serious golfers, beginning and pro alike.
Former titles (until 1991): Golf (New York) (1056-5485); (until 1986): Golf Magazine (0017-1808)
Related titles: Microform ed.: (from PQC); Online - full text ed.
Indexed: A01, A02, A03, A08, A11, A22, A25, A26, B04, BRD, C05, C11, C12, CPerl, ConsI, E08, G05, G06, G07, G08, G09, H03, I05, I06, I07, M01, M02, M04, M06, MASUSE, MagInd, P02, P10, P19, P48, P53, P54, PEI, PMR, PQC, R03, RGAb, RGPR, S08, S09, S23, SD, SPI, SportS, T02, U01, W03, W05, WBA, WMB.
—Ingenta. **CCC.**
Published by: Time Inc. (Subsidiary of: Time Warner Inc.), Time & Life Bldg, Rockefeller Center, 29th Fl, 1271 Ave of the Americas, New York, NY 10020-1393. TEL 212-522-1212, FAX 212-522-3684, information@timeinc.com, http://www.timeinc.com. Pub. Charlie Kammerer TEL 212-522-2076. adv.: B&W page USD 62,190, color page USD 93,350; trim 8 x 10.75. Circ: 1,400,000 (paid).

796.352 USA
GOLF MAGAZINE LIVING. Text in English. 2006. s-a. (Spr. & Fal.). **Document type:** *Magazine, Consumer.* **Description:** Covers luxury lifestyle, including homes, luxury communities, interior decor, electronics and cars.
Published by: Time Inc. (Subsidiary of: Time Warner Inc.), 1271 Ave of the Americas, New York, NY 10020. TEL 212-522-1212, information@timeinc.com, http://www.timeinc.com. Ed. David Clark. Pub. Christopher Wightman. Circ: 350,000.

796.352 USA
GOLF MANAGEMENT COMPANIES. Text in English. 2/m. **Document type:** *Newsletter, Trade.* **Description:** Contains in-depth coverage of the growing number of management companies in the golf industry.
Published by: Cypress Magazines, Inc, 5715 Kerny Villa Rd, Ste108, San Diego, CA 92123. TEL 800-296-9656, FAX 858-503-7588, info@cypressmagazines.com, http://www.cypressmagazines.com.

796.352069 GBR ISSN 1368-7727
GOLF MANAGEMENT EUROPE. Text in English. 1997. bi-m. GBP 30 domestic; GBP 36 in Europe; GBP 42 elsewhere (effective 2009). adv. bk.rev. illus.; mkt.; tr.lit.; stat. back issues avail. **Document type:** *Magazine, Trade.* **Description:** Covers all aspects of operating and managing a golf club.
Related titles: Online - full text ed.
Published by: Portman Publishing Co. Ltd., Deben House, Main Rd, Martlesham, Woodbridge, IP12 4SE, United Kingdom. TEL 44-1394-380800, FAX 44-1394-380594, info@portman.uk.com. adv.: page GBP 1,520; bleed 216 x 303. Circ: 5,200.

796.352 DEU
GOLF MANAGER. Text in German. 1995. bi-m. EUR 60 domestic; EUR 66 foreign (effective 2010). **Document type:** *Magazine, Trade.*
Published by: (Golf Management Verband Deutschland e.V.), Koellen Druck und Verlag GmbH, Ernst-Robert-Curtius-Str 14, Bonn, 53117, Germany. TEL 49-228-9898280, FAX 49-228-9898299, verlag@koellen.de, http://www.koellen.de. Ed. Franz-Josef Ungerechts. Adv. contact Norbert Hauser TEL 49-228-9898287. Circ: 4,200 (paid).

796.352 330 USA
GOLF MARKET TODAY. Text in English. 1972. bi-m. membership. **Document type:** *Newsletter.* **Description:** Publishes golf industry news, profiles of industry leaders, research findings and current trends in golf participation and golf course development and management in the US and around the world.
Published by: National Golf Foundation, 1150 S US Hwy 1, Jupiter, FL 33477. TEL 561-744-6006, FAX 561-744-6107. Ed., R&P Bill Burbaum. Circ: 9,000 (controlled).

796.352 USA
GOLF MARKETING & OPERATIONS. Text in English. 19??. 2/m. **Document type:** *Newsletter, Trade.* **Description:** Contains up-to-date information on what golf courses and clubs are doing to increase profits and cut costs in all aspects of the operation, from managing personnel and budgeting to employee training and improving customer service.
Published by: Cypress Magazines, Inc, 5715 Kerny Villa Rd, Ste108, San Diego, CA 92123. TEL 800-296-9656, FAX 858-503-7588, info@cypressmagazines.com, http://www.cypressmagazines.com.

910.2 796.352 USA
GOLF MEETINGS, RESORTS & DESTINATIONS. Text in English. 1983. a., latest 2008. free to qualified personnel (effective 2011). **Document type:** *Handbook/Manual/Guide, Trade.* **Description:** Contains a roundup of top golf destinations and properties in Florida and the U.S., the Caribbean and Mexico.
Related titles: Online - full text ed.: free (effective 2011).
Published by: Worth International Media Group, 5979 NW 151 St, Ste 120, Miami Lakes, FL 33014. TEL 305-828-0123, FAX 305-826-6950, info@worthit.com, http//www.worthit.com.

796.352 GBR ISSN 0017-1816
GOLF MONTHLY. Text in English. 1911. m. GBP 34.99 domestic; USD 107.50 in United States; USD 118.90 in Canada; EUR 83.20 in Europe; GBP 74.40 elsewhere; GBP 4 newsstand/cover (effective 2010). adv. illus. back issues avail. **Document type:** *Magazine, Consumer.* **Description:** Covers all the aspects of golf including articles on top players, equipment and instruction.
Related titles: Online - full text ed.
Indexed: SportS.
—BLDSC (4201.224500).
Published by: I P C Country & Leisure Media Ltd. (Subsidiary of: I P C Media Ltd.), The Blue Fin Bldg, 110 Southwark St, London, SE1 0SU, United Kingdom. TEL 44-20-31484530, http://www.ipcmedia.com. Ed. Michael Harris TEL 44-20-31484520. Adv. contact Andrew Boxer TEL 44-20-31484251. color page GBP 4,835; trim 210 x 286. **Subscr. to:** Rockwood House, Perrymount Rd, Haywards Heath RH16 3DH, United Kingdom. TEL 44-845-1231231, IPCsubs@quadrantsubs.com, http://www.magazinesdirect.co.uk. **Dist. by:** MarketForce UK Ltd. salesinnovation@marketforce.co.uk, http://www.marketforce.co.uk/.

796.352 KEN
GOLF NEWS. Text in English. bi-m. free.
Published by: Golf Publications, PO Box 31283, Nairobi, Kenya.

796.352 910.202 USA ISSN 1550-7939
GOLF ODYSSEY; the sophisticated guide to golf travel. Text in English. 1992. m. USD 79 (effective 1999). **Document type:** *Magazine, Consumer.*
Formerly: Golf Travel (1068-6142)
Published by: Travel Guide, Inc., PO Box 3485, Charlottesville, VA 22903-0485. TEL 804-295-1200, 800-225-7825, FAX 804-977-4885. Ed. William Irwin. Pub. Terence Sieg.

796.352 USA ISSN 1529-7721
GOLF ON CAPE COD. Text in English. 2000. q. USD 10.95; USD 4.25 newsstand/cover (effective 2001). adv. **Document type:** *Magazine, Consumer.*
Published by: Northeast Publications, Inc., 143A Upper County Rd, Dennisport, MA 02639. TEL 508-398-3101, FAX 508-398-4711, preiss@ma.ultranet.com, http://www.golfoncapecod.com. Ed. Geoff Converse. Pub. Paul W Reiss.

796.352 GBR ISSN 1359-9496
GOLF OWNERS, OPERATORS AND DEVELOPERS DIRECTORY. Text in English. 1995. a. GBP 15 in Europe; GBP 18 elsewhere. **Document type:** *Directory.*
Published by: Golf Business Communications Ltd., 5-7 High St, Dorchester-On-Thames, Oxfords OX10 7HH, United Kingdom. TEL 44-1865-341580, FAX 44-1865-341575. Ed. Geoffrey Russell.

796.352 USA ISSN 1941-0603
GOLF POWER ANNUAL (YEAR). Text in English. 2008 (Feb.). a. USD 9 per issue (effective 2011). adv. **Document type:** *Magazine, Consumer.* **Description:** Offers tips, product information, drills, stories and techniques to improve stroke distance on the fairway.
Published by: Werner Publishing Corporation, 12121 Wilshire Blvd, 12th Fl, Los Angeles, Los Angeles, CA 90025. TEL 310-820-1500, FAX 310-826-5008, http://www.golftipsmag.com.

796.352 ITA ISSN 1827-8604
GOLF PUNK (ITALIAN EDITION). Text in Italian. 2006. 10/yr. EUR 36 (effective 2009). adv. **Document type:** *Magazine, Consumer.*
Related titles: ◆ Regional ed(s).: Golf Punk (U K Edition). ISSN 1743-0968.
Published by: Play Media Company, Via di Santa Cornelia 5A, Formello, RM 00060, Italy. TEL 39-06-33221250, FAX 39-06-33221235, abbonamenti@playmediacompany.it, http://www.playmediacompany.it.

796.352 GBR ISSN 1743-0968
GOLF PUNK (U K EDITION). Text in English. 2004. 11/yr. GBP 29.95 domestic; GBP 49.10 in Europe; GBP 56.37 elsewhere (effective 2009). adv. **Document type:** *Magazine, Consumer.*
Related titles: ◆ Regional ed(s).: Golf Punk (Italian Edition). ISSN 1827-8604; Golf Punk (Indonesia Edition). 2006 (Mar.).
Published by: J F Media Ltd., Unit 10-13, The Sussex Innovation Centre, Science Park Sq, Brighton, East Sussex BN1 9SB, United Kingdom. editorial@jf-media.co.uk.

796.3 AUT ISSN 1017-8457
GOLF REVUE. Text in German. 1978. 7/yr. EUR 34.90; EUR 3.90 newsstand/cover (effective 2011). adv. back issues avail. **Document type:** *Magazine, Consumer.*
Formerly (until 1994): Golf Gazette
Related titles: Online - full text ed.
Published by: Verlagsgruppe News Gesellschaft mbH (Subsidiary of: Gruner + Jahr AG & Co), Taborstr 1-3, Vienna, W 1020, Austria. TEL 43-1-213129011, FAX 43-1-213121650, redaktion@news.at, http://www.news.at. Circ: 38,000 (paid).

796.352 DEU
GOLF SPIELEN. Text in German. 4/yr. EUR 16 (effective 2006). adv. **Document type:** *Magazine, Consumer.*
Published by: Sueddeutscher Verlag GmbH, Sendlinger Str 80, Munich, 80331, Germany. TEL 49-89-21830, FAX 49-89-2183787, szonnet@sueddeutsche.de, http://www.sueddeutsche.de. adv.: page EUR 13,200. Circ: 408,491 (paid and controlled).

796.352 LIE
GOLF STYLE; das Magazin fuer Golf und Gesellschaft. Text in German. 4/yr. adv. **Document type:** *Magazine, Consumer.*
Published by: A V A - Allgemeine Verlagsanstalt, In der Fina 18, Schaan, 9494, Liechtenstein. TEL 423-2334383, FAX 423-2334383. adv.: B&W page EUR 8,750, color page EUR 12,400. Circ: 59,525 (controlled).

796.352 USA ISSN 1051-7758
GOLF TIPS. Variant title: Golf Tips Magazine. Text in English. 1989. bi-m. USD 12.97 domestic; USD 27.97 foreign; USD 9 per issue (effective 2011). **Document type:** *Magazine, Consumer.* **Description:** Serves as an in-depth instruction and equipment magazine. Articles are written by teaching professionals who specialize in teaching amateurs. Includes equipment selection guides, instructions, tips, new techiques and information on challenging courses.
Related titles: Online - full text ed.; ◆ Cumulative ed(s).: Golf Tips Annual. ISSN 2151-8602.
Indexed: SPI.
Published by: Werner Publishing Corporation, 12121 Wilshire Blvd, 12th Fl, Los Angeles, Los Angeles, CA 90025. TEL 310-820-1500, FAX 310-826-5008, http://www.wernerpublishing.com.

796.352 USA ISSN 2151-8602
GV965
▼ **GOLF TIPS ANNUAL.** Text in English. 2010. a. USD 9 per issue (effective 2010). **Document type:** *Magazine, Consumer.* **Description:** A cumulative annual edition of Golf Tips Magazine.
Related titles: ◆ Cumulative ed. of: Golf Tips. ISSN 1051-7758.
Published by: Werner Publishing Corporation, 12121 Wilshire Blvd 1200, Los Angeles, CA 90025-1176. TEL 310-820-1500, FAX 310-826-5008, editors@planeandpilotmag.com, http://www.wernerpublishing.com.

796.352 USA ISSN 1524-2854
GOLF TODAY; golf magazine for the western United States. Text in English. 1987. m. USD 29 domestic (effective 2009). adv. bk.rev. illus. back issues avail. **Document type:** *Magazine, Consumer.* **Description:** Provides golfers and golf professionals with essential information on all aspects of the game.
Related titles: E-mail ed.; Online - full text ed.: free (effective 2009).
Published by: Golf Today, Inc., 25101 Bear Valley Rd, PMB 90, Tehachapi, CA 93561. TEL 661-823-7842, FAX 661-823-7942. Ed., Pub. Bob Koczor. Adv. contact Charley Coppola TEL 916-427-3441. page USD 2,890; 9.375 x 11.5.

796.352 MEX
GOLF TOURNAMENT. Text in Spanish. m. MXN 360; MXN 760 Including Hecho en Mexico (effective 2001). adv. back issues avail. **Document type:** *Trade.*
Related titles: Online - full text ed.: ISSN 1563-7573.
Published by: Grupo Internacional Editorial S A de C V, Rio Nazas 34, Col. Cuahutemoc, Mexico D F, 06500, Mexico. TEL 52-5-2099930, FAX 52-5-5660564, buzon@intermundo.com.mx. Ed. Ana Luisa Ochoa. Adv. contact Fabrizio Tavano. color page MXN 44,000. Circ: 15,000.

796.352 USA ISSN 0191-717X
GV975
GOLF TRAVELER. Text in English. 1976. bi-m. USD 12 to members; USD 2 newsstand/cover (effective 2001). adv. bk.rev. tr.lit. reprints avail. **Document type:** *Magazine, Consumer.* **Description:** Focuses on golf and travel for members of the Golf Card, an affiliation of 3,300 golf courses that offer discounted greens fees to members.
Published by: Golf Card International, 64 Inverness Drive E, Inverness, CO 80112. TEL 805-667-4333, 800-321-8269. Ed. Valerie Rogers. Pub. Robert Helms. Adv. contact Kerri Land. Circ: 130,000.

796.352 AUS ISSN 1837-0489
▼ **GOLF VACATIONS (AUSTRALIA & NEW ZEALAND EDITION).** Variant title: Golf Vacations. Text in English. 2009. q. AUD 34.95 domestic; AUD 44.95 in New Zealand; AUD 55 elsewhere (effective 2011). adv. back issues avail. **Document type:** *Magazine, Consumer.*
Published by: Global Publishing Pty Ltd., Ste F12 1-15 Barr St, Balmain, NSW 2041, Australia. TEL 61-2-95558100, FAX 61-2-98185625, info@globalpublishing.com.au. Ed. Jon Underwood. Adv. contact Julien Coste TEL 61-4-10171352.

796.352 AUS ISSN 0312-9195
GOLF VICTORIA. Text in English. 1959. bi-m. free to members (effective 2009). adv. back issues avail. **Document type:** *Magazine, Consumer.* **Description:** Provides the golf enthusiasts in Victoria with informative articles on golf.
Formerly (until 1975): Victorian Golf (0312-9187)
Related titles: Online - full text ed.
Indexed: SD.
Published by: Victorian Golf Association, 15 Bardolph St, Burwood, VIC 3125, Australia. TEL 61-3-98896731, FAX 61-3-98891077, vga@golfvic.org.au. Ed. Brian Meldrum. Adv. contact Ray Kelsall. color page AUD 2,250; trim 210 x 297.

796.352 USA
GOLF WEEK ROCHESTER NEWSPAPER. Text in English. 1989. w. (Fri.). USD 30 in county (effective 2008). adv. 24 p./no. 5 cols./p.; **Document type:** *Newspaper, Consumer.*
Formerly: Golf Week Newspaper
Published by: Expositor Ledger Newspapers, 2535 Brighton Henrietta Townline Rd, Rochester, NY 14623. TEL 585-427-2468. Ed. Dave Eaton. Pub. George Morgenstern. adv.: col. inch USD 30. Circ: 26,000 (controlled and free).

796.352 USA ISSN 0017-1891
GV961
GOLF WORLD; international news magazine of golf. Text in English. 1947. w. (Jan.-Sep., bi-w., Oct.-Dec.). USD 31.97 domestic; USD 51.97 in Canada; USD 126.85 elsewhere (effective 2009). adv. illus. reprints avail. **Document type:** *Magazine, Consumer.* **Description:** Covers news of the game and business of golf.
Formerly (19??): The International Golf World Newsweekly
Related titles: Online - full text ed.
Indexed: A11, C05, C12, CPerI, G05, G06, G07, G08, I05, I06, I07, M01, M02, MASUSE, P10, P48, P53, P54, PEI, PQC, S23, SD, SPI, SportS, T02, U01.
—CCC.
Published by: The Golf Digest Companies (Subsidiary of: Advance Publications, Inc.), 20 Westport Rd, Wilton, CT 06897. TEL 203-761-5100, 800-438-0491, FAX 203-761-5129, glscustserv@cdsfulfilment.com. Ed. Geoff Russell. Pub. Laura Sequenzia TEL 212-286-3884. Adv. contact Stephanie Olavarria TEL 203-761-5330. B&W page USD 20,480, color page USD 29,260; trim 7.875 x 10.5.

796.352 GBR ISSN 0017-1883
GOLF WORLD. Text in English. 1962. m. GBP 46 domestic; GBP 55 in Europe; GBP 60 elsewhere; GBP 3.99 newsstand/cover (effective 2009). adv. bk.rev. charts; illus.; stat.; tr.lit. back issues avail. **Document type:** *Magazine, Consumer.* **Description:** Contains articles and comments from the world's top professional golfers.
Incorporates: Golfing
Indexed: SD, SportS.
Published by: H. Bauer Publishing Ltd. (Subsidiary of: Bauer Media Group), Media House, Lynchwood, Peterborough, Cambridgeshire PE2 6EA, United Kingdom. TEL 44-1733-468243, FAX 44-1733-468843, http://www.bauer.co.uk. Ed. Chris Jones. Adv. contact Thomas Berkoe TEL 44-207-2955434. page GBP 4,510. **Subscr. to:** Tower House, Sovereign Park, Market Harborough, Leicestershire LE16 9EF, United Kingdom. TEL 44-1858-438866, subs@greatmagazines.co.uk.

796.352 USA ISSN 1530-8480
GOLF WORLD BUSINESS. Text in English. 1963. 2/yr. illus.; stat. **Document type:** *Magazine, Trade.* **Description:** Provides the Golf industry with relevant business information.
Former titles (until 2000): GolfShop Operations (0017-1824); Pro Shop Operations
Related titles: Online - full text ed.
Indexed: B02, B15, B17, B18, G04, G06, G07, G08, I05, SportS.
—CCC.
Published by: The Golf Digest Companies (Subsidiary of: Advance Publications, Inc.), 20 Westport Rd, Wilton, CT 06897. TEL 203-761-5100, 800-438-0491, FAX 203-761-5129, glscustserv@cdsfulfilment.com, http://www.golfdigest.com.

796.352 USA
GOLF YEARBOOK. Text in English. a. **Document type:** *Magazine, Consumer.*
Published by: Century Publishing Inc., E 5710 Seltice Way, Post Falls, ID 83854. TEL 208-765-6300, 800-824-1806, FAX 208-676-8476, privacy@CenturyPublishing.com, http://www.centurypublishing.com.

796.352 SWE ISSN 1653-4298
GOLFBLADET. Text in Swedish. 2005. q. SEK 99 (effective 2006). adv. **Document type:** *Magazine, Consumer.*
Published by: Fairway Golf Magazine, Skonertgraend 9, Torekov, 26093, Sweden. Ed. Fredrik Richter TEL 46-733-965488.

796.352 USA ISSN 1526-4270
GV975.5
GOLFDOM. Text in English. 1927-19??; resumed 1999. m. USD 30 domestic; USD 49 in Canada & Mexico; USD 89 elsewhere (effective 2009); Includes supplement: TurfGrass Trends. adv. software rev. charts; illus.; maps; stat.; tr.lit. back issues avail.; reprints avail. **Document type:** *Magazine, Trade.* **Description:** Provides golf information to golf course superintendents, management, developers, consultants, and owners.
Former titles (19??): Golf Business (0148-3706); (until 1976): Golfdom (0017-1905)
Related titles: Online - full text ed.; ◆ Supplement(s): TurfGrass Trends. ISSN 1076-7207.
Indexed: Agr, GardL, SD, SportS, T02.
—CCC.
Published by: Questex Media Group Inc., 275 Grove St, Bldg 2, Ste 130, Newton, MA 02466. TEL 617-219-8300, 888-552-4346, FAX 617-219-8310, questex@sunbeltfs.com, http://www.questex.com. Eds. David Frabotta TEL 800-669-1668 ext 3758, Larry Aylward TEL 800-669-1668 ext 3737. adv.: color page USD 6,824; trim 7.75 x 10.5. Circ: 30,000 (controlled).

796.352 USA
THE GOLFER. Text in English. 1994. bi-m. **Document type:** *Magazine, Consumer.*
Published by: Heather & Pine Publishing, 516 Fifth Ave, Ste 304, New York, NY 10036. TEL 212-867-7070, FAX 212-867-8550.

796.352 AUS ISSN 1835-1336
GOLFER PACIFIC.COM.AU. Text in English. 1977. m. AUD 59 domestic; AUD 5 newsstand/cover (effective 2009). adv. back issues avail. **Document type:** *Newspaper, Trade.* **Description:** Provides local coverage of news and events, plus an important mix of state, national and international news on a monthly basis.
Formerly (until 2007): The Golfer (N S W Edition) (1832-5858)
Related titles: Regional ed(s).: The Golfer (Western Australia & South Australia Edition). ISSN 1832-5866; The Golfer (Victoria & Tasmania Edition). ISSN 1447-9273; The Golfer (Queensland & Northern Territory Edition). ISSN 1447-9281.
Published by: Varsity Publishing Pty Ltd., Unit 6/175 Varsity Parade, Varsity Lakes, Gold Coast, QLD 4227, Australia. TEL 61-7-55535300, FAX 61-7-55535399, lisa@golferpacific.com.au. **Subscr. to:** iSubscribe Pty Ltd., 25 Lime St, Ste 303, Level 3, Sydney, NSW 2000, Australia. TEL 61-2-92621722, FAX 61-2-92625044, info@isubscribe.com.au, http://www.isubscribe.com.au.

796.352 IRL
THE GOLFERS GUIDE TO IRELAND. Text in English. a. adv. **Document type:** *Directory, Consumer.*
Published by: In Europe Publishing, 4 Cumberland St., Dun Laoghaire, Co. Dublin, Ireland. TEL 353-1-6604805, FAX 353-1-6604165, info@ineurope.ie. Adv. contact Eoin Doyle. page EUR 2,793; trim 210 x 297. Circ: 90,000 (paid and controlled).

796.352 USA
GOLFER'S GUIDE TO NORTH AMERICA. Text in English. 2001. q. USD 14.95 newsstand/cover (effective 2001). adv. **Document type:** *Magazine, Consumer.*
Published by: Frey Media, Inc., Box 5926, Hilton Head Island, SC 29938. Ed. Marc A Frey. Pub. Shawn P Grimes.

796.352 NLD ISSN 1381-8686
GOLFERS MAGAZINE. Text in Dutch. 1985. 11/yr. EUR 49.95; EUR 6.50 newsstand/cover (effective 2011). adv. bk.rev.; video rev. illus.; maps; stat. **Document type:** *Magazine, Consumer.* **Description:** Covers golfing news, tournaments, instruction, tourism and the golf business for the active Dutch golfer.
Published by: Sanoma Men's Magazines, Haaksbergweg 75, Amsterdam (ZO), 1101 BR, Netherlands. TEL 31-20-7518000, FAX 31-20-7518301, sales@smm.nl, http://www.smm.nl.

796.352 GBR ISSN 0953-0215
GOLFERS NEWS. Text in English. 1985. m. GBP 13.50. adv. bk.rev. tr.lit. back issues avail. **Document type:** *Magazine, Consumer.* **Description:** Covers golf with news, reviews, features, and competition results.
Address: Alcester Rd, Portway, Birmingham B48 7HX, United Kingdom. TEL 0564-822877, FAX 0564-824712. Ed. D Lawrenson. Circ: 75,000.

796.352 USA
GOLFEXTRA. Text in English. bi-m. USD 9.95; USD 2.95 newsstand/cover (effective 2001). adv. **Description:** Focuses on golf in Orange County, California, including instruction, course reviews, and information on golf vacations.
Published by: O C R Magazines, 625 N Grand Ave, Santa Ana, CA 92701. TEL 714-796-2444, FAX 714-796-6781, http://www.ocrmagazines.com. Ed. Chris Meyer. Pub. Christopher O Schulze. Adv. contact Stacey Basile TEL 714-796-2485. page USD 2,965.

796.352 NLD ISSN 0927-5304
GOLFJOURNAAL. Text in Dutch. 1988. 10/yr. EUR 5.50 newsstand/cover (effective 2011). adv. bk.rev.; video rev. charts; illus.; maps; stat. back issues avail. **Document type:** *Magazine, Consumer.* **Description:** News and information of the Dutch golfing world.
Published by: Sanoma Men's Magazines, Haaksbergweg 75, Amsterdam (ZO), 1101 BR, Netherlands. TEL 31-20-7518000, FAX 31-20-7518301, sales@smm.nl, http://www.smm.nl.

796.352 NLD ISSN 1874-9909
GOLFLIFE; a beautiful way of living. Text in Dutch. 200?. q. EUR 22.50; EUR 5.95 newsstand/cover (effective 2008). adv. **Document type:** *Magazine, Consumer.*
Published by: FK Media b.v., Gouverneurlaan 4, Postbus 155, Weert, 6000 AD, Netherlands. TEL 31-495-450105, FAX 31-495-539485. Ed. Ben van der Sommen TEL 31-6-53392367. Pub. Frank Stienissen. adv.: color page EUR 2,250; trim 230 x 297. Circ: 25,000.

796.352 DNK ISSN 1398-5213
GOLFMAGASINET. Variant title: Golf Magasinet. Text in Danish. 1997. m. DKK 594 (effective 2010). adv. **Document type:** *Magazine, Consumer.*
Related titles: Online - full text ed.
Published by: J S L Publications A/S, Dortheavej 59, Copenhagen NV, 2400, Denmark. TEL 45-32-711200, FAX 45-32-711212, info@jslpublications.dk, http://www.jslp.dk. Ed. Ole Hoej Hansen. Adv. contact Peter Hermann. color page DKK 28,500; 208 x 280.

796 DEU ISSN 0933-7415
GOLFMAGAZIN. Text in German. 1961. m. EUR 64.80; EUR 5.90 newsstand/cover (effective 2011). adv. bk.rev. **Document type:** *Magazine, Consumer.*
Formerly (until 1987): Golf (0017-1735)
Published by: Jahr Top Special Verlag, Troplowitzstr 5, Hamburg, 22529, Germany. TEL 49-40-389060, FAX 49-40-38906300, info@jahr-tsv.de, http://www.jahr-tsv.de. Ed. Dieter Genske. Adv. contact Wolfgang Vogler TEL 49-40-38906284. Circ: 28,276 (paid).

796.352 NLD ISSN 1568-8720
GOLFNIEUWS. Text in Dutch. 19??. 4/yr. adv. **Document type:** *Magazine, Consumer.*
Published by: Sanoma Men's Magazines, Haaksbergweg 75, Amsterdam (ZO), 1101 BR, Netherlands. TEL 31-20-7518000, FAX 31-20-7518301, sales@smm.nl, http://www.smm.nl. Circ: 132,146 (controlled).

796.352 DEU
GOLFPLUSONLINE. Text in German. d. adv. **Document type:** *Consumer.* **Description:** Covers golf leagues, tournaments, players and personalities throughout the world.
Published by: MSV Verlag Juergen Metzger, Windener Str 6, Einsbach, 85254, Germany. TEL 49-8135-9103, FAX 49-8135-8029. Ed., Pub. Juergen Metzger.

796.352 NOR ISSN 1504-937X
GOLFPOSTEN. Text in Norwegian. 2003. bi-m. NOK 290 (effective 2008). adv. **Document type:** *Magazine, Consumer.*
Published by: Golfposten AS, PO Box72, Vinderen, Oslo, 0319, Norway. TEL 47-22-492900, FAX 47-22-492901, hans.henrik@golfposten.no, http://www.golfposten.no. adv.: page NOK 28,000; 235 x 300.

796.352 DEU
GOLFPUNK. Text in German. 8/yr. EUR 32; EUR 4.50 newsstand/cover (effective 2008). adv. **Document type:** *Magazine, Consumer.*
Published by: b&d Media Network GmbH, Osterfeldstr 12-14, Hamburg, 22529, Germany. TEL 49-40-4800070, FAX 49-40-48000799, info@bdverlag.de, http://www.bdverlag.de. Adv. contact Cornelia Niemann. B&W page EUR 4,950, color page EUR 6,400; trim 230 x 280. Circ: 16,557 (paid and controlled).

796.352029 USA
GOLF'S YELLOW PAGE DIRECTORY. Text in English. 1994. a. USD 25 (effective 2000 & 2001). adv. Index. 300 p./no.; **Document type:** *Directory, Trade.* **Description:** Lists golf related businesses including courses, retailers, and manufacturers.
Supersedes (in 1999): Yellow Pages of Golf
Published by: Golf's Yellow Page Directory Inc., 7251 S W 152nd St, Miami, FL 33157. TEL 305-378-4100, FAX 305-378-1559. Ed., Adv. contact David Burnham. Circ: 50,000 (controlled).

796.352 NLD ISSN 1874-8686
GOLFSCHEURKALENDER. Text in Dutch. 2006. a. EUR 14.95 (effective 2009).
Published by: Uitgeverij Solo, Laurillardlaan 29, Bilthoven, 3723 DD, Netherlands. TEL 31-30-2288147, FAX 31-30-2284943, info@uitgeverij-solo.com, http://www.uitgeverij-solo.com.

796.352 LIE
GOLFSTYLE INTERNATIONAL; Magazin fuer Golf und Gesellschaft. Text in German. 4/yr. EUR 16.40 (effective 2006). adv. **Document type:** *Magazine, Consumer.*
Published by: Neue Verlagsanstalt, In der Fina 18, Schaan, 9494, Liechtenstein. TEL 423-233-4381, FAX 423-233-4382, info@neue-verlagsanstalt.li, http://www.neue-verlagsanstalt.li. Ed. Beate Juergens. Pub., Adv. contact Rita Quaderer. page EUR 12,990; trim 213 x 273. Circ: 32,584 (paid and controlled).

S

796.352 USA ISSN 1554-2629
GOLFSTYLES. Text in English. 1994. m. (except Jan., Jul., Oct. & Nov.). USD 19.95 for 2 yrs.; USD 5 newsstand/cover; free to qualified personnel (effective 2009). back issues avail. **Document type:** *Magazine, Consumer.* **Description:** Covers golf in the Washington DC area and the Mid-Atlantic. Includes tournament news, travel information, and other topics related to the golfing lifestyle.
Formerly (until 2005): Washington Golf Monthly (1076-0261)
Related titles: Online - full text ed.; ◆ Regional ed(s).: GolfStyles Ohio; ◆ GolfStyles New England; ◆ GolfStyles New Jersey; ◆ GolfStyles Philadelphia; ◆ GolfStyles Atlanta.
Published by: Newsworld Communications Inc., 3600 New York Ave, NE, Washington, DC 20002. TEL 202-379-2893, GS.Info@GolfStyles.net. Ed. Bill Kamenjar TEL 202-279-2893 ext 4. Pub. Michael Keating.

796.352 USA
GOLFSTYLES ATLANTA. Text in English. 2005. m. (except Jan., Jul., Oct. & Nov.). USD 19.95 for 2 yrs.; USD 5 per issue; free to qualified personnel (effective 2009). back issues avail.; reprints avail. **Document type:** *Magazine, Consumer.* **Description:** Aims to provide information and entertainment about the courses to play, the places to stay and the golf lifestyle in Atlanta.
Related titles: Online - full text ed.: free (effective 2009); ◆ Regional ed(s).: GolfStyles Ohio; ◆ GolfStyles New England; ◆ GolfStyles New Jersey; ◆ GolfStyles. ISSN 1554-2629; ◆ GolfStyles Philadelphia.
Published by: Newsworld Communications Inc., 3600 New York Ave, NE, Washington, DC 20002. TEL 202-379-2893, GS.Info@GolfStyles.net, http://www.golfstyles.net. Pub. Michael Keating. Adv. contact Franklin Riggins TEL 202-256-7949. **Subscr. to:** PO Box 3186, Van Nuys, CA 91407. TEL 800-318-4653.

796.352 USA
GOLFSTYLES NEW ENGLAND. Text in English. 1994. m. (except Jan., Jul., Oct. & Nov.). USD 19.95 for 2 yrs.; USD 5 per issue; free to qualified personnel (effective 2009). adv. back issues avail.; reprints avail. **Document type:** *Magazine, Consumer.* **Description:** Aims to provide information and entertainment about the courses to play, the places to stay and the golf lifestyle in New England.
Former titles (until 2006): GolfStyles Boston; (until 2005): New England Journal of Golf
Related titles: Online - full text ed.: free (effective 2009); ◆ Regional ed(s).: GolfStyles Ohio; ◆ GolfStyles Atlanta; ◆ GolfStyles New Jersey; ◆ GolfStyles. ISSN 1554-2629; ◆ GolfStyles Philadelphia.
Published by: Newsworld Communications Inc., 3600 New York Ave, NE, Washington, DC 20002. TEL 202-379-2893, GS.Info@GolfStyles.net, http://www.golfstyles.net. Ed. David DeSmith TEL 207-761-4653. Pub. Michael Keating. Adv. contact David Ekeland TEL 207-761-4653. color page USD 4,890; trim 8 x 10.5. Circ: 45,000. **Subscr. to:** PO Box 3186, Van Nuys, CA 91407. TEL 800-318-4653.

796.352 USA
GOLFSTYLES NEW JERSEY. Text in English. m. (except Jan., Jul., Oct. & Nov.). USD 19.95 for 2 yrs.; USD 5 per issue; free to qualified personnel (effective 2009). back issues avail.; reprints avail. **Document type:** *Magazine, Consumer.* **Description:** Aims to provide information and entertainment about the courses to play, the places to stay and the golf lifestyle in New Jersey.
Related titles: Online - full text ed.: free (effective 2009); ◆ Regional ed(s).: GolfStyles Ohio; ◆ GolfStyles Atlanta; ◆ GolfStyles New England; ◆ GolfStyles. ISSN 1554-2629; ◆ GolfStyles Philadelphia.
Published by: Newsworld Communications Inc., 3600 New York Ave, NE, Washington, DC 20002. TEL 202-379-2893, GS.Info@GolfStyles.net, http://www.golfstyles.net. Ed. Dave Raudenbush. Pub. Michael Keating. **Subscr. to:** PO Box 3186, Van Nuys, CA 91407. TEL 800-318-4653.

796.352 USA
GOLFSTYLES OHIO. Text in English. 1994. m. (except Jan., Jul., Oct. & Nov.). back issues avail.; reprints avail. **Document type:** *Magazine, Consumer.* **Description:** Aims to provide information and entertainment about the courses to play, the places to stay and the golf lifestyle in Ohio.
Related titles: Online - full text ed.: free (effective 2009); ◆ Regional ed(s).: GolfStyles New Jersey; ◆ GolfStyles Atlanta; ◆ GolfStyles New England; ◆ GolfStyles. ISSN 1554-2629; ◆ GolfStyles Philadelphia.
Published by: Newsworld Communications Inc., 3600 New York Ave, NE, Washington, DC 20002. TEL 202-379-2893, GS.Info@GolfStyles.net, http://www.golfstyles.net. Ed. T R Massey TEL 614-499-1305. Pub. Michael Keating.

796.352 USA
GOLFSTYLES PHILADELPHIA. Text in English. 2003. m. free to qualified personnel in DE, MD, NJ & PA; USD 5 per issue (effective 2008). adv. back issues avail. **Document type:** *Magazine, Consumer.* **Description:** Aims to provide information and entertainment about the courses to play, the places to stay and the golf lifestyle in Philadelphia.
Formerly: Philadelphia Golf Monthly
Related titles: Online - full text ed.: free; ◆ Regional ed(s).: GolfStyles Ohio; ◆ GolfStyles New England; ◆ GolfStyles New Jersey; ◆ GolfStyles. ISSN 1554-2629; ◆ GolfStyles Atlanta.
Published by: Newsworld Communications Inc., 3600 New York Ave, NE, Washington, DC 20002. TEL 202-636-3342, FAX 202-526-4212, http://www.golfstyles.net. Ed. Tony Leodora. Pub. Doug McDaniel. Adv. contact Mary Raimondo TEL 202-636-4956. color page USD 4,890; trim 8 x 10.5. Circ: 40,000.

796.352 USA ISSN 0890-3514
GOLFWEEK. Text in English. 1975. 45/yr. USD 34.65 domestic; USD 59.65 in Canada; USD 139.65 foreign (effective 2009). adv. charts; illus.; stat.; tr.lit. back issues avail.; reprints avail. **Document type:** *Magazine, Consumer.* **Description:** Covers all aspects of golf arena with information on the game and events, pros and amateurs, collegiate, equipment, courses and industry.
Formerly (until 19??): Florida Golfweek (0745-7464)
Related titles: E-mail ed.; Fax ed.
Published by: Turnstile Publishing Company, 1500 Park Center Dr, Orlando, FL 32835. TEL 407-563-7000, FAX 407-563-7077, rdaily@golfweek.com. Ed. Jeff Babineau. Pub. Terry Olson. Adv. contact Jason C Redditt TEL 619-546-8721.

796.352 DEU
GOLFWELT. Text in German. bi-m. EUR 18; EUR 3.50 newsstand/cover (effective 2006). adv. **Document type:** *Magazine, Consumer.*
Published by: Kern & Kern Media Verlag OHG, Simrockstr 5, Bonn, 53113, Germany. TEL 49-228-9354800, FAX 49-228-93548020. Ed. Ulrich Hauschild. Adv. contact Ruscha Kern. page EUR 7,950. Circ: 53,000 (paid and controlled).

GOLFWELT BUSINESS. *see* BUSINESS AND ECONOMICS

796.352 DEU
GOLFWELT REISE. Text in German. a. adv. **Document type:** *Magazine, Consumer.*
Published by: Kern & Kern Media Verlag OHG, Simrockstr 5, Bonn, 53113, Germany. TEL 49-228-9354800, FAX 49-228-93548020. adv.: color page EUR 6,880; trim 210 x 297. Circ: 45,000 (controlled).

976.357 USA
GOTHAM BASEBALL; the past, present and future of the New York game. Text in English. 2005. q. USD 14.95 domestic; USD 24.95 foreign; USD 5.95 per issue domestic (effective 2006). adv. **Document type:** *Magazine, Trade.* **Description:** Focuses on all aspects of the game as related to the New York City Mets, Yankees, fans, old-time ball and more.
Published by: Gotham Sports Media, PO Box 321, Lynbrook, NY 11563. FAX 215-790-6218. Ed. Mike McGann TEL 610-793-6712. adv.: color page USD 1,200; trim 8 x 10.875.

796.334 CHL ISSN 0718-3224
EL GRAFICO. Text in Spanish. 2006. m. CLP 19,500 (effective 2008).
Published by: Grupo Previa, S.A., Ave del Valle 937 Ofic. 551-A, Palo Mayor, Huechuraba, Santiago, Chile. info@elgrafico.cl, http://www.elgrafico.cl.

796.352 910.2 USA ISSN 1061-3544
GREAT GOLF RESORTS OF THE WORLD. Text in English. a. adv. **Description:** Covers golf resorts around the world.
Published by: Great Golf Resorts of the World, Inc, 2600 Philmont Ave, 201, Huntingdon Valley, PA 19006. TEL 215-914-2071, FAX 215-814-2076. Pub. Richard K Summers.

796.333 GBR ISSN 0965-4232
THE GREATEST GAME. Text in English. 1990. q. GBP 5. adv. bk.rev. back issues avail.
Published by: Rugby League Supporters' Association, 5 Wesley St, Cutsyke, Castleford, W Yorks WF10 5HQ, United Kingdom. Ed. Stuart Lake. Circ: 1,000 (paid).

796.352 USA ISSN 1554-1886
THE GREEN MAGAZINE (NEW YORK); golf beyond the links. Text in English. 2004 (Mar.). bi-m. USD 19.99 (effective 2005). adv. **Document type:** *Magazine, Consumer.* **Description:** Contains articles on the financial, travel, fashion and business-related activities of interest to middle- and upper-income multicultural golfers.
Published by: Vision Media and Communications, LLC, 48 W 37th St, 12th Fl, New York, NY 10018. TEL 212-629-4920, FAX 212-629-4932. adv.: color page USD 19,000; trim 9 x 12.

796.352 USA
GREEN MOUNTAIN LINKS. Text in English. irreg. adv. **Document type:** *Magazine, Consumer.* **Description:** Covers all news on golf in Vermont.
Related titles: Online - full text ed.
Address: 45 Killington Ave, Rutland, VT 05701. TEL 802-747-4801, FAX 802-747-4056.

796.334 GBR ISSN 2045-2276
▼ **THE GREEN SOCCER JOURNAL.** Text in English. 2010. q. GBP 7.50 per issue domestic; GBP 9.50 per issue in Europe; GBP 12.50 per issue elsewhere (effective 2011). **Document type:** *Journal, Trade.* **Description:** Includes an eclectic mix of football culture.
Published by: Junior Junior Media, 340 - 344 Kingsland Rd, London, E8 4DA, United Kingdom.

796.352 635 CAN ISSN 0380-3333
GV975
GREENMASTER. Text in English. 1966. 6/yr. CAD 36 domestic; CAD 46 foreign (effective 2005). adv. bk.rev. **Description:** Covers such topics as pest management, winter recovery, course architecture and design, nutrition techniques and programs, water management, continuing education, course construction, maintenance and remodeling, cultural techniques and turfgrass management.
Indexed: SD, SportS, T02.
Published by: (Canadian Golf Superintendents Association/Association Canadienne des Surintendants de Golf), Kenilworth Media Inc., 15 Wertheim Ct, Ste 710, Richmond Hill, ON L4B 3H7, Canada. TEL 905-771-7333, 800-409-8688, FAX 905-771-7336, production@kenilworth.com, http://www.kenilworth.com. adv.: B&W page CAD 1,250, color page CAD 2,000; trim 10.75 x 8.13. Circ: 2,000.

796.352 GBR
GREENSIDE; equipment & instruction direct from your PGA pro. Text in English. 3/yr. **Document type:** *Magazine, Consumer.*
Published by: Haymarket Network (Subsidiary of: Haymarket Media Group), Teddington Studios, Broom Rd, Teddington, TW11 9BE, United Kingdom. TEL 44-20-82675013, FAX 44-20-82675194, enquiries@haymarket.com, http://www.haymarketnetwork.com.

796.332 USA ISSN 1071-1902
GRIDIRON COACH. Text in English. 1991. 9/yr. USD 37 domestic; USD 47 in Canada & Mexico; USD 52 S. America & Europe; USD 56 elsewhere. adv. **Document type:** *Journal, Trade.*
Published by: Crystal Publications Company, PO Box 490087, Leesburg, FL 34749-0087. TEL 877-262-2464, FAX 320-734-4462.

796.332 USA
GRIDIRON GREATS; the quarterly digest of North American football history & its memorabilia. Text in English. 2002. q. USD 29.95 domestic; CAD 44 in Canada; USD 8 per issue (effective 2007). adv. 56 p./no.; **Document type:** *Magazine, Consumer.* **Description:** Contains articles and features on football players and events, both collegiate and professional, from the late nineteenth and early twentieth century up through 1979, with corresponding information on memorabilia where possible.
Published by: BiGG Publishing, 5082 4th Ln, Vero Beach, FL 32968. TEL 772-563-0425. Ed., Pub., Adv. contact Franklin Rose. color page USD 250, B&W page USD 175; trim 8.375 x 10.875.

796.352 NLD ISSN 1573-529X
GROEN & GOLF. Text in Dutch. 2003. bi-m. EUR 98.70 (effective 2008). adv. **Document type:** *Magazine, Trade.*
Published by: (Nederlandse Greenkeepers Associatie), AgriMedia BV, Postbus 42, Wageningen, 6700 AA, Netherlands. TEL 31-317-465670, FAX 31-317-465671, mail@agrimedia.info, http://www.agrimedia.info. Eds. Patrick Medema TEL 31-317-465676, Gertjan Zevenbergen. adv.: color page EUR 1,097; trim 180 x 264. Circ: 750.

796.323 CHN ISSN 1674-313X
GUANLAN/N B A INSIDE STUFF. Variant title: Inside Stuff. Text in Chinese. 1992. 3/m. **Document type:** *Magazine, Consumer.*
Formerly (until 2008): Huanqiu Tiyu/Global Sports (1005-085X)
Published by: (Huanqiu Xinwen Chuban Shiye Youxian Gongsi), Guanlan Zazhishe, 26, Guomao Dadao, 13/F, Huitong Dasha, Haikou, 510655, China.

796.352 USA ISSN 0889-4825
GULF COAST GOLFER. Text in English. 1984. 12/yr. USD 22 (effective 2000). adv. bk.rev. **Document type:** *Magazine, Consumer.* **Description:** Provides information to golfers in South Texas on quality of courses, better playing techniques, upcoming tournaments, and area tournament results. Includes an alphabetical list of golf courses in that region every other month.
Published by: Golfer Magazines, Inc., 10301 Northwest Fwy, Ste 418, Houston, TX 77092-8228. TEL 713-680-1680, FAX 713-680-0138. Ed. Bob Gray. Pub. Sommy L Ham. R&P David Widener. Adv. contact Sommy Ham. B&W page USD 1,850, color page USD 2,523; trim 10.25 x 13. Circ: 35,000 (controlled).

796.332 USA ISSN 1942-2717
GV958.U52863
HAIL TO THE VICTORS. Abbreviated title: H T T V. Text in English. 2007. a. USD 12.99 per issue (effective 2011). back issues avail. **Document type:** *Handbook/Manual/Guide, Consumer.*
Published by: Maple Street Press, 155 Webster St, Ste B, Hanover, MA 02339. TEL 781-347-4730, FAX 781-347-4732, info@maplestreetpress.com. Ed. Brian Cook.

796.334 NLD ISSN 2211-2057
▼ **HALF 3**; tijd voor voetbal. Text in Dutch. 2010. bi-m. EUR 39.75; EUR 7.95 newsstand/cover (effective 2011). **Document type:** *Magazine, Consumer.*
Published by: Parata Media, Postbus 217, Duiven, 6920 AE, Netherlands. TEL 31-6-29054444, FAX 31-316-281502. Ed. Ruud Doevendans.

796.3 USA ISSN 0046-6778
HANDBALL. Text in English. 1950. bi-m. free to members (effective 2010). adv. bk.rev. charts; illus. reprints avail. **Document type:** *Magazine, Consumer.*
Formerly (until 1971): Ace (0515-2488)
Related titles: Microform ed.: (from PQC).
Indexed: A22, PEI, SD, SPI, SportS, T02.
—Ingenta.
Published by: U.S. Handball Association, 2333 N Tucson Blvd, Tucson, AZ 85716. TEL 520-795-0434, FAX 520-795-0465, http://ushandball.org.

796.31 CHE
HANDBALL; die einzige schweizer Handball Zeitschrift. Text in German. 7/yr. illus. **Document type:** *Consumer.* **Description:** Publishes news, announcements and articles of interest to handball players and enthusiasts.
Published by: Zobrist Sport- und Freizeit - Agentur, Schachenallee 29, Aarau, 5000, Switzerland. TEL 41-62-822-9419, FAX 41-62-822-9460. Ed. Hans Hugentobler.

790 DEU ISSN 0178-2983
HANDBALL MAGAZIN. Text in German. 1984. m. EUR 45.60 domestic; EUR 52.80 foreign (effective 2011). adv. **Document type:** *Magazine, Consumer.*
Incorporates (1953-1990): Handball (0138-1296)
Indexed: SD.
Published by: Philippka-Sportverlag Konrad Honig, Rektoratsweg 36, Muenster, 48159, Germany. TEL 49-251-230050, FAX 49-251-2300579, info@philippka.de, http://www.philippka.de. Ed. Arnulf Beckmann. Adv. contact Peter Moellers TEL 49-251-2300528.

790 DEU
DER HANDBALL SCHIEDSRICHTER. Text in German. 1997. q. EUR 15 domestic; EUR 18 foreign (effective 2011). adv. **Document type:** *Magazine, Trade.*
Formerly (until 1998): Schiedsrichter-Brief
Published by: Philippka-Sportverlag Konrad Honig, Rektoratsweg 36, Muenster, 48159, Germany. TEL 49-251-230050, FAX 49-251-2300579, info@philippka.de, http://www.philippka.de. Ed. Christiane Spaete. Adv. contact Peter Moellers TEL 49-251-2300528. Circ: 6,930 (paid and controlled).

790.1 DEU ISSN 0930-5564
HANDBALLTRAINING. Text in German. 1979. m. EUR 45 domestic; EUR 48.60 foreign (effective 2011). adv. back issues avail. **Document type:** *Magazine, Trade.*
Formerly (until 1985): Lehre und Praxis des Handballspiels (0172-2476)
Published by: Philippka-Sportverlag Konrad Honig, Rektoratsweg 36, Muenster, 48159, Germany. TEL 49-251-230050, FAX 49-251-2300579, info@philippka.de, http://www.philippka.de. Ed. Dietrich Spaete. Adv. contact Peter Moellers TEL 49-251-2300528.

796.31 DEU ISSN 0947-8949
HANDBALLWOCHE. Text in German. 1954. w. EUR 93.60; EUR 2 newsstand/cover (effective 2009). adv. **Document type:** *Newspaper, Consumer.*
Formerly (until 1993): Deutsche Handball-Woche (0012-0243)
—**CCC.**
Published by: Handballwoche GmbH, Gaensemarkt 1-3, Neumuenster, 24534, Germany. TEL 49-4321-9465400, FAX 49-4321-9465419. Ed. Burchard Forth. Adv. contact Christian Arbien. page EUR 2,270; trim 228 x 322. Circ: 13,090 (paid).

796.325 SWE ISSN 1650-9382
HANDBOLLSMAGASINET. Variant title: Tidningen Handboll. Text in Swedish. 1961. q. (10/yr.). SEK 159 (effective 2004). adv.
Former titles (until 2001): Handboll (0345-4479); (until 1968): Handbollskontakten
Published by: Svenska Handbollfoerbundet, Idrottens Hus, Stockholm, 11473, Sweden. TEL 46-8-6996000, FAX 46-8-938574, http://www.handboll.info. adv.: B&W page SEK 7,900, color page SEK 9,900; 216 x 303. Circ: 11,700.

796.357 USA ISSN 1940-4484
GV877
THE HARDBALL TIMES BASEBALL ANNUAL. Text in English. 2005. a. USD 22.95 per issue (effective 2011). back issues avail. **Document type:** *Magazine, Consumer.*
Published by: A C T A Sports, 4848 N Clark St, Chicago, IL 60640. TEL 800-397-2282, info@actasports.com.

796.357 USA ISSN 1940-798X
GV877
THE HARDBALL TIMES SEASON PREVIEW. Text in English. 2008 (Feb.). a. USD 19.95 per issue (effective 2011). back issues avail. **Document type:** *Magazine, Consumer.* **Description:** Covers every major league team and player for the upcoming Major League Baseball season.
Published by: A C T A Sports, 5559 W Howard St, Skokie, IL 60077. info@actasports.com.

796.352 USA
HAWAII GOLF. Text in English. q. adv.
Published by: Pro Graphics Pacific, 55-090 Naupaka St., Laie, HI 96762-1127. TEL 808-262-0926, FAX 808-262-0926. Pub. Lee Prochaska.

796.352 USA ISSN 1947-6361
▼ **HAWAII GOLF JOURNAL.** Text in English. forthcoming 2010. m. USD 9.99 per issue (effective 2009). **Document type:** *Magazine, Consumer.* **Description:** Features articles on golf for Hawaii.
Published by: In Publishing, 9769 NW 45 Ln, Miami, FL 33178. TEL 736-314-0456, info@miamigolfjournal.com.

796.3 USA ISSN 1066-1239
HAWGS ILLUSTRATED. Text in English. 1992. 19/yr. USD 49.90; USD 2.95 newsstand/cover (effective 2001). adv. **Document type:** *Magazine, Consumer.* **Description:** Covers University of Arkansas sports.
Address: 17 1/2 East Center, 211, Fayetteville, AR 72702. TEL 501-582-2332, 501-582-2332. Ed. Clay Henry. Pub., R&P Bob Bennett. Adv. contact Dee Dee Vaughan. B&W page USD 800, color page USD 1,200; trim 10.88 x 8.25. Circ: 7,600.

796.332 USA ISSN 1942-1478
GV958.U54
HERE COME THE IRISH. Text in English. 2006. a. USD 12.99 per issue (effective 2011). back issues avail. **Document type:** *Handbook/Manual/Guide, Consumer.*
Published by: Maple Street Press, 155 Webster St, Ste B, Hanover, MA 02339. TEL 781-347-4730, FAX 781-347-4732, info@maplestreetpress.com. Ed. Pat Mitsch.

796.334 DEU
HESSEN FUSSBALL. Text in German. m. adv. **Document type:** *Magazine, Trade.*
Published by: Hessischer Fussball-Verband e.V., Otto-Fleck-Schneise 4, Frankfurt am Main, 60528, Germany. TEL 49-69-6772820, FAX 49-69-677282238, info@hfv-online.de, http://www.hfv-online.de. adv.: color page EUR 300. Circ: 8,000 (controlled).

HIDEAWAYS GOLF SPECIAL. *see* TRAVEL AND TOURISM

796.323 USA
HIGH SCHOOL BASKETBALL HANDBOOK. Text in English. 1943. biennial. USD 6.95 per issue (effective 2009). adv. **Document type:** *Handbook/Manual/Guide, Trade.* **Description:** Features the brief history of high school basketball, procedures followed in developing the rules and an emphasis on the philosophy of the rules committees.
Former titles (until 199?): Official High School Basketball Handbook; (until 1986): Basketball Handbook
Published by: National Federation of State High School Associations, PO Box 690, Indianapolis, IN 46206. TEL 317-972-6900, 800-776-3462, FAX 317-822-5700, info@nfhs.org, http://www.nfhs.org.

796.332 USA ISSN 1549-5639
HIGH SCHOOL FOOTBALL. Variant title: Sporting News High School Football. Text in English. 2003. a. 120 p./no.; **Document type:** *Magazine, Consumer.*
Published by: American City Business Journals, Inc. (Subsidiary of: Advance Publications, Inc.), 120 W Morehead St, Charlotte, NC 28202. TEL 704-973-1000, FAX 704-973-1001, http://www.acbj.com. **Co-publisher:** SchoolSports, Inc.

796.332 USA
GV955
HIGH SCHOOL FOOTBALL CASE BOOK. Text in English. 19??. a. USD 6.95 per issue (effective 2009). adv. **Document type:** *Handbook/Manual/Guide, Trade.* **Description:** Provides the high school football enthusiasts with in-depth information on the actual play situations.
Formerly (until 19??): Football Case Book (0163-6200)
Published by: National Federation of State High School Associations, PO Box 690, Indianapolis, IN 46206. TEL 317-972-6900, FAX 317-822-5700, info@nfhs.org, http://www.nfhs.org.

796.323 USA
HIGH SCHOOL HOOPS. Text in English. 2003 (Oct.). a. 132 p./no.; **Document type:** *Magazine, Consumer.* **Description:** Provides a guide to the nation's best high school players and teams for the coming season.
Published by: American City Business Journals, Inc. (Subsidiary of: Advance Publications, Inc.), 120 W Morehead St, Charlotte, NC 28202. TEL 704-973-1000, FAX 704-973-1001, http://www.acbj.com. Circ: 100,000. **Co-publisher:** SchoolSports, Inc.

796.3 IRL ISSN 1393-6158
HIGHBALL. Text in English. 1998. m. adv. **Document type:** *Magazine, Consumer.*
Related titles: Supplement(s): Highball Annual. ISSN 1649-1505. 1998.
Published by: (Gaelic Athletic Association), Hoson Company, 3-7 Camden Pl., Dublin, 2, Ireland. TEL 353-1-4784322, FAX 353-1-4781055, editor@hoson.com, http://www.hoson.com. Ed. Donal McAnallen. Adv. contact Dairmuid Ryan.

796.35 NLD ISSN 1876-0155
HOCKEY.NL. Text in Dutch. 2003. m. EUR 35; EUR 4.95 newsstand/cover (effective 2011). adv. **Document type:** *Magazine, Consumer.*
Formerly (until 2008): Hockey Magazine Special (1875-4015)
Published by: (Koninklijke Nederlandse Hockey Bond/Royal Netherlands Hockey Association), Sanoma Men's Magazines, Haaksbergweg 75, Amsterdam (ZO), 1101 BR, Netherlands. TEL 31-20-7518000, FAX 31-20-7518301, sales@smm.nl, http://www.smm.nl.

796.335 DEU ISSN 1439-5398
HOCKEY TRAINING. Text in German. 1999. 9/yr. EUR 2.60 newsstand/cover (effective 2006). adv. **Document type:** *Magazine, Trade.*
Published by: Sportverlag Schmidt und Dreisilker GmbH, Boeblinger Str 68/1, Sindelfingen, 71065, Germany. TEL 49-7031-862800, FAX 49-7031-862801. adv.: B&W page EUR 850, color page EUR 1,300. Circ: 3,382 (paid and controlled).

796.323 USA ISSN 0749-5285
GV885.515.N37
HOOP. Text in English. 19??. bi-m. USD 12 domestic; USD 24.99 foreign (effective 2009). adv. **Document type:** *Magazine, Consumer.* **Description:** Covers the lifestyle of NBA players and teams.
Formerly (until 1984): N B A Today (0279-1935)
Related titles: ◆ Supplement(s): Hoop Basketball Yearbook. ISSN 1042-9387.
Published by: (National Basketball Association), Professional Sports Publications (P S P), 519 8th Ave, Ste 2500, New York, NY 10018. TEL 212-697-1460, FAX 212-286-8154, http://www.pspsports.com. Ed. Ming Wong.

796 USA ISSN 1042-9387
GV885.515.N37
HOOP BASKETBALL YEARBOOK. Text in English. 19??. a. **Document type:** *Magazine, Consumer.*
Related titles: ◆ Supplement to: Hoop. ISSN 0749-5285.
Published by: Professional Sports Publications (P S P), 519 8th Ave, Ste 2500, New York, NY 10018. TEL 212-697-1460, FAX 212-286-8154, http://www.pspsports.com.

796.323 USA
HOOP GIRLS; fan mag. Text in English. irreg. **Document type:** *Newsletter.* **Description:** Covers the world of women's basketball from the fans' perspective.
Media: Online - full text.

796.323 USA
HOOP STARS BASKETBALL NEWSLETTER. Text in English. w. **Document type:** *Newsletter, Consumer.* **Description:** Contains the latest statistics and information on pro basketball teams and players.
Published by: Northcoast Sports, Inc., PO Box 35126, Cleveland, OH 44135. TEL 216-521-9467, 800-654-3448, CustomerSupport@ncsports.com, http://www.ncsports.com.

796.332 DEU ISSN 0948-3535
HUDDLE; American Football - die Wochenzeitung. Text in German. 1989. w. EUR 110 domestic; EUR 125 in Europe; EUR 140 elsewhere; EUR 2.30 newsstand/cover (effective 2010). adv. back issues avail. **Document type:** *Magazine, Consumer.*
Published by: Huddle Verlags GmbH, Laubacher Str 10, Berlin, 14197, Germany. TEL 49-30-82009341, FAX 49-30-82009353, huddle@huddle-verlag.de. Ed. Michael Auerbach. R&P, Adv. contact Gregor Wittig.

794.6 DEU
HUDDLE SPEZIAL. Text in German. 1994. 2/yr. **Document type:** *Magazine, Consumer.*
Formerly: German Bowl Magazin
Published by: Huddle Verlags GmbH, Laubacher Str 10, Berlin, 14197, Germany. TEL 49-30-82009341, FAX 49-30-82009353, huddle@huddle-verlag.de, http://www.huddle-verlag.de. Ed. Michael Auerbach. R&P, Adv. contact Gregor Wittig.

796.353 GBR ISSN 1750-0486
HURLINGHAM. Text in English. 2005. 3/yr. GBP 30; GBP 12.50 per issue (effective 2009). back issues avail. **Document type:** *Magazine, Consumer.*
Related titles: Online - full text ed.: ISSN 1750-0494. free (effective 2009).
Published by: (Hurlingham Polo Association), Hurlingham Media, 47-48 Chelsea Manor St, London, SW3 5RZ, United Kingdom. TEL 44-203-2399347, hurlingham@hpa-polo.co.uk, http://www.hurlinghampolo.com. Ed. Arabella Dickie. Pub. Roderick Vere Nicoll.

796.332 378.198 USA ISSN 0279-3474
HUSKERS ILLUSTRATED. Text in English. 1981. m. (Jan.-Jun., Aug.; w., Sep.-Nov.). adv. back issues avail. **Document type:** *Magazine, Consumer.* **Description:** Carries stories and information on athletics at the University of Nebraska, with special emphasis on football.
Related titles: Online - full text ed.
Published by: 247 Sports, PO Box 1498, Shelbyville, KY 40066. TEL 888-474-8669, info@247sports.com, http://247sports.com.

796.352 USA
I N G SCORECARD. Text in English. 1989. 6/yr. USD 50 (effective 2000). adv. **Document type:** *Magazine, Trade.* **Description:** Covers all aspects of the golf business and golf media.
Formerly (until 1991): Florida Golf Reporter
Published by: Jamison Communications Inc., PO Box 951422, Lake Mary, FL 32795-1422. TEL 407-328-0500, FAX 407-328-0599, mikej@jamisongolf.com. Ed. Michael Jamison. Pub. Michael W Jamison. R&P Linda Jamison. Circ: 2,000 (controlled).

796 SWE ISSN 0347-2744
IDROTTSBOKEN; aarets idrott. Spine title: Aarets Idrott. Text in Swedish. 1945. a. SEK 861 (effective 1990).
Incorporates (1962-1989): Aarets Idrott (0567-4573)
Published by: Stroemberg - Brunnhage, Fack 65, Vallingby, 16211, Sweden.

796 SWE ISSN 0348-9787
IDROTTSFORSKAREN; tidskrift foer svensk beteendevetenskaplig idrottsforskning. Text in Swedish. 1976. s-a. (plus a. cumulation). SEK 150 to individuals; SEK 300 to libraries (effective 2003). **Document type:** *Academic/Scholarly.*
Published by: S V E B I - Svensk Foerening foer Beteendevetenskaplig Idrottsforskning/Swedish Association for Behavioral Sport Science, Musketoersgranden 3, Lund, 22639, Sweden. TEL 46-46-2229411, FAX 46-46-2229412, http://www/psychology.lu.se/svebi. Ed. Anders Oestnaes.

796.077 370 SWE ISSN 1101-6892
IDROTTSLAERAREN. Text in Swedish. 1985-1986; resumed 1989. q. SEK 190 (effective 2011). adv. **Document type:** *Magazine, Trade.*
Former titles (until 1986): Idrottlaerarnas Riksfoerening - Medlemsblad; (until vol.2, 1985): Idrottlaerarnas Riksfoerening - Stockholmskretsens Medlemsblad
Related titles: Online - full text ed.
Published by: Laerarfoerbundet/The Swedish Teachers' Union, Segelbaatsvaegen 15, PO Box 12229, Stockholm, 10226, Sweden. TEL 46-8-7376500, FAX 46-8-6569415, kansli@lararforbundet.se, http://www.lararforbundet.se. Ed. Helena Gaardsaeter. Adv. contact Gun Thil. Circ: 2,100 (paid).

796.352 USA ISSN 1947-6442
▼ **ILLINOIS GOLF JOURNAL.** Text in English. forthcoming 2010 (Oct.). m. USD 9.99 per issue (effective 2010). **Document type:** *Magazine, Consumer.* **Description:** Features articles on golf for Illinois.
Published by: In Publishing, 9769 NW 45 Ln, Miami, FL 33178. TEL 736-314-0456, info@miamigolfjournal.com.

IN UNIFORM - THE MAGAZINE. *see* HOMOSEXUALITY

796.357 USA ISSN 1057-6398
GV875.C55
INDIANS INK. Text in English. 1990. irreg. USD 29.95. adv. **Document type:** *Newspaper, Consumer.*
Published by: Jet Media Inc., 539, Mentor, OH 44061-0539. TEL 440-953-2200, FAX 440-953-2202. Ed. Frank Derry. Adv. contact Donna Schreiber. Circ: 10,000. **Dist. by:** Newspaper Sales, 2635 Payne Ave, Cleveland, OH 44114.

796.323 USA
INNER NETS. Text in English. 6/yr. USD 30 (effective 2000). **Document type:** *Magazine, Consumer.* **Description:** Contains interesting information on Nets basketball players and coaches as well as other news from around the NBA.
Published by: New Jersey Nets Publications, 390 Murray Hill Pkwy, East Rutherford, NJ 07073. TEL 800-765-6387.

796.358 AUS
INSIDE CRICKET. Text in English. 2004. m. (during season). AUD 48.95 domestic; AUD 84.60 in New Zealand; AUD 85 elsewhere; AUD 6.95 newsstand/cover (effective 2008). adv. **Document type:** *Magazine, Consumer.* **Description:** Provides expert views, news, reviews and unparalleled insight about the stars of the sport.
Formerly (until 2001): Inside Edge (Sydney) (1442-794X)
Indexed: SD.
Published by: A C P Magazines Ltd. (Subsidiary of: P B L Media Pty Ltd.), 54-58 Park St, Sydney, NSW 2000, Australia. TEL 61-2-92828000, FAX 61-2-91263769. Ed. Nick Raman. Adv. contact Cameron Jones TEL 61-2-92889123. color page AUD 2,800; trim 210 x 275. **Subscr. to:** Magshop, Reply Paid 4967, Sydney, NSW 2001, Australia. TEL 61-2-136116, subs@magstore.com.au, http://shop.magstore.com.au.

796.323 796.332 USA ISSN 1061-480X
GV691.I6
INSIDE INDIANA; complete sports coverage of the Hoosiers. Text in English. 1991. 24/yr. (w. Oct.-March, m. in Dec.; bi-m. Apr.-Sept.;). USD 49.95 (effective 2011). 32 p./no. 4 cols./p.; back issues avail. **Document type:** *Magazine, Consumer.* **Description:** Coverage of Indiana University athletics, primarily basketball and football.
Related titles: Online - full text ed.
Published by: 247 Sports, PO Box 1498, Shelbyville, KY 40066. TEL 888-474-8669, info@247sports.com, http://247sports.com.

796.33305 AUS ISSN 1449-6674
INSIDE RUGBY. Text in English. 1998. m. AUD 36 domestic; AUD 48 in New Zealand; AUD 7.95 newsstand/cover (effective 2008). adv. **Document type:** *Magazine, Consumer.* **Description:** Provides indepth columns from leading rugby writers and personalities, along with comprehensive statistics and results.
Indexed: A11, G06, G07, G08, I05, SD.
Published by: A C P Magazines Ltd. (Subsidiary of: P B L Media Pty Ltd.), 54-58 Park St, Sydney, NSW 2000, Australia. TEL 61-2-92828000, FAX 61-2-91263769, research@acpaction.com.au. Ed. Mark Cashman. Adv. contact Cameron Jones TEL 61-2-92889123. color page AUD 2,800; bleed 216 x 285. **Subscr. to:** Magshop, Reply Paid 4967, Sydney, NSW 2001, Australia. TEL 61-2-136116, subs@magstore.com.au, http://shop.magstore.com.au.

796.342 USA ISSN 2153-1625
INSIDE TENNIS (ATLANTA EDITION). Text in English. 1981. 10/yr. USD 32 domestic to non-members; USD 75 foreign to non-members; free to members (effective 2010). adv. **Document type:** *Magazine, Consumer.* **Description:** Contains international, national, and local tennis news and features.
Related titles: ◆ Regional ed(s).: Inside Tennis (Northern California Edition). ISSN 2153-1587; ◆ Inside Tennis (Nevada Edition). ISSN 2153-1617; ◆ Inside Tennis (Southern California Edition). ISSN 2153-1595.
Published by: (United States Tennis Association in Atlanta), Inside Tennis Associates, 2220 Mountain Blvd, Ste 200, Oakland, CA 94611. TEL 510-530-2200, FAX 510-530-1483, info@insidetennis.com. Ed., Pub. Bill Simons.

796.342 USA ISSN 2153-1617
INSIDE TENNIS (NEVADA EDITION). Text in English. 1981. 10/yr. free to members (effective 2010). adv. **Document type:** *Magazine, Consumer.* **Description:** Contains international, national, and local tennis news and features.
Related titles: ◆ Regional ed(s).: Inside Tennis (Northern California Edition). ISSN 2153-1587; ◆ Inside Tennis (Atlanta Edition). ISSN 2153-1625; ◆ Inside Tennis (Southern California Edition). ISSN 2153-1595.
Published by: (United States Tennis Association in Nevada), Inside Tennis Associates, 2220 Mountain Blvd, Ste 200, Oakland, CA 94611. TEL 510-530-2200, FAX 510-530-1483, info@insidetennis.com. Ed., Pub. Bill Simons.

796.342 USA ISSN 2153-1587
INSIDE TENNIS (NORTHERN CALIFORNIA EDITION). Text in English. 1981. 10/yr. USD 32 domestic to non-members; USD 75 foreign to non-members; free to members (effective 2010). adv. **Document type:** *Magazine, Consumer.* **Description:** Contains international, national, and local tennis news and features.
Related titles: ◆ Regional ed(s).: Inside Tennis (Southern California Edition). ISSN 2153-1595; ◆ Inside Tennis (Atlanta Edition). ISSN 2153-1625; ◆ Inside Tennis (Nevada Edition). ISSN 2153-1617.
Published by: (United States Tennis Association in Northern California), Inside Tennis Associates, 2220 Mountain Blvd, Ste 200, Oakland, CA 94611. TEL 510-530-2200, FAX 510-530-1483, info@insidetennis.com. Ed., Pub. Bill Simons.

796.342 USA ISSN 2153-1595
INSIDE TENNIS (SOUTHERN CALIFORNIA EDITION). Text in English. 1981. 10/yr. USD 32 domestic to non-members; USD 75 foreign to non-members; free to members (effective 2010). adv. **Document type:** *Magazine, Consumer.* **Description:** Contains international, national, and local tennis news and features.
Related titles: ◆ Regional ed(s).: Inside Tennis (Northern California Edition). ISSN 2153-1587; ◆ Inside Tennis (Atlanta Edition). ISSN 2153-1625; ◆ Inside Tennis (Nevada Edition). ISSN 2153-1617.
Published by: (United States Tennis Association in Southern California), Inside Tennis Associates, 2220 Mountain Blvd, Ste 200, Oakland, CA 94611. TEL 510-530-2200, FAX 510-530-1483, info@insidetennis.com. Ed., Pub. Bill Simons.

796.334 GBR ISSN 1749-6497
INSIDE UNITED. Text in English. 1992. m. GBP 36; GBP 3.75 newsstand/cover (effective 2009). **Document type:** *Magazine, Consumer.* **Description:** Covers all aspects of the Manchester United football club and players as they compete within the Premier League and European championships.
Formerly (until 2006): Manchester United Magazine (0967-9308)
Related titles: International ed.: Inside United (Korean Edition). ISSN 1976-1988. 2007.
—CCC.
Published by: Haymarket Network (Subsidiary of: Haymarket Media Group), Teddington Studios, Broom Rd, Teddington, TW11 9BE, United Kingdom. TEL 44-20-82675013, FAX 44-20-82675194, enquiries@haymarket.com, http://www.haymarketnetwork.com.

796.334 ITA
INTER FOOTBALL CLUB. Text in Italian. 1962. m. (11/yr.). EUR 44 domestic (effective 2008). adv. **Document type:** *Magazine, Consumer.*
Published by: Cantelli Editore Srl, Via Saliceto 22c, Castelmaggiore, BO 40013, Italy. TEL 39-051-6328811, FAX 39-051-6328815, cantelli.editore@cantelli.net, http://www.cantelli.net.

793 DEU
INTERNATIONAL BASKETBALL FEDERATION. OFFICIAL REPORT OF THE WORLD CONGRESS. Text in English, French. 1932. biennial. looseleaf. **Document type:** *Proceedings, Corporate.*
Formerly: International Amateur Basketball Federation. Official Report of the World Congress (0534-6622)
Published by: International Basketball Federation/Federation Internationale de Basketball, Postfach 700607, Munich, 81306, Germany. TEL 49-89-7481580, FAX 49-89-74815833, secretariat@office.fiba.com, http://www.fiba.com. Ed. S Haunschild. R&P G Hartmann. Circ: 300 (controlled).

794.6 USA
INTERNATIONAL BOWLING INDUSTRY. Text in English. 1993. m. USD 50 domestic; USD 65 in Canada & Mexico; USD 80 elsewhere (effective 2005). adv. **Document type:** *Magazine, Trade.* **Description:** Devoted exclusively to the business of bowling. Reaches bowling center and pro shop owners, manufacturers and suppliers worldwide.
Published by: B 2 B Media, Inc., 660 Hampshire Rd, Ste 200, Westlake Village, CA 91361. TEL 805-371-7877, FAX 805-371-7885. Ed., Pub. Scott Frager. adv.: B&W page USD 2,240; trim 8.25 x 10.875. Circ: 10,750 (controlled).

796.333 GBR ISSN 1742-7908
INTERNATIONAL RUGBY NEWS. Text in English. 1988. m. GBP 30 (effective 2009). adv. **Document type:** *Magazine, Consumer.* **Description:** Covers rugby news and includes articles on fitness, junior clubs, and world rankings, as well as editorials.
Formerly (until 2002): Rugby News & Monthly (0954-7428)
Indexed: SD.
Address: 191 Marsh Wall, London, E14 9RS, United Kingdom. Ed. Jon Edwards TEL 44-20-70055077. Adv. contact Clare Hughes TEL 44-20-70055019.

796.357 USA
INTERNATIONAL SOFTBALL CONGRESS (YEAR) WORLD CHAMPIONSHIP GUIDE. Text in English. 1953. a. USD 5 (effective 1998). adv. **Document type:** *Directory.*
Formerly: International Softball Congress (Year) Official Yearbook and Guide
Published by: International Softball Congress, c/o Ken Hackmeister, Exec. Dir., 153 E. 200 S. #10, Farmington, UT 84025. TEL 801-447-8807, FAX 801-447-8793, KLSports@aol.com, http://www.iscfastpitch.com/. Ed. Ed Kirner. Pub., R&P, Adv. contact Milt Stark. Circ: 10,000.

796.3 GBR ISSN 2042-7611
INTERNATIONAL SQUASH MAGAZINE. Text in English. 2005. q. GBP 3, EUR 4.50, USD 5.50 per issue; free to qualified personnel (effective 2010). adv. back issues avail. **Document type:** *Magazine, Consumer.* **Description:** Provides information on world's most exciting sports squash.
Related titles: Online - full text ed.: free (effective 2010).
Published by: International Sport Group, No 4 The Spinney, Chester Rd, Poynton, Cheshire SK12 1HB, United Kingdom. TEL 44-7973-544719, info@isportgroup.com. Ed. Paul Walters. Adv. contact Dean Finegold TEL 44-7967-362589. page GBP 2,500; trim 210 x 297. Circ: 60,000.

796.343 ITA ISSN 1121-6581
INTERNATIONAL SQUASH MAGAZINE. Text in Multiple languages. 1987. q. **Document type:** *Magazine, Consumer.*
Formerly (until 1989): Squash Magazine (1121-6603)
Published by: Squash Eventi, Via Grazie 40, Brescia, BS 25100, Italy. TEL 39-030-3776924, FAX 39-030-2898602, http://www.squash.it.

796.342 GBR ISSN 2042-7336
INTERNATIONAL TENNIS MAGAZINE. Text in English. 2008. q. GBP 3, EUR 4.50, USD 5.50 per issue; free to qualified personnel (effective 2010). adv. back issues avail. **Document type:** *Magazine, Consumer.* **Description:** Provides information about the world of tennis with content presented in a modern, pictorial-led format, comprising tournament previews and reviews, rankings, player profiles, competitions, equipment/buyer guides and reader services/offers, coaching instructions, hints and tips.
Related titles: Online - full text ed.: free (effective 2010).
Published by: International Sport Group, No 4 The Spinney, Chester Rd, Poynton, Cheshire SK12 1HB, United Kingdom. TEL 44-7973-544719, info@isportgroup.com. Ed. Paul Walters. Adv. contact Dean Finegold TEL 44-7967-362589. page GBP 2,000; trim 210 x 297. Circ: 60,000.

796.352 USA ISSN 1947-6434
▼ **IOWA GOLF JOURNAL.** Text in English. forthcoming 2010. m. USD 9.99 per issue (effective 2009). **Document type:** *Magazine, Consumer.* **Description:** Features articles on golf for Iowa.
Published by: In Publishing, 9769 NW 45 Ln, Miami, FL 33178. TEL 736-314-0456, info@miamigolfjournal.com.

796.352 IRL ISSN 1649-0509
IRISH GOLF REVIEW. Text in English. 1997. q. adv. **Document type:** *Magazine, Consumer.*
Published by: Lacethorn Ltd., 11 Clare St, Dublin, 2, Ireland. TEL 353-1-6624887, FAX 353-1-6624886. Adv. contact Ciaran Vines. color page EUR 1,905; trim 213 x 303. Circ: 11,000 (paid and controlled).

796.352 IRL ISSN 1649-0517
IRISH GOLF WORLD. Text in English. 1998. m. adv. **Document type:** *Magazine, Consumer.*
Published by: Lacethorn Ltd., 11 Clare St, Dublin, 2, Ireland. TEL 353-1-6624887, FAX 353-1-6624886. Adv. contact Ciaran Vines. color page EUR 1,524; trim 266 x 342. Circ: 50,000 (paid and controlled).

796.352 IRL ISSN 1649-0169
IRISH LADY GOLFER. Text in English. 2000. bi-m. adv. **Document type:** *Magazine, Consumer.*
Address: Crannagh House, 198 Rathfranham Rd., Dublin, 14, Ireland. TEL 353-1-4900781, FAX 353-1-4906763. Adv. contact Mary McCarthy. color page EUR 2,412; trim 210 x 297. Circ: 20,000 (paid and controlled).

796.333 IRL ISSN 0790-228X
IRISH RUGBY REVIEW. Text in English. 1976. 9/yr. adv. **Document type:** *Magazine, Consumer.*
Formerly (until 1983): Irish Rugby (0790-2271)
Published by: Victory Irish Promotions, PO Box 7992, Dun Laoghaire, Co. Dublin, Ireland. TEL 353-1-2804481, FAX 353-1-2804481. Adv. contact Margaret Walsh. B&W page EUR 1,206, color page EUR 1,651; trim 210 x 297. Circ: 12,000 (paid and controlled).

796.332 USA ISSN 1069-7276
GV546.5
➤ **IRON GAME HISTORY**; the journal of physical culture. Text in English. 1990. 4/yr. USD 25 domestic; USD 30 foreign (effective 2011). back issues avail. **Document type:** *Journal, Academic/Scholarly.* **Description:** Examines physical culture.
Indexed: CA, SD, SportS, T02.
Published by: University of Texas at Austin, The H.J. Lutcher Stark Center for Physical Culture & Sports, NEZ 5.700, D3600, 1 University Station, Austin, TX 78712. TEL 512-471-4890, FAX 512-401-3447, terry@starkcenter.org, jan@starkcenter.org. Eds. Jan Todd, Terry Todd. R&P Jan Todd.

796.334 NLD ISSN 1879-7660
HET JAAR VAN A Z. (Alkmaar Zaanstreek) Variant title: A Z Jaarboek. Text in Dutch. 2007. a. EUR 19.95 (effective 2010).
Published by: HDC Media B.V., Postbus 2, Alkmaar, 1800 AA, Netherlands. TEL 31-72-5196196, FAX 31-72-5126183, http://www.hdcmedia.nl.

796.342 USA ISSN 1935-3278
JAX TENNIS; northeast Florida's tennis source. Text in English. 2007. 11/yr. USD 19.95 (effective 2007). adv. **Document type:** *Magazine, Consumer.* **Description:** Covers tennis from the Northeast Florida league and tournament level up to the pros. It features player profiles, gear and apparel guides, columns and more.
Related titles: Online - full text ed.
Published by: Jax Tennis Magazine, LLC, 2516 Chesterbrook Ct, Jacksonville, FL 32224. TEL 904-992-4332. Ed., Pub. Richard Vach. Adv. contact Steve Everly TEL 267-893-5686. color page USD 1,395, B&W page USD 975; trim 11 x 13.

796.3 USA ISSN 2150-5373
▼ **JAYHAWKS TIP-OFF.** Variant title: M S P Jayhawk Tip-Off. Text in English. 2009. a. USD 12.99 per issue (effective 2011). back issues avail. **Document type:** *Handbook/Manual/Guide, Consumer.* **Description:** Annual guide to the University of Kansas Jayhawks men's basketball team.
Published by: Maple Street Press, 155 Webster St, Ste B, Hanover, MA 02339. TEL 781-347-4730, FAX 781-347-4732, info@maplestreetpress.com. Ed. Eric Angevine.

796.343 CHN
JISU SPORT - SQUASH/VELOCITY SPORT - SQUASH. Text in Chinese. 2004 (Jun.). irreg. CNY 10 (effective 2005). **Document type:** *Magazine, Consumer.*
Published by: Zhongguo Biqiu Xiehui, 2, Tiyouguan Lu, Beijing, 100763, China. TEL 86-10-67111759, http://www.squash.com.cn/. Ed. Xiaoqian Zhou. Pub. Hongbin Wang.

796.332 USA
JOE MONTANA'S IN THE RED ZONE. Text in English. 2000. 10/yr. USD 3.95 newsstand/cover (effective 2000). adv. **Document type:** *Magazine, Consumer.* **Description:** Provides analyses and insight into all aspects of pro football.
Published by: Go Deep Inc., 30 Broad St, 43rd Fl, New York, NY 10004. rausch@aol.com. Ed. Joe Montana. Pub. Thomas Rausch.

796.352 USA ISSN 2161-3044
▼ ➤ **THE JOURNAL OF APPLIED GOLF RESEARCH.** Abbreviated title: J A G R. Text in English. 2011. q. USD 68 to non-members; USD 48 to members (effective 2011). **Document type:** *Journal, Academic/Scholarly.* **Description:** Designed to provide timely, practical and peer reviewed research on the teaching and learning of golf skills.
Media: Online - full text.
Published by: 3D Golf Labs Inc., 929 Lynaugh Rd, Victor, NY 14564. TEL 585-723-8034, dan@3dgolflabs.com, http://www.3dgolflabs.com. Ed. Dan Parks.

794 CAN ISSN 0849-1623
JOURNAL QUEBEC QUILLES. Text mainly in French; Text occasionally in English. 1988. 6/yr. CAD 9.95; USD 12.95 in United States; USD 24.95 elsewhere. adv. **Document type:** *Newspaper, Consumer.*
Published by: Quebec Quilles Inc., Succ Anjou, C P 126, Anjou, PQ H1K 4G6, Canada. TEL 514-351-5224, 800-588-9703, FAX 514-351-6818. Ed. Gilles Poulin. Pub., R&P Yves Larocque. Adv. contact Gil Legault. B&W page CAD 1,495; trim 15 x 11.38. Circ: 20,000.
Subscr. to: 2930 Desmarteau St, Montreal, PQ H1L 4N7, Canada.

796.332 ESP
JUGON!. Text in Spanish. 2005. m. EUR 2.95 newsstand/cover (effective 2010). **Document type:** *Magazine, Consumer.*
Published by: Panini Espana S.A., Calle Vallespi 20, Torroella de Montgri, Girona, 17257, Spain. TEL 34-972-757411, FAX 34-972-757711, http://www.panini.es.

796.357 USA ISSN 1522-8460
GV880.8
JUNIOR BASEBALL. Abbreviated title: J B. Text in English. 1996. bi-m. USD 17.70 domestic; USD 27.70 in Canada & Mexico; USD 47.70 elsewhere (effective 2010). adv. illus. back issues avail. **Document type:** *Magazine, Consumer.* **Description:** Aimed at youth baseball players, their parents, coaches, and associated organizations, regardless of league, park or school affiliation. Provides information to enhance the youth baseball experience for the entire family.
Formerly (until Jan.1999): Junior League Baseball (1089-7038)
Published by: JSAN Publishing LLC, 14 Woodway Ln, Wilton, CT 06897. TEL 203-210-5726, publisher@juniorbaseball.com. Ed. Jim Beecher.
Subscr. to: PO Box 3059, Langhorne, PA 19047.

JUST KICK-IT!. *see* CHILDREN AND YOUTH—For

796.352 USA ISSN 1947-6450
▼ **KENTUCKY GOLF JOURNAL.** Text in English. forthcoming 2010. m. USD 9.99 per issue (effective 2009). **Document type:** *Magazine, Consumer.* **Description:** Features articles on golf for Kentucky.
Published by: In Publishing, 9769 NW 45 Ln, Miami, FL 33178. TEL 736-314-0456, info@miamigolfjournal.com.

KEY NOTE MARKET REPORT: FOOTBALL CLUBS & FINANCE. *see* BUSINESS AND ECONOMICS—Production Of Goods And Services

796.333 GBR ISSN 1468-1935
KEY NOTE MARKET REPORT: RUGBY CLUBS & FINANCE. Text in English. 1999. irreg., latest 1999, Aug. GBP 235 per issue (effective 2008). **Document type:** *Report, Trade.* **Description:** Provides an overview of a specific UK market segment and includes executive summary, market definition, market size, industry background, competitor analysis, current issues, forecasts, company profiles, and more.
Published by: Key Note Ltd. (Subsidiary of: Bonnier Business Information), Field House, 72 Oldfield Rd, Hampton, Mddx TW12 2HQ, United Kingdom. TEL 44-20-84818750, FAX 44-20-87830049, info@keynote.co.uk, http://www.keynote.co.uk. Ed. Simon Howitt.

796.332 CAN
KICK OFF. Text in English. m. USD 25. adv.
Published by: Kick Off Publications, 28 88 South Park Dr, Winnipeg, MB R3T 2M1, Canada. TEL 204-269-5724. Ed. Will Oliver. Circ: 50,000.

796.334 USA
KICKOFF. Text in English. q. members only. **Description:** Covers collective bargaining of the league, player benefits, and soccer news.
Published by: Major Indoor Soccer League Players Association, 2021 L St, N W, Ste 407, Washington, DC 20036. Ed. Will Bray. Circ: 125.

796.334 ZAF ISSN 1022-3819
KICKOFF. Text in English. 1994. fortn. ZAR 125; ZAR 6.25 newsstand/cover (effective 2000). illus. **Document type:** *Magazine, Consumer.* **Description:** Covers professional local and international soccer.
Published by: Touchline Media, PO Box 16368, Vlaeberg, Cape Town 8018, South Africa. TEL 27-21-217810, FAX 27-21-215118, http://www.touchline.co.za. Ed. Richard Maguire. Pub. Rob Moore. R&P Stuart Lowe. Adv. contact Mike Allen. Circ: 80,000 (paid).

796.3 ZAF
KICKOFF (NIGERIA EDITION). Text in English. m. NGN 300, ZAR 240 (effective 2007). adv. **Document type:** *Magazine, Consumer.*
Related titles: Online - full text ed.: ISSN 1994-5515. 2007.
Published by: Touchline Media, PO Box 16368, Vlaeberg, Cape Town 8018, South Africa. TEL 27-21-4083800, FAX 27-21-4083811, http://www.touchline.co.za. Ed. Samm Audu. Adv. contact Ovie Obonna TEL 234-8-22920545.

796.323 HRV ISSN 1330-4895
KOSARKA. Text in Croatian. 1994. m. HRK 220 (effective 2002). adv. **Document type:** *Magazine, Consumer.*
Related titles: Online - full text ed.
Published by: Zri-Sport d.o.o., Prisavlje 2, Zagreb, 10000, Croatia. TEL 385-1-6060840, FAX 385-1-6159606, urednistvo@zri-sport.hr. Ed. Vladimir Radicevic.

796.323 CHN ISSN 1673-856X
KOULAN/SLAM. Text in Chinese. 2006. m. CNY 120; CNY 10 per issue (effective 2010). back issues avail. **Document type:** *Magazine, Consumer.*
Related titles: Online - full text ed.
Published by: Titan Chuanmei Jituan/Titan Culture - Express Co, ltd, Donghuashi Dajie Bei-li Xi-qu #22, Chongwen-qu, Beijing, 100062, China. TEL 86-10-51005876, http://www.titan24.com/.

796.334 DNK ISSN 0905-5320
KRIDTSTREGEN. Text in Danish. 1982. 4/yr. DKK 125 (effective 2008). adv. illus. **Document type:** *Magazine, Consumer.* **Description:** Soccer magazine for and about female players.
Formerly (until 1990): Focus Damefodbold (0108-4666)
Published by: Foreningen Kridtstregen, Lisesminde 10, Kolding, 8900, Denmark. TEL 45-86-407062, FAX 45-86-406679, http://www.kridtstregen.dk. Ed. John Witting TEL 45-86-404808.

796.355 USA
L C S: GUIDE TO HOCKEY. (Le Coq Sportif) Text in English. 1994. bi-w.
Formerly: Le Coq Sportif
Media: Online - full text.
Published by: Canadas Net, 632 Hempfield St, Greensburg, PA 15601. Ed. Michael Dell.

796.342 GBR
L T A HANDBOOK. Text in English. 1980. a. free to members. **Document type:** *Corporate.*
Former titles: Tennis Great Britain; Lawn Tennis Association Handbook
—BLDSC (4246.200000).

Published by: Lawn Tennis Association, The National Tennis Centre, 100 Priory Lane, Roehampton, London, SW15 5JQ, United Kingdom. TEL 44-20-84877000, FAX 44-20-84877301, Info@LTA.org.uk, http://www.lta.org.uk/. Ed. Stephen Holmes. Circ: 5,000.

796.347 GBR ISSN 0023-7086
LACROSSETALK. Text in English. 1948. q. free to members (effective 2009). adv. illus. **Document type:** *Magazine, Consumer.* **Description:** Includes articles and comment on both women's and men's lacrosse in the UK.
Formerly (until 1989): Lacrosse
Related titles: Online - full text ed.
Indexed: SPI, SportS.
Published by: English Lacrosse Association, Belle Vue Athletics Ctr, Pink Bank Ln, Manchester, M12 5GL, United Kingdom. TEL 44-161-2273626, FAX 44-161-2273625, info@englishlacrosse.co.uk. Eds. Ashley Tarran-Jones TEL 44-161-2273626, Neil Goulding. Adv. contact Caroline Royle TEL 44-161-2273626. B&W page GBP 750, color page GBP 1,000; 178 x 252. Circ: 10,000.

796.352 USA
LADIES GOLF JOURNEY. Text in English. 9/yr. adv.
Published by: R C M Productions, PO Box 923, Versailles, KY 40383. TEL 606-879-8822, FAX 606-873-3561.

796.352 051 ITA ISSN 1825-5124
LADY GOLF & STYLE. Text in Italian. 2005. m. EUR 28 (effective 2008). **Document type:** *Magazine, Consumer.*
Published by: Casa Editrice Scode SpA, Corso Monforte 36, Milan, 20122, Italy. TEL 39-02-76002874, FAX 39-02-76004905, info@scode.it, http://www.scode.it.

796.352 GBR ISSN 0307-4366
GV966
LADY GOLFER'S HANDBOOK. Text in English. 1893. a. free to members (effective 2009). **Document type:** *Directory, Trade.*
Published by: Ladies Golf Union, The Scores, St Andrews, Fife KY16 9AT, United Kingdom. TEL 44-1334-475811, FAX 44-1334-472818, http://www.lgu.org.

796.352 DEU
LADYS LOUNGE. Variant title: Golfwelt Ladys Lounge. Text in German. 4/yr. adv. **Document type:** *Magazine, Consumer.*
Published by: Kern & Kern Media Verlag OHG, Simrockstr 5, Bonn, 53113, Germany. TEL 49-228-9354800, FAX 49-228-93548020. adv.: color page EUR 7,450; trim 210 x 297. Circ: 25,000 (controlled).

796.323 CHN ISSN 1000-3460
LANQIU/BASKETBALL. Text in Chinese. 1981. m. USD 55.20 (effective 2009). **Document type:** *Magazine, Consumer.*
Related titles: Online - full content ed.
—East View.
Published by: (Zhongguo Lanqiu Xiehui/China Basketball Society), Zhongguo Tiyubao Yezongshe, 8, Tiyuguan Lu, Chongwen-qu, Beijing, 100061, China. TEL 86-10-67158591, FAX 86-10-67158590. **Dist. in U.S. by:** China International Book Trading Corp, 35 Chegongzhuang Xilu, Haidian District, PO Box 399, Beijing 100044, China. TEL 86-10-68412045, FAX 86-10-68412023, cibtc@mail.cibtc.com.cn, http://www.cibtc.com.cn.

796.323 CHN ISSN 1673-1115
LANQIU JULEBU/BASKETBALL CLUB. Text in Chinese. 2005. m. **Document type:** *Magazine, Consumer.*
Published by: Kelaibo Tiyu Wenhua Chuanmei Zhongxin, 310, Yangming Lu, 12/F, Chuban Dasha, Nanchang, 330006, China. TEL 86-791-6894727, FAX 86-791-6895190.

796.352 USA
LEADER BOARD. Text in English. 1991. q. free to members (effective 2011). adv. charts; illus. **Document type:** *Newsletter, Trade.*
Published by: (Center for Golf Course Management), Golf Course Superintendents Association of America, 1421 Research Park Dr, Lawrence, KS 66049. TEL 785-841-2240, 800-472-7878, FAX 785-832-3643, infobox@gcsaa.org, http://www.gcsaa.org.

796.332 USA
THE LEGEND (TULEPO); Mississippi Division I football guide. Text in English. 2000. a. USD 2.95 newsstand/cover (effective 2001). adv. **Document type:** *Magazine, Consumer.*
Published by: The Legend, Box 1388, Tupelo, MS 38802. Ed., Pub. Wesley Wells.

796.3 USA ISSN 0892-9440
LET'S PLAY SOFTBALL. Text in English. 1986. 12/yr. adv. **Document type:** *Newspaper, Consumer.* **Description:** For players, parents, coaches, fans and officials.
Published by: Let's Play, Inc., 2721 E 42nd St, Minneapolis, MN 55406. TEL 612-729-0023, FAX 612-729-0259. Ed. Steve Carroll. Pub., Adv. contact Doug Johnson. Circ: 5,000.

796.332 USA
LINDY'S A C C FOOTBALL ANNUAL. (Atlantic Coast Conference) Variant title: A C C Football Annual. Text in English. 1987. a. USD 9.50 per issue (effective 2009). adv. 180 p./no. 3 cols./p.; back issues avail. **Document type:** *Magazine, Consumer.* **Description:** Highlights ACC college football plus NCAA football as a whole.
Published by: D M D Publications, Inc., 2100 Centennial Dr, Ste 100, Birmingham, AL 35216. TEL 205-871-1182, FAX 205-871-1184, lindy@lindyssports.com, http://www.lindyssports.com/. Ed. Don Borst. Pub., R&P, Adv. contact Lindy Davis. page USD 1,500. Circ: 20,000.

796.357 USA
LINDY'S BASEBALL. Text in English. 2001. a. USD 9.50 per issue (effective 2009). 184 p./no. 3 cols./p.; **Document type:** *Magazine, Consumer.*
Published by: D M D Publications, Inc., 2100 Centennial Dr, Ste 100, Birmingham, AL 35216. TEL 205-871-1182, FAX 205-871-1184, lindy@lindyssports.com, http://www.lindyssports.com/.

796.357 USA ISSN 1546-6795
LINDY'S BASEBALL SCOUTING REPORT (YEAR). Variant title: Baseball Scouting Report (Year). Lindy's Scouting Report. Text in English. 2001. a. USD 9.50 per issue (effective 2008). adv. back issues avail. **Document type:** *Magazine, Consumer.* **Description:** Provides information on baseball game.
Published by: D M D Publications, Inc., 2100 Centennial Dr, Ste 100, Birmingham, AL 35216. TEL 205-871-1182, FAX 205-871-1184, lindy@lindyssports.com, http://www.lindyssports.com/. Pub., R&P, Adv. contact Lindy Davis.

796.332 USA
LINDY'S BIG 10 FOOTBALL ANNUAL. Text in English. 1987. a. USD 9.50 per issue (effective 2008). adv. 200 p./no.; back issues avail. **Document type:** *Magazine, Consumer.*
Published by: D M D Publications, Inc., 2100 Centennial Dr, Ste 100, Birmingham, AL 35216. TEL 205-871-1182, FAX 205-871-1184, lindy@lindyssports.com, http://www.lindyssports.com/. Ed. Mike Beacom. Pub., R&P, Adv. contact Lindy Davis. page USD 3,000. Circ: 35,000 (paid).

796.332 USA ISSN 1523-1852
LINDY'S BIG 12 FOOTBALL ANNUAL. Text in English. 1987. a. USD 9.50 per issue (effective 2008). adv. 200 p./no. 3 cols./p.; back issues avail. **Document type:** *Magazine, Consumer.*
Formed by the 1996 merger of: Lindy's Southwest Football Annual; Lindy's Big 8 Football Annual
Published by: D M D Publications, Inc., 2100 Centennial Dr, Ste 100, Birmingham, AL 35216. TEL 205-871-1182, FAX 205-871-1184, lindy@lindyssports.com, http://www.lindyssports.com/. Ed. Anthony Gimino. Pub., R&P, Adv. contact Lindy Davis. page USD 2,250. Circ: 30,000.

796.332 USA
LINDY'S COLLEGE BASKETBALL ANNUAL. Text in English. 1999. a. USD 9.50 per issue (effective 2009). adv. 206 p./no. 3 cols./p.; back issues avail. **Document type:** *Magazine, Consumer.*
Formerly (until 1995): Lindy's Basketball Annuals
Published by: D M D Publications, Inc., 2100 Centennial Dr, Ste 100, Birmingham, AL 35216. TEL 205-871-1182, FAX 205-871-1184, lindy@lindyssports.com, http://www.lindyssports.com/. Pub., R&P, Adv. contact Lindy Davis. page USD 5,250. Circ: 65,000 (paid).

796.332 USA
LINDY'S DRAFT GUIDE. Variant title: Draft Guide. Text in English. 2007. a. USD 9.50 per issue (effective 2008). adv. 152 p./no. 3 cols./p.; back issues avail. **Document type:** *Magazine, Consumer.*
Published by: D M D Publications, Inc., 2100 Centennial Dr, Ste 100, Birmingham, AL 35216. TEL 205-871-1182, FAX 205-871-1184, lindy@lindyssports.com, http://www.lindyssports.com/. Pub., R&P, Adv. contact Lindy Davis. page USD 4,750. Circ: 80,000 (paid).

796.357 USA ISSN 1554-3765
GV1202.F33
LINDY'S FANTASY BASEBALL. Text in English. 2001. a. USD 9.50 per issue (effective 2008). adv. 144 p./no. 3 cols./p.; back issues avail. **Document type:** *Magazine, Consumer.* **Description:** Contains fantasy player profiles, draft-day checklists and lots of great features.
Published by: D M D Publications, Inc., 2100 Centennial Dr, Ste 100, Birmingham, AL 35216. TEL 205-871-1182, FAX 205-871-1184, lindy@lindyssports.com, http://www.lindyssports.com/. Pub., R&P, Adv. contact Lindy Davis. page USD 3,375. Circ: 45,000 (paid).

796.332 USA ISSN 1542-5940
LINDY'S NATIONAL COLLEGE FOOTBALL ANNUAL. Variant title: Lindy's Football Annuals. National College Football Annual. Text in English. 1998. a. USD 9.50 per issue (effective 2008). adv. 216 p./no.; back issues avail. **Document type:** *Magazine, Consumer.* **Description:** Highlights the NCAA football as whole and contains recruiting, depth charts, schedules and team/player information.
Published by: D M D Publications, Inc., 2100 Centennial Dr, Ste 100, Birmingham, AL 35216. TEL 205-871-1182, FAX 205-871-1184, lindy@lindyssports.com, http://www.lindyssports.com/. Ed. Anthony Gimino. Pub., R&P, Adv. contact Lindy Davis. page USD 6,750. Circ: 90,000 (paid).

796.332 USA
LINDY'S PAC 10 FOOTBALL ANNUAL. Text in English. 1987. a. USD 9.50 per issue (effective 2008). adv. 180 p./no. 3 cols./p.; **Document type:** *Magazine, Consumer.* **Description:** Contains the highlights of PAC-10 college football plus NCAA football as a whole.
Published by: D M D Publications, Inc., 2100 Centennial Dr, Ste 100, Birmingham, AL 35216. TEL 205-871-1182, FAX 205-871-1184, lindy@lindyssports.com, http://www.lindyssports.com/. Ed. Anthony Gimino. Pub., Adv. contact Lindy Davis. page USD 1,125. Circ: 15,000.

796.323 USA ISSN 1077-9612
LINDY'S PRO BASKETBALL. Variant title: Pro Basketball. Text in English. 1994. a. USD 9.50 per issue (effective 2008). adv. 144 p./no.; back issues avail. **Document type:** *Magazine, Consumer.* **Description:** For serious pro basketball fans.
Published by: D M D Publications, Inc., 2100 Centennial Dr, Ste 100, Birmingham, AL 35216. TEL 205-871-1182, FAX 205-871-1184, lindy@lindyssports.com, http://www.lindyssports.com/. Ed. Ed Roland Lazenby. Adv. contact Lindy Davis. page USD 3,750; trim 8 x 10.5. Circ: 45,000 (paid).

796.332 USA ISSN 1062-4198
GV937
LINDY'S PRO EDITION FOOTBALL ANNUAL. Text in English. 1987. a. USD 9.50 per issue (effective 2008). adv. 224 p./no.; back issues avail. **Document type:** *Magazine, Consumer.* **Description:** For the serious pro football fan.
Published by: D M D Publications, Inc., 2100 Centennial Dr, Ste 100, Birmingham, AL 35216. TEL 205-871-1182, FAX 205-871-1184, lindy@lindyssports.com, http://www.lindyssports.com/. Ed. Howard Balzar. Pub., R&P, Adv. contact Lindy Davis. page USD 13,500. Circ: 18,000 (paid).

796.332 USA
LINDY'S PRO FANTASY FOOTBALL. Variant title: Pro Fantasy Football. Text in English. 2001. a. USD 9.50 per issue (effective 2008). adv. 160 p./no.; back issues avail. **Document type:** *Magazine, Consumer.* **Description:** Highlights the NFL fantasy football.
Published by: D M D Publications, Inc., 2100 Centennial Dr, Ste 100, Birmingham, AL 35216. TEL 205-871-1182, FAX 205-871-1184, lindy@lindyssports.com, http://www.lindyssports.com/. Pub., R&P, Adv. contact Lindy Davis. page USD 4,125. Circ: 55,000 (paid).

796.332 USA
LINDY'S SOUTHEASTERN FOOTBALL. Variant title: Southeastern Football. Text in English. 1982. a. USD 9.50 per issue (effective 2008). adv. 224 p./no. 3 cols./p.; back issues avail. **Document type:** *Magazine, Consumer.*
Formerly (until 199?): Lindy's S E C Football Annual
Published by: D M D Publications, Inc., 2100 Centennial Dr, Ste 100, Birmingham, AL 35216. TEL 205-871-1182, FAX 205-871-1184, lindy@lindyssports.com, http://www.lindyssports.com/. Ed. Anthony Gimino. Pub., Adv. contact Lindy Davis. page USD 6,000; trim 8 x 10.5. Circ: 80,000 (paid).

796.352 USA ISSN 1554-9151
LINKS (HILTON HEAD ISLAND); the best of golf. Text in English. 1993. 5/yr. USD 11.95 domestic; USD 21.95 in Canada; USD 37.95 elsewhere (effective 2009). adv. bk.rev. illus. back issues avail. **Document type:** *Magazine, Consumer.* **Description:** Contains information about preserving the history and traditions of golf. Covers highly regarded courses, resorts, and golf communities, and features essays and profiles.
Formed by the merger of (1988-1993): Southern Links (1043-6375); (1990-1993): Western Link (1052-3219)
Related titles: Online - full text ed.
Published by: Purcell Enterprises, Inc., 10 Executive Park Rd, Ste 202, PO Box 7628, Hilton Head Island, SC 29928. TEL 843-842-6200, FAX 843-842-6233, letters@linksmagazine.com. Eds. Hunki Yun, Nancy Purcell. Pub. Jack Purcell Jr. adv.: color page USD 29,165; trim 8 x 10.5. Circ: 250,000.

796.332 GBR ISSN 2046-3014
LIVERPOOL F C. (Football Club) Abbreviated title: L F C. Variant title: Liverpool F C Official Matchday Programme. Text in English. 2000. s-m. GBP 72 (effective 2011). back issues avail. **Document type:** *Magazine, Consumer.*
Former titles (until 2010): This is Anfield (1478-3037); (until 2002): Liverpool Official Matchday Magazine (1471-6127)
Published by: Sport Media, PO Box 1959, Liverpool, L69 3JY, United Kingdom. TEL 44-843-1705000.

796.334 GBR ISSN 1356-2231
LIVERPOOL F C OFFICIAL MAGAZINE. (Football Club) Text in English. 1994. w. GBP 117; GBP 58.50 for 6 mos. (effective 2009). **Document type:** *Magazine, Consumer.* **Description:** Features exclusive, up-to-date content, stunning photography, player interviews and regular columns from Anfield legends such as Alan Hansen and Kenny Dalglish.
Published by: (Liverpool Football Club), Northern & Shell Plc, The Northern & Shell Bldg, Number 10 Lower Thames St, London, EC3R 6EN, United Kingdom. TEL 44-870-0626620, http://www.northernandshell.co.uk.

LIVING IN GAUTENG. *see* LIFESTYLE

LIVING IN THE CAPE. *see* LIFESTYLE

796.323 USA ISSN 1531-4987
LONESTAR BASKETBALL; annual preseason magazine. Text in English. 2000. a. USD 4.95 newsstand/cover (effective 2002).
Published by: Grace Media, LLC, P. O. Box 4120, Houston, TX 77210. TEL 713-426-0347, FAX 713-426-0321, mail@lonestarbball.com. Ed. Sarah Hornaday.

196.332 USA
LOS ANGELES RAMS OFFICIAL YEARBOOK. Text in English. 1983. irreg., latest 1994. illus. **Document type:** *Magazine, Consumer.*
Published by: Woodford Publishing, Inc., PO Box 910, Tiburon, CA 94920. TEL 415-397-1853, FAX 415-399-0942. Ed. Jon Rochmis. Pub. Laurence J Hyman. R&P, Adv. contact David Lilienstein.

796.3 USA ISSN 1940-3178
M C L A; the lax mag. (Men's Collegiate Lacrosse Association) Text in English. 2007. 7/yr. USD 35 (effective 2008). adv. **Document type:** *Magazine, Consumer.* **Description:** Dedicated to all aspects of college men's lacrosse, including team spotlights, player profiles, conferences and coaching strategies.
Published by: M C L A the Lax Mag LLC, 3145 Geary Blvd, Castle 56, San Francisco, CA 94118. Ed. Karl F Lynch.

796.357 USA ISSN 1941-5060
GV862
M L B INSIDERS CLUB MAGAZINE. (Major League Baseball) Text mainly in English. 2008. q. USD 24 membership (effective 2010). adv. **Document type:** *Magazine, Consumer.*
Indexed: PEI.
Published by: North American Membership Group, Inc., 12301 Whitewater Dr, Minnetonka, MN 55343. TEL 952-936-9333, FAX 952-936-9169, 800-688-7611, namghq@namginc.com, http://www.namginc.com/.

796.334 SWE ISSN 1651-4459
MAGASINET FOTBOLL. Text in Swedish. 1982. q. SEK 200 domestic; SEK 300 in Europe; SEK 360 elsewhere (effective 2004). adv. **Document type:** *Magazine, Consumer.*
Formerly (until 2001): Fotbollmagasinet (0284-2319); Supersedes in part (in 1987): Fotboll (0280-2325)
Published by: Svenska Fotbollfoerbundet, Box 1216, Solna, 17123, Sweden. TEL 46-8-7350900, FAX 46-8-7350901, svff@svenskfotboll.se.

796.334 CZE ISSN 1802-1077
▼ **MAGAZIN JIHOCESKY FOTBAL.** Text in Czech. 2009. 32/yr. CZK 800; CZK 29 newsstand/cover (effective 2011). adv. **Document type:** *Magazine, Consumer.*
Published by: Fmedia s.r.o., Sportovni 401, Borsov nad Vltavou, 373 82, Czech Republic. Ed. Helena Kristkova.

796.334 ITA
MAGLIAZZURRA. Text in Italian. 1970. bi-m. membership. adv. **Document type:** *Magazine, Consumer.*
Published by: Associazione Nazionale Atleti Azzurri d'Italia (A N A A I), Foro Italico, Rome, 00194, Italy. TEL 39-06-36857410, FAX 39-06-36857687, azzurri@anaai.it, http://www.anaai.it.

796.334 USA ISSN 1939-0750
GV942
MAJOR LEAGUE SOCCER. Text in English. 2007. bi-m. USD 4.95 newsstand/cover (effective 2007). adv. **Document type:** *Magazine, Consumer.* **Description:** Devoted to all aspects of Major League Soccer in the United States, including players, teams, important games, fashion and fans.
Published by: Terry Moutter Publishing, Woodland Plaza, 21243 Ventura Blvd, Ste 226, Woodland Hills, CA 91364. TEL 818-577-6005. Pub. Terry Moutter.

S

796.352 USA
MAJORS OF GOLF. Text in English. q. USD 11.95; USD 3.50 newsstand/cover (effective 2001). adv. **Description:** Covers the P G A's major golf championships.
Published by: Great Golf Resorts of the World, Inc, 2600 Philmont Ave, 201, Huntingdon Valley, PA 19006. TEL 215-914-2071, FAX 215-814-2076. Pub. Richard K Summers.

796.332 USA ISSN 2155-0360
▼ **MAPLE STREET PRESS BRONCOS ANNUAL.** Text in English. 2010 (July). a. USD 12.99 per issue (effective 2011). **Document type:** *Consumer.* **Description:** Preview for the Denver Broncos football team.
Published by: Maple Street Press, 155 Webster St, Ste B, Hanover, MA 02339. info@maplestreetpress.com, http://www.maplestreetpress.com.

796.357 USA ISSN 1944-3889
GV875.S3
▼ **MAPLE STREET PRESS CARDINALS ANNUAL.** Variant title: Cardinals Annual. Text in English. 2009 (Mar.). a. USD 12.99 per issue (effective 2011). back issues avail. **Document type:** *Handbook/Manual/Guide, Consumer.*
Published by: Maple Street Press, 155 Webster St, Ste B, Hanover, MA 02339. TEL 781-347-4730, FAX 781-347-4732, info@maplestreetpress.com. Ed. Larry Borowsky.

796.357 USA ISSN 1948-5603
MAPLE STREET PRESS CORNHUSKER KICKOFF. Variant title: Cornhusker Kickoff. Text in English. 2008 (Jul.). a. USD 12.99 per issue (effective 2011). back issues avail. **Document type:** *Handbook/Manual/Guide, Consumer.*
Formerly (until 2009): Sea of Red (1941-7071)
Published by: Maple Street Press, 155 Webster St, Ste B, Hanover, MA 02339. TEL 781-347-4730, FAX 781-347-4732, info@maplestreetpress.com. Ed. Jon Johnston.

796.357 USA ISSN 2159-4058
GV875.C6
MAPLE STREET PRESS CUBS ANNUAL. Variant title: Cubs Annual. Text in English. 2007. a. USD 12.99 per issue (effective 2011). back issues avail. **Document type:** *Handbook/Manual/Guide, Consumer.*
Formerly (until 2009): Wrigley Season Ticket (1942-2369)
Published by: Maple Street Press, 155 Webster St, Ste B, Hanover, MA 02339. TEL 781-347-4730, FAX 781-347-4732, info@maplestreetpress.com. Ed. Al Yellon.

796.332 USA ISSN 2155-0352
GV956.N4
▼ **MAPLE STREET PRESS GIANTS ANNUAL.** Text in English. 2010 (July). a. USD 12.99 per issue (effective 2011). **Document type:** *Consumer.* **Description:** Presents a preview of the upcoming New York Giants football season.
Published by: Maple Street Press, 155 Webster St, Ste B, Hanover, MA 02339. info@maplestreetpress.com.

796.357 USA ISSN 1944-3897
GV875.C7
▼ **MAPLE STREET PRESS INDIANS ANNUAL.** Variant title: Indians Annual. Text in English. 2009 (Mar.). a. USD 12.99 per issue (effective 2011). **Document type:** *Handbook/Manual/Guide, Consumer.*
Published by: Maple Street Press, 155 Webster St, Ste B, Hanover, MA 02339. TEL 781-347-4730, FAX 781-347-4732, info@maplestreetpress.com. Ed. Jay Levin.

796.357 USA ISSN 2159-3868
GV875.N45
MAPLE STREET PRESS METS ANNUAL. Variant title: Mets Annual. Text in English. 2008. a. USD 12.99 per issue (effective 2011). back issues avail. **Document type:** *Handbook/Manual/Guide, Consumer.*
Formerly (until 2009): Meet the Mets (1942-0560)
Published by: Maple Street Press, 155 Webster St, Ste B, Hanover, MA 02339. TEL 781-347-4730, FAX 781-347-4732, info@maplestreetpress.com. Ed. Matthew Silverman.

796.332 USA ISSN 2155-0344
GV956.G7
▼ **MAPLE STREET PRESS PACKERS ANNUAL.** Text in English. 2010 (July). a. USD 12.99 per issue (effective 2011). **Description:** A preview for the Green Bay Packers football season.
Published by: Maple Street Press, 155 Webster St, Ste B, Hanover, MA 02339. info@maplestreetpress.com.

796.357 USA ISSN 1944-3870
GV875.P45
▼ **MAPLE STREET PRESS PHILLIES ANNUAL.** Variant title: Phillies Annual. Text in English. 2009 (Mar.). a. USD 12.99 per issue (effective 2011). back issues avail. **Document type:** *Handbook/Manual/Guide, Consumer.*
Published by: Maple Street Press, 155 Webster St, Ste B, Hanover, MA 02339. TEL 781-347-4730, FAX 781-347-4732, info@maplestreetpress.com, http://www.maplestreetpress.com. Ed. Peter Baker.

796.357 USA ISSN 1942-2016
GV875.B62
MAPLE STREET PRESS RED SOX ANNUAL. Text in English. 2007. a. USD 12.99 per issue (effective 2011). back issues avail. **Document type:** *Handbook/Manual/Guide, Consumer.*
Published by: Maple Street Press, 155 Webster St, Ste B, Hanover, MA 02339. TEL 781-347-4730, FAX 781-347-4732, info@maplestreetpress.com. Ed., Pub. Jim Walsh.

796.332 USA ISSN 2155-0336
▼ **MAPLE STREET PRESS REDSKINS ANNUAL.** Text in English. 2010 (July). a. USD 12.99 per issue (effective 2011). **Document type:** *Consumer.* **Description:** A preview of the Washington Redskins football season.
Published by: Maple Street Press, 155 Webster St, Ste B, Hanover, MA 02339. info@maplestreetpress.com.

796.357 USA ISSN 2159-5992
GV875.D6
MAPLE STREET PRESS TIGERS ANNUAL. Text in English. 2007. a. USD 12.99 per issue (effective 2011). back issues avail. **Document type:** *Handbook/Manual/Guide, Consumer.*
Formerly (until 2008): Tigers (Year) Corner (1942-1400)
Published by: Maple Street Press, 155 Webster St, Ste B, Hanover, MA 02339. TEL 781-347-4730, FAX 781-347-4732, info@maplestreetpress.com. Ed. Kurt Mensching.

796.357 USA ISSN 2157-555X
GV875.N4
MAPLE STREET PRESS YANKEES ANNUAL. Text in English. 2007. a. USD 12.99 per issue (effective 2011). back issues avail. **Document type:** *Handbook/Manual/Guide, Consumer.* **Description:** Focuses solely on the Bronx Bombers.
Formerly (until 2010): Bombers Broadside (1942-2377)
Published by: Maple Street Press, 155 Webster St, Ste B, Hanover, MA 02339. TEL 781-347-4730, FAX 781-347-4732, info@maplestreetpress.com. Ed. Cecilia Tan.

796.352 USA ISSN 1947-6590
▼ **MARYLAND GOLF JOURNAL.** Text in English. forthcoming 2010. m. USD 9.99 per issue (effective 2009). **Document type:** *Magazine, Consumer.* **Description:** Features articles on golf for Maryland.
Published by: In Publishing, 9769 NW 45 Ln, Miami, FL 33178. TEL 736-314-0456, info@miamigolfjournal.com.

796.352 USA ISSN 1947-6515
▼ **MASSACHUSETTS GOLF JOURNAL.** Text in English. forthcoming 2010. q. USD 9.99 per issue (effective 2009). **Document type:** *Magazine, Consumer.* **Description:** Features articles on golf for Massachusetts.
Published by: In Publishing, 9769 NW 45 Ln, Miami, FL 33178. TEL 736-314-0456, info@miamigolfjournal.com.

796.352 USA
MASSGOLFER. Text in English. q.
Formerly: Massachusetts Golfer
Published by: Massachusetts Golf Association, 300 Arnold Palmer Blvd, Norton, MA 02766. TEL 774-430-9100, 800-356-2201, FAX 774-430-9101. Ed. Rick Dunfey. Circ: 50,000.

796.352 USA ISSN 1933-3234
GV970.3.M37
MASTERS ANNUAL. Text in English. 2004. a., latest 2007. GBP 23.99, EUR 29.20 per issue (effective 2010). adv. reprints avail. **Document type:** *Magazine, Consumer.*
Published by: (Augusta National Golf Club), John Wiley & Sons, Inc., 111 River St, Hoboken, NJ 07030. TEL 201-748-6000, FAX 201-748-6088, info@wiley.com, http://www.wiley.com/WileyCDA/.

796.352 JPN
THE MASTERS OF GOLF. Text in Japanese. 1997 (Oct.). q. (Apr., Jun., Oct., & Dec.). adv. **Document type:** *Consumer.* **Description:** Provides techniques for golf, information on golf tournaments, and features on the history and culture of golf.
Formerly: Golf - Meijin
Published by: Nikkei Business Publications Inc. (Subsidiary of: Nihon Keizai Shimbun, Inc.), 2-7-6 Hirakawa-cho, Chiyoda-ku, Tokyo, 102-8622, Japan. TEL 81-3-5210-8311, FAX 81-3-5210-8530, info@nikkeibp-america.com. Ed. Noriho Okudera. Pub. Jun'ichi Ogino. adv.: B&W page JPY 1,100,000, color page JPY 1,680,000; trim 210 x 280. Circ: 270,000. **Dist. in America by:** Nikkei Business Publications America Inc., 575 Fifth Ave, 20th Fl, New York, NY 10017.

796.334 GBR ISSN 0955-4947
MATCH. Text in English. 1979. w. GBP 51 domestic; GBP 70 in Europe & USA; GBP 75 elsewhere (effective 2010). adv. illus.; stat. back issues avail. **Document type:** *Magazine, Consumer.* **Description:** Features articles about celebrities, interviews, and the latest football news every week.
Formerly (until 1983): Match Weekly (0262-5601)
Related titles: Supplement(s): Match! Collector's Special. ISSN 1753-8459.
Published by: H. Bauer Publishing Ltd. (Subsidiary of: Bauer Media Group), Media House, Lynchwood, Peterborough, Cambridgeshire PE2 6EA, United Kingdom. TEL 44-1733-468000, http://www.bauer.co.uk. Ed. Nikki Palmer TEL 44-1733-468008. Adv. contact Dave Elliott TEL 44-1733-468158.

796.3 GBR ISSN 1364-4521
MATCH OF THE DAY; superstars! action! gossip!. Text in English. 1996. w. GBP 91.80; GBP 1.90 per issue (effective 2010). adv. **Document type:** *Magazine, Consumer.* **Description:** Provides coverage of the players, teams and personalities competing in the Premier League.
Published by: B B C Worldwide Ltd., Media Centre, 201 Wood Ln, London, W12 7TQ, United Kingdom. bbcworldwide@bbc.co.uk, http://www.bbcworldwide.com.

796.323 USA
MEN'S BASKETBALL MEDIA GUIDE. Text in English. 19??. a. charts; illus.; stat. back issues avail. **Document type:** *Handbook/Manual/Guide, Consumer.*
Former titles (until 1998): Men's Basketball Guide; (until 1996): Men's Basketball Media Guide; (until 1992): Basketball (Big Ten Conference Men's Edition)
Related titles: Online - full text ed.: free (effective 2011).
Published by: Big Ten Conference, 1500 W Higgins Rd, Park Ridge, IL 60068. TEL 847-696-1010, FAX 847-696-1150.

796.352 USA ISSN 1042-7678
MET GOLFER. Text in English. 1983. bi-m. free to members (effective 2005). adv. **Document type:** *Magazine, Consumer.* **Description:** For amateur and professional golfers in the New York metropolitan area. Covers events, tournaments, travel, fashion and personalities.
Published by: T P G Sports, Inc., 6160 Summit Dr, Ste 375, Minneapolis, MN 55430. TEL 763-595-0808, 800-597-5656, FAX 763-595-0016, info@tpgsports.com, http://www.tpgsports.com/. Ed. Morin Bishop. Circ: 100,000 (paid).

796.333 ITA ISSN 1724-6792
LA META RUGBY. Text in Italian. 2000. m. EUR 52 domestic (effective 2008). **Document type:** *Magazine, Consumer.*
Published by: Cantelli Editore Srl, Via Saliceto 22c, Castelmaggiore, BO 40013, Italy. TEL 39-051-6328811, FAX 39-051-6328815, cantelli.editore@cantelli.net, http://www.cantelli.net.

796.352 USA ISSN 1063-2425
METRO GOLF; a magazine for area golfers. Text in English. 1991. 6/yr. USD 3 newsstand/cover (effective 2007). adv. bk.rev. **Document type:** *Magazine, Consumer.* **Description:** Covers people, places, events and tournaments important to the game.
Published by: Summerville Press, Inc., 3254 N St., NW, Washington, DC 20007. TEL 202-812-2750, FAX 202-625-9310. Ed. Margaret Heimbold. Pub. Margaret B Heimbold. Adv. contact Eric Gordon. page USD 5,000.

796.352 USA ISSN 1080-3874
METROLINA GOLF MAGAZINE; serving the Charlotte metropolitan area. Text in English. 1992. 8/yr. USD 8; USD 16 foreign. adv. bk.rev. back issues avail. **Document type:** *Magazine, Consumer.* **Description:** Covers news and events of interest to golfers living in or visiting North and South Carolina. Profiles local players and covers regional tournaments. Reviews area golf courses and travel destinations.
—CCC.
Address: PO Box 1027, Davidson, NC 28036-1027. TEL 704-895-9908, FAX 704-892-5899. Ed., Pub., Adv. contact Reid Spencer. Circ: 24,000.

796.352 USA ISSN 1071-2313
MICHIGAN GOLFER. Text in English. 1980. 6/yr. USD 15; USD 2.95 newsstand/cover (effective 2003). adv. **Document type:** *Magazine, Consumer.* **Description:** Covers golf events and news; includes calendar of events, technical advice, new products, and travel information.
Published by: Great Lakes Sports Publications, Inc., 3588 Plymouth Rd, Ste 245, Ann Arbor, MI 48105-2603. TEL 734-507-0241, FAX 734-434-4765, info@glsp.com, http://www.glsp.com. Ed. Terry Moore. Pub., Adv. contact Art McCafferty. Circ: 22,500.

796.352 USA ISSN 1531-1732
MICHIGAN LINKS MAGAZINE. Text in English. 1998. bi-m. USD 2.95 newsstand/cover (effective 2001). adv. 32 p./no.; back issues avail. **Document type:** *Magazine, Consumer.* **Description:** Includes news and trends, information on local courses and private clubs, tournament previews, personality profiles and history.
Published by: T P G Sports, Inc., 6160 Summit Dr, Ste 375, Minneapolis, MN 55430. TEL 763-595-0808, 800-597-5656, FAX 763-595-0016, info@tpgsports.com. Pub. Robert Fallen. Adv. contact Kevin Hartzell TEL 763-595-0808 ext 100. B&W page USD 3,163, color page USD 3,515; trim 8.25 x 11. Circ: 37,581 (paid).

796.352 USA ISSN 1058-8590
MID-OHIO GOLFER. Text in English. 1991. 18/yr. USD 13.95 (effective 2001). adv. **Description:** Covers golf in central Ohio.
Published by: C M Media Inc., 5255 Sinclair Rd, PO Box 29913, Columbus, OH 43229. TEL 614-848-4653, FAX 614-848-3838.

796.352 UAE ISSN 1816-1146
MIDDLE EAST GOLFER. Text mainly in English. 2005. m. AED 90 domestic; AED 109 GCC countries; AED 149 elsewhere (effective 2007). adv. **Document type:** *Magazine, Consumer.*
Published by: I T P Consumer Publishing (Subsidiary of: I T P Publishing Group), PO Box 500024, Dubai, United Arab Emirates. TEL 971-4-2108000, FAX 971-4-2108080, info@itp.com, http://www.itp.com. Ed. Robbie Greenfield. Adv. contact Samer Murad. page USD 5,500; trim 210 x 297.

796.33 FRA ISSN 0994-6187
MIDI OLYMPIQUE - RUGBYRAMA; le journal du rugby. Abbreviated title: Midol. Text in French. 1931. bi-w. EUR 139.50 (effective 2010). adv. illus. **Document type:** *Newspaper, Consumer.* **Description:** Covers rugby action in France and worldwide.
Formerly (until 1946): France Olympique (0994-6179); Which was formed by the merger of (1929-1931): Midi Olympique (0994-6160); (1920-1931): Auto et Sport (0994-6225)
Related titles: Online - full text ed.; ◆ Supplement(s): Midol Mag. ISSN 1274-5707.
Published by: Groupe La Depeche du Midi, Ave Jean Baylet, Toulouse, 31095, France. TEL 33-5-62113300, FAX 33-5-62113614, http://www.ladepeche.com.

796.333 FRA ISSN 1274-5707
MIDOL MAG. Text in French. m. illus. **Document type:** *Consumer.* **Description:** Covers all aspects of the world of rugby.
Related titles: ◆ Supplement to: Midi Olympique - Rugbyrama. ISSN 0994-6187.
Published by: Groupe La Depeche du Midi, Ave Jean Baylet, Toulouse, 31095, France. TEL 33-5-62113300, FAX 33-5-62113614, http://www.ladepeche.com.

796.352 USA
MIDWEST GOLF NEWS. Text in English. m.
Address: PO Box 529, Anna, IL 62906. TEL 618-833-2158. Ed. Mike Fitzgerald.

796.3522 DEU ISSN 1861-3276
MINIGOLF MAGAZIN. Text in German. 1973. 5/yr. EUR 12 (effective 2009). adv. bk.rev. **Document type:** *Magazine, Consumer.* **Description:** Contains information about competition in mini-golfing.
Formerly (until 2005): Bahnengolfer (0178-2436)
Published by: Deutscher Minigolfsport-Verband, Panzerleite 49, Bamberg, 96049, Germany. TEL 49-951-2974196, FAX 49-951-2974197, info@minigolfsport.de. Ed. Achim Braungart-Zink. Circ: 1,100 (controlled).

796.352 NLD ISSN 2210-8084
▼ **MINIGOLF NIEUWS.** Text in Dutch. 2010. q. **Document type:** *Newsletter.*
Published by: Nederlandse Minigolf Bond, Kloversdonk 305, Apeldoorn, 7326 AT, Netherlands. TEL 31-55-5411237, http://www.fnmb.nl.

796.352 USA ISSN 1062-1105
MINNESOTA GOLFER. Text in English. 1973. bi-m. USD 12 (effective 2001); USD 2.95. adv. 48 p./no.; **Document type:** *Magazine, Consumer.* **Description:** Reports on players, courses, events and news in the state.
Related titles: Online - full text ed.; Special ed(s).: Minnesota Golfer. Annual Directory. 2000.
Published by: (Minnesota Golf Association), T P G Sports, Inc., 6160 Summit Dr, Ste 375, Minneapolis, MN 55430. TEL 763-595-0808, 800-597-5656, info@tpgsports.com, http://www.tpgsports.com. Ed. W P Ryan. Pub. Robert Fallen. R&P Joseph Oberle TEL 763-595-0808 ext 114. Adv. contact Kevin Hartzell TEL 763-595-0808 ext 100. page USD 4,900; trim 11 x 8.5. Circ: 68,000.

796.334 USA
MINNESOTA SOCCER TIMES. Text in English. 1991. bi-m. free to members (effective 2011). adv. **Document type:** *Magazine, Consumer.* **Description:** Covers tournament rules and profiles outstanding players.
Related titles: Online - full text ed.: free (effective 2011).

Published by: (Minnesota Youth Soccer Association), Varsity Communications, Ltd. (Subsidiary of: Mavety Media Group), 12510 33rd Ave NE, Ste 300, Seattle, WA 98125. TEL 206-367-2420, 888-367-6420, FAX 206-363-9099, stephens@varsitycommunications.com, http://www.varsitycommunications.com/.

796.352 ITA ISSN 1128-0352
IL MONDO DEL GOLF. Text in Italian. 1979. m. EUR 42 (effective 2008). adv. bk.rev. illus. **Document type:** *Magazine, Consumer.*
Formerly: Golf Digest Italia
Published by: Casa Editrice Scode SpA, Corso Monforte 36, Milan, 20122, Italy. TEL 39-02-76002874, FAX 39-02-76004905, info@scode.it, http://www.scode.it.

796 FRA ISSN 1959-0164
MONDOSPORTS; l'information sportive vue par la presse etrangere. Variant title: Mondo Sports. Text in French. 2007. m. **Document type:** *Magazine, Consumer.*
Published by: Mondo Medias, 16 Rue des Charettes, Rouen, 76000, France.

796.352 USA
MOUNTAIN WEST GOLF. Variant title: M W Golf. Text in English. 1972. m. USD 21.95 (effective 2008). adv. back issues avail.; reprints avail. **Document type:** *Magazine, Trade.* **Description:** Covers golf courses, resort facilities, competitions, equipment, techniques and instruction, travel, on-course living and other aspects of golf in the Mountain West.
Formerly (until 2003): Idaho Golf
Related titles: Online - full text ed.
Published by: Harris Publishing, Inc. (Idaho Falls), 360 B St, Idaho Falls, ID 83402-3547. TEL 208-524-7000, 800-638-0135, FAX 208-522-5241, customerservice@harrispublishing.com, http://www.harrispublishing.com. Ed. Steve Smede TEL 208-542-2254. Pub. Jason Harris TEL 208-524-7000 ext 2222. Adv. contact Janet Chase TEL 208-542-2221. color page USD 3,071; trim 8 x 10.75. Circ: 25,000.

796.352 USA
MYRTLE BEACH GOLF. Text in English. 1992. m. USD 9. adv. back issues avail. **Document type:** *Newspaper.* **Description:** Informs visitors to Myrtle Beach golf courses on packages and events; profiles local golf pros.
Related titles: Microfilm ed.
Published by: Sun Publishing Company, 914 Frontage Rd E, Myrtle Beach, SC 29577. TEL 803-626-8555, FAX 803-626-0356. Ed. John Braiser. Adv. contact John Cioni.

MYRTLE BEACH GOLF HOLIDAY MAGAZINE. *see* TRAVEL AND TOURISM

796.352 USA
N A G A NEWSLETTER. Text in English. s-a. **Document type:** *Newsletter.*
Published by: National Amputee Golf Association, 11 Walnut Hill Rd, Amherst, NH 03031. TEL 800-633-6242, b1naga@aol.com. Ed. Bob Wilson. R&P Jim Coombes. Adv. contact Patty Johnson.

796 USA ISSN 0736-5209
GV877
N C A A BASEBALL RULES. Text in English. 19??. a. USD 7.80 per issue (effective 2011). adv. illus. Index. back issues avail. **Document type:** *Handbook/Manual/Guide, Trade.* **Description:** Covers official signals, interpretations, and rulings.
Supersedes in part (in 1983): N C A A Baseball; Which was formerly (until 1980): Official National Collegiate Athletic Association Baseball Guide (0466-1478); (until 1958): College Base Ball Guide
Related titles: Online - full text ed.: free (effective 2011).
Published by: National Collegiate Athletic Association, 700 W Washington St, PO Box 6222, Indianapolis, IN 46206. TEL 317-917-6222, FAX 317-917-6888, http://www.ncaa.org/. Ed. Ty Halpin.

796.323 USA
N C A A BASKETBALL. OFFICIAL (YEAR) MEN'S BASKETBALL RECORDS BOOK. Text in English. 1923. a. USD 12.50 per issue (effective 2009). stat. **Document type:** *Report, Trade.* **Description:** Contains individual and team records for all divisions, including coaching records, a timeline of rule changes, photos, statistical leaders, all-American teams, game results from the preceding year, and schedules for the current year.
Former titles (until 1999): Official N C A A Basketball. The Official (Year) Men's College Basketball Records Book (1089-5280); (until 1997): N C A A Basketball (1089-473X); (until 1995): Official N C A A Basketball (1063-1089); (until 1992): N C A A Basketball (0276-1017); Which incorporated (1981-1982): Basketball Records (0733-8376); Which was formerly (until 1980): Official National Collegiate Athletic Association Basketball Guide
Published by: National Collegiate Athletic Association, 700 W Washington St, PO Box 6222, Indianapolis, IN 46206. TEL 317-917-6222, FAX 317-917-6888, esummers@ncaa.org, http://www.ncaa.org/. Circ: 12,000.

796.332 USA ISSN 0738-1611
GV956.8
N C A A FOOTBALL RECORDS. Key Title: Football Records. Text in English. 19??. a. stat. **Document type:** *Report, Trade.*
Formerly (until 1979): The Official National Collegiate Athletic Association Football Records (0145-2630)
Published by: National Collegiate Athletic Association, 700 W Washington St, PO Box 6222, Indianapolis, IN 46206. TEL 317-917-6222, FAX 317-917-6888, esummers@ncaa.org, http://www.ncaa.org/.

796.33 USA ISSN 0736-5160
GV956.8
N C A A FOOTBALL RULES AND INTERPRETATIONS. Text in English. 19??. a. USD 7.80 per issue (effective 2011). adv. illus. back issues avail. **Document type:** *Handbook/Manual/Guide, Trade.* **Description:** Contains diagrams of playing areas, official signals, and official interpretations and rulings.
Formerly (until 1979): Official National Collegiate Athletic Association Football Rules and Interpretations (0094-5226)
Related titles: Online - full text ed.: free (effective 2011).
Published by: National Collegiate Athletic Association, 700 W Washington St, PO Box 6222, Indianapolis, IN 46206. TEL 317-917-6222, FAX 317-917-6888, http://www.ncaa.org/. Ed. Ty Halpin.

796.32 USA ISSN 1042-3877
GV885.45
N C A A MEN'S AND WOMEN'S BASKETBALL RULES AND INTERPRETATIONS. Text in English. 1988. a. USD 7.80 per issue (effective 2011). adv. illus. back issues avail. **Document type:** *Handbook/Manual/Guide, Trade.* **Description:** Contains diagrams of playing areas, official signals, and official interpretations and rulings.
Formed by the merger of (1986-1988): N C A A Women's Basketball Rules (0882-6293); (1983-1988): N C A A Men's Basketball Rules and Interpretations (0736-5187); Which was formerly (until 1983): N C A A Basketball Rules and Interpretations; (until 1980): Official National Collegiate Athletic Association Basketball Rules and Interpretations (0163-2817)
Related titles: Online - full text ed.: free (effective 2011).
Published by: National Collegiate Athletic Association, 700 W Washington St, PO Box 6222, Indianapolis, IN 46206. TEL 317-917-6222, FAX 317-917-6888, http://www.ncaa.org/.

796.32 USA ISSN 1042-3869
GV885.45
N C A A MEN'S AND WOMEN'S ILLUSTRATED BASKETBALL RULES. Text in English. 19??. a., latest 2006. illus. back issues avail. **Document type:** *Handbook/Manual/Guide, Trade.* **Description:** Contains diagrams of playing areas, official signals, and official interpretations and rulings.
Former titles (until 1988): N C A A Illustrated Men's Basketball Rules (0736-5179); (until 1983): N C A A Illustrated Basketball Rules (0272-5754); Official National Collegiate Athletic Association Basketball Rules (0094-5234)
Related titles: Online - full text ed.
Published by: National Collegiate Athletic Association, 700 W Washington St, PO Box 6222, Indianapolis, IN 46206. TEL 317-917-6222, FAX 317-917-6888, esummers@ncaa.org, http://www.ncaa.org/.

796.334 USA
GV943.4
N C A A MEN'S AND WOMEN'S SOCCER RULES AND INTERPRETATIONS. Text in English. 19??. a. USD 7.80 per issue (effective 2011). illus. back issues avail. **Document type:** *Handbook/Manual/Guide, Trade.* **Description:** Contains diagrams of playing areas, official signals, and official interpretations and rulings.
Supersedes: N C A A Men's Soccer Rules (0735-0368); Formerly: Official National Collegiate Athletic Association Soccer Guide
Related titles: Online - full text ed.: free (effective 2011).
Published by: National Collegiate Athletic Association, 700 W Washington St, PO Box 6222, Indianapolis, IN 46206. TEL 317-917-6222, FAX 317-917-6888, http://www.ncaa.org/.

796.323 USA
N C A A MEN'S BASKETBALL. Text in English. a. stat. **Document type:** *Report, Trade.* **Description:** Contains individual and team records for men's basketball and covers statistical leaders, conference standings, coaches' records, and much more.
Published by: National Collegiate Athletic Association, 700 W Washington St, PO Box 6222, Indianapolis, IN 46206. TEL 317-917-6222, FAX 317-917-6888, esummers@ncaa.org, http://www.ncaa.org/.

796 USA ISSN 0742-4361
N C A A MEN'S LACROSSE RULES. Text in English. 19??. a. USD 7.80 per issue (effective 2011). illus. back issues avail. **Document type:** *Handbook/Manual/Guide, Trade.* **Description:** Contains diagrams of playing areas, official signals, and official interpretations and rulings.
Former titles (until 1984): N C A A Lacrosse Rules (0736-7775); (until 1983): N C A A Lacrosse (0732-9059); (until 1980): Official N C A A Lacrosse Guide
Related titles: Online - full text ed.: free (effective 2011).
Published by: National Collegiate Athletic Association, 700 W Washington St, PO Box 6222, Indianapolis, IN 46206. TEL 317-917-6222, FAX 317-917-6888, http://www.ncaa.org/.

796.323 USA
N C A A WOMEN'S BASKETBALL. Text in English. a. stat. **Description:** Contains individual and team records for women's collegiate basketball, along with information on statistical leaders, conference standings, coaches' records, and much more.
Published by: National Collegiate Athletic Association, 700 W Washington St, PO Box 6222, Indianapolis, IN 46206. TEL 317-917-6222, FAX 317-917-6888, esummers@ncaa.org, http://www.ncaa.org/.

796.3 796.092 USA
N F H S COACHES' QUARTERLY. Text in English. 19??. q. USD 15 (effective 2009). adv. **Document type:** *Magazine, Trade.* **Description:** Provides the high school coaches with all the latest officials rules changes and interpretations, as well as regular features in the areas of health and safety, citizenship and risk management.
Published by: National Federation of State High School Associations, PO Box 690, Indianapolis, IN 46206. TEL 317-972-6900, 800-776-3462, FAX 317-822-5700, info@nfhs.org. Circ: 30,000.

796.077 USA
N F H S OFFICIALS' QUARTERLY. Text in English. 199?. q. USD 15 (effective 2009). adv. **Document type:** *Magazine, Trade.* **Description:** Provides the high school officials with all the latest officials rules changes and interpretations, as well as regular features in the areas of health and safety and citizenship.
Published by: National Federation of State High School Associations, PO Box 690, Indianapolis, IN 46206. TEL 317-972-6900, 800-776-3462, FAX 317-822-5700, info@nfhs.org. Circ: 135,000.

796.962 USA
N H L HOME ICE. (National Hockey League) Text in English. 2002. q. adv. **Document type:** *Magazine, Consumer.* **Description:** Takes you behind the scenes of the NHL and delivering the overall excitement of the league.
Published by: Professional Sports Publications (P S P), 519 8th Ave, Ste 2500, New York, NY 10018. TEL 212-697-1460, FAX 212-286-8154, mlewis@pspsports.com, http://www.pspsports.com. adv.: color page USD 55,000; trim 5.375 x 8.375.

796.33 NZL ISSN 1175-1088
N Z RUGBY WORLD. (New Zealand) Text in English. 1997. 10/yr. back issues avail. **Document type:** *Magazine, Consumer.*
Formerly (until 1999): N Z Rugby (1174-2046)
Related titles: Online - full content ed.
Indexed: SD, T02.
Published by: Image Centre Publishing, 34 Westmoreland St, P.O. Box 78070 Grey Lynn, Ponsonby, Auckland, New Zealand. TEL 64-9-360-5701, FAX 64-9-360-5702. Ed. Gregor Paul. Adv. contact Matthew Hewetson.

796.357 USA ISSN 0278-1867
GV863.A1
NATIONAL BASEBALL HALL OF FAME & MUSEUM YEARBOOK. Text in English. 1981. a. USD 9. adv. **Document type:** *Yearbook, Trade.* **Description:** Includes text and photographs on all 232 Hall of Famers.
Related titles: Online - full text ed.
Published by: National Baseball Hall of Fame, Main St, Box 590, Cooperstown, NY 13326. TEL 607-547-7200. Ed., R&P, Adv. contact John Ralph. Circ: 30,000.

794.7 USA ISSN 0747-3265
NATIONAL BILLIARD NEWS. Text in English. m.
Address: PO Box 807, Northville, MI 48167. TEL 313-348-0053, FAX 313-348-7828. Ed. Conrad J Burkman. Circ: 14,500.

796.35 USA ISSN 1047-6474
NATIONAL CROQUET CALENDAR. Text in English. 1988. bi-m. USD 35; USD 40 foreign. adv. **Document type:** *Magazine, Consumer.* **Description:** Covers championship croquet. Features national and international news, strategy articles, product information, and tournament schedules and results.
Published by: Garth Eliassen, Ed. & Pub., PO Box 208, Monmouth, OR 97361-0208. TEL 503-838-5697. Circ: 400 (paid).

NATIONAL FOOTBALL LEAGUE TEAM TRACKER. *see* CHILDREN AND YOUTH—For

796.352 ZAF ISSN 1992-2809
NATIONAL GOLF NETWORK. Text in English. 2006. a. adv.
Published by: Highbury Safika Media, PO Box 8145, Roggebaai, 8012, South Africa. TEL 27-21-4160141, FAX 27-21-4180132, info@hsm.co.za. adv.: color page ZAR 32,850. Circ: 160,000 (controlled).

NATIONAL HOCKEY LEAGUE. OFFICIAL GUIDE & RECORD BOOK. *see* SPORTS AND GAMES—Abstracting, Bibliographies, Statistics

796.357 USA ISSN 0734-6905
GV863.A1
NATIONAL PASTIME; baseball in the Peach State. Text in English. 1982. a. USD 14.95 per issue to non-members; free to members (effective 2010). adv. **Document type:** *Journal, Consumer.* **Description:** Provides articles on all aspects of baseball history.
Related titles: Online - full text ed.
Indexed: A26, E08, G06, G07, G08, I05, I06, I07, S09, S23, SD, SportS.
Published by: Society for American Baseball Research, Inc., 812 Huron Rd, Ste 719, Cleveland, OH 44115. TEL 216-575-0500, 800-969-7227, FAX 216-575-0502, info@sabr.org.

796.333 CAN
NATIONAL RUGBY POST. Text in English. 1985. 6/yr. CAD 20 domestic; CAD 27 in United States; CAD 39 elsewhere. adv. bk.rev. **Document type:** *Newspaper.*
Published by: (Canadian Rugby Union), National Rugby Post, 13228 76 St, Edmonton, AB T5C 1B6, Canada. TEL 403-476-0268, FAX 403-473-1066. Ed. Don Whidden. Pub. D Graham. Circ: 6,000.

796.323 USA
NATIONAL WHEELCHAIR BASKETBALL ASSOCIATION. DIRECTORY. Text in English. 1960. a. USD 50. **Document type:** *Directory.*
Published by: National Wheelchair Basketball Association, 110 Seaton Bldg, University of Kentucky, Lexington, KY 40506. Ed. Stan Labanowich. Circ: 350.

796.323 USA
NATIONAL WHEELCHAIR BASKETBALL ASSOCIATION. NEWSLETTER. Text in English. s-w. (Nov.-Mar.). membership only. **Document type:** *Newsletter.*
Published by: National Wheelchair Basketball Association, 110 Seaton Bldg, University of Kentucky, Lexington, KY 40506.

796.334 GBR
NATIONWIDE FOOTBALL ANNUAL. Text in English. 1887. a. GBP 6.99 per issue (effective 2010). **Description:** Features facts, stats and information relevant to the football game worldwide.
Former titles (until 2008): News of the World Football Annual (0305-4780); Which superseded in part: News of the World Football and Sports Annual; News of the World and Empire News Football Annual
Published by: Invincible Press, Flat 78, 85 Fulham Palace Rd, London, Mddx W6 8JA, United Kingdom. Ed. Stuart Barnes.

796.352 USA ISSN 1525-1268
NATURAL GOLFER. Text in English. 1999. 5/yr. adv.
Published by: Lineal Publishing Co., 2400 W Hassell Rd, Hoffman Estates, IL 60195. TEL 847-781-3000 ext 147, FAX 847-781-0280. Pub. Peter Lineal.

796.352 USA
NEBRASKA GOLF. Text in English. 2002. s-a. adv. **Document type:** *Magazine, Consumer.*
Published by: (Nebraska Golf Association), T P G Sports, Inc., 6160 Summit Dr, Ste 375, Minneapolis, MN 55430. TEL 763-595-0808, 800-597-5656, FAX 763-595-0016, info@tpgsports.com. adv.: color page USD 1,495; trim 8.25 x 10.875. Circ: 16,175.

796.333 NLD ISSN 1878-9269
NEDERLANDS RUGBY MAGAZINE. Text in Dutch. 2005. q. EUR 17.50 (effective 2011). adv. **Document type:** *Magazine, Consumer.*
Published by: Haagsche Rugby Club, Theo Maan Bouwmeesterlaan 800, The Hague, 2597 HM, Netherlands. TEL 31-70-3244955, FAX 31-70-3282573, info@haagscherugbyclub.com, http://www.haagscherugbyclub.nl.

796.342 USA
NET FRIEND NEWS. Text in English. 1978. bi-m. membership. **Document type:** *Newsletter.*
Published by: American Tennis Federation, 200 Castlewood Dr, North Palm Beach, FL 33408. TEL 407-848-1026, FAX 407-863-8984. Ed. Brad Patterson. Circ: 200 (controlled).

796.342 USA
NET NEWS. Text in English. 1992. bi-m. USD 5. adv. bk.rev. **Document type:** *Magazine, Trade.* **Description:** Covers leagues and scores and profiles personalities.

S

Published by: (Atlanta Lawn Tennis Association), New South Publishing, 1303 Hightower Trail, Ste 101, Atlanta, GA 30350-2919. TEL 770-650-1102, FAX 770-650-2848. Ed. Cheryl Fenton. Pub., Adv. contact John Hanna. R&P Larry Lebovitz. B&W page USD 3,320, color page USD 4,820; trim 10.88 x 8.13. Circ: 50,000 (paid).

796.32 GBR ISSN 0959-1117
NETBALL MAGAZINE. Text in English. 1933-1937; resumed 1944. bi-m. free to members (effective 2009). adv. bk.rev. back issues avail. **Document type:** *Magazine, Consumer.* **Description:** Covers all the latest Netball news and everything one needs to know about England's top female team sport.
Formerly (until 1989): Netball (0144-0810)
Related titles: Online - full text ed.
Indexed: SportS.
Published by: All England Netball Association, Netball House, 9 Paynes Park, Hitchin, Herts SG5 1EH, United Kingdom. TEL 44-1462-442344, FAX 44-1462-442343, info@englandnetball.co.uk. Ed. Nikki Richardson.

796.323 AUS ISSN 1324-8367
NETBALL WORLD. Text in English. 1995. 9/yr. **Document type:** *Magazine, Consumer.*
Indexed: SD.
Published by: J P Publications, PO Box 2805, Taren Point, NSW 2229, Australia. TEL 61-2-95427335, FAX 61-2-95427323, jppublic@ozemail.com.au, http://www.magna.com.au/~iphala.

796.323 AUS
NETBALLER ECONTACT. Text in English. 1981. 10/yr. **Document type:** *Newsletter.* **Description:** Covers administration, coaching, umpiring, junior development, talent identification, events and other news for all those interested in netball.
Former titles (until 2003): Netballer Contact (Online); (until 2002): Netballer Contact (Print) (1442-3316); (until 1999): Victorian Netballer (1324-8472); (until 1985): Victorian Netball News; (until 1984): Netball News Victoria
Media: Online - full text.
Published by: Netball Victoria, PO Box 60, North Melbourne, VIC 3051, Australia. TEL 61-3-93212222, FAX 61-3-93212233, reception@netballvic.com.au, http://www.netballvic.com.au. Ed. Kate Bentley. R&P, Adv. contact Marne James. Circ: 3,000.

796.333 GBR ISSN 1752-8186
NETWORKS MAGAZINE. Text in English. 2004. 3/yr. GBP 3 newsstand/cover (effective 2009). back issues avail. **Document type:** *Magazine, Consumer.* **Description:** Provides information about foot ball matches.
Related titles: Online - full text ed.: free (effective 2009).
Published by: Hampshire Football Association, William Pickford House, Winklebury Football Complex, Winklebury Way, Basingstoke, RG23 8BF, United Kingdom. TEL 44-1256-853000, FAX 44-1256-357973, Info@HampshireFA.com.

796.352 USA ISSN 1947-6531
▼ **NEVADA GOLF JOURNAL.** Text in English. forthcoming 2010. m. USD 9.99 per issue (effective 2009). **Document type:** *Magazine, Consumer.* **Description:** Features articles on golf for Nevada.
Published by: In Publishing, 9769 NW 45 Ln, Miami, FL 33178. TEL 736-314-0456, info@miamigolfjournal.com.

796.357 USA
▼ **NEW ENGLAND BASEBALL JOURNAL.** Text in English. 2010. 10/yr. USD 34.99 (effective 2011). adv. **Document type:** *Magazine, Consumer.*
Published by: Seamans Media, 1400 Hancock St, Seventh Fl, Quincy, MA 02169. TEL 617-773-9955, FAX 617-773-6688, michelle@seamansmedia.com, http://www.seamansmedia.com. Ed. Eric Beato. Pub., Adv. contact Eric Seamans.

796.352 USA
NEW ENGLAND GOLF MAGAZINE. Text in English. 1989. bi-m. USD 19.97 (effective 2005). adv. **Document type:** *Magazine, Consumer.* **Description:** Focuses on local events, tournaments, courses and players.
Published by: New England Golf Magazine, Inc., 20 Park Plaza, Ste. 630, Boston, MA 02116. TEL 800-627-7012, FAX 508-840-3209. Ed. Kevin Morris. Pubs. Gerald Sperry, Mark Mitchell. Circ: 50,000.

796.34 USA
NEW ENGLAND LACROSSE. Text in English. 2008. 10/yr. USD 34.99 (effective 2011). adv. **Document type:** *Magazine, Consumer.*
Published by: Seamans Media, 1400 Hancock St, Seventh Fl, Quincy, MA 02169. TEL 617-773-9955, FAX 617-773-6688, michelle@seamansmedia.com, http://www.seamansmedia.com. Ed. Eric Beato. Pub., Adv. contact Eric Seamans.

796.352 USA ISSN 1947-6418
▼ **NEW HAMPSHIRE GOLF JOURNAL.** Text in English. 2010 (Oct.). m. USD 9.99 per issue (effective 2009). **Document type:** *Magazine, Consumer.* **Description:** Features articles on golf for New Hampshire.
Published by: In Publishing, 9769 NW 45 Ln, Miami, FL 33178. TEL 736-314-0456, info@miamigolfjournal.com.

796.3 USA ISSN 1947-6388
▼ **NEW JERSEY GOLF JOURNAL.** Text in English. forthcoming 2010. m. USD 9.99 per issue (effective 2009). **Document type:** *Magazine, Consumer.* **Description:** Features articles on golf for New Jersey.
Published by: In Publishing, 9769 NW 45 Ln, Miami, FL 33178. TEL 736-314-0456, info@miamigolfjournal.com.

796.323 USA
NEW JERSEY NETS OFFICIAL YEARBOOK. Text in English. a. USD 12 newsstand/cover (effective 2000). **Document type:** *Magazine, Consumer.* **Description:** Filled with exciting color photos of Nets players and coaches along with interesting facts and trivia about the team.
Published by: New Jersey Nets Publications, 390 Murray Hill Pkwy, East Rutherford, NJ 07073. TEL 800-765-6387.

796.352 USA ISSN 1947-6523
▼ **NEW YORK GOLF JOURNAL.** Text in English. forthcoming 2010. m. USD 9.99 per issue (effective 2009). **Document type:** *Magazine, Consumer.* **Description:** Features articles on golf for New York.
Published by: In Publishing, 9769 NW 45 Ln, Miami, FL 33178. TEL 736-314-0456, info@miamigolfjournal.com.

796.332 USA
NEW YORK JETS OFFICIAL YEARBOOK. Text in English. 1971. a. USD 7. charts; illus.; stat. **Document type:** *Magazine, Consumer.*
Published by: (New York Jets Football Club Inc.), New York Jets, 26 Green St., Newbury, MA 01951-1708. Ed. Ken Ilchukmas. Circ: 100,000.

796.323 USA
NEW YORK KNICKS YEARBOOK; official guide and record book. Text in English. 1947. a. USD 10 per issue. adv. charts; illus.; stat. reprints avail.
Published by: (New York Knickerbockers Basketball Club), Madison Square Garden Corporation (Subsidiary of: Cablevision), 2 Pennsylvania Plaza, New York, NY 10121. TEL 212-465-6000, FAX 212-465-6498. Ed. Dennis D'Agostino. Circ: 20,000.

796.3 USA ISSN 1081-6461
NEW YORK SPORTSCENE. Text in English. m. USD 29.95; USD 2.95 newsstand/cover (effective 2001). adv. **Description:** Covers a wide range of sports for fans in the New York metropolitan area.
Published by: New York Sportscene Enterprises, 990 Motor Pkwy, Central Islip, NY 11722. TEL 631-435-8890, FAX 631-435-8925. Ed. Eric Justic. Pub. Mike Cutino. adv.: B&W page USD 2,900, color page USD 4,200; bleed 8.25 x 11.125.

796.352 NZL
NEW ZEALAND GOLF GAZETTE. Text in English. 1997 (Dec.). m. NZD 35 (effective 2008). adv. **Document type:** *Newspaper, Consumer.* **Description:** Contains club, provincial, national and international news, features, course reviews, and columns by professionals in the industry.
Address: Silverdale, PO Box 368, Auckland, New Zealand. Circ: 15,000 (paid and controlled).

796.352 NZL ISSN 1176-9556
NEW ZEALAND GOLF MAGAZINE. Text in English. 1994. 11/yr. NZD 79 domestic; NZD 169 South Pacific; NZD 270 elsewhere (effective 2008). adv. **Document type:** *Magazine, Consumer.*
Former titles (until 2005): Golf Update (1173-7158); (until 1995): New Zealand Golf Update (1173-017X)
Address: PO Box 36-257, Northcote, Auckland, New Zealand. TEL 64-9-4809264, FAX 64-9-4809266, http://www.nzgolfmagazine.co.nz. Ed. Ian Hepenstall. Pub., Adv. contact Geoff Witton.

NICKLAUS; enjoy the game of life. *see* LIFESTYLE

796.342 DEU
NIEDERRHEIN TENNIS. Text in German. 1998. 6/yr. EUR 21 (effective 2010). adv. **Document type:** *Magazine, Consumer.*
Published by: (Tennisverband Niederrhein e.V.), Vereinigte Verlagsanstalten GmbH, Hoeherweg 278, Duesseldorf, 40231, Germany. TEL 49-211-73570, FAX 49-211-7357123, info@vva.de, http://www.vva.de. Adv. contact Regina Pheiler. color page EUR 2,880. Circ: 20,395 (controlled).

796.357 USA ISSN 1188-9330
GV862.5 CODEN: NNENFS
➤ **NINE**; a journal of baseball history & culture. Text in English. 1992. s-a. USD 52 combined subscription domestic to individuals (print & online eds.); USD 72 combined subscription foreign to individuals (print & online eds.); USD 88 combined subscription domestic to institutions (print & online eds.); USD 108 combined subscription foreign to institutions (print & online eds.); USD 29 per issue to individuals; USD 48 per issue to institutions (effective 2011). adv. bk.rev.; film rev. illus.; stat. back issues avail. **Document type:** *Journal, Academic/Scholarly.* **Description:** Covers studies of all historical aspects of baseball, centering on the societal and cultural implications of the game wherever in the world it is played.
Related titles: Online - full text ed.: ISSN 1534-1844. 2000.
Indexed: A01, A03, A08, A22, A26, AmH&L, CA, E01, E08, G08, G09, HistAb, I05, I06, I07, MLA-IB, P02, P10, P48, P53, P54, PEI, PQC, S02, S03, S09, S23, SD, SOPODA, SociolAb, T02.
—IE. CCC.
Published by: University of Nebraska Press, 1111 Lincoln Mall, Lincoln, NE 68588. TEL 402-472-3581, FAX 402-472-6214, pressmail@unl.edu. Ed. Trey Strecker. Adv. contact Joyce Gettman TEL 402-472-8330. Circ: 250. **Subscr. to:** PO Box 84555, Lincoln, NE 68501. TEL 402-472-8536, 800-848-6224, FAX 800-272-6817, journals@unlnotes.unl.edu.

796.332 HRV ISSN 1331-4262
NOGOMET. Text in Croatian. 1998. m. HRK 240 (effective 2002). adv. **Document type:** *Magazine, Consumer.*
Related titles: Online - full text ed.
Published by: Zri-Sport d.o.o., Prisavlje 2, Zagreb, 10000, Croatia. TEL 385-1-6060840, FAX 385-1-6159606, urednistvo@zri-sport.hr. Ed. Leo Miler.

796.3 GBR ISSN 2042-2288
▼ **NON LEAGUE 24.** Text in English. 2009. m. **Document type:** *Magazine, Trade.* **Description:** Contains football news.
Published by: Non League News Ltd., c/o Express Motors, 282 Broadwater Cresecent, Stevenage, Hertfordshire SG2 8AQ, United Kingdom. TEL 44-1438-364460, news@nonleaguenews24.com. Ed. David Watters.

796.352 USA ISSN 1947-6493
▼ **NORTH CAROLINA GOLF JOURNAL.** Text in English. forthcoming 2010. m. USD 9.99 per issue (effective 2009). **Document type:** *Magazine, Consumer.* **Description:** Features articles on golf for North Carolina.
Published by: In Publishing, 9769 NW 45 Ln, Miami, FL 33178. TEL 736-314-0456, info@miamigolfjournal.com.

796.352 USA ISSN 0889-2377
NORTH TEXAS GOLFER. Text in English. 1986. 12/yr. USD 22 (effective 2000). adv. **Document type:** *Magazine, Consumer.* **Description:** Provides information to golfers in Texas above the 31st parallel on quality of courses, better playing techniques, upcoming tournaments, and tournament results. Includes an alphabetical list of golf courses in that area every other month.
Published by: Golfer Magazines, Inc., 10301 Northwest Fwy, Ste 418, Houston, TX 77092-8228. TEL 713-680-1680, FAX 713-680-0138. Ed. Bob Gray. Pub. Sommy L Ham. R&P David Widener. Adv. contact Sommy Ham. B&W page USD 1,730, color page USD 2,491; 13 x 10.25. Circ: 31,000 (controlled).

796.3 USA
NORTHCOAST SPORTS PRO FOOTBALL PREVIEW. Text in English. a. **Document type:** *Magazine, Consumer.* **Description:** Contains information and statistics on all National Football League teams and players.
Published by: Northcoast Sports, Inc., PO Box 35126, Cleveland, OH 44135. TEL 216-521-9467, 800-654-3448, CustomerSupport@ncsports.com, http://www.ncsports.com.

796.334 ITA ISSN 1121-3256
IL NUOVO CALCIO. Text in Italian. 1991. m. (11/yr.). EUR 44 domestic; EUR 98 in Europe; EUR 130 elsewhere (effective 2009). adv. **Document type:** *Magazine, Consumer.*
Published by: Editoriale Sport Italia, Via Masaccio 12, Milan, MI 20149, Italy. TEL 39-02-4815396, FAX 39-02-4690907, http://www.sportivi.it. Ed. Marco Marchei. Adv. contact Antonio Brazzit. Circ: 50,000.

796.357 USA
(YEAR) OAKLAND ATHLETIC MAGAZINE. Text in English. 1995. 3/yr. (during baseball season). index. back issues avail. **Document type:** *Magazine, Consumer.*
Published by: Woodford Publishing, Inc., PO Box 910, Tiburon, CA 94920. TEL 415-397-1853, FAX 514-399-0942. Ed. Kate Hanley. Pub. Laurence J Hyman. R&P David Lilienstein. Adv. contact Tony Khing.

796.357 USA
OFFICIAL (YEAR) N C A A BASEBALL RECORDS. Text in English. 1991. a. stat. back issues avail. **Document type:** *Report, Trade.* **Description:** Contains individual and team records and statistical leaders in collegiate baseball and softball.
Supersedes in part (in 2004): Official (Year) N C A A Baseball & Softball Records; Which was formerly (until 2001): Baseball & Softball; (until 2000): N C A A Baseball & Softball (1089-4551); (until 1996): Official (Year) N C A A Baseball and Softball
Related titles: Online - full text ed.: free (effective 2011).
Published by: National Collegiate Athletic Association, 700 W Washington St, PO Box 6222, Indianapolis, IN 46206. TEL 317-917-6222, FAX 317-917-6888, esummers@ncaa.org, http://www.ncaa.org/.

796.33 USA
OFFICIAL (YEAR) N C A A MEN'S FINAL FOUR RECORDS BOOK. (National Collegiate Athletic Association) Text in English. 19??. a. stat. back issues avail. **Document type:** *Report, Trade.* **Description:** Provides an official statistical history of the Final Four.
Supersedes in part: Official (Year) N C A A Final Four Tournament Records; Which was formerly (until 2001): Official N C A A Final Four Records Book; (until 2000): Final Four Records
Related titles: Online - full text ed.: free (effective 2011).
Published by: National Collegiate Athletic Association, 700 W Washington St, PO Box 6222, Indianapolis, IN 46206. TEL 317-917-6222, FAX 317-917-6888, http://www.ncaa.org/.

796.3 USA
OFFICIAL (YEAR) N C A A SOFTBALL RECORDS. Text in English. 1991. a. back issues avail. **Document type:** *Report, Trade.*
Supersedes in part (in 2004): Official (Year) N C A A Baseball & Softball Records; Which was formerly (until 2001): Baseball & Softball; (until 2000): N C A A Baseball & Softball (1089-4551); (until 1996): Official (Year) N C A A Baseball and Softball; (until 1992): N C A A Baseball and Softball
Related titles: Online - full text ed.: free (effective 2011).
Published by: National Collegiate Athletic Association, 700 W Washington St, PO Box 6222, Indianapolis, IN 46206. TEL 317-917-6222, FAX 317-917-6888, http://www.ncaa.org/.

796.3 USA
OFFICIAL (YEAR) N C A A WOMEN'S FINAL FOUR RECORDS BOOK. Text in English. 19??. a. back issues avail. **Document type:** *Report, Trade.*
Supersedes in part: Official (Year) N C A A Final Four Tournament Records; Which was formerly (until 2001): Official N C A A Final Four Records Book; (until 2000): Final Four Records
Related titles: Online - full text ed.: free (effective 2011).
Published by: National Collegiate Athletic Association, 700 W Washington St, PO Box 6222, Indianapolis, IN 46206. TEL 317-917-6222, FAX 317-917-6888, http://www.ncaa.org/.

796.334 GBR ISSN 1369-0868
OFFICIAL ARSENAL F C MAGAZINE. (Football Club) Text in English. 1997. m. GBP 33 domestic; GBP 42 in Europe; GBP 45 in North America; GBP 52 elsewhere (effective 2009). **Document type:** *Magazine, Consumer.* **Description:** Contains exclusive interviews, regular columnists, match stats and reports, competitions and all the news from Emirates Stadium.
Published by: Northern & Shell Plc, The Northern & Shell Bldg, Number 10 Lower Thames St, London, EC3R 6EN, United Kingdom. TEL 44-870-0626620, http://www.northernandshell.co.uk. **Subscr. to:** Johnson's International Media Services.

796.357 USA ISSN 0078-3846
GV877
OFFICIAL BASEBALL RULES. Text in English. 1950. a. **Document type:** *Magazine, Consumer.*
—CCC.
Published by: American City Business Journals, Inc. (Subsidiary of: Advance Publications, Inc.), 120 W Morehead St, Charlotte, NC 28202. http://www.acbj.com.

796.323 USA
(YEAR) OFFICIAL C B A GUIDE AND REGISTER. Text in English. 1978. a. USD 15.95. adv.
Formerly: C B A Media Guide Yearbook
Published by: Continental Basketball Association, 400 N Fifth St, Phoenix, AZ 85004-3902. TEL 602-254-6677. Eds. Brett Meister, Greg Anderson. Circ: 6,000.

796.352 USA
OFFICIAL CHAMPIONS TOUR GUIDE. Text in English. a. USD 24.95 (effective 2008). **Description:** Provides in-depth coverage of the P.G.A. Senior Tour.
Former titles (until 2003): Official Media Guide of the Senior P G A Tour (1555-8800); (until 199?): Senior P G A Tour Guide
Published by: (Professional Golfers Association of America), Golf Smart, 13100 Grass Valley Ave, Grass Valley, CA 95945. TEL 800-637-3557, FAX 530-272-2133, info@golfsmart.com, http://www.golfsmart.com.

796.352 USA ISSN 1543-4885
OFFICIAL GUIDEBOOK TO GOLFING TEXAS. Text in English. 2003. a. USD 7.95 newsstand/cover (effective 2003).

Published by: Golf Media Group, LLC, 7553 Holloran Ct., Las Vegas, NV 89128. TEL 702-256-6303, FAX 702-363-8542, info@golfmediagroup.com, http://www.golfmediagroup.com. Ed. Stephen Weeks. Pubs. Bret Enerson, Stephen Weeks.

796.3 USA
OFFICIAL LAWN BOWLS ALMANAC. Text in English. 1964. irreg. USD 1.50 to non-members.
Former titles (until 1984): Official Lawn Bowls Handbook (0065-9053); Lawn Bowler's Handbook
Published by: American Lawn Bowls Association, 445 Surfview Dr, Pacific Palisades, CA 90272. TEL 213-454-2775.

796.323 USA
GV886
OFFICIAL N C A A WOMEN'S BASKETBALL RECORDS BOOK (YEAR). Text in English. a. USD 12.50 per issue (effective 2009). stat.
Description: Contain single-game, season and career records, plus coaching records, collegiate records, conference standings, attendance leaders, and award winners.
Formerly (until 1999): N C A A Basketball. The Official Women's College Basketball Records Book (1089-5299)
Published by: National Collegiate Athletic Association, 700 W Washington St, PO Box 6222, Indianapolis, IN 46206. TEL 317-917-6222, FAX 317-917-6888, esummers@ncaa.org, http://www.ncaa.org/.

796.323 USA
OFFICIAL OHIO STATE UNIVERSITY MEN'S BASKETBALL PROGRAM. Text in English. irreg. (published for each men's home basketball game). adv. back issues avail. **Description:** The official game day program for the Ohio State University men's basketball team. Includes player and coach profiles, alumni news etc.
Published by: (The Ohio State University), Zimmerman Publishing Company, Inc., 4500 Mobile Dr #100, Columbus, OH 43220-3715. TEL 614-294-8878, FAX 614-294-4831.

796.357 CAN ISSN 0318-4714
OFFICIAL RULES OF BASEBALL. Text in English. 1971. a.
Former titles (until 1976): Official C F A B Baseball Rules (0834-5082); (until 1975): C F A B Official Baseball Rules (0318-4706); (until 1973): Official Playing Rules of the C F A B (0318-4692)
Published by: Baseball Canada, 2212 Gladwin Crescent, Suite A7, Ottawa, ON K1B 5N1, Canada. TEL 613-748-5606, FAX 613-748-5767, info@baseball.ca, http://www.baseball.ca.

796.323 USA
OFFICIAL RULES OF BASKETBALL (YEAR). Text in English. 199?. a.
Published by: National Collegiate Athletic Association, 700 W Washington St, PO Box 6222, Indianapolis, IN 46206. TEL 317-917-6222, FAX 317-917-6888, esummers@ncaa.org, http://www.ncaa.org/.

796.357 USA
OFFICIAL RULES OF MAJOR LEAGUE BASEBALL. Variant title: Official Rules of Baseball (Year). Text in English. 19??. a. USD 9.95 per issue (effective 2011). back issues avail. **Document type:** *Handbook/Manual/Guide, Consumer.* **Description:** Lays out all the rules of the game.
Published by: Triumph Books, 542 S Dearborn St, Ste 750, Chicago, IL 60605. TEL 312-939-3330, 800-335-5323, FAX 312-663-3557, S.Wilson@TriumphBooks.com.

796.334 USA
OFFICIAL RULES OF SOCCER. Text in English. 19??. a. USD 9.95 per issue (effective 2011). back issues avail. **Document type:** *Handbook/Manual/Guide, Consumer.*
Published by: Triumph Books, 542 S Dearborn St, Ste 750, Chicago, IL 60605. TEL 312-939-3330, 800-335-5323, FAX 312-663-3557, S.Wilson@TriumphBooks.com.

796.332 USA
OFFICIAL RULES OF THE N F L. (National Football League) Text in English. 1995. a. USD 9.95 per issue (effective 2011). back issues avail. **Document type:** *Handbook/Manual/Guide, Consumer.*
Published by: Triumph Books, 542 S Dearborn St, Ste 750, Chicago, IL 60605. TEL 312-939-3330, 800-335-5323, FAX 312-663-3557, S.Wilson@TriumphBooks.com.

796.345 FRA ISSN 1957-2417
L'OFFICIEL DU BADMINTON. Text in French. 2007. q. **Document type:** *Consumer.*
Related titles: Online - full text ed.: ISSN 1954-3603.
Published by: Federation Francaise de Badminton, 9-11 Av. Michelet, Saint-Ouen, 93583 Cedex, France. TEL 33-1-49450707, FAX 33-1-49451871, ffba@ffba.org.

796.334 SWE ISSN 1404-6822
OFFSIDE; fotbollsmagasinet. Text in Swedish. 2000. 6/yr. SEK 275 (effective 2005). adv. **Document type:** *Magazine, Consumer.*
Published by: Offside Press AB, Oestra Hamngatan 45, Goeteborg, 41110, Sweden. TEL 46-31-7115882, FAX 46-31-7742210. Eds. Tobias Regnell, Mattias Goeransson. Pub. Mattias Goeransson. Adv. contact Hermann Dill. page SEK 19,500; 170 x 242. Circ: 30,000.

796.358 NZL ISSN 1177-7591
OFFSPIN. Text in English. 2007. q. NZD 28 (effective 2008). adv. **Document type:** *Magazine, Consumer.* **Description:** Focuses on entertaining and informing readers with professional photography and great articles.
Address: PO Box 125 287, St Hellers, Auckland, 1740, New Zealand. info@offspinnz.co.nz.

796.352 USA ISSN 1947-6477
▼ **OHIO GOLF JOURNAL.** Text in English. 2009 (Oct.). m. USD 10.50 per issue (effective 2010). **Document type:** *Magazine, Consumer.* **Description:** Features articles on golf for Ohio.
Published by: In Publishing, 9769 NW 45 Ln, Miami, FL 33178. TEL 736-314-0456, info@miamigolfjournal.com.

796.342 CAN ISSN 0824-6629
ON COURT. Text in English. 1982. 8/yr. CAD 12. adv. bk.rev.
Published by: Fourhand II, Inc., 1200 Sheppard Ave E, Ste 400, Willowdale, ON M2K 2S5, Canada. TEL 416-497-1370, FAX 416-494-5343. Ed. Tom Mayenknecht. Circ: 50,000 (controlled).

796.352 USA
ONLINE GOLF SOLUTIONS NEWSLETTER. Text in English. 1999. m. adv. back issues avail. **Document type:** *Newsletter.* **Description:** Designed for anyone who loves golf. Geared for the golf pro and superintendent-type.
Media: Online - full text.
Address: 1908 Night Song Ct., Apt. 101, Schaumburg, IL 60194-2192. TEL 616-723-2245, 800-353-2245. Ed. Dan Perry.

796.352 CAN ISSN 1709-2922
ONTARIO GOLF. Text in English. 1980. 5/yr. CAD 10. adv. bk.rev. **Document type:** *Magazine, Consumer.* **Description:** Contains coverage of all the major tournaments played in Ontario and golf highlights across Canada. Lists all golf courses in Ontario plus instructional articles and golf rules.
Formerly (until 2002): Ontario Golf News (0710-2801)
Published by: Ontario Golf News Inc., 2 Billingham Rd, Ste 400, Toronto, ON M9B 6E1, Canada. TEL 416-232-2380, FAX 416-232-9291. Ed. Charles Halpin. Pub., R&P, Adv. contact Ken McKenzie. Circ: 40,000 (controlled).

796.342 CAN
ONTARIO TENNIS. Text in English. 1969. bi-m. CAD 9.95. adv. bk.rev. stat. back issues avail.
Published by: Ontario Tennis Association, 1 Shoreham Dr., Suite 200, Toronto, ON M3N 3A7, Canada. TEL 416-514-1100, 800-387-5066, FAX 416-514-1112, ota@tennisontario.com, http://www.tennisontario.com. Ed. David Dunkelman. Circ: 10,000.

796.334 FRA ISSN 0995-6921
ONZE MONDIAL. Text in French. 1989. m. EUR 30.90; EUR 3.20 newsstand/cover (effective 2008). adv. **Document type:** *Magazine, Consumer.* **Description:** Covers the world of soccer through interviews, in-depth coverage, and game results.
Formed by the 1989 merger of (1976-1989): Onze (0396-972X); (1977-1989): Mondial (0150-2913)
Published by: Hachette Filipacchi Medias S.A. (Subsidiary of: Lagardere Media), 149/151 Rue Anatole France, Levallois-Perret, 925340, France. TEL 33-1-413462, FAX 33-1-413469, lgardere@interdeco.fr, http://www.lagardere.com. Circ: 173,000.

OPERATING & FINANCIAL PERFORMANCE PROFILES OF 18-HOLE GOLF FACILITIES IN THE U.S. *see* BUSINESS AND ECONOMICS

796.352 USA ISSN 1044-1204
GV961
P G A MAGAZINE. Text in English. 1920. m. adv. bk.rev. illus. **Document type:** *Magazine, Trade.*
Former titles (until 1989): P G A (1042-6310); (until 1988): P G A Magazine (0161-1259); (until 1977): Professional Golfer (0033-0132)
Indexed: SPI, SportS.
Published by: Professional Golfers Association of America, 2600 Philmont Ave, Ste 119, Huntingdon Valley, PA 19006. TEL 215-914-2071, FAX 215-914-2076, rsummers@pgamagazine.com, http://www.pga.com. Ed. Matt Marsom. Adv. contact Scott Miller. page USD 9,075; trim 7.88 x 10.75. Circ: 40,000 (controlled).

796.352 GBR
P G A PROFILE. Text in English. m. adv. bk.rev. back issues avail. **Document type:** *Journal, Trade.*
Published by: Professional Golfers' Association, Centenary House, The De Vere Belfry, Sutton Coldfield, W Mids B76 9PT, United Kingdom. TEL 44-1675-470333, FAX 44-1675-477888, http://www.pga.info/. Circ: 5,500 (controlled).

796.352 USA ISSN 1093-6076
P G A TOUR PARTNERS. (Professional Golf Association) Text in English. 1997. bi-m. free to members (effective 2008). adv. back issues avail. **Document type:** *Magazine, Consumer.* **Description:** Provides coverage, equipment reviews, professional perspectives, instruction from tour pros and in-depth information on popular golf destinations.
Published by: (PGA Tour Partners Club), North American Media Group, Inc. (Subsidiary of: North American Membership Group, Inc.), 12301 Whitewater Dr, Minnetonka, MN 55343. TEL 952-936-9333, 800-922-4888, FAX 952-936-9755, namghq@namginc.com, http://www.northamericanmediagroup.com/. Ed. Tom Stine. Pub. Rich Sundberg TEL 320-846-6090. Adv. contact Mark Swanson TEL 952-352-7035. B&W page USD 27,775, color page USD 40,545; trim 7.75 x 10.5. Circ: 523,831.

796.357 USA
P O N Y BASEBALL RULES AND REGULATIONS. (Protect Our Nation's Youth) (In 3 editions: Shetland, Pinto & Rules Mustang; Bronco, Pony, Colt & Palomino Rules; Girls Softball) Text in English. 1951. a. free membership. **Document type:** *Magazine, Consumer.* **Description:** Rulebooks for different age level baseball and softball leagues.
Published by: P O N Y Baseball, Inc., 1951 Pony Pl, PO Box 225, Washington, PA 15301. TEL 724-225-1060, FAX 724-225-9852, info@pony.org, http://www.pony.org. Ed. Don Clawson. Circ: 150,000.

796.357 USA
P O N Y BASEBALL - SOFTBALL EXPRESS. (Protect Our Nation's Youth) Text in English. 1952. q. free membership. adv. illus. **Document type:** *Newspaper, Consumer.* **Description:** Covers current news in organized baseball and softball for boys and girls from ages 5-18, including items for organizers and teams.
Former titles: Pony Baseball Express; Pony Baseball Newsletter; Boys Baseball Newsletter; Boys Baseball Bulletin (0006-856X)
Published by: P O N Y Baseball, Inc., 1951 Pony Pl, PO Box 225, Washington, PA 15301. TEL 724-225-1060, FAX 724-225-9852, info@pony.org, http://www.pony.org. Ed. Chris Headley. Circ: 30,000.

P S A POPULATION REPORT AND PRICE GUIDE. (Professional Sports Authenticator) *see* HOBBIES

P S A VINTAGE POPULATION REPORT. (Professional Sports Authenticator) *see* HOBBIES

796.332 NLD
P S V FLITS. (Philips Sport Vereniging) Text in Dutch. 22/yr. adv.
Published by: (P S V Eindhoven), EFKA Uitgevers bv, Postbus 155, Weert, 6000 AD, Netherlands. TEL 31-495-450105, FAX 31-495-539485, info@efka-uitgevers.nl, http://www.efka-uitgevers.nl. adv.: color page EUR 850; 105 x 162. Circ: 35,000.

796.332 NLD
P S V INSIDE. (Philips Sport Vereniging) Text in Dutch. 5/yr. EUR 19.90 (effective 2008). adv. **Document type:** *Magazine, Consumer.*
Published by: (P S V Eindhoven), EFKA Uitgevers bv, Postbus 155, Weert, 6000 AD, Netherlands. TEL 31-495-450105, FAX 31-495-539485, info@efka-uitgevers.nl, http://www.efka-uitgevers.nl. adv.: color page EUR 2,200; trim 230 x 297. Circ: 27,500.

796.332 NLD
P S V INZAKE. (Philips Sport Vereniging) Text in Dutch. 3/yr. adv. **Document type:** *Magazine, Consumer.*
Published by: EFKA Uitgevers bv, Postbus 155, Weert, 6000 AD, Netherlands. TEL 31-495-450105, FAX 31-495-539485, info@efka-uitgevers.nl, http://www.efka-uitgevers.nl. adv.: color page EUR 1,950; trim 230 x 297. Circ: 3,500.

796.332 NLD
P S V PHOXYNIEUWS. (Philips Sport Vereniging) Text in Dutch. bi-m. adv.
Published by: (P S V Eindhoven), EFKA Uitgevers bv, Postbus 155, Weert, 6000 AD, Netherlands. TEL 31-495-450105, FAX 31-495-539485, info@efka-uitgevers.nl, http://www.efka-uitgevers.nl. adv.: color page EUR 850; 150 x 210. Circ: 22,000.

796.352 CAN
PACIFIC GOLF. Text in English. 1993. 4/yr. CAD 9.98. adv. **Document type:** *Magazine, Consumer.*
Published by: Canada Wide Media Ltd., 4180 Lougheed Hwy, 4th Fl, Burnaby, BC V5C 6A7, Canada. TEL 604-299-7311, FAX 604-299-9188, cwm@canadawide.com, http://www.canadawide.com. Ed. Ann Collette. Pub. Peter Legge. Adv. contact Stephen Thomas. B&W page CAD 2,475, color page CAD 3,250; trim 10.88 x 8.13. Circ: 20,000.

796.352 USA ISSN 1087-7045
PACIFIC NORTHWEST GOLFER. Text in English. q. USD 11.80; USD 2.95 newsstand/cover (effective 2001).
Published by: (Idaho Golf Association, British Columbia Golf Association CAN, Oregon Golf Asssociation, Washington State Golf Association, Northwest Golf Association), Varsity Sports Communications, 12510 33rd Ave, NE, Ste 300, Seattle, WA 98125. TEL 206-367-2420, FAX 206-367-2636. Ed. Dick Stephens. Pub. Ozzie Boyle.

796.332 USA ISSN 1064-4296
PACKER PLUS. Variant title: Milwaukee Sentinel Packer Plus. Text in English. 1991. w. **Document type:** *Magazine, Consumer.*
Related titles: Online - full content ed.
Published by: Journal Communications, Inc., 333 W State St, PO Box 661, Milwaukee, WI 53203. TEL 414-224-2000, http://www.jnlcom.com.

796.332 USA ISSN 1081-9851
PACKER REPORT. Text in English. 1972. 24/yr. (w. during football season). USD 42.95; USD 2 newsstand/cover (effective 2005). adv. stat. 32 p./no.; back issues avail. **Document type:** *Newspaper.* **Description:** Devoted to coverage of the Green Bay Packers and the NFL. Contains game stories, statistics, coaches' comments, player profiles, photos and line-ups.
Formerly (until 1995): Ray Nitschke's Packer Report (1049-1902)
Related titles: Online - full text ed.
Published by: (Green Bay Packers), Royle Publications, Inc., 726 Lois Ln, Sun Prairie, WI 53590. TEL 608-837-2200, FAX 608-825-3053. Ed. Todd Korth. Pub., R&P Jeffrey Royle. Adv. contact Ron Royle. B&W page USD 1,035; trim 14 x 11.38. Circ: 25,000 (paid); 10,000 (free). **Co-sponsor:** America's Pack Fan Club.

796.3 CAN
PADDLE NEWS. Text in English. q. looseleaf. CAD 10 to individuals; CAD 25 to institutions. adv. back issues avail. **Document type:** *Newsletter.* **Description:** Provides up-to-date table tenn is news from the province, country and world levels.
Published by: Alberta Table Tennis Association, 11759 Groat Rd, Edmonton, AB T5M 3K6, Canada. TEL 403-453-8657, FAX 403-453-8553. Ed. David Jackson. Adv. contact Rosanne Prinsen. page CAD 75. Circ: 150.

796.358 PAK
PAKISTAN BOOK OF CRICKET. Text in English. 1976. a. PKR 10. charts; illus.
Published by: Q. Ahmed, Pub., Spencers Bldg., 3rd Fl., I.I. Chundrigar Rd., G P O Box 3721, Karachi, Pakistan.

796.352 JPN
PAR GOLF. Text in Japanese. 1969. m. JPY 8,160.
Published by: Gakken Co. Ltd., 1-17-15, Nakaikegami, Otaku, Tokyo, 145-0064, Japan. Ed. Kenichi Shiono.

796.352 DEU ISSN 1618-5285
PARADISE GOLF. Text in German. 1997. q. EUR 7.50 newsstand/cover (effective 2003). adv. **Document type:** *Magazine, Consumer.*
Published by: Lady International Verlag, Salzmannweg 17, Stuttgart, 70192, Germany. TEL 49-711-2227722, FAX 49-711-2227723. adv.: B&W page EUR 5,840, color page EUR 9,700. Circ: 53,600 (paid and controlled).

796.33 IRL ISSN 1649-6876
PEIL. Text in English. 2005. q. EUR 2 newsstand/cover (effective 2006). **Document type:** *Magazine, Consumer.*
Published by: Cumann Peil Gael Na mBan, Level 6 Cusack Stand, Croke Park, Dublin, 3, Ireland. TEL 353-1-8363156. Eds. Alan Gunn, Fr. Liam Kelleher.

796.352 USA ISSN 1947-2293
▼ **PENNSYLVANIA GOLF JOURNAL.** Text in English. forthcoming 2010. m. USD 9.99 per issue (effective 2009). **Document type:** *Magazine, Consumer.* **Description:** Features articles on golf for Pennsylvania.
Published by: In Publishing, 9769 NW 45 Ln, Miami, FL 33178. TEL 736-314-0456, info@miamigolfjournal.com.

796.334 RUS
PERVYI TAIM. Text in Russian. bi-m. USD 95 in United States.
Published by: Obshchestvennaya Organizatsiya Detskaya Futbol'naya Liga, Ul Pravdy 24, etazh 6-i, Moscow, 125866, Russian Federation. TEL 7-095-9258387, FAX 7-095-9214191. Ed. V N Gorlov. **Dist. by:** East View Information Services, 10601 Wayzata Blvd, Minneapolis, MN 55305. TEL 952-252-1201, 800-477-1005, FAX 952-252-1202, info@eastview.com, http://www.eastview.com.

796.3 NZL ISSN 1177-2646
PETANQUE NEW ZEALAND. Text in English. 1994-2003; resumed 2005 (Sep.). q. NZD 20 domestic to individuals (effective 2008). back issues avail. **Document type:** *Magazine, Consumer.*
Former titles (until 1999): Boules Gazette; (until 1995): New Zealand Petanque Association. Newsletter
Address: PO Box 31127, Lower Hutt, New Zealand.

796.357 USA ISSN 0148-3153
GV875.A1
PETERSEN'S PRO BASEBALL. Text in English. 1977. a. USD 4.50 newsstand/cover. adv. **Document type:** *Magazine, Consumer.* **Description:** Includes predictions, ratings, draft review, schedules and stats. Reviews the past season.

S

Published by: Petersen Publishing Co. LLC, 6420 Wilshire Blvd, Los Angeles, CA 90048-5515. TEL 213-782-2000, FAX 213-782-2718. Circ: 196,000.

796.93 USA
PHIL STEELE'S COLLEGE FOOTBALL PREVIEW. Text in English. 2003. a. USD 8.95 newsstand/cover (effective 2009). adv. back issues avail. **Document type:** *Magazine, Consumer.* **Description:** Features in-depth articles, team statistics, rankings, schedules.
Published by: Northcoast Sports, Inc., PO Box 35126, Cleveland, OH 44135. TEL 216-521-9467, 800-654-3448, CustomerSupport@ncsports.com, http://www.ncsports.com.

796.352 USA
PHILADELPHIA GOLF MAGAZINE. Text in English. 1986. 5/yr. USD 8. adv. **Document type:** *Magazine, Consumer.* **Description:** Provides news, entertainment and information about Philadelphia area golf. Covers pro and amateur tournaments.
Published by: Philadelphia Golf Publishing Co., 1583 Maple Ave, Paoli, PA 19301-1249. TEL 215-647-4692. Circ: 70,000.

796.3 FRA ISSN 0991-3769
PILOTA. Text in French. q. EUR 15 (effective 2008). **Document type:** *Newsletter, Consumer.* **Description:** Dedicated to the game of pelota.
Published by: Federation Francaise de Pelote Basque, Trinquet Moderne, 60 av. Dubrocq, BP 816, Bayonne, Cedex 64108, France. TEL 33-5-59592234, FAX 33-5-59254982, ffpb@wanadoo.fr, http://www.ffpb.net. Ed. Louis Goyeneix. Pub. Jean Haritschelhar.

796.346 CHN ISSN 1000-3452
GV1004.9
PINGPANG SHIJIE/TABLE TENNIS WORLD. Text in Chinese. 1981. m. USD 74.40 (effective 2009). **Document type:** *Magazine, Consumer.*
Related titles: Online - full content ed.; Online - full text ed.
—East View.
Published by: (Zhongguo Pingpang Xiehui/China Table Tennis Association), Zhongguo Tiyubao Yezongshe, 8, Tiyuguan Lu, Chongwen-qu, Beijing, 100061, China. TEL 86-10-67158579. **Dist. by:** China International Book Trading Corp, 35 Chegongzhuang Xilu, Haidian District, PO Box 399, Beijing 100044, China. TEL 86-10-68412045, FAX 86-10-68412023, cibtc@mail.cibtc.com.cn, http://www.cibtc.com.cn.

796.334 USA
THE PITCH (CARROLLTON). Text in English. 1989. m. USD 18; USD 1.50 newsstand/cover (effective 2001). adv. **Document type:** *Newspaper.* **Description:** Contains association news, events, announcements and coaching hints for administrators and coaches.
Published by: (North Texas State Soccer Association), Varsity Sports Communications, 12510 33rd Ave, NE, Ste 300, Seattle, WA 98125. TEL 206-367-2420, FAX 206-367-2636. Ed., R&P Chuck Mozingo. adv.: B&W page USD 1,790, color page USD 2,690; trim 13.5 x 9.63. Circ: 120,000.

796.332 USA ISSN 2152-0526
▼ **PLANOFOOTBALL SPORTS NEWS.** Text in English. 2009. w. free (effective 2010). back issues avail. **Document type:** *Magazine, Consumer.*
Media: Online - full text.
Published by: Plano Football Sports News Ed. Brian Porter.

796.342 USA
PLATFORM TENNIS NEWS (ONLINE). Text in English. m. free (effective 2008). back issues avail. **Document type:** *Magazine, Consumer.*
Formerly: Platform Tennis News (Print)
Media: Online - full text.
Published by: American Platform Tennis Association, c/o Ann Sheedy, Exe.Director, 109 Wesport Dr, Pittsburgh, PA 15238. TEL 412-963-0176, FAX 412-963-1545, apta@platformtennis.org, mafischl@yahoo.com, http://www.platformtennis.org. Ed. James McCready. Circ: 3,000.

796.357 CAN ISSN 1718-2611
PLAY BALL!. Text in English. 2006. q. CAD 15 (effective 2007). **Document type:** *Magazine, Consumer.* **Description:** Profiles baseball in British Columbia.
Indexed: SD.
Published by: Play Ball! B C BASEBALL Magazine, 1226 Killarney St, Penticton, BC V2A 4R2, Canada. http://www.playballbc.com. Ed., Pub. Robyn Harden. Circ: 20,000.

796.352 BEL ISSN 0775-9878
PLAY GOLF (NEDERLANDSE EDITIE). Text in Dutch. 1988. m. adv. illus. **Document type:** *Consumer.*
Related titles: French ed.: Play Golf (Edition Francaise). ISSN 0776-023X.
Published by: Play Golf S.A., Rue du Chatelain 49, Brussels, 1050, Belgium. TEL 32-2-6471750, FAX 32-2-6482989. Ed. Bernard de Wasseige. Circ: (controlled).

796.334 USA
PLAY ON!. Text in English. 6/yr. USD 9; free to qualified personnel (effective 2009). **Document type:** *Newsletter, Consumer.* **Description:** Covers news of the Washington Youth Soccer Association.
Published by: (Washington State Youth Soccer Association), Varsity Sports Communications, 12510 33rd Ave, NE, Ste 300, Seattle, WA 98125. TEL 206-367-2420, FAX 206-367-2636.

796.358 GBR ISSN 0079-2314
PLAYFAIR CRICKET ANNUAL. Text in English. 1947. a. GBP 6.99 per issue (effective 2010). back issues avail. **Document type:** *Journal, Trade.* **Description:** Includes all the essential information required to follow events on the cricket field, with unrivalled up-to-the-minute statistical detail on all first-class players.
Published by: Headline Book Publishing, 338 Euston Rd, London, NW1 3BH, United Kingdom. TEL 44-207-8736000, enquiries@headline.co.uk, http://www.headline.co.uk.

796.3 GBR ISSN 0079-2322
PLAYFAIR FOOTBALL ANNUAL. Text in English. 1948. a. GBP 6.99 per issue (effective 2010). **Document type:** *Directory, Trade.* **Description:** Provides a directory of each English and Scottish League club with statistical details of the players in the 92 English clubs. Contains feature articles on players, matches and upcoming seasons.
Published by: Headline Book Publishing, 338 Euston Rd, London, NW1 3BH, United Kingdom. TEL 44-207-8736000, enquiries@headline.co.uk.

796.352 CAN ISSN 0821-2023
POCKET PRO GOLF MAGAZINE. Text in English. 1978. a. free. adv. **Document type:** *Magazine, Consumer.*
Formerly: Pro Pocket Guide Golf Magazine (0711-4079)
Published by: Longhurst Golf Corporation, 236 Wynchwood Ave, Tornoto, ON, Canada. TEL 416-654-9171. Ed., Pub., R&P, Adv. contact Bruce Longhurst. B&W page CAD 12,000, color page CAD 15,000. Circ: 200,000.

796.353 HKG ISSN 1997-454X
POLO/HUANGJIA MAQIU. Text in English. 2007 (Nov.). s-a. **Document type:** *Magazine, Consumer.* **Description:** Covers sport, fashion and lifestyle.
Related titles: Online - full content ed.
Published by: Blu Inc Media (HK) Ltd. (Subsidiary of: S P H Magazines Pte Ltd.), Ste 2901, 29/F Universal Trade Centre, No. 3 Arbuthnot Rd, Central, Hong Kong. TEL 852-2165-2800, FAX 852-2868-1799, queries@bluincmedia.com, http://www.bluincmedia.com.hk/.

796.353 USA ISSN 0146-4574
GV1010
POLO MAGAZINE; adventure - elegance - sport. Text in English. 1975. bi-m. USD 19.95; USD 32 in Canada; USD 37 elsewhere; USD 4.95 newsstand/cover; CAD 5.95 newsstand/cover in Canada. adv. bk.rev. illus. **Document type:** *Magazine, Consumer.* **Description:** Presents news on the sport of polo: tournament coverage, instructional articles and player profiles. Includes lifestyle articles of interest to upscale audiences.
Formerly: Polo News
Indexed: SPI, SportS.
Published by: (U S Polo Association), Winchester Media Company, 5075 Westheimer, Ste 840, Houston, TX 77056. TEL 214-369-3445, FAX 214-369-7987. Ed. Chris Kelly. Pub. James D Lonergan. Circ: 5,600 (paid). **Subscr. to:** PO Box 354, Mt Morris, IL 61054.

796.357 USA
PONY BASEBALL. BLUE BOOK. Text in English. 1959. triennial. USD 5 (effective 2000). **Description:** Guide for operating a youth baseball or softball program for the entire community.
Formerly: Boys Baseball. Blue Book (0068-0575)
Published by: P O N Y Baseball, Inc., 1951 Pony Pl, PO Box 225, Washington, PA 15301. TEL 724-225-1060, FAX 724-225-9852, info@pony.org. Circ: 20,000.

794.7 USA ISSN 1049-2852
POOL & BILLIARD MAGAZINE. Text in English. 1983. m. USD 34.95 domestic; USD 44.95 in Canada & Mexico; USD 74.95 elsewhere (effective 2008). adv. bk.rev. **Document type:** *Magazine, Consumer.* **Description:** Dedicated to the sport of pool and billiards with instructional articles, tournament coverage, and industry news. Also includes new products and trends.
Incorporates (in 1982): Games and Leisure Inc
Address: 115 S Main St, Summerville, SC 29483. TEL 843-875-5115, FAX 843-875-5171. Ed. Shari J Stauch. Pub. Harold L Simonsen. Adv. contact Paul Bennema. Circ: 15,000.

796.93 USA
POWER PLAYS NEWSLETTER (ONLINE). Text in English. w. USD 94 (effective 2009). back issues avail. **Document type:** *Newsletter, Consumer.* **Description:** Guides to predict the rushing and passing yards, game scores, turnovers and unique power rating for each team.
Formerly: Power Plays Newsletter (Print)
Media: Online - full text.
Published by: Northcoast Sports, Inc., PO Box 35126, Cleveland, OH 44135. TEL 216-521-9467, 800-654-3448, CustomerSupport@ncsports.com, http://www.ncsports.com.

796.3 USA
POWER SWEEP NEWSLETTER (ONLINE). Text in English. bi-w. USD 94 (effective 2009). back issues avail. **Document type:** *Newsletter, Consumer.* **Description:** Provides up-to-date and in-depth analysis on all pro and college football teams.
Formerly (until 200?): Power Sweep Newsletter (Print)
Media: Online - full text.
Published by: Northcoast Sports, Inc., PO Box 35126, Cleveland, OH 44135. TEL 216-521-9467, 800-654-3448, CustomerSupport@ncsports.com.

796.352 USA
PRACTICE WHILE YOU PLAY. Text in English. 1999. d. USD 29.95 domestic; USD 39.95 foreign (effective 2006). **Document type:** *Bulletin, Consumer.*
—CCC.
Published by: T N T Publishing, 13867 Foothill Blvd, no 105, Sylmar, CA 91342. TEL 818-581-1922, FAX 818-367-5413, ballhold@earthlink.net. Ed. Melodie Agin. Pub., R&P, Adv. contact Teresa Thomas. Circ: 100 (controlled).

796.352 910.2 CAN ISSN 1912-8002
PRINCE EDWARD ISLAND, CANADA. DESTINATION & GOLF GUIDE. Text in English. 1998. a. adv. **Document type:** *Magazine, Consumer.*
Former titles (until 2006): Golf Prince Edward Island (1912-7995); (until 2003): P E I Golf Guide (1497-4428)
Published by: Golf P E I, 565 North River Rd, Charlottetown, PE C1E 1J7, Canada. TEL 902-566-4653, FAX 902-629-1981, http://www.golfpei.ca/opening.html.

796.352 USA
PRIVATE COUNTRY CLUB GUEST POLICY DIRECTORY. Text in English. 1976. a. USD 25 per issue (effective 2008). adv. **Document type:** *Directory.*
Supersedes (1976-1979): Golf and Country Club Guest Policy Directory
Published by: Pazdur Publishing, Inc., 2171 Campus Dr, Ste 330, Irvine, CA 92715-1499. TEL 949-752-6474, 800-367-8653. Ed. Edward F Pazdur. Circ: 100,000.

796.332 CZE ISSN 1212-818X
PRO FOOTBALL. Text in Czech. 2000. 12/yr. CZK 663; CZK 65, EUR 2.69 newsstand/cover (effective 2011). adv. **Document type:** *Magazine, Consumer.*
Published by: Egmont CR s.r.o., Zirovnicka 3124, Prague 10, 10600, Czech Republic. TEL 420-224-800751, FAX 420-272-770044, egmontcr@egmont.cz. Adv. contact Ratislav Packo. Circ: 19,000 (paid and controlled).

796.93 USA
PRO FOOTBALL SCOREBOOK. Text in English. a. USD 34.95 per issue (effective 2008). **Document type:** *Magazine, Consumer.* **Description:** Features updated actual and ATS statistics on every pro team and their performance.
Published by: Northcoast Sports, Inc., PO Box 35126, Cleveland, OH 44135. TEL 216-521-9467, 800-654-3448, CustomerSupport@ncsports.com.

796.332 USA ISSN 0032-9053
PRO FOOTBALL WEEKLY. Abbreviated title: P F W. Text in English. 1967. 32/yr. (w. during football season, m. off-season). USD 44.95 for 15 issues; USD 79.95 for 30 issues (effective 2007). adv. bk.rev. charts; illus.; stat. back issues avail.; reprints avail. **Document type:** *Magazine, Consumer.* **Description:** Devoted exclusively to professional football.
Related titles: Online - full text ed.
—CCC.
Published by: Source Interlink Companies, 302 Saunders Rd, Ste 100, Riverwoods, IL 60015. TEL 847-940-1100, dheine@sourceinterlink.com, http://www.sourceinterlinkmedia.com. adv.: B&W page USD 2,300, color page USD 3,050. Circ: 125,262.

796.352 GBR ISSN 1355-2740
PRO SHOP EUROPE. Abbreviated title: P S E. Text in English. 1984. m. GBP 99 domestic; GBP 143 in Europe; free to qualified personnel (effective 2010). adv. back issues avail. **Document type:** *Magazine, Trade.* **Description:** Provides up to the minute news from the golf trade around Europe, detailed description and pictures of all the new golfing products, a wide range of in-depth features on the golf trade scene, and a comprehensive recruitment section.
Related titles: Online - full text ed.: free (effective 2010).
Published by: Mark Allen Publishing Ltd., Jesses Farm, Snow Hill, Dinton, Salisbury, Wiltshire SP3 5HN, United Kingdom. TEL 44-1722-716996, FAX 44-1722-716926, subscriptions@markallengroup.com, http://www.markallengroup.com. Ed. Geraldine Faulker. Pub. Jane Kennedy. Adv. contact Geoff Pullin.

796.352 BEL
PROGRAMME OFFICIEL DES CONCOURS DE GOLF. Text in Dutch, French. 1945. a. adv. **Document type:** *Directory.* **Description:** Lists Belgian golf competitions and information on Belgian golf courses.
Published by: Belgame S.A., Av Montjoie 167, Brussels, 1180, Belgium. TEL 32-2-3430845, FAX 32-2-3435772. Ed., R&P, Adv. contact Claire Rolin. Circ: 20,000.

796.352 USA
PUB LINKS GOLFER MAGAZINE. Text in English. 2000. bi-m. USD 22.10 (effective 2007). adv. **Document type:** *Magazine, Consumer.* **Description:** Targets the public, municipal, resort and semi-private course player. It provides nine regional editions further breaking down into over 56 local editions all sharing the same national section.
Published by: Golfer Magazine, Inc., 1077 Silas Deane Hwy #122, Wethersfield, CT 06109. TEL 860-563-1633, FAX 860-747-4226, 646-607-3001, tlanders@golfingmagazine.net, http://www.publinksgolfer.net. Ed. John Torsiello. Pub. H James Kuhe.

796.352 USA ISSN 1041-5785
PUTT-PUTT WORLD; forthefunofit!. Text in English. 1958. s-a. USD 4; USD 8 foreign. adv. **Document type:** *Magazine, Consumer.* **Description:** Deals with current trends, issues, stories, and lifestyles for families who enjoy outdoor entertainment and miniature golf, competitive putting, and updates on the Professional Putters Association.
Formerly: Putters World
Published by: Putt-Putt Golf Courses of America, Inc., 6350 Quadrangle Dr., Ste. 210, Chapel Hill, NC 27517-7803. TEL 910-485-7131, FAX 910-485-1122. Ed. Bobby Owens. R&P Christine Thompson. Adv. contact Kimberly Brewington. Circ: 75,000.

796.334 GBR ISSN 1759-6386
Q P R. (Queens Park Rangers) Text in English. 2008. q. GBP 14.99 domestic; GBP 23.99 in Europe; GBP 26.99 in North America; GBP 33.99 elsewhere; GBP 3.99 per issue (effective 2010). back issues avail. **Document type:** *Magazine, Trade.* **Description:** Contains variety of informative features, incorporating the past, present and future of the club.
Published by: Q P R Football Club, Loftus Rd Stadium, London, W12 7PA, United Kingdom. TEL 44-20-87430262, http://www.qpr.co.uk. Ed. Ian Taylor.

796.3 CHN
QIUBAO/BALLS WEEKLY. Text in Chinese. 1988. s-w. **Document type:** *Newspaper, Consumer.*
Formerly (until 1992): Meibao - Qiukan
Related titles: Online - full content ed.
Published by: Liaoning Ribao Baoye Jituan/Liaoning Daily Newspaper Group, 339, Zhongshan Lu, Chenyang, 110001, China. TEL 86-24-22872198, FAX 86-24-22865402.

796.334 CHN
QIUMI BAO/FOOTBALL FAN NEWS. Text in Chinese. w. CNY 30.12. **Document type:** *Newspaper, Consumer.*
Related titles: Online - full content ed.
Published by: Tianjin Ribao Baoye Jituan, 873, Dagu Nanlu, Tianjin, 300211, China. TEL 86-22-28201211. **Dist. by:** China International Book Trading Corp, 35 Chegongzhuang Xilu, Haidian District, PO Box 399, Beijing 100044, China. TEL 86-10-68412045, FAX 86-10-68412023, cibtc@mail.cibtc.com.cn, http://www.cibtc.com.cn.

796.335 CAN ISSN 0228-6351
QUEBEC SOCCER. Text in English. 1977. m. CAD 21 domestic; CAD 35 in United States; CAD 40 in Europe; CAD 2 newsstand/cover (effective 2000). **Document type:** *Newspaper.* **Description:** Coverage of soccer activities and related issues in Quebec, Canada and abroad from amateur to professional.
Published by: Promotions Soccer Inc., 6900 St Denis, 3rd Fl, Montreal, PQ H2S 2S2, Canada. TEL 514-278-6399, FAX 514-278-9737. Ed. Philippe Germain. R&P Pasquale Cifarelli. Adv. contact Laurence Petitraux. Circ: 40,000.

796.333 AUS
QUEENSLAND RUGBY LEAGUE NEWS. Text in English. 19??. irreg. **Document type:** *Monographic series, Trade.* **Description:** Official match program for selected Rugby League games.

Published by: (Queensland Rugby League), The Magazine Publishing Company Pty. Ltd., 34 Station St, PO Box 406, Nundah, QLD 4012, Australia. TEL 61-7-38660000, FAX 61-7-38660066, info@tmpc.com.au, https://www.tmpc.com.au.

RACING & FOOTBALL OUTLOOK FOOTBALL GUIDE (YEARS). *see* SPORTS AND GAMES

RACING & FOOTBALL OUTLOOK: RACING ANNUAL. *see* SPORTS AND GAMES

796.342 USA
RACQUET SPORTS INDUSTRY. Text in English. 1975. m. USD 25 (effective 2005). adv. charts; illus.; mkt.; tr.lit. 32 p./no.; back issues avail. **Document type:** *Magazine, Trade.* **Description:** Covers new products, industry trends, technical product information, and stringing techniques.
Former titles (until Jan. 2005): Racquet Tech (1536-4135); (until 1999): Stringer's Assistant
Indexed: SportS.
Published by: United States Racquet Stringers Association, 330 Main St, Vista, CA 92084-6011. TEL 760-536-1177, FAX 760-536-1171, usrsa@racquettech.com, http://www.racquettech.com. Ed. Crawford Lindsey. Pub. Patrick Curry. Circ: 8,012.

796.343 USA
RACQUETBALL AROUND OHIO. Text in English. 1982. bi-m. USD 10 (effective 2001). adv. **Document type:** *Magazine, Consumer.* **Description:** Features events, schedules and rankings. Includes national and professional news and event coverage.
Published by: Ohio Racquetball Association, 6449 Lake Trail Dr, Westerville, OH 43082. TEL 614-890-6073, FAX 614-890-9986. Ed. Maureen Persinger. Circ: 2,500.

796.343 USA ISSN 1060-877X
RACQUETBALL MAGAZINE. Text in English. 1990. 6/yr. USD 20 domestic membership; USD 35 foreign membership (effective 2005). adv. **Document type:** *Magazine, Trade.* **Description:** Covers international events, national championships, state and regional news. Includes industry reports, schedules and rankings.
Indexed: PEI, SD, T02.
Published by: United States Racquetball Association, 1685 W Uintah, Colorado Springs, CO 80904-2906. Ed., R&P Linda Mojer. Circ: 40,000.

796.334 DEU
▼ **RAN (BIELEFELD)**; Fussball, international, Champions League. Text in German. 2010. 8/yr. EUR 23.20 domestic; EUR 26.40 in Austria; EUR 31.25 in Switzerland; EUR 35 elsewhere; EUR 2.90 newsstand/cover (effective 2011). adv. **Document type:** *Magazine, Consumer.*
Published by: Delius Klasing Verlag GmbH, Siekerwall 21, Bielefeld, 33602, Germany. TEL 49-521-5590, FAX 49-521-559113, info@delius-klasing.de, http://www.delius-klasing.de. Adv. contact Melanie Schwarz. Circ: 40,000 (paid).

796.323 USA ISSN 2159-0826
GV885.47
▼ **THE REAL AAU BASKETBALL.** Text in English. 2009. q. free to qualified personnel (effective 2011). **Document type:** *Magazine, Trade.* **Description:** Provides full of editorial content of critical interest to basketball coach members, ensuring prolonged attention to advertising messages.
Published by: Lessiter Publications, 225 Regency Ct, Ste 200, Brookfield, WI 53045. TEL 262-782-4480, 800-645-8455, FAX 262-782-1252, info@lesspub.com, http://www.lesspub.com/. Pub. Todd Rank.

796.357 USA ISSN 1057-9540
REDS REPORT. Text in English. 1988. m. USD 24.95; USD 2.50 newsstand/cover (effective 2001). adv. **Document type:** *Magazine, Consumer.* **Description:** Includes extensive coverage of the Cincinnati Reds baseball club for fans.
Published by: Columbus Sports Publications, 1350 W 5th Ave, 30, Columbus, OH 43212. TEL 614-486-2202. Ed. Frank Moskowitz. adv.: B&W page USD 400, color page USD 600; 13 x 10. Circ: 7,200.

796.323 FRA ISSN 1774-0835
REVERSE; original basketbal magazine. Text in French. 2005. q. EUR 25 (effective 2007). back issues avail. **Document type:** *Magazine, Consumer.*
Published by: Les Editions Reverse, 14 rue Soleillet, Paris, 75020, France. TEL 33-1-40334476.

796.334 MEX ISSN 1605-5683
REVISTA MORELIA. Text in Spanish. irreg. **Description:** Includes notes and short articles about Mexican soccer league, with particular emphasis on Morelia's team.
Media: Online - full text.
Address: http://www.geocities.com/Baja/Mesa/4930/principal.html.

796.352 CAN ISSN 1713-2452
REVUE GOLF A G P INTERNATIONAL. (Association des Golfeurs Professionnels) Text in French. 2004. 5/yr. CAD 29.95 (effective 2008). adv. **Document type:** *Magazine, Consumer.*
Formed by the merger of (1992-2004): Golf International (1189-4830); (2002-2004): Revue Golf A G P (1702-4625)
Published by: Editions Gesca, C.P. 9425, Succ. Sainte-Foy, Sainte-Foy, PQ G1V 4B8, Canada. TEL 514-904-5537, 877-997-4653, contact@editionsgesca.ca.

796.352 DEU
RHEINGOLF MAGAZIN. Text in German. 2001. 3/yr. adv. **Document type:** *Magazine, Consumer.*
Formerly (until 2005): Rheingolf News
Published by: Agentur Michael Jacoby, Dieselstr 5, Pulheim, 50259, Germany. TEL 49-2238-30210, FAX 49-2238-302121. adv.: color page EUR 1,725. Circ: 20,000 (controlled).

796.352 USA ISSN 1947-6469
▼ **RHODE ISLAND GOLF JOURNAL.** Text in English. forthcoming 2010. m. USD 9.99 per issue (effective 2009). **Document type:** *Magazine, Consumer.* **Description:** Features articles on golf for Rhode Island.
Published by: In Publishing, 9769 NW 45 Ln, Miami, FL 33178. TEL 736-314-0456, info@miamigolfjournal.com.

796.352 USA
ROCHESTER GOLF WEEK & SPORTS LEDGER. Text in English. 1988. w. USD 20 (effective 2000). adv. bk.rev. illus. reprints avail. **Document type:** *Newspaper, Consumer.* **Description:** Serves the golf sport market.
Published by: Expositor Ledger Newspapers, 2535 Brighton Henrietta Town Line Rd, Rochester, NY 14623-2711. TEL 585-427-2468, FAX 585-271-8521. Ed., R&P Dave Eaton. Adv. contact Barbara Morgenstern. Circ: 26,000.

796.352 USA
ROCKY MOUNTAIN GOLF. Text in English. 2000. a. USD 5.95 (effective 2001). adv. **Description:** Covers the past, present, and future of golf in the Vail Valley.
Formerly (until Apr. 2002): Vail Valley Golf
Published by: Rocky Mountain Media LLC, 160 W Beaver Creek Blvd, Ste C-102, Avon, CO 81620. TEL 970-879-5250, FAX 970-879-4650, sjacobs@mtnmags.com, http://www.macmediaweb.com. Pub. Michael Barry TEL 970-926-5700. Adv. contact Lee DePaolo TEL 970-476-1019. color page USD 4,137; trim 8.375 x 10.875.

796.332 NLD
RODA JC KRANT. Text in Dutch. 2/yr. adv.
Published by: (Roda JC), EFKA Uitgevers bv, Postbus 155, Weert, 6000 AD, Netherlands. TEL 31-495-450105, FAX 31-495-539485, info@efka-uitgevers.nl, http://www.efka-uitgevers.nl. adv.: color page EUR 2,700; trim 289 x 415. Circ: 150,000.

796.332 NLD
RODACTION. Text in Dutch. 4/yr. EUR 16.50 (effective 2008). adv.
Published by: (Roda JC), EFKA Uitgevers bv, Postbus 155, Weert, 6000 AD, Netherlands. TEL 31-495-450105, FAX 31-495-539485, info@efka-uitgevers.nl, http://www.efka-uitgevers.nl. adv.: color page EUR 1,750; trim 230 x 297.

796.332 NLD
RODAPLAY. Text in Dutch. free (effective 2008). adv.
Published by: (Roda JC), EFKA Uitgevers bv, Postbus 155, Weert, 6000 AD, Netherlands. TEL 31-495-450105, FAX 31-495-539485, info@efka-uitgevers.nl, http://www.efka-uitgevers.nl. adv.: color page EUR 650; trim 120 x 160. Circ: 8,000 (free).

796.334 CHE ISSN 1660-0878
ROTBLAU. Text in German. 1921. m. CHF 8 newsstand/cover (effective 2008). adv. **Document type:** *Magazine, Consumer.*
Former titles (until 2002): Hattrick (1660-5845); (until 1996): Fussballclub Basel. Club-Organ (1660-5853)
Published by: Friedrich Reinhardt Verlag, Missionsstr 36, Basel, 4012, Switzerland. TEL 41-61-2646450, FAX 41-61-2646488, verlag@reinhardt.ch, http://www.reinhardt.ch.

796.334 CHE ISSN 1661-304X
ROTWEISS. Text in German. 2005. m. CHF 80 (effective 2008). adv. **Document type:** *Magazine, Consumer.*
Related titles: French ed.: Hop Suisse!. ISSN 1661-3031. 2005.
Published by: Friedrich Reinhardt Verlag, Missionsstr 36, Basel, 4012, Switzerland. TEL 41-61-2646450, FAX 41-61-2646488, verlag@reinhardt.ch, http://www.reinhardt.ch.

796.333 USA ISSN 0162-1297
GV944.8
RUGBY. Text in English. 1975. bi-m. USD 19.95 (effective 2010). adv. bk.rev. 64 p./no. 3 cols./p.; back issues avail. **Document type:** *Magazine, Consumer.* **Description:** Contains coverage of all U.S. championships and news on the world rugby scene, including Canada, Europe, South Africa, Australia, New Zealand and the South Pacific. Regular coverage of topics from fitness and nutrition to refereeing. Includes profiles of clubs, personalities and tournaments.
Indexed: SD, SportS.
Published by: American International Media, 33 Kings Hwy, Ste 1, Orangeburg, NY 10962. TEL 845-359-4225, FAX 845-359-4698, publisher@rugbymag.com. Ed., Pub. Stephen Hanks. adv.: B&W page USD 1,200, color page USD 1,500. Circ: 10,000 (paid).

796.333 CAN ISSN 1203-5793
RUGBY CATALOGUE OF INFORMATION SOURCES. Text in English. a. USD 20. **Document type:** *Abstract/Index.* **Description:** Reflects the latest literature and concerns about the sport from around the world.
Published by: (International Rugby Information Centre (IRIC)), Sport Information Resource Centre (SIRC)/Centre de Documentation pour le Sport, 180 Elgin St, Ste 1400, Ottawa, ON K2P 2K3, Canada. TEL 613-231-7472, FAX 613-231-3739.

796.3 GBR ISSN 0080-4827
RUGBY FOOTBALL LEAGUE OFFICIAL GUIDE. Text in English. 1980. a. GBP 8 (effective 1999). adv. **Document type:** *Directory.* **Description:** Directory listing contact details for all office holders, officials, clubs and organizations within the British Rugby League.
Published by: Rugby Football League, Red Hall, Red Hall Ln, Leeds, W Yorks LS17 8NB, United Kingdom. TEL 44-113-2329111, FAX 44-113-2323666. Ed., R&P, Adv. contact John Huxley. Circ: 500.

796.333 IRL ISSN 1393-7391
RUGBY IRELAND INTERNATIONAL. Text in English. 1993. 6/yr. adv. **Document type:** *Magazine, Consumer.*
Formerly (until 1997): Leinster Rugby Magazine (0791-9549)
Published by: New Century Publishing Ltd., 10b Lanesville, Monkstown, Co. Dublin, Ireland. TEL 353-1-8244844, FAX 353-1-2844522, century@indigo.ie. Adv. contact James Jackson. color page EUR 2,349. Circ: 20,000 (paid and controlled).

796.333 PNG
RUGBY LEAGUE NEWS. Text in English. 1979. 28/yr. (during season). adv. illus.
Published by: Word Publishing Co., PO Box 1982, Boroko, Papua New Guinea. Ed. Sikio Oyassi. Circ: 6,000.

796.333 AUS
RUGBY LEAGUE WEEK. Variant title: League Week. Text in English. 1970. 32/yr. (during rugby season). AUD 166.50 domestic; AUD 168.50 in New Zealand; AUD 201.60 elsewhere; AUD 5.50 newsstand/cover (effective 2008). adv. **Document type:** *Magazine, Consumer.* **Description:** Delivers news, opinion, in-depth features and essential information on the game of rugby and its personalities.
Former titles (until 2002): League Week (1445-2553); (until 2000): Rugby League Week (0035-9742)
Related titles: Online - full text ed.
Indexed: A11, SD, T02.
Published by: A C P Magazines Ltd. (Subsidiary of: P B L Media Pty Ltd.), 54-58 Park St, Sydney, NSW 2000, Australia. TEL 61-2-92828000, FAX 61-2-91263769, research@acpaction.com.au, http://www.acp.com.au. Ed. Martin Lenehan. Adv. contact Cameron Jones TEL 61-2-92889123. color page AUD 2,500; trim 275 x 312. Circ: 22,532. **Subscr. to:** Magshop, Reply Paid 4967, Sydney, NSW 2001, Australia. TEL 61-2-136116, subs@magstore.com.au, http://shop.magstore.com.au.

796.3338 GBR ISSN 1466-0105
RUGBY LEAGUE WORLD. Text in English. 1976. m. GBP 39 domestic; GBP 46 in Europe; GBP 60 elsewhere; GBP 3.50 per issue domestic; GBP 4.50 per issue in Europe; GBP 5.50 per issue elsewhere (effective 2009). back issues avail. **Document type:** *Magazine, Consumer.* **Description:** Features league news as well as trivia for the avid rugby fan.
Formerly (until 1999): Open Rugby (0958-5427)
Related titles: Online - full text ed.
Published by: League Publications Ltd., Wellington House, Briggate, Brighouse, W Yorks HD6 1DN, United Kingdom. TEL 44-1484-401895, FAX 44-1484-401995, info@totalrl.com. Ed. Richard de la Riviere. Adv. contact Honor James. Circ: 25,000.

796.333 GBR
RUGBY LEAGUER. Text in English. 1949. w. adv. bk.rev. illus.; stat. back issues avail. **Document type:** *Newspaper.* **Description:** Contains news and features on Rugby League teams and matches.
Published by: Lancashire Publications Ltd., Martland Mill Ln, Wigan, Lancs WN5 0LX, United Kingdom. TEL 44-1942-228000, FAX 44-1942-214004. Ed. Steve Brady. Adv. contact Richard Woods. Circ: 16,000.

796.333 JPN
RUGBY MAGAZINE. Text in Japanese. 1972. m. JPY 9,480 (effective 2000). **Document type:** *Consumer.*
Published by: Baseball Magazine Sha, 3-10-10 Misaki-cho, Chiyoda-ku, Tokyo, 101-0061, Japan. FAX 81-3-3238-0106. Ed. Kazuhiro Tamura.

796.333 FRA ISSN 2102-0477
▼ **LE RUGBY MAGAZINE.** Text in French. 2009. bi-m. EUR 25 (effective 2010). **Document type:** *Magazine, Consumer.*
Published by: Lafont Presse, 53 Rue du Chemin Vert, Boulogne-Billancourt, 92100, France. TEL 33-1-46102121, FAX 33-1-45792211.

796.522 NZL ISSN 0114-1406
RUGBY NEWS. Text in English. 1970. 36/yr. NZD 139 domestic; NZD 199 in Australia; NZD 229 elsewhere (effective 2008). **Document type:** *Magazine, Consumer.* **Description:** Showcases all the latest news, events, in-depth reporting, exclusive interviews and coverage of: Super 14, Tri Nations, Bledisloe Cup, All Blacks, Sevens and International rugby, plus grassroots reporting at club and school levels.
Former titles (until 1988): New Zealand Rugby News (0111-9672); (until 1981): Rugby News (0110-3679)
Published by: Rugby Press International, Level One, 3 Robert St, Ellerslie, PO Box 11553, Auckland, New Zealand. TEL 64-9-5255434, FAX 64-9-5255435. Ed. Dave Campbell. Pub. Margaret Mitchell.

796.333 NLD ISSN 0166-9648
RUGBY NIEUWS. Text in Dutch. 1977. 10/yr. adv. bk.rev. **Document type:** *Newspaper.* **Description:** Covers national rugby matches.
Published by: Dutch Rugby Union/Nederlandse Rugby Bond, Postbus 8811, Amsterdam, 1006 JA, Netherlands. TEL 31-20-4808100, FAX 31-20-4808101, info@rugby.nl, http://www.rugby.nl.

796.333 ZAF ISSN 1022-2499
RUGBY REVIEW. Cover title: South Africa Rugby Review. Text in English. 1993. a. ZAR 29.95. adv. bk.rev. illus.; maps. **Document type:** *Journal, Consumer.*
Published by: Rugby 15 International, PO Box 4003, Durban, KwaZulu-natal 4000, South Africa. TEL 27-31-3045326, FAX 27-31-3053067. Ed. Wynand Claassen. Circ: 11,000.

796.333 GBR ISSN 1363-9633
RUGBY WORLD. Text in English. 1960. m. GBP 34.99 domestic; USD 69.70 in US & Canada; EUR 47 in Europe; GBP 52.10 elsewhere; GBP 3.90 newsstand/cover (effective 2009). adv. bk.rev. illus. back issues avail. **Document type:** *Magazine, Consumer.* **Description:** Provides a comprehensive round-up of rugby action, results and fixtures as well as dynamic photography.
Formerly (until 1996): Rugby World and Post (0268-9804); Which was formed by the merger of (1960-1985): Rugby World (0035-9777); Rugby Post; Rugby Wales
Related titles: Online - full text ed.
Indexed: A11, SD, SportS, T02, U01, WBA, WMB.
—CCC.
Published by: I P C Country & Leisure Media Ltd. (Subsidiary of: I P C Media Ltd.), Westover House, West Quay Rd, Poole, Dorset, BH15 1JG, United Kingdom. http://www.ipcmedia.com. Ed. Paul Morgan TEL 44-20-31484702. Adv. contact Andrew Boxer TEL 44-20-31484251. color page GBP 2,995; trim 230 x 300. Circ: 46,047. **Dist. by:** MarketForce UK Ltd. salesinnovation@marketforce.co.uk, http://www.marketforce.co.uk/.

811 USA ISSN 0882-018X
RUNDY'S JOURNAL AND CONFEDERATION COURIER. Text in English. 1976. s-a. USD 10. back issues avail. **Document type:** *Newsletter.* **Description:** Covers baseball.
Published by: Rundy's Journal, 217 Elizabeth St, 7, New York, NY 10012. TEL 212-966-1233. Ed., R&P John A Craig. Circ: 350.

794.72 RUS
RUSSKII BIL'YARD. Text in Russian. bi-m. USD 95 in United States.
Published by: Izdatel'stvo Vityaz, Tikhvinskaya ul 39, str 2, Moscow, 103055, Russian Federation. TEL 7-095-9724450, FAX 7-095-9724450. Ed. V V Yunak. **Dist. by:** East View Information Services, 10601 Wayzata Blvd, Minneapolis, MN 55305. TEL 952-252-1201, 800-477-1005, FAX 952-252-1202, info@eastview.com, http://www.eastview.com.

796.357 USA
S A B R BULLETIN. Text in English. 1971. q. free to members (effective 2010). adv. back issues avail. **Document type:** *Bulletin, Trade.* **Description:** Instructs members committee and chapter events, book reviews, and conferences and other baseball-related events.
Related titles: Online - full text ed.: free (effective 2010).
Indexed: SD.

S

Published by: Society for American Baseball Research, Inc., 812 Huron Rd, Ste 719, Cleveland, OH 44115. TEL 216-575-0500, 800-969-7227, FAX 216-575-0502, info@sabr.org. Adv. contact Susan Petrone.

796.357 ZAF ISSN 1021-3570
S A BASEBALL DIGEST. (South African) Text in English. 1993. q. ZAR 37.40. illus. **Document type:** *Journal, Consumer.*
Published by: (Christian Media Network), K & F Colour, PO Box 260272, Excom, Johannesburg 2023, South Africa.

796.358 ZAF ISSN 1022-6478
S A CRICKETER. (South African) Text in English. 1993. irreg. ZAR 3 per issue; USD 5 per issue foreign. illus. **Document type:** *Monographic series, Consumer.*
Published by: S.A. Cricketer, PO Box 146, Germiston, 1400, South Africa. sac@ats.co.za, http://www.cricket.org/.

796.333 ZAF ISSN 1810-5742
S A RUGBY NEWS. (South African) Text in English. 2004. m. **Document type:** *Magazine, Consumer.*
Published by: Juiced Media (Pty) Ltd., 1 Rosebery Ave, Durban North, 4052, South Africa. TEL 27-31-5737240, FAX 27-31-5643999, mail@juicedmedia.co.za. Ed. Chris Schoeman.

796.352 305.4 ZAF ISSN 1996-1391
S A WOMAN GOLFER. (South African) Text in English. 2007. q. ZAR 239.40 for 3 yrs. (effective 2007). adv. **Document type:** *Magazine, Consumer.*
Published by: S A Woman Golfer cc, PO Box 2210, Jukskei Park, 2153, South Africa. FAX 27-86-5177395. Ed. Shelley Galliver. Adv. contact Lynda Coulentianos TEL 27-83-6274523. color page ZAR 18,000; trim 210 x 276.

796.352 GBR ISSN 1475-8636
S G B GOLF. (Sports Goods Buyer) Text in English. 2001. m. GBP 76 domestic; GBP 98 in Europe; GBP 128 elsewhere; free to qualified personnel (effective 2009). adv. back issues avail. **Document type:** *Magazine, Trade.* **Description:** Provides golf industry retail stock purchasers with the latest industry news, product information and market intelligence.
Related titles: Online - full text ed.: free to qualified personnel (effective 2009).
—CCC.
Published by: Datateam Publishing Ltd, 15a London Rd, Maidstone, Kent ME16 8LY, United Kingdom. TEL 44-1622-687031, FAX 44-1622-757646, info@datateam.co.uk, http://www.datateam.co.uk. Ed. Duncan Lennard TEL 44-1934-641417. Pub. Paul Ryder TEL 44-1622-699105. Adv. contact Roger Bourne. color page GBP 1,575; trim 229 x 306.

796.332 USA
(YEAR) SAN DIEGO CHARGERS OFFICIAL YEARBOOK. Text in English. 1994. irreg., latest 1995. illus. index. back issues avail. **Document type:** *Yearbook, Magazine, Consumer.*
Published by: Woodford Publishing, Inc., PO Box 910, Tiburon, CA 94920. TEL 415-397-1853, FAX 415-399-0942. Ed. Kate Hanley. Pub. Laurence J Hyman. R&P David Lilienstein. Adv. contact Tony Khing.

796.332 USA
SAN DIEGO PADRES OFFICIAL YEARBOOK. Text in English. 1984. irreg., latest 1993. illus. **Document type:** *Magazine, Consumer.*
Published by: Woodford Publishing, Inc., PO Box 910, Tiburon, CA 94920. TEL 415-397-1853, FAX 415-399-0942. Ed. Jon Rochmis. Pub. Laurence J Hyman. R&P, Adv. contact David Lilienstein.

196.332 USA
SAN FRANCISCO 49ERS GAMEDAY INSIDER MAGAZINE. Text in English. 1997. 10/yr. **Document type:** *Magazine, Consumer.*
Formerly: San Francisco 49ers GameDay Magazine
Published by: Woodford Publishing, Inc., 5900 Hollis St, Ste K, Emeryville, CA 94608. TEL 510-250-3006, 800-359-3373, FAX 510-250-3012, mail@woodfordpub.com, http://www.woodfordpub.com. Ed. C. David Burgin. Pubs. C David Burgin, Daniel C Ross. Adv. contact Tony Khing.

196.332 USA
SAN FRANCISCO 49ERS (YEAR) OFFICIAL YEARBOOK. Text in English. 1982. a. illus. index. back issues avail. **Document type:** *Yearbook, Magazine, Consumer.*
Published by: Woodford Publishing, Inc., PO Box 910, Tiburon, CA 94920. TEL 415-397-1853, FAX 415-399-0942. Ed. Kate Hanley. Pub. Laurence J Hyman. R&P David Lilienstein. Adv. contact Tony Khing.

796 QAT
AL-SAQR AL-RIYADI. Text in Arabic. 1977. m. USD 20 to individuals; USD 25 to institutions. adv. bk.rev. illus. back issues avail.
Formerly: Saqer - Falcon
Published by: Al- Saqr Magazine, P O Box 4925, Doha, Qatar. TEL 320476. Ed. M Kazem. Circ: 120,000.

796.334 GBR ISSN 1467-534X
SCENE@ ST. JAMES'. Text in English. 1994. q. GBP 9.99 in United Kingdom; GBP 14.99 in Europe; GBP 19.99 elsewhere; GBP 3.50 newsstand/cover in United Kingdom; GBP 4 newsstand/cover in Europe; GBP 5 newsstand/cover elsewhere (effective 2001). adv. **Document type:** *Magazine, Consumer.* **Description:** Football cub publication containing news and information concerning the Newcastle football (soccer) team and players.
Formerly (until 2000): Black and White (1353-6591)
Published by: Crystalspirit Ltd., Unit 4, Princes Park, Princeway, Team Valley, Gateshead, Tyne and Wear NE11 0NF, United Kingdom. TEL 44-191-491-1234, FAX 44-191-491-4730, subs@nufcpubs.co.uk, http://www.nufcpubs.co.uk. Ed. Paul Tully. Adv. contact Suzanne Williams. Circ: 50,000. **Subscr. to:** PO Box 17, Gateshead, Tyne & Wear NE11 0YU, United Kingdom. **Dist. by:** Seymour Distribution Ltd, 86 Newman St, London W1T 3EX, United Kingdom. FAX 44-207-396-8002, enquiries@seymour.co.uk.

796.332 DEU
SCHIEDSRICHTER-ZEITUNG. Text in German. 1928. bi-m. EUR 15 (effective 2009). **Document type:** *Magazine, Trade.*
Formerly (until 1996): D F B Schiedsricherzeitung
Published by: Deutscher Fussball-Bund/German Soccer Association, Otto-Fleck-Schneise 6, Frankfurt Am Main, 60528, Germany. TEL 49-69-67880, FAX 49-69-6788204, info@dfb.de.

796.352 CAN ISSN 0711-3226
SCORE; Canada's golf magazine. Text in English. 1981. bi-m. CAD 16. adv. bk.rev. illus. **Description:** Covers golf instruction, travel, profiles, tournament news, and equipment.
Published by: Canadian Controlled Media Communications, 287 MacPherson Ave, Toronto, ON M4V 1A4, Canada. TEL 416-928-2909, FAX 416-928-1357, weeksy@direct.com. Ed. Bob Weeks. Circ: 125,000.

796.333 ZAF ISSN 1811-315X
SCRUM. Text in English. 2003. bi-m. adv. **Document type:** *Magazine, Consumer.*
Published by: Imbongi Communications, PO Box 287, Woodstock, 7915, South Africa. TEL 27-21-4611705, FAX 27-21-4658512, info@imbongisa.com, http://www.imbongisa.com. Adv. contact Cullum Johnston. Circ: 25,000.

796.334 USA ISSN 1554-2416
SCUOLA CALCIO COACHING MAGAZINE. Text in English. 2005. 9/yr. **Document type:** *Magazine, Consumer.*
Address: PO Box 15669, Wilmington, NC 28408. TEL 910-686-7706, 800-954-7086, info@soccercoachingmagazine.com, http://www.soccercoachingmagazine.com.

796.357 USA ISSN 1934-922X
SENIOR SOFTBALL NEWS. Text in English. s-w. **Document type:** *Newspaper, Consumer.*
Formerly (until 200?): Senior Softball - USA News
Published by: Senior Softball - USA, 2701 K St, Ste 101A, Sacramento, CA 95816. TEL 916-326-5303, FAX 916-326-5304, info@seniorsoftball.com.

796.352 USA ISSN 1551-4145
GV961
SHIVAS IRONS SOCIETY. JOURNAL. Text in English. 2004. s-a. illus. 80 p./no.; back issues avail. **Document type:** *Journal, Academic/Scholarly.* **Description:** Covers all aspects of the literature and art of golf.
Published by: Shivas Irons Society, PO Box 222339, Carmel, CA 93922. TEL 831-899-8441, FAX 831-899-8453, MemberServices@shivas.org.

796.334 GBR ISSN 1758-4337
SHOOT (LONDON). Text in English. 1969. m. back issues avail. **Document type:** *Magazine, Consumer.* **Description:** Aims to bring its young readers closer to the game of soccer and is strongly biased towards the premier league clubs and top stars.
Former titles (until 2007): Shoot Monthly (1473-9453); (until 2001): Shoot (0308-5236); Which incorporated: Goal (0017-1492)
Published by: I P C Country & Leisure Media Ltd. (Subsidiary of: I P C Media Ltd.), The Blue Fin Bldg, 110 Southwark St, London, SE1 0SU, United Kingdom. magazinesales@ipcmedia.com, http://www.ipcmedia.com. **Dist. by:** MarketForce UK Ltd.

796.357 JPN
SHUKAN BASEBALL. Text in Japanese. 1958. w. JPY 18,870 (effective 2000).
Published by: Baseball Magazine Sha, 3-10-10 Misaki-cho, Chiyoda-ku, Tokyo, 101-0061, Japan. FAX 81-3-3238-0106. Ed. Motoharu Yanamoto.

796.357 USA
SIDEKICKS. Text in English. 1993. bi-m. USD 9.97. **Document type:** *Magazine, Consumer.* **Description:** Contains information on all aspects of soccer for players at all levels.
Published by: Southern Media Corporation, 9625 W. Sample Rd., Coral Springs, FL 33065. TEL 304-344-0332. Ed. Steve Hanks. Pub. Frank Genovese. adv.: B&W page USD 2,400, color page USD 3,000. Circ: 25,000.

796.3 GBR ISSN 1749-9720
SKY SPORTS FOOTBALL YEARBOOK. Text in English. 1970. a. GBP 40 per issue (effective 2010). adv. back issues avail. **Document type:** *Bulletin, Consumer.* **Description:** Covers the qualifying and final tournaments of the World Cup as well as a review of the three major European cup competitions.
Formerly (until 2003): Rothmans Football Yearbook (0080-4088)
Published by: Headline Book Publishing, 338 Euston Rd, London, NW1 3BH, United Kingdom. TEL 44-207-8736000, enquiries@headline.co.uk.

796.323 USA ISSN 1072-625X
SLAM (NEW YORK). Text in English. 1994. 10/yr. USD 12.97 (effective 2008). adv. back issues avail. **Document type:** *Magazine, Consumer.* **Description:** Offers the basketball fan news, views, and interviews with all the major teams and players.
Related titles: Online - full text ed.
—CCC.
Published by: Source Interlink Companies, 6420 Wilshire Blvd, 10th Fl, Los Angeles, CA 90048. TEL 323-782-2000, FAX 323-782-2585, dheine@sourceinterlink.com, http://www.sourceinterlinkmedia.com. Eds. Ryan Jones, Ben Osborne. Pub. Dennis Page. adv.: B&W page USD 7,460, color page USD 10,280. Circ: 200,000.

796.3 USA
SLO-PITCH GAME. Text in English. 1970. 7/yr. USD 11; USD 1.75 newsstand/cover (effective 2001). adv. **Document type:** *Newspaper.*
Published by: United States Slo-Pitch Softball Association, 13540 Lake City Way, N E, Ste 3, Seattle, WA 98125. TEL 206-367-2420, FAX 206-367-2636. Eds. Al Ramsey, Dick Stephens. Adv. contact Kirk Tortillotte. B&W page USD 3,995, color page USD 5,195; trim 13.31 x 10.31. Circ: 114,500 (paid).

796.333 NZL ISSN 2230-312X
▼ **SMALL BLACKS MAGAZINE.** Text in English. 2011. q. NZD 5.99 (effective 2011). **Document type:** *Magazine, Trade.* **Description:** Provides educational articles, player profiles and training tips for rugby kids.
Published by: Media Titles Group, Level 1, 3 Robert St, Ellerslie, Auckland, 1051, New Zealand. TEL 64-9-5255434, FAX 64-9-5255435, info@mediatitlesgroup.com, http://www.mediatitlesgroup.com/.

796.325 CAN
SMASH. Text in French. 1970. 2/yr. CAD 12.84 for 2 yrs. (effective 1999). adv. bk.rev. **Document type:** *Newsletter.*
Published by: Federation de Volley-Ball du Quebec, 4545 ave Pierre de Coubertin, C P 1000, Sta M, Montreal, PQ H1V 3R2, Canada. TEL 514-252-3065, FAX 514-252-3176. Ed., R&P Elaine Lauzon. Adv. contact Dominique Pepin. Circ: 2,500.

796.342 CHE ISSN 1424-9251
SMASH; Swiss tennis magazine. Text in English. 1971. 11/yr. CHF 89 domestic; CHF 111 foreign (effective 2003). adv. back issues avail. **Document type:** *Magazine, Consumer.*
Former titles (until 1990): Smash Tennis Magazin (1660-0932); (until 1977): Tennis
Published by: (Swiss Tennis Association), St. Galler Tagblatt AG, Fuerstenlandstr 122, St Gallen, 9001, Switzerland. TEL 41-71-2727439, FAX 41-71-2727449. Ed. Doris Rickenbacher. Pub. Thomas Muellerschoen. Adv. contact Paul Diethelm. B&W page CHF 4,328, color page CHF 6,998. Circ: 20,000 (paid and controlled).

796.342 USA ISSN 1930-2592
SMASH. Text in English. 2005. q. USD 9.97 domestic; USD 4.99 per issue (effective 2009). adv. **Document type:** *Magazine, Consumer.* **Description:** Covers tennis from a youthful perspective, including sports personalities, music, fashion and other sports topics.
Published by: Miller Publishing Group, Miller Sports Group LLC., 79 Madison Ave, 8th Fl, New York, NY 10016. TEL 212-636-2700, FAX 212-636-2730. Ed. James Martin TEL 212-636-2708. Adv. contact Jeff William TEL 212-636-2758. color page USD 16,550, B&W page USD 11,050; trim 9 x 10.875.

796.334 FRA ISSN 1765-9086
SO FOOT. Text in French. 2003. 10/yr. EUR 19 (effective 2011). adv. **Document type:** *Magazine, Consumer.*
Address: 13 bis rue de Versigny, Paris, 75018, France. Ed. Franck Annese.

796.334 USA ISSN 0163-4070
GV942
SOCCER AMERICA. Text in English. 1971. m. free to members (effective 2010). adv. bk.rev. illus. back issues avail.; reprints avail. **Document type:** *Magazine, Consumer.* **Description:** Provides comprehensive, national soccer news and information to soccer fans.
Supersedes (in 1972): Soccer West
Related titles: Microform ed.: (from PQC).
Indexed: A22, SPI, SportS.
Published by: Soccer America Communications LLC, 1140 Broadway, 4th Fl, New York, NY 10001. TEL 212-849-2901, FAX 212-204-2038. Ed. Paul Kennedy TEL 510-559-2211. Adv. contact Doug Murdock TEL 510-374-2967.

796.344 306.483 GBR ISSN 1466-0970
GV944.G7
➤ **SOCCER AND SOCIETY.** Text in English. 2000. bi-m. GBP 410 combined subscription in United Kingdom to institutions (print & online eds.); EUR 489, USD 610 combined subscription to institutions (print & online eds.) (effective 2012). adv. bk.rev. Index. back issues avail.; reprint service avail. from PSC. **Document type:** *Journal, Academic/Scholarly.* **Description:** Examines the historical, sociological, political, and economic aspects of soccer.
Related titles: Online - full text ed.: ISSN 1743-9590. GBP 369 in United Kingdom to institutions; EUR 440, USD 549 to institutions (effective 2012) (from IngentaConnect).
Indexed: A01, A03, A08, A22, C25, CA, CABA, E01, E12, GH, LT, P34, PEI, R12, RRTA, S02, S03, SCOPUS, SD, T02, T05, W11.
—IE, Ingenta. **CCC.**
Published by: Routledge (Subsidiary of: Taylor & Francis Group), 4 Park Sq, Milton Park, Abingdon, Oxon OX14 4RN, United Kingdom. TEL 44-20-70176000, FAX 44-20-70176336, subscriptions@tandf.co.uk, http://www.routledge.com. Adv. contact Linda Hann TEL 44-1344-779945. **Subscr. to:** Taylor & Francis Ltd., Journals Customer Service, Sheepen Pl, Colchester, Essex CO3 3LP, United Kingdom. TEL 44-20-70175544, FAX 44-20-70175198.

796.334 USA
SOCCER DIGEST ANNUAL GUIDE. Text in English. a. **Document type:** *Magazine, Consumer.*
Published by: Century Publishing Inc., E 5710 Seltice Way, Post Falls, ID 83854. TEL 208-765-6300, 800-824-1806, FAX 208-676-8476, privacy@CenturyPublishing.com, http://www.centurypublishing.com.

796.334 AUS ISSN 1321-7763
SOCCER INTERNATIONAL. Text in English. 1993. m. AUD 79 (effective 2008). adv. **Document type:** *Magazine, Consumer.*
Related titles: Online - full text ed.
Indexed: SD.
Published by: Blitz Publications, PO Box 4075, Mulgrave, VIC 3170, Australia. TEL 61-3-95748460, FAX 61-3-95748899, info@blitzmag.com.au. Ed. Mark van Aken TEL 61-3-95748999. Adv. contact Marcus Stergiopoulos TEL 61-3-95748999.

796.334 USA ISSN 0560-3617
GV942
SOCCER JOURNAL. Text in English. 1941. 7/yr. free to members (effective 2010). bk.rev. illus. back issues avail.; reprints avail. **Document type:** *Journal, Academic/Scholarly.* **Description:** Contains technical and tactical articles, news and updates on important events, thoughts from opinion leaders in the sport and features on the interesting people and issues of the game.
Related titles: Online - full text ed.
Indexed: PEI, SD, SPI, SportS, T02.
—BLDSC (8318.021640), IE, Ingenta.
Published by: National Soccer Coaches Association of America, 800 Ann Ave, Kansas City, KS 66101. TEL 913-362-1747, 800-458-0678, FAX 913-362-3439, info@nscaa.com. Ed. Martin Jay.

796.334 JPN
SOCCER MAGAZINE. Text in Japanese. 1966. w. JPY 21,420 (effective 2000).
Published by: Baseball Magazine Sha, 3-10-10 Misaki-cho, Chiyoda-ku, Tokyo, 101-0061, Japan. FAX 81-3-3238-0106. Ed. Takehiko Ito.

796.334 IRL ISSN 0790-3871
THE SOCCER MAGAZINE. Variant title: Irish Soccer Magazine. Text in English. 1984. 9/yr. adv. **Document type:** *Magazine, Consumer.*
Published by: Victory Irish Promotions, PO Box 7992, Dun Laoghaire, Co. Dublin, Ireland. TEL 353-1-2804481, FAX 353-1-2804481. Adv. contact Margaret Walsh. B&W page EUR 1,206, color page EUR 1,651; trim 210 x 297. Circ: 13,000 (paid and controlled).

796.334 USA
SOCCER NOW. Text in English. 1977. q. USD 9; USD 2 per issue (effective 2001). adv. **Description:** Membership magazine of the American Youth Soccer Organization.
Published by: American Youth Soccer Organization, 12501 S Isis Ave, Hawthorne, CA 90250. TEL 310-643-6455, 800-usa-ayso, FAX 310-643-5310. Ed. David Brown.

796.334 USA ISSN 1072-0170
GV943.4
SOCCER RULES BOOK. Text in English. 19??. a. USD 6.95 per issue (effective 2009). adv. **Document type:** *Handbook/Manual/Guide, Trade.* **Description:** Contains the official rules for soccer and is used by coaches, officials, players and many fans who wish to know more about the rules of the game.
Former titles (until 1994): Soccer Rule Book (0731-9541); (until 1980): National Federation of State High School Associations. Soccer Rules (0163-4763)
Published by: National Federation of State High School Associations, PO Box 690, Indianapolis, IN 46206. TEL 317-972-6900, 800-776-3462, FAX 317-822-5700, info@nfhs.org, http://www.nfhs.org.

796.3 ZAF ISSN 1729-973X
SOCCERLIFE. Variant title: Four Four Two. Text in English. 2004. m. ZAR 143.55 domestic; ZAR 320 foreign (effective 2006). adv. **Document type:** *Magazine, Consumer.*
Published by: Johnnic Communications Ltd., 4 Biermann Ave, Rosebank, Johannesburg, 2196, South Africa. TEL 27-11-2803000, FAX 27-11-2805151, http://www.johncom.co.za/. adv.: page ZAR 22,260; trim 230 x 280.

796.3 CAN ISSN 0849-5564
SOFTBALL B.C. MAGAZINE; the voice of the British Columbia Amateur Softball Association. Text in English. 1980. q. CAD 10. adv. back issues avail. **Description:** Contains membership information and articles of sport related interest.
Published by: Softball British Columbia, Sunnyside Mall, P O Box 45570, Surrey, BC V4A 9N3, Canada. TEL 604-531-0044, FAX 604-531-8831. Ed. Penny Gardner. Circ: 7,000.

796.357 USA ISSN 1543-8570
SOFTBALL MAGAZINE. Text in English. 1997 (Apr.). 10/yr. USD 20 domestic; USD 50 in Canada (effective 2003).
Published by: Brevard Softball Magazine, 38 Nevins Ct., Merritt Is, FL 32953-4657. info@softballmag.com. Pub. Gene Smith. Adv. contact Bob Grey.

796.357 USA
GV881
SOFTBALL RULES BOOK. Text in English. 199?. a. USD 6.95 per issue (effective 2009). adv. **Document type:** *Handbook/Manual/Guide, Trade.* **Description:** Contains the official rules for softball and is used by coaches, officials, players and many fans who wish to know more about the rules of the game.
Former titles (until 1983): National Federation of State High School Associations. Softball Rule Book (0732-2844); National Federation of State High School Associations. Softball Rules. 12-Inch Fast Pitch and 12-Inch Slow Pitch (0146-8286)
Published by: National Federation of State High School Associations, PO Box 690, Indianapolis, IN 46206. TEL 317-972-6900, 800-776-3462, FAX 317-822-5700, info@nfhs.org, http://www.nfhs.org.

796.357 USA
SOFTBALL WORLD. Text in English. 1977. m. USD 16.25. adv. bk.rev. **Document type:** *Newspaper.*
Published by: Sporting World, PO Box 10151, Oakland Lake Sta, Oakland, CA 94610. TEL 510-428-2000. Ed. George Epstein.

796.352 ESP
SOLO GOLF. Text in Spanish. m. EUR 40 domestic; EUR 60 in Europe; EUR 90 elsewhere (effective 2009). adv. **Document type:** *Magazine, Consumer.*
Published by: Alesport S.A., Gran Via 8-10, Hospitalet de Llobragat, Barcelona, 08902, Spain. TEL 34-93-4315533, FAX 34-93-2973905, http://www.alesport.com. Ed. Teresa Bagaria.

796.334 USA ISSN 1085-9705
GV942
SOLO SOCCER. Text in Spanish. 1991. m. USD 3.50 per issue. adv. **Document type:** *Magazine, Consumer.*
Formerly (until 1994): Soccer U S A
Related titles: Online - full text ed.
Indexed: I04.
Address: PO Box 742149, Houston, TX 77274-2149. TEL 713-774-4675, FAX 713-774-4666. Ed. Eduardo Beltramini. Pub., R&P Mario Duenas. Adv. contact Tracy Hall. B&W page USD 3,100, color page USD 4,250; trim 11 x 8.5. Circ: 60,000.

796.332 ITA ISSN 1826-3887
SOLOCALCIO. Text in Italian. 2005. m. adv. **Document type:** *Magazine, Consumer.*
Related titles: Online - full text ed.
Published by: Europress s.r.l., Via Donini, 33-35, San Lazzaro di Savena, 40068, Italy. TEL 39-051-6257700, FAX 39-051-6257573.

796.352 ZAF ISSN 1027-3476
SOUTH AFRICAN GOLFERS YEARBOOK. Text in English. 1996. a.
Published by: Picasso Headline (Pty) Ltd, Mill St, PO Box 12500, Gardens, 8010, South Africa. TEL 27-21-4621023, FAX 27-21-4621124, info@picasso.co.za, http://www.picasso.co.za. Ed. Jonathan Hobday.

796.333 ZAF
SOUTH AFRICAN RUGBY. Variant title: S.A. Rugby. Text in English. 1995. 10/yr. ZAR 103 (effective 2000). adv. illus. **Document type:** *Journal, Consumer.*
Published by: Strobe Communications, PO Box 2081, Capetown, South Africa. TEL 27-21-6855004, FAX 27-21-6855159, http://www.magzone.co.za. Ed. Chris Schoeman.

796.332 AUS ISSN 1834-5506
SOUTH AUSTRALIAN FOOTBALL BUDGET. Text in English. 1914. w. AUD 90. adv. bk.rev. back issues avail. **Document type:** *Report, Consumer.* **Description:** Contains statistics on football, and articles on players, clubs and current issues.
Published by: South Australian National Football League, PO Box 1, West Lakes, SA 5021, Australia. http://www.sanfl.com.au. Ed. Shane Fuller. Circ: 5,000.

796.352 USA ISSN 1947-6507
▼ **SOUTH CAROLINA GOLF JOURNAL.** Text in English. forthcoming 2010. m. USD 9.99 per issue (effective 2009). **Document type:** *Magazine, Consumer.* **Description:** Features articles on golf for South Carolina.
Published by: In Publishing, 9769 NW 45 Ln, Miami, FL 33178. TEL 736-314-0456, info@miamigolfjournal.com.

796.352 USA
SOUTHERN CALIFORNIA GOLF. Text in English. q. adv. **Document type:** *Magazine, Consumer.* **Description:** Contains information on the best golf courses in southern California as well as local amateurs and professionals.
Published by: Sunwest Publishing, 3769 Tibbetts Ave, Ste A, Riverside, CA 92506. TEL 909-682-3026, FAX 909-682-0246, iemail@pacbell.net, http://www.inlandempiremagazine.com/index.html.

796.352 USA
SOUTHLAND GOLF MAGAZINE. Text in English. m. USD 26 (effective 2008). adv. back issues avail. **Document type:** *Magazine, Consumer.* **Description:** Covers all things golf, from local courses and players to an expanded golf lifestyle section, including features on automotive, real estate, fine dining and resort destinations.
Published by: Churm Media, 1451 Quail St, Ste 201, Newport Beach, CA 92660. TEL 949-757-1404 ext 303, FAX 949-757-1996, http://www.churmmedia.com. Ed. Michael Miller. adv.: B&W page USD 3,945, color page USD 4,295; trim 8.375 x 10.75. Circ: 55,000.

796.352 USA
SOUTHPAW ACTIVITIES. Text in English. 1961. bi-m. membership. **Document type:** *Newsletter.* **Description:** Covers news of golf tournaments, golf courses, members' activities.
Published by: National Association of Left-Handed Golfers, 3249 Hazelwood Dr SW, Atlanta, GA 30311-3035. nalg@mindspring.com, http://www.nalg.org. Ed. Ken Ahrens.

796.334 ZAF ISSN 1028-2920
SOWETAN SOCCER GUIDE. Text in English. 1997. a. adv.
Published by: Highbury Safika Media, PO Box 8145, Roggebaai, 8012, South Africa. TEL 27-21-4160141, FAX 27-21-4180132, info@hsm.co.za, http://www.hsm.co.za. adv.: color page ZAR 29,950.

796.332 USA
SPARTAN. Text in English. 18/yr. **Description:** Focuses on Michigan State basketball and football.
Published by: Greenville News, Inc, 109 N Lafayette St, Greenville, MI 48838. TEL 800-732-6532, FAX 616-754-8559. Ed. Jim Companori. Pub. John Stafford.

SPITBALL; the literary baseball magazines. *see* LITERATURE

796.332 NLD ISSN 2211-9809
▼ **SPORT 1 VOETBALMAGAZINE.** Abbreviated title: Sport Een Voetbalmagazine. Text in Dutch. 2011. 10/yr. EUR 44.95 (effective 2011). adv. **Document type:** *Magazine, Consumer.*
Published by: Elf BV, Postbus 97843, The Hague, 2516 EH, Netherlands.

THE SPORT AMERICANA PRICE GUIDE TO BASEBALL COLLECTIBLES. *see* HOBBIES

THE SPORT AMERICANA TEAM BASEBALL CARD CHECKLIST. *see* HOBBIES

THE SPORT AMERICANA TEAM FOOTBALL AND BASKETBALL CARD CHECKLIST. *see* HOBBIES

796.334 GBR ISSN 1757-9902
SPORT IQ SOCCER. Text in English. 2008. bi-m. free (effective 2011). **Document type:** *Magazine, Trade.* **Description:** Features: futsal, street soccer, mini soccer, freestyling, women's football, 5-a-side, disability soccer, as well as the 11-a side game.
Media: Online - full text.
Published by: Sport IQ Publications Ltd., 101 Aberdeen Ave, Manadon Park, Plymouth, Devon PL5 3UN, United Kingdom. TEL 44-8459-569688, info@sport-iq.com.

796.357 USA ISSN 0275-0732
GV863.A1
THE SPORTING NEWS BASEBALL YEARBOOK. Variant title: Baseball Yearbook. Text in English. 1981. a. USD 7.99 (effective 2008). adv. back issues avail. **Document type:** *Magazine, Consumer.*
Published by: American City Business Journals, Inc. (Subsidiary of: Advance Publications, Inc.), 120 W Morehead St, Charlotte, NC 28202. TEL 704-973-1000, FAX 704-973-1001, http://www.acbj.com. Ed. Mike Nahrstedt.

796.3 USA ISSN 0078-3862
GV885
SPORTING NEWS BOOKS OFFICIAL N B A GUIDE. Text in English. 1958. a. USD 15.95 (effective 2007). stat. **Document type:** *Magazine, Consumer.*
Former titles (until 2004): The Sporting News Official N B A Guide; The Sporting News N B A Guide; (until 1992): Official N B A Guide; The Official N B A Guide
Published by: (National Basketball Association), American City Business Journals, Inc. (Subsidiary of: Advance Publications, Inc.), 120 W Morehead St, Charlotte, NC 28202. TEL 704-973-1000, FAX 704-973-1001, http://www.acbj.com. Ed. Craig Carter.

796.323 USA ISSN 0895-0598
THE SPORTING NEWS COLLEGE BASKETBALL YEARBOOK. Text in English. 1988. a. USD 7.99 per issue (effective 2008). back issues avail. **Document type:** *Magazine, Consumer.*
Supersedes in part (in 198?): Sporting News College and Pro Basketball Yearbook
Published by: American City Business Journals, Inc. (Subsidiary of: Advance Publications, Inc.), 120 W Morehead St, Charlotte, NC 28202. TEL 704-973-1000, FAX 704-973-1001, info@bizjournals.com, http://www.bizjournals.com.

796.332 USA ISSN 0733-2823
THE SPORTING NEWS COLLEGE FOOTBALL YEARBOOK. Variant title: College Football Yearbook. Text in English. 1982. a. USD 7.99 (effective 2008). adv. back issues avail. **Document type:** *Magazine, Consumer.*
Published by: American City Business Journals, Inc. (Subsidiary of: Advance Publications, Inc.), 120 W Morehead St, Charlotte, NC 28202. TEL 704-973-1000, FAX 704-973-1001, http://www.acbj.com. Ed. Mike Nahrstedt.

796.357 USA ISSN 1552-9304
GV1202.F33
THE SPORTING NEWS FANTASY BASEBALL. Text in English. 1991. a. USD 7.99 per issue (effective 2008). back issues avail. **Document type:** *Magazine, Consumer.*
Former titles (until 199?): The Sporting News Fantasy Baseball Owners Manual (1052-7591); Sporting News Fantasy Baseball Yearbook
Published by: American City Business Journals, Inc. (Subsidiary of: Advance Publications, Inc.), 120 W Morehead St, Charlotte, NC 28202. TEL 704-973-1000, FAX 704-973-1001, info@bizjournals.com, http://www.bizjournals.com.

796.332 USA ISSN 1552-9290
GV939.A1
THE SPORTING NEWS FANTASY FOOTBALL. Running title: T S N Fantasy Football. Text in English. 1994. a. USD 7.99 per issue (effective 2008). back issues avail. **Document type:** *Magazine, Consumer.*
Formerly (until 2001): The Sporting News Fantasy Football Owners Manual (1526-2707)
Published by: American City Business Journals, Inc. (Subsidiary of: Advance Publications, Inc.), 120 W Morehead St, Charlotte, NC 28202. TEL 704-973-1000, FAX 704-973-1001, info@bizjournals.com, http://www.bizjournals.com. Ed. Mike Nahrstedt.

796.323 USA ISSN 0739-3067
GV885.515.N37
THE SPORTING NEWS OFFICIAL N B A REGISTER. Variant title: N B A Register. Text in English. 1981. a. **Document type:** *Magazine, Consumer.*
Former titles (until 1983): Official N B A Register (0894-315X); (until 1982): Official National Basketball Association Register (0271-8170)
Published by: American City Business Journals, Inc. (Subsidiary of: Advance Publications, Inc.), 120 W Morehead St, Charlotte, NC 28202. TEL 704-973-1000, FAX 704-973-1001, http://www.acbj.com.

796.323 USA ISSN 0895-0601
GV885.7
THE SPORTING NEWS PRO BASKETBALL YEARBOOK. Text in English. 1988. a. USD 7.99 (effective 2008). adv. back issues avail. **Document type:** *Magazine, Consumer.*
Supersedes in part (in 198?): The Sporting News College and Pro Basketball Yearbook (0733-6047)
Published by: American City Business Journals, Inc. (Subsidiary of: Advance Publications, Inc.), 120 W Morehead St, Charlotte, NC 28202. TEL 704-973-1000, FAX 704-973-1001, http://www.acbj.com. Ed. Mike Nahrstedt.

796.332 USA ISSN 0732-1902
GV937
THE SPORTING NEWS PRO FOOTBALL GUIDE. Text in English. 1970. a. USD 7.99 (effective 2007). stat. **Document type:** *Magazine, Consumer.*
Formerly: Sporting News' National Football Guide (0081-3788)
Published by: American City Business Journals, Inc. (Subsidiary of: Advance Publications, Inc.), 120 W Morehead St, Charlotte, NC 28202. TEL 704-973-1000, FAX 704-973-1001, http://www.acbj.com. Ed. Craig Carter.

796.332 USA ISSN 0276-2307
GV937
THE SPORTING NEWS PRO FOOTBALL YEARBOOK. Text in English. 1981. a. USD 7.99 (effective 2008). adv. back issues avail. **Document type:** *Magazine, Consumer.*
Published by: American City Business Journals, Inc. (Subsidiary of: Advance Publications, Inc.), 120 W Morehead St, Charlotte, NC 28202. TEL 704-973-1000, FAX 704-973-1001, http://www.acbj.com.

796.357 USA ISSN 1930-3149
GV880.22
SPORTING NEWS ULTIMATE BASEBALL SCOUTING GUIDE. Variant title: Baseball Scouting Guide. Ultimate Baseball Scouting Guide. Text in English. 2004. a. **Document type:** *Guide, Consumer.*
Published by: American City Business Journals, Inc. (Subsidiary of: Advance Publications, Inc.), 120 W Morehead St, Charlotte, NC 28202. TEL 704-973-1000, FAX 704-973-1001, http://www.acbj.com.

796.3 FRA ISSN 1960-7857
SPORTMAG. Text in French. 2007. m. (11/yr). EUR 35 (effective 2009). **Document type:** *Magazine, Consumer.*
Published by: Even'dia, 15 Av. Charles Cros, Jacou, 34830, France. TEL 33-4-67541491, FAX 33-4-67574259.

SPORTS COLLECTORS DIGEST; voice for the hobby. *see* HOBBIES

SPORTS MARKET REPORT. *see* HOBBIES

794.6 USA
SPORTS REPORTER. Text in English. 1940. w. USD 25 (effective 2000). adv. **Document type:** *Newspaper.* **Description:** Covers bowling in the metropolitan New York region as well as nationally, with tournament results and announcements of upcoming competitions.
Address: PO Box 1491, Secaucus, NJ 07096-1491. TEL 973-875-4339, 888-838-2695, FAX 973-875-1247. Ed., Pub., R&P, Adv. contact Dan McDonough. Circ: 5,000 (paid and controlled).

796.357 USA
SPORTS WEEKLY NEWSLETTER - BASEBALL. Text in English. 1968. w. USD 200 (effective 1998). **Document type:** *Newsletter.*
Published by: R.W. Livingston, Ed. & Pub., PO Box 60008, North, SC 29419-0008. TEL 803-797-6173.

796.323 USA
SPORTS WEEKLY NEWSLETTER - BASKETBALL. Text in English. w. USD 100 (effective 1998). **Document type:** *Newsletter.*
Published by: R.W. Livingston, Ed. & Pub., PO Box 60008, North, SC 29419-0008. TEL 803-797-6173.

796.332 USA
SPORTS WEEKLY NEWSLETTER. FOOTBALL ANALYST. Text in English. 1968. w. USD 100 (effective 1998). charts; stat.
Published by: R.W. Livingston, Ed. & Pub., PO Box 60008, North, SC 29419-0008. TEL 803-797-6173. Circ: 3,000.

796.357 USA ISSN 1061-687X
SPORTSTURF. Text in English. 1985. m. USD 40 domestic; USD 65 foreign; free to qualified personnel (effective 2006). adv. 44 p./no.; **Document type:** *Magazine, Trade.* **Description:** Directed to owners and landscape/ground managers of athletic fields, golf courses, parks and schools, colleges and universities.
Former titles: Golf and Sportsturf (1049-0000); Sportsturf (0890-0167)
Related titles: Online - full text ed.
Indexed: G06, G07, G08, I05, I07, S23, SD, T02.
—CCC.

S

Published by: Green Media (Subsidiary of: M2Media360), 1030 West Higgins Rd., Suite 230, Park Ridge, IL 60068. Ed. John Kmitta TEL 630-499-1017. Pub. Douglas B Hebbard TEL 847-356-7675. adv.: B&W page USD 3,370, color page USD 4,270. Circ: 25,000 (controlled).

796.334 ITA ISSN 1970-0318
SPORTY CALCIO. Text in Italian. 2006. m. **Document type:** *Magazine, Consumer.*
Published by: Cantelli Editore Srl, Via Saliceto 22c, Castelmaggiore, BO 40013, Italy. TEL 39-051-6328811, FAX 39-051-6328815, cantelli.editore@cantelli.net, http://www.cantelli.net.

796.357 USA ISSN 0894-2889
GV875.A1
SPRING TRAINING; baseball yearbook. Text in English. 1988. a., latest 2001. USD 6 (effective 2001); USD9.50 for Pre-Order of 2002 Edition. adv. **Document type:** *Magazine, Consumer.* **Description:** Focuses on Major League Baseball's exhibition season in Florida and Arizona with team and schedule information. Gives full information about the upcoming regular season.
Related titles: Online - full text ed.
Published by: Spring Training, Inc., 107 W Poplar Ave, Carrboro, NC 27510. TEL 919-967-2420. Ed. Myles Friedman. Pub. Merle Thorpe. Circ: 150,000 (paid).

796.357 USA
SPRING TRAINING BASEBALL YEARBOOK. Text in English. a. adv. **Document type:** *Yearbook, Consumer.*
Published by: Vanguard Publications, 107 W Poplar Ave, Carboro, NC 27510. TEL 919-967-2420, FAX 919-967-6294, http://www.vanguardpublications.com. Ed. Myles Friedman. Pub. Merle Thorpe. Adv. contact Reem Nourallah TEL 202-333-8622. color page USD 2,900; trim 8.125 x 10.5. Circ: 136,000.

796.345 CAN ISSN 0821-025X
SQUASH LIFE. Text in English. 1977. 4/yr. CAD 15. adv. bk.rev. charts; illus. back issues avail. **Document type:** *Newsletter.* **Description:** News about squash tournaments and clubs; playing tips.
Formerly (until 1981): Let Point (0821-0241)
Related titles: ◆ Supplement(s): Squash Ontario Handbook. ISSN 1191-8624.
Indexed: SD, SportS.
Published by: Squash Ontario, 1185 Eglinton Ave E, North York, ON M3C 3C6, Canada. TEL 416-426-7201, FAX 416-426-7393. Ed., Adv. contact Sherry Funston. Pub. Roman Lehecka. Circ: 5,000.

796.345 CAN ISSN 1191-8624
SQUASH ONTARIO HANDBOOK. Text in English. 1982. a.
Formerly (until 1992): Squash Ontario Yearbook (0836-3552)
Related titles: ◆ Supplement to: Squash Life. ISSN 0821-025X.
Published by: Squash Ontario, 1185 Eglinton Ave E, North York, ON M3C 3C6, Canada. TEL 416-426-7201, FAX 416-426-7393. Ed. Sherry Funston. Pub. Roman Lehecka.

796 GBR ISSN 1356-7780
THE SQUASH PLAYER. Abbreviated title: S P. Text in English. 1971. bi-m. GBP 24 domestic; GBP 27 in Europe; GBP 30 elsewhere (effective 2009). adv. bk.rev. back issues avail. **Document type:** *Magazine, Consumer.* **Description:** Features informative articles on Squash.
Formed by the merger of: Squash Player International (0262-4338); Squash World (0952-8512)
Indexed: SportS.
Published by: McKenzie Publishing Ltd., Longhouse, 460 Bath Rd, Longford, Mddx UB7 0EB, United Kingdom. TEL 44-1753-775511, FAX 44-1753-775512. Ed. Ian McKenzie. Adv. contact Joe Loredo.

796.31 USA
SQUASHTALK. Text in English. irreg. **Document type:** *Magazine, Consumer.*
Media: Online - full text.
Published by: Squashtalk.com, 648, Concord, MA 01742-0648. TEL 978-371-3953, editor@squashtalk.com. Ed., Pub. Ron Beck.

796.332 GBR ISSN 1752-8534
STOKE CITY SOUTHERN SUPPORTERS CLUB. Text in English. 2006. a. (Sum.). free to members (effective 2009). **Document type:** *Magazine, Consumer.*
Formerly (until 2006): Potters Monthly (1363-6235)
Related titles: Online - full text ed.
Address: c/o Julia Zuk, Membership Secretary, 97 Blossom Way, W Drayton, Midds UB7 9HG, United Kingdom. TEL 44-1895-421650, membershipinfo@scssc.co.uk. Ed. Neil Chadwick TEL 44-118-9787905.

796.257 USA
GV877
STREET & SMITH'S BASEBALL. Text in English. 1941. a. USD 7.99 per issue domestic; USD 15 per issue foreign (effective 2008). adv. illus.; stat. **Document type:** *Yearbook, Consumer.* **Description:** All about baseball: the statistics and schedules, profiles of teams and players, commentary and forecasts.
Former titles (until 1987): Street and Smith's Official Yearbook. Baseball (0161-2018); Street and Smith's Baseball Yearbook (0491-1520)
Published by: Street & Smith's Sports Group (Subsidiary of: American City Business Journals, Inc.), 120 W Morehead St, Ste 230, Charlotte, NC 28202. TEL 704-973-1300, FAX 704-973-1576, annuals@streetandsmiths.com, http://www.streetandsmiths.com. Pub. Mike Kallay. Adv. contact Patrick Wood TEL 704-973-1358. page USD 9,275; trim 8 x 10.875.

796.323 USA ISSN 1522-5836
GV885.7
STREET & SMITH'S COLLEGE BASKETBALL. Text in English. a. USD 7.99 per issue domestic; USD 15 per issue foreign (effective 2008). adv. **Document type:** *Yearbook, Consumer.* **Description:** Covers major college teams, conferences, independents with over 450 scouting reports, team and conference schedules, and individual statistics, TV-radio listings, and pre-season ratings.
Supersedes in part (in 1988): Street and Smith's Official Yearbook. College, Pro, Prep Basketball (0272-6262); Which was formerly: Street and Smith's Official College, Pro, and Prep Yearbook. Basketball (0149-7103); Street and Smith's College and Pro Official Yearbook. Basketball (0092-511X)

Published by: Street & Smith's Sports Group (Subsidiary of: American City Business Journals, Inc.), 120 W Morehead St, Ste 230, Charlotte, NC 28202. TEL 704-973-1300, FAX 704-973-1576, annuals@streetandsmiths.com, http://www.streetandsmiths.com. Pub. Mike Kallay. Adv. contact Patrick Wood TEL 704-973-1358. page USD 6,725; trim 8 x 10.875.

796.33 USA
GV956.8
STREET & SMITH'S COLLEGE FOOTBALL. Text in English. 1940. a. USD 7.99 per issue domestic; USD 15 per issue foreign (effective 2008). adv. illus.; stat. **Document type:** *Yearbook, Consumer.* **Description:** Furnishes analyses of more than 270 college football teams. Schedules include teams from each major conference. Player and team profiles, historical and topical features, review of past season and preview of coming season.
Formerly (until 1986): Street and Smith's Official Yearbook. College Football (0091-9977)
Published by: Street & Smith's Sports Group (Subsidiary of: American City Business Journals, Inc.), 120 W Morehead St, Ste 230, Charlotte, NC 28202. TEL 704-973-1300, FAX 704-973-1576, annuals@streetandsmiths.com, http://www.streetandsmiths.com. Pub. Mike Kallay. Adv. contact Patrick Wood TEL 704-973-1358. page USD 10,325; trim 8 x 10.875.

796.32 USA
GV885.7
STREET & SMITH'S PRO BASKETBALL. Text in English. a. USD 5.99 per issue domestic; USD 15 per issue foreign (effective 2009). adv. illus. **Document type:** *Yearbook, Consumer.* **Description:** For coaches, players and avid basketball enthusiasts. Covers scouting reports, team and conference schedules, individual statistics, TV-radio listings, and pre-season ratings.
Supersedes in part (in 1988): Street and Smith's Official Yearbook. College, Pro, Prep Basketball (0272-6262); Which was formerly: Street and Smith's Official College, Pro and Prep Yearbook. Basketball (0149-7103); Street and Smith's College and Pro Official Yearbook. Basketball (0092-511X)
Published by: Street & Smith's Sports Group (Subsidiary of: American City Business Journals, Inc.), 120 W Morehead St, Ste 230, Charlotte, NC 28202. TEL 704-973-1300, FAX 704-973-1576, annuals@streetandsmiths.com, http://www.streetandsmiths.com. Pub. Mike Kallay. Adv. contact Patrick Wood TEL 704-973-1358. page USD 6,725; trim 8 x 10.875.

796.33 USA ISSN 1053-2641
GV937
STREET & SMITH'S PRO FOOTBALL. Text in English. 19??. a. USD 7.99 per issue domestic; USD 15 per issue foreign (effective 2008). adv. illus. reprints avail. **Document type:** *Yearbook, Consumer.* **Description:** Provides information regarding teams representing the National Football conference, American Football conference, and Canadian Football League. Includes NFL rosters, schedules, individual player records, review of past season and preview of coming season.
Formerly (until 1987): Street and Smith's Official Yearbook. Pro Football (0092-3214)
Published by: Street & Smith's Sports Group (Subsidiary of: American City Business Journals, Inc.), 120 W Morehead St, Ste 230, Charlotte, NC 28202. TEL 704-973-1300, FAX 704-973-1576, annuals@streetandsmiths.com, http://www.streetandsmiths.com. Pub. Mike Kallay. Adv. contact Patrick Wood TEL 704-973-1358. page USD 13,875; trim 8 x 10.875.

STREET TALK. *see* SOCIAL SERVICES AND WELFARE

796.334 USA
STRIKER MAGAZINE. Text in English. 2005. q. adv. **Document type:** *Magazine, Consumer.*
Published by: Harris Publications, Inc., 1115 Broadway, New York, NY 10010. TEL 212-807-7100, FAX 212-924-2352, subscriptions@harris-pub.com, http://www.harris-pub.com/. Ed. Lang Whitaker. Pub. Dennis S Page. Adv. contact Scott Nemeroff.

796.334 USA
STRIKER WEST. Text in English. q. **Document type:** *Magazine, Consumer.* **Description:** Includes association news and a calendar of events.
Published by: New York State West Youth Soccer Association, 41 Riverside Dr, Corning, NY 14830. TEL 607-962-9923, FAX 607-962-0525, office@nyswysa.org, http://www.nyswysa.org.

STUDENT PULSEN. *see* COLLEGE AND ALUMNI

796.352 USA
SUBURBAN GOLF. Text in English. 1990. 7/yr. adv. **Document type:** *Magazine, Consumer.*
Published by: Journal News Custom Publishing, One Gannett Dr, White Plains, NY 10604. TEL 914-694-5385, FAX 914-696-8418. Ed. Sean Mayer TEL 914-696-8527. Adv. contact Charlie Serra TEL 914-694-5157. B&W page USD 5,500; trim 8.25 x 10.875. Circ: 100,000 (free).

796.334 371.3 DEU ISSN 1438-0153
SUCCESS IN SOCCER; the teaching magazine for winning soccer. Text in English. 1998. bi-m. EUR 33 (effective 2011). adv. back issues avail. **Document type:** *Magazine, Consumer.*
Indexed: PEI, SD, T02.
Published by: Philippka-Sportverlag Konrad Honig, Rektoratsweg 36, Muenster, 48159, Germany. TEL 49-251-230050, FAX 49-251-2300579, info@philippka.de, http://www.philippka.de.

796.352 USA
SUN GOLF. Text in English. 8/yr. USD 12 (effective 2000). adv. **Document type:** *Magazine, Consumer.* **Description:** Covers all levels of golf throughout Arizona, including the PGA SWS.
Published by: Sun Magazine Group, 7237 N 31st Dr, Phoenix, AZ 85051-7401. TEL 602-242-5045, FAX 602-242-5016, http://www.sunmagazines.com/. Ed. Les McCook. Pub. Richard Bacon TEL 602-242-5045. adv.: B&W page USD 1,950, color page USD 2,400; trim 10.25 x 13.25. Circ: 50,000.

796.342 USA
SUN TENNIS MAGAZINE. Text in English. 1983. bi-m. USD 15 (effective 2007). adv. 28 p./no. 4 cols./p.; **Document type:** *Magazine, Consumer.* **Description:** Covers all levels of tennis throughout Arizona and the southwest. Includes tennis news, features, tournament results, and calendar of events.

Published by: Sun Magazine Group, 7237 N 31st Dr, Phoenix, AZ 85051-7401. TEL 602-242-5045, FAX 602-242-5016. Ed., Pub., R&P Richard Bacon TEL 602-242-5045. adv.: B&W page USD 1,550, color page USD 2,000; trim 10.25 x 13.25. Circ: 20,000.

796.352 FIN ISSN 0784-5502
SUOMEN GOLFLEHTI. Text in Finnish. 1987. 8/yr. adv. **Document type:** *Magazine, Consumer.*
Related titles: Online - full text ed.: 1999.
Published by: Suomen Golfliitto ry, Radiokatu 20, Helsinki, 00093, Finland. TEL 358-9-34812520, FAX 358-9-147145, office@golf.fi. adv.: color page EUR 5,500; 217 x 280.

796.342 ITA
SUPER TENNIS MAGAZINE. Text in Italian. 1978. m. (10/yr.). **Document type:** *Magazine, Consumer.*
Formerly: Tennis
Published by: Federazione Italiana Tennis, Viale dei Gladiatori 31, Rome, 00194, Italy. http://www.federtennis.it. Circ: 90,000.

796.323 ITA ISSN 0393-7852
SUPERBASKET. Text in Italian. 1978. 49/yr. EUR 130 domestic; EUR 240 foreign (effective 2008). adv. Supplement avail.; back issues avail. **Document type:** *Magazine, Consumer.*
Published by: Cantelli Editore Srl, Via Saliceto 22c, Castelmaggiore, BO 40013, Italy. TEL 39-051-6328811, FAX 39-051-6328815, cantelli.editore@cantelli.net, http://www.cantelli.net. Circ: 33,000.

796.334 FRA ISSN 1767-9966
SUPERFOOT MAG. Text in French. 2004. m. **Document type:** *Magazine, Consumer.*
Published by: Panini France S A, Z.I. Secteur D, Quartiers des Iscles, Saint-Laurent-du-Var, 06700, France. TEL 33-4-92125757.

796.334 NLD ISSN 1876-455X
SUPPORTERS MAGAZINE. Text in Dutch. 198?. 5/yr. EUR 14 membership (effective 2008).
Published by: Supportersvereniging van A Z, Postbus 9099, Alkmaar, 1800 GB, Netherlands. http://www.sv-az.nl. Ed. Jaap Hoeben. Circ: 4,000.

796.352 SWE ISSN 0346-2102
SVENSK GOLF; vi goer dig till en baetere golfare. Text in Swedish. 1946. 13/yr. SEK 395; SEK 40 newsstand/cover (effective 2004). adv. **Document type:** *Magazine, Consumer.*
Published by: (Svenska Golfoerbundet/Swedish Golf Federation), Svenska Golffoerbundets Affaersutveckling AB, Kevingestrand 20, PO Box 84, Danderyd, 18211, Sweden. TEL 46-8-6221500, FAX 46-8-6226930, http://www.svensk.golf.se. Ed. Stefan Cardner TEL 46-8-4445225. adv.: page SEK 66,000; 185 x 270. Circ: 350,000.

796.352 SWE ISSN 1100-3758
SVENSK GOLFGUIDE. Text in Swedish. 1988. a. SEK 75 (effective 1994).
Published by: Svenska Golffoerbundets Affaersutveckling AB, Kevingestrand 20, PO Box 84, Danderyd, 18211, Sweden.

796.352 HRV ISSN 1331-6117
SVIJET GOLFA. Text in Croatian. 1998. m. **Document type:** *Magazine, Consumer.*
Published by: R I M M Sport, Krajiska 20, Zagreb, 10000, Croatia. TEL 385-1-3701134, FAX 385-1-3704322, rimm.sport@zg.tel.hr. Ed. Drazen Slamar.

796.352 USA ISSN 1533-3434
T & L GOLF. (Travel & Leisure) Text in English. 1998. bi-m. free to qualified personnel (effective 2009); includes with subr. to Travel & Leisure. adv. illus.; tr.lit. 140 p./no.; **Document type:** *Magazine, Consumer.* **Description:** Provides the readers with information on world's best golf courses, superior hotels and restaurants and smart advice from top pros to keep their game in shape.
Formerly (until 2000): Travel & Leisure Golf (1097-4709)
Related titles: Online - full text ed.: Tlgolf.com.
Published by: American Express Publishing Corp., 1120 Ave of the Americas, New York, NY 10036. TEL 212-382-5600, FAX 212-764-2177, http://www.amexpub.com. Eds. Paul Rogers, John Atwood. adv.: B&W page USD 47,210, color page USD 65,000; trim 8 x 10.5. Circ: 600,000 (paid).

796.346 GBR ISSN 0039-8799
TABLE TENNIS NEWS. Abbreviated title: T T N. Text in English. 19??. 8/yr. GBP 2.95 per issue domestic to non-members; GBP 5.54 per issue in Europe to non-members; GBP 8.85 per issue elsewhere to non-members; free to members (effective 2009). adv. bk.rev. illus. 48 p./no.; back issues avail. **Document type:** *Magazine, Consumer.* **Description:** Gives up-to-date information on national and international table tennis events and activities.
Formerly (until 1966): Table Tennis
Published by: English Table Tennis Association, 3rd Fl, Queensbury House, Havelock Rd, Hastings, E Sussex TN34 1HF, United Kingdom. TEL 44-1424-722525, FAX 44-1424-422103, admin@ettahq.freeserve.co.uk. Ed. Ian Marshall.

796.334 GBR ISSN 1357-891X
TALK OF THE TYNE. Text in English. 1995. 8/yr. GBP 5.30; GBP 7.80 in Europe; GBP 8.80 elsewhere. adv. bk.rev. **Document type:** *Newsletter.* **Description:** A voice for the supporters of Newcastle United FC.
Related titles: Online - full text ed.
Address: PO Box 25, Spennymoor, Durham DL16 6GI, United Kingdom. TEL 44-1388-815878, FAX 44-1388-815878. Ed., Adv. contact Kevin Fletcher. Circ: 2,500 (paid).

796.334 IRN ISSN 1024-2244
TAMASHAGARAN; mahnameh futbol Iran. Text in Persian, Modern. 1992. m. IRR 36,000 newsstand/cover; IRR 98,000 newsstand/cover foreign. adv. illus. **Document type:** *Consumer.* **Description:** Covers the soccer scene inside Iran and at the international level. Publishes reports on domestic games and Asian tournaments, articles and commentary on the state of the game today, and interviews with players, coaches and officials.
Published by: Tamashagaran Publications, No.15, 3rd Fl., Golriz St., Mottahhari Ave., P O Box 15875-5564, Tehran, Iran. TEL 98-21-837060, FAX 98-21-832905. Ed., Pub., R&P Nader Davoodi. Adv. contact Souryeh Kabiri. Circ: 60,000 (paid).

796.323 USA ISSN 1942-0714
GV885.43.U54
TAR HEEL TIP-OFF. Variant title: M S P Tar Heel Tip-Off. Maple Street Press Tar Heel Tip-Off. Text in English. 2007. a. USD 12.99 per issue (effective 2011). back issues avail. **Document type:** *Handbook/ Manual/Guide, Consumer.*
Published by: Maple Street Press, 155 Webster St, Ste B, Hanover, MA 02339. TEL 781-347-4730, FAX 781-347-4732, info@maplestreetpress.com. Ed. Adrian Atkinson.

796.334 GBR ISSN 0963-049X
TEAM TALK. Text in English. 1991. m. GBP 29 domestic; GBP 37 foreign (effective 2000); GBP 2.50 newsstand/cover. adv. bk.rev. back issues avail. **Document type:** *Magazine, Consumer.*
Published by: Tony Williams Publications, Helland, North Curry, Somerset, Taunton TA3 6DU, United Kingdom. TEL 44-1823-490684, FAX 44-1823-490281. Ed., Pub., R&P Tony Williams. Adv. contact Forbes Chapman. color page GBP 1,200. Circ: 20,000 (paid).

796 FRA ISSN 1952-580X
TECHNIQUES & PRATIQUE DU SPORT. Text in French. 2006. irreg., latest 2007. back issues avail. **Document type:** *Monographic series, Consumer.*
Published by: Editions Solar, 12 av. d'Italie, Paris, 75627 Cedex 13, France. edito@solar.tm.fr, contact@solar.tm.fr, http://www.solar.tm.fr.

TEE TIME. *see* PHILATELY

796.342 CZE ISSN 0862-6766
TENIS; prvni cesky tenisovy magazin. Text in Czech, Slovak. 1990. m. CZK 312; CZK 39 newsstand/cover (effective 2010). adv. **Document type:** *Magazine, Consumer.*
Published by: T-Production s.r.o., Hudeckova 10, Prague 4, 140 00, Czech Republic. burians@volny.cz. Ed. Frantisek Kreuz.

796.342 JPN
➤ **TENISU JANARU/TENNIS JOURNAL.** Text in Japanese. 1982. m. illus. **Document type:** *Magazine, Consumer.*
Published by: Skui Janaru Kabushiki Kaisha/Ski Journal Publisher Inc., Araki-cho 20-Banchi, Shinjuku-ku, Intech 88 Bldg, Tokyo, 160-0007, Japan. TEL 81-3-33537092, FAX 81-3-33536633, sjsales@skijournal.co.jp. Ed. Seiji Miyashita.

796.334 GBR
THE TENNENT'S LAGER SCOTTISH FOOTBALL REVIEW. Text in English. 1980. a. GBP 6.95. adv. illus. **Document type:** *Journal, Consumer.*
Former titles (until 1998): Tennent's Lager Scottish Football League Review; Tartan Special Scottish Football League Review; Scottish Football League Review; B and Q Scottish Football League Review; Clydesdale Bank Scottish Football League Review (0260-8804)
Published by: Scottish Football League, 188 West Regent St, Glasgow, G2 4RY, United Kingdom. TEL 44-141-248-3844, FAX 44-141-221-7450. Ed. David C Thomson. Circ: 25,000.

796.332 USA
TENNESSEE FOOTBALL. Text in English. 2007. a. **Document type:** *Magazine, Consumer.*
Published by: Varsity Sports Media, 3401 Russ Circle, Ste E, Alcoa, TN 37701. TEL 865-379-0625, FAX 865-379-9653.

796.352 USA ISSN 1947-640X
▼ **TENNESSEE GOLF JOURNAL.** Text in English. forthcoming 2010. m. USD 9.99 per issue (effective 2009). **Description:** Features articles on golf for Tennessee.
Published by: In Publishing, 9769 NW 45 Ln, Miami, FL 33178. TEL 736-314-0456, info@miamigolfjournal.com.

796.342 USA ISSN 0040-3423
GV991
TENNIS. Text in English. 1965. 10/yr. USD 15 domestic; USD 35 in Canada; USD 50 elsewhere (effective 2009). adv. bk.rev. charts; illus. Index. back issues avail.; reprints avail. **Document type:** *Magazine, Consumer.* **Description:** Covers professional and amateur tennis, including playing instruction, the mental aspect of the game, courts, and equipment.
Related titles: Microfilm ed.: (from PQC); Online - full text ed.
Indexed: A11, A22, B04, BRD, C05, C11, C12, CPerI, ConsI, G05, G06, G07, G08, G09, H03, I05, I07, M01, M02, M04, MASUSE, MagInd, P02, P10, P48, P53, P54, PEI, PMR, PQC, R03, RGAb, RGPR, SD, SPI, SportS, T02, U01, W03, W05.
—IE, Infotrieve, Ingenta.
Published by: Miller Publishing Group, Miller Sports Group LLC., 79 Madison Ave, 8th Fl, New York, NY 10016. TEL 212-636-2700, FAX 212-636-2730. Ed. James Martin TEL 212-636-2708. Adv. contact Jeff William TEL 212-636-2758. B&W page USD 34,400, color page USD 51,610; trim 8 x 10.8125.

796.346 FRA ISSN 0984-421X
TENNIS DE TABLE MAGAZINE. Text in French. m. EUR 41 domestic; EUR 70 foreign (effective 2009). **Document type:** *Magazine, Consumer.* **Description:** Presents the world of ping-pong through interviews, in-depth coverage and game results.
Related titles: Online - full text ed.
Indexed: SD.
Published by: Federation Francaise de Tennis de Table, 3 Rue Dieudonne Costes, BP 40348, Paris, Cedex 13 75625, France. TEL 33-1-53945000, FAX 33-1-53945040, fftt@wanadoo.fr, http://www.fftt.com. Ed. Paul Courteau. Pub. Pierre Albertini.

796.342 BEL
TENNIS ECHO. Text in French. 1982. bi-m. USD 80. adv. illus. back issues avail. **Document type:** *Consumer.* **Description:** Covers international tennis matches and topics of interest to tennis players, including fitness and health, equipment, tactics, and how to improve your game.
Related titles: Dutch ed.
Published by: Tennis Promotion, Bergstraat 18, Grobbendonk, 2280, Belgium. TEL 32-13-522754, FAX 32-13-522472. Ed., R&P, Adv. contact Roger Vekemans. Circ: 50,000.

796.342 NLD ISSN 0928-9372
TENNIS & COACH. Text in Dutch. 1959. bi-m. EUR 34 (effective 2009). adv. **Document type:** *Magazine, Trade.*
Former titles (until 1992): Tennis en Coaching (0926-0145); (until 1990): Tennisleraar (0167-0093)
Published by: Tennis en Coach, Tegelstraat 1, Noord-Scharwoude, 1723 MJ, Netherlands. TEL 31-226-343436, FAX 31-226-343630. Ed. Marcel Crok. Adv. contact Mart Crok.

796.342 USA ISSN 1057-6851
GV991
TENNIS ILLUSTRATED (NEW YORK). Text in English. 1953. m. bk.rev. illus.
Formerly (until 1991): World Tennis (0043-910X); Which incorporated (in 1953): Raquet; Which was formerly (until 1951): American Lawn Tennis
Indexed: A25, A26, AcaI, B04, BRD, ConsI, E08, G05, G06, G07, G08, G09, HlthInd, M01, M02, MagInd, P02, P10, P53, P54, PMR, PQC, R03, R04, R06, RASB, RGAb, RGPR, S08, S09, SPI, SportS, W03.
Published by: Family Media, Inc., Men's and In-Home Group, PO Box 108, Miami, OK 74355. TEL 918-541-1934, FAX 918-541-1939, http://familymediainc.com.

796.342 FRA ISSN 0221-8127
TENNIS INFO. Text in French. m. (10/yr). EUR 17 domestic; EUR 29 foreign (effective 2009). **Document type:** *Magazine, Consumer.* **Description:** Presents the world of tennis through interviews, in-depth coverage and game results.
Published by: Federation Francaise de Tennis, 2 av. Gordon Bennett, Paris, 75016, France. TEL 33-1-47434800, FAX 33-1-47430494. Ed. Axel Labatiniere. Pub. Jacques Dupre. **Subscr. to:** Christian Bernard Abonnement (C B A), BP 6, Lille Cedex 9 59718, France. TEL 33-3-20121130.

796 ITA ISSN 0393-0890
TENNIS ITALIANO. Text in Italian. 1929. m. EUR 50 domestic; EUR 78 in the European Union; EUR 104 elsewhere (effective 2009). adv. bk.rev. illus. index. **Document type:** *Magazine, Consumer.* **Description:** Covers news about tennis, international and regional sports news, tests of rackets and shoes.
Related titles: Online - full text ed.
Published by: Edisport Editoriale SpA, Via Gradisca 11, Milan, MI 20151, Italy. TEL 39-02-38085, FAX 39-02-38010393, edisport@edisport.it, http://www.edisport.it. Circ: 70,000.

796.342 USA ISSN 1545-6609
TENNIS LIFE. Variant title: Tennis Life Magazine. Text in English. 19??. bi-m. USD 19.97 (effective 2010). adv. **Document type:** *Magazine, Consumer.*
Indexed: SD.
Published by: Goldman Group, Inc., PO Box 270, Lutz, FL 33559. TEL 813-949-0006, FAX 813-433-5181, deb@ggpubs.com. Adv. contact Todd Goldman TEL 813-949-0006 ext 222. Circ: 125,000.

796.342 USA ISSN 1548-8462
TENNIS LIFE EN ESPANOL. Text in Spanish. 2004 (Apr.). bi-m. **Document type:** *Magazine, Consumer.*
Published by: Goldman Group, Inc., PO Box 270, Lutz, FL 33559. TEL 813-949-0006, FAX 813-433-5181, deb@ggpubs.com, http://www.ggpubs.com.

796.342 DEU ISSN 0176-8794
TENNIS MAGAZIN. Text in German. 1976. 10/yr. EUR 49; EUR 4.90 newsstand/cover (effective 2011). adv. **Document type:** *Magazine, Consumer.*
Published by: Jahr Top Special Verlag, Troplowitzstr 5, Hamburg, 22529, Germany. TEL 49-40-389060, FAX 49-40-38906300, info@jahr-tsv.de, http://www.jahr-tsv.de. Ed. Dieter Genske. Adv. contact Holger Henopp. Circ: 21,176 (paid).

796.342 JPN
TENNIS MAGAZINE. Text in Japanese. 1970. w. JPY 6,840 (effective 2000). **Document type:** *Consumer.*
Indexed: MagInd.
Published by: Baseball Magazine Sha, 3-10-10 Misaki-cho, Chiyoda-ku, Tokyo, 101-0061, Japan. Ed. Masahiro Satoh.

796.342 NLD ISSN 1571-4284
TENNIS MAGAZINE. Text in Dutch. 2001. 8/yr. EUR 30 (effective 2009). **Document type:** *Magazine, Consumer.*
Formed by the merger of (2000-2001): Tennisrevue (1567-5297); Which superseded in part (in 2000): Tennis Revue (0928-5504); Which superseded in part (in 1993): Exclusive Sports & Resorts (0928-0766); Which was formerly (until 1992): Special Sports (0925-7470); (until 1990): Tennis Revue (0168-6488); (1981-1983): Tennisvaria (0167-921X); (1999-2001): Tennis (1566-4791); Which was formerly (until 1999): Tennis Magazine (0169-233X); (until 1985): Tennis (0167-0042); (19??-1978): Lawn Tennis (0023-9429)
Published by: Bohn Stafleu van Loghum B.V. (Subsidiary of: Springer Science+Business Media), Postbus 246, Houten, 3990 GA, Netherlands. TEL 31-30-6383872, FAX 31-30-6383991, boekhandels@bsl.nl, http://www.bsl.nl.

796.342 USA
TENNIS MIDWEST. Text in English. bi-m. adv.
Address: PO Box 24379, Edina, MN 55424-0379. TEL 612-920-8947, FAX 612-927-7155. Ed. Geoff Gorvin. Circ: 12,000.

796.342 DEU
TENNIS NORDWEST. Text in German. 4/yr. EUR 12 (effective 2009). adv. **Document type:** *Magazine, Consumer.*
Published by: (Tennisverband Nordwest e.V.), Pferdesport Verlag Rolf Ehlers GmbH, Rockwinkeler Landstr 20, Bremen-Oberneuland, 28355, Germany. TEL 49-421-2575544, FAX 49-421-2575543, info@ehlers-bremen.de, http://www.ehlers-bremen.de. Ed. Walter Marahrens. Adv. contact Maren Arndt.

796.342 ITA ISSN 1721-419X
TENNIS OGGI. Text in Italian. 1980. m. (10/yr.). EUR 25 domestic; EUR 52 in Europe; EUR 78 elsewhere (effective 2009). adv. **Document type:** *Magazine, Consumer.*
Formerly (until 1985): Tennis Lazio (1721-4203)
Published by: Edizioni Sportive Italiane, Via della Balduina 88, Rome, 00136, Italy. Ed. Michela Rossi. Circ: 30,000.

796.342 RUS ISSN 0130-9439
QA300
TENNIS PLUS. Text in Russian. m. USD 179.95 in United States.
—East View.
Address: Kropotkinskii per 4, Moscow, 119034, Russian Federation. TEL 7-095-2468047, FAX 7-095-2468047. **Dist. by:** East View Information Services, 10601 Wayzata Blvd, Minneapolis, MN 55305. TEL 952-252-1201, 800-477-1005, FAX 952-252-1202, info@eastview.com, http://www.eastview.com.

796.342 NLD ISSN 1879-4793
▼ **TENNIS SCHEURKALENDER.** Text in Dutch. 2009. a. EUR 14.95 (effective 2010).
Published by: Uitgeverij Solo, Laurillardlaan 29, Bilthoven, 3723 DD, Netherlands. TEL 31-30-2288147, FAX 31-30-2284943, info@uitgeverij-solo.com, http://www.uitgeverij-solo.com.

796.342 USA
TENNIS SERVER INTERACTIVE. Text in English. 1994. m. free. **Document type:** *Newsletter.* **Description:** News about tennis information on the Internet as well as other tennis information of general interest.
Media: Online - full text.
Published by: Tenagra Corporation, 1100 Hercules, Ste 120, Houston, TX 77058. Ed. Clifford Kurtzman.

796.342 GBR ISSN 0140-5497
TENNIS TODAY. Text in English. 1976. bi-m. adv. **Document type:** *Magazine, Consumer.*
—BLDSC (8790.761800).
Published by: Tennis Today Ltd., 14 Sykes Lane, Balderton, Newark, Notts, United Kingdom. TEL 44-1636-689169, FAX 44-1636-707952.

796.342 USA
TENNIS U S T A. (In 4 regional eds.) Text in English. 1990. m. membership. adv. **Document type:** *Magazine, Consumer.* **Description:** Includes news of the association's events on the national, regional and sectional level, with feature stories.
Published by: United States Tennis Association, PO Box 643767, Pittsburgh, PA 15264-3767. TEL 800-990-8782, http://www.usta.com. Circ: 440,000 (controlled).

796.342 305.4 USA ISSN 1937-7894
TENNIS VIEW. Text in English. 2008. q. USD 10 for 2 yrs. (effective 2008 - 2009). adv. **Document type:** *Magazine, Consumer.* **Description:** Promotes participation and growth of women's tennis through gear, strategy and health information for female tennis players.
Published by: T A Z Publications, PO Box 7282, Seminole, FL 33775. Ed., Pub. Teresa Thompson.

796.342 USA ISSN 0194-9098
TENNIS WEEK. Text in English. 1974. 6/yr. USD 19 domestic; USD 45 in Canada & Mexico; USD 80 elsewhere (effective 2007). adv. bk.rev. illus. back issues avail. **Document type:** *Magazine, Consumer.* **Description:** Provides instant coverage of Wimbledon, the Australian, French and US Opens, ATP and WTA pro tours, Davis Cup, Fed Cup, major collegiate, junior and senior events plus other international, national and regional tournaments. Business summaries focus on new products, retail stores, camps, tournament draws, schedules, scores, latest rankings and earnings.
Formerly: Tennis News
Related titles: Online - full text ed.
Address: 304 Park Ave S, 8th Fl, New York, NY 10010. TEL 646-871-2400, FAX 212-772-0899. Ed. Brandusa Niro. Pub. Andrea Leand. Adv. contact Carole Graebner. page USD 412,000. Circ: 110,470 (paid and controlled).

796.342 DNK ISSN 1902-4134
TENNISAVISEN. Text in Danish. 2006. 7/yr. **Document type:** *Magazine, Consumer.*
Published by: (Dansk Tennis Forbund), MagMedia, Auroravej 48, Roedovre, 2610, Denmark. TEL 45-20-901001, info@mag-media.dk, http://www.mag-media.dk. Circ: 19,000 (controlled).

796.342 GBR ISSN 2043-6688
▼ **TENNISHEAD.** Text in English. 2010. bi-m. GBP 20 domestic; GBP 40 in Europe; GBP 49 elsewhere (effective 2010). adv. **Document type:** *Magazine, Consumer.*
Published by: Advantage Publishing Ltd., Barry House, Ist Fl, 20-22 Worple Rd, London, SW19 4DH, United Kingdom. TEL 44-20-89470100, FAX 44-20-89470117, contact@advantagepub.com, http://www.advantagepub.com.

793.342 USA
TENNISPRO MAGAZINE; the international magazine for PTR tennis teachers and coaches. Text in English. 1988. bi-m. free to members (effective 2007). adv. bk.rev. 40 p./no.; **Document type:** *Magazine, Trade.* **Description:** Geared for the tennis teaching professionals. Covers sports science, programming, sports medicine, new drills and product reviews.
Published by: Professional Tennis Registry, 116 Shipyard Dr, Hilton Head Island, SC 29928. TEL 843-785-7244, FAX 843-686-2033, ptr@ptrtennis.org, http://www.usptr.org/. Ed., R&P Peggy Edwards. Adv. contact Julie Jilly. Circ: 15,000 (free).

796.342 DEU ISSN 0937-9681
TENNISSPORT; Tennistraining in Theorie und Praxis. Text in German. 1990. bi-m. EUR 34.80 (effective 2006). adv. charts; illus.; maps. back issues avail. **Document type:** *Magazine, Consumer.*
Published by: Sportverlag Schmidt und Dreisilker GmbH, Boeblinger Str 68/1, Sindelfingen, 71065, Germany. TEL 49-7031-862800, FAX 49-7031-862801. Ed. Brigitte Schurr. Adv. contact Yvonne Damast TEL 49-7031-862831. B&W page EUR 1,000, color page EUR 1,600. Circ: 3,947 (paid and controlled).

796.332 USA
TEXAS FOOTBALL MAGAZINE. Text in English. 1960. a. USD 8.95 newsstand/cover (effective 2006). back issues avail. **Document type:** *Magazine, Trade.* **Description:** A favorite for football fans as it provides complete college and high school previews and in depth features on the sport's biggest names in the state of Texas.
Published by: Host Communications, Inc., 2828 E Trinity Mills Rd., Ste 106, Carrollton, TX 75006. TEL 972-392-5753, 800-313-HOST, FAX 972-392-5880, info@hostcommunications.com, http://www.hostcommunications.com. Ed. Dave Campbell. R&P Dave Stephenson. Adv. contacts Dave Stephenson, Dawn Colvin. B&W page USD 2,660, color page USD 3,800; trim 8.375 x 10.875. Circ: 110,000 (paid and free).

796.352 USA ISSN 1947-637X
▼ **TEXAS GOLF JOURNAL.** Text in English. forthcoming 2010. m. USD 9.99 per issue (effective 2009). **Document type:** *Magazine, Consumer.* **Description:** Features articles on golf for Texas.
Published by: In Publishing, 9769 NW 45 Ln, Miami, FL 33178. TEL 736-314-0456, info@miamigolfjournal.com.

796.352 USA
TEXAS GOLFER MAGAZINE. Text in English. m. **Description:** Covers golf news in Texas. Features interviews and articles by tour professionals, tips on how to improve your game, resort information, course reviews, and a special section on courses across the state for those on a tighter budget. Also includes information on tournaments and junior golf.

S

Published by: Golfer Magazines, Inc., 10301 Northwest Fwy, Ste 418, Houston, TX 77092-8228. TEL 713-680-1680, FAX 713-680-0138, http://www.golfermagazines.com. Ed. Bob Gray. Pub. Sommy L Ham. Adv. contact Frances Dowling.

796.334 CHN
TICAI DAOKAN. Text in Chinese. 4/w. CNY 3 newsstand/cover (effective 2004). **Document type:** *Consumer.*
Related titles: Online - full content ed.
Published by: Zhongguo Tiyubao Yezongshe, 8, Tiyuguan Lu, Chongwen-qu, Beijing, 100061, China. TEL 86-10-67178651. **Dist. by:** China International Book Trading Corp, 35 Chegongzhuang Xilu, Haidian District, PO Box 399, Beijing 100044, China. TEL 86-10-68412045, FAX 86-10-68412023, cibtc@mail.cibtc.com.cn, http://www.cibtc.com.cn.

796.342 SWE ISSN 1653-2546
TIEBREAK/SWEDISH TENNIS. Text in Swedish. 1945-2004; resumed 2005. 5/yr. adv. **Document type:** *Magazine, Consumer.* **Description:** Covers tennis in Sweden and worldwide.
Former titles (until 2005): Tidningen Tennis (1651-0690); (until 2002): Svensk Tennis (1101-6469); (until 1991): Tennistidningen (0040-3431)
Published by: (Svenska Tennisfoerbundet/Swedish Tennis Union), Forma Publishing Group, PO Box 6630, Stockholm, 11384, Sweden. TEL 46-21-194000, FAX 46-21-194136, http://www.formapg.se. Ed. Magdalena Sekkenes. adv.: page SEK 33,000; trim 185 x 270. Circ: 75,000 (paid and controlled).

796.334 SRB ISSN 1451-1606
TIP NOVOSTI. Text in Serbian. 2002. w. adv. **Document type:** *Newspaper, Consumer.*
Published by: Kompanija Novosti, Trg Nikole Pasica 7, Belgrade, 11000. TEL 381-11-3398202, FAX 381-11-3398337, redakcija@novosti.co.yu, http://www.novosti.co.yu. Ed. Miodrag Stojanovic.

796.334 MEX
TIRO DE ESQUINA. Text in Spanish. w. USD 75 (effective 1997). adv. **Document type:** *Consumer.* **Description:** Presents news about soccer, with emphasis on Mexican teams.
Indexed: R15.
Published by: Consorcio Sayrols, Mier y Pesado 126, Mexico, Col del Valle, Mexico City, DF 03100, Mexico. TEL 52-5-6874699, FAX 525-523-7045. Ed. Javier Araiza. Adv. contact Beatriz Coria. color page USD 1,125. Circ: 45,000.

790 DEU
TISCHTENNIS. Text in German. 1946. m. EUR 45.60 domestic; EUR 51 foreign (effective 2011). adv. back issues avail. **Document type:** *Magazine, Consumer.*
Formerly (until 2004): Deutscher Tischtennis Sport (0930-0791)
Published by: Philippka-Sportverlag Konrad Honig, Rektoratsweg 36, Muenster, 48159, Germany. TEL 49-251-230050, FAX 49-251-2300579, info@philippka.de, http://www.philippka.de. Ed. Rahul Nelson. Adv. contact Peter Moellers TEL 49-251-2300528.

796.352 GBR ISSN 0955-4939
TODAY'S GOLFER. Text in English. 1988. 13/yr. GBP 51.87; GBP 3.99 newsstand/cover (effective 2009). adv. back issues avail. **Document type:** *Magazine, Consumer.* **Description:** Provides information on how to play golf better, buy better and choose the best places to play.
Published by: H. Bauer Publishing Ltd. (Subsidiary of: Bauer Media Group), Media House, Lynchwood, Peterborough, Cambridgeshire PE2 6EA, United Kingdom. TEL 44-1733-468243, FAX 44-1733-468843, http://www.bauer.co.uk. Ed. Andy Calton. Adv. contact Thomas Berkoe TEL 44-207-2955434. page GBP 5,500. **Subscr. to:** Tower House, Sovereign Park, Market Harborough, Leicestershire LE16 9EF, United Kingdom. TEL 44-1858-438866, subs@greatmagazines.co.uk.

796.31 IRL ISSN 2009-4019
TOP ACE; Irish handball annual. Text in English. 1996. a. GBP 8.50, EUR 9.95 per issue (effective 2011). **Document type:** *Magazine, Consumer.*
Formerly (until 2007): Irish Handball Yearbook (1649-0371)
Related titles: Online - full text ed.: free (effective 2011).
Published by: G A A Handball, C.L.G. Comhairle Liathroid Laimhe na Heireann, Pairc an Chrocaigh, Baile Atha Cliath, Dublin, 3, Ireland. TEL 353-1-8192384, nationalmanager.handball@gaa.ie.

796.342 DEU
TOPSPIN. Text in German. 1988. 10/yr. adv. **Document type:** *Magazine, Consumer.*
Published by: Hessischer Tennis Verband e.V., Auf der Rosenhoehe 68, Offenbach, 63069, Germany. TEL 49-69-984032-0, FAX 49-69-98403220, info@htv-tennis.de, http://www.htv-tennis.de. adv.: B&W page EUR 925, color page EUR 1,620. Circ: 4,900 (controlled).

796.357 USA ISSN 1935-0449
TOTAL TEXAS BASEBALL. Text in English. 2006. 10/yr. USD 29.95 (effective 2007). adv. **Document type:** *Magazine, Consumer.* **Description:** Features information about all aspects of baseball in Texas, from Major League to high school.
Address: PO Box 13270, Arlington, TX 76094. TEL 817-277-1966, FAX 817-277-1969, Info@TotalTexasBaseball.com. Ed. Kurt Daniels. Pub. Bennie Rooks. adv.: color page USD 1,150; 10.875 x 12.625. Circ: 50,000 (controlled).

796.332 USA
TOUCHDOWN ILLUSTRATED; college football gameday programs. Text in English. 1973. 45/yr. USD 65 per season (effective 2007). adv. **Document type:** *Magazine, Consumer.*
Former titles: Touchdown Publications; Pro Sports
Published by: Professional Sports Publications (P S P), 519 8th Ave, Ste 2500, New York, NY 10018. TEL 212-697-1460, FAX 212-286-8154, mlewis@pspsports.com, http://www.pspsports.com. Pub. Kevin Hahn. Circ: 3,000,000 (paid).

796.334 USA
TOUCHLINE. Text in English. 1971. a. free to members. adv. back issues avail. **Document type:** *Magazine, Consumer.* **Description:** Contains membership updates and new information about the world of scoccer.
Published by: Soccer Association for Youth U S A, 1 North Commerce Park Dr, Ste 306, Cincinnati, OH 45215. TEL 513-769-3800, 800-233-7291, FAX 513-769-0500, sayusa@saysoccer.org, http://www.saysoccer.org. Ed. Amanda Weiss. adv.: page USD 700. Circ: 5,000 (controlled).

TRADING CARDS. *see* HOBBIES

796.323 USA ISSN 1948-0725
TRAIN YOUR GAME; the newsletter for serious basketball players and coaches. Text in English. 2008. w. free (effective 2009). **Document type:** *Newsletter, Consumer.* **Description:** Features basketball articles, reports and drills, tips and training advice from expert players and coaches.
Published by: M V P Athletic Skills, LLC, 2213 W Aspen Wood Loop, Lehi, UT 84043. TEL 801-361-0639, http://mvpathleticskills.com.

796.332 NLD ISSN 0927-7293
DE TRAINER-COACH. Text in Dutch. 1992. 4/yr. EUR 39.50 (effective 2009). **Document type:** *Magazine, Trade.*
Published by: (Vereniging van Voetbaloefenmeesters in Nederland), Eisma Businessmedia bv, Celsiusweg 41, Postbus 340, Leeuwarden, 8901 BC, Netherlands. TEL 31-58-2954854, FAX 31-58-2954875, businessmedia@eisma.nl, http://www.eisma.nl/businessmedia/index.asp. Ed. Paul Geerars. Pub. Minne Hovenga.

796.332 NLD ISSN 1569-4623
TRAINERSMAGAZINE. Text in Dutch. 2002. 8/yr. EUR 51.75 domestic; EUR 61.75 in Europe; EUR 71.75 elsewhere (effective 2010). adv. **Document type:** *Magazine, Trade.*
Published by: Sportfacilities & Media BV, Postbus 952, Zeist, 3700 AZ, Netherlands. TEL 31-30-6977710, FAX 31-30-6977720, info@sportfacilities.com, http://www.sportfacilities.com. Ed. Paul van Veen. adv.: page EUR 1,250; trim 210 x 297. Circ: 6,000.

796.333 ZAF
TRANSVAAL RUGBY. Text in Afrikaans, English. 1972. 12/yr. USD 30. adv. bk.rev. **Document type:** *Magazine, Consumer.*
Published by: (Transvaal Rugby Football Union), Pieter Coetzee Promotions, PO Box 6842, Bracken Downs, 1454, South Africa. TEL 011-902-4656. Ed. P H Coetzee. Circ: 80,000.

796.334 ITA ISSN 1970-5220
LA TRIESTINA. Text in Italian. 2006. m. **Document type:** *Magazine, Consumer.*
Published by: Edizioni Luglio, Via Miani 5b, Trieste, 34148, Italy. TEL 39-040-381416, FAX 39-040-280215.

796.352 ESP
TROFEO GOLF. Text in Spanish. 1954. m. **Document type:** *Magazine, Consumer.* **Description:** Covers all aspects of golf.
Published by: Editorial America Iberica, C. Miguel Yuste 33bis, Madrid, 28037, Spain. TEL 34-91-3277950, FAX 34-91-3044746, editorial@eai.es, http://www.eai.es/.

796.333 ARG ISSN 1852-6284
TRY MUNDIAL. Text in Spanish. 2008. 3/yr. back issues avail. **Document type:** *Magazine, Consumer.*
Published by: Editorial Mundial, Diego Detang s-n, Catamarca Martinex, Buenos Aires, 2032, Argentina. TEL 54-11-47173009.

796.352 USA ISSN 1940-5812
TURFNET. Text in English. 1999. m. free to members (effective 2009). adv. back issues avail. **Document type:** *Magazine, Trade.* **Description:** Explores issues relating to golf course maintenance, development, design and construction.
Formerly (until 2007): Golfweek's Superintendent News (1530-7662)
Published by: Turnstile Publishing Company, 1500 Park Center Dr, Orlando, FL 32835. TEL 407-563-7000, FAX 407-563-7077, rdaily@golfweek.com. Ed. John Reitman TEL 407-563-7049. Pub. Terry Olson. Adv. contact Jason C Redditt TEL 619-546-8721.

796.334 CHE
U E F A FLASH. Text in English. 1991. m. free. **Document type:** *Newsletter.*
Related titles: German ed.; French ed.
Published by: Union of European Football Associations/Union des Associations Europeennes de Football, Chemin de la Redoute 54, Case Postale, Nyon 2, 1260, Switzerland. TEL 41-22-9944444, FAX 41-22-9944488.

796.334 ITA
U R B S INFORMAZIONI. Text in Italian. 1972. w. free. adv. bk.rev. **Document type:** *Newspaper, Consumer.*
Published by: Maurizio Longega, Ed. & Pub., Casella Postale 6291, Rome, RM 00195, Italy. TEL 39-06-330734215, FAX 39-06-39722092, mlongega@quipo.it. Ed., Pub. Maurizio Longega.

796.3 FRA ISSN 2107-2922
U S A P SAISON .. (Union Sportive Arlequins-Perpignan) Text in French. 2004. a., latest 2010. **Document type:** *Magazine, Consumer.*
Published by: Trabucaire Editions, 2 Rue Jouy d'Arnaud, Canet, 66140, France. http://fr.usap.fr/index.php.

796.35 USA
U S A SOFTBALL MAGAZINE. Text in English. 1933. bi-m. adv. bk.rev. illus.; stat. **Description:** Includes news and information about the programs of ASA-USA softball. Covers local, national and international events. Also includes regular updates on business and economic issues, as well as player and personality profiles.
Formerly (until 1995): Balls and Strikes (0199-2406)
Indexed: SPI, SportS.
Published by: Amateur Softball Association of America, 2801 N E 50th St, Oklahoma City, OK 73111. info@softball.org, http://www.softball.org.

796.346 USA ISSN 1089-1870
U S A TABLE TENNIS MAGAZINE. Text in English. 1933. bi-m. USD 20 domestic; USD 50 elsewhere (effective 2010). adv. bk.rev. charts; illus. 64 p./no.; back issues avail. **Document type:** *Magazine, Consumer.* **Description:** Contains feature articles, player profiles, coaching tips, club profiles and soft news.
Former titles (until 1996): Table Tennis Today (1068-5782); (until 1992): Table Tennis Topics (0887-6576); Spin Magazine (0746-1801); (until 1983): Table Tennis News (0273-8538)
Indexed: SportS.
Published by: U.S.A. Table Tennis, 1 Olympic Plaza, Colorado Springs, CO 80909-5769. TEL 719-866-4583, FAX 719-632-6071. Eds. Marie Hopkins, Steve Hopkins. adv.: page USD 450; 8.5 x 11. Circ: 7,000.

796.352 USA
U S A TODAY (YEAR) GOLF ALMANAC. Text in English. a.
Published by: Hyperion, 114 Fifth Ave, New York, NY 10011. Ed. Don Cronin.

796.357 USA ISSN 1541-5228
U S A TODAY SPORTS WEEKLY. Text in English. 1991. w. USD 44.95; USD 2 newsstand/cover (effective 2009). adv. illus.; stat. reprints avail. **Document type:** *Magazine, Consumer.* **Description:** Covers both major leagues and the minor leagues including reports on fantasy leagues, collectables and memorabilia, nostalgia, and personalities.
Formerly (until 2002): U S A Today Baseball Weekly (1057-9532)
Related titles: Online - full text ed.
Indexed: A22.
—CCC.
Published by: U S A Today (Subsidiary of: Gannett Company, Inc.), 7950 Jones Branch Dr, McLean, VA 22108. TEL 703-854-6319, FAX 703-854-2030, webads@usatoday.com. Adv. contact Richard Goldstein TEL 212-715-2198. B&W page USD 13,100, color page USD 15,700. Circ: 170,795.

796.323 USA ISSN 0041-5472
U S B W A TIP-OFF. Text in English. 1959. m. (Nov.-Apr.). membership.
Media: Duplicated (not offset).
Published by: United States Basketball Writers Association, c/o Joe Mitch, Ed., 803 Wildview Lane, St. Louis, MO 63011. TEL 703-780-8577. Circ: 1,000.

794.6 USA
U S BOWLER. Text in English. 2000 (Aug.). q. USD 21 membership (effective 2007). adv. 40 p./no.; **Document type:** *Magazine, Consumer.*
Formerly (until Fall 2005): American Bowler
Published by: United States Bowling Congress, 5301 S 76th St, Greendale, WI 53129. TEL 414-421-6400, 800-514-2695, FAX 414-421-3013. Eds. David Merline, Jim Arehart. Adv. contact Barbara Peltz. B&W page USD 19,000, color page USD 21,000; trim 6 x 9. Circ: 2,000,000.

796.354 USA
U S C A CROQUET DIRECTORY. Text in English. 1992. a. free. adv. **Document type:** *Directory, Consumer.* **Description:** Includes reports on U.S.C.A. events, facilities, and members; reviews croquet equipment; and discusses the history and other topics pertinent to the development, advancement, and promotion of croquet in the U.S.
Formerly: Croquet Annual
Published by: United States Croquet Association, 700 Florida Mango Rd, West Palm Beach, FL 33406. TEL 561-478-0760, USCA@msn.com, http://www.croquetamerica.com/. adv.: B&W page USD 2,800, color page USD 3,500; trim 11.75 x 8. Circ: 15,000.

796.354 USA
U S C A CROQUET NEWS. Text in English. q. membership. **Document type:** *Newsletter, Consumer.*
Published by: United States Croquet Association, 700 Florida Mango Rd, West Palm Beach, FL 33406. TEL 561-478-0760, USCA@msn.com, http://www.croquetamerica.com/.

U S G A GREEN SECTION RECORD (ONLINE). *see* GARDENING AND HORTICULTURE

U S G A TURFGRASS AND ENVIRONMENTAL RESEARCH ONLINE; using science to benefit golf. (United States Golf Association) *see* BIOLOGY—Botany

794.6 USA
U S YOUTH BOWLER. Text in English. 2003 (Fall). q. free to members (effective 2005). adv. 32 p./no.; **Document type:** *Magazine, Consumer.*
Related titles: Online - full content ed.
Published by: U S B C Communications, 5301 S 76th St, Greendale, WI 53129. TEL 414-421-3013. Ed. Tom Clark. Adv. contacts Barbara Peltz, Keith Hamilton. B&W page USD 10,500, color page USD 12,500; trim 8 x 10.5. Circ: 375,000 (paid).

796.334 USA
U S YOUTH SOCCER. Text in English. 2002. s-a. **Description:** Features stories on every aspect of youth soccer, profiles of amateurs and professional players and lifestyle stories about people involved with the game. It also includes skills development features, coaching and player tips and news on the latest equipment and technology. Interactive features will includes games, puzzles, contests and more.
Published by: T P G Sports, Inc., 505 N Hwy 169, Ste 465, Minneapolis, MN 55441. info@tpgsports.com, http://www.tpgsports.com.

796 CHE ISSN 0501-1590
UNION OF EUROPEAN FOOTBALL ASSOCIATIONS. BULLETIN. Text in English. q. **Document type:** *Bulletin.* **Description:** Includes association news, reports and results of events, championships, tournaments, international news, coming events, meetings, and new books.
Published by: Union of European Football Associations/Union des Associations Europeennes de Football, Chemin de la Redoute 54, Case Postale, Nyon 2, 1260, Switzerland. TEL 41-22-9944444, FAX 41-22-9944488, TELEX 419796-UEF-CH.

796 CHE ISSN 0570-2070
UNION OF EUROPEAN FOOTBALL ASSOCIATIONS. HANDBOOK OF U E F A. Text in English, French, German. 1959. base vol. plus irreg. updates. CHF 100 per vol. bk.rev. **Document type:** *Handbook/Manual/Guide, Trade.*
Published by: Union of European Football Associations/Union des Associations Europeennes de Football, Chemin de la Redoute 54, Case Postale, Nyon 2, 1260, Switzerland. TEL 41-22-9944444, FAX 41-22-9944488, TELEX 419706-UEF-CH. Circ: 2,500.

796.3 GBR ISSN 2044-2211
UNITED FRONT. Text in English. 2008. s-a. **Document type:** *Trade.*
Published by: N C J Media Ltd., Groat Market, Newcastle Upon Tyne, NE1 1ED, United Kingdom. TEL 44-191-2327500, http://www.trinity-mirror-north-east.co.uk.

796.334 GBR ISSN 1355-6983
UNITED REVIEW. Text in English. 192?. 15/yr. GBP 41.40 (effective 2009). **Document type:** *Magazine, Consumer.*
Published by: Haymarket Network (Subsidiary of: Haymarket Media Group), Teddington Studios, Broom Rd, Teddington, TW11 9BE, United Kingdom. TEL 44-20-82675013, FAX 44-20-82675194, enquiries@haymarket.com, http://www.haymarketnetwork.com.

796.353 USA ISSN 0083-3118
UNITED STATES POLO ASSOCIATION. YEARBOOK. Text in English. 1890. a. USD 25. adv.
Published by: United States Polo Association, 4059 Iron Works Pike, Lexington, KY 40511. FAX 606-231-9738. Circ: 3,000.

796.343 USA ISSN 0083-3398
UNITED STATES SQUASH RACQUETS ASSOCIATION. OFFICIAL YEAR BOOK. Text in English. 1925. a. USD 6. adv. index. **Document type:** *Bulletin.*
Published by: United States Squash Racquets Association, PO Box 1216, Bala Cynwyd, PA 19004-5216. TEL 610-667-4006, FAX 610-667-6539. Ed. Craig W Brand. Circ: 8,000.

796.342 USA ISSN 0196-5425
UNITED STATES TENNIS ASSOCIATION. YEARBOOK. Text in English. 1937. a. USD 16.45 to non-members; USD 12.45 to members (effective 1999). adv. **Description:** Reports of previous year's activities from all USTA sections. Includes player statistics, USTA officers and committees, national rankings for all agee groups, the official rules of the game, and reviews professional seasons, including Davis and Federation Cup play.
Formerly: United States Lawn Tennis Association. Yearbook (0083-1557)
Published by: (United States Lawn Tennis Association), H.O. Zimman, Inc., Seaport Landing, 152 The Lynnway, Lynn, MA 01902-3419. Ed., R&P John Donahue. Circ: 15,000.

796.33 AUS ISSN 1833-6051
UPROAR. Text in English. 2006. q. **Document type:** *Magazine, Consumer.*
Published by: Queensland Roar Football Club, Luxury Paints Stadium, 133 Pine Rd, Richlands, QLD 4077, Australia. TEL 61-7-37123333, FAX 61-7-32715785, admin@qldroar.com.au, http://www.qldroar.com.au.

796.352 USA ISSN 1947-2544
▼ **UTAH GOLF JOURNAL.** Text in English. forthcoming 2010. m. USD 9.99 per issue (effective 2009). **Document type:** *Magazine, Consumer.* **Description:** Features articles on golf for Utah.
Published by: In Publishing, 9769 NW 45 Ln, Miami, FL 33178. TEL 736-314-0456, info@miamigolfjournal.com.

V I P INTERNATIONAL GOLF EDITION. (Very Important Persons) *see* TRAVEL AND TOURISM

796.352 USA ISSN 1529-4781
VEGASGOLFER. Summaries in English; Text in English. 1996. bi-m. USD 14.95; USD 3.99 per issue (effective 2008). adv. bk.rev. charts; illus.; mkt.; maps; stat. back issues avail. **Document type:** *Magazine, Consumer.* **Description:** Revealing golf destination to locals and visitors by providing a variety of content and visito information. Publishes the Invensys Classic and Las Vegas Senior Classic program guides and the Wendy's Three Tour Challenge program guide.
Related titles: Online - full text ed.
Published by: Greenspun Media Group, 2360 Corporate Circle, Third Fl, Henderson, NV 89074. TEL 702-990-2550, FAX 702-990-2530, gmginfo@gmgvegas.com, http://www.greenspunmedia.com/. Ed. Bill Bowman TEL 702-990-2586. Pub. Ray Hurtado TEL 702-990-8996. R&P Steven Geiger TEL 702-990-2585. Adv. contact Karyn Hearn. page USD 9,141; trim 8.25 x 10.75. Circ: 80,000.

796.332 GBR ISSN 2044-1126
THE VIKING STORM. Text in English. 200?. bi-w. **Document type:** *Magazine, Consumer.* **Description:** Features football team news and game reports as well as player interviews and analysis.
Published by: Community Initiatives Associates, Magazine House, Egerton Mill, 25 Egerton St, Chester, CH1 3ND, United Kingdom. TEL 800-783-5805, FAX 800-783-5806, admin@communityinitiatives.co.uk.

THE VINTAGE & CLASSIC BASEBALL COLLECTOR; the journal of baseball's rare collectibles & its history. *see* HOBBIES

796.352 USA ISSN 1947-6426
▼ **VIRGINIA GOLF MAGAZINE.** Text in English. forthcoming 2010 (Oct.). m. USD 9.99 per issue (effective 2009). **Document type:** *Magazine, Consumer.* **Description:** Features articles on golf for Virginia.
Published by: In Publishing, 9769 NW 45 Ln, Miami, FL 33178. TEL 736-314-0456, info@miamigolfjournal.com.

796.352 USA ISSN 1094-3021
VIRGINIA GOLFER. Text in English. 1982. bi-m. adv. 44 p./no.; **Document type:** *Magazine, Consumer.*
Published by: T P G Sports, Inc., 6160 Summit Dr, Ste 375, Minneapolis, MN 55430. TEL 763-595-0808, 800-597-5656, FAX 763-595-0016, info@tpgsports.com, http://www.tpgsports.com. Ed. Andrew Blair. R&P Joseph Oberle TEL 763-595-0808 ext 114. Adv. contact Alan Bross. B&W page USD 2,330, color page USD 2,700; 8.25 x 10.875. Circ: 30,586 (paid).

796.334 NLD ISSN 0042-7977
VOETBAL INTERNATIONAL. Text in Dutch. 1965. w. EUR 104; EUR 2.99 newsstand/cover (effective 2010). adv. illus. **Document type:** *Magazine, Consumer.*
Related titles: ◆ Supplement(s): Voetbal International. Seizoengids. ISSN 1878-8904.
Published by: Weekbladpers Tijdschriften, Raamgracht 4, Amsterdam, 1011 KK, Netherlands. TEL 31-20-5518711, FAX 31-20-5518638, http://www.weekbladpers.nl. adv.: color page EUR 11,890; trim 215 x 285. Circ: 171,407.

796.332 NLD ISSN 1878-8904
VOETBAL INTERNATIONAL. SEIZOENGIDS. Text in Dutch. 1997. a. EUR 5.50 newsstand/cover (effective 2011).
Related titles: ◆ Supplement to: Voetbal International. ISSN 0042-7977.
Published by: Weekbladpers Tijdschriften, Raamgracht 4, Amsterdam, 1011 KK, Netherlands. TEL 31-20-5518711, FAX 31-20-5518638, http://www.weekbladpers.nl.

796.332 NLD ISSN 1872-0269
VOETBAL MAGAZINE. Text in Dutch. 1987. m. EUR 36 (effective 2009). adv. **Document type:** *Magazine, Consumer.*
Former titles (until 2005): F C (1572-7475); (until 2004): Voetbal Magazine (1386-2154); (until 1996): Voetbal (0921-7819)
Published by: BCM Publishing, Postbus 1392, Eindhoven, 5602 BJ, Netherlands. TEL 31-4998-98115, 31-40-8447644, FAX 31-40-8447655, http://www.bcm.nl. Ed. Steven Kooijman. Pub. Eric Bruger. Adv. contact Jeroen van der Linden.

796.332 NLD ISSN 1382-7065
DE VOETBALTRAINER. Text in Dutch. 1983. 8/yr. EUR 82.50 (effective 2009). adv. **Document type:** *Magazine, Trade.*
Published by: Eisma Businessmedia bv, Celsiusweg 41, Postbus 340, Leeuwarden, 8901 BC, Netherlands. TEL 31-58-2954854, FAX 31-58-2954875, businessmedia@eisma.nl, http://www.eisma.nl/businessmedia/index.asp.

796.3 USA ISSN 0892-7421
VOICE OF THE HAWKEYES. Text in English. 198?. 25/yr. USD 47.15 (effective 2011). adv. **Document type:** *Magazine, Consumer.* **Description:** Covers University of Iowa sports.
Published by: 247 Sports, PO Box 1498, Shelbyville, KY 40066. TEL 888-474-8669, info@247sports.com, http://247sports.com.

796.325 FRA ISSN 1282-691X
VOLLEY-BALL. Text in French. 194?. bi-m. EUR 15.25 domestic; EUR 18.30 foreign (effective 2009). **Document type:** *Magazine, Consumer.* **Description:** Presents the world of volleyball through interviews, in-depth coverage, game results.
Published by: Federation Francaise de Volley-Ball, 17 Rue Georges Clemenceau, Choisy-le-Roi, Cedex 94607, France. ffvolley@volley.asso.fr.

796.325 USA ISSN 1058-4668
VOLLEYBALL. Text in English. 1990. m. USD 24.97 domestic; USD 35 in Canada; USD 49 elsewhere (effective 2007). adv. illus. reprints avail. **Document type:** *Magazine, Consumer.* **Description:** Provides coverage of all facets of the game including indoor, beach, juniors, and college.
Related titles: Online - full text ed.
Indexed: B04, BRD, G05, G06, G07, G08, G09, I05, I07, P10, P48, P53, P54, PEI, PQC, R03, RGAb, RGPR, SD, T02, W03, W05.
—CCC.
Published by: Madavor Media, Llc., 420 Boylston St, 5th Fl, Boston, MA 02116. TEL 617-536-0100, FAX 617-536-0102, info@madavor.com, http://www.madavor.com. Ed. Mike Miazga. Pub. Susan Fitzgerald TEL 617-706-9086. adv.: B&W page USD 2,205, color page USD 3,465. Circ: 61,184 (paid).

796.325 USA
VOLLEYBALL ACE POWER TIPS. Key Title: Power Tips. Text in English. 1990. m. **Document type:** *Bulletin, Trade.* **Description:** Drill bulletin presenting volleyball coaches with tips on techniques and strategy. Includes latest news from around the country affecting volleyball.
Former titles: Dynamic Power Tips; American Volleyball Coaches Association. Power Tips (1051-7847)
Published by: American Volleyball Coaches Association, 2365 Harrodsburg Rd, Ste A325, Lexington, KY 40504. TEL 859-226-4315, 866-544-2822, FAX 859-226-4338, members@avca.org, http://www.avca.org. Ed., R&P Bill Kauffman. Adv. contact Brian Peterson.

790 DEU
VOLLEYBALL-MAGAZIN. Text in German. 1977. m. EUR 47.40 domestic; EUR 52.80 foreign (effective 2011). adv. back issues avail. **Document type:** *Magazine, Consumer.*
Formerly (until 2002): Deutsche Volleyball Zeitschrift (0170-1509)
Published by: Philippka-Sportverlag Konrad Honig, Rektoratsweg 36, Muenster, 48159, Germany. TEL 49-251-230050, FAX 49-251-2300579, info@philippka.de, http://www.philippka.de. Ed. Klaus Wegener. Circ: 7,090 (paid and controlled).

796.325 USA ISSN 0274-6662
GV1015
VOLLEYBALL MAGAZINE. Text in English. 1976. m. USD 19.95. adv. bk.rev.
Incorporates (in Dec. 1994): Volleyball Monthly (0889-1990)
Indexed: SportS.
Published by: (American National Volleyball Association), Straight Down, Inc., 774 Marsh St, Ste C, San Luis Obispo, CA 93401-3943. TEL 805-541-2294, 800-876-2509, FAX 805-541-2439. Ed. Dennis Steers. Circ: 40,000.

796.325 USA ISSN 0882-1372
GV1017.V6
VOLLEYBALL RULES BOOK. Cover title: Official High School Volleyball Rules for Boys and Girls Competition. Text in English. 19??. a. USD 6.95 per issue (effective 2009). adv. **Document type:** *Handbook/Manual/Guide, Trade.* **Description:** Contains the official rules for volleyball and is used by coaches, officials, players and many fans who wish to know more about the rules of the game.
Formerly (until 1980): National Federation of High School Associations. Volleyball Rules (0363-2156)
Published by: National Federation of State High School Associations, PO Box 690, Indianapolis, IN 46206. TEL 317-972-6900, 800-776-3462, FAX 317-822-5700, info@nfhs.org, http://www.nfhs.org.

796.325 NOR ISSN 1501-6978
VOLLEYBALLNYTT. Text in Norwegian. 1966. 6/yr. NOK 100 (effective 2000). adv. back issues avail. **Document type:** *Magazine, Consumer.*
Former titles (until 1999): Volleyball (0804-9033); (until 1994): Volleyballnytt (0804-9025); (until 1993): Volleyball (0803-3102); (until 1990): Volleyballnytt (0800-5699); (until 1970): Volleyball (0800-6385)
Published by: Norges Volleyballforbund, Ullevaal Stadion, PO Box 1, Oslo, 0840, Norway. TEL 47-21-02-90-00, FAX 47-21-02-96-91. Circ: 15,000.

796.325 USA
VOLLEYBALLUSA. Text in English. 1972. q. USD 10 domestic; USD 24 foreign (effective 2010). adv. bk.rev. illus. reprints avail. **Document type:** *Magazine, Trade.* **Description:** Reviews activities of the association, U.S. Olympic teams and volleyball in general.
Former titles (until 1992): Inside U S A Volleyball (1059-8227); Volleyball U S A
Published by: U S A Volleyball, 715 S Circle Dr, Colorado Springs, CO 80910. TEL 719-228-6800, 888-786-5539, FAX 719-228-6899, http://www.usavolleyball.org.

796.332 305.4 NLD ISSN 2211-1328
▼ **VROUWEN EN VOETBAL MAGAZINE.** Key Title: Vrouwen&Voetbal Magazine. Text in Dutch. 2011. 10/yr. EUR 34.95 (effective 2011). adv. **Document type:** *Magazine, Consumer.*
Published by: Accolade Pers en Publiciteit, Weerscheut 71/c, Vinkel, 5381 GT, Netherlands. TEL 31-73-5320035. Adv. contact Nico van Noland.

WALDVIERTEL UND GOLF. *see* SPORTS AND GAMES—Outdoor Life

796.342 CHN ISSN 1006-2300
WANGQIU TIANDI/TENNIS WORLD. Text in Chinese. 1990. m. USD 106.80 (effective 2009). adv. illus. **Document type:** *Magazine, Consumer.*
Formerly (until 1995): Yumaoqiu Wangqiu (1003-0018)
Related titles: Online - full content ed.; Online - full text ed.
—East View.
Published by: (Zhongguo Wangqiu Xiehui/China Tennis Association), Zhongguo Tiyubao Yezongshe, 8, Tiyuguan Lu, Chongwen-qu, Beijing, 100061, China. TEL 86-10-67158589. **Dist. by:** China International Book Trading Corp, 35 Chegongzhuang Xilu, Haidian District, PO Box 399, Beijing 100044, China. TEL 86-10-68412045, FAX 86-10-68412023, cibtc@mail.cibtc.com.cn, http://www.cibtc.com.cn.

796.334 USA ISSN 1933-5369
THE WARRIOR NATION. Text in English. 2007. q. **Document type:** *Magazine, Consumer.* **Description:** Celebrates game highlights, athletes and fans of Trinidad and Tobago soccer.
Published by: Soca Warriors Supporters Club, PO Box 566088, Miami, FL 33256. publishing@thewarriornation.com, http://thewarriornation.com/. Ed. Denzil Streete.

796.334 USA
WASHINGTON STATE YOUTH SOCCER NEWS. Text in English. 1985. m. free to members (effective 2011). adv. **Document type:** *Newsletter, Trade.* **Description:** Contains association news, events, and coaching hints for administrators, coaches, and players.
Published by: (Minnesota Youth Soccer Association), Varsity Publications, PO Box 825, Pekin, IL 61554. TEL 877-477-2056, sales@varsitypublications.net, http://varsitypublications.net/.

796.357 USA ISSN 1930-2282
GV867
WATCHING BASEBALL; discovering the game within the game. Text in English. 2004. a., latest 2008, 4th ed. USD 14.95 per issue (effective 2008). 400 p./no.; **Document type:** *Magazine, Consumer.*
Published by: The Globe Pequot Press, Inc., 246 Goose Ln, PO Box 480, Guilford, CT 06437. TEL 203-458-4500, 888-249-7586, FAX 203-458-4601, 800-820-2329, info@globepequot.com. Ed. Jerry Remy.

796.334 GBR ISSN 2043-7706
▼ **WELL RED.** Text in English. 2010. bi-m. GBP 15 domestic; GBP 22 in Europe & Ireland; GBP 30 elsewhere; GBP 3 per issue domestic; GBP 4 per issue in Europe & Ireland; GBP 5 per issue elsewhere (effective 2011). **Document type:** *Magazine, Trade.*
Published by: Well Red Publishing Ltd., Office 113, Imperial Ct, Exchange St E, Liverpool, L3 2AB, United Kingdom. advertising@wellredmag.co.uk.

796.334 DEU
WERDER BREMEN. Text in German. 20/yr. EUR 25 (effective 2010). adv. **Document type:** *Magazine, Consumer.*
Published by: Werder Bremen GmbH & Co. KG, Franz-Boehmert-Str 1c, Bremen, 28205, Germany. TEL 49-180-5937337, FAX 49-421-493555, info@werder.de. adv.: color page EUR 2,200; trim 210 x 297. Circ: 50,000 (controlled).

796.352 USA ISSN 1947-2552
▼ **WEST VIRGINIA GOLF MAGAZINE.** Text in English. forthcoming 2010. m. USD 9.99 per issue (effective 2009). **Document type:** *Magazine, Consumer.* **Description:** Features articles on golf for West Virginia.
Published by: In Publishing, 9769 NW 45 Ln, Miami, FL 33178. TEL 736-314-0456, info@miamigolfjournal.com.

794.6 DEU
WESTDEUTSCHE KEGLER RUNDSCHAU. Text in German. 1964. m. EUR 16.50; EUR 2 (effective 2010). adv. **Document type:** *Magazine, Consumer.*
Published by: Westdeutscher Kegel- und Bowling-Verband e.V., c/o Erich Schroeder, Im Kamp 53, Unna, 59427, Germany. TEL 49-2303-54992, FAX 49-2303-5731, erich.schroder@t-online.de, http://www.wkvkegeln.de. Ed. Werner Piede. adv.: page EUR 185. Circ: 2,700 (controlled).

796.342 DEU
WESTFALEN TENNIS. Text in German. 1982. m. EUR 22; EUR 2.05 newsstand/cover (effective 2007). adv. **Document type:** *Magazine, Consumer.*
Published by: Sportverlag Schmidt und Dreisilker GmbH, Boeblinger Str 68/1, Sindelfingen, 71065, Germany. TEL 49-7031-862800, FAX 49-7031-862801. adv.: B&W page EUR 1,000, color page EUR 1,900. Circ: 6,921 (paid and controlled).

796.3 GBR ISSN 0959-0048
GV944.G7
WHEN SATURDAY COMES. Text in English. 1986. m. GBP 20.15 domestic; GBP 36 in Europe; GBP 44 elsewhere (effective 2009). adv. bk.rev. back issues avail. **Document type:** *Magazine, Consumer.* **Description:** Presents football issues from both serious and humorous perspectives.
Related titles: Online - full text ed.
—CCC.
Published by: When Saturday Comes Ltd., The Old Fire Station, 140 Tabernacle St, London, EC2A 4SD, United Kingdom. orders@wsc.co.uk. Ed. Andy Lyons.

796.323 USA ISSN 2150-5357
▼ **WILDCAT TIP-OFF.** Variant title: M S P Wildcat Tip-Off. Maple Street Press Wildcat Tip-Off. Text in English. 2009. a. USD 12.99 per issue (effective 2011). back issues avail. **Document type:** *Handbook/Manual/Guide, Consumer.* **Description:** Provides analysis of Kentucky Wildcats' men's basketball team.
Published by: Maple Street Press, 155 Webster St, Ste B, Hanover, MA 02339. TEL 781-347-4730, FAX 781-347-4732, info@maplestreetpress.com.

796.334 DEU
WILDPARK LIVE. Text in German. 17/yr. EUR 1 newsstand/cover (effective 2007). adv. **Document type:** *Magazine, Consumer.*
Published by: Karlsruher Sport-Club Muehlburg-Phoenix e.V., Adenauerring 17, Karlsruhe, 76131, Germany. TEL 49-721-9643450, FAX 49-721-9643469, online@ksc.de, http://www.ksc.de.

794.6 USA ISSN 1066-596X
WINDY CITY BOWLING NEWS. Text in English. 1990. 24/yr. USD 15 domestic; USD 30 foreign (effective 2000). adv. **Document type:** *Newspaper.*
Address: N7788 Carver School Rd, East Troy, WI 53120-2541. TEL 262-642-3989, FAX 262-642-5138. Ed. Bill Vint. Pub., R&P Lisa Vint. adv.: B&W page USD 385; trim 14 x 11.38. Circ: 20,000.

S

796.323 USA ISSN 0893-6439
WINNING HOOPS. Text in English. 1986. m. USD 44.95 in North America; USD 66.95 elsewhere (effective 2011). adv. back issues avail. **Document type:** *Newsletter, Trade.* **Description:** Offers solid coaching skills, fully illustrated plays and drills, tips, techniques and innovative basketball management ideas.
Published by: Lessiter Publications, 225 Regency Ct, Ste 200, Brookfield, WI 53045. TEL 262-782-4480, 800-645-8455, FAX 262-782-1252, info@lesspub.com, http://www.lesspub.com/.

796.332 USA
WINNING POINTS. Text in English. 1972. 19/yr. USD 30. adv. charts; stat.
Published by: Star Publishing, 114 E 32nd St, Rm 1102, New York, NY 10016-5506. TEL 212-683-3668, FAX 212-683-1012. Circ: 20,000.

796.352 USA
WISCONSIN GOLF DIRECTORY OF COURSES. Text in English. a. adv. **Document type:** *Directory.* **Description:** Lists public access golf courses in Wisconsin.
Formerly: Wisconsin Golf Directory
Published by: Killarney Press, 211 S Paterson St, Suite 170, Madison, WI 53703. TEL 608-280-8800, FAX 608-280-8883. Ed., Pub., R&P, Adv. contact John Hughes. Circ: 150,000.

796.352 USA ISSN 1528-5421
WISCONSIN GOLFER. Text in English. 1989. 6/yr. USD 19.95; USD 3.95 newsstand/cover (effective 2001). adv. bk.rev. reprints avail. **Document type:** *Magazine, Consumer.* **Description:** Features local golf personalities, tournaments, and courses. Covers travel, environmental issues, equipment and apparel, and instruction.
Formerly: Wisconsin Golf (1042-6620)
Published by: (Wisconsin State Golf Association), Killarney Press, PO Box 14439, Madison, WI 53714. TEL 608-280-8800, FAX 608-280-8883. Ed., Pub., R&P, Adv. contact John Hughes. Circ: 43,500.

796.358 GBR ISSN 1740-9519
THE WISDEN CRICKETER. Text in English. 2003 (Sept.). m. GBP 39.99 domestic; GBP 48.99 foreign (effective 2009). **Document type:** *Magazine, Consumer.* **Description:** Reports in depth on international and domestic first class cricket. Also brings you features on UK club cricket with a special player's section, and provides comprehensive statistics, reviews and action photography.
Formed by the merger of (1979-2003): The Wisden Cricket Monthly (0263-9041); (1974-2003): Cricketer International (0266-7398); Which was formerly (until 1974): Cricketer (0011-1260)
Related titles: Online - full text ed.
—CCC.
Published by: Wisden & Co, Wisden Cricketers' Almanack, 13 Old Aylesfield, Golden Pot, Alton, Hampshire GU34 4BY, United Kingdom. TEL 44-1420-83415, FAX 44-1420-83056, almanack@wisden.com, http://www.wisden.com/. Ed. Scyld Berry. Pub. Christopher Lane.

796.358 ZAF ISSN 1813-0011
THE WISDEN CRICKETER (SOUTH AFRICAN EDITION). Text in English. 2004. 8/yr. ZAR 199 (effective 2006). adv. **Document type:** *Magazine, Consumer.*
Published by: Touchline Media, PO Box 16368, Vlaeberg, Cape Town 8018, South Africa. TEL 27-21-4083800, FAX 27-21-4083811, http://www.touchline.co.za. Ed. Rob Houwing TEL 27-21-4083812. Pub. Nic Wides. Adv. contact Anthony Evlambiou TEL 27-21-4083813. color page ZAR 17,850; trim 210 x 276.

796.358 GBR ISSN 0142-9213
WISDEN CRICKETERS' ALMANACK (YEAR). Text in English. 1864. a. GBP 45 per issue (effective 2009). **Document type:** *Handbook/Manual/Guide, Consumer.*
Formerly (until 1938): John Wisden's Cricketers' Almanack
—BLDSC (9325.950000).
Published by: Cricinfo U K, 3 Queen Caroline St, Hammersmith, London, W6 9PE, United Kingdom.

796.32 USA ISSN 1524-9204
GV886
WOMEN'S BASKETBALL. Text in English. 1999. bi-m. USD 19.97 domestic; USD 29 in Canada; USD 39 elsewhere (effective 2010). adv. 52 p./no.; back issues avail. **Document type:** *Magazine, Consumer.* **Description:** Provides coverage of all aspects of the sport from the expanding youth scene to the pros.
Related titles: Online - full text ed.
Indexed: B04, BRD, G05, G06, G07, G08, G09, I05, I07, P10, P53, P54, PQC, R03, RGAb, RGPR, SD, W03, W05.
—CCC.
Published by: Goldman Group, Inc., 4125 Gunn Hwy, Ste B1, Tampa, FL 33618. TEL 813-264-2772, 800-600-4364, FAX 813-264-2343, http://www.ggpubs.com. Pub., Adv. contact Todd Goldman TEL 813-949-0006 ext 222.

796.323 USA ISSN 1936-3990
GV886
WOMEN'S BASKETBALL FINEST. Text in English. 2007. a. **Document type:** *Yearbook, Consumer.*
Related titles: Online - full text ed.: ISSN 1936-4008.
Published by: National Collegiate Athletic Association, 700 W Washington St, PO Box 6222, Indianapolis, IN 46206. TEL 317-917-6222, FAX 317-917-6888, esummers@ncaa.org, http://www.ncaa.org/.

796.323 USA
WOMEN'S BASKETBALL MEDIA GUIDE. Text in English. 19??. a. charts; illus.; stat. back issues avail. **Document type:** *Handbook/Manual/Guide, Consumer.*
Former titles (until 1998): Women's Basketball Guide; (until 1996): Women's Basketball Media Guide; (until 1991): Basketball (Big Ten Conference Women's Edition)
Related titles: Online - full text ed.: free (effective 2011).
Published by: Big Ten Conference, 1500 W Higgins Rd, Park Ridge, IL 60068. TEL 847-696-1010, FAX 847-696-1150.

796.352 AUS
WOMENS GOLF. Text in English. 2005. q. **Document type:** *Magazine, Consumer.*
Formerly (until 2006): Australasian Womens Golf (1832-8040)
Published by: Reflections Media Pty. Ltd., PO Box 123, Southport, QLD 4217, Australia. TEL 61-7-5528-2222, FAX 61-7-5528-2211, http://www.reflectionsmedia.com.au.

796.325 659.1 USA
(YEAR) WOMEN'S VOLLEYBALL MEDIA GUIDE. Text in English. 19??. a. charts; illus.; stat. back issues avail. **Document type:** *Directory, Consumer.*
Related titles: Online - full text ed.
Published by: Big Ten Conference, 2 Corporate Park, Ste 206, Irvine, CA 92606. TEL 949-261-2525, FAX 949-261-2528, dfarrell@bigwest.org.

796.352 USA
WORLD AMATEUR GOLF COUNCIL. RECORD BOOK. Text in English. 1958. biennial. membership; also avail. upon request. **Description:** Covers world amateur team championships in golf.
Published by: World Amateur Golf Council, Golf House, Box 708, Far Hills, NJ 07931-0708. TEL 908-234-2300, FAX 908-234-2178, sparel@usga.org, http://www.wagc.org. Circ: 1,000.

796.31 CHE ISSN 1040-5216
GV862
WORLD BASEBALL. Variant title: I B A F World Baseball. Text in English, Spanish. 1983. 2/yr. membership. adv. charts; stat. back issues avail. **Document type:** *Magazine, Consumer.* **Description:** News on baseball around the world. Includes coverage of world tournaments and developments in the association's 109 member countries.
Published by: International BAseball Federation (IBAF), Ave de Mon Repos 24, Case Postale 609931, Lausanne 5, 1002, Switzerland. TEL 41-21-3188240, FAX 41-21-3188241. Ed. Miguel Ortin. adv.: color page CHF 2,500; trim 204 x 274. Circ: 8,000.

796.342 GBR ISSN 0305-6325
WORLD OF TENNIS. Text in English. 1969. a. GBP 12.99. adv. index. **Document type:** *Journal, Consumer.*
Published by: (International Tennis Federation), HarperCollins Publishers, Harper Collins Publishers, Flat 77, 58 Fulham Palace Rd, London, W6 8JB, United Kingdom. TEL 44-181-307-4362, FAX 44-181-307-4249. Ed. John Barrett. Circ: 5,000.

796.334 GBR ISSN 0043-9037
WORLD SOCCER. Text in English. 1960. m. GBP 36 domestic; USD 74.59 in United States; USD 69.19 in Canada; EUR 59.21 in Europe; GBP 62.36 elsewhere; GBP 3.70 newsstand/cover (effective 2010). adv. illus. back issues avail. **Document type:** *Magazine, Consumer.* **Description:** Features soccer news from around the world including a diary of soccer dates to remember and profiles of world soccer stars and teams.
Incorporates: Soccer Star (0037-7546)
Indexed: RASB, SD, SportS.
—IE.
Published by: I P C Country & Leisure Media Ltd. (Subsidiary of: I P C Media Ltd.), The Blue Fin Bldg, 110 Southwark St, London, SE1 0SU, United Kingdom. TEL 44-20-31484817, FAX 44-20-72617474, 44-20-31486439, http://www.ipcmedia.com. Ed. Gavin Hamilton TEL 44-20-31484810. Adv. contacts Dave Stone TEL 44-20-31482516, Wayne Lashley TEL 44-20-31482823. color page GBP 1,975; trim 210 x 286. Circ: 40,003. **Subscr. to:** Rockwood House, Perrymount Rd, Haywards Heath RH16 3DH, United Kingdom. TEL 44-845-1231231, IPCsubs@quadrantsubs.com, http://www.magazinesdirect.co.uk. **Dist. by:** MarketForce UK Ltd.

796.342 DEU
WUERTTEMBERG TENNIS. Text in German. 1974. m. adv. **Document type:** *Magazine, Consumer.*
Published by: Jahr Top Special Verlag, Troplowitzstr 5, Hamburg, 22529, Germany. TEL 49-40-389060, FAX 49-40-38906300, info@jahr-tsv.de, http://www.jahr-tsv.de. adv.: B&W page EUR 917, color page EUR 1,643. Circ: 21,215 (paid and controlled).

796.323 SRB ISSN 1365-8077
X X L BASKETBALL. Text in English. 1996. m. **Document type:** *Magazine, Consumer.* **Description:** Features news on the NBA, as well as articles on the game and those who play it.
Formerly (until 1996): Inside the N B A (1363-7789)
Related titles: Dutch ed.; French ed.; German ed.; Italian ed.; Portuguese ed.; Spanish ed.; Greek ed.; Chinese ed.; Korean ed.; Polish ed.
Published by: Alliance International Media Ltd., KnegInje Zorke 11b, Belgrade, 11000. TEL 381-11-3089977, FAX 381-11-3089988, office@allianceinternationalmedia.com.

796.357 USA ISSN 0744-0006
GV875.N45
YANKEES MAGAZINE. Text in English. 1980. 8/yr. USD 49.99 (effective 2005). adv. illus. **Document type:** *Magazine, Consumer.* **Description:** Constitutes the official publication of the New York Yankees baseball team. Covers baseball past and present.
Published by: New York Yankees, Yankee Stadium, 161st St & River Ave, Bronx, NY 10451. TEL 800-Go-Yanks. Ed. Stephanie J Geosits. Pub., R&P Dan Cahalane. Adv. contact Joe Perello. Circ: 38,000 (paid).

796.332 USA ISSN 1941-7063
YEA ALABAMA. Text in English. 2008 (Jul.). a. USD 12.99 per issue (effective 2011). back issues avail. **Document type:** *Handbook/Manual/Guide, Consumer.*
Published by: Maple Street Press, 155 Webster St, Ste B, Hanover, MA 02339. TEL 781-347-4730, FAX 781-347-4732, info@maplestreetpress.com, http://www.maplestreetpress.com. Eds. Joel Gamble, Todd Jones.

796.352 GBR ISSN 1352-4720
A YEAR AT ST. ANDREWS; the home of golf. Text in English. a. GBP 3.95 per issue (effective 2010). **Document type:** *Yearbook, Consumer.* **Description:** Reviews the previous season of golf and a preview of the forthcoming year, including photographs.
Published by: (St. Andrews Links Trust), Highbury Customer Publications, The Publishing House, 1-3 Highbury Station Rd, London, N1 1SE, United Kingdom. TEL 44-20-226-2222, FAX 44-20-77040758, customerpublishing@hhc.co.uk, http://www.hhc.co.uk/. Ed. Dan Hayes. Pub. Alan White. Circ: 500,000.

796.334 CHN
ZHONGGUO ZUQIU BAO/CHINA SOCCER. Text in Chinese. s-w. CNY 96 (effective 2004). **Document type:** *Newspaper, Consumer.*
Related titles: Online - full content ed.
Published by: Zhongguo Tiyubao Yezongshe, 8, Tiyuguan Lu, Chongwen-qu, Beijing, 100061, China. TEL 86-10-67143708. **Dist. by:** China International Book Trading Corp, 35 Chegongzhuang Xilu, Haidian District, PO Box 399, Beijing 100044, China. TEL 86-10-68412045, FAX 86-10-68412023, cibtc@mail.cibtc.com.cn, http://www.cibtc.com.cn.

ZIMBALI. *see* LIFESTYLE

796.334 CHN ISSN 1006-5814
ZUQIU JULEBU/FOOTBALL CLUB. Text in Chinese. 1993. s-m. **Document type:** *Magazine, Consumer.*
Related titles: Online - full text ed.
Published by: Kelaibo Tiyu Wenhua Chuanmei Zhongxin, 310, Yangming Lu, 12/F, Chuban Dasha, Nanchang, 330006, China. TEL 86-791-6894727, FAX 86-791-6895190.

796.33 CHN ISSN 1000-3517
ZUQIU SHIJIE/FOOTBALL WORLD. Text in Chinese. 1981. s-m. CNY 5.90 newsstand/cover (effective 2005). **Document type:** *Magazine, Consumer.*
Related titles: Online - full content ed.; Online - full text ed.
—East View.
Published by: (Zhongguo Zuqiu Xiehui/China Soccer Association), Zhongguo Tiyubao Yezongshe, 8, Tiyuguan Lu, Chongwen-qu, Beijing, 100061, China. TEL 86-10-67158573. **Dist. by:** China International Book Trading Corp, 35 Chegongzhuang Xilu, Haidian District, PO Box 399, Beijing 100044, China. TEL 86-10-68412045, FAX 86-10-68412023, cibtc@mail.cibtc.com.cn, http://www.cibtc.com.cn.

796.334 CHN ISSN 1671-0738
ZUQIU ZHOUKAN/SOCCER WEEKLY. Text in Chinese. 2001. w. CNY 8 per issue (effective 2010). back issues avail. **Document type:** *Magazine, Consumer.*
Related titles: Online - full text ed.
Published by: Titan Chuanmei Jituan/Titan Culture - Express Co, ltd, 1, Tiyuguan Lu, Changsha, 410005, China. TEL 86-731-4556749, http://www.titan24.com/.

796.334 CHN
ZUQIUBAO. Abbreviated title: Football. Text in Chinese. 1980. 3/w. CNY 228 (effective 2004). **Document type:** *Consumer.*
Related titles: Online - full content ed.
Published by: Guangzhou Ribao Baoye Jituan/Guangzhou Daily Newspaper Group, 10, Renmin Zhonglu Tongle Lu, Guangzhou, 510121, China. TEL 86-20-81883088. **Dist. by:** China International Book Trading Corp, 35 Chegongzhuang Xilu, Haidian District, PO Box 399, Beijing 100044, China. TEL 86-10-68412045, FAX 86-10-68412023, cibtc@mail.cibtc.com.cn, http://www.cibtc.com.cn.

796.3 GBR ISSN 2043-6327
▼ **3 LIONS.** Text in English. 2010. s-a. **Document type:** *Magazine, Trade.*
Published by: Bauer Media, Media House, Lynch Wood, Peterborough, PE2 6EA, United Kingdom. TEL 44-1733-468000, http://www.bauermedia.co.uk/.

796.334 DEU ISSN 1860-0255
11 FREUNDE; Magazin fuer Fussball Kultur. Text in German. 2000. m. EUR 47 domestic; EUR 57 in Europe; EUR 77 elsewhere; EUR 4.50 newsstand/cover (effective 2011). adv. **Document type:** *Magazine, Consumer.* **Description:** Covers professional soccer as a sport and business as well as a lifestyle.
Published by: 11 Freunde Verlag GmbH & Co. KG, Palisadenstr 48, Berlin, 10243, Germany. TEL 49-30-4039360, FAX 49-30-403936122. Ed. Philipp Koester. Adv. contact Oliver Bresch. Circ: 55,549 (paid and controlled).

796 CAN
20/20. Text in English, French. 1987. 4/yr. CAD 25 (effective 1997). adv. illus. back issues avail. **Document type:** *Newsletter.* **Description:** Contains articles on and results of Canadians involved in table tennis from local to international levels.
Related titles: Diskette ed.
Published by: Canadian Table Tennis Association, 2800 1125 Colonel By Dr, Ottawa, ON K1S 5R1, Canada. TEL 613-733-6272, FAX 613-733-7279. Ed. Cttc Bldg. Circ: 3,000 (controlled).

796.332 USA ISSN 0887-7084
49ERS REPORT. Text in English. 1987. 26/yr. USD 36.95 (effective 1999). adv. **Document type:** *Newspaper.* **Description:** Devoted to the San Francisco 49ers.
Address: 5819 Hwy 6 South, Ste 370, Missouri City, TX 77459. TEL 281-261-6077, FAX 281-261-5999. Ed. James Walden. Pub. McMillan. R&P Sir McMillan. Adv. contact Al Allen. Circ: 15,000 (paid).

796.334 USA
90 MINUTES. Text in English. 1981. q. USD 25. bk.rev. **Document type:** *Newsletter.*
Formerly: National Soccer Hall of Fame News
Published by: National Soccer Hall of Fame, 11 Ford Ave, Oneonta, NY 13820. TEL 607-432-3351, FAX 607-432-8429. Ed. Brett Buzzy. Circ: 4,000.

796.334 FRA ISSN 2105-6617
▼ **90 MINUTES.** Text in French. 2010. m. **Document type:** *Magazine, Consumer.*
Published by: Sports & Medias, 8, Rue Balzac, Tours, 37000To, France. redaction@sportsetmedias.fr. Ed. Alexandre Mazas.

796.357 USA ISSN 1937-285X
GV862
108. Text in English. 2006. q. USD 28.97 domestic; USD 38.97 in Canada; USD 48.97 in Mexico (effective 2007). **Document type:** *Magazine, Consumer.* **Description:** Focuses on baseball's contribution to American history, culture, and communities. Presents historical profiles, interviews, fiction, photos and illustrations to tell the stories of the people who have played, watched, or written about the sport.
Published by: Sandlot Media Inc, 517 N Mountain Ave, Ste 237, Upland, CA 91786. info@108mag.com. Ed. Randy Merritt.

796.3 USA ISSN 1933-2092
411 SPORTS AND ENTERTAINMENT. Text in English. 2004. s-m. adv. **Document type:** *Magazine, Consumer.*
Related titles: Online - full text ed.: 411 Sports. ISSN 1933-2084. 2005.
Published by: Cedric E Lyons, Sr, 1400 Elm St, Ste 1900, Dallas, TX 75202. TEL 214-744-1428, FAX 214-744-1435, http://www.411sportsnews.com.

SPORTS AND GAMES—Bicycles And Motorcycles

796.7 DEU
A D A C MOTORRADWELT. Text in German. 2/yr. adv. **Document type:** *Magazine, Consumer.*

Published by: (Allgemeiner Deutscher Automobil-Club e.V.), A D A C Verlag GmbH, Leonhard-Moll-Bogen 1, Munich, 81365, Germany. TEL 49-89-76760, FAX 49-89-76762500, verlag@adac.de, http://www.adac.de. adv.: color page EUR 17,600. Circ: 600,000 (controlled).

A T V 4-WHEEL ACTION. (All Terrain Vehicle) *see* TRANSPORTATION—Automobiles

796.7 USA ISSN 1537-1956
A T V ILLUSTRATED. Text in English. 2001. q. USD 18.95 domestic; USD 22.95 foreign (effective 2002). adv.
Related titles: Online - full text ed.
Published by: Tamarack Publications, R. R. 1, Box 274-B, Wapwallopen, PA 18660. TEL 570-868-6662, FAX 570-868-6122. Ed., Pub. Bob Davis.

796.7 USA
A T V - INDUSTRY MAGAZINE. (All Terrain Vehicle) Text in English. 2002. m. free in US & Canada to qualified personnel (effective 2005). adv. **Document type:** *Magazine, Trade.* **Description:** Provides the latest updates in market trends, news, segment reports, future purchase intentions, industry trends and more.
Published by: Industry Shopper Publishing, Inc., 1521 Church St., Gardnerville, NV 89410. TEL 775-782-0222, FAX 775-782-0266. Ed., Pub. Rick Campbell. Adv. contact Caroline Carr. B&W page USD 3,090, color page USD 3,730; trim 8.5 x 14.5.

796.7 USA ISSN 1548-6303
A T V RIDER. (All Terrain Vehicle) Text in English. 2002. m. USD 14.97 domestic; USD 26.97 in Canada; USD 38.97 elsewhere (effective 2008). adv. back issues avail. **Document type:** *Magazine, Consumer.* **Description:** Features the many ways enthusiasts can enjoy ATV riding.
Indexed: G06, G07, G08, I05, S23.
—CCC.
Published by: Source Interlink Companies, 2570 E Cerritos Ave, Anaheim, CA 92806. TEL 714-941-1400, FAX 714-978-6390, dheine@sourceinterlink.com, http://www.sourceinterlinkmedia.com. Ed. Thad Josey. Pub. Sean Finley. adv.: B&W page USD 5,110, color page USD 6,390. Circ: 25,192 (paid).

796.7 CAN ISSN 1912-4325
A T V TRAIL RIDER. (All Terrain Vehicle) Text in English. 2001. bi-m. **Document type:** *Magazine, Consumer.*
Formerly (until 2005): A T V Rider (1499-1829)
Indexed: H20.
Published by: L C Media, Inc., 4105 Matte Blvd., Ste G, Brossard, PQ J4Y 2P4, Canada. TEL 450-444-1103, FAX 450-444-6773.

338.347 613.7 362.1 GBR ISSN 1751-6943
ACTIVE TRAVEL CYMRU NEWS. Text in English, Welsh. 2006. 3/yr. back issues avail. **Document type:** *Magazine, Consumer.* **Description:** Highlights examples of best practice within Wades and aims to provide officers within the public and voluntary sectors with policy solutions and practical steps to increase opportunities for active travel.
Related titles: Online - full text ed.: ISSN 1751-6951.
—CCC.
Published by: Sustrans, 2 Cathedral Sq, College Green, Bristol, Avon BS1 5DD, United Kingdom. TEL 44-117-9268893, FAX 44-117-9294173, sustranscymru@sustrans.org.uk.

388.347 613.7 GBR ISSN 1745-0438
ACTIVE TRAVEL NEWS. Variant title: Sustrans Active Travel News. Text in English. 2001. q. back issues avail. **Document type:** *Newsletter, Consumer.* **Description:** Aims to promote walking and cycling as health-enhancing physical activity.
Former titles (until 2004): Healthy Travel (1478-5870); (until 2002): Active Travel (1476-8569)
Related titles: Online - full text ed.: ISSN 1745-0446.
—CCC.
Published by: Sustrans, 2 Cathedral Sq, College Green, Bristol, Avon BS1 5DD, United Kingdom. TEL 44-117-9268893, FAX 44-117-9294173, info@sustrans.org.uk.

796.6 910.09 USA
ADVENTURE CYCLIST. Text in English. 1975. 9/yr. USD 30 membership (effective 2005). adv. bk.rev. 44 p./no. 3 cols./p.; back issues avail. **Document type:** *Magazine, Consumer.* **Description:** Bicycle travel publication, including destinations, technical information, product news, and articles concerning nutrition and training.
Formerly: BikeReport
Related titles: Online - full text ed.
Indexed: SportS.
Published by: Adventure Cycling Association, 150 E Pine St, PO Box 8308, Missoula, MT 59807. TEL 406-721-1776, FAX 406-721-8754. Ed. Michael Deme. Adv. contact Kevin Condit. Circ: 41,000 (paid).

796.6 DEU ISSN 0940-4929
AKTIV RADFAHREN. Text in German. 1980. 8/yr. EUR 39.80 domestic; EUR 45.80 foreign; EUR 4.20 newsstand/cover (effective 2011). adv. **Document type:** *Magazine, Consumer.*
Formerly (until 1991): Radfahren (0720-8545)
Published by: B V A Bielefelder Verlag GmbH & Co. KG, Niederwall 53, Bielefeld, 33602, Germany. TEL 49-521-595514, FAX 49-521-595518, kontakt@bva-bielefeld.de, http://www.bva-bielefeld.de. Ed. Daniel Fikuart. Adv. contact Michael Wagner. Circ: 55,000 (paid and controlled).

388.347 USA ISSN 2162-3880
▼ **ALL ABOUT BIKES.** Text in English. 2010. bi-m. USD 12.95 (effective 2011). **Document type:** *Magazine, Trade.*
Related titles: Online - full text ed.: ISSN 2162-3899. free (effective 2011).
Published by: J V H Media Group, Llc., 438 Division St, Sewickley, PA 15143. http://www.jvhmediagroup.com/.

ALL-TERRAIN VEHICLE. *see* SPORTS AND GAMES—Outdoor Life

796.75 SWE ISSN 0345-0813
ALLT OM M C. (MotorCyclar) Text in Swedish. 1965. 10/yr. SEK 249 for 6 nos.; SEK 60 newsstand/cover (effective 2010). adv. bk.rev. back issues avail. **Document type:** *Magazine, Consumer.* **Description:** News for motor bike enthuthiasts.
Formerly (until 1974): Racingsport
Published by: Foerlags AB Albinsson & Sjoeberg, PO Box 529, Karlskrona, 37123, Sweden. TEL 46-455-335325, FAX 46-455-311715, fabas@fabas.se, http://www.fabas.se. Ed. Goeran Svensson. Adv. contact Frida Sanjiva. color page SEK 18,900; trim 190 x 275. Circ: 22,300 (controlled).

388.347 USA ISSN 2159-2810
AMERICAN BAGGER; the original American v-twin performance touring and customizing authority. Text in English. 2006. m. USD 21.95 domestic; USD 37.95 in Canada; USD 49.50 elsewhere (effective 2011). adv. **Document type:** *Magazine, Trade.* **Description:** Focuses on new products for riders, tech articles, custom baggers, and shows and personality coverage.
Published by: Maverick Publications, 3105 W Fairgrounds Loop, Ste 200, Spearfish, SD 57783. TEL 605-722-0112, 800-999-9718, FAX 605-722-0008, info@maverickpub.com, http://www.maverickpub.com.

629.227 USA ISSN 1095-7375
AMERICAN BICYCLIST. Text in English. 1879. m. USD 350; free to qualified personnel (effective 2006). adv. bk.rev. illus.; tr.lit. **Document type:** *Magazine, Trade.* **Description:** Trade publication for the bicycle industry: dealers, wholesale distributors, importers, and manufacturers.
Former titles (until Aug. 1994): American Bicyclist Magazine (1074-4983); (until Jan. 1994): American Bicyclist and Motorcyclist (0002-7677)
Indexed: SportS.
—Ingenta. CCC.
Published by: League of American Bicyclists, 1612 K St, N W, Ste 800, Washington, DC 20006-2850. TEL 202-822-1333, bikeleague@bikeleague.org, http://www.bikeleague.org. Ed. Elizabeth Preston. Circ: 30,000 (controlled).

388.347 USA ISSN 2159-4732
AMERICAN CYCLE; the Harley-Davidson performance and customizing authority. Text in English. 2006. m. USD 19.95 domestic; USD 49.95 in Canada; USD 74.95 elsewhere (effective 2011). **Document type:** *Magazine, Trade.* **Description:** Features new products, tech articles, the wildest customs and the shows and personalities that define the American V-Twin market.
Published by: Maverick Publications, 3105 W Fairgrounds Loop, Ste 200, Spearfish, SD 57783. TEL 605-722-0112, 800-999-9718, FAX 605-722-0008, info@maverickpub.com, http://www.maverickpub.com.

796.7 USA ISSN 1059-7891
AMERICAN IRON MAGAZINE; for people who love Harley-Davidsons. Text in English. 19??. m. USD 24.95 domestic; USD 39.95 in Canada; USD 120 foreign; USD 5.99 per issue (effective 2011). adv. 148 p./no.; back issues avail.; reprints avail. **Document type:** *Magazine, Consumer.* **Description:** Showcases restored and customized Harleys, tests new models and aftermarket products, covers club news throughout the U.S., technical and repair topics, as well as travel and touring items, and other issues of interest to Harley-Davidson enthusiasts.
Formerly (until 1989): American Iron (1052-0945)
Published by: T A M Communications Inc., 5610 Scotts Valley Dr, Ste B552, Scotts Valley, CA 95066. TEL 831-439-1500, FAX 866-390-1218, http://www.tamcom.com.

AMERICAN IRON RETAILER. *see* BUSINESS AND ECONOMICS—Management

796.7 338 GBR ISSN 1465-7627
AMERICAN MOTORCYCLE DEALER. Text in English. 1993. m. free to qualified personnel (effective 2009). adv. back issues avail. **Document type:** *Magazine, Trade.* **Description:** Provides international product information, industry news, events coverage, supplier profiles and technical features.
Formerly (until 1999): European Dealer News
Related titles: Online - full text ed.
Published by: Dealer-World.com, Kenwood House, 1 Upper Grosvenor Rd, Tunbridge Wells, TN1 2DU, United Kingdom. TEL 44-1892-511516, FAX 44-1892-511517. Pub., Adv. contact Robin Bradley. page GBP 1,895; 180 x 267.

796.7 USA ISSN 0277-9358
AMERICAN MOTORCYCLIST. Text in English. 1947. m. free to members (effective 2010). adv. bk.rev. illus. back issues avail.; reprints avail. **Document type:** *Magazine, Consumer.* **Description:** Focuses on the races and roadriding events sanctioned by the AMA each year, as well as motorcycle-related legislation at the various levels of government.
Former titles (until Sep.1977): A M A News (0003-0074); (until 19??): American Motorcycling
Related titles: Online - full text ed.
Published by: American Motorcyclist Association, 13515 Yarmouth Dr, Pickerington, OH 43147. TEL 614-856-1900, 800-AMA-JOIN, FAX 614-856-1935, http://www.ama-cycle.org/magazine/index.html. Adv. contact Ray Monroe TEL 815-885-4445.

796.7 USA ISSN 1072-4893
AMERICAN RIDER; Harley-Davidson riding at its best. Text in English. 1993. bi-m. USD 15.97 domestic; USD 21.97 in Canada; USD 27.97 elsewhere (effective 2008). adv. illus. 3 cols./p.; back issues avail.; reprints avail. **Document type:** *Magazine, Trade.* **Description:** Publishes articles, road tests, interviews, and features relating to Harley-Davidson motorcycles.
Related titles: Online - full text ed.
Indexed: G05, G06, G07, G08, I05.
Published by: Affinity Group Inc., 2575 Vista Del Mar, Ventura, CA 93001. TEL 805-667-4100, FAX 805-667-4419, info@affinitygroup.com, http://www.affinitygroup.com. Ed. Reg Kittrelle TEL 805-667-4100. Adv. contact Roland Haug. Circ: 61,186.

796.6 FRA ISSN 1955-0413
L'ANNEE DU CYCLISME. Text in French. 1974. a. price varies. illus.
Published by: Editions Calmann-Levy, 31 Rue de Fleurus, Paris, 75006, France. TEL 33-1-49543600, FAX 33-1-49543640, http://www.editions-calmann-levy.com.

796.6 ESP
ANUARIO URTEKARIA. Text in Spanish. 2000. a. adv. **Document type:** *Catalog, Consumer.*
Related titles: ◆ Supplement to: Ciclismo a Fondo. ISSN 0213-4179.
Published by: Motorpress Iberica (Subsidiary of: Gruner + Jahr AG & Co), Ancora 40, Madrid, 28045, Spain. TEL 34-91-3470100, FAX 34-91-3470152, http://www.motorpress-iberica.es.

796.6 USA ISSN 1542-5274
ASPHALT (REDONDO BEACH); the road cycling life. Text in English. 2003. q. USD 34.95 domestic; USD 52.95 foreign (effective 2005). **Document type:** *Magazine, Consumer.*
Published by: Daly/Brady Media, LLC, P. O. Box 1734, Redondo Beach, CA 90278. TEL 310-502-8076, info@asphaltmag.com. Eds., Pubs. Lorraine Daly, Patrick Brady.

796.6 USA
ASPHALT MAGAZINE. Text in English. q. USD 34.95 domestic; USD 52.95 in Canada; USD 72.95 foreign; USD 9.95 per issue (effective 2005). **Document type:** *Magazine, Consumer.*
Published by: Daly/Brady Media LLC, P.O. Box 1734, Redondo Beach, CA 90278. TEL 310-502-8076. Ed. Lorraine Daly. Pub. Patrick Brady.

796.7 AUS ISSN 0155-378X
AUSTRALASIAN DIRT BIKE. Abbreviated title: A D B. Text in English. 1972. m. AUD 40 domestic; AUD 95 in New Zealand; AUD 120 elsewhere; AUD 7.95 newsstand/cover (effective 2008). adv. **Document type:** *Magazine, Consumer.* **Description:** Provides definitive source of information bike tests, race reports, rider interviews, tech tips, riding tips, adventure ride reports, product reports, environmental issues, and awesome pictorials and posters, also give information about where to ride and what gear to wear.
Formerly (until 197?): Cycle Australia (0310-2122)
Related titles: Online - full text ed.
Indexed: Pinpoint.
Published by: A C P Magazines Ltd. (Subsidiary of: P B L Media Pty Ltd.), 54-58 Park St, Sydney, NSW 2000, Australia. TEL 61-2-92828000, FAX 61-2-91263769, research@acpaction.com.au, http://www.acp.com.au. Eds. Andy Wigan, Martin Child. Adv. contact Andrew Hobbs. page USD 2,560; bleed 215 x 285. Circ: 30,611.

AUSTRALIA. BUREAU OF STATISTICS. NEW MOTOR VEHICLE REGISTRATION, AUSTRALIA, MOTORCYCLES DATA ON SUPERTABLE (ONLINE). *see* SPORTS AND GAMES—Abstracting, Bibliographies, Statistics

796.75 AUS
AUSTRALIAN A T V ACTION. (All Terrain Vehicle) Text in English. 200?. q. AUD 39.95 in Australia & New Zealand; AUD 48.45 elsewhere; AUD 7.50 newsstand/cover (effective 2008). adv. **Document type:** *Magazine, Trade.* **Description:** Provides information on all terrain vehicles including new model tests and shootouts, interviews, race reports, technical articles on how to service and maintain ATVs, and trail riding stories.
Published by: A C P Trader International Group (Subsidiary of: P B L Media Pty Ltd.), 73 Atherton Rd, Oakleigh, VIC 3166, Australia. TEL 61-3-95674200, FAX 61-3-95634554. Ed. Greg Leech TEL 61-3-95674194. Adv. contact Justine Schuller. color page AUD 1,900; trim 215 x 300. Circ: 8,000. **Subscr. to:** Magshop, Reply Paid 4967, Sydney, NSW 2001, Australia. TEL 61-2-136116, subs@magstore.com.au, http://shop.magstore.com.au.

796.6 AUS ISSN 1034-3016
AUSTRALIAN CYCLIST; cycling for everyone. Text in English. 1976. bi-m. AUD 39 domestic; AUD 56 in Asia & the Pacific; AUD 67 elsewhere (effective 2008). adv. bk.rev. back issues avail. **Document type:** *Magazine, Consumer.* **Description:** Covers all aspects of cycling, emphasizing recreation and transportation.
Formerly (until 1989): Push On (0157-0994)
Indexed: SD.
Published by: (Bicycle Federation of Australia), Nuance Multimedia Australia Pty Ltd., Ste 2, Level 1, 10 Queens Rd, Melbourne, VIC 3004, Australia. TEL 61-3-98604500, FAX 61-3-98604508, info@nuancemultimedia.com, http://www.nuancemultimedia.com. Ed. Matt Johnson. Adv. contact David Sutcliffe TEL 61-2-85072429. color page AUD 1,525, B&W page AUD 985; trim 205 x 275. Circ: 14,350.

796.7 AUS ISSN 1320-2103
AUSTRALIAN MOTORCYCLE NEWS. Abbreviated title: A M C N. Text in English. 1951. bi-w. AUD 120; AUD 6.95 newsstand/cover (effective 2008). adv. back issues avail. **Document type:** *Magazine, Consumer.* **Description:** Contains motorcycle news and features, road tests, new products, new models, grand prix coverage, and competition reports.
Formerly (until 1963): Australian Motorcycle and Scooter News
Indexed: A11, SD.
Published by: A C P Magazines Ltd. (Subsidiary of: P B L Media Pty Ltd.), 54-58 Park St, Sydney, NSW 2000, Australia. TEL 61-2-92828000, FAX 61-2-91263769, research@acpaction.com.au. Ed. Mick Matheson. Adv. contact Iain Aitken. page AUD 2,350; trim 206 x 275. Circ: 21,911. **Subscr. to:** Magshop, Reply Paid 4967, Sydney, NSW 2001, Australia. TEL 61-2-136116, subs@magstore.com.au, http://shop.magstore.com.au.

796.75 AUS ISSN 1449-6232
AUSTRALIAN MOTORCYCLE TRADER. Text in English. 1994. 13/yr. AUD 59.95 in Australia & New Zealand; AUD 76.95 elsewhere; AUD 4.95 newsstand/cover (effective 2008). adv. **Document type:** *Magazine, Consumer.* **Description:** Provides articles about road tests of bikes and associated gear; offers a detailed color classified section for buying and selling motorcycles.
Published by: A C P Trader International Group (Subsidiary of: P B L Media Pty Ltd.), 73 Atherton Rd, Oakleigh, VIC 3166, Australia. TEL 61-3-95674200, FAX 61-3-95634554. Ed. Greg Leech TEL 61-3-95674194. Adv. contact Justine Schuller. color page AUD 2,120; trim 195 x 275. Circ: 30,140. **Subscr. to:** Magshop, Reply Paid 4967, Sydney, NSW 2001, Australia. TEL 61-2-136116, subs@magstore.com.au, http://shop.magstore.com.au.

796.6 AUS ISSN 1328-6854
AUSTRALIAN MOUNTAIN BIKE. Abbreviated title: A M B. Text in English. 1994. bi-m. AUD 34 domestic; AUD 45 in New Zealand; AUD 58 elsewhere; AUD 7.95 newsstand/cover (effective 2008). adv. **Document type:** *Magazine, Consumer.* **Description:** Covers all aspects of mountain biking. It provides access to an active, adventurous audience. It is about engaging riders of all levels - inspiring, educating and entertaining them.
Former titles (until 1997): Australasian Mountain Bike (1327-7952); (until 1996): Australian Mountain Bike (1323-6938)
Indexed: SD.

S

Published by: A C P Magazines Ltd. (Subsidiary of: P B L Media Pty Ltd.), 54-58 Park St, Sydney, NSW 2000, Australia. TEL 61-2-92828000, FAX 61-2-91263769, research@acpaction.com.au. Adv. contact Andrew Hobbs. page AUD 1,805; bleed 215 x 285. Circ: 20,000.

796.7 AUS
AUSTRALIAN TRAIL & TRACK MONTHLY. Text in English. 1973. m. bk.rev.
Former titles (until 1984): Trail & Track; (until 1982): Australian Trail & Track; (until 1978): Trail & Track (0312-388X); (until 1975): Australian Trail & Track (0310-5431)
Published by: L.W. & T.S. Nominees, Tootal Park, Tootal Rd, Dingley, VIC 3172, Australia. Ed. Les Swallow.

796.7 NLD ISSN 1877-8046
AUTOPED MAGAZINE. Text in Dutch. q. EUR 19 membership (effective 2011). adv. **Document type:** *Magazine, Consumer.*
Published by: Nederlandse Autoped Federatie, Kl. Benninkstraat 19, Genemuiden, 8281 ZV, Netherlands. TEL 31-38-3856747, FAX 3-84-2297741, secretariaat@autoped.nl, http://www.autoped.nl.

AUTORAMA; mensile d'informazione e cultura del mondo dei motori. *see* TRANSPORTATION—Automobiles

AUTOREVUU. *see* TRANSPORTATION—Automobiles

796.7 SVN
AVTO MAGAZIN. MOTO KATALOG. Variant title: Moto Katalog. Text in Slovenian. a. **Document type:** *Magazine, Consumer.*
Published by: Adria Media Ljubljana, Zaloznistvo in Trzenje, d.o.o., Vosnjakova ulica 3, Ljubljana, 1000, Slovenia. TEL 386-1-3000700, FAX 386-1-3000713, info@adriamedia.si, http://www.adriamedia.si. Circ: 8,000 (paid and controlled).

380.1 USA ISSN 1072-1061
HD9999.B43
B D S. Text in English. 1971. m. USD 35 (effective 1997). adv. bk.rev. illus.
Description: For bicycle and fitness equipment dealers with articles on selling and merchandizing.
Formerly: Bicycle Dealer Showcase (0361-381X)
Indexed: SportS.
Published by: Miramar Publishing Co., PO Box 15518, N. Hollywood, CA 91615-9773. Ed. Ron Piechota. Circ: 10,382.

796.6 USA ISSN 2154-2635
▼ **B M W MOTORCYCLE MAGAZINE.** (Bayerische Motoren Werke) Text in English. 2010 (May). q. USD 19.95 (effective 2010). **Description:** Features English content from BMW Motorrader as well as original articles for an American audience.
Related titles: ◆ German ed.: B M W Motorraeder.
Published by: Vivid Image Publications, LLC, 2647 W Arthur Pl, Tucson, AZ 85713. TEL 520-407-5546, FAX 520-204-1377, sandy@bmwmcmag.com.

796.7 DEU
B M W MOTORRAEDER. (Bayerische Motoren Werke) Text in German. 8/yr. EUR 48 domestic; EUR 59 foreign; EUR 6.20 newsstand/cover (effective 2007). adv. **Document type:** *Magazine, Consumer.*
Related titles: ◆ English ed.: B M W Motorcycle Magazine. ISSN 2154-2635.
Published by: Mo Medien Verlag GmbH, Schrempfstr 8, Stuttgart, 70597, Germany. TEL 49-711-24897600, FAX 49-711-24897628, redaktion@mo-web.de. adv.: B&W page EUR 3,655, color page EUR 6,140. Circ: 31,000 (paid and controlled).

629 USA ISSN 1080-5729
B M W - O N. (Bayerische Motoren Werke - Owners News) Text in English. 1972. m. USD 32 domestic membership; USD 47 foreign membership (effective 2002). adv. **Document type:** *Magazine, Consumer.* **Description:** Contains the latest BMW motorcycle information on new models, maintenance, technical expertise, touring, events, safety, accessories, new products, and contests.
Formerly (until 1995): B M W Owners News (8750-765X)
Published by: B M W Motorcycle Owners of America, PO Box 3982, Ballwin, MO 63022. TEL 636-394-7277, FAX 636-391-1811, comments@bmwmoa.org, http://www.bmwmoa.org. Ed. Sandy Cohen. Adv. contact Ted Moyer.

796.7 USA
B M X ACTION. Text in English. 2000. 4/yr. USD 15 domestic; USD 25 in Canada; USD 30 elsewhere (effective 2001). **Document type:** *Magazine, Consumer.* **Description:** Covers the local southern California BMX bicycle scene.
Address: 1300 S Lyon St, Santa Ana, CA 92705. TEL 714-547-5200, FAX 714-547-5200.

796.7 USA ISSN 0195-0320
GV1060.12
B M X PLUS. (Bicycle Motocross) Text in English. 1978. m. USD 13.99 domestic; USD 23.99 in Canada; USD 28.99 elsewhere (effective 2010). adv. illus. **Document type:** *Magazine, Consumer.* **Description:** Features product news and race coverage in the US and worldwide.
Related titles: Online - full text ed.
Indexed: A11, C05, G09, M01, M02, M04, MASUSE, P02, P10, P48, P53, P54, PQC, T02, U01.
Published by: Hi-Torque Publications, Inc., 25233 Anza Dr, Valencia, CA 91355. TEL 661-295-1910, FAX 661-295-1278, http://www.hi-torque.com. Adv. contact Robert Rex TEL 661-367-2109.

796.6 AUS
B M XPRESS. (Bicycle Motorcross) Text in English. 1999. bi-m. AUD 48.20 (effective 2008). back issues avail. **Document type:** *Magazine, Consumer.*
Address: PO Box 3537, Wamberal, NSW 2260, Australia. TEL 61-2-43859678. Ed. Warwick Wheeler.

796 GBR
B T I. (Bicycle Trade and Industry) Text in English. 1980. m. adv. bk.rev. back issues avail. **Document type:** *Magazine, Trade.* **Description:** Contains news and current affairs of interest to anyone dealing with the British bicycle trade.
Related titles: Online - full text ed.: free (effective 2009).
Address: 97 Front St, Whickham, Tyne & Wear, NE16 4JL, United Kingdom. TEL 091-488-1947, FAX 091-488-6718. Ed. Peter Lumley. Adv. contact Kate Spencer. Circ: 3,500 (controlled).

BACK STREET HEROES. *see* TRANSPORTATION—Automobiles

796.7 USA
BACKROADS; the local source for motorcycle enthusiasts. Text in English. 1995. m.
Published by: Backroads, Inc., Box 317, Branchville, NJ 07826. TEL 973-948-4176, FAX 973-948-0823, editor@backroadsusa.com, http://www.backroadsusa.com. Ed., Pub. Brian Rathjen. Circ: 40,000 (paid and controlled).

796.7 USA ISSN 2159-7782
BAGGERS. Text in English. 1994. m. USD 19.97 domestic; USD 31.97 in Canada; USD 43.97 elsewhere (effective 2011). adv. back issues avail. **Document type:** *Magazine, Consumer.* **Description:** Addresses the market of V-twin motorcycle with bags.
Former titles (until 2011): Hot Bike Baggers (1939-7968); (until 2007): Hot Rod's Bikeworks (1556-9764); (until 2005): Hot Rod Bikes (1086-8267); (until 1995): Hot Rod Harleys
Related titles: Online - full text ed.
Indexed: G06, G07, G08, I05, S23.
—CCC.
Published by: Source Interlink Companies, 27500 Riverview Ctr Blvd, Bonita Springs, FL 34134. TEL 239-949-4450, http://www.sourceinterlink.com.

796.75 DEU ISSN 0724-7192
BAHNSPORT AKTUELL; Speedway - Ice Speedway - Grasbahn - Langbahn. Text in German. 1971. m. EUR 42 domestic; EUR 52 foreign (effective 2010). adv. illus.; stat. back issues avail. **Document type:** *Magazine, Consumer.* **Description:** International sports magazine for motorcycle racing. Features racing on sand courses, grass courses, on ice and speedways. Includes reports and results of events and championships, news, letters from readers, and future events.
Supersedes in part (in 1983): Bahnsport Moto Cross und Enduro Aktuell (0723-2535); Which was formerly (until 1982): Bahnsport Aktuell (0171-8940)
Indexed: RASB.
Published by: Ziegler Verlags GmbH, Birkenweiherstr 14, Langenselbold, 63505, Germany. TEL 49-6184-923330, FAX 49-6184-923355, info@ziegler-verlag.de. Ed. Stefan Ziegler. Adv. contact Ralf Ziegler. B&W page EUR 1,460, color page EUR 2,634. Circ: 50,000 (paid and controlled).

796.6 CHE
BASLER VELOBLATT. Text in German. 1976. bi-m. CHF 30. **Document type:** *Newsletter.*
Published by: I G Velo, Dornacherstr 101, Basel, 4053, Switzerland. TEL 41-61-3633535, FAX 41-61-3633539. Ed. Nicholas Berger. Circ: 7,700.

796.7 USA
BATTLE 2WIN; buell & hi-performance sportster motorcycles. Text in English. q. USD 12.95; USD 16.95 in Canada; USD 25 elsewhere (effective 2000). adv. **Document type:** *Magazine, Consumer.* **Description:** Focuses on the latest information and personalities involving Buells and high-performance sportsters.
Published by: Thunder Press Inc., 4865 Scotts Valley Dr, Ste 200, Scotts Valley, CA 95066. TEL 831-438-7882, FAX 831-438-0993, advertising@thunderpressinc.com, http://thunderpressinc.com.

BEST MOTORING. *see* HOBBIES

796.7 JPN
BEST MOTORING HOT VERSION. Text in Japanese. bi-m. **Document type:** *Magazine, Consumer.*
Published by: Kodansha Ltd., 2-12-21 Otowa, Bunkyo-ku, Tokyo, 112-8001, Japan. TEL 81-3-3946-6201, FAX 81-3-3944-9915, http://www.kodansha.co.jp.

796.6 ITA ISSN 1123-9212
LA BICICLETTA; il giornale delle gran fondo. Text in Italian. 1984. m. EUR 56 domestic (effective 2009). adv. **Document type:** *Magazine, Consumer.*
Published by: La Cuba Srl, Via della Maratona 66, Rome, RM 00194, Italy. TEL 39-063-629021, FAX 39-063-6309950.

796.6 ITA ISSN 1593-9812
BICISPORT. Text in Italian. 1976. m. (plus 4/yr. special issues). EUR 57 domestic; EUR 105 foreign (effective 2008). adv. illus. **Document type:** *Magazine, Consumer.*
Published by: Compagnia Editoriale, Via Giuseppe Capogrossi 50, Rome, 00155, Italy. TEL 39-06-22857256, http://www.compagniaeditoriale.it. Circ: 62,000.

796.6 ITA ISSN 1970-4895
BICITECH. Text in Italian. 2006. bi-m. EUR 30 domestic; EUR 60 in Europe; EUR 80 elsewhere (effective 2011). **Document type:** *Magazine, Consumer.*
Published by: Tecniche Nuove SpA, Via Eritrea 21, Milan, MI 201, Italy. TEL 39-02-390901, FAX 39-02-7570364, info@tecnichenuove.com. Ed. Marina Temporal.

796.6 ESP
BICITECH (YEAR). Text in Spanish. 1995. a. **Document type:** *Consumer.*
Published by: Motorpress Iberica (Subsidiary of: Gruner + Jahr AG & Co), Ancora 40, Madrid, 28045, Spain. TEL 34-91-3470100, FAX 34-91-3470152, http://www.motorpress-iberica.es.

796.6 ESP
BICITECH A FONDO. Text in Spanish. 1995. irreg. **Document type:** *Catalog, Consumer.*
Related titles: ◆ Supplement to: Ciclismo a Fondo. ISSN 0213-4179; ◆ Supplement to: Bike. ISSN 1889-514X.
Published by: Motorpress Iberica (Subsidiary of: Gruner + Jahr AG & Co), Ancora 40, Madrid, 28045, Spain. TEL 34-91-3470100, FAX 34-91-3470152, http://www.motorpress-iberica.es. Circ: 19,000 (paid).

629.227 GBR ISSN 1758-8618
THE BICYCLE BUYER. Text in English. 2008. bi-m. GBP 23.99 domestic; EUR 45 in Europe; USD 70 elsewhere (effective 2010). adv. back issues avail. **Document type:** *Magazine, Consumer.* **Description:** Features include comparative test information, stand-alone reviews, accessory reviews, plus guidance on where and how to ride, in the city or out of the trails.
Published by: Factory Media, One W Smithfield, London, EC1A 9JU, United Kingdom. TEL 44-20-73329700, contact@factorymedia.com, http://www.factorymedia.com. Ed. David Hopkins. Adv. contact Kate Marley TEL 44-20-3329747.

796.6 CAN
BICYCLE HANDBOOK. Text in English. 1977. a. CAD 4. adv.
Published by: Cycling British Columbia, 332 1367 West Broadway, Vancouver, BC V6H 4A9, Canada. TEL 604-737-3034, FAX 604-738-7175. Ed. Tony Badger. Circ: 6,000.

796.6 USA ISSN 0742-8308
BICYCLE PAPER; the voice of Northwest cycling. Text in English. 1972. m. (Mar.-Sep.; plus winter issue). USD 14 domestic (effective 2001). adv. bk.rev. illus. **Document type:** *Newspaper, Consumer.* **Description:** Touring, racing, personality features. Includes calendar of events in the Northwest for bicycle enthusiasts.
Formerly: Great Bicycle Conspiracy
Related titles: Online - full text ed.
Indexed: SD.
Address: 12420 Gibson Rd, Everett, WA 98204. TEL 425-438-9031, FAX 425-355-9322, sales@bicyclepaper.com. Ed. David McNamara. Pub. Paul Clark. R&P Alison Bohan. Adv. contact Claire Bonin. B&W page USD 1,150. Circ: 2,500 (paid); 22,500 (controlled).

796.6 USA ISSN 1941-8809
BICYCLE QUARTERLY. Text in English. 2002. q. USD 30 domestic; USD 36 in Canada; USD 50 elsewhere (effective 2008). **Document type:** *Newsletter, Consumer.*
Formerly (until 2006): Vintage Bicycle Quarterly (1555-2942)
Address: 140 Lakeside Ave, Ste C, Seattle, WA 98122. TEL 206-297-1199, http://www.vintagebicyclepress.com. Ed. Jan Heine.

338.47 658 USA ISSN 1069-8493
BICYCLE RETAILER AND INDUSTRY NEWS. Abbreviated title: B R A I N. Text in English. 1992. 18/yr. USD 65 domestic; USD 78 in Canada & Mexico; USD 173 in Europe includes Pacific rim, far east; free to qualified personnel (effective 2009). adv. bk.rev. 56 p./no. 4 cols./p.; **Document type:** *Magazine, Trade.* **Description:** Keeps retailers current on industry trends, new technology and marketing strategies.
Related titles: Online - full text ed.
Indexed: A09, A10, A15, ABIn, B01, B06, B07, B09, G08, I05, P48, P51, PQC, T02, V02, V03, V04.
—CCC.
Published by: (National Bicycle Dealers Association), Nielsen Business Publications (Subsidiary of: Nielsen Business Media, Inc.), 25431 Cabot Rd, Ste 204, Laguna Hills, CA 92653. TEL 949-206-1677, FAX 949-206-1675, bmcomm@nielsen.com, http://www.nielsenbusinessmedia.com. Ed. Megan Tomkins TEL 949-206-1677 ext 203. Pub. Marc Sani TEL 949-206-1677 ext 205. adv.: B&W page USD 4,738, color page USD 5,575; trim 10.25 x 11.875. Circ: 12,473 (paid).

796.6 USA ISSN 1946-6366
▼ **BICYCLE TIMES.** Text in English. 2009. q. USD 10 domestic; USD 20 in Canada & Mexico; USD 25 elsewhere; USD 5 per issue (effective 2009). adv. back issues avail. **Document type:** *Magazine, Trade.* **Description:** Features about the joy of riding.
Published by: Dirt Rag Magazine Ltd., 3483 Saxonburg Blvd, Pittsburgh, PA 15238. TEL 412-767-9910, 800-762-7617, FAX 412-767-9920. Ed. Karen Brooks TEL 412-767-9910 ext 104. Pub. Maurice Tierney TEL 412-767-9910 ext 102. Adv. contact Andy Bruno TEL 412-767-9910 ext 107. B&W page USD 1,100, color page USD 1,500; trim 8 x 10.75. Circ: 42,530.

381.456 GBR ISSN 1476-1505
BICYCLEBUSINESS; for everyone in the bicycle business. Variant title: BikeBiz. Text in English. 2000. m. GBP 50 domestic; GBP 60 in Europe; GBP 90 elsewhere (effective 2009). adv. back issues avail. **Document type:** *Magazine, Trade.*
Related titles: Online - full text ed.: free (effective 2009).
—CCC.
Published by: Intent Media Ltd., Saxon House, 6a St Andrew St, Hertford, Hertfordshire SG14 1JA, United Kingdom. TEL 44-1992-535646, FAX 44-1992-535648, bike.subscriptions@c-cms.com, http://www.intentmedia.co.uk. Ed. Jonathon Harker. **Subscr. to:** PO Box 35, Robertsbridge TN32 5WN, United Kingdom. TEL 44-1580-883848, FAX 44-1580-883849.

796.6 USA ISSN 0006-2073
GV1040
BICYCLING. Text in English. 1962. 11/yr. USD 19.98 domestic; CAD 29.96 in Canada; USD 45 elsewhere (effective 2011). adv. bk.rev. illus. index. back issues avail.; reprints avail. **Document type:** *Magazine, Consumer.* **Description:** Features fitness, training, nutrition, touring, racing, equipment, clothing, bike maintenance and new-product review.
Incorporates: (1990-200?): Mountain Bike (0897-5213); (1972-1980): Bike World (0098-8650); Formerly (until 1968): American Cycling
Related titles: Microfiche ed.: (from NBI, PQC); Online - full text ed.
Indexed: A11, A22, A25, A26, ASIP, Acal, B04, BRD, C05, C11, C12, CPerI, ConsI, E08, G05, G06, G07, G08, G09, H03, HlthInd, I05, I06, I07, IHTDI, M01, M02, M04, M06, MASUSE, MagInd, P02, P10, P19, P48, P53, P54, PEI, PMR, PQC, R03, RGAb, RGPR, S08, S09, S23, SD, SportS, T02, TOM, U01, W03, W05, WBA, WMB.
—Ingenta. **CCC.**
Published by: Rodale, Inc., 33 E Minor St, Emmaus, PA 18098. TEL 610-967-5171, http://www.rodaleinc.com. Ed. Peer Flax. **Dist. in UK by:** MarketForce UK Ltd.

796.6 AUS ISSN 1034-8085
BICYCLING AUSTRALIA. Text in English. 1990. m. AUD 49 domestic (effective 2007); AUD 75 in New Zealand; AUD 85 elsewhere (effective 2004). adv. illus. back issues avail. **Document type:** *Magazine, Consumer.* **Description:** Covers road and track cycling, mountain biking. Includes equipment and training guides.
Indexed: A11, SD.
Published by: Lake Wangary Publishing Co. Pty. Ltd., Unit 1/36 Wentworth St, Port Kembla, NSW 2505, Australia. mail@bicyclingaustralia.com. Ed. Nick Raman. Pub. Gary Hunt. R&P Phil Latz. adv.: B&W page AUD 990, color page AUD 1,490; trim 195 x 265.

796.6 AUS ISSN 1832-0597
BICYCLING BUYERS' GUIDE. Text in English. 1999. a. **Document type:** *Handbook/Manual/Guide, Consumer.*
Indexed: A11.
Published by: Lake Wangary Publishing Co. Pty. Ltd., Unit 1/36 Wentworth St, Port Kembla, NSW 2505, Australia. mail@bicyclingaustralia.com, http://www.bicyclingaustralia.com. Pub. Gary Hunt.

796.6 FRA ISSN 1638-4083
BIG BIKE. Text in French. 2002. bi-m. (7/yr). EUR 32.50 (effective 2009). **Document type:** *Magazine, Consumer.*

Published by: Editions Niveales, 6 Rue Irvoy, Grenoble, 38000, France. TEL 33-4-76705411, FAX 33-4-76705412, http://www.dipresse.com/niveales. Ed. Laurent Belluard. **Dist. by:** Dipresse, 18-24 Quai de la Marne, Paris 75164, France. TEL 33-1-44848526, FAX 33-1-42005692, http://www.dipresse.com.

796.7 USA ISSN 1084-3183
BIG TWIN. Text in English. 1993. a. USD 5.95 newsstand/cover (effective 2007). adv. illus. **Document type:** *Magazine, Consumer.* **Description:** For Harley-Davidson enthusiasts.
Former titles (until 199?): Cycle World Big Twin (1075-6140); (until 1994): Cycle World's American Big Twin (1067-4470)
Related titles: Online - full text ed.
Published by: Hachette Filipacchi Media U.S., Inc. (Subsidiary of: Hachette Filipacchi Medias S.A.), 1633 Broadway, New York, NY 10019. TEL 212-767-6000, FAX 212-767-5600, saleshfmbooks@hfmus.com, http://www.hfmus.com.

796.7 SWE ISSN 1653-7173
BIGTWIN. Text in Swedish. 2006. m. SEK 699 (effective 2011). adv. **Document type:** *Magazine, Consumer.*
Published by: I D G AB (Subsidiary of: I D G Communications Inc.), Karlbergsvaegen 77-81, Stockholm, 10678, Sweden. TEL 46-8-4536000, FAX 46-8-4536005, kundservice@idg.se, http://www.idg.se. Ed. Bjorn Glansk.

796.6 796.7 ESP ISSN 1889-514X
BIKE. Text in Spanish. 1992. m. adv. **Document type:** *Magazine, Consumer.*
Former titles (until 2005): Bike a Fondo (1576-429X); (until 1997): Bike (1131-9585)
Related titles: ◆ Supplement(s): Bicitech a Fondo.
Published by: Motorpress Iberica (Subsidiary of: Gruner + Jahr AG & Co), Ancora 40, Madrid, 28045, Spain. TEL 34-91-3470100, FAX 34-91-3470152, http://www.motorpress-iberica.es. Ed. Julio Vicioso. Circ: 23,700 (paid).

796.6 DEU ISSN 0936-7624
BIKE; Das Mountainbike-Magazin. Text in German. 1989. 12/yr. EUR 47 in Germany & Austria; EUR 61 in Switzerland; EUR 75.20 elsewhere; EUR 4.50 newsstand/cover (effective 2011). adv. **Document type:** *Magazine, Consumer.*
Published by: Delius Klasing Verlag GmbH, Siekerwall 21, Bielefeld, 33602, Germany. TEL 49-521-5590, FAX 49-521-559113, info@delius-klasing.de, http://www.delius-klasing.de. Ed. Jochen Welz. Pub. Konrad Delius. Adv. contact Ingeborg Bockstette. Circ: 76,115 (paid).

796.6 GBR ISSN 0140-4547
BIKE; Britain's best-selling motorcycle magazine. Text in English. 1971. m. GBP 43 domestic; GBP 58.73 in United States; GBP 50.48 in Europe; GBP 75.60 elsewhere (effective 2009). adv. bk.rev. **Document type:** *Magazine, Consumer.* **Description:** Covers all types of bikes from tourers to dirt bikes, custom and street racers.
—CCC.
Published by: H. Bauer Publishing Ltd. (Subsidiary of: Bauer Media Group), Academic House, 24-28 Oval Rd, London, NW1 7DT, United Kingdom. TEL 44-20-72418000, FAX 44-20-72418030, http://www.bauer.co.uk. Ed. Tim Thompson. **Subscr. to:** Tower House, Sovereign Park, Market Harborough, Leicestershire LE16 9EF, United Kingdom. TEL 44-1858-438866, subs@greatmagazines.co.uk.

796.7 FRA ISSN 1638-7724
BIKE. Text in French. 2003. m. EUR 45 (effective 2009). **Document type:** *Magazine, Consumer.*
Published by: Editions Lariviere, 6 Rue Olof Palme, Clichy, 92587, France. TEL 33-1-47565400, http://www.editions-lariviere.fr.

796.6 BRA ISSN 1518-3963
BIKE ACTION. Text in Portuguese. 2000. m. BRL 97 (effective 2007). adv. **Document type:** *Magazine, Consumer.*
Published by: Adrenal Editora, Rua Antonio Comparato 164, Sao Paulo, 04605-030, Brazil. TEL 55-11-55433511, FAX 55-11-50414227.

796.6 DEU ISSN 1611-3438
BIKE & BUSINESS. Text in German. 1995. 11/yr. EUR 96 domestic; EUR 102 foreign (effective 2010). adv. **Document type:** *Magazine, Trade.*
Related titles: Online - full text ed.
Published by: Vogel Business Media GmbH & Co.KG, Max-Planck-Str 7-9, Wuerzburg, 97064, Germany. TEL 49-931-4180, FAX 49-931-4182750, info@vogel.de, http://www.vogel-media.de. Ed. Stephan Maderner. adv.: B&W page EUR 1,930, color page EUR 2,830. Circ: 7,400 (paid and controlled).

796.7 ZAF ISSN 1995-1353
BIKE AND QUAD MART. Text in English. 2007. s-m.
Published by: Alli-Cat Publishing, PO Box 3487, Parklands, 2121, South Africa. TEL 27-12-3423840.

796.7 USA ISSN 1932-2747
TL488
BIKE BUILDER'S HANDBOOK FOR HARLEY-DAVIDSON AND V-TWIN OWNERS. Variant title: V-Twin Magazine Presents the New Bike Builder's Handbook for Harley-Davidson and V-Twin Owners. Text in English. 1996. a., latest 2008. USD 12.99 newsstand/cover (effective 2009). adv. back issues avail. **Document type:** *Directory, Consumer.* **Description:** Designed to help build dream bikes.
Formerly (until 2006): Annual Buyer's Guide for Harley-Davidson & American Hybrid Owners (1092-8375)
Published by: Paisano Publications, Inc., 28210 Dorothy Dr, Box 3075, Agoura Hills, CA 91301. TEL 818-889-8740, 800-247-6246, FAX 818-735-6518, bulkmagazines@paisanopub.com. Adv. contact Tammy Porter TEL 818-889-8740 ext 1265.

796.6 NLD ISSN 1877-7961
▼ **BIKE & TREKKING;** fiets- en reismagazine. Text in Dutch. 2009. q. EUR 14.50 (effective 2010). adv. **Document type:** *Magazine, Consumer.*
Published by: Maruba b.v., Winthontlaan 200, Utrecht, 3526 KV, Netherlands. TEL 31-30-2891073, FAX 31-30-2887415, maruba@maruba.com, http://www.maruba.nl. Pub. Maas H van Drie. adv.: color page EUR 3,660; trim 240 x 300. Circ: 30,000.

388.347 NLD ISSN 1387-1366
BIKE EUROPE. Text in Dutch. 1997. m. (11/yr.). EUR 273.52 (effective 2009). adv. **Document type:** *Journal, Trade.* **Description:** For top and middle management of the European bicycle and scooter market.
Published by: Reed Business bv (Subsidiary of: Reed Business), Hanzestraat 1, Doetinchem, 7006 RH, Netherlands. info@reedbusiness.nl, http://www.reedbusiness.nl. Ed. Jack Oortwijn TEL 31-346-577390. Pub. Geert van de Bosch. adv.: B&W page EUR 3,050, color page EUR 5,611; 211 x 257. Circ: 12,000.

796.6 PRT
BIKE GUIA DO COMPRADOR. Text in Portuguese. 1995. a. EUR 15,382 newsstand/cover (effective 2005). adv. **Document type:** *Magazine, Consumer.* **Description:** Contains information and reviews of the latest bicycle models and accessories.
Published by: Motorpress Lisboa, SA (Subsidiary of: Gruner + Jahr AG & Co), Rua Policarpio Anjos No. 4, Cruz Quebrada, Dafundo 1495-742, Portugal. TEL 351-21-4154500, FAX 351-21-4154501, buzine@motorpress.pt, http://www.mpl.pt. Circ: 15,382 (paid).

388.347 GBR ISSN 1755-3415
BIKE IT PROJECT REVIEW. Text in English. 2005. a. **Document type:** *Magazine, Trade.*
Related titles: Online - full text ed.: ISSN 1755-3423. 2005.
—CCC.
Published by: Sustrans, 2 Cathedral Sq, College Green, Bristol, Avon BS1 5DD, United Kingdom. TEL 44-117-9268893, FAX 44-117-9294173, info@sustrans.org.uk, http://www.sustrans.org.uk.

796.6 PRT
BIKE MAGAZINE. Text in Portuguese. 1994. m. EUR 3.50 newsstand/cover (effective 2005). adv. **Document type:** *Magazine, Consumer.*
Published by: Motorpress Lisboa, SA (Subsidiary of: Gruner + Jahr AG & Co), Rua Policarpio Anjos No. 4, Cruz Quebrada, Dafundo 1495-742, Portugal. TEL 351-21-4154500, FAX 351-21-4154501, buzine@motorpress.pt, http://www.mpl.pt. Ed. Vitor Sousa. Pub. Fernando Pereira. Circ: 6,457 (paid).

796.6 USA ISSN 1072-4869
GV1040
BIKE MAGAZINE. Text in English. 1994. 8/yr. USD 11.97 domestic; USD 24.97 in Canada; USD 26.97 elsewhere (effective 2008). adv. back issues avail.; reprints avail. **Document type:** *Magazine, Consumer.* **Description:** Designed to inspire its readers to get on their bikes, pedal a little harder, climb a little higher and send it a little farther.
Related titles: Online - full text ed.
Indexed: A26, B04, E08, G06, G07, G08, I05, I06, I07, R03, RGAb, RGPR, S09, S23, W03, W05.
—CCC.
Published by: Source Interlink Companies, PO Box 1028, Dana Point, CA 92629. TEL 949-661-5150, FAX 949-496-7849, dheine@sourceinterlink.com, http://www.sourceinterlinkmedia.com. Ed. Lou Mazzante. Pub. Derek DeJonge. adv.: B&W page USD 5,540, color page USD 16,530; trim 8.375 x 10.875. Circ: 56,371 (paid).

796.6 USA ISSN 1940-5855
BIKE MONKEY MAGAZINE. Text in English. 2008. bi-m. USD 15 (effective 2007). **Document type:** *Magazine, Consumer.* **Description:** Dedicated to providing a voice for bicyclists and discussing community issues relevent to biking in Sonoma County and surrounding areas.
Published by: Bike Monkey, 1935 Knolls Dr, Santa Rosa, CA 95495. Editor@BikeMonkeyMag.com. Pub. Carlos Perez.

796.6 ZAF ISSN 0378-9128
BIKE S.A. Text in English. 1975. m. ZAR 100; ZAR 140 foreign (effective 1998). adv. bk.rev. illus. **Document type:** *Journal, Consumer.* **Description:** Information on motor bikes, bike gear and maintenance, courses and competitions.
Published by: Bike Promotions (Pty) Ltd., PO Box 894, Johannesburg, 2000, South Africa. TEL 27-11-782-5521, FAX 27-11-888-3431. Ed., Adv. contact Simon Fourie. B&W page ZAR 4,800, color page ZAR 6,400; trim 203 x 280. Circ: 24,000.

796.6 DEU ISSN 1437-9767
BIKE SPORT NEWS; das Magazin fuer echte Biker. Text in German. 1990. 10/yr. EUR 37.80 domestic; EUR 43.80 foreign; EUR 4.20 newsstand/cover (effective 2011). adv. **Document type:** *Magazine, Consumer.*
Published by: B V A Bielefelder Verlag GmbH & Co. KG, Niederwall 53, Bielefeld, 33602, Germany. TEL 49-521-595514, FAX 49-521-595518, kontakt@bva-bielefeld.de, http://www.bva-bielefeld.de. Ed. Martin Munker. Adv. contact Michael Wagner. Circ: 28,150 (paid and controlled).

796.7 ZAF ISSN 1992-092X
BIKE TALK. Text in English. 2006. m. ZAR 105 (effective 2006). adv. **Document type:** *Magazine, Consumer.*
Published by: Talk 2 Me, PO Box 902, Amanzimtoti, 4125, South Africa. TEL 27-31-9166902, FAX 27-31-9162140. Ed. Hein Jonker. adv.: page ZAR 1,140.

796.6 ITA ISSN 1824-0208
BIKE TOUR; il piacere di viaggiare in bicicletta. Text in Italian. 2004. m. **Document type:** *Magazine, Consumer.*
Published by: Techne Editore, Viale Piave 11, Milan, 20129, Italy. TEL 39-02-76002856, FAX 39-02-76004252, info@techneditore.it, http://www.techneditore.it.

796.7 GBR ISSN 1362-5640
BIKE TRADER. Text in English. 1996. fortn. GBP 70 (effective 2010). adv. **Document type:** *Magazine, Trade.* **Description:** Provides information and assistance to those wishing to buy or sell motorcycles and scooters.
Related titles: Online - full text ed.
Published by: Trader Media Group Ltd., Optimim House, Clippers Quay, Salford Quays, Manchester, M50 3XP, United Kingdom. enquiries@autotrader.co.uk, http://www.tradermediagroup.com/. Circ: 17,876.

794 DEU ISSN 0946-1698
BIKE WORKSHOP. Text in German. 1994. a. EUR 8.60 newsstand/cover (effective 2011). adv. **Document type:** *Magazine, Consumer.*
Published by: Delius Klasing Verlag GmbH, Siekerwall 21, Bielefeld, 33602, Germany. TEL 49-521-5590, FAX 49-521-559113, info@delius-klasing.de, http://www.delius-klasing.de. Adv. contact Ingeborg Bockstette. Circ: 75,000 (paid).

796.6 USA ISSN 1933-222X
BIKECULTURE MAGAZINE. Text in English. 1997. 8/yr. USD 18 (effective 2007). adv. **Document type:** *Magazine, Consumer.*
Formerly (until 2006): The Ride Magazine (1095-9165)
Address: PO Box 441, Lexington, MA 02420. TEL 781-641-9515, FAX 781-652-9575, bikeculture@bikeculture.com. Ed. Richard Fries. Pub. Deb Fries.

796.7 USA ISSN 1058-7926
GV1059.5
BIKER; lifestyle magazine of events, news and bikes. Text in English. 1987. 9/yr. USD 27.95; USD 6.99 newsstand/cover (effective 2009). adv. back issues avail. **Document type:** *Magazine, Consumer.* **Description:** Designed for dissenting adults who appreciate righteous motorcycles, pretty ladies and wild parties.
Former titles (until 19??): Easyriders Presents Biker (1046-1604); (until 198?): Biker Lifestyle (0745-3604)
Published by: Paisano Publications, Inc., 28210 Dorothy Dr, Box 3075, Agoura Hills, CA 91301. TEL 818-889-8740, 800-247-6246, FAX 818-735-6518, bulkmagazines@paisanopub.com. Adv. contact Tammy Porter TEL 818-889-8740 ext 1265. Circ: 44,898.

796.7 DEU
BIKER BOERSE. Text in German. 1993. m. adv. **Document type:** *Magazine, Consumer.* **Description:** Covers motorcycles and motorbiking.
Related titles: Online - full text ed.
Published by: Zweite Hand Verlag, Askanischer Platz 3, Berlin, 10963, Germany. TEL 49-30-290210, FAX 49-30-2902199935, service@zweitehand.de, http://www.zweitehand.de. Ed. Bernd Zimmerman. adv.: page EUR 2,408.

796.7 DEU
BIKER'S MOTORRAD KATALOG. Text in German. 1989. a. EUR 7.70 newsstand/cover (effective 2007). adv. back issues avail. **Document type:** *Magazine, Consumer.*
Formerly: Schermer's Motorrad Katalog
Published by: Mo Medien Verlag GmbH, Schrempfstr 8, Stuttgart, 70597, Germany. TEL 49-711-24897600, FAX 49-711-24897628, redaktion@mo-web.de, http://www.mo-web.de. adv.: B&W page EUR 4,250, color page EUR 7,140. Circ: 64,000 (paid and controlled).

796.7 DEU ISSN 1614-9157
BIKERS NEWS. Text in German. m. EUR 52 domestic; EUR 75 foreign; EUR 5 newsstand/cover (effective 2010). adv. **Document type:** *Magazine, Consumer.*
Published by: Huber Verlag GmbH & Co. KG, Markircher Str 9 a, Mannheim, 68229, Germany. TEL 49-621-483610, FAX 49-621-4836111, szeneshop@huber-verlag.de, http://www.huber-verlag.de. Ed. Michael Ahlsdorf. Adv. contact Nina Kropp.

796.6 USA ISSN 1943-9792
▼ **BIKES & GEAR.** Text in English. 2009. 2/yr. USD 7.99 newsstand/cover (effective 2009). adv. **Document type:** *Magazine, Consumer.* **Description:** Aims to introduce cyclists to the newest and most technologically advanced bicycles, wheels and gear available for the year.
Published by: Future U S, Inc. (Subsidiary of: Future Publishing Ltd.), 4000 Shoreline Ct, Ste 400, South San Francisco, CA 94080. TEL 650-872-1642, FAX 650-872-1643, http://www.futureus.com. Eds. Bruce Hildenbrand, Jon Phillips TEL 650-238-2490.

796.6 NLD ISSN 1879-5625
▼ **BIKESTYLE.** Text in Dutch. 2009. q. EUR 22.50 (effective 2010). **Document type:** *Magazine, Consumer.*
Published by: Blauw Media Uitgeverij B.V., Postbus 1043, Maarssen, 3600 BA, Netherlands. TEL 31-346-574040, FAX 31-346-576056, info@blauwmedia.com, http://blauwmedia.nl.

796.7 USA
BLACK BIKER MAGAZINE. Text in English. 2006 (Jun.). q. USD 19.99 (effective 2006). **Document type:** *Magazine, Consumer.* **Description:** Covers African American Bikers in a manner that is professional and dignified through pictures, interviews, and stories.
Address: PO Box 5778, Oakland, CA 94605 . Ed. Gary Hayes. Pub. Nai'l Karim.

BLACK BOOK. MOTORCYCLE XPRESS. *see* BUSINESS AND ECONOMICS—Trade And Industrial Directories

BLACK BOOK. OFFICIAL MOTORCYCLE AND POWERSPORTS VALUE GUIDE. *see* BUSINESS AND ECONOMICS—Trade And Industrial Directories

629.227 USA ISSN 2151-0776
▼ **BLINGROCKETS.COM.** Text in English. 2009. m. free (effective 2009). back issues avail. **Document type:** *Magazine, Trade.*
Media: Online - full content.

796.7 DEU
BOCK. Text in German. 2003. q. EUR 3.50 newsstand/cover (effective 2003). adv. **Document type:** *Magazine, Consumer.*
Published by: Schau Verlag GmbH, Gruener Deich 1, Hamburg, 20097, Germany. TEL 49-40-3287270, FAX 49-40-32872722, info@schauverlag.de, http://www.sp-m.de. Adv. contact Antje Sievert. page EUR 19,400; trim 240 x 340. Circ: 200,000 (controlled).

796.6 USA ISSN 1942-5597
BONESHAKER; a bicycling almanac. Text in English. 2008 (May). irreg. (Five times every two years). USD 5 newsstand/cover (effective 2008). **Document type:** *Guide, Consumer.* **Description:** Aims to provide relevant, interesting, and useful considerations of bicycle commuting. Geared towards anyone even remotely interested in going by bike, the collection gathers news, information, facts, figures, and fictions for the common cyclist.
Published by: Wolverine Farm Publishing, PO Box 814, Fort Collins, CO 80522. TEL 970-472-4284, wolverinefarm@yahoo.com. Pub. Todd Simmons.

629.227 GBR ISSN 1751-9322
BRIT CHOPPER MAGAZINE. Text in English. 2006. q. GBP 3.50 newsstand/cover (effective 2009). adv. back issues avail. **Document type:** *Magazine, Trade.*
Related titles: Optical Disk - DVD ed.: ISSN 1751-9330.
Address: PO Box 1184, Ormesby, Norfolk, United Kingdom. TEL 44-7793-671124, info@britchopper.co.uk. Ed. Chris Ireland. Adv. contact Mark Duckett. page GBP 450; 200 x 287. **Subscr. to:** PO Box 54, Tunbridge Wells, Kent TN2 9FJ, United Kingdom. subscriptions@britchopper.co.uk.

BRITISH CAR. *see* TRANSPORTATION—Automobiles

796.7 USA ISSN 1536-4925
C B R MAGAZINE. (Classic Bike Rider) Text in English. 2001 (Sept.). q. USD 48 in North America; USD 60 elsewhere (effective 2003). adv.

S

Published by: Too-Due Publishing, LLC, 8882 Timberchase Ct., West Chester, OH 45069. TEL 513-942-4019, http://www.cbr-mag.com. Ed. Mark Thompson.

796.7 USA ISSN 1525-9803
C C MOTORCYCLE NEWSMAGAZINE. (City Cycle) Text in English. 1989. m. USD 25 (effective 2001). adv. bk.rev.; film rev.; rec.rev.; tel.rev.; video rev.; Website rev. 68 p./no.; back issues avail. **Document type:** *Newspaper, Consumer.*
Published by: Motomag Corp., Box 808, Nyack, NY 10960. TEL 845-353-MOTO, FAX 845-353-5240. Ed., Pub., Adv. contact Mark Kalan. page USD 750; 10 x 14. Circ: 60,000.

629.118 FRA ISSN 1273-6600
CAFE RACER. Text in French. 1996. bi-m. EUR 25 (effective 2010). adv. **Document type:** *Magazine, Consumer.*
Related titles: Online - full text ed.; Supplement(s): Cafe Racer. Hors Serie. ISSN 1288-2496. 199?.
Published by: Les Editions du Dollar, 16 Rue Meslay, Paris, 75003, France. TEL 33-1-42710041. Ed. Bertrand Bussillet.

796.7 CAN ISSN 1196-7218
CANADIAN BIKER. Text in English. 1980. 8/yr. CAD 24.95 domestic; CAD 35 in United States; CAD 40 elsewhere; CAD 3.95 newsstand/cover (effective 2000). adv. back issues avail. **Description:** Covers touring, off-road cycling, and news for motorcycle enthusiasts.
Formerly (until 1992): Canadian Biker Magazine (0820-8344)
Published by: Western Biker Publications Ltd., 735 Market St, Victoria, BC V8T 2E2, Canada. TEL 604-384-0333, FAX 604-384-1832, canbike@canadianbiker.com, http://www.islandnet.com/~canbike/canbike.html. Ed. W L Creed. Circ: 16,000.

796.6 CAN ISSN 1923-1628
▼ **CANADIAN CYCLING MAGAZINE.** Abbreviated title: C C M. Text in English. 2010. bi-m. CAD 20.95 (effective 2010). adv. **Document type:** *Magazine, Consumer.*
Published by: Gripped Publishing Inc., 344 Bloor St, Unit 510, Toronto, ON M5S 3A7, Canada. TEL 416-927-0774, FAX 416-927-1491, info@gripped.com. Ed. Dan Dakin. Pub. Sam Cohen. Adv. contact Chris Lepik.

796.6 CAN ISSN 1180-1352
CANADIAN CYCLIST. Text in English. 1990. 5/yr. CAD 17.12 domestic; CAD 21 in United States; CAD 27 elsewhere (effective 1999). adv. **Document type:** *Magazine, Consumer.* **Description:** Covers al aspects of cycling in Canada by Canadians.
Related titles: Online - full text ed.
Address: 7 Barker St, Paris, ON N3L 2H4, Canada. TEL 519-442-7905, FAX 514-442-5259. Ed. Robert Jones. Pub. Tracy Harkness. Circ: 9,000.

796.7 658.8 CAN
CANADIAN POWERSPORT TRADE. Text in English. bi-m. free to qualified personnel. **Document type:** *Magazine, Trade.*
Formerly: Motorsport Dealer and Trade
Published by: Point One Media, #3-2232 Wilgress Rd, Nanaimo, BC V9S 4N4, Canada. TEL 877-755-2762, FAX 250-758-8665, info@pointonemedia.com, http://www.pointonemedia.com. Ed. Lara Perraton. Pub. Joe Perraton.

796.6 FRA ISSN 2105-7389
LE CANARD DE L'ARRAS CYCLO. Text in French. 2004. q. **Document type:** *Newsletter, Consumer.*
Former titles (until 2009): Le Canard de la Race Cyclo (1773-228X); (until 2005): Arras Cyclo Tourisme. Bulletin Trimestriel (1767-9109)
Published by: Arras Cyclo Tourisme, Complex Grimaldi, Rue E Zola, Arras, 62000, France. http://arrascyclo.free.fr.

796.6 AUS ISSN 1030-4770
CANBERRA CYCLIST. Text in English. 1975. bi-m. free to members (effective 2009). adv. bk.rev. illus. back issues avail. **Document type:** *Magazine, Trade.* **Description:** Includes rides calendar, ride reports, discounters list, new designs, letters to the editor, policy and planning reports.
Former titles (until 1987): Pedal Power (0313-4334); (until 1976): Pedal Power A C T. Newsletter (0313-4326)
Published by: Pedal Power A.C.T. Inc., GPO Box 581, Canberra, ACT 2601, Australia. TEL 61-2-62487995, FAX 61-2-62487774, office@pedalpower.org.au, http://sunsite.anu.edu.au/community/pedalpower/. Ed. Julia Widdup. Adv. contact Leon Arundell TEL 61-2-62480873. B&W page AUD 150, color page AUD 425. Circ: 2,000.

796 AUS ISSN 0311-1717
CAT-A-LOG. Text in English. 1971. 11/yr. AUD 5 (effective 2009). adv. bk.rev. **Document type:** *Magazine, Trade.*
Published by: Jaguar Car Club of Victoria Ltd., PO Box 4263, Mulgrave, VIC 3170, Australia. TEL 61-3-95585434, inquiry@jagvic.org.au.

796.6 ESP ISSN 1131-9593
CATALOGO BICISPORT. Text in Spanish. 1990. a. **Document type:** *Catalog, Trade.*
Published by: Motorpress Iberica (Subsidiary of: Gruner + Jahr AG & Co), Ancora 40, Madrid, 28045, Spain. TEL 34-91-3470100, FAX 34-91-3470152, http://www.motorpress-iberica.es. Circ: 18,000.

796.75 AUS ISSN 1837-218X
▼ **CHIX MOTO BIKES.** Text in English. 2010. q. USD 35 domestic; USD 52.50 in New Zealand; USD 70.90 in Asia & the Pacific; USD 107.20 elsewhere (effective 2010). adv. back issues avail. **Document type:** *Magazine, Trade.* **Description:** Contains articles from Australian best to tips on road bikes to dirt bikes. Provides stories of Australia's top female riders.
Published by: Power SS Media, PO Box 567, Gympie, QLD 4570, Australia. info@powerssmedia.com.

796.6 ITA ISSN 1123-9107
CICLISMO. Text in Italian. 1995. m. EUR 46 domestic; EUR 80 in the European Union; EUR 130 per issue elsewhere (effective 2009). adv. illus.; maps. back issues avail. **Document type:** *Magazine, Consumer.* **Description:** Contains technical news and accurate surveys about bicycles.
Related titles: Online - full text ed.
Published by: Edisport Editoriale SpA, Via Gradisca 11, Milan, MI 20151, Italy. TEL 39-02-38085, FAX 39-02-38010393, edisport@edisport.it, http://www.edisport.it.

796.6 ESP ISSN 0213-4179
CICLISMO A FONDO. Text in Spanish. 1985. m. adv. **Document type:** *Magazine, Consumer.*
Related titles: ◆ Supplement(s): Anuario Urtekaria; ◆ Bicitech a Fondo; ◆ Cicloturismo a Fondo. ISSN 1136-3134.
Published by: Motorpress Iberica (Subsidiary of: Gruner + Jahr AG & Co), Ancora 40, Madrid, 28045, Spain. TEL 34-91-3470100, FAX 34-91-3470152, http://www.motorpress-iberica.es. Ed. Miguel Angel Chico. Circ: 26,100 (paid).

796.6 ITA ISSN 1593-9820
CICLOTURISMO. Text in Italian. 1988. m. EUR 57 domestic; EUR 105 foreign (effective 2008). adv. illus. **Document type:** *Magazine, Consumer.*
Published by: Compagnia Editoriale, Via Giuseppe Capogrossi 50, Rome, 00155, Italy. TEL 39-06-22857256, http://www.compagniaeditoriale.it.

796.6 ESP ISSN 1136-3134
CICLOTURISMO A FONDO. Text in Spanish. 1996. q. **Document type:** *Consumer.*
Related titles: ◆ Supplement to: Ciclismo a Fondo. ISSN 0213-4179.
Published by: Motorpress Iberica (Subsidiary of: Gruner + Jahr AG & Co), Ancora 40, Madrid, 28045, Spain. TEL 34-91-3470100, FAX 34-91-3470152, http://www.motorpress-iberica.es. Circ: 10,000 (paid).

796.6 388.347 CAN ISSN 1183-7543
CITIZENS FOR SAFE CYCLING NEWSLETTER. Text in English. 1986. irreg. **Document type:** *Newsletter.*
Formerly (until 1986): Share the Road (1185-6513)
Published by: Citizens for Safe Cycling, P O BOX 248, Sta B, Ottawa, ON K1P 6C4, Canada. TEL 613-722-4454, FAX 613-729-2207. Ed. Brett Delmage.

796.6 USA
CITY CYCLIST. Text in English. 1974. bi-m. USD 10 to members (effective 2000). adv. bk.rev. **Document type:** *Newsletter.* **Description:** Covers bicycle transportation and environmental issues in New York City.
Formerly: New York City Cyclist (1063-0880)
Indexed: SportS.
Published by: Transportation Alternatives, 115 W 30th St, Ste 1207, New York, NY 10001-4010. TEL 212-629-8080, FAX 212-629-8334. Ed., Pub. John Kachny. R&P Sharon Soons. Adv. contact Catherine Fennell. Circ: 12,000.

THE CLASSIC AND ANTIQUE BICYCLE EXCHANGE. *see* HOBBIES

796 GBR ISSN 0142-890X
CLASSIC BIKE; real bikes for blokes with spanners. Text in English. 1978. m. GBP 45.60 domestic; GBP 50 in Europe; GBP 65 elsewhere; GBP 3.80, USD 9.99 newsstand/cover (effective 2009). adv. back issues avail. **Document type:** *Magazine, Consumer.* **Description:** Covers information on bikes from the 50's and 60's.
—CCC.
Published by: H. Bauer Publishing Ltd. (Subsidiary of: Bauer Media Group), Media House, Lynchwood, Peterborough, Cambridgeshire PE2 6EA, United Kingdom. TEL 44-1733-468000, http://www.bauer.co.uk. **Subscr. to:** Tower House, Sovereign Park, Market Harborough, Leicestershire LE16 9EF, United Kingdom. TEL 44-1858-438866, subs@greatmagazines.co.uk.

796.7 GBR ISSN 0959-7123
CLASSIC BIKE GUIDE. Abbreviated title: C B G. Text in English. 1990. m. GBP 37 domestic; GBP 44 in Europe; GBP 54 elsewhere (effective 2009). adv. bk.rev. back issues avail. **Document type:** *Magazine, Consumer.* **Description:** Presents a forum for the appreciation of old or classic British, European and Japanese motorcycles with stories, facts, figures, price guides, and free advertisements.
—CCC.
Published by: Mortons Media Group Ltd., Media Centre, Morton Way, Horncastle, Lincs LN9 6JR, United Kingdom. TEL 44-1507-529529, FAX 44-1507-529490, mortons@mortons.co.uk, http://www.mortonsmediagroup.com/. Ed. Nigel Clark TEL 44-1507-529402. Adv. contact Alexis Bain TEL 44-1507-524004. Circ: 34,000. **Dist. by:** Comag, Tavistock Rd, W Drayton, Middlesex UB7 7QE, United Kingdom. TEL 44-1895-444055, FAX 44-1895-433602.

796.756 GBR ISSN 1752-6558
CLASSIC DIRT BIKE MAGAZINE. Variant title: Classic Dirtbike. Text in English. 2006. q. GBP 20 domestic; GBP 25 in Europe; GBP 30 elsewhere (effective 2009). adv. back issues avail. **Document type:** *Magazine, Consumer.* **Description:** Covers pre-65 machines, classic and twin shocks, trials as well as scrambling/motocross and enduros.
Published by: Mortons Media Group Ltd., Media Centre, Morton Way, Horncastle, Lincs LN9 6JR, United Kingdom. TEL 44-1507-529529, FAX 44-1507-529490, mortons@mortons.co.uk, http://www.mortonsmediagroup.com/. Ed. Tim Britton TEL 44-1507-529404. Adv. contact Judy Kane TEL 44-1507-529541. page GBP 824.

769.7 GBR ISSN 0263-0850
CLASSIC MOTORCYCLE. Text in English. 1981. m. GBP 37 domestic; GBP 44 in Europe; GBP 54 elsewhere (effective 2009). adv. back issues avail. **Document type:** *Magazine, Consumer.* **Description:** Celebrates classic British motorcycles and their heritage, with analyses and reports.
Published by: Mortons Motorcycle Media (Subsidiary of: Mortons Media Group Ltd.), Media Centre, Morton Way, Horncastle, Lincs LN9 6JR, United Kingdom. TEL 44-1507-523456, http://www.mortonsmediagroup.com. Ed. James Robinson TEL 44-1507-529405. Adv. contact Gemma Larkin TEL 44-1507-524004.

796.7 GBR ISSN 0959-0900
CLASSIC MOTORCYCLE MECHANICS. Text in English. 1983. m. GBP 37 domestic; GBP 44 in Europe; GBP 54 elsewhere (effective 2009). adv. **Document type:** *Magazine, Consumer.*
Formerly (until 1990): Classic Mechanics (0266-8114)
—BLDSC (3274.503100).
Published by: Mortons Motorcycle Media (Subsidiary of: Mortons Media Group Ltd.), Media Centre, Morton Way, Horncastle, Lincs LN9 6JR, United Kingdom. TEL 44-1507-523456, http://www.mortonsmediagroup.com. Ed. Rod Gibson TEL 44-1507-529442. Adv. contact Andrew Catton TEL 44-1507-529538.

629.227 GBR ISSN 2042-1079
▼ **CLASSIC PORSCHE.** Text in English. 2009. q. GBP 15 domestic; GBP 20 in Europe; GBP 27 elsewhere (effective 2010). back issues avail. **Document type:** *Magazine, Trade.* **Description:** Covers ideas related to motoring and motorsports.
Published by: C H Publications Ltd., Nimax House, 20 Ullswater Cresent, Ullswater Business Park, Coulsdon, Surrey CR5 2HR, United Kingdom. TEL 44-20-86556400, FAX 44-20-87631001, chp@chpltd.com. Ed. Steve Bennett. Pub. Nigel Fryatt.

629.227 GBR ISSN 0266-8106
CLASSIC RACER. Text in English. 1982. bi-m. GBP 20 domestic; GBP 24 in Europe; GBP 29 elsewhere (effective 2009). adv. back issues avail. **Document type:** *Magazine, Consumer.* **Description:** Features articles about motorcycles and those who ride them.
Published by: Mortons Media Group Ltd., Media Centre, Morton Way, Horncastle, Lincs LN9 6JR, United Kingdom. TEL 44-1507-529529, FAX 44-1507-529490, mortons@mortons.co.uk, http://www.mortonsmediagroup.com/. Ed. Malcolm Wheeler TEL 44-1507-529529. Adv. contact Adam Holland TEL 44-1507-524004.

796 CAN
THE CLUB TREAD REPORT. Text in English. 1995. m. **Description:** Contains cycling industry information, product reviews and tech tips.
Media: Online - full text. **Related titles:** E-mail ed.
Published by: Braun's Bicycle & Fitness, 27 Scott St, Kitchener, ON N2H 2P8, Canada. TEL 519-579-BIKE, FAX 519-579-8723. Ed. Robert Braun.

CONTRACTSPELER. *see* SPORTS AND GAMES

796.6 388.347 USA ISSN 1060-085X
CRANKMAIL; cycling in northeastern Ohio. Text in English. 1975. 10/yr. USD 11; USD 1.25 newsstand/cover (effective 1999). adv. bk.rev. 28 p./no. 2 cols./p.; back issues avail. **Document type:** *Magazine, Consumer.* **Description:** Covers recreational and competitive on- and off-road bicycling activity and use of bicycles as practical transportation.
Published by: The Clockwork Press, PO Box 33249, Cleveland, OH 44133-0249. TEL 440-877-0373, FAX 440-877-0373. Ed., Pub., R&P, Adv. contact James Guilford. page USD 46; trim 8.5 x 5.5. Circ: 1,000.

CRUZIN' SOUTH MAGAZINE. *see* TRANSPORTATION—Automobiles

796.7 DEU ISSN 1614-9378
CUSTOMBIKE. Text in German. 1992. bi-m. EUR 27 domestic; EUR 39 foreign; EUR 4.90 newsstand/cover (effective 2010). adv. **Document type:** *Magazine, Consumer.*
Formerly (until 2005): Bikers Live
Published by: Huber Verlag GmbH & Co. KG, Markircher Str 9 a, Mannheim, 68229, Germany. TEL 49-621-483610, FAX 49-621-4836111, szeneshop@huber-verlag.de, http://www.huber-verlag.de. Ed. Dirk Mangartz. Adv. contact Bjoern Meissner.

388.347 FRA ISSN 0184-1238
LE CYCLE. Text in French. 1975. m. EUR 55 (effective 2008). **Document type:** *Magazine, Consumer.*
Formerly (until 1979): L' Officiel dy Cycle (0339-6762)
Indexed: Acal.
Published by: Mondadori France, 1 Rue du Colonel Pierre-Avia, Paris, Cedex 15 75754, France. TEL 33-1-41335001, contact@mondadori.fr, http://www.mondadori.fr. Circ: 47,000.

796.6 GBR ISSN 2042-9460
CYCLE. Text in English. 1967. bi-m. GBP 3 per issue to non-members; free to members (effective 2011). adv. bk.rev. illus. back issues avail. **Document type:** *Magazine, Consumer.* **Description:** Contains articles and other features for cycling enthusiasts.
Former titles (until 200?): Cycle Touring & Campaigning (0965-0776); (until 1989): Cycletouring
Related titles: Online - full text ed.: free (effective 2011).
Indexed: SportS.
Published by: (Cyclists Touring Club), James Pembroke Publishing, 90 Walcot St, Bath, BA1 5BG, United Kingdom. TEL 44-1225-337777, FAX 44-1225-339977, jamesp@jppublishing.co.uk, http://www.jppublishing.co.uk. Ed. Matt Bielby. Adv. contact Jolyon Bird TEL 44-20-74878408.

796.75 CAN ISSN 0835-0612
CYCLE 1. Text in English. 8/yr.
Published by: Jarco Publishing Co., 2021 Union St, Ste 1150, Montreal, PQ H3A 2S9, Canada. TEL 514-284-1732, FAX 514-289-9257. adv.: B&W page USD 2,500, color page USD 3,500. Circ: 59,473.

796 USA
CYCLE CALIFORNIA. Text in English. 1995. 11/yr. **Document type:** *Magazine, Consumer.* **Description:** Covers bicycling events and races in Northern California.
Published by: Advanced Project Management, Box 189, Mountain View, CA 94042. TEL 650-961-2663, FAX 650-968-9030, cycleca@cyclecalifornia.com, http://www.cyclecalifornia.com. Ed., Pub. Tracy L Corral. Circ: 25,500.

796 CAN ISSN 0319-2822
CYCLE CANADA. Text in English. 1971. 10/yr. CAD 29.95 domestic; CAD 39.95 in United States; CAD 54.95 elsewhere; CAD 3.50 newsstand/cover (effective 2000). adv. bk.rev. **Document type:** *Magazine, Consumer.*
Related titles: Microfiche ed.: (from MML); Microform ed.: (from MML); ◆ French ed.: Moto Journal. ISSN 0319-2865; English ed.
Indexed: C03, CBCARef, CBPI, CPerI, G08, P48, PQC.
Published by: Turbopress Inc., 411 Richmond St E, Ste 301, Toronto, ON M5A 3S5, Canada. TEL 416-362-7966, FAX 416-362-3950, cyclecan@aol.com. Ed. Bruce Reeve. Pub. Jean Pierre Belmonte. adv.: B&W page CAD 4,730, color page CAD 5,910; trim 10.75 x 8. Circ: 27,000.

796.6 USA ISSN 1545-0538
CYCLE SPORT AMERICA. Text in English. m. USD 49.95 domestic; USD 59.95 in Canada (effective 2003).
Formerly (until 2003): Cycle Sport (American edition) (1545-052X)
Published by: Cycle Sport USA, 2225 University Ave., St. Paul, MN 55114. TEL 888-329-2533, info@cyclesportmag.com. Ed. Robert Garbutt.

796.6 JPN
CYCLE SPORTS; for bikers only. Text in Japanese. 1970. m. JPY 5,520 domestic; JPY 12,360 in Asia; JPY 15,840 in N. America, Europe; JPY 21,360 in Oceania; JPY 20,760 elsewhere (effective 2000). adv. back issues avail. **Document type:** *Consumer.* **Description:** Covers all aspects of bicycling, including road races, mountain biking, touring, and biking for triathlons. Includes information on bike maintenance.

Published by: Yaesu Publishing Co. Ltd., 5-9 Haccho-Bori 4-chome, Chuo-ku, Tokyo, 104-0032, Japan. TEL 81-3-3552-8431, FAX 81-3-3552-0777. Ed. Shinobu Miyauchi. Pub. Masayasu Sakai. Adv. contact Akira Soma. color page JPY 450,000; trim 282 x 185. Circ: 200,000; (controlled).

796 016 USA ISSN 0011-4286
TL440
CYCLE WORLD. Text in English. 1961. m. USD 10 domestic; USD 18 foreign (effective 2008). adv. bk.rev. illus. back issues avail.; reprints avail. **Document type:** *Magazine, Consumer.* **Description:** Covers the full story of motorcycling where and when motorcycle enthusiasts are looking for it.
Incorporates: Cycle (0574-8135)
Related titles: Online - full text ed.: USD 8 (effective 2008).
Indexed: A11, A22, A25, A26, Acal, B04, B07, BRD, C05, C12, CPerl, Consl, E08, G05, G06, G07, G08, G09, I05, I07, M01, M02, M04, MASUSE, MagInd, P02, P10, P48, P53, P54, PMR, PQC, R03, R04, RGAb, RGPR, S08, S09, SportS, W03.
—BLDSC (3506.412000), IE, Ingenta.
Published by: Hachette Filipacchi Medias U.S., Inc. (Subsidiary of: Hachette Filipacchi Medias S.A.), 1633 Broadway, New York, NY 10019. TEL 212-767-6000, FAX 212-767-5600, flyedit@hfmus.com, http://www.hfmus.com. Pub. Larry Little. adv.: B&W page USD 31,595, color page USD 47,375; trim 7.88 x 10.5. Circ: 325,000 (paid).

796.7 USA ISSN 1534-5173
GV1059.5
CYCLE WORLD'S MOTORCYCLE TRAVEL & ADVENTURE. Text in English. 2001. m. USD 5.95 newsstand/cover (effective 2007). adv. **Document type:** *Magazine, Consumer.*
Published by: Hachette Filipacchi Media U.S., Inc. (Subsidiary of: Hachette Filipacchi Medias S.A.), 1633 Broadway, New York, NY 10019. TEL 212-767-6000, FAX 212-767-5600, saleshfmbooks@hfmus.com, http://www.hfmus.com. adv.: B&W page USD 7,335, color page USD 10,945.

796 USA ISSN 1532-5067
CYCLE WORLD'S POWER & PERFORMANCE HARLEY-DAVIDSON (YEAR) BUYER'S GUIDE. Text in English. 2000. a. USD 5.95 newsstand/cover (effective 2007). adv. **Document type:** *Magazine, Consumer.*
Published by: Hachette Filipacchi Media U.S., Inc. (Subsidiary of: Hachette Filipacchi Medias S.A.), 1633 Broadway, New York, NY 10019. TEL 212-767-6000, FAX 212-767-5600, saleshfmbooks@hfmus.com, http://www.hfmus.com. adv.: B&W page USD 7,700, color page USD 10,040.

796.6 GBR ISSN 2041-3858
▼ **CYCLING ACTIVE.** Text in English. 2009. m. GBP 39.95 domestic; EUR 51.80 foreign (effective 2010). **Document type:** *Magazine, Trade.* **Description:** Aims to inform and entertain with a mix of bike and tec reviews, commuting and health and fitness advice, how-to guides, routes to ride.
—CCC.
Published by: I P C Inspire Focus, Blue Fin Bldg, 110 Southwark St, London, SE1 0SU, United Kingdom. TEL 44-203-1485000.

796.6 CAN
CYCLING: B.C. NEWS. Text in English. q. membership. **Document type:** *Newsletter.*
Published by: Cycling British Columbia, 332 1367 West Broadway, Vancouver, BC V6H 4A9, Canada. TEL 604-737-3034, FAX 604-738-7175. Ed. Jeff Hohner.

796.6 USA ISSN 0000-0744
CYCLING ON ONE. Text in English. 1998. s-a. USD 4.99 newsstand/cover (effective 2001). **Document type:** *Magazine, Consumer.*
Related titles: ♦ Supplement to: Re-Unicycling the Past. ISSN 0566-778X.
Published by: One Wheel Good, Inc. (Subsidiary of: Consumer Collectibles Inc.), 147 Lake Valley Rd, Morristown, NJ 07960. TEL 908-219-0286, info@onewheelgood.com, http://www.onewheel.com. Circ: 50 (paid and controlled).

796.6 GBR ISSN 0964-6868
CYCLING PLUS; for people who love to ride. Text in English. 1992. m. GBP 39.99 domestic; GBP 45 in Europe; GBP 55 elsewhere; GBP 3.99 newsstand/cover (effective 2010). adv. back issues avail. **Document type:** *Magazine, Consumer.* **Description:** For anyone who appreciates the all-out effort of time-trialing, the freedom of touring, the cut-and-thrust of commuting, and the sheer joy of just being out on the road.
Related titles: Online - full text ed.: GBP 79.30; GBP 6.10 per issue (effective 2010).
—CCC.
Published by: Future Publishing Ltd., Beauford Ct, 30 Monmouth St, Bath, Avon BA1 2BW, United Kingdom. TEL 44-1225-442244, FAX 44-1225-446019, customerservice@subscription.co.uk, http://www.futureplc.com. Ed. Rob Spedding. **Subscr. to:** Tower House, Sovereign Park, Market Harborough, Leicestershire LE16 9EF, United Kingdom. TEL 44-844-8481602, FAX 44-1858-438795, future@subscription.co.uk.

796.6 USA ISSN 1535-9069
CYCLING UTAH. Text in English. 1993. 8/yr. (Mar. through Oct.). USD 15 (effective 2008). **Document type:** *Guide, Consumer.* **Description:** A source for Utah and Intermountain West bicycling information.
Address: PO Box 57980, Murray, UT 84157-0980. TEL 801-268-2652, FAX 801-263-1010, http://www.cyclingutah.com. Ed., Adv. contact Dave Iltis. Pub. Dave Ward.

796.6 GBR ISSN 0951-5852
CYCLING WEEKLY. Text in English. 1891. w. GBP 87.50 domestic; EUR 237.48 in Europe eurozone; GBP 152.24 in Europe non-eurozone; USD 187.49 in United States; GBP 151.87 in Canada; GBP 162.49 elsewhere (effective 2009). adv. bk.rev. illus. back issues avail. **Document type:** *Magazine, Consumer.* **Description:** Offers an exciting mix of fitness advice, bike tests, product reviews, news and ride guides for every cyclist, as well as coverage of the national and international racing scene.
Former titles (until 1986): Cycling (0011-4316); (until 1964): Cycling and Mopeds; Incorporates (1982-1985): Cyclist Monthly (0263-5550)
Related titles: Online - full text ed.
Indexed: RASB, SD, SportS.
Published by: I P C Country & Leisure Media Ltd. (Subsidiary of: I P C Media Ltd.), The Blue Fin Bldg, 110 Southwark St, London, SE1 0SU, United Kingdom. TEL 44-20-31485000, magazinesales@ipcmedia.com, http://www.ipcmedia.com. Ed. Robert Garbutt TEL 44-20-87268461. adv.: page GBP 1,350. Circ: 27,609 (paid). **Dist. by:** MarketForce UK Ltd, The Blue Fin Bldg, 3rd Fl, 110 Southwark St, London SE1 0SU, United Kingdom. TEL 44-20-31483300, FAX 44-20-31488105, salesinnovation@marketforce.co.uk, http://www.marketforce.co.uk/.

796.6029 USA
CYCLISTS' YELLOW PAGES. Text in English. a. membership only. maps. **Document type:** *Magazine, Consumer.* **Description:** Information resource for bicyclists covering all 50 states, all Canadian provinces and territories, and 58 foreign countries; includes listings of hostels, bike shops, tour operators, cycling books and videos, tips on transporting bicycles (including airline regulations), getting in shape, and places to go mountain biking.
Published by: Adventure Cycling Association, 150 E Pine St, PO Box 8308, Missoula, MT 59807. TEL 406-721-1776, 800-755-2453, FAX 406-721-8754, info@adventurecycling.org. Ed. Daniel D'Ambrosio. Pub. Gary MacFadden. R&P Bill Wiles. Adv. contact Paul Adkins.

796.6 FRA ISSN 1779-1480
CYCLOSPORT. Text in French. 200?. m. EUR 42 (effective 2009). **Document type:** *Magazine, Consumer.*
Published by: Editions Riva, 16 Rue de la Fontaine-au-Roi, Paris, 75011, France. info@cyclosport.com.

796.6 FRA ISSN 0981-101X
CYCLOTOURISME. Text in French. 1953. m. (11/yr). EUR 47 (effective 2009). adv. bk.rev. **Document type:** *Magazine, Consumer.* **Description:** Presents the regions of France to bicyclists.
Published by: Federation Francaise de Cyclotourisme (F F C T), 12 rue Louis Bertrand, Ivry-sur-Seine, 94207 Cedex, France. TEL 33-1-56208888, FAX 33-1-56208899. Ed. Sophie Le Dily TEL 33-1-56208871. Circ: 35,000.

CYCLOTOURISME SANTE. *see* MEDICAL SCIENCES—Sports Medicine

796.6 DNK ISSN 0106-3529
CYKELBRANCHEN; cykel- og knallertbranchen. Text in Danish. 1900. 6/yr. DKK 540 membership (effective 2009). adv. bibl.; mkt. index. **Document type:** *Magazine, Trade.*
Formerly (until 1978): Styret Cykelbranchen (0039-4319); Incorporates (1940-1974): Cykelhandleren (0106-3510)
Related titles: Online - full text ed.
Published by: Danske Cykelhandlere, Middelfartvej 123, PO Box 770, Odense V, 5200, Denmark. TEL 45-65-923300, FAX 45-65-923500, info@danskecykelhandlere.dk. Ed. Erik Oddershede. Adv. contact Grethe Fabrin. B&W page DKK 3,825, color page DKK 7,675; 297 x 210. Circ: 820.

796 SWE ISSN 0280-3038
CYKLING. Text in Swedish. 1935. q. SEK 225 domestic; SEK 290 in Scandinavia; SEK 330 in Europe; SEK 355 elsewhere (effective 2004). adv. bk.rev. illus. **Document type:** *Magazine, Consumer.*
Former titles (until 1981): Cykel- och Mopednytt (0011-4391); (until 1954): Cyklisten
Published by: Cykelfraemjandet/Swedish Cycling Promotion Institute, Tulegatan 43, Stockholm, 11353, Sweden. TEL 46-8-54591030, FAX 46-8-54591039, cyklamera@cykelframjandet.se, http://cykelframjandet.se. Ed. Bertil Karlen. Adv. contact Christine Fogelhorn. page SEK 8,200; 185 x 264. Circ: 11,000.

796.6 388.34 DNK ISSN 0109-2790
CYKLISTER. Text in Danish. 1933. bi-m. DKK 290 to individual members (effective 2008). **Document type:** *Magazine, Consumer.*
Published by: Dansk Cyklist Forbund/The Danish Cyclists Federation, Roemersgade 7, Copenhagen K, 1362, Denmark. TEL 45-33-323121, FAX 45-33-327683, dcf@dcf.dk, http://www.dcf.dk.

796.7 DNK ISSN 0109-3649
D M C - BLADET. Text in Danish. 1982. 5/yr. DKK 240 membership (effective 2008). adv. bk.rev. illus. 16 p./no. 3 cols./p.; **Document type:** *Magazine, Consumer.*
Formerly (until Nov. 1983): D M C Nyt (0107-8984)
Published by: Danske Motorcyklisters Raad/Danish Motorcycle Council, Haverslevsvej 47, Ersted, Skoerping, 9520, Denmark. TEL 45-98-373693, FAX 45-98-372881, skovloekke@dmc-org.dk, http://www.dmc-org.dk. Ed. Rolf Skovloekke.

DAZHONG QICHE (MOTUOCHE). *see* TRANSPORTATION

796.7 338 GBR ISSN 1746-5842
DEALER WORLD. Text in English. 2006 (Mar.). bi-m. free to qualified personnel (effective 2009). adv. back issues avail. **Document type:** *Magazine, Trade.*
Related titles: Online - full text ed.
Published by: Dealer-World.com, Kenwood House, 1 Upper Grosvenor Rd, Turnbridge Wells, TN1 2DU, United Kingdom. TEL 44-1892-511516, FAX 44-1892-511517. Pub., Adv. contact Robin Bradley. page USD 1,795; 177 x 250. **US dist.:** Dealer-World USA.

629.227 USA ISSN 0893-2522
TL440
DEALERNEWS; the voice of the powersports vehicle industry. Text in English. 1965. m. USD 50 domestic; USD 66.50 in Canada & Mexico; USD 103.25 elsewhere; USD 11 newsstand/cover domestic; USD 16 newsstand/cover in Canada & Mexico; USD 21 newsstand/cover elsewhere (effective 2011). adv. back issues avail.; reprints avail. **Document type:** *Magazine, Trade.* **Description:** For dealers in the powersport industry. Includes dealer profiles, comprehensive new product information, industry research.
Former titles (until 1987): Motorcycle DealerNews (0888-4234); (until 1986): Dealer News (0887-0950); (until 1985): Motorcycle Dealer News (0192-0219)
Related titles: Microform ed.: (from PQC); Online - full text ed.: ISSN 1939-1870. USD 40 (effective 2011).
Indexed: A09, A10, A15, ABIn, B01, B02, B03, B06, B07, B08, B09, B11, B15, B17, B18, BusI, C12, CWI, G04, G06, G07, G08, I05, M01, M02, P48, P51, PQC, T&II, T02, T03, V03, V04.
—CCC.
Published by: Advanstar Communications, Inc., 6200 Canoga Ave, 2nd Fl, Woodland Hills, CA 91367. TEL 818-593-5000, FAX 818-593-5020, info@advanstar.com, http://www.advanstar.com. Ed. Dennis Johnson. Adv. contact Angela Gibbs TEL 815-772-7871.

388.347 640.73 USA
DEALERNEWS BUYERS GUIDE. Text in English. 19??. a. adv. **Document type:** *Directory, Trade.*
Formerly (until 1985): Motorcycle Dealernews Buyers Guide
Related titles: Microform ed.: (from PQC).
Published by: Advanstar Communications, Inc., 6200 Canoga Ave, 2nd Fl, Woodland Hills, CA 91367. TEL 818-593-5000, FAX 818-593-5020, info@advanstar.com, http://www.advanstar.com.

DIANDONG ZIXINGCHE. *see* TRANSPORTATION

796.6 GBR
DIG B M X. Text in English. 1993. bi-m. GBP 18.35 domestic; USD 32 in United States; EUR 30 in Europe; USD 52 elsewhere (effective 2009). back issues avail. **Document type:** *Magazine, Consumer.* **Description:** Covers all aspects of the BMX racing industry.
Related titles: Online - full text ed.
Published by: Factory Media, Studio 153, 355 Byres Rd, Glasgow, G12 8QZ, United Kingdom. TEL 44-141-9455019, FAX 44-141-9455019, http://www.factorymedia.com. Adv. contact Ian Gunner. **Subscr. to:** Dovetail Services UK Ltd, 800 Guillat Ave, Kent Science Park, Sittingbourne, Kent ME9 8GU, United Kingdom. TEL 44-1795-414634, digbmx@servicehelpline.co.uk, http://www.dovetailservices.com/.

796.7 GBR ISSN 1364-8764
DIRT; mountainbike magazine. Text in English. 1996. m. GBP 29.99 domestic; USD 58 in United States; EUR 63 in Europe; USD 86 elsewhere; GBP 3 newsstand/cover (effective 2009). adv. **Document type:** *Magazine, Consumer.* **Description:** Provides action-packed downhill mountain bike coverage that includes racing results, interviews with the best riders, equipment and location reviews, and technical and tactical advice for downhillers of all levels.
Related titles: Online - full text ed.
Published by: Factory Media, Studio 153, 355 Byres Rd, Glasgow, G12 8QZ, United Kingdom. TEL 44-141-9455019, FAX 44-141-9455019, http://www.factorymedia.com. Adv. contact Ian Gunner. **Subscr. to:** Dovetail Services UK Ltd, 800 Guillat Ave, Kent Science Park, Sittingbourne, Kent ME9 8GU, United Kingdom. TEL 44-1795-414555, contact@dovetailservices.com, http://www.dovetailservices.com/.

796.75 BRA ISSN 1413-2796
DIRT ACTION; motocross, enduro, rally. Text in Portuguese. 1995. m. BRL 97 (effective 2007). adv. **Document type:** *Magazine, Consumer.*
Published by: Adrenal Editora, Rua Antonio Comparato 164, Sao Paulo, 04605-030, Brazil. TEL 55-11-55433511, FAX 55-11-50414227.

796.7 USA ISSN 0364-1546
TL440
DIRT BIKE. Text in English. 1971. m. USD 19.99 domestic; USD 32.99 in Canada; USD 39.99 elsewhere; USD 4.99 newsstand/cover (effective 2011). adv. back issues avail. **Document type:** *Magazine, Consumer.*
Related titles: Online - full text ed.
Indexed: G09, JHMA, M01, M02, M04, MASUSE, P02, P10, P53, P54, PQC, SD, SportS, T02.
Published by: Hi-Torque Publications, Inc., 25233 Anza Dr, Valencia, CA 91355. TEL 661-295-1910, FAX 661-295-1278, michelle@hi-torque.com, http://www.hi-torque.com. Adv. contact Robert Rex TEL 661-367-2109. Circ: 132,000 (paid).

796.7 GBR ISSN 0262-5628
DIRT BIKE RIDER. Text in English. 1982. m. GBP 30 domestic; GBP 49.50 in Europe; GBP 65 elsewhere (effective 2009). adv. illus. back issues avail. **Document type:** *Magazine, Trade.* **Description:** Contains the latest news and stories on the off-road motorcycle world.
Related titles: Online - full text ed.
Published by: Lancaster and Morecambe Newspapers Ltd., Victoria St, Morecambe, Lancs LA4 4AG, United Kingdom. TEL 44-1524-834030. Ed. Sean Lawless TEL 44-1524-834077. Adv. contact Phil Armitage TEL 44-1524-834012.

796.75 GBR ISSN 1748-5053
DIRT M X MAGAZINE. (Moto Cross) Text in English. 2005. bi-m. GBP 20 domestic; GBP 25 in Ireland (effective 2006). **Document type:** *Magazine, Consumer.*
Formerly: Racer M X; Supersedes in part: Irish Racer
Published by: Careva Publishing, D5 - Colvin House, Dundonald Enterprise Park, Carrowreagh Rd, Belfast, BT16 1QT, United Kingdom. TEL 44-28-90486430, FAX 44-28-90488954, info@carevapr.co.uk, http://www.carevapublishing.com/.

796.6 USA ISSN 1082-6785
DIRT RAG; the mountain bike forum. Text in English. 1989. 7/yr. USD 16.95 domestic; USD 21.95 in Canada; USD 26.95 elsewhere; USD 4.95 newsstand/cover domestic; USD 5.95 newsstand/cover in Canada (effective 2005). adv. bk.rev.; film rev.; music rev.; tel.rev.; video rev. abstr.; illus. back issues avail. **Document type:** *Magazine, Consumer.* **Description:** Published by mountain bikers for mountain bikers.
Published by: A K A Productions, 3483 Saxonburg Blvd, Pittsburgh, PA 15238. TEL 412-767-9910, FAX 412-767-9920. Ed. Michael Browne. Pub., R&P Maurice Tierney. Adv. contact Chris Cosby. B&W page USD 1,295, color page USD 1,875; trim 8 x 10.75. Circ: 30,000.

796.7 USA ISSN 0735-4355
DIRT RIDER MAGAZINE. Text in English. 1982. m. USD 12 domestic; USD 24 in Canada; USD 36 elsewhere (effective 2008). adv. bk.rev. illus. back issues avail.; reprints avail. **Document type:** *Magazine, Consumer.* **Description:** Provides high-quality, informative and entertaining coverage of all forms of off-road motorcycle recreation.
Related titles: Online - full text ed.
Indexed: G06, G07, G08, I05, I06, I07, IHTDI, S23.
—CCC.
Published by: Source Interlink Companies, 2570 E Cerritos Ave, Anaheim, CA 92806. TEL 714-941-1400, dheine@sourceinterlink.com, http://www.sourceinterlinkmedia.com. Ed. Jimmy Lewis. Pub. Sean Finley TEL 714-941-1403. adv.: B&W page USD 13,040, color page USD 16,300. Circ: 137,379 (paid).

796.6 USA ISSN 1060-4804
DIRT WHEELS. Text in English. 19??. m. USD 19.99 domestic; USD 32.99 in Canada; USD 44.99 elsewhere (effective 2011). adv. back issues avail. **Document type:** *Magazine, Consumer.*
Formerly (until 199?): Dirt Wheels Magazine (0745-0192)
Related titles: Online - full text ed.
Published by: Hi - Torque Publications, Inc., 25233 Amza Dr, Valencia, CA 91355. TEL 661-295-1910, FAX 661-295-1278, michelle@hi-torque.com, http://www.hi-torque.com. Adv. contact Robert Rex.

S

796.75 NZL ISSN 1176-9386
DIRTRIDER DOWNUNDER. Text in English. 2005. m. NZD 96 (effective 2008). adv. back issues avail. **Document type:** *Magazine, Consumer.*
Published by: Dirt Rider Downunder, PO Box 223, Paeroa, 2951, New Zealand. Eds. Fraser Davey, Paul Lance. Pub. Tracey Lance. adv.: color page NZD 1,100; 210 x 273.

796.6 AUT
DRAHTESEL. Text in German. 1984. bi-m. EUR 29 membership; EUR 18 to students (effective 2005). adv. bk.rev. back issues avail. **Document type:** *Magazine, Consumer.*
Published by: A R G U S - Arbeitsgemeinschaft Umweltfreundlicher Stadtverkehr, Frankenberggasse 11, Vienna, W 1040, Austria. TEL 43-1-5058435, FAX 43-1-505090719, service@argus.or.at, http://www.argus.or.at/argus/. Ed. Evelyne Doppel.

796.7 DEU ISSN 1613-0731
DREAM-MACHINES HARLEY-DAVIDSON. Text in German. 1998. 6/yr. EUR 27 domestic; EUR 39 foreign; EUR 5 newsstand/cover (effective 2010). adv. **Document type:** *Magazine, Consumer.*
Incorporates (1999-2002): V2 Machines (1439-5975)
—CCC.
Published by: Huber Verlag GmbH & Co. KG, Markircher Str 9 a, Mannheim, 68229, Germany. TEL 49-621-483610, FAX 49-621-4836111, szeneshop@huber-verlag.de, http://www.huber-verlag.de. Ed. Heinrich Christmann. Adv. contact Nina Kropp.

796.75 USA ISSN 8750-1732
DUSTY TIMES. Text in English. 1983. m. USD 25 domestic; USD 30 foreign (effective 2005). adv. 60 p./no. 5 cols./p.; back issues avail. **Document type:** *Newspaper, Consumer.* **Description:** Concerned with rallying and off road racing.
Published by: Hillside Racing Corp., 20761 Plummer St, Chatsworth, CA 91311. TEL 818-882-0004, FAX 818-882-0090. Ed. John B Calvin. Adv. contact Bekki Wikel. B&W page USD 950, color page USD 1,310; trim 10 x 14. Circ: 10,000 (paid).

796 USA ISSN 0046-0990
GV1059.5
EASYRIDERS. Text in English. 1971. m. USD 29.95; USD 6.99 newsstand/cover (effective 2009). adv. bk.rev. charts; illus.; tr.lit. 154 p./no.; back issues avail. **Document type:** *Magazine, Consumer.*
Published by: Paisano Publications, Inc., 28210 Dorothy Dr, Box 3075, Agoura Hills, CA 91301. TEL 818-889-8740, 800-247-6246, FAX 818-735-6518, bulkmagazines@paisanopub.com. Adv. contact Tammy Porter TEL 818-889-8740 ext 1265. Circ: 146,305.

796.7 CZE ISSN 1214-9543
EASYRIDERS. Text in Czech. 2005. bi-m. CZK 594 (effective 2011). adv. **Document type:** *Magazine, Consumer.*
Published by: Vydavatelstvi Taurus s.r.o., Preloucska 252, Pardubice, 530 06, Czech Republic. TEL 420-466-970296, info@etaurus.cz, http://www.etaurus.cz. Ed. Pavel Ruzek. Adv. contact Simona Skreptacova.

796.7 DEU
EASYRIDERS. Text in German. 1998. m. EUR 4.50 newsstand/cover (effective 2011). adv. **Document type:** *Magazine, Consumer.*
Published by: Vestische Mediengruppe Welke GmbH & Co. KG, Hertener Mark 7, Herten, 45699, Germany. TEL 49-2366-808400, FAX 49-2366-808499, info@vmw-verlag.de, http://vmw-verlag.de. Circ: 31,149 (paid and controlled).

388.347 GBR ISSN 2045-3183
▼ **ELECTRIC BIKE.** Text in English. 2010. q. GBP 10 domestic; GBP 20 in Europe; GBP 24 elsewhere (effective 2010). adv. **Document type:** *Magazine, Trade.* **Description:** Provides advice on all the makes and models of electric bike.
Related titles: Online - full text ed.: ISSN 2045-3191. free (effective 2010).
Published by: Velo Vision, York Eco Business Ctr, Amy Johnson Way, Clifton Moor, York, YO30 4AG, United Kingdom. TEL 44-1904-692800, peter@velovision.com, http://www.velovision.co.uk/. Ed., Pub. Peter Eland.

796.7 DEU ISSN 0948-2881
ENDURO. Text in German. 1981. m. EUR 38 domestic; EUR 44 foreign (effective 2009). adv. **Document type:** *Magazine, Consumer.*
Published by: Enduro Verlagsgesellschaft mbH, Parlerstr 24, Schwaebisch Gmuend, 73525, Germany. TEL 49-7171-18020, FAX 49-7171-180280, redaktion@enduro-press.de, http://www.enduro-press.de. Ed. Norbert Bauer. Adv. contact Ute Werner. B&W page EUR 1,940, color page EUR 3,435; trim 210 x 280. Circ: 16,619 (paid and controlled).

796.7 DEU
ENDURO ABENTEUER. Text in German. 2000. 6/yr. EUR 3.40 newsstand/cover (effective 2006). adv. **Document type:** *Magazine, Consumer.*
Published by: Moto Media GmbH, Severinstr 1, Rosenheim, 83026, Germany. TEL 49-8031-354970, FAX 49-8031-3549718. adv.: B&W page EUR 1,930, color page EUR 3,990. Circ: 25,000 (paid and controlled).

796.7 SVK ISSN 1336-331X
ENDURO AKTUAL. Text in Slovak. 2003. m. CZK 280; CZK 35 newsstand/cover (effective 2006). adv. **Document type:** *Magazine, Consumer.*
Published by: Ecce Rallye, o.z., Lesnicka 25, Kosice 25, 040 11, Slovakia. TEL 421-0905-413848. Ed. Alena Dudekova.

796.7 USA ISSN 0027-2167
ENTHUSIAST. Variant title: Motorcycle Enthusiast. Text in English. 1916. q. (3-4/yr). free to members (effective 2009). bk.rev. illus. 30 p./no.; **Document type:** *Magazine, Consumer.* **Description:** Provides up to date news and information on Harley-Davidson motorcycles, including a wide range of feature articles and stories.
Published by: Harley-Davidson Motor Co., Inc., 3700 W Juneau Ave, Milwaukee, WI 53208. TEL 414-343-4056.

796.7 PRT
ESPECIAL CUSTOM. Text in Portuguese. 2000. a. EUR 3.50 newsstand/cover (effective 2005). **Document type:** *Magazine, Consumer.*
Related titles: ◆ Supplement to: Motociclismo.
Published by: Motorpress Lisboa, SA (Subsidiary of: Gruner + Jahr AG & Co), Rua Policarpio Anjos No. 4, Cruz Quebrada, Dafundo 1495-742, Portugal. TEL 351-21-4154500, FAX 351-21-4154501, buzine@motorpress.pt, http://www.mpl.pt. Circ: 7,753 (paid).

796.6 ZAF ISSN 1991-6108
THE ESSENTIAL GUIDE TO CYCLING. Text in English. 2006. a. ZAR 49.95 (effective 2007).
Published by: Touchline Media, PO Box 16368, Vlaeberg, Cape Town 8018, South Africa. TEL 27-21-4083800, FAX 27-21-4083811, http://www.touchline.co.za.

796.7 FRA ISSN 1767-4883
L'ESSENTIEL DE LA MOTO. Text in French. 2004. q. EUR 44 for 2 yrs. (effective 2010). **Document type:** *Magazine, Consumer.*
Published by: Lafont Presse, 53 Rue du Chemin Vert, Boulogne-Billancourt, 92100, France. TEL 33-1-46102121, FAX 33-1-45792211. Ed. Bernard Pace.

796.7 FRA ISSN 1960-1964
L'ESSENTIEL DU QUAD. Text in French. 2007. q. EUR 44 for 2 yrs. (effective 2008). **Document type:** *Magazine, Consumer.*
Published by: Lafont Presse, 53 Rue du Chemin Vert, Boulogne-Billancourt, 92100, France. FAX 33-1-45792211, http://www.lafontpresse.fr.

796.7 ITA ISSN 1827-0131
EUROMOTO. Text in Italian. 2005. m. **Document type:** *Magazine, Consumer.*
Related titles: Spanish ed.: ISSN 1827-0166; English ed.: ISSN 1827-014X; French ed.: ISSN 1827-0158; German ed.: ISSN 1827-0174.
Address: Via Gallarate 230, Milan, 20151, Italy. TEL 39-02-365881, FAX 39-02-36588222, http://www.euromoto.eu.

796.7 ITA ISSN 1973-9524
FAST BIKES. Text in Italian. 2008. m. **Document type:** *Magazine, Consumer.*
Published by: Sprea Editori Srl, Via Torino 51, Cernusco sul Naviglio, MI 20063, Italy. TEL 39-02-92432222, FAX 39-02-92432236, editori@sprea.it, http://www.sprea.it.

796.7 GBR ISSN 0961-7981
FAST BIKES; truth knowledge knackered sliders. Abbreviated title: F B. Text in English. 1991. m. GBP 47.97 domestic; GBP 85 in Europe; GBP 75 in United States; GBP 110 elsewhere; GBP 4.10 newsstand/cover (effective 2010). adv. back issues avail. **Document type:** *Magazine, Consumer.* **Description:** Filled with information on motorcycles and motorcycle racing for fans and enthusiasts.
Related titles: Online - full text ed.: GBP 53.30; GBP 4.10 per issue (effective 2010).
Published by: Future Publishing Ltd., Beauford Ct, 30 Monmouth St, Bath, Avon BA1 2BW, United Kingdom. TEL 44-1225-442244, FAX 44-1225-446019, customerservice@subscription.co.uk, http://www.futureplc.com. Ed. Richard Newland. **Subscr. to:** Tower House, Sovereign Park, Market Harborough, Leicestershire LE16 9EF, United Kingdom. TEL 44-844-8481602, FAX 44-1858-438795, future@subscription.co.uk.

796 CHE ISSN 0071-4283
FEDERATION INTERNATIONALE MOTOCYCLISTE. ANNUAIRE. Text in English, French. 1912. a. CHF 27. adv. bk.rev. **Document type:** *Bulletin.*
Related titles: Supplement(s): International Motorcycle Sporting Calendar.
Published by: International Motorcycle Federation, 11 route Suisse, Mies, 1295, Switzerland. TEL 41-22-9509500, FAX 41-22-9509501. Circ: 10,000.

796.6 NLD ISSN 0922-1824
FIETS; het race & mtb magazine. Text in Dutch. 1982. m. EUR 36.95; EUR 4.95 newsstand/cover (effective 2011). adv. bk.rev. back issues avail. **Document type:** *Magazine, Consumer.* **Description:** Bicycle magazine with buyer's guide.
Incorporates (1979-1982): Fietsmagazine (0922-1832)
—IE, Infotrieve.
Published by: Sanoma Men's Magazines, Haaksbergweg 75, Amsterdam (ZO), 1101 BR, Netherlands. TEL 31-20-7518000, FAX 31-20-7518301, sales@smm.nl, http://www.smm.nl. Eds. Anja Janssen, Rodrick de Munnik.

796.6 NLD ISSN 1879-8918
▼ **FIETS SCHEURKALENDER.** Text in Dutch. 2009. a. EUR 14.95 (effective 2010).
Published by: Uitgeverij De Fontein - Tirion, Julianalaan 11, Baarn, 3743 JG, Netherlands. TEL 31-35-5486600, FAX 31-35-5486615, http://www.defonteintirion.nl.

796.61 NLD ISSN 1388-3836
FIETSACTIEF. Text in Dutch. 1996. bi-m. EUR 19.95; EUR 5.10 newsstand/cover (effective 2011). adv. **Document type:** *Magazine, Consumer.*
Published by: Sanoma Men's Magazines, Haaksbergweg 75, Amsterdam (ZO), 1101 BR, Netherlands. TEL 31-20-7518000, FAX 31-20-7518301, sales@smm.nl, http://www.smm.nl. Eds. Marte Schaap, Rodrick de Munnik.

796.6 NLD ISSN 1383-6684
FIETSMARKT; vakblad voor de tweewielerbranche. Text in Dutch. 1995. 8/yr. EUR 41.10; EUR 6.60 newsstand/cover (effective 2008). adv. **Document type:** *Magazine, Consumer.*
Published by: Blauw Media Uitgeverij B.V., Postbus 1043, Maarssen, 3600 BA, Netherlands. TEL 31-346-574040, FAX 31-346-576056, info@blauwmedia.com, http://www.blauwmediauitgeverij.nl. Circ: 3,500.

796.6 BEL
FIETSVAKANTIEINFO. Text in Dutch. 1991. a. USD 4. maps. **Description:** Contains information on bicycle vacations including guides and addresses.
Published by: Fietsvakanties, Gootstraat 15/17, Sint-Truiden, B-3800, Belgium. Ed. Diederik De Leersnyder.

388.347 NLD ISSN 1872-0870
FIETSVERKEER. Text in Dutch. 2001. 3/yr.
Published by: Fietsberaad, Postbus 24051, Utrecht, 3502 MB, Netherlands. TEL 31-10-2855000, info@fietsberaad.nl. Circ: 4,500.

796.7 CAN
FISHTAIL WEST. Text in English. bi-m. USD 18 (effective 1999).
Published by: Velocette Owners Club of North America, c/o Sam Jowett, 6630 Gilley Ave, Burnaby, BC V5H 3W9, Canada. Ed. Geof Blanthorn.

796.6 910.202 USA
FODOR'S SPORTS: CYCLING. Text in English. 1992. irreg. USD 12.
Published by: Fodor's Travel Publications, Inc. (Subsidiary of: Random House Inc.), 1745 Broadway, 15th Fl, New York, NY 10019. TEL 212-572-2313, editors@fodors.com, http://www.fodors.com. **Dist. by:** Random House Inc.

796.6 FRA ISSN 0245-0429
LA FRANCE CYCLISTE. Text in French. 1946. bi-m. EUR 55 domestic; EUR 62 foreign (effective 2009). **Document type:** *Magazine, Consumer.*
Indexed: SD.
Published by: Federation Francaise de Cyclisme, Batiment Jean-Monnet, 5 rue de Rome, Rosny, Cedex 93561, France. TEL 33-1-49356926, FAX 33-1-48940997, FFC@Wanadoo.fr. Ed., R&P Henri Montulet. Pub. Daniel Baal. Adv. contact Marie Claude Goutal.

796.7 DEU
FREEDOM B M X. Text in German. 1993. bi-m. EUR 3.20 newsstand/cover (effective 2008). adv. **Document type:** *Magazine, Consumer.* **Description:** Contains articles and information on all aspects and levels of BMX bicycle stunts and competitions.
Related titles: Online - full text ed.
Published by: b&d Media Network GmbH, Osterfeldstr 12-14, Hamburg, 22529, Germany. TEL 49-40-4800070, FAX 49-40-48000799, info@bdverlag.de, http://www.bdverlag.de. Adv. contact Denis Koenig. B&W page EUR 2,400, color page EUR 3,200; trim 210 x 280. Circ: 17,614 (paid).

796.7 USA
▼ **FREEHUB.** Text in English. 2010. s-a. USD 22.95 (effective 2010). adv. **Document type:** *Magazine, Consumer.*
Related titles: Online - full text ed.: free (effective 2010).
Published by: Freehub Media, Llc., P O Box 29831, Bellingham, WA 98228-1831. editor@freehubmag.com, info@freehubmag.com.

796.7 DEU ISSN 1866-7724
FREERIDE; das Magazin fuer Ueberflieger. Variant title: Bike Special Freeride. Text in German. 2005. 4/yr. EUR 24.50 domestic; EUR 32.50 foreign; EUR 4.90 newsstand/cover (effective 2011). adv. **Document type:** *Magazine, Consumer.*
Published by: Delius Klasing Verlag GmbH, Siekerwall 21, Bielefeld, 33602, Germany. TEL 49-521-5590, FAX 49-521-559113, info@delius-klasing.de, http://www.delius-klasing.de. Adv. contact Ingeborg Bockstette. Circ: 28,000 (paid).

796.7 AUS ISSN 1443-1998
FREERIDER M X MAGAZINE. Text in English. 2000. bi-m. AUD 43 domestic; AUD 73.40 in New Zealand; AUD 84.20 in Asia & the Pacific; AUD 124.45 elsewhere (effective 2007). adv. **Document type:** *Magazine, Consumer.* **Description:** Covers the broad spectrum of the motocross world, from the elite professionals right through to the average bush hacker.
Related titles: Alternate Frequency ed(s).: Freerider M X Photo Annual. ISSN 1833-1793. 2006. a.
Published by: Morrison Media Services Ltd., PO Box 823, Burleigh Heads, QLD 4220, Australia. TEL 61-7-55761388, FAX 61-7-55761527, pm@morrisonmedia.com.au, http://www.morrisonmedia.com.au. Ed. Ben Foster TEL 61-7-5576-1388. Pub. Peter Morrison. Circ: 72,000.

796.7 FRA ISSN 1634-3735
FREESTYLE MOTOCROSS. Text in French. 2002. bi-m. EUR 35 for 2 yrs. (effective 2008). **Document type:** *Magazine, Consumer.*
Published by: B & B Media, 40 Rue de Paradis, Paris, 75010, France. TEL 33-1-53249970, FAX 33-1-53249979, info@bandbmedia.com. **Subscr. to:** Viapresse, 7 Impasse Marie Blanche, Paris 75018, France. serviceclients@viapresse.com.

796.6 ITA ISSN 2038-1891
▼ **FREEWAY BIKE.** Text in Italian. 2010. m. **Document type:** *Magazine, Consumer.*
Published by: Acacia Edizioni, Via Copernico 3, Binasco, MI 20082, Italy. http://www.acaciaedizioni.com.

629.11 ITA ISSN 1125-4696
FREEWAY MAGAZINE. Text in Italian. 1995. m. adv. **Document type:** *Magazine, Consumer.*
Published by: Acacia Edizioni, Via Copernico 3, Binasco, MI 20082, Italy. http://www.acaciaedizioni.com.

796.72 FRA ISSN 1167-3559
FREEWAY MAGAZINE. Text in French. 1991. m. EUR 52 (effective 2009). adv. **Document type:** *Magazine, Consumer.*
Related titles: Supplement(s): Freeway Magazine. Hors Serie. ISSN 1169-4882. 1992.
Address: 65 Bd Cote Blatin, Clermont-Ferrand, Cedex 1 63008, France. TEL 33-4-73293235, FAX 33-4-73293249, infos@freewaymag.com, http://www.freewaymag.com.

796 IRL ISSN 1649-9875
FREEWHEEL. Text in English. 2007. bi-m. **Document type:** *Magazine, Consumer.*
Published by: Outsider Media, Guinness Enterprise Centre, Taylor's Lane, Dublin, 8, Ireland. TEL 353-1-4151209, FAX 353-1-4151267, http://www.outsider.ie.

FREIE FAHRT. *see* TRANSPORTATION—Automobiles

796 SWE
FRITID MAGASIN. Text in Swedish. 1935. bi-m. SEK 344 to non-members (effective 1999); SEK 25 newsstand/cover; SEK 125 to members (effective 1999). adv. charts; illus.; stat.; tr.lit. **Document type:** *Consumer.*
Former titles: Fritidshandlaren (1104-4535); (until 1993): Fritidshandlaren Cykel och Sport (1100-052X); (until 1988): Cykel och Sportfritidshandlaren (0283-6254); (until vol.4, 1984): Cykel- och Sporthandlaren
Published by: (Cykel- och Sporthandlarnas Riksfoerbund), C S R's Serviceaktiebolag, Vestagatan 2, Goeteborg, 41664, Sweden. TEL 46-8-791-54-40, FAX 46-8-24-96-16. Ed. Ingrid Hellgren. Pub. Olle Burstroem. Adv. contact Karin Hedman. B&W page SEK 8,700, color page SEK 13,800; trim 262 x 180. Circ: 1,500.

629.227 AUS ISSN 1838-515X
▼ **GASOLINE.** Text in English. 2011. bi-m. USD 79.50; AUD 7.95 per issue (effective 2011). adv. **Document type:** *Magazine, Trade.* **Description:** For traditional street machine enthusiasts.
Published by: Drive Publishing Pty. Ltd., Unit 3, 7 Gateway Ct, Coomera, QLD 4209, Australia. TEL 61-7-55194292, FAX 61-7-55194240, info@drivepublishing.com.au, http://www.drivepublishing.com.au.

796.7 FRA ISSN 1286-3661
GENERATION 125. Variant title: Generation Cent-Vingt-Cinq. Text in French. 1997. bi-m. EUR 23.50 (effective 2008). back issues avail. **Document type:** *Magazine, Consumer.*
Published by: Roadmedia, 1 Av. des Marguerites, Bonneuil-sur-Marne, 94380, France. TEL 33-6-29258971.

GENTE MOTORI. *see* TRANSPORTATION—Automobiles

GESAMTVERBAND AUTOTEILE-HANDEL. MITGLIEDERVERZEICHNIS. *see* TRANSPORTATION—Automobiles

338.476 GBR
GLASS'S GUIDE TO MOTORCYCLE VALUES. Text in English. 1950. m. adv. **Document type:** *Handbook/Manual/Guide, Trade.* **Description:** Offers motorcycle dealers data on the values of new and used machines.
Formerly (until 1985): Glass's Guide to Used Motor Cycle Values
Published by: Glass's Information Services Ltd., 1 Princes Rd, Weybridge, Surrey KT13 9TU, United Kingdom. TEL 44-1932-823823, FAX 44-1932-846564, customer@glass.co.uk, http://www.glass.co.uk. Ed. Randal Thomas.

388.347 GBR ISSN 0966-629X
GLASS'S MOTORCYCLE CHECKBOOK. Text in English. 1957. a. adv. **Document type:** *Handbook/Manual/Guide, Trade.* **Description:** Contains up-to-date information to help identify the exact year and model of a vehicle.
Published by: Glass's Information Services Ltd., 1 Princes Rd, Weybridge, Surrey KT13 9TU, United Kingdom. TEL 44-1932-823823, FAX 44-1932-846564, customer@glass.co.uk, http://www.glass.co.uk.

796 ITA ISSN 1970-0768
LE GRANDI SALITE DEL CICLISMO. Text in Italian. 2007. s-m. **Document type:** *Magazine, Consumer.*
Published by: De Agostini Editore, Via G da Verrazzano 15, Novara, 28100, Italy. TEL 39-0321-4241, FAX 39-0321-424305, info@deagostini.it, http://www.deagostini.it.

796.7 ITA ISSN 1971-0259
GUIDA ALL'ACQUISTO DELLO SCOOTER. Text in Italian. 2006. s-a. **Document type:** *Magazine, Consumer.*
Published by: Eurosport Editoriale, Via della Bufalotta 378, Rome, 00139, Italy. TEL 39-06-45231508, FAX 39-06-45231599, info@eurosporteditoriale.com, http://www.eurosporteditoriale.com.

796.6 FRA ISSN 1951-4581
LE GUIDE DU CYCLOTOURISTE. Text in French. 1948. irreg. **Document type:** *Magazine, Consumer.*
Former titles (until 200?): Guide des Bonnes Adresses (1290-2322); (until 1997): Guide du Cyclotouriste (1290-2314); (until 1960): Guide Cyclotouriste (1297-1812)
Published by: Federation Francaise de Cyclotourisme (F F C T), 12 rue Louis Bertrand, Ivry-sur-Seine, 94207 Cedex, France. TEL 33-1-56208888, FAX 33-1-56208899.

796.7 GBR ISSN 2043-7811
H O G MAGAZINE. (Harley Owners Group) Text in English. 1983. q. free to members (effective 2010). adv. 2 cols./p.; **Document type:** *Magazine, Trade.* **Description:** Aims to keep members up to date on HOG happenings around the world.
Former titles (until 2009): H O G Tales; (until 2007): H O G News; H O G Tales incorporated: Enthusiast
Published by: Harley-Davidson UK, Globe House, 1 Chertsey Rd, Twickenham, TW1 1LR, United Kingdom. TEL 800-1111-2223, FAX 800-7766-5566, customerservices@hog-europe.com.

796.7 USA ISSN 1055-033X
HACK'D; the magazine for and about sidecarists. Text in English. 1984. q. USD 29; USD 39 foreign. adv. bk.rev. index. back issues avail. **Document type:** *Magazine, Consumer.* **Description:** Covers motorcycle sidecars.
Published by: J & C Enterprises, PO Box 813, Buckhannon, WV 26201. TEL 304-472-6146, FAX 304-472-7027. Ed., R&P Jim Dodson. Circ: 3,000 (paid).

HANDBOEK FIETSEN. *see* TRAVEL AND TOURISM

796.6 DEU
HANNORAD. Text in German. q. EUR 3.30 to non-members (effective 2008). adv. **Document type:** *Magazine, Consumer.* **Description:** Contains recreational and membership information for bicycle enthusiasts in the Hannover area.
Published by: Allgemeiner Deutscher Fahrrad Club, Region Hannover e.V., Rambergstr 17, Hannover, 30161, Germany. TEL 49-511-3482322, FAX 49-511-3360504, adfc-hannover@t-online.de. Ed. Michael Holert. Adv. contact Jochen Pipetz.

629.118 DEU
HARLEY-DAVIDSON MAGAZIN. Text in German. 2000. 3/yr. EUR 3.50 newsstand/cover (effective 2006). adv. **Document type:** *Magazine, Consumer.*
Published by: Harley-Davidson GmbH, Starkenburgstr 12, Moerfelden, 64546, Germany. TEL 49-6105-2840, gmbhinfo@harley-davidson.com, http://www.harley-davidson.com. adv.: page EUR 3,900. Circ: 25,000 (paid and controlled).

796.7 USA
HOG TALES. Text in English. 1986. bi-m. free to members (effective 2009). **Document type:** *Magazine, Consumer.*
Published by: Harley-Davidson Motor Co., Inc., 3700 W Juneau Ave, Milwaukee, WI 53208. TEL 414-343-4056, http://www.harley-davidson.com.

796.7 USA ISSN 1523-8857
THE HORSE, BACKSTREET CHOPPERS. Text in English. 1999. m. USD 39.99 domestic; USD 48.99 in Canada; USD 59.99 elsewhere; USD 5.99 newsstand/cover domestic; USD 6.99 newsstand/cover in Canada (effective 2004). **Document type:** *Magazine, Consumer.* **Description:** Satisfies the craving for home-built chops, bobbers and creative customs.
Published by: Iron Cross, Ltd., PO Box 603, Centerport, NY 11721. TEL 631-261-6273, 877-286-0127, FAX 631-261-6532. Ed. Geno DiPol. Pub. Ralph Janus. Adv. contact Rod Anderson.

HORSELESS CARRIAGE GAZETTE. *see* ANTIQUES

796 USA ISSN 0046-8045
HOT BIKE; the Harley-Davidson enthusiast's magazine. Text in English. 1969. m. (13/yr.). USD 23 domestic; USD 62 in Canada; USD 88 elsewhere (effective 2008). adv. illus. back issues avail. **Document type:** *Magazine, Consumer.* **Description:** Written for Harley-Davidson motorcycle owners and enthusiasts, emphasizing the owner/rider's pride in and loyalty to America's only surviving motorcycle.
Former titles (until 198?): Street Chopper, Hot Bike Magazine (0746-2948); (until 1983): Street Chopper Custom Cycle (0744-0464); (until 19??): Street Chopper (0049-2329)
Related titles: Online - full text ed.: USD 11.50 (effective 2008).
Indexed: G06, G07, G08, I05, S23.
Published by: Source Interlink Companies, 2570 E Cerritos Ave, Anaheim, CA 92806. TEL 714-941-1400, FAX 714-978-6390, dheine@sourceinterlink.com, http://www.sourceinterlinkmedia.com. Ed. Eric Ellis TEL 714-941-1403. Pubs. Jeff Tinnion, Sean Finley. adv.: B&W page USD 5,555, color page USD 7,405; bleed 8.125 x 10.75. Circ: 92,638 (paid).

796.75 ITA ISSN 1971-0267
HOT BIKES. Text and summaries in Italian. 2006. 3/yr. **Document type:** *Magazine, Consumer.*
Published by: Eurosport Editoriale, Via della Bufalotta 378, Rome, 00139, Italy. TEL 39-06-45231508, FAX 39-06-45231599, info@eurosporteditoriale.com, http://www.eurosporteditoriale.com.

388.347 GBR ISSN 1755-3717
THE HUB. Text in English. 199?. 3/yr. **Document type:** *Newsletter, Trade.*
Formerly (until 2005): Sustrans. Supporters' Newsletter
Related titles: Online - full text ed.: ISSN 1755-3725; Regional ed(s).: The Hub. Northern Ireland and Ireland. ISSN 1755-4071. 200?; The Hub. East. ISSN 1755-4004. 2005; The Hub. East Midlands. ISSN 1755-3741. 2005; The Hub. Yorkshire and the North East. ISSN 1755-4012. 2005; The Hub. North West. ISSN 1755-4039. 2005; The Hub. Scotland. ISSN 1755-4047. 2005; The Hub. South East - South Central. ISSN 1755-4055. 2005; The Hub. South West. ISSN 1755-4020. 2005; The Hub. Midlands. ISSN 2044-4397. 2005; The Hub. Wales. ISSN 1755-3733. 2005; The Hub. London. ISSN 1755-408X. 2005.
—CCC.
Published by: Sustrans, 2 Cathedral Sq, College Green, Bristol, Avon BS1 5DD, United Kingdom. TEL 44-117-9268893, FAX 44-117-9294173, info@sustrans.org.uk, http://www.sustrans.org.uk.

338.347 USA
I B F NEWS. Text in English. 1986. s-a. free. **Document type:** *Newsletter.* **Description:** News on bicycle transportation policy, programs and philosophy.
Published by: International Bicycle Fund, 4887 Columbia Dr S, Seattle, WA 98108-1919. TEL 206-767-0848, ibike@ibike.org, http://www.ibike.org. Ed., R&P David Mozer. Circ: 3,000.

796.7 USA ISSN 1949-6583
▼ **III COUNTY.** Text in English. 2009. m. free (effective 2009). **Document type:** *Magazine, Consumer.* **Description:** For the members of the Mavericks Motorcycle Club.
Media: Online - full content.
Published by: Gary Jones, Ed. & Pub., 135 Deerwood Dr, Harleton, TX 75651. TEL 903-343-7181, wtmft@mavericksmciiicounty.com.

796.7 ITA ISSN 1122-1720
IN MOTO. Text in Italian. m. **Document type:** *Magazine, Consumer.* **Description:** Covers production and racing bikes.
Published by: Conti Editore SpA, Via del Lavoro 7, San Lazzaro di Savena, BO 40068, Italy. http://www.contieditore.it. Circ: 64,300.

796.7 ITA ISSN 1591-173X
IN SELLA; il mensile per chi va in moto. Text in Italian. 2000. m. EUR 19 domestic; EUR 88 in Europe; EUR 160 elsewhere (effective 2009). adv. charts; illus. **Document type:** *Magazine, Consumer.*
Published by: Unibeta S.r.l. (Subsidiary of: Casa Editrice Universo SpA), Corso di Porta Nuova 3A, Milan, 20121, Italy. TEL 39-02-636751, FAX 39-02-252007333. Circ: 200,000 (paid).

796.6 USA ISSN 1059-759X
IN THE WIND. Text in English. 1978. q. USD 16.95; USD 7.99 newsstand/cover (effective 2009). adv. back issues avail. **Document type:** *Magazine, Consumer.* **Description:** Contains photos of all the great biker bashes, bike shows, rodeos and events.
Formerly (until 199?): Easyriders in the Wind (0884-5131)
Published by: Paisano Publications, Inc., 28210 Dorothy Dr, Box 3075, Agoura Hills, CA 91301. TEL 818-889-8740, 800-247-6246, FAX 818-735-6518, bulkmagazines@paisanopub.com. Adv. contact Tammy Porter TEL 818-889-8740 ext 1265. Circ: 62,848.

388.347 USA ISSN 2157-9962
▼ **INLINE PERFORMANCE MAG**; the premier motorcycle media outlet. Text in English. 2010. a. **Document type:** *Magazine, Trade.* **Description:** Provides information about bikes.
Published by: I P M, 870 Market St, Ste 945, San Francisco, CA 94102.

796.72 FRA ISSN 1294-2200
L'INTEGRAL; la moto dans tous ses etats. Text in French. 1999. bi-m. EUR 28 (effective 2009). adv. **Document type:** *Magazine, Consumer.*
Published by: Editions Lariviere, 6 Rue Olof Palme, Clichy, 92587, France. TEL 33-1-47565400, http://www.editions-lariviere.fr.

796.7 338 GBR ISSN 1354-4047
INTERNATIONAL DEALER NEWS. Abbreviated title: I D N. Text in English. 1997. m. free to qualified personnel (effective 2009). adv. back issues avail. **Document type:** *Magazine, Trade.* **Description:** Provides readers with a unique mix of independently sourced international product information, industry news, events coverage, supplier profiles and technical features.
Formerly (until 1999): C T N. Customer Trade News (1362-0967)
Related titles: Online - full text ed.
Published by: Dealer-World.com, Kenwood House, 1 Upper Grosvenor Rd, Turnbridge Wells, TN1 2DU, United Kingdom. TEL 44-1892-511516, FAX 44-1892-511517. Pub., Adv. contact Robin Bradley. page GBP 1,895; 180 x 267.

THE INTERNATIONAL DIRECTORY OF BICYCLES, MOPEDS AND MOTORCYCLES IMPORTERS. *see* BUSINESS AND ECONOMICS—Trade And Industrial Directories

796.7 USA ISSN 1931-275X
➤ **INTERNATIONAL JOURNAL OF MOTORCYCLE STUDIES.** Abbreviated title: I J M S. Text in English. 2005 (Mar.). s-a. free (effective 2011). back issues avail. **Document type:** *Journal, Academic/Scholarly.* **Description:** Dedicated to the study and discussion of motorcycling culture in all its forms.
Media: Online - full text.
Indexed: A01, A39, C27, C29, CA, D03, D04, E13, MLA-IB, R14, S14, S15, S18, SD, T02.
—IE.
Address: c/o Suzanne Ferriss, Nova Southeastern University, 3301 College Ave, Fort Lauderdale, FL 33314. TEL 954-262-8219, FAX 954-262-3881. Eds. Steven Alford, Suzanne Ferriss.

796.6 IRL ISSN 0790-0600
IRISH CYCLING REVIEW. Text in English. 1983. q. adv. **Document type:** *Magazine, Consumer.*
Published by: Victory Irish Promotions, PO Box 7992, Dun Laoghaire, Co. Dublin, Ireland. TEL 353-1-2804481, FAX 353-1-2804481. Adv. contact Margaret Walsh.

796.7 USA ISSN 1063-5661
IRONWORKS; American street bike magazine. Abbreviated title: I W. Text in English. 1991. 9/yr. USD 19.95 domestic; USD 28 in Canada; USD 38 elsewhere; USD 4.99 newsstand/cover in US & Canada; free to qualified personnel (effective 2009). adv. bk.rev.; film rev. illus. back issues avail.; reprints avail. **Document type:** *Magazine, Consumer.* **Description:** Contains up-to-date information on all the latest trends in customizing, from bolt-ons to scratch-builds, big twins to sportsters, Harley to Indian to Buell.
Formerly (until 1992): Iron Trader News
—CCC.
Published by: Hatton-Brown Publishers, Inc., PO Box 2268, Montgomery, AL 36102. TEL 334-834-1170, FAX 334-834-4525, Dianne@hattonbrown.com, http://www.hattonbrown.com/. Ed. Dain Gingerilli. Adv. contacts David Ramsey, Fran Kokes TEL 847-934-0084. B&W page USD 3,290, color page USD 3,800; trim 8.125 x 10.875.

629.227 GBR ISSN 2042-1087
▼ **ITALIAN LEGENDS.** Text in English. 2009. q. GBP 6.99 per issue domestic; GBP 8.99 per issue in Europe; GBP 9.99 per issue elsewhere (effective 2010). **Document type:** *Magazine, Trade.* **Description:** Covers the cars, the people and the engines that make Italian cars special.
Published by: C H Publications Ltd., Nimax House, 20 Ullswater Cresent, Ullswater Business Park, Coulsdon, Surrey CR5 2HR, United Kingdom. TEL 44-20-86556400, FAX 44-20-87631001, chp@chpltd.com.

796.6 CHE ISSN 1022-3770
KATZENAUGE. Text in German. 1981. 17/yr. CHF 20. adv. bk.rev. **Document type:** *Bulletin.*
Address: Postfach, Zuerich, 8021, Switzerland. TEL 41-1-4629080. Ed. Rene Jacques Weber. Circ: 2,000.

796.7 629.2 USA ISSN 1092-4817
KEYSTONE MOTORCYCLE PRESS. Text in English. 1988. m. USD 15; USD 1.75 newsstand/cover (effective 1998). adv. bk.rev. charts; illus.; mkt.; maps; stat.; tr.lit. back issues avail. **Document type:** *Newspaper, Consumer.* **Description:** Covers events, tours, activities and interests of the motorcyclist interested in PA and its environs.
Published by: Blue Moon Publications, Inc., PO Box 296, Ambridge, PA 15003-0296. TEL 724-774-6542, FAX 724-774-5320, kmppress@aol.com. Ed., R&P Dan Faingnaert. Adv. contact Marilyn Shields. page USD 415. Circ: 12,500.

796.7 NZL ISSN 1177-0023
KIWI RIDER. Text in English. 1986. m. NZD 89 (effective 2008). adv. **Document type:** *Magazine, Consumer.*
Former titles (until 2005): Kiwi Motorcycle Rider (1174-491X); (until 1997): Kiwi Rider News (0113-0218); Which was formed by the merger of (1984-1986): Kiwi Motorcycle Rider (0112-5869); (1978-1986): New Zealand Motorcycle News (0111-9540); Which was formerly (until 1981): N Z M C N (0111-7300)
Published by: McStannic Publishing Ltd., PO Box 299, Kumeu, Auckland, New Zealand. TEL 64-9-4165307, FAX 64-9-4165308. Ed. Ross MacKay. Pub., Adv. contact Pete McPhee.

796.7 DEU
KLASSIK MOTORRAD. Text in German. 6/yr. EUR 29 domestic; EUR 40 foreign; EUR 5.50 newsstand/cover (effective 2007). adv. **Document type:** *Magazine, Consumer.*
Published by: Mo Medien Verlag GmbH, Schrempfstr 8, Stuttgart, 70597, Germany. TEL 49-711-24897600, FAX 49-711-24897628, redaktion@mo-web.de, http://www.mo-web.de. adv.: B&W page EUR 3,655, color page EUR 6,140. Circ: 26,000 (paid and controlled).

796.75 AUS ISSN 1838-6431
▼ **KNEE DOWN MAGAZINE.** Text in English. 2010. irreg. **Document type:** *Magazine, Trade.*
Published by: J P Media, PO Box 3197, Umina Beach, NSW 2257, Australia. TEL 61-3-43410666, http://www.rapidbikes.com.au.

796.7 DEU
KURVE. Text in German. 1981. m. EUR 19.20 (effective 2011). adv. **Document type:** *Magazine, Consumer.*
Published by: Syburger Verlag GmbH, Hertingerstr 60, Unna, 59423, Germany. TEL 49-2303-98550, FAX 49-2303-98559, info@syburger.de, http://www.syburger.de. Ed. Erik Foerster. Adv. contact Jessica Kwasny. Circ: 28,000 (paid and controlled).

629.118 ITA
KUSTOM. Text in Italian. 1998. bi-m. adv. **Document type:** *Magazine, Consumer.*
Formerly (until 2003): Custom Machines (1127-1310)
Published by: Acacia Edizioni, Via Copernico 3, Binasco, MI 20082, Italy. http://www.acaciaedizioni.com.

796.6 USA
GV1045
LEAGUE OF AMERICAN BICYCLISTS MAGAZINE. Text in English. 1965. q. USD 30 to individuals; USD 20 to libraries. adv. bk.rev. **Document type:** *Magazine, Consumer.*
Former titles: Bicycle U S A (0747-0371); (until 1984): American Wheelmen (0199-2139); (until 1979): League of American Wheelmen Bulletin (0192-6063)
Related titles: Special ed(s).: Bicycle U S A Almanac.
Indexed: SD, SportS.

S

Published by: League of American Bicyclists, 1612 K St, N W, Ste 800, Washington, DC 20006-2850. TEL 202-822-1333, FAX 202-822-1334. Ed., Adv. contact Patrick W McCormick. Circ: 40,000.

796.75 GBR ISSN 2044-821X
▼ **LEARNER LEGAL**; everything for the new rider. Text in English. 2010. bi-m. adv. **Document type:** *Magazine, Consumer.* **Description:** Provides novice riders with valuable advice and information to help them as they take their first steps as motorcyclists.
Related titles: Online - full text ed.
Published by: Evolution Media Communications, 66 Higher Brimley Rd, Teignmouth, Devon TQ14 8JU, United Kingdom. Pub., Adv. contact Mat Smith.

796.7 ITA ISSN 1121-7146
LEGEND BIKE/MOTOCICLETTE DA LEGGENDA; motociclette da leggenda. Text in Italian. 1992. m. EUR 62 domestic; EUR 124 foreign (effective 2008). adv. **Document type:** *Magazine, Consumer.*
Published by: Cantelli Editore Srl, Via Saliceto 22c, Castelmaggiore, BO 40013, Italy. TEL 39-051-6328811, FAX 39-051-6328815, cantelli.editore@cantelli.net, http://www.cantelli.net. Circ: 62,000.

388.347 AUS ISSN 1320-1220
LIVE TO RIDE. Text in English. 1989. m. AUD 69.95 domestic; AUD 101 in New Zealand; AUD 166 elsewhere; AUD 7.95 newsstand/cover (effective 2008). adv. **Document type:** *Magazine, Consumer.* **Description:** Covers all facets of the biker lifestyle.
Published by: News Magazines Pty Ltd., Level 3, 2 Holt St, Surry Hills, NSW 2010, Australia. TEL 61-2-92883000, http://www.newsspace.com.au/magazines. Ed. Miles Rangeley. Adv. contact Brett Cross TEL 61-2-80622701. color page AUD 2,350; trim 206 x 276. Circ: 24,055.

796.7 USA ISSN 1089-0076
LONG RIDERS; for people who love to ride. Text in English. 1996. 8/yr. USD 28 domestic; USD 42 in Canada & Mexico; USD 48 elsewhere; USD 4.99 newsstand/cover (effective 2001). adv. back issues avail. **Document type:** *Magazine, Consumer.* **Description:** Contains articles and features geared to motorcycle enthusiasts of all ages, genders and ethnicities.
Published by: Long Riders, Inc., 1223 N Cameron St, 2nd Fl, Ste B, Harrisburg, PA 17103. TEL 717-234-8705, FAX 717-232-2415. Ed., R&P Christine McGee. Pub., Adv. contact Charles McGee. Circ: 25,000 (paid and controlled). **Dist. by:** Curtis Circulation Co., 730 River Rd, New Milford, NJ 07646. TEL 201-634-7400, FAX 201-634-7499.

796.7 796.77 USA ISSN 2153-3547
▼ **LOWSIDE MAGAZINE**; garage built suicide machines. Text in English. 2010 (Feb.). q. USD 24 (effective 2010). **Document type:** *Magazine, Consumer.* **Description:** For motorcycle and custom car enthusiasts.
Published by: Lowside Syndicate, 8900 Yellow Brick Rd, Baltimore, MD 21237. TEL 443-865-3765, rich@lowsidesyn.com.

796.7 629.227 SWE ISSN 0281-7403
M C - FOLKET. Text in Swedish. 1964. 8/yr. SEK 375 membership (effective 2011). adv. back issues avail. **Document type:** *Magazine, Consumer.*
Formerly (until 1981): S M C - Bladet (0346-0517)
Published by: Sveriges Motorcyklisters Centralorganisation, Forskargatan 3, Borlaenge, 78170, Sweden. TEL 46-234-82280, smc@svmc.se, http://www.svmc.se.

796.7 629.227 SWE ISSN 0282-9134
M C M; motorcykelmagasinet. (Motorcykelmagasinet) Text in Swedish. 1985. bi-m. SEK 310 domestic; EUR 42 foreign; SEK 64 newsstand/cover (effective 2008). adv. bk.rev. 80 p./no. 4 cols./p.; back issues avail. **Document type:** *Magazine, Consumer.* **Description:** Covers all aspects of owning and riding a motocycle.
Related titles: E-mail ed.; Fax ed.
Published by: M C M Foerlag, Torsgatan 65, Stockholm, 11337, Sweden. TEL 46-8-340407, FAX 46-8-340422. Ed. Inge Persson Carleson. Pub. Inge Persson-Carleson. Adv. contact Annika Bath. B&W page SEK 9,850, color page SEK 13,100; trim 270 x 186. Circ: 22,000 (paid); 8,000 (controlled).

796 SWE ISSN 0024-7995
M C - NYTT. Text in Swedish. 1959. 10/yr. SEK 439 (effective 2007). adv. bk.rev. illus.; stat. **Document type:** *Magazine, Consumer.*
Incorporates (in 1975): M C - Sport (0025-6250)
Published by: Mediapress SN AB, Ynglingagatan 12, PO Box 23800, Stockholm, 10435, Sweden. TEL 46-8-7361200, FAX 46-8-7361221. Ed. Manfred Holz. Adv. contact Claes Jaurelius TEL 46-300-75782.

629.2275 DNK ISSN 0107-0606
M C REVYEN. (Motorcykel) Text in Danish. 1974. a. DKK 148 (effective 2009). mkt. **Document type:** *Catalog, Consumer.* **Description:** Catalogue of all motorbikes sold on the Danish market.
Published by: Benjamin Media A/S, Finsensvej 6 D, Frederiksberg, 2000, Denmark. TEL 45-70-220255, FAX 45-70-220056, http://www.benjamin.dk.

796.7 CAN
M D T. (Motorsport Dealer & Trade) Text in English. 1978. 6/yr. free to qualified personnel. adv. charts; stat.; tr.lit. back issues avail. **Document type:** *Journal, Trade.* **Description:** For dealers, distributors and manufacturers in the powersports industry.
Formerly: Motorcycle Dealer and Trade (0705-2030)
Related titles: Microfilm ed.: (from MML); Microform ed.: (from MML).
Indexed: C03, CBCABus, PQC.
Published by: Turbopress Inc., 411 Richmond St E, Ste 301, Toronto, ON M5A 3S5, Canada. TEL 416-362-7966, FAX 416-362-3950. Ed. Jim Aikins. Pub. J P Belmonte. Adv. contact Mike Moloney. B&W page CAD 1,800; trim 15.75 x 10.13. Circ: 4,000 (controlled).

796 GBR
M S A NEWSLINK. Text in English. 199?. m. free to members (effective 2010). adv. bk.rev. **Document type:** *Newspaper, Trade.* **Description:** Features significant information for the driving instructors.
Published by: (Motor Schools Association of Great Britain), Integral Publishing Co. Ltd., Castlefield Ho, Liverpool Rd, Castlefield, Manchester, Lancs M60 9BF, United Kingdom.

796.7 USA ISSN 1538-313X
M X MACHINE MAGAZINE. Text in English. 2002. bi-m. USD 9.99 domestic; USD 19.99 foreign (effective 2002). **Document type:** *Magazine, Consumer.*
Published by: L F P, Inc., 8484 Wilshire Blvd., Ste. 900, Beverly Hills, CA 90211. TEL 888-357-6313. Ed. Nick Ciotti. Pub. Larry Flynt. Adv. contact Angelo Ciotti.

796.75 GBR
M X U K. (Motor Cross United Kingdom) Text in English. 1998. m. GBP 24.99 in United Kingdom; GBP 33 in Europe; GBP 45 rest of world (effective 2000); GBP 2.95 newsstand/cover. adv. **Document type:** *Magazine, Consumer.* **Description:** Promotes dirt biking by featuring the world's top riders, as well as Britain's most talented stars.
Published by: Future Publishing Ltd., Beauford Ct, 30 Monmouth St, Bath, Avon BA1 2BW, United Kingdom. TEL 44-1225-442244, FAX 44-1225-446019, customerservice@subscription.co.uk, http://www.futureplc.com. Ed. Sean Hawker.

796.7 USA
MAIN STREET LOW RIDAZ. Text in English. 2001. q. USD 17; USD 3.99 newsstand/cover (effective 2002). adv. **Document type:** *Magazine, Consumer.*
Published by: B.L.I. Publishing Inc., 1020 Green Acres Rd, Eugene, OR 97408. http://www.LowRidazMagazine.com. Ed. Theresita Ingram.

796.7 AUS ISSN 1833-2609
MANUAL OF MOTORCYCLE SPORT. Text in English. 19??. a. **Document type:** *Handbook/Manual/Guide, Consumer.*
Published by: Motorcycling Australia, PO Box 134, South Melbourne, VIC 3205, Australia. TEL 61-3-9684-0500, FAX 61-3-9684-0555, mail@ma.org.au, http://www.ma.org.au//AM/Template.cfm?Section=Home.

388.347 640.73 USA
MASS CYCLIST. Text in English. 1979. q. USD 30; includes membership (effective 2000). bk.rev. charts; illus.; tr.lit. back issues avail. **Document type:** *Newsletter.* **Description:** Newsletter of the Coalition, a bicycle advocacy group working to promote the safe and practical use of the bicycle for both transportation and recreation.
Former titles (until 1993): Boston Cyclist; Spoke 'n Word
Published by: Massachusetts Bicycle Coalition, 20 Park Plaza, Ste 1028, Boston, MA 02116. TEL 617-491-RIDE. Ed. Jack W Johnson. Adv. contact Larry Slotnick. Circ: 1,000.

796.7 CAN
MASTERLINK. Text in English. 8/yr. CAD 19.95, USD 19.95 for 12 nos. adv. illus.
Published by: Western Biker Publications Ltd., 735 Market St, Victoria, BC V8T 2E2, Canada. TEL 604-384-0333, FAX 604-384-1832. Ed. Len Creed. **Subscr. to:** P O Box 4122, Sta. A, Victoria, BC V8X 3X4, Canada.

796.72 FRA ISSN 1628-2124
MAXIMOTO. Text in French. 2001. bi-m. EUR 79 for 2 yrs. (effective 2008). adv. back issues avail. **Document type:** *Magazine, Consumer.*
Published by: B & B Media, 40 Rue de Paradis, Paris, 75010, France. TEL 33-1-53249970, FAX 33-1-53249979, info@bandbmedia.com. **Subscr. to:** Viapresse, 7 Impasse Marie Blanche, Paris 75018, France. serviceclients@viapresse.com.

796.7 FRA ISSN 1778-8676
MINI MOTO MAGAZINE. Text in French. 2006. bi-m. **Document type:** *Magazine, Consumer.*
Address: 89 rue Carnot, Levallois-Perret, 92300, France. TEL 33-1-41050478, desk@minimoto-mag.com.

796.75 USA ISSN 1939-4209
MINI RIDER MAGAZINE. Text in English. 2004. s-m. USD 14.97 domestic; USD 20.97 in Canada; USD 26.97 elsewhere (effective 2007). adv. **Document type:** *Magazine, Consumer.*
—CCC.
Published by: Source Interlink Companies, 6420 Wilshire Blvd, 10th Fl, Los Angeles, CA 90048. TEL 323-782-2000, FAX 323-782-2585, dheine@sourceinterlink.com, http://www.sourceinterlinkmedia.com.

796.6 ITA ISSN 1593-0769
IL MONDO DEL CICLISMO. Text in Italian. 2001. w. EUR 80 domestic (effective 2008). **Document type:** *Magazine, Consumer.*
Published by: Cantelli Editore Srl, Via Saliceto 22c, Castelmaggiore, BO 40013, Italy. TEL 39-051-6328811, FAX 39-051-6328815, cantelli.editore@cantelli.net, http://www.cantelli.net.

629 FIN ISSN 1796-8968
MONKIJA. Text in Finnish. 2007. q. EUR 25 (effective 2008). adv. **Document type:** *Magazine, Consumer.*
Published by: RideMedia Oy, PO Box 140, Hyvinkaa, 05801, Finland. TEL 358-19-483490, FAX 358-19-483480, jukka.helminen@ridemedia.fi, http://www.ridemedia.fi. Ed. Arttu Toivonen. Adv. contact Ossi Sinisilta TEL 358-3-6715474. B&W page EUR 1,320, color page EUR 2,100.

388.347 796.7 ITA ISSN 0392-3681
MOTITALIA. Text in Italian. 1947. m. free to members. adv. bk.rev. **Document type:** *Magazine, Consumer.* **Description:** Deals with motorcycle racing in Italy; includes biographies of racers, activities of racing groups, and details of competitions.
Published by: Federazione Motociclistica Italiana, Viale Tiziano 70, Rome, 00196, Italy. http://www.federmoto.it. Circ: 110,000.

796.7 629.227 RUS
MOTO. Text in Russian. 1991. m. RUR 90 for 6 mos. adv. illus. **Document type:** *Consumer.* **Description:** Covers motorcycles and motorcycling: technique, new models, shows, history, and sport.
Related titles: Online - full text ed.
Published by: Izdatel'stvo Za Rulem, Seliverstov per 10, Moscow, 103045, Russian Federation. TEL 7-095-207-3349, FAX 7-095-208-0070. Ed. Petr Menshikh. Pub., R&P Victor V Panyarsky TEL 7-095-207-1827. Adv. contact A Mukhin. page USD 1,500. Circ: 40,000. **Dist. by:** East View Information Services, 10601 Wayzata Blvd, Minneapolis, MN 55305. TEL 952-252-1201, 800-477-1005, FAX 952-252-1202, info@eastview.com, http://www.eastview.com.

796.7 ESP
LA MOTO. Text in Spanish. 1990. m. adv. **Document type:** *Magazine, Consumer.*
Published by: Motorpress Iberica (Subsidiary of: Gruner + Jahr AG & Co), Ancora 40, Madrid, 28045, Spain. TEL 34-91-3470100, FAX 34-91-3470152, http://www.motorpress-iberica.es. Ed. Pepe Burgaleta. Circ: 20,000 (paid).

796.7 NLD ISSN 0165-8859
MOTO 73. Text in Dutch. 1973. 26/yr. EUR 75.40; EUR 3.95 newsstand/cover (effective 2009). adv. illus. **Document type:** *Magazine, Consumer.* **Description:** Dedicated to racing, touring, and street motorcycle enthusiasts.
Published by: Sanoma Men's Magazines, Haaksbergweg 75, Amsterdam (ZO), 1101 BR, Netherlands. TEL 31-20-7518000, FAX 31-20-7518301, sales@smm.nl, http://www.smm.nl. adv.: B&W page EUR 1,685, color page EUR 3,370; trim 230 x 300. Circ: 26,748.

796.7 BEL
MOTO 80. Text in French. 1980. bi-w. EUR 65 (effective 2005). **Document type:** *Consumer.* **Description:** Covers all types of motorcycle racing in Belgium and Europe, as well as road tests of new models, travel and other related topics.
Published by: Moto 80 s.p.r.l., 15, Rue Abbe Michel Renard, Nivelles, 1400, Belgium. TEL 32-67-493636, FAX 32-67-493639, moto80@moto80.be, http://www.moto80.be. Ed. Luc Paquier. Circ: 22,000.

796.7 GRC ISSN 1108-7846
MOTO ACCESSORIES. Text in German. 1997. a. EUR 7.98 newsstand/cover (effective 2006). adv. **Document type:** *Magazine, Consumer.*
Published by: Motorpress Hellas (Subsidiary of: Gruner + Jahr AG & Co), 132 Lefkis Str, Krioneri, 14568, Greece. TEL 30-210-6262000, FAX 30-210-6262401, info@motorpress.gr, http://www.motorpress.gr. Circ: 20,000 (paid and controlled).

796.7 USA ISSN 2153-2524
▼ **MOTO ADVENTURE.** Text in English. forthcoming 2010 (Apr.). bi-m. USD 5.99 per issue (effective 2010). **Document type:** *Magazine, Consumer.*
Published by: Werner Publishing Corporation, 12121 Wilshire Blvd 1200, Los Angeles, CA 90025-1176. TEL 310-820-1500, FAX 310-826-5008, editors@planeandpilotmag.com, http://www.wernerpublishing.com.

388.347 FRA ISSN 1950-8506
MOTO CONSO. Text in French. 2006. bi-m. EUR 25 (effective 2007). back issues avail. **Document type:** *Magazine, Consumer.*
Published by: Motor Presse France, 12 rue Rouget de Lisle, Issy-les-Moulineaux, 92442, France. http://www.motorpresse.fr.

796.7 FRA ISSN 0766-0847
MOTO CRAMPONS. Text in French. 1985. m. EUR 36 (effective 2008). adv. back issues avail. **Document type:** *Magazine, Consumer.* **Description:** For motorcycle enthusiasts. Contains tests, comparisons, and driving techniques.
Published by: B & B Media, 40 Rue de Paradis, Paris, 75010, France. TEL 33-1-53249970, FAX 33-1-53249979, info@bandbmedia.com. Circ: 68,240 (paid).

796.75 ITA ISSN 1826-316X
LE MOTO DEL CAMPIONE. Text in Italian. 2005. w. **Document type:** *Magazine, Consumer.*
Published by: R C S Libri (Subsidiary of: R C S Mediagroup), Via Mecenate 91, Milan, 20138, Italy. TEL 39-02-5095-2248, FAX 39-02-5095-2975, http://rcslibri.corriere.it/libri/index.htm.

388.347 ITA ISSN 1825-0270
MOTO G P COLLECTION. Text in Italian. 2005. 2/m. **Document type:** *Magazine, Consumer.*
Published by: De Agostini Editore, Via G da Verrazzano 15, Novara, 28100, Italy. TEL 39-0321-4241, FAX 39-0321-424305, info@deagostini.it, http://www.deagostini.it.

796 CAN ISSN 0319-2865
MOTO JOURNAL. Text in French. 1972. 10/yr. CAD 29.95 domestic; CAD 39.95 in United States; CAD 54.95 elsewhere; CAD 3.50 newsstand/cover (effective 2000). adv.
Related titles: ◆ English ed.: Cycle Canada. ISSN 0319-2822; English ed.
Published by: Turbopress Inc., 411 Richmond St E, Ste 301, Toronto, ON M5A 3S5, Canada. TEL 514-738-9439, FAX 738-4929, motojournal@accent.net. Ed. Claude Leonard. Pub. Jean Pierre Belmonte. adv.: B&W page CAD 3,490, color page CAD 4,360; trim 10.75 x 8. Circ: 11,000.

796.7 FRA ISSN 0751-591X
MOTO JOURNAL. Text in French. 1971. w. (48/yr.). EUR 109 (effective 2010). adv. **Document type:** *Magazine, Consumer.* **Description:** Features comparisons, and tests of various motorbikes and their performance.
Published by: Motor Presse France, 12 rue Rouget de Lisle, Issy-les-Moulineaux, 92442, France. http://www.motorpresse.fr.

796.7 028.5 FRA ISSN 1766-9553
MOTO KIDS. Text in French. 2004. m. (10/yr). back issues avail. **Document type:** *Magazine, Consumer.*
Published by: Moto Kids Magazine, 89 Rue Carnot, Levallois-Perret, 92300, France. TEL 33-1-41050478, FAX 33-1-41499251.

796.7 629.222 FRA ISSN 1155-2069
MOTO LEGENDE. Text in French. 1990. m. EUR 48 domestic; EUR 52 foreign (effective 2009). adv. cum.index. 80 p./no. 3 cols./p.; back issues avail. **Document type:** *Newspaper.* **Description:** Covers classic motorcycles.
Published by: Editions L V A, Chateau de la Magdeleine, Samois-sur-Seine, 77920, France. Circ: 45,000.

796 FRA ISSN 0047-8180
MOTO REVUE; le bimensuel de tous les motards. Text in French. 1913. 23/yr. EUR 59 (effective 2009). adv. abstr.; illus.; stat. **Document type:** *Magazine, Consumer.*
Published by: Editions Lariviere, 6 Rue Olof Palme, Clichy, 92587, France. TEL 33-1-47565400, http://www.editions-lariviere.fr. Ed. Jacques Tillier. Adv. contact Philippe Budillon. Circ: 100,000.

796.7 FRA ISSN 1633-2776
MOTO REVUE CLASSIC. Text in French. 2002. bi-m. EUR 30 (effective 2009). **Document type:** *Magazine, Consumer.*
Published by: Editions Lariviere, 6 Rue Olof Palme, Clichy, 92587, France. TEL 33-1-47565400.

796.7 CHE ISSN 1420-0457
MOTO SPORT SCHWEIZ. Text in German. 1972. fortn. CHF 119 (effective 2007). adv. **Document type:** *Magazine, Consumer.*
Former titles (until 1980): Moto-Sport (1421-1491); (until 1975): Moto-Sport Schweiz (1421-1505)
Related titles: ◆ French ed.: Moto Sport Suisse. ISSN 1420-0465.
Published by: Buechler Grafino AG, Dammweg 9, Bern, 3001, Switzerland. TEL 41-31-3303555, FAX 41-31-3303377, redaktion@espace.ch, http://www.espace.ch. Ed. Markus Schmid. Adv. contact Eva Fankhauser. Circ: 14,403 (paid).

796.7 CHE ISSN 1420-0465
MOTO SPORT SUISSE. Text in French. 1986. fortn. CHF 89 (effective 2007). adv. **Document type:** *Magazine, Consumer.*
Related titles: ◆ German ed.: Moto Sport Schweiz. ISSN 1420-0457.
Published by: Buechler Grafino AG, Dammweg 9, Bern, 3001, Switzerland. TEL 41-31-3303555, FAX 41-31-3303377, redaktion@espace.ch, http://www.espace.ch. Ed. Markus Schmid. Adv. contact Eva Fankhauser. Circ: 4,000.

796.7 ITA ISSN 1125-6400
MOTO STORICHE & D'EPOCA. Text in Italian. 1984. m. EUR 25 domestic (effective 2009). adv. 90 p./no.; back issues avail. **Document type:** *Magazine, Consumer.* **Description:** Devoted to classic and antique motorcycles. Intended for enthusiasts, collectors and dealers of classic motorcycles.
Published by: Nuovi Periodici Milanesi, Via Molise 3, Locate Triulzi, MI 20085, Italy. http://www.nuoviperiodicimilanesi.com. Circ: 45,000 (paid).

796.7 GRC ISSN 1108-7854
MOTO TRITI. Text in Greek. 1996. fortn. EUR 4.98 newsstand/cover (effective 2006). adv. **Document type:** *Magazine, Consumer.*
Published by: Motorpress Hellas (Subsidiary of: Gruner + Jahr AG & Co), 132 Lefkis Str, Krioneri, 14568, Greece. TEL 30-210-6262000, FAX 30-210-6262401, info@motorpress.gr, http://www.motorpress.gr. Circ: 20,000 (paid and controlled).

796.7 GRC
MOTO TRITI ON-OFF. Text in Greek. 2001. a. EUR 5.95 newsstand/cover (effective 2006). adv. **Document type:** *Magazine, Consumer.*
Published by: Motorpress Hellas (Subsidiary of: Gruner + Jahr AG & Co), 132 Lefkis Str, Krioneri, 14568, Greece. TEL 30-210-6262000, FAX 30-210-6262401, info@motorpress.gr, http://www.motorpress.gr. Circ: 20,000 (paid and controlled).

796.7 GRC
MOTO TRITI SCOOTER. Text in Greek. 2001. a. EUR 6.98 newsstand/cover (effective 2006). adv. **Document type:** *Magazine, Consumer.*
Published by: Motorpress Hellas (Subsidiary of: Gruner + Jahr AG & Co), 132 Lefkis Str, Krioneri, 14568, Greece. TEL 30-210-6262000, FAX 30-210-6262401, info@motorpress.gr, http://www.motorpress.gr. Circ: 20,000 (paid and controlled).

796.7 GRC
MOTO TRITI TEST BOOK. Text in Greek. 1997. a. EUR 6.98 newsstand/cover (effective 2006). adv. **Document type:** *Magazine, Consumer.*
Published by: Motorpress Hellas (Subsidiary of: Gruner + Jahr AG & Co), 132 Lefkis Str, Krioneri, 14568, Greece. TEL 30-210-6262000, FAX 30-210-6262401, info@motorpress.gr, http://www.motorpress.gr. Circ: 20,000 (paid and controlled).

796.7 ESP
MOTO VERDE. Text in Spanish. 1987. m. adv. **Document type:** *Magazine, Consumer.*
Published by: Motorpress Iberica (Subsidiary of: Gruner + Jahr AG & Co), Ancora 40, Madrid, 28045, Spain. TEL 34-91-3470100, FAX 34-91-3470152. Circ: 60,000 (paid).

796.75 FRA
MOTO VERTE; le leader de la presse tout-terrain. Text in French. m. EUR 53 (effective 2009). adv. **Document type:** *Magazine, Consumer.*
Published by: Editions Lariviere, 6 Rue Olof Palme, Clichy, 92587, France. TEL 33-1-47565400, http://www.editions-lariviere.fr. Ed. Jacques Tillier. Adv. contact Philippe Budillon.

796.77 DEU
MOTO X. Text in German. 1998. m. EUR 42; EUR 4.20 newsstand/cover (effective 2008). adv. **Document type:** *Magazine, Consumer.*
Related titles: Online - full text ed.
Published by: b&d Media Network GmbH, Osterfeldstr 12-14, Hamburg, 22529, Germany. TEL 49-40-4800070, FAX 49-40-48000799, info@bdverlag.de, http://www.bdverlag.de. Ed. Wolfgang Brandt. Adv. contact Denis Koenig. B&W page EUR 3,300, color page EUR 4,400; trim 230 x 300. Circ: 58,845 (paid).

796.7 ESP
MOTOCASION. Text in Spanish. m. EUR 1.95 newsstand/cover (effective 2009). adv. **Document type:** *Magazine, Consumer.*
Published by: Grupo V, C Valportillo Primera, 11, Alcobendas, Madrid, 28108, Spain. TEL 34-91-6622137, FAX 34-91-6622654, secretaria@grupov.es. Adv. contact Cristina Pelayo. page EUR 2,010; trim 21 x 25.5. Circ: 45,000.

796.7 ESP ISSN 1579-203X
MOTOCICLISMO. Text in Spanish. 1951. w. adv. **Document type:** *Magazine, Consumer.*
Related titles: ◆ Supplement(s): Motociclismo Catalogo. ISSN 1131-785X; ◆ Motociclismo Pruebas; ◆ Motociclismo. Especial Grandes Premios. ISSN 1579-4245.
Published by: Motorpress Iberica (Subsidiary of: Gruner + Jahr AG & Co), Ancora 40, Madrid, 28045, Spain. TEL 34-91-3470100, FAX 34-91-3470152, http://www.motorpress-iberica.es. Ed. Augusto Moreno de Carlos. Circ: 38,000 (paid).

796.7 PRT
MOTOCICLISMO. Text in Portuguese. 1991. m. EUR 3.50 newsstand/cover (effective 2005). adv. **Document type:** *Magazine, Consumer.*
Related titles: Online - full text ed.; ◆ Supplement(s): Especial Custom.
Published by: Motorpress Lisboa, SA (Subsidiary of: Gruner + Jahr AG & Co), Rua Policarpio Anjos No. 4, Cruz Quebrada, Dafundo 1495-742, Portugal. TEL 351-21-4154500, FAX 351-21-4154501, buzine@motorpress.pt, http://www.mpl.pt. Ed. Vitor Sousa. Adv. contact Fernando Pereira. Circ: 14,300 (paid).

796.7 ITA ISSN 0027-1691
MOTOCICLISMO. Text in Italian. 1914. m. EUR 48 domestic; EUR 92 in the European Union; EUR 152 elsewhere (effective 2009). adv. bk.rev. charts; illus.; mkt. index. **Document type:** *Magazine, Consumer.* **Description:** News about two and three-wheel motor vehicles including test results, industrial information, prices.
Related titles: Online - full text ed.
—IE.
Published by: Edisport Editoriale SpA, Via Gradisca 11, Milan, MI 20151, Italy. TEL 39-02-38085, FAX 39-02-38010393, edisport@edisport.it, http://www.edisport.it. Circ: 200,000.

796.6 ESP ISSN 1131-785X
MOTOCICLISMO CATALOGO. Text in Spanish. 1980. a. **Document type:** *Catalog, Consumer.* **Description:** Presents information on current motorcycle models.
Related titles: ◆ Supplement to: Motociclismo. ISSN 1579-203X.
Published by: Motorpress Iberica (Subsidiary of: Gruner + Jahr AG & Co), Ancora 40, Madrid, 28045, Spain. TEL 34-91-3470100, FAX 34-91-3470152, http://www.motorpress-iberica.es. Ed. Augusto Moreno de Carlos. Pub. Jose Luis Sarralde. Adv. contact Miguel Angel Aguado. Circ: 48,000 (paid).

796.7 PRT
MOTOCICLISMO CATALOGO (CRUZ QUEBRADA). Text in Portuguese. 1993. a. EUR 5 (effective 2005). adv. **Document type:** *Magazine, Consumer.* **Description:** Contains the latest reviews and technical specifications of motorcycle models available in the Portuguese market.
Formerly: Motociclismo Motocatalogo
Published by: Motorpress Lisboa, SA (Subsidiary of: Gruner + Jahr AG & Co), Rua Policarpio Anjos No. 4, Cruz Quebrada, Dafundo 1495-742, Portugal. TEL 351-21-4154500, FAX 351-21-4154501, buzine@motorpress.pt, http://www.mpl.pt. Circ: 14,856 (paid).

796.7 ITA ISSN 1123-4571
MOTOCICLISMO D'EPOCA. Text in Italian. 1995. 10/yr. EUR 58 domestic; EUR 92 in the European Union; EUR 140 elsewhere (effective 2009). adv. **Document type:** *Magazine, Consumer.* **Description:** Covers classic motorcycles.
Related titles: Online - full text ed.
Published by: Edisport Editoriale SpA, Via Gradisca 11, Milan, MI 20151, Italy. TEL 39-02-38085, FAX 39-02-38010393, edisport@edisport.it, http://www.edisport.it. Circ: 50,000 (paid).

796.7 ESP ISSN 1579-4245
MOTOCICLISMO. ESPECIAL GRANDES PREMIOS. Text in Spanish. 1988. a. **Document type:** *Magazine, Consumer.*
Related titles: ◆ Supplement to: Motociclismo. ISSN 1579-203X.
Published by: Motorpress Iberica (Subsidiary of: Gruner + Jahr AG & Co), Ancora 40, Madrid, 28045, Spain. TEL 34-91-3470100, FAX 34-91-3470152, http://www.motorpress-iberica.es. Circ: 6,000 (paid).

796.7 ESP ISSN 1579-4369
MOTOCICLISMO ESPECIAL PRUEBAS. Text in Spanish. 1981. a. **Document type:** *Consumer.* **Description:** Presents test results on over 100 motorcycles, grouped into 10 categories.
Published by: Motorpress Iberica (Subsidiary of: Gruner + Jahr AG & Co), Ancora 40, Madrid, 28045, Spain. TEL 34-91-3470100, FAX 34-91-3470152, http://www.motorpress-iberica.es. Circ: 35,000.

796.7 ITA ISSN 1722-3083
MOTOCICLISMO FUORISTRADA. Text in Italian. 2003. m. EUR 35 domestic; EUR 67 in the European Union; EUR 117 elsewhere (effective 2009). **Document type:** *Magazine, Consumer.*
Related titles: Online - full text ed.
Published by: Edisport Editoriale SpA, Via Gradisca 11, Milan, MI 20151, Italy. TEL 39-02-38085, FAX 39-02-38010393, edisport@edisport.it, http://www.edisport.it.

796.72 BRA ISSN 1415-1863
MOTOCICLISMO MAGAZINE. Text in Portuguese. 1998. m. BRL 4.90 newsstand/cover (effective 2001). adv. **Document type:** *Magazine, Consumer.*
Published by: MotorPress Brasil (Subsidiary of: Gruner + Jahr AG & Co), Rua Benjamin Mota 86, Sao Paulo, SP 04727-070, Brazil. TEL 55-11-56413454, FAX 55-11-56413858. Ed. Gabriel Marazzi. Pubs. Isabel Reis, Sergio Quintanilha. Adv. contact Dario Castilho. Circ: 12,000 (paid).

796.75 ESP
MOTOCICLISMO PRUEBAS. Text in Spanish. 1990. a. **Document type:** *Magazine, Consumer.*
Related titles: ◆ Supplement to: Motociclismo. ISSN 1579-203X.
Published by: Motorpress Iberica (Subsidiary of: Gruner + Jahr AG & Co), Ancora 40, Madrid, 28045, Spain. TEL 34-91-3470100, FAX 34-91-3470152, http://www.motorpress-iberica.es. Circ: 21,000 (paid).

388.347 GBR ISSN 0309-4642
MOTOCOURSE; the world's leading Grand Prix and Superbike annual. Text in English. 1976. a. GBP 29.75 per issue (effective 2010). adv. illus. **Document type:** *Magazine, Consumer.* **Description:** Provides detailed coverage of the previous year's motorcycle Grand Prix season and other championships and profiles championship riders.
Published by: Icon Publishing Ltd., Regent Lodge, 4 Hanley Rd, Malvern, WR14 4PQ, United Kingdom. TEL 44-1684-564511.

388.347 796.7 ITA
MOTOCROSS. Text in Italian. 1971. m. EUR 47 domestic; EUR 100 in Europe; EUR 120 elsewhere (effective 2009). adv. **Document type:** *Magazine, Consumer.* **Description:** The most important Italian magazine dedicated to off-road motorcycling.
Address: Via Cusani 10, Milan, MI 20121, Italy. Circ: 200,000.

796.77 USA ISSN 0146-3292
GV1060
MOTOCROSS ACTION. Text in English. 1973. m. USD 19.99 (effective 2009). adv. back issues avail. **Document type:** *Magazine, Consumer.*
Indexed: SD, SportS, T02.
Published by: Hi - Torque Publications, Inc., 25233 Anza Dr, Valencia, CA 91355. TEL 661-295-1910, FAX 661-295-1278, http://www.hi-torque.com.

796.7 DEU ISSN 1611-1184
MOTOCROSS ENDURO; Offroadmagazin. Text in German. 1971. m. EUR 42 domestic; EUR 52 foreign (effective 2010). adv. bk.rev. back issues avail. **Document type:** *Magazine, Consumer.* **Description:** Sports magazine for all motocross enthusiasts. Features reports, results and announcements of events, championships, national and international news, and new products.
Former titles (until 2002): M C E Aktuell (1430-760X); (until 1996): Moto Cross Enduro Aktuell (0947-6393); (until 1993): Moto Cross Aktuell und Enduro (0724-7206); Which superseded in part (in 1983): Bahnsport Moto Cross und Enduro Aktuell (0723-2535); Which was formerly (until 1982): Bahnsport Aktuell (0171-8940)
Published by: Ziegler Verlags GmbH, Birkenweiherstr 14, Langenselbold, 63505, Germany. TEL 49-6184-923330, FAX 49-6184-923355, info@ziegler-verlag.de. Ed. Stefan Ziegler. Adv. contact Ralf Ziegler. B&W page EUR 2,253, color page EUR 4,068. Circ: 36,100 (paid).

629.118 POL ISSN 1426-2932
MOTOCYKL. Text in Polish. 1994. m. PLZ 5.50 newsstand/cover (effective 2001). adv. **Document type:** *Magazine, Consumer.*
Published by: Motor-Presse Polska, ul Przyjazni 2-4, Wroclaw, 53 030, Poland. TEL 48-71-3397011, FAX 48-71-3397012. Ed. Wlodzimierz Kwas. Pub. Krzysztof Komar. Adv. contact Maciej Ignaczak. Circ: 50,000 (paid).

796.7 CZE ISSN 1210-1419
MOTOCYKL. Text in Czech. 1990. m. CZK 711 (effective 2009). adv. **Document type:** *Magazine, Consumer.*
Published by: Motor-Presse Bohemia, U Krcskeho Nadrazi 36, Prague 4, 14000, Czech Republic. TEL 420-2-24109340, FAX 420-2-41721905, motopresse@motorpresse.cz, http://www.motorpresse.cz. Ed. Richard Simer. Adv. contact Renata Ben. page CZK 55,000; trim 185 x 242. Circ: 17,000 (paid).

796.7 CZE ISSN 1214-6137
MOTOCYKL PRUVODCE. Text in Czech. 1996. a. CZK 229 per issue (effective 2009). adv. **Document type:** *Catalog, Consumer.*
Formerly (until 2004): Motocykl Katalog (1212-0537)
Published by: Motor-Presse Bohemia, U Krcskeho Nadrazi 36, Prague 4, 14000, Czech Republic. TEL 420-2-24109340, FAX 420-2-41721905, motopresse@motorpresse.cz, http://www.motorpresse.cz. Ed. Richard Simer. Adv. contact Renata Ben. Circ: 30,000 (paid).

629.118 POL ISSN 1426-2622
MOTOCYKLE KATALOG. Text in Polish. 1995. a. PLZ 19.50 newsstand/cover (effective 2001). adv. **Document type:** *Magazine, Consumer.*
Published by: Motor-Presse Polska, ul Przyjazni 2-4, Wroclaw, 53 030, Poland. TEL 48-71-3397011, FAX 48-71-3397012. Pub. Krzysztof Komar. Circ: 30,000 (paid).

796.7 USA
MOTOMAMA; magazine for biker chicks. Text in English. 1999. q. USD 20; USD 3.99 newsstand/cover (effective 2001). adv. **Document type:** *Magazine, Consumer.* **Description:** Contains articles, stories, photos and features devoted to motorcycles and the women who ride them.
Address: 452 W 19th St, Ste 1D, New York, NY 10011. TEL 646-486-1878. Ed. Jennifer Palmer.

796.7 BRA ISSN 1809-3825
MOTOMAX. Text in Portuguese. 2006. m. BRL 7.90 newsstand/cover (effective 2007). adv. **Document type:** *Magazine, Consumer.*
Published by: Editora Europa Ltda., Rua MMDC 121, Butanta, Sao Paulo, SP 05510-021, Brazil. TEL 55-11-30385050, FAX 55-11-38190538.

796.7 ITA ISSN 1824-7695
MOTOMONDIALE COLLECTION. Text in Italian. 2004. w. **Document type:** *Magazine, Consumer.*
Published by: R C S Libri (Subsidiary of: R C S Mediagroup), Via Mecenate 91, Milan, 20138, Italy. TEL 39-02-5095-2248, FAX 39-02-5095-2975, http://rcslibri.corriere.it/libri/index.htm.

MOTOR. *see* TRANSPORTATION—Air Transport

796.7 NLD ISSN 0027-1721
MOTOR. Text in Dutch. 1913. fortn. EUR 35 (effective 2008); EUR 3.95 newsstand/cover (effective 2007). adv. bk.rev. illus. **Document type:** *Magazine, Consumer.* **Description:** Publishes articles for motorcycle aficionados (all makes).
Incorporates (1979-1983): Motorvisie (0167-2886)
Related titles: Online - full text ed.
—IE.
Published by: (Koninklijke Nederlandse Motorrijders Vereniging/Royal Dutch Motorcycle Union), Sanoma Men's Magazines, Haaksbergweg 75, Amsterdam (ZO), 1101 BR, Netherlands. TEL 31-20-7518000, FAX 31-20-7518301, sales@smm.nl, http://www.smm.nl. adv.: B&W page EUR 1,605, color page EUR 3,210; trim 204 x 272. Circ: 28,310.

796.7 GBR ISSN 0027-1853
MOTOR CYCLE NEWS. Variant title: M C N. Text in English. 1952. w. GBP 120 domestic; GBP 176 in Europe; GBP 211 elsewhere (effective 2009). illus.; tr.lit. back issues avail. **Document type:** *Magazine, Consumer.* **Description:** Designed to inform, inspire, and educate bikers.
Related titles: Online - full text ed.
—CCC.
Published by: H. Bauer Publishing Ltd. (Subsidiary of: Bauer Media Group), Media House, Lynchwood, Peterborough, Cambridgeshire PE2 6EA, United Kingdom. TEL 44-1733-468000, http://www.bauer.co.uk. Ed. Marc Potter TEL 44-1733-468006. Adv. contact Sarah Nunn TEL 44-1733-468067. **Subscr. to:** Tower House, Sovereign Park, Market Harborough, Leicestershire LE16 9EF, United Kingdom. TEL 44-1858-438666, subs@greatmagazines.co.uk.

MOTOR JOURNAL; nestranny a nezavisly mesicnik vsech automobilistu a motocyklistu. *see* TRANSPORTATION—Automobiles

796.7 HUN ISSN 0865-7165
MOTOR KATALOGUS. Text in Hungarian. 1990. a., latest 2001. HUF 1,890 newsstand/cover (effective 2006). adv. 180 p./no.; back issues avail. **Document type:** *Magazine, Consumer.*
Published by: Motor-Presse Budapest Lapkiado kft, Hajogyari-sziget 307, Budapest, 1033, Hungary. TEL 36-1-4369244, FAX 36-1-4369248, mpb@motorpresse.hu, http://www.motorpresse.hu. Ed. Imre Paulovits. Pub. Dietmar Metzger. Adv. contact Andrea Poz. Circ: 25,000 (paid). **Dist. by:** Lapker Rt, 1097 Tablas utca, Budapest, Hungary.

796.7 HUN ISSN 0865-4131
MOTOR REVUE. Text in Hungarian. 1989. m. HUF 8,340; HUF 729 newsstand/cover (effective 2006). adv. 64 p./no.; **Document type:** *Magazine, Consumer.*
Published by: Motor-Presse Budapest Lapkiado kft, Hajogyari-sziget 307, Budapest, 1033, Hungary. TEL 36-1-4369244, FAX 36-1-4369248, mpb@motorpresse.hu, http://www.motorpresse.hu. Ed. Imre Paulovits. Pub. Dietmar Metzger. Adv. contacts Andrea Poz, Dietmar Metzger. Circ: 30,000 (paid).

796.77 DEU
MOTOR ROLLER KATALOG. Text in German. a. EUR 4.95 newsstand/cover (effective 2007). **Document type:** *Magazine, Consumer.*
Published by: Motoretta Verlagsgesellschaft mbH, Wickingstr 3a, Recklinghausen, 45657, Germany. TEL 49-2361-93580, FAX 49-2361-16495. adv.: B&W page EUR 2,000, color page EUR 3,565. Circ: 59,000 (paid and controlled).

388.347 796.7 ITA ISSN 1128-6210
MOTOR SUPER MARKET. Text in Italian. 1998. m. **Document type:** *Magazine, Consumer.*

S

Published by: Edizeta Srl, Via Lussinpiccolo 19, Mestre, VE 30174, Italy. TEL 39-041-5459500, FAX 39-041-5459555, redazione@edizeta.com, http://www.edizeta.it.

796.7 796.6 DNK ISSN 0107-7554
MOTORBLADET; officielt organ for DMU. Text in Danish. 1921. 10/yr. DKK 370 (effective 2008). adv. **Document type:** *Magazine, Consumer.*
Former titles (until 1951): Motor og Sport; (until 1946): Motorbladet
Published by: Danmarks Motor Union, Idraettens Hus, Broendby Stadion 20, Broendby, 2605, Denmark. TEL 45-43-262613, FAX 45-43-262615, dmu@dmusport.dk, http://www.dmusport.dk. Ed. Kenneth Majkjaer Mikkelsen. adv.: B&W page DKK 4,725, color page DKK 7,675; 190 x 269. Circ: 8,400.

380.1 USA ISSN 0091-3774
HD9710.5.U5
MOTORCYCLE BLUE BOOK. Variant title: Hap Jones Motorcycle Blue Book. Text in English. 1952. s-a. USD 22 (effective 2001). **Document type:** *Magazine, Trade.*
Address: 1040 Rock Ave, San Jose, CA 95131. TEL 408-432-1918, FAX 408-432-1926. Ed. Walter Buntin. Pub. Hap Jones. R&P Jackie Provost.

796.7 USA ISSN 1556-0880
MOTORCYCLE CLASSICS; ride 'em, don't hide 'em. Text in English. 2005 (Aug.). bi-m. USD 24.95 domestic; USD 34.95 in Canada; USD 39.95 elsewhere (effective 2008). adv. **Document type:** *Magazine, Consumer.* **Description:** Features exciting and evocative articles and photographs of the most brilliant, unusual and popular motorcycles ever made.
Published by: Ogden Publications, 1503 S W 42nd St, Topeka, KS 66609. TEL 785-274-4300, http://www.ogdenpubs.com. Ed. Richard Backus. Pub. Bryan Welch. adv.: B&W page USD 2,502, color page USD 3,575; trim 8.125 x 10.875. Circ: 35,547 (paid and controlled).

796.7 USA ISSN 1073-9408
TL440.5
MOTORCYCLE CONSUMER NEWS. Abbreviated title: M C N. Text in English. 1969. m. USD 22 domestic; USD 40 foreign (effective 2008). adv. bk.rev. illus. index. back issues avail.; reprints avail. **Document type:** *Newsletter, Consumer.* **Description:** Provides in-depth reporting for all types of riders. Covers cruisers, sportbikes, and sport tourers. Features product tests, model evaluations, riding tips, consumer issues and technical information.
Former titles (until 1994): Road Rider's Motorcycle Consumer News (1067-8697); (until 1993): Road Rider (0035-7243); (until 1970); Road Rider News (0161-4509)
Related titles: Online - full text ed.
Published by: BowTie, Inc., 2401 Beverly Blvd, PO Box 57900, Los Angeles, CA 90057. TEL 213-385-2222, FAX 213-385-8565, http://www.bowtieinc.com. Ed. Dave Searle. Pub. Norman Ridker. Circ: 60,000 (paid).

796.7 USA ISSN 1525-772X
MOTORCYCLE CRUISER. Variant title: Cruiser. Text in English. 1996. 8/yr. USD 14.97 domestic; USD 13.97 in Canada; USD 19.97 elsewhere (effective 2008). adv. back issues avail. **Document type:** *Magazine, Consumer.* **Description:** Contains information for people who enjoy classically styled bikes of all brands.
Indexed: G06, G07, G08, I05, S23.
—CCC.
Published by: Source Interlink Companies, 6420 Wilshire Blvd, 10th Fl, Los Angeles, CA 90048. TEL 323-782-2000, FAX 323-782-2585, dheine@sourceinterlink.com, http://www.sourceinterlinkmedia.com. Ed. Andrew Cherney. Pub. Marty Estes TEL 323-782-2489. adv.: B&W page USD 6,325, color page USD 9,440. Circ: 49,359 (paid).

796.75 ZAF ISSN 0258-5073
MOTORCYCLE DEALERS' GUIDE. Text in English. 1979. bi-m. ZAR 409.72. **Document type:** *Handbook/Manual/Guide, Trade.* **Description:** Provides trade and retail values of used motorcycles traded throughout South Africa.
Published by: Mead & McGrouther (Pty) Ltd., PO Box 1240, Randburg, Gauteng 2125, South Africa. TEL 27-11-789-3213, FAX 27-11-789-5218. adv.: B&W page ZAR 700, color page ZAR 1,150. Circ: 565.

796.7 USA ISSN 1099-0100
MOTORCYCLE EVENTS MAGAZINE. Text in English. 1998. s-a. USD 8.95 domestic; USD 12.95 in Canada; USD 16.50 elsewhere (effective 2002). adv. **Document type:** *Magazine, Consumer.* **Description:** Covers more than 300 motorcycle events in each issue for motorcyclists (street bike owners of all brands) that love to travel.
Published by: Motorcycle Events Association, Inc., 303 East Sioux Ave, PO Box 100, Pierre, SD 57501. TEL 605-224-8898, 800-675-4856, FAX 605-224-2063, info@motocycleevents.com. Ed. Mary Beth Crowe. Pub. Tom Roberts. adv.: B&W page USD 3,000, color page USD 5,000, online banner USD 450; trim 8.375 x 10.875. Circ: 60,000 (controlled).

796.7 687 338 GBR ISSN 1476-8747
MOTORCYCLE FASHION. Text in English. 2002. q. free to qualified personnel (effective 2009). back issues avail. **Document type:** *Magazine, Trade.* **Description:** Aims to help dealers to better market the product lines the stock, to help them add value to existing clothing and helmet sales, and through comprehensive information provision help them to select new brands, suppliers or products suitable for their local customer base.
Published by: Dealer-World.com, Kenwood House, 1 Upper Grosvenor Rd, Turnbridge Wells, TN1 2DU, United Kingdom. TEL 44-1892-511516, FAX 44-1892-511517, http://www.dealer-world.com/.

796.7 USA ISSN 0884-626X
MOTORCYCLE INDUSTRY MAGAZINE. Text in English. 1980. m. USD 180 foreign; free in US & Canada to qualified personnel (effective 2007). adv. bk.rev. 120 p./no.; back issues avail.; reprints avail. **Document type:** *Magazine, Trade.* **Description:** Contains columns and features that will inform, educate and entertain those who earn their living in the motorcycle industry.
Former titles: Motorcycle Industry Shopper (0274-5437); Motorcycle Industry Magazine
Published by: Industry Shopper Publishing, Inc., 1521 Church St., Gardnerville, NV 89410. TEL 775-782-0222, FAX 775-782-0266. Ed., Pub., R&P, Adv. contact Rick Campbell. B&W page USD 2,970, color page USD 4,245. Circ: 13,200 (controlled).

MOTORCYCLE JAPAN; annual guide to Japan's motorcycle industry. *see* TRANSPORTATION

796.7 GBR ISSN 1754-6478
MOTORCYCLE MONTHLY. Text in English. 2006. m. GBP 12 domestic; GBP 18 in Europe; GBP 23 elsewhere (effective 2009). adv. **Document type:** *Magazine, Consumer.* **Description:** Written by enthusiasts for enthusiasts and puts emphasis on real stories about real bikers.
Published by: Mortons Media Group Ltd., Media Centre, Morton Way, Horncastle, Lincs LN9 6JR, United Kingdom. TEL 44-1507-529529, FAX 44-1507-529490, mortons@mortons.co.uk, http://www.mortonsmediagroup.com/. Ed. Brian Tarbox TEL 44-1507-529529. Adv. contact Lee Buxton TEL 44-1507-524004.

796.7 USA
MOTORCYCLE ONLINE. Text in English. m.
Media: Online - full text.

796.7 USA ISSN 0164-8349
MOTORCYCLE PRODUCT NEWS. Variant title: M P N. Text in English. 1974. m. USD 15 in US & Canada includes Mexico; USD 130 elsewhere; USD 8 per issue (effective 2008). adv. illus. 100 p./no. 3 cols./p.; Supplement avail.; back issues avail.; reprints avail. **Document type:** *Magazine, Trade.* **Description:** Serves the trade selling, servicing, manufacturing, distributing, importing and exporting of motorcycles, motorscooters, mopeds, ATV's, personal watercraft, and parts and accessories.
Published by: Athletic Business Publications, Inc., 4130 Lien Rd, Madison, WI 53704-3602. TEL 608-249-0186, 800-722-8764, FAX 608-249-1153, http://www.athleticbusiness.com. Adv. contact Chad Wiggen TEL 866-616-1635 ext 129. B&W page USD 3,205, color page USD 4,370; trim 8.25 x 10.875. Circ: 17,250.

MOTORCYCLE PRODUCT NEWS TRADE DIRECTORY. *see* BUSINESS AND ECONOMICS—Trade And Industrial Directories

629.227 GBR ISSN 2042-5279
▼ **MOTORCYCLE RACE TECHNOLOGY.** Text in English. 2009. triennial. GBP 20 per issue domestic; GBP 24 per issue in Europe; GBP 25 per issue in US & Canada; GBP 26 per issue elsewhere (effective 2010). **Document type:** *Magazine, Trade.* **Description:** Features input from leading designers and race engineers this report presents a unique look at the engineering and mechanics of contemporary motorcycle road-race bikes.
Published by: High Power Media Ltd., Whitfield House, Cheddar Rd, Wedmore, Somerset BS28 4EJ, United Kingdom. TEL 44-1934-713811, FAX 44-208-4972102, info@highpowermedia.com.

388.347 USA
MOTORCYCLE SAFETY FOUNDATION. Text in English. q. **Document type:** *Magazine, Consumer.*
Address: 2 Jenner St, Ste 150, Irvine, CA 92718-3812. TEL 949-727-3227, FAX 949-727-3313.

796.7 USA ISSN 1075-2447
MOTORCYCLE SHOPPER. Text in English. 1990. m. USD 19.95; USD 42 in Canada & Mexico; USD 60 elsewhere. adv. bk.rev. **Document type:** *Magazine, Consumer.* **Description:** Marketplace for buyers, sellers and rebuilders of motorcycles of every make and model, including vintage, stock and custom.
Related titles: Online - full text ed.
Published by: Payne Corp., 243 River Village Dr., Debary, FL 32713-4006. TEL 407-860-1989, 800-982-4599, FAX 407-574-1014. Pub. Luis Hernandez Jr. adv.: B&W page USD 102,375; trim 10.75 x 8.13. Circ: 45,000 (paid).

796.7 GBR ISSN 1478-839X
MOTORCYCLE SPORT & LEISURE. Text in English. 1962. m. GBP 36 domestic; GBP 44 in Europe; GBP 56 elsewhere; GBP 3.75 per issue (effective 2009). adv. bk.rev. illus. back issues avail. **Document type:** *Magazine, Consumer.* **Description:** Explores the joys of owning and riding a motorcycle.
Incorporates (in Apr. 1999): Motorcycle Review (0956-1285); Motorcyclist Illustrated (0027-187X); (in 1997): Motorcyclist International (0268-7151); Supersedes (in 1996): Motorcycle Sport (0955-9116)
Indexed: BrTechI, E11, T04.
Published by: Mortons Media Group Ltd., Media Centre, Morton Way, Horncastle, Lincs LN9 6JR, United Kingdom. TEL 44-1507-529529, FAX 44-1507-529490, http://www.mortonsmediagroup.com/. Ed. Tony Carter TEL 44-1507-529529. Circ: 17,500. **Subscr. in the US to:** Motorsport, 7164 Cty Rd N #441, Bancroft, WI 54921. **Dist. by:** Comag, Tavistock Rd, W Drayton, Middlesex UB7 7QE, United Kingdom. TEL 44-1895-433600, http://www.comag.co.uk.

629.227 CAN ISSN 1924-2018
▼ **THE MOTORCYCLE TIMES.** Text in English. 2009. 10/yr. USD 11.50 in state; USD 15.50 in Canada; USD 22.50 in United States (effective 2010). adv. back issues avail. **Document type:** *Magazine, Trade.* **Description:** About the passion for riding and life experience on two wheels.
Formerly (until 2010): The Motorcycle News (1921-5525)
Related titles: Online - full text ed.: free (effective 2010).
Published by: Advantage Media, 105 W 25th St, Hamilton, ON L9C 4X3, Canada. TEL 905-962-1890. Ed. Tim Shamess. Adv. contact Laura McDonald.

796.7 NZL ISSN 1174-2747
MOTORCYCLE TRADER & NEWS. Text in English. 1997. fortn. NZD 60 (effective 2008). adv. **Document type:** *Magazine, Consumer.* **Description:** Features the latest bike releases and reports from around the world, as well as road tests of bikes available on the local market. All aspects of motorcycling are featured, including road racing, classic bikes, motocross and all off-road activity.
Published by: A C P Media New Zealand (Subsidiary of: A C P Magazines Ltd.), Private Bag 92512, Auckland, 1036, New Zealand. TEL 64-9-3082700, FAX 64-9-3082878, http://www.acpmedia.co.nz/. Adv. contact Cameron Mills.

796.7 GRC
MOTORCYCLE WORLD. Text in Greek. 1992. a. adv. mkt.; illus. back issues avail. **Document type:** *Magazine, Consumer.* **Description:** Contains a market guide to motorcycles and accessories.
Published by: Technical Press SA, 80 Ioannou Metaxa, Karelas, Koropi, 19400, Greece. TEL 30-210-9792500, FAX 30-210-9792528, info@technicalpress.gr, http://www.technicalpress.gr. Circ: 10,000 (paid).

796.7 USA ISSN 0027-2205
TL1
MOTORCYCLIST. Text in English. 1912. m. USD 10 domestic; USD 22 in Canada; USD 34 elsewhere (effective 2008). adv. bk.rev. illus. back issues avail. **Document type:** *Magazine, Consumer.* **Description:** Provides technical how-to stories, riding tips and useful gear information to professional bike-buying advice, specifications and prices on various machines.
Incorporates (1970-1988): Motorcycle Buyer's Guide (0077-1678)
Related titles: Online - full text ed.
Indexed: A22, ConsI, G05, G06, G07, G08, I05, I06, I07, IHTDI, S23, SportS.
—Ingenta. **CCC.**
Published by: Source Interlink Companies, 6420 Wilshire Blvd, 10th Fl, Los Angeles, CA 90048. TEL 323-782-2000, FAX 323-782-2585, dheine@sourceinterlink.com, http://www.sourceinterlinkmedia.com. Eds. Brian Catterson, Mitch Boehm. Pub. Marty Estes TEL 323-782-2489. adv.: page USD 32,810. Circ: 239,388 (paid).

796.75 USA ISSN 1946-9780
TL1
MOTORCYCLIST RETRO. Text in English. 2008. irreg. **Document type:** *Magazine, Consumer.*
Published by: Source Interlink Media, LLC, 6420 Wilshire Blvd, 10th Fl, Los Angeles, CA 90048. TEL 323-782-2000, FAX 323-782-2585, http://www.sourceinterlinkmedia.com.

796.7 USA ISSN 0164-9256
MOTORCYCLIST'S POST. Text in English. 1967. m. USD 25 (effective 2005). adv. bk.rev. back issues avail. **Document type:** *Newspaper, Consumer.*
Published by: Motorcyclists Post Publishing Co., c/o Leo Castell, 11 Haven Ln, Huntington, CT 06484. TEL 203-929-9409, FAX 203-926-9347. Ed., R&P, Adv. contact Leo P Castell. Circ: 9,895.

796.77 DEU ISSN 1610-5125
MOTORETTA. Text in German. 19??. 8/yr. EUR 18; EUR 3 newsstand/cover (effective 2007). adv. **Document type:** *Magazine, Consumer.*
Formerly (until 2002): Motoretta Scooter Magazine (1619-5949)
Published by: Motoretta Verlagsgesellschaft mbH, Wickingstr 3a, Recklinghausen, 45657, Germany. TEL 49-2361-93580, FAX 49-2361-16495. adv.: B&W page EUR 2,135, color page EUR 3,805. Circ: 61,000 (paid and controlled).

796.7 CZE ISSN 1801-0997
MOTOROUTE MAGAZIN. Text in Czech. 2005. bi-m. CZK 342 (effective 2009). adv. **Document type:** *Magazine, Consumer.*
Address: Tr T Bati 3761, Zlin, 760 01, Czech Republic. TEL 420-575-759871, FAX 420-575-759872. Ed. Ivo Klasek. Adv. contact Iveta Mackova.

388.3 DEU ISSN 0027-237X
DAS MOTORRAD. Text in German. 1903. fortn. EUR 93.80; EUR 3.50 newsstand/cover (effective 2008). adv. bk.rev. illus. **Document type:** *Magazine, Consumer.*
Indexed: RefZh.
Published by: Motor Presse Stuttgart GmbH und Co. KG, Leuschnerstr 1, Stuttgart, 70174, Germany. TEL 49-711-18201, FAX 49-711-1821779, cgolla@motorpresse.de, http://www.motorpresse.de. Ed. Michael Pfeiffer. Pub. Paul Pietsch. Adv. contact Sven Damson. color page EUR 16,100; trim 185 x 248. Circ: 139,664 (paid and controlled).

796.7 CHE
MOTORRAD. Text in German. 24/yr.
Address: Villa Mueslischreck, Dietwil, 6042, Switzerland. TEL 041-912950. Ed. Alfred Wepf. Circ: 25,000.

796.7 DEU ISSN 1619-4462
MOTORRAD ABENTEUER; das Reportage-Magazin. Text in German. 1997. bi-m. EUR 21.60; EUR 4.90 newsstand/cover (effective 2011). adv. **Document type:** *Magazine, Consumer.*
Formerly (until 1999): On Rout' (1434-2162)
Published by: Reiner H. Nitschke Verlags GmbH, Eifelring 28, Euskirchen, 53879, Germany. TEL 49-2251-650460, FAX 49-2251-6504699, service@nitschke-verlag.de, http://www.nitschke-verlag.de.

MOTORRAD ADRESSBUCH. *see* BUSINESS AND ECONOMICS—Trade And Industrial Directories

796.7 DEU ISSN 0937-9495
MOTORRAD CLASSIC. Text in German. 1987. bi-m. EUR 5.50 newsstand/cover (effective 2007). adv. illus. **Document type:** *Magazine, Consumer.*
Published by: Motor Presse Stuttgart GmbH und Co. KG, Leuschnerstr 1, Stuttgart, 70174, Germany. TEL 49-711-18201, FAX 49-711-1821779, cgolla@motorpresse.de, http://www.motorpresse.de. Ed. Michael Pfeiffer. Pub. Peter Paul Pietsch. Adv. contact Claus Schlosser. color page EUR 6,100; trim 185 x 248. Circ: 24,125 (paid and controlled).

796.7 AUT
MOTORRAD HAENDLER. Text in German. 8/yr. EUR 52 domestic; EUR 48 in Germany; EUR 56 in Europe; EUR 64 elsewhere (effective 2006). adv. **Document type:** *Magazine, Trade.*
Published by: Rede & Antwort Verlag und Handels GmbH, Hauptplatz 3, Neulengbach, 3040, Austria. TEL 43-2772-568230, FAX 43-2772-568235. Ed. Immo Dubies. adv.: B&W page EUR 2,700, color page EUR 3,000; trim 210 x 297. Circ: 9,773 (paid and controlled).

796.7 DEU
MOTORRAD HANDEL. Text in German. 1996. m. EUR 34.80; EUR 2.90 newsstand/cover (effective 2008). adv. **Document type:** *Magazine, Consumer.*
Published by: A M O Verlag GmbH, Sattlerstr 7, Luebeck, 23556, Germany. TEL 49-1805-151165, FAX 49-190-151050, info@amo-verlag.de, http://www.amo-verlag.de. Ed. Juergen Koslowski. adv.: B&W page EUR 400, color page EUR 500; trim 204 x 270.

796.7 DEU ISSN 0949-0892
MOTORRAD KATALOG. Text in German. 1970. a. EUR 8.50 newsstand/cover (effective 2007). adv. illus. **Document type:** *Magazine, Consumer.*
Published by: Motor Presse Stuttgart GmbH und Co. KG, Leuschnerstr 1, Stuttgart, 70174, Germany. TEL 49-711-18201, FAX 49-711-1821779, cgolla@motorpresse.de, http://www.motorpresse.de. Ed. Michael Pfeiffer. Pub. Peter Paul Pietsch. Adv. contact Marcus Schardt. color page EUR 10,800; trim 185 x 248. Circ: 150,000 (controlled).

796.7 DEU
MOTORRAD KONTAKTE. Text in German. 1999. m. EUR 19.20 (effective 2011). adv. **Document type:** *Magazine, Consumer.*
Published by: Syburger Verlag GmbH, Hertingerstr 60, Unna, 59423, Germany. TEL 49-2303-98550, FAX 49-2303-98559, info@syburger.de, http://www.syburger.de. Circ: 20,000 (paid and controlled).

796.7 DEU ISSN 0723-2616
MOTORRAD MAGAZIN M O. Text in German. 1978. m. EUR 39.80 domestic; EUR 46.50 foreign; EUR 3.90 newsstand/cover (effective 2007). adv. back issues avail. **Document type:** *Magazine, Consumer.*
Former titles (until 1982): Mofa, Motorrad, Test, Sport (0722-3196); (until 1981): Motorrad, Mokick, Mofa und Sport (0172-1410)
Published by: Mo Medien Verlag GmbH, Bopserstr 2, Stuttgart, 70180, Germany. Eds. Jochen Soppa, Wolf Martin Riedel. Pub. Andreas Illg. R&P Jochen Soppa. adv.: B&W page EUR 4,250, color page EUR 7,140. Circ: 41,287 (paid and controlled).

796.7 DEU
MOTORRAD MARKT. Text in German. 1991. m. EUR 34.80; EUR 2.90 newsstand/cover (effective 2008). adv. **Document type:** *Magazine, Consumer.*
Published by: A M O Verlag GmbH, Sattlerstr 7, Luebeck, 23556, Germany. TEL 49-1805-151165, FAX 49-190-151050, info@amo-verlag.de, http://www.amo-verlag.de. Ed. Juergen Koslowski. adv.: B&W page EUR 400, color page EUR 500; trim 204 x 270.

796.7 DEU
MOTORRAD NEWS; das Nachrichten-Magazin: Test, Technik, Szene, Regionales, Reise. Text in German. 1993. m. EUR 21 domestic; EUR 27 foreign; EUR 1.95 newsstand/cover (effective 2011). adv. **Document type:** *Magazine, Consumer.*
Published by: Syburger Verlag GmbH, Hertingerstr 60, Unna, 59423, Germany. TEL 49-2303-98550, FAX 49-2303-98559, info@syburger.de, http://www.syburger.de. Adv. contact Jessica Kwasny.

796.7 DEU
MOTORRAD OLDTIMER KATALOG; Europas groesster Marktfuehrer fuer Motorrad-Veteranen. Text in German. 1988. irreg., latest vol.12, 2010. EUR 14.95 (effective 2010). back issues avail. **Document type:** *Catalog, Consumer.*
Published by: Heel-Verlag GmbH, Gut Pottscheidt, Koenigswinter, 53639, Germany. TEL 49-2223-92300, FAX 49-2223-92301326, info@heel-verlag.de, http://www.heel-verlag.de. Ed. Guido Saliger. Pub. Franz Christoph Heel. R&P Karin Michelberger. Adv. contact Sabine Bluem.

796.7 DEU
MOTORRAD SPIEGEL; das Baden-Wuerttemberger Motorrad Magazin. Text in German. 1986. m. EUR 19.20 (effective 2011). adv. **Document type:** *Magazine, Consumer.*
Published by: Syburger Verlag GmbH, Hertingerstr 60, Unna, 59423, Germany. TEL 49-2303-98550, FAX 49-2303-98559, info@syburger.de, http://www.syburger.de. Ed. Erik Foerster. Adv. contact Jessica Kwasny.

796.7 DEU
MOTORRAD SZENE; das Magazin der Motorradfahrer. Text in German. 1988. m. EUR 19.20 (effective 2011). adv. **Document type:** *Magazine, Consumer.*
Published by: Syburger Verlag GmbH, Hertingerstr 60, Unna, 59423, Germany. TEL 49-2303-98550, FAX 49-2303-98559, info@syburger.de, http://www.syburger.de. Ed. Erik Foerster. Adv. contact Jessica Kwasny.

796.7 DEU
▼ **MOTORRAD-SZENE OESTERREICH.** Text in German. 2010. m. EUR 32.40; free newsstand/cover (effective 2011). adv. **Document type:** *Magazine, Consumer.*
Published by: Syburger Verlag GmbH, Hertingerstr 60, Unna, 59423, Germany. TEL 49-2303-98550, FAX 49-2303-98559, info@syburger.de, http://www.syburger.de. Ed. Erik Foerster. Adv. contact Jessica Kwasny.

796.75 DEU
MOTORRAD TEST (YEAR); Katalog. Text in German. 1983. a. EUR 4.90 newsstand/cover (effective 2007). adv. **Document type:** *Magazine, Consumer.*
Published by: Mo Medien Verlag GmbH, Schrempfstr 8, Stuttgart, 70597, Germany. TEL 49-711-24897600, FAX 49-711-24897628, redaktion@mo-web.de, http://www.mo-web.de. adv.: B&W page EUR 4,250, color page EUR 7,140. Circ: 48,000 (controlled).

796.7 DEU
MOTORRAD TREFF; das Magazin fuer Sachsen-Anhalt und Thueringen. Text in German. 1990. m. EUR 19.20 (effective 2011). adv. **Document type:** *Magazine, Consumer.*
Published by: Syburger Verlag GmbH, Hertingerstr 60, Unna, 59423, Germany. TEL 49-2303-98550, FAX 49-2303-98559, info@syburger.de, http://www.syburger.de. Ed. Erik Foerster. Adv. contact Jessica Kwasny.

796.7 DEU
MOTORRAD UND REISEN. Text in German. 2003. bi-m. EUR 10; EUR 1.95 newsstand/cover (effective 2009). adv. **Document type:** *Magazine, Consumer.*
Formerly (until 2007): MotoRoute
Address: Obere Harzstr 28, Osterode, 37520, Germany. TEL 49-5522-506485.

796.75 DEU ISSN 0935-7645
MOTORRADFAHRER; Test und Technik fuer die Praxis. Text in German. 1988. m. EUR 21.60; EUR 2 newsstand/cover (effective 2011). adv. **Document type:** *Magazine, Consumer.*
Published by: Reiner H. Nitschke Verlags GmbH, Eifelring 28, Euskirchen, 53879, Germany. TEL 49-2251-650460, FAX 49-2251-6504699, service@nitschke-verlag.de, http://www.nitschke-verlag.de. Ed. Guido Saliger. Adv. contact Martina Jonas.

388.3 DEU
MOTORRADMAGAZIN. Text in German. d. adv. **Document type:** *Consumer.* **Description:** Provides the latest information and news concerning motorcycles and related products.
Media: Online - full text.
Published by: Spessartweb Online Verlag, Buettnerstr 15, Triefenstein, 97855, Germany. TEL 49-9395-997914, FAX 49-9395-997915, verlag@motorradmagazin.de, info@spessartweb.de, http://www.spessartweb.de. Eds. Claudia Sollinger, Markus Sollinger. Pub. Petra Witzl. Adv. contact Markus Sollinger.

796.7 AUT
MOTORRADMAGAZIN. Text in German. 1995. 11/yr. EUR 29 (effective 2008). adv. bk.rev. back issues avail. **Document type:** *Magazine, Consumer.*
Published by: Sportverlag GmbH & Co. KG (Subsidiary of: Styria Medien AG), Kaiserstr 113-115, Vienna, W 1070, Austria. TEL 43-1-360850, FAX 43-1-36085200, office@vsm.at, http://www.vsm.at. Ed. Michael Bernleitner. Adv. contact Beate Kloda. color page EUR 5,600; trim 185 x 280. Circ: 32,000 (paid and controlled).

796.7 DEU
MOTORRADSZENE BAYERN. Text in German. 1989. m. EUR 19.20 (effective 2011). adv. **Document type:** *Magazine, Consumer.*
Published by: Syburger Verlag GmbH, Hertingerstr 60, Unna, 59423, Germany. TEL 49-2303-98550, FAX 49-2303-98559, info@syburger.de, http://www.syburger.de. Ed. Erik Foerster. Adv. contact Jessica Kwasny.

796.7 DEU
MOTORRADTREFF SPINNER; das Motorradmagazin fuer Berlin, Brandenburg und Mecklenburg. Text in German. 1990. m. EUR 19.20 (effective 2011). adv. **Document type:** *Magazine, Consumer.*
Published by: Syburger Verlag GmbH, Hertingerstr 60, Unna, 59423, Germany. TEL 49-2303-98550, FAX 49-2303-98559, info@syburger.de, http://www.syburger.de. Ed. Erik Foerster. Adv. contact Jessica Kwasny.

796.7 DEU
MOTORRAEDER. Text in German. 1992. a. EUR 6.80 newsstand/cover (effective 2011). adv. **Document type:** *Magazine, Consumer.*
Published by: Syburger Verlag GmbH, Hertingerstr 60, Unna, 59423, Germany. TEL 49-2303-98550, FAX 49-2303-98559, info@syburger.de, http://www.syburger.de.

796.7 DEU
MOTORRAEDER AUS ITALIEN. Text in German. a. EUR 6.20 newsstand/cover (effective 2007). adv. **Document type:** *Magazine, Consumer.*
Published by: Mo Medien Verlag GmbH, Schrempfstr 8, Stuttgart, 70597, Germany. TEL 49-711-24897600, FAX 49-711-24897628, redaktion@mo-web.de, http://www.mo-web.de. adv.: B&W page EUR 3,655, color page EUR 6,140. Circ: 21,000 (controlled).

796.7 CHE ISSN 1421-8488
MOTORSPORT AKTUELL. Text and summaries in German. 1963. w. EUR 2 newsstand/cover (effective 2007). adv. bk.rev. **Document type:** *Magazine, Consumer.* **Description:** Provides the "fastest" newspaper on motorsports in German speaking countries with all international and national car and motorcycle race series.
Formerly (until 1976): Powerslide (0032-6097)
Published by: Motor-Presse (Schweiz) AG, Bahnstr 24, Schwerzenbach, 8603, Switzerland. TEL 41-44-8065555, FAX 41-44-8065500, verlag@motorpresse.ch, http://www.motorpresse.ch. Ed. Guenther Wiesinger. Pub. August Hug. Adv. contact Stephen Brand. color page EUR 6,900; trim 206 x 291. Circ: 93,117 (paid).

796.75 GBR
MOTORSPORT NEWS. Text in English. 1955. w. GBP 89.25 (effective 2009). adv. **Document type:** *Newspaper, Consumer.* **Description:** Provides up-to-date, entertaining and reliable news, reports and results from all areas of motorsport.
Published by: Haymarket Publishing Ltd. (Subsidiary of: Haymarket Media Group), Teddington Studios, Broom Rd, Teddington, Middlesex, TW11 9BE, United Kingdom. TEL 44-20-82675630, FAX 44-20-82675759, info@haymarket.com, http://www.haymarket.com. Ed. Matt Burt TEL 44-20-82675363. Pub. Rob Aherne TEL 44-20-82675428. Adv. contact Simon Grayson TEL 44-20-82675389. Circ: 18,206. **Subscr. to:** PO Box 568, Haywards Heath RH16 3XQ, United Kingdom. TEL 44-8456-777800, Haymarket.subs@qss-uk.com, http://www.themagazineshop.com.

796.75 USA
MOTORSPORTS SPONSORSHIP MARKETING NEWS. Text in English. 1985. m. USD 89.95 domestic; USD 99.95 foreign (effective 2006). adv. 8 p./no. 2 cols./p.; **Document type:** *Newsletter.*
Published by: Ernie Saxton Communications, Inc., 1448 Hollywood Ave., Langhorne, PA 19047. TEL 215-752-7797, FAX 215-752-1518. Ed. Marilyn Saxton. adv.: page USD 500.

388.347 796.7 ITA ISSN 1122-1739
MOTOSPRINT. Text in Italian. 1976. w. (51/yr.). bk.rev. **Document type:** *Magazine, Consumer.*
Published by: Conti Editore SpA, Via del Lavoro 7, San Lazzaro di Savena, BO 40068, Italy. http://www.contieditore.it. Ed. Tommaso Valentinetti. Circ: 51,522.

629.227 ITA
MOTOTECNICA. Variant title: Super Moto Tecnica. Text in Italian, English. 1985. m. EUR 55 domestic (effective 2009). Website rev. 120 p./no.; back issues avail. **Document type:** *Magazine, Trade.* **Description:** Devoted to motorcycles. Intended for enthusiasts, collectors and dealers of classic motorcycles.
Formerly: Super MotoTecnica (1121-3892)
Published by: Nuovi Periodici Milanesi, Via Molise 3, Locate Triulzi, MI 20085, Italy. http://www.nuoviperiodicimilanesi.com. Circ: 65,000 (paid).

796.7 ITA ISSN 1128-3947
MOTOTURISMO; il piacere di andare in moto. Text in Italian. 1987. m. (10/yr.). EUR 34 domestic; EUR 60 in Europe; EUR 78 elsewhere (effective 2009). bk.rev. **Document type:** *Magazine, Consumer.* **Description:** Covers footage on motorcycle trips, history of motorbikes and includes information on organized tours for motorcyclists.
Related titles: Online - full text ed.
Published by: Editrice l'Isola, Casella Postale 65, Como, CO 22100, Italy. TEL 39-031-937736, FAX 39-031-937362. Circ: 45,000.

796.7 CHN ISSN 1002-6754
MOTUO CHE/MOTORCYCLE. Text in Chinese. 1985. m. USD 49.20 (effective 2009). **Document type:** *Consumer.*
Related titles: Online - full text ed.
—East View.
Published by: Renmin Youdian Chubanshe/People's Posts and Telecommunications Publishing House, 14 A Xizhaosi Street, Chongwen District, Beijing, 100061, China. TEL 86-10-67929931, abc@ptpress.com.cn. Ed. Yu Xiaochuan.

796.6 DEU ISSN 0946-2996
MOUNTAIN BIKE. Text in German. 1993. m. EUR 49.50; EUR 4.50 newsstand/cover (effective 2011). adv. **Document type:** *Magazine, Consumer.* **Description:** Presents new products, practical tests, repair tips, riding techniques, and the best trails.
Related titles: Online - full text ed.; ◆ Supplement(s): Mountain Bike Touren-Special. ISSN 1860-1715.
Published by: Motor Presse Stuttgart GmbH & Co. KG (Subsidiary of: Gruner + Jahr AG & Co), Leuschnerstr 1, Stuttgart, 70174, Germany. TEL 49-711-18201, FAX 49-711-1821779, cgolla@motorpresse.de, http://www.motorpresse.de. Ed. Jens Voegele. Adv. contact Bernd Holzhauer. Circ: 62,494 (paid).

796 USA ISSN 0895-8467
TL410.
MOUNTAIN BIKE ACTION. Text in English. 1986. m. USD 19.99 domestic; USD 34.99 in Canada; USD 44.99 elsewhere (effective 2009). adv. 140 p./no.; back issues avail. **Document type:** *Magazine, Consumer.* **Description:** Features the latest new bike tests, product and equipment tests and travel features.
Published by: Hi-Torque Publications, Inc., 25233 Anza Dr, Valencia, CA 91355. TEL 661-295-1910, http://www.mbaction.com/. Adv. contact Jennifer Edmonston TEL 661-367-2143.

796.6 ITA ISSN 1970-027X
MOUNTAIN BIKE ACTION. Text in Italian. 2006. m. EUR 46.50 domestic; EUR 86.50 in Europe (effective 2009). adv. **Document type:** *Magazine, Consumer.*
Published by: G P R Publishing s.a.s., Via Toniolo 1, Treviso, 31100, Italy. TEL 39-0422-543351, FAX 39-0422-549159, info@gprpublishing.com.

796.6 ISR
MOUNTAIN BIKE ACTION (TEL AVIV). Short title: M B A. Text in Hebrew. 2005. m. ILS 365 (effective 2008). **Document type:** *Magazine, Consumer.*
Related titles: Online - full text ed.: ILS 180 (effective 2008).
Published by: S B C Group, 8 Shefa Tal St., Tel Aviv, 67013, Israel. TEL 972-3-565-2100, FAX 972-3-562-6476, sherut@sbc.co.il, http://www.sbc.co.il/Index.asp.

796.6 GBR ISSN 1367-0824
MOUNTAIN BIKE RIDER. Text in English. 1997. m. GBP 54.60 domestic; USD 90.83 in US & Canada; EUR 84.26 in Europe; GBP 59.17 elsewhere; GBP 4.20 newsstand/cover (effective 2009). adv. illus. back issues avail. **Document type:** *Magazine, Consumer.* **Description:** Contains practical and technical content along with product ratings, best buys, equipment tests and consumer guidance.
Related titles: Online - full text ed.: GBP 20.31 (effective 2009).
Published by: I P C Country & Leisure Media Ltd. (Subsidiary of: I P C Media Ltd.), Leon House, 233 High St, Croydon, CR9 1HZ, United Kingdom. TEL 44-20-87268000, http://www.ipcmedia.com. Ed. John Kitchiner TEL 44-20-87268463. Adv. contact Kevin Attridge TEL 44-20-87268409. color page GBP 1,770. Circ: 33,918. **Subscr. to:** Rockwood House, Perrymount Rd, Haywards Heath RH16 3DH, United Kingdom. TEL 44-845-1231231, IPCsubs@quadrantsubs.com, http://www.magazinesdirect.co.uk. **Dist. by:** MarketForce UK Ltd, The Blue Fin Bldg, 3rd Fl, 110 Southwark St, London SE1 0SU, United Kingdom. TEL 44-20-31483300, FAX 44-20-31488105, salesinnovation@marketforce.co.uk, http://www.marketforce.co.uk/.

796 DEU ISSN 1860-1715
MOUNTAIN BIKE TOUREN-SPECIAL. Text in German. 2003. 2/yr. EUR 5 newsstand/cover (effective 2011). adv. **Document type:** *Magazine, Consumer.*
Related titles: ◆ Supplement to: Mountain Bike. ISSN 0946-2996.
Published by: Motor Presse Stuttgart GmbH & Co. KG (Subsidiary of: Gruner + Jahr AG & Co), Leuschnerstr 1, Stuttgart, 70174, Germany. TEL 49-711-18201, FAX 49-711-1821779, cgolla@motorpresse.de, http://www.motorpresse.de. Ed. Jens Voegele. Adv. contact Bernd Holzhauer. Circ: 45,000 (paid and controlled).

796.6 ITA
MOUNTAIN BIKE WORLD. Text in Italian. 1990. m. EUR 40 domestic (effective 2009). adv. **Document type:** *Magazine, Consumer.*
Formerly (until 200?): Bici da Montagna (1123-9220)
Related titles: Online - full text ed.
Published by: La Cuba Srl, Via della Maratona 66, Rome, RM 00194, Italy. TEL 39-063-629021, FAX 39-063-6309950.

796.6 USA ISSN 1062-2918
MOUNTAIN BIKING. Text in English. 1987. m. adv. **Document type:** *Magazine, Consumer.* **Description:** Covers all aspects of the sport and recreation of mountain biking, including product reviews, bike tests, racing coverage, how-tos, interviews with industry reps and racers, and travel.
Former titles (until 1992): Mountain and City Biking (1046-4875); (until 1989): Mountain Biking (0890-605X)
Indexed: G06, G07, G08, I05.
Published by: Challenge Publications, Inc., 9509 Vassar Ave, Unit A, Chatsworth, CA 91311. TEL 818-700-6868, FAX 818-700-6282, customerservice@challengeweb.com, http://www.challengeweb.com/. Ed. Chris Hatounian. Pub. Edwin Schnepf. R&P, Adv. contact Dave House. Circ: 103,257. **Dist. in UK by:** M M C Ltd., Octagon House, White Hart Meadows, Ripley, Woking, Surrey GU23 6HR, United Kingdom. TEL 44-1483-211222, FAX 44-1483-224541, enquiries@mmcltd.co.uk, http://www.mmcextranet.co.uk.

796.6 GBR ISSN 0954-8696
MOUNTAIN BIKING U K. Abbreviated title: M B U K. Variant title: Mountain Biking United Kingdom. Text in English. 1988. m. GBP 41.99 domestic; GBP 70 in Europe; GBP 85 elsewhere; GBP 4.20 newsstand/cover (effective 2010). adv. illus. back issues avail. **Document type:** *Magazine, Consumer.* **Description:** Tells the whole truth about radical mountain biking - the bikes, equipment, riders and places to ride.
—CCC.

S

Published by: Future Publishing Ltd., Beauford Ct, 30 Monmouth St, Bath, Avon BA1 2BW, United Kingdom. TEL 44-1225-442244, FAX 44-1225-446019, customerservice@subscription.co.uk, http://www.futureplc.com. Ed. Danny Walter. **Subscr. to:** Tower House, Sovereign Park, Market Harborough, Leicestershire LE16 9EF, United Kingdom. TEL 44-844-8481602, FAX 44-1858-438795, future@subscription.co.uk.

796.7 DEU
MOUNTAINBIKE RIDER. Text in German. 1997. 12/yr. EUR 42; EUR 4 newsstand/cover (effective 2011). adv. **Document type:** *Magazine, Consumer.*
Formerly (until 2001): Mountainbike Downhill
Published by: Delius Klasing Verlag GmbH, Siekerwall 21, Bielefeld, 33602, Germany. TEL 49-521-5590, FAX 49-521-559113, info@delius-klasing.de, http://www.delius-klasing.de. Ed. Frank Weckert.

388.347 GBR ISSN 2042-4337
THE MOVEMENT. Variant title: Sustrans Volunteer Rangers Newsletter. Text in English. 1999. s-a. back issues avail. **Document type:** *Newsletter, Consumer.*
Formerly (until 2008): The Ranger (1755-3709)
Related titles: Online - full text ed.: free (effective 2010).
—CCC.
Published by: Sustrans, 2 Cathedral Sq, College Green, Bristol, Avon BS1 5DD, United Kingdom. TEL 44-117-9268893, FAX 44-117-9294173, info@sustrans.org.uk, http://www.sustrans.org.uk.

796.6 NLD ISSN 1569-3090
DE MUUR. Text in Dutch. 2002. 4/yr. EUR 33.50 domestic; EUR 46 foreign (effective 2010).
Published by: L.J. Veen Uitgeversgroep, Herengracht 481, Amsterdam, 1017 BT, Netherlands. TEL 31-20-5249800, FAX 31-20-6276851, info@ljveen.nl, http://www.ljveen.nl. Eds. Bert Wagendorp, Mart Smeets, Peter Ouwerkerk.

796.6 NLD ISSN 1877-2234
DE MUUR WIELERSCHEURKALENDER. Text in Dutch. 2008. a. EUR 14.95 (effective 2011).
Published by: L.J. Veen Uitgeversgroep, Herengracht 481, Amsterdam, 1017 BT, Netherlands. TEL 31-20-5249800, FAX 31-20-6276851, info@ljveen.nl, http://www.ljveen.nl.

388.347 796.95 USA
N A D A MOTORCYCLE - SNOWMOBILE - A T V - PERSONAL WATERCRAFT APPRAISAL GUIDE. Text in English. 19??. 3/yr. USD 74 to non-members; USD 37 per issue to non-members; free to members (effective 2011). **Document type:** *Handbook/Manual/ Guide, Trade.*
Supersedes: N A D A Motorcycle Appraisal Guide (0095-6953)
Published by: (National Automobile Dealers Association), N.A.D.A. Appraisal Guides, PO Box 7800, Costa Mesa, CA 92628. http://www.nadaguides.com.

388.347 GBR ISSN 1755-3431
THE NATIONAL CYCLE NETWORK ROUTE USER MONITORING REPORT TO THE END OF (YEAR). Text in English. 2005. a. **Document type:** *Magazine, Trade.* **Description:** Provides statistics and information on usage of the National Cycle Network throughout the year.
Related titles: Online - full text ed.: ISSN 1755-344X. 2005.
—CCC.
Published by: Sustrans, 2 Cathedral Sq, College Green, Bristol, Avon BS1 5DD, United Kingdom. TEL 44-117-9268893, FAX 44-117-9294173, info@sustrans.org.uk, http://www.sustrans.org.uk.

N'EAST MAGAZINE; artist built, athlete driven, reader supported. *see* SPORTS AND GAMES—Outdoor Life

THE NETWORK. *see* TRANSPORTATION

796.7 DEU
NEUE & GEBRAUCHTE MOTORRAEDER; Strassenmaschinen; Enduros; Chopper; Roller; Zubehoer. Text in German. 1996. m. EUR 2.80 newsstand/cover (effective 2011). adv. **Document type:** *Magazine, Consumer.*
Formerly (until 2009): Motorrad Boerse
Published by: Der Heisse Draht Verlag GmbH und Co., Drostestr 14, Hannover, 30161, Germany. TEL 49-511-390910, FAX 49-511-39091196, zentrale@dhd.de, http://www.dhd.de. Pub. Curd Kitzelmann. Adv. contact Ruediger Gassmann. Circ: 46,000 (paid and controlled).

796.6 NZL ISSN 1179-884X
NEW ZEALAND ENDURANCE; endurance sport magazine. Text in English. 200?. bi-m. NZD 55 (effective 2010). **Document type:** *Magazine, Consumer.* **Description:** Features the latest news on triathlon, multisport, orienteering, running and adventure racing plus our regular columns, product reviews, training tips and race reports from international and local events.
Formerly (until 2005): Endurancesport New Zealand
Related titles: Online - full text ed.: NZD 35; NZD 7 per issue (effective 2010).
Published by: Media Unlimited, PO Box 98, Albert Town, Wanaka, 9344, New Zealand. TEL 64-3-4436295, FAX 64-3-4436294, team@mediaunlimited.co.nz, http://www.mediaunlimited.co.nz.

796.6 NZL ISSN 1179-920X
▼ **NEW ZEALAND ROAD CYCLIST.** Text in English. 2010. bi-m. NZD 49 domestic; NZD 75 foreign (effective 2011). adv. back issues avail. **Document type:** *Magazine, Consumer.* **Description:** Covers all aspects of road cycling from a distinctly Kiwi perspective in a format that aims to inform, inspire, educate and entertain the readers.
Published by: Spot On Publications, Unit F1, 27-29 William Pickering Dr, Albany, N Shore, Auckland, New Zealand. TEL 64-9-4185205, FAX 64-9-4185206, info@spoton.net.nz, http://www.spoton.net.nz. Ed. John McKenzie. Pub. Chris Gaskell. Adv. contact Simon Gladstone.

796.7 DEU
DER NUERBURGER. Text in German. 1991. m. EUR 19.20 (effective 2011). adv. **Document type:** *Magazine, Consumer.*
Published by: Syburger Verlag GmbH, Hertingerstr 60, Unna, 59423, Germany. TEL 49-2303-98550, FAX 49-2303-98559, info@syburger.de, http://www.syburger.de. Ed. Erik Foerster. Adv. contact Jessica Kwasny. Circ: 20,000 (controlled).

796.6 SWE ISSN 1102-8629
NYA CYKELTIDNINGEN. Variant title: Cykeltidningen. Text in Swedish. 1980. q. SEK 180 to individual members; SEK 360 to institutional members (effective 2004). adv. bk.rev. 3 cols./p.; **Document type:** *Consumer.*
Formerly (until 1992): Cykeltidningen (0280-302X)
Published by: Svenska Cykelsaellskapet, Torneaagatan 10, Kista, 16479, Sweden. TEL 46-8-7516204, FAX 46-8-7511935, info@svenska-cykelsallskapet.se.

796 SWE ISSN 0048-1211
NYA CYKLISTEN. Text in Swedish. 1964. 8/yr. SEK 337 domestic; SEK 537 in Scandinavia; SEK 637 elsewhere (effective 2004). adv. bk.rev. **Document type:** *Magazine, Consumer.*
Formerly (until 1970): Tidningen Cyklisten
Published by: (Svenska Cykelfoerbundet), Daus Tryck och Media, Daushuset, Bjaesta, 89380, Sweden. TEL 46-660-266100, FAX 46-660-266128, http://www.daus.se. Ed. Charlie Wedin. Adv. contact Leif Dylicki TEL 46-660-266107. B&W page SEK 6,865, color page SEK 8,930; 185 x 260.

796 FRA ISSN 1240-8751
L'OFFICIEL DU CYCLE ET DE LA MOTO. Variant title: L' Officiel du Cycle, de la Moto et du Quad. Text in French. 1891. m. EUR 119 (effective 2008). adv. bk.rev. charts; stat. **Document type:** *Magazine, Consumer.* **Description:** Reviews the cycle and motorcycle industry.
Former titles (until 1992): Officiel du Cycle et du Motocycle (0751-994X); (until 1982): Officiel du Cycle, du Motocycle et de la Motoculture (0030-0519); (until 1969): Officiel du Cycle, du Motocycle et du Camping (1769-2628)
Published by: Mondadori France, 1 Rue du Colonel Pierre-Avia, Paris, Cedex 15 75754, France. TEL 33-1-41335001, contact@mondadori.fr, http://www.mondadori.fr. Circ: 13,500.

796.75 CZE ISSN 1801-4526
OFFROAD QUAD. Text in Czech. 2005. q. CZK 445 (effective 2011). **Document type:** *Magazine, Consumer.*
Published by: Off Road Club s.r.o., Olomoucka 2332, Prague 9, 19800, Czech Republic. TEL 420-2-81933121, FAX 420-2-81933053. Ed. Dan Pejzl. Adv. contact Dagmar Kubinova.

629.227 AUS ISSN 1833-3249
OLD BIKE AUSTRALASIA. Text in English. 2006. bi-m. AUD 49.95 in Australia & New Zealand; AUD 89 elsewhere; AUD 15 per issue (effective 2008). back issues avail. **Document type:** *Magazine, Consumer.* **Description:** Provides latest news and results from recent events in race reports and rally roundup, along with new and old bike news and reviews, readers letters and club directory.
Published by: Chevron Publishing Group Pty. Ltd., PO Box 1421, Lane Cove, NSW 1595, Australia. TEL 61-2-94189225, FAX 61-2-94189641, sales@chevron.com.au, http://www.chevron.com.au. **Subscr. to:** my.magazine.com.au, PO Box 3355, St Leonards, NSW 1590, Australia. TEL 61-2-99016111, 800-227-236, FAX 61-2-99016110, subscribe@mymagazines.com.au, https://www.mymagazines.com.au.

OLDTIMER ANZEIGER; Klassische Automobile & Motorraeder - Zubehoer. *see* ADVERTISING AND PUBLIC RELATIONS

OLDTIMER BOERSE. *see* TRANSPORTATION—Automobiles

OLDTIMER HANDEL. *see* TRANSPORTATION—Automobiles

796.7 DEU
OLDTIMER MOTORRAD MARKT. Text in German. q. EUR 11.60; EUR 2.90 newsstand/cover (effective 2008). adv. **Document type:** *Magazine, Consumer.*
Published by: A M O Verlag GmbH, Sattlerstr 7, Luebeck, 23556, Germany. TEL 49-1805-151165, FAX 49-190-151050, info@amo-verlag.de, http://www.amo-verlag.de. Ed. Juergen Koslowski. adv.: B&W page EUR 400, color page EUR 500; trim 204 x 270.

796.6 USA ISSN 0893-4606
ON ONE WHEEL. Text in English. 1972. q. USD 15 domestic membership; USD 20 in Canada & Mexico; USD 25 elsewhere (effective 1999). adv. bk.rev. 20 p./no. 2 cols./p.; back issues avail. **Document type:** *Newsletter.* **Description:** Information about all phases of unicycling including building techniques, tricks, and meets.
Published by: Unicycling Society of America, Inc., PO Box 40534, Redford, MI 48240. Ed., Pub. Tammy Marsh. adv.: page USD 100. Circ: 500 (paid).

796.6 GBR
ON YOUR BIKE. Text in English. 1997. q. GBP 9.90 domestic; GBP 16 in Europe; GBP 24 elsewhere; GBP 3.20 newsstand/cover. adv. **Document type:** *Magazine, Consumer.* **Description:** Contains cycling information and features for the whole family.
Published by: Kindlife Ltd., 6a Kenton Park Centre, Gosforth, Newcastle upon Tyne, Tyne and Wear NE3 4NN, United Kingdom. TEL 44-191-213-2058, FAX 44-191-213-2052. Ed., Pub. Carlton Reid.

796.6 FRA ISSN 1961-3830
ONLYBIKE MAGAZINE; l'indispensable pour bien suivre la saison. Text in French. 2008. irreg. EUR 4.90 newsstand/cover (effective 2008). **Document type:** *Magazine, Consumer.*
Address: Chemin des Garennes, Chemellier, 49320, France. http://www.onlybike.com.

796.6 NLD ISSN 2210-4151
OP PAD BIKING. Variant title: Biking. Text in Dutch. s-a. EUR 5.50 newsstand/cover (effective 2010). **Document type:** *Magazine, Consumer.*
Published by: ANWB BV/Royal Dutch Touring Club, Wassenaarseweg 220, Postbus 93200, The Hague, 2509 BA, Netherlands. TEL 31-70-3146533, FAX 31-70-3147404, info@anwb.nl, http://www.anwb.nl.

796 USA ISSN 0885-2030
OUTLAW BIKER. Text in English. 1985. q. USD 16 domestic; USD 28 in Canada (effective 2008). adv. back issues avail. **Document type:** *Magazine, Consumer.*
Published by: Outlaw Biker Enterprises, Inc./Art & Ink, 1000 Seaboard St, Ste C6, Charlotte, NC 28206. TEL 704-333-3331, FAX 704-333-3433, webhead@outlawbiker.com. Pub. Casey Exton. Adv. contact Chris Jean Miller. Circ: 150,000.

796.6 USA
OUTSPOKIN'. Text in English. 10/yr. USD 125 (effective 2001). **Document type:** *Newsletter.* **Description:** Covers news and concerns of the bicycle trade.
Published by: National Bicycle Dealers Association, 777W 19th St, Ste O, Costa Mesa, CA 92627. TEL 949-722-6909, FAX 949-722-1747, info@nbda.com. Pub. Fred Clements. Circ: 1,300.

796.7 AUS ISSN 0155-4360
OZBIKE; thunder down under. Text in English. 1977. bi-m. AUD 80 (effective 2009). adv. back issues avail. **Document type:** *Magazine, Consumer.* **Description:** Covers custom motorcycles and Australian biker lifestyle.
Related titles: Supplement(s): Biker Business Directory.
Published by: U C P Publishing Pty Ltd., PO Box 62, Gladesville, NSW 1675, Australia. TEL 61-2-98104333. Ed. Roadkill . Pub. Skol . Adv. contact Stephen Seagull. page AUD 1,550; bleed 220 x 300.

796.6 NOR ISSN 0801-0986
PAA HJUL. Text in Norwegian. 1980. 6/yr. NOK 150. adv. bk.rev.
Published by: Norges Cykelforbund, Hanger Skolevei 1, Rud, 1351, Norway. FAX 02-132989, TELEX 78586 NIF. Ed. Per Furseth. Circ: 8,500.

796 CAN ISSN 1191-2685
PEDAL. Variant title: Canadian Cycling News. Text in English. 1986. 6/yr. CAD 23.70 domestic; USD 26 in United States; CAD 32 foreign; CAD 3.95 newsstand/cover (effective 2000). adv. bk.rev. **Document type:** *Magazine, Consumer.* **Description:** Provides wide-range coverage of cycling including competitive events both national and international for road and track - mountain biking, interviews, recreational stories, product reviews, training, technique, repair and maintenance tips.
Published by: (Canadian Cycling Association), Pedal Magazine, 317 Adelaide St W, Ste 703, Toronto, ON M5V 1P9, Canada. TEL 416-977-2100, FAX 416-977-9200, pedal@passport.ca, http://www.pedal.com. Ed., Pub., R&P Benjamin A Sadavoy. Adv. contact Jennifer Dixon. Circ: 20,000.

796.6 AUS ISSN 1321-1870
PEDAL UPDATE. Text in English. 1976. bi-m. looseleaf. free to members (effective 2008). back issues avail. **Document type:** *Newsletter.* **Description:** Advocates the use of bicycles. Informs and educates members on all the benefits of cycling for economical commuting, personal health and resource conservation.
Former titles (until 1989): Pedal; (until 1978): Cyclist Protection Association of South Australia. Newsletter
Related titles: Online - full text ed.
Published by: Bicycle Institute of South Australia Inc., GPO Box 792, Adelaide, SA 5001, Australia. TEL 61-8-84110233, secretary@bisa.asn.au. Ed. Sam Powrie TEL 61-4-84499902. Circ: 600.

796.75 USA ISSN 2159-4252
▼ **PELOTON**; fuel for the ride. Text in English. 2010. bi-m. USD 21.99 domestic; USD 36.99 in Canada; USD 46.99 elsewhere; USD 25.99 combined subscription domestic (print & online eds.); USD 40.99 combined subscription in Canada (print & online eds.); USD 50.99 combined subscription elsewhere (print & online eds.) (effective 2011). adv. **Document type:** *Magazine, Trade.*
Related titles: Online - full text ed.: USD 12.99 (effective 2011).
Published by: Move Press, Llc, 1000 Fremont Ave, Ste H, S Pasadena, CA 91030. TEL 626-441-2113, FAX 626-441-2316. Adv. contact Adam Reek TEL 626-441-2276.

796.7 GBR ISSN 0268-4942
PERFORMANCE BIKES. Text in English. 19??. m. price varies. adv. back issues avail. **Document type:** *Magazine, Consumer.* **Description:** Features information about high performance motorbikes.
Former titles (until 1985): Mechanics (0263-8274); Which incorporated (1980-1983): Biker (0260-5147); (until 1982): Motor Cycle Mechanics (0262-5822); (until 1972): Motor Cycle, Scooter and Three-Wheeler Mechanics (0027-2183)
Published by: H. Bauer Publishing Ltd. (Subsidiary of: Bauer Media Group), Media House, Lynchwood, Peterborough, Cambridgeshire PE2 6EA, United Kingdom. TEL 44-1733-468000, http://www.bauer.co.uk. Ed. Sally Barker TEL 44-1733-468099. Adv. contact Gareth Ashman TEL 44-1733-468118.

796.75 CAN ISSN 0834-809X
PERFORMANCE RACING NEWS. Text in English. 1989. 12/yr. CAD 14.99 domestic (effective 2007). adv. illus. back issues avail. **Document type:** *Magazine, Consumer.* **Description:** Provides complete coverage of all forms of motorsports on a regional, national and international basis.
Published by: Performance Publications Inc., 44 Prince Andrew Place, Toronto, ON M6P 3M9, Canada. TEL 416-922-7526, http://www.performancepublicationsinc.com. adv.: B&W page CAD 2,338; trim 14 x 10.5. Circ: 17,059 (paid).

796.7 USA ISSN 0162-3214
TL235.6
PETERSEN'S 4 WHEEL & OFF-ROAD. Variant title: 4 Wheel & Off-Road. Text in English. 1977. m. USD 12 domestic; USD 18 in Canada; USD 30 elsewhere (effective 2008). adv. illus. back issues avail. **Document type:** *Magazine, Consumer.* **Description:** Offers tips on driving and customizing off-road four-wheel-drive trucks.
Formerly: Hot Rod Magazine's 4 Wheel and Off-Road
Related titles: Online - full text ed.
Indexed: ConsI, G05, G06, G07, G08, I05, I06, I07, M04, S23.
—Ingenta. **CCC.**
Published by: Source Interlink Companies, 6420 Wilshire Blvd, 10th Fl, Los Angeles, CA 90048. TEL 323-782-2000, FAX 323-782-2585, dheine@sourceinterlink.com, http://www.sourceinterlinkmedia.com. Ed. Rick Pewe. Pub. Jeff Nasi TEL 323-782-2649. adv.: B&W page USD 23,975, color page USD 39,945. Circ: 345,777 (paid).

796.6 USA
PRACTICAL PEDAL; the journal of practical bicycling. Text in English. 2007. q. free. **Document type:** *Magazine, Consumer.* **Description:** Covers the use of bicycles as primary transportation.
Address: 701 1/2 S 14th Ave, Bozeman, MT 59715. TEL 760-443-3515.

796 CAN
PRAIRIE PEDALER. Text in English. 1985. q. free to members. adv. **Document type:** *Newsletter.*
Published by: Saskatchewan Cycling Association, 2205 Victoria Ave, Regina, SK S4P 0S4, Canada. TEL 306-780-9299, FAX 306-525-4009. Ed., Pub., Adv. contact Denise Eberle. Circ: 400.

796.6 NLD ISSN 1879-4424
PROCYCLING. Text in Dutch. 2008. m. EUR 49.80 (effective 2010). adv. **Document type:** *Magazine, Consumer.*

Published by: Sanoma Men's Magazines, Capellalaan 65, Hoofddorp, 2132 JL, Netherlands. TEL 31-88-7518380, sales@smm.nl, http://www.smm.nl. Adv. contact Gijsbert Goes. Circ: 35,000.

796.65 DEU ISSN 1613-0871
PROCYCLING; Europas grosses Radsport-Magazin. Text in German. 2004. m. EUR 59.40; EUR 4.80 newsstand/cover (effective 2009). adv. **Document type:** *Magazine, Consumer.*
Incorporates (2006-2007): Velomotion (1863-1487)
Published by: Bruckmann Verlag GmbH, Infanteriestr 11a, Munich, 80797, Germany. TEL 49-89-13069911, FAX 49-89-13069910, info@bruckmann-verlag.de, http://www.bruckmann-verlag.de. Ed. Chris Hauke. Adv. contact Judith Fischl. color page EUR 4,500; trim 210 x 280. Circ: 25,300 (paid).

796.65 GBR ISSN 1465-7198
PROCYCLING. Text in English. 1999. 13/yr. GBP 39.99 domestic; GBP 55 in Europe; GBP 75 elsewhere; GBP 3.99 newsstand/cover (effective 2010). adv. back issues avail. **Document type:** *Magazine, Consumer.* **Description:** Covers all aspects of professional bicycle road racing.
Published by: Future Publishing Ltd., Beauford Ct, 30 Monmouth St, Bath, Avon BA1 2BW, United Kingdom. TEL 44-1225-442244, FAX 44-1225-446019, customerservice@subscription.co.uk, http://www.futureplc.com. Ed. Cam Winstanley. **Subscr. to:** Tower House, Sovereign Park, Market Harborough, Leicestershire LE16 9EF, United Kingdom. TEL 44-844-8481602, FAX 44-1858-438795, future@subscription.co.uk.

796.7 NLD ISSN 1381-0154
PROMOTOR. Text in Dutch. 1990. 10/yr. EUR 53 to non-members; EUR 49.50 to members (effective 2008). adv. Website rev. illus. **Document type:** *Consumer.* **Description:** For motorcycle enthusiasts.
Published by: (ANWB BV/Royal Dutch Touring Club), Algemene Nederlandse Wielrijders Bond (A N W B) Media/Dutch Automobile Association Media, Postbus 93200, The Hague, 2509 BA, Netherlands. TEL 31-70-3141470, FAX 31-70-3146538, http://www.anwbmedia.nl. Eds. Rene van Tienhoven, Joyce Kuipers. Pub. Jacques Peters. adv.: B&W page EUR 3,150, color page EUR 3,900; bleed 230 x 300. Circ: 36,418.

796.7 NLD ISSN 1876-178X
PRUTTELPOT. Text in Dutch. 1979. bi-m.
Published by: MZ Club Holland, Julianalaan 6, Bennekom, 6721 EG, Netherlands. http://www.mzch.nl.

796.77 DEU
QUAD & A T V KATALOG. Text in German. a. EUR 4.95 newsstand/cover (effective 2007). adv. **Document type:** *Magazine, Consumer.*
Published by: Motoretta Verlagsgesellschaft mbH, Wickingstr 3a, Recklinghausen, 45657, Germany. TEL 49-2361-93580, FAX 49-2361-16495. adv.: B&W page EUR 2,000, color page EUR 3,565. Circ: 35,000 (paid and controlled).

796.7 DEU
QUAD MAGAZIN. Text in German. 6/yr. EUR 20 domestic; EUR 29 foreign; EUR 3.90 newsstand/cover (effective 2007). adv. **Document type:** *Magazine, Consumer.*
Published by: Mo Medien Verlag GmbH, Schrempfstr 8, Stuttgart, 70597, Germany. TEL 49-711-24897600, FAX 49-711-24897628, redaktion@mo-web.de. adv.: B&W page EUR 2,710, color page EUR 4,550. Circ: 14,000 (paid and controlled).

796.7 USA ISSN 1557-3559
TL235.6
QUAD OFF-ROAD MAGAZINE. Text in English. 2005 (Jul.). 10/yr. USD 16.97 domestic; USD 29.97 in Canada; USD 53.97 elsewhere; USD 4.99 newsstand/cover domestic (effective 2009). adv. back issues avail. **Document type:** *Magazine, Consumer.* **Description:** Offers news, product reviews, buyers guides, and travel information for both recreational and competitive riders.
Indexed: G08, I05.
—CCC.
Published by: TransWorld Media (Subsidiary of: Bonnier Magazine Group), 1421 Edinger Ave, Ste D, Tustin, CA 92780. TEL 714-247-0077, FAX 714-247-0078, http://www.transworldmatrix.com/twmatrix/. Pub. Pete Martini TEL 714-247-0077 ext 251. Adv. contact Mike Keller TEL 714-247-0077 ext 248. color page USD 9,195; trim 7.875 x 10.5. Circ: 70,000 (paid).

796.7 ZAF ISSN 1683-4984
QUAD S A. Text in English. 2002. m. ZAR 144 domestic; ZAR 339 in neighboring countries; ZAR 404 elsewhere (effective 2006). **Document type:** *Magazine, Consumer.*
Published by: Bike Promotions (Pty) Ltd., PO Box 894, Johannesburg, 2000, South Africa.

796.7 USA ISSN 1080-2428
QUICK THROTTLE. Text in English. 1995. m. USD 29.95; free (effective 2009). adv. illus. **Document type:** *Magazine, Consumer.* **Description:** Focuses on all aspects of the motorcycle riding community; covering local stories and related events.
Published by: Paisano Publications, Inc., PO Box 3062, Dana Point, CA 92629. TEL 888-770-9866, FAX 949-388-3696, bulkmagazines@paisanopub.com, http://www.paisanopub.com. Pub. Chris Dalgaard. Adv. contact Lisa Dalgaard. Circ: 150,000.

629.227 GBR ISSN 1356-2975
RACE TECH INTERNATIONAL; technology, business and mechanics. Variant title: Race Tech Magazine. Text in English. 200?. m. GBP 49.50 domestic; GBP 74 in Europe; GBP 84 in United States; GBP 80 elsewhere (effective 2010). adv. back issues avail. **Document type:** *Magazine, Consumer.*
Published by: Racecar Graphic Ltd., 841 High Rd, Finchley, London, N12 8PT, United Kingdom. TEL 44-20-84462100, FAX 44-20-84462191. Ed. William Kimberley. adv.: B&W page GBP 1,200, color page GBP 1,800; trim 210 x 297.

796.75 USA ISSN 1099-6729
RACER X ILLUSTRATED. Text in English. 1998. bi-m. USD 24; USD 4.95 newsstand/cover (effective 2001). adv. illus. **Document type:** *Magazine, Consumer.* **Description:** Covers all aspects of motocross motorcycle racing and recreation.
Related titles: Online - full text ed.
Address: 122 Vista Del Rio Dr., Morgantown, WV 26508-8832. TEL 304-284-0080, FAX 304-284-0081. Ed. Davey Coombs. Adv. contact Julie Kramer. **Dist. by:** Curtis Circulation Co., 730 River Rd, New Milford, NJ 07646. TEL 201-634-7400, FAX 201-634-7499.

629.227 DEU ISSN 0033-8540
RADMARKT; deutsche Fachzeitschrift der Zweiradwirtschaft. Text in German. 1879. m. EUR 91.80 domestic; EUR 114.60 foreign; EUR 8.40 newsstand/cover (effective 2008). adv. bk.rev. charts; illus.; mkt.; pat.; tr.lit.; tr.mk. index. **Document type:** *Magazine, Trade.* **Description:** Trade publication for the bicycle market. Covers the latest information concerning bicycles, motorcycles, scooters, and foreign trade. Includes letters to the editor and list of advertisers.
Published by: B V A Bielefelder Verlag GmbH & Co. KG, Niederwall 53, Bielefeld, 33602, Germany. TEL 49-521-595514, FAX 49-521-595518, kontakt@bva-bielefeld.de. Ed. Michael Bollschweiler. Adv. contact Barbara Goeppert. color page EUR 2,930; trim 210 x 297. Circ: 5,622 (paid and controlled).

796.6 DEU
RADSPORT. Text in German. 1912. w. (Tues.). EUR 109.20 domestic; EUR 124.80 foreign; EUR 2.30 newsstand/cover (effective 2008). adv. **Document type:** *Newspaper, Consumer.*
Published by: B V A Bielefelder Verlag GmbH & Co. KG, Niederwall 53, Bielefeld, 33602, Germany. TEL 49-521-595-520, 49-521-595514, FAX 49-521-595518, http://www.bva-bielefeld.de. adv.: B&W page EUR 1,850. Circ: 5,562 (paid and controlled).

796.6 910.202 DEU ISSN 1439-0671
RADTOUREN. Text in German. 1998. 6/yr. EUR 27.30 (effective 2010). adv. bk.rev. illus.; mkt.; maps. 64 p./no. 3 cols./p.; back issues avail. **Document type:** *Magazine, Consumer.* **Description:** Presents maps, information and practical advice for bike tours.
Published by: Maenken Kommunikation GmbH, Von-der-Wettern-Str 25, Cologne, 51149, Germany. TEL 49-2203-35840, FAX 49-2203-3584185, info@maenken.com, http://www.maenken.com. Ed. David Feist. Pub. Wieland Maenken. adv.: color page EUR 3,700; trim 181 x 270. Circ: 20,000 (paid).

796.6 DEU ISSN 1438-4612
RADWELT. Text in German. 1997. bi-m. free to members (effective 2010). adv. **Document type:** *Magazine, Consumer.*
Published by: (Allgemeiner Deutscher Fahrrad-Club e.V.), Zweiplus Medienagentur, Pallaswiesenstr. 109, Darmstadt, 64293, Germany. TEL 49-6151-81270, FAX 49-6151-893098. Ed. Alexandra Kirsch. Adv. contact Petra Wedel. B&W page EUR 3,650, color page EUR 5,300. Circ: 74,106 (paid and controlled).

796.7 AUT
RADWELT. Text in German. 7/yr. adv. **Document type:** *Magazine, Consumer.*
Address: Wengerweg 10, Postfach 80, Altheim, O 4950, Austria. TEL 43-7723-43739, FAX 43-7723-44899, urc.radwelt@telering.at, http://www.radwelt.at. Ed. Wolfgang Hirschl. Pub., Adv. contact Arnold Hirschl. Circ: 5,000.

796.6 DEU ISSN 1439-8702
RADZEIT. Text in German. 1983. bi-m. EUR 8; free newsstand/cover (effective 2008). adv. **Document type:** *Magazine, Consumer.*
Published by: A D F C Berlin e.V., Brunnenstr 28, Berlin, 10119, Germany. TEL 49-30-4484724, FAX 49-30-44340520, kontakt@adfc-berlin.de, http://www.adfc-berlin.de. Ed. Michaela Mueller. adv.: B&W page EUR 845, color page EUR 1,480. Circ: 46,224 (paid and controlled).

RE-UNICYCLING THE PAST; collecting antique unicycles. *see* ANTIQUES

796.6 USA
RECUMBENT & TANDEM RIDER. Text in English. 2001. q. USD 9.95 (effective 2001). **Document type:** *Magazine, Consumer.* **Description:** Provides a forum of communication for riders and enthusiasts of recumbent and tandem bicycles; Contains articles, reports, reports of ancillary equipment and tests.
Published by: Coyne Publishing, 1313 Paseo Alamos, PO Box 337, San Dimas, CA 91773. info@rtrmag.com, http://www.rtrmag.com/.

796 USA
RECUMBENT CYCLIST NEWS. Text in English. 1990. 6/yr. USD 40 domestic; USD 70 outside of UK or Canada (effective 2001). adv. back issues avail. **Document type:** *Magazine, Consumer.* **Description:** Fosters communication between recumbent bicycle enthusiasts, dealers and manufacturers.
Former titles (until June 1993): Recumbent Cyclist Magazine; (until 1991): Recumbent Cyclist Newsletter
Related titles: Special ed(s).: Recumbent Cyclist News. Buyers Guide.
Address: PO Box 2048, Port Townsend, WA 98368-0239. info@recumbentcyclistnews.com, http://www.recumbentcyclistnews.com/. Pubs. Bob Bryant, Marilyn Bryant. adv.: B&W page USD 550; trim 11 x 8.5. Circ: 4,500 (paid).

796.7 ZAF
REDLINE MAGAZINE; take it to the limit. Text in English. 1993. m. (11/yr.). ZAR 120. adv. illus. **Document type:** *Magazine, Consumer.* **Description:** Covers motorcycle news and events nationally and internationally, and includes road tests and price information.
Supersedes: Redline Motorcycle News (1022-4580)
Published by: Redline CC, PO Box 990429, Kibler Park, Gauteng 2053, South Africa. TEL 27-11-943-2729, FAX 27-11-943-1794. Ed., Pub., R&P Kenn Slater. Adv. contact Lee Slater. color page ZAR 3,800, B&W page ZAR 2,900; trim 210 x 275. Circ: 28,500.

796.7 DEU ISSN 0947-1375
REISE MOTORRAD. Text in German. 1991. bi-m. EUR 27 domestic; EUR 39 in Europe; EUR 60 elsewhere (effective 2010). adv. **Document type:** *Magazine, Consumer.*
Related titles: Online - full text ed.
Published by: Huber Verlag GmbH & Co. KG, Markircher Str 9 a, Mannheim, 68229, Germany. TEL 49-621-483610, FAX 49-621-4836111, szeneshop@huber-verlag.de, http://www.huber-verlag.de. Ed. Anton Sacher. Adv. contact Katrin Schumann.

796.7 AUT
DER REITWAGEN; Das schnelle oesterreichische Motorradmagazin. Text in German. 10/yr. EUR 29.50; EUR 3.30 newsstand/cover (effective 2005). adv. **Document type:** *Magazine, Consumer.*
Published by: Reitwagen Zeitschriftenverlagsgesellschaft mbH, Kammangasse 9/6, Wiener Neustadt, N 2700, Austria. TEL 43-2622-87101, FAX 43-2622-20534, verlag@reitwagen.at. Ed., Pub. Andreas Werth. Adv. contact Michael Maxa. Circ: 28,000.

796.6 DEU ISSN 1861-2733
RENNRAD. Text in German. 2005. 8/yr. EUR 27.80, EUR 31.80; EUR 3.50 newsstand/cover (effective 2011). adv. **Document type:** *Magazine, Consumer.*

Published by: B V A Bielefelder Verlag GmbH & Co. KG, Niederwall 53, Bielefeld, 33602, Germany. TEL 49-521-595514, FAX 49-521-595518, kontakt@bva-bielefeld.de, http://www.bva-bielefeld.de. Circ: 40,000 (paid and controlled).

796.7 USA
REV MAGAZINE. Text in English. 2002. 4/yr. USD 5.95 per month (effective 2005). adv. **Document type:** *Magazine, Consumer.*
Address: PO Box 1052, Pacific Palisades, CA 90272.

796.7 PRT ISSN 1647-7138
▼ **REV MOTORCYCLE CULTURE.** Text in Portuguese. 2010. q. **Document type:** *Magazine, Consumer.*
Published by: Fast Lane - Media e Eventos Lda, Rua Cintura do Porto, Lisbon, 1950-326, Portugal.

796.6 AUS ISSN 1832-1577
[R]EVOLUTION; the progressive Australian MTB magazine. Text in English. 2004. q. USD 37.50; USD 9.95 newsstand/cover (effective 2011). adv. back issues avail. **Document type:** *Magazine, Trade.* **Description:** Dedicated to document the changing face of mountain bike in Australia through progressive riding, the finest photography, passionate and expert editorial along with dedicated design.
Published by: [R]evolution MTB, PO Box 498, Newtown, NSW 2042, Australia. subs@revolutionmtb.com.au.

796.7 388.3 CAN ISSN 1913-0082
REVOLUTION MOTORCYCLE MAG (ENGLISH EDITION); the first Canadian magazine of custom bike. Text in English. 2007. q. CAD 25 (effective 2007). back issues avail. **Document type:** *Magazine, Consumer.*
Related titles: French ed.: Revolution Motorcycle Mag (French Edition). ISSN 1913-0090.
Published by: Revolution Motorcycle Magazine, 1302 Garden Av., Mascouche, PQ J7L 0A4, Canada. TEL 514-726-5742, FAX 450-477-9814.

629.227 FRA ISSN 0150-7214
REVUE MOTO TECHNIQUE. Text in French. 1969. q. EUR 97 (effective 2009). charts; illus. **Document type:** *Magazine, Trade.* **Description:** Each issue deals with 2 motorcycles and explains how to dismantle and repair them.
—CCC.
Published by: Editions Techniques pour l'Automobile et l'Industrie (E T A I), 20-22 rue de la Saussiere, Boulogne Billancourt, 92100, France. TEL 33-1-46992424, FAX 33-1-48255692, http://www.groupe-etai.com. Ed. Christian Rey. Circ: 15,000.

629.2275 GBR ISSN 1360-3507
RIDE. Text in English. 1995. m. GBP 41 domestic; GBP 50.47 in Europe; GBP 56.36 in United States; GBP 66.30 elsewhere (effective 2009). adv. **Document type:** *Magazine, Consumer.* **Description:** Covers information on new and used motorcycles as well as bike products.
Published by: H. Bauer Publishing Ltd. (Subsidiary of: Bauer Media Group), Media House, Lynchwood, Peterborough, Cambridgeshire PE2 6EA, United Kingdom. TEL 44-1733-468000, http://www.bauer.co.uk. Ed. Sally Barker TEL 44-1733-468099. Adv. contact Gareth Ashman TEL 44-1733-468118.

796.6 USA ISSN 1078-0084
GV1049.3
RIDE B M X. Text in English. 1991. m. USD 18.97 domestic; USD 30.97 in Canada; USD 47.97 elsewhere; USD 4.99 newsstand/cover (effective 2009). adv. illus. **Document type:** *Magazine, Consumer.* **Description:** Covers the world of BMX sports bike racing.
Incorporates (1994-2004): Transworld B M X (1534-035X); Which was formerly (until 2001): Snap B M X (1090-8579)
Related titles: Online - full text ed.
Indexed: A11, C05, G08, I05, I07, M01, M02, M04, MASUSE, T02.
—CCC.
Published by: TransWorld Media (Subsidiary of: Bonnier Magazine Group), 1421 Edinger Ave, Ste D, Tustin, CA 92780. TEL 714-247-0077, FAX 714-247-0078, http://www.transworldmatrix.com/twmatrix/. Adv. contact Bill Dies TEL 714-247-0077 ext 239. color page USD 9,895; trim 9 x 10.5. Circ: 40,476 (paid).

796.75 AUS ISSN 1838-4080
▼ **RIDE FOR TOMORROW**; respect the environment, respect others. Text in English. 2010. s-a. free (effective 2011). **Document type:** *Newsletter, Government.* **Description:** Contains information for riders about choosing a suitable bike, protective equipment, licence and registration requirements, general information on where to ride and some simple riding tips etc.
Media: Online - full text.
Published by: Victoria. Department of Sustainability and Environment, 8 Nicholson St, East Melbourne, VIC 3002, Australia. TEL 61-3-53325000, customer.service@dse.vic.gov.au, http://www.dse.vic.gov.au/dse/index.htm.

RIDE ON!. *see* CONSERVATION

796.6 AUS ISSN 1838-0387
RIDE ON. Text in English. 1976. bi-m. USD 50 domestic to non-members; USD 80 foreign to non-members; free to members (effective 2011). adv. charts; illus.; maps. 32 p./no.; **Document type:** *Magazine, Consumer.* **Description:** Provides information on bike-lifestyle features, reviews of hot new bikes and products, expert health and fitness advice.
Former titles (until 2004): B V News (1320-3959); (until 199?): Bicycle Victoria (0819-9159); (until 1987): Pedal Power (0157-4167)
Published by: Bicycle Institute of Victoria, Inc., PO Box 426, Collins St West, VIC 8007, Australia. TEL 61-3-86368888, 800-639-634, FAX 61-3-86368800, bicyclevic@bv.com.au. Circ: 50,000.

796.7 USA
RIDE TEXAS. Text in English. bi-m. USD 20; USD 4.50 newsstand/cover (effective 2003). adv. **Document type:** *Magazine, Consumer.* **Description:** Offers articles, rides, and news for Texas motorcyclists.
Related titles: Online - full text ed.
Address: PO Box 90374, Austin, TX 78709-1931. miguel@texmoto.com. Ed., Pub. Val Asensio. Adv. contact Reynolds Mansson.

796.6 USA
RIDE THE WEB. Text in English. m. adv. **Document type:** *Bulletin.* **Description:** Cycling Web-zine with stories about biking areas and rides, reviews of bicycling products and services, and issues of concern to both road and mountain bikers.
Media: Online - full text.

Published by: Tackett Management Solutions, 5564 N Osborne Ct, San Bernardino, CA 92407. TEL 909-886-3266, FAX 909-886-9348. Adv. contact Bill Tackett.

796.6 GBR ISSN 1757-7721
RIDE U K. Text in English. 1992. m. GBP 32.60 domestic; USD 58 in United States; EUR 50 in Europe; USD 86 elsewhere (effective 2009). adv. bk.rev. back issues avail. **Document type:** *Magazine, Consumer.* **Description:** Provides coverage of the personalities and products of the BMX biking scene featuring events, the top riders, product reviews, location descriptions and logistics, and tips and tricks.
Former titles (until 2007): Ride B M X Magazine (0967-1234); (until 1992): Invert
Related titles: Online - full text ed.
Published by: Factory Media, Studio 153, 355 Byres Rd, Glasgow, G12 8QZ, United Kingdom. TEL 44-141-9455019, FAX 44-141-9455019, http://www.factorymedia.com. Eds. Robin Fenlon TEL 44-207-3329700, Steve Bancroft. Adv. contact Ian Gunner. **Subscr. to:** Dovetail Services UK Ltd, 800 Guillat Ave, Kent Science Park, Sittingbourne, Kent ME9 8GU, United Kingdom. TEL 44-1795-414555, contact@dovetailservices.com, http://www.dovetailservices.com/.

796.7 USA ISSN 1522-9726
RIDER; motorcycle touring & sport touring. Text in English. 1974. m. USD 12 domestic (effective 2010). adv. illus. Index. back issues avail.; reprints avail. **Document type:** *Magazine, Consumer.* **Description:** Devoted to the motorcycle touring enthusiast. Examines bike tests, new-product evaluations, touring adventures, and buyer's guides.
Related titles: Online - full text ed.
Indexed: G06, G07, G08, I05.
Published by: Affinity Group Inc., 2575 Vista Del Mar, Ventura, CA 93001. TEL 805-667-4100, FAX 805-667-4419, info@affinitygroup.com, http://www.affinitygroup.com. Ed. Mark Tuttle. Circ: 122,000.

796.6 DEU
ROAD BIKE; Faszination Rennrad. Text in German. 2006. m. EUR 49.50; EUR 4.50 newsstand/cover (effective 2011). adv. **Document type:** *Magazine, Consumer.*
Published by: Motor Presse Stuttgart GmbH & Co. KG (Subsidiary of: Gruner + Jahr AG & Co), Leuschnerstr 1, Stuttgart, 70174, Germany. TEL 49-711-18201, FAX 49-711-1821779, cgolla@motorpresse.de, http://www.motorpresse.de. Ed. Jens Voegele. Adv. contact Bernd Holzhauer. Circ: 35,359 (paid and controlled).

796.6 USA ISSN 1069-2649
ROAD BIKE ACTION. Text in English. 1993. m. USD 15.99 domestic; USD 26.99 in Canada; USD 33.99 elsewhere; USD 4.99 newsstand/cover (effective 2011). adv. back issues avail. **Document type:** *Magazine, Consumer.*
Related titles: Online - full text ed.: USD 15.99 (effective 2011).
Published by: Hi - Torque Publications, Inc., 25233 Amza Dr, Valencia, CA 91355. TEL 661-295-1910, FAX 661-295-1278, michelle@hi-torque.com, http://www.hi-torque.com. Adv. contact Robert Rex.

796.6 ITA ISSN 1971-8594
ROAD BIKE ACTION MAGAZINE. Text in Italian. 2007. bi-m. EUR 22.90; EUR 7.50 newsstand/cover (effective 2009). adv. **Document type:** *Magazine, Consumer.*
Published by: G P R Publishing s.a.s., Via Toniolo 1, Treviso, 31100, Italy. TEL 39-0422-543351, FAX 39-0422-549159, info@gprpublishing.com.

796.6 USA ISSN 1555-4864
GV1045.5.F76
ROAD BIKING COLORADO'S FRONT RANGE; a guide to the greatest bike rides from Colorado Springs to Fort Collins. Text in English. 2005. biennial, latest 2005, 1st ed. USD 15.95 per issue (effective 2008). **Document type:** *Magazine, Consumer.* **Description:** Features thirty-two carefully designed rides between Colorado Springs and Fort Collins - from the cities to the foothills and everywhere in between.
Published by: Falcon Publishing (Subsidiary of: The Globe Pequot Press, Inc.), 246 Goose Ln, PO Box 480, Guilford, CT 06437. TEL 203-458-4500, http://www.falcon.com. Ed. Shelley Wolf.

796.75 USA ISSN 1542-4022
ROAD RACER X. Text in English. 2003 (Mar./Apr.). bi-m. USD 15 domestic; USD 21 in Canada; USD 36 elsewhere (effective 2003).
Published by: Filter Publications, LLC, 122 Vista Del Rio Dr., Morgantown, WV 26508-8832. Eds. Chris Jonnum, Davey Coombs. Pub., Adv. contact Scott Wallenberg.

388.347 796.6 796.75 USA ISSN 1939-7976
ROAD RUNNER MOTORCYCLE TOURING & TRAVEL. Text in English. 2001 (Spring). 6/yr. USD 24.95 (effective 2007). adv. back issues avail. **Document type:** *Magazine, Consumer.* **Description:** Get the inside track on exciting new places to go, the best ways to get there, and the right equipment to enhance the comfort and enjoyment of the ride.
Formerly (until 2007): Road Runner Motorcycle Cruising & Touring (1544-614X)
Published by: RoadRUNNER Publishing, 3601 Edgemoor Court, Clemmons, NC 27012. Christa@RRmotorcycling.com. Ed. Andy Seiler. Pub. Christian Neuhauser. Adv. contact Michael Miller TEL 336-721-0328. color page USD 7,950; trim 8.375 x 11.75.

ROAD TRIP. *see* TRAVEL AND TOURISM

796.7 910.202 USA ISSN 1538-4748
ROADBIKE. Text in English. 1993. m. USD 4.99 newsstand/cover (effective 2011). bk.rev. charts; illus.; tr.lit. reprints avail. **Document type:** *Magazine, Consumer.* **Description:** Upscale tour and travel magazine from a motorcyclists' perspective. Also discusses places to go and what to see there and contains information for the long-distance rider.
Former titles (until 2002): Motorcycle Tour & Cruiser (1093-815X); (until 199?): Motorcycle Tour and Travel (1069-2797)
Published by: T A M Communications Inc., 5610 Scotts Valley Dr, Ste B552, Scotts Valley, CA 95066. TEL 831-439-1500, FAX 866-390-1218, http://www.tamcom.com.

796.75 USA ISSN 1056-4845
ROADRACING WORLD & MOTORCYCLE TECHNOLOGY. Text in English. 1990. m. USD 17.95 domestic; USD 39.95 in Canada & Mexico; USD 74.95 elsewhere (effective 2003). adv. bk.rev. illus. **Document type:** *Magazine, Consumer.* **Description:** Covers high-performance motorcycles, road races and motorcycle technology for racers and enthusiasts.
Address: 581 Birch St, Unit C, Lake Elsinore, CA 92530. TEL 909-245-6411, FAX 909-245-6417. Ed. John D Ulrich. Pub., R&P Trudy C Ulrich. Adv. contact Robert Dragich. Circ: 18,000.

629.2275 IRL ISSN 1393-9211
ROADRUNNER. Text in English. q. adv. **Document type:** *Magazine, Consumer.* **Description:** Carries articles about motorcycles and all related issues and news affecting riders in Ireland.
Published by: Irish Motorcyclists' Action Group, 1b Ring Terrace, Inchicore, Dublin, 8, Ireland. TEL 353-1-4530797, FAX 353-1-4536343, magsupport@magireland.iol.ie, http://www.iol.ie/~maglink. adv.: color page EUR 350; 8 x 11.5. Circ: 5,000 (paid and controlled).

796.7 DEU ISSN 1860-1634
ROLLER KATALOG. Text in German. 1994. a. EUR 3.50 newsstand/cover (effective 2007). adv. **Document type:** *Magazine, Consumer.*
Published by: Motor Presse Stuttgart GmbH und Co. KG, Leuschnerstr 1, Stuttgart, 70174, Germany. TEL 49-711-18201, FAX 49-711-1821779, cgolla@motorpresse.de, http://www.motorpresse.de. Ed. Michael Pfeiffer. Pub. Peter Paul Pietsch. Adv. contact Marcus Schardt. B&W page EUR 4,000, color page EUR 6,400; trim 185 x 248. Circ: 50,000 (paid and controlled).

796.62 GBR ISSN 1752-962X
ROULEUR. Text in English. 200?. q. GBP 34; GBP 9 per issue (effective 2009). adv. back issues avail. **Document type:** *Magazine, Consumer.* **Description:** Aimed at those people who are interested in the road racing sport.
Published by: Rapha Racing Ltd., Imperial Works, Perren St, London, NW5 3ED, United Kingdom. TEL 44-20-74855000, enquiries@rapha.cc, http://www.rapha.cc/. Ed. Guy Andrews. Adv. contact Jon Cannings.

388.120 GBR ISSN 1755-3393
ROUTES TO ACTION. Text in English. 2003. 3/yr. free (effective 2009). **Document type:** *Magazine, Trade.*
Related titles: Online - full text ed.: ISSN 1755-3407. 2003.
—CCC.
Published by: Sustrans, 2 Cathedral Sq, College Green, Bristol, Avon BS1 5DD, United Kingdom. TEL 44-117-9268893, FAX 44-117-9294173, info@sustrans.org.uk, http://www.sustrans.org.uk.

796.7 USA ISSN 1051-0613
SAFE CYCLING. Text in English. 1980. q. USD 15 per issue (effective 2005). bk.rev. charts; illus.; stat.; tr.lit. **Document type:** *Newsletter, Trade.* **Description:** Motorcycle safety information for instructors and individuals.
Indexed: CLT&T, HRIS.
Published by: Motorcycle Safety Foundation, 2 Jenner St, Ste 150, Irvine, CA 92718-3812. TEL 949-727-3227. Circ: 6,500 (controlled).

388.347 GBR ISSN 1755-3660
SAFE ROUTES TO SCHOOL. NORTHERN IRELAND. Text in English. 2007. s-a. free (effective 2009). **Document type:** *Newsletter, Consumer.*
Related titles: Online - full text ed.: ISSN 1755-3679. 2007.
—CCC.
Published by: Sustrans, 2 Cathedral Sq, College Green, Bristol, Avon BS1 5DD, United Kingdom. TEL 44-117-9268893, FAX 44-117-9294173, info@sustrans.org.uk, http://www.sustrans.org.uk.

388.347 GBR ISSN 1755-3687
SAFE ROUTES TO SCHOOL. SCOTLAND. Text in English. 200?. s-a. **Document type:** *Magazine, Trade.*
Related titles: Online - full text ed.: ISSN 1755-3695.
—CCC.
Published by: Sustrans, 2 Cathedral Sq, College Green, Bristol, Avon BS1 5DD, United Kingdom. TEL 44-117-9268893, FAX 44-117-9294173, info@sustrans.org.uk, http://www.sustrans.org.uk.

629 USA ISSN 1940-3860
SAND ADDICTION. Text in English. 2003. bi-m. USD 16.95 domestic; USD 27.95 in Canada; USD 40.95 elsewhere (effective 2009). adv. back issues avail. **Document type:** *Magazine, Consumer.* **Description:** Provides a fix for dune junkies by providing an in-depth look at the action, trend, and lifestyle of this ever-growing sport.
Published by: P G I Media, Inc., 31599 Outer Hwy 10, Redlands, CA 92373. TEL 909-794-4601, 888-923-9035, FAX 909-794-4505, http://www.pgimedia.com. Pub. Nick Mcfayden. adv.: color page USD 2,250; trim 7.75 x 10.5. Circ: 20,000.

388 CAN ISSN 0705-1840
SANFORD EVANS GOLD BOOK OF MOTORCYCLE DATA & USED PRICES. Text in English. 1977. a. CAD 19.50. **Document type:** *Handbook/Manual/Guide, Trade.* **Description:** Valuation guide features trade-in value of motorcycles, vehicle identification numbers, weight, over-all length.
Published by: Sanford Evans Research Group A Subsidiary of Sun Media Corporation, 1700 Church Ave, Winnipeg, MB R2X 3A2, Canada. TEL 204-694-2022, FAX 204-632-4250. Ed. G B Henry. Pub. Gary Henry.

796.7 SWE ISSN 1400-5670
SCANBIKE. Text mainly in Swedish. 1993. bi-m. SEK 348 domestic; DKK 348 in Denmark; NOK 348 in Norway; SEK 460 foreign (effective 2009). adv. **Document type:** *Magazine, Consumer.*
Published by: Kuloert Kultur, Aelvgatan 9, Helsingborg, Sweden. TEL 46-42-206577, info@scanbike.se, http://www.scanbike.se. Ed. Mikael Blomdahl.

796.7 DEU
SCHWACKELISTE ZWEIRAD. Text in German. 1960. q. EUR 185; EUR 72 per issue (effective 2009). adv. **Document type:** *Magazine, Trade.*
Published by: EurotaxSchwacke GmbH, Wilhelm-Roentgen-Str 7, Maintal, 63477, Germany. TEL 49-6181-4050, FAX 49-6181-405111, info@schwacke.de, http://www.schwacke.de. adv.: B&W page EUR 700, color page EUR 1,600; trim 105 x 148. Circ: 3,205 (paid and controlled).

388.3475 USA
SCOOT! MAGAZINE. Text in English. 199?. bi-m. USD 24.95 domestic; USD 37.95 in Canada & Mexico; USD 54.95 elsewhere (effective 2008). music rev.; video rev. back issues avail. **Document type:** *Magazine, Consumer.* **Description:** Covers the fun, goofy side of scootering as well as the serious, technical issues; topics include scooter models, races, fan clubs and other related fields.
Formerly (until 2007): Scoot! Quarterly (1545-1356)
Published by: Scoot!, 9605, San Jose, CA 95157-0605. casey@scooter.com, http://www.scooter.com.

796.7 DEU
SCOOTER & SPORT. Text in German. 1995. bi-m. EUR 3 newsstand/cover (effective 2010). adv. **Document type:** *Magazine, Consumer.*
Published by: Wagner & Wimme Verlag, Ziegelstr. 24, Rednitzhembach, 91126, Germany. adv.: B&W page EUR 2,990, color page EUR 5,190. Circ: 16,128 (paid and controlled).

796.7 ITA ISSN 1128-9694
SCOOTER MAGAZINE. Text in Italian. 1991. q. adv. **Document type:** *Magazine, Consumer.* **Description:** Covers new, vintage, and custom scooters, accessories, trips, technical tips, and news from clubs.
Related titles: Online - full text ed.
Published by: EmmeK Editore, Via 1o Maggio 9, Fino Mornasco, CO 22073, Italy. TEL 39-031-881281, FAX 39-031-928898, http://www.emmekeditore.it. Circ: 50,000.

796.7 GBR ISSN 0268-7194
SCOOTERING MAGAZINE. Text in English. 1985. m. GBP 37 domestic; GBP 44 in Europe; GBP 56 elsewhere; GBP 3.60 per issue domestic; GBP 4.60 per issue in Europe; GBP 5.60 per issue elsewhere (effective 2009). back issues avail. **Document type:** *Magazine, Consumer.*
Address: PO Box 99, Horncastle, LN9 6LZ, United Kingdom. TEL 44-1507-529529, FAX 44-1507-529490. Ed. Andy Gillard. Adv. contact Sandra Fisher.

796.75 ESP
SCOOTERMANIA. Text in Spanish. 1994. m. adv. **Document type:** *Magazine, Consumer.*
Related titles: Supplement(s): Catalogo Scootermania. 2001. EUR 2.40 newsstand/cover (effective 2004).
Published by: Motorpress Iberica (Subsidiary of: Gruner + Jahr AG & Co), Ancora 40, Madrid, 28045, Spain. TEL 34-91-3470100, FAX 34-91-3470152, http://www.motorpress-iberica.es. Ed. Josep Maria Armengol. Circ: 25,750 (paid and controlled).

796.75 FRA ISSN 1258-8555
SCOOT'N SCOOT. Text in French. 1994. bi-m. EUR 39 domestic; EUR 60 foreign (effective 2009). **Document type:** *Magazine, Consumer.*
Related titles: Supplement(s): Booster & B W's. ISSN 1775-0067. 200?. EUR 4.95 per issue (effective 2006).
Published by: Editions Terre-Mars, 4 rue Pitois, Puteaux, 92800, France.

796.6 305.4 USA
▼ **SHE PEDALS;** the journal of women in cycling. Text in English. 2009. q. USD 30 domestic; USD 40 in Canada; USD 50 elsewhere (effective 2010). adv. illus. **Document type:** *Magazine, Consumer.* **Description:** For female bicycle racers. It focuses on race locations and on individual women who've made notable accomplishments in road- or mountain-bike racing.
Related titles: Online - full text ed.
Published by: She Pedals Publishing, 2888 E Walnut St, Studio 6, Pasadena, CA 91107. Ed. Dena Eaton.

629 USA
SIDE X SIDE ACTION MAGAZINE. Variant title: S X S. Text in English. 2006. 10/yr. USD 19.95 domestic; USD 27.95 in Canada; USD 40.95 elsewhere (effective 2009). adv. **Document type:** *Magazine, Consumer.* **Description:** Provides an up-close and personal look into the vehicles that are changing the face of off-road.and includes photography, trend-setting editorials and in-depth stories.
Published by: P G I Media, Inc., 31599 Outer Hwy 10, Redlands, CA 92373. TEL 909-794-4601, 888-923-9035, FAX 909-794-4505, http://www.pgimedia.com. Pub. Nick Mcfayden. adv.: color page USD 4,565; trim 7.75 x 10.5. Circ: 65,000.

796.7 ESP
SOLO MOTO 30. Text in Spanish. 1983. m. EUR 108 domestic; EUR 195 in Europe; EUR 255 elsewhere (effective 2008). adv. bk.rev.; video rev. bibl.; stat. back issues avail. **Document type:** *Magazine, Consumer.* **Description:** Dedicated to the motorcyclist, with reviews of new products and some sports coverage.
Published by: Alesport S.A., Gran Via 8-10, Hospitalet de Llobragat, Barcelona, 08902, Spain. TEL 34-93-4315533, FAX 34-93-2973905, http://www.alesport.com. Ed., R&P Jose Codina. Adv. contact Nelo Dreshite. Circ: 60,000.

796.7 ESP
SOLO MOTO ACTUAL. Text in Spanish. 1975. w. EUR 36 domestic; EUR 60 in Europe; EUR 90 elsewhere (effective 2008). adv. back issues avail. **Document type:** *Magazine, Consumer.* **Description:** Dedicated to the motorcyclist, includes reviews of new products and sports coverage.
Related titles: Online - full text ed.
Published by: Alesport S.A., Gran Via 8-10, Hospitalet de Llobragat, Barcelona, 08902, Spain. TEL 34-93-4315533, FAX 34-93-2973905, http://www.alesport.com. Ed. Francisco Comunas. Circ: 18,000.

796.7 ESP
SOLO MOTO OFF ROAD; todo sobre cross, enduro, trial motos acuaticas, quads, raids. Text in Spanish. m. EUR 28 domestic; EUR 60 in Europe; EUR 90 elsewhere (effective 2008). adv.
Published by: Alesport S.A., Gran Via 8-10, Hospitalet de Llobragat, Barcelona, 08902, Spain. TEL 34-93-4315533, FAX 34-93-2973905, http://www.alesport.com.

796.6 ESP
SOLO SCOOTER. Text in Spanish. 1994. q. EUR 36 domestic; EUR 60 in Europe; EUR 90 elsewhere (effective 2008). adv. bk.rev.; video rev. bibl.; stat. back issues avail. **Document type:** *Magazine, Consumer.* **Description:** Presents articles comparing and testing scooter models, and interviews with manufacturers and designers.
Related titles: Online - full text ed.
Published by: Alesport S.A., Gran Via 8-10, Hospitalet de Llobragat, Barcelona, 08902, Spain. TEL 34-93-4315533, FAX 34-93-2973905, http://www.alesport.com. Ed. Jose Codina. Pub. Jaime Alguersuari. Adv. contact Antonio Defebrer. Circ: 50,000.

796.7 USA ISSN 1930-8353
TL440
SOUL RYDAH MAGAZINE. Text in English. 2006. q. **Document type:** *Magazine, Consumer.*
Address: PO Box 451666, Los Angeles, CA 90045. TEL 310-902-8391, info@soulrydahmag.com.

796.6 USA
SOUTHERN CYCLIST. Text in English. 1998. irreg. illus. **Document type:** *Magazine, Consumer.* **Description:** Designed for bicycling interest in the South of the United States.
Media: Online - full text.

796.7 AUS ISSN 0310-446X
SPEEDWAY RACING NEWS. Text in English. 1972. fortn. AUD 150; AUD 5.95 newsstand/cover (effective 2009). adv. **Document type:** *Magazine, Consumer.* **Description:** Sporting magazine for speedway enthusiasts. Covers 150 speedway tracks in Australia and New Zealand.
Address: PO Box 473, Padstow, NSW 2211, Australia. TEL 61-2-97926111, FAX 61-2-97922680. Ed. Matt Payne. Pub. David Lander. Adv. contact Rod Colquhoun.

796.75 AUS
SPEEDWAY WORLD. Text in English. 1986. m. AUD 66 domestic; AUD 86 foreign; AUD 5.50 newsstand/cover (effective 2009). adv. **Document type:** *Newspaper, Consumer.* **Description:** Covers motorcycle and auto racing worldwide.
Formerly (until 1997): Peter White's Speedway World (1035-123X)
Related titles: Online - full text ed.: AUD 66 (effective 2009).
Published by: Peter White Publishing, PO Box 666, Chester Hill, NSW 2162, Australia. TEL 61-2-96449754, FAX 61-2-96446137. Ed., Pub. Peter White. adv.: page AUD 300. Circ: 6,200.

796.6 DEU
▼ **SPOKE;** Magazin fuer Singlespeed, Fashion & Lifestyle. Text in German. 2010. 4/yr. EUR 4.40 newsstand/cover (effective 2011). adv. **Document type:** *Magazine, Consumer.*
Published by: Delius Klasing Verlag GmbH, Siekerwall 21, Bielefeld, 33602, Germany. TEL 49-521-5590, FAX 49-521-559113, info@delius-klasing.de, http://www.delius-klasing.de. Adv. contact Ingeborg Bockstette. Circ: 34,000 (controlled).

796.63 NZL ISSN 1177-018X
SPOKE; New Zealand's mountain biking magazine. Text in English. 2001. q. NZD 26 domestic; NZD 58 in Australia; NZD 92 elsewhere (effective 2008). adv. **Document type:** *Magazine, Consumer.* **Description:** Provides an unbiased look at the lives and activities of mountain bikers in Aotearoa, consistently pushing the boundaries of mountain bike photography, and graphic design.
Published by: First Floor Publishing Ltd., Level 1, 27 Dixon St, PO Box 9912, Wellington, New Zealand. FAX 64-4-3845018. Adv. contact Caleb Smith.

796.7 USA ISSN 1065-7649
SPORT RIDER. Text in English. 1992. 10/yr. USD 15.95 (effective 2008). adv. illus. back issues avail. **Document type:** *Magazine, Consumer.* **Description:** Provides in-depth, detailed coverage of sport bikes and racing motorcycles.
Indexed: G06, G07, G08, I05, I07, S23.
—CCC.
Published by: Source Interlink Companies, 6420 Wilshire Blvd, 10th Fl, Los Angeles, CA 90048. TEL 323-782-2000, FAX 323-782-2585, dheine@sourceinterlink.com, http://www.sourceinterlink.com. Ed. Kent Kunitsugu. Pub. Marty Estes TEL 323-782-2489. adv.: B&W page USD 7,410, color page USD 11,055. Circ: 65,362 (paid).

796.6 USA ISSN 1060-8419
SPORTBIKE. Text in English. 1991. a. USD 5.95 newsstand/cover (effective 2007). adv. illus. reprints avail. **Document type:** *Magazine, Consumer.*
Published by: Hachette Filipacchi Media U.S., Inc. (Subsidiary of: Hachette Filipacchi Medias S.A.), 1633 Broadway, New York, NY 10019. TEL 212-767-6000, FAX 212-767-5600, saleshfmbooks@hfmus.com, http://www.hfmus.com. Ed. Paul Seredynski. adv.: B&W page USD 7,335, color page USD 10,945.

796.75 USA ISSN 2158-009X
▼ **SPORTBIKES INC.** Text in English. 2010. m. free (effective 2010). **Document type:** *Magazine, Trade.* **Description:** Features road racing, drag racing, custom bikes, stunt riding and also celebrates the motorcycle club and independent rider lifestyle, with contributions from authorities in each discipline.
Media: Online - full text.
Published by: Hard Knocks Motorcycle Entertainment, 1729 Calamia Dr, Norristown, PA 19401. Ed., Pub. Allan Lane.

SPORTS ETC; Seattle's outdoor magazine. *see* SPORTS AND GAMES—Outdoor Life

796.7 USA ISSN 1548-6540
STREET CHOPPER. Text in English. 2000. m. USD 20 domestic; USD 32 in Canada; USD 44 elsewhere (effective 2007). adv. back issues avail. **Document type:** *Magazine, Consumer.*
Published by: Source Interlink Companies, 2570 E Cerritos Ave, Anaheim, CA 92806. TEL 714-941-1400, FAX 714-978-6390, dheine@sourceinterlinkmedia.com, http://www.sourceinterlinkmedia.com. Ed. Courtney Halowell. Pub. Sean Finley TEL 714-941-1403.

796.75 USA ISSN 1949-3541
STREET DESIREZ MAGAZINE. Text in English. 2008. m. USD 14.99 (effective 2009). adv. **Document type:** *Magazine, Consumer.*
Address: PO Box 770272, Miami, FL 33177. TEL 800-763-9210.

796.7 FRA ISSN 1956-3841
STREET MONSTERS; bikes tricks and lifestyles. Text in French. 2007. bi-m. EUR 28 domestic (effective 2010); EUR 45 in Europe; EUR 53 in North America (effective 2007). **Document type:** *Magazine, Consumer.*
Address: 67 Rue Antonin Georges Belin, Argenteuil, 95100, France. TEL 33-1-39618199, streetmonstersmag@yahoo.com.

796.7 GBR ISSN 0961-9453
STREETFIGHTERS. Text in English. 1991. m. GBP 43.89 domestic; GBP 55.89 in Europe; GBP 67.89 elsewhere (effective 2010). adv. back issues avail. **Document type:** *Magazine, Consumer.* **Description:** Contains coverage of the world's top stunt riders and stunt events, regular product reviews, technical articles by the authors.
Related titles: Supplement(s): Streetfighters Xtra. ISSN 1749-7965. 2006.
Published by: Ocean Media Group Ltd. (Subsidiary of: Trinity Mirror Plc.), 1 Canada Sq, 19th Fl, Canary Wharf, London, E14 5AP, United Kingdom. TEL 44-20-77728300, FAX 44-20-77728599, Pamela.McSweeney@oceanmedia.co.uk, http://www.oceanmedia.co.uk. Adv. contact Justin Driver TEL 44-207-7728327.

388.347 DNK ISSN 0905-4766
STYRET. Text in Danish. 1990. m. **Document type:** *Newsletter, Trade.*
Published by: Koebenhavns Cykelhandlerforening, Ny Kongensgade 20, Copenhagen V, 1557, Denmark. TEL 45-33-114003, FAX 45-33-126419. Ed. Erik Sveboelle.

796.7 USA ISSN 1934-4996
SUPER STREETBIKE. Text in English. 2003. m. USD 18 domestic; USD 30 in Canada; USD 42 elsewhere (effective 2008). adv. back issues avail. **Document type:** *Magazine, Consumer.* **Description:** Explores the custom sportbike and stunting movement.
Indexed: G06, G07, G08, I05, S23.
—CCC.
Published by: Source Interlink Companies, 6420 Wilshire Blvd, 10th Fl, Los Angeles, CA 90048. TEL 323-782-2000, FAX 323-782-2585, dheine@sourceinterlink.com, http://www.sourceinterlinkmedia.com. Ed. David Sonsky. Pub. Marty Estes TEL 323-782-2489. adv.: B&W page USD 5,605, color page USD 8,785. Circ: 43,182 (paid).

796 GBR ISSN 0262-8457
SUPERBIKE. Text in English. 1977. m. GBP 37.76 domestic; USD 94.89 in United States; USD 97.41 in Canada; EUR 95.99 in Europe; GBP 60.89 elsewhere; GBP 4.15 newsstand/cover domestic; USD 10.50 newsstand/cover in US & Canada; USD 11.25 newsstand/cover in Australia (effective 2010). adv. back issues avail. **Document type:** *Magazine, Consumer.* **Description:** Focuses on serious testing, technical features and in-depth bike reviews.
Related titles: Online - full text ed.: GBP 15.23 (effective 2010).
Published by: I P C Country & Leisure Media Ltd. (Subsidiary of: I P C Media Ltd.), Leon House, 233 High St, Croydon, CR9 1HZ, United Kingdom. TEL 44-20-87268000, http://www.ipcmedia.com. Ed. Kenny Pryde TEL 44-20-87268445. Adv. contact Susan Bann TEL 44-20-87268412. color page GBP 3,060; trim 216 x 297. Circ: 38,951. **Subscr. to:** Rockwood House, Perrymount Rd, Haywards Heath RH16 3DH, United Kingdom. TEL 44-845-1231231, IPCsubs@quadrantsubs.com, http://www.magazinesdirect.co.uk. **Dist. by:** MarketForce UK Ltd, The Blue Fin Bldg, 3rd Fl, 110 Southwark St, London SE1 0SU, United Kingdom. TEL 44-20-31483300, FAX 44-20-31488105, salesinnovation@marketforce.co.uk, http://www.marketforce.co.uk/.

796.75 FRA ISSN 1779-5486
SUPERMOTO ONE. Text in French. 2006. m. EUR 34 (effective 2007). **Document type:** *Magazine, Consumer.*
Published by: A3KOM, 10 rue Lebouis, Paris, 75014, France. TEL 33-1-40640550, http://www.supermoto-one.com.

796.75 USA ISSN 1932-6068
SUPERMOTO RACER MAGAZINE. Text in English. 2005. q. USD 14.95 domestic; USD 35 in Canada; USD 60 elsewhere (effective 2007). **Document type:** *Magazine, Consumer.*
Published by: J A Media Group, 212 Alicante Aisle, Irvine, CA 92614. info@supermotoracer.com, http://www.supermotoracer.com/index2.html.

796.6 DEU ISSN 0947-8515
SURFERS; the soul magazine for surfing. Text in German. 1995. 6/yr. EUR 16; EUR 4 newsstand/cover (effective 2008). adv. **Document type:** *Magazine, Consumer.* **Description:** Covers all aspects of surfing personalities, places and products.
Published by: b&d Media Network GmbH, Osterfeldstr 12-14, Hamburg, 22529, Germany. TEL 49-40-4800070, FAX 49-40-48000799, info@bdverlag.de, http://www.bdverlag.de. Ed. Dirk Herpel. Pub. Wolfgang Block. Adv. contact Ingo Meyer. B&W page EUR 4,350, color page EUR 5,650; trim 230 x 300. Circ: 42,276 (paid). **Subscr. to:** ASV Vertriebs GmbH. TEL 49-40-2364830.

796.6 SWE ISSN 1651-162X
SVENSKA CYKELFOERBUNDETS OFFICIELLA KALENDER. Text in Swedish. 1946. a.
Former titles (until 2000): Cykelkalendern (1103-582X); (until 1989): Svenska Cykelkalendern (0347-2701); (until 1961): Svenska Cykelboken
Published by: Svenska Cykelfoerbundet, Drakslingan 1, Sigtuna, 19340, Sweden. TEL 46-8-59252550, FAX 46-8-59252936, kansli@scf.se, http://www.svenska-cykelforbundet.se.

796.7 DEU
DER SYBURGER; das nordrheinwestfaelische Motorrad-Magazin. Text in German. 1980. m. EUR 19.20 (effective 2011). adv. bk.rev. **Document type:** *Magazine, Consumer.*
Published by: Syburger Verlag GmbH, Hertingerstr 60, Unna, 59423, Germany. TEL 49-2303-98550, FAX 49-2303-98559, info@syburger.de, http://www.syburger.de. Ed. Erik Foerster. Adv. contact Jessica Kwasny. Circ: 33,000 (paid and controlled).

796.6 NOR ISSN 1503-6553
SYKKELMAGASINET. Text in Norwegian. 1993. 9/yr. NOK 400; NOK 54 per issue (effective 2006). adv. **Document type:** *Magazine, Consumer.*
Former titles (until 2000): Sykkelmagasinet Off Road (0805-7834); (until 1994): Det Norske Off Road og Mountain Bike Magasinet (0804-7863)
Address: Masteveien 3, PO Box 145, Skytte, 1483, Norway. TEL 47-67-062320, FAX 47-67-062321, post@sykkelmagasinet.no. Ed. Fritjof Iversen. adv.: B&W page NOK 12,950, color page NOK 15,950; 230 x 310.

796.7 USA ISSN 2154-333X
▼ **THROTTLE NATION.** Text in English. 2010. bi-m. USD 30 (effective 2010). **Document type:** *Magazine, Consumer.* **Description:** For freestyle motorcycle riders.
Related titles: Online - full text ed.: ISSN 2155-3904.
Published by: Pleasant Media, 3138 Custer Dr. Ste 220, Lexington, KY 40517. TEL 859-619-6856, jp@stuntersedgemagazine.com.

796.7 USA
THUNDER ALLEY. Text in English. 1993. bi-m. adv. **Document type:** *Magazine, Consumer.* **Description:** Covers high-performance Harley-Davidson bikes. Offers real-world comparisons of motorcycle products and publishes technical and how-to articles on how to improve a Harley's performance.
Formerly (until 1995): American Iron Magazine Presents .. (1068-8250)
Published by: T A M Communications Inc., 5610 Scotts Valley Dr, Ste B552, Scotts Valley, CA 95066. TEL 831-439-1500, FAX 866-390-1218, http://www.tamcom.com.

796.7 USA
THUNDER PRESS; harley-davidson and American motorcycle news. Text in English. 1992. m. USD 35 domestic; USD 85 foreign (effective 2007). adv. back issues avail. **Document type:** *Magazine, Consumer.* **Description:** Contains up-to-date news, product reviews and tests, interviews and rider profiles, and other information of interest to Harley and Buell motorcycle riders and enthusiasts.
Related titles: Regional ed(s).: Thunder Press South; Thunder Press North.
Published by: Affinity Group Inc., 2575 Vista Del Mar, Ventura, CA 93001. TEL 805-667-4100, FAX 805-667-4419, info@affinitygroup.com, http://www.affinitygroup.com. adv.: B&W page USD 3,740, color page USD 5,495. Circ: 123,000.

796.75 USA ISSN 1949-4238
THUNDER ROADS MAGAZINE. Text in English. 2003. m. USD 29; free to qualified personnel (effective 2009). adv. back issues avail. **Document type:** *Magazine, Trade.* **Description:** Provides information about rides, events, travel and other segments of the motorcycle market.
Related titles: Online - full text ed.: ISSN 1949-4246. free (effective 2009).
Published by: Thunder Roads Texas, 4631 Cashel Glen Dr, Houston, TX 77069. TEL 281-866-8149, FAX 281-817-7504. Ed. Shelly Horan. Adv. contact Jerry Knowles TEL 281-919-7167.

388.3 CHE ISSN 1424-0149
TOEFF; das schweizer Magazin fuer Motorrad und Sport. Text in German. 1994. m. CHF 4.50 newsstand/cover (effective 2001). adv. **Document type:** *Magazine, Consumer.*
Published by: Motor-Presse (Schweiz) AG, Bahnstr 24, Schwerzenbach, 8603, Switzerland. TEL 41-1-2662166, FAX 41-1-2662160, verlag@motorpresse.ch. Ed. Guenther Wiesinger. Pub., Adv. contact August Hug. Circ: 26,000 (paid).

796.75 DEU
TOP IN SPORT MOTO G P. Text in German. 10/yr. EUR 39.50 domestic; EUR 44 foreign (effective 2008). adv. **Document type:** *Magazine, Consumer.*
Published by: B P A Sportpresse GmbH, Leonhardtstr 2a, Hannover, 30175, Germany. TEL 49-511-1233280, FAX 49-511-12332811, verlag@bpa-sportpresse.de, http://www.bpa-sportpresse.de.

388.347 AUS ISSN 1837-0799
▼ **TOTALLY SPEEDWAY.** Text in English. 2009. m. AUD 80 (effective 2011). back issues avail. **Document type:** *Magazine, Trade.*
Published by: Daniel Powell, Ed. & Pub., PO Box 645, Glebe, NSW 2037, Australia. TEL 61-4-32126210, FAX 61-2-64572685, daniel@redlinemedia.com.au. **Subscr. to:** PO Box 46, Jindabyne, NSW 2627, Australia.

796.6 DEU ISSN 0936-0905
TOUR; Europas groesstes Rennrad-Magazin. Text in German. 1977. m. EUR 47 in Germany & Austria; EUR 61 in Switzerland; EUR 69 elsewhere; EUR 4.50 newsstand/cover (effective 2011). adv. **Document type:** *Magazine, Consumer.*
Published by: Delius Klasing Verlag GmbH, Siekerwall 21, Bielefeld, 33602, Germany. TEL 49-521-5590, FAX 49-521-559113, info@delius-klasing.de, http://www.delius-klasing.de. Ed. Thomas Musch. Adv. contact Ingeborg Bockstette. Circ: 91,000 (paid).

796.75 DEU ISSN 0933-4440
TOUREN-FAHRER; Reportagen - Test - Technik. Text in German. 1981. 12/yr. EUR 54; EUR 5 newsstand/cover (effective 2011). adv. **Document type:** *Magazine, Consumer.*
Published by: Reiner H. Nitschke Verlags GmbH, Eifelring 28, Euskirchen, 53879, Germany. TEL 49-2251-650460, FAX 49-2251-6504699, service@nitschke-verlag.de, http://www.nitschke-verlag.de.

796.7 DNK ISSN 0106-1925
TOURING NYT. Text in Danish. 1966. 9/yr. adv. bk.rev. **Document type:** *Magazine, Consumer.*
Published by: M C Touring Club, Markvangen 6, Viby J, 8260, Denmark. TEL 45-86-116200, FAX 45-86-116259, tn@mctc.dk, http://www.mctouringclub.dk. Ed. Gunnar Skrydstrup. Adv. contact Peter Krogh. Circ: 38,700.

388.347 FRA ISSN 1955-6926
TOUTE L'OCCASION MOTO. Text in French. 200?. bi-m. **Document type:** *Magazine, Consumer.*
Published by: Mape et Rouire, 66 Av du General Leclerc, L'Hay-les-Roses, 94240, France. TEL 33-1-41242929.

796.7 USA
TOY & HAULER BUSINESS. Abbreviated title: T H B. Text in English. 2005. m. free (effective 2009). adv. back issues avail.; reprints avail. **Document type:** *Magazine, Trade.* **Description:** Covers the toy hauler segment of the recreational vehicle industry and the closely related power sports industry.
Published by: National Business Media, Inc., PO Box 1416, Broomfield, CO 80038. TEL 303-469-0424, 800-669-0424, FAX 303-469-5730, rpmpublisher@nbm.com.

796.7 USA ISSN 0892-3922
THE TRAIL RIDER. Text in English. 19??. 8/yr. USD 19.97 domestic; USD 46 in Canada; USD 60 elsewhere (effective 2010). adv. back issues avail. **Document type:** *Magazine, Consumer.* **Description:** Covers off-road motorcycling throughout the Northeast.
Former titles (until 198?): Trail Rider (0890-9393); (until 1986): The New England Trail Rider (0747-3982)
Indexed: G06, G07, G08, I05.
Published by: Horse Media Group (Subsidiary of: Belvoir Media Group, LLC), 908 Main St, Ste 300, Louisville, CO 80027. TEL 303-661-9282, FAX 303-661-9298, http://www.horsemediagroup.com. Ed. Rene Riley. Adv. contact Nick Griggs. B&W page USD 1,945, color page USD 2,295; trim 8.25 x 10.5. Circ: 41,622 (paid). **Subscr. to:** Palm Coast Data, LLC, PO Box 420235, Palm Coast, FL 32142. TEL 866-343-1802, http://www.palmcoastdata.com.

S

796.7 USA ISSN 1524-6574
TRAIL RIDER MAGAZINE. Text in English. 1996. 8/yr. USD 25 domestic; USD 35 in Canada (effective 2011). adv. **Document type:** *Magazine, Consumer.* **Description:** Covers stories about trail rides and the people that run them, as well as the people who ride them, rides taking place all over the United States and elsewhere, horse care, trail riding vacations, wagon train rides, merchandise for sale, horses for sales, and much more.
Related titles: Online - full text ed.: USD 20 (effective 2011).
Address: PO Box 2038, Medford Lakes, NJ 08055. TEL 609-953-2922, FAX 609-953-7223. adv.: B&W page USD 469, color page USD 1,380; trim 8 x 10.75. Circ: 1,523 (controlled); 19,046 (paid).

796.77 USA ISSN 1533-6212
TRANSWORLD MOTOCROSS. Text in English. 2000 (Sept.). m. USD 16.97 domestic; USD 28.97 in Canada; USD 45.97 elsewhere; USD 4.99 newsstand/cover (effective 2009). adv. illus. **Document type:** *Magazine, Consumer.* **Description:** Covers the entire spectrum of motocross interests, including product reviews, how-tos, motorcycle tests, interviews with stars, and extensive race coverage.
Indexed: G08, I05.
—CCC.
Published by: TransWorld Media (Subsidiary of: Bonnier Magazine Group), 1421 Edinger Ave, Ste D, Tustin, CA 92780. TEL 714-247-0077, FAX 714-247-0078, http://www.transworldmatrix.com/twmatrix/. Ed. Donn Maeda. Adv. contact Marquita Braxton. color page USD 12,708; trim 7.875 x 10.5. Circ: 125,000.

796.6 DEU ISSN 1860-1421
TREKKINGBIKE; das moderne Fahrradmagazin. Text in German. 2002. bi-m. EUR 25.20 domestic; EUR 34.10 foreign; EUR 3.90 newsstand/cover (effective 2011). adv. **Document type:** *Magazine, Consumer.*
Related titles: Supplement(s): E-bike. 2010. EUR 4.90 newsstand/cover (effective 2011).
Published by: Delius Klasing Verlag GmbH, Siekerwall 21, Bielefeld, 33602, Germany. TEL 49-521-5590, FAX 49-521-559113, info@delius-klasing.de, http://www.delius-klasing.de. Ed. Tom Bierl. Adv. contact Ingeborg Bockstette.

796.7 GBR ISSN 0958-4226
TRIALS + MOTOCROSS NEWS. Variant title: Trials and Motocross News. Text in English. 1977. w. GBP 79.95 domestic; GBP 130 in Europe; GBP 169 elsewhere (effective 2009). adv. bk.rev. **Document type:** *Newspaper, Trade.* **Description:** Provides reviews, results, comments on all aspects of trails, motocross, enduro etc. Features on the stars, machines and competititons.
—CCC.
Published by: Lancaster and Morecambe Newspapers Ltd., Victoria St, Morecambe, Lancs LA4 4AG, United Kingdom. TEL 44-1524-834030. Ed. John Dickinson TEL 44-1524-834084. Adv. contact Debs Stuchbury TEL 44-1524-834007.

629.2 GBR ISSN 1756-2015
TRIKE MAGAZINE. Text in English. 2007. q. GBP 15.80 domestic; GBP 21.16 in Europe; GBP 23.52 elsewhere; GBP 3.95 per issue (effective 2009). adv. back issues avail. **Document type:** *Magazine, Consumer.* **Description:** Covers all things tricycular. Looks at both full custom builds and bike conversions, disabled options, legalities, trike events, news, products.
Related titles: Online - full text ed.: GBP 17; GBP 4.25 per issue (effective 2009).
Published by: Jazz Fashion Publishing Ltd., The Old School, Main Rd, Higher Kinnerton, Chester, Ches. CH4 9AJ, United Kingdom. TEL 44-1244-663400, FAX 44-1244-660611, info@jazzpublishing.co.uk, http://www.jazzpublishing.co.uk. Ed. Nik Samson TEL 44-7719-679078. Pub. David Gamble. Adv. contact Shelley Curry TEL 44-1244-663400 ext 303. Circ: 13,892.

796.75 ITA ISSN 1824-615X
TUNING BIKE. Text in Italian. 2004. a. **Document type:** *Magazine, Consumer.*
Published by: Eurosport Editoriale, Via della Bufalotta 378, Rome, 00139, Italy. TEL 39-06-45231508, FAX 39-06-45231599, info@eurosporteditoriale.com, http://www.eurosporteditoriale.com.

796.6 ITA ISSN 1120-5873
TUTTO MOUNTAIN BIKE. Text in Italian. 1989. m. (11/yr.). EUR 53 (effective 2008). adv. **Document type:** *Magazine, Consumer.*
Published by: Cantelli Editore Srl, Via Saliceto 22c, Castelmaggiore, BO 40013, Italy. TEL 39-051-6328811, FAX 39-051-6328815, cantelli.editore@cantelli.net, http://www.cantelli.net. Circ: 55,000.

796.7 ITA ISSN 1125-6141
TUTTO SCOOTER. Text in Italian. 1997. m. **Document type:** *Magazine, Consumer.*
Published by: Piscopo Editore Srl, Via di Villa Sacchetti 11, Rome, 00197, Italy. TEL 39-06-3200105, FAX 39-06-3200143, http://www.piscopoeditore.it. Ed. Alfonso Rago.

TUTTOFUORISTRADA OSSERVATORE MOTORISTICO. *see* TRANSPORTATION—Automobiles

338.347 796.7 ITA ISSN 0393-7879
TUTTOMOTO. Text in Italian. 1978. 11/yr. adv. **Document type:** *Magazine, Consumer.*
Published by: Hachette Rusconi SpA (Subsidiary of: Hachette Filipacchi Medias S.A.), Viale Sarca 235, Milan, 20126, Italy. TEL 39-02-66192629, FAX 39-02-66192469, dirgen@rusconi.it, http://portale.hachettepubblicita.it. Ed. Giulio Palumbo. Adv. contact Eduardo Giliberti. Circ: 98,000.

629.227 ITA ISSN 1124-5387
TUTTORALLY. Text in Italian. 1983. m. EUR 66 (effective 2008). adv. **Document type:** *Magazine, Consumer.*
Published by: Barbero Editori Srl, Via Galileo Galilei 3, Chieri, TO 10023, Italy. TEL 39-011-9470400, FAX 39-011-9470577. Ed. Nanni Barbero. Circ: 75,000.

629.227 NLD ISSN 0165-1943
TWEEWIELER; maandblad voor de tweewielerbranche. Text in Dutch. 1921. m. (11/yr.). EUR 135 (effective 2009). adv. abstr.; illus.; mkt.; stat. **Document type:** *Trade.* **Description:** Supplies information about current developments of interest to bicycle, scooter and motorcycle retailers.
Formerly (until 1973): F Vier
Indexed: KES.
Published by: Reed Business bv (Subsidiary of: Reed Business), Hanzestraat 1, Doetinchem, 7006 RH, Netherlands. TEL 31-314-349911, FAX 31-314-343839, info@reedbusiness.nl, http://www.reedbusiness.nl. Ed. Arnauld Hackmann TEL 31-314-349884. Pub. Geert van de Bosch. adv.: B&W page EUR 2,796, color page EUR 5,085; trim 230 x 300. Circ: 4,444.

796 AUS ISSN 0041-4700
TWO WHEELS. Text in English. 1968. m. AUD 78.70 domestic; AUD 116 in New Zealand; AUD 171 elsewhere; AUD 8.50 newsstand/cover (effective 2008). adv. **Document type:** *Magazine, Consumer.* **Description:** Provides the information on latest models, road tests and equipment for motorcycles.
Incorporates (1994-1995): Revs Motorcycle Sport (1323-6717); Which was formerly (1975-1994): Revs Motorcycle News (0027-2175)
Indexed: ARI, Pinpoint.
Published by: News Magazines Pty Ltd., Level 3, 2 Holt St, Surry Hills, NSW 2010, Australia. TEL 61-2-92883000, subscriptions@newsmagazines.com.au, http://www.newsspace.com.au/magazines. Ed. Jeremy Bowdler. Adv. contact Luke Finn TEL 61-2-80622738. color page AUD 2,645; trim 206 x 276. Circ: 32,182.

796.6 USA ISSN 1524-525X
GV1045
U S A CYCLING. Text in English. 1980. bi-m. USD 25 (effective 2005). adv. bk.rev. illus. **Document type:** *Magazine, Consumer.* **Description:** Offers association-related news reports and releases, feature articles on all aspects of bicycle racing, profiles of coaches and cyclists, and information on events and programs of interest to members.
Former titles (until 1999): Bike Racing Nation (1098-3724); Cycling U S A (0274-4813)
Address: One Olympic Plaza, Colorado Springs, CO 80909. TEL 719-866-4581, FAX 719-866-4628. Ed., R&P B J Hoeptner TEL 719-578-4581. Circ: 60,000.

796.75 GBR ISSN 2046-4282
ULSTER ROAD RACING IN FOCUS. Text in English. 1997. bi-m. GBP 25.80 domestic; GBP 31.50 in US, Europe & UK; GBP 39 elsewhere; GBP 4.80 per issue domestic; GBP 5.75 per issue in US, Europe & UK; GBP 7 per issue elsewhere (effective 2011). **Document type:** *Magazine, Trade.*
Former titles (until 2010): Motorcycle Road Racing in Focus (2045-0494); (until 2009): Ulster Road Racing in Focus (1742-4127)
Published by: Ulster Speed Promotions, 6 Parkland Ave, Lisburn, Antrim BT28 3JW, United Kingdom.

796.7 USA ISSN 1945-9580
ULTIMATE MOTORCYCLING. Text in English. 2004 (Spr). bi-m. USD 19.97 domestic; USD 29.97 in Canada; USD 59.97 elsewhere (effective 2009). adv. **Document type:** *Magazine, Consumer.* **Description:** Covers the luxury motorcycle market and the affluent enthusiasts.
Formerly (until 2008): Robb Report Motorcycling (1548-6281)
Related titles: Online - full text ed.
Published by: CurtCo Robb Media LLC., 29160 Heathercliff Rd, Ste 200, Malibu, CA 90265. TEL 310-589-7700, FAX 310-589-7723, support@robbreport.com, http://www.curtco.com. Ed. Don Williams. Pub. Arthur C Coldwells. Circ: 100,000.

796.6 GBR ISSN 1751-5408
UNI; the unicycle magazine. Text in English. 2006. q. GBP 30 domestic; EUR 50 in Europe; USD 72 in United States; GBP 36 elsewhere; GBP 5 per issue domestic; EUR 8 per issue in Europe; USD 12 per issue in United States; GBP 6 per issue elsewhere (effective 2009). adv. back issues avail. **Document type:** *Magazine, Consumer.* **Description:** Covers events across the globe and all aspects of unicycling, composing an authoritative information source for the international community.
Published by: Chaelpen Pulishing, 2 Ullswater Rd, London, SW13 JP, United Kingdom.

UNSER WANDERBOTE. *see* SPORTS AND GAMES

796.6 NLD ISSN 2211-2235
▼ **UP/DOWN.** Text in Dutch. 2010. q. EUR 10; EUR 4.95 newsstand/cover (effective 2011). adv. **Document type:** *Magazine, Consumer.*
Published by: Soul Media, Stetweg 43C, Castricum, 1901 JD, Netherlands. TEL 31-251-674911, FAX 31-251-674378, info@soulonline.nl, http://www.soulonline.nl. Circ: 10,000.

388.347 USA ISSN 2159-2802
▼ **URBAN BAGGER.** Text in English. 2010. bi-m. USD 19.95 domestic; USD 49.95 in Canada; USD 74.95 elsewhere (effective 2011). adv. **Document type:** *Magazine, Trade.*
Published by: Maverick Publications, 3105 W Fairgrounds Loop, Ste 200, Spearfish, SD 57783. TEL 605-722-0112, 800-999-9718, FAX 605-722-0008, info@maverickpub.com, http://www.maverickpub.com.

796.7 USA
URBAN BIKER. Text in English. m. USD 4.99 newsstand/cover domestic; USD 6.99 newsstand/cover in Canada (effective 2009). **Document type:** *Magazine, Consumer.*
Published by: Urban Bike Magazine, PO Box 21, New York, NY 10101-0021. TEL 212-971-1064, info@urbanbikemag.com. Ed. Elaine Gh'rael. Pub. Carl Broady.

796.7 USA ISSN 2154-4204
URBAN BURNOUT. Text in English. 2006. d. free (effective 2010). **Document type:** *Magazine, Consumer.* **Description:** For the urban motorcyclist.
Media: Online - full text.
Published by: Dionne H. Nichols, 688 Yorkshire Dr, Clayton, NC 27520. dionne@urbanburnout.com.

796.75 AUS ISSN 1838-644X
▼ **USED & CLASSIC BIKE ENTHUSIAST.** Text in English. 2010. q. USD 8.95 (effective 2011). **Document type:** *Magazine, Trade.*
Published by: J P Media, PO Box 3197, Umina Beach, NSW 2257, Australia. TEL 61-3-43410666, http://www.rapidbikes.com.au.

796.7 GBR ISSN 0969-6105
USED BIKE GUIDE. Text in English. 1988. bi-m. GBP 16 domestic; GBP 20 in Europe; GBP 24 elsewhere (effective 2009). adv. **Document type:** *Magazine, Consumer.* **Description:** Provides information on all aspects of buying and selling used motorcycles.
Formerly (until 1991): Used and Classic Bike Guide (0955-6362)
Published by: Mortons Media Group Ltd., Media Centre, Morton Way, Horncastle, Lincs LN9 6JR, United Kingdom. TEL 44-1507-529529, FAX 44-1507-529490, mortons@mortons.co.uk, http://www.mortonsmediagroup.com/.

796.7 GBR ISSN 0269-3828
USED MOTORCYCLE GUIDE. Text in English. 1986. q. USD 19.99; GBP 1.75 newsstand/cover (effective 1999). **Document type:** *Handbook/Manual/Guide, Consumer.* **Description:** Contains reports with photos on bikes, buyers' guides and travel.
Address: 5 Princes St, Cardiff, CF2 3PR, United Kingdom. info@net-motorcycles.com. Ed., Pub. Bill Fowler. **Dist. by:** Seymour Distribution Ltd, 86 Newman St, London W1T 3EX, United Kingdom. FAX 44-207-396-8002, enquiries@seymour.co.uk.

796.63 FRA ISSN 0299-4208
V T T MAGAZINE; l'officiel du velo tout terrain. (Velo Tout Terrain) Text in French. 1987. 11/yr. EUR 38 domestic; EUR 50 in Belgium; EUR 53 in United States (effective 2010).
Address: 40-50 bd. Senard, St Cloud, 92210, France. TEL 33-1-47112000, FAX 33-1-46022311. Ed. Francoise Merckling. Pub. Olivier Quesnel.

796.7 USA ISSN 1088-1557
V-TWIN. Text in English. 1989. m. USD 24.95; USD 6.99 newsstand/cover (effective 2009). adv. illus. back issues avail. **Document type:** *Magazine, Consumer.* **Description:** Features information on the new products, accessories and services for today's cruiser motorcycles.
Incorporates (1994-2001): V Q (1073-581X); Former titles (until 1995): Easyriders V-Twin Edition; (until 1992): V-Twin (1042-5365)
Published by: Paisano Publications, Inc., 28210 Dorothy Dr, Box 3075, Agoura Hills, CA 91301. TEL 818-889-8740, 800-247-6246, FAX 818-735-6518, bulkmagazines@paisanopub.com. Adv. contact Tammy Porter TEL 818-889-8740 ext 1265. Circ: 66,493.

796.7 USA ISSN 1932-8052
V-TWIN ANNUAL. Text in English. a. USD 9.99 per issue (effective 2008). **Document type:** *Magazine, Consumer.*
Published by: Paisano Publications, Inc., 28210 Dorothy Dr, Box 3075, Agoura Hills, CA 91301. TEL 818-889-8740, FAX 818-735-6518.

796.6 CAN ISSN 1180-1360
VELO MAG. Text in English. 6/yr. CAD 25.64 (effective 2000). adv.
Indexed: PdeR, SD.
Published by: Editions Tricycle, 1251 rue Rachel Est, Montreal, PQ H2J 2J9, Canada. TEL 514-521-8356, FAX 514-521-5711. Ed. Pierre Hamel. Adv. contact F Tremblay. B&W page CAD 2,010, color page CAD 2,680; trim 10 x 7.13.

796.6 USA ISSN 0161-1798
VELONEWS; the journal of competitive cycling. Text in English. 1972. 15/yr. USD 29.95 domestic; USD 53.95 in Canada; USD 81.95 elsewhere; USD 49.95 combined subscription domestic (print & online eds.); USD 73.95 combined subscription in Canada (print & online eds.); USD 101.95 combined subscription elsewhere (print & online eds.) (effective 2009). adv. bk.rev.; film rev. charts; illus.; stat. Index. 84 p./no.; back issues avail.; reprints avail. **Document type:** *Magazine, Consumer.* **Description:** Contains comprehensive news, exclusive rider interviews, expert training advice, unbiased gear reviews and best race analysis.
Former titles (until 1974): Cyclenews; (until 1972): Northeast Bicycle News
Related titles: Microfilm ed.: (from PQC); Online - full text ed.: USD 29.95 (effective 2009).
Indexed: SD, SPI, SportS.
Published by: Inside Communications Inc., 1830 N 55th St, Boulder, CO 80301. TEL 303-440-0601, FAX 303-444-6788, fmagowan@insideinc.com, http://www.insideinc.com/. Eds. Ben Delaney, John Wilcockson. Pub. Andy Pemberton TEL 303-245-2186. Circ: 49,233 (paid). **Subscr. to:** Publishers Creative Systems, 119 E Grand Ave, Escondido, CA 92025. TEL 800 847-9910, http://www.pcspublink.com.

VIE DE LA MOTO. *see* ANTIQUES

LA VIE DE L'AUTO. *see* ANTIQUES

796.7 GBR
VINTAGE MOTOR CYCLE. Text in English. 1948. m. GBP 18. adv. bk.rev. **Document type:** *Magazine, Consumer.*
Formerly: Vintage Motor Cycle Club Magazine
Published by: (Vintage Motor Cycle Club), Dalton Watson Fine Books Ltd., Belton, PO Box 2, Loughborough, Leics LE12 9UW, United Kingdom. TEL 01530-223569. Ed. David Styles. Circ: 10,600.

796.75 GBR ISSN 2041-4528
VISOR DOWN. Text in English. 2002. m. GBP 10.62 per quarter (effective 2010). adv. back issues avail. **Document type:** *Magazine, Consumer.*
Formerly (until 2009): Two Wheels Only (1473-9674)
Related titles: Online - full text ed.
—CCC.
Published by: Magicalia Ltd., 15-18 White Lion St, Islington, London, N1 9PG, United Kingdom. TEL 44-20-78438800, FAX 44-20-78438999, customer.services@magicalia.com, http://www.magicalia.com/. Ed. Ben Cope.

VOGELVRIJE FIETSER. *see* TRANSPORTATION

796.6 052 GBR
W O W MAGAZINE. (Women on Wheels) Text in English. 4/yr. **Document type:** *Newsletter.*
Published by: Women's Cycle Racing Association, 27 Parkhill Rd, Sidcup, Kent DA15 7NJ, United Kingdom. Ed. M Ivatts.

796.7 USA ISSN 1051-8088
WALNECK'S CLASSIC CYCLE TRADER. Text in English. 19??. m. illus. reprints avail. **Document type:** *Magazine, Trade.*
Related titles: Online - full text ed.
Published by: Trader Publishing Co., 150 Granby St, Norfolk, VA 23510. TEL 757-640-4020, http://www.traderonline.com/.

796.6 NLD ISSN 1382-7278
DE WERELDFIETSER; de vakantiefietser. Text in Dutch. 1994. q. EUR 15 (effective 2009). adv. illus. **Document type:** *Magazine, Consumer.* **Description:** Offers touring bicyclists stories, news, and travel information.
Published by: (Vereniging voor Wereldfietsers), Holcus, Sierpeerhof 10, Diemen, 1112 GE, Netherlands. TEL 31-20-6902125, FAX 31-20-6958085, post@holcus.nl, http://www.holcus.nl/. Circ: 5,000.

796.6 GBR ISSN 0955-4912
WHAT BIKE?. Text in English. 1982. q. adv. **Document type:** *Magazine, Consumer.*
Formerly (until 1986): Bike Buyer (0266-8092)
Published by: H. Bauer Publishing Ltd. (Subsidiary of: Bauer Media Group), Media House, Lynchwood, Peterborough, Cambridgeshire PE2 6EA, United Kingdom. TEL 44-1733-468000. Ed. Sally Barker TEL 44-1733-468099. Adv. contact Gareth Ashman TEL 44-1733-468118.

796.6 GBR ISSN 1469-9117
WHAT MOUNTAIN BIKE?. Text in English. 2000. 13/yr. GBP 41.99 domestic; GBP 60 in Europe; GBP 75 in United States; GBP 77 elsewhere; GBP 4.20 newsstand/cover (effective 2010). adv. back issues avail. **Document type:** *Magazine, Consumer.* **Description:** Features comprehensive tests, reviews and recommendations, buying advice, maintenance walkthroughs and route guides for mountain biking enthusiasts.
—CCC.
Published by: Future Publishing Ltd., Beauford Ct, 30 Monmouth St, Bath, Avon BA1 2BW, United Kingdom. TEL 44-1225-442244, FAX 44-1225-446019, customerservice@subscription.co.uk, http://www.futureplc.com. Ed. Matt Skinner. **Subscr. to:** Tower House, Sovereign Park, Market Harborough, Leicestershire LE16 9EF, United Kingdom. TEL 44-844-8481602, FAX 44-1858-438795, future@subscription.co.uk.

796.6 NLD ISSN 2211-6672
▼ **WIELERLAND MAGAZINE.** Text in Dutch. 2011. m. EUR 42 (effective 2011). adv. **Document type:** *Magazine, Consumer.*
Formed by the merger of (2006-2011): Wieler Magazine (1874-7124); (2007-2011): K N W U Wieler Magazine (1875-2403)
Published by: Wieler Magazine, Postbus 2, Raalte, 8100 AA, Netherlands. TEL 31-612-407514. Eds. Marcel Slagman, Roy Schriemer, Evert de Rooij. Adv. contact Dini Smeding TEL 31-6-12406393.

629 USA ISSN 0745-273X
WING WORLD; for the Gold Wing & Valkyrie rider. Text in English. 1982. m. USD 40 (effective 2002). adv. **Document type:** *Magazine, Consumer.* **Description:** Contains information and news specifically targeted to the interests of the Honda Gold Wing and Valkyrie motorcyclist.
Related titles: Online - full text ed.
Published by: Gold Wing Road Riders Association, 21423 N. 11th Ave., Phoeniz, AZ 85027. TEL 800-843-9460, FAX 623-581-3844, http://www.gwrra.org. Ed. Nick Hoppner.

796.7 DEU
WORLD OF BIKE. Text in German. 1999. m. adv. **Document type:** *Magazine, Trade.*
Published by: A. V. & M. Verlag - Klaus Huettinger, Ochsenfurter Str 56, Sommerhausen, 97286, Germany. TEL 49-9333-904990, FAX 49-9333-9049915, klaus.huettinger@motorrad2000.de, http://www.motorrad2000.de. Ed. Stefan Boehm. Adv. contact Daliah Wohlfeil. B&W page EUR 2,905, color page EUR 3,363. Circ: 8,924 (controlled).

796.6 NLD ISSN 1872-4264
6 DAAGSEN STATISTIEKEN. Text in Dutch. 1993. a.
Published by: J.D. van Reijendam, Ed. & Pub., Meent 157, Breda, 4817 NS, Netherlands.

629.227 CHN ISSN 1000-999X
ZHONGGUO ZIXINGCHE/CHINA BICYCLE. Text in Chinese. 1972. bi-m. CNY 100, USD 80. adv. software rev. illus.
Related titles: Online - full text ed.
Published by: Bicycle Information Centre of China, China Bicycle Association, No6, Alley 360, Anyuan Rd, Shanghai, 200060, China. TEL 021-2584696, FAX 021-2550918. Ed. Yang Huide. Pub. Sheng Aiguo. adv.: B&W page USD 400, color page USD 1,000. Circ: 10,000.

796.6 DEU
ZWANZIG ZOLL. Text in German. 4/yr. EUR 10; EUR 2.90 newsstand/cover (effective 2008). adv. **Document type:** *Magazine, Consumer.*
Published by: All Eins e.V., Friedrichshagender Str 10, Berlin, 12555, Germany. Eds. Hans Friedrich, Sascha Richter. Adv. contact Jens Werner. page EUR 2,400. Circ: 5,000 (paid and controlled).

ZWEIRAD ADRESSBUCH. *see* BUSINESS AND ECONOMICS—Trade And Industrial Directories

796.7 CHE ISSN 1421-6647
ZWEIRAD SCHWEIZ. Text in French, German. 1900. bi-m. adv. illus.; stat. index. **Document type:** *Magazine, Consumer.*
Former titles (until 1989): Fahrrad- und Motorrad Gewerbe; (until 1969): F M G Fachblatt (0014-5955); (until 1958): Haendler- und Mechaniker-Fachblatt (1421-6841); (until 1953): Schweizerisches Haendler- und Mechaniker-Fachblatt (1421-7414); (until 1929): Schweizerisches Velohaendler- und Mechaniker-Fachblatt (1421-7406)
Published by: Schweizerischer Fahrrad- und Motorrad-Gewerbe Verband/Union Suisse des Mecaniciens en Cycles et Motos, Entfelderstr 11, Aarau, 5001, Switzerland. TEL 41-62-8233785, FAX 41-62-8233784, sfmgv@swissonline.ch, http://www.sfmgv.ch. Ed. Daniel Schaerer. adv.: page CHF 1,134; trim 185 x 270. Circ: 2,100.

796.7 DEU
ZWEITE HAND BIKER BOERSE. Text in German. 1994. m. EUR 1.90 newsstand/cover (effective 2010). adv. **Document type:** *Magazine, Consumer.*
Published by: Zweite Hand Verlag, Askanischer Platz 3, Berlin, 10963, Germany. TEL 49-30-290210, FAX 49-30-2902199935, service@zweitehand.de, http://www.zweitehand.de. adv.: color page EUR 1,100. Circ: 19,400 (paid and controlled).

796.7 CHE
2 RAD SCHWEIZ (BERN). Text in German. m. **Document type:** *Consumer.*
Published by: S F M G V, Zentral Sekretariat, Weststr 9, Bern 6, 3000, Switzerland. TEL 031-3516660.

796.7 GRC ISSN 1105-1299
2 TROCHOI/2 WHEELS. Text in Greek. 1988. q. adv. illus. **Document type:** *Magazine, Consumer.* **Description:** Covers motorcycles in general.
Published by: Technical Press SA, 80 Ioannou Metaxa, Karelas, Koropi, 19400, Greece. TEL 30-210-9792500, FAX 30-210-9792528, info@technicalpress.gr, http://www.technicalpress.gr. Ed. Marinos Koulis. Adv. contact Chrisanthi Bitsori.

796.7 DEU
2RAEDER. Text in German. 2006. m. EUR 33; EUR 2.50 newsstand/cover (effective 2011). adv. **Document type:** *Magazine, Consumer.*
Published by: Motor Presse Stuttgart GmbH und Co. KG, Leuschnerstr 1, Stuttgart, 70174, Germany. TEL 49-711-18201, FAX 49-711-1821779, cgolla@motorpresse.de, http://www.motorpresse.de. Circ: 32,870 (paid).

796.75 USA ISSN 1548-1514
2WHEEL TUNER. Text in English. 2004. m. adv. **Document type:** *Magazine, Consumer.* **Description:** Geared toward hardcore sportbike enthusiasts who spend serious money and time building and modifying bikes for competition, racing and show. Editorial content covers street racing, road racing, drag racing, stunting and hitting the open road.
Published by: Advanstar Communications, Inc., 6200 Canoga Ave, 2nd Fl, Woodland Hills, CA 91367. TEL 818-593-5000, FAX 818-593-5020, info@advanstar.com, http://www.advanstar.com. Ed. Jamie Robinson. Pub. Sarah Timleck.

796.6 USA ISSN 2161-3087
▼ **3 GO TRIATHLON;** fuel for the modern triathlete. Text in English. 2011. bi-m. USD 21.99 domestic; USD 36.99 in Canada; USD 46.99 elsewhere; USD 25.99 combined subscription domestic (print & online eds.); USD 40.99 combined subscription in Canada (print & online eds.); USD 50.99 combined subscription elsewhere (print & online eds.); USD 7.99 per issue (effective 2011). adv. back issues avail. **Document type:** *Magazine, Consumer.*
Related titles: Online - full text ed.: USD 12.99 (effective 2011).
Published by: Move Press, Llc, 1000 Fremont Ave, Ste H, S Pasadena, CA 91030. TEL 626-441-2113, FAX 626-441-2316. Ed. Brad Roe. Adv. contact Adam Reek TEL 626-441-2276.

SPORTS AND GAMES—Boats And Boating

797.1 NLD
A N W B BOOT. (Algemene Nederlandse Wielrijders Bond) Text in Dutch. 8/yr. free. adv.
Published by: (ANWB BV/Royal Dutch Touring Club), Algemene Nederlandse Wielrijders Bond (A N W B) Media/Dutch Automobile Association Media, Postbus 93200, The Hague, 2509 BA, Netherlands. TEL 31-70-3141470, FAX 31-70-3146538, http://www.anwbmedia.nl. adv.: color page EUR 6,500; trim 260 x 385. Circ: 80,000.

797.14 USA ISSN 1542-3735
GV835.9
A P B A RULES FOR STOCK OUTBOARD, MODIFIED OUTBOARD, PRO OUTBOARD, OUTBOARD PERFORMANCE CRAFT, J CLASS, OUTBOARD DRAG, AND PERFORMANCE INFLATABLE RACING. (American Power Boat Association) Text in English. a. **Document type:** *Handbook/Manual/Guide, Trade.*
Formerly (until 2001): Rules for Stock Outboard, Pro Outboard, Modified Outboard (0272-3476)
Published by: American Power Boat Association, 17640 E Nine Mile Rd, Box 377, Eastpointe, MI 48021. TEL 810-773-9700, FAX 810-773-6490, apbahq@aol.com, http://www.apba-racing.com.

796.95 USA
A S A AFFILIATE AND INSTRUCTOR NEWS. Text in English. 1983. bi-m. looseleaf. membership only. back issues avail. **Document type:** *Newsletter.* **Description:** Business topics relating to boating businesses.
Published by: American Sailing Association, PO Box 12079, Marina Dl Rey, CA 90295-3079. TEL 310-822-7171, FAX 310-822-4741, info@american-sailing.com, http://www.american-sailing.com. Ed., R&P Harry Munns. Circ: 10,000.

796 GBR ISSN 1462-5849
A Y R S JOURNAL. Text in English. 1955. irreg. (approx. 2-3/yr). bk.rev. **Document type:** *Newsletter, Academic/Scholarly.*
Former titles (until 1997): A Y R S (1462-5830); (until 1976): A Y R S Journal (0144-1396)
—BLDSC (1841.289200).
Published by: Amateur Yacht Research Society, c/o Sheila Fishwick, Secretary, BCM - AYRS, London, WC1N 3XX, United Kingdom. TEL 44-1727-862268, FAX 44-8700-526657, office@ayrs.org, http://www.ayrs.org. Ed. Simon Fishwick. Circ: 1,400.

796.95 GBR ISSN 0964-0932
ADMARINE. Text in English. 1983. m. GBP 12. adv. bk.rev. **Document type:** *Journal, Trade.* **Description:** Reports on all aspects of the marine leisure industry.
Published by: Compass Rose Ltd., 92 The Avenue, Sunbury-on-Thames, Mddx TW16 5EX, United Kingdom. Circ: 20,000 (controlled).

797.122 CAN ISSN 1496-8894
ADVENTURE KAYAK; Canada's kayak touring magazine. Text in English. q. CAD 14 domestic; CAD 21 foreign (effective 2002). adv. back issues avail. **Document type:** *Magazine, Consumer.* **Description:** Includes boat and product reviews, features, news on kayak touring destinations, and a calendar of related events.
Published by: Rapid Media Inc., PO Box 70, Palmer Rapids, ON K0J 2E0, Canada. TEL 613-758-2042, FAX 613-758-2853, http://www.rapidmedia.com/home.

797.14 AUS ISSN 1034-6651
THE ALFRED'S YACHTSMAN. Text in English. 3/yr. adv. **Description:** Covers all club events plus major yachting and sailing news.
Formerly (until 1989): Alfred's Navigator's Notebook (0311-0990)
Published by: Royal Prince Alfred Yacht Club, 16 Mitala St, PO Box 99, Newport Beach, NSW, Australia. TEL 61-2-99971022, FAX 61-2-99978620, rpayc@rpayc.com.au, http://www.rpayc.com.au. Ed., Pub., Adv. contact Damian Devine. Circ: 3,000.

797.1 USA
AMERICAN POWER BOAT ASSOCIATION. A P B A REFERENCE BOOK. Text in English. 1903. a. (in 4 vols.), latest vol.55. USD 15 to non-members. adv. index. 96 p./no.;
Former titles: American Power Boat Association. A P B A Rule - Reference Book; American Power Boat Association. A P B A Rule Book (0065-9797)
Published by: American Power Boat Association, 17640 E Nine Mile Rd, Box 377, Eastpointe, MI 48021. TEL 810-773-9700, FAX 810-773-6490, apbahq@aol.com. Ed., R&P, Adv. contact Tana Moore. Pub. Gloria Urbin. page USD 300; 4.75 x 7.875. Circ: 7,000 (paid).

796.95 USA
AMERICAN SAILING. Text in English. bi-m. membership only. **Document type:** *Newsletter.*
Published by: American Sailing Association, PO Box 12079, Marina Dl Rey, CA 90295-3079. TEL 310-822-7171, FAX 310-822-4741, http://www.american-sailing.com. Ed., R&P Harry Munns.

797.1 USA ISSN 0279-9553
AMERICAN SAILOR. Text in English. 1980. m. membership. adv.
Indexed: SD, SportS.
Published by: U S Yacht Racing Union, PO Box 843, Franklin, TN 37064. TEL 615-791-1780. Circ: 28,000.

333.7845 USA ISSN 0300-7626
GV788
AMERICAN WHITEWATER. Text in English. 1967. bi-m. USD 35 domestic; USD 40 in Canada & Mexico; USD 45 elsewhere (effective 2005). adv. bk.rev. **Document type:** *Magazine, Consumer.* **Description:** Covers canoeing and kayaking and river conservation.
Indexed: SD, SportS.
—Ingenta.
Published by: American Whitewater Affiliation, 204 Philadelphia Ave., Takoma Park, MD 20912-4213. info@amwhitewater.org, http://www.americanwhitewater.org. Ed. Ambrose Tuscano. Adv. contact Phyllis B Horowitz. B&W page USD 465; trim 10.75 x 8.25. Circ: 11,000 (paid).

796.95 USA ISSN 1546-4806
AMERICAN YACHT REVIEW. Text in English. 1999. a. free to qualified personnel (effective 2009). back issues avail. **Document type:** *Magazine, Consumer.* **Description:** Provides an in-depth look at the year's top custom boats.
Related titles: Online - full text ed.
—CCC.
Published by: Navigator Publishing LLC., 58 Fore St, Portland, ME 04101-4842. TEL 207-772-2466, FAX 207-772-2879, subscriptions@oceannavigator.com. Ed. Tim Queeney TEL 207-822-4350 ext 211. Pub., Adv. contact Alex Agnew TEL 207-822-4350 ext 219. Circ: 50,000 (paid); 5,000 (controlled).

ANKER MAGAZIN. *see* SPORTS AND GAMES—Outdoor Life

797.1 FRA ISSN 2105-6447
L'ANNEE DE LA VOILE. Text in French. 19??. a. **Document type:** *Magazine, Consumer.*
Published by: Mer & Decouverte Editions, B P 16144, Saint-Gregoire, 35761, France. TEL 33-2-99238383, http://www.meretdecouverte.com.

797 FRA ISSN 0758-6639
ANNUAIRE NAUTISME. Text in French. 1963. a. adv.
Published by: Editions de Chabassol, 16-18 bd de Lagny, Bussy-St-Georges, Marne-la-Vallee Cedex 3, 77600, France. TEL 33-1-64766490, FAX 33-1-64766499.

797.1 ITA
ANNUARIO DELLA NAUTICA. Text in Italian. 1977. a. adv. illus. **Document type:** *Catalog.*
Related titles: Online - full text ed.
Published by: Nautica Editrice, Via Tevere 44, Rome, RM 00198, Italy. TEL 39-06-8413060, FAX 39-06-8543653, info@nautica.it, http://www.nautica.it. Circ: 41,000.

797.1 USA ISSN 0003-5904
ANTIQUE OUTBOARDER. Text in English. 1966. q. USD 50 for 2 yrs. domestic membership; USD 63 for 2 yrs. in Canada membership; USD 67 for 2 yrs. elsewhere membership (effective 2008). adv. illus.; stat. **Document type:** *Magazine, Consumer.* **Description:** Covers history, restoration, technical reports, antique outboard racing, special features, and chapter news.
Related titles: ♦ Supplement(s): Antique Outboard Motor Club Newsletter.
Published by: Antique Outboard Motor Club, Inc., PO Box 2526, Walla Walla, WA 99362. memberservices@aomci.org, http://www.aomci.org. Circ: 3,000.

797.1 FRA ISSN 1638-6272
L'ARGUS DU BATEAU. Text in French. bi-m. EUR 24.50 (effective 2009). adv. **Document type:** *Magazine, Consumer.*
Published by: Editions Lariviere, 6 Rue Olof Palme, Clichy, 92587, France. TEL 33-1-47565400, http://www.editions-lariviere.fr.

796.95 HKG
ASIA-PACIFIC BOATING. Text in Chinese. 1976. m. HKD 320 domestic (effective 2008); USD 60 in Indonesia & China; USD 28 in Malaysia in Malaysia & Philippines; USD 34 in Singapore; USD 36 in Thailand; USD 70 in United Arab Emirates; USD 80 elsewhere in Asia; USD 150 in United States; USD 190 elsewhere. **Document type:** *Magazine, Consumer.*
Formerly (until 1999): Asian Boating
Related titles: Online - full content ed.
Published by: Blu Inc Media (HK) Ltd. (Subsidiary of: S P H Magazines Pte Ltd.), Ste 2901, 29/F Universal Trade Centre, No. 3 Arbuthnot Rd, Central, Hong Kong. TEL 852-2165-2800, FAX 852-2868-1799, queries@bluincmedia.com, http://www.bluincmedia.com.hk/. Circ: 30,000.

623.88 CAN ISSN 1483-4723
ATLANTIC BOATING NEWS. Text in English. 1997. bi-m. CAD 3.07 domestic; CAD 3.70 foreign; CAD 2.95 newsstand/cover (effective 2000). **Document type:** *Magazine, Consumer.*
Published by: Diversity Special Interest Publishing Co, PO Box 2705, Halifax, NS B3S 3P7, Canada. TEL 902-453-6683, diversity@fox.nstn.ca.

796.95 AUS ISSN 1835-6060
AUSTRALASIAN YACHTING. Text in English. 1983. m. AUD 82.50 domestic; AUD 95 in New Zealand; AUD 110 in Asia; AUD 150 elsewhere; AUD 6.95 newsstand/cover (effective 2008). adv. bk.rev. **Document type:** *Magazine, Consumer.* **Description:** Covers boat reviews, news on yacht races, product information and feature articles.
Former titles (until 2007): Australian Yachting (1035-3852); (until 1990): Nautical News (1034-4179); (until 1989): Australian Nautical News (0812-163X)

S

Published by: Yaffa Publishing Group Pty Ltd., 17-21 Bellevue St, Surry Hills, NSW 2010, Australia. TEL 61-2-92812333, FAX 61-2-92812750, info@yaffa.com.au. Ed. Vanessa Dudley TEL 61-2-92138252. Adv. contact Peter Rendle TEL 61-2-92138259. color page AUD 2,560; trim 220 x 297. Circ: 2,229. **Subscr. to:** GPO Box 606, Sydney, NSW 2001, Australia.

797 AUS
AUSTRALIAN P W C MAGAZINE. (Australian Personal Watercraft Magazine) Text in English. 1996. q. **Description:** Includes articles and news on personal watercraft activities.
Media: Online - full text.
Published by: Trick Media, PO Box 33, Sylvania Waters, NSW 2224, Australia. TEL 61-2-95447820, info@ozpwc.com, http://www.ozpwc.com.

796.95 AUS ISSN 0313-766X
AUSTRALIAN POWERBOAT. Text in English. 1976. bi-m. adv. **Document type:** *Magazine, Consumer.* **Description:** For the informed enthusiast who owns a power boat or intends to acquire one.
Indexed: SD.
Published by: Yaffa Publishing Group Pty Ltd., 17-21 Bellevue St, Surry Hills, NSW 2010, Australia. TEL 61-2-92812333, FAX 61-2-92812750, yaffa@yaffa.com.au, http://www.yaffa.com.au. adv.: B&W page AUD 2,190, color page AUD 2,790; trim 220 x 273. Circ: 5,119. **Subscr. to:** GPO Box 606, Sydney, NSW 2001, Australia.

797.1 AUS ISSN 0726-5646
AUSTRALIAN SAILING. Text in English. 1976. m. AUD 77 domestic; AUD 90 in New Zealand; AUD 105 in Asia; AUD 140 elsewhere; AUD 6.50 newsstand/cover (effective 2008). adv. **Document type:** *Magazine, Consumer.* **Description:** Provides in-depth reports of major international events; offers information on latest innovations in kit, boat design and technology.
Related titles: CD-ROM ed.; Online - full text ed.; Supplement(s): Sailing Champs.
Indexed: SD.
Published by: Yaffa Publishing Group Pty Ltd., 17-21 Bellevue St, Surry Hills, NSW 2010, Australia. TEL 61-2-92812333, FAX 61-2-92812750, info@yaffa.com.au. Ed. Vanessa Dudley TEL 61-2-92138252. Adv. contact Peter Rendle TEL 61-2-92138259. color page AUD 2,510; trim 210 x 297. Circ: 4,533. **Subscr. to:** GPO Box 606, Sydney, NSW 2001, Australia.

797.1 FRA ISSN 0988-1956
AVIRON. Text in French. 1886. 6/yr. EUR 25 domestic; EUR 38 foreign (effective 2008). adv. bk.rev. illus. **Document type:** *Magazine, Consumer.*
Indexed: SportS.
Published by: Aviron France Promotion, 17 bd. de la Marne, Nogent Sur Marne, Cedex 94736, France. TEL 33-1-45142640, FAX 33-1-48757875, contact@avironfrance.fr, http://www.avironfrance.fr. Ed. D Roudy.

AVVISO AI NAVIGANTI. *see* TRANSPORTATION—Ships And Shipping

796.95 USA ISSN 1090-1272
B O A T - U S MAGAZINE. Text in English. 1966 (July). bi-m. free to members (effective 2009). adv. bk.rev. **Document type:** *Magazine, Consumer.* **Description:** Covers legislative, regulatory and consumer issues of interest to owners of recreational boats.
Formerly (until 1996): B O A T - U S Reports (0279-5949)
Related titles: Online - full text ed.
Indexed: G06, G07, G08, I05, I06, I07, S23.
Published by: Boat Owners Association of the United States, 880 S Pickett St, Alexandria, VA 22304. TEL 703-461-2864, FAX 703-461-2847, mail@boatus.com. Ed., Pub. Michael G Sciulla. Adv. contact John Bratten TEL 703-461-4389. B&W page USD 14,000, color page USD 28,000; trim 8 x 10.875. Circ: 600,000.

796.95 USA ISSN 0735-973X
HD9993.B633
B U C USED BOAT PRICE GUIDE. Text in English. 1961. s-a. USD 183 (effective 2000). stat. **Document type:** *Directory.*
Formerly (until 198?): Statistically Authenticated Used Boat Price Guide (0190-4795); Incorporates: Older Boat Price Guide (0197-212X)
Published by: B U C International Corp, 1314 N E 17th Ct, Ft Lauderdale, FL 33305. TEL 954-565-6715. Ed. Paul Rosetti. R&P Joan Alagna TEL 973-485-6000.

797.1 DNK
BAADMAGASINET MOTOR. Text in Danish. 1992. m. DKK 399 (effective 2008). adv. back issues avail. **Document type:** *Magazine, Consumer.*
Supersedes in part (in 2008): Baadmagasinet (0907-0559); Which incorporated (1993-1995): Sejlernyt (0908-5238)
Related titles: Online - full text ed.
Published by: Baadmagasinet ApS, Generatorvej 8 D, Herlev, 2730, Denmark. TEL 45-44-854400, FAX 45-44-854495. Ed. Soeren Oeverup. Adv. contact Lars Kiaer TEL 45-44-854496. color page DKK 20,500; 195 x 262.

797.1 DNK
BAADMAGASINET SEJL. Text in Danish. 1992. m. DKK 399 (effective 2008). adv. back issues avail. **Document type:** *Magazine, Consumer.*
Supersedes in part (in 2008): Baadmagasinet (0907-0559); Which incorporated (1993-1995): Sejlernyt (0908-5238)
Related titles: Online - full text ed.
Published by: Baadmagasinet ApS, Generatorvej 8 D, Herlev, 2730, Denmark. TEL 45-44-854400, FAX 45-44-854495. Ed. Soeren Oeverup. Adv. contact Lars Kiaer TEL 45-44-854496. color page DKK 20,500; 195 x 262.

796.95 DNK ISSN 1603-0907
BAADNYT. Text in Danish. 1999. m. DKK 594 (effective 2010). adv. **Document type:** *Magazine, Consumer.* **Description:** Contains tests, cruising articles and do-it-yourself material on boats in Denmark.
Formerly (until 2002): Baadnyt med Sejl og Motor (1600-924X); Which was formed by the merger of (1971-1999): Baadnyt (0108-0652); Which incorporated (1975-1980): Baaden i Dag (0108-0644); (1939-1999): Sejl og Motor (0037-1130)
Related titles: Online - full text ed.
Published by: J S L Publications A/S, Dortheavej 59, Copenhagen NV, 2400, Denmark. TEL 45-32-711200, FAX 45-32-711212, info@jslpublications.dk, http://www.jslp.dk. Ed. Morten Brandt TEL 45-32-711241. Adv. contact Lennart Le Fevre. page DKK 22,900; 223 x 297. Circ: 12,066.

796.95 SWE ISSN 1100-5580
BAATAR TIL SALU; koep, saelj, hyr allt foer sjoen. Text in Swedish. 1988. fortn. SEK 356. adv. **Document type:** *Trade.*
Address: Stockholm, 11285, Sweden. TEL 46-8-692-01-75, FAX 46-8-650-37-20. Ed. Emma Roos.

796.95 SWE ISSN 1101-1432
BAATBRANSCHEN. Text in Swedish. 1982. 6/yr. SEK 149 per issue (effective 2004). adv. back issues avail. **Document type:** *Yearbook, Consumer.* **Description:** Market guide for motor- and sailboats.
Former titles (until 1990): Baatvaerlden (0283-5770); (until 1986): Baatbranschen (0280-6312)
Published by: Baatbranchens Riksfoerbund, Box 279, Karlshamn, 37424, Sweden. TEL 46-8-4495590, FAX 46-8-4495595, info@sweboat.se, http://www.sweboat.se. Ed. Lars-Aake Redeen. Adv. contact Staffan Oester. page SEK 9,900; 190 x 275. Circ: 20,000.

797.1 NOR ISSN 1504-3452
BAATFOLKETS AARBOK. Text in Norwegian. 2004. a. NOK 198 per issue (effective 2006). **Document type:** *Consumer.* **Description:** Annual for the boating enthusiast.
Published by: Schibsted Forlagene AS, PO Box 6974, St. Olavs Plass, Oslo, 0130, Norway. TEL 47-24-146800, FAX 47-24-146801, schibstedforlagene@schibstedforlagene.no, http://www.schibstedforlagene.no. Ed. Jon Winge.

797.1 NOR ISSN 1503-7258
BAATFORENINGEN; medlemsblad for alle foreningsmedlemmer paa Vestlandet. Text in Norwegian. 2002. 7/yr. NOK 100 (effective 2006). adv. **Document type:** *Magazine, Consumer.*
Related titles: Online - full text ed.
Published by: Stavanger Avishus AS, PO Box 1091, Hillevaag, Stavanger, 4095, Norway. TEL 47-51-882690, FAX 47-51-882693, stavanger.avishus@online.no. Ed. Arne Nordmand Larsen. Adv. contact Sissel Meling. color page NOK 8,000.

797.125 NOR ISSN 1504-3908
BAATLIV. Text in Norwegian. 1994. 9/yr. NOK 545 (effective 2011). adv. **Document type:** *Magazine, Consumer.*
Former titles (until 2005): Praktisk Baatliv (0808-4688); (until 1997): Praktisk Smaabaatliv (0804-4996)
Published by: Norsk Maritimt Forlag AS, Leangbukta 40, Vettre, 1392, Norway. TEL 47-66-764950, FAX 47-66-764951, http://www.havna.com. Ed. Ole-Henrik Nissen-Lie. Adv. contact Anders Theodor Bye.

797.95 SWE ISSN 0282-3934
BAATLIV. Text in Swedish. 1971. 6/yr. SEK 200 domestic; SEK 380 foreign (effective 2010). adv. **Document type:** *Magazine, Consumer.*
Formerly (until vol.3, 1983): Fritidsbaaten (0349-389X)
Published by: Svenska Baatunionen/Swedish Yachting Association, af Pontins Vaeg 6, Stockholm, 11521, Sweden. TEL 46-8-54585960, FAX 46-8-54585969, info@batliv.se, http://www.batliv.se. Ed., Pub. Lars-Aake Redeen.

797.1 NOR ISSN 0801-1672
BAATMAGASINET. Text in Norwegian. 1985. m. NOK 698 (effective 2009). adv. **Document type:** *Magazine, Consumer.* **Description:** Covers all aspects of boats and boating from sail boats to motorboats.
Related titles: ◆ Online - full text ed.: Batmagasinet Online. ISSN 0806-8089.
Published by: Aller Forlag AS, Stenersgaten 2, Sentrum, Oslo, 0189, Norway. TEL 47-21-301000, FAX 47-21-301205, allerforlag@aller.no, http://www.aller.no. Adv. contact Vidar Borgen TEL 47-21-301255. color page NOK 23,000; bleed 222 x 299. Circ: 20,904 (paid).

797.1 SWE ISSN 1650-7320
BAATMARKNADEN. Text in Swedish. 2001. 12/yr. adv. mkt. **Document type:** *Magazine, Consumer.*
Published by: Foerlags AB Albinsson & Sjoeberg, PO Box 529, Karlskrona, 37123, Sweden. TEL 46-455-335325, FAX 46-455-311715, fabas@fabas.se, http://www.fabas.se. Ed., Adv. contact Stefan Janeld. page SEK 6,000; trim 190 x 275.

797.1 SWE ISSN 0005-6308
BAATNYTT/BOATING NEWS. Text in Swedish. 1958. m. (12/13 yr). SEK 599 (effective 2007). adv. bk.rev. illus.; mkt. index. **Document type:** *Magazine, Consumer.* **Description:** Features articles and stories on motorboat and sailing destinations and equipment.
Formerly (until 1962): Motorbaatsnytt; Incorporates (1969-1983): Baat foer Alla (0345-1976)
Published by: T T G Sverige AB (Subsidiary of: De Telegraaf Tijdschriftengroep), PO Box 26206, Stockholm, 10041, Sweden. TEL 46-8-50667800, FAX 46-8-50667859, info@ttg.se, http://www.ttg.se. Eds. Aasa Bonthelius, Elias Johansson. Adv. contact Henrik Salen. page SEK 28,000; 217 x 280.

797.14 SWE ISSN 1101-4253
BAATRACING. Text in Swedish. 1989-1999; resumed 2001. 3/yr. **Document type:** *Consumer.*
Published by: Svenska Racerbaatfoerbundet (SVERA), Idrottshuset Farsta, Farsta, 12343, Sweden. TEL 46-8-6833020, FAX 46-8-6833029, info@svera.org, http://www.svera.org.

796.95 SWE ISSN 0347-2647
BAATVAERLDEN (STOCKHOLM); baatar, motorer & tilbehoer. Text in Swedish. 1969. a., latest vol.37, 2007. SEK 99 (effective 2007). adv. back issues avail. **Document type:** *Yearbook, Consumer.*
Incorporates (1987-1991): Alla Baatar (0284-9437)
Related titles: Online - full text ed.
Published by: T T G Sverige AB (Subsidiary of: De Telegraaf Tijdschriftengroep), PO Box 26206, Stockholm, 10041, Sweden. TEL 46-8-50667800, FAX 46-8-50667859, info@ttg.se, http://www.ttg.se. Adv. contact Mats Linden TEL 46-498-245061.

797.1 ITA ISSN 1827-7004
LA BARCA PER TUTTI. Text in Italian. 2005. q. **Document type:** *Magazine, Consumer.*
Published by: Edisport Editoriale SpA, Via Gradisca 11, Milan, MI 20151, Italy. TEL 39-02-38085, FAX 39-02-38010393, edisport@edisport.it, http://www.edisport.it.

797.124 ITA ISSN 1971-1638
BARCHE A VELA. Text in Italian. 2007. w. **Document type:** *Magazine, Consumer.*
Published by: De Agostini Editore, Via G da Verrazzano 15, Novara, 28100, Italy. TEL 39-0321-4241, FAX 39-0321-424305, info@deagostini.it, http://www.deagostini.it.

796.95 ARG
BARCOS. Text in Spanish. 1976. m. free. bk.rev. **Document type:** *Consumer.* **Description:** Covers commercial craft, cruising, design, electronic equipment, engines, fishing, history, jetskis, yachts, maintenance, meteorology, ports, power cruisers, racing, sailboards, vacations, nautical technology and cartography.
Published by: Editorial Barcos S.R.L., Blanco Encalada, 121, San Isidro, Buenos Aires 1642, Argentina. TEL 54-114-7354404, FAX 54-114-7354407. Ed. Silvina Garcia Guevara. Pub. Roberto Garcia Guevara. adv.: B&W page USD 1,800, color page USD 2,400; 280 x 215. Circ: 10,000 (paid); 8,000 (controlled).

796.95 ESP
BARCOS A VAPOR & YACHTING. Text in Spanish. m. EUR 4 newsstand/cover (effective 2009). adv. **Document type:** *Magazine, Consumer.*
Published by: Grupo V, C Valportillo Primera, 11, Alcobendas, Madrid, 28108, Spain. TEL 34-91-6622137, FAX 34-91-6622654, secretaria@grupov.es. Ed. Miguel Sanchez. Adv. contact Aurora Perez-Olivares. page EUR 2,590; trim 18.5 x 26.5. Circ: 2,590.

796.95 ESP
BARCOS A VELA. Text in Spanish. m. EUR 4 newsstand/cover (effective 2009). adv. **Document type:** *Magazine, Consumer.*
Published by: Grupo V, C Valportillo Primera, 11, Alcobendas, Madrid, 28108, Spain. TEL 34-91-6622137, FAX 34-91-6622654, secretaria@grupov.es. Ed. Miguel Sanchez. Adv. contact Aurora Perez-Olivares. page EUR 2,590; trim 18.5 x 26.5. Circ: 12,100.

796.95 USA ISSN 1091-9341
BASS & WALLEYE BOATS; the magazine of performance fishing boats. Abbreviated title: B & W B. Text in English. 1994. 9/yr. USD 12.97 domestic; USD 21.97 foreign; USD 4.99 newsstand/cover (effective 2008). adv. back issues avail. **Document type:** *Magazine, Trade.* **Description:** Covers the boating platform of bass and walleye fishing on all levels. Includes boat tests, performance tips, industry news and more.
Related titles: Online - full text ed.
Indexed: G05, G06, G07, G08, I05.
Published by: Affinity Group Inc., 2575 Vista Del Mar, Ventura, CA 93001. TEL 805-667-4100, FAX 805-667-4419, info@affinitygroup.com, http://www.affinitygroup.com. Ed. Steve Fleming. Pub. Jim Hendricks. adv.: B&W page USD 5,115, color page USD 8,415; trim 7.875 x 10.5. Circ: 122,000.

BASSMASTER CLASSIC REPORT. *see* SPORTS AND GAMES—Outdoor Life

797.1 FRA ISSN 1155-8709
BATEAUX. Text in French. 1958. m. EUR 49 (effective 2008). adv. bk.rev. bibl.; charts; illus.; mkt.; tr.lit. index, cum.index. **Document type:** *Magazine, Consumer.* **Description:** Features true stories from the high seas, navigation guides, nautical instruction, marine charts, etc.
Indexed: SD.
Published by: Mondadori France, 1 Rue du Colonel Pierre-Avia, Paris, Cedex 15 75754, France. TEL 33-1-41335001, contact@mondadori.fr, http://www.mondadori.fr. Circ: 74,081.

797.1 NOR ISSN 0806-8089
BATMAGASINET ONLINE. Text in Norwegian. 1995. m. adv. **Document type:** *Consumer.*
Media: Online - full text. **Related titles:** ◆ Print ed.: Baatmagasinet. ISSN 0801-1672.
Published by: Aller Forlag AS, Stenersgaten 2, Sentrum, Oslo, 0189, Norway. allerforlag@aller.no, http://www.aller.no.

797.1 USA ISSN 1076-5557
BAY & DELTA YACHTSMAN. Text in English. 1965. m. USD 17.60. adv. illus. **Document type:** *Magazine, Consumer.*
Former titles (until 1993): Yachtsman (1065-7398); (until 1992): Bay and Delta Yachtsman (0191-4731)
Published by: Recreation Publications, 400 S McCarran Blvd, Ste E, Reno, NV 89502. customer.servive@yachtsforsale.com. Pub. Don Abbott. Circ: 20,000.

797.1 380.1029 AUS
BIG BOAT. Text in English. a. 128 p./no.; **Document type:** *Magazine, Consumer.* **Description:** Provides information, news and features on newest boats; offers classifieds section for buying and selling boats.
Published by: A C P Trader International Group (Subsidiary of: P B L Media Pty Ltd.), 73 Atherton Rd, Oakleigh, VIC 3166, Australia. TEL 61-3-95674200, FAX 61-3-95634554. Eds. Vanessa Dudley, Greg Leech TEL 61-3-95674194. Adv. contact Shane Aughterson. Circ: 15,000.

797.1 AUS ISSN 1832-231X
BIGONBLUE. Text in English. 2004. a. USD 7.95 per issue (effective 2009). adv. **Document type:** *Magazine, Consumer.* **Description:** Includes a national marina guide, international boat show calendar, extensive dealer list, entertaining editorial and complete list of Australian boat manufacturers and distributors.
Published by: Marine Media Group Pty. Ltd., First Fl, 222 St Kilda Rd, St Kilda, VIC 3182, Australia. TEL 613-95936888, 1800-1800-59, FAX 613-95936788, enquiries@marinemedia.com.au. adv.: page AUD 7,000; trim 215 x 270.

BLAKES HOLIDAY BOATING. *see* TRAVEL AND TOURISM

797.1 DEU ISSN 0006-4637
DER BLAUE PETER; Zeitschrift fuer Segeln und Segelausbildung. Text in German. 1925. 4/yr. EUR 11 (effective 2009). adv. illus. **Document type:** *Magazine, Consumer.*
Published by: Deutscher Hochseesportverband Hansa e.V., Rothenbaumchausee 58, Hamburg, 20148, Germany. TEL 49-40-44114250, FAX 49-40-444534, dhh@dhh.de, http://www.dhh.de. adv.: B&W page EUR 1,650, color page EUR 2,000; trim 215 x 280. Circ: 16,000 (paid).

796 DEU ISSN 1862-5444
BLAUWASSER; Leben Unter Segeln. Text in German. 2001. q. EUR 16; EUR 7 newsstand/cover (effective 2007). **Document type:** *Magazine, Consumer.*
Published by: Palstek Verlag GmbH, Eppendorfer Weg 57a, Hamburg, 20259, Germany. TEL 49-40-40196353, FAX 49-40-40196341, info@palstek.de. Ed., Pub., Adv. contact Ulrich Kronberg.

799.1 797.1 AUS ISSN 1449-8537
THE BLUE WATER BULLETIN. Text in English. 19??. bi-m. free to members (effective 2009). **Document type:** *Magazine, Consumer.*
Published by: Fremantle Sailing Club Inc., 151 Marine Terrace, Fremantle, W.A. 6160, Australia. TEL 61-8-94358800, FAX 61-8-94358873, info@fsc.com.au, http://www.fsc.com.au.

797.1 USA ISSN 1091-1979
BLUE WATER SAILING; the worlds best cruising magazine. Text in English. 1996. m. USD 29.95 domestic; USD 44.95 in Canada; USD 64.95 elsewhere (effective 2010). adv. back issues avail. **Document type:** *Magazine, Consumer.* **Description:** Contains articles and features on world cruising, passage making, racing and exploring the best cruising grounds.
Address: 747 Aquidneck Ave, Ste 201, Middletown, RI 02842. TEL 401-847-7612, 888-800-7245, FAX 401-845-8580. Pub. George Day. Adv. contact Tim Day. color page USD 4,900; trim 8.125 x 10.875. Circ: 52,000.

BLUEWATER BOATS & SPORTSFISHING. *see* SPORTS AND GAMES—Outdoor Life

796.95 GBR ISSN 0950-7337
BOARDS. Text in English. 1982. 10/yr. GBP 36 domestic; GBP 53 foreign; GBP 3.60 per issue (print or online ed.) (effective 2009). adv. bk.rev. **Document type:** *Magazine, Consumer.*
Related titles: Online - full text ed.: GBP 35 (effective 2009).
Published by: Yachting Press Ltd., 196 Eastern Esplanade, Southend-on-Sea, Essex SS1 3AB, United Kingdom. TEL 44-1702-588434, 44-1702-582245, info@yachtingpress.co.uk, http://www.yachtingpress.co.uk/. Ed. Dave White. **Dist. by:** Comag.

387.2029 USA ISSN 0006-5366
HF6201.B3
BOAT & MOTOR DEALER; business solutions for the boating trade. Abbreviated title: B M C. Text in English. 1958. w. bk.rev. back issues avail.; reprints avail. **Document type:** *Magazine, Trade.* **Description:** Dedicated to providing businesses in the recreational marine industry with the information, commentary and analysis needed to expand their businesses and improve profitability.
Former titles (until 19??): Boats & Motors; Boat & Motor Dealer
Related titles: Online - full text ed.
—CCC.
Published by: Preston Publications, 6600 W Touhy Ave, Niles, IL 60714-4588. TEL 847-647-2900, FAX 847-647-1155, circulation@prestonpub.com, http://www.prestonpub.com. Ed. Jerry Koncel. Pub. Janice Gordon.

796.95 658.8 USA
BOAT BROKER. Text in English. 19??. m. free (effective 2009). **Document type:** *Magazine, Trade.* **Description:** Designed for the southeast Alaskan boaters, outdoor enthusiasts and marine dealers.
Published by: Morris Multimedia, Inc., 725 Broad St, Augusta, GA 30901. TEL 706-724-0851.

797.1 DEU ISSN 1866-6922
BOAT EXCLUSIVE; the world of superyachts. Text in English. 2008. bi-m. GBP 32.50 in United Kingdom; EUR 50.40 in the European Union; EUR 54.90 elsewhere (effective 2011). adv. **Document type:** *Magazine, Consumer.*
Related titles: ◆ German ed.: Boote Exclusiv. ISSN 0935-2961.
Published by: Delius Klasing Verlag GmbH, Siekerwall 21, Bielefeld, 33602, Germany. TEL 49-521-5590, FAX 49-521-559113, info@delius-klasing.de, http://www.delius-klasing.de. Ed. Markus Krall. Adv. contact Stefanie Schwarz. Circ: 55,000 (paid and controlled).

797.1029 CAN ISSN 0826-2802
BOAT GUIDE. Text in English. 2/yr. adv. **Document type:** *Handbook/Manual/Guide, Consumer.* **Description:** Official program for Toronto and London boat show. Lists Canadian prices, photos, specifications on all new power boats and engines. Includes editorials covering sport fishing, boating trends, electronics and an index of manufacturers.
Published by: Formula Publications (Subsidiary of: Torstar Corp.), 447 Speers Rd, Ste 4, Oakville, ON L6K 3S7, Canada. TEL 905-842-6591, FAX 905-842-6843. Ed. Lizanne Madigan. Pub. J Scott Robinson. R&P J Robinson. Adv. contact Judy Richardson.

387 GBR ISSN 0264-9136
BOAT INTERNATIONAL. Text in English. 1983. m. GBP 50 (effective 2010). adv. bk.rev. back issues avail. **Document type:** *Magazine, Consumer.* **Description:** Covers luxury private yachts, both sail and power, worldwide.
—CCC.
Published by: Boat International Media, First Fl, 41-47 Hartfield Rd, London, SW19 3RQ, United Kingdom. TEL 44-208-5459330, FAX 44-208-5459333, info@boatinternational.co.uk, http://www.boatinternational.co.uk. Ed. Amanda McCracken. Pub. Tony Harris. adv.: page EUR 6,001, page GBP 5,219, page USD 8,611. Circ: 13,779.

797.1 UAE ISSN 1816-8442
BOAT OWNER MIDDLE EAST. Text in English. 2005. m. AED 90 domestic; AED 109 GCC countries; AED 149 elsewhere (effective 2007). adv. **Document type:** *Magazine, Consumer.*
Published by: I T P Consumer Publishing (Subsidiary of: I T P Publishing Group), PO Box 500024, Dubai, United Arab Emirates. TEL 971-4-2108000, FAX 971-4-2108080, info@itp.com, http://www.itp.com. Adv. contacts Andrew Wingrove, Karam Awad. page USD 5,500; trim 225 x 290.

797.102 GBR ISSN 1751-0872
BOAT TRADER. Text in English. 1993. m. GBP 29.90 domestic; GBP 48 in Europe; GBP 2.60 newsstand/cover (effective 2009). adv. back issues avail. **Document type:** *Catalog, Consumer.* **Description:** Lists boats for sale that cost less than 15,000 pounds.
Formerly (until 2006): Buy a Boat (1350-2913)
Published by: BoatShop24 Ltd., 44a N St, Chichester, W Sussex PO19 1NF, United Kingdom. TEL 44-1243-533394, FAX 44-1243-532025, sales@boatshop24.co.uk. adv.: page GBP 450; bleed 230 x 310. Circ: 18,000.

623.82 USA
BOATBUILDER'S INTERNATIONAL DIRECTORY; the boatbuilder's source book of designers, kit makers and suppliers. Text in English. 1980. a. USD 7.50. adv. bk.rev. **Document type:** *Directory.*
Published by: Saffron Publishing, 1001 Bridgeway, Dept 621, Sausalito, CA 94965. Ed. Peter Whyte. Circ: 10,000.

797.1 USA ISSN 0006-5374
GV771
BOATING. Text in English. 1956. m. USD 14 domestic; USD 24 foreign (effective 2008). adv. bk.rev. charts; illus. Index. back issues avail.; reprints avail. **Document type:** *Magazine, Consumer.* **Description:** Contains evaluations of new powerboats, accessories and equipment; feature stories that embody the adventure of the sport; and how-to service articles.
Incorporates (in 1980): Motorboat (0093-6782); Which incorporated (in 1975): Family Houseboating (0014-7273); Formerly: Popular Boating
Related titles: Online - full text ed.: USD 12 (effective 2008).
Indexed: A11, A22, A33, ASIP, C05, C12, CPerI, ConsI, G05, G06, G07, G08, G09, I05, M01, M02, MagInd, P02, P10, P53, P54, PQC, SPI.
—CCC.
Published by: Hachette Filipacchi Media U.S., Inc. (Subsidiary of: Hachette Filipacchi Medias S.A.), 1633 Broadway, New York, NY 10019. TEL 212-767-6000, flyedit@hfmus.com, http://www.hfmus.com. Pub. Wade Luce TEL 323-954-4820. Adv. contacts Natalie Rankin TEL 323-954-4835, Melissa Homant TEL 248-729-2142. B&W page USD 31,510, color page USD 45,505; trim 8 x 10.88. Circ: 201,536 (paid).

796.95 GBR ISSN 0260-9452
BOATING BUSINESS. Text in English. 1981. m. GBP 69.50 domestic; GBP 79 in Europe; GBP 105 elsewhere; free to qualified personnel (effective 2010). illus. **Document type:** *Magazine, Trade.* **Description:** Provides a medium through which suppliers to the trade can establish and maintain contact with their sales outlets.
Related titles: Online - full text ed.: free (effective 2010); ◆ Supplement(s): The Boating Business Directory. ISSN 1758-9096; Boating Business. Product Profile Pages (Farnham). ISSN 1466-4577.
—CCC.
Published by: Mercator Media Ltd., The Old Mill, Lower Quay, Fareham, Hampshire PO16 0RA, United Kingdom. TEL 44-1329-825335, FAX 44-1329-825330, corporate@mercatormedia.com, http://www.mercatormedia.com. Ed. Peter Nash TEL 44-1892-545696.

796.95 CAN ISSN 0702-7524
BOATING BUSINESS. Text in English. 1976. 6/yr. adv. **Document type:** *Magazine, Trade.*
Published by: Formula Publications (Subsidiary of: Torstar Corp.), 447 Speers Rd, Ste 4, Oakville, ON L6K 3S7, Canada. TEL 905-842-6591, FAX 905-842-6843. Ed. Lizanne Madigan. Pub. J Scott Robinson. R&P J Robinson. Adv. contact Judy Richardson. Circ: 5,000.

797.1 AUS ISSN 1834-142X
BOATING BUSINESS. Text in English. 2006. bi-m. **Document type:** *Magazine, Consumer.*
Published by: Go Boating Publications, PO Box 5646, Stafford Heights, QLD 4053, Australia. TEL 61-7-3359-2378, FAX 61-7-3359-2948, http://www.goboating.com.au.

796.95 GBR ISSN 1758-9096
THE BOATING BUSINESS DIRECTORY. Text in English. 1989. a. adv. **Document type:** *Directory, Trade.* **Description:** A comprehensive directory of the UK marine industry, indexed and written with both the trade and consumers in mind.
Formerly (until 200?): The Boating Directory (1466-2426); (until 1999): M P C Business to Business Marine Directory (1466-2418); (until 1998): Boating Business and Marine Buyers Guide (0967-5086); (until 1991): Boating Business and Marine Trades Directory (0957-5219)
Related titles: Online - full content ed.; ◆ Supplement to: Boating Business. ISSN 0260-9452.
—CCC.
Published by: Mercator Media Ltd., The Old Mill, Lower Quay, Fareham, Hampshire PO16 0RA, United Kingdom. TEL 44-1329-825335, FAX 44-1329-825330, corporate@mercatormedia.com, http://www.mercatormedia.com.

387.2 USA ISSN 1543-4400
HD9993.B633
BOATING INDUSTRY. Text in English. 1929. m. free in US & Canada; USD 129 elsewhere (effective 2008). adv. charts; illus.; tr.lit. back issues avail.; reprints avail. **Document type:** *Magazine, Trade.* **Description:** Presents ideas, role models, and guidance for boat retailers to operate their businesses more effectively and profitably. Includes information on marine management, merchandising and selling, market analysis, and industry trends.
Former titles (until 2003): Boating Industry International (1537-2685); (until 2000): Boating Industry (0006-5404); Which incorporated (in 198?): Marine Business (0147-8923)
Related titles: Microform ed.: (from PQC); Online - full text ed.; ◆ Supplement(s): Boating Industry Marine Buyers' Guide.
Indexed: A22, B02, B15, B17, B18, BusI, G04, G06, G07, G08, I05, SRI, T&II.
—CCC.
Published by: Affinity Group Inc., 2575 Vista Del Mar, Ventura, CA 93001. TEL 805-667-4100, FAX 805-667-4419, info@affinitygroup.com, http://www.affinitygroup.com. Eds. Liz Walz TEL 315-637-5726, Matt Gruhn TEL 763-383-4448. adv.: B&W page USD 4,930, color page USD 6,130; trim 7.875 x 10.75. Circ: 26,000.

BOATING INDUSTRY MARINE BUYERS' GUIDE. *see* BUSINESS AND ECONOMICS—Trade And Industrial Directories

796.95 USA ISSN 1092-8219
BOATING LIFE; the authority on recreational boating. Text in English. 1997. 9/yr. USD 19.97 domestic; USD 27.97 in Canada; USD 35.97 elsewhere (effective 2009). adv. illus. back issues avail. **Document type:** *Magazine, Consumer.* **Description:** Provides information and ideas on the recreational aspects of boating.
Related titles: Online - full text ed.
—CCC.
Published by: Bonnier Corp. (Subsidiary of: Bonnier Group), 460 N Orlando Ave, Ste 200, Winter Park, FL 32789. TEL 407-628-4802, FAX 407-628-7061, http://www.bonniercorp.com. Ed. Randy Vance. Pub. John McEver Jr. **Dist. in UK by:** Comag, Tavistock Rd, W Drayton, Middlesex UB7 7QE, United Kingdom.

797.1 NZL ISSN 0113-0838
BOATING NEW ZEALAND. Text in English. 1986. m. adv. **Document type:** *Magazine, Consumer.* **Description:** Covers all the latest in boating news including power, sail, cruising, racing, fishing, diving, stories of local, national and international interest.
Indexed: A11, A33, T02, WBA.
Published by: Fairfax Media (Subsidiary of: John Fairfax Holdings Ltd.), Level 1, 274 Church St, Penrose, PO Box 12965, Auckland, New Zealand. TEL 64-9-6341800, FAX 64-9-6342948. Ed. Kent Gray TEL 64-9-6341800. Circ: 16,705.

797.1 USA ISSN 1931-9126
BOATING SAFETY CIRCULAR. Text in English. 19??. irreg. **Document type:** *Bulletin, Consumer.*
Related titles: Online - full text ed.: ISSN 1931-9355. 1969.
—Linda Hall.
Published by: U.S. Coast Guard, 2100 Second St, SW, Washington, DC 20593. TEL 202-267-1061, FAX 202-267-4402, gchappell@comdt.uscg.mil, http://www.uscg.mil/default.asp.

797 USA ISSN 1059-5155
VM320
BOATING WORLD. Text in English. 1979. 8/yr. USD 12 domestic; USD 15 in Canada; USD 30 elsewhere; USD 4.95 per issue (effective 2010). adv. bk.rev. charts; illus. Index. back issues avail.; reprints avail. **Document type:** *Magazine, Consumer.* **Description:** Provides family boaters, fishermen, cruising boaters, and other watersports enthusiasts with information needed to select equipment, maintain, and enjoy their boats.
Former titles (until 1991): Boat Journal (1050-8945); (until 1990): Small Boat Journal (0192-7396)
Related titles: Online - full text ed.: free (effective 2010).
Indexed: A11, B04, BRD, C05, G06, G07, G08, H20, I05, IHTDI, M02, R03, RGAb, RGPR, T02, U01, W03, W05.
Published by: Duncan McIntosh Co. Inc., 17782 Cowan, Ste A, Irvine, CA 92614. TEL 949-660-6150, FAX 949-660-6172. Adv. contact Janette Hood.

796.95 USA ISSN 0739-2257
BOATS & HARBORS. Text in English. 1971. 36/yr. USD 4. adv. charts; illus.; tr.lit.
Address: 175 Fourth St, Crossville, TN 38555. TEL 931-484-6100. Ed. Edwin Donnelly.

796.95 GBR ISSN 1467-579X
BOATS & YACHTS FOR SALE. Text in English. 1985. m. GBP 36 domestic; GBP 53 in Europe; GBP 76 elsewhere; GBP 3.60 newsstand/cover (effective 2009). back issues avail. **Document type:** *Catalog, Trade.* **Description:** Covers the European second-hand boat and yacht market.
Formerly (until 1999): Boats & Planes for Sale (0955-0402)
Published by: BoatShop24 Ltd., 44a N St, Chichester, W Sussex PO19 1NF, United Kingdom. TEL 44-1243-533394, FAX 44-1243-532025, sales@boatshop24.co.uk. Circ: 9,400. **Dist. by:** Auto Trader National Magazines.

796.95 USA
BOATSAFEKIDS; boating courses, boating tips, boating safety, boating contests. Text in English. 19??. m.
Formerly: BoatSafe and BoatSafeKids
Media: Online - full text.
Published by: Nautical Know How, Inc., 51 N 3rd St #240, Philadelphia, PA 19106. TEL 772-382-7601, nkh@boatsafe.com, http://Boatsafe.com.

797.1 ITA ISSN 1121-3108
BOLINA; andar per mare. Text in Italian. 1985. m. EUR 37.50 domestic; EUR 47.50 in Europe; EUR 90 elsewhere (effective 2009). adv. **Document type:** *Magazine, Consumer.* **Description:** Covers sailing, yachts, classic boats and tourism.
Related titles: Online - full text ed.
Published by: Editrice Incontri Nautici, Largo Angelicum 6, Rome, 00184, Italy. TEL 39-06-6990100, FAX 39-06-6990137. Circ: 45,000 (paid).

797.1 NLD ISSN 1878-8688
▼ **BOOT EN AUTO.** Text in Dutch. 2009. m. EUR 19.95 domestic; EUR 39.95 in Belgium; EUR 39.95 in Spain (effective 2010). adv. **Document type:** *Magazine, Consumer.*
Formed by the merger of (2006-2009): Boot Journaal (1570-6346); (200?-2009): AutoMaand (1878-3589)
Published by: Publi Force, Postbus 229, Alblasserdam, 2950 AE, Netherlands. TEL 31-78-6522700, FAX 31-78-6522701, info@publiforce.nl, http://www.publiforce.nl. adv.: page EUR 2,500; trim 230 x 297. Circ: 22,087.

797.1 DEU ISSN 0006-7636
BOOTE; Europas groesstes Motorboot-Magazin. Text in German. 1965. m. EUR 49.50 in Germany & Austria; EUR 61 in Switzerland; EUR 74.70 elsewhere; EUR 4.50 newsstand/cover (effective 2011). adv. illus. **Document type:** *Magazine, Consumer.*
Related titles: ◆ Supplement(s): Boote Exclusiv. ISSN 0935-2961.
Indexed: RASB.
—CCC.
Published by: Delius Klasing Verlag GmbH, Siekerwall 21, Bielefeld, 33602, Germany. TEL 49-521-5590, FAX 49-521-559113, info@delius-klasing.de, http://www.delius-klasing.de. Ed. Torsten Moench. Pub. Konrad Delius. Adv. contact Annkristin Diekmayer. Circ: 30,880 (paid).

797.1 DEU ISSN 0935-2961
BOOTE EXCLUSIV; die Welt der grossen Yachten. Text in German. 1988. 6/yr. EUR 41 domestic; EUR 58 foreign; EUR 8 newsstand/cover (effective 2011). adv. **Document type:** *Magazine, Consumer.*
Related titles: ◆ English ed.: Boat Exclusive. ISSN 1866-6922; ◆ Supplement to: Boote. ISSN 0006-7636.
Published by: Delius Klasing Verlag GmbH, Siekerwall 21, Bielefeld, 33602, Germany. TEL 49-521-5590, FAX 49-521-559113, info@delius-klasing.de, http://www.delius-klasing.de. Ed. Markus Krall. Pub. Konrad Delius. Adv. contact Stefanie Schwarz. Circ: 25,000 (paid).

797.124 DEU ISSN 0949-4065
BOOTS BOERSE; aktuelle Maritime Angebote. Text in German. m. EUR 3.50 newsstand/cover (effective 2006). adv. **Document type:** *Magazine, Trade.*
Published by: S V G Service Verlag GmbH, Schwertfegerstr 1-3, Luebeck, 23556, Germany. TEL 49-451-898974, FAX 49-451-898557, gewerbe@segler-zeitung.de, http://www.svgverlag.de. Pub. Hermann Hell. Adv. contact Britta Stein. B&W page EUR 1,556, color page EUR 2,115; trim 192 x 270. Circ: 62,000 (paid and controlled).

797.1 DEU
BOOTSHANDEL; das Magazin fuer Motor- und Segelboote. Text in German. 1998. m. EUR 45 domestic; EUR 58 foreign (effective 2010). adv. **Document type:** *Magazine, Consumer.*

S

Formerly (until 2007): Zweite Hand Bootshandel
Published by: Zweite Hand Verlag, Askanischer Platz 3, Berlin, 10963, Germany. TEL 49-30-290210, FAX 49-30-2902199935, service@zweitehand.de, http://www.zweitehand.de. Ed. Stefan Gerhard TEL 49-30-2902135010. adv.: color page EUR 1,550. Circ: 12,637 (paid).

797 DEU ISSN 0947-7772
BOOTSMARKT. Text in German. 1968. a. EUR 12.90 newsstand/cover (effective 2011). adv. **Document type:** *Magazine, Consumer.*
Formerly (until 1994): Klasings Bootsmarkt International: Yachten und Boote Zubehoer, Ausruestung, Motoren (0075-627X)
Published by: Delius Klasing Verlag GmbH, Siekerwall 21, Bielefeld, 33602, Germany. TEL 49-521-5590, FAX 49-521-559113, info@delius-klasing.de, http://www.delius-klasing.de. Ed. Tom Dieck. Circ: 18,000 (paid).

623.82 DEU ISSN 0935-395X
BOOTWIRTSCHAFT AKTUELL. Text in German. 1988. 4/yr. free to members (effective 2008). **Document type:** *Newsletter, Consumer.*
Published by: Deutscher Boots- und Schiffbauer-Verband, Sternstr 108, Hamburg, 20357, Germany. TEL 49-40-30706790, FAX 49-40-344227, info@dbsv.de, http://www.dbsv.de.

797.123 GBR ISSN 0068-2446
BRITISH ROWING ALMANACK. Variant title: (Year) British Rowing Almanack. A R A Yearbook. Text in English. 1861. a. GBP 26 per issue to non-members; GBP 23 per issue to members (effective 2009). adv. bk.rev. index. **Document type:** *Directory, Trade.*
Formerly (until 1948): The Rowing Almanack and Oarsman's Companion for.
Published by: Amateur Rowing Association, 6 Lower Mall, Hammersmith, London, W6 9DJ, United Kingdom. TEL 44-20-82376700, FAX 44-20-82376749, info@britishrowing.org. Ed. Keith L Osborne. Adv. contact George Miller TEL 44-20-89718463.

797 GBR ISSN 0068-290X
BROWN'S NAUTICAL ALMANAC. Text in English. 1876. a. GBP 58 domestic; GBP 67.48 foreign (effective 2009). **Document type:** *Directory, Trade.* **Description:** Features astronomical data in daily use by navigators, explanations of its use, nautical tables and methods, tide tables for home and foreign waters, coastal courses and distances around the British Isles, and much more.
—CCC.
Published by: Brown, Son and Ferguson Ltd., 4-10 Darnley St, Glasgow, Scotland G41 2SD, United Kingdom. TEL 44-141-4291234, FAX 44-141-4201694, info@skipper.co.uk.

796.95 USA
BY-THE-SEA. Text in English. 1996. d. free (effective 2010). **Document type:** *Magazine, Trade.* **Description:** Contains articles and stories from various boating print publications, extensive classified ads and numerous interactive message boards.
Media: Online - full text.
Address: PO Box 2804, Orleans, MA 02653. TEL 508-240-2533, FAX 508-240-2677.

197.124 CAN ISSN 0832-8080
CANADIAN SAILING REVIEW/REVUE CANADIENNE DE VOILE. Text in English. 1983. q. membership. **Document type:** *Newsletter.*
Indexed: SportS.
Published by: Canadian Yachting Association/Association Canadienne de Yachting, 1600 James Naismith Dr, Gloucester, ON K1B 5N4, Canada. TEL 613-748-5687, FAX 613-748-5688. Ed. Shirley Joseph. Circ: 20,000.

796.95 CAN ISSN 0384-0999
CANADIAN YACHTING. Text in English. 1976. bi-m. CAD 20 domestic; USD 30 foreign; CAD 3.95 newsstand/cover (effective 2005). adv. bk.rev. **Document type:** *Magazine, Consumer.*
Related titles: Microfiche ed.: (from MML); Microform ed.: (from MML); Online - full text ed.
Indexed: C03, CBCARef, CBPI, CPerl, G08, P48, PQC, SportS.
—CIS.
Published by: Kerrwil Publications Ltd., 49 Bathurst St, Ste 201B, Toronto, ON M5V 2P2, Canada. TEL 416-703-7167, FAX 416-703-1330, info@kerrwil.com, http://www.kerrwil.com. Ed. Heather Ormerod. Pub. Michael Unger. adv.: B&W page CAD 2,725, color page CAD 3,760. Circ: 15,000.

386 797.109 GBR ISSN 1758-8987
CANAL BOAT; for everyone who enjoys the waterways. Text in English. 1996. m. GBP 29 (effective 2010). illus. back issues avail. **Document type:** *Magazine, Consumer.*
Formerly (until 2007): Canal Boat and Inland Waterways (1362-0312)
Related titles: Online - full text ed.
—CCC.
Published by: Archant Specialist Ltd. (Subsidiary of: Archant Group), Archant House, Oriel Rd, Cheltenham, GL50 1BB, United Kingdom. TEL 44-1242-216052, miller.hogg@archant.co.uk, http://www.archant.co.uk/business_specialist.aspx. Ed. Nick Wall TEL 44-118-9897215. Adv. contact Jennifer Bishop TEL 44-118-9897240.

797.1 GBR ISSN 2045-1326
CANALS, RIVERS + BOATS. Text in English. 1978. m. GBP 3.30 per issue (effective 2011). adv. bk.rev. illus. 96 p./no. 3 cols./p.; back issues avail.; reprints avail. **Document type:** *Magazine, Consumer.* **Description:** Presents colorful and informative descriptions of various boats and waterways located throughout the United Kingdom.
Former titles (until 2010): Canals & Rivers (1749-6942); Which incorporated (2007-2008): Broker; (until 2006): Canal & Riverboat Monthly (0141-2302)
Related titles: ◆ Supplement(s): Marinas, Maintenance & Moorings (Year).
—CCC.
Published by: A.E. Morgan Publications Ltd., 8A High St, Epsom, Surrey KT19 8AD, United Kingdom. TEL 44-1372-741411, FAX 44-1372-744493, info@aemorgan.co.uk, http://www.aemorgan.co.uk/. Ed. Chris Cattrall TEL 44-1603-708930. Adv. contact Doreen Reed TEL 44-1280-847038. **Dist. by:** Comag, Tavistock Rd, W Drayton, Middlesex UB7 7QE, United Kingdom. TEL 44-1895-433800, FAX 44-1895-433801.

797.122 ITA
CANOA FLUVIALE. Text in Italian. 1977. 4/yr. adv. bk.rev. **Description:** Provides information on Italian canoeing and kayaking, and tourist activity on rivers, lakes and seas. Includes canoeing club addresses and information about raids and rivers.
Published by: Associazione Italiana Canoa Fluviale, Via Ernesto Breda, 19-C, Milan, MI 20126, Italy. TEL 39-2-25-76638. Ed. Granacci Guglielmo. Circ: 5,000.

797.122 USA ISSN 1077-3258
GV781
CANOE & KAYAK; the #1 paddlesports resource. Text in English. 1973. bi-m. USD 14.95 domestic; USD 27.95 in Canada; USD 29.95 elsewhere (effective 2008). adv. bk.rev. charts; illus.; tr.lit. 124 p./no.; back issues avail.; reprints avail. **Document type:** *Magazine, Consumer.* **Description:** Reflects and leads paddling culture for the range of paddlesports - from wilderness canoeing and sea kayaking to whitewater kayaking and rafting.
Former titles (until 1993): Canoe (0360-7496); Which was Incorporated (in 1941): American Canoeist
Related titles: Online - full text ed.
Indexed: A22, B04, G06, G07, G08, I05, PEI, R03, RGAb, RGPR, S23, SD, SportS, W03, W05.
—Ingenta. **CCC.**
Published by: Source Interlink Companies, 950 Calle Amanecer, Ste C, San Clemente, CA 92673. dheine@sourceinterlink.com, http://www.sourceinterlinkmedia.com. Eds. Frederick Reimers, Ross Prather. Pubs. Glen Bernard, Jim Marsh. adv.: color page USD 6,025; trim 7.75 x 10.5. Circ: 47,330 (paid).

797.122 USA ISSN 1547-1144
CANOE AND KAYAK BEGINNER'S GUIDE. Variant title: Beginners Guide. Text in English. 1999. a. USD 4.99 (effective 2008). adv. **Document type:** *Magazine, Consumer.* **Description:** Provides basic information on getting started in paddlesports, including which boats are best for different kinds of paddling, choosing good used boats, how to pick proper paddles, and sections on some of the best North American paddling destinations.
Formerly: Beginner's Guide to Canoeing and Kayaking
Published by: Source Interlink Companies, 27500 Riverview Ctr Blvd, Bonita Springs, FL 34134. TEL 239-949-4450, dheine@sourceinterlink.com, http://www.sourceinterlinkmedia.com. Ed. Ross Prather. Pub. Glen Bernard.

797.122 GBR ISSN 0008-5626
CANOE - CAMPER. Text in English. 1938. 4/yr. free membership. adv. bk.rev. abstr.; charts; illus. **Document type:** *Magazine, Consumer.*
Published by: The Canoe Camping Club, Greenfields House, Westwood Way, Coventry, CV4 8JH, United Kingdom. TEL 44-24-76475448, http://www.windsor.canoe-club.co.uk/aspnuke14/. Ed. Nick Hodson. Adv. contact Rosemarie Green. Circ: 700.

797.122 GBR ISSN 0953-010X
CANOE FOCUS. Text in English. 1976. bi-m. GBP 21 domestic to non-members; GBP 24.50 foreign to non-members; free to members (effective 2009). adv. bk.rev.; video rev. **Document type:** *Magazine, Trade.* **Description:** Covers canoeing competition and recreation news, events, expeditions, and equipment.
Published by: British Canoe Union, 18 Market Pl, Bingham, Nottingham, NG13 8AP, United Kingdom. TEL 44-845-3709500, FAX 44-845-3709501, info@bcu.org.uk, http://www.bcu.org.uk. Ed., Adv. contact Peter Tranter TEL 44-1480-465081. page GBP 695; trim 210 x 297. Circ: 23,500.

797.122 USA ISSN 1540-8728
GV781
CANOE JOURNAL. Text in English. 1997. a. USD 4.99 newsstand/cover (effective 2008). adv. **Document type:** *Journal, Consumer.* **Description:** Provides information about current canoe gurus and paddlers from the past, as well as other engaging features and how-to articles.
Published by: Source Interlink Companies, 6420 Wilshire Blvd, 10th Fl, Los Angeles, CA 90048. TEL 323-782-2000, FAX 323-782-2585, dheine@sourceinterlink.com, http://www.sourceinterlinkmedia.com. Ed. Ross Prather. Pub. Glen Bernard.

797.122 FRA ISSN 1157-1101
CANOE KAYAK MAGAZINE. Text in French. 1970. 6/yr. (plus one special issue). EUR 38.20 (effective 2009). **Document type:** *Magazine, Consumer.*
Published by: Outdoor Editions, 1 Rue des Rivieres, Lyon, 69009, France. http://www.outdoor-editions.fr.

797.122 GBR ISSN 0269-9982
CANOEIST. Text in English. 1953. m. GBP 35.40 domestic; GBP 51.12 in Europe; GBP 49.08 elsewhere (effective 2001). adv. bk.rev.; film rev.; music rev.; software rev.; tel.rev.; video rev. bibl.; charts; illus.; maps; stat.; tr.lit. index. 60 p./no. 3 cols./p.; back issues avail. **Document type:** *Magazine, Consumer.* **Description:** For canoe and kayak paddlers with information on competitions, new equipment, water guides and safety suggestions, includes book reviews.
Formerly (until 1983): White Water Magazine
Published by: S.T. & R.J. Fisher, 4 Sinodun Row, Appleford on Thames, Abingdon, Oxon OX14 4PE, United Kingdom. TEL 44-1235-847270, FAX 44-1235-847520. Ed. S Fisher. Pubs. R J Fisher, S T Fisher. R&P R J Fisher. adv.: color page GBP 536. **Dist. by:** Comag Specialist Division, Tavistock Works, Tavistock Rd, W Drayton, Mddx UB7 7QX, United Kingdom. TEL 4401895-433800, FAX 44-1895-433801.

796.93 GBR ISSN 1359-1088
VM331
CAPITAL SHIP. Text in English. 1991. m. GBP 66, USD 132. bk.rev. charts. back issues avail. **Document type:** *Magazine, Trade.*
Published by: International Media Corporation Ltd., Empire House, Ste 1A, 175 Piccadilly, London, W1V 9DB, United Kingdom. TEL 44-171-491-2044, FAX 44-171-409-1923. Ed. Gregory Copley. Adv. contact Pamela Vongruber. B&W page GBP 700, color page GBP 1,400. Circ: 1,400 (paid).

797.124605 GBR ISSN 1469-6754
CATALYST (LONDON, 2000). Text in English. 2000. q. free to members. **Document type:** *Journal, Consumer.*
—BLDSC (3090.948400).
Published by: Amateur Yacht Research Society, c/o Sheila Fishwick, Secretary, BCM - AYRS, London, WC1N 3XX, United Kingdom. TEL 44-1727-862268, FAX 44-8700-526657, office@ayrs.org. Ed. Simon Fishwick.

797.124 USA
CATAMARAN SAILOR. Text in English. 1995. 10/yr. USD 15 (effective 2001). adv. bk.rev.; video rev. charts; illus.; mkt.; maps; stat. back issues avail. **Document type:** *Newspaper.* **Description:** For catamaran and multihull sailors. Contains news, how-to information, schedules, results and classifieds.
Related titles: Online - full text ed.
Published by: Ram Press, PO Box 2060, Key Largo, FL 33037. TEL 305-451-3287, FAX 305-453-0255, ram5@icanect.net. Ed., Pub. Mary Wells. R&P Mary A Wells. Adv. contact Rick White. B&W page USD 180; trim 11 x 8.5. Circ: 20,000 (paid).

797.1 658 USA
CHARTER INDUSTRY; management magazine for the marine charter industry. Text in English. 1985. bi-m. USD 26.50 (effective 1995 & 1996). adv. cum.index: 1985-1994. back issues avail. **Document type:** *Magazine, Trade.* **Description:** Informs the marine charter industry's professionals about ways to improve their business operations. Covers insurance, promotion, advertising, taxes, legal issues, and personnel issues.
Published by: Charter Industry Services, Inc., 43 Kindred St, Stuart, FL 34994. TEL 407-288-1066. Ed. Paul McElroy. Adv. contact Mich McElroy. Circ: 10,000 (paid); 750 (controlled).

797.122 CAN
CHE - MUN; the journal of Canadian wilderness canoeing. Text in English. q. **Description:** Covers trip reports, book reviews, northern news and historical accounts.
Address: P O Box 548, Stn O, Toronto, ON M5M 1M9, Canada. che-mun@canoemail.com, http://www.canoe.ca/che-mun. Ed. Michael Peake.

917 796.95 USA ISSN 0045-656X
CHESAPEAKE BAY MAGAZINE. Text in English. 1971. m. USD 22.95; USD 4.99 newsstand/cover (effective 2007). adv. bk.rev. charts; illus. back issues avail.; reprints avail. **Document type:** *Magazine, Consumer.* **Description:** Covers boating, history, environment, ecology and the culture of the bay from the C-and-D Canal to Norfolk, VA.
—Ingenta.
Published by: Chesapeake Bay Communications, Inc., 1819 Bay Ridge Ave, Annapolis, MD 21403. TEL 410-263-2662, FAX 410-267-6924, editor@cbmmag.net. Ed. Tim Sayles. Pub., R&P Richard Royer. Adv. contact John Stefancik. Circ: 46,000 (paid).

797.1 HKG ISSN 1816-8663
CHINA BOATING/ZHONGHUA BAOTING. Text in English. 2004. m. **Document type:** *Magazine, Consumer.* **Description:** Covers luxury yachting in China.
Related titles: Online - full content ed.
Published by: Blu Inc Media (HK) Ltd. (Subsidiary of: S P H Magazines Pte Ltd.), Ste 2901, 29/F Universal Trade Centre, No. 3 Arbuthnot Rd, Central, Hong Kong. TEL 852-2165-2800, FAX 852-2868-1799, queries@bluincmedia.com, http://www.bluincmedia.com.hk/. Circ: 35,000.

CIENCIA Y TECNOLOGIA DE BUQUES. *see* ENGINEERING—Mechanical Engineering

799.1 USA
CIRCLE HOOK; an online international fishing magazine. Text in English. irreg. back issues avail. **Description:** Includes news of all types of saltwater from offshore to inshore.
Media: Online - full text.
Published by: Fish-N-Net, 7107 S Indian River Dr, Ft Pierce, FL 34982. TEL 561-460-2779. Ed. John Schultz.

796.95 USA ISSN 1070-9290
CLASSIC BOATING; the magazine of vintage power boats. Text in English. 1984. bi-m. USD 28 domestic; USD 32 in Canada; USD 65 elsewhere (effective 2006). adv. bk.rev. illus. reprints avail. **Document type:** *Magazine, Consumer.*
Formerly (until 1987): Antique and Classic Boat
Address: 280 Lac la Belle Dr, Oconomowoc, WI 53066-1648. TEL 262-567-4800, FAX 262-567-5545. Ed. Jim Wangard. Pub. Norm Wangard. Adv. contact Terri Wangard. Circ: 9,300 (paid).

CLUB MARINE. *see* LIFESTYLE

796.95 910.202 USA ISSN 0897-750X
COASTAL CRUISING. Text in English. 1985. 6/yr. USD 19.75 (effective 2000). adv. bk.rev. **Document type:** *Magazine, Consumer.*
Formerly (until 1988): Carolina Cruising (0893-3723)
Address: 140 Littleton Rd, Ste 108, Parsippany, NJ 07054-1867. TEL 919-728-2233, FAX 919-728-6050. Ed. Ted Jones. Pub., R&P John S Ryan TEL 973-402-1892. Adv. contact Kelly S Lippe. Circ: 52,000.

797.140 FRA ISSN 1775-1268
COLLECTION COUREURS DES MERS. Text in French. 2005. irreg. **Document type:** *Monographic series, Consumer.*
Published by: Editions Menges, 6 rue du Mail, Paris, 75002, France. TEL 33-1-44553750, FAX 33-1-40209974, http://www.editions-menges.com.

797.122 USA ISSN 1527-4381
GV781
COMPLETE GUIDE TO KAYAK TOURING. Variant title: Kayak Touring. Text in English. 199?. a. USD 4.99 newsstand/cover (effective 2007). adv. **Document type:** *Magazine, Consumer.* **Description:** Provides an entry level guide on all the fundamentals of sea kayaking, including how to get started, where to go, and what to take.
Published by: Source Interlink Companies, 6420 Wilshire Blvd, 10th Fl, Los Angeles, CA 90048. TEL 323-782-2000, FAX 323-782-2585, dheine@sourceinterlink.com, http://www.sourceinterlink.com. Ed. Ross Prather. Pub. Glen Bernard.

796.95 GBR
CRUISING ASSOCIATION. HANDBOOK. Text in English. 1909. a. membership. **Document type:** *Handbook/Manual/Guide, Consumer.*
Formerly: Cruising Association. Yearbook
Published by: Cruising Association, CA House, 1 Northey St, Limehouse Basin, London, E14 8BT, United Kingdom. TEL 44-207-537-2828, FAX 44-207-537-2266, office@cruising.org.uk, http://www.cruising.org.uk. Circ: 5,000 (controlled).

796.95 GBR ISSN 1350-1321
CRUISING ASSOCIATION. MAGAZINE. Variant title: Cruising Magazine. Text in English. 1910. q. free to members (effective 2009). adv. bk.rev. **Document type:** *Magazine, Consumer.* **Description:** Contains the news about cruising.
Formerly (until 1989): Cruising Association. Bulletin (0952-7982)

Published by: Cruising Association, CA House, 1 Northey St, Limehouse Basin, London, E14 8BT, United Kingdom. TEL 44-20-75372828, FAX 44-20-75372266, office@cruising.org.uk. Ed. Fred Barter.

797.14 AUS ISSN 0812-4086
CRUISING HELMSMAN. Text in English. 1980. m. AUD 82.50 domestic; AUD 95 in New Zealand; AUD 110 in Asia; AUD 160 elsewhere; AUD 6.95 newsstand/cover (effective 2008). adv. **Document type:** *Magazine, Consumer.* **Description:** Provides reviews and advices on latest cruising boats, equipment, clothing and accessories, boat maintenance; offers real-life accounts from seasoned cruisers and their onboard experiences.
Published by: Yaffa Publishing Group Pty Ltd., 17-21 Bellevue St, Surry Hills, NSW 2010, Australia. TEL 61-2-92812333, FAX 61-2-92812750, info@yaffa.com.au. Ed. Caroline Strainig TEL 61-2-92138253. Adv. contact Peter Rendle TEL 61-2-92138259. color page AUD 3,160; trim 220 x 275. Circ: 8,624.

797.124 USA ISSN 0098-3519
GV771
CRUISING WORLD. Text in English. 1974. m. USD 28 domestic; USD 42 in Canada; USD 64 elsewhere; USD 4.99 newsstand/cover (effective 2011). adv. bk.rev. charts; illus.; tr.lit. index. back issues avail.; reprints avail. **Document type:** *Magazine, Consumer.*
Related titles: Microform ed.: (from PQC); Online - full text ed.: USD 24 (effective 2011).
Indexed: A22, CPerl, G05, G06, G07, G08, G09, I05, I07, MagInd, P02, P10, P48, P53, P54, PQC, SD.
—CCC.
Published by: Bonnier Corp. (Subsidiary of: Bonnier Group), 55 Hammarlund Way, Middletown, RI 02842. TEL 401-845-5100, FAX 401-845-5180, http://www.bonniercorp.com. Ed. Mark Pillsbury. Pub. Sally Helme TEL 401-845-4405. Adv. contact Greg Schumann TEL 212-779-5302. Circ: 130,000 (paid). **Subscr. to:** PO Box 420235, Palm Coast, FL 32142. TEL 386-246-3402, 866-436-2461.

656.61 ITA ISSN 1827-0611
THE CUP. Variant title: The Cup - Yacht Capital. Text in Italian. 2005. s-a. adv. **Document type:** *Magazine, Consumer.*
Published by: De Agostini Editore, Via G da Verrazzano 15, Novara, 28100, Italy. TEL 39-0321-4241, FAX 39-0321-424305, info@deagostini.it, http://www.deagostini.it. Circ: 76,000 (controlled).

797.1 USA
CURRENTS (COLORADO SPRINGS). Text in English. 1979. q. USD 20. adv. bk.rev. back issues avail. **Description:** Covers whitewater rivers and rivers running internationally, with emphasis on the United States.
Published by: National Organization for River Sports, 212 W Cheyenne Mountain Blvd, Colorado Springs, CO 80906-3712. TEL 719-473-2466, FAX 719-576-6238. Ed. Greg Moore. Circ: 5,000.

623.82 USA ISSN 1201-5598
D I Y BOAT OWNER; the marine maintenance magazine. (Do It Yourself) Text in English. 1995. q. USD 21 domestic; USD 26 in Canada (effective 2010). adv. back issues avail. **Document type:** *Magazine, Consumer.* **Description:** Focuses exclusively on maintenance, repairs and upgrades. Shows owners how to perform routine maintenance, install accessories, troubleshoot engines, electronics and more. Lists sources of maintenance products, new equipment, supply sources, replacement parts, service people and shops.
Related titles: Online - full text ed.: USD 15 (effective 2010).
Address: PO Box 15282, Washington, DC 20003. TEL 888-658-2628. Ed. Jan Mundy.

797.124 DEU
DEUTSCHE SEEREGATTEN. Text in German. 1984. a. adv. **Document type:** *Directory, Consumer.*
Published by: S V G Service Verlag GmbH, Schwertfegerstr 1-3, Luebeck, 23556, Germany. TEL 49-451-898974, FAX 49-451-898557, gewerbe@segler-zeitung.de, http://www.svgverlag.de. adv.: B&W page EUR 1,350, color page EUR 1,750. Circ: 6,300 (controlled).

797.1 USA
DOCKSIDE. Text in English. m. USD 14.95 (effective 1998).
Published by: Dockside Publications, 2082 Business Center Dr., Ste. 225, Irvine, CA 92612-1155. TEL 949-645-9100, 800-474-5733, FAX 949-650-4904. Ed., Pub. Scott Leigh. **Subscr. to:** Dockside, PO Box 2926, Newport Beach, CA 92659.

623.88 GBR
DOCKWALK. Text in English. 1998. m. adv. reprints avail. **Document type:** *Magazine, Consumer.* **Description:** Designed to enable captains and crew to become up to date of yachting industry news.
Incorporates (2001-2005): Captain's Log (1473-8767)
Published by: Boat International Media, First Fl, 41-47 Hartfield Rd, London, SW19 3RQ, United Kingdom. TEL 44-208-5459330, FAX 44-208-5459333, info@boatinternational.co.uk, http://www.boatinternational.co.uk. Ed. Kate Simpson Lardy TEL 954-522-2628. Pub. Tony Harris. adv.: page GBP 2,150, page EUR 3,225, page USD 4,300; trim 247 x 304.

797.1 USA ISSN 1931-4515
DOZIER'S WATERWAY GUIDE MAGAZINE. Text in English. 2006. q. **Document type:** *Magazine, Consumer.*
Published by: Waterway Guide Magazine, PO Box 4219, Annapolis, MD 21403. TEL 443-482-9377, FAX 443-482-9422, http://www.waterwayguide.com/index.php. Pub. Jack Dozier.

796.95 USA
DUCKWORKS MAGAZINE; written for and by those wacky homemade boat builders. Text in English. d.
Media: Online - full content.
Address: HC 63, Box 289, Harper, TX 78631.

796.95 USA ISSN 1091-6474
DUPONT REGISTRY: A BUYER'S GALLERY OF FINE BOATS. Variant title: Buyers Gallery of Fine Boats. Text in English. 1997. bi-m. USD 15.95 domestic; USD 30.95 in Canada; USD 45.95 elsewhere; USD 9.80 per issue domestic; USD 12.95 per issue in Canada; USD 14.95 per issue elsewhere (effective 2009). adv. illus. back issues avail. **Document type:** *Magazine, Consumer.* **Description:** Covers showcase of perfomance and luxury boats for sale.
Related titles: Online - full text ed.
Published by: DuPont Publishing, Inc., 3051 Tech Dr, Saint Petersburg, FL 33716. TEL 727-573-9339, 800-233-1731, dcsupport@dupontregistry.com, http://www2.dupontregistry.com. Pub. Thomas L Dupont.

623 USA ISSN 1058-3556
VM461
EGREGIOUS STEAMBOAT JOURNAL. Text in English. 1991. bi-m. **Description:** Covers steamboat history, technical studies, model building tips and current events.
Indexed: CLT&T.
Published by: Steamboat Masters & Associates, Box 3046, Louisville, KY 40201-3046. Eds. Jack Custer, Sandy Custer.

796.95 USA
ELECTRIC BOAT JOURNAL. Text in English. 1992. 6/yr. USD 35 domestic; USD 50 foreign (effective 2001). adv. bk.rev. 16 p./no.; **Document type:** *Newsletter, Consumer.*
Formerly: E B A A Current (1073-158X)
Published by: Electric Boat Association of the Americas, Inc., PO Box 4025, Lantana, FL 33465-4025. TEL 561-588-3242, elecboat@msn.com. Ed., R&P Kenneth Matthews. Circ: 1,000.

623.82 621.8 AUS ISSN 1448-9120
ENGINESONBLUE (YEAR). Text in English. 2004. a., latest 2006. adv. **Document type:** *Catalog, Trade.* **Description:** A marine engine guide that presents all available products on a level playing field.
Published by: Marine Media Group Pty. Ltd., First Fl, 222 St Kilda Rd, St Kilda, VIC 3182, Australia. TEL 613-95936888, 1800-1800-59, FAX 613-95936788, enquiries@marinemedia.com.au.

797.124 CAN ISSN 1201-5407
L'ESCALE NAUTIQUE; le leader de la presse nautique au Quebec. Text in French. 1995. q. (5/yr.). CAD 17.25 (effective 2005). **Document type:** *Magazine, Consumer.*
Incorporates (1974-1997): Voile Quebec Info (1483-5797); Which was formerly (until 1996): Voile Quebec (1193-1035); (until 1991): Revue Voile Quebec (0820-4969); (until 1986): Ecoute (0712-6557)
Published by: L' Escale Nautique, 175 Rue Saint-Paul, Quebec, PQ G1K 3W2, Canada. FAX 418-692-5198, http://www.escalenautique.qc.ca.

797.1 ITA ISSN 1591-8629
FARE VELA. Text in Italian. 1985. m. EUR 120 for 2 yrs. (effective 2009). adv. **Document type:** *Magazine, Consumer.*
Published by: Interlinea Editrice Scrl, Viale Parioli, 160, Roma, 00197, Italy. TEL 39-06-809-1111, FAX 39-06-809-11121. Circ: 20,000.

797 FRA ISSN 0071-4194
FEDERATION FRANCAISE DE NATATION. ANNUAIRE. Text in French. 1921. a.
Published by: Federation Francaise de Natation, 148 av. Gambetta, Paris, 75020, France. TEL 33-1-40311770, FAX 33-1-40311990, http://www.ffnatation.fr.

623.8 FIN ISSN 0789-7332
FINNBOAT NEWS. Text in English, Finnish, Swedish. 1991. q. free (effective 2001). adv. **Document type:** *Magazine, Trade.*
Formed by the merger of (1979-1991): Finnboat News (English Edition) (0358-3724); (1979-1991): Finnboat News (Suomenkielinen P.) (0358-3740); (1979-1991): Finnboat news (Svensk Utg.) (0358-3732)
Published by: Venelean Keskusliitto Finnboat ry/Finnish Marine Industries Federation Finnboat, Kaenkuja 8 A 47, Helsinki, 00500, Finland. TEL 358-9-6962160, FAX 358-9-69621611. Eds. Jouko Huju, Lena Mickelsson. adv.: color page EUR 565; 185 x 265. Circ: 2,300.

623.8 FIN ISSN 0356-7753
FINNISH BOATBUILDING INDUSTRY; Catalogue. Text in English, German. 1971. irreg. free. **Document type:** *Catalog, Corporate.*
Published by: Venelean Keskusliitto Finnboat ry/Finnish Marine Industries Federation Finnboat, Kaenkuja 8 A 47, Helsinki, 00500, Finland.

797.14 CAN ISSN 1202-0265
FISHBOATS. Text in English. 1993. a.
Related titles: ♦ Supplement to: Power Boating Canada. ISSN 0838-0872.
Published by: Taylor Publishing Group, 2585 Skymark Ave, Ste 306, Mississauga, ON L4W 4L5, Canada. TEL 905-624-8218, FAX 905-624-6764.

799.1 USA
FISHING FLORIDA MAGAZINE. Text in English. irreg. **Document type:** *Magazine, Consumer.* **Description:** Includes fishing reports, guides, tide charts, regulations and other related information designed for anglers and tourists.
Media: Online - full text.
Address: PO Box 263158, Tampa, FL 33685-3158. TEL 813-884-1878, FAX 813-889-7015. Ed. Mel Berman.

FISHING WORLD. *see* FISH AND FISHERIES

797.124 SWE ISSN 1654-6512
FLERSKROVSBLADET. Text in Swedish. 1966. q. SEK 190 membership (effective 2007). **Document type:** *Magazine, Consumer.*
Formerly (until 2007): Bladet
Published by: Sveriges Catamaran och Trimaran Seglare/Swedish Catamaran and Trimaran Sailors, c/o Tomas Eriksson, Johan Lundbergs Vaeg 1, Karlholmsbruk, 81064, Sweden. TEL 46-294-512800, syladybird@telia.com, http://www.multihulls.org. Ed. Rolf Karlsson.

797.14 USA
FLIGHT WORLD. Text in English. 1997. q. USD 19.95 domestic; USD 24.95 in Canada & Mexico; USD 34.95 elsewhere (effective 2000). adv. **Document type:** *Magazine, Consumer.* **Description:** Contains features, tips, news, and event coverage on the sport of hydrofoiling.
Address: 31566 Railroad Canyon Rd, PMB 101, Canyon Lake, CA 92587. TEL 909-244-6723, FAX 909-246-9640. Ed., Pub. Tony Klarich.

797.1 USA
FLORIDA MARINER. Text in English. 1995. bi-w. (Sun.). USD 6.50 newsstand/cover (effective 2005). **Document type:** *Newspaper.*
Published by: Journal Community Publishing Group, 600 Industrial Dr., PO Box 609, Waupaca, WI 54981. TEL 715-258-8450. Ed. Stacy Fulgieri. Pub. Ken Brothwell. Circ: 23,500 (paid and free).

797.124 910.202 USA
FODOR'S SPORTS: SAILING. Text in English. irreg. USD 12.
Published by: Fodor's Travel Publications, Inc. (Subsidiary of: Random House Inc.), 1745 Broadway, 15th Fl, New York, NY 10019. TEL 212-572-2313, editors@fodors.com, http://www.fodors.com. **Dist. by:** Random House Inc.

797.124 FIN ISSN 0359-6648
FRISK BRIS. Text in Finnish, Swedish. 1903. 7/yr. EUR 42; EUR 7 per issue (effective 2004). adv. bk.rev. illus. **Document type:** *Magazine, Consumer.* **Description:** Devoted to yachting, cruising, racing; old boats and life in the archipelago.
Published by: Grafiska Industri AB, Mannerheimvaegen 20 A, Helsingfors, 00100, Finland. TEL 358-9-54955500, FAX 358-9-54955577. Ed. Kari Wilen TEL 358-9-5023490. Adv. contact Sam Bjoerklund. B&W page EUR 620, color page EUR 920. Circ: 2,000.

796.95 SWE ISSN 1403-2252
GAESTHAMNSGUIDEN. Text in Swedish. 1990. a. **Document type:** *Yearbook, Consumer.* **Description:** Cruising guide to Swedish harbors.
Formerly (until 1998): Baatturist (1101-0088); Which incorporated (1957-1988): Gaesthamnar (0283-1384)
Related titles: Online - full text ed.
Published by: (Svenska Kryssarklubben/Swedish Cruising Association, Svenska Turistfoereningen/Swedish Touring Club, Svenska Baatunionen/Swedish Yachting Association), Gaesthamnsguiden AB, PO Box 20, Norrhult, 36071, Sweden. TEL 46-474-48285, FAX 46-474-48286, gasthamnsguiden@sxk.se, http://www.gasthamnsguiden.se.

797.1 CAN ISSN 0016-4259
GAM ON YACHTING. Text in English. 1957. 8/yr. CAD 12.84 domestic (effective 1999); CAD 2 newsstand/cover; USD 21 foreign (effective 1999). adv. bk.rev. mkt. back issues avail. **Document type:** *Magazine, Consumer.* **Description:** Covers sailing in Canada, forum where people can write of their racing, cruising experiences and pass them on to fellow sailors. Lists new and used sailboats for sale. Includes technical and how-to articles.
Related titles: Fax ed.
Indexed: SportS.
Published by: Gam on Yachting Inc., 250 The Esplanade, Ste 202, Toronto, ON M5A 1J2, Canada. TEL 416-368-1559, FAX 416-368-2831. Ed., Pub. Karin Larson. R&P Craig Green. Adv. contact Craig Greene. B&W page CAD 1,350, color page USD 1,950; trim 11 x 8.5. Circ: 9,500 (paid); 4,000 (controlled).

GENTE MOTORI. *see* TRANSPORTATION—Automobiles

623.8 USA ISSN 1932-1511
VM320
GETTING STARTED IN BOATS. Text in English. 2006. irreg. **Document type:** *Magazine, Consumer.* **Description:** Includes step-by-step instructions and diagrams for beginners to build, paint and maintain wooden boats and boating accessories.
Related titles: Online - full text ed.: ISSN 1932-152X.
Published by: WoodenBoat Publications, Inc., 41 WoodenBoat Ln, Brooklin, ME 04616. TEL 207-359-4651, FAX 207-359-8920, woodenboat@woodenboat.com, http://www.woodenboat.com. Ed. Matthew P Murphy. Pub. Carl Cramer.

797.124 ITA ISSN 1122-3073
IL GIORNALE DELLA VELA. Key Title: Vela. Text in Italian. 1975. m. (11/yr.). EUR 65 (effective 2009). adv. bk.rev. **Document type:** *Magazine, Consumer.*
Related titles: Online - full text ed.
Published by: Panama Editore SpA, Via Quaranta 52, Milan, 20139, Italy. TEL 39-02-5358111, FAX 39-02-56802965, http://www.panamaeditore.it. Circ: 30,000.

797.125 ITA ISSN 1120-799X
IL GIORNALE DELLE BARCHE A MOTORE. Key Title: Barche a Motore. Text in Italian. 1990. m. (11/yr.). EUR 65 (effective 2009). adv. **Document type:** *Magazine, Consumer.* **Description:** Contains general interest articles on motor boating. Also includes a classified section for motor boat traders.
Related titles: Online - full text ed.
Published by: Panama Editore SpA, Via Quaranta 52, Milan, 20139, Italy. TEL 39-02-5358111, FAX 39-02-56802965, http://www.panamaeditore.it. Circ: 28,000.

797.1 USA ISSN 1526-8519
GO BOATING. Text in English. 1997. 8/yr. USD 19.97 domestic; USD 29.97 in Canada; USD 39.97 elsewhere (effective 2007). **Document type:** *Magazine, Consumer.* **Description:** Covers a wide range of topics from selecting the next new boat to launching, operation and maintenance.
Published by: Duncan McIntosh Co. Inc., 17782 Cowan, Ste A, Irvine, CA 92614. TEL 949-660-6150, FAX 949-660-6172. Pubs. Duncan McIntosh Jr., Jeffrey Fleming. Adv. contact Janette Hood. Circ: 105,000 (paid).

797.152 NLD ISSN 1872-0080
GODEVAERT. Text in Dutch. 2006. 6/yr. EUR 19.95; EUR 4.95 newsstand/cover (effective 2009). adv.
Published by: GHS Uitgeverij BV, Postbus 1023, Noorden, 2430 AA, Netherlands. TEL 31-172-408558, FAX 31-172-407015, info@ghs-bv.nl, http://www.ghs-bv.nl. Eds. Carine Harting, Rens Groenendijk. Pub. J M van Smoorenburg. Circ: 15,000.

796.95 ITA ISSN 1120-2262
IL GOMMONE E LA NAUTICA PER TUTTI. Text in Italian. 1977. 10/yr. EUR 40 domestic; EUR 78 foreign (effective 2009). adv. **Document type:** *Magazine, Consumer.*
Former titles: Gommone; Gommone e le Piccole Barche
Published by: Koster Publishing, Via della Liberazione 1, Peschiera Borromeo, MI 20068, Italy. TEL 39-02-56306067, FAX 39-02-56306068, http://www.koster.it. Circ: 30,000.

797.1 USA ISSN 1099-6354
GOOD OLD BOAT. Text in English. 1998. bi-m. USD 39.95 in US & Canada; USD 49.95 elsewhere (effective 2010). adv. **Document type:** *Magazine, Consumer.* **Description:** Designed to bring sailors together by promoting the class associations and helping sailors make contacts with other sailors.
Published by: Partnership for Excellence, Inc., 7340 Niagara Ln N, Maple Grove, MN 55311. TEL 701-952-9433, FAX 701-952-9434. Ed. Karen Larson. Adv. contact Michael Facius. color page USD 1,898; 7 x 10.

S

796.95 USA ISSN 1063-7656
GORGE GUIDE. Text in English. 1983. a., latest vol.29, 2011. USD 4.95 per issue (effective 2011). adv. 120 p./no.; **Document type:** *Magazine, Consumer.* **Description:** Visitor and recreation guide to the Columbia River Gorge. Primarily west coast residents plus national and international visitors. Families and senior citizens, day visitors to weeklong vacationers, Sightseers and active recreation participants, skiers, windsurfers, hikers, kayakers and mountain bikers.
Incorporates: Columbia Gorge Magazine (1063-763X)
Published by: Gorge Publishing, Inc., PO Box 918, Hood River, OR 97031. TEL 541-386-7440, FAX 541-386-7480, http://www.gorgepublishing.com. Ed. Jeff Jones. Pub. Annisa Olsson Jones.

797.124 FRA ISSN 0994-4230
GRAND VOILE. Text in French. N.S. 1970. m. adv. bk.rev. bibl.; illus.; stat. back issues avail. **Document type:** *Newsletter, Consumer.*
Former titles (until 1988): Voile Magazine (0766-4796); (until 1984): Yachting a Voile (0337-4556)
Related titles: Online - full text ed.
Indexed: SportS.
Published by: Federation Francaise de Voile, 17 Rue Henri Bocquillon, Paris, 75015, France. TEL 33-1-40603700, FAX 33-1-40603737. Ed. Gilles Klein. Circ: 21,000.

797.124 FRA ISSN 1959-7118
GRAND VOILE MAGAZINE. Text in French. 2007. irreg. **Document type:** *Magazine, Consumer.*
Published by: Federation Francaise de Voile, 17 Rue Henri Bocquillon, Paris, 75015, France. TEL 33-1-40603700, FAX 33-1-40603737.

797.1 USA ISSN 1937-7274
GREAT LAKES BOATING. Text in English. 1982. bi-m. USD 15 (effective 2008). adv. **Document type:** *Magazine, Consumer.*
Address: 1032 LaSalle Dr, Chicago, IL 60610. TEL 312-266-8400, FAX 312-266-8470. Pub. F Dikmen.

GREAT LAKES CRUISER; the boater's travel guide. *see* TRAVEL AND TOURISM

797 USA ISSN 0017-4629
THE GROSSE POINTER. Text in English. 1939. bi-m. USD 25 (effective 1998). back issues avail.
Published by: Dorian Naughton Design Group, 74 Stanton Ln., Grosse Pointe, MI 48236-3744. TEL 313-881-8320. Ed. Jeanie Graham. adv.: B&W page USD 748, color page USD 1,265. Circ: 1,100.

797.1 ITA ISSN 1974-5567
GUIDA NAUTICA. Text in Italian. 2008. a. **Document type:** *Handbook/Manual/Guide, Consumer.*
Published by: Technipress Srl, Via Olindo Guerrini 20 D, Rome, 00139, Italy. TEL 39-06-8720331, FAX 39-06-87139141, http://www.technipress.it.

910.202 USA
GUIDE TO CRUISING THE CHESAPEAKE BAY. Text in English. 1974. a. USD 29.95 (effective 2007). adv. **Document type:** *Magazine, Consumer.* **Description:** Contains photographs, drawings and narratives to guide yachtsman to anchorages and ports of call along the bay from the C&D Canal to Norfolk, VA.
Published by: Chesapeake Bay Communications, Inc., 1819 Bay Ridge Ave, Annapolis, MD 21403. TEL 410-263-2662, FAX 410-267-6924. Ed. Marty LeGrand. Pub., R&P Richard Royer. Adv. contact Pam Harris.

796.95 USA
GULF COAST & TEXAS BOATING. Text in English. 1992. m. **Document type:** *Magazine, Consumer.*
Published by: Gulf Coast Boating, Box 1199, Boutte, LA 70039. TEL 504-758-7217, FAX 504-758-7000, boating@acadiacom.net. Ed. Todd Masson. Circ: 40,000.

797.124 ZAF ISSN 1814-2648
GUST. Text in English. 2005. bi-m. adv. **Document type:** *Magazine, Consumer.*
Published by: Nexor 349 cc, PO Box 633, Milnerton, 7435, South Africa. Ed., Adv. contact Janet LightBody.

797.1 DNK ISSN 1903-8771
▼ **HAVNELODSEN.** Text in Danish. 2009. irreg. DKK 280 per issue (effective 2010). **Document type:** *Guide, Consumer.* **Description:** information about Danish harbors and their facilities.
Published by: Iver C. Weilbach & Co. A/S, Toldbodgade 35, Copenhagen K, 1253, Denmark. TEL 45-33-343560, FAX 45-33-343561, nautical@weilbach.dk, http://www.weilbach.dk.

797.1 USA ISSN 1042-1009
HEARTLAND BOATING. Text in English. 1989. 8/yr. USD 16 (effective 2011). bk.rev. back issues avail. **Document type:** *Magazine, Consumer.* **Description:** Provides stories about boating on the Tennessee, Ohio, Cumberland and Mississippi rivers, the inland lakes and the Tenn-Tom waterway. Includes houseboating, sailing and cruising features, and marina profiles.
Published by: Waterways Journal, Inc., 319 N 4th St, Ste 650, St. Louis, MO 63102. TEL 314-241-4310, 800-366-9630, FAX 314-241-4207. Ed. Lee Braff. Pub. H Nelson Spencer.

797 AUS
HERON NEWSLETTER. Text in English. 1964. q. adv. **Document type:** *Newsletter.*
Published by: National Heron Sailing Association of Australia, 1 Ethel St, Balgowlah, NSW 2093, Australia. http://www.heronsailing.com.au/. Circ: 1,750.

797.1 FRA ISSN 1774-1505
HORS-BORD MAGAZINE. Text in French. 2005. bi-m. EUR 29 (effective 2007). **Document type:** *Magazine, Consumer.*
Published by: Glob'Eau Productions, 134 Rue Gallieni, Boulogne Billancourt, 92100, France. TEL 33-1-55601790, FAX 33-1-55600851, contact@globeau.com, http://www.globeau.com.

910.2 GBR
HOSEASONS BOATING HOLIDAYS IN UK AND EUROPE. Text in English. 1946. a. free. **Document type:** *Directory, Consumer.*
Formerly: Hoseasons Holiday Boats and Bungalows Hire (0073-3431)
Related titles: Online - full text ed.
Published by: Hoseasons Holidays, Sunway House, Raglan Rd, Lowestoft, Suffolk NR32 2LW, United Kingdom. TEL 44-1502-500505, FAX 44-1502-514298, mail@hoseasons.co.uk.

796.95 USA ISSN 0892-8320
HOT BOAT. Text in English. 1985 (vol.7). m. USD 27 domestic; USD 37 foreign; GBP 2.50 newsstand/cover (effective 2000). adv. **Document type:** *Magazine, Consumer.* **Description:** Focuses on motorized family water sporting events, personalities, "how-to" and technical data.
Formerly: Hot Boat Magazine (0745-6077)
Published by: Larry Flynt Publications, Inc., 8484 Wilshire Blvd, Ste 900, Beverly Hills, CA 90211. TEL 323-651-5400, FAX 310-274-7985. Circ: 30,000.

797.1 USA
HOUSEBOAT MAGAZINE; the family magazine for American houseboaters. Text in English. 1971. m. USD 29.95 domestic; USD 44.95 in Canada; USD 49.95 elsewhere (effective 2008). adv. illus. back issues avail.; reprints avail. **Document type:** *Magazine, Trade.* **Description:** Presents features of new boats to lifestyle stories, how-tos and product reviews about the house boat industry.
Published by: Harris Publishing, Inc (Idaho Falls), 360 B St, Idaho Falls, ID 83402-3547. TEL 208-524-7000, 800-638-0135, FAX 208-522-5241, customerservice@harrispublishing.com, http://www.harrispublishing.com. Adv. contact Greg Larsen TEL 208-542-2216. B&W page USD 2,666, color page USD 3,798; trim 8 x 10.75. Circ: 25,000.

797.1 USA
HOUSEBOATING ADVENTURES. Text in English. 2004. bi-m. USD 18.95 (effective 2005). **Document type:** *Magazine, Consumer.* **Description:** Features travel to fabulous houseboat destinations, gorgeous photos, resort reviews and vacation planning, personality interviews, houseboat reviews, factory tours, sport boat reviews, new water sports, galley and cooking advice, the latest in electronics and home entertainment, houseboat driving tips, gear reviews, and houseboat maintenance tips and updates.
Published by: Adventure Publications, Inc., 2710 Belmont Dr., PO Box 336, Hood River, OR 97031. TEL 541-386-3172, FAX 541-386-1405, custservice@adventurepublications.net, http://www.adventurepublications.net/. Pub. Michael McDonald Low.

797.1 347.75 JPN
I A P H WORLD PORTS CONFERENCE. PROCEEDINGS. Text in English. biennial. **Document type:** *Proceedings, Academic/Scholarly.*
Published by: International Association of Ports and Harbors/Kokusai Kowan Kyokai, 5th Fl. North Tower New Pier Takeshiba, 1-11-1 Kaigan, Minato-ku, Tokyo, 105-0022, Japan. TEL 81-3-5403-2770, FAX 81-3-5403-7651, info@iaphworldports.org, http://www.iaphworldports.org.

623.82 DEU ISSN 0020-921X
I B N; Das Magazin fuer Wassersport am Bodensee. (Internationale Bodensee & Boot Nachrichten) Text in German. 1964. m. EUR 57; EUR 5 newsstand/cover (effective 2009). adv. bk.rev. illus. index. **Document type:** *Magazine, Consumer.*
Published by: Druck & Verlagshaus Hermann Daniel GmbH & Co. KG, Gruenewaldstr 15, Balingen, 72336, Germany. TEL 49-7433-2660, FAX 49-7433-266236, info@hermann-daniel.de, http://www.hermann-daniel.de. Ed. Hans Dieter Moehlhenrich. adv.: B&W page EUR 1,315, color page EUR 1,615; trim 210 x 297. Circ: 7,650 (paid and controlled).

797.14 USA
I C Y R A N A DIRECTORY. Text in English. a. free. **Document type:** *Directory, Trade.*
Published by: Intercollegiate Yacht Racing Association of North America, c/o Eric Wallischeck, Yocum Sailing Center, US Merchant Marine Academy, Kings Point, NY 11024-1699. TEL 516-773-5232, FAX 516-773-5344, wallischecke@USMMA.edu, http://www.collegesailing.org. Circ: 400.

797.1 NLD ISSN 1872-7824
INFO 20M. Text in Dutch. 2006. bi-m.
Media: Online - full text.
Published by: Expertisebureau Bos, Hasebroekstraat 7, Heemskerk, 1962 SV, Netherlands. TEL 31-251-230050, bosq@xs4all.nl. Pubs. Henk Bos, Janneke Bos.

INFORMAZIONI NAUTICHE. *see* TRANSPORTATION—Ships And Shipping

387.2 GBR ISSN 0020-6172
HD9999.B5
INTERNATIONAL BOAT INDUSTRY. Text in English. 1968. 8/yr. free to qualified personnel (effective 2009). adv. bk.rev. back issues avail. **Document type:** *Magazine, Trade.* **Description:** Features articles relevant to the marine leisure industry.
Formerly (until 1970): International Boating
Related titles: Online - full text ed.
Published by: I P C Country & Leisure Media Ltd. (Subsidiary of: I P C Media Ltd.), Leon House, 233 High St, Croydon, CR9 1HZ, United Kingdom. http://www.ipcmedia.com. Ed. Ed Slack TEL 44-20-87268134. Pub. Nick Hopkinson TEL 44-20-87268119. Adv. contact Laurent Subra TEL 44-20-87268121. page GBP 3,360.

THE INTERNATIONAL DIRECTORY OF MARINE AND BOATING EQUIPMENT AND SUPPLIES IMPORTERS. *see* BUSINESS AND ECONOMICS—Trade And Industrial Directories

797.124 USA
INTERNATIONAL ETCHELLS CLASS NEWS. Text in English. 1970. q. membership. adv. 16 p./no. 3 cols./p.; back issues avail. **Document type:** *Proceedings.* **Description:** Aimed at owners of Etchells Class yachts in fleets worldwide.
Formerly: International E-22 Class Newsletter
Published by: International Etchells Class Association, PO BOX 534, WALL ST STA, New York, NY 10268. TEL 212-943-5757. Ed. Bunny Wayt. Circ: 1,800.

797.124 USA
INTERNATIONAL ETCHELLS CLASS YEARBOOK. Text in English. 1970. biennial. membership. adv. **Document type:** *Proceedings.* **Description:** Aimed at owners of Etchells Class yachts.
Formerly: International E-22 Class Yearbook
Published by: International Etchells Class Association, PO BOX 534, WALL ST STA, New York, NY 10268. TEL 212-943-5757. Ed. Catherine D Norton. Circ: 4,000.

797.124 GBR ISSN 0307-4706
INTERNATIONAL FIREBALL. Text in English. 1970. s-a. membership. adv.
Published by: Fireball International, 47 Chiswick Quay, London, W4 3UR, United Kingdom. FAX 44-1392-410432. Ed. Richard Hughes. Circ: 2,500.

797.124 USA ISSN 1550-9435
INTERNATIONAL YACHTSMAN. Text in English. bi-m. USD 9.95 (effective 2006). adv. **Document type:** *Magazine, Consumer.*
Formerly (until Mar. 2004): Fort Lauderdale Yachtsman
Published by: Perfect Vision Media Group, 420 Lincoln Rd Ste 221, Miami Beach, FL 33139. TEL 786-621-6270, FAX 786-621-6290, info@perfectvisionmedia.com, http://perfectvisionmedia.com/. adv.: color page USD 4,500; trim 10 x 12. Circ: 30,000 (paid).

796.95 DEU
INTERNATIONALES BODENSEE-JAHRBUCH DER SPORTSCHIFFAHRT. Text in German. 1959. a. EUR 13 (effective 2009). **Document type:** *Magazine, Consumer.*
Formerly (until 1971): Bodenseejahrbuch der Sportschiffahrt
Published by: (Bodensee Segler Verband), Druck & Verlagshaus Hermann Daniel GmbH & Co. KG, Gruenewaldstr 15, Balingen, 72336, Germany. TEL 49-7433-2660, FAX 49-7433-266236, info@hermann-daniel.de, http://www.hermann-daniel.de. Circ: 11,000 (paid). **Co-sponsor:** Bodensee Motorboot Verband.

INWATER. *see* SPORTS AND GAMES—Outdoor Life

797.1 IRL ISSN 0791-1459
IRELAND AFLOAT. Text in English. 1962. 10/yr. EUR 38 in Ireland & U.K.; EUR 89 elsewhere (effective 2002). adv. bk.rev. abstr.; charts; illus. **Document type:** *Magazine, Consumer.*
Former titles (until 1986): Afloat (0332-4486); (until 1982): Ireland Afloat (0791-1440); (until 1972): Irish Yachting and Motorboating (0021-1451); (until 1962): Irish Yachting (0791-1432)
Published by: Irish Marine Press, 2 Lower Glenageary Rd., Dun Laoghaire, Dublin, 4, Ireland. TEL 353-1-2846161, FAX 353-1-2846192. adv.: B&W page EUR 1,303, color page EUR 1,851. Circ: 10,000.

797.124 GBR
THE ISLAND; magazine of the Island Sailing Club. Text in English. 1985. s-a. free to members. **Document type:** *Magazine, Consumer.*
Published by: Island Sailing Club, 70 Hight St, Cowes, Isle of Wight, PO31 7RE, United Kingdom. TEL 44-1983-296621, FAX 44-1983-293214, admin@islandsc.org.uk, http://www.islandsc.org.uk/. Ed. Rosemary Joy. Adv. contact John Terry.

796.95 USA
JAVELIN CLASS ASSOCIATION YEARBOOK. Text in English. 1976. quinquennial. membership. Supplement avail.
Related titles: ◆ Supplement(s): Javelin Class Association Yearbook. Supplement.
Published by: Javelin Class Association, 874 Beecher's Rd., Mayfield Village, OH 44143. TEL 216-461-8511. Ed. G T Reiber. Circ: 250.

796.95 USA
JAVELIN CLASS ASSOCIATION YEARBOOK. SUPPLEMENT. Text in English. 1977. a. membership.
Related titles: ◆ Supplement to: Javelin Class Association Yearbook.
Published by: Javelin Class Association, 874 Beecher's Rd., Mayfield Village, OH 44143. TEL 216-461-8511. Ed. G T Reiber.

797.1 GBR
JET SKIER & PERSONAL WATERCRAFT. Text in English. m. GBP 25.20; GBP 2.10 newsstand/cover (effective 1999). adv. **Document type:** *Handbook/Manual/Guide, Consumer.* **Description:** Guide to all aspects of watercraft usage from racing and competitions to product and water site reviews.
Published by: C S L Publishing Ltd., S L House, 184 Histon Rd, Cambridge, Cambs CB4 3JP, United Kingdom. TEL 44-1223-460490, FAX 44-1223-315960. Ed. Damian McAuley. Pub. Graham Stuart. Adv. contact Jo White. **Dist. by:** M M C Ltd., Octagon House, White Hart Meadows, Ripley, Woking, Surrey GU23 6HR, United Kingdom. TEL 44-1483-211222, FAX 44-1483-224541.

796.95 387 CAN ISSN 1910-2232
JIB. Text in English. 1980. q. looseleaf. membership. adv. **Document type:** *Newsletter, Consumer.* **Description:** Contains current developments at the institution and projects underway; as well as comments on staff and volunteer projects.
Formerly (until 2006): Jib Gems (0839-105X)
Published by: Marine Museum Great Lakes at Kingston, 55 Ontario St, Kingston, ON K7L 2Y2, Canada. TEL 613-542-2261, FAX 613-542-0043, marmaus@marmuseum.ca, http://www.marmuseum.ca. Ed., R&P Maurice Smith. Circ: 600.

797.122 917.104 CAN ISSN 1198-9580
GV781
KANAWA; Canada's paddling magazine. Text in English. 1972. q. CAD 42.80 domestic; USD 40 foreign (effective 2006). adv. bk.rev. back issues avail. **Document type:** *Magazine, Consumer.* **Description:** Canoeing, kayaking and sea kayaking destinations, environmental issues, paddling events, equipment features, instruction, heritage, photography and more.
Former titles (until 1993): Kanawa Magazine for Recreational Paddling in Canada (1189-5152); (until 1990): Kanawa (0820-2990)
Indexed: SD.
Published by: Paddle Canada, 446 Main St W, PO Box 398, Merrickville, ON K0J 1N0, Canada. TEL 613-269-2910, 888-252-6292, FAX 613-269-2908, info@paddlingcanada.com, http://paddlingcanada.com. Circ: 15,000 (paid).

797.122 DNK ISSN 0900-8438
KANO & KAJAK. Text in Danish. 1959-2005; resumed 2010. bi-m. adv. **Document type:** *Magazine, Consumer.*
Related titles: Online - full text ed.: ISSN 1904-2108.
Published by: Dansk Kano og Kajak Forbund, Idraettens Hus, Broendby, 2605, Denmark. TEL 45-43-262094, dkf@kano-kajak.dk. Ed. Anders Krintel. Adv. contact Kim Sangild TEL 45-96-701120. Circ: 20,000 (controlled and free).

797.122 NLD ISSN 0928-1495
KANO-SPORT. Text in Dutch. 1980. q. EUR 36.50; EUR 9.75 newsstand/cover (effective 2009). adv. bk.rev. **Document type:** *Magazine, Consumer.*
Formerly: Kano-Bulletin
Published by: Nederlandse Kano Bond, Postbus 2656, Nieuwegein, 3430 GB, Netherlands. TEL 31-30-7513750, FAX 31-30-6564783, info@nkb.nl, http://www.nkb.nl. adv.: B&W page EUR 590, color page EUR 695; trim 210 x 297. Circ: 7,500.

797.122 AUS ISSN 1328-1801
KANU CULTURE. Text in English. 1995. a., latest vol.7, 2001. back issues avail. **Document type:** *Journal, Consumer.* **Description:** Covers the sport of outrigger canoeing, including photos, features covering techniques, equipment, major races, interviews, culture and history.
Published by: Batini Books, PO Box 506, Maroochydore, QLD 4558, Australia. steve@kanuculture.com.

797.122 DEU ISSN 0022-8923
KANU SPORT. Text in German. 1919. m. EUR 30 domestic; EUR 36 foreign; EUR 3 newsstand/cover (effective 2009). adv. bk.rev. illus.; bibl.; maps; mkt. 48 p./no.; back issues avail. **Document type:** *Magazine, Consumer.*
Published by: Deutscher Kanu Verband - Wirtschafts- und Verlags GmbH, Bertaallee 8, Duisburg, 47055, Germany. TEL 49-203-99759-0, FAX 49-203-9975961, verlag@kanu.de. Ed., R&P Dieter Reinmuth. Adv. contact Sabine Egermann. B&W page EUR 990, color page EUR 1,490; trim 210 x 297. Circ: 9,815 (controlled).

797.127 DEU ISSN 1436-7750
KANUMAGAZIN; Europas groesstes Magazin fuer Paddler. Text in German. 1994. 8/yr. EUR 46.50; EUR 6 newsstand/cover (effective 2011). adv. **Document type:** *Magazine, Consumer.*
Published by: Atlas Verlag GmbH, Brienner Str 41, Munich, 80333, Germany. TEL 49-89-552410, FAX 49-89-55241100, info@atlas-verlag.de, http://www.atlas-verlag.de. Ed. Michael Neumann. Adv. contact Thomas Obermaier.

797.1 RUS ISSN 0320-9199
KATERA I YAKHTY. Text in Russian. 1963. m. USD 48 foreign (effective 2003).
Indexed: RefZh.
Address: M Morskaya 8, St Petersburg, 191186, Russian Federation. TEL 812-3124078, FAX 812-3143360. Ed. K Konstantinov. **Dist. by:** M K - Periodica, ul Gilyarovskogo 39, Moscow 129110, Russian Federation. TEL 7-095-2845008, FAX 7-095-2813798, info@periodicals.ru, http://www.mkniga.ru; East View Information Services, 10601 Wayzata Blvd, Minneapolis, MN 55305. TEL 952-252-1201, 800-477-1005, FAX 952-252-1202, info@eastview.com, http://www.eastview.com.

797.122 USA ISSN 1527-4985
KAYAK MAGAZINE. Text in English. 2000. q. USD 14.95; USD 4.95 newsstand/cover (effective 2001). adv. **Document type:** *Magazine, Consumer.*
Address: PMB 25187, Jackson, WY 83001. editor@kayakmagazine.com, http://www.kayakmagazine.com. Ed. Kenny Unser. Pub. Njord Rota.

797.122 NZL
KAYAK NEW ZEALAND. Text in English. bi-m. NZD 35 (effective 2008). adv. **Document type:** *Magazine, Consumer.* **Description:** Contains heaps of great advice on kayaking techniques, paddling destinations, recent kayaking adventures by readers, weather and navigation and a comprehensive catalogue of the latest and greatest kayaks and gear.
Published by: Canoe & Kayak Ltd., 6 Tavern Rd, Silverdale, Auckland, New Zealand. TEL 64-9-4210662, FAX 64-9-4210663, info@canoeandkayak.co.nz.

797.1 JPN ISSN 0389-1771
KAZI/SAIL AND POWERBOAT MAGAZINE. Text in Japanese. 1932. m. JPY 1,000 per issue (effective 1998). adv. bk.rev. **Document type:** *Consumer.* **Description:** Covers everythin relating to sailing, boating, and fishing.
Published by: Kazi Co. Ltd., 2-17 Hamamatsu-cho 1-chome, Minato-ku, Tokyo, 105-0013, Japan. TEL 81-3-3434-5181, FAX 81-3-3434-5184. Ed. Masami Takubo. Pub. Yoshio Doi. Adv. contact Buko Negishi. Circ: 120,000.

797.1 FIN ISSN 0780-5373
KIPPARI. Text in English, Finnish, Swedish. 1982. 11/yr. EUR 56.80 (effective 2005). adv. **Document type:** *Magazine, Consumer.* **Description:** For users of motorboats, from small boats to luxury yachts. Has detailed, expert and wide-ranging tests and presentations of boats, motors and gear.
Published by: Yhtyneet Kuvalehdet Oy/United Magazines Ltd., Maistraatinportti 1, Helsinki, 00015, Finland. TEL 358-9-15661, FAX 358-9-145650, http://www.kuvalehdet.fi. Ed. Vesa Leppa. adv.: color page EUR 1,700; 217 x 280. Circ: 17,147.

797.124 ITA ISSN 1593-6392
KITEBOARD ITALIA. Text in Italian. 2001. bi-m. EUR 26 domestic; EUR 43 foreign (effective 2008). **Document type:** *Magazine, Consumer.*
Published by: Cantelli Editore Srl, Via Saliceto 22c, Castelmaggiore, BO 40013, Italy. TEL 39-051-6328811, FAX 39-051-6328815, cantelli.editore@cantelli.net, http://www.cantelli.net.

797.1 623.8 SWE ISSN 2000-8031
▼ **KLASSIAKA BAATAR.** Text in Swedish. 2011. q. adv. **Document type:** *Magazine, Consumer.*
Supersedes in part (in 2011): Nostalgia Special (2000-4001)
Related titles: Online - full text ed.
Published by: Foerlags AB Albinsson & Sjoeberg, PO Box 529, Karlskrona, 37123, Sweden. TEL 46-455-335325, FAX 46-455-311715.

797.1 USA ISSN 0744-9194
LAKELAND BOATING; the Great Lakes boating magazine. Text in English. 1946. m. USD 21.95 domestic; USD 27.95 in Canada; USD 55.90 elsewhere; USD 4.99 newsstand/cover (effective 2007). adv. bk.rev. illus. reprints avail. **Document type:** *Magazine, Consumer.* **Description:** Contains articles and features on all aspects of power boating on the Great Lakes.
Former titles (until 1983): Lakeland Boating Incorporating Sea (0274-9076); (until 1980): Lakeland Boating (0023-7345); Lakeland Yachting
Related titles: Microform ed.: 1946 (from PQC).
Indexed: A22, Consl, MMI, SportS.
—Linda Hall.
Published by: O'Meara - Brown Publications, Inc., 727 S Dearborn, Ste 812, Chicago, IL 60605. TEL 312-276-0610, 800-827-0289, FAX 312-276-0619. Ed. Matthew Wright. Pub. Walter B. O'Meara. Adv. contact Kirsten Moxley. B&W page USD 4,325, color page USD 6,835. Circ: 50,226 (paid).

LAKESTYLE. *see* LIFESTYLE

797.1 SWE ISSN 0347-4232
LASERNYTT. Text in Swedish. 1976. q. SEK 250 to members. **Document type:** *Consumer.*
Published by: Svenska Laserfoerbundet, Gisloevs Strandvaeg 1543, Trelleborg, 23192, Sweden. http://www.seglaglaser.nu. Ed. Ulla Halloff TEL 46-8-7471221.

797.1 USA ISSN 1094-4435
LATITUDES & ATTITUDES; world of the cruising sailor. Text in English. 1997. bi-m. USD 19.95 domestic; USD 24.95; USD 34.95 elsewhere; USD 4.99 newsstand/cover (effective 2001). adv. bk.rev. back issues avail. **Document type:** *Magazine, Consumer.* **Description:** Covers the cruising lifestyle. Includes information on new products and new designs, as well as accounts of those living at sea.
Published by: F T W Publishing, Inc., PO Box 668, Redondo Beach, CA 90277. TEL 310-798-3445, FAX 310-798-3448, editor@latsandatts.net. Ed., Pub., R&P Bob Bitchin. Adv. contact Vicki Snyder. color page USD 4,000, B&W page USD 3,500. Circ: 70,000 (paid).

623.829 GBR ISSN 0024-3086
VK1300
LIFEBOAT. Text in English. 1852. q. GBP 18 to members (effective 2000). adv. bk.rev. illus. **Document type:** *Newsletter.* **Description:** Contains a regular pattern of lifeboat service reports, fundraising news, and a variety of features and articles.
Published by: Royal National Lifeboat Institution, West Quay Rd, Poole, Dorset BH15 1HZ, United Kingdom. TEL 44-1202-663000, FAX 44-1202-663238. Ed. Mike Floyd. Adv. contact James Vaughan. B&W page GBP 1,845, color page GBP 2,310; trim 178 x 267. Circ: 260,000.

LIGHT LIST. *see* TRANSPORTATION—Ships And Shipping

797.1 GBR ISSN 0024-5062
THE LITTLE SHIP. Text in English. 1928. 3/yr. free to members. bk.rev. charts; illus. **Document type:** *Magazine, Consumer.* **Description:** Contains news, features and reports of Club activities.
Formerly (until 1957): Little Ship Club. Journal
Published by: Little Ship Club, Upper Thames St, Bell Wharf Ln, London, EC4R 3TB, United Kingdom. TEL 44-20-72367729, FAX 44-20-72369100.

797.1 USA ISSN 0897-2656
LIVING ABOARD. Text in English. 1973. bi-m. USD 18 domestic; USD 22 foreign (effective 2006). **Document type:** *Magazine, Consumer.* **Description:** Written by liveaboards for liveaboards to share stories, methods, tools, tips, to make life aboard watercraft more enjoyable and meaningful.
Address: PO Box 91299, Austin, TX 78709-1299. TEL 512-892-4446, FAX 512-892-4448. Ed. Linda Ridihalgh. Pub., R&P Fred C Walters. Adv. contact Paula Buchalla. Circ: 6,000 (paid).

051 USA
THE LOG (SAN DIEGO EDITION). Text in English. s-m. USD 29.90 (effective 2008). adv. **Document type:** *Newspaper, Consumer.*
Related titles: Regional ed(s).: Log (Los Angeles Edition); Log (Arizona Edition); Log (Northern California Edition); Log (Orange County Edition).
Published by: The Log Newspaper, 17782 Cowan, Ste A, Irvine, CA 92614. TEL 949-660-6150, FAX 949-660-6172. Ed. Eston Ellis. Pub. Daniel Teckenoff.

797.14 USA ISSN 0076-0455
LOG OF THE STAR CLASS; official rule book. Text in English. 1921. a. membership. adv.
Published by: International Star Class Yacht Racing Association, 1545 Waukegan Rd, Glenview, IL 60025. TEL 847-729-0630, FAX 847-729-0718. Circ: 3,970.

LOOKOUT!. *see* TRANSPORTATION—Ships And Shipping

797.1 USA
M R A A NEWSLETTER. Text in English. 1972. m. membership. adv. **Document type:** *Newsletter.* **Description:** For members who are experienced professional marine dealers, with up-to-date information on industry trends.
Published by: Marine Retailers Association of America, PO Box 1127, Oak Park, IL 60304-0127. TEL 312-938-0359, FAX 312-938-9035. Ed. Kermit Small. Circ: 16,000.

797.1 USA
MAINE COASTAL NEWS. Text in English. 1987. m. USD 10; USD 0.75 newsstand/cover (effective 1999). adv. bk.rev. tr.lit. back issues avail. **Document type:** *Newspaper.* **Description:** Concerned with all aspects of boating on the waters off the coast of Maine.
Address: 710, Winterport, ME 04496-0710. TEL 207-223-8846, FAX 207-223-9004. Ed., Pub. Jon B Johansen. adv.: page USD 500; trim 14.88 x 9.88. Circ: 5,000.

797.1 CHE ISSN 1662-1298
MARINA.CH. Text in German. 2007. 10/yr. CHF 74 (effective 2011). adv. **Document type:** *Magazine, Consumer.*
Related titles: French ed.: ISSN 1662-1301. 2007.
Published by: Los Media GmbH, Ralligweg 10, Bern, 3012, Switzerland. TEL 41-31-3010031, FAX 41-31-3010047. Ed., Pub. Lori Schuepbach. Adv. contact Ruedi Hilber. Circ: 12,000 (paid and controlled).

796.95 USA ISSN 1079-1930
MARINA DOCK AGE. Abbreviated title: M D A. Text in English. 1988. 8/yr. USD 75 domestic; USD 85 foreign; USD 8.95 per issue domestic; USD 11.95 per issue foreign; free to qualified personnel (effective 2009). adv. back issues avail. **Document type:** *Magazine, Trade.* **Description:** Covers the marina and boat-yard business.
—CCC.
Published by: Preston Publications, 6600 W Touhy Ave, Niles, IL 60714-4588. TEL 847-647-2900, FAX 847-647-1155, circulation@prestonpub.com, http://www.prestonpub.com. Ed. Jerry Koncel. Pub. Janice Gordon. adv.: B&W page USD 1,890, color page USD 2,775; bleed 8.375 x 11.125. Circ: 17,208.

797.14 USA ISSN 2152-2200
MARINALIFE. Text in English. 2007. q. free to members (effective 2010). adv. back issues avail. **Document type:** *Magazine, Consumer.* **Description:** Includes articles on where to cruise, new marina destinations, restaurants, recipes, events, cruising stories and much more.
Related titles: Online - full text ed.: ISSN 2152-2243.
Published by: Marinalife, LLC, 1414 Key Hwy, 3rd Fl, Baltimore, MD 21230. TEL 410-752-0505, FAX 410-752-0358, info@marinalife.com.

796.95 330 USA ISSN 1537-2766
MARINE BUSINESS JOURNAL; the voice of the marine industries nationwide. Text in English. 1986. 6/yr. free. adv. back issues avail. **Document type:** *Magazine, Trade.* **Description:** Trade magazine about the marine industry. Covers political issues, new technologies and products. Includes export, management and insurance.
Former titles: Southern Marine Business Journal; National Marine Business Journal
Published by: Southern Boating and Yachting, Inc., 330 N Andrews Ave, Fort Lauderdale, FL 33301. TEL 954-522-5515, FAX 954-522-2260. Ed. Bill Lindsey. Pub. Skip Allen Jr. adv.: B&W page USD 3,905, color page USD 5,220. Circ: 29,000 (paid and free).

MARINE SAFETY REVIEW. *see* TRANSPORTATION—Ships And Shipping

MARINE SAFETY UPDATE. *see* PUBLIC HEALTH AND SAFETY

797.1 USA
THE MARINER. Text in English. 1982. bi-w. (m. Dec.-Feb.; Mar.-Nov.). free (effective 2011). 80 p./no. 4 cols./p.; **Document type:** *Newspaper, Consumer.* **Description:** Recreational boating on the Chesapeake Bay.
Published by: Chesapeake Publishing Corp., 601 Bridge St, Elkton, Cecil, MD 21922. TEL 410-398-3311, FAX 410-398-4044, twinmill@chespub.com. Ed. Dan Meadows. Pub. David Fike.

MARITIME STUDIES. *see* TRANSPORTATION—Ships And Shipping

796.95 USA ISSN 0749-2006
MARLIN; the international sportfishing magazine. Text in English. 1982. 8/yr. USD 19.95 domestic; USD 31.95 per issue in Canada; USD 51.95 elsewhere (effective 2011). adv. bk.rev. illus. back issues avail. **Document type:** *Magazine, Consumer.* **Description:** Provides international coverage of the sport of offshore fishing.
Related titles: Online - full text ed.: USD 14.95 (effective 2011).
Indexed: G08, I05.
—CCC.
Published by: Bonnier Corp. (Subsidiary of: Bonnier Group), 460 N Orlando Ave, Ste 200, Orlando, FL 32789. TEL 407-628-4802, FAX 407-628-7061, http://www.bonniercorp.com. Ed. Dave Ferrell. Pub. Natasha Lloyd TEL 954-760-4602.

797.1 USA ISSN 1946-4657
THE MASIK. Text in English. 2003. quadrennial. free (effective 2009). back issues avail. **Document type:** *Newsletter.* **Description:** Contains information on traditional kayaking, including articles on home-built kayaks and paddles, traditional kayaking techniques, do-it-yourself ideas, and the happenings within Qajaq USA.
Media: Online - full content.
Published by: Qajaq USA, 1215 E. M113, Kingsley, MI 49649. publications@qajaqusa.org. Ed. Tom Milani.

798.177 DEU ISSN 1158-0437
MEER & YACHTEN. Text in German. 1991. bi-m. EUR 27; EUR 6 newsstand/cover (effective 2009). adv. **Document type:** *Magazine, Consumer.*
Published by: Edimer Verlag (Subsidiary of: Boat International Media), Flensburger Str 87, Kiel, 24106, Germany. TEL 49-431-336883, FAX 49-431-331485. Ed. Jochen Halbe. adv.: page EUR 5,685; trim 223 x 275. Circ: 17,000 (paid and controlled).

796.95 FRA ISSN 0999-7148
MER & BATEAUX. Text in French. 1977. m. adv. bk.rev. illus. index. **Document type:** *Magazine, Consumer.*
Formerly (until 1989): Annee Bateaux Magazine (0184-5055)
Published by: Edimer (Subsidiary of: Boat International Media), 83 bis, rue Thiers, Boulogne, 92100, France. TEL 33-1-46204040, FAX 33-1-46201413. Ed. Patrick Teboul. Circ: 32,000.

MESSENGER LINE. *see* MUSEUMS AND ART GALLERIES

796.95 USA
MESSING ABOUT IN BOATS. Text in English. 1983. s-m. USD 32 (effective 2007). adv. bk.rev. back issues avail. **Document type:** *Magazine, Consumer.* **Description:** Small boat owner news.
Published by: Cycle Sport Publishing, 29 Burley St, Wenham, MA 01984. TEL 978-774-0906. Ed., R&P, Adv. contact Bob Hicks. page USD 100; trim 8.5 x 11. Circ: 4,000 (paid).

629.12 ITA ISSN 1723-3658
LA MIA BARCA. Text in Italian. 2003. 11/yr. EUR 34.90 (effective 2008). adv. **Document type:** *Magazine, Consumer.*
Published by: Edizioni Master SpA, Contrada Lecco 64, Zona Industriale, Roges di Rende, CS 87036, Italy. TEL 39-0984-831900, FAX 39-0984-8319225, contact@edmaster.it, http://www.edmaster.it.

623.82 GBR ISSN 0144-2910
MODEL BOATS. Text in English. 1951. m. GBP 44.95 domestic; GBP 51.95 in Europe; GBP 48 in United States; GBP 55 elsewhere (effective 2010). adv. charts; illus. index. back issues avail. **Document type:** *Magazine, Consumer.* **Description:** Contains articles and plans for builders of working model boats.
Former titles (until 1977): Model Maker and Model Boats (0026-7333); (until 1964): Model Maker
Related titles: Online - full text ed.
Indexed: IHTDI.
Published by: MyHobbyStore Ltd., Berwick House, 8-10 Knoll Rise, Orpington, Kent BR6 0EL, United Kingdom. TEL 44-844-4122262, info@myhobbystore.com, http://www.myhobbystoregroup.com. Ed. Paul Freshney. Adv. contact Duncan Armstrong TEL 44-1689-869855.

797.1 AUS ISSN 1443-2838
MODERN BOATING. Text in English. 1965. 10/yr. AUD 50 domestic; AUD 90 in New Zealand; AUD 150 elsewhere; AUD 8.95 newsstand/cover (effective 2008). adv. bk.rev. illus. index. **Document type:** *Magazine, Consumer.* **Description:** Covers sail and power boats, basic hints to electronic navigation and all types of boating throughout Australia and New Zealand.
Former titles (until 1997): Modern Boating, Power and Sail (1443-282X); (until 1993): Modern Boating and Boat-Mart (1443-2811); (until 1988): Modern Boating (0811-0697); (until 1980): Modern Boating & Seacraft (0158-5606); (until 1965): Australian Seacraft Modern Boating (0026-752X)
Indexed: Pinpoint.
Published by: News Magazines Pty Ltd., Level 3, 2 Holt St, Surry Hills, NSW 2010, Australia. TEL 61-2-92883000, http://www.newsspace.com.au/magazines. Ed. Ian Macrae. Adv. contact Dominic Wiseman TEL 61-2-80622771. color page AUD 2,100; trim 220 x 276. Circ: 10,520.

S

797.1 ITA ISSN 1826-1914
MONDO BARCA. Text in English, Italian. 1988. m. adv. back issues avail. **Document type:** *Magazine, Consumer.* **Description:** Deals with sail and motor boats, yachts, new products, equipment and sports events.
Published by: Gruppo Editoriale Olimpia SpA, Via E Fermi 24, Loc Osmannoro, Sesto Fiorentino, FI 50129, Italy. TEL 39-055-30321, FAX 39-055-3032280, info@edolimpia.it, http://www.edolimpia.it.

797.1 HRV ISSN 1330-7088
MORE. Text in Croatian. 1995. m. HRK 260 (effective 2002). adv. **Document type:** *Magazine, Consumer.*
Published by: Fabra d.o.o., Savska 141, Zagreb, 10000, Croatia. TEL 385-1-6190476, FAX 385-1-6190742, fabra@zg.tel.hr.

797 FRA ISSN 0994-964X
MOTEUR BOAT MAGAZINE. Text in French. 1988. m. EUR 67 (effective 2009). adv. **Document type:** *Magazine, Consumer.*
Published by: Editions Lariviere, 6 Rue Olof Palme, Clichy, 92587, France. TEL 33-1-47565400, http://www.editions-lariviere.fr. Ed. William Borel. Pub. Fabien Darmon. Adv. contact Frederique Cazenava Tapie.

796.95 ITA ISSN 1825-988X
MOTONAUTICA. Text in Italian, English. 1981. m. (11/yr.). EUR 55 domestic; EUR 120 foreign (effective 2009). adv. illus.; tr.lit. back issues avail. **Document type:** *Magazine, Consumer.* **Description:** Provides the latest news about the national and international boating world.
Related titles: Online - full text ed.; Supplement(s): Guida agli Accessori e Componenti Nautici. ISSN 1825-9898. 2005; Guida Motonautica. ISSN 1825-9901. 2005.
Published by: Motonautica Editrice, Via IV Novembre 54, Settimo Milanese, MI 20019, Italy. TEL 39-02-335531, FAX 39-02-33501391.

MOTOR. *see* TRANSPORTATION—Automobiles

797.1 GBR ISSN 0027-1780
MOTOR BOAT & YACHTING. Text in English. 1904. m. GBP 36.98 domestic; USD 80.05 in United States; USD 121.06 in Canada; EUR 87.19 in Europe; GBP 75.66 elsewhere; GBP 4.30 newsstand/cover (effective 2009). adv. bk.rev. charts; illus.; tr.lit. s-a. index. back issues avail. **Document type:** *Magazine, Consumer.* **Description:** Contains boat tests, cruising guides, advice on seamanship and navigational information for the committed boater.
Former titles (until 1938): Motor Boat, Yachting and Commercial Craft; (until 1936): Motor Boat; (until 1920): Motor Ship and Motor Boat; (until 1912): Motor Boat and Marine Oil and Gas Engine; (until 1911): Motor Boat
Related titles: Microform ed.: (from PQC); Online - full text ed.: GBP 29.99 (effective 2009).
Indexed: A28, APA, BrCerAb, BrTechI, C&ISA, CA/WCA, CIA, CerAb, CivEngAb, CorrAb, E&CAJ, E11, EEA, EMA, H15, M&TEA, M09, MBF, METADEX, RASB, SolStAb, T04, WAA.
—Linda Hall.
Published by: I P C Country & Leisure Media Ltd. (Subsidiary of: I P C Media Ltd.), The Blue Fin Bldg, 110 Southwark St, London, SE1 0SU, United Kingdom. TEL 44-20-31484651, FAX 44-20-31488128, http://www.ipcmedia.com. Ed. Hugo Andreae TEL 44-20-31484643. Pub. Stephen Kendall TEL 44-20-31484281. Adv. contact Mike Wills TEL 44-20-31484898. B&W page GBP 1,716, color page GBP 3,615. Circ: 17,346. **Subscr. to:** Rockwood House, Perrymount Rd, Haywards Heath RH16 3DH, United Kingdom. TEL 44-845-1231231, IPCsubs@quadrantsubs.com, http://www.magazinesdirect.co.uk. **Dist. by:** MarketForce UK Ltd. salesinnovation@marketforce.co.uk, http://www.marketforce.co.uk/.

971 USA ISSN 1531-2623
VM320
MOTOR BOATING. Text in English. 1907. 10/yr. USD 14 domestic; USD 24 in Canada; USD 44 elsewhere (effective 2009). adv. bk.rev. charts; illus.; stat. index. Supplement avail.; back issues avail.; reprints avail. **Document type:** *Magazine, Consumer.* **Description:** Provides tips on how to get the most from one's power or sailboat.
Former titles (until 2000): Motor Boating & Sailing (0027-1799); (until 1970): Motor Boating; (until 1909): Motor Boating Magazine
Related titles: Microfiche ed.: (from NBI, PQC); Online - full text ed.: free (effective 2009).
Indexed: A11, A22, B04, BRD, C05, C12, CPerI, ConsI, G05, G06, G07, G08, G09, I05, I07, M01, M02, M06, MASUSE, MagInd, P02, P10, P48, P53, P54, PMR, PQC, R03, R04, RGAb, RGPR, S23, SPI, SportS, T02, W03.
—Ingenta. **CCC.**
Published by: Bonnier Corp. (Subsidiary of: Bonnier Group), 460 N Orlando Ave, Ste 200, Winter Park, FL 32789. TEL 407-628-4802, FAX 407-628-7061, http://www.bonniercorp.com. Ed. Peter A Janssen. Pub. John McEver Jr.

797.1 GBR ISSN 0958-1898
MOTOR BOATS MONTHLY. Text in English. 1987. m. GBP 38.31 domestic; USD 104.29 in US & Canada; EUR 72.28 in Europe; GBP 68.06 elsewhere; GBP 4.20 newsstand/cover (effective 2009). adv. illus. back issues avail. **Document type:** *Magazine, Consumer.* **Description:** Covers all types of motorboats 15 to 65 feet long, including oceangoing vessels.
Related titles: Online - full text ed.: GBP 29.99 (effective 2009).
Published by: I P C Country & Leisure Media Ltd. (Subsidiary of: I P C Media Ltd.), The Blue Fin Bldg, 110 Southwark St, London, SE1 0SU, United Kingdom. TEL 44-20-31484664, FAX 44-20-31486439, http://www.ipcmedia.com. Ed. Carl Richardson TEL 44-20-31484668. Pub. Stephen Kendall TEL 44-20-31484281. Adv. contact Mike Wills TEL 44-20-31484898. B&W page GBP 1,362, color page GBP 2,837. Circ: 16,117. **Subscr. to:** Rockwood House, Perrymount Rd, Haywards Heath RH16 3DH, United Kingdom. TEL 44-845-1231231, IPCsubs@quadrantsubs.com, http://www.magazinesdirect.co.uk. **Dist. by:** MarketForce UK Ltd. salesinnovation@marketforce.co.uk, http://www.marketforce.co.uk/.

797.1 NLD ISSN 1381-8708
MOTORBOOT; maandblad voor de motorvaart. Text in Dutch. 1983. m. EUR 52 domestic; EUR 95 in Europe; EUR 197.50 elsewhere (effective 2009). adv. charts; illus.; maps; stat. back issues avail. **Document type:** *Consumer.* **Description:** Covers all aspects of owning and operating a motorboat.
—Infotrieve.
Published by: Uitgeverij Motorboot, Kubus 181, Sliedrecht, 3364 DG, Netherlands. TEL 31-184-448950, FAX 31-184-618079, motorboot@bdu.nl. Ed. Hans Papenburg. Adv. contact Frank van Gils. B&W page EUR 1,295, color page EUR 1,945; bleed 230 x 310. Circ: 21,650.

797.124 FRA ISSN 1960-2014
MULTICOQUES MAG. HORS-SERIE. Text in French. 2005. biennial. EUR 7.50 newsstand/cover (effective 2007). **Document type:** *Magazine, Consumer.*
Published by: Aloha Editions, 36 Rue Moliere, Nice, 06100, France. TEL 33-4-92091618.

797.124 FRA ISSN 0296-0877
MULTICOQUES MAGAZINE. Text in French. 1985. bi-m. EUR 29 domestic; EUR 39 foreign (effective 2007 - 2008). **Document type:** *Magazine, Consumer.*
Related titles: English ed.: Multihulls World. ISSN 1161-3904. 199?.
Indexed: SD.
Published by: Aloha Editions, 36 Rue Moliere, Nice, 06100, France. TEL 33-4-92091618.

796.95 USA ISSN 0749-4122
GV810
MULTIHULLS. Text in English. 1975. bi-m. USD 5.95, CAD 8.60, GBP 4.95 newsstand/cover (effective 2010). adv. bk.rev.; film rev. charts; tr.lit.; illus. 92 p./no. 3 cols./p.; back issues avail. **Document type:** *Magazine, Consumer.* **Description:** Features articles covering catamaran/multihulls industry.
Related titles: Online - full text ed.: USD 19.95; USD 3.95 per issue (effective 2010).
Published by: Chiodi Advertising & Publishing, Inc., 421 Hancock St, PO Box 7, N Quincy, MA 02171. TEL 617-328-8181, 800-333-6858, FAX 617-471-0118. Pub. Charles Ke Chiodi.

797.1 GBR ISSN 2047-2110
N A B O NEWS. Text in English. 19??. bi-m. free to members (effective 2011). back issues avail. **Document type:** *Newsletter, Trade.*
Formerly (until 1997): N A B O Newsletter
Related titles: Online - full text ed.: ISSN 2047-2129.
Published by: National Association of Boat Owners, c/o Richard Carpenter, Birmingham, B31 2BR, United Kingdom. TEL 44-7989-441674.

796.95 USA
HD9993.B63
N A D A MARINE APPRAISAL GUIDE. Text in English. 1998. 3/yr. USD 140 to non-members; USD 70 per issue to non-members; free to members (effective 2011). **Document type:** *Handbook/Manual/Guide, Trade.*
Formed by the merger of (1990-1998): N A D A Small Boat Appraisal Guide (1055-1964); (1990-1998): N A D A Large Boat Appraisal Guide (1055-1972); Supersedes in part: N A D A Boat Appraisal Guide
Published by: (National Automobile Dealers Association), N.A.D.A. Appraisal Guides, PO Box 7800, Costa Mesa, CA 92628. http://www.nadaguides.com.

N A D A MOTORCYCLE - SNOWMOBILE - A T V - PERSONAL WATERCRAFT APPRAISAL GUIDE. *see* SPORTS AND GAMES—Bicycles And Motorcycles

797.1 USA
N M M A CERTIFICATION HANDBOOK. Text in English. 1956. a. USD 200 to members (effective 2008). index.
Former titles: B I A Certification Handbook (0067-9402); Boating Industry Associations Engineering Manual of Recommended Practices
Published by: National Marine Manufacturers Association, 200 E Randolph Dr, Ste 5100, Chicago, IL 60601-6436. TEL 312-946-6200, FAX 312-946-1461, orderdesk@nmma.org, http://www.nmma.org.

623.8 NZL ISSN 1179-9773
N Z MARINE NEWS. (New Zealand) Text in English. 19??. s-a. back issues avail. **Document type:** *Magazine, Trade.*
Former titles (until 2010): M I A News (1176-5526); (until 2003): B I A News
Related titles: Online - full text ed.: ISSN 1179-9781. free (effective 2011).
Published by: N Z Marine Industry Association, Victoria St W, PO Box 90-448, Auckland, 1142, New Zealand. TEL 64-9-3600056, 800-600-242, FAX 64-9-3600019, info@bia.org.nz, http://www.nzmarine.com. Ed. Rebecca Hayter.

797.121 NZL
N Z R A NEWSLETTER (ONLINE). (New Zealand Rafting Association) Text in English. 2002. q. **Document type:** *Newsletter, Consumer.*
Former titles (until 2006): Rafting News (Print) (1177-2204); (until 200?): N Z Rafting News (1176-1601)
Media: Online - full text.
Published by: New Zealand Rafting Association, 203 Orari River Rd, RD 22, Peel Forest, New Zealand. TEL 64-3-6963849, FAX 64-3-6963531, nzraftingassociation@xtra.co.nz, http://www.nz-rafting.co.nz.

NATIONAL MARINE BANKERS ASSOCIATION. SUMMARY ANNUAL REPORT. *see* BUSINESS AND ECONOMICS—Banking And Finance

797.1 NLD
DE NATIONALE BOTENBANK. Text in Dutch. 2002. m. EUR 2 newsstand/cover (effective 2009). adv. **Document type:** *Magazine, Consumer.*
Published by: Sanoma Men's Magazines, Haaksbergweg 75, Amsterdam (ZO), 1101 BR, Netherlands. TEL 31-20-7518000, FAX 31-20-7518301, sales@smm.nl, http://www.smm.nl. adv.: color page EUR 875; 215 x 285.

797.1 ITA ISSN 1825-6155
NAUTECH. Text in Italian. 2005. bi-m. (7/yr.). EUR 30 domestic; EUR 60 in Europe; EUR 80 elsewhere (effective 2011). **Document type:** *Magazine, Consumer.*
Published by: Tecniche Nuove SpA, Via Eritrea 21, Milan, MI 201, Italy. TEL 39-02-390901, FAX 39-02-7570364, info@tecnichenuove.com. Ed. Stefania Garancini.

NAUTIC SERVICE. *see* TRANSPORTATION—Ships And Shipping

797.1 ESP ISSN 0214-6983
NAUTICA. Text in Spanish. 1989. m. adv. **Document type:** *Magazine, Consumer.*
Published by: M C Ediciones, Paseo de Sant Gervasi 16-20, Barcelona, 08022, Spain. TEL 34-93-2541250, FAX 34-93-2541262, http://www.mcediciones.net.

797.1 ITA ISSN 0392-369X
NAUTICA; mensile internazionale di navigazione. Text in Italian. 1962. m. EUR 60 (effective 2010). bk.rev. charts; illus. back issues avail. **Document type:** *Magazine, Consumer.* **Description:** Meets the needs of all boatmen with articles covering not only boats but also technical information, didactics, rules, port information, travel tips, boat chartering and many occasions for whoever wants to buy, change and sell a boat.
Related titles: Online - full text ed.
Published by: Nautica Editrice, Via Tevere 44, Rome, RM 00198, Italy. TEL 39-06-8413060, FAX 39-06-8543653, info@nautica.it, http://www.nautica.it. Circ: 40,000.

797.125 GRC ISSN 1108-2712
NAUTICA. Text in Greek. 1998. m. adv. illus. back issues avail. **Document type:** *Magazine, Consumer.* **Description:** Describes motor boats, power cruisers, inflatable boats (eg, Zodiacs), along with related water sports, such as fishing, diving, waterskiing, and jet skiing.
Published by: International Marine Publications/Diethneis Nautikes Ekdosis, Akti Themistokleous 22, Piraeus, 185 36, Greece. TEL 30-1-4281-923, FAX 30-1-4286-553, info@nautica.gr, http://www.nautica.gr. Ed. Thanos Andronikos. Pub., R&P John Papadopoulos TEL 30-1-4183-111. adv.: B&W page GBP 1,300, color page GBP 1,560; trim 220 x 300. Circ: 22,500 (paid).

797.1 PRT ISSN 1647-0575
A NAUTICA DA MADEIRA. Text in Portuguese. 2008. s-a. **Document type:** *Magazine, Consumer.*
Published by: Associacao Nautica da Madeira, Marina do Funchal 12, Funchal, 9000-055, Portugal. http://anmadeira.wordpress.com.

797.1 ITA ISSN 1974-3262
▼ **NAUTICA INTERNATIONAL.** Text in English. 2009. bi-m. **Document type:** *Magazine, Consumer.*
Published by: Nautica Editrice, Via Tevere 44, Rome, RM 00198, Italy. TEL 39-06-8413060, FAX 39-06-8543653, info@nautica.it, http://www.nautica.it.

796.95 BRA ISSN 1413-1412
NAUTICA MAGAZINE. Text in Portuguese. 1976. m. USD 50 domestic; USD 60 foreign. adv. **Document type:** *Consumer.* **Description:** Covers power cruising, luxury yachts, sailing yachts, dinghies, sports boats, water skiing, personal motor crafts, and charters.
Formerly: Mar - Vela e Motor; Which was formed by the merger of: Vela e Motor; Mar
Published by: G R 1 Editora, Rua Mateus Grou, 282, Pinheiros, Sao Paulo, SP 05415-040, Brazil. TEL 55-11-2822355, FAX 55-11-8830991. Ed., R&P Denise Godoy. Pub., Adv. contact Ernani Paciornik. B&W page USD 3,465, color page USD 7,623; 245 x 185. Circ: 50,000.

NAUTICAL RESEARCH JOURNAL. *see* TRANSPORTATION—Ships And Shipping

797.1 USA ISSN 1947-6329
▼ ➤ **NAUTILUS (BUZZARDS BAY).** Text in English. forthcoming 2010 (June). a. USD 35 domestic to institutions; USD 40 elsewhere (effective 2010). **Document type:** *Journal, Academic/Scholarly.* **Description:** Features scholarly research on maritime history, literature and culture.
Published by: Massachusetts Maritime Academy, 101 Academy Dr, Buzzards Bay, MA 02532. TEL 508-830-5000, kmudgett@maritime.edu, http://www.maritime.edu/.

797.1 ESP
NAUTIOCASION. Text in Spanish. bi-m. EUR 2.95 newsstand/cover (effective 2009). adv. **Document type:** *Magazine, Consumer.*
Published by: Grupo V, C Valportillo Primera, 11, Alcobendas, Madrid, 28108, Spain. TEL 34-91-6622137, FAX 34-91-6622654, secretaria@grupov.es. Ed. Francisco Otero-Saez. Adv. contact Amador Moreno. page EUR 2,290; trim 19.5 x 25.5. Circ: 17,100.

797.124 NLD ISSN 1383-8067
NAUTIQUE. Text in Dutch. 1995. 4/yr. EUR 15 (effective 2011). adv. **Document type:** *Magazine, Consumer.*
Published by: Pelican Magazines Hearst, Delflandlaan 4, Amsterdam, 1062 EB, Netherlands. TEL 31-20-7581000, FAX 31-20-7581003, info@pelicanmags.nl, http://www.pelicanmags.nl.

NAVIGATION DOUCE; le magazine du tourisme fluvial. *see* TRAVEL AND TOURISM

797.1 SWE ISSN 0028-1603
NAVIS; navigationssaellskapets medlemsblad. Text in Swedish. 1926. q. illus. **Document type:** *Newsletter, Consumer.*
Published by: Navigationssaellskapet, Ryssviksvaegen 12, Djurgaarden, Stockholm, 11521, Sweden. TEL 46-8-6619494, FAX 46-8-6616991, navigationssallskapet@talia.com, http://www.navis.se.

796.95 FRA ISSN 1266-8184
NEPTUNE YACHTING MOTEUR. Text in French. 1962. 11/yr. EUR 60 (effective 2009). adv. illus. **Document type:** *Magazine, Consumer.*
Former titles (until 1995): Neptune Yachting (0762-7378); (until 1984): Neptune (0753-7794); (until 1982): Neptune Nautisme (0028-2782)
Related titles: ◆ Supplement(s): Neptune Moteur. Hors-Serie Special Essais. ISSN 1274-2988.
Indexed: SportS.
Published by: (Societe d'Etude et de Developpement de la Presse Periodique (SEDPP)), Editions Lariviere, 6 Rue Olof Palme, Clichy, 92587, France. TEL 33-1-47565400, http://www.editions-lariviere.fr. Circ: 50,000.

NEW HAMPSHIRE SELECTED MOTOR VEHICLE, BOATING AND RELATED LAWS ANNOTATED. *see* TRANSPORTATION—Automobiles

797.122 NZL ISSN 1176-3744
NEW ZEALAND PADDLER PASIFIKA. Variant title: Paddler Pasifika. Text in English. 2003. q. **Document type:** *Magazine, Consumer.*
Published by: John Papalii, Ed. & Pub., 50 Thatcher St, Mission Bay, Auckland, New Zealand. TEL 64-9-5217265, johnpapalii@nzpaddlerpasifika.com.

623.82 796.95 JPN
NIHON SHUTEI KOGYOKAIHO/JAPAN BOATING INDUSTRY ASSOCIATION. NEWS. Text in Japanese. 1970. bi-m.
Published by: Nihon Shutei Kogyokai/Japan Boating Industry Association, 5-1 Ginza 2-chome, Chuo-ku, Tokyo, 104-0061, Japan.

796.95 USA ISSN 1938-6354
GV776.N75
NORTHEAST BOATING. Text in English. 1976. m. USD 25.95 (effective 2008). adv. bk.rev. illus. reprints avail. **Description:** Targets the mid-Atlantic and New England boating enthusiast.
Former titles (until 200?): Offshore (Needham) (0274-9394); (until 19??): New England Offshore (0192-4885)
Published by: Offshore Communications, 500 Victory Rd., North Quincy, MA 02171-3139. TEL 617-221-1400, FAX 617-847-1871. Pub. Richard J Royer Jr. Adv. contact John Stefancik. Circ: 36,000 (paid).

796.95 USA
NORTHERN BREEZES; sailing magazine. Text in English. 1989. m. **Document type:** *Magazine, Consumer.*
Published by: Northern Breezes, Inc., 245 Brunswick Ave S, Golden Valley, MN 55416. TEL 612-542-9707, FAX 612-542-8998, thomnbreez@aol.com. Ed. Gloria Peck. Circ: 22,300.

NORTHERN MARINER. *see* HISTORY

797.1 USA ISSN 1541-9401
NORTHWEST YACHTING. Text in English. 1987. m. USD 20 domestic; USD 50 in Canada (effective 2002). adv.
Published by: S K T Publishers, Inc., 7342 15th Ave. NW, Seattle, WA 98117-5401. TEL 206-789-8116, FAX 206-781-1554. Pub. Dan Schworer. Adv. contact Bruce Hedrick.

796.95 USA ISSN 0739-747X
NOR'WESTING. Text in English. 1965. m. USD 15 (effective 2001). adv. bk.rev. charts; illus.; tr.lit. **Document type:** *Magazine, Consumer.* **Description:** Covers recreational boating, boat club news, racing and related activities and events in the Pacific Northwest, from Oregon to Alaska, with a focus on the Puget Sound area.
Published by: Nor'westing Publications Inc., 513 Bay St 7, Port Orchard, WA 95366. TEL 360-874-1992, FAX 360-874-1987. Circ: 6,500 (paid).

796.95 USA ISSN 0886-0149
VK555
OCEAN NAVIGATOR; marine navigation and ocean voyaging. Text in English. 1985. bi-m. USD 27.95 combined subscription domestic; USD 37.95 combined subscription in Canada; USD 42.95 combined subscription elsewhere (effective 2009). adv. bk.rev. illus. back issues avail.; reprints avail. **Document type:** *Magazine, Trade.* **Description:** Contains news and features covering navigation, marine weather, electronics, communications, boat maintenance, marine science and technology.
Formerly (until Dec. 1985): Navigator (0882-2670)
Related titles: Online - full content ed.
Indexed: ASFA.
—CCC.
Published by: Navigator Publishing LLC., 58 Fore St, Portland, ME 04101-4842. TEL 207-772-2466, FAX 207-772-2879. Ed. Tim Queeney TEL 207-822-4350 ext 211. Pub. Alex Agnew TEL 207-822-4350 ext 219. Adv. contact Susan Hadlock TEL 207-822-4350 ext 212. B&W page USD 3,122, color page USD 4,670; 7 x 10. Circ: 44,000 (paid and controlled).

796.95 USA ISSN 1546-4814
VK555
OCEAN VOYAGER; handbook of offshore sailing. Text in English. 1988. a. free to qualified personnel (effective 2008). adv. back issues avail. **Document type:** *Magazine, Consumer.* **Description:** Focuses on the skills and techniques of ocean passagemaking.
Related titles: Online - full text ed.
—CCC.
Published by: Navigator Publishing LLC., 58 Fore St, Portland, ME 04101-4842. TEL 207-772-2466, FAX 207-772-2879, subscriptions@oceannavigator.com, http://www.oceannavigator.com. Ed. Tim Queeney TEL 207-822-4350 ext 211. Pub., Adv. contact Alex Agnew TEL 207-822-4350 ext 219. Circ: 50,000 (paid); 5,000 (controlled).

797.124 AUT
OCEAN7; Das oesterreichische Yachtmagazin. Text in German. 2007. 10/yr. EUR 31.50 (effective 2008). adv. **Document type:** *Magazine, Consumer.*
Published by: Ocean7 GmbH & Co. KG (Subsidiary of: Styria Medien AG), Geiselbergstr 15, Vienna, 1110, Austria. TEL 43-1-60117828, FAX 43-1-60117830. Ed. Thomas Dobernigg. adv.: page EUR 5,500; trim 210 x 280. Circ: 25,000 (paid and controlled).

797.1 AUT
OESTERREICHS KANUSPORT. Text in German. 1948. 5/yr. adv. bk.rev. abstr.; bibl.; charts; illus.; stat.; tr.lit. **Document type:** *Newsletter, Consumer.* **Description:** News on canoes, sports events, canoe associations and canoe trips.
Formerly: Oesterreichs Paddelsport (0029-9995)
Published by: Oesterreichischer Kanu-Verband, GieBereistr 8, Braunau am Inn, W 5280, Austria. office@kanuverband.at, http://www.okv.at. Ed. Guenter Goldbach. Circ: 5,000.

797 AUS
OFFSHORE YACHTING. Text in English. 1969. bi-m. AUD 48 domestic; USD 78 in Asia including New Zealand; USD 108 elsewhere (effective 2009). adv. bk.rev. charts; illus. back issues avail. **Document type:** *Magazine, Consumer.* **Description:** Covers all local, national and international offshore and inshore yachting; yacht racing, yacht tests and reviews, boats and boating.
Former titles (until 19??): Offshore Australian Yachting; Offshore Yacht Racing and Cruising; (until 1987): Offshore (1036-9171)
Related titles: Online - full text ed.: free (effective 2009).
Indexed: G06, G07, T&II.
Published by: (Cruising Yacht Club of Australia), Ocean Media, Ste 67, The Lower Deck, Jones Bay Wharf 26 Pirrama Rd, Pyrmont Point, NSW 2009, Australia. TEL 61-2-95661777, FAX 61-2-95661333, ocean@oceanmedia.com.au. Pub. Anthony Twibill. Adv. contact Donna Betts TEL 61-4-29603533. page AUD 2,950; trim 230 x 277.

ON THE WATER. *see* SPORTS AND GAMES—Outdoor Life

797.1 SWE ISSN 1404-9597
PAA KRYSS. Text in Swedish. 1971. 9/yr. SEK 360 (effective 2004). adv. bk.rev. **Document type:** *Magazine, Consumer.* **Description:** Contains articles on yachting and motorboating; adventure, cruising and racing, people and equipment.
Former titles (until 2000): Paa Kryss Till Rors (0345-9667); (until vol.7, 1986): Paa Kryss och Till Rors; Which was formed by the merger of (1930-1971): Paa Kryss; (1947-1971): Till Rors med Segel och Motor (0040-7682); Which was formed by the merger of (1935-1947): Till Rors; (1935-1947): Segel och Motor
Published by: Svenska Kryssarklubben/Swedish Cruising Association, PO Box 1189, Nacka Strand, 13127, Sweden. TEL 46-8-4482880, FAX 46-8-4482889, info@sxk.se. Ed. Erling Matz. Pub. Hans Larson. Adv. contact William Blanck. B&W page SEK 20,300, color page SEK 25,950; trim 190 x 265. Circ: 34,000 (controlled).

797.1 USA
GV776.C2
PACIFIC BOATING ALMANAC. NORTHERN CALIFORNIA & THE DELTA. Text in English. 1965. a. illus. **Document type:** *Handbook/ Manual/Guide, Trade.*
Former titles (until 1998): Pacific Boating Almanac. Northern California; (until 1996): Pacific Boating Almanac. Northern California & Nevada (0193-3515); (until 1977): Sea Boating Almanac. Northern California & Nevada (0363-7700)
Published by: ProStar Publications, Inc., 8643 Hayden Pl, Culver City, CA 90232. TEL 800-481-6277, FAX 800-487-6277, editor@prostarpublications.com, http://www.prostarpublications.com.

797.9 USA
GV776.N76
PACIFIC BOATING ALMANAC. PACIFIC NORTHWEST. Text in English. 1976. a. illus. **Document type:** *Handbook/Manual/Guide, Trade.*
Former titles: Pacific Boating Almanac. Pacific Northwest and Alaska (0899-9368); (until 1985): Pacific Boating Almanac. Oregon, Washington, British Columbia and Southeastern Alaska Editon (0276-8771); (until 1981): Pacific Boating Almanac. Pacific Northwest and Alaska (0148-1177); (until 1976): Sea Boating Almanac. Pacific Northwest and Alaska (0363-7999)
Published by: ProStar Publications, Inc., 8643 Hayden Pl, Culver City, CA 90232. TEL 800-481-6277, FAX 800-487-6277, editor@prostarpublications.com, http://www.prostarpublications.com.

797.1 NZL ISSN 2230-2123
▼ **PACIFIC PASSAGEMAKER**; dedicated to trawlers, passage makers and cruising. Text in English. 2011. s-a. AUD 30 in Australia; NZD 18 elsewhere; NZD 10 per issue (effective 2011). adv. **Document type:** *Magazine, Consumer.*
Related titles: Online - full text ed.: ISSN 2230-2131. free (effective 2011).
Published by: D & B Publishing Ltd., Whangaparaoa, PO Box 132, Auckland, 0943, New Zealand. TEL 64-9-4282086, FAX 64-9-4242786. Ed. Barry Thompson. Adv. contact Mark Saville TEL 64-21-772202.

797.125099305 NZL ISSN 2230-4134
▼ **PACIFIC POWERBOAT.** Text in English. 2011. bi-m. NZD 50 domestic; AUD 55 in Australia (effective 2011). adv. **Document type:** *Magazine, Consumer.* **Description:** Covers up-to-date information on new boats, the latest trends in power options, towing tips, fishing, engine shootouts, and product guides and to places to visit and ways to enjoy Power Boat.
Formed by the merger of (2007-2011): Propeller (2230-2166); Which was formerly (until 2007): New Zealand Propeller (1173-809X); (2000-2011): Pacific MotorYacht (1175-4370); Which was formerly (until 2000): New Zealand Launch & Motor Yacht (1174-5312)
Related titles: Online - full text ed.: free (effective 2011).
Published by: D & B Publishing Ltd., Whangaparaoa, PO Box 132, Auckland, 0943, New Zealand. TEL 64-9-4282086, FAX 64-9-4242786. Ed. Barry Thompson. Adv. contact Doug Dukeson TEL 64-9-4282328.

797.1 CAN ISSN 0030-8986
PACIFIC YACHTING; Western Canada's premier boating magazine. Text in English. 1968. m. CAD 44; CAD 4.50 newsstand/cover (effective 2004). adv. bk.rev. charts; illus. **Document type:** *Magazine, Consumer.*
Formerly: Pacific Yachting Journal
Related titles: Microfiche ed.: (from MML); Microform ed.: (from MML).
Indexed: C03, CBCARef, CBPI, CPerI, G08, H20, P48, PQC.
Published by: O P Publishing Ltd., 1080 Howe St, Ste 900, Vancouver, BC V6Z 2T1, Canada. TEL 604-606-4644, FAX 604-687-1925, markyelic@oppublishing.com, http://www.oppub.com. Ed. Peter A Robson. Pub. Mark Yelic. Adv. contact Mark Collett. B&W page CAD 2,650, color page CAD 3,376; trim 273 x 203. Circ: 19,000 (paid).

797.122 USA
PADDLE DEALER; the trade magazine for paddlesports. Text in English. 1993. q. **Document type:** *Magazine, Trade.*
Published by: Paddlesport Publishing, Inc., 7432 Alban Station Blvd, Ste B-226, Springfield, VA 22150. TEL 703-455-3419. Ed. Tom Bie. Circ: 7,500.

797.122 USA
PADDLESPORTS PRO. Text in English. 1979. bi-m. free to members. adv. bk.rev. **Document type:** *Newsletter, Consumer.* **Description:** Promotes safety, protection of waterways, and public rights of access and use of waterways.
Former titles: Paddler's Print; Professional Paddlesports Association News; N A C L O News
Published by: Professional Paddlesports Association, 7432 Alban Station Blvd, Ste B-232, Springfield, VA 22150. TEL 703-451-3864, 800-789-2202, FAX 703-451-1015, ppa@propaddle.com, http://www.propaddle.com. Ed., R&P Jim Thaxton. Adv. contact Karen Warner. Circ: 750 (controlled).

797.122 SWE ISSN 1653-2503
PADDLING. Text in Swedish. 1950-1983; resumed 1985. q. SEK 140 (effective 2005). adv. bk.rev. illus. **Document type:** *Magazine, Consumer.*
Formerly (until 2005): Kanot-Nytt (0022-8397)
Published by: Svenska Kanotfoerbundet/Swedish Canoe Federation, Rosvalla, Nykoeping, 61162, Sweden. TEL 46-155-209080, FAX 46-155-209081, kanot@rf.se, http://www.kanot.com. Eds. Fredrik Fransson TEL 46-651-16555, Lars Larsson. Adv. contact Fredrik Fransson TEL 46-651-16555. Circ: 12,000.

797.122 USA ISSN 1934-8347
PADDLING LIFE. Text in English. 2007. 5/yr. free (effective 2007). adv. **Document type:** *Magazine, Consumer.* **Description:** Contains news about canoeing events, gear and places to canoe, including tides, surf and river information.
Published by: Recreation Publishing Inc, PO Box 775589, Steamboat Springs, CO 80477. TEL 970-870-0880. Ed. Eugene Buchanan.

796.95 DEU ISSN 0936-5877
PALSTEK; Technisches Magazin fuer Segler. Text in German. 1985. bi-m. EUR 30.60 domestic; EUR 34 in Europe; EUR 5.10 newsstand/cover (effective 2007). adv. **Document type:** *Magazine, Consumer.*
Related titles: Online - full text ed.
Published by: Palstek Verlag GmbH, Eppendorfer Weg 57a, Hamburg, 20259, Germany. TEL 49-40-40196353, FAX 49-40-40196341. Ed., Pub., R&P, Adv. contact Ulrich Kronberg. B&W page EUR 2,350, color page EUR 3,785; trim 165 x 265. Circ: 26,841 (paid and controlled).

797.125 USA ISSN 1095-7286
GV771
PASSAGEMAKER; the trawler & ocean motorboat magazine. Text in English. 1996. 8/yr. USD 34.95 domestic; USD 48.95 in Canada; USD 62.95 elsewhere; USD 43.95 combined subscription domestic (print & online eds.); USD 57.95 combined subscription in Canada (print & online eds.); USD 71.95 combined subscription elsewhere (print & online eds.) (effective 2010). adv. back issues avail. **Document type:** *Magazine, Consumer.* **Description:** Provides trawler owners and enthusiasts with significant information on cruising and voyaging with an emphasis on boats, people and lifestyle.
Related titles: Online - full text ed.: USD 15.95 (effective 2010).
Published by: PassageMaker Magazine, Inc., 105 Eastern Ave, Ste 103, Annapolis, MD 21403. TEL 410-990-9086, FAX 410-990-9094. Ed. John Wooldridge TEL 410-990-9086 ext 20. Pub. Rob Dorfmeyer TEL 410-990-9086 ext 19. **Dist. by:** Curtis Distributing Company.

PENNSYLVANIA ANGLER & BOATER. *see* SPORTS AND GAMES—Outdoor Life

797.1 USA ISSN 1941-9473
PERFORMANCE BOATS. Text in English. 2008. 6/yr. USD 17.95 (effective 2008). adv. **Document type:** *Magazine, Consumer.* **Description:** Focused on the personalities of the performance boat industry, with coverage of both east and west coast performance boats.
Related titles: Online - full text ed.
Published by: D C O Enterprises, 3620 N Rancho Dr, Ste 105, Las Vegas, NV 89130. TEL 702-313-1400, FAX 702-313-1405. Ed. Brett Bayne.

797.1 USA
PERFORMANCE SAILOR; the official newsletter for N A C R A, Prindle and Inter Class Associations. Text in English. bi-m. USD 20 domestic; USD 30 foreign (effective 2000). adv. back issues avail. **Document type:** *Newsletter.* **Description:** Covers boating news, schedules of regattas, race reports and member stories.
Published by: Nautical Promotions, 777 W 19th St, W, Costa Mesa, CA 92627. TEL 949-548-9322, FAX 949-548-8013. Ed., Adv. contact Amy Elliott. B&W page USD 150; trim 11 x 8.5. Circ: 500 (paid).
Co-sponsor: Performance Catamorans.

797.1 USA ISSN 1041-567X
PERSONAL WATERCRAFT ILLUSTRATED; the personal watercraft recreation magazine. Text in English. 1987. m. USD 18.95 domestic; USD 65 foreign (effective 2008). adv. illus. reprints avail. **Document type:** *Magazine, Consumer.* **Description:** Covers all aspects of the sport and recreational use of personal watercraft.
Published by: Cycle News Publishing Group, 3505-M Cadillac Ave, Costa Mesa, CA 92626. TEL 714-751-7433, FAX 714-436-9573. Ed. Paul Carruthers. Pub. Michael D Klinger. Adv. contact Mark Thome. Circ: 68,115.

PESCA E NAUTICA. *see* SPORTS AND GAMES—Outdoor Life

PESCA Y BARCOS. *see* FISH AND FISHERIES

796.95 CAN ISSN 0820-5086
PLAISANCIERS. Text in English. 1986. 5/yr. CAD 15 (effective 2000). adv. **Document type:** *Journal, Consumer.*
Published by: Roy C. Baird, Pub., 970 Montee de Liesse, Ste 310, St Laurent, PQ H4T 1W7, Canada. TEL 514-856-0787. Ed. Claude Leonard. R&P Roy C Baird. Circ: 20,000 (controlled).

797.1224 GBR
PLAYBOATING; whitewater kayaking magazine. Text in English. 1994. 5/yr. back issues avail. **Document type:** *Magazine, Abstract/Index.* **Description:** Includes news, competition reports, destination articles, technique clinics for whitewater kayakers.
Published by: Warners Group Publications Plc., The Maltings, Manor Ln, Bourne, Lincs PE10 9PH, United Kingdom. TEL 44-1778-391000, http://www.warnersgroup.co.uk. Ed. Jason Smith.

797.1 287.2 USA
PONTOON & DECK BOAT. Abbreviated title: P D B. Variant title: Pontoon. Text in English. 1971. 11/yr. USD 19.97 domestic; USD 34.97 in Canada; USD 39.97 elsewhere (effective 2008). adv. bk.rev. illus.; mkt.; maps. back issues avail.; reprints avail. **Document type:** *Magazine, Trade.* **Description:** Covers boat tests, performance issues, boating tips, technical advice and lifestyle features in the pontoon and deck boat world.
Related titles: Online - full text ed.
Published by: Harris Publishing, Inc. (Idaho Falls), 360 B St, Idaho Falls, ID 83402-3547. TEL 208-524-7000, 800-638-0135, FAX 208-522-5241, customerservice@harrispublishing.com, http://www.harrispublishing.com. Adv. contact Greg Larsen TEL 208-542-2216. B&W page USD 6,331, color page USD 9,258; bleed 8.25 x 11. Circ: 82,000.

796.95 CAN ISSN 0830-8705
PORT HOLE/HUBLOT. Text in English, French. q. CAD 8, USD 10. adv. bk.rev. **Document type:** *Newsletter.* **Description:** Promotes safe boating through education. Keeps members informed of CPS activities, legal and legislative matters, new products and equipment. Entertains with amusing cruising yarns, timely marine maintenance, safety articles. Serves as a forum for lively exchange of opinions and ideas.
Published by: Canadian Power & Sail Squadrons/Escadrilles Canadiennes de Plaisance, 26 Golden Gate Ct, Scarborough, ON M1P 3A5, Canada. TEL 416-293-2438, FAX 416-293-2445. Ed. Jane Theodore. Circ: 24,000.

797.1 ESP ISSN 0213-3059
PORT NAUTIC PRESS; nautica deportiva. Variant title: Nautic Press. Text in Spanish. 1982. m. EUR 37 domestic; EUR 47 foreign (effective 2009). **Document type:** *Magazine, Consumer.*

S

Published by: Grupo Editorial Men-Car, Passeig de Colom, 24, Barcelona, 08002, Spain. TEL 34-93-301-5749, FAX 34-93-302-1779, men-car@men-car.com, http://www.men-car.com. Circ: 32,000.

796.95 621.381 USA ISSN 0886-4411
POWER AND MOTORYACHT. Text in English. 1985. m. USD 11.97 domestic; USD 24.97 in Canada; USD 26.97 elsewhere (effective 2008). adv. illus. back issues avail.; reprints avail. **Document type:** *Magazine, Consumer.* **Description:** Contains information on boat tests, gear, electronics, maintenance, mega yachts, etc.
Formerly: Guide to Marine Electronics
Related titles: Online - full text ed.: USD 11.97 (effective 2008); Supplement(s): Big Game Tournament Guide. ISSN 1944-3633.
Indexed: A22, B04, G06, G07, G08, H20, I05, R03, RGAb, RGPR, S23, W03, W05.
—CCC.
Published by: Source Interlink Companies, 261 Madison Ave, 6th Fl, New York, NY 10016. TEL 212-915-4000, FAX 212-915-4422, dheine@sourceinterlink.com, http://www.sourceinterlinkmedia.com. Ed. Richard Thiel. adv.: B&W page USD 18,335, color page USD 27,685; bleed 8.875 x 11. Circ: 157,000 (controlled).

797.14 CAN ISSN 0838-0872
POWER BOATING CANADA. Text in English. 1986. 6/yr. CAD 19.26. adv. **Document type:** *Magazine, Consumer.*
Formerly: Power Boating Ontario (0827-7710)
Related titles: ◆ Supplement(s): FishBoats. ISSN 1202-0265.
Published by: Taylor Publishing Group, 2585 Skymark Ave, Ste 306, Mississauga, ON L4W 4L5, Canada. TEL 905-624-8218, FAX 905-624-6764. Ed. Karen Hill. Pub., Adv. contact Bill Taylor. Circ: 50,000.

796.95 USA ISSN 1545-3995
THE POWER OF MULTIHULLS. Text in English. 1998. q. USD 15 domestic; USD 21 foreign (effective 2006). adv. 64 p./no.; **Document type:** *Magazine, Consumer.*
Published by: Chiodi Advertising & Publishing, Inc., 421 Hancock St, PO Box 7, N Quincy, MA 02171. TEL 617-328-8181, 800-333-6858, FAX 617-471-0118. Ed., Pub. Charles K Chiodi. adv.: color page USD 2,600. Circ: 20,000.

797.122 CAN
POWER STROKE. Text in English. irreg. (3-5/yr.). looseleaf. membership. adv. bk.rev.; Website rev. **Document type:** *Newsletter.* **Description:** Covers upcoming events and reports on completed events. Relates to recreational canoeing, marathon canoe racing and whitewater kayaking.
Published by: Saskatoon Canoe Club, P O Box 7764, Saskatoon, SK S7K 4J1, Canada. Ed., Adv. contact Robin Karpan. Circ: 150.

797.1 USA ISSN 0032-6089
GV835.9
POWERBOAT; the world's leading performance boating magazine. Text in English. 1968. bi-m. USD 19.97 domestic; USD 25.97 in Canada; USD 31.97 elsewhere (effective 2010). adv. illus. back issues avail.; reprints avail. **Document type:** *Magazine, Consumer.* **Description:** Contains significant articles on performance boating.
Formerly (until 19??): Power Boat
Indexed: SportS.
Published by: Nordskog Publishing, Inc., 2575 Vista Del Mar, Ventura, CA 93001. TEL 805-667-4100, FAX 805-667-4336, http://nordskogpublishing.com. Ed. Gregg Mansfield. Adv. contact Ryan Johnson.

797.1 GBR ISSN 0032-6348
VM320
PRACTICAL BOAT OWNER. Text in English. 1967. m. GBP 36.57 domestic; USD 75.53 in United States; EUR 75.53 in Europe; GBP 70.76 elsewhere; GBP 3.95 newsstand/cover (effective 2010). adv. bk.rev. index. back issues avail. **Document type:** *Magazine, Consumer.* **Description:** Practical information for hands-on cruising skippers.
Related titles: Online - full text ed.: GBP 29.99 (effective 2010); Supplement(s): Cruising Magazine. ISSN 0267-047X.
—CCC.
Published by: I P C Country & Leisure Media Ltd. (Subsidiary of: I P C Media Ltd.), Westover House, West Quay Rd, Poole, Dorset, BH15 1JG, United Kingdom. TEL 44-1202-440820, FAX 44-1202-440860, http://www.ipcmedia.com. Ed. Sarah Norbury TEL 44-1202-440820. Adv. contact John Gaylord TEL 44-20-31484880. B&W page GBP 1,785, color page GBP 3,287. Circ: 47,406. **Subscr. to:** Rockwood House, Perrymount Rd, Haywards Heath RH16 3DH, United Kingdom. TEL 44-845-1231231, IPCsubs@quadrantsubs.com, http://www.magazinesdirect.co.uk. **Dist. by:** MarketForce UK Ltd, The Blue Fin Bldg, 3rd Fl, 110 Southwark St, London SE1 0SU, United Kingdom. TEL 44-20-31483300, FAX 44-20-31488105, salesinnovation@marketforce.co.uk, http://www.marketforce.co.uk/.

796.95 USA ISSN 0161-8059
PRACTICAL SAILOR; guide to sailing gear. Text in English. 1974. m. USD 84 combined subscription in US & Canada (print & online eds.); USD 120 combined subscription elsewhere (print & online eds.) (effective 2010). back issues avail. **Document type:** *Magazine, Trade.* **Description:** Contains independent product test report of sailboats, sailing equipment and gear.
Related titles: Online - full text ed.: Practical-Sailor.com.
Indexed: SD, SportS.
Published by: Belvoir Media Group, LLC, PO Box 5656, Norwalk, CT 06856. TEL 203-857-3100, 800-424-7887, FAX 203-857-3103, customer_service@belvoir.com, http://www.belvoir.com. Ed. Darrell Nicholson. **Subscr. to:** Palm Coast Data, LLC, PO Box 420235, Palm Coast, FL 32142. TEL 800-829-9087, http://www.palmcoastdata.com.

797.1 ZAF ISSN 1996-708X
PRESTIGE. Text in English. 2007. m. ZAR 299 (effective 2007). adv. **Document type:** *Magazine, Consumer.*
Published by: TCB Publishing, PO Box 11273, Hatfield, 0028, South Africa. TEL 27-12-4605600, FAX 27-12-3462367, mail@tcbpublishing.co.za, http://www.tcbpublishing.co.za/. Adv. contact Rui Barbosa. page ZAR 11,950; bleed 240 x 337.

623.82 USA ISSN 1043-2035
VM320
PROFESSIONAL BOATBUILDER. Text in English. 1989. bi-m. free to qualified personnel. adv. bk.rev.; software rev. back issues avail. **Document type:** *Magazine, Trade.* **Description:** Contains articles of interest to boat construction, repair, design and surveying company personnel.
Related titles: Online - full text ed.
Indexed: M01, M02, S22, T02.
Published by: WoodenBoat Publications, Inc., Naskeag Rd, PO Box 78, Brooklin, ME 04616-0078. TEL 207-359-4651, FAX 207-359-8920. Ed. Paul Lazarus. Pub., R&P Carl Cramer. Adv. contact Michele Corbeil. Circ: 25,000 (controlled).

796.95 USA ISSN 0194-6218
PROPELLER; official publication of the American Power Boat Association. Text in English. 1935. m. USD 25 to members (effective 2001). adv. tr.lit.; illus. 36 p./no.; **Document type:** *Magazine, Consumer.* **Description:** Features accounts of racing events, technology, safety and racing accomplishments.
Published by: American Power Boat Association, 17640 E Nine Mile Rd, Box 377, Eastpointe, MI 48021. TEL 810-773-9700, FAX 810-773-6490, apbahq@aol.com, http://www.goracing.com. Ed., R&P, Adv. contact Tana Moore. Pub. Gloria Urbin. page USD 508.30; 7.5 x 10. Circ: 7,000 (paid).

797.1 USA ISSN 1936-1890
GV836.15
PURELY PONTOONS. Text in English. 2007 (Apr.). s-a. USD 9.95 (effective 2007). **Document type:** *Magazine, Trade.*
Published by: Affinity Group Inc., 2575 Vista Del Mar, Ventura, CA 93001. TEL 805-667-4100, FAX 805-667-4419, info@affinitygroup.com, http://www.affinitygroup.com.

797.14 797.124 FIN ISSN 0355-6980
PURJEHTIJA/SEGLAREN. Text in Finnish, Swedish. 1974. bi-m. adv. bk.rev. back issues avail. **Document type:** *Magazine, Consumer.*
Published by: Suomen Purjehtijaliitto/Finnish Yachting Association, Vattuniemenkatu 13, Helsinki, 00210, Finland. TEL 358-207-338883, FAX 358-207-338888. Ed. Kurre Loennqvist TEL 358-40-7707594. Circ: 31,000 (controlled).

796.95 USA
QUIMBY'S CRUISING GUIDE. Text in English. 1986. a. USD 39 per issue (effective 2011). adv. **Document type:** *Handbook/Manual/Guide, Trade.* **Description:** Information on where to get gas and overnight dockage on inland waterways. Lists marinas, includes columns.
Formerly (until 1991): Quimby's Boating Guide; Which was formed by the 1986 merger of: Quimby's Harbor Guide (0749-3754); Three Rivers Boating Guide (0364-0353)
Published by: Waterways Journal, Inc., 319 N 4th St, Ste 650, St. Louis, MO 63102. TEL 314-241-7354, FAX 314-241-4207, http://www.waterwaysjournal.net.

797.1 GBR ISSN 2045-9297
R I B MAGAZINE. (Rigid Inflatable Boat) Text in English. 1994. bi-m. GBP 20 domestic; GBP 30 in Europe; GBP 34 elsewhere (effective 2011). adv. 3 cols./p.; back issues avail. **Document type:** *Magazine, Consumer.* **Description:** Features boat tests, multiple equipment reviews, cruising and event reports, features on boat handling, and special subjects such as, industry news, commercial reports and data, plus a whole lot more.
Former titles (until 2010): R I B International (1360-9408); (until 1995): R I B & Small Boat (1355-8390)
Published by: R I B International Ltd., Oyster House, Hunters Lodge, Kentisbeare, Devon EX15 2DY, United Kingdom. TEL 44-1884-266100, FAX 44-1884-266101, subs@ribmagazine.com.

RADIO CONTROL BOAT MODELER. *see* HOBBIES

796.95 USA
REFERENCE POINT (ANNAPOLIS). Text in English. 1954. q. free to members (effective 2007). bk.rev. tr.lit. **Document type:** *Magazine, Consumer.* **Description:** Articles on technical and safety issues related to recreational boating.
Formerly (until 200?): A B Y C News
Published by: American Boat & Yacht Council, Inc., 613 Third St, Ste 10, Annapolis, MD 21403-3248. TEL 410-990-4460, FAX 410-990-4466, http://www.abycinc.org. Ed. Judith Ramsey. Circ: 4,700 (controlled).

797.14 POL ISSN 1507-1308
REJS. Text in Polish. 1999. m. PLZ 90 domestic; PLZ 361 in Europe; PLZ 405 in United States; PLZ 585.40 in Australia (effective 2003). adv. **Document type:** *Magazine, Consumer.*
Related titles: Online - full text ed.: ISSN 1689-3956.
Published by: S P I T S S.A., ul Plocka 25, Warsaw, 01-231, Poland. TEL 48-22-6323567, FAX 48-22-6314103. Adv. contact Marta Korzeniowska.

797.1 NZL ISSN 1175-9968
RESCUES; the quarterly publication that supports the Royal New Zealand Coastguard. Text in English. 1994. q. bk.rev. **Document type:** *Newspaper.*
Formerly (until 2002): Coastguard New Zealand (1173-2202)
Published by: Royal New Zealand Coastguard Inc., Victoria St West, PO Box 91322, Auckland, 1142, New Zealand. TEL 64-9-4891510, FAX 64-9-4891506, http://www.nzcoastguard.org.nz/. Adv. contact Peter Hamling TEL 64-9-4860229. Circ: 15,000 (controlled).

797.1 USA
RIDE P W C MAGAZINE. (Personal Watercraft) Text in English. 1982. bi-m. USD 24 (effective 2009). **Document type:** *Magazine, Consumer.* **Description:** Includes reports and photo stories on competitions, personalities, safety articles and a directory to products and services.
Former titles (until 2003): Jet Sports; JetSkier Magazine
Published by: (American Watercraft Association), Hammock Publishing, Inc., 3322 W End Ave, Ste 700, Nashville, TN 37203. TEL 615-690-3400, FAX 615-690-3401, info@hammock.com. Circ: 40,515 (controlled).

797.122 CAN ISSN 1910-7196
THE RIPPLE. Text in English. 2000. q. **Document type:** *Newsletter, Consumer.*
Published by: Manitoba Recreational Canoeing Association, PO Box 2663, Winnipeg, MB R3C 4B3, Canada. TEL 204-338-6722, http://www.paddle.mb.ca/mrcawebsite/index.htm.

797.1 USA ISSN 1942-4752
RIVER TALK. Text in English. 200?. m. **Document type:** *Newsletter, Consumer.* **Description:** Features Assocation's news and member updates, and area airboating news.
Published by: (Nebraska Airboaters Association), Black Rhino Publishing Company, PO Box 44, Plattsmouth, NE 68048. TEL 402-290-5102, admin@blackrhinopublishing.com, http://www.blackrhinopublishing.com/contactus.html.

797.123 NLD ISSN 0048-8518
ROEIEN. Text in Dutch. 1938. m. EUR 25.96; EUR 3.94 newsstand/cover (effective 2009). adv. illus. index. **Document type:** *Bulletin.* **Description:** Reports on regattas in Holland and abroad including world championships and Olympic games (including results and records), and other rowing events, touring, rowing equipment, education and training.
Published by: Koninklijke Nederlandsche Roeibond, Bosbaan 6, Amstelveen, 1182 AG, Netherlands. TEL 31-20-6462740, FAX 31-20-6463881, info@knrb.nl, http://www.knrb.nl. Ed. Sybrand Treffers. Circ: 5,000.

796.95 GBR ISSN 0485-5175
ROVING COMMISSIONS; anthology of cruising logs. Text in English. 1880. a. price varies. bk.rev. **Document type:** *Bulletin, Trade.* **Description:** Features voyages and cruises of members of the Royal Cruising Club.
Published by: The R C C Pilotage Foundation, Whitehouse Barn, Hangram Ln, Sheffield, Yorkshire S11 7TQ, United Kingdom. TEL 44-1548-831070, FAX 44-1548-831196, james@chenecourt.com. Ed. Judy Lomax.

797 GBR
ROWING & REGATTA. Text in English. 1987. 10/yr. free to members (effective 2009). adv. **Document type:** *Magazine, Trade.*
Former titles (until 19??): Regatta; (until 1987): A.R.A. Club News
Indexed: SportS.
Published by: Amateur Rowing Association, 6 Lower Mall, Hammersmith, London, W6 9DJ, United Kingdom. TEL 44-20-82376700, FAX 44-20-82376749, info@ara-rowing.org. Adv. contact Luke Wyatt.

797.1 GBR ISSN 0035-9041
ROYAL NAVAL SAILING ASSOCIATION JOURNAL. Text in English. 1936. s-a. free members. adv. bk.rev. illus. **Document type:** *Journal, Academic/Scholarly.*
—BLDSC (4862.300000).
Published by: Royal Naval Sailing Association, 10 Haslar Marina, Haslar Road, Gosport, Hamps PO12 1NU, United Kingdom. TEL 44-23-92521100, FAX 44-23-92521122, gensecrnsa@btconnect.com, http://www.rnsa.net/. Ed. Cmdr. Mike Shrives. Circ: 6,800.

796.95 DEU ISSN 0342-8281
RUDERSPORT. Text in German. 1883. m. EUR 79.80 (effective 2010). adv. **Document type:** *Magazine, Consumer.*
Indexed: RASB.
Published by: (German Rowing Association), Sportverlag Schmidt und Dreisilker GmbH, Boeblinger Str 68/1, Sindelfingen, 71065, Germany. TEL 49-7031-862800, FAX 49-7031-862801. Ed. Brigitte Schurr. Adv. contact Yvonne Damast TEL 49-7031-862831. Circ: 6,000 (paid and controlled).

797.124 USA ISSN 0036-2700
GV811
SAIL. Text in English. 1970. m. USD 10 domestic; USD 23 in Canada; USD 25 elsewhere (effective 2008). adv. bk.rev. charts; illus.; tr.lit. 120 p./no. 3 cols./p.; back issues avail.; reprints avail. **Document type:** *Magazine, Consumer.* **Description:** Covers the total sailing experience, featuring articles on coastal and blue-water cruising, trailer-sailing, racing, multihulls and monohulls, daysailing, one-design racing, etc.
Related titles: Online - full text ed.: USD 5 (effective 2008); ◆ Supplement(s): Sailboat Buyers Guide.
Indexed: A22, B04, Consl, G05, G06, G07, G08, G09, H20, I05, MagInd, P02, P10, P53, P54, PMR, PQC, R03, RASB, RGAb, RGPR, S23, SPI, SportS, W03, W05.
—Ingenta. **CCC.**
Published by: Source Interlink Companies, 6420 Wilshire Blvd, 10th Fl, Los Angeles, CA 90048. TEL 323-782-2000, FAX 323-782-2585, dheine@sourceinterlink.com, http://www.sourceinterlinkmedia.com. Ed. Peter Nielsen TEL 617-720-8629. Pub. Josh Adams TEL 617-720-8605. Adv. contact Gregg Boersma. B&W page USD 14,395, color page USD 20,580. Circ: 170,000 (paid); 5,000 (controlled).

797.124 THA
SAIL THAILAND. Text in English. irreg. USD 31 per issue (effective 2003). adv. **Document type:** *Magazine, Consumer.*
Published by: Artasia Press Co., Ltd., 143/1-2 Soi Dumex, Charoen Nakorn Rd 13, Klong Tonsai, Klongsarn, Bangkok, 10600, Thailand. TEL 66-2-8613360, FAX 66-2-8613363, info@aapress.net, http://www.aapress.net/.

797.124 USA
SAILBOAT BUYERS GUIDE. Text in English. 1967. a. USD 6.99 per issue (effective 2008). adv. bk.rev. illus. 400 p./no.; back issues avail.; reprints avail. **Document type:** *Guide, Consumer.* **Description:** Provides the sailing community, the public and the trade with a reference guide to the sailboats and sailboat products available in the US and Canada.
Former titles (until 1994): Sailboat and Equipment Directory (0148-8732); (until 1970): Sailboat Directory (0581-3115)
Related titles: Online - full content ed.: ◆ Supplement to: Sail. ISSN 0036-2700.
Published by: Source Interlink Companies, 98 N Washington St, Boston, MA 02114. TEL 617-720-8600, FAX 617-723-0911, http://www.sourceinterlink.com. adv.: B&W page USD 5,445. Circ: 70,000 (paid).

797.1 ZAF ISSN 1605-6442
SAILING; incorporating S A yachting. Text in English. 1999. m. ZAR 135 domestic; ZAR 380 foreign; ZAR 15.50 newsstand/cover (effective 2005). adv. bk.rev.; software rev.; video rev. charts; illus.; maps. index. back issues avail. **Document type:** *Magazine, Consumer.* **Description:** Includes in-depth technical features on the art and science of sailing, analysis of advances in equipment design, and anecdotal coverage of all sailing events.
Formed by the merger of (1957-1999): S.A. Yachting (0256-7431); (1984-1999): Sailing Inland & Offshore (0259-9449); Which was formerly (1977-1984): Yachtsman R S A (0256-0453)
Published by: Sailing Publications, PO Box 1849, Westville, KwaZulu-Natal 3630, South Africa. TEL 27-31-709-6087, 27-31-709-6088, FAX 27-31-709-6143. Ed., Pub., R&P, Adv. contact Richard Crockett. B&W page ZAR 3,250, color page ZAR 4,000; trim 210 x 297. Circ: 5,000.

797.124 USA ISSN 0036-2719
SAILING; the beauty of sail. Text in English. 1966. m. USD 28 domestic; USD 39 in Canada; USD 70 elsewhere (effective 2010). adv. bk.rev. illus. back issues avail.; reprints avail. **Document type:** *Magazine, Consumer.*
Formerly: Lake Michigan Sailing
Related titles: Microform ed.: (from PQC); Online - full text ed.
Indexed: A22, BRI.
Published by: Port Publications, Inc., 125 E Main St, PO Box 249, Port Washington, WI 53074. TEL 262-284-3494, FAX 262-284-7764, ads@sailingmagazine.net. Ed., Pub. Bill Schanen. adv.: page USD 4,109; trim 10 x 12.875. Circ: 40,000.

797.1 DEU
SAILING JOURNAL. Text in German. bi-m. EUR 4.80 newsstand/cover (effective 2007). adv. **Document type:** *Magazine, Consumer.*
Published by: Terra Oceanis Verlag, Braunstr 32, Kiel, 24145, Germany. TEL 49-431-9969977, FAX 49-431-9969986, info@terraoceanisverlag.de, http://www.terraoceanisverlag.de. adv.: color page EUR 5,900. Circ: 40,000 (paid and controlled).

797.124 GBR ISSN 1367-5869
SAILING TODAY. Text in English. 1997. 13/yr. GBP 32.99 domestic; GBP 52.99 in Europe; GBP 63.69 elsewhere; GBP 2.37 per issue (effective 2010). adv. back issues avail. **Document type:** *Magazine, Consumer.*
Related titles: Online - full text ed.: GBP 22.75; GBP 1.75 per issue (effective 2010).
—CCC.
Published by: Sailing Today Magazine, Swanwick Marina, Lower Swanwick, Southampton, SO31 1ZL, United Kingdom. Ed. Jake Frith TEL 44-1489-585213. Adv. contact Jayne Bennett TEL 44-1489-585200.

797.1 USA ISSN 0889-4094
GV811.8
SAILING WORLD; the authority on performance sailing. Text in English. 1962. 9/yr. USD 14.97 domestic; USD 23.97 in Canada; USD 36.97 elsewhere (effective 2011). adv. bk.rev. illus. back issues avail.; reprints avail. **Document type:** *Magazine, Consumer.* **Description:** Publishes for the active sailor who races or cruises. Covers sailboat design, sailing technique and equipment, charter cruising and racing, seamanship, racing events and news.
Former titles (until 1986): Yacht Racing and Cruising (0190-7956); (until 1983): Yacht Racing (0276-2935); (until 1972): One-Design and Offshore Yachtsman (0030-2511); (until 1965): One-Design Yachtsman
Related titles: Microform ed.: (from PQC); Online - full text ed.
Indexed: CPerI, G05, G06, G07, G08, I05, I07, MASUSE, RASB, SportS.
—CCC.
Published by: Bonnier Corp. (Subsidiary of: Bonnier Group), 55 Hammarlund Way, Middletown, RI 02842. TEL 401-845-5100, FAX 401-845-5180, http://www.bonniercorp.com. Ed. Dave Reed. Pub. Sally Helme TEL 401-845-4405. **Subscr. to:** PO Box 420235, Palm Coast, FL 32142. TEL 386-246-3402, 866-436-2461.

797.1 USA
SANTANA; the So-Cal sailing rag. Text in English. 1987. m. USD 20 (effective 1998). adv. bk.rev. **Description:** Covers sailing, both cruising and racing.
Published by: NaCl-y Publications Inc., 15548 Graham St, Huntington Beach, CA 92649-1609. TEL 714-379-3070, FAX 714-379-9976. Ed., Pub. Kitty James. Adv. contact Lorin Weiss. Circ: 25,000.

623.82 USA
SAWDUST. Text in English. bi-m. USD 30 to individuals includes Shavings; USD 10 to students includes Shavings (effective 2001). **Document type:** *Newsletter.*
Published by: Center For Wooden Boats, 1010 Valley St, Seattle, WA 98109. TEL 206-382-2628. R&P Dick Wagner. Circ: 3,000 (paid).

SCALE & R C BOAT. *see* HOBBIES

797.1 USA ISSN 0746-8601
GV811.8
SEA; America's western boating magazine. Variant title: Sea Magazine. (Covers the 13 Western United States; British Columbia, Canada, and West Coast of Mexico.) Text in English. 1908. m. USD 19.97 domestic; USD 86.97 foreign; USD 4.95 newsstand/cover (effective 2007). adv. bk.rev. charts; illus.; tr.lit. reprints avail. **Document type:** *Magazine, Consumer.* **Description:** Profiles boating personalities, cruise destinations, boat reports, analysis of marine environmental issues, technical information, seamanship, and news from western harbors.
Incorporates (1993-1997): Waterfront Northwest News; (1993-1997): Waterfront Southern California News; Formerly (until 1984): Sea and Pacific Skipper (0274-905X); Incorporates (in 1977): Rudder (0274-9068); Which superseded: Sea, Eastern Edition (0163-7533); Sea and Pacific Motor Boat (0036-9969)
Indexed: A22, B04, PMR, R03, RGAb, RGPR, SportS, W03, W05.
Published by: Duncan McIntosh Co. Inc., 17782 Cowan, Ste A, Irvine, CA 92614. TEL 949-660-6150, FAX 949-660-6172. Pub. Duncan McIntosh Jr. Adv. contact Janette Hood. B&W page USD 3,660, color page USD 5,599. Circ: 50,000 (paid).

796.5 GRC ISSN 1106-8892
SEA & YACHTING; the Greek monthly yachting magazine. Text in Greek. 1977. m. USD 80 (effective 1999 - 2000). adv. back issues avail. **Document type:** *Consumer.* **Description:** Presents articles about pleasure boats and yachts. Includes information on racing, professional or pleasure yachting, technical features, presentation and tests concerning new models of yachts and equipment, reports on the major international Greek events, and other general information.
Related titles: Online - full text ed.
Published by: International Marine Publications/Diethneis Nautikes Ekdosis, Akti Themistokleous 22, Piraeus, 185 36, Greece. TEL 30-1-4281-923, FAX 30-1-4286-553, TELEX 21 2000 VAL GR, yachting@yachtingmag.gr, http://www.yachtingmag.gr. Ed. Kiki Pentheroudakis. Pub., R&P John Papadopoulos TEL 30-1-4183-111. Adv. contact George Helitsiotis. B&W page GBP 1,330, color page GBP 1,550; trim 220 x 300. Circ: 22,000.

797.122 NZL ISSN 1177-4177
SEA CANOEIST. Text in English. 1986. bi-m. free membership (effective 2009). **Document type:** *Newsletter, Consumer.* **Description:** Covers a range of topics pertaining to sea kayaking, and keeps paddlers up to date with what has been happening in sea kayaking around New Zealand and internationally.
Published by: Kiwi Association of Sea Kayakers New Zealand, PO Box 23, Runanga, West Coast, 7845, New Zealand. http://www.kask.co.nz/.

796.95 USA ISSN 0829-3279
GV788.5
SEA KAYAKER; experience the world's waterways. Text in English. 1984. bi-m. USD 23.95 domestic; USD 25.95 in Canada; USD 33.95 elsewhere (effective 2010). adv. bk.rev. illus. back issues avail.; reprints avail. **Document type:** *Magazine, Consumer.* **Description:** Explores kayak touring on sea and lakes, and covers safety techniques, health, destinations, history and much more.
Indexed: CA, SD, SportS, T02.
Published by: Sea Kayaker Inc., PO Box 17029, Seattle, WA 98127. TEL 206-789-9536, FAX 206-781-1141, sknewsletter@seakayakermag.com. Adv. contact Paul Riek.

797.1 NZL ISSN 1173-9479
SEA SPRAY. Text in English. 1992. m. NZD 55 domestic; NZD 90 in Australia; NZD 140 elsewhere (effective 2008). adv. bk.rev. charts; illus. Index. back issues avail. **Document type:** *Magazine, Consumer.* **Description:** Covers general boating, cruising, yachting, amateur boat building, race reports, test reports.
Formerly (until 1996): BoatingWorld (1171-7270); Which was formed by the merger of (1984-1992): New Zealand Powerboat (0112-4412); (1945-1992): Sea Spray (0037-0037); Which incorporated: Boating World (1171-7300)
Address: PO Box 55 199, Mission Bay, Auckland, New Zealand. TEL 64-9-5285561, FAX 64-9-5214887. Circ: 24,000.

797.1 USA ISSN 1546-010X
SEA TOW LIFELINES. Text in English. 1994. q.
Published by: Hachette Filipacchi Media U.S., Inc. (Subsidiary of: Hachette Filipacchi Medias S.A.), 1633 Broadway, New York, NY 10019. TEL 212-767-6000, FAX 212-767-5600, saleshfmbooks@hfmus.com, http://www.hfmus.com.

797.14 GBR
SEAHORSE INTERNATIONAL SAILING. Text in English. 1969. m. GBP 56 domestic; EUR 90 in Europe; USD 84 in US & Canada; GBP 76 elsewhere (effective 2009). adv. back issues avail. **Document type:** *Magazine, Consumer.* **Description:** Contains information on yacht design and technology, as well as international race coverage.
Formerly (until 200?): Seahorse (0143-246X)
Indexed: AES.
Published by: (Royal Ocean Racing Club), Seahorse Magazine, 5 Britannia Place, Station St, Lymington, Hampshire SO41 3BA, United Kingdom. TEL 44-1590-671899, FAX 44-1590-671116. Ed. Andrew Hurst TEL 44-1590-671898. Adv. contact Graham Beeson. Circ: 20,000.

796.5 CHE ISSN 1423-6729
SEEMEILE; Seefahrt - Nautik - Revier. Text in German. 1983. 6/yr. CHF 52 domestic; EUR 28.90 in Germany & Austria (effective 2001). adv. bk.rev.; Website rev. back issues avail. **Document type:** *Newspaper, Consumer.* **Description:** Presents information on nautical trips and tourism.
Related titles: ◆ Online - full text ed.: Seemeile Online.
Published by: DaKaeLag, Bergstr 51, Herrliberg, 8704, Switzerland. TEL 41-1-9916200, FAX 41-1-9916208, anzeigen@dakaelag.ch. Ed., Pub., R&P Daniel Heusser. Adv. contact Brigitte Weber. color page CHF 2,884, B&W page CHF 2,266; trim 196 x 265. Circ: 10,000 (paid).

796.5 CHE
SEEMEILE ONLINE. Text in German. 1999. d. adv. **Document type:** *Consumer.*
Media: Online - full text. **Related titles:** ◆ Print ed.: Seemeile. ISSN 1423-6729.
Published by: DaKaeLag, Bergstr 51, Herrliberg, 8704, Switzerland. TEL 41-1-9916200, FAX 41-1-9916208, anzeigen@dakaelag.ch, redaktion@seemeile.ch. Ed., Pub., R&P Daniel Heusser. Adv. contact Brigitte Weber. online banner CHF 433.

797.1 DEU
SEGEL JOURNAL. Text in German. bi-m. EUR 19.50; EUR 3 newsstand/cover (effective 2008). adv. **Document type:** *Magazine, Consumer.* **Description:** Covers all aspects of boating and yachting.
Published by: Atlas Verlag GmbH, Brienner Str 41, Munich, 80333, Germany. TEL 49-89-552410, FAX 49-89-55241100, info@atlas-verlag.de, http://www.atlas-verlag.de. Adv. contact Thomas Obermaier. B&W page EUR 3,500, color page EUR 5,900; trim 210 x 280. Circ: 25,000 (paid and controlled).

797.124 DEU ISSN 0342-7528
SEGELN; das Magazin fuer Fahrtensegler. Text in German. 1979. m. EUR 54; EUR 4.50 newsstand/cover (effective 2011). adv. **Document type:** *Magazine, Consumer.*
Published by: Jahr Top Special Verlag, Troplowitzstr 5, Hamburg, 22529, Germany. TEL 49-40-389060, FAX 49-40-38906300, info@jahr-tsv.de, http://www.jahr-tsv.de. Ed. Thorsten Hoege. Adv. contact Nadine Querfurth. Circ: 25,829 (paid).

797.1 SWE ISSN 0037-0916
SEGLARBLADET; Vaestkustens baattidning. Text in Swedish. 1911. 7/yr. SEK 200 (effective 1991). adv. bk.rev. charts; illus.
Published by: Goeteborgs Kungliga Segelsaellskap, Fack 5039, Vaestra Froelunda, 42105, Sweden. Ed. Malin Schroeder. Circ: 5,000.

797.124 DEU ISSN 0930-2891
SEGLER ZEITUNG; Informationen fuer Sport Skipper. Text in German. 1981. m. EUR 3 newsstand/cover (effective 2007). adv. illus. **Document type:** *Magazine, Consumer.*
Published by: S V G Service Verlag GmbH, Schwertfegerstr 1-3, Luebeck, 23556, Germany. TEL 49-451-898974, FAX 49-451-898557, gewerbe@segler-zeitung.de, http://www.svgverlag.de. Ed. Horst Schlichting. Pub. Hermann Hell. Adv. contact Britta Stein. B&W page EUR 1,380, color page EUR 2,292. Circ: 25,200 (paid and controlled).

796.95 SWE
SEGLING. Text in Swedish. 1982. 7/yr. SEK 278 domestic; SEK 300 in Norway; SEK 360 Denmark & Finland; SEK 430 in Europe Denmark & Finland; SEK 480 elsewhere Denmark & Finland (effective 1999). adv. **Document type:** *Consumer.* **Description:** Devoted to sailing, racing and cruising.
Published by: Nakterhuset Foerlags AB, Turingegatan 26, Sodertalje, 15136, Sweden. TEL 46-8-550-372-82, FAX 46-8-550-370-36. Ed., Pub., R&P Bengt Joernstedt. adv.: B&W page SEK 16,100, color page SEK 19,900; trim 265 x 190. Circ: 20,000.

797.124 SWE
SEGLING. Text in Swedish. 1983. 9/yr. SEK 370 (effective 2007). adv. back issues avail. **Document type:** *Magazine, Consumer.*
Formerly (until 2007): Race and Cruising Segling (0282-0900); Which incorporated (1986-1986): S S F Bulletiner (0283-3875); Which was formerly (1979-1986): Svensk Segelsport (0280-9915); (1977-1979): Svenska Seglarfoerbundet. Bulletin
Published by: T T G Sverige AB (Subsidiary of: De Telegraaf Tijdschriftengroep), PO Box 26206, Stockholm, 10041, Sweden. TEL 46-8-50667800, FAX 46-8-50667859, info@ttg.se, http://www.ttg.se. Ed. Joakim Hermansson TEL 46-8-50667500. Adv. contact William Blanck. page SEK 22,600; 180 x 251.

797.124 NOR ISSN 0803-0553
SEILAS. Text in Norwegian. 1906. 9/yr. NOK 595 (effective 2011). adv. **Document type:** *Magazine, Consumer.*
Supersedes in part (in 1991): Seilas og Baatliv (0800-0093); Which was formerly (until 1979): Seilas (0332-6462); Which incorporated (1981-1984): Fun Sport (0800-5052); Which was formerly (until 1983): Brettseilas (0333-2756)
Related titles: Online - full text ed.: 2006.
Published by: (Kongelig Norsk Seilforening/Royal Norwegian Yacht Club, Norges Seilforbund), Norsk Maritimt Forlag AS, Leangbukta 40, Vettre, 1392, Norway. TEL 47-66-764950, FAX 47-66-764951, http://www.havna.com. Ed. Ole-Henrik Nissen-Lie. Adv. contact Anders Theodor Bye.

797.124 NOR ISSN 1501-8105
SEILMAGASINET. Text in Norwegian. 1906. 10/yr. (11/yr.). NOK 569 (effective 2002). adv. bk.rev. back issues avail.; reprints avail. **Description:** Articles on yachting, motoring and sailing.
Former titles (until 2000): Baatnytt (0803-6187); (until 1992): Seiling og Baatliv (0803-0227); Which superseded in part (in 1991): Seilas og Baatliv (0800-0093); Which was formerly (until 1979): Seilas (0332-6462); Incorporates (1968-1990): Seilsport (0802-3018); Incorporates (in 1984): FunSport (0800-5052); Which was formerly (1981-1983): Brettseilas (0333-2756)
Related titles: Online - full content ed.
Published by: Medianavigering AS, Fekjan 15, Postboks 253, Nesbru, 1379, Norway. TEL 47-66-77-40-60, FAX 47-66-77-40-61. Ed., Pub. Morten Jensen. Adv. contact Martin Larsen TEL 47-66-77-40-64. color page NOK 17,900; 265 x 190.

797.1 DNK ISSN 1902-1925
SEJLER; sejlerbladet. Text in Danish. 2000. q. adv. **Document type:** *Magazine, Consumer.*
Formerly (until 2007): Sejlerbladet (1602-4842); Which superseded in part (in 2000): Baadmagasinet (0907-0559)
Related titles: Online - full text ed.: 2008.
Published by: Dansk Sejlunion, c/o Idraettens Hus, Broendby, 2605, Denmark. TEL 45-43-262182, FAX 45-43-262191, ds@sejlsport.dk. Eds. Christian M Borch, Dan Ipsen TEL 45-43-262189. Adv. contact Jens Greisen TEL 45-20-406947. Circ: 47,970 (controlled).

SELF-CATERING HOLIDAYS IN BRITAIN. *see* TRAVEL AND TOURISM

SERRA E MAR/MOUNTAINS AND SEA. *see* SPORTS AND GAMES—Outdoor Life

796.95 CHE
SEXTANT. Text in French, German. 1974. q. CHF 30 (effective 2001). adv. **Document type:** *Newsletter, Trade.* **Description:** Information on boatbuilding, boat maintenance, and boating watersports.
Published by: Schweizerischer Bootbauer-Verband, Gemeindehaus, Postfach 74, Faellanden, 8117, Switzerland. TEL 41-1-825-0388, FAX 41-1-825-2256, sbv@bootbauer.ch, http://www.bootbauer.ch. Ed. Roland Zaugg. Circ: 300 (paid).

623.82 USA ISSN 0734-0680
VM320
SHAVINGS (SEATTLE). Text in English. 1979. bi-m. USD 30 to individuals includes Sawdust; USD 10 to students includes Sawdust (effective 2001). adv. bk.rev. back issues avail. **Document type:** *Newsletter.* **Description:** Maritime museum preserving and passing on our small craft heritage.
Published by: Center For Wooden Boats, 1010 Valley St, Seattle, WA 98109. TEL 206-382-2628. Ed., Pub., R&P, Adv. contact Dick Wagner. Circ: 3,000.

SHIP & BOAT INTERNATIONAL. *see* TRANSPORTATION—Ships And Shipping

796.95 USA ISSN 0749-2952
SHOWBOATS INTERNATIONAL. Text in English. 1988. bi-m. USD 23.95 domestic; USD 38.95 in Canada; USD 63.95 elsewhere (effective 2009). adv. back issues avail.; reprints avail. **Document type:** *Magazine, Consumer.* **Description:** Covers the breadth of the megayacht industry from its rich history to the latest news.
Formerly (until 198?): Showboats
Related titles: Online - full text ed.
Indexed: A15, ABIn, B16, P10, P16, P48, P51, P53, P54, PQC.
Published by: CurtCo Robb Media LLC., 29160 Heathercliff Rd, Ste 200, Malibu, CA 90265. TEL 310-589-7700, FAX 310-589-7723, support@robbreport.com, http://www.curtco.com. Ed. Jill Bobrow TEL 802-496-7469. Pub. Gary DeSanctis TEL 212-201-1138. adv.: page USD 15,060; trim 9 x 10.813. Circ: 50,000.

797.1 DEU ISSN 0721-4472
SKIPPER. Text in German. 1978. m. EUR 44 domestic; EUR 50 foreign; EUR 4 newsstand/cover (effective 2010). **Document type:** *Magazine, Consumer.*
Published by: Freizeit und Wassersport Verlag GmbH, Am Windfeld 15, Miesbach, 83714, Germany. TEL 49-8025-294243, FAX 49-8025-294271. **Dist. by:** Moderner Zeitschriften Vertrieb, Breslauerstr 5, Eching 85386, Germany. TEL 49-89-31906125, FAX 49-89-31906161, mzv@mzv.de.

797.1 USA ISSN 1933-6152
VM351
SMALL BOATS. Text in English. 2006. a. USD 5.99 per issue domestic; USD 7.99 per issue in Canada (effective 2008). **Document type:** *Magazine, Consumer.*

S

Published by: WoodenBoat Publications, Inc., 41 WoodenBoat Ln, Brooklin, ME 04616. TEL 207-359-4651, FAX 207-359-8920, woodenboat@woodenboat.com, http://www.woodenboat.com. Pub. Carl Cramer.

343.09 797 USA ISSN 1066-2383
HV8080.W38
SMALL CRAFT ADVISORY. Text in English. 198?. bi-m. **Description:** Promotes boating safety.
Published by: National Association of State Boating Law Administrators, c/o Mississippi Department of Wildlife, Fisheries and Parks, P O Box 451, Jackson, MS 39205. TEL 601-362-9212, FAX 601-961-4337.

797.1 GBR
SOLENT BOOK; solent cruising & racing association year book. Text in English. 1910. a. free to members (effective 2009). charts. **Document type:** *Yearbook, Trade.* **Description:** Provides information to all yachting and boating users of the Solent Cruising & Racing Association; includes classes, programme of events, navigational information, tide tables and ferries.
Former titles (until 1992): Solent Cruising and Racing Association. Solent Year Book; (until 1974): Solent Clubs Racing Association. Year Book
Published by: (Solent Cruising & Racing Association), Isle of Wight County Press Ltd., Isle of Wight, Brannon House, 123 Pyle St, Newport, Isle of Wight PO30 1ST, United Kingdom. TEL 44-1983-521333.

796.95 USA ISSN 1526-8268
SOUNDINGS (ESSEX); real boats, real boaters. Text in English. 1963. m. USD 24.97 domestic; USD 36.97 in Canada; USD 66.97 elsewhere; USD 4.95 newsstand/cover domestic; USD 5.95 newsstand/cover in Canada (effective 2007). adv. bk.rev. illus. **Document type:** *Magazine, Consumer.* **Description:** Covers boating for recreational mariners and others interested in boats, the water and the waterfront in the US. Also covers local, state, and national legislative news, fishing news as it affects the recreational boatman, ecology and the environment, the Coast Guard, DNR, and other policy making and enforcing agencies.
Related titles: Online - full text ed.
Indexed: AmHI, CERDIC, GSS&RPL.
Published by: Soundings Publications, L L C, 10 Bokum Rd, Essex, CT 06426. TEL 860-767-3200, FAX 860-767-0642. Eds. William Sisson, Ian C. Bowen. Pub. Peter Mitchel. Adv. contact Kirk Carr. Circ: 65,000 (paid).

796.95 USA ISSN 0194-8369
SOUNDINGS TRADE ONLY. Text in English. 197?. m. USD 24.97; free to qualified personnel (effective 2005). adv. **Document type:** *Newspaper, Trade.* **Description:** The boating business newspaper.
Formerly: Trade Only
Related titles: Online - full text ed.
Indexed: PROMT.
Published by: Soundings Publications, L L C, 10 Bokum Rd, Essex, CT 06426. TEL 860-767-3200, FAX 860-767-0642. Circ: 35,000.

797.1 ZAF ISSN 1817-1931
SOUTH AFRICAN PADDLER. Text in English. 2004. bi-m. ZAR 100 domestic; ZAR 265 foreign (effective 2006). adv. **Document type:** *Magazine, Consumer.*
Published by: Atoll Media, PO Box 208, Umgeni Park, Durban 4098, South Africa. TEL 27-31-2632772, FAX 27-31-2632771. Ed. Marc Cloete. Pub. Iain Evans. Adv. contact Steve Woods. color page ZAR 7,500; 210 x 275.

796.95 USA ISSN 0192-3579
SOUTHERN BOATING; the South's largest boating magazine. Text in English. 1972. m. USD 22.95 domestic; USD 42.95 foreign; USD 4.50 newsstand/cover; USD 5.50 newsstand/cover in Canada (effective 2005). adv. bk.rev. illus. reprints avail. **Document type:** *Magazine, Consumer.* **Description:** Provides general boating and cruising information for the Southeastern U.S. and Caribbean.
Published by: Southern Boating and Yachting, Inc., 330 N Andrews Ave, Fort Lauderdale, FL 33301. mbj@marinebusinessjournal.com, http://www.marinebusinessjournal.com. Ed. Bill Lindsey. Pub. Skip Allen Jr. Adv. contact Vincent Scutellaro. B&W page USD 6,290, color page USD 8,555; trim 8.12 x 10.75. Circ: 40,000.

797.124 USA
SPEARHEAD (MAYFIELD). Text in English. 1970. bi-m. membership. illus. **Description:** Covers education and information about Javelin sailboats, including accepted and approved modifications, social activities as well as racing.
Published by: Javelin Class Association, 874 Beecher's Rd., Mayfield Village, OH 44143. TEL 216-461-8511. Ed. G T Reiber. Circ: 250.

797.1 NLD ISSN 1878-9978
SPEED!. Text in Dutch. 2005. 3/yr. EUR 12.95 (effective 2011). **Document type:** *Magazine, Consumer.*
Formerly (until 2008): H2O Bootaccessoires en Marine Equipment (1871-4447)
Published by: Uitgeverij Interdijk BV, Postbus 10, Uithoorn, 1420 AA, Netherlands. TEL 31-297-566385, FAX 31-297-531051, info@interdijk.nl, http://www.interdijk.nl.

797.124 NLD ISSN 0165-5132
SPIEGEL DER ZEILVAART. Text in Dutch. 1977. 10/yr. EUR 41; EUR 46 in Belgium; EUR 50 in Europe; EUR 55 elsewhere (effective 2010). adv. bk.rev. illus. **Document type:** *Magazine, Consumer.* **Description:** Covers topics in sailing and sail boats.
—IE.
Published by: Stichting Spiegel der Zeilvaart, PO Box 653, Haarlem, 2003 RR, Netherlands. TEL 31-23-5341801, FAX 31-23-5345803, spiegel@vaarvijzer.nl, http://www.vaarwijzer.nl.

796.95 USA ISSN 0898-8951
SPLASH (COSTA MESA); the complete personal watercraft magazine. Text in English. 1987. 9/yr. USD 14.95 domestic; USD 23.95 foreign; USD 3.99 newsstand/cover (effective 2001). adv. back issues avail. **Document type:** *Magazine, Consumer.* **Description:** Covers all makes and models of personal watercraft, equipment, accessories and personalities.
Published by: Personal Watercraft, 3505-M Cadillac Ave, Costa Mesa, CA 92626. adv.: B&W page USD 2,415, color page USD 3,390; bleed 8.125 x 10.75. Circ: 12,395 (paid). **Dist. in UK by:** Comag, Tavistock Rd, W Drayton, Middlesex UB7 7QE, United Kingdom. TEL 44-1895-444055, FAX 44-1895-433602.

797.1 USA
SPORTFISHING BOATS. Text in English. 2000. bi-m. USD 9.97; USD 3.95 newsstand/cover (effective 2001). adv. **Document type:** *Magazine, Consumer.*
Published by: Poole Publications, Inc. (Subsidiary of: Ehlert Publishing Group, Inc.), 20700 Belshaw Ave, Carson, CA 90746. TEL 310-537-6322, FAX 310-537-8735. Ed. Ron Eldridge.

797.1 GBR ISSN 0969-0727
SPORTSBOAT AND WATERSKI INTERNATIONAL. Text in English. 1993. m. GBP 30 domestic; GBP 36 in Europe; GBP 46 elsewhere; GBP 2.50 newsstand/cover. adv. **Document type:** *Handbook/Manual/Guide, Consumer.* **Description:** Takes an in-depth look at modern high-performance sportboats and the sport of waterskiing.
Published by: C S L Publishing Ltd., S L House, 184 Histon Rd, Cambridge, Cambs CB4 3JP, United Kingdom. TEL 44-1223-460490, FAX 44-1223-315960. Ed. Frances Barthorpe. Pub. Graham Stuart. Adv. contact Joanne White.

797.1 DEU
SPORTSCHIPPER. Text in German. m. adv. **Document type:** *Magazine, Consumer.*
Published by: S V G Service Verlag GmbH, Schwertfegerstr 1-3, Luebeck, 23556, Germany. TEL 49-451-898974, FAX 49-451-898557, gewerbe@segler-zeitung.de, http://www.svgverlag.de. adv.: color page EUR 1,040, B&W page EUR 650. Circ: 7,300 (controlled).

796.95 USA
STANDARDS AND RECOMMENDED PRACTICES FOR SMALL CRAFT. Text in English. 1965. base vol. plus a. updates. looseleaf. membership only. Supplement avail. **Document type:** *Handbook/Manual/Guide, Trade.* **Description:** Standards and recommended practices for the design and construction of recreational boats and their equipment.
Published by: American Boat & Yacht Council, Inc., 613 Third St, Ste 10, Annapolis, MD 21403-3248. TEL 410-990-4460, FAX 410-990-4466. Ed. Thomas Hale. Circ: 3,300.

797.1 DEU ISSN 0038-9706
STANDER; Boot und Motor und Wassersport. Text in German. 1959. m. adv. bk.rev. charts; illus. index. **Document type:** *Magazine, Consumer.* **Description:** Information about navigation techniques and accessories.
Published by: (Deutscher Motoryachtverband e.V.), Panorama Verlags- und Werbegesellschaft mbH, Sudbrackstr 14-18, Bielefeld, 33611, Germany. TEL 49-521-585540, FAX 49-521-585371. Ed. Claus Breitenfeld. adv.: B&W page EUR 4,000, color page EUR 7,000. Circ: 60,033.

797.1 USA ISSN 0038-9927
STARLIGHTS. Text in English. 1921. m. USD 8 (effective 1999). adv. bk.rev. charts; stat.; tr.lit. **Document type:** *Newsletter.*
Published by: International Star Class Yacht Racing Association, 1545 Waukegan Rd, Glenview, IL 60025. TEL 847-729-0630, FAX 847-729-0718. Circ: 3,970.

STATION LOG. *see* MUSEUMS AND ART GALLERIES

796.95 USA ISSN 1056-6422
STEAMBOATING; steamboater's handbook. Text in English. 1985. a. (plus 2 updates/yr.). USD 25 (effective 2000). adv. bk.rev. charts; illus. back issues avail. **Document type:** *Magazine, Consumer.* **Description:** Includes information about the members, their boat/s, their plans and ideas. Publishes articles, photos, plans, news items, clippings, stories, "how-to" material, questions and answers, or anything else that would interest other members.
Formerly: Steamboat News
Indexed: IHTDI.
Published by: International Steamboat Society, Rt. 1, Box 262, Middlebourne, WV 26149. TEL 304-386-4434. Ed., Pub., R&P, Adv. contact Bill Warren Mueller. Circ: 1,000 (paid).

387.105 GBR ISSN 1468-439X
SUPERPORTS. Text in English. 1996. a. GBP 65 per issue (effective 2010). adv. reprints avail. **Document type:** *Magazine, Consumer.* **Description:** Provides a comprehensive overview of almost 400 superyacht marinas and ports worldwide.
Published by: Boat International Media, First Fl, 41-47 Hartfield Rd, London, SW19 3RQ, United Kingdom. TEL 44-208-5459330, FAX 44-208-5459333, info@boatinternational.co.uk, http://www.boatinternational.co.uk. adv.: page GBP 5,219, page EUR 6,001, page USD 8,611; trim 153 x 227.

797.1 GBR ISSN 2046-4991
▼ **SUPERYACHT DESIGN.** Text in English. 2009. q. **Document type:** *Magazine, Trade.*
Published by: Yacht Report Group, 3-7 Northcote Rd, London, SW11 1NG, United Kingdom. TEL 44-20-79244004, FAX 44-20-79241004, info@theyachtreportgroup.com, http://www.theyachtreportgroup.com. Ed. Justin Ratcliffe.

797.1 GBR ISSN 2046-4975
▼ **THE SUPERYACHT INTELLIGENCE QUARTERLY.** Text in English. 2009. q. back issues avail. **Document type:** *Magazine, Trade.*
Published by: Yacht Report Group, 3-7 Northcote Rd, London, SW11 1NG, United Kingdom. TEL 44-20-79244004, FAX 44-20-79241004, info@theyachtreportgroup.com, http://www.theyachtreportgroup.com.

797.1 ITA ISSN 2035-5874
▼ **SUPERYACHT INTERNATIONAL (ITALIAN EDITION).** Text in Italian. 2009. q. **Document type:** *Magazine, Consumer.*
Published by: Nautica Editrice, Via Tevere 44, Rome, RM 00198, Italy. TEL 39-06-8413060, FAX 39-06-8543653, info@nautica.it, http://www.nautica.it.

797.1 CHE ISSN 1422-7703
SWISSBOAT - YACHTING; das schweizer yachtmagazin - le magazin du yachting. Text in German. 1995. 10/yr. CHF 77 domestic; CHF 95 foreign (effective 2003). adv. illus. back issues avail. **Document type:** *Magazine, Consumer.* **Description:** Consists of articles about people, travel, boat tests, technicals, news and advertising about boats.
Related titles: E-mail ed.; Fax ed.; French ed.: Swissboat. ISSN 1422-7681.
Published by: Boatmedia AG, Marktgasse 9, Postfach, Bern 7, 3000, Switzerland. TEL 41-31-311-51-52, FAX 41-31-3111-09-11. Ed. Martin Horisberger. adv.: B&W page CHF 5,720, color page CHF 7,430; trim 1960 x 260. Circ: 12,520 (paid).

796.95 CAN
TANZER TALK; newsletter of the Tanzer 22 class. Text in English. 1971. bi-m. USD 25 (effective 2009). back issues avail. **Document type:** *Newsletter.* **Description:** News and information related to yachts and yachting.
Formerly: Tanzer 22 Newsletter
Published by: Tanzer 22 Class Association, P.O. Box 11122, Station H, Nepean, ON K2H 7T9, Canada. TEL 450-227-3108, FAX 450-227-3276, jgcharters@compuserve.com. Ed. John G Charters. Circ: 500.

796.95 USA
THOROUGHBRED. Text in English. 1980. q. USD 25. bk.rev. cum.index. back issues avail. **Document type:** *Magazine, Trade.* **Description:** Covers classical and antique Century boats.
Published by: Century Boat Club, Inc., RR2 Box 438, Big Knob Rd, Rochester, PA 15074-9752. TEL 412-775-4849, FAX 412-775-6862. Ed., R&P Frank G Miklos. adv.: page USD 150. Circ: 1,500 (paid). **Subscr. to:** PO Box 761, Manistee, MI 49660.

797.125 ITA ISSN 1826-1825
TOP YACHTS. Text in Multiple languages. 2005. s-a. **Document type:** *Magazine, Consumer.*
Published by: Panama Editore SpA, Via Quaranta 52, Milan, 20139, Italy. TEL 39-02-5358111, FAX 39-02-56802965, http://www.panamaeditore.it.

797.1 AUS ISSN 1449-6305
TRADE-A-BOAT. Text in English. 1977. 13/yr. AUD 98 in Australia & New Zealand; AUD 126 elsewhere; AUD 7.95 newsstand/cover (effective 2008). adv. **Document type:** *Magazine, Consumer.* **Description:** Provides information on boats and boating equipment; offers a list of boats available for sale.
Published by: A C P Trader International Group (Subsidiary of: P B L Media Pty Ltd.), 73 Atherton Rd, Oakleigh, VIC 3166, Australia. TEL 61-3-95674200, FAX 61-3-95634554. Eds. Geoff Middleton, Greg Leech TEL 61-3-95674194. Adv. contact Justine Schuller. color page AUD 2,970; trim 195 x 275. Circ: 22,616. **Subscr. to:** Magshop, Reply Paid 4967, Sydney, NSW 2001, Australia. TEL 61-2-136116, subs@magstore.com.au, http://shop.magstore.com.au.

623.8 SWE ISSN 0347-0652
TRAEBITEN. Text in Swedish. 1970. q. SEK 225 to members (effective 2010). back issues avail. **Document type:** *Magazine, Consumer.* **Description:** Devoted to preserving the unique Old-Nordic style of boatbuilding.
Related titles: Online - full text ed.
Published by: Foereningen Allmogebaatar, Hjalmars Vaeg 15, Uddevalla, 45196, Sweden. TEL 46-31-120879. Ed. Sigvard Fjellsson.

387.2 AUS ISSN 1449-6542
TRAILER BOAT; Australia's small boat marketplace. Text in English. 1989. 13/yr. AUD 69 in Australia & New Zealand; AUD 85.50 elsewhere; AUD 6.50 newsstand/cover (effective 2008). adv. **Document type:** *Magazine, Consumer.* **Description:** Provides technical and informative reviews on boats, boating and fishing; offers a list of new and second hand boats available for sale.
Formerly (until 1991): Trailer Boat Supermarket
Published by: A C P Trader International Group (Subsidiary of: P B L Media Pty Ltd.), 73 Atherton Rd, Oakleigh, VIC 3166, Australia. TEL 61-3-95674200, FAX 61-3-95634554. Eds. Kevin Poulter TEL 61-3-95674158, Phil Kaberry, Greg Leech TEL 61-3-95674194. adv.: color page AUD 2,035; trim 195 x 275. Circ: 19,194. **Subscr. to:** Magshop, Reply Paid 4967, Sydney, NSW 2001, Australia. TEL 61-2-136116, subs@magstore.com.au, http://shop.magstore.com.au.

797.1 USA ISSN 0300-6557
GV776.A2
TRAILER BOATS; guiding avid boaters since 1971. Text in English. 1971. m. USD 16.97 domestic; USD 28.97 in Canada; USD 41.97 domestic (effective 2008). adv. bk.rev. illus. index. back issues avail.; reprints avail. **Document type:** *Magazine, Trade.* **Description:** Covers recreational boating topics, including boat and trailer tests, marine electronics, waterskiing, product evaluations, and boating destinations.
Related titles: Microform ed.: (from PQC); Online - full text ed.
Indexed: A22, Consl, G05, G06, G07, G08, G09, I05, MagInd, P02, P10, P48, P53, P54, PQC.
Published by: Affinity Group Inc., 2575 Vista Del Mar, Ventura, CA 93001. TEL 805-667-4100, FAX 805-667-4419, info@affinitygroup.com, http://www.affinitygroup.com. Ed. Ron Eldridge. Pub. Jim Hendricks. adv.: B&W page USD 7,910, color page USD 13,000; trim 7.875 x 10.5. Circ: 102,000 (paid).

797.124 DEU ISSN 1433-4798
TRANS-OCEAN. Text in German. 1968. q. adv. bk.rev. 60 p./no.; back issues avail. **Document type:** *Bulletin, Consumer.*
Related titles: Online - full text ed.
Published by: Verein zur Foerderung des Hochseesegelns e.V., Postfach 728, Cuxhaven, 27457, Germany. TEL 49-4721-51800, FAX 49-4721-51874. Ed. Helmut Bellmer. Circ: 5,600.

797.1 ESP ISSN 1699-2776
TROFEO NAUTICA. Text in Spanish. 2004. a. adv. **Document type:** *Magazine, Consumer.* **Description:** Covers all aspects of sailing.
Published by: Editorial America Iberica, C. Miguel Yuste 33bis, Madrid, 28037, Spain. TEL 34-91-3277950, FAX 34-91-3044746, editorial@eai.es, http://www.eai.es/. Ed. Jose Luis de la Vina. adv.: page EUR 4,960; trim 230 x 297.

797.1 NLD ISSN 1574-4159
TURFROUTE INFORMATIEBLAD. Text in Dutch. a.
Published by: Stichting de Nije Kompanjons, Bij de Leijwei 139, Hoornsterzwaag, 8412 SK, Netherlands. TEL 31-516-463777, http://www.turfroute.nl. Ed. S Mulder.

797.14 USA ISSN 1080-7586
THE TYPHOONER. Text in English. 1994. irreg. free. back issues avail. **Document type:** *Newsletter.* **Description:** Publishes information for owners of Cape Dory Typhoon sailboats.
Related titles: Diskette ed.
Published by: Typhooner, 23311 County Rd 88, Winters, CA 95694-9008. TEL 530-662-3364. Ed., R&P Noel Peattie. Circ: 225 (paid).

797.123 USA ISSN 1094-1231
GV790.6
U S ROWING. (United States) Text in English. 1969. bi-m. USD 25 to members (effective 2001). adv. bk.rev. illus. index. **Document type:** *Magazine, Trade.*

Former titles (until 1998): American Rowing (0888-1154); (until 1986): Rowing U.S.A. (0744-4788); Oarsman
Indexed: PEI, SD, SPI, SportS.
Published by: United States Rowing Association, 201 S Capitol Ave, Ste 400, Indianapolis, IN 46225-1054. TEL 317-237-5656, FAX 317-237-5646. Ed. Mo Merhoff. Adv. contact Brett Johnson. Circ: 15,000.

797.124 USA ISSN 1545-2794
U S SAILING. Text in English. 2003 (Spr.). 3/yr. free (effective 2003).
Indexed: SD.
Published by: United States Sailing Association, PO Box 1260, Portsmouth, RI 02871-0924. TEL 401-683-0800, FAX 401-683-0840, http://www.ussailing.org. Ed. Cynthia Goss.

797.1 USA
U S SAILING DIRECTORY. Text in English. 1925. a. membership. **Document type:** *Directory.* **Description:** Provides reference material and contains a list of all committee and council memebers, race officers, instructors & others.
Former titles: U S Y R U Directory; U S Y R U Yearbook; N A Y R U Yearbook
Published by: United States Sailing Association, PO Box 1260, Portsmouth, RI 02871-0924. TEL 401-683-0800, FAX 401-683-0840, TELEX 704592-USYRU-NORT-UD. Eds. Joy Shipman, Susan Cook. Circ: 40,000.

630 USA ISSN 1057-1779
UNIVERSITY OF ARKANSAS. COOPERATIVE EXTENSION SERVICE. FACT SHEET. Text in English. 1984. irreg., latest no.9600. free (effective 2011). **Document type:** *Monographic series, Trade.*
Related titles: Online - full text ed.
Indexed: Agr.
Published by: University of Arkansas, Cooperative Extension Service, 2301 S University Ave, Little Rock, AR 72204. TEL 501-671-2000, FAX 501-671-2209.

797.124 DEU
UNSERE ALTE LIEBE. Text in German. 1926. q. **Document type:** *Bulletin.*
Published by: Segler Vereinigung Cuxhaven, Postfach 672, Cuxhaven, 27456, Germany. TEL 04721-22280. Ed. Folker Weiss. Circ: 1,000.

796.95 USA
VAPOR TRAIL'S BOATING NEWS & INTERNATIONAL YACHTING & CRUISER AND MANUFACTURERS REPORT. Text in English. 1966. m. USD 24.
Formed by the merger of: Vapor Trail's Yachting and Cruiser News; Vapor Trail's Boating News and Manufacturing Report; Which was formerly: Vapor Trail's Competition News and Manufacturing Report (0042-2630)
Published by: Gemini Productions, Ltd., 8962 Bainford Dr, Huntington Beach, CA 92646. TEL 714-833-8003. Ed. Patricia Collins. Circ: 25,000.

796.95 BEL ISSN 0775-8553
VAREN; maandblad voor de watersport. Text in Dutch. 1969. 10/yr. EUR 27.20; EUR 3.70 per issue (effective 2005). adv. bk.rev. **Document type:** *Magazine, Consumer.* **Description:** Covers all aspects of yachting, sailing and motorboating.
Published by: Aquamedia NV, Emiel Claeyslaan 46, Ghent, 9050, Belgium. TEL 32-9-2111816, FAX 32-9-2111817, varen@aquamedia.be. Ed. Luk Hautekiet. Adv. contact Rik Vyncke. B&W page EUR 1,165, color page EUR 1,905. Circ: 30,000 (paid and free).

797.1 ITA ISSN 0042-3181
VELA E MOTORE. Text in Italian. 1923. 11/yr. EUR 48 domestic; EUR 78 in the European Union; EUR 118 elsewhere (effective 2009). adv. bk.rev. charts; illus. index. **Document type:** *Magazine, Consumer.* **Description:** News about sailboats and powerboats, instruments, regattas, marinas and ports.
Related titles: Online - full text ed.
Published by: Edisport Editoriale SpA, Via Gradisca 11, Milan, MI 20151, Italy. TEL 39-02-38085, FAX 39-02-38010393, edisport@edisport.it, http://www.edisport.it. Ed. A Vettese. Adv. contact Luigi Perego. Circ: 50,000.

797.1 BRA
VELA, MAR E MOTOR. Text in Portuguese. 1994. a. BRL 18, USD 13. **Document type:** *Consumer.*
Published by: Casa Editorial Ltda., Rua Sampaio Vidal, 652, Jd Paulistano, Sao Paulo, SP 01443-000, Brazil. TEL 55-11-30613688, FAX 55-11-852-9430. adv.: page USD 16,000. Circ: 30,000.

797.124 ITA ISSN 1828-9266
VELE E REGATE. Text in Italian. 2004. m. **Document type:** *Magazine, Consumer.*
Published by: Alfa Print Editore, Via Bellini 24, Busto Arsizio, VA 21052, Italy. TEL 39-0331-620100, FAX 39-0331-321116, mensil@alfaprint.com.

797.1 FIN ISSN 0042-3343
VENE. Text in Finnish. 1966. 11/yr. EUR 60.90 (effective 2005). adv. bk.rev. illus. index. **Document type:** *Magazine, Consumer.*
Published by: Yhtyneet Kuvalehdet Oy/United Magazines Ltd., Maistraatinportti 1, Helsinki, 00015, Finland. TEL 358-9-15661, FAX 358-9-145650, http://www.kuvalehdet.fi. Ed. Matti Murto. Circ: 30,466.

797.1 623.8 SWE ISSN 1401-3924
VI BAATAEGARE. Text in Swedish. 1973. m. SEK 559 (effective 2007). adv. back issues avail. **Document type:** *Magazine, Consumer.*
Former titles (until 1993): Baataegare (1101-4121); (until 1990): Vi Baataegare (0346-4229)
Published by: T T G Sverige AB (Subsidiary of: De Telegraaf Tijdschriftengroep), PO Box 26206, Stockholm, 10041, Sweden. TEL 46-8-50667800, FAX 46-8-50667859, info@ttg.se, http://www.ttg.se. Eds. Anders Jelving, Lasse Genberg. Adv. contact Magnus Norlen TEL 46-8-50667815. page SEK 23,900; 198 x 265.

797.1 NOR ISSN 1504-615X
VI MENN BAT. Text in Norwegian. 2000. 7/yr. NOK 299; NOK 65 newsstand/cover (effective 2009). adv. **Document type:** *Magazine, Consumer.*
Published by: Hjemmet Mortensen AS, Gullhaugveien 1, Nydalen, Oslo, 0441, Norway. TEL 47-22-585000, FAX 47-22-585959, firmapost@hm-media.no, http://www.hm-media.no. adv.: page NOK 27,600.

797.1 AUS ISSN 1834-5433
VICTORIAN RECREATIONAL BOATING SAFETY HANDBOOK. Text in English. 2001. a. **Document type:** *Handbook/Manual/Guide, Consumer.*
Related titles: Online - full text ed.: ISSN 1834-5441.
Published by: Marine Safety Victoria, PO Box 2797, Melbourne, VIC 3001, Australia. TEL 61-3-9655-3399, 1800-223-022, FAX 61-3-9655-6611, marinesafety@doi.vic.gov.au, http://www.marinesafety.vic.gov.au.

797.1 USA ISSN 1542-0248
VINTAGE BOATING LIFE. Text in English. 2002 (Nov./Dec.). bi-m. USD 36 domestic; USD 40 in Canada & Mexico; USD 72 elsewhere (effective 2002).
Published by: EBSCO Media, P. O. Box 130902, Birmingham, AL 35213-0902. TEL 205-803-4106, 877-244-2628, FAX 205-879-0766. Ed. Tom Schley.

797.124 FRA ISSN 0751-5405
VOILES ET VOILIERS. Text in French. m. EUR 55.60 domestic; EUR 75.10 in the European Union; EUR 91.60 in US & Canada (effective 2008). illus. **Document type:** *Magazine, Consumer.*
Indexed: RASB.
Published by: Societe d'Edition de Revues Nationales Specialisees, 21 rue du Fg. Saint Antoine, Paris, Cedex 11 75550, France. TEL 33-1-44878787, FAX 33-1-44878779. Ed. Daniel Allisy. Pub. Pierre Lavialle. Circ: 100,000. **Subscr. to:** BP 70, Perthes Cedex 77932, France.

797.1 USA ISSN 1930-3076
VOYAGING. (Formerly a supplement to Power & Motoryacht) Text in English. 2004. q. (a. until 2004). USD 9.95 (effective 2007). back issues avail. **Document type:** *Magazine, Consumer.* **Description:** Covers the lifestyle of cruising enthusiasts.
—CCC.
Published by: Source Interlink Companies, 6420 Wilshire Blvd, 10th Fl, Los Angeles, CA 90048. TEL 323-782-2000, FAX 323-782-2585, dheine@sourceinterlink.com, http://www.sourceinterlinkmedia.com. Ed. Richard Thiel. Pub. Dennis O'Neill.

796.95 DEU
WASSERSKI & WAKEBOARD MAGAZIN. Text in German. 1975. bi-m. EUR 25 in Europe; USD 38 elsewhere (effective 2010). adv. back issues avail. **Document type:** *Magazine, Consumer.* **Description:** News about waterskiing, jetboating and wakeboarding.
Formerly: Wasserski Magazin (0940-3183)
Published by: Wasserski Magazin, Weierbach 5, Schleich-Poelich, 54340, Germany. TEL 49-6507-99133, FAX 49-6507-99134. Pub. Franz Kirsch. adv.: page EUR 860; 180 x 270. Circ: 10,800 (paid and controlled).

797.124 DEU ISSN 1861-6534
WASSERSPORT. Text in German. 1986. m. EUR 30; EUR 3 newsstand/cover (effective 2007). adv. **Document type:** *Magazine, Consumer.*
Formerly (until 2004): Wassersport im Westen (1435-3504)
Published by: S V G Service Verlag GmbH, Schwertfegerstr 1-3, Luebeck, 23556, Germany. TEL 49-451-898974, FAX 49-451-898557, gewerbe@segler-zeitung.de. Pub. Hermann Hell. Adv. contact Britta Stein. B&W page EUR 1,278, color page EUR 2,183; trim 180 x 250. Circ: 16,100 (paid and controlled).

797.124 DEU ISSN 0945-8859
WASSERSPORT WIRTSCHAFT. Text in German. 1991. q. EUR 10 (effective 2006). adv. **Document type:** *Magazine, Trade.*
Published by: S V G Service Verlag GmbH, Schwertfegerstr 1-3, Luebeck, 23556, Germany. TEL 49-451-898974, FAX 49-451-898557, gewerbe@segler-zeitung.de, http://www.svgverlag.de. adv.: B&W page EUR 855, color page EUR 1,260; bleed 210 x 280. Circ: 10,000.

797.1 GBR ISSN 1367-0859
WATER CRAFT; better boats and boat building. Variant title: Peter Greenfield's Water Craft. Text in English. 1996. bi-m. GBP 21.50 domestic; GBP 23.50 in Europe includes USA & Canada; GBP 25.50 elsewhere; GBP 5 per issue (effective 2009). adv. 80 p./no. 2 cols./p.; back issues avail. **Document type:** *Magazine, Consumer.* **Description:** Covers information about practical boatwork, boatdesign and amateur and professional boatbuilding and renovation, with emphasis on smaller, affordable craft.
Published by: Pete Greenfield Publishing, Bridge Shop, Gweek, Helston, Cornwall TR12 6UD, United Kingdom. TEL 44-1326-221424, FAX 44-1326-221728, subs@watercraft-magazine.com. **Dist. by:** M M C Ltd., Octagon House, White Hart Meadows, Ripley, Woking, Surrey GU23 6HR, United Kingdom. TEL 44-1483-211222, FAX 44-1483-224541, enquiries@mmcltd.co.uk, http://www.mmcextranet.co.uk.

797.1 USA ISSN 1092-2784
WATER CRAFT POWER. Text in English. 1997. 8/yr. USD 3.50 newsstand/cover. **Document type:** *Magazine, Consumer.*
Published by: Petersen Publishing Co. LLC, 6420 Wilshire Blvd, Los Angeles, CA 90048-5515. TEL 213-782-2461, FAX 213-782-2263.

THE WATER SKIER; having fun today - building champions for tomorrow. *see* SPORTS AND GAMES—Outdoor Life

797.1 NLD ISSN 1872-0900
WATERALMANAK. Text in Dutch. 1975. a. EUR 17.50 (effective 2008).
Formerly (until 2002): Almanak voor Watertoerisme (0923-1692)
Published by: ANWB BV/Royal Dutch Touring Club, Wassenaarseweg 220, Postbus 93200, The Hague, 2509 BA, Netherlands. http://www.anwb.nl.

796.95 USA ISSN 1073-3191
WATERCRAFT WORLD. Text in English. 1987. bi-m. USD 11.97 domestic; USD 17.97 foreign (effective 2008). adv. back issues avail.; reprints avail. **Document type:** *Magazine, Trade.*
Formerly (until 1993): Water Scooter (0899-9775)
Related titles: Online - full text ed.
Indexed: G05, G06, G07, G08, I05.
Published by: Affinity Group Inc., 2575 Vista Del Mar, Ventura, CA 93001. TEL 805-667-4100, FAX 805-667-4419, info@affinitygroup.com, http://www.affinitygroup.com. Eds. Jeff Hemmel TEL 805-667-4100, Matt Gruhn TEL 763-383-4448. Adv. contact Jeff Johnston. Circ: 22,000 (paid); 119,000 (controlled).

796.95 917.504 USA ISSN 8756-0038
WATERFRONT NEWS; South Florida's nautical newspaper. Text in English. 1984. m. USD 12 domestic; USD 36 foreign (effective 2005). adv. bk.rev. 28 p./no. 3 cols./p.; back issues avail. **Document type:** *Newspaper.* **Description:** Covers South Florida's sailing, power boating, nautical history, diving, fishing and waterfront community news.
Published by: Ziegler Publishing Co., Inc., 1515 S.W. First Ave., Fort Lauderdale, FL 33315. TEL 954-524-9450, FAX 954-524-9464, h2onews@aol.com. Ed. Jennifer Heit. Pub., R&P John Ziegler. Adv. contact Elana Bryan. col. inch USD 30. Circ: 42,000 (controlled).

797.1 NLD ISSN 0043-1451
WATERKAMPIOEN. Text in Dutch. 1927. 20/yr. EUR 84.25 to non-members; EUR 72.95 to members (effective 2008). adv. bk.rev.; Website rev. charts; illus. index. **Document type:** *Consumer.* **Description:** Covers water sports and travel related topics.
Indexed: KES.
—IE, Infotrieve.
Published by: (ANWB BV/Royal Dutch Touring Club), Algemene Nederlandse Wielrijders Bond (A N W B) Media/Dutch Automobile Association Media, Postbus 93200, The Hague, 2509 BA, Netherlands. TEL 31-70-3141470, FAX 31-70-3146538, http://www.anwbmedia.nl. adv.: B&W page EUR 3,111, color page EUR 4,569; bleed 215 x 285. Circ: 41,039.

797.1 NLD
WATERKAMPIOEN 2EHANDS. Text in Dutch. m. EUR 34 to non-members; EUR 19.95 to members (effective 2008). **Document type:** *Magazine, Consumer.*
Published by: (ANWB BV/Royal Dutch Touring Club), Algemene Nederlandse Wielrijders Bond (A N W B) Media/Dutch Automobile Association Media, Postbus 93200, The Hague, 2509 BA, Netherlands. TEL 31-70-3141470, FAX 31-70-3146538, http://www.anwbmedia.nl.

387.2 USA ISSN 0509-917X
GV835
WATERWAY GUIDE - MID-ATLANTIC. Text in English. a. USD 39.95 newsstand/cover (effective 2005). adv. charts. **Document type:** *Magazine, Consumer.* **Description:** Navigation and travel guide for recreational boaters who cruise the Chesapeake Bay, Delmarva Coast, and the inter-coastal waterway from Norfolk to the Georgia - Florida border.
Published by: York Associates LLC, 326 First St., Ste. 400, PO Box 4219, Annapolis, MD 21403. TEL 443-482-9377, 800-233-3359, FAX 443-482-9422, http://www.waterwayguide.com/. Eds. Gary Reich, Ryan Stallings. Pub. Jack Dozier.

387.2 USA ISSN 0090-712X
VK994
WATERWAY GUIDE - NORTHERN. Text in English. a. USD 39.95 newsstand/cover (effective 2005). adv. charts. **Document type:** *Magazine, Consumer.* **Description:** Navigation and travel guide for recreational boaters who cruise the waters of the Delaware Bay, New Jersey coast, Long Island Sound, and the coasts of Connecticut, Massachusetts and Maine.
Published by: York Associates LLC, 326 First St., Ste. 400, PO Box 4219, Annapolis, MD 21403. TEL 443-482-9377, 800-233-3359, FAX 443-482-9422, http://www.waterwayguide.com/. Eds. Gary Reich, Ryan Stallings. Pub. Jack Dozier.

387.2 USA ISSN 0511-3806
Q917.6/W
WATERWAY GUIDE - SOUTHERN. Text in English. a. USD 39.95 newsstand/cover (effective 2005). adv. charts. **Document type:** *Magazine, Consumer.* **Description:** Navigation and travel guide for recreational boaters who cruise the east and west coast of Florida, Bahamas, Gulf Coast to Mexico and the Tenn-Tom Waterway.
Published by: York Associates LLC, 326 First St., Ste. 400, PO Box 4219, Annapolis, MD 21403. TEL 443-482-9377, 800-233-3359, FAX 443-482-9422, http://www.waterwayguide.com/. Pub. Jack Dozier. adv.: B&W page USD 1,770, color page USD 3,380.

796.95 GBR ISSN 0969-0654
WATERWAYS. Text in English. 1946. q. free to members (effective 2009). adv. bk.rev. back issues avail. **Document type:** *Magazine, Trade.*
Former titles (until 1991): I W A Waterways (0308-583X); (until 1976): Inland Waterways Association. Bulletin (0307-1227)
Related titles: Online - full text ed.: free (effective 2009).
Indexed: RICS.
Published by: Inland Waterways Association, Island House, Moor Rd, Chesham, HP5 1WA, United Kingdom. TEL 44-1494-783453, iwa@waterways.org.uk. Ed. Keith Goss TEL 44-1283-742951. Adv. contact Tony Preston TEL 44-1283-742965.

797.1 GBR ISSN 0309-1422
WATERWAYS WORLD. Text in English. 1972. m. GBP 37.80 (effective 2009). adv. bk.rev. charts; illus.; stat. index. back issues avail. **Document type:** *Magazine, Consumer.*
Published by: Waterways World Ltd., 151 Station St, Burton-on-Trent, DE14 1BG, United Kingdom. TEL 44-1283-742970, FAX 44-1283-742957, admin@wwonline.co.uk, subscriptions@wwonline.co.uk, http://www.wwmagazines.com/magazines.html. Ed. Richard Fairhurst TEL 44-1283-742950. Pub. Peter Johns. Adv. contact Ian Sharpe TEL 44-1283-742975. Circ: 17,007 (paid).

797.1 USA
WAVE SOUTH FLORIDA; on, in, around the water. Text in English. 2003. bi-m. USD 18 (effective 2004). adv. **Document type:** *Magazine, Consumer.*
Published by: Wave South Florida, LLC, Brickell Bayview Center, 80 S W 8th St, Ste 2230, Miami, FL 33130. TEL 786-425-2095, FAX 305-523-2255. Pub. Jose Chao. Adv. contact Jim Guthrie. B&W page USD 3,000, color page USD 3,900; trim 9.125 x 10.875. Circ: 95,700 (paid and controlled).

WESTCOAST MARINER. *see* TRANSPORTATION—Ships And Shipping

797.122 USA
WHITEWATER PADDLING. Text in English. 1997. a. USD 4.99 (effective 2008). adv. **Document type:** *Magazine, Consumer.* **Description:** Provides articles and information for whitewater enthusiasts, including whitewater spots, safety tips, and new products.
Published by: Source Interlink Companies, 6420 Wilshire Blvd, 10th Fl, Los Angeles, CA 90048. TEL 323-782-2000, FAX 323-782-2585, dheine@sourceinterlink.com, http://www.sourceinterlinkmedia.com. Ed. Ross Prather. Pub. Glen Bernard.

S

WILDLIFE AND BOATING SAFETY LAWS OF TENNESSEE. *see* LAW

797.1 CAN ISSN 0826-5003
WINDSPORT; north america's windsurfing magazine. Text in English. 1982. 4/yr. USD 25 in US & Canada; USD 50 elsewhere; USD 3.75 newsstand/cover (effective 2001). adv. bk.rev. charts; illus.; stat. back issues avail. **Document type:** *Magazine, Consumer.*
Indexed: SD, SportS.
Published by: S B C Media, 2255 B Queen St E, Ste 3266, Toronto, ON M4E 1G3, Canada. TEL 416-698-0138, FAX 416-698-8080, info@sbcmedia.com, http://www.sbcmedia.com. Ed., Pub. Steve Jarrett. Circ: 15,500. **Dist. by:** International Publishers Direct, 27500 Riverview Center Blvd, Bonita Springs, FL 34134. TEL 858-320-4563, FAX 858-677-3220.

797.1 GBR ISSN 0958-5508
WINDSURF. Text in English. 1980. 10/yr. GBP 34 domestic; GBP 50 in Europe; GBP 60 elsewhere; GBP 4.10 newsstand/cover (effective 2009). illus. back issues avail. **Document type:** *Magazine, Consumer.* **Description:** Promotes the sport of windsurfing. Includes tack tips, race events and new product information.
Former titles (until 1990): Windsurf and Boardsailing; (until 19??): Come Board Sailing
Indexed: RASB.
Address: The Blue Barns, Tew Ln, Wootton, Woodstock OX20 1HA, United Kingdom. TEL 44-1993-811181, FAX 44-1993-813438, subs@windsurf.co.uk. Adv. contact Dan Beechener.

797.1 ITA ISSN 1120-5865
WINDSURF ITALIA. Text in Italian. 1983. m. EUR 43 domestic; EUR 83 foreign (effective 2008). **Document type:** *Magazine, Consumer.*
Published by: Cantelli Editore Srl, Via Saliceto 22c, Castelmaggiore, BO 40013, Italy. TEL 39-051-6328811, FAX 39-051-6328815, cantelli.editore@cantelli.net, http://www.cantelli.net. Circ: 43,800.

797.124 USA
WINDWARD LEG. Text in English. 3/yr. USD 30 to members. adv. bk.rev. back issues avail. **Document type:** *Newsletter.* **Description:** Provides coverage of world and North American championships in all categories - men's, women's, and juniors' - as well as regional and local regattas.
Published by: United States Sunfish Class Association, 329 Central Ave, Sarasota, FL 34236. TEL 248-673-2750, FAX 248-673-2750. Ed., Adv. contact Cindy Clifton. Circ: 2,000. **Co-sponsor:** International Sunfish Class Association.

623.82 USA ISSN 0095-067X
VM320
THE WOODENBOAT; the magazine for wooden boat owners, builders and designers. Text in English. 1974. bi-m. USD 32 (effective 2010). adv. bk.rev. illus. index. back issues avail.; reprints avail. **Document type:** *Magazine, Consumer.* **Description:** Devoted to the building, design, history and maintenance of wooden boats.
Indexed: A22, H20, IHTDI, T02.
Published by: WoodenBoat Publications, Inc., 41 WoodenBoat Ln, Brooklin, ME 04616. TEL 207-359-4651, FAX 207-359-8920. Pub. Carl Cramer.

796.95 NLD ISSN 0928-4702
WOONBOOT MAGAZINE. Text in Dutch. 1992. bi-m. EUR 39.50; EUR 3.80 newsstand/cover (effective 2010). adv. **Document type:** *Magazine, Consumer.* **Description:** Covers all aspects of living on a houseboat, including technical, legal, and lifestyle concerns.
Published by: (Vereniging Landelijke Woonboten Organisatie), Stichting Uitgeverij Woonboot Publicaties, Postbus 8192, Utrecht, 3503 RD, Netherlands. TEL 31-30-2967698, FAX 31-30-2817561. Eds. Dave Schmalz, Frans Nuberg. Adv. contact Heleen Deurloo.

WORKBOAT. *see* TRANSPORTATION—Ships And Shipping

387.2 GBR ISSN 1756-0594
WORLD OF POWERBOATS; the premier publication for performance powerboating. Text in English. 2005. bi-m. GBP 26 domestic; EUR 45 in Europe; USD 73 elsewhere (effective 2009). adv. back issues avail. **Document type:** *Magazine, Consumer.*
Related titles: Online - full text ed.: ISSN 1756-0608.
Published by: Blue Media Group Ltd., Investment House, 178 Oatlands Dr, Weybridge, Surrey KT13 9ET, United Kingdom. TEL 44-1932-828060, FAX 44-1932-856444, info@blue-mediagroup.com, http://www.blue-mediagroup.co.uk/.

797.1 DEU ISSN 0043-9932
YACHT; Europas groesstes Segelmagazin. Text in German. 1904. fortn. EUR 90 in Germany & Austria; EUR 105 in Switzerland; EUR 129 elsewhere; EUR 4.20 newsstand/cover (effective 2011). adv. illus. **Document type:** *Magazine, Consumer.*
Indexed: RASB.
—CCC.
Published by: Delius Klasing Verlag GmbH, Siekerwall 21, Bielefeld, 33602, Germany. TEL 49-521-5590, FAX 49-521-559113, info@delius-klasing.de, http://www.delius-klasing.de. Ed. Jochen Rieker. Adv. contact Robin Aljoscha Doeberl.

797.1 ITA ISSN 1120-7663
YACHT CAPITAL. Text in Italian, English. 1990. m. adv. illus. **Document type:** *Magazine, Consumer.* **Description:** Covers sailing and motor yachts, along with sailing news and events worldwide.
Related titles: Online - full content ed.: Yacht Capital Online. 1990; Supplement(s): Crociere. ISSN 1591-6553. 2001.
Published by: De Agostini Editore, Via G da Verrazzano 15, Novara, 28100, Italy. TEL 39-0321-4241, FAX 39-0321-424305, info@deagostini.it, http://www.deagostini.it. Ed. Matteo Zaccagnino. Circ: 49,000 (paid). **Dist. in UK by:** Seymour Distribution Ltd, 86 Newman St, London W1T 3EX, United Kingdom. FAX 44-207-396-8002, enquiries@seymour.co.uk.

347.792 ITA
YACHT DESIGN. Text in Italian. 1997. bi-m. adv. **Document type:** *Magazine, Consumer.*
Published by: Hachette Rusconi SpA (Subsidiary of: Hachette Filipacchi Medias S.A.), Viale Sarca 235, Milan, 20126, Italy. TEL 39-02-66192629, FAX 39-02-66192469, dirgen@rusconi.it, http://portale.hachettepubblicita.it. Circ: 43,000 (paid and controlled).

797.1 ITA ISSN 0394-3143
YACHT DIGEST. Text in Italian. 1987. 6/yr. adv. bk.rev. illus. **Document type:** *Magazine, Consumer.*
Published by: De Agostini Editore, Via G da Verrazzano 15, Novara, 28100, Italy. TEL 39-0321-4241, FAX 39-0321-424305, info@deagostini.it, http://www.deagostini.it. Circ: 40,000 (paid and controlled).

796.95 USA
YACHT TRADER. Text in English. 19??. m. **Document type:** *Magazine, Trade.*
Published by: Trader Publishing Co., 150 Granby St, Norfolk, VA 23510. TEL 757-640-4020, http://www.traderonline.com/.

797.1 DEU
YACHT UND BOOT. Text in German. 6/yr. EUR 3 newsstand/cover (effective 2005). adv. **Document type:** *Magazine, Consumer.* **Description:** Contains information and listings for yachts and related accessories and destinations.
Published by: Michael E. Brieden Verlag GmbH, Gartroper Str 42, Duisburg, 47138, Germany. TEL 49-203-42920, FAX 49-203-4292149, info@brieden.de, http://www.brieden.de. adv.: color page EUR 1,533; trim 194 x 267. Circ: 170,000 (paid and controlled).

797.1 USA ISSN 0043-9940
GV771
YACHTING; power and sail. Text in English. 1907. m. USD 14 for 3 yrs. domestic; USD 26 in Canada; USD 46 elsewhere (effective 2009). adv. bk.rev. charts; illus.; tr.lit. reprints avail. **Document type:** *Magazine, Consumer.* **Description:** Provides reports on developments in marine electronics, and sails and engines for large power and sailing yachts. Covers chartering options and racing; lists yacht brokerages.
Related titles: Microform ed.: (from PQC); Online - full text ed.
Indexed: A11, A22, B14, BRI, C05, CBRI, CPerI, ConsI, G05, G06, G07, G08, G09, I05, I06, I07, M01, M02, MASUSE, MagInd, P02, P10, P48, P53, P54, PMR, PQC, R04, S23, SD, SPI, T02.
—Ingenta. **CCC.**
Published by: Bonnier Corp. (Subsidiary of: Bonnier Group), 2 Park Ave, 9th Fl, New York, NY 10016. TEL 212-779-5000, 800-999-0869, FAX 212-779-5479, http://www.bonniercorp.com. Ed. George Sass Jr. Pub. Ed Baker. adv.: B&W page USD 30,295, color page USD 33,655; trim 8.375 x 10.875.

797.1 DEU ISSN 1861-549X
YACHTING & STYLE. Text in German. 2006. 3/yr. EUR 24; EUR 8 newsstand/cover (effective 2007). adv. **Document type:** *Magazine, Consumer.*
Published by: Klocke Verlag GmbH, Hoefeweg 40, Bielefeld, 33619, Germany. TEL 49-521-911110, FAX 49-521-9111112, info@klocke-verlag.de, http://www.klocke-verlag.de. adv.: B&W page EUR 5,800, color page EUR 8,500. Circ: 48,510 (controlled).

796.95 GBR ISSN 0958-6393
YACHTING LIFE. Text in English. 1977. m. GBP 28 (effective 2009). adv. bk.rev. 64 p./no. 4 cols./p.; back issues avail. **Document type:** *Magazine, Trade.*
—CCC.
Published by: K A V Publicity (Glasgow) Ltd., Wheatsheaf House, Montgomery St, The Village, E Kilbride, G74 4JS, United Kingdom. TEL 44-1355-279077, FAX 44-1355-279088, info@kavpublicity.co.uk. Ed. Alistair M Vallance. Adv. contact Mary Connelly. B&W page GBP 675, color page GBP 990; trim 210 x 297. **Dist. by:** Warners Group Publications Plc., The Maltings, Manor Ln, Bourne, Lincs PE10 9PH, United Kingdom. TEL 44-1778-393652, FAX 44-1778-393668.

797.1 GBR ISSN 0043-9983
GV771
YACHTING MONTHLY. Text in English. 1906. m. GBP 40 domestic; USD 63.60 in United States; USD 104.30 in Canada; EUR 74.37 in Europe; GBP 72.75 elsewhere; GBP 4.30 newsstand/cover domestic; AUD 10.50 newsstand/cover in Australia; NZD 17 newsstand/cover in New Zealand (effective 2010). adv. bk.rev. charts; illus.; tr.lit. index. back issues avail. **Document type:** *Magazine, Consumer.* **Description:** Provides an entertaining mix of vital information for cruising yachtsmen with all levels of experience, which maximises their enjoyment, increases their skills and gives them the confidence to broaden their horizons.
Related titles: Online - full text ed.: GBP 29.99 (effective 2010).
—CCC.
Published by: I P C Country & Leisure Media Ltd. (Subsidiary of: I P C Media Ltd.), The Blue Fin Bldg, 110 Southwark St, London, SE1 0SU, United Kingdom. TEL 44-203-1484872, FAX 44-203-1488128, http://www.ipcmedia.com. Ed. Paul Gelder TEL 44-20-31484867. Adv. contact John Gaylord TEL 44-20-31484880. B&W page GBP 2,140, color page GBP 3,910. Circ: 34,103. **Subscr. to:** Rockwood House, Perrymount Rd, Haywards Heath RH16 3DH, United Kingdom. TEL 44-845-1231231, IPCsubs@quadrantsubs.com, http://www.magazinesdirect.co.uk. **Dist. by:** MarketForce UK Ltd.

797.14 CZE ISSN 1213-1601
YACHTING REVUE. Text in Czech. 2000. m. CZK 750; CZK 62.50 newsstand/cover (effective 2009). adv. **Document type:** *Magazine, Consumer.*
Published by: Petr Ehrlich, Novodvorska 1010/14, Prague 4, 14200, Czech Republic. TEL 420-2-33313274, FAX 420-2-33313275. Ed. Jan Langsadl.

797.1 BEL ISSN 0774-0670
YACHTING SUD SUR L'EAU. Text in French. 1923. 10/yr. EUR 22.50; EUR 2.50 per issue (effective 2005). adv. bk.rev. 32 p./no.; **Document type:** *Magazine, Consumer.* **Description:** Covers regional, national and international yachting developments.
Formerly (until 1982): Sur l'Eau (0039-5994)
Published by: (Ligue Regionale du Yachting Belge), Editions Bertels, avenue des Lilas 10, Rhode St.Genese, B-1640, Belgium. yachting.sud@skynet.be. Ed., R&P Charles Bertels. Adv. contact Caroline Rome TEL 32-478-365-449. B&W page EUR 609.82, color page EUR 867.63; trim 215 x 275. Circ: 8,000.

797.1 USA ISSN 2153-0831
▼ **YACHTING TIMES**; America's bilingual boating magazine. Text in English. 2010 (Feb.). q. USD 9 (effective 2010). adv. illus. **Document type:** *Magazine, Consumer.* **Description:** Provides articles, information and news on yachts and yacht racing.
Related titles: Online - full text ed.: ISSN 2153-084X. 2010 (Feb.).
Published by: Delores Barciela de Mrongowius, Ed. & Pub., PO Box 31-0725, Miami, FL 33231-0725. TEL 786-237-7830, info@yachtingtimesmagazine.com.

796.7 AUS
YACHTING WESTERN AUSTRALIA. YEAR BOOK. Text in English. 1965. a.
Former titles (until 2001): Yachting Association of Western Australia. Annual Reference Yearbook; (until 1989): Yachting Association of Western Australia. Year Book; (until 1985): Western Australian Yachting Association Yearbook (0811-3572)
Published by: Yachting Western Australia Inc, The Esplanade, Nedlands, W.A. 6009, Australia. TEL 61-8-93862438, FAX 61-8-93898686, ywa.office@wa.yachting.org.au, http://www.wa.yachting.org.au.

797.1 GBR ISSN 0043-9991
GV811.8
YACHTING WORLD. Text in English. 1894. m. GBP 41.60 domestic; USD 78.37 in United States; USD 117.98 in Canada; EUR 77.44 in Europe; GBP 79.47 elsewhere; GBP 4.50 newsstand/cover domestic; NZD 16 newsstand/cover in New Zealand; EUR 7.50 newsstand/cover in Spain (effective 2010). adv. bk.rev. illus. back issues avail. **Document type:** *Magazine, Consumer.* **Description:** Features nautical writing and photography, up-to-the-minute technical reports, equipment valuation, new boat tests and informed comment.
Former titles (until 1961): Yachting World, Power and Sail; (until 19??): Yachting World; (until 1945): Yachting World and Power Craft; (until 1939): Yachting World and Motor Boating Journal; (until 1929): Yachting World and Marine Motor Journal; Yachting World
Related titles: Microform ed.: (from PQC); Online - full text ed.: GBP 29.99 (effective 2010); Supplement(s): Supersail World. ISSN 1759-068X; Premiere Yachting World. ISSN 0961-9984.
Indexed: RASB, SportS.
—CCC.
Published by: I P C Country & Leisure Media Ltd. (Subsidiary of: I P C Media Ltd.), The Blue Fin Bldg, 110 Southwark St, London, SE1 0SU, United Kingdom. TEL 44-20-31484846, FAX 44-20-31488127, http://www.ipcmedia.com. Ed. Andrew Bray TEL 44-20-31484830. Adv. contact Alan Warren TEL 44-20-31484888. Circ: 27,649. **Subscr. to:** Rockwood House, Perrymount Rd, Haywards Heath RH16 3DH, United Kingdom. TEL 44-845-1231231, IPCsubs@quadrantsubs.com, http://www.magazinesdirect.co.uk. **Dist. by:** MarketForce UK Ltd.

797.1 USA ISSN 0094-8136
GV825
YACHTING YEARBOOK OF NORTHERN CALIFORNIA. Text in English. 1922. a. USD 10.95. adv. illus. **Document type:** *Directory.*
Published by: Pacific Inter-Club Yacht Association of Northern California, Publication Office, 530 Alemeda del Prado 200, Novato, CA 94949. TEL 415-823-6633, FAX 415-388-8361. Circ: 10,000.

796.95 AUT ISSN 1013-7823
YACHTREVUE. Text in German. 1976. m. EUR 30; EUR 3.10 newsstand/cover (effective 2006). adv. bk.rev. back issues avail. **Document type:** *Magazine, Consumer.*
Related titles: Online - full text ed.
Published by: Verlagsgruppe News Gesellschaft mbH (Subsidiary of: Gruner + Jahr AG & Co), Taborstr 1-3, Vienna, W 1020, Austria. TEL 43-1-213129011, FAX 43-1-213121650, redaktion@news.at, http://www.news.at. Ed. Luis Gazzari. adv.: page EUR 4,000; trim 210 x 280. Circ: 16,532 (paid).

797.1 GBR ISSN 0044-0000
YACHTS AND YACHTING; the UK's top performance sailing magazine. Text in English. 1947. m. GBP 42 domestic; GBP 63 foreign (effective 2009). adv. bk.rev.; Website rev. charts; illus. back issues avail. **Document type:** *Magazine, Consumer.* **Description:** Contains worldwide yachting news, products, competitions, boat tests and boat running features.
Related titles: Online - full text ed.: GBP 35; free to members (effective 2009).
Indexed: SportS.
—CCC.
Published by: Yachts & Yachting Ltd., 196 Eastern Esplanade, Southend-on-Sea, Essex SS1 3AB, United Kingdom. TEL 44-1702-582245 ext 107, FAX 44-1702-588434, subscriptions@yachtsandyachting.com. Ed. Gael Pawson TEL 44-7855-849273. **Dist. by:** Comag.

797.1246 623.82023 USA ISSN 1095-1091
YACHTS INTERNATIONAL. Text in English. 1997. bi-m. USD 24.95 domestic; USD 40 in Canada; USD 70 in Europe; USD 90 elsewhere (effective 2007). back issues avail. **Document type:** *Magazine, Consumer.*
Published by: Yachts International Magazine (Subsidiary of: Active Interest Media), 1850 SE 17th St, Ste 310, Fort Lauderdale, FL 33316. TEL 954-761-8777, FAX 954-761-8890. Ed. Jamie Welsh. Pub. Andy Clurman TEL 310-356-4129. Circ: 50,000.

656.6 ITA ISSN 1723-4107
YACHTSMAN. Text in Italian. 2003. q. adv. **Document type:** *Magazine, Consumer.*
Published by: Hachette Rusconi SpA (Subsidiary of: Hachette Filipacchi Medias S.A.), Viale Sarca 235, Milan, 20126, Italy. TEL 39-02-66192629, FAX 39-02-66192469, dirgen@rusconi.it, http://portale.hachettepubblicita.it. Circ: 42,000 (paid and controlled).

769.95 910.202 USA
YACHTSMAN'S GUIDE TO THE BAHAMAS. Text in English. 1950. a., latest vol.51. USD 34.95 (effective 2001). adv. **Document type:** *Directory, Consumer.* **Description:** Cruising guide with sketch charts, charter planning, resort, restaurant, diving and marina information. Covers the history of the islands.
Published by: Tropical Island Publishers, Inc., PO Box 12, Adelphia, NJ 07710-0012. TEL 732-544-1502, FAX 732-389-9139. Ed., Pub. Thomas J Daly. R&P, Adv. contact Linda Heden. Circ: 12,132.

797.14 USA ISSN 0084-327X
YACHTSMAN'S GUIDE TO THE GREAT LAKES. Text in English. 1956. a. USD 20 domestic; USD 25 in Canada (effective 2000). adv. index. **Document type:** *Handbook/Manual/Guide, Trade.* **Description:** Provides a guide to Great Lakes harbors.
Published by: Seaway Publishing Co., 18 22 S Elm St, Zeeland, MI 49464. TEL 616-772-2132. Ed. Paul E. Van Koevering. Pub., R&P, Adv. contact Paul E Van Koevering. Circ: 5,000 (paid).

796.95 USA
GV817.V5
YACHTSMAN'S GUIDE TO THE VIRGIN ISLANDS. Text in English. 1968. a. USD 15.95 (effective 2006). adv. **Document type:** *Magazine, Consumer.* **Description:** Cruising guide with sketch charts, charter planning, resorts, diving, restaurants, and marina information. Also covers the history of the islands.
Former titles: Yachtsman's Guide to the Virgin Islands and Puerto Rico (0735-9020); Which supersedes (in 1987): Yachtsman's Guide to the Greater Antilles (0162-7635)
Published by: Tropical Island Publishers, Inc., PO Box 12, Adelphia, NJ 07710-0012. TEL 732-544-1502, FAX 732-389-9139. Ed. Meredith H Fields. Pub. Thomas J Daly. Adv. contact Linda Heden.

796.95 ESP ISSN 1130-8516
YATE. Text in Spanish. 1965. m. adv. bk.rev. bibl.; charts; illus. back issues avail. **Document type:** *Magazine, Consumer.*
Formerly (until 1991): Yate y Motonautica (0210-0320)
Indexed: RASB.
Published by: M C Ediciones, Paseo de Sant Gervasi 16-20, Barcelona, 08022, Spain. TEL 34-93-2541250, FAX 34-93-2541262, http://www.mcediciones.net.

797.1 POL ISSN 0860-2670
ZAGLE; magazyn sportow wodnych. Text in Polish. 1959. m. PLZ 138; PLZ 11.50 newsstand/cover (effective 2011). adv. **Document type:** *Magazine, Consumer.*
Former titles (until 1985): Zagle i Jachting Motorowy (0137-4656); (until 1973): Zagle (0867-678X)
Related titles: Online - full text ed.
Published by: (Warszawskie Towarzystwo Wioslarskie), Wydawnictwo Murator Sp. z o.o., ul Deblinska 6, Warsaw, 04187, Poland. TEL 48-22-5905000, FAX 48-22-5905444, klienci@murator.com.pl, http://www.murator.com.pl. Ed. Waldemar Heflich. adv.: page PLZ 18,000; trim 175 x 255.

797.14 NLD ISSN 1382-8274
ZEILEN. Text in Dutch. 1985. m. EUR 46.40; EUR 5.50 newsstand/cover (effective 2009). adv. **Document type:** *Magazine, Consumer.*
Published by: Sanoma Men's Magazines, Haaksbergweg 75, Amsterdam (ZO), 1101 BR, Netherlands. TEL 31-20-7518000, FAX 31-20-7518301, sales@smm.nl, http://www.smm.nl. Ed. Cees van Dijk. Pub. Jan Paul de Wilt. adv.: color page EUR 2,940, B&W page EUR 1,940; trim 229 x 298. Circ: 27,653.

797.1 DEU
ZWEITE HAND BOOTE UND ZUBEHOER. Text in German. 2006. m. adv. **Document type:** *Magazine, Consumer.*
Published by: Zweite Hand Verlag, Askanischer Platz 3, Berlin, 10963, Germany. TEL 49-30-290210, FAX 49-30-2902199935, service@zweitehand.de, http://www.zweitehand.de. adv.: color page EUR 1,500. Circ: 21,500 (controlled).

797.1 USA
48 DEGREES NORTH; the sailing magazine. Text in English. 1981. m. USD 19.95 (effective 2005). adv. bk.rev. 940 p./no.; **Document type:** *Magazine, Consumer.* **Description:** Reports boating activities and racing for the Northwest.
Published by: Boundless Enterprises, Inc., 6327 Seaview Ave, N W, Seattle, WA 98107. TEL 206-789-7350, FAX 206-789-6392. Ed. Rich Hazelton. Pub. Charles Streatch. Adv. contact Michael Collins. B&W page USD 800; trim 7.25 x 10. Circ: 25,000 (paid and free).

SPORTS AND GAMES—Horses And Horsemanship

636.1 USA
A H C NEWS. (American Horse Council) Text in English. 1969. q. free to members (effective 2010). **Document type:** *Newsletter, Trade.* **Description:** Provides news of AHC activities.
Formerly: A H C Newsletter
Published by: American Horse Council, Inc., 1616 H St NW 7th Fl, Washington, DC 20006. TEL 202-296-4031, FAX 202-296-1970, ahc@horsecouncil.org.

636.1 USA
A H P A NEWS. (American Horse Protection Association) Text in English. 1966. s-a. USD 20 (effective 1999). **Document type:** *Newsletter.*
Formerly: American Horse Protection Association Newsletter
Published by: American Horse Protection Association, Inc., 1000 29th St, N W, Ste T100, Washington, DC 20007. TEL 202-965-0500. Ed., Pub., R&P Robin C Lohnes. Circ: 15,000.

636.1 NLD ISSN 1872-664X
A V S MAGAZINE. (Arabische Volbloedpaarden Stamboek) Text in Dutch. bi-m. adv.
Former titles (until 2006): Vereniging Arabische Volbloedpaarden Stamboek in Nederland. Nieuwsbrief (1872-0188); (until 2005): A V S Nieuwsbrief (0926-2490); (until 1990): Arabisch Volbloed (0926-2482)
Published by: Vereniging Het Arabische Volbloedpaarden Stamboek in Nederland, Postbus 40306, Utrecht, 3504 AC, Netherlands. TEL 31-30-2410001, FAX 31-30-2415544, info@arabier.com, http://www.avsweb.nl. adv.: color page EUR 417, B&W page EUR 245; trim 210 x 297. Circ: 1,500.

798.2 GBR ISSN 1358-8869
ABSOLUTE HORSE. Text in English. 1991. m. GBP 35.99; GBP 2.50 per issue (effective 2009). **Document type:** *Magazine, Consumer.* **Description:** Contains features on horse breeding, health, and racing and results.
Formerly (until 1995): Anglian Horse (0965-4119)
Published by: P C D Publishing, Home Barn, Grove Hill, Belstead, Ipswich, IP8 3LS, United Kingdom. TEL 44-1473-731220.

799 DEU ISSN 1618-3479
AKTUELLER VOLTIGIERZIRKEL. Text in German. 2000. 4/yr. EUR 10 per issue (effective 2010). adv. **Document type:** *Magazine, Consumer.*
Related titles: Online - full text ed.
Published by: Voltigierzirkel e.V., Reilsheimer Weg 7, Gaiberg bei Heidelberg, 69251, Germany. geschaeftsstelle@voltigierzirkel.de. Ed. Felix Bender. adv.: B&W page EUR 870, color page EUR 1,630. Circ: 2,000 (controlled).

798 USA
ALASKA HORSE JOURNAL. Text in English. 1996. 11/yr. (plus annual guide). USD 17.50; free horse related outlets (effective 2003). adv. **Document type:** *Journal, Consumer.*
Address: 310 N Harriette St, Wasilla, AK 99654-7627. adv.: page USD 220; 7 x 9.5.

798 CAN
THE ALBERTA THOROUGHBRED. Text in English. q. membership. adv. back issues avail. **Document type:** *Newsletter.* **Description:** Keeps membership up-to-date with the industry.
Formerly (until 1997): Horse Cents
Published by: Canadian Thoroughbred Horse Society, Alberta Division, 401, 255 17 Ave S W, Calgary, AB T2S 2T8, Canada. TEL 403-229-3609, FAX 403-244-6909, cthsalta@cadvision.com. Ed., R&P Rennie Gellner. Adv. contact Lindsay Ward. Circ: 3,000 (controlled).

798 CAN ISSN 1913-3537
ALBERTA'S HORSE COMMUNITY GUIDE; the annual consumers' guide to Alberta's horse community. Text in English. 2007. a. **Document type:** *Magazine, Consumer.*
Published by: Horse Community Journals Inc., P O Box 2190, Sidney, BC V8L 3S8, Canada. TEL 250-655-8883, FAX 250-655-8913, editor@horsejournals.com.

798 DNK ISSN 1902-7842
ALL HORSE; ridesportens gratis magasin. Text in Danish. 2007. 8/yr. adv. **Document type:** *Magazine, Consumer.*
Related titles: Online - full text ed.
Published by: Prier Petersen Publishing I/S, Lilleskovvej 5, Ugerloese, 4350, Denmark. TEL 45-59-172217. Adv. contact Claus Femerling. page DKK 12,000; 210 x 297. Circ: 20,000 (controlled and free).

798 USA ISSN 1930-5796
SF304.5
AMERICAN CARRIAGE DRIVER. Text in English. 2006. q. USD 20 domestic; USD 22 in Canada; USD 32 in United Kingdom (effective 2007). **Document type:** *Magazine, Consumer.*
Published by: American Carriage Driver, LLC, PO Box 25, Foster, RI 02825. TEL 401-647-5702, http://www.acdmag.com/home.html. Ed. Dorothy A Billington.

798.2 USA ISSN 1046-1361
AMERICAN CONNEMARA. Text in English. 1985. bi-m. USD 15 (effective 1999). adv. bk.rev. **Document type:** *Bulletin.* **Description:** Contains articles about the versatile Connemara pony and news from the American Connemara Pony Society.
Published by: American Connemara Pony Society, 32600 Fairmount Blvd., Pepper Pike, OH 44124-4834. FAX 440-442-1060. Ed., Pub., R&P, Adv. contact Patricia Lightbody. Circ: 1,000.

636.1 USA
AMERICAN FARRIER'S ASSOCIATION NEWSLETTER. Text in English. 1977. bi-m. membership. **Document type:** *Newsletter.* **Description:** Contains ongoing information regarding the American Farrier's Association and its activities.
Published by: American Farrier's Association, 4059 Iron Works Pkwy, Ste 2, Lexington, KY 40511. TEL 606-233-7411, FAX 606-231-7862. Ed. Kelly Werner. Circ: 2,500 (paid).

636.1 USA ISSN 0274-6565
AMERICAN FARRIERS JOURNAL. Abbreviated title: A F J. Text in English. 1974. 8/yr. USD 47.95 in North America; USD 79.95 elsewhere (effective 2010). adv. 120 p./no.; back issues avail. **Document type:** *Magazine, Trade.* **Description:** Contains articles on horse anatomy and physiology, leg pathology and therapy, shoeing, and horse handling.
—BLDSC (0814.780000), IE, Ingenta. **CCC.**
Published by: Lessiter Publications, 225 Regency Ct, Ste 200, Brookfield, WI 53045. TEL 262-782-4480, 800-645-8455, FAX 262-782-1252, info@lesspub.com, http://www.lesspub.com/. Ed., Pub. Frank Lessiter. adv.: B&W page USD 1,480, color page USD 2,845.

798 336.2 USA
AMERICAN HORSE COUNCIL TAX BULLETIN. Text in English. 1970. bi-m. free to members (effective 2010). **Document type:** *Bulletin, Trade.* **Description:** Presents reviews tax cases and other tax issues affecting those owning horses as a business.
Published by: American Horse Council, Inc., 1616 H St NW 7th Fl, Washington, DC 20006. TEL 202-296-4031, FAX 202-296-1970, ahc@horsecouncil.org.

636.1 USA ISSN 1538-3490
SF293.Q3
THE AMERICAN QUARTER HORSE JOURNAL. Text in English. 1948. m. USD 25 domestic; USD 50 in Canada; USD 80 elsewhere; USD 4.25 per issue (effective 2010). adv. bk.rev. illus. Index. reprints avail. **Document type:** *Journal, Trade.* **Description:** Covers horse show results, business opportunities, and all other news of interest relevant to the association.
Former titles (until Jun.2001): Quarter Horse Journal (0164-6656); (until 1953): Quarter Horse and the Quarter Horse Journal; Which was formed by the merger of (1948-1949): Quarter Horse Journal; (1946-1949): Quarter Horse
Related titles: Microfiche ed.: (from PQC).
Indexed: PMR.
—Ingenta.
Published by: American Quarter Horse Association, PO Box 200, Amarillo, TX 79168. TEL 806-376-4811. adv.: B&W page USD 1,625, color page USD 2,125; trim 8.25 x 10.5. Circ: 67,000.

798 USA ISSN 0746-6153
THE AMERICAN SADDLEBRED. Text in English. 1983. 5/yr. USD 50 in North America to non-members (effective 2008). adv. bk.rev. illus. index. reprints avail. **Document type:** *Magazine, Consumer.* **Description:** Provides information on equine health, international activities, legal issues, taxes, champions of the breed.
—Ingenta.
Published by: American Saddlebred Horse Association (A S H A), 4093 Iron Works Pike, Lexington, KY 40511. TEL 859-259-2742, FAX 859-259-1628, http://www.asha.net. Circ: 7,200.

791.8 USA
AMERICAN SHETLAND PONY CLUB. JOURNAL; American miniature horse registry. Text in English. 1948. bi-m. USD 30 domestic to members; USD 56 foreign to members (effective 2000). adv. bk.rev. back issues avail. **Document type:** *Journal, Trade.*
Formerly: Pony Journal (0199-5537)
Published by: American Shetland Pony Club, P O Box 887, Warrenville, IL 60555. TEL 630-585-7158, FAX 630-585-0259. Ed. Amy H Roberts. adv.: B&W page USD 135, color page USD 350; 9.75 x 7. Circ: 7,000 (paid).

636.1 USA ISSN 0730-2975
AMERICAN TRAKEHNER. Text in English. 1975. q. USD 20 domestic; USD 30 foreign (effective 2000). adv. back issues avail. **Document type:** *Magazine, Trade.* **Description:** Promotes the Trakehner breed of horse in North America.
Published by: American Trakehner Association, 1514 W. Church St., Newark, OH 43055-1532. TEL 740-344-1111, FAX 740-344-3225. Ed. Helen K Gibble. R&P Charee L Adams. Adv. contact Jim Bishop. Circ: 1,400 (paid). **Dist. by:** 631 N W Tyler Ct, Ste 301, Topeka, KS 66608.

798.4 USA ISSN 0003-1445
AMERICAN TURF MONTHLY. Text in English. 1946. m. USD 42 (effective 2006). adv. bk.rev. illus. **Document type:** *Magazine, Consumer.* **Description:** Helps horseplayers pick winners. Nurtures racing fans along the path to becoming confident handicappers—racetrack investors. Includes articles on angles, the best way to decipher class in thoroughbred, horses to watch, and money management.
Published by: Star Sports Corporation, 747 Middle Neck Rd, Great Neck, NY 11024. TEL 516-773-4075, 800-645-2240, FAX 516-773-2944. Ed., R&P James Corbett. Pub. Allen Hakim. Adv. contact Scott Romick. Circ: 28,000.

636 USA ISSN 1522-8983
SF293.Q3
AMERICA'S HORSE. Text in English. 1998. m. free membership. adv. **Document type:** *Magazine, Consumer.* **Description:** Includes ranch, rodeo and trail ride features as well as historical stories about the horses and people who helped build the Association.
Published by: American Quarter Horse Association, PO Box 200, Amarillo, TX 79168. TEL 806-376-4888, FAX 806-349-6400. adv.: color page USD 13,500; trim 8.25 x 10.625. Circ: 316,994 (paid and controlled).

798 ITA ISSN 1971-1883
AMICO CAVALLO. Text in Italian. 2007. m. **Document type:** *Magazine, Consumer.*
Published by: Sprea Editori Srl, Via Torino 51, Cernusco sul Naviglio, MI 20063, Italy. TEL 39-02-92432222, FAX 39-02-92432236, editori@sprea.it, http://www.sprea.it.

798 USA ISSN 2151-5190
ANDALUSIAN. Text in English. 1991. q. USD 30 to non-members; free to members (effective 2009). adv. back issues avail. **Document type:** *Magazine, Trade.* **Description:** Features news and beautiful pictures of horses.
Published by: (International Andalusian and Lusitano Horse Association), Lionheart Publishing, Inc., 506 Roswell St, Ste 220, Marietta, GA 30060. TEL 770-431-0867, FAX 770-432-6969, lpi@lionhrtpub.com, http://www.lionhrtpub.com. Ed. Sue Weakley TEL 662-238-2833. Adv. contact Aileen Kronke. B&W page USD 350, color page USD 500; bleed 8.75 x 11.125.

798 636.1 SWE ISSN 1653-9117
ANGLO NYTT. Text in Swedish. 2006. q. SEK 210 membership (effective 2007). **Document type:** *Magazine, Consumer.*
Published by: Svenska Angloarabfoereningen, c/o Lena Gaevert, Hinderstorp PL 202, Mullhyttan, 71694, Sweden. TEL 46-585-43272, http://hem.passagen.se/anglo.

798.2 NLD ISSN 0168-3608
SF294.2
L'ANNEE HIPPIQUE; international equestrian yearbook. Text in English, Dutch. 1983. a. EUR 53 (effective 2009). adv. illus. **Document type:** *Yearbook, Consumer.* **Description:** Reports the equestrian highlights of the preceding year.
Published by: (Federation Equestre Internationale), BCM Publishing, Postbus 245, Best, 5680 AE, Netherlands. bcm@bcm.nl, http://www.bcm.nl. Ed. Denise van der Net. Adv. contact Inge van der Net. B&W page EUR 3,325, color page EUR 4,807; 233 x 320. Circ: 44,000 (paid).

636.1 USA ISSN 0892-385X
APPALOOSA JOURNAL. Text in English. 1946. m. USD 39.95 domestic (effective 2008). adv. stat.; tr.lit. 2 cols./p.; back issues avail. **Document type:** *Magazine, Trade.* **Description:** Promotes the breed; provides informative articles; presents features and profiles that show all facets of the breed's talents.
Formerly: Appaloosa News (0003-665X)
Related titles: Microform ed.: (from PQC); Online - full text ed.
Indexed: A22.
—Ingenta.
Published by: Appaloosa Horse Club, 2720 W Pullman Rd, Moscow, ID 83843-0903. TEL 208-882-5578, FAX 208-882-8150, http://www.appaloosa.com. Ed., R&P Diane Rice. Pub. Roger Klamfoth. Adv. contact Katie Elliott. Circ: 21,340 (paid and free).

791.8 USA ISSN 0273-6519
SF293.A3
APPALOOSA WORLD. Text in English. 1980. m. index. back issues avail.
Address: Drawer 291310, Dayton Beach, FL 32029. TEL 904-767-6284. Ed. Gerald A Matacale.

798 USA
APPLES 'N OATS. Text in English. 1997. irreg. USD 10 (effective 2001). **Document type:** *Newsletter.* **Description:** Designed for Iowa equestrians; includes horse activities, news, rodeos, hunts, contests and other related activities.
Address: 5070 Northridge Pt SE, Cedar Rapids, IA 52403. TEL 319-365-7314, FAX 319-364-6548. Ed. Carol Eilers.

798 GBR ISSN 1746-3386
ARAB HORSE STUD BOOK. Text in English. 1919. quadrennial, latest vol.20. GBP 40 per vol. (effective 2009). adv. **Document type:** *Handbook/Manual/Guide, Trade.*
Published by: Arab Horse Society, Windsor House, The Square, Ramsbury, Marlborough, Wilts SN8 2PE, United Kingdom. TEL 44-1672-521411, FAX 44-1672-520880, areeves@reevesfinancial.co.uk, http://www.arabhorsesociety.com.

798 DEU ISSN 1614-192X
ARABER WELTWEIT. Text in German. 2004. bi-m. EUR 33.90 domestic; EUR 37.50 foreign; EUR 6.30 newsstand/cover (effective 2011). adv. **Document type:** *Magazine, Consumer.*
Incorporates (1984-2007): Araber Journal (0177-591X); Which incorporated (1979-1993): Arabische Pferde (0721-5169); (1990-1994): Arabian Horse Europe (0938-118X)

S

Published by: Paul Parey Zeitschriftenverlag GmbH, Erich Kaestner Str 2, Singhofen, 56379, Germany. TEL 49-2604-9780, FAX 49-2604-978190, online@paulparey.de, http://www.paulparey.de. Ed. Susanne Hennig. Adv. contact Guido Augustin.

636.1 USA
ARABIAN HORSE COUNTRY. Text in English. 1981. m. USD 20. bk.rev. reprints avail.
Published by: BeAnCa Publications, 4346 S E Division St, Portland, OR 97206. Circ: 39,504.

636.121 USA ISSN 0194-6803
SF293.A8
ARABIAN HORSE EXPRESS. Text in English. 1978. m. USD 25. bk.rev. **Document type:** *Magazine, Consumer.*
Address: 512 Green Bay Rd, Kenilworth, IL 60043-1073. TEL 847-256-7111, 800-533-9734, FAX 847-256-5898. Eds. Julie Kohn, Maureen Spurr. Pub. Frederick Goss. Circ: 7,500.

798.2 AUS ISSN 1445-9191
ARABIAN HORSE EXPRESS. Text in English. 1994. bi-m. AUD 21 domestic; AUD 32 in Asia & the Pacific; AUD 42 elsewhere (effective 2009). adv. **Document type:** *Magazine, Trade.* **Description:** Provides educational articles, show results, industry news and profiles of farms and horses.
Formerly (until 1996): Australian Arabian Horse Express (1329-7872)
Published by: Vink Publishing, PO Box 8369, Woolloongabba, QLD 4102, Australia. TEL 61-7-33348000, FAX 61-7-33915118, sue@vinkpub.com, http://www.vinkpub.com/. Ed. Sharon Meyers. Pub. Michael . Adv. contact Julie Russell TEL 61-7-33348008. B&W page AUD 352, color page AUD 660; trim 210 x 297.

798 USA ISSN 1545-6706
THE ARABIAN HORSE NEWSPAPER. Text in English. 1986. m. USD 15 (effective 2003). adv.
Formerly (until 1989): Arabian Newspaper
Published by: Arabian Resources, Inc., P. O. Box 380, Dublin, TX 76446-0380. TEL 254-785-2251, FAX 254-785-2252. Pub. Joanna Friebele.

798.4 USA ISSN 0279-8425
SF293.A8
ARABIAN HORSE TIMES. Text in English. 1970. m. USD 25. adv. bk.rev. **Document type:** *Magazine, Consumer.*
Published by: Adams Corp., 1050 8th St, N E, Waseca, MN 56093. TEL 507-835-3204, FAX 507-835-5138. Ed. Lynn Wright. Circ: 25,000.

636.1 USA ISSN 0003-7494
SF293.A8
ARABIAN HORSE WORLD; the magazine for owners, breeders and admirers of fine horses. Abbreviated title: A H W. Text in English. 1960. m. USD 40 domestic; USD 72 in Canada; USD 88 elsewhere (effective 2008). adv. bk.rev. illus. Index. back issues avail.; reprints avail. **Document type:** *Magazine, Consumer.* **Description:** Contains reports on horse shows, races and endurance events, as well as profiles on top breeders.
Related titles: Online - full text ed.
Indexed: B04, G06, G07, G08, H20, I05, I07, R03, RGAb, RGPR, W03, W05.
—CCC.
Published by: Source Interlink Companies, 1316 Tamson Dr, Ste 101, Cambria, CA 93428. TEL 805-771-2300, 800-955-9423, FAX 805-927-6522, dheine@sourceinterlink.com, http://www.sourceinterlinkmedia.com. Ed. Mary Jane Parkinson. Pub. Denise Hearst. adv.: B&W page USD 620, color page USD 1,385; bleed 8.125 x 10.75. Circ: 7,117.

798.2 AUS
ARABIAN STUDS & STALLIONS. Text in English. 1972. a. adv. bk.rev. back issues avail. **Document type:** *Journal, Trade.* **Description:** Contains stallion and client profiles, show reports, and educational articles.
Former titles (until 1987): Arabian Studs and Stallions Magazine (1324-9517); (until 1978): Arabian Stallions and Studs
Published by: Vink Publishing, PO Box 8369, Woolloongabba, QLD 4102, Australia. TEL 61-7-33348000, sue@vinkpub.com, http://www.vinkpub.com/. Ed. Sharon Meyers. Pub. Michael . Adv. contact Julie Russell TEL 61-7-33348008. B&W page AUD 435, color page AUD 765; trim 215 x 302.

798.2 USA
ARIZONA HORSE CONNECTION. Text in English. 1987. m. USD 15 (effective 2001). adv. back issues avail. **Document type:** *Magazine, Consumer.* **Description:** For all horse enthusiasts; features articles on ranches, trainers, horses of notable interest, and all types of riding disciplines.
Published by: Arizona Horse Connection, Inc., 14821 E Chandler Heights Rd, Chandler, AZ 85249. TEL 480-895-1870, FAX 602-530-4504. Ed., R&P, Adv. contact Patti E Trueba. Circ: 10,000.

798.2 USA
ASIDE WORLD. Text in English. 1974. bi-m. free to members (effective 2008). adv. bk.rev. index. back issues avail. **Document type:** *Magazine, Consumer.*
Formerly: Side-Saddle News (0744-3056)
Indexed: SD, SportS.
Published by: International Side-Saddle Organization, PO Box 161, Stevensville, MD 21666-0161. Info@sidesaddle.com, http://www.sidesaddle.org. Ed. Carol D Swanby. R&P Carol Swandby. adv.: B&W page USD 240. Circ: 450 (paid).

636.1 COL ISSN 2011-1428
ASOARABES. Text in Spanish. 2007. s-a.
Published by: Asociacion Colombiana de Criadores de Caballos Arabes, Calle 75 No. 14-37, Bogota, Colombia. TEL 57-1-5417390, FAX 57-1-3215763, asoarabes@usa.edu.co, http://www.unaga.org.co/asociados/arabes.htm.

798 ESP ISSN 2173-4682
▼ **ASSOCIACIO DE CRIADOS I PROPIETARIS DE CAVALS DE RACA MENORQUINA. ANUARI.** Text in Catalan. 2009. a. **Document type:** *Monographic series, Academic/Scholarly.*
Published by: Associacio de Criadors i Propietaris de Cavalls de Raca de Menorca, C bijuters, 17, Ciutadella de Menorca, 07760, Spain. TEL 34-971-480916, http://www.cavalls-menorca.com/index.php.

636.1 798 CAN
ASSOCIATION QUEBECOISE DU CHEVAL CANADIEN. JOURNAL. Text in French. 1999. q. **Document type:** *Magazine, Consumer.*
Published by: Association Quebecoise du Cheval Canadien, 15 Route Principale, Riviere-Eternite, PQ G0V 1P0, Canada. TEL 418-272-1264, FAX 418-272-1862, contact@chevalcanadien.org.

798.2 CAN ISSN 1182-5472
ATLANTIC HORSE & PONY. Text in English. 1987. bi-m. CAD 20 domestic; USD 30 foreign; USD 3.50 newsstand/cover (effective 2011). adv. bk.rev. **Document type:** *Magazine, Trade.* **Description:** For horse and pony owners, trainers and enthusiasts in the Atlantic region.
Formerly (until 1989): Eastern Horse and Pony (0848-8444)
Related titles: Online - full text ed.
Published by: D v L Publishing, PO Box 1509, Liverpool, NS B0T 1K0, Canada. TEL 902-354-5411, 877-354-3764, http://www.countrymagazines.com. Ed. Anne Gray. Pub. Dirk van Loon. Adv. contact Janie Smith-Clattenberg. Circ: 4,000.

798.4 CAN ISSN 0226-627X
ATLANTIC POST CALLS. Text in English. 1979. 40/yr. CAD 53.75 (effective 1999). adv. **Document type:** *Newsletter, Trade.*
—CCC.
Published by: Transcontinental Media, Inc., Cumberland Publishing Ltd. (Subsidiary of: Transcontinental, Inc.), 1100 Blvd Rene Levesque W, 24th Fl, Montreal, PQ H3B 4X9, Canada. TEL 514-392-9000, FAX 514-392-1489, info@transcontinental.ca, http://www.transcontinental-gtc.com/en/home.html. Ed., Adv. contact Doug Harkness. R&P Earl Gouchie. Circ: 1,800.

798 FRA ISSN 2112-1494
▼ **ATOUT CHEVAL.** Text in French. 2010. m. **Document type:** *Magazine, Consumer.*
Published by: Volta Sport, 109-111 Av. Gambetta, Paris, 75020, France. TEL 33-1-43152626, FAX 33-1-43664023, contact@volta-sports.com, http://www.volta-sports.com.

636.1 DEU
AUSGEWAEHLTE HENGSTE DEUTSCHLANDS; ein Jahrbuch der Hengste. Text in German. 1994. irreg., latest vol.10, 2010. EUR 70 per issue (effective 2011). **Document type:** *Handbook/Manual/Guide, Trade.*
Published by: FORUM Zeitschriften und Spezialmedien GmbH (Subsidiary of: FORUM Media Group GmbH), Mandichostr 18, Merching, 86504, Germany. TEL 49-8233-381361, FAX 49-8233-381212, service@forum-zeitschriften.de, http://www.forum-zeitschriften.de.

798.4 AUS
AUSTRALIA & NEW ZEALAND'S TURF MONTHLY. Text in English. 1951. m. AUD 121 domestic; AUD 132 in New Zealand; AUD 200 in Asia & the Pacific; AUD 250 elsewhere (effective 2009). adv. bk.rev. back issues avail. **Document type:** *Magazine, Consumer.* **Description:** Covers all aspects of horse racing: breeding, punting, personalities and topicalities.
Former titles (until 2007): Australasian Turf Monthly (1447-3925); (until Mar.2002): Turf Monthly (0726-8254)
Related titles: Online - full text ed.
Published by: Turf Monthly Pty. Ltd., 206 Kelly St, PO Box 486, Scone, NSW 2337, Australia. TEL 61-2-65459444, FAX 61-2-65459466. Ed. Paul Vettise TEL 64-6-3484902. Adv. contacts Paul Vettise TEL 64-6-3484902, Warren Wruck.

798.2 AUS ISSN 0727-4092
AUSTRALIAN ARABIAN HORSE NEWS. Abbreviated title: A H N. Text in English. 1967. q. AUD 26 domestic; AUD 50 in Asia & the Pacific; AUD 62 elsewhere (effective 2009). adv. bk.rev. back issues avail. **Document type:** *Magazine, Trade.* **Description:** Covers local and overseas shows, veterinary articles, horse and farm profiles, management practices and photographic forums.
Former titles (until 1976): Arabian Horse News (0312-0791); (until 1974): Arab Horse News (0312-0783)
Published by: (Australian Arabian Society), Vink Publishing, PO Box 8369, Woolloongabba, QLD 4102, Australia. TEL 61-7-33348000, FAX 61-7-33915118, sue@vinkpub.com, http://www.vinkpub.com/. Ed. Sharon Meyers. Pub. Michael . Adv. contact Julie Russell TEL 61-7-33348008. B&W page AUD 435, color page AUD 765; trim 210 x 297.

798 AUS ISSN 1834-0091
AUSTRALIAN CAMPDRAFTING MAGAZINE. Text in English. 2006. bi-m. **Document type:** *Magazine, Consumer.*
Published by: Sue Jones Campdrafting Promotions, PO Box 51, Willow Tree, NSW 2339, Australia. Pub. Sue Jones.

798 AUS ISSN 1833-0886
AUSTRALIAN HORSEWYSE. Variant title: Horsewyse. Text in English. 2001. q. AUD 26 domestic; AUD 52 includes USA, Canada, England, Europe & South Africa; AUD 43 includes New Zealand, Hong Kong, Norfolk Island, Asia Pacific & Fiji (effective 2009). adv. back issues avail. **Document type:** *Magazine, Consumer.* **Description:** Contains instructional articles, fiction, pen-pals, activities for all ages, competitions, the Official Saddle Club Fan Club, lift-out poster, cartoons, breed FAQ and more.
Formerly (until 2001): Horsewyse (1445-1794); Incorporates (2003-2006): Filly (1448-2401)
Related titles: Online - full text ed.
Published by: Filly & Horsewyse Magazines, Knox City Centre, PO Box 4144, Wantirna South, VIC 3152, Australia. TEL 61-3-98016800, FAX 61-3-98874898. Ed. Vicki Sach. adv.: page AUD 660; 185 x 250.

636.1 AUS ISSN 1446-5132
AUSTRALIAN PERFORMANCE HORSE. Text in English. 1968. bi-m. AUD 35 (effective 2008). adv. bk.rev.
Former titles (until 2001): Australian Quarter Horse and Western Breeds Magazine (1440-074X); (until 1995): Australian Quarter Horse Magazine
Published by: (Australian Quarter Horse Association), Prestige Publications, PO Box 8337, Woolloongabba, QLD 4102, Australia. TEL 61-7-38911299, FAX 61-7-33914033, enquiries@prespub.com. Ed. Janine Leichsenring. adv.: page AUD 550; trim 210 x 297.

798 AUS ISSN 1832-1704
AUSTRALIAN QUARTER HORSE NEWS. Text in English. 2002. 11/yr. AUD 69.50 to non-members; free to members (effective 2008). adv. **Document type:** *Magazine, Trade.*
Published by: Australian Quarter Horse Association, 131 Gunnedah Rd, PO Box 979, Tamworth, NSW 2340, Australia. TEL 61-2-67626444, FAX 61-2-67626422, qhorse@aqha.com.au. Eds. Jenna Bignell, Tara Gordon. adv.: color page AUD 620; 210 x 297. Circ: 6,000.

798.2 AUS ISSN 0817-8550
AUSTRALIAN STOCK HORSE JOURNAL. Abbreviated title: A S H Journal. Text in English. 1975. bi-m. AUD 60 (effective 2008). adv. **Document type:** *Journal, Consumer.* **Description:** Provides information and articles relevant to Australian Stock Horse lovers.
Formerly (until 1985): Australian Stock Horse (0314-9056)
Published by: Australian Stock Horse Society, 48 Guernsey St, PO Box 288, Scone, NSW 2337, Australia. TEL 61-2-65451122, FAX 61-2-65452165, info@ashs.com.au. Adv. contact Amanda Albury TEL 61-2-65451122. color page AUD 886; 220 x 307. Circ: 6,500 (controlled).

798 AUS ISSN 1832-0295
AUSTRALIAN THOROUGHBRED RECORD. Text in English. 2004. a. **Document type:** *Journal, Consumer.*
Formed by the merger of (1978-2003): Australian Thoroughbred Statistical Record (0157-8588); (199?-2003): Australian Race Results (0155-6231); Which was formerly (1882-1996): Victorian Racing Calendar
Published by: Racing Information Services Australia Pty. Ltd., Level 1 Racing Ctr,, 400 Epsom Rd,, Flemington, VIC 3031, Australia. TEL 61-3-92584711, FAX 61-3-92584273, customerservice@risa.com.au, http://www.risa.com.au.

798 CAN ISSN 1913-3545
B C'S HORSE COMMUNITY GUIDE; the annual consumer's guide to British Columbia's horse community. Text in English. 2007. a. **Document type:** *Magazine, Consumer.*
Published by: Horse Community Journals Inc., P O Box 2190, Sidney, BC V8L 3S8, Canada. TEL 250-655-8883, FAX 250-655-8913, editor@horsejournals.com.

798.2 DEU ISSN 0174-0512
BAYERNS PFERDE ZUCHT UND SPORT; Reiten - Pferdepraxis - Fahren. Text in German. 1980. m. EUR 66.60 domestic; EUR 73.70 foreign; EUR 6.50 newsstand/cover (effective 2009). adv. **Document type:** *Magazine, Consumer.*
Related titles: Online - full text ed.
—CCC.
Published by: Deutscher Landwirtschaftsverlag GmbH, Lothstr 29, Munich, 80797, Germany. TEL 49-89-127051, FAX 49-89-12705335, dlv.muenchen@dlv.de, http://www.dlv.de. Ed. Annegret Strehle. Adv. contact Henning Stemmler. B&W page EUR 1,868, color page EUR 3,186; trim 216 x 303. Circ: 13,331 (paid and controlled).

798.2 DEU
▼ **BELLA SARA**; Dein fantastisches Pferdemagazin!. Text in German. 2010. bi-m. EUR 2.99 newsstand/cover (effective 2011). adv. **Document type:** *Magazine, Consumer.*
Published by: Blue Ocean Entertainment AG, Breitscheidstr 6, Stuttgart, 70174, Germany. TEL 49-711-22021790, FAX 49-711-22021799, leserservice@blue-ocean-ag.de. Circ: 42,590 (paid).

798.4 NZL
BEST BETS. Text in English. s-w. adv. **Document type:** *Newspaper, Consumer.* **Description:** Provides horse racing information in New Zealand for people interest in horse racing/sports betting.
Published by: Fairfax Media (Subsidiary of: John Fairfax Holdings Ltd.), 155 New North Rd, Eden Terrace, PO Box 1327, Auckland, New Zealand. TEL 64-9-3021300, FAX 64-9-3664565. Ed., Adv. contact Alan Caddy TEL 64-9-3021300. Circ: 45,000.

798 NLD ISSN 1383-8342
BIT (DOETINCHEM); maandblad voor de paardenhouder. Text in Dutch. 1995. 10/yr. EUR 59.50; EUR 6.75 newsstand/cover (effective 2009). adv. **Document type:** *Magazine, Trade.* **Description:** Includes articles and reports on breeding and care of horses, equestrian sport, and devotes attention to all horse and pony breeds.
Published by: Reed Business bv (Subsidiary of: Reed Business), Hanzestraat 1, Doetinchem, 7006 RH, Netherlands. TEL 31-314-349911, FAX 31-314-343839, info@reedbusiness.nl, http://www.reedbusiness.nl. Ed. Dr. Marjan Tulp. adv.: B&W page EUR 1,266, color page EUR 1,941; trim 230 x 297. Circ: 22,165.

636.1 USA ISSN 1050-5741
BIT AND BRIDLE (NATIONAL EDITION). Text in English. 1964. m. USD 19 (effective 2007). adv. bk.rev. charts. **Document type:** *Newspaper, Consumer.*
Formerly (until Mar. 1989): Midwest Bridle and Bit (0006-3851); Incorporates: Separator
Related titles: Online - full content ed.; Regional ed(s).: Bit and Bridle (Arizona Edition); Supplement(s): Horse Property; Bit and Bridle (Directory Edition).
Published by: Bit and Bridle, 15203 N. Cave Creek Rd., Phoenix, AZ 85032. TEL 602-788-5108, 602-788-7100, FAX 602-788-3572. Ed. Wager Tracy. Pub. Rex Wager. Circ: 4,000.

636.1 798.4 USA ISSN 0006-4998
SF277
THE BLOOD-HORSE. Text in English. 1916. w. USD 99 domestic (effective 2008). adv. bk.rev. charts; illus.; stat. index. reprints avail. **Document type:** *Magazine, Consumer.* **Description:** Covers thoroughbred horse breeding and racing.
Related titles: Microform ed.: (from PQC).
Indexed: A22, SPI.
—Ingenta, Linda Hall.
Published by: (Thoroughbred Owners and Breeders Association), The Blood-Horse, Inc., PO Box 4030, Lexington, KY 40544. TEL 859-278-2361, FAX 859-276-4450. Ed. Raymond S Paulick. Pub. Stacy V Bearse. Adv. contact Jim Cox. Circ: 24,000 (paid).

798.2 USA ISSN 1068-8676
BLUEGRASS HORSEMAN. Text in English. 1972. s-m. USD 20 (effective 2000). adv. back issues avail. **Document type:** *Magazine, Trade.* **Description:** For owners, trainers, and horse show managers of American Saddlebred, Roadster, and Hackney horses and ponies.
Published by: Saddle Horse, Inc., PO Box 389, Lexington, KY 40585. TEL 606-258-9420, FAX 606-258-9422. Ed., Pub., Adv. contact Keith Cupp. B&W page USD 355; trim 13 x 10. Circ: 5,000 (paid).

798 USA ISSN 1523-7370
THE BRAYER; journal of the American donkey and mule society. Text in English. 1968. bi-m. USD 23 domestic membership; USD 30 in Canada membership; USD 35 elsewhere membership (effective 2007). adv. bk.rev.; video rev.; software rev. tr.lit.; illus. 112 p./no. 2 cols./p.; back issues avail.; reprints avail. **Document type:** *Journal, Trade.* **Description:** For owners and fanciers of donkeys and mules. Includes articles on the care, training and uses of these animals as well as international coverage, activities, history, art and photos.

Published by: American Donkey and Mule Society, Inc., PO Box 1210, Lewisville, TX 75067. TEL 972-219-0781, FAX 972-420-9980, adms@juno.com, http://www.lovelongears.com/. Ed. Lean Patton. adv.: B&W page USD 175; trim 11 x 8.5. Circ: 4,000 (paid).

798 GBR
BRITISH DRESSAGE. Abbreviated title: B D. Text in English. 1995. bi-m. free to members (effective 2010). adv. back issues avail. **Document type:** *Magazine, Consumer.* **Description:** Contains dressage schedules and results along with other information for members of the Dressage Group.
Formerly (until 2000): Dressage News
Published by: (British Dressage), Mannin Media Group Ltd., Media House, Cronkbourne, Douglas, Isle of Man, IM4 4SB, United Kingdom. TEL 44-1624-696565, FAX 44-1624-625623, mail@manninmedia.co.im, http://www.manninmedia.co.im. Circ: 9,500.

798 GBR ISSN 1466-9331
BRITISH EQUESTRIAN DIRECTORY. Text in English. 1979. a. adv. Supplement avail. **Document type:** *Directory, Trade.* **Description:** Lists 20,000 breeders, retailers, riding schools, vets, farriers, trainers and holidays in Great Britain.
Former titles (until 1999): British Horse World (1367-2428); (until 1996): British Equestrian Directory (0144-7203); Which incorporated: Changes: An Editorial Update of Important Equestrian Developments
Published by: Equestrian Management Consultants Ltd., Stockeld Park, Wetherby, West Yorkshire LS22 4AW, United Kingdom. FAX 44-1937-582778, sales@beta-int.com, 44-1937-582111.

798 GBR
BRITISH HORSE. Text in English. 1985. bi-m. free to members (effective 2010). adv. **Document type:** *Magazine, Trade.* **Description:** Contains news and views of activities of the British Horse Society. Advice and help to horse owners and riders.
Formerly (until 1992): Horseshoe
Published by: British Horse Society, Stoneleigh Deer Park, Kenilworth, Warks CV8 2XZ, United Kingdom. TEL 44-844-8481666, FAX 44-1926-707800, communications@bhs.org.uk.

798 GBR
BRITISH HORSE SOCIETY MEMBERS' HANDBOOK. Text in English. 1967. a. free to members (effective 2010). adv. **Document type:** *Directory, Trade.*
Former titles (until 19??): British Horse Society Members' Year Book (0951-1776); (until 1987): British Horse Society Year Book (0269-1000); (until 1983): British Horse Society Year Book and Diary (0068-2063)
Published by: British Horse Society, Stoneleigh Deer Park, Kenilworth, Warks CV8 2XZ, United Kingdom. TEL 44-844-8481666, FAX 44-1926-707800, communications@bhs.org.uk, http://www.bhs.org.uk. Circ: 56,000.

798.2 GBR ISSN 0969-5575
BRITISH HORSE SOCIETY. REGISTER OF INSTRUCTORS. Text in English. 1991. a. free to members (effective 2010). **Document type:** *Directory, Trade.*
—CCC.
Published by: British Horse Society, Stoneleigh Deer Park, Kenilworth, Warks CV8 2XZ, United Kingdom. TEL 44-844-8481666, FAX 44-1926-707800, communications@bhs.org.uk.

798.021 GBR
BRITISH RACING STATISTICS (YEARS). Text in English. 1987. a. back issues avail. **Document type:** *Journal, Trade.*
Formerly (until 2003): The Racing Industry Statistical Bureau Statistics (Year)
Related titles: Online - full text ed.: free (effective 2010).
Published by: (British Horseracing Board), Weatherbys Group Limited, Sanders Rd, Wellingborough, Northants NN8 4BX, United Kingdom. TEL 44-1933-440077, FAX 44-1933-440807, ihelp@weatherbys.co.uk, http://www.weatherbys.co.uk.

798 USA
CALIFORNIA HORSEMAN'S DIRECTORY. Text in English. 1990. a. adv. **Document type:** *Directory.*
Published by: Riding Publications, Inc., 9131 Chesapeake Dr, San Diego, CA 92123. TEL 858-503-7872, FAX 858-268-0397. Pub. Cheryl Erpelding. adv.: B&W page USD 2,177, color page USD 3,418; 7.5 x 9.75. Circ: 36,000 (free).

798 USA
CALIFORNIA RIDING MAGAZINE. Text in English. 1990. m. adv. **Document type:** *Magazine, Consumer.* **Description:** Contains information on local riders, training articles, events in the back country, and a calendar of upcoming events and horse shows.
Published by: (California Dressage Society, San Diego Chapter), Riding Publications, Inc., 9131 Chesapeake Dr, San Diego, CA 92123. TEL 858-503-7872, FAX 858-268-0397. Pub. Cheryl Erpelding. adv.: B&W page USD 516, color page USD 972; trim 8.875 x 11.25. Circ: 20,000.

636.1 798 USA ISSN 1092-7328
SF293.T5
CALIFORNIA THOROUGHBRED. Text in English. 1941. m. USD 45 (effective 2005). adv. bk.rev. charts; illus. Index. reprints avail. **Document type:** *Magazine, Trade.*
Formerly: Thoroughbred of California (0049-3821)
Related titles: Microform ed.: (from PQC).
—Ingenta.
Published by: California Thoroughbred Breeders Association, 201 Colorado Pl, Arcadia, CA 91007. TEL 800-573-2822, FAX 818-574-0852. Adv. contact Deanna Sparks-Kjorlien. Circ: 3,500 (paid).

636.1 CAN ISSN 0008-2864
CANADIAN ARABIAN NEWS. Text in English. 1960. q. CAD 26.75 domestic (effective 1999); CAD 6.25 newsstand/cover; USD 32 in United States; CAD 49.50 elsewhere (effective 1999). adv. bk.rev. illus. **Document type:** *Magazine, Consumer.* **Description:** For purebred and partbred Arabian owners and enthusiasts. Includes articles on bloodlines, Arabians and their trainers-owners, horse health, show results and training.
Indexed: SportS.
Published by: Canadian Arabian Horse Registry, 801 Terrace Plz, 4445 Calgary Tr S, Edmonton, AB T6H 5R7, Canada. TEL 780-436-4244, FAX 780-438-2971. Ed., Adv. contact Peggy Arthurs. B&W page CAD 310; 7.5 x 9.5. Circ: 2,200.

798 CAN
CANADIAN EQUINE. Text in English. 1996. 6/yr. CAD 12, USD 18 (effective 1998). **Document type:** *Magazine, Consumer.* **Description:** Information geared toward the English rider.
Published by: Dakota Design and Advertising, Bay 114, 3907-3A St N E, Calgary, AB T2E 6S7, Canada. FAX 403-250-1194, dka@telusplanet.net. Ed. Ingrid Schulz. Circ: 7,000.

636.1 CAN ISSN 0382-5795
CANADIAN HACKNEY STUD BOOK. Text in English. 1905. irreg. adv. illus.
Published by: Canadian Hackney Society, c/o Canadian Livestock Records Corporation, Ottawa, ON K1V 0M7, Canada. TEL 613-731-7110.

798.2 CAN
THE CANADIAN HORSE ANNUAL. Text in English. 1985. a. CAD 7.95 (effective 1999). adv. back issues avail. **Document type:** *Directory, Consumer.*
Formerly: Directory of the Canadian Horse Industry (0831-5183)
Related titles: ◆ Supplement to: Canadian Horseman. ISSN 0840-6200; ◆ Supplement to: Canadian Thoroughbred. ISSN 0830-0593.
Indexed: SD.
Published by: Horse Publications, 225 Industrial Pkwy S, P O Box 670, Aurora, ON L4G 4J9, Canada. TEL 905-727-0107, FAX 905-841-1530. Ed., Pub. Susan J Anstey. R&P Susan Stafford. Adv. contact Ron Faragher. Circ: 20,000.

798 CAN ISSN 1496-1733
CANADIAN HORSE JOURNAL. Text in English. 2000. bi-m. **Document type:** *Magazine, Consumer.*
Indexed: SD.
Published by: Horse Community Journals Inc., P O Box 2190, Sidney, BC V8L 3S8, Canada. TEL 250-655-8883, FAX 250-655-8913, editor@horsejournals.com.

636.1 CAN ISSN 1924-8636
CANADIAN HORSE JOURNAL (PACIFIC AND PRAIRIE EDITION). Text in English. 1999. 11/yr. CAD 27 to non-members; CAD 19 to members (effective 2011). adv. **Document type:** *Magazine, Consumer.* **Description:** Features local news, commentary, and a calendar of events, relevant to the horse community from BC to Manitoba.
Formerly (until 2010): Pacific & Prairie Horse Journal (1704-7978)
Published by: Horse Community Journals Inc., 201-2400 Bevan Ave, Sidney, BC V8L 1W1, Canada. TEL 250-655-8883, 800-299-3799, FAX 250-655-8913, sales@horsejournals.com.

791.8 CAN ISSN 0317-7785
CANADIAN RODEO NEWS. Text in English. 1964. m. CAD 21.40, USD 20 domestic; CAD 30 foreign; CAD 1.80 newsstand/cover (effective 2000). adv. bk.rev. **Document type:** *Newspaper.* **Description:** Promotion of professional rodeo in Canada.
Indexed: SportS.
Published by: (Canadian Professional Rodeo Association), Canadian Rodeo News Ltd., 223 2116 27th Ave N E, Calgary, AB T2E 7A6, Canada. TEL 403-250-7292, FAX 403-250-6926, rodeonews@iul-ccs.com. Ed. Lisa Cannady. R&P Vicki Mowat. Adv. contact Jennifer James. B&W page CAD 520; trim 13.75 x 10.625. Circ: 4,800.

791.8 CAN ISSN 0008-5073
CANADIAN SPORTSMAN (ONTARIO). Text in English. 1870. fortn. CAD 52 domestic; USD 65 in United States; CAD 120 foreign (effective 2000). adv. back issues avail. **Document type:** *Journal, Trade.*
Published by: Canadian Sportsman, 25 Old Plank Rd, P O Box 129, Straffordville, ON N0J 1Y0, Canada. TEL 519-866-5558, FAX 519-866-5596. Ed. Dave Briggs. Pub., R&P Gary Foerster. Adv. contact Wilma Haskett. Circ: 6,500.

798.4 CAN ISSN 0830-0593
CODEN: IRCCEP
CANADIAN THOROUGHBRED; journal of racing and breeding. Text in English. 1964. 6/yr. CAD 39.95 domestic; CAD 42.94 Atlantic; USD 49.95 elsewhere; CAD 5 newsstand/cover (effective 2000). adv. bk.rev. charts; pat.; stat.; tr.lit. index. back issues avail. **Document type:** *Journal, Consumer.* **Description:** Covers Canadian racing and breeding statistics, major races and profiles.
Former titles: Thoroughbred Review; Canadian Horse (0008-378X)
Related titles: ◆ Supplement(s): The Canadian Horse Annual.
Indexed: H20, SD, SportS.
Published by: Horse Publications, 225 Industrial Pkwy S, P O Box 670, Aurora, ON L4G 4J9, Canada. TEL 905-727-0107, FAX 905-841-1530, horsepower@horsenet.com. Ed., R&P Lee Benson. Pub. Susan Jane Anstey. Adv. contact Shirley Gill. B&W page CAD 1,150, color page CAD 2,045. Circ: 2,200 (paid).

798 BEL ISSN 1781-6718
CAP; het grootste paardenmagazine van Vlaanderen. Text in Dutch. 2003. m. (11/yr.). EUR 49.80; EUR 5.60 newsstand/cover (effective 2009). adv. **Document type:** *Magazine, Consumer.*
Published by: CAP Publishing NV, Sint-Jorisstr 20, Brugge, 8000, Belgium. TEL 32-50-368899, FAX 32-50-368890, info@cappublishing.net. Ed. Dorien van Dijk. Adv. contact Luc Van Isterdael. B&W page EUR 940, color page EUR 1,105; 240 x 320. Circ: 13,000.

798 GBR ISSN 0958-1820
CARRIAGE DRIVING. Text in English. 1986. m. GBP 41.40 domestic to individuals; EUR 75.60 in Europe to individuals; USD 131.40 elsewhere to individuals (effective 2009). adv. bk.rev. charts; illus. back issues avail. **Document type:** *Magazine, Consumer.* **Description:** Covers all types of carriage driving and related subjects.
Published by: Willingdon Management Ltd., Jesses Farm, Snow Hill, Dinton, Salisbury, Wiltshire SP3 5HN, United Kingdom. TEL 44-1722-716996, FAX 44-1722-716926. Ed. Richard James. Adv. contact Claire Burden TEL 44-1722-717021. page GBP 900; 186 x 255.

798.2 USA ISSN 0899-756X
CASCADE HORSEMAN. Text in English. 1986. m. USD 14.95 (effective 2005). adv. **Document type:** *Magazine, Trade.* **Description:** West Coast horse industry publication.
Published by: (Klamath Publishing), Pioneer Newspaper, 1301 Esplanade, Klamath Fall, OR 97601. TEL 541-885-4460, FAX 541-885-4447. Pub. John Walker. adv.: B&W page USD 460, color page USD 680. Circ: 10,000 (paid).

798.2 FRA ISSN 1959-7428
CAVALIERE. Text in French. 2006. bi-m. **Document type:** *Magazine, Consumer.*
Published by: Editions Riva, 16 Rue de la Fontaine-au-Roi, Paris, 75011, France.

798 ITA ISSN 1121-3809
CAVALLI E CAVALIERI. Text in Italian. 1989. m. EUR 42 (effective 2008). **Document type:** *Magazine, Consumer.*
Published by: Mio Cavallo, Via Giovanni Battista Pergolesi, 8, Milan, MI 20124, Italy. TEL 39-02-66715150, FAX 39-02-66715171.

798 DEU ISSN 1430-9270
CAVALLO; das Magazin fuer aktives Reiten. Text in German. 1996. m. EUR 42.50; EUR 3.90 newsstand/cover (effective 2011). adv. bk.rev. back issues avail. **Document type:** *Magazine, Consumer.* **Description:** Latest news on how to keep, feed, care for, manage and train horses.
Related titles: Online - full text ed.
Published by: Motor Presse Stuttgart GmbH & Co. KG (Subsidiary of: Gruner + Jahr AG & Co), Leuschnerstr 1, Stuttgart, 70174, Germany. TEL 49-711-18201, FAX 49-711-1821779, cgolla@motorpresse.de, http://www.motorpresse.de. Ed. Christine Felsinger. Adv. contact Michael Mueller. Circ: 70,353 (paid).

CAVALLO MAGAZINE; mensile di natura, politica e cultura. *see* ANIMAL WELFARE

798 BRA
CAVALOS DE RACA E ESPORTE. Text in Portuguese. 2000. m. BRL 6.90 newsstand/cover (effective 2006). adv. **Document type:** *Magazine, Consumer.*
Formerly: Cavalos de Raca (1517-8935)
Published by: Editora Escala Ltda., Av Prof Ida Kolb, 551, Casa Verde, Sao Paulo, 02518-000, Brazil. TEL 55-11-38552100, FAX 55-11-38579643, escala@escala.com.br, http://www.escala.com.br.

798 MEX
CENTAURO. Text in English, Spanish. 1990. 10/yr. MXN 160, USD 3. adv. **Document type:** *Magazine, Consumer.* **Description:** Covers equestrian events, art, fashion and gastronomy while focusing on horse lovers.
Published by: Editorial Cala S.A. de C.V., Ave. VERACRUZ 69-101, Col Condesa, Del. Cuauhtemoc, Mexico City, DF 06140, Mexico. TEL 52-5-256170, FAX 52-5-2560972. Ed. Adrea Villasenor. Adv. contact Ricardo Torres Inzunza. page USD 4,070. Circ: 10,000.

798 USA ISSN 1934-7642
CENTRAL TEXAS PONY EXPRESS MAGAZINE. Text in English. 2006. m. USD 20 (effective 2008). **Document type:** *Magazine, Consumer.*
Address: PO Box 1256, Lockhart, TX 78644-1256. Ed. Sharon Johnston. Pub. Hershell Johnston.

791.84 USA ISSN 1931-5619
CHARRO U S A MAGAZINE. Text in English, Spanish. 2006. q. USD 24 domestic; USD 40 in Canada & Mexico; USD 46 elsewhere (effective 2008). **Document type:** *Magazine, Consumer.*
Published by: Mis Altos Network, PO Box 786, Lindsay, CA 93247. TEL 650-464-4823, FAX 559-562-3070, magazine@charrousa.com.

796.42 GBR
CHASERS AND HURDLERS. Text in English. 1975. a. GBP 70 per issue (effective 2010). 1088 p./no. 1 cols./p.; back issues avail. **Document type:** *Yearbook, Consumer.* **Description:** Essays and notes on the performances of horses.
Published by: Portway Press Ltd., 25 Timeform House, Northgate, Halifax, W Yorks HX1 1XF, United Kingdom. TEL 44-1422-330330, FAX 44-1422-398017, timeform@timeform.com.

798.4 GBR ISSN 1470-3742
CHELTENHAM RACECOURSE. Text in English. 1999. a. adv. **Document type:** *Magazine, Consumer.*
Published by: Main Stream Magazines, Prestbury Park, Cheltenham, Gloucestershire GL50 4SH, United Kingdom. TEL 44-1242-513014. Adv. contact Peter McNeile TEL 44-1242-537600.

798 FRA ISSN 2103-3137
CHEVAL ARABE NEWS. Text in French. 2005. bi-m. EUR 28 domestic; EUR 33 foreign (effective 2009). **Document type:** *Magazine, Consumer.*
Formerly (until 2008): Cheval Arabe Sport (1779-5281)
Related titles: Supplement(s): Cheval Arabe News. Hors-serie. ISSN 2106-9050. 2010.
Published by: Editions C A N, 35 Rue des Chantiers, Versailles, 78000, France. TEL 33-9-61512883, http://www.chevalarabenews.com.

798 FRA ISSN 1779-8876
CHEVAL ATTITUDE. Text in French. 2006. 4/yr. EUR 19 (effective 2009). **Document type:** *Magazine, Consumer.*
Published by: Editions Bertrand-Nel, 7 rue Principale, Ritzing, 57480, France. TEL 33-3-82560442.

798.208 FRA ISSN 1774-5276
CHEVAL FAN. Text in French. 2005. irreg. EUR 3.90 per issue (effective 2006). **Document type:** *Magazine, Consumer.*
Published by: Go Multimedia, 60 rue Vitruve, Paris, 75020, France.

CHEVAL JUNIOR. *see* CHILDREN AND YOUTH—For

798.2 636.1 FRA ISSN 1959-2841
CHEVAL LUSITANIEN MAGAZINE. Text in French. 2007. bi-m. EUR 48 (effective 2009). back issues avail. **Document type:** *Magazine, Consumer.*
Address: Forges, Nassigny, 03190, France. TEL 33-4-70067519.

798.2 FRA ISSN 0245-3614
CHEVAL MAGAZINE. Text in French. 1971. m. EUR 39; EUR 4.90 per issue (effective 2009). adv. **Document type:** *Magazine, Consumer.*
Formerly (until 1979): Cheval (0339-9060)
Published by: Optipress, 3 Chemin Bluche, B.P. 60, Montfort-l'Amaury, Cedex 78490, France. TEL 33-1-34862922, FAX 33-1-34867879. Circ: 88,404.

798 FRA ISSN 1145-6000
CHEVAL PRATIQUE. Text in French. 1990. m. EUR 49.25 (effective 2009). adv. back issues avail. **Document type:** *Magazine, Consumer.* **Description:** Practical information and sports articles for young riders who own their own horses.
Published by: Editions Lariviere, 6 Rue Olof Palme, Clichy, 92587, France. TEL 33-1-47565400, http://www.editions-lariviere.fr. Ed. Pierre Miriski. Adv. contact Stephane Litas. Circ: 80,000.

798.2 FRA ISSN 1148-201X
CHEVAL STAR. Text in French. 1987. m. EUR 29 (effective 2009). adv. **Document type:** *Magazine, Consumer.* **Description:** Illustrated stories on horses and ponies for kids and adolescents.

S

Published by: Optipress, 3 Chemin Bluche, B.P. 60, Montfort-l'Amaury, Cedex 78490, France. TEL 33-1-34862909, FAX 33-1-34867879. Ed., R&P Jerome Chehu. Adv. contact Anita Horlon. Circ: 42,364.

798.4 USA ISSN 0009-5990
SF321
THE CHRONICLE OF THE HORSE. Text in English. 1937. w. USD 59 combined subscription domestic (print & online eds.); USD 79 combined subscription foreign (print & online eds.) (effective 2010). adv. bk.rev. illus. s-a. index. back issues avail.; reprints avail. **Document type:** *Magazine, Consumer.* **Description:** Provides news coverage of national and international sport horse competitions.
Former titles (until 1961): The Chronicle; (until 1939): Horse
Related titles: Microform ed.: (from PQC); Online - full text ed.: USD 35 (effective 2010).
Indexed: A22, SPI.
Published by: Chronicle of the Horse, Inc., PO Box 46, Middleburg, VA 20118. TEL 540-687-6341, FAX 540-687-3937, subscriptions@chronofhorse.com. Ed. Tricia Booker. Adv. contact Susan Lee. B&W page USD 1,296, color page USD 2,271; trim 8.25 x 10.75. Circ: 1,480 (paid).

636.1 GBR
CLYDESDALE STUD BOOK. Text in English. 1877. a. GBP 15 domestic; GBP 20 foreign. **Document type:** *Directory.*
Published by: Clydesdale Society of Great Britain and Ireland, 3 Grosvenor Gardens, Edinburgh, EH12 5JU, United Kingdom. TEL 44-1764-664925. Ed. Kate Stephen. Circ: 300.

636.1 798 613.71 GBR ISSN 1755-2540
➤ **COMPARATIVE EXERCISE PHYSIOLOGY**; the international journal of exercise physiology, biomechanics and nutrition. Text in English. 2004 (Jan.). q. GBP 330, USD 633 to institutions; GBP 351, USD 679 combined subscription to institutions (print & online eds.) (effective 2011). adv. back issues avail.; reprint service avail. from PSC. **Document type:** *Journal, Academic/Scholarly.* **Description:** Contains articles that specifically deal with the latest research in equine exercise physiology.
Formerly (until 2008): Equine and Comparative Exercise Physiology (1478-0615)
Related titles: Online - full text ed.: ISSN 1755-2559. GBP 273, USD 530 to institutions (effective 2011).
Indexed: A01, A22, A34, A35, A37, A38, AgBio, AgrForAb, CA, CABA, D01, E01, E12, F08, G11, GH, IndVet, LT, N02, N03, N04, P15, P48, PQC, RRTA, T02, VS, W11.
—BLDSC (3363.780650), IE, Ingenta. **CCC.**
Published by: Cambridge University Press, The Edinburgh Bldg, Shaftesbury Rd, Cambridge, CB2 8RU, United Kingdom. TEL 44-1223-312393, FAX 44-1223-315052, information@cambridge.org. Ed. David Marlin. Adv. contact Rebecca Roberts TEL 44-1223-325083. page GBP 610, page USD 1,160. **Subscr. to:** Cambridge University Press, 100 Brook Hill Dr, W Nyack, NY 10994. TEL 845-353-7500, 800-872-7423, FAX 845-353-4141, subscriptions_newyork@cambridge.org

798.4 ZAF ISSN 1016-6416
COMPUTAFORM. Variant title: Transvaal Computaform. Text in English. 1946. w. adv. stat. cum.index.
Former titles (until 1972): Duff's Turf Guide (Incorporating Computaform); Duff's Turf Guide (0012-7035)
Related titles: Regional ed(s).: Computaform (Eastern Cape Edition). ISSN 1017-1363.
Published by: Times Media Limited, PO Box 1746, Saxonwold, Johannesburg 2133, South Africa. TEL 27-11-280-3000, FAX 27-11-280-3773. Circ: 4,000.

798.2 FRA ISSN 2106-9719
CONNAITRE LES CHEVAUX. Text in French. 2006. q. **Document type:** *Magazine, Consumer.*
Formerly (until 2010): Cheval Lecture (1779-305X)
Published by: Go Multimedia, 60 rue Vitruve, Paris, 75020, France.

798 USA ISSN 1094-8651
CONQUISTADOR; the world of Spanish horses. Text in English. 1991. bi-m. USD 19.95 domestic; USD 31.95 in Canada & Mexico; USD 43.95 elsewhere; USD 3.95 newsstand/cover (effective 2000). adv. bk.rev. charts; illus.; maps; tr.lit. index. back issues avail. **Document type:** *Magazine, Consumer.* **Description:** Informs and educate horse owners and admirers about all aspects of horses of Spanish ancestry-Breeding, training, riding, history, events, travel and art.
Published by: Amigo Publications, Inc., PO Box 666, Los Olivos, CA 93441-0666. TEL 805-686-4616, 888-88A-MIGO, FAX 805-688-3427. Ed., Pub., R&P, Adv. contact Heinz Reusser. B&W page USD 595, color page USD 975; trim 10.88 x 8.38. Circ: 3,000 (paid); 4,000 (controlled).

636.009 FRA ISSN 1775-8114
CONTACT ELEVAGE; le journal des eleveurs. Text in French. 2004. q. EUR 2 per issue (effective 2006). **Document type:** *Magazine, Consumer.*
Published by: Association de Production Animale de l'Est, 870 rue Denis-Papin, Zone Industrielle, B.P. 30125, Ludres, 54715, France.

CONTRACTSPELER. *see* SPORTS AND GAMES

798.2 CAN ISSN 0829-2930
CORINTHIAN HORSE SPORT. Text in English. 1968. m. CAD 32.95 domestic; CAD 35.41 Atlantic; USD 42.95 elsewhere; CAD 3.95 newsstand/cover (effective 2000). adv. bk.rev. charts; pat.; stat.; tr.lit. back issues avail. **Document type:** *Magazine, Consumer.* **Description:** Features show results, training techniques, profiles, international news.
Former titles: Corinthian Horse Sport in Canada; Corinthian: Horse Sport; Corinthian (0319-7581)
Related titles: Microfiche ed.: (from MML); Microform ed.: (from MML).
Indexed: C03, CBCARef, CBPI, H20, P48, PQC, SD, SportS.
Published by: Horse Publications, 225 Industrial Pkwy S, P O Box 670, Aurora, ON L4G 4J9, Canada. TEL 905-727-0107, FAX 905-841-1530, info@horse-canada.com, http://www.horse-canada.com. Ed. Susan Stafford. Pub. Susan Jane Anstey. Adv. contact Vicki Mosher. B&W page CAD 1,150, color page CAD 2,045. Circ: 6,000.

COUNTRY ROAD CHRONICLES. *see* NATIVE AMERICAN STUDIES

798 CAN ISSN 0847-2173
COURRIER HIPPIQUE. Text in English. 1983. 6/yr. CAD 23. adv.
Published by: Sportam Inc., 4545 Pierre de Coubertin, P O Box 1000, Sta M, Montreal, PQ H1V 3R2, Canada. TEL 514-252-3053, FAX 514-252-3165. Ed. Jocelyne Lortie.

636.1 FRA ISSN 0300-5607
COURSES ET ELEVAGE. Text in French. 1954. 6/yr. bk.rev. illus. **Document type:** *Academic/Scholarly.* **Description:** Presents a technical magazine about racing and breeding in France, French flat and steeple chasing, racing season, pedigrees, and statistics.
Published by: Etalons, 24 rue Jean Mermoz, Paris, 75008, France. TEL 33-1-43599414, FAX 33-1-43599441. Ed. Gerard de Chevigny. Pub. Louis Giscard d'Estaing. Adv. contact Beatrice Villa. Circ: 5,000.

798 USA ISSN 1053-2633
F596
COWBOY MAGAZINE. Text in English. 1990. q. USD 20; USD 28 foreign (effective 1999). adv. bk.rev.; music rev.; video rev. illus. back issues avail. **Document type:** *Magazine, Consumer.* **Description:** For and about the working ranch cowboy.
—Ingenta.
Published by: Magpie Publishing, 124 N Main, PO Box 126, La Veta, CO 81055-0126. TEL 719-742-5250, FAX 719-742-3034. Ed. Darrell. Pub., R&P, Adv. contact Darrell Arnold. B&W page USD 893, color page USD 1,831; trim 10.63 x 8. Circ: 12,000 (paid).

798 USA ISSN 0887-2406
CURLY CUES. Text in English. 1975. q. USD 10 to members (effective 2000). adv. **Document type:** *Newsletter.* **Description:** Promotes the rare curly-coated horse.
Published by: American Bashkir Curly Registry, PO Box 246, Ely, NV 89301. TEL 775-289-4999, FAX 775-289-8579. Ed., Pub., R&P, Adv. contact Sue Chilson. Circ: 1,500.

798 USA ISSN 1081-0951
CUTTING HORSE CHATTER. Text in English. 1948. m. USD 70 (effective 2008). adv. bk.rev. illus. back issues avail.; reprints avail. **Document type:** *Magazine, Trade.*
Former titles (until Apr. 1993): Cutting Horse (1061-3986); (until 1991): Cuttin' Hoss Chatter (0090-8711)
Published by: National Cutting Horse Association, 260 Bailey Ave., Fort Worth, TX 76107-1862. TEL 817-244-6188, FAX 817-244-2015. Ed. Stacy Pigott. adv.: B&W page USD 532, color page USD 832; trim 8.5 x 11. Circ: 12,000.

798.46 SWE
D D GUIDEN. (Dagens Dubbel) Text in Swedish. w. SEK 995 (effective 2001). adv. **Document type:** *Magazine, Consumer.*
Published by: Guidenfoerlaget AB, Box 20002, Bromma, 16102, Sweden. TEL 46-8-506-660-00, FAX 46-8-28-82-40, guiden@guiden.se, http://www.guiden.se. Ed. Andreas Lidstroem. Pub. Bjoern Holmquist.

798.4 SWE
DD GUIDEN. Text in Swedish. w. SEK 945 (effective 2000). adv. **Document type:** *Magazine, Consumer.*
Published by: Guiden Foerlaget AB, Fack 20002, Bromma, 16102, Sweden. TEL 46-8-28-48-80, FAX 46-8-28-82-40, guiden@guiden.se, http://www.guiden.se. Ed. Mikael Nybrink. Pub. Bjoern Holmquist. adv.: B&W page SEK 5,000, color page SEK 7,000; trim 155 x 224.

798.2 DEU
DEUTSCHE REITERLICHE VEREINIGUNG. REPORT. Text in German. 1920. w. **Document type:** *Newsletter, Consumer.* **Description:** Reports and articles on horses and riding.
Published by: (Deutsche Reiterliche Vereinigung e.V.), F N - Verlag, Freiherr-von-Langen-Str 13, Warendorf, 48231, Germany. TEL 49-2581-6362115, FAX 49-2581-633146, http://www.fnverlag.de. Circ: 2,400.

796.029 GBR ISSN 1463-8460
THE DIRECTORY OF THE TURF (YEAR). Text in English. 1961. a. GBP 49.50 per issue (effective 2009). adv. **Document type:** *Directory.* **Description:** A-Z Listings of 10,000 Organisations & Businesses around the world involved in the racing and breeding industry.
Former titles (until 1998): The Turf Directory; (until 1992): Directory of the Turf (0419-3806); (until 1963): Directory of the British Turf
Related titles: Online - full text ed.: The Internet Directory of the Turf. ISSN 1475-1127. 2001.
—BLDSC (3595.260000).
Published by: Tomorrows Guides Ltd., PO Box 7677, Hungerford, RG17 0FX, United Kingdom. TEL 44-1488-684321, FAX 44-1488-681968. Adv. contact Giles Anderson TEL 44-1380-816777. B&W page GBP 1,240, color page GBP 1,760; trim 210 x 297. Circ: 3,000.

798 GBR
THE DIRECTORY OF THE TURF HANDBOOK (YEAR); guide to thoroughbred horse racing & breeding. Abbreviated title: D O T. Text in English. 1992. a. GBP 55 per issue (effective 2009). adv. **Document type:** *Directory, Trade.* **Description:** Provides informative and detailed listings of organizations, businesses and individuals around the world involved in the racing and breeding industry.
Formerly (until 2005): Telephone Directory of the Turf (1463-8479)
Published by: Tomorrows Guides Ltd., PO Box 7677, Hungerford, RG17 0FX, United Kingdom. TEL 44-1488-684321, FAX 44-1488-681968, info@directoryoftheturf.com. Adv. contact Paula Green. page GBP 1,760; trim 210 x 297.

798 USA ISSN 1558-1837
SF277
DISCOVER HORSES. Text in English. 2000. a. adv. **Document type:** *Magazine, Consumer.*
Indexed: G06, G07, G08, I05, I07, R03, RGPR.
—**CCC.**
Published by: Source Interlink Companies, 27500 Riverview Ctr Blvd, Bonita Springs, FL 34134. dheine@sourceinterlink.com, http://www.sourceinterlinkmedia.com. Ed. Mary Kay Kinnish. Pub. Susan Harding.

798 DEU
DISTANZ AKTUELL. Text in German. 1980. bi-m. EUR 3.50 newsstand/cover (effective 2006). adv. **Document type:** *Magazine, Consumer.*
Published by: (Verein Deutscher Distanzreiter und -fahrer e.V.), C. Kohlmann Druck & Verlag GmbH, Hauptstr 36-38, Bad Lauterberg, 37431, Germany. TEL 49-5524-85000, FAX 49-5524-850039, info@kohlmann-druck.de, http://www.kohlmann-druck.de. adv.: B&W page EUR 420, color page EUR 630; trim 185 x 271. Circ: 2,600 (controlled).

636.1 USA
DOC WARREN ONLINE. Text in English. irreg. **Document type:** *Bulletin.* **Description:** Covers horse health, horse care and horse management.
Media: Online - full text. Ed. David P Warren.

DONKEY DIGEST. *see* ANIMAL WELFARE

798.4 NLD ISSN 1567-908X
DRAF EN RENSPORT. Text in Dutch. 1880. w. EUR 165 (effective 2009). adv. bk.rev. charts. **Document type:** *Trade.*
Formerly (until 2000): Paardesport in Ren en Draf (0039-1387); Which was formed by the 1952 merger of: Paardesport en Fokkerij; Paardesport; Incorporates: Stichting Nederlandse Draf- en Rensport. Officieel Bulletin
Published by: (Nederlandse Draf- en Rensport), BCM Publishing, Postbus 1392, Eindhoven, 5602 BJ, Netherlands. TEL 31-40-8447644, FAX 31-40-8447655, bcm@bcm.nl, http://www.bcm.nl. Ed. Douwe Frerichs. Adv. contact Ton van den Oudenalder. color page EUR 721; 233 x 320. Circ: 8,500.

THE DRAFT HORSE JOURNAL. *see* AGRICULTURE—Poultry And Livestock

798.2 USA ISSN 1079-1167
SF309.5
DRESSAGE TODAY. Variant title: Dressage. Text in English. 1994. m. USD 19.95 domestic; USD 32.95 in Canada; USD 34.95 elsewhere (effective 2008). adv. bk.rev.; software rev.; video rev. charts; illus. back issues avail.; reprints avail. **Document type:** *Magazine, Consumer.* **Description:** Features articles covering both the practical and theoretical aspects of the sport.
Related titles: Online - full text ed.: USD 10 (effective 2008).
Indexed: B04, G06, G07, G08, I05, R03, RGAb, RGPR, SD, W03, W05.
—Ingenta. **CCC.**
Published by: Source Interlink Companies, 6420 Wilshire Blvd, 10th Fl, Los Angeles, CA 90048. TEL 323-782-2000, FAX 323-782-2585, dheine@sourceinterlink.com, http://www.sourceinterlinkmedia.com. Ed. Patricia Lasko. Adv. contact Debra Reinhardt. B&W page USD 2,010, color page USD 3,225; bleed 10.75 x 8.125. Circ: 47,610 (paid).

798 USA ISSN 2156-0315
SF277
ECLECTIC HORSEMAN. Text in English. 2001. bi-m. USD 24 (effective 2010). **Document type:** *Magazine, Consumer.* **Description:** Features detailed how-to articles from a number of top trainers and clinicians as well as thought-provoking philosophical stories.
Published by: Eclectic Horseman Communications, PO Box 174, Elbert, CO 80106. TEL 866-773-3537.

798.2 636.1 ESP ISSN 0212-3762
ECUESTRE. Text in Spanish. 1982. m. adv. **Document type:** *Magazine, Consumer.*
Formerly (until 1986): Revista Ecuestre (1136-9760)
Related titles: Online - full text ed.
Published by: Motorpress Iberica (Subsidiary of: Gruner + Jahr AG & Co), Ancora 40, Madrid, 28045, Spain. TEL 34-91-3470100, FAX 34-91-3470152, http://www.motorpress-iberica.es. Ed. Luis Poncela. Circ: 14,500 (paid).

798 ISL ISSN 1021-7169
EIDFAXI; hestafrettir. Text in Icelandic. 1977. m. USD 56; USD 11 per issue (effective 2005). adv. **Document type:** *Magazine, Consumer.* **Description:** Presents educational articles, travel stories, news from the horse world along with interviews and visits to horsefarms.
Incorporates (1960-1998): Hesturinn Okkar (1670-5475)
Published by: Eidfaxi ehf., Duggovogur 10, Reykjavik, 104, Iceland. TEL 354-588-2525, FAX 354-588-2528, eidfaxi@eidfaxi.is, http://www.eidfaxi.is. Ed. Jon Finnur Hansson. Adv. contact Kolbrun Olafsdottir. page ISK 135,000.

798 FRA ISSN 1951-252X
ENDURANCE EQUESTRE. Text in French. 2006. bi-m. EUR 30 (effective 2009). **Document type:** *Magazine, Consumer.*
Published by: Equimagazines, 10 Rue du Clos-Saint-Pierre, Villecresnes, 94440, France. TEL 33-9-54541828.

798 USA ISSN 1548-873X
EQUESTRIAN; the official magazine of American equestrian sports since 1937. Text in English. 1937. 10/yr. free to members (effective 2007). bk.rev. tr.lit.; bibl. back issues avail. **Document type:** *Magazine, Consumer.* **Description:** Provides information on ruling, policies and officials and profiles top horsemen and horsewomen who compete at USA Equestrian-recognized events.
Former titles: U S A Equestrian (1537-0968); (until July 2001): Horse Show (1095-3264)
Published by: United States Equestrian Federation, Inc. (U S E F), 4047 Iron Works Pkwy, Lexington, KY 40511-8483. TEL 859-225-6938, FAX 859-231-6662. Ed., R&P Christine E. Stafford TEL 859-225-6923. Adv. contact Sandy Lawson TEL 859-225-6991. Circ: 78,000.

798.2094205 GBR ISSN 1756-7254
THE EQUESTRIAN LIFESTYLE MAGAZINE. Text in English. 2004. bi-m. GBP 19.50 domestic; GBP 32.50 in Europe; GBP 42.50 elsewhere (effective 2010). adv. back issues avail. **Document type:** *Magazine, Consumer.* **Description:** Aims to promote Equestrian pursuits and enhance its profile within England.
Formerly (until 2008): England's Equestrian (1744-7542)
Related titles: Online - full text ed.: GBP 10.50 (effective 2010).
Published by: M A I Publications, Revenue Chambers, St. Peter's St, Huddersfield, W Yorkshire HD1 1DL, United Kingdom. TEL 44-1484-435011, FAX 44-1484-422177, martialartsltd@btconnect.com, http://www.martialartsltd.co.uk. Ed. Sue Porter TEL 44-1623-474227. Adv. contact Vickie Littlewood.

798 USA
THE EQUESTRIAN NEWS; uniting L.A.'s horsepower. Text in English. 2003. bi-m. USD 12 (effective 2006). adv. **Document type:** *Newspaper, Consumer.* **Description:** Includes a complete calendar of events for shows and clinics, plus stories about the people behind those events and coverage of local riders, reports on local riding areas and more.
Published by: The Equestrian News, 3940 Laurel Canyon Blvd, #632, Studio City, CA 91604. TEL 323-822-1864. Pub. Nancy Cole. adv.: B&W page USD 1,000, color page USD 1,500; trim 11 x 17.

798 USA ISSN 1528-5197
EQUESTRIAN RETAILER. Abbreviated title: E Q R. Text in English. 1998. bi-m. free to members (effective 2009). adv. **Document type:** *Magazine, Trade.* **Description:** Provides useful, timely business information to help retailers and manufacturers of equestrian products grow their businesses.
Related titles: Online - full text ed.

Published by: Morris Multimedia, Inc., 9266 Montgomery St, Fort Worth, TX 76107. TEL 817-737-6397, FAX 817-737-9266, http://www.morris.com/. Ed. Emily Esterson. Pub. Jodi Hendrickson.

798.2 NZL ISSN 2230-4312
EQUESTRIAN SPORTS NEW ZEALAND. BULLETIN. Text in English. 19??. 11/yr. NZD 60 to non-members; NZD 6 per issue to non-members; free to members (effective 2011). adv. **Document type:** *Bulletin, Consumer.*
Former titles (until 2006): New Zealand Equestrian Federation. Bulletin (1177-1410); (until Feb.2006): Equestrian N Z (1174-3972); (until 1998): New Zealand Equestrian Federation. Bulletin (1173-9053)
Published by: Equestrian Sports New Zealand, PO Box 6146, Marion Sq, Wellington, 6141, New Zealand. TEL 61-4-4998994, FAX 61-4-4992899, nzef@nzequestrian.org.nz. Ed. Jane Hunt. Adv. contact Maureen Callow TEL 61-6-3555993.

798 USA
THE EQUESTRIAN TIMES. Text in English. 1995. d. free to members (effective 2010). back issues avail. **Document type:** *Newspaper, Trade.* **Description:** Covers international equestrian events, show results, reports, feature articles, interviews, and photos. Comprehensive coverage of the international world of equine sport.
Media: Online - full text.
Published by: International Equestrian News Network, PO Box 227, Marshfield Hills, MA 02051. TEL 781-834-7137, ienn@equestriantimes.com. Ed. Nicole Graf.

798 GBR ISSN 1462-9526
EQUESTRIAN TRADE NEWS. Text in English. 1978. m. free to qualified personnel (effective 2009). adv. bk.rev. **Document type:** *Magazine, Trade.* **Description:** Provids news on trade matters relating to saddlery, riding, clothing, feedstuffs and equipment, both overseas and in the U.K.
Published by: Equestrian Management Consultants Ltd., Stockeld Park, Wetherby, West Yorkshire LS22 4AW, United Kingdom. FAX 44-1937-582778, sales@beta-int.com, 44-1937-582111.

798 USA ISSN 0013-9831
EQUESTRIAN TRAILS. Text in English. 1970 (vol.24). m. membership. adv. bk.rev. charts; illus.; tr.lit. **Document type:** *Newspaper.*
Published by: Equestrian Trails, Inc., 13741 Foothill Blvd, Ste 220, Sylmar, CA 91342-3105. FAX 818-362-9443. Ed. Holly E Carson. Circ: 5,000.

798 USA
EQUIJOURNAL. Text in English. d. **Description:** Features articles on horse care, and equestrian sports in the United States and the world.
Media: Online - full text.
Published by: A A O Internet Services, A division of AAA Enterprises Inc., 642 Peekskill Howoll Rd, Putnam Valley, NY 10579. FAX 914-528-1586.

798 CAN
EQUILIFE. Text in English, French. s-m.
Address: P O Box 164, Dalkeith, PQ K0B 1E0, Canada. TEL 613-874-2219. Ed. Diane Coombs. Circ: 7,000.

798 GBR
EQUINE BEHAVIOUR. Text in English. 1978. q. free to members (effective 2009). bk.rev. abstr.; bibl.; charts; illus. back issues avail. **Document type:** *Journal, Consumer.* **Description:** Contains letters, articles, views and experiences, requests for and offers of help and advice and more.
Indexed: E-psyche.
Published by: Equine Behaviour Forum, c/o Francis Burton, Chairman, 27 Grosvenor Ln, Glasgow, G12 9AA, United Kingdom. Eds. Alison Averis, Francis Burton.

798 AUS ISSN 1836-3229
EQUINE EXCELLENCE. Text in English. 2008. q. AUD 65; AUD 9.95 newsstand/cover (effective 2011). adv. back issues avail. **Document type:** *Magazine, Consumer.* **Description:** Covers all genres of horsemanship such as dressage, western, eventing, endurance, showing and show-jumping.
Published by: E D E E Publications, 39 Bates St, Cranbourne, VIC 3977, Australia. TEL 61-3-59966228, FAX 61-3-59966228. Ed. Daphne McNeill TEL 61-4-17030017. Adv. contact Andy Cole TEL 61-4-48501866.

636.1 USA
EQUINE JOURNAL. Text in English. 1988. m. USD 14 (effective 2000). adv. bk.rev. **Document type:** *Journal, Trade.* **Description:** Features articles on horses and horse lovers of all breeds and disciplines. Also contains a calendar of equestrian events, teaching and training techniques, information on equine healthcare, as well as letters from the New York, New Jersey, Pennsylvania, and New England regions.
Formerly: Northeast Equine Journal (1067-5884)
Published by: Turley Publications, Inc., 312 Marlboro St, Keene, NH 03431. TEL 603-357-4271, FAX 603-357-7851. Ed., R&P Kathleen Lyons. Pub. Natalee Roberts. Adv. contact Natalee S Roberts. Circ: 26,000 (paid).

636.1 USA ISSN 1056-8212
EQUINE TIMES. Text in English. 1980. m. USD 14.95. adv. bk.rev. **Document type:** *Newsletter.* **Description:** Serves the horse enthusiast in Michigan, Indiana and Ohio.
Published by: Camden Publications, Inc., 331 E Bell St, P O Box 130, Camden, MI 49232-0008. FAX 517-368-5131, http://www.farmersadvance.com. Ed. John Snyder. Pub. Kurt Greenhoe. Adv. contact Debbie Peiffer. Circ: 6,000 (paid).

798 USA ISSN 1087-8734
THE EQUINE TRADE JOURNAL. Text in English. 1993. bi-m. USD 24. **Document type:** *Journal, Trade.* **Description:** Provides a medium for trainers and breeders of sport horses to market their stock directly to the attention of other equine professionals.
Published by: Equine Trade Journal, PO Box 5299, Laguna Beach, CA 92652. TEL 714-494-2033, FAX 714-376-8891. Pub., R&P Ann Abbott.

EQUINE WELLNESS; for the natural horse. *see* VETERINARY SCIENCE

798 GBR
EQUINE WORLD UK ONLINE MAGAZINE. Text in English. m. adv. **Description:** Includes news and items of interest to equestrian businesses.
Media: E-mail.
Published by: Equine World UK Ltd, 18 Sheperds Close, Grove, Oxon, OX12 9NX, United Kingdom. Ed. Lorraine Hill.

798 636.089 CAN ISSN 0828-864X
EQUINEWS; serving the horse industry - all breeds, all disciplines. Text in English. 1980. m. CAD 15 domestic; CAD 22 foreign. adv. back issues avail.
Formerly (until 1984): Hoof Beats
Published by: John Whittle, Ed. & Pub. (Subsidiary of: Westview Publications), Site 15 C 5 R R 6, Vernon, BC V1T 6Y5, Canada. TEL 604-542-2002, FAX 604-549-7099.

798 FRA ISSN 1951-4115
EQUIT' INFOS. Variant title: Equitation Infos. Text in French. 1937. m. EUR 76.22 (effective 2009). **Document type:** *Bulletin.*
Former titles (until 2006): A Cheval (1256-9747); (until 1971): A Cheval..en Avant (1256-9542)
Published by: Groupement Hippique National, Parc Equestre, Lamotte, 41600, France. TEL 33-2-54830202, FAX 33-2-54830203, infos@ghn.com.fr.

794 DEU ISSN 0948-6119
EQUITRENDS; Das Magazin fuer Handel, Hersteller und Dienstleister im Pferdesport. Text in German. 1995. m. EUR 84.46 (effective 2011). adv. **Document type:** *Magazine, Trade.*
Published by: FORUM Zeitschriften und Spezialmedien GmbH (Subsidiary of: FORUM Media Group GmbH), Mandichostr 18, Merching, 86504, Germany. TEL 49-8233-381361, FAX 49-8233-381212, service@forum-zeitschriften.de, http://www.forum-zeitschriften.de. Ed. Guido Krisam. Circ: 2,000 (paid and controlled).

EQUUS. *see* BIOLOGY—Zoology

EQUUS INTERNATIONAL. *see* ART

798.2 GBR
EUROPEAN PATTERN BOOK. Text in English, French. 19??. a. GBP 44 per issue (effective 2010). **Document type:** *Handbook/Manual/Guide, Trade.* **Description:** Provides outlines all group-classified horse races in Europe and their requirements.
Published by: (British Horseracing Board), Weatherbys Group Limited, Sanders Rd, Wellingborough, Northants NN8 4BX, United Kingdom. TEL 44-1933-440077, FAX 44-1933-440807, ihelp@weatherbys.co.uk, http://www.weatherbys.co.uk. R&P Steve Cheney. Circ: 500 (controlled).

636.1 NZL
EXPRESSION. Text in English. q. free membership. adv. **Document type:** *Magazine, Consumer.* **Description:** Provides news, articles and other information about the arabian world in New Zealand.
Published by: New Zealand Arab Horse Breeders Society, Private Bag 1924, Dunedin, New Zealand. arabianz@horsetalk.co.nz, http://www.horsetalk.co.nz/arabianz/index.html. Ed. Lee Cox. adv.: B&W page NZD 35, color page NZD 90.

FARM 'N' EQUINE. *see* AGRICULTURE—Poultry And Livestock

636.1 DNK ISSN 0108-7738
FJORDHESTEN. Text in Danish. 1969. q. DKK 500 domestic to individual members; DKK 300 in Europe to individual members; DKK 350 elsewhere to individual members (effective 2009). adv. illus. **Document type:** *Magazine, Consumer.*
Published by: Fjordhesteavlen i Danmark, c/o Birgit Mortensen, Norddalen 9, Sankt Klemens, Odense S, 5260, Denmark. TEL 45-66-153908, birgit@fjordhest.dk, http://www.fjordhest.dk.

798 636.1 NLD ISSN 1569-7932
DE FORESTER. Text in Dutch. 196?. bi-m.
Published by: Nederlands New Forest Pony Stamboek, Postbus 190, Oosterwolde, 8430 AD, Netherlands. TEL 31-516-480627, FAX 31-516-480521, info@newforestpony.nl, http://www.newforestpony.nl. Circ: 1,700.

798.4 GBR
FORM BOOK FLAT ANNUAL. Text in English. 1899. a. GBP 30 per issue (effective 2009). adv. 1525 p./no.; **Document type:** *Handbook/Manual/Guide, Trade.* **Description:** Provides a record of racing from the previous year and a guide to future race winners.
Formerly: Raceform Up-to-Date Form Book Annual (0081-377X)
Published by: Racing Post, One Canada Sq, Canary Wharf, London, E14 5AP, United Kingdom. TEL 44-1635-898781, shop@racingpost.co.uk, http://www.racingpost.co.uk. Ed. Ashley Rumney.

798.2 DEU ISSN 0342-4758
FREIZEIT IM SATTEL; die Fachzeitschrift rund ums Reiten. Text in German. 1958. m. EUR 44 domestic; EUR 48 foreign; EUR 4.40 newsstand/cover (effective 2006). adv. bk.rev. **Document type:** *Magazine, Consumer.* **Description:** Covers all aspects of horses and horsemanship.
Published by: F S Verlag GmbH, Droste-Huelshoff-Str 3, Bonn, 53129, Germany. TEL 49-228-530120, FAX 49-228-5301260. Ed. Eva Wunderlich. Adv. contact Barbara Baerwolf. B&W page EUR 1,910, color page EUR 3,343; trim 185 x 260. Circ: 19,624 (paid).

798 636.1 FRA ISSN 1779-9163
FRENCH ANNUAL REVIEW. Text in English, French. 2006. a.
Formerly (until 2006): Racing and Breeding in France (0995-3019)
Published by: French Racing and Breeding Committee, 46 place Abel Gance, Boulogne, 92655 Cedex, France. TEL 33-1-49102332, FAX 33-1-49102333, info@frbc.net.

636.1 USA
GAITED HORSE INTERNATIONAL MAGAZINE. Text in English. 2001. q. USD 25 domestic; USD 34 in Canada; USD 45 elsewhere (effective 2001). **Document type:** *Magazine, Consumer.* **Description:** Dedicated to all gaited horse breeds worldwide. Each issue will feature an in-depth look at two breeds on a rotational basis.
Related titles: Online - full content ed.
Published by: Gaited Horse International Magazine, Inc., 507 N Sullivan Rd Ste A-3, Veradale, WA 99037-8531. TEL 509-232-2698, FAX 509-232-2665.

798 028.5 FRA ISSN 2108-114X
GALOP PASSION. Text in French. 2008. bi-m. **Document type:** *Magazine, Consumer.*
Formerly (until 2010): Poney Passion (2108-1131)
Published by: S A R L Alezan Editions, 3, Rue d'Abbeville, Paris, 75010, France. TEL 33-9-50500885, alezan.editions@gmail.com, http://www.galopassion.com. Ed. Sylvie Hennequin.

636.160 FRA ISSN 1635-4915
GALOPIN; pour les amoureux du poney des 5 ans. Text in French. 2002. bi-m. EUR 18 (effective 2009). **Document type:** *Magazine, Consumer.*
Related titles: ◆ Supplement(s): Galopin. Hors-Serie. ISSN 1775-8343.
Published by: Optipress, 3 Chemin Bluche, B.P. 60, Montfort-l'Amaury, Cedex 78490, France. TEL 33-1-34862909, FAX 33-1-34867879. Ed. Jerome Chehu.

636.160 FRA ISSN 1775-8343
GALOPIN. HORS-SERIE. Text in French. 2005. irreg. EUR 4.30 per issue (effective 2009). **Document type:** *Magazine, Consumer.*
Related titles: ◆ Supplement to: Galopin. ISSN 1635-4915.
Published by: Optipress, 3 Chemin Bluche, B.P. 60, Montfort-l'Amaury, Cedex 78490, France.

798 DEU
GALOPP (YEAR); der gruene Kalender. Text in German. 1998. a. EUR 13.70 newsstand/cover (effective 2009). adv. **Document type:** *Yearbook, Consumer.*
Published by: D S V Deutscher Sportverlag GmbH, Im Mediapark 8, Cologne, 50670, Germany. TEL 49-221-25870, FAX 49-221-2587212, kontakt@dsv-sportverlag.de, http://www.dsv-sportverlag.de.

798 DEU
GALOPP INTERN; Informationsdienst fuer Vollblutzucht und Galopprennen. Text in German. 1982. 20/w. adv. **Document type:** *Journal, Trade.*
Published by: Klaus Goentzsche, Am Pannesbusch 89, Wuppertal, 42281, Germany. TEL 49-202-706001, FAX 49-202-702824, giwup@aol.com. Ed. Patrick Buecheler. Pub. Klaus Goentzsche. adv.: B&W page EUR 490, color page EUR 770. Circ: 1,000 (controlled).

798 GBR ISSN 0072-078X
GENERAL STUD BOOK. Text in English. 1793. quadrennial (vol.46 due spring 2006). GBP 270 per issue (effective 2009). adv. stat. back issues avail. **Document type:** *Directory, Trade.* **Description:** Provide information to cattle breeders in Britain and Ireland.
Published by: Weatherbys Group Limited, Sanders Rd, Wellingborough, Northants NN8 4BX, United Kingdom. TEL 44-1933-440077, FAX 44-1933-440807, ihelp@weatherbys.co.uk, http://www.weatherbys.co.uk.

GOLF TENNIS POLO; magazine for sports, journeys, pastime, society and fashion. *see* SPORTS AND GAMES

798.4 FRA ISSN 1966-6756
GRAND PRIX INTERNATIONAL. Text in French. 1997. bi-m. **Document type:** *Magazine, Consumer.*
Published by: Volta Sport, 109-111 Av. Gambetta, Paris, 75020, France. TEL 33-1-43152626, FAX 33-1-43664023, contact@volta-sports.com. Ed. Daniel Koroloff.

798 FRA ISSN 1968-7265
GRAND PRIX MAGAZINE. Text in French. 2008. m. EUR 52 (effective 2011). **Document type:** *Magazine, Consumer.*
Published by: Volta Sport, 109-111 Av. Gambetta, Paris, 75020, France. TEL 33-1-43152626, FAX 33-1-43664023, contact@volta-sports.com. Ed. Daniel Koroloff.

636.1 GBR
HACKNEY HORSE SOCIETY YEAR BOOK. Text in English. 1966. a. free to members (effective 2009). **Description:** Covers information about Hackney horse society.
Published by: Hackney Horse Society, Fallow Fields, Little London, Heytesbury, Warminster, Wilts BA12 0ES, United Kingdom. TEL 44-1985-840717, FAX 44-1985-840616, dawn@hackney-horse.org.uk, http://www.hackney-horse.org.uk.

636.1 GBR
HACKNEY STUD BOOK. Text in English. quinquennial. GBP 25 (effective 2001).
Published by: Hackney Horse Society, Fallow Fields, Little London, Heytesbury, Warminster, Wilts BA12 0ES, United Kingdom. TEL 44-1985-840717, FAX 44-1985-840616.

798 SWE ISSN 1653-400X
HAEST & RYTTARE. Text in Swedish. 2005. bi-m. **Document type:** *Magazine, Consumer.*
Published by: (Svenska Ridsportfoerbundet/Swedish Equestrian Federation), Forma Publishing Group, PO Box 6630, Stockholm, 11384, Sweden. TEL 46-21-194000, FAX 46-21-194136, http://www.formapg.se. Ed. Hege Hellstroem TEL 46-21-194434. Adv. contact Christina Sjoeberg TEL 46-8-4445215.

798.2 636.1 SWE ISSN 0345-486X
HAESTEN/HORSE; foer avel och sport. Text in Swedish. 1920. 8/yr. SEK 350 domestic; SEK 480 foreign (effective 2001). adv. **Document type:** *Magazine, Consumer.*
Former titles (until 1945): Svensk Ryttartidning; Haesten
Published by: Tidskriften Haesten, Kampavall 566, Lerdala, 54017, Sweden. TEL 46-511-82230, FAX 46-511-82238, haesten@telia.com, http://www.haesten.nu. Ed. Maria Cidh. adv.: B&W page SEK 6,500, color page SEK 10,000. Circ: 10,000.

798 636 SWE ISSN 1404-7322
HAESTMAGASINET. Text in Swedish. 2000. 10/yr. SEK 395 (effective 2005). adv. **Document type:** *Magazine, Consumer.*
Published by: Peak Media AB, Skommarvaegen 3, Gustafs, 78300, Sweden. TEL 46-243-253900, FAX 46-243-240028. Ed., Pub. Robert Solin TEL 46-705-379630. Adv. contact Per Elvin. page SEK 14,900; 185 x 270.

798.2 SWE ISSN 0280-7777
HAESTSPORT; magasin foer trav och galopp. Text in Swedish. 1982. bi-m.
Address: Fack 28088, Malmo, 200 28, Sweden.

798 DEU
HAFLINGER AKTUELL. Text in German. bi-m. EUR 31.50 domestic; EUR 38.80 foreign (effective 2010). adv. **Document type:** *Magazine, Consumer.* **Description:** Contains a wide variety of items and features on the Haflinger breed of horses.
Published by: Zeitschriftenverlag Ulrich Wulf, Niehorster Str 16, Guetersloh, 33334, Germany. TEL 49-5241-35362, FAX 49-5241-37601. Ed. Ulrich Wulf. Adv. contact Denise Senkhorst-Wulf. B&W page EUR 755, color page EUR 1,120; 185 x 265. Circ: 12,000.

798.46 DEU
HAMBURGER DERBY-WOCHE. Text in German. 1978. a. adv. **Document type:** *Journal, Consumer.* **Description:** Covers all angles of the annual Hamburg Derby horse races.

S

Published by: Lokal-Anzeiger Verlag, Kattunbleiche 37-39, Hamburg, 22014, Germany. hb@lokal-anzeiger-verlag.de, http://lokal-anzeiger-verlag.de.

636.1 DEU ISSN 1433-3457
DER HANNOVERANER. Text in German. 1922. m. EUR 125 membership (effective 2007). adv. bk.rev. bibl.; charts; illus.; stat. **Document type:** *Magazine, Trade.*
Formerly: Hannoversches Pferd (0017-7474)
Published by: Verband Hannoverscher Warmblutzuechter e.V., Lindhooperstr 92, Verden, 27283, Germany. TEL 49-4231-6730, FAX 49-4231-67312. Ed. Dr. Ludwig Christmann. R&P Britta Zuengel. Adv. contact Monika Meyer. B&W page EUR 1,700, color page EUR 2,880. Circ: 19,747 (controlled).

798.2 AUS ISSN 1440-0057
HARNESS RACING WEEKLY. Abbreviated title: H R W. Text in English. 1975. w. AUD 320; AUD 4.30 newsstand/cover (effective 2008). adv. back issues avail. **Document type:** *Magazine, Consumer.* **Description:** Covers harness racing in all states of Australia.
Former titles (until 1997): National Trotting Weekly (1320-2081); (until 1979): Victorian Trotting Weekly (0312-9810)
Address: 68 Pennyroyal Cres, Melton, VIC 3337, Australia. TEL 61-3-97466788, FAX 61-3-97473667. Eds. Andrew Georgiou, Paul Courts. Adv. contact Trevor Perrin. page AUD 1,320; trim 260 x 375. Circ: 6,000.

636.1 GBR ISSN 0951-2640
HEAVY HORSE WORLD. Text in English. 1987. q. GBP 20 domestic; GBP 22 in Europe; GBP 24 elsewhere; GBP 5 newsstand/cover (effective 2009). adv. bk.rev. back issues avail. **Document type:** *Magazine, Consumer.* **Description:** Serves the buoyant and growing interest in heavy draft horses throughout the country.
Formerly: Heavy Horse
—BLDSC (4282.153000).
Address: Lindford Cottage, Church Ln, Cocking, Midhurst, West Sussex GU29 0HW, United Kingdom. TEL 44-1730-812419, FAX 44-1730-812419. Ed., Pub., Adv. contact Diana Zeuner. color page GBP 320; 190 x 250.

HEST. *see* AGRICULTURE—Poultry And Livestock

798.2 NOR ISSN 0806-5314
HESTESPORT. Text in Norwegian. 1963. 8/yr. NOK 390 to non-members; NOK 170 to members (effective 2007). adv. bk.rev. maps. **Document type:** *Magazine, Consumer.*
Formerly (until 1995): Rytterkontakt (0333-0338)
Published by: Norges Rytterforbund/Norwegian Equestrian Federation, Sognsveien 75, Serviceboks 1 u.s., Oslo, 0840, Norway. TEL 46-21-029000, FAX 46-21-029651. Ed. Anne Buvik. Adv. contact Merete Andersen TEL 46-32-88-33-81. B&W page NOK 14,900, color page NOK 18,900; trim 185 x 260.

636.1 DEU
HESTUR. Text in German. 1976. bi-m. EUR 28.50 domestic; EUR 35 foreign; EUR 4.75 newsstand/cover (effective 2009). adv. **Document type:** *Magazine, Consumer.*
Published by: Rathmann Verlag GmbH & Co. KG, Schlossgarten 3-4, Kiel, 24103, Germany. TEL 49-431-8881230, FAX 49-431-9828710. Ed. Jessica Bunjes. Adv. contact Philip Rathmann. B&W page EUR 510, color page EUR 924; trim 215 x 280. Circ: 3,350 (paid and controlled).

798 636.1 FIN ISSN 1239-856X
HEVOSET JA RATSASTUS. Text in Finnish. 1996. 8/yr. EUR 39 (effective 2006). adv. **Document type:** *Magazine, Consumer.*
Published by: RideMedia Oy, PO Box 140, Hyvinkaa, 05801, Finland. TEL 358-19-483490, FAX 358-19-483480, http://www.ridemedia.fi. Ed. Virpi Hyokki. Pub. Jukka Helminen. Adv. contact Etti Koivula TEL 358-40-5752917. B&W page EUR 1,050, color page EUR 1,850; 210 x 297.

798 FIN ISSN 1455-0547
HEVOSMAAILMA. Text in Finnish. 1997. bi-m. EUR 31 (effective 2007). adv. **Document type:** *Magazine, Consumer.*
Published by: Karprint Oy, Vanha Turunrie 371, Huhmari, 03150, Finland. TEL 358-9-41397300, FAX 358-9-41397405, http://www.karprint.fi. Ed. Anna-Leena Brannare. Adv. contact Arja Blom. page EUR 1,511. Circ: 13,500.

798 NLD
DE HIPPISCHE ONDERNEMER. Text in Dutch. 6/yr. EUR 20 (effective 2009). **Document type:** *Magazine, Trade.*
Published by: BCM Publishing, Postbus 1392, Eindhoven, 5602 BJ, Netherlands. TEL 31-40-8447644, FAX 31-40-8447655, bcm@bcm.nl, http://www.bcm.nl. Ed. Marlies Strik. Adv. contact Ton van den Oudenalder. Circ: 7,500.

798 BEL ISSN 1377-2201
HIPPO NEWS; la revue equestre Belgique et Luxembourg. Text in French. 1972. m. EUR 25 domestic; EUR 37.50 foreign (effective 2005). adv. bk.rev. bibl.; illus.
Published by: Federation Francophone d'Equitation et d'Attelage, Rue du Tienne 12, Ligny, 5140, Belgium. TEL 32-71-815052, FAX 32-71-817615, info@ffe.be. Ed. Roland Heldenbergh. adv.: B&W page EUR 425, color page EUR 695; bleed 210 x 297.

798.4 NLD ISSN 0046-7715
HOEFSLAG; geillustreerd weekblad voor paardenvrienden. Text in Dutch. 1949. w. EUR 115.50 domestic; EUR 127 in Belgium; EUR 171 elsewhere; EUR 4.50 newsstand/cover (effective 2009). adv. bk.rev. **Document type:** *Consumer.* **Description:** Covers all aspects of the equestrian world, for recreational riders, stable-owners, competition riders, stud owners.
Incorporates (1972-1982): Paard en Pony (0165-3326)
Related titles: ◆ Supplement(s): Paard en Sport. ISSN 1388-0047; Hoefslag Jaarboek; Paarden & Cap.
Published by: BCM Publishing, Postbus 1392, Eindhoven, 5602 BJ, Netherlands. TEL 31-40-8447644, FAX 31-40-8447655, bcm@bcm.nl, http://www.bcm.nl. Ed. Ton Corbeau. Pub. Eric Bruger. Adv. contact Jeroen van der Linden. B&W page EUR 1,559, color page EUR 1,833; 215 x 285. Circ: 45,000.

798.4 USA ISSN 0018-4683
SF321
HOOF BEATS. Text in English. 1933. m. USD 32.50 domestic to non-members; USD 49 in Canada to non-members; USD 70 elsewhere to non-members; USD 16.50 domestic to members; USD 33 in Canada to members; USD 54 elsewhere to members (effective 2010). adv. bk.rev. charts; stat.; illus. Index. back issues avail.; reprints avail. **Document type:** *Magazine, Trade.* **Description:** Provides the fans and participants of harness racing with information on the major events and trends in the sport.
—Ingenta.
Published by: United States Trotting Association, 750 Michigan Ave, Columbus, OH 43215. TEL 614-224-2291, 877-800-8782, FAX 614-222-6791, editorial@ustrotting.com, http://www.ustrotting.com. Adv. contact Heather Dodds TEL 877-800-8782 ext 3217. B&W page USD 766.50, color page USD 995; trim 8.125 x 10.75. Circ: 13,500.

HOOFCARE & LAMENESS; the journal of equine foot science. *see* VETERINARY SCIENCE

636.1 GBR ISSN 2042-4191
▼ **HOOKED ON HORSES.** Text in English. 2009. m. GBP 31.20; GBP 2.60 per issue (effective 2011). adv. back issues avail. **Document type:** *Magazine, Consumer.* **Description:** Features everything 'horse' in and around the East Anglia region.
Published by: M Paveley, Ed. & Pub., Woodside Farm, Rayleigh Ave, Eastwood, Leigh-on-Sea, Essex SS9 5DJ, United Kingdom. Ed. Abbey Wass TEL 44-7540-271870. Adv. contact Michael Paveley TEL 44-7802-647220.

636.12 798.2 USA ISSN 1081-9711
SF291
THE HORSE; your guide to equine health care. Text in English. 1984. m. USD 24 domestic; USD 37.80 in Canada; USD 65 elsewhere; USD 4.95 per issue (effective 2010). bk.rev. **Document type:** *Magazine, Consumer.* **Description:** Designed to bridge the gap from the research laboratory to the barn thereby helping horsemen to sort valuable new information from gimmicks and fads.
Formerly (until 1995): Modern Horse Breeding (0747-1424)
Related titles: Online - full text ed.: TheHorse.Com. USD 24 (effective 2010).
Indexed: F&GI.
—Ingenta.
Published by: The Blood-Horse, Inc., PO Box 919003, Lexington, KY 40591. Ed., Pub. Kimberly S Brown.

636.1 CAN
HORSE & COUNTRY CANADA. Text in English. 1994. 7/yr.
Published by: Equine Publications, Inc., P.O. Box 1051, Smith Falls, ON K7A 5A5, Canada. TEL 613-275-1684, FAX 613-275-1686. Ed. Judith H McCartney. Circ: 14,000 (paid and controlled).

636.1 798 GBR ISSN 0018-5140
HORSE AND HOUND. Text in English. 1884. w. GBP 89.99 domestic; USD 187.90 in United States; USD 225.50 in Canada; EUR 174.10 in Europe; GBP 165.40 elsewhere; GBP 2.40 newsstand/cover (effective 2009). adv. bk.rev. illus. back issues avail. **Document type:** *Magazine, Consumer.* **Description:** Covers all British equestrian sports and international championships, including racing, horse trials, dressage, polo, show jumping, showing, hunting, pony club.
—CCC.
Published by: I P C Country & Leisure Media Ltd. (Subsidiary of: I P C Media Ltd.), The Blue Fin Bldg, 110 Southwark St, London, SE1 0SU, United Kingdom. TEL 44-20-31485000, http://www.ipcmedia.com. Ed. Lucy Higginson TEL 44-20-31484562. Pub. Joanna Pieters TEL 44-203-1484448. Adv. contact Emma Sharp TEL 44-20-31484226. B&W page GBP 2,286, color page GBP 4,085; trim 210 x 297. Circ: 61,445. **Subscr. to:** Rockwood House, Perrymount Rd, Haywards Heath RH16 3DH, United Kingdom. TEL 44-845-1231231, IPCsubs@quadrantsubs.com, http://www.magazinesdirect.co.uk. **Dist. by:** MarketForce UK Ltd. salesinnovation@marketforce.co.uk, http://www.marketforce.co.uk/.

798 USA
HORSE & PONY. Text in English. 1969. s-m. USD 16 In Florida; USD 22 elsewhere in US; USD 35 foreign (effective 2007). adv. bk.rev. **Document type:** *Newspaper.* **Description:** Deals with the care and training of horses, riding tips and equine news.
Published by: Horse & Pony News Paper Inc., PO Box 2050, Seffner, FL 33583-2050. TEL 813-621-2510, FAX 813-621-7431, horsepony@mindspring.com. Ed., Pub. Louise Smith. R&P, Adv. contact Valerie J Hirvela. B&W page USD 220; trim 14 x 10. Circ: 11,100 (paid).

798 GBR
HORSE + PONY. Text in English. 1971-2001; N.S. 2005 (Oct.). m. GBP 28.80 domestic; GBP 42.40 in Europe; GBP 57.40 elsewhere (effective 2009). adv. bk.rev. illus. **Document type:** *Magazine, Consumer.*
Former titles (until 2004): H & P (1471-4019); (until 1999): Horse and Pony (0262-5814)
—CCC.
Published by: Bourne Publishing Group Ltd. (B P G), Roebuck House, 33 Broad St, Stamford, Lincs PE9 1RB, United Kingdom. TEL 44-1780-766199, FAX 44-1780-754774, info@bournepublishinggroup.co.uk, http://www.bournepublishinggroup.co.uk/. Ed. Sarah Whittington. Circ: 54,260 (paid).

636.1 GBR ISSN 0955-5366
HORSE & RIDER; a real passion for horses. Text in English. 1950. m. GBP 48.10 domestic; GBP 69.90 in Europe; GBP 86 elsewhere (effective 2009). adv. bk.rev.; Website rev. illus. back issues avail. **Document type:** *Magazine, Consumer.* **Description:** Covers all aspects of equestrianism in depth and actively promotes classical riding principles and humane horse care.
Former titles (until 1981): The Light Horse (0024-3329); (until 1951): Show Jumping and Horse News
Indexed: F&GI, JHMA, SportS.
Published by: D.J. Murphy Publishers Ltd., Headley House, Headley Rd, Grayshott, Surrey GU26 6TU, United Kingdom. TEL 44-1428-601020, info@signaturepl.co.uk, http://www.djmurphy.co.uk. Eds. Nicky Moffatt, Alison Bridge. Adv. contact Amanda Toms. **Subscr. to:** PO Box 464, Berkhamsted, Herts HP4 2UR, United Kingdom. TEL 44-1442-879097. **Dist. by:** Seymour Distribution Ltd.

798 636.1 USA ISSN 0018-5159
SF277
HORSE & RIDER. Text in English. 1968. m. USD 15.95 domestic; USD 28.95 in Canada; USD 30.95 elsewhere (effective 2008). adv. bk.rev. charts; illus.; tr.lit. Index. back issues avail.; reprints avail. **Document type:** *Magazine, Consumer.* **Description:** Provides readers with the expert advice they want.
Incorporates (1981-1991): Performance Horseman (0744-3633)
Related titles: Online - full text ed.: USD 8 (effective 2008).
Indexed: A09, A10, A11, A22, B04, C05, CPerI, G06, G07, G08, G09, H20, I05, I07, M01, M02, M04, MASUSE, P01, P02, P10, P16, P19, P48, P53, P54, PMR, PQC, R03, RASB, RGAb, RGPR, S23, SD, SportS, T02, U01, V02, V03, V04, W03, W05.
—Ingenta. **CCC.**
Published by: Source Interlink Companies, 2000 S Stemmons Freeway, Ste 101, Lake Dallas, TX 75065. TEL 940-497-4600, FAX 940-497-5749, dheine@sourceinterlink.com, http://www.sourceinterlinkmedia.com. Ed. Darrell Dodds. Pub. Susan Harding. Adv. contact Jim Hart. B&W page USD 5,325, color page USD 8,340; bleed 8.125 x 10.75. Circ: 161,596 (paid).

798 CAN ISSN 1702-8299
HORSE CANADA. (The title of the journal appears to be Horse-Canada.com or Horse Canada. I put Horse-Canada.com in the variant format field.) Text in English. 2002. bi-m. CAD 24.95 (effective 2005). **Document type:** *Magazine, Consumer.*
Formed by the merger of (1988-2002): Horsepower (0840-6715); (1982-2002): Canadian Horseman (0840-6200); Which was formerly (until 1989): Horse Sense (0829-3244); (until 1983): Horse Sense Press (0821-5073)
Indexed: H20, SD.
Published by: Horse Publications, 225 Industrial Pkwy S, P O Box 670, Aurora, ON L4G 4J9, Canada. TEL 905-727-0107, FAX 905-841-1530, info@horse-canada.com, http://www.horse-canada.com.

798 USA ISSN 2154-1434
▼ **HORSE CENTS.** Text in English. forthcoming 2011 (Jan.). a. **Document type:** *Magazine, Consumer.*
Published by: One Horse Press, 70883 39th St, Paw Paw, MI 49079. onehorsepress@aol.com.

798 AUS ISSN 1446-6287
HORSE DEALS. Text in English. 1986. m. AUD 95.70 for 6 mos. (effective 2009). adv. back issues avail. **Document type:** *Magazine, Consumer.* **Description:** Provides information about horses in Australia.
Former titles (until 2001): Horse Deals Australia (1442-9055); (until 1996): Horse Deals Australia, New Zealand (1323-3696); (until 1994): Horse Deals Around Australia
Related titles: Optical Disk - DVD ed.: AUD 19.50 per issue (effective 2009).
Published by: Horse Deals Australia, 7 Anthony St, PO Box 2049, Mount Gambier, SA 5290, Australia. TEL 61-8-87254744, FAX 61-8-87254711. adv.: B&W page AUD 572, color page AUD 85.

636.1 GBR ISSN 2046-0600
HORSE HEALTH. Text in English. 2005. bi-m. GBP 25 domestic; GBP 40 foreign; free to qualified personnel (effective 2011). adv. **Document type:** *Magazine, Trade.* **Description:** Designed for those whose profession is responsible for the health, well-being and treatment of horses every day.
Published by: Wharncliffe Publishing Ltd., 47 Church St, Barnsley, S Yorkshire S70 2AS, United Kingdom. TEL 44-1226-734639, FAX 44-1226-734478, editorial@wharncliffepublishing.co.uk, http://www.wharncliffepublishing.co.uk. Adv. contact Tony Barry TEL 44-1226-734333.

636.1 USA ISSN 0145-9791
SF277
HORSE ILLUSTRATED. Text in English. 1976. m. USD 10 domestic; USD 28 foreign (effective 2008). adv. bk.rev. illus. Index. back issues avail.; reprints avail. **Document type:** *Magazine, Consumer.* **Description:** For families caring for one or more pleasure horses and who ride both English and Western (all breeds). Covers the care, health and performance of the horse, as well as regular features on training, conditioning, feeding and showing.
Published by: BowTie, Inc., 2401 Beverly Blvd, PO Box 57900, Los Angeles, CA 90057. TEL 213-385-2222, FAX 213-385-8565, adtraffic@bowtieinc.com, http://www.bowtieinc.com. Eds. Elizabeth Moyer, Moira Harris. adv.: B&W page USD 7,530, color page USD 11,080; trim 8 x 10.875. Circ: 197,772 (paid and controlled).

636.1 USA ISSN 0890-233X
SF278.5 CODEN: AESSE8
HORSE INDUSTRY DIRECTORY. Text in English. 1972. a. USD 25 per issue to non-members; free to members (effective 2010). **Document type:** *Directory, Trade.* **Description:** Contains both national and international contacts covering every segment of the equine community and breed registries, racing, rodeo, show, sport, and trails organizations.
Formerly (until 1976): Horse Industry Trade Press Directory
Published by: American Horse Council, Inc., 1616 H St NW 7th Fl, Washington, DC 20006. TEL 202-296-4031, FAX 202-296-1970, ahc@horsecouncil.org.

798.2 NLD ISSN 1383-0732
HORSE INTERNATIONAL; sport & breeding. Text in English. 1993. 10/yr. EUR 60.50 in Europe; USD 85 elsewhere (effective 2009). adv. illus. **Document type:** *Magazine, Consumer.*
Formerly (until Dec. 1994): Horse Sport International (1352-6006)
Published by: BCM Publishing, Postbus 1392, Eindhoven, 5602 BJ, Netherlands. TEL 31-40-8447644, FAX 31-40-8447655, bcm@bcm.nl, http://www.bcm.nl. Ed. Denise van der Net. Adv. contact Inge van der Net. B&W page EUR 2,235, color page EUR 2,630; 233 x 320. Circ: 19,000.

798.2 USA ISSN 1097-6949
HORSE JOURNAL; the product, care and service guide for people who love horses. Text in English. 1994. m. USD 24 combined subscription domestic (print & online eds.); USD 29 combined subscription in Canada (print & online eds.); USD 42 combined subscription elsewhere (print & online eds.) (effective 2010). illus. Index. back issues avail.; reprints avail. **Document type:** *Journal, Consumer.* **Description:** Contains information about product, care and service guide for horse owners.
Formerly (until 199?): Michael Plumb's Horse Journal (1073-5704)
Related titles: Online - full text ed.: Horse-Journal.com.
Indexed: G06, G07, G08, I05, I07, R03, RGAb, RGPR, W03, W05.

Published by: Belvoir Media Group, LLC, PO Box 5656, Norwalk, CT 06856. TEL 203-857-3100, 800-424-7887, FAX 203-857-3103, customer_service@belvoir.com. Ed. Cynthia Foley. **Subscr. to:** Palm Coast Data, LLC, PO Box 420235, Palm Coast, FL 32142. TEL 800-829-9165, http://www.palmcoastdata.com.

798 USA ISSN 1935-2433
HORSE LOVER JOURNAL. Text in English. 2007. bi-m. **Document type:** *Newsletter, Consumer.*
Media: Online - full text.
Published by: Carolina Rag Company, 6914 Toogoodoo Rd, Hollywood, SC 29449. TEL 843-889-9286. Ed. David A Spooner.

798 GBR ISSN 1368-6453
HORSE MAGAZINE; inspiration for riders. Text in English. 1997. m. GBP 34.99 domestic; USD 78.80 in US & Canada; EUR 54.40 in Europe; GBP 60.90 elsewhere; GBP 3.50 newsstand/cover (effective 2009). adv. illus. back issues avail. **Document type:** *Magazine, Consumer.* **Description:** Provides lively, educational and entertaining articles for all levels of equestrian enthusiasts.
—BLDSC (4329.347500).
Published by: I P C Country & Leisure Media Ltd. (Subsidiary of: I P C Media Ltd.), The Blue Fin Bldg, 110 Southwark St, London, SE1 0SU, United Kingdom. TEL 44-20-31485000, http://www.ipcmedia.com. Eds. Jo Browne, Joanna Pyatt TEL 44-20-31484600. Adv. contact Emma Sharp TEL 44-20-31484226. B&W page GBP 1,800, color page GBP 2,400; trim 210 x 297. Circ: 18,268. **Subscr. to:** Rockwood House, Perrymount Rd, Haywards Heath RH16 3DH, United Kingdom. TEL 44-845-1231231, IPCsubs@quadrantsubs.com, http://www.magazinesdirect.co.uk. **Dist. by:** MarketForce UK Ltd. salesinnovation@marketforce.co.uk, http://www.marketforce.co.uk/.

798 USA
HORSE NEWS. Text in English. m. USD 12 (effective 2000). back issues avail. **Document type:** *Newspaper, Consumer.*
Related titles: Online - full text ed.
Published by: Hunterdon County Democrat Newspapers, Minneakoning Rd, PO Box 32, Flemington, NJ 08822-0032. TEL 908-782-4747, FAX 908-782-6572. Ed., R&P Jay Langley. Adv. contact Al Angelini. Circ: 12,000.

798 USA
THE HORSE OF DELAWARE VALLEY. Text in English. 1980. m. USD 35. adv. back issues avail. **Document type:** *Newspaper, Trade.* **Description:** Concerned with equestrian sports, including Olympic disciplines, show jumping, dressage, steeplechase racing, and horse breeding.
Related titles: Online - full text ed.
Published by: Sar Cavanagh, Ed., PO Box 223, Unionville, PA 19375. TEL 610-793-3119, FAX 610-793-3119. Pub. H L Schwartz III. Adv. contact Deb Vandenberg. page USD 800. Circ: 24,800.

798 336 USA
HORSE OWNERS AND BREEDERS TAX HANDBOOK. Text in English. 1978. irreg. USD 85 per issue (effective 2010). **Document type:** *Handbook/Manual/Guide, Trade.* **Description:** Explains the Internal Revenue Code as it pertains to the U.S. horse industry. Covers topics such as Business versus hobby-including summaries of important court decisions, and forms of doing business etc.
Formerly (until 1997): Horse Owners and Breeders Tax Manual
Published by: American Horse Council, Inc., 1616 H St NW 7th Fl, Washington, DC 20006. TEL 202-296-4031, FAX 202-296-1970, ahc@horsecouncil.org.

798 USA
HORSE PREVIEWS MAGAZINE. Text in English. m. USD 15 domestic; USD 18 in Canada (effective 2008); USD 40 elsewhere. adv.
Related titles: Online - full text ed.
Published by: Exchange Publishing, P O Box 427, Spokane, WA 99210-0427. TEL 509-922-3456, 800-326-2223. Ed., R&P Helen Boyd. Pub. Aaron R Spurway. Adv. contact Keri Marion. B&W page USD 125. Circ: 6,850.

798.4 AUS ISSN 1833-3427
HORSE RACING AUSTRALIA MAGAZINE. Abbreviated title: H R A. Text in English. 1997. q. AUD 49; AUD 7.70 per issue; free to members (effective 2009). adv. back issues avail. **Document type:** *Magazine, Consumer.* **Description:** Provides news about horse racing information in Australia.
Related titles: Online - full text ed.: ISSN 1833-3435. 1998.
Published by: Winform Publishing, PO BOX 375, Wallsend, NSW 2287, Australia. TEL 61-2-49501747, FAX 61-2-49517364, direct@hunterlink.net.au. Ed. Mr. Garry Robinson. Adv. contact Prue Hawkins. color page AUD 1,100; 200 x 270. Circ: 18,000.

THE HORSE REPORT. *see* VETERINARY SCIENCE

798 AUS ISSN 1832-4819
HORSE SHOWS. Text in English. 2005. bi-m. **Document type:** *Magazine, Consumer.*
Published by: Horse Media Pty. Ltd., PO Box 73, Kurmond, NSW 2757, Australia. TEL 61-2-45730811, FAX 61-2-45730666, horseshows@bigpond.com, www.horseshows.com.au.

798 CAN ISSN 1205-5433
HORSE SOURCE. Text in English. m. CAD 18; CAD 24 foreign (effective 1998).
Address: A2- 2285 St Laurent Blvd, Ottawa, ON K1G 4Z4, Canada. TEL 613-521-4392, FAX 613-521-5576.

636.1 USA ISSN 0018-5191
SF284.U5
HORSE WORLD; feature-oriented show-horse specialty publication. Text in English. 1933. m. USD 60 (effective 2005). adv. bk.rev. **Document type:** *Magazine, Consumer.*
Indexed: SportS.
Published by: Dabora, Inc., 730 Madison St, Shelbyville, TN 37160. TEL 931-684-8123, FAX 931-684-8196. Ed. David L Howard. Pub. Christy Howard Parsons. Circ: 5,000.

798 CAN ISSN 1495-5563
HORSELIFE. Text in English. 1978. bi-m. CAD 16 domestic; CAD 30 foreign (effective 2006). adv. **Document type:** *Newsletter.* **Description:** Covers rule changes, dates of clinics-seminars, current topics in coaching information, show dates, affiliate organization news.
Former titles (until 2000): Canadian Equestrian Federation. Federation Bulletin (1483-8419); (until 1996): Canadian Equestrian Federation. Bulletin (0838-1690); (until 1988): Canadian Equestrian Federation. Official Bulletin (0710-9156)
Indexed: SD, T02.
Published by: (Equine Canada), Post Publishers Ltd., 26730 56th Ave, Suite 105, Langley, BC V4W 3X5, Canada. TEL 604-607-5577, 800-663-4802, FAX 604-607-0533, http://www.postpublishers.com. Circ: 11,051 (controlled).

798.2 USA ISSN 0018-523X
HORSEMAN AND FAIR WORLD; devoted to the trotting and pacing horse. Text in English. 1877. w. USD 46 for 6 mos. domestic; USD 54 for 6 mos. foreign; USD 80 domestic; USD 98 foreign (effective 2005). adv. illus.; stat. **Document type:** *Magazine, Consumer.* **Description:** Discusses harness horse racing and breeding.
Related titles: Online - full text ed.
Published by: Horseman Publishing Co, Inc., PO Box 8480, Lexington, KY 40533-8480. TEL 859-276-4026, FAX 859-277-8100. Ed. Kathy Parker. Adv. contact Lynne Meyers. B&W page USD 580, color page USD 840. Circ: 6,500 (paid).

798 USA
HORSEMAN'S NEWS. Variant title: California Horseman's News. Text in English. m. USD 25.
Published by: Pacific Coast Publications, PO Box 893640, Temecula, CA 92589. TEL 909-699-2777. Ed. Virginia McClintock.

636.1 798.4 USA ISSN 0018-5256
HORSEMEN'S JOURNAL. Text in English. 1949-1993; resumed 1997. m. USD 14 (effective 2007). adv. bk.rev. bibl.; charts; illus.; stat. index. back issues avail. **Document type:** *Journal, Trade.* **Description:** Aimed chiefly at thoroughbred race horse owners and trainers who are members of the Horsemen's Benevolent and Protective Association. Seeks to keep them abreast of the latest racing industry issues.
Related titles: Microform ed.: (from PQC).
Indexed: G09, P02, P10, P48, P53, P54, PQC.
Published by: The National Horsemen's Benevolent and Protective Association, 4063 Iron Work Pkwy, Ste 2, Lexington, KY 40511-8905. TEL 859-259-0451, 866-245-1711, FAX 859-259-0452, racing@hbpa.org. adv.: B&W page USD 1,140; trim 10.88 x 8.13. Circ: 30,000.

798 USA
HORSE'N AROUND. Text in English. m. adv. **Document type:** *Magazine, Consumer.* **Description:** Written specifically for horse enthusiasts in the Midwest. Provides tips and news from top notch regional authorities and associations along with features from nationally recognized clinicians.
Published by: Horse'n Around Magazine, 279, Blue Earth, MN 56013-0279. TEL 800-657-4663, gkaraban@klapublishing.com. adv.: B&W page USD 685; trim 10.25 x 12.

636.1 USA ISSN 0046-7936
HORSES. Text in English. 1962. bi-m. USD 29.95; USD 39.95 foreign. adv. bk.rev.; film rev. stat. **Document type:** *Magazine, Consumer.* **Description:** Covers international equestrian events.
Indexed: SportS.
Published by: Horses Publishing Co., 21 Greenview, Carlsbad, CA 92009. TEL 619-931-9958, FAX 619-931-0650. Ed. John Quirk. Circ: 10,000.

798.2 CAN ISSN 0225-4913
HORSES ALL; the magazine dedicated to horses and their people. Text in English. 1977. m. CAD 24.61 domestic; USD 51 foreign (effective 2005). adv. bk.rev.; film rev. illus. **Document type:** *Newspaper, Consumer.* **Description:** Official publication of 39 national and regional associations including light horse, heavy horse, rodeo, and jumping. Includes health news, equine law, sports psychology and a kids page.
Address: 49 White Oak Crescent S W, Calgary, AB T3C 3J9, Canada. TEL 403-249-8770, FAX 403-249-8769. Ed. Cindy Mark. Pub. Steven Mark. adv.: B&W page CAD 545. Circ: 9,000.

798 GBR ISSN 0081-3761
HORSES IN TRAINING (YEAR). Text in English. 1891. a. GBP 15.99 per issue (effective 2009). adv. 800 p./no.; **Document type:** *Report, Trade.* **Description:** Lists the strings of over 600 Flat and Jumps trainers in Britain, along with leading Irish and French yards, in an A-Z format. Includes owner and breeding of each horse plus foaling dates and sale prices of two-year-olds. Fully indexed, it includes 200 pages of racing statistics.
Formerly: Sporting Chronicle "Horses in Training"
Published by: Racing Post, One Canada Sq, Canary Wharf, London, E14 5AP, United Kingdom. TEL 44-1635-898781, help@racingpost.com, http://www.racingpost.com. Ed. Richard Lowther.

798 GBR
HORSES TO FOLLOW. Text in English. 1969. s-a. ((flat edition published Mar.; jumps edition published Sep.)). GBP 7.95 per issue (effective 2010). **Document type:** *Journal, Consumer.* **Description:** Notes on fifty of the horses most likely to succeed in the coming season.
Published by: Portway Press Ltd., 25 Timeform House, Northgate, Halifax, W Yorks HX1 1XF, United Kingdom. TEL 44-1422-330330, FAX 44-1422-398017, timeform@timeform.com.

636.1 USA ISSN 1093-9385
HORSES U S A. Text in English. 1997. a. USD 6.99 per issue (effective 2008). adv. **Document type:** *Magazine, Trade.* **Description:** Geared for first-time buyer of a registered (purebred) horse and includes medical, breed, riding and training information, as well as a buyer's guide for must-have products.
Published by: BowTie, Inc., 2401 Beverly Blvd, PO Box 57900, Los Angeles, CA 90057. TEL 213-385-2222, FAX 213-385-8565, adtraffic@bowtieinc.com, http://www.bowtieinc.com. Ed. Moira Harris. adv.: B&W page USD 4,410, color page USD 6,600; trim 8 x 10.875. Circ: 93,336.

636.1 USA ISSN 0018-5264
THE HORSETRADER. Text in English. 1960. m. USD 45; USD 3 newsstand/cover (effective 2007). adv. illus. **Document type:** *Magazine, Trade.*
Published by: The Horsetrader, Inc. (Subsidiary of: Morris Multimedia, Inc.), 2112 Montgomery St, Fort Worth, TX 76107. TEL 817-426-4900, 800-837-0066, FAX 817-426-4644. Pub. Warren Wilson. adv.: B&W page USD 468. Circ: 36,255 (paid and controlled).

798 NLD ISSN 1570-6354
HORSIMO. Text in Dutch. 2006. m. EUR 19.95 domestic; EUR 39.95 in Belgium; EUR 39.95 in Spain (effective 2010). adv. **Document type:** *Magazine, Consumer.*
Published by: Publi Force, Postbus 229, Alblasserdam, 2950 AE, Netherlands. TEL 31-78-6522700, FAX 31-78-6522701, info@publiforce.nl, http://www.publiforce.nl. adv.: page EUR 2,500; trim 230 x 297. Circ: 24,415.

798 GBR
HOUNDS. Text in English. 1984. m. GBP 30 (effective 2009). adv. bk.rev. illus. 66 p./no. 2 cols./p.; back issues avail. **Document type:** *Magazine, Consumer.* **Description:** National publication serving the hunting fraternity, covers all hunting with hounds.
Published by: Ravensworld, Rose Cottage, Hughley, Shropshrie, Shrewsbury SY5 6NX, United Kingdom. TEL 44-1746-785637, linda.sagar@yahoo.co.uk. adv.: color page GBP 400. Circ: 10,800.

798 USA ISSN 1057-8501
HUNTER & SPORT HORSE. Text in English. 1989. 6/yr. USD 21.95; USD 5 newsstand/cover (effective 2005). adv. 92 p./no.; back issues avail. **Document type:** *Magazine, Consumer.* **Description:** Covers dressage, combined training, hunter-jumper, and related equestrian sports.
Formerly (until 1992): Midwest Hunter & Sport Horse (1056-8182)
Published by: Silver Square Tech, Inc., 12204 Covington Rd., Fort Wayne, IN 46814-9720. TEL 260-625-4030, FAX 260-625-3480. Ed., Pub. Laura Allen. Adv. contact Kerry Scarbough. B&W page USD 1,260, color page USD 1,680; trim 8.5 x 10.825. Circ: 29,000 (paid).

798.2 USA ISSN 1934-9475
HUNTER JUMPER. Text in English. 2007. m. USD 25 domestic; USD 40 in Canada (effective 2008). adv. **Document type:** *Magazine, Consumer.* **Description:** Highlights relevant issues, products and services for horse riders, trainers and show managers on the Pacific Coast.
Published by: Calvert Media Group, 12385 Pear Ln, Wilton, CA 95693. TEL 916-837-6214, FAX 916-687-0441, info@hunterjumpermag.com. Ed. Kym Calvert.

I.M. COWGIRL; the life of the western woman. *see* WOMEN'S INTERESTS

798 USA ISSN 1097-8380
ICELANDIC HORSE AND TRAVEL MAGAZINE. Text in English. q. USD 25 domestic; USD 35 in Canada; USD 45 elsewhere (effective 2001). adv. **Description:** Provides information on Icelandic horses and travel to Iceland or wherever the Icelandic Horse is found.
Formerly: Icelandic Horse Magazine of North America (1087-271X)
Related titles: Online - full content ed.
Address: 507 North Sullivan Rd, Ste A-4, Veradale, WA 99037. TEL 509-928-8389, FAX 50—928-2392, http://www.icemag.com. adv.: B&W page USD 135, color page USD 355.

636.16 798.2 NLD ISSN 1384-4334
IJSLANDSE PAARDEN. Text in Dutch. 1973. bi-m. EUR 45 domestic; EUR 62.50 foreign; EUR 10 newsstand/cover (effective 2009). bk.rev.; video rev. illus.; mkt. back issues avail. **Document type:** *Newsletter.* **Description:** For owners and riders of Icelandic horses. Covers care, breeding, sporting events and exhibitions, travel in Iceland.
Formerly (until 1996): Stamboekje (1382-1407)
Published by: Nederlandse Stamboek voor IJslandse Paarden, Postbus 84, Oosterwolde, 8430 AB, Netherlands. info@nsijp.nl, http://www.nsijp.nl.

798.4 USA ISSN 1083-8309
ILLINOIS RACING NEWS. Text in English. 1972. m. USD 24 (effective 2007). adv. bk.rev. **Document type:** *Magazine, Consumer.* **Description:** Covers thoroughbred horse racing and breeding.
Published by: (Illinois Thoroughbred Breeders and Owners Foundation), Midwest Outdoors Ltd., 111 Shore Dr, Burr Ridge, IL 60521. TEL 630-887-7722, 800-666-8878, FAX 630-887-1958. Ed. Joan Colby. Pub. Gene Laulunen.

798.2 NLD ISSN 0166-3607
IN DE STRENGEN. Text in Dutch. 1938. 25/yr. adv. **Document type:** *Magazine, Trade.*
Published by: (Koninklijk Warmbloed Paardenstamboek Nederland), BCM Publishing, Postbus 1392, Eindhoven, 5602 BJ, Netherlands. TEL 31-40-8447644, FAX 31-40-8447655, bcm@bcm.nl, http://www.bcm.nl. Ed. Charlotte Dekker. Adv. contact Alexander den Braber. B&W page EUR 1,251, color page EUR 2,058; 215 x 285. Circ: 30,500.

798.2 NLD
IN DE STRENGEN INTERNATIONAL. Text in English. bi-m. adv.
Published by: (Koninklijk Warmbloed Paardenstamboek Nederland), BCM Publishing, Postbus 1392, Eindhoven, 5602 BJ, Netherlands. TEL 31-40-8447644, FAX 31-40-8447655, bcm@bcm.nl, http://www.bcm.nl. Ed. Yvonne Buis-Franken. Adv. contact Moniek Kouwenberg. B&W page EUR 477, color page EUR 561; 215 x 285. Circ: 5,000.

798 BEL ISSN 0777-916X
INFOR MARECHALERIE-DER HUF/FARRIERS JOURNAL. Text in English, French, German. 1986. bi-m. EUR 50 in the European Union; USD 50 elsewhere (effective 2005). adv. bk.rev. illus. back issues avail. **Description:** Covers all aspects of horse locomotion, the life of the professional blacksmith, and the relationships between blacksmithing, horse ownership and veterinary medicine.
Formerly (until 1990): Infor Marechalerie (0774-4323)
Related titles: Spanish ed.: El Herrador; Italian ed.: Infor Mascalcia. ISSN 1376-425X. 1996.
Published by: Diasse S P R L, Rue d'Opprebais 16, Maleves-Ste-Marie, 1360, Belgium. TEL 32-10-888898, FAX 32-10-889934. Ed. Domique Falisse. R&P Dominique Falisse. adv.: B&W page USD 770, color page USD 1,450; trim 297 x 210. Circ: 3,400.

IPPOLOGIA. *see* VETERINARY SCIENCE

798 IRL
IRELAND'S EQUESTRIAN. Text in English. m. adv. **Document type:** *Magazine, Consumer.*
Published by: Mainstream Publications, Coolbracken House, Church Terrace, Bray, Co. Wicklow, Ireland. TEL 353-1-2868246, FAX 353-1-2868241. Adv. contact Leslie Magill. color page EUR 1,587; trim 210 x 297.

798 IRL ISSN 1393-4120
IRELAND'S HORSE REVIEW. Text in English. 1997. m. adv. **Document type:** *Magazine, Consumer.*
Related titles: Online - full text ed.

S

Published by: Review Publishing Group, Garden St., Ballina, Co. Mayo, Ireland. TEL 353-96-73500, FAX 353-96-72077, horserev@iol.ie. Ed. Liam Geddes. adv.: B&W page EUR 2,469, color page EUR 2,825; 10.25 x 14. Circ: 30,000.

798 IRL
IRISH BLOODHORSE; magazine for the thoroughbred industry. Text in English. 2005 (Sept.). m. **Document type:** *Magazine, Consumer.*
Published by: Bloodhorse Media Ltd., PO Box 907, Naas, County Kildare, Ireland. TEL 353-45-864890.

636.1 798.4 IRL ISSN 0021-1184
IRISH FIELD. Text in English. 1870. w. EUR 175 domestic; EUR 210 in United Kingdom; EUR 210 in Europe; EUR 250 elsewhere (effective 2004). adv. bk.rev. illus. **Document type:** *Newspaper, Consumer.* **Description:** Covers horse breeding, racing and show jumping.
Related titles: Microfilm ed.
Published by: Irish Times Ltd., Irish Farm Centre, Bluebell, Dublin, 12, Ireland. TEL 353-1-4051100, FAX 353-1-4554008, info@irishfield.ie. adv.: B&W page EUR 4,500. Circ: 11,256.

798.4 IRL ISSN 0791-9107
IRISH RACING CALENDAR. Text in English. 1986. a. adv. **Document type:** *Magazine, Consumer.*
Address: The Registry Office, The Turf Club, The Curragh, Co. Kildare, Ireland. TEL 353-45-445600, FAX 353-45-445699. Adv. contact Martin Murphy. B&W page EUR 381. Circ: 1,600 (paid and controlled).

798 SWE ISSN 0284-9607
ISLANDSHAESTEN/ICELANDIC HORSE. Text in Swedish. 1987. 9/yr. adv.
Published by: Svenska Islandshaestfoereningen, Stroemsholm, Ridsportens Hus, Kolbaeck, 73040, Sweden. TEL 46-220-45680, FAX 46-220-45683, kansli@icelandichorse.se. adv.: B&W page SEK 5,000, color page SEK 7,500. Circ: 5,000.

798 FIN ISSN 1797-3538
ISLANNINHEVONEN. Text in Finnish. 1984. bi-m. **Document type:** *Magazine, Consumer.*
Formerly (until 2008): Islanninhevoskuulumisia (0783-7828)
Published by: Suomen Islanninhevosyhdistys ry/Finnish Icelandic Horse Association, c/o Anne Backman, Leppapammemtie 210, Perttula, 01860, Finland. TEL 358-45-6716040, anne.backman@kolumbus.fi.

798.2 DEU ISSN 0173-8208
JAHRBUCH ZUCHT; Leistungen und Daten der Deutschen Pferdezucht. Text in German. 1911. a. EUR 64 (effective 2005). **Document type:** *Directory, Trade.* **Description:** German stallion data, including lists of breeders.
Former titles (until 1972): Jahrbuch fuer Pferdeleistungspruefungen. Tiel 2, Zucht (0173-8194); Leistunshengste der Deutschen Warmblutzucht (0173-8178)
Published by: (Deutsche Reiterliche Vereinigung), F N - Verlag, Freiherr-von-Langen-Str 13, Warendorf, 48231, Germany. TEL 49-2581-6362115, FAX 49-2581-633146, http://www.fnverlag.de. Circ: 3,000.

JESSY. *see* CHILDREN AND YOUTH—For

JESSY. *see* CHILDREN AND YOUTH—For

798.2 CZE ISSN 1210-5406
JEZDECTVI. Text in Czech. 1993. m. adv. **Document type:** *Magazine, Consumer.*
Published by: K4K Publishing, Prokopova 15, Prague 3, 13000, Czech Republic. TEL 420-222-317809. Ed. Zdena Motyginova. Adv. contact Marketa Vosatkova.

798.4 ARG ISSN 0329-6598
JOCKEY CLUB BIBLIOTECA. BOLETIN. Key Title: Boletin de la Biblioteca del Jockey Club. Text in Spanish. 1935. irreg.
Published by: Jockey Club of Buenos Aires, Ave. Alvear 1345, Buenos Aires, 1014, Argentina. info@eljockeyclub.com, http://www.jockeyclub.com.ar. Ed. Robert D Muller.

798.2 USA ISSN 1949-9787
JOIN-UP JOURNAL. Text in English. 19??. q. USD 45 domestic; USD 55 foreign (effective 2009). **Document type:** *Journal, Trade.* **Description:** Provides information that will assist readers on the path to force-free training and encourage them to bring understanding and trust to their horses, family members and others.
Published by: Monty & Pat Roberts, Inc., PO Box 1700, Solvang, CA 93464. TEL 805-688-6288, FAX 805-688-9709, info@montyroberts.com, http://www.montyroberts.com. Ed. Monty Roberts.

798 JPN ISSN 1340-3516
SF277
JOURNAL OF EQUINE SCIENCE. Text in English, Japanese. 1994. q. **Document type:** *Journal, Academic/Scholarly.*
Formed by the merger of (1990-1993): Japanese Journal of Equine Science (0917-1967); (1977-1993): Kyosoba Sogo Kenkyujo Hokoku (0386-4634); Which was formerly (1961-1976): Kyosoba Hoken Kenkyusho Hokoku (0368-5543)
Related titles: Online - full content ed.: free (effective 2011); Online - full text ed.: ISSN 1347-7501.
Indexed: A34, A35, A36, A37, A38, A39, AgBio, B20, B21, B25, BIOSIS Prev, C27, C29, CABA, D03, D04, E12, E13, ESPM, G11, GH, GenetAb, H17, IndVet, MycolAb, N04, P33, P39, PN&I, R08, R14, RM&VM, RefZh, S13, S14, S15, S16, S18, SCOPUS, TAR, VS, ViroIAbstr, W11.
—BLDSC (4979.491000), INIST.
Published by: Japanese Society of Equine Science, 321-4 Tokami-cho, Utsunomiya-shi, Tochigi 320-0856, Japan. TEL 81-28-647-0656, FAX 81-28-647-0686, jes@center.equinst.go.jp, http://www.equinst.go.jp/JSES/top.html. Ed. Hirokazu Tsubone.

798 USA
JUST HORSES. Text in English. m. **Document type:** *Newspaper, Consumer.* **Description:** Lists equine businesses in Connecticut, Massachusetts, Rhode Island and eastern New York.
Contact Owner: Krahn Publishing, Inc. Circ: 6,000 (paid).

798 CHE ISSN 1420-5696
KAVALLO; Zeitschrift fuer Pferdesport und Pferdezucht. Text in German. 1911. 20/yr. CHF 99.80 (effective 1999 & 2000). adv. bk.rev. illus. back issues avail. **Document type:** *Consumer.*
Former titles (until 1993): Kavallerist (1420-5874); (until 1990): Schweizer Kavallerist (0036-7389)
Address: Postfach 25, Pfaeffikon ZH, 8330, Switzerland. TEL 41-1-9531180, FAX 41-1-9531183. Ed. Karin Tropper. Pub. Kavallo GmbH. R&P Kavallo Gambh. Adv. contact Andre Bolliger. Circ: 17,200.

798 USA
KEENELAND. Text in English. 2000. 3/yr. USD 5 newsstand/cover (effective 2001). adv. **Document type:** *Magazine, Consumer.*
Published by: The Blood-Horse, Inc., 3101 Beaumont Centre Circle, Lexington, KY 40513. TEL 859-278-2361, FAX 859-276-4450, http://www.bloodhorse.com. Ed. Jacqueline Duke. Pub. Stacy V Bearse.

798 636.1 POL ISSN 0137-1487
KON POLSKI. Text in Polish. 1966. m. USD 68 in Europe; USD 90 elsewhere (effective 2003). adv. bk.rev. **Document type:** *Newspaper, Consumer.*
Indexed: AgrLib.
Published by: Kon Polski Sp. z o.o., ul Kaniowska 132, Warsaw, 01529, Poland. TEL 48-22-8699320, FAX 48-22-8699318. Ed., R&P Jan Krauze. Adv. contact Anna Chmieliwska. B&W page USD 386, color page USD 579. Circ: 10,000.

636.1 798 RUS ISSN 0023-3285
KONEVODSTVO I KONNYI SPORT. Text in Russian. 1842. bi-m. USD 60 foreign (effective 2004). bk.rev. index.
—East View, INIST.
Address: Sadovaya-Spasskaya 18, Moscow, 107807, Russian Federation. TEL 7-095-2072071. Ed., R&P, Adv. contact Nikolai A Moiseenko. Circ: 15,000. **Dist. by:** M K - Periodica, ul Gilyarovskogo 39, Moscow 129110, Russian Federation. TEL 7-095-2845008, FAX 7-095-2813798, info@periodicals.ru, http://www.mkniga.ru.

798.2 USA ISSN 0047-4088
THE LARIAT. Text in English. 1949. m. USD 14 (effective 1999). adv. bk.rev. illus. back issues avail. **Document type:** *Newspaper.* **Description:** Constitutesa general tabloid for Northwest horsepeople. Covers all breeds of horses, news of individuals, clubs, and competitions.
Published by: Lariat, PO Box 229, Beaverton, OR 97075-0229. TEL 503-644-2233, FAX 503-644-2213. Ed. Barbara Zellner. Circ: 5,500.

798.2 028.5 DEU
LISSY; ein Herz fuer Pferde. Text in German. 1992. m. EUR 28.80; EUR 2.40 newsstand/cover (effective 2010). adv. **Document type:** *Magazine, Consumer.*
Published by: Pabel-Moewig Verlag KG (Subsidiary of: Bauer Media Group), Karlsruherstr 31, Rastatt, 76437, Germany. TEL 49-7222-130, FAX 49-7222-13218, empfang@vpm.de, http://www.vpm-online.de. Ed. Susanne Stegbauer. adv.: page EUR 4,900. Circ: 90,561 (paid).

798.2 028.5 CZE ISSN 1804-7912
▼ **LISSY.** Text in Czech. 2011. bi-m. CZK 28 newsstand/cover (effective 2011). adv. **Document type:** *Magazine, Consumer.* **Description:** Aimed at girls ages 7 to 13 who have an interest in horses and animals.
Published by: Bauer Media v.o.s. (Subsidiary of: Bauer Media Group), Viktora Huga 6, Prague 5, 150 00, Czech Republic. TEL 420-2-25008111, FAX 420-2-57327103, info@bauermedia.cz, http://www.bauermedia.cz. Ed. Andrea Behounkova. Adv. contact Dagmar Schoenova.

636.1 798 USA ISSN 0892-6271
LONE STAR HORSE REPORT. Text in English. 1983. m. USD 15 domestic (effective 2007). bk.rev. 76 p./no. 3 cols./p.; back issues avail. **Document type:** *Magazine, Consumer.* **Description:** Distributes information about horses, horsemen, events and places in the Texas-Oklahoma horse market.
Published by: Dan Talbot, Ed. & Pub., P O Box 470215, Fort Worth, TX 76147-0215. TEL 817-877-3050, FAX 817-877-3060. Ed., Pub. Dan Talbot. Circ: 12,000 (paid and controlled).

354 CAN ISSN 0317-7262
SF335.C2
MANITOBA. HORSE RACING COMMISSION. ANNUAL REPORT. Text in English. a. free. stat. **Document type:** *Government.*
Published by: Horse Racing Commission, P O Box 46086, Winnipeg, MB R3R 3S3, Canada. TEL 204-885-7770, FAX 204-831-0942. Circ: 200.

636.1 USA ISSN 0025-4274
SF277
THE MARYLAND HORSE. Text in English. 1936. m. membership only. adv. bk.rev. charts; illus.; stat. **Document type:** *Newsletter.* **Description:** Promotes Maryland's equine industry, covering the entire, diverse spectrum with concentration on the breeding and racing of thoroughbreds. Intended both as information and entertainment for all those interested in equestrian activities and events in Maryland.
Indexed: SportS.
Published by: Maryland Horse Breeders Association, 30 E Padonia Rd, 303, Timonium, MD 21093. TEL 410-252-2100, FAX 410-560-0503. Ed., R&P Timothy Capps. Adv. contact Barrie Reightler. Circ: 1,000.

798 USA ISSN 1945-1393
MASSACHUSETTS HORSE. Text in English. 1998. bi-m. USD 15 (effective 2008). adv. **Document type:** *Magazine, Consumer.* **Description:** Covers local horses, horsepeople, horse-related products and services, 4-H and other group activities and volunteer opportunities in western Massachusetts.
Published by: Stephanie Sanders-Ferris, Ed. & Pub., 99 Bissell Rd, PO Box 524, Goshen, MA 01032. TEL 413-268-3302, FAX 413-268-0050, info@mahorse.com. Pub. Stephanie Sanders-Ferris. adv.: color page USD 449.

636.1 DEU
MECKLENBURGER PFERDE. Text in German. 1990. m. **Document type:** *Magazine, Trade.*
Former titles (until 2007): Mecklenburger Pferde Journal (1613-656X); (until 2001): Das Mecklenburger Pferd
Published by: (Verband der Pferdezuechter Mecklenburg-Vorpommern e.V.), Delego Wirtschaftsverlag, Kloeresgang 5, Schwerin, 19053, Germany. TEL 49-385-485630, FAX 49-385-4856324, info@delego-verlag.de, http://delego-verlag.net.

798.2 DEU ISSN 1861-4205
MEIN PFERD; Das Magazin fuer aktive Reiter. Text in German. 2005. m. EUR 39.60 domestic; EUR 64.80 in Europe; EUR 106.80 elsewhere; EUR 3.50 newsstand/cover (effective 2011). adv. **Document type:** *Magazine, Consumer.*
Incorporates (2000-2008): Pferde Heute (1868-1220); Which was formerly (until 2000): Pferde Heute, Rund um den Paddock (1435-537X)
Published by: Jahr Top Special Verlag, Troplowitzstr 5, Hamburg, 22529, Germany. TEL 49-40-389060, FAX 49-40-38906300, info@jahr-tsv.de, http://www.jahr-tsv.de. Ed. Ilja van de Kasteele. Adv. contact Melanie Hausmann TEL 49-40-38906468. Circ: 32,871 (paid).

798.4 AUS ISSN 1449-8731
MELBOURNE CUP CARNIVAL. Text in English. 1996. a. free to members (effective 2009). 116 p./no.; Supplement avail.; back issues avail. **Document type:** *Magazine, Consumer.* **Description:** Features information on the Melbourne Cup Carnival, including fashion forecasts and ideas, plus interviews with world-renowned trainers and jockeys.
Published by: (Victoria Racing Club Ltd.), Text Pacific Publishing, Level 7, 620 Bourke St., Melbourne, VIC 3000, Australia. TEL 61-3-90380500, FAX 61-3-90380599, http://www.textpacific.com.au/.

798 AUT
MENSCH UND PFERD. Text in German. 1986. bi-m. adv. bk.rev. back issues avail. **Document type:** *Newsletter, Consumer.*
Formerly: Haflingersport (1018-3698)
Published by: Reitclub St. Erhard, Haymogasse 19, Vienna, W 1230, Austria. TEL 43-1-8884698. Ed. Erika Bruhns. Circ: 1,500 (controlled).

636.1 DEU ISSN 1867-6456
▼ **MENSCH UND PFERD INTERNATIONAL**; Zeitschrift fuer Foerderung und Therapie mit dem Pferd. Text in German. 2009. q. EUR 49.90; EUR 14 newsstand/cover (effective 2011). **Document type:** *Journal, Trade.*
Published by: Ernst Reinhardt Verlag, Kemnatenstr 46, Munich, 80639, Germany. TEL 49-89-1780160, FAX 49-89-17801630, webmaster@reinhardt-verlag.de.

798.2 NLD ISSN 0922-2499
MENSPORT. Text in Dutch. 1985. 9/yr. adv. **Document type:** *Magazine, Consumer.*
Published by: Media Primair, Anthonie Fokkerstraat 2, Barneveld, 3772 MR, Netherlands. TEL 31-342-400279, FAX 31-342-421580, info@mediaprimair.nl, http://www.mediaprimair.nl. adv.: B&W page EUR 820, color page EUR 1,044; 230 x 297.

798 USA
MICHIGAN QUARTER HORSE JOURNAL. Text in English. 1955. m. USD 35 to members. adv. illus. back issues avail. **Document type:** *Journal, Trade.* **Description:** Articles on the advancement and improvement of the breeding and performance of the quarter horse.
Published by: Michigan Quarter Horse Association, PO Box 278, Greenville, MI 48838. TEL 616-225-8211, FAX 616-225-8313, http://www.mich-qh.org. Ed. Diane Graves. Circ: 2,500.

636.1 USA ISSN 1056-3245
SF293.T5
MID-ATLANTIC THOROUGHBRED. Text in English. 1991. m. USD 30 domestic; USD 42 foreign (effective 2001). adv. bk.rev. **Document type:** *Newsletter, Trade.* **Description:** Promotes thoroughbred racing and breeding in the Mid-Atlantic region. Directed to horse breeders, trainers, owners and enthusiasts.
Published by: Maryland Horse Breeders Association, 30 E Padonia Rd, 303, Timonium, MD 21093. TEL 410-252-2100, FAX 410-560-0503. Ed., Pub. Timothy Capps. Adv. contacts Barrie Reightler, Brian Magness. B&W page USD 600, color page USD 1,200. Circ: 10,000.

798 USA
MID-SOUTH HORSE REVIEW. Text in English. 1992. m. USD 29 (effective 2007). adv. bk.rev. 64 p./no. 4 cols./p.; back issues avail. **Document type:** *Magazine, Consumer.* **Description:** Reporting news of interest to horse owners in mid-south area.
Published by: The Mid-South Horse Review, PO Box 423, Somerville, TN 38068. TEL 901-465-1905, FAX 901-465-1905, sales@midsouthhorsereview.com. Ed., R&P, Adv. contact Don Dowdle. B&W page USD 595. Circ: 11,000.

798.2 SWE ISSN 0345-7990
MIN HAEST. Text in Swedish. 1972. fortn. SEK 589 (effective 2009). adv. **Document type:** *Magazine, Consumer.*
Published by: Egmont Serieforlaget AB, Stora Varvsgatan 19A, Malmo, 20507, Sweden. TEL 46-40-385200, FAX 46-40-385396, tord.joensson@egmont.se, http://www.egmont.se. adv.: page SEK 20,400; trim 170 x 270. Circ: 35,000 (controlled).

798 ITA ISSN 1121-3183
IL MIO CAVALLO. Text in Italian. 1990. m. EUR 40 (effective 2009). **Document type:** *Magazine, Consumer.*
Published by: Mio Cavallo, Via Giovanni Battista Pergolesi, 8, Milan, MI 20124, Italy. TEL 39-02-66715150, FAX 39-02-66715171. Circ: 31,600.

636.1 USA ISSN 1942-4183
MODERN ARABIAN HORSE; the magazine for people who love Arabian horses. Text in English. 1979. 6/yr. USD 25 (effective 2008). adv. **Document type:** *Magazine, Consumer.* **Description:** Official publication of the Arabian, Half-Arabian and Anglo-Arabian horse. Promotes the three breeds as the versatile horse of choice for competition, recreation and enjoyment. Includes articles on training; horsemanship; horse care, feeding and health; successful amateur and junior owners; and lifestyle pieces.
Former titles (until 200?): Arabian Horse Magazine (1543-8597); (until 200?): International Arabian Horse (1082-2984); (until 1994): Inside International (0894-0614)
Published by: Arabian Horse Association, 10805 E Bethany Dr, Aurora,, CO 80014. TEL 303-696-4500, 303-696-4599. Ed. Amy Train. Circ: 30,000.

636.1 USA
MORAB PERSPECTIVE. Text in English. 1993. q. USD 30 membership (effective 2003). adv. **Document type:** *Newsletter, Consumer.*
Published by: International Morab Breeders Association, 732 S. Miller Ct., Decatur, IL 62521-3245. imba@morab.com, http://www.morab.com. Ed. Jane Licht. R&P, Adv. contact Linda Konichek.

636.1 USA ISSN 0027-1098
SF293.M8
THE MORGAN HORSE. Abbreviated title: T M H. Text in English. 1941. m. USD 31.50 domestic; USD 53.50 in Canada & Mexico; USD 61.50 elsewhere; USD 9.50 per issue; USD 4 newsstand/cover (effective 2010). adv. bk.rev. illus. Index. back issues avail.; reprints avail. **Document type:** *Magazine, Consumer.* **Description:** Focuses on all aspects of the Morgan's horse including significant articles, how-to's, profiles of horses or trainers and much more.
Formerly (until 1951): Morgan Horse Magazine
Related titles: Online - full text ed.
—Ingenta.
Published by: American Morgan Horse Association, 122 Bostwick Rd, Shelburne, VT 05482. TEL 802-985-4944, FAX 802-985-8897, info@morganhorse.com. Ed. Stephen Kinney TEL 401-450-9006. adv.: B&W page USD 405, color page USD 735. Circ: 15,000.

798.2 362.4 USA ISSN 1067-5876
N A R H A NEWS. Text in English. 1970. 8/yr. USD 45 in North America membership; USD 85 elsewhere membership (effective 2005). adv. bk.rev. **Document type:** *Newsletter, Consumer.* **Description:** Provides news and technical information for people who assist the physically and mentally disabled to ride horses for therapy and recreation.
Indexed: IAB, SportS.
Published by: North American Riding for the Handicapped Association, Inc., PO Box 33150, Denver, CO 80233. TEL 303-452-1212, 800-369-7433, FAX 303-252-4610, narha@narha.org, http://www.narha.org. Circ: 4,500.

798.2 362.4 USA ISSN 1541-0188
N A R H A STRIDES. Text in English. 1995. q. free to members (effective 2010). bk.rev. illus. **Document type:** *Magazine, Trade.* **Description:** Provides feature articles and news of interest for people who assist the mentally and physically disabled to ride horses for therapy and recreation.
Published by: North American Riding for the Handicapped Association, Inc., PO Box 33150, Denver, CO 80233. TEL 303-452-1212, 800-369-7433, FAX 303-252-4610, narha@narha.org, http://www.narha.org.

798.2 USA ISSN 0199-6762
N R H A REINER. Text in English. 1980. bi-m. USD 35 domestic to non-members; USD 60 in Canada to non-members (effective 2008). adv. illus. reprints avail. **Document type:** *Magazine, Consumer.* **Description:** Covers major reining events, awards and championships.
Related titles: Online - full content ed.: USD 35 to non-members (effective 2008).
Published by: National Reining Horse Association, 3000 NW Tenth St, Oklahoma, OK 73107-5302. TEL 405-946-7400, dwall@nrha.com. Adv. contact Sharon Barr. Circ: 6,000.

798.2 NLD ISSN 1879-5463
N R P S NIEUWS. (Nederlands Rijpaarden- en Pony Stamboek) Text in Dutch. 1998. m. EUR 20 to alumni; EUR 2 newsstand/cover to alumni (effective 2010). adv. **Document type:** *Magazine, Consumer.*
Published by: Nederlands Rijpaarden- en Pony Stamboek, Postbus 3072, Ermelo, 3850 CB, Netherlands. TEL 31-577-401150, FAX 31-577-401145, info@nrps.nl. Circ: 5,500.

798.4 AUS ISSN 0726-1799
NATIONAL BUCKSKIN SOCIETY. NEWSLETTER. Text in English. 1973. q. AUD 60 membership (effective 2008). adv. bk.rev. back issues avail. **Document type:** *Newsletter.* **Description:** Provides information on dressage, turnout, showing, and caring for horses.
Formerly (until 1983): National Buckskin Society. Journal
Published by: National Buckskin Society Inc., c/o Sue Emeny, Membership Co-ordinator, 2939 Warburton Hwy, Wesburn, VIC 3799, Australia. http://www.nbs.org.au/. Ed. Anna Thirkell. adv.: page AUD 20. Circ: 200.

798 USA
NATIONAL CUTTING HORSE ASSOCIATION. RULE BOOK. Text in English. 1946. a. membership. adv. **Document type:** *Handbook/Manual/Guide, Trade.*
Published by: National Cutting Horse Association, 260 Bailey Ave., Fort Worth, TX 76107-1862. TEL 817-244-6188, FAX 817-244-2015. Ed., R&P Peggy Riggle. Adv. contact Shawn McCoy. Circ: 12,000.

636.1 USA ISSN 0027-9455
SF295.185
THE NATIONAL HORSEMAN. Text in English. 1865. 14/yr. USD 56; USD 146 newsstand/cover foreign; USD 6.50 newsstand/cover (effective 2000). adv. illus. **Description:** Includes interviews, articles, calendars, and coverage of horse shows for American saddlebreds and Hackney ponies.
—Ingenta.
Published by: National Horseman, 16101 N 82nd St, Ste 10, Scottsdale, AZ 85260-1830. TEL 480-922-5202, FAX 480-922-5212. Ed. John Owens. Pub., R&P Karen Owens. Circ: 3,400 (paid).

798 GBR ISSN 1751-8393
NATIONAL HORSEMART. Text in English. 1998. m. GBP 30 (effective 2010). adv. back issues avail. **Document type:** *Magazine, Trade.* **Description:** Contains thousands of horses, horseboxes and trailers for sale.
Formerly (until 2006): National Horsemart Weekly (1750-8665)
Related titles: Online - full text ed.
Published by: Friday-Ad Ltd., London Rd, Sayers Common, W Sussex BN6 9HS, United Kingdom. TEL 44-1646-680720, support@friday-ad.co.uk, http://www.friday-ad.co.uk/.

798.029 USA ISSN 0886-5647
SF285.35
NATIONWIDE OVERNIGHT STABLING DIRECTORY & EQUESTRIAN VACATION GUIDE. Key Title: Nationwide Overnight Stabling Directory. Variant title: Equestrian Vacation Guide. Text in English. 1982. a., latest vol.20. USD 26.95 (effective 2010). adv. maps. 224 p./no. 1 cols./p.; **Document type:** *Directory.*
Published by: Equine Travelers of America, Inc., PO Box 322, Arkansas City, KS 67005. TEL 620-442-8131, FAX 620-442-8215, eta@hit.net. Ed. James L McDaniel. R&P, Adv. contact Janice J Nelson TEL 620-442-8131. page USD 50,050; 3.75 x 4.38. Circ: 5,000.

NATURAL HORSE. *see* ANIMAL WELFARE

798 USA
THE NETWORK. Text in English. m. looseleaf. free membership (effective 2005). adv. **Document type:** *Newsletter.*
Formerly (until 1999): A M H A News & Morgan Sales Network; Incorporates (1975-1994): Morganizer; Former titles: Morgan Sales Network; (until 1992): A M H A Newsletter
Published by: American Morgan Horse Association, 122 Bostwick Rd, Shelburne, VT 05482. TEL 802-985-4944, FAX 802-985-8897. Ed., R&P Christina Kollander. Pub. Fred Braden. Adv. contact Lisa Peterson. Circ: 15,000.

798 USA
NEW YORK THOROUGHBRED LIFE. Text in English. 2006 (Jul.). bi-m. USD 24.95 (effective 2006). **Document type:** *Magazine, Consumer.*
Published by: Thoroughbred Life, Inc., 46 Grange St., New York City, NY 11010 . Ed. Bill Heller.

798.4 NZL ISSN 0113-0641
NEW ZEALAND HARNESS RACING WEEKLY. Variant title: Harness Racing. Text in English. 1938. w. adv. illus.; stat. **Document type:** *Handbook/Manual/Guide, Consumer.*
Former titles (until 1986): New Zealand Trotting Calendar (0028-8799); (until 1977): New Zealand Trotguide; (until 1974): New Zealand Trotting; (until 1972): New Zealand Trotting Calendar
—CCC.
Published by: (N.Z. Trotting Conference), Harness Racing New Zealand, 135 Lincoln Rd, PO Box 459, Christchurch, New Zealand. TEL 64-3-9641200, FAX 64-3-9641205, admin@hrnz.co.nz. Ed. Mike Grainger. Adv. contact John Robinson. Circ: 5,000.

636.1 NZL ISSN 0028-8209
NEW ZEALAND HORSE & PONY. Text in English. 1959. m. NZD 69.50 domestic; NZD 125 in Australia; NZD 190 elsewhere; NZD 7.50 newsstand/cover (effective 2008). adv. bk.rev. **Document type:** *Magazine, Consumer.* **Description:** Covers equestrian sports in New Zealand - eventing, show jumping, dressage, endurance, polo, polocrosse, driving etc. Also covers sport horse breeding; major international competitions featuring New Zealand; profiles and personality stories; instructional articles; veterinary and horse health topics.
Related titles: Online - full text ed.
—CCC.
Published by: (New Zealand Pony Clubs Association), Fairfax Magazines (Subsidiary of: Fairfax Media), Level 1, 274 Church St, Penrose, PO Box 12965, Auckland, New Zealand. TEL 64-9-6341800, FAX 64-9-6342948, info@fairfaxmedia.co.nz, http://www.fairfaxnz.co.nz. Ed. Rowan Dixon. Adv. contact Tanya Nicholson TEL 64-9-6349853. color page NZD 1,400; trim 210 x 297. Circ: 12,428.

NEW ZEALAND MONTHLY HORSE TRADER. *see* BUSINESS AND ECONOMICS—Small Business

798.2 GBR ISSN 1748-5770
NEWS. ARAB HORSE SOCIETY. Text in English. 1935. s-a. free to members (effective 2009). adv. illus. **Document type:** *Newsletter, Trade.*
Former titles (until 2003): Arab Horse (1473-2068); (until 2000): Arab Horse Society News (0402-7493)
Published by: Arab Horse Society, Windsor House, The Square, Ramsbury, Marlborough, Wilts SN8 2PE, United Kingdom. TEL 44-1672-521411, FAX 44-1672-520880, areeves@reevesfinancial.co.uk, http://www.arabhorsesociety.com.

636.1 NOR ISSN 0809-8697
NORSK ARABERHEST. Text in Norwegian. 2005. q. NOK 400 domestic; NOK 500 foreign (effective 2006). **Document type:** *Magazine, Trade.*
Published by: Norsk Araberhestforening, c/o Tore Nikkerud, Braataveien 1, Mjoendalen, 3050, Norway.

636.1 NOR ISSN 1504-4351
NORSK-SVENSK TRAVERSTAMBOK FOR KALDBLODSHESTER. Text in Norwegian. triennial. NOK 300 per issue (effective 2006). back issues avail. **Document type:** *Consumer.*
Formerly (until 2004): Norsk Traverstambok for Kaldblodshester (1502-7120)
Published by: Det Norske Travselskap, PO Box 194, Oekern, Oslo, 0510, Norway. TEL 47-22-956000, FAX 47-22-956060, dnt@rikstoto.no, http://www.travsport.no.

798 CAN ISSN 1202-3116
NORTHERN HORSE REVIEW. Text in English. 1993. 10/yr. CAD 32; CAD 3.95 newsstand/cover (effective 2005). **Document type:** *Magazine, Consumer.* **Description:** For western horse persons, reaching northwestern states and Canada.
Formerly (until 1993): Horse Review (1202-3108)
Published by: Dakota Design and Advertising, Bay 114, 3907-3A St N E, Calgary, AB T2E 6S7, Canada. TEL 800-566-1722, dka@telusplanet.net. Ed. Ingrid Schulz. Circ: 10,000.

798 ITA ISSN 1724-2959
I NOSTRI AMICI CAVALLI. Text in Italian. 2003. m. EUR 34.90 (effective 2009). **Document type:** *Magazine, Consumer.*
Related titles: Alternate Frequency ed(s).: I Nostri Amici Cavalli Collection. ISSN 1971-2715. s-a.
Published by: Sprea Editori Srl, Via Torino 51, Cernusco sul Naviglio, MI 20063, Italy. TEL 39-02-92432222, FAX 39-02-92432236, editori@sprea.it, http://www.sprea.it.

798.2 USA
NUESTRO CABALLO. Text in English. 1970. q. membership only. bk.rev. **Document type:** *Newsletter.*
Published by: Peruvian Paso Horse Registry of North America, 3077 Wiljan Ct, Ste A, Santa Rosa, CA 95407-5702. TEL 707-579-4394, FAX 707-579-1038. Circ: 1,400.

798 USA
OHIO THOROUGHBRED. Text in English. 1971. q. USD 25 (effective 1998 & 1999). bk.rev. back issues avail. **Document type:** *Magazine, Trade.* **Description:** Contains information pertaining to the thoroughbred industry in Ohio.
Published by: (Ohio Thoroughbred Breeders and Owners), Centaurus, Inc., 6024 Harrison Ave, Ste 13, Cincinnati, OH 45248-1621. TEL 513-574-5888, FAX 513-574-2313. Ed. Gayle Babst. Circ: 1,500.

798 USA ISSN 0882-9624
P O A. (Pony of the Americas) Text in English. 1956. m. USD 35 (effective 2010). bk.rev. **Document type:** *Magazine, Trade.* **Description:** Covers horse care, training, show results, and club events.
Formerly (until 1985): Pony of the Americas
Published by: Pony of the Americas Club Inc., 3828 S Emerson Avenue, Indianapolis, IN 46203. TEL 317-788-0107, FAX 317-788-8974, poac@poac.org.

791.8 798.2 USA
P R C A MEDIA GUIDE. Text in English. a. **Document type:** *Handbook/Manual/Guide, Trade.* **Description:** Covers the personalities and drama of professional rodeo events across the nation.
Formerly: Professional Rodeo U S A
Published by: Professional Rodeo Cowboy Association, 101 Pro Rodeo Dr, Colorado Spings, CO 80919. TEL 719-593-8840, FAX 719-548-4889, http://www.proodeo.com.

798.2 NLD ISSN 2211-3290
▼ **PAARD EN LEVEN.** Key Title: Paard&leven. Text in Dutch. 2010. q. EUR 2.95 newsstand/cover (effective 2011). adv. **Document type:** *Magazine, Consumer.*
Published by: (Koninklijke Nederlandse Hippische Sportfederatie, Federatie van Nederlandse Ruitersportcentra), BCM Publishing, Postbus 1392, Eindhoven, 5602 BJ, Netherlands. TEL 31-40-8447644, FAX 31-40-8447655, bcm@bcm.nl, http://www.bcm.nl. Circ: 125,000.

798.2 NLD ISSN 1388-0047
PAARD EN SPORT. Text in Dutch. 1998. m. adv. illus. **Document type:** *Trade.*
Related titles: ◆ Supplement to: Hoefslag. ISSN 0046-7715.
Published by: BCM Publishing, Postbus 1392, Eindhoven, 5602 BJ, Netherlands. TEL 31-40-8447644, FAX 31-40-8447655, bcm@bcm.nl, http://www.bcm.nl. Ed. Carmen Nagtegaal. Adv. contact Jeroen van der Linden. B&W page EUR 1,676, color page EUR 1,999; 215 x 285. Circ: 49,000.

636.1 NLD ISSN 1380-4537
DE PAARDENKRANT. Text in Dutch. 1989. s-w. EUR 189.50 (effective 2010). adv. **Document type:** *Newspaper, Consumer.*
Published by: Reed Business bv (Subsidiary of: Reed Business), Postbus 4, Doetinchem, 7000 BA, Netherlands. info@reedbusiness.nl, http://www.reedbusiness.nl. Ed. Roel Leferink. Circ: 10,031.

636.1 NLD ISSN 2210-402X
▼ **DE PAARDENKRANT. EXTRA.** Text in Dutch. 2010. bi-m. EUR 29.50 (effective 2010). **Document type:** *Magazine, Consumer.*
Published by: Reed Business bv (Subsidiary of: Reed Business), Postbus 4, Doetinchem, 7000 BA, Netherlands. info@reedbusiness.nl, http://www.reedbusiness.nl.

798 USA
PACIFIC & SOUTHWEST ARABIAN. Text in English. 8/yr. USD 30 (effective 1998). **Document type:** *Magazine, Consumer.* **Description:** Covers all aspects of Arabian horses.
Related titles: Online - full text ed.
Address: 33783 Temecula Creek Rd, Temecula, CA 92592. TEL 909-695-2524, FAX 909-695-2873. adv.: B&W page USD 345, color page USD 645.

798 USA ISSN 0894-4458
PACIFIC COAST JOURNAL (TEMECULA). Text in English. 1963. m. USD 15. adv. **Document type:** *Newspaper.* **Description:** Focuses on equine breeding, taxes and laws, coverage of upcoming events and championship standings.
Formerly (until 1985): Quarter Horse of the Pacific Coast (0093-8238)
Published by: Pacific Coast Publications, PO Box 893640, Temecula, CA 92589. TEL 909-699-2777. Ed., R&P Virginia McClintock. Pub. Kevin Wickstrom. Adv. contact Denise Munson. Circ: 5,082.

798.4 CZE ISSN 1801-6812
PADDOCK REVUE. Text in Czech. 2004. 11/yr. EUR 30 (effective 2009). **Document type:** *Magazine, Trade.*
Address: Plostilova 15/1886, Prague 4, 143 00, Czech Republic. Ed. Petr Guth.

636.1 798 USA ISSN 0164-5706
PAINT HORSE JOURNAL. Text in English. 1962. m. USD 75 (effective 2008). adv. bk.rev. illus. Index. back issues avail.; reprints avail. **Document type:** *Magazine, Trade.* **Description:** For those interested in riding, training, breeding, exhibiting or racing American Paint Horses.
Published by: American Paint Horse Association, PO Box 961023, Ft. Worth, TX 76161-0023. TEL 817-834-2742, FAX 817-834-3152, ddodds@apha.com, http://www.apha.com. Ed. Jennifer Nice. Adv. contact Michelle Stone. Circ: 32,000 (paid).

636.1 NLD ISSN 2210-2582
▼ **PAINTS AND QUARTERS.** Text in Dutch. 2010. q. EUR 17 domestic; EUR 22 foreign (effective 2010). **Document type:** *Magazine, Consumer.*
Published by: Astrid Klomp Graphic Design, Bijsterveld 12, Winteire, 5513 NN, Netherlands. TEL 31-40-2545636, astrid.klomp@zonnet.nl, http://www.astrid-klomp.nl.

636.1 USA ISSN 0031-045X
SF293.P3
PALOMINO HORSES. Text in English. 1942 (Apr.). m. USD 40 to non-members; USD 30 domestic to members; USD 55 in Canada to members; USD 145 elsewhere to members (effective 2005). adv. bk.rev. **Document type:** *Magazine, Trade.*
—Ingenta.
Published by: Palomino Horse Breeders of America, Inc., 15253 E Skelly Dr, Tulsa, OK 74116-2637. TEL 918-438-1234, 800-846-8959, FAX 918-438-1232, yellahrses@aol.com. Pub. Carol Butler Gwaltney. Circ: 6,663 (controlled).

798.2 USA
PALOMINO PARADE. Text in English. 1936. bi-m. looseleaf. USD 15; USD 20 foreign (effective 1999). adv. back issues avail. **Document type:** *Newsletter.* **Description:** News and information of interest to Palomino horse owners.
Published by: Palomino Horse Association, HC 63, Box 24, Dornsife, PA 17823. TEL 570-758-3067. Ed. Jean Plankenhorn. Adv. contact Raelene Rebuck.

798.4 ZAF ISSN 1819-8759
PARADE. Text in English. 2003. bi-m. adv.
Related titles: Online - full text ed.: ISSN 1819-8767.
Published by: Gold Circle, PO Box 40, Durban, 4000, South Africa. TEL 27-31-3141500, FAX 27-31-3141626, info@goldcircle.co.za. Ed. Lance Benson TEL 27-31-3141599.

S

798 USA ISSN 1054-3201
CODEN: STLAEI
PASO FINO HORSE WORLD. Text in English. m. USD 20; USD 3 newsstand/cover (effective 1995). adv. back issues avail. **Document type:** *Newsletter.* **Description:** Geared to current and future owners of Paso Fino horses. Gives tips on care, show schedules, and regional news.
Published by: (Paso Fino Horse Association, Inc.), Southern Publishing, 3839 Business Hwy, 45 N, Box 71, Meridian, MS 39302-0071. TEL 800-647-6672. Ed. Vicki Dwight. Circ: 2,650 (paid).

798.2 CHE
PEGASUS PFERDE MAGAZIN. Text in German. 1989. m. CHF 88; CHF 8.80 newsstand/cover. adv. bk.rev. index. back issues avail. **Document type:** *Consumer.* **Description:** All aspects of horse riding, horse and rider training, breeding, and horse care.
Published by: Pegasus Pferde Verlag AG, Chellenstr 27, Goldach, 9403, Switzerland. TEL 41-71-8585656, FAX 41-71-8585657. Ed. Brenda Zuckschwerdt. Pub. Ruth Zuckschwerdt. Adv. contact Sybil Schoenbaechler. Circ: 50,000.

791 USA
PENNSYLVANIA EQUESTRIAN. Text in English. bi-m. adv. **Document type:** *Newspaper.* **Description:** Covers news important to horse owners in Pennsylvania.
Published by: Lawson - Shertzer Marketing & Publishing, PO Box 8412, Lancaster, PA 17604. TEL 717-898-5874, FAX 717-898-1458. Adv. contact Debbie Hocke.

798 028.5 NLD ISSN 1572-624X
PENNY. Text in Dutch. 198?. m. EUR 69 incl. Penny Plus (effective 2009). adv. **Document type:** *Magazine, Consumer.*
Published by: Holco Publications B.V., Postbus 267, Alkmaar, 1800 AG, Netherlands. TEL 31-72-5121616, FAX 31-84-7517131. adv.: color page EUR 3,740; bleed 210 x 280. Circ: 50,000.

636.1 NLD ISSN 1569-7703
PENNY PLUS. Text in Dutch. 198?. m. EUR 69 incl. Penny (effective 2009). adv. **Document type:** *Magazine, Consumer.*
Published by: Holco Publications B.V., Postbus 267, Alkmaar, 1800 AG, Netherlands. TEL 31-72-5121616, FAX 31-84-7517131. adv.: color page EUR 2,750; bleed 210 x 280. Circ: 40,000.

PFERD&CO. *see* CHILDREN AND YOUTH—For

636.1 DEU ISSN 0932-3570
PFERD UND SPORT IN SCHLESWIG-HOLSTEIN UND HAMBURG. Text in German. 1960. m. EUR 61.20 domestic; EUR 103 foreign; EUR 5.10 newsstand/cover (effective 2010). adv. bk.rev. illus.; stat. **Document type:** *Magazine, Consumer.* **Description:** Covers all aspects of horse breeding.
Former titles (until 1986): Pferde (0932-3562); (until 1971): Holsteiner Pferd (0018-3709)
Related titles: Online - full text ed.
Published by: (Verband der Zuechter des Holsteiner Pferdes), Rathmann Verlag GmbH & Co. KG, Schlossgarten 3-4, Kiel, 24103, Germany. TEL 49-431-8881230, FAX 49-431-9828710, philip@rathmaenner.de, http://www.rathmann-verlag.de. Ed. Donata von Preussen. Adv. contact Philip Rathmann. B&W page EUR 2,110, color page EUR 2,710; trim 215 x 280. Circ: 14,726 (paid and controlled).

798.2 DEU
PFERD UND WAGEN. Text in German. 2007. bi-m. EUR 58.80 domestic; EUR 76.80 foreign (effective 2010). **Document type:** *Magazine, Consumer.*
Published by: Fachverlag Sagkob, von-Ketteler-Str 16, Taufkirchen, 85456, Germany. TEL 49-8084-4133660, FAX 49-8084-4133661, info@fs-on.de. Ed. Anja Sagkob. Pub. Thomas Sagkob. Adv. contact Volker Sagkob.

798 DEU
PFERDE-ANZEIGER. Text in German. 1996. m. EUR 42 domestic; EUR 96 foreign; EUR 3.50 newsstand/cover (effective 2011). adv. **Document type:** *Magazine, Consumer.*
Published by: Der Heisse Draht Verlag GmbH und Co., Drostestr 14, Hannover, 30161, Germany. TEL 49-511-390910, FAX 49-511-39091196, zentrale@dhd.de, http://www.dhd.de. Adv. contact Lars Schnatmann. Circ: 60,000 (paid and controlled).

636.1 DEU
PFERDE FIT & VITAL. Text in German. s-a. EUR 12 domestic; EUR 15 foreign; EUR 6 newsstand/cover (effective 2007). adv. **Document type:** *Magazine, Consumer.* **Description:** Provides information on caring for and nurturing horses.
Published by: Pferdesport Verlag Rolf Ehlers GmbH, Rockwinkeler Landstr 20, Bremen-Oberneuland, 28355, Germany. TEL 49-421-2575544, FAX 49-421-2575543, info@ehlers-bremen.de, http://www.ehlers-bremen.de. Adv. contact Maren Arndt. B&W page EUR 2,196, color page EUR 3,144; trim 210 x 297.

PFERDE - FREUNDE FUERS LEBEN. *see* CHILDREN AND YOUTH—For

798.2 DEU
PFERDE SAISON. Text in German. m. EUR 48 domestic; EUR 65 foreign; EUR 6 newsstand/cover (effective 2007). adv. **Document type:** *Magazine, Consumer.*
Published by: Pferdesport Verlag Rolf Ehlers GmbH, Rockwinkeler Landstr 20, Bremen-Oberneuland, 28355, Germany. TEL 49-421-2575544, FAX 49-421-2575543, info@ehlers-bremen.de, http://www.ehlers-bremen.de. Adv. contact Maren Arndt. B&W page EUR 2,196, color page EUR 3,144; trim 210 x 297.

PFERDE SPIEGEL. *see* VETERINARY SCIENCE

636.1 DEU
PFERDE ZUCHT UND HALTUNG. Text in German. 2/yr. EUR 23.80 (effective 2008). adv. **Document type:** *Magazine, Trade.*
Published by: A V A - Agrar Verlag Allgaeu GmbH, Porschestr 2, Kempten, 87437, Germany. TEL 49-831-571420, FAX 49-831-79008, info@ava-verlag.de, http://www.ava-verlag.de. Ed. Harald Stroehlein. Pub. Wolfgang Kuehnle. Adv. contact Karl Koenig. B&W page EUR 1,555.20, color page EUR 2,106; trim 185 x 270.

798.2 DEU ISSN 1437-3866
PFERDEBETRIEB. Text in German. 1999. bi-m. EUR 42.59 (effective 2011). adv. **Document type:** *Magazine, Trade.*
Published by: FORUM Zeitschriften und Spezialmedien GmbH (Subsidiary of: FORUM Media Group GmbH), Mandichostr 18, Merching, 86504, Germany. TEL 49-8233-381361, FAX 49-8233-381212, service@forum-zeitschriften.de, http://www.forum-zeitschriften.de. Ed. Guido Krisam. Adv. contact Sabine Konhaeuser. Circ: 6,000 (paid).

636.1 DEU ISSN 1617-8289
PFERDEBOERSE. Text in German. 2000. bi-m. EUR 20 domestic; EUR 21.90 in Austria; CHF 39 in Switzerland; EUR 23 elsewhere; EUR 4 newsstand/cover (effective 2007). adv. **Document type:** *Magazine, Consumer.* **Description:** Provides information on buying and selling a wide variety of horses.
Related titles: Online - full text ed.
Published by: Hannes Scholten Verlag GmbH & Co. KG (Subsidiary of: Motor Presse Stuttgart GmbH und Co. KG), Olgastr 86, Stuttgart, 70180, Germany. TEL 49-711-2108078, FAX 49-711-2108075, redaktion@cavallo.de, http://www.motorpresse.de/de/verlag/Scholten_Verlag.php. adv.: B&W page EUR 2,812, color page EUR 3,306; trim 230 x 297. Circ: 32,811 (paid and controlled).

636.1 798 DEU ISSN 1619-5167
PFERDEFORUM; Oldenburg - Weser-Ems. Text in German. 2001. 12/yr. EUR 62 domestic; EUR 83.35 foreign; EUR 5.80 newsstand/cover (effective 2009). adv. bk.rev. illus.; stat. **Document type:** *Magazine, Consumer.*
Formed by the merger of (1969-2001): Das Oldenburger Sportpferd (0030-2066); (1976-2001): Reitsport in Weser-Elms (0344-4295)
Published by: (Verband der Zuechter des Oldenburger Pferdes e.V.), Deutscher Landwirtschaftsverlag GmbH, Kabelkamp 6, Hannover, 30179, Germany. TEL 49-511-678060, FAX 49-511-67806200, dlv.hannover@dlv.de, http://www.dlv.de. Eds. Heiko Meinardus, Susanne Posch. Adv. contact Heike Breckweg TEL 49-4431-6767. B&W page EUR 2,000, color page EUR 2,830; trim 216 x 303. Circ: 13,234 (paid and controlled).

798 DEU ISSN 1432-3230
PFERDEMARKT; Fachblatt fuer alle Pferdefreunde. Text in German. 1977. bi-m. EUR 35.50 (effective 2010). adv. illus. back issues avail. **Document type:** *Magazine, Consumer.* **Description:** Contains articles and features on horses and horsemanship as a hobby.
Related titles: Online - full text ed.
Published by: Landwirtschaftsverlag GmbH, Huelsebrockstr 2, Muenster, 48165, Germany. TEL 49-2501-27500, FAX 49-2501-27551, zentrale@lv-h.de, http://www.lv-h.de. Ed. Markus Woermann. Adv. contact Christiane Strauchs. Circ: 33,968 (controlled).

798.2 AUT ISSN 1016-9733
PFERDEREVUE. Text in German. 1990. m. EUR 33 domestic; EUR 45 foreign (effective 2005). adv. back issues avail. **Document type:** *Magazine, Consumer.*
Published by: Verlagsgruppe News Gesellschaft mbH (Subsidiary of: Gruner + Jahr AG & Co), Schlossgasse 10-12, Vienna, N 1050, Austria. TEL 43-1-5452577420, FAX 43-1-5452577421. Ed. Leopold Pingitzer. adv.: B&W page EUR 2,736, color page EUR 4,651; trim 185 x 250. Circ: 49,200.

798.2 DEU
PFERDESPORT BREMEN. Text in German. 1986. bi-m. adv. **Document type:** *Magazine, Consumer.*
Published by: Pferdesport Verlag Rolf Ehlers GmbH, Rockwinkeler Landstr 20, Bremen-Oberneuland, 28355, Germany. TEL 49-421-2575544, FAX 49-421-2575543, info@ehlers-bremen.de, http://www.ehlers-bremen.de. adv.: B&W page EUR 786, color page EUR 992; trim 210 x 280.

798.2 DEU
PFERDESPORT INTERNATIONAL. Text in German. fortn. EUR 65.80 (effective 2011). adv. **Document type:** *Magazine, Consumer.*
Published by: MG Marketing GmbH, Holzheimer Str 67, Limburg, 65549, Germany. TEL 49-6431-4090533, FAX 49-6431-4090511. Ed. Karolin Behrens. adv.: B&W page EUR 2,100, color page EUR 3,000. Circ: 32,280 (paid and controlled).

798 NLD ISSN 1381-8538
PHRYSO. Text in Dutch. 1950. m. EUR 65 domestic to non-members; EUR 37 domestic to members; EUR 89 in Europe to non-members; EUR 62 in Europe to members; EUR 102 elsewhere to non-members; EUR 74 elsewhere to members (effective 2009). adv. **Document type:** *Magazine, Trade.*
Published by: (Koninklijke Vereniging "Het Friesch Paarden-Stamboek"), BCM Publishing, Postbus 1392, Eindhoven, 5602 BJ, Netherlands. TEL 31-40-8447644, FAX 31-40-8447655, bcm@bcm.nl, http://www.bcm.nl. Ed. Ineke Jensen. Adv. contact Samantha Munoz. B&W page EUR 667, color page EUR 1,232; trim 210 x 297. Circ: 10,200.

636.1 USA ISSN 8750-7269
THE PINTO HORSE. Text in English. bi-m. USD 25 to non-members; USD 20 to members (effective 2000). adv. charts; illus.; stat. **Document type:** *Magazine, Consumer.*
Former titles (until 1985): Pinto Horse International (0744-8287); (until 1982): Pinto Horse (0031-9937)
Published by: Pinto Horse Association of America Inc., 7330 NW 23rd St., Bethany, OK 73008-5134. TEL 817-336-7842, FAX 817-336-7416. Ed., R&P Joe E Grissom. Adv. contact Carol Butler-Gwaltney. Circ: 2,800.

POLO MAGAZINE; adventure - elegance - sport. *see* SPORTS AND GAMES—Ball Games

796 DEU ISSN 1614-2810
POLO + 10. Text in German. 2004. 3/yr. adv. **Document type:** *Magazine, Consumer.*
Published by: RegJo Verlag fuer Regionales Marketing GmbH, Bahnhofsallee 1B, Goettingen, 37081, Germany. TEL 49-551-507510, FAX 49-551-5075150, hallo@regjo.de, http://www.regjo.de. adv.: color page EUR 4,300; trim 235 x 303. Circ: 25,000 (controlled).

798.2 USA
PONY ENTHUSIAST. Text in English. q. USD 6 newsstand/cover. adv. **Document type:** *Magazine, Consumer.*
Address: PO Box 220, Lebanon, OR 97355. TEL 321-288-0235, FAX 888-697-3586.

636.1 798.2 GBR ISSN 0032-4256
PONY MAGAZINE. Text in English. 1949. m. GBP 35.10 domestic; GBP 44.40 in Europe; GBP 62.20 elsewhere (effective 2009). adv. bk.rev.; video rev. illus. back issues avail. **Document type:** *Magazine, Consumer.*
Published by: D.J. Murphy Publishers Ltd., Headley House, Headley Rd, Grayshott, Surrey GU26 6TU, United Kingdom. TEL 44-1428-601020, info@djmurphy.co.uk, http://www.djmurphy.co.uk. Ed. Janet Rising. Adv. contact Amanda Toms. **Subscr. to:** PO Box 464, Berkhamsted, Herts HP4 2UR, United Kingdom. TEL 44-1442-879097. **Dist. by:** Seymour Distribution Ltd, 86 Newman St, London W1T 3EX, United Kingdom. TEL 44-20-73968000, FAX 44-20-73968002.

636.1 GBR ISSN 2046-3928
▼ **PONY PALS.** Text in English. 2011. m. GBP 35.80; GBP 2.99 per issue (effective 2011). **Document type:** *Magazine, Consumer.* **Description:** Encourages learning about ponies in a fun and playful way.
Published by: Signature Publishing Ltd., Headley House, Headley Rd, Grayshott, Surrey GU26 6TU, United Kingdom. TEL 44-1428-601020, FAX 44-1428-601030, info@signaturepl.co.uk.

798.2 USA ISSN 0090-8762
SF277
PRACTICAL HORSEMAN. Text in English. 1973. m. USD 19.95 domestic; USD 32.95 in Canada; USD 34.95 elsewhere (effective 2008). adv. illus. back issues avail.; reprints avail. **Document type:** *Magazine, Consumer.* **Description:** Contains how-to articles for the dressage, eventing and hunter/jumper disciplines, as well as periodic articles on endurance and driving.
Incorporates (in 1972): Pennsylvania Horse
Related titles: Online - full text ed.: USD 10 (effective 2008).
Indexed: A09, A10, A26, B04, E08, G05, G06, G07, G08, G09, H20, I05, I07, M01, M02, P10, P16, P19, P48, P53, P54, PQC, R03, RASB, RGAb, RGPR, S09, S23, SD, SPI, SportS, T02, V02, V03, V04, W03, W05.
—Ingenta. **CCC.**
Published by: Source Interlink Companies, 656 Quince Orchard Rd, Ste 600, Gaithersburg, MD 20878. TEL 301-977-3900, FAX 301-990-9015, dheine@sourceinterlink.com, http://www.sourceinterlinkmedia.com. Ed. Sandra Oliynyk. Adv. contact Kathy Dando. B&W page USD 4,585, color page USD 6,875; bleed 8.125 x 10.75. Circ: 65,195 (paid).

791.8 USA ISSN 1080-031X
PRO RODEO WORLD. Text in English. 1994. m. USD 25 domestic; USD 28 foreign; USD 2 newsstand/cover (effective 2001). bk.rev. tr.lit. back issues avail. **Document type:** *Magazine, Trade.* **Description:** Includes rodeo listings and results, features and standing of contestants.
Published by: International Professional Rodeo Association, 2304 Exchange Ave, Oklahoma City, OK 73108. TEL 405-235-6540, FAX 405-235-6577. Ed., R&P, Adv. contact Todd Newville. Circ: 5,700.

PRORODEO SPORTS NEWS. *see* SPORTS AND GAMES

798 SGP ISSN 0218-8813
PUNTERS' WAY. Text in English. 1977. s-w. SGD 3.50 newsstand/cover. adv. illus. back issues avail. **Document type:** *Journal, Consumer.* **Description:** Contains racing information for specific race days.
Related titles: Chinese ed.: ISSN 0218-8821.
Published by: Pioneers & Leaders (Publishers) Pte. Ltd., Pioneers & Leaders Centre, 4 Ubi View (off Ubi Rd 3), Singapore, 408557, Singapore. TEL 65-68485481, FAX 65-67412321, http://www.winner21.com/winner/Mainpage. Ed. Ts Phan. Adv. contact Ho Keat. B&W page SGD 500, color page SGD 1,450; trim 215 x 148. Circ: 30,000.

798.4 ITA
IL PUROSANGUE IN ITALIA. Text in Italian. 1969. 6/yr. free to members (effective 2008). adv. bk.rev. illus.; stat. index. back issues avail. **Document type:** *Magazine, Consumer.* **Description:** Covers thoroughbred horses. Profiles racing personalities, covers races and their results, includes breeding and veterinary news.
Published by: Associazione Nazionale Allevatori Cavalli Purosangue, Via del Caravaggio 3, Milan, MI 20144, Italy. TEL 39-02-48012002, FAX 39-02-48194547, anacity@tin.it, http://www.anacpurosangue.com. Ed. Franco Castelfranchi. Circ: 2,500 (controlled).

798.2 DEU
QUARTER HORSE JOURNAL. Text in German. 1991. m. EUR 48 domestic; EUR 65 foreign; EUR 4 newsstand/cover (effective 2007). adv. **Document type:** *Magazine, Consumer.* **Description:** Covers all aspects of riding and taking care of horses.
Related titles: Online - full text ed.
Published by: Pferdesport Verlag Rolf Ehlers GmbH, Rockwinkeler Landstr 20, Bremen-Oberneuland, 28355, Germany. TEL 49-421-2575544, FAX 49-421-2575543, info@ehlers-bremen.de, http://www.ehlers-bremen.de. Adv. contact Maren Arndt. B&W page EUR 952, color page EUR 1,464; trim 210 x 280. Circ: 23,000 (paid and controlled).

636.1 USA ISSN 0273-8597
QUARTER HORSE NEWS. Text in English. 1978. s-m. USD 39.95 domestic; USD 69.95 in Canada; USD 240 elsewhere (effective 2007). adv. back issues avail. **Document type:** *Newspaper, Consumer.* **Description:** Covers all facets and interests of the quarter horse industry, includes both professional and amateur aspects.
Published by: Cowboy Publishing Group (Subsidiary of: Morris Multimedia, Inc.), PO Box 9707, Ft. Worth, TX 76147. TEL 817-569-7116, karen.ficklin@cowboypublishing.com. Ed. Katie Tims. Pub., R&P Carl Mullins. Adv. contact Ed Tavender. B&W page USD 625, color page USD 1,000; 13.5 x 10.25. Circ: 13,000 (paid).

636.1 USA ISSN 1529-2983
QUARTER HORSES U S A. Text in English. 2000. a. USD 9.99 per issue (effective 2008). adv. **Document type:** *Magazine, Consumer.* **Description:** Provides a complete guide to American quarter horses.
Published by: BowTie, Inc., 2401 Beverly Blvd, PO Box 57900, Los Angeles, CA 90057. TEL 213-385-2222, FAX 213-385-8565, adtraffic@bowtieinc.com, http://www.bowtieinc.com.

798.4 USA ISSN 0899-3130
THE QUARTER RACING JOURNAL. Text in English. 1988. m. USD 25; USD 80 foreign (effective 1998). adv. bk.rev. back issues avail. **Document type:** *Journal, Trade.* **Description:** Records and preserves the pedigree of the American quarter horse. Covers the American quarter horse racing industry.
—Ingenta.
Published by: American Quarter Horse Association, PO Box 200, Amarillo, TX 79168. TEL 806-376-4811, FAX 806-349-6400. R&P Jim Jennings TEL 806-376-4811. adv.: B&W page USD 605, color page USD 1,090; trim 8.25 x 10.875. Circ: 10,000.

798.4 AUS
QUEENSLAND RACING MAGAZINE. Text in English. 1886. m. AUD 110 domestic; AUD 195 foreign; free to qualified personnel (effective 2008). adv. **Document type:** *Magazine, Trade.* **Description:** Covers news and legislation pertaining to the horse racing industry. Includes events, lists trainers, jockeys, etc.
Formerly (until 2002): Queensland Racing Calendar
Published by: (Queensland Racing Ltd.), The Magazine Publishing Company Pty. Ltd., 34 Station St, PO Box 406, Nundah, QLD 4012, Australia. TEL 61-7-38660000, FAX 61-7-38660066, info@tmpc.com.au. adv.: color page AUD 1,725; trim 210 x 297. Circ: 5,100.

798 GBR ISSN 0079-9408
RACEHORSES. Text in English. 1948. a. ((Mar.)). GBP 75 per issue (effective 2010). adv. **Document type:** *Journal, Consumer.* **Description:** Essays and notes on the performances of horses in the flat racing category.
Published by: Portway Press Ltd., 25 Timeform House, Northgate, Halifax, W Yorks HX1 1XF, United Kingdom. TEL 44-1422-330330, FAX 44-1422-398017, timeform@timeform.com.

798.2 GBR ISSN 1743-551X
RACING AHEAD (LIVERPOOL). Text in English. 2004. m. GBP 28 domestic; GBP 38 in Europe & Ireland; GBP 48 elsewhere (effective 2009). adv. **Document type:** *Magazine, Consumer.* **Description:** Contains interviews, race tips, horses to follow, systems etc.
Related titles: Online - full text ed.: GBP 17 (effective 2009); Supplement(s): Racing Ahead Weekend. ISSN 1755-6775.
Published by: Racing Ahead Ltd., Office 113, Imperial Ct, Exchange St E, Liverpool, L3 2AB, United Kingdom. TEL 44-845-6380704, FAX 44-845-6380704.

798.2 GBR ISSN 1746-1901
RACING AHEAD. IRELAND. Text in English. 2005. m. adv. **Document type:** *Magazine, Consumer.*
Published by: Racing Ahead Ltd., PO Box 118, Liverpool, L37 3WW, United Kingdom. info@racingahead.net, http://www.racingahead.net/.

798 GBR ISSN 0968-3364
RACING POST. Text in English. 1986. d. (Mon.-Sat.). adv. bk.rev. 70 p./no. 6 cols./p.; back issues avail. **Document type:** *Newspaper, Consumer.* **Description:** Covers horse racing, greyhound racing and general sports betting.
Formerly (until 1986): Sporting Life (0956-3121)
Related titles: Online - full text ed.
Indexed: I05.
—CIS. **CCC.**
Address: One Canada Sq, Canary Wharf, London, E14 5AP, United Kingdom. TEL 44-1635-898781, shop@racingpost.co.uk, http://www.racingpost.com. **Subscr. to:** Johnson's International Media Services.

798.2 USA
RACING UPDATE. Text in English. 1977. s-m. USD 200. adv. back issues avail. **Document type:** *Newsletter, Trade.*
Published by: Racing Update, Inc. (Subsidiary of: Rockbridge Enterprises Inc.), PO Box 11052, Lexington, KY 40512. TEL 606-231-7966, 888-329-8729, FAX 606-276-3150. Ed. April Gaither. Pub. Michael S Brown. R&P, Adv. contact Martha Seagram. Circ: 1,500.

636.1 USA ISSN 0744-6829
THE RACKING REVIEW. Text in English. 1975. s-m. USD 20. illus.
Published by: Racking Review, c/o Ann O Yeiser, Box 777, Waynesboro, TN 38485. TEL 615-722-3688, FAX 615-722-3689.

798.2 USA
RANGERBRED NEWS. Text in English. 1965. bi-m. free to members. adv. **Document type:** *Newsletter.* **Description:** Contains information about CRHA, and happenings elsewhere in the horseworld.
Published by: Colorado Ranger Horse Association, Inc., Rd 1, Box 1290, Wampum, PA 16157. TEL 412-535-4841. Ed. Laurel Kosior. Circ: 450.

636.1 USA ISSN 8750-5630
RECORD HORSEMAN. Text in English. 1966. bi-w. USD 35. adv. **Document type:** *Newspaper.* **Description:** General interest, all-breed publication for the Rocky Mountain area horse enthusiast.
Incorporates: Capital Horseman (8750-152X); Straight from the Horse's Mouth
Published by: R S Livestock Publishers, 4800 Wadsworth, Ste 320, PO Box 1209, Wheat Ridge, CO 80034-1209. TEL 303-425-5777, FAX 303-431-7545. Ed. Dan Green. Pub. Harry Green Jr. Adv. contact Ann Meyers. Circ: 10,000.

791.8 658 USA
REGISTRY NEWS. Text in English. 1968. q. membership only. tr.lit. **Document type:** *Newsletter.* **Description:** Updates the members on rules and policy changes related to registration and transfer records of purebred Arabian horses, as well as on the activities of the registry.
Published by: Arabian Horse Registry of America, Inc., 10805 E. Bethany Dr., Aurora, CO 80014-2605. TEL 303-450-4748. Eds. Jennifer Ashton TEL 303-450-4715, Jennifer Horan. R&P Jennifer Ashton TEL 303-450-4715. Circ: 25,000.

798.4 DEU ISSN 0944-5854
REITEN UND FAHREN ST. GEORG; Magazin fuer Pferdesport und Pferdezucht. Text in German. 1993. m. EUR 60; EUR 4.90 newsstand/cover (effective 2011). adv. back issues avail. **Document type:** *Magazine, Consumer.*
Formed by the merger of (1980-1993): Reiten und Fahren (0720-5104); (1900-1993): Reiten - St. Georg (0720-1524); Which was formerly (until 1980): St. Georg (0344-0222)
Published by: Jahr Top Special Verlag, Troplowitzstr 5, Hamburg, 22529, Germany. TEL 49-40-389060, FAX 49-40-38906300, info@jahr-tsv.de, http://www.jahr-tsv.de. Ed. Gabriele Pochhammer. Adv. contact Jasmin Seitter. Circ: 40,900 (paid and controlled).

636.1 DEU
REITEN UND ZUCHT IN BERLIN-BRANDENBURG. Text in German. m. EUR 4.30 newsstand/cover (effective 2007). adv. **Document type:** *Magazine, Trade.*
Published by: Moeller Druck und Verlag GmbH, Oraniendamm 48, Berlin, 13469, Germany. TEL 49-30-419090, FAX 49-30-41909299, info@moellerdruck.de, http://www.moellerdruck.de. adv.: B&W page EUR 710, color page EUR 1,349. Circ: 5,375 (paid).

798.2 DEU ISSN 0722-0731
REITER PRISMA; Fachmagazin fuer Pferdesport und -zucht in Rheinland-Pfalz, Saarland und Luxemburg. Text in German. 1979. m. EUR 55.80 domestic; EUR 68.40 foreign; EUR 4.90 newsstand/cover (effective 2008). adv. **Document type:** *Magazine, Consumer.*
Published by: Fachverlag Dr. Fraund GmbH, Weberstr 9, Mainz, 55130, Germany. TEL 49-6131-62050, FAX 49-6131-620544, info@fraund.de, http://www.fraund.de. adv.: B&W page EUR 1,435, color page EUR 2,515. Circ: 5,784 (paid and controlled).

798 DEU ISSN 0034-3692
REITER REVUE INTERNATIONAL. Text in German. 1958. m. EUR 57 domestic; EUR 60.30 foreign; EUR 5 newsstand/cover (effective 2011). adv. bk.rev. tr.lit. index. **Document type:** *Magazine, Consumer.* **Description:** Covers all aspects of horse sports from the recreational to the professional.
Incorporates (1956-1970): Reiter- und Fahrer-Magazin (0034-3706); (1957-1990): Pferd und Sport (0138-1342); Which superseded in part (1955-1956): Sportschiessen und Pferdesport (0490-5504); Which superseded in part (1954-1955): Sport und Technik. Ausgabe E: Sportschiessen, Sporttauben, Reit- und Hundesport (0232-6841); Which superseded in part (1952-1954): Sport und Technik (0490-5105)
—CCC.
Published by: Paul Parey Zeitschriftenverlag GmbH, Erich Kaestner Str 2, Singhofen, 56379, Germany. TEL 49-2604-9780, FAX 49-2604-978190, online@paulparey.de, http://www.paulparey.de. Ed. Susanne Hennig. Adv. contact Ulrike Scheuermann.

636.1 DEU ISSN 0343-6861
REITER UND PFERDE IN WESTFALEN. Text in German. 1976. m. EUR 52.80 (effective 2010). adv. **Document type:** *Journal, Trade.* **Description:** Horse breeding and riding information.
Published by: Landwirtschaftsverlag GmbH, Huelsebrockstr 2, Muenster, 48165, Germany. TEL 49-2501-27500, FAX 49-2501-27551, zentrale@lv-h.de, http://www.lv-h.de. Ed. Jasmin Wiedemann. Adv. contact Friedrich Deckert. Circ: 27,086 (paid and controlled).

798.2 DEU ISSN 1869-4209
▼ **DIE REITERIN**; Reiten, Lieben, Leben, Mode, Wohnen. Text in German. 2009 (Dec.). bi-m. EUR 27; EUR 3.50 newsstand/cover (effective 2011). adv. **Document type:** *Magazine, Consumer.*
Published by: FORUM Zeitschriften und Spezialmedien GmbH (Subsidiary of: FORUM Media Group GmbH), Mandichostr 18, Merching, 86504, Germany. TEL 49-8233-381361, FAX 49-8233-381212, service@forum-zeitschriften.de, http://www.forum-zeitschriften.de. Ed. Dagmar Sauer. Adv. contact Sabine Konhaeuser. Circ: 50,000 (paid).

798.2 DEU ISSN 0173-2404
REITERJOURNAL; Fachmagazin fuer Pferdezucht und Reitsport in Baden-Wuerttemberg. Text in German. 1980. m. EUR 5.20 newsstand/cover (effective 2007). adv. index. **Document type:** *Magazine, Trade.*
Published by: Matthaes Verlag GmbH, Silberburgstr 122, Stuttgart, 70176, Germany. TEL 49-711-2133245, FAX 49-711-2133350, kontaktm@matthaes.de, http://www.matthaes.de. Ed. Hugo Matthaes. adv.: B&W page EUR 1,905, color page EUR 3,085. Circ: 18,023 (paid and controlled).

798.2 DEU
REITPONY.INFO. Text in German. 2007. m. EUR 15 (effective 2010). adv. **Document type:** *Magazine, Consumer.*
Incorporates (2000-2008): Kleinpferde; Which was formerly (until 2004): Kleinpferde und Ponys; Kleinpferde incorporated (1979-2004): Haflinger-Magazin
Media: Online - full text.
Published by: Kretzschmar Verlagsgesellschaft mbH, Huelsebrockstr 101, Muenster, 48165, Germany. TEL 49-2501-27500, FAX 49-2501-27551, kretzschmarverlag@t-online.de. Ed. Helga Kretzschmar.

798.2 DEU ISSN 1862-782X
REITSPORT MAGAZIN FUER DAS PFERDELAND NIEDERSACHSEN. Text in German. 1983. m. EUR 60; EUR 5.50 newsstand/cover (effective 2008). adv. **Document type:** *Magazine, Consumer.*
Former titles (until 2005): Reitsport Magazin fuer Hannover-Bremen (0940-8282); (until 1991): Reitsport-Magazin (0936-9074)
Published by: (Reiterverbandes Hannover - Bremen), Paragon Verlagsgesellschaft mbH, Misburger Str 119, Hannover, 30625, Germany. TEL 49-511-56059930, FAX 40-511-56059939, verlag@paragon.de. Adv. contact Martina Ruehl-Berend. B&W page EUR 1,740, color page EUR 2,960. Circ: 9,655 (paid and controlled).

798.2 DEU
REITSPORT WESER-EMS. Text in German. 1975. m. adv. **Document type:** *Consumer.*
Formerly: Reitsport in Weser-Ems (0344-4295)
Published by: (Pferdesportverband Weser-Ems e.V.), Landwirtschaftsverlag Weser-Ems GmbH, Mars-la-Tour-Str 4, Oldenburg, 26121, Germany. TEL 49-441-8012-0, FAX 49-441-801269. Ed. Bernd Kiene. Adv. contact Ute Lienemann. Circ: 7,800.

798.2 DEU ISSN 2191-7590
▼ **REITZEIT**; Menschen und Pferde im Norden. Text in German. 2011. m. EUR 34.80 (effective 2011). adv. **Document type:** *Magazine, Consumer.*
Published by: Paragon Verlagsgesellschaft mbH, Misburger Str 119, Hannover, 30625, Germany. TEL 49-511-56059930, FAX 40-511-56059939, verlag@paragon.de.

798 GBR
THE RETURN OF MARES. Text in English. 1971. a. GBP 44 per issue (effective 2010). **Document type:** *Report, Trade.* **Description:** Covers resulting foals, sex, colour and date of birth of mares.
Supersedes in part (in 2003): Statistical Record (0307-0093); Which superseded in part (in 1971): Statistical Abstract; (in 1971): General Stud book. Weatherbys Statistical Supplement
Published by: Weatherbys Group Limited, Sanders Rd, Wellingborough, Northants NN8 4BX, United Kingdom. TEL 44-1933-440077, FAX 44-1933-440807, ihelp@weatherbys.co.uk, http://www.weatherbys.co.uk. Circ: 1,000.

798.4 FRA ISSN 1769-8138
LA REVUE DU GALOP; le bimestriel des acteurs des courses au galop. Text in French. 2004. bi-m. EUR 60 (effective 2009). back issues avail. **Document type:** *Magazine.*
Published by: Hippodrome Edition et Communication, 92 Av. du General de Gaulle, La Garenne Colombes, 92250, France. TEL 33-1-46491840.

798.2 DEU
RHEINLANDS REITER-PFERDE. Text in German. 1969. m. EUR 48; EUR 5 newsstand/cover (effective 2007). adv. **Document type:** *Magazine, Consumer.* **Description:** Contains articles and features on all aspects of equestrian riding, training and competition.
Published by: Neusser Druckerei und Verlag GmbH, Moselstr 14, Neuss, 41464, Germany. TEL 49-2131-40402, FAX 49-2131-404283, info@ndv.de, http://www.ndv.de. Ed. Uwe Xanke. Adv. contact Sandra Lehmann. B&W page EUR 1,560, color page EUR 2,355. Circ: 15,083 (paid and controlled).

798.2309481 DNK ISSN 1600-0927
RIDEHESTEN; Norges store hesteblad. Text in Danish, Norwegian. 1998. m. DKK 670 domestic; NOK 615 in Norway; DKK 620 in Europe; DKK 710 in the European Union; DKK 660 elsewhere (effective 2009). adv. **Document type:** *Magazine, Consumer.*
Formerly (until 1999): Ridehesten Hippologisk Nytt (1398-7488)
Published by: Mediehuset Wiegaarden, Blaakildevej 15, PO Box 315, Hobro, 9500, Denmark. TEL 45-98-512066, FAX 45-98-512006, mediahuset@wiegaarden, http://www.wiegaarden.dk. Ed. Britt Carlsen. Adv. contact Joergen Bak Rasmussen. color page DKK 7,980; 210 x 297. Circ: 9,800.

798 DNK ISSN 1396-0377
RIDEHESTEN, HIPPOLOGISK I AVL & SPORT. Text in Danish. 1996. m. DKK 776 domestic; DKK 970 in Europe; DKK 1,100 in the European Union; DKK 1,276 elsewhere (effective 2009). adv. bk.rev. **Document type:** *Magazine, Consumer.*
Incorporates (1923-2001): Dansk Ride Kalender (1399-9141); Formed by the merger of (1995-1996): Ridehesten i Avl og Sport (1395-2536); (1888-1996): Hippologisk (1395-4334); Which was formerly (until 1995): Hippologisk Tidsskrift (0018-201X)
Published by: (Sportsrideklubben i Koebenhavn, Dansk Varmblod), Mediehuset Wiegaarden, Blaakildevej 15, PO Box 315, Hobro, 9500, Denmark. TEL 45-98-512066, FAX 45-98-512006, mediahuset@wiegaarden, http://www.wiegaarden.dk. Ed. Britt Carlsen. Adv. contact Joergen Bak Rasmussen. color page DKK 10,850; 210 x 297. Circ: 15,000.

798 DNK ISSN 1903-7880
RIDEHESTEN JUNIOR. Text in Danish. 1997. m. DKK 350 (effective 2009). adv. **Document type:** *Magazine, Consumer.*
Former titles (until 2009): Ridehesten, Hippoloisk Junior (1398-2567); (until 1998): Ridehesten, Hippologisk Pony (1397-6311)
Published by: Mediehuset Wiegaarden, Blaakildevej 15, PO Box 315, Hobro, 9500, Denmark. TEL 45-98-512066, FAX 45-98-512006, mediahuset@wiegaarden, http://www.wiegaarden.dk. Ed. Britt Carlsen. Adv. contact Joergen Bak Rasmussen. color page DKK 8,778; 210 x 297. Circ: 10,200.

798.2 DNK ISSN 1603-6123
RIDEMAGASINET EQUIPAGE. Text in Danish. 2003. m. DKK 384 (effective 2011). adv. **Document type:** *Magazine, Consumer.*
Published by: Oxygen Magasiner A/S, Thoravej 13, 3 sal, Copenhagen, 2400, Denmark. hl@oxygen.dk, http://www.oxygen.dk. Ed. Peter Bennett. Adv. contact Nina Thygesen Gjoerup.

798.2 CAN ISSN 1910-2275
THE RIDER.COM. Text in English. 1994. m. (10/yr.). CAD 25; CAD 40 foreign (effective 1999). adv. bk.rev. **Document type:** *Journal, Trade.* **Description:** Covers all aspects of horsemanship, primarily in Ontario and the U.S. Midwest, but also elsewhere.
Formerly (until 2005): The Rider (1209-3955); Which was formed by the merger of (1990-1994): English Rider (1182-9958); (1987-1994): Western Rider (0820-571X); Which was formerly (until 1987): Canadian Rider (0702-9071); (until 1976): Canadian Western Rider (Ancaster, 1970) (0045-5555); Canadian Rider incorporated (in 1983): Canadian Western Rider (Ancaster, 1983) (0823-4582); (1973-1979): Canadian Quarter Horse Journal (0319-6348)
Indexed: SportS.
Published by: Golden Arc Publishing and Typesetting Ltd., 491 Book Rd W, Ancaster, ON L9G 3L1, Canada. TEL 905-648-2035, FAX 905-648-6977. Ed., Pub. Aidan W Finn. Adv. contact Barry Finn. Circ: 10,000.

636.1 USA
RIDING HOLIDAYS MAGAZINE. Text in English. 1999. m. free. adv. illus.
Media: Online - full text.
Address: http://www.ridingholidays.com/magazine.

798 USA
RIDING INSTRUCTOR. Text in English. 1985. q. USD 35 (effective 2000). adv. bk.rev. **Document type:** *Magazine, Trade.*
Published by: American Riding Instructors Association, 28801 Trenton Ct, Bonita Springs, FL 34134. TEL 239-948-3232, FAX 239-948-5053. Ed., Pub. Charlotte Brailey Kneeland. adv.: B&W page USD 265; trim 9.75 x 7.

798.2 SWE ISSN 0345-973X
RIDSPORT. Text in Swedish. 1973. bi-m. SEK 670; includes Ridsport Special. **Document type:** *Newsletter.*
Published by: Tidnings AB Ridsport, Fack 14, Trosa, 61921, Sweden. TEL 46-156-132-40, FAX 46-156-120-29.

798.2 SWE ISSN 1100-9721
RIDSPORT SPECIAL. Text in Swedish. 1989. s-a. SEK 670; includes Ridsport. **Document type:** *Newsletter.*
Published by: Tidnings AB Ridsport, Fack 14, Trosa, 61921, Sweden. TEL 46-156-132-40, FAX 46-156-120-29.

798.2 USA ISSN 0738-8381
ROCKY MOUNTAIN QUARTER HORSE MAGAZINE. Text in English. 1963. m. USD 25; USD 3 per issue (effective 2007). adv. back issues avail. **Document type:** *Magazine, Trade.* **Description:** Regional affiliate for American Quarter Horse Association providing information update results and articles on reginal shows, races, sales, contests, and members of the Quarter Horse.
Published by: Rocky Mountain Quarter Horse Association, 4701 Marion St., Ste. 307, Denver, CO 80216-2140. TEL 303-296-1143, FAX 303-297-8576, rmqha1@mindspring.com, http://www.rmqha.com/. Ed. Karen Karvonen. Adv. contact Melissa Nankervis. B&W page USD 200, color page USD 300. Circ: 1,100 (paid and free).

S

636.1 USA ISSN 1536-3007
ROCKY MOUNTAIN RIDER MAGAZINE; regional all-breed horse magazine. Text in English. 1993. m. USD 15 (effective 2001). back issues avail. **Document type:** *Magazine, Consumer.* **Description:** Covers all breeds of horses for northern Rocky Mountain Horse lovers.
Address: Box 1011, Hamilton, MT 59840. TEL 406-363-4085, FAX 406-363-1056. Ed., Pub. Natalie Riehl. Adv. contact Sam Walsh. Circ: 14,000 (paid and controlled).

791.84 USA ISSN 1934-5224
RODEO NEWS (LAPORTE). Text in English. 1993. irreg. USD 25 (effective 2008). adv. **Document type:** *Magazine, Trade.*
Published by: Rodeo News, PO Box 842, LaPorte, CO 80535. TEL 970-419-4747, FAX 970-494-2125, info@therodeonews.com, http://therodeonews.com/index.php?pid=rodeo_news&spid=home. Ed. Rebecca Lasich. Pub. Siri Stevens. adv.: B&W page USD 340.

798 NLD ISSN 1570-6257
ROS PAARDENMAGAZINE. Text in Dutch. 2007. bi-m. EUR 27.95; EUR 4.95 newsstand/cover (effective 2011). adv. **Document type:** *Magazine, Consumer.*
Published by: Vipmedia Publishing en Services, Takkebijsters 57a, Breda, 4817 BL, Netherlands. TEL 31-76-5301717, FAX 31-76-5144531, info@vipmedia.nl, http://www.vipmedia.nl. Ed. Frank Stienissen. Adv. contact Edwin Fijnaut. Circ: 22,000. **Subscr. to:** Postbus 7272, Breda 4800 GG, Netherlands; Vipmedia, Bredabaan 852, Merksem 2170, Belgium. TEL 32-3-6455618, FAX 32-3-6450500.

636.1 USA ISSN 0036-2271
SF277
SADDLE & BRIDLE; the oldest name in show horse magazine. Text in English. 1927. m. USD 79 (effective 2008). adv. bk.rev. illus.; abstr.; bibl.; tr.lit. 320 p./no. 3 cols./p.; back issues avail. **Document type:** *Magazine, Trade.* **Description:** Directed to owners and trainers of various breeds of English show horses. Provides information on training, management, veterinary care and horse show history.
Published by: Saddle and Bridle, Inc., 375 Jackson Ave., St. Louis, MO 63130-4243. TEL 314-725-9115, FAX 314-725-6440. Ed. Mary Bernhardt. Pub. Jeffrey Thomson. R&P Jeff Thompson TEL 314-725-9115. Adv. contact Christopher Thompson TEL 314-725-9115. B&W page USD 595. Circ: 5,200 (paid).

798 USA ISSN 0161-7842
SADDLE HORSE REPORT. Text in English. 1976. w. USD 60 domestic; USD 70 foreign (effective 2005); includes Horse World. adv. **Document type:** *Magazine, Consumer.*
Published by: Dabora, Inc., 730 Madison St, Shelbyville, TN 37160. TEL 931-684-8123, FAX 931-684-8196. Pub. Christy Howard Parsons. Circ: 3,500 (paid).

791.8 636.1 NLD ISSN 1384-0568
DE SHETLAND PONY. Text in Dutch. 1952. m. EUR 62 domestic; EUR 67 foreign (effective 2009). adv. 32 p./no. 3 cols./p.; back issues avail. **Document type:** *Newspaper.* **Description:** Publishes articles on Shetland ponies.
Published by: Nederlandse Shetland Pony Stamboek, Nieuwstad 89, Zutphen, 7201 NM, Netherlands. TEL 31-575-518063, FAX 31-575-542384, info@shetlandponystamboek.nl, http://www.shetlandponystamboek.nl. Circ: 4,300.

636.1 GBR
SHETLAND PONY STUD-BOOK SOCIETY MAGAZINE. Text in English. 1968. a. GBP 10 domestic; GBP 14.50 in Europe; GBP 18.50 elsewhere (effective 2009). adv. back issues avail. **Document type:** *Directory, Trade.*
Published by: Shetland Pony Stud-Book Society, Shetland House, 22 York Pl, Perth, PH2 8EH, United Kingdom. TEL 44-1738-623471, FAX 44-1738-442274, enquiries@shetlandponystudbooksociety.co.uk, http://www.shetlandponystudbooksociety.co.uk/.

798.2 636.16 SWE ISSN 1104-7860
SHETLANDSPONNYN. Text in Swedish. 1987. q. SEK 350 domestic to members; SEK 400 elsewhere to members (effective 2011). adv. **Document type:** *Magazine, Consumer.*
Published by: Sveriges Shetlandssaellskap, c/o S Gustafsson, Vintervaegen 2, Holmsjoe, 37034, Sweden. glantansponny@tele2.se, http://www.shetlandsponny.se. Ed. Aasa Petersson.

798 GBR
SHIRE HORSE SHOW CATALOGUE. Text in English. 1897. a. adv. **Document type:** *Catalog.*
Published by: Shire Horse Society, East of England Showground, Oundle Rd, Alwalton, Peterborough, Cambs PE2 6XE, United Kingdom. info@shire-horse.org.uk, http://www.shire-horse.org.uk/. Circ: 3,000.

636.1 GBR
SHIRE HORSE SOCIETY. STUD BOOK. Text in English. 1930. a. **Document type:** *Directory.*
Formerly (until 1964): Shire Horse Stud Book
Published by: Shire Horse Society, East of England Showground, Oundle Rd, Alwalton, Peterborough, Cambs PE2 6XE, United Kingdom. info@shire-horse.org.uk, http://www.shire-horse.org.uk/. Circ: 3,000.

798 USA
SHOW CIRCUIT. Text in English. 1994. q. USD 43.20 (effective 2005). adv. illus. **Document type:** *Magazine, Consumer.*
Address: 33603 Pacific Coast Hwy, Malibu, CA 90265. Ed. Jill Brooke.

798 USA
SOUTHEAST EQUINE MONTHLY. Text in English. m. USD 19.95 (effective 2003). adv. **Document type:** *Magazine, Consumer.* **Description:** Written specifically for horse enthusiasts in Virginia, North Carolina, South Carolina, Georgia, Florida and Tennessee. Combines horse-related information from throughout the nation and the region it serves into a single source that both amateurs and professionals can use to stay on top of news and information in the field.
Published by: Horse'n Around Magazine, 279, Blue Earth, MN 56013-0279. TEL 800-657-4663, gkaraban@klapublishing.com. adv.: B&W page USD 738; trim 10.75 x 13.

798 USA ISSN 1931-7131
SOUTHERN HORSE AND RIDER. Text in English. 2006. m. adv. **Document type:** *Magazine, Consumer.*
Address: P.O. Box 618, Flora, MS 39071. TEL 601-624-3484, http://www.southernhorseandrider.com/index.htm. Pub. Daryl Watkins. Adv. contact Trey Burton.

798 USA ISSN 0093-3929
SF277
SOUTHERN HORSEMAN. Text in English. 1962. m. USD 15. adv. **Document type:** *Magazine, Consumer.*
Published by: Southern Publishing, 3839 Business Hwy, 45 N, Box 71, Meridian, MS 39302-0071. TEL 601-693-6607. Ed. Tracy Thompson. Pub., R&P Thelma Thompson. Adv. contact Jeanette Pinkham. B&W page USD 528, color page USD 935. Circ: 26,000.

798.4 FRA ISSN 1632-0700
SPECIAL DERNIERE - LE MEILLEUR. Text in French. 2002. w. EUR 1.10 newsstand/cover (effective 2008). adv. **Document type:** *Magazine, Consumer.*
Formed by the merger of (1969-2002): Special Derniere (0750-3458); (1971-2002): Le Meilleur. Edition Rouge (0395-5915); Which was formerly (until 1971): Le Meilleur Tierce. Edition Rouge (0395-5923)
Published by: Groupe Alain Ayache, 117 rue de la Tour, Paris, 75116, France. TEL 33-1-45038000, FAX 33-1-45038020, kparent@groupe-ayache.com, http://www.groupe-ayache.com.

798.4 USA
SF321
SPEEDHORSE - RACING REPORT. Text in English. 1969. w. USD 39; USD 70 foreign (effective 1999). adv. bk.rev. **Document type:** *Newspaper.*
Incorporates (in 1990): Racing Report; Which was formerly: Speedhorse Tabloid; Incorporates (in 1990): Speedhorse (0364-9237); Which was formerly: Quarter Racing World (0048-6124)
Published by: Speedhorse, Inc., PO Box 1000, Norman, OK 73070-1000. TEL 405-573-1050, FAX 405-573-1059. Ed. Diane Carloni. Pub. Constance Golden. Adv. contact Andrew Golden. Circ: 5,600; 6,000 (paid).

791.84 USA ISSN 2160-1151
SPIN TO WIN RODEO. Variant title: Spin to Win Rodeo Magazine. Text in English. 1997. m. USD 24 domestic; USD 36 in Canada; USD 48 elsewhere (effective 2011). adv. back issues avail. **Document type:** *Magazine, Trade.* **Description:** Contains independent voice of team roping educates and entertains readers who actively participate in the sport.
Formerly (until 2011): Spin to Win (1096-9772)
Indexed: B04, G06, G07, G08, I05, R03, RGAb, RGPR, W03, W05.
Published by: Horse Media Group (Subsidiary of: Belvoir Media Group, LLC), 908 Main St, Ste 300, Louisville, CO 80027. TEL 303-661-9282, FAX 303-661-9298, http://www.horsemediagroup.com. Adv. contact Nick Griggs. **Subscr. to:** Palm Coast Data, LLC.

798 AUS ISSN 1038-9601
SPORTSMAN. Text in English. 1901. s-w. bk.rev. **Document type:** *Newspaper.*
Incorporates (in 1996): Weekend Sporting Globe; and: Midweek Sporting Globe; Both of which superseded in part (1922-1988): Sporting Globe (1030-0317); Formerly (until 1960): Sydney Sportsman
Related titles: Online - full text ed.
Indexed: I05.
—CIS.
Published by: Wayne Hickson News Ltd., 2 Holt St, Surry Hills, NSW 2010, Australia. TEL 61-2-2882528, FAX 61-2-2883453.

798 658 USA ISSN 1539-1256
STABLE MANAGEMENT. Text in English. 2000 (June). bi-m. free domestic to qualified personnel. adv. **Document type:** *Magazine, Trade.* **Description:** Trade publication for owners and operators of horse stables.
Related titles: Online - full content ed.
Published by: Beardsley Publishing Corp, 45 Main St N, Box 644, Woodbury, CT 06798. TEL 203-263-0888, FAX 203-266-0452. Ed. Jennifer Rowan. Adv. contacts Linda Humbert, Roger Humbert. page USD 2,280. Circ: 20,000 (free).

636.1 USA ISSN 1055-2979
SF293.T5
STALLION DIRECTORY. Text in English. a. included with subscr. to Thoroughbred Times. illus. **Document type:** *Directory.* **Description:** Lists throughbred stallions available for racing.
Incorporates: Sire Book (0272-3786)
Related titles: Online - full text ed.; ◆ Special ed. of: Thoroughbred Times. ISSN 0887-2244.
Published by: Thoroughbred Times Co, Inc. (Subsidiary of: BowTie, Inc.), 2008 Mercer Rd, Lexington, KY 40511. TEL 859-260-9800, FAX 859-260-9812, letters@thoroughbredtimes.com, http://www.thoroughbredtimes.com/. **Subscr. to:** PO Box Box 8237, Lexington, KY 40533.

636.1 ISL ISSN 1670-4789
STODHESTAR/HENGSTE/STALLIONS. Text in English, Icelandic, German. 1998. a. ISK 1,500, EUR 18, USD 19 per issue (effective 2005). adv. **Document type:** *Directory, Consumer.*
Formerly (until 2001): Stodhestar a Islands (1670-4800)
Published by: Eidfaxi ehf., Duggovogur 10, Reykjavik, 104, Iceland. TEL 354-588-2525, FAX 354-588-2528, eidfaxi@eidfaxi.is, http://www.eidfaxi.is. Ed. Jon Finnur Hansson. Adv. contact Kolbrun Olafsdottir. page ISK 135,000.

798 AUS ISSN 0311-8215
STUD AND STABLE. Text in English. 1971. irreg.
Formerly (until 1974): Australasian Stud and Stable (0310-6403)
Published by: Percival Publishing Company Pty Ltd., 862-870 Elizabeth St, Waterloo Dc, NSW 2017, Australia. TEL 61-2-93196231.

636.1 GBR
SUFFOLK STUD BOOK. Text in English. 1880. a. adv. **Document type:** *Directory.* **Description:** Comprises of the pedigree register also known as the pure-bred register; the section X non-breeding register; the grade register; and the international register.
Published by: Suffolk Horse Society, The Market Hill, Woodbridge, Suffolk IP12 4LU, United Kingdom. see@suffolkhorsesociety.org.uk.

798 USA
T E A M CLUB NEWSLETTER. (Tellington-Jones Equine Awareness Method) Text in English. 1981. q. USD 25 to members. **Document type:** *Newsletter.*
Published by: T.E.A.M News International, PO Box 3793, Santa Fe, NM 87501-0793. TEL 505-455-2945. Ed. Robyn Hood. Circ: 4,000.

798.4 USA
T Q H A NEWSLETTER. Text in English. 10/yr. Membership only (effective 2003). **Document type:** *Newsletter.*
Published by: Texas Quarter Horse Association, P O Box 9449, Austin, TX 78766-9449. TEL 512-485-5202, 800-945-6157, FAX 512-458-1713, tqha@nabi.net, http://www.tqha.com.

798.2 USA
TACK 'N TOGS BUYERS GUIDE; the international directory to products for the horse and rider. Text in English. 1971. a. USD 60 per issue (effective 2012). adv. charts; stat.; tr.lit. reprints avail. **Document type:** *Directory, Trade.* **Description:** List companies, products, manufacturers representatives and distributors.
Formerly: Tack 'n Togs Book
Related titles: Online - full text ed.: free (effective 2011).
Published by: Miller Publishing Co., 12400 Whitewater Dr, Ste 160, Minnetonka, MN 55343. TEL 952-930-4390, FAX 952-930-4362. Ed., Pub. Sarah Muirhead TEL 630-462-2466. Adv. contact Cindy Miller Johnson TEL 217-459-2710.

688.76 USA ISSN 0149-3442
SF285.3
TACK 'N TOGS MERCHANDISING; for retailers of apparel, equipment and supplies for horse and rider. Text in English. 1970. m. USD 50 domestic; USD 60 foreign; USD 3 per issue domestic; USD 5 per issue foreign; free to qualified personnel (effective 2011). adv. charts; illus.; stat.; tr.lit. reprints avail. **Document type:** *Magazine, Trade.* **Description:** Their mission is to connect the equine merchandising industry by providing cutting-edge information on new product launches, proven merchandising techniques, store management tips and industry trends.
Related titles: Microform ed.: (from PQC); Online - full text ed.: free (effective 2011).
—CCC.
Published by: Miller Publishing Co., 12400 Whitewater Dr, Ste 160, Minnetonka, MN 55343. TEL 952-930-4390, FAX 952-930-4362. Ed., Pub. Sarah Muirhead TEL 630-462-2466. Adv. contact Cindy Miller Johnson TEL 217-459-2710.

798.4 USA ISSN 0164-6168
THE TEXAS THOROUGHBRED. Text in English. 1979 (vol.4). bi-m. USD 40. adv. illus. **Document type:** *Magazine, Trade.* **Description:** Covers issues and topics of interest to the owners, breeders and fans of Texas Thoroughbreds.
Published by: Texas Thoroughbred Association, PO Box 14967, Austin, TX 78761. TEL 512-458-6133, FAX 512-453-5919. Ed., R&P Jim Cullen. Adv. contact Elizabeth Garza. Circ: 2,800.

798.2 615.8 DEU ISSN 0942-7546
THERAPEUTISCHES REITEN. Text in German. 1982. q. free to members (effective 2009). adv. **Document type:** *Magazine, Trade.*
Formerly (until 1992): Therapeutisches Reiten in Medizin, Paedagogik, Sport (0935-5804)
Indexed: IAB.
Published by: Deutsches Kuratorium fuer Therapeutisches Reiten e.V., Freiherr-von-Langen-Str 8a, Warendorf, 48231, Germany. TEL 49-2581-9279191, FAX 49-2581-9279199, dkthr@fn-dokr.de. Ed. Susanne Hennig. Adv. contact Elke Lindner. page EUR 450; trim 181 x 260. Circ: 3,500 (controlled).

798 USA ISSN 0082-4240
THOROUGHBRED RACING ASSOCIATIONS. DIRECTORY AND RECORD BOOK. Text in English. 1955. a. USD 17 to non-members (effective 2000). **Document type:** *Directory.*
Published by: Thoroughbred Racing Associations, 420 Fair Hill Dr, 1, Elkton, MD 21921-2573. FAX 410-398-1366. Ed. Christopher N Scherf. Circ: 3,000 (controlled).

798.4 USA ISSN 0887-2244
THOROUGHBRED TIMES; the weekly newsmagazine of thoroughbred racing. Text in English. 1985. w. USD 104.94 in state; USD 99 out of state; USD 279 elsewhere; USD 3.95 newsstand/cover (effective 2006); includes Stallion Directory. adv. bk.rev. illus. back issues avail. **Document type:** *Magazine, Consumer.* **Description:** Covers breeding, racing and public auction news of the thoroughbred industry.
Related titles: Microform ed.; ◆ Special ed(s).: Stallion Directory. ISSN 1055-2979.
Published by: Thoroughbred Times Co, Inc. (Subsidiary of: BowTie, Inc.), 2008 Mercer Rd, Lexington, KY 40511. TEL 859-260-9800, FAX 859-260-9812, http://www.thoroughbredtimes.com/. Ed. Mark Simon. Adv. contact Ken Ward. B&W page USD 3,460, color page USD 5,080; trim 10.875 x 14.75. Circ: 19,685 (paid).

798 GBR
TIMEFORM BLACK BOOK. Text in English. 1940. w. price varies. 2 cols./p.; **Document type:** *Journal, Consumer.* **Description:** Contains individual dossiers of facts and opinions for every racehorse in Britain.
Formerly: Timeform
Published by: Portway Press Ltd., 25 Timeform House, Northgate, Halifax, W Yorks HX1 1XF, United Kingdom. TEL 44-1422-330330, FAX 44-1422-398017, timeform@timeform.com.

798.46 USA
TIMES: ALMANAC. Text in English. a. adv. **Document type:** *Newspaper, Trade.* **Description:** Reviews public auctions, major races, statistics for breeders, owners and horsemen, pedigree pages for the upcoming breeding season and a directory of industry-related services and products.
Published by: TIMES: standard inc., 8125 Jonestown Rd, Harrisburg, PA 17112. TEL 717-469-2000, FAX 717-469-2005. Ed., R&P David M Dolezal. Adv. contact Shannon Butterfield.

798.46 USA ISSN 1046-9974
TIMES: IN HARNESS. Text in English. 1989. bi-w. USD 49.95; includes TIMES: Almanac. adv. **Document type:** *Newspaper, Trade.* **Description:** Covers national and international harness racing. Includes major harness racing events, race previews, and controversial topics.
Related titles: Online - full text ed.
Published by: TIMES: standard inc., 8125 Jonestown Rd, Harrisburg, PA 17112. TEL 717-469-2000, FAX 717-469-2005. Ed., R&P David M Dolezal. Adv. contact Shannon Butterfield. Circ: 7,000.

798.4 DEU ISSN 1865-5165
TRABER-JOURNAL; Fachzeitung fuer Trabersport und -zucht mit offiziellem Rennprogramm. Text in German. 1981. 120/yr. EUR 2.90 per issue (effective 2010). adv. **Document type:** *Newspaper, Consumer.*

Formerly (until 2007): Bayerisches Traber-Journal (0179-4272); Which incorporated (1927-1987): Herold (0018-0807)
Published by: Verlag fuer Trabrennsport GmbH, Stahlgruberring 7a, Munich, 81829, Germany. TEL 49-89-4201163, FAX 49-89-425441. adv.: B&W page EUR 500, color page EUR 800. Circ: 4,250 (paid and controlled).

798 USA ISSN 1527-5035
TRACK MAGAZINE. Text in English. 1975. m. USD 25 domestic; USD 50 foreign (effective 2008). 124 p./no. 3 cols./p.; **Document type:** *Magazine, Trade.*
Former titles (until 1999): Southwest Horse Track (1079-3534); (until 1994): Quarter Horse Track (1054-7525)
Published by: Quarter Horse Track Publishers, Inc., PO Box 222, Morgan Mill, TX 76465. TEL 254-965-9667, FAX 254-965-3936. Pub. Ben Hudson. Circ: 6,000 (paid).

798 AUS ISSN 1832-360X
TRACK TO TRACK. Text in English. 2005. m. back issues avail. **Document type:** *Magazine, Consumer.*
Published by: R I U Publishing, PO Box 1533, Subiaco, W.A. 6904, Australia. TEL 61-8-93823955, FAX 61-8-93881025, http://www.riu.com.au.

798.46 USA
TRACK TOPICS. Text in English. 1961. s-m. looseleaf. free to members, press and legislators. back issues avail. **Document type:** *Magazine, Trade.* **Description:** Concerned with the management and legislative issues concerning the harness racing pari-mutuel industry worldwide.
Formerly: Weekly Track Topics
Related titles: Online - full text ed.
Published by: Harness Tracks of America, Inc., 4640 E Sunrise Dr, Ste 200, Tucson, AZ 85718-4576. TEL 520-529-2525, FAX 520-529-3235. Ed. Stanley F Bergstein. R&P Stanley Bergstein. Circ: 2,000 (controlled and free).

798 USA
TRACK'S MONDAY REPORT. Text in English. 1998. w. USD 195 (effective 2007). adv. 14 p./no.; **Document type:** *Magazine, Trade.*
Published by: Quarter Horse Track Publishers, Inc., PO Box 222, Morgan Mill, TX 76465. TEL 254-965-9667, FAX 254-965-3936. Ed., Pub. Ben Hudson. adv.: page USD 400. Circ: 500 (controlled).

798.2 CAN
TRAIL RIDERS OF THE CANADIAN ROCKIES NEWSLETTER. Text in English. 1962. 3/yr. looseleaf. membership. adv. **Document type:** *Newsletter.*
Published by: Trail Riders of the Canadian Rockies, P O Box 6742, Sta D, Calgary, AB T2P 2E6, Canada. TEL 403-264-8656, FAX 403-264-8657. Ed. Nancy Maguire. Pub. Shel Bercouich. R&P Penny Egeland. Adv. contact Dean Newhouse. Circ: 230.

798.2 DEU ISSN 1865-1232
DER TRAKEHNER. Text in German. 195?. m. EUR 60 domestic; EUR 103 foreign; EUR 5 newsstand/cover (effective 2010). adv. **Document type:** *Magazine, Consumer.*
Former titles (until 2006): Trakehner Hefte (0720-9150); (until 1980): Trakehner Pferde (0720-9142); (until 1966): Trakehner Edelpferde (0496-0653)
Related titles: Online - full text ed.
—CCC.
Published by: (Trakehner Verband e.V.), Rathmann Verlag GmbH & Co. KG, Schlossgarten 3-4, Kiel, 24103, Germany. TEL 49-431-8881230, FAX 49-431-9828710, philip@rathmaenner.de, http://www.rathmann-verlag.de. Ed. Imke Eppers. Adv. contact Philip Rathmann. B&W page EUR 1,010, color page EUR 1,835; trim 215 x 280. Circ: 4,996 (paid).

798.4 SWE ISSN 0346-332X
TRAV- OCH GALOPPRONDEN. Text in Swedish. 1932. s-w.
Published by: Trav- och Galoppronden AB, Fack 20046, Bromma, 16102, Sweden. TEL 46-8-98-43-60, FAX 46-8-29-63-37. Ed. Claes Freidenvall. Pub. Thorbjoern Ericson. adv.: B&W page SEK 9,880, color page SEK 14,320; trim 277 x 190. Circ: 27,200.

798.2 910.91 USA
THE TRIAL RIDER; America's premier trial & pleasure riding magazine. Text in English. 19??. 8/yr. USD 19.97 domestic; CAD 29 in Canada; USD 35 elsewhere (effective 2010). adv. **Document type:** *Magazine, Consumer.* **Description:** Covers information about how and where to enjoy trail and recreational riding. Includes recommendations on destinations, previews of great trail rides, guidance for effective horse care and training, tips for buying tack and equipment.
Published by: Belvoir Media Group, LLC, PO Box 5656, Norwalk, CT 06856. TEL 203-857-3100, 800-424-7887, FAX 203-857-3103, customer_service@belvoir.com, http://www.belvoir.com. Ed. Rene E Riley. Adv. contact Nick Griggs TEL 806-622-2225. **Subscr. to:** PO Box 420235, Palm Coast, FL 33142. TEL 866-343-1802.

798 ESP
TROFEO DOMA CLASICA. Text in Spanish. bi-m. adv. **Document type:** *Magazine, Consumer.*
Published by: Editorial America Iberica, C. Miguel Yuste 33bis, Madrid, 28037, Spain. TEL 34-91-3277950, FAX 34-91-3044746, editorial@eai.es, http://www.eai.es/. Ed. Katharina Braren. adv.: page EUR 1,200; trim 230 x 297.

798 ESP ISSN 1579-234X
TROFEO TODO CABALLO. Text in Spanish. 1998. m. adv. **Document type:** *Magazine, Consumer.* **Description:** Covers all aspects of horsemanship, horseback riding and the equestrian world.
Published by: Editorial America Iberica, C. Miguel Yuste 33bis, Madrid, 28037, Spain. TEL 34-91-3277950, FAX 34-91-3044746, editorial@eai.es, http://www.eai.es/. Ed. Raquel Benjumeda. adv.: page EUR 2,500; trim 230 x 297.

798.4 CAN ISSN 0704-0733
TROT. Text in English, French. 1975. m. CAD 22 to non-members. bk.rev.
Former titles: Maple Leaf Trot; Canadian Trot Canadien (0045-5504)
Indexed: SportS.
Published by: Canadian Trotting Association, 2150 Meadowvale Blvd, Mississauga, ON L5N 6R6, Canada. TEL 416-858-3060, FAX 416-858-3111. Ed. Harold Howe. adv.: B&W page CAD 600; trim 10.88 x 8.13. Circ: 25,000.

798 ITA
IL TROTTATORE. Text in Italian. 1953. m. free to members. charts; illus.; stat. back issues avail. **Document type:** *Magazine, Consumer.*
Published by: Associazione Nazionale Allevatori del Cavallo Trottatore, Viale del Policlinico 131, Rome, 00161, Italy. TEL 39-06-4416421, FAX 39-06-44164237, info@anact.it, http://www.anact.it. Circ: 2,300.

798 USA ISSN 0083-3509
TROTTING AND PACING GUIDE; official handbook of harness racing. Text in English. 1947. a. USD 18 to non-members (effective 2001). index.
Published by: United States Trotting Association, 750 Michigan Ave, Columbus, OH 43215. TEL 614-224-2291. Ed. John Pawlak. Circ: 3,500.

798.4 NZL
TURF DIGEST. Variant title: Turf digest Weekender. Text in English. 1925. s-w. adv. **Document type:** *Handbook/Manual/Guide, Consumer.*
Incorporates (in 1982): Racetrack
Published by: Fairfax Media (Subsidiary of: John Fairfax Holdings Ltd.), 155 New North Rd, Eden Terrace, PO Box 1327, Auckland, New Zealand. TEL 64-9-3021300, FAX 64-9-3664565. Ed., Adv. contact Alan Caddy TEL 64-9-3021300. B&W page NZD 368; 125 x 200. Circ: 22,000.

798 USA ISSN 0744-0103
U S C T A NEWS. Text in English. 1973. bi-m. USD 20. adv. bk.rev. back issues avail. **Document type:** *Magazine, Trade.* **Description:** Informs members of proper treatment and training of horses, features rider and horse profiles, and provides updates of national and international rules for the equine sport of evening and combined training.
Indexed: SD.
Published by: United States Combined Training Association, 525 Old Waterford Rd NW, Leesburg, VA 20176. TEL 703-779-0440, FAX 703-779-0550. Ed., R&P, Adv. contact Jo Whitehouse. Circ: 10,000.

798 USA
U S E T FOUNDATION NEWS. Text in English. 1956. irreg. (5-6/yr.). membership. **Document type:** *Newsletter.*
Published by: United States Equestrian Team, 1040 Pottersville Rd, PO Box 355, Gladstone, NJ 07934-9955. TEL 908-234-1251, FAX 908-234-0670, http://www.uset.org/. Ed. Bill Landsman. Circ: 15,000.

798 USA
U S T A SIRES AND DAMS; the register. Text in English. 1948. a. USD 90 to non-members (effective 2001). index. **Document type:** *Directory.*
Formerly: Sires and Dams (0083-3495)
Published by: United States Trotting Association, 750 Michigan Ave, Columbus, OH 43215. TEL 614-224-2291. Ed. David Carr. Circ: 3,500.

798 USA ISSN 0083-3517
SF325
U S T A YEAR BOOK. Text in English. 1939. a. USD 60 to non-members (effective 1999). index.
Published by: United States Trotting Association, 750 Michigan Ave, Columbus, OH 43215. TEL 614-224-2291. Ed. David Carr. Circ: 3,000.

798.2 636.1 DEU ISSN 0342-7331
UNSER PFERD; Magazin fuer Pferdezucht und Pferdesport in Hessen. Text in German. 1966. m. EUR 57.80 domestic; EUR 69.90 foreign (effective 2010). adv. **Document type:** *Magazine, Consumer.*
Published by: Fachverlag Dr. Fraund GmbH, Weberstr 9, Mainz, 55130, Germany. TEL 49-6131-62050, FAX 49-6131-620544, info@fraund.de, http://www.fraund.de. Circ: 8,425 (paid and controlled).

798.46 SWE
V64-GUIDEN. Text in Swedish. w. SEK 995 (effective 2001). adv. **Document type:** *Magazine, Consumer.*
Published by: Guidenfoerlaget AB, Box 20002, Bromma, 16102, Sweden. TEL 46-8-506-660-00, FAX 46-8-28-82-40, guiden@guiden.se, http://www.guiden.se. Ed. Stefan Berglund. Pub. Bjoern Holmquist.

798.46 SWE
V75-GUIDEN. Text in Swedish. w. SEK 995 (effective 2001). adv. **Document type:** *Magazine, Consumer.*
Published by: Guidenfoerlaget AB, Box 20002, Bromma, 16102, Sweden. TEL 46-8-506-660-00, FAX 46-8-28-82-40, guiden@guiden.se, http://www.guiden.se. Ed. Mikael Nybrink. Pub. Bjoern Holmquist. Adv. contact Lars Sjoeblom. B&W page SEK 9,900, color page SEK 11,900; trim 175 x 248.

792.4 DNK ISSN 0042-2118
VAEDDELOEBSBLADET. Variant title: V6 Magasinet. Vseks Magasinet. Text in Danish. 1913. m. DKK 800 (effective 2010). adv. illus. **Document type:** *Magazine, Consumer.*
Address: Hestesportens Hus, Traverbanevej 10, Charlottenlund, 2920, Denmark. TEL 45-39-962020, vb@trav.dk, http://www.travoggalop.dk. Ed. Henrik Ebbesen. Adv. contact Mads M Jensen. Circ: 6,000.

636.1 FIN ISSN 0781-5638
VILLIVARSA. Text in Finnish. 1984. m. EUR 29 (effective 2005). adv. **Document type:** *Magazine, Consumer.*
Published by: Yhtyneet Kuvalehdet Oy/United Magazines Ltd., Maistraatinportti 1, Helsinki, 00015, Finland. TEL 358-9-15661, FAX 358-9-145650, http://www.kuvalehdet.fi. Ed. Sirkku Kuusava. adv.: B&W page EUR 205, color page EUR 520; trim 265 x 190. Circ: 15,396.

630 USA
VIRGINIA HORSE COUNCIL NEWSLETTER. Text in English. 1973. 6/yr. USD 10 to members. adv. **Document type:** *Newsletter, Consumer.* **Description:** Features articles on horse health; includes updates, 4-H recognitions, legislative issues, and industry events in Virginia.
Formerly: Virginia Horse
Published by: Virginia Horse Council, PO Box 665, Mineral, VA 23117. TEL 888-467-7382, FAX 540-854-7827, http://www.virginiahorsecouncil.org/. Ed., Adv. contact Alice Alley. Circ: 550.

798.4 USA ISSN 0505-8813
SF293.T4
VOICE OF THE TENNESSEE WALKING HORSE; a national publication devoted exclusively to the breed. Text in English. 1962. m. (except Sep.). USD 30 domestic; USD 40 in Canada; USD 50 elsewhere (effective 2000). adv. **Document type:** *Magazine, Trade.* **Description:** Provides information for those who own, breed, train, or ride Tennessee Walking Horses, whether for show or pleasure. Covers industry events, personality profiles, health care, and farm management and includes training-related articles.
Published by: Tennessee Walking Horse Breeders' & Exhibitors' Association, PO Box 286, Lewisburg, TN 37091. TEL 931-359-1567, 800-467-0232, FAX 931-270-8618. Ed. P J Wamble. R&P P.J. Wamble. Adv. contact David Kranich. Circ: 20,000.

798 DEU ISSN 0504-7064
VOLLBLUT; Rennsport - Zucht - Szene. Text in German. 1957. 4/yr. EUR 35.60; EUR 9.50 newsstand/cover (effective 2009). adv. **Document type:** *Magazine, Consumer.*
Published by: D S V Deutscher Sportverlag GmbH, Im Mediapark 8, Cologne, 50670, Germany. TEL 49-221-25870, FAX 49-221-2587212, kontakt@dsv-sportverlag.de, http://www.dsv-sportverlag.de. Ed. Peter Scheid. Adv. contact Werner Loof. page EUR 1,200; trim 184 x 240. Circ: 10,000 (paid and controlled).

798 USA ISSN 0093-6928
WALKING HORSE REPORT. Text in English. 1971. w. USD 50 domestic; USD 60 foreign (effective 2005). adv. **Document type:** *Magazine, Trade.*
Published by: Dabora, Inc., 730 Madison St, Shelbyville, TN 37160. Pub. Christy Howard Parsons. Circ: 5,500.

798 USA ISSN 1079-4433
WARMBLOOD NEWS. Text in English. 1989. bi-m. USD 24 domestic; USD 37 foreign (effective 2000). adv. bk.rev.; video rev. charts; illus.; stat. back issues avail. **Document type:** *Newsletter, Trade.* **Description:** Presents auction results, sales statistics, performance results, breed and registry news, breed profiles, pedigree analysis, government regulations.
Published by: American Warmblood Registry, Inc., PO Box 127, Davis, CA 95617. TEL 530-757-1377, FAX 530-756-0892. Ed., Adv. contact Gail Miller. Pub. Sonja K Lowenfish. R&P Laurie Campoy. Circ: 4,129. **Dist. by:** Sonoma Valley Publishing, Sonoma Valley Publishing, Box C, Sonoma, CA 95476.

636.1 USA
WELARA JOURNAL. Text in English. 1982. s-a. USD 4 domestic; USD 5.50 foreign (effective 2001). adv. bk.rev.; software rev. back issues avail. **Document type:** *Magazine, Trade.* **Description:** Covers the Welsh-Arabian (Welara) breed, along with breeders, show and events.
Related titles: Diskette ed.; Online - full text ed.
Published by: Welara Pony Society, PO Box 401, Yucca Valley, CA 92286. TEL 760-364-2048, FAX 760-364-2048. Ed., Adv. contact John H Collins. R&P Olivia G Collins. B&W page USD 30, color page USD 50. Circ: 1,500 (paid).

636.1 798 ZAF ISSN 1815-9117
WELSH PONY AND COB SOCIETY. JOURNAL. Text in English. 2005. a. ZAR 45 (effective 2006). **Document type:** *Journal, Trade.*
Published by: Welsh Pony and Cob Society of South Africa, PO Box 1029, Halfway House, 1685, South Africa. FAX 27-11-8003903.

798 GBR
WELSH PONY AND COB SOCIETY JOURNAL. Text in English. 1962. a. free to members (effective 2009). adv. back issues avail. **Document type:** *Journal, Trade.* **Description:** Provides information about Welsh Pony and Cob Society.
Published by: Welsh Pony and Cob Society/Cymdeithas y Merlod a'r Cobiau Cymreig, 6 Chalybeate St, Aberystwyth, Dyfed, Wales SY23 1HP, United Kingdom. TEL 44-1970-617501, FAX 44-1970-625401, info@wpcs.uk.com, http://www.wpcs.uk.com. Ed. David Blair TEL 44-1383-851732. Adv. contact E Wynne Davies TEL 44-1443-224317.

WENDY. *see* CHILDREN AND YOUTH—For
▼ **WENDY.** *see* CHILDREN AND YOUTH—For
WENDY. *see* CHILDREN AND YOUTH—For
WENDY. *see* CHILDREN AND YOUTH—For
WENDY. *see* CHILDREN AND YOUTH—For
▼ **WENDY FANTASIE PFERDE.** *see* CHILDREN AND YOUTH—For

798 CAN ISSN 1914-0835
WESTERN CANADIAN STALLION EDITION. Text in English. 1982. a., latest 2007. **Document type:** *Directory, Trade.* **Description:** Canadian sire list through October 15.
Former titles (until 2007): Western Canada Stallion Edition (1910-0582); (until 2005): Western Canada Stallion Directory (1209-322X); (until 199?): Stallion Directory (0829-0342); (until 1985): Western Canada Stallion Directory (0826-0850)
Published by: Canadian Thoroughbred Horse Society, British Columbia Division, 17687 - 56a Ave, Surrey, BC V3S 1G4, Canada. TEL 604-574 -0145, FAX 604-574-5868, cthsbc@uniserve.com, http://www.cthsbc.org.

798 USA ISSN 1062-3914
THE WESTERN HORSE; adventure & sport out West. Text in English. 1980. bi-m. USD 14.97 domestic; USD 20.22 in Canada; USD 22.97 elsewhere; USD 2.50 newsstand/cover (effective 1999). adv. illus. **Document type:** *Magazine, Consumer.* **Description:** Reports on world-class Western equine sporting events. Profiles top trainers and riders and covers related sightseeing, fashion, books, music, and art.
Former titles (until 199?): The Western Horse Magazine (1045-5957); (until 198?): The Western Horse (0746-1143)
Published by: BowTie, Inc., 2401 Beverly Blvd, PO Box 57900, Los Angeles, CA 90057. TEL 213-385-2222, FAX 213-385-8565, adtraffic@bowtieinc.com, http://www.bowtieinc.com. Ed. Richard Gibson. Pub. Lew Fay II. Circ: 70,000.

798.2 DEU ISSN 0933-9345
WESTERN HORSE; Zucht - Haltung - Western Reiten. Text in German. 1988. m. EUR 48 domestic; EUR 52 foreign (effective 2011). adv. bk.rev. back issues avail. **Document type:** *Magazine, Consumer.*
Published by: Verlag Ute Kierdorf, Im Mediapark 8, Cologne, 50670, Germany. TEL 49-221-55405445, FAX 49-221-5540545, kierdorf-verlag@t-online.de. Circ: 29,000.

798 AUS ISSN 1449-7581
WESTERN HORSE BREEDERS ANNUAL. Abbreviated title: W H B A. Text in English. 2004. a., latest no.6, 2009. AUD 13.50 per issue domestic; AUD 15.50 per issue in New Zealand (effective 2009). adv. back issues avail. **Document type:** *Magazine, Consumer.* **Description:** Provides information about horse and horse breeds.
Published by: MacoMedia, 16 Scrub Rd, Coolum Beach, QLD 4573, Australia. Ed., Pub., Adv. contact Margaret Oakden. B&W page AUD 360, color page AUD 660.

S

636.1 GBR ISSN 2040-5197
WESTERN HORSE UK. Text in English. 200?. bi-m. GBP 22 domestic; GBP 35 in Europe; GBP 43 elsewhere; GBP 3.99 per issue (effective 2010). adv. **Document type:** *Magazine, Consumer.*
Formerly (until 2009): FreeRein
Related titles: Online - full text ed.: free (effective 2010).
Published by: T. Wade, Ed. & Pub., The House on the Hill, Friezley Ln, Cranbrook, Kent TN17 2LL, United Kingdom. TEL 44-1580-714968, FAX 44-7753-757891. Ed., Pub. Tally Wade.

636.1 USA ISSN 0043-3837
SF277
WESTERN HORSEMAN. Text in English. 1936. m. USD 24; USD 2 per issue (effective 2009). bk.rev. illus. index. back issues avail.; reprints avail. **Document type:** *Magazine, Consumer.* **Description:** Covers western riding, training, veterinary care, saddles and equipment, endurance riding, reining, rodeo, cowboy history and poetry, working ranches, western art, packing and outfitting.
Related titles: Microform ed.: (from PQC); Online - full text ed.
Indexed: A22, G09, M01, M02, P02, P10, P53, P54, PMR, PQC, SPI, SportS.
—Ingenta, Linda Hall.
Published by: Western Horseman, Inc. (Subsidiary of: Cowboy Publishing Group), PO Box 7980, Colorado Springs, CO 80933. TEL 719-633-5524, FAX 719-473-0997. Ed. A J Mangum.

798.2 USA ISSN 1937-6405
SF309.3
WESTERN SHOOTING HORSE. Text in English. 2007 (Nov.). bi-m. USD 19.95 domestic; USD 34.95 in Canada; USD 54.95 elsewhere (effective 2009). adv. **Document type:** *Magazine, Consumer.* **Description:** Dedicated to promoting the sport of Mounted Shooting, including techniques, equipment, horses and riders.
Related titles: Online - full text ed.: ISSN 1937-6413. 2007 (Nov.).
Published by: Western Shooting Horse Association, 870 Historic Rte 66, Tijeras, NM 87059. TEL 505-286-0100, FAX 505-286-0501, wsha@westernshootinghorse.com, http://www.westernshootinghorse.com. Ed. Ken Amorosano. adv.: B&W page USD 1,370, color page USD 2,322; trim 8 x 10.875.

798.2 USA
WHIP. Text in English. 1974. q. USD 55 (effective 1999). adv. back issues avail. **Document type:** *Newsletter.*
Indexed: SD.
Published by: American Driving Society, PO Box 160, Metamora, MI 48455. TEL 810-664-8666. Ed. Ann L Pringle. Circ: 2,500.

798 305.4 USA
WOMEN & HORSES MAGAZINE. Text in English. 2005 (Jun./Jul.). bi-m. USD 24.95 (effective 2006). **Document type:** *Magazine, Consumer.*
Published by: W&H Media, PO Box 2660, Niagara Falls, NY 14302.

791.8 USA ISSN 1093-9202
WOMEN'S PRO RODEO NEWS. Text in English. 1964. m. illus. **Document type:** *Magazine, Trade.*
Formerly: Girls' Rodeo Association News
Published by: Women's Professional Rodeo Association, c/o Dolli Lautaret, 3840 Cheyenne, Kingman, AZ 86401. TEL 928-753-0053, FAX 928-718-5872, dolli@wpra.com, http://www.wpra.com.

798 USA ISSN 1098-2442
YOUNG RIDER; the magazine for horse and pony lovers. Text in English. 1994. bi-m. USD 12.99 domestic; USD 21.99 foreign; USD 3.99 per issue (effective 2008). adv. bk.rev. illus. **Document type:** *Magazine, Consumer.* **Description:** For children who are learning to ride horses, western and English styles. Covers the care, training and grooming of horses. Includes tips for showing, competing and general riding skills.
Published by: BowTie, Inc., 2401 Beverly Blvd, PO Box 57900, Los Angeles, CA 90057. TEL 213-385-2222, FAX 213-385-8565, adtraffic@bowtieinc.com, http://www.bowtieinc.com. Ed. Lesley Ward. Pub. Norman Ridker. adv.: B&W page USD 3,760, color page USD 5,680; trim 8 x 10.875. Circ: 82,699 (paid).

636.1 GBR ISSN 0266-4119
YOUR HORSE. Text in English. 1983. m. GBP 41.50 domestic; GBP 55 foreign (effective 2009). adv. back issues avail. **Document type:** *Magazine, Consumer.* **Description:** Provides a step-by-step guide on all aspects of riding and stable management. Helps you to care for and enjoy your horse.
Published by: H. Bauer Publishing Ltd. (Subsidiary of: Bauer Media Group), Bushfield House, Orton Centre, Peterborough, PE2 5UW, United Kingdom. TEL 44-1733-395052, http://www.bauer.co.uk. Ed. Julie Brown. Adv. contact Iain Grundy TEL 44-1733-468000. **Subscr. to:** Tower House, Sovereign Park, Market Harborough, Leicestershire LE16 9EF, United Kingdom. TEL 44-1858-438866, subs@greatmagazines.co.uk.

798 SVK ISSN 1337-1037
ZIVOTNY STYL A KON. Text in Slovak. 2007. m. adv. **Document type:** *Magazine, Consumer.*
Published by: E U Press, s.r.o., Desiata 16, Bratislava, 831 01, Slovakia. TEL 421-905-843945, FAX 421-2-54771956. Ed. Olga Kasova.

798 DEU
ZUECHTERFORUM. Text in German. 1997. m. EUR 55; EUR 5 newsstand/cover (effective 2006). adv. **Document type:** *Magazine, Trade.*
Published by: Matthaes Verlag GmbH, Silberburgstr 122, Stuttgart, 70176, Germany. TEL 49-711-2133245, FAX 49-711-2133350, kontaktm@matthaes.de, http://www.matthaes.de. adv.: B&W page EUR 1,210, color page EUR 2,010. Circ: 4,100 (paid and controlled).

798.4 GBR
100 WINNERS HORSES TO FOLLOW (YEAR). Text in English. 1963. a. GBP 2.50 per issue (effective 2009). **Document type:** *Journal, Trade.* **Description:** Compiles information on the leading horse candidates predicted to win races.
Formerly (until 2003): 100 Winners for (0955-0445)
Published by: Racing Post, One Canada Sq, Canary Wharf, London, E14 5AP, United Kingdom. TEL 44-1635-898781, help@racingpost.com, http://www.racingpost.com. Ed. Ashley Rumney.

SPORTS AND GAMES—Outdoor Life

796.42 USA ISSN 0361-347X
GV1060.67
A A U OFFICIAL TRACK AND FIELD HANDBOOK. Text in English. a. USD 10 (effective 1998). **Document type:** *Handbook/Manual/Guide, Trade.*
Published by: Amateur Athletic Union of the United States, 1910 Hotal Plaza Blvd, P O Box 22409, Lake Buena Vista, FL 32830. TEL 407-934-7200, FAX 407-934-7242, anita@aausports.org, http://aausports.org.

A C AUTOCARAVAN. *see* TRAVEL AND TOURISM

796.54 GBR ISSN 1750-5984
A C C E O MATTERS. Text in English. 199?. q. **Document type:** *Newsletter, Trade.*
Published by: (Association of Caravan & Camping Exempted Organisations), Leeds Media, White Rose House, 28a York Place, Leeds, LS1 2EZ, United Kingdom. info@leedsmedia.co.uk, http://www.leedsmedia.co.uk.

796 USA ISSN 1521-0189
A C O N A OUTDOOR ADVENTURE. Text in English. 1997. bi-m. **Document type:** *Magazine, Consumer.*
Published by: (Adventure Club of North America), The Pohly Co., 99 Bedford St, Fl 5, Boston, MA 02111. TEL 617-451-1700, 800-383-0888, FAX 617-338-7767, info@pohlyco.com, http://www.pohlyco.com.

796.5 910 DEU ISSN 1618-6281
A D A C CAMPING-CARAVANING-FUEHRER. BAND 2: DEUTSCHLAND, NORDEUROPA. Text in German. 1963. a. EUR 17.90 (effective 2008). adv. **Document type:** *Magazine, Consumer.*
Former titles (until 1997): A D A C Campingfuehrer. Band 2: Deutschland, Nordeuropa (0179-6062); (until 1985): A D A C Campingfuehrer. Band 2: Deutschland, Mittel- und Nordeuropa (0179-6046); (until 1971): Internationaler Campingfuehrer. Band 2: Deutschland, Mittel- und Nordeuropa (0179-6038); Which was formed by the merger of (1961-1963): A D A C Campingfuehrer Deutschland (0179-6011); (1959-1963): Internationaler Campingfuehrer. Zwischen Main und Eismeer (0179-6178); (1959-1963): Internationaler Campingfuehrer. Benelux, England, Nordeuropa (0179-6186)
Related titles: CD-ROM ed.
Published by: (Allgemeiner Deutscher Automobil-Club e.V.), A D A C Verlag GmbH, Leonhard-Moll-Bogen 1, Munich, 81365, Germany. TEL 49-89-76760, FAX 49-89-76762500, verlag@adac.de, http://www.adac.de. adv.: B&W page EUR 5,100, color page EUR 7,700. Circ: 75,573 (controlled).

796.5 910 DEU ISSN 1618-6273
A D A C CAMPING-CARAVANING-FUEHRER. SUEDEUROPA. Text in German. 1963. a. EUR 17.90 (effective 2008). adv. **Document type:** *Magazine, Consumer.*
Former titles (until 1997): A D A C Campingfuehrer. Band 1: Suedeuropa (0179-6089); (until 1971): Internationaler Campingfuehrer (0179-6070); Which was formed by the merger of (195?-1963): Internationaler Campingfuehrer. Zwischen Main und Mittelmeer (0179-6151); (19??-1963): Internationaler Campingfuehrer. Hamburg, Muenchen, Palermo, Gibraltar (0535-4250); Which was formerly (until 195?): Internationaler Zeltwanderfuehrer. Muenchen, Marseille, Palermo (0444-3241)
Related titles: CD-ROM ed.
Published by: (Allgemeiner Deutscher Automobil-Club e.V.), A D A C Verlag GmbH, Leonhard-Moll-Bogen 1, Munich, 81365, Germany. TEL 49-89-76760, FAX 49-89-76762500, verlag@adac.de, http://www.adac.de. adv.: B&W page EUR 5,350, color page EUR 8,080. Circ: 88,351 (controlled).

796.5 910 DEU
A D A C FREIZEIT MOBIL. Text in German. 2/yr. adv. **Document type:** *Magazine, Consumer.*
Published by: (Allgemeiner Deutscher Automobil-Club e.V.), A D A C Verlag GmbH, Leonhard-Moll-Bogen 1, Munich, 81365, Germany. TEL 49-89-76760, FAX 49-89-76762500, verlag@adac.de, http://www.adac.de. adv.: B&W page EUR 10,500, color page EUR 15,150. Circ: 455,000 (controlled).

796.93 DEU ISSN 1862-1651
A D A C SKI AND SNOWBOARD. Text in German. 2003. a. adv. **Document type:** *Magazine, Consumer.*
Formerly (until 2005): A D A C PistenAtlas (1618-372X)
Published by: (Allgemeiner Deutscher Automobil-Club e.V.), A D A C Verlag GmbH, Leonhard-Moll-Bogen 1, Munich, 81365, Germany. TEL 49-89-76760, FAX 49-89-76762500, verlag@adac.de, http://www.adac.de. adv.: color page EUR 4,400. Circ: 20,000 (controlled).

796.93 DEU ISSN 1866-5616
A D A C SKI-GUIDE. Text in German. 1984. a. EUR 19.95 (effective 2008). adv. **Document type:** *Magazine, Consumer.*
Former titles (until 2007): A D A C Ski-Guide Alpen (1616-2110); (until 2000): A D A C Ski-Atlas Alpen (0936-5192); (until 1988): Grosser A D A C Ski Atlas (0179-5538)
Published by: (Allgemeiner Deutscher Automobil-Club e.V.), A D A C Verlag GmbH, Leonhard-Moll-Bogen 1, Munich, 81365, Germany. TEL 49-89-76760, FAX 49-89-76762500, verlag@adac.de, http://www.adac.de. adv.: color page EUR 8,990. Circ: 50,000 (controlled).

796.552 USA ISSN 1067-5604
G505
A M C OUTDOORS. Text in English. 1907. 10/yr. free to members (effective 2010). adv. bk.rev. illus. back issues avail.; reprints avail. **Document type:** *Magazine, Trade.* **Description:** Provides club members and the public with coverage of how to protect and enjoy the Northeast outdoors.
Former titles (until 1993): Appalachia Bulletin issue (1052-5319); (until 1974): Appalachia Bulletin
Related titles: Online - full text ed.
Indexed: E04, E05.
—Ingenta.
Published by: Appalachian Mountain Club, 5 Joy St, Boston, MA 02108. TEL 617-523-0655, FAX 617-523-0722, information@outdoors.org. Pub. Heather Stephenson.

796.522 GBR ISSN 2044-754X
A M I MAGAZINE. Text in English. 2006. q. GBP 20 to non-members; free to members (effective 2011). adv. **Document type:** *Magazine, Consumer.* **Description:** For everyone interested in the outdoors, climbing and mountaineering.
Formerly (until 2010): A M I News (1757-6253)
Published by: Association of Mountaineering Instructors, Siabod Cottage, Capel Curig, Conwy, LL24 0ES, United Kingdom. TEL 44-1690-720123, FAX 44-1690-720248, enquiries@ami.org.uk. Ed. Ed Chard.

A N S O M. (Army - Navy Store & Outdoor Merchandiser) *see* CLOTHING TRADE

796.54 NLD ISSN 1871-9597
A N W B CAMPINGGIDS NEDERLAND. (Algemene Nederlandse Wielrijders Bond) Cover title: A N W B Campinggids Nederland-Belgie-Luxemburg. Text in Dutch. 1987. a. EUR 9.50 (effective 2008).
Former titles (until 2001): Camping Nederland (1385-0725); (until 1994): Campinggids Nederland (1385-0717)
Published by: ANWB BV/Royal Dutch Touring Club, Wassenaarseweg 220, Postbus 93200, The Hague, 2509 BA, Netherlands. info@anwb.nl, http://www.anwb.nl.

799.2 AUS ISSN 1443-5713
A S J (KENT TOWN). (Australian Shooters Journal) Text in English. 1999. a., latest vol.11, 2009. free to members (effective 2009). back issues avail. **Document type:** *Journal, Consumer.* **Description:** Contains vital issues concerning gun ownership and ever-changing firearm laws.
Supersedes in part (in 1999): Australian Shooters Journal (0005-0245)
Related titles: Online - full text ed.; ◆ Supplement to: Australian Shooter. ISSN 1442-7354.
Published by: Sporting Shooters Association of Australia, PO Box 906, St. Marys, NSW 1790, Australia. TEL 61-2-9623-4900, FAX 61-2-9623-5900, as@ssaa.org.au.

796.5 USA ISSN 1556-2751
F106
A T JOURNEYS. (Appalachian Trail) Text in English. 1939. bi-m. free to members (effective 2010). bk.rev. illus. back issues avail.; reprints avail. **Document type:** *Magazine, Trade.* **Description:** Contains Appalachian Trail news and features.
Formerly (until Aug.2005): Appalachian Trailway News (0003-6641)
Indexed: GeoRef, SpeleolAb.
Published by: Appalachian Trail Conservancy, 799 Washington St, PO Box 807, Harpers Ferry, WV 25425. TEL 304-535-6331, FAX 304-535-2667, info@appalachiantrail.org.

796 SWE ISSN 0348-1379
AAKA SKIDOR; ski & adventure magazine. Variant title: Aaka Skidor - Skid och Fjaellmagazinet. Nya Aaka Skidor. Text in Swedish. 1974. 7/yr. SEK 343 (effective 2005). adv. bk.rev. **Document type:** *Magazine, Consumer.* **Description:** Devoted to Alpine skiing, mountain biking, mountain climbing, and adventure sports.
Incorporates (1988-1989): Skid och Flaellmagazinet (1100-0120); (1982-1988): Ski Alp (0281-8175)
Published by: Hjemmet Mortensen AB (Subsidiary of: Hjemmet-Mortensen AS), PO Box 164, Aare, 83013, Sweden. TEL 46-647-51440, FAX 46-647-51444, info@hjemmetmortensen.se, http://www.hjemmetmortensen.se. Eds. Maarten Pettersson, Patrik Leje. adv.: color page SEK 33,000. Circ: 56,000 (controlled).

796.552 USA
ACCESS NOTES. Text in English. q.
Published by: Access Fund, Box 17010, Boulder, CO 80308. Ed. Sally Moser.

796.52 USA ISSN 0065-082X
GV199.8
ACCIDENTS IN NORTH AMERICAN MOUNTAINEERING. Text in English. 1948. a. USD 10 (effective 2000). reprints avail. **Document type:** *Report, Trade.*
Formerly: Accidents in American Mountaineering
Published by: American Alpine Club, 710 10th St, Ste 100, Golden, CO 80401. TEL 303-384-0110, FAX 303-384-0111. Ed. John E Williamson. R&P Lloyd Athearn TEL 303-384-0110 ext 13. Circ: 15,000.

796 DEU ISSN 2191-2890
▼ **ACTIVE;** wandern, erleben, geniessen. Text in German. 2010. bi-m. EUR 26.50 domestic; EUR 29.40 foreign (effective 2011). adv. **Document type:** *Magazine, Consumer.*
Published by: DoldeMedien Verlag GmbH, Postwiesenstr 5A, Stuttgart, 70327, Germany. TEL 49-711-134660, FAX 49-711-1346638, info@doldemedien.de, http://www.doldemedien.de. Adv. contact Sylke Wohlschiess.

796 DEU
▼ **ACTIVE LIFE;** Fitness, Natur, Genuss. Text in German. 2010. 4/yr. EUR 2.90 newsstand/cover (effective 2011). adv. **Document type:** *Magazine, Consumer.*
Published by: Motor Presse Stuttgart GmbH & Co. KG (Subsidiary of: Gruner + Jahr AG & Co), Leuschnerstr 1, Stuttgart, 70174, Germany. TEL 49-711-18201, FAX 49-711-1821779, cgolla@motorpresse.de, http://www.motorpresse.de. Ed. Olaf Beck. Adv. contact Bernd Holzhauer. Circ: 130,000 (paid).

796.522 USA ISSN 0001-8236
F127.A2
ADIRONDAC. Text in English. 1945. 6/yr. USD 20 domestic to non-members; USD 22.50 foreign to non-members (effective 2002). adv. bk.rev. illus. index. 32 p./no. 3 cols./p.; reprints avail. **Document type:** *Magazine, Consumer.* **Description:** Features articles on conservation, nature, history, wilderness trips, use of equipment, places to go in Adirondack and Catskill Parks, New York state parks and open space, and club-sponsored outings and workshops.
Indexed: APD, EIA, EnerInd, EnvAb.
—Ingenta.
Published by: Adirondack Mountain Club, Inc., 814 Goggins Rd, Lake George, NY 12845-4117. TEL 518-668-4447, FAX 518-668-3746, pubs@adk.org, http://www.adk.org. Ed. Neal Burdick. R&P, Adv. contact John Kettlewell TEL 518-668-4447 ext. 12. B&W page USD 540; trim 8.13 x 10.88. Circ: 18,500 (controlled).

917 USA ISSN 0001-8252
F127.A2
ADIRONDACK LIFE. Text in English. 1970. 8/yr. USD 24.95; USD 4.95 newsstand/cover (effective 2005). adv. bk.rev. bibl.; charts; illus. cum.index: 1970-1984, 1985-1999. back issues avail.; reprints avail. **Document type:** *Magazine, Consumer.* **Description:** Provides news and information about the Adirondack region.
Indexed: APD, AmH&L, RILM.
Address: PO Box 410, Jay, NY 12941. TEL 518-946-2191, FAX 518-946-7461, aledit@primelinkl.net. Ed., R&P Galen Crane. Pub. Tom Hughes. Adv. contact Jo'el P Kramer. B&W page USD 2,210, color page USD 2,980. Circ: 51,079 (paid and free).

796.552 USA
ADIRONDACK TRAIL IMPROVEMENT SOCIETY NEWSLETTER. Text in English. 1897. s-a.
Published by: Adirondack Trail Improvement Society, PO Box 565, Keene Valley, NY 12943. TEL 518-576-9949. Ed. Tony Goodwin.

799.1 GBR ISSN 1475-6315
ADVANCED CARP FISHING. Text in English. 1995. m. GBP 35.52 domestic; GBP 50 in Europe; GBP 65 elsewhere; GBP 3.25 newsstand/cover (effective 2009). adv. back issues avail. **Document type:** *Magazine, Consumer.* **Description:** Covers all aspects of carp fishing.
Formerly (until 1999): David Hall's Advanced Carp Fishing (1360-3086)
Published by: David Hall Publishing Ltd. (Subsidiary of: DHP Holdings Ltd.), 2 Stephenson Close, Drayton Fields, Daventry, Northants NN11 8RF, United Kingdom. TEL 44-1327-311999, FAX 44-1327-311190, info@dhpub.co.uk, http://www.davidhallpublishing.com. Ed. Richard Stewart TEL 44-1327-315447. Pub. David Hall TEL 44-1327-315402. Adv. contact Dean Rothery TEL 44-1327-315432. color page GBP 787; 210 x 297. **Dist. by:** M M C Ltd.

796 USA
ADVANCED DIVER MAGAZINE. Text in English. bi-m. adv.
Address: PO Box 21222, Bradenton, FL 34204-1222. adv.: B&W page USD 810, color page USD 1,305.

796 GBR
ADVENTURE COACHING. Text in English. 2005. irreg. free. **Document type:** *Magazine, Trade.* **Description:** Combines personal development with outdoor adventures.
Media: Online - full content.
Address: TEL 44-870-1620802, peter@adventurecoaching.co.uk, clay@adventurecoaching.co.uk.

799.1 GBR ISSN 2044-2793
▼ **ADVENTURE FISHING.** Text in English. 2010. bi-m. GBP 22.95 domestic; GBP 32.95 in Europe; GBP 38.95 elsewhere; GBP 4.85 per issue (effective 2010). adv. **Document type:** *Magazine, Consumer.* **Description:** Covers the process of angling, fishing experiences, amazing destinations, advices from experts in fishing.
Published by: Newsquest Specialist Media Ltd., 30 Cannon St, London, EC4M 6YJ, United Kingdom. TEL 44-20-76183456, FAX 44-20-76183459, info@newsquestspecialistmedia.com, http://www.newsquestspecialistmedia.com. Ed. Paul Beasley TEL 44-20-76183073. Adv. contact Rob Price TEL 44-20-76183418.

796 AUS ISSN 1832-8393
ADVENTURE GEAR GUIDE. Text in English. 2005. a., latest vol.1, 2005. AUD 9.95 (effective 2008). adv. back issues avail. **Document type:** *Magazine, Consumer.* **Description:** Contains gear facts and advice for Australian bushwalkers, campers, mountain bikers, paddlers, adventure racers, skiers, snowshoers, travellers and four wheel drivers.
Published by: Adventure Publishing, 2 Victoria St, Leura, NSW 2780, Australia. TEL 61-2-47841029, FAX 61-2-82128163, admin@adventurepublishing.com.au. Ed. Carl Roe. Adv. contact Lucas Trihey. page AUD 2,195; trim 210 x 297.

796 USA
ADVENTURE RACING MAGAZINE; the ultimate multi-sport endurance challenge. Text in English. 2001. q. USD 4.95 newsstand/cover (effective 2002). back issues avail. **Document type:** *Magazine, Consumer.*
Published by: Adventure Media, Inc, PO Box 2654, Oneco, FL 34264. TEL 941-545-5865.

796 USA ISSN 1949-1174
▼ **ADVENTURE RACING NAVIGATION SUPPLIES**; table top adventure race & navigation challenge, 12 navigation challenges for map and compass navigation. Text in English. 2009. q. USD 70; USD 19.95 per issue (effective 2009). **Document type:** *Catalog, Consumer.* **Description:** Includes navigation challenges for adventure racing.
Published by: A R Navigation Supplies, Inc., 2340 Pacific Ave, Ste 402, San Francisco, CA 94115. TEL 408-420-3883, info@ARNavSupplies.com, http://www.arnavsupplies.com.

ADVENTURE TRAVEL. *see* TRAVEL AND TOURISM

796 CAN
ADVENTUROUS. Text in English. 2005. q. CAD 15 domestic; CAD 21 foreign (effective 2005). **Document type:** *Magazine, Consumer.* **Description:** Covers various outdoors adventure activities and locations.
Published by: O P Publishing Ltd., 1080 Howe St, Ste 900, Vancouver, BC V6Z 2T1, Canada. TEL 604-606-4644, FAX 604-687-1925, http://www.oppub.com. Ed. David Webb. Adv. contact Derek Nyrose TEL 604-678-2583.

797.55 FRA ISSN 1292-2412
AERIAL; le magazine du vol libre et des sports aeriens. Text in French. 1997. q. EUR 27 domestic; EUR 27 DOM-TOM; EUR 30 in the European Union; EUR 40 elsewhere (effective 2009). **Document type:** *Magazine, Consumer.*
Published by: Cadre Plein Ciel, 3 Rue de le Trefilerie, Chamesson, 21400, France. TEL 33-9-54542966, http://www.cadre-plein-ciel.com.

799.2 ZAF ISSN 1817-1958
AFRICAN OUTFITTER. Text in English. 2005. bi-m. ZAR 100 domestic; ZAR 210 neighboring countries; USD 45 elsewhere (effective 2006). adv.
Published by: Game and Hunt Africa (Pty) Ltd, PO Box 35299, Menlo Park, 0102, South Africa. TEL 27-12-3485550, FAX 27-12-3485551. Ed. Mauritz Coetzee. Adv. contact Salome van Niekerk. page ZAR 10,000.

797.55 AUS ISSN 0158-8346
AIRFLOW. Text in English. 1947. m. free to qualified personnel (effective 2008). adv. back issues avail. **Document type:** *Magazine, Trade.*
Related titles: Online - full text ed.: free (effective 2008).
Published by: Gliding Club of Victoria, Samaria Rd, PO Box 46, Benalla, VIC 3672, Australia. TEL 61-3-57621058, FAX 61-3-57625599, gliding@benalla.net.au, http://www.glidingclub.org.au. Ed. Amanda Penrose.

796.79 USA
AIRSTREAM LIFE; the official Airstream lifestyle magazine. Text in English. 2004. q. USD 16 in US & Canada; USD 46 in Western Europe, Japan, Australia & New Zealand (effective 2008). adv. **Document type:** *Magazine, Consumer.* **Description:** Explores a broad range of topics related to the traveling lifestyle of Airstream travelk trailer and motor home owners.
Published by: Church Street Publishing, Inc., PO Box 74, Ferrisburg, VT 05456. TEL 802-877-2900, FAX 802-610-1013. Ed., Pub. Rich Luhr TEL 802-877-2900 ext 3. adv.: color page USD 2,850. Circ: 1,000 (controlled); 24,000 (paid).

799.2 SWE ISSN 1404-8434
AKILA. Text in Swedish. 2000. 6/yr. SEK 150 (effective 2004). adv. **Document type:** *Consumer.* **Description:** Hunting magazine for young readers.
Published by: Svenska Jaegarefoerbundet/Swedish Hunters Association, Oester-Malma, Nykoeping, 61191, Sweden. TEL 46-155-246200, FAX 46-155-246250. Ed. Marie Gadolin. Circ: 15,000.

799.3 USA ISSN 0279-6783
ALABAMA GAME & FISH. Text in English. 19??. m. USD 12.99 domestic; USD 25.99 in Canada; USD 27.99 elsewhere (effective 2011). adv. illus. **Document type:** *Magazine, Consumer.* **Description:** Informs sportsmen of hunting and fishing, as well as environmental and conservation issues in Alabama.
Related titles: Online - full text ed.; ◆ Regional ed(s).: Game & Fish; ◆ Louisiana Game & Fish. ISSN 0744-3692; ◆ Florida Game & Fish. ISSN 0889-3322; ◆ Mississippi-Louisiana Game & Fish. ISSN 1947-2358; ◆ North Carolina Game & Fish. ISSN 0897-8816; ◆ South Carolina Game & Fish. ISSN 0897-9154; ◆ West Virginia Game & Fish. ISSN 0897-9162; ◆ Missouri Game & Fish. ISSN 0889-3799; ◆ New York Game & Fish. ISSN 0897-9189; ◆ California Game & Fish. ISSN 1056-0122; ◆ Great Plains Game & Fish. ISSN 1055-6532; ◆ Illinois Game & Fish. ISSN 0897-9014; ◆ Indiana Game & Fish. ISSN 0897-8980; ◆ Iowa Game & Fish. ISSN 0897-9197; ◆ Mid-Atlantic Game & Fish. ISSN 1055-6540; ◆ Oklahoma Game & Fish. ISSN 0746-6013; ◆ Rocky Mountain Game & Fish. ISSN 1056-0114; ◆ Pennsylvania Game & Fish. ISSN 0897-8808; ◆ Virginia Game & Fish. ISSN 0897-8794; ◆ Washington - Oregon Game & Fish. ISSN 1056-0106; ◆ Ohio Game & Fish. ISSN 0897-9170; New England Game & Fish. ISSN 0897-8972. 1988. USD 12 domestic; USD 25 in Canada; USD 27 elsewhere (effective 2010).
Published by: Intermedia Outdoors, Inc., 512 7th Ave, 11th Fl, New York, NY 10018. TEL 212-852-6600, 800-260-6397, FAX 212-302-4472, customerservice@imoutdoors.com, http://www.imoutdoorsmedia.com. Ed. Ken Dunwoody. Pub., Adv. contact Peter Gross.

ALABAMA WILDLIFE. *see* CONSERVATION

799.1 USA ISSN 1047-5176
THE ALASKA ANGLER. Text in English. 1986. bi-m. looseleaf. USD 49; USD 59 in Canada; USD 69 elsewhere. adv. bk.rev. charts; illus.; stat. back issues avail. **Document type:** *Magazine, Consumer.* **Description:** Covers Alaska sportfishing.
Published by: Alaska Angler Publications, PO Box 83550, Fairbanks, AK 99708. TEL 907-455-8000, FAX 907-455-6691. Ed. Chris Batin.

ALASKA DEPARTMENT OF FISH AND GAME. DIVISION OF WILDLIFE CONSERVATION. ANNUAL PERFORMANCE REPORT. *see* FISH AND FISHERIES

ALASKA DEPARTMENT OF FISH AND GAME. DIVISION OF WILDLIFE CONSERVATION. FEDERAL AID IN WILDLIFE RESTORATION. ANNUAL RESEARCH PERFORMANCE REPORT. *see* FISH AND FISHERIES

ALASKA DEPARTMENT OF FISH AND GAME. DIVISION OF WILDLIFE CONSERVATION. FEDERAL AID IN WILDLIFE RESTORATION. RESEARCH PROGRESS REPORT. *see* FISH AND FISHERIES

ALASKA DEPARTMENT OF FISH AND GAME. DIVISION OF WILDLIFE CONSERVATION. FEDERAL AID IN WILDLIFE RESTORATION. SURVEY-INVENTORY MANAGEMENT REPORT. *see* FISH AND FISHERIES

ALASKA DEPARTMENT OF FISH AND GAME. DIVISION OF WILDLIFE CONSERVATION. FINAL REPORT. *see* FISH AND FISHERIES

799.2 USA ISSN 1047-5184
THE ALASKA HUNTER. Text in English. 1987. bi-m. looseleaf. USD 49; USD 59 in Canada; USD 69 elsewhere. adv. bk.rev. charts; illus.; stat. back issues avail. **Document type:** *Magazine, Consumer.* **Description:** Provides information on where to hunt in Alaska.
Published by: Alaska Angler Publications, PO Box 83550, Fairbanks, AK 99708. TEL 907-455-8000, FAX 907-455-6691. Ed. Chris Batin.

799 CAN ISSN 0318-4943
ALBERTA FISHING GUIDE. Text in English. 1972. a. CAD 4.95. adv. bk.rev. illus. **Document type:** *Handbook/Manual/Guide, Consumer.* **Description:** Includes a comprehensive guide to 1300 sportfishing waters in Alberta, comes with current and detailed directions, species, size of fish, and facilities.
Published by: Barry Mitchell Publications Ltd., 6C 5571 45 St, Red Deer, AB T4N 1L2, Canada. TEL 403-347-5079, FAX 403-341-5454. Ed. Ann Mitchell. Adv. contact Barry Mitchell. B&W page CAD 1,565, color page CAD 2,035; trim 10.75 x 8.25. Circ: 30,000.

796.93 USA ISSN 2162-3953
▼ **ALL ABOUT SNOW.** Text in English. 2010. q. **Document type:** *Magazine, Trade.*
Related titles: Online - full text ed.: ISSN 2162-3961.
Published by: J V H Media Group, Llc., 438 Division St, Sewickley, PA 15143. http://www.jvhmediagroup.com/. Ed. Rodney Burrell.

ALL AROUND KENTUCKY. *see* AGRICULTURE

796.75 USA
ALL-TERRAIN VEHICLE. Text in English. q. adv. **Document type:** *Magazine, Consumer.* **Description:** Aimed at the outdoor motorsports enthusiast.
Published by: All Terrain Vehicle, LLC, 9445 Minnetonka Blvd., Minneapolis, MN 55426-2900. Pub. Mark Lester TEL 705-286-2135. adv.: B&W page USD 3,455, color page USD 6,250; trim 8.25 x 10.875. Circ: 21,000 (paid); 75,000 (free).

ALLMOUNTAIN; Bergsport - Reisen - Ausruestung. *see* TRAVEL AND TOURISM

799.1 SWE ISSN 1650-6812
ALLT OM FLUGFISKE. Text in Swedish. 2001. bi-m. SEK 398 (effective 2006). adv. **Document type:** *Magazine, Consumer.* **Description:** Fly-fishing for all.
Published by: L R F Media AB, Bergdorffsgatan 5B, Karlstad, 65224, Sweden. TEL 46-54-7752520, lrfmedia@lrfmedia.lrf.se. Ed. Matts Gyllsand TEL 46-54-7752503. Adv. contact Ulla Jonsson TEL 46-54-7752521. page SEK 23,400; 190 x 265.

796.5 SWE ISSN 0346-9190
ALLT OM HUSVAGN & CAMPING. Text in Swedish. 1976. 11/yr. SEK 419; SEK 49.50 per issue (effective 2005). adv. bk.rev. **Document type:** *Magazine, Consumer.* **Description:** Provides news and consumer tests of caravans and mobile homes. Informs on travel in Sweden, Nordic countries and elsewhere in Europe.
Formerly (until 2001): Husvagn & Camping
Published by: Hjemmet Mortensen AB (Subsidiary of: Hjemmet-Mortensen AS), Gaevlegatan 22, Stockholm, 11378, Sweden. TEL 46-8-6920100, FAX 46-8-6509705, info@hjemmetmortensen.se, http://www.hjemmetmortensen.se. Eds. Susanne Landin TEL 46-8-6920110, Ulla Carle TEL 46-8-6920114. Adv. contact Kenneth Svensson TEL 46-31-478650. color page SEK 14,800; 193 x 255. Circ: 23,300 (controlled).

796.93 ITA ISSN 1722-7828
ALP G M. (Grandi Montagne) Text in Italian. 1985. bi-m. EUR 39 (effective 2008). cum.index: nos.1-100. **Document type:** *Magazine, Consumer.* **Description:** Covers mountaineering.
Supersedes in part (1985-2000): Alp (1122-6668)
Published by: C D A Vivalda Editori Srl, Via Invorio 24-A, Turin, TO 10146, Italy. TEL 39-011-7720444, FAX 39-011-7732170, abbonamenti@cdavivalda.it, http://www.cdavivalda.it. Ed. Enrico Camanni. Pub., Adv. contact Mario Dalmaviva.

796.93 ITA ISSN 1972-683X
ALP SPECIALI. Text in Italian. 1985. bi-m. **Document type:** *Magazine, Consumer.*
Formerly (until 2007): Alp Wall (1722-6902); Which superseded in part (in 2001): Alp (1122-6668)
Published by: C D A Vivalda Editori Srl, Via Invorio 24-A, Turin, TO 10146, Italy. TEL 39-011-7720444, FAX 39-011-7732170, abbonamenti@cdavivalda.it, http://www.cdavivalda.it.

796.522 CHE ISSN 0002-6336
DQ821
DIE ALPEN/ALPES/ALPI. Text in French, German. 1892. m. CHF 50 domestic; CHF 66 foreign (effective 2001). adv. bk.rev. charts; illus. **Document type:** *Magazine, Consumer.* **Description:** Contains articles on mountaineering.
Indexed: A33, GeoRef.
—CCC.
Published by: Schweizer Alpen Club/Club Alpin Suisse, Monbijoustr 61, Bern 23, 3000, Switzerland. TEL 41-31-3701818, FAX 41-31-3701890, alpen@sac-cas.ch. Ed. Gross Etienne. R&P Etienne Gross. adv.: B&W page CHF 4,800, color page CHF 7,200. Circ: 80,000.

796 AUT
ALPENVEREIN GRAZ. NACHRICHTEN. Text in German. s-a. adv. **Document type:** *Newsletter, Consumer.* **Description:** Covers events and activities in the Graz Alpine region.
Published by: Oesterreichischer Alpenverein, Sektion Graz, Sackstr 16, Graz, St 8010, Austria. TEL 43-316-822266, FAX 43-316-812474, graz@sektion.aplenverein.at. Circ: 9,000.

796.510 FRA ISSN 1957-3219
ALPES MAGAZINE BALADES ET RANDONNEES. Text in French. 1991. a. **Document type:** *Magazine, Consumer.*
Former titles (until 2007): Rando Alpes (1950-4136); (until 2006): Balades et Randonnees (1292-3966)
Published by: Milan Presse, 300 Rue Leon Joulin, Toulouse, 31101, France. TEL 33-5-61766495, http://www.milanpresse.com.

796.522 ITA ISSN 0002-6468
LE ALPI VENETE; rivista di montagna. Text in Italian. 1947. s-a. EUR 4.50 per issue (effective 2008). adv. bk.rev. bibl.; charts; illus. **Document type:** *Magazine, Consumer.*
Published by: Club Alpino Italiano, Sezioni Trivenete, C.P. 514, Mestre, PT 30170, Italy.

796.522 796.93 DEU ISSN 0177-3542
ALPIN; das Bergweltmagazin. Text in German. 1963. m. EUR 49.80; EUR 4.60 newsstand/cover (effective 2006). adv. **Document type:** *Magazine, Consumer.*
Former titles (until 1984): Alpin-Magazin (0722-7884); (until 1982): Alpinismus (0002-6484); Incorporates (1974-1988): Bergwelt (0340-1294); Which was formerly (1971-1973): Winter, Bergkamerad (0005-8939); Which was formed by the merger of (1949-1971): Der Bergkamerad (0340-1340); (1906-1971): Der Winter (0340-1391); Which incorporated (1906-1907): Alpinismus und Wintersport (1421-0762); Which was formerly (1903-1906): Alpiner Wintersport (1421-0754); (1902-1903): Winter im Bernerland (1421-0789)
Indexed: RASB.
—CCC.
Published by: Olympia Verlag GmbH, Badstr 4-6, Nuernberg, 90402, Germany. TEL 49-911-2160, FAX 49-911-2162741, 49-911-2162741, anzeigen@olympia-verlag.de. Ed. Georg Schimke. Adv. contact Alexander Herrmann. B&W page EUR 3,000, color page EUR 3,800; trim 210 x 280. Circ: 31,646 (paid and controlled).

796.552 GBR ISSN 0065-6569
DQ821
THE ALPINE JOURNAL; a record of mountain adventure and scientific observation. Text in English. 1863. a., latest vol.105. GBP 26 per issue; free to members (effective 2009). bk.rev. illus. index. back issues avail.; reprints avail. **Document type:** *Journal, Academic/Scholarly.* **Description:** Covers whom and what's been going on in the world of mountaineering and alpinism during the last 12 months.
Incorporates (in 1982): Alpine Climbing; (in 1961): Ladies Alpine Club. Journal
Indexed: GeoRef, SpeleolAb, SportS.

S

—BLDSC (0802.150000), IE, Ingenta, INIST.
Published by: Alpine Club, 55/56 Charlotte Rd, London, EC2A 3QF, United Kingdom. TEL 44-20-76130755, admin@alpine-club.org.uk. Ed. Steve Goodwin.

796.552 FRA ISSN 1254-714X
ALPINISME & RANDONNEE. Text in French. 1978. m. adv. bk.rev.
Former titles (until 1994): Alpirando (0759-2167); (until 1984): Alpinisme et Randonnee (0154-1757)
Related titles: Supplement(s): Guides Alpinisme et Randonnee. ISSN 1271-0172.
Published by: Alpinisme et Randonnee, 48-50 bd. Senart, Saint Cloud, 92210, France. FAX 33-1-46022311. Ed. Christine Grosjean. Circ: 35,000.

796.52 USA ISSN 1540-725X
ALPINIST MAGAZINE. Text in English. q. USD 46 domestic; USD 52 in Canada; USD 58 elsewhere; USD 12.95 newsstand/cover (effective 2007). **Description:** Dedicated to world alpinism and adventure climbing. It captures the art of ascent in its most powerful manifestations, presenting an articulation of climbing and its lifestyle that matches the intensity of the pursuit itself. Features of the magazine include first-person accounts of the hottest new routes, spectacular photography from the lenses of the world's best climbing photographers, and compelling reportage on climbs from the four corners of the globe.
Published by: Alphanist, 1160 Alpine Ln Ste 2G, PO Box 4956, Jackson, WY 83001. TEL 877-960-0600, info@hatsoff.net. Ed. Christian Beckwith. Pub. Marc Ewing.

796.552 DEU
ALPINWELT. Text in German. 2000. q. adv. **Document type:** *Magazine, Consumer.*
Published by: Deutscher Alpenverein, Sektion Muenchen, Bayerstr 21, Munich, 80335, Germany. TEL 49-89-5517000, FAX 49-89-55170099, service@alpenverein-muenchen.de, http://www.alpenverein-muenchen-oberland.de. Ed. Frank Martin Siefarth. Adv. contact Thomas Obermaier TEL 49-89-55241272. B&W page EUR 3,253, color page EUR 4,631; trim 210 x 280. Circ: 85,000 (controlled).

799.1 NOR ISSN 0804-5887
ALT OM FISKE. Text in Norwegian. 1994. 10/yr. NOK 349; NOK 75 newsstand/cover (effective 2009). adv. **Document type:** *Magazine, Consumer.*
Published by: Hjemmet Mortensen AS, Gullhaugveien 1, Nydalen, Oslo, 0441, Norway. TEL 47-22-585000, FAX 47-22-585959, firmapost@hm-media.no, http://www.hm-media.no. Ed. Jon Lenas. adv.: page NOK 23,800.

799.31 USA ISSN 0065-6747
AMATEUR TRAPSHOOTING ASSOCIATION. OFFICIAL TRAPSHOOTING RULES. Text in English. 1923. a. USD 25 to members. index.
Published by: Amateur Trapshooting Association, 601 W National Rd, Vandalia, OH 45377. TEL 937-898-4638, FAX 937-898-5472. Circ: 100,000.

799.1 DNK ISSN 0900-2650
AMATOERFISKEREN. Text in Danish. 1979. 6/yr. membership. illus. **Document type:** *Magazine, Consumer.*
Published by: Dansk Amatoerfiskerforening, c/o Vagn Gram, Kildetoften 1, Faaborg, 5600, Denmark. TEL 45-62-611800, FAX 45-62-611817, vgram@stofanet.dk, http://www.fritidsfiskeri.dk. Ed. Henning Nielsen.

796.52 USA ISSN 0065-6925
G505
AMERICAN ALPINE JOURNAL. Abbreviated title: A A J. Text in English. 1929. a. free to members (effective 2010). bk.rev. illus. index. back issues avail.; reprints avail. **Document type:** *Journal, Trade.* **Description:** Features articles devoted to mountaineering and rock climbing, the conservation and study of mountainous regions, and representing the interests of the American climbing community.
Related titles: Microform ed.: (from PQC); Online - full text ed.: free (effective 2010).
Indexed: A33, GeoRef, MLA-IB, SpeleolAb.
—Ingenta.
Published by: American Alpine Club, 710 10th St, Ste 100, Golden, CO 80401. TEL 303-384-0110, FAX 303-384-0111, info@americanalpineclub.org, http://www.americanalpineclub.org. Ed. Gene Ellis.

796.552 USA ISSN 0147-9288
AMERICAN ALPINE NEWS. Text in English. 1950. q. USD 5 domestic; USD 10 foreign (effective 2000). adv. bk.rev. illus. reprints avail. **Document type:** *Newsletter, Consumer.* **Description:** Contains articles on mountaineering and maps.
Formerly: A A C News
Indexed: SportS.
Published by: American Alpine Club, 710 10th St, Ste 100, Golden, CO 80401. TEL 303-384-0110. Eds. Gene Ellis, Hilary Maitland. R&P Lloyd Athearn TEL 303-384-0110 ext 13. Circ: 6,000.

799.1 USA ISSN 1055-6737
SH451
AMERICAN ANGLER. Text in English. 1978. bi-m. USD 19.95 combined subscription domestic (print & online eds); USD 29.95 combined subscription in Canada (print & online eds); USD 39.95 combined subscription elsewhere (print & online eds) (effective 2009). bk.rev. stat.; tr.lit. back issues avail. **Document type:** *Magazine, Consumer.*
Former titles (until 1991): American Angler and Fly Tyer; (until 1988): Fly Tyer (0164-730X)
Related titles: Online - full text ed.
Indexed: B21, PEI.
Published by: Morris Multimedia, Inc., PO Box 34, Boulder, CO 80329. TEL 706-724-0851, 800-458-4010, http://www.morris.com. Ed. Phil Monahan. Adv. contact Michael Floyd TEL 706-823-3739. Circ: 41,164 (paid).

799.2 USA ISSN 0002-807X
AMERICAN COONER. Text in English. 1970. m. USD 17. adv. illus.
Address: 16 E Franklin, Sesser, IL 62884. TEL 618-625-2711. Ed., Pub. George O Slankard. Circ: 17,000 (paid).

799.2 USA ISSN 0002-8452
SK1
AMERICAN FIELD. Text in English. 1874. w. USD 49; USD 3 newsstand/cover (effective 2005). adv. bk.rev. illus. **Document type:** *Newspaper, Consumer.* **Description:** Devoted to pointing dog field trials and upland game bird hunting, conservation and propagation.
Published by: American Field Publishing Co., 542 S Dearborn St, Chicago, IL 60605-1508. Pub. V.E. Brown. Adv. contact Jeffrey C. Olson. Circ: 8,000 (paid).

799.1 USA
AMERICAN FLY FISHER. Text in English. 1974. q. free. **Document type:** *Journal, Consumer.* **Description:** Contains features on the collection with articles written by some of the most respected fly-fishing historians in the world today, the journal also reprints rare, interesting and often amusing pieces of literature from a vast body of often-neglected fishing writers. It also keeps readers apprised of the museum's latest acquisitions and events.
Published by: The American Museum of Fly Fishing, 4104 Main St, Manchester, VT 05254 . TEL 802-362-3300, FAX 802-362-3308, amff@amff.com. Ed. Kate Achor.

799.3 USA ISSN 1060-0892
TS535
AMERICAN GUNSMITH; technical journal of firearms repair and maintenance. Text in English. 1986. m. USD 34 in US & Canada; USD 52 elsewhere (effective 2010). illus. reprints avail. **Document type:** *Journal, Consumer.* **Description:** Covers the tools and techniques of gunsmithing.
Related titles: Online - full text ed.
Indexed: A26, G05, G06, G07, G08, I05.
Published by: (American Gunsmithing Association), A G Media Inc. (Subsidiary of: Belvoir Media Group, LLC), PO Box 540638, Merritt Island, FL 32954. TEL 321-459-1558. Ed. Keith Lawrence. **Subscr. to:** Palm Coast Data, LLC, PO Box 420235, Palm Coast, FL 32142. TEL 800-829-5119, http://www.palmcoastdata.com.

799 USA
AMERICAN HANDGUNNER'S ANNUAL BOOK OF HANDGUNS. Text in English. 19??. a. adv. illus. **Document type:** *Magazine, Consumer.* **Description:** Contains detailed specifications, photos, catalog guides, prices and editorial descriptions and information on firearms that qualify as handguns.
Published by: Publishers Development Corp., F M G Publications, 12345 World Trade Dr, San Diego, CA 92128. TEL 858-605-0202, 800-826-2216, FAX 858-605-0247. Ed. Lisa Parsons Wraith. R&P Thomas Hollander TEL 619-297-8032. Adv. contact Steve Evatt TEL 858-605-0218. Circ: 90,000.

796.5 USA ISSN 0279-9472
GV199.4
AMERICAN HIKER. Text in English. 1977. q. free to members (effective 2010). adv. illus. back issues avail.; reprints avail. **Document type:** *Magazine, Trade.* **Description:** Features interesting articles covering hiking, trails, new products as well as camping.
Formerly (until 1993): American Hiker News (0164-5722)
Published by: American Hiking Society, 1422 Fenwick Ln, Silver Spring, MD 20910. TEL 301-565-6704, 800-972-8608, FAX 301-565-6714, info@americanhiking.org. Adv. contact Margie Cohen TEL 404-873-0403. page USD 1,600; 7.25 x 9.625.

799.2 USA ISSN 0092-1068
SK1
AMERICAN HUNTER. Text in English. 1973. m. USD 9.95 to members (effective 2009). adv. bk.rev. illus. reprints avail. **Document type:** *Magazine, Consumer.* **Description:** Covers hunting, technique, equipment, places to hunt, wildlife management and Second Amendment issues.
Related titles: Online - full text ed.
Indexed: A22, Consl, G09, P02, P10, P19, P48, P53, P54, PQC.
—Ingenta.
Published by: National Rifle Association of America, 11250 Waples Mill Rd, Fairfax, VA 22030. TEL 800-672-3888, membership@nrahq.org, http://www.nra.org. Eds. J Scott Olmstead TEL 703-267-1335, John Zent TEL 703-267-1332. adv.: B&W page USD 32,685, color page USD 49,040; trim 7.625 x 10.5.

796.42 USA ISSN 1091-482X
AMERICAN RUNNER; the magazine for the dedicated runner and racer. Text in English. 1995. s-m. USD 15.95; USD 2.95 newsstand/cover (effective 1998). adv. bk.rev. **Document type:** *Magazine, Consumer.* **Description:** For competitive middle and long distance runners. Features personality profiles, event reports and statistics, training advice, news and product reviews.
Related titles: Online - full text ed.
Published by: American Runner Magazine Inc., 233 Fourth St., Roy, NY 12180. TEL 518-274-1899, FAX 518-274-5959. Ed., Pub. James O'Brien. Adv. contact Lenore Melagrano. page USD 2,735; trim 10.88 x 8.13. Circ: 30,000.

799.21 USA
AMERICAN SHOOTING MAGAZINE. Text in English. 1996. m. **Description:** Provides informative and entertaining articles pertaining to the shooting sports and peripherals.
Media: Online - full text.
Published by: Silver Bullet Industries, Inc., 45303 Margate, Macomb, MI 45304. Ed. David A Pierce.

388.3 USA ISSN 1078-6414
AMERICAN SNOWMOBILER. Text in English. 1986. 6/yr. USD 14.95 domestic; USD 19.95 in Canada; USD 22.95 foreign (effective 2008). adv. back issues avail. **Document type:** *Magazine, Consumer.* **Description:** Features straight-talk reviews and honest tests, real world shoot-out results, performance tips, how-to ideas, travel destinations and news.
Related titles: Online - full text ed.
Indexed: A33, M01, M02, T02.
Published by: Kalmbach Publishing Co., 21027 Crossroads Circle, PO Box 1612, Waukesha, WI 53187. TEL 262-796-8776, 888-350-2413, FAX 262-796-1615, customerservice@kalmbach.com, http://www.kalmbach.com. Eds. Mark Boncher, Mark Savage. Pub. Scott Stollberg. Circ: 90,000 (paid).

796.42 USA ISSN 1098-6464
GV1060.6
AMERICAN TRACK & FIELD. Text in English. 1994. q. free to qualified personnel (effective 2010). adv. **Document type:** *Magazine, Consumer.* **Description:** Dedicated to the improvement of both the image and the performance of American athletes in the disciplines of track and field, cross country, and race walking.
Published by: Shooting Star Media, Inc., PO Box 67, Fort Atkinson, WI 53538. TEL 608-239-3785, FAX 920-563-7298, shootingstarmediabiz@gmail.com, http://www.shootingstarmediainc.com/. Pub. Larry Eder TEL 608-239-3785.

796.42 USA
AMERICAN TRACK & FIELD ATHLETE. Variant title: Athletes Only. Text in English. 1995. 5/yr. free to qualified personnel (effective 2010). adv. **Document type:** *Magazine, Consumer.* **Description:** Aimed at 14-19 year olds, or track & field, and cross country athletes involved in high school, college or club teams in North America. Focuses on helping the developing athlete learn about training, footwear, apparel, competition opportunities and the singular enjoyment of achieving personal goals.
Published by: Shooting Star Media, Inc., PO Box 67, Fort Atkinson, WI 53538. TEL 608-239-3785, FAX 920-563-7298, shootingstarmediabiz@gmail.com, http://www.shootingstarmediainc.com/. Pub. Larry Eder TEL 608-239-3785.

796 USA
AMERICAN TRAILS MAGAZINE. Text in English. 2006. 3/yr. USD 25 to individuals; USD 35 to libraries; USD 100 to institutions (effective 2008).
Published by: American Trails, PO Box 491797, Redding, CA 96049-1797. TEL 530-547-2060, FAX 530-547-2035, trailhead@americantrails.org, http://americantrails.org.

797.33 USA ISSN 1092-6909
GV811.63.W56
AMERICAN WINDSURFER. Text in English. 1993. m. USD 25 domestic; USD 40 in Canada; USD 55 elsewhere (effective 2005). adv. **Document type:** *Magazine, Consumer.*
Published by: Grapho, Inc., PO Box 1310, Hood River, OR 97031. TEL 541-386-3905, FAX 541-386-3606. Ed. John Chao.

796.7 USA
AMERICAN WOMAN ROAD & TRAVEL. Text in English. 1989. bi-m. USD 12. adv. **Document type:** *Magazine, Consumer.* **Description:** An automotive lifestyle magazine geared towards working and active women.
Former titles: American Woman Motorscene; American Woman Motorsports; American Woman Magazine; American Woman Road Riding; American Woman Road Rider
Indexed: CWI, GW.
Published by: American Woman Motorscene, 2424 Coolidge Rd, Ste 203, Troy, MI 48084. TEL 248-614-0017, FAX 248-614-8929, courtney@americanwomanmag.com, http://www.americanwomanmag.com. Ed. Courtney Caldwell. adv.: B&W page USD 1,750, color page USD 3,550; trim 10.5 x 7.88. Circ: 500,000.

799 AUT ISSN 0003-2824
ANBLICK; Zeitschrift fuer Jagd und Natur in den Alpen. Text in German. 1946. m. EUR 45.60 domestic; EUR 64.20 foreign; EUR 4.10 newsstand/cover (effective 2005). adv. bk.rev. illus. index. **Document type:** *Magazine, Consumer.* **Description:** Focuses on fishing and hunting.
Indexed: KWIWR, W08.
Published by: Steirische Landesjaegerschaft, Rottalgasse 24, Graz, St 8010, Austria. TEL 43-316-3212480, FAX 43-316-3212483. Ed., Pub. Hannes Kollar. Adv. contact Martin Ossmann. B&W page EUR 1,750; trim 170 x 252. Circ: 23,500 (paid and controlled).

799.1 DEU ISSN 0179-843X
ANGELWOCHE; deutsche Sportfischer-Zeitung. Text in German. 1984. fortn. EUR 59.80; EUR 2.30 newsstand/cover (effective 2011). adv. **Document type:** *Magazine, Consumer.*
Incorporates (1983-198?): Deutsche Sportfischer-Zeitung (0179-2210)
Published by: Jahr Top Special Verlag, Troplowitzstr 5, Hamburg, 22529, Germany. TEL 49-40-389060, FAX 49-40-38906300, info@jahr-tsv.de, http://www.jahr-tsv.de. Ed. Rolf Schwarzer. Adv. contact Christopher Zippert TEL 49-40-38906267. Circ: 66,052 (paid).

ANGLERS GUIDE TO IRELAND. *see* TRAVEL AND TOURISM

799.1 GBR ISSN 0003-3243
ANGLER'S MAIL. Text in English. 1964. w. GBP 69.84 domestic; EUR 132.78 in Europe eurozone; GBP 95.27 in Europe non-eurozone; USD 195.41 in United States; GBP 127.72 in Canada; GBP 124.69 rest of world (effective 2009). adv. bk.rev. illus. Supplement avail. **Document type:** *Magazine, Consumer.* **Description:** Britain's only all color angling weekly.
—CCC.
Published by: I P C Country & Leisure Media Ltd. (Subsidiary of: I P C Media Ltd.), The Blue Fin Bldg, 110 Southwark St, London, SE1 0SU, United Kingdom. TEL 44-20-31485000, http://www.ipcmedia.com. Ed. Tim Knight TEL 44-20-31484150. Pub. Hazel Eccles TEL 44-20-31484312. Adv. contact Lee Morris TEL 44-20-31482517. Circ: 32,639. **Dist. by:** MarketForce UK Ltd, The Blue Fin Bldg, 3rd Fl, 110 Southwark St, London SE1 0SU, United Kingdom. TEL 44-20-31483300, FAX 44-20-31488105, salesinnovation@marketforce.co.uk, http://www.marketforce.co.uk/.

799.1 USA ISSN 1045-3539
CODEN: VMIKDG
THE ANGLING REPORT. Text in English. 1988. m. looseleaf. USD 39 domestic; USD 50 in Canada & Mexico; USD 68 elsewhere. adv. back issues avail. **Document type:** *Newsletter.* **Description:** Serves the angler who travels.
Published by: Oxpecker Enterprises, Inc., 9300 S Dadeland Blvd, Ste 605, Miami, FL 33156-2721. TEL 305-670-1361, FAX 305-670-1376. Ed., Pub., R&P Don Causey. Adv. contact Milton Aquino. Circ: 3,800.

799.1 GBR ISSN 0003-3308
ANGLING TIMES. Text in English. 1953. w. GBP 59.99 domestic; GBP 86.70 foreign (effective 2009). adv. bk.rev. illus.; tr.lit. back issues avail. **Document type:** *Magazine, Consumer.* **Description:** Features the latest news in the world of coarse fishing.
Related titles: Supplement(s): UK Carp. ISSN 1751-5424.
—CCC.

Published by: H. Bauer Publishing Ltd. (Subsidiary of: Bauer Media Group), Academic House, 24-28 Oval Rd, London, NW1 7DT, United Kingdom. TEL 44-20-72418000, FAX 44-20-72418030, http://www.bauer.co.uk. Ed. Richard Lee TEL 44-1733-395106. Adv. contact Donna Harris TEL 44-1733-288054. **Subscr. to:** Tower House, Sovereign Park, Market Harborough, Leicestershire LE16 9EF, United Kingdom. TEL 44-1858-438866, subs@greatmagazines.co.uk.

799.1 GBR ISSN 1741-6051
ANGLING TIMES ADVANCED. Text in English. 1993. m. GBP 80 domestic; GBP 86 foreign (effective 2009). adv. back issues avail. **Document type:** *Magazine, Consumer.*
Former titles (until 2003): Match Angling Plus (1468-5868); (until 1998): Angling Plus (0969-9945)
Published by: Emap Media Ltd. (Subsidiary of: Emap Communications Ltd.), Bushfield House, Orton Ctr, Peterborough, PE2 5UW, United Kingdom. TEL 44-1733-237111, FAX 44-1733-465658, http://www.emap.com. Ed. Steve Cole TEL 870-062-3364. Adv. contact Donna Harris TEL 870-062-6067.

792.113 DEU
ANKER MAGAZIN. Text in German. bi-m. EUR 36 for 2 yrs. domestic; EUR 55 for 2 yrs. foreign; EUR 3 newsstand/cover (effective 2008). adv. **Document type:** *Magazine, Consumer.* **Description:** Contains items of interest to participants in all the various types of water sports.
Published by: Anker Wassersport Verlag Schuhmann, Frankenthalerstr 196, Ludwigshafen, 67059, Germany. TEL 49-621-591370, FAX 49-621-512315. adv.: B&W page EUR 1,800, color page EUR 2,400. Circ: 35,000 (paid and controlled).

799.1 FRA ISSN 1956-7545
L'ANNUAIRE DE LA PECHE DE LOISIR. Text in French. 2007. a., latest 2010. EUR 22 per issue (effective 2010). **Document type:** *Monographic series, Consumer.*
Published by: Vac Editions, 38 Rue Truffaut, Paris, 75017, France. TEL 33-1-42940101, FAX 33-1-42940155.

799.3 USA ISSN 0072-906X
TS532
ANNUAL GUNS & AMMO. Variant title: Guns & Ammo Annual. Text in English. 1969. a. USD 14.97 domestic; USD 27.97 in Canada; USD 29.97 elsewhere (effective 2007). adv. **Document type:** *Magazine, Consumer.* **Description:** Features articles on the application and history of various types of firearms. Reports on field tests and outdoor accessories.
Related titles: ◆ Supplement to: Guns & Ammo. ISSN 0017-5684.
Published by: Source Interlink Companies, 6420 Wilshire Blvd, 10th Fl, Los Angeles, CA 90048. TEL 323-782-2000, FAX 323-782-2585, dheine@sourceinterlink.com, http://www.sourceinterlinkmedia.com. Ed. Scott Rupp. Pub. Kevin Steele. Adv. contact David Fireman. B&W page USD 5,540, color page USD 10,915; trim 10.5 x 7.75. Circ: 575,000.

799 CAN ISSN 0840-9560
ANNUEL DE CHASSE. Text in English. 1987. a. CAD 5.49 (effective 2000). adv. back issues avail. **Document type:** *Journal, Consumer.* **Description:** Publishes articles on hunting, outdoor life and the environment.
Published by: Groupe Polygone Editeurs, Inc., 11450 Blvd Albert Hudon, Montreal, PQ H1G 3J9, Canada. TEL 514-327-4464, FAX 514-327-0602. Ed. Jeannot Ruel. Pub. Luc Lemay. Adv. contact Campbell Martin. Circ: 40,000.

799 CAN ISSN 1208-6878
ANNUEL DE PECHE. Text in English. 1988. a. CAD 5.49 (effective 2000). adv. back issues avail. **Document type:** *Journal, Consumer.* **Description:** Publishes articles on fishing, outdoor life and the environment.
Published by: Groupe Polygone Editeurs, Inc., 11450 Blvd Albert Hudon, Montreal, PQ H1G 3J9, Canada. TEL 514-327-4464, FAX 514-327-0602. Ed. Jeannot Ruel. Pub. Luc Lemay. Adv. contact Campbell Martin. Circ: 40,000.

799.1 745.1 USA ISSN 0744-3749
ANTIQUE ANGLER; a quarterly newsletter-history of fishing-collectible tackle, etc. Text in English. 1979. q. USD 7.50. adv. bk.rev. **Description:** Provides a forum for exchanging information among fishing tackle collectors of U.S. and abroad.
Published by: Antique Angler, Inc., 2295 State Highway 166., Cooperstown, NY 13326-4600. TEL 609-397-1577. Ed. Paul J Webber. Circ: 2,000.

796 USA
APEX. Text in English. 1999. q. USD 14; USD 3.95 newsstand/cover (effective 1999). illus. **Document type:** *Magazine, Consumer.* **Description:** Covers camping and other outdoor recreational activities.
Published by: Apex Publishing, LLC., PO Box 1721, Vail, CO 81658.

796.552 USA
APEX TO ZENITH. Text in English. q. **Document type:** *Newsletter, Consumer.*
Published by: Highpointers Club, PO Box 1496, Golden, CO 80402. webmaster@highpointers.org. Eds. Dave Covill, John Mitchler.

796.522 USA ISSN 0003-6587
G505
APPALACHIA JOURNAL. Text in English. 1876. s-a. USD 15 (effective 2008). adv. bk.rev. abstr.; bibl.; illus.; stat. Index. reprints avail. **Document type:** *Magazine, Consumer.* **Description:** Covers articles on mountaineering and conservation.
Indexed: GeoRef, MLA-IB, SpeleolAb.
—Ingenta.
Published by: Appalachian Mountain Club, 5 Joy St, Boston, MA 02108. TEL 617-523-0636, FAX 617-523-0722. Ed. Christine Woodside. Circ: 13,000 (paid).

796.93 ITA ISSN 0392-2375
L'APPENNINO. Text in Italian. 1873. m. free to members. adv. **Document type:** *Magazine, Consumer.*
Published by: Club Alpino Italiano, Sezione di Roma, Via Galvani 10, Rome, 00153, Italy. TEL 39-06-57287143, FAX 39-06-57287143, http://www.cairoma.it. Ed. Carlo Alberto Pinelli.

799.32 USA ISSN 1541-7506
ARCHERY FOCUS. Text in English. 1997 (Mar.). bi-m. USD 20 domestic (effective 2002). adv.
Published by: (National Archery Association of the United States), Satchmo Productions, 664A Freeman Ln., PMB 395, Grass Valley, CA 95949-9630. TEL 800-671-1140, FAX 530-477-8384. Ed. Steve Ruis. Pub. Claudia Stevenson. Adv. contact Ty Pelfrey.

799.2 ITA ISSN 1593-0386
ARCO. Text in Italian. 1989. bi-m. EUR 24 (effective 2009). adv. 66 p./no.; **Document type:** *Magazine, Consumer.*
Related titles: Online - full text ed.
Published by: Greentime SpA, Via Barberia 11, Bologna, BO 40123, Italy. TEL 39-051-584020, FAX 39-051-585000, info@greentime.it, http://www.greentime.it. Circ: 46,000 (paid).

799 USA ISSN 0888-840X
ARIZONA HUNTER AND ANGLER. Text in English. 1984. m. USD 19 (effective 2000). adv. **Document type:** *Magazine, Consumer.* **Description:** Features where-to-go and how-to-do-it articles on fishing and hunting in the state.
Published by: Allstar Bass Fishing Tournaments, PO Box 859, Mesa, AZ 85211-0859. TEL 480-894-2775. Ed. Harry Morgan. Pub., R&P, Adv. contact Tom Stiles. Circ: 38,810.

ARIZONA WILDLIFE VIEWS. *see* CONSERVATION

ARKANSAS OUTDOORS. *see* CONSERVATION

799.3 USA ISSN 0744-4184
ARKANSAS SPORTSMAN. Text in English. 198?. m. USD 14.97 domestic; USD 27.97 in Canada; USD 29.97 elsewhere (effective 2008). adv. illus. **Document type:** *Magazine, Consumer.* **Description:** Discusses the wheres, hows, and whens of hunting and fishing, as well as environmental and conservation issues in Arkansas.
Published by: Intermedia Outdoors, Inc., 512 7th Ave, 11th Fl, New York, NY 10018. TEL 212-852-6600, 800-260-6397, FAX 212-302-4472, customerservice@imoutdoors.com, http://www.imoutdoorsmedia.com. adv.: B&W page USD 13,830, color page USD 19,360; trim 7.875 x 10.75. Circ: 33,000.

ARKANSAS WILDLIFE. *see* CONSERVATION

799.2 FRA ISSN 1627-3184
ARMES DE CHASSE. Text in French. 2001. q. EUR 23 (effective 2009). adv. **Document type:** *Magazine, Consumer.*
Published by: Editions Lariviere, 6 Rue Olof Palme, Clichy, 92587, France. TEL 33-1-47565400, http://www.editions-lariviere.fr.

799.2 ITA ISSN 1970-0776
ARMI DA CACCIA. Text in Italian. 2006. s-m. **Document type:** *Magazine, Consumer.*
Published by: De Agostini Editore, Via G da Verrazzano 15, Novara, 28100, Italy. TEL 39-0321-4241, FAX 39-0321-424305, info@deagostini.it, http://www.deagostini.it.

799.2 ITA
▼ **ARMI E MUNIZIONI.** Text in Italian. 2009. m. adv. illus. 144 p./no.; back issues avail. **Document type:** *Magazine, Consumer.*
Formed by the merger of (1967-2009): Diana Armi (0012-2351); (1964-2009): Tacarmi (1594-1108)
Related titles: ◆ Supplement to: Diana. ISSN 0012-2343.
Published by: Gruppo Editoriale Olimpia SpA, Via E Fermi 24, Loc Osmannoro, Sesto Fiorentino, FI 50129, Italy. TEL 39-055-30321, FAX 39-055-3032280, http://www.edolimpia.it. **Dist. by:** Parrini & C, Piazza Colonna 361, Rome, RM 00187, Italy. TEL 39-06-695141.

799 ITA ISSN 1122-6560
ARMI E TIRO; rivista di armi tiro, caccia e turismo. Text in Italian. 1988. m. EUR 55 domestic; EUR 85 in the European Union; EUR 120 elsewhere (effective 2009). adv. bk.rev. charts; illus. index. **Document type:** *Magazine, Consumer.* **Description:** Covers weapon tests and archery used in hunting.
Related titles: Online - full text ed.
Published by: Edisport Editoriale SpA, Via Gradisca 11, Milan, MI 20151, Italy. TEL 39-02-38085, FAX 39-02-38010393, edisport@edisport.it, http://www.edisport.it. Circ: 70,000.

799.2 ITA ISSN 1125-551X
ARMI MAGAZINE. Text in Italian. 1995. m. adv. **Document type:** *Magazine, Consumer.* **Description:** Devoted primarily to firearms. Contains information on hunting rifles, pistols, gun shows, and relevant legal issues.
Published by: Caff Editrice, Via Sabatelli 1, Milan, 20154, Italy. TEL 39-02-34537504, FAX 39-02-34537513, segreteria@caffeditrice.it, http://www.caffeditrice.net.

799.1 USA ISSN 1536-9536
SH401
ART OF ANGLING JOURNAL. Text in English. 2001. q. USD 35 domestic; USD 55 foreign (effective 2002). adv.
Published by: The Complete Sportsman, P. O. Box 826, Westborough, MA 01581. TEL 508-898-2990, FAX 508-898-3379. Eds. Ingrid Sils, Paul Schmookler.

799.2 683.4 FIN ISSN 0781-2124
ASE & ERA/GUN AND GAME. Text in Finnish. 1984. 8/yr. EUR 49 (effective 2007). adv. bk.rev. back issues avail. **Document type:** *Magazine, Consumer.* **Description:** Oriented towards hunters, gun enthusiasts, collectors.
Published by: Karprint Oy, Vanha Turunrie 371, Huhmari, 03150, Finland. TEL 358-9-41397300, FAX 358-9-41397405, http://www.karprint.fi. Ed. Juha Ahola. Adv. contact Arja Blom. page EUR 1,605. Circ: 22,000.

797.23095 SGP ISSN 0218-3064
ASIAN DIVER. Text in English. 1992. 7/yr. SGD 50 domestic; SGD 60 ASEAN countries; SGD 75 rest of Asia; SGD 88 elsewhere (effective 2005). adv. **Document type:** *Magazine, Consumer.*
Published by: MediaCorp Publishing, Caldecott Broadcast Centre, Andrew Road, Singapore, 299939, Singapore. TEL 65-64837118, FAX 65-64812098, subhelp@mediacorppub.com.sg, http://corporate.mediacorpsingapore.com/index.htm. Ed. Carol Lim. Circ: 40,000 (paid).

796.5 296 USA
ASSOCIATION OF JEWISH SPONSORED CAMPS. CAMP DIRECTORY. Text in English. 1963. a. free. **Document type:** *Directory.*
Published by: Association of Jewish Sponsored Camps, 130 E 59th St, New York, NY 10022. TEL 212-751-0477. Ed. Rahel Goldberg. Circ: 2,000.

796.93 USA ISSN 0199-1574
ATLANTA SKIER. Text in English. 1967. 8/yr. USD 10 to non-members; USD 5 to members.
Published by: Atlanta Ski Club, Inc., 6255 Barfield Rd, Ste 206, Atlanta, GA 30328-4236. TEL 404-303-1460, FAX 404-303-8159, admin@atlantaskiclub.org, http://www.atlantaskiclub.com. Ed. Joe Hatchell.

ATLANTIC INFLIGHT. *see* AERONAUTICS AND SPACE FLIGHT

ATLANTIC SALMON JOURNAL. *see* FISH AND FISHERIES

796.42 ESP
ATLETISMO ESPANOL. Text in Spanish. 1951. m. EUR 42 domestic; EUR 81 foreign (effective 2010). adv. bk.rev. bibl. back issues avail. **Document type:** *Consumer.* **Description:** Provides results of track and field events, calendar of events, interviews with athletes, and training techniques.
Published by: Real Federacion Espanola de Atletismo, Avda Valladolid, 81, Esq. Dcha. 1o., Madrid, 28008, Spain. TEL 34-91-5411927, publicaciones@rfea.es. Ed., R&P Juan Carlos Garcia de Polavieja. Adv. contacts Elena Cabezas, Juan Carlos Garcia de Polavieja. Circ: 15,000.

796 AUS
AUSSIE BACKPACKER ACCOMMODATION GUIDE. Text in English. 1990. includes with subscr. to Aussie Backpacker. **Document type:** *Handbook/Manual/Guide, Consumer.* **Description:** Contains a listing of best budget accommodation throughout Australia.
Related titles: ◆ Special ed. of: Aussie Backpacker.
Published by: North Australian Publishing Co. Pty. Ltd., PO Box 1264, Townsville, QLD 4810, Australia. TEL 61-7-47723244, FAX 61-7-47723250, info@aussiebackpacker.com.au. Ed. Marie Erker. Pub. Warren Gardner.

799.2 AUS ISSN 1835-6923
AUSTRALASIAN SPORTING SHOOTER. Text in English. 1961. 13/yr. AUD 83.60 domestic; AUD 96 in New Zealand; AUD 110 in Asia; AUD 152 elsewhere; AUD 6.50 newsstand/cover (effective 2008). adv. bk.rev. illus. **Document type:** *Magazine, Consumer.* **Description:** Designed for enthusiasts who love the outdoors and the thrill of hunting.
Former titles (until 2007): Sporting Shooter (1325-9075); (until 1995): Australasian Sporting Shooter (0810-5928); (until 1982): Sporting Shooter (0038-8076)
Related titles: Supplement(s): Sporting Shooter Hunting Special.
Indexed: SD, SportS.
Published by: (Sporting Shooters Association of Australia), Yaffa Publishing Group Pty Ltd., 17-21 Bellevue St, Surry Hills, NSW 2010, Australia. TEL 61-2-92812333, FAX 61-2-92812750, info@yaffa.com.au. Ed. Marcus O'Dean TEL 61-2-92138258. Adv. contact Michelle Carneiro TEL 61-2-92138219. B&W page AUD 2,580, color page AUD 3,280; trim 210 x 275. Circ: 14,397. **Subscr. to:** GPO Box 606, Sydney, NSW 2001, Australia.

799.2 AUS ISSN 1837-6487
▼ **AUSTRALIA NEW ZEALAND BOWHUNTER MAGAZINE.** Text in English. 2010. bi-m. AUD 55 domestic; AUD 70 in New Zealand; AUD 110 elsewhere (effective 2011). adv. back issues avail. **Document type:** *Magazine, Trade.* **Description:** Presents a broad coverage of the use of the bow and arrow and all disciplines of archery and bowhunting in Australia and New Zealand.
Published by: Cooee X Press Pty Ltd, 6 Tram Rd, Gundiah, QLD 4650, Australia. TEL 61-7-41293218, FAX 61-7-41293218.

799.1 AUS
AUSTRALIAN ADVENTURE ANGLER. Cover title: Fishing Tips & Techniques. Text in English. 2006. bi-m. AUD 33.39; AUD 7.95 newsstand/cover (effective 2008). back issues avail. **Document type:** *Magazine, Consumer.* **Description:** Provides fishing tips, features on fishing destinations around Australia, tips on forwarding techniques, and guides on caravan and camping adventures.
Published by: Express Publications Pty. Ltd., 2-4 Stanley St, Locked Bag 111, Silverwater, NSW 2168, Australia. TEL 61-2-97413800, 800-801-647, FAX 61-2-97378017, subs@magstore.com.au, http://www.expresspublications.com.au. **Subscr. to:** iSubscribe Pty Ltd., 25 Lime St, Ste 303, Level 3, Sydney, NSW 2000, Australia. TEL 61-2-92621722, FAX 61-2-92625044, info@isubscribe.com.au, http://www.isubscribe.com.au.

796.93 AUS
AUSTRALIAN AND NEW ZEALAND SKIING. Text in English. 1969. a. AUD 50. adv. bk.rev. **Document type:** *Magazine, Consumer.* **Description:** Explores the world of Australian skiing.
Former titles (until 1997): Australian Skiing (0818-9307); (until 1986): Fall-Line Ski Magazine (0818-9315)
Indexed: SD.
Published by: (N.S.W. Ski Association), A C P Magazines Ltd. (Subsidiary of: P B L Media Pty Ltd.), 54-58 Park St, Sydney, NSW 2000, Australia. TEL 61-2-92828000, FAX 61-2-91263769, research@acpaction.com.au, http://www.acp.com.au. Adv. contact Marcus Hucker TEL 61-2-81149485. page AUD 2,835; bleed 242 x 310. Circ: 16,000.

AUSTRALIAN JOURNAL OF OUTDOOR EDUCATION. *see* EDUCATION

796.9 AUS ISSN 1442-6757
AUSTRALIAN LONGBOARDING MAGAZINE. Abbreviated title: A L B. Text in English. 199?. bi-m. AUD 53.95 domestic; AUD 78.50 in New Zealand; AUD 89.35 in Asia & the Pacific; AUD 134.40 elsewhere (effective 2008). adv. back issues avail. **Document type:** *Magazine, Consumer.*
Published by: Morrison Media Services Ltd., PO Box 823, Burleigh Heads, QLD 4220, Australia. TEL 61-7-55761388, FAX 61-7-55761527, subs@morrisonmedia.com.au, http://www.morrisonmedia.com.au. Ed. Bruce Channon TEL 61-2-99972657. Pub. Peter Morrison. Adv. contact Terry Williams TEL 61-7-55209126. page AUD 2,121; trim 210 x 297.

796 AUS ISSN 0818-6510
AUSTRALIAN ORIENTEER. Text in English. 1979. q. AUD 40 domestic; AUD 44 in Asia & the Pacific; AUD 49 elsewhere (effective 2008). adv. bk.rev. back issues avail. **Document type:** *Newsletter.* **Description:** Covers the sport of orienteering in Australia.
Indexed: SD.
—BLDSC (1817.030000).

S

Published by: Orienteering Federation of Australia Inc., PO Box 284, Mitchell, ACT 2911, Australia. TEL 61-2-61621200, orienteering@netspeed.com.au. Ed. Mike Hubbert. adv.: B&W page AUD 770, color page AUD 990; bleed 216 x 303. Circ: 1,400.

797.32 AUS ISSN 1837-2066
▼ **AUSTRALIAN PADDLE SURFER.** Text in English. 2010. q. AUD 9.99 per issue (effective 2010). back issues avail. **Document type:** *Magazine, Consumer.*
Published by: Australian Paddle Surfer Magazine, PO Box 1015, Mona Vale, NSW 1660, Australia. TEL 44-2-99402255.

799.2 AUS ISSN 1442-7354
AUSTRALIAN SHOOTER. Text in English. 1999. m. free to members (effective 2009). adv. back issues avail. **Document type:** *Magazine, Consumer.*
Supersedes in part (in 1999): Australian Shooters Journal (0005-0245)
Related titles: ◆ Supplement(s): A S J (Kent Town). ISSN 1443-5713.
Indexed: SD.
Published by: Sporting Shooters Association of Australia, PO Box 906, St. Marys, NSW 1790, Australia. TEL 61-2-9623-4900, FAX 61-2-9623-5900, as@ssaa.org.au. Adv. contact Karoline Minicozzi. B&W page AUD 4,125, color page AUD 5,275; 205 x 270. Circ: 100,714.

796.93 AUS ISSN 1321-5914
AUSTRALIAN SNOWBOARDER MAGAZINE. Key Title: Snowboarder. Text in English. 1994. m. AUD 22.80 domestic; AUD 37.65 in New Zealand; AUD 43.15 in Asia & the Pacific; AUD 63.50 elsewhere (effective 2008). adv. illus. Supplement avail. **Document type:** *Magazine, Consumer.*
Published by: Morrison Media Services Ltd., PO Box 823, Burleigh Heads, QLD 4220, Australia. TEL 61-7-55761388, FAX 61-7-55761527, subs@morrisonmedia.com.au, http://www.morrisonmedia.com.au. Ed. Ryan Willmott TEL 61-4-21524296. Pub. Peter Morrison. Adv. contact Ben Salkeld TEL 61-4-02432165. color page AUD 2,963; trim 240 x 297.

796.172 AUS ISSN 1832-2956
AUSTRALIAN SURFRIDER. Text in English. 2002. bi-m. **Document type:** *Newsletter, Consumer.*
Published by: Surfrider Foundation Ltd., PO Box 271, Coolangatta, QLD 4225, Australia. TEL 61-7-56071217, FAX 61-7-55342866, info@surfrider.org.au, http://www.surfrider.org.au.

796 AUS ISSN 1832-3944
AUSTRALIAN TARGET RIFLE. Text in English. 1996. bi-m. AUD 39 domestic to non-members; AUD 45 in New Zealand to non-members; AUD 60 elsewhere to non-members; free to members (effective 2009). **Document type:** *Magazine, Consumer.*
Indexed: SD.
Published by: National Rifle Association of Australia, PO Box 414, Carina, QLD 4152, Australia. TEL 617-33981228, FAX 617-33983515, nraa@bigpond.com.

799.1 AUS ISSN 1838-4358
▼ **AUSTRALIAN TRAVELLING ANGLER.** Abbreviated title: A T A. Text in English. 2010. bi-m. AUD 49.90; AUD 9.95 newsstand/cover (effective 2011). adv. **Document type:** *Magazine, Consumer.* **Description:** Designed for people with a passion and love of fishing. Covers the adventure and excitement of travelling and fishing in Australia.
Published by: On the Road Publishing, PO Box 90, Dingley, VIC 3172, Australia. TEL 61-3-97690999. Adv. contact Travis Wyeth TEL 61-4-00120789.

796.172 AUS ISSN 1036-3491
AUSTRALIA'S SURFING LIFE. Abbreviated title: A S L. Text in English. 1985. m. (plus a. cumulation). AUD 89.95 domestic; AUD 110 in New Zealand; AUD 130 elsewhere (effective 2008). adv. music rev.; video rev. illus. **Document type:** *Magazine, Consumer.*
Related titles: Online - full text ed.; Optical Disk - DVD ed.
Published by: Morrison Media Services Ltd., PO Box 823, Burleigh Heads, QLD 4220, Australia. TEL 61-7-55761388, FAX 61-7-55761527, subs@morrisonmedia.com.au, http://www.morrisonmedia.com.au. Ed. Tim Fisher. Pub. Peter Morrison. Adv. contact Terry Williams TEL 61-7-55209126. color page AUD 3,444; trim 210 x 297.

796.54 CHE ISSN 1662-8020
AUTOCARAVANE. Text in French. 2007. 5/yr. CHF 64 for 2 yrs.; CHF 8 newsstand/cover (effective 2011). adv. **Document type:** *Magazine, Consumer.*
Published by: Etzel-Verlag AG, Knonauerstr 56, Cham, 6330, Switzerland. TEL 41-41-7855085, FAX 41-41-7855088, info@etzel-verlag.ch, http://www.etzel-verlag.ch. Ed. Christoph Hostettler. Pub. Thomas Staehli.

799.1 USA
B A S S FISHING TECHNIQUES. Text in English. 1995. a. illus. **Document type:** *Magazine, Consumer.* **Description:** Provides a facts you need about bass fishing.
Published by: (Bass Anglers Sportsman Society), B.A.S.S., Inc. (Subsidiary of: E S P N, Inc.), PO Box 17900, Montgomery, AL 36141-0900. TEL 334-272-9530, FAX 334-279-7148, customerservice@bassmaster.com. Circ: 125,000.

799.1 USA ISSN 0274-7936
B A S S TIMES. Text in English. 1970. m. USD 12 domestic to members; USD 17 in Canada to members; USD 20.50 elsewhere to members; USD 1 per issue (effective 2009). adv. illus. back issues avail. **Document type:** *Magazine, Consumer.* **Description:** Features articles on techniques, new products, and tournaments for the serious expert and beginner bass angler.
Published by: (Bass Anglers Sportsman Society), E S P N Publishing, Inc., PO Box 17900, Montgomery, AL 36141. TEL 334-272-9530, FAX 334-279-7148, editorial@bassmaster.com.

799.1 CAN
B C FISHING DIRECTORY & ATLAS; B C lakes & streams. (British Columbia) (Freshwater and Saltwater editions avail.) Text in English. 1984. a. CAD 10.95. adv.
Former titles: Okay Angler's B C Fishing Directory and Atlas (0839-7791); (until 1987): Okay Anglers Fishing Directory and Atlas (0827-570X)
Published by: A. Belhumeur Ent. Ltd., 1640 Western Dr, Port Coquitlam, BC V3C 2X3, Canada. TEL 604-942-5671, FAX 604-942-7395. Ed. A Belhumeur. Circ: 20,000.

799.2 CAN ISSN 1496-7642
B C OUTDOORS HUNTING AND SHOOTING. Text in English. 1967. s-a. free with subsc. to B C Outdoors Sport Fishing. **Document type:** *Magazine, Consumer.*
Supersedes in part (in 2001): B C Outdoors (0045-3013)
Related titles: ◆ Supplement to: B C Outdoors Sport Fishing and Outdoor Adventure. ISSN 1496-7634.
Indexed: C03, CBCARef, H20, P48, PQC.
—CCC.
Published by: O P Publishing Ltd., 1080 Howe St, Ste 900, Vancouver, BC V6Z 2T1, Canada. TEL 604-606-4644, FAX 604-687-1925, http://www.oppub.com.

796.5 CAN ISSN 1496-7634
SH572.B8
B C OUTDOORS SPORT FISHING AND OUTDOOR ADVENTURE. Text in English. 1967. bi-m. CAD 25 (effective 2004). **Document type:** *Magazine, Consumer.*
Supersedes in part (in 2001): B C Outdoors (0045-3013)
Related titles: ◆ Supplement(s): B C Outdoors Hunting and Shooting. ISSN 1496-7642.
Indexed: C03, CBCARef, CPerI, G08, H20, P48, P52, P56, PQC.
Published by: O P Publishing Ltd., 1080 Howe St, Ste 900, Vancouver, BC V6Z 2T1, Canada. TEL 604-606-4644, FAX 604-687-1925, http://www.oppub.com.

796.522 GBR ISSN 2046-5629
B M C SUMMIT. Text in English. 19??. q. back issues avail. **Document type:** *Magazine, Trade.*
Published by: (British Mountaineering Council), Warners Group Publications Plc., The Maltings, Manor Ln, Bourne, Lincs PE10 9PH, United Kingdom. TEL 44-1778-391010, http://www.warnersgroup.co.uk. Adv. contact Emma Howl TEL 44-1778-392443.

796 USA ISSN 1083-5350
BACKCOUNTRY. Text in English. 1994. q. USD 11.50 (effective 2001); USD 3.95 newsstand/cover. adv. bk.rev. illus. **Document type:** *Magazine, Consumer.* **Description:** Contains features on remote skiing areas for those who like to stay off the beaten track.
Incorporates (in 2007): Couloir (1080-4455)
Address: 7065 Dover Way, Arvada, CO 80004. TEL 303-424-5858, FAX 303-424-4063. Ed., Pub., R&P, Adv. contact David Harrower. Circ: 16,000 (paid).

796.5 USA ISSN 0277-867X
GV199.6
BACKPACKER; the outdoor at your doorsteps. Text in English. 1973. 9/yr. USD 15.95 domestic; USD 23.95 in Canada; USD 36.95 elsewhere; USD 4.99 per issue in US & Canada (effective 2009). adv. bk.rev. illus. back issues avail.; reprints avail. **Document type:** *Magazine, Consumer.* **Description:** Includes articles on the latest equipment, destinations and how to get the most out of a trip.
Incorporates (1977 -198?): Backpacker Footnotes (0271-6534); (19??-1979): Wilderness Camping (0043-5430)
Related titles: Microform ed.: (from PQC); Online - full text ed.
Indexed: A11, A22, A25, A26, AcaI, B04, BRD, C05, C12, CPerI, ConsI, E08, G05, G06, G07, G08, G09, H20, I05, I06, I07, M01, M02, M06, MASUSE, MagInd, P02, P10, P19, P48, P53, P54, PEI, PMR, PQC, R03, RGAb, RGPR, S08, S09, S23, SD, SportS, T02, TOM, U01, W03, W05, WBA, WMB.
—Ingenta.
Published by: Active Interest Media, 2520 55th St, Ste 210, Boulder, CO 80301. FAX 303-413-1602, http://www.aimmedia.com/. Eds. Anthony Cerretani, Jonathan Dorn. Pub. Kent Ebersole TEL 303-625-1605. adv.: B&W page USD 32,975, color page USD 45,480; bleed 8.125 x 10.75. Circ: 500,000 (paid).

796.552 USA ISSN 1550-4417
BACKPACKING LIGHT; pack less, be more. Abbreviated title: B P L. Text in English. 2004. q. USD 24.99 to non-members; USD 19.99 to members; USD 9.95 per issue to non-members; USD 9.45 per issue to members (effective 2010). adv. **Document type:** *Magazine, Bibliography.* **Description:** Features articles essential for lightweight backpacking enthusiasts.
Related titles: Online - full text ed.: Backpacking.com. ISSN 1537-0364. 2001. USD 5.99 per issue (effective 2010).
Published by: Beartooth Mountain Press, 1627 W Main St, Ste 310, Bozeman, MT 59715. FAX 406-522-0948, sales@beartoothmountainpress.com, http://www.beartoothmountainpress.com. Pub. Ryan Jordan.

769.552 USA
BACKPACKING NEWSLETTER. Text in English. 1976. m. looseleaf. USD 20. bk.rev. **Document type:** *Newsletter.*
Published by: Frank Ashley, Ed. & Pub., PO Box 79, Spickard, MO 64679-0079. TEL 816-485-6648.

799.2 AUS ISSN 1441-4368
BACON BUSTERS; pig hunting guide. Text in English. 1995. q. AUD 29.70 domestic; AUD 37 in New Zealand; AUD 42 in Asia; AUD 55 elsewhere; AUD 7.50 newsstand/cover (effective 2008). adv. **Document type:** *Magazine, Consumer.* **Description:** Includes readers' short stories, how-to articles, pig hunting features, technical advice, pig dog profiles and Australia's biggest collection of pig hunting photos.
Published by: Yaffa Publishing Group Pty Ltd., 17-21 Bellevue St, Surry Hills, NSW 2010, Australia. TEL 61-2-92812333, FAX 61-2-92812750, info@yaffa.com.au. Ed. Clint Magro TEL 61-2-92138287. Adv. contact Michelle Carneiro TEL 61-2-92138219. page AUD 3,120; trim 210 x 297. Circ: 19,000. **Subscr. to:** GPO Box 606, Sydney, NSW 2001, Australia.

799 USA ISSN 0005-3775
BADGER SPORTSMAN. Text in English. 1943. m. USD 12 (effective 1998). adv. **Document type:** *Magazine, Trade.* **Description:** Covers the outdoors in Wisconsin.
Published by: Vercauteren Publishing Inc., 19 E Main St, Chilton, WI 53014. TEL 920-849-7036, FAX 920-849-4651. Ed. Gary Vercauteren. Pub., R&P Kay Schaefer. Adv. contact Robert Trude. Circ: 26,800.

BAILY'S HUNTING DIRECTORY. *see* BUSINESS AND ECONOMICS—Trade And Industrial Directories

799.1 USA
BAIT FISHERMAN. Text in English. 1995. bi-m. USD 15, USD 21 domestic (effective 2001). adv. **Document type:** *Magazine, Consumer.* **Description:** Covers natural bait fishing, including techniques of bait use, offbeat and uncommon baits; everything from minnows and earthworm to scents and chum. Also covers game fish, including panfish, catfish, carp, bowfin, and other fresh and saltwater species.
Published by: Beaver Pond Publishing, Box 224, Greenville, PA 16125. TEL 724-588-3492, FAX 724-588-2486, beaverpond@pathway.net, http://www.beaverpondpublishing.com. Ed. Rich Faler. adv.: B&W page USD 300, color page USD 500; 7.25 x 9.75. Circ: 5,000 (paid).

796 FRA ISSN 2106-9697
BALADES. Text in French. 1995. bi-m. **Document type:** *Magazine, Consumer.*
Formerly (until 2007): Balades en France (1270-8941)
Published by: Promo-Presse SARL, 1 Rue Bourbon le Chateau, Paris, 75006, France. TEL 33-8-11094004.

BALADES NATURE. *see* TRAVEL AND TOURISM

796.22 USA
BALANCE (PHILADELPHIA); an online skateboarding presentation. Text in English. irreg. **Document type:** *Magazine, Consumer.* **Description:** Presents skateboarding images and articles.
Media: Online - full text.
Published by: Balance, 4251 Ridge Ave, Philadelphia, PA 19129. TEL 267-679-6813, david@rizzio.net. Ed. Joseph M Peleckis.

796 FRA ISSN 2108-4432
BALISES 31. Text in French. 2000. q. **Document type:** *Magazine, Consumer.*
Related titles: Online - full text ed.: ISSN 2107-7061. 2010.
Published by: Le Comite Departemental Randonnee Pedestre de la Haute-Garonne, 5 Port St Sauveur, Midi-Pyrenees - Haute Garonne, Toulouse, 31000, France. cdrp31@free.fr, http://cdrp31.free.fr/rando.

797.51 DEU
BALLONSPORT MAGAZIN. Text in German. 1984. bi-m. EUR 40 domestic; EUR 60 foreign (effective 2009). adv. **Document type:** *Magazine, Consumer.*
Published by: (Deutscher Freiballonsport-Verband e.V.), Verlag Hephaistos, Gnadenberger Weg 4, Immenstadt, 87509, Germany. TEL 49-8379-728016, FAX 49-8379-728018. Ed. Marita Krafczyk. Pub. Peter Elgass. Adv. contact Sven Christian Elgass. B&W page EUR 735, color page EUR 1,500; trim 170 x 262. Circ: 3,396 (paid and controlled).

799.1 USA ISSN 2156-4604
BASS ANGLER MAGAZINE. Abbreviated title: B A G. Text in English. 2002. q. USD 24; USD 7.95 per issue (effective 2010). adv. back issues avail. **Document type:** *Magazine, Consumer.* **Description:** Helps anglers at every level become better at their craft.
Formerly (until 2010): Bass Angler's Guide (2152-1778)
Address: PO Box 2805, San Ramon, CA 94583. TEL 925-362-3190, FAX 925-362-3039. Ed., Pub., Adv. contact Mark Lassagne TEL 925-362-3190. page USD 799.

799.1 USA
BASS CLUB DIGEST. Abbreviated title: B C D. Text in English. 1992. 3/yr. (Jan. & Mar.). free to members (effective 2009). adv. **Document type:** *Magazine, Consumer.* **Description:** Designed for the management and advancement of organized bass fishing.
Published by: EBSCO Publishing (Subsidiary of: EBSCO Industries, Inc.), 10 Estes St, PO Box 682, Ipswich, MA 01938. TEL 978-356-6500, 800-653-2726, FAX 978-356-6565, information@ebscohost.com, http://www.ebscohost.com. Ed. John Gallaspy. Pub. Brian Thurston. adv.: B&W page USD 5,055, color page USD 6,595; trim 8 x 10.875.

796.5 USA ISSN 1538-7984
BASS GUIDE. Text in English. 1996. a. USD 5 newsstand/cover (effective 2007). adv. back issues avail. **Document type:** *Magazine, Consumer.* **Description:** Provides a comprehensive guide to the applications and techniques necessary to help anglers catch more fish.
Published by: Source Interlink Companies, 6420 Wilshire Blvd, 10th Fl, Los Angeles, CA 90048. TEL 323-782-2000, FAX 323-782-2585, dheine@sourceinterlink.com, http://www.sourceinterlinkmedia.com. adv.: B&W page USD 3,500, color page USD 4,725; trim 10.5 x 7.88. Circ: 100,000 (paid and controlled).

799.1 ZAF ISSN 1815-6746
BASSAFRICA; official magazine of S A B A A. Text in English. 2005. bi-m. ZAR 145 (effective 2006). adv. **Document type:** *Magazine, Consumer.*
Published by: (South African Bass Angling Association), Associated Media International, PO Box 519, Cramerview, 2060, South Africa. TEL 27-11-4677007, FAX 27-11-4677003, info@amint.co.za, http://www.technikons.co.za. adv.: page ZAR 9,000.

BASSIN'. *see* FISH AND FISHERIES

799.1 796.95 USA
BASSMASTER CLASSIC REPORT. Text in English. 1981. a. (July). USD 2.95. illus.; stat. **Document type:** *Magazine, Consumer.* **Description:** Press guide and program of the Bass Masters Classic, the world championship of bass fishing. Profiles professional bass anglers and their techniques.
Published by: (Bass Anglers Sportsman Society), B.A.S.S., Inc. (Subsidiary of: E S P N, Inc.), PO Box 17900, Montgomery, AL 36141-0900. TEL 334-272-9530, FAX 334-279-7148. Ed. Dave Precht. adv.: B&W page USD 4,185, color page USD 6,110; trim 10.5 x 7.88. Circ: 100,000 (paid).

779.1 USA ISSN 0199-3291
SH681
BASSMASTER MAGAZINE. Text in English. 1968. 11/yr. USD 25 domestic; USD 40 in Canada; USD 50 elsewhere (effective 2008). adv. bk.rev. charts; illus. **Document type:** *Magazine, Consumer.* **Description:** Presents how-to, where-to and when-to information for bass anglers.
Published by: (Bass Anglers Sportsman Society), E S P N Publishing, Inc., PO Box 10000, Lake Buena Vista, FL 32830. TEL 407-566-BASS, FAX 407-566-2072. Adv. contact Don McPherson. B&W page USD 22,235, color page USD 32,540. Circ: 600,000 (paid).

799.1 USA
THE BASSMASTER TOUR. Text in English. 1994. a. (July). illus.; mkt.; tr.lit. reprints avail. **Document type:** *Magazine, Consumer.*
Description: Provides in-depth information on each stop on the bassmaster trail and each angler fishing along it.
Published by: (Bass Anglers Sportsman Society), B.A.S.S., Inc. (Subsidiary of: E S P N, Inc.), PO Box 17900, Montgomery, AL 36141-0900. TEL 334-272-9530, FAX 334-279-7148, customerservice@bassmaster.com.

799.1 910.2 USA
BASSMASTER'S TOP BASS DESTINATIONS; the travel guide for bass fishermen. Text in English. 1996. a. (Apr.). USD 2.95 newsstand/ cover. illus.; tr.lit. **Document type:** *Magazine, Consumer.*
Description: Describes travel destinations of interest to bass anglers. Comments on family vacation destinations, where to find trophy bass, and exotic fishing locales.
Published by: (Bass Anglers Sportsman Society), B.A.S.S., Inc. (Subsidiary of: E S P N, Inc.), PO Box 17900, Montgomery, AL 36141-0900. TEL 334-272-9530, FAX 334-279-7148. adv.: B&W page USD 3,755, color page USD 5,490; trim 10.5 x 7.88. Circ: 125,000.

796 JPN
BE-PAL. Text in Japanese. 1981. m. JPY 390 newsstand/cover (effective 2002). adv. **Document type:** *Magazine, Consumer.* **Description:** Provides information on the latest outdoor products, the environment and year-round camping.
Published by: Shogakukan Inc., 3-1 Hitotsubashi 2-chome, Chiyoda-ku, Tokyo, 101-8001, Japan. TEL 81-3-3230-5211, FAX 81-3-3264-8471, http://www.shogakukan.co.jp.

796.5 DEU ISSN 0179-1419
BERG (YEAR); Alpenvereins-Jahrbuch. Text in German. 1970. a. EUR 22.90 (effective 2009). index. **Document type:** *Magazine, Consumer.*
Formerly (until 1984): Alpenvereins-Jahrbuch (0065-6534); Which was formed by the merger of (1951-1970): Deutscher Alpenverein. Jahrbuch (0179-1400); (1953-1970): Oesterreichischer Alpenverein. Jahrbuch (0257-9340)
Indexed: GeoRef, SpeleolAb.
Published by: Deutscher Alpenverein, Von-Kahr-Str 2-4, Munich, 80997, Germany. TEL 49-89-140030, FAX 49-89-1400323, info@alpenverein.de, http://www.alpenverein.de. **Co-sponsor:** Oesterreichischer Alpenverein.

796.522 LIE ISSN 0572-6220
DQ821
BERGHEIMAT. Text in German. 19??. a. CHF 15 (effective 2007). **Document type:** *Journal, Academic/Scholarly.*
Published by: Liechtensteiner Alpenverein, In der Stein-Egerta 26, Schaan, 9494, Liechtenstein. TEL 423-2329812, FAX 423-2329813, liechtensteiner@alpenverein.li, http://www.alpenverein.li.

796 DEU ISSN 1435-8905
G505
BERGSTEIGER; Das Tourenmagazin. Text in German. 1923. m. EUR 73; EUR 5.30 newsstand/cover (effective 2009). adv. bk.rev. **Document type:** *Magazine, Consumer.* **Description:** Covers mountaineering and skiing.
Former titles (until 1997): Bergsteiger und Bergwanderer (1431-097X); (until 1983): Bergsteiger (0005-8963)
Published by: Bruckmann Verlag GmbH, Infanteriestr 11a, Munich, 80797, Germany. TEL 49-89-13069911, FAX 49-89-13069910, info@bruckmann-verlag.de, http://www.bruckmann-verlag.de. Ed. Andreas Kubin. Adv. contact Judith Fischl. color page EUR 3,650; trim 210 x 280. Circ: 23,045 (paid).

796 910.91 USA ISSN 1553-2232
GV199.42.U82
BEST EASY DAY HIKES CANYONLANDS AND ARCHES. Text in English. 1997. biennial, latest 2005, 2nd ed. USD 7.95 per issue (effective 2008). 80 p./no.; **Document type:** *Guide, Consumer.*
Description: Provides information about past tranquil waterfalls, up mountains offering spectacular vistas and through groves of giant sequoias, the largest living organisms on the planet.
Published by: The Globe Pequot Press, Inc., 246 Goose Ln, PO Box 480, Guilford, CT 06437. TEL 203-458-4500, 888-249-7586, FAX 203-458-4603, 800-820-2329, info@globepequot.com, http://www.globepequot.com.

799.1 JPN
BEST FISHING. Text in Japanese. 1977. m. JPY 3,970.
Published by: Nihon Journal Press, 11-8 Higashi-Shinbashi 2-chome, Minato-ku, Tokyo, 105-0021, Japan. Ed. Ichitaro Midorigawa.

796.93 USA
BEST OF CROSS COUNTRY SKIING AND SNOWSHOEING. Text in English. 1990. a. USD 3. **Document type:** *Directory.* **Description:** Lists over 200 cross country ski areas in the US and selected areas in Canada. Includes information on groomed kilometers, ski services, lodging, and ski areas amenities and programs.
Formerly: Best of Cross Country Skiing
Related titles: Online - full text ed.
Published by: Cross Country Ski Areas Association, 259 Bolton Rd, Winchester, NH 03470. TEL 603-239-4341, 877-779-2754, FAX 603-239-6387, ccsaa@xcski.org, http://www.xcski.org. Ed. Chris Frado. Circ: 10,000.

BICYCLING. *see* SPORTS AND GAMES—Bicycles And Motorcycles

051 USA ISSN 1073-1504
BIG BROTHER; skate boarding magazine. Text in English. 1999 (no.46). m. USD 19.95; USD 3.99 newsstand/cover (effective 2004). adv. **Document type:** *Magazine, Consumer.*
Published by: L F P, Inc., 8484 Wilshire Blvd., Ste. 900, Beverly Hills, CA 90211. TEL 323-651-5400, 888-357-6313, FAX 323-651-0651. Ed. Sean Cliver. Pub. Larry Flynt. Adv. contact David Lutzke. **Subscr. to:** PO Box 15187, Beverly Hills, CA 90209-1187.

799.1 DNK ISSN 1904-2116
▼ **BIGGAME MAGAZINE.** Text in Danish. 2010. q. DKK 276; DKK 69 per issue (effective 2010). adv. **Document type:** *Magazine, Consumer.*
Published by: Fisk og Fri Aps, Christians Brygge 28, Copenhagen V, 1559, Denmark. TEL 45-33-111488, FAX 45-33-111489, fiskogfri@fiskogfri.dk, http://fiskogfri.dk.

796 USA
BIKELEAGUE NEWS. Text in English. bi-m. adv. **Document type:** *Newsletter.*
Media: E-mail.
Published by: League of American Bicyclists, 1612 K St, N W, Ste 800, Washington, DC 20006-2850. TEL 202-822-1333, FAX 202-822-1334.

796.93 CHN ISSN 1002-3488
BINGXUE YUNDONG/CHINA WINTER SPORTS. Text in Chinese. 1981. q. CNY 16 newsstand/cover (effective 2006). **Document type:** *Magazine, Consumer.*
Related titles: Online - full text ed.
Address: 7, Xuanxin Jie, Ha'erbin, 150008, China. TEL 86-451-82618531.

799.2 USA
THE BIRD HUNTING REPORT; serving bird hunters and waterfowlers who travel. Text in English. 1995. a. USD 59 (effective 2011). back issues avail. **Document type:** *Report, Trade.* **Description:** Independent guide to bird hunting and waterfowling in the US and abroad. Evaluates lodges and hunting destinations, outfitters, and reports on hunting conditions.
Formerly: Hunting Report for Birdshooters and Waterfowlers (1053-4466)
Related titles: Online - full text ed.: USD 49 (effective 2011).
Published by: Brunson Publishing, 588 Linwood St, Apt 1, Brooklyn, NY 11208. Pub. Stuart Brunson.

796.93 NOR ISSN 0804-1326
BIRKEBEINER'N. Variant title: Mosjonsmagasinet Birkebeiner'n. Text in Norwegian. 1989. 6/yr. NOK 150 (effective 2001). adv. back issues avail. **Document type:** *Magazine, Consumer.*
Formerly (until 1992): Turrenmagasinet Birkebeiner'n (0802-426X)
Published by: Sport Media AS, Vestre Ringvei 5, PO Box A, Askim, 1801, Norway. TEL 47-69-81-97-00, FAX 47-69-88-99-80, http://www.sportmedia.no. Eds. Eivind Bye, Erik Unaas TEL 47-69-819703. Adv. contact Terje Lund Olsen. Circ: 15,000.

799.21 USA
THE BLACK POWDER JOURNAL. Text in English. 1996. bi-m. free. adv.
Description: Dedicated to black powder shooting, muzzle loading and associated activities.
Media: Online - full text.
Published by: C R Labs, Inc., 12440 New London Eastern Rd, Homerville, OH 44235. TEL 330-648-2707, FAX 330-648-2707. Ed., Adv. contact Joseph Cindric II.

799.2 USA ISSN 1931-6275
BLACKPOWDER GUNS & HUNTING. Text in English. 200?. q. USD 9.99 domestic; USD 19.99 in Canada; USD 24.99 elsewhere (effective 2008). adv. back issues avail. **Document type:** *Magazine, Trade.*
Description: Covers muzzleloading enthusiasts with the specifics needed to harvest trophy wild game.
Related titles: Online - full text ed.
Indexed: H20.
Published by: Grand View Media Group, Inc. (Subsidiary of: EBSCO Industries, Inc.), 200 Croft St, Ste 1, Birmingham, AL 35242. TEL 888-431-2877, FAX 205-408-3797, webmaster@grandviewmedia.com, http://www.gvmg.com. Ed. Chad Schearer TEL 406-799-7984. Pub. Mike Kizzire TEL 205-408-3716. adv.: B&W page USD 2,750, color page USD 3,440; trim 7.75 x 10.625.

791 USA ISSN 1093-7897
BLACKPOWDER HUNTING. Text in English. q. USD 20 domestic; USD 40 foreign (effective 2002). **Document type:** *Magazine, Trade.*
Published by: International Blackpowder Hunting Association, PO Box 1180, Glenrock, WY 82637. TEL 307-436-9817.

DER BLAUE PETER; Zeitschrift fuer Segeln und Segelausbildung. *see* SPORTS AND GAMES—Boats And Boating

799.1 DEU ISSN 0720-4116
BLINKER; Europas groesste Anglerzeitschrift. Text in German. 1969. m. EUR 50.40; EUR 4.20 newsstand/cover (effective 2011). adv. back issues avail. **Document type:** *Magazine, Consumer.* **Description:** Provides information and advice on all matters related to recreational fishing.
Published by: Jahr Top Special Verlag, Troplowitzstr 5, Hamburg, 22529, Germany. TEL 49-40-389060, FAX 49-40-38906300, info@jahr-tsv.de, http://www.jahr-tsv.de. Ed. Henning Stilke. Adv. contact Christopher Zippert TEL 49-40-38906267. Circ: 73,112 (paid).

796.93 914 USA ISSN 1067-3938
GV854.8.E9
BLUE BOOK OF EUROPEAN SKI RESORTS. Text in English. 1993. biennial. USD 21.95 (effective 2000). adv. **Document type:** *Directory, Consumer.* **Description:** Complete listing of European ski areas with facilities, rates, statistics and telephone numbers.
Published by: (Austrian Tourist Office Company Des Alpes), Publishers Group International, PO Box 3775, Washington, DC 20007. TEL 202-342-0886, FAX 202-338-1940. Ed. Robert G Enzel. R&P Emily Enzel. Adv. contact David Bruce Schissler. Circ: 10,000.

BLUE LAKE INFORMATION GUIDE. *see* TRAVEL AND TOURISM

THE BLUE WATER BULLETIN. *see* SPORTS AND GAMES—Boats And Boating

796 797.1 AUS ISSN 1449-6321
BLUEWATER BOATS & SPORTSFISHING. Text in English. 1997. bi-m. AUD 74.95 in Australia & New Zealand; AUD 99.95 elsewhere (effective 2008). adv. **Document type:** *Magazine, Trade.*
Address: Ste 4, 2nd Fl, Runaway Bay Marina, 247 Bayview St, Runaway Bay, QLD 4216, Australia. TEL 61-7-55015400, FAX 61-7-55015411. Ed. Tim Simpson. Adv. contact Rowan Wyeth.

799.1 USA
BOAR HUNTER. Text in English. 2001. bi-m. USD 22; USD 3.25 newsstand/cover (effective 2001). adv. **Document type:** *Magazine, Consumer.*
Published by: Boar Hunter Magazine, Box 129, Baxley, GA 31515. TEL 912-366-8062, http://www.boarhuntermagazine.com. Ed. K G Smith. Pub. Pat Aycock.

796.93 USA
BOARDTEST MAGAZINE; snowboard equipment buyers' guide. Text in English. 1995. a. USD 8.95. adv. illus.; maps; stat. **Document type:** *Magazine, Consumer.*
Published by: Arboreal Publishing Ltd., 118 W 29th St, Vancouver, WA 98660. TEL 360-695-9975, FAX 360-695-9975. Ed., Pub. Gordon Smith. Adv. contact B O'Neill. B&W page USD 1,750; trim 11 x 8.5. Circ: 60,000. **Dist. by:** 3400 Dunde Rd, Northbrook, IL 60062.

BOATWORKS; how to rewire your boat. *see* TRANSPORTATION—Ships And Shipping

799 USA
BOB ELLSBERG'S HUNTER & FISHERMAN'S PLANNING YEARBOOK; a complete guidebook, calendar & journal for the outdoorsman. Text in English. a. USD 12.95. illus.
Published by: Outdoor Enterprises, 1048 Valley St, Astoria, OR 97103. TEL 503-325-5573. Ed. Paul F Barnum.

796.5 NOR ISSN 1500-3051
BOBIL & CARAVAN; fritidsmagasinet. Text in Norwegian. 1994. 6/yr. NOK 150 (effective 2001). adv. **Document type:** *Magazine, Consumer.*
Published by: Sport Media AS, Vestre Ringvei 5, PO Box A, Askim, 1801, Norway. TEL 47-69-81-97-00, FAX 47-69-88-99-80, http://www.sportmedia.no. Ed. Eivind Bye. Adv. contact Terje Lund Olsen. Circ: 11,000 (controlled).

797.32 FRA ISSN 1764-5549
BODYBOARD MAGAZINE. Text in French. 1993. bi-m. EUR 20 domestic; EUR 33 in the European Union; EUR 45 elsewhere (effective 2008). **Document type:** *Magazine, Consumer.*
Former titles (until 2003): Surf Session. Bodyboard (1288-7250); (until 1998): Bodyboard Air Force (1246-1601)
Published by: Surf Session, 20 rue Maryse Bastie, Anglet, 64600, France. TEL 33-5-59417000, FAX 33-5-59412412, surf@atlantel.fr, http://www.surfsession.com.

799.32 USA ISSN 0894-7856
GV1183
BOW AND ARROW HUNTING; the world's leading archery magazine. Text in English. 1963. 9/yr. USD 19.95 (effective 2011). adv. bk.rev. illus. back issues avail.; reprints avail. **Document type:** *Magazine, Consumer.* **Description:** Concentrates on bowhunting, with emphasis on hunting North American species.
Formerly (until 1985): Bow and Arrow (0006-8403)
Indexed: SD, SportS, T02.
—Ingenta.
Published by: Beckett Media Llc, 4635 McEwen Rd, Dallas, TX 75244. TEL 714-939-9991, FAX 714-456-0146, customerservice@beckett.com, http://www.beckett.com.

799.2 USA ISSN 1949-0364
▼ **THE BOWFISHER.** Text in English. 2009. bi-m. USD 20.65 (effective 2009). **Document type:** *Magazine, Consumer.* **Description:** Features the sport of bowfishing.
Published by: The Bowfisher, LLC, HC 79 Box 3240, Pittsburg, MO 65724. TEL 417-399-1608, pswearingin@thebowfisher.com.

799.2 USA ISSN 1947-3745
SK36
BOWHUNT AMERICA. Text in English. 2008. 8/yr. USD 9.95 domestic; USD 29.95 in Canada; USD 39.95 elsewhere (effective 2009). adv. back issues avail. **Document type:** *Magazine, Consumer.*
Description: Features significant information on Bow hunting.
Published by: Zebra Publishing Inc, 2960 N Academy Blvd, Ste 101, Colorado Springs, CO 80917. TEL 719-495-9999, FAX 719-495-8899, info@zebrapub.com. Ed. Bill Krenz TEL 719-495-9999 ext 111. Pub. Sherry Krenz TEL 719-495-9999 ext 112. adv.: B&W page USD 3,497, color page USD 5,290; trim 8.125 x 10.75. Circ: 101,428.

799.32 USA ISSN 0273-7434
BOWHUNTER; the magazine for the hunting archer. Text in English. 1971. 9/yr. USD 12.97 domestic; USD 25.97 in Canada; USD 27.97 elsewhere (effective 2009). adv. bk.rev. reprints avail. **Document type:** *Magazine, Consumer.* **Description:** Features interesting articles on bow hunting.
Related titles: Microform ed.: (from PQC); Online - full text ed.
Indexed: A22, A33, G06, G07, G08, G09, H20, I05, M01, M02, P02, P10, P19, P48, P53, P54, PQC, SD, SportS, T02.
—CCC.
Published by: Intermedia Outdoors, Inc., 6405 Flank Dr, Harrisburg, PA 17112. TEL 717-657-9555, FAX 717-657-9552, customerservice@imoutdoors.com, http://www.imoutdoorsmedia.com. Ed. Dwight Schuh. Pub. Jeff Waring TEL 717-695-8080. Adv. contact Jeff Millar TEL 717-695-8081. B&W page USD 5,635, color page USD 9,009; trim 7.75 x 10.5. Circ: 143,085.
Subscr. to: PO Box 420235, Palm Coast, FL 32142. TEL 386-447-6318, 800-829-2543, bowhunter@palmcoastd.com.

799.32 USA ISSN 1049-9768
BOWHUNTING. Variant title: Petersen's Bowhunting. Text in English. 198?. 9/yr. USD 12.97 domestic; USD 25.97 in Canada; USD 27.97 elsewhere (effective 2008). adv. illus. **Document type:** *Magazine, Consumer.* **Description:** Features hunting articles, equipment tests, and the tactics, techniques and tools needed to be a successful bowhunter.
Related titles: Online - full text ed.
Indexed: G06, G07, G08, I05.
—CCC.
Published by: Intermedia Outdoors, Inc., 512 7th Ave, 11th Fl, New York, NY 10018. TEL 212-852-6600, 800-260-6397, FAX 212-302-4472, customerservice@imoutdoors.com, http://www.imoutdoorsmedia.com. adv.: B&W page USD 5,418, color page USD 8,663. Circ: 156,000 (paid).

799.32 USA ISSN 1043-5492
BOWHUNTING WORLD; the archery equipment authority. Text in English. 1952. 9/yr. USD 12.97 domestic; USD 21.97 foreign (effective 2008). adv. bk.rev. charts; illus.; mkt.; pat.; tr.lit.; tr.mk. index. back issues avail.; reprints avail. **Document type:** *Magazine, Trade.* **Description:** Contains information about bowhunters and their successful hunting experience.
Formerly (until 1989): Archery World (0003-827X)
Related titles: Online - full text ed.
Indexed: A22, Consl, G06, G07, G08, MagInd, PEI, SD, SPI, SportS, T02.
—Ingenta.
Published by: Grand View Media Group, Inc. (Subsidiary of: EBSCO Industries, Inc.), 200 Croft St, Ste 1, Birmingham, AL 35242. TEL 888-431-2877, FAX 205-408-3797, webmaster@grandviewmedia.com, http://www.gvmg.com. Ed. Mike Strandlund TEL 952-405-2280 ext 101. Pub. Derrick Nawrocki TEL 205-408-3732. adv.: B&W page USD 4,795, color page USD 6,313; trim 8 x 10.5. Circ: 96,590.

THE BOWYER'S JOURNAL. *see* ARTS AND HANDICRAFTS

799.2 POL ISSN 1429-7698
BRAC LOWIECKA. Text in Polish. 1998. m. PLZ 102; PLZ 11 newsstand/ cover (effective 2011). adv. **Document type:** *Magazine, Consumer.*

S

Indexed: AgrLib.
Published by: Oficyna Wydawnicza OIKOS, ul Kaliska 1/7, Warsaw, 02316, Poland. TEL 48-22-8220334, FAX 48-22-8226649, oikos@oikos.net.pl, http://www.oikos.net.pl. Ed. Bogdan Zlotorzynski. Adv. contact Pawel Szustkiewicz.

799.2 362.1 CAN ISSN 1910-2615
BRITISH COLUMBIA. MINISTRY OF PUBLIC SAFETY AND SOLICITOR GENERAL. GAMING POLICY AND ENFORCEMENT BRANCH. ANNUAL REPORT. Text in English. 2005. a. **Document type:** *Government.*
Published by: British Columbia, Ministry of Public Safety and Solicitor General, PO Box 9310, Stn. Prov. Govt., Victoria, BC V8W 9N1, Canada. TEL 250-387-5311, FAX 250-356-8149, Gaming.Branch@gov.bc.ca, http://www.gov.bc.ca/bvprd/bc/channel.do?action=ministry&channelID=-8391&navId=NAV_ID_province.

796.522 CAN ISSN 0045-2998
BRITISH COLUMBIA MOUNTAINEER. Text in English. 1917. biennial. CAD 12 (effective 2000). adv. bk.rev. illus. reprints avail. **Document type:** *Journal, Consumer.*
Published by: British Columbia Mountaineering Club, PO Box 2674, Vancouver, BC V6B 3W8, Canada. TEL 604-737-3050. Ed. M C Feller. Circ: 500.

796.552 CAN ISSN 0829-0504
BRITISH COLUMBIA MOUNTAINEERING CLUB NEWSLETTER. Key Title: B.C. Mountaineering Club Newsletter. Text in English. 10/yr. **Document type:** *Newsletter.*
Former titles (until 1982): B.C. Mountaineer. Newsletter (0227-6275); (until 1978): B.C.M.C. News (0708-7713); (until 1977): B.C.M.C. Newsletter (0700-7361); (until 1969): British Columbia Mountaineering Club. Newsletter (0700-7345)
Published by: British Columbia Mountaineering Club, PO Box 2674, Vancouver, BC V6B 3W8, Canada. TEL 604-268-9502, info@bcmc.ca, http://bcmc.ca.

796 CAN ISSN 0711-0014
BRITISH COLUMBIA SUMMER GAMES. GENERAL RULES. Text in English. 1978. a.
Published by: British Columbia Games Society, 990 Fort St, Suite 200, Victoria, BC V8V 3K2, Canada. TEL 250-387-1375, FAX 250-387-4489, info@bcgames.org.

799.1 CAN ISSN 0837-4899
SH572.B7
BRITISH COLUMBIA TIDAL WATERS SPORT FISHING GUIDE. Text in English. biennial.
—CCC.
Published by: Fisheries and Oceans Canada, Pacific Region, 200-401 Burrard St, Vancouver, BC V6C 3S4, Canada. TEL 604-666-0384, FAX 604-666-1847, http://www.pac.dfo-mpo.gc.ca.

796.5 CAN ISSN 0383-9249
BRUCE TRAIL NEWS. Text in English. 1963. q. CAD 12, USD 12. adv. bk.rev. illus. back issues avail.; reprints avail. **Description:** News about outdoor life, camping and the environment.
Published by: (Bruce Trail Association), Trail News Inc., 17 Marlborough Ave, Toronto, ON M5R 1X5, Canada. TEL 416-964-7281. Ed. Norman Day. adv.: B&W page USD 600, color page USD 9,000; trim 11 x 8.25. Circ: 10,000 (controlled).

797.2 ESP ISSN 1579-3583
BUCEADORES. Text in Spanish. 1998. bi-m. **Document type:** *Magazine, Consumer.*
Related titles: ◆ Supplement(s): El Buceo. ISSN 2174-0208.
Published by: Sofimav Ediciones Espana, C FAstenrath, 12, Barcelona, Spain. TEL 34-93-2122610, FAX 34-93-4173876.

797.2 ESP ISSN 2174-0208
EL BUCEO. Text in Spanish. 1995. a. **Document type:** *Magazine, Consumer.*
Related titles: ◆ Supplement to: Buceadores. ISSN 1579-3583.
Published by: Sofimav Ediciones Espana, C FAstenrath, 12, Barcelona, Spain. TEL 34-93-2122610, FAX 34-93-4173876.

796.552 USA
BUCKEYE TRAILBLAZER. Text in English. bi-m.
Published by: Buckeye Trail Association, Box 254, Worthington, OH 43085. Ed. James W Sprague.

799.2 USA ISSN 1936-0819
BUCKMASTERS GUNHUNTER MAGAZINE. Text in English. 2004. bi-m. USD 20.95 (effective 2011). adv. back issues avail. **Document type:** *Magazine, Consumer.* **Description:** Covers in detail the best guns, ammo and accessories for a wide variety of hunting applications, from antelope to zebra.
Published by: Buckmasters, Inc., 10350 Hwy 80 E, Montgomery, AL 36117. TEL 334-215-3337, FAX 334-215-3535, customerservice@buckmasters.com.

BUCKSKINNER. *see* HISTORY—History Of North And South America

BUGLE (MISSOULA); journal of elk and the hunt. *see* CONSERVATION

796 910.91 NLD ISSN 1571-408X
BUITENLEVEN. Text in Dutch. 2003. 8/yr. EUR 34.95 to members; EUR 36.95 to non-members; EUR 4.95 newsstand/cover (effective 2008). adv. **Document type:** *Magazine, Consumer.*
Published by: Algemene Nederlandse Wielrijders Bond (A N W B) Media/Dutch Automobile Association Media, Postbus 93200, The Hague, 2509 BA, Netherlands. TEL 31-70-3141470, FAX 31-70-3146538, http://www.anwbmedia.nl. adv.: B&W page EUR 3,166, color page EUR 4,225; bleed 230 x 300.

796 910.2 NLD ISSN 0007-3768
BUITENSPOOR. Text in Dutch. 1918. 10/yr. free membership (effective 2009). adv. bk.rev. charts; illus. index.
Published by: Nederlandse Toeristen Kampeerclub, Ebrodreef 87, Utrecht, 3561 JM, Netherlands. TEL 31-30-2618118, clubburreau@kampeerclub.nl, http://www.kampeerclub.nl. Circ: 4,000.

799.1 AUS ISSN 1832-4517
BUSH 'N BEACH FISHING; location reports & tips. Text in English. 19??. m. AUD 40 domestic (effective 2008). adv. **Document type:** *Newspaper, Consumer.* **Description:** Covers Australia's east coast and inland recreational fisheries.
Published by: Collins Media, No 38 120 Bloomfield St, PO Box 387, Cleveland, QLD 4163, Australia. TEL 61-7-32861833, FAX 61-7-38212637. Adv. contact Debbie Voisey. B&W page AUD 925, color page AUD 1,270; 26 x 38. Circ: 13,500.

C T P A NEWS. *see* TRAVEL AND TOURISM

799.1 USA ISSN 1931-6259
CABELA'S OUTFITTER JOURNAL. Abbreviated title: C O J. Text in English. 2000. bi-m. USD 12.99 domestic; USD 22.90 in Canada; USD 27.99 elsewhere (effective 2008). adv. back issues avail. **Document type:** *Magazine, Trade.*
Related titles: Online - full text ed.
Indexed: H20.
Published by: Grand View Media Group, Inc. (Subsidiary of: EBSCO Industries, Inc.), 200 Croft St, Ste 1, Birmingham, AL 35242. TEL 888-431-2877, FAX 205-408-3797, webmaster@grandviewmedia.com, http://www.gvmg.com. Ed. Chuck Smock. Pub. Stephen Statham TEL 205-408-3724. adv.: B&W page USD 4,944, color page USD 6,174; trim 7.75 x 10.625.

799.2 ITA
IL CACCIATORE ITALIANO. Text in Italian. bi-m. free to members (effective 2008). 72 p./no.; back issues avail. **Document type:** *Magazine, Consumer.*
Published by: (Federazione Italiana Caccia), Greentime SpA, Via Barberia 11, Bologna, BO 40123, Italy. TEL 39-051-584020, FAX 39-051-585000, info@greentime.it. Ed. Rodolfo Grassi. Pub., R&P Olga Misley. Circ: 450,000.

799.2 ITA ISSN 1828-4825
IL CACCIATORE TRENTINO. Text in Italian. 1947. q. EUR 15.50 (effective 2008). **Document type:** *Magazine, Consumer.*
Published by: Federazione Italiana della Caccia, Associazione Cacciatori Trentini, Via Guardini 41, Trent, 38100, Italy. TEL 39-0461-825834, FAX 39-0461-825558, http://www.cacciatoritrentini.it.

799.2 FRA ISSN 1962-8366
▼ **LES CAHIERS CYNEGETIQUES DU NATURALISTE.** Text in French. 2009. irreg. EUR 25 per issue (effective 2010). **Document type:** *Monographic series, Academic/Scholarly.*
Published by: Editions Montbel, 8, Rue de Courcelles, Paris, 75008, France. TEL 33-1-45630404, livres@montbel.com, http://www.montbel.com/boutique/liste_rayons.cfm.

CALIFORNIA. DEPARTMENT OF FISH AND GAME. FISH BULLETIN. *see* FISH AND FISHERIES

796 975 USA ISSN 0164-8748
F856 C2
CALIFORNIA EXPLORER. Text in English. 1978. bi-m. USD 28.50 (effective 1999). adv. cum.index. back issues avail. **Document type:** *Magazine, Consumer.* **Description:** Covers the backroads, hiking trails and history of the West.
Published by: J B K Enterprises Inc., 1404 Simpson Ct., Marina, CA 93933-5045. TEL 707-942-6249, FAX 707-942-6249. Ed. Kay Graves. Pub., R&P, Adv. contact Harold Chevrier. Circ: 7,509 (paid).

CALIFORNIA FISH AND GAME. *see* BIOLOGY—Zoology

799.1 USA ISSN 1071-5673
CALIFORNIA FLY FISHER; good stories! good fishing! good tips!. Text in English. 1992. bi-m. USD 14.95 (effective 2008). adv. bk.rev. index. **Document type:** *Magazine, Consumer.* **Description:** Dedicated to exploring fly fishing opportunities in and around California.
Address: 10550 Olympic Blvd, Truckee, CA 96161-1743. TEL 415-284-0313, FAX 415-284-0321, calflyfisher@compuserve.com. Ed., Pub., R&P, Adv. contact Richard Anderson. Circ: 10,000 (paid).

799 USA ISSN 1056-0122
CALIFORNIA GAME & FISH. Text in English. 19??. m. USD 12.99 domestic; USD 25.99 in Canada; USD 27.99 elsewhere (effective 2011). adv. illus. **Document type:** *Magazine, Consumer.* **Description:** Informs sportsmen of hunting and fishing, as well as environmental and conservation issues in California.
Related titles: Online - full text ed.; ◆ Regional ed(s).: Game & Fish; ◆ Louisiana Game & Fish. ISSN 0744-3692; ◆ Florida Game & Fish. ISSN 0889-3322; ◆ Alabama Game & Fish. ISSN 0279-6783; ◆ Mississippi-Louisiana Game & Fish. ISSN 1947-2358; ◆ North Carolina Game & Fish. ISSN 0897-8816; ◆ South Carolina Game & Fish. ISSN 0897-9154; ◆ West Virginia Game & Fish. ISSN 0897-9162; ◆ Missouri Game & Fish. ISSN 0889-3799; ◆ New York Game & Fish. ISSN 0897-9189; ◆ Great Plains Game & Fish. ISSN 1055-6532; ◆ Illinois Game & Fish. ISSN 0897-9014; ◆ Indiana Game & Fish. ISSN 0897-8980; ◆ Iowa Game & Fish. ISSN 0897-9197; ◆ Mid-Atlantic Game & Fish. ISSN 1055-6540; ◆ Oklahoma Game & Fish. ISSN 0746-6013; ◆ Rocky Mountain Game & Fish. ISSN 1056-0114; ◆ Pennsylvania Game & Fish. ISSN 0897-8808; ◆ Virginia Game & Fish. ISSN 0897-8794; ◆ Washington - Oregon Game & Fish. ISSN 1056-0106; ◆ Ohio Game & Fish. ISSN 0897-9170; New England Game & Fish. ISSN 0897-8972. 1988. USD 12 domestic; USD 25 in Canada; USD 27 elsewhere (effective 2010).
Published by: Intermedia Outdoors, Inc., 512 7th Ave, 11th Fl, New York, NY 10018. TEL 212-852-6600, 800-260-6397, FAX 212-302-4472, customerservice@imoutdoors.com, http://www.imoutdoorsmedia.com. Ed. Ken Dunwoody. Pub., Adv. contact Peter Gross.

796.42 USA
CALIFORNIA TRACK & RUNNING NEWS. Text in English. 1974. bi-m. free to qualified personnel (effective 2010). adv. **Document type:** *Magazine, Consumer.* **Description:** Covers race walking, road running, prep track & cross country, college cross country, and ultra-running.
Published by: Shooting Star Media, Inc., PO Box 67, Fort Atkinson, WI 53538. TEL 608-239-3785, FAX 920-563-7298, shootingstarmediabiz@gmail.com, http://www.shootingstarmediainc.com/. Pub. Larry Eder TEL 608-239-3785. adv.: B&W page USD 1,505, color page USD 2,740; trim 8.125 x 10.875.

CALL OUT. *see* PUBLIC HEALTH AND SAFETY

OS CAMINHOS DA TERRA. *see* CONSERVATION

796.5 DEU ISSN 0724-4215
CAMP; Magazin fuer Caravan und Reisemobil. Text in German. 1977. m. adv. **Document type:** *Consumer.*
Published by: Top Special Verlag GmbH, Nebendahlstr 16, Hamburg, 22041, Germany. TEL 040-3470-0, FAX 040-34725588. Ed. Joachim Kalkowsky. Adv. contact Beate Asmus Fuegert. Circ: 37,924.

CAMPBOOK: CALIFORNIA - NEVADA. *see* TRAVEL AND TOURISM
CAMPBOOK: EASTERN CANADA. *see* TRAVEL AND TOURISM
CAMPBOOK: GREAT LAKES. *see* TRAVEL AND TOURISM
CAMPBOOK: MIDEASTERN. *see* TRAVEL AND TOURISM
CAMPBOOK: NORTH CENTRAL. *see* TRAVEL AND TOURISM
CAMPBOOK: NORTHWESTERN. *see* TRAVEL AND TOURISM
CAMPBOOK: SOUTH CENTRAL. *see* TRAVEL AND TOURISM
CAMPBOOK: SOUTHEASTERN. *see* TRAVEL AND TOURISM
CAMPBOOK: SOUTHWESTERN. *see* TRAVEL AND TOURISM

796.5 ITA ISSN 0008-2325
CAMPEGGIO ITALIANO. Text in Italian. 1957. m. free to members. adv. back issues avail. **Document type:** *Magazine, Consumer.*
Published by: Confederazione Italiana Campeggiatori, Via Vittorio Emanuele 11, Calenzano, FI 50041, Italy. TEL 39-055-882391, FAX 39-055-8825918, federcampeggio@tin.it. Ed. Giancarlo Ceci. Circ: 25,000.

796.54 ITA ISSN 2038-6443
▼ **CAMPER MAGAZINE.** Text in Italian. 2010. m. **Document type:** *Magazine, Consumer.*
Published by: Sprea Editori Srl, Via Torino 51, Cernusco sul Naviglio, MI 20063, Italy. TEL 39-02-92432222, FAX 39-02-92432236, editori@sprea.it, http://www.sprea.it.

796.54 NLD ISSN 1573-0220
CAMPERGIDS FACILE-EN-ROUTE. Cover title: Facile en Route Campergids. Text in Dutch. 1998. a. EUR 24.95 (effective 2009).
Published by: Facile Media, Postbus 555, Oss, 5340 AN, Netherlands. TEL 31-412-656885, FAX 31-412-656886, info@facilemedia.nl, http://www.facilemedia.nl.

796.54 NLD ISSN 1574-2644
CAMPERKRIEBELS. Text in Dutch. 2005. 8/yr. EUR 37.50 (effective 2009).
Published by: Camper Club Nederland, Postbus 70, Lochem, 7240 AB, Netherlands. TEL 31-643-582790, ccn@campervriendelijk.nl, http://www.campervriendelijk.nl.

▼ **CAMPERREISMAGAZINE.** *see* TRAVEL AND TOURISM

796.54 NLD ISSN 1879-6354
▼ **CAMPERVARIA.** Text in Dutch. 2009. 3/yr. EUR 7.50 (effective 2010). **Document type:** *Newspaper, Consumer.*
Published by: B & B Provice, Postbus 330, Stadskanaal, 9500 AH, Netherlands. TEL 31-599-652346, FAX 31-599-652273. Ed. Mariette Bos. Circ: 20,000.

796 USA ISSN 0410-4889
CAMPFIRE CHATTER. Text in English. 1957. m. USD 23 membership (effective 2008). adv. **Document type:** *Newsletter.*
Published by: North American Family Camps Association, Inc., PO Box 318, Lunenburg, MA 01462. http://www.nafca.org. Ed. Pat O'Malley. Circ: 2,500.

796.5 DEU
CAMPING; illustrierte Zeitschrift fuer Caravan-, Zelt-, Motor-Touristik und Wassersport. Text in German. 1952. m. adv. **Document type:** *Magazine, Consumer.*
Published by: (Deutscher Camping Club e.V.), D C C - Wirtschaftsdienst und Verlag GmbH, Mandlstr 28, Munich, 80802, Germany. TEL 49-89-3801420, FAX 49-89-334737, info@campingpresse.de, http://www.campingpresse.de. adv.: B&W page EUR 3,210, color page EUR 6,095; 192 x 251. Circ: 33,765 (controlled).

796.5 GBR ISSN 0957-851X
CAMPING & CARAVANNING. Text in English. 1907. m. free to members (effective 2009). adv. bk.rev. illus. **Document type:** *Magazine, Consumer.* **Description:** Provides a useful tips, interesting articles, holiday ideas and road tests of new units, tents and equipment.
Formerly (until 1971): Camping and Outdoor Life
Published by: Camping and Caravanning Club, Greenfields House, Westwood Way, Coventry, Warks CV4 8JH, United Kingdom. TEL 44-24-76475448. Ed. Simon McGrath. Adv. contact Matthew Styrka TEL 44-20-73060300 ext 2121.

796 CAN ISSN 1485-2985
CAMPING CANADA'S R V LIFESTYLE. Text in English. 1975. 7/yr. CAD 17.12 (effective 2000). adv. tr.lit. **Document type:** *Magazine, Consumer.*
Formerly: Camping Canada (0384-9856)
Indexed: SportS, T&II.
Published by: Taylor Publishing Group, 2585 Skymark Ave, Ste 306, Mississauga, ON L4W 4L5, Canada. TEL 905-624-8218, FAX 905-624-6764. Ed. Howard Elmer. Pub., Adv. contact Bill Taylor.

CAMPING-CAR MAGAZINE SPECIAL FOURGONS. *see* TRANSPORTATION—Automobiles

796.5 DEU ISSN 2191-2718
CAMPING, CARS UND CARAVANS. Text in German. 1994. m. EUR 34.80 domestic; EUR 39 foreign; EUR 3 newsstand/cover (effective 2011). adv. **Document type:** *Magazine, Consumer.*
Related titles: Online - full text ed.
Published by: DoldeMedien Verlag GmbH, Postwiesenstr 5A, Stuttgart, 70327, Germany. TEL 49-711-134660, FAX 49-711-1346638, info@doldemedien.de, http://www.doldemedien.de. Adv. contact Sylke Wohlschiess. Circ: 55,000 (paid and controlled). **Subscr. to:** Zenit Pressevertrieb, Postfach 810640, Stuttgart 70523, Germany. TEL 49-711-7252197, FAX 49-711-7252333, kundenservice@zenit-presse.de.

796.54 NLD ISSN 2211-6605
▼ **CAMPING CHEQUEGIDS. EUROPE.** Text in Dutch. 2010. a. EUR 6 (effective 2011).
Published by: (ANWB BV/Royal Dutch Touring Club), Algemene Nederlandse Wielrijders Bond (A N W B) Media/Dutch Automobile Association Media, Postbus 93200, The Hague, 2509 BA, Netherlands. TEL 31-70-3141470, FAX 31-70-3146538, http://www.anwbmedia.nl.

674.9448908 DNK ISSN 0108-7355
GV191.48.D4
CAMPING DANMARK; godkendte campingpladser i Danmark. (Forms part of: Nordiske Officielle Campingfortegnelser) Text in Danish, English, German. 1968. a. DKK 99 (effective 2008). illus. **Document type:** *Catalog, Consumer.*
Formerly (until 1983): Godkendte Campingpladser i Danmark (0108-7347)

Published by: Campingraadet/Danish Camping Board, Mosedalsvej 15, Valby, 2500, Denmark. TEL 45-39-278844, FAX 45-39-278044, info@campingraadet.dk, http://www.campingraadet.dk.

680 796 FRA ISSN 1779-3599
CAMPING ET CARAVANING. Text in French. 1965. 8/yr. EUR 23 (effective 2010). adv. illus. **Document type:** *Magazine, Consumer.*
Formerly (until 2002): Le Caravanier (0399-7715)
Published by: Motor Presse France, 12 rue Rouget de Lisle, Issy-les-Moulineaux, 92442, France. http://www.motorpresse.fr.

796.5 CAN ISSN 0829-4844
CAMPING IN ONTARIO. Text in English. 1975. a. free. adv. **Document type:** *Directory.*
Former titles (until 1985): Ontario Private Campground Association. Camping Directory (0827-4223); (until 1981): Camp Ontario (0827-4231)
Published by: Ontario Private Campground Association, R R 5, Owen Sound, ON N4K 5N7, Canada. TEL 519-371-3393, FAX 519-371-0080. Ed. Marcel Gobeil. Circ: 175,000.

796.5 AUS
CAMPING IN VICTORIA. Text in English. biennial. AUD 6.95 newsstand/cover (effective 2001). bk.rev. maps. back issues avail. **Document type:** *Directory, Consumer.* **Description:** Lists group camping facilities, accomodations, and camping facilities for all types of families or groups. Includes articles for the first time camper, recipes, bushwalking for beginners and where to camp in Victoria's national parks.
Formerly: The Where-to Book
Published by: Nicholson Media Group Pty. Ltd., PO Box 1206, Hawksburn, VIC 3142, Australia. TEL 61-3-98268448, FAX 61-3-98278808.

796.54 USA ISSN 1529-5664
GV191.4
CAMPING LIFE. Text in English. 199?. every 8 yrs. USD 14.97 domestic; USD 22.97 in Canada; USD 30.97 elsewhere (effective 2008). adv. **Document type:** *Magazine, Consumer.* **Description:** Covers the outdoor life style, camp equipment, trailers, camp sites and other related fields.
Related titles: Online - full text ed.
Indexed: G05, G06, G07, G08, I05.
Published by: Affinity Group Inc., 2575 Vista Del Mar, Ventura, CA 93001. TEL 805-667-4100, FAX 805-667-4419, info@affinitygroup.com, http://www.affinitygroup.com. Ed. Stuart Bourdon. Adv. contact Angela van Hover TEL 310-537-6322 ext 135. B&W page USD 4,790, color page USD 7,860; trim 7.875 x 10.5. Circ: 83,000 (paid and controlled).

CAMPING MAGAZINE. *see* CHILDREN AND YOUTH—About

796.5 GBR ISSN 1350-1453
CAMPING MAGAZINE. Text in English. 1961. m. GBP 29.99 domestic; GBP 34 in Europe; GBP 44 elsewhere (effective 2009). adv. bk.rev. illus. back issues avail. **Document type:** *Magazine, Consumer.* **Description:** Offers family-oriented information about camping and walking.
Former titles (until 1992): Camping and Walking (0952-5106); (until 1986): Camping and Trailer (0266-7878); (until 1984): Camping (0032-4469); (until 1970): Popular Camping (0551-5041)
—CCC.
Published by: Warners Group Publications Plc., The Maltings, Manor Ln, Bourne, Lincs PE10 9PH, United Kingdom. TEL 44-1778-391000, FAX 44-1778-425437, wgpsubs@warnersgroup.co.uk, http://www.warnersgroup.co.uk. Ed. Clive Garrett TEL 44-1778-392442. Pub. Rob McDonnell TEL 44-1778-391181. Adv. contact Darren Webb TEL 44-1778-391119.

796.5 DNK ISSN 0907-4856
CAMPING & FRITID. Text in Danish. 1926. 8/yr. DKK 310 to individual members (effective 2008). adv. bk.rev.; film rev. charts; illus. back issues avail. **Document type:** *Magazine, Consumer.*
Formerly (until 1991): Camping (0045-4125)
Related titles: Online - full text ed.: ISSN 1901-4066. 2001.
Published by: Dansk Camping Union, Korsdalsvej 134, Broendby, 2605, Denmark. TEL 45-33-210600, FAX 45-33-210608, info@dcu.dk. Ed. Joergen W G Froehlich. adv.: page DKK 18,000; 220 x 300. Circ: 65,000.

796.5 CHE ISSN 1422-5786
CAMPING-REVUE. Text in French, German, Italian. 1937. 10/yr. CHF 25 (effective 2001). adv. bk.rev. 32 p./no.; **Document type:** *Magazine, Consumer.*
Former titles (until 1998): Camping-Caravanning-Revue (0008-2414); (until 1960): Camping-Revue (1421-6442); (until 1950): Camping und Canoe (1421-6434); (until 1947): Camping-Revue (1421-6450)
Published by: Schweizerischer Camping- und Caravanning-Verband/ Federation Suisse de Camping et de Caravanning, Case Postale 42, Basel 4, 4027, Switzerland. TEL 41-61-3022626, FAX 41-61-3022481, info@sccv.ch. Circ: 11,093.

796.5 AUT
CAMPING REVUE; Magazin des Oesterreichischen Camping Clubs. Text in German. 1951. 6/yr. membership. adv. bk.rev. abstr.; charts; illus.; stat. **Document type:** *Magazine, Consumer.*
Former titles: Sport Review; Oesterreichische Camping Revue; Oesterreichische Camping and Caravaning Revue (0029-8972); Camping und Sport Revue
Published by: (Oesterreichischer Camping Club), Oe A M T C Verlag GmbH, Tauchnergasse 5, Klosterneuburg, N 3400, Austria. TEL 43-2243-4042700, FAX 43-2243-4042721, autotouring.verlag@oeamtc.at, http://www.oeamtc.at. Ed. Horst S Duernsteiner. R&P, Adv. contact Reinhart Rosner TEL 43-1-8898995. Circ: 15,000.

796 USA ISSN 8750-1465
CAMPING TODAY. Text in English. 1983. m. USD 25 to members. adv. **Document type:** *Newsletter.* **Description:** For camper and RV owners. Also covers wildlife and conservation.
Formerly: Tent and Trail
Published by: Family Campers & R Vers, 4804 Transit Rd, Bldg 2, Depew, NY 14043. TEL 716-668-6242. Ed., R&P DeWayne Johnston TEL 724-283-7401. Adv. contact Cheryl Fields. Circ: 15,000 (paid).

796.54 DEU ISSN 2191-2726
CAMPINGIMPULSE; Das Manager-Magazin fuer innovative Camping-Unternehmer. Text in German. 2000. bi-m. EUR 59.40 domestic; EUR 66 foreign (effective 2011). adv. **Document type:** *Magazine, Trade.*
Published by: DoldeMedien Verlag GmbH, Postwiesenstr 5A, Stuttgart, 70327, Germany. TEL 49-711-134660, FAX 49-711-1346638, info@doldemedien.de, http://www.doldemedien.de. Adv. contact Sylke Wohlschiess. Circ: 1,700 (paid).

796.54 NLD ISSN 1879-9884
CAMPINGLIFE MAGAZINE. Text in Dutch. 2008. bi-m. EUR 15; EUR 3.95 newsstand/cover (effective 2010). adv. **Document type:** *Magazine, Consumer.*
Published by: (RTL Nederland), Rise Media, Aambeeldstraat 2-b, Edam, 1135 GC, Netherlands. TEL 31-299-714229, FAX 31-299-714220, http://www.risemedia.nl. adv.: online banner EUR 1,495; trim 210 x 297. Circ: 20,000.

796.5 ESP ISSN 1132-0389
CAMPITUR; guia profesional de camping y ocio al aire libre. Text in Spanish. 1991. 2/yr. EUR 8 newsstand/cover domestic; EUR 9 newsstand/cover foreign (effective 2009). **Document type:** *Magazine, Trade.*
Published by: TPI Edita, Ave Manoteras, 26 3a Planta, Madrid, 28050, Spain. TEL 34-91-3396807, FAX 34-91-3396096, info@grupotpi.es.

796.54 CAN ISSN 1911-5040
CANADA CAMPS; the magazine for Canadian camp professionals. Text in English. 1983. 3/yr. **Document type:** *Magazine, Trade.*
Address: 1054 Centre St., Suite 199, Thornhill, ON L4J 8E5, Canada. TEL 905-370-0736, FAX 905-747-0409, paul@canadacampsmag.com.

799.2 CAN ISSN 1493-4450
CANADA'S OUTDOOR SPORTSMAN. Text in English. 1997. 6/yr. CAD 23.95 domestic; CAD 29.95 foreign; CAD 4.95 newsstand/cover (effective 2000). **Document type:** *Magazine, Consumer.* **Description:** Covers the best hunting and fishing in the country.
Formerly (until 1999): Canadian Sportsman (Saskatchewan) (1206-4637)
Published by: Canadian Outdoor Publications, PO Box 21036, Brandon, MB R7B 3W8, Canada. TEL 800-575-2674, sportsman@westman.wave.ca. Ed. George Gruenefeld.

796.52 CAN ISSN 0068-8207
F1090 CODEN: CNAJA6
CANADIAN ALPINE JOURNAL. Abbreviated title: C A J. Text in English. 1907. a. free to members (effective 2010). adv. bk.rev. illus. index, cum.index: 1907-1987. back issues avail.; reprints avail. **Document type:** *Journal, Consumer.* **Description:** Provides a record of the Canadian mountain ethos and mindset.
Indexed: GeoRef, SpeleolAb, SportS.
—Ingenta.
Published by: Alpine Club of Canada, Indian Flats Rd, P O Box 8040, Canmore, AB T1W 2T8, Canada. TEL 403-678-3200, FAX 403-678-3224, info@AlpineClubofCanada.ca, http://www.AlpineClubfCanada.ca. Ed. Sean Isaac.

799.1 CAN ISSN 1496-1717
THE CANADIAN FLY FISHER. Text in English. q. CAD 19.95 domestic; USD 19.95 in United States; CAD 38 elsewhere; USD 6.95 newsstand/cover (effective 2001). adv. **Document type:** *Magazine, Consumer.* **Description:** Filled with information on Canadian fly fishing destinations and techniques.
Published by: The Canadian Fly Fisher, 389 Bridge St W, RR 2, Belleville, ON K8N 4Z2, Canada. TEL 613-966-8017, 888-805-5608, FAX 613-966-5002. Ed., Pub. Chris Marshall. Adv. contact Jutta Witteveen. **Dist. by:** International Publishers Direct, 27500 Riverview Center Blvd, Bonita Springs, FL 34134. TEL 858-320-4563, FAX 858-677-3220.

CANADIAN GUIDER. *see* CHILDREN AND YOUTH—About

797.56 CAN ISSN 0319-3896
CANPARA. Text in English. 1961. 6/yr. CAD 26.75; CAD 35 foreign. adv. bk.rev. **Document type:** *Newsletter.*
Former titles: Canadian Parachutist (0045-5245); Parachute Club of Canada. Newsletter
Indexed: CA, SD, SportS, T02.
Published by: Canadian Sport Parachuting Association, 4185 Dunning Rd, Navan, ON K4B 1J1, Canada. TEL 613-835-3731, FAX 613-835-3731, office@cspa.ca, http://www.cspa.ca. Adv. contact Pierre Carpentier. B&W page CAD 250, color page CAD 600. Circ: 4,500.

796.5 DEU ISSN 0930-0309
CARAVAN; Zeitschrift fuer Camper, Caravaner, Touristen. Text in German. 1957. m. adv. illus. **Document type:** *Consumer.* **Description:** Information about travelling, new accessories and techniques.
Former titles: Caravan Camping-Journal (0343-2912); Camping Journal (0008-2449)
Published by: Panorama Verlags- und Werbegesellschaft mbH, Sudbrackstr 14-18, Bielefeld, 33611, Germany. TEL 49-521-585540, FAX 49-521-585371. Ed. Norbert M Hoyer. Circ: 40,000.

796.5 GBR
CARAVAN AND CAMPING GUIDE - BRITAIN & IRELAND (YEAR). Text in English. 19??. a. GBP 7.99 per issue (effective 2009). **Document type:** *Handbook/Manual/Guide, Consumer.* **Description:** Contains over 1,000 annually inspected caravan and camping parks with each site inspected by the AA and graded.
Former titles (until 1996): Britain's Best Camping and Caravanning Parks; Camping and Caravanning in Britain; Camping and Caravanning in the U.K.
Published by: (Automobile Association), A A Publishing, Contact Ctr, Lambert House, Stockport Rd, Cheadle, Hants SK8 2DY, United Kingdom. TEL 44-161-4958945, FAX 44-161-4887544, customer.services@theAA.com, http://www.theaa.com.

CARAVAN AND OUTDOOR LIFE. *see* TRAVEL AND TOURISM

796.5 SWE ISSN 0008-6169
CARAVAN BLADET. Text in Swedish. 1958. bi-m. SEK 225 domestic; SEK 375 foreign (effective 2007). adv. illus. **Document type:** *Magazine, Consumer.*
Published by: Caravan Club of Sweden, Kyrkvaegen 25, Oerebro, 70375, Sweden. TEL 46-19-234610, FAX 46-19-234425, kansli@caravanclub.se, http://www.caravanclub.se. Pub. Stig E Stenberg. Adv. contact Meta Hagsten. B&W page SEK 5,500, color page SEK 7,600; trim 265 x 185. Circ: 14,000.

796.5 GBR ISSN 1369-5088
THE CARAVAN CLUB MAGAZINE. Text in English. 1974. m. free to members (effective 2009). adv. bk.rev. back issues avail. **Document type:** *Magazine, Consumer.* **Description:** Contains full of news and views about touring features, not just about club events and services.
Formerly (until 1997): En Route
Related titles: Online - full text ed.
Published by: Caravan Club, East Grinstead House, East Grinstead, W Sussex RH19 1UA, United Kingdom. TEL 44-1342-336804, FAX 44-1342-410258, enquiries@caravanclub.co.uk, http://www.caravanclub.co.uk. Ed. Gray Martin. Adv. contact Richard Cochrane TEL 44-20-78782318. B&W page GBP 4,626, color page GBP 6,431.

CARAVAN E CAMPER. *see* TRAVEL AND TOURISM

796.93 GBR ISSN 1479-7615
CARAVAN, MOTORHOME AND CAMPING MART. Text in English. 1988. m. GBP 16.99 domestic (effective 2009). adv. illus. back issues avail. **Document type:** *Magazine, Consumer.* **Description:** Helps in choosing/buying a used motorhome, caravan or camping equipment.
Formerly (until 2003): Caravan, Motorcaravan & Camping Mart (0956-6562)
—CCC.
Published by: Warners Group Publications Plc., The Maltings, Manor Ln, Bourne, Lincs PE10 9PH, United Kingdom. TEL 44-1778-391000, wgpsubs@warnersgroup.co.uk, http://www.warnersgroup.co.uk. Ed. Peter Sharpe TEL 44-1778-392059.

CARAVANING & CAMPING. *see* TRAVEL AND TOURISM

796.54 910.91 NLD ISSN 1571-4403
CARAVANNEN!. Text in Dutch. 1990. q. EUR 14.95 (effective 2010). **Document type:** *Magazine, Consumer.*
Formerly (until 2002): Caravan en Motorhome Sport (1386-1778)
Published by: Uitgeverij Interdijk BV, Postbus 10, Uithoorn, 1420 AA, Netherlands. TEL 31-297-566385, FAX 31-297-531051, info@interdijk.nl.

799.1 ITA ISSN 2036-9697
▼ **CARP & CATFISHING.** Text in Italian. 2010. bi-m. **Document type:** *Magazine, Consumer.*
Published by: Ediservice Casa Editrice Firenze, Via XX Settembre 60, Florence, 50129, Italy. TEL 39-055-4625293, FAX 39-055-4633331, info@ediservice.it, http://www.ediservice.it.

799.1 GBR
CARP - TALK; the only weekly news magazine for carp anglers. Text in English. 1994. w. GBP 90 domestic; GBP 110 foreign; GBP 1.70 newsstand/cover (effective 2009). adv. **Document type:** *Magazine, Consumer.* **Description:** Contains information about carp fishing.
Related titles: Online - full text ed.
Published by: Carp Fishing News Ltd., Newport, East Yorkshire HU15 2QG, United Kingdom. TEL 44-1430-440624, FAX 44-1430-441319, carper@btconnect.com. Eds. Kevin Clifford, Simon Crow. Adv. contact Chris Ball TEL 44-1590-678400. **Dist. by:** Comag, Tavistock Rd, W Drayton, Middlesex UB7 7QE, United Kingdom.

799.1 FRA ISSN 2107-4909
▼ **CARPE NATURE**; le magazine des carpistes amoureux de la nature. Text in French. 2010. bi-m. EUR 4.90 per issue (effective 2011). **Document type:** *Magazine, Consumer.*
Published by: Edipeche, 31 Rue Bapst, Asnieres-sur-Seine, 92600, France. Ed. Nicolas Beroud.

799.1 ITA ISSN 1123-9670
CARPFISHING. Cover title: Pescare Carpfishing. Text in Italian. 1994. bi-m. EUR 27 domestic (effective 2008). adv. video rev. 96 p./no.; back issues avail. **Document type:** *Magazine, Consumer.* **Description:** Includes techniques for carp fishing, as well as information on tools and clubs.
Published by: Gruppo Editoriale Olimpia SpA, Via E Fermi 24, Loc Osmannoro, Sesto Fiorentino, FI 50129, Italy. TEL 39-055-30321, FAX 39-055-3032280, http://www.edolimpia.it. Circ: 25,000. **Dist. by:** Parrini & C, Piazza Colonna 361, Rome, RM 00187, Italy. TEL 39-06-695141.

799.1 ITA ISSN 1828-5511
CARPFISHING MAGAZINE. Text in Italian. 2006. m. **Document type:** *Magazine, Consumer.*
Published by: Acacia Edizioni, Via Copernico 3, Binasco, MI 20082, Italy. http://www.acaciaedizioni.com.

799.1 GBR ISSN 0957-8528
CARPWORLD. Text in English. 1988. m. GBP 50; GBP 4.40 newsstand/cover (effective 2009). adv. back issues avail. **Document type:** *Magazine, Consumer.* **Description:** Features the most technical in carp fishing rigs and tactics.
Related titles: Online - full text ed.
Published by: Angling Publications Ltd., Regent House, 101 Broadfield Rd, Sheffield, S8 0XH, United Kingdom. TEL 44-114-2580812, FAX 44-114-2582728, info@anglingpublications.co.uk. Eds. Lewis Porter TEL 44-114-2580812 ext 209, Martin Ford TEL 44-114-2580812 ext 214. Adv. contact Philippa Dean TEL 44-114-2580812 ext 202. **Dist. by:** Comag Magazine Marketing.

796.172 GBR ISSN 1354-5086
CARVE SURFING MAGAZINE. Text in English. 19??. 9/yr. GBP 29.99 domestic; GBP 36.99 in Europe; GBP 53.99 elsewhere (effective 2009). adv. back issues avail. **Document type:** *Magazine, Consumer.* **Description:** Aimed at surfers, includes travel photo stories, news, international and British competition coverage, and 'how to' features.
Formerly (until 1994): Groundswell
Published by: Orca Publications Ltd., Berry Rd Studios, Berry Rd, Newquay, Cornwall TR7 1AT, United Kingdom. TEL 44-1637-878074, FAX 44-1637-850226, info@orcasurf.co.uk, http://www.orcasurf.co.uk. Adv. contact Steve England. **Dist. by:** USM.

CATALOGUE OF CANADIAN RECREATION AND LEISURE RESEARCH. *see* LEISURE AND RECREATION

799.1 USA ISSN 1088-3029
CATFISH GUIDE. Text in English. 1996. a. price varies. adv. back issues avail. **Document type:** *Magazine, Consumer.* **Description:** Recommends prime areas for angling for catfish. Offers tips on techniques and equipment, as well as information on fisheries and boats, and recipes.

S

Published by: Source Interlink Companies, 6420 Wilshire Blvd, 10th Fl, Los Angeles, CA 90048. TEL 323-782-2000, FAX 323-782-2585, dheine@sourceinterlink.com, http://www.sourceinterlinkmedia.com. adv.: B&W page USD 3,500; color page USD 4,725; trim 10.5 x 7.88. Circ: 200,000 (paid).

799.1 USA ISSN 1544-709X
SH691.C35
CATFISH IN-SIDER. GUIDE. Text in English. 199?. 8/yr. USD 16 domestic; USD 29 in Canada; USD 31 elsewhere (effective 2007). **Document type:** *Magazine, Consumer.*
Formerly (until 2000): Catfish In-sider (1537-1298)
Published by: Source Interlink Companies, 6420 Wilshire Blvd, 10th Fl, Los Angeles, CA 90048. TEL 323-782-2000, FAX 323-782-2585, dheine@sourceinterlink.com, http://www.sourceinterlink.com. Eds. Steve Quinin, Doug Stange. Pub. Steve Hoffman.

799.2 ESP
CAZA FEDER. Text in Spanish. m. EUR 3.95 newsstand/cover (effective 2009). adv. **Document type:** *Magazine, Consumer.*
Published by: Grupo V, C Valportillo Primera, 11, Alcobendas, Madrid, 28108, Spain. TEL 34-91-6622137, FAX 34-91-6622654, secretaria@grupov.es, http://www.grupov.es/. Ed. Jose Carlos Garcia. Adv. contact Rafael Morillo. page EUR 3,900; trim 18.5 x 26.5. Circ: 52,954.

799.2 ESP
CAZA MAYOR. Text in Spanish. m. adv. **Document type:** *Magazine, Consumer.* **Description:** Dedicated to the enthusiast hunters and safari lovers.
Published by: Grupo V, C Valportillo Primera, 11, Alcobendas, Madrid, 28108, Spain. TEL 34-91-6622137, FAX 34-91-6622654. Ed. Jose Carlos Garcia. Adv. contact Rafael Morillo. page EUR 2,420; bleed 19.5 x 26.7. Circ: 25,310.

799.2 ESP
CAZA OCASION. Text in Spanish. bi-m. EUR 2.95 newsstand/cover (effective 2009). adv. **Document type:** *Magazine, Consumer.*
Published by: Grupo V, C Valportillo Primera, 11, Alcobendas, Madrid, 28108, Spain. TEL 34-91-6622137, FAX 34-91-6622654, secretaria@grupov.es, http://www.grupov.es/. Ed. Jose Carlos Garcia. Adv. contact Rafael Morillo. page EUR 1,030; trim 18.5 x 25.5. Circ: 50,000.

799 VEN
CAZA Y PESCA NAUTICA. Text in Spanish. 1954. m. USD 25. adv. **Description:** Cover fishing, hunting and water sports.
Address: P.O. Box 60.764, Caracas, 1060 A, Venezuela. Ed. Heinz R Doebbel. Circ: 25,500.

799.2 ESP
CAZAR MAS. Text in Spanish. m. EUR 5.95 newsstand/cover (effective 2009). adv. **Document type:** *Magazine, Consumer.*
Published by: Grupo V, C Valportillo Primera, 11, Alcobendas, Madrid, 28108, Spain. TEL 34-91-6622137, FAX 34-91-6622654, secretaria@grupov.es. Ed. Jose Carlos Garcia. Adv. contact Rafael Morillo. page EUR 1,815; trim 19.5 x 26.7. Circ: 35,400.

796.54 CAN ISSN 1911-9437
LES CENTRES DE VACANCES FAMILIALES. Text in French. 1994. a. **Document type:** *Journal, Consumer.*
Former titles (until 2007): Camps Familiaux (1711-8042); (until 2004): Repertoire du Mouvement Quebecois des Camps Familiaux (1196-5517)
Published by: Mouvement Quebecois des Vacances Familiales, 4545 Av. Pierre De Coubertin, B P 1000, Montreal, PQ H1V 3R2, Canada. TEL 514-252-3118, FAX 514-252-4302, mqvf@vacancesfamiliales.qc.ca, http://www.vacancesfamiliales.qc.ca.

799.2 FRA ISSN 1770-443X
CHARC; le magazine de la chasse a l'arc. Text in French. 2005. q. EUR 25 domestic; EUR 32 foreign (effective 2009). back issues avail. **Document type:** *Magazine, Consumer.*
Published by: Editions Crepin-Leblond, 14 rue du Patronage Laique, Chaumont, 52000, France. TEL 33-3-25038748, FAX 33-3-25038740, crepin-leblond@graphycom.com.

799.2 USA ISSN 0009-1952
SK284
THE CHASE; a full cry of hunting. Text in English. 1920. 11/yr. USD 30 domestic; USD 32 in Canada; USD 34 elsewhere (effective 2006). adv. bk.rev. tr.lit.; illus. 130 p./no. 4 cols./p.; **Document type:** *Magazine, Trade.* **Description:** Includes listings, registrations, results of field trials, plus articles and stories.
Published by: Chase Publishing Co., Inc., 1150 Industry Rd, PO Box 55090, Lexington, KY 40555. TEL 859-254-4262, FAX 859-254-3145, chasepubl@aol.com. Ed., R&P, Adv. contact JoAnn Stone. B&W page USD 177. Circ: 3,300 (paid).

799.2 FRA ISSN 1774-9700
CHASSE INFO 03. Text in French. 2002. s-a. **Document type:** *Bulletin, Consumer.*
Published by: Federation Departementale des Chasseurs de l'Allier, 6 av Victor Hugo, Moulins, 03000, France.

799.2 FRA ISSN 1283-6478
CHASSE SANGLIER PASSION. Text in French. 1998. bi-m. EUR 28 domestic; EUR 41 DOM-TOM; EUR 41 in the European Union; EUR 46 elsewhere (effective 2011). **Document type:** *Magazine, Consumer.*
Related titles: Supplement(s): Chasse Sanglier Passion. Hors-serie. ISSN 2105-6005. 2009.
Published by: Editions du Marcassin, 32 Rue de Paradis, Paris, 75010, France. TEL 33-1-44799770, FAX 33-1-40229994, sanglierpassion@editions-versicolor.com, http://www.sanglier-passion.com. Ed. Pierre Vincent TEL 33-5-81331081.

796 FRA ISSN 0750-3334
LE CHASSEUR FRANCAIS. Text in French. 1885. m. EUR 27.90 (effective 2008). **Document type:** *Magazine, Consumer.* **Description:** Publishes articles on the joys of the outdoors, including fishing and hunting.
Published by: Mondadori France, 1 Rue du Colonel Pierre-Avia, Paris, Cedex 15 75754, France. TEL 33-1-46484848, contact@mondadori.fr, http://www.mondadori.fr. Circ: 504,887 (paid).

CHATAR & CHALUPAR; casopis pro kutily, chatare a chalupare. *see* ARCHITECTURE

796 USA
CHEVY OUTDOORS SPORTING JOURNAL. Text in English. 2008. q. USD 29.95 (effective 2008). adv. **Document type:** *Magazine, Consumer.* **Description:** Delivers the outdoors experience through a combination of storytelling and photography. Covers hunting, fishing, camping and boating. Also explores key issues, such as conservation efforts to preserve the environments.
Published by: Campbell - Ewald Publishing, 30400 Van Dyke, Warren, MI 48093-2316. TEL 586-558-5202, FAX 586-558-5870, http://www.campbell-ewald.com/. Adv. contact Tom Krempel TEL 586-558-4502. color page USD 12,927; trim 8 x 10.5. Circ: 300,000.

796.552 USA
CHICAGO MOUNTAINEER. Text in English. 1945. s-a. USD 10. bk.rev. bibl. **Description:** Covers technical rock climbing. Includes reports on expeditions and personal experiences.
Published by: (Chicago Mountaineering Club), Data Base Management Services, 998 Lake Country Ct, Oconomowoc, WI 53066. TEL 414-567-1110. Ed. David L Harrison. Circ: 350. **Subscr. to:** Chicago Mountaineering Club, 22 S Thurlow St, Hinsdale, IL 60921.

796.93 305.4 FRA ISSN 1952-7586
CHICKS POWER. Text in French. 200?. bi-m. **Document type:** *Magazine, Consumer.*
Formerly (until 2006): Girl Power (1950-3830)
Published by: Blink Editions, 18 Rue de Sully, Biarritz, 64200, France.

CHIEN DE CHASSE MAGAZINE. *see* PETS

796 USA
CHOCONUT FOUNDATION NEWSLETTER. Text in English. 1985. 4/yr. looseleaf. USD 10 to members. **Document type:** *Newsletter.* **Description:** News of foundation activities in outdoor education and recreation, with announcements of meetings and reports from members.
Supersedes (1896-1985): Choconut News
Published by: Choconut Foundation, H C R 19, Stephentown, NY 12168. Ed. Dan Lorber. **Subscr. to:** Urko Wood, Treas, 105 S Narberth Ave, Narberth, PA 19072. TEL 215-668-9397.

799.1 CHN ISSN 1009-7910
CHUIDIAO. Text in Chinese. 2001. m. **Document type:** *Magazine, Consumer.*
Published by: Chuidiao Zazhishe, 15, Ningshen Zhong Lu, Shenyang, 110031, China. TEL 86-24-86863100.

796.42 JPN
CITY RUNNER. Text in Japanese. 1983. m. JPY 4,560.
Published by: Gakken Co. Ltd., 1-17-15, Nakaikegami, Otaku, Tokyo, 145-0064, Japan. Ed. Masahiro Onuma.

796.95 USA
CIY SLEDDER. Text in English. q.
Published by: Midwest Sports Publishing Network, 3432 Hwy 101 S, Minnetonka, MN 55345. TEL 952-473-7870, FAX 952-473-7805.

CLAY SHOOTING; for the sporting clays, five stand and parcours de chasse shooter. *see* SPORTS AND GAMES

799.313 GBR ISSN 1479-2885
CLAY SHOOTING USA. Variant title: ClayShootingUSA. Text in English. 2002. bi-m. USD 31.95 in United States; USD 62.95 elsewhere (effective 2010). adv. **Document type:** *Magazine, Consumer.*
Published by: Brunton Business Publications Ltd., 1 Salisbury Office Park, London Rd, Salisbury, Wiltshire SP1 3HP, United Kingdom. TEL 44-1722-337038, publications@brunton.co.uk, http://www.brunton.co.uk. Pub. Dan Brunton. Adv. contact Ben Brunton. **Subscr. to:** 1100 NW Loop 410, Ste 102, San Antonio, TX 78213. TEL 210-377-1117, FAX 210-377-1119, subscriptions@clayshootingusa.com.

796.522 DEU ISSN 1867-9854
CLIMB!; Klettern drinnen und draussen. Text in German. 2006. q. EUR 18.64; EUR 4.90 newsstand/cover (effective 2009). adv. **Document type:** *Magazine, Consumer.*
Published by: Bruckmann Verlag GmbH, Infanteriestr 11a, Munich, 80797, Germany. TEL 49-89-13069911, FAX 49-89-13069910, info@bruckmann-verlag.de, http://www.bruckmann-verlag.de. Ed. Andreas Kubin. Adv. contact Judith Fischl. color page EUR 2,950; trim 210 x 280. Circ: 11,658 (paid).

796.522 GBR ISSN 1745-2775
GV199.8
CLIMB MAGAZINE. Text in English. 2005. m. GBP 35 domestic; GBP 50 in Europe; GBP 70 elsewhere; GBP 4 per issue domestic; GBP 6 per issue in Europe; GBP 8 per issue elsewhere (effective 2009). adv. back issues avail. **Document type:** *Magazine, Consumer.* **Description:** Covers hiking, climbing and outdoor recreation.
Related titles: Online - full text ed.
Published by: Greenshires Publishing Limited, 160-164 Barkby Rd, Leicester, LE16 8FZ, United Kingdom. TEL 44-116-2022600, FAX 44-116-2769002, subscriptions@climbmagazine.com, http://www.greenshires.com. Ed. Neil Pearsons TEL 44-1298-72801.

796.522 GBR ISSN 1358-5207
CLIMBER. Text in English. 1961. m. GBP 35 domestic; GBP 47 in Europe; GBP 60 elsewhere (effective 2009). adv. bk.rev. charts; illus.; tr.lit. reprints avail. **Document type:** *Magazine, Consumer.* **Description:** Reports on competitions, news and new equipment and gear for the climbing enthusiast.
Former titles (until 1995): Climber and Hillwalker (0955-3045); (until 1988): Climber (0953-1319); (until 1986): Climber and Rambler (0009-8973); (until 1969): Climber (0529-9578)
Indexed: SD, SportS.
—Ingenta.
Published by: Warners Group Publications Plc., The Maltings, Manor Ln, Bourne, Lincs PE10 9PH, United Kingdom. TEL 44-1778-391000, wgpsubs@warnersgroup.co.uk, http://www.warnersgroup.co.uk. Ed. Andy McCue TEL 44-1778-392425. Adv. contact Emma Howl TEL 44-1778-392443.

796.552 NZL ISSN 1174-216X
CLIMBER; New Zealand's climbing magazine. Text in English. 1992. q. NZD 28; NZD 8.95 newsstand/cover (effective 2008). adv. back issues avail. **Document type:** *Magazine, Consumer.* **Description:** Covers new routes, access, people, huts, environmental issues, new products, safety issues, training, techniques, and books, as well as New Zealand Alpine Club news. Guides to new areas are a regular feature, together with in-depth feature articles.
Formerly (until 1997): New Zealand Climber (1171-4328)
Published by: New Zealand Alpine Club Inc., Christchurch Mail Centre 8140, PO Box 786, Christchurch, New Zealand. TEL 64-3-3777595, FAX 64-3-3777594. Ed., Adv. contact Kester Brown. Circ: 3,000.

796.522 USA ISSN 0045-7159
GV199.4
CLIMBING. Text in English. 1970. 9/yr. USD 14.97 domestic; USD 29.97 in Canada; USD 34.97 elsewhere (effective 2008). adv. bk.rev. charts; illus. 174 p./no.; back issues avail.; reprints avail. **Document type:** *Magazine, Consumer.* **Description:** Every issue contains practical information about climbing destinations, equipment, training and techniques, as well as compelling first-hand accounts, fascinating profiles and great photography.
Related titles: Online - full text ed.
Indexed: B04, G09, P02, P10, P19, P48, P53, P54, PQC, R03, RGAb, RGPR, SportS, W03, W05.
—IE, Ingenta. **CCC.**
Published by: Source Interlink Companies, 1260 Yellow Pine Ave, Boulder, CO 80304. TEL 303-225-4628, FAX 303-417-1371, dheine@sourceinterlink.com, http://www.sourceinterlinkmedia.com. Ed. Douglas Glad. Pub. John Gallagher TEL 323-782-2733. adv.: B&W page USD 5,195, color page USD 7,095. Circ: 38,263 (paid).

796.522 USA
CLIMBING EYEWITNESS. Text in English. 2001. 9/yr. USD 29.95; USD 5.95 newsstand/cover (effective 2002). adv. **Document type:** *Magazine, Consumer.*
Published by: Climbing Magazine, 326 Hwy 133, Ste 190, Carbondale, CO 81623. Ed. Michael Benge. Pub. Duane Raleigh.

▼ **CLOSE-UP (DUTCH EDITION).** *see* LEISURE AND RECREATION

799.1 GBR ISSN 0309-8281
COARSE FISHERMAN; the magazine for serious anglers. Text in English. 1975. m. GBP 35.40 domestic; GBP 46 in Europe; GBP 53 elsewhere; GBP 2.95 per issue (effective 2009). adv. back issues avail. **Document type:** *Magazine, Trade.*
Published by: MetroCrest Ltd., 67 Tyrrell St, Leicester, Leics LE3 5SB, United Kingdom. Ed. Stu Dexter TEL 44-116-2894567. Adv. contact Ross O'Loughlin TEL 44-1778-392459. **Dist. by:** Comag.

799.1 ITA ISSN 2038-8454
▼ **COLLEZIONE ABC DELLA PESCA.** Text in Italian. 2010. a.
Published by: Corrado Tedeschi Editore, Via Guglielmo Massaia 98, Florence, FI 50134, Italy. TEL 39-055-495213, FAX 39-055-4627290, http://www.tedeschi-net.it.

799.1 ITA ISSN 2036-7112
▼ **COLLEZIONE PESCA IN MARE.** Text in Italian. 2009. q. **Document type:** *Magazine, Consumer.*
Published by: Ediservice Casa Editrice Firenze, Via XX Settembre 60, Florence, 50129, Italy. TEL 39-055-4625293, FAX 39-055-4633331, info@ediservice.it, http://www.ediservice.it.

796 636.596 BEL ISSN 0773-1825
LA COLOMBOPHILIE BELGE. Text in French. 1945. w. adv. bibl.; illus. **Document type:** *Newspaper.*
Former titles (until 1959): La Nouvelle Colombophilie Belge (0773-1817); (until 1954): La Colombophilie Belge (0010-1427)
Published by: Herbots Family, Dungelstr 35, Halle-Booienhoven, 3440, Belgium. TEL 32-11-789190, FAX 32-11-780738, jo@herbots.com, http://www.herbots.be/en/index.asp. Circ: 15,000.

796 USA
COLORADO EXPLORER MAGAZINE. Text in English. 2007 (Jan.). bi-m. (m. in 2007). **Document type:** *Magazine, Consumer.* **Description:** Contains articles and photographs of the Rocky Mountain region, including travel, advanture, places and people stories.
Address: 16316 Prairie Farm Circle, Parker, CO 80134. Ed. Jon Thiessen.

799 USA ISSN 0010-1699
SK351
COLORADO OUTDOORS. Text in English. 1938. bi-m. USD 10.50 (effective 2011). charts; illus. index. **Document type:** *Magazine, Government.* **Description:** Contains information about Colorado and its hunting, fishing and wildlife viewing opportunities.
Former titles (until 1956): Colorado Conservation; (until 1950): Colorado Conservation Comments
Indexed: KWIWR, W08, WildRev.
—Ingenta.
Published by: Division of Wildlife, 6060 Broadway, Denver, CO 80216. TEL 303-297-1192.

796.552 ITA ISSN 0391-1764
COMMISSIONE GROTTE EUGENIO BOEGAN. ATTI E MEMORIE. Text in Italian. 1960. a. **Document type:** *Monographic series, Academic/Scholarly.*
Indexed: GeoRef, Z01.
Published by: Club Alpino Italiano, Societa Alpina delle Giulie, Via Donata 2, Trieste, 34121, Italy. TEL 39-040-630464, http://www.caisag.ts.it.

796.5 PRT ISSN 0010-3969
COMPANHEIROS. Text in Portuguese. 6/yr. free. bk.rev. illus.
Published by: Clube de Campismo de Lisboa, Rua da Misericordia, 137 Andar 2, Lisbon, 1200, Portugal. Ed. Armando Almeida Henriques.

799.1 ZAF
THE COMPLETE FLY FISHERMAN; South Africa's fresh and salt water fly fishing magazine. Text in English. 1993. m. ZAR 120; ZAR 10.95 newsstand/cover. adv. illus.; maps. back issues avail. **Document type:** *Magazine, Consumer.* **Description:** Offers high-quality, stimulating articles on fly fishing for people from all walks of life.
Published by: Complete Fly Fisherman, PO Box 3083, Pretoria, 0001, South Africa. TEL 27-12-322-6774, FAX 27-12-320-4579. Ed., Pub. P.J. Jacobs. R&P P J Jacobs. Adv. contact Frank Burton. color page ZAR 8,475; trim 280 x 210. Circ: 11,000 (paid); 3,000 (controlled). **Dist. by:** Junkmail, PO Box 6574, Pretoria 0001, South Africa. TEL 27-11-804-1299, FAX 27-11-804-6008.

799.1 ZAF ISSN 1819-1991
THE COMPLETE GUIDE TO BASS FISHING SOUTHERN AFRICA. Text in English. 2006. biennial. ZAR 265 per issue (effective 2007).
Published by: (South African Bass Angling Association), Associated Media International, PO Box 519, Cramerview, 2060, South Africa. TEL 27-11-4677007, FAX 27-11-4677003, info@amint.co.za, http://www.technikons.co.za.

799.2 FRA ISSN 0396-5678
CONNAISSANCE DE LA CHASSE. Text in French. 1976. m. EUR 55 (effective 2009). adv. **Document type:** *Magazine, Consumer.*
Indexed: RASB.
Published by: Editions Lariviere, 6 Rue Olof Palme, Clichy, 92587, France. TEL 33-1-47565400, http://www.editions-lariviere.fr. Ed. Jacques Tillier. Adv. contact Marc Defougerolles.

333.7 USA ISSN 0092-5764
SD1
CONNECTICUT WALK BOOK. Text in English. 1937. irreg., latest vol.18, 1997. USD 18 (effective 1999). adv. illus. **Document type:** *Magazine, Consumer.* **Description:** Presents a guide to hiking trails in Connecticut.
Published by: Connecticut Forest and Park Association, Inc., Middlefield, 16 Meriden Rd, Rockfall, CT 06481-2961. http://www.ctwoodlands.org. Ed. John Barrett. Adv. contact Kathy Rankin.

799.3 USA
COON-HOUND CORNER. Text in English. bi-m.
Address: 2298 S Elliott Rd, S W, Stockport, OH 43787. TEL 614-557-3248, FAX 614-557-3253. Ed. Katherine A Janson. Circ: 9,000.

636.7 799.2 USA ISSN 1067-0920
COONHOUND BLOODLINES. Text in English. 1973. m. USD 25 domestic; USD 35 foreign; USD 4.50 per issue (effective 2005). adv. bk.rev. **Document type:** *Magazine, Consumer.* **Description:** Contains information about raccoon, bobcat and bear hunting, and coonhound field trials.
Published by: United Kennel Club, Inc., 100 E Kilgore Rd, Kalamazoo, MI 49002-5584. TEL 269-343-9020, FAX 269-343-7037. Ed., R&P Vicki Rand. Adv. contacts Kairee Thayer, Rosie Reeves. Circ: 17,000 (paid).

799.1 LVA ISSN 1407-3269
COPES LIETAS. Text in Latvian. 1997. m. LVL 18.90 (effective 2011). adv. **Document type:** *Magazine, Consumer.*
Published by: Izdevnieciba Lilita SIA, Mukusala Business Centre, Mukusalas Str 41B, Riga, 1004, Latvia. TEL 371-67061600, FAX 371-67616050, izdevnieciba@lilita.lv, http://www.lilita.lv. Ed. Aldis Miesnieks. Adv. contact Ilze Ozola.

790 CRI
COSTA RICA OUTDOORS. Text in English. bi-m. **Document type:** *Magazine, Consumer.*
Published by: Jerda S.A. Pub., PO Box 199-6150, San Jose, Costa Rica. TEL 506-282-6743, 506-282-7241, 506-282-6260, 506-282-6514. Ed. A Koutnik. Adv. contact Alfonso Acosta.

COUNTRY ILLUSTRATED. *see* LIFESTYLE

796 GBR ISSN 0953-2757
COUNTRY WALKING. Text in English. 1987. 13/yr. GBP 45 domestic; GBP 60 foreign; GBP 3.90 newsstand/cover (effective 2009). adv. bk.rev. back issues avail. **Document type:** *Magazine, Consumer.* **Description:** Provides guidance to the countryside including over 27 planned walks every month.
Published by: H. Bauer Publishing Ltd. (Subsidiary of: Bauer Media Group), Academic House, 24-28 Oval Rd, London, NW1 7DT, United Kingdom. TEL 44-20-72418000, FAX 44-20-72418030, http://www.bauer.co.uk. Ed. Jonathan Manning TEL 44-1733-468208. Adv. contact Justin Gould TEL 44-1733-468330. **Subscr. to:** Tower House, Sovereign Park, Market Harborough, Leicestershire LE16 9EF, United Kingdom. TEL 44-1858-438866, subs@greatmagazines.co.uk.

799.2 GBR ISSN 1350-9683
THE COUNTRYMAN'S WEEKLY; Britain's countrysports newspaper. Text in English. 1985. w. GBP 81; GBP 9.99 per issue domestic; GBP 11.50 per issue in Europe (effective 2009). adv. bk.rev. **Document type:** *Newspaper, Consumer.* **Description:** Covers ferreting, trapping, stalking, gundogs, lurchers and terriers, horses, wildfowling, game shooting, clay shooting and other topics.
Former titles (until 19??): Shooting News and Country Weekly; (until 1993): Shooting News and Weekly (0954-8718); Which was formed by the merger of (19??-1985): Shooting Weekly; (1983-1985): Shooting News (0955-579X)
Published by: Countrywide Periodical Publishing Ltd., PO Box 258, Plymouth, PL5 9AE, United Kingdom. TEL 44-1752-762990, FAX 44-1752-762990. Adv. contact Tracy Allan TEL 44-1822-855281. color page GBP 560.

796 GBR
COUNTRYSIDE ALLIANCE. UPDATE. Variant title: Country Sports Campaign Update. Text in English. 1999. q. GBP 51 membership (effective 2009). adv. 20 p./no.; **Document type:** *Newsletter.* **Description:** Promotes the Alliance's interests and shares news, developments and information about upcoming events with its members.
Former titles (until 2006): Campaign Update; (until 2003): Real Countryside; (until 2002): Country Sports
Published by: (Countryside Alliance), Archant Dialogue Ltd. (Subsidiary of: Archant Group), Prospect House, Rouen Rd, Norwich, NR1 1RE, United Kingdom. TEL 44-1603-664242, FAX 44-1603-627823. adv.: page GBP 3,360; trim 210 x 297. Circ: 76,000 (controlled).

CRAPPIE WORLD. *see* FISH AND FISHERIES

796.93 USA
CROSS COUNTRY SKI AREA OPERATIONS SURVEY. Text in English. 1985. a. USD 100. back issues avail. **Document type:** *Guide, Consumer.* **Description:** For the industry covering revenue, skier visits, growth, and grooming patterns.
Published by: Cross Country Ski Areas Association, 259 Bolton Rd, Winchester, NH 03470. TEL 603-239-4341, 877-779-2754, FAX 603-239-6387, ccsaa@xcski.org, http://www.xcski.org. Circ: 250.

796.93 USA ISSN 0278-9213
GV854.4
CROSS COUNTRY SKIER. Text in English. 1976. q. USD 14.95 (effective 2010). adv. bk.rev. illus. back issues avail.; reprints avail. **Document type:** *Magazine, Consumer.* **Description:** Devoted to cross country skiing. Provides information for both novice and expert skiers in tuning up techniques, buying equipment, and finding new places to ski.
Formerly (until 1981): Nordic Skiing (0164-6974)
Related titles: Online - full text ed.; Supplement(s): Cross Country Annual.
Indexed: A22, G06, G07, G08, I05, I06, I07, S23, SD, SPI, SportS.
—Ingenta.
Published by: Country Skier, LLC, PO Box 550, Cable, WI 54821. TEL 715-798-5500, FAX 715-798-3599. Ed., Pub. Ron Bergin.

796.93 FIN ISSN 1795-7818
CROSSCOUNTRY; maastohiihdon erikoislehti. Text in Finnish. 2005. q. **Document type:** *Magazine, Consumer.*
Published by: Egmont Kustannus Oy, PO Box 317, Tampere, 33101, Finland. TEL 358-201-332222, FAX 358-201-332278, info@egmont-kustannus.fi, http://www.egmont-kustannus.fi. Adv. contact Tommy Tenhunen TEL 358-201-332266. Circ: 14,000.

CYCLE. *see* SPORTS AND GAMES—Bicycles And Motorcycles

CYCLE SPORTS; for bikers only. *see* SPORTS AND GAMES—Bicycles And Motorcycles

796.522 DEU ISSN 1437-5923
D A V PANORAMA. Text in German. 1948. bi-m. free to members (effective 2011). adv. bk.rev. illus. index. back issues avail. **Document type:** *Magazine, Consumer.* **Description:** Covers mountaineering in the Alps.
Formerly (until 1999): Deutscher Alpenverein (0012-1088)
Related titles: Online - full text ed.
Indexed: SpeleolAb.
Published by: Deutscher Alpenverein, Von-Kahr-Str 2-4, Munich, 80997, Germany. TEL 49-89-140030, FAX 49-89-1400323, http://www.alpenverein.de. Ed., R&P Georg Hohenester. Adv. contact Silvia Schreck TEL 49-89-55241252. Circ: 529,092 (paid and controlled). **Subscr. to:** DAV Service GmbH, Postfach 600303, Munich 81203, Germany. TEL 49-89-8299940, FAX 49-89-82999414. **Dist. by:** Konzept Verlagsgesellschaft mbH, Ludwigstr 33-37, Frankfurt Am Main 60327, Germany. TEL 49-69-97460340, FAX 49-69-974608340.

D C C - CARAVAN UND MOTORCARAVAN MODELLFUEHRER. *see* TRANSPORTATION—Automobiles

D C C - TOURISTIK SERVICE. *see* TRAVEL AND TOURISM

796 DEU ISSN 0177-7149
D V V - KURIER. (Deutscher Volkssportverband) Text in German. 1971. 6/yr. EUR 2.30 newsstand/cover (effective 2010). adv. back issues avail. **Document type:** *Magazine, Consumer.*
Published by: Deutscher Volkssportverband e.V., Fabrikstr 8, Altoetting, 84503, Germany. TEL 49-8671-96310, FAX 49-8671-963131, geschaeftsstelle@dvv-wandern.de.

790.1 USA ISSN 1086-9557
DAILY BREAD MAGAZINE; inline skate magazine. Text in English. 1993. m. USD 21.95 domestic; USD 33.95 in Canada; USD 51.95 elsewhere (effective 2005). adv. **Document type:** *Magazine, Consumer.* **Description:** Covers the complete street skater's package - gear, clothes and lifestyle.
Formerly (until 1994): Daily Bread Skate Magazine (1086-9549)
Address: PO Box 121910, San Diego, CA 92112. TEL 619-744-0848 Ext 14, publisher@dbmag.com. Ed. Justin Eisinger. Pub. Angie Walton. adv.: B&W page USD 1,327, color page USD 2,250; trim 8.125 x 10.75. Circ: 15,420 (paid).

796.93 GBR ISSN 0960-6157
DAILY MAIL SKI. Text in English. m. GBP 35.40 domestic; GBP 45 foreign; GBP 2.95 newsstand/cover. adv. **Document type:** *Magazine, Consumer.* **Description:** Offers the ski enthusiast a range of articles and material on the issues that are at the heart of the skiing world.
Published by: D M G Pinnacle Ltd., Equitable House, Lyon Rd, Harrow, Middx HA1 2EW, United Kingdom. TEL 44-181-515-2000, FAX 44-181-515-2080. Ed. Dave Watts. Pub. Marie Francis. Adv. contact Sergei Sollo. Circ: 25,095 (paid).

796.42 USA ISSN 1069-8795
DAILY RACING FORM (GARDENA). Text in English. 1894. d. USD 5 newsstand/cover; USD 167.75 subscr - mailed (effective 2005). **Document type:** *Newspaper, Consumer.*
Published by: Daily Racing Form LLC, 100 Broadway, 7th Fl., New York, NY 10005-1902. TEL 212-366-7600. Pub. Steven Crist. Adv. contacts Arthur Krawitz, Gary Dworet. Circ: 26,000 morning (paid). Wire service: RN.

799 USA ISSN 0194-5769
DAKOTA COUNTRY. Text in English. 1979. m. USD 16.95 (effective 2007). bk.rev. 80 p./no.; **Document type:** *Magazine, Consumer.* **Description:** Focuses on fishing and hunting in the Dakotas.
Published by: Mitzel Outdoor Publications, Inc., PO Box 2714, Bismarck, ND 58502. TEL 701-255-3031, FAX 701-255-5038. Ed., R&P, Adv. contact William A Mitzel. Circ: 14,500 (paid).

799 USA ISSN 0891-902X
DAKOTA OUTDOORS. Text in English. 1976. m. USD 10 (effective 2000). adv. bk.rev. tr.lit. back issues avail. **Document type:** *Guide, Consumer.* **Description:** Covers all aspects of hunting and fishing as well as outdoor news, legislative, governmental and regulatory concerns. Also provides product information, hints, tips.
Formerly (until 1986): Dakota Fisherman
Related titles: Microfilm ed.
Published by: Hipple Publishing Co., Inc., 333 W Dakota, Box 669, Pierre, SD 57501-0669. TEL 605-224-7301, FAX 605-224-9210. Ed., Pub. Kevin Hipple. R&P Rachel Engbrecht. Adv. contact Alice Burgess. Circ: 8,200 (paid).

DATA; national newsletter for campground buyers & owners. *see* BUSINESS AND ECONOMICS—Small Business

799.1 GBR ISSN 0958-9023
DAVID HALL'S MATCH FISHING MAGAZINE. Variant title: Match Fishing. Text in English. 1986. m. GBP 33.60 domestic; GBP 50 in Europe; GBP 65 elsewhere; GBP 3.15 newsstand/cover (effective 2009). adv. bk.rev. illus. back issues avail. **Document type:** *Magazine, Consumer.*
Published by: David Hall Publishing Ltd. (Subsidiary of: DHP Holdings Ltd.), 2 Stephenson Close, Drayton Fields, Daventry, Northants NN11 8RF, United Kingdom. TEL 44-1327-311999, FAX 44-1327-311190, info@dhpub.co.uk, http://www.davidhallpublishing.com. Ed. Dave Harrell TEL 44-1327-315422. Pub. David Hall TEL 44-1327-315402. Adv. contact Dean Rothery TEL 44-1327-315432. color page GBP 700; 210 x 297. **Dist. by:** M M C Distribution Ltd.

658.91 FRA ISSN 1286-1952
DECISIONS. Text in French. 1998. m. EUR 59 (effective 2009). adv. **Document type:** *Magazine, Trade.*
Published by: Editions Lariviere, 6 Rue Olof Palme, Clichy, 92587, France. TEL 33-1-47565400, http://www.editions-lariviere.fr.

799.2 USA ISSN 0164-7318
DEER & DEER HUNTING; practical & comprehensive information for white-tailed deer hunters. Text in English. 1977. m. USD 23.99; USD 6.99 newsstand/cover (effective 2012); subscr. includes Deer Hunter's Almanac. adv. bk.rev. illus. back issues avail.; reprints avail. **Document type:** *Magazine, Trade.* **Description:** Edited for serious, year-round whitetail hunting enthusiasts and focuses on hunting techniques, deer biology and behavior, deer management, habitat requirements, the natural history of deer, and hunting ethics. Contains how-to articles designed to help hunters be successful, book reviews, unusual observations by deer hunters, new products, photos of deer killed by hunters, letters from readers, and many questions and answers that pertain to today's deer hunter.
Indexed: G08, I05.
—CCC.
Published by: F + W Media Inc., 4700 E Galbraith Rd, Cincinnati, OH 45236. TEL 513-531-2690, contact_us@fwmedia.com, http://www.fwmedia.com/. Ed. Dan Schmidt TEL 715-445-2214 ext 13472. Pub. Brad Rucks TEL 715-445-2214 ext 13486.

799.2 USA
DEER HUNTER'S ALMANAC. Text in English. a. USD 6.95 (effective 2008). 208 p./no.; **Document type:** *Magazine, Consumer.* **Description:** Covers information on how to identify and interpret deer signs, buying a used firearm and state and provincial harvest data.
Published by: Krause Publications, Inc. (Subsidiary of: F + W Media Inc.), 700 E State St, Iola, WI 54990. TEL 715-445-2214, 888-457-2873, FAX 715-445-2164, info@krause.com, http://www.krause.com. Ed. Ryan Gilligan. **Subscr. to:** PO Box 420235, Palm Coast, FL 32142. TEL 386-246-3414, 800-250-9159.

799.2 USA ISSN 1931-3934
DELTA WATERFOWL MAGAZINE. Text in English. 2004. irreg. **Document type:** *Magazine, Consumer.*
Published by: Delta Waterfowl Foundation, PO Box 3128, Bismarck, ND 58502. TEL 888-987-3695, http://www.deltawaterfowl.org/index.php.

796.525 GBR ISSN 0046-0036
DESCENT; the magazine of underground exploration. Text in English. 1969. bi-m. GBP 26.40 domestic; GBP 29.25 in Europe; USD 58.50 elsewhere (effective 2009). adv. bk.rev.; Website rev. charts; illus. cum. index. 40 p./no.; back issues avail. **Document type:** *Magazine, Consumer.* **Description:** Covers the sport of caving, speleology and mine exploration.
Indexed: SportS.
—BLDSC (3555.750000), IE, Ingenta, INIST.
Published by: Wild Places Publishing, PO Box 100, Abergavenny, NP7 9WY, United Kingdom. TEL 44-1873-737707. Ed. Chris Howes. Adv. contact Alan Jones TEL 44-29-20218091.

796.552 USA
DESERT TRAILS. Text in English. 1975. q.
Published by: Desert Trail Association, Box 34, Madras, OR 97741. Ed. Anne Garrison.

796.54094405 GBR ISSN 1749-8465
DESTINATION FRANCE; the magazine with a passion for France. Text in English. 2005. m. GBP 12.95 (effective 2009). **Document type:** *Magazine, Consumer.* **Description:** For anyone with a passion for France, whether they are looking for a holiday, a holiday home or to re-locate to France.
Formerly: Camping in France (1744-3423)
Published by: Waterways World Ltd., 151 Station St, Burton-on-Trent, DE14 1BG, United Kingdom. TEL 44-1283-742970, FAX 44-1283-742957, subscriptions@wwonline.co.uk, admin@wwonline.co.uk, http://www.wwmagazines.com/magazines.html. Ed. Carmen Konopka.

799.2 DEU ISSN 0724-2654
DEUTSCHE JAGD-ZEITUNG; der Spiegel der Jagd. Text in German. 1983. m. EUR 46 domestic; EUR 54.30 foreign; EUR 4.40 newsstand/cover (effective 2011). adv. **Document type:** *Magazine, Consumer.*
Indexed: W08.
Published by: Paul Parey Zeitschriftenverlag GmbH, Erich Kaestner Str 2, Singhofen, 56379, Germany. TEL 49-2604-9780, FAX 49-2604-978190, online@paulparey.de, http://www.paulparey.de. Ed. Karl-Heinz Betz. Adv. contact Peter Zins.

796.552 DEU
DEUTSCHER ALPENVEREIN - SEKTION LUDWIGSBURG. MITTEILUNGSBLATT. Text in German. 1972. a. back issues avail. **Document type:** *Bulletin, Consumer.* **Description:** Covers mountaineering and hiking.
Published by: Deutscher Alpenverein - Sektion Ludwigsburg, Imbroederstr 14, Ludwigsburg, 71634, Germany. TEL 49-7141-927893, FAX 49-7141-924042, info@alpenverein-ludwigsburg.de, http://www.alpenverein-ludwigsburg.de. Circ: 2,500 (controlled).

799.2 ITA ISSN 0012-2343
DIANA; la caccia, la natura. Text in Italian. 1906. s-m. adv. illus. index. 112 p./no.; back issues avail. **Document type:** *Magazine, Consumer.* **Description:** Features articles and information about hunting.
Former titles (until 1944): Diana Venatoria (1125-2405); (until 1939): Venatoria Diana (1125-2391); (until 1938): Diana (1125-2383)
Related titles: ◆ Supplement(s): Armi e Munizioni.
Published by: Gruppo Editoriale Olimpia SpA, Via E Fermi 24, Loc Osmannoro, Sesto Fiorentino, FI 50129, Italy. TEL 39-055-30321, FAX 39-055-3032280, http://www.edolimpia.it. Circ: 45,629. **Dist. by:** Parrini & C, Piazza Colonna 361, Rome, RM 00187, Italy. TEL 39-06-695141.

796.54 NZL ISSN 1177-0392
DIRECTORY OF RESIDENTIAL CAMPS. NEW ZEALAND. Text in English. a. NZD 12.95 per issue (effective 2008). adv. **Document type:** *Directory.*
Formed by the merger of (2002-2005): Directory of Residential Camps. Upper North Island (1176-5577); (2004-2005): Directory of Residential Camps. Lower North Island and South Island (1176-9521); Which was formed by the merger of (2002-2004): Directory of Residential Camps. Lower North Island (1176-5585); (2003-2004): Directory of Residential Camps. South Island, New Zealand (1176-5593); Which superseded in part (in 2002): Directory of Residential Camps
Published by: Ed-Media, PO Box 376, Thames, New Zealand. TEL 64-7-8682670, FAX 64-7-8682279. Pub. Ian Meredith. adv.: B&W page NZD 390, color page NZD 690; trim 210 x 297. Circ: 6,000.

DIRTSPORTS. *see* TRANSPORTATION—Automobiles

S

796 362.4 USA ISSN 1067-098X
DISABLED OUTDOORS MAGAZINE. Text in English. 1987. q. USD 14; USD 20 in Canada. adv. bk.rev. illus. reprints avail. **Document type:** *Magazine, Consumer.* **Description:** Covers outdoor sports such as fishing, camping, sky diving and water skiing for disabled people.
Published by: John Kopchik, Jr., HC 80, Box 395, Grand Marais, MN 55604. TEL 218-387-9100, FAX 218-387-9100. Ed. Carolyn Dohme. Circ: 7,800.

796.352 USA ISSN 0892-2357
DISC GOLF WORLD NEWS. Text in English. 1984 (July). q. USD 20 domestic to individuals; USD 28 in Canada to individuals; USD 41 in Europe to individuals; USD 44 elsewhere to individuals; USD 15 to libraries (effective 2005). adv. bk.rev.; software rev.; Website rev. charts; illus.; stat.; tr.lit. 80 p./no. 3 cols./p.; back issues avail. **Document type:** *Magazine, Consumer.* **Description:** Review and preview of disc golf events, equipment and promotions, results, interviews, cartoons, and instructional pieces.
Formerly: Columbia Disc Golf News
Published by: Disc Golf World, 509 E 18th St, Kansas City, MO 64108. TEL 816-471-3472, 888-237-6884, FAX 816-471-4653, rick@discgolfworld.com, http://www.discgolfworld.com. Pub., R&P, Adv. contact Rick Rothstein. Circ: 6,000 (paid).

799.2 USA ISSN 0737-0105
TS536.6.M8
DIXIE GUN WORKS BLACKPOWDER ANNUAL. Text in English. a. USD 3.95 (effective 1999). adv. back issues avail. **Document type:** *Magazine, Consumer.* **Description:** Covers hunting, history, modern uses of black powder, and topics relating to the black powder era.
Published by: Dixie Gun Works, PO Box 684, Union City, TN 38281. TEL 901-885-0374, FAX 901-885-0440. Ed. Butch Winter. Circ: 100,000.

942.33005 GBR ISSN 1355-7521
DORSET; the magazine for people who like to explore. Text in English. 1994. m. GBP 30 domestic; GBP 40 foreign; GBP 2.75 newsstand/cover (effective 2010). adv. illus. back issues avail. **Document type:** *Magazine, Consumer.* **Description:** Explores the past, present and future for those with an interest in Dorset. Informs and entertains, covering landscape and history, the arts and lifestyle.
Related titles: Online - full text ed.: free (effective 2010).
Published by: Archant Life Ltd (Subsidiary of: Archant Group), Archant House, Babbage Rd, Totnes, Devon TQ9 5JA, United Kingdom. TEL 44-1803-860910, FAX 44-1803-860922, http://www.archant.co.uk/. Ed. Helen Stiles TEL 44-1803-860920. Pub. Tim Randell TEL 44-1803-860761. adv.: page GBP 1,140; 216 x 303.

799.2 683.4 USA ISSN 1050-2262
THE DOUBLE GUN JOURNAL. Text in English. 1989. q. USD 39; USD 12.95 newsstand/cover (effective 2000). adv. bk.rev. **Document type:** *Magazine, Consumer.* **Description:** Dedicated to double barreled shot guns and rifles and to what we do with them.
Published by: Double Gun Journal, PO Box 550, East Jordan, MI 49727. TEL 616-536-7439, 800-447-1658, FAX 616-536-7450. Ed., R&P, Adv. contact Daniel Philip Cote. B&W page USD 2,300, color page USD 2,900. Circ: 31,000 (paid).

799.1 USA
THE DRAKE; for people who fish. Text in English. 1998. a. USD 8 newsstand/cover (effective 2007). **Document type:** *Magazine, Consumer.* **Description:** Contains information and stories for flyfishing enthusiasts.
Published by: Paddlesport Publishing, Inc., 7432 Alban Station Blvd, Ste B-226, Springfield, VA 22150. TEL 703-455-3419. Ed., Pub. Tom Bie.

797.32 GBR ISSN 1755-9545
DRIFT (BRISTOL). Text in English. 200?. bi-m. back issues avail. **Document type:** *Magazine, Consumer.*
Published by: Polestar Publishing, 22 Church Ln, Cliftonwood, Bristol, BS8 4TR, United Kingdom. TEL 44-1179-291390, Sales@polestar-publishing.co.uk, http://www.polestar-publishing.com. Ed., Pub. Howard Swanwick.

797.2 NLD ISSN 0923-7607
DUIKEN. Text in Dutch. 1986. m. EUR 54.45; EUR 4.95 newsstand/cover (effective 2011). adv. illus. **Document type:** *Magazine, Consumer.* **Description:** Discusses all aspects of scuba diving.
Published by: Vipmedia Publishing en Services, Takkebijsters 57a, Breda, 4817 BL, Netherlands. TEL 31-76-5301721, FAX 31-76-5144531, info@vipmedia.nl, http://www.vipmedia.nl. Eds. Judith Rietveld, Rene Lipmann. Adv. contact Rob Keersmaekers TEL 31-76-5301716. Circ: 22,000. **Subscr. in Belgium to:** Vipmedia, Bredabaan 852, Merksem 2170, Belgium. TEL 32-3-6455618, FAX 32-3-6450500; **Subscr. to:** Postbus 7272, Breda 4800 GG, Netherlands.

354.35 USA
DWELLING PORTABLY. Text in English. 1980. 3/yr. USD 2 domestic; USD 3 foreign (effective 2004). adv. bk.rev. illus. 16 p./no.; back issues avail. **Document type:** *Newsletter, Consumer.*
Former titles: Portable Dwelling; Message Post
Published by: Light Living Library, c/o Lisa Ahne, POB 181, Alsea, OR 97324. Ed. Holly Davis. Circ: 1,300.

769.93 USA
E W S R A ANNUAL BUYER'S GUIDE. Text in English. a. **Document type:** *Guide, Trade.* **Description:** Listing of sales reps who represent ski and snowboard related products; member reps' name, address, phone, fax, and the lines they represent.
Formerly: E S R Buyers' Guide
Related titles: Online - full text ed.: free (effective 2010).
Published by: Eastern Winter Sports Reps Association, 5142 State St, P O Box 88, White Haven, PA 18661. TEL 570-443-7180, FAX 570-443-0388, ewsra@uplink.net.

796.93 USA
E W S R A NEWSLETTER. Text in English. irreg. **Document type:** *Newsletter.*
Formerly: E S R Newsletter
Related titles: Online - full text ed.
Published by: Eastern Winter Sports Reps Association, 5142 State St, P O Box 88, White Haven, PA 18661. TEL 570-443-7180, FAX 570-443-0388, ewsra@uplink.net, http://www.ewsra.org/.

799.124 USA
EASTERN FLY FISHING. Text in English. 2005 (Spring). bi-m. USD 29.95 domestic; USD 36.95 in Canada; USD 44.95 elsewhere (effective 2010). adv. **Document type:** *Magazine, Consumer.* **Description:** Contains the latest news about fly fishing, conservation, new products, and Eastern adventures; detailed, step-by-step fly tying instructions of patterns specifically for Eastern angling; pioneers and legends; innovative fly tiers; excerpts from books; fish tales and more.
Related titles: ◆ Regional ed(s).: Southwest Fly Fishing. ISSN 1536-8505; ◆ Northwest Fly Fishing. ISSN 1527-8255.
Published by: Northwest Fly Fishing, LLC., PO Box 708, Raymond, WA 98577. TEL 206-667-9359, FAX 206-667-9364. Ed. Steve Probasco. Adv. contact Peter Crumbaker TEL 206-667-3059. B&W page USD 1,970, color page USD 2,415; trim 7.875 x 10.875. Circ: 30,457 (paid).

799 USA
EASTMANS' BOWHUNTING JOURNAL. Text in English. bi-m. USD 19.95 (effective 2002).
Published by: Eastmans, c/o Kevin Stump, 5695 Black Bear Rd, Helena, MT 59602. TEL 307-754-5584, 800-842-6887.

799 USA ISSN 1524-3168
EASTMANS' HUNTING JOURNAL. Text in English. m. USD 19.95 (effective 2002); includes Mule Deer Stalker IV video. **Document type:** *Magazine, Consumer.*
Published by: Eastmans, c/o Kevin Stump, 5695 Black Bear Rd, Helena, MT 59602. TEL 307-754-5584, 800-842-6887.

796 AUT
EDELWEISS AKTUELL. Text in English. 1946. bi-m. bk.rev. **Document type:** *Magazine, Consumer.* **Description:** News for members of the Austrian Alpine Association.
Published by: Oesterreichischer Alpenverein, Sektion Edelweiss, Walfischgasse 12, Vienna, W 1010, Austria. TEL 43-1-5138500, FAX 43-1-513850019, office@edelweiss.oeav.at, http://www.oeav-events.at/edelweiss/. Ed. Csaba Szepfalusi. R&P B Stummer TEL 43-1-5138500. Circ: 10,000 (controlled).

796.9 DEU ISSN 1610-8477
EISKANAL. Text in German. 2002. 2/yr. EUR 15 domestic; EUR 16.50 in Austria; EUR 18.40 in Italy; CHF 28 in Switzerland (effective 2004). **Document type:** *Magazine, Consumer.* **Description:** Covers all aspects of bobsledding and other downhill ice track sports.
Published by: Treffpunkt-Media Verlag fuer Buch und Neue Medien, Jaegerhausstr 52, Heilbronn, 74074, Germany. TEL 49-7131-2039422, FAX 49-7131-2039427, n.winckler@treffpunkt-media.de, http://www.treffpunkt-media.de. Pub. Bernd Wonneberger. Adv. contact Thomas Hibler.

796.522 LIE
ENZIAN. Text in German. 4/yr. **Document type:** *Magazine, Consumer.*
Published by: Liechtensteiner Alpenverein, In der Stein-Egerta 26, Schaan, 9494, Liechtenstein. TEL 423-2329812, FAX 423-2329813, liechtensteiner@alpenverein.li, http://www.alpenverein.li.

796 799 FIN ISSN 0356-3464
ERA. Text in Finnish. 1977. m. EUR 73.60 (effective 2005). adv. **Document type:** *Magazine, Consumer.* **Description:** Focuses on camping, fishing and hunting. Each issue carries a special theme.
Related titles: ◆ Supplement(s): Eravaeltaja. ISSN 1459-952X.
Published by: Yhtyneet Kuvalehdet Oy/United Magazines Ltd., Maistraatinportti 1, Helsinki, 00015, Finland. TEL 358-9-15661, FAX 358-9-145650, http://www.kuvalehdet.fi. Ed. Seppo Suuronen. adv.: color page EUR 2,460; trim 280 x 217. Circ: 52,088.

796 799 FIN ISSN 1459-952X
ERAVAELTAJA. Text in Finnish. 2004. a. **Document type:** *Yearbook, Consumer.*
Related titles: ◆ Supplement to: Era. ISSN 0356-3464.
Published by: Yhtyneet Kuvalehdet Oy/United Magazines Ltd., Maistraatinportti 1, Helsinki, 00015, Finland. TEL 358-9-15661, FAX 358-9-145650, http://www.kuvalehdet.fi.

ESCAPEES. *see* TRANSPORTATION—Automobiles

ESCAPEES CLUB. ANNUAL DIRECTORY. *see* TRANSPORTATION—Automobiles

799.1 DEU
ESOX. Text in German. 1992. m. EUR 24; EUR 2 newsstand/cover (effective 2011). adv. **Document type:** *Magazine, Consumer.*
Published by: Jahr Top Special Verlag, Troplowitzstr 5, Hamburg, 22529, Germany. TEL 49-40-389060, FAX 49-40-38906300, info@jahr-tsv.de, http://www.jahr-tsv.de. Ed. Henning Stilke. Adv. contact Christopher Zippert TEL 49-40-38906267. Circ: 46,168 (paid).

799.1 USA ISSN 1545-1925
ESOX ANGLER. Variant title: The Next Bite. Text in English. 2000. q. USD 22; USD 6.95 newsstand/cover (effective 2007). adv. 116 p./no.; **Document type:** *Magazine, Consumer.*
Published by: Esox Angler, Inc., PO Box 280, Stone Lake, WI 54876. Ed. Jack Burns.

910.09 796 FRA ISSN 0336-1446
ESPACES; tourisme et loisirs. Text in French. 1970. m. (11/yr). EUR 275 combined subscription domestic print & online eds.; EUR 295 combined subscription foreign print & online eds. (effective 2009). adv. illus. **Document type:** *Journal, Trade.*
Related titles: Online - full text ed.
Indexed: AgrForAb, BA, CABA, E12, F08, F12, FR, GH, LT, N02, OR, R12, RRTA, S13, S16, T05, W11.
—BLDSC (3811.329000), IE, Ingenta.
Published by: Espaces Tourisme & Loisirs, 6 Rue Cels, Paris, 75014, France. TEL 33-1-43275590, FAX 33-1-45387101, info@revue-espaces.com, http://www.revue-espaces.com. Ed. Pierre Defert.

796.52 FRA ISSN 1779-3904
ESPRIT TRAIL. Text in French. 2003. bi-m. EUR 24 (effective 2007). **Document type:** *Magazine, Consumer.*
Published by: Editions Riva, 16 Rue de la Fontaine-au-Roi, Paris, 75011, France.

797.173 VEN
ESQUI ACUATICO Y OTROS DEPORTES. Text in Spanish. 1975. 6/yr. adv.
Address: Av. Lisboa, Ota La Caromotana 5-01-19-28, Calif. Norte, Caracas, 1070, Venezuela. Circ: 10,000.

796.54 FRA ISSN 2107-0059
▼ **L'ESSENTIEL DU CAMPING-CAR.** Text in French. 2010. q. EUR 11.66; EUR 4.80 per issue (effective 2010). **Document type:** *Magazine, Consumer.*
Published by: Lafont Presse, 53 Rue du Chemin Vert, Boulogne-Billancourt, 92100, France. TEL 33-1-46102121.

796.54 NLD ISSN 1871-9783
EUROCAMP.NL. Text in Dutch. 2005. s-a. free (effective 2009).
Published by: Eurocamp, Postbus 1071, Amersfoort, 3800 BB, Netherlands. TEL 31-33-4602700, FAX 31-33-4612811, info@eurocamp.nl, http://www.eurocamp.nl.

796.5 DEU ISSN 0071-2272
EUROPA CAMPING UND CARAVANING. INTERNATIONALER FUEHRER. Text in English, French, German. 1959. a. EUR 14.90 per issue (effective 2009). adv. 1040 p./no.; **Document type:** *Journal, Consumer.*
Published by: Drei Brunnen Verlag GmbH und Co., Heusee 19, Pluederhausen, 73655, Germany. TEL 49-7181-86020, FAX 49-7181-860229, mail@drei-brunnen-verlag.de, http://www.drei-brunnen-verlag.de. Ed. Emmerich Mueller. adv.: B&W page EUR 2,420, color page EUR 4,480. Circ: 80,000 (paid and controlled).

796.52 CZE ISSN 1213-1849
EVEREST; casopis o horach a lidech. Text in Czech. 2000. q. CZK 155 (effective 2008). adv. **Document type:** *Magazine, Consumer.*
Published by: Czech Press Group a.s., Klisska 1432-18, Usti nad Labem, 400 01, Czech Republic. TEL 420-47-5211088, FAX 420-47-5216182, inzerce@koktejl.cz, http://www.czech-press.cz. Ed. Ludmila Vesela. adv.: page CZK 65,000; trim 195 x 260.

621.932 FRA ISSN 1274-0950
EXCALIBUR. Text in French. q. EUR 25 domestic; EUR 32 foreign (effective 2009). **Document type:** *Magazine, Consumer.* **Description:** Dedicated to french and Foreign knives; technical, historical and latest news.
Published by: Editions Crepin-Leblond, 14 rue du Patronage Laique, Chaumont, 52000, France. TEL 33-3-25038748, FAX 33-3-25038740, crepin-leblond@graphycom.com. Ed. Jean-Jacques Pietraru. Adv. contact Laurent Picard. Circ: 40,000.

790.1 CAN ISSN 0714-816X
EXPLORE (CALGARY); Canada's outdoor magazine. Text in English. 1979. 7/yr. USD 24 domestic; USD 34 in United States; USD 39 elsewhere (effective 2010). adv. bk.rev. back issues avail.; reprints avail. **Document type:** *Magazine, Consumer.* **Description:** Focuses on back packing, bicycling, canoeing and skiing featuring Canadian destinations.
Formerly (until 1982): Explore Alberta! Magazine (0706-8174); Incorporates (1979-1982): Whiskey Jack Magazine (0226-7462); Which was formerly (1977-1979): Whiskey Jack (0704-7312)
Related titles: Microfiche ed.: (from MML); Online - full text ed.
Indexed: C03, CBCARef, CBPI, CPerI, G08, I05, P48, PQC, SD.
Published by: Quarto Communications, 54 St. Patrick St, Toronto, ON M5T 1V1, Canada. TEL 416-599-2000, clmag@cottagelife.com. Ed. James Little. Pub. Al Zikovitz. Adv. contact Randy Craig.

790 USA
EXPLORE (CARROLTON). Text in English. irreg. **Description:** Focuses on adventure entertainment. Includes features on hiking, biking, skiing, snowboarding, paddling, adventure travel, and climbing. Also covers environmental issues, the latest gear, and more.
Media: Online - full content.
Published by: iValue, 2045 Chenault, Carrolton, TX 75006.

EXPLORE MINNESOTA CAMPGROUNDS AND R V PARKS GUIDE. *see* TRAVEL AND TOURISM

EXPLORER MAGAZIN. *see* TRAVEL AND TOURISM

799.1 ZAF ISSN 1990-3022
EXTREME SPORTS ANGLING. Text in English. 2006. m. ZAR 199 (effective 2008). **Document type:** *Magazine, Consumer.* **Description:** Covers all aspects of shore and off-shore angling.
Published by: Picasso Headline (Pty) Ltd, Mill St, PO Box 12500, Gardens, 8010, South Africa. FAX 27-21-4621124, info@picasso.co.za, http://www.picasso.co.za.

796.93 CHE ISSN 0425-5291
F I S BULLETIN. Text in English, French, German. q. CHF 70 (effective 1998). back issues avail. **Document type:** *Bulletin.*
Indexed: SportS.
Published by: (International Ski Federation), Hallwag AG, Nordring 4, Bern, 3001, Switzerland. TEL 41-31-3323131, FAX 41-31-3314133. Circ: 1,709.

799.1 USA ISSN 1543-6179
F L W OUTDOORS. (Forrest L Wood) Text in English. 2002. 8/yr. USD 25 (effective 2007). **Document type:** *Magazine, Consumer.* **Description:** Features information for sport fishermen about techniques, lures, bait, boating, and places for the best fishing.
Address: 30 Gamble Ln, Benton, KY 42025. TEL 270-252-1000, info@flwoutdoors.com. Ed. Chris Eubanks.

FAIR CHASE. *see* CONSERVATION

796 910.91 USA ISSN 1553-1597
F832.D5
A FALCONGUIDE TO DINOSAUR NATIONAL MONUMENT. Text in English. 2002. biennial, latest 2005, 2nd ed. USD 14.95 per issue (effective 2008). **Document type:** *Guide, Consumer.* **Description:** Provides the information and acts as a guide to unique places.
Formerly (until 2002): Exploring Dinosaur National Monument (1553-3220)
Published by: The Globe Pequot Press, Inc., 246 Goose Ln, PO Box 480, Guilford, CT 06437. TEL 203-458-4500, 888-249-7586, FAX 203-458-4603, 800-820-2329, info@globepequot.com, http://www.globepequot.com.

796 910.91 USA ISSN 1553-958X
F897.W57
A FALCONGUIDE TO THE MOUNT BAKER-MOUNT SHUKSAN AREA. Text in English. 2005. biennial, latest 2005, 1st ed. USD 15.95 per issue (effective 2008). **Document type:** *Guide, Consumer.* **Description:** Provides the information and acts as a guide to unique places.
Published by: The Globe Pequot Press, Inc., 246 Goose Ln, PO Box 480, Guilford, CT 06437. TEL 203-458-4500, 888-249-7586, FAX 203-458-4603, 800-820-2329, info@globepequot.com, http://www.globepequot.com.

796 USA
FAMILY CAMPING; International Camping Magazine for the entire family. Text in English. 1999. m. USD 24 domestic; USD 36 foreign (effective 2000); USD 3.50 newsstand/cover. bk.rev. illus.; maps. back issues avail. **Document type:** *Magazine, Consumer.* **Description:** Provides current information on camping and family activities.
Published by: M A K Publishing, Inc., 6196 Garden Grove Blvd, Westminster, CA 92683. TEL 714-799-0062, FAX 714-799-0042. Ed., Pub., R&P Michael Kadletz. adv.: B&W page USD 3,130, color page USD 4,960; trim 10.75 x 8.25. Circ: 100,000.

647.944109 GBR ISSN 0957-7327
FAMILY SITES. Text in English. 1989. a. **Document type:** *Directory.* **Description:** Lists and evaluates more than 1500 camper sites.
Former titles: Camper Sites Guide; Practical Camper's Sites Guide; Camping Sites in Britain and France (0068-6980)
—BLDSC (3865.576204). **CCC.**
Published by: Haymarket Publishing Ltd. (Subsidiary of: Haymarket Media Group), 174 Hammersmith Rd, London, W6 7JP, United Kingdom. TEL 44-20-82674210, info@haymarket.com, http://www.haymarket.com.

FANG; Fuehrungszeitschrift. *see* FORESTS AND FORESTRY

FARM POND HARVEST. *see* FISH AND FISHERIES

797.2 USA ISSN 1547-0881
GV838.672
FATHOMS; adventure for serious divers. Text in English. 2001. q. USD 30 (effective 2003).
Published by: G2 Publishing, P. O. Box 34180, Pensacola, FL 32507. TEL 850-492-0649. Eds. Brett C. Gilliam, Fred D. Garth.

639.11 799.2 AUS ISSN 1323-4854
FEATHERS & FUR. Text in English. 1995. q. free to members (effective 2009). bk.rev. **Document type:** *Magazine, Consumer.* **Description:** Contains general hunting information and hunting stories.
Related titles: Online - full text ed.
Published by: Field and Game Australia Inc., 65 Anzac Ave, PO Box 464, Seymour, VIC 3661, Australia. TEL 61-3-57990960, FAX 61-3-57990961, fga@fga.net.au, http://www.fga.net.au. Ed. Graeme Eames.

796 GBR ISSN 0015-0649
GV1
THE FIELD. Text in English. 1853. m. GBP 34.49 domestic; USD 62.50 in United States; USD 87.40 in Canada; EUR 94.30 in Europe; GBP 60.10 elsewhere (effective 2010). adv. bk.rev. illus. back issues avail. **Document type:** *Magazine, Consumer.* **Description:** Revels in the pleasures and pursuits of the English countryside and its participants.
Incorporates (19??-1920): Land and Water; Which was formerly (until 19??): County Gentleman and Land and Water
Related titles: Online - full text ed.
—BLDSC (3918.900000), IE, Ingenta.
Published by: I P C Country & Leisure Media Ltd. (Subsidiary of: I P C Media Ltd.), The Blue Fin Bldg, 110 Southwark St, London, SE1 0SU, United Kingdom. TEL 44-20-31484772, FAX 44-20-31488179, http://www.ipcmedia.com. Ed. Jonathan Young TEL 44-20-31484772. Pub. Fiona Mercer TEL 44-20-31484311. Adv. contact Rosmary Archer TEL 44-20-31484214. color page GBP 3,318. Circ: 31,292. **Subscr. to:** PO Box 272, Haywards Heath, W Sussex RH16 3FS, United Kingdom. TEL 44-845-6767778, FAX 44-1444-445599, IPCsubs@quadrantsubs.com, http://www.magazinesdirect.co.uk. **Dist. by:** MarketForce UK Ltd, The Blue Fin Bldg, 3rd Fl, 110 Southwark St, London SE1 0SU, United Kingdom. TEL 44-20-31483300, FAX 44-20-31488105, salesinnovation@marketforce.co.uk, http://www.marketforce.co.uk/.

799 USA ISSN 1554-8066
SK1
FIELD & STREAM. Text in English. 2003. m. USD 12 domestic; USD 26 in Canada; USD 45 elsewhere; USD 1 per issue domestic; USD 2.17 per issue in Canada; USD 3.75 per issue elsewhere (effective 2011). adv. **Document type:** *Magazine, Consumer.*
Formed by the 2003 merger of: Field & Stream. Northeast Edition (8755-8580); Field & Stream. Far West Edition (8755-8572); Field & Stream. West Edition (8755-8610); Field & Stream. South Edition (8755-8602); Field & Stream. Midwest Edition (8755-8599); All of which superseded in part (in 1984): Field & Stream (0015-0673); Which incorporated: Living Outdoors; Which was formerly: Western Field and Stream; Which incorporated: Field and Stream
Related titles: ♦ Online - full text ed.: Field & Stream (Online).
Indexed: A01, A09, A10, A11, A25, A26, C05, C12, E08, G05, G06, G07, G08, I05, I06, I07, M01, M02, M04, M05, MASUSE, P02, P10, P19, P48, P53, P54, PQC, S23, T02, U01, V02, V03, V04.
Published by: Bonnier Corp. (Subsidiary of: Bonnier Group), 2 Park Ave, 9th Fl, New York, NY 10016. TEL 212-779-5047, FAX 212-779-5108, http://www.bonniercorp.com. Ed. Anthony Licata.

799 USA
FIELD & STREAM (ONLINE). Text in English. m. USD 10 (effective 2011). back issues avail. **Document type:** *Magazine, Consumer.* **Description:** Provides full-text articles relating to hunting, fishing, camping and other outdoor pursuits.
Media: Online - full text. **Related titles:** ♦ Print ed.: Field & Stream. ISSN 1554-8066.
Published by: Bonnier Corp. (Subsidiary of: Bonnier Group), 2 Park Ave, 9th Fl, New York, NY 10016. TEL 212-779-5000, http://www.bonniercorp.com. Ed. Anthony Licata. Pub. Eric Zinczenko.

796.6 FIN ISSN 1236-7966
FILLARI. Text in Finnish. 1993. 7/yr. EUR 40 (effective 2006). adv. **Document type:** *Magazine, Consumer.*
Published by: RideMedia Oy, PO Box 140, Hyvinkaa, 05801, Finland. TEL 358-19-483490, FAX 358-19-483480, http://www.ridemedia.fi. Ed. Janne Lehti TEL 358-19-483427. Pub. Jukka Helminen. Adv. contact Ossi Sinisilta TEL 358-3-6715474. B&W page EUR 1,380, color page EUR 2,100; 210 x 297.

799.1 USA
FINE FISHING. Text in English. 1995. w. adv. **Document type:** *Magazine, Consumer.* **Description:** Contains articles, new links to sites, recipes, and contests for all kinds of anglers.
Media: Online - full text.
Address: 1230 Yew Ct., Florence, OR 97439-7629. TEL 208-883-0802, FAX 208-883-3498. Ed., Pub. Louis Bignami. R&P Annette Lucido. Adv. contact Robert Benson.

796.552 USA
FINGER LAKES TRAIL NEWS. Text in English. 1962. q. free to qualified personnel (effective 2003). adv. 2 cols./p.; back issues avail. **Document type:** *Newsletter, Consumer.* **Description:** Covers hiking & backpacking for the Finger Lakes Trail area.
Published by: Finger Lakes Trail Conference, 6111 Visitor Center Rd, Mt. Morris, NY 14510. TEL 585-658-9320, FAX 585-658-2390, information@fingerlakestrail.org, http://www.fingerlakestrail.org. Ed. Jo H Taylor. Adv. contact Gene Bavis, Exec. Dir. Circ: 1,200 (paid); 750 (controlled).

796.54 790.019 USA ISSN 2154-5545
▼ **FINN CAMP NEWSLETTER.** Text in English. 2009. m. free (effective 2010). back issues avail. **Document type:** *Newsletter, Consumer.* **Description:** Contains information on camp activities, including swimming lessons, swim meets, track meets, and stage productions.
Media: Online - full text.
Published by: Detroit Finnish Cooperative Summer Camp Association, 2524 Loon Lake Rd, Wixom, MI 48393. TEL 248-624-2550, Secretary@finncamp.org.

799.1 DEU ISSN 0015-2838
FISCH UND FANG; das Erlebnis Magazin fuer Angler. Text in German. 1960. m. EUR 45.50 domestic; EUR 50 foreign; EUR 4.20 newsstand/cover (effective 2011). bk.rev. illus. index. **Document type:** *Magazine, Consumer.* **Description:** Covers all techniques, products and places related to recreational fishing.
Published by: Paul Parey Zeitschriftenverlag GmbH, Erich Kaestner Str 2, Singhofen, 56379, Germany. TEL 49-2604-9780, FAX 49-2604-978190, online@paulparey.de, http://www.paulparey.de. Ed. Henning Stuehring. Adv. contact Fabine Jacobs. Circ: 64,190 (paid).

799.1 DEU
FISCH UND FLIEGE. Text in German. 1990. 2/yr. EUR 13 (effective 2007). adv. **Document type:** *Magazine, Consumer.*
Published by: Moeller Neue Medien Verlags GmbH, Heidenkampsweg 76A, Hamburg, 20097, Germany. TEL 49-40-2361300, FAX 49-40-23613022, kloeer@ruteundrolle.de, http://www.ruteundrolle.de. adv.: B&W page EUR 2,840, color page EUR 3,630. Circ: 11,000 (paid and controlled).

799.1 DEU ISSN 0722-706X
FISCHWAID. Text in German. 1970. bi-m. EUR 15.40 (effective 2002). adv. **Document type:** *Magazine, Consumer.*
Formerly (until 1982): A F Z Fischwaid (0342-5320); Which was formed by the merger of (1886-1970): Allgemeine Fischerei Zeitung (0374-5392); (1947-1970): Fischwaid (0342-5312)
Published by: Verband Deutscher Sportfischer e.V., Siemensstr. 11-13, Offenbach, 63071, Germany. TEL 49-69-855006, FAX 49-69-873770, vdsf.ev@t-online.de, http://www.vdsf.de. adv.: B&W page EUR 910; trim 213 x 301.

799.1 USA ISSN 1535-6353
FISH & FLY; for the adventure angler. Text in English. 4/yr. USD 16.95 domestic; USD 24.95 in Canada; USD 36.95 elsewhere; USD 5.99 newsstand/cover domestic; USD 7.99 newsstand/cover in Canada (effective 2008). adv. **Document type:** *Magazine, Consumer.* **Description:** Covers all aspects of flyfishing including equipment reviews, stories from readers, and places to go.
Published by: Turnstile Publishing Company, 1500 Park Center Dr, Orlando, FL 32835. TEL 407-563-7000, FAX 407-563-7077. Ed. Thomas R Pero.

799.1 NZL ISSN 1172-434X
FISH & GAME NEW ZEALAND. Text in English. q. NZD 30 domestic; NZD 38 in Australia (effective 2008); NZD 81 in Asia, US & UK (effective 2005); NZD 55 elsewhere; NZD 8.90 newsstand/cover (effective 2008). adv. **Document type:** *Magazine, Consumer.* **Description:** Aimed specifically at the person who fishes freshwater trout and salmon and who hunts upland game birds in New Zealand.
Published by: Fairfax Media (Subsidiary of: John Fairfax Holdings Ltd.), Level 1, 274 Church St, Penrose, PO Box 12965, Auckland, New Zealand. TEL 64-9-6341800, FAX 64-9-6342948, info@fairfaxmedia.co.nz. Ed. Tim Porter. Circ: 18,061.

799.1 USA ISSN 0747-3397
THE FISH SNIFFER; for the northern California, Nevada, and Oregon angler. Text in English. 1982. bi-w. USD 35. adv. back issues avail. **Description:** Up-to-date news and features covering recreational fishing and conservation in the West.
Related titles: Supplement(s): Gamefishing West.
Published by: Northern California Angler Publications, Inc., PO Box 994, Elk, CA 95759-0994. TEL 916-685-2245, FAX 916-685-1498. Ed. Daniel K Bacher. Circ: 21,500 (paid).

799.1 GBR ISSN 1750-4023
FISH UPDATE. Text in English. 2006. m. **Document type:** *Newspaper, Consumer.*
Formed by the merger of (1997-2006): Fishing Monthly (1367-6601); Which was formerly (until 1997): Scottish Fishing Monthly; (19??-2006): Fish Farming Today; European Fish Trader
Related titles: Online - full text ed.: free (effective 2009).
—CCC.
Published by: Oban Times Ltd., Craigcrook Castle, Craigcrook Rd, Edinburgh, EH4 3PE, United Kingdom. TEL 44-131-3124550, FAX 44-131-3124551, letters@obantimes.co.uk, http://www.obantimes.co.uk/. Ed. Bob Kennedy. Adv. contact William Dowds.

799.1 USA ISSN 1040-0109
SH401
THE FISHERMAN (LONG ISLAND, METROPOLITAN NEW YORK EDITION). Text in English. 196?. w. adv. **Document type:** *Magazine, Trade.*
Formerly (until 1983): Long Island Fisherman
Related titles: ♦ Regional ed(s).: The Fisherman (Florida Edition). ISSN 1059-5295; ♦ The Fisherman (New England Edition). ISSN 1040-0125; ♦ The Fisherman (New Jersey, Delaware Bay, Edition). ISSN 1040-0117; ♦ The Fisherman (Delaware, Maryland, Virgina Edition). ISSN 1040-0133.
Published by: L I F Publishing Corp., 14 Ramsey Rd, Shirley, NY 11967. TEL 631-345-5200, FAX 631-345-5304. Pub. Michael Caruso TEL 631-345-5200 ext 204. Circ: 91,200.

799.1 USA ISSN 1040-0125
THE FISHERMAN (NEW ENGLAND EDITION). Text in English. 19??. w. adv. **Document type:** *Magazine, Consumer.*
Formerly: New England Fisherman
Related titles: ♦ Regional ed(s).: The Fisherman (Florida Edition). ISSN 1059-5295; ♦ The Fisherman (Delaware, Maryland, Virgina Edition). ISSN 1040-0133; ♦ The Fisherman (New Jersey, Delaware Bay, Edition). ISSN 1040-0117; ♦ The Fisherman (Long Island, Metropolitan New York Edition). ISSN 1040-0109.
Published by: L I F Publishing Corp., 14 Ramsey Rd, Shirley, NY 11967. TEL 631-345-5200, FAX 631-345-5304. Ed. Zach Harvey TEL 860-572-0564. Pub. Michael Caruso TEL 631-345-5200 ext 204. Circ: 69,300.

799.1 USA ISSN 1040-0117
THE FISHERMAN (NEW JERSEY, DELAWARE BAY, EDITION). Text in English. 1973. w. adv. **Document type:** *Magazine, Consumer.*
Formerly (until 19??): New Jersey Fisherman
Related titles: ♦ Regional ed(s).: The Fisherman (Florida Edition). ISSN 1059-5295; ♦ The Fisherman (Delaware, Maryland, Virgina Edition). ISSN 1040-0133; ♦ The Fisherman (New England Edition). ISSN 1040-0125; ♦ The Fisherman (Long Island, Metropolitan New York Edition). ISSN 1040-0109.
Published by: L I F Publishing Corp., 14 Ramsey Rd, Shirley, NY 11967. TEL 631-345-5200, FAX 631-345-5304. Pub. Michael Caruso TEL 631-345-5200 ext 204. Circ: 92,700.

796 AUS
FISHIN' BOATS. Text in English. a. AUD 6.95 newsstand/cover (effective 2008). **Document type:** *Magazine, Trade.* **Description:** Provides latest boat reviews and tests on trailer boat. It offers update on marine engines.
Published by: A C P Trader International Group (Subsidiary of: P B L Media Pty Ltd.), 73 Atherton Rd, Oakleigh, VIC 3166, Australia. TEL 61-3-95674200, FAX 61-3-95634554. Ed. Greg Leech TEL 61-3-95674194. Adv. contact Justine Schuller. **Subscr. to:** Magshop, Reply Paid 4967, Sydney, NSW 2001, Australia. TEL 61-2-136116, subs@magstore.com.au, http://shop.magstore.com.au.

799.1 AUS ISSN 1833-7430
THE FISHING ALMANAC. Text in English. 2007. a. USD 29.95 per issue (effective 2009). **Description:** Contains useful fishing tips for both the beginner and more experienced angler's.
Media: CD-ROM.
Published by: HAL Computing Pty Ltd., PO BOX 3004, Lindfield West, NSW 2070, Australia. TEL 61-2-94994226, http://www.halcomputing.com.

799 USA ISSN 0015-301X
SK1
FISHING AND HUNTING NEWS; the nation's largest outdoor newspaper . (Seven editions avail. covering 15 Western states and Michigan) Text in English. 1944. 24/yr. USD 39.95; USD 3.50 newsstand/cover (effective 2007). adv. bk.rev. charts; illus.; stat. reprints avail. **Document type:** *Magazine, Consumer.*
Published by: Outdoor Empire Publishing, Inc., 21415 87th St, Woodinville, WA 98072. TEL 206-624-3845, 800-645-5489, FAX 206-695-8467, mliang@outdoorempire.com, http://www.outdoorempire.com. Ed. John Marsh. Pub. Mark Fisher. R&P Mark Raio. Adv. contact Mike Oseth. Circ: 85,000 (paid).

799.1 USA
FISHING FACTS. Text in English. 1963. 6/yr. USD 23.95 domestic; USD 29.95 in Canada (effective 2007). adv. charts; stat.; illus. 64 p./no.; back issues avail. **Document type:** *Magazine, Consumer.*
Formed by the merger of: Fishing Facts (Northern Edition) (0899-9597); Fishing Facts (Southern Edition) (0899-9589); Which was formerly: Fishing News
Related titles: ♦ Regional ed(s).: Fishing Facts (Southern Edition). ISSN 0899-9589.
Indexed: SPI.
Published by: Midwest Outdoors Ltd., 111 Shore Dr, Burr Ridge, IL 60521. TEL 630-887-7722, FAX 630-887-1958. Ed., Pub. Gene Laulunen. Circ: 29,500.

799.1 USA
FISHING GURU. Text in English. 2002. bi-m. **Description:** Designed to serve those consumers with strong interest in recreational fishing and boating, in both freshwater and saltwater environments.
Published by: United Fishing Association, 66 Kewanee Dr, New Rochelle, NY 10804. TEL 914-576-2150, FAX 914-576-0409, fisherman@fishufa.com, http://www.fichufa.com. Ed. Vin Sparano. Pub. Michael E Horne. Circ: 1,011,017 (controlled).

799.1 USA ISSN 0164-0941
SH505
FISHING IN MARYLAND. Text in English. 1953. a. USD 9.85 per issue in state; USD 9.45 per issue out of state (effective 2006). adv. illus. **Document type:** *Magazine, Consumer.* **Description:** Contains informative articles, tide tables, forecasts, where-to go and how-to. Stimulates fishing interest through its award and citation programs.
Supersedes in part: Fishing in the Mid-Atlantic; Fishing in Maryland and Virginia (0363-8898)
Published by: Fishing in Maryland, Inc., 10 Shanney Brook Ct, Box 201, Phoenix, MD 21131. TEL 401-561-3720, FAX 401-561-3720, http://www.mdangler.net/. Ed. Bill Burton. Pub. W Cary de Russy. R&P, Adv. contact W. Cary de Russy. Circ: 26,500 (paid).

799.1 ZAF ISSN 1562-9120
THE FISHING JOURNAL. Text in English. 1998. bi-m. ZAR 54 domestic; ZAR 79 in Southern Africa; ZAR 86 elsewhere (effective 2000). adv. bk.rev. illus. **Document type:** *Journal, Consumer.* **Description:** Covers all sport fishing disciplines in both fresh and saltwater, concertrating on the spiritual values of angling, infoormation regarding fish and their habitats, conservation of fishes.
Published by: The Fishing Journal, PO Box 2152, Port Alfred, 6170, South Africa. TEL 27-46-624-3004, FAX 27-46-624-3004, fishjournal@xsinet.co.za. Ed., Pub. Bruce Truter. Circ: 1,300 (paid).

FISHING MAGAZINE FOR YOUNG BOY. *see* CHILDREN AND YOUTH—For

799.1 CAN ISSN 1488-0717
THE FISHING NETWORK WEB-ZINE. Text in English. 1995. bi-w. **Description:** Contains worldwide angling topics.
Media: Online - full text.
Published by: Fishing Network Web-Zine, 117 Fern Valley Cres, Richmond Hill, ON L4E 2K3, Canada. Ed. Scott M Binnie.

799.1 AUS ISSN 1447-2228
FISHING QUEENSLAND. Text in English. 199?. a., latest 2006. **Document type:** *Magazine, Consumer.*

S

Published by: Fishing Monthly Group, PO Box 621, Hamilton, QLD 4007, Australia. TEL 61-7-3268-3992, FAX 61-7-3268-3993, http://www.fishingmonthly.com.au.

799.1 USA ISSN 8750-1287
FISHING TACKLE RETAILER. Abbreviated title: F T R. Text in English. 1980. m. (11/yr.). free to qualified personnel (effective 2009). adv. back issues avail. **Document type:** *Magazine, Trade.* **Description:** Provides to them valuable information for managing their businesses and increasing profits.
Former titles (until 198?): Fishing Tackle Retailer Magazine (0745-8169); (until 198?): Fishing Tackle Retailer (0274-788X)
Published by: E S P N Publishing, Inc., PO Box 10000, Lake Buena Vista, FL 32830. FAX 407-566-2214, editorial@bassmaster.com. Adv. contact Clem Dippel TEL 715-543-8427. B&W page USD 3,927, color page USD 6,237; trim 7.875 x 10.5.

799.1 AUS ISSN 1448-756X
FISHING VICTORIA ANNUAL; the east coast fishing annual. Text in English. 2003. a. AUD 19.95 per issue (effective 2009). adv. back issues avail. **Document type:** *Magazine, Consumer.* **Description:** Contains articles that describe where to fish and how to fish, this glossy, full colour publication has almost 40 technique, location and species articles from Queensland, New South Wales and Victoria.
Published by: Fishing Monthly Group, PO Box 3172, Loganholme, QLD 4129, Australia. TEL 61-7-33870800, FAX 61-7-33870801, subscribe@fishingmonthly.com.au, http://www.fishingmonthly.com.au. Adv. contact Heatha Nicholas. Circ: 20,000.

799.1 DNK ISSN 0108-2000
FISK & FRI; magasinet for lystfiskere. Text in Danish. 1982. 10/yr. DKK 450 (effective 2009). adv. **Document type:** *Magazine, Consumer.*
Published by: Fisk og Fri Aps, Christians Brygge 28, Copenhagen V, 1559, Denmark. TEL 45-33-111488, FAX 45-33-111489, fiskogfri@fiskogfri.dk, http://fiskogfri.dk. Eds. Jens Bursell TEL 45-33-938170, Gordon P Henriksen, Peter Kirkby. adv.: page DKK 15,500; 210 x 297. Circ: 12,600 (paid).

799.1 DNK ISSN 1600-1664
FISKE-FEBER (COPENHAGEN); magasinet om flue, spin og rovfisk!. Text in Danish. 2000. 6/yr. DKK 298 (effective 2009). adv. back issues avail. **Document type:** *Magazine, Consumer.*
Published by: Fiske-Feber Aps, Gunnekaer 8 Baghuset, Roedovre, 2610, Denmark. TEL 45-70-213121, FAX 45-70-213321, fisk@fiske-feber.dk, http://www.fiske-feber.dk.

799.1 SWE ISSN 1652-2540
FISKE-FEBER (HELSINGBORG). Text in Swedish. 2004. biennial. SEK 239 (effective 2005). adv. **Document type:** *Magazine, Consumer.*
Published by: Fiske-Feber AB, Karl Johans Gata 2, Helsingborg, 25267, Sweden. TEL 46-42-211122, FAX 46-42-211137, info@fiske-feber.se. Ed. Joergen Larsson. Adv. contact Robin Ekman. page SEK 22,500; 210 x 280.

799.1 SWE ISSN 1100-3626
FISKE FOER ALLA. Text in Swedish. 1988. 8/yr. SEK 388 (effective 2006). adv. **Document type:** *Magazine, Consumer.*
Published by: L R F Media AB, Bergdorffsgatan 5B, Karlstad, 65224, Sweden. TEL 46-54-7752520, lrfmedia@lrfmedia.lrf.se, http://www.online.lrf.se. Ed. Matts Gyllsand TEL 46-54-7752503. Adv. contact Ulla Jonsson TEL 46-54-7752521. page SEK 23,400; trim 265 x 190.

799.1 SWE ISSN 1403-7300
FISKEJOURNALEN. Variant title: Nya Fiskejournalen. Text in Swedish. 1988. 9/yr. SEK 410 (effective 2005). adv. bk.rev. abstr.; charts; illus. index. Supplement avail. **Document type:** *Magazine, Consumer.*
Supersedes in part (in 1999): Sportfiske (1101-0045); Which was formerly (until 1990): Fiskejournalen, Sportsfiskaren; Which was formed by the merger of(1974-1989): Fiskejournalen (0345-3367); (1985-1989): Sportfiskaren (0282-499X); Which was formerly (1970-1985): Svenskt Fiske (0039-694X)
Published by: Allers Foerlag AB, Landskronavaegen 23, Helsingborg, 25185, Sweden. TEL 46-42-173500, FAX 46-42-173682. Ed. Martin Falklind. Adv. contact Haakon Otterberg TEL 46-302-24446. B&W page SEK 19,700, color page SEK 26,900; trim 210 x 297. Circ: 28,200 (controlled).

796 CHE ISSN 1423-5137
FIT FOR LIFE. Text in German. 1985. 10/yr. CHF 79; CHF 8 newsstand/cover (effective 2006). adv. **Document type:** *Magazine, Consumer.*
Formerly (until 1997): Der Laeufer (1423-5218); Which incoporated (1983-1990): Loipe (1423-5226)
Published by: A Z Fachverlage AG, Neumattstr 1, Aarau, 5001, Switzerland. TEL 41-58-2005650, FAX 41-58-2005651, vertrieb@azag.ch, http://www.azmediengruppe.ch. Ed. Andi Gonseth. Pub. Christoph Marty. Adv. contact Mathias Schenk. color page CHF 5,300. Circ: 20,301 (paid and controlled).

796 USA ISSN 1046-1701
FITNESS CYCLING. Text in English. 2000. q. adv. **Document type:** *Magazine, Consumer.*
Published by: Challenge Publications, Inc., 9509 Vassar Ave, Unit A, Chatsworth, CA 91311. TEL 818-700-6868, FAX 818-700-6282, customerservice@challengeweb.com, http://www.challengeweb.com/. Ed. Chris Hatounian. Pub. Edwin Schnepf.

796.5 SWE ISSN 1104-6503
FJAELLET. Text in Swedish. 1956. q. SEK 290 domestic membership; SEK 360 foreign membership (effective 2010). adv. bk.rev. back issues avail. **Document type:** *Magazine, Consumer.* **Description:** All aspects of backpacking and mountaineering.
Formerly (until 1994): Fjaellklubbsnytt (0348-5013)
Published by: Svenska Fjaellklubben/Swedish Alpine Club, Skogvaktargatan 6 B, Stockholm, 11542, Sweden. info@fjallklubben.se, http://www.fjallklubben.se. Ed. Kenneth Westerlund.

796.552 NOR ISSN 0332-8775
FJELL OG VIDDE. Text in Norwegian. 1967. 6/yr. NOK 530 membership; NOK 295 to students; NOK 62 newsstand/cover (effective 2011). adv. bk.rev. **Document type:** *Magazine, Consumer.*
Published by: Den Norske Turistforening, Youngstorget 1, Oslo, 0181, Norway. TEL 47-40-001868, FAX 47-42-426427, info@turistforeningen.no, http://www.turistforeningen.no. Ed. Helle Andresen. Adv. contact Geir Bentsen. Circ: 142,000 (paid and free).

796.9 NOR ISSN 0809-6198
FJOEL BIBELEN; best paa skate og snowboard. Text in Norwegian. 1996. 3/yr. free. adv. **Document type:** *Magazine, Consumer.*
Former titles (until 2000): Fjoel (1502-377X); (until 1997): Wax Magazine (0806-6841)
Published by: Mediafabrikken, Mariedalsveien 87, Oslo, 0461, Norway. TEL 47-22-040600, FAX 47-22-040610. Ed. Lars Gaartaa TEL 47-22-040611. Adv. contact Jan P B Rutgersen TEL 47-22-040606. color page NOK 16,500; 235 x 296.

799.1 DEU ISSN 0178-0409
FLIEGENFISCHEN; internationales Magazin fuer Flugangler. Text in German. 1984. 6/yr. EUR 51; EUR 8.50 newsstand/cover (effective 2011). adv. back issues avail. **Document type:** *Magazine, Consumer.*
Published by: Jahr Top Special Verlag, Troplowitzstr 5, Hamburg, 22529, Germany. TEL 49-40-389060, FAX 49-40-38906300, info@jahr-tsv.de, http://www.jahr-tsv.de. Ed. Michael Werner. Adv. contact Christopher Zippert TEL 49-40-38906267. Circ: 12,214 (paid).

799.1 DEU
DER FLIEGENFISCHER (ONLINE). Text in German. 1975. bi-m. free. bk.rev. index. back issues avail. **Document type:** *Magazine, Consumer.* **Description:** Covers fly fishing.
Formerly (until 2007): Der Fliegenfischer (Print) (0176-2087)
Media: Online - full text.
Published by: Verlag J. Schueck, Lohhofer Str 11, Nuernberg, 90453, Germany. TEL 49-911-635055, FAX 49-911-6324338. Circ: 5,000.

799.1 USA ISSN 1081-910X
FLORIDA FISH AND GAME FINDER MAGAZINE. (In 24 regional editions: Arkansas, California, Florida, Georgia, Illinois, Indiana, Louisiana, Michigan, Minnesota, Missouri, New England, New Jersey, New York, North Carolina, Ohio, Oklahoma, Pennsylvania, Rocky Mountain, South Carolina, Tennessee, Texas, Virginia, Washington, Wisconsin) Text in English. 1973. m. USD 24 (effective 2008). adv. illus. reprints avail. **Document type:** *Magazine, Consumer.* **Description:** Promotes the various types of fishing and hunting for the active outdoorsman. Contains local, regional and statewide reports.
Formerly: Florida Fish Finder Magazine (0279-7879)
Related titles: Online - full text ed.: 1973.
Published by: Outdoor Sports Marketing Inc., 4270 Aloma Ave, Ste 124, PMB 55J, Winter Park, FL 32792. TEL 800-741-0045, FAX 407-677-1878, publisher@floridafishandgamerfinder.com. Pub. Ted Ensminger. adv.: page USD 49,250; trim 10 x 7. Circ: 720,000 (controlled).

799 USA ISSN 0889-3322
FLORIDA GAME & FISH. Text in English. 1986. m. USD 12.99 domestic; USD 25.99 in Canada; USD 27.99 elsewhere (effective 2011). adv. illus. back issues avail. **Document type:** *Magazine, Consumer.* **Description:** Informs sportsmen of hunting and fishing, as well as environmental and conservation issues in Florida.
Related titles: Online - full text ed.; ◆ Regional ed(s).: Game & Fish; ◆ Louisiana Game & Fish. ISSN 0744-3692; ◆ Alabama Game & Fish. ISSN 0279-6783; ◆ Mississippi-Louisiana Game & Fish. ISSN 1947-2358; ◆ North Carolina Game & Fish. ISSN 0897-8816; ◆ South Carolina Game & Fish. ISSN 0897-9154; ◆ West Virginia Game & Fish. ISSN 0897-9162; ◆ Missouri Game & Fish. ISSN 0889-3799; ◆ New York Game & Fish. ISSN 0897-9189; ◆ California Game & Fish. ISSN 1056-0122; ◆ Great Plains Game & Fish. ISSN 1055-6532; ◆ Illinois Game & Fish. ISSN 0897-9014; ◆ Indiana Game & Fish. ISSN 0897-8980; ◆ Iowa Game & Fish. ISSN 0897-9197; ◆ Mid-Atlantic Game & Fish. ISSN 1055-6540; ◆ Oklahoma Game & Fish. ISSN 0746-6013; ◆ Rocky Mountain Game & Fish. ISSN 1056-0114; ◆ Pennsylvania Game & Fish. ISSN 0897-8808; ◆ Virginia Game & Fish. ISSN 0897-8794; ◆ Washington - Oregon Game & Fish. ISSN 1056-0106; ◆ Ohio Game & Fish. ISSN 0897-9170; New England Game & Fish. ISSN 0897-8972. 1988. USD 12 domestic; USD 25 in Canada; USD 27 elsewhere (effective 2010).
Published by: Intermedia Outdoors, Inc., 512 7th Ave, 11th Fl, New York, NY 10018. TEL 212-852-6682, 800-260-6397, FAX 212-302-4472, customerservice@imoutdoors.com, http://www.imoutdoorsmedia.com. Ed. Ken Dunwoody. Pub., Adv. contact Peter Gross.

799 USA ISSN 0015-3885
FLORIDA SPORTSMAN. Text in English. 1969. m. USD 19.95 domestic; USD 32.95 in Canada; USD 34.95 elsewhere (effective 2009). adv. bk.rev. charts; illus. **Document type:** *Magazine, Consumer.* **Description:** Contains information on sport fish, conservation issues, regional fishing within Florida and all fishing gear including fishing tackle, fishing rods and reels, and boating equipment of all kinds.
Formerly (until 1971): Florida and Tropic Sportsman
Related titles: Online - full text ed.; ◆ Supplement(s): Florida Sportsman's Redfish & Trout Annual Guide.
Indexed: EnvAb, EnvInd, G08, I05.
—CCC.
Published by: Intermedia Outdoors, Inc., 2700 S Kanner Hwy, Stuart, FL 34994. TEL 772-219-7400, FAX 772-219-6900, customerservice@imoutdoors.com, http://www.imoutdoorsmedia.com. Eds. Jeff Weakley TEL 772-219-7400 ext 116, Karl Wickstrom. adv.: B&W page USD 4,820, color page USD 6,500; trim 8 x 10.875. Circ: 96,776 (paid). **Subscr. to:** PO Box 420235, Palm Coast, FL 32142. TEL 800-274-6386.

799 USA
FLORIDA SPORTSMAN'S REDFISH & TROUT ANNUAL GUIDE. Key Title: Redfish & Trout Annual Guide. Text in English. 19??. a. **Document type:** *Magazine, Consumer.*
Related titles: ◆ Supplement to: Florida Sportsman. ISSN 0015-3885.
Published by: Intermedia Outdoors, Inc., 512 7th Ave, 11th Fl, New York, NY 10018. TEL 212-852-6682, FAX 212-302-4472, customerservice@imoutdoors.com, http://www.imoutdoorsmedia.com.

FLORIDA WILDLIFE. *see* CONSERVATION

796 USA ISSN 1947-797X
▼ **FLOWBOARDER MAGAZINE.** Text in English. 2009. q. USD 3.99 per issue (effective 2009). **Document type:** *Magazine, Consumer.* **Description:** Features athletes in flowboarding and bodyboarding.
Published by: Apex Propaganda, PO Box 64, Wisconsin Dells, WI 53965. TEL 608-566-9160, jason@flowboardermag.com.

799.1 SWE ISSN 0349-3849
FLUGFISKE I NORDEN. Text in Swedish. 1979. bi-m. SEK 280 domestic; SEK 310 in Norway; SEK 295 in Denmark; EUR 41 in Finland; EUR 49 in Europe; SEK 495 elsewhere (effective 2002). adv.
Published by: Foerlags AB Flugfiske i Norden, c/o Anne Marie Skarp, Soedra Parkgatan 8, Aelmhult, 34331, Sweden. Adv. contact Pelle Klippinge TEL 46-491 913 23. **Subscr. to:** A.M. Skarp, Soedra Parkgatan 8, Aelmhult 34331, Sweden.

796.172 BRA ISSN 0104-155X
FLUIR. Text in Portuguese. 1987. m. USD 54. adv. charts; illus. **Document type:** *Consumer.* **Description:** Covers surfing: championships, equipment and fashions.
Related titles: Supplement(s): Fluir Bodyboard.
Published by: Editora Azul, S.A., Ave. NACOES UNIDAS, 5777, Sao Paulo, SP 05479-900, Brazil. TEL 55-11-867300, FAX 55-11-8673311. Ed. Felipe Zobaran. R&P Benjamin Goncalvez TEL 55-11-8673304. Adv. contact Enio Vergeiro. color page USD 8,096; 274 x 208. Circ: 41,802 (paid).

799.1 AUS
FLY ANGLER AUSTRALIA (ONLINE). Text in English. 2006. q. adv. back issues avail. **Document type:** *Magazine, Trade.*
Formerly (until 200?): Fly Angler Australia (Print) (1833-4806)
Media: Online - full text.
Published by: Fly Angler Publishing, PO Box 1251, Tewantin, QLD 4565, Australia. TEL 61-7-54853066, FAX 61-7-54853077. Ed., Pub. Mark Bantich.

799.1 USA ISSN 0015-4741
SH401
FLY FISHERMAN; the leading magazine of fly fishing. Text in English. 1969. bi-m. USD 18.99 domestic; USD 31.99 in Canada; USD 33.99 elsewhere (effective 2011). adv. bk.rev. illus. cum.index: vols.1-16. reprints avail. **Document type:** *Magazine, Consumer.* **Description:** Provides readers with expert advice on the latest fly fishing techniques, the newest tackle, and the hottest new fly patterns.
Related titles: Online - full text ed.
Indexed: A11, A22, C05, CPerI, G05, G06, G07, G08, G09, H20, I05, I07, M01, M02, P10, P19, P48, P52, P53, P54, P56, PQC, S23, T02, U01.
—Ingenta. **CCC.**
Published by: Intermedia Outdoors, Inc., 512 7th Ave, 11th Fl, New York, NY 10018. TEL 212-852-6682, 800-260-6397, FAX 212-302-4472, customerservice@imoutdoors.com, http://www.imoutdoorsmedia.com.

799.12 GBR ISSN 0959-8383
FLY FISHING AND FLY TYING; for the progressive game angler and fly tyer. Text in English. 1990. m. GBP 36 domestic; GBP 49 in Europe; GBP 56.50 subscr - carrier delivery elsewhere; GBP 3.10 per issue (effective 2009). adv. illus. back issues avail. **Document type:** *Magazine, Consumer.* **Description:** Informative articles, tips and reviews for fly fishing anglers and fly tyers.
Published by: Rolling River Publications Ltd., The Locus Ctr, The Sq, Aberfeldy, Perthshire PH15 2DD, United Kingdom. TEL 44-1887-829868, FAX 44-1887-829856. Ed. Mark Bowler. **Dist. by:** M M C Ltd., Octagon House, White Hart Meadows, Ripley, Woking, Surrey GU23 6HR, United Kingdom.

799.1 USA
FLY FISHING MADE EASY. Text in English. 1984. irreg., latest vol.4, 2006. USD 16.95 (effective 2008). adv. **Document type:** *Magazine, Consumer.*
Published by: Falcon Publishing (Subsidiary of: The Globe Pequot Press, Inc.), 246 Goose Ln, PO Box 480, Guilford, CT 06437. TEL 203-458-4500, http://www.falcon.com. Circ: 130,000.

799.1 USA ISSN 1045-0149
FLY ROD & REEL; the magazine of American fly-fishing. Text in English. 1979. 6/yr. USD 19.97 domestic; USD 26.97 foreign; USD 4.99 newsstand/cover (effective 2008). adv. bk.rev. illus. back issues avail.; reprints avail. **Document type:** *Magazine, Consumer.* **Description:** Covers conservation and fly-fishing how-to, equipment reviews and travel.
Formerly (until 1989): Rod and Reel (0194-925X)
Published by: Down East Enterprise, Inc., 680 Commercial St., Rockport, ME 04856. TEL 207-594-9544, 800-727-7422, FAX 207-594-7215. Ed., R&P Paul Guernsey. Pub. Kit Parker. Adv. contact Bill Anderson. Circ: 63,400 (paid).

799.1 USA ISSN 1082-1309
SH451
FLY TYER. Text in English. 1978. q. USD 21.95 domestic; USD 31.95 in Canada & Mexico; USD 41.95 elsewhere (effective 2008). adv. back issues avail. **Document type:** *Magazine, Consumer.*
Published by: Morris Multimedia, Inc., 725 Broad St, Augusta, GA 30901. TEL 800-726-4707, http://www.morris.com. Ed. David Klausmeyer. Pub. William S Morris III. Adv. contact Michael Floyd TEL 706-823-3739.

799.1 USA ISSN 1947-4539
SH456
▼ **THE FLYFISH JOURNAL.** Text in English. 2009 (Fall). q. USD 39.99; USD 12.99 newsstand/cover (effective 2010). adv. illus. **Document type:** *Magazine, Consumer.* **Description:** Covers fly fishing's icons, environment, and global culture.
Published by: Funny Feelings, LLC, PO Box 2806, Bellingham, WA 98227. TEL 360-671-7386, http://www.funnyfeelingsllc.com/.

799.1 USA ISSN 0147-8834
SH456
FLYFISHER. Text in English. 1968. q. membership. adv. bk.rev. tr.lit. back issues avail. **Document type:** *Magazine, Consumer.* **Description:** Covers articles on fly fishing, where, how, why, and news from what's happening in the Federation.
Indexed: H20.
Published by: Federation of Fly Fishers, Richard Wentz, Keokee Publishing, PO Box 722, Sandpoint, ID 83864. TEL 208-263-3573, FAX 208-263-4045. Ed., Adv. contact Richard Wentz. R&P Chris Bessler. page USD 1,035. Circ: 15,000. **Subscr. to:** 215 E. Lewis St., Ste. 305, Livingston, MT 59047-3145.

799.1 GBR ISSN 0046-4228
FLYFISHERS JOURNAL. Text in English. 1911. s-a. GBP 18 (effective 2000). adv. bk.rev. illus. index. **Document type:** *Bulletin, Consumer.*
—BLDSC (4754.230000).
Published by: Flyfishers' Club, 69 Brook St, London, W1Y 2ER, United Kingdom. TEL 44-20-7629-5958. Ed., Pub., R&P, Adv. contact Kenneth Robson. Circ: 700.

799.1 USA ISSN 1521-7361
FLYFISHING & TYING JOURNAL. Text in English. 1978. q. USD 18.95 (effective 2010). adv. bk.rev. back issues avail.; reprints avail. **Document type:** *Magazine, Consumer.* **Description:** Covers casting, fly tying, knots, best places to fish, conservation, new product services and domestic and foreign news.
Former titles (until 1998): Flyfishing (1097-8763); (until 1997): Western Flyfishing (1086-8194); (until 1996): Flyfishing (0744-7191)
Published by: Frank Amato Publications, Inc, PO Box 82112, Portland, OR 97282. TEL 503-653-8108, 800-541-9498, FAX 503-653-2766, info@amatobooks.com. Ed. Mr. Frank W Amato. Adv. contact Mr. Robert Crandall.

799.1 USA
FLYFISHING.COM. Text in English. 1995. d.
Media: Online - full content.
Published by: AnglersWeb, Inc. noc@w3works.com, http://www.flyfishing.com.

799.1 AUS ISSN 1324-2288
FLYLIFE; salt and freshwater fly fishing. Text in English. 1995. q. AUD 45 in Australia & New Zealand; AUD 70 elsewhere; AUD 11.95 newsstand/cover (effective 2009). adv. back issues avail. **Document type:** *Magazine, Consumer.* **Description:** Covers flyfishing, fly-tying for trout and saltwater species in Australia, New Zealand and the South Pacific.
Published by: FlyLife Publishing, 45 Bridge St, Richmond, TAS 7025, Australia. TEL 61-3-62602409, FAX 61-3-62602751. Ed., Pub. Robert Sloane. Adv. contact Ian Ainslie.

333.95416 USA
FOCUS ON FISH AND WILDLIFE. Text in English. q. free. **Document type:** *Newsletter, Government.*
Formerly: Focus (Indianapolis)
Published by: Indiana Department of Natural Resources, 402 W Washington, Rm W273, Indianapolis, IN 46204. TEL 317-232-4080, FAX 317-232-8150. Ed., Pub., R&P Michael Ellis. Circ: 34,000.

FODOR'S SKIING IN THE U S A & CANADA. *see* TRAVEL AND TOURISM

796.5 910.202 USA
FODOR'S SPORTS: HIKING. Text in English. 1992. irreg. USD 12.
Published by: Fodor's Travel Publications, Inc. (Subsidiary of: Random House Inc.), 1745 Broadway, 15th Fl, New York, NY 10019. TEL 212-572-2313, editors@fodors.com, http://www.fodors.com. **Dist. by:** Random House Inc.

796.42 910.202 USA
FODOR'S SPORTS: RUNNING. Text in English. 1992. irreg. USD 12.
Published by: Fodor's Travel Publications, Inc. (Subsidiary of: Random House Inc.), 1745 Broadway, 15th Fl, New York, NY 10019. TEL 212-572-2313, editors@fodors.com, http://www.fodors.com. **Dist. by:** Random House Inc.

796 USA ISSN 1553-6114
GV199.42.M2
FOGHORN OUTDOORS. MAINE HIKING. Text in English. 2005. biennial, latest 2005. USD 12.95 per issue (effective 2009). **Document type:** *Guide, Consumer.*
Published by: Avalon Travel Publishing, 1400 65th St, Ste 250, Emeryville, CA 94608. avalon.publicity@perseusbooks.com, http://www.avalontravelbooks.com.

796 USA ISSN 1553-6106
GV199.42.N4
FOGHORN OUTDOORS. NEW HAMPSHIRE HIKING. Text in English. 2005. biennial, latest 2005. USD 12.95 per issue (effective 2009). **Document type:** *Guide, Consumer.*
Published by: Avalon Travel Publishing, 1400 65th St, Ste 250, Emeryville, CA 94608. avalon.publicity@perseusbooks.com, http://www.avalontravelbooks.com.

796 910.2 USA ISSN 1553-9075
GV199.42.W2
FOGHORN OUTDOORS. WASHINGTON HIKING. Text in English. 2005. biennial, latest 2005. USD 17.95 per issue (effective 2009). **Document type:** *Guide, Consumer.*
Published by: Avalon Travel Publishing, 1700 4th St, Berkeley, CA 94710. TEL 510-595-3664, avalon.publicity@perseusbooks.com, http://www.avalontravelbooks.com.

FOOTPATH WORKER. *see* CONSERVATION

796.552 790.1 USA ISSN 1064-0681
THE FOOTPRINT; the official newsletter of the Florida trail association. Text in English. 1966. bi-m. USD 25 membership. adv. bk.rev. **Document type:** *Newsletter.* **Description:** Provides Florida trail policy, items affecting the trail, upcoming events and activities, announcements, notices and articles for and by about members reflecting a topic of interest to FTA members.
Published by: Florida Trail Association, PO Box 13708, Gainesville, FL 32604. TEL 325-378-8823, 800-343-1882, FAX 352-378-4550. Ed. Peter Durnell. Pub. Judy Trotta. adv.: B&W page USD 325; trim 9.5 x 7.5. Circ: 3,500 (paid). **Dist. by:** Ship Right Plus Inc., 2937 N E 19th Dr, Gainesville, FL 32609. TEL 352-377-4525, FAX 352-372-6729.

796.172 USA
FOREVERSKIM. Text in English. 2004. bi-m. free. **Document type:** *Magazine, Consumer.* **Description:** Covers the watersport of skimboarding, including locations, gears, and personalities.
Media: Online - full content.
Published by: 20/30 North Studios, PO Box 2021, Fort Walton Beach, FL 32549. TEL 850-225-1858, 850-225-1858, 2030north@gmail.com, http://www.2030northstudios.com/. Ed. Derek Makekau.

FREE FLIGHT/VOL LIBRE. *see* AERONAUTICS AND SPACE FLIGHT

796.04605 GBR ISSN 1747-048X
FREEFLOW; Ireland's soul of extreme sports. Text in English. 2005. bi-m. GBP 15, EUR 25 (effective 2006). adv. **Document type:** *Magazine, Consumer.*
Related titles: Online - full text ed.: free (effective 2009).
Published by: Freeflow Magazine, Thomas House, Belfast, BT71JJ, United Kingdom. TEL 44-28-90621122, FAX 44-28-90430606.

796.93 USA
FREQUENCY. Text in English. 2001. q. USD 39.95 domestic; USD 49.99 in Canada; USD 59.99 elsewhere (effective 2002). illus. back issues avail. **Description:** Focused on the personalities, landscapes, and opinions which drive snowboarding forward.
Published by: Funny Feelings, LLC, 814 Lakeway Drive, Number 172, Bellingham, WA 98226. http://www.funnyfeelingsllc.com/. Ed. Jeff Galbraith.

799.1 CAN ISSN 1208-8722
FRESHWATER FISHING REGULATIONS SYNOPSIS. Text in English. 197?. a.
Formerly (until 1988): British Columbia Sport Fishing Regulations Synopsis (0701-9742)
Published by: British Columbia Ministry of Environment, Fish and Wildlife Branch, PO Box 9374, Stn Prov Govt, Victoria, BC V8W 9M4, Canada.

796 SWE ISSN 0283-9571
FRILUFTSLIV, I ALLA VAEDER. Text in Swedish. 1947. q. adv. bk.rev. **Document type:** *Magazine, Consumer.* **Description:** Articles for the whole family on outdoor life; trekking, canoing, walking, skiing, skating, etc.
Formerly (until 1987): I Alla Vaeder (0345-5017)
Related titles: Audio cassette/tape ed.
Published by: Friluftsfraemjandet, Instrumentvaegen 14, Haegersten, 11392, Sweden. TEL 46-8-447-44-40, FAX 46-8-30-25-54. Ed., Pub. Per Goethlin. adv.: color page SEK 31,000; trim 185 x 270. Circ: 39,300.

FRITID & KULTUR I SVERIGE. *see* LEISURE AND RECREATION

796.5 ESP ISSN 1134-0762
FUERZA 7 BEAUFORT. Text in Spanish. 1994. bi-m. adv. back issues avail. **Document type:** *Magazine, Consumer.*
Published by: Punta Usaje S.L., Gl Lopez de Hoyos, 168 4o C Int, Madrid, 28002, Spain. TEL 34-91-4159950, FAX 34-91-4151529, fuerza7@arrauis.es. Circ: 15,000 (controlled).

799.2 USA ISSN 0016-2620
FULL CRY; published exclusively for the American coon hound and trail hound enthusiast. Text in English. 1939. m. USD 23; USD 3 newsstand/cover (effective 2005). adv. bk.rev. illus. reprints avail. **Document type:** *Magazine, Consumer.* **Description:** Offers raccoon, bear, lion, bobcat and squirrel hunters tips and information.
Published by: C & H Publishing, PO Box 777, Sesser, IL 62884. TEL 618-625-2711, FAX 618-626-6221. Ed. Terry Walker. adv.: B&W page USD 250. Circ: 20,200 (paid).

799.1 USA
FUR-FISH-GAME. Text in English. m. **Document type:** *Magazine, Consumer.*
Address: 2878 E Main, Columbus, OH 43209-9947. Ed. Mitch Cox. Circ: 111,000 (paid).

799 USA ISSN 0016-2922
TS1060
FUR - FISH - GAME. HARDING'S MAGAZINE. Text in English. 1925. m. USD 16.95 (effective 2005). adv. bk.rev. illus.; tr.lit. reprints avail. **Document type:** *Magazine, Consumer.* **Description:** Presents hunting, trapping and fishing advice for practical outdoorsmen.
Published by: A.R. Harding Publishing Co., 2878 E Main St, Columbus, OH 43209. TEL 614-231-9585, FAX 614-231-5735, ffgservice@ameritech.net. Ed. Mitch Cox. Pub. Jeff Kirn. Adv. contact Eric Schweinhagen. B&W page USD 3,349, color page USD 4,980. Circ: 113,000 (paid).

796.939 USA ISSN 1554-8511
GV857.S57
FUTURE SNOWBOARDING. Variant title: Snowboarding. Text in English. 2005 (Nov.). bi-m. USD 5 domestic; USD 15 in Canada; USD 19 elsewhere (effective 2008). **Document type:** *Magazine, Consumer.* **Description:** Designed to expand the enjoyment of snowboarding through jaw-dropping photography with a mission of bringing the readers closer to the products, places and personalities.
Related titles: CD-ROM ed.
Published by: Future U S, Inc. (Subsidiary of: Future Publishing Ltd.), 4000 Shoreline Ct, Ste 400, South San Francisco, CA 94080. TEL 650-872-1642, FAX 650-872-1643, http://www.futureus.com. Eds. Larry Nunez, Jeff Baker. Adv. contact Jeff Baker. Circ: 116,827.

799.1 USA ISSN 1930-0468
G A F F MAGAZINE. (Gulf Atlantic Florida Fishing) Text in English. 2003. bi-m. **Document type:** *Magazine, Consumer.*
Address: P.O. Box 15066, Tallahassee, FL 32317. TEL 850-570-9600, 866-457-0757, http://www.gaffmag.net. Pub. Matt Draper.

796.93 USA ISSN 1930-2479
G I E MEDIA'S SNOW. Variant title: Snow Magazine. Text in English. 2000. bi-m. free to qualified personnel (effective 2008). adv. back issues avail.; reprints avail. **Document type:** *Magazine, Trade.*
Related titles: Online - full text ed.
Published by: G I E Media Inc., 4020 Kinross Lakes Pky, Richfield, OH 44286. TEL 330-523-5400, 800-456-0707, FAX 330-659-0823, http://www.giemedia.com/pages/home/default.aspx. Ed. Michael Zawacki TEL 330-523-5381. Pub. Kevin Gilbride TEL 330-523-5368. Adv. contact Samantha Gilbride TEL 330-523-5386. page USD 5,563, color page USD 6,286; trim 8.125 x 10.875. Circ: 30,462.

796.5 BEL ISSN 0776-3646
G R INFOS SENTIERS. Text in French. 1964. q. EUR 15 domestic; EUR 18 foreign (effective 2005). **Document type:** *Bulletin.* **Description:** Includes information on footpaths, hiking, and trekking.
Formerly (until 1988): G R Informations (0775-7344)
Published by: Les Sentiers de Grande Randonnee, Rue Pierre Fontaine 32, Papignies, 7861, Belgium. TEL 32-68-333337, FAX 32-19-588767. Ed. Jean-Marie Maquet. Circ: 2,000.

796 SWE ISSN 1651-9655
GAANGSPORT MED VANDRING. Text in Swedish. 1979. 6/yr.
Former titles (until 2001): Gaang och Vandring (1400-8858); (until 1995): Gaangsport (1400-2574); (until 1991): Gaang och Vandring (0349-2354)
Published by: Svenska Gaang- och Vandrarfoerbundet/Swedish Walking Association, c/o Kvibergs Idrottscenter, Goeteborg, 41582, Sweden. TEL 46-31-7266110, http://www.gangsport.com.

796.552 JPN
GAKUJIN/ALPINIST. Text in Japanese. 1947. m.
Published by: Tokyo Shimbun Publications Dept., 2-3-13 Ko-Unan, Minato-ku, Tokyo, 108-0075, Japan. Ed. Takao Nakazono. Circ: 150,000.

799 USA
GAME & FISH. Text in English. 19??. m. USD 12 domestic; USD 25 in Canada; USD 27 elsewhere (effective 2011). adv. **Document type:** *Magazine, Consumer.*
Related titles: Online - full text ed.; ♦ Regional ed(s).: Oklahoma Game & Fish. ISSN 0746-6013; ♦ Louisiana Game & Fish. ISSN 0744-3692; ♦ Florida Game & Fish. ISSN 0889-3322; ♦ Alabama Game & Fish. ISSN 0279-6783; ♦ Mississippi-Louisiana Game & Fish. ISSN 1947-2358; ♦ North Carolina Game & Fish. ISSN 0897-8816; ♦ South Carolina Game & Fish. ISSN 0897-9154; ♦ West Virginia Game & Fish. ISSN 0897-9162; ♦ Missouri Game & Fish. ISSN 0889-3799; ♦ New York Game & Fish. ISSN 0897-9189; ♦ California Game & Fish. ISSN 1056-0122; ♦ Great Plains Game & Fish. ISSN 1055-6532; ♦ Illinois Game & Fish. ISSN 0897-9014; ♦ Indiana Game & Fish. ISSN 0897-8980; ♦ Iowa Game & Fish. ISSN 0897-9197; ♦ Mid-Atlantic Game & Fish. ISSN 1055-6540; ♦ Rocky Mountain Game & Fish. ISSN 1056-0114; ♦ Pennsylvania Game & Fish. ISSN 0897-8808; ♦ Virginia Game & Fish. ISSN 0897-8794; ♦ Washington - Oregon Game & Fish. ISSN 1056-0106; ♦ Ohio Game & Fish. ISSN 0897-9170; New England Game & Fish. ISSN 0897-8972. 1988. USD 12 domestic; USD 25 in Canada; USD 27 elsewhere (effective 2010).
Published by: Intermedia Outdoors, Inc., 512 7th Ave, 11th Fl, New York, NY 10018. TEL 212-852-6682, 800-260-6397, FAX 212-302-4472, customerservice@imoutdoors.com, http://www.imoutdoorsmedia.com. Ed. Ken Dunwoody. Pub., Adv. contact Peter Gross.

799 USA ISSN 1066-0577
SK351
THE GAME MANAGER. Text in English. 1987. q. USD 20 (effective 2004). adv. **Document type:** *Newsletter.* **Description:** Designed for land owners and game managers.
Formerly (until 1989): Hunting Ranch Business
Published by: Multiple Use Managers, Inc., PO Box 669, Los Molinos, CA 96055. TEL 530-527-3588, FAX 530-527-3246. Ed. Wayne Long. Circ: 400 (paid and free).

796.552 CAN ISSN 0833-0778
GAZETTE OF THE ALPINE CLUB OF CANADA. Text in English. 1986. q.
Published by: Alpine Club of Canada, Indian Flats Rd, P O Box 8040, Canmore, AB T1W 2T8, Canada. Ed. Zac Bolan.

GENERATION CAMPING CAR; Le Magazine de l'art de vivre en camping-car. *see* TRANSPORTATION—Automobiles

796 CAN ISSN 1194-5303
GEO PLEIN-AIR; magazine quebecois de l'aventure. Variant title: Magazine Geo Plein Air. Text in English. bi-m. CAD 22.50, USD 30; CAD 3.95 newsstand/cover (effective 1999). adv. back issues avail. **Description:** Offers a price list for skiing, biking and other sporting equipment.
Formerly (until 1992): Plein Air (0843-8552)
Indexed: PdeR.
Published by: Editions Tricycle, 1251 rue Rachel Est, Montreal, PQ H2J 2J9, Canada. TEL 514-521-8356, FAX 514-521-5711. Ed. Simon Kretz. Pub. Pierre Hamel. Adv. contact Andre Dalpe. B&W page CAD 2,445, color page CAD 3,260; trim 10 x 7.13. Circ: 25,000.

799 USA ISSN 0895-3295
SK662.G4
GEORGIA OUTDOOR NEWS. Text in English. 1986. m. USD 11.95. adv. **Document type:** *Magazine, Consumer.* **Description:** Focuses on fishing and hunting throughout Georgia.
Published by: Georgia Outdoor News, Inc., 1086 Ward Rd., Madison, GA 30650-2008. TEL 404-425-0990, FAX 404-425-0998. Adv. contact Phil Barnet. B&W page USD 725, color page USD 1,075; trim 10.88 x 7.75. Circ: 34,145.

799 USA ISSN 0199-6517
GEORGIA SPORTSMAN. Text in English. 1976. m. USD 14.97 domestic; USD 27.97 in Canada; USD 29.97 elsewhere (effective 2008). adv. illus. **Document type:** *Magazine, Consumer.* **Description:** Reports on all aspects of hunting and fishing, as well as environmental and conservation matters.
Published by: Intermedia Outdoors, Inc., 512 7th Ave, 11th Fl, New York, NY 10018. TEL 212-852-6600, 800-260-6397, FAX 212-302-4472, customerservice@imoutdoors.com, http://www.imoutdoorsmedia.com. Pub. Jimmy Stewart. adv.: B&W page USD 13,830, color page USD 19,360. Circ: 42,000 (paid).

796 USA ISSN 1939-5418
GEORGIA'S OUTDOOR ADVENTURES. Text in English. 2000. m. USD 24 for 2 yrs. (effective 2007). adv. **Document type:** *Magazine, Consumer.* **Description:** Features hunting and fishing news and stories from around Georgia.
Published by: Outdoor Adventures Inc, PO Box 55, Perry, GA 31069. TEL 478-987-1200. Pub. Terry Todd.

796 CAN ISSN 1912-0443
GET OUT THERE (BRITISH COLUMBIA EDITION). Text in English. 2006. bi-m. free (effective 2007). **Document type:** *Magazine, Consumer.*
Related titles: Regional ed(s).: Get Out There (Ontario Edition). ISSN 1912-0435. 2004.
Published by: Get Out There Communications Inc., Suite 1200 - 1 Aberfoyle Crescent, Toronto, ON M8X 2X8, Canada. TEL 416-239-1590, FAX 416-840-4943, info@getouttheremag.com, http://www.getouttheremag.com. Eds. Karen Shim, Terri Dewar TEL 604-947-0033. Pub. Marissa Schroder. Circ: 80,000.

GETAWAY. *see* TRAVEL AND TOURISM

796.54 NLD ISSN 2211-422X
▼ **GLAMPING MAGAZINE.** Text in Dutch. 2010. a. EUR 2.95 newsstand/cover (effective 2011). adv. **Document type:** *Magazine, Consumer.*
Published by: (ANWB BV/Royal Dutch Touring Club), Algemene Nederlandse Wielrijders Bond (A N W B) Media/Dutch Automobile Association Media, Postbus 93200, The Hague, 2509 BA, Netherlands. TEL 31-70-3141470, FAX 31-70-3146538, http://www.anwbmedia.nl.

629.1 AUT
GLEITSCHIRM, FLY AND GLIDE. Text in German. 2008. 10/yr. EUR 55 (effective 2009). adv. **Document type:** *Magazine, Consumer.*

S

Formed by the merger of (2004-2008): Schlechtflieger-Magazin; (1998-2008): Gleitschirm; (1994-2008): Fly and Glide (0947-627X); Which was formerly (until 1994): Drachenflieger-Magazin (0175-1492); (until 1983): Drachenflieger (0722-8589); (1975-1980): Drachenflieger-Magazin (0343-3447)
Published by: Thermik Verlag, Stelzhamerstr 18, Wels, 4600, Austria. TEL 43-7242-452240, FAX 43-7242-4522422. Eds. Norbert Aprissnig, Sascha Burkhardt. Adv. contact Elisabeth Rauchenberger.

796.93 SWE ISSN 1652-2737
GLID. Text in Swedish. 2004. bi-m. SEK 289 (effective 2006). adv. **Document type:** *Magazine, Consumer.*
Published by: Baangman&Oernborg Foerlag AB, Raaslavaegen 14, Solna, 16954, Sweden. TEL 46-8-7352451, info@glidmagazine.se. Ed. Mary Oernborg TEL 46-736-200810. Pub. Karin Baangman. Adv. contact Marlene Stenwall.

796.93 SWE ISSN 1653-5553
GLID. LAANGFAERDSSKRIDSKOR. Text in Swedish. 2004. a. **Document type:** *Consumer.*
Published by: Baangman&Oernborg Foerlag AB, Raaslavaegen 14, Solna, 16954, Sweden. TEL 46-8-7352451, info@glidmagazine.se, http://www.glidmagazine.se.

GO! (CAPE TOWN, 2006). *see* TRAVEL AND TOURISM

796.52 USA ISSN 1533-709X
GV200.2
GO CLIMB!. Text in English. 2001. a.
Published by: North South Publications, 5455 Spine Rd. Mezz. A, Boulder, CO 80301. TEL 303-499-8410, FAX 303-530-3729. Pub. Dougald MacDonald.

796.93 BEL ISSN 0774-6849
GO SKIING (NEDERLAND EDITION). Text in Flemish. 1983. a. adv. illus. **Document type:** *Consumer.* **Description:** Covers all aspects of skiing, for beginners and pros, including competition results, travel features, interviews and more.
Related titles: French ed.: Go Skiing (France Edition). ISSN 0774-6830.
Published by: Event S.A., Chaussee de Waterloo, 1455, Brussels, 1180, Belgium. TEL 32-2-3792990, FAX 32-2-3792999, play.tennis@skynet.be. Ed. Marie Dominique Spinoit. Adv. contact Vanessa Coupe. color page EUR 1,710.46; trim 216 x 146.

GOLD PROSPECTOR. *see* MINES AND MINING INDUSTRY

GOLDEN DOLPHIN VIDEO C D MAGAZINE. (Compact Disc) *see* EARTH SCIENCES—Oceanography

GOOD BEACH GUIDE (ONLINE). *see* ENVIRONMENTAL STUDIES—Pollution

GOOD CAMPS GUIDE BRITAIN (YEAR). *see* TRAVEL AND TOURISM

GOOD CAMPS GUIDE EUROPE (YEAR). *see* TRAVEL AND TOURISM

GOOD CAMPS GUIDE FRANCE (YEAR). *see* TRAVEL AND TOURISM

796.93 GBR ISSN 0958-0689
GOOD SKI GUIDE. Text in English. 1983. q. GBP 15 combined subscription (print & online eds.) (effective 2009); subscr. includes Mountain Magic Magazine. adv. charts; illus.; stat.; tr.lit. back issues avail. **Document type:** *Magazine, Consumer.*
Related titles: Online - full text ed.
Published by: Good Ski Guide Ltd., Parman House, 30-36 Fife Rd, Kingston-upon-Thames, Surrey KT1 1SY, United Kingdom. TEL 44-20-85479822, FAX 44-20-85460984, edit@goodholidayideas.com. Ed., Pub. John Hill. Adv. contact Gideon Reeves.

796.93 RUS
GORNYE LYZHI/MOUNTAIN-SKIING. Text in Russian. 1992. 4/yr. USD 98 foreign (effective 2006). **Document type:** *Magazine, Consumer.* **Description:** Contains advice to beginners and pros on vacationing in the mountains. Covers ski slopes, vacation spots and downhill lessons.
Address: Novodmitrovskaya ul 5-a, Moscow, 125015, Russian Federation. TEL 7-095-2851687, FAX 7-095-2341678. Ed. A N Perevozchikov. Circ: 17,000 (paid). **Dist. by:** East View Information Services, 10601 Wayzata Blvd, Minneapolis, MN 55305. TEL 952-252-1201, 800-477-1005, FAX 952-252-1202, info@eastview.com, http://www.eastview.com.

799.2 FRA ISSN 1285-3909
GRAND GIBIER. Text in French. 1998. q. EUR 17.50 (effective 2008). **Document type:** *Magazine, Consumer.*
Related titles: ◆ Supplement to: La Revue Nationale de la Chasse. ISSN 1961-0890.
Published by: Mondadori France, 1 Rue du Colonel Pierre-Avia, Paris, Cedex 15 75754, France. TEL 33-1-46484848, contact@mondadori.fr, http://www.mondadori.fr.

GRAND TOUR EMOZIONI IN VIAGGIO. SCI SULLE ALPI. *see* TRAVEL AND TOURISM

799 USA ISSN 0273-6691
GV191.2
GRAY'S SPORTING JOURNAL. Abbreviated title: G S J. Text in English. 1976. 7/yr. USD 29.95 domestic; USD 49.95 in Canada; USD 69.95 elsewhere (effective 2009). bk.rev. illus. back issues avail.; reprints avail. **Document type:** *Magazine, Consumer.* **Description:** Covers hunting and fishing. Includes recipes, history, tradition, poems, and other hunting entries.
Published by: Morris Multimedia, Inc., 725 Broad St, Augusta, GA 30901. TEL 800-458-4010, http://www.morris.com. Ed. James R Babb. Pub. William S Morris III. Circ: 31,316 (paid).

799.1 USA ISSN 1524-0355
GREAT LAKES ANGLER. Text in English. 1999. 9/yr. USD 19.95 domestic; USD 27.95 in Canada (effective 2007). back issues avail.; reprints avail. **Document type:** *Magazine, Consumer.* **Description:** Deals with angling on the Great Lakes and their connecting waters: how, where, and other feature stories.
Published by: O'Meara - Brown Publications, Inc., 727 S Dearborn, Ste 812, Chicago, IL 60605. TEL 312-276-0610, 800-827-0289, FAX 312-276-0619, glangler@omeara-brown.com. Ed. Dave Mull. Pub. Walter B. O'Meara. Circ: 30,000 (controlled).

796.5 GBR ISSN 0140-7570
THE GREAT OUTDOORS. Text in English. 1978. m. adv. back issues avail. **Document type:** *Magazine, Consumer.* **Description:** Features articles on new and exciting places to hike and backpack, as well as new and improved gear and equipment for the outdoor lover.
Indexed: SD.
—**CCC.**
Published by: Caledonian Magazines Ltd., 6th Fl, 195 Albion St, Glasgow, G1 1QQ, United Kingdom. TEL 44-20-77344784, FAX 44-20-77344975, info@calmags.co.uk. Ed. Cameron McNeish TEL 44-141-3027735. Pub. Darren Bruce TEL 44-141-3027721.

799 USA ISSN 1055-6532
GREAT PLAINS GAME & FISH. Text in English. 1991. m. USD 12.99 domestic; USD 25.99 in Canada; USD 27.99 elsewhere (effective 2011). adv. illus. **Document type:** *Magazine, Consumer.* **Description:** Informs sportsmen of hunting and fishing, as well as environmental and conservation issues in the Great Plains region.
Formerly (until 1991): Kansas Game and Fish (0897-9200); Incorporates: Dakota Game and Fish (0897-8883); Nebraska Game and Fish (0897-8999)
Related titles: Online - full text ed.; ◆ Regional ed(s).: Game & Fish; ◆ Louisiana Game & Fish. ISSN 0744-3692; ◆ Florida Game & Fish. ISSN 0889-3322; ◆ Alabama Game & Fish. ISSN 0279-6783; ◆ Mississippi-Louisiana Game & Fish. ISSN 1947-2358; ◆ North Carolina Game & Fish. ISSN 0897-8816; ◆ South Carolina Game & Fish. ISSN 0897-9154; ◆ West Virginia Game & Fish. ISSN 0897-9162; ◆ Missouri Game & Fish. ISSN 0889-3799; ◆ New York Game & Fish. ISSN 0897-9189; ◆ California Game & Fish. ISSN 1056-0122; ◆ Illinois Game & Fish. ISSN 0897-9014; ◆ Indiana Game & Fish. ISSN 0897-8980; ◆ Iowa Game & Fish. ISSN 0897-9197; ◆ Mid-Atlantic Game & Fish. ISSN 1055-6540; ◆ Oklahoma Game & Fish. ISSN 0746-6013; ◆ Rocky Mountain Game & Fish. ISSN 1056-0114; ◆ Pennsylvania Game & Fish. ISSN 0897-8808; ◆ Virginia Game & Fish. ISSN 0897-8794; ◆ Washington - Oregon Game & Fish. ISSN 1056-0106; ◆ Ohio Game & Fish. ISSN 0897-9170; New England Game & Fish. ISSN 0897-8972. 1988. USD 12 domestic; USD 25 in Canada; USD 27 elsewhere (effective 2010).
Published by: Intermedia Outdoors, Inc., 512 7th Ave, 11th Fl, New York, NY 10018. TEL 212-852-6682, 800-260-6397, FAX 212-302-4472, customerservice@imoutdoors.com, http://www.imoutdoorsmedia.com. Ed. Ken Dunwoody. Pub., Adv. contact Peter Gross.

796.63 GBR ISSN 1750-7103
THE GREAT SKIING AND SNOWBOARDING GUIDE (YEAR). Text in English. 1985. a. GBP 15.99, USD 22.95 per issue (effective 2006). **Document type:** *Directory, Consumer.* **Description:** Covers 500 ski resorts on five continents.
Former titles (until 2006): The Good Skiing and Snowboarding Guide (1467-9027); (until 1998): Good Skiing Guide (0955-8748)
Published by: (Consumers Association), Cadogan Guides (Subsidiary of: The Globe Pequot Press, Inc.), 2nd Fl, 233 High Holborn, London, WC1V 7DN, United Kingdom. TEL 44-20-76114660, FAX 44-20-76614665, info@cadoganguides.co.uk, http://www.cadoganguides.com/.

796 AUS ISSN 1835-0321
GREAT WALKS; the fresh air magazine. Text in English. 2007. bi-m. (plus a. cumulation). AUD 55; AUD 7.95 newsstand/cover (effective 2008). adv. **Document type:** *Magazine, Consumer.* **Description:** Provides extensive, independent and authoritative walking gear guides, plus practical information on specific walks, with accompanying maps.
Published by: Yaffa Publishing Group Pty Ltd., 17-21 Bellevue St, Surry Hills, NSW 2010, Australia. TEL 61-2-92812333, FAX 61-2-92812750, info@yaffa.com.au. Ed. Brent McKean TEL 61-2-92138274. Adv. contact Mike Ford TEL 61-2-92138262. color page AUD 2,685; trim 210 x 297. Circ: 20,000.

796.5 SVN ISSN 1580-3783
GREMO!. Text in Slovenian. 2000. m. adv. **Document type:** *Magazine, Consumer.*
Published by: Delo Revije d.o.o., Dunajska 5, Ljubljana, 1509, Slovenia. TEL 386-1-4737000, FAX 386-1-4737352, narocnine@delo-revije.si, http://www.delo-revije.si.

796.352 NOR ISSN 0804-8665
GRESS-FORUM. Text in Norwegian. 1992. q. NOK 400 (effective 2006). **Document type:** *Magazine, Trade.*
Formerly (until 1993): N G A-Nytt (0804-8657)
Published by: Norwegian Greenkeepers Association, Luksefjellveien 861, Skien, 3721, Norway. TEL 47-35-590499, FAX 47-35-594929, adm@nga.no. Adv. contact Kjell Sandager.

796.552 FRA ISSN 1251-4187
GRIMPER. Text in French. 1994. bi-m. (8/yr). EUR 36 (effective 2009). **Document type:** *Magazine, Consumer.*
Published by: Editions Niveales, 6 Rue Irvoy, Grenoble, 38000, France. TEL 33-4-76705411, FAX 33-4-76705412, http://www.dipresse.com/niveales. Ed. Jean-Marc Chenevier.

796.522 CAN ISSN 1488-0814
GRIPPED; the climbing magazine. Text in English. 1999. bi-m. USD 25.95 (effective 2010). adv. back issues avail. **Document type:** *Magazine, Consumer.*
Related titles: Online - full text ed.: USD 29.70 (effective 2010).
Published by: Gripped Publishing Inc., 344 Bloor St, Unit 510, Toronto, ON M5S 3A7, Canada. TEL 416-927-0774, FAX 416-927-1491, info@gripped.com. Ed. David Chaundy-Smart. Pub. Sam Cohen. Adv. contact Chris Lepik.

635.9642 GBR ISSN 0017-4696
GROUNDSMAN. Text in English. 1947. m. free membership (effective 2009). adv. bk.rev. illus. **Document type:** *Magazine, Trade.*
Indexed: SD, SportS.
—BLDSC (4220.150000).
Published by: Institute of Groundsmanship, 28 Stratford Office Village, Walker Ave, Wolverton Mill East, Milton Keynes, MK12 5TW, United Kingdom. TEL 44-1908-312511, FAX 44-1908-311140, http://www.iog.org. Circ: 6,000 (controlled).

796 914.5 ITA ISSN 0072-792X
GUIDA CAMPING D'ITALIA. Text in Italian. 1958. a. free to members. adv. **Document type:** *Catalog, Consumer.*
Published by: Confederazione Italiana Campeggiatori, Via Vittorio Emanuele 11, Calenzano, FI 50041, Italy. TEL 39-055-882391, FAX 39-055-8825918, federcampeggio@tin.it, http://www.federcampeggio.it.

796.522 ITA ISSN 1972-2427
GUIDA DELLA MONTAGNA. Variant title: Bell'Italia. Le Guide. Guida della Montagna. Text in Italian. 2000. a. **Document type:** *Magazine, Consumer.*
Published by: Editoriale Giorgio Mondadori SpA (Subsidiary of: Cairo Communication SpA), Via Tucidide 56, Torre 3, Milan, 20134, Italy. TEL 39-02-748111, FAX 39-02-70100102, info@cairocommunication.it, http://www.cairocommunication.it.

GUIDE DES MERVEILLES DE LA NATURE. *see* TRAVEL AND TOURISM

796.5 FRA
GUIDE OFFICIEL DES ETAPES DE CAMPING-CAR. Text in French. a. adv. **Document type:** *Directory, Consumer.*
Formerly: Guide Officiel Camping - Caravaning (0765-7005)
Published by: (Federation Francaise de Camping et de Caravaning), Motor Presse France, 12 rue Rouget de Lisle, Issy-les-Moulineaux, 92442, France. http://www.motorpresse.fr. Circ: 135,000.

799.1 FRA ISSN 1951-4034
LE GUIDE PRATIQUE DU CHASSEUR SOUS-MARIN. Text in French. 2006. a. EUR 21.90 newsstand/cover (effective 2009). back issues avail. **Document type:** *Yearbook, Consumer.*
Published by: Editions Le Monde de Neptune, 13 rue Georges Courteline, Tours, 37000, France. TEL 33-6-71314488.

GUIDE TO CARAVAN AND CAMPING HOLIDAYS. *see* TRAVEL AND TOURISM

GUIDE TO EATING ONTARIO SPORT FISH. *see* FISH AND FISHERIES

796.42 ZAF ISSN 1991-6116
GUIDE TO RUNNING. Text in English. 2006. a.
Published by: Touchline Media, PO Box 16368, Vlaeberg, Cape Town 8018, South Africa. TEL 27-21-4083800, FAX 27-21-4083811, http://www.touchline.co.za.

799.1 USA ISSN 0164-3746
GULF COAST FISHERMAN. Variant title: Harold Wells Gulf Coast Fisherman. Text in English. 1976. q. USD 11.75 (effective 2000). adv. bk.rev. **Document type:** *Magazine, Consumer.* **Description:** Covers all aspects of saltwater fishing from Florida to Texas. Features the Wells Daily Fishing Forecast, used by fisherman for over 40 years to plan their fishing.
Published by: Harold Wells Gulf Coast Fisherman, Inc., Drawer P, Port Lavaca, TX 77979. TEL 361-552-8864, FAX 361-552-8864. Ed., Pub. Gary M Ralston. R&P Gary Ralston. Adv. contact Janna Ralston. Circ: 19,000 (paid).

799.2 636.7 USA ISSN 0279-5086
GUN DOG; upland bird and waterfowl dogs. Text in English. 1981. 7/yr. USD 24.97 domestic; USD 37.97 in Canada; USD 39.97 elsewhere (effective 2008). adv. bk.rev. illus. reprints avail. **Document type:** *Magazine, Consumer.* **Description:** Provides tips for upland bird and waterfowl hunter-gunners involved with pointing, flushing, and retrieving breeds of bird dogs.
Indexed: G08, I05.
—**CCC.**
Published by: Intermedia Outdoors, Inc., 512 7th Ave, 11th Fl, New York, NY 10018. TEL 212-852-6600, 800-260-6397, FAX 212-302-4472, customerservice@imoutdoors.com, http://www.imoutdoorsmedia.com. Ed. Rick Van Etten. adv.: B&W page USD 3,390, color page USD 4,597. Circ: 41,005 (paid).

GUN-KNIFE SHOW CALENDAR. *see* ANTIQUES

799.202 USA ISSN 1042-6450
TS534.5
GUN TESTS; the consumer resource for the serious shooter. Text in English. 1989. m. USD 24 combined subscription in US & Canada (print & online eds.); USD 42 combined subscription elsewhere (print & online eds.) (effective 2010). adv. back issues avail. **Document type:** *Magazine, Consumer.* **Description:** Examines tests and rates all types of firearms, ammunition and accessories.
Related titles: Online - full text ed.: Gun-Tests.com.
Published by: A G Media Inc. (Subsidiary of: Belvoir Media Group, LLC), PO Box 5656, Norwalk, CT 06856. TEL 203-857-3100, FAX 203-857-3103, customer_service@belvoir.com, http://www.belvoir.com. Ed. W Todd Woodard. **Subscr. to:** Palm Coast Data, LLC, PO Box 420235, Palm Coast, FL 32142. TEL 800-829-9084, http://www.palmcoastdata.com.

799.3 USA ISSN 0017-5684
TS535
GUNS & AMMO. Abbreviated title: G & A. Text in English. 1958. m. USD 14.97 domestic; USD 27.97 in Canada; USD 29.97 elsewhere (effective 2008). adv. bk.rev. charts; illus. index. back issues avail.; reprints avail. **Document type:** *Magazine, Consumer.* **Description:** Addresses the practical application of sporting firearms, with an emphasis on their safe and proper use.
Incorporates (1995-1996): Performance Shooter (1083-804X)
Related titles: Microform ed.: (from PQC); Online - full text ed.; ◆ Supplement(s): Annual Guns & Ammo. ISSN 0072-906X.
Indexed: A22, G06, G07, G08, I05, MagInd, PMR, SPI.
—IE, Infotrieve. **CCC.**
Published by: Intermedia Outdoors, Inc., 512 7th Ave, 11th Fl, New York, NY 10018. TEL 800-260-6397, FAX 212-302-4472, customerservice@imoutdoors.com, http://www.imoutdoorsmedia.com. Ed. Richard Venola. adv.: B&W page USD 21,990, color page USD 36,005; trim 10.5 x 7.75. Circ: 462,154 (paid).

799.3 USA ISSN 0883-9468
SK274
GUNS & AMMO ACTION SERIES. Text in English. 1983. bi-m. USD 14.97 (effective 2007). **Document type:** *Magazine, Consumer.*
Published by: Source Interlink Companies, 6420 Wilshire Blvd, 10th Fl, Los Angeles, CA 90048. TEL 323-782-2000, FAX 323-782-2585, dheine@sourceinterlink.com, http://www.sourceinterlinkmedia.com. Ed. Lee Hoots. Pub. Michael Cassidy.

799.1 USA ISSN 1521-0138
SK1
GUNS & GEAR; the newsmonthly & equipment guide for hunters & shooters. Text in English. 1952. m. bk.rev. illus. **Document type:** *Magazine, Consumer.* **Description:** Publishes for hunters and professional shooters and offers information on hunting, archery, outdoor gear, and trophies.
Former titles (until 1998): Southern Outdoors (0199-3372); Southern Outdoors - Gulf Coast Fisherman
Indexed: PMR.

Published by: (Bass Anglers Sportsman Society), B.A.S.S., Inc. (Subsidiary of: E S P N, Inc.), PO Box 17900, Montgomery, AL 36141-0900. TEL 334-272-9530, FAX 334-279-7148, customerservice@bassmaster.com.

799.2028 USA
SK274
GUNS & HUNTING. Text in English. 1987. bi-m. **Document type:** *Magazine, Consumer.*
Formerly (until 1993): The Complete Sportsman: Guns & Hunting (1058-3785)
Published by: Harris Publications, Inc., 1115 Broadway, New York, NY 10010. TEL 212-807-7100, FAX 212-924-2352, subscriptions@harris-pub.com, http://www.harris-pub.com.

683.4 739.4 USA
GUNS OF THE OLD WEST. Text in English. 1997. q. USD 18.97 in US & Canada; USD 37.94 elsewhere (effective 2009). adv. back issues avail. **Document type:** *Magazine, Consumer.* **Description:** Covers antique guns of the old west.
Published by: Harris Publications, Inc., 1115 Broadway, New York, NY 10010. TEL 212-807-7100, FAX 212-924-2352, subscriptions@harris-pub.com, http://www.harris-pub.com.

GUNSHOT. *see* SPORTS AND GAMES

796.54 NLD
HANDBOEK KAMPEREN. Text in Dutch. a. free (effective 2008). adv.
Published by: Algemene Nederlandse Wielrijders Bond (A N W B) Media/Dutch Automobile Association Media, Postbus 93200, The Hague, 2509 BA, Netherlands. TEL 31-70-3141470, FAX 31-70-3146538, http://www.anwbmedia.nl. adv.: color page EUR 2,820. Circ: 130,000.

HANDBOOK OF RECORDS AND RESULTS. *see* SPORTS AND GAMES—Abstracting, Bibliographies, Statistics

739.7 USA ISSN 1068-2635
HANDGUNS. Text in English. 1987. bi-m. USD 15.97 domestic; USD 28.97 in Canada; USD 30.97 elsewhere (effective 2008). adv. **Document type:** *Magazine, Consumer.*
Former titles (until 199?): Handguns for Sport and Defense (1054-4135); (until 1990): Petersen's Handguns (1040-1865)
Related titles: Online - full text ed.
Indexed: G06, G07, G08, I05, M06.
Published by: Intermedia Outdoors, Inc., 512 7th Ave, 11th Fl, New York, NY 10018. TEL 212-852-6600, 800-260-6397, FAX 212-302-4472, customerservice@imoutdoors.com, http://www.imoutdoorsmedia.com. Pub. Chris Agnes TEL 972-392-1892. Adv. contact Matt Johnson. B&W page USD 5,960, color page USD 9,550. Circ: 118,843 (paid).

799.2 SWE
HANDVAPENGUIDEN. Text in Swedish. 1996. a. SEK 159 (effective 2002). adv. back issues avail. **Document type:** *Yearbook.* **Description:** Guide to hand weapons.
Published by: Jakt & Skyttefoerlaget AB, Grubbensringen 20 D, Stockholm, 11269, Sweden. FAX 46-8-441-18-99. Ed. Clas Johansson.

797 USA ISSN 1936-2552
HANG GLIDING AND PARAGLIDING. Text in English. 2003. m. **Document type:** *Magazine, Consumer.* **Description:** Contains news and information about the U.S. Hang Gliding and Paragliding Association and its activities and features on all aspects of free flight.
Formerly (until 2007): U S H P A. Aero (1936-2137); (until 200?): Hang Gliding & Paragliding (1543-5989); Which was formed by the Merger of (1970-2003): Hang Gliding (0895-433X); (19??-2003): Paragliding (1089-1846)
Published by: U.S. Hang Gliding Association, Inc., PO Box 1330, Colorado Springs, CO 80933-1330. ushga@shga.org, http://www.ushga.org. Ed. Gil Dodgen.

799.1 USA ISSN 0194-651X
HAWAII FISHING NEWS. Text in English. 1977. m. USD 35 in Hawaii; USD 40 mainland US; USD 60 elsewhere; USD 4.50 newsstand/cover (effective 2000). adv. back issues avail. **Document type:** *Magazine, Consumer.* **Description:** Covers all types of fishing in the Hawaiian islands. Includes diving and hiking.
Address: 6650 Hawaii Kai Dr, Ste 201, Honolulu, HI 96825. TEL 808-395-4499, FAX 808-396-3474. Ed., Pub., Adv. contact Chuck Johnston. color page USD 2,600, page USD 2,000; trim 11 x 15.5. Circ: 10,000 (paid). **Subscr. to:** PO Box 25488, Honolulu, HI 96825-0488.

796 USA ISSN 8756-310X
SB486.V64
HELPING OUT IN THE OUTDOORS; a directory of volunteer jobs and internships in parks and forests nationwide. Text in English. 1980. a. USD 10 per issue (effective 2000). **Document type:** *Directory, Consumer.*
Published by: American Hiking Society, PO Box 20160, Washington, DC 20041-2160. TEL 301-565-6704, FAX 301-565-6714. Ed. Shirley Hearn. Circ: 15,000.

799.2 DEU ISSN 0931-8879
HESSENJAEGER. Text in German. 1982. m. adv. **Document type:** *Magazine, Consumer.*
Published by: Landwirtschaftsverlag Hessen GmbH, Taunusstr 151, Friedrichsdorf, 61381, Germany. TEL 49-6172-7106193, FAX 49-6172-7106199, harald.niese@lv-hessen.de. adv.: B&W page EUR 2,311.20, color page EUR 3,758.40. Circ: 20,242 (controlled).

796.552 GBR
HIGH MOUNTAIN. Text in English. 1982. m. GBP 28 domestic; GBP 45 foreign; GBP 2.99 newsstand/cover (effective 2003). adv. bk.rev.; video rev. illus. back issues avail.; reprints avail. **Document type:** *Magazine, Consumer.* **Description:** Contains international and UK coverage of rock climbing, mountaineering, serious hill walking and related mountain sports.
Former titles: High Mountain Sports (0962-2667); High Magazine (0951-8940)
Related titles: Online - full text ed.
—Ingenta. **CCC.**
Published by: (British Mountaineering Council), Greenshires Publishing Limited, Telford Way, Kettering, Northants NN16 8UN, United Kingdom. TEL 44-1536-382500, FAX 44-1536-382501, http://www.greenshires.com. Ed. Geoff Birtles. R&P Andrew Carter TEL 44-1536-382400. Adv. contacts Gill Wootton, Jane Harris. B&W page GBP 950, color page GBP 1,590; trim 190 x 273. Circ: 14,000. **Dist. by:** Comag, Tavistock Rd, W Drayton, Middlesex UB7 7QE, United Kingdom. FAX 44-189-543-3606.

796 USA
HIGHWAYS. Text in English. 1966. m. USD 3.99 newsstand/cover; free to members (effective 2009). adv. 96 p./no.; back issues avail. **Document type:** *Magazine, Consumer.* **Description:** Provides an insight of Northern California's uncrowded sea to sky loop, from the wave-swept Pacific coast to the towering Sierra Range.
Formerly (until 1989): Good Sam's Hi-Way Herald (0194-9764)
Related titles: Online - full text ed.; ◆ Regional ed(s).: Highways (Region 6 Southeast Edition). ISSN 1047-0875; ◆ Highways (Region 3, 4 Central Edition). ISSN 1047-0859; ◆ Highways (Region 5 Northeast Edition). ISSN 1047-0867; ◆ Highways (Region 1 Northwest Edition). ISSN 1045-5922; ◆ Highways (Region 2 Southwest Edition). ISSN 1047-0840.
Published by: (Good Sam Club), Affinity Group Inc., 2575 Vista Del Mar, Ventura, CA 93001. TEL 805-667-4100, FAX 805-667-4484, info@affinitygroup.com, http://www.affinitygroup.com. Ed. John Sullaway. Adv. contact Terry Thompson TEL 206-283-9545. B&W page USD 22,530, color page USD 32,570. Circ: 958,916.

796 USA ISSN 1045-5922
HIGHWAYS (REGION 1 NORTHWEST EDITION). Text in English. 19??. m.
Formerly (until 1989): Good Sam's Hi-Way Herald (Region 1 Northwest Edition)
Related titles: ◆ Regional ed(s).: Highways; ◆ Highways (Region 6 Southeast Edition). ISSN 1047-0875; ◆ Highways (Region 5 Northeast Edition). ISSN 1047-0867; ◆ Highways (Region 2 Southwest Edition). ISSN 1047-0840; ◆ Highways (Region 3, 4 Central Edition). ISSN 1047-0859.
Published by: (Good Sam Club), Affinity Group Inc., 2575 Vista Del Mar, Ventura, CA 93001. TEL 805-667-4100, FAX 805-667-4419, info@affinitygroup.com, http://www.affinitygroup.com.

796 USA ISSN 1047-0840
HIGHWAYS (REGION 2 SOUTHWEST EDITION). Text in English. 19??. m.
Formerly (until 1989): Good Sam's Hi-Way Herald (Region 2 Southwest Edition)
Related titles: ◆ Regional ed(s).: Highways; ◆ Highways (Region 6 Southeast Edition). ISSN 1047-0875; ◆ Highways (Region 5 Northeast Edition). ISSN 1047-0867; ◆ Highways (Region 1 Northwest Edition). ISSN 1045-5922; ◆ Highways (Region 3, 4 Central Edition). ISSN 1047-0859.
Published by: Affinity Group Inc., 2575 Vista Del Mar, Ventura, CA 93001. TEL 805-667-4100, FAX 805-667-4419, info@affinitygroup.com, http://www.affinitygroup.com.

796 USA ISSN 1047-0859
HIGHWAYS (REGION 3, 4 CENTRAL EDITION). Text in English. 19??. m.
Formerly (until 1989): Good Sam's Hi-Way Herald (Region 3, 4 Central Edition)
Related titles: ◆ Regional ed(s).: Highways; ◆ Highways (Region 6 Southeast Edition). ISSN 1047-0875; ◆ Highways (Region 5 Northeast Edition). ISSN 1047-0867; ◆ Highways (Region 1 Northwest Edition). ISSN 1045-5922; ◆ Highways (Region 2 Southwest Edition). ISSN 1047-0840.
Published by: Affinity Group Inc., 2575 Vista Del Mar, Ventura, CA 93001. TEL 805-667-4100, FAX 805-667-4419, info@affinitygroup.com, http://www.affinitygroup.com.

796 USA ISSN 1047-0867
HIGHWAYS (REGION 5 NORTHEAST EDITION). Text in English. 19??. m.
Formerly (until 1989): Good Sam's Hi-Way Herald (Region 5 Northeast Edition)
Related titles: ◆ Regional ed(s).: Highways; ◆ Highways (Region 6 Southeast Edition). ISSN 1047-0875; ◆ Highways (Region 3, 4 Central Edition). ISSN 1047-0859; ◆ Highways (Region 1 Northwest Edition). ISSN 1045-5922; ◆ Highways (Region 2 Southwest Edition). ISSN 1047-0840.
Published by: Affinity Group Inc., 2575 Vista Del Mar, Ventura, CA 93001. TEL 805-667-4100, FAX 805-667-4419, info@affinitygroup.com, http://www.affinitygroup.com.

796 USA ISSN 1047-0875
HIGHWAYS (REGION 6 SOUTHEAST EDITION). Text in English. 1989. m.
Formerly (until 1989): Good Sam's Hi-Way Herald (Region 6 Southeast Edition)
Related titles: ◆ Regional ed(s).: Highways; ◆ Highways (Region 5 Northeast Edition). ISSN 1047-0867; ◆ Highways (Region 3, 4 Central Edition). ISSN 1047-0859; ◆ Highways (Region 1 Northwest Edition). ISSN 1045-5922; ◆ Highways (Region 2 Southwest Edition). ISSN 1047-0840.
Published by: Affinity Group Inc., 2575 Vista Del Mar, Ventura, CA 93001. TEL 805-667-4100, FAX 805-667-4419, info@affinitygroup.com, http://www.affinitygroup.com.

799.2 DEU
HIRSCHMANNBRIEF. Text in German. 1961. a. USD 5.
Published by: Verein Hirschmann e.V., c/o Dr Wolf-Eberhard Barth, Oderhaus Post, St Andreasberg, 37444, Germany. Circ: 550.

HOLIDAY RESORTS & DESTINATIONS. *see* TRAVEL AND TOURISM

HOMES & GARDENS. *see* INTERIOR DESIGN AND DECORATION—Furniture And House Furnishings

HONDENSPORT & SPORTHONDEN; het tijdschrift voor liefhebbers van hondensport en africhting. *see* PETS

796.522 NLD ISSN 1387-862X
HOOGTELIJN. Text in Dutch. 1998. 5/yr. EUR 20 (effective 2009). adv. bk.rev.; video rev. charts; illus.; mkt.; maps; tr.lit. back issues avail. **Document type:** *Magazine, Consumer.* **Description:** Concerns mountaineering, climbing, sports, environment, safety, equipment, information for the members of the Dutch Climbing and Mountaineering Association.
Formed by the merger of (1952-1998): Bergvriend (0005-898X); (1933-1998): Berggids (1381-7418)
Published by: Nederlandse Klim- en Bergsportvereniging/Dutch Climbing and Mountaineering Association, Postbus 225, Woerden, 3440 AE, Netherlands. TEL 31-348-409521, FAX 31-348-409534, info@nkbv.nl.

799.2 NZL ISSN 1178-234X
HOOKED ON BOARS MAGAZINE. Text in English. 2005. bi-m. NZD 49.95 domestic; NZD 89.95 in Australia; NZD 129.95 elsewhere (effective 2011). **Document type:** *Magazine, Consumer.*
Supersedes in part (in 2008): Bowhunting New Zealand Magazine (1177-0511)
Published by: M W Magazines, PO Box 838, Blenheim, 724, New Zealand. TEL 64-27-4466496. Ed. Matt Willis.

799.1 USA
HOOKS AND LINES. Text in English. bi-m. membership. **Document type:** *Newsletter.*
Published by: International Women's Fishing Association, Drawer 3125, Palm Beach, FL 33480. Ed. Joan Willmott.

796.07 GBR ISSN 1462-0677
HORIZONS (CUMBRIA); news, reviews, practice and policy in outdoor learning. Text in English. 1984. q. GBP 35 domestic to non-members; GBP 40 in Europe to non-members; GBP 45 elsewhere to non-members; GBP 20 domestic to members; GBP 25 in Europe to members; GBP 35 elsewhere to members; free to institutional members (effective 2009). adv. bk.rev. illus. 44 p./no. 2 cols./p.; back issues avail. **Document type:** *Magazine, Consumer.* **Description:** Provides outdoor professionals with informative articles on professional development.
Former titles (until 1997): Journal of Adventure Education and Outdoor Leadership (0966-7652); (until 1991): Adventure Education and Outdoor Leadership (1463-6980); (until 1988): Adventure Education (0265-5802)
Indexed: CPE, SD.
—BLDSC (4326.794170), IE, Ingenta. **CCC.**
Published by: Institute for Outdoor Learning, Warwick Mill Business Ctr, Warwick Bridge, Cumbria, Carlisle CA4 8RR, United Kingdom. TEL 44-1228-564580, FAX 44-1228-564581, institute@outdoor-learning.org. Adv. contact Fiona Exon. color page GBP 620.

HOSEASONS HOLIDAY PARKS AND LODGES. *see* TRAVEL AND TOURISM

HOUNDS. *see* SPORTS AND GAMES—Horses And Horsemanship

796.552 HRV ISSN 0354-0650
G505
HRVATSKI PLANINAR/CROATIAN MOUNTAINEER. Text in Croatian. 1898. m. adv. bk.rev. charts; illus. index; cum.index.
Former titles (until Mar. 1991): Nase Planine (0027-819X); (until 1944): Hrvatski Planinar
Indexed: RILM.
Published by: Hrvatski Planinarski Savez/Croatian Mountaineering Association, Kozarceva 22, Zagreb, 10000, Croatia. TEL 385-1-4824142, TELEX 385-1-4824142. Ed., R&P Dr. Zeljko Poljak. Circ: 1,300.

796 CHN ISSN 1673-7881
HUIWAI/OUTSIDE. Text in Chinese. 2006. m. CNY 240; CNY 20 per issue (effective 2010). **Document type:** *Magazine, Consumer.*
Related titles: Online - full text ed.
Published by: Titan Chuanmei Jituan/Titan Culture - Express Co, ltd, Donghuashi Dajie Bei-li Xi-qu #22, Chongwen-qu, Beijing, 100062, China. TEL 86-10-51005876, http://www.titan24.com/.

799.2 USA ISSN 1932-1082
HUNT CLUB DIGEST. Text in English. 2000. q. USD 9.99 domestic; USD 19.99 in Canada; USD 24.99 elsewhere (effective 2008). adv. Supplement avail.; back issues avail. **Document type:** *Magazine, Trade.*
Related titles: Online - full text ed.
Indexed: H20, M02, T02.
Published by: Grand View Media Group, Inc. (Subsidiary of: EBSCO Industries, Inc.), 200 Croft St, Ste 1, Birmingham, AL 35242. TEL 888-431-2877, FAX 205-408-3797, webmaster@grandviewmedia.com, http://www.gvmg.com. Ed. Wayne J Fears. Pub. Mike Kizzire TEL 205-408-3716. adv.: B&W page USD 4,860, color page USD 6,075; trim 7.75 x 10.625.

799.2 USA
HUNT FOREVER. Text in English. 2003. bi-m. USD 14.95 (effective 2011). adv. **Document type:** *Magazine, Consumer.* **Description:** Covers hunting advocacy, equipment, tips, reviews, wildlife conservation projects and legal issues.
Published by: Safari Club International, 4800 W Gates Pass Rd, Tucson, AZ 85745. http://www.scifirstforhunters.org/. Circ: 250,000.

799.2 USA
HUNTER & SHOOTING SPORTS EDUCATION JOURNAL. Text in English. 1973. 3/yr. USD 25 to members volunteer; USD 100 to corporations member (effective 2004). adv. film rev. charts; illus.; stat.; tr.lit. index. **Document type:** *Journal, Consumer.* **Description:** The purpose of the journal is to increase the skill and effectiveness of hunter education instructors and administrators, and ultimately to make hunter education training courses more fun and effective for students.
Former titles (until 2004): Hunter Education Journal (1521-5970); (until 1998): Hunter Education Instructor (1066-3460); (until 1989): Hunter Safety Instructor (0737-6227); (until 1983): Hunter Safety News
Published by: International Hunter Education Assocation (I H E A), 3725 Cleveland Ave, PO Box 490, Wellington, CO 80549. TEL 970-568-7954, FAX 970-568-7955, info@ihea.com. Circ: 65,000 (controlled).

799.2 CAN ISSN 0846-104X
HUNTER EDUCATION NEWS. Text in English. 1990. q. free to qualified personnel. adv. **Document type:** *Newsletter.*
Published by: Ontario Federation of Anglers & Hunters, 4601 Guthrie Dr, P O Box 2800, Peterborough, ON K9J 8L5, Canada. TEL 705-748-6324, FAX 705-748-9577. Adv. contact Mark Holmes. Circ: 1,000.

796.93 USA
HUNTER MOUNTAIN NEWS. Text in English. 1970. 12/yr. USD 15. adv. bk.rev. charts; illus.
Published by: (Hunter Mountain Ski Bowl), Hunter Mt. News Corp., PO Box 110, Syosset, NY 11791. TEL 516-496-4588. Ed. Paul E Pepe. Circ: 25,000.

799.2 USA ISSN 0018-7860
HUNTER'S HORN. Text in English. 1921. m. USD 25 (effective 2006). adv. bk.rev. illus. 120 p./no. 3 cols./p.; back issues avail. **Document type:** *Magazine, Consumer.* **Description:** Describes fox and wolf hunting.
Address: 117 N Garfield, Sand Springs, OK 74063-0426. Ed., Pub. Terry Walker. adv.: page USD 140. Circ: 8,021 (paid).

799.1 799.2 USA ISSN 1539-9079
SK41
HUNTING & FISHING COLLECTIBLES; history and artifacts from america's sporting past. Text in English. 2000. bi-m. USD 39 domestic; USD 44 in Canada; USD 71 in Asia; USD 71 in Europe (effective 2002). adv.
Published by: Hunting & Fishing Collectibles, Inc., 704 Hwy. W., Lawsonville, NC 27022-9988. TEL 336-593-9477, FAX 336-593-8085, hfcollectibles@aol.com. Pub. Stanley L. Van Etten. Adv. contact Bob Woollens.

799.2 658.8 USA
HUNTING BUSINESS. Text in English. q. **Document type:** *Magazine, Trade.*
Published by: SportsOneSource Group, 2151 Hawkins St, Ste 200, Charlotte, NC 28269. TEL 704-987-3450, FAX 704-987-3455, info@sportsonesource.com, http://www.sportsonesource.com. Circ: 10,000.

799.2 USA ISSN 1558-8866
SK1
HUNTING CAMP JOURNAL. Text in English. 2006 (Spr.). q. USD 19.95 (effective 2006). adv. **Document type:** *Magazine, Consumer.* **Description:** Covers hunting related issues, techniques, lifestyle, profiles, including issues in conservation and land management.
Published by: J N E Publishing, Inc., PO Box 5647, Huntsville, AL 35814. TEL 800-250-1528, http://www.jnepublishing.com/. Ed. J. Wayne Fears.

799.2 USA
HUNTING ILLUSTRATED. Text in English. 2001. bi-m. USD 24.95 domestic; USD 34.95 foreign (effective 2004). 100 p./no.; **Document type:** *Magazine, Consumer.* **Description:** Contains hunting stories, articles, adventure, how-to, photo spreads and more.
Published by: King's Outdoor Ventures, LLC., PO Box 307, Mt. Pleasant, UT 84647. TEL 800-447-6897, FAX 435-462-7436, http://www.kingsoutdoorworld.com/. Ed. David King.

799.2 USA ISSN 1052-4746
THE HUNTING REPORT FOR BIG GAME HUNTERS; serving the hunter who travels. Text in English. 1981. m. looseleaf. USD 60 domestic; USD 71 in Canada & Mexico; USD 89 elsewhere. adv. bk.rev. back issues avail. **Document type:** *Newsletter.*
Published by: Oxpecker Enterprises, Inc., 9300 S Dadeland Blvd, Ste 605, Miami, FL 33156-2721. TEL 305-670-1361, FAX 305-670-1376. Ed., Pub., R&P Don Causey. Adv. contact Milton Aquino. Circ: 3,500.

799.2 USA ISSN 1932-135X
SK1
HUNTING THE COUNTRY. Variant title: Mossy Oak's Hunting the Country. Text in English. 1998. q. USD 9.95 (effective 2004). adv. **Document type:** *Magazine, Consumer.*
Indexed: H20, M02, T02.
Published by: Grand View Media Group, Inc. (Subsidiary of: EBSCO Industries, Inc.), 200 Croft St, Ste 1, Birmingham, AL 35242. TEL 888-431-2877, FAX 205-408-3797, webmaster@grandviewmedia.com, http://www.gvmg.com. Ed. Eddie Lee Rider. Pub. Scott Fowler. Adv. contact Chris Elliott. B&W page USD 2,832, color page USD 3,840; trim 7.75 x 10.625.

799.2 USA ISSN 1556-3960
HUNTING THE WEST. Text in English. 2005 (Fall). q. USD 19.95 (effective 2006). **Document type:** *Magazine, Consumer.* **Description:** Covers the hunting techniques and technical details of games.
Published by: Frank Amato Publications, PO Box 82112, Portland, OR 97282. TEL 800-541-9498. Ed. Scott Haugen.

HUNTING WITH COUNTRY ILLUSTRATED. *see* LIFESTYLE

796 CHN ISSN 1673-9434
HUWAI ZHUANGBEI/OUTDOOR GEARS. Text in Chinese. 2007. m. **Document type:** *Magazine, Consumer.*
Published by: Diannao Aihaozhe Zazhishe, PO Box 9615, Beijing, 100086, China.

711 GBR ISSN 1814-3709
I F P R A WORLD. Text in English. 1988. q. free to members (effective 2009). **Document type:** *Magazine, Trade.*
Formerly (until 2003): I F P R A Bulletin (1012-7720)
—CCC.
Published by: International Federation of Park and Recreation Administration, Globe House, Crispin Close, Caversham, Reading, RG4 7JS, United Kingdom. TEL 44-118-9461680, FAX 44-118-9461680, ifpraworld@aol.com. Ed. Alan Smith.

796.93 USA
I LOVE NEW YORK WINTER TRAVEL AND SKI GUIDE. Text in English. a. free. illus.; maps. **Document type:** *Magazine, Consumer.* **Description:** Lists downhill and cross-country skiing centers and facilities, events, festivals and package tours.
Formerly: I Love New York Skiing and Winter Adventures
Media: Online - full text.
Published by: Department of Economic Development, 30 South Pearl St., Albany, NY 12245. TEL 518-474-4116, FAX 518-486-6416. Ed. Mary Ellen Walsh.

799.1 USA
I W F A YEARBOOK. Text in English. 1955. a. membership. adv.
Published by: International Women's Fishing Association, Drawer 3125, Palm Beach, FL 33480. Ed. Joan S Willmott. Circ: 300.

799.1 USA ISSN 1523-1879
ICE FISHING GUIDE. Variant title: In-Fisherman Ice Fishing Guide. Text in English. 1998. a. USD 4.99 newsstand/cover domestic; USD 5.50 newsstand/cover in Canada (effective 2007). illus. **Document type:** *Magazine, Consumer.* **Description:** Provides location and presentation techniques for specific species, as well as a look at all the necessary equipment.
Published by: Source Interlink Companies, 6420 Wilshire Blvd, 10th Fl, Los Angeles, CA 90048. TEL 323-782-2000, FAX 323-782-2585, dheine@sourceinterlink.com, http://www.sourceinterlinkmedia.com. Circ: 100,000.

799 USA ISSN 0897-9014
ILLINOIS GAME & FISH. Text in English. 19??. m. USD 12.99 domestic; USD 25.99 in Canada; USD 27.99 elsewhere (effective 2011). adv. illus. **Document type:** *Magazine, Consumer.* **Description:** Informs sportsmen of hunting and fishing, as well as environmental and conservation issues in Illinois.
Related titles: Online - full text ed.; ◆ Regional ed(s).: Game & Fish; ◆ Louisiana Game & Fish. ISSN 0744-3692; ◆ Florida Game & Fish. ISSN 0889-3322; ◆ Alabama Game & Fish. ISSN 0279-6783; ◆ Mississippi-Louisiana Game & Fish. ISSN 1947-2358; ◆ North Carolina Game & Fish. ISSN 0897-8816; ◆ South Carolina Game & Fish. ISSN 0897-9154; ◆ West Virginia Game & Fish. ISSN 0897-9162; ◆ Missouri Game & Fish. ISSN 0889-3799; ◆ New York Game & Fish. ISSN 0897-9189; ◆ California Game & Fish. ISSN 1056-0122; ◆ Great Plains Game & Fish. ISSN 1055-6532; ◆ Indiana Game & Fish. ISSN 0897-8980; ◆ Iowa Game & Fish. ISSN 0897-9197; ◆ Mid-Atlantic Game & Fish. ISSN 1055-6540; ◆ Oklahoma Game & Fish. ISSN 0746-6013; ◆ Rocky Mountain Game & Fish. ISSN 1056-0114; ◆ Pennsylvania Game & Fish. ISSN 0897-8808; ◆ Virginia Game & Fish. ISSN 0897-8794; ◆ Washington - Oregon Game & Fish. ISSN 1056-0106; ◆ Ohio Game & Fish. ISSN 0897-9170; New England Game & Fish. ISSN 0897-8972. 1988. USD 12 domestic; USD 25 in Canada; USD 27 elsewhere (effective 2010).
Published by: Intermedia Outdoors, Inc., 512 7th Ave, 11th Fl, New York, NY 10018. TEL 212-852-6682, 800-260-6397, FAX 212-302-4472, customerservice@imoutdoors.com, http://www.imoutdoorsmedia.com. Ed. Ken Dunwoody. Pub., Adv. contact Peter Gross.

796 USA ISSN 1942-6461
ILLINOIS OUTDOOR NEWS. Text mainly in English. 2008. bi-w. USD 18 (effective 2008). adv. **Document type:** *Magazine, Consumer.* **Description:** Features articles about fishing, hunting, resorts outdoor life and events in the Illinois area.
Published by: Outdoor News, Inc., PO Box 389, Troy, IL 62294. TEL 800-975-3474. Ed. Ralph Loos. Pub. Glenn Meyer. Adv. contact Jeff Bast. B&W page USD 1,050; trim 11 x 17. Circ: 20,000 (paid).

333.783 USA ISSN 0019-2155
SB481.A1
ILLINOIS PARKS & RECREATION. Text in English. 1970. bi-m. free to qualified personnel (effective 2005). adv. bk.rev. illus.; stat. **Document type:** *Magazine, Consumer.*
Formerly: Illinois Park and Recreation Quarterly
Published by: Illinois Association of Park Districts, 211 E Monroe, Springfield, IL 62701. TEL 217-523-4554, FAX 217-523-4273, iapd@ILparks.org, http://www.ILparks.org. Ed. Ann M Londrigan. R&P Ann Londrigan. Adv. contact David Stumph. Circ: 5,500.
Co-sponsor: Illinois Park and Recreation Association.

796.95 USA ISSN 0745-0915
ILLINOIS SNOWMOBILER. Text in English. 1982. 6/yr. (Sep.-Mar.). free to members (effective 2009). adv. **Document type:** *Magazine, Consumer.* **Description:** Contains information about the activities of the association, club events and legislative issues.
Published by: (Illinois Association of Snowmobile Clubs'), PrintComm, Inc., PO BOX 182, Rio, WI 53960. TEL 920-992-6370, 800-380-3767, FAX 920-992-6369, http://www.printcomm.com/. Pub. Kevin Naughton. Adv. contact Branda Poe. B&W page USD 1,389, color page USD 1,655; trim 8.375 x 10.875. Circ: 10,000 (paid).

796.54 ITA ISSN 1970-6065
ILMIOCAMPER. Text in Italian. 2006. m. **Document type:** *Magazine, Consumer.*
Published by: Marco Sabatelli Editore, Piazza Vescovado 11, Savona, SV 17100, Italy. http://www.sabatelli.it.

799.1 GBR ISSN 0959-9606
IMPROVE YOUR COARSE FISHING. Text in English. 1990. m. GBP 39.99 domestic; GBP 55 in Europe; GBP 60 elsewhere (effective 2009). adv. back issues avail. **Document type:** *Magazine, Consumer.* **Description:** Designed for coarse anglers who want to improve their fishing.
Published by: H. Bauer Publishing Ltd. (Subsidiary of: Bauer Media Group), Academic House, 24-28 Oval Rd, London, NW1 7DT, United Kingdom. TEL 44-20-72418000, FAX 44-20-72418030, http://www.bauer.co.uk. Ed. Kevin Green TEL 44-1733-395138. Adv. contact Donna Harris TEL 44-1733-288054. **Subscr. to:** Tower House, Sovereign Park, Market Harborough, Leicestershire LE16 9EF, United Kingdom. TEL 44-1858-438866, subs@greatmagazines.co.uk.

796.522 ITA ISSN 1827-353X
IN ALTO. Text in Italian. 1878. a. **Document type:** *Magazine, Consumer.*
Published by: Societa Alpina Friulana, Via B Odorico 3, 1o Piano, Udine, 33100, Italy. safcai@tin.it.

799.1 USA ISSN 0276-9905
SH401
IN-FISHERMAN. Text in English. 1979. 8/yr. USD 12.99 domestic; USD 25.99 in Canada; USD 27.99 elsewhere (effective 2011). adv. illus. reprints avail. **Document type:** *Magazine, Consumer.* **Description:** For freshwater anglers from beginners to professionals.
Related titles: Online - full text ed.
Indexed: ASIP, G08, I05, SPI.
Published by: Intermedia Outdoors, Inc., 512 7th Ave, 11th Fl, New York, NY 10018. TEL 212-852-6682, 800-260-6397, FAX 212-302-4472, customerservice@imoutdoors.com, http://www.imoutdoorsmedia.com. Ed. Ken Dunwoody. Pub., Adv. contact Peter Gross.

796.552 IND ISSN 0971-426X
INDIAN MOUNTAINEER. Text in English. 1978. s-a. free to members (effective 2011). bk.rev. 176 p./no.; back issues avail. **Document type:** *Journal, Academic/Scholarly.*
Published by: Indian Mountaineering Foundation, 6, Benito Juarez Rd, New Delhi, 110 021, India. TEL 91-11-24111211, FAX 91-11-24113412, indmount@bol.net.in.

799 USA ISSN 0897-8980
INDIANA GAME & FISH. Text in English. 19??. m. USD 12.99 domestic; USD 25.99 in Canada; USD 27.99 elsewhere (effective 2011). adv. illus. **Document type:** *Magazine, Consumer.* **Description:** Informs sportsmen of hunting and fishing, as well as environmental and conservation issues in Indiana.
Related titles: Online - full text ed.; ◆ Regional ed(s).: Game & Fish; ◆ Louisiana Game & Fish. ISSN 0744-3692; ◆ Florida Game & Fish. ISSN 0889-3322; ◆ Alabama Game & Fish. ISSN 0279-6783; ◆ Mississippi-Louisiana Game & Fish. ISSN 1947-2358; ◆ North Carolina Game & Fish. ISSN 0897-8816; ◆ South Carolina Game & Fish. ISSN 0897-9154; ◆ West Virginia Game & Fish. ISSN 0897-9162; ◆ Missouri Game & Fish. ISSN 0889-3799; ◆ New York Game & Fish. ISSN 0897-9189; ◆ California Game & Fish. ISSN 1056-0122; ◆ Great Plains Game & Fish. ISSN 1055-6532; ◆ Illinois Game & Fish. ISSN 0897-9014; ◆ Iowa Game & Fish. ISSN 0897-9197; ◆ Mid-Atlantic Game & Fish. ISSN 1055-6540; ◆ Oklahoma Game & Fish. ISSN 0746-6013; ◆ Rocky Mountain Game & Fish. ISSN 1056-0114; ◆ Pennsylvania Game & Fish. ISSN 0897-8808; ◆ Virginia Game & Fish. ISSN 0897-8794; ◆ Washington - Oregon Game & Fish. ISSN 1056-0106; ◆ Ohio Game & Fish. ISSN 0897-9170; New England Game & Fish. ISSN 0897-8972. 1988. USD 12 domestic; USD 25 in Canada; USD 27 elsewhere (effective 2010).
Published by: Intermedia Outdoors, Inc., 512 7th Ave, 11th Fl, New York, NY 10018. TEL 212-852-6682, 800-260-6397, FAX 212-302-4472, customerservice@imoutdoors.com, http://www.imoutdoorsmedia.com. Ed. Ken Dunwoody. Pub., Adv. contact Peter Gross.

DIE INFO; Mitteilungen des Bundesverbandes. *see* FORESTS AND FORESTRY

799.1 FRA ISSN 1965-183X
▼ **INFO PECHE.** Text in French. 2010. 11/yr. EUR 29.50 (effective 2011). back issues avail. **Document type:** *Magazine, Consumer.*
Published by: Edipeche, 31 Rue Bapst, Asnieres-sur-Seine, 92600, France. TEL 33-1-74633840.

797.2 ESP
INMERSION; la revista practica de buceo. Text in Spanish. m. EUR 3.95 newsstand/cover (effective 2009). adv. **Document type:** *Magazine, Consumer.*
Published by: Grupo V, C Valportillo Primera, 11, Alcobendas, Madrid, 28108, Spain. TEL 34-91-6622137, FAX 34-91-6622654, secretaria@grupov.es. Ed. Nora Camara. Adv. contact Carmina Ferrer. page EUR 2,700; trim 22 x 29.7. Circ: 14,000.

799.2 USA ISSN 1940-3879
INSIDE ARCHERY. Text in English. 200?. m. USD 39.95 (effective 2007). **Document type:** *Magazine, Consumer.*
Published by: Zebra Publishing Inc, 2960 N Academy Blvd, Ste 101, Colorado Springs, CO 80917. TEL 719-495-9999, FAX 719-495-8899, info@zebrapub.com, http://www.zebrapub.com. Ed. Bill Krenz TEL 719-495-9999 ext 111. Pub. Sherry Krenz TEL 719-495-9999 ext 112.

796.42 USA ISSN 1042-3664
INSIDE TEXAS RUNNING. Text in English. 1977. 10/yr. adv. **Document type:** *Magazine, Consumer.* **Description:** Covers running and running-related events in Texas.
Published by: Runner Triathlete News, 2470 Gray Falls Dr, Ste 110, Houston, TX 77077. TEL 281-759-0555, FAX 281-759-7766. Ed. Lance Phegley. Pub. Loren Sheffer. Circ: 10,000 (paid).

796.4257 USA ISSN 1070-6070
INSIDE TRIATHLON. Text in English. 1986. bi-m. USD 19.95 domestic; USD 31.95 in Canada; USD 44.95 elsewhere (effective 2009). adv. bk.rev.; tel.rev.; video rev. charts; illus.; maps. back issues avail. **Document type:** *Magazine, Consumer.* **Description:** Features informative articles on Triathlon.
Formerly (until 1993): Triathlon Today (1051-9564)
Indexed: SD.
Published by: Inside Communications Inc., 1830 N 55th St, Boulder, CO 80301. TEL 303-440-0601, FAX 303-444-6788, fmagowan@insideinc.com, http://www.insideinc.com/. Pub. Greg Thomas TEL 303-440-0601 ext 170. Adv. contact Lars Finanger TEL 303-440-0601 ext 144. **Subscr. to:** Publishers Creative Systems, 119 E Grand Ave, Escondido, CA 92025. TEL 800 847-9910, http://www.pcspublink.com.

796.93 USA ISSN 1070-2172
INSIDERS SKI LETTER. Text in English. 1989. 10/yr. USD 33. **Document type:** *Newsletter.* **Description:** Covers skiing for serious skiers.
Related titles: Online - full text ed.
Published by: Skiletter, Inc., 115 Lilly Pond Ln, Katonah, NY 10536. TEL 914-232-5094. Ed. Greg Berry.

796.5 USA ISSN 1554-2246
INSITE (COLORADO SPRINGS). Text in English. 1969. bi-m. USD 26.95 domestic; USD 36.95 foreign (effective 2005). adv. bk.rev. illus.; stat. index. **Description:** For all who are in the Christian camping arena, primarily for those who serve in camps, conference centers, and retreat centers in the Association.
Former titles (until 2005): Christian Camp and Conference Journal (1094-3455); (until 1997): Journal of Christian Camping (0021-9649); Camps and Conference Magazine
Indexed: ChrPI.
Published by: Christian Camping International, PO Box 62189, Colorado Springs, CO 80962-2189. TEL 719-260-9400, FAX 719-260-6398. Ed. Dean Ridings.

799.1 USA ISSN 0257-1420
SH401
INTERNATIONAL ANGLER. Text in English. 1973. bi-m. USD 40 membership (effective 2007). adv. bk.rev. illus.; stat. reprints avail. **Document type:** *Newsletter, Consumer.* **Description:** Game fish world records, articles relating to recreational fishing, conservation and statistics on fishing.
Formerly: International Marine Angler
Published by: International Game Fish Association, IGFA World Fishing Center, 300 Gulf Stream Way, Dania, FL 33004. TEL 954-927-2628, FAX 954-924-4299, hq@igfa.org, http://www.igfa.org. Ed. Ray Crawford. Circ: 33,000.

THE INTERNATIONAL DIRECTORY OF GARDEN, LAWN AND PATIO EQUIPMENT AND SUPPLIES IMPORTERS. *see* BUSINESS AND ECONOMICS—Trade And Industrial Directories

799.14 AUS ISSN 1446-3636
INTERNATIONAL FREEDIVING AND SPEARFISHING NEWS. Text in English. 1994. q. AUD 35 domestic; ZAR 240 in South Africa; AUD 49.50 elsewhere (effective 2009). adv. back issues avail. **Document type:** *Magazine, Consumer.* **Description:** Covers spearfishing competitions, equipment, articles on fish.

Formerly (until 1998): Australian Free Diving and Spearfishing News (1323-7071)
Published by: Mountain Ocean & Travel Publications Pty Ltd., PO Box 355, Upper Beaconsfield, VIC 3808, Australia. TEL 61-3-59443774, FAX 61-3-59444024, sportdiving@motpub.com.au, http://www.divetheblue.net. Ed. Robert Torelli. Pub. Barry Andrewartha. Adv. contact Leanne Wylie. B&W page AUD 638, color page AUD 913; bleed 275 x 395. Circ: 28,000.

796 CAN
INTERNATIONAL LONGBOARDER MAGAZINE. Text in English. 1999. bi-m. adv.
Published by: I L B Publishing, 1054 Centre St, 293, Thornhill, ON L4J 8E5, Canada. TEL 905-738-0804, FAX 905-761-5295. Pub. Michael Brooke.

796.93 USA
INTERNATIONAL SNOWSURFING. Text in English. 1999. m. USD 35 domestic; USD 50 foreign (effective 2000). adv. bk.rev. **Document type:** *Magazine, Consumer.* **Description:** Covers snowsurfing, also known as snowboarding, in all its aspects worldwide.
Published by: International Surfing Federation, PO Box 2893, Palm Beach, FL 33480. isfworldsrnfing@aol.com. Ed. Hank Rockefeller. Pub. Gary Filosa. Circ: 250,000 (controlled).

INTERNATIONAL SPORT CULT. *see* CLOTHING TRADE—Fashions

INTERNATIONAL UNION OF ALPINE ASSOCIATIONS. BULLETIN/ UNION INTERNATIONALE DES ASSOCIATIONS D'ALPINISME. BULLETIN. *see* TRAVEL AND TOURISM

796 AUS ISSN 0815-077X
INTO THE BLUE. Text in English. m.
Published by: Coast and Mountain Walkers of New South Wales, PO Box 2449, Sydney, NSW 2001, Australia. http://www.cmw.asn.au. Ed. R Nivison Smith.

799.1 797.1 ZAF ISSN 1727-3382
INWATER. Text in English. 2003. m. ZAR 126.25 (effective 2006). adv. **Document type:** *Magazine, Consumer.*
Related titles: Optical Disk - DVD ed.: Inwater Africa. ISSN 1994-022X.
Published by: Associated Media International, PO Box 519, Cramerview, 2060, South Africa. TEL 27-11-4677007, FAX 27-11-4677003. Ed. Roger Donaldson. adv.: color page ZAR 12,950, B&W page ZAR 5,820; trim 210 x 276. Circ: 7,000.

799 USA ISSN 0897-9197
IOWA GAME & FISH. Text in English. 198?. m. USD 12.99 domestic; USD 25.99 in Canada; USD 27.99 elsewhere (effective 2011). adv. illus. **Document type:** *Magazine, Consumer.* **Description:** Informs sportsmen of hunting and fishing, as well as environmental and conservation issues in Iowa.
Related titles: Online - full text ed.; ◆ Regional ed(s).: Game & Fish; ◆ Louisiana Game & Fish. ISSN 0744-3692; ◆ Florida Game & Fish. ISSN 0889-3322; ◆ Alabama Game & Fish. ISSN 0279-6783; ◆ Mississippi-Louisiana Game & Fish. ISSN 1947-2358; ◆ North Carolina Game & Fish. ISSN 0897-8816; ◆ South Carolina Game & Fish. ISSN 0897-9154; ◆ West Virginia Game & Fish. ISSN 0897-9162; ◆ Missouri Game & Fish. ISSN 0889-3799; ◆ New York Game & Fish. ISSN 0897-9189; ◆ California Game & Fish. ISSN 1056-0122; ◆ Great Plains Game & Fish. ISSN 1055-6532; ◆ Illinois Game & Fish. ISSN 0897-9014; ◆ Indiana Game & Fish. ISSN 0897-8980; ◆ Mid-Atlantic Game & Fish. ISSN 1055-6540; ◆ Oklahoma Game & Fish. ISSN 0746-6013; ◆ Rocky Mountain Game & Fish. ISSN 1056-0114; ◆ Pennsylvania Game & Fish. ISSN 0897-8808; ◆ Virginia Game & Fish. ISSN 0897-8794; ◆ Washington - Oregon Game & Fish. ISSN 1056-0106; ◆ Ohio Game & Fish. ISSN 0897-9170; New England Game & Fish. ISSN 0897-8972. 1988. USD 12 domestic; USD 25 in Canada; USD 27 elsewhere (effective 2010).
Published by: Intermedia Outdoors, Inc., 512 7th Ave, 11th Fl, New York, NY 10018. TEL 212-852-6682, 800-260-6397, FAX 212-302-4472, http://www.imoutdoorsmedia.com. Ed. Ken Dunwoody. Pub., Adv. contact Peter Gross.

796.5 IRL ISSN 0790-8008
IRISH MOUNTAIN LOG. Text in English. 1986. q. adv. **Document type:** *Magazine, Consumer.* **Description:** Covers all aspects of Irish mountaineering and hillwalking.
Published by: Mountaineering Council of Ireland, House of Sport, Longmile Rd., Dublin, 12, Ireland. TEL 353-1-4507376, FAX 353-1-4502805, mci@eircom.net, http://www.mountaineering.ie. Ed. Chris Avison. adv.: color page EUR 1,428; bleed 216 x 303. Circ: 8,578 (paid and controlled).

799.1 IRL ISSN 1649-6841
IRISH SPECIMEN FISH. Variant title: Irish Specimen Fish Committee. Annual Report. Text in English. 1956. a. free (effective 2006).
Formerly (until 2000): Irish Specimen Fish Committee. Report (1649-7597)
Published by: Irish Specimen Fish Committee, c/o CFB, Swords Business Campus, Balheary Rd, Swords, Co. Dublin, Ireland. TEL 353-1-8842600, FAX 353-1-8360060, isfc@cfb.ie, http://www.irish-trophy-fish.com.

IRON DOG TRACKS. *see* ANTIQUES

796.52 ISL ISSN 1021-108X
ISALP; arsrit Islenska Alpaklubbsins. Text in Icelandic. 1985. a. ISK 2,700. adv. illus. back issues avail.
Published by: Islenski Alpaklubburinn, PO Box 1054, Reykjavik, 121, Iceland. TEL 354-581-1700. Ed. Torfi Hjaltason. Circ: 300.

797 AUS
IT. Text in English. 1965. m. free to members (effective 2008). **Document type:** *Newsletter, Consumer.*
Former titles (until 1967): Monthly Circular; (until 1966): Walks Programme; (until 1965): Canberra Walking and Touring Club
Related titles: Online - full text ed.
Published by: Canberra Bushwalking Club, PO Box 160, Canberra, ACT 2601, Australia. info@canberrabushwalkingclub.org.au, http://www.canberrabushwalkingclub.org.au.

796.552 JPN
IWA-TO-YUKI/ROCK AND SNOW. Text in Japanese. 1958. bi-m. JPY 7,700. adv.
Published by: Yama-Kei (Publishers) Co. Ltd., 1-1-33 Shiba-Daimon, Minato-ku, Tokyo, 105-0000, Japan. TEL 03-3436-4026, FAX 03-5472-4430. Ed. Tsunemichi Ikeda. Adv. contact Isamu Arai. Circ: 50,000.

796.552 796.93 FRA ISSN 1272-9183
J A M E S. JOURNAL DES AMOUREUX DE LA MONTAGNE, DE L'ESCALADE ET DU SKI. Text in French. 1994. s-a. **Document type:** *Magazine, Consumer.*
Formerly (until 1995): Club Alpin Francais de l'Ain. Journal (1263-574X)
Published by: Club Alpin Francais, Section Ain, Maison de la Vie Associative, Boulevard Joliot Curie, Bourg en Bresse, France. TEL 33-4-74223280, FAX 33-4-74226676.

799.2 DEU ISSN 0720-4523
JAEGER; Zeitschrift fuer das Jagdrevier. Text in German. 1883. m. EUR 62.40; EUR 5.20 newsstand/cover (effective 2011). adv. illus. **Document type:** *Magazine, Consumer.* **Description:** Discusses all aspects of hunting.
Formerly (until 1974): Deutsche Jaeger-Zeitung (0012-0324)
Indexed: KWIWR.
Published by: Jahr Top Special Verlag, Troplowitzstr 5, Hamburg, 22529, Germany. TEL 49-40-389060, FAX 49-40-38906300, info@jahr-tsv.de, http://www.jahr-tsv.de. Ed. Roland Korioth. Adv. contact Rainer Propp TEL 49-40-38906285. Circ: 32,604 (paid and controlled).

799.2 DNK ISSN 0906-415X
JAEGER. Text in Danish. 1991. m. DKK 736 membership (effective 2009). adv. bk.rev. charts; illus.; stat. index. **Document type:** *Magazine, Consumer.* **Description:** Articles on all aspects of hunting.
Formed by the merger of (1974-1991): Dansk Jagt (0106-9500); Which was formerly (1885-1973): Dansk Jagttidende (0011-6327); (1942-1991): Strandjaegeren (0039-212X); (1923-1991): Jagt og Fiskeri (0021-3977)
Published by: Danmarks Jaegerforbund, Hoejnaesvej 56, Roedovre, 2610, Denmark. TEL 45-88-887500, FAX 45-36-720911, post@jaegerne.dk. Eds. Stig Trellegaard Moeller TEL 45-88-887540, Steen Axel Hansen TEL 45-88-887550. Adv. contact Leif B Thomassen TEL 45-88-887553. color page DKK 30,503; 210 x 297.

799.2 DEU ISSN 0720-1702
DER JAEGER IN BADEN-WUERTTEMBERG. Text in German. 1956. m. free to members (effective 2009). adv. back issues avail. **Document type:** *Magazine, Consumer.*
Published by: (Landesjagdverband Baden-Wuerttemberg e.V.), Dr. Neinhaus Verlag AG, Wollgrasweg 31, Stuttgart, 70599, Germany. TEL 49-711-451275, FAX 49-711-456603, info@neinhaus-verlag.de, http://www.neinhaus-verlag.de. Ed. Ulrich Baade. Adv. contact Mirjana Staniura. B&W page EUR 2,322; trim 187 x 270. Circ: 28,735 (controlled).

799.2 DEU ISSN 1861-6747
JAEGER IN SCHLESWIG-HOLSTEIN. Text in German. 1954. 10/yr. EUR 4.20; EUR 0.70 newsstand/cover (effective 2011). adv. **Document type:** *Magazine, Trade.*
Formerly (until 2005): Jaeger und Fischer (0949-6351); Which incorporated (1994-2000): Hamburger Jaeger (0949-6343)
Published by: (Landesjagdverband Schleswig-Holstein e.V.), Max Schmidt-Roemhild KG, Mengstr 16, Luebeck, 23552, Germany. TEL 49-451-703101, FAX 49-451-7031253, info@schmidt-roemhild.de, http://www.beleke.de/unternehmen/verlage/schmidtroemhild/index.html.

799.2 DEU ISSN 0949-9563
JAGD IN BAYERN. Text in German. 1952. m. adv. **Document type:** *Magazine, Consumer.* **Description:** Examines wild animal welfare, guns, and pistols for the hunter.
Published by: Landesjagdverband Bayern e.V., Hohenlindner Str 12, Feldkirchen, 85622, Germany. TEL 49-89-9902340, FAX 49-89-99023435, info@jagd-bayern.de. Ed. Alfred Preisser. adv.: B&W page EUR 1,990, color page EUR 3,785. Circ: 43,601 (controlled).

799.2 DEU ISSN 0021-3926
JAGD UND JAEGER IN RHEINLAND-PFALZ. Text in German. 1964. m. membership. adv. bk.rev. **Document type:** *Magazine, Consumer.* **Description:** Emphasis is on hunting.
Published by: (Landesjagdverband Rheinland-Pfalz), Verlag Dieter Hoffmann (Mainz), Senefelderstr 25, Mainz, 55129, Germany. TEL 49-6136-95100, FAX 49-6136-951037, online@verlag-hoffmann.de, http://www.verlag-hoffmann.de. Ed. Nis Wagner. adv.: B&W page EUR 1,360.80, color page EUR 2,410.80; trim 185 x 252. Circ: 18,200 (controlled).

799.2 DEU ISSN 0021-3942
DER JAGDGEBRAUCHSHUND. Text in German. 1965. m. EUR 44.80 domestic; EUR 49.80 foreign; EUR 4.40 newsstand/cover (effective 2009). adv. bk.rev. abstr.; illus. **Document type:** *Magazine, Consumer.*
—CCC.
Published by: (Jagdgebrauchshundverband), Deutscher Landwirtschaftsverlag GmbH, Lothstr 29, Munich, 80797, Germany. TEL 49-89-127051, FAX 49-89-12705335, dlv.muenchen@dlv.de, http://www.dlv.de. adv.: B&W page EUR 1,231, color page EUR 2,538; trim 216 x 303. Circ: 6,519 (paid and controlled).

799.2 DEU ISSN 0943-9773
JAGEN WELTWEIT. Text in German. 1990. bi-m. EUR 47 domestic; EUR 50.50 foreign; EUR 8.90 newsstand/cover (effective 2011). adv. **Document type:** *Magazine, Consumer.*
Published by: Paul Parey Zeitschriftenverlag GmbH, Erich Kaestner Str 2, Singhofen, 56379, Germany. TEL 49-2604-9780, FAX 49-2604-978190, online@paulparey.de, http://www.paulparey.de. Ed. Karl-Heinz Betz. Adv. contact Peter Zins.

799.2 DNK ISSN 1902-3650
JAGT, VILDT & VAABEN. Text in Danish. 2006. 11/yr. DKK 699 (effective 2010). adv. **Document type:** *Magazine, Consumer.*
Formerly (until 2006): L D+ (1604-3707)
Related titles: Online - full text ed.
Published by: J S L Publications A/S, Dortheavej 59, Copenhagen NV, 2400, Denmark. TEL 45-32-711200, FAX 45-32-711212, info@jslpublications.dk, http://www.jslp.dk. Ed. Ole Hoej Hansen. Adv. contact Preben Henrichsen. color page DKK 21,200; 208 x 280.

799.2 DNK ISSN 0900-0488
JAGTHUNDEN. Text in Danish. 1942. 8/yr. membership. adv. **Document type:** *Magazine, Consumer.*
Published by: Faellesrepraesentationen for Specialklubber for Staaende Jagthunde i Danmark, c/o Flemming Thune-Stephensen, Moellebakken 47, Hinnerup, 8382, Denmark. TEL 45-86-988325, http://www.fjd.dk. Ed., Adv. contact Joern Christiansen.

799.2 NOR ISSN 1503-1233
JAKT; ekte jaktglede - hele aret. Text in Norwegian. 1996. 10/yr. NOK 349; NOK 79 newsstand/cover (effective 2009). adv. **Document type:** *Magazine, Consumer.*
Formerly (until 2002): Jakt, Hund og Vapen (0807-9374)
Published by: Hjemmet Mortensen AS, Gullhaugveien 1, Nydalen, Oslo, 0441, Norway. TEL 47-22-585000, FAX 47-22-585959, firmapost@hm-media.no, http://www.hm-media.no. Ed. Knut Brevik. adv.: page NOK 21,400.

799 SWE ISSN 1401-8306
JAKT OCH JAEGARE. Text in Swedish. 1969. m. SEK 210 (effective 1998). adv. bk.rev. **Document type:** *Magazine, Consumer.* **Description:** Focuses on hunting and hunting politics.
Formerly (until 1980): Jakt och Jaegare. Kring Laegerelden (0345-5629); Which was formed by the merger of (19??-1969): Kring Laegerelden; (1940-1969): Jakt och Jaegare
Published by: Jaegarnas Riksfoerbund - Landsbygdens Jaegare, Saltsjoegatan 15, Soedertaelje, 15171, Sweden. TEL 46-8-550-336-59, FAX 46-8-550-651-77. Ed. Bengt Tandberg. Adv. contact Bo Gunnarsson. Circ: 14,500.

799.1 NOR ISSN 0809-6201
JAKT & FISKE, FRILUFTSLIV; medlemsblad for Troms og Svalbard. Text in Norwegian. 1998. 3/yr. **Document type:** *Magazine, Consumer.*
Published by: Norges Jeger- og Fiskerforbund Troms/Norwegian Association of Hunters and Anglers in Troms, Gratangen, 9470, Norway. TEL 47-77-021188, FAX 47-77-021189, troms@njff.no, http://www.njff.no.

799.2 SWE ISSN 1102-5026
JAKTDEBATT. Text in Swedish. 1988. q. SEK 75 membership.
Published by: Riksfoereningen Haensynsfull Jakt, c/o A Ekholm, Parkvagen 11 B, Sandviken, 81136, Sweden.

799.2 SWE ISSN 0345-5637
JAKTJOURNALEN. Text in Swedish. 1970. 11/yr. SEK 455 (effective 2005). adv. bk.rev. **Document type:** *Magazine, Consumer.* **Description:** Covers all aspects of hunting.
Published by: Allers Foerlag AB, Landskronavaegen 23, Helsingborg, 25185, Sweden. TEL 46-42-173500, FAX 46-42-173682, http://www.allersforlag.se. Ed. Holger Nilsson. Adv. contact Marie Edlund TEL 46-40-408692. B&W page SEK 15,900, color page SEK 19,200; trim 260 x 185. Circ: 29,700.

799.2 SWE ISSN 1102-1217
JAKTKAMRATEN. Text in Swedish. 1954. a. price varies. **Description:** New and classical hunting stories.
Published by: Poem Foerlag, Arvika, 67193, Sweden. TEL 46-571-341 95, FAX 46-571-341 71.

799 SWE ISSN 0021-406X
JAKTMARKER OCH FISKEVATTEN. Text in Swedish. 1913. 11/yr. SEK 495 (effective 2005). adv. bk.rev. 100 p./no. 4 cols./p.; **Document type:** *Magazine, Consumer.* **Description:** Covers all aspects of fishing and hunting.
Formerly (until vol.3, 1962): Fraan Jaktmarker och Fiskevatten
Related titles: Supplement(s): Jakt och Fiske.
Published by: L R F Media AB, Gaevlegatan 22, Stockholm, 11392, Sweden. TEL 46-8-58836600, FAX 46-8-58836989, lrfmedia@lrfmedia.lrf.se, http://www.online.lrf.se. Ed. Matts Gyllsand TEL 46-54-7752503. Adv. contact Ulla Jonsson TEL 46-54-7752521. B&W page SEK 25,850, color page SEK 27,900; trim 185 x 267. Circ: 46,800.

799.2028 SWE ISSN 1103-2731
JAKTVAPENGUIDEN. Text in Swedish. 1993. a. SEK 167 (effective 2002). adv. **Document type:** *Yearbook.* **Description:** Guide to hunting weapons.
Published by: Jakt & Skyttefoerlaget AB, Grubbensringen 20 D, Stockholm, 11269, Sweden. FAX 46-8-441-18-99. Ed. Clas Johansson. Adv. contact Bo-Goeran Edstroem.

799.2 ESP
JARA Y SEDAL. Text in Spanish. m. adv. **Document type:** *Magazine, Consumer.*
Published by: Editorial America Iberica, C. Miguel Yuste 33bis, Madrid, 28037, Spain. TEL 34-91-3277950, FAX 34-91-3044746, editorial@eai.es, http://www.eai.es/. Ed. Israel Hernandez. adv.: page EUR 1,800; trim 210 x 285.

799.2 NOR ISSN 0809-3539
JEGER, HUND OG VAPEN. Text in Norwegian. 1996. 10/yr. NOK 449 (effective 2009). adv. **Document type:** *Magazine, Consumer.* **Description:** Covers all aspects of hunting and shooting, including equipment, gamekeeping and hunting dogs.
Published by: Aller Forlag AS, Stenersgaten 2, Sentrum, Oslo, 0189, Norway. TEL 47-21-301000, FAX 47-21-301205, allerforlag@aller.no, http://www.aller.no. Adv. contact Bjorn Trangsrud. color page NOK 21,500; bleed 234 x 305. Circ: 17,830 (paid).

799.1 799.2 NOR ISSN 1504-4025
JEGER & FISKER; medlemsblad for NJFF Vest-Agder. Text in Norwegian. 2000. s-a. **Document type:** *Monographic series, Consumer.*
Published by: Norges Jeger- og Fiskerforbund Vest-Agder/Norwegian Association of Hunters and Anglers in Vest-Agder, Skippergaten 21, Kristiansand, 4611, Norway. TEL 47-38-024251, vestagdar@njff.org.

JERSEY SIERRAN. *see* CONSERVATION

796 USA ISSN 2154-4778
▼ **JIM STRADER'S KENTUCKY OUTDOORS.** Variant title: Kentucky Outdoors. Text in English. 2010 (May). m. USD 19.95 (effective 2011). **Document type:** *Magazine, Consumer.* **Description:** Kentucky hunting and fishing tips and advice by Jim Strader.
Related titles: Online - full text ed.: ISSN 2154-476X. 2010 (May).
Published by: Kentucky Outdoors Magazine, 5103 Preston Hwy, Ste 4, Louisville, KY 40213. TEL 502-966-3661, FAX 502-966-3662, knclark@insightbb.com.

796.93 CHN
JISU SKEE/VELOCITY SKI. Text in Chinese. 2005. 7/yr. CNY 16 (effective 2005). **Document type:** *Magazine, Consumer.*
Related titles: Online - full content ed.
Published by: (Zhongguo Huaxue Xiehui/Chinese Ski Association), Luyou Zazhishe, 13 Xiagongfu Jie, Dongcheng-qu, Beijing, China.

S

796.42 POL ISSN 1231-4854
JOGGING. Text in Polish. 1992. bi-m. PLZ 40 domestic; USD 104 foreign (effective 2002). adv. **Document type:** *Magazine, Consumer.* **Description:** Publishes articles about jogging for health and satisfaction.
Published by: MenupSport, Ul Reymonta 10-127, Warsaw, 01842, Poland. TEL 48-22-6636828, FAX 48-22-6636828. Ed., Pub., Adv. contact Zbigniew Zaremba.

796.939 USA
THE JOURNAL. Text in English. 2004. q. USD 27; USD 5 newsstand/cover (effective 2006). **Document type:** *Magazine, Consumer.*
Published by: The Journal, 619 East 6th St, New York, NY 10009.

799 FRA ISSN 0755-7140
JOURNAL DU CHASSEUR. Text in French. 1950. bi-m. EUR 12.20 (effective 2009). adv. bk.rev. **Document type:** *Magazine, Consumer.*
Published by: Groupe Hugo Edition, La Boutique d'Hugo, 70 Av. du 10eme Dragon, Montauban, 82000, France. TEL 33-5-63242286, FAX 33-5-63242268, http://www.groupehugoedition.com. Circ: 14,000.

796.07 GBR ISSN 1472-9679
LB1047
➤ **JOURNAL OF ADVENTURE EDUCATION AND OUTDOOR LEARNING.** Text in English. 1984. s-a. GBP 149 combined subscription in United Kingdom to institutions (print & online eds.); EUR 248, USD 311 combined subscription to institutions (print & online eds.) (effective 2012). adv. bk.rev. 80 p./no. 1 cols./p.; back issues avail.; reprint service avail. from PSC. **Document type:** *Journal, Academic/Scholarly.* **Description:** Aims to promote dialogue, research, thinking, teaching and practice from critical perspectives in the fields of adventure education and outdoor learning.
Supersedes in part (in 2000): Horizons (1462-0677); Which was formerly (until 1997): Journal of Adventure Education and Outdoor Leadership (0966-7652); (until 1991): Adventure Education and Outdoor Leadership (1463-6980); (until 1988): Adventure Education (0265-5802)
Related titles: Online - full text ed.: ISSN 1754-0402. GBP 134 in United Kingdom to institutions; EUR 223, USD 280 to institutions (effective 2012).
Indexed: B29, CA, CPE, E03, ERI, ERIC, IBR, IBZ, P03, P10, P18, P48, P53, P54, PQC, PsycInfo, T02.
—BLDSC (4918.948500), IE. **CCC.**
Published by: (Institute for Outdoor Learning), Routledge (Subsidiary of: Taylor & Francis Group), 4 Park Sq, Milton Park, Abingdon, Oxon OX14 4RN, United Kingdom. TEL 44-20-70176000, FAX 44-20-70176336, subscriptions@tandf.co.uk, http://www.routledge.com. Adv. contact Linda Hann TEL 44-1344-779945. Circ: 7,500. **Subscr. to:** Taylor & Francis Ltd., Journals Customer Service, Sheepen Pl, Colchester, Essex CO3 3LP, United Kingdom. TEL 44-20-70175544, FAX 44-20-70175198.

➤ **JOURNAL OF LEISURE RESEARCH.** *see* LEISURE AND RECREATION

796 USA ISSN 1948-5123
▼ ➤ **JOURNAL OF OUTDOOR RECREATION, EDUCATION, AND LEADERSHIP.** Text in English. 2009. s-a. (2 or 3 times a yr.). USD 25 to individual members; USD 50 to non-members; USD 125 to institutions (effective 2009). **Document type:** *Journal, Academic/Scholarly.* **Description:** Research on outdoor recreation, education, and leadership.
Media: Online - full content.
Published by: (Association of Outdoor Recreation and Education, Wilderness Education Association), Western Kentucky University, 1906 College Heights Blvd, Bowling Green, KY 42101. TEL 502-745-6278, FAX 502-745-2697, western@wku.edu, http://www.wku.edu.

333.783 USA ISSN 2160-6862
GV181.5
JOURNAL OF PARK AND RECREATION ADMINISTRATION (ONLINE). Abbreviated title: J P R A. Text in English. 2002. q. bk.rev. 100 p./no. 1 cols./p.; back issues avail. **Document type:** *Journal, Academic/Scholarly.* **Description:** Scholarly articles for the leisure service practitioner, focusing on planning, finance, organizational practice, personnel evaluation, programming, and marketing and promotion.
Media: Online - full text.
Indexed: SportS.
Published by: (American Academy for Park and Recreation Administration), Sagamore Publishing, 1807 N Federal Dr, Urbana, IL 61801. TEL 217-359-5940, FAX 217-359-5975, books@sagamorepub.com, http://www.sagamorepub.com. Ed. James A Busser TEL 702-895-0942.

JOURNAL OF SPORT AND TOURISM. *see* LEISURE AND RECREATION

799.2 USA
JOURNAL OF THE TEXAS TROPHY HUNTERS. Text in English. bi-m. USD 29.70 (effective 2002).
Published by: Texas Trophy Hunting Association, PO Box 791107, San Antonio, TX 78279-1107. TEL 210-523-8500, 800-800-3207, FAX 210-523-8871, info@ttha.com.

799.2 FRA ISSN 1622-8979
JOURS DE CHASSE. Text in French. 2000. q. EUR 26 domestic; EUR 32.10 foreign (effective 2008). back issues avail. **Document type:** *Magazine, Consumer.*
Published by: Valmonde & Cie, 3-5, rue St. Georges, Paris, 75009, France. TEL 33-1-40541100, FAX 33-1-40541285, http://www.valmonderegie.fr.

799.1 DEU
JUNGJAEGERINFO. Text in German. 4/yr. adv. **Document type:** *Magazine, Consumer.*
Published by: Paul Parey Zeitschriftenverlag GmbH, Erich Kaestner Str 2, Singhofen, 56379, Germany. TEL 49-2604-9780, FAX 49-2604-978190, online@paulparey.de, http://www.paulparey.de. adv.: B&W page EUR 1,189, color page EUR 1,885. Circ: 17,000 (controlled).

796.4 796.9 FIN ISSN 1796-1483
JUOKSU & HIIHTO. Text in Finnish. 2006. bi-m. EUR 35 (effective 2006). adv. **Document type:** *Magazine, Consumer.*
Published by: RideMedia Oy, PO Box 140, Hyvinkaa, 05801, Finland. TEL 358-19-483490, FAX 358-19-483480, http://www.ridemedia.fi. Ed. Jari Hemmila TEL 358-400-928110. Pub. Jukka Helminen. Adv. contact Ossi Sinisilta TEL 358-3-6715474. B&W page EUR 1,380, color page EUR 2,100; 210 x 297.

K O A DIRECTORY. (Kampgrounds of America) *see* BUSINESS AND ECONOMICS—Trade And Industrial Directories

799 AUT
KAERNTNER JAEGER. Text in German. 1971. q. membership. adv. bk.rev. illus. **Description:** Covers all aspects of hunting.
Indexed: KWIWR.
Published by: Kaerntner Jaegerschaft, Bahnhofstrasse 38 B, Klagenfurt, K 9020, Austria. Ed. G Anderluh.

799.1 CZE ISSN 1211-5924
KAJMAN; rybarsky casopis. Text in Czech. 1994. m. CZK 592; CZK 49.33 newsstand/cover (effective 2009). adv. **Document type:** *Magazine, Consumer.*
Formerly (until 1994): Rybarske Noviny (1210-826X)
Published by: Kajman Czech s.r.o., Budejovicka 1542, Tabor, 390 02, Czech Republic. TEL 420-381-256666, FAX 420-381-256667, kajman@telecom.cz. Ed. Tomas Rozsypal.

796.5 BEL ISSN 0775-8545
KAMPEERTOERIST. Text in Dutch. 1953. m. (11/yr.). bk.rev. **Description:** For campers and outdoor sports enthusiasts.
Published by: (Vlaamse Kampeertoeristen vzw), Making Magazines, Blekersdijk, 14, Gent, 9000, Belgium. TEL 32-9-2338463, FAX 32-9-2338087. Circ: 13,700. **Co-sponsor:** Sportfederatie Vlaamse Kampeerders.

KANSAS WILDLIFE & PARKS. *see* CONSERVATION

799.1 NLD ISSN 1568-1998
KARPER. Text in Dutch. 1997. bi-m. EUR 49.25; EUR 8.95 newsstand/cover (effective 2011). adv. **Document type:** *Magazine, Consumer.*
Published by: Vipmedia Publishing en Services, Takkebijsters 57a, Breda, 4817 BL, Netherlands. TEL 31-76-5301721, FAX 31-76-5144531, info@vipmedia.nl, http://www.vipmedia.nl. Ed. Pierre Bronsgeest. Adv. contact John Huussen TEL 31-76-5301725.

799.1 DEU
▼ **KARPFEN;** internationales Karpfenmagazin. Text in German. 2009. 4/yr. EUR 31.80; EUR 7.95 newsstand/cover (effective 2011). adv. **Document type:** *Magazine, Consumer.*
Published by: Jahr Top Special Verlag, Troplowitzstr 5, Hamburg, 22529, Germany. TEL 49-40-389060, FAX 49-40-38906300, info@jahr-tsv.de, http://www.jahr-tsv.de. Ed. Gregor Bradler. Adv. contact Cord Schumann. Circ: 6,000 (paid).

KASHSHAFAT AL-IMARAT/EMIRATES BOY SCOUTS. *see* CLUBS

796.42 NLD ISSN 1877-0290
KEEP ON RUNNING. Text in Dutch. 2008. s-a. EUR 2.50 newsstand/cover (effective 2011). **Document type:** *Magazine, Consumer.*
Published by: Uitgeverij Marken, Kaldenkerkerweg 223, Venlo, 5915 PP, Netherlands. TEL 31-77-3207000, FAX 31-77-3207008, info@uitgeverijmarken.nl, http://www.uitgeverijmarken.nl.

KENTUCKY AFIELD. *see* CONSERVATION

799 USA ISSN 0889-3802
KENTUCKY GAME & FISH. Text in English. 1986. m. USD 12.99 domestic; USD 25.99 in Canada; USD 27.99 elsewhere (effective 2011). adv. illus. **Document type:** *Magazine, Consumer.* **Description:** Informs sportsmen of hunting and fishing, as well as environmental and coservation issues in Kentucky.
Related titles: Online - full text ed.
Published by: Intermedia Outdoors, Inc., 512 7th Ave, 11th Fl, New York, NY 10018. TEL 212-852-6682, 800-260-6397, FAX 212-302-4472, customerservice@imoutdoors.com, http://www.imoutdoorsmedia.com. Ed. Ken Dunwoody. Pub., Adv. contact Peter Gross.

KEY NOTE MARKET REPORT: CAMPING & CARAVANNING. *see* LEISURE AND RECREATION

797 FRA ISSN 1624-8570
KITEBOARDER. Text in French. 2000. bi-m. **Document type:** *Magazine, Consumer.*
Published by: Editions Niveales, 6 Rue Irvoy, Grenoble, 38000, France. TEL 33-4-76705411, FAX 33-4-76705412, http://www.dipresse.com/niveales. Ed. Gilles Debrix.

796 USA ISSN 1534-4282
GV840.K49
KITEBOARDING. Text in English. 2000. bi-m. USD 29.97 domestic; USD 41.97 in Canada; USD 65.97 elsewhere (effective 2011). adv. illus. back issues avail. **Document type:** *Magazine, Consumer.* **Description:** Contains ground-breaking techniques and the inside scoop on the latest of the rapidly developing gear.
Related titles: Online - full text ed.
Indexed: G08, I05.
—**CCC.**
Published by: Bonnier Corp. (Subsidiary of: Bonnier Group), 460 N Orlando Ave, Ste 200, Orlando, FL 32789. http://www.bonniercorp.com. Ed. Aaron Sales. Pub. David Combe TEL 503-417-7934.

790 USA ISSN 0192-3439
TL759.A1
KITELINES; the international kite journal. Text in English. 1977. q. USD 18 domestic; USD 27 foreign; USD 6 newsstand/cover (effective 2000). adv. bk.rev. charts; illus. index. back issues avail. **Document type:** *Magazine, Consumer.* **Description:** Comprehensive full-color international magazine of kite news, reviews, plans, tips and in-depth feature articles.
Supersedes: Kite Tales (0192-3420)
Related titles: Microfiche ed.
Indexed: IHTDI.
Published by: Aeolus Press, Inc., 8807 Liberty Rd, PO Box 466, Randallstown, MD 21133-0466. TEL 410-922-1212, FAX 410-922-4262. Ed., Pub., R&P, Adv. contact Valerie Govig. Circ: 13,000 (paid).

796.158 GBR ISSN 1477-1314
KITEWORLD. Variant title: Kite World. Text in English. 2002. bi-m. GBP 22 domestic includes United States; GBP 60 elsewhere; GBP 3.75 newsstand/cover (effective 2009). adv. **Document type:** *Magazine, Consumer.* **Description:** Features adventurous travel stories from the ocean, mountains, backcountry and beaches, inspirational galleries from the world's best photographers as well as techniques and advice from the kiting sport's most gifted riders and instructors.
Related titles: Online - full text ed.: GBP 15 (effective 2009).
Published by: 328 Media Ltd., 5 St Georges Pl, Brighton, BN1 4GA, United Kingdom. TEL 44-1273-808601, FAX 44-5600-655815, http://www.328media.com/. Ed. Jim Gaunt. Adv. contact Rob Darling.

797.32099305 AUS ISSN 1170-6139
KIWI SURF. Text in English. 1990. bi-m. NZD 82.50 domestic; NZD 41.80 in New Zealand; NZD 118.50 elsewhere; NZD 6.99 newsstand/cover (effective 2008). adv. back issues avail. **Document type:** *Magazine, Consumer.* **Description:** Aims to promote the New Zealand surfing lifestyle.
Published by: Morrison Media Services Ltd., PO Box 823, Burleigh Heads, QLD 4220, Australia. TEL 61-7-55761388, FAX 61-7-55761527, subs@morrisonmedia.com.au, http://www.morrisonmedia.com.au. Ed. Chris Millet TEL 64-9-4117834. Pub. Peter Morrison. Adv. contact Nick Towner TEL 64-2-1802024. color page AUD 2,362; trim 210 x 297. **Subscr. to:** ISubscribe Pty Ltd., 25 Lime St, Ste 303, Level 3, Sydney, NSW 2000, Australia. TEL 61-2-92621722, FAX 61-2-92625044, info@isubscribe.com.au, http://www.isubscribe.com.au.

796.522 DEU ISSN 1437-7462
KLETTERN; hot rocks - cold ice - big walls. Text in German. 1995. 8/yr. EUR 5.50 newsstand/cover (effective 2011). adv. **Document type:** *Magazine, Consumer.* **Description:** Contains articles and features on all aspects of outdoor climbing.
Related titles: Online - full text ed.
Published by: Motor Presse Stuttgart GmbH & Co. KG (Subsidiary of: Gruner + Jahr AG & Co), Leuschnerstr 1, Stuttgart, 70174, Germany. TEL 49-711-18201, FAX 49-711-1821779, cgolla@motorpresse.de, http://www.motorpresse.de. Ed. Volker Leuchsner. Adv. contact Bernd Holzhauer. Circ: 18,668 (paid).

799.2 USA
KNIGHT & HALE ULTIMATE TEAM HUNTING. Text in English. 2002. s-a. USD 5.95 (effective 2004). adv. **Document type:** *Magazine, Consumer.*
Related titles: Online - full text ed.
Published by: Grand View Media Group, Inc. (Subsidiary of: EBSCO Industries, Inc.), 200 Croft St, Ste 1, Birmingham, AL 35242. TEL 888-431-2877, FAX 205-408-3797, webmaster@grandviewmedia.com, http://www.grandviewmedia.com. adv.: B&W page USD 2,750, color page USD 3,440; trim 8 x 10.875.

796.93 330 USA ISSN 1079-5839
GV854.A1
KOTTKE NATIONAL END OF SEASON SURVEY. Text in English. 1979. a. USD 175 to non-members; USD 75 to members (effective 2000). **Description:** Examines changes and trends in skier visits for the domestic ski industry. Analyzes influence of season length, lift capacity, night skiing, and snow-making on business volume.
Formerly (until 1993): End of Season National Business Survey
Published by: National Ski Areas Association, 133 S Van Gordon St, Ste 300, Lakewood, CO 80288. TEL 303-987-1111, FAX 303-986-2345. R&P Tim White.

796.552 DEU
KREUZ & QUER. Text in German. q. EUR 12; EUR 2.25 newsstand/cover (effective 2007). adv. **Document type:** *Magazine, Consumer.*
Published by: Sauerlaendischer Gebirgsverein e.V., Hasenwinkel 4, Arnsberg, 59821, Germany. TEL 49-2931-524813, FAX 49-2931-524815, info@sgv.de. Ed. Thomas Reunert. Adv. contact Andrea Hoelcke. page EUR 1,900.80. Circ: 46,000 (controlled).

799.1 DEU ISSN 1431-9551
KUTTER UND KUESTE; das Meeresangler-Magazin. Text in German. 1996. q. EUR 22; EUR 5.50 newsstand/cover (effective 2011). adv. **Document type:** *Magazine, Consumer.* **Description:** Contains articles and features on all aspects of sea fishing.
Published by: Jahr Top Special Verlag, Troplowitzstr 5, Hamburg, 22529, Germany. TEL 49-40-389060, FAX 49-40-38906300, info@jahr-tsv.de, http://www.jahr-tsv.de. Ed. Michael Werner. Adv. contact Christopher Zippert TEL 49-40-38906267. Circ: 16,605 (paid).

LAND AND WATER CONSERVATION FUND GRANTS MANUAL. *see* CONSERVATION

796 FIN ISSN 0356-2395
LATU JA POLKU. Text in Finnish. 1945. 8/yr. EUR 35 (effective 2005). adv. **Document type:** *Magazine, Consumer.* **Description:** Devoted to outdoor sports and the adventure of hiking.
Formerly (until 1973): Latu
Published by: Suomen Latu, Fabianinkatu 7, Helsinki, 00130, Finland. TEL 358-9-170101, FAX 358-9-663376, http://www.suomenlatu.fi. Ed. Tuomo Jantunen. adv.: B&W page EUR 1,595, color page EUR 2,485; 210 x 297. Circ: 55,000 (paid).

796.79 388.346 USA
LAZYDAYS R V SHOWCASE. (Recreational Vehicle) Text in English. 2005. q. free to qualified personnel (effective 2009). back issues avail. **Document type:** *Magazine, Consumer.* **Description:** Informs, inspires and entertains the community of people who are passionate about RVs.
Formerly (until 200?): Lazydays R V Living (1555-1822)
Published by: (Lazy Days RV Center, Inc.), Rodale, Inc., 33 E Minor St, Emmaus, PA 18098. TEL 610-967-5171, FAX 610-967-8963, customer_service@rodale.com, http://www.rodaleinc.com. Ed. Tina Richey.

797.21 DEU ISSN 1617-8009
LEBENSRETTER; Wir in der DLRG. Text in German. 2000. 4/yr. EUR 7.50 (effective 2009). adv. **Document type:** *Magazine, Trade.*
Formed by the merger of (1991-2000): Delphin. Ausgabe Mitte-West (0945-411X); (1991-2000): Delphin. Ausgabe Nord-West (0945-4098); (1991-2000): Delphin. Ausgabe West (0945-4101); (1991-2000): Delphin. Ausgabe Schleswig-Holstein - Hamburg (1432-5950); (1991-2000): Delphin. Ausgabe Wuerttemberg (1432-5969); Which all superseded in part (19??-1991): D L R G Magazin (0938-7013); Which was formerly (until 1990): Der Lebensretter (0938-7005)

Published by: Deutsche Lebens-Rettungs-Gesellschaft e.V., Im Niedernfeld 2, Bad Nenndorf, 31542, Germany. TEL 49-5723-955440, FAX 49-5723-955549, admin-info@dlrg.de, http://www.dlrg.de. adv.: page EUR 2,200; trim 177 x 265. Circ: 35,000 (controlled).

796.42 DEU ISSN 0343-5369
LEICHTATHLETIK. Text in German. 1926. w. EUR 115; EUR 3 newsstand/cover (effective 2011). adv. bk.rev. index. **Document type:** *Magazine, Consumer.*
Incorporates (1952-1990): Leichtathlet (0323-4134); Which was formerly (until 1953): Leichtathletik (0323-7346)
Indexed: A22, RASB.
—IE, Infotrieve.
Published by: Marken Verlag GmbH, Hansaring 97, Cologne, 50670, Germany. TEL 49-221-9574270, FAX 49-221-95742777, marken-info@markenverlag.de, http://www.markenverlag.de. Adv. contact Frank Krauthaeuser. Circ: 6,000 (paid).

796.42 DEU
LEICHTATHLETIK SPECIAL. Text in German. 1912. 3/yr. adv. **Document type:** *Newspaper, Trade.*
Published by: Marken Verlag GmbH, Hansaring 97, Cologne, 50670, Germany. TEL 49-221-9574270, FAX 49-221-95742777, marken-info@markenverlag.de, http://www.markenverlag.de. Adv. contact Frank Krauthaeuser. Circ: 13,650 (paid and controlled).

796.42 DEU ISSN 0939-8392
LEICHTATHLETIKTRAINING. Text in German. 1990. m. EUR 46.80 domestic; EUR 51.60 foreign (effective 2011). adv. **Document type:** *Magazine, Trade.*
Indexed: DIP, IBR, IBZ.
Published by: Philippka-Sportverlag Konrad Honig, Rektoratsweg 36, Muenster, 48159, Germany. TEL 49-251-230050, FAX 49-251-2300579, info@philippka.de, http://www.philippka.de. Ed. Frank Mueller. Adv. contact Peter Moellers TEL 49-251-2300528.

LEISURE/LOISIR. *see* LEISURE AND RECREATION

796 NLD ISSN 2211-6311
LIFT. Text in Dutch. 1993. 8/yr. EUR 29 (effective 2011). adv. **Document type:** *Magazine, Consumer.*
Formerly (until 2011): Outdoor Magazine (0928-5709)
Related titles: ◆ Supplement(s): Outdoor Buyer's Guide.
Published by: Maruba b.v., Winthontlaan 200, Utrecht, 3526 KV, Netherlands. TEL 31-30-2891073, FAX 31-30-2887415, maruba@maruba.com, http://www.maruba.nl. Circ: 35,000.

LIGHT SPORT AND ULTRALIGHT FLYING!; the magazine for sport pilots. *see* AERONAUTICS AND SPACE FLIGHT

796 USA
THE LIGHTNIN' RIDGE OUTDOOR JOURNAL. Text in English. 2003. irreg. (hunting/gaming seasons). illus. 48 p./no.; **Document type:** *Magazine, Consumer.*
Published by: The Lightnin' Ridge Outdoor Journal, PO Box 22, Bolivar, MO 65613. lightninridge@alltel.net.

796.552 USA
LINCOLN HERITAGE TRAIL FOUNDATION. Text in English. 1963. 5/yr.
Address: PO Box 1507, Springfield, IL 62705. Ed. Bryan Marshall.

796.172 ZAF ISSN 1816-2436
LIQUID; girls surfing magazine. Text in English. 2005. q. ZAR 70 (effective 2006). adv.
Published by: Blue Mountain Publishers, 28 Harries St, Plumstead, Cape Town 7800, South Africa. Ed. Shannon McLaughlin. Adv. contact Alex Molde.

799.2 634.9 UKR
LISOVYI I MYSLYVS'KYI ZHURNAL/FOREST AND HUNTING MAGAZINE. Text in Ukrainian. 1995. bi-m. 48 p./no.; **Document type:** *Magazine, Consumer.*
Address: c/o Valentina Maksimenko, Vul Khreschatyk 5, Room 403, Kyiv, 252601, Ukraine. Ed. Valentina Maksimenko.

796.93 USA
LONG ISLAND SKI. Text in English. 1981. irreg. free. adv.
Published by: Leah S. Dunaief, Ed. & Pub., PO Box V.T., Setauket, NY 11733. TEL 516-751-1550. Circ: 60,000.

796 USA
LONG TRAIL NEWS. Text in English. 1922. q. USD 27; membership or exchange basis. adv. bk.rev. **Document type:** *Newsletter.*
Description: News, information, letters, and announcements pertaining to the members and activities of the Green Mountain Club, which promotes, protects and maintains hiking and conservation activities in Vermont.
Formerly (until 1925): Green Mountain News
Published by: Green Mountain Club, Inc., Rte 100 RR 1 Box 650, Waterbury, VT 05677-9735. TEL 802-244-7037, FAX 802-244-5867. Ed., Adv. contact Sylvia L Plumb. Circ: 8,500.

796 GBR ISSN 2042-0250
▼ **LONGBOARDING & FREERIDE.** Text in English. 2010. q. **Document type:** *Trade.*
Related titles: Online - full text ed.
Published by: Endless Summer Media, Ste 3, Kerns House Unit 11, Threemilestone Industrial Estate, Turo, TR4 9LD, United Kingdom. Ed. Tim Nunn. Adv. contact Mel Eden TEL 44-1872-224030.

796.172 AUS ISSN 1832-2115
LONGBREAK. Text in English. 2004. q. AUD 30 (effective 2008). adv. 80 p./no.; **Document type:** *Magazine, Consumer.*
Related titles: Online - full text ed.
Published by: Cambridge Media, 17 Northwood St, West Leederville, W.A. 6007, Australia. TEL 61-8-93823911, mail@cambridgemedia.com.au, http://www.cambridgemedia.com.au.

799 USA ISSN 1060-7617
LONGHUNTER JOURNAL. Text in English. 1989. q. USD 15. adv. bk.rev. **Document type:** *Newsletter.*
Published by: National Muzzle Loading Rifle Association, PO Box 67, Friendship, IN 47021. TEL 812-667-5131, 800-745-1493, FAX 812-667-5136. Ed. Jon Uithol. Adv. contact Joyce Vogel.

796.5 NLD ISSN 1567-3804
LOPENDE ZAKEN. Text in Dutch. 1997. q.
Published by: Stichting Wandelplatform-LAW, Postbus 846, Amersfoort, 3800 AV, Netherlands. TEL 31-33-4653660, FAX 31-33-4654377, slaw@wandelnet.nl, http://www.wandelnet.nl.

LOUISIANA CONSERVATIONIST. *see* CONSERVATION

799.2 USA ISSN 0744-3692
LOUISIANA GAME & FISH. Text in English. 1981. m. USD 12.99 domestic; USD 25.99 in Canada; USD 27.99 elsewhere (effective 2011). adv. illus. **Document type:** *Magazine, Consumer.*
Description: Informs sportsmen of hunting and fishing, as well as environmental and conservation issues in Louisiana.
Related titles: Online - full text ed.; ◆ Regional ed(s).: Game & Fish; ◆ Florida Game & Fish. ISSN 0889-3322; ◆ Alabama Game & Fish. ISSN 0279-6783; ◆ Mississippi-Louisiana Game & Fish. ISSN 1947-2358; ◆ North Carolina Game & Fish. ISSN 0897-8816; ◆ South Carolina Game & Fish. ISSN 0897-9154; ◆ West Virginia Game & Fish. ISSN 0897-9162; ◆ Missouri Game & Fish. ISSN 0889-3799; ◆ New York Game & Fish. ISSN 0897-9189; ◆ California Game & Fish. ISSN 1056-0122; ◆ Great Plains Game & Fish. ISSN 1055-6532; ◆ Illinois Game & Fish. ISSN 0897-9014; ◆ Indiana Game & Fish. ISSN 0897-8980; ◆ Iowa Game & Fish. ISSN 0897-9197; ◆ Mid-Atlantic Game & Fish. ISSN 1055-6540; ◆ Oklahoma Game & Fish. ISSN 0746-6013; ◆ Rocky Mountain Game & Fish. ISSN 1056-0114; ◆ Pennsylvania Game & Fish. ISSN 0897-8808; ◆ Virginia Game & Fish. ISSN 0897-8794; ◆ Washington - Oregon Game & Fish. ISSN 1056-0106; ◆ Ohio Game & Fish. ISSN 0897-9170; New England Game & Fish. ISSN 0897-8972. 1988. USD 12 domestic; USD 25 in Canada; USD 27 elsewhere (effective 2010).
Published by: Intermedia Outdoors, Inc., 512 7th Ave, 11th Fl, New York, NY 10018. TEL 212-852-6682, 800-260-6397, FAX 212-302-4472, customerservice@imoutdoors.com, http://www.imoutdoorsmedia.com. Ed. Ken Dunwoody. Pub., Adv. contact Peter Gross.

799.2 BGR ISSN 0324-0541
LOV I RIBOLOV. Text in Bulgarian. 1895. m. BGL 490, USD 35. adv. charts; illus. **Document type:** *Consumer.* **Description:** Includes articles, short stories about hunting, animals, predominantly wild animals and nature, conservation, ecology, international hunting tourism.
Published by: Nasluka Ltd., Lov i Ribolov, 31-33 Vitosha blvd, Sofia, 1040, Bulgaria. TEL 00359-02-881492, FAX 00359-02-803633. Ed., Adv. contact Stefan Landjev. Circ: 15,000. **Subscr. to:** Klokotnitsa ul 24, Sofia, Bulgaria.

799.2 SVN ISSN 0024-7014
LOVEC; revija za lovstvo, lovsko kinologijo in varstvo narove. Text in Slovenian. 1918. m. EUR 92 (effective 2007). **Document type:** *Magazine, Consumer.* **Description:** Discusses hunting.
Related titles: Online - full content ed.
Indexed: RASB.
Published by: Lovska Zveza Slovenije, Zupanciceva 9, pp 505, Ljubljana, 1001, Slovenia. TEL 386-1-2410922, FAX 386-1-2410927, info@lovstvo.net, http://www.lovstvo.net. Ed. Boris Leskovic.

799.2 SVK ISSN 1337-9860
▼ **LOVU ZDAR!;** polovnicky magazin. Text in Slovak. 2009. bi-m. EUR 2.35 newsstand/cover (effective 2011). adv. **Document type:** *Magazine, Consumer.*
Published by: ITF Press, s.r.o., Hviezdna 8, Samorin, 93101, Slovakia. TEL 421-918-529825.

796.9 FIN ISSN 0788-3749
M K-LEHTI. (Moottorikelkka) Text in Finnish. 1990. 5/yr. EUR 31 (effective 2006). adv. **Document type:** *Magazine, Consumer.*
Published by: RideMedia Oy, PO Box 140, Hyvinkaa, 05801, Finland. TEL 358-19-483490, FAX 358-19-483480, http://www.ridemedia.fi. Ed. Virpi Hyokki. Pub. Jukka Helminen. Adv. contact Ossi Sinisilta TEL 358-3-6715474. B&W page EUR 1,320, color page EUR 2,100; 210 x 297.

799 SWE ISSN 1404-921X
MAGASINET VILDMARK; jakt, fiske, uteliv. Text in Swedish. 1989. bi-m. SEK 195; SEK 280 foreign (effective 1997). adv.
Formerly (until 2000): Vildmarks Nytt (1101-5012)
Published by: Daus Tryck och Media, Daushuset, Bjaesta, 89380, Sweden. TEL 46-660-266100. adv.: B&W page SEK 13,800, color page SEK 14,300; trim 275 x 192. Circ: 30,000.

799.2 FRA ISSN 1957-6455
LE MAGAZINE DU PIEGEUR & PETIT GIBIER. Text in French. 2007. q. **Document type:** *Magazine, Consumer.*
Formed by the merger of (2002-2007): Le Magazine du Piegeur (1769-3519); (1999-2007): Le Chasseur de Petit Gibier (1293-9420)
Published by: Editions Chasse Nature, B P 12, Quissac, 30260, France. TEL 33-4-66773806.

799 USA ISSN 0199-0365
SK85
MAINE SPORTSMAN. Text in English. 1977. 20/yr. USD 22. adv.
Description: Covers hunting and fishing in Maine.
Published by: All Outdoors, PO Box 365, Augusta, ME 04330. TEL 207-626-3315. Ed. Harry Vanderweide. Pub. Jon Lynd. Adv. contact George Pulkhinen. Circ: 30,000 (paid). **Subscr. to:** PO Box 507, Yarmouth, ME 04096.

799.2 ZAF
MAN MAGNUM; the shooters' magazine. Text mainly in English; Section in Afrikaans. 1976. m. ZAR 165 domestic; ZAR 240 foreign (effective 2003). adv. bk.rev. index. back issues avail. **Document type:** *Magazine.*
Formerly: Man
Indexed: ISAP.
Published by: South Africa Man Pty. Ltd., PO Box 35204, Northway, 4065, South Africa. TEL 27-31-5726551, FAX 27-31-5628389. Ed., Pub., R&P Ronald K Anger. Adv. contact Meridan Creak. B&W page ZAR 7,204.80, color page ZAR 11,599.50; trim 185 x 253. Circ: 30,000 (paid).

796.42 DEU ISSN 0179-5597
MARATHON AKTUELL. Text in German. 1981. m. USD 25. adv. bk.rev. back issues avail.
Published by: Sportverlag, Derfflingerstr 34, Duesseldorf, 40470, Germany. Ed. Burkhard Swara. Circ: 6,000.

MASSACHUSETTS SIERRAN. *see* CONSERVATION

MATKAILU/TOURISM. *see* TRAVEL AND TOURISM

796.172 USA
THE MAUI WINDSURFING REPORT. Text in English. 1995. irreg. **Document type:** *Magazine, Consumer.*
Media: Online - full text.
Published by: Maui Windsurfing Report, PO Box 1202, Kula, HI 96790. Ed. Tm Orden.

796.42 GBR ISSN 2042-972X
▼ **MEN'S RUNNING;** for runners with balls. Text in English. 2010. m. GBP 29 (effective 2010). back issues avail. **Document type:** *Magazine, Consumer.* **Description:** Provides advice, inspiration and guidance to all levels of runners. Covers topics such as fitness, sports, lifestyle, health, nutrition for runners.
Published by: Wild Bunch Media Ltd., 4th Fl, 26-28 Hammersmith Grove, London, W6 7BA, United Kingdom. TEL 44-20-88341650. Ed. Christina Neal.

796.552 ITA ISSN 1721-5072
MERIDIANI MONTAGNE. Text in Italian. 2002. bi-m. **Document type:** *Magazine, Consumer.*
Published by: Editoriale Domus, Via Gianni Mazzocchi 1/3, Rozzano, MI 20089, Italy. TEL 39-02-824721, editorialedomus@edidomus.it, http://www.edidomus.it.

MERIDIANI MONTAGNE. GLI SPECIALI. *see* TRAVEL AND TOURISM

796.552 ITA ISSN 1824-2731
MERIDIANI MONTAGNE. RIFUGI E BIVACCHI. Text in Italian. 2004. bi-m. **Document type:** *Magazine, Consumer.*
Published by: Editoriale Domus, Via Gianni Mazzocchi 1/3, Rozzano, MI 20089, Italy. TEL 39-02-824721, editorialedomus@edidomus.it, http://www.edidomus.it.

799.2 ITA ISSN 0392-3665
IL MESE DI CACCIA. Text in Italian. 1964. m. (10/yr.). adv. **Document type:** *Magazine, Consumer.*
Published by: Associazione Nazionale Libera Caccia, Via Cavour, 183-B, Rome, RM 00184, Italy. Ed. Mario Pagnoncelli. Circ: 150,000.

796 639.2 346 USA ISSN 0896-3290
THE MESSAGE (NORTHBOROUGH). Text in English. 1979. m. USD 6 membership (effective 2000). adv. bk.rev. 36 p./no.; back issues avail. **Document type:** *Newspaper.* **Description:** Contains information on firearms issues and legislative issues in Massachusetts and Rhode Island of interest to members.
Published by: Outdoor Message Cooperative, 37 Pierce St, PO Box 567, Northborough, MA 01532. TEL 508-393-5136, FAX 508-393-5222. Ed., Adv. contact Michelle Siudut TEL 603-642-4628. Pub. Michael Yacino. page USD 653.44. Circ: 30,000.

796.93 AUT
METHODMAG. Text in English. 2003 (Fall). q. **Document type:** *Magazine, Consumer.*
Related titles: Optical Disk - DVD ed.; German ed.; French ed.
Published by: Methodmedia Publishing AB, Kapuzinergasse 45, Innsbruck, 6020, Austria. TEL 43-676-6906794.

METSASTAJA. *see* CONSERVATION

799 FIN ISSN 0026-1629
METSASTYS JA KALASTUS. Text in Finnish. 1911. 13/yr. EUR 72.20 (effective 2005). adv. illus. **Document type:** *Magazine, Consumer.*
Description: Concerns hunting and fishing.
Published by: Yhtyneet Kuvalehdet Oy/United Magazines Ltd., Maistraatinportti 1, Helsinki, 00015, Finland. TEL 358-9-15661, FAX 358-9-145650, http://www.kuvalehdet.fi. Ed. Jussi Soikkanen. adv.: color page EUR 2,300; 217 x 280. Circ: 36,178.

MICHIGAN NATURAL RESOURCES MAGAZINE. *see* CONSERVATION

799 USA ISSN 1529-5486
MICHIGAN OUTDOOR NEWS; the sportsman's choice for news and information. Text in English. 19??. bi-w. USD 20 (effective 2008). adv. back issues avail. **Document type:** *Newspaper, Consumer.*
Description: Provides the sportsmen/women in Michigan with the statewide hunting/fishing report, a lake profile complete with map, statewide calendar of events, season and permit dates and in-depth fishing and hunting news.
Related titles: Online - full text ed.
Published by: Outdoor News, Inc., PO Box 199, Lake Orion, MI 48361-0199. TEL 269-651-9293, FAX 269-651-9295, subscribe@outdoornews.com. Ed. Bill Parker. Pub. Glenn Meyer. Adv. contact Jeff Wenzel. B&W page USD 1,102, color page USD 1,477; 10 x 16.

796.42 USA ISSN 0279-1773
MICHIGAN RUNNER. Text in English. 1979. 6/yr. USD 15 domestic; USD 20 foreign; USD 3 newsstand/cover (effective 2003). adv. **Document type:** *Magazine, Consumer.* **Description:** Includes medical advice, calendar of running events and news.
Published by: Great Lakes Sports Publications, Inc., 3588 Plymouth Rd, Ste 245, Ann Arbor, MI 48105-2603. TEL 734-507-0241, FAX 734-434-4765, info@glsp.com, http://www.glsp.com. Ed. Jennie McCafferty. Pub. Art McCafferty. Adv. contact Ann Neff. Circ: 10,000.

S

796.95 USA ISSN 0193-2632
MICHIGAN SNOWMOBILE NEWS. Text in English. 197?. 7/yr. (Sep.-Mar.). free to members (effective 2009). adv. **Document type:** *Magazine, Consumer.* **Description:** Contains timely updates on local and state matters, as well as activities of the snowmobile association in Michigan, club events and legislative action.
Published by: (Michigan Snowmobile Association), PrintComm, Inc., 2929 Davison Rd, Flint, MI 48506. TEL 810-239-5763, 800-935-1592, FAX 810-239-8642, http://www.printcomm.com/. Pub. Kevin Naughton. Adv. contact Shannon Kubiak. B&W page USD 1,964, color page USD 2,282; trim 8.375 x 10.875.

796.94 USA ISSN 0746-2298
MICHIGAN SNOWMOBILER. Text in English. 1967. 6/yr. (Sep-Feb). USD 12; USD 2.50 per issue (effective 2005). 108 p./no.; **Document type:** *Magazine, Consumer.* **Description:** Covers all aspects of snowmobiling from trail riding to racing.
Address: PO Box 417, E. Jordan, MI 49727-0417. TEL 231-536-2371, FAX 231-536-7691, michsnow@unet.com. Ed., Pub. Lyle K Shipe. Adv. contact Stella Shisler. Circ: 30,000 (paid and controlled).

799 USA ISSN 0539-8908
SK91
MICHIGAN SPORTSMAN. Text in English. 1976. m. USD 14.97 domestic; USD 27.97 in Canada; USD 29.97 elsewhere (effective 2008). adv. illus. **Document type:** *Magazine, Consumer.* **Description:** Discusses all aspects of hunting and fishing, along with environmental and conservation issues in Michigan.
Indexed: MMI.
Published by: Intermedia Outdoors, Inc., 512 7th Ave, 11th Fl, New York, NY 10018. TEL 212-852-6600, 800-260-6397, FAX 212-302-4472, customerservice@imoutdoors.com, http://www.imoutdoorsmedia.com. Circ: 33,000.

799 USA ISSN 1055-6540
MID-ATLANTIC GAME & FISH. Text in English. 1991. m. USD 12.99 domestic; USD 25.99 in Canada; USD 27.99 elsewhere (effective 2011). adv. illus. **Document type:** *Magazine, Consumer.* **Description:** Informs sportsmen of hunting and fishing, as well as environmental and conservation issues in the Mid-Atlantic states.
Formerly (until 1991): Maryland - Delaware Game and Fish (0897-9022); Incorporates: New Jersey Game and Fish (0897-9006)
Related titles: Online - full text ed.; ◆ Regional ed(s).: Game & Fish; ◆ Louisiana Game & Fish. ISSN 0744-3692; ◆ Florida Game & Fish. ISSN 0889-3322; ◆ Alabama Game & Fish. ISSN 0279-6783; ◆ Mississippi-Louisiana Game & Fish. ISSN 1947-2358; ◆ North Carolina Game & Fish. ISSN 0897-8816; ◆ South Carolina Game & Fish. ISSN 0897-9154; ◆ West Virginia Game & Fish. ISSN 0897-9162; ◆ Missouri Game & Fish. ISSN 0889-3799; ◆ New York Game & Fish. ISSN 0897-9189; ◆ California Game & Fish. ISSN 1056-0122; ◆ Great Plains Game & Fish. ISSN 1055-6532; ◆ Illinois Game & Fish. ISSN 0897-9014; ◆ Indiana Game & Fish. ISSN 0897-8980; ◆ Iowa Game & Fish. ISSN 0897-9197; ◆ Oklahoma Game & Fish. ISSN 0746-6013; ◆ Rocky Mountain Game & Fish. ISSN 1056-0114; ◆ Pennsylvania Game & Fish. ISSN 0897-8808; ◆ Virginia Game & Fish. ISSN 0897-8794; ◆ Washington - Oregon Game & Fish. ISSN 1056-0106; ◆ Ohio Game & Fish. ISSN 0897-9170; New England Game & Fish. ISSN 0897-8972. 1988. USD 12 domestic; USD 25 in Canada; USD 27 elsewhere (effective 2010).
Published by: Intermedia Outdoors, Inc., 512 7th Ave, 11th Fl, New York, NY 10018. TEL 212-852-6682, 800-260-6397, FAX 212-302-4472, customerservice@imoutdoors.com, http://www.imoutdoorsmedia.com. Ed. Ken Dunwoody. Pub., Adv. contact Peter Gross.

799 USA ISSN 0894-7767
MID-SOUTH HUNTING & FISHING NEWS. Text in English. 1987. m. USD 14.95 (effective 2008). adv. **Description:** Covers hunting and fishing in the Mid-South region.
Address: PO Box 198, Brownsville, TN 38012. TEL 731-772-9962, 800-625-6397. Ed. Taylor Wilson. Pub. Carlton Veirs. Adv. contact Joe Sills TEL 731-443-0811. color page USD 675; 7.375 x 9.5.

799.2 USA
MIDWEST BOWHUNTER. Text in English. 1985. bi-m. USD 8.95; USD 15.95 foreign (effective 1997). adv. bk.rev. **Document type:** *Newspaper.* **Description:** For the hunting archer. Provides hunter success stories and photos, conservation news and information on new products.
Address: 405 Pearl St, Sioux City, IA 51101. TEL 712-255-5132. Ed., R&P Ritch A Stolpe. Circ: 5,000.

799 USA ISSN 0747-3648
MIDWEST OUTDOORS. Text in English. 1967. m. USD 14.95; USD 2.99 newsstand/cover (effective 2007). adv. bk.rev. charts; illus. 4 cols./p.; **Document type:** *Magazine, Consumer.*
Published by: Midwest Outdoors Ltd., 111 Shore Dr, Burr Ridge, IL 60521. TEL 630-887-7722, 800-666-8878, FAX 630-887-1958. Ed., Pub. Gene Laulunen. Adv. contact Dan Ferris TEL 630-887-7722. Circ: 34,000 (paid).

799 USA
MINNESOTA OUTDOOR NEWS; the sportsman's weekly. Variant title: Outdoor News. Text in English. 1968. w. USD 36 (effective 2008). adv. back issues avail. **Document type:** *Newspaper, Consumer.* **Description:** Provides the sportsmen/women in Minnesota with the statewide hunting/fishing report, a lake profile complete with map, statewide calendar of events, season and permit dates and in-depth fishing and hunting news.
Related titles: Online - full text ed.
Published by: Outdoor News, Inc., 9850 51st Ave N, Ste 130, Plymouth, MN 55442. TEL 800-535-5191, subscribe@outdoornews.com. Ed. Rob Drieslein. Pub. Glenn Meyer. Adv. contact Eric Meyer. B&W page USD 1,820, color page USD 2,195; 10 x 16.

799 USA ISSN 0274-8622
MINNESOTA SPORTSMAN. Text in English. 1977. m. USD 14.97 domestic; USD 27.97 in Canada; USD 29.97 elsewhere (effective 2008). adv. illus. **Document type:** *Magazine, Consumer.* **Description:** Reports on all aspects of fishing and hunting, as well as environmental and conservation matters in Minnesota.
Published by: Intermedia Outdoors, Inc., 512 7th Ave, 11th Fl, New York, NY 10018. TEL 212-852-6600, 800-260-6397, FAX 212-302-4472, customerservice@imoutdoors.com, http://www.imoutdoorsmedia.com. adv.: color page USD 19,360, B&W page USD 13,830; trim 7.875 x 10.75. Circ: 33,000.

799 USA ISSN 1947-2358
MISSISSIPPI-LOUISIANA GAME & FISH. Text in English. 198?. m. adv. illus. back issues avail. **Document type:** *Magazine, Consumer.* **Description:** Informs sportsmen of hunting and fishing, as well as environmental and conservation issues in Mississippi.
Formerly (until 2009): Mississippi Game & Fish (0744-4192)
Related titles: ◆ Regional ed(s).: Game & Fish; ◆ Rocky Mountain Game & Fish. ISSN 1056-0114; ◆ Louisiana Game & Fish. ISSN 0744-3692; ◆ Florida Game & Fish. ISSN 0889-3322; ◆ Alabama Game & Fish. ISSN 0279-6783; ◆ North Carolina Game & Fish. ISSN 0897-8816; ◆ South Carolina Game & Fish. ISSN 0897-9154; ◆ West Virginia Game & Fish. ISSN 0897-9162; ◆ Missouri Game & Fish. ISSN 0889-3799; ◆ New York Game & Fish. ISSN 0897-9189; ◆ California Game & Fish. ISSN 1056-0122; ◆ Great Plains Game & Fish. ISSN 1055-6532; ◆ Illinois Game & Fish. ISSN 0897-9014; ◆ Indiana Game & Fish. ISSN 0897-8980; ◆ Iowa Game & Fish. ISSN 0897-9197; ◆ Mid-Atlantic Game & Fish. ISSN 1055-6540; ◆ Pennsylvania Game & Fish. ISSN 0897-8808; ◆ Oklahoma Game & Fish. ISSN 0746-6013; ◆ Virginia Game & Fish. ISSN 0897-8794; ◆ Washington - Oregon Game & Fish. ISSN 1056-0106; ◆ Ohio Game & Fish. ISSN 0897-9170; New England Game & Fish. ISSN 0897-8972. 1988. USD 12 domestic; USD 25 in Canada; USD 27 elsewhere (effective 2010).
Published by: Intermedia Outdoors, Inc., 2250 Newmarket Pky, Ste 110, Marietta, GA 30067. TEL 770-953-9222, 800-448-0756, FAX 770-933-9510, http://www.imoutdoorsmedia.com.

MISSISSIPPI OUTDOORS. *see* CONSERVATION

MISSOURI CONSERVATIONIST. *see* CONSERVATION

799 USA ISSN 0889-3799
MISSOURI GAME & FISH. Text in English. 1986. m. USD 12 domestic; USD 25 in Canada; USD 27 elsewhere (effective 2011). adv. illus. **Document type:** *Magazine, Consumer.* **Description:** Informs sportsmen of hunting and fishing, as well as environmental and conservation issues in Missouri.
Related titles: Online - full text ed.; ◆ Regional ed(s).: Game & Fish; ◆ Louisiana Game & Fish. ISSN 0744-3692; ◆ Florida Game & Fish. ISSN 0889-3322; ◆ Alabama Game & Fish. ISSN 0279-6783; ◆ Mississippi-Louisiana Game & Fish. ISSN 1947-2358; ◆ North Carolina Game & Fish. ISSN 0897-8816; ◆ South Carolina Game & Fish. ISSN 0897-9154; ◆ West Virginia Game & Fish. ISSN 0897-9162; ◆ New York Game & Fish. ISSN 0897-9189; ◆ California Game & Fish. ISSN 1056-0122; ◆ Great Plains Game & Fish. ISSN 1055-6532; ◆ Illinois Game & Fish. ISSN 0897-9014; ◆ Indiana Game & Fish. ISSN 0897-8980; ◆ Iowa Game & Fish. ISSN 0897-9197; ◆ Mid-Atlantic Game & Fish. ISSN 1055-6540; ◆ Oklahoma Game & Fish. ISSN 0746-6013; ◆ Rocky Mountain Game & Fish. ISSN 1056-0114; ◆ Pennsylvania Game & Fish. ISSN 0897-8808; ◆ Virginia Game & Fish. ISSN 0897-8794; ◆ Washington - Oregon Game & Fish. ISSN 1056-0106; ◆ Ohio Game & Fish. ISSN 0897-9170; New England Game & Fish. ISSN 0897-8972. 1988. USD 12 domestic; USD 25 in Canada; USD 27 elsewhere (effective 2010).
Published by: Intermedia Outdoors, Inc., 512 7th Ave, 11th Fl, New York, NY 10018. TEL 212-852-6682, 800-260-6397, FAX 212-302-4472, customerservice@imoutdoors.com, http://www.imoutdoorsmedia.com. Ed. Ken Dunwoody. Pub., Adv. contact Peter Gross.

796.42 617.1 AUS ISSN 0047-7672
MODERN ATHLETE & COACH. Text in English. 1962. q. AUD 60 domestic to non-members; AUD 75 foreign to non-members; free to members (effective 2008). bk.rev. **Document type:** *Journal, Trade.* **Description:** Contains articles about technical preparation, planning and a conditioning nature for all levels of athletic coaching abilities. Also features articles by renowned coaches, dieticians, physiotherapists and academics.
Indexed: SD, SportS, T02.
—BLDSC (5883.690000), IE, Ingenta. **CCC.**
Published by: Australian Track & Field Coaches Association, Ste 25B, 207 Currumburra Rd, PO Box 430, Ashmore, QLD 4214, Australia. TEL 61-7-55974499, FAX 61-7-55975544, enquiries@atfca.com.au. Ed., Adv. contact Jess Jarver. Circ: 3,200.

796.54 FRA ISSN 1638-3494
LE MONDE DU PLEIN AIR. Text in French. 1994. bi-m. EUR 22 (effective 2009). adv. **Document type:** *Magazine, Consumer.* **Description:** Contains information and advice for foreign trips.
Formerly (until 2003): Caravane Magazine (1261-467X)
Published by: Editions Lariviere, 6 Rue Olof Palme, Clichy, 92587, France. TEL 33-1-47565400, http://www.editions-lariviere.fr. Ed. Olivier Lemaire. Pub. Fabien Darmon. Adv. contact Karim Khaldi.

799.2 ITA ISSN 2038-2588
▼ **MONDO CACCIA E CINOFILIA**; international hunting magazine. Text in Italian. 2010. q. **Document type:** *Magazine, Consumer.*
Published by: Vecchiarelli Editore, Piazza dell'Olmo 27, Manziana, RM, Italy. vecchiarellieditore@inwind.it, http://www.vecchiarellieditore.com.

799.1 ITA ISSN 2038-0542
▼ **MONDO CARPA.** Text in Italian. 2010. q. **Document type:** *Magazine, Consumer.*
Published by: Vecchiarelli Editore, Piazza dell'Olmo 27, Manziana, RM, Italy. vecchiarellieditore@inwind.it, http://www.vecchiarellieditore.com.

796.522 FRA ISSN 0047-7923
DQ821
LA MONTAGNE ET L'ALPINISME. Text in French. 1955. q. EUR 29 domestic; EUR 34 foreign (effective 2009). adv. bk.rev. illus.; charts. **Document type:** *Magazine, Consumer.* **Description:** Covers all aspects of mountaineering.
Formed by the merger of (1926-1954): Alpinisme (1157-0709); (1905-1954): Montagne (1157-0725); Which was formed by the merger of (1875-1904): Club Alpin Francais. Annuaire (1157-0687); (1874-1904): Club Alpin Francais. Bulletin (1157-0695)
Indexed: GeoRef, RASB.
Published by: Federation Francaise des Clubs Alpins et de Montagne, 24 Av. de la Laumiere, Paris, 75019, France. TEL 33-1-53728700, FAX 33-1-42035560. Circ: 35,000 (paid).

796.552 FRA ISSN 0184-2595
MONTAGNES MAGAZINE. Text in French. 1978. m. (11/yr). EUR 49.50 domestic; EUR 58 in Europe; EUR 66 in North America; EUR 66 in the Middle East; EUR 72 elsewhere (effective 2008). **Document type:** *Magazine, Consumer.*
Indexed: SD.
Published by: Editions Niveales, 6 Rue Irvoy, Grenoble, 38000, France. TEL 33-4-76705411, FAX 33-4-76705412. Ed. Philippe Descamps. **Dist. by:** Dipresse, 18-24 Quai de la Marne, Paris 75164, France.

796 USA ISSN 2151-1799
▼ **MONTANA HEADWALL**; outdoor adventure under the big sky. Text in English. 2009. q. adv. back issues avail. **Document type:** *Magazine, Consumer.*
Related titles: Online - full text ed.
Published by: Independent Publishing Inc., 317 S Orange St, Missoula, MT 59801. TEL 406-543-6609, FAX 406-543-4367. Ed. Matt Gibson. Adv. contact Peter Kearns.

639.9 USA ISSN 0027-0016
SK417
MONTANA OUTDOORS. Text in English. 1970. bi-m. USD 9 domestic; USD 12 in Canada; USD 25 elsewhere (effective 2005). bk.rev. charts; illus. back issues avail. **Description:** For hunters, fishermen, nature lovers, photographers and all who are interested in wildlife.
Indexed: WildRev.
—Ingenta.
Published by: Department of Fish, Wildlife and Parks, 1420 E Sixth Ave, PO Box 200701, Helena, MT 59620-0701. TEL 406-444-2474, http://fwp.mt.gov/resource/submtout.htm. Ed. Dave Books. Circ: 40,000.

796 ITA ISSN 1128-0204
MONTEBIANCO. Text in Italian. 1998. m. (10/yr.). EUR 22.50 domestic; EUR 102 in the European Union; EUR 132 newsstand/cover elsewhere (effective 2009). adv. illus.; maps. **Document type:** *Magazine, Consumer.* **Description:** Covers winter sports and outdoor activities in the snow.
Related titles: Online - full text ed.
Published by: Leditore Srl, Via Gadames 123, Milan, 20151, Italy. Circ: 120,000.

▼ **MOON OUTDOORS: MINNESOTA CAMPING.** *see* TRAVEL AND TOURISM

796.54 USA ISSN 1557-7236
GV191.42.W2
MOON OUTDOORS: WASHINGTON CAMPING. Text in English. 2002. biennial, latest 2nd ed. USD 19.95 2nd ed. (effective 2008). **Document type:** *Guide, Consumer.*
Formerly (until 2006): Foghorn Outdoors. Washington Camping (1537-8551)
Published by: Avalon Travel Publishing, 1700 4th St, Berkeley, CA 94710. TEL 510-595-3664, avalon.publicity@perseusbooks.com, http://www.avalontravelbooks.com. Ed. Tom Stienstra.

796.5109489 DNK ISSN 0107-8976
MOTIONSGANG. Text in Danish. 1982. bi-m. DKK 85 membership (effective 2009). **Document type:** *Magazine, Consumer.*
Published by: De Sjaellandske Gangsport Foreninger, c/o Finn Henriksen, Strandmoellevej 156, Holbaek, 4300, Denmark. TEL 45-59-431687. Ed. Karen Lindtner TEL 45-32-513185.

796.5 GBR ISSN 0268-6120
MOTOR CARAVAN. Text in English. 1985. m. GBP 29.99 domestic; USD 93.90 in US & Canada; EUR 62.50 in Europe; GBP 58.70 elsewhere; GBP 3.40 newsstand/cover (effective 2009). adv. illus. back issues avail. **Document type:** *Magazine, Consumer.* **Description:** Features a buyer's guide and road tests of trailers and recreational vehicles.
Published by: I P C Country & Leisure Media Ltd. (Subsidiary of: I P C Media Ltd.), Leon House, 233 High St, Croydon, CR9 1HZ, United Kingdom. http://www.ipcmedia.com. Ed. Victoria Bentley TEL 44-20-87268245. Pub. Clive Birch TEL 44-20-87268235. Adv. contact Sue Tannatt TEL 44-20-87268221. page GBP 992; trim 210 x 298. **Subscr. to:** Rockwood House, Perrymount Rd, Haywards Heath RH16 3DH, United Kingdom. TEL 44-845-1231231, IPCsubs@quadrantsubs.com, http://www.magazinesdirect.co.uk. **Dist. by:** MarketForce UK Ltd, The Blue Fin Bldg, 3rd Fl, 110 Southwark St, London SE1 0SU, United Kingdom. TEL 44-20-31483300, FAX 44-20-31488105, salesinnovation@marketforce.co.uk, http://www.marketforce.co.uk/.

796.5 GBR
MOTOR CARAVANNER. Text in English. 1960. m. free to members (effective 2009). adv. bk.rev. **Document type:** *Magazine, Consumer.* **Description:** Contains articles and correspondence of interest to Motor Caravanners with road tests, travel reports, technical and news items as well as trade announcements and adverts.
Published by: Motor Caravanners' Club, c/o Colin Reay, 22 Evelyn Close, Twickenham, Middlesex, TW2 7BN, United Kingdom. TEL 44-20-88933883, FAX 44-20-88938324, info@motorcaravanners.eu.

796.5 GBR ISSN 0141-9269
MOTORCARAVAN & MOTORHOME MONTHLY. Abbreviated title: M M M. Text in English. 1966. m. adv. bk.rev.; Website rev. illus.; mkt. 256 p./no.; back issues avail. **Document type:** *Magazine, Consumer.*
Formerly (until 1978): Motor Caravan and Camping (0027-1829)
Published by: Warners Group Publications Plc., The Maltings, Manor Ln, Bourne, Lincs PE10 9PH, United Kingdom. TEL 44-1778-391000, wgpsubs@warnersgroup.co.uk, http://www.warnersgroup.co.uk. Eds. Jane Jago, Mike Jago. Pub. Stehpen Warner.

796.5 388.346 USA ISSN 0744-074X
TX1100
MOTORHOME; travel tech lifestyle for the RV enthusiast. Text in English. 1963. m. USD 19.97 domestic (print or online ed.); USD 31.97 foreign (print or online ed.) (effective 2009). adv. illus.; mkt.; tr.mk.; tr.lit. 130 p./no.; back issues avail.; reprints avail. **Document type:** *Magazine, Consumer.* **Description:** Features the latest news on financing, prime campgrounds and RV spots, product advice and tips.
Former titles (until 1982): Motorhome Life (0164-503X); (until 1978): Motorhome Life and Camper Coachman (0361-1043); Which was formed by the merger of: Motorhome Life (0027-2221); Camper Coachman (0008-2333); Which was formerly (until 197?): The Camper Coachman and Motorhome Sportsman; Incorporates: Van Life and Family Trucking (0160-6107)
Related titles: Online - full text ed.
Indexed: Consl, G06, G07, G08, I05.
Published by: Affinity Group Inc., 2575 Vista Del Mar, Ventura, CA 93001. TEL 805-667-4100, FAX 805-667-4419, info@affinitygroup.com, http://www.affinitygroup.com. Ed. Eileen Hubbard. Pub. Bill Estes. Adv. contact Scott Oakes. B&W page USD 10,445, color page USD 15,035; trim 7.875 x 10.5. Circ: 141,287 (paid).

MOTORHOME MONTHLY. *see* TRANSPORTATION

MOUNT BULLER NEWS. *see* TRAVEL AND TOURISM

796.552 USA
MOUNTAIN ATHLETICS. Text in English. 2000. q. USD 3 newsstand/cover (effective 2001). **Document type:** *Magazine, Consumer.*
Published by: Timberland Company, 200 Domain Dr, Stratham, NH 03885. Ed. Scott Landry. Pub. Andrew Dawson.

MOUNTAIN BIKE RIDER. *see* SPORTS AND GAMES—Bicycles And Motorcycles

796.552 ZAF ISSN 0258-0101
MOUNTAIN CLUB OF SOUTH AFRICA. JOURNAL. Text in Afrikaans, English. 1894. a. ZAR 35. adv. bk.rev.
Published by: Mountain Club of South Africa, 97 Hatfield St, Cape Town, 8001, South Africa. TEL 021-453-412. Ed. A Hutton. Circ: 2,800.

796.93 USA ISSN 0160-726X
GV191.2
MOUNTAIN GAZETTE. Text in English. 1966. m. USD 20 (effective 2007). adv. bk.rev.; film rev. **Document type:** *Newspaper, Consumer.*
Formerly (until 1972): Skiers Gazette (0037-6256)
Published by: Mountain Gazette Publishing, LLC, 5th & Main St., PO Box 585, Frisco, CO 80443. TEL 970-513-9865, FAX 970-513-9887. Ed. M John Fayhee. Circ: 6,000.

796.552 CAN
MOUNTAIN LIFE. Text in English. q. CAD 19.95 (effective 2005). **Document type:** *Magazine, Consumer.*
Published by: Calgary Publishing Ltd., 1902K-11 St S E, Calgary, AB, Canada. TEL 403-240-9055, FAX 403-240-9059, gdavies@calgarypubishing.com, http://www.calgarypublishing.com.

796.93 USA ISSN 2152-4637
GV191.4
▼ **MOUNTAIN SPORTS + LIVING.** Variant title: Mountain Sports plus Living. Text in English. 2009. q. free to members (effective 2010). adv. **Document type:** *Magazine, Consumer.*
Published by: High Country Media, 3121-A Longhorn Rd, Boulder, CO 80302. TEL 303-815-1080, rob@highcmedia.com, http://highcmedia.com. Ed. Marc Peruzzi. Pub. James E Pentz.

796.522 USA ISSN 0027-2620
F886
MOUNTAINEER (SEATTLE); to explore, study, preserve and enjoy the natural beauty of the Northwest and beyond. Text in English. 1907. m. (plus special issues). looseleaf. USD 20 (effective 2001). adv. bk.rev. illus. reprints avail. **Document type:** *Bulletin.*
Indexed: GeoRef, SpeleolAb.
—Ingenta.
Published by: Mountaineers, Inc., 300 Third Ave W, Seattle, WA 98119-4117. TEL 206-284-6310, FAX 206-284-4977. Ed., R&P, Adv. contact Brad Stracener. Circ: 15,000.

796 USA ISSN 1524-2579
MOUNTAINFREAK. Text in English. 1996. q. USD 16; USD 5.95 newsstand/cover; CAD 7.25 newsstand/cover in Canada (effective 2000). **Document type:** *Magazine, Consumer.* **Description:** Contains features on mountain living, culture, sports, art, music, politics, alternative health, and sustainable living.
Related titles: Online - full content ed.
Published by: Lungta, LLC, PO Box 4149, Telluride, CO 81435. TEL 970-728-9731, FAX 970-728-9821. Ed., R&P John Kula. Pub., Adv. contact Hilary White. Circ: 10,000 (controlled); 15,000 (paid). **Dist. by:** International Publishers Direct, 27500 Riverview Center Blvd, Bonita Springs, FL 34134. TEL 858-320-4563.

799.8 USA ISSN 0895-9668
MUSHING; the magazine of dog-powered sports. Text in English. 1988. bi-m. USD 24; USD 33 in Canada; USD 45 elsewhere. adv. back issues avail. **Document type:** *Magazine, Consumer.* **Description:** Provides information and entertainment year-round on the growing sports of dogsledding, skijoring, carting, dog packing and weight pulling.
Related titles: Online - full text ed.
Indexed: SD.
Published by: Stellar Communications, Inc., PO Box 149, Ester, AK 99725-0149. TEL 907-479-0454, FAX 907-479-3137. Ed. Erica Iseri. Pub. Todd Hoener. R&P, Adv. contact Carey Brink.

MUSKIE. *see* FISH AND FISHERIES

799.3 USA ISSN 1079-3402
MUSKY HUNTER MAGAZINE. Text in English. 1989. bi-m. USD 21.95 domestic; USD 24.95 foreign (effective 2008). adv. **Document type:** *Magazine, Consumer.* **Description:** Contains articles designed to educate and entertain musk-fishing enthusiasts.
Published by: Esox Promotions, Inc, 7978 Hwy 70 East, St Germain, WI 54558. TEL 715-477-2178, FAX 715-477-8858, info@muskyhunter.com, http://www.muskyhunter.com. Ed. Jim Saric. Circ: 32,000 (paid).

799.3 USA ISSN 0027-5360
GV1151
MUZZLE BLASTS. Text in English. 1939. m. USD 40 membership (effective 2007). adv. bk.rev. bibl.; charts; illus. Index. 72 p./no.; back issues avail.; reprints avail. **Document type:** *Magazine, Consumer.*
Related titles: Online - full text ed.
Published by: National Muzzle Loading Rifle Association, PO Box 67, Friendship, IN 47021. TEL 800-745-1493. Eds. Eric Bye, Terri Trowbridge. Adv. contact Denise Goodpaster. B&W page USD 768. Circ: 21,000 (controlled).

796.552 USA ISSN 0274-5720
TS536.6.M8
MUZZLELOADER; publication for black powder shooters. Text in English. 1974. bi-m. USD 23 domestic; USD 29 foreign (effective 2007). adv. bk.rev. illus. index. 84 p./no.; back issues avail.; reprints avail. **Document type:** *Magazine, Consumer.* **Description:** Focuses on building, shooting, and hunting with muzzleloading guns, and on the history of America during the 18th century.
Published by: Scurlock Publishing Co., Inc., 1293 Myrtle Springs Rd, Texarkana, TX 75503-9403. TEL 903-832-4726, 800-228-6389, FAX 903-831-3177, jason@scurlockpublishing.com. Ed., Pub., R&P Bill Scurlock. Adv. contact Jason Dempsey. Circ: 15,000 (paid).

799.2 CZE ISSN 0323-214X
MYSLIVOST. Text in Czech. 1923. m. CZK 600 domestic; CZK 50 per issue domestic (effective 2009). charts; illus. **Document type:** *Magazine, Consumer.* **Description:** Brings professional information from the field of game management, game keeping, hunting and sports shooting, and also from the branch of forest management and nature protection.
Published by: Myslivost s.r.o., Seifertova 81, Prague 1, 13000tel, Czech Republic. TEL 420-2-22781524, FAX 420-2-22783056. Ed. Jiri Kasina. Adv. contact Martina Jungova. Circ: 48,000 (paid and controlled).

796.93 USA ISSN 0741-9279
GV854.A1
N C A A MEN'S AND WOMEN'S SKIING RULES. Text in English. 19??. a. USD 7.80 per issue (effective 2011). adv. illus. back issues avail. **Document type:** *Handbook/Manual/Guide, Trade.* **Description:** Contains diagrams of playing areas, official signals, and official interpretations and rulings.
Former titles (until 1984): N C A A Men's Skiing Rules (0736-5136); (until 1983): N C A A Skiing Rules; (until 1980): National Collegiate Athletic Association. Official Skiing Rules (0469-8592); (until 1964): Official National Collegiate Athletic Association Boxing, Gymnastics, Skiing Rules
Related titles: Online - full text ed.: free (effective 2011).
Published by: National Collegiate Athletic Association, 700 W Washington St, PO Box 6222, Indianapolis, IN 46206. TEL 317-917-6222, FAX 317-917-6888, http://www.ncaa.org/. Ed. Teresa Smith.

796.42 USA
GV1060.6
N C A A MEN'S AND WOMEN'S TRACK AND FIELD AND CROSS COUNTRY RULES. Text in English. 1922. a. USD 7.80 per issue (effective 2011). illus. back issues avail. **Document type:** *Handbook/Manual/Guide, Trade.* **Description:** Covers official signals, interpretations, and rulings.
Former titles (until 1993): N C A A Men's and Women's Cross Country and Track & Field Rules (0882-3170); (until 1984): N C A A Men's and Women's Track and Field Rules (0736-7783); (until 1983): N C A A Track and Field (0277-6677); (until 1980): Official National Collegiate Athletic Association Track and Field Guide (0196-9358)
Related titles: Online - full text ed.: free (effective 2011).
Published by: National Collegiate Athletic Association, 700 W Washington St, PO Box 6222, Indianapolis, IN 46206. TEL 317-917-6222, FAX 317-917-6888, http://www.ncaa.org/.

799 GBR ISSN 0028-0070
N R A JOURNAL. Text in English. 1860. 3/yr. free to members (effective 2009). adv. bk.rev. back issues avail. **Document type:** *Journal, Trade.* **Description:** Contains news and informational articles pertaining to the activities and membership of the NRA with results of competitions, personal profiles, agendas of meetings, and announcements of events.
Related titles: Online - full text ed.: free (effective 2009).
Indexed: SportS.
Published by: National Rifle Association, Bisley Camp, Brookwood, Woking, Surrey GU24 0PB, United Kingdom. TEL 44-1483-797777, FAX 44-1483-797285, info@nra.org.uk. Ed. Karen Robertson TEL 44-1483-797777 ext 146.

N R M A DRIVE TRAVEL TOURIST PARKS GUIDE. (National Roads and Motorists Association) *see* BUSINESS AND ECONOMICS—Trade And Industrial Directories

N S S R A NEWSLETTER. *see* BUSINESS AND ECONOMICS—Marketing And Purchasing

N Z OUTSIDE. COASTAL LIFE; the complete guide to the NZ outdoor experience. (New Zealand) *see* ARCHITECTURE

NA SZLAKU; gory - turystyka - alphinizm. *see* TRAVEL AND TOURISM

796.172 USA ISSN 1557-7953
NALU UNDERGROUND. Text in English. 2005. q. USD 20 (effective 2007). 106 p./no.; **Document type:** *Magazine, Consumer.* **Description:** Cover surfing events, profiles, and other topics related to the sport.
Published by: C S Group, 4734 Lae Rd., Kalaheo, HI 96741. Ed. Curt Smith.

797.21 FRA ISSN 1268-631X
NATATION MAGAZINE. Text in French. 1992. 8/yr. EUR 30 (effective 2009). **Document type:** *Magazine, Consumer.*
Indexed: SD.
Published by: Federation Francaise de Natation, 148 av. Gambetta, Paris, 75020, France. TEL 33-1-44126010, FAX 33-1-44126019. Ed. Bernard Rayaume.

796.42 USA ISSN 0744-2416
NATIONAL MASTERS NEWS. Text in English. 1977. m. USD 28; USD 3 per issue (effective 2007). adv. bk.rev. stat. 38 p./no.; back issues avail. **Document type:** *Magazine, Consumer.* **Description:** Covers running and track and field for athletes forty and over.
Formerly: National Masters Newsletter (0194-5505)
Address: PO Box 1117, Orangevale, CA 95662-117. TEL 916-989-6667, http://members.aol.com/natmanews/index.html. Ed. Jerry Wojcik. Pub. Suzanne Hess. Circ: 6,000 (paid).

799.31 USA ISSN 0077-5738
NATIONAL SKEET SHOOTING ASSOCIATION. RECORDS ANNUAL. Text in English. 1947. a. USD 15. adv. index.
Published by: National Skeet Shooting Association, 5931 Roft Rd, San Antonio, TX 78253. TEL 210-688-3371, FAX 210-688-3632. Ed. Susie Fluckiger. Circ: 18,000.

NATIONAL WILDLIFE; dedicated to the conservation of our nation's natural resources. *see* CONSERVATION

791 USA ISSN 1931-6267
NATION'S BEST SPORTS. Variant title: N B S Fish & Hunt. Nation's Best Sports Fish & Hunt. Text in English. 2002. q. USD 9.99 (effective 2006). adv. **Document type:** *Magazine, Consumer.* **Description:** Delivers balanced coverage of each sport, including in-depth profiles and the newest in equipment and gear to help hook or bag your top trophies.
Formerly (until 200?): Fish & Hunt (1544-659X)
Related titles: Online - full text ed.
Indexed: H20, M02, SD, T02.
Published by: Grand View Media Group, Inc. (Subsidiary of: EBSCO Industries, Inc.), 200 Croft St, Ste 1, Birmingham, AL 35242. TEL 888-431-2877, FAX 205-408-3797, webmaster@grandviewmedia.com, http://www.grandviewmedia.com. Ed. Eddie Lee Rider. Pub. Scott Fowler. Adv. contact David Farlow. B&W page USD 4,080, color page USD 5,095; trim 7.75 x 10.625.

796 CHE ISSN 1423-5129
NATUERLICH. Text in German. 1981. 12/yr. CHF 84; CHF 8 newsstand/cover (effective 2006). adv. **Document type:** *Magazine, Consumer.*
Incorporates (1980-1985): Chrueteregge (1423-520X)
Published by: A Z Fachverlage AG, Neumattstr 1, Aarau, 5001, Switzerland. TEL 41-58-2005650, FAX 41-58-2005651, vertrieb@azag.ch, http://www.azmediengruppe.ch. Ed. Thomas Vogel. Adv. contact Christian Becker. B&W page CHF 4,550, color page CHF 6,300; trim 185 x 268. Circ: 85,000 (paid and controlled).

796 BEL ISSN 1379-2652
NATURE ETHIQUE; la revue qui est dans le vent pour une meilleure qualite de vie. Text in French. 1972. 10/yr. EUR 40 (effective 2006). **Document type:** *Magazine, Consumer.* **Description:** Covers topics relating to outdoor recreation, hunting, fishing, conservation and matters of interest to land and forest owners.
Former titles (until 2003): Euro Gicef (1379-0366); (until 2001): Euro-Union Gicef (1379-0358); (until 1989): Foret Chasse Peche Environnement (1379-034X)
Published by: Fondation Saint-Hubert, Rue de le Converserie, 44, Saint-Hubert, 6870, Belgium. TEL 32-61-293084, FAX 32-61-612732, info@fondation-saint-hubert.be.

333.72 DEU
NATURFREUNDIN. Text in German. 1949. q. EUR 20 (effective 2011). adv. bk.rev. **Document type:** *Magazine, Consumer.*
Former titles: Naturfreunde (0943-4607); (until 1992): Wandern und Bergsteigen (0342-6432)
Related titles: Online - full text ed.
Published by: (Naturfreunde Bundesgruppe Deutschland e.V.), Verlag NaturFreunde Freizeit und Wandern GmbH, Warschauer Str 58a, Berlin, 10243, Germany. TEL 49-30-29773260, FAX 49-30-29773280, info@naturfreunde.de, http://www.naturfreunde.de. Ed. Hans-Gerd Marian. adv.: B&W page EUR 2,350, color page EUR 3,650; trim 185 x 241. Circ: 60,000 (controlled).

NAUTICA. *see* SPORTS AND GAMES—Boats And Boating

796.75 796.9 USA
N'EAST MAGAZINE; artist built, athlete driven, reader supported. Text in English. 2004. 4/yr. USD 25 (effective 2007). adv. **Document type:** *Magazine, Consumer.* **Description:** Focuses on surfing, snowboarding, skiing, skateboarding and biking and the personalities, art, music and fashions that stem from these sports.
Address: 164 Middle St, Ste 2 & 3, Portland, ME 04101. TEL 207-772-3255, FAX 207-347-3573. Ed., Pub. Jim McGinley. Adv. contact Ryan Montani. color page USD 1,800; trim 9 x 10.875. Circ: 27,000 (paid).

NEBRASKALAND MAGAZINE. *see* CONSERVATION

333.95416 NLD ISSN 0166-0004
DE NEDERLANDSE JAGER; tijdschrift over natuur, wildbeheer en jachthonden. Text in Dutch. 1895. 24/m. EUR 151 membership (effective 2009). adv. illus. **Document type:** *Consumer.* **Description:** Provides information about hunting, the outdoors, wildlife management, hunting dogs, travel, and country clothing.
Published by: Koninklijke Nederlandse Jagersvereniging, Postbus 1165, Amersfoort, 3800 BD, Netherlands. TEL 31-33-4619841, FAX 31-33-4651355, info@knjv.nl, http://www.knjv.nl.

799.1 NLD ISSN 1384-8054
DE NEDERLANDSE VLIEGVISSER. Text in Dutch. 1985. q. EUR 27.50 domestic; EUR 30 in Belgium; EUR 36.50 in Europe; EUR 45.50 elsewhere (effective 2010). adv. bk.rev. bibl.; charts; illus.; mkt.; maps. 80 p./no. 3 cols./p.; back issues avail. **Document type:** *Magazine, Consumer.* **Description:** Contains items of interest to the fly fishing community in the Netherlands and northern Belgium, including conservation of fish habitats, fly fishing locations throughout the world, fly tying, and fly fishing equipment.
Published by: Vereniging Nederlandse Vliegvissers, Dunantstraat 1041, Zoetermeer, 2713 TL, Netherlands. TEL 31-79-3163356, http://www.vnv.nu. Ed. Peter Luitze TEL 31-35-6037285. Adv. contact Herman Wissink. Circ: 4,500.

NEIGE ET AVALANCHES. *see* METEOROLOGY

NEW ANGLER. *see* FISH AND FISHERIES

796.42 USA ISSN 1041-4800
NEW ENGLAND RUNNER. Text in English. 1983. 7/yr. USD 19.97 domestic; USD 24.97 in Canada; USD 34.97 elsewhere; USD 3.95 newsstand/cover (effective 2008). adv. **Document type:** *Magazine, Consumer.* **Description:** Covers running, triathlons, and track and field events in the six New England states and New York.
Formerly (until 198?): Boston Running News (8750-8621); Which incorporates (1978-1987): New England Running (0737-0385)
Published by: New England Sports Publications, PO Box 205, South Weymouth, MA 02190-0002. TEL 339-499-6022, FAX 339-499-6041. Ed. Bob Fitzgerald. Pubs. Bob Fitzgerald, Michelle Le Brun TEL 617-232-8778. Adv. contact Michelle Le Brun TEL 617-232-8778. Circ: 14,575.

796.93 USA
NEW ENGLAND SKI JOURNAL. Text in English. 1995. 8/yr. USD 27.99 (effective 2011). adv. **Document type:** *Magazine, Consumer.*
Published by: Seamans Media, 1400 Hancock St, Seventh Fl, Quincy, MA 02169. TEL 617-773-9955, FAX 617-773-6688, michelle@seamansmedia.com, http://www.seamansmedia.com. Ed. Eric Beato. Pub., Adv. contact Eric Seamans.

797.124 USA
NEW ENGLAND WINDSURFING JOURNAL. Text in English. 1983. 9/yr. USD 12 (effective 2005). **Document type:** *Magazine, Consumer.*
Formerly (until 1991): New England Sailboard Journal
Published by: Buzzwords, PO Box 371, Milford, CT 06460-0371. TEL 203-876-2001, FAX 203-876-2868. Ed., Pub. Peter Bogucki. Circ: 8,000 (paid).

NEW HAMPSHIRE FISH AND GAME LAWS ANNOTATED. *see* LAW—Judicial Systems

333.95416 USA ISSN 1066-1379
NEW HAMPSHIRE WILDLIFE JOURNAL. Text in English. 1969. 6/yr. USD 10 (effective 1997). **Document type:** *Government.* **Description:** Publishes stories and information about wildlife, fishing, hunting, conservation department programs and subjects of interest to outdoor enthusiasts.
Former titles (until Nov. 1992): Fish and Game Highlights of New Hampshire (1041-4762); (until 1986): New Hampshire Natural Resources (0028-5285); Which superseded: Field Notes (Concord) (0739-5663)
Published by: Fish and Game Department, 2 Hazen Dr, Concord, NH 03301. TEL 603-271-3211, 800-735-2964, FAX 603-271-1438. Ed. Judy Stokes. R&P Eric Aldrich. Circ: 4,000.

799 USA
NEW JERSEY FISH & GAME FINDER MAGAZINE. Text in English. 1997. m. USD 18; USD 1.50 newsstand/cover. adv. back issues avail. **Document type:** *Magazine, Consumer.* **Description:** Includes features and articles dealing with hunting, fresh and salt water fishing, and diving in the state of New Jersey, as well as travelogues.
Address: 8 Navesink Ct, Long Branch, NJ 07740. TEL 888-501-4979, FAX 732-229-0712. Ed. George J Meringold. Adv. contact Michael Formichella. page USD 525. Circ: 18,000.

799.1 USA ISSN 0897-9189
NEW YORK GAME & FISH. Text in English. 1986. m. USD 12 domestic; USD 25 in Canada; USD 27 elsewhere (effective 2011). adv. illus. **Document type:** *Magazine, Consumer.* **Description:** Informs sportsmen of hunting and fishing, as well as environmental and conservation issues in New York.
Formerly (until 1987): New York in the Field (0893-1445)

S

Related titles: Online - full text ed.; ◆ Regional ed(s).: Game & Fish; ◆ Louisiana Game & Fish. ISSN 0744-3692; ◆ Florida Game & Fish. ISSN 0889-3322; ◆ Alabama Game & Fish. ISSN 0279-6783; ◆ Mississippi-Louisiana Game & Fish. ISSN 1947-2358; ◆ North Carolina Game & Fish. ISSN 0897-8816; ◆ South Carolina Game & Fish. ISSN 0897-9154; ◆ West Virginia Game & Fish. ISSN 0897-9162; ◆ Missouri Game & Fish. ISSN 0889-3799; ◆ California Game & Fish. ISSN 1056-0122; ◆ Great Plains Game & Fish. ISSN 1055-6532; ◆ Illinois Game & Fish. ISSN 0897-9014; ◆ Indiana Game & Fish. ISSN 0897-8980; ◆ Iowa Game & Fish. ISSN 0897-9197; ◆ Mid-Atlantic Game & Fish. ISSN 1055-6540; ◆ Oklahoma Game & Fish. ISSN 0746-6013; ◆ Rocky Mountain Game & Fish. ISSN 1056-0114; ◆ Pennsylvania Game & Fish. ISSN 0897-8808; ◆ Virginia Game & Fish. ISSN 0897-8794; ◆ Washington - Oregon Game & Fish. ISSN 1056-0106; ◆ Ohio Game & Fish. ISSN 0897-9170; New England Game & Fish. ISSN 0897-8972. 1988. USD 12 domestic; USD 25 in Canada; USD 27 elsewhere (effective 2010).
Published by: Intermedia Outdoors, Inc., 512 7th Ave, 11th Fl, New York, NY 10018. TEL 212-852-6682, 800-260-6397, FAX 212-302-4472, customerservice@imoutdoors.com, http://www.imoutdoorsmedia.com. Ed. Ken Dunwoody. Pub., Adv. contact Peter Gross.

799 USA ISSN 1557-0177
NEW YORK OUTDOOR NEWS; the sportsman's choice for news and information. Text in English. 2004. bi-w. USD 22 (effective 2008). adv. back issues avail. **Document type:** *Newspaper, Consumer.* **Description:** Provides the sportsmen/women in New York with the statewide hunting/fishing report, a lake profile complete with map, statewide calendar of events, season and permit dates and in-depth fishing and hunting news.
Published by: Outdoor News, Inc., PO Box 248, Elizabethtown, NY 12932-0248. TEL 877-705-5303, FAX 763-546-5913, subscribe@outdoornews.com. Ed. Steve Piatt. Pub. Glenn Meyer. Adv. contact Craig Turner. B&W page USD 1,214, color page USD 1,589; 10 x 16.

796.95 USA
NEW YORK SNOWMOBILE NEWS. Text in English. 2000. 7/yr. (Sep.-Mar.). **Document type:** *Magazine, Consumer.* **Description:** Contains information about the activities of the association, club events and legislative issues.
Published by: (New York State Snowmobile Association), PrintComm, Inc., PO BOX 182, Rio, WI 53960. TEL 920-992-6370, 800-380-3767, FAX 920-992-6369, http://www.printcomm.com/.

THE NEW YORK STATE CONSERVATIONIST. *see* CONSERVATION

796.552 NZL ISSN 0110-1080
NEW ZEALAND ALPINE JOURNAL. Text in English. 1892. a. free to members; NZD 20 to non-members (effective 2008). back issues avail. **Document type:** *Journal, Consumer.* **Description:** Provides annual account of mountaineering, exploration and mountain studies in New Zealand and by New Zealanders.
Indexed: GeoRef, SpeleolAb.
Published by: New Zealand Alpine Club Inc., Christchurch Mail Centre 8140, PO Box 786, Christchurch, New Zealand. TEL 64-3-3777595, FAX 64-3-3777594. Ed. Kester Brown. Circ: 2,000.

799.1 NZL ISSN 0110-8476
NEW ZEALAND FISHING NEWS. Text in English. m. NZD 69 domestic; NZD 119.50 in Australia; NZD 200 elsewhere; NZD 7.70 newsstand/cover (effective 2008). adv. **Document type:** *Magazine, Consumer.*
Indexed: GeoRef.
Published by: Fairfax Magazines (Subsidiary of: Fairfax Media), Level 1, 274 Church St, Penrose, PO Box 12965, Auckland, New Zealand. TEL 64-9-6341800, FAX 64-9-6342948, info@fairfaxmedia.co.nz, http://www.fairfaxnz.co.nz. Ed. Grant Dixon. Adv. contact Brett Patterson TEL 64-9-6341800. Circ: 26,094 (paid).

799.10993 NZL ISSN 1175-3374
NEW ZEALAND FISHING WORLD. Text in English. 2000. bi-m. NZD 45 domestic; NZD 76 in Australia; NZD 115 elsewhere (effective 2008). adv. **Document type:** *Magazine, Consumer.*
Published by: Image Centre Publishing, 34 Westmoreland St, P.O. Box 78070 Grey Lynn, Ponsonby, Auckland, New Zealand. TEL 64-9-360-5701, FAX 64-9-360-5702, http://www.image-centre.com. Ed. Geoff Thomas.

799.1 351 NZL
NEW ZEALAND GAZETTE. SUPPLEMENT. ANGLERS NOTICES. Text in English. irreg. NZD 216 combined subscription inclds. Gazette, supplements & special eds. (effective 2005). **Document type:** *Government.*
Related titles: ◆ Supplement to: New Zealand Gazette. ISSN 0111-5650.
Published by: Department of Internal Affairs, New Zealand Gazette Office, Level 13, Prime Property Tower, 86-90 Lambton Quay, PO Box 805, Wellington, 6011, New Zealand. TEL 64-4-4702930, FAX 64-4-4702932, gazette@parliament.govt.nz, http://www.gazette.govt.nz/diawebsite.nsf.

799.2 NZL ISSN 1175-1649
NEW ZEALAND GUNS & HUNTING. Text in English. 1990. bi-m. NZD 45 domestic; NZD 65 in Australia & Pacific Islands; NZD 85 elsewhere (effective 2008). adv. back issues avail. **Document type:** *Magazine, Consumer.*
Formerly (until 1999): New Zealand Guns (1170-3857)
Address: RD 2, Waihi, 3682, New Zealand.

799.2 NZL ISSN 1171-6568
NEW ZEALAND HUNTING & WILDLIFE. Text in English. 1962. q. free to members. adv. bk.rev. charts; illus. cum.index. **Document type:** *Magazine, Consumer.* **Description:** Provides hunting articles on instruction, memories and conservation issues.
Formerly: New Zealand Wildlife (0028-8802)
—CCC.
Published by: New Zealand Deerstalkers' Association Inc., Te Aro, PO Box 6514, Wellington, 6035, New Zealand. TEL 64-4-8017367, FAX 64-4-8017368, deerstalkers@paradise.net.nz, http://www.deerstalkers.org.nz/. Ed. Blake Abernethy. Adv. contact Ursula Barnard. Circ: 7,500 (paid).

796 NZL ISSN 1176-9149
NEW ZEALAND JOURNAL OF OUTDOOR EDUCATION. Variant title: Ko Tane Mahuta Pupuke. Text in English. 2001. 2/yr. free to members. **Document type:** *Journal, Consumer.* **Description:** Contains information on all aspects of outdoor education and recreation.
Published by: Outdoors New Zealand, PO Box 11-776, Manners Mall, Wellington, New Zealand. TEL 64-4-3857287, FAX 64-4-3859680, info@outdoorsnz.org.nz, http://www.outdoorsnz.org.nz. Ed. M.A. Boyes. Circ: 1,500 (controlled).

796 NZL ISSN 1174-2666
NEW ZEALAND OUTSIDE; wilderness annual and directory. Text in English. 1993. a. **Document type:** *Magazine, Consumer.* **Description:** Contains information and guides to New Zealand's outdoor life.
Formerly (until 1996): New Zealand Adventure Annual & Directory (1172-3386)
Published by: Lifestyle Publishing Ltd., 51a Riverlea Ave, Pakuranga, Panmure, PO Box 14-109, Auckland, New Zealand. TEL 64-9-5702658, FAX 64-9-5702684, admin@nzoutside.com. Ed. David Hall.

796.93 NZL ISSN 1177-7559
NEW ZEALAND SKI & SNOW. Text in English. 2002. s-a. NZD 9.90 newsstand/cover (effective 2008). adv. **Document type:** *Magazine, Consumer.*
Published by: Pacific Media Ltd, 114 Swann Beach Rd, Manly, PO Box 562, Whangaparaoa, New Zealand. TEL 64-9-4282441, p.media@xtra.co.za, http://www.pacificmedia.co.nz. Adv. contact Angela Jolly TEL 64-9-4285676. Circ: 15,000.

796.9099305 NZL ISSN 1172-5257
NEW ZEALAND SNOWBOARDER. Text in English. 1993 (May). q. NZD 34 domestic; NZD 60 in Australia; NZD 95 elsewhere (effective 2008). adv. back issues avail. **Document type:** *Magazine, Consumer.*
Address: 119 Wairere Rd, Gisborne, New Zealand. TEL 64-6-8687974, FAX 64-6-8687971, hq@nzsnowboarder.nzl.com. Adv. contacts Phil Erickson, Ste'en Webster.

797 NZL ISSN 0114-8966
NEW ZEALAND SURFING. Text in English. 1988. bi-m. adv. **Document type:** *Magazine, Consumer.*
Published by: Lifestyle Publishing Ltd., 51a Riverlea Ave, Pakuranga, Panmure, PO Box 14-109, Auckland, New Zealand. TEL 64-9-5702658, FAX 64-9-5702684. Ed. Craig Levers. Adv. contact Luke Millen TEL 64-9-8648979.

799.1755099305 NZL ISSN 1173-1761
THE NEW ZEALAND TROUTFISHER. Text in English. 1992. 10/yr. NZD 50 domestic; NZD 55 in Australia; NZD 60 elsewhere (effective 2009). adv. **Document type:** *Magazine, Consumer.* **Description:** Dedicated to New Zealand trout fishing.
Formerly (until 1994): New Zealand Adipose Fin (1172-4455)
Related titles: Online - full content ed.: NZD 24 (effective 2009).
Published by: P.W. Storey & Associates, 1 Ronald Rd, Lake Tarawera, RD5 Rotorua, 1330, New Zealand. TEL 64-7-3628914, peter@nztroutfisher.co.nz. Ed., Pub. Peter Storey. adv.: color page NZD 1,250, B&W page NZD 400.

799 DEU ISSN 0048-0339
NIEDERSAECHSISCHER JAEGER. Text in German. 1950. s-m. EUR 84.90 domestic; EUR 103.20 foreign; EUR 3.90 newsstand/cover (effective 2009). adv. bk.rev. **Document type:** *Magazine, Consumer.* **Description:** Covers cultural, historical, social, economical and ecological aspects of hunting and natural conservation in the Lower Saxony region of Germany.
Indexed: GeoRef, SpeleolAb.
—CCC.
Published by: (Landesjagdverband Niedersachsen), Deutscher Landwirtschaftsverlag GmbH, Kabelkamp 6, Hannover, 30179, Germany. TEL 49-511-678060, FAX 49-511-67806200, dlv.hannover@dlv.de, http://www.dlv.de. Ed. Dieter Bartsch. Adv. contact Jens Riegamer. B&W page EUR 2,430, color page EUR 3,370; trim 216 x 303. Circ: 20,663 (paid and controlled).

796 SVN ISSN 1408-8347
NON-STOP. Text in Slovenian. 1994. 2/yr. adv. **Document type:** *Magazine, Consumer.*
Formerly (until 1998): Rekreacijski Non-Stop (1318-3443)
Related titles: Online - full content ed.: ISSN 1581-0143.
Published by: Delo Revije d.o.o., Dunajska 5, Ljubljana, 1509, Slovenia. TEL 386-1-4737000, FAX 386-1-4737352, narocnine@delo-revije.si, http://www.delo-revije.si.

796 DEU
NORDIC FITNESS MAGAZIN; aktiv, gesund und besser leben. Text in German. 2005. bi-m. EUR 18; EUR 3.50 newsstand/cover (effective 2005). adv. **Document type:** *Magazine, Consumer.*
Address: Ahornweg 3, Aitrang, 87648, Germany. TEL 49-8343-9239940, FAX 49-8343-923179. Ed. Ulrich Pramann. Adv. contact Sylvia Schreck. B&W page EUR 4,100, color page EUR 5,800.

380.1029 USA
NORDIC NETWORK. Text in English. 1976. q. USD 25. adv. bk.rev. **Document type:** *Newsletter.*
Formerly: Cross Country Ski Areas of America Newsletter
Published by: Cross Country Ski Areas Association, 259 Bolton Rd, Winchester, NH 03470. TEL 603-239-4341, 877-779-2754, FAX 603-239-6387, ccsaa@xcski.org, http://www.xcski.org. Ed., R&P, Adv. contact Chris Frado. Circ: 450.

796.93 DEU
NORDIC SPORTS MAGAZIN; das Magazin fuer Ausdauersportler. Text in German. 1979. 6/yr. EUR 24.30 domestic; EUR 34 foreign; EUR 4.50 newsstand/cover (effective 2011). adv. **Document type:** *Magazine, Consumer.*
Former titles: Skilanglauf - Triathlon - Marathon (0944-6281); (until 1991): Skilanglauf - Triathlon (0178-1901); (until 1984): Skilanglauf Magazin (0724-3448)
Published by: Brinkmann Henrich Medien GmbH, Heerstr 5, Meinerzhagen, 58540, Germany. TEL 49-2354-77990, FAX 49-2354-779977, info@bhmg.de, http://www.bhmg.de. Ed. Arnd Hemmersbach. Adv. contact Hans Martin Brinkmann. Circ: 32,304 (paid).

796 DEU
NORR; Das Outdoor-Magazin aus Skandinavien. Text in German. 4/yr. EUR 15; EUR 4.50 newsstand/cover (effective 2008). adv. **Document type:** *Magazine, Consumer.*
Published by: Atlas Verlag GmbH, Brienner Str 41, Munich, 80333, Germany. TEL 49-89-552410, FAX 49-89-55241100, info@atlas-verlag.de, http://www.atlas-verlag.de. Ed. Gabriel Arthur. Adv. contact Thomas Obermaier. B&W page EUR 2,850, color page EUR 3,800; trim 210 x 280.

NORSK FISKARALMANAKK. *see* FISH AND FISHERIES

799.1 USA ISSN 1043-2450
NORTH AMERICAN FISHERMAN. Text in English. 1988. 7/yr. free to members (effective 2008). adv. bk.rev. illus. back issues avail.; reprints avail. **Document type:** *Magazine, Consumer.* **Description:** Takes readers beyond the basics by sharing advanced tactics, the latest tips, proper techniques and new products.
Incorporates (1955-1996): Fishing World (0015-3079)
Related titles: Online - full text ed.
Indexed: C05, M01, M02, MASUSE.
Published by: (North American Fishing Club), North American Media Group, Inc. (Subsidiary of: North American Membership Group, Inc.), 12301 Whitewater Dr, Minnetonka, MN 55343. TEL 952-936-9333, 800-922-4888, FAX 952-936-9755, namghq@namginc.com, http://www.northamericanmediagroup.com/. Ed. Steve Pennaz. Pub. Rich Sundberg TEL 320-846-6090. Adv. contact Mark Swanson TEL 952-352-7035. B&W page USD 18,720, color page USD 24,335; trim 7.75 x 10.5. Circ: 467,908.

799.2 USA ISSN 0194-4320
SK40
NORTH AMERICAN HUNTER. Abbreviated title: N A H. Text in English. 1979. 8/yr. free to members (effective 2008). adv. bk.rev. illus. back issues avail.; reprints avail. **Document type:** *Magazine, Consumer.* **Description:** Contains tactics, equipment tips, product ratings and information from the hunting industry's recognized outdoor writers.
—Ingenta.
Published by: (North American Hunting Club), North American Media Group, Inc. (Subsidiary of: North American Membership Group, Inc.), 12301 Whitewater Dr, Minnetonka, MN 55343. TEL 952-936-9333, 800-922-4888, FAX 952-936-9755, namghq@namginc.com, http://www.northamericanmediagroup.com/. Pub. Rich Sundberg TEL 320-846-6090. Adv. contact Mark Swanson TEL 952-352-7035. B&W page USD 22,715, color page USD 33,160; trim 7.75 x 10.5. Circ: 783,053.

NORTH AMERICAN PYLON; dedicated to sports car autocrossing. *see* TRANSPORTATION—Automobiles

NORTH AMERICAN SKI JOURNALISTS ASSOCIATION NEWSLETTER. *see* JOURNALISM

799.2 USA ISSN 0746-6250
NORTH AMERICAN WHITETAIL; the magazine devoted to the serious trophy deer hunter. Text in English. 1982. 8/yr. USD 15 domestic; USD 28 in Canada; USD 30 elsewhere (effective 2011). adv. illus. reprints avail. **Document type:** *Magazine, Consumer.* **Description:** Delivers information about deer hunting, including tips and favorable locations. Discusses deer management and other conservation issues.
Related titles: Online - full text ed.
Indexed: G08, I05.
—CCC.
Published by: Intermedia Outdoors, Inc., 512 7th Ave, 11th Fl, New York, NY 10018. TEL 212-852-6682, 800-260-6397, FAX 212-302-4472, customerservice@imoutdoors.com, http://www.imoutdoorsmedia.com. Ed. Ken Dunwoody. Pub., Adv. contact Peter Gross.

799 USA ISSN 0897-8816
NORTH CAROLINA GAME & FISH. Text in English. 198?. m. USD 12.99 domestic; USD 25.99 in Canada; USD 27.99 elsewhere (effective 2011). adv. illus. **Document type:** *Magazine, Consumer.* **Description:** Informs sportsmen of hunting and fishing, as well as environmental and conservation issues in North Carolina.
Supersedes in part (in 198?): Carolina Game and Fish (0744-4176)
Related titles: Online - full text ed.; ◆ Regional ed(s).: Game & Fish; ◆ Louisiana Game & Fish. ISSN 0744-3692; ◆ Florida Game & Fish. ISSN 0889-3322; ◆ Alabama Game & Fish. ISSN 0279-6783; ◆ Mississippi-Louisiana Game & Fish. ISSN 1947-2358; ◆ South Carolina Game & Fish. ISSN 0897-9154; ◆ West Virginia Game & Fish. ISSN 0897-9162; ◆ Missouri Game & Fish. ISSN 0889-3799; ◆ New York Game & Fish. ISSN 0897-9189; ◆ California Game & Fish. ISSN 1056-0122; ◆ Great Plains Game & Fish. ISSN 1055-6532; ◆ Illinois Game & Fish. ISSN 0897-9014; ◆ Indiana Game & Fish. ISSN 0897-8980; ◆ Iowa Game & Fish. ISSN 0897-9197; ◆ Mid-Atlantic Game & Fish. ISSN 1055-6540; ◆ Oklahoma Game & Fish. ISSN 0746-6013; ◆ Rocky Mountain Game & Fish. ISSN 1056-0114; ◆ Pennsylvania Game & Fish. ISSN 0897-8808; ◆ Virginia Game & Fish. ISSN 0897-8794; ◆ Washington - Oregon Game & Fish. ISSN 1056-0106; ◆ Ohio Game & Fish. ISSN 0897-9170; New England Game & Fish. ISSN 0897-8972. 1988. USD 12 domestic; USD 25 in Canada; USD 27 elsewhere (effective 2010).
Published by: Intermedia Outdoors, Inc., 512 7th Ave, 11th Fl, New York, NY 10018. TEL 212-852-6682, 800-260-6397, FAX 212-302-4472, customerservice@imoutdoors.com, http://www.imoutdoorsmedia.com. Ed. Ken Dunwoody. Pub., Adv. contact Peter Gross.

NORTH DAKOTA OUTDOORS; official journal of the game and fish department. *see* CONSERVATION

799.1 AUS ISSN 1325-3204
NORTH EAST ANGLER. Text in English. 199?. bi-m. AUD 4.20 newsstand/cover (effective 2009). adv. **Document type:** *Magazine, Consumer.*
Published by: East Gippsland Newspapers, Cnr Macleod & Bailey St, PO Box 465, Bairnsdale, VIC 3875, Australia. TEL 61-3-51502300, FAX 61-3-51526257, events@eastvicmedia.com.au, http://www.eastvicmedia.com.au/index.php?module=Website&action=Home&content=home.

796.552 USA
NORTH STAR (GRAND RAPIDS). Text in English. 1981. q. **Document type:** *Newsletter.*
Published by: North Country Trail Association, 49 Monroe Center, Ste 200B, Grand Rapids, MI 49503. Ed. Robert Papp.

799 USA
NORTHEAST WOODS & WATERS. Text in English. 1987. m. USD 16; USD 2.95 newsstand/cover. adv. back issues avail. **Document type:** *Magazine, Consumer.*
Related titles: Online - full text ed.
Published by: Northeast Woods & Waters Inc., 707, Granby, MA 01033-0707. TEL 413-594-6613, FAX 413-598-0340. Ed. Frank Sousa. Pub. Dianne Gordon. Adv. contact Tory Gordon. B&W page USD 900, color page USD 2,000; trim 17 x 11. Circ: 20,500 (paid).

NORTHERN CALIFORNIA EXPLORE. *see* TRAVEL AND TOURISM

799.1 USA ISSN 1087-2760
SH559
NORTHWEST FISHING HOLES. Text in English. 1974. bi-m. USD 14.95; USD 2.95 newsstand/cover. adv. maps. **Document type:** *Guide, Consumer.* **Description:** Provides information on all aspects of fishing in the Northwest US and Canada, from Northern California to Southern Alaska.
Former titles (until 1991): Washington Fishing Holes (0194-7729); (until 1994): Fishing Holes (1063-1577)
Published by: Fishing Holes Magazine, 14505 N E 91st St, Redmond, WA 98052-6585. TEL 425-883-1919, FAX 425-869-8239. Ed., Adv. contact Ramon Vanden Brulle. R&P Russ Cooley. Circ: 6,000.

799.124 USA ISSN 1527-8255
SH464.N6
NORTHWEST FLY FISHING. Text in English. 199?. bi-m. USD 29.95 domestic; USD 36.95 in Canada; USD 44.95 elsewhere (effective 2007). adv. back issues avail. **Document type:** *Magazine, Consumer.* **Description:** Covers 6 Northwest angling destinations in each issue, including practical traveling information, angling history, description of the fishery, in-depth description of conditions and species, seasonal changes, detailed descriptions of angling techniques, gear and flies for each locale, maps and hatch charts, names, addresses and phone numbers of guide services, fly shops and accommodations.
Related titles: ◆ Regional ed(s).: Eastern Fly Fishing; ◆ Southwest Fly Fishing. ISSN 1536-8505.
Published by: Northwest Fly Fishing, LLC., PO Box 708, Raymond, WA 98577. TEL 206-667-9359, FAX 206-667-9364. Ed. Steve Probasco. adv.: B&W page USD 1,970, color page USD 2,415; trim 7.875 x 10.875. Circ: 27,272 (paid).

799.1 USA ISSN 2150-1955
SH464.N6
NORTHWEST SPORTSMAN; your hunting & fishing resource. Text in English. 193?. m. USD 19.95; USD 1.66 per issue (effective 2009). adv. back issues avail. **Document type:** *Magazine, Trade.* **Description:** Contains information on hunting and fishing.
Published by: Media Index Publishing, Inc., PO Box 24365, Seattle, WA 98124. TEL 206-382-9220, 800-332-1736, FAX 206-382-9437, media@media-inc.com, http://www.media-inc.com. Ed. Andy Walgamott. Pub. James Baker. Adv. contact Brian Lull. Circ: 73,613.

796.522 GBR ISSN 2042-826X
O E RETAILER. (Outdoor Enthusiast) Abbreviated title: O E R. Text in English. 2005. q. adv. back issues avail. **Document type:** *Magazine, Trade.*
Related titles: Online - full text ed.: ISSN 2042-8278. free (effective 2010).
—CCC.
Published by: Target Publishing Ltd., The Old Dairy, Hudsons Farm, Fieldgate Ln, Ugley Green, Bishops Stortford, Essex CM22 6HJ, United Kingdom. TEL 44-1279-810080, FAX 44-1279-810081, info@targetpublishing.com, http://www.targetpublishing.com. Ed. Rebecca Corbally.

OESTERREICHISCHE TOURISTENZEITUNG. *see* TRAVEL AND TOURISM

796 AUT ISSN 0029-8840
OESTERREICHISCHER ALPENVEREIN. AKADEMISCHE SEKTION GRAZ. MITTEILUNGEN. Text in German. 1892. a. free to members (effective 2011). adv. bk.rev. illus. **Document type:** *Bulletin, Trade.*
Published by: Oesterreichischer Alpenverein, Akademische Sektion Graz, Schoergelgasse 28a, Graz, St 8010, Austria. TEL 43-316-822266, alpenverein@inode.at, http://www.alpenverein.at/akad-sektion-graz. Ed. Maria Schmikl.

796.522 AUT ISSN 0029-9715
OESTERREICHISCHER ALPENVEREIN. MITTEILUNGEN. Text in German. 1863. bi-m. bk.rev. index. back issues avail. **Document type:** *Magazine, Consumer.* **Description:** Covers mountain climbing and hiking, tourism, travel reports, expeditions, skiing, forestry, environmental planning and protection, history, and new publications. Includes readers' letters.
Indexed: BibCart.
Published by: Oesterreichischer Alpenverein, Olympiastr 37, Innsbruck, 6020, Austria. TEL 43-512-595470, FAX 43-512-575528, office@alpenverein.at, http://www.alpenverein.at.

799.1 USA
OHIO FISHWRAPPER. Text in English. 1986. m. USD 8.95. adv.
Published by: Fremont Messenger Co. (Subsidiary of: Gannett Company, Inc.), 1700 Cedar St, Fremont, OH 43420. TEL 419-332-5511, FAX 419-332-9750. Circ: 40,000.

799 USA ISSN 0897-9170
OHIO GAME & FISH. Text in English. 198?. m. USD 12.99 domestic; USD 25.99 in Canada; USD 27.99 elsewhere (effective 2011). adv. illus. **Document type:** *Magazine, Consumer.* **Description:** Informs sportsmen of hunting and fishing, as well as environmental and conservation issues in Ohio.
Related titles: Online - full text ed.; ◆ Regional ed(s).: Game & Fish; ◆ Louisiana Game & Fish. ISSN 0744-3692; ◆ Florida Game & Fish. ISSN 0889-3322; ◆ Alabama Game & Fish. ISSN 0279-6783; ◆ Mississippi-Louisiana Game & Fish. ISSN 1947-2358; ◆ North Carolina Game & Fish. ISSN 0897-8816; ◆ South Carolina Game & Fish. ISSN 0897-9154; ◆ West Virginia Game & Fish. ISSN 0897-9162; ◆ Missouri Game & Fish. ISSN 0889-3799; ◆ New York Game & Fish. ISSN 0897-9189; ◆ California Game & Fish. ISSN 1056-0122; ◆ Great Plains Game & Fish. ISSN 1055-6532; ◆ Illinois Game & Fish. ISSN 0897-9014; ◆ Indiana Game & Fish. ISSN 0897-8980; ◆ Iowa Game & Fish. ISSN 0897-9197; ◆ Mid-Atlantic Game & Fish. ISSN 1055-6540; ◆ Oklahoma Game & Fish. ISSN 0746-6013; ◆ Rocky Mountain Game & Fish. ISSN 1056-0114; ◆ Pennsylvania Game & Fish. ISSN 0897-8808; ◆ Virginia Game & Fish. ISSN 0897-8794; ◆ Washington - Oregon Game & Fish. ISSN 1056-0106; New England Game & Fish. ISSN 0897-8972. 1988. USD 12 domestic; USD 25 in Canada; USD 27 elsewhere (effective 2010).
Published by: Intermedia Outdoors, Inc., 512 7th Ave, 11th Fl, New York, NY 10018. TEL 212-852-6682, 800-260-6397, FAX 212-302-4472, customerservice@imoutdoors.com, http://www.imoutdoorsmedia.com. Ed. Ken Dunwoody. Pub., Adv. contact Peter Gross.

799 USA ISSN 1935-0392
OHIO OUTDOOR NEWS; the sportsman's online choice for news and information. Text in English. 2005. bi-w. USD 20 (effective 2009). adv. back issues avail. **Document type:** *Newspaper, Consumer.* **Description:** Provides the sportsmen/women in Ohio with the statewide hunting/fishing report, a lake profile complete with map, statewide calendar of events, season and permit dates and in-depth fishing and hunting news.
Related titles: Online - full text ed.
Published by: Outdoor News, Inc., PO Box 1010, Delaware, OH 43015. TEL 740-363-2374, 800-960-7476, FAX 763-546-5913, subscribe@outdoornews.com, http://www.outdoornews.com. Ed. Mike Moore. Pub. Glenn Meyer. Adv. contact Aaron Wolf. B&W page USD 1,102, color page USD 1,477; 10 x 16.

796 USA
OHIO OUTDOORS. Text in English. 1996. bi-m.
Media: Online - full text.
Published by: Firelands.Net, 12440 New London Eastern Rd, Homerville, OH 44235. Ed. Joseph Cindric Jr.

799.2 799.1 RUS ISSN 1727-5539
OKHOTA I RYBALKA XXI VEK. Variant title: Okhota i Rybalka Dvadtsat' Pervyi Vek. Text in Russian. 2003. m. **Document type:** *Newspaper, Consumer.*
Published by: Moskovskii Komsomolets, ul 1905 goda, dom 7, Moscow, 123995, Russian Federation. TEL 7-095-2532094, podpiska@mk.ru, http://www.mk.ru.

799.2 RUS ISSN 0134-9244
OKHOTNIK. Text in Russian. bi-m. USD 124 foreign (effective 2005). **Document type:** *Journal.*
—East View.
Published by: Voenno-Okhotnich'ye Obshchestvo, ul Burdenko 14, Moscow, 119121, Russian Federation. TEL 7-095-2484067. **Dist. by:** East View Information Services, 10601 Wayzata Blvd, Minneapolis, MN 55305. TEL 952-252-1201, 800-477-1005, FAX 952-252-1202, info@eastview.com, http://www.eastview.com.

796 JPN
OKINAWA DIVER. Text in English. 1998. a. adv. **Description:** Features diving in Okinawa, targeting US military personnel. Provides descriptions of diving sites and discusses diver safety.
Published by: M C C S Marketing, MCB Camp SD Butler, Unit 35023, FPO AP OKINAWA, 96373, Japan. Adv. contact Roy Forster.

799 USA ISSN 0746-6013
OKLAHOMA GAME & FISH. Text in English. 1982. m. USD 12.99 domestic; USD 25.99 in Canada; USD 27.99 elsewhere (effective 2011). adv. illus. **Document type:** *Magazine, Consumer.* **Description:** Informs sportsmen of hunting and fishing, as well as environmental and conservation issues in Oklahoma.
Related titles: Online - full text ed.; ◆ Regional ed(s).: Game & Fish; ◆ Florida Game & Fish. ISSN 0889-3322; ◆ Alabama Game & Fish. ISSN 0279-6783; ◆ Mississippi-Louisiana Game & Fish. ISSN 1947-2358; ◆ North Carolina Game & Fish. ISSN 0897-8816; ◆ South Carolina Game & Fish. ISSN 0897-9154; ◆ West Virginia Game & Fish. ISSN 0897-9162; ◆ Missouri Game & Fish. ISSN 0889-3799; ◆ New York Game & Fish. ISSN 0897-9189; ◆ California Game & Fish. ISSN 1056-0122; ◆ Great Plains Game & Fish. ISSN 1055-6532; ◆ Illinois Game & Fish. ISSN 0897-9014; ◆ Indiana Game & Fish. ISSN 0897-8980; ◆ Iowa Game & Fish. ISSN 0897-9197; ◆ Mid-Atlantic Game & Fish. ISSN 1055-6540; ◆ Louisiana Game & Fish. ISSN 0744-3692; ◆ Rocky Mountain Game & Fish. ISSN 1056-0114; ◆ Pennsylvania Game & Fish. ISSN 0897-8808; ◆ Virginia Game & Fish. ISSN 0897-8794; ◆ Washington - Oregon Game & Fish. ISSN 1056-0106; ◆ Ohio Game & Fish. ISSN 0897-9170; New England Game & Fish. ISSN 0897-8972. 1988. USD 12 domestic; USD 25 in Canada; USD 27 elsewhere (effective 2010).
Published by: Intermedia Outdoors, Inc., 512 7th Ave, 11th Fl, New York, NY 10018. TEL 212-852-6682, 800-260-6397, FAX 212-302-4472, customerservice@imoutdoors.com, http://www.imoutdoorsmedia.com. Ed. Ken Dunwoody. Pub., Adv. contact Peter Gross.

799.1 USA ISSN 1935-0856
SH449
OLD FISHING LURES & TACKLE. Text in English. 1980. irreg., latest 8th ed. USD 23.09 per issue (effective 2011). **Document type:** *Handbook/Manual/Guide, Consumer.*
Published by: Krause Publications, Inc. (Subsidiary of: F + W Media Inc.), 700 E State St, Iola, WI 54990. TEL 715-445-2214, 888-457-2873, FAX 715-445-2164, info@krause.com, http://www.krause.com. Ed. Carl F Luckey.

796.421 DNK ISSN 1902-7885
OLYMPIA; teknik, traening, inspiration, forskning. Text in Danish. 2007. q. DKK 30 per issue (effective 2008). **Document type:** *Magazine, Consumer.*
Published by: Dansk Atletik Forbund/Danish Athletic Federation, Idraettens Hus, Broendby Stadion 20, Brondby, 2605, Denmark. TEL 45-43-262626, FAX 45-43-262325, daf@dansk-atletik.dk, http://www.dansk-atletik.dk.

ON SCENE (LAKEWOOD); the journal of outdoor emergency care. *see* PUBLIC HEALTH AND SAFETY

ON THE LINE (PENSACOLA). *see* LEISURE AND RECREATION

796 USA
ON THE TRAIL. Text in English. 1974. m. USD 15 domestic; CAD 22 in Canada. **Document type:** *Newspaper.*
Published by: On the Trail, Inc, PO Box 456, E Syracuse, NY 13057-0456. TEL 315-437-9296. Ed. Janel Hansen.

796.95 USA
ON THE TRAILS WITH S A M. Text in English. 2000. 7/yr. (Sep.-Mar.). free to members (effective 2009). adv. **Document type:** *Magazine, Consumer.* **Description:** Contains information about the activities of the association, club events and legislative issues.
Published by: (Snowmobile Association of Massachusetts), PrintComm, Inc., 2929 Davison Rd, Flint, MI 48506. TEL 810-239-5763, 800-935-1592, FAX 810-239-8642, http://www.printcomm.com/. Pub. Kevin Naughton. Adv. contact Branda Poe. B&W page USD 1,806, color page USD 2,098; trim 8.375 x 10.875.

799.1 797.1 USA ISSN 1090-963X
ON THE WATER. Text in English. 1996. m. USD 25; USD 4.95 newsstand/cover (effective 2007). adv. **Document type:** *Magazine, Consumer.*
Published by: On the Water LLC, 35 Technology Park Dr, Ste 2, E Falmouth, MA 02536. TEL 508-299-8383 ext 205, FAX 508-299-8386. Pub. Chris Megan. Adv. contact John Burke. color page USD 2,402; trim 10 x 12.5. Circ: 28,500 (paid and free).

796.21 796.22 USA
ONE (SAN DIEGO). Text in English. 2006. bi-m. USD 9.95; USD 3.95 newsstand/cover domestic; USD 5.95 newsstand/cover in Canada (effective 2007). **Document type:** *Magazine, Consumer.*
Published by: Molotov Media, Llc, P O Box 40458, San Diego, CA 92164. Ed. Justin Eisinger.

ONTARIO FARM & COUNTRY ACCOMMODATIONS. BED & BREAKFAST FARM VACATION DIRECTORY. *see* TRAVEL AND TOURISM

799 CAN ISSN 0707-3178
SK152.O5
ONTARIO OUT OF DOORS. Text in English. 1969. 10/yr. CAD 22 domestic; USD 41 in United States (effective 2007). adv. bk.rev. illus. **Document type:** *Magazine, Consumer.* **Description:** Directed to the Ontario outdoor enthusiasts of with information about fishing, hunting, and camping activities. Includes where-to and how-to articles, and examines conservation of natural resources.
Related titles: Microfiche ed.: (from MML); Microform ed.: (from MML); Online - full text ed.
Indexed: C03, C04, C05, CBCARef, CBPI, CPerI, G08, G09, I05, M02, P10, P19, P53, P54, PQC, T02.
Published by: Rogers Publishing Ltd./Les Editions Rogers Limitee, One Mount Pleasant Rd, 11th Fl, Toronto, ON M4Y 2Y5, Canada. TEL 416-764-2000, FAX 416-764-3941, http://www.rogerspublishing.ca. Ed. Burton Myers. Pub. Ron Goodman. adv.: B&W page USD 3,326, color page USD 3,655; 11 x 8.25. Circ: 100,000.

796.95 CAN ISSN 0383-7009
ONTARIO SNOWMOBILER. Text in English. 1986. 5/yr. CAD 17, USD 22 (effective 1998). adv. maps. back issues avail. **Document type:** *Magazine, Consumer.* **Description:** News about snowmobiling and the snowmobile industry.
Published by: (Ontario Federation of Snowmobile Clubs), Ontario Snowmobiler Publishing Inc., 78 Main St South, Newmarket, ON L3Y 3Y6, Canada. TEL 905-898-8585, FAX 905-898-8071. Ed. Mark Lester. Pub. Terrence D Kehoe. R&P Kent Lester. Adv. contact John Hildebrandt. Circ: 87,000 (paid).

797.1 CAN ISSN 0226-5702
THE ONTARIO WATER SKIER. Text in English. 1974. 4/yr. CAD 15 (effective 1999). adv. bk.rev. illus. back issues avail. **Document type:** *Newsletter.* **Description:** Covers articles on waterskiing, equipment, techniques, events and activities on both recreational and competitive aspects of the sport.
Indexed: SD, SportS.
Published by: Ontario Water Ski Association, 1185 Eglinton Ave E, Toronto, ON M3C 3C6, Canada. TEL 416-426-7092, FAX 416-426-7378, owsa@owsa.com, http://www.owsa.com. Ed., R&P, Adv. contact Nazneen Dhalla. B&W page CAD 240; trim 10 x 7.5. Circ: 2,000.

796.51 NLD ISSN 0168-9126
OP LEMEN VOETEN. Text in Dutch. 1979. q. EUR 27.50 (effective 2010). adv.
Published by: Virtumedia, Postbus 595, Zeist, 3700 AN, Netherlands. TEL 31-30-6920677, FAX 31-30-6913312, info@virtumedia.nl, http://www.virtumedia.nl. adv.: B&W page EUR 825, color page EUR 1,495; 182 x 260.

796 NLD ISSN 0168-3845
OP PAD. Text in Dutch. 1983. 8/yr. EUR 42.95 to non-members; EUR 40.95 to members (effective 2008). adv. Website rev. illus. **Document type:** *Consumer.* **Description:** For well-to-do campers, hikers, cyclists, canoeists and mountaineers.
Published by: (ANWB BV/Royal Dutch Touring Club), Algemene Nederlandse Wielrijders Bond (A N W B) Media/Dutch Automobile Association Media, Postbus 93200, The Hague, 2509 BA, Netherlands. TEL 31-70-3141470, FAX 31-70-3146538, http://www.anwbmedia.nl. adv.: B&W page EUR 3,162, color page EUR 4,650; bleed 215 x 300. Circ: 37,178 (paid).

OPEN SPACE. *see* CONSERVATION

796 USA ISSN 1083-9348
OREGON OUTSIDE. Text in English. 1993. q. USD 12.95; USD 3.50 newsstand/cover. adv. bk.rev. illus.; maps. back issues avail. **Document type:** *Magazine, Consumer.* **Description:** For residents and visitors involved in outdoor activities in Oregon from walking to mountain climbing, diving, and hot air ballooning.
Formerly (until 1995): Oregon Parks (1081-4493)
Published by: Northwest Regional Magazines, PO Box 18000, Florence, OR 97439. TEL 541-997-8401, 800-348-8401, FAX 541-997-1124, rob@presys.com. Ed. Jim Frost. Pub. Rob Spooner. R&P, Adv. contact Alicia Spooner.

796.93 USA
OREGON SNOWSPORTS GUIDE. Text in English. 1998. a. free. adv. bk.rev. **Document type:** *Directory, Magazine, Consumer.* **Description:** The official directory to Oregon's ski and snowboard resorts and winter recreation areas.
Published by: Gorge Publishing, Inc., PO Box 918, Hood River, OR 97031. TEL 541-386-7440, FAX 541-386-7480, info@gorgepublishing.com. Ed. Carol York. Pub., R&P, Adv. contact Pete Fotheringham. page USD 5,260; trim 8.375 x 10.875. Circ: 120,000 (free).

796.5 CAN ISSN 0227-6658
ORIENTEERING CANADA. Text in English. 1973. q.
Indexed: SD.
Published by: Canadian Orienteering Federation, Box 62062, Convent Glen P.O., Orleans, ON K1C 2R9, Canada. TEL 613-830-1147, FAX 613-830-0456, canadianorienteering@rogers.com, http://www.orienteering.ca.

790.1 USA ISSN 0886-1080
GV200.4
ORIENTEERING NORTH AMERICA; covering map & compass sports in the US and Canada. Text in English. 1985. 8/yr. UZS 23; USD 26 in Canada; USD 29 elsewhere (effective 2001). adv. bk.rev. maps. back issues avail. **Document type:** *Magazine, Consumer.* **Description:** Covers all aspects of the sport of orienteering. Geared towards all levels of interest.

S

Published by: (United States Orienteering Federation), D M B Publishing, 488 Thayer Pond Rd, Wilton, CT 06897. TEL 203-762-0737, http://www.us.orienteering.org. Ed. Donna Benevento Fluegel. Circ: 1,500.

796.442 FIN ISSN 1015-4965
ORIENTEERING WORLD. Text in English. bi-m. EUR 13.50 in Europe; EUR 18 elsewhere (effective 2002).
Indexed: SD.
Published by: International Orienteering Federation, Radiokatu 20, Slu, 00093, Finland. TEL 358-9-34813112, FAX 358-9-34813113.

OUT WEST. *see* TRAVEL AND TOURISM

796.5 DEU ISSN 0935-3356
OUTDOOR; Reisen, Wandern, Abenteuer. Text in German. 1988. m. EUR 57.30 domestic; EUR 65.30 in Austria; CHF 119.90 in Switzerland; EUR 5 newsstand/cover (effective 2011). adv. bk.rev. index. back issues avail. **Document type:** *Magazine, Consumer.*
Indexed: TM.
Published by: Motor Presse Stuttgart GmbH & Co. KG (Subsidiary of: Gruner + Jahr AG & Co), Leuschnerstr 1, Stuttgart, 70174, Germany. TEL 49-711-18201, FAX 49-711-1821779, cgolla@motorpresse.de, http://www.motorpresse.de. Ed. Olaf Beck. Adv. contact Bernd Holzhauer. Circ: 40,111 (paid).

OUTDOOR ALABAMA. *see* CONSERVATION

796.505 AUS ISSN 1324-5643
OUTDOOR AUSTRALIA. Text in English. 1995. q. AUD 38 domestic; AUD 45 in New Zealand; AUD 58 elsewhere; AUD 7.95 newsstand/cover (effective 2008). adv. **Document type:** *Magazine, Consumer.* **Description:** Provides adventure travel guide to the readers and also give information about finest trails, rivers, mountains and landscapes.
Related titles: Online - full text ed.
Indexed: SD.
Published by: A C P Magazines Ltd. (Subsidiary of: P B L Media Pty Ltd.), 54-58 Park St, Sydney, NSW 2000, Australia. TEL 61-2-92828000, FAX 61-2-91263769, research@acpaction.com.au, http://www.acp.com.au. Adv. contact Marc Connors TEL 61-2-81149426. page AUD 2,685; bleed 454 x 285. Circ: 20,000.

796 NLD
OUTDOOR BUYER'S GUIDE. Text in Dutch. s-a. EUR 3.95 newsstand/cover (effective 2010). adv.
Related titles: ◆ Supplement to: Lift. ISSN 2211-6311.
Published by: Maruba b.v., Winthontlaan 200, Utrecht, 3526 KV, Netherlands. TEL 31-30-2891073, FAX 31-30-2887415, maruba@maruba.com, http://www.maruba.nl. adv.: color page EUR 4,135; 240 x 300. Circ: 35,000 Summer; 50,000 Winter.

333.95416 CAN ISSN 0315-0542
SK601.6
OUTDOOR CANADA; the total outdoor experience. Text in English. 1972. 8/yr. CAD 20.97 domestic; CAD 34.97 in United States (effective 2008). adv. illus.; tr.lit. back issues avail.; reprints avail. **Document type:** *Magazine, Consumer.* **Description:** For active, outdoor Canadians and their families. Covers fishing, canoeing, hiking, hunting, exploring, boating, photography, wildlife and winter sports.
Related titles: Microfiche ed.: (from MML); Microform ed.: (from MML); Online - full text ed.
Indexed: C03, C04, C05, CBCARef, CBPI, CPerl, G08, P48, PQC, SportS, WildRev.
—CIS, Ingenta. **CCC.**
Published by: Transcontinental Media, Inc. (Subsidiary of: Transcontinental, Inc.), 25 Sheppard Ave West, Ste 100, Toronto, ON M2N 6S7, Canada. TEL 416-733-7600, FAX 416-218-3544, info@transcontinental.ca, http://www.medias-transcontinental.com. Ed. Patrick Walsh. adv.: B&W page CAD 6,790, color page CAD 7,900; trim 10 x 7. Circ: 93,000 (paid).

799.06 CAN ISSN 0700-9909
OUTDOOR CREST. Text in English. 1975. irreg. free. illus. **Document type:** *Newsletter.*
Formerly: Outdoor Crest Newsletter (0700-9895)
Published by: Toronto Sportsmen's Association, 17 Mill St, Willowdale, ON M2P 1B3, Canada. TEL 416-487-4477. Ed. Peter Edwards. Circ: 1,200.

796 CAN ISSN 1186-8023
OUTDOOR EDGE. Text in English. 1955. bi-m. CAD 25 (effective 2004). adv. back issues avail. **Document type:** *Magazine, Consumer.*
Formerly (until 1991): Wildlife Crusader (0043-5457)
Published by: O P Publishing Ltd., 1080 Howe St, Ste 900, Vancouver, BC V6Z 2T1, Canada. TEL 604-606-4644, FAX 604-687-1925, markyelic@oppublishing.com, http://www.oppub.com. adv.: B&W page CAD 3,170, color page CAD 3,985; trim 10.75 x 7.88. Circ: 53,000.

OUTDOOR EDUCATION AND RECREATION LAW QUARTERLY; a resource for outdoor & adventure program decision makers. *see* LAW—Corporate Law

796.505 GBR ISSN 1744-9898
OUTDOOR ENTHUSIAST. Text in English. 2004. q. GBP 9.99 domestic; GBP 18 in Europe; GBP 28 elsewhere; GBP 2.49 per issue domestic; GBP 4.50 per issue in Europe (effective 2009). adv. back issues avail. **Document type:** *Magazine, Consumer.* **Description:** Contains product reviews, interviews, news and information on a wide variety of exciting outdoor pursuits.
Related titles: Online - full text ed.: free (effective 2009).
Published by: Target Publishing Ltd., The Old Dairy, Hudsons Farm, Fieldgate Ln, Ugley Green, Bishops Stortford, Essex CM22 6HJ, United Kingdom. TEL 44-1279-810080, FAX 44-1279-810081, info@targetpublishing.com, http://www.targetpublishing.com. Ed. Richard Madden.

796 GBR
▼ **OUTDOOR FITNESS**; get out, get fitter, live more. Text in English. 2011 (Jul.). bi-m. GBP 3.99 newsstand/cover (effective 2011). **Document type:** *Magazine, Consumer.*
Published by: Bauer Consumer Media Ltd., Mappin House, 4 Winsley St, London, W1W 8HF, United Kingdom. TEL 44-20-71828000, http://www.bauermedia.co.uk. Ed. Jonathan Manning. Adv. contact Charlie Brookes.

796 GBR ISSN 2043-8591
OUTDOOR FOCUS. Abbreviated title: O F. Text in English. q. free to members (effective 2010). back issues avail. **Document type:** *Magazine, Trade.* **Description:** Contains full of news, advice and tips, writing and photography in the outdoors, which helps to improve skills or understand the market.
Formerly (until 2007): Bootprint
Related titles: Online - full text ed.: ISSN 2043-8605.
Published by: Outdoor Writers and Photographers Guild, 1 Waterside Close, Garstang, Lancashire PR3 1HJ, United Kingdom. TEL 44-1995-605340, FAX 44-871-2668621, secretary@owg.org.uk. Ed. John Manning.

796 USA
OUTDOOR GUIDES NEWS. Text in English. 1991. bi-m. USD 50. adv. bk.rev. back issues avail. **Document type:** *Newsletter, Trade.*
Related titles: Online - full text ed.
Published by: Outdoor Guides Association, 401 E. Gulf Beach Dr., St. George Island, FL 32328. TEL 904-927-3536, FAX 904-927-3532. Ed. Richard Farren. Adv. contact Casey Madigan. page USD 1,300. Circ: 15,000; 15,000 (paid).

799 USA ISSN 0030-7076
SK1
OUTDOOR LIFE; the source for hunting and fishing adventure. Text in English. 1898. m. USD 39.90 domestic; USD 26 in Canada; USD 45 elsewhere; USD 3.99 newsstand/cover (effective 2011). adv. illus. reprints avail. **Document type:** *Magazine, Consumer.* **Description:** Contains articles on hunting and fishing as well as other outdoor activities.
Incorporates: Fisherman; (in 1927): Outdoor Recreation; Which was formerly (until 1924): Outer's Recreation; (until 1919): Outer's Book-Recreation; Incorporates (in 1907): Pacific Sportsman; Which was formerly (until 1904): Pacific Coast Sportman
Related titles: CD-ROM ed.; Diskette ed.; Microfiche ed.: (from NBI, PQC); Online - full text ed.
Indexed: A01, A02, A03, A08, A11, A22, A26, A33, ARG, B04, BRD, C05, C12, CPerl, ConsI, G05, G06, G07, G08, G09, I05, I06, I07, JHMA, M01, M02, M04, M05, M06, MASUSE, MagInd, P02, P10, P19, P34, P47, P48, P53, P54, PMR, PQC, R03, R04, R06, RGAb, RGPR, S23, SPI, T02, TOM, U01, W03, W05.
—Ingenta. **CCC.**
Published by: Bonnier Corp. (Subsidiary of: Bonnier Group), 2 Park Ave, 9th Fl, New York, NY 10016. http://www.bonniercorp.com. Ed. Todd W Smith. Circ: 750,000 (paid). **Subscr. to:** Outdoor Life Customer Service, PO Box 60001, Tampa, FL 33660-0001.

796 DEU ISSN 1865-1216
OUTDOOR.MARKT. Text in German. 2007. m. EUR 40 (effective 2011). adv. **Document type:** *Magazine, Trade.*
Published by: Jahr Top Special Verlag, Troplowitzstr 5, Hamburg, 22529, Germany. TEL 49-40-389060, FAX 49-40-38906300, info@jahr-tsv.de, http://www.jahr-tsv.de. Ed. Andreas Mayer. Adv. contact Holger Henopp. Circ: 10,000 (paid and controlled).

OUTDOOR NEWS. *see* CONSERVATION

OUTDOOR NEWS BULLETIN. *see* CONSERVATION

OUTDOOR OKLAHOMA. *see* CONSERVATION

THE OUTDOOR RECREATION REPORT. *see* LEISURE AND RECREATION

790.1 AUS ISSN 1440-3900
OUTDOOR SHOWMAN. Text in English. 1947. q. **Document type:** *Handbook/Manual/Guide, Trade.*
Published by: Victorian Showmen's Guild, PO Box 36, Ascot Vale, VIC 3032, Australia. TEL 61-3-93768544, FAX 61-3-93760505.

OUTDOOR SINGLES NETWORK. *see* SINGLES' INTERESTS AND LIFESTYLES

796 GBR
THE OUTDOOR SOURCE BOOK (YEAR). Text in English. 1984. a., latest 2005. GBP 9.95 per issue; GBP 13 combined subscription per issue (print & CDROM eds.) (effective 2009). **Document type:** *Directory.* **Description:** Contains information on careers in outdoor learning,activities for people with disabilities, HE and FE in outdoor learning, corporate and adult development outdoors, outdoor therapy, art and drama, first aid outdoors, etc.
Related titles: CD-ROM ed.: GBP 4.50 per issue (effective 2009).
Published by: Adventure Education Ltd, Warwick Mill Business Centre, Warwick Bridge, Carlisle, Cumbria CA4 8RR, United Kingdom. TEL 44-1228-564580, FAX 44-1228-564581, institute@outdoor-learning.org.

796.5 GBR
OUTDOOR TRADE AND INDUSTRY. Text in English. 1984. bi-m. GBP 20. adv. **Document type:** *Magazine, Trade.*
Incorporates: Camping and Outdoor Leisure Trader
Address: 97 Front St, Whickham, Newcastle upon Tyne, NE16 4JL, United Kingdom. Ed. Peter Lumley. Circ: (controlled).

796 USA ISSN 1936-3796
OUTDOOR WOMAN MAGAZINE. Text in English. 2007 (Jul.). bi-m. adv. **Document type:** *Magazine, Consumer.* **Description:** Features articles that offer encouragement to women hesitant to explore new activities as well as provides solid information for women already involved in outdoor recreation.
Published by: Outdoor Woman Publishing, Inc, PO Box 65519, Vancouver, WA 98665.

799 USA ISSN 1931-8294
OUTDOORS MAGAZINE. Text in English. 1996. m. USD 18.95 (effective 2006). adv. maps; stat. back issues avail. **Document type:** *Magazine, Consumer.* **Description:** Serves as a guide to hunting, fishing and outdoor life in Vermont.
Formerly (until 2005?): Vermont Outdoors Magazine (1096-1976)
Published by: Lake Iroquois Publishing, Inc., 2 Church St, Burlington, VT 05401. TEL 802-860-0003, FAX 802-863-8069. Ed. Lawrence Pyne. Pub. John Boutin. Adv. contact Danielle Livellara. Circ: 8,000.

796.5 USA
OUTDOORS NETWORK. Text in English. m.
Media: Online - full content.
Address: publishers@outdoors.net, http://www.outdoors.net. Ed. Joe Reynolds.

796.5 USA
OUTDOORS ONLINE. Text in English. 1996. w.
Media: Online - full content.
Address: http://www.ool.com/homepage.html.

OUTDOORS UNLIMITED. *see* CONSERVATION

799 USA
THE OUTDOORSMEN. Text in English. 1980. m. USD 12 (effective 2000). adv. bk.rev. back issues avail. **Document type:** *Newspaper.* **Description:** Covers the outdoors in North and South Dakota, Nebraska, Iowa, southwest Minnesota, northern Kansas, and Missouri including fishing, hunting, camping and boating.
Published by: Outdoorsmen Publications, 109 N Broadway, PO Box 354, Hartington, NE 68739-0354. TEL 402-254-3268, 800-279-4780, FAX 402-254-3266. Ed., Pub. Gary Howey. Adv. contact Cindy Howey. B&W page USD 750; trim 12.5 x 9.75. Circ: 17,100.

796 SWE ISSN 1652-4624
OUTSIDE. Text in Swedish. 2004. m. SEK 579 (effective 2006). adv. **Document type:** *Magazine, Consumer.*
Published by: First Publishing Group AB, Deltavaegen 3, PO Box 3187, Vaexjoe, 35043, Sweden. TEL 46-470-762400, FAX 46-470-762425, info@firstpublishing.se, http://www.firstpublishing.se.

796 USA ISSN 0278-1433
GV191.2
OUTSIDE (SANTA FE). Text in English. 1979. m. USD 19.95 domestic; CAD 35 in Canada; USD 1.66 per issue domestic (effective 2009). adv. bk.rev. illus. back issues avail.; reprints avail. **Document type:** *Magazine, Consumer.* **Description:** Aims to inspire people to enjoy fuller, more rewarding lives through year-round participation in sports, travel, events, photography, and politics of the world.
Formerly (until 1980): Mariah - Outside (0194-4371); Which was formed by the merger of (1976-1979): Mariah (0149-7790); (1977-1979): Outside (San Francisco) (0276-1211)
Related titles: Microfilm ed.: (from PQC); Online - full text ed.
Indexed: A01, A02, A03, A08, A11, A21, A22, A33, ASIP, C05, CA, ERI, G09, M02, P02, P10, P34, P48, P53, P54, PQC, RI-1, RI-2, SD, SportS, T02, U01.
—Ingenta.
Published by: Mariah Media Inc., 400 Market St, Santa Fe, NM 87501. TEL 505-989-7100, FAX 505-989-4700, letters@outsidemag.com. Ed. Lawrence J Burke TEL 505-989-7100 ext 200. adv.: B&W page USD 82,280, color page USD 85,255; trim 8 x 10.875. Circ: 687,916. **Subscr. to:** PO Box 7785, Red Oak, IA 51541. TEL 515-246-6917, 800-678-113, FAX 712-623-5731.

796 USA ISSN 1079-6258
GV191.623
OUTSIDE BUYER'S GUIDE. Text in English. 1995. s-a. included with subsc. to Outside (Santa Fe). adv. **Document type:** *Guide, Consumer.* **Description:** Features tips on running, cycling, skiing and triathlon training.
Published by: Mariah Media Inc., 400 Market St, Santa Fe, NM 87501. TEL 505-989-7100, FAX 505-989-4700, letters@outsidemag.com, http://outside.away.com/index.html. Ed. Lawrence J Burke TEL 505-989-7100 ext 200. adv.: page USD 32,585.

796 USA ISSN 1933-5628
GV191.2
OUTSIDE TRAVELER. Text in English. 1996. s-a. adv. illus. **Document type:** *Magazine, Consumer.* **Description:** Provides travelers with essential information.
Formerly (until 200?): Outside Travel Guide (1079-6274)
Published by: Mariah Media Inc., 400 Market St, Santa Fe, NM 87501. TEL 505-989-7100, FAX 505-989-4700, outsideonline@outsidemag.com, http://outside.away.com/index.html.

796 USA ISSN 1092-6674
GV182.8
OUTSIDE'S GUIDE TO FAMILY VACATIONS. Variant title: Guide to Family Vacations. Text in English. 1997. a. adv. **Document type:** *Magazine, Consumer.*
Published by: Mariah Media Inc., 400 Market St, Santa Fe, NM 87501. TEL 505-989-7100, FAX 505-989-4700, outsideonline@outsidemag.com, http://outside.away.com/index.html.

796 USA
OVERLAND JOURNAL (PRESCOTT). Text in English. 2007. 5/yr. USD 45 in US & Canada; USD 60 elsewhere (effective 2007). **Document type:** *Magazine, Consumer.*
Published by: Overland Journal, LLC, PO Box 1150, Prescott, AZ 86302. TEL 928-308-2158.

796.552 USA
OZARK HIGHLANDS TRAIL ASSOCIATION NEWSLETTER. Text in English. m.
Published by: Ozark Highlands Trail Association, 411 Patricia, Fayetteville, AR 72703. Ed. Tim Ernst.

796 USA
P E - W O W. (Press - Enterprise Wheels - Offroad - Waves) Text in English. 2007. w. (Wed.). **Document type:** *Magazine, Newspaper-distributed.* **Description:** Covers the active outdoor lifestyle, including RV, camping, boating, off road vehicle, and motorcycle.
Published by: Press - Enterprise Company, 3512 14th St., Riverside, CA 92501. http://www.enterpe.com/.

799.1 USA ISSN 1544-7480
PACIFIC COAST SPORTFISHING. Text in English. 198?. m. USD 26.95; USD 3.95 newsstand/cover (effective 2002). adv. **Description:** Contains columns and features on electronics, rods, reels and fishing gear that can help our readers boat more fish, in addition to monthly boat reviews from "battleship" sized sport fishers to walk-arounds to bay boats, and helpful articles on the engines that power them. It also contains how to articles on fishing techniques for virous west coast gamefish, including species found offshore, inshore and in bays and harbors.
Formerly (until 1993): South Coast Sportfishing (0279-2249)
Published by: Abundant Life Media, Inc., 901 Dover Dr, Ste 101, Newport Beach, CA 92660. TEL 714-258-2344, FAX 714-258-3448. Pub. Drew Lawler. adv.: B&W page USD 3,490; trim 8 x 10.75. Circ: 5,750 (controlled); 9,320 (paid).

799.1 USA ISSN 1069-0689
PACIFIC FISHERMAN. Text in English. 1989. m. free (effective 2008). adv. back issues avail. **Document type:** *Magazine, Consumer.* **Description:** Covers saltwater fishing in Alaska, Washington, Oregon, California and Baja California. Includes how-to techniques and travel.
Media: Online - full text.

Published by: Barana Publishing, 23182 Alcalde, Ste K, Laguna Hills, CA 92653. TEL 714-830-2290, FAX 714-830-5108, rhod@pacificfisherman.com. Ed. Rhod Santiago. R&P Monica Cole. Adv. contact Jim Yant. Circ: 16,846 (paid).

799.3 GBR ISSN 0955-9124
PAINTBALL ADVENTURES. Text in English. 1989. m. GBP 20.50. adv. bk.rev. back issues avail. **Document type:** *Magazine, Consumer.*
Published by: Penn Publishing Co., 20 Hill Farm Way, Hazlemere, High Wycombe, Bucks HP15 7SY, United Kingdom. TEL 44-1494-814418, FAX 44-1494-812746. Ed. Stuart Wall. Adv. contact David Smith.

799.2 FRA ISSN 2106-8178
PALOMBE & TRADITION. Text in French. 2003. q. **Document type:** *Magazine, Consumer.*
Published by: Edipassion, 4, Rue des Pinsons, Casteljaloux, 47700, France. contact@palombe-tradition.com, http://www.palombe-tradition.com.

799.1 USA
▼ **PANFISH GUIDE**; the world's foremost authority on panfish. Text in English. 2009 (Mar.). a. USD 5 per issue (effective 2011). adv. back issues avail. **Document type:** *Handbook/Manual/Guide, Consumer.* **Description:** Features exclusive location and presentation tactics for crappies, bluegills, perch, white bass and more. Edited for anglers that persue panfish, includes education and information on boat rigging and new products.
Published by: Intermedia Outdoors, Inc., 512 7th Ave, 11th Fl, New York, NY 10018. TEL 212-852-6682, 800-260-6397, FAX 212-302-4472, customerservice@imoutdoors.com, http://www.imoutdoorsmedia.com.

797.55 FRA ISSN 1156-9743
PARAPENTE MAG. Text in French. 1989. bi-m. EUR 29; EUR 5.80 per issue (effective 2009). **Document type:** *Magazine, Consumer.*
Published by: Societe Sports Loisirs Presse, 50 bd. Senard, St Cloud, 92210, France. TEL 33-1-47112000, FAX 33-1-47112995. Ed. Pierre Pagani. Pub. Michel Hommell.

796.552 FRA ISSN 1269-4339
PARIS-CHAMONIX. Text in French. 1934. 5/yr. adv. bk.rev. illus. back issues avail. **Document type:** *Magazine, Consumer.*
Formerly (until 1975): Club Alpin Francais. Section de Paris (1269-4347)
Published by: Federation Francaise des Clubs Alpins et de Montagne, 24 Av. de la Laumiere, Paris, 75019, France. Ed. Monique Rebiffe. Circ: 10,000.

363.68 790.068 658 USA ISSN 1539-9990
PARKS & REC BUSINESS; common sense solutions to everyday problems. Abbreviated title: P R B. Text in English. 2002. m. free in US & Canada to qualified personnel; USD 67 foreign; USD 5 per issue (effective 2011). adv. back issues avail. **Document type:** *Magazine, Trade.*
Related titles: Online - full text ed.: ISSN 2161-2684. free (effective 2011).
Published by: Northstar Publishing, Inc., PO Box 1166, Medina, OH 44258. TEL 330-721-9126, FAX 330-723-6598, info@northstarpubs.com, http://www.northstarpubs.com/. Ed. Christine Sima TEL 866-444-4216 ext 221. Pub. Rodney J Auth TEL 866-444-4216 ext 226.

799.1 ITA ISSN 1826-395X
PASSIONE PESCA IN ACQUA DOLCE. Text in Italian. 2005. m. **Document type:** *Magazine, Consumer.*
Published by: Edizioni La Traccia, Via Columella 36, Milan, 20128, Italy. FAX 36-02-89078188.

799.1 ITA ISSN 1826-3968
PASSIONE PESCA IN MARE. Text in Italian. 2005. m. **Document type:** *Magazine, Consumer.*
Published by: Edizioni La Traccia, Via Columella 36, Milan, 20128, Italy. FAX 36-02-89078188.

PATHWAYS; the Ontario journal of outdoor education. *see* CONSERVATION

796 USA
PATHWAYS ACROSS AMERICA; a newsletter for national scenic and historic trails. Text in English. q. **Document type:** *Newsletter.*
Published by: American Hiking Society, PO Box 20160, Washington, DC 20041-2160. TEL 301-565-6704, FAX 301-565-6714.

796.552 DEU ISSN 1613-8775
PEAK; ueber alle Berge. Text in German. 2004. bi-m. adv. **Document type:** *Magazine, Consumer.*
Published by: Olympia Verlag GmbH, Badstr 4-6, Nuernberg, 90402, Germany. TEL 49-911-2160, FAX 49-911-2162741, anzeigen@olympia-verlag.de, http://www.olympia-verlag.de. Adv. contact Alexander Herrmann. B&W page EUR 2,246, color page EUR 3,853. Circ: 47,400 (controlled).

PEAK AND PRAIRIE. *see* CONSERVATION

799.1 FRA ISSN 1282-5220
PECHE MOUCHE. Text in French. 1997. bi-m. EUR 25 (effective 2008). **Document type:** *Magazine, Consumer.*
Published by: Mondadori France, 1 Rue du Colonel Pierre-Avia, Paris, Cedex 15 75754, France. TEL 33-1-41335001, contact@mondadori.fr, http://www.mondadori.fr.

799.1 FRA ISSN 1779-9651
PECHES ET BATEAUX. Text in French. 200?. q. EUR 24.10 domestic; EUR 40.60 foreign (effective 2010). back issues avail. **Document type:** *Magazine, Consumer.*
Formerly (until 2006): Le Pecheur de France. Peche pour Tous (1636-0605)
Published by: Le Pecheur de France, 21 Rue du Faubourg Saint-Antoine, Paris, 75550 Cedex 11, France. TEL 33-1-44878787, FAX 33-1-44878729, boutique@lepecheurdefrance.com, http://www.lepecheurdefrance.com.

799.1 FRA ISSN 0154-6953
LE PECHEUR DE FRANCE. Text in French. 1977. 10/yr. EUR 40.50 domestic; EUR 54.60 foreign (effective 2010). back issues avail. **Document type:** *Magazine, Consumer.*
Published by: Le Pecheur de France, 21 Rue du Faubourg Saint-Antoine, Paris, 75550 Cedex 11, France. TEL 33-1-44878787, FAX 33-1-44878729, boutique@lepecheurdefrance.com, http://www.lepecheurdefrance.com.

796.5 USA ISSN 1093-0574
SH1
PENNSYLVANIA ANGLER & BOATER. Text in English. 1931. bi-m. USD 9; USD 3 newsstand/cover (effective 2005). bk.rev. **Document type:** *Magazine, Consumer.* **Description:** Covers fishing, boating and camping.
Formerly (until 1997): Pennsylvania Angler (0031-434X)
Indexed: WildRev.
—Ingenta.
Published by: Pennsylvania Fish & Boat Commission, 1601 Elmorton Ave, Harrisburg, Dauphin, PA 17110. TEL 717-705-7800, FAX 717-705-7831, amichaels@state.pa.us, http://www.fish.state.pa.us/. Ed. Art Michaels. Circ: 40,000 (paid and controlled).

799 USA ISSN 0897-8808
PENNSYLVANIA GAME & FISH. Text in English. 1982. m. USD 12 domestic; USD 25 in Canada; USD 27 elsewhere (effective 2011). adv. illus. **Document type:** *Magazine, Consumer.* **Description:** Informs sportsmen of hunting and fishing, as well as environmental and conservation issues in Pennsylvania.
Formerly (until 198?): Pennsylvania Outdoors (0745-225X)
Related titles: Online - full text ed.; ♦ Regional ed(s).: Game & Fish; ♦ Florida Game & Fish. ISSN 0889-3322; ♦ Alabama Game & Fish. ISSN 0279-6783; ♦ Mississippi-Louisiana Game & Fish. ISSN 1947-2358; ♦ North Carolina Game & Fish. ISSN 0897-8816; ♦ South Carolina Game & Fish. ISSN 0897-9154; ♦ West Virginia Game & Fish. ISSN 0897-9162; ♦ Missouri Game & Fish. ISSN 0889-3799; ♦ New York Game & Fish. ISSN 0897-9189; ♦ California Game & Fish. ISSN 1056-0122; ♦ Great Plains Game & Fish. ISSN 1055-6532; ♦ Illinois Game & Fish. ISSN 0897-9014; ♦ Indiana Game & Fish. ISSN 0897-8980; ♦ Iowa Game & Fish. ISSN 0897-9197; ♦ Mid-Atlantic Game & Fish. ISSN 1055-6540; ♦ Louisiana Game & Fish. ISSN 0744-3692; ♦ Rocky Mountain Game & Fish. ISSN 1056-0114; ♦ Oklahoma Game & Fish. ISSN 0746-6013; ♦ Virginia Game & Fish. ISSN 0897-8794; ♦ Washington - Oregon Game & Fish. ISSN 1056-0106; ♦ Ohio Game & Fish. ISSN 0897-9170; New England Game & Fish. ISSN 0897-8972. 1988. USD 12 domestic; USD 25 in Canada; USD 27 elsewhere (effective 2010).
Published by: Intermedia Outdoors, Inc., 512 7th Ave, 11th Fl, New York, NY 10018. TEL 212-852-6682, 800-260-6397, FAX 212-302-4472, customerservice@imoutdoors.com, http://www.imoutdoorsmedia.com. Ed. Ken Dunwoody. Pub., Adv. contact Peter Gross.

799.2 USA ISSN 0031-451X
SK351
PENNSYLVANIA GAME NEWS. Text in English. 1931. m. USD 12 (effective 2000). bk.rev. illus. index. reprints avail. **Document type:** *Government.*
Related titles: Microform ed.: (from PQC).
Indexed: A22, W08.
Published by: Pennsylvania Game Commission, 2001 Elmerton Ave, Harrisburg, PA 17110-9797. TEL 717-787-3745, FAX 717-772-0542. Ed. Bob Mitchell. Circ: 150,000.

799 USA ISSN 1548-4637
PENNSYLVANIA OUTDOOR NEWS; the sportsman's online choice for news and information. Text in English. 2004. bi-w. USD 22 (effective 2009). adv. back issues avail. **Document type:** *Newspaper, Consumer.* **Description:** Provides the sportsmen/women in Pennsylvania with the statewide hunting/fishing report, a lake profile complete with map, statewide calendar of events, season and permit dates and in-depth fishing and hunting news.
Related titles: Online - full text ed.
Published by: Outdoor News, Inc., PO Box 1393, Altoona, PA 16603. TEL 740-363-2374, 800-353-1393, FAX 763-546-5913, subscribe@outdoornews.com, http://www.outdoornews.com. Ed. Jeff Mulhollem. Pub. Glenn Meyer. Adv. contact Aaron Wolf. B&W page USD 1,214, color page USD 1,589; 10 x 16.

796 USA ISSN 1534-0589
PENNSYLVANIA OUTDOOR TIMES. Text in English. 1993. m. USD 18 (effective 2009). adv. back issues avail. **Document type:** *Magazine, Consumer.* **Description:** Provides the sportsmen/women in Pennsylvania with the statewide hunting/fishing report, statewide calendar of events, season and permit dates and in-depth fishing and hunting news.
Formerly (until 199?): Pennsylvania Afield
Related titles: Online - full text ed.
Published by: Ogden Publications, PO Box 930, Altoona, PA 16603. TEL 800-854-8228, FAX 814-946-7410, http://www.ogdenpubs.com. Ed. Ken Piper. Pub. Ed Kruger. R&P Angie Harbst TEL 814-946-7546. Adv. contact Kelly Cooper TEL 570-584-4612. B&W page USD 425, color page USD 570. Circ: 100,000. **Subscr. to:** 1503 S W 42nd St, Topeka, KS 66609.

799.2 ESP
PERROS CAZA. Text in Spanish. m. EUR 5.95 newsstand/cover (effective 2009). adv. **Document type:** *Magazine, Consumer.*
Published by: Grupo V, C Valportillo Primera, 11, Alcobendas, Madrid, 28108, Spain. TEL 34-91-6622137, FAX 34-91-6622654, secretaria@grupov.es. Ed. Jose Maria Garcia-Medina. Adv. contact Rafael Morillo. page EUR 1,760; trim 19.5 x 26.7.

799.1 ITA ISSN 1827-0743
PESCA CHE PASSIONE. Text in Italian. 2006. w. **Document type:** *Magazine, Consumer.*
Published by: De Agostini Editore, Via G da Verrazzano 15, Novara, 28100, Italy. TEL 39-0321-4241, FAX 39-0321-424305, info@deagostini.it, http://www.deagostini.it.

799.1 ITA ISSN 1972-3385
PESCA DA TERRA. Text in Italian. 2007. m. **Document type:** *Magazine, Consumer.*
Published by: Ediservice Casa Editrice Firenze, Via XX Settembre 60, Florence, 50129, Italy. TEL 39-055-4625293, FAX 39-055-4633331, info@ediservice.it, http://www.ediservice.it.

799.1 797.1 ITA ISSN 1971-2731
PESCA E NAUTICA. Text in Italian. 2007. m. **Document type:** *Magazine, Consumer.*
Published by: Sprea Editori Srl, Via Torino 51, Cernusco sul Naviglio, MI 20063, Italy. TEL 39-02-92432222, FAX 39-02-92432236, editori@sprea.it, http://www.sprea.it.

799.1 ITA ISSN 0394-090X
PESCA IN FIUMI, LAGHI E TORRENTI. Text in Italian. m. EUR 50 domestic; EUR 88 in Europe; EUR 112 elsewhere (effective 2009). **Document type:** *Magazine, Consumer.* **Description:** Covers freshwater fishing. Contains competition reports, scientific articles, tourist itineraries and environmental issues.
Published by: Ediservice Casa Editrice Firenze, Via XX Settembre 60, Florence, 50129, Italy. TEL 39-055-4625293, FAX 39-055-4633331, info@ediservice.it, http://www.ediservice.it.

799.1 ITA ISSN 0394-0918
PESCA IN MARE. Text in Italian. m. EUR 50 domestic; EUR 88 in Europe; EUR 112 elsewhere (effective 2009). adv. **Document type:** *Magazine, Consumer.* **Description:** Covers sea fishing, fishing boats, nautical and environmental issues and tourism itineraries.
Published by: Ediservice Casa Editrice Firenze, Via XX Settembre 60, Florence, 50129, Italy. TEL 39-055-4625293, FAX 39-055-4633331, info@ediservice.it, http://www.ediservice.it.

PESCA MARINA Y EL BARCO PESQUERO. *see* FISH AND FISHERIES

799.1 ITA ISSN 1590-3583
LA PESCA MOSCA E SPINNING. Text in Italian. 1990. bi-m. EUR 28 (effective 2009). adv. **Document type:** *Magazine, Consumer.*
Published by: Petra Srl, Via Ridolfi 4, Empoli, 50053, Italy. Circ: 18,000.

799.1 ESP ISSN 2174-0143
PESCA SUBMARINA Y APNEA. Text in Spanish. 1991. bi-m. **Document type:** *Magazine, Consumer.*
Formerly (until 2010): Apnea (1136-7083)
Published by: Sofimav Ediciones Espana, C FAstenrath, 12, Barcelona, Spain. TEL 34-93-2122610, FAX 34-93-4173876.

799.1 ITA ISSN 0031-6091
PESCARE; la rivista dei pescatori. Text in Italian. 1962. m. EUR 48 domestic (effective 2008). adv. video rev. index. 128 p./no.; back issues avail. **Document type:** *Magazine, Consumer.* **Description:** Contains techniques, tools, itineraries and news about sea and fly fishing. Also includes editorials and correspondence with readers.
Published by: Gruppo Editoriale Olimpia SpA, Via E Fermi 24, Loc Osmannoro, Sesto Fiorentino, FI 50129, Italy. TEL 39-055-30321, FAX 39-055-3032280, http://www.edolimpia.it. Circ: 43,000. **Dist. by:** Parrini & C, Piazza Colonna 361, Rome, RM 00187, Italy. TEL 39-06-695141.

799.1 ITA ISSN 2035-4495
▼ **PESCARE APNEA.** Text in Italian. 2009. m. **Document type:** *Magazine, Consumer.*
Published by: Gruppo Editoriale Olimpia SpA, Via E Fermi 24, Loc Osmannoro, Sesto Fiorentino, FI 50129, Italy. TEL 39-055-30321, FAX 39-055-3032280, info@edolimpia.it, http://www.edolimpia.it.

799.1 ITA ISSN 1121-3833
PESCARE MARE. Text in Italian. 1989. m. EUR 48 domestic (effective 2008). adv. video rev. 144 p./no.; back issues avail. **Document type:** *Magazine, Consumer.* **Description:** Contains articles about various techniques of sea-fishing, tools, contests, and exhibitions.
Published by: Gruppo Editoriale Olimpia SpA, Via E Fermi 24, Loc Osmannoro, Sesto Fiorentino, FI 50129, Italy. TEL 39-055-30321, FAX 39-055-3032280, http://www.edolimpia.it. Circ: 28,500. **Dist. by:** Parrini & C, Piazza Colonna 361, Rome, RM 00187, Italy. TEL 39-06-695141.

799.1 ITA
PESCASPORT. Text in Italian. bi-m. EUR 18 (effective 2009). **Document type:** *Magazine, Consumer.*
Published by: Greentime SpA, Via Barberia 11, Bologna, BO 40123, Italy. TEL 39-051-584020, FAX 39-051-585000, info@greentime.it, http://www.greentime.it. Circ: 11,000 (controlled).

799.1 ITA ISSN 1122-6978
IL PESCATORE D'ACQUA DOLCE. Text in Italian. 1994. m. adv. back issues avail. **Document type:** *Magazine, Consumer.* **Description:** Includes freshwater fishing techniques and information on tools, accessories and itineraries.
Published by: Gruppo Editoriale Olimpia SpA, Via E Fermi 24, Loc Osmannoro, Sesto Fiorentino, FI 50129, Italy. TEL 39-055-30321, FAX 39-055-3032280, info@edolimpia.it, http://www.edolimpia.it. Circ: 45,700.

799.1 ITA ISSN 1828-4817
IL PESCATORE TRENTINO. Text in Italian. 1978. 3/yr. **Document type:** *Magazine, Consumer.*
Published by: Associazione Pescatori Dilettanti Trentini (A P D T), 2 Via del Ponte a Ravina, Trent, TN, Italy. apdt@apdt.net, http://www.apdt.net.

799.2 USA ISSN 1059-1737
SK1
PETERSEN'S ANNUAL HUNTING. Variant title: Petersen's Hunting. Text in English. 1975. a. adv. **Document type:** *Magazine, Consumer.*
Formerly (until 19??): Petersen's Hunting Annual (0095-5124)
—CCC.
Published by: Source Interlink Companies, 6420 Wilshire Blvd, 10th Fl, Los Angeles, CA 90048. TEL 323-782-2000, FAX 323-782-2585, dheine@sourceinterlink.com, http://www.sourceinterlinkmedia.com.

799.2 USA ISSN 1065-6006
SK301
PETERSEN'S DEER HUNTING. Text in English. 1977. a. **Document type:** *Magazine, Consumer.*
Formerly (until 1990): Deer Hunting (0270-0069)
Published by: Source Interlink Companies, 6420 Wilshire Blvd, 10th Fl, Los Angeles, CA 90048. TEL 323-782-2000, FAX 323-782-2585, dheine@sourceinterlink.com, http://www.sourceinterlinkmedia.com.

799.2 USA ISSN 0146-4671
SK1
PETERSEN'S HUNTING. Text in English. 1973. 10/yr. USD 14 domestic; USD 27 in Canada; USD 29 elsewhere (effective 2010). adv. bk.rev. illus. reprints avail. **Document type:** *Magazine, Consumer.* **Description:** Covers all areas and aspects of hunting. Reviews outdoor clothing, accessories, bows, and firearms.
Related titles: Online - full text ed.
Indexed: G06, G07, G08, I05.
—CCC.
Published by: Intermedia Outdoors, Inc., 512 7th Ave, 11th Fl, New York, NY 10018. TEL 800-260-6397, FAX 212-302-4472, customerservice@imoutdoors.com, http://www.imoutdoorsmedia.com. adv.: B&W page USD 17,420, color page USD 28,922. Circ: 363,106 (paid).

S

799.1 CHE ISSN 0031-6318
PETRI-HEIL; Schweizerische Fischereizeitung. Text in German. 1950. m. CHF 72.20. **Document type:** *Newspaper.*
Published by: V I P Media Verlag, Alte Landstr 19, Scherzingen, 8596, Switzerland. Ed. H Dietiker. Circ: 20,000.

799.2 USA ISSN 1079-7041
SK325.P5
PHEASANTS FOREVER; journal of upland game conservation. Text in English. 1982. 5/yr. USD 25 (effective 2003). adv. illus. reprints avail. **Description:** For pheasant hunters and enthusiasts. Focuses on conservation and the importance of wildlife, specifically upland birds.
Published by: Pheasants Forever Inc., 1783 Buerkle Circle, St. Paul, MN 55110-5254. TEL 877-773-2070. Ed. Mark Herwig. Circ: 100,000.

799.1 USA
PIKE & MUSKIE GUIDE. Text in English. 2008. a. USD 5 per issue (effective 2011). back issues avail. **Document type:** *Handbook/ Manual/Guide, Consumer.*
Published by: Intermedia Outdoors, Inc., 512 7th Ave, 11th Fl, New York, NY 10018. TEL 800-260-6397, FAX 212-302-0472, customerservice@imoutdoors.com, http://www.imoutdoorsmedia.com.

PINEWOOD-MUNDS PARK, ARIZONA COMMUNITY GUIDE & DIRECTORY; a relocation guide for the communities of northern Arizona. *see* TRAVEL AND TOURISM

799.2 DEU ISSN 0340-7829
DIE PIRSCH; Magazin fuer Jagd und Natur. Text in German. 1948. fortn. EUR 99.80 domestic; CHF 202.40 in Switzerland; EUR 110.50 elsewhere; EUR 4.80 newsstand/cover (effective 2009). adv. bk.rev. illus. **Document type:** *Magazine, Consumer.* **Description:** Contains articles on all aspects of hunting as well as nature and land conservation.
Formed by merger of: Pirsch (0032-0269); Deutscher Jaeger (0012-1118)
Related titles: Online - full text ed.
Indexed: KWIWR, W08.
—CCC.
Published by: Deutscher Landwirtschaftsverlag GmbH, Lothstr 29, Munich, 80797, Germany. TEL 49-89-127051, FAX 49-89-12705335, dlv.muenchen@dlv.de, http://www.dlv.de. Ed. Jost Doerenkamp. Adv. contact Henning Stemmler. B&W page EUR 2,840, color page EUR 5,519; trim 210 x 297. Circ: 35,743 (paid and controlled).

796.5 FRA ISSN 0048-427X
PLAISIRS DE LA CHASSE. Text in French. 1952. m. EUR 35 domestic; EUR 50 foreign (effective 2009). adv. **Document type:** *Magazine, Consumer.*
Published by: Editions Crepin-Leblond, 14 rue du Patronage Laique, Chaumont, 52000, France. TEL 33-3-25038748, FAX 33-3-25038740, crepin-leblond@graphycom.com. Ed. Jean Bletner. Adv. contact Laurent Picard. Circ: 48,000.

796 FRA ISSN 0764-3055
PLANCHE MAG. Text in French. 1980. m. EUR 34 domestic; EUR 50 DOM-TOM; EUR 50 in Europe (effective 2008). **Document type:** *Magazine, Consumer.*
Former titles (until 1985): Planche Magazine (0242-6986); (until 1981): Force 6 (0246-8603)
Indexed: SportS.
Published by: Expression Media, Passage du Cheval-Blanc, 2 rue de la Roquette, Paris, 75011, France.

796.93 DEU ISSN 1860-1685
PLANETSNOW; ski & wintersports. Text in German. 2000. 4/yr. EUR 6.50 newsstand/cover (effective 2011). adv. **Document type:** *Magazine, Consumer.* **Description:** Covers the latest trends and products in a variety of winter sports.
Related titles: Online - full text ed.
Published by: Motor Presse Stuttgart GmbH & Co. KG (Subsidiary of: Gruner + Jahr AG & Co), Leuschnerstr 1, Stuttgart, 70174, Germany. TEL 49-711-18201, FAX 49-711-1821779, cgolla@motorpresse.de, http://www.motorpresse.de. Ed. Florian Schmidt. Adv. contact Bernd Holzhauer. Circ: 35,000 (paid).

796.2 DEU
PLAYBOARD; skateboard - snowboard - music. Text in German. 2004. bi-m. EUR 20 domestic; EUR 25 in Europe (effective 2009). adv. **Document type:** *Magazine, Consumer.*
Published by: Beatnuts GmbH & Co. KG, Bahnweg 4, Regenstauf, 93128, Germany. TEL 49-9402-504747, FAX 49-9402-9489190. Ed. Jochen Bauer. Adv. contact Helge Zirkl. page EUR 3,300. Circ: 41,928 (paid and controlled).

796.5 910.202 ITA ISSN 1124-0202
PLEINAIR; turismo secondo natura, camper, caravan, tenda, escursioni. Text in Italian. 1971. m. (11/yr.). EUR 40 domestic; EUR 100 in the European Union (effective 2009). adv. bk.rev. **Document type:** *Magazine, Consumer.* **Description:** Includes nature, vacations, traveling, outdoor sports and life.
Former titles (until 1993): Plein Air 2C Caravan Camping (1124-0245); (until 1988): 2C Caravan Camping (1124-0253)
Related titles: ◆ Supplement(s): PleinAir Market.
Published by: Edizioni PleinAir, Piazza Imerio 11, Rome, 00165, Italy. http://www.pleinair.it. Circ: 78,000.

796.5 ITA
PLEINAIR MARKET. Text in Italian. 1994. m. (11/yr.). included in Plein Air. adv. bk.rev. **Document type:** *Newsletter, Consumer.* **Description:** Presents technical and commercial information about motorcaravans, motorhomes, caravans, tents, camping and accessories.
Related titles: ◆ Supplement to: PleinAir. ISSN 1124-0202.
Published by: Edizioni PleinAir, Piazza Imerio 11, Rome, 00165, Italy. http://www.pleinair.it. Circ: 78,000.

799.202 USA ISSN 2152-9450
TS537
▼ **POCKET PISTOLS.** Variant title: Harris Outdoor Group Presents Pocket Pistols. Text mainly in English. 2010 (Feb.). a. adv. **Document type:** *Magazine, Consumer.* **Description:** Includes articles and information about new pocket pistols.
Published by: Harris Publications, Inc., 1115 Broadway, New York, NY 10010. TEL 212-807-7100, FAX 212-610-7787, harrismags@aol.com.

799.2 636.5 USA ISSN 1067-0947
THE POINTING DOG JOURNAL. Text in English. 1993. bi-m. USD 26.95 domestic; USD 37.95 in Canada; USD 47.95 elsewhere; USD 5 newsstand/cover (effective 2006). adv. bk.rev.; video rev. 106 p./no. 3 cols./p.; back issues avail. **Document type:** *Magazine, Consumer.* **Description:** Caters to outdoor sports enthusiasts who hunt upland game birds with pointers.
Published by: Village Press, PO Box 509, Traverse City, MI 49685-0968. editor@villagepress.com, http://www.villagepress.com. Ed., R&P Steve Smith. Pub. David G Meisner. Adv. contact James Dietsch. B&W page USD 1,900, color page USD 2,790; trim 8.5 x 11. Circ: 22,095 (paid).

799.1 GBR ISSN 2041-1235
POLE FISHING. Text in English. 1995. m. GBP 29.76 domestic; GBP 50 in Europe; GBP 65 elsewhere; GBP 3.10 newsstand/cover (effective 2010). adv. Website rev. illus. 100 p./no. 3 cols./p.; back issues avail. **Document type:** *Magazine, Consumer.* **Description:** Offers pole anglers tips on bait, angling techniques, and where to fish. Reviews the latest equipment and competitions.
Former titles (until 2009): Advanced Pole Fishing (1473-2874); (until 1999): Advanced Pole Fishing Techniques (1470-0727); David Hall's Advanced Pole Fishing Techniques (1356-6350)
Published by: David Hall Publishing Ltd. (Subsidiary of: DHP Holdings Ltd.), 2 Stephenson Close, Drayton Fields, Daventry, Northants NN11 8RF, United Kingdom. TEL 44-1327-311999, FAX 44-1327-311190, info@dhpub.co.uk, http://www.davidhallpublishing.com. Ed. Jon Arthur TEL 44-1327-315442. Adv. contact Dean Rothery TEL 44-1327-315432. color page GBP 682; 210 x 297.

POLISIDROTT. *see* CRIMINOLOGY AND LAW ENFORCEMENT

799 SVK ISSN 0231-8768
POL'OVNICTVO A RYBARSTVO/HUNTING AND FISHING. Text in Slovak. 1949. m. EUR 16.45; EUR 1.52 newsstand/cover (effective 2011). adv. **Document type:** *Magazine, Consumer.*
—BLDSC (6545.200000).
Published by: (Slovensky Polovnicky Zvaz/Slovak Hunters' Union, Slovensky Rybarsky Zvaz/Slovak Fishermen's Union), Spolocnost 7 Plus s.r.o., Panonska cesta 7, Bratislava 5, 85232, Slovakia. TEL 421-2-32153111, FAX 421-2-32153376, predplatne@7plus.sk, http://www.7plus.sk. Adv. contact Adriena Griesbachova. Circ: 45,000 (paid and controlled).

643.556 GBR ISSN 1748-5185
POOL & SPA INDUSTRY. Text in English. 2005. bi-m. GBP 20 domestic; GBP 30 foreign (effective 2009). adv. back issues avail. **Document type:** *Magazine, Trade.* **Description:** Provides a shop window on products and services within wet leisure sector.
Published by: Waterland Publishing Ltd., 17 Sedgeway Business Park, Witchford, Ely, Cambs CB6 2HY, United Kingdom. TEL 44-1353-666663, FAX 44-1353-666664, info@thewaterlandgroup.com, http://www.thewaterlandgroup.com. Ed. Christina Connor. Circ: 9,000.

643.556 GBR ISSN 1748-5193
POOL & SPA LIFESTYLE. Text in English. 2005. s-a. GBP 6 domestic; GBP 10 foreign (effective 2009). adv. back issues avail. **Document type:** *Magazine, Consumer.* **Description:** Provides information for existing and prospective owners of home swimming pools, hot tubs and related products.
Published by: (British Swimming Pool Federation), Waterland Publishing Ltd., 17 Sedgeway Business Park, Witchford, Ely, Cambs CB6 2HY, United Kingdom. TEL 44-1353-666663, FAX 44-1353-666664, info@thewaterlandgroup.com, http://www.thewaterlandgroup.com. Ed. Christina Connor. Circ: 30,000 (controlled).

796.522 USA ISSN 0098-8154
POTOMAC APPALACHIAN. Text in English. 1932. m. USD 6 (effective 2000). bk.rev. illus. 18 p./no. 3 cols./p.; back issues avail. **Document type:** *Newsletter.* **Description:** Covers hiking, mountaineering and outdoor recreation.
Incorporates (in 1972): Potomac Appalachian Forecast; Formerly (until 1971): Potomac Appalachian Trail Club. Bulletin (0032-5635)
Related titles: Online - full text ed.
Indexed: BRI, SportS.
Published by: Potomac Appalachian Trail Club, Inc., 118 Park St, S E, Vienna, VA 22180-4609. TEL 703-242-0693, FAX 703-242-0968. Ed. Linda Shannon-Beaver. R&P Wilson Riley. Circ: 5,500 (paid).

796.93 USA ISSN 0145-4471
GV854.A1
POWDER. Text in English. 1971. bi-m. USD 10.97 domestic; USD 23.97 in Canada; USD 25.97 elsewhere (effective 2008). adv. illus. back issues avail. **Document type:** *Magazine, Consumer.* **Description:** Designed for advanced skiers seeking the on-mountain experience, motivating them to ski.
Related titles: Online - full text ed.: USD 5 (effective 2008).
Indexed: B04, G06, G07, G08, I05, I07, R03, RGAb, RGPR, S23, SD, SPI, SportS, W03, W05.
—Ingenta. **CCC.**
Published by: Source Interlink Companies, 6420 Wilshire Blvd, 10th Fl, Los Angeles, CA 90048. TEL 323-782-2000, FAX 323-782-2585, dheine@sourceinterlink.com, http://www.sourceinterlinkmedia.com. Eds. Derek Taylor, Tom Bie. Pub. Joshua Weis. Adv. contact Kevin Back. color page USD 10,175; trim 9 x 10.875. Circ: 70,000.

796.93 AUS ISSN 1321-7003
POWDERHOUND. Text in English. 1976. q. AUD 16.20 for 2 yrs. domestic; AUD 21.30 in New Zealand; AUD 23.10 in Asia; AUD 36.90 elsewhere (effective 2008). adv. bk.rev. illus. back issues avail. **Document type:** *Magazine, Consumer.*
Formerly (until 1989): Powderhound Ski Magazine (0726-0474)
Published by: Morrison Media Services Ltd., PO Box 823, Burleigh Heads, QLD 4220, Australia. TEL 61-7-55761388, FAX 61-7-55761527, subs@morrisonmedia.com.au. Ed. Christie Dowling TEL 61-4-04077669. Pub. Peter Morrison. Adv. contact Scott Chapman. color page AUD 2,633; trim 240 x 297.

POWER STROKE. *see* SPORTS AND GAMES—Boats And Boating

796.95 USA ISSN 1097-850X
POWERSPORTS BUSINESS. Text in English. 1997. 16/yr. free in US & Canada; USD 74.95 elsewhere (effective 2008). adv. charts; illus.; stat. back issues avail.; reprints avail. **Document type:** *Magazine, Trade.*
Formed by the merger of (1987-1997): Watercraft Business (1079-3119); Which was formerly: Water Scooter Business (1061-3196); (1985-1997): Snowmobile Business (0883-8259); Which was formerly (1967-1985): Snow Goer Trade (0279-3873)
Related titles: Online - full text ed.
Indexed: B02, B15, B17, B18, G04, G08, I05.
Published by: Affinity Group Inc., 2575 Vista Del Mar, Ventura, CA 93001. TEL 805-667-4100, FAX 805-667-4419, info@affinitygroup.com, http://www.affinitygroup.com. Ed. Neil Pascale TEL 763-383-4400 ext 422. Adv. contact David Voll TEL 763-383-4400 ext 421. Circ: 12,000.

796 GBR ISSN 0269-9427
PRACTICAL CARAVAN; Britain's best selling caravan magazine. Text in English. 1967. m. GBP 39.52 (effective 2009). adv. illus.; maps; mkt. 200 p./no. 4 cols./p.; back issues avail. **Document type:** *Magazine, Consumer.* **Description:** Contains articles regarding caravaning in Britain and abroad. Also includes caravan Q & A, puzzles, a buyers' guide and plenty of tips and advice on all aspects of caravaning.
—CCC.
Published by: Haymarket Publishing Ltd. (Subsidiary of: Haymarket Media Group), Teddington Studios, Broom Rd, Teddington, Middlesex, TW11 9BE, United Kingdom. TEL 44-20-82675629, FAX 44-20-82675725, info@haymarket.com, http://www.haymarket.com. Ed. Nigel Donnelly TEL 44-20-82675767. Circ: 41,515. **Subscr. to:** PO Box 568, Haywards Heath RH16 3XQ, United Kingdom. Haymarket.subs@qss-uk.com, http://www.themagazineshop.com.

629.229 GBR ISSN 1474-1830
PRACTICAL MOTORHOME. Text in English. 2001. m. GBP 34.56 (effective 2009). adv. **Document type:** *Magazine, Consumer.* **Description:** Contains travel features, product reviews, advice and columns, to bring essential information to motorhome owners and potential buyers.
Published by: Haymarket Publishing Ltd. (Subsidiary of: Haymarket Media Group), Teddington Studios, Broom Rd, Teddington, Middlesex, TW11 9BE, United Kingdom. TEL 44-20-82675629, FAX 44-20-82675725, info@haymarket.com, http://www.haymarket.com. Ed. Rob Ganley TEL 44-20-82675535. Circ: 15,225. **Subscr. to:** PO Box 568, Haywards Heath RH16 3XQ, United Kingdom. TEL 44-8456-777800, Haymarket.subs@qss-uk.com, http://www.themagazineshop.com.

799 USA ISSN 1067-5914
PRACTICAL SPORTSMAN; hunting, fishing and the shooting sports. Key Title: Fred Trost's Practical Sportsman. Text in English. bi-m. USD 20 membership. adv. back issues avail. **Document type:** *Magazine, Consumer.* **Description:** Information, news and events of interest to active hunters and sportsmen.
Former titles (until 1992): Fred Trost's Outdoor Digest (0884-9137); (until 1985): Michigan Outdoors Club. Club Digest (8750-1996)
Published by: (Practical Sportsman Club), Practical Sportsman, Inc., 14099 Webster Rd, Bath, MI 48808. TEL 517-641-6701, FAX 517-641-6061. Ed. Jo Ann Cribley. Pub. Fred Trost. Adv. contact Matt Radzialowski. Circ: 25,000. **Subscr. to:** PO Box 1001, Bath, MI 48808-1001.

796 USA
PREDATOR & PREY. Text in English. 5/yr. USD 19.95 (effective 2006). adv. **Document type:** *Magazine, Consumer.* **Description:** Covers hunting techniques and expert advise in various situations and scenarios.
Published by: J N E Publishing, Inc., PO Box 5647, Huntsville, AL 35814. TEL 800-250-1528, http://www.jnepublishing.com/. Ed. Bill Bynum.

799 USA ISSN 1535-3982
PREDATOR XTREME; America's #1 source for year-round hunting and shooting information. Text in English. 1995. bi-m. USD 13.95 (effective 2005). adv. back issues avail. **Document type:** *Magazine, Trade.*
Formerly (until 2001): Varmint Masters Magazine (1097-2951)
Indexed: H20, M02, T02.
Published by: Grand View Media Group, Inc. (Subsidiary of: EBSCO Industries, Inc.), 200 Croft St, Ste 1, Birmingham, AL 35242. TEL 888-431-2877, FAX 205-408-3797, webmaster@grandviewmedia.com, http://www.gvmg.com. Ed. Ralph Lermayer TEL 505-671-4889. Adv. contact Mike Kizzire TEL 205-408-3716. B&W page USD 4,165, color page USD 5,025; trim 7.75 x 10.625. Circ: 76,231.

799.1 AUS ISSN 1834-2388
PRO-ANGLER. Text in English. 2006. s-a. AUD 12.95 (effective 2007). **Document type:** *Magazine, Consumer.*
Published by: Pro-Angler Australia, 489 South Rd, Bentleigh, VIC 3204, Australia. TEL 61-3-9532-1583, FAX 61-3-9532-2604.

796.939 USA ISSN 1536-3953
THE PRO RIDER; the official publication of the American Association of Snowboard Instructors. Text in English. 1998. a. adv.
Indexed: SD.
Published by: American Association of Snowboard Instructors, 133 S. Van Gordon St., Ste. 102, Lakewood, CO 80228. TEL 303-987-2700, aasi@aasi.org, http://www.aasi.org. Eds. John Armstrong, Rebecca W. Ayers. Adv. contact Mark Dorsey.

796.91 NLD ISSN 1879-565X
PRO SKATING. Text in Dutch. 1996. bi-m. EUR 20.50 (effective 2010). **Document type:** *Magazine, Consumer.*
Formerly (until 2009): Schaatsmarathon (1389-126X)
Published by: Media Collectief, Postbus 157, Sneek, 8600 AD, Netherlands. TEL 31-515-438830, FAX 31-515-431361, info@mediacollectief.com, http://www.mediacollectief.com.

PSYCHOLOGY AND SOCIOLOGY OF SPORT: CURRENT SELECTED RESEARCH. *see* PSYCHOLOGY

QUALITY WHITETAILS. *see* CONSERVATION

799 CAN
GV585.3.Q4
QUEBEC (PROVINCE). MINISTERE DE L'ENVIRONNEMENT ET FAUNE. RAPPORT ANNUEL. Text in English. 1980. a. price varies.
Former titles: Quebec (Province). Ministere du Loisir de la Chasse et de la Peche. Rapport Annuel (0229-3811); Quebec (Province). Department of Tourism, Fish and Game. Annual Report (0481-2786)
Published by: (Quebec (Province). Ministere de l'Environnement et Faune), Publications du Quebec, C P 1005, Quebec, PQ G1K 7B5, Canada. TEL 418-643-5150, FAX 418-643-6177.

333.95416 USA
R G S MAGAZINE. Text in English. 1989. 4/yr. USD 20 (effective 2001). adv. bk.rev. 40 p./no.; back issues avail. **Document type:** *Magazine, Consumer.* **Description:** Contains articles and advertisements intended for wildlife conservationists and upland bird hunters.
Published by: Ruffed Grouse Society, 451 McCormick Rd, Coraopolis, PA 15108. TEL 412-262-4044, FAX 412-262-9207, rgshq@aol.com, http://www.ruffedgrousesociety.org. Ed., Adv. contact Paul Carson. B&W page USD 750, color page USD 1,235; trim 10.875 x 8.25. Circ: 25,000.

388.346 910 796.79 USA ISSN 1541-7395
R V AMERICA; the rvers guide to the open road. (Recreational Vehicle) Text in English. 2003. q. USD 8 (effective 2009).
Published by: Passport America, 602 S Main St, Crestview, FL 32536. TEL 800-844-3969, manager@passportamerica.com. Adv. contact Ginny Bauman.

R V EXTREME MAGAZINE. (Recreational Vehicle) *see* TRANSPORTATION

796.54 USA
R V PARK & CAMPGROUND REPORT. (Recreational Vehicle) Text in English. 1981. m. USD 25. adv. bk.rev. **Description:** Covers news in the commercial campground and resort park industry.
Formerly (until 1993): N C O A News
Published by: National Association of R V Parks & Campgrounds, 113 Park Ave, Falls Church, VA 22046-4308. TEL 703-241-8801, FAX 703-241-1004, arvc@erols.com, http://www.gocampingamerica.com. Ed. Dina Lewis. Circ: 3,300.

796.42 GBR ISSN 1351-833X
RACE WALKING RECORD. Text in English. 1941. m. GBP 30 domestic; GBP 40 foreign (effective 2009). back issues avail. **Document type:** *Magazine, Consumer.*
Related titles: E-mail ed.: GBP 20 (effective 2009).
Published by: Race Walking Association, c/o Peter Cassidy, Hufflers, Heard's Ln, Shenfield, Brentwood, CM15 0SF, United Kingdom. TEL 44-1277-220687, RaceWalkingAssociation@btinternet.com, http://www.racewalkingassociation.btinternet.co.uk/. Ed. John Constandinou.

799.2 USA ISSN 1072-9208
RACK. Text in English. 199?. bi-m. USD 20.95 (effective 2011). adv. back issues avail. **Document type:** *Magazine, Consumer.*
Published by: Buckmasters, Inc., 10350 Hwy 80 E, Montgomery, AL 36117. TEL 334-215-3337, FAX 334-215-3535, customerservice@buckmasters.com.

796.552 USA ISSN 1523-4126
QH58
RAILS TO TRAILS MAGAZINE. Text in English. 1985. q. **Document type:** *Magazine, Consumer.*
Formerly (until 1998): Trailblazer (Washington)
Published by: Rails-to-Trails Conservancy, 1100 17th St N W, 10th Fl, Washington, DC 20036, Washington, DC 20036. TEL 202-331-9696, FAX 202-331-9680, railtrails@transact.org. Ed. Keith Laughlin.

798.23 FRA ISSN 1772-8932
RANDONNER A CHEVAL; le magazine des cavaliers d'exterieur. Text in French. 2005. bi-m. back issues avail. **Document type:** *Magazine, Consumer.*
Published by: Mobil Media Presse, 12 Rue du 8 Mai 1945, Fraze, 28160, France.

797.1224 CAN ISSN 1494-9172
RAPID; Canada's whitewater mag. Text in English. 1999. q. CAD 14 domestic; USD 14 in United States; USD 20 elsewhere; USD 3.95 newsstand/cover (effective 2001). adv. **Document type:** *Magazine, Consumer.* **Description:** Provides informative and comprehensive coverage of whitewater paddling news, issues and events.
Related titles: Online - full text ed.
Published by: Rapid Media Inc., PO Box 70, Palmer Rapids, ON K0J 2E0, Canada. TEL 613-758-2042, FAX 613-758-2853, http://www.rapidmedia.com/home.

796.5 CAN ISSN 0845-4418
RATHERBY. Text in English. 9/yr. CAD 10. adv. **Description:** Calendar, folklore and nature magazine for Muskoka Cottagers.
Published by: Keeper Publications, 28 Fairy Ave, P O Box 2849, Huntsville, ON P0A 1K0, Canada. TEL 705-789-6600, FAX 705-789-6600. Circ: 14,000.

799.1 DEU ISSN 1433-1233
DER RAUBFISCH; das Magazin mit Biss. Text in German. 1996. bi-m. EUR 21.50 domestic; EUR 24.50 foreign; EUR 3.70 newsstand/cover (effective 2011). adv. **Document type:** *Magazine, Consumer.*
Published by: Paul Parey Zeitschriftenverlag GmbH, Erich Kaestner Str 2, Singhofen, 56379, Germany. TEL 49-2604-9780, FAX 49-2604-978190, online@paulparey.de, http://www.paulparey.de. Ed. Thomas Wendt. Adv. contact Marianne Wolff.

333.78 NLD ISSN 0165-4179
RECREATIE EN TOERISME; tijdschrift voor management in de leisure. Text in Dutch. 1968. bi-m. EUR 145 (effective 2009). adv. bk.rev. illus. **Document type:** *Magazine, Trade.* **Description:** Offers management information for professionals working in the leisure, tourism, and recreation industries. Offers research, marketing, and political analysis.
Formerly (until 1983): Recreatievoorzieningen (0926-6941); Incorporates (1963-1990): Recreatie (0165-8581)
Indexed: DokStr, HRIS.
—BLDSC (7326.760000), IE, Ingenta.
Published by: Arko Sports Media (Subsidiary of: Arko Uitgeverij BV), Postbus 393, Nieuwegein, 3430 AJ, Netherlands. TEL 31-30-6051090, FAX 31-30-6052618, info@arko.nl, http://www.arko.nl.

RECREATION EXECUTIVE REPORT. *see* LEISURE AND RECREATION

RECREATION NEWS. *see* TRAVEL AND TOURISM

799.1 305.4 AUS ISSN 1449-3012
REEL WOMEN. Text in English. 2004. q. **Document type:** *Magazine, Consumer.*
Published by: Reel Women Fishing and Adventure, PO Box 708, Sanderson, N.T. 0813, Australia. http://www.reelwomen.com.

796 SWE ISSN 1654-2169
REFEREE; domarmagazin. Text in Swedish. 2007. 10/yr. SEK 495 (effective 2007). **Document type:** *Magazine, Consumer.*
Published by: Sport Marketing, Norre Esplanaden 14, Sala, 73330, Sweden. TEL 46-224-86500, info@refereemagazin.se. Ed., Pub. Mattias Johanssen TEL 46-70-9747310.

REGARDS - SPELEO INFO. *see* EARTH SCIENCES—Geology

796.54 CAN ISSN 0316-1226
REPERTOIRE DES CAMPS DE VACANCES/DIRECTORY OF ACCREDITED CAMPS. Text in English, French. 1963. a. free. adv. **Document type:** *Directory.*
Published by: Quebec Camping Association, 4545 ave Pierre de Coubertin, Montreal, PQ H1V 3R2, Canada. TEL 514-252-3113, FAX 514-252-1650. R&P Louis Jean. Adv. contact Sophie Latour.

796 FRA ISSN 1958-5101
RESEAU NATIONAL DES SPORTS DE NATURE. LA LETTRE. Text in French. 2004. m. **Document type:** *Newsletter.*
Media: Online - full text.
Published by: Pole Ressources National Sports de Nature, B P 38, Vallon Pont d'Arc, 07150, France. TEL 33-4-75881510, prn.sportsnature@jeunesse-sports.gouv.fr.

799.2 636.5 USA ISSN 1084-4198
THE RETRIEVER JOURNAL. Text in English. 1997. bi-m. USD 26.95 domestic; USD 37.95 in Canada; USD 46.95 elsewhere; USD 5.50 per issue (effective 2006). adv. bk.rev.; video rev. 72 p./no.; back issues avail. **Document type:** *Magazine, Consumer.*
Published by: Village Press, PO Box 509, Traverse City, MI 49685-0968. TEL 616-946-3712, FAX 616-946-3289, http://www.villagepress.com. Ed., R&P Steve Smith. Pub. Robert Goff. adv.: B&W page USD 1,625, color page USD 2,395; trim 11 x 8.5. Circ: 12,300.

796.552 DEU
REUTLINGER ALPINIST; Magazin der Sektion Reutlingen im Deutschen Alpenverein. Text in German. 1984. q. bibl.; charts; stat. index. **Document type:** *Magazine, Consumer.* **Description:** Description of mountain adventures, climbing and tourist excursions.
Published by: Deutscher Alpenverein, Sektion Reutlingen e.V., Weingaertnerstr 6, Reutlingen, 72764, Germany. TEL 49-7121-330940, FAX 49-7121-380070, alpenverein@dav-reutlingen.de, http://www.cnsweb.de:8080/cms/sites/dav/dyncon?cid=1&sid=0&usr=0.

796.42 PRT
REVISTA ATLETISMO; mundo da corrida. Text in Portuguese. 1981. m. EUR 43.89 in Europe; EUR 59.36 elsewhere (effective 2001). adv. bk.rev. 80 p./no.; **Document type:** *Magazine.* **Description:** Covers track and field.
Address: Calcada da Tapada, 67A, Lisbon, 1349-012, Portugal. TEL 351-21-3616160, FAX 351-21-3616169, revistas-ra@clix.pt. Ed. Antonio Manuel Fernandes. Adv. contact Antonio Campos. Circ: 5,000.

799.1 BRA ISSN 1413-6554
REVISTA PESCADOR. Text in Portuguese. 1996. m. BRL 5.90 newsstand/cover (effective 2006). adv. **Document type:** *Magazine, Consumer.*
Published by: Editora Escala Ltda., Av Prof Ida Kolb, 551, Casa Verde, Sao Paulo, 02518-000, Brazil. TEL 55-11-38552100, FAX 55-11-38579643, escala@escala.com.br, http://www.escala.com.br.

799.2 FRA ISSN 1961-0890
LA REVUE NATIONALE DE LA CHASSE. Text in French. 1947. m. EUR 4.50 newsstand/cover (effective 2008). adv. illus.; bibl. **Document type:** *Magazine, Consumer.* **Description:** Publishes articles of interest to the hunting enthusiast.
Formerly (until 2001): La Chasse (1276-1303); Which superseded in part (in 1997): La Revue Nationale de la Chasse (0035-3752); Which incorporated (1936-1952): Sauvagine (1142-4842)
Related titles: ◆ Supplement(s): Grand Gibier. ISSN 1285-3909.
Published by: Mondadori France, 1 Rue du Colonel Pierre-Avia, Paris, Cedex 15 75754, France. TEL 33-1-41332225, http://www.mondadori.fr. Circ: 62,521 (paid).

796.552 FRA ISSN 0241-0311
REVUE PYRENEENNE. Text in French. 1953. q. EUR 12.50 (effective 2009). adv. bk.rev. **Document type:** *Magazine, Consumer.*
Published by: Club Alpin Francais* Section Bordeaux, 3 Rue de l'Orient, Toulouse, 31000, France. http://clubalpin.crmipy.free.fr. Ed. Stienne Noel. Circ: 5,000.

799.2 DEU ISSN 0171-0796
RHEINISCH-WESTFAELISCHER JAEGER. Text in German. 1947. m. EUR 52.80 (effective 2010). adv. back issues avail. **Document type:** *Magazine, Consumer.*
Published by: (Landesjagdverband Nordrhein - Westfalen e.V.), Landwirtschaftsverlag GmbH, Huelsebrockstr 2, Muenster, 48165, Germany. TEL 49-2501-27500, FAX 49-2501-27551, zentrale@lv-h.de, http://www.lv-h.de. Ed. Matthias Kruse. Adv. contact Friedrich Deckert. Circ: 63,848 (paid and controlled).

796.552 USA
RIDGELINE. Text in English. bi-m.
Published by: Superior Hiking Trail Association, 731 Seventh Ave., Two Harbors, MN 55616-0004. Ed. Nancy Odden.

796 USA ISSN 0162-3583
SK274
RIFLE; the sporting firearms journal. Text in English. 1968. bi-m. USD 19.97 domestic; USD 26 foreign (effective 2010). adv. bk.rev. charts; illus.; mkt.; pat.; stat. index, cum.index every 2 yrs. 96 p./no. 3 cols./p.; reprints avail. **Document type:** *Magazine, Consumer.*
Formerly: Rifle Magazine (0035-5216)
Published by: Wolfe Publishing Co., 2625 Stearman Rd., Ste. A, Prescott, AZ 86301-6155. TEL 928-445-7810, FAX 928-778-5124. Ed. Dave Scovill. Pub. Mark Harris. Adv. contact Don Polacek. B&W page USD 2,667, color page USD 3,410. Circ: 113,000.

799 USA
RIFLE & SHOTGUN ANNUAL. Text in English. a. adv. illus. **Document type:** *Magazine, Consumer.*
Published by: Source Interlink Companies, 6420 Wilshire Blvd, 10th Fl, Los Angeles, CA 90048. TEL 323-782-2000, FAX 323-782-2585, dheine@sourceinterlink.com, http://www.sourceinterlinkmedia.com.

799.202 790.023 USA ISSN 1933-2750
RIFLE'S HANDLOADER AMMUNITION RELOADING JOURNAL. Text in English. 1966. bi-m. USD 22.97 domestic; USD 29 foreign; USD 4.99 newsstand/cover (effective 2007). adv. bk.rev. charts; illus.; mkt.; tr.lit. cum.index. 104 p./no. 3 cols./p.; reprints avail. **Document type:** *Magazine, Consumer.*
Formerly: Handloader (0017-7393)
Published by: Wolfe Publishing Co., 2625 Stearman Rd., Ste. A, Prescott, AZ 86301-6155. TEL 928-445-7810, FAX 928-778-5124. Ed. Dave Scovill. Pub. Mark Harris. Adv. contact Don Polacek. B&W page USD 2,667, color page USD 3,410. Circ: 110,000 (paid).

RING JUNGER BUENDE. MITTEILUNGEN. *see* CHILDREN AND YOUTH—About

796.3205 AUS ISSN 1034-2346
RIPTIDE; a mag about bodyboarding. Text in English. 1989. bi-m. AUD 42.65 domestic; AUD 72.90 in New Zealand; AUD 83.70 in Asia & the Pacific; AUD 121.70 elsewhere (effective 2008). adv. music rev.; video rev. illus. back issues avail. **Document type:** *Magazine, Consumer.* **Description:** Dedicated to covering every aspect of the bodyboarding lifestyle in Australia.
Related titles: Supplement(s): Riptide. Photo Annual. ISSN 1329-4709.
Published by: Morrison Media Services Ltd., PO Box 823, Burleigh Heads, QLD 4220, Australia. TEL 61-7-55761388, FAX 61-7-55761527, subs@morrisonmedia.com.au, http://www.morrisonmedia.com.au. Ed. Nick Lawrence. Pub. Peter Morrison. Adv. contact Warren Randell TEL 61-2-99760361. color page AUD 2,226; trim 210 x 297.

333.7845 USA ISSN 1098-5956
RIVER; the journal of paddlesports and river adventure. Text in English. 1998. 8/yr. USD 23.95 domestic; CAD 43.87 in Canada; USD 3.95 newsstand/cover domestic; CAD 4.50 newsstand/cover in Canada. adv. bk.rev. illus. **Document type:** *Magazine, Consumer.* **Description:** Covers America's wild rivers for water lovers, from conservationists to adventure travelers.
Published by: MacLeod Publishing, LLC., PO Box 15637, Hattiesburg, MS 39404-5637. TEL 406-582-5440. Ed., Pub. Mike MacLeod. R&P Dena Foltz. Adv. contact Graham Neale. Circ: 50,000. **Dist. by:** Curtis CIRC Company, 641 Lexington Ave, New York, NY 10022. TEL 212-705-4600, FAX 212-705-4666.

796.522 ITA ISSN 1825-8743
LA RIVISTA. Text in Italian. 1874. bi-m. free to members; includes Lo Scarpone. adv. bk.rev. abstr.; bibl.; charts; illus.; stat.; tr.lit. index. **Document type:** *Magazine, Consumer.*
Former titles (until 2003): Club Alpino Italiano. La Rivista (0392-9221); (until 1978): Club Alpino Italiano. Rivista Mensile (0009-9511); (until 1944): Le Alpi (0392-9272); (until 1938): Centro Alpinistico Italiano. Rivista (0392-9299); (until 1937): Club Alpino Italiano. Rivista (0392-9280); (until 1907): Club Alpino Italiano. Rivista Mensile (0392-9302); (until 1884): Rivista Alpina Italiana (0392-9310); (until 1875): Alpinista (1825-8735)
Related titles: ◆ Supplement(s): Lo Scarpone. ISSN 1590-7716.
Indexed: BAS, GeoRef, SpeleolAb.
Published by: Club Alpino Italiano, Via Petrella 19, Milan, MI 20124, Italy. TEL 39-02-2057231, FAX 39-02-205723201, http://www.cai.it. Circ: 200,000.

796.552 ITA ISSN 0393-4217
RIVISTA DELLA MONTAGNA. Abbreviated title: R d M. Text in Italian. 1970. bi-m. EUR 25 (effective 2008). adv. bk.rev. illus. index, cum.index. back issues avail. **Document type:** *Magazine, Consumer.* **Description:** Giorgio/Mantovani.
Related titles: Online - full text ed.
Published by: C D A Vivalda Editori Srl, Via Invorio 24-A, Turin, TO 10146, Italy. TEL 39-011-7720444, FAX 39-011-7732170, abbonamenti@cdavivalda.it, http://www.cdavivalda.it.

796.42 USA ISSN 0739-3784
ROAD RACE MANAGEMENT NEWSLETTER. Text in English. 1982. 11/yr. USD 97 domestic; USD 112 foreign (effective 2001). adv. back issues avail. **Document type:** *Newsletter.* **Description:** For sponsors, directors and organizers of long-distance running events.
Indexed: SD, SportS.
Published by: Road Race Management, Inc., 4904 Glen Cove Pkwy, Bethesda, MD 20816-3006. TEL 301-320-6865, FAX 301-320-9164. Ed., Pub. Phil Stewart. Circ: 500.

796.522 AUS ISSN 1034-215X
ROCK (PRAHRAN); Australia's climbing magazine. Text in English. 1978-1980; resumed 1983. q. AUD 35.95 domestic; AUD 49.95 foreign; AUD 8.99 per issue (effective 2009). adv. back issues avail. **Document type:** *Magazine, Consumer.* **Description:** Covers rock climbing.
Formerly (until 1987): Australian Rock (0816-2425)
Published by: Wild Publications Pty. Ltd., PO Box 415, Prahran, VIC 3181, Australia. TEL 61-3-98268482, FAX 61-3-98263787, http://www.wild.com.au. Ed. Mr. Ross Taylor. Adv. contact Stephen Hamilton.

796.552 USA
ROCK & GROOVE. Text in English. 1997. irreg. illus.
Published by: Rock and Groove, 3333 24th St., San Francisco, CA 94110-3869.

796.552 USA ISSN 0885-5722
ROCK & ICE; the climber's magazine. Text in English. 1984. 8/yr. USD 29.95 combined subscription domestic (print & online eds.) (effective 2010). adv. bk.rev. charts; illus. back issues avail.; reprints avail. **Document type:** *Magazine, Consumer.* **Description:** Covers rock climbing, ice climbing and mountaineering worldwide.
Related titles: Online - full text ed.
—Ingenta.
Published by: Big Stone Publishing, 417 Main St, Unit N, Carbondale, CO 81623. TEL 970-704-1442, FAX 970-963-4965, http://www.bigstonepub.com. Pub. Duane Raleigh TEL 970-704-1442 ext 26. Adv. contact Shannon Votruba TEL 970-704-1442 ext 23. B&W page USD 2,640, color page USD 3,740; trim 9 x 10.875.

796 CAN
ROCKIES; rocky mountain living. Text in English. q. CAD 18 domestic; CAD 24 in United States; CAD 28 elsewhere; USD 3.95 newsstand/cover (effective 2002). adv. **Document type:** *Magazine, Consumer.* **Description:** Focuses on outdoor recreation, land-use and wildlife for those living in, visiting, or dreaming of the Rockies.
Published by: Elk Valley Publishing, 112 2nd Ave., Box 2650, Fernie, BC V0B 1M0, Canada. TEL 250-423-6693, FAX 250-423-6874. Ed. Steve Short. Pub. Bernie Palmer.

S

799 USA ISSN 1056-0114
ROCKY MOUNTAIN GAME & FISH. Text in English. 19??. m. USD 12 domestic; USD 25 in Canada; USD 27 elsewhere (effective 2011). adv. illus. **Document type:** *Magazine, Consumer.* **Description:** Informs sportsmen of hunting and fishing, as well as environmental and conservation issues in the Rocky Mountain states.
Related titles: Online - full text ed.; ◆ Regional ed(s).: Game & Fish; ◆ Louisiana Game & Fish. ISSN 0744-3692; ◆ Florida Game & Fish. ISSN 0889-3322; ◆ Alabama Game & Fish. ISSN 0279-6783; ◆ Mississippi-Louisiana Game & Fish. ISSN 1947-2358; ◆ North Carolina Game & Fish. ISSN 0897-8816; ◆ South Carolina Game & Fish. ISSN 0897-9154; ◆ West Virginia Game & Fish. ISSN 0897-9162; ◆ Missouri Game & Fish. ISSN 0889-3799; ◆ New York Game & Fish. ISSN 0897-9189; ◆ California Game & Fish. ISSN 1056-0122; ◆ Great Plains Game & Fish. ISSN 1055-6532; ◆ Illinois Game & Fish. ISSN 0897-9014; ◆ Indiana Game & Fish. ISSN 0897-8980; ◆ Iowa Game & Fish. ISSN 0897-9197; ◆ Mid-Atlantic Game & Fish. ISSN 1055-6540; ◆ Oklahoma Game & Fish. ISSN 0746-6013; ◆ Ohio Game & Fish. ISSN 0897-9170; ◆ Pennsylvania Game & Fish. ISSN 0897-8808; ◆ Virginia Game & Fish. ISSN 0897-8794; ◆ Washington - Oregon Game & Fish. ISSN 1056-0106; New England Game & Fish. ISSN 0897-8972. 1988. USD 12 domestic; USD 25 in Canada; USD 27 elsewhere (effective 2010).
Published by: Intermedia Outdoors, Inc., 512 7th Ave, 11th Fl, New York, NY 10018. TEL 212-852-6682, 800-260-6397, FAX 212-302-4472, customerservice@imoutdoors.com, http://www.imoutdoorsmedia.com. Ed. Ken Dunwoody. Pub., Adv. contact Peter Gross.

688.7912 USA ISSN 1542-1023
RODMAKER MAGAZINE. Text in English. 1998. bi-m. USD 24.95 (effective 2002).
Address: P. O. Box 1322, High Point, NC 27261. TEL 336-882-3226, rodmaker@earthlink.net. Ed. Tom Kirkman.

ROMANIAN TRAVEL GUIDE. *see* TRAVEL AND TOURISM

799.1 NLD ISSN 1568-2013
DE ROOFVIS. Text in Dutch. 2000. bi-m. adv. **Document type:** *Magazine, Consumer.*
Published by: Publishing House & Facilities B.V., Postbus 119, Doetinchem, 7000 AC, Netherlands. TEL 31-314-340150, FAX 31-314-346675, info@publishinghouse.nl, http://www.publishinghouse.nl. adv.: B&W page EUR 775, color page EUR 1,275; 184 x 252. Circ: 12,500.

799.2 RUS ISSN 1682-6981
ROSSIISKAYA OKHOTNICH'YA GAZETA. Text in Russian. 1994. w. **Document type:** *Newspaper, Consumer.* **Description:** Covers activities of hunting associations, materials about the protection of Russia's wildlife and plant life.
Related titles: Online - full text ed.: ISSN 1682-699X.
Published by: Moskovskii Komsomolets, ul 1905 goda, dom 7, Moscow, 123995, Russian Federation. TEL 7-095-2532094, podpiska@mk.ru.

799.1 NLD
ROVERS. Text in Dutch. 8/yr. EUR 49.50; EUR 6.95 newsstand/cover (effective 2011). adv. **Document type:** *Magazine, Consumer.*
Published by: Vipmedia Publishing en Services, Takkebijsters 57a, Breda, 4817 BL, Netherlands. TEL 31-76-5301721, FAX 31-76-5144531, info@vipmedia.nl, http://www.vipmedia.nl. Ed. Pierre Bronsgeest. Adv. contact John Huussen TEL 31-76-5301725.

796.42 AUS ISSN 1832-7079
RUN FOR YOUR LIFE. Variant title: R 4 L Y. Text in English. 2005. bi-m. AUD 70; AUD 7.50 per issue (effective 2009). adv. back issues avail. **Document type:** *Magazine, Trade.* **Description:** Provides information for runners at all levels, from beginners through to the elite.
Indexed: SD.
Address: 6A Fenner St, Downer, ACT 2602, Australia. TEL 61-431-412478. Ed. Andrew Letherby. Pub. Dr. Daniel Green. adv.: page AUD 2,290; 210 x 297. Circ: 15,000.

796.42 NLD ISSN 1879-5102
▼ **RUN2DAY MAGAZINE.** Text in Dutch. 2009. s-a. EUR 10 (effective 2010). adv. **Document type:** *Magazine, Consumer.*
Published by: Supertroopers, Postbus 69654, Amsterdam, 1060 CS, Netherlands. TEL 31-20-4085511, FAX 31-20-4082280. Ed., Pub. Peter van Rhoon. Adv. contact Patrick Holland. Circ: 50,000.

796.42 NLD ISSN 1382-3779
RUNNER'S WORLD. Text in Dutch. 1982. m. (11/yr.). EUR 52; EUR 5.25 newsstand/cover (effective 2010). adv. **Document type:** *Magazine, Consumer.*
Former titles (until 1995): Runners (0929-8983); (until 1985): European Runners Magazine (0168-2288)
Published by: Weekbladpers Tijdschriften, Raamgracht 4, Amsterdam, 1011 KK, Netherlands. TEL 31-20-5518711, FAX 31-20-5518638, http://www.weekbladpers.nl. adv.: color page EUR 3,385; 215 x 285. Circ: 36,393.

796.42 FRA ISSN 1962-445X
RUNNER'S WORLD. Text in French. 2008. bi-m. EUR 24.75 (effective 2008). **Document type:** *Magazine, Consumer.*
Published by: Euro Services Internet, 60 rue Vitruve, Paris, 75020, France. FAX 33-1-55253101.

796.42 USA ISSN 0892-5038
RUNNING JOURNAL. Text in English. 1984. m. USD 19.95 domestic; USD 29.95 foreign (effective 2007). adv. **Document type:** *Magazine, Consumer.* **Description:** Covers running in the Southeast, along with race walking, bi- and triathloning. Includes a calendar of events covering 13 states.
Formerly (until 1986): Carolina Runner (0883-1629); Incorporated (in 198?): Racing South Magazine (8750-507X); Which was formerly: Racing South (0164-5129)
Published by: Media Services Group, Inc., PO Box 157, Greeneville, TN 37744. TEL 423-638-4177, FAX 423-638-3328. Circ: 15,000.

796.42 FRA ISSN 2108-8276
▼ **RUNNING POUR ELLES.** Text in French. 2010. q. **Document type:** *Magazine, Consumer.*
Published by: Editions Riva, 16 Rue de la Fontaine-au-Roi, Paris, 75011, France. TEL 33-1-40218200, FAX 33-1-40210021.

RUNNING WILD; the trailrunner's magazine. *see* LEISURE AND RECREATION

796.42 AUS ISSN 1440-9062
RUNNING WRITING. Text in English. 1997. m. AUD 25. back issues avail. **Description:** Contains articles about and interviews with runners and track and field athletes by a variety of authors.
Related titles: Online - full text ed.
Address: 41 Chippindall Ct, Theodore, ACT 2905, Australia. TEL 61-6-2926553, ewen@atrax.net.au.

799.1 DEU ISSN 0863-4750
RUTE UND ROLLE; der deutsche Angler Magazin. Text in German. 1949. m. EUR 36; EUR 3.20 newsstand/cover (effective 2007). adv. **Document type:** *Magazine, Consumer.*
Former titles (until 1990): Deutscher Angelsport (0323-3472); (until 1956): Fischen und Angeln (0323-6099); (until 1954): Fischen und Angeln. Fuer Angler und Aquarianer (0863-1441)
Related titles: Online - full text ed.
Published by: Moeller Neue Medien Verlags GmbH, Heidenkampsweg 76A, Hamburg, 20097, Germany. TEL 49-40-2361300, FAX 49-40-23613022. Ed., Adv. contact Matthias Six. Pub. Eugen Karau. B&W page EUR 3,200, color page EUR 5,360; trim 196 x 260. Circ: 63,961 (paid and controlled).

RYBARSTVI. *see* FISH AND FISHERIES

799.1 CZE ISSN 1802-7520
RYBOLOV. Text in Czech. 2000. m. CZK 270; CZK 45 newsstand/cover (effective 2009). **Document type:** *Magazine, Consumer.*
Formerly (until 2001): Sportovni Rybolov (1213-015X)
Published by: Vaclav Ehrlich, Kozinova 1, Podebrady, 290 01, Czech Republic. TEL 420-603-289635.

796.552 ZAF ISSN 1683-7444
S A MOUNTAIN MAGAZINE. (South Africa) Variant title: South Africa Mountain Magazine. Text in English. 2002. q. ZAR 70 domestic; ZAR 150 in Africa; ZAR 200 elsewhere (effective 2006). **Document type:** *Magazine, Consumer.* **Description:** Covers climbing, mountaineering and trekking in South Africa and around the world.
Published by: Blue Mountain Publishers, Suite 88, Private Bag X7, Sea Point, Cape Town 8060, South Africa. info@bluemountainpublishers.com, http://www.samountainmag.com/bluemountain/. Ed. Tony Lourens.

333.95416 799.2 ZAF
S.A. WILD & JAG/S.A. GAME & HUNT. (South Africa) Text in Afrikaans, English. 1994. m. ZAR 115 domestic; ZAR 211 foreign; ZAR 12 newsstand/cover (effective 2000). adv. **Document type:** *Magazine, Consumer.* **Description:** Covers game ranching, hunting, and wildlife conservation.
Formerly: S.A. Wild
Indexed: ISAP.
Published by: Jan Louis Enterprises, PO Box 4722, Pretoria, 0001, South Africa. TEL 27-12-320-0691, FAX 27-12-320-5561. Ed. Jan L van der Walt. Circ: 12,000 (paid).

797.32 CAN ISSN 1913-1690
S B C SURF. (Snow Board Canada) Variant title: Canada's New Surf Magazine. Text in English. 2007. s-a. **Document type:** *Magazine, Consumer.*
Published by: S B C Media, 2255 B Queen St E, Ste 3266, Toronto, ON M4E 1G3, Canada. TEL 416-406-2400, FAX 416-406-0656, info@sbcmedia.com, http://www.sbcmedia.com.

796.5 790.01 GBR ISSN 1757-7276
S G B SPORTS AND OUTDOOR. (Sports Goods Buyer) Text in English. 1930. m. GBP 76 domestic; GBP 98 in Europe; GBP 128 elsewhere; free to qualified personnel (effective 2009). adv. bk.rev.; film rev. back issues avail. **Document type:** *Magazine, Trade.* **Description:** Provides news and trends from core sports trade to action sports and emerging style.
Incorporates (2002-2007): S G B Outdoor (1743-1425); Which was formerly (1997-2001): Outdoor Update (1475-8628); Former titles (until 2007): S G B UK (1465-6930); (until 1999): Harpers Sports & Leisure (0263-8134); (until 1982): Harpers Sports (0141-142X); (until 1978): Harpers Sports and Camping
Related titles: Online - full text ed.: free to qualified personnel (effective 2009); ◆ Supplement(s): S G B UK - Guide to the Trade. ISSN 1466-0709.
—CCC.
Published by: Datateam Publishing Ltd, 15a London Rd, Maidstone, Kent ME16 8LY, United Kingdom. TEL 44-1622-687031, FAX 44-1622-757646, info@datateam.co.uk, http://www.datateam.co.uk. Ed. Jon Bruford TEL 44-1584-877177. Pub. Paul Ryder TEL 44-1622-699105. adv.: color page GBP 1,400; trim 229 x 306.

796 GBR ISSN 1466-0709
S G B UK - GUIDE TO THE TRADE. (Sports Goods Buyer) Text in English. 19??. a. GBP 76 per issue (effective 2009). **Document type:** *Handbook/Manual/Guide, Trade.* **Description:** Provides a guide to the entire UK sports industry and provides detailed information on UK buying groups and multiples; manufacturers and distributors, brand names and their suppliers, equipment, wholesalers, independent sales agents, trade and sports associations, governing bodies and exhibition organizers.
Former titles (until 1999): Harpers Sports & Leisure Guide to the Trade (1368-048X); (until 1983): Harpers Guide to the Sports Trade
Related titles: ◆ Supplement to: S G B Sports and Outdoor. ISSN 1757-7276.
Published by: Datateam Publishing Ltd, 15a London Rd, Maidstone, Kent ME16 8LY, United Kingdom. TEL 44-1622-687031, FAX 44-1622-757646, info@datateam.co.uk, http://www.datateam.co.uk.

799 USA ISSN 1081-8618
S H O T BUSINESS; shooting, hunting & outdoor trade. (Shooting, Hunting & Outdoor Trade) Text in English. 1993. m. USD 25; USD 5 per issue; free domestic to qualified personnel (effective 2011). adv. bk.rev. illus. reprints avail. **Document type:** *Magazine, Trade.* **Description:** Designed to equip retailers, manufacturers and sales representatives with expert "real time" information that will help them run better, more profitable businesses.
Indexed: B01, B07.
—CCC.
Published by: (National Shooting Sports Foundation), Bonnier Corp. (Subsidiary of: Bonnier Group), 2 Park Ave, 9th Fl, New York, NY 10016. TEL 212-779-5047, FAX 212-779-5108, http://www.bonniercorp.com. Ed. Slaton L White.

797 AUS
S W: SURFING WORLD. Text in English. 1962. bi-m. AUD 59.95 domestic; AUD 150 foreign (effective 2008). adv. **Document type:** *Magazine, Consumer.* **Description:** Provides articles and photographs on surfing.
Former titles (until 2001): Australian Surfing World (1322-5375); (until 1978): Surfing World
Published by: Breaker Publications, PO Box 747, Manly, NSW 2095, Australia. Ed. Adam Blakey. Adv. contact Doug Lees. page AUD 2,995; trim 230 x 297.

799.2 USA
SAFARI CLUB INTERNATIONAL. RECORD BOOK. Variant title: Safari Club International Record Book of Animals. Text in English. 19??. irreg. (in 3 vols.). adv. **Document type:** *Monographic series, Consumer.* **Description:** Provides information on hundreds of big game species, including behavior, habitat, distribution, hunting pointers, and listings of record-setting animals confirmed by SCI Master Measurers.
Published by: Safari Club International, 4800 W Gates Pass Rd, Tucson, AZ 85745.

799.2 USA ISSN 0199-5316
SK1
SAFARI MAGAZINE. Text in English. 1975. 7/yr. free to members (effective 2011). adv. bk.rev. illus. back issues avail. **Document type:** *Magazine, Consumer.* **Description:** Features big game hunt stories, SCI news-activities related to conservation, new product reviews, hunting reports, club-convention reports.
Published by: Safari Club International, 4800 W Gates Pass Rd, Tucson, AZ 85745. TEL 520-620-1220, FAX 520-622-1205. Adv. contact Angela Sagi TEL 910-875-8781.

799.2 USA ISSN 1085-1011
SK1
SAFARI TIMES. Text in English. 198?. m. free to members (effective 2011). adv. back issues avail. **Document type:** *Newspaper, Consumer.* **Description:** Covers hunting trends, issues in the sport, tips and news about SCI programs and many SCI Chapter activities.
Published by: Safari Club International, 4800 W Gates Pass Rd, Tucson, AZ 85745. TEL 520-620-1220, FAX 520-622-1205. Adv. contact Angela Sagi TEL 910-875-8781.

799.1 CAN ISSN 0703-5810
SALMO SALAR. Text in English. 1976. bi-m.
Published by: Association des Pecheurs Sportifs de Saumons du Quebec, 7525 place Martin, Charlesbourg, PQ, Canada.

799.1 USA ISSN 0029-3431
SALMON TROUT STEELHEADER. Text in English. 1967. 10/yr. USD 24.95 in North America to individuals (effective 2007). adv. bk.rev. illus. reprints avail. **Document type:** *Magazine, Consumer.* **Description:** For serious fishermen. Covers fishing techniques, good fishing locations, and conservation. Includes fly tying instructions and in-depth fishing articles.
Formerly: Northwest Salmon - Trout Steelheader
Published by: Frank Amato Publications, Inc, 4040 S E Wister St, Portland, OR 97222. TEL 503-653-8108, 800-541-9498. Ed. Mr. Nick S Amato. Pub. Mr. Frank W Amato. R&P Ms. Kim Koch. Adv. contacts Mr. David Eng, Mr. Robert Crandall. B&W page USD 1,440, color page USD 1,755; trim 10.875 x 8.125. Circ: 23,604 (paid).

799.1 USA ISSN 0036-3618
SH401
SALT WATER SPORTSMAN. Text in English. 1939. m. USD 18 domestic (print or online ed.); USD 30 in Canada; USD 50 elsewhere (effective 2011). adv. bk.rev. illus. index. back issues avail.; reprints avail. **Document type:** *Magazine, Consumer.* **Description:** Covers marine sport fishing.
Related titles: Diskette ed.; Online - full text ed.
Indexed: A11, A22, C05, CPerI, ConsI, G06, G07, G08, I05, M01, M02, PMR, SD, SportS, T02, U01.
—CCC.
Published by: (Salt Water Sportsman, Inc.), Bonnier Corp. (Subsidiary of: Bonnier Group), 2 Park Ave, 9th Fl, New York, NY 10016. TEL 212-779-5047, FAX 212-779-5108, http://www.bonniercorp.com. Ed. John Brownlee. Pub. Dave Morel.

799.1 AUS
SALTWATER FISHING; tips & techniques straight from the experts. Text in English. bi-m. AUD 33.39; AUD 7.95 newsstand/cover (effective 2008). back issues avail. **Document type:** *Magazine, Consumer.* **Description:** Provides information on key locations, latest gear, best techniques and features on saltwater angling.
Published by: Express Publications Pty. Ltd., 2-4 Stanley St, Locked Bag 111, Silverwater, NSW 2168, Australia. TEL 61-2-97413800, 800-801-647, FAX 61-2-97378017, subs@magstore.com.au, http://www.expresspublications.com.au. **Subscr. to:** ISubscribe Pty Ltd., 25 Lime St, Ste 303, Level 3, Sydney, NSW 2000, Australia. TEL 61-2-92621722, FAX 61-2-92625044, info@isubscribe.com.au, http://www.isubscribe.com.au.

797.178 028.5 ZAF ISSN 1605-7759
SALTWATER GIRL. Text in English. 2000. 10/yr. ZAR 175 (effective 2006). adv. **Document type:** *Magazine, Consumer.*
Related titles: ◆ Supplement(s): Saltwater Girl Surf Magazine. ISSN 1818-9253.
Published by: Atoll Media, PO Box 208, Umgeni Park, Durban 4098, South Africa. TEL 27-31-2631603, FAX 27-31-2362068. Ed. Lari Brown. Pub. John McCarthy. adv.: page ZAR 19,500; trim 210 x 275. Circ: 45,360.

797.178 ZAF ISSN 1818-9253
SALTWATER GIRL SURF MAGAZINE. Text in English. 2006. q. adv. **Document type:** *Magazine, Consumer.*
Related titles: ◆ Supplement to: Saltwater Girl. ISSN 1605-7759.
Published by: Atoll Media, PO Box 208, Umgeni Park, Durban 4098, South Africa. TEL 27-31-2631603, FAX 27-31-2362068. Pub. John McCarthy. Adv. contact Joanna Carlson.

SANFORD EVANS GOLD BOOK OF SNOWMOBILE DATA AND USED PRICES. *see* SPORTS AND GAMES—Abstracting, Bibliographies, Statistics

799.2 AUT ISSN 0036-2875
ST. HUBERTUS; Oesterreichs unabhaengiges Magazin fuer Jagd, Fischerei und Natur. Text in German. 1915. m. EUR 59 domestic; EUR 73 foreign (effective 2004). adv. bk.rev. illus. cum.index. **Document type:** *Magazine, Consumer.*

Published by: Oesterreichischer Agrarverlag GmbH, Sturzgasse 1a, Vienna, N 1140, Austria. TEL 43-1-981770, FAX 43-1-98177111, office@agrarverlag.at. Ed. Rainer Wernisch. Adv. contact Ingrid Urban. B&W page EUR 3,106, color page EUR 3,856; trim 175 x 260. Circ: 15,000 (paid and controlled).

799 FRA ISSN 1775-0253
LA SAUVAGINE. Text in French. 1935. m. EUR 38 (effective 2008). adv. bk.rev. **Document type:** *Magazine.*
Former titles (until 1998): La Sauvagine et Sa Chasse (0751-9907); (until 1967): La Sauvagine (1142-4834); Which superseded in part (in 1997): La Revue Nationale de La Casse (0035-3752); Which incorporated (1936-1952): La Sauvagine (1142-4842)
Published by: Association Nationale des Chasseurs de Gibier d'Eau, 4 Av. des Chasseurs, Paris, 75017, France. TEL 33-1-47646490, FAX 33-1-46228253, ancge@ancge.asso.fr. Ed. Raymond Pouget. Circ: 30,000.

796.93 ITA ISSN 1590-7716
LO SCARPONE. Text in Italian. 1931. m. free to members; included with Rivista del Club Alpino Italiano. adv. **Document type:** *Newsletter, Consumer.*
Related titles: ◆ Supplement to: La Rivista. ISSN 1825-8743.
Indexed: GeoRef.
Published by: Club Alpino Italiano, Via Petrella 19, Milan, MI 20124, Italy. TEL 39-02-2057231, FAX 39-02-205723201, http://www.cai.it. Ed. Teresio Valsesia. Circ: 200,000.

796.9 NLD ISSN 1567-7508
SCHAATSSPORT. Text in Dutch. 1984. 10/yr. EUR 32.25 (effective 2010). **Document type:** *Magazine, Consumer.*
Former titles (until 1998): Schaatsmagazine (0929-7952); (until 1993): Schaats en Kroniek (0921-8432); (until 1987): Schaats (0168-9495)
Published by: Koninklijke Nederlandsche Schaatsenrijders Bond, Postbus 1120, Amersfoort, 3800 BC, Netherlands. TEL 31-33-4892000, FAX 31-33-4620823, bondsbureau@knsb.nl. Circ: 30,000.

798.8 DEU
SCHLITTENHUND MAGAZIN. Text in German. 8/yr. EUR 27.50 domestic; EUR 32 foreign (effective 2005). adv. **Document type:** *Magazine, Consumer.* **Description:** Contains articles and features on all aspects of sled dog racing and breeding.
Published by: Goldrausch Verlag, Goethestr 1a, Kleinblittersdorf, 66271, Germany. TEL 49-6805-99099, FAX 49-6805-99090. Ed. Karl-Heinz Raubach.

DER SCHUETZE. *see* SPORTS AND GAMES

799 CHE ISSN 0036-8016
SCHWEIZER JAEGER. Text in German. 1915. 12/yr. CHF 90 (effective 1999). adv. bk.rev. illus.; stat. index. **Document type:** *Consumer.*
Indexed: KWIWR.
Published by: (Schweizerischer Patentjaeger- und Wildschutzverband), Druckerei Marcel Kuerzi AG, Werner Kaelin Str 11, Einsiedeln, 8840, Switzerland. Ed. Wendelin Fuchs. Adv. contact Marcel Kurzi. Circ: 10,000.

796.93 ITA ISSN 0036-8040
SCI; rivista degli sport invernali. Text in Italian. 1957. 10/yr. EUR 41 (effective 2008). adv. bk.rev. illus. **Document type:** *Magazine, Consumer.*
Published by: Casa Editrice Scode SpA, Corso Monforte 36, Milan, 20122, Italy. TEL 39-02-76002874, FAX 39-02-76004905, info@scode.it, http://www.scode.it. Circ: 18,400.

796.93 ITA ISSN 1128-0344
SCI FONDO. Text in Italian. 1978. 5/yr. EUR 12.50 (effective 2008). bk.rev. illus. **Document type:** *Magazine, Consumer.*
Published by: Casa Editrice Scode SpA, Corso Monforte 36, Milan, 20122, Italy. TEL 39-02-76002874, FAX 39-02-76004905, info@scode.it, http://www.scode.it. Circ: 10,000.

796.93 ITA ISSN 1124-5522
SCIARE. Text in Italian. 1966. 10/yr. adv. **Document type:** *Magazine, Consumer.*
Related titles: Online - full text ed.
Published by: Ottis Srl, Via Winkelmann 2, Milan, 20146, Italy. TEL 39-02-424191, FAX 39-02-47710278. Circ: 85,000.

796.422 FIN ISSN 1012-0602
SCIENTIFIC JOURNAL OF ORIENTEERING. Text in English. 1995. s-a.
Indexed: CA, T02.
—Ingenta.
Published by: International Orienteering Federation, Radiokatu 20, Slu, 00093, Finland. TEL 358-9-34813112, FAX 358-9-34813113.

917.1 CAN ISSN 0225-8315
SCOPE CAMPING NEWS. Text in English. 1965. 4/yr. CAD 24 (effective 1998). adv. illus. **Document type:** *Magazine, Consumer.* **Description:** Provides travel articles and camping activities for the recreational vehicle user in Canada.
Formerly: Scope: Recreational Vehicle and Camping News (0048-9743)
Published by: Merton Publications Ltd., Hyde Park Centre, P O Box 39, London, ON N6H 5M8, Canada. Ed., Pub., Adv. contact Harold Merton. Circ: 30,000.

796.522 GBR ISSN 0080-813X
G505
SCOTTISH MOUNTAINEERING CLUB. JOURNAL. Text in English. 1890. a. GBP 13.95 newsstand/cover; free to members (effective 2009). adv. bk.rev. **Document type:** *Journal, Consumer.*
—BLDSC (8210.930000).
Published by: (Scottish Mountaineering Club), Cordee Ltd., 11 Jacknell Rd, Dodwell's Bridge Industrial Estate, Hinckley, Leics LE10 3BS, United Kingdom. TEL 44-1455-611185, http://www.cordee.co.uk. Ed. D Noel Williams.

796.5 DEU ISSN 0176-4624
SCOUTING; Zeitschrift fuer Pfadfinderinnen und Pfadfinder. Text in German. 1984. 5/yr. EUR 4 newsstand/cover (effective 2007). adv. bk.rev. back issues avail. **Document type:** *Magazine, Consumer.* **Description:** Independent German scout and guide magazine.
Published by: Spurbuchverlag, Am Eichenhuegel 4, Baunach, 96148, Germany. TEL 49-9544-1561, FAX 49-9544-809, info@spurbuch.de, http://www.spurbuch.de. Ed. Paul Thomas Hinkel. Pub. Klaus Hinkel. adv.: B&W page EUR 3,600, color page EUR 3,600; trim 185 x 275. Circ: 4,000 (controlled).

SCOUTING SPIRIT. *see* CHILDREN AND YOUTH—About

797.2 USA ISSN 1553-7919
GV840.S78
SCUBA DIVING; the magazine divers trust. Text in English. 1992. m. (11/yr.). USD 21.98; USD 4.99 newsstand/cover (effective 2009). adv. illus. back issues avail. **Document type:** *Magazine, Consumer.* **Description:** Provides information about the practice of diving, dive travel opportunities, the marine environment, the reader's health and safety and the dive equipment on which they depend. Travel editorial focuses on both domestic and international dive travel. Equipment editorial offers readers comparative product reviews.
Formerly (until 2004): Rodale's Scuba Diving (1060-9563); Incorporates (1987-1992): Fisheye View Scuba Magazine
Related titles: Online - full text ed.
Indexed: A25, A26, E08, G06, G07, G08, I05, S08, S09, S23.
Published by: F + W Media Inc., 6600 Abercorn St, Ste 208, Savannah, GA 31405. TEL 912-351-0855, 800-283-0963, FAX 912-351-0890, http://www.fwpublications.com. Ed., Pub. Keith Phillips TEL 912-351-6234. Adv. contact Travis Gainsley TEL 212-447-1400 ext 12150. B&W page USD 11,950, color page USD 17,950; bleed 9 x 10.1875. Circ: 174,288. **Dist. in UK by:** MarketForce UK Ltd, The Blue Fin Bldg, 3rd Fl, 110 Southwark St, London SE1 0SU, United Kingdom. TEL 44-20-31483300, FAX 44-20-31488105.

799.1 GBR ISSN 0306-6568
SEA ANGLER. Text in English. 1972. m. GBP 38 domestic; GBP 50 in Europe; GBP 55 elsewhere (effective 2009). adv. bk.rev. charts; illus.; stat.; tr.lit. **Document type:** *Magazine, Consumer.* **Description:** Contains news, fishing stories, tackle tests, where to fish guides, and tips from the experts.
Incorporates (1980-1983): Sea Angling Monthly (0260-728X)
—CCC.
Published by: H. Bauer Publishing Ltd. (Subsidiary of: Bauer Media Group), Academic House, 24-28 Oval Rd, London, NW1 7DT, United Kingdom. TEL 44-20-72418000, FAX 44-20-72418030, http://www.bauer.co.uk. Ed. Mel Russ TEL 44-1733-395147. Adv. contact Donna Harris TEL 44-1733-288054. **Subscr. to:** Tower House, Sovereign Park, Market Harborough, Leicestershire LE16 9EF, United Kingdom. TEL 44-1858-438866, subs@greatmagazines.co.uk.

796.42 DEU ISSN 1860-2118
SENIOREN LEICHTATHLETIK. Text in German. 2005. 10/yr. EUR 48; EUR 5 newsstand/cover (effective 2011). adv. **Document type:** *Magazine, Trade.*
Published by: Meyer & Meyer Verlag, Von-Coels-Str 390, Aachen, 52080, Germany. TEL 49-241-958100, FAX 49-241-9581010, verlag@m-m-sports.com, http://m-m-sports.de. Circ: 8,000 (paid and controlled).

799 CAN ISSN 0711-7957
SK1S46
SENTIER CHASSE - PECHE. Text in English. 1971. m. (11/yr.). CAD 38.18 domestic; CAD 75 foreign (effective 2000). adv. back issues avail. **Description:** Articles on fishing, hunting, outdoor life and the environment.
Formerly: Quebec Chasse et Peche (0315-260X)
Indexed: PdeR.
Published by: Groupe Polygone Editeurs, Inc., 11450 Blvd Albert Hudon, Montreal, PQ H1G 3J9, Canada. TEL 514-327-4464, FAX 514-327-0514. Ed. Jeannot Ruel. Pub. Luc Lemay. Adv. contact Robert Ferland. Circ: 70,000.

796.552 797.1 PRT
SERRA E MAR/MOUNTAINS AND SEA. Text in Portuguese. 12/yr.
Address: Rua Dr. Antonio Menano, Fornos De Algodres, 6370, Portugal. TEL 71-99476. Ed. Paulo Menano.

799.1 USA ISSN 1932-5304
SHALLOW WATER ANGLER. Text in English. 2005. bi-m. adv. **Document type:** *Magazine, Consumer.* **Description:** Provides you with regional reports for fishing the shallow waters stretching from Texas to Cape Cod.
Related titles: Online - full text ed.
Indexed: G08.
Published by: Intermedia Outdoors, Inc., 512 7th Ave, 11th Fl, New York, NY 10018. TEL 212-852-6682, 800-260-6397, FAX 212-302-4472, customerservice@imoutdoors.com, http://www.imoutdoorsmedia.com.

799.2 GBR ISSN 0957-4182
SHOOTING GAZETTE. Text in English. 1989. m. GBP 34.49 domestic; USD 105.30 in US & Canada; EUR 69 in Europe; GBP 66.70 elsewhere; GBP 3.75 newsstand/cover (effective 2010). adv. bk.rev. 5 cols./p.; back issues avail. **Document type:** *Magazine, Consumer.* **Description:** Covers every aspect of game and rough shooting and reviews good places to hunt.
Published by: I P C Media Ltd. (Subsidiary of: Time Inc.), PO Box 225, Stamford, Lincs PE9 2HS, United Kingdom. TEL 44-1780-485350, http://www.ipcmedia.com/. Ed. William Hetherington. Pub. Fiona Mercer TEL 44-20-31484311. Adv. contact David Thomas TEL 44-203-1484212. page GBP 1,280. Circ: 14,765. **Subscr. to:** Rockwood House, Perrymount Rd, Haywards Heath RH16 3DH, United Kingdom. TEL 44-845-1231231, IPCsubs@quadrantsubs.com, http://www.magazinesdirect.co.uk. **Dist. by:** MarketForce UK Ltd.

683.4 799.2 USA ISSN 1544-3000
SHOOTING ILLUSTRATED. Abbreviated title: S I. Text in English. 2002. m. USD 9.95 domestic; USD 14.95 in Canada; USD 19.95 elsewhere (effective 2009). adv. **Document type:** *Magazine, Consumer.* **Description:** Features the latest information on rifles, pistols or shotguns.
Published by: National Rifle Association of America, 11250 Waples Mill Rd, Fairfax, VA 22030. TEL 800-672-3888, membership@nrahq.org, http://www.nra.org. Eds. Guy Sagi TEL 703-267-1375, John Zent TEL 703-267-1332. adv.: B&W page USD 1,910, color page USD 2,900; trim 7.625 x 10.5.

799.21 GBR ISSN 1367-6997
SHOOTING SPORTS. Text in English. 1993. m. GBP 29.99 domestic; GBP 34.95 in Europe; GBP 47.95 elsewhere (effective 2010). adv. **Document type:** *Magazine, Consumer.* **Description:** Contains articles on shooting, guns and gun laws.
Formerly (until 1997): Guns and Shooting (0966-1247)
—CCC.
Published by: Aceville Publications Ltd., 21-23 Phoenix Ct, Hawkins Rd, Colchester, Essex CO2 8JY, United Kingdom. TEL 44-1206-505962, FAX 44-1206-505915, aceville@servicehelpline.co.uk, http://www.aceville.com. Ed. Pete Moore TEL 44-1206-525697. Adv. contact Vanessa Green TEL 44-1206-506247. **Subscr. to:** 800 Guillat Ave, Kent Science Park, Sittingbourne, Kent ME9 8GU, United Kingdom. TEL 44-844-8440381, FAX 44-845-4567143.

799.2 USA ISSN 1050-5717
SK313
SHOOTING SPORTSMAN; magazine of wingshooting and fine guns. Text in English. 1988. bi-m. USD 32 domestic; USD 5.95 newsstand/cover (effective 2005). adv. bk.rev. illus. back issues avail.; reprints avail. **Document type:** *Magazine, Consumer.* **Description:** Features fine double shotguns and wingshooting. Each issue is illustrated with hunting destination stories, gun reviews, etc.
Published by: Down East Enterprise, Outdoor Group Publications, PO Box 1357, Camden, ME 04843. TEL 207-594-9544, FAX 207-594-7215. Ed., R&P Ralph P Stuart. Pub. Kit Parker. Adv. contact Bill Anderson. B&W page USD 2,300, color page USD 3,175. Circ: 31,000 (paid). **Subscr. to:** PO Box 37048, Boone, IA 50037.

799.2 USA ISSN 0744-3773
SHOTGUN SPORTS; America's leading shotgun magazine. Text in English. 1976. m. USD 32.95 domestic; USD 39.95 foreign; USD 4.95 newsstand/cover (effective 2007). adv. illus. reprints avail. **Document type:** *Magazine, Consumer.*
Address: PO Box 6810, Auburn, CA 95604. TEL 530-889-2220, FAX 530-889-9106. Ed., R&P Frank Kodl. Adv. contact Lynn Berger. Circ: 108,000.

796.93 AUT
SICHERHEIT IM BERGLAND. Text in German. 1972. a. **Document type:** *Journal, Trade.*
Formerly: Fuer die Sicherheit im Bergland
Published by: Oesterreichisches Kuratorium fuer Alpine Sicherheit, Olympiastr 10, Innsbruck, W 6020, Austria. TEL 43-512-365451, FAX 43-512-361998, office@alpinesicherheit.at, http://www.alpinesicherheit.at. Circ: 2,000.

SIERRA ATLANTIC. *see* CONSERVATION

796.552 USA
SIERRA CARRIERS NEWSLETTER. Text in English. 1978. a.
Published by: Sierra Carriers and Mountaineering Group, 1637 McCollum Pike, Los Angeles, CA 90026. Ed. James C Keene.

SIERRA REPORT. *see* CONSERVATION

796.5 917.9 USA ISSN 8750-1600
GV199.42.N69
SIGNPOST FOR NORTHWEST TRAILS. Text in English. 1966. m. USD 25. adv. bk.rev. illus. index. reprints avail. **Document type:** *Magazine, Consumer.*
Formerly: Signpost for Northwest Hikers (0583-2594)
Published by: Washington Trails Association, 2019 3rd Ave., Ste. 100, Seattle, WA 98121-2430. TEL 206-625-1367. Ed., R&P Dan Nelson. adv.: B&W page USD 285, color page USD 850; trim 9.75 x 7. Circ: 3,500 (paid).

796 ITA ISSN 1825-215X
SKATEBOARD FREESTYLE MAGAZINE. Variant title: Skateboard. Text in Italian. 1997. bi-m. **Document type:** *Magazine, Consumer.*
Formerly (until 2005): Freestyler (1724-272X)
Published by: Life Edizioni, Via Stazione 2, Baveno, VB 28831, Italy. TEL 39-0323-924644, FAX 39-0323-925197, http://www.lifed.it.

796.22 USA ISSN 1099-842X
SKATEDORK. Text in English. 1997. irreg. free. **Document type:** *Magazine, Consumer.* **Description:** Features original columns, photographs, and scene reports on skateboarding.
Media: Online - full text.
Address: 221 Spring Ridge Dr, Berkeley Heights, NJ 07922. steve@skatedork.org. Ed., Pub. Steve Voss.

796.93 USA ISSN 0037-6159
GV854.A1
SKI. Text in English. 1936. 7/yr. USD 10 (effective 2011). adv. illus. reprints avail. **Document type:** *Magazine, Consumer.* **Description:** Covers ski equipment, instruction, resorts, and lifestyle issues and products for avid skiers.
Incorporates: Ski Life
Related titles: Microform ed.: (from PQC); Online - full text ed.
Indexed: A11, A22, A33, C05, CPerI, ConsI, G08, G09, I05, I06, I07, M01, M02, M04, MASUSE, P02, P10, P19, P48, P53, P54, PEI, PMR, PQC, RASB, S23, SD, SPI, SportS, T02, U01.
—Ingenta. **CCC.**
Published by: Bonnier Corp. (Subsidiary of: Bonnier Group), 5720 Flatiron Pky, Boulder, CO 80301. TEL 303-253-6300, http://www.bonniercorp.com. Ed. Kendall Hamilton.

796.93 CHE ISSN 1420-0333
SKI; die schweizer Skisport-Zeitschrift. Text in French, German, Italian. 1968. 7/yr. CHF 29 (effective 2000). adv. bk.rev. **Document type:** *Magazine, Consumer.*
Former titles (until 1994): Skijournal (1421-0819); (until 1992): Ski - Schweizer Skisport (0037-623X)
—CCC.
Published by: (Schweizerischer Ski-Verbandes), Vogt-Schild AG, Zuchwilerstr 21, Solothurn, 4501, Switzerland. TEL 41-32-6247111, FAX 41-32-6247251. Ed. Joseph Weibel. Adv. contact Urs Roelli. B&W page CHF 7,320, color page CHF 10,270; trim 210 x 280. Circ: 89,902 (controlled).

796.93 FRA ISSN 1763-5535
SKI. Text in French. 1940. bi-m. adv. bk.rev. illus. back issues avail. **Document type:** *Consumer.* **Description:** Covers leisure and competition skiing.
Formerly (until 2003): Ski Francais (0399-2055)
Indexed: RASB.
Published by: Editions Jacques Glenat, 37 Rue Servan, Grenoble, 38000, France. TEL 33-4-76887575, FAX 33-4-76887570, http://www.glenat.com. Circ: 55,000.

796.93 GBR ISSN 1369-8826
SKI + BOARD. Text in English. 1972. 4/yr. free to members; GBP 16 domestic; GBP 20 in Europe; GBP 28 elsewhere (effective 2011). adv. bk.rev. cum.index every 3 yrs. back issues avail. **Document type:** *Magazine, Consumer.*
Formerly (until 1997): Ski Survey (0955-8225)
Indexed: SD, SportS.

S

—BLDSC (8295.375350).
Published by: Ski Club of Great Britain, The White House, 57-63 Church Rd, Wimbledon, London, SW19 5SB, United Kingdom. TEL 44-20-84102000, FAX 44-20-84102001, skiers@skiclub.co.uk. Ed. Arnie Wilson. Adv. contact Jo Peskett. Circ: 20,973.

796.93 DEU
SKI & SPORTMAGAZIN. Text in German. 1970. 6/yr. adv. **Document type:** *Magazine, Consumer.*
Former titles (until 2009): D S V Aktiv Ski & Sportmagazin (2190-8621); (until 2005): Aktiv (1616-8712); (until 2001): Ski (1615-1895); (until 1977): Inter-Ski
Published by: (Deutscher Skilehrerverband e.V.), Motor Presse Stuttgart GmbH & Co. KG (Subsidiary of: Gruner + Jahr AG & Co), Leuschnerstr 1, Stuttgart, 70174, Germany. TEL 49-711-18201, FAX 49-711-1821779, internet-redaktion@motor-presse-stuttgart.de, http://www.motorpresse.de. Ed. Florian Schmidt. Adv. contact Bernd Holzhauer. Circ: 183,100 (controlled).

796.93 USA ISSN 0037-6175
GV854.A1
SKI AREA MANAGEMENT. Text in English. 1962. bi-m. USD 42 domestic; USD 48 in Canada; USD 64 elsewhere (effective 2005). adv. bk.rev. index. back issues avail.; reprints avail. **Document type:** *Magazine, Trade.* **Description:** Covers new equipment and management practices for mountain resorts, equipment for maintenance, cafeteria, lighting, office, summer recreation, ski area design and planning and marketing.
Related titles: Online - full content ed.
Indexed: H&TI, H06, Hospl, SD, SportS, T02.
—BLDSC (8295.375450), IE, Ingenta.
Published by: Beardsley Publishing Corp, 45 Main St N, Box 644, Woodbury, CT 06798. TEL 203-263-0888, FAX 203-266-0452. Ed. Rick Kahl. Adv. contact Sharon Walsh. page USD 2,280. Circ: 3,711 (paid).

796 AUT
SKI AUSTRIA. Text in German. 9/yr. EUR 23.70 domestic; EUR 30 foreign (effective 2005). adv. **Document type:** *Magazine, Consumer.*
Published by: Oesterreichischer Skiverband, Olympiastr 10, Innsbruck, T 6010, Austria. TEL 43-512-335010, FAX 43-512-361998, sandhofer@oesv.at, http://www.oesv.at. adv.: B&W page EUR 4,040, color page EUR 5,657; trim 188 x 243. Circ: 91,500 (paid and controlled).

796.93 CAN ISSN 0702-701X
SKI CANADA. Text in English. 1972. 6/yr. CAD 14.99 domestic; CAD 23.99 in United States; CAD 44.95 foreign; USD 4.95 newsstand/cover (effective 2000). adv. bk.rev.; video rev.; software rev. **Document type:** *Magazine, Consumer.*
Formerly: Ski Canada Journal (0316-2648)
Related titles: Microfiche ed.: (from MML); Microform ed.: (from MML).
Indexed: C03, CBCARef, CBPI, CPerI, G08, P48, PQC, SD, SportS.
—CCC.
Published by: Solstice Publishing Inc., 47 Soho Square, Toronto, ON M5T 2Z2, Canada. TEL 416-595-1252, FAX 416-595-7255. Ed. Iain MacMillan. Pub., R&P, Adv. contact Paul Green. color page CAD 5,400. Circ: 45,581.

796.93 CAN
SKI CANADA BUYER'S GUIDE. Text in English. a. USD 5.95 newsstand/cover (effective 2001). adv. **Document type:** *Magazine, Consumer.*
Published by: Solstice Publishing Inc., 47 Soho Square, Toronto, ON M5T 2Z2, Canada. TEL 416-595-1252, FAX 416-595-7255, info@skicanadamag.com. Circ: 39,900 (paid); 7,649 (controlled).

796.93 USA ISSN 0197-3479
GV854.A1
SKI INDUSTRY LETTER. Text in English. 1979. m. USD 298; USD 349 foreign. bk.rev. **Document type:** *Newsletter.* **Description:** Covers the ski trade.
Related titles: Fax ed.
Published by: Skiletter, Inc., 115 Lilly Pond Ln, Katonah, NY 10536. TEL 914-232-5094. Ed. Greg Berry.

796.93 DEU
SKI JOURNAL. Text in German. a. adv. **Document type:** *Magazine, Consumer.*
Published by: Atlas Verlag GmbH, Brienner Str 41, Munich, 80333, Germany. TEL 49-89-552410, FAX 49-89-55241100, info@atlas-verlag.de, http://www.atlas-verlag.de. Adv. contact Thomas Obermaier. B&W page EUR 8,900, color page EUR 11,500; trim 210 x 280. Circ: 680,000 (controlled).

796.93 USA ISSN 1935-3219
GV854.A1
THE SKI JOURNAL. Text in English. 2007. q. USD 39.99 domestic; USD 50.99 in Canada; USD 89.99 elsewhere (effective 2008). adv. illus. **Document type:** *Magazine, Consumer.* **Description:** Covers slopes around the world, ski stories, and major players in competative skiing.
Published by: Funny Feelings, LLC, PO Box 2806, Bellingham, WA 98227. TEL 360-671-7386, http://www.funnyfeelingsllc.com/. Ed. Jeff Galbraith.

796.93 CAN ISSN 1490-7755
SKI PRESS. Text in English, French. 1998. 3/yr. adv. back issues avail. **Document type:** *Magazine, Consumer.*
Related titles: Online - full content ed.: free (effective 2004).
Indexed: SD.
Published by: Ski Press News, Inc., 850 Bernard Pilon, McMasterville, PQ JG 5X7, Canada. Pub. Patrick Wells TEL 819-216-5312. adv.: color page USD 31,250; trim 10.5 x 13.

796.93 CAN
SKI THE WEST. Text in English. 1987. a. CAD 5. **Document type:** *Handbook/Manual/Guide, Consumer.* **Description:** For visitors who wish to ski in Southeast B.C., Northwest Montana and Northern Idaho.
Published by: Kootenay Advertiser Ltd., 1510 2nd St N, Cranbrook, BC V1C 3L2, Canada. FAX 604-489-3743. Ed. Daryl Shellborn. Circ: 40,450.

796.93 CAN
SKI TRAX; North America's nordic ski magazine. Text in English. m. CAD 13 domestic; USD 14 in United States; CAD 17 elsewhere (effective 2010). illus. **Document type:** *Magazine, Consumer.*
Address: 260 Spadina Ave, Ste 200, Toronto, ON M5T 2E4, Canada. TEL 416-977-2100, 866-754-8729, FAX 416-977-9200.

796.93 USA
SKI WATCH ATLAS. Text in English. a. USD 3.95 (effective 2001). adv. **Document type:** *Directory.*
Published by: C R N International, Inc., One Circular Ave, Hamden, CT 06514. TEL 203-288-2002, FAX 203-281-3291. Ed. Gary Zenobia. Pubs. Barry Beeman, Richard Kalt. Adv. contact Patrick Kane. B&W page USD 4,000, color page USD 5,000; trim 10.88 x 8.38. Circ: 100,000 (controlled).

SKI WRITERS BULLETIN. *see* JOURNALISM

796.93 GBR ISSN 1475-7451
THE SKIER AND SNOWBOARDER. Text in English. 1983. q. GBP 10 (effective 2009). adv. bk.rev. **Document type:** *Magazine, Consumer.* **Description:** All aspects of ski and snowboard related subjects; racing, equipment and travel.
Formerly (until 199?): Skier (0951-5941); Which incorporates: British Ski Magazine
Indexed: SportS.
Published by: Mountain Marketing Ltd., PO Box 386, Sevenoaks, Kent TN13 1AQ, United Kingdom. TEL 44-845-3108303.

796.93 USA ISSN 1094-0960
SKIER NEWS. Text in English. 1988. 3/yr. free at select ski shops. adv. bk.rev. 32 p./no.; **Document type:** *Magazine, Consumer.* **Description:** For recreational skiers. Content is family-oriented.
Related titles: Online - full text ed.
Published by: Skier News, Inc., PO Box 77327, W Trenton, NJ 08628-6327. TEL 609-882-1111, FAX 609-882-2700. Eds. Jennifer Hawkins, Lorraine Leonardi. Pub., R&P, Adv. contact David Leonardi. page USD 3,199; trim 16 x 10. Circ: 70,000 (controlled).

796.93 FRA ISSN 1266-9210
SKIEUR MAGAZINE. Text in French. 1995. bi-m. EUR 39.50 domestic (effective 2007). adv. **Document type:** *Magazine, Consumer.*
Published by: Editions Niveales, 6 Rue Irvoy, Grenoble, 38000, France. TEL 33-4-76705411, FAX 33-4-76705412, http://www.dipresse.com/niveales. Ed. Laurent Belluard. **Dist. by:** Dipresse, 18-24 Quai de la Marne, Paris 75164, France. TEL 33-1-44848526, FAX 33-1-42005692, http://www.dipresse.com.

796.93 DEU
SKIING. Text in German. bi-m. EUR 17; EUR 3.80 newsstand/cover (effective 2008). adv. **Document type:** *Magazine, Consumer.*
Published by: b&d Media Network GmbH, Osterfeldstr 12-14, Hamburg, 22529, Germany. TEL 49-40-4800070, FAX 49-40-48000799, info@bdverlag.de, http://www.bdverlag.de. Adv. contact Jennifer Stracke. B&W page EUR 3,600, color page EUR 4,800; trim 230 x 290. Circ: 44,137 (paid and controlled).

796.93 USA ISSN 0037-6264
GV854.A1
SKIING MAGAZINE. Text in English. 1948. 6/yr. USD 6.99 newsstand/cover (effective 2011). adv. bk.rev. illus. index. reprints avail. **Document type:** *Magazine, Consumer.* **Description:** Brings winter adventure alive for young, active skiers. Highlights great ski destinations, unusual personalities, and noteworthy gear. Provides practical information to help you squeeze maximum pleasure from your time in the mountains.
Former titles (until 1958): National Skiing; (until 1954): National Newspaper of Skiing; (until 1950): Rocky Mountain Skiing
Related titles: Microform ed.: (from PQC); Online - full text ed.: USD 4.99 per issue (effective 2011); Supplement(s): Women's Skiing. ISSN 1938-4157.
Indexed: A01, A02, A03, A08, A11, A22, A25, A26, Acal, B04, BRD, C05, C12, CPerI, ConsI, E08, G05, G06, G07, G08, G09, I05, I06, I07, M01, M02, M04, MASUSE, MagInd, P02, P10, P19, P48, P53, P54, PEI, PMR, PQC, R03, R04, R06, RGAb, RGPR, S08, S09, S23, SD, SPI, SportS, T02, TOM, U01, W03, W05.
—Ingenta. **CCC.**
Published by: Bonnier Corp. (Subsidiary of: Bonnier Group), 5720 Flatiron Pky, Boulder, CO 80301. TEL 303-253-6300, http://www.bonniercorp.com. Eds. Sam Bass, Greg Ditrinco. Pub. Merri Lee Kingsly.

796.93 DEU ISSN 0583-4724
SKIMAGAZIN. Text in German. 1966. 6/yr. EUR 25.10 domestic; EUR 34.50 foreign; EUR 4.50 newsstand/cover (effective 2009). adv. **Document type:** *Magazine, Consumer.*
Incorporates (1994-1998): Ski-Supertest (0944-7156); Formerly (until 1967): Der Skilehrer und seine Schueler
Published by: Brinkmann Henrich Medien GmbH, Heerstr 5, Meinerzhagen, 58540, Germany. TEL 49-2354-77990, FAX 49-2354-779977, info@bhmg.de, http://www.bhmg.de. Ed. Florian Schmidt. adv.: color page EUR 11,230, B&W page EUR 6,737; trim 180 x 250. Circ: 112,291 (paid and controlled).

796.93 FIN ISSN 0359-0569
SKIMBAAJA. Text in Finnish. 1977. 6/yr. EUR 29.65 (effective 2005). adv. **Document type:** *Magazine, Consumer.*
Published by: Egmont Kustannus Oy, PO Box 317, Tampere, 33101, Finland. TEL 358-201-332222, FAX 358-201-332278, info@egmont-kustannus.fi, http://www.egmont-kustannus.fi. Adv. contact Tommy Tenhunen TEL 358-201-332266. B&W page EUR 1,900, color page EUR 2,700; 210 x 273. Circ: 14,000.

796.93 NOR ISSN 0333-3973
SKISPORT. Variant title: Ski-Sport. Text in Norwegian. 1948. 8/yr. NOK 320 domestic; NOK 380 in Europe; NOK 400 elsewhere (effective 2002). adv. back issues avail. **Document type:** *Magazine, Consumer.* **Description:** Devoted to everything relevant to skiing in Norway.
Supersedes in part (in 1981): Alpin-Sport (0332-8252); Ski-Idrett (0332-9720)
Published by: (Norges Skiforbund), Skiforum A-S, Postboks 6, Baerum Postterminal, 1306, Norway. TEL 47-67-13-46-46, FAX 47-67-13-46-47. Ed. Allan Aabecn. Adv. contact Per Stenberg. B&W page NOK 9,500, color page NOK 15,000. Circ: 13,000 (paid).

796.42 333.78 SWE ISSN 0346-1297
SKOGSSPORT. Text in Swedish. 1947. 10/yr. SEK 360 domestic; SEK 420 in Scandinavia; SEK 450 elsewhere (effective 2004). adv. 58 p./no. 4 cols./p.; **Document type:** *Consumer.*
Formerly (until 1969): Tidning foer Skogssport
Published by: Svenska Orienteringsfoerbundet, PO Box 22, Solna, 17118, Sweden. TEL 46-8-58772000, FAX 46-8-58772088, info@orientering.se. Ed. Ola Gustafsson. Pub. Jan Eric Goth. adv.: color page SEK 15,900; trim 267 x 185. Circ: 10,300 (controlled).

796.93 JPN
SKUI JANARU/SKI JOURNAL. Text in Japanese. 1966. m. illus. **Document type:** *Consumer.*
Published by: Skui Janaru Kabushiki Kaisha/Ski Journal Publisher Inc., Araki-cho 20-Banchi, Shinjuku-ku, Intech 88 Bldg, Tokyo, 160-0007, Japan. TEL 81-3-33535541, FAX 81-3-33536633, sjsales@skijournal.co.jp, http://www.skijournal.co.jp.

797 GBR ISSN 1470-5249
SKYDIVE. Text in English. 1964. bi-m. GBP 22 in UK & USA; EUR 33 in Europe; GBP 30 elsewhere; free to members (effective 2009). adv. bk.rev. illus. back issues avail. **Document type:** *Magazine, Consumer.* **Description:** Features articles that cover all the aspects of the sport of parachuting.
Formerly (until 1999): Sport Parachutist (0584-9217)
Related titles: Online - full text ed.: free (effective 2009).
Indexed: SD, SportS.
Published by: British Parachute Association, 5 Wharf Way, Glen Parva, Leicester, LE2 9TF, United Kingdom. TEL 44-116-2785271, FAX 44-116-2477662, http://www.bpa.org.uk. Ed. Lesley Gale TEL 44-1733-380568. Adv. contact Ross O'Loughlin TEL 44-1778-392459. color page GBP 670; trim 210 x 297.

796.552 790.1 CAN
SKYLINER. Text in English. 1972. m. membership.
Published by: Skyline Hikers of the Canadian Rockies, 114 Brantford Crescent, N W, Calgary, AB T2L 1N8, Canada. Ed. Virginia Klatzel.

797.5 GBR ISSN 1475-5440
SKYWINGS. Text in English. 19??. m. GBP 32 domestic to non-members; EUR 36 in Europe to non-members; USD 49 in United States to non-members; CAD 57 in Canada to non-members; AUD 64 in Australia to non-members; GBP 49 elsewhere to non-members; free to members (effective 2009). adv. bk.rev. back issues avail. **Document type:** *Magazine, Consumer.* **Description:** Publishes national and international news from the world of free-flying and features on related sports equipment, new product reviews, aircraft tests, competition reports, interviews with personalities within the sport, safety advice and pilots discussion forum.
Former titles (until 1983): Wings! (0951-5712); (until 1975): Illustrated Monthly Flypaper
Related titles: Online - full text ed.
Published by: British Hang Gliding and Paragliding Association Ltd., Old Schoolroom, Loughborough Rd, Leicester, Leics LE4 5PJ, United Kingdom. TEL 44-116-2611322, FAX 44-116-2611323, office@bhpa.co.uk, http://www.bhpa.co.uk/. Ed. Joe Schofield TEL 44-1379-855021. Circ: 7,500 (paid).

796 AUS ISSN 1036-3483
SLAM; skateboarding magazine. Text in English. 1988. m. (plus a. cumulation). AUD 79.60 domestic; AUD 145.65 in New Zealand; AUD 167.60 in Asia & the Pacific; AUD 246.55 elsewhere (effective 2008). adv. music rev.; video rev. illus. back issues avail. **Document type:** *Magazine, Consumer.*
Published by: Morrison Media Services Ltd., PO Box 823, Burleigh Heads, QLD 4220, Australia. TEL 61-7-55761388, FAX 61-7-55761527, subs@morrisonmedia.com.au, http://www.morrisonmedia.com.au. Ed. Jake Frost. Pub. Peter Morrison. Adv. contact Rob Henry TEL 61-3-92142704. color page AUD 2,020; trim 210 x 275.

796.9 FIN ISSN 1239-9035
SLAMMER; ostajan opas. Text in Finnish. 1997. 6/yr. EUR 31.40 (effective 2005). adv. illus. **Document type:** *Magazine, Consumer.* **Description:** A specialist snowboarding magazine made by experts.
Published by: Yhtyneet Kuvalehdet Oy/United Magazines Ltd., Maistraatinportti 1, Helsinki, 00015, Finland. TEL 358-9-15661, FAX 358-9-145650, http://www.kuvalehdet.fi. Ed. Juha Mustonen. Circ: 7,057.

796.95 USA
SLEDHEADS. Text in English. bi-m. free to members (effective 2008). adv. reprints avail. **Document type:** *Magazine, Trade.* **Description:** Contains in-depth mod sled bios, technical how-to articles and entertaining stories, outstanding photography and a unique focus on the snowmobile industry.
Published by: (American Sledhead Association), Harris Publishing, Inc. (Idaho Falls), 360 B St, Idaho Falls, ID 83402-3547. TEL 208-524-7000, 800-638-0135, FAX 208-522-5241, customerservice@harrispublishing.com, http://www.harrispublishing.com.

796.93 NOR ISSN 0332-9682
SNOE OG SKI. Text in Norwegian. 1972. q. NOK 560 membership; NOK 270 to students (effective 2011). adv. illus. **Document type:** *Magazine, Consumer.*
Published by: Foreningen til Ski-Idrettens Fremme/Association for the Promotion of Skiing, Kongeveien 5, Oslo, 0787, Norway. TEL 47-22-923200, FAX 47-22-923250, post@skiforeningen.no.

796.95 SWE ISSN 2000-1797
SNOESKOTER. Text in Swedish. 2003. 6/yr. SEK 289 domestic; NOK 420 in Norway; SEK 470 in Scandinavia; SEK 570 elsewhere (effective 2011). adv. 86 p./no. 4 cols./p.; **Document type:** *Magazine, Consumer.*
Formerly (until 2008): Snoeskoter med Racing (1652-9154); Which was formed by the merger of (1978-2003): Snoeskoter (0348-1867); (1992-2003): Skoter Racing (1651-4890); Which was formerly (until 2002): Snoeskoter Racing (1400-4194)
Related titles: Online - full text ed.
Published by: (Sveriges Snoeskoteraegares Riksorganisation), Liwall Foerlags AB, PO Box 6064, Umea, 90602, Sweden. TEL 46-90-189250, FAX 46-90-188118.

796.93 USA ISSN 1942-1249
SNOW. Text in English. 2007 (Nov.). 3/yr. USD 19.97 domestic (print or online ed.); USD 28.97 in Canada (effective 2011). adv. **Document type:** *Magazine, Consumer.* **Description:** Covers luxury snowsports lifestyle, including equipment, travel, food, fashion, nightlife, and shopping.
Related titles: Online - full text ed.
Published by: Bonnier Corp. (Subsidiary of: Bonnier Group), 460 N Orlando Ave, Ste 200, Winter Park, FL 32789. TEL 407-628-4802, FAX 407-628-7061, http://www.bonniercorp.com. Ed. David K Gibson. Pub. Barbara Sanders.

796.93 NLD ISSN 1574-1427
SNOW. Text in Dutch. 2004. q. EUR 14.50 (effective 2009). adv. **Document type:** *Magazine, Consumer.*

Published by: Maruba b.v., Winthontlaan 200, Utrecht, 3526 KV, Netherlands. TEL 31-30-2891073, FAX 31-30-2887415, maruba@maruba.com, http://www.maruba.nl. Pub. Maas H van Drie. adv.: color page EUR 3,660; trim 240 x 300. Circ: 30,000.

796.93 USA ISSN 2155-2576
TD868
SNOW BUSINESS. Text in English. 2000. q. **Document type:** *Magazine, Trade.* **Description:** Provides news and information on the snow and ice business.
Published by: (Snow & Ice Management Association), Questex Media Group Inc., 275 Grove St, Bldg 2, Ste 130, Newton, MA 02466. TEL 617-219-8300, FAX 617-219-8310, questex@sunbeltfs.com, http://www.questex.com.

796.95 CAN ISSN 0711-6454
SNOW GOER; snowmobiling. Text in English. 1979. 4/yr. adv. **Document type:** *Magazine, Consumer.*
Published by: Snow Goer Media, 230 Bayview Dr, Unit 20, Barrie, ON L4N 4Y8, Canada. TEL 705-735-6868, FAX 705-735-4994, island@snowgoercanada.com. Circ: 150,000 (controlled).

796.95 USA ISSN 1056-4209
CODEN: PWORE4
SNOW GOER. Text in English. 1990. 7/yr. USD 14.97 domestic; USD 21.97 in Canada; USD 28.97 elsewhere (effective 2008). adv. back issues avail. **Document type:** *Magazine, Trade.* **Description:** Provides information on the world of snowmobiling, new machines, travel, new products, performance, personalities, do-it-yourself projects and events.
Related titles: Online - full text ed.
Indexed: G05, G06, G07, G08, I05.
Published by: Affinity Group Inc., 2575 Vista Del Mar, Ventura, CA 93001. TEL 805-667-4100, FAX 805-667-4419, info@affinitygroup.com, http://www.affinitygroup.com. Ed. Tim Erickson TEL 763-383-4400. Circ: 68,044.

796.93 DEU
SNOW PRODUCT GUIDE. Text in German. a. EUR 5.90 newsstand/cover (effective 2009). adv. **Document type:** *Magazine, Consumer.*
Published by: Brinkmann Henrich Medien GmbH, Heerstr 5, Meinerzhagen, 58540, Germany. TEL 49-2354-77990, FAX 49-2354-779977, info@bhmg.de, http://www.bhmg.de. Ed. Florian Schmidt. adv.: B&W page EUR 5,176, color page EUR 8,626. Circ: 59,987 (paid).

796.53 DEU
SNOW SPORT. Text in German. 3/yr. free to members (effective 2008). adv. **Document type:** *Magazine, Trade.*
Published by: Deutscher Skilehrerverband e.V., Buergermeister-Finsterwalder-Ring 1, Wolfratshausen, 82515, Germany. TEL 49-8171-34720, FAX 49-8171-347210, info@skilehrerverband.de, http://www.skilehrerverband.de. adv.: B&W page EUR 1,100, color page EUR 1,800. Circ: 13,000 (controlled).

796.93 FRA ISSN 1243-5554
SNOW SURF. Text in French. 1992. bi-m. (7/yr). EUR 38.50 (effective 2009). **Document type:** *Magazine, Consumer.*
Published by: Editions Niveales, 6 Rue Irvoy, Grenoble, 38000, France. TEL 33-4-76705411, FAX 33-4-76705412, http://www.dipresse.com/niveales. Ed. Denis Bertrand. **Dist. by:** Dipresse, 18-24 Quai de la Marne, Paris 75164, France. TEL 33-1-44848526, FAX 33-1-42005692, http://www.dipresse.com.

796.95 USA ISSN 0164-7342
SNOW WEEK; the snowmobile news and racing weekly. Text in English. 1973. q. adv. back issues avail. **Document type:** *Magazine, Consumer.* **Description:** Delivers year-round information on the competition and high-performance aspects of snowmobiling.
Formerly (until 1977): Snowmobile Week
Related titles: Online - full text ed.
Indexed: G05, G06, G07, G08, I05.
Published by: Affinity Group Inc., 2575 Vista Del Mar, Ventura, CA 93001. TEL 805-667-4100, FAX 805-667-4419, info@affinitygroup.com, http://www.affinitygroup.com. adv.: B&W page USD 4,840, color page USD 7,035. Circ: 20,132.

796 USA
SNOWACTION. Text in English. 1987. 7/yr. USD 14.95 (effective 2000). adv. **Document type:** *Magazine, Consumer.*
Published by: Harris Publishing, Inc. (Idaho Falls), 360 B St, Idaho Falls, ID 83402-3547. TEL 208-524-7000, 800-638-0135, FAX 208-522-5241, customerservice@harrispublishing.com, http://www.harrispublishing.com. Ed. Lane Lindstrom. Pub. Steve James. Adv. contact Gregg Manwaring. Circ: 22,000.

796.93 CAN ISSN 1192-3776
SNOWBOARD CANADA. Text in English. 1992. 4/yr. USD 3.95 newsstand/cover. adv. bk.rev. charts; illus. **Document type:** *Magazine, Consumer.* **Description:** Contains extensive reviews and information on all aspects of snowboarding and the personalities and places associated with it.
Published by: S B C Media, 2255 B Queen St E, Ste 3266, Toronto, ON M4E 1G3, Canada. TEL 416-698-0138, FAX 416-698-8080, info@sbcmedia.com, http://www.sbcmedia.com. Ed. Steve Jarrett. Adv. contact Leslie Atkin. **Dist. by:** International Publishers Direct, 27500 Riverview Center Blvd, Bonita Springs, FL 34134. TEL 858-320-4563, FAX 858-677-3220.

796.93 USA ISSN 1546-9778
THE SNOWBOARD JOURNAL; snowboarding for everyone. Text in English. q. USD 30 domestic; USD 40 in Canada; USD 55 elsewhere (effective 2006). adv. **Document type:** *Magazine, Consumer.*
Related titles: Online - full text ed.
Published by: The Snowboard Journal, 420 Stevens Ave, Ste 350, Solanan Beach, CA 92075. TEL 858-876-1100, 800-839-4544, FAX 858-755-4195. Ed. Scooter Leonard. Pub. Jason Ford.

796.93 NLD ISSN 1383-8652
SNOWBOARD MAGAZINE. Text in Dutch. 1995. a. adv. illus. **Document type:** *Magazine, Consumer.* **Description:** Presents articles and product information relating to snowboarding.
Published by: (Snowboard Holland), ManagementMedia B.V., PO Box 1932, Hilversum, 1200 BX, Netherlands. TEL 31-35-6232756, FAX 31-35-6232401, info@managementmedia.nl, http://www.managementmedia.nl.

796.93 GBR ISSN 0964-0231
SNOWBOARD UK. Text in English. 1991. m. GBP 45.60 domestic; GBP 90 in Europe; GBP 120 elsewhere (effective 2010). adv. back issues avail. **Document type:** *Magazine, Consumer.* **Description:** Promotes the sport of snowboarding in the UK.
Published by: Freestyle Publications Ltd., Alexander House, Ling Rd, Tower Park, Poole, Dorset BH12 4NZ, United Kingdom. TEL 44-1202-735090, FAX 44-1202-733969.

796.93 USA ISSN 1046-0403
GV857.S57
SNOWBOARDER. Text in English. 1988. 8/yr. USD 11.97 domestic; USD 24.97 in Canada; USD 26.97 elsewhere (effective 2008). adv. back issues avail. **Document type:** *Magazine, Consumer.* **Description:** Presents information on the sport of snowboarding and uses professional snowboarders as the conduit to inspire riders to go out and shred, indulge in their passion and progress their riding to the fullest.
Related titles: Online - full text ed.
Indexed: B04, G06, G07, G08, H11, I05, I07, R03, RGAb, RGPR, S23, SD, W03, W05.
—Ingenta. **CCC.**
Published by: Source Interlink Companies, 261 Madison Ave, 6th Fl, New York, NY 10016. TEL 212-915-4000, FAX 212-915-4422, dheine@sourceinterlink.com, http://www.sourceinterlink.com. Ed. Pat Bridges. Pub. Chris Engelsman. adv.: B&W page USD 7,353, color page USD 10,502; trim 8 x 10.5. Circ: 72,826 (paid).

796.93 ITA ISSN 1123-8429
SNOWBOARDER MAGAZINE. Text in Italian. 1995. 7/yr. **Document type:** *Magazine, Consumer.*
Related titles: Online - full text ed.
Published by: Life Edizioni, Via Stazione 2, Baveno, VB 28831, Italy. TEL 39-0323-924644, FAX 39-0323-925197, http://www.lifed.it.

796.93 DEU
SNOWBOARDER MONSTER BACKSIDE MAGAZIN. Variant title: Snowboarder MBM. Text in German. 1990. 9/yr. EUR 29.70; EUR 3.90 newsstand/cover (effective 2008). adv. **Document type:** *Magazine, Consumer.* **Description:** Covers the events, places and products of the snowboarding world.
Published by: b&d Media Network GmbH, Osterfeldstr 12-14, Hamburg, 22529, Germany. TEL 49-40-4800070, FAX 49-40-48000799, info@bdverlag.de, http://www.bdverlag.de. Adv. contact Jennifer Stracke. B&W page EUR 4,500, color page EUR 5,815; trim 230 x 300. Circ: 64,297 (paid and controlled). **Subscr. to:** ASV Vertriebs GmbH. TEL 49-40-2364830.

796.9 NLD ISSN 1871-6857
SNOWBOARDERMAG. Text in Dutch. 1989. q. EUR 14.50 (effective 2009). adv. **Document type:** *Magazine, Consumer.*
Formerly (until 2005): FunSports Snowboarder (1574-8456); Which superseded in part (in 1994): FunSports (0925-0743)
Published by: Maruba b.v., Winthontlaan 200, Utrecht, 3526 KV, Netherlands. TEL 31-30-2891073, FAX 31-30-2887415, maruba@maruba.com, http://www.maruba.nl. Pub. Maas H van Drie. adv.: color page EUR 3,660; trim 170 x 240. Circ: 27,500.

790.1 USA
SNOWEST; western snowmobile authority. Text in English. 1974. 9/yr. USD 19.95 domestic; USD 29.95 in Canada; USD 34.95 elsewhere (effective 2008). adv. back issues avail.; reprints avail. **Document type:** *Magazine, Trade.* **Description:** Provides in-depth information and a better perspective on how to make snowmobiling experience more enjoyable.
Formerly: Snowmobile West Magazine (0164-6540)
Related titles: Special ed(s).: Mod-Stock Competition.
Published by: Harris Publishing, Inc. (Idaho Falls), 360 B St, Idaho Falls, ID 83402-3547. TEL 208-524-7000, 800-638-0135, FAX 208-522-5241, customerservice@harrispublishing.com, http://www.harrispublishing.com. Adv. contact Gregg Manwaring. B&W page USD 13,865, color page USD 17,636; trim 8 x 10.75. Circ: 161,000 (paid and controlled).

796.9 USA ISSN 0274-8363
GV856.4
SNOWMOBILE. Text in English. 1980. s-a. USD 6.97 domestic; USD 8.97 foreign; USD 3.99 newsstand/cover domestic; USD 4.99 newsstand/cover foreign (effective 2007). adv. bk.rev. back issues avail.; reprints avail. **Document type:** *Magazine, Consumer.*
Incorporates (1966-1985): Snow Goer (0191-8095); Formed by the 1980 merger of: SnoTrack (0049-0822); Midwest Snowmobiler
Published by: Affinity Group Inc., 2575 Vista Del Mar, Ventura, CA 93001. TEL 805-667-4100, FAX 805-667-4419, http://www.affinitygroup.com. adv.: B&W page USD 31,100, color page USD 43,900. Circ: 480,935 (controlled).

796.95 SWE ISSN 1103-0844
SNOWMOBILE; largest snowmobile magazine in Europe. Text in Swedish, Norwegian. 1986. m. SEK 33 domestic; USD 50 foreign; SEK 44 newsstand/cover. adv. back issues avail. **Document type:** *Consumer.* **Description:** Presents information on the testing of snowmobiles, technical specifications, touring, racing and testing of products related to snowmobiles.
Formerly (until 1992): Snoe och Terraeng Skoter Magasinet (0284-3390)
Related titles: Online - full text ed.
Published by: Tima Press AB, Fack 2027, Oestersund, 80102, Sweden. TEL 063-1010210-21, FAX 063-101012. Ed., Pub. Jan Engstroem. adv.: color page SEK 16,200; trim 190 x 270. Circ: 12,100.

796.93 USA ISSN 0892-9963
SNOWSHOE (CORINTH). Text in English. 19??. a. USD 5. adv. **Document type:** *Newspaper, Consumer.* **Description:** Covers snowshoe related books, outdoor products and gifts.
Published by: United States Snowshoe Association, 678 County Route 25, Corinth, NY 12822 . TEL 518-654-7648, http://www.snowshoeracing.com/.

796 USA
SNOWSHOE MAGAZINE (EMAIL). Text in English. 2005. m. free (effective 2010). **Document type:** *Newsletter, Consumer.* **Description:** Covers the sport of snowshoeing through reviews, blogs and other written testimonies of gear, products and services.
Formerly: Snowshoe Magazine (Print)
Media: E-mail.
Published by: Alford Publishing, Inc., 10285 Sedalia St, Commerce City, CO 80022. TEL 303-332-4993, FAX 303-635-0392, ryan@snowshoemag.com.

796.93 DEU
SNOWSPORT. Text in German. 1980. bi-m. illus. **Document type:** *Magazine, Trade.*
Former titles (until 1999): Skilehrer Magazin; (until 1983): Deutscher Skilehrerverband. Magazin
Published by: Deutscher Skilehrerverband e.V., Buergermeister-Finsterwalder-Ring 1, Wolfratshausen, 82515, Germany. TEL 49-8171-34720, FAX 49-8171-347210, info@skilehrerverband.de, http://www.skilehrerverband.de. Circ: 8,000.

796.95 USA
SNOWTECH MAGAZINE. Text in English. 1968. 5/yr. USD 15 domestic; USD 22 in Canada; USD 40 elsewhere (effective 2006). 128 p./no.; back issues avail. **Document type:** *Magazine, Consumer.* **Description:** Provides information to technically oriented snowmobilers. Articles explaining snowmobile components, testing of aftermarket products; a "what's new" section, engineering theory, new model reports, step by step articles on how to tune a snowmobile for maximum performance, other "how to" features, with adventurous picture features also included.
Formerly: Race & Rally
Published by: Field Clean Inc., 630 Hiawatha Circle, NW, Alexandria, MN 56308. TEL 320-763-5411, FAX 320-763-1775. Pub., Adv. contact Jim Beilke. Circ: 65,000 (paid); 2,500 (free).

796.63 ESP
SOLO SNOWBOARD. Text in Spanish. m. EUR 12.80 domestic; EUR 22 in Europe; EUR 25 elsewhere (effective 2009). adv. back issues avail. **Document type:** *Magazine, Consumer.*
Published by: Alesport S.A., Gran Via 8-10, Hospitalet de Llobragat, Barcelona, 08902, Spain. TEL 34-93-4315533, FAX 34-93-2973905, http://www.alesport.com.

799.1 799.2 NZL ISSN 1177-5807
SOLUNAR BITE TIMES. Text in English. 2006. a. NZD 8 (effective 2007). **Description:** Forecasts the time of the day when animals are most active.
Published by: OceanFun Publishing Ltd, PO Box 26, Kaikoura, New Zealand. publish@ofu.co.nz, http://www.ofu.co.nz.

SOUTH AFRICAN 4 X 4. *see* TRANSPORTATION—Automobiles

799 USA ISSN 0897-9154
SOUTH CAROLINA GAME & FISH. Text in English. 198?. m. USD 12 domestic; USD 25 in Canada; USD 27 elsewhere (effective 2011). adv. illus. **Document type:** *Magazine, Consumer.* **Description:** Informs sportsmen of hunting and fishing, as well as environmental and conservation issues in South Carolina.
Supersedes in part (in 198?): Carolina Game and Fish (0744-4176)
Related titles: Online - full text ed.; ◆ Regional ed(s).: Game & Fish; ◆ Louisiana Game & Fish. ISSN 0744-3692; ◆ Florida Game & Fish. ISSN 0889-3322; ◆ Alabama Game & Fish. ISSN 0279-6783; ◆ Mississippi-Louisiana Game & Fish. ISSN 1947-2358; ◆ North Carolina Game & Fish. ISSN 0897-8816; ◆ West Virginia Game & Fish. ISSN 0897-9162; ◆ Missouri Game & Fish. ISSN 0889-3799; ◆ New York Game & Fish. ISSN 0897-9189; ◆ California Game & Fish. ISSN 1056-0122; ◆ Great Plains Game & Fish. ISSN 1055-6532; ◆ Illinois Game & Fish. ISSN 0897-9014; ◆ Indiana Game & Fish. ISSN 0897-8980; ◆ Iowa Game & Fish. ISSN 0897-9197; ◆ Mid-Atlantic Game & Fish. ISSN 1055-6540; ◆ Oklahoma Game & Fish. ISSN 0746-6013; ◆ Rocky Mountain Game & Fish. ISSN 1056-0114; ◆ Pennsylvania Game & Fish. ISSN 0897-8808; ◆ Virginia Game & Fish. ISSN 0897-8794; ◆ Washington - Oregon Game & Fish. ISSN 1056-0106; ◆ Ohio Game & Fish. ISSN 0897-9170; New England Game & Fish. ISSN 0897-8972. 1988. USD 12 domestic; USD 25 in Canada; USD 27 elsewhere (effective 2010).
Published by: Intermedia Outdoors, Inc., 512 7th Ave, 11th Fl, New York, NY 10018. TEL 212-852-6682, 800-260-6397, FAX 212-302-4472, customerservice@imoutdoors.com, http://www.imoutdoorsmedia.com. Ed. Ken Dunwoody. Pub., Adv. contact Peter Gross.

SOUTH CAROLINA OUT-OF-DOORS. *see* CONSERVATION

SOUTH CAROLINA WILDLIFE. *see* CONSERVATION

799.1 AUS
SOUTH EAST & WEST FISHING. Text in English. 199?. bi-m. adv. **Document type:** *Magazine, Consumer.* **Description:** Provides up to date information with what is happening in the saltwater scene with what's biting and where.
Formed by the merger of (1995-2007): South East Fishing (1324-3853); Which was formerly (until 1995): Fishing Gippsland (1323-0123); (199?-2006): South West Fishing (1329-6507)
Published by: East Gippsland Newspapers, Cnr Macleod & Bailey St, PO Box 465, Bairnsdale, VIC 3875, Australia. TEL 61-3-51502300, FAX 61-3-51526257, events@eastvicmedia.com.au, http://www.eastvicmedia.com.au/index.php?module=Website&action=Home&content=home. adv.: color page AUD 280.

796 USA
SOUTH FLORIDA ADVENTURES. Text in English. 2005 (May/Jun.). m. USD 21.95 (effective 2007); dist. free in some locations. adv. 60 p./no.; **Document type:** *Magazine, Consumer.* **Description:** Contain regular features on paddling, biking, diving, hiking, traveling and various locations for adventure sports.
Address: PO Box 21051, Fort Lauderdale, FL 33335. TEL 954-683-5336, FAX 954-767-6294. Ed., Pub. David Raterman. adv.: page USD 1,000; trim 8.375 x 10.875. Circ: 10,000.

SOUTHERN FISHERIES; your magazine for South Australian fishing news and issues. *see* FISH AND FISHERIES

SOUTHERN SIERRAN. *see* CONSERVATION

799.2 USA ISSN 1097-2978
GV561
SOUTHERN SPORTING JOURNAL. Text in English. 1996. bi-m. USD 9.99 domestic; USD 19.99 in Canada; USD 24.99 elsewhere (effective 2008). adv. Supplement avail.; back issues avail. **Document type:** *Magazine, Trade.* **Description:** Focuses on hunters, shooters and anglers in the southern region of the United States.
Related titles: Online - full text ed.
Indexed: H20, M02, SD, T02.

S

Published by: Grand View Media Group, Inc. (Subsidiary of: EBSCO Industries, Inc.), 200 Croft St, Ste 1, Birmingham, AL 35242. TEL 888-431-2877, FAX 205-408-3797, webmaster@grandviewmedia.com, http://www.gvmg.com. Ed. Doug Howlett TEL 609-638-2810. Pub. Stephen Statham TEL 205-408-3724. adv.: B&W page USD 2,714, color page USD 2,924; trim 7.75 x 10.625. Circ: 35,000.

799.124 USA ISSN 1536-8505
SOUTHWEST FLY FISHING. Text in English. 2000. bi-m. USD 29.95 domestic; USD 36.95 in Canada; USD 44.95 elsewhere (effective 2007). adv. **Document type:** *Magazine, Consumer.* **Description:** Contains the latest news about fly fishing, conservation, new products and Southwest adventures; detailed, step-by-step fly tying instructions of patterns specifically for Southwest fishing; excerpts from books that will move and inspire readers; humorous anecdotes and fish stories from our writers and readers.
Related titles: ◆ Regional ed(s).: Eastern Fly Fishing; ◆ Northwest Fly Fishing. ISSN 1527-8255.
Published by: Northwest Fly Fishing, LLC., PO Box 708, Raymond, WA 98577. TEL 206-667-9359, FAX 206-667-9364. Ed. Steve Probasco. Adv. contact Pete Crumbaker TEL 206-667-3059. B&W page USD 1,555, color page USD 1,935; trim 8.875 x 10.875. Circ: 17,009 (paid).

799.2 ITA ISSN 1123-9662
GLI SPECIALI DI OLIMPIA. Text in Italian. 1996. bi-m. price varies. adv. 94 p./no.; back issues avail. **Document type:** *Magazine, Consumer.* **Description:** Covers weapons, hunting, dogs and birds.
Published by: Gruppo Editoriale Olimpia SpA, Via E Fermi 24, Loc Osmannoro, Sesto Fiorentino, FI 50129, Italy. TEL 39-055-30321, FAX 39-055-3032280, info@edolimpia.it, http://www.edolimpia.it. Circ: 60,000. **Dist. by:** Parrini & C, Piazza Colonna 361, Rome, RM 00187, Italy. TEL 39-06-695141.

799.1 NLD ISSN 2210-2329
SPIEGEL. Text in Dutch. 2006. bi-m. EUR 44.50 (effective 2010). adv. **Document type:** *Magazine, Consumer.*
Published by: Spiegel Magazine, Industrieweg 92a, Zutphen, 7202 CB, Netherlands. TEL 31-575-544461, FAX 31-575-544487, info@spiegelmagazine.nl, http://www.spiegelmagazine.nl. Eds. Arjen Uitbeijerse, Roelof Schut.

799.1 ITA ISSN 1828-9460
SPINNING MAGAZINE. Text in Italian. 2006. m. EUR 54 (effective 2009). **Document type:** *Magazine, Consumer.*
Published by: Acacia Edizioni, Via Copernico 3, Binasco, MI 20082, Italy. http://www.acaciaedizioni.com.

797.32 AUS
SPLASH. Text in English. s-a. adv. **Document type:** *Magazine, Consumer.* **Description:** Provides tips and advice to girls who are just discovering their love for surfing.
Published by: A C P Magazines Ltd. (Subsidiary of: P B L Media Pty Ltd.), 54-58 Park St, Sydney, NSW 2000, Australia. TEL 61-2-92828000, FAX 61-2-91263769, research@acpaction.com.au. Ed. Jade Harrison. Adv. contact Marcus Hucker TEL 61-2-81149485. page AUD 2,965; trim 205 x 275. Circ: 30,000.

SPORT AVIATION. *see* AERONAUTICS AND SPACE FLIGHT

796.5 FRA ISSN 0397-4707
SPORT ET PLEIN AIR. Text in French. 1952. m. (10/yr.). EUR 25 domestic; EUR 41 foreign (effective 2009). adv. **Document type:** *Magazine, Consumer.*
Indexed: SportS.
Published by: Federation Sportive et Gymnique du Travail, 14 rue de Scandicci, Pantin, Cedex 93508, France. TEL 33-1-49422316. Circ: 70,000.

799.1 USA ISSN 0896-7369
SPORT FISHING; the magazine of saltwater fishing. Text in English. 1986. 10/yr. USD 19.97 for 3 yrs. domestic; USD 31.97 for 3 yrs. in Canada; USD 55.97 for 3 yrs. elsewhere (effective 2011). adv. illus. **Document type:** *Magazine, Consumer.* **Description:** Get tips on baiting, rigging and live-bait selections, instruction on saltwater fly fishing, and tips on boat maintenance.
Related titles: Online - full text ed.: USD 9.97 per issue (effective 2011).
Indexed: G08, I05.
—CCC.
Published by: Bonnier Corp. (Subsidiary of: Bonnier Group), 460 N Orlando Ave, Ste 200, Orlando, FL 32789. TEL 407-628-4802, FAX 407-628-7061, http://www.bonniercorp.com. Eds. Chris Woodward, Doug Olander.

799 AUS ISSN 1322-4883
SPORTDIVING MAGAZINE. Text in English. 1968. bi-m. AUD 46.20 domestic; MYR 90 in Malaysia; SGD 42 in Singapore; AUD 84 elsewhere (effective 2009). adv. bk.rev. illus. Index. back issues avail. **Document type:** *Magazine, Consumer.* **Description:** Provides diving news and in-depth coverage of famous dive destinations from across the globe.
Former titles (until 1993): Sportdiving in Australia and the South Pacific (1033-7458); (until 1986): Skindiving (0726-3112); (until 1980): Skindiving in Australia and the South Pacific (0313-4954); (until 1974): Skindiving in Australia (0313-4946)
Published by: Mountain Ocean & Travel Publications Pty Ltd., PO Box 355, Upper Beaconsfield, VIC 3808, Australia. TEL 61-3-59443774, FAX 61-3-59444024. Ed. Belinda Barnes. Pub. Barry Andrewartha. Adv. contact Leanne Wylie. page AUD 2,488; bleed 210 x 276.

799 USA ISSN 0279-0998
SK1
SPORTING CLASSICS. Text in English. 1981. bi-m. USD 23.95 (effective 2004). adv. bk.rev. back issues avail. **Document type:** *Magazine, Consumer.* **Description:** Features on-location hunting and fishing adventures around the world; articles on fine-quality sporting equipment, collectibles and wildlife artists.
Published by: Sporting Classics Inc., PO Box 23707, Columbia, SC 29224. TEL 803-736-2424, 800-849-1004, FAX 803-736-3404. Ed. Chuck Wechsler. Adv. contact Brian Raley. B&W page USD 2,250, color page USD 2,835; trim 8.125 x 10.75. Circ: 32,000 (paid and controlled).

799.2 GBR ISSN 0141-7053
SPORTING GUN. Text in English. 1977. m. GBP 29.99 domestic; USD 98.10 in United States; USD 124.30 in Canada; EUR 73.10 in Europe; GBP 71.90 elsewhere; GBP 3.40 newsstand/cover (effective 2009). adv. bk.rev. illus.; tr.lit. back issues avail. **Document type:** *Magazine, Consumer.* **Description:** Designed for the rough game and clay shooter.
Published by: I P C Country & Leisure Media Ltd. (Subsidiary of: I P C Media Ltd.), The Blue Fin Bldg, 110 Southwark St, London, SE1 0SU, United Kingdom. TEL 44-20-31485000, http://www.ipcmedia.com. Ed. Robin Scott TEL 44-1780-481077. Pub. Fiona Mercer TEL 44-20-31484311. Adv. contact David Thomas TEL 44-20-31484212. color page GBP 3,045. Circ: 32,886. **Subscr. to:** Rockwood House, Perrymount Rd, Haywards Heath RH16 3DH, United Kingdom. TEL 44-845-1231231, IPCsubs@quadrantsubs.com, http://www.magazinesdirect.co.uk. **Dist. by:** MarketForce UK Ltd. salesinnovation@marketforce.co.uk, http://www.marketforce.co.uk/.

791 RUS
SPORTIVNAYA MOSKVA; informatsionno-sportivnoe izdanie. Text in Russian. w.
Address: Bumazhnyi pr-d 14, Moscow, 101462, Russian Federation. TEL 7-095-2573684. Ed. G A Rogov. Circ: 20,000.

797.56 NLD ISSN 0921-8017
SPORTPARACHUTIST. Text in Dutch. 1959. q. EUR 30 domestic to non-members; EUR 33 foreign to non-members (effective 2009). adv. bk.rev.; software rev.; Website rev. illus. 32 p./no. 4 cols./p.; back issues avail. **Document type:** *Magazine, Consumer.* **Description:** Covers technical (equipment, instruction, regulations) and social (competitions, shows, clubs and people) aspects of skydiving.
Formerly (until 1972): Swing Through the Air (0039-7458)
Published by: Koninklijke Nederlandse Vereniging voor Luchtvaart, Afdeling Parachutespringen/Royal Netherlands Aeronautical Association, Department of Parachuting, Houttuinlaan 16A, Woerden, 3447 GM, Netherlands. TEL 31-348-437060, FAX 31-348-437069, hbp@parachute.nl, http://www.parachute.nl. adv.: color page EUR 885; bleed 210 x 297. Circ: 2,100.

796 USA ISSN 0038-8149
SPORTS AFIELD. Text in English. 1887-2002 (Jun.); resumed 2003 (Jan.). bi-m. USD 24.97 domestic; USD 49.97 foreign (effective 2010). adv. bk.rev. charts; illus. back issues avail. **Document type:** *Magazine, Consumer.* **Description:** Hands-on magazine for outdoor enthusiasts. Covers hiking, fishing, biking, paddeling and off-road activities, nature and conservation issues and practical tips.
Former titles (until 1940): Sports Afield with Rod and Gun; Sports Afield
Related titles: Online - full text ed.
Indexed: A01, A22, C12, ConsI, G05, G06, G07, G08, G09, I05, I07, M01, M02, MagInd, P02, P07, P10, P19, P48, P53, P54, PMR, PQC, S23, SPI.
—Ingenta.
Published by: Sports Afield, Inc., 15621 Chemical Ln, Bldg B, Huntington Beach, CA 92649. TEL 714-373-4910, 800-451-4788, FAX 714-894-4949, letters@sportsafield.com. Ed. Diana Rupp. Pub. Ludo J Wurfbain. Adv. contact James Reed TEL 714-373-4910 ext 20. B&W page USD 2,670, color page USD 4,265; trim 210 x 276.

796 USA ISSN 1521-2114
SPORTS ETC; Seattle's outdoor magazine. Text in English. 1988. m. USD 18 (effective 2001). adv. bk.rev. back issues avail. **Document type:** *Magazine, Consumer.* **Description:** Covers non-motorized outdoor pursuits and "adventure" sports such as cycling, kayaking, running, skiing, snowboarding, and hiking.
Supersedes (in Oct. 1995): Northwest Cyclist
Published by: Price Media Inc., 11715 Greenwood Ave N, Seattle, WA 98133. TEL 206-418-0747, FAX 206-418-0746. Eds. Carolyn Price, Joe Zauner. Pubs. Carolyn Price, Greg Price. R&P Carolyn Price. Adv. contact Greg Price. page USD 1,950; trim 8.25 x 10.75. Circ: 40,000.

338.76359 GBR
▼ **SPORTS TURF, AMENITY & LEISURE.** Text in English. 2009 (Jan.). bi-m. GBP 60 domestic; GBP 72 in Europe; GBP 98 elsewhere (effective 2009). adv. **Document type:** *Journal, Trade.*
—BLDSC (8419.839910).
Published by: Institute of Groundsmanship, 28 Stratford Office Village, Walker Ave, Wolverton Mill East, Milton Keynes, MK12 5TW, United Kingdom. TEL 44-1908-312511, FAX 44-1908-311140, http://www.iog.org. Ed. Siobhan Harper. Adv. contact Clare Johnson TEL 44-1962-736989.

796 DNK ISSN 1396-8521
SPORTSHOP; magasin for sports- og fritidsbranchen. Text in Danish. 1996. q. DKK 264 domestic; DKK 324 foreign; DKK 75 per issue (effective 2008). adv. back issues avail. **Document type:** *Magazine, Trade.* **Description:** Trends in sports clothing and equipment.
Related titles: Online - full text ed.
Published by: Danmarks Sportshandler Forening, Naverland 34, Glostrup, 2600, Denmark. TEL 45-43-434646, FAX 45-43-435532, dsfweb@dsfweb.dk, http://www.dsfweb.dk. Ed. Pia Finne TEL 45-35-824551. Adv. contact Erik Nielsen. B&W page DKK 12,500, color page DKK 14,750; 265 x 176. Circ: 2,001.

799.1 HRV ISSN 1330-9056
SPORTSKI RIBOLOV. Text in Croatian. 1953. bi-m. adv. **Document type:** *Magazine, Consumer.*
Former titles (until 1995): Ribolov (0038-8289); (until 1972): Sportski Ribolov (1330-2027)
Published by: Hrvatski Sportsko Ribolovni Savez/Croatian Sportfishing Association, Samoborska cesta b.b., Sveta Nedjelja, 10431, Croatia. TEL 385-1-3372350, FAX 385-1-3372350. Ed. Aleksandar Puskadija. Circ: 30,000.

799 NLD ISSN 1380-2135
SPORTVISSERSMAGAZINE BEET. Text in Dutch. 1989. m. EUR 49.50; EUR 4.95 newsstand/cover (effective 2011). adv. illus. **Document type:** *Magazine, Consumer.* **Description:** Covers all aspects of sport fishing and angling.
Formerly (until 1992): Sportvissers Magazine (0924-3763); Which was formed by the merger of (1984-1989): Visblad Extra (0921-7010); Which was formerly (until 1986): Sportvissers Journaal (0921-7088); (1976-1989): Beet (0166-6827); Which incorporates (1970-1985): Vissport (0165-3431)
Related titles: Online - full content ed.

Published by: Vipmedia Publishing en Services, Takkebijsters 57a, Breda, 4817 BL, Netherlands. TEL 31-76-5301717, FAX 31-76-5144531, info@vipmedia.nl, http://www.vipmedia.nl. Ed. Pierre Bronsgeest. Adv. contact John Huussen TEL 31-76-5301725. **Subscr. in Belgium to:** Vipmedia, Bredabaan 852, Merksem 2170, Belgium. TEL 32-53-810480, FAX 32-53-810490; **Subscr. to:** Postbus 7272, Breda 4800 GG, Netherlands.

799.1 NZL ISSN 1177-6463
SPOT X; New Zealand fishing guide news. Variant title: N Z Fishing Guide Book. Text in English. 1988. a. NZD 39.99 per vol. (effective 2008). **Document type:** *Handbook/Manual/Guide, Consumer.*
Formerly (until 2006): New Zealand Fishing News. Map Guide Annual (1174-8737)
Address: 274 Church St, Penrose, PO Box 12965, Auckland, New Zealand. TEL 64-9-6341800, FAX 64-9-6342948, http://www.spotx.com.

796 USA ISSN 1945-7723
THE STANDERD WAKE QUARTERLY. Text in English. 2007. q. USD 35 domestic; USD 65 in Canada; USD 85 elsewhere (effective 2008). adv. **Document type:** *Magazine, Consumer.*
Published by: Standerd Media, 2875 S Orange Ave, Ste 500-2710, Orlando, FL 32806.

796.522 NOR ISSN 0049-2248
STI OG VARDE. Text in Norwegian. 1970. q. NOK 90 (effective 1996). adv. bk.rev. illus. **Document type:** *Bulletin.*
—CCC.
Published by: Bergen Turlag, C Sundts Gate 3, Bergen, 5004, Norway. FAX 47-55-32-81-15. Ed. Torill Refsdal Aase. Circ: 10,000.

STIHL POST. *see* FORESTS AND FORESTRY

796 ZAF
STRAIGHT 25; clay shooting, fly fishing, equestrian. Text in English. 1995. bi-m. illus. **Document type:** *Magazine, Consumer.*
Published by: Advisory Bureau for Development, PO Box 95020, Pretoria, 0145, South Africa.

796 ZAF ISSN 1818-6904
STUFF U NEED!. Text in English. 2006. m. free (effective 2006). adv. **Document type:** *Magazine, Consumer.* **Description:** Covers all sports and events, health and nutrition, sports equipment, clothing and footwear, new products, places to stay, restaurants, and interviews with up-and-coming sports personalities.
Published by: ProImage Media cc, PO Box 371, Gillitts, 3603, South Africa. adv.: color page ZAR 5,000; trim 185 x 310.

799.1 ZAF ISSN 0040-7399
STYWE LYNE/TIGHT LINES. Text in Afrikaans, English. 1960. m. adv.
Published by: Outdoor Pages, PO Box 12270, Brandhof, Bloemfontein, 9324, South Africa. TEL 27-12-8041496, FAX 27-12-8049861, info@outdoorpages.co.za, http://www.outdoorpages.co.za. Ed. Ettene Kriel. Adv. contact Craig Lesser.

796 ITA ISSN 0390-4415
IL SUBACQUEO. Text in Italian. 1973. m. (11/yr.). EUR 56 domestic (effective 2009). adv. **Document type:** *Magazine, Consumer.*
Published by: La Cuba Srl, Via della Maratona 66, Rome, RM 00194, Italy. TEL 39-063-629021, FAX 39-063-6309950. Circ: 70,000.

797 FRA ISSN 0990-0845
SUBAQUA. Text in French. 1958. bi-m. adv. bk.rev.; film rev. illus.; charts. index. **Document type:** *Magazine, Consumer.*
Formerly: Etudes et Sports Sous-Marins (0425-5054); Incorporates (in 1981): Aventure Sous-Marine (0005-1977)
Indexed: SportS.
Published by: Federation Francaise d'Etudes et de Sports Sous-Marins, 24 quai de Rive Neuve, Marseille, Cedex 7 13007, France. TEL 33-4-91339970, FAX 33-4-91547743. Ed. Pierre Martin Razi. Pub. Francis Imbert. Adv. contact Max Walker. Circ: 35,000.

799.2 USA ISSN 1541-6259
SUCCESSFUL HUNTER. Text in English. 2003. bi-m. USD 19.97 domestic; USD 26 foreign (effective 2007). adv. 76 p./no. 3 cols./p.; **Document type:** *Magazine, Consumer.*
Published by: Wolfe Publishing Co., 2625 Stearman Rd., Ste. A, Prescott, AZ 86301-6155. TEL 928-445-7810, FAX 928-778-5124. Pub. Mark Harris. Adv. contact Don Polacek. B&W page USD 2,667, color page USD 3,410; trim 8.5 x 10.875. Circ: 107,000.

799.1 FIN ISSN 0789-6638
SUOMEN KALAPAIKKAOPAS. Variant title: Kalapaikat. Text in Finnish; Summaries in English, German, Swedish. 1966. irreg. adv. index. **Document type:** *Magazine, Consumer.* **Description:** Guide to angling in Finland.
Formerly (until 1988): Kalastuspaikkaopas (0075-4684)
Related titles: ◆ Series of: Kalatalouden Keskusliiton Julkaisu. ISSN 0783-3954.
Published by: Kalatalouden Keskusliitto/Federation of Finnish Fisheries Associations, Koeydenpunojankatu 7 B 23, Helsinki, 00180, Finland. TEL 358-9-6844590, FAX 358-9-68445959, kalustus@ahven.net, http://www.ahven.fi. Ed. Markku Myllyae. Adv. contact Jouko Poutanen. Circ: 10,000.

796 USA ISSN 1069-5508
SUPER LOOPER MAGAZINE. Text in English. 1992. m. USD 20 (effective 2005). **Document type:** *Magazine, Consumer.* **Description:** For members of the United States Team Roping Championships.
Published by: Equibrand Entertainment Group, 2340 Meanul, Ste 400, Albuquerque, NM 87107. TEL 505-899-1870, FAX 505-792-5678. Ed. Robin Davis. Circ: 30,000 (paid).

796.95 CAN ISSN 1195-4965
SUPERTRAX INTERNATIONAL. Text in English, French. 1989. 4/yr. CAD 14.99, USD 11 (effective 2005). adv. **Document type:** *Magazine, Consumer.* **Description:** News, tests and specifications about snowmobiles and the industry across Canada and the US.
Formerly: Supertrax
Published by: Supertrax Publishing Inc., 856 Upper James Street, Box 20219, Hamilton, ON L9C 7M8, Canada. TEL 705-286-2135, 800-905-8729, FAX 705-286-6308, info@supertraxmag.com. Ed. Kent Lester. Pub. Terrence D Kehoe. Adv. contact John Hildebrandt. B&W page USD 15,390, color page USD 20,750. Circ: 220,000 (controlled).

796.172 DEU ISSN 1436-5618
SURF. Text in German. 1977. 10/yr. EUR 42 in Germany & Austria; EUR 45 in Switzerland; EUR 55.50 elsewhere; EUR 4.50 newsstand/cover (effective 2011). adv. bk.rev. illus. **Document type:** *Magazine, Consumer.*
Former titles (until 1994): Surf-Magazin (0944-9159); (until 1988): Surf (0342-7560)
—CCC.
Published by: Delius Klasing Verlag GmbH, Siekerwall 21, Bielefeld, 33602, Germany. TEL 49-521-5590, FAX 49-521-559113, info@delius-klasing.de, http://www.delius-klasing.de. Ed. Andreas Erbe.

796.3 ESP ISSN 1135-3775
SURF A VELA; revista mensual de windsurfing. Text in Spanish. 1984. m. adv. illus. back issues avail. **Document type:** *Magazine, Consumer.* **Description:** Covers the world of windsurfing: travel, races, equipment, people and industry. Includes snowboarding in the wintertime.
Published by: Editorial Noray, S.A., Cardeenal Vives i Tuto 59, Barcelona, 08034, Spain. TEL 34-93-4146496, info@noray.es, http://www.noray.es. Ed. Panxo Pi Suner Canellas. Pub. Pablo Zendrera Zariquiey. Adv. contact Irene Cereceda. Circ: 20,000.

797.172 USA ISSN 0270-2630
GV840.S8
SURF REPORT; journal of international surfing destinations. Text in English. 1980. m. USD 35; USD 42 foreign. adv. back issues avail. **Document type:** *Newsletter.*
Address: PO Box 1028, Dana Point, CA 92629. TEL 714-496-5922, FAX 714-496-7849. Ed., Pub., R&P Chris Dixon. Adv. contact Beth Gessner.

799.1 ITA ISSN 1828-7948
SURFCASTING MAGAZINE. Text in Italian. 2006. m. **Document type:** *Magazine, Consumer.*
Published by: Acacia Edizioni, Via Copernico 3, Binasco, MI 20082, Italy. http://www.acaciaedizioni.com.

797.172 USA ISSN 0039-6036
GV840.S8
SURFER. Text in English. 1960. m. USD 14.97 domestic; USD 27.97 in Canada; USD 29.97 foreign (effective 2008). adv. back issues avail. **Document type:** *Magazine, Consumer.* **Description:** Covers a wide spectrum of the sport from important amateur and professional competitions, along with profiles of the pros and soon-to-be pros, to far-ranging environmental concerns and special coverage of female athletes in the sport.
Related titles: Online - full text ed.
Indexed: A22, B04, G05, G06, G07, G08, I05, I06, I07, MagInd, R03, RGAb, RGPR, S23, SD, SPI, SportS, W03, W05.
—CCC.
Published by: Source Interlink Companies, 6420 Wilshire Blvd, 10th Fl, Los Angeles, CA 90048. TEL 323-782-2000, FAX 323-782-2585, dheine@sourceinterlink.com, http://www.sourceinterlinkmedia.com. Eds. Chris Mauro, Joel Patterson. Pub. Rick Irons. Adv. contact Inna Cazares. color page USD 14,470; trim 8 x 10.5. Circ: 106,048 (paid).

797.172 USA
SURFERGIRL. Text in English. bi-m. USD 14.95; USD 24.95 foreign (effective 1998). **Document type:** *Magazine, Consumer.*
Address: PO Box 3618, Half Moon Bay, CA 94019. FAX 650-726-3299.

797.172 USA ISSN 1062-3892
GV840.S8 CODEN: OCMEE8
THE SURFER'S JOURNAL. Text in English. 1992. q. USD 39; USD 55 foreign. adv. bk.rev. illus. back issues avail. **Document type:** *Magazine, Consumer.* **Description:** Includes information on the sport, art, lifestyle, and culture of surfing for experienced surfers.
Related titles: Online - full text ed.
Published by: Steve Pezman, Ed. & Pub., 1010 Calle Cordillera, Ste 102, San Clemente, CA 92673-6243. TEL 714-361-0331, 800-666-2121, FAX 714-361-2417. R&P Steve Pezman. Adv. contact Debbee Pezman. color page USD 4,200. Circ: 22,000 (paid).

797.32 FRA ISSN 1257-8576
SURFER'S JOURNAL. Text in French. 1994. bi-m. EUR 55 domestic; EUR 68 in the European Union; EUR 80 elsewhere (effective 2008). **Document type:** *Magazine, Consumer.*
Published by: Surf Session, 20 rue Maryse Bastie, Anglet, 64600, France. TEL 33-5-59417000, FAX 33-5-59412412, surf@atlantel.fr, http://www.surfsession.com.

796.172 GBR ISSN 1366-2678
THE SURFER'S PATH. Text in English. 1997. bi-m. GBP 24.95 domestic; GBP 33 in Europe; GBP 45 elsewhere; GBP 3.95 newsstand/cover; USD 7.95 newsstand/cover in United States. back issues avail. **Document type:** *Handbook/Manual/Guide, Consumer.* **Description:** Provides a wealth of information for the traveling surfer. Every two months, the editors will feature a region, an area or break that they think is worth a trip, giving information about the waves, getting there, and staying there,.
Published by: Permanent Publishing Ltd., 1 Stert St, Abingdon, Oxon OX14 3JF, United Kingdom. TEL 44-1235-536229, FAX 44-1235-536230. Ed. Alex Dick Read. Pub. Jim Peskett.

797.32 305.4 FRA ISSN 1960-2464
SURFEUSES. Text in French. 2003. q. EUR 17 domestic; EUR 27 in the European Union; EUR 42 elsewhere (effective 2008). **Document type:** *Magazine, Consumer.* **Description:** For the woman surfer.
Formerly (until 2007): Session (1761-9432)
Published by: Surf Session, 20 rue Maryse Bastie, Anglet, 64600, France. TEL 33-5-59417000, FAX 33-5-59412412, surf@atlantel.fr, http://www.surfsession.com.

797.172 USA ISSN 0194-9314
SURFING. Text in English. 1964. m. USD 12 domestic; USD 25 in Canada; USD 27 elsewhere (effective 2008). adv. bk.rev. illus. back issues avail.; reprints avail. **Document type:** *Magazine, Consumer.* **Description:** Educates readers on new and emerging trends and ideas within the sport and empowers them to be better surfers.
Related titles: Online - full text ed.: USD 6 (effective 2008); ♦ Supplement(s): S G: Surf Snow Skate Girl.
Indexed: B04, CalPI, G06, G07, G08, H11, I05, R03, RGAb, RGPR, S23, SD, SportS, W03, W05.
—CCC.
Published by: Source Interlink Companies, 6420 Wilshire Blvd, 10th Fl, Los Angeles, CA 90048. TEL 323-782-2000, FAX 323-782-2585, dheine@sourceinterlink.com, http://www.sourceinterlinkmedia.com. Ed. Evan Slater. Pubs. James Lynch, Tony Perez. adv.: B&W page USD 10,268, color page USD 14,286. Circ: 97,842.

796.22 PRT ISSN 1647-6271
▼ **SURGE SKATEBOARD MAGAZINE.** Text in Portuguese. 2010. bi-m. free (effective 2011). **Document type:** *Magazine, Consumer.*
Address: Avenida 1o de Maio 42, Costa de Caparica, 2825-394, Portugal. info@surgeskateboard.com, http://www.surgeskateboard.com.

796 POL ISSN 1730-5241
SURVIVAL. Text in Polish. 2003. m. PLZ 103.20 domestic; PLZ 117.60 in Europe; PLZ 235.20 in United States; PLZ 5.60 newsstand/cover (effective 2004). adv. **Document type:** *Magazine, Consumer.*
Published by: Oficyna Wydawnicza OIKOS, ul Kaliska 1/7, Warsaw, 02316, Poland. TEL 48-22-8220334, oikos@oikos.net.pl, http://www.oikos.net.pl. Adv. contact Agnieszka Lobik-Przejsz.

796.96 SWE ISSN 0346-2048
SVENSK CURLING. Text in Swedish. 1961. q. SEK 80 in Sweden; SEK 100 in Scandinavia; SEK 120 in Europe; SEK 140 elsewhere (effective 2001). adv. illus. **Document type:** *Consumer.*
Formerly (until vol.4, 1971): Curling (0011-3107)
Published by: Svenska Curlingfoerbundet, Farsta, 12387, Sweden. FAX 46-86-04-70-78. Ed., Pub. Haakan Sundstroem. Circ: 5,000.

799 SWE ISSN 0039-6583
SVENSK JAKT. Text in Swedish. 1832. m. SEK 375 (effective 2001). adv. bk.rev. charts; illus. Supplement avail. **Document type:** *Magazine, Consumer.* **Description:** Focuses on nature. Covers shooting, hunting and dog-breeding.
Related titles: Supplement(s): Svensk Jakt Nyheter. 1998.
Published by: Svenska Jaegarefoerbundet/Swedish Hunters Association, Oester-Malma, Nykoeping, 61191, Sweden. TEL 46-155-246200, FAX 46-155-246250. Ed., Pub. Jan Henricson. Adv. contact Lennart Aastroem TEL 46-8-54021597. B&W page SEK 28,875, color page SEK 38,850; trim 183 x 250. Circ: 174,100 (controlled).

796.93 SWE
SVENSK SKIDSPORTSKI & BOARD MAGAZINE. Text in Swedish. 1969. 15/yr. SEK 320 domestic; SEK 520 in Scandinavia; SEK 620 elsewhere (effective 2004). adv. bk.rev.
Former titles (until 2005): Svensk Skidsport (0049-2671); (until 2002): Svenska Skidfoerbundet. Nyheter och Meddelandens; Which incorporated (1966-1988): Alpin Skidsport (0349-800X)
Published by: (Svenska Skidfoerbundet), Daus Tryck och Media, Daushuset, Bjaesta, 89380, Sweden. TEL 46-660-266100, FAX 46-660-266128. Adv. contact Solveig Engstrand TEL 46-660-166108. B&W page SEK 103,000, color page SEK 12,900; 185 x 260.

SVENSKT FISKE (BROMMA). *see* FISH AND FISHERIES

797.21 613.7 USA
SWIMMING POOLS TODAY. Text in English. 1985. q. looseleaf. USD 5. bk.rev. **Document type:** *Newsletter.* **Description:** Featuring the swimming pool: safety, chemistry, cleaning, repair, and new products; swimming for fitness and health; entertainment at the poolside.
Published by: National Swimming Pool Owner's Association (NSPOA), 1213 Ridgecrest Circle, Denton, TX 76205-5421. Ed., Pub. Tom A Doron. Circ: 36,000.

SYLVANIAN. *see* CONSERVATION

796 USA ISSN 1559-3568
SYNCHRONIZED SKATING MAGAZINE. Text in English. 2003. q. USD 35.50 (effective 2007). back issues avail. **Document type:** *Magazine, Consumer.*
Address: PO Box 646, Royal Oak, MI 48068-0646. custserv@synchronizedskatingmag.com, http://synchronizedskatingmag.com.

796.42 JPN
T. TENNIS; tennis magazine. Text in Japanese. 1983. m. JPY 4,200.
Published by: Gakken Co. Ltd., 1-17-15, Nakaikegami, Otaku, Tokyo, 145-0064, Japan. Ed. Kunio Suganuma.

688.7 GBR ISSN 0955-7695
TACKLE & GUNS. Text in English. 1957. m. free to qualified personnel. adv. bk.rev. illus.; stat.; tr.lit. **Document type:** *Magazine, Trade.* **Description:** Contains the latest news on what is happening to suppliers, agents and retailers, not to mention in-depth features on the vital issues of the day.
Former titles (until 1988): Shooting and Fishing Trade News (0953-086X); (until 1987): Tackle and Guns (0015-3052)
—BLDSC (8598.170000). **CCC.**
Published by: David Hall Publishing Ltd. (Subsidiary of: DHP Holdings Ltd.), 2 Stephenson Close, Drayton Fields, Daventry, Northants NN11 8RF, United Kingdom. TEL 44-1327-311999, FAX 44-1327-311190, info@dhpub.co.uk. Ed. John Hunter TEL 44-1327-315412. Pub. Sean O'Driscoll.

796 CAN ISSN 1183-7950
TAMARACK MAGAZINE. Text in English. 1991. a. **Document type:** *Magazine, Consumer.*
Related titles: Online - full content ed.
Published by: Mackenzie High School, c/o Mr. John Steer, 82 Brookhouse Way, PO Box 397, Deep River, ON K0J 1P0, Canada. TEL 613-584-3361 ext 33, FAX 613-584-1706.

796 AUS
TANDANYA. Text in English. 1971. q. AUD 10 to members (effective 2008). adv. illus. **Document type:** *Magazine, Consumer.* **Description:** Provides information and articles related to bush walking, offers conservation reports, walks reports and food recipes.
Related titles: Online - full text ed.
Published by: Adelaide Bushwalkers Inc., PO Box 178, Unley, SA 5061, Australia. TEL 61-8-82265525, FAX 61-8-82265523, info@adelaidebushwalkers.org. Ed., R&P, Adv. contact David Evans. Circ: 220.

797 AUS ISSN 0157-2938
THE TASMANIAN TRAMP. Text in English. 1933. biennial, latest no.38. AUD 20 per issue (effective 2010). adv. cum.index: 1933-1963; 1966-1979. back issues avail. **Document type:** *Magazine, Consumer.* **Description:** Covers articles of general interest to bushwalkers, photographs and sketches, as well as descriptions of walking trips in various parts of Tasmania and sometimes interstate or overseas.
Published by: Hobart Walking Club, GPO Box 753, Hobart, TAS 7001, Australia. secretary@hobartwalkingclub.org.au. Circ: 1,300.

796.939 NLD ISSN 1574-7549
TASTE SNOWBOARD MAGAZINE. Text in Dutch. 1999. s-a. EUR 11.90 (effective 2010). adv. **Document type:** *Magazine, Consumer.*
Published by: Soul Media, Stetweg 43C, Castricum, 1901 JD, Netherlands. TEL 31-251-674911, FAX 31-251-674378, info@soulonline.nl, http://www.soulonline.nl. Circ: 20,000.

TEAM AND TRAIL; the musher's monthly news. *see* PETS

799.2 USA
TED NUGENT ADVENTURE OUTDOORS. Text in English. 1989. bi-m. USD 26. adv.
Former titles (until 1996): World Bowhunters; Ted Nugent United Sportsmen of America
Address: 4133 W Michigan Ave, Jackson, MI 49202. TEL 517-750-9060, FAX 517-750-3640. Ed. Ted Nugent. Adv. contact Cyndy Brogdon. Circ: 15,000.

796.42 FRA ISSN 1766-9057
TEMPS COURSE MAG. Text in French. 2004. m. **Document type:** *Magazine, Consumer.*
Published by: Temps Course, 8 Rue de la Republique, Montpellier, 34000, France. TEL 33-4-67585287, FAX 33-4-67583292.

THE TENNESSEE CONSERVATIONIST; nature, environmental issues. *see* CONSERVATION

790.1 USA
TENNESSEE SPORTSMAN. Text in English. 1980. m. USD 14.97 domestic; USD 27.97 in Canada; USD 29.97 elsewhere (effective 2008). illus. **Document type:** *Magazine, Consumer.* **Description:** Discusses all aspects of hunting and fishing, as well as environmental and conservation issues in Tennessee.
Published by: Intermedia Outdoors, Inc., 512 7th Ave, 11th Fl, New York, NY 10018. TEL 212-852-6600, 800-260-6397, FAX 212-302-4472, customerservice@imoutdoors.com, http://www.imoutdoorsmedia.com. Pub. Jimmy Stewart. Circ: 18,475.

799 USA ISSN 1077-4572
TENNESSEE VALLEY OUTDOORS; the enthusiast's guide to fishing, hunting, boating and recreation. Text in English. 1993. m. USD 14.95 (effective 2007). adv. **Document type:** *Magazine, Consumer.* **Description:** Contains features on fishing, hunting, boating, and issues of concern to outdoors enthusiasts in Tennessee and the Tennessee Valley.
Related titles: Online - full text ed.
Published by: Media Services Group, Inc., PO Box 157, Greeneville, TN 37744. TEL 423-638-4177, FAX 423-638-3328. Ed. Doug Morris. Adv. contact Barry Wilson.

799 USA ISSN 0887-4174
SK131
TEXAS FISH & GAME. Text in English. 1973. 12/yr. USD 19 (effective 2005). **Document type:** *Magazine, Consumer.* **Description:** Covers hunting and fishing activities.
Incorporates (1973-1991): Texas Fisherman
Related titles: Online - full text ed.
Indexed: M01, M02, P34, T02.
Published by: Highland Publishing Co., 1745 Greens Rd, Houston, TX 77032-3132. TEL 281-227-3001, FAX 281-227-3002. Pub. Roy Neves. Adv. contact Ardia Neves. Circ: 105,000 (paid).

799.2 USA
TEXAS HUNTING DIRECTORY. Text in English. s-a. USD 19.95 (effective 2001). **Document type:** *Magazine, Consumer.* **Description:** Provides extensive and up-to-date information on hunting in Texas.
Address: PO Box1787, Fredericksburg, TX 78624. TEL 800-676-5703, FAX 830-997-6873, http://www.texashunting.com.

796 USA ISSN 1082-5940
TEXAS OUTDOORS JOURNAL. Text in English. 1992. m. USD 13.95 (effective 2002). **Document type:** *Magazine, Consumer.*
Published by: Texas Outdoors Journal, Inc., 1706 W. Sam Houston Pkwy N, Houston, TX 77043.

799.1 USA
TEXAS RECREATIONAL FRESH AND SALTWATER FISHING GUIDE (YEAR). Text in English. a. free. adv. **Document type:** *Government.* **Description:** Summary of fishing regulations.
Published by: Texas Parks and Wildlife Department, 3000 S IH35, Ste 120, Austin, TX 78704. TEL 512-389-4800, FAX 512-389-4894.

799.16 USA ISSN 1935-9586
TEXAS SALTWATER FISHING MAGAZINE. Text mainly in English. 2007. m. USD 34 (effective 2007). **Document type:** *Magazine, Consumer.* **Description:** Features information about boating, lures, competitions, conservation advice from professionals and for saltwater fishermen.
Related titles: Online - full text ed.: ISSN 1937-0970.
Address: PO Box 429, Seadrift, TX 77983. TEL 361-785-3420. Ed. Everett Johnson.

799.2 799.1 USA
TEXAS SPORTING JOURNAL. Text in English. 2003 (Oct.). bi-m. USD 19.95; USD 53.95 newsstand/cover (effective 2005). adv. **Document type:** *Journal, Magazine, Consumer.* **Description:** Covers hunting, fishing and adventure for discriminating sportsman and women.
Published by: Wildlife Publishing LLC, World Head Quarters, 34 Herff Rd, Boerne, TX 78006. TEL 830-816-2548, rbiles@texassportingjournal.com. Ed. Marc McDonald. adv.: color page USD 4,400; trim 8.5 x 10.875.

799 USA ISSN 0279-8875
TEXAS SPORTSMAN. Text in English. 19??. m. USD 14.97 domestic; USD 27.97 in Canada; USD 29.97 elsewhere (effective 2008). adv. illus. **Document type:** *Magazine, Consumer.* **Description:** Provides the sportsman with in-depth information on the whens, wheres, and hows of hunting and fishing. Covers environmental and conservation issues in Texas.
Formerly (until 19??): Texas Sportsman Magazine

S

Published by: Intermedia Outdoors, Inc., 512 7th Ave, 11th Fl, New York, NY 10018. TEL 212-852-6600, 800-260-6397, FAX 212-302-4472, customerservice@imoutdoors.com, http://www.imoutdoorsmedia.com. adv.: B&W page USD 13,830, color page USD 19,360; trim 7.875 x 10.75. Circ: 33,000.

796.552 JPN
THE-YAMA-TO-KEIKOKU/MOUNTAIN AND VALLEY. Text in Japanese. 1930. m.
Published by: Yama-Kei (Publishers) Co. Ltd., 1-1-33 Shiba-Daimon, Minato-ku, Tokyo, 105-0000, Japan. TEL 03-3436-4023. Ed. Akira Yamaguchi. Circ: 230,000.

796.172 GBR ISSN 1352-9471
THREESIXTY BODYBOARD MAGAZINE. Text in English. 1992. q. GBP 12.99 domestic; GBP 14.99 in Europe; GBP 16.99 elsewhere (effective 2009). adv. back issues avail. **Document type:** *Magazine, Consumer.* **Description:** Aimed at bodyboarders aged 13-25, includes travel photo series, news, international and British competition coverage, and how-to features.
Published by: Orca Publications Ltd., Berry Rd Studios, Berry Rd, Newquay, Cornwall TR7 1AT, United Kingdom. TEL 44-1637-878074, FAX 44-1637-850226, info@orcasurf.co.uk, http://www.orcasurf.co.uk. Ed. Rob Barber. Pub. Louise Searle. **Dist. by:** Seymour Distribution Ltd.

799.2 DEU
THUERINGER JAEGER. Text in German. 1989. m. adv. **Document type:** *Magazine, Consumer.*
Published by: (Landesjagdverband Thueringen e.V.), Deutscher Landwirtschaftsverlag GmbH, Kabelkamp 6, Hannover, 30179, Germany. TEL 49-511-678060, FAX 49-511-67806200, dlv.hannover@dlv.de, http://www.dlv.de. adv.: B&W page EUR 1,685, color page EUR 2,279; trim 203 x 292. Circ: 9,500 (controlled).

796.42 CHN ISSN 1000-3509
TIANJING/TRACK & FIELD. Text in Chinese. 1981. m. USD 62.40 (effective 2009). **Document type:** *Magazine, Consumer.*
Related titles: Online - full content ed.; Online - full text ed.
—East View.
Published by: (Zhongguo Tianjing Xiehui/China track and Field Association), Zhongguo Tiyubao Yezongshe, 8, Tiyuguan Lu, Chongwen-qu, Beijing, 100061, China. TEL 86-10-67167788 ext 279, FAX 86-10-67158575. **Dist. in U.S. by:** China International Book Trading Corp, 35 Chegongzhuang Xilu, Haidian District, PO Box 399, Beijing 100044, China. TEL 86-10-68412045, FAX 86-10-68412023, cibtc@mail.cibtc.com.cn, http://www.cibtc.com.cn.

TIDE. *see* CONSERVATION

796.5 SWE ISSN 0348-5617
TILL FJAELLS. Text in Swedish. 1929. biennial. adv. back issues avail. **Document type:** *Consumer.*
Indexed: GeoRef.
Published by: Svenska Fjaellklubben/Swedish Alpine Club, Skogvaktargatan 6 B, Stockholm, 11542, Sweden. info@fjallklubben.se, http://www.fjallklubben.se.

799.32 FRA ISSN 1269-5475
LE TIR A L'ARC. Text in French. 1927. bi-m. EUR 27 domestic to members; EUR 40 domestic to non-members; EUR 54 foreign to non-members (effective 2009). **Document type:** *Magazine, Consumer.*
Formerly (until 1926): Vrai Chevalier (1269-5483)
Published by: Federation Francaise du Tir a l'Arc, 268-270 rue de Brement, Rosny-sous-Bois, Cedex 93561, France. TEL 33-1-48121220, FAX 33-1-48942348, ffta@ffta.fr, http://www.ffta.fr. Ed. Philippe Bouclet. Adv. contact Didier Aubin.

799.32 FRA ISSN 1964-9576
TIR A L'ARC MAGAZINE. Text in French. 2008. q. EUR 25 domestic; EUR 32 foreign (effective 2009). **Document type:** *Magazine, Consumer.*
Published by: Editions Crepin-Leblond, 14 rue du Patronage Laique, Chaumont, 52000, France. TEL 33-3-25038748, FAX 33-3-25038740, crepin-leblond@graphycom.com.

TODAY'S PLAYGROUND. *see* CHILDREN AND YOUTH—About

799.1 GBR ISSN 1467-7938
TOTAL CARP. Text in English. 1999. m. GBP 36 domestic; GBP 50 in Europe; GBP 65 elsewhere; GBP 3.40 newsstand/cover (effective 2009). adv. illus. 132 p./no. 3 cols./p.; back issues avail. **Document type:** *Magazine, Consumer.* **Description:** Discusses carp fishing, with emphasis on techniques and tips, new tackle and equipment and competitions.
Former titles (until 1999): Catchmore Carp (1360-3213); (until 1995): Carp News & Angling Techniques (1354-0238)
Published by: David Hall Publishing Ltd. (Subsidiary of: DHP Holdings Ltd.), 2 Stephenson Close, Drayton Fields, Daventry, Northants NN11 8RF, United Kingdom. TEL 44-1327-311999, FAX 44-1327-311190, info@dhpub.co.uk, http://www.davidhallpublishing.com. Ed. Marc Coulson TEL 44-1327-315425. Pub. David Hall TEL 44-1327-315402. Adv. contact Dean Rothery TEL 44-1327-315432. color page GBP 845; 210 x 297. **Dist. by:** Magazine Marketing Co.

796.42 USA ISSN 1042-878X
GV1060.67
TRACK AND FIELD AND CROSS COUNTRY RULES BOOK. Cover title: Official High School Track and Field and Cross Country Rules. Text in English. a. USD 6.95 per issue (effective 2009). adv. **Document type:** *Handbook/Manual/Guide, Trade.* **Description:** Contains the official rules for track and field & cross country, and is used by coaches, officials, players and many fans who wish to know more about the rules of the game.
Former titles: National Federation Track and Field Rule Book (0270-4129); Track and Field Rules and Records
Published by: National Federation of State High School Associations, PO Box 690, Indianapolis, IN 46206. TEL 317-972-6900, 800-776-3462, FAX 317-822-5700, info@nfhs.org, http://www.nfhs.org.

796.42 USA
TRACK AND FIELD CASE BOOK. Text in English. 19??. a. USD 6.95 per issue (effective 2009). adv. **Document type:** *Handbook/Manual/Guide, Trade.* **Description:** Provides the track and field enthusiasts with in-depth information on the actual play situations.
Published by: National Federation of State High School Associations, PO Box 690, Indianapolis, IN 46206. TEL 317-972-6900, 800-776-3462, FAX 317-822-5700, info@nfhs.org, http://www.nfhs.org.

796.42 USA ISSN 0041-0284
GV1060.5
TRACK & FIELD NEWS; the bible of the sports. Text in English. 1948. m. USD 43.95 domestic; USD 55 in Canada; USD 69 elsewhere (effective 2010). adv. bk.rev. illus.; mkt. back issues avail.; reprints avail. **Document type:** *Magazine, Consumer.* **Description:** Provides complete coverage of the sport of track and field from high school to the Olympic level including news, features, interviews, and action photos.
Related titles: Microform ed.: (from PQC); Online - full text ed.
Indexed: A22, RASB, SD, SPI, SportS.
—IE, Infotrieve, Ingenta.
Address: 2570 El Camino Real, Ste 480, Mountain View, CA 94040. TEL 650-943-8188, FAX 650-948-9445, tjordan@trackandfieldnews.com. Ed. E Garry Hill. Pub. Ed Fox.

796.42 USA
TRACK AND FIELD OFFICIALS MANUAL. Text in English. 19??. biennial. USD 6.95 per issue (effective 2009). **Document type:** *Handbook/Manual/Guide, Trade.* **Description:** Designed for those who wish to enter the field of officiating or to those who are interested in improving their competence in the field of track and field.
Formerly: National Federation Track and Field Officials Manual (0271-1680)
Published by: National Federation of State High School Associations, PO Box 690, Indianapolis, IN 46206. TEL 317-972-6900, 800-776-3462, FAX 317-822-5700, info@nfhs.org, http://www.nfhs.org.

796.42 USA ISSN 1085-8792
GV561
TRACK COACH. Text in English. 1960-1981; resumed 1983. q. USD 20 domestic; USD 24 foreign (effective 2004). bk.rev. bibl.; charts; illus. back issues avail.; reprints avail. **Document type:** *Magazine, Consumer.* **Description:** Covers track and field technique and training for all events, injury care and prevention, biomechanics and physiology, motivation and coaching psychology, diet and nutrition, strength training, racing tactics.
Former titles (until 1995): Track Technique: Official Technical Publication (0742-3918); (until 1981): Track Technique
Related titles: Microform ed.: (from PQC).
Indexed: A22, E03, ERI, RASB, SD, SPI, SportS, T02.
—BLDSC (8877.352000), IE, Infotrieve, Ingenta.
Published by: (U S A Track & Field), Track & Field News, 2570 El Camino Real, Ste 480, Mountain View, CA 94040. TEL 650-948-8188, FAX 650-948-9445, subs@trackandfieldnews.com, http://www.trackandfieldnews.com. Pub. Ed Fox. Circ: 3,000 (paid).

796.42 USA ISSN 0041-0306
TRACK NEWSLETTER. Text in English. 1955. 25/yr. USD 39; USD 55 foreign (effective 1999). adv. **Document type:** *Newsletter.* **Description:** Latest track and field, results and summaries.
Indexed: SportS.
Published by: Track & Field News, 2570 El Camino Real, Ste 480, Mountain View, CA 94040. TEL 650-948-8188, FAX 650-949-9445, subs@trackandfieldnews.com. Ed. E Garry Hill. R&P Janet Vitu. Adv. contact Pete Koch Weser. Circ: 450 (paid).

797.172 AUS ISSN 1032-3317
TRACKS. Text in English. 1970. m. AUD 85 domestic; AUD 110 in New Zealand; AUD 130 elsewhere; AUD 7.95 newsstand/cover (effective 2008). adv. **Document type:** *Magazine, Consumer.* **Description:** Provides information for surfers and give most exotic surfing locations.
Related titles: ◆ Supplement(s): Australian and New Zealand Snowboarding.
Published by: A C P Magazines Ltd. (Subsidiary of: P B L Media Pty Ltd.), 54-58 Park St, Sydney, NSW 2000, Australia. TEL 61-2-92828000, FAX 61-2-91263769, research@acpaction.com.au, http://www.acp.com.au. Ed. Luke Kennedy TEL 61-2-81149419. Adv. contacts Marcus Hucker TEL 61-2-81149485, Danny Lavell TEL 61-2-95819521. page AUD 3,640; bleed 235 x 310. Circ: 38,000.

796.15 USA
TRADEWINDS. Text in English. 1981. q. membership only. **Document type:** *Newsletter.* **Description:** For persons involved in various aspects of the kite industry.
Published by: Kite Trade Association International, PO Box 115, Rose Lodge, OR 97372-0115. TEL 541-994-3453, FAX 541-994-3459, info@kitetrade.org, http://www.kitetrade.org/. Ed. Maggie Vohs.

796.5 GBR ISSN 1361-9748
TRAIL. Text in English. 1990. 13/yr. GBP 49.50; GBP 3.99 newsstand/cover (effective 2011). adv. back issues avail. **Document type:** *Magazine, Consumer.* **Description:** Contains information on routes, advice and reviews joy the mountains and hills.
Formerly (until 1996): Trail Walker (0959-9037)
Published by: Bauer Consumer Media Ltd., Mappin House, 4 Winsley St, London, W1W 8HF, United Kingdom. TEL 44-20-71828000, http://www.bauermedia.co.uk. Ed. Matt Swaine. Adv. contact Jayne Phillips.

796.522 USA ISSN 0041-0756
F782.R6
TRAIL AND TIMBERLINE. Text in English. 1918. m. USD 15 to non-members; USD 20 foreign to non-members. adv. bk.rev. charts; illus.; maps. index, cum.index every 10 yrs. reprints avail. **Document type:** *Magazine, Consumer.* **Description:** Membership magazine for the Colorado Mountain Club with news on mountain sports and conservation.
—Ingenta.
Published by: Colorado Mountain Club, 710 10th St, Ste 200, Golden, CO 80401-1022. TEL 303-279-3080, FAX 303-279-9690. Ed. Scott Stebbinson. adv.: B&W page USD 230; 11 x 8.5. Circ: 7,500.

▼ **TRAIL OF THE COEUR D'ALENES**; unofficial guidebook with frequently asked questions. *see* TRAVEL AND TOURISM

796.5 USA ISSN 1526-3134
TRAIL RUNNER; one dirty magazine. Text in English. 1999. bi-m. USD 19.95 combined subscription (print & online eds.) (effective 2010). back issues avail. **Document type:** *Magazine, Consumer.* **Description:** Covers all aspects of off-road running, including features and briefs on trail-runner personalities, training, nutrition, racing, adventure travel, gear, and related news.
Related titles: Online - full text ed.
Published by: Big Stone Publishing, 417 Main St, Unit N, Carbondale, CO 81623. TEL 970-704-1442, FAX 970-963-4965, http://www.bigstonepub.com. Ed. Michael Benge TEL 970-704-1442 ext 24. Adv. contact Cynthia Bruggeman TEL 970-704-1442 ext 13. Circ: 2,900 (paid).

796 USA ISSN 0749-1352
TRAIL WALKER; news of hiking and conservation. Text in English. 1963. bi-m. USD 21 membership; USD 15 to libraries (effective 2000). adv. bk.rev. **Document type:** *Newspaper.*
Published by: New York - New Jersey Trail Conference, Inc., 156 Ramapo Valley Rd., Mahwah, NJ 07430-1199. TEL 212-685-9699, FAX 212-779-8102. Ed. Jan Hesbon. R&P Anne Lutkanhouse. Adv. contact Paul Leikin. Circ: 10,000 (paid).

796 388 AUS ISSN 1832-7745
TRAIL ZONE; trail, enduro & adventure riding magazine. Text in English. 2005. bi-m. AUD 45 (effective 2009). adv. back issues avail. **Document type:** *Magazine, Trade.* **Description:** Provides the bike enthusiasts with interesting articles on adventurous riding.
Published by: Trail Zone Pty. Ltd., PO Box 68, Narrabeen, NSW 2101, Australia. TEL 61-2-99829444, FAX 61-2-99729577. Ed., Pub. Andrew Clubb. adv.: page AUD 1,200; trim 210 x 275. Circ: 21,000.

TRAILBLAZER. *see* TRAVEL AND TOURISM

796.5 388.344 USA ISSN 0041-0780
TX1100
TRAILER LIFE; follow the road to adventure. Text in English. 1941. m. USD 15.97 domestic (print or online ed.); USD 27.97 foreign (print or online ed.) (effective 2009). adv. illus.; mkt.; tr.lit. back issues avail.; reprints avail. **Document type:** *Magazine, Consumer.* **Description:** Provides detailed information about vehicle tests, travel articles, product reviews and more.
Related titles: Microform ed.: (from PQC); Online - full text ed.
Indexed: A22, ConsI, G05, G06, G07, G08, G09, I05, M01, M02, MagInd, P02, P10, P19, P48, P53, P54, PMR, PQC.
—Ingenta.
Published by: Affinity Group Inc., 2575 Vista Del Mar, Ventura, CA 93001. TEL 805-667-4100, FAX 805-667-4484, info@affinitygroup.com, http://www.affinitygroup.com. Pub. Bill Estes. Adv. contacts Barbara Keig, Terry Thompson TEL 206-283-9545. B&W page USD 14,220, color page USD 20,600; trim 7.875 x 10.5. Circ: 268,605 (paid).

796.42 FRA ISSN 2107-5506
TRAILS ENDURANCE. Text in French. 1997. bi-m. EUR 33 (effective 2011); incl. Endurance Book 2012.
Formerly (until 2010): Endurance (1280-2174)
Related titles: Supplement(s): Endurance Book (Year). ISSN 1772-0567. 1998.
Published by: Outdoor Editions, 1 Rue des Rivieres, Lyon, 69009, France. http://www.outdoor-editions.fr.

796 USA ISSN 0748-7401
GV859.8
TRANSWORLD SKATEBOARDING. Text in English. 1982. m. USD 16.97 domestic; USD 34.97 in Canada; USD 74.97 elsewhere; USD 3.99 newsstand/cover (effective 2009). adv. music rev. illus. back issues avail. **Document type:** *Magazine, Consumer.* **Description:** Contains interviews with leading skaters, contests, features about the local skating scene, worldwide travel stories, and trick tips.
Related titles: Online - full text ed.
Indexed: G08, I05, M02, M04, T02.
—CCC.
Published by: TransWorld Media (Subsidiary of: Bonnier Magazine Group), 2052 Corte del Nogal Ste B, Carlsbad, CA 92011. TEL 760-722-7777, http://www.transworldmatrix.com/twmatrix/. Adv. contact Lauren N Machen TEL 760-722-7777 ext 227. color page USD 22,271; trim 8 x 10.5. Circ: 93,591 (paid).

796.93 USA ISSN 1046-4611
TRANSWORLD SNOWBOARDING. Text in English. 1986. 9/yr. USD 16.97 domestic; USD 29.97 in Canada; USD 59.97 elsewhere; USD 4.99 newsstand/cover (effective 2009). adv. illus. back issues avail. **Document type:** *Magazine, Consumer.* **Description:** Contains interviews with leading snowboarders, contest news, features about the local snow scene, worldwide travel stories, and snowboarding skills.
Related titles: Online - full text ed.; Supplement(s): Snowboard Resort Guide. USD 3.99 newsstand/cover domestic; GBP 2.50 newsstand/cover in United Kingdom (effective 2000).
Indexed: G08, I05.
—CCC.
Published by: TransWorld Media (Subsidiary of: Bonnier Magazine Group), 2052 Corte del Nogal Ste B, Carlsbad, CA 92011. TEL 760-722-7777, FAX 760-722-0653, http://www.transworldmatrix.com/twmatrix/. Adv. contact Lauren N Machen TEL 760-722-7777 ext 227. color page USD 20,472; trim 8 x 10.5. Circ: 115,125.

799 USA ISSN 0041-1760
SK1
TRAP & FIELD. Text in English. 1890. m. USD 29 domestic; USD 41 foreign (effective 2010). adv. illus. back issues avail.; reprints avail. **Document type:** *Magazine, Consumer.*
Related titles: Online - full text ed.
Indexed: SD, SportS.
Published by: (Amateur Trapshooting Association), Curtis Magazine Group, Inc., 1000 Waterway Blvd, Indianapolis, IN 46202. TEL 317-633-8800, FAX 317-633-2084. Ed. Terry Heeg. Adv. contact Valerie Kinsey.

799.2 GBR ISSN 1946-7613
▼ **TRAP SHOOTING U S A.** Text in English. 2009. bi-m. USD 31.95; USD 5.99 per issue (effective 2009). **Document type:** *Magazine, Consumer.* **Description:** Dedicated to all aspects of the American and international trap disciplines.
Related titles: Online - full text ed.: ISSN 1946-7621.
Published by: Brunton Business Publications Ltd., 1 Salisbury Office Park, London Rd, Salisbury, Wiltshire SP1 3HP, United Kingdom. TEL 44-1722-337038, publications@brunton.co.uk, http://www.brunton.co.uk.

799.2 USA ISSN 8750-233X
TRAPPER & PREDATOR CALLER; practical information for experienced dedicated trappers & predator callers. Text in English. 1975. 10/yr. USD 19.95; USD 3.99 newsstand/cover (effective 2012). adv. illus. back issues avail.; reprints avail. **Document type:** *Magazine, Trade.* **Description:** Contains news, in-depth features, and how-to tips on trapping, the art of predatory calling, and animal damage control. Regular columns and departments include: Regular columns and departments include: The fur shed, lets swap ideas, market report, questions & answers, and news from state trapping associations nationwide.
Formerly (until 1984): Trapper (0739-0599)
Indexed: G08, I05.
—CCC.
Published by: F + W Media Inc., 4700 E Galbraith Rd, Cincinnati, OH 45236. Ed. Jared Blohm TEL 715-445-2214 ext 13439. Pub. Brad Rucks TEL 715-445-2214 ext 13486.

799.2 USA ISSN 1541-826X
THE TRAVELING WINGSHOOTER. Text in English. 2004. a. **Document type:** *Magazine, Trade.*
Published by: Village Press, Inc., 2779 Aero Park Dr, PO Box 968, Traverse City, MI 49685. TEL 231-946-3712, 800-327-7377, FAX 231-946-3289, info@villagepress.com, http://www.villagepress.com.

799.1 DEU ISSN 2191-7655
▼ **TRAVELLING FISHERMEN.** Text in German. 2011. 2/yr. EUR 19.95 (effective 2011). adv. **Document type:** *Magazine, Consumer.*
Published by: Bronk & Boden Outdoorpress Verlags GbR, Steig 15, Lehrensteinsfeld, 74251, Germany. TEL 49-7134-915365. Eds. Ben Boden, Karsten Bronk.

796.42 FRA ISSN 2109-5639
▼ **TRI-MAX/TRIATHLON MAGAZINE.** Text in French. 2010. m. **Document type:** *Magazine, Consumer.*
Published by: Sports Event Mag, 3 Rue des Champs, Saint Marcel, 27950, France. TEL 33-2-32215615, sportmagevents@gmail.com, http://s-m-e.fr/site/?cat=7.

796.42 DEU ISSN 0931-3850
TRIATHLON UND SPORTWISSENSCHAFT. Text in German. 1987. irreg., latest vol.19, 2008. price varies. **Document type:** *Proceedings, Academic/Scholarly.*
Published by: (Sportwissenschaftlicher Beirat der Deutschen Triathlon Union), Czwalina Verlag, Bei der Neuen Muenze 4a, Hamburg, 22145, Germany. TEL 49-40-6794300, FAX 49-40-67943030, post@feldhaus-verlag, http://www.edition-czwalina.de.

TRIATLON DUATLON SPORT. *see* SPORTS AND GAMES

797.32 FRA ISSN 1250-7571
TRIP SURF. Text in French. 1994. bi-m. EUR 29 domestic; EUR 49 in the European Union; EUR 69 elsewhere (effective 2008). **Document type:** *Magazine, Consumer.*
Published by: Surf Session, 20 rue Maryse Bastie, Anglet, 64600, France. TEL 33-5-59417000, FAX 33-5-59412412, surf@atlantel.fr, http://www.surfsession.com.

799.2 ESP ISSN 1886-2233
TROFEO ARMAS DE CAZA. Text in Spanish. a. adv. **Document type:** *Magazine, Consumer.*
Published by: Editorial America Iberica, C. Miguel Yuste 33bis, Madrid, 28037, Spain. TEL 34-91-3277950, FAX 34-91-3044746, editorial@eai.es, http://www.eai.es/. Ed. Juan Francisco Paris. adv.: page EUR 3,200; trim 230 x 297.

333.72 ESP ISSN 1699-7492
TROFEO CAZA; caza - naturaleza. Text in Spanish. 1970. m. EUR 55 (effective 2009). adv. **Document type:** *Magazine, Consumer.* **Description:** Covers hunting and nature conservation.
Published by: Editorial America Iberica, C. Miguel Yuste 33bis, Madrid, 28037, Spain. TEL 34-91-3277950, FAX 34-91-3044746, editorial@eai.es, http://www.eai.es/. Ed. Jose Ignacio Nudi Marianas. adv.: page EUR 3,200; trim 230 x 297. Circ: 40,000.

799.2 ESP
TROFEO CAZA MAYOR. Text in Spanish. m. adv. **Document type:** *Magazine, Consumer.*
Published by: Editorial America Iberica, C. Miguel Yuste 33bis, Madrid, 28037, Spain. TEL 34-91-3277950, FAX 34-91-3044746, editorial@eai.es, http://www.eai.es/. Ed. Jose Ignacio Nudi Marianas. adv.: page EUR 3,200; trim 230 x 297.

796.93 ESP ISSN 1886-2136
TROFEO NIEVE. Text in Spanish. a. adv. **Document type:** *Directory, Consumer.* **Description:** All about skiing, ski places, ski products.
Published by: Editorial America Iberica, C. Miguel Yuste 33bis, Madrid, 28037, Spain. TEL 34-91-3277950, FAX 34-91-3044746, editorial@eai.es, http://www.eai.es/. Ed. Nacho Ferrer. adv.: page EUR 4,960; trim 230 x 297.

799.2 ESP
TROFEO PERROS DE CAZA. Text in Spanish. m. adv. **Document type:** *Magazine, Consumer.*
Published by: Editorial America Iberica, C. Miguel Yuste 33bis, Madrid, 28037, Spain. TEL 34-91-3277950, FAX 34-91-3044746, editorial@eai.es, http://www.eai.es/. Ed. Antonio Lopez. adv.: page EUR 3,000; trim 230 x 297.

799.1 ESP ISSN 1699-2768
TROFEO PESCA. Text in Spanish. 1993. 8/yr. adv. **Document type:** *Magazine, Consumer.* **Description:** Covers fishing in freshwater and saltwater.
Published by: Editorial America Iberica, C. Miguel Yuste 33bis, Madrid, 28037, Spain. TEL 34-91-3277950, FAX 34-91-3044746, editorial@eai.es, http://www.eai.es/. Ed. Enrique Aguado. adv.: page EUR 3,000; trim 230 x 297. Circ: 40,000 (paid).

799.1 ESP ISSN 1889-0695
TROFEO PESCA MAR. Text in Spanish. 2007. q. adv. **Document type:** *Magazine, Consumer.*
Published by: Editorial America Iberica, C. Miguel Yuste 33bis, Madrid, 28037, Spain. TEL 34-91-3277950, editorial@eai.es, http://www.eai.es/. Ed. Enrique Aguado. adv.: page EUR 3,000; trim 230 x 297.

TROPI-TIES E-ZINE & CATALOG. *see* TRAVEL AND TOURISM

799.1 GBR ISSN 0041-3372
TROUT AND SALMON. Text in English. 1955. m. GBP 35 domestic; GBP 55 in Europe; GBP 60 elsewhere (effective 2009). adv. illus. **Document type:** *Magazine, Consumer.* **Description:** Provides news and information on game fishing.
—CCC.
Published by: H. Bauer Publishing Ltd. (Subsidiary of: Bauer Media Group), Academic House, 24-28 Oval Rd, London, NW1 7DT, United Kingdom. TEL 44-20-72418000, FAX 44-20-72418030, http://www.bauer.co.uk. Ed. Andrew Flitcroft TEL 44-1733-395143. Adv. contact Donna Harris TEL 44-1733-288054. **Subscr. to:** Tower House, Sovereign Park, Market Harborough, Leicestershire LE16 9EF, United Kingdom. TEL 44-1858-438866, subs@greatmagazines.co.uk.

799.1 GBR ISSN 0142-9108
TROUT FISHERMAN. Text in English. 1977. m. GBP 37 domestic; GBP 55 in Europe; GBP 60 elsewhere (effective 2009). adv. bk.rev. illus. **Document type:** *Magazine, Consumer.* **Description:** Designed for stillwater game anglers including up-to-date news, match and fishery information, tackle reviews, expert advice, flytying and essential prospects guide to fish the nation's trout waters.
Published by: H. Bauer Publishing Ltd. (Subsidiary of: Bauer Media Group), Academic House, 24-28 Oval Rd, London, NW1 7DT, United Kingdom. TEL 44-20-72418000, FAX 44-20-72418030, http://www.bauer.co.uk. Ed. Russell Hill TEL 44-1733-395131. Adv. contact Donna Harris TEL 44-1733-288054. **Subscr. to:** Tower House, Sovereign Park, Market Harborough, Leicestershire LE16 9EF, United Kingdom. TEL 44-1858-438866, subs@greatmagazines.co.uk.

799.1 FRA ISSN 1292-6078
TRUITE MAG. Text in French. 1997. q. EUR 18 (effective 2007).
Supersedes in part (in 1998): Carnassiers Salmonides (1281-0940)
Published by: Editions Chasse Nature, B P 12, Quissac, 30260, France. TEL 33-4-66773806.

TURISTA. *see* TRAVEL AND TOURISM

799.2 USA ISSN 1067-4942
TURKEY & TURKEY HUNTING; practical & comprehensive information for wild turkey hunters. Text in English. 1983. bi-m. USD 16.95; USD 3.95 newsstand/cover (effective 2012). adv. bk.rev. illus. back issues avail.; reprints avail. **Document type:** *Magazine, Trade.* **Description:** Articles focus on hunting, scouting, turkey behavior and biology, hunting ethics, new equipment, methodologies, turkey management, and current research. Regular columns include: Tree call, turkey biology, decision time, bad birds, gobbler shots, favorite calls, turkey tools, hunters library, and readers shots.
Incorporates (in 1992): Turkey Hunter (0896-1786); Which was formerly (until 198?): Turkey (8750-0205)
Related titles: Online - full text ed.; Optical Disk - DVD ed.
—CCC.
Published by: F + W Media Inc., 4700 E Galbraith Rd, Cincinnati, OH 45236. TEL 513-531-2690, contact_us@fwmedia.com, http://www.fwmedia.com/. Ed. Brian Lovett TEL 715-445-2214 ext 13484. Pub. Brad Rucks TEL 715-445-2214 ext 13486.

199.2 USA ISSN 1949-9086
TURKEY COUNTRY. Text in English. 1973. bi-m. free membership. **Document type:** *Magazine, Consumer.* **Description:** The official magazine of the National Wild Turkey Federation, featuring articles on turkey hunting.
Formerly (until 2009): Turkey Call (1064-6094); Incorporates (2000-2009): Women in the Outdoors (1526-8217); (2005-2009): Get In the Game (1554-2211); (2002-2009): Wheelin' Sportsmen (1538-1218)
Published by: National Wild Turkey Federation, Inc., 770 Augusta Rd, Edgefield, SC 29824-0530. TEL 803-637-3106, FAX 803-637-0034, kroop@nwtf.net, http://www.nwtf.net. Ed. Karen Lee.

799.246 USA
TURKEY HUNTING STRATEGIES. Text in English. a. **Document type:** *Magazine, Consumer.*
Published by: Harris Publications, Inc., 1115 Broadway, New York, NY 10010. TEL 212-807-7100, FAX 212-924-2352, subscriptions@harris-pub.com, http://www.harris-pub.com.

799.1 ITA ISSN 1826-4239
TUTTOPESCE. Text in Italian. 2005. bi-w. **Document type:** *Magazine, Consumer.*
Published by: De Agostini Editore, Via G da Verrazzano 15, Novara, 28100, Italy. TEL 39-0321-4241, FAX 39-0321-424305, info@deagostini.it, http://www.deagostini.it.

U.S. FISH AND WILDLIFE SERVICE. NATIONAL SURVEY OF FISHING, HUNTING AND WILDLIFE - ASSOCIATED RECREATION. *see* SPORTS AND GAMES—Abstracting, Bibliographies, Statistics

796.54 USA ISSN 1938-9981
GV191.42.E19
U.S. NATIONAL FOREST CAMPGROUND GUIDE. EASTERN REGION. Text in English. 2003. irreg. **Document type:** *Guide, Consumer.*
Related titles: CD-ROM ed.; Online - full text ed.
Published by: Moon Canyon Publishing LLC, PO Box 1575, Bisbee, AZ 85603. TEL 520-432-5783, sf@forestcamping.com.

796.54 USA ISSN 1940-3917
GV198.65.W47
U.S. NATIONAL FOREST CAMPGROUND GUIDE. INTERMOUNTAIN REGION. Text in English. 2004. triennial. **Document type:** *Guide, Consumer.*
Related titles: CD-ROM ed.; Online - full text ed.
Published by: Moon Canyon Publishing LLC, PO Box 1575, Bisbee, AZ 85603. TEL 520-432-5783, sf@forestcamping.com.

796.54 USA ISSN 1945-5887
GV191.42.C2
U.S. NATIONAL FOREST CAMPGROUND GUIDE. PACIFIC SOUTHWEST REGION, SOUTH SECTION. Text in English. 200?. irreg. **Document type:** *Handbook/Manual/Guide, Consumer.*
Related titles: CD-ROM ed.; Online - full text ed.
Published by: Moon Canyon Publishing LLC, PO Box 1575, Bisbee, AZ 85603. TEL 520-432-5783, sf@forestcamping.com.

796.54 USA ISSN 1940-6886
GV191.42.P17
U.S. NATIONAL FOREST CAMPGROUND GUIDE. PACIFIC SOUTHWESTERN REGION, NORTH SECTION. Text in English. 200?. irreg. **Document type:** *Guide, Consumer.*
Related titles: CD-ROM ed.; Online - full text ed.
Published by: Moon Canyon Publishing LLC, PO Box 1575, Bisbee, AZ 85603. TEL 520-432-5783, sf@forestcamping.com.

796.54 369 NLD ISSN 1877-5292
DE UITLAATKLEP. Text in Dutch. 1999. q. **Document type:** *Magazine, Consumer.*
Published by: Mercedes-Hanomag Kampeersautoclub "Dubbellucht", c/o Ron Cretier, Sec., Keurvorstenplein 4, Ravenstein, 5371 CM, Netherlands. secretariaat@dubbellucht.nl, http://www.dubbellucht.nl. Ed. Hans van Leur. Circ: 1,500.

796 GBR ISSN 1759-1783
▼ **UK ADVENTURE SPORTS**; adventure / endurance / lifestyle magazine. Text in English. 2009. q. GBP 15 domestic; GBP 20 in Europe; GBP 25 elsewhere (effective 2010). adv. **Document type:** *Magazine, Trade.* **Description:** Features competitive adventure sports in UK. It includes any form of outdoor adventure sports.
Published by: UK Adventure Sports Magazine, 2 Kerry Gardens, Sandleheath, Fordingbridge, Hants SP6 1QW, United Kingdom. TEL 44-7841-832778. Ed., Adv. contact Paul Pickering.

796.42 USA ISSN 0744-3609
GV1065.2
ULTRARUNNING. Text in English. 1981. 10/yr. USD 40 domestic; USD 75 in Canada & Mexico; USD 90 elsewhere (effective 2010). adv. bk.rev. back issues avail. **Document type:** *Magazine, Consumer.* **Description:** Covers the North American ultrarunning community with complete results of all ultra races. Also features an extensive schedule of races.
Related titles: Online - full text ed.
Indexed: SD, SportS.
Published by: UltraRunning Magazine, 5825 W Dry Creek Rd, Healdsburg, CA 95448. TEL 707-431-9898. Ed. Tia Bodington. Pub. John Medinger. Adv. contact Lisa Henson.

796.334 GBR ISSN 1369-9202
UNITED WE STAND. Text in English. 1989. m. GBP 24.50 domestic; GBP 29 in Europe; GBP 33 elsewhere; GBP 2.50 newsstand/cover (effective 2009). adv. bk.rev. **Document type:** *Magazine, Consumer.* **Description:** The independent voice of Manchester United fans.
Address: PO Box 45, Manchester, Lancs M41 9GQ, United Kingdom.
Dist. by: M M C Ltd.

799.2 DEU ISSN 0566-2621
UNSERE JAGD; die Zeitschrift fuer Jaeger und alle Naturfreunde. Text in German. 1951. m. EUR 45.90 domestic; EUR 51.80 foreign; EUR 4.40 newsstand/cover (effective 2009). adv. illus. **Document type:** *Magazine, Consumer.*
Indexed: KWIWR, W08.
Published by: Deutscher Landwirtschaftsverlag GmbH, Berliner Str 112A, Berlin, 13189, Germany. TEL 49-30-29397450, FAX 49-30-29397459, dlv.berlin@dlv.de, http://www.dlv.de. Adv. contact Henning Stemmler. B&W page EUR 2,840, color page EUR 5,519; trim 216 x 303. Circ: 41,539 (paid and controlled).

796.552 USA
UP ROPE. Text in English. 1944. m. USD 15 (effective 2003). **Description:** Newsletter for the Mountaineering Section of the Potomac Appalachian Trail Club.
Published by: Potomac Appalachian Trail Club, Inc., 118 Park St, S E, Vienna, VA 22180-4609. TEL 703-242-0693, FAX 703-242-0968, info@patc.net, http://patc.net. Ed. T Isaacson.

799.2 USA ISSN 1541-597X
THE UPLAND ALMANAC. Text in English. 1998 (Sum.). q. USD 19.95; USD 5.95 per issue (effective 2007). adv. **Document type:** *Magazine, Consumer.*
Formerly (until Spr. 2003): The Grouse Point Almanac (1536-4437)
Published by: Upland Publishing Group, 20 Delorme Rd., Fairfax, VT 05454. TEL 802-849-9000, FAX 802-849-6452. Pub. John C. Gosselin.

796 USA
URBAN CLIMBER MAGAZINE. Text in English. 2004. 8/yr. USD 24.97 (effective 2010). **Document type:** *Magazine, Consumer.*
Published by: Skram Media, 2291 Arapahoe Av, Boulder, CO 80302. TEL 303-225-4628, FAX 303-417-1371, info@skrammedia.com. Ed. Andrew Tower.

796 SWE ISSN 0281-2932
UTEMAGASINET. Text in Swedish. 1980. 8/yr. SEK 529 (effective 2005). adv. bk.rev. **Document type:** *Magazine, Consumer.*
Published by: Hjemmet Mortensen AB (Subsidiary of: Hjemmet-Mortensen AS), PO Box 164, Aare, 83013, Sweden. TEL 46-647-51440, FAX 46-647-51444, info@hjemmetmortensen.se, http://www.hjemmetmortensen.se. Eds. Erika Wilner, Ingalill Forslund. adv.: page SEK 32,000; trim 200 x 253. Circ: 35,000.

UTIVIST. *see* TRAVEL AND TOURISM

910.2 NLD ISSN 1388-8927
VAKANTIEKRIEBELS & VRIJE TIJD. Text in Dutch. 1998. bi-m. EUR 7.50 (effective 2009).
Published by: B & B Provice, Postbus 330, Stadskanaal, 9500 AH, Netherlands. TEL 31-599-652346.

799.2028 SWE ISSN 1400-8092
VAPENTIDNINGEN; Skandinaviens ledande magasin foer jaegere, skytter och samlare. Text in Swedish. 1993. 5/yr. SEK 49 per issue (effective 2004). adv. **Document type:** *Consumer.*
Formerly (until 1994): Jakt- and Handvapen (1104-389X)
Published by: Tidningen HiFi Musik AB, PO Box 23084, Stockholm, 10435, Sweden. TEL 46-8-342970, FAX 46-8-342971.

799.2 USA ISSN 1555-2640
THE VARMINT HUNTER MAGAZINE. Text in English. 1992. q. USD 30 domestic; USD 40 in Canada; USD 50 elsewhere (effective 2008). adv. **Document type:** *Magazine, Consumer.*
Published by: Varmint Hunters Association, PO Box 759, Pierre, SD 57501. TEL 605-224-6665, 800-528-4868, FAX 605-224-6544, info@varminthunter.org. Ed. John Anderson.

796.42 SWE ISSN 0283-5533
VASALOEPAREN; tidningen foer dig som aaker laanglopp. Text in Swedish. 1985. q. SEK 90 (effective 1994).
Published by: Vasaloppets Marknads AB, Vasaloppets Hus, Mora, 79232, Sweden.

799.1 799.2 ISL ISSN 1670-0112
VEIDIMADURINN. Text in Icelandic. 1940. 3/yr. **Document type:** *Magazine, Consumer.* **Description:** Focuses on sport fishing, hunting and shooting.

S

Incorporates (1984-1993): A Veidum (1017-3625)
Published by: Strangaveitifelag Reykjavikur/The Angling Club of Reykjavik, Haaleitisbraut 68, Reykjavik, 103, Iceland. TEL 354-568-6050, FAX 354-553-2060, svfr@svfr.is. Ed. Eggert Skulason.

796.552 NOR ISSN 1502-1823
VEIVALG. Text in Norwegian. 1959. 6/yr. NOK 525 (effective 2001). adv.
Document type: *Magazine, Consumer.*
Former titles (until 1999): Orientering (0800-6067); (until 1984): Norges Orienteringsforbund Posten (0333-1490)
Published by: Sport Media AS, Vestre Ringvei 5, PO Box A, Askim, 1801, Norway. TEL 47-69-81-97-00, FAX 47-69-88-99-80. Eds. Erik Unaas TEL 47-69-819703, Svein Kvalheim. Adv. contact Terje Lund Olsen. Circ: 4,700 (controlled).

799.2 683.4 USA ISSN 1547-0113
TS532
VELOCITY (EXETER). Text in English. 2003 (Feb.). q. USD 19.95 (effective 2003).
Published by: Sigarms, Inc., 18 Industrial Dr., Exeter, NH 03833. TEL 603-772-2302, FAX 603-772-9082, http://www.sigarms.com. Ed., Pub. Laura S. Burgess.

796.172 PRT ISSN 0873-8025
VERT; Bodyboard Magazine. Text in Portuguese. 1994. bi-m. music rev.; video rev. back issues avail. **Document type:** *Consumer.*
Description: Concerns bodyboarding and accompanying lifestyles, and features music, cartoons and Internet articles for a young audience.
Published by: M S T Z Edicoes e Publicidade Lda., Apartado 21 Santa Cruz, Silveria, 2560-996, Portugal. boogietime@clix.pt. Ed. Antonio Fonseca. R&P A Fonseca. Adv. contact Pedro Crispim. **Dist. by:** V A S P, Lda. Rua da Tascoa, 40 piso, Massama, Queluz 2745, Portugal. TEL 35-1-439-8500, FAX 35-1-1-430-2499.

796.522 ESP ISSN 0042-4420
VERTEX. Text in Catalan; Summaries in French, Spanish. 1966. bi-m. EUR 25.30 (effective 2009). adv. bk.rev. bibl.; charts; illus. index; cum.index. back issues avail. **Document type:** *Magazine, Consumer.*
Published by: Federacio d'Entitats Excursionistes de Catalunya, Rambla 41 Pral., Barcelona, 08002, Spain. TEL 34-93-4120777, FAX 34-93-4126353, feec@feec.org. Circ: 4,000.

796.52 FRA ISSN 1764-6243
VERTICAL. Text in French. 1985. m. **Document type:** *Magazine, Consumer.*
Formerly (until 2003): Vertical, Roc (1299-2968); Which was formed by the merger of (1985-2000): Vertical (0769-6205); (1995-1999): Roc'n Wall (1260-9986)
Published by: Editions Niveales, 6 Rue Irvoy, Grenoble, 38000, France. TEL 33-4-76705411, FAX 33-4-76705412, http://www.dipresse.com/niveales.

796.522 ARG ISSN 1851-9954
VERTICAL ARGENTINAL; revista de montana. Text in Spanish. 2008. q. back issues avail. **Document type:** *Magazine, Consumer.*
Published by: Vertical Argentina, Mar de la Plata s-n, Buenos Aires, 7600, Argentina. info@verticalargentina.com, http://www.verticalargentina.com/.

799.1 AUS ISSN 1449-9525
VICTORIA FISHING MONTHLY; the recreational anglers voice. Text in English. 2004. m. AUD 55; AUD 4.95 per issue (effective 2009). adv. back issues avail. **Document type:** *Magazine, Consumer.*
Description: Dedicated to fishing around Victoria.
Published by: Fishing Monthly Group, PO Box 3172, Loganholme, QLD 4129, Australia. TEL 61-7-33870800, FAX 61-7-33870801, subscribe@fishingmonthly.com.au, http://www.fishingmonthly.com.au. Adv. contact Heatha Nicholas. Circ: 13,000.

799.1 ITA ISSN 1826-3984
LE VIE DELLA PESCA IN ACQUA DOLCE. Text in Italian. 2005. m. EUR 45 (effective 2009). **Document type:** *Magazine, Consumer.*
Published by: Acacia Edizioni, Via Copernico 3, Binasco, MI 20082, Italy. http://www.acaciaedizioni.com.

799.1 ITA ISSN 1826-3976
LE VIE DELLA PESCA IN MARE. Text in Italian. 2005. m. EUR 54 (effective 2009). **Document type:** *Magazine, Consumer.*
Published by: Acacia Edizioni, Via Copernico 3, Binasco, MI 20082, Italy. http://www.acaciaedizioni.com.

796.5 CAN ISSN 0844-1804
VIE EN PLEIN AIR. Text in French. 1970. q. adv. **Document type:** *Journal, Consumer.*
Published by: Roy C. Baird, Pub., 970 Montee de Liesse, Ste 310, St Laurent, PQ H4T 1W7, Canada. TEL 514-856-0787. Ed. Claude Leonard. R&P Roy C Baird. Adv. contact Roy J Baird.

799.29489 DNK ISSN 0906-4907
VILDTINFORMATION. Text in Danish. 1986. a. free. back issues avail.
Document type: *Government.* **Description:** Information for hunters.
Related titles: Online - full content ed.: ISSN 1602-558X. 200?.
Published by: Miljoeministeriet, Skov- og Naturstyrelsen/Ministry of the Environment. Danish Forest & Nature Agency, Haraldsgade 53, Copenhagen OE, 2100, Denmark. TEL 45-39-472000, FAX 45-39-279899, sns@sns.dk. Ed. Sandor Hestbaek Markus.

796.5 799 NOR ISSN 0332-7442
VILLMARKSLIV. Text in Norwegian. 1972. m. NOK 349; NOK 69 newsstand/cover (effective 2009). adv. bk.rev. **Document type:** *Magazine, Consumer.* **Description:** Contains articles and features for people interested in outdoor life, fishing and hunting.
Published by: Hjemmet Mortensen AS, Gullhaugveien 1, Nydalen, Oslo, 0441, Norway. TEL 47-22-585000, FAX 47-22-585959, firmapost@hm-media.no, http://www.hm-media.no. Ed. Knut Brevik. adv.: page NOK 29,900.

799 ROM ISSN 1220-4617
VINATORUL SI PESCARUL ROMAN. Text in Romanian. 1948. m. ROL 30,000, USD 18 (effective 1997). adv. bk.rev. **Document type:** *Consumer.*
Published by: Association of Hunters and Anglers, Calea Mosilor 128, Bucharest, 70344, Romania. TEL 401-3235637, FAX 401-6136804. Ed. Gabriel Cheriou. Circ: 25,000 (paid).

051 USA
VIRGINIA CAMPGROUND DIRECTORY. Text in English. 1997. a. adv.
Published by: (Virginia Campground Association), Vista Graphics, Inc, 1264 Perimeter Pkwy, Virginia Beach, VA 23454. TEL 757-422-8979, 800-422-0742, FAX 757-422-9092, http://www.vgnet.com/. Pub. Randy Thompson.

799 USA ISSN 0897-8794
VIRGINIA GAME & FISH. Text in English. 198?. m. USD 12 domestic; USD 25 in Canada; USD 27 elsewhere (effective 2011). adv. illus.
Document type: *Magazine, Consumer.* **Description:** Informs sportsmen of hunting and fishing, as well as environmental and conservation issues in Virginia.
Supersedes in part (in 198?): Virginia - West Virginia Game and Fish (0889-3314)
Related titles: Online - full text ed.; ◆ Regional ed(s).: Game & Fish; ◆ Louisiana Game & Fish. ISSN 0744-3692; ◆ Florida Game & Fish. ISSN 0889-3322; ◆ Alabama Game & Fish. ISSN 0279-6783; ◆ Mississippi-Louisiana Game & Fish. ISSN 1947-2358; ◆ North Carolina Game & Fish. ISSN 0897-8816; ◆ South Carolina Game & Fish. ISSN 0897-9154; ◆ West Virginia Game & Fish. ISSN 0897-9162; ◆ Missouri Game & Fish. ISSN 0889-3799; ◆ New York Game & Fish. ISSN 0897-9189; ◆ California Game & Fish. ISSN 1056-0122; ◆ Great Plains Game & Fish. ISSN 1055-6532; ◆ Illinois Game & Fish. ISSN 0897-9014; ◆ Indiana Game & Fish. ISSN 0897-8980; ◆ Iowa Game & Fish. ISSN 0897-9197; ◆ Mid-Atlantic Game & Fish. ISSN 1055-6540; ◆ Oklahoma Game & Fish. ISSN 0746-6013; ◆ Rocky Mountain Game & Fish. ISSN 1056-0114; ◆ Pennsylvania Game & Fish. ISSN 0897-8808; ◆ Washington - Oregon Game & Fish. ISSN 1056-0106; ◆ Ohio Game & Fish. ISSN 0897-9170; New England Game & Fish. ISSN 0897-8972. 1988. USD 12 domestic; USD 25 in Canada; USD 27 elsewhere (effective 2010).
Published by: Intermedia Outdoors, Inc., 512 7th Ave, 11th Fl, New York, NY 10018. TEL 212-852-6682, 800-260-6397, FAX 212-302-4472, customerservice@imoutdoors.com, http://www.imoutdoorsmedia.com. Ed. Ken Dunwoody. Pub., Adv. contact Peter Gross.

VIRGINIA WILDLIFE. *see* CONSERVATION

VIRGINIA WILDLIFE FEDERATION. FEDERATION RECORD. *see* CONSERVATION

799.1 USA
VIRTUAL FLYSHOP. Text in English. 1994. d. **Description:** Internet flyfishing resource containing news stories, feautres, travel advice, product reviews, and fly tying tips.
Media: Online - full text.
Published by: Fly Fisherman Magazine, 223 Linden, Ste 203, Fort Collins, CO 80525. Ed. Greg McDermid.

799.1 NLD ISSN 0920-4199
HET VISBLAD. Text in Dutch. 1976. m. EUR 11.95; EUR 2.50 newsstand/cover (effective 2010). adv. **Document type:** *Magazine, Consumer.*
Formerly (until 1986): Hengelsport (0166-9494); Incorporates (1979-2005): O V B - Bericht (0921-3147)
Published by: Sportvisserij Nederland, Leijenseweg 115, Postbus 162, Bilthoven, 3720 AD, Netherlands. TEL 31-30-6058400, info@sportvisserijnederland.nl, http://www.sportvisserijnederland.nl. Ed. Juul Steyn. adv.: B&W page EUR 1,750, color page EUR 2,400; trim 210 x 297. Circ: 90,000.

797.23 USA ISSN 1084-4228
VISIBILITY. Text in English. 1959. bi-m. USD 20 to individual members; USD 50 to institutional members (effective 2000). adv. bk.rev. bibl.
Document type: *Newsletter.* **Description:** Covers all issues of underwater diving.
Formerly: Underwater Reporter (0199-5189)
Published by: Underwater Society of America, PO Box 628, Daly City, CA 94017. TEL 650-583-8492, FAX 650-583-0614, http://www.underwater-society.org. Ed., Adv. contact Carol Rose. B&W page USD 150; trim 11 x 8.5. Circ: 2,500.

799 DEU ISSN 0933-4491
VISIER. Text in German. 1987. m. EUR 64.50 (effective 2010). adv.
Document type: *Magazine, Consumer.*
Incorporates (1975-1990): Visier (Berlin) (0138-1601)
Published by: V S Medien GmbH, Wipsch 1, Bad Ems, 56130, Germany. TEL 49-2603-5060201, FAX 49-2603-5060202, vertrieb@vsmedien.de. Ed. Sven Helmes. Pub. David Schiller. adv.: B&W page EUR 2,460, color page EUR 3,275. Circ: 34,450 (paid).

799 DEU ISSN 0948-0528
VISIER SPECIAL. Text in German. 1994. q. EUR 9.50 per issue (effective 2010). adv. **Document type:** *Magazine, Consumer.*
Published by: V S Medien GmbH, Wipsch 1, Bad Ems, 56130, Germany. TEL 49-2603-5060201, FAX 49-2603-5060202, vertrieb@vsmedien.de, http://www.visier.de. adv.: B&W page EUR 1,970, color page EUR 2,625. Circ: 28,500 (paid and controlled).

799.1 NLD ISSN 1569-7533
VISIONAIR. Text in Dutch. 2006. q. EUR 24.95; EUR 6.95 newsstand/cover (effective 2009).
Published by: Sportvisserij Nederland, Leijenseweg 115, Postbus 162, Bilthoven, 3720 AD, Netherlands. TEL 31-30-6058400, FAX 31-30-6039874, http://www.sportvisserijnederland.nl. Eds. Juul Steyn, Marco Kraal. Circ: 5,000.

799.1 NLD ISSN 2210-5271
VISTRIPS EN REIZEN. Variant title: Trips & Reizen. Text in Dutch. 2008. a. EUR 2.95 (effective 2010).
Published by: Publishing House & Facilities B.V., Postbus 119, Doetinchem, 7000 AC, Netherlands. TEL 31-314-340150, FAX 31-314-346675, info@publishinghouse.nl, http://www.publishinghouse.nl.

796 FRA ISSN 1268-2888
VOILE MAGAZINE. Text in French. 1995. m. EUR 50 (effective 2009). adv. **Document type:** *Magazine, Consumer.*
Published by: Editions Lariviere, 6 Rue Olof Palme, Clichy, 92587, France. TEL 33-1-47565400, http://www.editions-lariviere.fr. Ed. William Borel. Pub. Fabien Darmon. Adv. contact Christine Lhuillery.

797.55 FRA ISSN 0766-4877
VOL LIBRE. Text in French. 1976. m. EUR 70 (effective 2009). **Document type:** *Magazine, Consumer.*
Formerly (until 1982): Vol Libre Magazine (0397-0272)
Published by: Editions Retine, 3 rue Ampere, Ivry-sur-Seine, 94200, France. TEL 33-1-46701482, FAX 33-1-46589752, vollibre@compuserve.com. Ed. Noel Bertrand. Pub. Martine Coulon. Circ: 10,000 (paid); 3,000 (controlled).

797.5 FRA ISSN 1274-2007
VOL PASSION. Text in French. q.
Formerly: Ascendances (0299-1713)
Published by: (Federation Francaise de Vol Libre), Editions Retine, 3 rue Ampere, Ivry-sur-Seine, 94200, France. TEL 33-1-46701482, FAX 33-1-46589752. Circ: 14,000.

799.2 FRA ISSN 1953-5546
VOYAGES DE CHASSE. Key Title: Le Magazine des Voyages de Chasse. Text in French. 2004. q. EUR 24 domestic; EUR 28 in Europe; EUR 31 DOM-TOM; EUR 34 elsewhere (effective 2010). back issues avail. **Document type:** *Magazine, Consumer.*
Published by: M V P Editions, 17 Place du General de Gaulle, Montreuil, 93100, France. TEL 33-1-42875363, FAX 33-1-42875191.

VOYAGEUR TRAIL NEWS. *see* LEISURE AND RECREATION

796.172 USA
WAHINE; a girl's guide to water sports & beach culture. Text in English. 1995. 4/yr. USD 2.95 newsstand/cover. **Document type:** *Magazine, Consumer.* **Description:** Offers insightful travel, profiles, beach fashion, environmental notes, and food and fitness for both body and mind.
Related titles: Online - full text ed.
Address: TEL 562-434-9444.

799.2 639.1 NLD ISSN 2210-4267
▼ **WAIDMANNSHEIL.** Text in Dutch. 2010. bi-m. EUR 30 (effective 2011).
Document type: *Magazine, Consumer.*
Published by: Uitgeverij Hubertus, Postbus 382, Bergen op Zoom, Netherlands. TEL 31-164-854529, FAX 31-87-7847689.

797.35 797.1 FRA ISSN 1628-285X
WAKE & SKI MAGAZINE. Text in French. 2001. 8/yr. EUR 42 (effective 2009). **Document type:** *Magazine, Consumer.*
Published by: Federation Francaise de Ski Nautique, 18 Rue de la Michodiere, Paris, 75002, France. TEL 33-1-53201919, FAX 33-1-53201940, http://www.ffsn.fr.

796.172 USA
WAKESURFING. Text in English. 2006. q. USD 14.99 domestic; USD 29 foreign (effective 2006). adv. **Document type:** *Magazine, Consumer.*
Description: Covers destinations, personalities, board design and selection, and technique.
Address: PO Box 129, Templeton, CA 93465. TEL 805-434-1174, FAX 805-643-7789. adv.: B&W page USD 1,860, color page USD 2,825.

796 796.352 AUT
WALDVIERTEL UND GOLF. Text in German. 2/yr. **Document type:** *Magazine, Consumer.*
Published by: (Waldviertel Tourismus Marketing), Verlagsgruppe News Gesellschaft mbH (Subsidiary of: Gruner + Jahr AG & Co), Schlossgasse 10-12, Vienna, N 1050, Austria. TEL 43-1-8696536, FAX 43-1-8696536, http://www.news.at. Circ: 50,000 (controlled).

WALK (LONDON). *see* CONSERVATION

796.51 IRL ISSN 0791-8801
WALKING WORLD IRELAND. Text in English. 1993. bi-m. adv.
Document type: *Magazine, Consumer.*
Published by: Athletic Promotions, Cherrywood House, Garville Dr., Garville Ave., Rathgar, Dublin, 6, Ireland. TEL 353-1-4968344, FAX 353-1-4968359. adv.: color page EUR 1,900; trim 210 x 297. Circ: 13,600 (paid and controlled).

799.1 USA ISSN 2162-1667
WALLEYE (BENTON). Text in English. 20??. bi-m. USD 15 to non-members; free to members (effective 2011). adv. **Document type:** *Magazine, Trade.*
Formerly (until 2011): F L W Outdoors (1936-1971)
Related titles: Online - full text ed.: USD 8 (effective 2011).
Published by: F L W Outdoors, 30 Gamble Ln, Benton, KY 42025. TEL 270-252-1000, info@flwoutdoors.com, http://www.flwoutdoors.com. Ed. Colin Moore TEL 270-252-1606. Adv. contact Al Chapman TEL 270-252-1628.

799.1 USA
WALLEYE GUIDE. Text in English. 1983. a. USD 5 newsstand/cover (effective 2007). adv. **Document type:** *Magazine, Consumer.*
Description: Contains features on the nature of walleyes, tactical fishing traditions and trends, state notes, plus what's new in tackle, boats, motors, electronics and more.
Formerly (until 19??): In-Fisherman Walleye Guide
Published by: Source Interlink Companies, 6420 Wilshire Blvd, 10th Fl, Los Angeles, CA 90048. TEL 323-782-2000, FAX 323-782-2585, dheine@sourceinterlink.com, http://www.sourceinterlinkmedia.com. adv.: B&W page USD 3,500, color page USD 4,725. Circ: 204,000.

796 USA ISSN 1068-2112
WALLEYE IN-SIDER. Text in English. 1989. bi-m. adv. charts; illus.; maps. back issues avail. **Document type:** *Magazine, Consumer.*
Description: Features fishing techniques and tackle tips, trip tips and area-by-area evaluations and recommendations of prime walleye fishing locations.
Formerly (until 199?): The In-Fisherman Walleye In-Sider
Indexed: G08.
—CCC.
Published by: Intermedia Outdoors, Inc., 512 7th Ave, 11th Fl, New York, NY 10018. TEL 212-852-6682, 800-260-6397, FAX 212-302-4472, customerservice@imoutdoors.com, http://www.imoutdoorsmedia.com.

796 CHE
WANDER REVUE. Text in German. 1982. bi-m. CHF 40 (effective 2000).
Document type: *Magazine, Consumer.*
Related titles: French ed.: Revue Sentiers. 1982.
Published by: Schweizer Wanderwege, Im Hirshalm 49, Riehen, 4125, Switzerland. TEL 41-61-6069340, FAX 41-61-6069345. Ed. Sam Junker. Circ: 25,000.

796.5 DEU ISSN 0178-1677
WANDERMAGAZIN. Text in German. 1985. bi-m. EUR 22.25; EUR 4.90 newsstand/cover (effective 2008). adv. bk.rev. back issues avail.
Document type: *Magazine, Consumer.*
Published by: W & A Marketing und Verlag GmbH, Rudolf-Diesel-Str 14, Niederkassel, 53859, Germany. TEL 49-228-459510, FAX 49-228-4595199. Ed. Michael Saenger. Adv. contact Sandra Feld. B&W page EUR 1,530, color page EUR 2,645; trim 175 x 250. Circ: 24,000 (paid).

796.93 USA
WARREN MILLER SNOWORLD. Text in English. 1983. a. free (effective 2005). adv. **Document type:** *Magazine, Consumer.*
Formerly: Warren Miller'S Ski World
Published by: Mountain Sports Media, 2540 Frontier Ave, Ste 104, Boulder, CO 80301-2400. TEL 303-442-3430, FAX 303-442-3402. adv.: page USD 13,000. Circ: 200,000 (controlled).

799 USA ISSN 1056-0106
WASHINGTON - OREGON GAME & FISH. Text in English. 19??. m. USD 12 domestic; USD 25 in Canada; USD 27 elsewhere (effective 2011). adv. illus. **Document type:** *Magazine, Consumer.* **Description:** Informs sportsmen of hunting and fishing, as well as environmental and conservation issues in Oregon and Washington.
Related titles: Online - full text ed.; ◆ Regional ed(s).: Game & Fish; ◆ Louisiana Game & Fish. ISSN 0744-3692; ◆ Florida Game & Fish. ISSN 0889-3322; ◆ Alabama Game & Fish. ISSN 0279-6783; ◆ Mississippi-Louisiana Game & Fish. ISSN 1947-2358; ◆ North Carolina Game & Fish. ISSN 0897-8816; ◆ South Carolina Game & Fish. ISSN 0897-9154; ◆ West Virginia Game & Fish. ISSN 0897-9162; ◆ Missouri Game & Fish. ISSN 0889-3799; ◆ New York Game & Fish. ISSN 0897-9189; ◆ California Game & Fish. ISSN 1056-0122; ◆ Great Plains Game & Fish. ISSN 1055-6532; ◆ Illinois Game & Fish. ISSN 0897-9014; ◆ Indiana Game & Fish. ISSN 0897-8980; ◆ Iowa Game & Fish. ISSN 0897-9197; ◆ Mid-Atlantic Game & Fish. ISSN 1055-6540; ◆ Oklahoma Game & Fish. ISSN 0746-6013; ◆ Rocky Mountain Game & Fish. ISSN 1056-0114; ◆ Pennsylvania Game & Fish. ISSN 0897-8808; ◆ Virginia Game & Fish. ISSN 0897-8794; ◆ Ohio Game & Fish. ISSN 0897-9170; New England Game & Fish. ISSN 0897-8972. 1988. USD 12 domestic; USD 25 in Canada; USD 27 elsewhere (effective 2010).
Published by: Intermedia Outdoors, Inc., 512 7th Ave, 11th Fl, New York, NY 10018. TEL 212-852-6682, 800-260-6397, FAX 212-302-4472, customerservice@imoutdoors.com, http://www.imoutdoorsmedia.com. Ed. Ken Dunwoody. Pub., Adv. contact Peter Gross.

WASHINGTON SEA GRANT PROGRAM. PUBLICATION. *see* FISH AND FISHERIES

796.172 USA
WATER; pure surfing enjoyment. Text in English. 2001. q. USD 28 domestic; USD 34 Hawaiian Islands; USD 50 elsewhere (effective 2002). **Description:** Covers extensive interviews, photog and artist profiles, unique travel pieces, and features on towns that continue to shape American surf culture. Revisit certain eras where modern surfing was influenced, bringing readers the surfers' lifestyle through the eyes of those really living it.
Published by: Bluewater Publishing, P O Box 1338, Newport Beach, CA 92659. TEL 888-881-7873, FAX 949-645-8860, zeldo@waterzine.com, http://www.waterzine.com. Ed. Steve Zeldin.

797.173 USA ISSN 0049-7002
GV840.S5
THE WATER SKIER; having fun today - building champions for tomorrow. Text in English. 1951. 7/yr. USD 35 domestic to non-members; USD 40 foreign to non-members; free to members (effective 2010). adv. charts; illus.; tr.lit. Index. back issues avail.; reprints avail. **Document type:** *Magazine, Consumer.* **Description:** Features athlete profiles, instructional articles, tournament reports and results, trends in the water ski sport and classified advertisements.
Related titles: Microfiche ed.; Online - full text ed.
Indexed: ConsI, G05, G06, G07, G08, I05, MagInd, RASB, SportS.
Published by: U S A Water Ski, 1251 Holy Cow Rd, Polk City, FL 33868. TEL 863-324-4341, 800-533-2972, FAX 863-325-8259, memberservices@usawaterski.org. Ed., Pub. Scott Atkinson. adv.: B&W page USD 1,340, color page USD 2,060; bleed 8.5 x 11.125.

799.2 USA ISSN 1931-6240
WATERFOWL & RETRIEVER; hunting tactics, retriever training, conservation. Text in English. 2005. a. adv. back issues avail. **Document type:** *Magazine, Trade.* **Description:** Provides information on advanced decoying and hunting strategies, including reviews of new shotguns and loads, dog training and dog care products, regional hunting reports, outfitter and guide spotlights; boat, blind and game call buyer's guides and more.
Related titles: Online - full text ed.
Indexed: H20.
Published by: Grand View Media Group, Inc. (Subsidiary of: EBSCO Industries, Inc.), 200 Croft St, Ste 1, Birmingham, AL 35242. TEL 888-431-2877, FAX 205-408-3797, webmaster@grandviewmedia.com, http://www.gvmg.com. Ed. Bob Robb. Adv. contact Scott Fowler. color page USD 2,950; trim 7.75 x 10.625. Circ: 50,000.

799.2 USA
WATERFOWL HUNTER. Text in English. 2000. a. adv. **Document type:** *Magazine, Consumer.*
Published by: Harris Publications, Inc., 1115 Broadway, New York, NY 10010. TEL 212-807-7100, FAX 212-924-2352, subscriptions@harris-pub.com, http://www.harris-pub.com/. Ed. Gerald C Bethge. Pub. Stanley R Harris. adv.: B&W page USD 2,970, color page USD 3,190; trim 8 x 10.875.

799.1 GBR ISSN 1365-7585
WATERLOG; the world's finest angling magazine. Text in English. 1996. bi-m. GBP 34 domestic; GBP 46 in Europe; GBP 54 elsewhere (effective 2009). **Document type:** *Magazine, Consumer.*
Published by: The Medlar Press, The Grange, Ellesmere, Shrops SY12 9DE, United Kingdom. TEL 44-1691-623225, books@medpress.demon.co.uk, http://www.medlarpress.com. **Dist. by:** Comag Specialist Division, Tavistock Works, Tavistock Rd, W Drayton, Mddx UB7 7QX, United Kingdom.

797.173 USA ISSN 0883-7813
WATERSKI. Text in English. 1978. 8/yr. USD 9.97 domestic; USD 17.97 in Canada; USD 29.97 elsewhere; USD 4.99 newsstand/cover (effective 2009). adv. illus. back issues avail.; reprints avail. **Document type:** *Magazine, Consumer.* **Description:** Provides the most complete boat tests, equipment reviews and instructional articles on the market, all accompanied by outstanding photography.
Formed by the 198? merger of: World Waterskiing Magazine (0194-6633); Spray's Water Ski (8750-5509); Which incorporated: Spray's Water Ski Magazine (0273-7892); Which was formerly (until vol.4, no.7, 1980): Spray (0164-9922)
Related titles: Online - full text ed.: USD 9.97 (effective 2009).
Indexed: G08, I05.
—CCC.
Published by: World Publications LLC (Subsidiary of: Bonnier Magazine Group), 460 N Orlando Ave, Ste 200, Winter Park, FL 32789. TEL 407-628-4802, FAX 407-628-7061, info@worldpub.net, http://www.bonniercorp.com. Ed. Todd Ristorcelli. Pub. Jim Emmons. Adv. contact Jason Bingham. B&W page USD 8,745, color page USD 13,090; trim 8.125 x 10.75. Circ: 92,060 (paid). **Dist. in the UK by:** Comag, Tavistock Rd, W Drayton, Middlesex UB7 7QE, United Kingdom. TEL 44-1895-433800, FAX 44-1895-433602.

796.172 GBR ISSN 0967-2079
WAVELENGTH; Europe's premier surfing magazine. Variant title: Wavelength Magazine. Text in English. 1981. 9/yr. GBP 27 domestic; GBP 49.50 in Europe; GBP 74.80 elsewhere (effective 2009). adv. bk.rev.; film rev.; software rev.; video rev.; Website rev. 100 p./no.; back issues avail. **Document type:** *Magazine, Consumer.* **Description:** Features interviews and reports on the top surfers from the UK, both men and women as well as advice on board design from some of the UK's top shapers.
Related titles: Online - full text ed.
Published by: Anzar Ltd., 19 Esplanade Rd, Newquay, Cornwall TR7 1QB, United Kingdom. mail@wavelengthmag.co.uk. Ed. Tim Nunn TEL 44-1872-247456. **Dist. by:** Odyssey Publisher Services Ltd.

797.32 GBR ISSN 2044-7620
▼ **WAVELENGTH PHOTO ANNUAL.** Text in English. 2010. a. GBP 2.95 per issue (effective 2011). **Document type:** *Magazine, Consumer.*
Related titles: Online - full text ed.: free (effective 2011).
Published by: Endless Summer Media, Ste 3, Kerns House Unit 11, Threemilestone Industrial Estate, Turo, TR4 9LD, United Kingdom. Ed. Tim Nunn. Adv. contact Mel Eden TEL 44-1872-224030.

797.32 AUS
WAVES. Text in English. m. AUD 80 domestic; AUD 110 in New Zealand; AUD 125 elsewhere; AUD 7.95 newsstand/cover (effective 2008). adv. **Document type:** *Magazine, Consumer.* **Description:** Strives to provide the latest information on surfing and on surfers, in and out of the water.
Published by: A C P Magazines Ltd. (Subsidiary of: P B L Media Pty Ltd.), 54-58 Park St, Sydney, NSW 2000, Australia. TEL 61-2-92828000, FAX 61-2-91263769. Ed. Roghan McKerlie. Adv. contact Marcus Hucker TEL 61-2-81149485. color page AUD 3,260; trim 205 x 275. Circ: 30,000.

796 ARG ISSN 0328-4271
WEEKEND. Text in Spanish. 1971. m. adv. **Document type:** *Magazine, Consumer.* **Description:** Contains articles and features on outdoor and leisure recreation, including fishing, water sports, boating, trekking, and camping.
Related titles: Online - full text ed.; Supplement(s): Weekend Guia de Camping. ISSN 0328-9036. 1990.
Published by: Editorial Perfil S.A., Chacabuco 271, Buenos Aires, Buenos Aires 1069, Argentina. TEL 54-11-43419000, FAX 54-11-43418988, perfilcom@perfil.com.ar, http://www.perfil.com.ar. Ed. Jose Luis Aldorisio. Circ: 88,000 (paid).

WEG!. *see* TRAVEL AND TOURISM

WEGBREEK. *see* TRAVEL AND TOURISM

799.2 DEU
WEIDWERK IN MECKLENBURG-VORPOMMERN. Text in German. 1990. m. adv. **Document type:** *Magazine, Consumer.*
Published by: Landesjagdverband Mecklenburg-Vorpommern e.V., Forsthof 1, Damm, 19374, Germany. TEL 49-3871-6312-0, FAX 49-3871-631212, info@ljv-mecklenburg-vorpommern.de, http://www.ljv-mecklenburg-vorpommern.de. Ed. Henning Voigt. adv.: B&W page EUR 850, color page EUR 1,360. Circ: 10,500 (paid and controlled).

799 USA ISSN 0897-9162
WEST VIRGINIA GAME & FISH. Text in English. 198?. m. USD 12 domestic; USD 25 in Canada; USD 27 elsewhere (effective 2011). adv. **Document type:** *Magazine, Consumer.* **Description:** Informs sportsmen of hunting and fishing, as well as environmental and conservation issues in West Virginia.
Supersedes in part (in 198?): Virginia - West Virginia Game and Fish (0889-3314)
Related titles: Online - full text ed.; ◆ Regional ed(s).: Game & Fish; ◆ Louisiana Game & Fish. ISSN 0744-3692; ◆ Florida Game & Fish. ISSN 0889-3322; ◆ Alabama Game & Fish. ISSN 0279-6783; ◆ Mississippi-Louisiana Game & Fish. ISSN 1947-2358; ◆ North Carolina Game & Fish. ISSN 0897-8816; ◆ South Carolina Game & Fish. ISSN 0897-9154; ◆ Missouri Game & Fish. ISSN 0889-3799; ◆ New York Game & Fish. ISSN 0897-9189; ◆ California Game & Fish. ISSN 1056-0122; ◆ Great Plains Game & Fish. ISSN 1055-6532; ◆ Illinois Game & Fish. ISSN 0897-9014; ◆ Indiana Game & Fish. ISSN 0897-8980; ◆ Iowa Game & Fish. ISSN 0897-9197; ◆ Mid-Atlantic Game & Fish. ISSN 1055-6540; ◆ Oklahoma Game & Fish. ISSN 0746-6013; ◆ Rocky Mountain Game & Fish. ISSN 1056-0114; ◆ Pennsylvania Game & Fish. ISSN 0897-8808; ◆ Virginia Game & Fish. ISSN 0897-8794; ◆ Washington - Oregon Game & Fish. ISSN 1056-0106; ◆ Ohio Game & Fish. ISSN 0897-9170; New England Game & Fish. ISSN 0897-8972. 1988. USD 12 domestic; USD 25 in Canada; USD 27 elsewhere (effective 2010).
Published by: Intermedia Outdoors, Inc., 512 7th Ave, 11th Fl, New York, NY 10018. TEL 212-852-6682, 800-260-6397, FAX 212-302-4472, customerservice@imoutdoors.com, http://www.imoutdoorsmedia.com. Ed. Ken Dunwoody. Pub., Adv. contact Peter Gross.

799.1 AUS ISSN 1443-4814
WESTERN AUSTRALIA. RECREATIONAL FISHING ADVISORY COMMITTEE. PAPER. Text in English. 2000. irreg. **Document type:** *Monographic series, Consumer.* **Description:** Discusses fishers community.
Indexed: ASFA, B21.
Published by: Western Australia, Department of Fisheries, Locked Bag 39, Cloisters Square, W.A. 6850, Australia. TEL 61-8-94827333, 800-815-507, FAX 61-8-94827389, http://www.fish.wa.gov.au.

799.1 AUS ISSN 1832-3251
THE WESTERN AUSTRALIAN FISHING MAGAZINE. Text in English. 2005. bi-m. AUD 39.95 (effective 2007). **Document type:** *Magazine, Consumer.*
Published by: The Western Australian Fishing Magazine, PO Box 1504, Applecross, W.A. 6953, Australia. TEL 61-8-9364-8448, FAX 61-8-9364-4834, wafm@westnet.com.au.

799 USA ISSN 0049-7479
WESTERN OUTDOOR NEWS. Text in English. 1953. w. (Wed.). USD 39.95; USD 2.25 per issue (effective 2005). adv. **Document type:** *Newspaper, Consumer.*
Published by: Western Outdoors Publications, 185 Avenida La Pata, San Clemente, CA 92673. TEL 949-366-0030, FAX 949-366-0804. Ed. Pat McDonell. Pub., Adv. contact Joe Higgins. Circ: 75,000.

796.5 USA ISSN 0043-4000
SK1
WESTERN OUTDOORS. Text in English. 1960. 9/yr. USD 14.95; USD 3.50 newsstand/cover (effective 2001). adv. bk.rev. illus. **Document type:** *Magazine, Consumer.*
Indexed: CalPI, PMR.
—Ingenta.
Published by: Western Outdoors Publications, 185 Avenida La Pata., San Clemente, CA 92673-6307. Eds. Jack Brown, Lew Carpenter. Pub., Adv. contact Joe Higgins. Circ: 91,000.

799 CAN ISSN 0709-1532
WESTERN SPORTSMAN. Text in English. 1969. bi-m. CAD 25 (effective 2004). adv. bk.rev. charts; illus.; stat. **Document type:** *Magazine, Consumer.*
Formerly: Fish and Game Sportsman (0015-2897); Which was formed by the merger of: Fish and Game of Alberta; Saskatchewan Sportsman
Indexed: H20.
Published by: O P Publishing Ltd., 1080 Howe St, Ste 900, Vancouver, BC V6Z 2T1, Canada. TEL 604-606-4644, FAX 604-687-1925, markyelic@oppublishing.com, http://www.oppub.com. Circ: 28,000.

WHEELERS R V RESORT AND CAMPGROUND GUIDE: NORTH AMERICAN EDITION. *see* TRAVEL AND TOURISM

799.1 GBR ISSN 1362-3842
WHERE TO FISH. Text in English. 1922. biennial. GBP 22.50 hardback ed.; GBP 17.99 paperback ed. (effective 2000). adv. **Document type:** *Directory.* **Description:** Directory of fishing in the rivers, lakes, and reservoirs of England, Scotland, Wales, and Northern Ireland and overseas.
Published by: Thomas Harmsworth Publishing Co., Old Rectory Offices, Stoke Abbott, Beaminster, Dorset DT8 3JT, United Kingdom. TEL 44-1308-868118, FAX 44-1308-868995, thpc@thomasharmsworth.demon.co.uk. Pub., R&P, Adv. contact Thomas Harmsworth. Circ: 12,000.

WHICH MOTORCHOME. *see* TRANSPORTATION—Automobiles

796.93 917 USA ISSN 0163-9684
GV854.4
WHITE BOOK OF SKI AREAS. U S AND CANADA. Text in English. 1976. a. USD 18.95 (effective 2001). maps. 300 p./no.; back issues avail. **Document type:** *Directory, Consumer.* **Description:** Complete listing of ski areas in US and Canada with facilities, rates, statistics, and telephone numbers.
Formerly: White Book of U S Ski Areas (0145-6075)
Related titles: CD-ROM ed.
Published by: Inter-Ski Services, Inc., PO Box 3775, Georgetown Sta, Washington, DC 20007. TEL 202-342-0886, FAX 202-338-1940. Ed. Robert G Enzel. Circ: 10,000.

796.93 NLD ISSN 1875-4961
WHITE FREESKI MAG. Variant title: White. Text in Dutch. 200?. s-a. EUR 9; EUR 5.50 newsstand/cover (effective 2008). adv. **Document type:** *Magazine, Consumer.*
Formerly (until 2006): White Skiing Magazine (1574-7557)
Published by: Soul Media, Stetweg 43C, Castricum, 1901 JD, Netherlands. TEL 31-251-674911, FAX 31-251-674378, info@soulonline.nl, http://www.soulonline.nl. Circ: 22,000.

796.9 GBR ISSN 1359-0111
WHITE LINES; snowboarding magazine. Text in English. 1995. 5/yr. GBP 14.95; GBP 2.95 newsstand/cover (effective 1999). adv. **Document type:** *Magazine, Consumer.* **Description:** Covers all aspects of snowboarding and those who participate.
Published by: Permanent Publishing Ltd., 1 Stert St, Abingdon, Oxon OX14 3JF, United Kingdom. TEL 44-1235-536229, FAX 44-1235-536230. Ed. Tudor Thomas. Pub. Jim Preskett. **Dist. by:** Seymour Distribution Ltd, 86 Newman St, London W1T 3EX, United Kingdom. FAX 44-207-396-8002, enquiries@seymour.co.uk.

799.2 USA ISSN 1537-3126
THE WHITETAIL FANATIC; custom made for deer hunting enthusiasts. Text in English. 2001 (November). 9/yr. USD 20 (effective 2002).
Published by: Fanatic Enterprisese, 103 Lessing Street, P.O. Box 225, Guttenberg, IA 52052g. TEL 563-252-3981, editor@whitetailfanatic.com. Pub. Tom Fassbinder.

799.2 USA
WHITETAIL HUNTING STRATEGIES. Text in English. 19??. bi-m. adv. **Document type:** *Magazine, Consumer.* **Description:** Presents the advanced strategies of serious hunters who bag the giant bucks, season after season.
Published by: Harris Publications, Inc., 1115 Broadway, New York, NY 10010. TEL 212-807-7100, FAX 212-610-7787, subscriptions@harris-pub.com. adv.: B&W page USD 2,600, color page USD 3,250; trim 8 x 10.875.

799.2 USA ISSN 1097-296X
SK1
WHITETAIL JOURNAL; america's complete deer-hunting source. Variant title: White Tail Journal. Text in English. 1993. bi-m. USD 9.99 domestic; USD 19.99 in Canada; USD 24.99 elsewhere (effective 2008). adv. Supplement avail.; back issues avail. **Document type:** *Magazine, Trade.* **Description:** Covers all aspects of whitetail deer hunting, including the latest product information pertaining to guns, ammo, camo, bows and accessories.
Related titles: Online - full text ed.
Indexed: H20, M02, T02.
Published by: Grand View Media Group, Inc. (Subsidiary of: EBSCO Industries, Inc.), 200 Croft St, Ste 1, Birmingham, AL 35242. TEL 888-431-2877, FAX 205-408-3797, webmaster@grandviewmedia.com, http://www.gvmg.com. Ed. Bob Robb. Pub. Derrick Nawrocki TEL 205-408-3732. adv.: B&W page USD 3,845, color page USD 4,820; trim 7.75 x 10.625. Circ: 65,000.

799.2 USA ISSN 1085-7281
WHITETAILS UNLIMITED MAGAZINE. Text in English. 1983. s-a. USD 14 membership. adv. **Document type:** *Magazine, Consumer.*
Formerly (until 1993): Deer Trail

S

Published by: Whitetails Unlimited, Inc., PO Box 720, Sturgeon Bay, WI 54235-0720. TEL 920-743-6777. Ed. Kevin Haze. Circ: 40,000.

799.2 USA
WHITETALE JOURNAL. Text in English. 8/yr. USD 2.95 newsstand/cover. **Document type:** *Magazine, Consumer.*
Formerly: Buckhunter's Whitetail
Published by: Thickets Publishing, 2700 2nd Ave S, #3, Birmingham, AL 35233-2704. TEL 205-987-6007, FAX 205-987-2882.

799 USA
WHOOP 'N' HOLLER. Text in English. q. free membership. 8 p./no.; **Document type:** *Newsletter, Consumer.* **Description:** Covers hiking, backpacking, and club news.
Published by: West Virginia Scenic Trails Association, PO Box 4042, Charleston, WV 25364. wvscenictrailsassn@yahoo.com, http://wvscenictrails.org/. Ed. George L Rosier. Circ: 200.

796 AUS ISSN 1030-469X
WILD; Australia's wilderness adventure magazine. Text in English. 1981. q. AUD 31.95 domestic; AUD 56.95 foreign (effective 2009). adv. film rev. charts; illus. index. back issues avail. **Document type:** *Magazine, Consumer.* **Description:** Covers hiking, cross-country skiing, canoeing, mountaineering and caving in Australia.
Formerly (until 1987): Australian Wild (0726-2809)
Indexed: A11, CPerl, T02, WBA, WMB.
Published by: Wild Publications Pty. Ltd., PO Box 415, Prahran, VIC 3181, Australia. TEL 61-3-98268482, FAX 61-3-98263787. Adv. contact Stephen Hamilton.

333.95416 USA
WILD ALABAMA; a guide for hikers, hunters, fishermen, backpackers, campers, and outdoor people. Text in English. 1995. q. USD 24.95; USD 3.95 newsstand/cover; USD 29.95 foreign (effective 2000). adv. bk.rev. charts; illus.; maps. back issues avail. **Document type:** *Magazine, Consumer.* **Description:** For environmental and outdoors enthusiasts. Contains information on outdoor activities and skills. Also includes trail maps and descriptions of wild places in Alabama, local history and folklore, environmental reports on local issues, forest service management activities, and fiction and non-fiction stories about experiences in the wild.
Address: PO Box 117, Moulton, AL 35650. TEL 256-974-6166. Ed., Pub., R&P, Adv. contact Lamar Marshall TEL 256-974-6166. B&W page USD 600, color page USD 800; trim 10.75 x 8.25. Circ: 7,000 (controlled).

799.2 ZAF ISSN 1025-4226
WILD & JAG/GAME & HUNT. Text in Afrikaans, English. 1995. m. ZAR 300 domestic; ZAR 390 foreign (effective 2006). adv. **Document type:** *Magazine, Consumer.*
Indexed: ISAP.
Published by: JLO Publishing, PO Box 35299, Menlo Park, 0102, South Africa. TEL 27-12-3485550, FAX 27-12-3485551. Ed., Pub. Jan van der Walt. Adv. contact Ann Olivier. B&W page ZAR 5,100, color page ZAR 8,500; 185 x 270.

796 USA ISSN 1934-0443
WILD IDAHO NEWS. Text in English. 2005. bi-w. USD 27.95 (effective 2007). **Document type:** *Magazine, Consumer.* **Description:** Features local information about hunting, fishing and outdoor pursuits in Idaho.
Address: 200 N 4th St, Ste 101, Boise, ID 83702. TEL 208-939-8845, FAX 208-939-7038. Pub. Doug Schleis.

799.1 DEU ISSN 0043-5422
WILD UND HUND; das Jagdmagazin. Text in German. 1895. fortn. EUR 103 domestic; EUR 110 foreign; EUR 4.90 newsstand/cover (effective 2011). adv. bk.rev. illus. reprints avail. **Document type:** *Magazine, Consumer.*
Related titles: ◆ Supplement(s): Wild und Hund Exklusiv. ISSN 0948-1052.
Indexed: KWIWR, RASB, W08.
—CCC.
Published by: Paul Parey Zeitschriftenverlag GmbH, Erich Kaestner Str 2, Singhofen, 56379, Germany. TEL 49-2604-9780, FAX 49-2604-978190, online@paulparey.de, http://www.paulparey.de. Circ: 68,504 (paid).

799.1 DEU ISSN 0948-1052
WILD UND HUND EXKLUSIV. Text in German. 1995. 2/yr. adv. **Document type:** *Magazine, Consumer.*
Related titles: ◆ Supplement to: Wild und Hund. ISSN 0043-5422.
Published by: Paul Parey Zeitschriftenverlag GmbH, Erich Kaestner Str 2, Singhofen, 56379, Germany. TEL 49-2604-9780, FAX 49-2604-978190, online@paulparey.de, http://www.paulparey.de. Circ: 13,500 (controlled).

796.5 NZL ISSN 1177-0171
WILDERNESS. Text in English. 1991. m. NZD 79.50 domestic; NZD 140 in Australia & the Pacific; NZD 160 elsewhere (effective 2009). adv. back issues avail. **Document type:** *Magazine, Consumer.*
Formerly (until 2003): New Zealand Wilderness (1171-4174)
Published by: Lifestyle Publishing Ltd., 51a Riverlea Ave, Pakuranga, Panmure, PO Box 14-109, Auckland, New Zealand. TEL 64-9-5702658, FAX 64-9-5702684.

WILDERNESS AND ENVIRONMENTAL MEDICINE. *see* MEDICAL SCIENCES

796 USA
WILDERNESS WAY. Text in English. q. USD 16 domestic; CAD 26 in Canada; USD 33 elsewhere (effective 2002). back issues avail. **Document type:** *Magazine, Consumer.*
Related titles: Online - full content ed.
Published by: Wilderness Way Magazine, PO Box 621, Bellaire, TX 77402-0621. TEL 713-667-0128, FAX 801-730-3329. Ed. Steve Hulsey. Pub. Kelly Lilly.

799.2 USA ISSN 0886-0637
WILDFOWL; the magazine for duck & goose hunters. Text in English. 1985. 7/yr. USD 24.97 domestic; USD 37.97 in Canada; USD 39.97 elsewhere (effective 2008). adv. illus. back issues avail.; reprints avail. **Document type:** *Magazine, Consumer.* **Description:** For waterfowl hunters.
Indexed: A33, G08, I05, W08.
—CCC.
Published by: Intermedia Outdoors, Inc., 512 7th Ave, 11th Fl, New York, NY 10018. TEL 212-852-6600, 800-260-6397, FAX 212-302-4472, customerservice@imoutdoors.com, http://www.imoutdoorsmedia.com. Ed. Jay Michael Strangis. adv.: B&W page USD 2,850, color page USD 4,160. Circ: 39,522 (paid).

799.2 USA ISSN 0886-3458
WILDLIFE HARVEST; the magazine for gamebird production & improved hunting. Text in English. 1970. m. USD 35 (effective 2006). adv. bk.rev. illus. 70 p./no.; reprints avail. **Document type:** *Magazine, Trade.* **Description:** Covers the market for shooting and hunting supplies, clothing and equipment, shotguns, shotshells, clay-targets and sporting clay traps.
Published by: (North American Gamebird Association, Inc.), Wildlife Harvest Publications, PO Box 96, Goose Lake, IA 52750. TEL 563-259-4000, FAX 563-677-2400. adv.: B&W page USD 440. Circ: 2,500 (paid).

797.33 FRA ISSN 0241-1393
WIND MAGAZINE; le magazine du windsurf. Text in French. 1980. m. **Document type:** *Magazine, Consumer.*
Published by: Editions du Solaise, 6 rue Irvoy, Grenoble, 38000, France. TEL 33-4-76705720. Ed. Pierre Bigorgne. Pub. Pascal Maltherre.

796.172 USA ISSN 1057-0799
GV811.63.W56
WINDSURFING; the nation's leading windsurfing magazine. Text in English. 1981. bi-m. USD 9.97 domestic; USD 15.97 in Canada; USD 24.97 elsewhere; USD 4.99 newsstand/cover (effective 2009). adv. illus. back issues avail.; reprints avail. **Document type:** *Magazine, Consumer.* **Description:** Provides information on windsurfing with the latest gear, the windiest destinations, the hottest sailors and the best tips.
Formerly (until 1991): WindRider (0279-4659)
Related titles: Online - full text ed.: USD 9.99 (effective 2008).
Indexed: G08, I05.
—Ingenta. **CCC.**
Published by: World Publications LLC (Subsidiary of: Bonnier Magazine Group), 460 N Orlando Ave, Ste 200, Winter Park, FL 32789. TEL 407-628-4802, FAX 407-628-7061, info@worldpub.net, http://www.bonniercorp.com. Ed. Josh Sampiero. Pub., Adv. contact David Combe TEL 541-308-0559. B&W page USD 3,595, color page USD 5,385; trim 8.125 x 10.75. Circ: 27,569 (paid).

797.14 POL ISSN 1509-8710
WINDSURFING. Text in Polish. 2000. bi-m. PLZ 65 domestic; PLZ 96 in Europe; PLZ 126 in United States (effective 2003). adv. **Document type:** *Magazine, Consumer.*
Published by: Atol s.c., ul Bitwy pod Plowcami 63-65, Sopot, 81-731, Poland. Ed. Magda Puciata. Adv. contact Michal Surdykowski.

796.93 GBR ISSN 2045-6328
▼ **WINTER SPORTS TECHNOLOGY INTERNATIONAL.** Text in English. 2010. s-a. GBP 60, USD 98; free to qualified personnel (effective 2010). adv. **Document type:** *Magazine, Trade.* **Description:** Designed for the publication of ski resort and snowdome design, operation and technology. Features interviews with the industry's key figures, plus case studies on the latest venues and technologies.
Related titles: Online - full text ed.: ISSN 2045-6336. free (effective 2010).
Published by: UKIP Media & Events Ltd, Abinger House, Church St, Dorking, Surrey RH4 1DF, United Kingdom. TEL 44-1306-743744, FAX 44-1306-887546, info@ukintpress.com. Ed. Anthony James. Adv. contact Damien de Roche.

796.93 NLD ISSN 1879-5129
WINTERSPORT MAGAZINE. Text in Dutch. 1953. 5/yr. EUR 30 (effective 2010). adv. **Document type:** *Magazine, Consumer.* **Description:** Contains articles on skiing and winter sports activities, travel suggestions, product information.
Former titles (until 2009): Ski Magazine (0169-2364); (until 1983): Ski (0165-6902); Ski Magazine incorporated (1988-1991): Ski Plus (0923-3237)
Published by: Nederlandse Ski Vereniging, Postbus 82100, The Hague, 2508 EC, Netherlands. TEL 31-70-4273113, info@ski.nl, http://www.ski.nl.

WISCONSIN NATURAL RESOURCES. *see* CONSERVATION

799 USA ISSN 1076-0067
WISCONSIN OUTDOOR NEWS; the sportsman's online choice for news and information. Text in English. 1994. bi-w. USD 26 (effective 2009). adv. back issues avail. **Document type:** *Newspaper, Consumer.* **Description:** Provides the sportsmen/women in Wisconsin with the statewide hunting/fishing report, a lake profile complete with map, statewide calendar of events, season and permit dates and in-depth fishing and hunting news.
Related titles: Online - full text ed.
Published by: Outdoor News, Inc., 125 Kettle Moraine Dr S, Slinger, WI 53086. TEL 740-363-2374, 800-960-7476, FAX 763-546-5913, subscribe@outdoornews.com, http://www.outdoornews.com. Ed. Dean Bortz. Adv. contact Jeff Bast. B&W page USD 1,668, color page USD 2,043; 10 x 16.

796.95 USA ISSN 0745-161X
WISCONSIN SNOWMOBILE NEWS. Abbreviated title: W S N. Text in English. 1987. 7/yr. (Sep.-Mar.). free to members (effective 2010). adv. **Document type:** *Magazine, Trade.* **Description:** Contains information about the activities of the association, club events and legislative issues.
Published by: (Association of Wisconsin Snowmobile Clubs), PrintComm, Inc., PO BOX 182, Rio, WI 53960. TEL 920-992-6370, 800-380-3767, FAX 920-992-6369, http://www.printcomm.com/. Adv. contact Cathy Hanson. B&W page USD 2,629, color page USD 3,470; 7.5 x 10. Circ: 28,000.

796 USA ISSN 0361-9451
SK143
WISCONSIN SPORTSMAN. Text in English. 1972. m. USD 12 domestic; USD 25 in Canada; USD 27 elsewhere (effective 2011). adv. bk.rev. illus. **Document type:** *Magazine, Consumer.* **Description:** Reports on all aspects of hunting and fishing, as well as environmental and conservation issues in Wisconsin.
Related titles: Online - full text ed.
Published by: Intermedia Outdoors, Inc., 512 7th Ave, 11th Fl, New York, NY 10018. TEL 212-852-6682, 800-260-6397, FAX 212-302-4472, customerservice@imoutdoors.com, http://www.imoutdoorsmedia.com. Ed. Ken Dunwoody. Pub., Adv. contact Peter Gross.

796.54 DEU
WOHNMOBIL & REISEN. Text in German. 1993. 3/yr. EUR 14.70; EUR 4.90 newsstand/cover (effective 2009). adv. **Document type:** *Magazine, Consumer.*
Published by: Besser Bauen Verlag GmbH, Moerikestr 67, Stuttgart, 70199, Germany. TEL 49-711-96666999, FAX 49-711-96666980, info@besserbauen.de. Eds. Angela Koerbs, Klaus Vetterle. Adv. contact Ralph Ross. B&W page EUR 3,800, color page EUR 5,320; trim 185 x 254. Circ: 55,000 (paid and controlled).

796.54 CHE ISSN 1422-8459
WOHNMOBIL & CARAVAN. Text in German. 1995. 5/yr. CHF 64 for 2 yrs.; CHF 8 newsstand/cover (effective 2011). adv. **Document type:** *Magazine, Consumer.* **Description:** Contains reviews and tests on a wide variety of campers and mobile homes.
Formerly (until 1998): Wohnmobil, Reisen und Camping (1423-7024)
Published by: Etzel-Verlag AG, Knonauerstr 56, Cham, 6330, Switzerland. TEL 41-41-7855085, FAX 41-41-7855088, info@etzel-verlag.ch, http://www.etzel-verlag.ch. Ed. Christoph Hostettler. Circ: 20,400 (paid).

796.54 DEU
WOHNMOBIL, WOHNWAGEN-MARKT. Text in German. 19??. m. EUR 36 domestic; EUR 93.60 foreign; EUR 3 newsstand/cover (effective 2011). adv. **Document type:** *Magazine, Consumer.*
Former titles (until 2006): Wohnmobil, Wohnwagen-Markt International; (until 2004): Wohnmobil-Markt International; (until 2001): Wohnmobil Markt
Published by: Der Heisse Draht Verlag GmbH und Co., Drostestr 14, Hannover, 30161, Germany. TEL 49-511-390910, FAX 49-511-39091196, zentrale@dhd.de, http://www.dhd.de. Adv. contact Lars Schnatmann. Circ: 76,000 (paid and controlled).

799.2 305.4 USA ISSN 1944-6756
SK41
WOMAN HUNTER. Text in English. 2007. bi-m. USD 15.99; USD 2.99 newsstand/cover (effective 2009). adv. **Document type:** *Magazine, Consumer.*
Related titles: Online - full text ed.: ISSN 1944-6764.
Address: 4225 Miller Rd B-9, #255, Flint, MI 48507. Pub. Lisa Snelling.

WOMEN OUTDOORS MAGAZINE. *see* WOMEN'S INTERESTS

WOMEN'S ADVENTURE. *see* WOMEN'S INTERESTS

796 AUS
WOMEN'S GOLF AUSTRALIA. OFFICIAL YEARBOOK. Text in English. 1932. a. adv. **Document type:** *Directory.*
Formerly: Australian Ladies Golf Union. Official Yearbook
Published by: Women's Golf Australia Inc., Level 3, 95 Coventry St, South Melbourne, VIC 3205, Australia. TEL 61-3-96265050, FAX 61-3-96265095, info@golfaustralia.org.au, http://www.wga.com.au.

796 GBR ISSN 2042-0242
▼ **WOMEN'S RUNNING;** it's your time!. Text in English. 2010. m. GBP 44.40 (effective 2011). back issues avail. **Document type:** *Magazine, Consumer.* **Description:** Offers friendly, straightforward advice, inspiration and guidance to all levels of runner.
Published by: Wild Bunch Media Ltd., 4th Fl, 26-28 Hammersmith Grove, London, W6 7BA, United Kingdom. TEL 44-20-88341650.

797.32 USA ISSN 2158-7515
WOMEN'S SURF STYLE MAGAZINE. Abbreviated title: W S S M. Text in English. 2004. s-a. USD 19.99 domestic; USD 45.99 foreign; USD 9.99 per issue domestic; USD 22.99 per issue foreign (effective 2011). adv. back issues avail. **Document type:** *Magazine, Consumer.* **Description:** Explores eclectic mix of women's interests such as health, beauty, fitness,word finds, recipes, etc.
Related titles: Online - full text ed.: ISSN 2158-7523. free (effective 2011).
Published by: ChickSurf, PO Box 22853, Honolulu, HI 96823. Ed. Debbie L Olson. Circ: 10,000.

WONDERFUL WEST VIRGINIA. *see* CONSERVATION

WOODALL'S CAMPERWAYS; the Middle Atlantic campers' newspaper. *see* TRAVEL AND TOURISM

796.5 USA ISSN 0162-3796
WOODALL'S CAMPGROUND MANAGEMENT; the voice of the North American campground business. Text in English. 1970. m. free to qualified personnel (effective 2009). adv. bk.rev. charts; illus.; stat.; tr.lit. 30 p./no. 4 cols./p.; back issues avail. **Document type:** *Magazine, Trade.* **Description:** Contains information for the development, rehabilitation, maintenance, operation and management of a campground.
Formerly: Campground Management and R V Park Management
Published by: Woodall Publications Corp. (Subsidiary of: Affinity Group Inc.), PO Box 276, Syracuse, IN 46567. TEL 574-457-3370, FAX 574-457-8295, info@woodallpub.com, http://www.woodalls.com. Eds. Jeff Crider, Steve Bibler. Pub. Sherman Goldenberg. adv.: page USD 3,530, color page USD 3,980; 9.75 x 13. Circ: 14,000.

796.5 USA
GV191.35
WOODALL'S CAMPING LIFE MAGAZINE; America's family camping magazine. Text in English. 2008. 8/yr. USD 14.97 domestic; USD 22.97 in Canada; USD 30.97 elsewhere (effective 2009). adv. tr.lit. **Document type:** *Magazine, Trade.* **Description:** Lists all the campgrounds in the US and Canada that welcome tent campers; includes editorials on tenting accessories and tents, cooking recommendations, travel tips, and attractions, as well as checklists explaining how to pack.
Incorporates (in 2008): Woodall's Tenting Directory (1548-3711); Which was formerly (until 2008): Woodall's Plan It - Pack It - Go; (until 1993): Woodall's Tent Camping Guide (0742-3950); (until 1990): Woodall's Tenting Directory (0742-3977)
Published by: Woodall Publications Corp. (Subsidiary of: Affinity Group Inc.), 20700 Belshaw Ave, Carson, CA 90746. TEL 310-537-6322, FAX 310-537-8735, info@woodallpub.com, http://www.woodalls.com. Ed. Stuart Bourdon. Adv. contact Angela van Hover TEL 310-537-6322 ext 135. B&W page USD 4,790, color page USD 7,860; bleed 8.125 x 10.75.

917.59 USA ISSN 1545-8997
GV191.35
WOODALL'S EASTERN AMERICA CAMPGROUND DIRECTORY; the complete guide to campgrounds, RV parks, service centers & attractions. Text in English. a. USD 17.95 per issue (effective 2009). **Document type:** *Directory, Consumer.* **Description:** Covers the Eastern-most states and provinces in the U.S., Mexico and Canada and provides information on campground, service center and attraction available.
Formerly (until 2003): Woodall's Campground Directory. Eastern Edition (0162-7406); Supersedes in part: Woodall's Campground Directory; Which was formerly: Woodall's Trailering Parks and Campgrounds (0084-1110)
Published by: Woodall Publications Corp. (Subsidiary of: Affinity Group Inc.), 2575 Vista Del Mar Dr, Ventura, CA 93001. TEL 877-667-4100, 877-680-6155, FAX 805-667-4122, info@woodallpub.com.

917.59 USA ISSN 1547-6340
GV198.56
WOODALL'S NORTH AMERICA CAMPGROUND DIRECTORY; the complete guide to campgrounds, RV parks, service centers & attractions. (Also avail. in regional eds.: New York & New England; The South; Great Plains & Mountain States; Far West; Mid-Atlantic; Great Lakes; Frontier West; Canada) Text in English. a. USD 25.95 per issue (effective 2009). adv. bk.rev. bibl.; charts; illus.; tr.lit. **Document type:** *Directory, Consumer.* **Description:** Covers the U.S., Mexico and Canada and provides information on campground, service center and attraction available.
Former titles (until 2003): Woodall's Campground Directory. North American Edition; Woodall's Campground Directory. North American - Canadian Edition (0146-1362); Woodall's Campground Directory. North American Edition; Which superseded in part: Woodall's Campground Directory (0362-3823); Which was formerly: Woodall's Trailering Parks and Campgrounds (0084-1110)
Related titles: CD-ROM ed.
Published by: Woodall Publications Corp. (Subsidiary of: Affinity Group Inc.), 2575 Vista Del Mar Dr, Ventura, CA 93001. TEL 877-667-4100, 877-680-6155, FAX 805-667-4122, info@woodallpub.com. Ed. Barbara Tinucci. Pub. Deborah A Spriggs. adv.: B&W page USD 11,615, color page USD 13,765; trim 10.88 x 8.13. Circ: 421,000.

796.5 USA ISSN 1093-4189
WOODALL'S NORTHEAST OUTDOORS. Text in English. 1968. bi-m. USD 20 (effective 2009). adv. bk.rev. **Document type:** *Magazine, Consumer.* **Description:** Focuses on the Northeastern US, featuring NY, CT, MA, RI, VT, NH and ME.
Formerly (until 1997): Northeast Outdoors (0199-8463)
Published by: Woodall Publications Corp. (Subsidiary of: Affinity Group Inc.), 2575 Vista Del Mar Dr, Ventura, CA 93001. TEL 805-667-4100, 877-680-6155, FAX 805-667-4122, info@woodallpub.com. Eds. Brent Peterson, Malina Baccanari. Pub. Ann Emerson. adv.: color page USD 2,465, B&W page USD 1,695.

388 USA
WOODALL'S SOUTHERN R V. Text in English. 1981. m. adv. **Document type:** *Magazine, Consumer.*
Published by: Woodall Publications Corp. (Subsidiary of: Affinity Group Inc.), 2575 Vista Del Mar Dr, Ventura, CA 93001. TEL 805-667-4100, 877-680-6155, FAX 805-667-4122, info@woodallpub.com, http://www.woodalls.com.

917.59 USA ISSN 0162-7414
WOODALL'S WESTERN CAMPGROUND DIRECTORY; the complete guide to campgrounds, RV parks, service centers & attractions. Variant title: Campground Directory. Woodall's Campground Directory. Western Edition. Text in English. 1977. a. USD 17.95 per issue (effective 2009). **Document type:** *Directory, Consumer.* **Description:** Covers the Western-most states and provinces in the U.S., Mexico and Canada and provides information on campground, service center and attraction available.
Supersedes in part: Woodall's Campground Directory (0362-3823); Which was formerly: Woodall's Trailering Parks and Campgrounds (0084-1110)
Published by: Woodall Publications Corp. (Subsidiary of: Affinity Group Inc.), 2575 Vista Del Mar Dr, Ventura, CA 93001. TEL 877-667-4100, 877-680-6155, FAX 805-667-4122, info@woodallpub.com. Pub. Deborah A Spriggs.

WOODS, WATER & WILDLIFE. *see* CONSERVATION

WORLD RECORD GAME FISHES. *see* FISH AND FISHERIES

WYOMING WILDLIFE NEWS. *see* CONSERVATION

796 USA
XPLOR. Text in English. 2005 (Spring). 3/yr. (q. in 2006, bi-m. in 2007). free (effective 2005). **Document type:** *Magazine, Consumer.* **Description:** Covers regional outdoor activities, the newest places to hike or mountain bike, and the latest gears. Also covers environmental conservation and protection.
Published by: True North Custom Publishing, LLC (Subsidiary of: Sunshine Media, Inc.), 735 Broad St., Ste. 708, Chattanooga, TN 37402-9935. sheryl@xplormag.com, http://www.truenorthcustom.com/.

▼ **XPLOR (JEFFERSON CITY)**; adventures in nature. *see* CHILDREN AND YOUTH—For

796 028.5 DNK ISSN 1902-1666
XSPORT; ung handicapidraet. Text in Danish. 2003. q. DKK 75 (effective 2008). adv. **Document type:** *Magazine, Consumer.*
Formerly (until 2006): Handikids Sport (1604-0295)
Published by: Dansk Handicap Idraets Forbund, Idraettens Hus, Broendby, 2605, Denmark. TEL 45-43-262626, FAX 45-43-262470, handicapidraet@dhif.dk, http://www.dhif.dk. Ed. Kristian Bang Larsen.

796.54 GBR ISSN 1355-7491
YOUR BIG SITES BOOK; camping and caravanning club sites list. Text in English. 1920. biennial. free to members (effective 2009). adv. **Document type:** *Directory, Consumer.* **Description:** Contains listing of nearly 4,000 camp sites nationwide.
Supersedes in part (in 1989): Camping and Caravanning Club Handbook and Sites List; Which was formerly (until 19??): Camping Club Handbook and Sites List; (until 19??): Camping Club of Great Britain and Ireland. Year Book with List of Camp Sites (0068-6956)
Published by: Camping and Caravanning Club, Greenfields House, Westwood Way, Coventry, Warks CV4 8JH, United Kingdom. TEL 44-24-76475448. Ed. Simon McGrath. Adv. contact Matthew Styrka TEL 44-20-73060300 ext 2121.

796.54 GBR ISSN 1355-3348
YOUR PLACE IN THE COUNTRY: A GUIDE TO CAMPING AND CARAVANNING CLUB SITES. Text in English. 1920. a. free to members (effective 2009). adv. **Document type:** *Directory, Consumer.* **Description:** Contains information on all UK club sites.
Supersedes in part (in 1989): Camping and Caravanning Club Handbook and Sites List; Which was formerly (until 19??): Camping Club Handbook and Sites List; (until 19??): Camping Club of Great Britain and Ireland. Year Book with List of Camp Sites (0068-6956)
Published by: Camping and Caravanning Club, Greenfields House, Westwood Way, Coventry, Warks CV4 8JH, United Kingdom. TEL 44-24-76475448. Ed. Simon McGrath. Adv. contact Matthew Styrka TEL 44-20-73060300 ext 2121.

799.1 CZE ISSN 1212-5210
ZBRANE & NABOJE. Text in Czech. 1999. m. CZK 991; CZK 82.58 newsstand/cover (effective 2009). adv. **Document type:** *Magazine, Consumer.*
Published by: R F Hobby s.r.o., Bohdalecka 6, Prague 10, 110 00, Czech Republic. TEL 420-281-090610, FAX 420-281-090623, sekretariat@rf-hobby.cz, http://www.rf-hobby.cz. Ed. Zdenek Kastak. Adv. contact Petr Doul. Circ: 25,500 (paid and controlled).

799.16 NLD ISSN 1381-9976
ZEEHENGELSPORT; het einige zoute hengelsportmagazine. Text in Dutch. 1982. 8/yr. EUR 35; EUR 4.95 newsstand/cover (effective 2010). adv. bk.rev.; video rev. charts; illus.; maps; tr.lit. back issues avail. **Document type:** *Magazine, Consumer.* **Description:** Covers sea angling for Dutch and Belgian readers.
Published by: Publishing House & Facilities B.V., Postbus 119, Doetinchem, 7000 AC, Netherlands. TEL 31-314-340150, FAX 31-314-346675, info@publishinghouse.nl, http://www.publishinghouse.nl. adv.: B&W page EUR 775, color page EUR 1,275; 184 x 252. Circ: 15,000.

799.1 CHN ISSN 1000-3487
ZHONGGUO DIAOYU/CHINA ANGLING. Text in Chinese. 1984. m. USD 62.40 (effective 2009). adv. **Document type:** *Magazine, Consumer.*
Related titles: Online - full text ed.
—East View.
Published by: (Zhongguo Diaoyu Xiehui/China Angling Association), Zhongguo Tiyubao Yezongshe, 8, Tiyuguan Lu, Chongwen-qu, Beijing, 100061, China. TEL 86-10-67158577, FAX 86-10-67158584. Circ: 200,000.

ZIP LINES; the voice for adventure education. *see* EDUCATION

796.522 POL ISSN 1896-0294
3 ZYWIOLY. Text in Polish. 2006. q. PLZ 20 domestic (effective 2011). **Document type:** *Magazine, Consumer.*
Related titles: Online - full text ed.
Published by: Wydawnictwo Elamed, Al Rozdzienskiego 188, Katowice, 40203, Poland. TEL 48-32-2580361, FAX 48-32-2039356, elamed@elamed.com.pl, http://www.elamed.com.pl.

796.172 ESP
3SESENTA; el mejor surf. Text in Spanish. 1987. bi-m. adv. music rev. back issues avail. **Document type:** *Magazine, Consumer.*
Formerly (until 2000): Tres 60 Surf (0214-7440)
Address: Iparraguirre 59, 2o, Santurzi, Vizcaya 48980, Spain. TEL 34-944-614470, info@3sesenta.com, http://www.3sesenta.com. Circ: 10,000.

4 WHEEL ACTION; the 4wd adventure magazine. *see* TRANSPORTATION—Automobiles

796.172 NLD ISSN 1574-7417
6 SURFING MAGAZINE. Variant title: Zes Surf Magazine. Text in Dutch. 2005. 4/yr. EUR 23.80 (effective 2010). adv. **Document type:** *Magazine, Consumer.*
Published by: Soul Media, Stetweg 43C, Castricum, 1901 JD, Netherlands. TEL 31-251-674911, FAX 31-251-674378, info@soulonline.nl, http://www.soulonline.nl. Circ: 12,500.

796.939 USA ISSN 1943-7463
GV857.S57
32 DEGREES. Text in English. 2008. 3/yr. free to members (effective 2009). adv. back issues avail. **Document type:** *Magazine, Consumer.* **Description:** Provides articles relating to snowsports instruction in various disciplines such as alpine, nordic, snowboarding, and adaptive.
Related titles: Online - full text ed.
Published by: American Snowsports Education Association, 133 S Van Gordon St, Ste 200, Lakewood, CO 80228. TEL 303-987-9390, FAX 303-987-9489. Circ: 35,500.

796.552 TWN
523 WOAISHAN. Text in Chinese. q. TWD 1,000 membership (effective 2007). **Document type:** *Magazine, Consumer.*
Published by: Zhonghua Minguo 523 Dengshanhui/523 Mountaineering Association, Taiwan, No.28-2, Chihfong St., Datong District, Taipei, 103, Taiwan. TEL 886-2-25557523, FAX 886-2-25582292, 523@523.org.tw, http://www.523.org.tw/.

SPORTS MEDICINE

see MEDICAL SCIENCES—Sports Medicine

STATISTICS

see also MATHEMATICS ; POPULATION STUDIES ; and also Abstracting, Bibliographies, Statistics subheadings under specific subjects

A A M A INDUSTRY STATISTICAL REVIEW AND FORECAST. *see* BUILDING AND CONSTRUCTION—Abstracting, Bibliographies, Statistics

A F C O M'S ANNUAL SURVEY OF DATA PROCESSING OPERATIONS SALARIES. *see* BUSINESS AND ECONOMICS—Abstracting, Bibliographies, Statistics

A M C SOLUTIONS AND STATISTICS (YEAR) (JUNIOR INTERMEDIATE SENIOR). (Australian Mathematics Competition) *see* MATHEMATICS

A N F I A NOTIZIARIO STATISTICO. (Associazione Nazionale fra le Industrie Automobilistiche) *see* TRANSPORTATION—Abstracting, Bibliographies, Statistics

A P D U NEWSLETTER. *see* ENGINEERING—Computer Applications

A R L PRESERVATION STATISTICS. *see* LIBRARY AND INFORMATION SCIENCES—Abstracting, Bibliographies, Statistics

A R L STATISTICS. *see* LIBRARY AND INFORMATION SCIENCES—Abstracting, Bibliographies, Statistics

314 DEU ISSN 1863-8171
HA1 CODEN: ALSAAX
➤ **A ST A - ADVANCES IN STATISTICAL ANALYSIS.** Text in German; Summaries in English. 1890. q. EUR 262, USD 282 combined subscription to institutions (print & online eds.) (effective 2012). adv. bk.rev. bibl.; charts. index. reprints avail. **Document type:** *Journal, Academic/Scholarly.* **Description:** Provides a scientific forum for researchers and users from all branches of statistics.
Formerly (until 2007): Allgemeines Statistisches Archiv (0002-6018)
Related titles: Online - full text ed.: ISSN 1863-818X (from IngentaConnect).
Indexed: A22, A26, CCMJ, CIS, E01, E08, EconLit, IBR, IBSS, IBZ, JCQM, JEL, MSN, MathR, P30, PAIS, RASB, S09, SCI, SCOPUS, ST&MA, W07, Z02.
—IE, Infotrieve, Ingenta, INIST. **CCC.**
Published by: (Vorstand der Deutschen Statistischen Gesellschaft), Springer (Subsidiary of: Springer Science+Business Media), Tiergartenstr 17, Heidelberg, 69121, Germany. TEL 49-6221-4870, FAX 49-6221-345229, subscriptions@springer.com. **Subscr. in the Americas to:** Springer New York LLC, Journal Fulfillment, PO Box 2485, Secaucus, NJ 07096. TEL 800-777-4643, 201-348-4033, FAX 201-348-4505, journals-ny@springer.com, http://www.springer.com; **Subscr. to:** Springer Distribution Center, Kundenservice Zeitschriften, Haberstr 7, Heidelberg 69126, Germany. TEL 49-6221-3454303, FAX 49-6221-3454229, subscriptions@springer.com.

314 DEU ISSN 1863-8155
HA5
A ST A - WIRTSCHAFTS- UND SOZIALSTATISTISCHES ARCHIV. Text in German. 2007. q. EUR 185, USD 226 combined subscription to institutions (print & online eds.) (effective 2012). reprint service avail. from PSC. **Document type:** *Journal, Academic/Scholarly.*
Related titles: Online - full text ed.: ISSN 1863-8163. 2007 (from IngentaConnect).
Indexed: A22, A26, E01, E08, SCOPUS.
—IE. **CCC.**
Published by: Springer (Subsidiary of: Springer Science+Business Media), Tiergartenstr 17, Heidelberg, 69121, Germany. TEL 49-6221-4870, FAX 49-6221-345229, orders-hd-individuals@springer.com. Ed. Hans-Wolfgang Brachinger.

310 GBR
HA1161
A STATISTICAL FOCUS ON WALES THE UK AND OTHER COUNTRIES. Variant title: A Statistical Focus on Wales and the UK. Text in English. 1996. irreg., latest 2007. free (effective 2009). **Document type:** *Government.* **Description:** Features statistics about Wales as well as point of reference for students, researchers, business or public administrators.
Formerly (until 2007): Statistical Focus on Wales (1362-3575)
Related titles: Online - full text ed.
Published by: Welsh Assembly Government, Statistical Directorate, Cathays Park, Cardiff, CF10 3NQ, United Kingdom. TEL 44-1443-845500, stats.info.desk@wales.gsi.gov.uk, http://wales.gov.uk/?lang=en.

A W E X WOOL STATISTICS YEARBOOK. (Australian Wool Exchange) *see* TEXTILE INDUSTRIES AND FABRICS—Abstracting, Bibliographies, Statistics

AARSBOK FOER SVERIGES KOMMUNER/STATISTICAL YEARBOOK OF ADMINISTRATIVE DISTRICTS OF SWEDEN. *see* PUBLIC ADMINISTRATION—Abstracting, Bibliographies, Statistics

ABGEURTEILTE UND VERURTEILTE IN BAYERN. *see* LAW—Abstracting, Bibliographies, Statistics

ABU DHABI. DA'IRAT AT-TAKHTIT. AL-KITAB AL-IHSA'I AS-SANAWI/ ABU DHABI. DEPARTMENT OF PLANNING. STATISTICAL YEARBOOK. *see* PUBLIC ADMINISTRATION—Abstracting, Bibliographies, Statistics

ACCIDENT - INCIDENT REPORTING A D R E P. *see* TRANSPORTATION—Abstracting, Bibliographies, Statistics

310 FIN ISSN 1235-7936
ACTA WASAENSIA. STATISTICS. Text in English. 1979. irreg. price varies. back issues avail. **Document type:** *Monographic series, Academic/Scholarly.*
Related titles: ◆ Series of: Acta Wasaensia. ISSN 0355-2667.
Published by: Vaasan Yliopisto/University of Vaasa, PO Box 700, Vaasa, 65101, Finland. TEL 358-6-3248111, FAX 358-6-3248187, http://lipas.uwasa.fi/.

ACTUALITES HABITATION. PROVINCE DE QUEBEC/HOUSING NOW (PROVINCE OF QUEBEC). *see* HOUSING AND URBAN PLANNING—Abstracting, Bibliographies, Statistics

ACTUALITES HABITATION. QUEBEC/HOUSING NOW (QUEBEC). *see* HOUSING AND URBAN PLANNING—Abstracting, Bibliographies, Statistics

ACTUALITES HABITATION. REGINA/HOUSING NOW (REGINA). *see* HOUSING AND URBAN PLANNING—Abstracting, Bibliographies, Statistics

ACTUALITES HABITATION. SAGUENAY/HOUSING NOW (SAGUENAY). *see* HOUSING AND URBAN PLANNING—Abstracting, Bibliographies, Statistics

ACTUALITES HABITATION. SAINT JOHN, MONCTON ET FREDERICTON/HOUSING NOW (SAINT JOHN, MONCTON AND FREDERICTON). *see* HOUSING AND URBAN PLANNING—Abstracting, Bibliographies, Statistics

ACTUALITES HABITATION. SASKATOON/HOUSING NOW (SASKATOON). *see* HOUSING AND URBAN PLANNING—Abstracting, Bibliographies, Statistics

S

ACTUELE ONTWIKKELING VAN BEDRIJFSRESULTATEN EN INKOMENS. *see* AGRICULTURE—Abstracting, Bibliographies, Statistics

ADAJUR; Die juristische Datenbank des ADAC. *see* LAW—Abstracting, Bibliographies, Statistics

ADMINISTRATIVE OFFICE OF THE UNITED STATES COURTS. STATISTICS DIVISION. STATISTICAL TABLES FOR THE FEDERAL JUDICIARY (ONLINE). *see* LAW—Abstracting, Bibliographies, Statistics

ADVANCED STUDIES IN THEORETICAL AND APPLIED ECONOMETRICS. *see* BUSINESS AND ECONOMICS—Economic Systems And Theories, Economic History

310 IND ISSN 0972-3617
➤ **ADVANCES AND APPLICATIONS IN STATISTICS.** Text in English. 2001. m. (in 6 vols.). INR 9,000 domestic to institutions; EUR 595 combined subscription foreign to institutions (print & online eds.) (effective 2010). **Document type:** *Journal, Academic/Scholarly.* **Description:** Publishes original research papers in any area of current interest in statistics.
Related titles: Online - full text ed.: EUR 475 to institutions (effective 2010).
Indexed: CCMJ, CIS, MSN, MathR, P30, Z02.
Published by: Pushpa Publishing House, Vijaya Niwas, 198 Mumfordganj, Allahabad, Uttar Pradesh 211 002, India. TEL 91-532-2250078, FAX 91-532-2641508, sub@pphmj.com, arun@pphmj.com, http://www.pphmj.com. Ed. K K Azad. R&P, Adv. contact Arun Azad. **Dist. by:** Vijaya Books and Journals Distributors, Vijaya Niwas, 198, Mumfordganj, Allahabad 211 002, India.

➤ **ADVANCES IN DATA ANALYSIS AND CLASSIFICATION.** *see* COMPUTERS—Information Science And Information Theory

➤ **ADVANCES IN RISK ANALYSIS.** *see* PUBLIC HEALTH AND SAFETY—Abstracting, Bibliographies, Statistics

310 SGP ISSN 2010-1317
▼ **ADVANCES IN STATISTICS, PROBABILITY AND ACTUARIAL SCIENCE.** Text in English. forthcoming 2011. irreg. **Document type:** *Monographic series, Academic/Scholarly.* **Description:** Aims to publish monographs, advanced texts, and international conference proceedings on the methodological and/or applied aspects of statistics, probability and actuarial science.
Published by: World Scientific Publishing Co. Pte. Ltd., 5 Toh Tuck Link, Singapore, 596224, Singapore. TEL 65-6466-5775, FAX 65-6467-7667, wspc@wspc.com.sg, http://www.worldscientific.com. Eds. Hailiang Yang, Wai Keung Li, Wing Kam Fung. **Dist. by:** World Scientific Publishing Co., Inc., 27 Warren St, Ste 401-402, Hackensack, NJ 07601. TEL 201-487-9655, 800-227-7562, FAX 201-487-9656, 888-977-2665, wspc@wspc.com; World Scientific Publishing Ltd., 57 Shelton St, London WC2H 9HE, United Kingdom. TEL 44-207-8360888, FAX 44-207-8362020, sales@wspc.co.uk.

ADVERTISING EXPENDITURE FORECASTS. *see* ADVERTISING AND PUBLIC RELATIONS

ADVERTISING STATISTICS YEARBOOK (YEAR). *see* ADVERTISING AND PUBLIC RELATIONS—Abstracting, Bibliographies, Statistics

AEROSPACE AND ELECTRONICS COST INDICES (ONLINE). *see* BUSINESS AND ECONOMICS—Domestic Commerce

AG UPDATE. *see* AGRICULTURE—Abstracting, Bibliographies, Statistics

318 MEX ISSN 0186-0453
AGENDA ESTADISTICA. Text in Spanish. 1967. a. USD 20 (effective 1999). **Document type:** *Government.*
Published by: Instituto Nacional de Estadistica, Geografia e Informatica, Secretaria de Programacion y Presupuesto, Prol. Heroe de Nacozari 2301 Sur, Puerta 11, Acceso, Aguascalientes, 20270, Mexico. TEL 52-4-918-1948, FAX 52-4-918-07389. Circ: 11,000.

AGRARSTATISTIK. VIERTELJAHRESBULLETIN/AGRICULTURAL STATISTICS. QUARTERLY BULLETIN/STATISTIQUES AGRICOLES. BULLETIN TRIMESTRIEL. *see* AGRICULTURE

AGRICULTURAL PRICES IN INDIA. *see* AGRICULTURE—Abstracting, Bibliographies, Statistics

AGRICULTURAL REGIONS OF CYPRUS. *see* AGRICULTURE—Abstracting, Bibliographies, Statistics

AGRICULTURAL STATISTICS OF GREECE. *see* AGRICULTURE—Abstracting, Bibliographies, Statistics

AGRICULTURAL STATISTICS OF SARAWAK. *see* AGRICULTURE—Abstracting, Bibliographies, Statistics

AGRICULTURAL STATISTICS SERIES NO.2: ANIMAL PRODUCTION. *see* AGRICULTURE—Abstracting, Bibliographies, Statistics

AGRICULTURAL STATISTICS SERIES NO.3: EUROPEAN COMMUNITIES INDEX OF AGRICULTURAL PRICES. *see* AGRICULTURE—Abstracting, Bibliographies, Statistics

AGRICULTURE ECONOMIC STATISTICS. *see* AGRICULTURE—Agricultural Economics

AGRICULTURE IN DENMARK: FACTS AND FIGURES. *see* AGRICULTURE—Abstracting, Bibliographies, Statistics

AGRICULTURE IN DENMARK: STATISTICS ON DANISH AGRICULTURE. *see* AGRICULTURE—Abstracting, Bibliographies, Statistics

AGRIDEV WEEKLY BULLETIN. *see* AGRICULTURE—Abstracting, Bibliographies, Statistics

AIR CARRIER INDUSTRY SCHEDULE SERVICE TRAFFIC STATISTICS. MEDIUM REGIONAL CARRIERS. *see* TRANSPORTATION—Abstracting, Bibliographies, Statistics

AIR CARRIER TRAFFIC AT CANADIAN AIRPORTS. *see* TRANSPORTATION—Abstracting, Bibliographies, Statistics

AIR QUALITY DATA. *see* ENVIRONMENTAL STUDIES—Pollution

AIRCRAFT MOVEMENT STATISTICS. MONTHLY REPORT. *see* TRANSPORTATION—Abstracting, Bibliographies, Statistics

ALABAMA CITIES & COUNTIES GRAPHIC PERFORMANCE ANALYSIS. *see* PUBLIC ADMINISTRATION—Abstracting, Bibliographies, Statistics

ALABAMA LABOR MARKET NEWS. *see* BUSINESS AND ECONOMICS—Abstracting, Bibliographies, Statistics

304.6 USA ISSN 0095-3431
HA221
ALABAMA'S VITAL EVENTS. Text in English. 1971. a. (in 4 vols.). USD 10 per vol. illus. **Document type:** *Government.*
Related titles: Microfiche ed.: (from CIS).
Indexed: SRI.
Published by: Department of Public Health, Center for Health Statistics, 201 Monroe St, RSA Tower, Montgomery, AL 36104. TEL 334-206-5429, FAX 334-206-2666. Ed. Dale Quinney. Circ: 450.

ALASKA AGRICULTURAL STATISTICS. *see* AGRICULTURE—Abstracting, Bibliographies, Statistics

ALASKA FARM REPORTER. *see* AGRICULTURE—Abstracting, Bibliographies, Statistics

ALASKA WEEKLY CROP WEATHER. *see* AGRICULTURE—Abstracting, Bibliographies, Statistics

ALBERTA ELECTRIC INDUSTRY, ANNUAL STATISTICS. *see* ENERGY—Electrical Energy

316 DZA ISSN 1111-7680
ALGERIA. OFFICE NATIONAL DES STATISTIQUES. ANNUAIRE STATISTIQUE DES WILAYATE DE L'EST. Key Title: Annuaire Statistique des Wilayate de l'Est. Text in French. 1983. a. price varies. **Document type:** *Government.*
Published by: Office National des Statistiques/Al-Diwan al-Watani lil-Ihsa'iyat, 8 & 10 rue des Moussebiline, Ferhat Boussad, B P 202, Algiers, Algeria. TEL 213-64-77-90.

316 DZA ISSN 1111-0368
ALGERIA. OFFICE NATIONAL DES STATISTIQUES. ANNUAIRE STATISTIQUE DES WILAYATE DE L'OUEST. Key Title: Annuaire Statistique des Wilayate de l'Ouest. Text in French. 1981. a. price varies. **Document type:** *Government.*
Published by: Office National des Statistiques/Al-Diwan al-Watani lil-Ihsa'iyat, 8 & 10 rue des Moussebiline, Ferhat Boussad, B P 202, Algiers, Algeria. TEL 213-64-77-90.

316 DZA ISSN 1111-0376
ALGERIA. OFFICE NATIONAL DES STATISTIQUES. ANNUAIRE STATISTIQUE DES WILAYATE DU CENTRE. Key Title: Annuaire Statistique des Wilayate du Centre. Text in French. 1982. a. price varies. **Document type:** *Government.*
Published by: Office National des Statistiques/Al-Diwan al-Watani lil-Ihsa'iyat, 8 & 10 rue des Moussebiline, Ferhat Boussad, B P 202, Algiers, Algeria. TEL 213-64-77-90.

316 DZA ISSN 1111-5696
HA4683
ALGERIA. OFFICE NATIONAL DES STATISTIQUES. BULLETIN DE STATISTIQUES COURANTES. Text in French. 1987. 6/yr. DZD 500. back issues avail. **Document type:** *Government.*
Published by: Office National des Statistiques/Al-Diwan al-Watani lil-Ihsa'iyat, 8 & 10 rue des Moussebiline, Ferhat Boussad, B P 202, Algiers, Algeria. TEL 213-64-77-90.

316 DZA ISSN 1111-0392
ALGERIA. OFFICE NATIONAL DES STATISTIQUES. COLLECTIONS STATISTIQUES. Text in French. 1985. irreg. price varies. back issues avail. **Document type:** *Government.*
Published by: Office National des Statistiques/Al-Diwan al-Watani lil-Ihsa'iyat, 8 & 10 rue des Moussebiline, Ferhat Boussad, B P 202, Algiers, Algeria. TEL 213-64-77-90.

316 DZA ISSN 1111-5939
HA4683
ALGERIA. OFFICE NATIONAL DES STATISTIQUES. DONNEES STATISTIQUES. Text in French. 1985. m. DZD 500. back issues avail. **Document type:** *Government.*
Related titles: ◆ Series of: Algeria. Office National des Statistiques. Indices des Prix a la Consommation.
Published by: Office National des Statistiques/Al-Diwan al-Watani lil-Ihsa'iyat, 8 & 10 rue des Moussebiline, Ferhat Boussad, B P 202, Algiers, Algeria. TEL 213-64-77-90.

ALGERIA. OFFICE NATIONAL DES STATISTIQUES. INDICES DES PRIX A LA CONSOMMATION. *see* BUSINESS AND ECONOMICS—Abstracting, Bibliographies, Statistics

316 DZA ISSN 1111-7001
HC815.A1
ALGERIA. OFFICE NATIONAL DES STATISTIQUES. INFORMATIONS STATISTIQUES SUR LA CONJONCTURE. Text in French. 1989. q. DZD 250; DZD 1,250 foreign. back issues avail. **Document type:** *Government.*
Published by: Office National des Statistiques/Al-Diwan al-Watani lil-Ihsa'iyat, 8 & 10 rue des Moussebiline, Ferhat Boussad, B P 202, Algiers, Algeria. TEL 213-64-77-90.

316 DZA ISSN 1010-1284
L'ALGERIE EN QUELQUES CHIFFRES. Text in French. irreg. (approx a.). DZD 150. **Document type:** *Government.*
Related titles: ◆ Supplement to: Annuaire Statistique de l'Algerie. ISSN 1111-035X.
Published by: Office National des Statistiques/Al-Diwan al-Watani lil-Ihsa'iyat, 8 & 10 rue des Moussebiline, Ferhat Boussad, B P 202, Algiers, Algeria. TEL 213-64-77-90.

315.4 IND ISSN 0971-0388
➤ **ALIGARH JOURNAL OF STATISTICS.** Text in English. 1981. a. **Document type:** *Journal, Academic/Scholarly.*
Indexed: Biostat, CCMJ, CIS, MSN, MathR, ORMS, QC&AS, ST&MA.
Published by: Aligarh Muslim University, Administrative Block, Aligarh Muslim University, Aligarh, Uttar Pradesh 202 002, India. TEL 91-571-2703038, FAX 91-571-2702331.

➤ **THE ALMANAC OF AMERICAN EDUCATION.** *see* EDUCATION—Abstracting, Bibliographies, Statistics

➤ **AMELIORATIONS APPORTEES A L'ENQUETE SUR LA POPULATION ACTIVE, EPA.** *see* BUSINESS AND ECONOMICS—Abstracting, Bibliographies, Statistics

➤ **AMERICA VOTES**; election returns by state. *see* POLITICAL SCIENCE—Abstracting, Bibliographies, Statistics

➤ **AMERICAN IRON AND STEEL INSTITUTE. ANNUAL STATISTICAL REPORT.** *see* ENGINEERING—Abstracting, Bibliographies, Statistics

➤ **AMERICAN JOURNAL OF MATHEMATICAL AND MANAGEMENT SCIENCES.** *see* MATHEMATICS

➤ **AMERICAN PETROLEUM INSTITUTE. MONTHLY STATISTICAL REPORT.** *see* PETROLEUM AND GAS—Abstracting, Bibliographies, Statistics

➤ **AMERICAN RADIO.** *see* COMMUNICATIONS—Abstracting, Bibliographies, Statistics

➤ **AMERICAN SALARIES AND WAGES SURVEY.** *see* BUSINESS AND ECONOMICS—Abstracting, Bibliographies, Statistics

310 ASM
AMERICAN SAMOA CONSUMER PRICE INDEX. Text in English. q. **Document type:** *Government.*
Published by: (American Samoa. Statistics Division USA), American Samoa Government, Department of Commerce, Pago Pago, 97699, American Samoa. TEL 684-633-5155, FAX 684-633-4195.

310 ASM
AMERICAN SAMOA STATISTICAL YEARBOOK (YEAR). Text in English. a. USD 15; USD 20 foreign. adv. **Document type:** *Government.* **Description:** Details both historic and current economic and social characteristics to serve as a summary of aggregated statistics about American Samoa, and also as a guide to source references of information and detailed subject-matter specifications.
Formerly: American Samoa Statistical Digest (Year)
Published by: (Tennessee. Research and Statistics Division USA), American Samoa Government, Department of Commerce, Pago Pago, 96799, American Samoa. TEL 684-633-5155, FAX 684-633-4195. Ed., R&P, Adv. contact Vai Filiga.

519.5 USA ISSN 0162-1459
HA1 CODEN: JSTNAL
➤ **AMERICAN STATISTICAL ASSOCIATION. JOURNAL.** Abbreviated title: J A S A. Text in English. 1888. q. GBP 398 combined subscription in United Kingdom to institutions (print & online eds.); EUR 526, USD 646 combined subscription to institutions (print & online eds.) (effective 2012). adv. bk.rev. bibl.; illus. Index. back issues avail.; reprints avail. **Document type:** *Journal, Academic/Scholarly.* **Description:** Focuses on statistical applications, theory, and methods in economic, social, physical, engineering, and health sciences and on new methods of statistical education.
Former titles (until 1922): American Statistical Association. Quarterly Publications (1522-5445); (until 1912): American Statistical Association. Publications (1522-5437)
Related titles: Microform ed.: (from PMC, PQC); Online - full text ed.: ISSN 1537-274X. GBP 364 in United Kingdom to institutions; EUR 481, USD 601 to institutions (effective 2012).
Indexed: A12, A13, A20, A22, A23, A24, A25, A26, A34, A35, A36, A38, ABIn, ASCA, AgBio, B01, B02, B06, B07, B08, B09, B13, B15, B17, B18, Biostat, BusI, C12, C33, CA, CABA, CCMJ, CDA, CIS, CMCI, CPM, CompR, CurCont, E06, E08, E12, EconLit, F08, F12, FR, G04, G06, G07, G08, GH, H09, H10, H16, H17, I05, I11, IBR, IBSS, IBZ, ISR, IndVet, Inspec, JCQM, JEL, LT, MResA, MSN, MathR, N02, N03, ORMS, P02, P06, P10, P19, P21, P26, P30, P32, P33, P39, P40, P48, P50, P51, P52, P53, P54, PCI, PHN&I, PQC, PopulInd, PsycholAb, QC&AS, R07, R08, R12, R13, RASB, RM&VM, RRTA, S05, S06, S08, S09, S10, S13, S16, SCI, SCOPUS, ST&MA, T&II, T02, T05, VS, W07, W10, W11, WBA, Z02.
—BLDSC (4694.000000), IE, Infotrieve, Ingenta, INIST, Linda Hall. **CCC.**
Published by: American Statistical Association, 732 N Washington St, Alexandria, VA 22314. TEL 703-684-1221, 888-231-3473, FAX 703-684-2037, asainfo@amstat.org. Circ: 12,000. **Subscr. to:** Department 79081, Baltimore, MD 21279. TEL 888-231-3473, FAX 703-684-2037.

310 USA ISSN 1543-3218
HA12
AMERICAN STATISTICAL ASSOCIATION. PROCEEDINGS. Text in English. 2001. a. **Document type:** *Proceedings, Academic/Scholarly.*
Supersedes in part (in 2001): American Statistical Association. Biometrics Section. Proceedings (1093-2763); (in 2001): American Statistical Association. Biopharmaceutical Section. Proceedings (0898-4654); (in 2001): American Statistical Association. Business and Economic Statistics Section. Proceedings (0066-0736); (in 2001): American Statistical Association. Government Statistics Section. Proceedings of the Section of Government Statistics; Which was formed by the merger of (1958-1997): American Statistical Association. Social Statistics Section. Proceedings (0066-0752); (1995-1997): American Statistical Association. Section on Government Statistics. Proceedings; Which was formerly (19??-1995): American Statistical Association. Government Statistics Section. Proceedings; (in 2001): American Statistical Association. Section on Statistical Education, the Section on Teaching Statistics in the Health Sciences and the Section on Statistical Consulting. Proceedings; Which was formerly (19??-1999): American Statistical Association. Section on Statistical Education. Proceedings (0733-1282); (in 2001): American Statistical Association. Statistical Computing Section and Section on Statistical Graphics. Proceedings; Which was formed by the merger of (1975-1999): American Statistical Association. Statistical Computing Section. Proceedings (0149-9963); (19??-1999): American Statistical Association. Section on Statistical Graphics. Proceedings (1048-5635); (in 2001): American Statistical Association. Bayesian Statistical Science. Proceedings; (in 2001): American Statistical Association. Section on Physical and Engineering Sciences. Proceedings; (in 2001): American Statistical Association. Section on Quality and Productivity. Proceedings; (in 2001): American Statistical Association. Section on Statistics and the Environment. Proceedings (1093-1880); (in 2001): American Statistical Association. Section on Statistics in Epidemiology and the Health Policy Statistics Section. Proceedings; Which was formerly (until 199?): American Statistical Association. Section of Statistics in Epidemiology. Proceedings; (until 1998): American Statistical Association. Epidemiology Section. Proceedings (1093-3484); (until 1995): American Statistical Association. Section on Epidemiology. Proceedings; (in 2001): American Statistical Association. Section on Statistics in Sports. Proceedings; (in 2001): American Statistical Association. Section on Survey Research Methods. Proceedings (0733-5830)
Media: CD-ROM.
Indexed: CIS.
—Linda Hall. **CCC.**
Published by: American Statistical Association, 732 N Washington St, Alexandria, VA 22314. TEL 703-684-1221, 888-231-3473, FAX 703-684-2037, asainfo@amstat.org, http://www.amstat.org.

001.42 USA ISSN 1053-8607
AMERICAN STATISTICAL ASSOCIATION. STATS; the magazine for students of statistics. Variant title: Stats. Text in English. 1989. 3/yr. USD 25 to institutions; USD 15 combined subscription to members (print & online eds.); USD 20 combined subscription to non-members (print & online eds.) (effective 2009). adv. **Document type:** *Journal, Academic/Scholarly.* **Description:** Discusses careers in statistics, student experiences, current problems, and case studies.
Related titles: Online - full text ed.: free to members (effective 2009).
Indexed: A01, A03, A08, CIS, T02.
—CCC.
Published by: American Statistical Association, 732 N Washington St, Alexandria, VA 22314. TEL 703-684-1221, 888-231-3473, FAX 703-684-2037, asainfo@amstat.org, http://www.amstat.org. **Subscr. to:** Department 79081, Baltimore, MD 21279.

310.92 USA ISSN 0003-1305
HA1 CODEN: ASTAAJ
THE AMERICAN STATISTICIAN. Abbreviated title: T A S. Text in English. 1947. q. GBP 121 combined subscription in United Kingdom to institutions (print & online eds.); EUR 160, USD 189 combined subscription to institutions (print & online eds.) (effective 2012). adv. bk.rev. illus. back issues avail.; reprints avail. **Document type:** *Journal, Academic/Scholarly.* **Description:** Provides timely general-interest articles addressing current national and international statistical problems and programs, public policy matters of direct interest to the statistical profession, and the teaching of statistics.
Formerly (until 1947): American Statistical Association. Bulletin
Related titles: Microform ed.: (from MIM, PMC, PQC); Online - full text ed.: ISSN 1537-2731. GBP 101 in United Kingdom to institutions; EUR 134, USD 167 to institutions (effective 2012).
Indexed: A01, A02, A03, A08, A12, A13, A22, A25, A26, A36, ABIn, ASCA, B01, B04, B06, B07, B08, B09, BRD, Biostat, C12, C23, CA, CABA, CCMJ, CDA, CIS, CMCI, ChemAb, CompAb, CurCont, E02, E03, E07, E08, E12, ERI, EdA, EdI, FR, G01, G05, G06, G07, G08, GH, GeoRef, H01, H02, H09, I05, IBR, IBZ, ISR, Inspec, JCQM, JEL, M01, M02, M05, MSN, MathR, ORMS, P02, P06, P10, P19, P21, P26, P27, P30, P33, P34, P47, P48, P50, P51, P52, P53, P54, PAIS, PQC, QC&AS, RASB, RM&VM, S01, S02, S03, S05, S06, S08, S09, S10, S23, SCI, SCOPUS, SSAI, SSAb, SSI, ST&MA, SpeleolAb, T02, W01, W02, W03, W07, Z02.
—BLDSC (0857.650000), IE, Infotrieve, Ingenta, INIST, Linda Hall. **CCC.**
Published by: American Statistical Association, 732 N Washington St, Alexandria, VA 22314. TEL 703-684-1221, 888-231-3473, FAX 703-684-2037, asainfo@amstat.org. Ed. John Stufken. adv.: B&W page USD 1,000; 7 x 10. Circ: 11,500. **Subscr. to:** Department 79081, Baltimore, MD 21279. TEL 888-231-3473, FAX 703-684-2037.

016 USA ISSN 0091-1658
Z7554.U5
AMERICAN STATISTICS INDEX; a comprehensive guide and index to the statistical publications of the U.S. Government. Abbreviated title: A S I. Text in English. 1974. a. abstr.; stat.; illus. index; cum.index: 1974-79; 1980-84; 1985-88; 1989-92; 1993-96. back issues avail.; reprints avail. **Document type:** *Abstract/Index.* **Description:** Abstracts and index of U.S. government statistical publications by subject, name, type of data breakdown, title and report number.
Related titles: CD-ROM ed.; Microform ed.: ISSN 1050-1568. USD 39,750 domestic; USD 43,730 foreign (effective 2005); Online - full text ed.: ISSN 1064-4695.
—BLDSC (0857.656000), Linda Hall.
Published by: Congressional Information Service, Inc. (Subsidiary of: ProQuest), 789 E Eisenhower Pky, PO Box 1346, Ann Arbor, MI 48106. TEL 734-761-4700, academicinfo@proquest.com, http://www.proquest.com.

THE AMERICAN WOMAN (YEAR); a status report. *see* WOMEN'S STUDIES—Abstracting, Bibliographies, Statistics

AMERICA'S FAMILIES AND LIVING ARRANGEMENTS. *see* POPULATION STUDIES—Abstracting, Bibliographies, Statistics

659.021 GBR ISSN 1364-0267
HC94.A1
AMERICAS MARKET & MEDIAFACT. Text in English. 1996. a. GBP 100, EUR 110.02, USD 164.47 per issue (effective 2009). stat. **Document type:** *Report, Trade.* **Description:** Contains media statistics for TV & radio audiences, press circulation & readership, cinema screens & admissions, etc.
—CCC.
Published by: Zenith Optimedia, 24 Percy St, London, W1T 2BS, United Kingdom. TEL 44-20-79611000, FAX 44-20-79611113, info@zenithoptimedia.com.

AMERICA'S TOP-RATED CITIES: A STATISTICAL HANDBBOOK (YEAR). VOLUME 1 - SOUTHERN REGION. *see* HOUSING AND URBAN PLANNING—Abstracting, Bibliographies, Statistics

AMERICA'S TOP-RATED CITIES: A STATISTICAL HANDBOOK (YEAR). VOLUME 2 - WESTERN REGION. *see* HOUSING AND URBAN PLANNING—Abstracting, Bibliographies, Statistics

AMERICA'S TOP-RATED CITIES: A STATISTICAL HANDBOOK (YEAR). VOLUME 3 - CENTRAL REGION. *see* HOUSING AND URBAN PLANNING—Abstracting, Bibliographies, Statistics

AMERICA'S TOP-RATED CITIES: A STATISTICAL HANDBOOK (YEAR). VOLUME 4 - EASTERN REGION. *see* HOUSING AND URBAN PLANNING—Abstracting, Bibliographies, Statistics

AMERICA'S TOP-RATED SMALLER CITIES (YEARS); a statisitical profile. *see* HOUSING AND URBAN PLANNING—Abstracting, Bibliographies, Statistics

310 519.54 USA ISSN 0163-9617
HA1
AMSTAT NEWS. Text in English. 1974. m. USD 50; free to members (effective 2009). adv. back issues avail. **Document type:** *Magazine, Trade.* **Description:** Contains news and notices of the ASA, its chapters, its sections, and its members.
Related titles: Microform ed.: (from PQC); Online - full text ed.
Indexed: A22, ABIPC, CIS.
—IE, Infotrieve. **CCC.**
Published by: American Statistical Association, 732 N Washington St, Alexandria, VA 22314. TEL 703-684-1221, 888-231-3473, FAX 703-684-2037, asainfo@amstat.org. Adv. contact Claudine Donovan. **Subscr. to:** Department 79081, Baltimore, MD 21279. TEL 888-231-3473, FAX 703-684-2037.

AMTLICHES ORTSVERZEICHNIS FUER BAYERN. *see* PUBLIC ADMINISTRATION—Abstracting, Bibliographies, Statistics

316.6 AGO ISSN 0066-5193
ANGOLA. DIRECCAO DOS SERVICOS DE ESTATISTICA. ANUARIO ESTATISTICO. Text in Portuguese. 1933. a.
Related titles: Microfiche ed.: (from PQC).
Published by: Direccao dos Servicos de Estatistica, Luanda, 1215, Angola. Circ: 1,000.

316 AGO ISSN 0003-3413
ANGOLA. DIRECCAO DOS SERVICOS DE ESTATISTICA. BOLETIM MENSAL. Text in Portuguese. N.S. 1942. m. adv. stat. **Document type:** *Bulletin, Government.*
Published by: Direccao dos Servicos de Estatistica, Luanda, 1215, Angola. Circ: 15,200.

316.6 AGO
ANGOLA. DIRECCAO DOS SERVICOS DE ESTATISTICA. INFORMACOES ESTATISTICAS. Text in Portuguese. 1970. a. free. stat.
Published by: Direccao dos Servicos de Estatistica, Luanda, 1215, Angola. Circ: 7,000.

310 USA ISSN 1932-6157
QA276.A1
➤ **THE ANNALS OF APPLIED STATISTICS.** Text in English. 2007. q. USD 390 combined subscription to institutions (print & online eds.) (effective 2012). illus. **Document type:** *Journal, Academic/Scholarly.* **Description:** Provides a timely and unified forum for all areas of applied statistics.
Related titles: Online - full text ed.: ISSN 1941-7330. free to members (effective 2012).
Indexed: A20, CCMJ, CurCont, MSN, MathR, P30, SCI, W07, Z02.
—INIST, Linda Hall.
Published by: Institute of Mathematical Statistics, PO Box 22718, Beachwood, OH 44122. TEL 216-295-2340, 877-557-4674, FAX 216-295-5661, ims@imstat.org. Ed. Bradley Efron. **Subscr. to:** 9650 Rockville Pike, Ste L3503A, Bethesda, MD 20814. TEL 301-634-7029, FAX 301-634-7099.

519.5 USA ISSN 0090-5364
HA1 CODEN: ASTSC7
➤ **ANNALS OF STATISTICS.** Text in English. 1973. bi-m. USD 425 combined subscription to institutions (print & online eds.) (effective 2012). illus. Index. back issues avail.; reprints avail. **Document type:** *Journal, Academic/Scholarly.* **Description:** Features research papers of the highest quality reflecting the various facets of contemporary statistics.
Supersedes in part (in 1973): Annals of Mathematical Statistics (0003-4851)
Related titles: Microform ed.: (from PQC); Online - full text ed.
Indexed: A12, A17, A22, ABIn, ASCA, Biostat, CCMJ, CIS, CMCI, CurCont, IBR, IBZ, ISR, JCQM, MSN, MathR, ORMS, P30, P48, P49, P50, P51, P53, P54, PQC, QC&AS, RASB, SCI, SCOPUS, ST&MA, W07, Z02.
—BLDSC (1044.400000), IE, Infotrieve, Ingenta, INIST, Linda Hall. **CCC.**
Published by: Institute of Mathematical Statistics, PO Box 22718, Beachwood, OH 44122. TEL 216-295-2340, 877-557-4674, FAX 216-295-5661, ims@imstat.org. Eds. Peter Buhlmann TEL 41-44-6327338, T Tony Cai TEL 215-898-8224. **Subscr. to:** 9650 Rockville Pike, Ste L3503A, Bethesda, MD 20814. TEL 301-634-7029, FAX 301-634-7099.

➤ **UN ANNO DI BRUNA**; statistiche della Razza Bruna. *see* AGRICULTURE—Abstracting, Bibliographies, Statistics

➤ **ANNUAIRE DES STATISTIQUES DU COMMERCE EXTERIEUR DU TOGO.** *see* BUSINESS AND ECONOMICS—Abstracting, Bibliographies, Statistics

316.6 BEN
ANNUAIRE STATISTIQUE DE BENIN. Text in French. a., latest 1975. XOF 2,000.
Formerly: Annuaire Statistique du Dahomey
Related titles: Microfiche ed.: (from PQC).
Published by: Institut National de la Statistique et de l'Analyse Economique, BP 323, Cotonou, Benin.

314 FRA ISSN 2105-2972
HA1213
ANNUAIRE STATISTIQUE DE LA FRANCE (ONLINE). Text in French. 1878. a. free. reprint service avail. from SCH. **Document type:** *Government.* **Description:** Presents statistics showing trends in demographics, the economy and society. Includes commentary, definitions and methodology.
Former titles (until 200?): Annuaire Statistique de la France (Print) (0066-3654); (until 1952): Annuaire Statistique (0150-8822); (until 1900): Annuaire Statistique de la France (0150-8830)
Media: Online - full text. **Related titles:** CD-ROM ed.: FRF 710 (effective 1999); Microfiche ed.: (from BHP).
Indexed: RASB.
—INIST.
Published by: Institut National de la Statistique et des Etudes Economiques, INSEE-Info Service, Tour Gamma A, 195 rue de Bercy, Paris, Cedex 1 75582, France. TEL 33-1-41176611, FAX 33-1-53178809. Circ: 3,000. **Subscr. to:** Institut National de la Statistique et des Etudes Economiques, INSEE-CNGP, 1 rue Vincent Auriol, Amiens Cedex 1 80027, France. TEL 33-3-22927322, FAX 33-3-22979295.

316 TUN ISSN 0066-3689
HA2071
ANNUAIRE STATISTIQUE DE LA TUNISIE. Text in French. a. TND 10,000 (effective 2000). **Document type:** *Government.*
Related titles: Microfiche ed.: (from PQC).
Published by: Institut National de la Statistique, 70 Rue Ech-Cham, B P 260, Tunis, Tunisia. TEL 216-1-891002, FAX 216-1-792559.

316 DZA ISSN 1111-035X
HA2071
ANNUAIRE STATISTIQUE DE L'ALGERIE/STATISTICAL YEARBOOK OF ALGERIA. Text in French. a. DZD 2,750. **Document type:** *Government.*
Related titles: Microfiche ed.: (from PQC); ◆ Supplement(s): L'Algerie en Quelques Chiffres. ISSN 1010-1284.
Published by: Office National des Statistiques/Al-Diwan al-Watani lil-Ihsa'iyat, 8 & 10 rue des Moussebiline, Ferhat Boussad, B P 202, Algiers, Algeria. TEL 213-64-77-90.

316 MAR ISSN 0851-089X
ANNUAIRE STATISTIQUE DU MAROC. Text in French. 1917. a. MAD 220 (effective 2000). **Document type:** *Government.*
Incorporates: Morocco. Direction de la Statistique. Statistiques Retrospectives; Parc Automobile du Maroc
Related titles: Microfiche ed.: (from PQC); ◆ Arabic ed.: Nasrat al-Ihsa'iyyat al-Sanawiyyat li-i-Magrib. ISSN 0851-0903.
Indexed: RASB.
Published by: Morocco. Direction de la Statistique, B P 178, Rabat, Morocco. TEL 212-7-77-36-06, FAX 212-7-77-32-17.

316.6 TGO
ANNUAIRE STATISTIQUE DU TOGO. Text in French. 1966. a., latest 1987. XOF 4,000. illus.; stat. **Document type:** *Government.*
Related titles: Microfiche ed.: (from PQC).
Published by: Direction de la Statistique, BP 118, Lome, Togo.

ANNUAL BULLETIN OF HOUSING AND BUILDING STATISTICS FOR EUROPE. *see* HOUSING AND URBAN PLANNING—Abstracting, Bibliographies, Statistics

ANNUAL BULLETIN OF TRANSPORT STATISTICS FOR EUROPE AND NORTH AMERICA. *see* TRANSPORTATION—Abstracting, Bibliographies, Statistics

ANNUAL EMPLOYMENT SURVEY (YEAR). *see* BUSINESS AND ECONOMICS—Abstracting, Bibliographies, Statistics

ANNUAL REPORT OF MUNICIPAL STATISTICS. *see* PUBLIC ADMINISTRATION—Abstracting, Bibliographies, Statistics

ANNUAL STAINLESS STEEL STATISTICS. *see* METALLURGY—Abstracting, Bibliographies, Statistics

ANNUAL STATISTICAL REPORT ON PROFIT, SALES & PRODUCTION TRENDS FOR THE MEN'S & BOY'S TAILORED CLOTHING INDUSTRY (YEAR). *see* CLOTHING TRADE—Abstracting, Bibliographies, Statistics

ANNUAL SURVEY OF MANUFACTURES. GEOGRAPHIC AREA STATISTICS (ONLINE). *see* BUSINESS AND ECONOMICS—Abstracting, Bibliographies, Statistics

ANNUAL SURVEY OF MANUFACTURES. STATISTICS FOR INDUSTRY GROUPS AND INDUSTRIES (ONLINE). *see* BUSINESS AND ECONOMICS—Abstracting, Bibliographies, Statistics

ANNUAL SURVEY OF MANUFACTURES. VALUE OF PRODUCT SHIPMENTS (ONLINE). *see* BUSINESS AND ECONOMICS—Abstracting, Bibliographies, Statistics

314.5 ITA ISSN 1972-9677
ANNUARIO DELLO SPETTACOLO. Text in Italian. 1936. a. price varies. bk.rev. back issues avail. **Document type:** *Directory, Consumer.*
Former titles (until 2005): Il Quaderno dello Spettacolo in Italia (1972-8395); (until1998): Lo Spettacolo in Italia (1126-8581)
Published by: Societa Italiana degli Autori ed Editori (S I A E), Viale della Letteratura 30, Rome, 00144, Italy. TEL 39-06-59901, FAX 39-06-59647050, http://www.siae.it.

ANNUARIO GEOECONOMICO MONDIALE; commercio e produzioni. *see* BUSINESS AND ECONOMICS—Abstracting, Bibliographies, Statistics

ANNUARIO STATISTICO. *see* POPULATION STUDIES—Abstracting, Bibliographies, Statistics

314 ITA ISSN 0066-4545
HA1367
ANNUARIO STATISTICO ITALIANO. Text in Italian. 1878. a. **Document type:** *Government.*
Related titles: CD-ROM ed.: ISSN 1722-0696 (from PQC).
Indexed: RASB.
Published by: Istituto Nazionale di Statistica (I S T A T), Via Cesare Balbo 16, Rome, 00184, Italy. TEL 39-06-46731, http://www.istat.it.

ANNUARIUM STATISTICUM ECCLESIAE/STATISTICAL YEARBOOK OF THE CHURCH/STATISTIQUE DE L'EGLISE. *see* RELIGIONS AND THEOLOGY—Abstracting, Bibliographies, Statistics

314.6 ESP ISSN 1130-166X
HA1558.C3
ANUARI ESTADISTIC DE CATALUNYA. Text in Catalan. 1984. a., latest vol.200. Website rev. back issues avail. **Document type:** *Yearbook, Consumer.*
Related titles: CD-ROM ed.; Online - full content ed.
Published by: Generalitat de Catalunya, Institut d'Estadistica de Catalunya, Via Laietana, 58, Barcelona, 08003, Spain. TEL 34-934-120088, FAX 34-934-123145. Circ: 4,000.

ANUARIO DE ESTADISTICAS CULTURALES. *see* SOCIAL SERVICES AND WELFARE—Abstracting, Bibliographies, Statistics

317.2 MEX
ANUARIO DE ESTADISTICAS ESTATALES. Text in Spanish. 1984. a. MXN 2,000, USD 5.50. **Document type:** *Government.*
Published by: Instituto Nacional de Estadistica, Geografia e Informatica, Secretaria de Programacion y Presupuesto, Prol. Heroe de Nacozari 2301 Sur, Puerta 11, Acceso, Aguascalientes, 20270, Mexico. TEL 52-4-918-1948, FAX 52-4-918-0739. Circ: 1,000.

ANUARIO DE MIGRACIONES. *see* POPULATION STUDIES—Abstracting, Bibliographies, Statistics

318 CHL ISSN 1014-0697
HA751
ANUARIO ESTADISTICO DE AMERICA LATINA Y EL CARIBE/ STATISTICAL YEARBOOK FOR LATIN AMERICA AND THE CARIBBEAN. Text in Spanish. 1969. a. USD 75. charts. back issues avail.
Former titles (until 1985): Anuario Estadistico de America Latina (0251-9445); (until 1973): Boletin Estadistico de America Latina (0041-6401)
Related titles: Microfiche ed.: (from CIS); Online - full text ed.
Indexed: C32, FR, IIS, RASB.
Published by: Comision Economica para America Latina y el Caribe/ Economic Commission for Latin America and the Caribbean, Ave Dag Hammarskjold 3477, Vitacura, Santiago de Chile, Chile. TEL 56-2-4712000, FAX 56-2-2080252. **Subscr. to:** United Nations Publications, 2 United Nations Plaza, Rm DC2-853, New York, NY 10017. TEL 212-754-8302; United Nations Publications, Sales Office and Bookshop, Bureau E4, Geneva 10 1211, Switzerland.

ANUARIO ESTADISTICO DE ANDALUCIA. *see* POPULATION STUDIES—Abstracting, Bibliographies, Statistics

S

317.2 MEX ISSN 0188-8609
HA767.B34
ANUARIO ESTADISTICO DE BAJA CALIFORNIA. Text in Spanish. a. MXN 89 (effective 1999). **Document type:** *Government.*
Published by: Instituto Nacional de Estadistica, Geografia e Informatica, Secretaria de Programacion y Presupuesto, Prol. Heroe de Nacozari 2301 Sur, Puerta 11, Acceso, Aguascalientes, 20270, Mexico. TEL 52-4-918-1948, FAX 52-4-918-0739.

317.2 MEX ISSN 0188-8595
HA767.B36
ANUARIO ESTADISTICO DE BAJA CALIFORNIA SUR. Text in Spanish. a. MXN 83 (effective 1999). **Document type:** *Government.*
Published by: Instituto Nacional de Estadistica, Geografia e Informatica, Secretaria de Programacion y Presupuesto, Prol. Heroe de Nacozari 2301 Sur, Puerta 11, Acceso, Aguascalientes, 20270, Mexico. TEL 52-4-918-1948, FAX 52-4-918-0739. Circ: 600.

317 CUB ISSN 0574-6132
HA871
ANUARIO ESTADISTICO DE CUBA. Text in Spanish. 1952. a. USD 15 in North America; USD 17 in South America; USD 18 in Europe; USD 20 elsewhere. **Document type:** *Government.*
Related titles: ◆ English ed.: Statistical Yearbook Compendium of the Republic of Cuba.
Published by: Comite Estatal de Estadisticas, Centro de Informacion Cientifico-Tecnica, Almendares No. 156, esq. a Desague, Gaveta Postal 6016, Havana, Cuba. Circ: 1,000. **Dist. by:** Ediciones Cubanas, Obispo 527, Havana, Cuba.

317.2 MEX ISSN 0188-8641
ANUARIO ESTADISTICO DE DURANGO. Text in Spanish. a. MXN 95 (effective 1999). **Document type:** *Government.*
Published by: Instituto Nacional de Estadistica, Geografia e Informatica, Secretaria de Programacion y Presupuesto, Prol. Heroe de Nacozari 2301 Sur, Puerta 11, Acceso, Aguascalientes, 20270, Mexico. TEL 52-4-918-1948, FAX 52-4-918-0739.

ANUARIO ESTADISTICO DE EXISTENCIAS, FAENA Y EXPORTACION. *see* FOOD AND FOOD INDUSTRIES—Abstracting, Bibliographies, Statistics

ANUARIO ESTADISTICO DE EXTRANJERIA. *see* POPULATION STUDIES—Abstracting, Bibliographies, Statistics

ANUARIO ESTADISTICO DE LA SIDERURGIA Y MINERIA DE HIERRO EN AMERICA LATINA. *see* METALLURGY—Abstracting, Bibliographies, Statistics

317.2 MEX ISSN 0185-7126
ANUARIO ESTADISTICO DE LOS ESTADOS UNIDOS MEXICANOS. Text in Spanish. 1894. a. USD 145 (effective 1999). **Document type:** *Government.*
Formerly (until 1938): Anuario Estadistico de la Republica Mexicana (0187-8581)
Related titles: Microfiche ed.: (from PQC).
Published by: Instituto Nacional de Estadistica, Geografia e Informatica, Secretaria de Programacion y Presupuesto, Prol. Heroe de Nacozari 2301 Sur, Puerta 11, Acceso, Aguascalientes, 20270, Mexico. TEL 52-4-918-1948, FAX 52-4-918-0739. Circ: 5,000.

317.2 MEX ISSN 0188-848X
ANUARIO ESTADISTICO DE NAYARIT. Text in Spanish. a. MXN 95 (effective 1999). **Document type:** *Government.*
Published by: Instituto Nacional de Estadistica, Geografia e Informatica, Secretaria de Programacion y Presupuesto, Prol. Heroe de Nacozari 2301 Sur, Puerta 11, Acceso, Aguascalientes, 20270, Mexico. TEL 52-4-918-1948, FAX 52-4-918-0739.

317.2 MEX ISSN 0188-8633
HA767.S6
ANUARIO ESTADISTICO DE SONORA. Text in Spanish. a. MXN 110 (effective 1999). **Document type:** *Government.*
Published by: Instituto Nacional de Estadistica, Geografia e Informatica, Secretaria de Programacion y Presupuesto, Prol. Heroe de Nacozari 2301 Sur, Puerta 11, Acceso, Aguascalientes, 20270, Mexico. TEL 52-4-918-1948, FAX 52-4-918-0739. Circ: 1,000.

317.2 MEX ISSN 0187-4756
HA767.T62
ANUARIO ESTADISTICO DE TLAXCALA. Text in Spanish. a. MXN 100 (effective 1999). **Document type:** *Government.*
Published by: Instituto Nacional de Estadistica, Geografia e Informatica, Secretaria de Programacion y Presupuesto, Prol. Heroe de Nacozari 2301 Sur, Puerta 11, Acceso, Aguascalientes, 20270, Mexico. TEL 52-4-918-1948, FAX 52-4-918-0739.

317.2 MEX ISSN 0187-4748
HA767.Z33
ANUARIO ESTADISTICO DE ZACATECAS. Text in Spanish. a. MXN 92 (effective 1999). **Document type:** *Government.*
Published by: Instituto Nacional de Estadistica, Geografia e Informatica, Secretaria de Programacion y Presupuesto, Prol. Heroe de Nacozari 2301 Sur, Puerta 11, Acceso, Aguascalientes, 20270, Mexico. TEL 52-4-918-1948, FAX 52-4-918-1948.

314.6 ESP
ANUARIO ESTADISTICO DEL AREA METROPOLITANA DE L'HORTA. Text in Spanish. 1990. a. **Document type:** *Yearbook, Consumer.*
Formerly (until 1996): Anuario Estadistico del Area Metropolitana de Valencia (1133-4258)
Published by: Camara Oficial de Comercio Industria y Navegacion de Valencia, Jesus 19, Valencia, 46007, Spain. TEL 34-963-103900, FAX 34-963-531742, info@camaravalencia.com, http://www.camaravalencia.com/.

317.2 MEX ISSN 0188-8544
ANUARIO ESTADISTICO DEL DISTRITO FEDERAL. Text in Spanish. a. MXN 82 (effective 1999). **Document type:** *Government.*
Published by: Instituto Nacional de Estadistica, Geografia e Informatica, Secretaria de Programacion y Presupuesto, Prol. Heroe de Nacozari 2301 Sur, Puerta 11, Acceso, Aguascalientes, 20270, Mexico. TEL 52-4-918-1948, FAX 52-4-918-0739.

317.2 MEX ISSN 0188-8676
HA767.A35
ANUARIO ESTADISTICO DEL ESTADO DE AGUASCALIENTES. Text in Spanish. a. MXN 80 (effective 1999). **Document type:** *Government.*
Published by: Instituto Nacional de Estadistica, Geografia e Informatica, Secretaria de Programacion y Presupuesto, Prol. Heroe de Nacozari 2301 Sur, Puerta 11, Acceso, Aguascalientes, 20270, Mexico. TEL 52-4-918-1948, FAX 52-4-918-0739.

317.2 MEX ISSN 0188-8587
HA767.C35
ANUARIO ESTADISTICO DEL ESTADO DE CAMPECHE. Text in Spanish. a. MXN 82 (effective 1999). **Document type:** *Government.*
Published by: Instituto Nacional de Estadistica, Geografia e Informatica, Secretaria de Programacion y Presupuesto, Prol. Heroe de Nacozari 2301 Sur, Puerta 11, Acceso, Aguascalientes, 20270, Mexico. TEL 52-4-918-1948, FAX 52-4-918-0739.

317.2 MEX ISSN 0188-8552
HA767.C48
ANUARIO ESTADISTICO DEL ESTADO DE CHIAPAS. Text in Spanish. a. MXN 97, USD 22 (effective 1999). **Document type:** *Government.*
Published by: Instituto Nacional de Estadistica, Geografia e Informatica, Secretaria de Programacion y Presupuesto, Prol. Heroe de Nacozari 2301 Sur, Puerta 11, Acceso, Aguascalientes, 20270, Mexico. TEL 52-4-918-19488, FAX 52-4-918-0739.

317.2 MEX ISSN 0188-8668
HA767.C5
ANUARIO ESTADISTICO DEL ESTADO DE CHIHUAHUA. Text in Spanish. a. (in 2 vols.). MXN 105, USD 28.50 (effective 1999). **Document type:** *Government.*
Published by: Instituto Nacional de Estadistica, Geografia e Informatica, Secretaria de Programacion y Presupuesto, Prol. Heroe de Nacozari 2301 Sur, Puerta 11, Acceso, Aguascalientes, 20270, Mexico. TEL 52-4-918-1948, FAX 52-4-918-0739.

317.2 MEX ISSN 0188-8560
HA767.C55
ANUARIO ESTADISTICO DEL ESTADO DE COAHUILA. Text in Spanish. a. MXN 90 (effective 1999). **Document type:** *Government.*
Published by: Instituto Nacional de Estadistica, Geografia e Informatica, Secretaria de Programacion y Presupuesto, Prol. Heroe de Nacozari 2301 Sur, Puerta 11, Acceso, Aguascalientes, 20270, Mexico. TEL 52-4-918-1948, FAX 52-4-918-0739.

317.2 MEX ISSN 0188-8579
HA767.C6
ANUARIO ESTADISTICO DEL ESTADO DE COLIMA. Text in Spanish. a. MXN 90 (effective 1999). **Document type:** *Government.*
Published by: Instituto Nacional de Estadistica, Geografia e Informatica, Secretaria de Programacion y Presupuesto, Prol. Heroe de Nacozari 2301 Sur, Puerta 11, Acceso, Aguascalientes, 20270, Mexico. TEL 52-4-918-1948, FAX 52-4-918-0739.

317.2 MEX ISSN 0188-8536
HA767.G69
ANUARIO ESTADISTICO DEL ESTADO DE GUANAJUATO. Text in Spanish. a. MXN 100 (effective 1999). **Document type:** *Government.*
Published by: Instituto Nacional de Estadistica, Geografia e Informatica, Secretaria de Programacion y Presupuesto, Prol. Heroe de Nacozari 2301 Sur, Puerta 11, Acceso, Aguascalientes, 20270, Mexico. TEL 52-4-918-1948, FAX 52-4-918-0739.

317.2 MEX ISSN 0188-865X
HA767.G8
ANUARIO ESTADISTICO DEL ESTADO DE GUERRERO. Text in Spanish. a. MXN 100 (effective 1999). **Document type:** *Government.*
Published by: Instituto Nacional de Estadistica, Geografia e Informatica, Secretaria de Programacion y Presupuesto, Prol. Heroe de Nacozari 2301 Sur, Puerta 11, Acceso, Aguascalientes, 20270, Mexico. TEL 52-4-918-1948, FAX 52-4-918-0739. Circ: 750.

317.2 MEX ISSN 0188-8625
HA767.H53
ANUARIO ESTADISTICO DEL ESTADO DE HIDALGO. Text in Spanish. a. MXN 120 (effective 1999). **Document type:** *Government.*
Published by: Instituto Nacional de Estadistica, Geografia e Informatica, Secretaria de Programacion y Presupuesto, Prol. Heroe de Nacozari 2301 Sur, Puerta 11, Acceso, Aguascalientes, 20270, Mexico. TEL 52-4-918-1948, FAX 52-4-918-0739.

317.2 MEX ISSN 0188-8528
HA767.J34
ANUARIO ESTADISTICO DEL ESTADO DE JALISCO. Text in Spanish. a. MXN 110 (effective 1999). **Document type:** *Government.*
Published by: Instituto Nacional de Estadistica, Geografia e Informatica, Secretaria de Programacion y Presupuesto, Prol. Heroe de Nacozari 2301 Sur, Puerta 11, Acceso, Aguascalientes, 20270, Mexico. TEL 52-4-918-1948, FAX 52-4-918-0739.

317.2 MEX ISSN 0188-851X
ANUARIO ESTADISTICO DEL ESTADO DE MEXICO. Text in Spanish. a. MXN 115 (effective 1999). **Document type:** *Government.*
Published by: Instituto Nacional de Estadistica, Geografia e Informatica, Secretaria de Programacion y Presupuesto, Prol. Heroe de Nacozari 2301 Sur, Puerta 11, Acceso, Aguascalientes, 20270, Mexico. TEL 52-4-918-1948, FAX 52-4-918-0739.

317.2 MEX ISSN 0188-8498
HA767.M67
ANUARIO ESTADISTICO DEL ESTADO DE MORELOS. Text in Spanish. a. MXN 86 (effective 1999). **Document type:** *Government.*
Published by: Instituto Nacional de Estadistica, Geografia e Informatica, Secretaria de Programacion y Presupuesto, Prol. Heroe de Nacozari 2301 Sur, Puerta 11, Acceso, Aguascalientes, 20270, Mexico. TEL 52-4-918-1948, FAX 52-4-918-0739.

317.2 MEX ISSN 0188-8471
ANUARIO ESTADISTICO DEL ESTADO DE NUEVO LEON. Text in Spanish. a. MXN 110 (effective 1999). **Document type:** *Government.*
Published by: Instituto Nacional de Estadistica, Geografia e Informatica, Secretaria de Programacion y Presupuesto, Prol. Heroe de Nacozari 2301 Sur, Puerta 11, Acceso, Aguascalientes, 20270, Mexico. TEL 52-4-918-1948, FAX 52-4-918-0739.

317.2 MEX ISSN 0188-8463
ANUARIO ESTADISTICO DEL ESTADO DE OAXACA. Text in Spanish. a. MXN 125 (effective 1999). **Document type:** *Government.*
Published by: Instituto Nacional de Estadistica, Geografia e Informatica, Secretaria de Programacion y Presupuesto, Prol. Heroe de Nacozari 2301 Sur, Puerta 11, Acceso, Aguascalientes, 20270, Mexico. TEL 52-4-918-19488, FAX 52-4-918-0739.

317.2 MEX ISSN 0188-8684
HA767.P85
ANUARIO ESTADISTICO DEL ESTADO DE PUEBLA. Text in Spanish. a. MXN 135 (effective 1999). **Document type:** *Government.*
Published by: Instituto Nacional de Estadistica, Geografia e Informatica, Secretaria de Programacion y Presupuesto, Prol. Heroe de Nacozari 2301 Sur, Puerta 11, Acceso, Aguascalientes, 20270, Mexico. TEL 52-4-918-19488, FAX 52-4-918-0739. Circ: 1,000.

317.2 MEX ISSN 0188-8455
HA767.Q4
ANUARIO ESTADISTICO DEL ESTADO DE QUERETARO. Text in Spanish. a. MXN 100 (effective 1999). **Document type:** *Government.*
Published by: Instituto Nacional de Estadistica, Geografia e Informatica, Secretaria de Programacion y Presupuesto, Prol. Heroe de Nacozari 2301 Sur, Puerta 11, Acceso, Aguascalientes, 20270, Mexico. TEL 52-4-918-1948, FAX 52-4-918-0739.

317.2 MEX ISSN 0188-8617
HA767.Q55
ANUARIO ESTADISTICO DEL ESTADO DE QUINTANA ROO. Text in Spanish. a. MXN 80 (effective 1999). **Document type:** *Government.*
Published by: Instituto Nacional de Estadistica, Geografia e Informatica, Secretaria de Programacion y Presupuesto, Prol. Heroe de Nacozari 2301 Sur, Puerta 11, Acceso, Aguascalientes, 20270, Mexico. TEL 52-4-918-1948, FAX 52-4-918-0739.

317.2 MEX ISSN 0188-8447
ANUARIO ESTADISTICO DEL ESTADO DE SAN LUIS POTOSI. Text in Spanish. a. MXN 110 (effective 1999). **Document type:** *Government.*
Published by: Instituto Nacional de Estadistica, Geografia e Informatica, Secretaria de Programacion y Presupuesto, Prol. Heroe de Nacozari 2301 Sur, Puerta 11, Acceso, Aguascalientes, 20270, Mexico. TEL 52-4-918-1948, FAX 52-4-918-0739.

317.2 MEX ISSN 0188-8439
HA767.S5
ANUARIO ESTADISTICO DEL ESTADO DE SINALOA. Text in Spanish. a. MXN 100 (effective 1999). **Document type:** *Government.*
Published by: Instituto Nacional de Estadistica, Geografia e Informatica, Secretaria de Programacion y Presupuesto, Prol. Heroe de Nacozari 2301 Sur, Puerta 11, Acceso, Aguascalientes, 20270, Mexico. TEL 52-4-918-1948, FAX 52-4-918-0739.

317.2 MEX ISSN 0188-8420
ANUARIO ESTADISTICO DEL ESTADO DE TABASCO. Text in Spanish. a. MXN 97 (effective 1999). **Document type:** *Government.*
Published by: Instituto Nacional de Estadistica, Geografia e Informatica, Secretaria de Programacion y Presupuesto, Prol. Heroe de Nacozari 2301 Sur, Puerta 11, Acceso, Aguascalientes, 20270, Mexico. TEL 52-4-918-1948, FAX 52-4-918-0739.

317.2 MEX ISSN 0188-8412
HA767.T36
ANUARIO ESTADISTICO DEL ESTADO DE TAMAULIPAS. Text in Spanish. a. MXN 115 (effective 1999). **Document type:** *Government.*
Published by: Instituto Nacional de Estadistica, Geografia e Informatica, Secretaria de Programacion y Presupuesto, Prol. Heroe de Nacozari 2301 Sur, Puerta 11, Acceso, Aguascalientes, 20270, Mexico. TEL 52-4-918-1948, FAX 52-4-918-0739. Circ: 750.

317.2 MEX ISSN 0187-4764
HA767.V4
ANUARIO ESTADISTICO DEL ESTADO DE VERACRUZ. Text in Spanish. a. MXN 190 (effective 1999). **Document type:** *Government.*
Published by: Instituto Nacional de Estadistica, Geografia e Informatica, Secretaria de Programacion y Presupuesto, Prol. Heroe de Nacozari 2301 Sur, Puerta 11, Acceso, Aguascalientes, 20270, Mexico. TEL 52-4-918-1948, FAX 52-4-918-0739.

317.2 MEX ISSN 0188-8404
HA767.Y8
ANUARIO ESTADISTICO DEL ESTADO DE YUCATAN. Text in Spanish. a. MXN 109 (effective 1999). **Document type:** *Government.*
Published by: Instituto Nacional de Estadistica, Geografia e Informatica, Secretaria de Programacion y Presupuesto, Prol. Heroe de Nacozari 2301 Sur, Puerta 11, Acceso, Aguascalientes, 20270, Mexico. TEL 52-4-918-1948, FAX 52-4-918-0739.

318 PRY ISSN 0252-8932
HA1045
ANUARIO ESTADISTICO DEL PARAGUAY. Text in Spanish. 1886. a. per issue exchange basis. **Document type:** *Government.*
Related titles: Microfiche ed.: (from PQC); ◆ Supplement(s): Paraguay. Direccion General de Estadistica y Censos. Boletin Estadistico. ISSN 0031-1677.
Published by: Direccion General de Estadistica y Censos, HUMAITA, 463, Casilla de Correos 1118, Asuncion, Paraguay. Ed. Jose Diaz de Bedoya. Circ: 1,500.

ANUARIO ESTADISTICO DEL TRANSPORTE AEREO ESPANA - (YEAR). *see* TRANSPORTATION—Abstracting, Bibliographies, Statistics

ANUARIO ESTADISTICO - SEGUROS Y PREVISION SOCIAL. *see* INSURANCE—Abstracting, Bibliographies, Statistics

318 BRA ISSN 0102-0676
HA988.B3
ANUARIO ESTATISTICO DA BAHIA. Text in Portuguese. 1972. a. BRL 50 (effective 2002).
Published by: Superintendencia de Estudos Economicos e Sociais da Bahia, Ave Luiz Vianna Filho s/n, Salvador, Bahia 41 750-300, Brazil. TEL 55-71-3704847, FAX 55-71-371853, http://www.sei.ba.gov.br.

318 BRA
ANUARIO ESTATISTICO DA CIDADE DO RIO DE JANEIRO. Text in Portuguese. 1991. a. maps.
Published by: Instituto de Planejamento Municipal, Rua Gago Coutinho, 52 Andar 4, Laranjeiras, Rio De Janeiro, RJ 22221-070, Brazil. TEL 55-21-2054576, FAX 55-21-2852098. Circ: 1,000.

314 PRT ISSN 0871-8741
HA1575
ANUARIO ESTATISTICO DE PORTUGAL. Text in French, Portuguese. 1875. a. **Document type:** *Government.* **Description:** Provides an overview of Portugal's situation regarding to social, economic and population aspects.

Formerly (until 1990): Portugal. Instituto Nacional de Estatistica. Anuario Estatistico (0079-4112); Which incorporated (1943-1960): Anuario Estatistico do Ultramar (0872-4431); Which was formerly (until 1949): Anuario Estatistico do Imperio Colonial (0872-4423)
Related titles: ◆ Supplement(s): Portugal. Instituto Nacional de Estatistica. Contas Nacionais. ISSN 0870-2659.
Published by: Instituto Nacional de Estatistica, Av Antonio Jose de Almeida 2, Lisbon, 1000-043, Portugal. TEL 351-21-8426100, FAX 351-21-8426380, ine@ine.pt, http://www.ine.pt.

318 BRA ISSN 0100-1299
HA971
ANUARIO ESTATISTICO DO BRASIL/STATISTICAL YEARBOOK OF BRAZIL. Text in Portuguese. 1908. a. USD 100. bk.rev. charts; maps. **Document type:** *Government.* **Description:** Presents statistics on the physical, demographic, economic, social, cultural and political administrative situation of Brazil.
Related titles: CD-ROM ed.: USD 80; Microfiche ed.: (from PQC).
Indexed: RASB.
—Linda Hall.
Published by: Fundacao Instituto Brasileiro de Geografia e Estatistica, Centro de Documentacao e Disseminacao de Informacoes, Rua General Canabarro, 706 Andar 2, Maracana, Rio de Janeiro, RJ 20271-201, Brazil. TEL 55-21-2645424, FAX 55-21-2841959. Circ: 5,000.

318 BRA ISSN 0100-8730
HA988.S2
ANUARIO ESTATISTICO DO ESTADO DE SAO PAULO. Text in Portuguese. 1979. a. USD 69.10. charts. **Document type:** *Government.* **Description:** Characterizes the social, economic, demographic and physical aspects of the state.
Published by: Fundacao Sistema Estadual de Analise de Dados, Av Casper Libero, 464, Centro, Caixa Postal 8223, Sao Paulo, SP 01033-000, Brazil. Circ: 1,000.

318.11 BRA ISSN 0103-5274
ANUARIO ESTATISTICO DO ESTADO DO PARA. Text in Portuguese. 1977. a. USD 1. bibl.; charts; stat. **Description:** Discusses socio-economic issues of the state.
Published by: (Para. Coordenadoria de Estatistica Estadual), Instituto do Desenvolvimento Economico Social do Para, Av Nazare, 871, Nazare, Belem, Para 66035170, Brazil. TEL 55-91-2244411, FAX 55-91-2253414.

ANUARIO SOCIAL DE ESPANA. *see* POPULATION STUDIES—Abstracting, Bibliographies, Statistics

314 ROM ISSN 1220-3246
HA1641
ANUARUL STATISTIC AL ROMANIEI/STATISTICAL YEARBOOK OF ROMANIA. Text in English, Romanian. 1902. a. ROL 300,000, USD 65 (effective 1997). **Document type:** *Government.* **Description:** Presents statistical data in many areas. Includes comments, explanations and graphs.
Related titles: Microfiche ed.: (from PQC).
Published by: Comisia Nationala pentru Statistica/National Commission for Statistics, Bd. Libertatii 16, Sector 5, Bucharest, 70542, Romania. TEL 40-1-3363370, FAX 40-1-3124873.

310 DEU ISSN 1431-7982
ANWENDUNGSORIENTIERTE STATISTIK. Text in German. 1997. irreg., latest vol.9, 2005. price varies. **Document type:** *Monographic series, Academic/Scholarly.*
Indexed: MSN, Z02.
Published by: Peter Lang GmbH (Subsidiary of: Peter Lang Publishing Group), Eschborner Landstr 42-50, Frankfurt Am Main, 60489, Germany. TEL 49-69-7807050, FAX 49-69-78070550, zentrale.frankfurt@peterlang.com. Ed. Helge Toutenburg.

310 363.7 USA
APPLIED ENVIRONMENTAL STATISTICS. Variant title: Chapman & Hall/CRC Applied Environmental Statistics. Text in English. 2001. irreg. **Document type:** *Monographic series, Academic/Scholarly.* **Description:** Features monographs on applied statistics for environmental science and management.
Related titles: Online - full text ed.: ISSN 2154-4069.
Published by: C R C Press, LLC (Subsidiary of: Taylor & Francis Group), 6000 Broken Sound Pky, NW, Ste 300, Boca Raton, FL 33487. TEL 561-994-0555, FAX 561-989-9732, journals@crcpress.com, http://www.crcpress.com.

310 JOR
ARAB INSTITUTE FOR TRAINING & RESEARCH IN STATISTICS. STATISTICAL BULLETIN. Text in Arabic. q. free. **Document type:** *Newsletter, Academic/Scholarly.*
Media: Online - full text.
Published by: Arab Institute for Training & Research in Statistics, PO Box :851104, Amman, 11185, Jordan. TEL 962-6-5823405, FAX 962-6-5820327.

310 JOR
▼ ➤ **ARAB STATISTICAL SCIENCES JOURNAL.** Text in Arabic. 2009 (Apr.). s-a. USD 25 to individuals; USD 50 to institutions; free to members (effective 2009). **Document type:** *Journal, Academic/Scholarly.*
Published by: Arab Institute for Training & Research in Statistics, PO Box :851104, Amman, 11185, Jordan. http://www.aitrs.org/.

➤ **ARBEITSKOSTEN IM PRODUZIERENDEN GEWERBE UND IM DIENSTLEISTUNGSBEREICH IN BAYERN.** *see* BUSINESS AND ECONOMICS—Abstracting, Bibliographies, Statistics

314.95 FRO ISSN 0906-3323
ARBOK FYRI FOEROYAR/STATISTICAL YEARBOOK FOR THE FAROE ISLANDS. Text in English, Icelandic. 1976. irreg. price varies. **Document type:** *Government.* **Description:** Official statistics for the Faroe Islands.
Formerly (until 1990): Arsfragreiding fyri Foeroyar (0105-6794)
Published by: Hagstova Foeroyar/Statistics Faroe Islands, Glyvursvegur 1, PO Box 2068, Argir, FO-165, Faeroe Islands. TEL 298-352028, FAX 298-352038. Ed. Hans Pauli Stroem.

318 ARG
ARGENTINA. CENTRAL DE ESTADISTICAS NACIONALES. INFORME. Text in Spanish. 1976. irreg. USD 240. **Document type:** *Newsletter.*
Published by: Central de Estadisticas Nacionales, Avda 5 de Mayo 953, Buenos Aires, 1084, Argentina. TEL 54-114-3453500. Ed. Carlos A Canta Yoy. Circ: 10,500.

ARGENTINA. INSTITUTO NACIONAL DE ESTADISTICA Y CENSOS. ANUARIO ESTADISTICO. *see* POPULATION STUDIES—Abstracting, Bibliographies, Statistics

ARGENTINA. INSTITUTO NACIONAL DE ESTADISTICA Y CENSOS. CENSO NACIONAL AGROPECUARIO (YEAR); resultados generales - caracteristicas basicas. *see* AGRICULTURE—Abstracting, Bibliographies, Statistics

ARGENTINA. INSTITUTO NACIONAL DE ESTADISTICA Y CENSOS. CENSO NACIONAL ECONOMICO (YEAR). AVANCE DE RESULTADOS. *see* BUSINESS AND ECONOMICS—Abstracting, Bibliographies, Statistics

ARGENTINA. INSTITUTO NACIONAL DE ESTADISTICA Y CENSOS. CENSO NACIONAL ECONOMICO (YEAR). SERIE A. RESULTADOS DEFINITIVOS. *see* BUSINESS AND ECONOMICS—Abstracting, Bibliographies, Statistics

ARGENTINA. INSTITUTO NACIONAL DE ESTADISTICA Y CENSOS. ENCUESTA INDUSTRIAL ANUAL (YEAR). *see* BUSINESS AND ECONOMICS—Abstracting, Bibliographies, Statistics

ARGENTINA. INSTITUTO NACIONAL DE ESTADISTICA Y CENSOS. ENCUESTA NACIONAL AGROPECUARIA. *see* AGRICULTURE—Abstracting, Bibliographies, Statistics

ARGENTINA. INSTITUTO NACIONAL DE ESTADISTICA Y CENSOS. ESTADISTICA DE PRODUCTOS INDUSTRIALES. *see* BUSINESS AND ECONOMICS—Abstracting, Bibliographies, Statistics

ARGENTINA. INSTITUTO NACIONAL DE ESTADISTICA Y CENSOS. SERIE ESTRUCTURA OCCUPACIONAL. *see* BUSINESS AND ECONOMICS—Abstracting, Bibliographies, Statistics

ARGENTINA. INSTITUTO NACIONAL DE ESTADISTICA Y CENSOS. SERIE NOMENCLADORES Y CORRESPONDENCIAS. *see* BUSINESS AND ECONOMICS—Abstracting, Bibliographies, Statistics

ARGENTINA. JUNTA NACIONAL DE CARNES. SINTESIS ESTADISTICA. *see* AGRICULTURE—Abstracting, Bibliographies, Statistics

ARGENTINA. SECRETARIA DE AGRICULTURA GANADERIA Y PESCA. SITUACION DEL MERCADO DE CARNES. *see* AGRICULTURE—Abstracting, Bibliographies, Statistics

ARGENTINA. SECRETARIA DE ESTADO DE AGRICULTURA Y GANADERIA. AREA DE TRABAJO DE LECHERIA. RESENA ESTADISTICA. *see* AGRICULTURE—Abstracting, Bibliographies, Statistics

ARIZONA. AGRICULTURAL STATISTICS SERVICE. CATTLE. *see* AGRICULTURE—Abstracting, Bibliographies, Statistics

ARIZONA STATISTICAL ABSTRACT. *see* BUSINESS AND ECONOMICS—Abstracting, Bibliographies, Statistics

ARKANSAS CITIES & COUNTIES GRAPHIC PERFORMANCE ANALYSIS. *see* PUBLIC ADMINISTRATION—Abstracting, Bibliographies, Statistics

ARKANSAS. EMPLOYMENT SECURITY DEPARTMENT. STATISTICAL REVIEW. *see* BUSINESS AND ECONOMICS—Abstracting, Bibliographies, Statistics

ARKANSAS VITAL STATISTICS. *see* POPULATION STUDIES—Abstracting, Bibliographies, Statistics

ARTIST EMPLOYMENT IN (YEAR). *see* OCCUPATIONS AND CAREERS—Abstracting, Bibliographies, Statistics

315 THA ISSN 1014-3750
HA4551
ASIA - PACIFIC IN FIGURES. Text in English. 1987. a., latest 2001. USD 12 (effective 2001).
Indexed: IIS.
Published by: United Nations Economic and Social Commission for Asia and the Pacific, United Nations Bldg., Rajadamnern Ave., Bangkok, 10200, Thailand. unescap@unescap.org, http://www.unescap.org. **Dist. by:** Conference Services Unit, Conference Services Unit, ESCAP, Bangkok 10200, Thailand. TEL 662-288-1174, 662-288-2313, FAX 662-288-3022.

659.021 GBR ISSN 0968-2171
ASIA PACIFIC MARKET & MEDIAFACT. Text in English. 1988. a. GBP 100, EUR 110.02, USD 164.47 per issue (effective 2009). stat. **Document type:** *Report, Trade.* **Description:** Contains media statistics for TV & radio audiences, press cirulation & readership, cinema screens & admissions, etc.
—CCC.
Published by: Zenith Optimedia, 24 Percy St, London, W1T 2BS, United Kingdom. TEL 44-20-79611000, FAX 44-20-79611113, info@zenithoptimedia.com.

ASIAN JOURNAL OF MATHEMATICS & STATISTICS. *see* MATHEMATICS

ASSOCIATION OF FOOTBALL STATISTICIANS. ANNUAL. *see* SPORTS AND GAMES—Ball Games

ASSOCIATIONS SECTORIELLES PARITAIRES, LESIONS PROFESSIONNELLES, STATISTIQUES. TOME 1. ASSOCIATION PARITAIRE POUR LA SANTE ET LA SECURITE DU TRAVAIL DU SECTEUR AFFAIRES SOCIALES. *see* OCCUPATIONAL HEALTH AND SAFETY—Abstracting, Bibliographies, Statistics

ASSOCIATIONS SECTORIELLES PARITAIRES, LESIONS PROFESSIONNELLES, STATISTIQUES. TOME 11. ASSOCIATION PARITAIRE POUR LA SANTE ET LA SECURITE DU TRAVAIL DU SECTEUR MINIER. *see* OCCUPATIONAL HEALTH AND SAFETY—Abstracting, Bibliographies, Statistics

ASSOCIATIONS SECTORIELLES PARITAIRES, LESIONS PROFESSIONNELLES, STATISTIQUES. TOME 12. ASSOCIATION PARITAIRE POUR LA SANTE ET LA SECURITE DU TRAVAIL DU SECTEUR DES AFFAIRES MUNICIPALES. *see* OCCUPATIONAL HEALTH AND SAFETY—Abstracting, Bibliographies, Statistics

ASSOCIATIONS SECTORIELLES PARITAIRES, LESIONS PROFESSIONNELLES, STATISTIQUES. TOME 13. ASSOCIATION PARITAIRE POUR LA SANTE ET LA SECURITE DU TRAVAIL DU SECTEUR DE L'HABILLEMENT. *see* OCCUPATIONAL HEALTH AND SAFETY—Abstracting, Bibliographies, Statistics

ASSOCIATIONS SECTORIELLES PARITAIRES, LESIONS PROFESSIONNELLES, STATISTIQUES. TOME 2. PREVENTEX - ASSOCIATION PARITAIRE DU TEXTILE. *see* OCCUPATIONAL HEALTH AND SAFETY—Abstracting, Bibliographies, Statistics

ASSOCIATIONS SECTORIELLES PARITAIRES, LESIONS PROFESSIONNELLES, STATISTIQUES. TOME 3. ASSOCIATION PARITAIRE POUR LA SANTE ET LA SECURITE DU TRAVAIL DU SECTEUR TRANSPORT ET ENTREPOSAGE. *see* OCCUPATIONAL HEALTH AND SAFETY—Abstracting, Bibliographies, Statistics

ASSOCIATIONS SECTORIELLES PARITAIRES, LESIONS PROFESSIONNELLES, STATISTIQUES. TOME 4. ASSOCIATION PARITAIRE POUR LA SANTE ET LA SECURITE DU TRAVAIL DU SECTEUR DE L'IMPRIMERIE ET ACTIVITES CONNEXES. *see* OCCUPATIONAL HEALTH AND SAFETY—Abstracting, Bibliographies, Statistics

ASSOCIATIONS SECTORIELLES PARITAIRES, LESIONS PROFESSIONNELLES, STATISTIQUES. TOME 5. ASSOCIATION PARITAIRE POUR LA SANTE ET LA SECURITE DU TRAVAIL DU SECTEUR ADMINISTRATION PROVINCIALE. *see* OCCUPATIONAL HEALTH AND SAFETY—Abstracting, Bibliographies, Statistics

ASSOCIATIONS SECTORIELLES PARITAIRES, LESIONS PROFESSIONNELLES, STATISTIQUES. TOME 6. ASSOCIATION PARITAIRE POUR LA SANTE ET LA SECURITE DU TRAVAIL DU SECTEUR FABRICATION D'EQUIPEMENT DE TRANSPORT ET DE MACHINES. *see* OCCUPATIONAL HEALTH AND SAFETY—Abstracting, Bibliographies, Statistics

ASSOCIATIONS SECTORIELLES PARITAIRES, LESIONS PROFESSIONNELLES, STATISTIQUES. TOME 7. ASSOCIATION PARITAIRE POUR LA SANTE ET LA SECURITE DU TRAVAIL DU SECTEUR DE LA FABRICATION DE PRODUITS EN METAL ET DE PRODUITS ELECTRIQUES. *see* OCCUPATIONAL HEALTH AND SAFETY—Abstracting, Bibliographies, Statistics

ASSOCIATIONS SECTORIELLES PARITAIRES, LESIONS PROFESSIONNELLES, STATISTIQUES. TOME 8. ASSOCIATION PARITAIRE POUR LA SANTE ET LA SECURITE DU TRAVAIL DU SECTEUR DES SERVICES AUTOMOBILES. *see* OCCUPATIONAL HEALTH AND SAFETY—Abstracting, Bibliographies, Statistics

ASSOCIATIONS SECTORIELLES PARITAIRES, LESIONS PROFESSIONNELLES, STATISTIQUES. TOME 9. ASSOCIATION PARITAIRE POUR LA SANTE ET LA SECURITE DU TRAVAIL DU SECTEUR DE LA CONSTRUCTION. *see* OCCUPATIONAL HEALTH AND SAFETY—Abstracting, Bibliographies, Statistics

AUCKLAND DISTRICT CRIME STATISTICS. *see* CRIMINOLOGY AND LAW ENFORCEMENT—Abstracting, Bibliographies, Statistics

AUDIT BUREAU OF CIRCULATIONS. ANNUAL REPORT. *see* ADVERTISING AND PUBLIC RELATIONS—Abstracting, Bibliographies, Statistics

AUDIT BUREAU OF CIRCULATIONS. PUBLISHER'S STATEMENTS. *see* ADVERTISING AND PUBLIC RELATIONS—Abstracting, Bibliographies, Statistics

AUDIT BUREAU OF CIRCULATIONS. SUPPLEMENTAL DATA REPORTS. *see* ADVERTISING AND PUBLIC RELATIONS—Abstracting, Bibliographies, Statistics

AUSGEWAEHLTE ZAHLEN FUER DIE BAUWIRTSCHAFT. *see* BUILDING AND CONSTRUCTION—Abstracting, Bibliographies, Statistics

AUSTRALIA. AIR TRANSPORT STATISTICS. AIRPORT TRAFFIC DATA. *see* TRANSPORTATION—Abstracting, Bibliographies, Statistics

AUSTRALIA. AIR TRANSPORT STATISTICS. DOMESTIC AIRLINE ACTIVITY (MAJOR AUSTRALIAN AIRLINES) MONTHLY STATUS REPORT. *see* TRANSPORTATION—Abstracting, Bibliographies, Statistics

AUSTRALIA. AIR TRANSPORT STATISTICS. GENERAL AVIATION. *see* TRANSPORTATION—Abstracting, Bibliographies, Statistics

AUSTRALIA. AIR TRANSPORT STATISTICS. MONTHLY PROVISIONAL STATISTICS OF INTERNATIONAL SCHEDULED AIR TRANSPORT (ONLINE). *see* TRANSPORTATION—Abstracting, Bibliographies, Statistics

AUSTRALIA. BUREAU OF STATISTICS. (YEAR) CENSUS OF POPULATION AND HOUSING - A B S VIEWS ON CENSUS CLASSIFICATIONS. *see* POPULATION STUDIES—Abstracting, Bibliographies, Statistics

AUSTRALIA. BUREAU OF STATISTICS. 4-SITE CONSULTANCY. *see* POPULATION STUDIES—Abstracting, Bibliographies, Statistics

AUSTRALIA. BUREAU OF STATISTICS. A DIRECTORY OF EDUCATION AND TRAINING STATISTICS (ONLINE). *see* EDUCATION—Abstracting, Bibliographies, Statistics

AUSTRALIA. BUREAU OF STATISTICS. A GUIDE TO MAJOR A.B.S. CLASSIFICATIONS (ONLINE). *see* PUBLIC ADMINISTRATION—Abstracting, Bibliographies, Statistics

AUSTRALIA. BUREAU OF STATISTICS. A GUIDE TO THE AUSTRALIAN NATIONAL ACCOUNTS (ONLINE). *see* BUSINESS AND ECONOMICS—Abstracting, Bibliographies, Statistics

AUSTRALIA. BUREAU OF STATISTICS. A GUIDE TO THE CONSUMER PRICE INDEX. *see* BUSINESS AND ECONOMICS—Abstracting, Bibliographies, Statistics

AUSTRALIA. BUREAU OF STATISTICS. A GUIDE TO THE CONSUMER PRICE INDEX (ONLINE). *see* BUSINESS AND ECONOMICS—Abstracting, Bibliographies, Statistics

AUSTRALIA. BUREAU OF STATISTICS. A PORTRAIT OF AUSTRALIAN EXPORTERS: A REPORT BASED ON THE BUSINESS LONGITUDINAL SURVEY (ONLINE). *see* BUSINESS AND ECONOMICS—Abstracting, Bibliographies, Statistics

AUSTRALIA. BUREAU OF STATISTICS. A PROVISIONAL FRAMEWORK FOR HOUSEHOLD INCOME, CONSUMPTION, SAVING AND WEALTH (ONLINE). *see* BUSINESS AND ECONOMICS—Abstracting, Bibliographies, Statistics

AUSTRALIA. BUREAU OF STATISTICS. ACCOMMODATION SERVICES, AUSTRALIA (ONLINE). *see* HOTELS AND RESTAURANTS—Abstracting, Bibliographies, Statistics

AUSTRALIA. BUREAU OF STATISTICS. ACCOUNTING SERVICES, AUSTRALIA. *see* BUSINESS AND ECONOMICS—Abstracting, Bibliographies, Statistics

S

AUSTRALIA. BUREAU OF STATISTICS. ADULT LITERACY AND LIFE SKILLS SURVEY, SUMMARY RESULTS, AUSTRALIA (ONLINE). see EDUCATION—Abstracting, Bibliographies, Statistics

AUSTRALIA. BUREAU OF STATISTICS. AGRICULTURAL COMMODITIES, AUSTRALIA (ONLINE). see AGRICULTURE—Abstracting, Bibliographies, Statistics

AUSTRALIA. BUREAU OF STATISTICS. AGRICULTURE, AUSTRALIA (ONLINE). see AGRICULTURE—Abstracting, Bibliographies, Statistics

AUSTRALIA. BUREAU OF STATISTICS. AGSTATS MANUAL. see AGRICULTURE—Abstracting, Bibliographies, Statistics

AUSTRALIA. BUREAU OF STATISTICS. AN EVALUATION OF THE CENSUS OF POPULATION AND HOUSING. see POPULATION STUDIES—Abstracting, Bibliographies, Statistics

001.433 AUS
AUSTRALIA. BUREAU OF STATISTICS. AN INTRODUCTION TO SAMPLE SURVEYS: A USER'S GUIDE (ONLINE). Text in English. 1999. irreg., latest 1999. free (effective 2009). **Document type:** *Government.* **Description:** Features as a basic guide on the use of sample surveys, for the purpose of conducting all types of research.
Formerly: Australia. Bureau of Statistics. An Introduction to Sample Surveys: A User's Guide (Print)
Media: Online - full text.
Published by: Australian Bureau of Statistics, Locked Bag 10, Belconnen, ACT 2616, Australia. TEL 61-2-92684909, 300-135-070, FAX 61-2-92684654, client.services@abs.gov.au.

AUSTRALIA. BUREAU OF STATISTICS. ANNUAL STATISTICS ON FINANCIAL INSTITUTIONS (ONLINE). see BUSINESS AND ECONOMICS—Abstracting, Bibliographies, Statistics

AUSTRALIA. BUREAU OF STATISTICS. ARTS AND CULTURE IN AUSTRALIA: A STATISTICAL OVERVIEW. see HUMANITIES: COMPREHENSIVE WORKS—Abstracting, Bibliographies, Statistics

AUSTRALIA. BUREAU OF STATISTICS. ASPECTS OF LITERACY: PROFILES AND PERCEPTIONS, AUSTRALIA (ONLINE). see EDUCATION—Abstracting, Bibliographies, Statistics

AUSTRALIA. BUREAU OF STATISTICS. ATTENDANCE AT SELECTED CULTURAL VENUES, AUSTRALIA (ONLINE). see SOCIAL SCIENCES: COMPREHENSIVE WORKS—Abstracting, Bibliographies, Statistics

AUSTRALIA. BUREAU OF STATISTICS. AUDIOLOGY AND AUDIOMETRY SERVICES, AUSTRALIA (ONLINE). see PHYSICS—Abstracting, Bibliographies, Statistics

AUSTRALIA. BUREAU OF STATISTICS. AUSPEND. see BUSINESS AND ECONOMICS—Abstracting, Bibliographies, Statistics

319.4 AUS ISSN 1031-0541
AUSTRALIA. BUREAU OF STATISTICS. AUSTRALIA AT A GLANCE. Text in English. 1971. a. free (effective 2009). **Document type:** *Government.* **Description:** Contains information about demography and manpower, finance, production and retail sales, price indexes, national accounts, overseas transactions, transport and building.
Related titles: Online - full text ed.
Published by: Australian Bureau of Statistics, Locked Bag 10, Belconnen, ACT 2616, Australia. TEL 61-2-62527037, FAX 61-2-92684654, client.services@abs.gov.au. Circ: 2,409.

AUSTRALIA. BUREAU OF STATISTICS. AUSTRALIAN AND NEW ZEALAND STANDARD CLASSIFICATION OF OCCUPATIONS. see OCCUPATIONS AND CAREERS—Abstracting, Bibliographies, Statistics

AUSTRALIA. BUREAU OF STATISTICS. AUSTRALIAN AND NEW ZEALAND STANDARD INDUSTRIAL CLASSIFICATION. see BUSINESS AND ECONOMICS—Abstracting, Bibliographies, Statistics

AUSTRALIA. BUREAU OF STATISTICS. AUSTRALIAN AND NEW ZEALAND STANDARD INDUSTRIAL CLASSIFICATION - ALPHABETIC CODING INDEX (ONLINE). see BUSINESS AND ECONOMICS—Abstracting, Bibliographies, Statistics

AUSTRALIA. BUREAU OF STATISTICS. AUSTRALIAN AND NEW ZEALAND STANDARD INDUSTRIAL CLASSIFICATION CODER. see BUSINESS AND ECONOMICS—Abstracting, Bibliographies, Statistics

AUSTRALIA. BUREAU OF STATISTICS. AUSTRALIAN AND NEW ZEALAND STANDARD RESEARCH CLASSIFICATION. see BUSINESS AND ECONOMICS—Abstracting, Bibliographies, Statistics

AUSTRALIA. BUREAU OF STATISTICS. AUSTRALIAN BUSINESS REGISTER, A N Z S I C INDUSTRY CLASS BY STATE (ONLINE). see BUSINESS AND ECONOMICS—Abstracting, Bibliographies, Statistics

319.4 AUS
AUSTRALIA. BUREAU OF STATISTICS. AUSTRALIAN CAPITAL TERRITORY AT A GLANCE (ONLINE). Text in English. 1984. a., latest 2007. free (effective 2009). **Document type:** *Government.* **Description:** Contains information about population, vital statistics, education, health, welfare, crime and justice, income, labor force, prices, retail, trade, building, agriculture, tourist, finance, manufacturing, transport and climate.
Formerly (until 2005): Australia. Bureau of Statistics. Australian Capital Territory at a Glance (Print) (0815-3523)
Media: Online - full text.
Published by: Australian Bureau of Statistics, Locked Bag 10, Belconnen, ACT 2616, Australia. TEL 61-2-62527037, FAX 61-2-92684654, client.services@abs.gov.au.

AUSTRALIA. BUREAU OF STATISTICS. AUSTRALIAN CAPITAL TERRITORY'S YOUNG PEOPLE (ONLINE). see REAL ESTATE—Abstracting, Bibliographies, Statistics

AUSTRALIA. BUREAU OF STATISTICS. AUSTRALIAN CLASSIFICATION FRAMEWORK FOR CULTURE AND LEISURE STATISTICS. see SPORTS AND GAMES—Abstracting, Bibliographies, Statistics

AUSTRALIA. BUREAU OF STATISTICS. AUSTRALIAN CONSUMER PRICE INDEX: CONCEPTS, SOURCES AND METHODS (ONLINE). see BUSINESS AND ECONOMICS—Abstracting, Bibliographies, Statistics

AUSTRALIA. BUREAU OF STATISTICS. AUSTRALIAN CULTURE AND LEISURE CLASSIFICATIONS (ONLINE). see SPORTS AND GAMES—Abstracting, Bibliographies, Statistics

AUSTRALIA. BUREAU OF STATISTICS. AUSTRALIAN DEMOGRAPHIC (ONLINE). see POPULATION STUDIES—Abstracting, Bibliographies, Statistics

AUSTRALIA. BUREAU OF STATISTICS. AUSTRALIAN DEMOGRAPHIC STATISTICS (ONLINE). see POPULATION STUDIES—Abstracting, Bibliographies, Statistics

AUSTRALIA. BUREAU OF STATISTICS. AUSTRALIAN ECONOMIC INDICATORS (ONLINE). see BUSINESS AND ECONOMICS—Abstracting, Bibliographies, Statistics

AUSTRALIA. BUREAU OF STATISTICS. AUSTRALIAN FARMING IN BRIEF. see AGRICULTURE—Abstracting, Bibliographies, Statistics

AUSTRALIA. BUREAU OF STATISTICS. AUSTRALIAN HARMONIZED EXPORT COMMODITY CLASSIFICATION (ONLINE). see BUSINESS AND ECONOMICS—Abstracting, Bibliographies, Statistics

AUSTRALIA. BUREAU OF STATISTICS. AUSTRALIAN HISTORICAL POPULATION STATISTICS (ONLINE). see POPULATION STUDIES—Abstracting, Bibliographies, Statistics

AUSTRALIA. BUREAU OF STATISTICS. AUSTRALIAN HOSPITAL STATISTICS. see HEALTH FACILITIES AND ADMINISTRATION—Abstracting, Bibliographies, Statistics

AUSTRALIA. BUREAU OF STATISTICS. AUSTRALIAN HOUSING SURVEY: ABORIGINAL AND TORRES STRAIT ISLANDER RESULTS (ONLINE). see HOUSING AND URBAN PLANNING—Abstracting, Bibliographies, Statistics

AUSTRALIA. BUREAU OF STATISTICS. AUSTRALIAN HOUSING SURVEY: CONFIDENTIALISED UNIT RECORD FILE ON FLOPPY DISK. see HOUSING AND URBAN PLANNING—Abstracting, Bibliographies, Statistics

AUSTRALIA. BUREAU OF STATISTICS. AUSTRALIAN HOUSING SURVEY: CONFIDENTIALISED UNIT RECORD FILE ON MAGNETIC TAPE. see HOUSING AND URBAN PLANNING—Abstracting, Bibliographies, Statistics

AUSTRALIA. BUREAU OF STATISTICS. AUSTRALIAN HOUSING SURVEY: HOUSING CHARACTERISTICS, COSTS AND CONDITIONS, AUSTRALIA (ONLINE). see HOUSING AND URBAN PLANNING—Abstracting, Bibliographies, Statistics

AUSTRALIA. BUREAU OF STATISTICS. AUSTRALIAN HOUSING SURVEY: SELECTED FINDINGS (ONLINE). see HOUSING AND URBAN PLANNING—Abstracting, Bibliographies, Statistics

AUSTRALIA. BUREAU OF STATISTICS. AUSTRALIAN HOUSING SURVEY: USER GUIDE (ONLINE). see HOUSING AND URBAN PLANNING—Abstracting, Bibliographies, Statistics

AUSTRALIA. BUREAU OF STATISTICS. AUSTRALIAN INDIGENOUS GEOGRAPHICAL CLASSIFICATION. see GEOGRAPHY—Abstracting, Bibliographies, Statistics

AUSTRALIA. BUREAU OF STATISTICS. AUSTRALIAN INDIGENOUS STATISTICS CATALOGUE ON FLOPPY DISK. see POLITICAL SCIENCE—Abstracting, Bibliographies, Statistics

AUSTRALIA. BUREAU OF STATISTICS. AUSTRALIAN INDUSTRY (ONLINE). see BUSINESS AND ECONOMICS—Abstracting, Bibliographies, Statistics

AUSTRALIA. BUREAU OF STATISTICS. AUSTRALIAN LABOUR MARKET STATISTICS (ONLINE). see BUSINESS AND ECONOMICS—Abstracting, Bibliographies, Statistics

AUSTRALIA. BUREAU OF STATISTICS. AUSTRALIAN NATIONAL ACCOUNTS: FINANCIAL ACCOUNTS (ONLINE). see BUSINESS AND ECONOMICS—Abstracting, Bibliographies, Statistics

AUSTRALIA. BUREAU OF STATISTICS. AUSTRALIAN NATIONAL ACCOUNTS: INPUT-OUTPUT TABLES (ONLINE). see BUSINESS AND ECONOMICS—Abstracting, Bibliographies, Statistics

AUSTRALIA. BUREAU OF STATISTICS. AUSTRALIAN NATIONAL ACCOUNTS: INPUT-OUTPUT TABLES (PRODUCT DETAILS) (ONLINE). see BUSINESS AND ECONOMICS—Abstracting, Bibliographies, Statistics

AUSTRALIA. BUREAU OF STATISTICS. AUSTRALIAN NATIONAL ACCOUNTS: NATIONAL INCOME, EXPENDITURE AND PRODUCT (ONLINE). see BUSINESS AND ECONOMICS—Abstracting, Bibliographies, Statistics

AUSTRALIA. BUREAU OF STATISTICS. AUSTRALIAN NATIONAL ACCOUNTS: NON-PROFIT INSTITUTIONS SATELLITE ACCOUNT (ONLINE). see BUSINESS AND ECONOMICS—Abstracting, Bibliographies, Statistics

AUSTRALIA. BUREAU OF STATISTICS. AUSTRALIAN NATIONAL ACCOUNTS: STATE ACCOUNTS (ANNUAL) (ONLINE). see BUSINESS AND ECONOMICS—Abstracting, Bibliographies, Statistics

AUSTRALIA. BUREAU OF STATISTICS. AUSTRALIAN NATIONAL ACCOUNTS: TOURISM SATELLITE ACCOUNT (ONLINE). see TRAVEL AND TOURISM—Abstracting, Bibliographies, Statistics

AUSTRALIA. BUREAU OF STATISTICS. AUSTRALIAN SMALL BUSINESS OPERATORS - FINDINGS FROM THE 2005 AND 2006 CHARACTERISTICS OF SMALL BUSINESS SURVEYS (ONLINE). see BUSINESS AND ECONOMICS—Abstracting, Bibliographies, Statistics

AUSTRALIA. BUREAU OF STATISTICS. AUSTRALIAN SOCIAL TRENDS. see SOCIAL SCIENCES: COMPREHENSIVE WORKS—Abstracting, Bibliographies, Statistics

AUSTRALIA. BUREAU OF STATISTICS. AUSTRALIAN STANDARD CLASSIFICATION OF CULTURAL AND ETHNIC GROUPS (ONLINE). see POPULATION STUDIES—Abstracting, Bibliographies, Statistics

AUSTRALIA. BUREAU OF STATISTICS. AUSTRALIAN STANDARD CLASSIFICATION OF DRUGS OF CONCERN (ONLINE). see DRUG ABUSE AND ALCOHOLISM—Abstracting, Bibliographies, Statistics

AUSTRALIA. BUREAU OF STATISTICS. AUSTRALIAN STANDARD CLASSIFICATION OF EDUCATION. see EDUCATION—Abstracting, Bibliographies, Statistics

AUSTRALIA. BUREAU OF STATISTICS. AUSTRALIAN STANDARD CLASSIFICATION OF LANGUAGES (ONLINE). see LINGUISTICS—Abstracting, Bibliographies, Statistics

AUSTRALIA. BUREAU OF STATISTICS. AUSTRALIAN STANDARD CLASSIFICATION OF OCCUPATION, LINK FILE. see OCCUPATIONS AND CAREERS—Abstracting, Bibliographies, Statistics

AUSTRALIA. BUREAU OF STATISTICS. AUSTRALIAN STANDARD CLASSIFICATION OF OCCUPATIONS - MANUAL CODING SYSTEM: OCCUPATION LEVEL. see OCCUPATIONS AND CAREERS—Abstracting, Bibliographies, Statistics

AUSTRALIA. BUREAU OF STATISTICS. AUSTRALIAN STANDARD CLASSIFICATION OF RELIGIOUS GROUPS (ONLINE). see RELIGIONS AND THEOLOGY—Abstracting, Bibliographies, Statistics

AUSTRALIA. BUREAU OF STATISTICS. AUSTRALIAN STANDARD CLASSIFICATION OF VISITOR ACCOMMODATION (ONLINE). see HOTELS AND RESTAURANTS—Abstracting, Bibliographies, Statistics

AUSTRALIA. BUREAU OF STATISTICS. AUSTRALIAN STANDARD GEOGRAPHICAL CLASSIFICATION (ASGC) DIGITAL BOUNDARIES (INTERCENSAL), AUSTRALIA (ONLINE). see GEOGRAPHY—Abstracting, Bibliographies, Statistics

AUSTRALIA. BUREAU OF STATISTICS. AUSTRALIAN STANDARD GEOGRAPHICAL CLASSIFICATION (ONLINE). see GEOGRAPHY—Abstracting, Bibliographies, Statistics

AUSTRALIA. BUREAU OF STATISTICS. AUSTRALIAN STANDARD OFFENCE CLASSIFICATION (ONLINE). see CRIMINOLOGY AND LAW ENFORCEMENT—Abstracting, Bibliographies, Statistics

AUSTRALIA. BUREAU OF STATISTICS. AUSTRALIAN SYSTEM OF GOVERNMENT FINANCE STATISTICS: CONCEPTS, SOURCES AND METHODS (ONLINE). see BUSINESS AND ECONOMICS—Abstracting, Bibliographies, Statistics

AUSTRALIA. BUREAU OF STATISTICS. AUSTRALIAN SYSTEM OF NATIONAL ACCOUNTS (ONLINE). see BUSINESS AND ECONOMICS—Abstracting, Bibliographies, Statistics

AUSTRALIA. BUREAU OF STATISTICS. AUSTRALIAN SYSTEM OF NATIONAL ACCOUNTS: CONCEPTS, SOURCES AND METHODS (ONLINE). see BUSINESS AND ECONOMICS—Abstracting, Bibliographies, Statistics

AUSTRALIA. BUREAU OF STATISTICS. AUSTRALIAN TRANSPORT FREIGHT COMMODITY CLASSIFICATION AND AUSTRALIAN PACK CLASSIFICATION (ONLINE). see TRANSPORTATION—Abstracting, Bibliographies, Statistics

AUSTRALIA. BUREAU OF STATISTICS. AUSTRALIAN TRANSPORT FREIGHT COMMODITY CLASSIFICATION ON FLOPPY DISK. see TRANSPORTATION—Abstracting, Bibliographies, Statistics

AUSTRALIA. BUREAU OF STATISTICS. AUSTRALIAN WINE AND GRAPE INDUSTRY (ONLINE). see AGRICULTURE—Abstracting, Bibliographies, Statistics

AUSTRALIA. BUREAU OF STATISTICS. AUSTRALIANS AND THE ENVIRONMENT (ONLINE). see ENVIRONMENTAL STUDIES—Abstracting, Bibliographies, Statistics

AUSTRALIA. BUREAU OF STATISTICS. AUSTRALIA'S CHILDREN: THEIR HEALTH AND WELLBEING. see SOCIAL SERVICES AND WELFARE—Abstracting, Bibliographies, Statistics

AUSTRALIA. BUREAU OF STATISTICS. AUSTRALIA'S ENVIRONMENT: ISSUES AND TRENDS. see ENVIRONMENTAL STUDIES—Abstracting, Bibliographies, Statistics

AUSTRALIA. BUREAU OF STATISTICS. AUSTRALIA'S YOUNG PEOPLE: THEIR HEALTH AND WELLBEING. see SOCIAL SERVICES AND WELFARE—Abstracting, Bibliographies, Statistics

AUSTRALIA. BUREAU OF STATISTICS. AVERAGE RETAIL PRICES OF SELECTED ITEMS, EIGHT CAPITAL CITIES (ONLINE). see BUSINESS AND ECONOMICS—Abstracting, Bibliographies, Statistics

AUSTRALIA. BUREAU OF STATISTICS. AVERAGE WEEKLY EARNINGS, AUSTRALIA (ONLINE). see BUSINESS AND ECONOMICS—Abstracting, Bibliographies, Statistics

AUSTRALIA. BUREAU OF STATISTICS. BALANCE OF PAYMENTS AND INTERNATIONAL INVESTMENT POSITION, AUSTRALIA (QUARTERLY) (ONLINE). see BUSINESS AND ECONOMICS—Abstracting, Bibliographies, Statistics

AUSTRALIA. BUREAU OF STATISTICS. BALANCE OF PAYMENTS AND INTERNATIONAL INVESTMENT POSITION, AUSTRALIA - CONCEPTS, SOURCES AND METHODS (ONLINE). see BUSINESS AND ECONOMICS—Abstracting, Bibliographies, Statistics

AUSTRALIA. BUREAU OF STATISTICS. BALANCE OF PAYMENTS, AUSTRALIA - QUARTERLY FORWARD SEASONAL FACTORS SERVICE (ONLINE). see BUSINESS AND ECONOMICS—Abstracting, Bibliographies, Statistics

AUSTRALIA. BUREAU OF STATISTICS. BIRTHS, AUSTRALIA (ONLINE). see POPULATION STUDIES—Abstracting, Bibliographies, Statistics

AUSTRALIA. BUREAU OF STATISTICS. BOOK PUBLISHERS, AUSTRALIA (ONLINE). see PUBLISHING AND BOOK TRADE—Abstracting, Bibliographies, Statistics

AUSTRALIA. BUREAU OF STATISTICS. BOOK RETAILERS, AUSTRALIA (ONLINE). see PUBLISHING AND BOOK TRADE—Abstracting, Bibliographies, Statistics

AUSTRALIA. BUREAU OF STATISTICS. BOTANIC GARDENS, AUSTRALIA (ONLINE). see GARDENING AND HORTICULTURE—Abstracting, Bibliographies, Statistics

AUSTRALIA. BUREAU OF STATISTICS. BUILDING ACTIVITY, AUSTRALIA (ONLINE). see HOUSING AND URBAN PLANNING—Abstracting, Bibliographies, Statistics

AUSTRALIA. BUREAU OF STATISTICS. BUILDING ACTIVITY, AUSTRALIAN CAPITAL TERRITORY (ONLINE). see BUILDING AND CONSTRUCTION—Abstracting, Bibliographies, Statistics

AUSTRALIA. BUREAU OF STATISTICS. BUILDING APPROVALS, AUSTRALIA (ONLINE). see HOUSING AND URBAN PLANNING—Abstracting, Bibliographies, Statistics

AUSTRALIA. BUREAU OF STATISTICS. BUSINESS EVENTS VENUES INDUSTRY, AUSTRALIA (ONLINE). *see* BUSINESS AND ECONOMICS—Abstracting, Bibliographies, Statistics

AUSTRALIA. BUREAU OF STATISTICS. BUSINESS EXITS, AUSTRALIA. *see* BUSINESS AND ECONOMICS—Abstracting, Bibliographies, Statistics

AUSTRALIA. BUREAU OF STATISTICS. BUSINESS INDICATORS, AUSTRALIA (ONLINE). *see* BUSINESS AND ECONOMICS—Abstracting, Bibliographies, Statistics

AUSTRALIA. BUREAU OF STATISTICS. BUSINESS OPERATIONS AND INDUSTRY PERFORMANCE, AUSTRALIA (ONLINE). *see* BUSINESS AND ECONOMICS—Abstracting, Bibliographies, Statistics

AUSTRALIA. BUREAU OF STATISTICS. BUSINESS OPERATIONS AND INDUSTRY PERFORMANCE, AUSTRALIA, PRELIMINARY (ONLINE). *see* BUSINESS AND ECONOMICS—Abstracting, Bibliographies, Statistics

AUSTRALIA. BUREAU OF STATISTICS. BUSINESS REGISTER CONSULTANCY - LOCATIONS (ONLINE). *see* BUSINESS AND ECONOMICS—Abstracting, Bibliographies, Statistics

AUSTRALIA. BUREAU OF STATISTICS. BUSINESS REGISTER CONSULTANCY - MANAGEMENT UNITS (ONLINE). *see* BUSINESS AND ECONOMICS—Abstracting, Bibliographies, Statistics

AUSTRALIA. BUREAU OF STATISTICS. BUSINESS SPONSORSHIP, AUSTRALIA (ONLINE). *see* BUSINESS AND ECONOMICS—Abstracting, Bibliographies, Statistics

AUSTRALIA. BUREAU OF STATISTICS. BUSINESS USE OF INFORMATION TECHNOLOGY (ONLINE). *see* COMPUTERS—Abstracting, Bibliographies, Statistics

AUSTRALIA. BUREAU OF STATISTICS. BUSINESS USE OF INFORMATION TECHNOLOGY, PRELIMINARY (ONLINE). *see* COMPUTERS—Abstracting, Bibliographies, Statistics

AUSTRALIA. BUREAU OF STATISTICS. CAFES, RESTAURANTS AND CATERING SERVICES, AUSTRALIA (ONLINE). *see* HOTELS AND RESTAURANTS—Abstracting, Bibliographies, Statistics

AUSTRALIA. BUREAU OF STATISTICS. CANBERRA. A SOCIAL ATLAS. *see* POPULATION STUDIES—Abstracting, Bibliographies, Statistics

AUSTRALIA. BUREAU OF STATISTICS. CANCER IN AUSTRALIA. *see* MEDICAL SCIENCES—Oncology

AUSTRALIA. BUREAU OF STATISTICS. CAREER EXPERIENCE, AUSTRALIA (ONLINE). *see* OCCUPATIONS AND CAREERS—Abstracting, Bibliographies, Statistics

AUSTRALIA. BUREAU OF STATISTICS. CARING IN THE COMMUNITY, AUSTRALIA (ONLINE). *see* SOCIAL SERVICES AND WELFARE—Abstracting, Bibliographies, Statistics

AUSTRALIA. BUREAU OF STATISTICS. CASINOS, AUSTRALIA (ONLINE). *see* SPORTS AND GAMES—Abstracting, Bibliographies, Statistics

AUSTRALIA. BUREAU OF STATISTICS. CAUSES OF DEATH, AUSTRALIA (ONLINE). *see* POPULATION STUDIES—Abstracting, Bibliographies, Statistics

AUSTRALIA. BUREAU OF STATISTICS. CENSUS DICTIONARY (ONLINE). *see* POPULATION STUDIES—Abstracting, Bibliographies, Statistics

AUSTRALIA. BUREAU OF STATISTICS. CENSUS OF POPULATION AND HOUSING: (YEAR) CENSUS SNAPSHOTS. *see* POPULATION STUDIES—Abstracting, Bibliographies, Statistics

AUSTRALIA. BUREAU OF STATISTICS. CENSUS OF POPULATION AND HOUSING: ABORIGINAL AND TORRES STRAIT ISLANDER PEOPLE, AUSTRALIA (ONLINE). *see* POPULATION STUDIES—Abstracting, Bibliographies, Statistics

AUSTRALIA. BUREAU OF STATISTICS. CENSUS OF POPULATION AND HOUSING: ABORIGINAL AND TORRES STRAIT ISLANDER PEOPLE, AUSTRALIAN CAPITAL TERRITORY (ONLINE). *see* POPULATION STUDIES—Abstracting, Bibliographies, Statistics

AUSTRALIA. BUREAU OF STATISTICS. CENSUS OF POPULATION AND HOUSING: AUSTRALIA IN PROFILE - A REGIONAL ANALYSIS (ONLINE). *see* POPULATION STUDIES—Abstracting, Bibliographies, Statistics

AUSTRALIA. BUREAU OF STATISTICS. CENSUS OF POPULATION AND HOUSING: BASIC COMMUNITY PROFILE. *see* POPULATION STUDIES—Abstracting, Bibliographies, Statistics

AUSTRALIA. BUREAU OF STATISTICS. CENSUS OF POPULATION AND HOUSING: CDATA 2001 ADD-ON DATAPACK - EXPANDED COMMUNITY PROFILE (ONLINE). *see* POPULATION STUDIES—Abstracting, Bibliographies, Statistics

AUSTRALIA. BUREAU OF STATISTICS. CENSUS OF POPULATION AND HOUSING: CDATA2001 ADD-ON DATAPACK - ESTIMATED RESIDENT POPULATION. *see* POPULATION STUDIES—Abstracting, Bibliographies, Statistics

AUSTRALIA. BUREAU OF STATISTICS. CENSUS OF POPULATION AND HOUSING: CDATA2001 ADD-ON DATAPACK - EXPANDED COMMUNITY PROFILE. *see* POPULATION STUDIES—Abstracting, Bibliographies, Statistics

AUSTRALIA. BUREAU OF STATISTICS. CENSUS OF POPULATION AND HOUSING: CDATA2001 ADD-ON DATAPACK - INDIGENOUS PROFILE. *see* POPULATION STUDIES—Abstracting, Bibliographies, Statistics

AUSTRALIA. BUREAU OF STATISTICS. CENSUS OF POPULATION AND HOUSING: CDATA2001 ADD-ON DATAPACK - S E I F A. *see* POPULATION STUDIES—Abstracting, Bibliographies, Statistics

AUSTRALIA. BUREAU OF STATISTICS. CENSUS OF POPULATION AND HOUSING: CDATA2001 ADD-ON DATAPACK - USUAL RESIDENTS PROFILE. *see* POPULATION STUDIES—Abstracting, Bibliographies, Statistics

AUSTRALIA. BUREAU OF STATISTICS. CENSUS OF POPULATION AND HOUSING: CDATA2001 ADD-ON DATAPACK - WORKING POPULATION COMMUNITY PROFILE. *see* POPULATION STUDIES—Abstracting, Bibliographies, Statistics

AUSTRALIA. BUREAU OF STATISTICS. CENSUS OF POPULATION AND HOUSING: CDATA2001 - FULL GIS, AUSTRALIA (CD-ROM). *see* POPULATION STUDIES—Abstracting, Bibliographies, Statistics

AUSTRALIA. BUREAU OF STATISTICS. CENSUS OF POPULATION AND HOUSING: CDATA2001 - QUICKBUILD. *see* POPULATION STUDIES—Abstracting, Bibliographies, Statistics

AUSTRALIA. BUREAU OF STATISTICS. CENSUS OF POPULATION AND HOUSING: CDATA96 ADD-ON DATAPAKS. *see* POPULATION STUDIES—Abstracting, Bibliographies, Statistics

AUSTRALIA. BUREAU OF STATISTICS. CENSUS OF POPULATION AND HOUSING: CDATA96 ADD-ON DATAPAKS, AUSTRALIA. *see* POPULATION STUDIES—Abstracting, Bibliographies, Statistics

AUSTRALIA. BUREAU OF STATISTICS. CENSUS OF POPULATION AND HOUSING: CENSUS BASICS, AUSTRALIA. *see* POPULATION STUDIES—Abstracting, Bibliographies, Statistics

AUSTRALIA. BUREAU OF STATISTICS. CENSUS OF POPULATION AND HOUSING: CENSUS BASICS, AUSTRALIAN CAPITAL TERRITORY. *see* POPULATION STUDIES—Abstracting, Bibliographies, Statistics

AUSTRALIA. BUREAU OF STATISTICS. CENSUS OF POPULATION AND HOUSING: CENSUS GEOGRAPHIC AREAS DIGITAL BOUNDARIES, AUSTRALIA (ONLINE). *see* POPULATION STUDIES—Abstracting, Bibliographies, Statistics

AUSTRALIA. BUREAU OF STATISTICS. CENSUS OF POPULATION AND HOUSING: CENSUS GUIDE. *see* POPULATION STUDIES—Abstracting, Bibliographies, Statistics

AUSTRALIA. BUREAU OF STATISTICS. CENSUS OF POPULATION AND HOUSING: CLASSIFICATION COUNTS, AUSTRALIA. *see* POPULATION STUDIES—Abstracting, Bibliographies, Statistics

AUSTRALIA. BUREAU OF STATISTICS. CENSUS OF POPULATION AND HOUSING: COLLECTION DISTRICT AND STATISTICAL LOCAL AREA REFERENCE MAPS, AUSTRALIA. *see* POPULATION STUDIES—Abstracting, Bibliographies, Statistics

AUSTRALIA. BUREAU OF STATISTICS. CENSUS OF POPULATION AND HOUSING: COMMUNITY PROFILES, AUSTRALIA (ONLINE). *see* POPULATION STUDIES—Abstracting, Bibliographies, Statistics

AUSTRALIA. BUREAU OF STATISTICS. CENSUS OF POPULATION AND HOUSING: CUSTOMIZED TABLES, AUSTRALIA. *see* POPULATION STUDIES—Abstracting, Bibliographies, Statistics

AUSTRALIA. BUREAU OF STATISTICS. CENSUS OF POPULATION AND HOUSING: DIGITAL BOUNDARIES, AUSTRALIA. *see* POPULATION STUDIES—Abstracting, Bibliographies, Statistics

AUSTRALIA. BUREAU OF STATISTICS. CENSUS OF POPULATION AND HOUSING: EXPANDED COMMUNITY PROFILE. *see* POPULATION STUDIES—Abstracting, Bibliographies, Statistics

AUSTRALIA. BUREAU OF STATISTICS. CENSUS OF POPULATION AND HOUSING: HOUSEHOLD SAMPLE FILE. *see* POPULATION STUDIES—Abstracting, Bibliographies, Statistics

AUSTRALIA. BUREAU OF STATISTICS. CENSUS OF POPULATION AND HOUSING: INDIGENOUS PROFILE. *see* POPULATION STUDIES—Abstracting, Bibliographies, Statistics

AUSTRALIA. BUREAU OF STATISTICS. CENSUS OF POPULATION AND HOUSING: NATURE AND CONTENT (ONLINE). *see* POPULATION STUDIES—Abstracting, Bibliographies, Statistics

AUSTRALIA. BUREAU OF STATISTICS. CENSUS OF POPULATION AND HOUSING: OCCASIONAL PAPER - COUNTING THE HOMELESS (ONLINE). *see* SOCIAL SERVICES AND WELFARE—Abstracting, Bibliographies, Statistics

AUSTRALIA. BUREAU OF STATISTICS. CENSUS OF POPULATION AND HOUSING: PLACE OF ENUMERATION PROFILE. *see* POPULATION STUDIES—Abstracting, Bibliographies, Statistics

AUSTRALIA. BUREAU OF STATISTICS. CENSUS OF POPULATION AND HOUSING: POPULATION GROWTH AND DISTRIBUTION, AUSTRALIA (ONLINE). *see* POPULATION STUDIES—Abstracting, Bibliographies, Statistics

AUSTRALIA. BUREAU OF STATISTICS. CENSUS OF POPULATION AND HOUSING: SELECTED CHARACTERISTICS FOR URBAN CENTRES AND LOCALITIES, NEW SOUTH WALES AND AUSTRALIAN CAPITAL TERRITORY (ONLINE). *see* POPULATION STUDIES—Abstracting, Bibliographies, Statistics

AUSTRALIA. BUREAU OF STATISTICS. CENSUS OF POPULATION AND HOUSING: SELECTED CHARACTERISTICS FOR URBAN CENTRES, AUSTRALIA (ONLINE). *see* POPULATION STUDIES—Abstracting, Bibliographies, Statistics

AUSTRALIA. BUREAU OF STATISTICS. CENSUS OF POPULATION AND HOUSING: SELECTED EDUCATION AND LABOUR FORCE CHARACTERISTICS, AUSTRALIA (ONLINE). *see* POPULATION STUDIES—Abstracting, Bibliographies, Statistics

AUSTRALIA. BUREAU OF STATISTICS. CENSUS OF POPULATION AND HOUSING: SELECTED EDUCATION AND LABOUR FORCE CHARACTERISTICS FOR STATISTICAL LOCAL AREAS, AUSTRALIAN CAPITAL TERRITORY (ONLINE). *see* POPULATION STUDIES—Abstracting, Bibliographies, Statistics

AUSTRALIA. BUREAU OF STATISTICS. CENSUS OF POPULATION AND HOUSING: SELECTED SOCIAL AND HOUSING CHARACTERISTICS, AUSTRALIA (ONLINE). *see* POPULATION STUDIES—Abstracting, Bibliographies, Statistics

AUSTRALIA. BUREAU OF STATISTICS. CENSUS OF POPULATION AND HOUSING: SELECTED SOCIAL AND HOUSING CHARACTERISTICS FOR STATISTICAL LOCAL AREAS, AUSTRALIAN CAPITAL TERRITORY (ONLINE). *see* POPULATION STUDIES—Abstracting, Bibliographies, Statistics

AUSTRALIA. BUREAU OF STATISTICS. CENSUS OF POPULATION AND HOUSING: SOCIO-ECONOMIC INDEXES FOR AREAS, AUSTRALIA. *see* POPULATION STUDIES—Abstracting, Bibliographies, Statistics

AUSTRALIA. BUREAU OF STATISTICS. CENSUS OF POPULATION AND HOUSING: THEMATIC PROFILE SERVICE, AUSTRALIA. *see* POPULATION STUDIES—Abstracting, Bibliographies, Statistics

AUSTRALIA. BUREAU OF STATISTICS. CENSUS OF POPULATION AND HOUSING: TIME SERIES PROFILE. *see* POPULATION STUDIES—Abstracting, Bibliographies, Statistics

AUSTRALIA. BUREAU OF STATISTICS. CENSUS OF POPULATION AND HOUSING: WORKING POPULATION PROFILE. *see* POPULATION STUDIES—Abstracting, Bibliographies, Statistics

AUSTRALIA. BUREAU OF STATISTICS. CHILD CARE, AUSTRALIA (ONLINE). *see* CHILDREN AND YOUTH—Abstracting, Bibliographies, Statistics

AUSTRALIA. BUREAU OF STATISTICS. CHILDREN, AUSTRALIA: A SOCIAL REPORT (ONLINE). *see* CHILDREN AND YOUTH—Abstracting, Bibliographies, Statistics

AUSTRALIA. BUREAU OF STATISTICS. CHILDREN'S HEALTH SCREENING (ONLINE). *see* MEDICAL SCIENCES—Abstracting, Bibliographies, Statistics

AUSTRALIA. BUREAU OF STATISTICS. CHILDREN'S IMMUNISATION, AUSTRALIA (ONLINE). *see* MEDICAL SCIENCES—Abstracting, Bibliographies, Statistics

AUSTRALIA. BUREAU OF STATISTICS. CHILDREN'S PARTICIPATION IN CULTURAL AND LEISURE ACTIVITIES, AUSTRALIA (ONLINE). *see* LEISURE AND RECREATION—Abstracting, Bibliographies, Statistics

AUSTRALIA. BUREAU OF STATISTICS. CHIROPRACTIC AND OSTEOPATHIC SERVICES, AUSTRALIA (ONLINE). *see* MEDICAL SCIENCES—Abstracting, Bibliographies, Statistics

AUSTRALIA. BUREAU OF STATISTICS. CLEANING SERVICES INDUSTRY, AUSTRALIA (ONLINE). *see* HOME ECONOMICS—Abstracting, Bibliographies, Statistics

AUSTRALIA. BUREAU OF STATISTICS. CLUBS, PUBS, TAVERNS AND BARS, AUSTRALIA (ONLINE). *see* HOTELS AND RESTAURANTS—Abstracting, Bibliographies, Statistics

AUSTRALIA. BUREAU OF STATISTICS. COLLECTION DISTRICT COMPARABILITY LISTING, AUSTRALIA. *see* POPULATION STUDIES—Abstracting, Bibliographies, Statistics

AUSTRALIA. BUREAU OF STATISTICS. COLONIAL MICROFICHE SERIES - COLONIAL STATISTICS. *see* HISTORY—Abstracting, Bibliographies, Statistics

AUSTRALIA. BUREAU OF STATISTICS. COMMERCIAL ART GALLERIES, AUSTRALIA (ONLINE). *see* MUSEUMS AND ART GALLERIES—Abstracting, Bibliographies, Statistics

AUSTRALIA. BUREAU OF STATISTICS. COMMUNITY ATTITUDES TO CRIME AND POLICING, AUSTRALIA. *see* CRIMINOLOGY AND LAW ENFORCEMENT—Abstracting, Bibliographies, Statistics

AUSTRALIA. BUREAU OF STATISTICS. COMMUNITY SERVICES, AUSTRALIA (ONLINE). *see* SOCIAL SERVICES AND WELFARE—Abstracting, Bibliographies, Statistics

AUSTRALIA. BUREAU OF STATISTICS. COMMUNITY SERVICES, AUSTRALIA, PRELIMINARY (ONLINE). *see* SOCIAL SERVICES AND WELFARE—Abstracting, Bibliographies, Statistics

AUSTRALIA. BUREAU OF STATISTICS. COMPLETE SET OF SOCIAL ATLASES. *see* POPULATION STUDIES—Abstracting, Bibliographies, Statistics

AUSTRALIA. BUREAU OF STATISTICS. COMPUTING SERVICES INDUSTRY, AUSTRALIA. *see* COMPUTERS—Abstracting, Bibliographies, Statistics

AUSTRALIA. BUREAU OF STATISTICS. CONCEPTS, SOURCES AND METHODS FOR AUSTRALIA'S WATER AND GREENHOUSE GAS EMISSIONS ACCOUNTS. *see* ENERGY—Abstracting, Bibliographies, Statistics

AUSTRALIA. BUREAU OF STATISTICS. CONSTRUCTION ACTIVITY: CHAIN VOLUME MEASURES, AUSTRALIA (ONLINE). *see* HOUSING AND URBAN PLANNING—Abstracting, Bibliographies, Statistics

AUSTRALIA. BUREAU OF STATISTICS. CONSTRUCTION WORK DONE, AUSTRALIA, PRELIMINARY (ONLINE). *see* HOUSING AND URBAN PLANNING—Abstracting, Bibliographies, Statistics

AUSTRALIA. BUREAU OF STATISTICS. CONSULTANT ENGINEERING SERVICES, AUSTRALIA (ONLINE). *see* ENGINEERING—Abstracting, Bibliographies, Statistics

AUSTRALIA. BUREAU OF STATISTICS. CONSUMER PRICE INDEX, AUSTRALIA (ONLINE). *see* BUSINESS AND ECONOMICS—Abstracting, Bibliographies, Statistics

AUSTRALIA. BUREAU OF STATISTICS. CONSUMER PRICE INDEX: CONCORDANCE WITH HOUSEHOLD EXPENDITURE CLASSIFICATION, AUSTRALIA (ONLINE). *see* BUSINESS AND ECONOMICS—Abstracting, Bibliographies, Statistics

AUSTRALIA. BUREAU OF STATISTICS. CONSUMER PRICE INDEX STANDARD DATA REPORT: CAPITAL CITIES INDEX NUMBERS BY EXPENDITURE CLASS. *see* BUSINESS AND ECONOMICS—Abstracting, Bibliographies, Statistics

AUSTRALIA. BUREAU OF STATISTICS. CORRECTIVE SERVICES, AUSTRALIA (ONLINE). *see* LAW—Abstracting, Bibliographies, Statistics

AUSTRALIA. BUREAU OF STATISTICS. CRIME AND SAFETY, AUSTRALIA (ONLINE). *see* CRIMINOLOGY AND LAW ENFORCEMENT—Abstracting, Bibliographies, Statistics

AUSTRALIA. BUREAU OF STATISTICS. CRIMINAL COURTS, AUSTRALIA (ONLINE). *see* LAW—Abstracting, Bibliographies, Statistics

AUSTRALIA. BUREAU OF STATISTICS. CULTURAL FUNDING BY GOVERNMENT, AUSTRALIA (ONLINE). *see* ART—Abstracting, Bibliographies, Statistics

AUSTRALIA. BUREAU OF STATISTICS. CULTURAL INDUSTRIES, AUSTRALIA, PRELIMINARY. *see* BUSINESS AND ECONOMICS—Abstracting, Bibliographies, Statistics

AUSTRALIA. BUREAU OF STATISTICS. DEATHS, AUSTRALIA (ONLINE). *see* POPULATION STUDIES—Abstracting, Bibliographies, Statistics

AUSTRALIA. BUREAU OF STATISTICS. DEATHS DUE TO DISEASES AND CANCERS OF THE RESPIRATORY SYSTEM, AUSTRALIA (ONLINE). *see* MEDICAL SCIENCES—Abstracting, Bibliographies, Statistics

AUSTRALIA. BUREAU OF STATISTICS. DEMOGRAPHIC VARIABLES. *see* POPULATION STUDIES—Abstracting, Bibliographies, Statistics

S

AUSTRALIA. BUREAU OF STATISTICS. DENTAL SERVICES, AUSTRALIA (ONLINE). *see* MEDICAL SCIENCES—Abstracting, Bibliographies, Statistics

AUSTRALIA. BUREAU OF STATISTICS. DETAILED INDUSTRY PERFORMANCE, INCORPORATING BUSINESS INCOME TAX DATA, AUSTRALIA. *see* BUSINESS AND ECONOMICS—Abstracting, Bibliographies, Statistics

AUSTRALIA. BUREAU OF STATISTICS. DIRECTORY OF AGRICULTURAL AND RURAL STATISTICS (ONLINE). *see* AGRICULTURE—Abstracting, Bibliographies, Statistics

AUSTRALIA. BUREAU OF STATISTICS. DIRECTORY OF CAPITAL EXPENDITURE DATA SOURCES AND RELATED STATISTICS. *see* BUSINESS AND ECONOMICS—Abstracting, Bibliographies, Statistics

AUSTRALIA. BUREAU OF STATISTICS. DIRECTORY OF CENSUS STATISTICS (ONLINE). *see* POPULATION STUDIES—Abstracting, Bibliographies, Statistics

AUSTRALIA. BUREAU OF STATISTICS. DIRECTORY OF CHILD AND FAMILY STATISTICS (ONLINE). *see* POPULATION STUDIES—Abstracting, Bibliographies, Statistics

AUSTRALIA. BUREAU OF STATISTICS. DIRECTORY OF CONSTRUCTION STATISTICS. *see* BUILDING AND CONSTRUCTION—Abstracting, Bibliographies, Statistics

AUSTRALIA. BUREAU OF STATISTICS. DIRECTORY OF CULTURE AND LEISURE STATISTICS - WEB SITE VERSION. *see* SPORTS AND GAMES—Abstracting, Bibliographies, Statistics

AUSTRALIA. BUREAU OF STATISTICS. DIRECTORY OF ELECTRICITY, GAS, WATER AND SEWERAGE STATISTICS (ONLINE). *see* ENERGY—Electrical Energy

AUSTRALIA. BUREAU OF STATISTICS. DIRECTORY OF ENERGY STATISTICS (ONLINE). *see* ENERGY—Abstracting, Bibliographies, Statistics

AUSTRALIA. BUREAU OF STATISTICS. DIRECTORY OF HOUSING RELATED STATISTICS. *see* HOUSING AND URBAN PLANNING—Abstracting, Bibliographies, Statistics

AUSTRALIA. BUREAU OF STATISTICS. DIRECTORY OF INDUSTRIAL RELATIONS STATISTICS (ONLINE). *see* BUSINESS AND ECONOMICS—Abstracting, Bibliographies, Statistics

AUSTRALIA. BUREAU OF STATISTICS. DIRECTORY OF LABOUR MARKET AND SOCIAL SURVEY DATA (ONLINE). *see* BUSINESS AND ECONOMICS—Abstracting, Bibliographies, Statistics

AUSTRALIA. BUREAU OF STATISTICS. DIRECTORY OF MINING STATISTICS (ONLINE). *see* MINES AND MINING INDUSTRY—Abstracting, Bibliographies, Statistics

AUSTRALIA. BUREAU OF STATISTICS. DIRECTORY OF SUPERANNUATION RELATED STATISTICS. *see* BUSINESS AND ECONOMICS—Abstracting, Bibliographies, Statistics

AUSTRALIA. BUREAU OF STATISTICS. DIRECTORY OF TOURISM STATISTICS (ONLINE). *see* TRAVEL AND TOURISM—Abstracting, Bibliographies, Statistics

AUSTRALIA. BUREAU OF STATISTICS. DIRECTORY OF TRANSPORT STATISTICS (ONLINE). *see* TRANSPORTATION—Abstracting, Bibliographies, Statistics

AUSTRALIA. BUREAU OF STATISTICS. DISABILITY, AGEING AND CARERS, AUSTRALIA: DISABILITY AND LONG-TERM HEALTH CONDITIONS (ONLINE). *see* SOCIAL SERVICES AND WELFARE—Abstracting, Bibliographies, Statistics

AUSTRALIA. BUREAU OF STATISTICS. DISABILITY, AGEING AND CARERS, AUSTRALIA: HEARING IMPAIRMENT (ONLINE). *see* SOCIAL SERVICES AND WELFARE—Abstracting, Bibliographies, Statistics

AUSTRALIA. BUREAU OF STATISTICS. DISABILITY, AGEING AND CARERS, AUSTRALIA: SUMMARY OF FINDINGS (ONLINE). *see* SOCIAL SERVICES AND WELFARE—Abstracting, Bibliographies, Statistics

AUSTRALIA. BUREAU OF STATISTICS. DISABILITY, AGEING AND CARERS, AUSTRALIA: VISUAL IMPAIRMENT (ONLINE). *see* SOCIAL SERVICES AND WELFARE—Abstracting, Bibliographies, Statistics

AUSTRALIA. BUREAU OF STATISTICS. DISABILITY, AGEING AND CARERS, SUMMARY TABLES, AUSTRALIAN CAPITAL TERRITORY (ONLINE). *see* SOCIAL SERVICES AND WELFARE—Abstracting, Bibliographies, Statistics

AUSTRALIA. BUREAU OF STATISTICS. DISABILITY, AGEING AND CARERS: USER GUIDE, AUSTRALIA (ONLINE). *see* SOCIAL SERVICES AND WELFARE—Abstracting, Bibliographies, Statistics

AUSTRALIA. BUREAU OF STATISTICS. DISABILITY AND DISABLING CONDITIONS (ONLINE). *see* SOCIAL SERVICES AND WELFARE—Abstracting, Bibliographies, Statistics

AUSTRALIA. BUREAU OF STATISTICS. EDUCATION AND TRAINING EXPERIENCE, AUSTRALIA (ONLINE). *see* BUSINESS AND ECONOMICS—Abstracting, Bibliographies, Statistics

AUSTRALIA. BUREAU OF STATISTICS. EDUCATION AND TRAINING INDICATORS, AUSTRALIA (ONLINE). *see* EDUCATION—Abstracting, Bibliographies, Statistics

AUSTRALIA. BUREAU OF STATISTICS. EDUCATION AND WORK, AUSTRALIA (ONLINE). *see* OCCUPATIONS AND CAREERS—Abstracting, Bibliographies, Statistics

AUSTRALIA. BUREAU OF STATISTICS. ELECTRICITY, GAS, WATER AND WASTE SERVICES, AUSTRALIA (ONLINE). *see* ENERGY—Abstracting, Bibliographies, Statistics

AUSTRALIA. BUREAU OF STATISTICS. EMPLOYEE EARNINGS AND HOURS, AUSTRALIA (ONLINE). *see* BUSINESS AND ECONOMICS—Abstracting, Bibliographies, Statistics

AUSTRALIA. BUREAU OF STATISTICS. EMPLOYEE EARNINGS AND HOURS, AUSTRALIA, PRELIMINARY (ONLINE). *see* BUSINESS AND ECONOMICS—Abstracting, Bibliographies, Statistics

AUSTRALIA. BUREAU OF STATISTICS. EMPLOYEE EARNINGS AND HOURS, STATES AND AUSTRALIA - DATA SERVICE. *see* BUSINESS AND ECONOMICS—Abstracting, Bibliographies, Statistics

AUSTRALIA. BUREAU OF STATISTICS. EMPLOYEE EARNINGS, BENEFITS AND TRADE UNION MEMBERSHIP, AUSTRALIA (ONLINE). *see* BUSINESS AND ECONOMICS—Abstracting, Bibliographies, Statistics

AUSTRALIA. BUREAU OF STATISTICS. EMPLOYER TRAINING EXPENDITURE AND PRACTICES, AUSTRALIA (ONLINE). *see* BUSINESS AND ECONOMICS—Abstracting, Bibliographies, Statistics

AUSTRALIA. BUREAU OF STATISTICS. EMPLOYMENT ARRANGEMENTS, RETIREMENT AND SUPERANNUATION, AUSTRALIA. *see* BUSINESS AND ECONOMICS—Abstracting, Bibliographies, Statistics

AUSTRALIA. BUREAU OF STATISTICS. EMPLOYMENT IN CULTURE, AUSTRALIA (ONLINE). *see* BUSINESS AND ECONOMICS—Abstracting, Bibliographies, Statistics

AUSTRALIA. BUREAU OF STATISTICS. EMPLOYMENT IN SELECTED SPORT AND RECREATION OCCUPATIONS, AUSTRALIA (ONLINE). *see* BUSINESS AND ECONOMICS—Abstracting, Bibliographies, Statistics

AUSTRALIA. BUREAU OF STATISTICS. EMPLOYMENT IN SPORT AND RECREATION, AUSTRALIA (ONLINE). *see* SPORTS AND GAMES—Abstracting, Bibliographies, Statistics

AUSTRALIA. BUREAU OF STATISTICS. EMPLOYMENT SERVICES, AUSTRALIA (ONLINE). *see* BUSINESS AND ECONOMICS—Abstracting, Bibliographies, Statistics

AUSTRALIA. BUREAU OF STATISTICS. ENGINEERING CONSTRUCTION ACTIVITY, AUSTRALIA (ONLINE). *see* BUILDING AND CONSTRUCTION—Abstracting, Bibliographies, Statistics

AUSTRALIA. BUREAU OF STATISTICS. ENVIRONMENT EXPENDITURE, LOCAL GOVERNMENT, AUSTRALIA (ONLINE). *see* ENVIRONMENTAL STUDIES—Abstracting, Bibliographies, Statistics

AUSTRALIA. BUREAU OF STATISTICS. ENVIRONMENT PROTECTION, MINING AND MANUFACTURING INDUSTRIES, AUSTRALIA (ONLINE). *see* ENVIRONMENTAL STUDIES—Abstracting, Bibliographies, Statistics

AUSTRALIA. BUREAU OF STATISTICS. EXPERIMENTAL ESTIMATES AND PROJECTIONS OF INDIGENOUS AUSTRALIANS. *see* POPULATION STUDIES—Abstracting, Bibliographies, Statistics

AUSTRALIA. BUREAU OF STATISTICS. EXPERIMENTAL ESTIMATES, AUSTRALIAN INDUSTRY, A STATE PERSPECTIVE (ONLINE). *see* BUSINESS AND ECONOMICS—Abstracting, Bibliographies, Statistics

AUSTRALIA. BUREAU OF STATISTICS. EXPERIMENTAL ESTIMATES OF THE ABORIGINAL AND TORRES STRAIT ISLANDER POPULATION (ONLINE). *see* POPULATION STUDIES—Abstracting, Bibliographies, Statistics

AUSTRALIA. BUREAU OF STATISTICS. EXPERIMENTAL ESTIMATES, REGIONAL SMALL BUSINESS STATISTICS, AUSTRALIA (ONLINE). *see* BUSINESS AND ECONOMICS—Abstracting, Bibliographies, Statistics

AUSTRALIA. BUREAU OF STATISTICS. EXPERIMENTAL ESTIMATES, REGIONAL WAGE AND SALARY EARNER STATISTICS, AUSTRALIA. *see* BUSINESS AND ECONOMICS—Abstracting, Bibliographies, Statistics

AUSTRALIA. BUREAU OF STATISTICS. EXPERIMENTAL PROJECTIONS OF THE ABORIGINAL AND TORRES STRAIT ISLANDER POPULATION (ONLINE). *see* POPULATION STUDIES—Abstracting, Bibliographies, Statistics

AUSTRALIA. BUREAU OF STATISTICS. FAMILY CHARACTERISTICS AND TRANSITIONS, AUSTRALIA (ONLINE). *see* SOCIAL SERVICES AND WELFARE—Abstracting, Bibliographies, Statistics

AUSTRALIA. BUREAU OF STATISTICS. FAMILY, HOUSEHOLD AND INCOME UNIT VARIABLES. *see* SOCIOLOGY—Abstracting, Bibliographies, Statistics

AUSTRALIA. BUREAU OF STATISTICS. FINANCE ESTIMATES OF COMMONWEALTH PUBLIC TRADING ENTERPRISES, AUSTRALIA (ONLINE). *see* BUSINESS AND ECONOMICS—Abstracting, Bibliographies, Statistics

AUSTRALIA. BUREAU OF STATISTICS. FISH ACCOUNT, AUSTRALIA (ONLINE). *see* FISH AND FISHERIES—Abstracting, Bibliographies, Statistics

AUSTRALIA. BUREAU OF STATISTICS. FOCUS ON FAMILIES - A STATISTICAL SERIES: CARING IN FAMILIES: SUPPORT FOR PERSONS WHO ARE OLDER OR HAVE DISABILITIES (ONLINE). *see* SOCIAL SERVICES AND WELFARE—Abstracting, Bibliographies, Statistics

AUSTRALIA. BUREAU OF STATISTICS. FOREST ACCOUNT, AUSTRALIA. *see* FORESTS AND FORESTRY—Abstracting, Bibliographies, Statistics

AUSTRALIA. BUREAU OF STATISTICS. FORMS OF EMPLOYMENT, AUSTRALIA (ONLINE). *see* BUSINESS AND ECONOMICS—Abstracting, Bibliographies, Statistics

AUSTRALIA. BUREAU OF STATISTICS. FREIGHT MOVEMENTS, AUSTRALIA, SUMMARY (ONLINE). *see* TRANSPORTATION—Abstracting, Bibliographies, Statistics

AUSTRALIA. BUREAU OF STATISTICS. GAMBLING INDUSTRIES, AUSTRALIA, PRELIMINARY (ONLINE). *see* SPORTS AND GAMES—Abstracting, Bibliographies, Statistics

AUSTRALIA. BUREAU OF STATISTICS. GAMBLING SERVICES, AUSTRALIA (ONLINE). *see* SPORTS AND GAMES—Abstracting, Bibliographies, Statistics

AUSTRALIA. BUREAU OF STATISTICS. GENERAL SOCIAL SURVEY: SUMMARY RESULTS, AUSTRALIA (ONLINE). *see* SOCIAL SCIENCES: COMPREHENSIVE WORKS—Abstracting, Bibliographies, Statistics

AUSTRALIA. BUREAU OF STATISTICS. GENEROSITY OF AUSTRALIAN BUSINESSES (ONLINE). *see* BUSINESS AND ECONOMICS—Abstracting, Bibliographies, Statistics

AUSTRALIA. BUREAU OF STATISTICS. GOVERNMENT BENEFITS, TAXES AND HOUSEHOLD INCOME, AUSTRALIA (ONLINE). *see* BUSINESS AND ECONOMICS—Abstracting, Bibliographies, Statistics

AUSTRALIA. BUREAU OF STATISTICS. GOVERNMENT FINANCE STATISTICS, AUSTRALIA (ONLINE). *see* BUSINESS AND ECONOMICS—Abstracting, Bibliographies, Statistics

AUSTRALIA. BUREAU OF STATISTICS. GOVERNMENT FINANCE STATISTICS, EDUCATION, AUSTRALIA (ONLINE). *see* BUSINESS AND ECONOMICS—Abstracting, Bibliographies, Statistics

AUSTRALIA. BUREAU OF STATISTICS. GOVERNMENT FINANCIAL ESTIMATES, AUSTRALIAN CAPITAL TERRITORY, ELECTRONIC DELIVERY (EMAIL). *see* BUSINESS AND ECONOMICS—Abstracting, Bibliographies, Statistics

AUSTRALIA. BUREAU OF STATISTICS. GOVERNMENT TECHNOLOGY, AUSTRALIA (ONLINE). *see* COMPUTERS—Abstracting, Bibliographies, Statistics

AUSTRALIA. BUREAU OF STATISTICS. HEALTH AND COMMUNITY SERVICES LABOUR FORCE. *see* BUSINESS AND ECONOMICS—Abstracting, Bibliographies, Statistics

AUSTRALIA. BUREAU OF STATISTICS. HEALTH IN RURAL AND REMOTE AUSTRALIA. *see* SOCIAL SERVICES AND WELFARE—Abstracting, Bibliographies, Statistics

AUSTRALIA. BUREAU OF STATISTICS. HEALTH INSURANCE SURVEY, AUSTRALIA (ONLINE). *see* INSURANCE—Abstracting, Bibliographies, Statistics

AUSTRALIA. BUREAU OF STATISTICS. HEART, STROKE AND VASCULAR DISEASES AUSTRALIAN FACTS. *see* MEDICAL SCIENCES—Abstracting, Bibliographies, Statistics

AUSTRALIA. BUREAU OF STATISTICS. HIRE INDUSTRIES, AUSTRALIA, PRELIMINARY (ONLINE). *see* BUSINESS AND ECONOMICS—Abstracting, Bibliographies, Statistics

AUSTRALIA. BUREAU OF STATISTICS. HIRE SERVICES, AUSTRALIA (ONLINE). *see* BUSINESS AND ECONOMICS—Abstracting, Bibliographies, Statistics

AUSTRALIA. BUREAU OF STATISTICS. HISTORIC AUSTRALIAN STANDARD GEOGRAPHICAL CLASSIFICATION, DIGITAL BOUNDARY FILES, AUSTRALIA. *see* GEOGRAPHY—Abstracting, Bibliographies, Statistics

AUSTRALIA. BUREAU OF STATISTICS. HOME PRODUCTION OF SELECTED FOODSTUFFS, AUSTRALIA (ONLINE). *see* AGRICULTURE—Abstracting, Bibliographies, Statistics

AUSTRALIA. BUREAU OF STATISTICS. HOSPITALITY INDUSTRIES, AUSTRALIA (ONLINE). *see* BUSINESS AND ECONOMICS—Abstracting, Bibliographies, Statistics

AUSTRALIA. BUREAU OF STATISTICS. HOSPITALS, AUSTRALIA (ONLINE). *see* HEALTH FACILITIES AND ADMINISTRATION—Abstracting, Bibliographies, Statistics

AUSTRALIA. BUREAU OF STATISTICS. HOUSE PRICE INDEXES: EIGHT CAPITAL CITIES (ONLINE). *see* REAL ESTATE—Abstracting, Bibliographies, Statistics

AUSTRALIA. BUREAU OF STATISTICS. HOUSEHOLD AND FAMILY PROJECTIONS, AUSTRALIA (ONLINE). *see* SOCIOLOGY—Abstracting, Bibliographies, Statistics

AUSTRALIA. BUREAU OF STATISTICS. HOUSEHOLD EXPENDITURE SURVEY, AUSTRALIA: CONFIDENTIALISED UNIT RECORD FILE ON CD-ROM. *see* BUSINESS AND ECONOMICS—Abstracting, Bibliographies, Statistics

AUSTRALIA. BUREAU OF STATISTICS. HOUSEHOLD EXPENDITURE SURVEY, AUSTRALIA: DETAILED EXPENDITURE ITEMS (ONLINE). *see* BUSINESS AND ECONOMICS—Abstracting, Bibliographies, Statistics

AUSTRALIA. BUREAU OF STATISTICS. HOUSEHOLD EXPENDITURE SURVEY, AUSTRALIA: HOUSEHOLD CHARACTERISTICS (ONLINE). *see* BUSINESS AND ECONOMICS—Abstracting, Bibliographies, Statistics

AUSTRALIA. BUREAU OF STATISTICS. HOUSEHOLD EXPENDITURE SURVEY, AUSTRALIA: SUMMARY OF RESULTS (ONLINE). *see* BUSINESS AND ECONOMICS—Abstracting, Bibliographies, Statistics

AUSTRALIA. BUREAU OF STATISTICS. HOUSEHOLD EXPENDITURE SURVEY, AUSTRALIA: USER GUIDE (ONLINE). *see* BUSINESS AND ECONOMICS—Abstracting, Bibliographies, Statistics

AUSTRALIA. BUREAU OF STATISTICS. HOUSEHOLD USE OF INFORMATION TECHNOLOGY, AUSTRALIA (ONLINE). *see* COMPUTERS—Abstracting, Bibliographies, Statistics

AUSTRALIA. BUREAU OF STATISTICS. HOUSING AND INFRASTRUCTURE IN ABORIGINAL AND TORRES STRAIT ISLANDER COMMUNITIES, AUSTRALIA (ONLINE). *see* HOUSING AND URBAN PLANNING—Abstracting, Bibliographies, Statistics

AUSTRALIA. BUREAU OF STATISTICS. HOUSING OCCUPANCY AND COSTS, AUSTRALIA (ONLINE). *see* HOUSING AND URBAN PLANNING—Abstracting, Bibliographies, Statistics

AUSTRALIA. BUREAU OF STATISTICS. HOW AUSTRALIA TAKES A CENSUS (ONLINE). *see* POPULATION STUDIES—Abstracting, Bibliographies, Statistics

AUSTRALIA. BUREAU OF STATISTICS. HOW AUSTRALIANS MEASURE UP (ONLINE). *see* PHYSICAL FITNESS AND HYGIENE—Abstracting, Bibliographies, Statistics

AUSTRALIA. BUREAU OF STATISTICS. HOW AUSTRALIANS USE THEIR TIME (ONLINE). *see* HUMANITIES: COMPREHENSIVE WORKS—Abstracting, Bibliographies, Statistics

AUSTRALIA. BUREAU OF STATISTICS. HUMAN RESOURCES BY SELECTED QUALIFICATIONS AND OCCUPATIONS, AUSTRALIA (ONLINE). *see* BUSINESS AND ECONOMICS—Abstracting, Bibliographies, Statistics

AUSTRALIA. BUREAU OF STATISTICS. INDUSTRIAL DISPUTES, AUSTRALIA (MONTHLY) (ONLINE). *see* BUSINESS AND ECONOMICS—Abstracting, Bibliographies, Statistics

AUSTRALIA. BUREAU OF STATISTICS. INFORMATION AND COMMUNICATION TECHNOLOGY, AUSTRALIA (ONLINE). *see* COMPUTERS—Abstracting, Bibliographies, Statistics

AUSTRALIA. BUREAU OF STATISTICS. INFORMATION PAPER: A.B.S. STATISTICS AND THE NEW TAX SYSTEM (ONLINE). *see* BUSINESS AND ECONOMICS—Abstracting, Bibliographies, Statistics

AUSTRALIA. BUREAU OF STATISTICS. INFORMATION PAPER: A B S VIEWS ON REMOTENESS (ONLINE). *see* GEOGRAPHY—Abstracting, Bibliographies, Statistics

001.433 AUS

AUSTRALIA. BUREAU OF STATISTICS. INFORMATION PAPER: A GUIDE TO INTERPRETING TIME SERIES - MONITORING TRENDS (ONLINE). Text in English. 2003. irreg., latest 2003. free (effective 2009). **Document type:** *Government.* **Description:** Explains the main features and commentaries sections concerning most time series are increasingly emphasising the trend series rather than the seasonally adjusted or original data.
Formerly: Australia. Bureau of Statistics. Information Paper: A Guide to Interpreting Time Series - Monitoring Trends (Print)
Media: Online - full text.
Published by: Australian Bureau of Statistics, Locked Bag 10, Belconnen, ACT 2616, Australia. TEL 61-2-92684909, 300-135-070, FAX 61-2-92684654, client.services@abs.gov.au.

AUSTRALIA. BUREAU OF STATISTICS. INFORMATION PAPER: A N Z S C O - AUSTRALIAN AND NEW ZEALAND STANDARD CLASSIFICATION OF OCCUPATIONS. *see* OCCUPATIONS AND CAREERS—Abstracting, Bibliographies, Statistics

AUSTRALIA. BUREAU OF STATISTICS. INFORMATION PAPER: AUSTRALIAN CONSUMER PRICE INDEX 13TH SERIES REVIEW (ONLINE). *see* BUSINESS AND ECONOMICS—Abstracting, Bibliographies, Statistics

AUSTRALIA. BUREAU OF STATISTICS. INFORMATION PAPER: AUSTRALIAN NATIONAL ACCOUNTS, INTRODUCTION OF CHAIN VOLUME AND PRICE INDEXES (ONLINE). *see* BUSINESS AND ECONOMICS—Abstracting, Bibliographies, Statistics

AUSTRALIA. BUREAU OF STATISTICS. INFORMATION PAPER: AUSTRALIAN NATIONAL ACCOUNTS: INTRODUCTION TO INPUT - OUTPUT MULTIPLIERS (ONLINE). *see* BUSINESS AND ECONOMICS—Abstracting, Bibliographies, Statistics

AUSTRALIA. BUREAU OF STATISTICS. INFORMATION PAPER: AUSTRALIAN STANDARD CLASSIFICATION OF EDUCATION (ONLINE). *see* EDUCATION—Abstracting, Bibliographies, Statistics

AUSTRALIA. BUREAU OF STATISTICS. INFORMATION PAPER: AVAILABILITY OF STATISTICS RELATED TO MANUFACTURING (ONLINE). *see* BUSINESS AND ECONOMICS—Abstracting, Bibliographies, Statistics

AUSTRALIA. BUREAU OF STATISTICS. INFORMATION PAPER: CENSUS OF POPULATION AND HOUSING - A B S VIEWS ON CENSUS OUTPUT STRATEGY (ONLINE). *see* POPULATION STUDIES—Abstracting, Bibliographies, Statistics

AUSTRALIA. BUREAU OF STATISTICS. INFORMATION PAPER: CENSUS OF POPULATION AND HOUSING, A.B.S. VIEWS ON CONTENT AND PROCEDURES (ONLINE). *see* POPULATION STUDIES—Abstracting, Bibliographies, Statistics

AUSTRALIA. BUREAU OF STATISTICS. INFORMATION PAPER: CENSUS OF POPULATION AND HOUSING - DETAILS OF UNDERCOUNT. *see* POPULATION STUDIES—Abstracting, Bibliographies, Statistics

AUSTRALIA. BUREAU OF STATISTICS. INFORMATION PAPER - CENSUS OF POPULATION AND HOUSING: LINK BETWEEN AUSTRALIAN STANDARD CLASSIFICATION OF OCCUPATIONS (ASCO) SECOND EDITION AND AUSTRALIAN AND NEW ZEALAND STANDARD CLASSIFICATION OF OCCUPATIONS (ANZSCO). *see* POPULATION STUDIES—Abstracting, Bibliographies, Statistics

AUSTRALIA. BUREAU OF STATISTICS. INFORMATION PAPER: CENSUS OF POPULATION AND HOUSING - PROPOSED PRODUCTS AND SERVICES (ONLINE). *see* POPULATION STUDIES—Abstracting, Bibliographies, Statistics

AUSTRALIA. BUREAU OF STATISTICS. INFORMATION PAPER: CHANGES TO LABOUR FORCE STATISTICS PRODUCTS (ONLINE). *see* BUSINESS AND ECONOMICS—Abstracting, Bibliographies, Statistics

AUSTRALIA. BUREAU OF STATISTICS. INFORMATION PAPER: DEVELOPMENTS IN GOVERNMENT FINANCE STATISTICS (ONLINE). *see* BUSINESS AND ECONOMICS—Abstracting, Bibliographies, Statistics

AUSTRALIA. BUREAU OF STATISTICS. INFORMATION PAPER: EDUCATION, TRAINING AND INFORMATION TECHNOLOGY, AUSTRALIA, (YEAR) - CONFIDENTIALISED UNIT RECORD FILE (ONLINE). *see* EDUCATION—Abstracting, Bibliographies, Statistics

AUSTRALIA. BUREAU OF STATISTICS. INFORMATION PAPER: EXPANDED USE OF BUSINESS INCOME TAX DATA IN A.B.S. ECONOMIC STATISTICS - EXPERIMENTAL ESTIMATES FOR SELECTED INDUSTRIES (ONLINE). *see* BUSINESS AND ECONOMICS—Abstracting, Bibliographies, Statistics

AUSTRALIA. BUREAU OF STATISTICS. INFORMATION PAPER: IMPACT OF REVISED INTERNATIONAL STANDARDS IN THE AUSTRALIAN NATIONAL ACCOUNTS (ONLINE). *see* BUSINESS AND ECONOMICS—Abstracting, Bibliographies, Statistics

AUSTRALIA. BUREAU OF STATISTICS. INFORMATION PAPER: IMPLEMENTATION OF REVISED INTERNATIONAL STANDARDS IN THE AUSTRALIAN NATIONAL ACCOUNTS (ONLINE). *see* BUSINESS AND ECONOMICS—Abstracting, Bibliographies, Statistics

AUSTRALIA. BUREAU OF STATISTICS. INFORMATION PAPER: IMPLEMENTING NEW INTERNATIONAL STATISTICAL STANDARDS IN A.B.S. INTERNATIONAL ACCOUNTS STATISTICS (ONLINE). *see* BUSINESS AND ECONOMICS—Abstracting, Bibliographies, Statistics

AUSTRALIA. BUREAU OF STATISTICS. INFORMATION PAPER: IMPLEMENTING THE REDESIGNED LABOUR FORCE SURVEY QUESTIONNAIRE (ONLINE). *see* BUSINESS AND ECONOMICS—Abstracting, Bibliographies, Statistics

AUSTRALIA. BUREAU OF STATISTICS. INFORMATION PAPER: INTERNATIONAL MERCHANDISE TRADE STATISTICS, AUSTRALIA: DATA CONFIDENTIALITY (ONLINE). *see* BUSINESS AND ECONOMICS—Abstracting, Bibliographies, Statistics

AUSTRALIA. BUREAU OF STATISTICS. INFORMATION PAPER: INTRODUCTION OF CONCURRENT SEASONAL ADJUSTMENT INTO THE RETAIL TRADE SERIES (ONLINE). *see* BUSINESS AND ECONOMICS—Abstracting, Bibliographies, Statistics

AUSTRALIA. BUREAU OF STATISTICS. INFORMATION PAPER: INTRODUCTION OF THE 13TH SERIES AUSTRALIAN CONSUMER PRICE INDEX (ONLINE). *see* BUSINESS AND ECONOMICS—Abstracting, Bibliographies, Statistics

AUSTRALIA. BUREAU OF STATISTICS. INFORMATION PAPER: ISSUES TO BE CONSIDERED DURING THE 13TH SERIES AUSTRALIAN CONSUMER PRICE INDEX REVIEW (ONLINE). *see* BUSINESS AND ECONOMICS—Abstracting, Bibliographies, Statistics

AUSTRALIA. BUREAU OF STATISTICS. INFORMATION PAPER: LABOUR FORCE SURVEY, AUSTRALIA: REVISIONS TO HISTORICAL ANZSIC INDUSTRY DATA. *see* BUSINESS AND ECONOMICS—Abstracting, Bibliographies, Statistics

AUSTRALIA. BUREAU OF STATISTICS. INFORMATION PAPER: LABOUR FORCE SURVEY QUESTIONNAIRE REDESIGN (ONLINE). *see* BUSINESS AND ECONOMICS—Abstracting, Bibliographies, Statistics

AUSTRALIA. BUREAU OF STATISTICS. INFORMATION PAPER: LABOUR FORCE SURVEY SAMPLE DESIGN (ONLINE). *see* BUSINESS AND ECONOMICS—Abstracting, Bibliographies, Statistics

AUSTRALIA. BUREAU OF STATISTICS. INFORMATION PAPER: MEASURING EMPLOYMENT AND UNEMPLOYMENT. *see* BUSINESS AND ECONOMICS—Abstracting, Bibliographies, Statistics

AUSTRALIA. BUREAU OF STATISTICS. INFORMATION PAPER: MEASURING REGION OF ORIGIN MERCHANDISE EXPORTS. *see* BUSINESS AND ECONOMICS—Abstracting, Bibliographies, Statistics

AUSTRALIA. BUREAU OF STATISTICS. INFORMATION PAPER: MENTAL HEALTH AND WELLBEING OF ADULTS, AUSTRALIA, CONFIDENTIALISED UNIT RECORD FILE (ONLINE). *see* SOCIAL SERVICES AND WELFARE—Abstracting, Bibliographies, Statistics

319.4 AUS

AUSTRALIA. BUREAU OF STATISTICS. INFORMATION PAPER: NATIONAL HEALTH SURVEY - CONFIDENTIALISED UNIT RECORD FILES (ONLINE). Text in English. 1978. irreg., latest 2005. free (effective 2009). **Document type:** *Government.* **Description:** Provides technical details of the sample file, information about the data content together with conditions of issue and how to order.
Formerly (until 2001): Australia. Bureau of Statistics. Information Paper: National Health Survey, Sample File on Magnetic Media (Magnetic Tape)
Media: Online - full text.
Published by: Australian Bureau of Statistics, Locked Bag 10, Belconnen, ACT 2616, Australia. TEL 61-2-92684909, 61-2-62527037, 300-135-070, FAX 61-2-62528103, client.services@abs.gov.au.

AUSTRALIA. BUREAU OF STATISTICS. INFORMATION PAPER: NATIONAL NUTRITION SURVEY, CONFIDENTIALISED UNIT RECORD FILE (ONLINE). *see* NUTRITION AND DIETETICS—Abstracting, Bibliographies, Statistics

AUSTRALIA. BUREAU OF STATISTICS. INFORMATION PAPER: OUTCOME OF THE 13TH SERIES AUSTRALIAN CONSUMER PRICE INDEX REVIEW (ONLINE). *see* BUSINESS AND ECONOMICS—Abstracting, Bibliographies, Statistics

AUSTRALIA. BUREAU OF STATISTICS. INFORMATION PAPER: OUTCOMES OF A B S VIEWS ON REMOTENESS CONSULTATION, AUSTRALIA (ONLINE). *see* POPULATION STUDIES—Abstracting, Bibliographies, Statistics

AUSTRALIA. BUREAU OF STATISTICS. INFORMATION PAPER: PRICE INDEXES AND THE NEW TAX SYSTEM (ONLINE). *see* BUSINESS AND ECONOMICS—Abstracting, Bibliographies, Statistics

AUSTRALIA. BUREAU OF STATISTICS. INFORMATION PAPER: PRODUCER PRICE INDEX DEVELOPMENTS (ONLINE). *see* BUSINESS AND ECONOMICS—Abstracting, Bibliographies, Statistics

AUSTRALIA. BUREAU OF STATISTICS. INFORMATION PAPER: QUALITY OF AUSTRALIAN BALANCE OF PAYMENTS STATISTICS (ONLINE). *see* BUSINESS AND ECONOMICS—Abstracting, Bibliographies, Statistics

AUSTRALIA. BUREAU OF STATISTICS. INFORMATION PAPER: QUESTIONNAIRES IN THE LABOUR FORCE. *see* BUSINESS AND ECONOMICS—Abstracting, Bibliographies, Statistics

AUSTRALIA. BUREAU OF STATISTICS. INFORMATION PAPER: REGIONAL LABOUR FORCE STATISTICS (ONLINE). *see* BUSINESS AND ECONOMICS—Abstracting, Bibliographies, Statistics

AUSTRALIA. BUREAU OF STATISTICS. INFORMATION PAPER: REVIEW OF THE IMPORT PRICE INDEX AND EXPORT PRICE INDEX, AUSTRALIA (ONLINE). *see* BUSINESS AND ECONOMICS—Abstracting, Bibliographies, Statistics

AUSTRALIA. BUREAU OF STATISTICS. INFORMATION PAPER: SEASONAL INFLUENCES ON RETAIL TRADE (ONLINE). *see* BUSINESS AND ECONOMICS—Abstracting, Bibliographies, Statistics

AUSTRALIA. BUREAU OF STATISTICS. INFORMATION PAPER: UPGRADED AUSTRALIAN NATIONAL ACCOUNTS (ONLINE). *see* BUSINESS AND ECONOMICS—Abstracting, Bibliographies, Statistics

AUSTRALIA. BUREAU OF STATISTICS. INFORMATION PAPER: UPGRADED AUSTRALIAN NATIONAL ACCOUNTS: FINANCIAL ACCOUNTS (ONLINE). *see* BUSINESS AND ECONOMICS—Abstracting, Bibliographies, Statistics

AUSTRALIA. BUREAU OF STATISTICS. INFORMATION PAPER: UPGRADED BALANCE OF PAYMENTS AND INTERNATIONAL INVESTMENT POSITION STATISTICS (ONLINE). *see* BUSINESS AND ECONOMICS—Abstracting, Bibliographies, Statistics

AUSTRALIA. BUREAU OF STATISTICS. INFORMATION PAPER: USE OF INDIVIDUAL INCOME TAX DATA FOR REGIONAL STATISTICS (ONLINE). *see* BUSINESS AND ECONOMICS—Abstracting, Bibliographies, Statistics

AUSTRALIA. BUREAU OF STATISTICS. INFORMATION PAPER: USING THE A S G C REMOTENESS STRUCTURE TO ANALYSE CHARACTERISTICS OF WAGE AND SALARY EARNERS OF AUSTRALIA. *see* BUSINESS AND ECONOMICS—Abstracting, Bibliographies, Statistics

AUSTRALIA. BUREAU OF STATISTICS. INFORMATION TECHNOLOGY, AUSTRALIA, PRELIMINARY (ONLINE). *see* COMPUTERS—Abstracting, Bibliographies, Statistics

AUSTRALIA. BUREAU OF STATISTICS. INJURIES, AUSTRALIA. *see* MEDICAL SCIENCES—Abstracting, Bibliographies, Statistics

AUSTRALIA. BUREAU OF STATISTICS. INNOVATION IN MANUFACTURING, AUSTRALIA (ONLINE). *see* BUSINESS AND ECONOMICS—Abstracting, Bibliographies, Statistics

AUSTRALIA. BUREAU OF STATISTICS. INNOVATION IN MINING, AUSTRALIA (ONLINE). *see* MINES AND MINING INDUSTRY—Abstracting, Bibliographies, Statistics

AUSTRALIA. BUREAU OF STATISTICS. INNOVATION IN SELECTED INDUSTRIES, AUSTRALIA (ONLINE). *see* BUSINESS AND ECONOMICS—Abstracting, Bibliographies, Statistics

AUSTRALIA. BUREAU OF STATISTICS. INTERNATIONAL HEALTH - HOW AUSTRALIA COMPARES. *see* SOCIAL SERVICES AND WELFARE—Abstracting, Bibliographies, Statistics

AUSTRALIA. BUREAU OF STATISTICS. INTERNATIONAL INVESTMENT POSITION. AUSTRALIA: AUSTRALIAN SECURITIES HELD BY NOMINEES ON BEHALF OF NON-RESIDENTS. *see* BUSINESS AND ECONOMICS—Abstracting, Bibliographies, Statistics

AUSTRALIA. BUREAU OF STATISTICS. INTERNATIONAL INVESTMENT POSITION, AUSTRALIA: SUPPLEMENTARY COUNTRY STATISTICS (ONLINE). *see* BUSINESS AND ECONOMICS—Abstracting, Bibliographies, Statistics

AUSTRALIA. BUREAU OF STATISTICS. INTERNATIONAL MERCHANDISE IMPORTS, AUSTRALIA (ONLINE). *see* BUSINESS AND ECONOMICS—Abstracting, Bibliographies, Statistics

AUSTRALIA. BUREAU OF STATISTICS. INTERNATIONAL MERCHANDISE TRADE, AUSTRALIA: CONCEPTS, SOURCES AND METHODS (ONLINE). *see* BUSINESS AND ECONOMICS—Abstracting, Bibliographies, Statistics

AUSTRALIA. BUREAU OF STATISTICS. INTERNATIONAL TRADE, AUSTRALIA - INFORMATION CONSULTANCY AD HOC SERVICE. *see* BUSINESS AND ECONOMICS—Abstracting, Bibliographies, Statistics

AUSTRALIA. BUREAU OF STATISTICS. INTERNATIONAL TRADE IN GOODS AND SERVICES, AUSTRALIA (ONLINE). *see* BUSINESS AND ECONOMICS—Abstracting, Bibliographies, Statistics

AUSTRALIA. BUREAU OF STATISTICS. INTERNATIONAL TRADE IN GOODS AND SERVICES, AUSTRALIA: MONTHLY FORWARD SEASONAL FACTORS (ONLINE). *see* BUSINESS AND ECONOMICS—Abstracting, Bibliographies, Statistics

AUSTRALIA. BUREAU OF STATISTICS. INTERNATIONAL TRADE IN GOODS AND SERVICES, MONTHLY FORWARD SEASONAL FACTORS SERVICE, AUSTRALIA. *see* BUSINESS AND ECONOMICS—Abstracting, Bibliographies, Statistics

AUSTRALIA. BUREAU OF STATISTICS. INTERNATIONAL TRADE PRICE INDEXES, AUSTRALIA (ONLINE). *see* BUSINESS AND ECONOMICS—Abstracting, Bibliographies, Statistics

AUSTRALIA. BUREAU OF STATISTICS. INTERNET ACTIVITY, AUSTRALIA (ONLINE). *see* COMPUTERS—Abstracting, Bibliographies, Statistics

AUSTRALIA. BUREAU OF STATISTICS. INVOLVEMENT IN ORGANISED SPORT AND PHYSICAL ACTIVITY, AUSTRALIA (ONLINE). *see* BUSINESS AND ECONOMICS—Abstracting, Bibliographies, Statistics

AUSTRALIA. BUREAU OF STATISTICS. INVOLVEMENT IN ORGANIZED SPORT AND PHYSICAL ACTIVITY, AUSTRALIA (ONLINE). *see* SPORTS AND GAMES—Abstracting, Bibliographies, Statistics

AUSTRALIA. BUREAU OF STATISTICS. JOB SEARCH EXPERIENCE, AUSTRALIA (ONLINE). *see* OCCUPATIONS AND CAREERS—Abstracting, Bibliographies, Statistics

AUSTRALIA. BUREAU OF STATISTICS. LABOUR COSTS, AUSTRALIA (ONLINE). *see* BUSINESS AND ECONOMICS—Abstracting, Bibliographies, Statistics

AUSTRALIA. BUREAU OF STATISTICS. LABOUR FORCE, AUSTRALIA (ONLINE). *see* BUSINESS AND ECONOMICS—Abstracting, Bibliographies, Statistics

AUSTRALIA. BUREAU OF STATISTICS. LABOUR FORCE, AUSTRALIA - SEASONAL FACTORS. *see* BUSINESS AND ECONOMICS—Abstracting, Bibliographies, Statistics

AUSTRALIA. BUREAU OF STATISTICS. LABOUR FORCE EXPERIENCE, AUSTRALIA (ONLINE). *see* BUSINESS AND ECONOMICS—Abstracting, Bibliographies, Statistics

AUSTRALIA. BUREAU OF STATISTICS. LABOUR FORCE PROJECTIONS, AUSTRALIA (ONLINE). *see* BUSINESS AND ECONOMICS—Abstracting, Bibliographies, Statistics

AUSTRALIA. BUREAU OF STATISTICS. LABOUR FORCE, SELECTED SUMMARY TABLES, AUSTRALIA (ONLINE). *see* BUSINESS AND ECONOMICS—Abstracting, Bibliographies, Statistics

AUSTRALIA. BUREAU OF STATISTICS. LABOUR FORCE STATUS AND OTHER CHARACTERISTICS OF FAMILIES, AUSTRALIA (ONLINE). *see* BUSINESS AND ECONOMICS—Abstracting, Bibliographies, Statistics

AUSTRALIA. BUREAU OF STATISTICS. LABOUR FORCE STATUS AND OTHER CHARACTERISTICS OF MIGRANTS, AUSTRALIA (ONLINE). *see* BUSINESS AND ECONOMICS—Abstracting, Bibliographies, Statistics

AUSTRALIA. BUREAU OF STATISTICS. LABOUR FORCE SURVEY STANDARD ERRORS (ONLINE). *see* BUSINESS AND ECONOMICS—Abstracting, Bibliographies, Statistics

AUSTRALIA. BUREAU OF STATISTICS. LABOUR MOBILITY, AUSTRALIA (ONLINE). *see* BUSINESS AND ECONOMICS—Abstracting, Bibliographies, Statistics

AUSTRALIA. BUREAU OF STATISTICS. LABOUR PRICE INDEX: CONCEPTS, SOURCES AND METHODS. *see* BUSINESS AND ECONOMICS—Abstracting, Bibliographies, Statistics

AUSTRALIA. BUREAU OF STATISTICS. LABOUR STATISTICS: CONCEPTS, SOURCES AND METHODS (ONLINE). *see* BUSINESS AND ECONOMICS—Abstracting, Bibliographies, Statistics

AUSTRALIA. BUREAU OF STATISTICS. LABOUR STATISTICS IN BRIEF, AUSTRALIA (ONLINE). *see* BUSINESS AND ECONOMICS—Abstracting, Bibliographies, Statistics

AUSTRALIA. BUREAU OF STATISTICS. LEGAL PRACTICES, AUSTRALIA (ONLINE). *see* LAW—Abstracting, Bibliographies, Statistics

AUSTRALIA. BUREAU OF STATISTICS. LENDING FINANCE, AUSTRALIA (ONLINE). *see* BUSINESS AND ECONOMICS—Abstracting, Bibliographies, Statistics

AUSTRALIA. BUREAU OF STATISTICS. LIBRARIES, AUSTRALIA. *see* LIBRARY AND INFORMATION SCIENCES—Abstracting, Bibliographies, Statistics

AUSTRALIA. BUREAU OF STATISTICS. LIVESTOCK AND MEAT, AUSTRALIA (ONLINE). *see* AGRICULTURE—Abstracting, Bibliographies, Statistics

AUSTRALIA. BUREAU OF STATISTICS. LIVESTOCK PRODUCTS, AUSTRALIA (ONLINE). *see* AGRICULTURE—Abstracting, Bibliographies, Statistics

AUSTRALIA. BUREAU OF STATISTICS. LOCATIONS OF WORK, AUSTRALIA (ONLINE). *see* BUSINESS AND ECONOMICS—Abstracting, Bibliographies, Statistics

AUSTRALIA. BUREAU OF STATISTICS. MANAGED FUNDS, AUSTRALIA (ONLINE). *see* BUSINESS AND ECONOMICS—Abstracting, Bibliographies, Statistics

AUSTRALIA. BUREAU OF STATISTICS. MANUFACTURING INDUSTRY, AUSTRALIA (ONLINE). *see* BUSINESS AND ECONOMICS—Abstracting, Bibliographies, Statistics

AUSTRALIA. BUREAU OF STATISTICS. MANUFACTURING INDUSTRY, AUSTRALIA, PRELIMINARY (ONLINE). *see* BUSINESS AND ECONOMICS—Abstracting, Bibliographies, Statistics

AUSTRALIA. BUREAU OF STATISTICS. MANUFACTURING PRODUCTION, AUSTRALIA (ONLINE). *see* BUSINESS AND ECONOMICS—Abstracting, Bibliographies, Statistics

AUSTRALIA. BUREAU OF STATISTICS. MARKET RESEARCH SERVICES, AUSTRALIA (ONLINE). *see* BUSINESS AND ECONOMICS—Abstracting, Bibliographies, Statistics

AUSTRALIA. BUREAU OF STATISTICS. MEASURING AUSTRALIA'S ECONOMY (ONLINE). *see* BUSINESS AND ECONOMICS—Abstracting, Bibliographies, Statistics

AUSTRALIA. BUREAU OF STATISTICS. MEASURING AUSTRALIA'S PROGRESS (ONLINE). *see* BUSINESS AND ECONOMICS—Abstracting, Bibliographies, Statistics

AUSTRALIA. BUREAU OF STATISTICS. MEASURING WELLBEING: FRAMEWORKS FOR AUSTRALIAN SOCIAL STATISTICS (ONLINE). *see* SOCIOLOGY—Abstracting, Bibliographies, Statistics

AUSTRALIA. BUREAU OF STATISTICS. MEDICAL LABOUR FORCE. *see* MEDICAL SCIENCES—Abstracting, Bibliographies, Statistics

AUSTRALIA. BUREAU OF STATISTICS. MENTAL HEALTH AND WELLBEING: PROFILE OF ADULTS, AUSTRALIA (ONLINE). *see* SOCIAL SERVICES AND WELFARE—Abstracting, Bibliographies, Statistics

AUSTRALIA. BUREAU OF STATISTICS. MIGRATION, AUSTRALIA (ONLINE). *see* POPULATION STUDIES—Abstracting, Bibliographies, Statistics

AUSTRALIA. BUREAU OF STATISTICS. MINERAL AND PETROLEUM EXPLORATION, AUSTRALIA (ONLINE). *see* MINES AND MINING INDUSTRY—Abstracting, Bibliographies, Statistics

AUSTRALIA. BUREAU OF STATISTICS. MINING OPERATIONS AUSTRALIA (ONLINE). *see* MINES AND MINING INDUSTRY—Abstracting, Bibliographies, Statistics

AUSTRALIA. BUREAU OF STATISTICS. MODELLERS' DATABASE. *see* BUSINESS AND ECONOMICS—Abstracting, Bibliographies, Statistics

AUSTRALIA. BUREAU OF STATISTICS. MOTION PICTURE EXHIBITION, AUSTRALIA (ONLINE). *see* MOTION PICTURES—Abstracting, Bibliographies, Statistics

AUSTRALIA. BUREAU OF STATISTICS. MOTOR VEHICLE CENSUS, AUSTRALIA (ONLINE). *see* TRANSPORTATION—Abstracting, Bibliographies, Statistics

AUSTRALIA. BUREAU OF STATISTICS. MOTOR VEHICLE HIRE INDUSTRY, AUSTRALIA (ONLINE). *see* TRANSPORTATION—Abstracting, Bibliographies, Statistics

AUSTRALIA. BUREAU OF STATISTICS. MULTIPLE JOBHOLDING, AUSTRALIA (ONLINE). *see* BUSINESS AND ECONOMICS—Abstracting, Bibliographies, Statistics

AUSTRALIA. BUREAU OF STATISTICS. MUSEUMS, AUSTRALIA (ONLINE). *see* MUSEUMS AND ART GALLERIES—Abstracting, Bibliographies, Statistics

AUSTRALIA. BUREAU OF STATISTICS. NATIONAL ABORIGINAL AND TORRES STRAIT ISLANDER SOCIAL SURVEY. *see* POPULATION STUDIES—Abstracting, Bibliographies, Statistics

AUSTRALIA. BUREAU OF STATISTICS. NATIONAL ABORIGINAL AND TORRES STRAIT ISLANDER SURVEY: UNIT RECORD FILE (ONLINE). *see* POPULATION STUDIES—Abstracting, Bibliographies, Statistics

AUSTRALIA. BUREAU OF STATISTICS. NATIONAL HEALTH SURVEY: ABORIGINAL AND TORRES STRAIT ISLANDER RESULTS, AUSTRALIA (ONLINE). *see* POPULATION STUDIES—Abstracting, Bibliographies, Statistics

AUSTRALIA. BUREAU OF STATISTICS. NATIONAL HEALTH SURVEY: ASTHMA AND OTHER RESPIRATORY CONDITIONS, AUSTRALIA (ONLINE). *see* MEDICAL SCIENCES—Abstracting, Bibliographies, Statistics

AUSTRALIA. BUREAU OF STATISTICS. NATIONAL HEALTH SURVEY: CANCER SCREENING, AUSTRALIA (ONLINE). *see* MEDICAL SCIENCES—Abstracting, Bibliographies, Statistics

AUSTRALIA. BUREAU OF STATISTICS. NATIONAL HEALTH SURVEY: CARDIOVASCULAR AND RELATED CONDITIONS, AUSTRALIA (ONLINE). *see* MEDICAL SCIENCES—Abstracting, Bibliographies, Statistics

AUSTRALIA. BUREAU OF STATISTICS. NATIONAL HEALTH SURVEY: DIABETES, AUSTRALIA (ONLINE). *see* MEDICAL SCIENCES—Abstracting, Bibliographies, Statistics

AUSTRALIA. BUREAU OF STATISTICS. NATIONAL HEALTH SURVEY: HEALTH RISK FACTORS, AUSTRALIA (ONLINE). *see* PUBLIC HEALTH AND SAFETY—Abstracting, Bibliographies, Statistics

AUSTRALIA. BUREAU OF STATISTICS. NATIONAL HEALTH SURVEY: INJURIES, AUSTRALIA (ONLINE). *see* PUBLIC HEALTH AND SAFETY—Abstracting, Bibliographies, Statistics

AUSTRALIA. BUREAU OF STATISTICS. NATIONAL HEALTH SURVEY: PRIVATE HEALTH INSURANCE, AUSTRALIA (ONLINE). *see* INSURANCE—Abstracting, Bibliographies, Statistics

AUSTRALIA. BUREAU OF STATISTICS. NATIONAL HEALTH SURVEY: SF36 POPULATION NORMS, AUSTRALIA (ONLINE). *see* POPULATION STUDIES—Abstracting, Bibliographies, Statistics

AUSTRALIA. BUREAU OF STATISTICS. NATIONAL HEALTH SURVEY: SUMMARY OF RESULTS (ONLINE). *see* PUBLIC HEALTH AND SAFETY—Abstracting, Bibliographies, Statistics

AUSTRALIA. BUREAU OF STATISTICS. NATIONAL HEALTH SURVEY: USE OF MEDICATIONS, AUSTRALIA (ONLINE). *see* MEDICAL SCIENCES—Abstracting, Bibliographies, Statistics

AUSTRALIA. BUREAU OF STATISTICS. NATIONAL NUTRITION SURVEY: FOODS EATEN, AUSTRALIA (ONLINE). *see* NUTRITION AND DIETETICS—Abstracting, Bibliographies, Statistics

AUSTRALIA. BUREAU OF STATISTICS. NATIONAL NUTRITION SURVEY: NUTRIENT INTAKES AND PHYSICAL MEASUREMENTS, AUSTRALIA (ONLINE). *see* NUTRITION AND DIETETICS—Abstracting, Bibliographies, Statistics

AUSTRALIA. BUREAU OF STATISTICS. NATIONAL SURVEY OF MENTAL HEALTH AND WELLBEING: USER'S GUIDE (ONLINE). *see* SOCIAL SERVICES AND WELFARE—Abstracting, Bibliographies, Statistics

AUSTRALIA. BUREAU OF STATISTICS. NATURAL RESOURCE ACCOUNTING - AUSTRALIAN ENERGY ACCOUNTS (ONLINE). *see* ENERGY—Abstracting, Bibliographies, Statistics

AUSTRALIA. BUREAU OF STATISTICS. NEW MOTOR VEHICLE REGISTRATION, AUSTRALIA, MOTORCYCLES DATA ON SUPERTABLE (ONLINE). *see* SPORTS AND GAMES—Abstracting, Bibliographies, Statistics

AUSTRALIA. BUREAU OF STATISTICS. NEW SOUTH WALES OFFICE. AUSTRALIAN HOUSING SURVEY: NEW SOUTH WALES - DATA REPORT (ONLINE). *see* POPULATION STUDIES—Abstracting, Bibliographies, Statistics

AUSTRALIA. BUREAU OF STATISTICS. NEW SOUTH WALES OFFICE. CENSUS OF POPULATION AND HOUSING: ABORIGINAL AND TORRES STRAIT ISLANDER PEOPLE, NEW SOUTH WALES (ONLINE). *see* POPULATION STUDIES—Abstracting, Bibliographies, Statistics

AUSTRALIA. BUREAU OF STATISTICS. NEW SOUTH WALES OFFICE. CENSUS OF POPULATION AND HOUSING: CENSUS BASICS, NEW SOUTH WALES. *see* POPULATION STUDIES—Abstracting, Bibliographies, Statistics

AUSTRALIA. BUREAU OF STATISTICS. NEW SOUTH WALES OFFICE. CENSUS OF POPULATION AND HOUSING: SELECTED CHARACTERISTICS FOR URBAN CENTRES AND LOCALITIES, NEW SOUTH WALES AND AUSTRALIAN CAPITAL TERRITORY (ONLINE). *see* POPULATION STUDIES—Abstracting, Bibliographies, Statistics

AUSTRALIA. BUREAU OF STATISTICS. NEW SOUTH WALES OFFICE. CENSUS OF POPULATION AND HOUSING: SELECTED EDUCATION AND LABOUR FORCE CHARACTERISTICS FOR STATISTICAL LOCAL AREAS, NEW SOUTH WALES AND JERVIS BAY (ONLINE). *see* POPULATION STUDIES—Abstracting, Bibliographies, Statistics

AUSTRALIA. BUREAU OF STATISTICS. NEW SOUTH WALES OFFICE. CHILD CARE, NEW SOUTH WALES, DATA REPORT (ONLINE). *see* SOCIAL SERVICES AND WELFARE—Abstracting, Bibliographies, Statistics

AUSTRALIA. BUREAU OF STATISTICS. NEW SOUTH WALES OFFICE. CRIME AND SAFETY, NEW SOUTH WALES (ONLINE). *see* LAW—Abstracting, Bibliographies, Statistics

AUSTRALIA. BUREAU OF STATISTICS. NEW SOUTH WALES OFFICE. DISABILITY, AGEING AND CARERS, SUMMARY TABLES, NEW SOUTH WALES (ONLINE). *see* SOCIAL SERVICES AND WELFARE—Abstracting, Bibliographies, Statistics

AUSTRALIA. BUREAU OF STATISTICS. NEW SOUTH WALES OFFICE. DISABILITY, NEW SOUTH WALES (ONLINE). *see* SOCIAL SERVICES AND WELFARE—Abstracting, Bibliographies, Statistics

AUSTRALIA. BUREAU OF STATISTICS. NEW SOUTH WALES OFFICE. GOVERNMENT FINANCIAL ESTIMATES, NEW SOUTH WALES, ELECTRONIC DELIVERY. *see* BUSINESS AND ECONOMICS—Abstracting, Bibliographies, Statistics

AUSTRALIA. BUREAU OF STATISTICS. NEW SOUTH WALES OFFICE. HOME SECURITY PRECAUTIONS, NEW SOUTH WALES (ONLINE). *see* CRIMINOLOGY AND LAW ENFORCEMENT—Abstracting, Bibliographies, Statistics

AUSTRALIA. BUREAU OF STATISTICS. NEW SOUTH WALES OFFICE. MANUFACTURING INDUSTRY, NEW SOUTH WALES AND AUSTRALIAN CAPITAL TERRITORY (ONLINE). *see* BUSINESS AND ECONOMICS—Abstracting, Bibliographies, Statistics

AUSTRALIA. BUREAU OF STATISTICS. NEW SOUTH WALES OFFICE. MENTAL HEALTH AND WELLBEING: PROFILE OF ADULTS, NEW SOUTH WALES, DATA REPORT. *see* SOCIAL SERVICES AND WELFARE—Abstracting, Bibliographies, Statistics

AUSTRALIA. BUREAU OF STATISTICS. NEW SOUTH WALES OFFICE. NEW SOUTH WALES AT A GLANCE (ONLINE). *see* POPULATION STUDIES—Abstracting, Bibliographies, Statistics

AUSTRALIA. BUREAU OF STATISTICS. NEW SOUTH WALES OFFICE. NEW SOUTH WALES' YOUNG PEOPLE. *see* REAL ESTATE—Abstracting, Bibliographies, Statistics

AUSTRALIA. BUREAU OF STATISTICS. NEW SOUTH WALES OFFICE. OLDER PEOPLE, NEW SOUTH WALES (ONLINE). *see* SOCIAL SERVICES AND WELFARE—Abstracting, Bibliographies, Statistics

AUSTRALIA. BUREAU OF STATISTICS. NEW SOUTH WALES OFFICE. RETAILING IN NEW SOUTH WALES (ONLINE). *see* BUSINESS AND ECONOMICS—Abstracting, Bibliographies, Statistics

AUSTRALIA. BUREAU OF STATISTICS. NEW SOUTH WALES OFFICE. SYDNEY. A SOCIAL ATLAS. *see* POPULATION STUDIES—Abstracting, Bibliographies, Statistics

AUSTRALIA. BUREAU OF STATISTICS. NEW SOUTH WALES OFFICE. TOURIST ACCOMMODATION, SMALL AREA DATA, NEW SOUTH WALES (ONLINE). *see* HOTELS AND RESTAURANTS—Abstracting, Bibliographies, Statistics

AUSTRALIA. BUREAU OF STATISTICS. NORTHERN TERRITORY OFFICE. CENSUS OF POPULATION AND HOUSING: ABORIGINAL AND TORRES STRAIT ISLANDER PEOPLE, NORTHERN TERRITORY (ONLINE). *see* POPULATION STUDIES—Abstracting, Bibliographies, Statistics

AUSTRALIA. BUREAU OF STATISTICS. NORTHERN TERRITORY OFFICE. CENSUS OF POPULATION AND HOUSING: CENSUS BASICS, NORTHERN TERRITORY. *see* POPULATION STUDIES—Abstracting, Bibliographies, Statistics

AUSTRALIA. BUREAU OF STATISTICS. NORTHERN TERRITORY OFFICE. CENSUS OF POPULATION AND HOUSING: SELECTED CHARACTERISTICS FOR URBAN CENTRES AND LOCALITIES, NORTHERN TERRITORY (ONLINE). *see* POPULATION STUDIES—Abstracting, Bibliographies, Statistics

AUSTRALIA. BUREAU OF STATISTICS. NORTHERN TERRITORY OFFICE. CENSUS OF POPULATION AND HOUSING: SELECTED EDUCATION AND LABOUR FORCE CHARACTERISTICS FOR STATISTICAL LOCAL AREAS, NORTHERN TERRITORY (ONLINE). *see* POPULATION STUDIES—Abstracting, Bibliographies, Statistics

AUSTRALIA. BUREAU OF STATISTICS. NORTHERN TERRITORY OFFICE. CENSUS OF POPULATION AND HOUSING: SELECTED SOCIAL AND HOUSING CHARACTERISTICS FOR STATISTICAL LOCAL AREAS, NORTHERN TERRITORY (ONLINE). *see* POPULATION STUDIES—Abstracting, Bibliographies, Statistics

AUSTRALIA. BUREAU OF STATISTICS. NORTHERN TERRITORY OFFICE. CENSUS OF POPULATION AND HOUSING: SOCIO-ECONOMIC INDEXES FOR AREAS, NORTHERN TERRITORY. *see* POPULATION STUDIES—Abstracting, Bibliographies, Statistics

AUSTRALIA. BUREAU OF STATISTICS. NORTHERN TERRITORY OFFICE. DARWIN AND PALMERSTON. A SOCIAL ATLAS. *see* POPULATION STUDIES—Abstracting, Bibliographies, Statistics

AUSTRALIA. BUREAU OF STATISTICS. NORTHERN TERRITORY OFFICE. DISABILITY, AGEING AND CARERS, SUMMARY TABLES, NORTHERN TERRITORY (ONLINE). *see* SOCIAL SERVICES AND WELFARE—Abstracting, Bibliographies, Statistics

AUSTRALIA. BUREAU OF STATISTICS. NORTHERN TERRITORY OFFICE. GOVERNMENT FINANCIAL ESTIMATES, NORTHERN TERRITORY, ELECTRONIC DELIVERY. *see* BUSINESS AND ECONOMICS—Abstracting, Bibliographies, Statistics

AUSTRALIA. BUREAU OF STATISTICS. NORTHERN TERRITORY OFFICE. NATIONAL HEALTH SURVEY: DARWIN-PALMERSTON AND ALICE SPRINGS (ONLINE). *see* PUBLIC HEALTH AND SAFETY—Abstracting, Bibliographies, Statistics

319.4 AUS
AUSTRALIA. BUREAU OF STATISTICS. NORTHERN TERRITORY OFFICE. NORTHERN TERRITORY AT A GLANCE (ONLINE). Text in English. 1983. a. free (effective 2009). back issues avail.
Document type: *Catalog, Government.* **Description:** Contains a wide range of statistical information on the Northern Territory, including physical data, population, vitals, employment and wages, price indices, agriculture and fishing, mineral production, manufacturing, building, foreign trade and tourism.
Formerly: Australia. Bureau of Statistics. Northern Territory Office. Northern Territory at a Glance (Print) (0815-3809)
Media: Online - full text.
Published by: Australian Bureau of Statistics, Northern Territory Office, GPO BOX 3796, Darwin, N.T. 0801, Australia. TEL 61-2-92684909, 300-135-070. Circ: 9,000.

AUSTRALIA. BUREAU OF STATISTICS. NORTHERN TERRITORY OFFICE. NORTHERN TERRITORY'S YOUNG PEOPLE (ONLINE). *see* REAL ESTATE—Abstracting, Bibliographies, Statistics

AUSTRALIA. BUREAU OF STATISTICS. NORTHERN TERRITORY OFFICE. POPULATION PROJECTIONS, NORTHERN TERRITORY (ONLINE). *see* POPULATION STUDIES—Abstracting, Bibliographies, Statistics

AUSTRALIA. BUREAU OF STATISTICS. NORTHERN TERRITORY OFFICE. REGIONAL STATISTICS, NORTHERN TERRITORY (ONLINE). *see* POPULATION STUDIES—Abstracting, Bibliographies, Statistics

AUSTRALIA. BUREAU OF STATISTICS. NORTHERN TERRITORY OFFICE. TOURIST ACCOMMODATION, SMALL AREA DATA, NORTHERN TERRITORY (ONLINE). *see* HOTELS AND RESTAURANTS—Abstracting, Bibliographies, Statistics

AUSTRALIA. BUREAU OF STATISTICS. OCCASIONAL PAPER: A RISK INDEX APPROACH TO UNEMPLOYMENT - AN APPLICATION USING THE SURVEY OF EMPLOYMENT AND UNEMPLOYMENT PATTERNS (ONLINE). *see* BUSINESS AND ECONOMICS—Abstracting, Bibliographies, Statistics

AUSTRALIA. BUREAU OF STATISTICS. OCCASIONAL PAPER: AUSTRALIAN BUSINESS REGISTER - A SNAPSHOT (ONLINE). *see* BUSINESS AND ECONOMICS—Abstracting, Bibliographies, Statistics

AUSTRALIA. BUREAU OF STATISTICS. OCCASIONAL PAPER: CIGARETTE SMOKING AMONG INDIGENOUS AUSTRALIANS (ONLINE). *see* PHYSICAL FITNESS AND HYGIENE—Abstracting, Bibliographies, Statistics

AUSTRALIA. BUREAU OF STATISTICS. OCCASIONAL PAPER: DYNAMICS OF EARNED INCOME - AN APPLICATION USING THE SURVEY OF EMPLOYMENT AND UNEMPLOYMENT PATTERNS (ONLINE). *see* BUSINESS AND ECONOMICS—Abstracting, Bibliographies, Statistics

AUSTRALIA. BUREAU OF STATISTICS. OCCASIONAL PAPER: HOSPITAL STATISTICS, ABORIGINAL AND TORRES STRAIT ISLANDER AUSTRALIANS (ONLINE). *see* HEALTH FACILITIES AND ADMINISTRATION—Abstracting, Bibliographies, Statistics

AUSTRALIA. BUREAU OF STATISTICS. OCCASIONAL PAPER: INDIGENOUS LANGUAGES, AUSTRALIA. *see* LINGUISTICS—Abstracting, Bibliographies, Statistics

AUSTRALIA. BUREAU OF STATISTICS. OCCASIONAL PAPER: INNOVATION, PRODUCTIVITY AND PROFITABILITY OF AUSTRALIAN MANUFACTURERS. *see* COMPUTERS—Abstracting, Bibliographies, Statistics

AUSTRALIA. BUREAU OF STATISTICS. OCCASIONAL PAPER: JOB QUALITY AND CHURNING OF THE POOL OF THE UNEMPLOYED (ONLINE). *see* BUSINESS AND ECONOMICS—Abstracting, Bibliographies, Statistics

AUSTRALIA. BUREAU OF STATISTICS. OCCASIONAL PAPER: LABOUR FORCE CHARACTERISTICS OF ABORIGINAL AND TORRES STRAIT ISLANDER AUSTRALIANS (ONLINE). *see* BUSINESS AND ECONOMICS—Abstracting, Bibliographies, Statistics

AUSTRALIA. BUREAU OF STATISTICS. OCCASIONAL PAPER: LABOUR MARKET DYNAMICS IN AUSTRALIA - AN APPLICATION USING THE SURVEY OF EMPLOYMENT AND UNEMPLOYMENT PATTERNS (ONLINE). *see* BUSINESS AND ECONOMICS—Abstracting, Bibliographies, Statistics

AUSTRALIA. BUREAU OF STATISTICS. OCCASIONAL PAPER: LABOUR MARKET OUTCOMES OF LOW PAID ADULT WORKERS (ONLINE). *see* BUSINESS AND ECONOMICS—Abstracting, Bibliographies, Statistics

AUSTRALIA. BUREAU OF STATISTICS. OCCASIONAL PAPER: LABOUR MARKET PROGRAMS, UNEMPLOYMENT AND EMPLOYMENT HAZARDS (ONLINE). *see* BUSINESS AND ECONOMICS—Abstracting, Bibliographies, Statistics

AUSTRALIA. BUREAU OF STATISTICS. OCCASIONAL PAPER: MORTALITY OF INDIGENOUS AUSTRALIANS (ONLINE). *see* REAL ESTATE—Abstracting, Bibliographies, Statistics

AUSTRALIA. BUREAU OF STATISTICS. OCCASIONAL PAPER: OVERWEIGHT AND OBESITY, INDIGENOUS AUSTRALIANS (ONLINE). *see* PHYSICAL FITNESS AND HYGIENE—Abstracting, Bibliographies, Statistics

AUSTRALIA. BUREAU OF STATISTICS. OCCASIONAL PAPER: POPULATION ISSUES, INDIGENOUS AUSTRALIANS (ONLINE). *see* POPULATION STUDIES—Abstracting, Bibliographies, Statistics

AUSTRALIA. BUREAU OF STATISTICS. OCCASIONAL PAPER: SELF-ASSESSED HEALTH STATUS, INDIGENOUS AUSTRALIANS (ONLINE). *see* PHYSICAL FITNESS AND HYGIENE—Abstracting, Bibliographies, Statistics

AUSTRALIA. BUREAU OF STATISTICS. OCCASIONAL PAPER: THE DYNAMICS OF WELFARE RECEIPT AND LABOUR MARKET STATUS. *see* BUSINESS AND ECONOMICS—Abstracting, Bibliographies, Statistics

AUSTRALIA. BUREAU OF STATISTICS. OLDER PEOPLE, AUSTRALIA: A SOCIAL REPORT (ONLINE). *see* SOCIAL SERVICES AND WELFARE—Abstracting, Bibliographies, Statistics

AUSTRALIA. BUREAU OF STATISTICS. OPTOMETRY AND OPTICAL DISPENSING SERVICES, AUSTRALIA (ONLINE). *see* MEDICAL SCIENCES—Abstracting, Bibliographies, Statistics

AUSTRALIA. BUREAU OF STATISTICS. ORIGIN OF GUESTS, AUSTRALIA (ONLINE). *see* TRAVEL AND TOURISM—Abstracting, Bibliographies, Statistics

AUSTRALIA. BUREAU OF STATISTICS. OVERSEAS ARRIVALS AND DEPARTURES, AUSTRALIA (MONTHLY) (ONLINE). *see* POPULATION STUDIES—Abstracting, Bibliographies, Statistics

AUSTRALIA. BUREAU OF STATISTICS. PERFORMING ARTS, AUSTRALIA (ONLINE). *see* THEATER—Abstracting, Bibliographies, Statistics

AUSTRALIA. BUREAU OF STATISTICS. PERSONS NOT IN THE LABOUR FORCE, AUSTRALIA (ONLINE). *see* BUSINESS AND ECONOMICS—Abstracting, Bibliographies, Statistics

AUSTRALIA. BUREAU OF STATISTICS. PHYSIOTHERAPY SERVICES, AUSTRALIA (ONLINE). *see* MEDICAL SCIENCES—Abstracting, Bibliographies, Statistics

AUSTRALIA. BUREAU OF STATISTICS. POPULATION BY AGE AND SEX, AUSTRALIAN STATES AND TERRITORIES (ONLINE). *see* POPULATION STUDIES—Abstracting, Bibliographies, Statistics

AUSTRALIA. BUREAU OF STATISTICS. POPULATION CHARACTERISTICS, ABORIGINAL AND TORRES STRAIT ISLANDER AUSTRALIANS (ONLINE). *see* POPULATION STUDIES—Abstracting, Bibliographies, Statistics

AUSTRALIA. BUREAU OF STATISTICS. POPULATION DISTRIBUTION, ABORIGINAL AND TORRES STRAIT ISLANDER AUSTRALIANS (ONLINE). *see* POPULATION STUDIES—Abstracting, Bibliographies, Statistics

AUSTRALIA. BUREAU OF STATISTICS. POPULATION DISTRIBUTION, AUSTRALIA. *see* POPULATION STUDIES—Abstracting, Bibliographies, Statistics

AUSTRALIA. BUREAU OF STATISTICS. POPULATION PROJECTIONS, AUSTRALIA (ONLINE). *see* POPULATION STUDIES—Abstracting, Bibliographies, Statistics

AUSTRALIA. BUREAU OF STATISTICS. POSTAL AREA TO STATISTICAL LOCAL AREA CONCORDANCE, AUSTRALIA. *see* COMMUNICATIONS—Abstracting, Bibliographies, Statistics

AUSTRALIA. BUREAU OF STATISTICS. PRINCIPAL AGRICULTURAL COMMODITIES, AUSTRALIA, PRELIMINARY (ONLINE). *see* AGRICULTURE—Abstracting, Bibliographies, Statistics

AUSTRALIA. BUREAU OF STATISTICS. PRIVATE HOSPITALS, AUSTRALIA (ONLINE). *see* HEALTH FACILITIES AND ADMINISTRATION—Abstracting, Bibliographies, Statistics

AUSTRALIA. BUREAU OF STATISTICS. PRIVATE MEDICAL PRACTICES, AUSTRALIA (ONLINE). *see* MEDICAL SCIENCES—Abstracting, Bibliographies, Statistics

AUSTRALIA. BUREAU OF STATISTICS. PRIVATE MEDICAL PRACTITIONERS, AUSTRALIA (ONLINE). *see* MEDICAL SCIENCES—Abstracting, Bibliographies, Statistics

AUSTRALIA. BUREAU OF STATISTICS. PRIVATE NEW CAPITAL EXPENDITURE AND EXPECTED EXPENDITURE, AUSTRALIA (ONLINE). *see* BUSINESS AND ECONOMICS—Abstracting, Bibliographies, Statistics

AUSTRALIA. BUREAU OF STATISTICS. PRIVATE SECTOR CONSTRUCTION INDUSTRY, AUSTRALIA (ONLINE). *see* BUILDING AND CONSTRUCTION—Abstracting, Bibliographies, Statistics

AUSTRALIA. BUREAU OF STATISTICS. PRIVATE SECTOR CONSTRUCTION INDUSTRY, AUSTRALIA, PRELIMINARY. *see* BUILDING AND CONSTRUCTION—Abstracting, Bibliographies, Statistics

AUSTRALIA. BUREAU OF STATISTICS. PRODUCER PRICE INDEXES, AUSTRALIA (ONLINE). *see* BUSINESS AND ECONOMICS—Abstracting, Bibliographies, Statistics

AUSTRALIA. BUREAU OF STATISTICS. PUBLIC LIBRARIES, AUSTRALIA (ONLINE). *see* MUSEUMS AND ART GALLERIES—Abstracting, Bibliographies, Statistics

AUSTRALIA. BUREAU OF STATISTICS. QUEENSLAND OFFICE. BRISBANE. A SOCIAL ATLAS. *see* POPULATION STUDIES—Abstracting, Bibliographies, Statistics

AUSTRALIA. BUREAU OF STATISTICS. QUEENSLAND OFFICE. CATTLE BREEDS, QUEENSLAND. *see* AGRICULTURE—Abstracting, Bibliographies, Statistics

AUSTRALIA. BUREAU OF STATISTICS. QUEENSLAND OFFICE. CENSUS OF POPULATION AND HOUSING: ABORIGINAL AND TORRES STRAIT ISLANDER PEOPLE, QUEENSLAND (ONLINE). *see* POPULATION STUDIES—Abstracting, Bibliographies, Statistics

AUSTRALIA. BUREAU OF STATISTICS. QUEENSLAND OFFICE. CENSUS OF POPULATION AND HOUSING: CDATA2001, QUEENSLAND - FULL GIS. *see* POPULATION STUDIES—Abstracting, Bibliographies, Statistics

AUSTRALIA. BUREAU OF STATISTICS. QUEENSLAND OFFICE. CENSUS OF POPULATION AND HOUSING: CDATA2001 - QUICKBUILD, QUEENSLAND. *see* POPULATION STUDIES—Abstracting, Bibliographies, Statistics

AUSTRALIA. BUREAU OF STATISTICS. QUEENSLAND OFFICE. CENSUS OF POPULATION AND HOUSING: CENSUS BASICS, QUEENSLAND. *see* POPULATION STUDIES—Abstracting, Bibliographies, Statistics

AUSTRALIA. BUREAU OF STATISTICS. QUEENSLAND OFFICE. CENSUS OF POPULATION AND HOUSING: SELECTED CHARACTERISTICS FOR URBAN CENTRES AND LOCALITIES, QUEENSLAND (ONLINE). *see* POPULATION STUDIES—Abstracting, Bibliographies, Statistics

AUSTRALIA. BUREAU OF STATISTICS. QUEENSLAND OFFICE. CENSUS OF POPULATION AND HOUSING: SELECTED EDUCATION AND LABOUR FORCE CHARACTERISTICS FOR STATISTICAL LOCAL AREAS, QUEENSLAND (ONLINE). *see* POPULATION STUDIES—Abstracting, Bibliographies, Statistics

AUSTRALIA. BUREAU OF STATISTICS. QUEENSLAND OFFICE. CENSUS OF POPULATION AND HOUSING: SELECTED SOCIAL AND HOUSING CHARACTERISTICS FOR STATISTICAL LOCAL AREAS, QUEENSLAND (ONLINE). *see* POPULATION STUDIES—Abstracting, Bibliographies, Statistics

AUSTRALIA. BUREAU OF STATISTICS. QUEENSLAND OFFICE. CENSUS OF POPULATION AND HOUSING: SOCIO-ECONOMIC INDEXES FOR AREAS, QUEENSLAND. *see* POPULATION STUDIES—Abstracting, Bibliographies, Statistics

AUSTRALIA. BUREAU OF STATISTICS. QUEENSLAND OFFICE. DISABILITY, AGEING AND CARERS, SUMMARY TABLES, QUEENSLAND (ONLINE). *see* SOCIAL SERVICES AND WELFARE—Abstracting, Bibliographies, Statistics

AUSTRALIA. BUREAU OF STATISTICS. QUEENSLAND OFFICE. ESTIMATED RESIDENT POPULATION, QUEENSLAND. *see* POPULATION STUDIES—Abstracting, Bibliographies, Statistics

AUSTRALIA. BUREAU OF STATISTICS. QUEENSLAND OFFICE. FERTILITY TRENDS IN QUEENSLAND. *see* POPULATION STUDIES—Abstracting, Bibliographies, Statistics

AUSTRALIA. BUREAU OF STATISTICS. QUEENSLAND OFFICE. GOVERNMENT FINANCIAL ESTIMATES, QUEENSLAND (ONLINE). *see* BUSINESS AND ECONOMICS—Abstracting, Bibliographies, Statistics

AUSTRALIA. BUREAU OF STATISTICS. QUEENSLAND OFFICE. HOUSEHOLD EXPENDITURE SURVEY, QUEENSLAND. *see* HOME ECONOMICS—Abstracting, Bibliographies, Statistics

AUSTRALIA. BUREAU OF STATISTICS. QUEENSLAND OFFICE. MANUFACTURING INDUSTRY, QUEENSLAND (ONLINE). *see* BUSINESS AND ECONOMICS—Abstracting, Bibliographies, Statistics

AUSTRALIA. BUREAU OF STATISTICS. QUEENSLAND OFFICE. MENTAL HEALTH AND WELLBEING: PROFILE OF ADULTS, QUEENSLAND, DATA REPORT (ONLINE). *see* SOCIAL SERVICES AND WELFARE—Abstracting, Bibliographies, Statistics

AUSTRALIA. BUREAU OF STATISTICS. QUEENSLAND OFFICE. MIGRATION, QUEENSLAND. *see* POPULATION STUDIES—Abstracting, Bibliographies, Statistics

AUSTRALIA. BUREAU OF STATISTICS. QUEENSLAND OFFICE. NATIONAL ABORIGINAL AND TORRES STRAIT ISLANDER SURVEY: QUEENSLAND (ONLINE). *see* POPULATION STUDIES—Abstracting, Bibliographies, Statistics

AUSTRALIA. BUREAU OF STATISTICS. QUEENSLAND OFFICE. PERSONS AGED FIFTY YEARS AND OVER, QUEENSLAND (ONLINE). *see* SOCIAL SERVICES AND WELFARE—Abstracting, Bibliographies, Statistics

AUSTRALIA. BUREAU OF STATISTICS. QUEENSLAND OFFICE. POPULATION MOBILITY, QUEENSLAND (ONLINE). *see* POPULATION STUDIES—Abstracting, Bibliographies, Statistics

319 AUS
AUSTRALIA. BUREAU OF STATISTICS. QUEENSLAND OFFICE. QUEENSLAND AT A GLANCE (ONLINE). Text in English. 1978. a. free (effective 2009). back issues avail. **Document type:** *Catalog, Government.* **Description:** Provides statistics on all aspects of Queensland life: population, labor, wages, health, welfare services, law and crime, education, agriculture, mining, construction, transportation, communication, tourism, prices and finance.
Formerly (until 1994): Australia. Bureau of Statistics. Queensland Office. Queensland at a Glance (Print) (0157-3713)
Media: Online - full text.
Published by: Australian Bureau of Statistics, Queensland Office, GPO Box 9817, Brisbane, QLD 4001, Australia. TEL 61-2-92684909, 300-135-070.

AUSTRALIA. BUREAU OF STATISTICS. QUEENSLAND OFFICE. QUEENSLAND'S YOUNG PEOPLE (ONLINE). *see* REAL ESTATE—Abstracting, Bibliographies, Statistics

AUSTRALIA. BUREAU OF STATISTICS. QUEENSLAND OFFICE. RECENT POPULATION AND HOUSING TRENDS IN QUEENSLAND. *see* POPULATION STUDIES—Abstracting, Bibliographies, Statistics

AUSTRALIA. BUREAU OF STATISTICS. QUEENSLAND OFFICE. RETAIL INDUSTRY: SMALL AREA STATISTICS, QUEENSLAND. *see* BUSINESS AND ECONOMICS—Abstracting, Bibliographies, Statistics

AUSTRALIA. BUREAU OF STATISTICS. QUEENSLAND OFFICE. SAFETY IN THE HOME, QUEENSLAND (ONLINE). *see* NUTRITION AND DIETETICS—Abstracting, Bibliographies, Statistics

AUSTRALIA. BUREAU OF STATISTICS. QUEENSLAND OFFICE. TOURIST ACCOMMODATION, SMALL AREA DATA, QUEENSLAND (ONLINE). *see* HOTELS AND RESTAURANTS—Abstracting, Bibliographies, Statistics

AUSTRALIA. BUREAU OF STATISTICS. QUEENSLAND OFFICE. WORKING HOURS OF WAGE AND SALARY EARNERS, QUEENSLAND. *see* BUSINESS AND ECONOMICS—Abstracting, Bibliographies, Statistics

AUSTRALIA. BUREAU OF STATISTICS. REAL ESTATE SERVICES, AUSTRALIA (ONLINE). *see* REAL ESTATE—Abstracting, Bibliographies, Statistics

AUSTRALIA. BUREAU OF STATISTICS. REGIONAL POPULATION GROWTH. AUSTRALIA. *see* POPULATION STUDIES—Abstracting, Bibliographies, Statistics

AUSTRALIA. BUREAU OF STATISTICS. RENTERS IN AUSTRALIA (ONLINE). *see* REAL ESTATE—Abstracting, Bibliographies, Statistics

310 AUS
AUSTRALIA. BUREAU OF STATISTICS. RESEARCH AND EXPERIMENTAL DEVELOPMENT, ALL SECTOR SUMMARY, AUSTRALIA (ONLINE). Text in English. 1978. biennial. free (effective 2009). back issues avail. **Document type:** *Government.* **Description:** Presents summary statistics on the level and distribution of expenditure and human resources devoted to research and experimental development carried out by business enterprises, government, higher education and private non-profit sectors.
Formerly (until 2003): Australia. Bureau of Statistics. Research and Experimental Development, All Sector Summary, Australia (Print) (0729-5022)
Media: Online - full text.
Published by: Australian Bureau of Statistics, Locked Bag 10, Belconnen, ACT 2616, Australia. TEL 61-2-62527037, 61-2-92684909, 300-135-070, FAX 61-2-62528103, client.services@abs.gov.au.

AUSTRALIA. BUREAU OF STATISTICS. RESEARCH AND EXPERIMENTAL DEVELOPMENT, BUSINESSES, AUSTRALIA (ONLINE). *see* BUSINESS AND ECONOMICS—Abstracting, Bibliographies, Statistics

AUSTRALIA. BUREAU OF STATISTICS. RESEARCH AND EXPERIMENTAL DEVELOPMENT, GOVERNMENT AND PRIVATE NON-PROFIT ORGANISATIONS, AUSTRALIA (ONLINE). *see* BUSINESS AND ECONOMICS—Abstracting, Bibliographies, Statistics

AUSTRALIA. BUREAU OF STATISTICS. RESEARCH AND EXPERIMENTAL DEVELOPMENT, HIGHER EDUCATION ORGANISATIONS, AUSTRALIA (ONLINE). *see* EDUCATION—Abstracting, Bibliographies, Statistics

AUSTRALIA. BUREAU OF STATISTICS. RETAIL AND WHOLESALE INDUSTRIES, AUSTRALIA (ONLINE). *see* BUSINESS AND ECONOMICS—Abstracting, Bibliographies, Statistics

AUSTRALIA. BUREAU OF STATISTICS. RETAIL AND WHOLESALE INDUSTRIES, AUSTRALIA: COMMODITIES (ONLINE). *see* BUSINESS AND ECONOMICS—Abstracting, Bibliographies, Statistics

S

AUSTRALIA. BUREAU OF STATISTICS. RETAIL TRADE, AUSTRALIA (ONLINE). *see* BUSINESS AND ECONOMICS—Abstracting, Bibliographies, Statistics

AUSTRALIA. BUREAU OF STATISTICS. RETAIL TRADE SPECIAL DATA SERVICE: CUSTOMISED REPORTS - DATA REPORT (ONLINE). *see* BUSINESS AND ECONOMICS—Abstracting, Bibliographies, Statistics

AUSTRALIA. BUREAU OF STATISTICS. RETAILING IN AUSTRALIA. *see* BUSINESS AND ECONOMICS—Abstracting, Bibliographies, Statistics

AUSTRALIA. BUREAU OF STATISTICS. RETIREMENT AND RETIREMENT INTENTIONS, AUSTRALIA (ONLINE). *see* BUSINESS AND ECONOMICS—Abstracting, Bibliographies, Statistics

AUSTRALIA. BUREAU OF STATISTICS. RETRENCHMENT AND REDUNDANCY, AUSTRALIA (ONLINE). *see* BUSINESS AND ECONOMICS—Abstracting, Bibliographies, Statistics

AUSTRALIA. BUREAU OF STATISTICS. SALES OF AUSTRALIAN WINE AND BRANDY BY WINEMAKERS (ONLINE). *see* BEVERAGES—Abstracting, Bibliographies, Statistics

AUSTRALIA. BUREAU OF STATISTICS. SALINITY ON AUSTRALIAN FARMS (ONLINE). *see* ENVIRONMENTAL STUDIES—Abstracting, Bibliographies, Statistics

AUSTRALIA. BUREAU OF STATISTICS. SCHOOLS, AUSTRALIA (ONLINE). *see* EDUCATION—Abstracting, Bibliographies, Statistics

AUSTRALIA. BUREAU OF STATISTICS. SECURITY SERVICES, AUSTRALIA (ONLINE). *see* CRIMINOLOGY AND LAW ENFORCEMENT—Abstracting, Bibliographies, Statistics

AUSTRALIA. BUREAU OF STATISTICS. SELECTED AMUSEMENT AND LEISURE INDUSTRIES, AUSTRALIA (ONLINE). *see* SPORTS AND GAMES—Abstracting, Bibliographies, Statistics

AUSTRALIA. BUREAU OF STATISTICS. SELECTED BUSINESS SERVICES, AUSTRALIA (ONLINE). *see* BUSINESS AND ECONOMICS—Abstracting, Bibliographies, Statistics

AUSTRALIA. BUREAU OF STATISTICS. SELECTED MUSEUMS, AUSTRALIA (ONLINE). *see* MUSEUMS AND ART GALLERIES—Abstracting, Bibliographies, Statistics

AUSTRALIA. BUREAU OF STATISTICS. SMALL BUSINESS IN AUSTRALIA (ONLINE). *see* BUSINESS AND ECONOMICS—Abstracting, Bibliographies, Statistics

AUSTRALIA. BUREAU OF STATISTICS. SOUND RECORDING STUDIOS, AUSTRALIA (ONLINE). *see* PHYSICS—Abstracting, Bibliographies, Statistics

AUSTRALIA. BUREAU OF STATISTICS. SOUTH AUSTRALIAN OFFICE. ADELAIDE. A SOCIAL ATLAS. *see* POPULATION STUDIES—Abstracting, Bibliographies, Statistics

AUSTRALIA. BUREAU OF STATISTICS. SOUTH AUSTRALIAN OFFICE. AUSTRALIAN HOUSING SURVEY: SOUTH AUSTRALIA. *see* HOUSING AND URBAN PLANNING—Abstracting, Bibliographies, Statistics

AUSTRALIA. BUREAU OF STATISTICS. SOUTH AUSTRALIAN OFFICE. CENSUS OF POPULATION AND HOUSING: ABORIGINAL AND TORRES STRAIT ISLANDER PEOPLE, SOUTH AUSTRALIA (ONLINE). *see* POPULATION STUDIES—Abstracting, Bibliographies, Statistics

AUSTRALIA. BUREAU OF STATISTICS. SOUTH AUSTRALIAN OFFICE. CENSUS OF POPULATION AND HOUSING: CDATA2001, SOUTH AUSTRALIA - FULL GIS. *see* POPULATION STUDIES—Abstracting, Bibliographies, Statistics

AUSTRALIA. BUREAU OF STATISTICS. SOUTH AUSTRALIAN OFFICE. CENSUS OF POPULATION AND HOUSING: CENSUS BASICS, SOUTH AUSTRALIA. *see* POPULATION STUDIES—Abstracting, Bibliographies, Statistics

AUSTRALIA. BUREAU OF STATISTICS. SOUTH AUSTRALIAN OFFICE. CENSUS OF POPULATION AND HOUSING: SELECTED CHARACTERISTICS FOR URBAN CENTRES AND LOCALITIES, SOUTH AUSTRALIA (ONLINE). *see* POPULATION STUDIES—Abstracting, Bibliographies, Statistics

AUSTRALIA. BUREAU OF STATISTICS. SOUTH AUSTRALIAN OFFICE. CENSUS OF POPULATION AND HOUSING: SELECTED EDUCATION AND LABOUR FORCE CHARACTERISTICS FOR STATISTICAL LOCAL AREAS, SOUTH AUSTRALIA (ONLINE). *see* POPULATION STUDIES—Abstracting, Bibliographies, Statistics

AUSTRALIA. BUREAU OF STATISTICS. SOUTH AUSTRALIAN OFFICE. CENSUS OF POPULATION AND HOUSING: SELECTED SOCIAL AND HOUSING CHARACTERISTICS FOR STATISTICAL LOCAL AREAS, SOUTH AUSTRALIA (ONLINE). *see* POPULATION STUDIES—Abstracting, Bibliographies, Statistics

AUSTRALIA. BUREAU OF STATISTICS. SOUTH AUSTRALIAN OFFICE. CRIME AND SAFETY, SOUTH AUSTRALIA (ONLINE). *see* CRIMINOLOGY AND LAW ENFORCEMENT—Abstracting, Bibliographies, Statistics

AUSTRALIA. BUREAU OF STATISTICS. SOUTH AUSTRALIAN OFFICE. DISABILITY, AGEING AND CARERS, SUMMARY TABLES, SOUTH AUSTRALIA (ONLINE). *see* SOCIAL SERVICES AND WELFARE—Abstracting, Bibliographies, Statistics

AUSTRALIA. BUREAU OF STATISTICS. SOUTH AUSTRALIAN OFFICE. GOVERNMENT FINANCIAL ESTIMATES, SOUTH AUSTRALIA, ELECTRONIC DELIVERY. *see* BUSINESS AND ECONOMICS—Abstracting, Bibliographies, Statistics

AUSTRALIA. BUREAU OF STATISTICS. SOUTH AUSTRALIAN OFFICE. MANUFACTURING INDUSTRY, SOUTH AUSTRALIA (ONLINE). *see* BUSINESS AND ECONOMICS—Abstracting, Bibliographies, Statistics

AUSTRALIA. BUREAU OF STATISTICS. SOUTH AUSTRALIAN OFFICE. MENTAL HEALTH AND WELLBEING: PROFILE OF ADULTS, SOUTH AUSTRALIA, DATA REPORT (ONLINE). *see* SOCIAL SERVICES AND WELFARE—Abstracting, Bibliographies, Statistics

319.4 AUS
AUSTRALIA. BUREAU OF STATISTICS. SOUTH AUSTRALIAN OFFICE. REGIONAL STATISTICS, SOUTH AUSTRALIA (ONLINE). Text in English. 1999. a., latest 2004. free (effective 2009). back issues avail. **Document type:** *Government.* **Description:** Presents a statistical summary of key economic and social information for local government areas, statistical subdivisions and statistical divisions in South Australia.
Former titles: Australia. Bureau of Statistics. South Australian Office. Regional Statistics, South Australia (Print) (1444-0989); (until 2000): Australia. Bureau of Statistics. South Australian Office. Regional Indicators, South Australia (1440-320X)
Media: Online - full text.
Published by: Australian Bureau of Statistics, South Australian Office, GPO Box 2272, Adelaide, SA 5001, Australia. TEL 61-2-92684909, 300-135-070, client.services@abs.gov.au.

AUSTRALIA. BUREAU OF STATISTICS. SOUTH AUSTRALIAN OFFICE. SALES OF GOODS AND SERVICES BY BUSINESSES INVOLVED IN WATER RELATED ACTIVITY IN SOUTH AUSTRALIA (ONLINE). *see* BUSINESS AND ECONOMICS—Abstracting, Bibliographies, Statistics

319.4 AUS ISSN 0814-0871
AUSTRALIA. BUREAU OF STATISTICS. SOUTH AUSTRALIAN OFFICE. SOUTH AUSTRALIA AT A GLANCE. Text in English. 1979. a. back issues avail. **Document type:** *Government.* **Description:** Brochure contains information on South Australia compared with Australia, tourist accommodation, population, education, welfare services, prices, labor force, finance, trade, transport, agriculture, mining and building, etc.
Published by: Australian Bureau of Statistics, South Australian Office, GPO Box 2272, Adelaide, SA 5001, Australia. TEL 61-2-92684909, 300-135-070, client.services@abs.gov.au.

AUSTRALIA. BUREAU OF STATISTICS. SOUTH AUSTRALIAN OFFICE. SOUTH AUSTRALIA'S YOUNG PEOPLE (ONLINE). *see* REAL ESTATE—Abstracting, Bibliographies, Statistics

AUSTRALIA. BUREAU OF STATISTICS. SOUTH AUSTRALIAN OFFICE. TOURIST ACCOMMODATION, SMALL AREA DATA, SOUTH AUSTRALIA (ONLINE). *see* TRAVEL AND TOURISM—Abstracting, Bibliographies, Statistics

AUSTRALIA. BUREAU OF STATISTICS. SOUTH AUSTRALIAN OFFICE. TRAVEL TO WORK AND PLACE OF EDUCATION, ADELAIDE STATISTICAL DIVISION (ONLINE). *see* TRANSPORTATION—Abstracting, Bibliographies, Statistics

AUSTRALIA. BUREAU OF STATISTICS. SPORT AND RECREATION FUNDING BY GOVERNMENT, AUSTRALIA (ONLINE). *see* SPORTS AND GAMES—Abstracting, Bibliographies, Statistics

AUSTRALIA. BUREAU OF STATISTICS. SPORT, RECREATION AND GAMBLING INDUSTRIES, AUSTRALIA, PRELIMINARY (ONLINE). *see* SPORTS AND GAMES—Abstracting, Bibliographies, Statistics

AUSTRALIA. BUREAU OF STATISTICS. SPORTS AND PHYSICAL RECREATION: A STATISTICAL OVERVIEW, AUSTRALIA. *see* SPORTS AND GAMES—Abstracting, Bibliographies, Statistics

AUSTRALIA. BUREAU OF STATISTICS. SPORTS AND PHYSICAL RECREATION SERVICES, AUSTRALIA (ONLINE). *see* SPORTS AND GAMES—Abstracting, Bibliographies, Statistics

AUSTRALIA. BUREAU OF STATISTICS. SPORTS ATTENDANCE, AUSTRALIA (ONLINE). *see* SPORTS AND GAMES—Abstracting, Bibliographies, Statistics

AUSTRALIA. BUREAU OF STATISTICS. STANDARD AUSTRALIAN CLASSIFICATION OF COUNTRIES (ONLINE). *see* POPULATION STUDIES—Abstracting, Bibliographies, Statistics

AUSTRALIA. BUREAU OF STATISTICS. STANDARD ECONOMIC SECTOR CLASSIFICATIONS OF AUSTRALIA (ONLINE). *see* BUSINESS AND ECONOMICS—Abstracting, Bibliographies, Statistics

336.021 AUS
AUSTRALIA. BUREAU OF STATISTICS. STANDARDS FOR CASH INCOME STATISTICS (ONLINE). Text in English. 1997. irreg., latest 1997. free (effective 2009). **Document type:** *Government.* **Description:** Covers ABS standards for the collection, processing, storage and dissemination of statistics on income.
Formerly: Australia. Bureau of Statistics. Standards for Cash Income Statistics (Print)
Media: Online - full text.
Published by: Australian Bureau of Statistics, Locked Bag 10, Belconnen, ACT 2616, Australia. TEL 61-2-62527037, 61-2-92684909, 300-135-070, FAX 61-2-62528103, client.services@abs.gov.au.

AUSTRALIA. BUREAU OF STATISTICS. STANDARDS FOR LABOUR FORCE STATISTICS (ONLINE). *see* BUSINESS AND ECONOMICS—Abstracting, Bibliographies, Statistics

AUSTRALIA. BUREAU OF STATISTICS. STANDARDS FOR STATISTICS ON CULTURAL AND LANGUAGE DIVERSITY (ONLINE). *see* SOCIAL SCIENCES: COMPREHENSIVE WORKS—Abstracting, Bibliographies, Statistics

AUSTRALIA. BUREAU OF STATISTICS. STATISTICAL GEOGRAPHY: VOLUME 2 - CENSUS GEOGRAPHIC AREAS, AUSTRALIA (ONLINE). *see* POPULATION STUDIES—Abstracting, Bibliographies, Statistics

AUSTRALIA. BUREAU OF STATISTICS. STATISTICAL GEOGRAPHY: VOLUME 3 - AUSTRALIAN STANDARD GEOGRAPHICAL CLASSIFICATION. URBAN CENTRES AND LOCALITIES (ONLINE). *see* POPULATION STUDIES—Abstracting, Bibliographies, Statistics

001.422 AUS
AUSTRALIA. BUREAU OF STATISTICS. STATISTICS - A POWERFUL EDGE! (ONLINE). Text in English. 1994. irreg., latest 2004. free (effective 2009). back issues avail. **Document type:** *Government.* **Description:** Published for middle school students of mathematics and information studies.
Formerly: Australia. Bureau of Statistics. Statistics - A Powerful Edge! (Print)
Media: Online - full text. **Related titles:** Diskette ed.
Published by: Australian Bureau of Statistics, Locked Bag 10, Belconnen, ACT 2616, Australia. TEL 61-2-92684909, 61-2-62527037, 300-135-070, FAX 61-2-62528103, client.services@abs.gov.au.

AUSTRALIA. BUREAU OF STATISTICS. SUCCESSFUL AND UNSUCCESSFUL JOB SEARCH EXPERIENCE, AUSTRALIA (ONLINE). *see* BUSINESS AND ECONOMICS—Abstracting, Bibliographies, Statistics

AUSTRALIA. BUREAU OF STATISTICS. SUPERANNUATION: COVERAGE AND FINANCIAL CHARACTERISTICS, AUSTRALIA (ONLINE). *see* BUSINESS AND ECONOMICS—Abstracting, Bibliographies, Statistics

AUSTRALIA. BUREAU OF STATISTICS. SURVEY OF INCOME AND HOUSING: CONFIDENTIALISED UNIT RECORD FILE. *see* BUSINESS AND ECONOMICS—Abstracting, Bibliographies, Statistics

AUSTRALIA. BUREAU OF STATISTICS. SURVEY OF MOTOR VEHICLE USE, AUSTRALIA TWELVE MONTHS ENDED (ONLINE). *see* TRANSPORTATION—Abstracting, Bibliographies, Statistics

AUSTRALIA. BUREAU OF STATISTICS. TASMANIAN OFFICE. BALANCING WORK AND CARING RESPONSIBILITIES, TASMANIA (ONLINE). *see* BUSINESS AND ECONOMICS—Abstracting, Bibliographies, Statistics

AUSTRALIA. BUREAU OF STATISTICS. TASMANIAN OFFICE. CENSUS OF POPULATION AND HOUSING: ABORIGINAL AND TORRES STRAIT ISLANDER PEOPLE, TASMANIA (ONLINE). *see* POPULATION STUDIES—Abstracting, Bibliographies, Statistics

AUSTRALIA. BUREAU OF STATISTICS. TASMANIAN OFFICE. CENSUS OF POPULATION AND HOUSING: BURNIE AND DEVONPORT SUBURBS (ONLINE). *see* POPULATION STUDIES—Abstracting, Bibliographies, Statistics

AUSTRALIA. BUREAU OF STATISTICS. TASMANIAN OFFICE. CENSUS OF POPULATION AND HOUSING: CENSUS BASICS, AUSTRALIA. *see* POPULATION STUDIES—Abstracting, Bibliographies, Statistics

AUSTRALIA. BUREAU OF STATISTICS. TASMANIAN OFFICE. CENSUS OF POPULATION AND HOUSING: LAUNCESTON SUBURBS (ONLINE). *see* POPULATION STUDIES—Abstracting, Bibliographies, Statistics

AUSTRALIA. BUREAU OF STATISTICS. TASMANIAN OFFICE. CENSUS OF POPULATION AND HOUSING: SELECTED CHARACTERISTICS FOR URBAN CENTRES AND LOCALITIES, TASMANIA (ONLINE). *see* POPULATION STUDIES—Abstracting, Bibliographies, Statistics

AUSTRALIA. BUREAU OF STATISTICS. TASMANIAN OFFICE. CENSUS OF POPULATION AND HOUSING: SELECTED EDUCATION AND LABOUR FORCE CHARACTERISTICS FOR STATISTICAL LOCAL AREAS, TASMANIA (ONLINE). *see* POPULATION STUDIES—Abstracting, Bibliographies, Statistics

AUSTRALIA. BUREAU OF STATISTICS. TASMANIAN OFFICE. CENSUS OF POPULATION AND HOUSING: SELECTED SOCIAL AND HOUSING CHARACTERISTICS FOR STATISTICAL LOCAL AREAS, TASMANIA (ONLINE). *see* POPULATION STUDIES—Abstracting, Bibliographies, Statistics

AUSTRALIA. BUREAU OF STATISTICS. TASMANIAN OFFICE. CENSUS OF POPULATION AND HOUSING: SOCIO-ECONOMIC INDEXES FOR AREAS, TASMANIA. *see* POPULATION STUDIES—Abstracting, Bibliographies, Statistics

AUSTRALIA. BUREAU OF STATISTICS. TASMANIAN OFFICE. COMMUNITY SAFETY, TASMANIA. *see* CRIMINOLOGY AND LAW ENFORCEMENT—Abstracting, Bibliographies, Statistics

AUSTRALIA. BUREAU OF STATISTICS. TASMANIAN OFFICE. DISABILITY, AGEING AND CARERS, SUMMARY TABLES, TASMANIA (ONLINE). *see* SOCIAL SERVICES AND WELFARE—Abstracting, Bibliographies, Statistics

AUSTRALIA. BUREAU OF STATISTICS. TASMANIAN OFFICE. HOBART. A SOCIAL ATLAS. *see* POPULATION STUDIES—Abstracting, Bibliographies, Statistics

AUSTRALIA. BUREAU OF STATISTICS. TASMANIAN OFFICE. MANUFACTURING INDUSTRY, TASMANIA (ONLINE). *see* BUSINESS AND ECONOMICS—Abstracting, Bibliographies, Statistics

AUSTRALIA. BUREAU OF STATISTICS. TASMANIAN OFFICE. POPULATION PROJECTIONS, TASMANIA (ONLINE). *see* POPULATION STUDIES—Abstracting, Bibliographies, Statistics

319.4 AUS
AUSTRALIA. BUREAU OF STATISTICS. TASMANIAN OFFICE. TASMANIA AT A GLANCE (ONLINE). Text in English. 1982. a. free (effective 2009). **Document type:** *Government.* **Description:** Contains information on Tasmania's geography, population, social and vital statistics, labor force, wages, price indexes, agriculture, mining, manufacturing, building, trade, transport, finance, and tourism.
Formerly (until 19??): Australia. Bureau of Statistics. Tasmanian Office. Tasmania at a Glance (Print) (0813-5487)
Media: Online - full text.
Published by: Australian Bureau of Statistics, Tasmanian Office, GPO Box 66A, Hobart, TAS 7001, Australia. TEL 61-2-92684909, 300-135-070, client.services@abs.gov.au.

AUSTRALIA. BUREAU OF STATISTICS. TASMANIAN OFFICE. TASMANIA'S YOUNG PEOPLE (ONLINE). *see* REAL ESTATE—Abstracting, Bibliographies, Statistics

AUSTRALIA. BUREAU OF STATISTICS. TASMANIAN OFFICE. TOURIST ACCOMMODATION, SMALL AREA DATA, TASMANIA. *see* HOTELS AND RESTAURANTS—Abstracting, Bibliographies, Statistics

AUSTRALIA. BUREAU OF STATISTICS. TASMANIAN POPULATION CENSUS DATA: HOBART SUBURBS (ONLINE). *see* POPULATION STUDIES—Abstracting, Bibliographies, Statistics

AUSTRALIA. BUREAU OF STATISTICS. TAXATION REVENUE, AUSTRALIA (ONLINE). *see* BUSINESS AND ECONOMICS—Abstracting, Bibliographies, Statistics

AUSTRALIA. BUREAU OF STATISTICS. TELECOMMUNICATION SERVICES, AUSTRALIA, PRELIMINARY (ONLINE). *see* COMMUNICATIONS—Abstracting, Bibliographies, Statistics

AUSTRALIA. BUREAU OF STATISTICS. TELEVISION, FILM AND VIDEO PRODUCTION AND POST-PRODUCTION SERVICES, AUSTRALIA (ONLINE). *see* COMMUNICATIONS—Abstracting, Bibliographies, Statistics

AUSTRALIA. BUREAU OF STATISTICS. TELEVISION SERVICES, AUSTRALIA (ONLINE). *see* COMMUNICATIONS—Abstracting, Bibliographies, Statistics

AUSTRALIA. BUREAU OF STATISTICS. THE HEALTH AND WELFARE OF AUSTRALIA'S ABORIGINAL AND TORRES STRAIT ISLANDER PEOPLES. *see* PHYSICAL FITNESS AND HYGIENE—Abstracting, Bibliographies, Statistics

AUSTRALIA. BUREAU OF STATISTICS. TIME USE ON CULTURE-LEISURE ACTIVITIES (ONLINE). *see* HUMANITIES: COMPREHENSIVE WORKS—Abstracting, Bibliographies, Statistics

AUSTRALIA. BUREAU OF STATISTICS. TIME USE SURVEY, AUSTRALIA - CONFIDENTIALISED UNIT RECORD FILE. *see* HUMANITIES: COMPREHENSIVE WORKS—Abstracting, Bibliographies, Statistics

AUSTRALIA. BUREAU OF STATISTICS. TIME USE SURVEY, AUSTRALIA - USER'S GUIDE (ONLINE). *see* HUMANITIES: COMPREHENSIVE WORKS—Abstracting, Bibliographies, Statistics

AUSTRALIA. BUREAU OF STATISTICS. TOURISM INDICATORS, AUSTRALIA (ONLINE). *see* TRAVEL AND TOURISM—Abstracting, Bibliographies, Statistics

AUSTRALIA. BUREAU OF STATISTICS. TOURISM MARKETING EXPENDITURE, AUSTRALIA. *see* TRAVEL AND TOURISM—Abstracting, Bibliographies, Statistics

AUSTRALIA. BUREAU OF STATISTICS. TOURIST ACCOMMODATION, AUSTRALIA (ONLINE). *see* HOTELS AND RESTAURANTS—Abstracting, Bibliographies, Statistics

AUSTRALIA. BUREAU OF STATISTICS. TOURIST ACCOMMODATION, SMALL AREA DATA, WESTERN AUSTRALIA (ONLINE). *see* HOTELS AND RESTAURANTS—Abstracting, Bibliographies, Statistics

AUSTRALIA. BUREAU OF STATISTICS. TOWNS IN TIME: ANALYSIS AND DATA, CENSUS STATISTICS FOR VICTORIA'S TOWNS AND RURAL AREAS. *see* POPULATION STUDIES—Abstracting, Bibliographies, Statistics

AUSTRALIA. BUREAU OF STATISTICS. TRAVEL AGENCY SERVICES, AUSTRALIA (ONLINE). *see* TRAVEL AND TOURISM—Abstracting, Bibliographies, Statistics

AUSTRALIA. BUREAU OF STATISTICS. TREASURY MODEL OF THE AUSTRALIAN ECONOMY - DOCUMENTATION (ONLINE). *see* BUSINESS AND ECONOMICS—Abstracting, Bibliographies, Statistics

AUSTRALIA. BUREAU OF STATISTICS. TREASURY MODEL OF THE AUSTRALIAN ECONOMY - TSP VERSION. *see* BUSINESS AND ECONOMICS—Abstracting, Bibliographies, Statistics

AUSTRALIA. BUREAU OF STATISTICS. UNDEREMPLOYED WORKERS, AUSTRALIA (ONLINE). *see* BUSINESS AND ECONOMICS—Abstracting, Bibliographies, Statistics

AUSTRALIA. BUREAU OF STATISTICS. UNPAID WORK AND THE AUSTRALIAN ECONOMY (ONLINE). *see* HOME ECONOMICS—Abstracting, Bibliographies, Statistics

AUSTRALIA. BUREAU OF STATISTICS. USE OF INFORMATION TECHNOLOGY ON FARMS, AUSTRALIA (ONLINE). *see* COMPUTERS—Abstracting, Bibliographies, Statistics

AUSTRALIA. BUREAU OF STATISTICS. USE OF INFORMATION TECHNOLOGY ON FARMS, AUSTRALIA, PRELIMINARY (ONLINE). *see* COMPUTERS—Abstracting, Bibliographies, Statistics

AUSTRALIA. BUREAU OF STATISTICS. VALUE OF PRINCIPAL AGRICULTURAL COMMODITIES PRODUCED, AUSTRALIA, PRELIMINARY (ONLINE). *see* AGRICULTURE—Abstracting, Bibliographies, Statistics

AUSTRALIA. BUREAU OF STATISTICS. VETERINARY SERVICES, AUSTRALIA (ONLINE). *see* VETERINARY SCIENCE—Abstracting, Bibliographies, Statistics

AUSTRALIA. BUREAU OF STATISTICS. VICTORIAN OFFICE. BUILDING APPROVALS BY STATISTICAL LOCAL AREAS, VICTORIA - SMALL AREA SUMMARY DATA REPORTS. *see* HOUSING AND URBAN PLANNING—Abstracting, Bibliographies, Statistics

AUSTRALIA. BUREAU OF STATISTICS. VICTORIAN OFFICE. CENSUS OF POPULATION AND HOUSING: ABORIGINAL AND TORRES STRAIT ISLANDER PEOPLE, VICTORIA (ONLINE). *see* POPULATION STUDIES—Abstracting, Bibliographies, Statistics

AUSTRALIA. BUREAU OF STATISTICS. VICTORIAN OFFICE. CENSUS OF POPULATION AND HOUSING: CENSUS BASICS, VICTORIA. *see* POPULATION STUDIES—Abstracting, Bibliographies, Statistics

AUSTRALIA. BUREAU OF STATISTICS. VICTORIAN OFFICE. CENSUS OF POPULATION AND HOUSING: SELECTED CHARACTERISTICS FOR URBAN CENTRES AND LOCALITIES, VICTORIA (ONLINE). *see* POPULATION STUDIES—Abstracting, Bibliographies, Statistics

AUSTRALIA. BUREAU OF STATISTICS. VICTORIAN OFFICE. CENSUS OF POPULATION AND HOUSING: SELECTED EDUCATION AND LABOUR FORCE CHARACTERISTICS FOR STATISTICAL LOCAL AREAS, VICTORIA (ONLINE). *see* POPULATION STUDIES—Abstracting, Bibliographies, Statistics

AUSTRALIA. BUREAU OF STATISTICS. VICTORIAN OFFICE. CENSUS OF POPULATION AND HOUSING: SELECTED SOCIAL AND HOUSING CHARACTERISTICS FOR STATISTICAL LOCAL AREAS, VICTORIA (ONLINE). *see* POPULATION STUDIES—Abstracting, Bibliographies, Statistics

AUSTRALIA. BUREAU OF STATISTICS. VICTORIAN OFFICE. DISABILITY, AGEING AND CARERS, SUMMARY TABLES, VICTORIA. *see* SOCIAL SERVICES AND WELFARE—Abstracting, Bibliographies, Statistics

AUSTRALIA. BUREAU OF STATISTICS. VICTORIAN OFFICE. MANUFACTURING INDUSTRY, VICTORIA (ONLINE). *see* BUSINESS AND ECONOMICS—Abstracting, Bibliographies, Statistics

AUSTRALIA. BUREAU OF STATISTICS. VICTORIAN OFFICE. MELBOURNE. A SOCIAL ATLAS. *see* POPULATION STUDIES—Abstracting, Bibliographies, Statistics

AUSTRALIA. BUREAU OF STATISTICS. VICTORIAN OFFICE. MELBOURNE IN FACT - (YEAR) CENSUS STATISTICS FOR MELBOURNE'S NEW LOCAL GOVERNMENT AREAS. *see* POPULATION STUDIES—Abstracting, Bibliographies, Statistics

AUSTRALIA. BUREAU OF STATISTICS. VICTORIAN OFFICE. MENTAL HEALTH AND WELLBEING: PROFILE OF ADULTS, VICTORIA, DATA REPORT (ONLINE). *see* SOCIAL SERVICES AND WELFARE—Abstracting, Bibliographies, Statistics

AUSTRALIA. BUREAU OF STATISTICS. VICTORIAN OFFICE. POPULATION MOBILITY, VICTORIA. *see* POPULATION STUDIES—Abstracting, Bibliographies, Statistics

319 AUS

AUSTRALIA. BUREAU OF STATISTICS. VICTORIAN OFFICE. REGIONAL STATISTICS, VICTORIA (ONLINE). Text in English. 1997. irreg., latest 2002. free (effective 2009). back issues avail. **Document type:** *Government.* **Description:** Contains recent summary demographic, economic, social and environmental statistics for Victoria's local government areas including population, agriculture and industry, education and training, health, labour force local government finance, and environmental protection and assets statistics.

Formerly: Australia. Bureau of Statistics. Victorian Office. Regional Statistics, Victoria (Print) (1443-8070)

Media: Online - full text.

Published by: Australian Bureau of Statistics, Victorian Office, GPO Box 2796Y, Melbourne, VIC 3001, Australia. TEL 61-2-62524909, 300-135-070, client.services@abs.gov.au.

AUSTRALIA. BUREAU OF STATISTICS. VICTORIAN OFFICE. REGIONAL VICTORIA IN FACT: CENSUS STATISTICS FOR REGIONAL VICTORIA'S NEW LOCAL GOVERNMENT AREAS. *see* POPULATION STUDIES—Abstracting, Bibliographies, Statistics

AUSTRALIA. BUREAU OF STATISTICS. VICTORIAN OFFICE. RETAIL INDUSTRY: DETAILS OF OPERATIONS, VICTORIA. *see* BUSINESS AND ECONOMICS—Abstracting, Bibliographies, Statistics

319.4 AUS

AUSTRALIA. BUREAU OF STATISTICS. VICTORIAN OFFICE. STATE AND REGIONAL INDICATORS, VICTORIA (ONLINE). Text in English. 2001. q. free (effective 2009). back issues avail. **Document type:** *Government.* **Description:** Contains recently released statistical information about the whole of Victoria. Data is sourced from ABS and non-ABS collections. It provides measures according to a triple bottom line of economic, social and environment elements.

Formerly: Australia. Bureau of Statistics. Victorian Office. State and Regional Indicators, Victoria (Print) (1445-6710)

Media: Online - full text.

Published by: Australian Bureau of Statistics, Victorian Office, GPO Box 2796Y, Melbourne, VIC 3001, Australia. TEL 61-2-62524909, 300-135-070, client.services@abs.gov.au.

AUSTRALIA. BUREAU OF STATISTICS. VICTORIAN OFFICE. TOURIST ACCOMMODATION, SMALL AREA DATA, VICTORIA. *see* HOTELS AND RESTAURANTS—Abstracting, Bibliographies, Statistics

AUSTRALIA. BUREAU OF STATISTICS. VICTORIAN OFFICE. VICTORIA IN FUTURE: OVERVIEW. THE VICTORIAN GOVERNMENT'S POPULATION PROJECTIONS (ONLINE). *see* POPULATION STUDIES—Abstracting, Bibliographies, Statistics

AUSTRALIA. BUREAU OF STATISTICS. VICTORIAN OFFICE. VICTORIA IN TIME - (YEAR) CENSUS STATISTICS FOR VICTORIA'S NEW LOCAL GOVERNMENT AREAS. *see* POPULATION STUDIES—Abstracting, Bibliographies, Statistics

AUSTRALIA. BUREAU OF STATISTICS. VICTORIAN OFFICE. VICTORIA'S YOUNG PEOPLE. *see* REAL ESTATE—Abstracting, Bibliographies, Statistics

AUSTRALIA. BUREAU OF STATISTICS. VIDEO HIRE INDUSTRY, AUSTRALIA (ONLINE). *see* BUSINESS AND ECONOMICS—Abstracting, Bibliographies, Statistics

AUSTRALIA. BUREAU OF STATISTICS. VIDEO HIRE OUTLETS, AUSTRALIA (ONLINE). *see* COMMUNICATIONS—Abstracting, Bibliographies, Statistics

AUSTRALIA. BUREAU OF STATISTICS. VOLUNTARY WORK, AUSTRALIA (ONLINE). *see* SOCIAL SERVICES AND WELFARE—Abstracting, Bibliographies, Statistics

AUSTRALIA. BUREAU OF STATISTICS. VOLUNTARY WORK, AUSTRALIA, PRELIMINARY (ONLINE). *see* SOCIAL SERVICES AND WELFARE—Abstracting, Bibliographies, Statistics

AUSTRALIA. BUREAU OF STATISTICS. WATER ACCOUNT, AUSTRALIA (ONLINE). *see* WATER RESOURCES—Abstracting, Bibliographies, Statistics

AUSTRALIA. BUREAU OF STATISTICS. WESTERN AUSTRALIAN OFFICE. CENSUS OF POPULATION AND HOUSING: CENSUS BASICS, WESTERN AUSTRALIA. *see* POPULATION STUDIES—Abstracting, Bibliographies, Statistics

AUSTRALIA. BUREAU OF STATISTICS. WESTERN AUSTRALIAN OFFICE. CENSUS OF POPULATION AND HOUSING: SELECTED CHARACTERISTICS FOR URBAN CENTRES AND LOCALITIES, WESTERN AUSTRALIA, COCOS (KEELING) AND CHRISTMAS ISLANDS (ONLINE). *see* POPULATION STUDIES—Abstracting, Bibliographies, Statistics

AUSTRALIA. BUREAU OF STATISTICS. WESTERN AUSTRALIAN OFFICE. CENSUS OF POPULATION AND HOUSING: SELECTED EDUCATION AND LABOUR FORCE CHARACTERISTICS FOR STATISTICAL LOCAL AREAS, WESTERN AUSTRALIA, COCOS (KEELING) AND CHRISTMAS ISLANDS (ONLINE). *see* POPULATION STUDIES—Abstracting, Bibliographies, Statistics

AUSTRALIA. BUREAU OF STATISTICS. WESTERN AUSTRALIAN OFFICE. CENSUS OF POPULATION AND HOUSING: SELECTED SOCIAL AND HOUSING CHARACTERISTICS FOR STATISTICAL LOCAL AREAS, WESTERN AUSTRALIA, COCOS (KEELING) AND CHRISTMAS ISLANDS (ONLINE). *see* POPULATION STUDIES—Abstracting, Bibliographies, Statistics

AUSTRALIA. BUREAU OF STATISTICS. WESTERN AUSTRALIAN OFFICE. CENSUS OF POPULATION AND HOUSING: SELECTED SOCIAL AND HOUSING CHARACTERISTICS FOR SUBURBS AND POSTAL AREAS, WESTERN AUSTRALIA (ONLINE). *see* POPULATION STUDIES—Abstracting, Bibliographies, Statistics

AUSTRALIA. BUREAU OF STATISTICS. WESTERN AUSTRALIAN OFFICE. CRIME AND SAFETY, WESTERN AUSTRALIA (ONLINE). *see* CRIMINOLOGY AND LAW ENFORCEMENT—Abstracting, Bibliographies, Statistics

AUSTRALIA. BUREAU OF STATISTICS. WESTERN AUSTRALIAN OFFICE. GOVERNMENT FINANCIAL ESTIMATES, WESTERN AUSTRALIA, ELECTRONIC DELIVERY. *see* BUSINESS AND ECONOMICS—Abstracting, Bibliographies, Statistics

AUSTRALIA. BUREAU OF STATISTICS. WESTERN AUSTRALIAN OFFICE. MANUFACTURING INDUSTRY, WESTERN AUSTRALIA (ONLINE). *see* BUSINESS AND ECONOMICS—Abstracting, Bibliographies, Statistics

AUSTRALIA. BUREAU OF STATISTICS. WESTERN AUSTRALIAN OFFICE. MENTAL HEALTH AND WELLBEING OF ADULTS, WESTERN AUSTRALIA: CONFIDENTIALISED UNIT RECORD FILE ON CD-ROM. *see* SOCIAL SERVICES AND WELFARE—Abstracting, Bibliographies, Statistics

AUSTRALIA. BUREAU OF STATISTICS. WESTERN AUSTRALIAN OFFICE. PERTH. A SOCIAL ATLAS. *see* POPULATION STUDIES—Abstracting, Bibliographies, Statistics

AUSTRALIA. BUREAU OF STATISTICS. WESTERN AUSTRALIAN OFFICE. STATSEARCH, A REFERENCE GUIDE TO WESTERN AUSTRALIAN STATISTICS (ONLINE). *see* POPULATION STUDIES—Abstracting, Bibliographies, Statistics

319.4 AUS

AUSTRALIA. BUREAU OF STATISTICS. WESTERN AUSTRALIAN OFFICE. WESTERN AUSTRALIA AT A GLANCE (ONLINE). Text in English. 1979. a. free (effective 2009). back issues avail. **Document type:** *Government.* **Description:** Provide condensed information about Western Australia.

Former titles: Australia. Bureau of Statistics. Western Australian Office. Western Australia at a Glance (1329-1351); (until 1997): Australia. Bureau of Statistics. Western Australian Office. Western Australia in Brief (0727-2022)

Media: Online - full text.

Published by: Australian Bureau of Statistics, Western Australian Office, GPO Box K881, Perth, W.A. 6842, Australia. TEL 61-2-62524909, 300-135-070, client.services@abs.gov.au.

319.4 AUS

AUSTRALIA. BUREAU OF STATISTICS. WESTERN AUSTRALIAN OFFICE. WESTERN AUSTRALIAN STATISTICAL INDICATORS (ONLINE). Text in English. 1958. q. free (effective 2009). back issues avail. **Document type:** *Government.* **Description:** Covers business activities, population, employment, wages and prices, building, production, finance, trade, tourism and transport.

Former titles: Australia. Bureau of Statistics. Western Australian Office. Western Australian Statistical Indicators (Print) (1443-993X); (until 2000): Australia. Bureau of Statistics. Western Australian Office. Monthly Summary of Statistics, Western Australia (0727-2367); (until 1997): Australia. Bureau of Statistics. Monthly Statistical Summary, Western Australia (0004-8542); Incorporates (1989-1993): Australia. Bureau of Statistics. Economic Indicators, Western Australia (1031-7155)

Media: Online - full text.

Published by: Australian Bureau of Statistics, Western Australian Office, GPO Box K881, Perth, W.A. 6842, Australia. TEL 61-2-62524909, 300-135-070, client.services@abs.gov.au.

319.4 AUS

AUSTRALIA. BUREAU OF STATISTICS. WESTERN AUSTRALIAN OFFICE. WESTERN AUSTRALIA'S ABORIGINAL PEOPLE (ONLINE). Text in English. 1993. irreg., latest 1993. free (effective 2009). **Document type:** *Government.* **Description:** Presents a range of statistics on Western Australia's Aboriginal population.

Formerly: Australia. Bureau of Statistics. Western Australian Office. Western Australia's Aboriginal People (Print)

Media: Online - full text.

Published by: Australian Bureau of Statistics, Western Australian Office, GPO Box K881, Perth, W.A. 6842, Australia. TEL 61-2-62524909, 300-135-070, client.services@abs.gov.au.

AUSTRALIA. BUREAU OF STATISTICS. WESTERN AUSTRALIAN OFFICE. WESTERN AUSTRALIA'S SENIORS. *see* POPULATION STUDIES—Abstracting, Bibliographies, Statistics

AUSTRALIA. BUREAU OF STATISTICS. WESTERN AUSTRALIAN OFFICE. WESTERN AUSTRALIA'S YOUNG PEOPLE. *see* REAL ESTATE—Abstracting, Bibliographies, Statistics

AUSTRALIA. BUREAU OF STATISTICS. WORK IN SELECTED CULTURE AND LEISURE ACTIVITIES, AUSTRALIA (ONLINE). *see* BUSINESS AND ECONOMICS—Abstracting, Bibliographies, Statistics

AUSTRALIA. BUREAU OF STATISTICS. WORK-RELATED INJURIES, AUSTRALIA (ONLINE). *see* BUSINESS AND ECONOMICS—Labor And Industrial Relations

AUSTRALIA. BUREAU OF STATISTICS. WORKING PAPERS IN ECONOMETRICS AND APPLIED STATISTICS (ONLINE). *see* BUSINESS AND ECONOMICS—Abstracting, Bibliographies, Statistics

AUSTRALIA. BUREAU OF STATISTICS. WORKING TIME ARRANGEMENTS, AUSTRALIA (ONLINE). *see* BUSINESS AND ECONOMICS—Abstracting, Bibliographies, Statistics

S

319.4 AUS ISSN 0810-8633
HA3001
AUSTRALIA. BUREAU OF STATISTICS. YEAR BOOK AUSTRALIA. Text in English. 1908. a., latest 2008. AUD 99 per issue (effective 2009). **Document type:** *Government.* **Description:** General statistical reference work, containing comprehensive information on demography, prices and household expenditures, labor and industry, social welfare, public health, law and order, education, agriculture and rural industry, and more.
Former titles (until 1977): Official Year Book of Australia (0312-4746); (until 1973): Official Year Book of the Commonwealth of Australia (0078-3927)
Related titles: CD-ROM ed.; Microfiche ed.: (from BHP); Online - full text ed.: free (effective 2009).
Indexed: AEI, GeoRef.
—BLDSC (9411.613600).
Published by: Australian Bureau of Statistics, Locked Bag 10, Belconnen, ACT 2616, Australia. TEL 61-2-92684909, 61-2-62527037, 300-135-070, FAX 61-2-62528103, client.services@abs.gov.au. Circ: 1,861.

AUSTRALIA. BUREAU OF STATISTICS. YOUTH, AUSTRALIA: A SOCIAL REPORT (ONLINE). *see* CHILDREN AND YOUTH—Abstracting, Bibliographies, Statistics

AUSTRALIA. DEPARTMENT OF FAMILIES, COMMUNITY SERVICES AND INDIGENOUS AFFAIRS. STATISTICAL PAPER. *see* POPULATION STUDIES—Abstracting, Bibliographies, Statistics

310 AUS ISSN 1369-1473
HA1
➤ **AUSTRALIAN & NEW ZEALAND JOURNAL OF STATISTICS.** Abbreviated title: A N Z J S. Text in English. 1998. q. GBP 206 in United Kingdom to institutions; EUR 262 in Europe to institutions; USD 297 in the Americas to institutions; USD 405 elsewhere to institutions; GBP 238 combined subscription in United Kingdom to institutions (print & online eds.); EUR 303 combined subscription in Europe to institutions (print & online eds.); USD 342 combined subscription in the Americas to institutions (print & online eds.); USD 467 combined subscription elsewhere to institutions (print & online eds.) (effective 2012). adv. bk.rev. charts; illus. index. back issues avail.; reprint service avail. from PSC. **Document type:** *Journal, Academic/Scholarly.* **Description:** Provides papers containing original contributions to the theory and methodology of statistics, econometrics and probability.
Formed by the merger of (1966-1997): New Zealand Statistician (0111-9176); (1959-1997): Australian Journal of Statistics (0004-9581); Which was formerly (until 1958): Statistical Society of New South Wales. Bulletin
Related titles: Online - full text ed.: ISSN 1467-842X. GBP 206 in United Kingdom to institutions; EUR 262 in Europe to institutions; USD 297 in the Americas to institutions; USD 405 elsewhere to institutions (effective 2012) (from IngentaConnect).
Indexed: A01, A02, A03, A08, A11, A22, A26, Biostat, CA, CCMJ, CIS, CMCI, E01, H05, JCQM, MSN, MathR, ORMS, P06, P30, PAIS, QC&AS, RASB, S01, SCI, SCOPUS, ST&MA, T02, W07, Z02.
—BLDSC (1796.898000), IE, Infotrieve, Ingenta. **CCC.**
Published by: (Statistical Society of Australia, New Zealand Statistical Association NZL), Wiley-Blackwell Publishing Asia (Subsidiary of: Wiley-Blackwell Publishing Ltd.), 155 Cremorne St, Richmond, VIC 3121, Australia. TEL 61-3-92743100, FAX 61-3-92743101, melbourne@wiley.com, http://www.wiley.com/WileyCDA/. Circ: 1,369.

➤ **AUSTRALIAN BUREAU OF AGRICULTURAL AND RESOURCE ECONOMICS. AUSTRALIAN COMMODITY STATISTICS.** *see* BUSINESS AND ECONOMICS—Abstracting, Bibliographies, Statistics

➤ **AUSTRALIAN BUREAU OF AGRICULTURAL AND RESOURCE ECONOMICS. AUSTRALIAN FISHERIES STATISTICS (YEAR) (ONLINE).** *see* FISH AND FISHERIES—Abstracting, Bibliographies, Statistics

➤ **AUSTRALIAN BUREAU OF AGRICULTURAL AND RESOURCE ECONOMICS. AUSTRALIAN MINERAL STATISTICS.** *see* MINES AND MINING INDUSTRY—Abstracting, Bibliographies, Statistics

➤ **AUSTRALIAN GAMBLING STATISTICS (ONLINE).** *see* SPORTS AND GAMES—Abstracting, Bibliographies, Statistics

➤ **AUSTRALIAN PROPERTY MARKET INDICATORS.** *see* HOUSING AND URBAN PLANNING—Abstracting, Bibliographies, Statistics

➤ **AUSTRALIAN SEA FREIGHT.** *see* TRANSPORTATION—Abstracting, Bibliographies, Statistics

➤ **AUSTRALIAN VOCATIONAL EDUCATION AND TRAINING STATISTICS. APPRENTICES AND TRAINEES. EARLY TREND ESTIMATES TO ..** *see* OCCUPATIONS AND CAREERS—Abstracting, Bibliographies, Statistics

➤ **AUSTRALIA'S ECONOMIC STATISTICS**; a student's guide to current economic conditions. *see* BUSINESS AND ECONOMICS—Abstracting, Bibliographies, Statistics

310 AUT
AUSTRIA. STATISTISCHES ZENTRALAMT. PUBLIKATIONSANGEBOT. Text in German. 1960. a. free. back issues avail. **Document type:** *Government.* **Description:** Publications list and prices.
Published by: Statistik Austria, Guglgasse 13, Vienna, W 1110, Austria. TEL 43-1-71128-0, FAX 43-1-7156828. Ed. Marion Bretterecker.

310 AUT
➤ **AUSTRIAN JOURNAL OF STATISTICS.** Text in German. 1972. s-a. **Document type:** *Journal, Academic/Scholarly.* **Description:** Promotes and extends the use of statistical methods in all kinds of theoretical and applied disciplines.
Former titles: Oesterreichische Zeitschrift fuer Statistik (1026-597X); (until 1995): Oesterreichische Zeitschrift fuer Statistik und Informatik (1015-0811); Oesterreichische Statistische Gesellschaft. Mitteilungsblatt (1015-695X); (until 198?): Oesterreichische Gesellschaft fuer Statistik und Informatik. Mitteilungsblatt (1015-6801)
Related titles: Online - full text ed.
Indexed: CIS, P30, RefZh, ST&MA.
Published by: Oesterreichische Statistische Gesellschaft/Austrian Statistical Society, Wirtschaftsuniversitaet Wien, Augasse 2-6, Vienna, W 1090, Austria. TEL 43-1-313364751, http://www.osg.or.at. Ed. Rudolf Dutter. Circ: 3,200.

➤ **AUTOMOBILE IN CIFRE (YEAR)/MOTOR INDUSTRY IN FIGURES (YEAR).** *see* TRANSPORTATION—Abstracting, Bibliographies, Statistics

➤ **AUTOMOTIVE TRADE.** *see* BUSINESS AND ECONOMICS—Abstracting, Bibliographies, Statistics

➤ **AVANCE DE INFORMACION ECONOMICA. EMPLEO.** *see* BUSINESS AND ECONOMICS—Abstracting, Bibliographies, Statistics

➤ **AVANCE DE INFORMACION ECONOMICA. INDUSTRIA DE LA CONSTRUCCION.** *see* BUILDING AND CONSTRUCTION—Abstracting, Bibliographies, Statistics

➤ **AVERAGE DAILY TRAFFIC VOLUMES WITH VEHICLE CLASSIFICATION DATA ON INTERSTATE, ARTERIAL AND PRIMARY ROUTES.** *see* TRANSPORTATION—Abstracting, Bibliographies, Statistics

➤ **AVERAGE RETAIL PRICES OF GOODS AND SERVICES BY RURAL AREAS.** *see* BUSINESS AND ECONOMICS—Abstracting, Bibliographies, Statistics

316.3 ETH
AVERAGE RETAIL PRICES OF GOODS AND SERVICES BY URBAN CENTER. Text in English. q. ETB 92, USD 13. back issues avail. **Document type:** *Government.* **Description:** Presents the average retail price of cereals milled and unmilled, oil seeds, meat, fish, vegetables, fruit, spices, coffee, tea, beverages, other food items, cigarettes, tobacco, cloth and clothing.
Related titles: CD-ROM ed.; Diskette ed.
Published by: Central Statistical Authority, PO Box 1143, Addis Ababa, Ethiopia. TEL 115470, FAX 550334.

B D E W - WASSERSTATISTIK. (Bundesverband der Energie- und Wasserwirtschaft) *see* WATER RESOURCES—Abstracting, Bibliographies, Statistics

B F S AKTUELL/ACTUALITES O F S. *see* PUBLIC ADMINISTRATION—Abstracting, Bibliographies, Statistics

B G W GASSTATISTIK. *see* PETROLEUM AND GAS—Abstracting, Bibliographies, Statistics

B L S RELEASES: DEMOGRAPHIC DATA BOOK FOR STATES AND LARGE METROPOLITAN AREAS. *see* BUSINESS AND ECONOMICS—Economic Situation And Conditions

B L S UPDATE. *see* BUSINESS AND ECONOMICS—Abstracting, Bibliographies, Statistics

B N L BASIC STATISTICS ON THE ITALIAN ECONOMY. (Banca Nazionale del Lavoro) *see* BUSINESS AND ECONOMICS—Abstracting, Bibliographies, Statistics

B P I STATISTICAL HANDBOOK. *see* MUSIC—Abstracting, Bibliographies, Statistics

B S R I A STATISTICS BULLETIN. *see* HEATING, PLUMBING AND REFRIGERATION—Abstracting, Bibliographies, Statistics

314 DEU
BADEN-WUERTTEMBERG. STATISTISCHES LANDESAMT. VEROEFFENTLICHUNGSVERZEICHNIS. Text in German. 1973. a. **Document type:** *Government.*
Published by: Statistisches Landesamt Baden-Wuerttemberg, Boeblinger Str 68, Stuttgart, 70199, Germany. TEL 49-711-6410, FAX 49-711-6412440, poststelle@stala.bwl.de, http://www.statistik.baden-wuerttemberg.de.

304.6 BHS
THE BAHAMAS IN FIGURES. Text in English. 1976. a. USD 13 (effective 2001). stat. **Document type:** *Government.*
Related titles: Diskette ed.; E-mail ed.
Published by: Department of Statistics, PO Box N 3904, Nassau, Bahamas. TEL 242-502-1251, FAX 242-325-5149, dpsdp@batelnet.bs. Ed. Violet Duacombe.

BAHIA ANALISE & DADOS. *see* BUSINESS AND ECONOMICS—Abstracting, Bibliographies, Statistics

BAHRAIN. MONETARY AGENCY. QUARTERLY STATISTICAL BULLETIN. *see* BUSINESS AND ECONOMICS—Abstracting, Bibliographies, Statistics

BALANCE SHEETS. *see* BUSINESS AND ECONOMICS—Abstracting, Bibliographies, Statistics

BALANCO ENERGETICO NACIONAL. *see* ENERGY—Abstracting, Bibliographies, Statistics

318 PRT ISSN 0870-4422
BALANCOS DE APROVISIONAMENTO. Text in Portuguese. 1987. bi-m. EUR 3.24.
Published by: Instituto Nacional de Estatistica, Av Antonio Jose de Almeida 2, Lisbon, 1000-043, Portugal. TEL 351-21-8426100, FAX 351-21-8426380, ine@ine.pt, http://www.ine.pt.

BANCA D'ITALIA. IL QUADRO DI SINTESI DEL BOLLETTINO STATISTICO; dati territoriali sul credito, la finanza e i tassi di interesse bancari. *see* BUSINESS AND ECONOMICS—Abstracting, Bibliographies, Statistics

BANCO CENTRAL DE VENEZUELA. ANUARIO DE BALANZA DE PAGOS. *see* BUSINESS AND ECONOMICS—Abstracting, Bibliographies, Statistics

BANCO CENTRAL DE VENEZUELA. ANUARIO DE CUENTAS NACIONALES. *see* BUSINESS AND ECONOMICS—Abstracting, Bibliographies, Statistics

BANCO CENTRAL DE VENEZUELA. ANUARIO DE ESTADISTICAS INTERNACIONALES. *see* BUSINESS AND ECONOMICS—Abstracting, Bibliographies, Statistics

BANCO CENTRAL DE VENEZUELA. ANUARIO DE ESTADISTICAS: PRECIOS Y MERCADO LABORAL. *see* BUSINESS AND ECONOMICS—Abstracting, Bibliographies, Statistics

BANCO CENTRAL DE VENEZUELA. ANUARIO DE ESTADISTICAS: SECTOR FINANCIERO. *see* BUSINESS AND ECONOMICS—Abstracting, Bibliographies, Statistics

BANCO CENTRAL DE VENEZUELA. BOLETIN DE INDICADORES SEMANALES. *see* BUSINESS AND ECONOMICS—Abstracting, Bibliographies, Statistics

BANCO CENTRAL DE VENEZUELA. BOLETIN MENSUAL. *see* BUSINESS AND ECONOMICS—Abstracting, Bibliographies, Statistics

BANCO CENTRAL DEL PARAGUAY. GERENCIA DE ESTUDIOS ECONOMICOS. ESTADISTICAS ECONOMICAS. *see* BUSINESS AND ECONOMICS—Abstracting, Bibliographies, Statistics

BANCO DE MEXICO. INDICADORES DEL SECTOR EXTERNO. *see* BUSINESS AND ECONOMICS—Abstracting, Bibliographies, Statistics

BANCO DE MEXICO. INDICE DE PRECIOS. *see* BUSINESS AND ECONOMICS—Abstracting, Bibliographies, Statistics

BANCO DE PORTUGAL. BOLETIM ESTATISTICO. *see* BUSINESS AND ECONOMICS—Abstracting, Bibliographies, Statistics

BANGLADESH AGRICULTURAL SCIENCES ABSTRACTS. *see* AGRICULTURE—Abstracting, Bibliographies, Statistics

BANGLADESH BANK. STATISTICS DEPARTMENT. ANNUAL BALANCE OF PAYMENTS. *see* BUSINESS AND ECONOMICS—Abstracting, Bibliographies, Statistics

BANGLADESH BANK. STATISTICS DEPARTMENT. BALANCE OF PAYMENTS. *see* BUSINESS AND ECONOMICS—Abstracting, Bibliographies, Statistics

BANGLADESH EDUCATION IN STATISTICS (YEAR). *see* EDUCATION—Abstracting, Bibliographies, Statistics

BANK FOR INTERNATIONAL SETTLEMENTS. CONSOLIDATED INTERNATIONAL BANKING STATISTICS. *see* BUSINESS AND ECONOMICS—Abstracting, Bibliographies, Statistics

BANK FOR INTERNATIONAL SETTLEMENTS. STATISTICS ON PAYMENT AND SETTLEMENT SYSTEMS IN SELECTED COUNTRIES. *see* BUSINESS AND ECONOMICS—Abstracting, Bibliographies, Statistics

BANK NEGARA MALAYSIA. STATISTICAL BULLETIN. *see* BUSINESS AND ECONOMICS—Abstracting, Bibliographies, Statistics

BANK OF ENGLAND. STATISTICAL CODE OF PRACTICE. *see* BUSINESS AND ECONOMICS—Banking And Finance

BANK OF GREECE. MONTHLY STATISTICAL BULLETIN. *see* BUSINESS AND ECONOMICS—Abstracting, Bibliographies, Statistics

BANK OF ISRAEL. ANNUAL INFORMATION ON THE BANKING CORPORATIONS/MEDA' SHNATI 'AL HATTA'AGIDIM HABBANQA'IYYIM. *see* BUSINESS AND ECONOMICS—Abstracting, Bibliographies, Statistics

BANK OF ISRAEL. CURRENT INFORMATION ON BANKS. *see* BUSINESS AND ECONOMICS—Abstracting, Bibliographies, Statistics

BANK OF ISRAEL. EXCHANGE RATES. *see* BUSINESS AND ECONOMICS—Abstracting, Bibliographies, Statistics

BANK OF ISRAEL. MAIN ISRAELI ECONOMIC DATA. *see* BUSINESS AND ECONOMICS—Abstracting, Bibliographies, Statistics

BANK OF KOREA. MONTHLY STATISTICAL BULLETIN. *see* BUSINESS AND ECONOMICS—Abstracting, Bibliographies, Statistics

BANQUE NATIONALE DE BELGIQUE. BELGOSTAT (YEAR). *see* BUSINESS AND ECONOMICS—Abstracting, Bibliographies, Statistics

BANQUE NATIONALE DE BELGIQUE. INDICATEURS ECONOMIQUES POUR LA BELGIQUE. *see* BUSINESS AND ECONOMICS—Abstracting, Bibliographies, Statistics

BANQUE NATIONALE DE BELGIQUE. INSTITUT DES COMPTES NATIONAUX. AGREGATS ANNUELS. *see* BUSINESS AND ECONOMICS—Abstracting, Bibliographies, Statistics

BANQUE NATIONALE DE BELGIQUE. INSTITUT DES COMPTES NATIONAUX. COMPTES NATIONAUX: AGREGATS TRIMESTRIELS. *see* BUSINESS AND ECONOMICS—Abstracting, Bibliographies, Statistics

BANQUE NATIONALE DE BELGIQUE. INSTITUT DES COMPTES NATIONAUX. COMPTES REGIONAUX. *see* BUSINESS AND ECONOMICS—Abstracting, Bibliographies, Statistics

BANQUE NATIONALE DE BELGIQUE. INSTITUT DES COMPTES NATIONAUX. STATISTIQUES DES EXPORTATIONS BELGES: RESULTATS REGIONAUX. *see* BUSINESS AND ECONOMICS—Abstracting, Bibliographies, Statistics

BANQUE NATIONALE DE BELGIQUE. INSTITUT DES COMPTES NATIONAUX. STATISTIQUES DU COMMERCE EXTERIEUR. *see* BUSINESS AND ECONOMICS—Abstracting, Bibliographies, Statistics

BANQUE NATIONALE DE BELGIQUE. INSTITUT DES COMPTES NATIONAUX. STATISTIQUES DU COMMERCE EXTERIEUR. ANNUAIRE. *see* BUSINESS AND ECONOMICS—Abstracting, Bibliographies, Statistics

BANQUE NATIONALE DE BELGIQUE. LA CENTRALE DES BILANS. STATISTIQUES. *see* BUSINESS AND ECONOMICS—Abstracting, Bibliographies, Statistics

BANQUE NATIONALE DE BELGIQUE. LA CENTRALE DES CREDITS AUX PARTICULIERS. *see* BUSINESS AND ECONOMICS—Abstracting, Bibliographies, Statistics

BARBADOS. REGISTRATION OFFICE. REPORT ON VITAL STATISTICS & REGISTRATIONS. *see* PUBLIC ADMINISTRATION—Abstracting, Bibliographies, Statistics

BARBADOS. STATISTICAL SERVICE. BULLETIN. OVERSEAS TRADE. *see* BUSINESS AND ECONOMICS—Abstracting, Bibliographies, Statistics

317.29 BRB ISSN 0378-8873
HA865
BARBADOS. STATISTICAL SERVICE. MONTHLY DIGEST OF STATISTICS. Text in English. 1974. m. BBD 0.50. illus. **Document type:** *Government.* **Description:** Figures on population and labour force, tourism transport, industrial production, overseas trade, finance, price and interest rates.
Published by: Statistical Service, National Insurance Bldg. 3rd Fl., Fairchild St., Bridgetown, Barbados. Circ: 300.

310 BRB
BARBADOS. STATISTICAL SERVICE. SURVEY OF ACCOMMODATION ESTABLISHMENTS. Text in English. irreg. **Document type:** *Government.*

Published by: Statistical Service, National Insurance Bldg. 3rd Fl., Fairchild St., Bridgetown, Barbados.

BAROMETRE OMT DU TOURISME MONDIAL. (Organisation Mondiale du Tourisme) *see* TRAVEL AND TOURISM—Abstracting, Bibliographies, Statistics

332.1 ITA
BASE INFORMATIVA PUBBLICA; statistiche sull'intermediazione, gli indicatori monetari, finanziari e di bilancia dei pagamenti. Text in Italian. 1998. m. **Document type:** *Directory, Trade.*
Media: Online - full text.
Published by: Banca d'Italia, Via Nazionale 187, Rome, 00184, Italy. TEL 39-06-47922333, FAX 39-06-47922059, http://www.bancaditalia.it.

BASIC AND CLINICAL BIOSTATISTICS. *see* MATHEMATICS

314 LUX
BASIC STATISTICS OF THE EUROPEAN UNION. Text in Dutch. 1961. a., latest no.33. EUR 13 per issue (effective 2005).
Former titles: Basic Statistics of the European Community; Statistical Office of the European Communities. Basic Statistics (0081-4873)
Related titles: Microfiche ed.: (from CIS); Spanish ed.: EUR 13 per issue (effective 2005); Danish ed.: EUR 13 per issue (effective 2005); Portuguese ed.: EUR 13 per issue (effective 2005); Greek ed.: EUR 13 per issue (effective 2005); French ed.: EUR 13 per issue (effective 2005); Italian ed.: EUR 13 per issue (effective 2005); English ed.: EUR 13 per issue (effective 2005); German ed.: EUR 13 per issue (effective 2005).
Indexed: IIS.
Published by: (European Commission, Statistical Office of the European Communities (E U R O S T A T)), European Commission, Office for Official Publications of the European Union, 2 Rue Mercier, Luxembourg, L-2985, Luxembourg. **Dist. in the U.S. by:** Bernan Associates, Bernan, 4611-F Assembly Dr., Lanham, MD 20706-4391. TEL 301-459-2255, 800-274-4447, FAX 301-459-0056.

BAU- UND WOHNBAUSTATISTIK IN DER SCHWEIZ. *see* BUILDING AND CONSTRUCTION—Abstracting, Bibliographies, Statistics

BAUSTATISTISCHES JAHRBUCH. *see* BUILDING AND CONSTRUCTION—Abstracting, Bibliographies, Statistics

BAY OF PLENTY DISTRICT CRIME STATISTICS. *see* CRIMINOLOGY AND LAW ENFORCEMENT—Abstracting, Bibliographies, Statistics

BAYERISCHES LANDESAMT FUER STATISTIK UND DATENVERARBEITUNG. STATISTISCHE BERICHTE A: BEVOELKERUNG, GESUNDHEITSWESEN, GEBIET, ERWERBSTAETIGKEIT. *see* PUBLIC ADMINISTRATION—Abstracting, Bibliographies, Statistics

BAYERISCHES LANDESAMT FUER STATISTIK UND DATENVERARBEITUNG. STATISTISCHE BERICHTE B: BILDUNG, RECHTSPFLEGE, WAHLEN UND VOLKSENTSCHEIDE. *see* PUBLIC ADMINISTRATION—Abstracting, Bibliographies, Statistics

BAYERISCHES LANDESAMT FUER STATISTIK UND DATENVERARBEITUNG. STATISTISCHE BERICHTE C: LAND- UND FORSTWIRTSCHAFT. *see* FORESTS AND FORESTRY—Abstracting, Bibliographies, Statistics

BAYERISCHES LANDESAMT FUER STATISTIK UND DATENVERARBEITUNG. STATISTISCHE BERICHTE D: GEWERBEANZEIGEN, UNTERNEHMEN, INSOLVENZEN. *see* BUSINESS AND ECONOMICS—Abstracting, Bibliographies, Statistics

BAYERISCHES LANDESAMT FUER STATISTIK UND DATENVERARBEITUNG. STATISTISCHE BERICHTE E: PRODUZIERENDES GEWERBE, HANDWERK. *see* BUSINESS AND ECONOMICS—Abstracting, Bibliographies, Statistics

BAYERISCHES LANDESAMT FUER STATISTIK UND DATENVERARBEITUNG. STATISTISCHE BERICHTE F: WOHNUNGSWESEN, BAUTAETIGKEIT. *see* HOUSING AND URBAN PLANNING—Abstracting, Bibliographies, Statistics

BAYERISCHES LANDESAMT FUER STATISTIK UND DATENVERARBEITUNG. STATISTISCHE BERICHTE G: HANDEL, TOURISMUS, GASTGEWERBE. *see* TRAVEL AND TOURISM—Abstracting, Bibliographies, Statistics

BAYERISCHES LANDESAMT FUER STATISTIK UND DATENVERARBEITUNG. STATISTISCHE BERICHTE H: VERKEHR. *see* TRANSPORTATION—Abstracting, Bibliographies, Statistics

BAYERISCHES LANDESAMT FUER STATISTIK UND DATENVERARBEITUNG. STATISTISCHE BERICHTE J: DIENSTLEISTUNGEN, GELD UND KREDIT. *see* BUSINESS AND ECONOMICS—Abstracting, Bibliographies, Statistics

BAYERISCHES LANDESAMT FUER STATISTIK UND DATENVERARBEITUNG. STATISTISCHE BERICHTE K: OEFFENTLICHE SOZIALLEISTUNGEN. *see* SOCIAL SERVICES AND WELFARE—Abstracting, Bibliographies, Statistics

BAYERISCHES LANDESAMT FUER STATISTIK UND DATENVERARBEITUNG. STATISTISCHE BERICHTE L: OEFFENTLICHE FINANZEN, PERSONAL, STEUERN. *see* BUSINESS AND ECONOMICS—Abstracting, Bibliographies, Statistics

BAYERISCHES LANDESAMT FUER STATISTIK UND DATENVERARBEITUNG. STATISTISCHE BERICHTE M: PREISE UND PREISINDIZES. *see* BUSINESS AND ECONOMICS—Abstracting, Bibliographies, Statistics

BAYERISCHES LANDESAMT FUER STATISTIK UND DATENVERARBEITUNG. STATISTISCHE BERICHTE N: LOEHNE UND GEHAELTER, ARBEITSKOSTEN, ARBEITSZEITEN. *see* BUSINESS AND ECONOMICS—Abstracting, Bibliographies, Statistics

BAYERISCHES LANDESAMT FUER STATISTIK UND DATENVERARBEITUNG. STATISTISCHE BERICHTE O: EINNAHMEN, AUSGABEN UND VERMOEGEN PRIVATER HAUSHALTE. *see* BUSINESS AND ECONOMICS—Abstracting, Bibliographies, Statistics

BAYERISCHES LANDESAMT FUER STATISTIK UND DATENVERARBEITUNG. STATISTISCHE BERICHTE P: VOLKSWIRTSCHAFTLICHE GESAMTRECHNUNGEN. *see* SOCIAL SCIENCES: COMPREHENSIVE WORKS—Abstracting, Bibliographies, Statistics

BAYERISCHES LANDESAMT FUER STATISTIK UND DATENVERARBEITUNG. STATISTISCHE BERICHTE Q: UMWELT. *see* ENVIRONMENTAL STUDIES—Abstracting, Bibliographies, Statistics

314 DEU
HA1261
BAYERISCHES LANDESAMT FUER STATISTIK UND DATENVERARBEITUNG. ZEITSCHRIFT - BAYERN IN ZAHLEN. Variant title: Bayern in Zahlen. Text in German. 1869. m. EUR 46; EUR 4.80 newsstand/cover (effective 2011). adv. charts; tr.lit. index. back issues avail. **Document type:** *Government.*
Formerly: Bayern in Zahlen (0005-7215)
Indexed: PAIS, RASB.
Published by: Bayerisches Landesamt fuer Statistik und Datenverarbeitung, Neuhauser Str 8, Munich, 80331, Germany. TEL 49-89-2119205, FAX 49-89-2119410, poststelle@statistik.bayern.de, http://www.statistik.bayern.de. Ed. Peter Englitz. Circ: 1,000.

310 USA ISSN 1931-6690
QA279.5
BAYESIAN ANALYSIS. Text in English. 2006. q. free (effective 2011). back issues avail. **Document type:** *Journal, Academic/Scholarly.*
Media: Online - full text. **Related titles:** Print ed.: ISSN 1936-0975.
Indexed: CCMJ, CurCont, MSN, MathR, P30, SCI, W07.
Published by: International Society for Bayesian Analysis, Department Of Statistics, Carnegie Mellon University, Pittsburgh, PA 15213. ba-mged@stat.cmu.edu, http://www.bayesian.org/. Ed. Herbie Lee.

519.5 GBR ISSN 0959-2083
BAYESIAN STATISTICS. Variant title: Valencia International Meeting. Proceedings. Text in English. 198?. irreg., latest vol.7, 2003. price varies. **Document type:** *Proceedings.*
Indexed: CIS.
—BLDSC (1871.234000). **CCC.**
Published by: Oxford University Press, Great Clarendon St, Oxford, OX2 6DP, United Kingdom. TEL 44-1865-556767, FAX 44-1865-556646, enquiry@oup.co.uk, http://www.oup.co.uk/. Eds. James O Berger, Jose M Bernardo, Mike West.

BEER STATISTICS NEWS. *see* BEVERAGES

BEFOLKNINGSSTATISTIK. DEL 2, INRIKES OCH UTRIKES FLYTTNINGAR. *see* POPULATION STUDIES—Abstracting, Bibliographies, Statistics

BEFOLKNINGSSTATISTIK. DEL 3, FOLKMANGDEN EFTER KON, ALDER OCH MEDBORGARSKAP M M. *see* POPULATION STUDIES—Abstracting, Bibliographies, Statistics

BEGRIFFSBESTIMMUNGEN; fuer die Bundesstatistiken der oesterreichischen Elektrizitaetswirtschaft. *see* ENERGY—Abstracting, Bibliographies, Statistics

314 AUT ISSN 0067-2319
BEITRAEGE ZUR OESTERREICHISCHEN STATISTIK. Text in German. 1953. irreg. price varies. **Document type:** *Government.* **Description:** Publications from all branches of statistics collection.
Related titles: ◆ Series: Statistik Austria. Wohnen; ◆ Statistik Austria. Ergebnisse der Landwirtschaftlichen Statistik; ◆ Demographisches Jahrbuch Oesterreichs. ISSN 0258-8676; ◆ Oesterreichische Hochschulstatistik. ISSN 0067-2343; ◆ Tourismus in Oesterreich; ◆ Austria. Statistisches Zentralamt. Baustatistik. ISSN 1018-0265; ◆ Statistik Austria. Mikrozensus Jahresergebnisse; ◆ Statistik Austria. Landwirtschaftliche Maschinenzaehlung; ◆ Austria. Statistisches Zentralamt. Industrie und Gewerbestatistik Part 1; ◆ Statistik Austria. Gewerbestatistik Part 2; ◆ Statistik Austria. Krippen, Kindergaerten und Horte (Kindertagesheime); ◆ Statistik Austria. Statistik der Jugendwohlfahrt.
Published by: Statistik Austria, Guglgasse 13, Vienna, W 1110, Austria. TEL 43-1-71128-0, FAX 43-1-7156828.

BEITRAEGE ZUR STATISTIK BAYERNS. *see* PUBLIC ADMINISTRATION—Abstracting, Bibliographies, Statistics

BELGIUM. COMMUNAUTE FRANCAISE DE BELGIQUE. INSTITUT NATIONAL DE STATISTIQUE. ANNUAIRE STATISTIQUE. *see* BUSINESS AND ECONOMICS—Abstracting, Bibliographies, Statistics

BELGIUM. FEDERAAL MINISTERIE VAN SOCIALE ZAKEN, VOLKSGEZONDHEID EN LEEFMILIEU. STATISTISCH JAARBOEK VAN DE SOCIALE ZEKERHEID/STATISTICS SOCIAL SECURITY YEARBOOK. *see* INSURANCE—Abstracting, Bibliographies, Statistics

BELGIUM. INSTITUT NATIONAL D'ASSURANCES SOCIALES POUR TRAVAILLEURS INDEPENDANTS. STATISTIQUE DES ENFANTS BENEFICIAIRES D'ALLOCATIONS FAMILIALES/BELGIUM. RIJKSINSTITUUT VOOR DE SOCIALE VERZEKERINGEN DER ZELFSTANDIGEN. STATISTIEK VAN DE KINDEREN DIE RECHT GEVEN OP KINDERBIJSLAG. *see* INSURANCE—Abstracting, Bibliographies, Statistics

BELGIUM. INSTITUT NATIONAL D'ASSURANCES SOCIALES POUR TRAVAILLEURS INDEPENDANTS. STATISTIQUES DES BENEFICIAIRES DE PRESTATIONS DE RETRAITE ET DE SURVIE/BELGIUM. RIJKSINSTITUUT VOOR DE SOCIALE VERZEKERINGEN DER ZELFSTANDIGEN. STATISTIEK VAN DE PERSONEN DIE EEN RUST- EN OVERLEVINGSPRESTATIE GENIETEN. *see* INSURANCE—Abstracting, Bibliographies, Statistics

BELGIUM. INSTITUT NATIONAL D'ASSURANCES SOCIALES POUR TRAVAILLEURS INDEPENDANTS. STATISTIQUES DES PERSONNES ASSUJETTIES AU STATUT SOCIAL DES TRAVAILLEURS INDEPENDANTS/BELGIUM. RIJKSINSTITUUT VOOR DE SOCIALE VERZEKERINGEN DER ZELFSTANDIGEN. STATISTIEK VAN DE PERSONEN DIE ONDER DE TOEPASSING VALLEN VAN HET SOCIAAL STATUUT VAN DE ZELFSTANDIGEN. *see* INSURANCE—Abstracting, Bibliographies, Statistics

BELGIUM. INSTITUT NATIONAL DE STATISTIQUE. AGRICULTURE. STATISTIQUES AGRICOLES. *see* AGRICULTURE—Abstracting, Bibliographies, Statistics

BELGIUM. INSTITUT NATIONAL DE STATISTIQUE. ANNUAIRE DE STATISTIQUES REGIONALES. *see* BUSINESS AND ECONOMICS—Abstracting, Bibliographies, Statistics

BELGIUM. INSTITUT NATIONAL DE STATISTIQUE. BULLETIN DE STATISTIQUE. *see* BUSINESS AND ECONOMICS—Abstracting, Bibliographies, Statistics

330.021 BEL
BELGIUM. INSTITUT NATIONAL DE STATISTIQUE. CATALOGUE DES PRODUITS ET SERVICES. Key Title: Catalogue des Produits et Services. Text in French. a. free. charts; illus. **Document type:** *Catalog, Government.*
Supersedes: Belgium. Institut National de Statistique. Catalogue des Publications (0376-7736)
Related titles: ◆ Dutch ed.: Belgium. Nationaal Instituut voor de Statistiek. Catalogus van de Produkten en Diensten.
Published by: Institut National de Statistique/Nationaal Instituut voor de Statistiek (Subsidiary of: Ministere des Affaires Economiques), Rue de Louvain 44, Brussels, 1000, Belgium. TEL 32-2-548-6211, FAX 32-2-548-6367.

BELGIUM. INSTITUT NATIONAL DE STATISTIQUE. COMMUNIQUE HEBDOMADAIRE. *see* BUSINESS AND ECONOMICS—Abstracting, Bibliographies, Statistics

BELGIUM. INSTITUT NATIONAL DE STATISTIQUE. DEMOGRAPHIE MATHEMATIQUE. TABLES DE MORTALITE. *see* POPULATION STUDIES—Abstracting, Bibliographies, Statistics

BELGIUM. INSTITUT NATIONAL DE STATISTIQUE. EMPLOI ET CHOMAGE. ENQUETE SUR LES FORCES DE TRAVAIL (YEAR). *see* BUSINESS AND ECONOMICS—Abstracting, Bibliographies, Statistics

310 BEL ISSN 0069-8075
HA1399
BELGIUM. INSTITUT NATIONAL DE STATISTIQUE. ETUDES STATISTIQUES. Key Title: Etudes Statistiques - Institut National de Statistique. Text in French. 1961. irreg. (2-4/yr). price varies. charts. **Document type:** *Government.*
Formerly (until 1966): Belgium. Institut National de Statistique. Etudes Statistiques et Econometriques (0772-1846)
Related titles: ◆ Dutch ed.: Belgium. Nationaal Instituut voor de Statistiek. Statistische Studien. ISSN 0772-1838.
Indexed: PAIS.
Published by: Institut National de Statistique/Nationaal Instituut voor de Statistiek (Subsidiary of: Ministere des Affaires Economiques), Rue de Louvain 44, Brussels, 1000, Belgium. TEL 32-2-548-6211, FAX 32-2-548-6367.

BELGIUM. INSTITUT NATIONAL DE STATISTIQUE. INDUSTRIE ET CONSTRUCTION. *see* BUSINESS AND ECONOMICS—Abstracting, Bibliographies, Statistics

BELGIUM. INSTITUT NATIONAL DE STATISTIQUE. INDUSTRIE ET CONSTRUCTION. CONSTRUCTION ET LOGEMENT. *see* HOUSING AND URBAN PLANNING—Abstracting, Bibliographies, Statistics

BELGIUM. INSTITUT NATIONAL DE STATISTIQUE. MEDIA. NOMBRE DE LICENCES D'APPAREILS DE RADIO SUR VEHICULE ET DE TELEVISION. *see* BUSINESS AND ECONOMICS—Abstracting, Bibliographies, Statistics

BELGIUM. INSTITUT NATIONAL DE STATISTIQUE. NOUVELLES ECONOMIQUES. *see* BUSINESS AND ECONOMICS—Abstracting, Bibliographies, Statistics

BELGIUM. INSTITUT NATIONAL DE STATISTIQUE. PERSPECTIVES DE POPULATION. *see* POPULATION STUDIES—Abstracting, Bibliographies, Statistics

BELGIUM. INSTITUT NATIONAL DE STATISTIQUE. SANTE. ACCIDENTS DE LA CIRCULATION SUR LA VOIE PUBLIQUE AVEC TUES ET BLESSES EN (ANNEE). *see* TRANSPORTATION—Abstracting, Bibliographies, Statistics

BELGIUM. INSTITUT NATIONAL DE STATISTIQUE. SANTE. CAUSES DE DECES. *see* POPULATION STUDIES—Abstracting, Bibliographies, Statistics

BELGIUM. INSTITUT NATIONAL DE STATISTIQUE. STATISTIQUE DU TOURISME ET DE L'HOTELLERIE. *see* TRAVEL AND TOURISM—Abstracting, Bibliographies, Statistics

BELGIUM. INSTITUT NATIONAL DE STATISTIQUE. STATISTIQUE DU TRAFIC INTERNATIONAL DES PORTS (U E B L). *see* TRANSPORTATION—Abstracting, Bibliographies, Statistics

BELGIUM. INSTITUT NATIONAL DE STATISTIQUE. STATISTIQUES DU TRANSPORT. PARC DES VEHICULES A MOTEUR AU (YEAR). *see* TRANSPORTATION—Abstracting, Bibliographies, Statistics

BELGIUM. INSTITUT NATIONAL DE STATISTIQUE. STATISTIQUES SOCIALES. *see* SOCIAL SERVICES AND WELFARE—Abstracting, Bibliographies, Statistics

BELGIUM. INSTITUT NATIONAL DE STATISTIQUE. TRANSPORT. NAVIGATION INTERIEURE. *see* TRANSPORTATION—Abstracting, Bibliographies, Statistics

BELGIUM. INSTITUT NATIONAL DE STATISTIQUE. TRANSPORT. VEHICULES A MOTEUR NEUFS ET D'OCCASION MIS EN CIRCULATION EN (ANNEE). *see* TRANSPORTATION—Abstracting, Bibliographies, Statistics

BELGIUM. MINISTERE DE L'EDUCATION, DE LA RECHERCHE ET DE LA FORMATION. ANNUAIRE STATISTIQUE. *see* EDUCATION—Abstracting, Bibliographies, Statistics

BELGIUM. MINISTERE DES AFFAIRES SOCIALES DE LA SANTE PUBLIQUE ET DE L'ENVIRONNEMENT. ADMINISTRATION DES SOINS DE SANTE. ANNUAIRE STATISTIQUE DES HOPITAUX/ BELGIUM. MINISTERIE VAN VOLKSGEZONDHEID EN LEEFMILIEU. BESTUUR VOOR DE VERZORGINGSINSTELLINGEN. STATISTISCH JAARBOEK VAN DE ZIEKENHUIZEN. *see* PUBLIC HEALTH AND SAFETY—Abstracting, Bibliographies, Statistics

BELGIUM. MINISTERE FEDERAL DES AFFAIRES SOCIALES DE LA SANTE PUBLIQUE ET DE L'ENVIRONNEMENT. ANNUAIRE STATISTIQUE DE SECURITE SOCIALE/STATISTICS SOCIAL SECURITY YEARBOOK. *see* INSURANCE—Abstracting, Bibliographies, Statistics

330.9 BEL
BELGIUM. NATIONAAL INSTITUUT VOOR DE STATISTIEK. CATALOGUS VAN DE PRODUKTEN EN DIENSTEN. Text in Dutch. a. free. charts; illus. **Document type:** *Catalog, Government.*

S

Supersedes: Belgium. Nationaal Instituut voor de Statistiek. Catologus van Publicaties
Related titles: ◆ French ed.: Belgium. Institut National de Statistique. Catalogue des Produits et Services.
Published by: Institut National de Statistique/Nationaal Instituut voor de Statistiek (Subsidiary of: Ministere des Affaires Economiques), Rue de Louvain 44, Brussels, 1000, Belgium. TEL 32-2-548-6211, FAX 32-2-548-6367.

BELGIUM. NATIONAAL INSTITUUT VOOR DE STATISTIEK. ECONOMISCHE NIEUWS. *see* BUSINESS AND ECONOMICS—Abstracting, Bibliographies, Statistics

BELGIUM. NATIONAAL INSTITUUT VOOR DE STATISTIEK. GEZONDHEID. DOODSOORZAKEN. *see* POPULATION STUDIES—Abstracting, Bibliographies, Statistics

BELGIUM. NATIONAAL INSTITUUT VOOR DE STATISTIEK. GEZONDHEID. VERKEERSONGEVALLEN OP DE OPENBARE WEG MET DODEN EN GEWONDEN IN (YEAR). *see* PUBLIC HEALTH AND SAFETY—Abstracting, Bibliographies, Statistics

BELGIUM. NATIONAAL INSTITUUT VOOR DE STATISTIEK. INDUSTRIE EN BOUWNIJVERHEID. *see* BUSINESS AND ECONOMICS—Abstracting, Bibliographies, Statistics

BELGIUM. NATIONAAL INSTITUUT VOOR DE STATISTIEK. INDUSTRIE EN BOUWNIJVERHEID. BOUWNIJVERHEID EN HUISVESTING. *see* HOUSING AND URBAN PLANNING—Abstracting, Bibliographies, Statistics

BELGIUM. NATIONAAL INSTITUUT VOOR DE STATISTIEK. LANDBOUW. LANDBOUWSTATISTIEKEN. *see* AGRICULTURE—Abstracting, Bibliographies, Statistics

BELGIUM. NATIONAAL INSTITUUT VOOR DE STATISTIEK. MATHEMATISCHE DEMOGRAFIE. STERFTETAFELS. *see* POPULATION STUDIES

BELGIUM. NATIONAAL INSTITUUT VOOR DE STATISTIEK. MEDIA. AANTAL VERGUNNINGEN VOOR AUTORADIO'S EN TELEVISIETOESTELLEN. *see* BUSINESS AND ECONOMICS—Abstracting, Bibliographies, Statistics

BELGIUM. NATIONAAL INSTITUUT VOOR DE STATISTIEK. REGIONAAL STATISTISCH JAARBOEK. *see* BUSINESS AND ECONOMICS—Abstracting, Bibliographies, Statistics

BELGIUM. NATIONAAL INSTITUUT VOOR DE STATISTIEK. SOCIALE STATISTIEKEN. *see* SOCIAL SERVICES AND WELFARE—Abstracting, Bibliographies, Statistics

BELGIUM. NATIONAAL INSTITUUT VOOR DE STATISTIEK. STATISTIEK VAN HET TOERISME EN HET HOTELWEZEN. *see* TRAVEL AND TOURISM—Abstracting, Bibliographies, Statistics

BELGIUM. NATIONAAL INSTITUUT VOOR DE STATISTIEK. STATISTISCH TIJDSCHRIFT. *see* BUSINESS AND ECONOMICS—Abstracting, Bibliographies, Statistics

BELGIUM. NATIONAAL INSTITUUT VOOR DE STATISTIEK. STATISTISCH ZAKJAARBOEK. *see* BUSINESS AND ECONOMICS—Abstracting, Bibliographies, Statistics

310 BEL ISSN 0772-1838
BELGIUM. NATIONAAL INSTITUUT VOOR DE STATISTIEK. STATISTISCHE STUDIEN. Text in Dutch. 1961. irreg. (2-4/yr). price varies. stat. **Document type:** *Government.*
Formerly (until 1966): Belgium. Nationaal Instituut voor de Statistiek. Statistische en Econometrische Studien (0772-1927)
Related titles: ◆ French ed.: Belgium. Institut National de Statistique. Etudes Statistiques. ISSN 0069-8075.
Published by: Institut National de Statistique/Nationaal Instituut voor de Statistiek (Subsidiary of: Ministere des Affaires Economiques), Rue de Louvain 44, Brussels, 1000, Belgium. TEL 32-2-548-6211, FAX 32-2-548-6367.

BELGIUM. NATIONAAL INSTITUUT VOOR DE STATISTIEK. VERVOER. BINNENSCHEEPVAART (JAAR). *see* TRANSPORTATION—Abstracting, Bibliographies, Statistics

BELGIUM. NATIONAAL INSTITUUT VOOR DE STATISTIEK. VERVOER. IN HET VERKEER GEBRACHTE NIEUWE EN TWEEDEHANDS MOTORVOERTUIGEN IN (YEAR). *see* TRANSPORTATION—Abstracting, Bibliographies, Statistics

BELGIUM. NATIONAAL INSTITUUT VOOR DE STATISTIEK. VERVOERSTATISTIEKEN. MOTORVOERTUIGENPARK OP (YEAR). *see* TRANSPORTATION—Abstracting, Bibliographies, Statistics

BELGIUM. NATIONAAL INSTITUUT VOOR DE STATISTIEK. WEEKBERICHT. *see* BUSINESS AND ECONOMICS—Abstracting, Bibliographies, Statistics

BELGIUM. NATIONAAL INSTITUUT VOOR DE STATISTIEK. WERKGELEGENHEID EN WERKLOOSHEID. ENQUETE NAAR DE ARBEIDSKRACHTEN (YEAR). *see* BUSINESS AND ECONOMICS—Abstracting, Bibliographies, Statistics

BELIZE. CENTRAL STATISTICAL OFFICE. ABSTRACT OF STATISTICS. *see* POPULATION STUDIES—Abstracting, Bibliographies, Statistics

(YEAR) BELIZE LABOUR FORCE INDICATORS. *see* BUSINESS AND ECONOMICS—Abstracting, Bibliographies, Statistics

BENCHMARKING; statistik. *see* HEATING, PLUMBING AND REFRIGERATION—Abstracting, Bibliographies, Statistics

BERNOULLI; a journal of mathematical statistics and probability. *see* MATHEMATICS

BERUFSCHULEN IN BAYERN. *see* EDUCATION—Abstracting, Bibliographies, Statistics

BERUFSSCHULEN ZUR SONDERPAEDAGOGISCHEN FOERDERUNG IN BAYERN. *see* EDUCATION—Abstracting, Bibliographies, Statistics

BETRIEBSKLASSIFIKATION UND SOZIALOEKONOMISCHE GLIEDERUNG DER LANDWIRTSCHAFTLICHEN BETRIEBE IN BAYERN. *see* AGRICULTURE—Abstracting, Bibliographies, Statistics

BETRIEBSSTATISTIK; Erzeugung und Verbrauch elektrischer Energie in Oesterreich. *see* ENERGY—Abstracting, Bibliographies, Statistics

BETRIEBSSTRUKTUR DER LANDWIRTSCHAFT IN BAYERN. AUSGEWAEHLTE ERGEBNISSE FUER KREISE. *see* AGRICULTURE—Abstracting, Bibliographies, Statistics

BETRIEBSSTRUKTUR IN DER LANDWIRTSCHAFT BAYERNS. AUSGEWAEHLTE ERGEBNISSE FUER GEMEINDEN. *see* AGRICULTURE—Abstracting, Bibliographies, Statistics

BIBLIOGRAFIA DE POLITICA INDUSTRIAL. *see* BUSINESS AND ECONOMICS—Abstracting, Bibliographies, Statistics

BIBLIOGRAPHISCHES JAHRBUCH FUER ERZAEHLBAENDE. *see* LITERATURE—Abstracting, Bibliographies, Statistics

BIOMEDICAL STATISTICS AND CLINICAL EPIDEMIOLOGY. *see* MEDICAL SCIENCES—Abstracting, Bibliographies, Statistics

570.15195 USA ISSN 8750-0434
BIOMETRIC BULLETIN. Text in English. 1984. q. USD 40 to non-members; free to members (effective 2004). abstr. back issues avail. **Document type:** *Bulletin.* **Description:** Contains news about membership activities, letters to the editor, and membership and editorial commentaries.
Related titles: Online - full content ed.
Indexed: CIS.
—CCC.
Published by: International Biometric Society, 1444 I St, N W, Ste 700, Washington, DC 20005. TEL 202-712-9049, FAX 202-216-9646, ibs@bostromdc.com. Ed. Tom Ten Have TEL 215-573-4885. Circ: 6,400 (paid).

570.15195 GBR ISSN 0006-341X
QH301 CODEN: BIOMB6
➤ **BIOMETRICS.** Text in English, French. 1945. q. GBP 293 in United Kingdom to institutions; EUR 370 in Europe to institutions; USD 426 in the Americas to institutions; USD 573 elsewhere to institutions; GBP 331 combined subscription in United Kingdom to institutions (print & online eds.); EUR 420 combined subscription in Europe to institutions (print & online eds.); USD 482 combined subscription in the Americas to institutions (print & online eds.); USD 647 combined subscription elsewhere to institutions (print & online eds.) (effective 2012). adv. bk.rev. charts; illus.; stat.; abstr. index, cum.index: vols.1-20, 1945-1964. back issues avail.; reprint service avail. from PSC. **Document type:** *Journal, Academic/Scholarly.* **Description:** Emphasizes the role of statistics and mathematics in the biosciences.
Formerly (until 1947): Biometrics Bulletin (0099-4987)
Related titles: Microfiche ed.: (from BHP); Microform ed.: (from PMC, PQC); Online - full text ed.: ISSN 1541-0420. GBP 293 in United Kingdom to institutions; EUR 371 in Europe to institutions; USD 426 in the Americas to institutions; USD 573 elsewhere to institutions (effective 2012) (from IngentaConnect).
Indexed: A01, A03, A05, A08, A22, A26, A32, A34, A35, A36, A38, AS&TA, AS&TI, ASCA, AbAn, AgBio, Agr, ApMecR, B&AI, B&BAb, B04, B10, B19, B21, B25, BIOSIS Prev, BioEngAb, Biostat, C10, C25, C30, CA, CABA, CCMJ, CIS, CISA, CMCI, ChemAb, CompAb, CompC, CurCont, D01, DentInd, E01, E12, EMBASE, ExcerpMed, F08, F12, FCA, FR, FS&TA, G11, GEOBASE, GH, GeoRef, H05, H12, H16, I05, IBR, IBZ, ISR, IndMed, IndVet, Inpharma, Inspec, JCQM, MEDLINE, MSN, MathR, MycolAb, N02, N03, N05, O01, ORMS, P02, P06, P20, P22, P26, P30, P32, P33, P39, P40, P48, P49, P50, P52, P54, P56, PGegResA, PQC, QC&AS, R07, R08, R09, R10, R12, RM&VM, Reac, S&MA, S01, S13, S16, SCI, SCOPUS, SD, ST&MA, T02, T05, TriticAb, VS, W07, W08, W10, WildRev, Z01, Z02.
—BLDSC (2088.000000), GNLM, IE, Infotrieve, Ingenta, INIST, Linda Hall. **CCC.**
Published by: (International Biometric Society USA), Wiley-Blackwell Publishing Ltd. (Subsidiary of: John Wiley & Sons, Inc.), 9600 Garsington Rd, Oxford, OX4 2DQ, United Kingdom. TEL 44-1865-776868, FAX 44-1865-714591, customerservices@blackwellpublishing.com. Adv. contact Kristin McCarthy. Circ: 8,000.

➤ **BIOMETRIKA.** *see* BIOLOGY—Abstracting, Bibliographies, Statistics

➤ **BIOTECHNOLOGY IN NEW ZEALAND.** *see* BIOLOGY—Abstracting, Bibliographies, Statistics

310 BGR ISSN 1311-2244
HD7045
BIUDZHETI NA DOMAKINSTVATA V REPUBLIKA BULGARIA. Text in Bulgarian. a. BGL 16.84 (effective 2002). 164 p./no.; **Description:** Publishes results of the researches of Bulgarian household income, expenditure and their budget.
Published by: Natsionalen Statisticheski Institut/National Statistical Institute, ul P Volov, # 2, Sofia, 1038, Bulgaria. FAX 359-2-9803319, publikacii@nsi.bg, http://www.nsi.bg. **Dist. by:** Sofia Books, ul Silivria 16, Sofia 1404, Bulgaria. TEL 359-2-9586257, info@sofiabooks-bg.com, http://www.sofiabooks-bg.com.

BLICKPUNKT SOEDRA AFRIKA. *see* HISTORY—History Of Africa

BLUE BOOK OF FOOD STORE OPERATORS & WHOLESALERS. *see* FOOD AND FOOD INDUSTRIES—Abstracting, Bibliographies, Statistics

BOATING REGISTRATION STATISTICS. *see* SPORTS AND GAMES—Abstracting, Bibliographies, Statistics

BOATING STATISTICS. *see* SPORTS AND GAMES—Abstracting, Bibliographies, Statistics

BOLETIN DE ESTADISTICAS DE SEGUROS. *see* INSURANCE—Abstracting, Bibliographies, Statistics

BOLETIN DE ESTADISTICAS LABORALES. *see* BUSINESS AND ECONOMICS—Abstracting, Bibliographies, Statistics

314 PRT ISSN 0032-5082
BOLETIN MENSAL DE ESTADISTICA. Text in English, Portuguese. 1929. m. EUR 80.64 (effective 2005). bibl.; stat. **Document type:** *Government.* **Description:** Provides up-to-date statistical data.
Published by: Instituto Nacional de Estatistica, Av Antonio Jose de Almeida 2, Lisbon, 1000-043, Portugal. TEL 351-21-8426100, FAX 351-21-8426380, ine@ine.pt. Circ: 1,450.

318 BOL
BOLIVIA. CAMARA DE DIPUTADOS. ESTADISTICAS SOCIO-ECONOMICAS. Text in Spanish. 198?. a.
Published by: Muller & Asociados, Edif. Camara de Comercio Ofc. 1305, Casilla 608, La Paz, Bolivia. TEL 378970.

318 BOL ISSN 0302-5217
HA965
BOLIVIA EN CIFRAS. Text in Spanish. 1972. a.
Related titles: Microfiche ed.: (from PQC).
Published by: Instituto Nacional de Estadistica, Casilla de Correos 6129, La Paz, Bolivia.

BOLIVIA. INSTITUTO NACIONAL DE ESTADISTICA. ANUARIO DE COMERCIO EXTERIOR. *see* BUSINESS AND ECONOMICS—Abstracting, Bibliographies, Statistics

BOLIVIA. INSTITUTO NACIONAL DE ESTADISTICA. ANUARIO DE ESTADISTICAS INDUSTRIALES. *see* BUSINESS AND ECONOMICS—Abstracting, Bibliographies, Statistics

BOLIVIA. INSTITUTO NACIONAL DE ESTADISTICA. ESTADISTICAS REGIONALES DEPARTAMENTALES. *see* POPULATION STUDIES—Abstracting, Bibliographies, Statistics

BOLSA MEXICANA DE VALORES. ANUARIO FINANCIERO (YEAR). *see* BUSINESS AND ECONOMICS—Abstracting, Bibliographies, Statistics

BOTSWANA. CENTRAL STATISTICS OFFICE. AGRICULTURE STATISTICS. *see* AGRICULTURE—Abstracting, Bibliographies, Statistics

BOTSWANA. CENTRAL STATISTICS OFFICE. CONSUMER PRICE STATISTICS. *see* BUSINESS AND ECONOMICS—Abstracting, Bibliographies, Statistics

BOTSWANA. CENTRAL STATISTICS OFFICE. DEMOGRAPHIC AND HEALTH SURVEY. *see* BUSINESS AND ECONOMICS—Abstracting, Bibliographies, Statistics

BOTSWANA. CENTRAL STATISTICS OFFICE. EDUCATION STATISTICS. *see* EDUCATION—Abstracting, Bibliographies, Statistics

BOTSWANA. CENTRAL STATISTICS OFFICE. ENVIRONMENT STATISTICS. *see* ENVIRONMENTAL STUDIES—Abstracting, Bibliographies, Statistics

BOTSWANA. CENTRAL STATISTICS OFFICE. EXTERNAL TRADE STATISTICS. *see* BUSINESS AND ECONOMICS—Abstracting, Bibliographies, Statistics

BOTSWANA. CENTRAL STATISTICS OFFICE. HEALTH STATISTICS REPORT. *see* MEDICAL SCIENCES—Abstracting, Bibliographies, Statistics

BOTSWANA. CENTRAL STATISTICS OFFICE. HOUSEHOLD INCOME AND EXPENDITURE SURVEY. *see* BUSINESS AND ECONOMICS—Abstracting, Bibliographies, Statistics

BOTSWANA. CENTRAL STATISTICS OFFICE. INDUSTRIAL STATISTICS. *see* BUSINESS AND ECONOMICS—Abstracting, Bibliographies, Statistics

BOTSWANA. CENTRAL STATISTICS OFFICE. LABOUR FORCE SURVEY. *see* BUSINESS AND ECONOMICS—Abstracting, Bibliographies, Statistics

BOTSWANA. CENTRAL STATISTICS OFFICE. LABOUR STATISTICS. *see* BUSINESS AND ECONOMICS—Abstracting, Bibliographies, Statistics

BOTSWANA. CENTRAL STATISTICS OFFICE. POPULATION AND HOUSING CENSUS. *see* POPULATION STUDIES—Abstracting, Bibliographies, Statistics

BOTSWANA. CENTRAL STATISTICS OFFICE. STATISTICAL BULLETIN. *see* BUSINESS AND ECONOMICS—Abstracting, Bibliographies, Statistics

BOTSWANA. CENTRAL STATISTICS OFFICE. TOURIST STATISTICS. *see* TRAVEL AND TOURISM—Abstracting, Bibliographies, Statistics

BOTSWANA. CENTRAL STATISTICS OFFICE. TRANSPORT STATISTICS. *see* TRANSPORTATION

BOTSWANA. MINISTRY OF AGRICULTURE. AGRICULTURAL STATISTICS. *see* AGRICULTURE—Abstracting, Bibliographies, Statistics

BOTSWANA. MINISTRY OF AGRICULTURE. FARM MANAGEMENT SURVEY RESULTS. *see* AGRICULTURE—Agricultural Economics

BOTSWANA. MINISTRY OF AGRICULTURE. LIVESTOCK MANAGEMENT SURVEY RESULTS. *see* AGRICULTURE—Poultry And Livestock

318.1 BRA ISSN 0103-9288
HA984
BRASIL EM NUMEROS/BRAZIL IN FIGURES. Text in Portuguese. 1960-1977; N.S. 1993. a. USD 30. **Description:** Presents a comprehensive view of Brazil through information presented in texts, maps, graphs and tables.
Supersedes (in 1993): Brasil: Series Estatisticas Retrospectivas (0068-0842); Which was formerly (until 1970): Brasil em Numeros (0524-2010)
Related titles: English ed.: N.S.
Published by: Fundacao Instituto Brasileiro de Geografia e Estatistica, Centro de Documentacao e Disseminacao de Informacoes, Rua General Canabarro, 706 Andar 2, Maracana, Rio de Janeiro, RJ 20271-201, Brazil. TEL 55-21-2645424, FAX 55-21-2841959.

BRAZIL. FUNDACAO INSTITUTO BRASILEIRO DE GEOGRAFIA E ESTADISTICA. ESTATISTICAS DO REGISTRO CIVIL. *see* POPULATION STUDIES—Abstracting, Bibliographies, Statistics

BRAZIL. SERVICO DE ESTATISTICA DA EDUCACAO E CULTURA. SINOPSE ESTATISTICA DA EDUCACAO PRE-ESCOLAR. *see* EDUCATION—Abstracting, Bibliographies, Statistics

BRAZIL. SERVICO DE ESTATISTICA DA EDUCACAO E CULTURA. SINOPSE ESTATISTICA DO ENSINO SUPERIOR. *see* EDUCATION—Abstracting, Bibliographies, Statistics

BRAZIL. SERVICO DE ESTATISTICA DA EDUCACAO. SINOPSE ESTATISTICA DO ENSINO REGULAR DE 1O GRAU. *see* EDUCATION—Abstracting, Bibliographies, Statistics

BRAZIL. SERVICO SOCIAL DO COMERCIO. ANUARIO ESTATISTICO. *see* PUBLIC ADMINISTRATION—Abstracting, Bibliographies, Statistics

BRAZILIAN JOURNAL OF PROBABILITY AND STATISTICS. *see* MATHEMATICS

BRICKS & BLOCKS. *see* BUILDING AND CONSTRUCTION—Abstracting, Bibliographies, Statistics

BRITISH BEER & PUB ASSOCIATION. STATISTICAL HANDBOOK (YEAR). *see* BEVERAGES—Abstracting, Bibliographies, Statistics

BRITISH COLUMBIA. DIVISION OF VITAL STATISTICS AGENCY. QUARTERLY DIGEST. *see* PUBLIC HEALTH AND SAFETY—Abstracting, Bibliographies, Statistics

BRITISH COLUMBIA FINANCIAL AND ECONOMIC REVIEW (ONLINE EDITION). *see* BUSINESS AND ECONOMICS—Abstracting, Bibliographies, Statistics

BRITISH COLUMBIA. MINISTRY OF AGRICULTURE AND FOOD. ANNUAL STATISTICS (YEAR). *see* AGRICULTURE—Abstracting, Bibliographies, Statistics

BRITISH COLUMBIA. MINISTRY OF MUNICIPAL AFFAIRS, RECREATION AND HOUSING. MUNICIPAL STATISTICS, INCLUDING REGIONAL DISTRICTS. *see* PUBLIC ADMINISTRATION—Abstracting, Bibliographies, Statistics

BRITISH COLUMBIA. POLICE SERVICES DIVISION. SUMMARY STATISTICS. *see* CRIMINOLOGY AND LAW ENFORCEMENT—Abstracting, Bibliographies, Statistics

BRITISH COLUMBIA POPULATION FORECAST. *see* POPULATION STUDIES—Abstracting, Bibliographies, Statistics

BRITISH JOURNAL OF MATHEMATICAL AND STATISTICAL PSYCHOLOGY. *see* PSYCHOLOGY

BRITISH VIRGIN ISLANDS. STATISTICS OFFICE. BALANCE OF PAYMENTS. *see* BUSINESS AND ECONOMICS—Abstracting, Bibliographies, Statistics

BRITISH VIRGIN ISLANDS. STATISTICS OFFICE. NATIONAL INCOME AND EXPENDITURE. *see* BUSINESS AND ECONOMICS—Abstracting, Bibliographies, Statistics

BROADCASTING AND TELECOMMUNICATIONS. *see* COMMUNICATIONS—Abstracting, Bibliographies, Statistics

947 314 HUN ISSN 0521-4882
HA1208
BUDAPEST STATISZTIKAI EVKONYVE. Text in Hungarian. a. HUF 325. stat. **Document type:** *Government.*
Indexed: RASB.
Published by: Kozponti Statisztikai Hivatal, Marketing Oszta'ly, Keleti Karoly utca 5-7, Budapest, 1024, Hungary. TEL 36-1-345-6000, FAX 36-1-345-6699. Circ: 800.

947 314 HUN ISSN 0438-2242
HA1208
BUDAPEST STATISZTIKAI ZSEBKONYVE. Text in Hungarian. a. HUF 99. stat. **Document type:** *Government.*
Indexed: P30, RASB.
Published by: Kozponti Statisztikai Hivatal, Marketing Oszta'ly, Keleti Karoly utca 5-7, Budapest, 1024, Hungary. TEL 36-1-345-6000, FAX 36-1-345-6699. Circ: 1,000.

314 HUN ISSN 0133-2449
HA1208.B8
BUDAPESTI STATISZTIKAI TAJEKOZTATO. Text in Hungarian. q. stat. **Document type:** *Government.*
Indexed: RASB.
Published by: (Hungary. Kozponti Statisztikai Hivatal, Hungary. Marketing Oszta'ly/Marketing Department), Statisztikai Kiado Vallalat, Keleti Karoly utca 5-7, Budapest, 1024, Hungary. TEL 36-1-345-6000, FAX 36-1-345-6699.

BUILDING NOTICES RECEIVED AND BUILDING PERMITS GRANTED. *see* BUILDING AND CONSTRUCTION—Abstracting, Bibliographies, Statistics

310 304.6 BGR
BULGARIA - (YEAR). Text in Bulgarian, English. a. USD 18 foreign (effective 2002). **Description:** Presents demographic, social and economic views of Bulgaria.
Published by: Natsionalen Statisticheski Institut/National Statistical Institute, ul P Volov, # 2, Sofia, 1038, Bulgaria. FAX 359-2-9803319, publikacii@nsi.bg, http://www.nsi.bg. **Dist. by:** Sofia Books, ul Silivria 16, Sofia 1404, Bulgaria. TEL 359-2-9586257, info@sofiabooks-bg.com, http://www.sofiabooks-bg.com.

310 304.6 BGR ISSN 1311-3364
BULGARIA: SOTSIALNO-IKONOMICHESKO RAZVITIE. Text in Bulgarian; Summaries in English. a. BGL 14.10 (effective 2002). 250 p./no.; **Description:** Investigates specific problems of the processes which characterize general tendencies related to: population, social levels, life standards and general economic conditions.
Published by: Natsionalen Statisticheski Institut/National Statistical Institute, ul P Volov, # 2, Sofia, 1038, Bulgaria. FAX 359-2-9803319, publikacii@nsi.bg, http://www.nsi.bg.

BULLETIN FLASH; revenu personnel. *see* BUSINESS AND ECONOMICS—Abstracting, Bibliographies, Statistics

BULLETIN FLASH; produit interieur brut regional. *see* PETROLEUM AND GAS—Abstracting, Bibliographies, Statistics

BULLETIN OF INFORMATICS AND CYBERNETICS. *see* MATHEMATICS

BULLETIN ON VITAL STATISTICS IN THE E S C W A REGION/NASRAT AL-IHSA'AT AL HAYAWIYYAT F MINTAQAT AL-LAGNAT AL-IQTISADIYYAT WA-AL-IGTIMA'IYYAT LI-GARBI ASIYA. *see* POPULATION STUDIES—Abstracting, Bibliographies, Statistics

BULLETIN STATISTIQUE REGIONAL. ABITIBI-TEMISCAMINGUE. *see* PUBLIC ADMINISTRATION—Abstracting, Bibliographies, Statistics

BULLETIN STATISTIQUE REGIONAL. BAS-SAINT-LAURENT. *see* PUBLIC ADMINISTRATION—Abstracting, Bibliographies, Statistics

BULLETIN STATISTIQUE REGIONAL. CAPITALE-NATIONALE. *see* PUBLIC ADMINISTRATION—Abstracting, Bibliographies, Statistics

BULLETIN STATISTIQUE REGIONAL. CENTRE-DU-QUEBEC. *see* PUBLIC ADMINISTRATION—Abstracting, Bibliographies, Statistics

BULLETIN STATISTIQUE REGIONAL. CHAUDIERE-APPALACHES. *see* PUBLIC ADMINISTRATION—Abstracting, Bibliographies, Statistics

BULLETIN STATISTIQUE REGIONAL. COTE-NORD. *see* PUBLIC ADMINISTRATION—Abstracting, Bibliographies, Statistics

BULLETIN STATISTIQUE REGIONAL. ESTRIE. *see* PUBLIC ADMINISTRATION—Abstracting, Bibliographies, Statistics

BULLETIN STATISTIQUE REGIONAL. GASPESIE-ILES-DE-LA-MADELEINE. *see* PUBLIC ADMINISTRATION—Abstracting, Bibliographies, Statistics

BULLETIN STATISTIQUE REGIONAL. LANAUDIERE. *see* PUBLIC ADMINISTRATION—Abstracting, Bibliographies, Statistics

BULLETIN STATISTIQUE REGIONAL. LAURENTIDES. *see* PUBLIC ADMINISTRATION—Abstracting, Bibliographies, Statistics

BULLETIN STATISTIQUE REGIONAL. LAVAL. *see* PUBLIC ADMINISTRATION—Abstracting, Bibliographies, Statistics

BULLETIN STATISTIQUE REGIONAL. MAURICIE. *see* PUBLIC ADMINISTRATION—Abstracting, Bibliographies, Statistics

BULLETIN STATISTIQUE REGIONAL. MONTEREGIE. *see* PUBLIC ADMINISTRATION—Abstracting, Bibliographies, Statistics

BULLETIN STATISTIQUE REGIONAL. MONTREAL. *see* PUBLIC ADMINISTRATION—Abstracting, Bibliographies, Statistics

BULLETIN STATISTIQUE REGIONAL. NORD-DU-QUEBEC. *see* PUBLIC ADMINISTRATION—Abstracting, Bibliographies, Statistics

BULLETIN STATISTIQUE REGIONAL. OUTAOUAIS. *see* PUBLIC ADMINISTRATION—Abstracting, Bibliographies, Statistics

BULLETIN STATISTIQUE REGIONAL. SAGUENAY-LAC-SAINT-JEAN. *see* PUBLIC ADMINISTRATION—Abstracting, Bibliographies, Statistics

BUNDESAMT FUER STATISTIK. INFO. *see* PUBLIC ADMINISTRATION—Abstracting, Bibliographies, Statistics

310 DEU
BUNDESMINISTERIUM FUER ERNAEHRUNG, LANDWIRTSCHAFT UND VERBRAUCHERSCHUTZ. STATISTISCHER MONATSBERICHT. Text in German. 1949. m. 80 p./no.; back issues avail. **Document type:** *Bulletin, Trade.*
Former titles (until 2006): Bundesministerium fuer Verbraucherschutz, Ernaehrung und Landwirtschaft. Statistischer Monatsbericht; (until 2001): Germany. Bundesministerium fuer Ernaehrung, Landwirtschaft und Forsten. Statistischer Monatsbericht (0433-7344); Which incorporated (195?-1996): Die Futterwirtschaft in Deutschland (0944-3495); Which was formerly (until 1992): Die Futterwirtschaft in der Bundesrepublik Deutschland (0178-9031); (until 1969): Statistische Unterlagen zur Futterwirtschaft in der Bundesrepublik Deutschland (0435-7361)
Published by: Bundesministerium fuer Ernaehrung, Landwirtschaft und Verbraucherschutz, Rochusstr 1, Bonn, 53123, Germany. TEL 49-228-995290, FAX 49-228-995293179, poststelle@bmelv.bund.de, http://www.bmelv.de. Circ: 900.

316 316 BDI
BURUNDI. INSTITUT DE STATISTIQUES ET D'ETUDES ECONOMIQUES. ANNUAIRE STATISTIQUE. Text in French. a. USD 45. **Document type:** *Bulletin.*
Formerly: Burundi. Departement des Etudes et Statistiques. Bulletin Annuaire
Related titles: Microfiche ed.: (from PQC).
Published by: Institut de Statistiques et d'Etudes Economiques, BP 1156, Bujumbura, Burundi.

316 BDI
BURUNDI. INSTITUT DE STATISTIQUES ET D'ETUDES ECONOMIQUES. BULLETIN MENSUEL DES PRIX. Text in French. m. USD 270. **Document type:** *Bulletin.*
Formerly: Burundi. Departement des Etudes et Statistiques. Informations Statistiques Mensuelles
Published by: Institut de Statistiques et d'Etudes Economiques, BP 1156, Bujumbura, Burundi.

316 BDI
BURUNDI. INSTITUT DE STATISTIQUES ET D'ETUDES ECONOMIQUES. BULLETIN STATISTIQUE TRIMESTRIEL. Text in French. 1965. q. USD 60. stat. Supplement avail. **Document type:** *Bulletin.*
Formerly: Burundi. Departement des Etudes et Statistiques. Bulletin Trimestriel; Supersedes: Burundi. Ministere du Plan. Departement des Statistiques. Bulletin de Statistique (0525-2539)
Published by: Institut de Statistiques et d'Etudes Economiques, BP 1156, Bujumbura, Burundi.

BUSINESS INDICATORS. *see* BUSINESS AND ECONOMICS—Abstracting, Bibliographies, Statistics

BYTOVA VYSTAVBA. *see* BUILDING AND CONSTRUCTION—Abstracting, Bibliographies, Statistics

C A B AIR CARRIER TRAFFIC STATISTICS. (Civil Aeronautics Board) *see* TRANSPORTATION—Abstracting, Bibliographies, Statistics

C D M O T A. (Compact Disc Monitor of Tourism Activity) *see* TRAVEL AND TOURISM—Abstracting, Bibliographies, Statistics

C H S DEMOGRAPHY/STATISTIQUE DU LOGEMENT AU CANADA: DEMOGRAPHIE. (Canadian Housing Statistics) *see* HOUSING AND URBAN PLANNING—Abstracting, Bibliographies, Statistics

C H S RENTAL MARKET SURVEY/STATISTIQUE DU LOGEMENT AU CANADA: ENQUETE SUR LE MARCHE LOCATIF. (Canadian Housing Statistics) *see* REAL ESTATE—Abstracting, Bibliographies, Statistics

C H S RESIDENTIAL BUILDING ACTIVITY/STATISTIQUE DU LOGEMENT AU CANADA: CONSTRUCTION RESIDENTIELLE. (Canadian Housing Statistics) *see* BUSINESS AND ECONOMICS—Abstracting, Bibliographies, Statistics

C I P F A FIRE AND RESCUE SERVICE STATISTICS. *see* FIRE PREVENTION—Abstracting, Bibliographies, Statistics

319 TTO
C.S.O. STATISTICAL BULLETINS. Text in English. 1972. irreg. price varies. **Document type:** *Government.*
Published by: Central Statistical Office, 35-41 Queen St, PO Box 98, Port-of-Spain, Trinidad, Trinidad & Tobago. TEL 868-623-6495, FAX 868-625-3802.

314 CZE
C Z S O MONTHLY STATISTICS. (Czech Statistical Office) Text in English. m. EUR 255, USD 266 foreign (effective 2008). **Document type:** *Government.*
Formerly (until 2004): Current C S O News
Related titles: ◆ Czech ed.: Cesky Statisticky Urad. Aktuality. ISSN 1214-1461.
Published by: Cesky Statisticky Urad, Na padesatem 81, Prague 10, 10082, Czech Republic. TEL 420-2-74051111, infoservis@czso.cz. **Dist. by:** Myris Trade Ltd., V Stihlach 1311, PO Box 2, Prague 4 14201, Czech Republic.

CABELL'S DIRECTORY OF PUBLISHING OPPORTUNITIES IN ACCOUNTING. *see* BUSINESS AND ECONOMICS—Abstracting, Bibliographies, Statistics

CABELL'S DIRECTORY OF PUBLISHING OPPORTUNITIES IN ECONOMICS AND FINANCE. *see* BUSINESS AND ECONOMICS—Abstracting, Bibliographies, Statistics

CABELL'S DIRECTORY OF PUBLISHING OPPORTUNITIES IN EDUCATIONAL CURRICULUM AND METHODS (ONLINE). *see* EDUCATION—Abstracting, Bibliographies, Statistics

CABELL'S DIRECTORY OF PUBLISHING OPPORTUNITIES IN EDUCATIONAL PSYCHOLOGY AND ADMINISTRATION (ONLINE). *see* EDUCATION—Abstracting, Bibliographies, Statistics

CABELL'S DIRECTORY OF PUBLISHING OPPORTUNITIES IN MANAGEMENT. *see* BUSINESS AND ECONOMICS—Abstracting, Bibliographies, Statistics

CABELL'S DIRECTORY OF PUBLISHING OPPORTUNITIES IN MARKETING. *see* BUSINESS AND ECONOMICS—Abstracting, Bibliographies, Statistics

CABELL'S DIRECTORY OF PUBLISHING OPPORTUNITIES IN PSYCHOLOGY AND PSYCHIATRY. *see* PSYCHOLOGY—Abstracting, Bibliographies, Statistics

CABLE T V ADVERTISING STATISTICS; a best-in-class study on the business of cable t v advertising. *see* COMMUNICATIONS—Abstracting, Bibliographies, Statistics

310 IND ISSN 0008-0683
HA1 CODEN: CSTBAA
➤ **CALCUTTA STATISTICAL ASSOCIATION. BULLETIN.** Text in English. 1947. q. USD 80 foreign (effective 2011). adv. bk.rev. charts; stat. index. **Document type:** *Journal, Academic/Scholarly.*
Indexed: A22, CCMJ, CIS, JCQM, MSN, MathR, P06, ST&MA, Z02. —IE, Infotrieve, Ingenta.
Published by: Calcutta Statistical Association, c/o, Department of Statistics, Calcutta University, 35, Bullygunge Circular Rd, Kolkata, West Bengal 700 019, India. Ed. B K Sinha. Circ: 350. **Subscr. to:** I N S I O Scientific Books & Periodicals, PO Box 7234, Indraprastha HPO, New Delhi 110 002, India. iihm@ap.nic.in, http://iihm.ap.nic.in/.

➤ **CALIFORNIA. AGRICULTURAL STATISTICS SERVICE. CROP WEATHER REPORT.** *see* AGRICULTURE—Abstracting, Bibliographies, Statistics

➤ **CALIFORNIA. AGRICULTURAL STATISTICS SERVICE. DAIRY INDUSTRY STATISTICS.** *see* AGRICULTURE—Abstracting, Bibliographies, Statistics

➤ **CALIFORNIA. AGRICULTURAL STATISTICS SERVICE. FIELD CROP REVIEW.** *see* AGRICULTURE—Abstracting, Bibliographies, Statistics

➤ **CALIFORNIA. AGRICULTURAL STATISTICS SERVICE. FRUIT AND NUT REVIEW.** *see* AGRICULTURE—Abstracting, Bibliographies, Statistics

➤ **CALIFORNIA. AGRICULTURAL STATISTICS SERVICE. GRAPE ACREAGE.** *see* AGRICULTURE—Abstracting, Bibliographies, Statistics

➤ **CALIFORNIA. AGRICULTURAL STATISTICS SERVICE. GRAPE CRUSH REPORT.** *see* AGRICULTURE—Abstracting, Bibliographies, Statistics

➤ **CALIFORNIA. AGRICULTURAL STATISTICS SERVICE. LIVESTOCK REVIEW.** *see* AGRICULTURE—Abstracting, Bibliographies, Statistics

➤ **CALIFORNIA. AGRICULTURAL STATISTICS SERVICE. POULTRY REPORT.** *see* AGRICULTURE—Abstracting, Bibliographies, Statistics

➤ **CALIFORNIA. AGRICULTURAL STATISTICS SERVICE. VEGETABLE REVIEW.** *see* AGRICULTURE—Abstracting, Bibliographies, Statistics

➤ **CALIFORNIA. AGRICULTURAL STATISTICS SERVICE. WALNUTS, RAISINS AND PRUNES (PRICE REPORT).** *see* AGRICULTURE—Abstracting, Bibliographies, Statistics

➤ **CALIFORNIA CITIES & COUNTIES GRAPHIC PERFORMANCE ANALYSIS.** *see* PUBLIC ADMINISTRATION—Abstracting, Bibliographies, Statistics

➤ **CALIFORNIA CITIES, TOWNS AND COUNTIES.** *see* SOCIOLOGY—Abstracting, Bibliographies, Statistics

➤ **CALIFORNIA COUNTY PROJECTIONS (YEAR).** *see* BUSINESS AND ECONOMICS—Abstracting, Bibliographies, Statistics

➤ **CALIFORNIA DAIRY INFORMATION BULLETIN (ONLINE).** *see* AGRICULTURE—Abstracting, Bibliographies, Statistics

➤ **CALIFORNIA ECONOMIC GROWTH (YEAR).** *see* BUSINESS AND ECONOMICS—Abstracting, Bibliographies, Statistics

➤ **CALIFORNIA FARM NEWS.** *see* AGRICULTURE—Abstracting, Bibliographies, Statistics

➤ **CALIFORNIA STATISTICAL ABSTRACTS.** *see* BUSINESS AND ECONOMICS—Banking And Finance

318 COL ISSN 0120-6338
HC196
CAMBIO Y PROGRESO. Text in Spanish. 1985. irreg. USD 30. **Document type:** *Government.*
Indexed: IBR, IBZ.
Published by: Departamento Administrativo Nacional de Estadistica (D A N E), Bancos de Datos, Centro Administrativo Nacional (CAN), Avenida Eldorado, Apartado Aereo 80043, Bogota, CUND, Colombia. TEL 57-1-222-3273, FAX 57-1-222-2305.

310 CMR
CAMEROON. DIRECTION DE LA STATISTIQUE ET DE LA COMPTABILITE NATIONALE. BULLETIN MENSUEL DE STATISTIQUE. Text in French. 1974. m. XAF 12,000.
Published by: Direction de la Statistique et de la Comptabilite Nationale/ Department of Statistics and National Accounts, BP 660, Yaounde, Cameroon. TEL 220-445. Circ: 500.

CAMEROON. DIRECTION DE LA STATISTIQUE ET DE LA COMPTABILITE NATIONALE. BULLETIN TRIMESTRIEL DE CONJONCTURE. *see* PUBLIC ADMINISTRATION—Abstracting, Bibliographies, Statistics

S

CAMEROON. DIRECTION DE LA STATISTIQUE ET DE LA COMPTABILITE NATIONALE. NOTE ANNUELLE DE STATISTIQUE. *see* BUSINESS AND ECONOMICS—Abstracting, Bibliographies, Statistics

316 CMR

CAMEROON. PROVINCIAL STATISTICAL SERVICE OF THE SOUTH WEST. ANNUAL STATISTICAL REPORT, SOUTH WEST PROVINCE. Text in English. a.

Published by: Service Provincial de la Statistique du Sud-Ouest, BP 93, Buea, Cameroon.

971 CAN ISSN 0840-6014

CANADA, A PORTRAIT. Text in English. 1930. biennial. CAD 49.95 (effective 2005). **Description:** Presents current and historical information to form a portrait of Canada.

Former titles (until 1989): Canada Handbook (0705-5331); (until 1977): Canada (English Edition) (0318-9015)

Related titles: Microfiche ed.: (from MML); Microform ed.: (from MML); French ed.: Portrait du Canada. ISSN 0840-6022.

—CCC.

Published by: Statistics Canada, Operations and Integration Division (Subsidiary of: Statistics Canada/Statistique Canada), Circulation Management, 120 Parkdale Ave, Ottawa, ON K1A 0T6, Canada. TEL 613-951-7277, 800-267-6677, FAX 613-951-1584.

CANADA. DEPARTMENT OF FINANCE. FISCAL REFERENCE TABLES. *see* BUSINESS AND ECONOMICS—Abstracting, Bibliographies, Statistics

CANADA. GRAIN COMMISSION. CORPORATE SERVICES. CANADIAN GRAIN EXPORTS. *see* AGRICULTURE—Abstracting, Bibliographies, Statistics

CANADA. GRAIN COMMISSION. CORPORATE SERVICES. EXPORTS OF CANADIAN GRAIN AND WHEAT FLOUR. *see* AGRICULTURE—Abstracting, Bibliographies, Statistics

CANADA GRAINS COUNCIL. STATISTICAL HANDBOOK. *see* AGRICULTURE—Abstracting, Bibliographies, Statistics

CANADA. HEALTH CANADA. REPORT ON OCCUPATIONAL RADIATION EXPOSURES IN CANADA. *see* PUBLIC HEALTH AND SAFETY—Abstracting, Bibliographies, Statistics

CANADA MORTGAGE AND HOUSING CORPORATION. MONTHLY HOUSING STATISTICS/SOCIETE CANADIENNE D'HYPOTHEQUES ET DE LOGEMENT. STATISTIQUES MENSUELLES SUR L'HABITATION. *see* HOUSING AND URBAN PLANNING—Abstracting, Bibliographies, Statistics

CANADA PENSION PLAN, OLD AGE SECURITY, STATISTICAL BULLETIN. *see* SOCIAL SERVICES AND WELFARE

CANADA REVENUE AGENCY. INCOME STATISTICS. *see* BUSINESS AND ECONOMICS—Abstracting, Bibliographies, Statistics

CANADA. STATISTICS CANADA. ADULT CORRECTIONAL SERVICES IN CANADA. *see* CRIMINOLOGY AND LAW ENFORCEMENT—Abstracting, Bibliographies, Statistics

CANADA. STATISTICS CANADA. ADULT CRIMINAL COURT STATISTICS. *see* CRIMINOLOGY AND LAW ENFORCEMENT—Abstracting, Bibliographies, Statistics

CANADA. STATISTICS CANADA. AIR CHARTER STATISTICS. *see* TRANSPORTATION—Abstracting, Bibliographies, Statistics

CANADA. STATISTICS CANADA. AIR PASSENGER ORIGIN AND DESTINATION. CANADA - UNITED STATES REPORT. *see* TRANSPORTATION—Abstracting, Bibliographies, Statistics

CANADA. STATISTICS CANADA. ANNUAL DEMOGRAPHIC STATISTICS. *see* POPULATION STUDIES—Abstracting, Bibliographies, Statistics

CANADA. STATISTICS CANADA. ASPHALT ROOFING/PAPIER-TOITURE ASPHALTE. *see* BUILDING AND CONSTRUCTION—Abstracting, Bibliographies, Statistics

CANADA. STATISTICS CANADA. AVIATION STATISTICS CENTRE. SERVICE BULLETIN/CANADA. CENTRE DES STATISTIQUES DE L'AVIATION. BULLETIN DE SERVICE. *see* TRANSPORTATION—Abstracting, Bibliographies, Statistics

CANADA. STATISTICS CANADA. BEVERAGE AND TOBACCO PRODUCTS INDUSTRIES/INDUSTRIES DES BOISSONS ET DU TABAC. *see* TOBACCO—Abstracting, Bibliographies, Statistics

CANADA. STATISTICS CANADA. BUILDING PERMITS/PERMIS DE BATIR. *see* BUILDING AND CONSTRUCTION—Abstracting, Bibliographies, Statistics

CANADA. STATISTICS CANADA. BUILDING PERMITS, ANNUAL SUMMARY/PERMIS DE BATIR, SOMMAIRE ANNUEL. *see* BUILDING AND CONSTRUCTION—Abstracting, Bibliographies, Statistics

CANADA. STATISTICS CANADA. BUSINESS SERVICES/CANADA. STATISTIQUE CANADA. SERVICES AUX ENTREPRISES. *see* BUSINESS AND ECONOMICS—Abstracting, Bibliographies, Statistics

CANADA. STATISTICS CANADA. CABLE TELEVISION/CANADA. STATISTIQUE CANADA. TELEDISTRIBUTION. *see* COMMUNICATIONS—Abstracting, Bibliographies, Statistics

CANADA. STATISTICS CANADA. CANADA AT A GLANCE. *see* TRAVEL AND TOURISM

CANADA. STATISTICS CANADA. CANADA FOOD STATS. *see* AGRICULTURE—Abstracting, Bibliographies, Statistics

971 317 CAN ISSN 0068-8142
HA744 CODEN: BIBUBX

CANADA. STATISTICS CANADA. CANADA YEAR BOOK. Text in English. 1867. biennial. CAD 54.95 domestic; USD 77 foreign (effective 1999). **Document type:** *Government.* **Description:** Offers comprehensive and timely data on economy, arts, sports, government, geography, demography.

Related titles: CD-ROM ed.: USD 74.95 (effective 1999); Microform ed.: (from MML); French ed.: Annuaire du Canada.

Published by: Statistics Canada, Operations and Integration Division (Subsidiary of: Statistics Canada/Statistique Canada), Circulation Management, 120 Parkdale Ave, Ottawa, ON K1A 0T6, Canada. TEL 613-951-7277, 800-267-6677, FAX 613-951-1584.

CANADA. STATISTICS CANADA. CANADA'S BALANCE OF INTERNATIONAL PAYMENTS/CANADA. STATISTIQUE CANADA. BALANCE DES PAIEMENTS INTERNATIONAUX DU CANADA. *see* BUSINESS AND ECONOMICS—Abstracting, Bibliographies, Statistics

CANADA. STATISTICS CANADA. CANADA'S BALANCE OF INTERNATIONAL PAYMENTS (FINAL EDITION). *see* BUSINESS AND ECONOMICS—Abstracting, Bibliographies, Statistics

CANADA. STATISTICS CANADA. CANADA'S INTERNATIONAL TRANSACTIONS IN SECURITIES/OPERATIONS INTERNATIONALES DU CANADA EN VALEURS MOBILIERES. *see* BUSINESS AND ECONOMICS—Abstracting, Bibliographies, Statistics

CANADA. STATISTICS CANADA. CANADA'S MINERAL PRODUCTION, PRELIMINARY ESTIMATE/PRODUCTION MINERALE DU CANADA, CALCUL PRELIMINAIRE. *see* MINES AND MINING INDUSTRY—Abstracting, Bibliographies, Statistics

CANADA. STATISTICS CANADA. CANADIAN CULTURE IN PERSPECTIVE: A STATISTICAL OVERVIEW/CANADA. STATISTIQUE CANADA. LE CANADA, SA CULTURE, SON PATRIMOINE ET SON IDENTITE: PERSPECTIVE STATISTIQUE. *see* PUBLIC ADMINISTRATION—Abstracting, Bibliographies, Statistics

CANADA. STATISTICS CANADA. CANADIAN TRAVEL SURVEY. DOMESTIC TRAVEL/CANADA. STATISTIQUE CANADA. ENQUETE SUR LES VOYAGES DES CANADIENS. VOYAGES INTERIEURS. *see* TRAVEL AND TOURISM—Abstracting, Bibliographies, Statistics

CANADA. STATISTICS CANADA. CAPITAL AND REPAIR EXPENDITURES, MANUFACTURING SUB-INDUSTRIES, INTENTIONS. *see* BUSINESS AND ECONOMICS—Abstracting, Bibliographies, Statistics

CANADA. STATISTICS CANADA. CAPITAL EXPENDITURE PRICE STATISTICS/CANADA. STATISTIQUE CANADA. STATISTIQUES DES PRIX DE LA CONSTRUCTION RAPPORT TRIMESTRIEL. *see* BUILDING AND CONSTRUCTION—Abstracting, Bibliographies, Statistics

CANADA. STATISTICS CANADA. CAPITAL EXPENDITURES BY TYPE OF ASSET. *see* BUILDING AND CONSTRUCTION—Abstracting, Bibliographies, Statistics

CANADA. STATISTICS CANADA. CAUSES OF DEATH (OTTAWA, 1997) (ONLINE EDITION). *see* POPULATION STUDIES—Abstracting, Bibliographies, Statistics

CANADA. STATISTICS CANADA. CLOTHING INDUSTRIES/CANADA. STATISTIQUE CANADA. INDUSTRIES DE L'HABILLEMENT. *see* CLOTHING TRADE—Abstracting, Bibliographies, Statistics

CANADA. STATISTICS CANADA. COAL AND COKE STATISTICS/ CANADA. STATISTIQUE CANADA. STATISTIQUE DU CHARBON ET DU COKE. *see* MINES AND MINING INDUSTRY—Abstracting, Bibliographies, Statistics

CANADA. STATISTICS CANADA. COAL MINING/CANADA. STATISTIQUE CANADA. MINES DE CHARBON. *see* MINES AND MINING INDUSTRY—Abstracting, Bibliographies, Statistics

CANADA. STATISTICS CANADA. CORPORATIONS, ASPECTS OF BUSINESS ORGANIZATION. *see* BUSINESS AND ECONOMICS—Abstracting, Bibliographies, Statistics

CANADA. STATISTICS CANADA. CORPORATIONS, ASPECTS OF FOREIGN CONTROL. *see* BUSINESS AND ECONOMICS—Abstracting, Bibliographies, Statistics

CANADA. STATISTICS CANADA. CRIMINAL PROSECUTIONS: PERSONNEL AND EXPENDITURES (ONLINE EDITION). *see* LAW—Abstracting, Bibliographies, Statistics

CANADA. STATISTICS CANADA. DAIRY REVIEW/CANADA. STATISTIQUE CANADA. REVUE LAITIERE. *see* AGRICULTURE—Abstracting, Bibliographies, Statistics

CANADA. STATISTICS CANADA. DIRECT SELLING IN CANADA/ CANADA. STATISTIQUE CANADA. VENTE DIRECTE AU CANADA. *see* BUSINESS AND ECONOMICS—Abstracting, Bibliographies, Statistics

CANADA. STATISTICS CANADA. DIVORCES. SHELF TABLES. *see* POPULATION STUDIES—Abstracting, Bibliographies, Statistics

CANADA. STATISTICS CANADA. ECONOMIC OVERVIEW OF FARM INCOMES. *see* AGRICULTURE—Abstracting, Bibliographies, Statistics

CANADA. STATISTICS CANADA. EDUCATION IN CANADA/CANADA. STATISTIQUE CANADA. L'EDUCATION AU CANADA. *see* EDUCATION—Abstracting, Bibliographies, Statistics

CANADA. STATISTICS CANADA. ELECTRIC POWER GENERATION, TRANSMISSION AND DISTRIBUTION/CANADA. STATISTIQUE CANADA. PRODUCTION, TRANSPORT ET DISTRIBUTION D'ELECTRICITE. *see* ENERGY—Abstracting, Bibliographies, Statistics

CANADA. STATISTICS CANADA. EMPLOYMENT, EARNINGS AND HOURS/CANADA. STATISTIQUE CANADA. EMPLOI, GAINS ET DUREE DU TRAVAIL. *see* BUSINESS AND ECONOMICS—Abstracting, Bibliographies, Statistics

CANADA. STATISTICS CANADA. ENVIRONMENTAL PERSPECTIVES, STUDIES AND STATISTICS. *see* ENVIRONMENTAL STUDIES—Abstracting, Bibliographies, Statistics

CANADA. STATISTICS CANADA. EXPORTS BY COMMODITY/ CANADA. STATISTIQUE CANADA. EXPORTATIONS PAR MARCHANDISES. *see* BUSINESS AND ECONOMICS—Abstracting, Bibliographies, Statistics

CANADA. STATISTICS CANADA. EXPORTS, MERCHANDISE TRADE/CANADA. STATISTIQUE CANADA. EXPORTATIONS, COMMERCE DE MARCHANDISES. *see* BUSINESS AND ECONOMICS—Abstracting, Bibliographies, Statistics

CANADA. STATISTICS CANADA. FABRICATED METAL PRODUCTS INDUSTRIES (ONLINE)/CANADA. STATISTIQUE CANADA. INDUSTRIES DE LA FABRICATION DES PRODUITS METALLIQUES. *see* METALLURGY—Abstracting, Bibliographies, Statistics

CANADA. STATISTICS CANADA. FAMILY VIOLENCE IN CANADA, A STATISTICAL PROFILE. *see* SOCIAL SERVICES AND WELFARE—Abstracting, Bibliographies, Statistics

CANADA. STATISTICS CANADA. FARM CASH RECEIPTS. *see* AGRICULTURE—Abstracting, Bibliographies, Statistics

CANADA. STATISTICS CANADA. FIELD CROP REPORTING SERIES/CANADA. STATISTIQUE CANADA. SERIE DE RAPPORTS SUR LES GRANDES CULTURES. *see* AGRICULTURE—Abstracting, Bibliographies, Statistics

CANADA. STATISTICS CANADA. FIXED CAPITAL FLOWS AND STOCKS/CANADA. STATISTIQUE CANADA. FLUX ET STOCKS DE CAPITAL FIXE. *see* PUBLIC ADMINISTRATION—Abstracting, Bibliographies, Statistics

CANADA. STATISTICS CANADA. FOOD CONSUMPTION IN CANADA. PART I. *see* FOOD AND FOOD INDUSTRIES—Abstracting, Bibliographies, Statistics

CANADA. STATISTICS CANADA. FOOD CONSUMPTION IN CANADA. PART II. *see* FOOD AND FOOD INDUSTRIES—Abstracting, Bibliographies, Statistics

CANADA. STATISTICS CANADA. FRUIT AND VEGETABLE PRODUCTION/CANADA. STATISTIQUE CANADA. PRODUCTIONS DE FRUITS ET LEGUMES. *see* AGRICULTURE—Abstracting, Bibliographies, Statistics

CANADA. STATISTICS CANADA. GENERAL REVIEW OF THE MINERAL INDUSTRIES, MINES, QUARRIES AND OIL WELLS/ CANADA. STATISTIQUE CANADA. REVUE GENERALE SUR LES INDUSTRIES MINERALES, MINES, CARRIERES ET PUITS DE PETROLE. *see* MINES AND MINING INDUSTRY—Abstracting, Bibliographies, Statistics

310 CAN

CANADA. STATISTICS CANADA. GUIDE TO STATISTICS CANADA'S PROGRAMS AND PRODUCTS. Text in English. irreg. CAD 91; USD 91 foreign. **Document type:** *Government.* **Description:** Profiles over 400 individual surveys conducted by Statistics Canada, providing survey content, frequency and the resulting products.

Related titles: Microform ed.: (from MML); French ed.: Guide d'Acces aux Programmes et Produits de Statistique Canada.

Published by: Statistics Canada, Operations and Integration Division (Subsidiary of: Statistics Canada/Statistique Canada), Circulation Management, 120 Parkdale Ave, Ottawa, ON K1A 0T6, Canada. TEL 613-951-7277, 800-267-6677, FAX 613-951-1584.

310 CAN ISSN 1710-5285

CANADA. STATISTICS CANADA. HEALTH DIVISION. BIRTHS. Text in English. 1996. a. **Document type:** *Government.*

Supersedes in part (in 1999): Births. Shelf Tables (Print, English & French Edition) (1706-8266); Which superseded in part (in 1997): Births and Deaths. Shelf Tables (1491-8552); Which was formerly (until 1995): Births and Deaths (1201-7353); Which was formed by the merger of (1991-1992): Deaths (1195-4132); (1991-1992): Births (1195-4124); Which was formerly (until 1990): Health Reports. Supplement. Births (1180-3088); Which superseded in part (in 1986): Births and Deaths (0825-2971); Which was formerly (until 1981): Vital Statistics. Volume 1, Births and Deaths (0225-7386); (until 1977): Vital Statistics. Volume 1, Births (0700-1452); Which superseded in part (in 1970): Vital Statistics (Annual Edition) (0527-6438); (in 1970): Vital Statistics. Preliminary Annual Report (0317-3143); Which was formerly (until 1951): Vital Statistics. Preliminary Annual Report and Fourth Quarter

Media: Online - full text. **Related titles:** French ed.: Statistique Canada. Division des Statistiques sur la Sante. Naissance. ISSN 1710-5293.

Published by: Statistics Canada, Health Division (Subsidiary of: Statistics Canada/Statistique Canada), R H Coats Bldg, 18th floor, Ottawa, ON K1A 0T6, Canada. TEL 613-951-8569.

310 CAN ISSN 1708-654X

CANADA. STATISTICS CANADA. HEALTH DIVISION. DEATHS. Text in English. 1993. irreg. **Document type:** *Government.*

Supersedes in part (in 1999): Deaths. Shelf Tables (Print, English & French Edition) (1706-8274); Which superseded in part (in 1997): Births and Deaths. Shelf Tables (1491-8552); Which was formerly (until 1996): Births and Deaths (1201-7353); Which was formed by the merger of (1991-1992): Deaths (1195-4132); (1991 -1992): Births (1195-4124); Which was formerly (until 1991): Health Reports. Supplement. Births (1180-3088); Which superseded in part (in 1986): Births and Deaths (0825-2971); Which was formerly (until 1981): Vital Statistics. Volume 1, Births and Deaths (0225-7386); (until 1977): Vital Statistics. Volume 1, Births (0700-1452); Which superseded in part (in 1970): Vital Statistics (Annual Edition) (0527-6438); (in 1970): Vital Statistics. Preliminary Annual Report (0317-3143); Which was formerly (until 1951): Vital Statistics. Preliminary Annual Report and Fourth Quarter

Media: Online - full text. **Related titles:** Ed.: Canada. Statistique Canada. Division des Statistiques sur la Sante. Deces. ISSN 1708-6558.

Published by: Statistics Canada, Health Division (Subsidiary of: Statistics Canada/Statistique Canada), R H Coats Bldg, 18th floor, Ottawa, ON K1A 0T6, Canada. TEL 613-951-8569.

CANADA. STATISTICS CANADA. HELP-WANTED INDEX/CANADA. STATISTIQUE CANADA. INDICE DE L'OFFRE D'EMPLOI. *see* BUSINESS AND ECONOMICS—Abstracting, Bibliographies, Statistics

CANADA. STATISTICS CANADA. HERITAGE INSTITUTIONS/ CANADA. STATISTIQUE CANADA. ESTABLISSEMENTS DU PATRIMOINE; data tables. *see* MUSEUMS AND ART GALLERIES—Abstracting, Bibliographies, Statistics

CANADA. STATISTICS CANADA. HERITAGE INSTITUTIONS; data tables. *see* MUSEUMS AND ART GALLERIES—Abstracting, Bibliographies, Statistics

CANADA. STATISTICS CANADA. HISTORICAL LABOUR FORCE STATISTICS/CANADA. STATISTIQUE CANADA. STATISTIQUES CHRONOLOGIQUES SUR LA POPULATION ACTIVE. *see* BUSINESS AND ECONOMICS—Abstracting, Bibliographies, Statistics

CANADA. STATISTICS CANADA. HOMEOWNER REPAIR AND RENOVATION EXPENDITURE/CANADA. STATISTIQUE CANADA. DEPENSES SUR LES REPARATIONS ET RENOVATIONS EFFECTUEES PAR LES PROPRIETAIRES DE LOGEMENT AU CANADA. *see* BUILDING AND CONSTRUCTION—Abstracting, Bibliographies, Statistics

CANADA. STATISTICS CANADA. HOSPITALS STATISTICS, PRELIMINARY ANNUAL REPORT/STATISTIQUE HOSPITALIERE, RAPPORT ANNUEL PRELIMINAIRE. *see* HEALTH FACILITIES AND ADMINISTRATION

CANADA. STATISTICS CANADA. HOUSEHOLD FACILITIES AND EQUIPMENT/CANADA. STATISTIQUE CANADA. EQUIPEMENT MENAGER. *see* HOME ECONOMICS—Abstracting, Bibliographies, Statistics

CANADA. STATISTICS CANADA. IMPORTS, MERCHANDISE TRADE/CANADA. STATISTIQUE CANADA. IMPORTATIONS, COMMERCE DE MARCHANDISES. *see* BUSINESS AND ECONOMICS—Abstracting, Bibliographies, Statistics

CANADA. STATISTICS CANADA. INCOME TRENDS IN CANADA/ CANADA. STATISTIQUE CANADA. TENDANCES DU REVENU AU CANADA. *see* BUSINESS AND ECONOMICS—Abstracting, Bibliographies, Statistics

CANADA. STATISTICS CANADA. INDUSTRIAL RESEARCH AND DEVELOPMENT (YEAR) INTENTIONS/CANADA. STATISTIQUE CANADA. RECHERCHE ET DEVELOPPEMENT INDUSTRIELS (ANNEE) PERSPECTIVE. *see* SHOES AND BOOTS—Abstracting, Bibliographies, Statistics

310 CAN ISSN 0380-0547

CANADA. STATISTICS CANADA. INFOMAT; a weekly review. Text in English. 1932. w. CAD 145 domestic; USD 145 foreign (effective 1999). **Document type:** *Government.* **Description:** Highlights major Statistics Canada reports, reference papers and other releases.

Formerly: Statistics Canada Weekly (0380-0555)

Related titles: Microform ed.: (from MML); Online - full text ed.; French ed.: ISSN 0380-0563.

Published by: Statistics Canada, Operations and Integration Division (Subsidiary of: Statistics Canada/Statistique Canada), Circulation Management, 120 Parkdale Ave, Ottawa, ON K1A 0T6, Canada. TEL 613-951-7277, 800-267-6677, FAX 613-951-1584.

CANADA. STATISTICS CANADA. INTERNATIONAL TRAVEL. *see* TRAVEL AND TOURISM—Abstracting, Bibliographies, Statistics

CANADA. STATISTICS CANADA. INTERNATIONAL TRAVEL, ADVANCE INFORMATION/CANADA. STATISTIQUE CANADA. VOYAGES INTERNATIONAUX, RENSEIGNEMENTS PRELIMINAIRES. *see* TRAVEL AND TOURISM—Abstracting, Bibliographies, Statistics

CANADA. STATISTICS CANADA. LABOUR FORCE INFORMATION/ CANADA. STATISTIQUE CANADA. INFORMATION POPULATION ACTIVE. *see* BUSINESS AND ECONOMICS—Abstracting, Bibliographies, Statistics

CANADA. STATISTICS CANADA. MARKET RESEARCH HANDBOOK/ CANADA. STATISTIQUE CANADA. MANUEL STATISTIQUE POUR ETUDES DE MARCHE. *see* BUSINESS AND ECONOMICS—Abstracting, Bibliographies, Statistics

CANADA. STATISTICS CANADA. MARRIAGES (ONLINE EDITION). *see* POPULATION STUDIES—Abstracting, Bibliographies, Statistics

CANADA. STATISTICS CANADA. METAL ORE MINING/CANADA. STATISTIQUE CANADA. EXTRACTION DE MINERAIS METALLIQUES. *see* MINES AND MINING INDUSTRY—Abstracting, Bibliographies, Statistics

CANADA. STATISTICS CANADA. MINERAL WOOL INCLUDING FIBROUS GLASS INSULATION/CANADA. STATISTIQUE CANADA. LAINE MINERALE Y COMPRIS LES ISOLANTS EN FIBRE DE VERRE. *see* BUILDING AND CONSTRUCTION—Abstracting, Bibliographies, Statistics

CANADA. STATISTICS CANADA. MINORITY AND SECOND LANGUAGE EDUCATION, ELEMENTARY AND SECONDARY LEVELS/CANADA. STATISTIQUE CANADA. LANGUE DE LA MINORITE ET LANGUE SECONDE DANS L'ENSEIGNEMENT, NIVEAUX ELEMENTAIRE ET SECONDAIRE. *see* LINGUISTICS—Abstracting, Bibliographies, Statistics

CANADA. STATISTICS CANADA. MORTALITY, SUMMARY LIST OF CAUSES. SHELF TABLES. *see* POPULATION STUDIES—Abstracting, Bibliographies, Statistics

CANADA. STATISTICS CANADA. NATIONAL INCOME AND EXPENDITURE ACCOUNTS, QUARTERLY ESTIMATES/CANADA. STATISTIQUE CANADA. COMPTES ECONOMIQUES ET FINANCIERS NATIONAUX, ESTIMATIONS TRIMESTRIELLES. *see* BUSINESS AND ECONOMICS—Abstracting, Bibliographies, Statistics

CANADA. STATISTICS CANADA. NATIONAL TOURISM INDICATORS. HISTORICAL ESTIMATES. *see* TRAVEL AND TOURISM—Abstracting, Bibliographies, Statistics

CANADA. STATISTICS CANADA. OIL AND GAS EXTRACTION. *see* PETROLEUM AND GAS—Abstracting, Bibliographies, Statistics

CANADA. STATISTICS CANADA. OIL AND GAS EXTRACTION. *see* PETROLEUM AND GAS—Abstracting, Bibliographies, Statistics

CANADA. STATISTICS CANADA. OILS AND FATS/CANADA. STATISTIQUE CANADA. HUILES ET CORPS GRAS. *see* FOOD AND FOOD INDUSTRIES—Abstracting, Bibliographies, Statistics

CANADA. STATISTICS CANADA. OTHER MANUFACTURING INDUSTRIES/CANADA. STATISTIQUE CANADA. AUTRES INDUSTRIES MANUFACTURIERES. *see* BUSINESS AND ECONOMICS—Abstracting, Bibliographies, Statistics

CANADA. STATISTICS CANADA. PASSENGER BUS AND URBAN TRANSIT STATISTICS/CANADA. STATISTIQUE CANDA. STATISTIQUE DU TRANSPORT DES VOYAGEURS PAR AUTOBUS ET DU TRANSPORT URBAIN. *see* TRANSPORTATION—Abstracting, Bibliographies, Statistics

CANADA. STATISTICS CANADA. PENSION PLANS IN CANADA/ CANADA. STATISTICS CANADA. REGIMES DE PENSION AU CANADA. *see* INSURANCE—Abstracting, Bibliographies, Statistics

CANADA. STATISTICS CANADA. PIPELINE TRANSPORTATION OF CRUDE OIL AND REFINED PETROLEUM PRODUCTS (ONLINE EDITION). *see* BUSINESS AND ECONOMICS—Abstracting, Bibliographies, Statistics

CANADA. STATISTICS CANADA. POLICE RESOURCES IN CANADA (ONLINE EDITION). *see* CRIMINOLOGY AND LAW ENFORCEMENT—Abstracting, Bibliographies, Statistics

CANADA. STATISTICS CANADA. POSTCENSAL ANNUAL ESTIMATES OF POPULATION BY MARITAL STATUS, AGE, SEX AND COMPONENTS OF GROWTH FOR CANADA, PROVINCES AND TERRITORIES. *see* POPULATION STUDIES—Abstracting, Bibliographies, Statistics

CANADA. STATISTICS CANADA. PRIMARY IRON AND STEEL/ CANADA. STATISTIQUE CANADA. FER ET ACIER PRIMAIRE. *see* METALLURGY—Abstracting, Bibliographies, Statistics

CANADA. STATISTICS CANADA. PRINTING, PUBLISHING AND ALLIED INDUSTRIES/CANADA. STATISTIQUE CANADA. IMPRIMERIE, EDITION ET INDUSTRIES CONNEXES. *see* PUBLISHING AND BOOK TRADE—Abstracting, Bibliographies, Statistics

CANADA. STATISTICS CANADA. PRIVATE AND PUBLIC INVESTMENT IN CANADA. INTENTIONS/CANADA. STATISTIQUE CANADA. INVESTISSEMENTS PRIVES ET PUBLICS AU CANADA. PERSPECTIVE. *see* BUSINESS AND ECONOMICS—Abstracting, Bibliographies, Statistics

CANADA. STATISTICS CANADA. PRIVATE AND PUBLIC INVESTMENT IN CANADA. REVISED INTENTIONS/CANADA. STATISTIQUE CANADA. INVESTISSEMENTS PRIVES ET PUBLICS AU CANADA, PERSPECTIVE REVISEE. *see* BUSINESS AND ECONOMICS—Abstracting, Bibliographies, Statistics

CANADA. STATISTICS CANADA. PRODUCTION AND VALUE OF HONEY AND MAPLE (ONLINE EDITION). *see* AGRICULTURE—Abstracting, Bibliographies, Statistics

CANADA. STATISTICS CANADA. PRODUCTION OF POULTRY AND EGGS/CANADA. STATISTIQUE CANADA. PRODUCTION DE VOLAILLE ET OEUFS. *see* AGRICULTURE—Abstracting, Bibliographies, Statistics

CANADA. STATISTICS CANADA. PRODUCTIVITY GROWTH IN CANADA. *see* BUSINESS AND ECONOMICS—Abstracting, Bibliographies, Statistics

CANADA. STATISTICS CANADA. PRODUCTS SHIPPED BY CANADIAN MANUFACTURERS/CANADA. STATISTIQUE CANADA. PRODUITS LIVRES PAR LES FABRICANTS CANADIENS. *see* BUSINESS AND ECONOMICS—Abstracting, Bibliographies, Statistics

CANADA. STATISTICS CANADA. PROVINCIAL ECONOMIC ACCOUNTS. ANNUAL ESTIMATES, TABLES AND ANALYTICAL DOCUMENT/CANADA. STATISTIQUE CANADA. COMPTES ECONOMIQUES PROVINCIAUX ESTIMATIONS ANNUELLES. *see* BUSINESS AND ECONOMICS—Abstracting, Bibliographies, Statistics

CANADA. STATISTICS CANADA. PUBLIC SECTOR STATISTICS. *see* BUSINESS AND ECONOMICS—Abstracting, Bibliographies, Statistics

CANADA. STATISTICS CANADA. QUARTERLY DEMOGRAPHIC ESTIMATES. *see* POPULATION STUDIES

CANADA. STATISTICS CANADA. QUARTERLY DEMOGRAPHIC STATISTICS. *see* POPULATION STUDIES—Abstracting, Bibliographies, Statistics

CANADA. STATISTICS CANADA. QUARTERLY ESTIMATES OF TRUSTEED PENSION FUNDS/CANADA. STATISTIQUE CANADA. ESTIMATIONS TRIMESTRIELLES SUR LES REGIMES DE PENSIONS EN FIDUCIE. *see* BUSINESS AND ECONOMICS—Abstracting, Bibliographies, Statistics

CANADA. STATISTICS CANADA. QUARTERLY REPORT ON ENERGY SUPPLY - DEMAND IN CANADA/CANADA. STATISTIQUE CANADA. BULLETIN TRIMESTRIEL, DISPONIBILITE ET ECOULEMENT D'ENERGIE AU CANADA. *see* ENERGY—Abstracting, Bibliographies, Statistics

CANADA. STATISTICS CANADA. RADIO AND TELEVISION BROADCASTING/CANADA. STATISTIQUE CANADA. RADIODIFFUSION ET TELEVISION. *see* COMMUNICATIONS—Abstracting, Bibliographies, Statistics

CANADA. STATISTICS CANADA. RAIL IN CANADA. *see* TRANSPORTATION—Abstracting, Bibliographies, Statistics

CANADA. STATISTICS CANADA. RAILWAY CARLOADINGS/ CANADA. STATISTIQUE CANADA. CHARGEMENTS FERROVIAIRES. *see* TRANSPORTATION—Abstracting, Bibliographies, Statistics

CANADA. STATISTICS CANADA. REFINED PETROLEUM AND COAL PRODUCTS INDUSTRIES/CANADA. STATISTIQUE CANADA. INDUSTRIES DES PRODUITS RAFFINES DU PETROLE ET DU CHARBON. *see* PETROLEUM AND GAS—Abstracting, Bibliographies, Statistics

CANADA. STATISTICS CANADA. RESTAURANT, CATERER AND TAVERN STATISTICS/CANADA. STATISTIQUE CANADA. STATISTIQUES DES RESTAURANTS, TRAITEURS ET TAVERNES. *see* HOTELS AND RESTAURANTS—Abstracting, Bibliographies, Statistics

CANADA. STATISTICS CANADA. RETAIL CHAIN AND DEPARTMENT STORES/CANADA. STATISTIQUE CANADA. MAGASINS DE DETAIL A SUCCURSALES ET LES GRANDES MAGASINS. *see* BUSINESS AND ECONOMICS—Abstracting, Bibliographies, Statistics

CANADA. STATISTICS CANADA. ROAD MOTOR VEHICLES, FUEL SALES/CANADA. STATISTIQUE CANADA. VEHICULES AUTOMOBILES, VENTES DE CARBURANTS. *see* TRANSPORTATION—Abstracting, Bibliographies, Statistics

CANADA. STATISTICS CANADA. ROAD MOTOR VEHICLES, REGISTRATIONS/CANADA. STATISTIQUE CANADA. VEHICULES AUTOMOBILES, IMMATRICULATIONS. *see* TRANSPORTATION—Abstracting, Bibliographies, Statistics

CANADA. STATISTICS CANADA. RUBBER AND PLASTIC PRODUCTS INDUSTRIES (ONLINE)/CANADA. STATISTIQUE CANADA. INDUSTRIES DES PRODUITS EN CAOUTCHOUC ET EN MATIERE PLASTIQUE. *see* RUBBER—Abstracting, Bibliographies, Statistics

CANADA. STATISTICS CANADA. SERVICES PRICE INDEXES. *see* BUSINESS AND ECONOMICS—Abstracting, Bibliographies, Statistics

CANADA. STATISTICS CANADA. SHIPPING IN CANADA/CANADA. STATISTIQUES CANADA. TRANSPORT MARITIME AU CANADA. *see* TRANSPORTATION—Abstracting, Bibliographies, Statistics

CANADA. STATISTICS CANADA. SMALL BUSINESS PROFILES. *see* BUSINESS AND ECONOMICS—Abstracting, Bibliographies, Statistics

CANADA. STATISTICS CANADA. SMALL BUSINESS PROFILES, ALBERTA. *see* BUSINESS AND ECONOMICS—Abstracting, Bibliographies, Statistics

CANADA. STATISTICS CANADA. SMALL BUSINESS PROFILES, BRITISH COLUMBIA. *see* BUSINESS AND ECONOMICS—Abstracting, Bibliographies, Statistics

CANADA. STATISTICS CANADA. SMALL BUSINESS PROFILES, MANITOBA. *see* BUSINESS AND ECONOMICS—Abstracting, Bibliographies, Statistics

CANADA. STATISTICS CANADA. SMALL BUSINESS PROFILES, NEW BRUNSWICK. *see* BUSINESS AND ECONOMICS—Abstracting, Bibliographies, Statistics

CANADA. STATISTICS CANADA. SMALL BUSINESS PROFILES, NEWFOUNDLAND. *see* BUSINESS AND ECONOMICS—Abstracting, Bibliographies, Statistics

CANADA. STATISTICS CANADA. SMALL BUSINESS PROFILES, NORTHWEST TERRITORIES. *see* BUSINESS AND ECONOMICS—Abstracting, Bibliographies, Statistics

CANADA. STATISTICS CANADA. SMALL BUSINESS PROFILES, NOVA SCOTIA. *see* BUSINESS AND ECONOMICS—Abstracting, Bibliographies, Statistics

CANADA. STATISTICS CANADA. SMALL BUSINESS PROFILES, ONTARIO. *see* BUSINESS AND ECONOMICS—Abstracting, Bibliographies, Statistics

CANADA. STATISTICS CANADA. SMALL BUSINESS PROFILES, PRINCE EDWARD ISLAND. *see* BUSINESS AND ECONOMICS—Abstracting, Bibliographies, Statistics

CANADA. STATISTICS CANADA. SMALL BUSINESS PROFILES, QUEBEC. *see* BUSINESS AND ECONOMICS—Abstracting, Bibliographies, Statistics

CANADA. STATISTICS CANADA. SMALL BUSINESS PROFILES, SASKATCHEWAN. *see* BUSINESS AND ECONOMICS—Abstracting, Bibliographies, Statistics

CANADA. STATISTICS CANADA. SMALL BUSINESS PROFILES, YUKON. *see* BUSINESS AND ECONOMICS—Abstracting, Bibliographies, Statistics

CANADA. STATISTICS CANADA. SPENDING PATTERNS IN CANADA. *see* BUSINESS AND ECONOMICS—Abstracting, Bibliographies, Statistics

CANADA. STATISTICS CANADA. STATISTIQUES SUR LE SECTEUR PUBLIC. *see* BUSINESS AND ECONOMICS—Abstracting, Bibliographies, Statistics

CANADA. STATISTICS CANADA. SURFACE AND MARINE TRANSPORT/CANADA. STATISTIQUE CANADA. TRANSPORTS TERRESTRE ET MARITIME. *see* TRANSPORTATION—Abstracting, Bibliographies, Statistics

CANADA. STATISTICS CANADA. SYSTEM OF NATIONAL ACCOUNTS, CANADA'S INTERNATIONAL INVESTMENT POSITION/CANADA. STATISTIQUE CANADA. BILAN DES INVESTISSEMENTS INTERNATIONAUX DU CANADA. *see* BUSINESS AND ECONOMICS—Abstracting, Bibliographies, Statistics

CANADA. STATISTICS CANADA. TELEPHONE STATISTICS/CANADA. STATISTIQUE CANADA. STATISTIQUE DU TELEPHONE. *see* COMMUNICATIONS—Abstracting, Bibliographies, Statistics

CANADA. STATISTICS CANADA. TEXTILE PRODUCTS INDUSTRIES/ CANADA. STATISTIQUE CANADA. INDUSTRIE DE PRODUITS TEXTILES. *see* TEXTILE INDUSTRIES AND FABRICS—Abstracting, Bibliographies, Statistics

317 CAN ISSN 0827-0465
HC111

CANADA. STATISTICS CANADA. THE DAILY. Text in English. 1932. d. CAD 120 (effective 1999). back issues avail. **Description:** Contains news summaries and announcements of reports, reference papers and a list of titles of the publications released.

Related titles: E-mail ed.; Online - full text ed.: 1995.

Indexed: P30.

Published by: Statistics Canada, Operations and Integration Division (Subsidiary of: Statistics Canada/Statistique Canada), Circulation Management, 120 Parkdale Ave, Ottawa, ON K1A 0T6, Canada. TEL 613-951-7277, 800-267-6677, FAX 613-951-1584.

CANADA. STATISTICS CANADA. TRUSTEED PENSION FUNDS - FINANCIAL STATISTICS/CANADA. STATISTIQUE CANADA. CAISSES DE RETRAITE EN FIDUCIE, STATISTIQUES FINANCIERES. *see* BUSINESS AND ECONOMICS—Abstracting, Bibliographies, Statistics

CANADA. STATISTICS CANADA. UNEMPLOYMENT INSURANCE STATISTICS. ANNUAL SUPPLEMENT/CANADA. STATISTIQUE CANADA. STATISTIQUES SUR L'ASSURANCE-CHOMAGE. SUPPLEMENT ANNUEL. *see* INSURANCE—Abstracting, Bibliographies, Statistics

CANADA. STATISTICS CANADA. VENDING MACHINE OPERATORS/ CANADA. STATISTIQUE CANADA. EXPLOITANTS DE DISTRIBUTEURS AUTOMATIQUES. *see* MACHINERY—Abstracting, Bibliographies, Statistics

CANADA. STATISTICS CANADA. VITAL STATISTICS COMPENDIUM. *see* POPULATION STUDIES—Abstracting, Bibliographies, Statistics

CANADA. STATISTICS CANADA. WHOLESALE TRADE/CANADA. STATISTIQUE CANADA. COMMERCE DE GROS. *see* BUSINESS AND ECONOMICS—Abstracting, Bibliographies, Statistics

CANADA. STATISTICS CANADA. YOUTH COURT DATA TABLES (ONLINE EDITION). *see* CRIMINOLOGY AND LAW ENFORCEMENT—Abstracting, Bibliographies, Statistics

CANADA. STATISTIQUE CANADA. CAUSES DE DECES. *see* POPULATION STUDIES—Abstracting, Bibliographies, Statistics

S

310 CAN ISSN 1911-0936
CANADA. STATISTIQUE CANADA. ESTIMATIONS DEMOGRAPHIQUES TRIMESTRIELLES. Text in French. 2005. q. **Document type:** *Government.*
Formerly (until 2006): Statistiques Demographiques Trimestrielles (1718-3081)
Media: Online - full text. **Related titles:** ◆ English ed.: Canada. Statistics Canada. Quarterly Demographic Estimates. ISSN 1911-0928.
Published by: Statistics Canada, Demography Division (Subsidiary of: Statistics Canada/Statistique Canada), Statistical Reference Centre, Rm 1500, Main Building, Holland Avenue, Ottawa, ON K1A 0T6, Canada.

304.21 CAN ISSN 0715-9307
CANADA. STATISTIQUES CANADA. RAPPORT SUR L'ETAT DE LA POPULATION DU CANADA. Text in French. 1983. a. **Document type:** *Government.*
Related titles: Online - full text ed.: ISSN 1718-7796; ◆ English ed.: Canada. Statistics Canada. Report on the Demographic Situation in Canada. ISSN 0715-9293.
Published by: (Statistics Canada, Demography Division), Statistics Canada/Statistique Canada, Communications Division, 3rd Fl, R H Coats Bldg, Ottawa, ON K1A 0A6, Canada. TEL 800-263-1136, http://www.statcan.gc.ca.

CANADA. STATISTIQUES CANADA. STATISTIQUES SUR LE SECTEUR PUBLIC. *see* BUSINESS AND ECONOMICS—Abstracting, Bibliographies, Statistics

CANADA. TREASURY BOARD. EMPLOYMENT STATISTICS FOR THE FEDERAL PUBLIC SERVICE. *see* PUBLIC ADMINISTRATION—Abstracting, Bibliographies, Statistics

CANADIAN CIRCULATION OF U S MAGAZINES. *see* ADVERTISING AND PUBLIC RELATIONS—Abstracting, Bibliographies, Statistics

CANADIAN CRIME STATISTICS. *see* LAW—Abstracting, Bibliographies, Statistics

CANADIAN ECONOMIC OBSERVER/OBSERVATEUR ECONOMIQUE CANADIEN. *see* BUSINESS AND ECONOMICS—Abstracting, Bibliographies, Statistics

CANADIAN ENVIRONMENTAL SUSTAINABILITY INDICATORS (ONLINE). *see* ENVIRONMENTAL STUDIES—Abstracting, Bibliographies, Statistics

CANADIAN ENVIRONMENTAL SUSTAINABILITY INDICATORS (PRINT). *see* ENVIRONMENTAL STUDIES—Abstracting, Bibliographies, Statistics

CANADIAN FISHERIES ANNUAL STATISTICAL REVIEW. *see* FISH AND FISHERIES

310 CAN ISSN 1708-0142
CANADIAN FOREIGN POST INDEXES. Text in English. 2003. m. **Document type:** *Government.*
Published by: Statistics Canada/Statistique Canada, Communications Division, 3rd Fl, R H Coats Bldg, Ottawa, ON K1A 0A6, Canada. TEL 800-263-1136, infostats@statcan.ca, http://www.statcan.gc.ca.

CANADIAN FOREST FIRE STATISTICS. *see* FORESTS AND FORESTRY—Abstracting, Bibliographies, Statistics

CANADIAN GRAINS INDUSTRY STATISTICAL HANDBOOK. *see* AGRICULTURE—Abstracting, Bibliographies, Statistics

CANADIAN HOUSING STATISTICS. *see* HOUSING AND URBAN PLANNING—Abstracting, Bibliographies, Statistics

310 USA ISSN 0319-5724
QA276.A1
➤ **CANADIAN JOURNAL OF STATISTICS/REVUE CANADIENNE DE STATISTIQUE.** Text in English, French. 1973. q. GBP 179 in United Kingdom to institutions; EUR 225 in Europe to institutions; USD 349 elsewhere to institutions; GBP 206 combined subscription in United Kingdom to institutions (print & online eds.); EUR 259 combined subscription in Europe to institutions (print & online eds.); USD 402 combined subscription elsewhere to institutions (print & online eds.) (effective 2012). adv. abstr.; bibl.; charts; illus.; stat. index. back issues avail.; reprint service avail. from PSC. **Document type:** *Journal, Academic/Scholarly.* **Description:** Publishes original articles on both theoretical and applied statistics.
Related titles: Online - full text ed.: ISSN 1708-945X. GBP 179 in United Kingdom to institutions; EUR 225 in Europe to institutions; USD 349 elsewhere to institutions (effective 2012).
Indexed: A01, A12, A17, A22, A28, ABIn, APA, ASCA, B21, Biostat, BrCerAb, C&ISA, C03, CA/WCA, CBCABus, CCMJ, CIA, CIS, CMCI, CerAb, CivEngAb, CorrAb, E&CAJ, E11, EEA, EMA, ESPM, EnvEAb, H05, H15, IBSS, JCQM, M&TEA, M09, MBF, METADEX, MSN, MathR, ORMS, P30, P48, P51, P53, P54, PAIS, PQC, QC&AS, RefZh, SCI, SCOPUS, ST&MA, SolStAb, T02, T04, W07, WAA, Z02.
—BLDSC (3035.760000), IE, Infotrieve, Ingenta, Linda Hall. **CCC.**
Published by: (Statistical Society of Canada CAN), Wiley-Blackwell Publishing, Inc. (Subsidiary of: Wiley-Blackwell Publishing Ltd.), 111 River St, Hoboken, NJ 07030. TEL 201-748-6000, FAX 201-748-6088, info@wiley.com, http://www.wiley.com/WileyCDA/. Ed. Jiahua Chen.

➤ **CANADIAN MEDICAL EDUCATION STATISTICS.** *see* MEDICAL SCIENCES—Abstracting, Bibliographies, Statistics

➤ **CANADIAN PULP AND PAPER ASSOCIATION. MONTHLY NEWSPRINT STATISTICS/ASSOCIATION CANADIENNE DES PATES ET PAPIERS. STATISTIQUES MENSUELLES SUR LE PAPIER JOURNAL.** *see* PAPER AND PULP

➤ **CANCER IN CANADA.** *see* MEDICAL SCIENCES—Oncology

➤ **CANCER SURVIVAL STATISTICS.** *see* PUBLIC HEALTH AND SAFETY—Abstracting, Bibliographies, Statistics

➤ **CANTERBURY DISTRICT CRIME STATISTICS.** *see* CRIMINOLOGY AND LAW ENFORCEMENT—Abstracting, Bibliographies, Statistics

➤ **CAPITAL PUNISHMENT (YEAR).** *see* CRIMINOLOGY AND LAW ENFORCEMENT—Abstracting, Bibliographies, Statistics

➤ **CARIBBEAN TOURISM ORGANIZATION. STATISTICAL NEWS.** *see* TRAVEL AND TOURISM—Abstracting, Bibliographies, Statistics

➤ **CAROLINAS CITIES & COUNTIES GRAPHIC PERFORMANCE ANALYSIS.** *see* PUBLIC ADMINISTRATION—Abstracting, Bibliographies, Statistics

310 USA ISSN 2152-372X
HF1017
CASE STUDIES IN BUSINESS, INDUSTRY AND GOVERNMENT STATISTICS. Text in English. 2006. s-a. **Document type:** *Journal, Academic/Scholarly.* **Description:** Covers case studies in modern data analysis ready to use for instruction, training or self-study.
Related titles: Online - full text ed.: free (effective 2011).
Published by: Bentley University, 175 Forest St, Waltham, MA 02452. TEL 781-891-2000, FAX 781-891-3165. Ed. Dominique Haughton.

CATALOGUE OF STATISTICAL MATERIALS OF DEVELOPING COUNTRIES. *see* BUSINESS AND ECONOMICS—Abstracting, Bibliographies, Statistics

CAUSE DI MORTE. *see* POPULATION STUDIES—Abstracting, Bibliographies, Statistics

319 CYM
CAYMAN ISLANDS. ECONOMICS & STATISTICS OFFICE. COMPENDIUM OF STATISTICS. Text in English. 1975. a. **Document type:** *Abstract/Index.*
Former titles: Cayman Islands. Statistics Office. Compendium of Statistics; Statistical Abstract of the Cayman Islands; Statistical Abstract of the Government of the Cayman Islands
Published by: Cayman Islands Government, Economics & Statistics Office, Government Administration Bldg., Grand Cayman, Cayman Isl. TEL 345-949-0940, FAX 345-949-8782, TELEX 4260 CIGOVT.

CENSO AGROPECUARIO. *see* AGRICULTURE—Abstracting, Bibliographies, Statistics

CENSO DA CONSTRUCAO. *see* BUILDING AND CONSTRUCTION—Abstracting, Bibliographies, Statistics

CENSO DE POBLACION Y VIVIENDAS. *see* POPULATION STUDIES—Abstracting, Bibliographies, Statistics

CENSUS OF AGRICULTURE. VOLUME 3: SPECIAL STUDIES. FARM AND RANCH IRRIGATION SURVEY. *see* AGRICULTURE—Abstracting, Bibliographies, Statistics

CENSUS OF GOVERNMENTS (ONLINE). *see* PUBLIC ADMINISTRATION—Abstracting, Bibliographies, Statistics

CENSUS OF MANUFACTURING INDUSTRIES OF PUERTO RICO. *see* BUSINESS AND ECONOMICS—Production Of Goods And Services

(YEAR) CENSUS OF POPULATION AND HOUSING. *see* POLITICAL SCIENCE—Abstracting, Bibliographies, Statistics

CENSUS OF PRIVATE NON-PROFIT MAKING INSTITUTIONS IN FIJI. A REPORT. *see* BUSINESS AND ECONOMICS—Abstracting, Bibliographies, Statistics

CENTRAL & EASTERN EUROPEAN MARKET & MEDIAFACT. *see* COMMUNICATIONS—Abstracting, Bibliographies, Statistics

CENTRAL BANK OF BELIZE. ANNUAL STATISTICAL DIGEST. *see* BUSINESS AND ECONOMICS—Abstracting, Bibliographies, Statistics

CENTRAL BANK OF JORDAN. MONTHLY STATISTICAL BULLETIN. *see* BUSINESS AND ECONOMICS—Abstracting, Bibliographies, Statistics

CENTRAL BANK OF KUWAIT. MONTHLY MONETARY STATISTICS. *see* BUSINESS AND ECONOMICS—Abstracting, Bibliographies, Statistics

CENTRAL BANK OF KUWAIT. QUARTERLY STATISTICAL BULLETIN/ BANK AL-KUWAYT AL-MARKAZI. AL-NASHRAH AL-IHSA'IYYAH AL-FASLIYYAH. *see* BUSINESS AND ECONOMICS—Abstracting, Bibliographies, Statistics

CENTRAL BANK OF RUSSIAN FEDERATION. BULLETIN OF BANKING STATISTICS. *see* BUSINESS AND ECONOMICS—Abstracting, Bibliographies, Statistics

CENTRAL BANK OF SRI LANKA. SOCIO ECONOMIC DATA. *see* BUSINESS AND ECONOMICS—Abstracting, Bibliographies, Statistics

CENTRAL BANK OF THE BAHAMAS. QUARTERLY STATISTICAL DIGEST. *see* BUSINESS AND ECONOMICS—Abstracting, Bibliographies, Statistics

CENTRAL BANK OF TRINIDAD AND TOBAGO. ECONOMIC BULLETIN. *see* BUSINESS AND ECONOMICS—Abstracting, Bibliographies, Statistics

310 ANT
CENTRAL BUREAU OF STATISTICS. STATISTICAL QUARTERLY BULLETIN. Text and summaries in English. 1953. q. ANG 30. **Document type:** *Government.*
Former titles (until 1986): Statistical Monthly Bulletin; (until 1986): Statistische Mededelingen
Published by: Central Bureau of Statistics, Fort Amsterdam z/n, Willemstad, Curacao, Netherlands Antilles. TEL 599-9-611031, FAX 599-9-611696. Circ: 250.

CENTRAL DISTRICT CRIME STATISTICS. *see* CRIMINOLOGY AND LAW ENFORCEMENT—Abstracting, Bibliographies, Statistics

314 POL ISSN 0554-436X
HA1451
CENTRAL STATISTICAL OFFICE. CONCISE STATISTICAL YEAR BOOK OF POLAND. Text in English. 1962. a.
Published by: Zaklad Wydawnictw Statystycznych, Al Niepodleglosci 208, Warsaw, 00925, Poland. TEL 48-22-6083145, zws-sprzedaz@stat.gov.pl, http://www.stat.gov.pl/zws.

318 URY
CENTRO DE ESTADISTICAS NACIONALES Y COMERCIO INTERNACIONAL DEL URUGUAY. COSTO DE LA VIDA. Text in Spanish. s-a. USD 35 per issue (effective 2001). **Document type:** *Bulletin.* **Description:** Provides indices and comparative percentage variations of prices, services, salaries, and the value of the dollar.
Published by: Centro de Estadisticas Nacionales y Comercio Internacional del Uruguay, Misiones, 1361, Montevideo, 11000, Uruguay. TEL 598-2-952930, FAX 598-2-954578, cenci@adinet.com.uy.

CEREALS AND OILSEEDS REVIEW. *see* AGRICULTURE—Abstracting, Bibliographies, Statistics

310 CZE ISSN 1214-1461
HC270.283
CESKY STATISTICKY URAD. AKTUALITY. Text in Czech. 1967. m. CZK 1,080 domestic (effective 2008). **Document type:** *Government.* **Description:** The first volume includes the results of price statistics, developments in the cost of living, unemployment, agriculture, tourism and cash receipts and expenditures of the state budget. The second volume covers the results of industry, construction, transport, internal and external expenditures of the population, and the preliminary results of financial performance. Also includes the latest results from business cycle surveys.
Formerly (until 2003): Czech Republic. Cesky Statisticky Urad. Statisticke Prehledy (0322-7537)
Related titles: ◆ English ed.: C Z S O Monthly Statistics.
Published by: Cesky Statisticky Urad, Na padesatem 81, Prague 10, 10082, Czech Republic. TEL 420-2-74051111, infoservis@czso.cz.

CESKY STATISTICKY URAD. ENERGETIKA/CZECH STATISTICAL OFFICE. ENERGY. *see* ENERGY

CESKY STATISTICKY URAD. STATISTICKA ROCENKA CESKE REPUBLIKY/CZECH STATISTICAL OFFICE. STATISTICAL YEARBOOK. *see* BUSINESS AND ECONOMICS—Abstracting, Bibliographies, Statistics

314 CZE ISSN 1210-6550
CESKY STATISTICKY URAD. ZPRAVODAJ. Text in Czech. 1960. m. **Document type:** *Journal, Government.*
Formerly (until 1993): Ustredni Statisticky Organ. Zpravodaj (0322-8134)
Published by: Cesky Statisticky Urad, Na padesatem 81, Prague 10, 10082, Czech Republic. TEL 420-2-74051111, infoservis@czso.cz, http://www.czso.cz.

519.5 004 USA ISSN 0933-2480
QA276.A1 CODEN: CNDCE4
➤ **CHANCE (NEW YORK, 1988).** Text in English. 1987. q. (in 1 vol., 4 nos./vol.). EUR 95, USD 96 combined subscription to institutions (print & online eds.) (effective 2011). adv. illus. Index. back issues avail.; reprint service avail. from PSC. **Document type:** *Magazine, Academic/Scholarly.* **Description:** Features articles aimed at persons using statistical methods and approaches in market research, demographic, social sciences, and medicine.
Related titles: Microform ed.: (from PQC); Online - full text ed.: ISSN 1867-2280. 2009 (from IngentaConnect).
Indexed: A01, A03, A08, A12, A22, A26, ABIn, ASFA, Biostat, CA, CCMJ, CIS, E01, ESPM, Inspec, M05, MSN, MathR, P10, P17, P26, P30, P48, P50, P51, P53, P54, PQC, S10, T02, Z02.
—BLDSC (3129.632370), IE, Infotrieve, Ingenta. **CCC.**
Published by: (American Statistics Association), Springer New York LLC (Subsidiary of: Springer Science+Business Media), 233 Spring St, New York, NY 10013. TEL 212-460-1500, 800-777-4643, FAX 212-460-1575, service-ny@springer.com. **Subscr. outside the Americas to:** Springer Distribution Center, Kundenservice Zeitschriften, Haberstr 7, Heidelberg 69126, Germany. TEL 49-6221-3454303, FAX 49-6221-3454229, subscriptions@springer.com; **Subscr. to:** Journal Fulfillment, PO Box 2485, Secaucus, NJ 07096. TEL 201-348-4033, FAX 201-348-4505.

➤ **CHARTERED INSTITUTE OF PUBLIC FINANCE AND ACCOUNTANCY. ARCHIVE SERVICES STATISTICS. ACTUALS.** *see* BUSINESS AND ECONOMICS—Public Finance, Taxation

➤ **CHARTERED INSTITUTE OF PUBLIC FINANCE AND ACCOUNTANCY. CAPITAL EXPENDITURE AND TREASURY MANAGEMENT STATISTICS. ACTUALS (ONLINE).** *see* BUSINESS AND ECONOMICS—Abstracting, Bibliographies, Statistics

➤ **CHARTERED INSTITUTE OF PUBLIC FINANCE AND ACCOUNTANCY. CEMETERIES STATISTICS. ACTUALS.** *see* PUBLIC HEALTH AND SAFETY—Abstracting, Bibliographies, Statistics

➤ **CHARTERED INSTITUTE OF PUBLIC FINANCE AND ACCOUNTANCY. CHILDREN'S SERVICES STATISTICS. ACTUALS.** *see* EDUCATION—Abstracting, Bibliographies, Statistics

➤ **CHARTERED INSTITUTE OF PUBLIC FINANCE AND ACCOUNTANCY. CHILDREN'S SERVICES STATISTICS. ESTIMATES (ONLINE).** *see* EDUCATION—Abstracting, Bibliographies, Statistics

➤ **CHARTERED INSTITUTE OF PUBLIC FINANCE AND ACCOUNTANCY. COUNTY FARMS AND RURAL ESTATES STATISTICS. ACTUALS.** *see* AGRICULTURE—Abstracting, Bibliographies, Statistics

➤ **CHARTERED INSTITUTE OF PUBLIC FINANCE AND ACCOUNTANCY. CREMATORIA STATISTICS. ACTUALS.** *see* PUBLIC HEALTH AND SAFETY—Abstracting, Bibliographies, Statistics

➤ **CHARTERED INSTITUTE OF PUBLIC FINANCE AND ACCOUNTANCY. CULTURAL STATISTICS IN SCOTLAND (ONLINE).** *see* BUSINESS AND ECONOMICS—Abstracting, Bibliographies, Statistics

➤ **CHARTERED INSTITUTE OF PUBLIC FINANCE AND ACCOUNTANCY. CULTURE, SPORT AND RECREATION STATISTICS. ESTIMATES (ONLINE).** *see* SPORTS AND GAMES—Abstracting, Bibliographies, Statistics

➤ **CHARTERED INSTITUTE OF PUBLIC FINANCE AND ACCOUNTANCY. ENVIRONMENTAL HEALTH STATISTICS. ACTUALS.** *see* PUBLIC HEALTH AND SAFETY—Abstracting, Bibliographies, Statistics

➤ **CHARTERED INSTITUTE OF PUBLIC FINANCE AND ACCOUNTANCY. FINANCE AND GENERAL STATISTICS. ACTUALS.** *see* BUSINESS AND ECONOMICS—Public Finance, Taxation

➤ **CHARTERED INSTITUTE OF PUBLIC FINANCE AND ACCOUNTANCY. FINANCE AND GENERAL STATISTICS. ESTIMATES (ONLINE).** *see* BUSINESS AND ECONOMICS—Abstracting, Bibliographies, Statistics

➤ **CHARTERED INSTITUTE OF PUBLIC FINANCE AND ACCOUNTANCY. HIGHWAYS AND TRANSPORTATION STATISTICS. ESTIMATES.** *see* TRANSPORTATION—Abstracting, Bibliographies, Statistics

➤ **CHARTERED INSTITUTE OF PUBLIC FINANCE AND ACCOUNTANCY. HOMELESSNESS STATISTICS. ACTUALS (ONLINE).** *see* HOUSING AND URBAN PLANNING—Abstracting, Bibliographies, Statistics

➤ **CHARTERED INSTITUTE OF PUBLIC FINANCE AND ACCOUNTANCY. HOUSING RENTS AND SERVICE CHARGES SATISTICS.** *see* HOUSING AND URBAN PLANNING—Abstracting, Bibliographies, Statistics

➤ **CHARTERED INSTITUTE OF PUBLIC FINANCE AND ACCOUNTANCY. HOUSING REVENUE ACCOUNT STATISTICS. ESTIMATES & ACTUALS.** *see* HOUSING AND URBAN PLANNING—Abstracting, Bibliographies, Statistics

➤ **CHARTERED INSTITUTE OF PUBLIC FINANCE AND ACCOUNTANCY. LOCAL AUTHORITY ASSETS STATISTICS (ONLINE).** *see* BUSINESS AND ECONOMICS—Abstracting, Bibliographies, Statistics

➤ **CHARTERED INSTITUTE OF PUBLIC FINANCE AND ACCOUNTANCY. LOCAL GOVERNMENT COMPARATIVE STATISTICS. ESTIMATES.** *see* PUBLIC ADMINISTRATION—Abstracting, Bibliographies, Statistics

➤ **CHARTERED INSTITUTE OF PUBLIC FINANCE AND ACCOUNTANCY. PLANNING AND DEVELOPMENT STATISTICS. ACTUALS.** *see* HOUSING AND URBAN PLANNING—Abstracting, Bibliographies, Statistics

➤ **CHARTERED INSTITUTE OF PUBLIC FINANCE AND ACCOUNTANCY. POLICE STATISTICS. ACTUALS.** *see* CRIMINOLOGY AND LAW ENFORCEMENT—Abstracting, Bibliographies, Statistics

➤ **CHARTERED INSTITUTE OF PUBLIC FINANCE AND ACCOUNTANCY. POLICE STATISTICS. ESTIMATES (ONLINE).** *see* CRIMINOLOGY AND LAW ENFORCEMENT—Abstracting, Bibliographies, Statistics

➤ **CHARTERED INSTITUTE OF PUBLIC FINANCE AND ACCOUNTANCY. PUBLIC LIBRARIES STATISTICS. ESTIMATES & ACTUALS.** *see* LIBRARY AND INFORMATION SCIENCES—Abstracting, Bibliographies, Statistics

➤ **CHARTERED INSTITUTE OF PUBLIC FINANCE AND ACCOUNTANCY. RATING REVIEW (SCOTLAND) STATISTICS. ACTUALS.** *see* BUSINESS AND ECONOMICS—Abstracting, Bibliographies, Statistics

➤ **CHARTERED INSTITUTE OF PUBLIC FINANCE AND ACCOUNTANCY. RATING REVIEW (SCOTLAND) STATISTICS. ESTIMATES.** *see* BUSINESS AND ECONOMICS—Abstracting, Bibliographies, Statistics

➤ **CHARTERED INSTITUTE OF PUBLIC FINANCE AND ACCOUNTANCY. REVENUE COLLECTION STATISTICS. ACTUALS (ONLINE).** *see* BUSINESS AND ECONOMICS—Abstracting, Bibliographies, Statistics

➤ **CHARTERED INSTITUTE OF PUBLIC FINANCE AND ACCOUNTANCY. TRADING STANDARDS STATISTICS. ACTUALS & ESTIMATES.** *see* BUSINESS AND ECONOMICS—Abstracting, Bibliographies, Statistics

➤ **CHARTERED INSTITUTE OF PUBLIC FINANCE AND ACCOUNTANCY. WASTE COLLECTION & DISPOSAL STATISTICS. ACTUALS.** *see* ENVIRONMENTAL STUDIES—Abstracting, Bibliographies, Statistics

314 FRA ISSN 2102-6378

▼ **CHIFFRES & STATISTIQUES.** Text in French. 2009. irreg. back issues avail. **Document type:** *Magazine, Government.*

Formed by the merger of (1997-2009): S E S P Infos Rapides. Construction (1779-2061); (1980-2009): S E S P Infos Rapides. Transport (1777-7372); Which was formerly (until 2005): France. Ministere de l'Equipement, des Transports et du Logement. S E S Infos Rapides. Transport (1277-4561); (until 1996): France. Ministere des Transports et de la Mer. Note de Conjoncture des Transports (1169-2553); Which superseded in part: France. Ministere de l'Equipement, du Logement, des Transports et du Tourisme. Note de Conjoncture; Which was formerly (1980-1997): France. Direction des Affaires Economiques et Internationales. Informations Rapides (0291-8897)

Media: Online - full text. **Related titles:** Microfiche ed.

Published by: France. Ministere de l'Equipement et du Logement, 34 Ave Marceau, Paris, 75008, France. cnt@cnt.fr, http://www.cnt.fr.

CHIFFRES-CLES (YEAR) DES RETRAITES DE L'ETAT. *see* BUSINESS AND ECONOMICS—Labor And Industrial Relations

▼ **CHIFFRES CLES DU TRANSPORT.** *see* TRANSPORTATION—Abstracting, Bibliographies, Statistics

CHIIKI HOKEN ROUJIN HOKEN JIGYOU HOUKOKU/JAPAN. MINISTRY OF HEALTH, LABOUR AND WELFARE. REPORT ON ACTIVITIES OF PUBLIC HEALTH CENTERS. *see* MEDICAL SCIENCES—Abstracting, Bibliographies, Statistics

CHILD SUPPORT AGENCY. QUARTERLY SUMMARY STATISTICS (ONLINE). *see* CHILDREN AND YOUTH—Abstracting, Bibliographies, Statistics

A CHILD'S DAY: (YEAR) (SELECTED INDICATORS OF CHILD WELL-BEING) (ONLINE). *see* CHILDREN AND YOUTH—Abstracting, Bibliographies, Statistics

CHILDSTATS. *see* CHILDREN AND YOUTH—Abstracting, Bibliographies, Statistics

CHILE. INSTITUTO NACIONAL DE ESTADISTICAS. ANUARIO DE JUSTICIA. *see* LAW—Abstracting, Bibliographies, Statistics

CHILE. INSTITUTO NACIONAL DE ESTADISTICAS. ANUARIO DE TRANSPORTE Y COMUNICACIONES. *see* TRANSPORTATION—Abstracting, Bibliographies, Statistics

CHILE. INSTITUTO NACIONAL DE ESTADISTICAS. ANUARIO DE TURISMO; estadisticas de turismo y movimiento internacional de viajeros. *see* TRAVEL AND TOURISM—Abstracting, Bibliographies, Statistics

318 CHL ISSN 0717-1463

CHILE. INSTITUTO NACIONAL DE ESTADISTICAS. CIUDADES, PUEBLOS Y ALDEAS. Text in Spanish. a.?.

Published by: Instituto Nacional de Estadisticas, Casilla 498, Correo 3, Ave. Bulnes, 418, Santiago, Chile. TEL 56-2-6991441, FAX 56-2-6712169.

318 CHL ISSN 0716-0607
HA991

CHILE. INSTITUTO NACIONAL DE ESTADISTICAS. COMPENDIO ESTADISTICO. Text in Spanish. 1971. a. CLP 3,000 domestic; USD 18.60 in United States; USD 23.60 elsewhere (effective 1999). stat.

Published by: Instituto Nacional de Estadisticas, Casilla 498, Correo 3, Ave. Bulnes, 418, Santiago, Chile. TEL 56-2-6991441, FAX 56-2-6712169.

CHILE. INSTITUTO NACIONAL DE ESTADISTICAS. CONSUMO REGIONAL DE ENERGIA EN LA INDUSTRIA MANUFACTURERA. *see* ENERGY—Abstracting, Bibliographies, Statistics

CHILE. INSTITUTO NACIONAL DE ESTADISTICAS. CULTURA Y MEDIOS DE COMUNICACION. *see* SOCIOLOGY—Abstracting, Bibliographies, Statistics

310 CHL ISSN 0717-1978
JS2462.L7

CHILE. INSTITUTO NACIONAL DE ESTADISTICAS. DIVISION POLITICO - ADMINISTRATIVA. Text in Spanish. every 10 yrs. CLP 2,000; USD 13.50 in United States; USD 15.90 elsewhere.

Published by: Instituto Nacional de Estadisticas, Casilla 498, Correo 3, Ave. Bulnes, 418, Santiago, Chile. TEL 56-2-6991441, FAX 56-2-6712169.

CHILE. INSTITUTO NACIONAL DE ESTADISTICAS. EDIFICACION. *see* BUILDING AND CONSTRUCTION—Abstracting, Bibliographies, Statistics

CHILE. INSTITUTO NACIONAL DE ESTADISTICAS. ENCUESTA NACIONAL DEL EMPLEO. *see* BUSINESS AND ECONOMICS—Abstracting, Bibliographies, Statistics

310 330 CHL

CHILE. INSTITUTO NACIONAL DE ESTADISTICAS. ESTADISTICA Y ECONOMIA. Text in Spanish. 1990. s-a. CLP 2,550; USD 17.40 in United States; USD 20.40 elsewhere.

Published by: Instituto Nacional de Estadisticas, Casilla 498, Correo 3, Ave. Bulnes, 418, Santiago, Chile. TEL 56-2-6991441, FAX 56-2-6712169.

CHILE. INSTITUTO NACIONAL DE ESTADISTICAS. ESTADISTICAS AGROPECUARIAS. *see* AGRICULTURE—Abstracting, Bibliographies, Statistics

CHILE. INSTITUTO NACIONAL DE ESTADISTICAS. ESTADISTICAS PECUARIAS. *see* AGRICULTURE—Abstracting, Bibliographies, Statistics

CHILE. INSTITUTO NACIONAL DE ESTADISTICAS. FINANZAS. *see* BUSINESS AND ECONOMICS—Abstracting, Bibliographies, Statistics

CHILE. INSTITUTO NACIONAL DE ESTADISTICAS. INDICADORES DE EMPLEO, POR SEXO Y GRUPOS DE EDAD, TOTAL NACIONAL. *see* BUSINESS AND ECONOMICS—Abstracting, Bibliographies, Statistics

CHILE. INSTITUTO NACIONAL DE ESTADISTICAS. INDICE DE PRECIOS AL CONSUMIDOR. *see* BUSINESS AND ECONOMICS—Abstracting, Bibliographies, Statistics

CHILE. INSTITUTO NACIONAL DE ESTADISTICAS. INDICE DE PRECIOS AL POR MAYOR. *see* BUSINESS AND ECONOMICS—Abstracting, Bibliographies, Statistics

CHILE. INSTITUTO NACIONAL DE ESTADISTICAS. INDUSTRIA MOLINERA. TRIGO. *see* AGRICULTURE—Abstracting, Bibliographies, Statistics

318 CHL

CHILE. INSTITUTO NACIONAL DE ESTADISTICAS. INFORMATIVO ESTADISTICO V REGION. Text in Spanish. 1974. a. CLP 1,200; USD 8.20 in North America; USD 9.40 elsewhere.

Published by: Instituto Nacional de Estadisticas, Casilla 498, Correo 3, Ave. Bulnes, 418, Santiago, Chile. TEL 56-2-6991441, FAX 56-2-6712169.

CHILE. INSTITUTO NACIONAL DE ESTADISTICAS. TRANSPORTE, COMUNICACIONES, TURISMO. *see* TRANSPORTATION—Abstracting, Bibliographies, Statistics

CHILE. SERVICIO NACIONAL DE PESCA. ANUARIO ESTADISTICO DE PESCA. *see* FISH AND FISHERIES

CHILE. SUPERINTENDENCIA DE SEGURIDAD SOCIAL. SEGURIDAD SOCIAL: ESTADISTICAS. *see* INSURANCE—Abstracting, Bibliographies, Statistics

310 CHL ISSN 0718-7912

CHILEAN JOURNAL OF STATISTICS. Text in English. 1984. s-a. **Document type:** *Journal, Academic/Scholarly.*

Formerly (until 2000): Sociedad Chilena de Estadistica. Revista (0716-1514)

Related titles: Online - full text ed.: ISSN 0718-7920. free (effective 2011).

Indexed: CIS.

Published by: Sociedad Chilena de Estadistica (S O C H E), Casilla 306, Correo 22, Santiago, Chile. http://www.soche.cl. Ed. Aureliano Arellano-Valle.

CHINA MONTHLY STATISTICS. *see* BUSINESS AND ECONOMICS—Abstracting, Bibliographies, Statistics

315 HKG ISSN 1052-9225
HA4631

CHINA STATISTICAL YEARBOOK. Text in English. 1981. a. HKD 895 domestic; USD 115 elsewhere. back issues avail. **Description:** Provides up-to-date statistics on China's social and economic development at national and local levels of provinces, autonomous regions and cities directly under the central government.

Formerly: Statistical Yearbook of China (0255-6766)

Related titles: Chinese ed.: Zhongguo Tongji Nianjian.

Indexed: RASB.

—BLDSC (3180.234633).

Published by: (State Statistics Bureau), China Phone Book Company Ltd., 24-F Citicorp Centre, 18 Whitfield Rd, GPO Box 11581, Hong Kong, Hong Kong. FAX 852-2503-1526. **Dist. by:** Current Pacific Ltd., 7 La Roche Pl, Northcote, PO Box 36-536, Auckland 0627, New Zealand. TEL 64-9-4801388, FAX 64-9-4801387, info@cplnz.com, http://www.cplnz.com.

CHINA WOOL FACTS & FIGURES. *see* BUSINESS AND ECONOMICS

CHISLENNOST' I MIGRATSIYA NASELENIYA ROSSIISKOI FEDERATSII (YEAR)/POPULATION SIZE AND MIGRATION IN THE RUSSIAN FEDERATION (YEAR). *see* POPULATION STUDIES—Abstracting, Bibliographies, Statistics

CHISLENNOST' NASELENIYA ROSSIISKOI FEDERATSII PO GORODAM, POSELKAM GORODSKOGO TIPA I RAYONAM (YEAR). *see* POPULATION STUDIES—Abstracting, Bibliographies, Statistics

CHISLENNOST' NASELENIYA ROSSIISKOI FEDERATSII PO POLU I VOZRASTU (YEAR)/POPULATION SIZE IN THE RUSSIAN FEDERATION BY SEX AND AGE (YEAR). *see* POPULATION STUDIES—Abstracting, Bibliographies, Statistics

CITY CRIME RANKINGS; crime in metropolitan America. *see* CRIMINOLOGY AND LAW ENFORCEMENT—Abstracting, Bibliographies, Statistics

CIVIL AVIATION STATISTICS OF THE WORLD (YEAR). *see* TRANSPORTATION—Abstracting, Bibliographies, Statistics

CLASIFICACION MEXICANA DE OCUPACIONES. *see* OCCUPATIONS AND CAREERS—Abstracting, Bibliographies, Statistics

CLIMATOLOGICAL DATA. PUERTO RICO AND VIRGIN ISLANDS. *see* METEOROLOGY—Abstracting, Bibliographies, Statistics

COLLEGE OF NURSES OF ONTARIO. MEMBERSHIP STATISTICS REPORT. *see* MEDICAL SCIENCES—Nurses And Nursing

COLOMBIA. DEPARTAMENTO ADMINISTRATIVO NACIONAL DE ESTADISTICA. ANUARIO DE INDUSTRIA MANUFACTURERA. *see* BUSINESS AND ECONOMICS—Abstracting, Bibliographies, Statistics

318 COL ISSN 0120-6281
HA1011

COLOMBIA. DEPARTAMENTO ADMINISTRATIVO NACIONAL DE ESTADISTICA. BOLETIN DE ESTADISTICA. Text in Spanish. 1951. m. COP 4,000, USD 450. charts; illus.; stat. index. Supplement avail. **Document type:** *Government.*

Formerly (until Dec. 1984): Colombia. Direccion General de Estadistica. Boletin Mensual de Estadistica (0120-0836); (until 1952): Colombia. Direccion General de Estadistica. Boletin Informativo

Indexed: PAIS.

Published by: Departamento Administrativo Nacional de Estadistica (D A N E), Bancos de Datos, Centro Administrativo Nacional (CAN), Avenida Eldorado, Apartado Aereo 80043, Bogota, CUND, Colombia. TEL 57-1-2221100, FAX 57-1-222107, TELEX 44573. Ed. Jorge Enrique Gomez Vallejo. Circ: 3,000.

COLOMBIA. DEPARTAMENTO ADMINISTRATIVO NACIONAL DE ESTADISTICA. DIVISION POLITICO-ADMINISTRATIVA. *see* PUBLIC ADMINISTRATION—Abstracting, Bibliographies, Statistics

318 COL

COLOMBIA. DEPARTAMENTO ADMINISTRATIVO NACIONAL DE ESTADISTICA. ESTADISTICAS HISTORICAS. Text in Spanish. irreg. **Document type:** *Government.*

Published by: Departamento Administrativo Nacional de Estadistica (D A N E), Bancos de Datos, Centro Administrativo Nacional (CAN), Avenida Eldorado, Apartado Aereo 80043, Bogota, CUND, Colombia.

318 COL ISSN 0120-6443
HA1011

COLOMBIA ESTADISTICA. Text in Spanish. 1979. a. USD 98 (effective 2000). **Document type:** *Government.*

Published by: Departamento Administrativo Nacional de Estadistica (D A N E), Bancos de Datos, Centro Administrativo Nacional (CAN), Avenida Eldorado, Apartado Aereo 80043, Bogota, CUND, Colombia. FAX 57-1-222-2107.

COLORADO CITIES & COUNTIES GRAPHIC PERFORMANCE ANALYSIS. *see* PUBLIC ADMINISTRATION—Abstracting, Bibliographies, Statistics

COLORADO CROP PROGRESS. *see* AGRICULTURE—Abstracting, Bibliographies, Statistics

COMERCIO EXTERIOR DE MEXICO. INFORMACION PRELIMINAR. *see* BUSINESS AND ECONOMICS—Abstracting, Bibliographies, Statistics

COMERTUL EXTERIOR AL ROMANIEI/FOREIGN TRADE OF ROMANIA. *see* BUSINESS AND ECONOMICS—Abstracting, Bibliographies, Statistics

COMMERCE EXTERIEUR DE LA GRECE/EXOTERIKON EMPORION TES ELLADOS. *see* BUSINESS AND ECONOMICS—Abstracting, Bibliographies, Statistics

COMMERCIAL FERTILIZERS REPORT. *see* AGRICULTURE—Abstracting, Bibliographies, Statistics

COMMODITY PRICE STATISTICS MONTHLY IN TAIWAN AREA. *see* BUSINESS AND ECONOMICS—Abstracting, Bibliographies, Statistics

COMMODITY TRADE STATISTICS; according to the Standard International Trade Classification. *see* BUSINESS AND ECONOMICS—Abstracting, Bibliographies, Statistics

COMMODITY YEARBOOK UPDATE SERVICE. *see* AGRICULTURE—Abstracting, Bibliographies, Statistics

318 BHS

COMMONWEALTH OF THE BAHAMAS STATISTICAL ABSTRACT ANNUAL REPORT. Text in English. 1969. a. USD 10 (effective 2005). stat. **Document type:** *Abstract/Index.*

Formerly (until 1999): Bahamas. Department of Statistics. Statistical Abstract

Related titles: E-mail ed.; Microfiche ed.: (from PQC).

Published by: Department of Statistics, PO Box N 3904, Nassau, Bahamas. TEL 242-502-1251, FAX 242-325-5149, dpsdp@batelnet.bs. Ed. Violet Duacombe.

318 BHS

THE COMMONWEALTH OF THE BAHAMAS. THE BAHAMAS IN FIGURES. Text in English. 1976. a., latest 1998. USD 3 (effective 2001). stat. **Document type:** *Government.*

Formerly: Bahamas. Department of Statistics. Statistical Summary

Related titles: Diskette ed.; E-mail ed.

Published by: Department of Statistics, PO Box N 3904, Nassau, Bahamas.

S

310 IDN
COMMUNICATION STATISTICS. Text in Indonesian. 1965. a. IDR 8,000, USD 3.50. **Document type:** *Government.*
Published by: Central Bureau of Statistics/Biro Pusat Statistik, Jalan Dr. Sutomo No. 8, PO Box 3, Jakarta Pusat, Indonesia. TEL 62-21-372808. Circ: 300.

COMMUNICATIONS IN STATISTICS: SIMULATION AND COMPUTATION. *see* COMPUTERS—Abstracting, Bibliographies, Statistics

519.5 USA ISSN 0361-0926
QA276.A1 CODEN: CSTMDC
➤ **COMMUNICATIONS IN STATISTICS: THEORY AND METHODS.** Text in English. 1976. 20/yr. GBP 5,360 combined subscription in United Kingdom to institutions (print & online eds.); EUR 7,075, USD 8,844 combined subscription to institutions (print & online eds.) (effective 2012). adv. charts; illus. Index. back issues avail.; reprint service avail. from PSC. **Document type:** *Journal, Academic/Scholarly.* **Description:** Focuses primarily on new applications of known statistical methods to actual problems in industry and government, and has a strong mathematical orientation to statistical studies.
Supersedes in part (in 1976): Communications in Statistics (0090-3272)
Related titles: Microform ed.: (from RPI); Online - full text ed.: ISSN 1532-415X. GBP 4,825 in United Kingdom to institutions; EUR 6,368, USD 7,960 to institutions (effective 2012) (from IngentaConnect).
Indexed: A22, A34, A36, ASCA, B01, B06, B07, B09, Biostat, C25, CA, CABA, CCMJ, CIS, CMCI, CPEI, CompLI, E01, E12, EngInd, FCA, FR, GH, GeoRef, ISR, Inspec, JCQM, LT, MSN, MathR, N02, N03, N04, ORMS, P30, P33, P39, P52, QC&AS, R12, RASB, RRTA, S13, S16, SCI, SCOPUS, ST&MA, SpeleolAb, T02, T05, VS, W07, W11, Z02.
—BLDSC (3363.432000), AskIEEE, IE, Infotrieve, Ingenta, INIST, Linda Hall. **CCC.**
Published by: Taylor & Francis Inc. (Subsidiary of: Taylor & Francis Group), 325 Chestnut St, Ste 800, Philadelphia, PA 19106. TEL 215-625-8900, 800-354-1420, FAX 215-625-8914, orders@taylorandfrancis.com, http://www.taylorandfrancis.com. Ed. N Balakrishnan. **Subscr. to:** Taylor & Francis Ltd., Journals Customer Service, Sheepen Pl, Colchester, Essex CO3 3LP, United Kingdom. TEL 44-20-70175544, FAX 44-20-70175198, subscriptions@tandf.co.uk.

314.6 ESP ISSN 1577-161X
COMMUNIDAD DE MADRID DATOS BASICOS. Text in Spanish. 2000. a. free (effective 2009). **Document type:** *Bulletin, Consumer.*
Related titles: Online - full text ed.; ◆ English ed.: Region of Madrid Data Guide. ISSN 1577-1628.
Published by: Comunidad de Madrid, Instituto de Estadistica, Principe de Vargara 108, Madrid, 28002, Spain. TEL 34-91-5802540, jestadis@madrid.org, http://www.madrid.org/iestadis/index.htm.

COMPANHIA PARANAENSE DE ENERGIA. INFORME ESTATISTICO ANUAL. *see* ENERGY—Abstracting, Bibliographies, Statistics

COMPANY R E F S (CD-ROM). (Really Essential Financial Statistics) *see* BUSINESS AND ECONOMICS—Abstracting, Bibliographies, Statistics

COMPANY R E F S (PRINT). (Really Essential Financial Statistics) *see* BUSINESS AND ECONOMICS—Abstracting, Bibliographies, Statistics

COMPARABLE HEALTH INDICATORS, CANADA, PROVINCES AND TERRITORIES. *see* PUBLIC HEALTH AND SAFETY—Abstracting, Bibliographies, Statistics

318 GTM
COMPENDIO ESTADISTICO SOBRE VARIABLES ECONOMICO-SOCIALES. Text in Spanish. a.
Published by: Instituto Nacional de Estadistica, Ministerio de Economia, 8A Calle no. 9-55, Guatemala City Zona, Guatemala.

COMPENDIO STATISTICO FERRARESE. *see* BUSINESS AND ECONOMICS—Abstracting, Bibliographies, Statistics

314 ITA ISSN 0069-7958
COMPENDIO STATISTICO ITALIANO. Text in Italian. 1927. a. **Document type:** *Government.* **Description:** Contains national and regional economic and demographic data.
Formerly (until 1931): Compendio Statistico (0390-640X)
Published by: Istituto Nazionale di Statistica (I S T A T), Via Cesare Balbo 16, Rome, 00184, Italy. TEL 39-06-46731, http://www.istat.it.

COMPENDIUM OF CANADIAN FORESTRY STATISTICS. *see* FORESTS AND FORESTRY—Abstracting, Bibliographies, Statistics

COMPENDIUM OF IRISH ECONOMIC AND AGRICULTURE STATISTICS (YEAR). *see* AGRICULTURE—Abstracting, Bibliographies, Statistics

COMPENDIUM OF NEW ZEALAND FARM PRODUCTION STATISTICS. *see* AGRICULTURE—Abstracting, Bibliographies, Statistics

519.5 NLD ISSN 0253-018X
COMPSTAT. Variant title: Computational Statisticst Symposium. Proceedings. Text in English. 1974. biennial. price varies. abstr. back issues avail. **Document type:** *Proceedings, Academic/Scholarly.* **Description:** Publishes papers reflecting current interests in computational statistics.
Indexed: ST&MA.
—BLDSC (3368.400000).
Published by: (International Association for Statistical Computing), International Statistical Institute, PO Box 24070, The Hague, 2490 AB, Netherlands. TEL 31-70-3375737, FAX 31-70-3860025, isi@cbs.nl, http://www.cbs.nl/. **Subscr. to:** Springer Netherlands.

519.5 DEU ISSN 0943-4062
QA276.4 CODEN: CSTAEB
➤ **COMPUTATIONAL STATISTICS.** Text in English. 1982. q. EUR 682, USD 818 combined subscription to institutions (print & online eds.) (effective 2012). bk.rev.; software rev. illus. reprint service avail. from PSC. **Document type:** *Journal, Academic/Scholarly.* **Description:** Covers computational aspects of new and existing statistical techniques.
Formerly (until 1992): C S Q - Computational Statistics Quarterly (0723-712X)
Related titles: Microform ed.: (from PQC); Online - full text ed.: ISSN 1613-9658 (from IngentaConnect).
Indexed: A12, A22, A26, ABIn, ASCA, CCMJ, CIS, CMCI, CybAb, E01, I05, IBR, IBZ, Inspec, JCQM, MSN, MathR, P10, P17, P26, P30, P48, P49, P50, P51, P53, P54, PQC, SCI, SCOPUS, ST&MA, W07, Z02.
—BLDSC (3390.624200), AskIEEE, IE, Infotrieve, Ingenta, Linda Hall. **CCC.**
Published by: Physica-Verlag GmbH und Co. (Subsidiary of: Springer), Postfach 105280, Heidelberg, 69042, Germany. TEL 49-6221-487492, FAX 49-6221-487177, physica@springer.de. Eds. J Symanzik, Y Mori, Friedrich Leisch. **Subscr. in the Americas to:** Springer New York LLC, Journal Fulfillment, PO Box 2485, Secaucus, NJ 07096. TEL 800-777-4643, 201-348-4033, FAX 201-348-4505, journals-ny@springer.com, http://www.springer.com; **Subscr. to:** Springer Distribution Center, Kundenservice Zeitschriften, Haberstr 7, Heidelberg 69126, Germany. TEL 49-6221-3454303, FAX 49-6221-3454229, subscriptions@springer.com.

➤ **COMPUTER AND INTERNET USE IN THE UNITED STATES.** *see* POPULATION STUDIES—Abstracting, Bibliographies, Statistics

310.004 JPN ISSN 0911-3878
COMPUTER SCIENCE MONOGRAPHS. Text in English. 1973. irreg., latest no.31, 2005. **Document type:** *Monographic series, Academic/Scholarly.* **Description:** Covers computer programs and software for statistical science.
Published by: Institute of Statistical Mathematics/Tokei Suri Kenkyujo, 4-6-7 Minami-Azabu, Minato-ku, Tokyo, 106-8569, Japan.

COMUNE DI PISA. ANNUARIO STATISTICO. *see* POPULATION STUDIES—Abstracting, Bibliographies, Statistics

COMUNE DI ROMA. ANNUARIO STATISTICO. *see* POPULATION STUDIES—Abstracting, Bibliographies, Statistics

314 ESP ISSN 1139-6407
HA1559.M3
COMUNIDAD DE MADRID. ANUARIO ESTADISTICO. Key Title: Anuario Estadistico de la Comunidad de Madrid. Text in Spanish. 1984. a., latest 2008. back issues avail. **Document type:** *Yearbook, Consumer.*
Related titles: CD-ROM ed.: ISSN 1578-4789. 2000; Online - full text ed.
Published by: Comunidad de Madrid, Instituto de Estadistica, Principe de Vargara 108, Madrid, 28002, Spain. TEL 34-91-5802540, jestadis@madrid.org, http://www.madrid.org/iestadis/index.htm.

314.6 ESP ISSN 1139-8434
LA COMUNIDAD DE MADRID EN CIFRAS. Text in Spanish. 1995. a. free (effective 2008). **Document type:** *Bulletin, Consumer.*
Related titles: Online - full text ed.
Published by: Comunidad de Madrid, Instituto de Estadistica, Principe de Vargara 108, Madrid, 28002, Spain. TEL 34-91-5802540, FAX 34-91-5802664, jestadis@madrid.org, http://www.madrid.org/iestadis/index.htm.

COMUNIDAD INFORMATICA. *see* COMPUTERS—Abstracting, Bibliographies, Statistics

314 GRC ISSN 0069-8245
CODEN: ASUTDG
CONCISE STATISTICAL YEARBOOK OF GREECE. Text in English, Greek. 1954. irreg., latest 2001. back issues avail. **Document type:** *Government.*
Published by: National Statistical Service of Greece, Statistical Information and Publications Division/Ethniki Statistiki Ypiresia tes Ellados, 14-16 Lykourgou St, Athens, 101 66, Greece. TEL 30-1-3289-397, FAX 30-1-3241-102.

THE CONDITION OF EDUCATION. *see* EDUCATION—Abstracting, Bibliographies, Statistics

CONGO. CENTRE NATIONAL DE LA STATISTIQUE ET DES ETUDES ECONOMIQUES. ANNUAIRE STATISTIQUE. *see* BUSINESS AND ECONOMICS—Abstracting, Bibliographies, Statistics

CONGO. CENTRE NATIONAL DE LA STATISTIQUE ET DES ETUDES ECONOMIQUES. BULLETIN DE STATISTIQUE. *see* BUSINESS AND ECONOMICS—Abstracting, Bibliographies, Statistics

316 COG ISSN 0010-5805
CONGO. CENTRE NATIONAL DE LA STATISTIQUE ET DES ETUDES ECONOMIQUES. BULLETIN MENSUEL DE LA STATISTIQUE. Text in French. 1958. m. XAF 3,000 per issue. charts; mkt.
Media: Duplicated (not offset).
Published by: Centre National de la Statistique et des Etudes Economiques, BP 2031, Brazzaville, Congo, Republic. Circ: 500.

CONGO. CENTRE NATIONAL DE LA STATISTIQUE ET DES ETUDES ECONOMIQUES. BULLETIN TRIMESTRIEL DE LA CONJONCTURE. *see* BUSINESS AND ECONOMICS—Abstracting, Bibliographies, Statistics

310 MAR ISSN 1113-9048
HC810.A1
CONJONCTURE: EVOLUTIONS ET PERSPECTIVES. Text in French. q. MAD 66 (effective 2000). **Document type:** *Government.*
Former titles (until 1997): Etudes de Conjoncture: Evolutions et Tendances; (until 1991): Conjoncture Economique (0851-5921); (until 1988): Conjoncture Economique au Maroc (0851-0989); Morocco. Direction de la Statistique. Etude de Conjoncture
Indexed: RASB.
Published by: Morocco. Direction de la Statistique, B P 178, Rabat, Morocco. TEL 212-7-77-36-06, FAX 212-7-77-32-17.

CONNECTICUT CITIES & COUNTIES GRAPHIC PERFORMANCE ANALYSIS. *see* PUBLIC ADMINISTRATION—Abstracting, Bibliographies, Statistics

CONSEJERIA DE OBRAS PUBLICAS Y ORDENACION DEL TERRITORIO. BOLETIN ESTADISTICO. *see* BUSINESS AND ECONOMICS—Economic Situation And Conditions

CONSTRUCTION REVIEW. *see* BUILDING AND CONSTRUCTION—Abstracting, Bibliographies, Statistics

CONSTRUCTION SPENDING. *see* BUILDING AND CONSTRUCTION—Abstracting, Bibliographies, Statistics

CONSUMER EXPENDITURE SURVEY. *see* BUSINESS AND ECONOMICS—Economic Situation And Conditions

CONSUMER EXPENDITURES IN (YEAR). *see* BUSINESS AND ECONOMICS—Economic Situation And Conditions

CONSUMER PRICE INDEX (VICTORIA). *see* BUSINESS AND ECONOMICS—Abstracting, Bibliographies, Statistics

CONSUMER PRICE INDEX. PACIFIC CITIES & U.S. AVERAGE. *see* BUSINESS AND ECONOMICS—Abstracting, Bibliographies, Statistics

CONSUMER PRICE INDICES OF ETHIOPIA AT COUNTRY, RURAL AND URBAN LEVELS. *see* BUSINESS AND ECONOMICS—Abstracting, Bibliographies, Statistics

I CONSUMI ENERGETICI DELLE IMPRESE INDUSTRIALI. *see* ENERGY—Abstracting, Bibliographies, Statistics

CONSUMO PECUARIO NACIONAL. *see* AGRICULTURE—Abstracting, Bibliographies, Statistics

▼ **CONTAS DO AMBIENTE/ENVIRONMENTAL ACCOUNTS.** *see* ENVIRONMENTAL STUDIES—Abstracting, Bibliographies, Statistics

CONTI DEGLI ITALIANI. *see* BUSINESS AND ECONOMICS—Abstracting, Bibliographies, Statistics

CONTINU ONDERZOEK BURGERPERSPECTIEVEN. *see* SOCIOLOGY—Abstracting, Bibliographies, Statistics

CONZOOM; klassifikation Danmark. *see* BUSINESS AND ECONOMICS—Abstracting, Bibliographies, Statistics

CORRECTIONAL POPULATIONS IN THE U S (YEAR). *see* CRIMINOLOGY AND LAW ENFORCEMENT—Abstracting, Bibliographies, Statistics

COST OF DOING BUSINESS REPORT: OPERATING PERFORMANCE COMPARISONS FOR MUSIC PRODUCT DEALERS. *see* MUSIC—Abstracting, Bibliographies, Statistics

COSTA RICA. DIRECCION GENERAL DE ESTADISTICA Y CENSOS. ENCUESTA DE HOGARES DE PROPOSITOS MULTIPLES. *see* BUSINESS AND ECONOMICS—Abstracting, Bibliographies, Statistics

317.2 CRI ISSN 1409-018X
HA801
COSTA RICA. DIRECCION GENERAL DE ESTADISTICA Y CENSOS. ESTADISTICAS VITALES; poblacion, nacimientos, defunciones, matrimonios. Text in Spanish. a.
Published by: Ministerio de Economia Industria y Comercio, Direccion General de Estadistica y Censos, Apdo 10163, San Jose, 1000, Costa Rica.

310 CRI ISSN 0589-8544
COSTA RICA. DIRECCION GENERAL DE ESTADISTICA Y CENSOS. INVENTARIO DE LAS ESTADISTICAS NACIONALES. Text in Spanish. 1964. irreg., latest 1970. per issue exchange basis.
Published by: Ministerio de Economia Industria y Comercio, Direccion General de Estadistica y Censos, Apdo 10163, San Jose, 1000, Costa Rica.

COSTA RICA. ESTADISTICAS DE COMERCIO EXTERIOR. *see* BUSINESS AND ECONOMICS—Abstracting, Bibliographies, Statistics

972.00021 CRI ISSN 1409-1941
HA802
COSTA RICA. INSTITUTO NACIONAL DE ESTADISTICA Y CENSOS. ANUARIO ESTADISTICO. Text in Spanish. quinquennial.
Published by: Ministerio de Economia Industria y Comercio, Direccion General de Estadistica y Censos, Apdo 10163, San Jose, 1000, Costa Rica.

COTTON: WORLD STATISTICS. *see* AGRICULTURE—Abstracting, Bibliographies, Statistics

COUNCIL OF ONTARIO UNIVERSITIES. APPLICATION STATISTICS. *see* EDUCATION—Abstracting, Bibliographies, Statistics

310 USA ISSN 0890-1627
COUNCIL OF PROFESSIONAL ASSOCIATION ON FEDERAL STATISTICS. NEWS. Key Title: New from C O P A F S. Text in English. 1982. q. USD 30. **Document type:** *Newsletter.*
Published by: Council of Professional Association on Federal Statistics, 1429 Duke St., Ste. 402, Alexandria, CA 22314-3402. Ed. Edward J Spar. Circ: 500.

COUNTIES / MANUKAU DISTRICT CRIME STATISTICS. *see* CRIMINOLOGY AND LAW ENFORCEMENT—Abstracting, Bibliographies, Statistics

317 USA ISSN 0082-9455
HA202
COUNTY AND CITY DATA BOOK. Text in English. 1944. irreg., latest 2007, 14th ed. USD 75 per issue (effective 2009). stat.; abstr. **Document type:** *Government.* **Description:** Presents states, counties, cities, and places in the United States statistics on: agriculture, banking, climate, crime, education, Federal funds and grants, government finances and employment, households, housing, income, labor force, land area, manufacturing, population, poverty, retail and wholesale trade, service industries, unemployment, and vital statistics.
Formed by the merger of: Cities Supplement; County Databook
Related titles: Online - full text ed.
Published by: U.S. Census Bureau (Subsidiary of: U.S. Department of Commerce), 4600 Silver Hill Rd, Washington, DC 20233. **Subscr. to:** U.S. Government Printing Office, Superintendent of Documents, PO Box 371954, Pittsburgh, PA 15250. TEL 202-512-1800, FAX 202-512-2250.

310 USA ISSN 1059-9096
HA203
COUNTY AND CITY EXTRA; annual metro, city and county data book. Text in English. 1992. a. price varies. charts. back issues avail. **Document type:** *Journal, Trade.* **Description:** General reference that lists a wide range of statistical data for every state, county, city, and metropolitan area in the United States. Incorporates data obtained from the Census Bureau, Bureau of Economic Analysis, FBI, National Weather Service, and others.
Related titles: CD-ROM ed.
—**CCC.**
Published by: (Kraus Organization, Ltd.), Bernan Press, 15200 NBN Way, PO Box 191, Blue Ridge Summit, PA 17214. TEL 301-459-7666, 800-865-3457, FAX 301-459-6988, 800-865-3450, customercare@bernan.com.

COUNTY BUSINESS PATTERNS (ONLINE). *see* BUSINESS AND ECONOMICS—Abstracting, Bibliographies, Statistics

COUNTY PENETRATION REPORTS; a tabulation of county circulation data for daily and weekly newspapers. *see* ADVERTISING AND PUBLIC RELATIONS—Abstracting, Bibliographies, Statistics

CRACKING THE A P STATISTICS EXAM. (Advanced Placement) *see* EDUCATION—Higher Education

CRICKET STATISTICIAN. *see* SPORTS AND GAMES—Abstracting, Bibliographies, Statistics

CRIME IN CALIFORNIA. *see* CRIMINOLOGY AND LAW ENFORCEMENT—Abstracting, Bibliographies, Statistics

CRIME STATE RANKINGS; crime in the 50 United States. *see* CRIMINOLOGY AND LAW ENFORCEMENT—Abstracting, Bibliographies, Statistics

CROATIAN OPERATIONAL RESEARCH REVIEW. *see* MATHEMATICS

CROP PROGRESS AND CONDITION. *see* AGRICULTURE—Abstracting, Bibliographies, Statistics

CROP PROGRESS & CONDITION. *see* AGRICULTURE—Abstracting, Bibliographies, Statistics

CROP WEATHER BULLETIN. *see* AGRICULTURE—Abstracting, Bibliographies, Statistics

318 CHL ISSN 0251-9437
CUADERNOS ESTADISTICOS DE LA C E P A L. Text in Spanish. 1976. irreg., latest vol.26, 1998. price varies.
Published by: Comision Economica para America Latina y el Caribe/ Economic Commission for Latin America and the Caribbean, Ave Dag Hammarskjold 3477, Vitacura, Santiago de Chile, Chile. TEL 56-2-4712000, FAX 56-2-2080252.

317.28 CUB
CUBA. COMITE ESTATAL DE ESTADISTICAS. REVISTA ESTADISTICA. Text in Spanish; Summaries in English, Russian. 1979. s-a. bk.rev. bibl.; charts.
Published by: Comite Estatal de Estadisticas, Centro de Informacion Cientifico-Tecnica, Almendares No. 156, esq. a Desague, Gaveta Postal 6016, Havana, Cuba. Ed. Ramon Sabadi Rodriquez.

CUBA EN CIFRAS. *see* BUSINESS AND ECONOMICS—Abstracting, Bibliographies, Statistics

CUBA. MINISTERIO DE SALUD PUBLICA. DIRECCION NACIONAL DE ESTADISTICAS. ANUARIO ESTADISTICO. *see* MEDICAL SCIENCES—Abstracting, Bibliographies, Statistics

CUBA QUARTERLY ECONOMIC REPORT. *see* BUSINESS AND ECONOMICS—Abstracting, Bibliographies, Statistics

CULTURAL INDICATORS FOR NEW ZEALAND/TOHU AHUREA MO AOTEAROA. *see* SOCIOLOGY—Abstracting, Bibliographies, Statistics

CURRENT INDEX TO STATISTICS (ONLINE); applications - methods - theory. *see* MATHEMATICS—Abstracting, Bibliographies, Statistics

CURRENT INDUSTRIAL REPORTS (ONLINE). *see* BUSINESS AND ECONOMICS—Abstracting, Bibliographies, Statistics

CURRENT INDUSTRIAL REPORTS. M3-1, MANUFACTURERS' SHIPMENTS, INVENTORIES, AND ORDERS (ONLINE). *see* BUSINESS AND ECONOMICS—Abstracting, Bibliographies, Statistics

CURRENT INDUSTRIAL REPORTS. M3-3, BENCHMARK REPORT FOR MANUFACTURERS' SHIPMENTS, INVENTORIES, AND ORDERS. *see* BUSINESS AND ECONOMICS—Abstracting, Bibliographies, Statistics

CURRENT INDUSTRIAL REPORTS. M311K, FATS AND OILS: PRODUCTION, CONSUMPTION, AND STOCKS (ONLINE). *see* FOOD AND FOOD INDUSTRIES—Abstracting, Bibliographies, Statistics

CURRENT LEGAL SOCIOLOGY; a periodical publication of abstracts and bibliography in law and society. *see* LAW—Abstracting, Bibliographies, Statistics

CURRENT STATISTICS. *see* BUSINESS AND ECONOMICS—Abstracting, Bibliographies, Statistics

CYPRUS. DEPARTMENT OF STATISTICS AND RESEARCH. AGRICULTURAL STATISTICS. *see* AGRICULTURE—Abstracting, Bibliographies, Statistics

CYPRUS. DEPARTMENT OF STATISTICS AND RESEARCH. CENSUS OF AGRICULTURE. *see* AGRICULTURE—Abstracting, Bibliographies, Statistics

CYPRUS. DEPARTMENT OF STATISTICS AND RESEARCH. CENSUS OF COTTAGE INDUSTRY. *see* BUSINESS AND ECONOMICS—Abstracting, Bibliographies, Statistics

CYPRUS. DEPARTMENT OF STATISTICS AND RESEARCH. CENSUS OF INDUSTRIAL PRODUCTION. *see* BUSINESS AND ECONOMICS—Abstracting, Bibliographies, Statistics

CYPRUS. DEPARTMENT OF STATISTICS AND RESEARCH. CENSUS OF POULTRY. *see* AGRICULTURE—Abstracting, Bibliographies, Statistics

CYPRUS. DEPARTMENT OF STATISTICS AND RESEARCH. CONSTRUCTION AND HOUSING STATISTICS. *see* BUILDING AND CONSTRUCTION—Abstracting, Bibliographies, Statistics

CYPRUS. DEPARTMENT OF STATISTICS AND RESEARCH. CRIMINAL STATISTICS. *see* CRIMINOLOGY AND LAW ENFORCEMENT—Abstracting, Bibliographies, Statistics

CYPRUS. DEPARTMENT OF STATISTICS AND RESEARCH. DEMOGRAPHIC SURVEY (YEARS). *see* POPULATION STUDIES—Abstracting, Bibliographies, Statistics

CYPRUS. DEPARTMENT OF STATISTICS AND RESEARCH. ECONOMIC REPORT. *see* BUSINESS AND ECONOMICS—Abstracting, Bibliographies, Statistics

CYPRUS. DEPARTMENT OF STATISTICS AND RESEARCH. EDUCATION STATISTICS. *see* EDUCATION—Abstracting, Bibliographies, Statistics

CYPRUS. DEPARTMENT OF STATISTICS AND RESEARCH. FUNCTIONS AND SERVICES. *see* PUBLIC ADMINISTRATION—Abstracting, Bibliographies, Statistics

CYPRUS. DEPARTMENT OF STATISTICS AND RESEARCH. HOUSEHOLD INCOME AND EXPENDITURE SURVEY. *see* BUSINESS AND ECONOMICS—Abstracting, Bibliographies, Statistics

CYPRUS. DEPARTMENT OF STATISTICS AND RESEARCH. IMPORTS AND EXPORTS STATISTICS. *see* BUSINESS AND ECONOMICS—Abstracting, Bibliographies, Statistics

CYPRUS. DEPARTMENT OF STATISTICS AND RESEARCH. INDUSTRIAL STATISTICS. *see* BUSINESS AND ECONOMICS—Abstracting, Bibliographies, Statistics

CYPRUS. DEPARTMENT OF STATISTICS AND RESEARCH. MONTHLY ECONOMIC INDICATORS. *see* BUSINESS AND ECONOMICS—Economic Situation And Conditions

CYPRUS. DEPARTMENT OF STATISTICS AND RESEARCH. MULTI-ROUND DEMOGRAPHIC SURVEY. MIGRATION IN CYPRUS. *see* POPULATION STUDIES—Abstracting, Bibliographies, Statistics

310 CYP
CYPRUS. DEPARTMENT OF STATISTICS AND RESEARCH. QUESTIONNAIRES FOR CENSUSES AND SURVEYS. Text in English, Greek. 1983. irreg. **Document type:** *Government.*
Description: Summarizes all questionnaires used by the Department of Statistics and Research in conducting censuses, surveys, and other statistical inquiries.
Published by: Ministry of Finance, Department of Statistics and Research, 13 Andreas Araouzos St, Nicosia, 1444, Cyprus. TEL 357-2-309318, FAX 357-2-37483.

CYPRUS. DEPARTMENT OF STATISTICS AND RESEARCH. STATISTICS OF IMPORTS AND EXPORTS. *see* BUSINESS AND ECONOMICS—Abstracting, Bibliographies, Statistics

CYPRUS. DEPARTMENT OF STATISTICS AND RESEARCH. TOURISM, MIGRATION AND TRAVEL STATISTICS. *see* TRAVEL AND TOURISM—Abstracting, Bibliographies, Statistics

CYPRUS. MINISTRY OF HEALTH. ANNUAL REPORT. *see* PUBLIC HEALTH AND SAFETY—Abstracting, Bibliographies, Statistics

CZECH CONSTRUCTION INDUSTRY IN FIGURES (YEAR). *see* BUILDING AND CONSTRUCTION—Abstracting, Bibliographies, Statistics

CZECH STATISTICAL OFFICE. INDICATORS OF SOCIAL AND ECONOMIC DEVELOPMENT IN THE CZECH REPUBLIC/CESKY STATISTICKY URAD. UKAZATELE SOCIALNIHO A HOSPODARSKEHO VYVOJE CESKE REPUBLIKY. *see* BUSINESS AND ECONOMICS—Abstracting, Bibliographies, Statistics

D A LOENSTATISTIK (ONLINE). (Dansk Arbejdsgiverforening) *see* BUSINESS AND ECONOMICS—Abstracting, Bibliographies, Statistics

D H B HOSPITAL BENCHMARK INFORMATION. (District Health Board) *see* HEALTH FACILITIES AND ADMINISTRATION—Abstracting, Bibliographies, Statistics

THE D V D STATISTICAL REPORT. (Digital Video Disc) *see* COMMUNICATIONS—Abstracting, Bibliographies, Statistics

THE D V D STATISTICAL REPORT. (Digital Video Disc) *see* COMMUNICATIONS—Abstracting, Bibliographies, Statistics

DAILY-FROM STATS CAN. *see* BUSINESS AND ECONOMICS—Abstracting, Bibliographies, Statistics

DAILY GRAIN REVIEW. *see* AGRICULTURE—Abstracting, Bibliographies, Statistics

DAIRY FACTS AND FIGURES AT A GLANCE. *see* AGRICULTURE—Abstracting, Bibliographies, Statistics

DAIRY MARKET STATISTICS: ANNUAL SUMMARY. *see* AGRICULTURE—Abstracting, Bibliographies, Statistics

DAIRY MONTHLY IMPORTS. *see* AGRICULTURE—Abstracting, Bibliographies, Statistics

DAIRY STATISTICS. *see* AGRICULTURE—Abstracting, Bibliographies, Statistics

001.4 190 DNK ISSN 1399-8897
DANISH CENTRE FOR STUDIES IN RESEARCH AND RESEARCH POLICY. WORKING PAPERS. Text mainly in English. 1999. irreg., latest 2008. charts; stat. back issues avail. **Document type:** *Monographic series, Academic/Scholarly.*
Related titles: Online - full text ed.
Published by: Dansk Center for Forskningsanalyse/Danish Centre for Studies in Research and Research Policy, Aarhus Universitet, Finlandsgade 4, Aarhus N, 8200, Denmark. TEL 45-89-422394, FAX 45-89-422399, cfa@cfa.au.dk.

DATA LINKAGE SERIES. *see* PUBLIC HEALTH AND SAFETY

310 PRI ISSN 1933-7868
HA1
➤ **DATACRITICA**; international journal of critical statistics. Text in English, Spanish. 2007. irreg. free (effective 2011). **Document type:** *Journal, Academic/Scholarly.* **Description:** Publishes articles that promote a critical perspective of specific statistical facts, concepts, methods and practices, examines the views of professional statisticians and promote the use of statistics for social and scientific criticism.
Media: Online - full text.
Indexed: A01, CA, T02.
Published by: Universidad de Puerto Rico a Mayaguez, PO Box 9041, Mayaguez, 00681, Puerto Rico. TEL 787-265-3815, http://www.uprm.edu.

➤ **DATI STATISTICI SULL' ENERGIA ELETTRICA IN ITALIA.** *see* ENERGY—Abstracting, Bibliographies, Statistics

318 COL
DATOS DE COLOMBIA. Text in Spanish. a.
Published by: A B C Editores, Carrera 14, 83-26 Of. 308, Apdo Aereo 59797, Bogota, CUND, Colombia. TEL 57-1-2567234, FAX 57-1-6100471.

DEMOGRAFICHESKII EZHEGODNIK ROSSII (YEAR)/DEMOGRAPHIC YEARBOOK OF RUSSIA. *see* POPULATION STUDIES—Abstracting, Bibliographies, Statistics

DEMOGRAFIE/DEMOGRAPHY; revue pro vyzkum populacniho vyvoje - review of research into population. *see* POPULATION STUDIES—Abstracting, Bibliographies, Statistics

DEMOGRAPHIC ANALYSIS (YEARS). *see* POPULATION STUDIES

DEMOGRAPHISCHES JAHRBUCH OESTERREICHS. *see* POPULATION STUDIES—Abstracting, Bibliographies, Statistics

DEMOGRAPHY OF SMALL AND MEDIUM ENTERPRISES. *see* POPULATION STUDIES

314.89 DNK ISSN 0107-7139
HA1473
DENMARK. DANMARKS STATISTIK. DANMARK I TAL. Text in Danish. 1981. a. free. illus. **Document type:** *Government.* **Description:** Contains all principal figures for Denmark. The publication contains tables with some of the most important figures within each subject-group.
Related titles: Online - full text ed.: ISSN 1601-1023. 200?; ◆ English ed.: Denmark. Danmarks Statistik. Denmark in Figures. ISSN 1901-5232.
Published by: Danmarks Statistik/Statistics Denmark, Sejroegade 11, Copenhagen OE, 2100, Denmark. TEL 45-39-173917, FAX 45-39-173939, dst@dst.dk. Ed. Margrethe Pihl Bisgaard TEL 45-39-173166.

314.89 DNK ISSN 1901-5232
DENMARK. DANMARKS STATISTIK. DENMARK IN FIGURES. Text in English. 1981. a. free. **Document type:** *Government.*
Formerly (until 2006): Data on Denmark (0107-7961)
Related titles: Online - full text ed.: ISSN 1901-5240. 200?; ◆ Danish ed.: Denmark. Danmarks Statistik. Danmark i Tal. ISSN 0107-7139.
Published by: Danmarks Statistik/Statistics Denmark, Sejroegade 11, Copenhagen OE, 2100, Denmark. TEL 45-39-173917, FAX 45-39-173939, dst@dst.dk. Ed. Margrethe Pihl Bisgaard TEL 45-39-173166.

001.409489 DNK ISSN 1399-4522
DENMARK. DANMARKS STATISTIK. FORSKNING OG UDVIKLINGSARBEJDE I DEN OFFENTLIGE SEKTOR (ONLINE). Text in Danish. 199?-1997; resumed 2008. irreg.
Media: Online - full text.
Published by: Danmarks Statistik/Statistics Denmark, Sejroegade 11, Copenhagen OE, 2100, Denmark. TEL 45-39-173917, FAX 45-39-173939, dst@dst.dk.

314.89 DNK ISSN 1398-9111
DENMARK. DANMARKS STATISTIK. KONJUNKTURSTATISTIK. SUPPLEMENT/DENMARK. STATISTICS DENMARK. MAIN INDICATORS. SUPPLEMENT. Text in Danish, English. 1983. a. **Document type:** *Government.*
Formerly (until 1999): Denmark. Danmarks Statistik. Statistisk Maanedsoversigt. Supplement (0108-5611)
Related titles: Online - full text ed.: ISSN 1601-9431. 1983; ◆ Supplement to: Denmark. Danmarks Statistik. Konjunkturstatistik. ISSN 1398-9103.
Published by: Danmarks Statistik/Statistics Denmark, Sejroegade 11, Copenhagen OE, 2100, Denmark. TEL 45-39-173917, FAX 45-39-173939, dst@dst.dk. Ed. Kamillla Elkjaer Nielsen TEL 45-39-173707.

DENMARK. DANMARKS STATISTIK. LANDBRUG/DENMARK. STATISTICS DENMARK. AGRICULTURAL STATISTICS; statistik om landbrug, gartneri og skovbrug. *see* AGRICULTURE—Abstracting, Bibliographies, Statistics

DENMARK. DANMARKS STATISTIK. NATIONALREGNSKAB/ DENMARK. STATISTICS DENMARK. NATIONAL ACCOUNTS. *see* BUSINESS AND ECONOMICS—Abstracting, Bibliographies, Statistics

DENMARK. DANMARKS STATISTIK. NATIONALREGNSKAB OG BETALINGSBALANCE (ONLINE). *see* BUSINESS AND ECONOMICS—Abstracting, Bibliographies, Statistics

DENMARK. DANMARKS STATISTIK. PRISSTATISTIK (ONLINE). *see* BUSINESS AND ECONOMICS—Abstracting, Bibliographies, Statistics

314.89 DNK ISSN 0070-3567
HA1477
DENMARK. DANMARKS STATISTIK. STATISTISK AARBOG/ DENMARK. STATISTICS DENMARK. STATISTICAL YEARBOOK/ DENMARK. STATISTIQUE DE DANEMARK. ANNUAIRE STATISTIQUE. Cover title: Statistisk Aarbog, Danmark. Text in Multiple languages. 1896. a. DKK 350 per issue (effective 2008). cum.index: 1769-1972. reprints avail. **Document type:** *Government.* **Description:** Statistics describing the annual developments in Denmark, the Faroe Islands, and Greenland in areas such as education, cultural life, elections, transportation, etc.
Related titles: Microfiche ed.: (from PQC); Online - full text ed.: ISSN 1601-104X; Danish ed.: Denmark. Danmarks Statistik. Statistical Yearbook (Year).
Indexed: RASB.
Published by: Danmarks Statistik/Statistics Denmark, Sejroegade 11, Copenhagen OE, 2100, Denmark. TEL 45-39-173917, FAX 45-39-173939, dst@dst.dk. Eds. Margrethe Pihl Bisgaard TEL 45-39-173166, Stefan Jul Gunnersen TEL 45-39-173167.

314.89 DNK ISSN 0070-3583
HA1472
DENMARK. DANMARKS STATISTIK. STATISTISK TIAARSOVERSIGT. Text in Danish. 1961. a. DKK 170 print ed.; DKK 113 online ed.; DKK 213 combined subscription print & online eds. (effective 2008). **Document type:** *Government.* **Description:** Presents comparable annual statistics for the past ten years, thus revealing both trends and structural changes. Adapted to the educational sector. Each issue also treats a special subject in details.
Related titles: CD-ROM ed.: ISSN 1398-8697; Online - full text ed.: ISSN 1602-3943; Ed.: Denmark. Danmarks Statistik. Statistical Ten-Year Review (Online). ISSN 1901-6395.
Published by: Danmarks Statistik/Statistics Denmark, Sejroegade 11, Copenhagen OE, 2100, Denmark. TEL 45-39-173917, FAX 45-39-173939, dst@dst.dk.

314.89 DNK
DENMARK. DANMARKS STATISTIK. STATISTISKE EFTERRETNINGER. INDHOLD (ONLINE). Text in Danish. 1983. irreg. **Document type:** *Government.*
Former titles (until 2007): Denmark. Danmarks Statistik. Statistiske Efterretninger. Indhold (Print) (1396-8173); (until 1989): Denmark. Danmarks Statistik. Statistiske Efterretninger. Indholdsfortegnelse (0109-0283)
Media: Online - full content. **Related titles:** ◆ Series: Denmark. Danmarks Statistik. Udenrigshandel (Online). ISSN 1601-1007; ◆ Denmark. Danmarks Statistik. Penge- og Kapitalmarked (Online). ISSN 1601-0957; ◆ Denmark. Danmarks Statistik. Byggeri og Boligforhold (Online). ISSN 1601-0876; ◆ Denmark. Danmarks Statistik. Arbejdsmarked (Online). ISSN 1601-085X; ◆ Denmark. Danmarks Statistik. Befolkning og Valg (Online). ISSN 1601-0868; ◆

S

Denmark. Danmarks Statistik. Generel Erhvervsstatistik (Online). ISSN 1601-0884; ◆ Denmark. Danmarks Statistik. Uddannelse og Kultur (Online). ISSN 1601-099X; ◆ Denmark. Danmarks Statistik. Industri (Online). ISSN 1603-9181; ◆ Denmark. Danmarks Statistik. Landbrug (Online). ISSN 1601-0914; ◆ Denmark. Danmarks Statistik. Offentlige Finanser (Online). ISSN 1601-0949; ◆ Denmark. Danmarks Statistik. Transport (Online). ISSN 1601-0981; ◆ Denmark. Danmarks Statistik. Sociale Forhold, Sundhed og Retsvaesen (Online). ISSN 1601-0973; ◆ Denmark. Danmarks Statistik. Indkomst, Forbrug og Priser (Online). ISSN 1601-0892.
Published by: Danmarks Statistik/Statistics Denmark, Sejroegade 11, Copenhagen OE, 2100, Denmark. TEL 45-39-173917, FAX 45-39-173939, dst@dst.dk.

314.89 DNK ISSN 0039-0682
DENMARK. DANMARKS STATISTIK. STATISTISKE UNDERSOEGELSER. Text in Danish. 1958. irreg. price varies. **Document type:** *Monographic series, Government.*
Published by: Danmarks Statistik/Statistics Denmark, Sejroegade 11, Copenhagen OE, 2100, Denmark. TEL 45-39-173917, FAX 45-39-173939, dst@dst.dk, http://www.dst.dk.

DENMARK. DANMARKS STATISTIK. UDENRIGSHANDEL, DETALJERET VAREHANDEL (ONLINE)/DENMARK. STATISTICS DENMARK. EXTERNAL TRADE OF DENMARK, DETAILED STATISTICS ON TRADE IN GOODS. see BUSINESS AND ECONOMICS—Abstracting, Bibliographies, Statistics

DENMARK. FINANSTILSYNET. PENGEINSTITUTTER. see BUSINESS AND ECONOMICS—Banking And Finance

DENMARK. FINANSTILSYNET. REALKREDITINSTITUTTER. see BUSINESS AND ECONOMICS—Abstracting, Bibliographies, Statistics

DENMARK. UNDERVISNINGSMINISTERIET. FACTS AND FIGURES; education indicators in Denmark. see EDUCATION—Abstracting, Bibliographies, Statistics

DEPARTMENT STORE INVENTORIES. see BUSINESS AND ECONOMICS—Economic Situation And Conditions

DEUTSCHE BUNDESBANK. DEVISENKURSSTATISTIK. see BUSINESS AND ECONOMICS—Abstracting, Bibliographies, Statistics

310 CHN ISSN 1004-7794
DIAO-YAN SHIJIE/WORLD OF SURVEY AND RESEARCH. Text in Chinese. 1988. m. **Document type:** *Journal, Academic/Scholarly.*
Formerly (until 1992): Nong-diao zhi You
Related titles: Online - full text ed.
Published by: Zhonghua Renmin Gongheguo Guojia Tongjiju/National Bureau of Statistics of China, 57, Yuetan Nan Jie, Beijing, 100826, China. TEL 86-10-63266600 ext 30203, info@stats.gov.cn.

DIASPORA STUDIES. see POLITICAL SCIENCE—International Relations

316 NGA ISSN 0029-0017
HA1977.N5
DIGEST OF STATISTICS. Text in English. 1952. q. USD 60 (effective 1997). stat. **Document type:** *Government.*
Indexed: RASB.
Published by: Federal Office of Statistics, Dissemination Division, c/o Mrs. M.T. Osita, 36-38 Broad St, PMB 12528, Lagos, Nigeria. TEL 234-1-2601710-4.

DIGEST OF UNITED KINGDOM ENERGY STATISTICS. see ENERGY—Abstracting, Bibliographies, Statistics

DIMENSIONS. see SOCIAL SERVICES AND WELFARE—Abstracting, Bibliographies, Statistics

I DIPLOMATI UNIVERSITARI E IL MERCATO DEL LAVORO. see OCCUPATIONS AND CAREERS—Abstracting, Bibliographies, Statistics

DIRECCAO GERAL DE VETERINARIA. BOLETIM ESTATISTICO. see VETERINARY SCIENCE—Abstracting, Bibliographies, Statistics

DIRECTORIO NACIONAL DE UNIDADES DE INFORMACION (BIBLIOTECAS). see LIBRARY AND INFORMATION SCIENCES—Abstracting, Bibliographies, Statistics

317.2 MEX
DIRECTORIO SECTOR PUBLICO. Text in Spanish. a. MXN 295. **Document type:** *Directory.*
Published by: Directorios Especiales S.A. de C.V., Ave. COYOACAN 1836, Col Del Valle, Mexico City, DF 03100, Mexico. TEL 525-5346168, FAX 525-5245288.

DIRECTORY AND STATISTICS OF AGRICULTURAL CO-OPERATIVES AND OTHER FARMER CONTROLLED BUSINESSES IN THE U K. see AGRICULTURE—Abstracting, Bibliographies, Statistics

310 NLD
DIRECTORY OF NATIONAL STATISTICAL OFFICES AND SOCIETIES (YEAR). Text in English. a. **Document type:** *Directory, Academic/Scholarly.* **Description:** Lists the names, addresses, telephone and fax numbers, e-mail addresses, and Web sites of national and international statistical agencies worldwide.
Former titles: Directory of Official Statistical Agencies (Year) (Online Edition); (until 2000): Directory of Official Statistical Agencies (Year) (Print Edition)
Media: Online - full text.
Published by: International Statistical Institute, PO Box 24070, The Hague, 2490 AB, Netherlands. TEL 31-70-3375737, FAX 31-70-3860025, isi@cbs.nl, http://www.cbs.nl/.

DISPLACED WORKERS. see BUSINESS AND ECONOMICS—Abstracting, Bibliographies, Statistics

DISTRIBUTION OF HIGH SCHOOL GRADUATES AND COLLEGE GOING RATE, NEW YORK STATE. see EDUCATION—Abstracting, Bibliographies, Statistics

DIVISION D'AIDE ET DE COOPERATION FRANCAISE. BULLETIN TRIMESTRIEL DE STATISTIQUE. see BUSINESS AND ECONOMICS—Abstracting, Bibliographies, Statistics

316 DJI
DJIBOUTI. DIRECTION NATIONALE DE LA STATISTIQUE. BULLETIN DE STATISTIQUE ET DE DOCUMENTATION. Text in French. 1970. q. DJF 500.
Former titles: Djibouti. Service de Statistique et de Documentation. Bulletin de Statistique et de Documentation; (until 1976): French Territory of the Afars and Issas. Service de Statistique et de Documentation. Bulletin de Statistique et de Documentation
Published by: Ministere du Commerce des Transports et du Tourisme, Direction Nationale de la Statistique, BP 1846, Djibouti, Djibouti.

DJIBOUTI. MINISTERE DE L'EDUCATION NATIONALE. ANNUAIRE STATISTIQUE. see EDUCATION—Abstracting, Bibliographies, Statistics

310 BGR ISSN 1311-2287
DOCHODI, RASCHODI I POTREBLENIE NA DOMAKINSTVATA. Text in Bulgarian. q. BGL 17.44 (effective 2002). 44 p./no.; **Description:** Offers statistical information on the household budgets in Bulgaria.
Published by: Natsionalen Statisticheski Institut/National Statistical Institute, ul P Volov, # 2, Sofia, 1038, Bulgaria. FAX 359-2-9803319, publikacii@nsi.bg, http://www.nsi.bg.

314 LUX ISSN 0251-2998
DOCUMENTATION EUROPEENE. Text in French. 19??. q. **Document type:** *Trade.*
Related titles: Portuguese ed.: Documentacao Europeia. ISSN 1017-4796. 19??; Spanish ed.: Documentation Europea. ISSN 1017-480X. 19??; Italian ed.: Documentazione Europea. ISSN 1017-4818. 19??; Danish ed.: Europaeisk Dokumentation. ISSN 1017-4826. 19??; Finnish ed.: Tietoa Euroopasta. ISSN 1609-4123. 19??; German ed.: Europaeische Dokumentation. ISSN 1017-4842. 19??; English ed.: European Documentation. ISSN 1017-4850. 19??; Dutch ed.: Europese Documentatie. ISSN 1017-4869. 19??; Swedish ed.: Europeisk Dokumentation. ISSN 1606-3457. 19??; Greek ed.: Europaika Keimena. ISSN 1017-4834. 19??.
Indexed: KES.
—CCC.
Published by: European Commission, Office for Official Publications of the European Union, 2 Rue Mercier, Luxembourg, L-2985, Luxembourg. TEL 352-29291, FAX 352-29291, info@publications.europa.eu, http://europa.eu.

310 330.1 ESP ISSN 1134-8984
DOCUMENTOS DE TRABAJO BILTOKI. Variant title: Biltoki. Text in Spanish. 1989. q. free (effective 2009). **Document type:** *Journal, Academic/Scholarly.*
Formerly (until 1994): Universidad del Pais Vasco. Facultad de Ciencias Economicas. Documentos de Trabajo (1134-8976)
Related titles: Online - full text ed.: 1997. free (effective 2011).
—CCC.
Published by: Universidad del Pais Vasco, Facultad de Ciencias Economicas, Avenida Lehendakari Aguirre 83, Bilbao, 48015, Spain.

DOKHODY, RASKHODY I POTREBLENIE DOMASHNIKH KHOZYAISTV/INCOMES, EXPENDITURES AND CONSUMPTION OF HOUSEHOLDS. see BUSINESS AND ECONOMICS—Abstracting, Bibliographies, Statistics

DOMINICA. MINISTRY OF FINANCE. CENTRAL STATISTICAL OFFICE. ANNUAL EDUCATION STATISTICS. see EDUCATION—Abstracting, Bibliographies, Statistics

DOMINICA. MINISTRY OF FINANCE. CENTRAL STATISTICAL OFFICE. ANNUAL OVERSEAS TRADE REPORT. see BUSINESS AND ECONOMICS—Abstracting, Bibliographies, Statistics

DONNEES STATISTIQUES SUR LE LIVRE BELGE DE LANGUE FRANCAISE. see PUBLISHING AND BOOK TRADE—Abstracting, Bibliographies, Statistics

DOSI GAGYEI YENBO/KOREA (REPUBLIC). NATIONAL STATISTICAL OFFICE. ANNUAL REPORT ON THE HOUSEHOLD INCOME AND EXPENDITURE SURVEY. see BUSINESS AND ECONOMICS—Abstracting, Bibliographies, Statistics

DOSSIERS SOLIDARITE ET SANTE (ONLINE). see SOCIAL SERVICES AND WELFARE—Abstracting, Bibliographies, Statistics

DREWRY SHIPPING INSIGHT. see TRANSPORTATION—Abstracting, Bibliographies, Statistics

DRINKWATERSTATISTIEKEN. see WATER RESOURCES—Abstracting, Bibliographies, Statistics

▼ **THE DUTCH GROWTH ACCOUNTS.** see BUSINESS AND ECONOMICS—Abstracting, Bibliographies, Statistics

DWELLING UNIT COMMENCEMENTS, AUSTRALIA, PRELIMINARY (ONLINE). see BUILDING AND CONSTRUCTION—Abstracting, Bibliographies, Statistics

E-DIGEST OF ENVIRONMENTAL STATISTICS. see ENVIRONMENTAL STUDIES—Abstracting, Bibliographies, Statistics

E S A I M: PROBABILITY & STATISTICS/E S A I M: PROBABILITES ET STATISTIQUE. (European Series in Applied and Industrial Mathematics) see MATHEMATICS

EARNINGS AND EMPLOYMENT TRENDS. see BUSINESS AND ECONOMICS—Abstracting, Bibliographies, Statistics

EARNINGS - INDUSTRY AND SERVICES. see BUSINESS AND ECONOMICS—Abstracting, Bibliographies, Statistics

EAST AFRICAN COMMUNITY. ECONOMIC AND STATISTICAL REVIEW. see BUSINESS AND ECONOMICS—Abstracting, Bibliographies, Statistics

310 USA
EAST TENNESSEE DEVELOPMENT DISTRICT ECONOMIC STATISTICS. Text in English. 1981. s-a. USD 1 per county; USD 10 per book. **Document type:** *Government.* **Description:** Summarizes various federal, state and local sources which provide economic data for East Tennessee Development District region.
Published by: East Tennessee Development District, PO Box 19806, Knoxville, TN 37919. TEL 423-584-8553, FAX 423-584-5159.

EASTERN DISTRICT CRIME STATISTICS. see CRIMINOLOGY AND LAW ENFORCEMENT—Abstracting, Bibliographies, Statistics

ECONNECTIONS: LINKING THE ENVIRONMENT AND THE ECONOMY. INDICATORS AND DETAILED STATISTICS. see CONSERVATION—Abstracting, Bibliographies, Statistics

ECONOMIC AND SOCIAL STATISTICS OF SRI LANKA. see BUSINESS AND ECONOMICS—Abstracting, Bibliographies, Statistics

ECONOMIC RESULTS OF INDUSTRY IN THE CZECH REPUBLIC (YEARS). see BUSINESS AND ECONOMICS—Abstracting, Bibliographies, Statistics

ECONOMIC RESULTS OF SMALL AND MEDIUM ENTERPRISES IN THE CZECH REPUBLIC (YEARS). see BUSINESS AND ECONOMICS—Abstracting, Bibliographies, Statistics

317 CAN ISSN 1206-6184
CA2PQBS11Q001
L'ECOSTAT. Text in English. 1962. q. CAD 125; CAD 35 newsstand/cover (effective 2006). index. 114 p./no.; **Document type:** *Government.*
Former titles (until 1997): Quebec (Province). Bureau de la Statistique. Statistiques (0227-0668); (until Apr. 1981): Revue Statistique du Quebec (0383-4603); (until 1973): Bureau de la Statistique du Quebec. Statistiques (0039-0550); (until 1963): Statistiques de la Province de Quebec (0383-459X)
Related titles: Online - full text ed.: ISSN 1715-6386.
Indexed: PdeR.
Published by: Institut de la Statistique du Quebec, 200 chemin Ste Foy, Quebec, PQ G1R 5T4, Canada. TEL 418-691-2401, direction@stat.gouv.qc.ca. Circ: 1,850.

304.6 ECU
ECUADOR. INSTITUTO NACIONAL DE ESTADISTICA Y CENSOS. ANUARIO ESTADISTICO. Text in Spanish. 1996. a. **Document type:** *Government.*
Related titles: Online - full text ed.
Published by: Instituto Nacional de Estadistica y Censos, Juan Larrea N15-36 y Jose Riofrio, Quito, Ecuador. TEL 593-2-529858, FAX 593-2-509836, inec1@ecnet.ec, http://www.inec.gov.ec.

ECUADOR. INSTITUTO NACIONAL DE ESTADISTICA Y CENSOS. CUENTAS NACIONALES DE LA SALUD. see PUBLIC HEALTH AND SAFETY—Abstracting, Bibliographies, Statistics

ECUADOR. INSTITUTO NACIONAL DE ESTADISTICA Y CENSOS. ENCUESTA ANUAL DE COMERCIO INTERNO. see BUSINESS AND ECONOMICS—Abstracting, Bibliographies, Statistics

ECUADOR. INSTITUTO NACIONAL DE ESTADISTICA Y CENSOS. ENCUESTA ANUAL DE EDIFICACIONES. see BUILDING AND CONSTRUCTION—Abstracting, Bibliographies, Statistics

ECUADOR. INSTITUTO NACIONAL DE ESTADISTICA Y CENSOS. ENCUESTA ANUAL DE MIGRACION INTERNACIONAL. see POPULATION STUDIES—Abstracting, Bibliographies, Statistics

ECUADOR. INSTITUTO NACIONAL DE ESTADISTICA Y CENSOS. ENCUESTA ANUAL DE RECURSOS Y ACTIVIDADES DE SALUD. see EDUCATION—Abstracting, Bibliographies, Statistics

ECUADOR. INSTITUTO NACIONAL DE ESTADISTICA Y CENSOS. ENCUESTA ANUAL DE RESTAURANTES, HOTELES Y SERVICIOS. see HOTELS AND RESTAURANTS—Abstracting, Bibliographies, Statistics

ECUADOR. INSTITUTO NACIONAL DE ESTADISTICA Y CENSOS. INDICE DE EMPLEO Y REMUNERACIONES. see BUSINESS AND ECONOMICS—Labor And Industrial Relations

ECUADOR. INSTITUTO NACIONAL DE ESTADISTICAS Y CENSOS. SISTEMA ARMONIZADO DE NOMENCLATURAS DE CARACTER ECONOMICO. see BUSINESS AND ECONOMICS—Abstracting, Bibliographies, Statistics

EDUCACAO (RIO DE JANIERO); indicadores sociais. see EDUCATION—Abstracting, Bibliographies, Statistics

EDUCATION MATTERS; insights on education, learning and training in Canada. see EDUCATION

EDUCATION STATISTICS, NEW YORK STATE; prepared especially for members of the Legislature. see EDUCATION—Abstracting, Bibliographies, Statistics

310 EST ISSN 1406-1783
HA1448.E8
EESTI STATISTIKA AASTARAAMAT/STATISTICAL YEARBOOK OF ESTONIA. Text in English, Estonian. 1991. a. EUR 22.37 per issue (effective 2011).
Published by: Statistikaamet/Statistical Office of Estonia, Endla 15, Tallinn, 15174, Estonia. TEL 372-62-59300, FAX 372-62-59370, stat@stat.ee, http://www.stat.ee.

L'EGYPTE CONTEMPORAINE. see POLITICAL SCIENCE—Abstracting, Bibliographies, Statistics

519.5 EGY ISSN 0542-1748
THE EGYPTIAN STATISTICAL JOURNAL/MAJALLAH AL-IHSA'IYYAH AL-MISRIYYAH. Abbreviated title: E S J. Text and summaries in Arabic, English. 1957. s-a. USD 30 (effective 1999). back issues avail. **Document type:** *Journal, Academic/Scholarly.* **Description:** Constitutes an Egyptian journal on Statistics.
Indexed: CCMJ, CIS, MSN, MathR, ST&MA, Z02.
Published by: Cairo University, Institute of Statistical Studies and Research, 5 Tharwat St, Orman, Giza, Egypt. dean@issr.cu.edu.eg, http://issr.cu.edu.eg. Ed. Dr. Elham Shoukri Mohamed.

EINRICHTUNGEN FUER AELTERE MENSCHEN IN BAYERN. see GERONTOLOGY AND GERIATRICS—Abstracting, Bibliographies, Statistics

EISEN UND STAHL - JAEHRLICHE STATISTIKEN. see METALLURGY—Abstracting, Bibliographies, Statistics

EKONOMETRI VE ISTATISTIK E-DERGISI/ISTANBUL UNIVERSITY ECONOMETRICS AND STATISTICS E-JOURNAL. see BUSINESS AND ECONOMICS

EKONOMICHESKIE POKAZATELI RAZVITIYA RAYONOV KRAINEGO SEVERA I PRIRAVNENNYKH K NIM MESTNOSTEI/ECONOMIC INDICATORS OF THE DEVELOPMENT OF THE FAR NORTH AND OTHER SIMILAR AREAS. see BUSINESS AND ECONOMICS—Abstracting, Bibliographies, Statistics

EKONOMICHESKOE I SOTSIAL'NOE RAZVITIE KORENNYKH MALOCHISLENNYKH NARODOV SEVERA/ECONOMIC AND SOCIAL DEVELOPMENT OF INDIGENOUS SMALL NATIONALITIES OF THE FAR NORTH. see BUSINESS AND ECONOMICS—Abstracting, Bibliographies, Statistics

EKONOMICKE VYSLEDKY PRUMYSLU C R V LETECH (YEARS). (Ceska Republika) see BUSINESS AND ECONOMICS—Abstracting, Bibliographies, Statistics

318 SLV ISSN 0080-5661
EL SALVADOR. DIRECCION GENERAL DE ESTADISTICA Y CENSOS. ANUARIO ESTADISTICO. Text in Spanish. a. free or exchange basis.
Related titles: Microfiche ed.: (from PQC).

Published by: Direccion General de Estadistica y Censos, 1 Calle Poniente y 43 Avenida Sur, San Salvador, El Salvador.

317.284 SLV ISSN 0013-404X
EL SALVADOR. DIRECCION GENERAL DE ESTADISTICA Y CENSOS. BOLETIN ESTADISTICO. Text in Spanish. 1951. q. free or exchange basis. mkt.; stat.
Published by: Direccion General de Estadistica y Censos, 1 Calle Poniente y 43 Avenida Sur, San Salvador, El Salvador.

EL SALVADOR. MINISTERIO DE PLANIFICACION Y COORDINACION DEL DESARROLLO ECONOMICO Y SOCIAL. ENCUESTA NACIONAL DE INGRESOS Y GASTOS DE LOS HOGARES URBANOS. see HOME ECONOMICS—Abstracting, Bibliographies, Statistics

318 SLV ISSN 0581-4111
EL SALVADOR. MINISTERIO DE PLANIFICACION Y COORDINACION DEL DESARROLLO ECONOMICO Y SOCIAL. INDICADORES ECONOMICOS Y SOCIALES. Text in Spanish. 1962. irreg., latest 1987-89. stat.; charts. **Description:** Covers El Salvador's public health, education, social security, employment, commerce, banking, public finance, construction, transportation, communication, agriculture and manufacture.
Published by: (El Salvador. Seccion de Investigaciones Estadisticas), Ministerio de Planificacion y Coordinacion del Desarrollo Economico y Social, Casa Presidential, San Salvador, El Salvador.

EL SALVADOR. MINISTERIO DE TRABAJO Y PREVISION SOCIAL. ESTADISTICAS DEL TRABAJO. see BUSINESS AND ECONOMICS—Abstracting, Bibliographies, Statistics

ELECTRIC POWER CAPABILITY AND LOAD. see ENERGY—Electrical Energy

001.422 ITA ISSN 2070-5948
QA276.A1
➤ **ELECTRONIC JOURNAL OF APPLIED STATISTICAL ANALYSIS.** Text in Arabic, English. 2008. a. free (effective 2011). **Document type:** *Journal, Academic/Scholarly.* **Description:** Publishes articles in all fields of applied statistics and related topics.
Media: Online - full text.
Published by: (Universita degli Studi del Salento, Coordinamento S I B A), Universita degli Studi del Salento, Edificio "Studium 2000", Via di Valesio, Lecce, 73100, Italy.

310 ITA ISSN 2037-3627
▼ **ELECTRONIC JOURNAL OF APPLIED STATISTICAL ANALYSIS. DECISION SUPPORT SYSTEMS AND SERVICES EVALUATION.** Text in English. 2009. a. free (effective 2011). **Document type:** *Journal, Academic/Scholarly.*
Media: Online - full text.
Published by: (Universita degli Studi del Salento, Coordinamento S I B A), Universita degli Studi del Salento, Edificio "Studium 2000", Via di Valesio, Lecce, 73100, Italy. Eds. Amjad D Al-Nassar, Giuseppe Boari.

519.5 USA ISSN 1935-7524
➤ **ELECTRONIC JOURNAL OF STATISTICS.** Abbreviated title: E J S. Text in English. 2007 (Jan.). a. free (effective 2012). **Document type:** *Journal, Academic/Scholarly.* **Description:** Features research articles and short notes in theoretical, computational and applied statistics.
Media: Online - full text.
Indexed: A39, C27, C29, CCMJ, CurCont, D03, D04, E13, MSN, MathR, P30, R14, S14, S15, S18, SCI, W07, Z02.
Published by: Institute of Mathematical Statistics, PO Box 22718, Beachwood, OH 44122. TEL 216-295-2340, 877-557-4674, FAX 216-295-5661, ims@imstat.org, http://www.imstat.org. Ed. David Ruppert TEL 607-255-9136. **Co-sponsor:** Bernoulli Society for Mathematical Statistics and Probability.

➤ **EMANCIPATIEMONITOR.** see SOCIOLOGY—Abstracting, Bibliographies, Statistics

➤ **EMPLOYER COSTS FOR EMPLOYEE COMPENSATION.** see BUSINESS AND ECONOMICS—Abstracting, Bibliographies, Statistics

➤ **EMPLOYMENT AND EARNINGS: CHARACTERISTICS OF FAMILIES.** see BUSINESS AND ECONOMICS—Economic Situation And Conditions

➤ **EMPLOYMENT AND PAYROLLS IN WASHINGTON STATE BY COUNTY AND INDUSTRY**; industries covered by the Employment Security Act and federal employment covered by Title 5, U.S.C. 85. see BUSINESS AND ECONOMICS—Abstracting, Bibliographies, Statistics

➤ **EMPLOYMENT AND WAGES ANNUAL AVERAGES.** see BUSINESS AND ECONOMICS—Abstracting, Bibliographies, Statistics

➤ **ENCUESTA CONTINUA DE HOGARES.** see HOUSING AND URBAN PLANNING—Abstracting, Bibliographies, Statistics

➤ **ENCUESTA INDUSTRIAL TRIMESTRAL.** see BUSINESS AND ECONOMICS—Abstracting, Bibliographies, Statistics

➤ **ENCUESTA NACIONAL AGROPECUARIA. RESULTADOS DE LA PRODUCCION AGRICOLA.** see AGRICULTURE—Abstracting, Bibliographies, Statistics

317.2 MEX
ENCUESTA NACIONAL DE INGRESOS Y GASTOS DE LOS HOGARES. Text in Spanish. irreg. MXN 86 (effective 1999).
Published by: Instituto Nacional de Estadistica, Geografia e Informatica, Secretaria de Programacion y Presupuesto, Prol. Heroe de Nacozari 2301 Sur, Puerta 11, Acceso, Aguascalientes, 20270, Mexico. TEL 52-4-918-1948, FAX 52-4-918-0739.

ENCUESTA NACIONAL DEL EMPLEO TOTAL PAIS. see BUSINESS AND ECONOMICS—Abstracting, Bibliographies, Statistics

ENCUESTA TRIMESTRAL SOBRE LA INDUSTRIA DE LA CONSTRUCCION. see BUILDING AND CONSTRUCTION—Abstracting, Bibliographies, Statistics

ENERGETICKE BILANCE C R. (Ceska Republika) see ENERGY—Abstracting, Bibliographies, Statistics

ENERGIEVERSORGUNG OESTERREICHS. see ENERGY—Abstracting, Bibliographies, Statistics

310 333.80 BGR
ENERGIINI BALANSI. Text in Bulgarian, English. a. BGL 4.20 (effective 2002). **Description:** Covers the balance of energy production and consumption in Bulgaria.
Related titles: Diskette ed.
Published by: Natsionalen Statisticheski Institut/National Statistical Institute, ul P Volov, # 2, Sofia, 1038, Bulgaria. FAX 359-2-9803319, publikacii@nsi.bg, http://www.nsi.bg. **Dist. by:** Sofia Books, ul Silivria 16, Sofia 1404, Bulgaria. TEL 359-2-9586257, info@sofiabooks-bg.com, http://www.sofiabooks-bg.com.

ENERGY BALANCE OF THE CZECH REPUBLIC. see ENERGY—Abstracting, Bibliographies, Statistics

ENERGY BALANCE SHEETS. see ENERGY—Abstracting, Bibliographies, Statistics

ENERGY BALANCES OF O E C D COUNTRIES/BILANS ENERGETIQUES DES PAYS DE L'O C D E (ORGANISATION DE COOPERATION ET DE DEVELOPPEMENT ECONOMIQUES). (Organisation for Economic Cooperation and Development) see ENERGY

ENERGY, TRANSPORT AND ENVIRONMENT INDICATORS. see ENERGY—Abstracting, Bibliographies, Statistics

ENQUETE ANNUELLE SUR L'ACTIVITE DES ORGANISMES DE SECURITE SOCIALE. see SOCIAL SERVICES AND WELFARE—Abstracting, Bibliographies, Statistics

310 658.3 CAN ISSN 1710-7490
L'ENQUETE SUR LA DYNAMIQUE DU TRAVAIL ET DU REVENU, DICTIONNAIRE ELECTRONIQUE DES DONNEES. Text in French. 2004. a. **Document type:** *Government.*
Media: Online - full text.
Published by: Statistics Canada/Statistique Canada, Communications Division, 3rd Fl, R H Coats Bldg, Ottawa, ON K1A 0A6, Canada. TEL 800-263-1136, infostats@statcan.ca, http://www.statcan.gc.ca.

314 DEU
ENTWICKLUNGEN IN NORDRHEIN-WESTFALEN IM JAHRE (YEAR). Text in German. 1972. a. **Document type:** *Government.* **Description:** Statistics of all areas of life in Nordrhein-Westfalen: population, employment, industry, agriculture, schools, traffic, etc.
Published by: Information und Technik Nordrhein-Westfalen, Mauerstr 51, Duesseldorf, 40476, Germany. TEL 49-211-94492494, FAX 49-211-442006, internet-redaktion@it.nrw.de. Circ: 7,000.

ENVIRONMENT CANADA. NATIONAL POLLUTANT RELEASE INVENTORY. NATIONAL OVERVIEW. see ENVIRONMENTAL STUDIES—Abstracting, Bibliographies, Statistics

ENVIRONMENTAL AND ECOLOGICAL STATISTICS. see ENVIRONMENTAL STUDIES—Abstracting, Bibliographies, Statistics

EOEOB CHONG JO'SA BUNSEOG BO'GO'SEO/KOREA (REPUBLIC). NATIONAL STATISTICAL OFFICE. FISHERIES CENSUS REPORT. see FISH AND FISHERIES—Abstracting, Bibliographies, Statistics

ESPANA EN CIFRAS. see POPULATION STUDIES—Abstracting, Bibliographies, Statistics

ESTABLECIMIENTOS MANUFACTUREROS EN PUERTO RICO. see BUSINESS AND ECONOMICS—Abstracting, Bibliographies, Statistics

ESTADISTICA BASICA DEL SISTEMA EDUCATIVO NACIONAL. see EDUCATION—Abstracting, Bibliographies, Statistics

ESTADISTICA DE ACCIDENTES DE TRABAJO. see BUSINESS AND ECONOMICS—Abstracting, Bibliographies, Statistics

ESTADISTICA DE HUELGA Y CIERRES PATRONALES. see BUSINESS AND ECONOMICS—Abstracting, Bibliographies, Statistics

ESTADISTICA DE LA INDUSTRIA DE ENERGIA ELECTRICA. see ENERGY—Abstracting, Bibliographies, Statistics

ESTADISTICA DE LA PRODUCCION EDITORIAL DE LIBROS. see LIBRARY AND INFORMATION SCIENCES—Abstracting, Bibliographies, Statistics

ESTADISTICA DE PROSPECCION Y PRODUCCION DE HIDROCARBUROS. see PETROLEUM AND GAS—Abstracting, Bibliographies, Statistics

ESTADISTICA DE REGULACION DE EMPLEO. see LAW—Abstracting, Bibliographies, Statistics

ESTADISTICA DEL SUICIDIO EN ESPANA. see POPULATION STUDIES—Abstracting, Bibliographies, Statistics

ESTADISTICA MENSUAL DE FAENA Y EXPORTACION. see FOOD AND FOOD INDUSTRIES—Abstracting, Bibliographies, Statistics

ESTADISTICA MINERA DE ESPANA. see MINES AND MINING INDUSTRY—Abstracting, Bibliographies, Statistics

319 PAN
ESTADISTICA PANAMENA. AVANCE DE CIFRAS. Text in Spanish. 1963. irreg. PAB 0.25 domestic (effective 2000). **Document type:** *Government.* **Description:** Presents preliminary data from the regular series, or a study on a specific theme.
Formerly: Estadistica Panamena. Boletin (0259-6725)
Published by: Direccion de Estadistica y Censo, Contraloria General, Apdo. 5213, Panama City, 5, Panama. FAX 507-210-4801. Circ: 850.

ESTADISTICA PANAMENA. INDICADORES ECONOMICOS. SECCION 011. see BUSINESS AND ECONOMICS—Abstracting, Bibliographies, Statistics

ESTADISTICA PANAMENA. INDICADORES SOCIALES. SECCION 012. see SOCIAL SERVICES AND WELFARE—Abstracting, Bibliographies, Statistics

ESTADISTICA PANAMENA. SITUACION CULTURAL. SECCION 511. EDUCACION. see EDUCATION—Abstracting, Bibliographies, Statistics

ESTADISTICA PANAMENA. SITUACION DEMOGRAFICA. SECCION 221. ESTADISTICAS VITALES. see POPULATION STUDIES—Abstracting, Bibliographies, Statistics

ESTADISTICA PANAMENA. SITUACION DEMOGRAFICA. SECCION 231. MOVIMIENTO INTERNACIONAL DE PASAJEROS. see POPULATION STUDIES—Abstracting, Bibliographies, Statistics

ESTADISTICA PANAMENA. SITUACION ECONOMICA. SECCION 312. PRODUCCION PECUARIA. see AGRICULTURE—Abstracting, Bibliographies, Statistics

ESTADISTICA PANAMENA. SITUACION ECONOMICA. SECCION 312. SUPERFICIE SEMBRADA Y COSECHA DE ARROZ, MAIZ Y FRIJOL DE BEJUCO. see AGRICULTURE—Abstracting, Bibliographies, Statistics

ESTADISTICA PANAMENA. SITUACION ECONOMICA. SECCION 312. SUPERFICIE SEMBRADA Y COSECHA DE CAFE Y CANA DE AZUCAR. see AGRICULTURE—Abstracting, Bibliographies, Statistics

ESTADISTICA PANAMENA. SITUACION ECONOMICA. SECCION 314, 323, 324, 325, 353. INDUSTRIA. see BUSINESS AND ECONOMICS—Abstracting, Bibliographies, Statistics

ESTADISTICA PANAMENA. SITUACION ECONOMICA. SECCION 321. INDUSTRIA MANUFACTURERA. see BUSINESS AND ECONOMICS—Abstracting, Bibliographies, Statistics

ESTADISTICA PANAMENA. SITUACION ECONOMICA. SECCION 323. INDICE DE LA PRODUCCION DE LA INDUSTRIA MANUFACTURERA. see BUSINESS AND ECONOMICS—Abstracting, Bibliographies, Statistics

ESTADISTICA PANAMENA. SITUACION ECONOMICA. SECCION 331. COMERCIO. ANUARIO DE COMERCIO EXTERIOR. see BUSINESS AND ECONOMICS—Abstracting, Bibliographies, Statistics

ESTADISTICA PANAMENA. SITUACION ECONOMICA. SECCION 333. TRANSPORTE. see TRANSPORTATION

ESTADISTICA PANAMENA. SITUACION ECONOMICA. SECCION 334. COMUNICACIONES. see COMMUNICATIONS—Abstracting, Bibliographies, Statistics

ESTADISTICA PANAMENA. SITUACION ECONOMICA. SECCION 341. BALANZA DE PAGOS. see BUSINESS AND ECONOMICS—Abstracting, Bibliographies, Statistics

ESTADISTICA PANAMENA. SITUACION ECONOMICA. SECCION 342. CUENTAS NACIONALES. see BUSINESS AND ECONOMICS—Abstracting, Bibliographies, Statistics

ESTADISTICA PANAMENA. SITUACION ECONOMICA. SECCION 343. HACIENDA PUBLICA. see BUSINESS AND ECONOMICS—Abstracting, Bibliographies, Statistics

ESTADISTICA PANAMENA. SITUACION ECONOMICA. SECCION 344. FINANZAS. see BUSINESS AND ECONOMICS—Abstracting, Bibliographies, Statistics

ESTADISTICA PANAMENA. SITUACION ECONOMICA. SECCION 351. INDICE DE PRECIOS AL POR MAYOR Y AL CONSUMIDOR. see BUSINESS AND ECONOMICS—Abstracting, Bibliographies, Statistics

ESTADISTICA PANAMENA. SITUACION ECONOMICA. SECCION 351. PRECIOS PAGADOS POR EL PRODUCTOR AGROPECUARIO. see AGRICULTURE—Abstracting, Bibliographies, Statistics

ESTADISTICA PANAMENA. SITUACION ECONOMICA. SECCION 351. PRECIOS RECIBIDOS POR EL PRODUCTOR AGROPECUARIO. see AGRICULTURE—Abstracting, Bibliographies, Statistics

ESTADISTICA PANAMENA. SITUACION ECONOMICA. SECCION 351. PRECIOS RECIBIDOS POR EL PRODUCTOR AGROPECUARIO. COMPENDIO. see AGRICULTURE—Abstracting, Bibliographies, Statistics

ESTADISTICA PANAMENA. SITUACION ECONOMICA. SECCION 352. HOJA DE BALANCE DE ALIMENTOS. see AGRICULTURE—Abstracting, Bibliographies, Statistics

ESTADISTICA PANAMENA. SITUACION FISICA. SECCION 121. METEOROLOGIA. see METEOROLOGY—Abstracting, Bibliographies, Statistics

ESTADISTICA PANAMENA. SITUACION POLITICA, ADMINISTRATIVA Y JUSTICIA. SECCION 631. JUSTICIA. see LAW—Abstracting, Bibliographies, Statistics

ESTADISTICA PANAMENA. SITUACION SOCIAL. SECCION 431. SERVICIOS DE SALUD. see SOCIAL SERVICES AND WELFARE—Abstracting, Bibliographies, Statistics

ESTADISTICA PANAMENA. SITUACION SOCIAL. SECCION 441. ESTADISTICAS DEL TRABAJO. see BUSINESS AND ECONOMICS—Abstracting, Bibliographies, Statistics

ESTADISTICA PANAMENA. SITUACION SOCIAL. SECCION 451. ACCIDENTES DE TRANSITO. see TRANSPORTATION—Abstracting, Bibliographies, Statistics

ESTADISTICAS BANCA INTERNET. see BUSINESS AND ECONOMICS—Abstracting, Bibliographies, Statistics

ESTADISTICAS DE CONVENIOS COLECTIVOS DE TRABAJO. see BUSINESS AND ECONOMICS—Abstracting, Bibliographies, Statistics

ESTADISTICAS DE EDUCACION EXTRAESCOLAR. see EDUCATION—Abstracting, Bibliographies, Statistics

ESTADISTICAS DE PERMISOS DE TRABAJO A ESTRANJEROS. see POPULATION STUDIES—Abstracting, Bibliographies, Statistics

ESTADISTICAS DEL COBRE Y OTROS MINERALES ANUARIO. see MINES AND MINING INDUSTRY—Abstracting, Bibliographies, Statistics

ESTADISTICAS DEL MOVIMIENTO NATURAL DE LA POBLACION DE LA COMUNIDAD DE MADRID. DEFUNCIONES. see POPULATION STUDIES—Abstracting, Bibliographies, Statistics

ESTADISTICAS POLICIALES. POLICIA DE INVESTIGACIONES DE CHILE. see CRIMINOLOGY AND LAW ENFORCEMENT—Abstracting, Bibliographies, Statistics

ESTADOS FINANCIEROS ANUALES DE SOCIEDADES FILIALES. see BUSINESS AND ECONOMICS—Abstracting, Bibliographies, Statistics

314 PRT ISSN 1646-9771
ESTATISTICA MENSAL. Text in Portuguese. 2008. m. **Document type:** *Report, Government.*
Media: Online - full text.
Published by: Instituto Nacional de Propriedade Industrial (I N P I), Campo das Cebolas, Lisbon, 1149-035, Portugal. TEL 351-21-8818100, FAX 351-21-8869859, http://www.inpi.pt.

ESTATISTICAS DA CONSTRUCAO DE EDIFICIOS. see BUILDING AND CONSTRUCTION—Abstracting, Bibliographies, Statistics

▼ **ESTATISTICAS DA CULTURA.** see EDUCATION—Abstracting, Bibliographies, Statistics

ESTATISTICAS DA SAUDE: ASSISTENCIA MEDICO-SANITARIA. see MEDICAL SCIENCES—Abstracting, Bibliographies, Statistics

S

ESTATISTICAS DE PROTECCAO SOCIAL. ASSOCIACOES SINDICAIS E PATRONAIS. *see* SOCIOLOGY—Abstracting, Bibliographies, Statistics

ESTATISTICAS DOS TRANSPORTES E COMUNICACOES. *see* TRANSPORTATION—Abstracting, Bibliographies, Statistics

ESTATISTICAS DOS TRANSPORTES RODOVIARIOS DE PASSAGEIROS E DE MERCADORIAS. *see* TRANSPORTATION—Abstracting, Bibliographies, Statistics

ESTATISTICAS EM SINTESE. BALANCO SOCIAL. *see* POPULATION STUDIES—Abstracting, Bibliographies, Statistics

ESTATISTICAS EM SINTESE. DEMOGRAFIA DE EMPRESAS, FLUXOS DE EMPREGO. *see* POPULATION STUDIES—Abstracting, Bibliographies, Statistics

ESTATISTICAS EM SINTESE. GREVES. *see* POPULATION STUDIES—Abstracting, Bibliographies, Statistics

ESTATISTICAS EM SINTESE. INQUERITO A EXECUCAO DAS ACCOES DE FORMACAO PROFISSIONAL. *see* POPULATION STUDIES—Abstracting, Bibliographies, Statistics

ESTATISTICAS EM SINTESE. INQUERITO AO EMPREGO NO SECTOR ESTRUTURADO. *see* POPULATION STUDIES—Abstracting, Bibliographies, Statistics

▼ **ESTATISTICAS EM SINTESE. INQUERITO AOS SALARIOS POR PROFISSOES NA CONTRUCAO.** *see* POPULATION STUDIES—Abstracting, Bibliographies, Statistics

ESTATISTICAS EM SINTESE. MOBILIDADE DOS TRABALHADORES EM PORTUGAL. *see* POPULATION STUDIES—Abstracting, Bibliographies, Statistics

ESTATISTICAS EM SINTESE. QUADROS DE PESSOAL. *see* POPULATION STUDIES—Abstracting, Bibliographies, Statistics

ESTATISTICAS EM SINTESE. SEGURANCA, HIGIENE E SAUDE NO TRABALHO. *see* POPULATION STUDIES—Abstracting, Bibliographies, Statistics

ESTATISTICAS REGIONAIS DA PRODUCCAO VEGETAL E ANIMAL. *see* AGRICULTURE—Abstracting, Bibliographies, Statistics

ESTESTVENNOE DVIZHENIE NASELENIYA ROSSIISKOI FEDERATSII. *see* POPULATION STUDIES—Abstracting, Bibliographies, Statistics

ESTIMATIONS DEMOGRAPHIQUES ANNUELLES, CANADA, PROVINCES ET TERRITOIRES. *see* POPULATION STUDIES—Abstracting, Bibliographies, Statistics

ETESIA STATISTIKE. EREVNA TOU KARKINOU/ANNUAL STATISTICAL SURVEY OF CANCER. *see* MEDICAL SCIENCES—Abstracting, Bibliographies, Statistics

EURO-MEDITERRANEAN STATISTICS. *see* BUSINESS AND ECONOMICS—Abstracting, Bibliographies, Statistics

314 FIN ISSN 1237-203X

EUROAVAIN. Text in Finnish. 1994. a. EUR 329.40 (effective 2005). **Document type:** *Government.*
Media: CD-ROM.
Published by: Tilastokeskus/Statistics Finland, Typopajakatu 13, Statistics Finland, Helsinki, 00022, Finland. TEL 358-9-17341, FAX 358-9-17342279, http://www.stat.fi.

EUROPEAN CEMENT ASSOCIATION. WORLD STATISTICAL REVIEW. *see* BUILDING AND CONSTRUCTION—Abstracting, Bibliographies, Statistics

EUROPEAN MARKETING FORECASTS. *see* BUSINESS AND ECONOMICS—Abstracting, Bibliographies, Statistics

EUROPEAN SOCIAL STATISTICS. SOCIAL PROTECTION. EXPENDITURE AND RECEIPTS. *see* SOCIAL SERVICES AND WELFARE—Abstracting, Bibliographies, Statistics

EUROPEAN SOURCEBOOK OF CRIME AND CRIMINAL JUSTICE STATISTICS. *see* CRIMINOLOGY AND LAW ENFORCEMENT—Abstracting, Bibliographies, Statistics

EUROSTAT AGRICULTURAL PRICES. PRICE INDICES AND ABSOLUTE PRICES./EUROSTAT. AGRARPREISE. PREISINDIZES UND ABSOLUTE PREISE/EUROSTAT. PRIX AGRICOLES. INDICES DE PRIX ET PRIX ABSOLUS; quarterly statistics. *see* AGRICULTURE

EUROSTAT GELD, FINANZEN UND DER EURO: STATISTIKEN. *see* BUSINESS AND ECONOMICS—Abstracting, Bibliographies, Statistics

EUROSTAT. GEONOMENCLATURE. *see* BUSINESS AND ECONOMICS—Abstracting, Bibliographies, Statistics

EUROSTAT. METHODS AND NOMENCLATURES. *see* BUSINESS AND ECONOMICS—Abstracting, Bibliographies, Statistics

EUROSTAT STATISTICS IN FOCUS. AGRICULTURE AND FISHERIES. *see* AGRICULTURE—Abstracting, Bibliographies, Statistics

EUROSTAT STATISTICS IN FOCUS. ECONOMY AND FINANCE. *see* BUSINESS AND ECONOMICS—Abstracting, Bibliographies, Statistics

EUROSTAT STATISTICS IN FOCUS. ENVIRONMENT AND ENERGY. *see* ENVIRONMENTAL STUDIES—Abstracting, Bibliographies, Statistics

EUROSTAT STATISTICS IN FOCUS. EXTERNAL TRADE. *see* BUSINESS AND ECONOMICS—Abstracting, Bibliographies, Statistics

EUROSTAT STATISTICS IN FOCUS. GENERAL STATISTICS. *see* BUSINESS AND ECONOMICS—Abstracting, Bibliographies, Statistics

EUROSTAT STATISTICS IN FOCUS. INDUSTRY, TRADE AND SERVICES. *see* BUSINESS AND ECONOMICS—Abstracting, Bibliographies, Statistics

EUROSTAT STATISTICS IN FOCUS. SCIENCE AND TECHNOLOGY. *see* BUSINESS AND ECONOMICS—Abstracting, Bibliographies, Statistics

EUROSTAT STATISTICS IN FOCUS. TRANSPORT. *see* TRANSPORTATION—Abstracting, Bibliographies, Statistics

EUROSTAT STATISTIK KURZ GEFASST. INDUSTRIE, HANDEL UND DIENSTLEISTUNGEN. *see* BUSINESS AND ECONOMICS—Abstracting, Bibliographies, Statistics

EUROSTAT STATISTIK KURZ GEFASST. LANDWIRTSCHAFT UND FISCHEREI. *see* AGRICULTURE—Abstracting, Bibliographies, Statistics

EUROSTAT STATISTIK KURZ GEFASST. WIRTSCHAFT UND FINANZEN. *see* BUSINESS AND ECONOMICS—Abstracting, Bibliographies, Statistics

EUROSTAT STATISTIK KURZ GEFASST. WISSENSCHAFT UND TECHNOLOGIE. *see* BUSINESS AND ECONOMICS—Abstracting, Bibliographies, Statistics

EUROSTAT STATISTIQUES EN BREF. AGRICULTURE ET PECHE. *see* AGRICULTURE—Abstracting, Bibliographies, Statistics

EUROSTAT STATISTIQUES EN BREF. ECONOMIE ET FINANCES. *see* BUSINESS AND ECONOMICS—Abstracting, Bibliographies, Statistics

EUROSTAT STATISTIQUES EN BREF. INDUSTRIE, COMMERCE ET SERVICES. *see* BUSINESS AND ECONOMICS—Abstracting, Bibliographies, Statistics

EUROSTAT STATISTIQUES EN BREF. SCIENCE ET TECHNOLOGIE. *see* BUSINESS AND ECONOMICS—Abstracting, Bibliographies, Statistics

314 LUX ISSN 1681-4789
HA1107

EUROSTAT YEARBOOK. Text in English. 2001. a. EUR 30 (effective 2011). maps. **Document type:** *Yearbook, Trade.* **Description:** Provides a statistical guide to the major issues relating to the evolution of the European Union.
Indexed: SSciA.
—BLDSC (3830.444000).
Published by: European Commission, Office for Official Publications of the European Union, 2 Rue Mercier, Luxembourg, L-2985, Luxembourg. TEL 352-29291, FAX 352-29291, info@publications.europa.eu, http://publications.europa.eu.

338 LUX ISSN 0252-8266

EUROSTATISTIK. DATEN ZUER KONJUNKTURANALYSE. Text in English. 1982. 11/yr. charts; stat. **Document type:** *Journal, Trade.*
Formed by the merger of (1979-1981): Eurostatistiken. Daten zur Konjunkturanalyse (0250-393X); (1979-1981): Eurostatistik. Data til Konjunkturanalyse (Mangesprogige Udg.) (0250-3921); Both of which superseded in part (1976-1978): EUROSTAT. Bulletin Mensuel des Statistiques Generales (0378-3456); Which was formerly (1969-1976): EUROSTAT. Statistiques Generales. Bulletin Mensuel (0377-3299); (1961-1969): Statistical Office of the European Communities. General Statistical Bulletin (0002-6026)
Published by: (European Commission, Statistical Office of the European Communities (E U R O S T A T)), European Commission, Office for Official Publications of the European Union, 2 Rue Mercier, Luxembourg, L-2985, Luxembourg. TEL 352-29291, FAX 352-29291, info@publications.europa.eu, http://publications.europa.eu. Circ: 3,800. **Dist. in the U.S. by:** European Commission, Information Service, 2100 M St, NW Ste 707, Washington, DC 20037.

EXPORTS. *see* BUSINESS AND ECONOMICS—Abstracting, Bibliographies, Statistics

EXPORTS BY COUNTRIES. *see* BUSINESS AND ECONOMICS—Abstracting, Bibliographies, Statistics

EXTERNAL AND INTRA-EUROPEAN UNION TRADE. MONTHLY STATISTICS. *see* BUSINESS AND ECONOMICS—Abstracting, Bibliographies, Statistics

EXTERNAL AND INTRA-EUROPEAN UNION TRADE. STATISTICAL YEARBOOK. *see* BUSINESS AND ECONOMICS—Abstracting, Bibliographies, Statistics

EXTERNAL TRADE STATISTICS OF GHANA (ANNUAL). *see* BUSINESS AND ECONOMICS—Abstracting, Bibliographies, Statistics

EXTERNAL TRADE STATISTICS OF GHANA (HALF-YEARLY). *see* BUSINESS AND ECONOMICS—Abstracting, Bibliographies, Statistics

EXTERNAL TRADE STATISTICS OF GHANA (QUARTERLY). *see* BUSINESS AND ECONOMICS—Abstracting, Bibliographies, Statistics

EXTRACTION SYSTEM OF AGRICULTURAL STATISTICS/SYSTEME D'EXTRACTION DES STATISTIQUES AGRICOLES. *see* AGRICULTURE—Abstracting, Bibliographies, Statistics

001.422 USA ISSN 1386-1999
QA276.A1 CODEN: EREMFM

➤ **EXTREMES**; statistical theory and applications in science, engineering and economics. Text in English. 1998. q. EUR 459, USD 459 combined subscription to institutions (print & online eds.) (effective 2012). adv. reprint service avail. from PSC. **Document type:** *Journal, Academic/Scholarly.* **Description:** Publishes original research on statistical extreme value theories and its aapplication in science, engineering, economics and other fields.
Related titles: Online - full text ed.: ISSN 1572-915X (from IngentaConnect).
Indexed: A12, A13, A17, A22, A26, ABIn, B01, B07, B21, BibLing, C10, CA, CCMJ, CIS, CurCont, E01, ESPM, ICEA, M&GPA, MSN, MathR, P26, P48, P50, P51, P52, P53, P54, PQC, RiskAb, SCI, SCOPUS, ST&MA, T02, W07, Z02.
—BLDSC (3854.505620), IE, Infotrieve, Ingenta, INIST. **CCC.**
Published by: Springer New York LLC (Subsidiary of: Springer Science+Business Media), 233 Spring St, New York, NY 10013. TEL 212-460-1500, FAX 212-460-1575, journals-ny@springer.com, http://www.springer.com. Ed. Juerg Huesler.

➤ **F A A STATISTICAL HANDBOOK OF AVIATION.** *see* TRANSPORTATION—Abstracting, Bibliographies, Statistics

310 ITA ISSN 1014-3378

F A O STATISTICAL DEVELOPMENT SERIES. (Food and Agriculture Organization) Text in English. 1986. irreg. price varies. stat. **Document type:** *Monographic series, Trade.*
Related titles: French ed.: Collection F A O, Developpement Statistique. ISSN 1014-3394; Arabic ed.: Silsilat Tatwir al-Ihsa'At. ISSN 1020-6574; Spanish ed.: Coleccion F A O, Desarrollo Estadistico. ISSN 1014-3386.
Indexed: A34, ASFA, B21, CABA, E12, ESPM, W11.
Published by: Food and Agriculture Organization of the United Nations (F A O), Viale delle Terme di Caracalla, Rome, RM 00153, Italy. TEL 39-06-5705-1, FAX 39-06-5705-3360, publications-sales@fao.org.

F A O YEARBOOK. FISHERY STATISTICS. CAPTURE PRODUCTION. *see* FISH AND FISHERIES—Abstracting, Bibliographies, Statistics

F A O YEARBOOK. FISHERY STATISTICS. COMMODITIES. *see* FISH AND FISHERIES—Abstracting, Bibliographies, Statistics

F A S - F A X: CANADIAN DAILY NEWSPAPERS. *see* ADVERTISING AND PUBLIC RELATIONS—Abstracting, Bibliographies, Statistics

F A S - F A X: UNITED STATES AND CANADIAN WEEKLY NEWPAPERS. *see* ADVERTISING AND PUBLIC RELATIONS—Abstracting, Bibliographies, Statistics

F A S - F A X: UNITED STATES DAILY NEWSPAPERS. *see* ADVERTISING AND PUBLIC RELATIONS—Abstracting, Bibliographies, Statistics

F D I C STATE PROFILE, ALABAMA. (Federal Deposit Insurance Corporation) *see* BUSINESS AND ECONOMICS—Abstracting, Bibliographies, Statistics

F D I C STATE PROFILE, ALASKA. (Federal Deposit Insurance Corporation) *see* BUSINESS AND ECONOMICS—Abstracting, Bibliographies, Statistics

F D I C STATE PROFILE, ARIZONA. (Federal Deposit Insurance Corporation) *see* BUSINESS AND ECONOMICS—Abstracting, Bibliographies, Statistics

F D I C STATE PROFILE, ARKANSAS. (Federal Deposit Insurance Corporation) *see* BUSINESS AND ECONOMICS—Abstracting, Bibliographies, Statistics

F D I C STATE PROFILE, CALIFORNIA. (Federal Deposit Insurance Corporation) *see* BUSINESS AND ECONOMICS—Abstracting, Bibliographies, Statistics

F D I C STATE PROFILE, COLORADO. (Federal Deposit Insurance Corporation) *see* BUSINESS AND ECONOMICS—Abstracting, Bibliographies, Statistics

F D I C STATE PROFILE, CONNECTICUT. (Federal Deposit Insurance Corporation) *see* BUSINESS AND ECONOMICS—Abstracting, Bibliographies, Statistics

F D I C STATE PROFILE, DELAWARE. (Federal Deposit Insurance Corporation) *see* BUSINESS AND ECONOMICS—Abstracting, Bibliographies, Statistics

F D I C STATE PROFILE, FLORIDA. (Federal Deposit Insurance Corporation) *see* BUSINESS AND ECONOMICS—Abstracting, Bibliographies, Statistics

F D I C STATE PROFILE, GEORGIA. (Federal Deposit Insurance Corporation) *see* BUSINESS AND ECONOMICS—Abstracting, Bibliographies, Statistics

F D I C STATE PROFILE, HAWAII. (Federal Deposit Insurance Corporation) *see* BUSINESS AND ECONOMICS—Abstracting, Bibliographies, Statistics

F D I C STATE PROFILE, IDAHO. (Federal Deposit Insurance Corporation) *see* BUSINESS AND ECONOMICS—Abstracting, Bibliographies, Statistics

F D I C STATE PROFILE, ILLINOIS. (Federal Deposit Insurance Corporation) *see* BUSINESS AND ECONOMICS—Abstracting, Bibliographies, Statistics

F D I C STATE PROFILE, INDIANA. (Federal Deposit Insurance Corporation) *see* BUSINESS AND ECONOMICS—Abstracting, Bibliographies, Statistics

F D I C STATE PROFILE, IOWA. (Federal Deposit Insurance Corporation) *see* BUSINESS AND ECONOMICS—Abstracting, Bibliographies, Statistics

F D I C STATE PROFILE, KANSAS. (Federal Deposit Insurance Corporation) *see* BUSINESS AND ECONOMICS—Abstracting, Bibliographies, Statistics

F D I C STATE PROFILE, KENTUCKY. (Federal Deposit Insurance Corporation) *see* BUSINESS AND ECONOMICS—Abstracting, Bibliographies, Statistics

F D I C STATE PROFILE, LOUISIANA. (Federal Deposit Insurance Corporation) *see* BUSINESS AND ECONOMICS—Abstracting, Bibliographies, Statistics

F D I C STATE PROFILE, MAINE. (Federal Deposit Insurance Corporation) *see* BUSINESS AND ECONOMICS—Abstracting, Bibliographies, Statistics

F D I C STATE PROFILE, MARYLAND AND WASHINGTON, D.C. (Federal Deposit Insurance Corporation) *see* BUSINESS AND ECONOMICS—Abstracting, Bibliographies, Statistics

F D I C STATE PROFILE, MASSACHUSETTS. (Federal Deposit Insurance Corporation) *see* BUSINESS AND ECONOMICS—Abstracting, Bibliographies, Statistics

F D I C STATE PROFILE, MICHIGAN. (Federal Deposit Insurance Corporation) *see* BUSINESS AND ECONOMICS—Abstracting, Bibliographies, Statistics

F D I C STATE PROFILE, MINNESOTA. (Federal Deposit Insurance Corporation) *see* BUSINESS AND ECONOMICS—Abstracting, Bibliographies, Statistics

F D I C STATE PROFILE, MISSISSIPPI. (Federal Deposit Insurance Corporation) *see* BUSINESS AND ECONOMICS—Abstracting, Bibliographies, Statistics

F D I C STATE PROFILE, MISSOURI. (Federal Deposit Insurance Corporation) *see* BUSINESS AND ECONOMICS—Abstracting, Bibliographies, Statistics

F D I C STATE PROFILE, MONTANA. (Federal Deposit Insurance Corporation) *see* BUSINESS AND ECONOMICS—Abstracting, Bibliographies, Statistics

F D I C STATE PROFILE, NEBRASKA. (Federal Deposit Insurance Corporation) *see* BUSINESS AND ECONOMICS—Abstracting, Bibliographies, Statistics

F D I C STATE PROFILE, NEVADA. (Federal Deposit Insurance Corporation) *see* BUSINESS AND ECONOMICS—Abstracting, Bibliographies, Statistics

F D I C STATE PROFILE, NEW HAMPSHIRE. (Federal Deposit Insurance Corporation) *see* BUSINESS AND ECONOMICS—Abstracting, Bibliographies, Statistics

F D I C STATE PROFILE, NEW JERSEY. (Federal Deposit Insurance Corporation) *see* BUSINESS AND ECONOMICS—Abstracting, Bibliographies, Statistics

F D I C STATE PROFILE, NEW MEXICO. (Federal Deposit Insurance Corporation) *see* BUSINESS AND ECONOMICS—Abstracting, Bibliographies, Statistics

F D I C STATE PROFILE, NEW YORK. (Federal Deposit Insurance Corporation) *see* BUSINESS AND ECONOMICS—Abstracting, Bibliographies, Statistics

F D I C STATE PROFILE, NORTH CAROLINA. (Federal Deposit Insurance Corporation) *see* BUSINESS AND ECONOMICS—Abstracting, Bibliographies, Statistics

F D I C STATE PROFILE, NORTH DAKOTA. (Federal Deposit Insurance Corporation) *see* BUSINESS AND ECONOMICS—Abstracting, Bibliographies, Statistics

F D I C STATE PROFILE, OHIO. (Federal Deposit Insurance Corporation) *see* BUSINESS AND ECONOMICS—Abstracting, Bibliographies, Statistics

F D I C STATE PROFILE, OKLAHOMA. (Federal Deposit Insurance Corporation) *see* BUSINESS AND ECONOMICS—Abstracting, Bibliographies, Statistics

F D I C STATE PROFILE, OREGON. (Federal Deposit Insurance Corporation) *see* BUSINESS AND ECONOMICS—Abstracting, Bibliographies, Statistics

F D I C STATE PROFILE, PENNSYLVANIA. (Federal Deposit Insurance Corporation) *see* BUSINESS AND ECONOMICS—Abstracting, Bibliographies, Statistics

F D I C STATE PROFILE, PUERTO RICO AND THE U.S. VIRGIN ISLANDS. (Federal Deposit Insurance Corporation) *see* BUSINESS AND ECONOMICS—Abstracting, Bibliographies, Statistics

F D I C STATE PROFILE, RHODE ISLAND. (Federal Deposit Insurance Corporation) *see* BUSINESS AND ECONOMICS—Abstracting, Bibliographies, Statistics

F D I C STATE PROFILE, SOUTH CAROLINA. (Federal Deposit Insurance Corporation) *see* BUSINESS AND ECONOMICS—Abstracting, Bibliographies, Statistics

F D I C STATE PROFILE, SOUTH DAKOTA. (Federal Deposit Insurance Corporation) *see* BUSINESS AND ECONOMICS—Abstracting, Bibliographies, Statistics

F D I C STATE PROFILE, TENNESSEE. (Federal Deposit Insurance Corporation) *see* BUSINESS AND ECONOMICS—Abstracting, Bibliographies, Statistics

F D I C STATE PROFILE, TEXAS. (Federal Deposit Insurance Corporation) *see* BUSINESS AND ECONOMICS—Abstracting, Bibliographies, Statistics

F D I C STATE PROFILE, UTAH. (Federal Deposit Insurance Corporation) *see* BUSINESS AND ECONOMICS—Abstracting, Bibliographies, Statistics

F D I C STATE PROFILE, VERMONT. (Federal Deposit Insurance Corporation) *see* BUSINESS AND ECONOMICS

F D I C STATE PROFILE, VIRGINIA. (Federal Deposit Insurance Corporation) *see* BUSINESS AND ECONOMICS—Abstracting, Bibliographies, Statistics

F D I C STATE PROFILE, WASHINGTON. (Federal Deposit Insurance Corporation) *see* BUSINESS AND ECONOMICS—Abstracting, Bibliographies, Statistics

F D I C STATE PROFILE, WEST VIRGINIA. (Federal Deposit Insurance Corporation) *see* BUSINESS AND ECONOMICS—Abstracting, Bibliographies, Statistics

F D I C STATE PROFILE, WISCONSIN. (Federal Deposit Insurance Corporation) *see* BUSINESS AND ECONOMICS—Abstracting, Bibliographies, Statistics

F D I C STATE PROFILE, WYOMING. (Federal Deposit Insurance Corporation) *see* BUSINESS AND ECONOMICS—Abstracting, Bibliographies, Statistics

FACSIMILE FACTS AND FIGURES. *see* COMMUNICATIONS—Abstracting, Bibliographies, Statistics

FACT BOOK; a statistical handbook. *see* EDUCATION—Abstracting, Bibliographies, Statistics

FACT BOOK ON THEOLOGICAL EDUCATION. *see* RELIGIONS AND THEOLOGY—Abstracting, Bibliographies, Statistics

FACTS ON BOTSWANA. *see* GENERAL INTEREST PERIODICALS—Botswana

310 330.9 ARG ISSN 1668-5008
FACULTAD DE CIENCIAS ECONOMICAS Y ESTADISTICAS. ACTAS DE LAS JORNADAS ANUALES INVESTIGACIONES. Text in Spanish. 1998. a. back issues avail. **Document type:** *Proceedings, Academic/Scholarly.*
Formerly (until 2003): Actas - Jornadas Investigaciones en la Facultad de Ciencias Economicas y Estadistica (1666-3543)
Media: Online - full text.
Published by: Universidad Nacional de Rosario, Facultad de Ciencias Economicas y Estadistica, Blvd Orono 1261, Rosario, Santa Fe, 2000, Argentina. TEL 54-341-4802791, FAX 54-341-4802783, http://www.fcecon.unr.edu.ar/presenta.htm.

FAR EAST JOURNAL OF THEORETICAL STATISTICS. *see* MATHEMATICS

FARMS, LAND IN FARMS, AND LIVESTOCK OPERATIONS. *see* AGRICULTURE—Abstracting, Bibliographies, Statistics

FATAL OCCUPATIONAL INJURIES AND ILLNESSES IN CALIFORNIA. *see* OCCUPATIONAL HEALTH AND SAFETY—Abstracting, Bibliographies, Statistics

FATAL OCCUPATIONAL INJURIES IN MAINE. *see* OCCUPATIONAL HEALTH AND SAFETY—Abstracting, Bibliographies, Statistics

FEDERAL CIVILIAN WORKFORCE STATISTICS. EMPLOYMENT AND TRENDS. *see* BUSINESS AND ECONOMICS—Abstracting, Bibliographies, Statistics

FEDERAL CIVILIAN WORKFORCE STATISTICS. WORK YEARS AND PERSONNEL COSTS. EXECUTIVE BRANCH, UNITED STATES GOVERNMENT. *see* BUSINESS AND ECONOMICS—Abstracting, Bibliographies, Statistics

FEDERAL EMPLOYMENT STATISTICS. BIENNIAL REPORT OF EMPLOYMENT BY GEOGRAPHIC AREA. *see* PUBLIC ADMINISTRATION

FEDERAL MILK ORDER MARKET STATISTICS. *see* AGRICULTURE—Abstracting, Bibliographies, Statistics

FEDERAL R & D FUNDING BY BUDGET FUNCTION (ONLINE). (Research & Development) *see* BUSINESS AND ECONOMICS—Abstracting, Bibliographies, Statistics

FEDERAL SENTENCING STATISTICS BY STATE, CIRCUIT & DISTRICT. *see* LAW—Abstracting, Bibliographies, Statistics

FEDERATION PROFESSIONNELLE DU SECTEUR ELECTRIQUE. ANNUAIRE STATISTIQUE (YEAR). *see* ENERGY—Abstracting, Bibliographies, Statistics

FERTILISER ASSOCIATION OF INDIA. FERTILISER STATISTICS. *see* AGRICULTURE—Abstracting, Bibliographies, Statistics

FERTILIZER FINANCIAL FACTS. *see* AGRICULTURE—Abstracting, Bibliographies, Statistics

FERTILIZER INSTITUTE. ANNUAL SUMMARY. *see* AGRICULTURE—Abstracting, Bibliographies, Statistics

FERTILIZER INSTITUTE. MONTHLY EXPORTS AND IMPORTS. *see* AGRICULTURE—Abstracting, Bibliographies, Statistics

FERTILIZER INSTITUTE. PRODUCTION SURVEY. *see* AGRICULTURE—Abstracting, Bibliographies, Statistics

▼ **FERTILIZER SHIPMENTS SURVEY.** *see* AGRICULTURE

001.422 378.0021 DNK ISSN 1901-1830
FIGURES FOR RESEARCH; statistics. Text in English. 2006. a.
Related titles: Online - full text ed.: ISSN 1901-1849. 2006; ◆ Danish ed.: Tal om Forskning. ISSN 1601-7196.
Published by: Forsknings- og Innovationsstyrelsen/Danish Agency for Science, Technology and Innovation, Bredgade 40, Copenhagen K, 1260, Denmark. TEL 45-35-446200, FAX 45-35-446201, fi@fi.dk, http://www.fi.dk.

FIJI. BUREAU OF STATISTICS. AIRCRAFT STATISTICS. *see* AERONAUTICS AND SPACE FLIGHT—Abstracting, Bibliographies, Statistics

310 FJI
FIJI. BUREAU OF STATISTICS. ANNUAL REPORT. Text in English. irreg., latest 1994. **Document type:** *Government.*
Published by: Bureau of Statistics, c/o Librarian, Govt. Bldg. 5, PO Box 2221, Suva, Fiji. TEL 679-315-822, FAX 679-303-656.

FIJI. BUREAU OF STATISTICS. CENSUS OF BUILDING AND CONSTRUCTION. *see* BUILDING AND CONSTRUCTION—Abstracting, Bibliographies, Statistics

FIJI. BUREAU OF STATISTICS. CENSUS OF DISTRIBUTION AND SERVICES. *see* BUSINESS AND ECONOMICS—Abstracting, Bibliographies, Statistics

FIJI. BUREAU OF STATISTICS. CENSUS OF INDUSTRIES. *see* BUSINESS AND ECONOMICS—Abstracting, Bibliographies, Statistics

FIJI. BUREAU OF STATISTICS. CURRENT ECONOMIC STATISTICS. *see* BUSINESS AND ECONOMICS—Abstracting, Bibliographies, Statistics

FIJI. BUREAU OF STATISTICS. ECONOMIC AND FUNCTIONAL CLASSIFICATION OF GOVERNMENT ACCOUNTS. *see* BUSINESS AND ECONOMICS—Abstracting, Bibliographies, Statistics

FIJI. BUREAU OF STATISTICS. EMPLOYMENT SURVEY OF FIJI. *see* BUSINESS AND ECONOMICS—Abstracting, Bibliographies, Statistics

FIJI. BUREAU OF STATISTICS. FIJI FERTILITY SURVEY. *see* POPULATION STUDIES—Abstracting, Bibliographies, Statistics

FIJI. BUREAU OF STATISTICS. FIJI HOUSEHOLD INCOME AND EXPENDITURE SURVEY. *see* BUSINESS AND ECONOMICS—Abstracting, Bibliographies, Statistics

315 FJI
FIJI. BUREAU OF STATISTICS. NATIONAL ACCOUNTS. Text in English. irreg., latest 1993. **Document type:** *Government.*
Description: Provides an economic and functional classification of government accounts for 1990-93.
Published by: Bureau of Statistics, c/o Librarian, Govt. Bldg. 5, PO Box 2221, Suva, Fiji. TEL 679-315-822, FAX 679-303-656.

FIJI. BUREAU OF STATISTICS. NATIONWIDE UNEMPLOYMENT SURVEY. *see* BUSINESS AND ECONOMICS—Abstracting, Bibliographies, Statistics

FIJI. BUREAU OF STATISTICS. OVERSEAS TRADE (YEAR). *see* BUSINESS AND ECONOMICS—Abstracting, Bibliographies, Statistics

FIJI. BUREAU OF STATISTICS. POPULATION OF FIJI; monograph for the U N World population. *see* POPULATION STUDIES—Abstracting, Bibliographies, Statistics

310 FJI ISSN 0256-4149
FIJI. BUREAU OF STATISTICS. STATISTICAL NEWS. Text in English. 1979. m. USD 33 (effective 2000 - 2001). **Document type:** *Government.*
Published by: Bureau of Statistics, c/o Librarian, Govt. Bldg. 5, PO Box 2221, Suva, Fiji. TEL 679-315-822, FAX 679-303-656.

FIJI. BUREAU OF STATISTICS. SURVEY OF DISTRIBUTIVE TRADE. *see* BUSINESS AND ECONOMICS—Abstracting, Bibliographies, Statistics

FIJI. BUREAU OF STATISTICS. TOURISM AND MIGRATION STATISTICS. *see* TRAVEL AND TOURISM—Abstracting, Bibliographies, Statistics

FIJI. BUREAU OF STATISTICS. TRADE REPORT. *see* BUSINESS AND ECONOMICS—Abstracting, Bibliographies, Statistics

FIJI. BUREAU OF STATISTICS. VITAL STATISTICS. *see* BUSINESS AND ECONOMICS—Abstracting, Bibliographies, Statistics

FIJI FACTS AND FIGURES. *see* BUSINESS AND ECONOMICS—Abstracting, Bibliographies, Statistics

FINANCIAL STATISTICS. *see* BUSINESS AND ECONOMICS—Abstracting, Bibliographies, Statistics

FINANCIAL STATISTICS EXPLANATORY HANDBOOK (YEAR). *see* BUSINESS AND ECONOMICS

330.9 310 BGR
FINANSI NA PREDPRIATIATA. Text in Bulgarian. a. USD 18 foreign (effective 2002). **Description:** Covers the financial and economic state of non-financial companies; the results are shown in branches and economic sectors.
Related titles: Diskette ed.
Published by: Natsionalen Statisticheski Institut/National Statistical Institute, ul P Volov, # 2, Sofia, 1038, Bulgaria. FAX 359-2-9803319, publikacii@nsi.bg, http://www.nsi.bg. **Dist. by:** Sofia Books, ul Silivria 16, Sofia 1404, Bulgaria. TEL 359-2-9586257, info@sofiabooks-bg.com, http://www.sofiabooks-bg.com.

FINANZAS PUBLICAS ESTATALES Y MUNICIPALES DE MEXICO. *see* BUSINESS AND ECONOMICS—Abstracting, Bibliographies, Statistics

FINLAND. KANSANELAKELAITOS. KELAN TILASTOLLINEN VUOSIKIRJA/FINLAND. FOLKPENSIONSANSTALTEN. F P AS STATISTISKA AARSBOK/FINLAND. SOCIAL INSURANCE INSTITUTION. STATISTICAL YEARBOOK. *see* INSURANCE—Abstracting, Bibliographies, Statistics

FINLAND. MAA- JA METSATALOUSMINISTERIO. TIETOPALVELUKESKUS TIETOKAPPA (ONLINE); maataloustilastollinen kuukausikatsaus. *see* AGRICULTURE—Abstracting, Bibliographies, Statistics

FINLAND. MINISTRY OF AGRICULTURE AND FORESTRY. INFORMATION CENTRE. STATISTICS. MAATILATILASTOLLINEN VUOSIKIRJA/YEARBOOK OF FARM STATISTICS. *see* AGRICULTURE—Abstracting, Bibliographies, Statistics

FINLAND. SOSIAALI- JA TERVEYSALAN TUTKIMUS- JA KEHITTAMISKESKUS. IKAANTYNEIDEN SOSIAALI- JA TERVEYSPALVELUT/FINLAND. FORSKNINGS- OCH UTVECKLINGSCENTRALEN FOER SOCIAL- OCH HAELSOVAARDEN. AELDREOMSORGEN/FINLAND. NATIONAL RESEARCH AND DEVELOPMENT CENTRE FOR WELFARE AND HEALTH. CARE AND SERVICES FOR OLDER PEOPLE. *see* GERONTOLOGY AND GERIATRICS—Abstracting, Bibliographies, Statistics

FINLAND. SOSIAALI- JA TERVEYSALAN TUTKIMUS- JA KEHITTAMISKESKUS. YKSITYINEN PALVELUTUOTANTO SOSIAALI- JA TERVEYDENHUOLLOSSA/FINLAND. FORSKNINGS- OCH UTVECLINGSCENTRALEN FOER SOCIAL- OCH HAELSOEVAARDEN. PRIVAT SERVICEPRODUKTION INOM SOCIALVAARDEN OCH HAELSO- OCH SJUKVAARDEN/ FINLAND. NATIONAL RESEARCH AND DEVELOPMENT CENTRE FOR WELFARE AND HEALTH. PRIVATE SERVICE PROVISION IN SOCIAL AND HEALTH CARE. *see* SOCIAL SERVICES AND WELFARE—Abstracting, Bibliographies, Statistics

FINLAND. STATISTICS FINLAND. ENERGY IN FINLAND. *see* ENERGY—Abstracting, Bibliographies, Statistics

FINLAND. TILASTOKESKUS. ANSIOTASOINDEKSI/FINLAND. STATISTICS FINLAND. INDEX OF WAGE AND SALARY EARNINGS/FINLAND. STATISTIKCENTRALEN. FOERTJAENSTNIVAAINDEX. *see* BUSINESS AND ECONOMICS—Abstracting, Bibliographies, Statistics

FINLAND. TILASTOKESKUS. ASUNTOJEN HINNAT. VUOSITILASTO/ FINLAND. STATISTICS FINLAND. HOUSE PRICES/FINLAND. STATISTIKCENTRALEN. BOSTADSPRISERNA. *see* HOUSING AND URBAN PLANNING—Abstracting, Bibliographies, Statistics

FINLAND. TILASTOKESKUS. EDUSKUNTAVAALIT/FINLAND. STATISTICS FINLAND. PARLIAMENTARY ELECTIONS/FINLAND. STATISTIKCENTRALEN. RIKSDAGSVALET. *see* POLITICAL SCIENCE—Abstracting, Bibliographies, Statistics

FINLAND. TILASTOKESKUS. ENERGIAENNAKKO/FINLAND. STATISTICS FINLAND. PRELIMINARY ENERGY STATISTICS/ FINLAND. STATISTIKCENTRALEN. PRELIMINAERA ENERGISTATISTIK. *see* ENERGY—Abstracting, Bibliographies, Statistics

FINLAND. TILASTOKESKUS. ENERGIAN TIOTANTO JA VESIHUOLTO. *see* ENERGY—Abstracting, Bibliographies, Statistics

FINLAND. TILASTOKESKUS. ETELA-SUOMEN KATSAUS. *see* PUBLIC ADMINISTRATION—Abstracting, Bibliographies, Statistics

FINLAND. TILASTOKESKUS. EUROPARLAMENTTIVAALIT/FINLAND. STATISTICS FINLAND. ELECTIONS FOR THE EUROPEAN PARLIAMENT/FINLAND. STATISTIKCENTRALEN. VALET TILL EUROPAPARLAMENTET. *see* POLITICAL SCIENCE—Abstracting, Bibliographies, Statistics

FINLAND. TILASTOKESKUS. EUROPARLAMENTTIVAALIT, ENNAKKOTILASTO/FINLAND. STATISTICS FINLAND. ELECTIONS FOR THE EUROPEAN PARLIAMENT/FINLAND. STATISTIKCENTRALEN. VALET TILL EUROPAPARLAMENTET. *see* POLITICAL SCIENCE—Abstracting, Bibliographies, Statistics

314 FIN ISSN 0357-4962
FINLAND. TILASTOKESKUS. FINLAND I SIFFROR. Text in Swedish. 1978. a. **Document type:** *Government.*
Formerly (until 1979): Finland. Tilastokeskus. Siffror om Finland (0357-038X)
Related titles: Online - full text ed.; ◆ Finnish ed.: Finland. Tilastokeskus. Suomi Lukuina. ISSN 1795-732X; ◆ English ed.: Finland. Tilastokeskus. Finland in Figures. ISSN 0357-0371; ◆ French ed.: Finland. Tilastokeskus. La Finlande en Chiffres. ISSN 0782-7326; ◆ German ed.: Finland. Tilastokeskus. Finnland in Zahlen. ISSN 0781-657X; Russian ed.: Finland. Tilastokeskus. Finlyandiya v Tsifrakh. ISSN 0358-8998. 1981; Spanish ed.: Finland. Tilastokeskus. Finlandia en Cifras. ISSN 0782-5196. 1986; Arabic ed.: Finland. Tilastokeskus. Finlanda Bil- Arqam. ISSN 0783-2699. 1986.
Published by: Tilastokeskus/Statistics Finland, Tyopajakatu 13, Statistics Finland, Helsinki, 00022, Finland. TEL 358-9-17341, FAX 358-9-17342279.

314 FIN ISSN 0357-0371
HA1450.5
FINLAND. TILASTOKESKUS. FINLAND IN FIGURES. Text in English. 1977. a. EUR 3 (effective 2008). **Document type:** *Government.*

S

Related titles: Online - full text ed.; ◆ Finnish ed.: Finland. Tilastokeskus. Suomi Lukuina. ISSN 1795-732X; ◆ Swedish ed.: Finland. Tilastokeskus. Finland i Siffror. ISSN 0357-4962; ◆ French ed.: Finland. Tilastokeskus. La Finlande en Chiffres. ISSN 0782-7326; ◆ German ed.: Finland. Tilastokeskus. Finnland in Zahlen. ISSN 0781-657X; Russian ed.: Finland. Tilastokeskus. Finlyandiya v Tsifrakh. ISSN 0358-8998. 1981; Spanish ed.: Finland. Tilastokeskus. Finlandia en Cifras. ISSN 0782-5196. 1986; Arabic ed.: Finland. Tilastokeskus. Finlanda Bil- Arqam. ISSN 0783-2699. 1986.
Published by: Tilastokeskus/Statistics Finland, Tyopajakatu 13, Statistics Finland, Helsinki, 00022, Finland. TEL 358-9-17341, FAX 358-9-17342279.

314 FIN ISSN 0781-657X
FINLAND. TILASTOKESKUS. FINNLAND IN ZAHLEN. Text in German. 1984. a. **Document type:** *Government.*
Related titles: Online - full text ed.; ◆ English ed.: Finland. Tilastokeskus. Finland in Figures. ISSN 0357-0371; ◆ Swedish ed.: Finland. Tilastokeskus. Finland i Siffror. ISSN 0357-4962; ◆ Finnish ed.: Finland. Tilastokeskus. Suomi Lukuina. ISSN 1795-732X; ◆ French ed.: Finland. Tilastokeskus. La Finlande en Chiffres. ISSN 0782-7326; Spanish ed.: Finland. Tilastokeskus. Finlandia en Cifras. ISSN 0782-5196. 1986; Russian ed.: Finland. Tilastokeskus. Finlyandiya v Tsifrakh. ISSN 0358-8998. 1981; Arabic ed.: Finland. Tilastokeskus. Finlanda Bil- Arqam. ISSN 0783-2699. 1986.
Published by: Tilastokeskus/Statistics Finland, Tyopajakatu 13, Statistics Finland, Helsinki, 00022, Finland. TEL 358-9-17341, FAX 358-9-17342279.

FINLAND. TILASTOKESKUS. HENKILOSTOKOULUTUS (ONLINE). *see* EDUCATION—Abstracting, Bibliographies, Statistics

FINLAND. TILASTOKESKUS. HINTA- JA PALKKATIEDOTE/FINLAND. STATISTICS FINLAND. PRICES AND WAGES REVIEW. *see* BUSINESS AND ECONOMICS—Abstracting, Bibliographies, Statistics

FINLAND. TILASTOKESKUS. ITA-SUOMEN KATSAUS. *see* PUBLIC ADMINISTRATION—Abstracting, Bibliographies, Statistics

FINLAND. TILASTOKESKUS. JOUKKOVIESTIMET/FINLAND. STATISTICS FINLAND. FINNISH MASS MEDIA/FINLAND. STATISTIKCENTRALEN. MASSMEDIER. *see* SOCIOLOGY—Abstracting, Bibliographies, Statistics

FINLAND. TILASTOKESKUS. JULKISYHTEISOJEN ALIJAAMA JA BRUTTOVELKA EMU-KRITEERIEN MUKAISINA (ONLINE)/ FINLAND. STATISTICS FINLAND. GENERAL GOVERNMENT DEFICIT AND GROSS DEBT ACCORDING TO EMU CRITERIA/ FINLAND. STATISTIKCENTRALEN. DE OFFENTLIGA SAMFUNDENS UNDERSKOTT OCH BRUTTOSKULD ENLIGT EMU-KRITERIER. *see* BUSINESS AND ECONOMICS—Abstracting, Bibliographies, Statistics

FINLAND. TILASTOKESKUS. KANSANEDUSTAJAIN VAALIT, ENNAKKOTILASTO/FINLAND. STATISTIKCENTRALEN. RIKSDAGSVALET, FOERHANDSSTATISTIK. *see* POLITICAL SCIENCE—Abstracting, Bibliographies, Statistics

FINLAND. TILASTOKESKUS. KANSANTALOUDEN TILINPITO (ONLINE)/FINLAND. CENTRAL STATISTICAL OFFICE. NATIONAL ACCOUNTS/FINLAND. STATISTIKCENTRALEN. NATIONAL RAEKENSKAPER. *see* BUSINESS AND ECONOMICS—Abstracting, Bibliographies, Statistics

314 FIN ISSN 0355-2063
QH178.F5
FINLAND. TILASTOKESKUS. KASIKIRJOJA/FINLAND. STATISTICS FINLAND. HANDBOOKS/FINLAND. STATISTIKCENTRALEN. HANDBOECKER. Text in Finnish, English, Swedish. 1971. irreg. price varies. **Document type:** *Monographic series, Government.*
Published by: Tilastokeskus/Statistics Finland, Tyopajakatu 13, Statistics Finland, Helsinki, 00022, Finland. TEL 358-9-17341, FAX 358-9-17342279, http://www.stat.fi.

FINLAND. TILASTOKESKUS. KESAMOKIT/FINLAND. STATISTICS FINLAND. FREE-TIME RESIDENCES/FINLAND. STATISTIKCENTRALEN. FRITIDSHUS. *see* HOUSING AND URBAN PLANNING—Abstracting, Bibliographies, Statistics

FINLAND. TILASTOKESKUS. KIINTEISTON YLLAPIDON KUSTANNUSINDEKSI/FINLAND. STATISTICS FINLAND. INDEX OF REAL ESTATE MAINTENANCE COSTS/FINLAND. STATISTIKCENTRALEN. KOSTNADSINDEX FOER FASTIGHETSUNDERHAALL. *see* HOUSING AND URBAN PLANNING—Abstracting, Bibliographies, Statistics

FINLAND. TILASTOKESKUS. KULTTUURITILASTO/FINLAND. STATISTICS FINLAND. CULTURAL STATISTICS. *see* SOCIOLOGY—Abstracting, Bibliographies, Statistics

FINLAND. TILASTOKESKUS. KULUTTAJABAROMETRI/FINLAND. STATISTICS FINALND. CONSUMER BAROMETER/FINLANF. STATISTIKCENTRALEN. KONSUMENTBAROMETERN. *see* BUSINESS AND ECONOMICS—Abstracting, Bibliographies, Statistics

FINLAND. TILASTOKESKUS. KULUTTAJABAROMETRI MAAKUNNITTAIN. *see* BUSINESS AND ECONOMICS—Abstracting, Bibliographies, Statistics

FINLAND. TILASTOKESKUS. KULUTTAJAHINTAINDEKSI/FINLAND. STATISTICS FINLAND. CONSUMER PRICE INDEX/FINLAND. STATISTIKCENTRALEN. KONSUMENTPRISINDEX. *see* BUSINESS AND ECONOMICS—Abstracting, Bibliographies, Statistics

FINLAND. TILASTOKESKUS. KUNNALLISVAALIT/FINLAND. STATISTICS FINLAND. MUNICIPAL ELECTIONS/FINLAND. STATISTIKCENTRALEN. KOMMUNALVALEN. *see* PUBLIC ADMINISTRATION—Abstracting, Bibliographies, Statistics

FINLAND. TILASTOKESKUS. KUNNALLISVAALIT, ENNAKKOTILASTO. *see* POLITICAL SCIENCE—Abstracting, Bibliographies, Statistics

FINLAND. TILASTOKESKUS. KUNTAFAKTA. *see* PUBLIC ADMINISTRATION—Abstracting, Bibliographies, Statistics

FINLAND. TILASTOKESKUS. KUNTAKATSAUS. *see* PUBLIC ADMINISTRATION—Abstracting, Bibliographies, Statistics

314 FIN ISSN 1238-3546
HN531
FINLAND. TILASTOKESKUS. KUNTAPUNTARI. Text in Finnish. 1995. 5/yr. EUR 197; EUR 46 per issue (effective 2008). stat. back issues avail. **Document type:** *Magazine, Government.*
Published by: Tilastokeskus/Statistics Finland, Tyopajakatu 13, Statistics Finland, Helsinki, 00022, Finland. TEL 358-9-17341, FAX 358-9-17342279.

FINLAND. TILASTOKESKUS. KUNTASEKTORIN PALKAT/FINLAND. STATISTIKCENTRALEN. MAANADSLOENER FOER KOMMUNALANSTAELLDA. *see* BUSINESS AND ECONOMICS—Abstracting, Bibliographies, Statistics

FINLAND. TILASTOKESKUS. KUNTASEKTORIN PALKAT AMMATEITTAIN/FINLAND. STATISTIKCENTRALEN. LOENER FOER KOMMUNALANSTAELLDA EFTER YRKE. *see* BUSINESS AND ECONOMICS—Abstracting, Bibliographies, Statistics

FINLAND. TILASTOKESKUS. KUNTASEKTORIN TUNTIPALKAT/ FINLAND. STATISTIKCENTRALEN. TIMLOENER I KOMMUNERNA. *see* BUSINESS AND ECONOMICS—Abstracting, Bibliographies, Statistics

FINLAND. TILASTOKESKUS. KUNTAYHTYMIEN TALOUS/FINLAND. STATISTIKCENTRALEN. SAMKOMMUNERNAS EKONOMI. *see* PUBLIC ADMINISTRATION—Abstracting, Bibliographies, Statistics

FINLAND. TILASTOKESKUS. KUNTIEN TALOUS JA TOIMINTA/ FINLAND. STATISTIKCENTRALEN. KOMMUNERNAS EKONOMI OCH VERKSAMHET. *see* BUSINESS AND ECONOMICS—Abstracting, Bibliographies, Statistics

FINLAND. TILASTOKESKUS. KUOLEMANSYYT/FINLAND. STATISTICS FINLAND. CAUSES OF DEATH/FINLAND. STATISTIKCENTRALEN. DOEDSORSAKER. *see* POPULATION STUDIES—Abstracting, Bibliographies, Statistics

FINLAND. TILASTOKESKUS. KUORMA-AUTOLIIKENTEEN KUSTANNUSINDEKSI/FINLAND. STATISTICS FINLAND. COST INDEX FOR ROAD TRANSPORT OF GOODS/FINLAND. STATISTIKCENTRALEN. KOSTNADSINDEX FOER LASTBILTRAFIK. *see* TRANSPORTATION—Abstracting, Bibliographies, Statistics

FINLAND. TILASTOKESKUS. L Y - TUNNUSKIRJA. *see* BUSINESS AND ECONOMICS—Abstracting, Bibliographies, Statistics

FINLAND. TILASTOKESKUS. LANSI-SUOMEN KATSAUS. *see* PUBLIC ADMINISTRATION—Abstracting, Bibliographies, Statistics

FINLAND. TILASTOKESKUS. LIIKENNETILASTOLLINEN VUOSIKIRJA/FINLAND. STATISTICS FINLAND. TRANSPORT AND COMMUNICATIONS STATISTICAL YEARBOOK FOR FINLAND/FINLAND. STATISTIKCENTRALEN. SAMFAERDSELSTATISTISKAARSBOK. *see* TRANSPORTATION—Abstracting, Bibliographies, Statistics

FINLAND. TILASTOKESKUS. LUONNONVARAT JA YMPARISTO. *see* ENVIRONMENTAL STUDIES—Abstracting, Bibliographies, Statistics

FINLAND. TILASTOKESKUS. LUOTTOKANTA/FINLAND. STATISTICS FINLAND. OUTSTANDING CREDIT/FINLAND. STATISTIKCENTRALEN. KREDITBESTAANDET. *see* BUSINESS AND ECONOMICS—Abstracting, Bibliographies, Statistics

FINLAND. TILASTOKESKUS. LUOTTOKORTIT/FINLAND. STATISTIKCENTRALEN. KREDITKORT. *see* BUSINESS AND ECONOMICS—Abstracting, Bibliographies, Statistics

FINLAND. TILASTOKESKUS. MAA- JA METSATALOUSYRITYSTEN TALOUSTILASTO/FINLAND. STATISTICS FINLAND. FINANCES OF AGRICULTURAL AND FORESTRY ENTERPRISES/FINLAND. STATISTIKCENTRALEN. JORD- OCH SKOGSBRUKSFOERETAGENS EKONOMI. *see* AGRICULTURE—Abstracting, Bibliographies, Statistics

310 FIN ISSN 0787-8516
FINLAND. TILASTOKESKUS. MAAILMA NUMEROINA. SUOMEN TILASTOLLINEN VUOSIKIRJAN..KANSAINVALINEN OSA/ FINLAND. STATITIKCENTRALEN. VAERLDEN I SIFFROR. STATISTICAL YEARBOOK OF FINLAND..INTERNATIONELLA OEVERSIKTER. Text in English, Finnish, Swedish. 1987. a. **Document type:** *Government.*
Related titles: Online - full text ed.; ◆ Supplement to: Finland. Tilastokeskus. Suomen Tilastollinen Vuosikirja. ISSN 0081-5063.
Published by: Tilastokeskus/Statistics Finland, Tyopajakatu 13, Statistics Finland, Helsinki, 00022, Finland. TEL 358-9-17341, FAX 358-9-17342279.

FINLAND. TILASTOKESKUS. MAARAKENNUSKUSTANNUSINDEKSI/ FINALND. STATISTIKCENTRALEN. JORDBYGGNADSKOSTNADSINDEX/FINLAND. STATISTICS FINLAND. COST INDEX OF CIVIL ENGINEERING WORKS. *see* BUILDING AND CONSTRUCTION—Abstracting, Bibliographies, Statistics

FINLAND. TILASTOKESKUS. MATKAILUTILASTO (KUUKAUSITILASTO)/FINLAND. STATISTICS FINLAND. TOURISM STATISTICS (MONTHLY). *see* TRAVEL AND TOURISM—Abstracting, Bibliographies, Statistics

FINLAND. TILASTOKESKUS. MATKAILUTILASTO (VUOSITILASTO)/ FINLAND. STATISTICS FINLAND. TOURISM STATISTICS (ANNUAL)/FINLAND. STATISTIKCENTRALEN. TURISMSTATISTIK. *see* TRAVEL AND TOURISM—Abstracting, Bibliographies, Statistics

FINLAND. TILASTOKESKUS. NAISET JA MIEHET SUOMESSA. *see* SOCIOLOGY—Abstracting, Bibliographies, Statistics

FINLAND. TILASTOKESKUS. OIKEUSTILASTOLLINEN VUOSIKIRJA/ FINLAND. STATISTICS FINLAND. YEARBOOK OF JUSTICE STATISTICS/FINLAND. STATISTIKCENTALEN. RAETTSSTATISTISK AARSBOK. *see* CRIMINOLOGY AND LAW ENFORCEMENT—Abstracting, Bibliographies, Statistics

FINLAND. TILASTOKESKUS. OPPILAITOSTILASTOT. *see* EDUCATION—Abstracting, Bibliographies, Statistics

FINLAND. TILASTOKESKUS. OULUN ALUEPALVELU. POHJOIS-SUOMEN KATSAUS. *see* PUBLIC ADMINISTRATION—Abstracting, Bibliographies, Statistics

FINLAND. TILASTOKESKUS. PALKKARAKENNE/FINLAND. STATISTICS FINLAND. STRUCTURE OF EARNINGS/FINLAND. STATISTIKCENTRALEN. LOENESTRUKTURSTATISTIK. *see* BUSINESS AND ECONOMICS—Abstracting, Bibliographies, Statistics

FINLAND. TILASTOKESKUS. PERHEET/FINLAND. STATISTICS FINLAND. FAMILIES/FINLAND. STATISTIKCENTRALEN. FAMILJER. *see* POPULATION STUDIES—Abstracting, Bibliographies, Statistics

FINLAND. TILASTOKESKUS. POLIISIN TIETOON TULLUT RIKOLLISUUS/FINLAND. STATISTIKCENTRALEN. BROTTSLIGHET SOM KOMMIT TILL POLISENS KAENNEDOM. *see* CRIMINOLOGY AND LAW ENFORCEMENT—Abstracting, Bibliographies, Statistics

FINLAND. TILASTOKESKUS. PRESIDENTIN VAALIT/FFINLAND. STATISTIKCENTRALEN. PRESIDENTVALET/FINLAND. STATISTICS FINLAND. PRESIDENTIAL ELECTION. *see* POLITICAL SCIENCE—Abstracting, Bibliographies, Statistics

FINLAND. TILASTOKESKUS. RAHALAITOKSET/FINLAND. STATISTICS FINLAND. MONETARY FINANCIAL INSTITUTIONS/ FINLAND. STATISTIKCENTRALEN. MONETAERA FINANSINSTITUT. *see* BUSINESS AND ECONOMICS—Abstracting, Bibliographies, Statistics

FINLAND. TILASTOKESKUS. RAHOITUSLEASING/FINLAND. STATISTICS FINLAND. FINANCIAL LEASING/FINLAND. STATISTIKCENTRALEN. FINANSIERINGSLEASING. *see* BUSINESS AND ECONOMICS—Abstracting, Bibliographies, Statistics

FINLAND. TILASTOKESKUS. RAKENNUKSET, ASUNNOT JA ASUINOLOT/FINLAND. STATISTICS FINLAND. BUILDINGS, DWELLINGS AND HOUSING CONDITIONS/FINLAND. STATISTIKCENTRALEN. BYGGNADER, BOSTAEDER OCH BOENDEFOERHAALLANDEN. *see* HOUSING AND URBAN PLANNING—Abstracting, Bibliographies, Statistics

FINLAND. TILASTOKESKUS. RAKENNUS- JA ASUNTOTUOTANTO/ FINLAND. STATISTICS FINLAND. BUILDING AND DWELLING PRODUCTION/FINLAND. STATISTIKCENTRALEN. BYGGNADS-OCH BOSTADSPRODUKTION. *see* BUILDING AND CONSTRUCTION—Abstracting, Bibliographies, Statistics

FINLAND. TILASTOKESKUS. RAKENNUSKUSTANNUSINDEKSI (KUUKAUSITILASTO)/FINLAND. STATISTICS FINLAND. BUILDING COST INDEX/FINLAND. STATISTIKCENTRALEN. BYGGNADSKOSTNADSINDEX. *see* BUILDING AND CONSTRUCTION—Abstracting, Bibliographies, Statistics

FINLAND. TILASTOKESKUS. RAKENTAMINEN JA ASUMINEN: VUOSIKIRJA/FINLAND. STATISTICS FINLAND. CONSTRUCTION AND HOUSING. YEARBOOK. *see* HOUSING AND URBAN PLANNING—Abstracting, Bibliographies, Statistics

FINLAND. TILASTOKESKUS. SCIENCE AND TECHNOLOGY IN FINLAND. *see* SCIENCES: COMPREHENSIVE WORKS

314 FIN ISSN 1456-2480
FINLAND. TILASTOKESKUS. SEUTUKUNTA- JA MAAKUNTAKATSAUS. Text in Finnish. 1997. a. price varies. stat. **Document type:** *Government.*
Formerly (until 1998): Finland. Tilastokeskus. Seutukuntakatsaus (1239-7490)
Published by: Tilastokeskus/Statistics Finland, Tyopajakatu 13, Statistics Finland, Helsinki, 00022, Finland. TEL 358-9-17341, FAX 358-9-17342279, http://www.stat.fi.

FINLAND. TILASTOKESKUS. SIJOITTUMISCD. *see* EDUCATION—Abstracting, Bibliographies, Statistics

FINLAND. TILASTOKESKUS. SIJOITUSPALVELUYRITTYKSET/ FINLAND. STATISTICS FINLAND. INVESTMENT SERVICE COMPANIES/FINLAND. STATISTIKCENTRALEN. VAERDEPAPPERSFOERETAG. *see* BUSINESS AND ECONOMICS—Abstracting, Bibliographies, Statistics

FINLAND. TILASTOKESKUS. SIJOITUSRAHASTOT/FINLAND. STATISTICS FINLAND. MUTUAL FUNDS/FINLAND. STATISTIKCENTRALEN. INVESTERINGSFONDER. *see* BUSINESS AND ECONOMICS—Abstracting, Bibliographies, Statistics

FINLAND. TILASTOKESKUS. SUKUPUOLTEN TASA-ARVO/FINALND. STATISTIKCENTRALEN. JAEMSTAELLDHETEN MELLAN KVINNOR OCH MAEN I FINLAND/FINLAND. STATISTICS FINLAND. GENDER EQUALITY IN FINLAND. *see* SOCIOLOGY—Abstracting, Bibliographies, Statistics

FINLAND. TILASTOKESKUS. SUOMALAISTEN MATKAILU/FINLAND. STATISTICS FINLAND. FINNISH TRAVEL/FINLAND. TRAFIKCENTRALEN. FINLAENDARNAS RESOR. *see* TRAVEL AND TOURISM—Abstracting, Bibliographies, Statistics

FINLAND. TILASTOKESKUS. SUOMEN LAHIALUEET. *see* BUSINESS AND ECONOMICS—Abstracting, Bibliographies, Statistics

314 FIN ISSN 0081-5063
HA1448
FINLAND. TILASTOKESKUS. SUOMEN TILASTOLLINEN VUOSIKIRJA/FINLAND. STATISTICS FINLAND. STATISTICAL YEARBOOK OF FINLAND/FINLAND. STATISTIKCENTRALEN. STATISTISK AARSBOK FOER FINLAND. Text in English, Finnish, Swedish. 1879. a. EUR 110 includes CD (effective 2008). **Document type:** *Government.*
Formerly (until 1903): Suomenmaan Tilastollinen Vuosikirja
Related titles: Microfiche ed.: (from PQC); Online - full text ed.; ◆ Series of: Finland. Tilastokeskus. Suomen Virallinen Tilasto. ISSN 1795-5165; ◆ Supplement(s): Finland. Tilastokeskus. Maailma Numeroina. Suomen Tilastollinen Vuosikirjan..Kansainvalinen Osa. ISSN 0787-8516.
Indexed: RASB.
—BLDSC (8452.850000).
Published by: Tilastokeskus/Statistics Finland, Tyopajakatu 13, Statistics Finland, Helsinki, 00022, Finland. TEL 358-9-17341, FAX 358-9-17342279. Circ: 5,000.

310 FIN ISSN 1795-5165
FINLAND. TILASTOKESKUS. SUOMEN VIRALLINEN TILASTO/ FINLAND. STATISTICS FINLAND. OFFICIAL STATISTICS OF FINLAND/FINLAND. STATISTIKCENTRALEN. FINLANDS OFFICIELLA STATISTIK. Text in English, Finnish, Swedish. 2005. irreg. back issues avail. **Document type:** *Monographic series, Government.*
Related titles: CD-ROM ed.: ISSN 1796-7082; ◆ Online - full text ed.: Finland. Tilastokeskus. Suomen Virallinen Tilasto. ISSN 1796-0479; ◆ Series: Finland. Tilastokeskus. Julkisyhteisojen Alijaama ja Bruttovelka EMU-Kriteerien Mukaisina (Online); ◆ Finland. Tilastokeskus. Tilastokatsauksia. ISSN 0015-2390; ◆ Finland. Tullihallitus. Tavaroiden Ulkomaankauppa. ISSN 1796-9344; ◆ Finland. Tilastokeskus. Ansiotasoindeksi. ISSN 0784-8218; ◆ Finland. Kansanelakelaitos. Kelan Tilastollinen Vuosikirja. ISSN 1796-5659; ◆ Finland. Tilastokeskus. Suomen Tilastollinen Vuosikirja. ISSN 0081-5063; ◆ Metsatilastollinen Vuosikirja. ISSN 0359-968X; ◆ Finland. Tilastokeskus. Eduskuntavaalit. ISSN 1457-0904; ◆ Finland. Tilastokeskus. Kunnallisvaalit. ISSN 0787-7153; ◆ Finland. Tilastokeskus. Kuntien Talousarviot. ISSN 0784-9737; ◆ Finland. Tilastokeskus. Kuolemansyyt. ISSN 0787-0132; ◆ Finland. Tilastokeskus. Liikennetilastollinen Vuosikirja. ISSN 0785-6172; ◆ Finland. Tilastokeskus. Tulo- ja Varallisuustilasto. ISSN 0785-6016; ◆ Finland. Tilastokeskus. Rakennuskustannusindeksi (Kuukausitilasto). ISSN 0784-8196; ◆ Finland. Tilastokeskus. Tyovoimatilasto (Annual Edition). ISSN 0785-0050; ◆ Finland. Tilastokeskus. Energiatilastot. ISSN 0785-3165; ◆ Finland. Tilastokeskus. Moottoriajoneuvot. ISSN 0785-613X; ◆ Finland. Tilastokeskus. Kiinteiston Yllapidon Kustannusindeksi. ISSN 1455-6413; ◆ Finland. Tilastokeskus. Kuluttajahintaindeksi. ISSN 0784-820X; ◆ Finland. Tilastokeskus. Kuorma-Autoliikenteen Kustannusindeksi. ISSN 0786-0366; ◆ Finland. Tilastokeskus. Maarakennuskustannusindeksi. ISSN 1236-9942; ◆ Finland. Tilastokeskus. Tuottajahintaindeksit. ISSN 0784-817X; ◆ Finland. Ministry of Agriculture and Forestry. Information Centre. Statistics. Maatilatilastollinen Vuosikirja. ISSN 0786-2857; ◆ Finland. Tilastokeskus. Tulonjakotilasto. ISSN 0785-9880; ◆ Finland. Tilastokeskus. Asuntojen Hinnat. Vuositilasto. ISSN 0788-0308; ◆ Finland. Tilastokeskus. Vuokratilasto. ISSN 0784-9346; ◆ Finland. Tilastokeskus. Kesamokit. ISSN 0789-0168; ◆ Finland. Tilastokeskus. Rakennukset, Asunnot ja Asuinolot. ISSN 1455-3724; ◆ Finland. Tilastokeskus. Kuntayhtymien Talous. ISSN 1238-4909; ◆ Finland. Tilastokeskus. Kuntayhtymien Talousarviot. ISSN 1236-6595; ◆ Finland. Tilastokeskus. Kuntien Talous ja Toiminta. Kunnittaisia Tietoja. ISSN 1456-4408; ◆ Finland. Tilastokeskus. Kuntien Talous ja Toiminta. ISSN 1239-1980; ◆ Finland. Tilastokeskus. Kansantalouden Tilinpito. Taulukot. ISSN 0784-9613; ◆ Finland. Tilastokeskus. Rahoitustilinpito. ISSN 0784-9672; ◆ Finland. Tilastokeskus. Oppilaitostilastot. ISSN 1455-4402; ◆ Finland. Tilastokeskus. Koulutuksen Jarjestajat ja Oppilaitokset. ISSN 1457-5183; ◆ Finland. Tilastokeskus. Vaeston Koulutusrakenne Kunnittain. ISSN 0785-0743; ◆ Finland. Tilastokeskus. Kulttuuritilasto. ISSN 1456-825X; ◆ Finland. Tilastokeskus. Suomalaisten Matkailu. ISSN 1239-7342; ◆ Finland. Tilastokeskus. Tieliikenteen Tavarankuljetustilasto. ISSN 0786-1877; ◆ Finland. Tilastokeskus. Matkailutilasto (Vuositilasto). ISSN 1238-7150; ◆ Finland. Tilastokeskus. Kuntasektorin Tuntipalkat. ISSN 1457-5590; ◆ Finland. Tilastokeskus. Kuntasektorin Palkat. ISSN 1459-6369; ◆ Finland. Tilastokeskus. Hinta- ja Palkkatiedote. ISSN 0789-2462; ◆ Finland. Tilastokeskus. Valtion Kuukausipalkat. ISSN 0785-8884; ◆ Finland. Tilastokeskus. Yksityisen Sektorin Palkat. ISSN 1797-0776; ◆ Finland. Tilastokeskus. Kuntasektorin Palkat Ammateittain. ISSN 1459-6377; ◆ Finland. Tilastokeskus. Palkkarakenne. ISSN 1457-5973; ◆ Finland. Tilastokeskus. Tyotunnin Kustannus. Tyovoimakustannusindeksi. ISSN 1457-084X; ◆ Finland. Tilastokeskus. Rahalaitokset. ISSN 1795-2050; ◆ Finland. Tilastokeskus. Luottokortit. ISSN 0785-7934; ◆ Finland. Tilastokeskus. Luottokanta. ISSN 1459-5451; ◆ Finland. Tilastokeskus. Rakentaminen ja Asuminen: Vuosikirja. ISSN 0787-572X; ◆ Finland. Tilastokeskus. Tyotapaturmat. ISSN 0789-1180; ◆ Finland. Tilastokeskus. Vaestorakenne ja Vaestonmuutokset Kunnittain. ISSN 1795-1887; ◆ Finland. Tilastokeskus. Perheet. ISSN 0785-8205; ◆ Finland. Tilastokeskus. Ulkomaalaiset ja Siirtolaisuus. ISSN 1239-9663; ◆ Finland. Tilastokeskus. Vaestoennusteet. ISSN 1236-5483; ◆ Finland. Tilastokeskus. Luonnonvarat ja Ymparisto. ISSN 1238-0261; ◆ Finland. Tilastokeskus. Ymparistotilasto. ISSN 0785-0387; ◆ Finland. Tilastokeskus. Suomen Yritykset. ISSN 0788-1738; ◆ Finland. Tilastokeskus. Tieliikenneonnettomuudet. ISSN 0785-6245; ◆ Finland. Tilastokeskus. Oikeustilastollinen Vuosikirja. ISSN 1236-2638; ◆ Finland. Tilastokeskus. Tiede ja Teknologia. ISSN 0785-0719; ◆ Finland. Tilastokeskus. Science and Technology in Finland. ISSN 0785-885X; ◆ Finland. Tilastokeskus. Kansanedustajain Vaalit, Ennakkotilasto. ISSN 0788-9178; ◆ Finland. Tilastokeskus. Europarlamenttivaalit. ISSN 1239-7415; ◆ Finland. Tilastokeskus. Kunnallisvaalit, Ennakkotilasto. ISSN 1235-9777; ◆ Finland. Tilastokeskus. Presidentin Vaalit. ISSN 1237-6779; ◆ Finland. Tilastokeskus. Suomessa Liikkuvat Liikkuvat Kuvat. ISSN 1237-4407; ◆ Finland. Tilastokeskus. Joukkoviestimet. ISSN 1455-9447; ◆ Ammattikalastus Merialueella Vuonna. ISSN 1236-6641; ◆ Finland. Maa- ja Metsatalousministerio. Tietopalvelukeskus. Eurojyva. ISSN 1795-3898; ◆ Finland. Statistics Finland. Energy in Finland. ISSN 1457-0491; ◆ Finland. Tilastokeskus. Rakennus- ja Asuntotuotanto. ISSN 1238-4623; ◆ Finland. Tilastokeskus. Naiset ja Miehet Suomessa. ISSN 1456-2618; ◆ Finland. Tilastokeskus. Kuluttajabarometri Maakunnittain. ISSN 1456-3886; ◆ Finland. Tilastokeskus. Kuluttajabarometri. ISSN 1456-0151; ◆ Finland. Sosiaali- ja Terveysalan Tutkimus- ja Kehittamiskeskus. Ikaantyneiden Sosiaali- ja Terveyspalvelut. ISSN 1459-7071; ◆ Finland. Sosiaali- ja Terveysalan Tutkimus- ja Kehittamiskeskus. Yksityinen Palvelutuotanto Sosiaali- ja Terveydenhuollossa. ISSN 1796-7848; ◆ Finland. Tilastokeskus. Tutkimus- ja Kehittamisrahoitus Valtion Talousarviossa. ISSN 1459-9066; ◆ Finland. Tilastokeskus. Tyovoimatilasto (Monthly Edition). ISSN 0784-7998.
Published by: Tilastokeskus/Statistics Finland, Tyopajakatu 13, Statistics Finland, Helsinki, 00022, Finland. TEL 358-9-17341, FAX 358-9-17342279, viestinta@tilastokeskus.fi.

314 FIN ISSN 1796-0479
FINLAND. TILASTOKESKUS. SUOMEN VIRALLINEN TILASTO. Text in English, Finnish, Swedish. 2005. irreg. **Document type:** *Government.*
Media: Online - full text. **Related titles:** CD-ROM ed.: ISSN 1796-7082; ◆ Print ed.: Finland. Tilastokeskus. Suomen Virallinen Tilasto. ISSN 1795-5165; Seasonal ed(s).: ISSN 1796-8666. 2007; ◆ Series: Metsatilastotiedote (Online). ISSN 1797-3074; ◆ Finland. Tilastokeskus. Maa- ja Metsatalousyritysten Taloustilasto. ISSN 1797-304X; Finland. Tilastokeskus. Financial Accounts (Online). ISSN 1458-8145. 1999. EUR 38 (effective 2008); ISSN 1796-2196. 2006; ISSN 1796-5195. 2006; ISSN 1796-4040. 2006; ISSN 1796-7015. 2006; ISSN 1796-3796. 2006; ISSN 1796-332X. 2006; ISSN 1795-4282. 2004; ISSN 1796-1246; ISSN 1796-3621. 2006; ISSN 1796-3613. 2006; ISSN 1459-9074. 2005; Finland. Statistics Finland. Labour Force Statistics. ISSN 1797-0415. 2007; ISSN 1796-864X. 2007.
Published by: Tilastokeskus/Statistics Finland, Tyopajakatu 13, Statistics Finland, Helsinki, 00022, Finland. TEL 358-9-17341, FAX 358-9-17342279.

FINLAND. TILASTOKESKUS. SUOMEN YRITYKSET/FINLAND. STATISTICS FINLAND. CORPORATE ENTERPRISES AND PERSONAL BUSINESSES IN FINLAND/FINLAND. STATISTIKCENTRALEN. FINLANDS FOERETAG. *see* BUSINESS AND ECONOMICS—Abstracting, Bibliographies, Statistics

FINLAND. TILASTOKESKUS. SUOMESSA LIIKKUVAT LIIKKUVAT KUVAT/FINLAND. STATISTICS FINLAND. MOVING IMAGES IN FINLAND; tilastoja televisio-, elokuva- ja videotarjonnasta ja televisio-ohjelmien viennista. *see* COMMUNICATIONS—Abstracting, Bibliographies, Statistics

314 FIN ISSN 1236-7877
FINLAND. TILASTOKESKUS. SUOMI CD. Text in Finnish. 1992. biennial. stat. **Document type:** *Government.*
Media: CD-ROM.
Indexed: RASB.
Published by: Tilastokeskus/Statistics Finland, Tyopajakatu 13, Statistics Finland, Helsinki, 00022, Finland. TEL 358-9-17341, FAX 358-9-17342279, http://www.stat.fi.

314 FIN ISSN 1795-732X
FINLAND. TILASTOKESKUS. SUOMI LUKUINA. Text in Finnish. 1976. a., latest 2007. **Document type:** *Government.* **Description:** Contains key statistical data about Finland on 25 different statistical topics. International comparison data are also included.
Formerly (until 2005): Finland. Tilastokeskus. Taskutilasto (0357-0363)
Related titles: ◆ German ed.: Finland. Tilastokeskus. Finnland in Zahlen. ISSN 0781-657X; ◆ English ed.: Finland. Tilastokeskus. Finland in Figures. ISSN 0357-0371; ◆ French ed.: Finland. Tilastokeskus. La Finlande en Chiffres. ISSN 0782-7326; ◆ Swedish ed.: Finland. Tilastokeskus. Finland i Siffror. ISSN 0357-4962; Russian ed.: Finland. Tilastokeskus. Finlyandiya v Tsifrakh. ISSN 0358-8998. 1981; Arabic ed.: Finland. Tilastokeskus. Finlanda Bil- Arqam. ISSN 0783-2699. 1986; Spanish ed.: Finland. Tilastokeskus. Finlandia en Cifras. ISSN 0782-5196. 1986.
Published by: Tilastokeskus/Statistics Finland, Tyopajakatu 13, Statistics Finland, Helsinki, 00022, Finland. TEL 358-9-17341, FAX 358-9-17342279, http://www.stat.fi.

FINLAND. TILASTOKESKUS. TASA-ARVOBAROMETRI. *see* SOCIAL SERVICES AND WELFARE—Abstracting, Bibliographies, Statistics

FINLAND. TILASTOKESKUS. TIEDE JA TEKNOLOGIA. *see* SCIENCES: COMPREHENSIVE WORKS

FINLAND. TILASTOKESKUS. TIEDE, TEKNOLOGIA JA TIETOYHTEISKUNTA/FINLAND. STATISTICS FINLAND. SCIENCE, TECHNOLOGY, AND INFORMATION SOCIETY/ FINLAND. STATISTIKCENTRALEN. VETENSKAP, TEKNOLOGI OCH INFORMATIONSSAMHAELLE. *see* SCIENCES: COMPREHENSIVE WORKS

FINLAND. TILASTOKESKUS. TIELIIKENNEONNETTOMUUDET/ FINLAND. STATISTICS FINLAND. ROAD ACCIDENTS IN FINLAND/FINLAND. STATISTIKCENTRALEN. VAEGTRAFIKOLYKOR. *see* TRANSPORTATION—Abstracting, Bibliographies, Statistics

FINLAND. TILASTOKESKUS. TIELIIKENTEEN TAVARANKULJETUSTILASTO/FINLAND. STATISTICS FINLAND. ROAD FREIGHT TRANSPORT/FINLAND. STATISTIKCENTRALEN. VARUTRANSPORTER MED LASTBIL. *see* TRAVEL AND TOURISM—Abstracting, Bibliographies, Statistics

314.71 FIN ISSN 0015-2390
HA1450.5
FINLAND. TILASTOKESKUS. TILASTOKATSAUKSIA/FINLAND. STATISTICS FINLAND. BULLETIN OF STATISTICS/FINLAND. STATISTIKCENTRALEN. STATISTISKA OEVERSIKTER. Variant title: Finland. Tilastokeskus. Tilastokatsaus. Text in English, Finnish, Swedish. 1924. q. charts; stat. **Document type:** *Bulletin, Government.*
Formerly (until 1971): Finland. Tilastokeskus. Tilastokatsauksia/ Tilastollinen Paatoimisto
Related titles: ◆ Series: Finland. Tilastokeskus. Suomen Virallinen Tilasto. ISSN 1795-5165.
Indexed: RASB.
Published by: Tilastokeskus/Statistics Finland, Tyopajakatu 13, Statistics Finland, Helsinki, 00022, Finland. TEL 358-9-17341, FAX 358-9-17342279, http://www.stat.fi. Circ: 2,350 (controlled).

311.4 FIN ISSN 0355-208X
HC340.2.Z9
FINLAND. TILASTOKESKUS. TILASTOLLISIA TIEDONANTOJA/ FINLAND. CENTRAL STATISTICAL OFFICE. STATISTICAL SURVEYS/FINLAND. STATISTIKCENTRALEN. STATISTISKA MEDDELANDEN. Text in English, Finnish, Swedish. 1906. irreg. price varies. back issues avail. **Document type:** *Monographic series, Government.*
Published by: Tilastokeskus/Statistics Finland, Tyopajakatu 13, Statistics Finland, Helsinki, 00022, Finland. TEL 358-9-17341, FAX 358-9-17342279, http://www.stat.fi.

FINLAND. TILASTOKESKUS. TUKKU- JA VAHITTAISKAUPPA/ FINLAND. STATISTICS FINLAND. WHOLESALE AND RETAIL TRADE/FINLAND. STATISTIKCENTRALEN. PARTI- OCH DETALJHANDELN. *see* BUSINESS AND ECONOMICS—Abstracting, Bibliographies, Statistics

FINLAND. TILASTOKESKUS. TULO- JA VARALLISUUSTILASTO/ FINLAND. STATISTICS FINLAND. STATISTICS OF INCOME AND PROPERTY/FINLAND. STATISTIKCENTRALEN. INKOMST- OCH FOERMOEGENHETSTATISTIK. *see* BUSINESS AND ECONOMICS—Abstracting, Bibliographies, Statistics

FINLAND. TILASTOKESKUS. TULONJAKOTILASTO/FINLAND. STATISTICS FINLAND. INCOME DISTRIBUTION STATISTICS/ FINLAND. STATISTIKCENTRALEN. INKOMSTFOERDELNINGSSTATISTIK. *see* BUSINESS AND ECONOMICS—Abstracting, Bibliographies, Statistics

FINLAND. TILASTOKESKUS. TUOTTAJAHINTAINDEKSIT/FINLAND. STATISTICS FINLAND. PRODUCER PRICE INDICES/FINLAND. STATISTIKCENTRALEN. PRODUCENTPRISINDEX. *see* BUSINESS AND ECONOMICS—Abstracting, Bibliographies, Statistics

314 FIN ISSN 0355-2071
HC337.F5
FINLAND. TILASTOKESKUS. TUTKIMUKSIA/FINLAND. STATISTICS FINLAND. STUDIES/FINLAND. STATISTIKCENTRALEN. UNDERSOEKNINGAR. Text in Finnish, English, Swedish. 1966. irreg. price varies. **Document type:** *Monographic series, Government.*
Formerly (until 1971): Tilastollisen Paatoimiston Tutkimuksia (0532-9884)
Published by: Tilastokeskus/Statistics Finland, Tyopajakatu 13, Statistics Finland, Helsinki, 00022, Finland. TEL 358-9-17341, FAX 358-9-17342279, http://www.stat.fi.

FINLAND. TILASTOKESKUS. TUTKIMUS- JA KEHITTAMISRAHOITUS VALTION TALOUSARVIOSSA/FINLAND. STATISTICS FINLAND. GOVERNMENT R&D FUNDING IN THE STATE BUDGET/ FINLAND. STATISTIKCENTRALEN. FORSKNINGS- OCH UTVECKLINGSFINANSIERING I STATSBUDGETEN. *see* BUSINESS AND ECONOMICS—Abstracting, Bibliographies, Statistics

FINLAND. TILASTOKESKUS. TUTKIMUS- JA KEHITTAMISTOIMINTA SUOMESSA/FINLAND. CENTRAL STATISTICAL OFFICE. RESEARCH ACTIVITY/FINLAND. STATISTIKCENTRALEN. FORSKNINGSVERKSAMHETEN. *see* SCIENCES: COMPREHENSIVE WORKS—Abstracting, Bibliographies, Statistics

FINLAND. TILASTOKESKUS. TYOSSAKAYNTI/FINAND. STATISTICS FINLAND. EMPLOYMENT STATISTICS/FINLAND. STATISTIKCENTRALEN. SYSSELSAETTNINGSSTATISTIK. *see* BUSINESS AND ECONOMICS—Abstracting, Bibliographies, Statistics

FINLAND. TILASTOKESKUS. TYOTAISTELUT (NELJANNESVUOSITILASTO). *see* BUSINESS AND ECONOMICS—Abstracting, Bibliographies, Statistics

FINLAND. TILASTOKESKUS. TYOTAPATURMAT/FINLAND. STATISTICS FINLAND. OCCUPATIONAL ACCIDENT STATISTICS/ FINLAND. STATISTIKCENTRALEN. OLYCKSFALL I ARBETE. *see* BUSINESS AND ECONOMICS—Abstracting, Bibliographies, Statistics

FINLAND. TILASTOKESKUS. TYOTUNNIN KUSTANNUS. TYOVOIMAKUSTANNUSINDEKSI/FINLAND. STATISTICS FINLAND. COST OF HOUR WORKED. LABOUR COST INDEX/ FINLAND. STATISTIKCENTRALEN. ARBETSKRAFTSKOSTNADSINDEX. *see* BUSINESS AND ECONOMICS—Abstracting, Bibliographies, Statistics

FINLAND. TILASTOKESKUS. TYOVOIMATILASTO (ANNUAL EDITION)/FINLAND. STATISTICS FINLAND. LABOUR FORCE STATISTICS/FINLAND. STATISTIKCENTRALEN. ARBETSKRAFTSSTATISTIK. *see* BUSINESS AND ECONOMICS—Abstracting, Bibliographies, Statistics

FINLAND. TILASTOKESKUS. TYOVOIMATILASTO (MONTHLY EDITION)/FINLAND. STATISTIKCENTRALEN. ARBETSKRAFTSSTATISTIK. *see* BUSINESS AND ECONOMICS—Abstracting, Bibliographies, Statistics

FINLAND. TILASTOKESKUS. ULKOMAALAISET JA SIIRTOLAISUUS/ FINLAND. STATISTICS FINLAND. ALIENS AND INTERNATIONAL MIGRATION. *see* POPULATION STUDIES—Abstracting, Bibliographies, Statistics

FINLAND. TILASTOKESKUS. VAESTOENNUSTEET/FINLAND. STATISTICS FINLAND. POPULATION PROJECTION/FINLAND. STATISTIKCENTRALEN. BEFOLKNINGSPROGNOSER. *see* POPULATION STUDIES—Abstracting, Bibliographies, Statistics

FINLAND. TILASTOKESKUS. VAESTON KOULUTUSRAKENNE KUNNITTAIN. *see* EDUCATION—Abstracting, Bibliographies, Statistics

FINLAND. TILASTOKESKUS. VAESTONMUUTOKSET/FINLAND. STATISTICS FINLAND. VITAL STATISTICS/FINLAND. STATISTIKCENTRALEN. BEFOLKNINGSROERELSEN. *see* POPULATION STUDIES—Abstracting, Bibliographies, Statistics

FINLAND. TILASTOKESKUS. VAESTORAKENNE JA VAESTONMUUTOKSET KUNNITTAIN/FINLAND. STATISTICS FINLAND. POPULATION STRUCTURE AND VITAL STATISTICS BY MUNICIPALITY/FINLAND. STATISTIKCENTRALEN. BEFOLKNINGENS SAMMANSAETTNING OCH BEFOLKNINGSFOERAENDRINGAR KOMMUNVIS. *see* POPULATION STUDIES—Abstracting, Bibliographies, Statistics

FINLAND. TILASTOKESKUS. VALTION KUUKAUSIPALKAT/FINLAND. STATISTIKCENTRALEN. MAANADSLOENER INOM STATEN. *see* BUSINESS AND ECONOMICS—Abstracting, Bibliographies, Statistics

FINLAND. TILASTOKESKUS. VUOKRATILASTO/FINLAND. STATISTICS FINLAND. RENTS/FINLAND. STATISTIKCENTRALEN. HYRESSTATISTIK. *see* HOUSING AND URBAN PLANNING—Abstracting, Bibliographies, Statistics

FINLAND. TILASTOKESKUS. YKSITYISEN SEKTORIN PALKAT/ FINLAND. STATISTIKCENTRALEN. LOENER INOM DEN PRIVATA SEKTORN. *see* BUSINESS AND ECONOMICS—Abstracting, Bibliographies, Statistics

FINLAND. TILASTOKESKUS. YMPARISTOTILASTO/FINLAND. STATISTICS FINLAND. ENVIRONMENT STATISTICS. *see* ENVIRONMENTAL STUDIES—Abstracting, Bibliographies, Statistics

S

FINLAND. TILASTOKESKUS. YRITYSTEN KANSAINVALISTYMINEN/ FINLAND. STATISTICS FINLAND. INTERNATIONALISATION OF ENTERPRISES/FINLAND. STATISTIKCENTRALEN. FOERETAGENS INTERNATIONALISERING. *see* BUSINESS AND ECONOMICS—Abstracting, Bibliographies, Statistics

FINLAND TILASTOKESKUS. YRITYSTEN RAKENTEET - TILASTOPALVELU/FINLAND. STATISTICS FINLAND. BUSINESS ENTERPRISES - NET RESULTS AND BALANCE SHEETS/ FINLAND. STATISTIKCENTRALEN. FOERETAGSVERKSAMHETENS RESULTAT OCH BALANSRAEKNIG. *see* BUSINESS AND ECONOMICS—Abstracting, Bibliographies, Statistics

FINLAND. TULLIHALLITUS. TAVAROIDEN ULKOMAANKAUPPA/ FINLAND. NATIONAL BOARD OF CUSTOMS. FOREIGN TRADE OF GOODS/FINLAND. TULLSTYRELSEN. UTRIKESHANDEL MED VAROR. *see* BUSINESS AND ECONOMICS—Abstracting, Bibliographies, Statistics

314 FIN ISSN 0782-7326
FINLAND. TILASTOKESKUS. LA FINLANDE EN CHIFFRES. Text in French. 1985. a. **Document type:** *Government.*
Related titles: Online - full text ed.; ◆ English ed.: Finland. Tilastokeskus. Finland in Figures. ISSN 0357-0371; ◆ Swedish ed.: Finland. Tilastokeskus. Finland i Siffror. ISSN 0357-4962; ◆ Finnish ed.: Finland. Tilastokeskus. Suomi Lukuina. ISSN 1795-732X; ◆ German ed.: Finland. Tilastokeskus. Finnland in Zahlen. ISSN 0781-657X; Russian ed.: Finland. Tilastokeskus. Finlyandiya v Tsifrakh. ISSN 0358-8998. 1981; Spanish ed.: Finland. Tilastokeskus. Finlandia en Cifras. ISSN 0782-5196. 1986; Arabic ed.: Finland. Tilastokeskus. Finlanda Bil- Arqam. ISSN 0783-2699. 1986.
Published by: Tilastokeskus/Statistics Finland, Tyopajakatu 13, Statistics Finland, Helsinki, 00022, Finland. TEL 358-9-17341, FAX 358-9-17342279.

FIRE COMMISSIONER'S STATISTICAL REPORT. *see* FIRE PREVENTION

FIRE LOSSES IN GOVERNMENT OF CANADA PROPERTIES. REPORT/PERTES DUES A L'INCENDIE DE BIENS IMMOBILIERS DE L'ADMINISTRATION FEDERALE. *see* FIRE PREVENTION—Abstracting, Bibliographies, Statistics

FISHERIES. YEARBOOK/FISCHEREI. JAHRBUCH/PECHE. ANNUAIRE. *see* FISH AND FISHERIES—Abstracting, Bibliographies, Statistics

FISKEOPDRETT/FISH FARMING. *see* FISH AND FISHERIES—Abstracting, Bibliographies, Statistics

310 DEU
FLENSBURGER ZAHLENSPIEGEL (YEAR). Text in German. 1951. a. **Document type:** *Government.* **Description:** Contains current and historical information on the city of Flensburg.
Published by: Stadt Flensburg, Amt fuer Stadtentwicklung, Postfach 2742, Flensburg, 24917, Germany. TEL 49-461-852208, FAX 49-461-852973. Circ: 500.

FLORIDA CITIES & COUNTIES GRAPHIC PERFORMANCE ANALYSIS. *see* PUBLIC ADMINISTRATION—Abstracting, Bibliographies, Statistics

FLORIDA LIME ADMINISTRATIVE COMMITTEE. SHIPMENTS REPORT. *see* AGRICULTURE—Abstracting, Bibliographies, Statistics

FLORIDA STATISTICAL ABSTRACT. *see* BUSINESS AND ECONOMICS—Abstracting, Bibliographies, Statistics

FLORIDA VITAL STATISTICS. *see* POPULATION STUDIES—Abstracting, Bibliographies, Statistics

519.23 SGP ISSN 0219-4775
Q380 CODEN: FNLLAW
➤ **FLUCTUATION AND NOISE LETTERS**; an interdisciplinary scientific journal on random processes in physical, biological and technological systems. Abbreviated title: F N L. Text in English. 2001. q. SGD 1,019, USD 640, EUR 516 combined subscription to institutions (print & online eds.) (effective 2012). adv. back issues avail. **Document type:** *Journal, Academic/Scholarly.* **Description:** Contains articles on random fluctuations, including: Noise enhanced phenomena including stochastic resonance; 1/f noise; shot noise; fluctuation-dissipation; ion channels; single molecules; neural systems; quantum fluctuations etc.
Related titles: Online - full text ed.: ISSN 1793-6780. SGD 926, USD 582, EUR 469 to institutions (effective 2012).
Indexed: A01, A02, A03, A08, A22, A28, APA, BrCerAb, C&ISA, C23, CA, CA/WCA, CCMJ, CIA, CMCI, CerAb, CivEngAb, CorrAb, CurCont, E&CAJ, E01, E11, EEA, EMA, ESPM, EnvEAb, H15, Inspec, M&TEA, M09, MBF, METADEX, MSN, MathR, S&VD, S01, SCI, SCOPUS, SolStAb, T02, T04, W07, WAA.
—BLDSC (3959.654000), IE, Linda Hall. **CCC.**
Published by: World Scientific Publishing Co. Pte. Ltd., 5 Toh Tuck Link, Singapore, 596224, Singapore. TEL 65-6466-5775, FAX 65-6467-7667, wspc@wspc.com.sg, http://www.worldscientific.com. Ed. P V E McClintock. **Dist. by:** World Scientific Publishing Co., Inc., 27 Warren St, Ste 401-402, Hackensack, NJ 07601. TEL 201-487-9655, 800-227-7562, FAX 201-487-9656, 888-977-2665, wspc@wspc.com; World Scientific Publishing Ltd., 57 Shelton St, London WC2H 9HE, United Kingdom. TEL 44-207-8360888, FAX 44-207-8362020, sales@wspc.co.uk.

➤ **FOOD AND AGRICULTURE ORGANIZATION OF THE UNITED NATIONS. ASIA AND THE PACIFIC COMMISSION ON AGRICULTURAL STATISTICS. PERIODIC REPORT.** *see* AGRICULTURE—Abstracting, Bibliographies, Statistics

➤ **FOREIGN PRODUCTION, SUPPLY AND DISTRIBUTION OF AGRICULTURAL COMMODITIES.** *see* AGRICULTURE—Abstracting, Bibliographies, Statistics

➤ **FOREIGN TRADE STATISTICS OF AFRICA. SERIES A: DIRECTION OF TRADE.** *see* BUSINESS AND ECONOMICS—Abstracting, Bibliographies, Statistics

➤ **FOREIGN TRADE STATISTICS OF ASIA AND THE PACIFIC.** *see* BUSINESS AND ECONOMICS—Abstracting, Bibliographies, Statistics

➤ **FOREIGN TRADE STATISTICS OF THE PHILIPPINES.** *see* BUSINESS AND ECONOMICS—Abstracting, Bibliographies, Statistics

➤ **FRANCE. DIRECTION DE L'ANIMATION DE LA RECHERCHE, DES ETUDES ET DES STATISTIQUES. DOSSIERS.** *see* BUSINESS AND ECONOMICS—Abstracting, Bibliographies, Statistics

➤ **FRANCE. DIRECTION GENERALE DE L'AVIATION CIVILE. BULLETIN STATISTIQUE.** *see* AERONAUTICS AND SPACE FLIGHT—Abstracting, Bibliographies, Statistics

314.4 FRA ISSN 0151-9514
FRANCE. INSTITUT NATIONAL DE LA STATISTIQUE ET DES ETUDES ECONOMIQUES. COURRIER DES STATISTIQUES. Text in French. 1977. 4/yr. **Document type:** *Bulletin, Government.* **Description:** Presents a global image of the life of the public statistical system.
Related titles: Online - full text ed.: ISSN 2107-0903. 200?; English ed.: ISSN 1259-475X. 1995.
Indexed: FR.
Published by: Institut National de la Statistique et des Etudes Economiques/National Institute for Statistics and Economic Studies, 18 bd. Adolphe Pinard, Paris, Cedex 14 75675, France. TEL 33-1-41175050, inseeactualites@insee.fr.

FRANCE. MINISTERE DE L'AGRICULTURE ET DE LA PECHE. AGRESTE; la statistique agricole. *see* AGRICULTURE—Abstracting, Bibliographies, Statistics

FRANCE. MINISTERE DE L'AGRICULTURE ET DE LA PECHE. AGRESTE. LES DOSSIERS. *see* AGRICULTURE—Abstracting, Bibliographies, Statistics

FRANCE. MINISTERE DE L'AGRICULTURE ET DE LA PECHE. GRAPH-AGRI; annuaire de graphiques agricoles. *see* AGRICULTURE—Agricultural Economics

FRANCE. MINISTERE DE L'EDUCATION NATIONALE, DE L'ENSEIGNEMENT SUPERIEUR ET DE LA RECHERCHE. DIRECTION DE L'EVALUATION, DE LA PROSPECTIVE ET DE LA PERFORMANCE. NOTE D'INFORMATION ENSEIGNEMENT SUPERIEUR ET RECHERCHE. *see* EDUCATION—Abstracting, Bibliographies, Statistics

FRANCE. MINISTERE DE L'EQUIPEMENT, DES TRANSPORTS, DU LOGEMENT ET DU TOURISME. DONNEES DETAILLEES DU S E S. CONSTRUCTION. *see* HOUSING AND URBAN PLANNING—Abstracting, Bibliographies, Statistics

314 DEU
FRANKFURT AM MAIN. BUERGERAMT, STATISTIK UND WAHLEN. STATISTISCHES JAHRBUCH. Text in German. 1951. a. **Document type:** *Yearbook, Government.* **Description:** Covers complete statistical information of the town. Includes population, economy, housing, public health, finance, culture and elections.
Former titles: Frankfurt am Main. Amt fuer Statistik, Wahlen und Einwohnerwesen. Statistisches Jahrbuch; Frankfurt am Main. Statistisches Amt und Wahlamt. Statistisches Jahrbuch (0071-9218)
Published by: Stadt Frankfurt am Main, Buergeramt, Statistik, Wahlen, Zeil 3, Frankfurt Am Main, 60313, Germany. TEL 49-69-21230600, FAX 49-69-21230898, infoservice.statistik@stadt-frankfurt.de, http://www.frankfurt.de/sis/rathaus.html. Circ: 600.

310 DEU ISSN 0177-7351
FRANKFURTER STATISTISCHE BERICHTE. Text in German. 1936. q. **Document type:** *Government.* **Description:** Covers complete statistics of the town: vital, population, economical, financial, public health, cultural, housing and more.
Published by: Stadt Frankfurt am Main, Buergeramt, Statistik, Wahlen, Zeil 3, Frankfurt Am Main, 60313, Germany. TEL 49-69-21230600, FAX 49-69-21230898, infoservice.statistik@stadt-frankfurt.de, http://www.frankfurt.de/sis/rathaus.html. Circ: 600.

FRESH FACTS. *see* GARDENING AND HORTICULTURE—Abstracting, Bibliographies, Statistics

FUEL AND ENERGY CONSUMPTION IN THE CZECH REPUBLIC (YEAR). *see* ENERGY—Abstracting, Bibliographies, Statistics

310 DEU
FULDA. STATISTISCHER BERICHT. Text in German. 1974. a. free.
Published by: Magistrat der Stadt Fulda, Abt 103, Postfach 1020, Fulda, 36010, Germany. TEL 0661-102198, FAX 0661-79153, TELEX 6619707-STDFD. Circ: 1,000.

310 ITA ISSN 2037-7738
G R A S P A WORKING PAPERS. (Gruppo di Ricerca per le Applicazioni della Statistica ai Problemi Ambientali) Text in English. 1999. irreg. **Document type:** *Journal, Trade.*
Media: Online - full text.
Published by: Gruppo di Ricerca per le Applicazioni della Statistica ai Problemi Ambientali

GA-CROP-WEATHER, STATE GEORGIA CROP WEATHER. *see* AGRICULTURE—Abstracting, Bibliographies, Statistics

310 GAB
GABON. DIRECTION GENERALE DE L'ECONOMIE. BULLETIN MENSUEL DE STATISTIQUE. Text in French. m.
Former titles: Gabon. Direction de la Statistique et des Etudes Economique. Bulletin Mensuel de Statistique; Gabon. Service National de la Statistique. Bulletin Mensuel de Statistique
Published by: Direction de la Statistique et des Etudes Economiques, BP 179, Libreville, Gabon.

GAMBIA. CENTRAL STATISTICS DEPARTMENT. EDUCATION STATISTICS. *see* EDUCATION—Abstracting, Bibliographies, Statistics

GAMBIA. CENTRAL STATISTICS DEPARTMENT. MONTHLY SUMMARY OF EXTERNAL TRADE STATISTICS. *see* BUSINESS AND ECONOMICS—Abstracting, Bibliographies, Statistics

GAMBIA. CENTRAL STATISTICS DEPARTMENT. QUARTERLY SURVEY OF EMPLOYMENT AND EARNINGS. *see* BUSINESS AND ECONOMICS—Abstracting, Bibliographies, Statistics

GAMBIA. CENTRAL STATISTICS DEPARTMENT. SUMMARY OF TOURIST STATISTICS. *see* TRAVEL AND TOURISM—Abstracting, Bibliographies, Statistics

GAMBIA. CENTRAL STATISTICS DEPARTMENT. TOURIST STATISTICS. *see* TRAVEL AND TOURISM—Abstracting, Bibliographies, Statistics

304.6 GMB
GAMBIA. MINISTRY OF TRADE, INDUSTRY & EMPLOYMENT. Text in English. 1992 (no.2). irreg. **Document type:** *Monographic series, Government.*
Published by: Ministry of Trade, Industry & Employment, Central Bank Bldg., Buckle St., Banjul, Gambia.

GARTNERI - REGNSKABSSTATISTIK/HORTICULTURAL ACCOUNTS STATISTICS. *see* AGRICULTURE—Abstracting, Bibliographies, Statistics

GAS STATISTICS AUSTRALIA. *see* PETROLEUM AND GAS—Abstracting, Bibliographies, Statistics

GELSENKIRCHEN IM SPIEGEL DER STATISTIK. *see* PUBLIC ADMINISTRATION—Abstracting, Bibliographies, Statistics

314 NLD ISSN 1871-4854
GEMEENTE AMSTERDAM. DIENST ONDERZOEK EN STATISTIEK. KERNCIJFERS AMSTERDAM. Text in Dutch. 1991. a.
Published by: Gemeente Amsterdam, Dienst Onderzoek en Statistiek, Postbus 658, Amsterdam, 1000 AR, Netherlands. TEL 31-20-2510333, FAX 31-20-2510444, algemeen@os.amsterdam.nl.

GEMEENTE AMSTERDAM. DIENST ONDERZOEK EN STATISTIEK. METROPOOLREGIO AMSTERDAM IN BEELD. *see* POPULATION STUDIES

▼ **GEMEENTE AMSTERDAM. DIENST ONDERZOEK EN STATISTIEK. METROPOOLREGIO AMSTERDAM IN CIJFERS.** *see* BUSINESS AND ECONOMICS

GEMEINDEFREIEN GEBIETE BAYERNS. *see* PUBLIC ADMINISTRATION—Abstracting, Bibliographies, Statistics

314 DEU
GEMEINDEN NORDRHEIN-WESTFALENS; Informationen aus der amtlichen Statistik. Text in German. 1976. a. EUR 10.50 (effective 2006). back issues avail. **Document type:** *Journal, Government.*
Related titles: Diskette ed.
Published by: Information und Technik Nordrhein-Westfalen, Mauerstr 51, Duesseldorf, 40476, Germany. TEL 49-211-944901, FAX 49-211-442006, poststelle@lds.nrw.de, http://www.it.nrw.de. Circ: 1,200.

GENERAL SOCIAL SURVEYS. *see* SOCIOLOGY—Abstracting, Bibliographies, Statistics

314 CHE ISSN 1423-1387
GENEVE. OFFICE CANTONAL DE LA STATISTIQUE. BULLETIN STATISTIQUE MENSUEL. Text in French. 1993. m. **Document type:** *Journal, Government.*
Formed by the merger of (1955-1993): Chambre de Commerce et d'Industrie de Geneve. Informations Statistiques (1423-1468); Which was formerly (until 1978): Chambre de Commerce de Geneve. Bulletin Statistique et Communications (1423-1433); (1963-1993): Geneve. Departement de l'Economie Publique. Service Contonal de Statistique. Bulletin Statistique (1013-5782); Which was formerly (until 1977): Informations Statistiques Geneve (1423-1425)
Published by: Geneve. Office Cantonal de la Statistique, CP 1735, Geneva 26, 1211, Switzerland. TEL 41-22-327-85-00, FAX 41-22-327-85-10, statistique@etat.ge.ch.

GEOGRAPHICAL CODE OF GREECE; by eparchy, municipality, commune and locality. *see* PUBLIC ADMINISTRATION—Abstracting, Bibliographies, Statistics

GEOGRAPHICAL MOBILITY. *see* POPULATION STUDIES—Abstracting, Bibliographies, Statistics

GEORGIA CITIES & COUNTIES GRAPHIC PERFORMANCE ANALYSIS. *see* PUBLIC ADMINISTRATION—Abstracting, Bibliographies, Statistics

317.58 USA ISSN 1044-0976
HA321
THE GEORGIA COUNTY GUIDE. Text in English. 1981. a. USD 15 (effective 2000). charts; maps; stat. back issues avail. **Description:** Covers demographic and economic variables for all counties in Georgia. Includes information on education, agriculture, and a broad range of other topics.
Related titles: Diskette ed.: USD 90.
Published by: University of Georgia, Cooperative Extension Service, Lumpkin House, Athens, GA 30602-4356. sboatri@uga.edu, http://www.agecon.uga.edu/~countyguide/. Eds. D C Bachtel, Susan R Boatright. Circ: 4,000. **Subscr. to:** AG Business Office, 203 Conner Hall, University of Georgia, Athens, GA 30602-7506. TEL 706-542-8938, FAX 706-542-8934.

GEORGIA STATISTICAL ABSTRACT. *see* BUSINESS AND ECONOMICS—Abstracting, Bibliographies, Statistics

GERMANY. STATISTISCHES BUNDESAMT. FACHSERIE 16: VERDIENSTE UND ARBEITSKOSTEN, REIHE 3: ARBEITERVERDIENSTE IM HANDWERK. *see* BUSINESS AND ECONOMICS—Abstracting, Bibliographies, Statistics

GERMANY. STATISTISCHES BUNDESAMT. WARENVERZEICHNIS FUER DIE AUSSENHANDELSSTATISTIK. *see* BUSINESS AND ECONOMICS—Abstracting, Bibliographies, Statistics

GESAMTSTATISTIK DER KRAFTFAHRTVERSICHERUNG. *see* INSURANCE—Abstracting, Bibliographies, Statistics

GEZONDHEID EN ZORG IN CIJFERS. *see* MEDICAL SCIENCES—Abstracting, Bibliographies, Statistics

GHANA INDUSTRIAL CENSUS. DIRECTORY OF INDUSTRIAL ESTABLISHMENTS. *see* BUSINESS AND ECONOMICS—Abstracting, Bibliographies, Statistics

GHANA INDUSTRIAL CENSUS. PHASE II REPORT. *see* BUSINESS AND ECONOMICS—Abstracting, Bibliographies, Statistics

GHANA LIVING STANDARDS SURVEY. ROUND REPORT. *see* BUSINESS AND ECONOMICS—Abstracting, Bibliographies, Statistics

GHANA LIVING STANDARDS SURVEY. RURAL COMMUNITIES IN GHANA. *see* BUSINESS AND ECONOMICS—Abstracting, Bibliographies, Statistics

GHANA. STATISTICAL SERVICE. ECONOMIC SURVEY. *see* BUSINESS AND ECONOMICS—Abstracting, Bibliographies, Statistics

GHANA. STATISTICAL SERVICE. MOTOR VEHICLE REGISTRATION. *see* TRANSPORTATION—Abstracting, Bibliographies, Statistics

GHANA. STATISTICAL SERVICE. POPULATION CENSUS - DEMOGRAPHIC AND ECONOMIC CHARACTERISTICS. *see* POPULATION STUDIES—Abstracting, Bibliographies, Statistics

GHANA. STATISTICAL SERVICE. POPULATION CENSUS - SPECIAL REPORT ON LOCALITIES. *see* POPULATION STUDIES—Abstracting, Bibliographies, Statistics

316 GHA ISSN 0855-0662
HC1060.A1
GHANA. STATISTICAL SERVICE. QUARTERLY DIGEST OF STATISTICS. Text in English. 1952. q. USD 60. **Document type:** *Government.*
Formerly: Ghana. Central Bureau of Statistics. Quarterly Digest of Statistics (0435-8864)
Published by: Statistical Service, Information Section, PO Box 1098, Accra, Ghana. TEL 233-21-663578, FAX 233-21-667069.

GOBERNO DA REGIAO ADMINISTRATIVA ESPECIAL DE MACAU. DIRECCAO DOS SERVICOS DE ESTATISTICA E CENSOS. CONTAS DO SECTOR PUBLICO/GOVERNMENT OF MACAO SPECIAL ADMINISTRATIVE REGION. STATISTICS AND CENSUS SERVICE. PUBLIC SECTOR ACCOUNTS. *see* BUSINESS AND ECONOMICS—Abstracting, Bibliographies, Statistics

310 SWE ISSN 0072-5110
GOETEBORGS UNIVERSITET. STATISTISKA INSTITUTIONEN. SKRIFTSERIE. PUBLICATIONS. Text in English, Swedish. 1954. irreg. price varies. back issues avail. **Document type:** *Monographic series, Academic/Scholarly.*
Published by: (Goeteborgs Universitet, Statistiska Institutionen), Almqvist & Wiksell International, P O Box 7634, Stockholm, 10394, Sweden. FAX 46-8-24-25-43. Ed. Sture Holm.

GOETTINGER STATISTIK. *see* PUBLIC ADMINISTRATION—Abstracting, Bibliographies, Statistics

318.1 BRA
GOIAS, BRAZIL. SECRETARIA DO PLANEJAMENTO E COORDENACAO. BOLETIM ESTADISTICO. Text in Portuguese. irreg.?.
Continues: Goias, Brazil. Departamento Estadual de Estatistica. Boletim Estatistico
Published by: Secretaria do Planejamento e Coordenacao, Goiania, Brazil.

310 MAC ISSN 0870-5615
HA1950.M3
GOVERNO DA REGIAO ADMINISTRATIVA ESPECIAL DE MACAU. DIRECCAO DOS SERVICOS DE ESTATISTICA E CENSOS. ANUARIO ESTATISTICO/MACAO. CENSUS AND STATISTICS DEPARTMENT. YEARBOOK OF STATISTICS. Key Title: Anuario Estadistico de Macau. Text in Chinese, English, Portuguese. 1932. a. free. **Document type:** *Government.*
Published by: Direccao dos Servicos de Estatistica e Censos, Alameda Dr Carlos d'Assumcao 411-417, Macao, Macau. TEL 853-3995311, FAX 853-307825, info@dsec.gov.mo, http://www.dsec.gov.mo.

GOVERNO DA REGIAO ADMINISTRATIVA ESPECIAL DE MACAU. DIRECCAO DOS SERVICOS DE ESTATISTICA E CENSOS. BALANCO ENERGETICO/GOVERNMENT OF MACAO SPECIAL ADMINISTRATIVE REGION. STATISTICS AND CENSUS SERVICE. BALANCE OF ENERGY. *see* ENERGY—Abstracting, Bibliographies, Statistics

314 MAC
GOVERNO DA REGIAO ADMINISTRATIVA ESPECIAL DE MACAU. DIRECCAO DOS SERVICOS DE ESTATISTICA E CENSOS. BOLETIM MENSAL DE ESTATISTICA/GOVERNMENT OF MACAO SPECIAL ADMINISTRATIVE REGION. STATISTICS AND CENSUS SERVICE. MONTHLY BULLETIN OF STATISTICS. Text in Chinese, Portuguese, English. 1976. m. free. **Document type:** *Government.*
Former titles: Macao. Direccao dos Servicos de Estatistica e Censos. Boletim Mensal (0872-461X); (until 1986): Macao. Direccao dos Servicos de Estatistica e Censos. Boletim Mensal de Estatistica (0870-5569)
Published by: Direccao dos Servicos de Estatistica e Censos, Alameda Dr Carlos d'Assumcao 411-417, Macao, Macau. TEL 853-3995311, FAX 853-307825, info@dsec.gov.mo, http://www.dsec.gov.mo.

GOVERNO DA REGIAO ADMINISTRATIVA ESPECIAL DE MACAU. DIRECCAO DOS SERVICOS DE ESTATISTICA E CENSOS. ESTATISTICAS DO COMERCIO EXTERNO/GOVERNMENT OF MACAO SPECIAL ADMINISTRATIVE REGION. STATISTICS AND CENSUS SERVICE EXTERNAL TRADE STATISTICS. *see* BUSINESS AND ECONOMICS—Abstracting, Bibliographies, Statistics

GOVERNO DA REGIAO ADMINISTRATIVA ESPECIAL DE MACAU. DIRECCAO DOS SERVICOS DE ESTATISTICA E CENSOS. INQUERITO AOS ORCAMENTOS FAMILIARES/GOVERNMENT OF MACAO SPECIAL ADMINISTRATIVE REGION. STATISTICS AND CENSUS SERVICE. HOUSEHOLD BUDGET SURVEY. *see* BUSINESS AND ECONOMICS—Abstracting, Bibliographies, Statistics

GOVERNO DA REGIAO ADMINISTRATIVA ESPECIAL DE MACAU. DIRECCAO DOS SERVICOS DE ESTATISTICA E CENSOS. INQUERITO AOS RESTAURANTES E SIMILARES/GOVERNMENT OF MACAO SPECIAL ADMINISTRATIVE REGION. STATISTICS AND CENSUS SERVICE. RESTAURANTS AND SIMILAR ESTABLISHMENTS SURVEY. *see* HOTELS AND RESTAURANTS—Abstracting, Bibliographies, Statistics

GOVERNO DA REGIAO ADMINISTRATIVA ESPECIAL DE MACAU. DIRECCAO DOS SERVICOS DE ESTATISTICA E CENSOS. REVISAO DO PERIODO BASE DO INDICE DE PRECOS NO CONSUMIDOR/GOVERNMENT OF MACAO SPACIAL ADMINISTRATIVE REGION. STATISTICS AND CENSUS SERVICE. REBASING OF CONSUMER PRICE INDEX. *see* BUSINESS AND ECONOMICS—Abstracting, Bibliographies, Statistics

GRADUATE MARKET TRENDS. *see* OCCUPATIONS AND CAREERS—Abstracting, Bibliographies, Statistics

GRANDE AREA METROPOLITANA DO PORTO. *see* BUSINESS AND ECONOMICS—Abstracting, Bibliographies, Statistics

GRANT ASSISTANCE PROGRAM. FISCAL YEAR STATISTICAL SUMMARIES. *see* TRANSPORTATION—Abstracting, Bibliographies, Statistics

GREAT BRITAIN. CIVIL AVIATION AUTHORITY. ANNUAL PUNCTUALITY STATISTICS - FULL AND SUMMARY ANALYSIS (YEAR). *see* TRANSPORTATION—Abstracting, Bibliographies, Statistics

GREAT BRITAIN. CIVIL AVIATION AUTHORITY. PUNCTUALITY STATISTICS HEATHROW, GATWICK, MANCHESTER, BIRMINGHAM, LUTON AND STANSTEAD - FULL ANALYSIS. *see* TRANSPORTATION—Abstracting, Bibliographies, Statistics

GREAT BRITAIN. CIVIL AVIATION AUTHORITY. PUNCTUALITY STATISTICS HEATHROW, GATWICK, MANCHESTER, BIRMINGHAM, LUTON AND STANSTEAD - SUMMARY ANALYSIS. *see* TRANSPORTATION—Abstracting, Bibliographies, Statistics

GREAT BRITAIN. CIVIL AVIATION AUTHORITY. U.K. AIRLINES ANNUAL OPERATING, TRAFFIC & FINANCIAL STATISTICS. *see* TRANSPORTATION—Abstracting, Bibliographies, Statistics

GREAT BRITAIN. CIVIL AVIATION AUTHORITY. U.K. AIRLINES MONTHLY OPERATING & TRAFFIC STATISTICS. *see* TRANSPORTATION—Abstracting, Bibliographies, Statistics

GREAT BRITAIN. CIVIL AVIATION AUTHORITY. U.K. AIRPORTS ANNUAL STATEMENTS OF MOVEMENTS, PASSENGERS AND CARGO (YEAR). *see* TRANSPORTATION—Abstracting, Bibliographies, Statistics

GREAT BRITAIN. CIVIL AVIATION AUTHORITY. U.K. AIRPORTS MONTHLY STATEMENTS OF MOVEMENTS, PASSENGERS AND CARGO. *see* TRANSPORTATION—Abstracting, Bibliographies, Statistics

GREAT BRITAIN. DEPARTMENT FOR BUSINESS, INNOVATION AND SKILLS. STATISTICAL FIRST RELEASE. *see* EDUCATION—Abstracting, Bibliographies, Statistics

GREAT BRITAIN. DEPARTMENT OF COMMUNITIES AND LOCAL GOVERNMENT. COMMERCIAL AND INDUSTRIAL FLOORSPACE AND RATEABLE VALUE STATISTICS (ONLINE). *see* HOUSING AND URBAN PLANNING—Abstracting, Bibliographies, Statistics

GREAT BRITAIN. DEPARTMENT OF COMMUNITIES AND LOCAL GOVERNMENT. DEVELOPMENT CONTROL STATISTICS (ONLINE). *see* HOUSING AND URBAN PLANNING—Abstracting, Bibliographies, Statistics

GREAT BRITAIN. DEPARTMENT OF COMMUNITIES AND LOCAL GOVERNMENT. FIRE STATISTICS UNITED KINGDOM. *see* FIRE PREVENTION—Abstracting, Bibliographies, Statistics

GREAT BRITAIN. DEPARTMENT OF COMMUNITIES AND LOCAL GOVERNMENT. HOUSING AND PLANNING STATISTICS. *see* HOUSING AND URBAN PLANNING—Abstracting, Bibliographies, Statistics

GREAT BRITAIN. DEPARTMENT OF COMMUNITIES AND LOCAL GOVERNMENT. LOCAL GOVERNMENT FINANCIAL STATISTICS: ENGLAND. *see* PUBLIC ADMINISTRATION—Abstracting, Bibliographies, Statistics

GREAT BRITAIN. GENERAL HOUSEHOLD SURVEY. *see* POPULATION STUDIES—Abstracting, Bibliographies, Statistics

GREAT BRITAIN. GOVERNMENT STATISTICAL SERVICE. ABORTION STATISTICS, ENGLAND AND WALES (YEAR) (ONLINE). *see* BIRTH CONTROL—Abstracting, Bibliographies, Statistics

GREAT BRITAIN. GOVERNMENT STATISTICAL SERVICE. BIRTH STATISTICS. ENGLAND AND WALES. *see* POPULATION STUDIES—Abstracting, Bibliographies, Statistics

GREAT BRITAIN. GOVERNMENT STATISTICAL SERVICE. CANCER STATISTICS REGISTRATIONS. ENGLAND AND WALES. *see* MEDICAL SCIENCES—Abstracting, Bibliographies, Statistics

GREAT BRITAIN. H M TREASURY. CIVIL SERVICE STATISTICS (ONLINE). *see* PUBLIC ADMINISTRATION—Abstracting, Bibliographies, Statistics

314 GBR
HA1122
GREAT BRITAIN. OFFICE FOR NATIONAL STATISTICS. ANNUAL ABSTRACT OF STATISTICS. Text in English. 1948. a. GBP 52 per issue (effective 2010). stat. reprints avail. **Document type:** *Government.* **Description:** Compiles the latest economic, financial, and social figures from the C.S.O. monthly and annual publications.
Formerly (until 1997): Great Britain. Central Statistical Office. Annual Abstract of Statistics (0072-5730)
Related titles: Microfiche ed.: (from PQC).
Indexed: RASB.
—Linda Hall. **CCC.**
Published by: (Great Britain. Office for National Statistics), Palgrave Macmillan Ltd. (Subsidiary of: Macmillan Publishers Ltd.), Houndmills, Basingstoke, Hants RG21 6XS, United Kingdom. TEL 44-1256-329242, FAX 44-1256-810526, bookenquiries@palgrave.com, http://www.palgrave.com. Circ: 5,500.

GREAT BRITAIN. OFFICE FOR NATIONAL STATISTICS. CONSUMER TRENDS (ONLINE). *see* BUSINESS AND ECONOMICS

GREAT BRITAIN. OFFICE FOR NATIONAL STATISTICS. FAMILY SPENDING. *see* BUSINESS AND ECONOMICS—Macroeconomics

GREAT BRITAIN. OFFICE FOR NATIONAL STATISTICS. MORTALITY STATISTICS. DEATHS REGISTERED IN (YEAR); review of the registrar general on deaths in England and Wales (Year). *see* POPULATION STUDIES—Abstracting, Bibliographies, Statistics

304.6 325 GBR ISSN 0261-1783
HA1123
GREAT BRITAIN. OFFICE FOR NATIONAL STATISTICS. REGIONAL TRENDS. Text in English. 1965. a. GBP 55 (effective 2010). charts; stat. **Document type:** *Government.* **Description:** Compiles detailed demographic statistics for each standard region of the UK.
Former titles (until 1981): Great Britain. Central Statistical Office. Regional Statistics (0308-146X); (until 1975): Great Britain. Central Statistical Office Abstracts of Regional Statistics (0072-5749)
Related titles: Online - full text ed.: ISSN 2040-1655.
—BLDSC (7336.786500). **CCC.**
Published by: (Great Britain. Office for National Statistics), Palgrave Macmillan Ltd. (Subsidiary of: Macmillan Publishers Ltd.), Houndmills, Basingstoke, Hants RG21 6XS, United Kingdom. TEL 44-1256-329242, FAX 44-1256-810526, bookenquiries@palgrave.com, http://www.palgrave.com.

GREAT BRITAIN. OFFICE FOR NATIONAL STATISTICS. SOCIAL TRENDS. *see* SOCIOLOGY—Abstracting, Bibliographies, Statistics

GREECE. NATIONAL STATISTICAL SERVICE. AGRICULTURAL AND LIVESTOCK PRODUCTION (YEAR). *see* AGRICULTURE—Abstracting, Bibliographies, Statistics

GREECE. NATIONAL STATISTICAL SERVICE. ANNUAL STATISTICAL SURVEY ON MINES, QUARRIES AND SALTERNS. *see* MINES AND MINING INDUSTRY—Abstracting, Bibliographies, Statistics

GREECE. NATIONAL STATISTICAL SERVICE. BUILDING ACTIVITY STATISTICS. *see* BUILDING AND CONSTRUCTION—Abstracting, Bibliographies, Statistics

GREECE. NATIONAL STATISTICAL SERVICE. CULTURAL STATISTICS. *see* ART—Abstracting, Bibliographies, Statistics

GREECE. NATIONAL STATISTICAL SERVICE. ENVIRONMENTAL STATISTICS. *see* ENVIRONMENTAL STUDIES—Abstracting, Bibliographies, Statistics

GREECE. NATIONAL STATISTICAL SERVICE. HOUSEHOLD EXPENDITURE SURVEY. *see* BUSINESS AND ECONOMICS—Abstracting, Bibliographies, Statistics

GREECE. NATIONAL STATISTICAL SERVICE. LABOUR FORCE SURVEY. *see* BUSINESS AND ECONOMICS—Abstracting, Bibliographies, Statistics

314 GRC ISSN 0028-0240
GREECE. NATIONAL STATISTICAL SERVICE. MONTHLY STATISTICAL BULLETIN. Text in English, Greek. 1955. m. **Document type:** *Bulletin, Government.*
Published by: National Statistical Service of Greece, Statistical Information and Publications Division/Ethniki Statistiki Ypereisa tes Ellados, 14-16 Lykourgou St, Athens, 101 66, Greece. TEL 30-1-3289-397, FAX 30-1-3241-102, http://www.statistics.gr/Main_eng.asp, http://www.statistics.gr.

GREECE. NATIONAL STATISTICAL SERVICE. PRODUCTION OF MANUFACTURED ITEMS. *see* BUSINESS AND ECONOMICS—Abstracting, Bibliographies, Statistics

GREECE. NATIONAL STATISTICAL SERVICE. PROVISIONAL NATIONAL ACCOUNTS OF GREECE. *see* BUSINESS AND ECONOMICS—Abstracting, Bibliographies, Statistics

GREECE. NATIONAL STATISTICAL SERVICE. PUBLIC FINANCE STATISTICS. *see* BUSINESS AND ECONOMICS—Abstracting, Bibliographies, Statistics

GREECE. NATIONAL STATISTICAL SERVICE. QUARTERLY NATIONAL ACCOUNTS OF GREECE. *see* BUSINESS AND ECONOMICS—Abstracting, Bibliographies, Statistics

GREECE. NATIONAL STATISTICAL SERVICE. RESULTS OF SEA FISHERY SURVEY BY MOTOR VESSELS/APOTELESMATA EREUNES THALASSIAS ALIEIAS DIA MEHANOKINETON SKAFON. *see* FISH AND FISHERIES—Abstracting, Bibliographies, Statistics

GREECE. NATIONAL STATISTICAL SERVICE. REVISED AGRICULTURAL PRICE INDICES. *see* AGRICULTURE—Abstracting, Bibliographies, Statistics

GREECE. NATIONAL STATISTICAL SERVICE. REVISED CONSUMER PRICE INDEX. *see* BUSINESS AND ECONOMICS—Abstracting, Bibliographies, Statistics

GREECE. NATIONAL STATISTICAL SERVICE. REVISED PRICE INDICES OF NEW BUILDING DWELLINGS CONSTRUCTION (YEAR). *see* BUILDING AND CONSTRUCTION—Abstracting, Bibliographies, Statistics

GREECE. NATIONAL STATISTICAL SERVICE. SHIPPING STATISTICS. *see* TRANSPORTATION—Abstracting, Bibliographies, Statistics

GREECE. NATIONAL STATISTICAL SERVICE. SOCIAL WELFARE AND HEALTH STATISTICS. *see* SOCIAL SERVICES AND WELFARE—Abstracting, Bibliographies, Statistics

GREECE. NATIONAL STATISTICAL SERVICE. STANDARD CLASSIFICATION OF THE BRANCHES OF ECONOMIC ACTIVITY. *see* BUSINESS AND ECONOMICS—Abstracting, Bibliographies, Statistics

GREECE. NATIONAL STATISTICAL SERVICE. STATISTICS OF THE DECLARED INCOME OF LEGAL ENTITIES AND ITS TAXATION. *see* BUSINESS AND ECONOMICS—Abstracting, Bibliographies, Statistics

GREECE. NATIONAL STATISTICAL SERVICE. STATISTICS ON CIVIL, CRIMINAL AND REFORMATORY JUSTICE. *see* CRIMINOLOGY AND LAW ENFORCEMENT—Abstracting, Bibliographies, Statistics

GREECE. NATIONAL STATISTICAL SERVICE. STATISTICS ON THE DECLARED INCOME OF PHYSICAL PERSONS AND ITS TAXATION. *see* BUSINESS AND ECONOMICS—Abstracting, Bibliographies, Statistics

GREECE. NATIONAL STATISTICAL SERVICE. STATISTIQUES DU TRAVAIL. *see* BUSINESS AND ECONOMICS—Abstracting, Bibliographies, Statistics

GREECE. NATIONAL STATISTICAL SERVICE. TOURIST STATISTICS. *see* TRAVEL AND TOURISM—Abstracting, Bibliographies, Statistics

GREECE. NATIONAL STATISTICAL SERVICE. TRANSPORT AND COMMUNICATION STATISTICS. *see* TRANSPORTATION—Abstracting, Bibliographies, Statistics

GREEK ECONOMY IN FIGURES (YEAR). *see* BUSINESS AND ECONOMICS—Abstracting, Bibliographies, Statistics

319.82 GRL ISSN 1397-0682
GREENLAND. GROENLANDS STATISTIK. BYGDESTATISTIK. Text in Multiple languages. 1996. a. **Document type:** *Government.*
Published by: Groenlands Statistik/Kalaallit Nunaanni Naatsorsueqqissaartarfik, PO Box 1025, Nuuk, 3900, Greenland. TEL 299-345564, FAX 299-322954.

319.82 GRL ISSN 0907-9432
GREENLAND. GROENLANDS STATISTIK. GREENLAND (YEAR) - STATISTICAL YEARBOOK/KALAALLIT NUNAAT. Text in English. 1992. a. DKK 275 (effective 2002).
Related titles: ◆ Danish ed.: Greenland. Groenlands Statistik. Groenland (Year) - Statistisk Aarbog. ISSN 0106-228X.
Published by: Atuagkat AS, Imaneq 9, Nuuk, 3900, Greenland. TEL 299-321-737, FAX 299-322-444. **Co-sponsor:** Groenlands Statistik/Kalaallit Nunaanni Naatsorsueqqissaartarfik.

319.82 GRL ISSN 0106-228X
HC110.5
GREENLAND. GROENLANDS STATISTIK. GROENLAND (YEAR) - STATISTISK AARBOG/KALAALLIT NUNAAT. Text in Danish, English. 1968. a. DKK 275 (effective 2002).

S

Related titles: ◆ English ed.: Greenland. Groenlands Statistik. Greenland (Year) - Statistical Yearbook. ISSN 0907-9432.
Published by: Atuagkat AS, Imaneq 9, Nuuk, 3900, Greenland. TEL 299-321-737, FAX 299-322-444. Circ: 3,800. **Co-sponsor:** Groenlands Statistik/Kalaallit Nunaanni Naatsorsueqqissaartarfik.

319.82 378.489 GRL ISSN 0907-2225
LA2280
GREENLAND. GROENLANDS STATISTIK. UDDANNELSE. Text in Danish. 1992. a. **Document type:** *Government.*
Related titles: Eskimo ed.: Greenland. Groenlands Statistik. Ilinniartitaaneq. ISSN 1396-4666. 1994.
Published by: Groenlands Statistik/Kalaallit Nunaanni Naatsorsueqqissaartarfik, PO Box 1025, Nuuk, 3900, Greenland. TEL 299-345564, FAX 299-322954.

GRENADA SCHOOL DIRECTORY AND BASIC EDUCATIONAL STATISTICS. *see* EDUCATION—Abstracting, Bibliographies, Statistics

GREY BOOK (ONLINE). *see* AGRICULTURE—Abstracting, Bibliographies, Statistics

001.422 190 DNK ISSN 1901-4198
GROENLANDSRELATERET FORSKNING OG UDVIKLING; forskningsstatistik. Text in Danish. 2004. irreg. charts; stat. back issues avail. **Document type:** *Academic/Scholarly.* **Description:** Greenland related research and development.
Related titles: Online - full text ed.: ISSN 1901-4201.
Published by: Dansk Center for Forskningsanalyse/Danish Centre for Studies in Research and Research Policy, Aarhus Universitet, Finlandsgade 4, Aarhus N, 8200, Denmark. TEL 45-89-422394, FAX 45-89-422399, cfa@cfa.au.dk, http://www.cfs.au.dk.

317 CAN ISSN 0711-852X
GROSS DOMESTIC PRODUCT BY INDUSTRY/PRODUIT INTERIEUR BRUT PAR INDUSTRIE. Text in English. 1987. m. CAD 127, USD 152 domestic; USD 178 foreign. **Description:** Contains monthly, quarterly, and annual estimates of GDP for 183 industries, including aggregates and special industry groupings.
Related titles: Alternate Frequency ed(s).: ISSN 0710-7269. 1974. a.
Published by: Statistics Canada, Operations and Integration Division (Subsidiary of: Statistics Canada/Statistique Canada), Circulation Management, 120 Parkdale Ave, Ottawa, ON K1A 0T6, Canada. TEL 613-951-7277, 800-267-6677, FAX 613-951-1584.

GUANGDONG SOCIOECONOMIC STATISTICS MONTHLY. *see* BUSINESS AND ECONOMICS—Abstracting, Bibliographies, Statistics

310 CHN
GUANGXI TONGJI/GUANGXI STATISTICS. Text in Chinese. bi-m.
Published by: Guangxi Tongji Ju/Guangxi Bureau of Statistics, 22 Xinzhu Lu, Nanning, Guangxi 530022, China. TEL 22368. Ed. Su Xiaohan.

318 GTM
GUATEMALA. DIRECCION GENERAL DE ESTADISTICA. ENCUESTA DE LA INDUSTRIA MANUFACTURERA FABRIL. Variant title: Encuesta Industrial. Text in Spanish. 1972. a., latest 1987. USD 15.
Formerly: Guatemala. Direccion General de Estadistica. Departamento de Estudios Especiales y Estadisticas Continuas. Produccion, Venta y Otros Ingresos de la Encuesta Anual de la Industria Manufacturera Fabril
Published by: (Guatemala. Departamento de Estudios Especiales y Estadisticas Continuas), Instituto Nacional de Estadistica, Ministerio de Economia, 8A Calle no. 9-55, Guatemala City Zona, Guatemala.

GUIDE TO THE CLASSIFICATION FOR OVERSEAS TRADE STATISTICS. *see* BUSINESS AND ECONOMICS—Abstracting, Bibliographies, Statistics

THE GUIDE TO THE POST INDEX. *see* BUSINESS AND ECONOMICS—Abstracting, Bibliographies, Statistics

GUYANA. NATIONAL INSURANCE BOARD. ANNUAL REPORT: GUYANA NATIONAL INSURANCE SCHEME. *see* INSURANCE—Abstracting, Bibliographies, Statistics

GUYANA. STATISTICAL BUREAU. ANNUAL ACCOUNT RELATING TO EXTERNAL TRADE. *see* BUSINESS AND ECONOMICS—Abstracting, Bibliographies, Statistics

GYEONG'GI JONGHAB JI'SU/KOREA (REPUBLIC). NATIONAL STATISTICAL OFFICE. COMPOSITE INDEXES OF BUSINESS INDICATORS. *see* BUSINESS AND ECONOMICS—Abstracting, Bibliographies, Statistics

GYEONGJE HWALDONG INGU YEONBO/KOREA (REPUBLIC). NATIONAL STATISTICAL OFFICE. ANNUAL REPORT ON THE ECONOMICALLY ACTIVE POPULATION SURVEY. *see* BUSINESS AND ECONOMICS—Abstracting, Bibliographies, Statistics

314.912 ISL ISSN 0254-4733
HAGSKYRSLUR ISLANDS/STATISTICS OF ICELAND. Text in Icelandic. 1914. irreg. back issues avail. **Document type:** *Government.*
Related titles: CD-ROM ed.
Published by: Hagstofa Islands/Statistics Iceland, Borgartuni 12 A, Reykjavik, 150, Iceland. TEL 354-528-1000, FAX 354-528-1099. Ed. Rut Jonsdottir.

314.912 ISL ISSN 0019-1078
HA1491
HAGTIDINDI/STATISTICAL SERIES. Text in Icelandic; Summaries in English. 1914. m. stat. index. back issues avail. **Document type:** *Monographic series, Government.*
Related titles: Online - full text ed.: ISSN 1670-4770. 2001.
Indexed: RASB.
Published by: Hagstofa Islands/Statistics Iceland, Borgartuni 12 A, Reykjavik, 150, Iceland. TEL 354-528-1000, FAX 354-528-1099. Ed. Sigurborg Steingrimsdottir.

317.29 HTI ISSN 0017-6788
HA881
HAITI. INSTITUT HAITIEN DE STATISTIQUE. BULLETIN TRIMESTRIEL DE STATISTIQUE. Text in French. 1952. a. free. charts; mkt.; stat. Supplement avail.
Published by: Institut Haitien de Statistique et d'Informatique, Departement des Finances et des Affaires Economique, Bd. Harry Truman, Port-au-Prince, Haiti. Ed. Raymond Gardiner. Circ: 500.

HAND BOOK ON SUGAR STATISTICS. *see* FOOD AND FOOD INDUSTRIES—Abstracting, Bibliographies, Statistics

315 IND ISSN 0072-9728
HANDBOOK OF BASIC STATISTICS OF MAHARASHTRA STATE. Text in English. 1960. a., latest 2007. back issues avail. **Document type:** *Handbook/Manual/Guide, Government.*
Formerly (until 1974): Handbook of Basic Statistics
Related titles: Online - full text ed.; Marathi ed.
Published by: Directorate of Economics and Statistics, 8th Fl, Administrative Bldg, Government Colony, Bandra (E), Mumbai, 400 051, India. TEL 91-22-26400205, dir_eco_stat@maharashtra.gov.in.

HANDBOOK OF NUMERICAL ANALYSIS. *see* MATHEMATICS

310 NLD ISSN 0169-7161
HANDBOOK OF STATISTICS. Text in English. 1980. irreg., latest vol.26, 2007. price varies. **Document type:** *Monographic series.*
Related titles: Online - full text ed.: ISSN 1875-7448.
Indexed: CCMJ, CIS, Inspec, MSN, MathR, SCOPUS.
—BLDSC (4253.080000). **CCC.**
Published by: Elsevier BV, North-Holland (Subsidiary of: Elsevier Science & Technology), Sara Burgerhartstraat 25, Amsterdam, 1055 KV, Netherlands. TEL 31-20-4853911, FAX 31-20-4852457, JournalsCustomerServiceEMEA@elsevier.com, http://www.elsevier.nl/homepage/about/us/regional_sites.htt. Ed. C R Rao. **Subscr. to:** Elsevier BV, Radarweg 29, PO Box 211, Amsterdam 1000 AE, Netherlands. TEL 31-20-4853757, FAX 31-20-4853432.

HANDBUCH DER OESTERREICHISCHEN SOZIALVERSICHERUNG. *see* INSURANCE—Abstracting, Bibliographies, Statistics

315.19 KOR ISSN 1228-8101
HAN'GUG TONG'GYE WOLBO/MONTHLY STATISTICS OF KOREA. Text in English, Korean. 1958. m. USD 11 (effective 2009). stat. Index. **Document type:** *Government.* **Description:** Provides wide ranges of current statistical data on demographic, social and economic situations of Korea.
Formerly: Han' Guk T'onggye Wolbo (0027-0563)
Related titles: Online - full text ed.: ISSN 2005-2499.
Published by: Tong'gyecheong/Korea National Statistical Office, Government Complex Daejeon, 139 Seonsaro (920 Dunsan 2-dong), Seo-gu, Daejeon, 302-701, Korea, S. TEL 82-42-4814114. **Subscr. to:** The Korean Statistical Association, Rm. 103, Seoul Statistical Branch Office Bldg. 71, Nonhyun-Dong, Kangnam-Ku, Seoul 135701, Korea, S. TEL 82-2-34437954, FAX 82-2-34437957, kosa@nso.go.kr.

HAN'GUG TONG'GYE YEON'GAM/KOREA STATISTICAL YEARBOOK. *see* POPULATION STUDIES—Abstracting, Bibliographies, Statistics

HAWAII AGRICULTURAL LABOR. *see* AGRICULTURE—Abstracting, Bibliographies, Statistics

HAWAII. DEPARTMENT OF BUSINESS, ECONOMIC DEVELOPMENT & TOURISM. QUARTERLY STATISTICAL & ECONOMIC REPORT. *see* BUSINESS AND ECONOMICS—Abstracting, Bibliographies, Statistics

HAWAII WEEKLY CROP WEATHER REPORT. *see* AGRICULTURE—Abstracting, Bibliographies, Statistics

310 610 CAN ISSN 1496-3922
HEALTH INDICATORS. Text in English. 2000. a. **Document type:** *Journal, Trade.*
Related titles: CD-ROM ed.: ISSN 1481-2495; Ed.: Indicateurs de la Sante. ISSN 1496-3930. 2000.
Published by: (Canadian Institute for Health Information/Institut Canadien d'Information sur la Sante), Statistics Canada/Statistique Canada, Communications Division, 3rd Fl, R H Coats Bldg, Ottawa, ON K1A 0A6, Canada. TEL 800-263-1136, infostats@statcan.ca, http://www.statcan.gc.ca.

HEALTH STATISTICS WALES/YSTADEGAU IECHYD CYMRU. *see* HEALTH FACILITIES AND ADMINISTRATION—Abstracting, Bibliographies, Statistics

HELSINGIN KAUPUNGIN TIETOKESKUKSEN NELJANNESVUOSIJULKAISU. KVARTTI/CITY OF HELSINKI URBAN FACTS. QUARTERLY/HELSINGFORS STADS FAKTACENTRAL. KVARTALSPUBLIKATION. *see* PUBLIC ADMINISTRATION

HELSINGIN KAUPUNGIN TIETOKESKUS. TILASTOJA/CITY OF HELSINKI URBAN FACTS. STATISTICS/HELSINGFORS STADS FAKTACENTRAL. STATISTIK. *see* PUBLIC ADMINISTRATION—Abstracting, Bibliographies, Statistics

310 FIN ISSN 0785-8736
HA1449.H4
HELSINGIN KAUPUNGIN TILASTOLLINEN VUOSIKIRJA; Helsingfors stads statistiska aarsbok/statistical yearbook of the City of Helsinki. Text in Finnish, Swedish. 1908. a. EUR 20 (effective 2006). stat. back issues avail. **Document type:** *Monographic series.*
Formerly (until 1988): Helsingin Kaupunki Tilastollinen Vuosikirja (0356-9489)
Published by: (Helsingfors Stads Faktacentral), Helsingin Kaupungin Tietokeskus/City of Helsinki Urban Facts, PO Box 5500, Helsinki, 00099, Finland. TEL 358-9-3101612, FAX 358-9-31036601, tietokeskus.kirjaamo@hel.fi, http://www.hel2.fi/tietokeskus/kaupunkitilastot/index.html. Ed. Aila Perttila. Circ: 1,300.

HEPATITIS C. *see* PUBLIC HEALTH AND SAFETY—Abstracting, Bibliographies, Statistics

314 DEU ISSN 0018-1021
HA1320.H6
HESSISCHE KREISZAHLEN. Text in German. 1951. s-a. EUR 11.90 (effective 2005). Website rev. **Document type:** *Government.* **Description:** Government publication covering extensive vital statistics.
Related titles: Diskette ed.; Online - full text ed.
Published by: Hessisches Statistisches Landesamt, Rheinstr 35-37, Wiesbaden, 65175, Germany. TEL 49-611-3802950, FAX 49-611-3802992, vertrieb@statistik-hessen.de, http://www.statistik-hessen.de.

HISTORICAL METHODS; a journal of quantitative and interdisciplinary history . *see* SOCIOLOGY—Abstracting, Bibliographies, Statistics

317 USA ISSN 0073-2664
HISTORICAL STATISTICS OF THE UNITED STATES. Text in English. 1949. irreg. (in 5 vols.). USD 1,225 in the Americas & Asia; USD 1,310.75 in Singapore; AUD 1,499 in Australia & New Zealand; GBP 593 elsewhere; GBP 1,947 combined subscription in Europe, Middle East & Africa (print & online eds.); AUD 4,500 combined subscription in Australasia (print & online eds.) (effective 2009). stat. **Document type:** *Monographic series, Academic/Scholarly.*
Related titles: Online - full text ed.: ISSN 1751-1216. GBP 1,800 in Europe, Middle East & Africa; AUD 4,999 in Australia & New Zealand (effective 2009).
Published by: (U.S. Census Bureau), Cambridge University Press, 32 Ave of the Americas, New York, NY 10013. TEL 212-337-5000, FAX 212-691-3239, http://us.cambridge.org.

HOME OFFICE. RESEARCH AND STATISTICS DIRECTORATE. STATISTICAL BULLETIN (ONLINE). *see* PUBLIC ADMINISTRATION—Abstracting, Bibliographies, Statistics

HOMENS E MULHERES EM PORTUGAL. *see* POPULATION STUDIES—Abstracting, Bibliographies, Statistics

HOMICIDE IN CALIFORNIA. *see* CRIMINOLOGY AND LAW ENFORCEMENT

318 HND
HONDURAS EN CIFRAS. Text in Spanish. 1965. a. free. charts; stat.
Published by: Banco Central de Honduras, Departamento de Estudios Economicos, 6a y 7a Avda., 1a Calle, Tegucigalpa D C, Honduras. TEL 37-2270, TELEX 1121.

318 HND
HONDURAS. SECRETARIA DE HACIENDA Y CREDITO PUBLICO. DIRECCION GENERAL DE PRESUPUESTO. PRESUPUESTO GENERAL DE INGRESOS Y EGRESOS DE LA REPUBLICA. Text in Spanish. a.
Published by: Secretaria de Hacienda y Credito Publico, Direccion General de Presupuesto, Tegucigalpa D.C, Honduras.

318 HND
HONDURAS. SECRETARIA DE PLANIFICACION, COORDINACION Y PRESUPUESTO. ANUARIO ESTADISTICO. Text in Spanish. a. **Document type:** *Government.*
Published by: Secretaria de Planificacion, Coordinacion y Presupuesto, Direccion General de Estadistica y Censos, Tegucigalpa DC, Honduras.

HONDURAS. SECRETARIA DE PLANIFICACION COORDINACION Y PRESUPUESTO. DIRECCION GENERAL DE ESTADISTICA Y CENSOS. ENCUESTA PERMANENTE DE HOGARES DE PROPOSITOS MULTIPLES. *see* HOUSING AND URBAN PLANNING—Abstracting, Bibliographies, Statistics

310 HKG
HONG KONG. BUILDING DEVELOPMENT DEPARTMENT. BUILDING STATISTICS. Text in English. m. HKD 20.
Published by: (Hong Kong. Building Development Department, Hong Kong. Buildings Ordinance Office), Government Publications Centre, G.P.O. Bldg, Ground Fl, Connaught Pl, Hong Kong, Hong Kong. TEL 5-8428801. **Subscr. to:** Director of Information Services, Information Services Dept., 1 Battery Path G-F, Central, Hong Kong, Hong Kong.

HONG KONG ECONOMIC TRENDS. *see* BUSINESS AND ECONOMICS—Abstracting, Bibliographies, Statistics

315 HKG
HONG KONG IN FIGURES. Text in English. 1976. a. free. stat. **Document type:** *Government.*
Related titles: Online - full text ed.; Chinese ed.: Hong Kong Tongjishu Yilan. 1983.
Published by: Census and Statistics Department/Zhengfu Tongjichu, General Statistics Section 1(B), 19/F Wanchai Tower, 12 Harbour Rd, Wan Chai, Hong Kong. TEL 852-2582-4068, FAX 852-2827-1708, genenq@censtatd.gov.hk, http://www.statisticalbookstore.gov.hk. **Subscr. to:** Government Publications Centre, Low Block, Ground Fl, Queensway Government Offices, 66 Queensway, Hong Kong, Hong Kong.

310 657 HKG
HONG KONG SPECIAL ADMINISTRATIVE REGION OF CHINA. AUDIT COMMISSION. DIRECTOR OF AUDIT'S REPORTS. Text in English. irreg., latest no.37, 2001, Oct. price varies. back issues avail. **Document type:** *Government.*
Related titles: Online - full content ed.; Chinese ed.
Published by: Audit Commission, 26/F, Immigration Tower, 7 Gloucester Rd, Wanchai, Hong Kong. TEL 852-2829-4210, FAX 852-2824-2087, enquiry@aud.gov.hk, http://www.info.gov.hk/aud/.

HONG KONG SPECIAL ADMINISTRATIVE REGION OF CHINA. CENSUS AND STATISTICS DEPARTMENT. AN OUTLINE OF STATISTICAL DEVELOPMENT. *see* POPULATION STUDIES—Abstracting, Bibliographies, Statistics

310 330.9 HKG
HONG KONG SPECIAL ADMINISTRATIVE REGION OF CHINA. CENSUS AND STATISTICS DEPARTMENT. ANNUAL REPORT ON THE CONSUMER PRICE INDEX. Text in Chinese, English. a., latest 2001. HKD 34 newsstand/cover (effective 2002). stat. back issues avail. **Document type:** *Government.* **Description:** Presents statistics on price index movements of various consumer goods and services and analysis on major movements of indices during the reference year.
Related titles: Online - full text ed.
Published by: Census and Statistics Department/Zhengfu Tongjichu, Consumer Price Index Section, 22/F Chuang's Hung Hom Plaza, 83 Wuhu St, Hung Hom, Wowloon, Hong Kong. TEL 852-2805-6403, FAX 852-2577-6253, cpi_1@censtatd.gov.hk, http://www.statisticalbookstore.gov.hk, http://www.info.gov.hk/censtatd. **Subscr. to:** Information Services Department, Publications Sales Unit, Rm 402, 4th Fl, Murray Bldg, Garden Rd, Hong Kong, Hong Kong. TEL 852-2842-8844, FAX 852-2598-7482, puborder@isd.gcn.gov.hk, http://www.info.gov.hk/isd/book_e.htm. **Dist. by:** Government Publications Centre, Low Block, Ground Fl, Queensway Government Offices, 66 Queensway, Hong Kong, Hong Kong. TEL 852-2537-1910, FAX 852-2523-7195.

HONG KONG SPECIAL ADMINISTRATIVE REGION OF CHINA. CENSUS AND STATISTICS DEPARTMENT. GROSS DOMESTIC PRODUCT (QUARTERLY EDITION). *see* BUSINESS AND ECONOMICS—Abstracting, Bibliographies, Statistics

HONG KONG SPECIAL ADMINISTRATIVE REGION OF CHINA. CENSUS AND STATISTICS DEPARTMENT. INDEX NUMBERS OF THE COSTS OF LABOUR AND SELECTED MATERIALS USED IN GOVERNMENT CONTRACTS. *see* POPULATION STUDIES—Abstracting, Bibliographies, Statistics

310 330.9 HKG
HONG KONG SPECIAL ADMINISTRATIVE REGION OF CHINA. CENSUS AND STATISTICS DEPARTMENT. MONTHLY REPORT ON THE CONSUMER PRICE INDEX. Text in Chinese, English. m. HKD 34 newsstand/cover (effective 2002). stat. back issues avail. **Document type:** *Government.* **Description:** Presents month-to-month and year-on-year movements of the monthly Consumer Price Indices, and analysis by commodity and service groups.
Related titles: Online - full text ed.
Published by: Census and Statistics Department/Zhengfu Tongjichu, Consumer Price Index Section, 22/F Chuang's Hung Hom Plaza, 83 Wuhu St, Hung Hom, Kowloon, Hong Kong. TEL 852-2805-6403, FAX 852-2577-6253, cpi_1@censtatd.gov.hk, http://www.info.gov.hk/censtatd, http://www.statisticalbookstore.gov.hk. **Subscr. to:** Information Services Department, Publications Sales Unit, Rm 402, 4th Fl, Murray Bldg, Garden Rd, Hong Kong, Hong Kong. TEL 852-2842-8844, FAX 852-2598-7482, puborder@isd.gcn.gov.hk, http://www.info.gov.hk/isd/book_e.htm. **Dist. by:** Government Publications Centre, Low Block, Ground Fl, Queensway Government Offices, 66 Queensway, Hong Kong, Hong Kong. TEL 852-2537-1910, FAX 852-2523-7195.

HONG KONG SPECIAL ADMINISTRATIVE REGION OF CHINA. CENSUS AND STATISTICS DEPARTMENT. QUARTERLY REPORT OF EMPLOYMENT AND VACANCIES AT CONSTRUCTION SITES. *see* BUILDING AND CONSTRUCTION—Abstracting, Bibliographies, Statistics

HONG KONG SPECIAL ADMINISTRATIVE REGION OF CHINA. CENSUS AND STATISTICS DEPARTMENT. QUARTERLY REPORT ON GENERAL HOUSEHOLD SURVEY. *see* BUSINESS AND ECONOMICS—Abstracting, Bibliographies, Statistics

HONG KONG SPECIAL ADMINISTRATIVE REGION OF CHINA. CENSUS AND STATISTICS DEPARTMENT. REPORT OF SALARIES AND EMPLOYEE BENEFITS STATISTICS MANAGERIAL AND PROFESSIONAL EMPLOYEES (EXCLUDING TOP MANAGEMENT). *see* BUSINESS AND ECONOMICS—Abstracting, Bibliographies, Statistics

HONG KONG SPECIAL ADMINISTRATIVE REGION OF CHINA. CENSUS AND STATISTICS DEPARTMENT. REPORT ON ANNUAL SURVEY OF BUILDING, CONSTRUCTION AND REAL ESTATE SECTORS. *see* BUILDING AND CONSTRUCTION—Abstracting, Bibliographies, Statistics

310 330.9 HKG
HONG KONG SPECIAL ADMINISTRATIVE REGION OF CHINA. CENSUS AND STATISTICS DEPARTMENT. REPORT ON MONTHLY SURVEY OF RETAIL SALES. Text in Chinese, English. 1981. m. HKD 60; HKD 5 newsstand/cover (effective 2001). stat. **Document type:** *Government.* **Description:** Publishes statistics on value of retail sales by type of retail outlet, in addition to those on value index of retail sales by type of retail outlet. Statistics on volume index of retail sales by type of retail outlet, which measure the volume change in real terms, are also released.
Related titles: Online - full text ed.
Published by: Census and Statistics Department/Zhengfu Tongjichu, Distribution and Services Statistics Section 1(A), 19/F Chuang's Hung Hom Plaza, 83 Wuhu St, Hung Hom, Kowloon, Hong Kong. TEL 852-2802-1264, FAX 852-2827-0551, asw@censtatd.gov.hk, http://www.statisticalbookstore.gov.hk. **Subscr. to:** Information Services Department, Publications Sales Unit, Rm 402, 4th Fl, Murray Bldg, Garden Rd, Hong Kong, Hong Kong. TEL 852-2842-8844, FAX 852-2598-7482, puborder@isd.gcn.gov.hk, http://www.info.gov.hk/isd/book_e.htm. **Dist. by:** Government Publications Centre, Low Block, Ground Fl, Queensway Government Offices, 66 Queensway, Hong Kong, Hong Kong. TEL 852-2537-1910, FAX 852-2523-7195.

HOUSEHOLD INCOME AND INCOME DISTRIBUTION, AUSTRALIA (ONLINE). *see* BUSINESS AND ECONOMICS—Abstracting, Bibliographies, Statistics

314 ROM ISSN 1223-7566
HD5811.8
HOUSEHOLD LABOUR FORCE SURVEY. Text in English, Romanian; Summaries in English, Romanian. a. ROL 60,000; USD 20 foreign. stat. **Document type:** *Government.* **Description:** Presents data and commentaries regarding the active employed and unemployed population and the in-active population.
Published by: Comisia Nationala pentru Statistica/National Commission for Statistics, Bd. Libertatii 16, Sector 5, Bucharest, 70542, Romania. TEL 40-1-3363370, FAX 40-1-3124873. Ed. Ivan Ungureanu Clementina.

HOUSING AFFORDABILITY REPORT. *see* HOUSING AND URBAN PLANNING—Abstracting, Bibliographies, Statistics

HOUSING CONSTRUCTION. *see* BUILDING AND CONSTRUCTION—Abstracting, Bibliographies, Statistics

HOUSING FINANCE, AUSTRALIA (ONLINE). *see* BUSINESS AND ECONOMICS—Abstracting, Bibliographies, Statistics

HOUSING INFORMATION MONTHLY/BULLETIN MENSUEL D'INFORMATION SUR LE LOGEMENT. *see* HOUSING AND URBAN PLANNING

HOUSING STATISTICS. *see* HOUSING AND URBAN PLANNING—Abstracting, Bibliographies, Statistics

HUMAN SETTLEMENTS BASIC STATISTICS. *see* HOUSING AND URBAN PLANNING—Abstracting, Bibliographies, Statistics

HUNGARY. KOZPONTI STATISZTIKAI HIVATAL. BERUHAZASI, EPITOIPARI, LAKASEPITESI EVKONYV. *see* BUILDING AND CONSTRUCTION—Abstracting, Bibliographies, Statistics

HUNGARY. KOZPONTI STATISZTIKAI HIVATAL. GAZDASAG ES STATISZTIKA. *see* BUSINESS AND ECONOMICS—Abstracting, Bibliographies, Statistics

HUNGARY. KOZPONTI STATISZTIKAI HIVATAL. MEZOGAZDASAGI ELELMISZERIPARI STATISZTIKAI EVKONYV/HUNGARY. CENTRAL STATISTICAL OFFICE. YEARBOOK OF AGRICULTURAL STATISTICS. *see* AGRICULTURE—Abstracting, Bibliographies, Statistics

HUNGARY. KOZPONTI STATISZTIKAI HIVATAL. MEZOGAZDASAGI ELELMISZERIPARI STATISZTIKAI ZSEBKONYV. *see* AGRICULTURE—Abstracting, Bibliographies, Statistics

310 HUN ISSN 0441-4713
HA162
HUNGARY. KOZPONTI STATISZTIKAI HIVATAL. NEMZETKOZI STATISZTIKAI EVKONYV. Text in Hungarian. quadrennial. HUF 371. stat. **Document type:** *Government.*
Published by: Kozponti Statisztikai Hivatal, Marketing Oszta'ly, Keleti Karoly utca 5-7, Budapest, 1024, Hungary. TEL 36-1-345-6000, FAX 36-1-345-6699. Circ: 3,000.

314 HUN ISSN 0018-781X
HA1201
HUNGARY. KOZPONTI STATISZTIKAI HIVATAL. STATISZTIKAI HAVI KOZLEMENYEK. Text in English, Hungarian. 1897. m. HUF 3,480, USD 66. adv. charts; stat. **Document type:** *Bulletin, Government.*
Indexed: RASB.
Published by: Kozponti Statisztikai Hivatal, Marketing Oszta'ly, Keleti Karoly utca 5-7, Budapest, 1024, Hungary. TEL 36-1-345-6000, FAX 36-1-345-6699. Ed. Lorinc Soos. Adv. contact Peter Zoltan. Circ: 1,350.

314 HUN ISSN 0039-0690
HA1
HUNGARY. KOZPONTI STATISZTIKAI HIVATAL. STATISZTIKAI SZEMLE. Text in Hungarian. 1923. m. HUF 396, USD 52. cum.index 1923-1962.
Formerly (until 1949): Magyar Statisztikai Szemle (0200-0261)
Indexed: IBSS, P30, PopulInd, RASB, SCOPUS.
Published by: Kozponti Statisztikai Hivatal, Marketing Oszta'ly, Keleti Karoly utca 5-7, Budapest, 1024, Hungary. TEL 36-1-345-6000, FAX 36-1-345-6699. Ed. Maria Visi Lakatos. Circ: 1,500.

HUNGARY. KOZPONTI STATISZTIKAI HIVATAL. SZAMITASTECHNIKAI STATISZTIKAI ZSEBKONYV. *see* COMPUTERS—Abstracting, Bibliographies, Statistics

314.391 HUN ISSN 0018-7828
HUNGARY. KOZPONTI STATISZTIKAI HIVATAL. TERULETI STATISZTIKA. Text in Hungarian; Contents page in English, Russian. 1957. bi-m. HUF 198, USD 21.50. bk.rev. charts; stat. **Document type:** *Government.*
Formerly: Megyei es Varosi Statisztikai Ertesito
Indexed: RASB.
—BLDSC (8796.170000).
Published by: Kozponti Statisztikai Hivatal, Marketing Oszta'ly, Keleti Karoly utca 5-7, Budapest, 1024, Hungary. TEL 31-1-345-6000, FAX 36-1-345-6699. Ed. Tibor Kordcs. Circ: 1,320. **Subscr. to:** Kultura, PO Box 149, Budapest 1389, Hungary.

947 314 HUN ISSN 0303-5344
HA1201
HUNGARY. KOZPONTI STATISZTIKAI HIVATAL. TERULETI STATISZTIKAI EVKONYV. Text in Hungarian. a. HUF 201. stat. **Document type:** *Government.*
Indexed: RASB.
Published by: Kozponti Statisztikai Hivatal, Marketing Oszta'ly, Keleti Karoly utca 5-7, Budapest, 1024, Hungary. TEL 36-1-345-6000, FAX 36-1-345-6699.

314 HUN ISSN 0133-9184
HA1205
HUNGARY. KOZPONTI STATISZTIKAI HIVATAL. TORTENETI STATISZTIKAI TANULMANYOK. Text in Hungarian. 1975. irreg., latest 2000. **Description:** Includes statistical history studies.
Supersedes in part: Torteneti Statisztikai Evkonyv
Indexed: P30.
Published by: (Hungary. Kozponti Statisztikai Hivatal), Statisztikai Kiado Vallalat, Kaszas utca 10-12, PO Box 99, Budapest 3, 1300, Hungary. **Subscr. to:** Kultura, PO Box 149, Budapest 1389, Hungary.

319.4 333.91 330.9 AUS ISSN 0729-5030
HUNTER VALLEY RESEARCH FOUNDATION. WORKING PAPERS. Text in English. 1969. irreg. free to qualified personnel (effective 2008). charts. back issues avail.
Published by: Hunter Valley Research Foundation, PO Box 3023, Hamilton DC, NSW 2303, Australia. TEL 61-2-49694566, FAX 61-2-49614981, info@hvrf.com.au, http://www.hvrf.com.au.

I B S NEWSLETTER BALTIC STATES. (International Business Statistics) *see* BUSINESS AND ECONOMICS—Abstracting, Bibliographies, Statistics

I B S NEWSLETTER CENTRAL AND WESTERN EUROPE. (International Business Statistics) *see* BUSINESS AND ECONOMICS—Abstracting, Bibliographies, Statistics

I B S NEWSLETTER RUSSIA. (International Business Statistics) *see* BUSINESS AND ECONOMICS—Abstracting, Bibliographies, Statistics

I D E STATISTICAL DATA SERIES. *see* BUSINESS AND ECONOMICS—Abstracting, Bibliographies, Statistics

I F L A SECTION ON STATISTICS AND EVALUATION. NEWSLETTER. (International Federation of Library Associations and Institutions) *see* LIBRARY AND INFORMATION SCIENCES

310 BRA ISSN 1413-9022
I M E. CADERNOS. SERIE ESTATISTICA. (Instituto de Matematica e Estatistica) Text in Portuguese, English, Spanish. 1996. s-a. **Document type:** *Journal, Academic/Scholarly.*
Related titles: Online - full text ed.: free (effective 2011).
Published by: Universidade do Estado do Rio de Janeiro, Instituto de Matematica e Estatistica, Rua Sao Francisco Xavier 524, Pavilhao Reitor Joao Lyra Filho, Rio de Janeiro, 20559-900, Brazil. Ed. Jose Fabiano da Serra Costa.

519.5 003 DNK ISSN 1601-2321
I M M-T R; teknisk rapport. (Informatik og Matematisk Modellering - Teknisk Rapport) Text in Danish, English. 1992. irreg., latest 2007. illus. back issues avail. **Document type:** *Monographic series, Academic/Scholarly.*
Former titles (until 2001): I M M. Technical Report (0909-6264); (until 1994): I M S O R. Technical Report (0906-9992); Which was formed by the merger of (1978-1992): Technical University of Denmark. Institute of Mathematical Statistics and Operations Research. Research Report (0107-3826); (1988-1992): Technical University of Denmark. Institute of Mathematical Statistics and Operations Research. Preprint (0904-7751)
Related titles: Online - full text ed.
Published by: Danmarks Tekniske Universitet, Informatik og Matematisk Modellering/Technical University of Denmark. Informatics and Mathematical Modelling, Bldg 321, Lyngby, 2800, Denmark. TEL 45-45-253351, FAX 45-45-882673, reception@imm.dtu.dk.

I N A I L DATI. (Istituto Nazionale per l'Assicurazione Contro gli Infortuni sul Lavoro) *see* OCCUPATIONAL HEALTH AND SAFETY—Abstracting, Bibliographies, Statistics

I N A I L NOTIZIARIO STATISTICO. (Istituto Nazionale per l'Assicurazione Contro gli Infortuni sul Lavoro) *see* OCCUPATIONAL HEALTH AND SAFETY—Abstracting, Bibliographies, Statistics

318.2 ARG ISSN 0326-6230
I N D E C DOCUMENTOS DE TRABAJO. Text in Spanish. irreg., latest vol.21, 1995. ARS 5, USD 10 (effective 1999). **Document type:** *Monographic series, Government.* **Description:** Presents methodological works or research in the field of applied theoretical statistics.
Published by: Instituto Nacional de Estadistica y Censos, Presidente Julio A Roca 615, Buenos Aires, 1067, Argentina. TEL 54-114-3499662, FAX 54-114-3499621.

318.2 ARG ISSN 0326-6249
I N D E C ESTUDIOS. Text in Spanish. 1984. irreg., latest vol.31, 1998. ARS 15, USD 45 (effective 1999). **Document type:** *Monographic series, Government.* **Description:** Presents results of special research in sociodemographic and economic areas.
Published by: Instituto Nacional de Estadistica y Censos, Presidente Julio A Roca 615, Buenos Aires, 1067, Argentina. TEL 54-114-3499662, FAX 54-114-3499621.

318 ARG ISSN 0328-5804
HB235.A7
I N D E C INFORMA. Text in Spanish. m. ARS 80, USD 120; ARS 9 newsstand/cover; USD 12 newsstand/cover in United States (effective 1999). **Document type:** *Government.* **Description:** Includes socioeconomic statistics on public services, employment, industrial activities, foreign trade and prices.
Formerly (until 1996): Argentina. Instituto Nacional de Estadistica y Censos. Estadistica Mensual (0326-6214); (until 1984): Argentina. Instituto Nacional de Estadistica y Censos. Boletin de Estadistica y Censos (0325-1950); Argentina. Direccion Nacional de Estadistica y Censos. Boletin Mensual de Estadistica (0518-4673)
Published by: Instituto Nacional de Estadistica y Censos, Presidente Julio A Roca 615, Buenos Aires, 1067, Argentina. TEL 54-11-43499200, ces@indec.mecon.ar.

318 ARG
I N D E C INFORMACION DE PRENSA. (Booklets in 15 subseries.) Text in Spanish. m. price varies. **Document type:** *Government.*
Published by: Instituto Nacional de Estadistica y Censos, Presidente Julio A Roca 615, Buenos Aires, 1067, Argentina. TEL 54-114-3499662, FAX 54-114-3499621.

318.2 ARG ISSN 0326-6222
I N D E C METODOLOGIAS. Text in Spanish. 1978. irreg., latest vol.10, 1995. ARS 15, USD 22 (effective 1999). **Document type:** *Monographic series, Government.* **Description:** Presents procedures and methods used in the production of statistical information.
Published by: Instituto Nacional de Estadistica y Censos, Presidente Julio A Roca 615, Buenos Aires, 1067, Argentina. TEL 54-114-3499662, FAX 54-114-3499621.

318.2 ARG
I N D E C NORMAS. Text in Spanish. 1988. irreg., latest vol.3, 1991. ARS 5, USD 14 (effective 1999). **Document type:** *Monographic series, Government.* **Description:** Includes rules, classifications and base codes for preparing statistics.
Published by: Instituto Nacional de Estadistica y Censos, Presidente Julio A Roca 615, Buenos Aires, 1067, Argentina. TEL 54-114-3499662, FAX 54-114-3499621.

318.2 ARG
I N D E C RECOPILACIONES. Text in Spanish. 1996 (no.5). irreg., latest vol.6, 1997. ARS 25, USD 40 (effective 1999). **Document type:** *Government.* **Description:** Recopiles data from other series.
Published by: Instituto Nacional de Estadistica y Censos, Presidente Julio A Roca 615, Buenos Aires, 1067, Argentina. TEL 54-114-3499662, FAX 54-114-3499621.

310 ESP ISSN 1579-2277
I N E. CIFRAS. (Instituto Nacional de Estadistica) Text in Spanish. 2001. irreg. EUR 26 (effective 2010). **Document type:** *Bulletin, Government.*
Published by: Instituto Nacional de Estadistica (I N E), Paseo de la Castellana 183, Madrid, 28071, Spain. TEL 34-91-5839100, http://www.ine.es/.

I N S E E PICARDIE ANALYSES. *see* BUSINESS AND ECONOMICS—Abstracting, Bibliographies, Statistics

I N S E E PICARDIE DOSSIERS. *see* BUSINESS AND ECONOMICS—Abstracting, Bibliographies, Statistics

I N S E E RESULTATS. ECONOMIE (ONLINE). *see* BUSINESS AND ECONOMICS—Abstracting, Bibliographies, Statistics

I N S E E STATISTIQUES ET ETUDES: MIDI-PYRENEES. (Institut National de la Statistique et des Etudes Economiques) *see* BUSINESS AND ECONOMICS—Abstracting, Bibliographies, Statistics

I R I S RATIO RESULTS. *see* INSURANCE—Abstracting, Bibliographies, Statistics

I T U STATISTICAL YEARBOOK/ANNUAIRE STATISTIQUE DES L'U I T. *see* COMMUNICATIONS—Abstracting, Bibliographies, Statistics

314.912 ISL ISSN 1025-6903
ICELAND IN FIGURES. Text in English. 1996. a. USD 4 per issue (effective 2005). back issues avail. **Document type:** *Government.*
Related titles: Online - full text ed.; ◆ Icelandic ed.: Island i Toelum. ISSN 1025-6911.

S

Published by: Hagstofa Islands/Statistics Iceland, Borgartuni 12 A, Reykjavik, 150, Iceland. TEL 354-528-1000, FAX 354-528-1099. Ed. Bjorgvin Sigurdsson.

IDAHO CROP PROGRESS AND CONDITION. *see* AGRICULTURE—Abstracting, Bibliographies, Statistics

IDAHO. DEPARTMENT OF HEALTH AND WELFARE. VITAL STATISTICS (YEAR). *see* PUBLIC HEALTH AND SAFETY—Abstracting, Bibliographies, Statistics

310 339 BGR ISSN 1311-2376
HC403.A1
IKONOMIKA I FINANSI. Text in Bulgarian, English. a. BGL 10.79 domestic; USD 23 foreign (effective 2002). 120 p./no.; **Description:** Contains basic macroeconomic indexes.
Published by: Natsionalen Statisticheski Institut/National Statistical Institute, ul P Volov, # 2, Sofia, 1038, Bulgaria. FAX 359-2-9803319, publikacii@nsi.bg, http://www.nsi.bg.

314 FRA ISSN 1775-0326
HC277.I47
ILE-DE-FRANCE REGARDS SUR.. Text in French. 1979. irreg. adv. **Document type:** *Government.* **Description:** Concentrates on one particular economic or social theme per publication, such as housing, salaries, health, etc.
Former titles (until 2003): I N S E E Ile-de-France Regards (Institut National de la Statistique et des Etudes Economiques) (1281-1122); (until 1996): Regards sur l'Ile-de-France (0990-2562); (until 1988): Aspects Statistiques de l'Ile de France
Related titles: Online - full text ed.: free.
Published by: Institut National de la Statistique et des Etudes Economiques, Direction Regionale d'Ile-de-France, 7 rue Stephenson, Saint-quentin-en-yvelines, Cedex 78188, France. TEL 33-1-30969000, FAX 33-1-30969001. Ed. Annie Etienne. Adv. contact Francoise Charbonnier. Circ: 1,500.

ILLINOIS CITIES & COUNTIES GRAPHIC PERFORMANCE ANALYSIS. *see* PUBLIC ADMINISTRATION—Abstracting, Bibliographies, Statistics

ILLINOIS. DEPARTMENT OF HUMAN SERVICES. DIVISION OF DISABILITY AND BEHAVIORAL HEALTH SERVICES. ILLINOIS STATISTICS. *see* SOCIAL SERVICES AND WELFARE—Abstracting, Bibliographies, Statistics

310 USA ISSN 1933-5709
ILLINOIS STATISTICAL ABSTRACT (ONLINE). Text in English. 1987. a. free (effective 2007). **Description:** Presents a wide range of statistics for the state, counties, metropolitan areas and the US.
Formerly (until 2002): Illinois Statistical Abstract (Print) (1053-3443)
Related titles: CD-ROM ed.: USD 75 for CD ed.; USD 120 for CD & Print eds. (effective 2000); Diskette ed.: USD 60 per issue for Disk ed.; USD 110 per issue for Print & Disk eds. (effective 2000).
Published by: University of Illinois, Institute of Government & Public Affairs, 1007 W Nevada St, Urbana, IL 61801. TEL 217-333-3340. Eds. Hilal Yilmaz, Melike Bulu.

IMMIGRATION HIGHLIGHTS. *see* POPULATION STUDIES—Abstracting, Bibliographies, Statistics

319.4 AUS ISSN 1034-5051
IMMIGRATION UPDATE. Text in English. 1989. biennial. free (effective 2008). back issues avail. **Document type:** *Government.* **Description:** Provides current immigration statistics including settler arrivals, permanent departures, visitors, students and business data.
Former titles (until 1989): Australia. Department of Immigration and Ethnic Affairs. Statistics Monthly; (until 1982): Australian Immigration. Commonwealth Department of Immigration. Quarterly Statistical Bulletin (0004-9336); (until 1959): Commonwealth of Australia. Department of Immigration. Statistical Bulletin; New South Wales. Quarterly Statistical Bulletin; New South Wales. Monthly Statistical Bulletin
Related titles: Online - full text ed.: free (effective 2008).
Published by: Australian Government. Department of Immigration and Multicultural and Indigenous Affairs, PO Box 25, Belconnen, ACT 2616, Australia. TEL 61-2-62641111, FAX 61-2-62644466.

IMPACT OF INTERNATIONAL VISITOR SPENDING ON STATE ECONOMICS. *see* TRAVEL AND TOURISM

IMPORTS & EXPORTS OF CRUDE OIL AND PETROLEUM PRODUCTS. *see* PETROLEUM AND GAS

IMPORTS BY COMMODITIES/IMPORTATIONS PAR MARCHANDISE. *see* BUSINESS AND ECONOMICS—Abstracting, Bibliographies, Statistics

IMPORTS BY COUNTRIES. *see* BUSINESS AND ECONOMICS—Abstracting, Bibliographies, Statistics

310 USA ISSN 0737-4461
Z7552
INDEX TO INTERNATIONAL STATISTICS. Text in English. 1983. m. abstr. index, cum.index: 1983-87, 1988-91, 1992-95. back issues avail. **Document type:** *Abstract/Index.* **Description:** Identifies, catalogues, describes and indexes statistical publications of international and intergovernmental organizations.
Related titles: CD-ROM ed.
—BLDSC (4380.455200).
Published by: Congressional Information Service, Inc. (Subsidiary of: ProQuest), 789 E Eisenhower Pky, PO Box 1346, Ann Arbor, MI 48106. TEL 734-761-4700, academicinfo@proquest.com, http://www.proquest.com.

317 CAN ISSN 0843-6142
CA1BS12C205
INDEX TO STATISTICS CANADA SURVEYS AND QUESTIONNAIRES. Text in English, French. 1975. a. CAD 26, USD 31 domestic; USD 36 foreign. **Description:** Lists all the questionnaire-based surveys of Statistics Canada and the questionnaires used in conducting the surveys, under the Division of Statistics Canada that is responsible for the survey.
Former titles (until 1987): Index to the Inventory of Statistics Canada Questionnaires on Microfiche (0713-9349); (until 1980): Index to Statistics Canada Questionnaires (0228-5126); (until 1979): Index to Microfiche of Statistics Canada Surveys (0848-6255); (until 1978): Index and Reference Guide to the Microfiche Base (0848-6247); (until 1975): Inventory of Schedules and Reference Guide to the Microfilm Base (0848-6239)
Published by: Statistics Canada, Operations and Integration Division (Subsidiary of: Statistics Canada/Statistique Canada), Circulation Management, 120 Parkdale Ave, Ottawa, ON K1A 0T6, Canada. TEL 613-951-7277, 800-267-6677, FAX 613-951-1584.

INDIA. DEPARTMENT OF SCIENCE AND TECHNOLOGY. RESEARCH AND DEVELOPMENT STATISTICS. *see* SCIENCES: COMPREHENSIVE WORKS—Abstracting, Bibliographies, Statistics

INDIA. MINISTRY OF AGRICULTURE. BULLETIN ON FOOD STATISTICS. *see* AGRICULTURE—Abstracting, Bibliographies, Statistics

INDIA. MINISTRY OF HOME AFFAIRS. VITAL STATISTICS DIVISION. SURVEY OF CAUSES OF DEATH (RURAL). *see* POPULATION STUDIES—Abstracting, Bibliographies, Statistics

INDIA. OFFICE OF THE REGISTRAR GENERAL. SAMPLE REGISTRATION SYSTEM - STATISTICAL REPORT. *see* POPULATION STUDIES—Abstracting, Bibliographies, Statistics

INDIAN AND NORTHERN AFFAIRS CANADA. BASIC DEPARTMENTAL DATA. *see* SOCIOLOGY—Abstracting, Bibliographies, Statistics

INDIAN AND NORTHERN AFFAIRS CANADA. NORTHERN INDICATORS. *see* BUSINESS AND ECONOMICS—Abstracting, Bibliographies, Statistics

INDIAN FERTILISER STATISTICS. *see* AGRICULTURE—Abstracting, Bibliographies, Statistics

310 IND ISSN 0537-2585
HA1 CODEN: ISAJB6
INDIAN STATISTICAL ASSOCIATION. JOURNAL. Text in English. 1963. s-a. INR 500 domestic to non-members; USD 55 foreign to non-members; free to members (effective 2011). **Document type:** *Journal, Academic/Scholarly.*
Indexed: CCMJ, CIS, MSN, MathR.
—Ingenta.
Published by: Indian Statistical Association, c/o A P Gore, Department of Statistics, University of Pune, Pune, 411 007, India. Ed. V Naik Nimbalkar.

310 IND ISSN 0073-6686
INDIAN STATISTICAL INSTITUTE. ANNUAL REPORT. Text in English. 1933. a. free (effective 2011). **Document type:** *Report, Trade.*
Published by: Indian Statistical Institute, 203 Barrackpore Trunk Rd, Kolkata, West Bengal 700 108, India. TEL 91-33-25752001. Circ: 2,000.

INDIAN SUGAR YEARBOOK. *see* AGRICULTURE—Abstracting, Bibliographies, Statistics

INDIANA CITIES & COUNTIES GRAPHIC PERFORMANCE ANALYSIS. *see* PUBLIC ADMINISTRATION—Abstracting, Bibliographies, Statistics

INDICADORES BASICOS DE SALUD PROVINCIALES. *see* MEDICAL SCIENCES—Abstracting, Bibliographies, Statistics

INDICADORES DA PRODUCAO VEGETAL. *see* AGRICULTURE—Abstracting, Bibliographies, Statistics

INDICADORES DE ACTIVIDAD. INDUSTRIA MANUFACTURERA. *see* BUSINESS AND ECONOMICS—Abstracting, Bibliographies, Statistics

INDICADORES DE ACTIVIDADES. PRODUCCION DE VIVIENDAS NUEVAS. *see* HOUSING AND URBAN PLANNING—Abstracting, Bibliographies, Statistics

INDICADORES DE CONFORTO DAS FAMILIAS. *see* HOUSING AND URBAN PLANNING—Abstracting, Bibliographies, Statistics

318.61 COL ISSN 0120-9299
HC196
INDICADORES DE COYUNTURA. Text in Spanish. 1987. m. USD 120. **Document type:** *Government.*
Published by: Departamento Administrativo Nacional de Estadistica (D A N E), Bancos de Datos, Centro Administrativo Nacional (CAN), Avenida Eldorado, Apartado Aereo 80043, Bogota, CUND, Colombia. TEL 57-1-2221100, FAX 57-1-4444107. Ed. Dora Sanchez de Aponte.

INDICADORES DEL MERCADO DE PRODUCTOS DERIVADOS. *see* BUSINESS AND ECONOMICS—Abstracting, Bibliographies, Statistics

INDICADORES ECONOMICOS Y SOCIALES DE PANAMA. *see* BUSINESS AND ECONOMICS—Abstracting, Bibliographies, Statistics

INDICADORES MUNICIPALES. *see* PUBLIC ADMINISTRATION—Municipal Government

INDICADORES SOCIALES DE ESPANA. *see* POPULATION STUDIES—Abstracting, Bibliographies, Statistics

310 CRI
INDICE DE PRECIOS AL CONSUMIDOR. BOLETIN MENSUAL. Text in Spanish. 1989. m. free. charts; stat. **Document type:** *Trade.* **Description:** Monitors the prices of major consumer goods, by region, for the previous month, comparing various indices with those of previous months over the past year.
Formerly: Indice de Precios al Consumidor de Ingresos Medios y Bajos del Area Metropolitana de San Jose
Published by: Ministerio de Economia Industria y Comercio, Area de Estadistica y Censos, Apdo 10163, San Jose, 1000, Costa Rica. TEL 506-258-0033, FAX 506-223-0813.

339 PRI
INDICE DE PRECIOS AL CONSUMIDOR PARA TODAS LAS FAMILIAS EN PUERTO RICO. Text in English, Spanish. 1966. m. free. charts; stat. **Document type:** *Government.*
Formerly: Indice de Precios al Consumidor para Familias Obreras en Puerto Rico (0019-7017)
Media: Duplicated (not offset).
Published by: Department of Labor, Bureau of Labor Statistics, 505 Munoz Rivera Ave., Hato Rey, 00918, Puerto Rico. Ed. Guillermo Solla Velez.

INDICE DE PRECO AO CONSUMIDOR. *see* BUSINESS AND ECONOMICS—Abstracting, Bibliographies, Statistics

▼ **INDICE SINTETICO DE DESENVOLVIMENTO REGIONAL.** *see* BUSINESS AND ECONOMICS—Abstracting, Bibliographies, Statistics

INDICES DE PRECIOS DE LOS INSUMOS BASICOS DE LA INDUSTRIA DE LA CONSTRUCCION. *see* BUILDING AND CONSTRUCTION—Abstracting, Bibliographies, Statistics

INDONESIA OIL STATISTICS/STATISTIK PERMINYAKAN INDONESIA. *see* PETROLEUM AND GAS—Abstracting, Bibliographies, Statistics

310 IDN
INDONESIA. WELFARE INDICATORS. Text in English, Indonesian. 1972. a. IDR 20,000, USD 8.70. **Document type:** *Government.*
Formerly: Indonesia. Social Welfare Indicators
Published by: Central Bureau of Statistics/Biro Pusat Statistik, Jalan Dr. Sutomo No. 8, PO Box 3, Jakarta Pusat, Indonesia. TEL 62-21-372808. Circ: 200.

INDUSTRIA ASEGURADORA COLOMBIANA. ESTADISTICAS ANUALES. *see* INSURANCE—Abstracting, Bibliographies, Statistics

INDUSTRIAL MONITOR ON CD-ROM/HORIZON INDUSTRIEL SUR CD-ROM. *see* BUSINESS AND ECONOMICS—Abstracting, Bibliographies, Statistics

INDUSTRIAL TRENDS. *see* BUSINESS AND ECONOMICS—Abstracting, Bibliographies, Statistics

INDUSTRIE- UND HANDELSKAMMER ZU DORTMUND. STATISTISCHES JAHRBUCH. *see* BUSINESS AND ECONOMICS—Abstracting, Bibliographies, Statistics

INDUSTRIES DE SERVICE. BULLETIN. *see* BUSINESS AND ECONOMICS

INDUSTRY CANADA. CANADIAN I C T SECTOR. QUARTERLY MONITOR. (Information and Communications Technologies) *see* TECHNOLOGY: COMPREHENSIVE WORKS

INDUSTRY CANADA. MICRO-ECONOMIC POLICY ANALYSIS BRANCH. MONTHLY ECONOMIC INDICATORS. *see* BUSINESS AND ECONOMICS—Abstracting, Bibliographies, Statistics

INDUSTRY OF THE CZECH REPUBLIC. *see* BUSINESS AND ECONOMICS—Abstracting, Bibliographies, Statistics

001.422 ITA ISSN 1120-690X
INDUZIONI. Text in Italian. 1990. s-a. EUR 245 combined subscription domestic to institutions (print & online eds.); EUR 295 combined subscription foreign to institutions (print & online eds) (effective 2009). **Document type:** *Journal, Academic/Scholarly.* **Description:** For students and teachers of math, statistics, economy, history and geography.
Related titles: Online - full text ed.: ISSN 1724-0476.
Published by: Fabrizio Serra Editore (Subsidiary of: Accademia Editoriale), c/o Accademia Editoriale, Via Santa Bibbiana 28, Pisa, 56127, Italy. TEL 39-050-542332, FAX 39-050-574888, accademiaeditoriale@accademiaeditoriale.it, http://www.libraweb.net.

INEBASE. (Instituto Nacional de Estadistica) *see* POPULATION STUDIES—Abstracting, Bibliographies, Statistics

318 BOL
INFORMACION ESTADISTICA REGIONAL COCHABAMBA. Text in Spanish. a.?. free.
Published by: Instituto Nacional de Estadistica, Casilla de Correos 6129, La Paz, Bolivia. Circ: 1,000.

318 URY
INFORMACIONES Y ESTADISTICAS NACIONALES AND INTERNACIONALES. Text in Spanish. bi-m. USD 140 (effective 2001). **Document type:** *Bulletin.* **Description:** Provides data on production, demographics, economic indicators and trade.
Published by: Centro de Estadisticas Nacionales y Comercio Internacional del Uruguay, Misiones, 1361, Montevideo, 11000, Uruguay. TEL 598-2-952930, FAX 598-2-954578, cenci@adinet.com.uy.

INFORMATION AND COMMUNICATION TECHNOLOGY IN NEW ZEALAND. *see* COMMUNICATIONS—Abstracting, Bibliographies, Statistics

INFORMATION PAPER: SURVEY OF INCOME AND HOUSING, USER GUIDE, AUSTRALIA (ONLINE). *see* BUSINESS AND ECONOMICS—Abstracting, Bibliographies, Statistics

INFORMATSIYA O SOTSIAL'NO-EKONOMICHESKOM POLOZHENII ROSSII/INFORMATION ON SOCIAL AND ECONOMIC SITUATION OF RUSSIA. *see* BUSINESS AND ECONOMICS—Abstracting, Bibliographies, Statistics

310 CHL
INFORME SOBRE CHILE. Text in Spanish. 1975. s-a. CLP 99,000; USD 260 foreign. adv. stat.
Related titles: CD-ROM ed.
Published by: Editorial Gestion Ltda., Casilla 16485 Correo 9, Rafael Canas, 114, Santiago, Chile. TEL 56-2-2361313, FAX 56-2-2361114. Ed. Francisco Argote. Adv. contact Rodrigo Sepulveda. Circ: 10,000.

IN'GU IDONG TONG'GYE YEONBO/KOREA (REPUBLIC). NATIONAL STATISTICAL OFFICE. ANNUAL REPORT ON THE INTERNAL MIGRATION STATISTICS. *see* POPULATION STUDIES—Abstracting, Bibliographies, Statistics

IN'GU JUTAEG CHONG JO'SA JAMJEONG BO'GO'SEO/KOREA (REPUBLIC). NATIONAL STATISTICAL OFFICE. POPULATION AND HOUSING CENSUS REPORT. *see* POPULATION STUDIES—Abstracting, Bibliographies, Statistics

INJURY EXPERIENCE IN SAND AND GRAVEL MINING. *see* OCCUPATIONAL HEALTH AND SAFETY—Abstracting, Bibliographies, Statistics

INNOVATION IN NEW ZEALAND. *see* BUSINESS AND ECONOMICS—Abstracting, Bibliographies, Statistics

▼ **INQUERITO AO TRANSPORTE RODOVIARIO TRANSFRONTERICO.** *see* TRANSPORTATION—Abstracting, Bibliographies, Statistics

INQUERITO AS DESPESAS DAS FAMILIAS. *see* POPULATION STUDIES—Abstracting, Bibliographies, Statistics

INQUERITO MENSAL DE CONJUNTURA A CONSTRUCAO E OBRAS PUBLICAS. *see* PUBLIC ADMINISTRATION—Abstracting, Bibliographies, Statistics

▼ **INQUERITO NACIONAL DE SAUDE.** *see* PUBLIC HEALTH AND SAFETY—Abstracting, Bibliographies, Statistics

021 PRT ISSN 0250-4251
HD5809
INQUERITO PERMANENTE AO EMPREGO. Text in Portuguese. 1978. s-a.
Published by: Instituto Nacional de Estatistica, Av Antonio Jose de Almeida 2, Lisbon, 1000-043, Portugal. TEL 351-21-8426100, FAX 351-21-8426380, http://www.ine.pt.

INSIGHTS ON. see BUSINESS AND ECONOMICS—Abstracting, Bibliographies, Statistics

310 USA
HA1
INSTITUTE OF MATHEMATICAL STATISTICS. JOINT DIRECTORY OF MEMBERS. Variant title: The B S and I M S Joint Membership Directory. Text in English. 1961. triennial. free (effective 2009). **Document type:** *Directory, Trade.* **Description:** Contains a membership details.
Supersedes in part (in 1999): American Statistical Association, Biometric Society. Eastern North American Region, Biometric Society. Western North American Region. Members Directory (0740-7181); Which was formerly (until 1981): Directory of Statisticians (0278-405X); (until 1978): Statisticians and Others in Allied Professions (0081-508X); (until 1967): Directory of Statisticians and Others in Allied Professions; Members Directory incorporated (in 1981): The Institute of Mathematical Statistics Directory (0883-444X); Which was formerly (until 1984): Institute of Mathematical Statistics. Membership Directory
Related titles: Online - full text ed.: free (effective 2009).
Published by: (Bernoulli Society for Mathematical Statistics and Probability GBR), Institute of Mathematical Statistics, PO Box 22718, Beachwood, OH 44122. TEL 216-295-2340, FAX 216-295-5661, ims@imstat.org, http://www.imstat.org.

INSTITUTE OF PETROLEUM STATISTICS SERVICE. see PETROLEUM AND GAS—Abstracting, Bibliographies, Statistics

INSTITUTE OF STATISTICAL MATHEMATICS. ANNALS. see MATHEMATICS

310.510 JPN
INSTITUTE OF STATISTICAL MATHEMATICS. RESEARCH MEMORANDUM. Text in English. 1986 (no.300). irreg. (freq. varies between 1 to many issues a month). **Document type:** *Monographic series, Academic/Scholarly.*
Published by: Institute of Statistical Mathematics/Tokei Suri Kenkyujo, 4-6-7 Minami-Azabu, Minato-ku, Tokyo, 106-8569, Japan. http://www.ism.ac.jp.

310 URY ISSN 1688-101X
INSTITUTO NACIONAL DE ESTADISTICA. ANUARIO ESTADISTICO. Text in Spanish. 2000. a. back issues avail.
Media: Online - full content.
Published by: Instituto Nacional de Estadistica, Rio Negro 1520, Montevideo, 11100, Uruguay. TEL 598-2-9027303.

314 ESP ISSN 0066-5177
INSTITUTO NACIONAL DE ESTADISTICA. ANUARIO ESTADISTICO DE ESPANA: EDICION EXTENSA. Text in Spanish. 1912. a. EUR 36.95 combined subscription both print & CD eds. (effective 2009).
Related titles: CD-ROM ed.: ISSN 1579-2722.
Indexed: GeoRef.
Published by: Instituto Nacional de Estadistica (I N E), Paseo de la Castellana 183, Madrid, 28071, Spain. TEL 34-91-5839100.

INSTITUTO NACIONAL DE ESTADISTICA. BOLETIM MENSAL DE ESTADISTICA. see PUBLIC ADMINISTRATION—Abstracting, Bibliographies, Statistics

314 ESP ISSN 1132-0516
INSTITUTO NACIONAL DE ESTADISTICA. BOLETIN MENSUAL DE ESTADISTICA. Text in Spanish. 1918. m. EUR 161.91 (effective 2009). charts; stat. index. **Document type:** *Government.*
Former titles (until 1990): Instituto Nacional de Estadistica. Boletin de Estadistica (0212-6664); (until 1979): Instituto Nacional de Estadistica. Boletin Mensual de Estadistica (0038-6391); (until 1964): Instituto Nacional de Estadistica. Boletin de Estadistica (0210-5128); (until 1945): Direccion General de Estadistica. Boletin de Estadistica (1696-3172); (until 1939): Servicio Nacional de Estadistica. Boletin de Estadistica (1696-3164); (until 1935): Centro de Investigaciones Especiales o Laboratorio de Estadistica. Boletin (0210-5136); (until 1932): Direccion General del Instituto Geografico, Catastral y de Estadistica. Boletin de Estadistica (1696-3121); (until 1931): Servicio General de Estadistica. Boletin de Estadistica (1696-3091); (until 1926): Jefatura Superior de Estadistica. Boletin de Estadistica (1696-3105); (until 1924): Direccion General de Estadistica. Boletin de Estadistica (0210-5144); (until 1923): Direccion General del Instituto Geografico y Estadistico. Boletin de Estadistica (1697-2414)
Related titles: ◆ Supplement(s): Instituto Nacional de Estadistica. Estadistica Espanola. ISSN 0014-1151.
Indexed: RASB.
Published by: Instituto Nacional de Estadistica (I N E), Paseo de la Castellana 183, Madrid, 28071, Spain. TEL 34-91-5839100. Circ: 3,100.

INSTITUTO NACIONAL DE ESTADISTICA. ENCUESTA DE POBLACION ACTIVA (CD-ROM EDITION). see POPULATION STUDIES—Abstracting, Bibliographies, Statistics

314 ESP ISSN 0014-1151
HA1 CODEN: ESTEA7
INSTITUTO NACIONAL DE ESTADISTICA. ESTADISTICA ESPANOLA. Key Title: Estadistica Espanola. Text in Spanish. 1958. 3/yr. EUR 16.61 (effective 2009). bk.rev. bibl.; charts; illus.; stat. **Document type:** *Bulletin, Government.*
Formerly (until 1957): Instituto Nacional de Estadistica. Suplemento al Buletin de Estadistica (0490-3048)
Related titles: ◆ Supplement to: Instituto Nacional de Estadistica. Boletin Mensual de Estadistica. ISSN 1132-0516.
Indexed: CIS, IECT, PAIS, ST&MA.
Published by: Instituto Nacional de Estadistica (I N E), Paseo de la Castellana 183, Madrid, 28071, Spain. TEL 34-91-5839100. Circ: 1,000.

016 MEX ISSN 0186-0437
INSTITUTO NACIONAL DE ESTADISTICA, GEOGRAFIA E INFORMATICA. CATALOGO DE PUBLICACIONES. Text in Spanish. 1987. a. free. **Document type:** *Catalog.*
Former titles (until 1977): Catalogo de Informacion Estadistica y Geografica; (until 1976): Sistema Nacional de Informacion. Catalog Historico de Publicasione
Published by: Instituto Nacional de Estadistica, Geografia e Informatica, Secretaria de Programacion y Presupuesto, Prol. Heroe de Nacozari 2301 Sur, Puerta 11, Acceso, Aguascalientes, 20270, Mexico. TEL 52-4-918-1948, FAX 52-4-918-0739. Circ: 4,000.

INSURANCE INFORMATION INSTITUTE. FACT BOOK. see INSURANCE—Abstracting, Bibliographies, Statistics

INSURANCE REPORT AND STATISTICS OF FIJI. see INSURANCE—Abstracting, Bibliographies, Statistics

INSURANCE STATISTICS YEARBOOK. see INSURANCE—Abstracting, Bibliographies, Statistics

INTEGRALE VEILIGHEIDSMONITOR. LANDELIJKE RAPPORTAGE. see LAW—Abstracting, Bibliographies, Statistics

INTERFAX. RUSSIA & C I S STATISTICS WEEKLY. (Commonwealth of Independent States) see BUSINESS AND ECONOMICS—Abstracting, Bibliographies, Statistics

INTERNAL TRADE OF IRAN. see BUSINESS AND ECONOMICS—Domestic Commerce

310.519 NLD ISSN 1874-7655
HA1 CODEN: SJUED4
➤ **INTERNATIONAL ASSOCIATION FOR OFFICIAL STATISTICS. STATISTICAL JOURNAL.** Text in English. 1982. q. USD 761 combined subscription in North America (print & online eds.); EUR 545 combined subscription elsewhere (print & online eds.) (effective 2012). adv. bk.rev. back issues avail. **Document type:** *Journal, Academic/Scholarly.* **Description:** Provides information for the professional world of statisticians and establishes a forum for critical discussion of the entire range of problems facing statistical services.
Formerly (until 2007): United Nations. Economic Commission for Europe. Statistical Journal (0167-8000)
Related titles: Online - full text ed.: ISSN 1875-9254 (from IngentaConnect).
Indexed: A01, A02, A03, A08, A22, B01, B06, B07, B08, B09, C12, CA, CIS, CPEI, E01, ESPM, EconLit, EngInd, IIS, Inspec, JCQM, JEL, M01, M02, P30, RiskAb, SCOPUS, SSciA, ST&MA, T02, WBA, WMB.
—BLDSC (8448.552100), AskIEEE, IE, Infotrieve, Ingenta, INIST. **CCC.**
Published by: (International Association for Official Statistics), I O S Press, Nieuwe Hemweg 6B, Amsterdam, 1013 BG, Netherlands. TEL 31-20-6883355, FAX 31-20-6870019, info@iospress.nl, http://www.iospress.nl. Ed. Frank Nolan. **Subscr. to:** I O S Press, Inc, 4502 Rachael Manor Dr, Fairfax, VA 22032-3631. sales@iospress.com; Globe Publication Pvt. Ltd., C-62 Inderpuri, New Delhi 100 012, India. TEL 91-11-579-3211, 91-11-579-3212, FAX 91-11-579-8876, custserve@globepub.com, http://www.globepub.com; Kinokuniya Co Ltd., Shinjuku 3-chome, Shinjuku-ku, Tokyo 160-0022, Japan. FAX 81-3-3439-1094, journal@kinokuniya.co.jp, http://www.kinokuniya.co.jp.

➤ **INTERNATIONAL AUTO STATISTICS.** see TRANSPORTATION—Abstracting, Bibliographies, Statistics

➤ **INTERNATIONAL CIVIL AVIATION ORGANIZATION. DIGESTS OF STATISTICS. SERIES AF. AIRPORT AND ROUTE FACILITIES. FINANCIAL DATA AND SUMMARY TRAFFIC DATA/ MEZHDUNARODNAYA ORGANIZATSIYA GRAZHDANSKOI AVIATSII. STATISTICHESKII SBORNIK. SERIYA AF. AEROPORTNOE I MARSHRUTNOE OBORUDOVANIE. FINANSOVYE IZLOZHENIYA DANNYKH PO PEREVOZKAM/ ORGANISATION DE L'AVIATION CIVILE. RECUEIL DE STATISTIQUES. SERIE AF. INSTALLATIONS ET SERVICES D'AEROPORT ET DE ROUTE. DONNES FINANCIERES ET STATISTIQUES DE TRAFFIC SOMMAIRES/ORGANIZACION DE AVIACION CIVIL INTERNACIONAL. COMPENDIO ESTADISTICO. SERIE AF. INSTALACIONES Y SERVICIOS DE AEROPUERTO Y EN RUTA. DATOS FINANCIEROS Y RESUMEN DE DATOS DE TRAFICO.** see TRANSPORTATION—Abstracting, Bibliographies, Statistics

➤ **INTERNATIONAL CIVIL AVIATION ORGANIZATION. DIGESTS OF STATISTICS. SERIES AT. AIRPORT TRAFFIC.** see TRANSPORTATION—Abstracting, Bibliographies, Statistics

➤ **INTERNATIONAL CIVIL AVIATION ORGANIZATION. DIGESTS OF STATISTICS. SERIES F. FINANCIAL DATA - COMMERCIAL AIR CARRIERS.** see TRANSPORTATION—Abstracting, Bibliographies, Statistics

➤ **INTERNATIONAL CIVIL AVIATION ORGANIZATION. DIGESTS OF STATISTICS. SERIES FP. FLEET - PERSONNEL - COMMERCIAL AIR CARRIERS.** see TRANSPORTATION—Abstracting, Bibliographies, Statistics

➤ **INTERNATIONAL CIVIL AVIATION ORGANIZATION. DIGESTS OF STATISTICS. SERIES OFOD. ON-FLIGHT ORIGIN AND DESTINATION/MEZHDUNARODNAYA ORGANIZATSIYA GRAZHDANSKOI AVIATSII. STATISTICHESKII SBORNIK. SERIYA OFOD. NACHALNYI I KONECHNYI PUNKTY POLETA/ ORGANISATION DE L'AVIATION CIVILE INTERNATIONALE. RECUEIL DE STATISTIQUES. SERIE OFOD. ORIGINE ET DESTINATION PAR VOL/ORGANIZACION DE AVIACION CIVIL INTERNACIONAL. COMPENDIO ESTADISTICO. SERIE OFOD. ORIGEN Y DESTINO POR VUELO.** see TRANSPORTATION—Abstracting, Bibliographies, Statistics

➤ **INTERNATIONAL CIVIL AVIATION ORGANIZATION. DIGESTS OF STATISTICS. SERIES T. TRAFFIC, COMMERCIAL AIR TRAFFIC.** see TRANSPORTATION—Abstracting, Bibliographies, Statistics

➤ **INTERNATIONAL CIVIL AVIATION ORGANIZATION. DIGESTS OF STATISTICS. SERIES TF. TRAFFIC BY FLIGHT STAGE.** see TRANSPORTATION—Abstracting, Bibliographies, Statistics

➤ **INTERNATIONAL COMMISSION FOR THE CONSERVATION OF ATLANTIC TUNAS. STATISTICAL BULLETIN/COMISION INTERNACIONAL PARA LA CONSERVACION DEL ATUN ATLANTICO. BOLETIN ESTADISTICO/COMMISSION INTERNATIONALE POUR LA CONSERVATION DES THONIDES DE L'ATLANTIQUE. BULLETIN STATISTIQUE.** see FISH AND FISHERIES—Abstracting, Bibliographies, Statistics

➤ **INTERNATIONAL CONFERENCE ON TEACHING STATISTICS. PROCEEDINGS.** see EDUCATION—Teaching Methods And Curriculum

➤ **INTERNATIONAL COTTON INDUSTRY STATISTICS.** see TEXTILE INDUSTRIES AND FABRICS—Abstracting, Bibliographies, Statistics

➤ **INTERNATIONAL GRAINS COUNCIL. WORLD GRAIN STATISTICS (YEAR) (ONLINE).** see AGRICULTURE—Abstracting, Bibliographies, Statistics

310.004 USA ISSN 2152-5080
▼ ➤ **INTERNATIONAL JOURNAL FOR UNCERTAINTY QUANTIFICATIONS.** Text in English. 2010 (Apr.). q. USD 646; USD 655 combined subscription (print & online eds.) (effective 2010). **Document type:** *Journal, Academic/Scholarly.* **Description:** Features information and research on the analysis, modeling, design and control of complexity systems in the presence of uncertainity, including cross stochastic analysis, statistical modeling and scientific computing.
Related titles: Online - full text ed.: ISSN 2152-5099. 2010 (Apr.).
Published by: Begell House Inc., 50 Cross Hwy, Redding, CT 06896. TEL 203-938-1300, FAX 203-938-1304, orders@begellhouse.com, http://www.begellhouse.com. Ed. Nocholas Zabaras.

➤ **INTERNATIONAL JOURNAL OF AGRICULTURAL AND STATISTICS SCIENCES.** see AGRICULTURE

➤ **INTERNATIONAL JOURNAL OF APPLIED MATHEMATICS & STATISTICS.** see MATHEMATICS

➤ **INTERNATIONAL JOURNAL OF ECOLOGICAL ECONOMICS & STATISTICS.** see BIOLOGY

➤ **INTERNATIONAL JOURNAL OF INTELLIGENT TECHNOLOGIES AND STATISTICS.** see MATHEMATICS

➤ **INTERNATIONAL JOURNAL OF MATHEMATICS AND STATISTICS.** see MATHEMATICS

310 MYS ISSN 2180-1339
▼ ➤ **INTERNATIONAL JOURNAL OF SCIENTIFIC AND STATISTICAL COMPUTING.** Text in English. 2010. bi-m. MYR 3,700 domestic to individuals; USD 1,200 foreign to individuals; MYR 4,642 domestic to institutions; USD 1,500 foreign to institutions (effective 2011). bk.rev. abstr.; bibl. Index. back issues avail. **Document type:** *Journal, Academic/Scholarly.* **Description:** Publishes research articles on numerical methods and techniques for scientific and statistical computation, focusing on new methodology on new computational and statistical modeling ideas; practical applications on interesting problems, which are addressed using an existing or a novel adaptation of an computational and statistical modeling techniques; and tutorials & reviews with papers on recent topics in computational and statistical concepts.
Related titles: Online - full text ed.
Published by: Computer Science Journals, M-3-19 Plaza Damas, Sri Hartamas, Kuala Lumpur, 50480, Malaysia. TEL 60-3-62071607, FAX 60-3-62071697, info@cscjournals.org. Pub. M.N. Tahir.

310.330 IND ISSN 0975-556X
➤ **INTERNATIONAL JOURNAL OF STATISTICS AND ECONOMICS.** Text in English. 2007. s-a. EUR 400 domestic to individuals; USD 600 in United States to institutions; USD 500 SAARC to institutions; EUR 550 elsewhere to institutions; USD 950 combined subscription in United States to institutions (print & online eds.); USD 800 combined subscription SAARC to institutions (print & online eds.); EUR 900 combined subscription elsewhere to institutions (print & online eds.) (effective 2011). back issues avail. **Document type:** *Journal, Academic/Scholarly.* **Description:** Publishes papers in all areas of statistics and economics with an emphasis on the practical importance, theoretical interest and policy-relevance of their substantive results.
Formerly (until 2009): Bulletin of Statistics and Economics (0973-7022)
Related titles: Online - full text ed.
Indexed: A26, B01, B07, CA, EconLit, I05, MSN, T02, Z02.
Published by: Centre for Environment, Social and Economic Research Publications, PO Box 113, Roorkee, Uttarakhand 247 667, India. http://www.ceser.res.in. Eds. Dr. Kaushal k Srivastava, Mrs. Tanuja Srivastava.

519.5 IND ISSN 0973-7359
INTERNATIONAL JOURNAL OF STATISTICS AND MANAGEMENT SYSTEM. Abbreviated title: I J S M S. Text in English. 2006. s-a. INR 3,000, USD 150 to institutions (effective 2011). **Document type:** *Journal, Academic/Scholarly.* **Description:** Publishes research and review articles in statistics and management systems.
Indexed: MSN.
Published by: Serials Publications, 4830/24, Ansari Rd, Darya Ganj, New Delhi, 110 002, India. TEL 91-11-23245225, FAX 91-11-23272135, serialspublications.india@gmail.com. Ed. Jiming Jiang.

310 IND ISSN 0973-2675
➤ **INTERNATIONAL JOURNAL OF STATISTICS AND SYSTEMS.** Abbreviated title: I J S S. Text in English. 2006. q. INR 3,000 domestic to libraries; USD 480 foreign to libraries; USD 520 combined subscription foreign to libraries (print & online eds.) (effective 2011). back issues avail. **Document type:** *Journal, Academic/Scholarly.* **Description:** Covers all disciplines and branches of statistics and management systems.
Related titles: Online - full text ed.: ISSN 0974-4851. USD 460 to libraries (effective 2011).
Indexed: A01, CA, T02.
Published by: Research India Publications, D1/71, Top Fl, Rohini Sec-16, New Delhi, 110 089, India. TEL 91-11-65394240, FAX 91-11-27297815, info@ripublication.com.

➤ **INTERNATIONAL MARKETING FORECASTS.** see BUSINESS AND ECONOMICS—Abstracting, Bibliographies, Statistics

➤ **INTERNATIONAL MONETARY FUND. DIRECTION OF TRADE STATISTICS.** see BUSINESS AND ECONOMICS—Abstracting, Bibliographies, Statistics

➤ **INTERNATIONAL NARCOTICS CONTROL BOARD. PSYCHOTROPIC SUBSTANCES;** assessments of medical and scientific requirements. see PHARMACY AND PHARMACOLOGY—Abstracting, Bibliographies, Statistics

➤ **INTERNATIONAL PHOTO PROCESSING INDUSTRY REPORT.** see PHOTOGRAPHY—Abstracting, Bibliographies, Statistics

➤ **INTERNATIONAL RAYON AND SYNTHETIC FIBRES COMMITTEE. STATISTICAL YEARBOOK.** see TEXTILE INDUSTRIES AND FABRICS—Abstracting, Bibliographies, Statistics

S

➤ **INTERNATIONAL STATISTICAL CLASSIFICATION OF DISEASES & RELATED HEALTH PROBLEMS.** *see* MEDICAL SCIENCES—Communicable Diseases

➤ **INTERNATIONAL STATISTICAL HANDBOOK OF URBAN PUBLIC TRANSPORT/INTERNATIONALES STATISTIK-HANDBUCH FUER DEN OEFFENTLICHEN STADTVERKEHR/RECUEIL INTERNATIONAL DE STATISTIQUES DES TRANSPORTS PUBLICS URBAINS.** *see* TRANSPORTATION—Abstracting, Bibliographies, Statistics

310 NLD ISSN 0074-8609
HA11 CODEN: BIISAR
INTERNATIONAL STATISTICAL INSTITUTE. BULLETIN. PROCEEDINGS OF THE BIENNIAL SESSIONS. Text in English. 1885. biennial. EUR 102 (effective 2009). back issues avail. **Document type:** *Proceedings, Academic/Scholarly.* **Description:** Publishes the proceedings of the biennial sessions of the ISI, including the text of all invited papers covering the spectrum of the statistical profession: statistical theory and method, applied statistics, and other topics.
Related titles: CD-ROM ed.: 2001. EUR 84 (effective 2003).
Indexed: AESIS, CIS, GeoRef, MathR, ST&MA.
—Linda Hall.
Published by: International Statistical Institute, PO Box 24070, The Hague, 2490 AB, Netherlands. TEL 31-70-3375737, FAX 31-70-3860025, isi@cbs.nl, http://www.cbs.nl/.

INTERNATIONAL STATISTICAL INSTITUTE. NEWSLETTER. *see* MATHEMATICS

519.5 GBR ISSN 0306-7734
HA11 CODEN: ISTRDP
➤ **INTERNATIONAL STATISTICAL REVIEW/REVUE INTERNATIONALE DE STATISTIQUE.** Abbreviated title: I S R. Text in English. 1920. 3/yr. GBP 245 combined subscription in United Kingdom to institutions (print & online eds.); EUR 311 combined subscription in Europe to institutions (print & online eds.); USD 441 combined subscription in the Americas to institutions (print & online eds.); USD 480 combined subscription elsewhere to institutions (print & online eds.) (effective 2012). adv. charts; illus.; stat. index. 170 p./no.; back issues avail.; reprints avail. **Document type:** *Journal, Academic/Scholarly.* **Description:** Provides a view of work in statistics, covering the spectrum of the statistical profession and including the most relevant aspects of probability.
Incorporates (1980-2007): Short Book Reviews (0254-7694); Former titles (until 1972): International Statistical Institute Review (0373-1138); (until 1933): Institut International de Statistique. Office Permanent. Bulletin Mensuel (1872-972X)
Related titles: Online - full text ed.: ISSN 1751-5823. GBP 223 in United Kingdom to institutions; EUR 282 in Europe to institutions; USD 401 in the Americas to institutions; USD 436 elsewhere to institutions (effective 2012) (from IngentaConnect).
Indexed: A01, A20, A22, ASCA, BibInd, Biostat, CA, CIS, CMCI, CPM, CurCont, E01, GeoRef, H05, ISR, Inspec, JCQM, MathR, ORMS, P03, P06, P30, P33, P50, PsycInfo, QC&AS, R08, RASB, SCI, SCOPUS, ST&MA, SpeleolAb, T02, T05, W07, Z02.
—BLDSC (4549.660000), IE, Infotrieve, Ingenta, INIST, Linda Hall. **CCC.**
Published by: (International Statistical Institute NLD), Wiley-Blackwell Publishing Ltd. (Subsidiary of: John Wiley & Sons, Inc.), 9600 Garsington Rd, Oxford, OX4 2DQ, United Kingdom. TEL 44-1865-776868, FAX 44-1865-714591, customerservices@blackwellpublishing.com. Eds. Marc Hallin, Vijay Nair.

➤ **INTERNATIONAL STEEL STATISTICS - AUSTRALIA.** *see* METALLURGY—Abstracting, Bibliographies, Statistics

➤ **INTERNATIONAL STEEL STATISTICS - AUSTRIA.** *see* METALLURGY—Abstracting, Bibliographies, Statistics

➤ **INTERNATIONAL STEEL STATISTICS - BELGIUM, LUXEMBOURG.** *see* METALLURGY—Abstracting, Bibliographies, Statistics

➤ **INTERNATIONAL STEEL STATISTICS - BRAZIL.** *see* METALLURGY—Abstracting, Bibliographies, Statistics

➤ **INTERNATIONAL STEEL STATISTICS - CANADA.** *see* METALLURGY—Abstracting, Bibliographies, Statistics

➤ **INTERNATIONAL STEEL STATISTICS - CHINA.** *see* METALLURGY—Abstracting, Bibliographies, Statistics

➤ **INTERNATIONAL STEEL STATISTICS - DENMARK.** *see* METALLURGY—Abstracting, Bibliographies, Statistics

➤ **INTERNATIONAL STEEL STATISTICS - FINLAND.** *see* METALLURGY—Abstracting, Bibliographies, Statistics

➤ **INTERNATIONAL STEEL STATISTICS - FRANCE.** *see* METALLURGY—Abstracting, Bibliographies, Statistics

➤ **INTERNATIONAL STEEL STATISTICS - GERMANY.** *see* METALLURGY—Abstracting, Bibliographies, Statistics

➤ **INTERNATIONAL STEEL STATISTICS - GREECE.** *see* METALLURGY—Abstracting, Bibliographies, Statistics

➤ **INTERNATIONAL STEEL STATISTICS - IRISH REPUBLIC.** *see* METALLURGY—Abstracting, Bibliographies, Statistics

➤ **INTERNATIONAL STEEL STATISTICS - ITALY.** *see* METALLURGY—Abstracting, Bibliographies, Statistics

➤ **INTERNATIONAL STEEL STATISTICS - JAPAN.** *see* METALLURGY—Abstracting, Bibliographies, Statistics

➤ **INTERNATIONAL STEEL STATISTICS - NETHERLANDS.** *see* METALLURGY—Abstracting, Bibliographies, Statistics

➤ **INTERNATIONAL STEEL STATISTICS - NORWAY.** *see* METALLURGY—Abstracting, Bibliographies, Statistics

➤ **INTERNATIONAL STEEL STATISTICS - PORTUGAL.** *see* METALLURGY—Abstracting, Bibliographies, Statistics

➤ **INTERNATIONAL STEEL STATISTICS - RUSSIA.** *see* METALLURGY—Abstracting, Bibliographies, Statistics

➤ **INTERNATIONAL STEEL STATISTICS - SOUTH KOREA.** *see* METALLURGY—Abstracting, Bibliographies, Statistics

➤ **INTERNATIONAL STEEL STATISTICS - SPAIN.** *see* METALLURGY—Abstracting, Bibliographies, Statistics

➤ **INTERNATIONAL STEEL STATISTICS - SUMMARY TABLES.** *see* METALLURGY—Abstracting, Bibliographies, Statistics

➤ **INTERNATIONAL STEEL STATISTICS - SWEDEN.** *see* METALLURGY—Abstracting, Bibliographies, Statistics

➤ **INTERNATIONAL STEEL STATISTICS - SWITZERLAND.** *see* METALLURGY—Abstracting, Bibliographies, Statistics

➤ **INTERNATIONAL STEEL STATISTICS - TAIWAN.** *see* METALLURGY—Abstracting, Bibliographies, Statistics

➤ **INTERNATIONAL STEEL STATISTICS - U S A.** *see* METALLURGY—Abstracting, Bibliographies, Statistics

➤ **INTERNATIONAL STEEL STATISTICS - UNITED KINGDOM.** *see* METALLURGY—Abstracting, Bibliographies, Statistics

➤ **INTERNATIONAL SUGAR ORGANIZATION. MARKET REPORT AND PRESS SUMMARY.** *see* FOOD AND FOOD INDUSTRIES

➤ **INTERNATIONAL SUGAR ORGANIZATION. PROCEEDINGS.** *see* FOOD AND FOOD INDUSTRIES

➤ **INTERNATIONAL SUGAR ORGANIZATION. STATISTICAL BULLETIN.** *see* FOOD AND FOOD INDUSTRIES—Abstracting, Bibliographies, Statistics

➤ **INTERNATIONAL TEXTILE MACHINERY SHIPMENT STATISTICS.** *see* TEXTILE INDUSTRIES AND FABRICS—Abstracting, Bibliographies, Statistics

➤ **INTERNATIONAL TRADE BY COMMODITIES STATISTICS/ STATISTIQUES DU COMMERCE INTERNATIONAL PAR PRODUIT.** *see* BUSINESS AND ECONOMICS—Abstracting, Bibliographies, Statistics

➤ **INTERNATIONAL VISITOR ARRIVALS TO NEW ZEALAND (ONLINE).** *see* TRAVEL AND TOURISM—Abstracting, Bibliographies, Statistics

➤ **INTERNATIONAL VISITORS IN AUSTRALIA (ONLINE).** *see* TRAVEL AND TOURISM—Abstracting, Bibliographies, Statistics

➤ **INTERNATIONAL YEARBOOK OF INDUSTRIAL STATISTICS (YEAR).** *see* BUSINESS AND ECONOMICS—Abstracting, Bibliographies, Statistics

310 USA ISSN 1941-689X
QA276.A1
➤ **INTERSTAT.** Text in English. 1995. irreg. free (effective 2011). stat. index. back issues avail. **Document type:** *Journal, Academic/Scholarly.* **Description:** Features articles that covering a wide range of topics related to statistics.
Media: Online - full text.

➤ **INVESTITSIONNAYA DEYATEL'NOST' V ROSSII: USLOVIYA, FAKTORY, TENDENTSII (YEAR)/INVESTMENT ACTIVITY IN RUSSIA: CONDITIONS, FACTORS AND TENDENCIES.** *see* BUSINESS AND ECONOMICS—Abstracting, Bibliographies, Statistics

➤ **IOWA. AGRICULTURAL STATISTICS SERVICE. AGRI-NEWS.** *see* AGRICULTURE—Abstracting, Bibliographies, Statistics

➤ **IOWA CITIES & COUNTIES GRAPHIC PERFORMANCE ANALYSIS.** *see* PUBLIC ADMINISTRATION—Abstracting, Bibliographies, Statistics

➤ **IOWA CROPS & WEATHER.** *see* AGRICULTURE—Abstracting, Bibliographies, Statistics

➤ **IOWA OFFICIAL REGISTER.** *see* PUBLIC ADMINISTRATION—Abstracting, Bibliographies, Statistics

➤ **IOWA STATE UNIVERSITY. STATISTICAL LABORATORY. ANNUAL REPORT.** *see* MATHEMATICS—Abstracting, Bibliographies, Statistics

310 IRN ISSN 1010-9633
HA4570.2
IRAN DAR A'INAH-I AMAR. Text in Persian, Modern. 1981. a.
Related titles: ◆ English ed.: Statistical Pocket Book of the Islamic Republic of Iran.
Published by: Statistical Centre of Iran, Dr. Fatemi Ave., Tehran, 14144, Iran. TEL 98-21-655061, FAX 98-21-653451.

IRAN. MINISTRY OF ECONOMY. BUREAU OF STATISTICS. SERIES. *see* BUSINESS AND ECONOMICS—Abstracting, Bibliographies, Statistics

319.55 IRN ISSN 1017-2564
HA4570.2
IRAN STATISTICAL YEARBOOK. Key Title: Salnamah-i Amari-i Kishvar. Text in Persian, Modern, English. 1967. a. GBP 49 (effective 2006). charts; illus.; stat. **Document type:** *Government.*
Published by: Statistical Centre of Iran, Dr. Fatemi Ave., Tehran, 14144, Iran. TEL 98-21-655061, FAX 98-21-653451. Circ: 3,500.

IRANIAN INDUSTRIAL STATISTICS. *see* BUSINESS AND ECONOMICS—Abstracting, Bibliographies, Statistics

IRANIAN MINERAL STATISTICS. *see* MINES AND MINING INDUSTRY—Abstracting, Bibliographies, Statistics

IRELAND. CENTRAL STATISTICAL OFFICE. AGRICULTURAL LAND SALES. *see* AGRICULTURE—Abstracting, Bibliographies, Statistics

IRELAND. CENTRAL STATISTICS OFFICE. ADVERTISING AGENCIES INQUIRY. *see* ADVERTISING AND PUBLIC RELATIONS—Abstracting, Bibliographies, Statistics

IRELAND. CENTRAL STATISTICS OFFICE. AGRICULTURAL LABOUR INPUT. *see* AGRICULTURE—Abstracting, Bibliographies, Statistics

IRELAND. CENTRAL STATISTICS OFFICE. AGRICULTURAL PRICE INDICES. *see* AGRICULTURE—Abstracting, Bibliographies, Statistics

IRELAND. CENTRAL STATISTICS OFFICE. AGRICULTURAL PRICE INDICES. PRELIMINARY ESTIMATES. *see* AGRICULTURE—Abstracting, Bibliographies, Statistics

IRELAND. CENTRAL STATISTICS OFFICE. ANNUAL SERVICES INQUIRY. *see* BUSINESS AND ECONOMICS—Abstracting, Bibliographies, Statistics

IRELAND. CENTRAL STATISTICS OFFICE. BALANCE OF INTERNATIONAL PAYMENTS. *see* BUSINESS AND ECONOMICS—Abstracting, Bibliographies, Statistics

IRELAND. CENTRAL STATISTICS OFFICE. BUILDING AND CONSTRUCTION PLANNING PERMISSIONS. *see* HOUSING AND URBAN PLANNING—Abstracting, Bibliographies, Statistics

IRELAND. CENTRAL STATISTICS OFFICE. CAPITAL ASSETS IN INDUSTRY. *see* BUSINESS AND ECONOMICS—Abstracting, Bibliographies, Statistics

IRELAND. CENTRAL STATISTICS OFFICE. CENSUS OF INDUSTRIAL PRODUCTION. *see* BUSINESS AND ECONOMICS—Abstracting, Bibliographies, Statistics

IRELAND. CENTRAL STATISTICS OFFICE. CENSUS OF INDUSTRIAL PRODUCTION. PROVISIONAL RESULTS. *see* BUSINESS AND ECONOMICS—Abstracting, Bibliographies, Statistics

IRELAND. CENTRAL STATISTICS OFFICE. CENSUS OF POPULATION. PRINCIPAL DEMOGRAPHIC RESULTS. *see* POPULATION STUDIES—Abstracting, Bibliographies, Statistics

IRELAND. CENTRAL STATISTICS OFFICE. CENSUS OF POPULATION. PRINCIPAL SOCIOECONOMIC RESULTS. *see* POPULATION STUDIES—Abstracting, Bibliographies, Statistics

IRELAND. CENTRAL STATISTICS OFFICE. CENSUS OF POPULATION. VOLUME 1: POPULATION CLASSIFIED BY AREA. *see* POPULATION STUDIES—Abstracting, Bibliographies, Statistics

IRELAND. CENTRAL STATISTICS OFFICE. CENSUS OF POPULATION. VOLUME 10: EDUCATION AND QUALIFICATIONS. *see* POPULATION STUDIES—Abstracting, Bibliographies, Statistics

IRELAND. CENTRAL STATISTICS OFFICE. CENSUS OF POPULATION. VOLUME 12: TRAVEL TO WORK, SCHOOL AND COLLEGE. *see* POPULATION STUDIES—Abstracting, Bibliographies, Statistics

IRELAND. CENTRAL STATISTICS OFFICE. CENSUS OF POPULATION. VOLUME 2: AGES AND MARITAL STATUS. *see* POPULATION STUDIES—Abstracting, Bibliographies, Statistics

IRELAND. CENTRAL STATISTICS OFFICE. CENSUS OF POPULATION. VOLUME 3: HOUSEHOLD COMPOSITION, FAMILY UNITS AND FERTILITY. *see* POPULATION STUDIES—Abstracting, Bibliographies, Statistics

IRELAND. CENTRAL STATISTICS OFFICE. CENSUS OF POPULATION. VOLUME 4: USUAL RESIDENCE, MIGRATION, BIRTHPLACES AND NATIONALITIES. *see* POPULATION STUDIES—Abstracting, Bibliographies, Statistics

IRELAND. CENTRAL STATISTICS OFFICE. CENSUS OF POPULATION. VOLUME 7: PRINCIPAL ECONOMIC STATUS AND INDUSTRIES. *see* POPULATION STUDIES—Abstracting, Bibliographies, Statistics

IRELAND. CENTRAL STATISTICS OFFICE. CENSUS OF POPULATION. VOLUME 8: OCCUPATIONS. *see* POPULATION STUDIES—Abstracting, Bibliographies, Statistics

IRELAND. CENTRAL STATISTICS OFFICE. CENSUS OF POPULATION. VOLUME 9: IRISH LANGUAGE. *see* POPULATION STUDIES—Abstracting, Bibliographies, Statistics

IRELAND. CENTRAL STATISTICS OFFICE. CEREALS SUPPLY BALANCE. *see* AGRICULTURE—Abstracting, Bibliographies, Statistics

IRELAND. CENTRAL STATISTICS OFFICE. CONSUMER PRICE INDEX. *see* BUSINESS AND ECONOMICS—Abstracting, Bibliographies, Statistics

IRELAND. CENTRAL STATISTICS OFFICE. CONSUMER PRICE INDEX DETAILED SUB-INDICES RELEASE. *see* BUSINESS AND ECONOMICS—Abstracting, Bibliographies, Statistics

IRELAND. CENTRAL STATISTICS OFFICE. COUNTY INCOMES AND REGIONAL GDP. *see* BUSINESS AND ECONOMICS—Abstracting, Bibliographies, Statistics

IRELAND. CENTRAL STATISTICS OFFICE. CROPS AND LIVESTOCK SURVEY - FINAL ESTIMATES. *see* AGRICULTURE—Abstracting, Bibliographies, Statistics

IRELAND. CENTRAL STATISTICS OFFICE. CROPS AND LIVESTOCK SURVEY, JUNE - PROVISIONAL RESULTS. *see* AGRICULTURE—Abstracting, Bibliographies, Statistics

IRELAND. CENTRAL STATISTICS OFFICE. DECEMBER LIVESTOCK SURVEY. *see* AGRICULTURE—Abstracting, Bibliographies, Statistics

IRELAND. CENTRAL STATISTICS OFFICE. EARNINGS AND HOURS WORKED IN CONSTRUCTION. *see* BUILDING AND CONSTRUCTION—Abstracting, Bibliographies, Statistics

IRELAND. CENTRAL STATISTICS OFFICE. EARNINGS AND LABOUR COSTS. *see* BUSINESS AND ECONOMICS—Abstracting, Bibliographies, Statistics

IRELAND. CENTRAL STATISTICS OFFICE. EARNINGS OF AGRICULTURAL WORKERS. *see* AGRICULTURE—Abstracting, Bibliographies, Statistics

IRELAND. CENTRAL STATISTICS OFFICE. EXTERNAL TRADE. *see* BUSINESS AND ECONOMICS—Abstracting, Bibliographies, Statistics

IRELAND. CENTRAL STATISTICS OFFICE. FARM STRUCTURES SURVEY. *see* AGRICULTURE—Abstracting, Bibliographies, Statistics

IRELAND. CENTRAL STATISTICS OFFICE. FISHERY STATISTICS. *see* FISH AND FISHERIES—Abstracting, Bibliographies, Statistics

IRELAND. CENTRAL STATISTICS OFFICE. HEADLINE CRIME STATISTICS. *see* CRIMINOLOGY AND LAW ENFORCEMENT—Abstracting, Bibliographies, Statistics

IRELAND. CENTRAL STATISTICS OFFICE. HOUSEHOLD BUDGET SURVEY. *see* HOME ECONOMICS—Abstracting, Bibliographies, Statistics

IRELAND. CENTRAL STATISTICS OFFICE. INDEX OF EMPLOYMENT IN CONSTRUCTION. *see* BUILDING AND CONSTRUCTION—Abstracting, Bibliographies, Statistics

IRELAND. CENTRAL STATISTICS OFFICE. INDUSTRIAL DISPUTES. *see* BUSINESS AND ECONOMICS—Abstracting, Bibliographies, Statistics

IRELAND. CENTRAL STATISTICS OFFICE. INDUSTRIAL EARNINGS AND HOURS WORKED. *see* BUSINESS AND ECONOMICS—Abstracting, Bibliographies, Statistics

IRELAND. CENTRAL STATISTICS OFFICE. INDUSTRIAL EMPLOYMENT. *see* BUSINESS AND ECONOMICS—Abstracting, Bibliographies, Statistics

IRELAND. CENTRAL STATISTICS OFFICE. INDUSTRIAL PRODUCTION AND TURNOVER. *see* BUSINESS AND ECONOMICS—Abstracting, Bibliographies, Statistics

IRELAND. CENTRAL STATISTICS OFFICE. INDUSTRIAL STOCKS. *see* BUSINESS AND ECONOMICS—Abstracting, Bibliographies, Statistics

IRELAND. CENTRAL STATISTICS OFFICE. INFORMATION SOCIETY AND TELECOMMUNICATIONS. *see* COMPUTERS—Computer Systems

IRELAND. CENTRAL STATISTICS OFFICE. INFORMATION SOCIETY STATISTICS, FIRST RESULTS. *see* COMPUTERS—Computer Systems

IRELAND. CENTRAL STATISTICS OFFICE. INSTITUTIONAL SECTOR ACCOUNTS, NON-FINANCIAL. *see* BUSINESS AND ECONOMICS—Abstracting, Bibliographies, Statistics

IRELAND. CENTRAL STATISTICS OFFICE. IRISH BABIES' NAMES. *see* CHILDREN AND YOUTH—Abstracting, Bibliographies, Statistics

IRELAND. CENTRAL STATISTICS OFFICE. LABOUR COSTS SURVEY - IN INDUSTRY, DISTRIBUTION, CREDIT AND INSURANCE. *see* BUSINESS AND ECONOMICS—Abstracting, Bibliographies, Statistics

IRELAND. CENTRAL STATISTICS OFFICE. LIVE REGISTER. *see* BUSINESS AND ECONOMICS—Abstracting, Bibliographies, Statistics

IRELAND. CENTRAL STATISTICS OFFICE. LIVE REGISTER AGE BY DURATION. *see* POPULATION STUDIES—Abstracting, Bibliographies, Statistics

IRELAND. CENTRAL STATISTICS OFFICE. LIVESTOCK SLAUGHTERINGS. *see* AGRICULTURE—Abstracting, Bibliographies, Statistics

IRELAND. CENTRAL STATISTICS OFFICE. MEAT SUPPLY BALANCE. *see* AGRICULTURE—Abstracting, Bibliographies, Statistics

IRELAND. CENTRAL STATISTICS OFFICE. MILK AND MILK PRODUCTS SUPPLY BALANCE. *see* AGRICULTURE—Abstracting, Bibliographies, Statistics

IRELAND. CENTRAL STATISTICS OFFICE. MILK STATISTICS. *see* AGRICULTURE—Abstracting, Bibliographies, Statistics

IRELAND. CENTRAL STATISTICS OFFICE. NATIONAL EMPLOYMENT SURVEY. *see* OCCUPATIONS AND CAREERS

IRELAND. CENTRAL STATISTICS OFFICE. NATIONAL INCOME AND EXPENDITURE. *see* BUSINESS AND ECONOMICS—Abstracting, Bibliographies, Statistics

IRELAND. CENTRAL STATISTICS OFFICE. NATIONAL INCOME AND EXPENDITURE. FIRST RESULTS. *see* BUSINESS AND ECONOMICS—Abstracting, Bibliographies, Statistics

IRELAND. CENTRAL STATISTICS OFFICE. OUTPUT, INPUT AND INCOME IN AGRICULTURE. *see* AGRICULTURE—Abstracting, Bibliographies, Statistics

IRELAND. CENTRAL STATISTICS OFFICE. OUTPUT, INPUT AND INCOME IN AGRICULTURE. ADVANCE ESTIMATE. *see* AGRICULTURE—Abstracting, Bibliographies, Statistics

IRELAND. CENTRAL STATISTICS OFFICE. OUTPUT, INPUT AND INCOME IN AGRICULTURE. PRELIMINARY ESTIMATE. *see* AGRICULTURE—Abstracting, Bibliographies, Statistics

IRELAND. CENTRAL STATISTICS OFFICE. PIG SURVEY - JUNE. *see* AGRICULTURE—Abstracting, Bibliographies, Statistics

IRELAND. CENTRAL STATISTICS OFFICE. POPULATION AND LABOUR FORCE PROJECTIONS. *see* POPULATION STUDIES

IRELAND. CENTRAL STATISTICS OFFICE. POPULATION AND MIGRATION ESTIMATES. *see* POPULATION STUDIES—Abstracting, Bibliographies, Statistics

IRELAND. CENTRAL STATISTICS OFFICE. PRODCOM PRODUCT SALES. *see* BUSINESS AND ECONOMICS—Abstracting, Bibliographies, Statistics

IRELAND. CENTRAL STATISTICS OFFICE. PRODUCTION IN BUILDING AND CONSTRUCTION INDEX. *see* BUILDING AND CONSTRUCTION—Abstracting, Bibliographies, Statistics

IRELAND. CENTRAL STATISTICS OFFICE. PUBLIC SECTOR EMPLOYMENT EARNINGS. *see* BUSINESS AND ECONOMICS—Abstracting, Bibliographies, Statistics

IRELAND. CENTRAL STATISTICS OFFICE. QUARTERLY NATIONAL HOUSEHOLD SURVEY. *see* BUSINESS AND ECONOMICS—Abstracting, Bibliographies, Statistics

IRELAND. CENTRAL STATISTICS OFFICE. QUARTERLY REPORT ON VITAL STATISTICS/TUARASCAIL CINN RAITHE AR STAIDREAMH BEATHA. *see* POPULATION STUDIES—Abstracting, Bibliographies, Statistics

IRELAND. CENTRAL STATISTICS OFFICE. REPORT ON VITAL STATISTICS - TUARASCAIL AR STAIDREAMH BEATHA. *see* POPULATION STUDIES—Abstracting, Bibliographies, Statistics

IRELAND. CENTRAL STATISTICS OFFICE. RETAIL SALES INDEX. *see* BUSINESS AND ECONOMICS—Abstracting, Bibliographies, Statistics

IRELAND. CENTRAL STATISTICS OFFICE. ROAD FREIGHT TRANSPORT SURVEY. *see* BUSINESS AND ECONOMICS—Abstracting, Bibliographies, Statistics

IRELAND. CENTRAL STATISTICS OFFICE. SERVICE EXPORTS AND IMPORTS. *see* BUSINESS AND ECONOMICS—International Commerce

IRELAND. CENTRAL STATISTICS OFFICE. SIZE OF HERD. *see* AGRICULTURE—Abstracting, Bibliographies, Statistics

IRELAND. CENTRAL STATISTICS OFFICE. STATISTICAL BULLETIN/ FEASCHAN STAIDRIMH. *see* BUSINESS AND ECONOMICS—Abstracting, Bibliographies, Statistics

IRELAND. CENTRAL STATISTICS OFFICE. STATISTICS OF PORT TRAFFIC. *see* TRANSPORTATION—Abstracting, Bibliographies, Statistics

IRELAND. CENTRAL STATISTICS OFFICE. SUPPLY AND USE TABLES FOR IRELAND. *see* BUSINESS AND ECONOMICS—Abstracting, Bibliographies, Statistics

IRELAND. CENTRAL STATISTICS OFFICE. TOURISM AND TRAVEL. *see* TRAVEL AND TOURISM—Abstracting, Bibliographies, Statistics

IRELAND. CENTRAL STATISTICS OFFICE. TOURISM AND TRAVEL (YEAR). *see* TRAVEL AND TOURISM—Abstracting, Bibliographies, Statistics

IRELAND. CENTRAL STATISTICS OFFICE. TRADE STATISTICS. *see* BUSINESS AND ECONOMICS—Abstracting, Bibliographies, Statistics

IRELAND. CENTRAL STATISTICS OFFICE. TRADE WITH NON - E U COUNTRIES. *see* BUSINESS AND ECONOMICS—Abstracting, Bibliographies, Statistics

IRELAND. CENTRAL STATISTICS OFFICE. VEHICLES LICENSED FOR THE FIRST TIME (MONTH). *see* BUSINESS AND ECONOMICS—Abstracting, Bibliographies, Statistics

IRELAND. CENTRAL STATISTICS OFFICE. VEHICLES LICENSED FOR THE FIRST TIME (YEAR). *see* TRANSPORTATION—Abstracting, Bibliographies, Statistics

IRELAND. CENTRAL STATISTICS OFFICE. WHOLESALE PRICE INDEX. *see* BUSINESS AND ECONOMICS—Abstracting, Bibliographies, Statistics

IRELAND. CENTRAL STATISTICS OFFICE. WOMEN AND MEN IN IRELAND. *see* SOCIOLOGY—Abstracting, Bibliographies, Statistics

IRON AND STEEL YEARLY STATISTICS. *see* METALLURGY—Abstracting, Bibliographies, Statistics

314.912 ISL ISSN 1025-6911
ISLAND I TOELUM. Text in Icelandic. 1995. a. ISK 300 per issue (effective 2005). **Document type:** *Government.*
Related titles: Online - full text ed.; ◆ English ed.: Iceland in Figures. ISSN 1025-6903.
Published by: Hagstofa Islands/Statistics Iceland, Borgartuni 12 A, Reykjavik, 150, Iceland. TEL 354-528-1000, FAX 354-528-1099. Ed. Bjorgvin Sigurdsson.

ISRAEL. CENTRAL BUREAU OF STATISTICS. CONSTRUCTION IN ISRAEL/HA-BINUI BE-YISRAEL. *see* BUILDING AND CONSTRUCTION—Abstracting, Bibliographies, Statistics

ISRAEL. CENTRAL BUREAU OF STATISTICS. ENERGY IN ISRAEL. *see* ENERGY—Abstracting, Bibliographies, Statistics

ISRAEL. CENTRAL BUREAU OF STATISTICS. FOREIGN TRADE STATISTICS (ANNUAL) - EXPORTS. *see* BUSINESS AND ECONOMICS—Abstracting, Bibliographies, Statistics

ISRAEL. CENTRAL BUREAU OF STATISTICS. FOREIGN TRADE STATISTICS (ANNUAL) - IMPORTS. *see* BUSINESS AND ECONOMICS—Abstracting, Bibliographies, Statistics

315 ISR ISSN 0021-1982
HA1931
ISRAEL. CENTRAL BUREAU OF STATISTICS. MONTHLY BULLETIN OF STATISTICS/YARHON STATISTI L'YISRA'EL. Text in English, Hebrew. 1949. m. ILS 30 per issue (effective 2008). stat. **Document type:** *Bulletin, Government.*
Related titles: Diskette ed.
Published by: Central Bureau of Statistics/Ha-Lishka Ha-Merkazit L'Statistiqa, PO Box 13015, Jerusalem, 91130, Israel. TEL 972-2-6553364, FAX 972-2-6521340.

ISRAEL. CENTRAL BUREAU OF STATISTICS. NATIONAL ACCOUNTS OF ISRAEL. *see* BUSINESS AND ECONOMICS—Abstracting, Bibliographies, Statistics

ISRAEL. CENTRAL BUREAU OF STATISTICS. NATIONAL EXPENDITURE ON CULTURE, RECREATION AND SPORTS/HA-HOTSA'A HA-L'UMIT L'TARBUT, L'VIDDUR, U-L'SPORT. *see* PUBLIC ADMINISTRATION—Abstracting, Bibliographies, Statistics

310 016 ISR ISSN 0334-3278
ISRAEL. CENTRAL BUREAU OF STATISTICS. NEW STATISTICAL PROJECTS AND PUBLICATIONS IN ISRAEL/PE'ULOT UFIRSUIMIM STATISTIYYIM HADASHIM B'YISRA'EL. Text in Hebrew; Summaries in English. 1970. q. USD 21. bibl. index. back issues avail. **Document type:** *Government.*
Published by: Central Bureau of Statistics/Ha-Lishka Ha-Merkazit L'Statistiqa, PO Box 13015, Jerusalem, 91130, Israel. TEL 972-2-6553364, FAX 972-2-6521340.

315.69 ISR ISSN 0081-4679
HA1931
ISRAEL. CENTRAL BUREAU OF STATISTICS. STATISTICAL ABSTRACT OF ISRAEL/SHENATON STATISTI LE-YISRAEL. Text in English, Hebrew. 1949. a., latest 2007. ILS 200 (effective 2008); incl. CD. **Document type:** *Report, Government.*
Published by: Central Bureau of Statistics/Ha-Lishka Ha-Merkazit L'Statistiqa, PO Box 13015, Jerusalem, 91130, Israel. TEL 972-2-6553364, FAX 972-2-6521340.

ISRAEL. CENTRAL BUREAU OF STATISTICS. SURVEY OF TRUCKS/ SEQER MASA'IYOT. *see* TRANSPORTATION—Abstracting, Bibliographies, Statistics

ISRAEL. CENTRAL BUREAU OF STATISTICS. TOURISM/TAYYARUT. *see* TRAVEL AND TOURISM—Abstracting, Bibliographies, Statistics

ISRAEL. CENTRAL BUREAU OF STATISTICS. VICTIMIZATION SURVEY. *see* CRIMINOLOGY AND LAW ENFORCEMENT—Abstracting, Bibliographies, Statistics

ISRAEL. CENTRAL BUREAU OF STATISTICS. VITAL STATISTICS. *see* POPULATION STUDIES—Abstracting, Bibliographies, Statistics

310 362.1 CAN ISSN 1712-4085
ISSUES DE LA GROSSESSE. Text in French. 2001. a., latest 2003. **Document type:** *Journal, Trade.*
Media: Online - full text.
Published by: Statistics Canada, Health Division (Subsidiary of: Statistics Canada/Statistique Canada), R H Coats Bldg, 18th floor, Ottawa, ON K1A 0T6, Canada. TEL 613-951-8569.

315.61 TUR ISSN 1300-431X
ISTATISTIKLERLE TURKIYE (YEAR). Text in Turkish. 1938. a. free (effective 2009). index, cum.index. **Document type:** *Government.* **Description:** Provides brief statistical information on Turkey, including finance and national accounts, foreign trade, industrial production, agriculture, energy, population, climate and geography.
Formerly (until 1991): Turkiye Istatistik Cep Yilligi
Related titles: ◆ English ed.: Turkey in Statistics (Year). ISSN 1300-4328.
Indexed: ST&MA.
Published by: T.C. Basbakanlik, Turkiye Istatistik Kurumu/Prime Ministry Republic of Turkey, Turkish Statistical Institute, Yucetepe Mah. Necatibey Cad No.114, Cankaya, Ankara, 06100, Turkey. TEL 90-312-4100410, FAX 90-312-4175886, bilgi@tuik.gov.tr, ulka.unsal@tuik.gov.tr, http://www.tuik.gov.tr.

314 ITA ISSN 1126-8603
ITALIAN STATISTICAL ABSTRACT. Text in English. 1953. a. **Document type:** *Government.* **Description:** Provides results of principal statistical works on the social and economic situation in Italy.
Published by: Istituto Nazionale di Statistica (I S T A T), Via Cesare Balbo 16, Rome, 00184, Italy. TEL 39-06-46731, http://www.istat.it.

ITALY. ISTITUTO NAZIONALE DI STATISTICA. ANNUARIO. DECESSI. *see* POPULATION STUDIES—Abstracting, Bibliographies, Statistics

ITALY. ISTITUTO NAZIONALE DI STATISTICA. ANNUARIO. NASCITE. *see* POPULATION STUDIES—Abstracting, Bibliographies, Statistics

ITALY. ISTITUTO NAZIONALE DI STATISTICA. ANNUARIO. STATISTICHE GIUDIZIARIE CIVILI. *see* LAW—Abstracting, Bibliographies, Statistics

ITALY. ISTITUTO NAZIONALE DI STATISTICA. ANNUARIO. STATISTICHE GIUDIZIARIE PENALI. *see* LAW—Abstracting, Bibliographies, Statistics

314 ITA ISSN 0021-3136
HA1360
ITALY. ISTITUTO NAZIONALE DI STATISTICA. BOLLETTINO MENSILE DI STATISTICA. Text in Italian. 1925. m. charts; stat. index. **Document type:** *Government.* **Description:** Detailed data of demographic, social, economic and financial phenomena.
Incorporates (1988-1952): Casi di Malattie Infettive e Diffusive Denunziati (1124-0911); Which was formerly (until 1945): Casi di Malattie dell'Uomo Denunciati (1124-0903); (until 1941): Bollettino delle Malattie Infettive del Regno (1124-089X); (until 1914): Bollettino Sanitario (1124-0776); Former titles (until 1949): Repubblica Italiana. Istituto Centrale di Statistica. Bollettino Mensile di Statistica (1124-0857); (until 1945): Regno d'Italia. Istituto Centrale di Statistica. Bollettino Mensile di Statistica (1124-0849)
Indexed: PAIS, RASB.
Published by: Istituto Nazionale di Statistica (I S T A T), Via Cesare Balbo 16, Rome, 00184, Italy. TEL 39-06-46731, http://www.istat.it. Circ: 5,000.

314 ITA ISSN 1120-8953
HA1363
ITALY. ISTITUTO NAZIONALE DI STATISTICA. COLLANA D'INFORMAZIONE. Text in Italian. 1977. irreg. price varies. **Document type:** *Government.*
Published by: Istituto Nazionale di Statistica (I S T A T), Via Cesare Balbo 16, Rome, 00184, Italy. TEL 39-06-46731, http://www.istat.it.

ITALY. ISTITUTO NAZIONALE DI STATISTICA. COLLANA D'INFORMAZIONE. STATISTICA ANNUALE DELLA PRODUZIONE INDUSTRIALE. *see* BUSINESS AND ECONOMICS—Abstracting, Bibliographies, Statistics

314 ITA ISSN 1594-3135
HA1361
ITALY. ISTITUTO NAZIONALE DI STATISTICA. RAPPORTO ANNUALE: LA SITUAZIONE DEL PAESE NEL (YEAR). Text in Italian. 1932. a. **Document type:** *Government.*
Incorporates (1992-1993): Istituto Nazionale di Statistica. Rapporto Annuale. L'Attivita e le Risorse della Statistica Ufficiale (1594-3127); Supersedes in part (in 1992): Istituto Nazionale di Statistica. L'Attivita (1594-3100); Which was formerly (until 1990): Istituto Centrale di Statistica. L'Attivita nell'Anno (Year) (1594-3097)
Published by: Istituto Nazionale di Statistica (I S T A T), Via Cesare Balbo 16, Rome, 00184, Italy. TEL 39-06-46731, http://www.istat.it.

ITALY. ISTITUTO NAZIONALE DI STATISTICA. STATISTICA ANNUALE DEL COMMERCIO CON L'ESTERO. TOMO 1. DATI GENERALI E RIASSUNTIVI. *see* BUSINESS AND ECONOMICS—Abstracting, Bibliographies, Statistics

ITALY. ISTITUTO NAZIONALE DI STATISTICA. STATISTICA ANNUALE DEL COMMERCIO CON L'ESTERO. TOMO 2: MERCI PER PAESI. *see* BUSINESS AND ECONOMICS—Abstracting, Bibliographies, Statistics

ITALY. ISTITUTO NAZIONALE DI STATISTICA. STATISTICA DEGLI INCIDENTI STRADALI. *see* TRANSPORTATION—Abstracting, Bibliographies, Statistics

ITALY. ISTITUTO NAZIONALE DI STATISTICA. STATISTICHE CULTURALI. *see* HUMANITIES: COMPREHENSIVE WORKS—Abstracting, Bibliographies, Statistics

ITALY. ISTITUTO NAZIONALE DI STATISTICA. STATISTICHE DEI TRASPORTI MARITTIMI. *see* TRANSPORTATION—Abstracting, Bibliographies, Statistics

ITALY. ISTITUTO NAZIONALE DI STATISTICA. STATISTICHE DEL COMMERCIO INTERNO. *see* BUSINESS AND ECONOMICS—Abstracting, Bibliographies, Statistics

ITALY. ISTITUTO NAZIONALE DI STATISTICA. STATISTICHE DELLA CACCIA E DELLA PESCA. *see* AGRICULTURE—Abstracting, Bibliographies, Statistics

ITALY. ISTITUTO NAZIONALE DI STATISTICA. STATISTICHE DELL'ATTIVITA EDILIZIA (YEAR). *see* BUILDING AND CONSTRUCTION—Abstracting, Bibliographies, Statistics

ITALY. ISTITUTO NAZIONALE DI STATISTICA. STATISTICHE DELLE AMMINISTRAZIONI PUBBLICHE (YEAR). *see* PUBLIC ADMINISTRATION—Abstracting, Bibliographies, Statistics

ITALY. ISTITUTO NAZIONALE DI STATISTICA. STATISTICHE DEMOGRAFICHE. *see* POPULATION STUDIES—Abstracting, Bibliographies, Statistics

ITALY. ISTITUTO NAZIONALE DI STATISTICA. STATISTICHE METEOROLOGICHE. *see* METEOROLOGY—Abstracting, Bibliographies, Statistics

ITALY. ISTITUTO NAZIONALE DI STATISTICA. STATISTICHE OPERE PUBBLICHE (YEAR). *see* BUILDING AND CONSTRUCTION—Abstracting, Bibliographies, Statistics

IVORY COAST. DIRECTION DE LA STATISTIQUE. BULLETIN MENSUEL DE STATISTIQUES. *see* BUSINESS AND ECONOMICS—Abstracting, Bibliographies, Statistics

S

IVORY COAST. MINISTERE DE L'AGRICULTURE. ANNUAIRE DES STATISTIQUES AGRICOLES. see AGRICULTURE—Abstracting, Bibliographies, Statistics

310 382 BGR ISSN 1311-2252
IZNOS I VNOS/EXPORT AND IMPORT. Text in Bulgarian, English. q. BGL 8.76 (effective 2002). 25 p./no.; **Description:** Presents data of the foreign trade statistics.
Published by: Natsionalen Statisticheski Institut/National Statistical Institute, ul P Volov, # 2, Sofia, 1038, Bulgaria. FAX 359-2-9803319, publikacii@nsi.bg, http://www.nsi.bg.

570.15195 IND ISSN 0973-5143
➤ **J P JOURNAL OF BIOSTATISTICS.** Abbreviated title: J P J B. Text in English. 2007. 3/yr. INR 4,000 domestic to institutions; EUR 298 combined subscription foreign to institutions (print & online eds.) (effective 2011). back issues avail. **Document type:** *Journal, Academic/Scholarly.* **Description:** Publishes original research papers and survey articles in all aspects of (theory and applications) of Biostatistics.
Related titles: Online - full text ed.: EUR 240 to institutions (effective 2011).
Indexed: CCMJ, MSN, MathR, Z02.
Published by: Pushpa Publishing House, Vijaya Niwas, 198 Mumfordganj, Allahabad, Uttar Pradesh 211 002, India. TEL 91-532-2250078, FAX 91-532-2641508, sub@pphmj.com, http://www.pphmj.com. **Dist. by:** Vijaya Books and Journals Distributors.

314 NLD ISSN 0927-4634
HA1381
JAAR IN CIJFERS (YEAR). Text in Dutch. 1968. a., latest 2004, for the year 2003.
Former titles (until 1991): In Cijfers (Year) (0925-790X); (until 1990): Jaar in Cijfers (0925-7896)
Related titles: ◆ Supplement to: Netherlands. Centraal Bureau voor de Statistiek. Statistisch Bulletin. ISSN 0166-9680.
Published by: Centraal Bureau voor de Statistiek, Henri Faasdreef 312, The Hague, 2492 JP, Netherlands. TEL 31-70-3373800, infoserv@cbs.nl, http://www.cbs.nl. **Orders to:** Sdu Uitgevers bv, Christoffel Plantijnstraat, The Hague 2515 TZ, Netherlands.

JAMI'AT QATAR. AL-TAQRIR AL-IHSA'I AL-SANAWI LIL-AAM AL-JAMI'I/UNIVERSITY OF QATAR. ANNUAL STATISTICAL REPORT FOR THE SCHOOL YEAR. see EDUCATION—Abstracting, Bibliographies, Statistics

315 JPN ISSN 0389-3502
HC461
JAPAN: AN INTERNATIONAL COMPARISON. Variant title: Japan (Year). Text in English. a. JPY 900, USD 9. adv. **Document type:** *Abstract/Index.* **Description:** Provides a statistical profile of Japan in comparison with other nations. Covers population and area, national income, agriculture and food supply, industry and services, foreign trade, balance of payments, exchange rates, employment, wages, and productivity.
Published by: Keizai Koho Center, Otemachi Bldg, 6-1 Ote-machi 1-chome, Chiyoda-ku, Tokyo, 100, Japan. TEL 81-3-3201-1415, FAX 81-3-3201-1418. Ed. Atsuo Ueda. Pub. Hiroshi Endo. Adv. contact Yoshitaka Arai.

JAPAN BANANA IMPORTERS ASSOCIATION. ANNUAL REPORT OF BANANA STATISTICS. see AGRICULTURE—Abstracting, Bibliographies, Statistics

JAPAN BANANA IMPORTERS ASSOCIATION. MONTHLY BULLETIN OF BANANA STATISTICS. see AGRICULTURE—Abstracting, Bibliographies, Statistics

JAPAN EXPORTS & IMPORTS: COMMODITY BY COUNTRY. see BUSINESS AND ECONOMICS—Abstracting, Bibliographies, Statistics

JAPAN. MINISTRY OF INTERNAL AFFAIRS AND COMMUNICATIONS. STATISTICS BUREAU. NEWS BULLETIN. see POPULATION STUDIES—Abstracting, Bibliographies, Statistics

JAPAN. POCKET SIZE STATISTICS OF SUGAR PRODUCTS. see FOOD AND FOOD INDUSTRIES—Abstracting, Bibliographies, Statistics

519.5 510.28 JPN ISSN 0915-2350
➤ **JAPANESE SOCIETY OF COMPUTATIONAL STATISTICS. JOURNAL.** Text in English. 1988. a. subscr. incld. with membership. **Document type:** *Journal, Academic/Scholarly.* **Description:** Publishes papers on new statistical methods in which computation plays an important role, new computational techniques in statistics, new philosophy, development or evaluation of statistical software.
Indexed: CCMJ, CIS, MSN, MathR, Z02.
—BLDSC (4809.419300). **CCC.**
Published by: Japanese Society of Computational Statistics, c/o Statistical Information Institute for Consulting and Analysis, Daiwa Bldg 2F, 6-3-9 Minami Aoyama, Minato-kui, Tokyo, 107-0062, Japan. office@jscs.or.jp. Ed. Yoshihiro Ochi. Circ: 400.

310 JPN ISSN 0910-9684
JIDOSHA HOYU SHARYOSU. Text in Japanese. 1973. m. JPY 7,080; JPY 6,480 foreign (effective 2000). bk.rev. back issues avail. **Document type:** *Newsletter.*
Published by: Jidosha Kensa Toroku Kyoryokukai, 35 Sankyo Bldg, 7-2 Irifune 3-chome, Chuo-ku, Tokyo, 104-0042, Japan. TEL 81-3-5542-5101, FAX 81-3-5542-5106. Ed., R&P Yukio Narita. Circ: 1,500 (controlled).

JOINT ASSOCIATION SURVEY ON DRILLING COSTS. see PETROLEUM AND GAS—Abstracting, Bibliographies, Statistics

JORDAN. DEPARTMENT OF STATISTICS. AGRICULTURAL STATISTICAL YEARBOOK AND AGRICULTURAL SAMPLE SURVEY. see AGRICULTURE

315 JOR ISSN 0075-4013
HA4561
JORDAN. DEPARTMENT OF STATISTICS. ANNUAL STATISTICAL YEARBOOK. Text in Arabic, English. 1950. a. USD 25 (effective 2000). **Document type:** *Government.*
Incorporates (1960-1988): Jordan. Department of Statistics. National Accounts (0449-1513)
Published by: Department of Statistics, P O Box 2015, Amman, Jordan. TEL 962-6-842171, FAX 962-6-833518.

JORDAN. DEPARTMENT OF STATISTICS. CONSTRUCTION STATISTICS. see BUILDING AND CONSTRUCTION—Abstracting, Bibliographies, Statistics

JORDAN. DEPARTMENT OF STATISTICS. EMPLOYMENT SURVEY FOR ESTABLISHMENTS ENGAGING FIVE PERSONS OR MORE. see BUSINESS AND ECONOMICS—Abstracting, Bibliographies, Statistics

JORDAN. DEPARTMENT OF STATISTICS. EMPLOYMENT, UNEMPLOYMENT AND INCOME SURVEY. see BUSINESS AND ECONOMICS—Abstracting, Bibliographies, Statistics

JORDAN. DEPARTMENT OF STATISTICS. EXTERNAL TRADE STATISTICS. see BUSINESS AND ECONOMICS—Abstracting, Bibliographies, Statistics

JORDAN JOURNAL OF MATHEMATICS AND STATISTICS. see MATHEMATICS

310 314 519 FRA ISSN 1962-5197
➤ **JOURNAL DE LA SOCIETE FRANCAISE DE STATISTIQUE & REVUE DE STATISTIQUE APPLIQUEE.** Text in French. 2007. q. back issues avail. **Document type:** *Journal, Academic/Scholarly.*
Formed by the merger of (1953-2006): Revue de Statistique Appliquee (0035-175X); (1998-2006): Journal de la societe francaise de statistique (1625-7421); Which was formerly (until 1998): Journal de la societe de statistique de Paris (0037-914X)
Indexed: MSN.
—Infotrieve, INIST.
Published by: (Societe Francaise de Statistique), Association Recherche Statistique et Applications, Institut Henri Poincare, 11 Rue Pierre et Marie Curie, Paris, Cedex 05 75231, France.

310 FRA ISSN 1773-0074
QA273.A1
➤ **JOURN@L ELECTRONIQUE D'HISTOIRE DES PROBABILITES ET DE LA STATISTIQUE/ELECTRONIC JOURNAL FOR HISTORY OF PROBABILITY AND STATISTICS.** Text in French, English. 2005. s-a. free (effective 2011). **Document type:** *Journal, Academic/Scholarly.* **Description:** Publishes original papers on probability and statistics including older documents of exceptional interest and makes them available as downloadable files.
Media: Online - full text.
Indexed: Z02.
Published by: College de France, Ecole des Hautes Etudes en Sciences Sociales (E H E S S), 96 Boulevard Raspail, Paris, 75006, France. TEL 33-1-53635658, FAX 33-1-49542428, editions@ehess.fr, http://www.ehess.fr.

310 519 USA ISSN 1943-2399
▼ ➤ **JOURNAL OF ADVANCED RESEARCH IN STATISTICS AND PROBABILITY.** Text in English. 2009. q. free. back issues avail. **Document type:** *Journal, Academic/Scholarly.* **Description:** Publishes high quality research articles that make original contributions to the theory and methodology of statistics and probability.
Media: Online - full text.
Indexed: C10, T02.
Published by: Institute of Advanced Scientific Research, Inc., 65 Palatine, Ste 232, Irvine, CA 92612. inquiry@i-asr.org.

➤ **JOURNAL OF AGRICULTURAL, BIOLOGICAL, AND ENVIRONMENTAL STATISTICS.** see BIOLOGY—Abstracting, Bibliographies, Statistics

310 USA ISSN 1930-6792
QA273.A1
JOURNAL OF APPLIED PROBABILITY AND STATISTICS. Abbreviated title: J A P S. Text in English. 2006 (Nov.). s-a. back issues avail. **Document type:** *Journal, Academic/Scholarly.* **Description:** Brings out research articles in areas of applied probability as well as diverse statistical methods and techniques covering both theory and applications.
Related titles: Online - full text ed.
Indexed: CCMJ, MSN, MathR, Z02.
—BLDSC (4946.750000), IE.
Published by: Dixie W Publishing Corporation, PO Box 241901, Montgomery, AL 36124. TEL 334-462-6919, info@dixiewpublishing.com, http://www.dixiewpublishing.com/. Ed. Shahjahan Khan.

JOURNAL OF APPLIED STATISTICAL SCIENCE. see MATHEMATICS

519.5 GBR ISSN 0266-4763
QA276.A1
➤ **JOURNAL OF APPLIED STATISTICS.** Abbreviated title: J A S. Text in English. 1975. m. GBP 2,291 combined subscription in United Kingdom to institutions (print & online eds.); EUR 3,026, USD 3,802 combined subscription to institutions (print & online eds.) (effective 2012). adv. bk.rev. back issues avail.; reprint service avail. from PSC. **Document type:** *Journal, Academic/Scholarly.* **Description:** Provides a forum for communication between both applied statisticians and users of applied statistical techniques across a wide range of disciplines.
Formerly (until 1984): Bulletin in Applied Statistics
Related titles: Microfiche ed.; Online - full text ed.: ISSN 1360-0532. GBP 2,062 in United Kingdom to institutions; EUR 2,723, USD 3,422 to institutions (effective 2012) (from IngentaConnect).
Indexed: A12, A17, A22, A34, A36, A37, A38, ABIn, ASCA, B01, B06, B07, B08, B09, Biostat, C12, C25, CA, CABA, CCMJ, CIS, CMCI, CPM, CompAb, D01, E01, E12, EconLit, F08, F12, FCA, GH, H16, IndVet, Inspec, JCQM, JEL, LT, MSN, MathR, N02, N03, N04, O01, ORMS, P02, P10, P27, P30, P32, P33, P39, P40, P46, P48, P49, P50, P51, P52, P53, P54, PQC, R08, R12, RASB, RRTA, S10, S12, S13, S16, SCI, SCOPUS, ST&MA, T02, T05, TriticAb, VS, W07, W08, W10, W11, Z02.
—IE, Infotrieve, Ingenta. **CCC.**
Published by: Routledge (Subsidiary of: Taylor & Francis Group), 4 Park Sq, Milton Park, Abingdon, Oxon OX14 4RN, United Kingdom. TEL 44-20-70176000, FAX 44-20-70176336, subscriptions@tandf.co.uk, http://www.routledge.com. Ed. Dr. Robert G Aykroyd TEL 44-113-3435167. Adv. contact Linda Hann TEL 44-1344-779945. **Subscr. to:** Taylor & Francis Ltd., Journals Customer Service, Sheepen Pl, Colchester, Essex CO3 3LP, United Kingdom. TEL 44-20-70175544, FAX 44-20-70175198, tf.enquiries@tfinforma.com.

➤ **JOURNAL OF BIOPHARMACEUTICAL STATISTICS.** see PHARMACY AND PHARMACOLOGY—Abstracting, Bibliographies, Statistics

➤ **JOURNAL OF BUSINESS AND ECONOMIC STATISTICS.** see BUSINESS AND ECONOMICS—Abstracting, Bibliographies, Statistics

➤ **JOURNAL OF CHOICE MODELLING.** see BUSINESS AND ECONOMICS

➤ **JOURNAL OF COMPUTATIONAL AND GRAPHICAL STATISTICS.** see MATHEMATICS

310 USA ISSN 1680-743X
JOURNAL OF DATA SCIENCE. Text in English. 2003. q. **Document type:** *Journal, Academic/Scholarly.*
Related titles: Online - full text ed.: ISSN 1683-8602. free (effective 2011).
Indexed: CIS, P30.
Published by: Columbia University, Department of Statistics, 618 Mathematics Bldg, MC 4403, 2990 Broadway, New York, NY 10027. TEL 212-854-3652, FAX 212-663-2454, http://www.stat.columbia.edu.

JOURNAL OF ECONOMETRICS. see BUSINESS AND ECONOMICS—Economic Systems And Theories, Economic History

519.5 NLD ISSN 0747-9662
H62.A1 CODEN: JEMEEZ
➤ **JOURNAL OF ECONOMIC AND SOCIAL MEASUREMENT.** Abbreviated title: J E S M. Text in English. 1974. q. USD 666 combined subscription in North America (print & online eds.); EUR 475 combined subscription elsewhere (print & online eds.) (effective 2012). **Document type:** *Journal, Academic/Scholarly.* **Description:** Investigates all aspects of data production, distribution, and use, with primary focus on economic and sociological data.
Formerly (until 1985): Review of Public Data Use (0092-2846)
Related titles: Online - full text ed.: ISSN 1875-8932.
Indexed: A01, A03, A08, A12, A13, A17, A22, A25, A26, ABIn, ASCA, B01, B06, B07, B08, B09, B16, C12, CA, CIS, ChPerI, E01, E08, ESPM, EconLit, G08, GEOBASE, HospLI, I05, IBR, IBSS, IBZ, JEL, M01, M02, P02, P06, P10, P30, P34, P48, P51, P53, P54, PAIS, PQC, PopulInd, RASB, RiskAb, S01, S02, S03, S08, S09, SCOPUS, SOPODA, SSA, SSciA, ST&MA, SociolAb, T02, UAA.
—BLDSC (4972.607000), IE, Infotrieve, Ingenta. **CCC.**
Published by: I O S Press, Nieuwe Hemweg 6B, Amsterdam, 1013 BG, Netherlands. TEL 31-20-6883355, FAX 31-20-6870019, info@iospress.nl. Ed. Charles G Renfro TEL 212-531-4448. Circ: 200. **Subscr. to:** I O S Press, Inc, 4502 Rachael Manor Dr, Fairfax, VA 22032-3631. iosbooks@iospress.com; Globe Publication Pvt. Ltd., C-62 Inderpuri, New Delhi 100 012, India. TEL 91-11-579-3211, 91-11-579-3212, FAX 91-11-579-8876, custserve@globepub.com, http://www.globepub.com; Kinokuniya Co Ltd., Shinjuku 3-chome, Shinjuku-ku, Tokyo 160-0022, Japan. FAX 81-3-3439-1094, journal@kinokuniya.co.jp, http://www.kinokuniya.co.jp.

➤ **JOURNAL OF EDUCATIONAL AND BEHAVIORAL STATISTICS.** see EDUCATION—Abstracting, Bibliographies, Statistics

▼ ➤ **JOURNAL OF ENVIRONMENTAL STATISTICS.** see ENVIRONMENTAL STUDIES—Abstracting, Bibliographies, Statistics

➤ **JOURNAL OF MATHEMATICAL SOCIOLOGY.** see SOCIOLOGY—Abstracting, Bibliographies, Statistics

➤ **JOURNAL OF MATHEMATICS AND STATISTICS.** see MATHEMATICS

001.433 USA ISSN 1538-9472
QA276.A1
➤ **JOURNAL OF MODERN APPLIED STATISTICAL METHODS.** Text in English. 2002. s-a. free (effective 2011). **Document type:** *Journal, Academic/Scholarly.* **Description:** Provides an outlet for the scholoarly works of applied nonparametric or parametric statisticians, data analysts, researchers, classical or modern psychometricians, quantitative or qualitative evaluators, and methodologists.
Media: Online - full text.
Indexed: A39, C27, C29, D03, D04, E13, P30, R14, S14, S15, S18, SCOPUS.
Published by: Wayne State University, College of Education, 5425 Gullen Mall, Detroit, MI 48202. TEL 313-577-2424, http://www.coe.wayne.edu.

➤ **JOURNAL OF MODERN MATHEMATICS AND STATISTICS.** see MATHEMATICS

▼ ➤ **JOURNAL OF NON-SIGNIFICANT RESULTS IN THE BEHAVIORAL SCIENCES.** see PSYCHOLOGY

519.5 GBR ISSN 1048-5252
QA278.8 CODEN: NOSTEK
➤ **JOURNAL OF NONPARAMETRIC STATISTICS.** Text in English. 1991. 8/yr. GBP 1,252 combined subscription in United Kingdom to institutions (print & online eds.); EUR 1,317, USD 1,654 combined subscription to institutions (print & online eds.) (effective 2012). adv. back issues avail.; reprint service avail. from PSC. **Document type:** *Journal, Academic/Scholarly.* **Description:** Provides a medium for the publication of research and survey work in the area of nonparametric statistics.
Related titles: CD-ROM ed.: ISSN 1026-7654. 1995; Microform ed.; Online - full text ed.: ISSN 1029-0311. 1996. GBP 1,127 in United Kingdom to institutions; EUR 1,185, USD 1,488 to institutions (effective 2012) (from IngentaConnect).
Indexed: A01, A03, A08, A22, A28, A36, APA, BrCerAb, C&ISA, CA, CA/WCA, CABA, CCMJ, CIA, CIS, CMCI, CerAb, CivEngAb, CorrAb, CurCont, E&CAJ, E01, E11, E12, EEA, EMA, ESPM, EnvEAb, F08, F12, GH, H05, H15, M&TEA, M09, MBF, METADEX, MSN, MathR, N02, N03, P17, P26, P30, P50, P53, P54, PQC, S01, S13, S16, SCI, SCOPUS, SolStAb, T02, T04, W07, WAA, Z02.
—IE, Infotrieve, Ingenta, Linda Hall. **CCC.**
Published by: Taylor & Francis Ltd. (Subsidiary of: Taylor & Francis Group), 4 Park Sq, Milton Park, Abingdon, Oxfordshire OX14 4RN, United Kingdom. TEL 44-20-70176000, FAX 44-20-70176336, subscriptions@tandf.co.uk, http://www.taylorandfrancis.com. Eds. Dimitris Politis, Michael Akritas. **Subscr. in N America to:** Taylor & Francis Inc., Customer Services Dept, 325 Chestnut St, 8th Fl, Philadelphia, PA 19106. TEL 215-625-8900, 800-354-1420, FAX 215-625-2940, customerservice@taylorandfrancis.com; **Subscr. to:** Journals Customer Service, Sheepen Pl, Colchester, Essex CO3 3LP, United Kingdom. TEL 44-20-70175544, FAX 44-20-70175198, tf.enquiries@tfinforma.com.

001.422 SWE ISSN 0282-423X
HA1523 CODEN: JOFSEA
JOURNAL OF OFFICIAL STATISTICS; an international quarterly. Text in English. 1860. q. adv. bk.rev. charts; illus.; stat. index. back issues avail. **Document type:** *Journal, Academic/Scholarly.* **Description:** Specializes in issues pertinent to survey sampling with emphasis on the methodology and applications used by statistical agencies in the production of official statistics.
Formerly (until 1985): Sweden. Statistiska Centralbyraan. Statistisk Tidskrift (0039-7261)
Related titles: Online - full text ed.: free (effective 2011).
Indexed: A22, Biostat, CIS, CurCont, DIP, IBR, IBZ, INIS AtomInd, JCQM, ORMS, P06, P30, P50, PopulInd, QC&AS, RASB, SCI, SCOPUS, SSCI, ST&MA, SociolAb, W07.
—BLDSC (5026.235000), IE, Infotrieve, Ingenta.
Published by: Statistiska Centralbyraan/Statistics Sweden, Publishing Unit, Orebro, 70189, Sweden. sbc@scb.se, http://www.scb.se. Ed. Lars Lyberg. **Subscr. to:** Journal of Official Statistics.

319.14 PHL ISSN 0022-3603
HA1821
JOURNAL OF PHILIPPINE STATISTICS. Text in English. 1940. q. USD 30 per issue (effective 1997). charts; stat. 114 p./no.; **Document type:** *Journal, Academic/Scholarly.* **Description:** Provides essential statistical information on population, education, health, vital statistics, travel, social welfare, foreign trade, prices and law enforcement.
Indexed: APEL, BAS, IPP, P06, P30, PAIS.
Published by: National Statistics Office, Ramon Magsaysay Blvd, PO Box 779, Manila, Philippines. FAX 63-2-610794. Ed. Preciosa Astillero. Circ: 250.

310 TWN ISSN 1726-3328
JOURNAL OF PROBABILITY AND STATISTICAL SCIENCE; a comprehensive journal of probability and statistics for theorists, methodologists, practitioners, teachers, and others. Text in English. 2000. s-a. **Document type:** *Journal, Academic/Scholarly.*
Formerly: Tongji Xinchuan/Journal of Propagations in Probability and Statistics (1607-7083)
Indexed: CCMJ, MSN, MathR.
—BLDSC (5042.478000).
Published by: Susan Rivers' Cultural Institute, 26, Lane 2, Chien Mei Road, Hsinchu, Taiwan. TEL 886-3-5716594, FAX 886-3-5712524.

JOURNAL OF REGISTRY MANAGEMENT. *see* MEDICAL SCIENCES—Abstracting, Bibliographies, Statistics

001.422 USA ISSN 2150-8143
Q179.9
JOURNAL OF RESEARCH METHODS AND METHODOLOGICAL ISSUES. Text in English. 2007. s-a. free (effective 2009). **Document type:** *Journal, Academic/Scholarly.*
Media: Online - full content.
Published by: Scientific Journals International (Subsidiary of: Global Commerce & Communication, Inc), 1407 33rd St S, Saint Cloud, MN 56301. TEL 320-217-6019, info@scientificjournals.org.

JOURNAL OF RISK AND UNCERTAINTY. *see* BUSINESS AND ECONOMICS—Economic Systems And Theories, Economic History

JOURNAL OF STATISTICAL COMPUTATION AND SIMULATION. *see* COMPUTERS—Abstracting, Bibliographies, Statistics

JOURNAL OF STATISTICAL PHYSICS. *see* PHYSICS

519.5 NLD ISSN 0378-3758
QA276.A1 CODEN: JSPIDN
➤ **JOURNAL OF STATISTICAL PLANNING AND INFERENCE.** Text in English. 1977. 12/yr. EUR 4,030 in Europe to institutions; JPY 536,100 in Japan to institutions; USD 4,508 elsewhere to institutions (effective 2012). abstr.; illus. back issues avail.; reprints avail. **Document type:** *Journal, Academic/Scholarly.* **Description:** Provides information on statistics, with special emphasis on statistical planning and the related areas of combinatorial mathematics and probability theory.
Related titles: Microform ed.: (from PQC); Online - full text ed.: ISSN 1873-1171 (from IngentaConnect, ScienceDirect).
Indexed: A01, A03, A08, A22, A26, ASCA, BPIA, Biostat, BusI, C10, CA, CCMJ, CIS, CJA, CMCI, CompAb, CompLI, FR, G08, ISR, Inspec, JCQM, MSN, MathR, ORMS, P30, QC&AS, S01, S02, S03, SCI, SCOPUS, ST&MA, T02, W07, Z02.
—BLDSC (5066.842000), AskIEEE, IE, Infotrieve, Ingenta, INIST. **CCC.**
Published by: Elsevier BV, North-Holland (Subsidiary of: Elsevier Science & Technology), Sara Burgerhartstraat 25, Amsterdam, 1055 KV, Netherlands. TEL 31-20-4853911, FAX 31-20-4852457, JournalsCustomerServiceEMEA@elsevier.com. **Subscr. to:** Elsevier BV, Radarweg 29, PO Box 211, Amsterdam 1000 AE, Netherlands. TEL 31-20-4853757, FAX 31-20-4853432.

001.422 BGD ISSN 0256-422X
QA276.A1
➤ **JOURNAL OF STATISTICAL RESEARCH.** Text in English. 1970. 2/yr. USD 50 (effective 2001 & 2002). bk.rev. charts; stat. 200 p./no.; back issues avail. **Document type:** *Journal, Academic/Scholarly.* **Description:** Contains papers on statistical research.
Supersedes: University of Dhaka. Institute of Statistical Research and Training. Bulletin (0020-3165)
Indexed: CCMJ, CIS, MSN, MathR, ST&MA.
Published by: (Institute of Statistical Research and Training), University of Dhaka, Ramna, Dhaka, 1000, Bangladesh. FAX 880-2-8615583, duregstr@bangla.net, http://www.univdhaka.edu. Eds. Ehsanes Saleh, M. Sekandve Hayat Khan.

310.285 USA ISSN 1548-7660
QA276.4
➤ **JOURNAL OF STATISTICAL SOFTWARE (ONLINE).** Text in English. 1996. irreg. free (effective 2011). back issues avail. **Document type:** *Journal, Academic/Scholarly.* **Description:** Contains articles focusing on improving statistics education at all levels, including elementary, secondary, post-secondary, post-graduate, continuing, and workplace.
Media: Online - full text.
Indexed: A39, C27, C29, CMCI, D03, D04, E13, P30, R14, S14, S15, S18, SCI, SCOPUS, W07.
—**CCC.**
Published by: American Statistical Association, 732 N Washington St, Alexandria, VA 22314. TEL 703-684-1221, 888-231-3473, FAX 703-684-2037, asainfo@amstat.org, http://www.amstat.org. Ed. Jan de Leeuw.

310 BGD ISSN 1022-4734
JOURNAL OF STATISTICAL STUDIES. Text in English. 1980. a.
Indexed: CCMJ, CIS, MSN, MathR.
—BLDSC (5066.843500).
Published by: Jahangirnagar University, Department of Statistics, Savar, Dhaka, 1342, Bangladesh. stat@juniv.edu, http://www.juniv.edu/stat.htm.

310.13 USA ISSN 1538-7887
QA276.A1
➤ **JOURNAL OF STATISTICAL THEORY AND APPLICATIONS.** Text in English. 2002. q. USD 45 to individuals; USD 80 to institutions; USD 15 per issue (effective 2011). adv. back issues avail. **Document type:** *Journal, Academic/Scholarly.*
Indexed: CCMJ, CIS, MSN, MathR.
Published by: Gowas Publishers, 274 Sydney Rd, Holland, PA 18955. TEL 267-364-5266, FAX 215-944-3928. Eds. Gholamhossein G Hamedani TEL 414-288-6348, M Ahsanullah TEL 609-895-5539.

310 USA ISSN 1559-8608
QA276.A1
➤ **JOURNAL OF STATISTICAL THEORY AND PRACTICE.** Text in English. 2007. q. GBP 414 combined subscription in United Kingdom to institutions (print & online eds.); EUR 546, USD 683 combined subscription to institutions (print & online eds.) (effective 2012). **Document type:** *Journal, Academic/Scholarly.* **Description:** Aims to explore new areas of knowlege in the fields of statistical mathematics, theory and their applications.
Related titles: Online - full text ed.: ISSN 1559-8616. GBP 372 in United Kingdom to institutions; EUR 491, USD 614 to institutions (effective 2012).
Indexed: CCMJ, MSN, MathR, P30, Z02.
—BLDSC (5066.843620), IE.
Published by: Grace Scientific Publishing, 20 Middlefield Ct, Greensboro, NC 27155. managingeditor@gracescientific.com. Ed. Sat Gupta.

310 IND ISSN 0973-4600
JOURNAL OF STATISTICS AND APPLICATIONS. Text in English. 2006. q. INR 1,000 domestic; USD 100 foreign; INR 1,500 combined subscription domestic (print & online eds.); USD 200 combined subscription foreign (print & online eds.) (effective 2010). **Document type:** *Journal, Academic/Scholarly.* **Description:** Covers new developments in probability and statistics and their applications in medical, agricultural, econometrics, physical or social sciences, industry, commerce, and government.
Related titles: Online - full text ed.: INR 750 domestic; USD 100 foreign (effective 2010).
Indexed: P10, P48, P50, P53, P54, PQC.
Published by: (Forum for Interdisciplinary Mathematics), M D Publications Pvt Ltd, 11 Darya Ganj, New Delhi, 110 002, India. TEL 91-11-41563325, FAX 91-11-23275542, contact@mdppl.com. Eds. Rameshwar D Gupta, Ravindra Khattree, Sudhir Gupta.

519.5 IND ISSN 0972-0510
➤ **JOURNAL OF STATISTICS & MANAGEMENT SYSTEMS.** Text in English. 1998. bi-m. INR 4,000 domestic (print or online ed.); INR 5,000 combined subscription domestic (print & online eds.) (effective 2011); USD 555 combined subscription in US & Canada (print & online eds.); EUR 400 combined subscription elsewhere (print & online eds.) (effective 2012). back issues avail. **Document type:** *Journal, Academic/Scholarly.* **Description:** Covers original research papers, survey articles, book reviews, dissertation abstracts etc. devoted to all theoretical and applicable topics in statistics, management systems and related areas viz. optimization.
Related titles: Online - full text ed.: USD 410 in US & Canada; EUR 320 elsewhere (effective 2011).
Indexed: CCMJ, CIS, Inspec, MSN, MathR, ST&MA, Z02.
—BLDSC (5066.840200), IE, Ingenta, Linda Hall.
Published by: Taru Publications, G-159, Pushkar Enclave, Paschim Vihar, New Delhi, 110 063, India. TEL 91-11-42331159, FAX 91-11-42321126, info@tarupublications.com. Ed. Dr. Bal Kishan Dass. **outside India:** I O S Press.

001.422 USA ISSN 1069-1898
QA276.18
➤ **JOURNAL OF STATISTICS EDUCATION**; an international journal on the teaching and learning of statistics. Abbreviated title: J S E. Text in English. 1993. 3/yr. free (effective 2011). adv. back issues avail. **Document type:** *Journal, Academic/Scholarly.* **Description:** Focuses on improving statistics education at all levels, including elementary, secondary, post-secondary, post-graduate, continuing, nd workplace.
Media: Online - full text.
Indexed: A39, C27, C29, CIS, D03, D04, E13, R14, S14, S15, S18, SCOPUS.
—**CCC.**
Published by: American Statistical Association, 732 N Washington St, Alexandria, VA 22314. TEL 703-684-1221, 888-231-3473, FAX 703-684-2037, asainfo@amstat.org. Ed. William Notz.

➤ **JOURNAL OF THEORETICAL PROBABILITY.** *see* MATHEMATICS

310 GBR ISSN 0143-9782
QA280 CODEN: JTSADL
➤ **JOURNAL OF TIME SERIES ANALYSIS.** Text in English. 1980. bi-m. GBP 1,140 in United Kingdom to institutions; EUR 1,447 in Europe to institutions; USD 2,104 in the Americas to institutions; USD 2,455 elsewhere to institutions; GBP 1,311 combined subscription in United Kingdom to institutions (print & online eds.); EUR 1,665 combined subscription in Europe to institutions (print & online eds.); USD 2,420 combined subscription in the Americas to institutions (print & online eds.); USD 2,824 combined subscription elsewhere to institutions (print & online eds.) (effective 2012). adv. illus. index. back issues avail.; reprint service avail. from PSC. **Document type:** *Journal, Academic/Scholarly.* **Description:** Its fields of application range from neurophysiology to astrophysics and it covers such well-known areas as economic forecasting, study of biological data, control systems, signal processing and communications and vibrations engineering.
Related titles: Online - full text ed.: ISSN 1467-9892. GBP 1,140 in United Kingdom to institutions; EUR 1,447 in Europe to institutions; USD 2,104 in the Americas to institutions; USD 2,455 elsewhere to institutions (effective 2012) (from IngentaConnect).
Indexed: A01, A03, A08, A12, A17, A22, A26, ABIn, Biostat, CA, CCMJ, CIS, CMCI, E01, ESPM, IBSS, ISR, Inspec, JCQM, MSN, MathR, ORMS, P48, P51, P53, P54, PQC, QC&AS, RiskAb, S01, SCI, SCOPUS, ST&MA, T02, W07, Z02.
—BLDSC (5069.400000), IE, Infotrieve, Ingenta. **CCC.**
Published by: Wiley-Blackwell Publishing Ltd. (Subsidiary of: John Wiley & Sons, Inc.), 9600 Garsington Rd, Oxford, OX4 2DQ, United Kingdom. TEL 44-1865-776868, FAX 44-1865-714591, customerservices@blackwellpublishing.com. Ed. M Priestley TEL 44-1612-003660. Adv. contact Craig Pickett TEL 44-1865-476267. **Co-sponsor:** Bernoulli Society for Mathematical Statistics and Probability.

➤ **JUSTICE EXPENDITURE AND EMPLOYMENT IN THE UNITED STATES.** *see* CRIMINOLOGY AND LAW ENFORCEMENT—Abstracting, Bibliographies, Statistics

➤ **JUSTIZ IN ZAHLEN.** *see* LAW—Abstracting, Bibliographies, Statistics

➤ **JUTAKU, TOCHI TOKEI CHOSA HOKOKU/HOUSING AND LAND SURVEY OF JAPAN (YEAR).** *see* HOUSING AND URBAN PLANNING—Abstracting, Bibliographies, Statistics

➤ **JUVENILE COURT STATISTICS.** *see* LAW—Abstracting, Bibliographies, Statistics

➤ **JYVASKYLAN YLIOPISTO. MATEMATIIKAN JA TILASTOTIETEEN LAITOS. VAITOKSET/UNIVERSITY OF JYVASKYLA. DEPARTMENT OF MATHEMATICS AND STATISTICS. DISSERTATIONS.** *see* MATHEMATICS

316 NGA
KADUNA STATE STATISTICAL YEARBOOK. Text in English. 1975. a. **Document type:** *Government.*
Formerly: North Central State Statistical Yearbook
Published by: Ministry of Economic Planning and Rural Development, Economic Planning Division, PMB 2032, Kaduna, Nigeria.

KAKEI CHOUSA NEMPOU. CHOCHIKU, FUSAI HEN/ANNUAL REPORT ON THE FAMILY INCOME AND EXPENDITURE SURVEY. 2, SAVINGS AND LIABILITIES. *see* BUSINESS AND ECONOMICS—Abstracting, Bibliographies, Statistics

KAKEI CHOUSA NEMPOU. KAKEI SHUUSHI HEN. *see* HOME ECONOMICS—Abstracting, Bibliographies, Statistics

KANO (STATE). MOTOR VEHICLE STATISTICS. *see* TRANSPORTATION—Abstracting, Bibliographies, Statistics

KANO (STATE). PUBLIC FINANCE STATISTICS OF KANO STATE & LOCAL GOVERNMENT COUNCILS. *see* BUSINESS AND ECONOMICS—Abstracting, Bibliographies, Statistics

KANO (STATE). STATISTICAL YEAR - BOOK. *see* BUSINESS AND ECONOMICS—Abstracting, Bibliographies, Statistics

316.69 NGA
KANO (STATE). STATISTICS DIVISION. AREA CODES. Text in English. a. price varies. **Document type:** *Directory, Government.*
Formerly: Northern Nigeria Area Code Publication
Published by: Statistics Division, Budget Department, Director of Statistics, PMB 3219, Kano, Nigeria.

KANSAS. AGRICULTURAL STATISTICS SERVICE. AGRICULTURAL PRICES. *see* AGRICULTURE—Abstracting, Bibliographies, Statistics

KANSAS. AGRICULTURAL STATISTICS SERVICE. CATTLE. *see* AGRICULTURE—Abstracting, Bibliographies, Statistics

KANSAS. AGRICULTURAL STATISTICS SERVICE. CROPS. *see* AGRICULTURE—Abstracting, Bibliographies, Statistics

KANSAS. AGRICULTURAL STATISTICS SERVICE. HOGS & PIGS. *see* AGRICULTURE—Abstracting, Bibliographies, Statistics

KANSAS CITIES & COUNTIES GRAPHIC PERFORMANCE ANALYSIS. *see* PUBLIC ADMINISTRATION—Abstracting, Bibliographies, Statistics

317 USA ISSN 1934-9319
KANSAS STATISTICAL ABSTRACT (ONLINE). Text in English. 1965. a., latest 2006, 41st ed.
Formerly (until 2002): Kansas Statistical Abstract (Print) (0453-2600)
Media: Online - full text.
Published by: University of Kansas, Institute for Policy & Social Research, 1541 Lilac Lane, 607 Blake Hall, Lawrence, KS 66044-3177. TEL 785-864-3701, FAX 785-864-3683, ipsr@ku.edu.

KANTONE UND STAEDTE DER SCHWEIZ. STATISTISCHE UEBERSICHTEN/CANTONS ET VILLES SUISSES. DONNEES STATISTIQUES. *see* PUBLIC ADMINISTRATION—Abstracting, Bibliographies, Statistics

KASSELER STATISTIK. *see* PUBLIC ADMINISTRATION—Abstracting, Bibliographies, Statistics

KAUKOLAMPOTILASTO. *see* ENERGY—Abstracting, Bibliographies, Statistics

KAYHAN-I SAL/KAYHAN YEARBOOK. *see* HISTORY—History Of The Near East

519.5 JPN ISSN 0914-8930
KEISANKI TOKEIGAKU/BULLETIN OF THE COMPUTATIONAL STATISTICS OF JAPAN. Text in Japanese; Summaries in English, Japanese. 1988. a. JPY 3,000 (effective 2000). adv. bk.rev. abstr. Index. **Document type:** *Journal, Academic/Scholarly.*
Indexed: CIS, ST&MA.
—**CCC.**
Published by: Nihon Keisanki Tokei Gakkai/Japanese Society of Computational Statistics, c/o Department of Environmental and Mathematical Science, Okayama University, Okayama, 700-8530, Japan. TEL 81-86-251-8509, FAX 81-86-251-8552. Ed., Adv. contact Yoshiharu Sato. Circ: 500.

KENSETSU TOKEI GEPPO/MONTHLY OF CONSTRUCTION STATISTICS. *see* BUILDING AND CONSTRUCTION—Abstracting, Bibliographies, Statistics

KENTUCKY AGRICULTURAL STATISTICS. *see* AGRICULTURE—Abstracting, Bibliographies, Statistics

KENTUCKY ANNUAL VITAL STATISTICS REPORT. *see* PUBLIC HEALTH AND SAFETY—Abstracting, Bibliographies, Statistics

KENTUCKY CITIES & COUNTIES GRAPHIC PERFORMANCE ANALYSIS. *see* PUBLIC ADMINISTRATION—Abstracting, Bibliographies, Statistics

KENTUCKY WEEKLY CROP & WEATHER REPORT. *see* AGRICULTURE—Abstracting, Bibliographies, Statistics

KENYA. CENTRAL BUREAU OF STATISTICS. AGRICULTURAL CENSUS (LARGE FARM AREAS). *see* AGRICULTURE—Abstracting, Bibliographies, Statistics

S

KENYA. CENTRAL BUREAU OF STATISTICS. DEVELOPMENT ESTIMATES. *see* BUSINESS AND ECONOMICS—Abstracting, Bibliographies, Statistics

KENYA. CENTRAL BUREAU OF STATISTICS. EMPLOYMENT AND EARNINGS IN THE MODERN SECTOR. *see* BUSINESS AND ECONOMICS—Abstracting, Bibliographies, Statistics

KENYA. CENTRAL BUREAU OF STATISTICS. ESTIMATES OF RECURRENT EXPENDITURES. *see* BUSINESS AND ECONOMICS—Abstracting, Bibliographies, Statistics

KENYA. CENTRAL BUREAU OF STATISTICS. ESTIMATES OF REVENUE EXPENDITURES. *see* BUSINESS AND ECONOMICS—Abstracting, Bibliographies, Statistics

316.76 KEN
KENYA. CENTRAL BUREAU OF STATISTICS. KENYA CONSUMER PRICE INDEX. Text in English. 1956. m. KES 1,200 (effective 2001). stat. back issues avail. **Document type:** *Government.*
Former titles: Kenya. Central Bureau of Statistics. Statistical Abstract; Kenya. Ministry of Economic Planning and Development. Statistics Division. Statistical Abstract (0075-5850)
Related titles: Microfiche ed.: (from PQC).
Published by: Ministry of Finance and Planning, Central Bureau of Statistics, PO Box 30266, Nairobi, Kenya. TEL 254-2-333970, 254-2-317011, FAX 254-2-333030, http://www.treasury.go.ke.cbs. **Subscr. to:** Government Press, Haile Selaissie Ave., PO Box 30128, Nairobi, Kenya. TEL 254-2-334075.

KENYA. CENTRAL BUREAU OF STATISTICS. SURVEYS OF INDUSTRIAL PRODUCTION. *see* BUSINESS AND ECONOMICS—Abstracting, Bibliographies, Statistics

316.76 KEN ISSN 0453-6002
KENYA STATISTICAL DIGEST. Text in English. 1963. q. price varies. stat. **Document type:** *Government.*
Published by: Ministry of Finance and Planning, Central Bureau of Statistics, PO Box 30266, Nairobi, Kenya. **Subscr. to:** Government Press, Haile Selaissie Ave., PO Box 30128, Nairobi, Kenya. TEL 254-2-334075.

314 NLD
KERNCIJFERS EINDHOVEN. Text in Dutch. 1957. a. stat.; illus. index. **Document type:** *Government.*
Formerly (until 1997): Jaarboek Eindhoven
Published by: Gemeente Eindhoven, Afdeling Bestuurlijke Informatie en Onderzoek, PO Box 90150, Eindhoven, 5600 RB, Netherlands. TEL 31-40-2386060, http://www.eindhoven.nl.

KERNCIJFERS TWEEWIELERS. *see* SPORTS AND GAMES—Abstracting, Bibliographies, Statistics

KEY DATA ON EDUCATION IN EUROPE. *see* EDUCATION—Abstracting, Bibliographies, Statistics

KEY DATA ON TEACHING LANGUAGES AT SCHOOL IN EUROPE. *see* EDUCATION—Abstracting, Bibliographies, Statistics

KEY POPULATION AND VITAL STATISTICS (ONLINE). *see* POPULATION STUDIES—Abstracting, Bibliographies, Statistics

KEY SCOTTISH ENVIRONMENT STATISTICS (ONLINE). *see* ENVIRONMENTAL STUDIES—Abstracting, Bibliographies, Statistics

KEY SMALL BUSINESS FINANCING STATISTICS (ONLINE). *see* BUSINESS AND ECONOMICS—Abstracting, Bibliographies, Statistics

KEY SMALL BUSINESS FINANCING STATISTICS (PRINT). *see* BUSINESS AND ECONOMICS—Abstracting, Bibliographies, Statistics

KEY SMALL BUSINESS STATISTICS (ONLINE). *see* BUSINESS AND ECONOMICS—Small Business

KEY SMALL BUSINESS STATISTICS (PRINT). *see* BUSINESS AND ECONOMICS—Small Business

KEY STATISTICS OF THAILAND (YEAR). *see* BUSINESS AND ECONOMICS—Abstracting, Bibliographies, Statistics

KEY STUDENT OUTCOMES INDICATORS FOR B.C. COLLEGE AND INSTITUTIONS. ANALYSIS BY INSTITUTION. *see* EDUCATION—Abstracting, Bibliographies, Statistics

KINDERTAGESEINRICHTUNGEN IN BAYERN. *see* EDUCATION—Abstracting, Bibliographies, Statistics

314.97 SVN ISSN 1408-9114
KLASIFIKACIJE/CLASSIFICATIONS. Text in Slovenian, English. 1998. a. price varies. stat. **Document type:** *Government.* **Description:** Publishes various classifications and nomenclatures that were adopted as national standards in Slovenia. Nomenclatures and classifications are used in preparing and implementing statistical surveys.
Related titles: Online - full content ed.
Published by: Statisticni Urad Republike Slovenije/Statistical Office of the Republic of Slovenia, Vozarski pot 12, Ljubjana, 1000, Slovenia. TEL 386-1-2415104, FAX 386-1-2415344, info.stat@gov.si. Ed. Ana Antoncic. Pub. Tomaz Banovec.

310 070.5 BGR
KNIGOIZDAVANE I PECHAT. Text in Bulgarian. a. BGL 4.56 (effective 2002).
Related titles: Diskette ed.
Published by: Natsionalen Statisticheski Institut/National Statistical Institute, ul P Volov, # 2, Sofia, 1038, Bulgaria. FAX 359-2-9803319, publikacii@nsi.bg, http://www.nsi.bg.

KNITSTATS; yearly statistical bulletin for the hosiery and knitwear industry. *see* TEXTILE INDUSTRIES AND FABRICS—Abstracting, Bibliographies, Statistics

KODO KEIRYOGAKU/JAPANESE JOURNAL OF BEHAVIORMETRICS. *see* SOCIOLOGY—Abstracting, Bibliographies, Statistics

KOELNER STATISTISCHE NACHRICHTEN. SONDERHEFTE. *see* PUBLIC ADMINISTRATION—Abstracting, Bibliographies, Statistics

KOMPENDIUM DER FINANZSTATISTIK. *see* PUBLIC ADMINISTRATION—Abstracting, Bibliographies, Statistics

310 NLD ISSN 1226-3192
HA1
KOREAN STATISTICAL SOCIETY. JOURNAL. Text in English. 1973. q. EUR 259 in Europe to institutions; JPY 56,500 in Japan to institutions; USD 346 elsewhere to institutions (effective 2012). stat. **Document type:** *Journal, Academic/Scholarly.* **Description:** Focuses on the development of statistics and research in related fields.
Formerly (until 1996): Tong'gyehag Yeon'gu (1225-0678)
Related titles: Online - full text ed.: ISSN 1876-4231 (from ScienceDirect).
Indexed: CA, CCMJ, CIS, MSN, MathR, P30, SCI, SCOPUS, T02, W07, Z02.
—BLDSC (4812.348700), IE. **CCC.**
Published by: (Han'gug Tong'gye Haghoe/Korean Statistical Society KOR), Elsevier BV (Subsidiary of: Elsevier Science & Technology), Radarweg 29, PO Box 211, Amsterdam, 1000 AE, Netherlands. TEL 31-20-4853911, FAX 31-20-4852457, JournalsCustomerServiceEMEA@elsevier.com, http://www.elsevier.nl. Ed. Byeong U Park TEL 82-2-8806576.

KOSEI NO SHIHYO/JOURNAL OF HEALTH AND WELFARE STATISTICS. *see* PUBLIC HEALTH AND SAFETY

KOUSEIROUDOUSHOU. JINKO DOTAI SHAKAI KEIZAIMEN CHOSA HOKOKU/JAPAN. MINISTRY OF HEALTH, LABOUR AND WELFARE. REPORT ON SURVEY OF SOCIO-ECONOMIC ASPECTS ON VITAL EVENTS. *see* POPULATION STUDIES—Abstracting, Bibliographies, Statistics

304.6 JPN ISSN 0075-3270
KOUSEIROUDOUSHOU. JINKO DOTAI TOKEI/JAPAN. MINISTRY OF HEALTH, LABOUR AND WELFARE. VITAL STATISTICS. Text in Japanese. 1899. a. (in 3 vols.). JPY 10,500 v.1; JPY 12,075 v.2; JPY 13,125 v.3. **Document type:** *Government.*
Formerly: Nihon Teikoku Jinko Dotai Tokei - Vital Statistics of the Japanese Empire
Published by: Kouseiroudoushou/Ministry of Health, Labour and Welfare, 1-2-2 Kasumigaseki Chiyoda-ku, Tokyo, 100-8916, Japan. TEL 81-3-52531111, http://www.mhlw.go.jp/. R&P Yoke Kanegae.

315 JPN ISSN 0385-969X
KOUSEIROUDOUSHOU. JINKO DOTAI TOKEI GEPPO, GAISU/JAPAN. MINISTRY OF HEALTH, LABOUR AND WELFARE. MONTHLY REPORT ON VITAL STATISTICS. Text in Japanese. m. JPY 735. **Document type:** *Government.*
Formerly (until 1970): Jinko Dotai Tokei Maigetsu Gaisu (0385-9681)
Published by: Kouseiroudoushou/Ministry of Health, Labour and Welfare, 1-2-2 Kasumigaseki Chiyoda-ku, Tokyo, 100-8916, Japan. TEL 81-3-52531111, http://www.mhlw.go.jp/. R&P Yoke Kanegae.

KOUSEIROUDOUSHOU. JINKOU DOUTAI SHOKUGUON. SANGYOUTOUKEI: JINKOU DOUTAI TOUKEI TOKUSHU HOUKOKU/JAPAN. MINISTRY OF HEALTH, LABOUR AND WELFARE. OCCUPATIONAL AND INDUSTRIAL ASPECTS: SPECIAL REPORT OF VITAL STATISTICS IN (YEAR). *see* OCCUPATIONS AND CAREERS—Abstracting, Bibliographies, Statistics

KOUSEIROUDOUSHOU. KOSEI TOKEI YORAN/JAPAN. MINISTRY OF HEALTH, LABOUR AND WELFARE. HANDBOOK OF HEALTH AND WELFARE STATISTICS. *see* PUBLIC HEALTH AND SAFETY—Abstracting, Bibliographies, Statistics

KOUSEIROUDOUSHOU. SEIKATSU HOGO DOTAI CHOSA HOKOKU/JAPAN. MINISTRY OF HEALTH, LABOUR AND WELFARE. REPORT ON SURVEY OF PUBLIC ASSISTANCE. *see* SOCIAL SERVICES AND WELFARE—Abstracting, Bibliographies, Statistics

KOUSEIROUDOUSHOU. SHAKAI FUKUSHI GYOSEI GYOMU HOKOKU/JAPAN. MINISTRY OF HEALTH, LABOUR AND WELFARE. STATISTICAL REPORT ON SOCIAL WELFARE ADMINISTRATION AND SERVICES. *see* SOCIAL SERVICES AND WELFARE—Abstracting, Bibliographies, Statistics

KOUSEIROUDOUSHOU. SHAKAI FUKUSHI SHISETSU TOU CHOSA HOKOKU/JAPAN. MINISTRY OF HEALTH, LABOUR AND WELFARE. REPORT ON SURVEY OF SOCIAL WELFARE INSTITUTIONS. *see* SOCIAL SERVICES AND WELFARE—Abstracting, Bibliographies, Statistics

KOUSEIROUDOUSHOU. SHAKAI IRYO SHINRYO KOIBETSU CHOSA HOKOKU/JAPAN. MINISTRY OF HEALTH, LABOUR AND WELFARE. REPORT ON SURVEY OF NATIONAL MEDICAL CARE INSURANCE SERVICES. *see* INSURANCE—Abstracting, Bibliographies, Statistics

KOUSEIROUDOUSHOU. SHOKUCHUDOKU TOKEI/JAPAN. MINISTRY OF HEALTH, LABOUR AND WELFARE. STATISTICAL REPORT ON FOOD POISONINGS. *see* PUBLIC HEALTH AND SAFETY—Abstracting, Bibliographies, Statistics

KRATKOSROCHNYE EKONOMICHESKIE POKAZATELI ROSSIISKOI FEDERATSII/SHORT-TERM INDICATORS OF THE RUSSIA'S ECONOMY. *see* BUSINESS AND ECONOMICS—Abstracting, Bibliographies, Statistics

314 DEU
KREFELD. AMT FUER STATISTIK UND STADTENTWICKLUNG. STATISTISCHES JAHRBUCH. Text in German. 1926. a. EUR 20 (effective 2005). bk.rev. **Document type:** *Yearbook, Government.*
Published by: Stadt Krefeld, Abteilung Statistik und Wahlen, Von-der-Leyen-Platz 1, Krefeld, 47798, Germany. TEL 49-2151-861353, FAX 49-2151-861360, statistik@krefeld.de, http://www.krefeld.de. Circ: 450.

314 DEU
KREISSTANDARDZAHLEN NORDRHEIN-WESTFALEN; statistische Angaben fuer kreisfreie Staedte und Kreise. Text in German. 1951. a. EUR 5.10 (effective 2006). back issues avail. **Document type:** *Yearbook, Government.*
Published by: Information und Technik Nordrhein-Westfalen, Mauerstr 51, Duesseldorf, 40476, Germany. TEL 49-211-944901, FAX 49-211-442006, poststelle@lds.nrw.de, http://www.it.nrw.de. Circ: 1,300.

KULTUR- UND STADTNACHRICHTEN AUS WEITRA. *see* HISTORY

KULTURSTATISTIKK/CULTURAL STATISTICS. *see* SOCIAL SCIENCES: COMPREHENSIVE WORKS—Abstracting, Bibliographies, Statistics

KUWAIT. CENTRAL STATISTICAL OFFICE. AGRICULTURAL STATISTICS BULLETIN/KUWAIT. AL-IDARAH AL-MARKAZIYYAH LIL-IHSA'. NASHRAH AL-IHSA'AT AL-ZIRA'IYYAH. *see* AGRICULTURE—Abstracting, Bibliographies, Statistics

KUWAIT. CENTRAL STATISTICAL OFFICE. ANNUAL BULLETIN OF FOREIGN TRADE STATISTICS/KUWAIT. AL-IDARAH AL-MARKAZIYYAH LIL-IHSA'. AL-NASHRAH AL-SANAWIYYAH LI-IHSA'AT AL-TIJARAH AL-KHARIJIYYAH. *see* BUSINESS AND ECONOMICS—Abstracting, Bibliographies, Statistics

315.367 KWT ISSN 0259-532X
KUWAIT. CENTRAL STATISTICAL OFFICE. ANNUAL STATISTICAL ABSTRACT. Key Title: Al-Majmu'ah al-Ihsa'iyyah al-Sanawiyyah - Wizarat al-Takhtit, al-Idarah al-Markaziyyah. Text in Arabic, English. 1964. a., latest 1996. KWD 0.50. **Document type:** *Government.*
Published by: Central Statistical Office/Al-Idarah al-Markaziyyah lil-Ihsa', P O Box 26188, Safat, 13122, Kuwait. TEL 965-2428200, FAX 965-2430464, TELEX 22468 TAKHTET KT. Circ: 450.

KUWAIT. CENTRAL STATISTICAL OFFICE. ANNUAL STATISTICAL BULLETIN FOR TRANSPORT AND COMMUNICATION/KUWAIT. AL-IDARAH AL-MARKAZIYYAH LIL-IHSA'. AL-NASHRAH AL-IHSA'IYYAH AL-SANAWIYYAH LIL-NAQL WAL-MUWASALAT. *see* TRANSPORTATION—Abstracting, Bibliographies, Statistics

KUWAIT. CENTRAL STATISTICAL OFFICE. ANNUAL SURVEY OF ESTABLISHMENTS - CONSTRUCTION/KUWAIT. AL-IDARAH AL-MARKAZIYYAH LIL-IHSA'. AL-BAHTH AL-SANAWI LIL-MANSHAAT - AL-TASHYID WAL-BINA'. *see* BUILDING AND CONSTRUCTION—Abstracting, Bibliographies, Statistics

KUWAIT. CENTRAL STATISTICAL OFFICE. ANNUAL SURVEY OF ESTABLISHMENTS - INDUSTRIAL/KUWAIT. AL-IDARAH AL-MARKAZIYYAH LIL-IHSA'. AL-BAHTH AL-SANAWI LIL-MANSHAAT - AL-SINA'AH. *see* BUSINESS AND ECONOMICS—Abstracting, Bibliographies, Statistics

KUWAIT. CENTRAL STATISTICAL OFFICE. ANNUAL SURVEY OF ESTABLISHMENTS - SERVICES/KUWAIT. AL-IDARAH AL-MARKAZIYYAH LIL-IHSA'. AL-BAHTH AL-SANAWI LIL-MANSHAAT - AL-KHADAMAT. *see* BUSINESS AND ECONOMICS—Abstracting, Bibliographies, Statistics

KUWAIT. CENTRAL STATISTICAL OFFICE. ANNUAL SURVEY OF ESTABLISHMENTS - WHOLESALE & RETAIL TRADE/KUWAIT. AL-IDARAH AL-MARKAZIYYAH LIL-IHSA'. AL-BAHTH AL-SANAWI LIL-MANSHAAT - TIJARAH AL-JUMLAH WAL-TAJZI'AH. *see* BUSINESS AND ECONOMICS—Abstracting, Bibliographies, Statistics

KUWAIT. CENTRAL STATISTICAL OFFICE. BUILDINGS AND DWELLINGS CENSUS/KUWAIT. AL-IDARAH AL-MARKAZIYYAH LIL-IHSA'. TA'DAD AL-MABANI WAL-MASAKIN. *see* BUSINESS AND ECONOMICS—Abstracting, Bibliographies, Statistics

KUWAIT. CENTRAL STATISTICAL OFFICE. CONSTRUCTION STATISTICS RESULTS/KUWAIT. AL-IDARAH AL-MARKAZIYYAH LIL-IHSA'. NATA'IJ IHSA'AT AL-TASHYID WAL-BINA'. *see* BUILDING AND CONSTRUCTION—Abstracting, Bibliographies, Statistics

KUWAIT. CENTRAL STATISTICAL OFFICE. ESTABLISHMENT CENSUS/KUWAIT. AL-IDARAH AL-MARKAZIYYAH LIL-IHSA'. TA'DAD AL-MUNSHAAT. *see* BUSINESS AND ECONOMICS—Abstracting, Bibliographies, Statistics

KUWAIT. CENTRAL STATISTICAL OFFICE. FAMILY BUDGET SURVEY - FINAL RESULTS/KUWAIT. AL-IDARAH AL-MARKAZIYYAH LIL-IHSA'. MIZANIYYAT AL-USRAH - AL-NATA'IJ AL-TAJMI'IYYAH AL-NIHA'IYYAH. *see* BUSINESS AND ECONOMICS—Abstracting, Bibliographies, Statistics

KUWAIT. CENTRAL STATISTICAL OFFICE. FINANCIAL STATISTICS/KUWAIT. AL-IDARAH AL-MARKAZIYYAH LIL-IHSA'. AL-IHSA'AT AL-MAALIYYAH. *see* BUSINESS AND ECONOMICS—Abstracting, Bibliographies, Statistics

KUWAIT. CENTRAL STATISTICAL OFFICE. FISHING STATISTICS BULLETIN/KUWAIT. AL-IDARAH AL-MARKAZIYYAH LIL-IHSA'. NASHRAH IHSA'AT AL-THARWAH AL-SAMAKIYYAH. *see* FISH AND FISHERIES—Abstracting, Bibliographies, Statistics

KUWAIT. CENTRAL STATISTICAL OFFICE. GENERAL POPULATION CENSUS/KUWAIT. AL-IDARAH AL-MARKAZIYYAH LIL-IHSA'. AL-TA'DAD AL-AAM LIL-SUKKAN. *see* POPULATION STUDIES—Abstracting, Bibliographies, Statistics

KUWAIT. CENTRAL STATISTICAL OFFICE. GOVERNMENT FINANCIAL STATISTICS/KUWAIT. AL-IDARAH AL-MARKAZIYYAH LIL-IHSA'. AL-IHSA'AT AL-MAALIYYAH LIL-HUKUMAH. *see* BUSINESS AND ECONOMICS—Abstracting, Bibliographies, Statistics

KUWAIT. CENTRAL STATISTICAL OFFICE. MONTHLY BULLETIN OF FOREIGN TRADE STATISTICS/KUWAIT. AL-IDARAH AL-MARKAZIYYAH LIL-IHSA'. AL-NASHRAH AL-SHAHRIYYAH LI-IHSA'AT AL-TIJARAH AL-KHARIJIYYAH. *see* BUSINESS AND ECONOMICS—Abstracting, Bibliographies, Statistics

KUWAIT. CENTRAL STATISTICAL OFFICE. MONTHLY CONSUMER PRICE INDEX NUMBERS. *see* BUSINESS AND ECONOMICS—Abstracting, Bibliographies, Statistics

310 KWT ISSN 0023-5768
KUWAIT. CENTRAL STATISTICAL OFFICE. MONTHLY DIGEST OF STATISTICS/KUWAIT. AL-IDARAH AL-MARKAZIYYAH LIL-IHSA'. AL-NASHRAH AL-IHSA'IYYAH AL-SHAHRIYYAH. Text in Arabic, English. 1965; N.S. 1980. m. KWD 0.50 (effective 1998). **Document type:** *Government.*
Supersedes: Kuwait. Central Statistical Office. Monthly Statistical Bulletin
Published by: Central Statistical Office/Al-Idarah al-Markaziyyah lil-Ihsa', P O Box 26188, Safat, 13122, Kuwait. TEL 965-2428200, FAX 965-2430464.

KUWAIT. CENTRAL STATISTICAL OFFICE. NATIONAL ACCOUNTS STATISTICS/KUWAIT. AL-IDARAH AL-MARKAZIYYAH LIL-IHSA'. IHSA'AT AL-HISABAT AL-QAWMIYYAH. *see* BUSINESS AND ECONOMICS—Abstracting, Bibliographies, Statistics

KUWAIT. CENTRAL STATISTICAL OFFICE. PRELIMINARY RESULTS OF LABOUR FORCE BY SAMPLE. *see* BUSINESS AND ECONOMICS—Abstracting, Bibliographies, Statistics

KUWAIT. CENTRAL STATISTICAL OFFICE. PROVISIONAL ESTIMATES - NATIONAL ACCOUNTS. *see* BUSINESS AND ECONOMICS—Abstracting, Bibliographies, Statistics

KUWAIT. CENTRAL STATISTICAL OFFICE. QUARTERLY BULLETIN FOR RETAIL PRICES. *see* BUSINESS AND ECONOMICS—Abstracting, Bibliographies, Statistics

KUWAIT. CENTRAL STATISTICAL OFFICE. QUARTERLY BULLETIN FOR WHOLESALE PRICES. *see* BUSINESS AND ECONOMICS—Abstracting, Bibliographies, Statistics

KUWAIT. CENTRAL STATISTICAL OFFICE. SOCIAL STATISTICS BULLETIN/KUWAIT. AL-IDARAH AL-MARKAZIYYAH LIL-IHSA'. NASHRAT AL-IHSA'AT AL-IJTIMA'IYYAH. *see* SOCIAL SERVICES AND WELFARE—Abstracting, Bibliographies, Statistics

KUWAIT. CENTRAL STATISTICAL OFFICE. VITAL STATISTICS - A SUMMARISED ANALYSIS BULLETIN/KUWAIT. AL-IDARAH AL-MARKAZIYYAH LIL-IHSA'. TAHLIL AL-IHSA'AT AL-HAYAWIYYAH. *see* POPULATION STUDIES—Abstracting, Bibliographies, Statistics

KUWAIT. CENTRAL STATISTICAL OFFICE. VITAL STATISTICS - BIRTHS AND DEATHS/KUWAIT. AL-IDARAH AL-MARKAZIYYAH LIL-IHSA'. AL-IHSA'AT AL-HAYAWIYYAH - AL-MAWALID WAL-WAFAYAT. *see* POPULATION STUDIES—Abstracting, Bibliographies, Statistics

KUWAIT. CENTRAL STATISTICAL OFFICE. VITAL STATISTICS - MARRIAGE AND DIVORCE/KUWAIT. AL-IDARAH AL-MARKAZIYYAH LIL-IHSA'. AL-IHSA'AT AL-HAYAWIYYAH - AL-ZAWAJ WAL-TALAQ. *see* MATRIMONY—Abstracting, Bibliographies, Statistics

KUWAIT. CENTRAL STATISTICAL OFFICE. WHOLESALE PRICE INDEX NUMBERS/KUWAIT. AL-IDARAH AL-MARKAZIYYAH LIL-IHSA'. AL-ARQAM AL-QIYASIYYAH LI-AS'AR AL-JUMLAH. *see* BUSINESS AND ECONOMICS—Abstracting, Bibliographies, Statistics

KUWAIT. CENTRAL STATISTICAL OFFICE. YEARLY BULLETIN OF TRANSIT STATISTICS/KUWAIT. AL-IDARAH AL-MARKAZIYYAH LIL-IHSA'. NASHRAH IHSA'AT AL-TRANSIT. *see* BUSINESS AND ECONOMICS—Abstracting, Bibliographies, Statistics

LABOR FORCE AND NONAGRICULTURAL EMPLOYMENT ESTIMATES. *see* BUSINESS AND ECONOMICS—Abstracting, Bibliographies, Statistics

LABOUR FORCE AND MIGRATION SURVEY. *see* POPULATION STUDIES—Abstracting, Bibliographies, Statistics

LABOUR FORCE SITUATION IN INDONESIA: PRELIMINARY FIGURES/KEADAAN ANGKATAN KERJA DE INDONESIA: ANGKA SEMENTARA. *see* BUSINESS AND ECONOMICS—Abstracting, Bibliographies, Statistics

LABOUR FORCE STATISTICS. *see* BUSINESS AND ECONOMICS—Abstracting, Bibliographies, Statistics

LABOUR FORCE SURVEY. *see* BUSINESS AND ECONOMICS—Abstracting, Bibliographies, Statistics

LABOUR PRICE INDEX (ONLINE). *see* BUSINESS AND ECONOMICS—Abstracting, Bibliographies, Statistics

LAKE HURON COMMERCIAL FISH HARVEST SUMMARY. *see* FISH AND FISHERIES

LAND- EN TUINBOUWCIJFERS. *see* GARDENING AND HORTICULTURE—Abstracting, Bibliographies, Statistics

LANDBOUW-ECONOMISCH INSTITUUT. DIENST LANDBOUWKUNDIG ONDERZOEK. PERIODIEKE RAPPORTAGE. *see* AGRICULTURE—Abstracting, Bibliographies, Statistics

LANDBRUGSREGNSKABSSTATISTIK/AGRICULTURAL ACCOUNTS STATISTICS/ECONOMIC RESULTS IN DANISH AGRICULTURE. *see* AGRICULTURE—Abstracting, Bibliographies, Statistics

▼ **LANDELIJK VERSPREIDINGSONDERZOEK.** *see* BIOLOGY—Abstracting, Bibliographies, Statistics

LANDELIJKE JEUGDMONITOR. *see* CHILDREN AND YOUTH—Abstracting, Bibliographies, Statistics

314.912 ISL ISSN 1017-6683
HA1491
LANDSHAGIR/STATISTICAL YEARBOOK OF ICELAND. Text in Icelandic. 1991. a. USD 45 (effective 2001). back issues avail. **Document type:** *Yearbook, Government.*
Related titles: CD-ROM ed.: 1997. USD 45 (effective 2001).
Published by: Hagstofa Islands/Statistics Iceland, Borgartuni 12 A, Reykjavik, 150, Iceland. TEL 354-560-9800, FAX 354-562-3312, hagstofa@hag.stjr.is, http://www.statice.is/stat/e-mail.htm. Ed. Bjorgvin Sigurdsson. Circ: 2,500.

LARGE AND MEDIUM SCALE MANUFACTURING AND ELECTRICITY INDUSTRY SURVEY. *see* BUSINESS AND ECONOMICS—Abstracting, Bibliographies, Statistics

LATEST DEVELOPMENTS IN THE CANADIAN ECONOMIC ACCOUNTS. *see* BUSINESS AND ECONOMICS—Abstracting, Bibliographies, Statistics

LAW ENFORCEMENT MANAGEMENT AND ADMINISTRATIVE STATISTICS (YEAR). *see* CRIMINOLOGY AND LAW ENFORCEMENT—Abstracting, Bibliographies, Statistics

LAW, PROBABILITY AND RISK; a journal of reasoning under uncertainty. *see* LAW

315.692 LBN
LEBANON. ADMINISTRATION CENTRALE DE LA STATISTIQUE. BULLETIN STATISTIQUE. Text in Arabic, French. 1963. m. free. mkt.; stat. 68 p./no.; **Document type:** *Bulletin.*
Former titles: Lebanon. Direction Centrale de la Statistique. Bulletin Statistique Mensuel (0023-9860); Lebanon. Service de Statistique Generale. Bulletin Statistique Mensuel
Published by: Administration Centrale de la Statistique, Presidence de Conseil, Kantari St., Commerce and Finance Bldg. 5th Fl., Beirut, Lebanon. TEL 961-1-373160, FAX 961-1-373161, cas@sedetel.com.lb, http://www.cas.gov.lb. Circ: 1,900.

310 USA ISSN 0930-0325
LECTURE NOTES IN STATISTICS. Abbreviated title: L N S. Text in English. 1980. irreg., latest vol.199, 2010. price varies. back issues avail.; reprints avail. **Document type:** *Monographic series.* **Description:** Contains research work on topics that are more specialized than volumes in Springer Series in Statistics (SSS).
Indexed: A22, CCMJ, CIS, Inspec, MSN.
—BLDSC (5180.422000), IE, Ingenta, Linda Hall. **CCC.**
Published by: Springer New York LLC (Subsidiary of: Springer Science+Business Media), 233 Spring St, New York, NY 10013. TEL 212-460-1500, FAX 212-460-1575, service-ny@springer.com.

LEGAL AID IN CANADA: RESOURCE AND CASELOAD STATISTICS. *see* LAW—Abstracting, Bibliographies, Statistics

315.126 MAC
LEGISLACAO DO SISTEMA DE INFORMACAO ESTATISTICA DE MACAU/LAW OF MACAO STATISTICAL INFORMATION SYSTEM. Text in Chinese, Portuguese. 1989. irreg. free. **Document type:** *Government.*
Published by: Direccao dos Servicos de Estatistica e Censos, Alameda Dr Carlos d'Assumcao 411-417, Macao, Macau. TEL 853-3995311, FAX 853-307825, info@dsec.gov.mo, http://www.dsec.gov.mo.

LENGTH OF STAY BY DIAGNOSIS & OPERATION, UNITED STATES. *see* HEALTH FACILITIES AND ADMINISTRATION—Abstracting, Bibliographies, Statistics

LENGTH OF STAY BY DIAGNOSIS & OPERATION, UNITED STATES, NORTH CENTRAL REGION. *see* HEALTH FACILITIES AND ADMINISTRATION—Abstracting, Bibliographies, Statistics

LENGTH OF STAY BY DIAGNOSIS & OPERATION, UNITED STATES, NORTHEASTERN REGION. *see* HEALTH FACILITIES AND ADMINISTRATION—Abstracting, Bibliographies, Statistics

LENGTH OF STAY BY DIAGNOSIS & OPERATION, UNITED STATES, SOUTHERN REGION. *see* HEALTH FACILITIES AND ADMINISTRATION—Abstracting, Bibliographies, Statistics

LENGTH OF STAY BY DIAGNOSIS & OPERATION, UNITED STATES, WESTERN REGION. *see* HEALTH FACILITIES AND ADMINISTRATION—Abstracting, Bibliographies, Statistics

LENGTH OF STAY BY PROCEDURE, UNITED STATES. *see* HEALTH FACILITIES AND ADMINISTRATION—Abstracting, Bibliographies, Statistics

LEVANTAMENTO SISTEMATICO DA PRODUCAO AGRICOLA/SYSTEMATIC SURVEY OF AGRICULTURAL PRODUCTION. *see* AGRICULTURE—Agricultural Economics

LIBRARY AND INFORMATION SCIENCE EDUCATION STATISTICAL REPORT. *see* LIBRARY AND INFORMATION SCIENCES—Abstracting, Bibliographies, Statistics

LIBYA. CENSUS AND STATISTICS DEPARTMENT. AGRICULTURAL CENSUS. *see* AGRICULTURE—Abstracting, Bibliographies, Statistics

LIBYA. CENSUS AND STATISTICS DEPARTMENT. EXTERNAL TRADE INDEX. *see* BUSINESS AND ECONOMICS—Abstracting, Bibliographies, Statistics

LIBYA. CENSUS AND STATISTICS DEPARTMENT. EXTERNAL TRADE STATISTICS. *see* BUSINESS AND ECONOMICS—Abstracting, Bibliographies, Statistics

339.42 LBY ISSN 0023-1630
LIBYA. CENSUS AND STATISTICS DEPARTMENT. MONTHLY COST OF LIVING INDEX FOR TRIPOLI TOWN. Text in Arabic, English. 1964. m. free. charts; stat. **Document type:** *Government.*
Published by: Lybia. Secretariat of Planning, Census and Statistics Department, P O Box 600, Tripoli, Libya.

LIBYA. CENSUS AND STATISTICS DEPARTMENT. REPORT OF THE ANNUAL SURVEY OF PETROLEUM MINING INDUSTRY. *see* PETROLEUM AND GAS—Abstracting, Bibliographies, Statistics

LIBYA. CENSUS AND STATISTICS DEPARTMENT. REPORT OF THE ANNUAL SURVEY OF UNITS PROVIDING TECHNICAL SERVICES TO THE PETROLEUM MINING INDUSTRY. *see* PETROLEUM AND GAS—Abstracting, Bibliographies, Statistics

LIBYA. CENSUS AND STATISTICS DEPARTMENT. REPORT OF THE SURVEY OF LICENSED CONSTRUCTION UNITS. *see* BUILDING AND CONSTRUCTION—Abstracting, Bibliographies, Statistics

315 LBY ISSN 0075-9287
HA4685
LIBYA. CENSUS AND STATISTICS DEPARTMENT. STATISTICAL ABSTRACT. Text in Arabic, English. 1958. a. free. **Document type:** *Government.*
Related titles: Microfiche ed.: (from PQC).
Published by: Lybia. Secretariat of Planning, Census and Statistics Department, P O Box 600, Tripoli, Libya.

LIBYA. CENSUS AND STATISTICS DEPARTMENT. TRENDS OF EXTERNAL TRADE. *see* BUSINESS AND ECONOMICS—Abstracting, Bibliographies, Statistics

310 CAN ISSN 1910-3484
LIFE TABLES, CANADA, PROVINCES AND TERRITORIES. Text in English. 1962. irreg. **Document type:** *Monographic series, Trade.*
Former titles (until 1998): Health Reports. Supplement. Life Tables, Canada and Provinces (Print) (1180-307X); (until 1982): Life Tables, Canada and Provinces (0827-990X); Which was formed by the merger of (1957-1962): Provincial and Regional Life Tables (0829-6294); (1951-1962): Canadian Life Table (0829-6286); (1945-1951): Life Tables for Canada (0840-2965); (1941-1945): Canadian Life Table (0840-2957); (1931-1941): Life Table of Canada (0840-2892); (1931-1931): Canadian Abridged Life Tables (0840-2884)
Media: Online - full text. **Related titles:** French ed.: Tables de Mortalite, Canada, Provinces et Territoires. ISSN 1910-3492; ◆ Supplement to: Health Reports (Online). ISSN 1209-1367.
Published by: Statistics Canada/Statistique Canada, Communications Division, 3rd Fl, R H Coats Bldg, Ottawa, ON K1A 0A6, Canada. TEL 800-263-1136, infostats@statcan.ca, http://www.statcan.gc.ca.

310 USA ISSN 1380-7870
QA276.A1 CODEN: LDANFI
➤ **LIFETIME DATA ANALYSIS**; an international journal devoted to the methods and applications of reliability and survival analysis. Text in English. 1995. q. EUR 702, USD 740 combined subscription to institutions (print & online eds.) (effective 2012). adv. illus. reprint service avail. from PSC. **Document type:** *Journal, Academic/Scholarly.* **Description:** Covers statistical science in the various applied fields that dealwith lifetime data, including: Actuarial Science - Economics - Engineering Sciences - Environmental Sciences - Management Science - Medicine - Operations Research - Public Health -Social and Behavioral Sciences.
Related titles: Online - full text ed.: ISSN 1572-9249 (from IngentaConnect).
Indexed: A12, A13, A17, A22, A26, A36, ABIn, B01, B07, BibLing, C06, C07, CA, CABA, CCMJ, CIS, CMCI, E01, EMBASE, ESPM, ExcerpMed, GH, H05, INI, IndMed, Inspec, MEDLINE, MSN, MathR, N02, N03, P20, P21, P22, P26, P30, P32, P48, P50, P51, P52, P53, P54, PQC, R12, RiskAb, SCI, SCOPUS, T02, T05, W07, W11, Z02.
—BLDSC (5208.966600), AskIEEE, IE, Infotrieve, Ingenta. **CCC.**
Published by: Springer New York LLC (Subsidiary of: Springer Science+Business Media), 233 Spring St, New York, NY 10013. TEL 212-460-1500, FAX 212-460-1575, journals@springer-ny.com, http://www.springer.com. Ed. Mei-Ling Ting Lee.

318 PER
LIMA - CALLAO COMPENDIO ESTADISTICO. Text in Spanish. irreg., latest vol.2, 1991.
Published by: Instituto Nacional de Estadistica, Ave. 28 de Julio 1056, Lima, Peru.

LOCAL HOUSING STATISTICS. ENGLAND (ONLINE). *see* HOUSING AND URBAN PLANNING—Abstracting, Bibliographies, Statistics

LOST-TIME CLAIMS. YOUNG WORKERS. *see* PUBLIC HEALTH AND SAFETY—Abstracting, Bibliographies, Statistics

LOUISIANA. AGRICULTURAL STATISTICS SERVICE. CROP WEATHER SUMMARY. *see* AGRICULTURE—Abstracting, Bibliographies, Statistics

LOUISIANA CITIES & COUNTIES GRAPHIC PERFORMANCE ANALYSIS. *see* PUBLIC ADMINISTRATION—Abstracting, Bibliographies, Statistics

LUFTFART/CIVIL AVIATION. *see* TRANSPORTATION—Abstracting, Bibliographies, Statistics

LUTHERAN CHURCH OF CENTRAL AFRICA. STATISTICAL REPORT. *see* RELIGIONS AND THEOLOGY—Abstracting, Bibliographies, Statistics

LE LUXEMBOURG EN CHIFFRES (YEAR). *see* POPULATION STUDIES—Abstracting, Bibliographies, Statistics

LUXEMBOURG. SERVICE CENTRAL DE LA STATISTIQUE ET DES ETUDES ECONOMIQUES. ANNUAIRE STATISTIQUE. *see* BUSINESS AND ECONOMICS—Abstracting, Bibliographies, Statistics

LUXEMBOURG. SERVICE CENTRAL DE LA STATISTIQUE ET DES ETUDES ECONOMIQUES. BULLETIN DU STATEC. *see* BUSINESS AND ECONOMICS—Abstracting, Bibliographies, Statistics

LUXEMBOURG. SERVICE CENTRAL DE LA STATISTIQUE ET DES ETUDES ECONOMIQUES. CAHIERS ECONOMIQUES. *see* BUSINESS AND ECONOMICS—Abstracting, Bibliographies, Statistics

LUXEMBOURG. SERVICE CENTRAL DE LA STATISTIQUE ET DES ETUDES ECONOMIQUES. COLLECTION RP: RECENSEMENT DE LA POPULATION ET MOUVEMENT DE LA POPULATION. *see* POPULATION STUDIES—Abstracting, Bibliographies, Statistics

LUXEMBOURG. SERVICE CENTRAL DE LA STATISTIQUE ET DES ETUDES ECONOMIQUES. CONJONCTURE ACTUELLE. *see* BUSINESS AND ECONOMICS—Abstracting, Bibliographies, Statistics

LUXEMBOURG. SERVICE CENTRAL DE LA STATISTIQUE ET DES ETUDES ECONOMIQUES. INDICATEURS RAPIDES. SERIE A1: INDICES DES PRIX A LA COMSOMMATION. *see* BUSINESS AND ECONOMICS—Abstracting, Bibliographies, Statistics

LUXEMBOURG. SERVICE CENTRAL DE LA STATISTIQUE ET DES ETUDES ECONOMIQUES. INDICATEURS RAPIDES. SERIE A2: INDICES DES PRIX DE LA CONSTRUCTION. *see* BUILDING AND CONSTRUCTION—Abstracting, Bibliographies, Statistics

LUXEMBOURG. SERVICE CENTRAL DE LA STATISTIQUE ET DES ETUDES ECONOMIQUES. INDICATEURS RAPIDES. SERIE A3: INDICES DES PRIX A LA PRODUCTION DES PRODUITS INDUSTRIELS. *see* BUSINESS AND ECONOMICS—Abstracting, Bibliographies, Statistics

LUXEMBOURG. SERVICE CENTRAL DE LA STATISTIQUE ET DES ETUDES ECONOMIQUES. INDICATEURS RAPIDES. SERIE B1: INDICES DE L'ACTIVITE INDUSTRIELLE. *see* BUSINESS AND ECONOMICS—Abstracting, Bibliographies, Statistics

LUXEMBOURG. SERVICE CENTRAL DE LA STATISTIQUE ET DES ETUDES ECONOMIQUES. INDICATEURS RAPIDES. SERIE B2: INDICES DE L'ACTIVITE DANS LA CONSTRUCTION. *see* BUILDING AND CONSTRUCTION—Abstracting, Bibliographies, Statistics

LUXEMBOURG. SERVICE CENTRAL DE LA STATISTIQUE ET DES ETUDES ECONOMIQUES. INDICATEURS RAPIDES. SERIE C: EMPLOI ET CHOMAGE - SIDERURGIE - FINANCES- TRANSPORT ET COMMERCE. *see* BUSINESS AND ECONOMICS—Abstracting, Bibliographies, Statistics

LUXEMBOURG. SERVICE CENTRAL DE LA STATISTIQUE ET DES ETUDES ECONOMIQUES. INDICATEURS RAPIDES. SERIE D. IMMATRICULATIONS DE VEHICULES AUTOMOTEURS. *see* TRANSPORTATION—Abstracting, Bibliographies, Statistics

LUXEMBOURG. SERVICE CENTRAL DE LA STATISTIQUE ET DES ETUDES ECONOMIQUES. INDICATEURS RAPIDES. SERIE E: NAISSANCES, MARIAGES, DIVORCES, DECES. *see* POPULATION STUDIES—Abstracting, Bibliographies, Statistics

LUXEMBOURG. SERVICE CENTRAL DE LA STATISTIQUE ET DES ETUDES ECONOMIQUES. INDICATEURS RAPIDES. SERIE G: AUTORISATIONS DE BATIR - BATIMENTS, LOGEMENTS ET VOLUME BATI. *see* BUILDING AND CONSTRUCTION—Abstracting, Bibliographies, Statistics

LUXEMBOURG. SERVICE CENTRAL DE LA STATISTIQUE ET DES ETUDES ECONOMIQUES. INDICATEURS RAPIDES. SERIE H: COMMERCE EXTERIEUR DU LUXEMBOURG. *see* BUSINESS AND ECONOMICS—Abstracting, Bibliographies, Statistics

LUXEMBOURG. SERVICE CENTRAL DE LA STATISTIQUE ET DES ETUDES ECONOMIQUES. INDICATEURS RAPIDES. SERIE J: RESULTATS DE L'ENQUETE DE CONJONCTURE. *see* POPULATION STUDIES—Abstracting, Bibliographies, Statistics

LUXEMBOURG. SERVICE CENTRAL DE LA STATISTIQUE ET DES ETUDES ECONOMIQUES. INDICATEURS RAPIDES. SERIE M: METEOROLOGIE. *see* METEOROLOGY—Abstracting, Bibliographies, Statistics

LUXEMBOURG. SERVICE CENTRAL DE LA STATISTIQUE ET DES ETUDES ECONOMIQUES. NOTE DE CONJONCTURE. *see* BUSINESS AND ECONOMICS—Abstracting, Bibliographies, Statistics

S

LUXEMBOURG. SERVICE CENTRAL DE LA STATISTIQUE ET DES ETUDES ECONOMIQUES. STATISTIQUES HISTORIQUES. *see* BUSINESS AND ECONOMICS—Abstracting, Bibliographies, Statistics

M S O R CONNECTIONS. (Maths, Stats & Operational Research) *see* MATHEMATICS

MACAO. DIRECCAO DOS SERVICOS DE ESTATISTICA E CENSOS. CENSOS DA POPULACAO/MACAO. CENSUS AND STATISTICS DEPARTMENT. POPULATION CENSUS. *see* POPULATION STUDIES—Abstracting, Bibliographies, Statistics

MACAO. DIRECCAO DOS SERVICOS DE ESTATISTICA E CENSOS. ESTATISTICAS DA CONSTRUCAO/MACAO. CENSUS AND STATISTICS DEPARTMENT. CONSTRUCTION STATISTICS. *see* REAL ESTATE—Abstracting, Bibliographies, Statistics

MACAO. DIRECCAO DOS SERVICOS DE ESTATISTICA E CENSOS. ESTATISTICAS DAS SOCIEDADES/MACAO. CENSUS AND STATISTICS DEPARTMENT. STATISTICAL DATA CONCERNING COMPANIES. *see* REAL ESTATE—Abstracting, Bibliographies, Statistics

MACAO. DIRECCAO DOS SERVICOS DE ESTATISTICA E CENSOS. ESTATISTICAS DEMOGRAFICAS/MACAO. CENSUS AND STATISTICS DEPARTMENT. DEMOGRAPHIC STATISTICS. *see* POPULATION STUDIES—Abstracting, Bibliographies, Statistics

MACAO. DIRECCAO DOS SERVICOS DE ESTATISTICA E CENSOS. ESTATISTICAS DO COMERCIO EXTERNO. EXPORTACAO/ MACAO. CENSUS AND STATISTICS DEPARTMENT. STATISTICS ON EXTERNAL TRADE. *see* BUSINESS AND ECONOMICS—Abstracting, Bibliographies, Statistics

MACAO. DIRECCAO DOS SERVICOS DE ESTATISTICA E CENSOS. ESTATISTICAS DO COMERCIO EXTERNO. IMPORTACAO/ MACAO. CENSUS AND STATISTICS DEPARTMENT. EXTERNAL TRADE INDICATORS. *see* BUSINESS AND ECONOMICS—Abstracting, Bibliographies, Statistics

MACAO. DIRECCAO DOS SERVICOS DE ESTATISTICA E CENSOS. ESTATISTICAS DO TURISMO/MACAO. CENSUS AND STATISTICS DEPARTMENT. TOURISM STATISTICS. *see* TRAVEL AND TOURISM—Abstracting, Bibliographies, Statistics

MACAO. DIRECCAO DOS SERVICOS DE ESTATISTICA E CENSOS. ESTIMATIVAS DA POPULACAO RESIDENTE DE MACAU/ MACAO. CENSUS AND STATISTICS DEPARTMENT. POPULATION ESTIMATES IN MACAO. *see* POPULATION STUDIES—Abstracting, Bibliographies, Statistics

MACAO. DIRECCAO DOS SERVICOS DE ESTATISTICA E CENSOS. ESTIMATIVAS DO PRODUTO INTERNO BRUTO/MACAO. CENSUS AND STATISTICS DEPARTMENT. GROSS DOMESTIC PRODUCT ESTIMATES. *see* BUSINESS AND ECONOMICS—Abstracting, Bibliographies, Statistics

MACAO. DIRECCAO DOS SERVICOS DE ESTATISTICA E CENSOS. INDICADORES DO TURISMO/MACAO. CENSUS AND STATISTICS DEPARTMENT. TOURISM INDICATORS. *see* TRAVEL AND TOURISM—Abstracting, Bibliographies, Statistics

MACAO. DIRECCAO DOS SERVICOS DE ESTATISTICA E CENSOS. INDICE DE PRECOS NO CONSUMIDOR/MACAO. CENSUS AND STATISTICS DEPARTMENT. CONSUMER PRICE INDEX. *see* BUSINESS AND ECONOMICS—Abstracting, Bibliographies, Statistics

MACAO. DIRECCAO DOS SERVICOS DE ESTATISTICA E CENSOS. INDICE DE PRECOS NO CONSUMIDOR (RELATORIO ANUAL)/ MACAO. CENSUS AND STATISTICS DEPARTMENT. CONSUMER PRICE INDEX (ANNUAL REPORT). *see* BUSINESS AND ECONOMICS—Abstracting, Bibliographies, Statistics

MACAO. DIRECCAO DOS SERVICOS DE ESTATISTICA E CENSOS. INDICES E PRECOS DOS MATERIAS DE CONSTRUCAO/MACAO. CENSUS AND STATISTICS DEPARTMENT. INDEXES AND PRICES OF CONSTRUCTION MATERIALS. *see* BUILDING AND CONSTRUCTION—Abstracting, Bibliographies, Statistics

MACAO. DIRECCAO DOS SERVICOS DE ESTATISTICA E CENSOS. INDICES E SALARIOS NA CONSTRUCAO CIVIL/MACAO. CENSUS AND STATISTICS DEPARTMENT. INDEXES AND WAGES IN CIVIL CONTRUCTION. *see* BUSINESS AND ECONOMICS—Abstracting, Bibliographies, Statistics

MACAO. DIRECCAO DOS SERVICOS DE ESTATISTICA E CENSOS. INQUERITO AO EMPREGO/MACAO. CENSUS AND STATISTICS DEPARTMENT. EMPLOYMENT SURVEY. *see* BUSINESS AND ECONOMICS—Abstracting, Bibliographies, Statistics

MACAO. DIRECCAO DOS SERVICOS DE ESTATISTICA E CENSOS. INQUERITO AO ENSINO/MACAO. CENSUS AND STATISTICS DEPARTMENT. EDUCATION SURVEY. *see* EDUCATION—Abstracting, Bibliographies, Statistics

MACAO. DIRECCAO DOS SERVICOS DE ESTATISTICA E CENSOS. INQUERITO INDUSTRIAL/MACAO. CENSUS AND STATISTICS DEPARTMENT. INDUSTRIAL SURVEY. *see* BUSINESS AND ECONOMICS—Abstracting, Bibliographies, Statistics

MACAO. DIRECCAO DOS SERVICOS DE ESTATISTICA E CENSOS. INQUERITOS AS NECESSIDADES DE MAO-DE-OBRA E AS REMUNERACOES/MACAO. CENSUS AND STATISTICS DEPARTMENT. MANPOWER NEEDS AND WAGES SURVEY. *see* BUSINESS AND ECONOMICS—Abstracting, Bibliographies, Statistics

315 MAC
MACAO. DIRECCAO DOS SERVICOS DE ESTATISTICA E CENSOS. PLANO DE ACTIVIDADES/MACAO. CENSUS AND STATISTICS DEPARTMENT. ACTIVITIES PLAN. Text in Chinese, Portuguese. 1988. a. free. **Document type:** *Government.*
Published by: Direccao dos Servicos de Estatistica e Censos, Alameda Dr Carlos d'Assumcao 411-417, Macao, Macau. TEL 853-3995311, FAX 853-307825, info@dsec.gov.mo, http://www.dsec.gov.mo.

315 MAC
MACAO. DIRECCAO DOS SERVICOS DE ESTATISTICA E CENSOS. PRINCIPAIS INDICADORES ESTATISTICOS/MACAO. CENSUS AND STATISTICS DEPARTMENT. PRINCIPAL STATISTICAL INDICATORS. Text in Chinese, English, Portuguese. 1993. q. free. **Document type:** *Government.*
Published by: Direccao dos Servicos de Estatistica e Censos, Alameda Dr Carlos d'Assumcao 411-417, Macao, Macau. TEL 853-3995311, FAX 853-307825, info@dsec.gov.mo, http://www.dsec.gov.mo.

MACAO. DIRECCAO DOS SERVICOS DE ESTATISTICA E CENSOS. RECENSEAMENTO A CONSTRUCAO/MACAO. CENSUS AND STATISTICS DEPARTMENT. CONSTRUCTION SURVEY. *see* BUILDING AND CONSTRUCTION—Abstracting, Bibliographies, Statistics

315 MAC ISSN 0872-4237
MACAO. DIRECCAO DOS SERVICOS DE ESTATISTICA E CENSOS. RELATORIO DE ACTIVIDADES/MACAO. CENSUS AND STATISTICS DEPARTMENT. ACTIVITIES REPORT. Text in Chinese, Portuguese. 1986. a. free. **Document type:** *Government.*
Published by: Direccao dos Servicos de Estatistica e Censos, Alameda Dr Carlos d'Assumcao 411-417, Macao, Macau. TEL 853-3995311, FAX 853-307825, info@dsec.gov.mo, http://www.dsec.gov.mo.

MACAO. DIRECCAO DOS SERVICOS DE ESTATISTICA E CENSOS. TRANSACCOES DE IMOVEIS/MACAO. CENSUS AND STATISTICS DEPARTMENT. TRANSACTIONS ON REAL ESTATE. *see* REAL ESTATE—Abstracting, Bibliographies, Statistics

310 MAC ISSN 0870-6778
HA4641
MACAU EM NUMEROS/MACAO IN FIGURES. Text in Chinese, English, Portuguese. 1985. a. free. **Document type:** *Government.*
Published by: Direccao dos Servicos de Estatistica e Censos, Alameda Dr Carlos d'Assumcao 411-417, Macao, Macau. TEL 853-3995311, FAX 853-307825, info@dsec.gov.mo, http://www.dsec.gov.mo.

MACHINERY INDUSTRIES, EXCEPT ELECTRICAL MACHINERY. *see* MACHINERY

MADAGASCAR. MINISTERE DE LA PRODUCTION AGRICOLE ET DU PATRIMOINE FONCIER. STATISTIQUES AGRICOLES. ANNUAIRE. *see* AGRICULTURE—Abstracting, Bibliographies, Statistics

314.9 PRT
MADEIRA. DIRECCAO REGIONAL DE ESTATISTICA. ANUARIO ESTATISTICO DA MADEIRA. Text in Portuguese. 1972. q. **Document type:** *Bulletin, Government.*
Former titles (until 1990): Madeira. Direccao Regional de Estatistica. Boletim Trimestral de Estatistica; Portugal. Instituto Nacional de Estatistica. Delegacao do Funchal. Anuario Estatistico - Regiao Autonoma de Madeira; Portugal. Instituto Nacional de Estatistica. Delegacao do Funchal. Boletim Trimestral de Estatistica - Arquipelago de Madeira (0303-1705)
Published by: Direccao Regional de Estatistica da Madeira, Rua de Joao Gao 4, Funchal, Madeira 9000-071, Portugal. http://estatistica.gov-madeira.pt.

MADHYA PRADESH. DIRECTORATE OF AGRICULTURE. AGRICULTURAL STATISTICS. *see* AGRICULTURE—Abstracting, Bibliographies, Statistics

MAGAZINE MARKET COVERAGE REPORT. *see* ADVERTISING AND PUBLIC RELATIONS—Abstracting, Bibliographies, Statistics

MAGAZINE TREND REPORT. *see* ADVERTISING AND PUBLIC RELATIONS—Abstracting, Bibliographies, Statistics

314 HUN ISSN 1215-7864
HA1201 CODEN: STEVEC
MAGYAR STATISZTIKAI EVKONYV/STATISTICAL YEARBOOK OF HUNGARY. Text and summaries in English, Hungarian. 1871. a. USD 37. **Document type:** *Government.*
Formerly (until 1990): Hungary. Kozponti Statisztikai Hivatal. Statisztikai Evkonyv (0073-4039)
Related titles: CD-ROM ed.; Microfiche ed.: (from BHP, PQC).
Published by: Kozponti Statisztikai Hivatal, Marketing Oszta'ly, Keleti Karoly utca 5-7, Budapest, 1024, Hungary. TEL 36-1-345-6000, FAX 36-1-345-6699.

314 HUN ISSN 0133-5847
HA1201
MAGYAR STATISZTIKAI ZSEBKONYV. Text in Hungarian. 1933. a. USD 15. charts; stat. **Document type:** *Government.* **Description:** Gives comprehensive information on the development of the social and economic processes of the previous year.
Related titles: English ed.: Statistical Pocketbook of Hungary. ISSN 0441-473X.
Indexed: RASB.
Published by: Kozponti Statisztikai Hivatal, Marketing Oszta'ly, Keleti Karoly utca 5-7, Budapest, 1024, Hungary. TEL 36-1-180-3311, FAX 36-1-345-6000, TELEX 36-1-345-6699. Circ: 1,200.

310 HUN ISSN 0230-5828
MAGYARORSZAG. Text in Hungarian. 1964. a. USD 41. stat. **Document type:** *Government.*
Related titles: English ed.: Hungary. ISSN 0230-5755; Russian ed.: Vengria v Godu. ISSN 0230-5925; German ed.: Ungarn. ISSN 0230-5909.
Indexed: RASB.
Published by: Kozponti Statisztikai Hivatal, Marketing Oszta'ly, Keleti Karoly utca 5-7, Budapest, 1024, Hungary. TEL 36-1-345-6000, FAX 36-1-345-6699. Ed. Jozsef Palfy. Circ: 200,000. **Subscr. to:** Kultura, PO Box 149, Budapest 1389, Hungary.

MAIL ADVERTISING SERVICE ASSOCIATION INTERNATIONAL. WAGE AND SALARY, AND FRINGE BENEFITS SURVEY. *see* ADVERTISING AND PUBLIC RELATIONS—Abstracting, Bibliographies, Statistics

MAIN ECONOMIC INDICATORS. *see* BUSINESS AND ECONOMICS—Abstracting, Bibliographies, Statistics

MAINE CITIES & COUNTIES GRAPHIC PERFORMANCE ANALYSIS. *see* PUBLIC ADMINISTRATION—Abstracting, Bibliographies, Statistics

MAINE. DEPARTMENT OF HUMAN SERVICES. POPULATION ESTIMATES FOR MINOR CIVIL DIVISIONS BY COUNTY. *see* POPULATION STUDIES—Abstracting, Bibliographies, Statistics

MAINE. DEPARTMENT OF HUMAN SERVICES. VITAL STATISTICS. *see* POPULATION STUDIES—Abstracting, Bibliographies, Statistics

MALAWI. NATIONAL STATISTICAL OFFICE. ANNUAL STATEMENT OF EXTERNAL TRADE. *see* BUSINESS AND ECONOMICS—Abstracting, Bibliographies, Statistics

MALAWI. NATIONAL STATISTICAL OFFICE. ANNUAL SURVEY OF ECONOMIC ACTIVITIES. *see* BUSINESS AND ECONOMICS—Abstracting, Bibliographies, Statistics

MALAWI. NATIONAL STATISTICAL OFFICE. BALANCE OF PAYMENTS. *see* BUSINESS AND ECONOMICS—Abstracting, Bibliographies, Statistics

MALAWI. NATIONAL STATISTICAL OFFICE. EMPLOYMENT AND EARNINGS: ANNUAL REPORT. *see* BUSINESS AND ECONOMICS—Abstracting, Bibliographies, Statistics

MALAWI. NATIONAL STATISTICAL OFFICE. FAMILY FORMATION SURVEY (YEAR). *see* SOCIOLOGY—Abstracting, Bibliographies, Statistics

316 MWI
MALAWI. NATIONAL STATISTICAL OFFICE. MONTHLY STATISTICAL BULLETIN. Text in English. m. MWK 50 per issue. **Document type:** *Bulletin, Government.*
Published by: (Malawi. Commissioner for Census and Statistics), National Statistical Office, PO Box 333, Zomba, Malawi. TEL 265-50-522377, FAX 265-50-523130, TELEX 44015 CENSUS MI.

310 MWI ISSN 0076-3284
MALAWI. NATIONAL STATISTICAL OFFICE. NATIONAL ACCOUNTS REPORT. Text in English. 1967. a. MWK 200. **Document type:** *Government.*
Published by: (Malawi. Commissioner for Census and Statistics), National Statistical Office, PO Box 333, Zomba, Malawi. TEL 265-50-522377, FAX 265-50-523130.

MALAWI. NATIONAL STATISTICAL OFFICE. NATIONAL SAMPLE SURVEY OF AGRICULTURE. *see* AGRICULTURE—Abstracting, Bibliographies, Statistics

MALAWI. NATIONAL STATISTICAL OFFICE. POPULATION CENSUS FINAL REPORT. *see* POPULATION STUDIES—Abstracting, Bibliographies, Statistics

MALAWI. NATIONAL STATISTICAL OFFICE. SURVEY OF HANDICAPPED PERSONS. *see* HANDICAPPED—Abstracting, Bibliographies, Statistics

MALAWI. NATIONAL STATISTICAL OFFICE. TRANSPORT STATISTICS. *see* TRANSPORTATION—Abstracting, Bibliographies, Statistics

MALAWI. NATIONAL STATISTICAL OFFICE. URBAN HOUSEHOLD EXPENDITURE SURVEY. *see* POPULATION STUDIES—Abstracting, Bibliographies, Statistics

MALAWI. NATIONAL STATISTICAL OFFICE. URBAN HOUSING SURVEY. *see* HOUSING AND URBAN PLANNING—Abstracting, Bibliographies, Statistics

316 MWI
MALAWI STATISTICAL YEARBOOK. Text in English. 1965. a. MWK 300. **Document type:** *Government.*
Supersedes: Malawi. National Statistical Office. Compendium of Statistics (0076-3268)
Related titles: Microfiche ed.: (from PQC).
Published by: (Malawi. Commissioner for Census and Statistics), National Statistical Office, PO Box 333, Zomba, Malawi. TEL 265-50-522377, FAX 265-50-523130.

MALAWI TOURISM REPORT. *see* TRAVEL AND TOURISM—Abstracting, Bibliographies, Statistics

MALAYSIA. DEPARTMENT OF MINES. STATISTICS RELATING TO THE MINING INDUSTRY OF MALAYSIA. *see* MINES AND MINING INDUSTRY—Abstracting, Bibliographies, Statistics

MALAYSIA. DEPARTMENT OF STATISTICS. COCOA, COCONUT AND TEA STATISTICS HANDBOOK, MALAYSIA/MALAYSIA. JABATAN PERANGKAAN. BUKU MAKLUMAT PERANGKAAN KOKO, KELAPA DAN TEH, MALAYSIA. *see* AGRICULTURE—Abstracting, Bibliographies, Statistics

MALAYSIA. DEPARTMENT OF STATISTICS. EXTERNAL TRADE STATISTICS, MALAYSIA/MALAYSIA. JABATAN PERANGKAAN. PERANGKAAN PERDAGANGAN LUAR NEGERI, MALAYSIA. *see* BUSINESS AND ECONOMICS—Abstracting, Bibliographies, Statistics

MALAYSIA. DEPARTMENT OF STATISTICS. EXTERNAL TRADE STATISTICS, SABAH/MALAYSIA. JABATAN PERANGKAAN. PERANGKAAN PERDANGANGAN LUAR NEGERI. SABAH. *see* BUSINESS AND ECONOMICS—Abstracting, Bibliographies, Statistics

MALAYSIA. DEPARTMENT OF STATISTICS. FRAMEWORK FOR THE DEVELOPMENT OF ENVIRONMENT STATISTICS (F D E S) IN MALAYSIA. *see* ENVIRONMENTAL STUDIES—Abstracting, Bibliographies, Statistics

MALAYSIA. DEPARTMENT OF STATISTICS. INDEX OF INDUSTRIAL PRODUCTION, MALAYSIA/MALAYSIA. JABATAN PERANGKAAN. INDEKS PENGELUARAN PERIDUSTRIAN, MALAYSIA. *see* BUSINESS AND ECONOMICS—Abstracting, Bibliographies, Statistics

MALAYSIA. DEPARTMENT OF STATISTICS. LABOUR FORCE SURVEY REPORT, MALAYSIA/MALAYSIA. JABATAN PERANGKAAN. LAPORAN PENYIASATAN TENAGA BURUH, MALAYSIA. *see* POPULATION STUDIES—Abstracting, Bibliographies, Statistics

MALAYSIA. DEPARTMENT OF STATISTICS. MALAYSIAN ECONOMY IN BRIEF/MALAYSIA. JABATAN PERANGKAAN. EKONOMI MALAYSIA SEPINTAS LALU. *see* BUSINESS AND ECONOMICS—Abstracting, Bibliographies, Statistics

315 MYS
MALAYSIA. DEPARTMENT OF STATISTICS. MONTHLY BULLETIN OF STATISTICS, SABAH/MALAYSIA. JABATAN PERANGKAAN. SIARAN PERANGKAAN BULANAN, SABAH. Text in English. m. MYR 10 per issue. **Document type:** *Government.*
Published by: Malaysia. Department of Statistics/Jabatan Perangkaan, Jalan Cenderasari, Kuala Lumpur, 50514, Malaysia. TEL 60-3-294-4264, FAX 60-3-291-4535. **Subscr. to:** Department of Statistics (Sabah Branch), 1st Fl, Federal House, Jalan Mat Salleh, Kota Kinabalu, Sabah 88000, Malaysia. TEL 60-88-232277.

315 330 MYS
MALAYSIA. DEPARTMENT OF STATISTICS. MONTHLY CONSUMER PRICE INDEX, MALAYSIA/MALAYSIA. JABATAN PERANGKAAN. INDEKS HARGA PENGGUNA, MALAYSIA. Key Title: Indeks Harga Pengguna Bagi Malaysia. Text in English, Malay. 1983. m. MYR 5. **Document type:** *Government.*
Published by: Malaysia. Department of Statistics/Jabatan Perangkaan, Jalan Cenderasari, Kuala Lumpur, 50514, Malaysia. TEL 60-3-294-4264, FAX 60-3-291-4535.

MALAYSIA. DEPARTMENT OF STATISTICS. MONTHLY EXTERNAL TRADE STATISTICS, MALAYSIA/MALAYSIA. JABATAN PERANGKANN. PERANGKAAN PERDAGANGAN LUAR NEGERI BULANAN, MALAYSIA. *see* BUSINESS AND ECONOMICS—Abstracting, Bibliographies, Statistics

MALAYSIA. DEPARTMENT OF STATISTICS. MONTHLY MANUFACTURING STATISTICS, MALAYSIA. *see* BUSINESS AND ECONOMICS—Abstracting, Bibliographies, Statistics

MALAYSIA. DEPARTMENT OF STATISTICS. MONTHLY RUBBER STATISTICS, MALAYSIA/MALAYSIA. JABATAN PERANGKAAN. PERANGKAAN GETAH BULANAN, MALAYSIA. *see* RUBBER—Abstracting, Bibliographies, Statistics

310 MYS
MALAYSIA. DEPARTMENT OF STATISTICS. MONTHLY STATISTICAL BULLETIN, MALAYSIA/SIARAN PERANGKAAN BULANAN SEMENANJUNG MALAYSIA. Text in English, Malay. 1949. m. MYR 15 per issue. **Document type:** *Government.*
Former titles (until 1990): Monthly Statistical Bulletin, Peninsular Malaysia; (until 1977): Monthly Statistical Bulletin of West Malaysia (0542-3686)
Indexed: R18, RASB.
Published by: Malaysia. Department of Statistics/Jabatan Perangkaan, Jalan Cenderasari, Kuala Lumpur, 50514, Malaysia. TEL 60-3-294-4264, FAX 60-3-291-4535.

315 MYS ISSN 0127-9238
MALAYSIA. DEPARTMENT OF STATISTICS. MONTHLY STATISTICAL BULLETIN, SARAWAK/MALAYSIA. JABATAN PERANGKAAN. SIARAN PERANGKAAN BULANAN, SARAWAK. Text in English. m. MYR 12 per issue. **Document type:** *Government.*
Published by: Malaysia. Department of Statistics/Jabatan Perangkaan, Jalan Cenderasari, Kuala Lumpur, 50514, Malaysia. TEL 60-3-294-4264, FAX 60-3-291-4535.

315 MYS ISSN 0126-7086
HC445.5.Z9
MALAYSIA. DEPARTMENT OF STATISTICS. NATIONAL ACCOUNTS STATISTICS, MALAYSIA/MALAYSIA. JABATAN PERANGKAAN. PERANGKAAN AKAUN NEGARA, MALAYSIA. Text in English. 1982. irreg. MYR 14. **Document type:** *Government.*
Published by: Malaysia. Department of Statistics/Jabatan Perangkaan, Jalan Cenderasari, Kuala Lumpur, 50514, Malaysia. TEL 60-3-294-4264, FAX 30-3-291-4535.

MALAYSIA. DEPARTMENT OF STATISTICS. QUARTERLY BALANCE OF PAYMENTS REPORT, MALAYSIA/MALAYSIA. JABATAN PERANGKAAN. LAPORAN IMBANGAN PEMBAYARAN SUKU TAHUNAN, MALAYSIA. *see* BUSINESS AND ECONOMICS—Abstracting, Bibliographies, Statistics

MALAYSIA. DEPARTMENT OF STATISTICS. QUARTERLY REVIEW OF MALAYSIAN POPULATION STATISTICS/MALAYSIA. JABATAN PERANGKAAN. SARAN PERANGKAAN PENDUDUK SUKU TAHUNAN, MALAYSIA. *see* POPULATION STUDIES—Abstracting, Bibliographies, Statistics

MALAYSIA. DEPARTMENT OF STATISTICS. REPORT OF THE FINANCIAL SURVEY OF LIMITED COMPANIES, MALAYSIA/MALAYSIA. JABATAN PERANGKAAN. LAPORAN PENYIASATAN KEWANGAN SYARIKAT - SYARIKAT BHD., MALAYSIA. *see* BUSINESS AND ECONOMICS—Abstracting, Bibliographies, Statistics

MALAYSIA. DEPARTMENT OF STATISTICS. RUBBER STATISTICS HANDBOOK, MALAYSIA/MALAYSIA. JABATAN PERANGKAAN. BUKU MAKLUMAT PERANGKAAN GETAH, MALAYSIA. *see* RUBBER—Abstracting, Bibliographies, Statistics

MALAYSIA. DEPARTMENT OF STATISTICS. SPECIAL RELEASE 1 - FOR CIVIL ENGINEERING WORKS, MALAYSIA/MALAYSIA. JABATAN PERANGKAAN. SIARAN KHAS 1 - UNTUK KERJA-KERJA KEJ. AWAM, MALAYSIA. *see* ENGINEERING—Abstracting, Bibliographies, Statistics

MALAYSIA. DEPARTMENT OF STATISTICS. SPECIAL RELEASE 1 - FOR CIVIL ENGINEERING WORKS, SABAH/MALAYSIA. JABATAN PERANGKAAN. SIARAN KHAS 1 - UNTUK KERJA-KERJA KEJ. AWAM, SABAH. *see* ENGINEERING—Abstracting, Bibliographies, Statistics

MALAYSIA. DEPARTMENT OF STATISTICS. SPECIAL RELEASE 1 - FOR CIVIL ENGINEERING WORKS, SARAWAK/MALAYSIA. JABATAN PERANGKAAN. SIARAN KHAS 1 - UNTUK KERJA-KERJA KEJ. AWAM, SARAWAK. *see* ENGINEERING—Abstracting, Bibliographies, Statistics

MALAYSIA. DEPARTMENT OF STATISTICS. SPECIAL RELEASE 2 - FOR BUILDING WORKS, PENINSULAR MALAYSIA/MALAYSIA. JABATAN PERANGKAAN. SIARAN KHAS 2 - UNTUK KERJA-KERJA PEMBINAAN, SEM. MALAYSIA. *see* BUILDING AND CONSTRUCTION—Abstracting, Bibliographies, Statistics

MALAYSIA. DEPARTMENT OF STATISTICS. SPECIAL RELEASE 2 - FOR BUILDING WORKS, SABAH/MALAYSIA. JABATAN PERANGKAAN. SIARAN KHAS 2 - UNTUK KERJA-KERJA PEMBINAAN, SABAH. *see* BUILDING AND CONSTRUCTION—Abstracting, Bibliographies, Statistics

MALAYSIA. DEPARTMENT OF STATISTICS. SPECIAL RELEASE 2 - FOR BUILDING WORKS, SARAWAK/MALAYSIA. JABATAN PERANGKAAN. SIARAN KHAS 2 - UNTUK KERJA-KERJA PEMBINAAN, SARAWAK. *see* BUILDING AND CONSTRUCTION—Abstracting, Bibliographies, Statistics

MALAYSIA. DEPARTMENT OF STATISTICS. STATISTICS OF EXTERNAL TRADE. SARAWAK/MALAYSIA. JABATAN PERANGKAAN. PERANGKAAN PERDAGANGAN LUAR NEGERI. SARAWAK. *see* BUSINESS AND ECONOMICS—Abstracting, Bibliographies, Statistics

MALAYSIA. DEPARTMENT OF STATISTICS. VITAL STATISTICS, MALAYSIA (YEAR)/MALAYSIA. JABATAN PERANGKAAN. PERANGKAAN PENTING, MALAYSIA. *see* POPULATION STUDIES—Abstracting, Bibliographies, Statistics

315.95 MYS
HA1791
MALAYSIA. DEPARTMENT OF STATISTICS. YEARBOOK OF STATISTICS/MALAYSIA. JABATAN PERANGKAAN. BUKU TAHNAN PERANGKAAN, MALAYSIA. Text in English. 1965. a. MYR 25. **Document type:** *Government.*
Formerly (until 1984): Malaysia. Department of Statistics. Annual Bulletin of Statistics (0542-3570)
Published by: Malaysia. Department of Statistics/Jabatan Perangkaan, Jalan Cenderasari, Kuala Lumpur, 50514, Malaysia. TEL 60-3-294-4264, FAX 60-3-291-4535.

MALAYSIA. DEPARTMENT OF STATISTICS. YEARBOOK OF STATISTICS, SABAH/MALAYSIA. JABATAN PERANGKAAN. BUKU TAHUNAN PERANGKAAN, SABAH. *see* BUSINESS AND ECONOMICS—Abstracting, Bibliographies, Statistics

MALAYSIA. DEPARTMENT OF STATISTICS. YEARBOOK OF STATISTICS, SARAWAK/MALAYSIA. JABATAN PERANGKAAN. BUKU TAHUNAN PERANGKAAN, SARAWAK. *see* BUSINESS AND ECONOMICS—Abstracting, Bibliographies, Statistics

MALAYSIA. JABATAN PERANGKAAN. DIREKTORI SUMBER DATA SEKTOR AWAM, MALAYSIA. *see* WATER RESOURCES—Abstracting, Bibliographies, Statistics

MALOE PREDPRINIMATEL'STVO V ROSSII (YEAR). *see* BUSINESS AND ECONOMICS—Abstracting, Bibliographies, Statistics

314 MLT ISSN 0256-8047
HA1117.M3
MALTA. CENTRAL OFFICE OF STATISTICS. ANNUAL ABSTRACT OF STATISTICS. Text in English. a. **Document type:** *Government.*
Formerly: Statistical Abstract of the Maltese Islands (0081-4733)
Published by: Central Office of Statistics, Auberge d'Italie, Merchants' St., Valletta, Malta. FAX 356-248483. **Subscr. to:** Publications Bookshop, Castille Place, Valletta, Malta.

MALTA. CENTRAL OFFICE OF STATISTICS. DEMOGRAPHIC REVIEW OF THE MALTESE ISLANDS. *see* POPULATION STUDIES—Abstracting, Bibliographies, Statistics

MALTA. CENTRAL OFFICE OF STATISTICS. EDUCATION STATISTICS. *see* EDUCATION—Abstracting, Bibliographies, Statistics

314.585 MLT ISSN 0025-1437
MALTA. CENTRAL OFFICE OF STATISTICS. QUARTERLY DIGEST OF STATISTICS. Text in English. 1960. s-a. **Document type:** *Government.*
Media: Duplicated (not offset).
Published by: Central Office of Statistics, Auberge d'Italie, Merchants' St., Valletta, Malta. FAX 356-248483. **Subscr. to:** Publications Bookshop, Castille Place, Valletta, Malta.

MALTA. CENTRAL OFFICE OF STATISTICS. SHIPPING AND AVIATION STATISTICS. *see* TRANSPORTATION—Abstracting, Bibliographies, Statistics

MALTA. DEPARTMENT OF INFORMATION. REPORTS ON THE WORKING OF GOVERNMENT DEPARTMENTS. *see* PUBLIC ADMINISTRATION—Abstracting, Bibliographies, Statistics

MANITOBA AGRICULTURAL FINANCIAL STATISTICS. *see* AGRICULTURE—Abstracting, Bibliographies, Statistics

317.127 CAN ISSN 0700-2971
MANITOBA STATISTICAL REVIEW. Text in English. 1972. q. CAD 55 (effective 2000). illus. **Document type:** *Government.*
Incorporates (in Jan. 1979): Manitoba Price Statistics; Formerly: Manitoba Digest of Statistics
Indexed: CSI.
Published by: Bureau of Statistics, 824 155 Carlton St, Winnipeg, MB R3C 3H8, Canada. TEL 204-945-2988, FAX 204-945-0695. Circ: 220.

MARKET TRENDS. *see* AGRICULTURE—Abstracting, Bibliographies, Statistics

330.9 316 MAR ISSN 0851-0946
LE MAROC EN CHIFFRES. Text in French. 1961. a. **Document type:** *Government.*
Related titles: Microfiche ed.; Arabic ed.: ISSN 0851-1519.
Published by: (Banque Marocaine du Commerce Exterieur), Morocco. Direction de la Statistique, B P 178, Rabat, Morocco. TEL 212-7-77-36-06, FAX 212-7-773042, dirstat@wizarat.sukkan.sukkan.gov.ma, http://sukkan.gov.ma. Circ: 14,000.

MARYLAND GRAIN & LIVESTOCK REPORT. *see* AGRICULTURE—Abstracting, Bibliographies, Statistics

MASSACHUSETTS CITIES & COUNTIES GRAPHIC PERFORMANCE ANALYSIS. *see* PUBLIC ADMINISTRATION—Abstracting, Bibliographies, Statistics

MASSACHUSETTS TAXPAYERS FOUNDATION. STATE BUDGET TRENDS. *see* PUBLIC ADMINISTRATION—Abstracting, Bibliographies, Statistics

316.6 MRT ISSN 0543-1433
MAURITANIA. DIRECTION DE LA STATISTIQUE ET DES ETUDES ECONOMIQUES. BULLETIN MENSUEL STATISTIQUE. Text in French. m. illus.
Published by: Direction de la Statistique et des Etudes Economiques, B.P. 240, BP 240, Nouakchott, Mauritania.

310 MRT
MAURITANIA. OFFICE NATIONAL DE LA STATISTIQUE. BULLETIN STATISTIQUE ET ECONOMIQUE. Text in French. irreg. **Document type:** *Bulletin, Government.*
Published by: Mauritanie. Office National de la Statistique/Mauritania. National Bureau of Statistics, BP 240, Nouakchott, Mauritania. TEL 222-5253070, FAX 222-5255170, webmaster@ons.mr, http://www.ons.mr.

MAURITIUS. CENTRAL STATISTICAL OFFICE. ANNUAL DIGEST OF STATISTICS. *see* BUSINESS AND ECONOMICS—Abstracting, Bibliographies, Statistics

MAURITIUS. CENTRAL STATISTICAL OFFICE. BUSINESS ACTIVITY STATISTICS. *see* BUSINESS AND ECONOMICS—Abstracting, Bibliographies, Statistics

MAURITIUS. CENTRAL STATISTICAL OFFICE. DIGEST OF AGRICULTURAL STATISTICS. *see* AGRICULTURE—Abstracting, Bibliographies, Statistics

MAURITIUS. CENTRAL STATISTICAL OFFICE. DIGEST OF DEMOGRAPHIC STATISTICS. *see* POPULATION STUDIES—Abstracting, Bibliographies, Statistics

MAURITIUS. CENTRAL STATISTICAL OFFICE. DIGEST OF EDUCATIONAL STATISTICS. *see* EDUCATION—Abstracting, Bibliographies, Statistics

MAURITIUS. CENTRAL STATISTICAL OFFICE. DIGEST OF EXTERNAL TRADE STATISTICS. *see* BUSINESS AND ECONOMICS—Abstracting, Bibliographies, Statistics

MAURITIUS. CENTRAL STATISTICAL OFFICE. DIGEST OF INDUSTRIAL STATISTICS. *see* BUSINESS AND ECONOMICS—Abstracting, Bibliographies, Statistics

MAURITIUS. CENTRAL STATISTICAL OFFICE. DIGEST OF INTERNATIONAL TRAVEL AND TOURISM STATISTICS. *see* TRAVEL AND TOURISM—Abstracting, Bibliographies, Statistics

MAURITIUS. CENTRAL STATISTICAL OFFICE. DIGEST OF LABOUR STATISTICS. *see* BUSINESS AND ECONOMICS—Abstracting, Bibliographies, Statistics

MAURITIUS. CENTRAL STATISTICAL OFFICE. DIGEST OF PRODUCTIVITY AND COMPETITIVENESS STATISTICS. *see* BUSINESS AND ECONOMICS—Abstracting, Bibliographies, Statistics

MAURITIUS. CENTRAL STATISTICAL OFFICE. DIGEST OF PUBLIC FINANCE STATISTICS. *see* BUSINESS AND ECONOMICS—Abstracting, Bibliographies, Statistics

MAURITIUS. CENTRAL STATISTICAL OFFICE. DIGEST OF ROAD TRANSPORT & ROAD ACCIDENTS STATISTICS. *see* TRANSPORTATION—Abstracting, Bibliographies, Statistics

MAURITIUS. CENTRAL STATISTICAL OFFICE. HOUSEHOLD BUDGET SURVEY. *see* HOME ECONOMICS—Abstracting, Bibliographies, Statistics

MAURITIUS. CENTRAL STATISTICAL OFFICE. HOUSING AND POPULATION CENSUS (YEAR). RESULTS. *see* HOUSING AND URBAN PLANNING—Abstracting, Bibliographies, Statistics

MAURITIUS. CENTRAL STATISTICAL OFFICE. HOUSING AND POPULATION CENSUS. ANALYSIS REPORTS. *see* HOUSING AND URBAN PLANNING—Abstracting, Bibliographies, Statistics

MAURITIUS. CENTRAL STATISTICAL OFFICE. HOUSING AND POPULATION CENSUS. CENSUS OF ECONOMIC ACTIVITIES (YEAR). *see* BUSINESS AND ECONOMICS—Abstracting, Bibliographies, Statistics

MAURITIUS. CENTRAL STATISTICAL OFFICE. NATIONAL ACCOUNTS OF MAURITIUS. *see* BUSINESS AND ECONOMICS—Abstracting, Bibliographies, Statistics

MAURITIUS. CENTRAL STATISTICAL OFFICE. STATISTICS ON RODRIGUES. *see* BUSINESS AND ECONOMICS—Abstracting, Bibliographies, Statistics

310 MUS
MAURITIUS. CENTRAL STATISTICS OFFICE. LABOUR FORCE SAMPLE SURVEY (YEAR). Text in English. irreg. MUR 150 (effective 2001).
Published by: Mauritius. Central Statistical Office, L.I.C. Centre, President John Kennedy St, Port Louis, Mauritius. TEL 230-212-2316, FAX 230-211-4150, cso@intnet.mu, http://statsmauritius.gov.mu. **Subscr. to:** Mauritius. Government Printing Office, Ramtoolah Bldg, Sir S Ramgoolam St, Port Louis, Mauritius. TEL 230-234-5294, 230-242-0234, FAX 230-234-5322.

MEANS CONSTRUCTION COST INDEXES. *see* BUILDING AND CONSTRUCTION—Abstracting, Bibliographies, Statistics

MEASUREMENT METHODS FOR THE SOCIAL SCIENCES. *see* METROLOGY AND STANDARDIZATION

MEASURING IRELAND'S PROGRESS. *see* HISTORY—Abstracting, Bibliographies, Statistics

MEDITSINSKI PREGLED. MEDITSINSKI MENIDZHMENT I ZDRAVNA POLITIKA. *see* PUBLIC HEALTH AND SAFETY—Abstracting, Bibliographies, Statistics

MERCOSUL: SINOPSE ESTATISTICA/MERCOSUR: SINOPSIS ESTADISTICA. *see* BUSINESS AND ECONOMICS—Abstracting, Bibliographies, Statistics

MERCOSUR; sinopsis estadistica. *see* BUSINESS AND ECONOMICS—Abstracting, Bibliographies, Statistics

MERGENT'S INDUSTRY REVIEW. *see* BUSINESS AND ECONOMICS—Abstracting, Bibliographies, Statistics

310 BGR ISSN 1311-2325
MESTNI ORGANI NA UPRAVLENIE. Text in Bulgarian. a. BGL 5.81 (effective 2002). 50 p./no.
Published by: Natsionalen Statisticheski Institut/National Statistical Institute, ul P Volov, # 2, Sofia, 1038, Bulgaria. FAX 359-2-9803319, publikacii@nsi.bg, http://www.nsi.bg.

METHODEN, DATEN, ANALYSEN. *see* SOCIOLOGY—Abstracting, Bibliographies, Statistics

001.422 RUS
METODOLOGICHESKIE POLOZHENIYA PO STATISTIKE. Text in Russian. a. RUR 275 per issue (effective 2005). **Document type:** *Government.*
Related titles: E-mail ed.: RUR 295 per issue (effective 2005).
Published by: Gosudarstvennyi Komitet Rossiiskoi Federatsii po Statistike/Federal State Statistics Office, ul Myasnitskaya 39, Moscow, 107450, Russian Federation. TEL 7-095-2074902, FAX 7-095-2074087, stat@gks.ru, http://www.gks.ru.

310 SVN ISSN 1408-1482
METODOLOSKO GRADIVO/METHODOLOGICAL MATERIAL. Text in Slovenian. 1947. irreg. stat. **Document type:** *Government.*
Description: Contains comprehensive information on used sources and methods of data collection, on coverage, on definitions of statistical surveys and other necessary explanations. Intended for performers of statistical surveys and for reporting units as well as for users of statistical data.
Formerly (until 1996): Zavod S R Slovenije za Statistiko. Metodolosko Gradivo (0489-1589)

S

Related titles: Online - full content ed.
Published by: Statisticni Urad Republike Slovenije/Statistical Office of the Republic of Slovenia, Vozarski pot 12, Ljubjana, 1000, Slovenia. TEL 386-1-2415104, FAX 386-1-2415344, info.stat@gov.si. Ed. Ana Antoncic. Pub. Tomaz Banovec.

519.5 DEU ISSN 0026-1335
QA276.A1 CODEN: MTRKA8
➤ **METRIKA**; international journal for theoretical and applied statistics. Text in English. 1958. bi-m. (in 2 vols., 3 nos./vol.). EUR 838, USD 1,049 combined subscription to institutions (print & online eds.) (effective 2012). adv. bk.rev. charts; illus. index. back issues avail.; reprint service avail. from PSC. **Document type:** *Journal, Academic/ Scholarly.* **Description:** Covers statistical methods and mathematical statistics. Includes statistical quality control, sampling control, sampling theory, design of experiments.
Formed by the merger of (1948-1958): Universitaet Wien. Institut fuer Statistik. Statistische Vierteljahresschrift (0255-7479); (1949-1958): Mitteilungsblatt fuer Mathematische Statistik und ihre Anwendungsgebiete (0176-5531); Which was formerly (until 1955): Mitteilungsblatt fuer Mathematische Statistik (0176-6074)
Related titles: Microform ed.: (from PQC); Online - full text ed.: ISSN 1435-926X (from IngentaConnect).
Indexed: A01, A03, A08, A22, A26, Biostat, CA, CCMJ, CIS, CMCI, E01, EconLit, IAOP, IBR, IBZ, Inspec, JEL, MSN, MathR, P30, RASB, SCI, SCOPUS, ST&MA, T02, W07, Z02.
—BLDSC (5748.700000), IE, Infotrieve, Ingenta, INIST, Linda Hall. **CCC.**
Published by: Springer (Subsidiary of: Springer Science+Business Media), Tiergartenstr 17, Heidelberg, 69121, Germany. TEL 49-6221-4870, FAX 49-6221-345229. Eds. Holger Dette, Udo Kamps. adv.: B&W page EUR 700, color page EUR 1,740. Circ: 360 (paid and controlled). **Subscr. in the Americas to:** Springer New York LLC, Journal Fulfillment, PO Box 2485, Secaucus, NJ 07096. TEL 800-777-4643, 201-348-4033, FAX 201-348-4505, journals-ny@springer.com, http://www.springer.com; **Subscr. to:** Springer Distribution Center, Kundenservice Zeitschriften, Haberstr 7, Heidelberg 69126, Germany. TEL 49-6221-3454303, FAX 49-6221-3454229, subscriptions@springer.com.

519.5 ITA ISSN 0026-1424
HA1 CODEN: MRONAM
➤ **METRON**; international journal of statistics. Text in English. 1920. 3/yr. EUR 106 domestic; EUR 113 foreign (effective 2008). adv. bk.rev. abstr.; charts; stat. index, cum.index. reprints avail. **Document type:** *Journal, Academic/Scholarly.* **Description:** Publishes original articles on statistical methodology, statistical applications or discussions of results achieved by statistical methods in different branches of science.
Indexed: A22, AIAP, CCMJ, CIS, MSN, MathR, SCOPUS, ST&MA, Z02.
—IE, Ingenta, INIST.
Published by: (Universita degli Studi di Roma "La Sapienza", Facolta di Scienze Statistiche Demografiche ed Attuariali), E S I A Books and Journals, Via Palestro 30, Rome, 00185, Italy. FAX 39-06-4747743, esia@esia.it, http://www.esia.it. Ed. Mario Badaloni. Circ: 1,000.

➤ **METSATILASTOTIEDOTE (ONLINE).** *see* FORESTS AND FORESTRY—Abstracting, Bibliographies, Statistics

➤ **MEXICO. COMISION NACIONAL DE SEGUROS Y FIANZAS. ANUARIO ESTADISTICO DE SEGUROS.** *see* INSURANCE—Abstracting, Bibliographies, Statistics

➤ **MEXICO. INSTITUTO NACIONAL DE ESTADISTICA, GEOGRAFIA E INFORMATICA. ENCUESTA INDUSTRIAL MENSUAL**; 129 clases de actividad. *see* BUSINESS AND ECONOMICS—Abstracting, Bibliographies, Statistics

➤ **MEXICO. INSTITUTO NACIONAL DE ESTADISTICA, GEOGRAFIA E INFORMATICA. ENCUESTA NACIONAL DE EDUCACION CAPACITACION Y EMPLEO.** *see* EDUCATION—Abstracting, Bibliographies, Statistics

➤ **MEXICO. INSTITUTO NACIONAL DE ESTADISTICA, GEOGRAFIA E INFORMATICA. ESTADISTICAS DEL MEDIO AMBIENTE.** *see* ENVIRONMENTAL STUDIES—Abstracting, Bibliographies, Statistics

317 MEX ISSN 0186-2707
HA37
MEXICO. INSTITUTO NACIONAL DE ESTADISTICA, GEOGRAFIA E INFORMATICA. REVISTA DE ESTADISTICA. Text in Spanish. 1938. irreg. MXN 18 per issue (effective 1999). mkt.; stat. index.
Formerly: Mexico. Direccion General de Estadistica. Revista de Estadistica y Geografia (0026-1769)
Indexed: CIS, JEL.
Published by: Instituto Nacional de Estadistica, Geografia e Informatica, Secretaria de Programacion y Presupuesto, Prol. Heroe de Nacozari 2301 Sur, Puerta 11, Acceso, Aguascalientes, 20270, Mexico. TEL 52-4-918-1948, FAX 52-4-918-0739. Circ: 1,000. **Subscr. to:** Direccion General de Estudios del Territorio Nacional, BALDERAS 71, Col Centro, Mexico City, DF 12400, Mexico.

MICHIGAN CITIES & COUNTIES GRAPHIC PERFORMANCE ANALYSIS. *see* PUBLIC ADMINISTRATION—Abstracting, Bibliographies, Statistics

MICHIGAN CROP-WEATHER. *see* AGRICULTURE—Abstracting, Bibliographies, Statistics

659.021 GBR ISSN 2042-6887
MIDDLE EAST AND NORTH AFRICA MARKET & MEDIAFACT. Text in English. 1996. a. GBP 50, EUR 55.97, USD 81.21 per issue (effective 2010). stat. **Document type:** *Report, Trade.* **Description:** Contains media statistics for TV & radio audiences, press circulation & readership, cinema screens & admissions, etc.
Formerly (until 200?): Africa & Middle East Market & MediaFact (1364-0275)
—CCC.
Published by: Zenith Optimedia, 24 Percy St, London, W1T 2BS, United Kingdom. TEL 44-20-79611000, FAX 44-20- 79611199, info@zenithoptimedia.com.

MIGRATION HIGHLIGHTS. *see* POPULATION STUDIES—Abstracting, Bibliographies, Statistics

▼ **MIGRATION STATISTICS QUARTERLY REPORT.** *see* POPULATION STUDIES—Abstracting, Bibliographies, Statistics

MINAS GERAIS, BRAZIL. DEPARTAMENTO DE ESTRADAS DE RODAGEM. SERVICO DE TRANSITO. ESTATISTICA DE TRAFEGO E ACIDENTES. *see* TRANSPORTATION—Abstracting, Bibliographies, Statistics

MINNESOTA AG NEWS .. CROP-WEATHER. *see* AGRICULTURE—Abstracting, Bibliographies, Statistics

MINNESOTA CITIES & COUNTIES GRAPHIC PERFORMANCE ANALYSIS. *see* PUBLIC ADMINISTRATION—Abstracting, Bibliographies, Statistics

MINNESOTA HEALTH STATISTICS. *see* PUBLIC HEALTH AND SAFETY—Abstracting, Bibliographies, Statistics

310 331 CAN ISSN 1708-0932
MISE A JOUR DES ETUDES ANALYTIQUES. Text in French. 2005. irreg.
Document type: *Newsletter, Trade.*
Media: Online - full text. **Related titles:** English ed.: Update on Analytical Studies Research. ISSN 1708-0924.
Published by: Statistics Canada/Statistique Canada, Communications Division, 3rd Fl, R H Coats Bldg, Ottawa, ON K1A 0A6, Canada. TEL 800-263-1136, infostats@statcan.ca, http://www.statcan.gc.ca.

MISSISSIPPI CITIES & COUNTIES GRAPHIC PERFORMANCE ANALYSIS. *see* PUBLIC ADMINISTRATION—Abstracting, Bibliographies, Statistics

MISSOURI CITIES & COUNTIES GRAPHIC PERFORMANCE ANALYSIS. *see* PUBLIC ADMINISTRATION—Abstracting, Bibliographies, Statistics

MISSOURI CROP & LIVESTOCK REPORTER. *see* AGRICULTURE—Abstracting, Bibliographies, Statistics

MISSOURI. DEPARTMENT OF INSURANCE. ANNUAL REPORT AND STATISTICAL DATA. *see* INSURANCE—Abstracting, Bibliographies, Statistics

MISSOURI MONTHLY VITAL STATISTICS. *see* POPULATION STUDIES—Abstracting, Bibliographies, Statistics

MISSOURI VITAL STATISTICS. *see* POPULATION STUDIES—Abstracting, Bibliographies, Statistics

316 MOZ
MOCAMBIQUE - INFORMACAO ESTATISTICA. Text in Portuguese. 1982. m.
Published by: (Mozambique. Comissao Nacional do Plano), Centro de Documentacao Economica, C.P. 2051, Maputo, Mozambique.

310 NLD ISSN 1574-1699
➤ **MODEL ASSISTED STATISTICS AND APPLICATIONS**; an international journal. Text in English. 2005. q. USD 441 combined subscription in North America (print & online eds.); EUR 315 combined subscription elsewhere (print & online eds.) (effective 2012). **Document type:** *Journal, Academic/Scholarly.* **Description:** Publishes in the field of sampling theory, econometrics, time-series, design of experiments and multivariate analysis.
Related titles: Online - full text ed.: ISSN 1875-9068.
Indexed: A22, C10, CA, CCMJ, E01, MSN, MathR, SCOPUS, T02, Z02.
—BLDSC (5880.280000), IE.
Published by: I O S Press, Nieuwe Hemweg 6B, Amsterdam, 1013 BG, Netherlands. TEL 31-20-6883355, FAX 31-20-6870019, info@iospress.nl. Eds. Sardinjer Singh, Stan Lipovetsky.

➤ **MODERN PROBABILITY AND STATISTICS.** *see* MATHEMATICS

➤ **MONEY STOCK MEASURES.** *see* BUSINESS AND ECONOMICS—Abstracting, Bibliographies, Statistics

▼ ➤ **MONITOR DUURZAAM NEDERLAND.** *see* ENVIRONMENTAL STUDIES—Abstracting, Bibliographies, Statistics

➤ **MONITOR, POPULATION AND HEALTH. ABORTION.** *see* POPULATION STUDIES

➤ **MONTANA CROP & LIVESTOCK REPORTER.** *see* AGRICULTURE—Abstracting, Bibliographies, Statistics

➤ **MONTANA CROP WEATHER REPORT.** *see* AGRICULTURE—Abstracting, Bibliographies, Statistics

➤ **MONTANA. DEPARTMENT OF SOCIAL AND REHABILITATION SERVICES. STATISTICAL REPORT.** *see* SOCIAL SERVICES AND WELFARE—Abstracting, Bibliographies, Statistics

➤ **MONTHLY BANKING STATISTICS.** *see* BUSINESS AND ECONOMICS—Banking And Finance

314 GBR ISSN 0308-6666
HC251
➤ **MONTHLY DIGEST OF STATISTICS.** Abbreviated title: M D S. Text in English. 1946. m. USD 473 in North America to institutions; GBP 249 elsewhere to institutions (effective 2011). adv. stat. back issues avail.; reprints avail. **Document type:** *Journal, Government.* **Description:** Provides the monthly and quarterly statistics for UK businesses, economy and society. Covers topics such as national accounts, including gross domestic product (GDP), population and vital statistics, labour market etc.
Related titles: Online - full text ed.: ISSN 2040-1582.
Indexed: G08, I05, RASB.
—CCC.
Published by: (Great Britain. Office for National Statistics), Palgrave Macmillan Ltd. (Subsidiary of: Macmillan Publishers Ltd.), Houndmills, Basingstoke, Hants RG21 6XS, United Kingdom. TEL 44-1256-329242, FAX 44-1256-479476, orders@palgrave.com, http://www.palgrave.com. Eds. Dilys Rosen TEL 44-1633-455850, Tammy Powell TEL 44-1633-456885. Pub. David Bull TEL 44-1256-329242. **Subscr. to:** Subscription Department, Brunel Rd, Houndmills, Basingstoke, Hants RG21 2XS, United Kingdom. TEL 44-1256-357893, FAX 44-1256-328339, subscriptions@palgrave.com.

➤ **MONTHLY REPORT ON TOURISM - REPUBLIC OF CHINA/KUAN KUANG TZU LIAO.** *see* TRAVEL AND TOURISM—Abstracting, Bibliographies, Statistics

315 BGD ISSN 0377-1555
HA1730.8
MONTHLY STATISTICAL BULLETIN OF BANGLADESH. Text in English. 1972. m. BDT 1,200, USD 240. Supplement avail.
Document type: *Government.* **Description:** Presents current data on performance of family planning, labor and employment, wages, agriculture, meteorology, industrial production, transport and communication, foreign trade, national income accounts, as well as public finance and accounting.
Supersedes: Bangladesh. Bureau of Statistics. Monthly Bulletin of Statistics (0012-849X)
Published by: (Bangladesh. Bureau of Statistics), Ministry of Planning, Statistics Division, Secretariat, Dhaka, 2, Bangladesh. TEL 868695. Ed. Tajul Islam. Circ: 300.

MONTHLY STATISTICS OF INTERNATIONAL TRADE/STATISTIQUES MENSUELLES DU COMMERCE INTERNATIONAL. *see* BUSINESS AND ECONOMICS—Abstracting, Bibliographies, Statistics

MONTHLY WHOLESALE TRADE: SALES AND INVENTORIES (ONLINE). *see* BUSINESS AND ECONOMICS—Abstracting, Bibliographies, Statistics

304.6 MAR ISSN 1113-7207
HC810.A1
MOROCCO. DIRECTION DE LA STATISTIQUE. BULLETIN STATISTIQUE. Text in Arabic, French. q. MAD 363 (effective 2000).
Document type: *Bulletin, Government.*
Formerly (until 1996): Morocco. Direction de la Statistique. Bulletin Mensuel des Statistiques (0256-9159)
Published by: Morocco. Direction de la Statistique, B P 178, Rabat, Morocco. TEL 212-7-77-36-06, FAX 212-7-77-32-17.

MOROCCO. DIRECTION DE LA STATISTIQUE. INDICE DES PRIX A LA PRODUCTION INDUSTRIELLE, ENERGETIQUE ET MINIERE. *see* BUSINESS AND ECONOMICS—Abstracting, Bibliographies, Statistics

MOROCCO. DIRECTION DE LA STATISTIQUE. INDICE DU COUT DE LA VIE. *see* BUSINESS AND ECONOMICS—Abstracting, Bibliographies, Statistics

MOROCCO. DIRECTION DE LA STATISTIQUE. POPULATION ACTIVE URBAINE, ACTIVITE, EMPLOI ET CHOMAGE. *see* POPULATION STUDIES—Abstracting, Bibliographies, Statistics

MOTOR VEHICLE CRASHES IN NEW ZEALAND. *see* TRANSPORTATION—Abstracting, Bibliographies, Statistics

MOTORFAHRZEUGE IN DER SCHWEIZ. BESTAND AM 30. SEPTEMBER (YEAR)/VEHICULES A MOTEUR EN SUISSE. EFFECTIF AU 30 SEPTEMBRE (YEAR). *see* TRANSPORTATION—Abstracting, Bibliographies, Statistics

MOTORFAHRZEUGE IN DER SCHWEIZ. EINGEFUEHRTE MOTORFAHRZEUGE/VEHICULES A MOTEUR EN SUISSE. VEHICULES A MOTEUR IMPORTES. *see* TRANSPORTATION—Abstracting, Bibliographies, Statistics

MOUNTAIN STATE REPORTER. *see* AGRICULTURE—Abstracting, Bibliographies, Statistics

MOVING INDUSTRY TRANSPORTATION STATISTICS (YEAR); demographic, economic and financial data of the moving industry. *see* TRANSPORTATION—Abstracting, Bibliographies, Statistics

316.8 MOZ
MOZAMBIQUE STATISTICAL YEARBOOK/ANUARIO ESTATISTICO DE MOCAMBIQUE. (Editions avail. by province: Gaza, Sofala, Zambezia, Nampula) Text in Portuguese. a.
Published by: Instituto Nacional de Estatistica, Av Ahmed Sekou Toure 21, Maputo, Mozambique. TEL 258-1-491054, FAX 258-1-493547, info@ine.gov.mz, http://www.ine.gov.mz.

MUELHEIMER STATISTIK. *see* PUBLIC ADMINISTRATION—Abstracting, Bibliographies, Statistics

318 CHL ISSN 0717-1900
MUJERES Y HOMBRES EN CHILE. CIFRAS Y REALIDADES. Text in Spanish. a.?.
Published by: Instituto Nacional de Estadisticas, Casilla 498, Correo 3, Ave. Bulnes, 418, Santiago, Chile. TEL 56-2-6991441, FAX 56-2-6712169.

MUNICIPAL STATISTICS. ANNUAL REPORT; for New Brunswick. *see* PUBLIC ADMINISTRATION

MUSIC U S A; annual statistical review of the musical instrument industry. *see* MUSIC

N C A A BASKETBALL. OFFICIAL (YEAR) MEN'S BASKETBALL RECORDS BOOK. *see* SPORTS AND GAMES—Ball Games

N C H S DATA BRIEF. (National Center for Health Statistics) *see* PUBLIC HEALTH AND SAFETY—Abstracting, Bibliographies, Statistics

N C U A (YEAR) YEAREND STATISTICS FOR FEDERALLY INSURED CREDIT UNIONS (ONLINE). (National Credit Union Administration) *see* BUSINESS AND ECONOMICS—Abstracting, Bibliographies, Statistics

N F H S BULLETIN. (National Family Health Survey) *see* PUBLIC HEALTH AND SAFETY

N P R A STATISTICAL REPORT. ANNUAL SURVEY OF OCCUPATIONAL INJURIES & INJURIES. *see* OCCUPATIONAL HEALTH AND SAFETY—Abstracting, Bibliographies, Statistics

N P R A STATISTICAL REPORT. LUBRICATING OIL AND WAX CAPACITY. *see* PETROLEUM AND GAS—Abstracting, Bibliographies, Statistics

N P R A STATISTICAL REPORT. U S LUBRICATING OIL & WAX SALES. *see* PETROLEUM AND GAS—Abstracting, Bibliographies, Statistics

N P R A STATISTICAL REPORT. U S REFINING CAPACITY. *see* PETROLEUM AND GAS—Abstracting, Bibliographies, Statistics

310 PHL ISSN 0115-2092
HA1821
N S O MONTHLY BULLETIN OF STATISTICS. Text in English. m. USD 12 per issue (effective 1997). 102 p./no.; **Description:** Provides the latest available monthly data on social, demographic, and economic variables.
Indexed: IPP.
Published by: National Statistics Office, Ramon Magsaysay Blvd, PO Box 779, Manila, Philippines. FAX 63-2-610794. Circ: 250.

N W T AIRPORT STATISTICS REPORT. (Northwest Territories) *see* TRANSPORTATION—Air Transport

N W T TRAFFIC COLLISION FACTS. (Northwest Territories) *see* TRANSPORTATION—Roads And Traffic

NARCOTIC DRUGS: ESTIMATED WORLD REQUIREMENTS FOR (YEAR). *see* PHARMACY AND PHARMACOLOGY—Abstracting, Bibliographies, Statistics

NARODNA BANKA SRBIJE. STATISTICKI BILTEN. *see* BUSINESS AND ECONOMICS—Abstracting, Bibliographies, Statistics

310 RUS
NARODNOE KHOZYAISTVO ALTAISKOGO KRAYA. Text in Russian. 1967. every 5 yrs. stat.

Published by: (Russia. Tsentral'noe Statisticheskoe Upravlenie), Redaktsionno-Poligraficheskoe Proizvodstvennoe Ob'edinenie "Soyuzblankoizdat", Altaiskoe Redaktsionno-Proizvodstve, B Olonskaya 28, Barnaul, Russian Federation. Ed. Olga Zamiatina. Circ: 5,000.

NARODOWY BANK POLSKI. INFORMACJA WSTEPNA/NATIONAL BANK OF POLAND. PRELIMINARY INFORMATION. *see* BUSINESS AND ECONOMICS—Abstracting, Bibliographies, Statistics

310 304.6 BGR ISSN 1311-2341
HA1621

NASELENIE I DEMOGRAFSKI PROTSESI. Text in Bulgarian, English. a. BGL 26.95; USD 40 foreign (effective 2002). 330 p./no.; **Description:** Contains results of the demographic statistical investigation of the levels of births, deaths, marriages, divorces, and migration of the population of Bulgaria.
Published by: Natsionalen Statisticheski Institut/National Statistical Institute, ul P Volov, # 2, Sofia, 1038, Bulgaria. FAX 359-2-9803319, publikacii@nsi.bg, http://www.nsi.bg. **Dist. by:** Sofia Books, ul Silivria 16, Sofia 1404, Bulgaria. TEL 359-2-9586257, info@sofiabooks-bg.com, http://www.sofiabooks-bg.com.

316 MAR ISSN 0851-0903

NASRAT AL-IHSA'IYYAT AL-SANAWIYYAT LI-I-MAGRIB. Text in Arabic. 1982. a.
Related titles: ◆ French ed.: Annuaire Statistique du Maroc. ISSN 0851-089X.
Published by: Morocco. Direction de la Statistique, B P 178, Rabat, Morocco.

NATIONAL ACCOUNTS OF THE MALTESE ISLANDS. *see* BUSINESS AND ECONOMICS—Abstracting, Bibliographies, Statistics

NATIONAL AUTOMOTIVE SAMPLING SYSTEM. *see* TRANSPORTATION—Abstracting, Bibliographies, Statistics

NATIONAL BANK OF LIBERIA. QUARTERLY STATISTICAL BULLETIN. *see* BUSINESS AND ECONOMICS—Banking And Finance

NATIONAL BANK OF SERBIA. STATISTICAL BULLETIN. *see* BUSINESS AND ECONOMICS—Abstracting, Bibliographies, Statistics

NATIONAL COMPENSATION SURVEY. AUSTIN-ROUND ROCK, TX. (Texas) *see* BUSINESS AND ECONOMICS—Abstracting, Bibliographies, Statistics

NATIONAL COMPENSATION SURVEY. BIRMINGHAM, AL. (Alabama) *see* BUSINESS AND ECONOMICS—Abstracting, Bibliographies, Statistics

NATIONAL COMPENSATION SURVEY. BOSTON-WORCESTER-LAWRENCE, MA - NH - ME - CT. *see* BUSINESS AND ECONOMICS—Abstracting, Bibliographies, Statistics

NATIONAL COMPENSATION SURVEY. CINCINNATI - HAMILTON, OH - KY - IN. (Ohio - Kentucky - Indiana) *see* BUSINESS AND ECONOMICS—Abstracting, Bibliographies, Statistics

NATIONAL COMPENSATION SURVEY. DAYTON-SPRINGFIELD, OH. (Ohio) *see* BUSINESS AND ECONOMICS—Abstracting, Bibliographies, Statistics

NATIONAL COMPENSATION SURVEY. FORT COLLINS-LOVELAND, CO. (Colorado) *see* BUSINESS AND ECONOMICS—Abstracting, Bibliographies, Statistics

NATIONAL COMPENSATION SURVEY. HICKORY-MORGANTON-LENOIR, NC. (North Carolina) *see* BUSINESS AND ECONOMICS—Abstracting, Bibliographies, Statistics

NATIONAL COMPENSATION SURVEY. KALAMAZOO-BATTLE CREEK, MI. (Michigan) *see* BUSINESS AND ECONOMICS—Abstracting, Bibliographies, Statistics

NATIONAL COMPENSATION SURVEY. LOUISVILLE, KY-IN. (Kentucky - Indiana) *see* BUSINESS AND ECONOMICS—Abstracting, Bibliographies, Statistics

NATIONAL COMPENSATION SURVEY. MOBILE, AL. (Alabama) *see* BUSINESS AND ECONOMICS—Abstracting, Bibliographies, Statistics

NATIONAL COMPENSATION SURVEY. NORFOLK-VIRGINIA BEACH-NEWPORT NEWS, VA-NC. (Virginia - North Carolina) *see* BUSINESS AND ECONOMICS—Abstracting, Bibliographies, Statistics

NATIONAL COMPENSATION SURVEY. OCCUPATIONAL WAGES IN THE UNITED STATES. *see* BUSINESS AND ECONOMICS—Abstracting, Bibliographies, Statistics

NATIONAL COMPENSATION SURVEY. OCCUPATIONAL WAGES IN THE WEST SOUTH CENTRAL CENSUS DIVISION. *see* BUSINESS AND ECONOMICS—Abstracting, Bibliographies, Statistics

NATIONAL COMPENSATION SURVEY. PORTLAND-SALEM, OR - WA. (Oregon - Washington) *see* BUSINESS AND ECONOMICS—Abstracting, Bibliographies, Statistics

NATIONAL COMPENSATION SURVEY: WASHINGTON-BALTIMORE, DC - MD - VA - WV. *see* BUSINESS AND ECONOMICS—Abstracting, Bibliographies, Statistics

310 JPN

NATIONAL FEDERATION OF STATISTICAL ASSOCIATIONS OF JAPAN. MONTHLY STATISTICS OF JAPAN/TOKEI JOHO. Text in Japanese. m. JPY 760 (effective 1999). **Document type:** *Government.*
Published by: National Federation of Statistical Associations of Japan, Sanshin Bldg 1-14-15, Okubo, Shinjuku-ku, Tokyo, 169-0072, Japan. TEL 81-3-3205-7951, FAX 81-3-5291-5471.

310 JPN ISSN 0561-922X
HA37

NATIONAL FEDERATION OF STATISTICAL ASSOCIATIONS OF JAPAN. STATISTICAL NOTES OF JAPAN. Text in English. 1953. irreg., latest vol.45, 1991. free. **Document type:** *Government.*
Indexed: P06, P30.
Published by: National Federation of Statistical Associations of Japan, Sanshin Bldg 1-14-15, Okubo, Shinjuku-ku, Tokyo, 169-0072, Japan. TEL 81-3-3205-7951, FAX 31-3-5291-5471. Circ: 550 (controlled).
Co-sponsor: Management and Coordination Agency. Statistics Bureau.

NATIONAL HEALTH INFORMATION MODEL. VERSION 2 (ONLINE). *see* PUBLIC HEALTH AND SAFETY—Abstracting, Bibliographies, Statistics

NATIONAL HOSPITAL DISCHARGE SURVEY. *see* PUBLIC HEALTH AND SAFETY—Abstracting, Bibliographies, Statistics

NATIONAL HOUSEWARES MANUFACTURERS ASSOCIATION. STATE OF THE INDUSTRY REPORT. *see* BUSINESS AND ECONOMICS—Abstracting, Bibliographies, Statistics

NATIONAL MINING ASSOCIATION. WEEKLY STATISTICAL SUMMARY. *see* MINES AND MINING INDUSTRY—Abstracting, Bibliographies, Statistics

318 ARG

NATIONAL TERRITORY OF TIERRA DEL FUEGO, ANTARCTICA AND ISLANDS OF THE SOUTH ATLANTIC. MINISTERIO DE ECONOMIA Y HACIENDA. ANUARIO ESTADISTICO. Text in Spanish. a. free.
Published by: Ministerio de Economia y Produccion, Hipolito Yrigoyen 250, Buenos Aires, CP1086AAB, Argentina. TEL 54-114-3495079, FAX 54-114-3495730, mpqonz@mecon.gov.ar, http://www.mecon.gov.ar/.

NATIONALRATSWAHLEN (YEAR)/ELECTIONS AU CONSEIL NATIONAL (YEAR); Uebersicht und Analyse. *see* PUBLIC ADMINISTRATION—Abstracting, Bibliographies, Statistics

NATSIONAL'NYE SCHETA ROSSII. *see* BUSINESS AND ECONOMICS—Abstracting, Bibliographies, Statistics

NATURAL GAS TRANSPORTATION AND DISTRIBUTION/CANADA. STATISTIQUE CANADA. SERVICES DE GAZ. *see* PETROLEUM AND GAS—Abstracting, Bibliographies, Statistics

NEBRASKA CITIES & COUNTIES GRAPHIC PERFORMANCE ANALYSIS. *see* PUBLIC ADMINISTRATION—Abstracting, Bibliographies, Statistics

NEBRASKA WEATHER & CROPS. *see* AGRICULTURE—Abstracting, Bibliographies, Statistics

DE NEDERLANDSE GROEIREKENINGEN. *see* BUSINESS AND ECONOMICS—Abstracting, Bibliographies, Statistics

HET NEDERLANDSE ONDERNEMINGSKLIMAAT IN CIJFERS. *see* BUSINESS AND ECONOMICS—Abstracting, Bibliographies, Statistics

DE NEDERLANDSE SAMENLEVING. *see* SOCIOLOGY—Abstracting, Bibliographies, Statistics

NEKAZAL ELIKAGAI SEKTOREAREN ESTATISTIKA URTEKARIA E.A.E./ANUARIO ESTADISTICO DEL SECTOR AGROALIMENTARIO C.A.P.V. *see* AGRICULTURE—Abstracting, Bibliographies, Statistics

310 NPL

NEPAL AND THE WORLD; a statistical profile. Text in English. 1992. a. USD 20 (effective 2000). **Document type:** *Journal, Trade.* **Description:** Contains wide range of statistics related to trade, industry, tourism and planning of Nepal. Compares Nepal's economy with the South Asian nations and the rest of the world.
Published by: Federation of Nepalese Chambers of Commerce and Industry, Teku, P O Box 269, Kathmandu, Nepal. TEL 977-1-262061, FAX 977-1-261022, fncci@mos.com.np, http://www.fncci.org. Ed. Binod H Joshi. R&P Badri P Ojha.

315.49 NPL

NEPAL. CENTRAL BUREAU OF STATISTICS. STATISTICAL POCKET BOOK. Text in English. 1974. biennial. USD 1. illus. **Document type:** *Government.*
Published by: Central Bureau of Statistics, Ramshah Path, Thapathali, Kathmandu, Nepal. TEL 977-1-245947, FAX 977-1-227720. Circ: 7,000.

NETENDANCES (VERSION INTEGRALE). *see* COMPUTERS—Internet

317 ANT

NETHERLANDS ANTILLES. CENTRAL BUREAU OF STATISTICS. STATISTICAL YEARBOOK. Text and summaries in English. 1956. a. ANG 15. **Document type:** *Government.*
Formerly: Netherlands Antilles. Bureau voor de Statistiek. Statistisch Jaarboek (0077-6661)
Related titles: Microfiche ed.: (from PQC).
Published by: Central Bureau of Statistics, Fort Amsterdam z/n, Willemstad, Curacao, Netherlands Antilles. TEL 599-9-611031, FAX 599-9-611696. Circ: 450.

NETHERLANDS. CENTRAAL BUREAU VOOR DE STATISTIEK. BEVOKLINGSTRENDS; statistisch kwartaalblad over de demografie van Nederland. *see* POPULATION STUDIES—Abstracting, Bibliographies, Statistics

NETHERLANDS. CENTRAAL BUREAU VOOR DE STATISTIEK. DEMOGRAFISCHE KERNCIJFERS PER GEMEENTE. *see* POPULATION STUDIES—Abstracting, Bibliographies, Statistics

NETHERLANDS. CENTRAAL BUREAU VOOR DE STATISTIEK. SOCIAAL-ECONOMISCHE TRENDS. *see* SOCIAL SERVICES AND WELFARE—Abstracting, Bibliographies, Statistics

NETHERLANDS. CENTRAAL BUREAU VOOR DE STATISTIEK. STATISTIEK FINANCIEN VAN ONDERNEMINGEN. *see* BUSINESS AND ECONOMICS—Abstracting, Bibliographies, Statistics

NETHERLANDS. CENTRAAL BUREAU VOOR DE STATISTIEK. STATISTISCH BULLETIN. *see* BUSINESS AND ECONOMICS—Abstracting, Bibliographies, Statistics

NETHERLANDS. CENTRAAL BUREAU VOOR DE STATISTIEK. STATISTISCH JAARBOEK/NETHERLANDS. CENTRAL BUREAU OF STATISTICS. POCKET YEARBOOK. *see* POPULATION STUDIES—Abstracting, Bibliographies, Statistics

314 NLD ISSN 0922-5897

NETHERLANDS. CENTRALE COMMISSIE VOOR DE STATISTIEK. JAARVERSLAG. Text in Dutch. 1899. a. free (effective 2008). **Document type:** *Government.* **Description:** Covers activities and meetings of the commission and its sub-commissions.
Published by: Centrale Commissie voor de Statistiek, Postbus 24500, The Hague, 2490 HA, Netherlands. TEL 31-70-3375361, http://www.cbs.nl.

NEVADA AG STATS NEWSLETTER. *see* AGRICULTURE—Abstracting, Bibliographies, Statistics

NEVADA CROP PROGRESS & CONDITIONS. *see* AGRICULTURE—Abstracting, Bibliographies, Statistics

NEW BRUNSWICK. TOURISM RECREATION & HERITAGE. TECHNICAL SERVICES BRANCH. PROVINCIAL PARK STATISTICS. *see* CONSERVATION—Abstracting, Bibliographies, Statistics

NEW BRUNSWICK. VITAL STATISTICS. ANNUAL STATISTICAL REPORT/NOUVEAU-BRUNSWICK. STATISTIQUES DE L'ETAT CIVIL. RAPPORT STATISTIQUE ANNUEL. *see* POPULATION STUDIES—Abstracting, Bibliographies, Statistics

NEW CALEDONIA. INSTITUT DE LA STATISTIQUE ET DES ETUDES ECONOMIQUES. INDICE ET INDEX DU B T P. *see* BUILDING AND CONSTRUCTION—Abstracting, Bibliographies, Statistics

330.9 319 NCL
HA4007.N4

NEW CALEDONIA. INSTITUT DE LA STATISTIQUE ET DES ETUDES ECONOMIQUES. INFORMATIONS STATISTIQUES. Text in French. 1972. q. XPF 500 domestic; EUR 587 foreign (effective 2005). adv. stat. 77 p./no.; **Document type:** *Government.*
Former titles: New Caledonia. Institut Territorial de la Statistique et des Etudes Economiques. Informations Statistiques (1623-1791); (until 1999): New Caledonia. Institut Territorial de la Statistique et des Etudes Economiques. Informations Statistiques Rapides (0336-4062); (until 1973): New Caledonia. Service de la Statistique. Nouvelle Caledonie et Dependences. Bulletin de Statistique. (0336-3945)
Published by: Institut de la Statistique et des Etudes Economiques, BP 823, Noumea, 98845, New Caledonia. TEL 687-283156, FAX 687-288148, dp@itsee.nc. Ed. Gerard Baudchon. Circ: 1,200.

NEW CALEDONIA. INSTITUT DE LA STATISTIQUE ET DES ETUDES ECONOMIQUES. POINT ECONOMIQUE. *see* BUSINESS AND ECONOMICS—Abstracting, Bibliographies, Statistics

NEW CALEDONIA. INSTITUT DE LA STATISTIQUE ET DES ETUDES ECONOMIQUES. TABLEAUX DE L'ECONOMIE CALEDONIENNE. *see* BUSINESS AND ECONOMICS—Abstracting, Bibliographies, Statistics

NEW CALEDONIA. INSTITUT TERRITORIAL DE LA STATISTIQUE ET DES ETUDES ECONOMIQUES. INDICES DES PRIX A LA CONSOMMATION. *see* BUSINESS AND ECONOMICS—Abstracting, Bibliographies, Statistics

NEW HAMPSHIRE VITAL STATISTICS. *see* POPULATION STUDIES—Abstracting, Bibliographies, Statistics

NEW JERSEY CITIES & COUNTIES GRAPHIC PERFORMANCE ANALYSIS. *see* PUBLIC ADMINISTRATION—Abstracting, Bibliographies, Statistics

NEW JERSEY PUBLIC LIBRARY STATISTICS FOR (YEAR). *see* LIBRARY AND INFORMATION SCIENCES—Abstracting, Bibliographies, Statistics

NEW JERSEY WEATHER AND CROP BULLETIN. *see* AGRICULTURE—Abstracting, Bibliographies, Statistics

NEW LOCAL GOVERNMENT AREA MONITOR. *see* POPULATION STUDIES—Abstracting, Bibliographies, Statistics

NEW MEXICO AGRICULTURAL STATISTICS. *see* AGRICULTURE—Abstracting, Bibliographies, Statistics

NEW RESIDENTIAL CONSTRUCTION IN .. *see* BUILDING AND CONSTRUCTION—Abstracting, Bibliographies, Statistics

NEW SOUTH WALES CRIMINAL COURTS STATISTICS. *see* LAW—Criminal Law

319.4 AUS ISSN 1838-0190

NEW SOUTH WALES. PARLIAMENTARY LIBRARY RESEARCH SERVICE. STATISTICAL INDICATORS. Text in English. 1993. q. free (effective 2011). back issues avail. **Document type:** *Report, Government.*
Formerly (until 1995): New South Wales. Parliamentary Library. Briefing Note (Print) (1321-2559)
Media: Online - full text.
Published by: New South Wales, Parliamentary Library Research Service, Department of Parliamentary Services, Parliament House, Macquarie St, Sydney, NSW 2000, Australia. TEL 61-2-92302111, FAX 61-2-92303370, assembly@parliament.nsw.gov.au, http://www.parliament.nsw.gov.au.

NEW SOUTH WALES RECORDED CRIME STATISTICS. *see* LAW—Criminal Law

NEW YORK (STATE). DIVISION OF CRIMINAL SERVICES. OFFICE OF JUSTICE SYSTEMS ANALYSIS. STATISTICAL INDICATOR BULLETIN. *see* CRIMINOLOGY AND LAW ENFORCEMENT—Abstracting, Bibliographies, Statistics

NEW YORK (STATE). OFFICE OF TEMPORARY AND DISABILITY ASSISTANCE. TEMPORARY AND DISABILITY ASSISTANCE STATISTICS (ONLINE). *see* SOCIAL SERVICES AND WELFARE—Abstracting, Bibliographies, Statistics

NEW YORK AGRICULTURAL STATISTICS. *see* AGRICULTURE—Abstracting, Bibliographies, Statistics

NEW YORK CITIES AND COUNTIES GRAPHIC PERFORMANCE ANALYSIS. *see* PUBLIC ADMINISTRATION—Abstracting, Bibliographies, Statistics

317 USA ISSN 0077-9334
HA541

NEW YORK STATE STATISTICAL YEARBOOK. Text in English. 1967. a. USD 66.30 per issue (effective 2010). index. back issues avail. **Document type:** *Yearbook, Government.* **Description:** Contains statistical information on New York State, as well as select US data.
Related titles: Online - full text ed.: free (effective 2010) (from CIS).
Indexed: SRI.
Published by: Nelson A. Rockefeller Institute of Government, 411 State St, Albany, NY 12203. TEL 518-443-5522, FAX 518-443-5788, info@rockinst.org.

NEW ZEALAND CRIME STATISTICS. *see* CRIMINOLOGY AND LAW ENFORCEMENT—Abstracting, Bibliographies, Statistics

NEW ZEALAND HEALTH INFORMATION SERVICE. CANCER: NEW REGISTRATIONS AND DEATHS. *see* MEDICAL SCIENCES—Abstracting, Bibliographies, Statistics

NEW ZEALAND HEALTH INFORMATION SERVICE. FETAL AND INFANT DEATHS (CD-ROM). *see* POPULATION STUDIES—Abstracting, Bibliographies, Statistics

NEW ZEALAND HEALTH INFORMATION SERVICE. MORTALITY AND DEMOGRAPHIC DATA. *see* POPULATION STUDIES—Abstracting, Bibliographies, Statistics

NEW ZEALAND HEALTH INFORMATION SERVICE. SELECTED MORBIDITY DATA FOR PRIVATELY FUNDED HOSPITALS (ONLINE). *see* HEALTH FACILITIES AND ADMINISTRATION—Abstracting, Bibliographies, Statistics

NEW ZEALAND QUALIFICATIONS AUTHORITY. SECONDARY QUALIFICATION STATISTICS. *see* EDUCATION—School Organization And Administration

NEW ZEALAND. STATISTICS NEW ZEALAND. ABORTION STATISTICS (YEAR). *see* MEDICAL SCIENCES—Obstetrics And Gynecology

NEW ZEALAND. STATISTICS NEW ZEALAND. ACCOMMODATION SURVEY. *see* HOTELS AND RESTAURANTS

NEW ZEALAND. STATISTICS NEW ZEALAND. AGRICULTURAL PRODUCTION STATISTICS. *see* AGRICULTURE

NEW ZEALAND. STATISTICS NEW ZEALAND. ALCOHOL AND TOBACCO AVAILABLE FOR CONSUMPTION. *see* BEVERAGES

NEW ZEALAND. STATISTICS NEW ZEALAND. CENSUS OF INTERNATIONAL TRADE IN SERVICES AND ROYALTIES. *see* BUSINESS AND ECONOMICS—International Commerce

NEW ZEALAND. STATISTICS NEW ZEALAND. CENSUS REPORTS. BIRTHPLACES AND ETHNIC ORIGIN. *see* POPULATION STUDIES—Abstracting, Bibliographies, Statistics

NEW ZEALAND. STATISTICS NEW ZEALAND. CENSUS REPORTS. FAMILIES AND HOUSEHOLDS. *see* POPULATION STUDIES—Abstracting, Bibliographies, Statistics

NEW ZEALAND. STATISTICS NEW ZEALAND. CENSUS REPORTS. INCOMES. *see* POPULATION STUDIES—Abstracting, Bibliographies, Statistics

NEW ZEALAND. STATISTICS NEW ZEALAND. CENSUS REPORTS. POPULATION AND DWELLING STATISTICS. *see* POPULATION STUDIES—Abstracting, Bibliographies, Statistics

NEW ZEALAND. STATISTICS NEW ZEALAND. CENSUS REPORTS. POPULATION STRUCTURE AND INTERNAL MIGRATION. *see* POPULATION STUDIES—Abstracting, Bibliographies, Statistics

NEW ZEALAND. STATISTICS NEW ZEALAND. CENSUS REPORTS. WORK. *see* POPULATION STUDIES—Abstracting, Bibliographies, Statistics

NEW ZEALAND. STATISTICS NEW ZEALAND. CONSUMER EXPENDITURE. *see* BUSINESS AND ECONOMICS—Abstracting, Bibliographies, Statistics

NEW ZEALAND. STATISTICS NEW ZEALAND. DEMOGRAPHIC TRENDS. *see* POPULATION STUDIES—Abstracting, Bibliographies, Statistics

310 NZL

NEW ZEALAND. STATISTICS NEW ZEALAND. DIRECT INVESTMENT STATISTICS BY COUNTRY (YEAR). Text in English. a., latest 1998. **Document type:** *Government.*

Published by: Statistics New Zealand/Te Tari Tatau, Statistics House, The Blvd, Harbour Quays, PO Box 2922, Wellington, 6140, New Zealand. TEL 64-4-9314600, FAX 64-4-9314610, info@stats.govt.nz, http://www.stats.govt.nz.

NEW ZEALAND. STATISTICS NEW ZEALAND. DISTRICT HEALTH BOARD FINANCIAL STATISTICS. *see* BUSINESS AND ECONOMICS—Public Finance, Taxation

NEW ZEALAND. STATISTICS NEW ZEALAND. ECONOMIC SURVEY OF MANUFACTURING. *see* BUSINESS AND ECONOMICS—Production Of Goods And Services

NEW ZEALAND. STATISTICS NEW ZEALAND. FIGURES AND FACTS (YEAR); a resource for schools. *see* EDUCATION

NEW ZEALAND. STATISTICS NEW ZEALAND. FISH MONETARY STOCK ACCOUNT. *see* FISH AND FISHERIES—Abstracting, Bibliographies, Statistics

NEW ZEALAND. STATISTICS NEW ZEALAND. FOOD PRICE INDEX. *see* FOOD AND FOOD INDUSTRIES

NEW ZEALAND. STATISTICS NEW ZEALAND. HOUSEHOLD HEALTH SURVEY. *see* PUBLIC HEALTH AND SAFETY—Abstracting, Bibliographies, Statistics

NEW ZEALAND. STATISTICS NEW ZEALAND. HOUSEHOLD LABOUR FORCE SURVEY. *see* BUSINESS AND ECONOMICS—Labor And Industrial Relations

NEW ZEALAND. STATISTICS NEW ZEALAND. INTERNATIONAL TRAVEL AND MIGRATION. *see* POPULATION STUDIES

NEW ZEALAND. STATISTICS NEW ZEALAND. KEY STATISTICS. *see* BUSINESS AND ECONOMICS—Abstracting, Bibliographies, Statistics

NEW ZEALAND. STATISTICS NEW ZEALAND. LABOUR COST INDEX (ALL LABOUR COSTS). *see* BUSINESS AND ECONOMICS—Labor And Industrial Relations

NEW ZEALAND. STATISTICS NEW ZEALAND. LABOUR COST INDEX (SALARY AND WAGE RATES). *see* BUSINESS AND ECONOMICS—Labor And Industrial Relations

NEW ZEALAND. STATISTICS NEW ZEALAND. LABOUR MARKET STATISTICS. *see* BUSINESS AND ECONOMICS—Abstracting, Bibliographies, Statistics

310 NZL ISSN 1178-0304

NEW ZEALAND. STATISTICS NEW ZEALAND. LOCAL AUTHORITY STATISTICS (ONLINE). Text in English. q.

Media: Online - full text.

Published by: Statistics New Zealand/Te Tari Tatau, Statistics House, The Blvd, Harbour Quays, PO Box 2922, Wellington, 6140, New Zealand. TEL 64-4-9314600, FAX 64-4-9314610, info@stats.govt.nz.

310 NZL

NEW ZEALAND. STATISTICS NEW ZEALAND. MARRIAGES, CIVIL UNIONS AND DIVORCES. Text in English. a. stat. **Document type:** *Government.* **Description:** Contains statistics on the number of marriages and divorces (marriage dissolutions) registered in New Zealand, and selected marriage and divorce indices.

Former titles (until 2005): New Zealand. Statistics New Zealand. Marriage and Divorces; (until 2002): New Zealand. Statistics New Zealand. Marriage and Divorce Statistics

Related titles: Online - full text ed.

Published by: Statistics New Zealand/Te Tari Tatau, Statistics House, The Blvd, Harbour Quays, PO Box 2922, Wellington, 6140, New Zealand. TEL 64-4-9314600, FAX 64-4-9314610, info@stats.govt.nz.

NEW ZEALAND. STATISTICS NEW ZEALAND. NATIONAL ACCOUNTS. *see* BUSINESS AND ECONOMICS—Abstracting, Bibliographies, Statistics

NEW ZEALAND. STATISTICS NEW ZEALAND. NEW ZEALAND INCOME SURVEY. *see* BUSINESS AND ECONOMICS—Abstracting, Bibliographies, Statistics

NEW ZEALAND. STATISTICS NEW ZEALAND. NEW ZEALAND LIFE TABLES. *see* INSURANCE—Abstracting, Bibliographies, Statistics

NEW ZEALAND. STATISTICS NEW ZEALAND. OVERSEAS MERCHANDISE TRADE. *see* BUSINESS AND ECONOMICS—International Commerce

NEW ZEALAND. STATISTICS NEW ZEALAND. OVERSEAS TRADE IN SERVICES PRICE INDEX. *see* BUSINESS AND ECONOMICS—International Commerce

NEW ZEALAND. STATISTICS NEW ZEALAND. PRODUCERS PRICE INDEX. *see* BUSINESS AND ECONOMICS—Abstracting, Bibliographies, Statistics

NEW ZEALAND. STATISTICS NEW ZEALAND. PRODUCTIVITY STATISTICS. *see* BUSINESS AND ECONOMICS—Production Of Goods And Services

NEW ZEALAND. STATISTICS NEW ZEALAND. QUARTERLY EMPLOYMENT SURVEY. *see* BUSINESS AND ECONOMICS—Abstracting, Bibliographies, Statistics

NEW ZEALAND. STATISTICS NEW ZEALAND. RETAIL TRADE SURVEY. *see* BUSINESS AND ECONOMICS—Abstracting, Bibliographies, Statistics

NEW ZEALAND. STATISTICS NEW ZEALAND. SCREEN INDUSTRY IN NEW ZEALAND. *see* MOTION PICTURES—Abstracting, Bibliographies, Statistics

NEW ZEALAND. STATISTICS NEW ZEALAND. WHOLESALE TRADE SURVEY. *see* BUSINESS AND ECONOMICS—Abstracting, Bibliographies, Statistics

NEW ZEALAND. STATISTICS NEW ZEALAND. WORK STOPPAGES. *see* BUSINESS AND ECONOMICS—Abstracting, Bibliographies, Statistics

NEWS. REAL EARNINGS IN (YEAR). *see* BUSINESS AND ECONOMICS—Economic Situation And Conditions

NEWSPAPER CIRCULATION RATE BOOK. *see* ADVERTISING AND PUBLIC RELATIONS—Abstracting, Bibliographies, Statistics

318.6 NIC

NICARAGUA EN CIFRAS. Text in Spanish. irreg., latest 1991. **Document type:** *Government.*

Published by: Instituto Nacional de Estadisticas y Censos, Apartado Postal 4031, Managua, Nicaragua. Circ: 2,000.

316.6 NER

NIGER. DIRECTION DE LA STATISTIQUE ET DES COMPTES NATIONAUX. BULLETIN TRIMESTRIEL DE STATISTIQUE. Text in French. q. illus.

Former titles: Niger. Ministere du Developpement et de la Cooperation. Direction de la Statistique. Bulletin de Statistique; Niger. Service de la Statistique. Bulletin Trimestriel de Statistique (0545-9516)

Published by: Direction de la Statistique et des Comptes Nationaux, Ministere du Plan, Niamey, Niger.

NIGERIA. FEDERAL MINISTRY OF LABOUR AND PRODUCTIVITY. QUARTERLY BULLETIN OF LABOUR STATISTICS. *see* BUSINESS AND ECONOMICS—Abstracting, Bibliographies, Statistics

316 NGA ISSN 0078-0626
HA1977.N5

NIGERIA. FEDERAL OFFICE OF STATISTICS. ANNUAL ABSTRACT OF STATISTICS. Text in English. a. USD 65 (effective 1997). **Document type:** *Government.*

Related titles: Microfiche ed.: (from PQC).

Published by: Federal Office of Statistics, Dissemination Division, c/o Mrs. M.T. Osita, 36-38 Broad St, PMB 12528, Lagos, Nigeria. TEL 234-1-2601710-4.

NIGERIA. FEDERAL OFFICE OF STATISTICS. REVIEW OF EXTERNAL TRADE. *see* BUSINESS AND ECONOMICS—Abstracting, Bibliographies, Statistics

NIGERIA. NATIONAL INTEGRATED SURVEY OF HOUSEHOLDS. INDUSTRIAL SURVEY. *see* BUSINESS AND ECONOMICS—Abstracting, Bibliographies, Statistics

NIGERIA. NATIONAL INTEGRATED SURVEY OF HOUSEHOLDS. REPORT ON GENERAL CONSUMER SURVEY. *see* BUSINESS AND ECONOMICS—Abstracting, Bibliographies, Statistics

NIGERIA. NATIONAL INTEGRATED SURVEY OF HOUSEHOLDS. REPORT ON GENERAL HOUSEHOLD. *see* BUSINESS AND ECONOMICS—Abstracting, Bibliographies, Statistics

NIGERIA. NATIONAL INTEGRATED SURVEY OF HOUSEHOLDS. REPORT ON GENERAL HOUSEHOLD SURVEY. *see* HOUSING AND URBAN PLANNING—Abstracting, Bibliographies, Statistics

NIGERIA. NATIONAL INTEGRATED SURVEY OF HOUSEHOLDS. REPORT ON NATIONAL CONSUMER SURVEY. *see* BUSINESS AND ECONOMICS—Abstracting, Bibliographies, Statistics

NIGERIA. NATIONAL INTEGRATED SURVEY OF HOUSEHOLDS. REPORT ON URBAN HOUSEHOLD SURVEY. *see* HOUSING AND URBAN PLANNING—Abstracting, Bibliographies, Statistics

NIGERIA. NATIONAL UNIVERSITIES COMMISSION. STATISTICAL DIGEST. *see* EDUCATION—Abstracting, Bibliographies, Statistics

NIGERIA TRADE SUMMARY. *see* BUSINESS AND ECONOMICS—International Commerce

NIHON ENGEI NOGYO KYODOKUMIAI RENGOKAI. KAJU TOKEI/ JAPAN FRUIT GROWERS COOPERATIVE ASSOCIATION. FRUIT TREE STATISTICS. *see* AGRICULTURE—Abstracting, Bibliographies, Statistics

NIHON KODO KEIRYO GAKKAI TAIKAI HAPPYO RONBUN SHOROKUSHU. *see* SOCIOLOGY—Abstracting, Bibliographies, Statistics

NIHON NO JINKO/POPULATION CENSUS OF JAPAN. *see* POPULATION STUDIES—Abstracting, Bibliographies, Statistics

315.2 JPN ISSN 0286-1402
HA1841

NIHON NO TOKEI (YEAR)/STATISTICS OF JAPAN (YEAR). Text in Japanese. 1956. m. JPY 1,848 (effective 2000). **Document type:** *Government.*

Related titles: Diskette ed.: JPY 10,500 per issue (effective 2000).

Published by: Japan. Ministry of Internal Affairs and Communications. Statistics Bureau/Somucho. Tokeikyoku, 19-1 Wakamatsu-cho, Shinjyuku-ku, Tokyo, 162-8668, Japan. TEL 81-3-5273-2020. **Subscr. to:** Japan Statistical Association, Meito Shinjuku Bldg, 6th Fl, 2-4-6 Shinjuku-ku, Tokyo 169-0073, Japan. TEL 81-3-53323151, http://www.jstat.or.jp/.

315 JPN ISSN 0389-9004

NIHON TOKEI NENKAN. Text in English, Japanese. 1949. a. **Document type:** *Yearbook, Government.*

Related titles: Online - full text ed.: free.

Indexed: RASB.

Published by: (Japan. Ministry of Internal Affairs and Communications. Statistical Research and Training Institute/Somucho. Tokeikenshujo), Japan. Ministry of Internal Affairs and Communications. Statistics Bureau/Somucho. Tokeikyoko, 19-1 Wakamatsu-cho, Shinjyuku-ku, Tokyo, 162-8668, Japan. TEL 81-3-5273-2020. R&P Akihiko Ito. Circ: 800. **Subscr. to:** Japan Statistical Association, Meito Shinjuku Bldg, 6th Fl, 2-4-6 Shinjuku-ku, Tokyo 169-0073, Japan. TEL 81-3-53323151, http://www.jstat.or.jp/.

NOEKKELTALL FOR HELSESEKTOREN. *see* SOCIAL SERVICES AND WELFARE—Abstracting, Bibliographies, Statistics

NONFATAL OCCUPATIONAL INJURIES AND ILLNESSES IN CALIFORNIA. *see* OCCUPATIONAL HEALTH AND SAFETY—Abstracting, Bibliographies, Statistics

314.8 DNK ISSN 0908-4339

NORDEN I TAL. Text in Swedish. 1985. a. **Document type:** *Government.*

Formerly (until 1993): Norden (0903-7721)

Related titles: Online - full text ed.; ◆ English ed.: The Nordic Countries in Figures. ISSN 0908-4398; ◆ Finnish ed.: Pohjola Numeroina. ISSN 1601-622X.

Published by: Nordisk Ministerraad/Nordic Council of Ministers, Store Strandstraede 18, Copenhagen K, 1255, Denmark. TEL 45-33-960200, FAX 45-33-960202, nmr@norden.org.

314.8 DNK ISSN 0908-4398

THE NORDIC COUNTRIES IN FIGURES. Text in English. 1987. a. free. back issues avail. **Document type:** *Government.*

Formerly (until 1993): The Nordic Countries (0903-773X)

Related titles: Online - full text ed.; ◆ Swedish ed.: Norden i Tal. ISSN 0908-4339; ◆ Finnish ed.: Pohjola Numeroina. ISSN 1601-622X.

Published by: Nordisk Ministerraad/Nordic Council of Ministers, Store Strandstraede 18, Copenhagen K, 1255, Denmark. TEL 45-33-960200, FAX 45-33-960202, nmr@norden.org.

314 DNK ISSN 1398-0017
HA1461

NORDIC STATISTICAL YEARBOOK/NORDISK STATISTISK AARSBOK. Text in English, Swedish. 1962. a. price varies. **Document type:** *Government.* **Description:** Presents statistical information on the Nordic countries and regions of Denmark, Finland, Iceland, Norway and Sweden, Greenland, the Faroe Islands and Aaland.

Formerly (until 1997): Yearbook of Nordic Statisticks (0078-1088)

Related titles: CD-ROM ed.; Microfiche ed.: (from CIS); Online - full text ed.

Indexed: IIS, RASB.

Published by: Nordisk Ministerraad/Nordic Council of Ministers, Store Strandstraede 18, Copenhagen K, 1255, Denmark. TEL 45-33-960200, FAX 45-33-960202, nmr@norden.org.

310 DEU ISSN 0468-656X
HA1320.N6

NORDRHEIN-WESTFALEN. STATISTISCHES JAHRBUCH. Text in German. 1949. a. price varies. **Document type:** *Yearbook, Government.*

Formerly: Duesseldorf. Statistisches Jahrbuch

—BLDSC (8454.826000), GNLM.

Published by: Information und Technik Nordrhein-Westfalen, Mauerstr 51, Duesseldorf, 40476, Germany. TEL 49-211-944901, FAX 49-211-442006, poststelle@lds.nrw.de, http://www.it.nrw.de. Circ: 2,000.

NORGES OFFISIELLE STATISTIKK/OFFICIAL STATISTICS OF NORWAY. *see* BUSINESS AND ECONOMICS—Abstracting, Bibliographies, Statistics

NORIN SUISAN TOKEI GEPPO/MONTHLY STATISTICS ON AGRICULTURE, FORESTRY AND FISHERIES. *see* AGRICULTURE—Abstracting, Bibliographies, Statistics

NORIN SUISAN TOSHO SHIRYO GEPPO. *see* AGRICULTURE—Abstracting, Bibliographies, Statistics

NORMTALLSUNDERSOEKELSEN. *see* PUBLISHING AND BOOK TRADE—Abstracting, Bibliographies, Statistics

001.4021 NOR ISSN 1500-0869
Q180.N6

DET NORSKE FORSKNINGS- OG INNOVASJONSSYSTEMET - STATISTIKK OG INDIKATORER. Text in Norwegian. 1997. biennial. free. back issues avail. **Document type:** *Government.*

Related titles: Online - full text ed.; ◆ English ed.: Report on Science & Technology Indicators for Norway. ISSN 1503-0857.

Published by: Norges Forskningsraad/The Research Council of Norway, P O Box 2700, St Hanshaugen, Oslo, 0131, Norway. TEL 47-22-037000, FAX 47-22-037001, post@forskningsradet.no, http://www.forskningsradet.no.

NORTH CAROLINA VITAL STATISTICS. *see* POPULATION STUDIES—Abstracting, Bibliographies, Statistics

NORTH CAROLINA WEATHER & CROPS REPORT. *see* AGRICULTURE—Abstracting, Bibliographies, Statistics

NORTH DAKOTA AGRICULTURAL STATISTICS. *see* AGRICULTURE—Abstracting, Bibliographies, Statistics

NORTH DAKOTA CITIES & COUNTIES GRAPHIC PERFORMANCE ANALYSIS. *see* PUBLIC ADMINISTRATION—Abstracting, Bibliographies, Statistics

NORTH DAKOTA CROP, LIVESTOCK & WEATHER REPORT. *see* AGRICULTURE—Abstracting, Bibliographies, Statistics

NORTH DAKOTA. DEPARTMENT OF PUBLIC INSTRUCTION. BIENNIAL REPORT OF THE SUPERINTENDENT OF PUBLIC INSTRUCTION. *see* EDUCATION—Abstracting, Bibliographies, Statistics

NORTH DAKOTA GRAIN AND OILSEED TRANSPORTATION STATISTICS. *see* AGRICULTURE—Abstracting, Bibliographies, Statistics

NORTH DAKOTA. JUDICIAL SYSTEM. ANNUAL REPORT. *see* LAW—Abstracting, Bibliographies, Statistics

NORTH PACIFIC ANADROMOUS FISH COMMISSION. STATISTICAL YEARBOOK. *see* FISH AND FISHERIES—Abstracting, Bibliographies, Statistics

NORTHEAST CITIES & COUNTIES GRAPHIC PERFORMANCE ANALYSIS. *see* PUBLIC ADMINISTRATION—Abstracting, Bibliographies, Statistics

NORTHERN IRELAND. DEPARTMENT OF EDUCATION. EDUCATION STATISTICS. *see* EDUCATION—Abstracting, Bibliographies, Statistics

NORTHERN TERRITORY. DEPARTMENT OF LANDS AND PLANNING. ANNUAL TRAFFIC REPORT. *see* TRANSPORTATION—Roads And Traffic

NORTHLAND DISTRICT CRIME STATISTICS. *see* CRIMINOLOGY AND LAW ENFORCEMENT—Abstracting, Bibliographies, Statistics

NORTHWEST CITIES & COUNTIES GRAPHIC PERFORMANCE ANALYSIS. *see* PUBLIC ADMINISTRATION—Abstracting, Bibliographies, Statistics

310 CAN ISSN 1707-5025
NORTHWEST TERRITORIES (YEAR) BY THE NUMBERS. Text in English. 19??. a.
Formerly (until 1998): Western N W T (Year) by the Numbers (1493-8669); Which superseded in part (in 1997): Northwest Territories (Year) by the Numbers (0847-1886)
Published by: Bureau of Statistics, Northwest Territories, Box 1320, Yellowknife, NT X1A 2L9, Canada. TEL 867-873-7147, FAX 867-873-0275, info@stats.gov.nt.ca.

NORTHWEST TERRITORIES. BUREAU OF STATISTICS. STATISTICS QUARTERLY. *see* BUSINESS AND ECONOMICS—Abstracting, Bibliographies, Statistics

NORWAY. STATISTISK SENTRALBYRAA. ARBEIDSUNDERSOEKELSEN. *see* BUSINESS AND ECONOMICS—Abstracting, Bibliographies, Statistics

NORWAY. STATISTISK SENTRALBYRAA. FISKERISTATISTIKK. *see* FISH AND FISHERIES—Abstracting, Bibliographies, Statistics

330.021 NOR ISSN 0809-733X
NORWAY. STATISTISK SENTRALBYRAA. FORSKNINGSAVDELINGEN. DISCUSSION PAPERS. Text in Norwegian, English. 1985. irreg. back issues avail. **Document type:** *Monographic series, Government.*
Formerly (until 1993): Norway. Statistisk Sentralbyraa. Discussion Paper (0803-074X)
Related titles: Online - full text ed.
Indexed: ASFA, B21, ESPM.
Published by: Statistisk Sentralbyraa/Statistics Norway, Kongensgate 6, P O Box 8131, Dep, Oslo, 0033, Norway. TEL 47-21-090000, FAX 47-21-094973, ssb@ssb.no.

NORWAY. STATISTISK SENTRALBYRAA. FRAMSKRIVING AV FOLKEMENGDEN/NORWAY. CENTRAL BUREAU OF STATISTICS. POPULATION PROJECTIONS: REGIONAL FIGURES. *see* POPULATION STUDIES—Abstracting, Bibliographies, Statistics

NORWAY. STATISTISK SENTRALBYRAA. HELSESTATISTIKK/ STATISTICS NORWAY. HEALTH STATISTICS. *see* PUBLIC HEALTH AND SAFETY—Abstracting, Bibliographies, Statistics

NORWAY. STATISTISK SENTRALBYRAA. INNENLANDSKE TRANSPORTYTELSER. *see* TRANSPORTATION—Abstracting, Bibliographies, Statistics

NORWAY. STATISTISK SENTRALBYRAA. JORDBRUKSSTATISTIKK/ STATISTICS NORWAY. AGRICULTURAL STATISTICS. *see* AGRICULTURE—Abstracting, Bibliographies, Statistics

NORWAY. STATISTISK SENTRALBYRAA. KOMMUNESTYREVALGET/ STATISTICS NORWAY. MUNICIPAL AND COUNTY ELECTIONS. *see* PUBLIC ADMINISTRATION—Abstracting, Bibliographies, Statistics

NORWAY. STATISTISK SENTRALBYRAA. KRIMINALSTATISTIKK/ STATISTICS NORWAY. CRIME STATISTICS. *see* CRIMINOLOGY AND LAW ENFORCEMENT—Abstracting, Bibliographies, Statistics

NORWAY. STATISTISK SENTRALBYRAA. KVARTALSVIS NASJONALREGNSKAP. *see* PUBLIC ADMINISTRATION—Abstracting, Bibliographies, Statistics

NORWAY. STATISTISK SENTRALBYRAA. LEVEKAARSUNDERSOEKELSEN. *see* SOCIOLOGY—Abstracting, Bibliographies, Statistics

NORWAY. STATISTISK SENTRALBYRAA. LOENNSSTATISTIKK/ STATISTICS NORWAY. WAGE STATISTICS. *see* BUSINESS AND ECONOMICS—Abstracting, Bibliographies, Statistics

NORWAY. STATISTISK SENTRALBYRAA. NASJONALREGNSKAPSSTATISTIKK. INSTITUSJONELT SEKTORREGNSKAP/NATIONAL ACCOUNTS STATISTICS. *see* BUSINESS AND ECONOMICS—Abstracting, Bibliographies, Statistics

NORWAY. STATISTISK SENTRALBYRAA. NASJONALREGNSKAPSSTATISTIKK. PRODUKSJON, ANVENDELSE OG SYSSELSETTING. *see* PUBLIC ADMINISTRATION—Abstracting, Bibliographies, Statistics

314 NOR ISSN 1891-5906
▼ **NORWAY. STATISTISK SENTRALBYRAA. NOTATER/DOCUMENTS.** Text in English. 2010. irreg. price varies. back issues avail. **Document type:** *Monographic series, Government.*
Formed by the merger of (1994-2010): Norway. Statistisk Sentralbyraa. Documents (0805-9411); (1993-2010): Norway. Statistisk Sentralbyraa. Notater (0806-3745); Which was formerly (1979-1993): Norway. Statistisk Sentralbyraa. Interne Notater (0806-3753)
Related titles: Online - full text ed.
Published by: Statistisk Sentralbyraa/Statistics Norway, Kongensgate 6, P O Box 8131, Dep, Oslo, 0033, Norway. TEL 47-21-090000, FAX 47-21-094973, ssb@ssb.no.

NORWAY. STATISTISK SENTRALBYRAA. OEKONOMISKE ANALYSER. *see* BUSINESS AND ECONOMICS—Economic Situation And Conditions

NORWAY. STATISTISK SENTRALBYRAA. PASIENTSTATISTIKK/ PATIENT STATISTICS. *see* HEALTH FACILITIES AND ADMINISTRATION—Abstracting, Bibliographies, Statistics

314.822 NOR
NORWAY. STATISTISK SENTRALBYRAA. REGIONALSTATISTIKK. AKERSHUS OG OSLO (ONLINE). Text in Norwegian. 1974. m. free. back issues avail. **Document type:** *Government.*
Former titles (until 2001): Norway. Statistisk Sentralbyraa. Regionalstatistikk. Akershus og Oslo (Print) (0804-2829); (until 1989): Norway. Statistisk Sentralyraa. Nye Distriktstall. Akershus og Oslo (0800-8175)
Media: Online - full content.
Published by: Statistisk Sentralbyraa/Statistics Norway, Kongensgate 6, P O Box 8131, Dep, Oslo, 0033, Norway. TEL 47-22-86-45-00, FAX 47-22-86-49-73.

314.831 NOR
NORWAY. STATISTISK SENTRALBYRAA. REGIONALSTATISTIKK. AUST-AGDER (ONLINE). Text in Norwegian. 1974. m. free. charts. back issues avail. **Document type:** *Government.*
Former titles (until 2001): Norway. Statistisk Sentralbyraa. Regionalstatistikk. Aust-Agder (Print) (0804-2837); (until 1989): Norway. Statistisk Sentralbyraa. Nye Distriktstall. Aust-Agder (0800-8183)
Media: Online - full content.
Published by: Statistisk Sentralbyraa/Statistics Norway, Kongensgate 6, P O Box 8131, Dep, Oslo, 0033, Norway. TEL 47-21-090000, FAX 47-21-094973, ssb@ssb.no.

314.826 NOR
NORWAY. STATISTISK SENTRALBYRAA. REGIONALSTATISTIKK. BUSKERUD (ONLINE). Text in Norwegian. 1974. m. free. charts, back issues avail. **Document type:** *Government.*
Former titles (until 2001): Norway. Statistisk Sentralbyraa. Regionalstatistikk. Buskerud (Print) (0804-2845); (until 1989): Norway. Statistisk Sentralbyraa. Nye Distriktstall. Buskerud (0800-8191)
Media: Online - full content.
Published by: Statistisk Sentralbyraa/Statistics Norway, Kongensgate 6, P O Box 8131, Dep, Oslo, 0033, Norway. TEL 47-21-090000, FAX 47-21-094973, ssb@ssb.no.

314.846 NOR
NORWAY. STATISTISK SENTRALBYRAA. REGIONALSTATISTIKK. FINNMARK (ONLINE). Text in Norwegian. 1974. m. charts. back issues avail. **Document type:** *Government.*
Former titles (until 2001): Norway. Statistisk Sentralbyraa. Regionalstatistikk. Finnmark (Print) (0804-287X); (until 1989): Norway. Statistisk Sentralbyraa. Nye Distriktstall. Finnmark (0800-8221)
Media: Online - full content.
Published by: Statistisk Sentralbyraa/Statistics Norway, Kongensgate 6, P O Box 8131, Dep, Oslo, 0033, Norway. TEL 47-21-090000, FAX 47-21-094973, ssb@ssb.no.

314.824 NOR
NORWAY. STATISTISK SENTRALBYRAA. REGIONALSTATISTIKK. HEDMARK (ONLINE). Text in Norwegian. 1974. m. free. charts. back issues avail. **Document type:** *Government.*
Former titles (until 2001): Norway. Statistisk Sentralbyraa. Regionalstatistikk. Hedmark (Print) (0804-2853); (until 1989): Norway. Statistisk Sentralbyraa. Nye Distriktstall. Hedmark (0800-8205)
Media: Online - full content.
Published by: Statistisk Sentralbyraa/Statistics Norway, Kongensgate 6, P O Box 8131, Dep, Oslo, 0033, Norway. TEL 47-21-090000, FAX 47-21-094973, ssb@ssb.no.

314.836 NOR
NORWAY. STATISTISK SENTRALBYRAA. REGIONALSTATISTIKK. HORDALAND (ONLINE). Text in Norwegian. 1974. m. free. charts. back issues avail. **Document type:** *Government.*
Former titles (until 2001): Norway. Statistisk Sentralbyraa. Regionalstatistikk. Hordaland (Print) (0804-2861); (until 1989): Norway. Statistisk Sentralbyraa. Nye Distriktstall. Hordaland (0800-8213)
Media: Online - full content.
Published by: Statistisk Sentralbyraa/Statistics Norway, Kongensgate 6, P O Box 8131, Dep, Oslo, 0033, Norway. TEL 47-21-090000, FAX 47-21-094973, ssb@ssb.no.

314.839 NOR
NORWAY. STATISTISK SENTRALBYRAA. REGIONALSTATISTIKK. MOERE OG ROMSDAL (ONLINE). Text in Norwegian. 1974. m. free. charts. back issues avail. **Document type:** *Government.*
Former titles (until 2001): Norway. Statistisk Sentralbyraa. Regionalstatistikk. Moere og Romsdal (Print) (0804-2888); (until 1989): Norway. Statistisk Sentralbyraa. Nye Distriktstall. Moere og Romsdal (0800-823X)
Media: Online - full content.
Published by: Statistisk Sentralbyraa/Statistics Norway, Kongensgate 6, P O Box 8131, Dep, Oslo, 0033, Norway. TEL 47-21-090000, FAX 47-21-094973, ssb@ssb.no.

314.842 NOR
NORWAY. STATISTISK SENTRALBYRAA. REGIONALSTATISTIKK. NORD-TROENDELAG (ONLINE). Text in Norwegian. 1974. m. free. charts. back issues avail. **Document type:** *Government.*
Former titles (until 2001): Norway. Statistisk Sentralbyraa. Regionalstatistikk. Nord-Troendelag (Print) (0804-290X); (until 1989): Norway. Statistisk Sentralbyraa. Nye Distriktstall. Nord-Troendelag (0800-8256)
Media: Online - full content.
Published by: Statistisk Sentralbyraa/Statistics Norway, Kongensgate 6, P O Box 8131, Dep, Oslo, 0033, Norway. TEL 47-21-090000, FAX 47-21-094973.

314.844 NOR
NORWAY. STATISTISK SENTRALBYRAA. REGIONALSTATISTIKK. NORDLAND (ONLINE). Text in Norwegian. 1974. m. free. back issues avail. **Document type:** *Government.*
Former titles (until 2001): Norway. Statistisk Sentralbyraa. Regionalstatistikk. Nordland (Print) (0804-2896); (until 1989): Norway. Statistisk Sentralbyraa. Nye Distriktstall. Nordland (0800-8248)
Media: Online - full content.
Published by: Statistisk Sentralbyraa/Statistics Norway, Kongensgate 6, P O Box 8131, Dep, Oslo, 0033, Norway. TEL 47-21-090000, FAX 47-21-094973.

314.823 NOR
NORWAY. STATISTISK SENTRALBYRAA. REGIONALSTATISTIKK. OESTFOLD (ONLINE). Text in Norwegian. 1974. m. free. back issues avail. **Document type:** *Government.*
Former titles (until 2001): Norway. Statistisk Sentralbyraa. Regionalstatistikk. Oestfold (Print) (0804-2985); (until 1989): Norway. Statistisk Sentralbyraa. Nye Distriktstall. Oestfold (0800-8345)
Media: Online - full text.
Published by: Statistisk Sentralbyraa/Statistics Norway, Kongensgate 6, P O Box 8131, Dep, Oslo, 0033, Norway. TEL 47-21-090000, FAX 47-21-094973, ssb@ssb.no.

314.825 NOR
NORWAY. STATISTISK SENTRALBYRAA. REGIONALSTATISTIKK. OPPLAND (ONLINE). Text in Norwegian. 1974. m. free. charts. back issues avail. **Document type:** *Government.*
Former titles (until 2001): Norway. Statistisk Sentralbyraa. Regionalstatistikk. Oppland (Print) (0804-2918); (until 1989): Norway. Statistisk Sentralbyraa. Nye Distriktstall. Oppland (0800-8264)
Media: Online - full content.
Published by: Statistisk Sentralbyraa/Statistics Norway, Kongensgate 6, P O Box 8131, Dep, Oslo, 0033, Norway. TEL 47-21-090000, FAX 47-21-094973, ssb@ssb.no.

314.834 NOR ISSN 0804-2926
NORWAY. STATISTISK SENTRALBYRAA. REGIONALSTATISTIKK. ROGALAND. Text in Norwegian. 1974. m. free. back issues avail. **Document type:** *Government.*
Formerly (until 1989): Norway. Statistisk Sentralbyraa. Nye Distriktstall. Rogaland (0800-8272)
Media: Online - full content.
Published by: Statistisk Sentralbyraa/Statistics Norway, Kongensgate 6, P O Box 8131, Dep, Oslo, 0033, Norway. TEL 47-21-090000, FAX 47-21-094973, ssb@ssb.no.

314.841 NOR
NORWAY. STATISTISK SENTRALBYRAA. REGIONALSTATISTIKK. SOER-TROENDELAG (ONLINE). Text in Norwegian. 1974. m. free. charts. **Document type:** *Government.*
Former titles (until 2001): Norway. Statistisk Sentralbyraa. Regionalstatistikk. Soer-Troendelag (Print) (0804-3302); (until 1989): Norway. Statistisk Sentralbyraa. Nye Distriktstall. Soer-Troendelag (0800-8299)
Media: Online - full content.
Published by: Statistisk Sentralbyraa/Statistics Norway, Kongensgate 6, P O Box 8131, Dep, Oslo, 0033, Norway. TEL 47-21-090000, FAX 47-21-094973, ssb@ssb.no.

314.838 NOR
NORWAY. STATISTISK SENTRALBYRAA. REGIONALSTATISTIKK. SOGN OG FJORDANE (ONLINE). Text in Norwegian. 1974. m. free. back issues avail. **Document type:** *Government.*
Former titles (until 2001): Norway. Statistisk Sentralbyraa. Regionalstatistikk. Sogn og Fjordane (Print) (0804-2934); (until 1989): Norway. Statistisk Sentralbyraa. Nye Distriktstall. Sogn og Fjordane (0800-8280)
Media: Online - full content.
Published by: Statistisk Sentralbyraa/Statistics Norway, Kongensgate 6, P O Box 8131, Dep, Oslo, 0033, Norway. TEL 47-21-090000, FAX 47-21-094973, ssb@ssb.no.

314.828 NOR
NORWAY. STATISTISK SENTRALBYRAA. REGIONALSTATISTIKK. TELEMARK (ONLINE). Text in Norwegian. 1974. m. free. **Document type:** *Government.*
Former titles (until 2001): Norway. Statistisk Sentralbyraa. Regionalstatistikk. Telemark (Print) (0804-2942); (until 1989): Norway. Statistikal Sentralbyraa. Nye Distriktstall. Telemark (0800-8302)
Media: Online - full content.
Published by: Statistisk Sentralbyraa/Statistics Norway, Kongensgate 6, P O Box 8131, Dep, Oslo, 0033, Norway. TEL 47-21-090000, FAX 47-21-094973, ssb@ssb.no.

314.845 NOR
NORWAY. STATISTISK SENTRALBYRAA. REGIONALSTATISTIKK. TROMS (ONLINE). Text in Norwegian. 1974. m. free. back issues avail. **Document type:** *Government.*
Former titles (until 2001): Norway. Statistisk Sentralbyraa. Regionalstatistikk. Troms (Print) (0804-2950); (until 1998): Norway. Statistisk Sentralbyraa. Nye Distriktstall. Troms (0800-8310)
Media: Online - full content.
Published by: Statistisk Sentralbyraa/Statistics Norway, Kongensgate 6, P O Box 8131, Dep, Oslo, 0033, Norway. TEL 47-21-090000, FAX 47-21-094973, ssb@ssb.no.

314.832 NOR
NORWAY. STATISTISK SENTRALBYRAA. REGIONALSTATISTIKK. VEST-AGDER (ONLINE). Text in Norwegian. 1974. m. free. back issues avail. **Document type:** *Government.*
Former titles (until 2001): Norway. Statistisk Sentralbyraa. Regionalstatistikk. Vest-Agder (Print) (0804-2969); (until 1989): Norway. Statistisk Sentralbyraa. Nye Distriktstall. Vest-Agder (0800-8329)
Media: Online - full content.
Published by: Statistisk Sentralbyraa/Statistics Norway, Kongensgate 6, P O Box 8131, Dep, Oslo, 0033, Norway. TEL 47-21-090000, FAX 47-21-094973, ssb@ssb.no.

S

314.827 NOR
NORWAY. STATISTISK SENTRALBYRAA. REGIONALSTATISTIKK. VESTFOLD (ONLINE). Text in Norwegian. 1974. m. free. charts. back issues avail. **Document type:** *Government.*
Former titles (until 2001): Norway. Statistisk Sentralbyraa. Regionalstatistikk. Vestfold (Print) (0804-2977); (until 1989): Norway. Statistisk Sentralbyraa. Nye Distriktstall. Vestfold (0800-8337)
Media: Online - full content.
Published by: Statistisk Sentralbyraa/Statistics Norway, Kongensgate 6, P O Box 8131, Dep, Oslo, 0033, Norway. TEL 47-21-090000, FAX 47-21-094973, ssb@ssb.no.

NORWAY. STATISTISK SENTRALBYRAA. SKOGSTATISTIKK/ FORESTRY STATISTICS. *see* FORESTS AND FORESTRY—Abstracting, Bibliographies, Statistics

NORWAY. STATISTISK SENTRALBYRAA. SOSIALHJELP, BARNEVERN OG FAMILIEVERN/STATISTICS NORWAY. SOCIAL ASSISTANCE, CHILD WELFARE STATISTICS AND FAMILY COUNSELING SERVICES. *see* SOCIOLOGY—Abstracting, Bibliographies, Statistics

314.81 NOR ISSN 0377-8908
HA1501
NORWAY. STATISTISK SENTRALBYRAA. STATISTISK AARBOK/ STATISTICS NORWAY. STATISTICAL YEARBOOK. Text in Norwegian. 1880. a., latest vol.122, 2003. NOK 260 (effective 2004). back issues avail. **Document type:** *Government.*
Former titles (until 1964): Norway. Statistisk Sentralbyraa. Statistisk Aarbok for Norge (0801-0420); (until 1934): Norway. Statistisk Sentralbyraa. Statistisk Aarbok for Kongeriket Norge (0801-0439)
Related titles: Microfiche ed.: (from PQC); Online - full text ed.; English ed.: ISSN 0809-1919. 1996; ◆ Series of: Norges Offisielle Statistikk. ISSN 0300-5585.
Indexed: RASB.
Published by: Statistisk Sentralbyraa/Statistics Norway, Kongensgate 6, P O Box 8131, Dep, Oslo, 0033, Norway. TEL 47-21-090000, FAX 47-21-094973, ssb@ssb.no. Circ: 35,000.

310 NOR
NORWAY. STATISTISK SENTRALBYRAA. STATISTISK MAANEDSHEFTE. Text in English, Norwegian. 1998. irreg. back issues avail. **Document type:** *Government.*
Media: Online - full content.
Published by: Statistisk Sentralbyraa/Statistics Norway, Kongensgate 6, P O Box 8131, Dep, Oslo, 0033, Norway. TEL 47-21-090000, FAX 47-21-094973, ssb@ssb.no.

314.81 NOR ISSN 0804-3221
NORWAY. STATISTISK SENTRALBYRAA. STATISTISKE ANALYSER. Text in Norwegian. 1993. irreg. price varies. back issues avail. **Document type:** *Monographic series, Government.*
Supersedes in part: Sociale og Oekonomiske Studier (0801-3845); Incorporates: Sosialt Utsyn
Related titles: Online - full text ed.
Indexed: ASFA, B21.
Published by: Statistisk Sentralbyraa/Statistics Norway, Kongensgate 6, P O Box 8131, Dep, Oslo, 0033, Norway. TEL 47-21-090000, FAX 47-21-094973, ssb@ssb.no. Circ: 6,000.

NORWAY. STATISTISK SENTRALBYRAA. STORTINGSVALGET/ STATISTICS NORWAY. PARLIAMENTARY ELECTIONS. *see* PUBLIC ADMINISTRATION—Abstracting, Bibliographies, Statistics

NORWAY. STATISTISK SENTRALBYRAA. STRUKTURSTATISTIKK FOR SAMFERSEL OG REISELIV/STATISTICS NORWAY. STRUCTURAL TRANSPORT AND TOURISM STATISTICS. *see* TRANSPORTATION—Abstracting, Bibliographies, Statistics

NORWAY. STATISTISK SENTRALBYRAA. UTENRIKSHANDEL (ONLINE)/STATISTICS NORWAY. EXTERNAL TRADE. *see* BUSINESS AND ECONOMICS—Abstracting, Bibliographies, Statistics

NORWAY. STATISTISK SENTRALBYRAA. VAREHANDELSSTATISTIKK/STATISTICS NORWAY. WHOLESALE AND RETAIL TRADE STATISTICS. *see* BUSINESS AND ECONOMICS—Abstracting, Bibliographies, Statistics

NOTAS SOBRE POLITICA ESTADISTICA EN EL MUNDO. *see* POLITICAL SCIENCE—Abstracting, Bibliographies, Statistics

NOTIZIARIO STATISTICO (YEAR)/STATISTICAL BULLETIN (YEAR). *see* TRANSPORTATION—Abstracting, Bibliographies, Statistics

LES NOUVEAUTES EN MATIERE DE COMPTES ECONOMIQUES CANADIENS. *see* BUSINESS AND ECONOMICS

NUERNBERGER STATISTIK AKTUELL. *see* PUBLIC ADMINISTRATION—Abstracting, Bibliographies, Statistics

NURSING HOME STATISTICAL YEARBOOK. *see* MEDICAL SCIENCES—Nurses And Nursing

314.89 DNK ISSN 0106-9799
NYT FRA DANMARKS STATISTIK. Variant title: Denmark. Danmarks Statistik. Nyt. Text in Danish. 1967. d. (550/yr). 2 p./no.; **Document type:** *Newsletter, Government.* **Description:** Daily updates of the very latest research in Danish statistics.
Related titles: E-mail ed.; Fax ed.; Online - full content ed.: ISSN 1601-1015. 199?.
Published by: Danmarks Statistik/Statistics Denmark, Sejroegade 11, Copenhagen OE, 2100, Denmark. TEL 45-39-173917, FAX 45-39-173939, dst@dst.dk.

O E C D AGRICULTURE AND FOOD ILIBRARY. (Organisation for Economic Cooperation and Development) *see* AGRICULTURE—Abstracting, Bibliographies, Statistics

O E C D BANKING STATISTICS/SOURCE O C D E RENTABILITE DES BANQUES. (Organisation for Economic Cooperation and Development) *see* BUSINESS AND ECONOMICS—Abstracting, Bibliographies, Statistics

O E C D ECONOMIC OUTLOOK: STATISTICS AND PROJECTIONS/ SOURCE O C D E STATISTIQUES DES PERSPECTIVES ECONOMIQUES DE L'O C D E. (Organisation for Economic Cooperation and Development) *see* BUSINESS AND ECONOMICS—Abstracting, Bibliographies, Statistics

O E C D EDUCATION STATISTICS/SOURCE O C D E STATISTIQUES DE L'EDUCATION. (Organisation for Economic Cooperation and Development) *see* EDUCATION—Abstracting, Bibliographies, Statistics

O E C D EMPLOYMENT AND LABOUR MARKET STATISTICS/ STATISTIQUES DE L'O C D E SUR L'EMPLOI ET LE MARCHE DU TRAVAIL. (Organisation for Economic Cooperation and Development) *see* BUSINESS AND ECONOMICS—Abstracting, Bibliographies, Statistics

O E C D INSURANCE STATISTICS. (Organisation for Economic Cooperation and Development) *see* INSURANCE—Abstracting, Bibliographies, Statistics

O E C D INTERNATIONAL DEVELOPMENT STATISTICS (ONLINE)/ STATISTIQUES DE L'O C D E SUR LE DEVELOPPEMENT INTERNATIONAL. (Organisation for Economic Cooperation and Development) *see* BUSINESS AND ECONOMICS—Abstracting, Bibliographies, Statistics

O E C D INTERNATIONAL DIRECT INVESTMENT STATISTICS (ONLINE). (Organisation for Economic Cooperation and Development) *see* BUSINESS AND ECONOMICS—Abstracting, Bibliographies, Statistics

O E C D INTERNATIONAL MIGRATION STATISTICS/SOURCE O C D E STATISTIQUES DES MIGRATIONS INTERNATIONALES. (Organisation for Economic Cooperation and Development) *see* BUSINESS AND ECONOMICS—Abstracting, Bibliographies, Statistics

O E C D INTERNATIONAL TRADE BY COMMODITIES STATISTICS/O E C D STATISTIQUES DU COMMERCE INTERNATIONAL PAR PRODUITS. (Organisation for Economic Cooperation and Development) *see* BUSINESS AND ECONOMICS—Abstracting, Bibliographies, Statistics

O E C D LABOUR FORCE STATISTICS/O C D E STATISTIQUES DE LA POPULATION ACTIVE. (Organisation for Economic Cooperation and Development) *see* BUSINESS AND ECONOMICS—Abstracting, Bibliographies, Statistics

O E C D SOCIAL EXPENDITURE STATISTICS/STATISTIQUES DE L'O C D E SUR LES DEPENSES SOCIALES. (Organisation for Economic Cooperation and Development) *see* BUSINESS AND ECONOMICS—Abstracting, Bibliographies, Statistics

O E C D STATISTICS ON INTERNATIONAL TRADE IN SERVICES/ SOURCE O C D E STATISTIQUES DES SERVICES. (Organisation for Economic Cooperation and Development) *see* BUSINESS AND ECONOMICS—Abstracting, Bibliographies, Statistics

O E C D STATISTICS ON MEASURING GLOBALISATION. *see* BUSINESS AND ECONOMICS—Abstracting, Bibliographies, Statistics

O E C D TELECOMMUNICATIONS AND INTERNET STATISTICS/ SOURCE O C D E BASE DE DONNEES DES TELECOMMUNICATIONS DE L'O C D E. (Organisation for Economic Cooperation and Development) *see* COMMUNICATIONS—Abstracting, Bibliographies, Statistics

310 330.9 ATG ISSN 1021-7274
O E C S ANNUAL DIGEST OF STATISTICS. (Organisation of Eastern Caribbean States) Text in English. 1984. irreg. XEC 25, USD 10. stat. **Document type:** *Bulletin.* **Description:** Summarizes statistics in the member countries.
Published by: Organisation of Eastern Caribbean States, Economic Affairs Secretariat, PO Box 822, St John's, Antigua. TEL 809-462-3500, FAX 809-462-1537. Circ: 350.

O E C S ENERGY REVIEW. (Organisation of Eastern Caribbean States) *see* ENERGY—Abstracting, Bibliographies, Statistics

310 330.9 ATG ISSN 1021-7339
O E C S NATIONAL ACCOUNTS DIGEST. (Organisation of Eastern Caribbean States) Text in English. 1985. irreg. XEC 160, USD 60. charts; stat. **Document type:** *Bulletin.* **Description:** Covers the national income and expenditure of OECS member countries.
Published by: Organisation of Eastern Caribbean States, Economic Affairs Secretariat, PO Box 822, St John's, Antigua. TEL 809-462-3500, FAX 809-462-1537. Circ: 350.

310 330.9 ATG ISSN 1021-7290
O E C S STATISTICAL POCKET DIGEST. (Organisation of Eastern Caribbean States) Text in English. 1983. irreg. XEC 5, USD 2. stat. **Document type:** *Bibliography.* **Description:** Reference guide to statistics and basic information about OECS member countries.
Published by: Organisation of Eastern Caribbean States, Economic Affairs Secretariat, PO Box 822, St John's, Antigua. TEL 809-462-3500, FAX 809-462-1537. Circ: 1,500.

O M T. BAROMETRO DEL TURISMO MUNDIAL. (Organizacion Mundial de Turismo) *see* TRAVEL AND TOURISM—Abstracting, Bibliographies, Statistics

310 BGR ISSN 1311-235X
HA1621
OBLASTI I OBSHCHINI V REPUBLIKA BULGARIA. Text in Bulgarian. a. BGL 12.48; USD 27 foreign (effective 2002). 220 p./no.; **Description:** Publishes statistical information about demographic, social and economic development of the different regions in Bulgaria.
Published by: Natsionalen Statisticheski Institut/National Statistical Institute, ul P Volov, # 2, Sofia, 1038, Bulgaria. FAX 359-2-9803319, publikacii@nsi.bg, http://www.nsi.bg. **Dist. by:** Sofia Books, ul Silivria 16, Sofia 1404, Bulgaria. TEL 359-2-9586257, info@sofiabooks-bg.com, http://www.sofiabooks-bg.com.

370 310 BGR
OBRAZOVANIE V REPUBLIKA BULGARIA/EDUCATION IN THE REPUBLIC OF BULGARIA. Text in Bulgarian. a. BGL 7.65 (effective 2002). 100 p./no.; **Description:** Publishes detailed statistical information about all kinds of education in Bulgaria.
Published by: Natsionalen Statisticheski Institut/National Statistical Institute, ul P Volov, # 2, Sofia, 1038, Bulgaria. FAX 359-2-9803319, publikacii@nsi.bg, http://www.nsi.bg. **Dist. by:** Sofia Books, ul Silivria 16, Sofia 1404, Bulgaria. TEL 359-2-9586257, info@sofiabooks-bg.com, http://www.sofiabooks-bg.com.

OBSLEDOVANIE NASELENIYA PO PROBLEMAM ZANYATOSTI/ SURVEY ON EMPLOYMENT OF POPULATION. *see* BUSINESS AND ECONOMICS—Abstracting, Bibliographies, Statistics

OCCUPATIONAL COMPENSATION SUMMARIES. *see* BUSINESS AND ECONOMICS—Abstracting, Bibliographies, Statistics

OCCUPATIONAL OUTLOOK HANDBOOK. *see* OCCUPATIONS AND CAREERS—Abstracting, Bibliographies, Statistics

OCCUPATIONAL OUTLOOK QUARTERLY. *see* OCCUPATIONS AND CAREERS—Abstracting, Bibliographies, Statistics

310 SWE ISSN 1651-8608
OEREBRO STUDIES IN STATISTICS. Text in English. 2003. irreg., latest vol.2, 2004. price varies. back issues avail. **Document type:** *Monographic series, Academic/Scholarly.*
Published by: Oerebro Universitet, Universitetsbiblioteket/University of Oerebro. University Library, Fakultetsgatan 1, Oerebro, 70182, Sweden. TEL 46-19-303240, FAX 46-19-331217, biblioteket@ub.oru.se. Ed. Joanna Jansdotter.

OESTERREICHISCHE HOCHSCHULSTATISTIK. *see* EDUCATION—Abstracting, Bibliographies, Statistics

OFFICE FOR NATIONAL STATISTICS. INTERNATIONAL TRADE IN SERVICES. *see* BUSINESS AND ECONOMICS—Abstracting, Bibliographies, Statistics

OFFICE FOR NATIONAL STATISTICS. NEWS RELEASE. *see* POPULATION STUDIES—Abstracting, Bibliographies, Statistics

OFFICE FOR NATIONAL STATISTICS. TECHNICAL NOTE. *see* BUSINESS AND ECONOMICS—Abstracting, Bibliographies, Statistics

OFFICE FOR NATIONAL STATISTICS. U.K. SERVICE SECTOR. *see* PUBLIC ADMINISTRATION—Abstracting, Bibliographies, Statistics

OFFICIAL N C A A WOMEN'S BASKETBALL RECORDS BOOK (YEAR). *see* SPORTS AND GAMES—Ball Games

OHIO CITIES & COUNTIES GRAPHIC PERFORMANCE ANALYSIS. *see* PUBLIC ADMINISTRATION—Abstracting, Bibliographies, Statistics

OHIO CROP WEATHER. *see* AGRICULTURE—Abstracting, Bibliographies, Statistics

OHIO. DEPARTMENT OF HUMAN SERVICES. CHILD WELFARE STATISTICS. *see* SOCIAL SERVICES AND WELFARE—Abstracting, Bibliographies, Statistics

OHIO HIGHER EDUCATION. BASIC DATA SERIES. *see* EDUCATION—Abstracting, Bibliographies, Statistics

OIL AND ENERGY TRENDS: ANNUAL STATISTICAL REVIEW. *see* ENERGY—Abstracting, Bibliographies, Statistics

OIL AND GAS STATISTICS REPORT. *see* PETROLEUM AND GAS—Abstracting, Bibliographies, Statistics

OIL, GAS, COAL & ELECTRICITY QUARTERLY STATISTICS/O C D E STATISTIQUES TRIMESTRIELLES. ELECTRICITE, CHARBON, GAZ & PETROLE. *see* PETROLEUM AND GAS—Abstracting, Bibliographies, Statistics

OIL MARKET INTELLIGENCE. *see* PETROLEUM AND GAS—Abstracting, Bibliographies, Statistics

OKLAHOMA BUSINESS BULLETIN. *see* BUSINESS AND ECONOMICS—Abstracting, Bibliographies, Statistics

OKLAHOMA CITIES & COUNTIES GRAPHIC PERFORMANCE ANALYSIS. *see* PUBLIC ADMINISTRATION—Abstracting, Bibliographies, Statistics

OKLAHOMA CROP WEATHER. *see* AGRICULTURE—Abstracting, Bibliographies, Statistics

OKLAHOMA HEALTH STATISTICS. *see* PUBLIC HEALTH AND SAFETY—Abstracting, Bibliographies, Statistics

310 363.7 BGR ISSN 1311-2368
GE190.B9
OKOLNA SREDA/ENVIRONMENT. Text in Bulgarian, English. a. BGL 11.25 (effective 2002). 90 p./no.; **Document type:** *Bulletin.* **Description:** Presents statistical research on the environment and its protection.
Published by: Natsionalen Statisticheski Institut/National Statistical Institute, ul P Volov, # 2, Sofia, 1038, Bulgaria. FAX 359-2-9803319, publikacii@nsi.bg, http://www.nsi.bg. **Dist. by:** Sofia Books, ul Silivria 16, Sofia 1404, Bulgaria. TEL 359-2-9586257, info@sofiabooks-bg.com, http://www.sofiabooks-bg.com.

THE OLDER POPULATION IN THE UNITED STATES. *see* POPULATION STUDIES—Abstracting, Bibliographies, Statistics

▼ **OPEN ACCESS MEDICAL STATISTICS.** *see* MEDICAL SCIENCES—Abstracting, Bibliographies, Statistics

310 USA ISSN 2161-718X
▼ **OPEN JOURNAL OF STATISTICS.** Abbreviated title: O J S. Text in English. 2011. q. USD 117 (effective 2011). **Document type:** *Journal, Academic/Scholarly.* **Description:** Provides a platform for scientists and academicians all over the world to promote, share, and discuss various new issues and developments in different areas of statistics.
Related titles: Online - full text ed.: ISSN 2161-7198. free (effective 2011).
Published by: Scientific Research Publishing, Inc., PO Box 54821, Irvine, CA 92619. service@scirp.org. Ed. Qihua Wang.

OPERANT SUBJECTIVITY; the international journal of Q methodology. *see* SOCIOLOGY—Abstracting, Bibliographies, Statistics

OREGON CROP WEATHER. *see* AGRICULTURE—Abstracting, Bibliographies, Statistics

OREGON PROPERTY TAX STATISTICS. *see* BUSINESS AND ECONOMICS—Abstracting, Bibliographies, Statistics

OREGON. PUBLIC UTILITY COMMISSIONER. OREGON UTILITY STATISTICS. *see* PUBLIC ADMINISTRATION—Abstracting, Bibliographies, Statistics

OREGON VITAL STATISTICS ANNUAL REPORT. *see* PUBLIC HEALTH AND SAFETY—Abstracting, Bibliographies, Statistics

OREGON VITAL STATISTICS COUNTY DATA. *see* PUBLIC HEALTH AND SAFETY—Abstracting, Bibliographies, Statistics

314.891 DNK ISSN 1903-2498
ORIENTERING. Text in Danish. 1972. irreg. stat. **Document type:** *Government.*
Former titles (until 2006): Orientering fra Koebenhavns Kommune, Statistisk Kontor (Print) (1397-6346); (until 1997): Orientering fra Koebenhavns Statistiske Kontor (0900-5218)
Media: Online - full text.
Published by: Center for Raadgivning og Udvikling, Statistik, Ottilliavej 1, Valby, 2500, Denmark. TEL 45-70-808000, statistik@ks.kk.dk, http://www.kk.dk/statistik.aspx.

318.4 BOL
ORURO EN CIFRAS. Text in Spanish. irreg. BOB 5, USD 2.50. adv. charts. **Document type:** *Bulletin.* **Description:** Reflects economic, socio-cultural, and population aspects of Oruro.
Published by: Universidad Boliviana Tecnica de Oruro, Instituto de Investigaciones Economicas, Casilla 441, Oruro, Bolivia. TEL 591-52-55503.

OSNOVNYE POKAZATELI INVESTITSIONNOI I STROITEL'NOI DEYATEL'NOSTI V ROSSIISKOI FEDERATSII/MAIN INDICATORS OF CONSTRUCTION AND INVESTMENT ACTIVITIES IN THE RUSSIAN FEDERATION. *see* BUSINESS AND ECONOMICS—Abstracting, Bibliographies, Statistics

OSNOVNYE POKAZATELI OKHRANY OKRUZHAYUSHCHEI SREDY/MAIN INDICATORS OF ENVIRONMENTAL PROTECTION. *see* ENVIRONMENTAL STUDIES—Abstracting, Bibliographies, Statistics

OSTEOPATHIC MEDICAL EDUCATION. ANNUAL REPORT. *see* MEDICAL SCIENCES—Abstracting, Bibliographies, Statistics

OVERSEAS TRADE STATISTICS. U K TRADE WITH COUNTRIES WITHIN THE EUROPEAN UNION (INTRA-EC TRADE: INTRASTAT). *see* BUSINESS AND ECONOMICS—Abstracting, Bibliographies, Statistics

OVERSEAS TRADE STATISTICS: U K TRADE WITH THE EUROPEAN UNION AND THE WORLD. *see* BUSINESS AND ECONOMICS—Abstracting, Bibliographies, Statistics

OXFORD BULLETIN OF ECONOMICS AND STATISTICS. *see* BUSINESS AND ECONOMICS

519.5 GBR ISSN 0952-9942
OXFORD STATISTICAL SCIENCE SERIES. Text in English. 1987. irreg., latest vol.34, 2007. price varies. back issues avail. **Document type:** *Monographic series, Academic/Scholarly.*
Indexed: CCMJ, CIS.
—BLDSC (6321.021300), IE, Ingenta.
Published by: Oxford University Press, Great Clarendon St, Oxford, OX2 6DP, United Kingdom. TEL 44-1865-556767, FAX 44-1865-556646, enquiry@oup.co.uk, http://www.oup-usa.org/catalogs/general/series/. **Orders in N. America to:** Oxford University Press, 2001 Evans Rd, Cary, NC 27513. TEL 919-677-0977 ext 5777, 800-852-7323, FAX 919-677-1714, jnlorders@oup-usa.org, http://www.us.oup.com.

519.5 JPN ISSN 0285-0370
➤ **OYO TOKEIGAKU/JAPANESE JOURNAL OF APPLIED STATISTICS.** Text in Japanese. 1971. 3/yr. JPY 5,000 membership (effective 2005). adv. **Document type:** *Journal, Academic/Scholarly.*
Indexed: CIS, CPM, ST&MA.
—CCC.
Published by: Oyo Tokei Gakkai/Japanese Society of Applied Statistics, Sinfonica, Daiwa Bldg., 6-3-9 Minami-Aoyama, Minato-ku, Tokyo, 107-0062, Japan. FAX 81-3-54670484, applstat@sinfonica.or.jp, http://www.applstat.gr.jp. Ed., R&P Kunio Shimizu. Adv. contact Yoshiyasu Tamura. Circ: 780.

318 331 BRA
P E D. INFORME. (Pesquisa de Emprego e Desemprego) Text in Portuguese. 1992. m. free (effective 2003). charts; stat. **Document type:** *Bulletin.* **Description:** Presents data on employment, unemployment and earnings in the metropolitan region.
Related titles: Online - full content ed.: 1999.
Published by: Fundacao de Economia e Estatistica Siegfried Emanuel Heuser, Rua Duque de Caxias 1691, Centro, Porto Alegre, RS 90010-283, Brazil. TEL 55-51-32169000, FAX 55-51-32250006, diretoria@fee.tche.br, http://www.fee.rs.gov.br. Circ: 1,100.

PACIFIC ASIA TRAVEL ASSOCIATION. ANNUAL STATISTICAL REPORT. *see* TRAVEL AND TOURISM—Abstracting, Bibliographies, Statistics

PACIFIC ASIA TRAVEL ASSOCIATION. QUARTERLY STATISTICAL REPORT. *see* TRAVEL AND TOURISM—Abstracting, Bibliographies, Statistics

PAKISTAN. CENTRAL BUREAU OF EDUCATION. EDUCATIONAL STATISTICS BULLETIN SERIES. *see* EDUCATION—Abstracting, Bibliographies, Statistics

PAKISTAN. FOOD AND AGRICULTURE DIVISION. AGRICULTURAL STATISTICS OF PAKISTAN. *see* AGRICULTURE—Abstracting, Bibliographies, Statistics

PAKISTAN INSTITUTE OF DEVELOPMENT ECONOMICS. STATISTICAL PAPERS SERIES. *see* BUSINESS AND ECONOMICS—Abstracting, Bibliographies, Statistics

PAKISTAN JOURNAL OF STATISTICS AND OPERATION RESEARCH. *see* MATHEMATICS

315 PAK ISSN 0078-8473
PAKISTAN STATISTICAL ASSOCIATION. PROCEEDINGS. Text in English. a. PKR 2. **Document type:** *Proceedings.*
Published by: Pakistan Statistical Association, Institute of Statistics, University of the Punjab, Lahore, Pakistan.

PANAMA EN CIFRAS. *see* BUSINESS AND ECONOMICS—Abstracting, Bibliographies, Statistics

PANORAMA OF TRANSPORT; statistical overview of road, rail and inland waterway transport in the European Union. *see* TRANSPORTATION—Abstracting, Bibliographies, Statistics

PAPUA NEW GUINEA. DEPARTMENT OF LABOUR AND EMPLOYMENT. WORKER'S COMPENSATION CLAIMS. *see* INSURANCE—Abstracting, Bibliographies, Statistics

PAPUA NEW GUINEA INTERNATIONAL ARRIVALS AND DEPARTURES. *see* POPULATION STUDIES—Abstracting, Bibliographies, Statistics

319 PNG ISSN 0310-5377
PAPUA NEW GUINEA. NATIONAL STATISTICAL OFFICE. ABSTRACT OF STATISTICS. Text in English. 1967. q. PGK 12 domestic; PGK 20 foreign (effective 2005). stat. **Document type:** *Abstract/Index.* **Description:** Includes monthly or quarterly figures drawn from most of the economic statistical series compiled by the NSO and some by the Bank of Papua New Guinea.
Formerly: Papua and New Guinea. Monthly Abstracts of Statistics
Published by: National Statistical Office, Waigani, National Capital District, PO Box 337, Port Moresby, Papua New Guinea. TEL 675-3011200, FAX 675-3251869, http://www.nso.gov.pg/. Ed. Francis K Kasau. Circ: 500.

PAPUA NEW GUINEA. NATIONAL STATISTICAL OFFICE. ANNUAL BUSINESS CENSUS. *see* BUSINESS AND ECONOMICS—Abstracting, Bibliographies, Statistics

PAPUA NEW GUINEA. NATIONAL STATISTICAL OFFICE. BUILDING STATISTICS. *see* BUILDING AND CONSTRUCTION—Abstracting, Bibliographies, Statistics

339 319 PNG ISSN 1017-6500
PAPUA NEW GUINEA. NATIONAL STATISTICAL OFFICE. CONSUMER PRICE INDEX. Text in English. 1964. q. PGK 14 domestic; PGK 22 foreign (effective 2005). **Document type:** *Government.* **Description:** Covers six urban areas and contains price indexes, for groups and major subgroups of household 3xpenditures, and retail prices of major domestic commodities.
Supersedes: Papua New Guinea. Bureau of Statistics. Quarterly Retail Price Index (0031-1529)
Published by: National Statistical Office, Waigani, National Capital District, PO Box 337, Port Moresby, Papua New Guinea. TEL 675-3011226, FAX 675-3251869. Ed. Francis K Kasau. Circ: 440.

PAPUA NEW GUINEA. NATIONAL STATISTICAL OFFICE. DOMESTIC FACTOR INCOMES, BY REGION AND PROVINCE. *see* BUSINESS AND ECONOMICS—Abstracting, Bibliographies, Statistics

PAPUA NEW GUINEA. NATIONAL STATISTICAL OFFICE. EXPORT PRICE INDEXES. *see* BUSINESS AND ECONOMICS—Abstracting, Bibliographies, Statistics

PAPUA NEW GUINEA. NATIONAL STATISTICAL OFFICE. GOVERNMENT FINANCE STATISTICS. *see* BUSINESS AND ECONOMICS—Abstracting, Bibliographies, Statistics

PAPUA NEW GUINEA. NATIONAL STATISTICAL OFFICE. GROSS DOMESTIC PRODUCT AND EXPENDITURE. *see* BUSINESS AND ECONOMICS—Abstracting, Bibliographies, Statistics

PAPUA NEW GUINEA. NATIONAL STATISTICAL OFFICE. IMPORT PRICE INDEXES. *see* BUSINESS AND ECONOMICS—Abstracting, Bibliographies, Statistics

PAPUA NEW GUINEA. NATIONAL STATISTICAL OFFICE. INTERNATIONAL TRADE - EXPORTS. *see* BUSINESS AND ECONOMICS—Abstracting, Bibliographies, Statistics

PAPUA NEW GUINEA. NATIONAL STATISTICAL OFFICE. INTERNATIONAL TRADE - IMPORTS. *see* BUSINESS AND ECONOMICS—Abstracting, Bibliographies, Statistics

PAPUA NEW GUINEA. NATIONAL STATISTICAL OFFICE. STATISTICAL BULLETIN: REGISTERED MOTOR VEHICLES. *see* TRANSPORTATION—Abstracting, Bibliographies, Statistics

318.92 PRY ISSN 0031-1677
PARAGUAY. DIRECCION GENERAL DE ESTADISTICA Y CENSOS. BOLETIN ESTADISTICO. Text in Spanish. 1957. s-a. free. mkt.; stat.
Related titles: ◆ Supplement to: Anuario Estadistico del Paraguay. ISSN 0252-8932.
Published by: Direccion General de Estadistica y Censos, HUMAITA, 463, Casilla de Correos 1118, Asuncion, Paraguay. Ed. Jose Diaz de Bedoya. Circ: 1,000.

PEDIATRIC LENGTH OF STAY BY DIAGNOSIS & OPERATION, UNITED STATES. *see* HEALTH FACILITIES AND ADMINISTRATION—Abstracting, Bibliographies, Statistics

PENNSYLVANIA. AGRICULTURAL STATISTICS SERVICE. CROP AND LIVESTOCK ANNUAL SUMMARY. *see* AGRICULTURE—Crop Production And Soil

PENNSYLVANIA. BOARD OF PROBATION AND PAROLE. MONTHLY STATISTICAL REPORT. *see* CRIMINOLOGY AND LAW ENFORCEMENT—Abstracting, Bibliographies, Statistics

PENNSYLVANIA CITIES & COUNTIES GRAPHIC PERFORMANCE ANALYSIS. *see* PUBLIC ADMINISTRATION—Abstracting, Bibliographies, Statistics

PENNSYLVANIA VITAL STATISTICS. *see* POPULATION STUDIES—Abstracting, Bibliographies, Statistics

PERFILES DE SALUD DE LAS COMUNIDADES HERMANAS DE LA FRONTERA MEXICO - ESTADOS UNIDOS/SISTER COMMUNITIES HEALTH PROFILES OF THE U S - MEXICO BORDER. *see* PUBLIC HEALTH AND SAFETY—Abstracting, Bibliographies, Statistics

310 ESP ISSN 1134-0444
PERSPECTIVA ECONOMICA DE CATALUNYA. Text in Spanish. 1963. bi-m. adv. stat. **Document type:** *Bulletin, Consumer.*
Former titles (until 1993): Boletin de Estadistica y Coyuntura (0210-1580); (until 1972): Boletin Estadistico Coyuntural (0522-3806)
Published by: Cambra Oficial de Comerc Industria i Navegacio de Barcelona, Avinguda Diagonal, 452, Barcelona, 08006, Spain. TEL 34-93-4169300, FAX 34-93-4169301, premsa@cambrabcn.org, http://www.cambrabcn.es/. Ed. Carmen Miro. Adv. contact Oriol Prats.

PESQUISA ANUAL DO TRANSPORTE RODOVIARIO. *see* TRANSPORTATION—Abstracting, Bibliographies, Statistics

PESQUISA DE ESTOQUES. *see* AGRICULTURE—Abstracting, Bibliographies, Statistics

318 BRA ISSN 0101-6822
HD7323.A3
PESQUISA NACIONAL POR AMOSTRA DE DOMICILIOS. (In 2 parts: Sintese de Indicadores; Mobilidade Social) Text in Portuguese. 1967. a. USD 40. charts; stat. **Document type:** *Government.* **Description:** Provides information on the main characteristics of the population, housing, labor force, fertility, family income and other aspects of the socioeconomic conditions of the population.
Published by: Fundacao Instituto Brasileiro de Geografia e Estatistica, Centro de Documentacao e Disseminacao de Informacoes, Rua General Canabarro, 706 Andar 2, Maracana, Rio de Janeiro, RJ 20271-201, Brazil. TEL 55-21-2645424, FAX 55-21-2841959.

PESSOAS EM NUMEROS. *see* POPULATION STUDIES—Abstracting, Bibliographies, Statistics

PETROLEUM, PETROLEUM PRODUCTS AND NATURAL GAS. *see* PETROLEUM AND GAS—Abstracting, Bibliographies, Statistics

PHARMACEUTICAL STATISTICS; the journal of applied statistics in the pharmaceutical industry. *see* PHARMACY AND PHARMACOLOGY

PHILIPPINE STATISTICAL YEARBOOK. *see* BUSINESS AND ECONOMICS—Abstracting, Bibliographies, Statistics

PHILIPPINES. BUREAU OF LABOR AND EMPLOYMENT STATISTICS. CURRENT LABOR STATISTICS. *see* BUSINESS AND ECONOMICS—Abstracting, Bibliographies, Statistics

PHILIPPINES. BUREAU OF LABOR AND EMPLOYMENT STATISTICS. LABOR AND EMPLOYMENT STATISTICAL REPORT. *see* BUSINESS AND ECONOMICS—Abstracting, Bibliographies, Statistics

PHILIPPINES. BUREAU OF LABOR AND EMPLOYMENT STATISTICS. OCCUPATIONAL WAGES SURVEY. *see* BUSINESS AND ECONOMICS—Abstracting, Bibliographies, Statistics

PHILIPPINES. BUREAU OF LABOR AND EMPLOYMENT STATISTICS. YEARBOOK OF LABOR STATISTICS. *see* BUSINESS AND ECONOMICS—Abstracting, Bibliographies, Statistics

PHILIPPINES. DEPARTMENT OF AGRICULTURE. BUREAU OF AGRICULTURAL STATISTICS. DEVELOPMENT INDICATORS IN PHILIPPINE AGRICULTURE. *see* AGRICULTURE—Abstracting, Bibliographies, Statistics

PHILIPPINES. DEPARTMENT OF AGRICULTURE. BUREAU OF AGRICULTURAL STATISTICS. LIVESTOCK AND POULTRY PERFORMANCE REPORT. *see* AGRICULTURE—Abstracting, Bibliographies, Statistics

PHILIPPINES. DEPARTMENT OF AGRICULTURE. BUREAU OF AGRICULTURAL STATISTICS. RICE AND CORN SITUATION OUTLOOK. *see* AGRICULTURE—Abstracting, Bibliographies, Statistics

PHILIPPINES. DEPARTMENT OF AGRICULTURE. BUREAU OF AGRICULTURAL STATISTICS. SELECTED STATISTICS IN AGRICULTURE. *see* AGRICULTURE—Abstracting, Bibliographies, Statistics

PHILIPPINES. NATIONAL STATISTICS OFFICE. ANNUAL SURVEY OF ESTABLISHMENTS. *see* BUSINESS AND ECONOMICS—Abstracting, Bibliographies, Statistics

PHILIPPINES. NATIONAL STATISTICS OFFICE. CENSUS OF ESTABLISHMENTS. *see* BUSINESS AND ECONOMICS—Abstracting, Bibliographies, Statistics

PHILIPPINES. NATIONAL STATISTICS OFFICE. CENSUS OF POPULATION AND HOUSING. *see* HOUSING AND URBAN PLANNING—Abstracting, Bibliographies, Statistics

PHILIPPINES. NATIONAL STATISTICS OFFICE. CONSUMER PRICE INDEX IN THE PHILIPPINES. *see* BUSINESS AND ECONOMICS—Abstracting, Bibliographies, Statistics

PHILIPPINES. NATIONAL STATISTICS OFFICE. DIRECTORY OF LARGE ESTABLISHMENTS. *see* BUSINESS AND ECONOMICS—Abstracting, Bibliographies, Statistics

PHILIPPINES. NATIONAL STATISTICS OFFICE. FAMILY INCOME AND EXPENDITURES SURVEY. *see* HOME ECONOMICS—Abstracting, Bibliographies, Statistics

315 PHL ISSN 0116-2624
HD8711
PHILIPPINES. NATIONAL STATISTICS OFFICE. INTEGRATED SURVEY OF HOUSEHOLDS BULLETIN. Text in English. q. USD 100. **Document type:** *Government.* **Description:** Deals with Philippine labor force and its socioeconomic characteristics.
Formerly: Philippines. National Census and Statistics Office. Sample Survey of Households Bulletin.
Published by: National Statistics Office, Ramon Magsaysay Blvd, PO Box 779, Manila, Philippines. FAX 63-2-610794. Circ: 300.

PHILIPPINES. NATIONAL STATISTICS OFFICE. NATIONAL DEMOGRAPHIC SURVEY. *see* POPULATION STUDIES—Abstracting, Bibliographies, Statistics

310 PHL
PHILIPPINES. NATIONAL STATISTICS OFFICE. PHILIPPINES IN FIGURES. Text in English. a. **Document type:** *Government.* **Description:** Summarizes various statistics generated by the NSO and other government and private agencies.
Published by: National Statistics Office, Ramon Magsaysay Blvd, PO Box 779, Manila, Philippines. FAX 63-2-610794.

310 PHL
PHILIPPINES. NATIONAL STATISTICS OFFICE. PROVINCIAL PROFILE. Text in English. every 5 yrs. **Document type:** *Government.* **Description:** An individual account of each of the country's 74 provinces. Serves as a convenient statistical reference on the geographic, economic, social and demographic features of every province and of the National Capital Region.
Published by: National Statistics Office, Ramon Magsaysay Blvd, PO Box 779, Manila, Philippines. FAX 63-2-610794.

310 PHL ISSN 0116-2640
PHILIPPINES. NATIONAL STATISTICS OFFICE. SPECIAL RELEASES. Text in English. irreg., latest 1996. **Document type:** *Government.* **Description:** Features recent reports on the results of surveys, censuses, or special studies conducted by the NSO.
Indexed: IPP.
Published by: National Statistics Office, Ramon Magsaysay Blvd, PO Box 779, Manila, Philippines. FAX 63-2-610794.

PHILIPPINES. NATIONAL STATISTICS OFFICE. VITAL STATISTICS REPORT. *see* POPULATION STUDIES—Abstracting, Bibliographies, Statistics

PHRMA ANNUAL REPORT. *see* PHARMACY AND PHARMACOLOGY—Abstracting, Bibliographies, Statistics

PHYSICIAN COMPENSATION AND PRODUCTION SURVEY. *see* MEDICAL SCIENCES—Abstracting, Bibliographies, Statistics

PIRMASENS ZAHLEN UND FAKTEN: STATISTISCHE JAHRBUCH STADT PIRMASENS. *see* PUBLIC ADMINISTRATION—Abstracting, Bibliographies, Statistics

310 USA ISSN 1073-0001
HA203
PLACES, TOWNS AND TOWNSHIPS. Text in English. 1993. a., latest 2007, 4th ed. USD 95 per issue (effective 2011). charts. back issues avail. **Document type:** *Journal, Trade.* **Description:** Provides an in-depth look at a wide range of statistical data for US towns and townships.

S

Published by: (Kraus Organization, Ltd.), Bernan Press, 15200 NBN Way, PO Box 191, Blue Ridge Summit, PA 17214. TEL 301-459-7666, 800-865-3457, FAX 301-459-6988, 800-865-3450, customercare@bernan.com.

318 CHL ISSN 0717-2028
PLAN NACIONAL DE RECOPILACION ESTADISTICA. Text in Spanish. 1983. a.
Published by: Instituto Nacional de Estadisticas, Casilla 498, Correo 3, Ave. Bulnes, 418, Santiago, Chile.

314.81 NOR
PLANER OG MELDINGER. Text in Norwegian. 1977. irreg., latest 2007. back issues avail. **Document type:** *Monographic series, Consumer.*
Former titles (until 199?): Norway. Statistisk Sentralbyraa. Publikasjonsoversikt (0802-4405); (until 1988): Fortegnelse over Norges Offisielle Statistikk og andre Publikasjoner
Published by: Statistisk Sentralbyraa/Statistics Norway, Kongensgate 6, P O Box 8131, Dep, Oslo, 0033, Norway. TEL 47-21-090000, FAX 47-21-094973, ssb@ssb.no, http://www.ssb.no.

310 338.1 BGR
PLOSHTI, DOBIVI I PROIZVODSTVO NA ZEMEDELSKITE KULTURI. Text in Bulgarian. a. **Description:** Presents data and tables about agricultural land, annual income and production of main crops.
Related titles: CD-ROM ed.
Published by: Natsionalen Statisticheski Institut/National Statistical Institute, ul P Volov, # 2, Sofia, 1038, Bulgaria. FAX 359-2-9803319, publikacii@nsi.bg, http://www.nsi.bg. **Dist. by:** Sofia Books, ul Silivria 16, Sofia 1404, Bulgaria. TEL 359-2-9586257, info@sofiabooks-bg.com, http://www.sofiabooks-bg.com.

PLUMBING FIXTURES & FITTINGS IN CHINA. *see* HEATING, PLUMBING AND REFRIGERATION—Abstracting, Bibliographies, Statistics

POBLACION DE LOS MUNICIPIOS ESPANOLES. *see* POPULATION STUDIES—Abstracting, Bibliographies, Statistics

314.8 DNK ISSN 1601-622X
POHJOLA NUMEROINA. Text in Finnish. 1998. a. **Document type:** *Government.*
Related titles: Online - full text ed.; ◆ Swedish ed.: Norden i Tal. ISSN 0908-4339; ◆ English ed.: The Nordic Countries in Figures. ISSN 0908-4398.
Published by: Nordisk Ministerraad/Nordic Council of Ministers, Store Strandstraede 18, Copenhagen K, 1255, Denmark. TEL 45-33-960200, FAX 45-33-960202, nmr@norden.org.

310 POL ISSN 0006-4025
HA1451 CODEN: BSTAEY
POLAND. GLOWNY URZAD STATYSTYCZNY. BIULETYN STATYSTYCZNY. Contents page in English, Russian. 1957. m. EUR 178 foreign (effective 2006). charts; stat. index.
Indexed: RASB.
Published by: (Poland. Glowny Urzad Statystyczny/Polish Statistical Association), Zaklad Wydawnictw Statystycznych, Al Niepodleglosci 208, Warsaw, 00925, Poland. TEL 48-22-6083145, FAX 48-22-6083183, http://www.stat.gov.pl/zws. Circ: 2,500. **Dist. by:** Ars Polona, Obroncow 25, Warsaw 03933, Poland. TEL 48-22-5098609, FAX 48-22-5098610, arspolona@arspolona.com.pl, http://www.arspolona.com.pl.

314 POL ISSN 1640-3630
HA1451 CODEN: MRSTEU
POLAND. GLOWNY URZAD STATYSTYCZNY. MALY ROCZNIK STATYSTYCZNY POLSKI/POLAND. CENTRAL STATISTICS OFFICE. CONCISE STATISTICAL YEARBOOK. Text in Polish. 1958. a. USD 20. **Document type:** *Government.*
Formerly (until 2000): Poland. Glowny Urzad Statystyczny. Maly Rocznik Statystyczny (0079-2608)
Related titles: CD-ROM ed.: ISSN 1640-5919.
Published by: (Poland. Glowny Urzad Statystyczny/Polish Statistical Association), Zaklad Wydawnictw Statystycznych, Al Niepodleglosci 208, Warsaw, 00925, Poland. TEL 48-22-6083210, FAX 48-22-6083867.

POLAND. GLOWNY URZAD STATYSTYCZNY. RAPORT O STANIE, ZAGROZENIU I OCHRONIE SRODOWISKA (YEAR). *see* ENVIRONMENTAL STUDIES—Abstracting, Bibliographies, Statistics

314 POL ISSN 1506-0632
HA1451 CODEN: RSTAE6
POLAND. GLOWNY URZAD STATYSTYCZNY. ROCZNIK STATYSTYCZNY RZECZYPOSPOLITEJ POLSKIEJ/POLAND. CENTRAL STATISTICS OFFICE. STATISTICAL YEARBOOK OF THE REPUBLIC OF POLAND. Text in Polish; Summaries in English, Russian. 1921. a. USD 36 foreign (effective 2000). **Document type:** *Government.*
Formerly (until 1998): Poland. Glowny Urzad Statystyczny. Rocznik Statystyczny (0079-2780)
Related titles: CD-ROM ed.; Microfiche ed.: (from PQC).
Indexed: FR.
Published by: (Poland. Glowny Urzad Statystyczny/Polish Statistical Association), Zaklad Wydawnictw Statystycznych, Al Niepodleglosci 208, Warsaw, 00925, Poland. TEL 48-22-6083210, FAX 48-22-6083867, c.cwetkow@stat.gov.pl, http://www.stat.gov.pl/zws. Ed. Andrzej Stasiun. Circ: 13,000 (controlled).

POLAND. GLOWNY URZAD STATYSTYCZNY. UZYTKOWANIE GRUNTOW, POWIERZCHNIA ZASIEWOW I POGLOWIE ZWIERZAT GOSPODARSKICH. *see* AGRICULTURE—Abstracting, Bibliographies, Statistics

314 POL ISSN 0043-518X
HA1451
POLAND. GLOWNY URZAD STATYSTYCZNY. WIADOMOSCI STATYSTYCZNE. Text in Polish; Abstracts and contents page in English, Russian. 1985. m. charts; stat. index. **Document type:** *Government.*
Indexed: AgrLib, P30, PopulInd, RASB, SCOPUS.
Published by: (Polskie Towarzystwo Statystyczne, Poland. Glowny Urzad Statystyczny/Polish Statistical Association), Zaklad Wydawnictw Statystycznych, Al Niepodleglosci 208, Warsaw, 00925, Poland. TEL 48-22-6083145, FAX 48-22-6083183, zws-sprzedaz@stat.gov.pl, http://www.stat.gov.pl/zws. Ed. Tadeusz Walczak. Circ: 3,400.

POLLING REPORT. *see* POLITICAL SCIENCE—Abstracting, Bibliographies, Statistics

314.97 SVN ISSN 1854-4657
HA1188.S54
POMEMBNEJSI STATISTICNI PODATKI O SLOVENIJI/SOME IMPORTANT STATISTICS ON SLOVENIA. Text in Slovenian, English. 2006. m. **Document type:** *Government.*
Incorporates (1981-2006): Mesecni Statisticni Pregled Republike Slovenije (0353-8591); Which was formerly (until 1991): Mesecni Statisticni Pregled S R Slovenije. Druzbeni Razvoj S R Slovenije (0352-0633); Which was formed by the merger of (1966-1981): Mesecni Statisticni Pregled S R Slovenije (0543-5471); (1966-1981): Druzbeni Razvoj S R Slovenije (0583-5747)
Related titles: Online - full content ed.
Published by: Statisticni Urad Republike Slovenije/Statistical Office of the Republic of Slovenia, Vozarski pot 12, Ljubljana, 1000, Slovenia. TEL 386-1-2415104, FAX 386-1-2415344, info.stat@gov.si.

310 USA ISSN 1041-3782
POPULAR STATISTICS SERIES. Text in English. 1983. irreg., latest vol.7, 1998. price varies. back issues avail. **Document type:** *Monographic series.*
Indexed: CIS.
Published by: C R C Press, LLC (Subsidiary of: Taylor & Francis Group), 6000 Broken Sound Pky, NW, Ste 300, Boca Raton, FL 33487. TEL 800-272-7737, FAX 800-374-3401, orders@crcpress.com.

316.3 ETH
POPULATION AND HOUSING CENSUS OF ETHIOPIA. Text in English. 1984. every 10 yrs. ETB 32, USD 4.30. back issues avail. **Document type:** *Government.* **Description:** Presents data on population size and characteristics, education, economic activity, migration, fertility, mortality, housing characteristics and conditions, and population projections.
Related titles: CD-ROM ed.; Diskette ed.
Published by: Central Statistical Authority, PO Box 1143, Addis Ababa, Ethiopia. TEL 115470, FAX 550334.

▼ **O PORTAL DE ESTATISTICAS OFICIAIS.** *see* PUBLIC ADMINISTRATION—Abstracting, Bibliographies, Statistics

UN PORTRAIT STATISTIQUE DES FAMILLES AU QUEBEC. *see* SOCIOLOGY—Abstracting, Bibliographies, Statistics

314 PRT ISSN 0871-8725
PORTUGAL EM NUMEROS. Text in Portuguese. 1969. a.
Former titles: Portugal (Year) (0377-2470); (until 1977): Sinopse de Dados Estatisticos (0871-9500)
Related titles: English ed.: Portugal in Figures. ISSN 0871-8733. 1977.
Published by: Instituto Nacional de Estatistica, Av Antonio Jose de Almeida 2, Lisbon, 1000-043, Portugal. TEL 351-21-8426100, FAX 351-21-8426380, ine@ine.pt, http://www.ine.pt.

314.6 PRT ISSN 0873-9811
HC391
PORTUGAL EM NUMEROS. SITUACAO SOCIO-ECONOMICA. Text in Portuguese. 1983. a. free. stat.; charts. back issues avail.; reprints avail. **Document type:** *Yearbook, Government.*
Formerly (until 1990): Portugal. Situacao Economica en Numeros (0871-4614)
Related titles: Online - full content ed.; Ed.: Portugal. Economic and Social Indicators. ISSN 0873-982X. 1989.
Published by: Ministerio do Ambiente e do Ordenamento do Territorio, Rua de "O Seculo", Lisbon, 1249-079, Portugal. http://www.maotdr.gov.pt.

PORTUGAL. INSTITUTO NACIONAL DE ESTATISTICA. ESTATISTICAS AGRICOLAS. *see* AGRICULTURE—Abstracting, Bibliographies, Statistics

PORTUGAL. INSTITUTO NACIONAL DE ESTATISTICA. INQUERITO AO GANHO DOS TRABALHADORES AGRICOLAS. *see* AGRICULTURE—Abstracting, Bibliographies, Statistics

314 PRT ISSN 0378-3227
PORTUGAL. INSTITUTO NACIONAL DE ESTATISTICA. SERIE ESTATISTICAS REGIONAIS. Text in Portuguese. 1970. irreg. stat.
Published by: Instituto Nacional de Estatistica, Av Antonio Jose de Almeida 2, Lisbon, 1000-043, Portugal. TEL 351-21-8426100, FAX 351-21-8426380, http://www.ine.pt. Circ: (controlled).

310 PRT ISSN 0378-3235
HA1571
PORTUGAL. INSTITUTO NACIONAL DE ESTATISTICA. SERIE ESTIMATIVAS PROVISORIAS. Text in Portuguese. 1956. irreg.
Published by: Instituto Nacional de Estatistica, Av Antonio Jose de Almeida 2, Lisbon, 1000-043, Portugal. TEL 351-21-8426100, FAX 351-21-8426380, http://www.ine.pt.

310 PRT
PORTUGAL. INSTITUTO NACIONAL DE ESTATISTICA. SERIE ESTUDOS. Text in Portuguese. 1942. irreg.
Published by: Instituto Nacional de Estatistica, Av Antonio Jose de Almeida 2, Lisbon, 1000-043, Portugal. TEL 351-21-8426100, FAX 351-21-8426380, http://www.ine.pt.

▼ **PORTUGUESE JOURNAL OF QUANTITATIVE METHODS.** *see* MATHEMATICS

310 SVN
POSEBNE PUBLIKACIJE/SPECIAL PUBLICATIONS. Text in Slovenian. 1998. irreg. stat. **Document type:** *Government.* **Description:** Presents a detailed analysis of an individual field of statistics or various fields of statistics. Also publises results and analysis of important projects implemented by the Statistical Office of the Republic of Slovenia.
Related titles: Online - full content ed.
Published by: Statisticni Urad Republike Slovenije/Statistical Office of the Republic of Slovenia, Vozarski pot 12, Ljubljana, 1000, Slovenia. TEL 386-1-2415104, FAX 386-1-2415344, info.stat@gov.si. Ed. Ana Antoncic. Pub. Tomaz Banovec.

POSTHARVEST NEWS AND INFORMATION. *see* AGRICULTURE—Abstracting, Bibliographies, Statistics

POSTVERKSAMHET/POSTAL SERVIES. *see* COMMUNICATIONS—Abstracting, Bibliographies, Statistics

PRECOS E RENDIMENTOS NA AGRICULTURA. *see* AGRICULTURE—Abstracting, Bibliographies, Statistics

PREGNANCY OUTCOMES. *see* PUBLIC HEALTH AND SAFETY

PREHLED VYDANYCH STAVEBNICH OHLASENI A POVOLENI. *see* BUILDING AND CONSTRUCTION—Abstracting, Bibliographies, Statistics

PRESS NEWS-SUGAR INDUSTRY. *see* AGRICULTURE—Abstracting, Bibliographies, Statistics

PRESS RELEASE - BUILDING SOCIETIES ASSOCIATION. *see* BUILDING AND CONSTRUCTION—Abstracting, Bibliographies, Statistics

310 364.1 BGR
PRESTUPLENIA I OSUDENI LITSA. Text in Bulgarian. a. BGL 5.40 (effective 2002). **Description:** Presents statistical information on different kinds of crimes in Bulgaria.
Related titles: Diskette ed.
Published by: Natsionalen Statisticheski Institut/National Statistical Institute, ul P Volov, # 2, Sofia, 1038, Bulgaria. FAX 359-2-9803319, publikacii@nsi.bg, http://www.nsi.bg. **Dist. by:** Sofia Books, ul Silivria 16, Sofia 1404, Bulgaria. TEL 359-2-9586257, info@sofiabooks-bg.com, http://www.sofiabooks-bg.com.

PRICE ADJUSTMENT FORMULAE INDICES ONLINE. *see* BUILDING AND CONSTRUCTION—Abstracting, Bibliographies, Statistics

PRINCE EDWARD ISLAND. DEPARTMENT OF AGRICULTURE. AGRICULTURAL STATISTICS. *see* AGRICULTURE—Abstracting, Bibliographies, Statistics

PROBABILITY AND MATHEMATICAL STATISTICS. *see* MATHEMATICS

PRODUCAO AGRICOLA MUNICIPAL; culturas temporarias e permanentes. *see* AGRICULTURE—Abstracting, Bibliographies, Statistics

PRODUCAO DA PECUARIA MUNICIPAL. *see* AGRICULTURE—Abstracting, Bibliographies, Statistics

PRODUCCION AGRICOLA - PERIODO DE INVIERNO. *see* AGRICULTURE—Abstracting, Bibliographies, Statistics

PRODUCCION AGRICOLA - PERIODO DE VERANO. *see* AGRICULTURE—Abstracting, Bibliographies, Statistics

PRODUCER PRICE INDEXES. *see* BUSINESS AND ECONOMICS—Abstracting, Bibliographies, Statistics

PRODUCTION OF CANADA'S LEADING MINERALS/PRODUCTION DES PRINCIPAUX MINERAUX DU CANADA. *see* MINES AND MINING INDUSTRY—Abstracting, Bibliographies, Statistics

PRODUCTION OF SELECTED INDUSTRIAL PRODUCTS (YEAR). *see* BUSINESS AND ECONOMICS—Abstracting, Bibliographies, Statistics

PRODUCTIVITY AND COSTS; business, nonfarm business, manufacturing, and nonfinancial corporations. *see* BUSINESS AND ECONOMICS—Economic Situation And Conditions

PRODUCTIVITY STATISTICS; productivity indexes and levels in APO member countries. *see* BUSINESS AND ECONOMICS—Abstracting, Bibliographies, Statistics

LA PRODUZIONE DELL'INDUSTRIA SIDERURGICA. *see* METALLURGY—Abstracting, Bibliographies, Statistics

PROFILE OF ELECTORAL DISTRICTS (ONLINE EDITION). *see* PUBLIC ADMINISTRATION—Abstracting, Bibliographies, Statistics

PROFILES OF EARNINGS IN CYPRUS: BY EDUCATION, OCCUPATION, EXPERIENCE, AGE, SEX AND SECTOR. *see* BUSINESS AND ECONOMICS—Abstracting, Bibliographies, Statistics

PROFITABILITY BY LINE BY STATE. *see* INSURANCE—Abstracting, Bibliographies, Statistics

PROGRESS OF EDUCATION IN SAUDI ARABIA; a statistical review. *see* EDUCATION—Abstracting, Bibliographies, Statistics

PROIZVODSTVO I OBOROT ETILIVOGO SPIRTA I ALKOGOL'NOI PRODUKTSII V ROSSIISKOI FEDERATSII/PRODUCTION AND TURNOVER OF ALCOHOLIC PRODUCTS IN RUSSIAN FEDERATION. *see* BEVERAGES—Abstracting, Bibliographies, Statistics

PROPANE MARKET FACTS; statistical handbook of the LP-gas industry. *see* PETROLEUM AND GAS—Abstracting, Bibliographies, Statistics

PRUMYSL CESKE REPUBLIKY. *see* BUSINESS AND ECONOMICS—Abstracting, Bibliographies, Statistics

314.97 SVN ISSN 1580-4216
PRVA STATISTICNA OBJAVA/FIRST RELEASE. Text in Slovenian, English. 1997. m. charts; stat. **Document type:** *Government.* **Description:** Covers only the most topical fields of statistics. Contains the most basic data and charts which are important as short-term indicators for various marcoeconomic analyses.
Related titles: Online - full content ed.
Published by: Statisticni Urad Republike Slovenije/Statistical Office of the Republic of Slovenia, Vozarski pot 12, Ljubljana, 1000, Slovenia. TEL 386-1-2415104, FAX 386-1-2415344, info.stat@gov.si. Eds. Avgustina Kuhar de Domizio, Ana Antoncic. Pub. Tomaz Banovec.

310 POL ISSN 0033-2372
HA1 CODEN: PZSTAD
➤ **PRZEGLAD STATYSTYCZNY/STATISTICAL REVIEW.** Text in Polish, English. 1954. q. EUR 77 foreign (effective 2011). bk.rev. charts; illus. index. 100 p./no.; **Document type:** *Journal, Academic/Scholarly.* **Description:** Contains scientific articles in the area of statistics, econometrics and other scientific disciplines where mathematics is applied for the purposes of research into economic phenomena.
Indexed: CIS, IAOP, Inspec, MathR, RASB, Z02. —AskIEEE.
Published by: Polska Akademia Nauk, Komitet Statystyki i Ekonometrii, c/o Dr. Krzysztof Najman, Katedra Statystyki, Wydzial Zarzadzania, Uniwersytet Gdanski, ul Armii Krajowej 101, Sopot, 81824, Poland. TEL 48-12-2935256, FAX 48-12-2935046, krzysztof.najman@wzr.ug.edu.pl, http://www.ksie.pan.pl. Ed. Miroslaw Szreder. Circ: 1,000. **Dist. by:** Ars Polona, Obroncow 25, Warsaw 03933, Poland. TEL 48-22-5098609, FAX 48-22-5098610, arspolona@arspolona.com.pl, http://www.arspolona.com.pl.

➤ **PUBLIC LIBRARY STATISTICS.** *see* LIBRARY AND INFORMATION SCIENCES

➤ **PUBLIC TRANSPORTATION FACT BOOK.** *see* TRANSPORTATION—Abstracting, Bibliographies, Statistics

➤ **PUERTO RICO. DEPARTMENT OF HEALTH. OFFICE OF HEALTH STATISTICS. DIVISION OF STATISTICS AND REPORTS. ANNUAL VITAL STATISTICS REPORT/INFORME ANUAL DE ESTADISTICAS VITALES.** *see* POPULATION STUDIES—Abstracting, Bibliographies, Statistics

➤ **PUERTO RICO. DEPARTMENT OF LABOR. DIRECTORIO DE ORGANIZACIONES DEL TRABAJO.** *see* LABOR UNIONS

➤ **PUERTO RICO. DEPARTMENT OF LABOR. EMPLEO, ASALARIADO NO AGRICOLA EN PUERTO RICO.** *see* BUSINESS AND ECONOMICS—Abstracting, Bibliographies, Statistics

➤ **PUERTO RICO. OFICINA DE ESTADISTICAS AGRICOLAS. BOLETIN SEMESTRAL DE ESTADISTICAS AGRICOLAS.** *see* AGRICULTURE—Abstracting, Bibliographies, Statistics

310 388 BGR
PUTNOTRANSPORTNI PROIZSHESTVIA V REPUBLIKA BULGARIA. Text in Bulgarian. a. BGL 4.80 (effective 2002).
Related titles: Diskette ed.
Published by: Natsionalen Statisticheski Institut/National Statistical Institute, ul P Volov, # 2, Sofia, 1038, Bulgaria. FAX 359-2-9803319, publikacii@nsi.bg, http://www.nsi.bg.

Q P A STATISTICAL YEARBOOK. *see* BUILDING AND CONSTRUCTION—Abstracting, Bibliographies, Statistics

QUADERNI STATISTICI E INFORMATIVI. *see* BUSINESS AND ECONOMICS—Abstracting, Bibliographies, Statistics

QUALITY AND QUANTITY; international journal of methodology. *see* SOCIOLOGY—Abstracting, Bibliographies, Statistics

QUALITY CONTROL AND APPLIED STATISTICS; international literature digest service. *see* BUSINESS AND ECONOMICS—Abstracting, Bibliographies, Statistics

QUARTERLY BULLETIN OF COCOA STATISTICS. *see* FOOD AND FOOD INDUSTRIES

QUARTERLY OPERATING STATISTICS; of major household goods carriers. *see* TRANSPORTATION—Abstracting, Bibliographies, Statistics

QUARTERLY PANORAMA OF EUROPEAN BUSINESS STATISTICS. *see* BUSINESS AND ECONOMICS—Abstracting, Bibliographies, Statistics

QUARTERLY REGIONAL STATISTICS. *see* BUSINESS AND ECONOMICS—Abstracting, Bibliographies, Statistics

310 IND
QUARTERLY STATISTICAL ABSTRACT OF TAMIL NADU. Text in English. 1956. q. back issues avail. **Document type:** *Report, Government.*
Formerly (until 198?): Abstract of Statistics for Tamil Nadu
Published by: Department of Economics and Statistics, Central Administrative Bldg, Block II, No 259, Anna Salai, Teynampet, Chennai, Tamilnadu 600 006, India. TEL 91-44-24321189, FAX 91-44-24322871, stats@tn.nic.in, http://www.tnstat.gov.in.

QUEBEC (PROVINCE). REGIE DE L'ASSURANCE-MALADIE. STATISTIQUES ANNUELLES. *see* INSURANCE—Abstracting, Bibliographies, Statistics

317 CAN ISSN 0834-5252
HA747
QUEBEC STATISTIQUE. Text in English. 1914-1980; resumed 1985. irreg., latest 1995. CAD 14.95. index. **Document type:** *Government.*
Former titles (until 1986): Annuaire du Quebec - Quebec Yearbook (0066-3018); (until 1962): Annuaire Statistique. Quebec (0704-3651); Which incorporated (1914-1934): Statistical Year Book (Quebec. English Edition) (0704-3643)
Published by: Publications du Quebec, P O Box 1005, Quebec, PQ G1K 7B5, Canada. TEL 418-643-5150, FAX 418-643-6177. Circ: 6,000.

QUELLEN, FINDBUECHER UND INVENTARE DES BRANDENBURGISCHEN LANDESHAUPTARCHIVS. *see* HISTORY—Abstracting, Bibliographies, Statistics

310 SWE ISSN 0283-3654
QVARTILEN. Text in Swedish. 1986. q. SEK 130, SEK 1,300 to institutional members (effective 2007). adv. stat. back issues avail. **Document type:** *Newsletter, Trade.*
Published by: Svenska Statistikersamfundet/Swedish Statistical Society, c/o Maria Wiberg, Statistiska Institutionen, Umeaa University, Umeaa, 90187, Sweden. TEL 46-90-7869524, folksekrsamf@gmail.com, http://www.statistikersamfundet.se. Eds. Jens Olofsson, Joakim Malmdin. adv.: page SEK 4,000.

001.422 001.433 CAN ISSN 1923-7448
R D C@ WESTERN RESEARCH HIGHLIGHTS. (Research Data Centre) Abbreviated title: R D C A Western Research Highlights. Text in English. 2007. 5/yr. back issues avail. **Document type:** *Newsletter, Trade.*
Related titles: Online - full text ed.: free (effective 2010).
Published by: University of Western Ontario, Research Data Centre, Rm 1030, Social Science Ctr, London, ON N6A 5C2, Canada. TEL 519-850-2971, rdc@uwo.ca, http://rdc.uwo.ca.

R I A QUARTERLY STATISTICS REPORT - ROBOTICS. *see* COMPUTERS—Robotics

310 AUT ISSN 1609-3631
R NEWS. Text in English. 2001. q. free (effective 2011). **Document type:** *Journal, Academic/Scholarly.*
Media: Online - full text.
Published by: Technische Universitaet Wien, Institut fuer Statistik und Wahrscheinlichkeitstheorie, Wiedner Haupstr 8-10/107, Vienna, 1040, Austria. TEL 43-1-58801, institut@statistik.tuwien.ac.at, http://www.statistik.tuwien.ac.at. Ed. John Fox.

316.8 ZAF
R S A STATISTICS IN BRIEF (YEAR). (Republic of South Africa) Text in English. a., latest 2000. free. **Document type:** *Government.*
Published by: Statistics South Africa/Statistieke Suid-Afrika, Private Bag X44, Pretoria, 0001, South Africa. TEL 27-12-3108911, FAX 27-12-3108500, info@statssa.gov.za, http://www.statssa.gov.za.

310 GBR ISSN 1351-0657
R S S NEWS. Text in English. 1974. m. (10/yr). free to members (effective 2009). adv. **Document type:** *Newsletter, Trade.* **Description:** News of events in the field of statistics and of the Royal Statistical Society.
Formerly (until 1993): News & Notes - R S S (0954-5530)
Related titles: Online - full text ed.
Indexed: CIS.
—CCC.
Published by: Royal Statistical Society, 12 Errol St, London, EC1Y 8LX, United Kingdom. TEL 44-20-76388998, FAX 44-20-76143905, rss@rss.org.uk. Ed. Frank Duckworth. Adv. contact Jonelle Lewis Chamberlain TEL 44-20-76143947. B&W page GBP 985, color page GBP 1,585; 180 x 145. Circ: 7,000.

R V BUSINESS. (Recreational Vehicle) *see* SPORTS AND GAMES—Abstracting, Bibliographies, Statistics

310 GBR ISSN 0268-6376
RADICAL STATISTICS. Variant title: Radstats. Text in English. 1975. 3/yr. GBP 7.50 per issue to non-members; free to members (effective 2009). bk.rev. back issues avail. **Document type:** *Journal, Academic/Scholarly.* **Description:** A forum for radical ideas in the political development and exploitation of statistical methods and in the uses and abuses of statistics.
—BLDSC (7228.098800), IE.
Published by: Radical Statistics Group, c/o London Hazards Centre, Interchange Studios, Dalby St, London, NW5 3NQ, United Kingdom. Eds. Jane Galbraith, Janet Shapiro.

RADIO ADVERTISING BUREAU. RADIO FACTS. *see* ADVERTISING AND PUBLIC RELATIONS—Abstracting, Bibliographies, Statistics

RAJASTHAN, INDIA. DIRECTORATE OF ECONOMICS AND STATISTICS. BASIC STATISTICS. *see* BUSINESS AND ECONOMICS—Abstracting, Bibliographies, Statistics

RAPPORT STATISTIQUE A L'INTENTION DES AGENTS IMMOBILIERS. REGION METROPOLITAINE DE SAGUENAY. *see* REAL ESTATE—Abstracting, Bibliographies, Statistics

RAPPORT STATISTIQUE A L'INTENTION DES AGENTS IMMOBILIERS. REGION METROPOLITAINE DE TROIS-RIVIERES, AGGLOMERATION DE SHAWINIGAN. *see* REAL ESTATE—Abstracting, Bibliographies, Statistics

RATINGS OF CONGRESS. *see* POLITICAL SCIENCE—Abstracting, Bibliographies, Statistics

RAUMFORSCHUNG UND RAUMORDNUNG. *see* HOUSING AND URBAN PLANNING—Abstracting, Bibliographies, Statistics

310 338 BGR
RAZVITIE NA CHASTNIA SEKTOR. Text in Bulgarian. a. USD 18 foreign (effective 2002). **Description:** Presents statistical information on the private sector of Bulgarian economy in the period of transition to a market economy.
Published by: Natsionalen Statisticheski Institut/National Statistical Institute, ul P Volov, # 2, Sofia, 1038, Bulgaria. FAX 359-2-9803319, publikacii@nsi.bg, http://www.nsi.bg. **Dist. by:** Sofia Books, ul Silivria 16, Sofia 1404, Bulgaria. TEL 359-2-9586257, info@sofiabooks-bg.com, http://www.sofiabooks-bg.com.

314.97 SVN ISSN 0354-0278
RAZVOJNA VPRASANJA STATISTIKE/DEVELOPMENT ISSUES OF STATISTICS. Text in Slovenian, English. 1991. irreg. price varies. stat. **Document type:** *Government.* **Description:** Contains a thorough professional analysis of methodological issues and solutions.
Related titles: Online - full content ed.
Published by: Statisticni Urad Republike Slovenije/Statistical Office of the Republic of Slovenia, Vozarski pot 12, Ljubljana, 1000, Slovenia. TEL 386-1-2415104, FAX 386-1-2415344, info.stat@gov.si. Eds. Avgustina Kuhar de Domizio, Ana Antoncic. Pub. Tomaz Banovec.

RECREATIECIJFERS BIJ DE HAND. *see* LEISURE AND RECREATION—Abstracting, Bibliographies, Statistics

318 PER
REGION ANDRES AVELINO CACERES COMPENDIO ESTADISTICO. Text in Spanish. irreg. **Document type:** *Government.*
Published by: Instituto Nacional de Estadistica, Ave. 28 de Julio 1056, Lima, Peru. Circ: 200.

318 PER
REGION AREQUIPA COMPENDIO ESTADISTICO. Text in Spanish. a.
Published by: Instituto Nacional de Estadistica, Ave. 28 de Julio 1056, Lima, Peru.

318 PER
REGION CHAVIN COMPENDIO ESTADISTICO. Text in Spanish. a.?. **Description:** Contains geographical, demographical, social and economic statistics of the region.
Published by: Instituto Nacional de Estadistica, Ave. 28 de Julio 1056, Lima, Peru. Circ: 200.

318 PER
REGION INKA COMPENDIO ESTADISTICO. Text in Spanish. irreg. **Document type:** *Government.*
Published by: Instituto Nacional de Estadistica, Ave. 28 de Julio 1056, Lima, Peru. Circ: 200.

318 PER
REGION JOSE CARLOS MARIATEGUI COMPENDIO ESTADISTICO. Text in Spanish. irreg., latest vol.3, 1991. **Document type:** *Government.*
Published by: Instituto Nacional de Estadistica, Ave. 28 de Julio 1056, Lima, Peru.

318 PER
REGION LORETO COMPENDIO ESTADISTICO. Text in Spanish. irreg., latest vol.3, 1991. **Document type:** *Government.*
Published by: Instituto Nacional de Estadistica, Ave. 28 de Julio 1056, Lima, Peru.

318 PER
REGION LOS LIBERTADORES - WARI COMPENDIO ESTADISTICO. Text in Spanish. irreg., latest vol.2, 1991. **Document type:** *Government.*
Published by: Instituto Nacional de Estadistica, Ave. 28 de Julio 1056, Lima, Peru. Circ: 200.

318 PER
REGION NOR ORIENTAL DEL MARANON COMPENDIO ESTADISTICO. Text in Spanish. irreg. **Document type:** *Government.*
Published by: Instituto Nacional de Estadistica, Ave. 28 de Julio 1056, Lima, Peru.

314.6 ESP ISSN 1577-1628
REGION OF MADRID DATA GUIDE. Text in English. 2000. a. free (effective 2009). back issues avail.
Related titles: ◆ Spanish ed.: Communidad de Madrid Datos Basicos. ISSN 1577-161X.
Published by: Comunidad de Madrid, Instituto de Estadistica, Principe de Vargara 108, Madrid, 28002, Spain. TEL 34-91-5802540, jestadis@madrid.org, http://www.madrid.org/iestadis/index.htm.

314.6 ESP ISSN 1577-1350
THE REGION OF MADRID IN FIGURES. Text in English. 1999. a. free (effective 2008). back issues avail. **Document type:** *Bulletin, Consumer.*
Formerly (until 2000): Community of Madrid in Figures (1578-5874)
Published by: Comunidad de Madrid, Instituto de Estadistica, Principe de Vargara 108, Madrid, 28002, Spain. TEL 34-91-5802540, FAX 34-91-5802664, jestadis@madrid.org, http://www.madrid.org/iestadis/index.htm.

318 PER
REGION SAN MARTIN - LA LIBERTAD COMPENDIO ESTADISTICO. Text in Spanish. irreg. **Document type:** *Government.*
Published by: Instituto Nacional de Estadistica, Ave. 28 de Julio 1056, Lima, Peru.

314 LUX ISSN 1681-9292
REGIONEN: STATISTISCHES JAHRBUCH (YEAR). Text in German. 2001. a. **Document type:** *Government.*
Related titles: CD-ROM ed.; ◆ French ed.: Regions: Annuaire Statistique (Year). ISSN 1681-9314; ◆ English ed.: Regions: Statistical Yearbook (Year). ISSN 1681-9306.
Published by: European Commission, Office for Official Publications of the European Union, 2 Rue Mercier, Luxembourg, L-2985, Luxembourg. TEL 352-29291, FAX 352-29291, http://publications.europa.eu.

314 LUX ISSN 1681-9314
REGIONS: ANNUAIRE STATISTIQUE (YEAR). Text in French. 2001. a. **Document type:** *Government.*
Related titles: CD-ROM ed.; ◆ German ed.: Regionen: Statistisches Jahrbuch (Year). ISSN 1681-9292; ◆ English ed.: Regions: Statistical Yearbook (Year). ISSN 1681-9306.
Published by: European Commission, Office for Official Publications of the European Union, 2 Rue Mercier, Luxembourg, L-2985, Luxembourg. TEL 352-29291, FAX 352-29291, http://publications.europa.eu.

314 LUX ISSN 1681-9306
HA1107.5
REGIONS: STATISTICAL YEARBOOK (YEAR). Text in English. 1971. a. EUR 30 (effective 2007). **Document type:** *Journal, Trade.*
Supersedes in part (in 2000): Regionen: Statistisches Jahrbuch (1609-5057); Which was formerly (until 1999): EUROSTAT. Regioner. Statistisk Arbog (1013-0381); (until 1986): EUROSTAT. Regionalstatistisk Arbog (0255-3945); (until 1981): EUROSTAT. Regional Statistics. Main Regional Indicators (0255-3937); (until 1979): EUROSTAT. Regionalstatistik. Befolkning, Erhverv, Levevilkar (0255-3708); (1971-1975): EUROSTAT. Regionalstatistik. Jahrbuch (1015-7603)
Related titles: CD-ROM ed.; ◆ French ed.: Regions: Annuaire Statistique (Year). ISSN 1681-9314; ◆ German ed.: Regionen: Statistisches Jahrbuch (Year). ISSN 1681-9292; Alternate Frequency ed(s).
—BLDSC (7336.856700).
Published by: (European Commission, Statistical Office of the European Communities (E U R O S T A T)), European Commission, Office for Official Publications of the European Union, 2 Rue Mercier, Luxembourg, L-2985, Luxembourg. TEL 352-29291, FAX 352-29291, info@publications.europa.eu, http://publications.europa.eu.

REGIONY ROSSII. SOTSIAL'NO-EKONOMICHESKIE POKAZATELI (YEAR). *see* BUSINESS AND ECONOMICS—Abstracting, Bibliographies, Statistics

REGULATORY REVIEW (YEAR). *see* BUSINESS AND ECONOMICS—Abstracting, Bibliographies, Statistics

310 PRT ISSN 1646-7221
RELATORIO DE ACTIVIDADES DO I N E DAS OUTRAS ENTIDADES INTERVENIENTES NA PRODUCCAO ESTATISTICA. (Instituto Nacional de Estatistica) Text in Portuguese. 2008. a. **Document type:** *Report, Government.*
Published by: Instituto Nacional de Estatistica, Av Antonio Jose de Almeida 2, Lisbon, 1000-043, Portugal. TEL 351-21-8426100, FAX 351-21-8426380, ine@ine.pt, http://www.ine.pt.

REPORT ON AVERAGE PRODUCERS' PRICE - AGRICULTURAL PRODUCTS. *see* AGRICULTURE—Abstracting, Bibliographies, Statistics

REPORT ON PASSENGER ROAD TRANSPORT IN ZAMBIA. *see* TRANSPORTATION—Abstracting, Bibliographies, Statistics

310 NOR ISSN 1503-0857
REPORT ON SCIENCE & TECHNOLOGY INDICATORS FOR NORWAY. Text in English. 2001. biennial. back issues avail. **Document type:** *Government.* **Description:** This is an abridged English version of the Norwegian indicator report. The report describes the research and innovation system in Norway with the aid of statistics and indicators for science and technology.
Related titles: Online - full text ed.; ◆ Norwegian ed.: Det Norske Forsknings- og Innovasjonssystemet - Statistikk og Indikatorer. ISSN 1500-0869.
Published by: (N I F U S T E P/Norwegian Institute for Studies in Research and Education, Centre for Innovation Research), Norges Forskningsraad/The Research Council of Norway, P O Box 2700, St Hanshaugen, Oslo, 0131, Norway. TEL 47-22-037000, FAX 47-22-037001, post@forskningsradet.no.

REPORT ON SMALL SCALE MANUFACTURING INDUSTRIES SURVEY. *see* BUSINESS AND ECONOMICS—Abstracting, Bibliographies, Statistics

REPORT ON TOURISM STATISTICS IN TANZANIA. *see* TRAVEL AND TOURISM—Abstracting, Bibliographies, Statistics

314 SRB ISSN 0354-205X
HA1631
REPUBLIKA SRBIJA. MESECNI STATISTICKI PREGLED/MONTHLY STATISTICAL REVIEW. Text in Serbian. 1952. m.
Formerly (until 1991): Mesecni Statisticki Pregled (0350-4247)
Indexed: RASB.
Published by: Republicki Zavod za Statistiku Srbije, Milana Rakica 5, Belgrade, 11000. TEL 381-11-411832, FAX 381-11-411260, dir@statserb.sr.gov.yu. Ed. Andreja Stokic. Circ: 310.

RESEARCH AND DEVELOPMENT IN NEW ZEALAND. *see* SCIENCES: COMPREHENSIVE WORKS—Abstracting, Bibliographies, Statistics

S

RESEARCH AND STUDIES. *see* EDUCATION—Abstracting, Bibliographies, Statistics

001.422 600 500 ROM
RESEARCH DEVELOPMENT AND TECHNOLOGICAL INNOVATION. Text in English, Romanian; Summaries in English, Romanian. 1999. a. ROL 50,000; USD 15 foreign. stat. back issues avail. **Document type:** *Government.* **Description:** Contains statistical data regarding science and technology.
Published by: Comisia Nationala pentru Statistica/National Commission for Statistics, Bd. Libertatii 16, Sector 5, Bucharest, 70542, Romania. TEL 40-1-3363370, FAX 40-1-3124873. R&P Ivan Ungureanu Clementina.

RESERVE BANK OF AUSTRALIA. BULLETIN. *see* BUSINESS AND ECONOMICS—Abstracting, Bibliographies, Statistics

RESIDENTIAL CARE HOMES SCOTLAND. STATISTICAL INFORMATION NOTE. *see* SOCIAL SERVICES AND WELFARE—Abstracting, Bibliographies, Statistics

▼ **RESIDENTIAL INFILL DEVELOPMENT.** *see* HOUSING AND URBAN PLANNING

314.97 SVN ISSN 0352-0226
HA1634.S58
RESULTATI RAZISKOVANJ/RESULTS OF SURVEYS. Text in Slovenian, English. 1967. a. price varies. bibl.; stat. **Document type:** *Government.* **Description:** Shows the results of individual statistical surveys or groups of related statistical surveys. Contains a detailed tabular review of results of statistical surveys, often with long time series of important data, methodological explanations describing definitions, standards and methods of implementing the surveys and usually also a comment.
Related titles: Online - full content ed.
Published by: Statisticni Urad Republike Slovenije/Statistical Office of the Republic of Slovenia, Vozarski pot 12, Ljubjana, 1000, Slovenia. TEL 386-1-2415104, FAX 386-1-2415344, info.stat@gov.si. Eds. Avgustina Kuhar de Domizio, Ana Antoncic. Pub. Tomaz Banovec.

RESULTS AND PERFORMANCES OF CONSTRUCTION, TRADE AND SERVICES ENTERPRISES. *see* BUSINESS AND ECONOMICS—Abstracting, Bibliographies, Statistics

314 310 ROM ISSN 1454-4490
RESULTS AND PERFORMANCES OF INDUSTRIAL ENTERPRISES (YEAR). Text in English, Romanian; Summaries in English. 1999. a. ROL 100,000; USD 20 foreign. stat. **Document type:** *Government.* **Description:** Contains data on turnover, volume, staffing, investments, assets, as well as, efficiency indicators on Rumanian social capital structure.
Published by: Comisia Nationala pentru Statistica/National Commission for Statistics, Bd. Libertatii 16, Sector 5, Bucharest, 70542, Romania. TEL 40-1-3363370, FAX 40-1-3124873. R&P Ivan Ungureanu Clementina.

RETAIL FOOD PRICE INDEX: WASHINGTON, D.C. *see* BUSINESS AND ECONOMICS—Economic Situation And Conditions

316.3 ETH
RETAIL PRICE INDEX FOR ADDIS ABABA (EXCLUDING RENT). Text in English. 1963. m. free. **Document type:** *Government.*
Published by: Central Statistical Authority, PO Box 1143, Addis Ababa, Ethiopia. TEL 553011, FAX 550334, TELEX 2167 STAT ET.

RETAIL SALES (ONLINE). *see* BUSINESS AND ECONOMICS—Abstracting, Bibliographies, Statistics

THE REVIEW OF ECONOMICS AND STATISTICS. *see* BUSINESS AND ECONOMICS

314 BRA ISSN 0034-7175
HA984
REVISTA BRASILEIRA DE ESTATISTICA/BRAZILIAN STATISTICAL JOURNAL. Text in Portuguese; Summaries in English. 1936. s-a. bk.rev. bibl.; charts; illus.; stat. index. back issues avail. **Document type:** *Magazine, Trade.* **Description:** Presents articles of great technical value that promote and enlarge the use of statistical methods in the area of economic and social sciences.
Formerly (until 1939): Revista de Economia e Estatistica (0100-1795)
Indexed: C01, CIS, P30, PAIS, PopulInd, RASB, SCOPUS.
—Linda Hall.
Published by: Fundacao Instituto Brasileiro de Geografia e Estatistica, Centro de Documentacao e Disseminacao de Informacoes, Rua General Canabarro, 706 Andar 2, Maracana, Rio de Janeiro, RJ 20271-201, Brazil. TEL 55-21-2645424, FAX 55-21-2841959. Circ: 1,000.

310 COL ISSN 0120-1751
REVISTA COLOMBIANA DE ESTADISTICA. Text in Spanish. 1968. irreg. COP 20,000 domestic; USD 20 foreign (effective 2010). **Document type:** *Journal, Academic/Scholarly.*
Related titles: Online - full text ed.: (from SciELO).
Indexed: CCMJ, CIS, MSN, MathR, SCI, SCOPUS, W07, Z02.
Published by: Universidad Nacional de Colombia, Departamento de Matematicas, Carrera 30 No. 45-03, Bogota, Colombia. TEL 57-1-3165207, FAX 57-1-3165247, http://www.matematicas.unal.edu.co.

REVISTA DE ECONOMIA Y ESTADISTICA. *see* BUSINESS AND ECONOMICS

REVISTA ECONOMIA; nueva etapa. *see* BUSINESS AND ECONOMICS

314.98 ROM ISSN 1018-046X
HA1
REVISTA ROMANA DE STATISTICA. Text in Romanian; Summaries in English. 1952. m. **Document type:** *Journal, Academic/Scholarly.* **Description:** Provides official figures from the commission's papers.
Formerly (until 1989): Revista de Statistica (0556-6398)
Related titles: Online - full text ed.: ISSN 1844-7694. free (effective 2011).
Indexed: CIS, P30, RASB, SCOPUS, T02.
Published by: Comisia Nationala pentru Statistica/National Commission for Statistics, Bd. Libertatii 16, Sector 5, Bucharest, 70542, Romania. TEL 40-1-4106744, FAX 40-1-3124873.

310 PRT ISSN 1645-6726
➤ **REVSTAT STATISTICAL JOURNAL.** Text in English. 1996. 3/yr. **Document type:** *Journal, Academic/Scholarly.* **Description:** Aims to publish articles of high scientific content, developing innovative statistical scientific methods and introducing original research, grounded in substantive problems.
Related titles: Online - full text ed.: free (effective 2011).
Indexed: CCMJ, MSN, MathR, SCI, W07, Z02.
Published by: Instituto Nacional de Estatistica, Av Antonio Jose de Almeida 2, Lisbon, 1000-043, Portugal. TEL 351-21-8426100, FAX 351-21-8426380, ine@ine.pt. Ed. Ivette Gomes.

➤ **REVUE DROMOISE.** *see* ARCHAEOLOGY

➤ **REVUE INFORMATIQUE ET STATISTIQUE DANS LES SCIENCES HUMAINES.** *see* HUMANITIES: COMPREHENSIVE WORKS—Abstracting, Bibliographies, Statistics

310 FRA ISSN 1769-7387
LA REVUE MODULAD (ONLINE). Text in French, English. 1988. irreg. free (effective 2011). **Document type:** *Journal, Academic/Scholarly.*
Formerly (until 2004): La Revue de Modulad (Print) (1145-895X)
Media: Online - full text.
—INIST.
Published by: Institut National de Recherche en Informatique et en Automatique (I N R I A), BP 105, Le Chesnay, Cedex 78153, France. TEL 33-1-39635511, FAX 33-1-39635330, http://www.inria.fr.

RHEINLAND AKTUELL; Analysen - Daten - Informationen. *see* AGRICULTURE—Abstracting, Bibliographies, Statistics

RHEINLAND-PFALZ HEUTE. *see* PUBLIC ADMINISTRATION—Abstracting, Bibliographies, Statistics

RHODE ISLAND. DEPARTMENT OF LABOR & TRAINING. CHARACTERISTICS OF THE INSURED UNEMPLOYED IN RHODE ISLAND. *see* BUSINESS AND ECONOMICS—Labor And Industrial Relations

RHODE ISLAND. DEPARTMENT OF LABOR & TRAINING. ESTABLISHMENT EMPLOYMENT IN RHODE ISLAND. *see* BUSINESS AND ECONOMICS—Labor And Industrial Relations

RHODE ISLAND. DEPARTMENT OF LABOR & TRAINING. LOCAL AREA UNEMPLOYMENT STATISTICS. *see* BUSINESS AND ECONOMICS—Labor And Industrial Relations

RHODE ISLAND. DEPARTMENT OF LABOR & TRAINING. OCCUPATIONAL EMPLOYMENT STATISTICS. *see* BUSINESS AND ECONOMICS—Labor And Industrial Relations

RHODE ISLAND. DEPARTMENT OF LABOR & TRAINING. RHODE ISLAND EMPLOYMENT BULLETIN. *see* BUSINESS AND ECONOMICS—Labor And Industrial Relations

RHODE ISLAND. DEPARTMENT OF LABOR & TRAINING. RHODE ISLAND STATISTICAL & FISCAL DIGEST. *see* BUSINESS AND ECONOMICS—Labor And Industrial Relations

310 ITA ISSN 1828-1982
RIVISTA DI STATISTICA UFFICIALE. Text in Italian. 1992. 3/yr. **Document type:** *Government.*
Formerly (until 1999): Quaderni di Ricerca I S T A T (1125-128X)
Related titles: Online - full text ed.: free.
Published by: Istituto Nazionale di Statistica (I S T A T), Via Cesare Balbo 16, Rome, 00184, Italy. TEL 39-06-46731.

RIVISTA ITALIANA DI ECONOMIA DEMOGRAFIA E STATISTICA. *see* POPULATION STUDIES—Abstracting, Bibliographies, Statistics

ROAD DEATHS AUSTRALIA. *see* TRANSPORTATION—Roads And Traffic

ROADS GOODS VEHICLES TRAVELLING TO MAINLAND EUROPE (QUARTERLY). *see* TRANSPORTATION—Abstracting, Bibliographies, Statistics

RODORIOKU CHOSA HOKOKU/MONTHLY REPORT ON THE LABOUR FORCE SURVEY. *see* BUSINESS AND ECONOMICS—Abstracting, Bibliographies, Statistics

314 ITA ISSN 0035-7960
ROMA E PROVINCIA ATTRAVERSO LA STATISTICA. Text in Italian. 1956. a. bk.rev. charts; stat. index, cum.index. **Document type:** *Magazine, Trade.*
Published by: Camera di Commercio Industria Artigianato e Agricoltura di Roma, Via De'Burro 147, Rome, 00186, Italy.

ROPA, ROPNE PRODUKTY A ZEMNI PLYN. *see* PETROLEUM AND GAS—Abstracting, Bibliographies, Statistics

ROSSIISKII STATISTICHESKII YEZHEGODNIK/RUSSIAN STATISTICAL YEARBOOK. *see* BUSINESS AND ECONOMICS—Abstracting, Bibliographies, Statistics

ROSSIYA (YEAR). *see* BUSINESS AND ECONOMICS—Abstracting, Bibliographies, Statistics

ROSSIYA I STRANY MIRA/RUSSIA AND COUNTRIES OF THE WORLD. *see* BUSINESS AND ECONOMICS—Abstracting, Bibliographies, Statistics

ROSSIYA I STRANY S N G/RUSSIA AND C I S COUNTRIES. (Sodruzhestvo Nezavisimykh Gosudarstv) *see* BUSINESS AND ECONOMICS—Abstracting, Bibliographies, Statistics

ROSSIYA V TSIFRAKH (YEAR); kratkii statisticheskii zbornik. *see* BUSINESS AND ECONOMICS—Abstracting, Bibliographies, Statistics

▼ **ROUDOURYOKU CHOUSA NEMPOU/ANNUAL REPORT ON THE LABOUR FORCE SURVEY.** *see* BUSINESS AND ECONOMICS—Abstracting, Bibliographies, Statistics

310 GBR ISSN 0964-1998
HA1 CODEN: JSSAEF
➤ **ROYAL STATISTICAL SOCIETY. JOURNAL. SERIES A: STATISTICS IN SOCIETY.** Text in English. 1838. q. GBP 362 combined subscription domestic to institutions (print & online eds.); EUR 458 combined subscription in Europe to institutions (print & online eds.); USD 739 combined subscription in the Americas to institutions (print & online eds.); USD 786 combined subscription elsewhere to institutions (print & online eds.) (effective 2011); subscr. includes Significance. adv. bk.rev. bibl.; illus. index. back issues avail.; reprint service avail. from PSC. **Document type:** *Journal, Academic/Scholarly.* **Description:** Contains papers on economic, social and governmental issues; historical, biographical, philosophical, demographical and medical statistics.
Incorporates in part (1950-2004): Royal Statistical Society. Journal. Series D: The Statistician (0039-0526); Which was formerly (until 1961): Incorporated Statistician (1466-9404); Former titles (until 1988): Royal Statistical Society. Journal. Series A: General (0035-9238); (until 1948): Royal Statistical Society. Journal (0952-8385); (until 1887): Statistical Society. Journal (0959-5341)
Related titles: Microfilm ed.: (from BHP); Online - full text ed.: ISSN 1467-985X. GBP 279 domestic to institutions; EUR 354 in Europe to institutions; USD 571 in the Americas to institutions; USD 608 elsewhere to institutions (effective 2009) (from IngentaConnect).
Indexed: A12, A20, A22, A23, A24, A26, A34, A36, A38, ABIn, ASCA, Agr, ApMecR, B01, B06, B07, B09, B13, Biostat, CA, CABA, CCMJ, CIS, CMCI, CPM, CurCont, D01, E01, E12, EconLit, FR, GH, GeoRef, H09, H10, HECAB, I11, I13, IBSS, ISR, IndVet, JCQM, JEL, LT, MResA, MSN, MathR, N02, N03, ORMS, P06, P30, P34, P42, P50, P53, P54, PCI, PN&I, PQC, PhilInd, PopulInd, QC&AS, R12, RASB, RRTA, RefZh, S02, S03, S05, S13, S16, SCI, SCOPUS, SSCI, ST&MA, SociolAb, T02, T05, VS, W07, W11, WBA, Z02.
—BLDSC (4866.000000), IE, Infotrieve, Ingenta, INIST, Linda Hall. **CCC.**
Published by: (Royal Statistical Society), Wiley-Blackwell Publishing Ltd. (Subsidiary of: John Wiley & Sons, Inc.), 9600 Garsington Rd, Oxford, OX4 2DQ, United Kingdom. TEL 44-1865-776868, FAX 44-1865-714591, customerservices@blackwellpublishing.com. Eds. A Chevalier, S Day. Adv. contact Craig Pickett TEL 44-1865-476267.

001.42 GBR ISSN 1369-7412
HA1
➤ **ROYAL STATISTICAL SOCIETY. JOURNAL. SERIES B: STATISTICAL METHODOLOGY.** Text in English. 1934. 5/yr. GBP 250 in United Kingdom to institutions; EUR 315 in Europe to institutions; USD 521 in the Americas to institutions; USD 555 elsewhere to institutions; GBP 288 combined subscription in United Kingdom to institutions (print & online eds.); EUR 363 combined subscription in Europe to institutions (print & online eds.); USD 599 combined subscription in the Americas to institutions (print & online eds.); USD 639 combined subscription elsewhere to institutions (print & online eds.) (effective 2012). adv. bibl.; illus. index. back issues avail.; reprint service avail. from PSC. **Document type:** *Journal, Academic/Scholarly.* **Description:** Addresses theory and development of new statistical methods and applications of established methods.
Former titles (until 1998): Royal Statistical Society. Journal. Series B: Methodological (0035-9246); (until 1948): Royal Statistical Society. Journal. Supplement (1466-6162)
Related titles: Online - full text ed.: ISSN 1467-9868. GBP 250 in United Kingdom to institutions; EUR 315 in Europe to institutions; USD 521 in the Americas to institutions; USD 555 elsewhere to institutions (effective 2012) (from IngentaConnect).
Indexed: A12, A17, A20, A22, A26, A36, ABIn, ASCA, Agr, ApMecR, B01, B06, B07, B09, Biostat, C23, CA, CABA, CCMJ, CIS, CMCI, CurCont, D01, E01, E12, F08, F12, FR, GH, GeoRef, I11, IBSS, ISR, JCQM, MResA, MSN, MathR, N02, N03, P06, P30, P48, P50, P51, P53, P54, PCI, PHN&I, PQC, PhilInd, R07, RASB, S13, S16, SCI, SCOPUS, ST&MA, T02, T05, VS, W07, Z02.
—BLDSC (4867.020000), IE, Infotrieve, Ingenta, INIST, Linda Hall. **CCC.**
Published by: (Royal Statistical Society), Wiley-Blackwell Publishing Ltd. (Subsidiary of: John Wiley & Sons, Inc.), 9600 Garsington Rd, Oxford, OX4 2DQ, United Kingdom. TEL 44-1865-776868, FAX 44-1865-714591, customerservices@blackwellpublishing.com. Eds. C P Robert, G Casella. Adv. contact Craig Pickett TEL 44-1865-476267.

519.5 GBR ISSN 0035-9254
HA1 CODEN: APSTAG
➤ **ROYAL STATISTICAL SOCIETY. JOURNAL. SERIES C: APPLIED STATISTICS.** Text in English. 1952. 5/yr. GBP 250 in United Kingdom to institutions; EUR 315 in Europe to institutions; USD 521 in the Americas to institutions; USD 555 elsewhere to institutions; GBP 288 combined subscription in United Kingdom to institutions (print & online eds.); EUR 363 combined subscription in Europe to institutions (print & online eds.); USD 599 combined subscription in the Americas to institutions (print & online eds.); USD 639 combined subscription elsewhere to institutions (print & online eds.) (effective 2012). adv. bk.rev. bibl.; illus. index. back issues avail.; reprint service avail. from PSC. **Document type:** *Journal, Academic/Scholarly.* **Description:** Discusses the application of statistical methods to practical problems including computer algorithms.
Incorporates in part (in 2004): Royal Statistical Society. Journal. Series D. The Statistician (0039-0526); Which was formerly (1950-1961): Incorporated Statistician (1466-9404)
Related titles: Online - full text ed.: ISSN 1467-9876. GBP 250 in United Kingdom to institutions; EUR 315 in Europe to institutions; USD 521 in the Americas to institutions; USD 555 elsewhere to institutions (effective 2012) (from IngentaConnect).
Indexed: A12, A17, A20, A22, A26, A34, A36, ABIn, Agr, B01, B06, B07, B09, Biostat, BrArAb, C23, C25, CA, CABA, CCMJ, CIS, CISA, CMCI, CurCont, D01, E01, E12, ESPM, FCA, FR, GH, GeoRef, H16, I11, IBR, IBSS, IBZ, ISR, IndVet, Inspec, JCQM, MResA, MSN, MathR, N02, ORMS, P06, P30, P33, P39, P48, P50, P51, P53, P54, PCI, PHN&I, PQC, QC&AS, R07, R13, RASB, RiskAb, S13, S16, SCI, SCOPUS, ST&MA, SociolAb, SpeleolAb, T02, T05, TriticAb, VS, W07, W10, Z02.
—BLDSC (1580.000000), IE, Infotrieve, Ingenta, INIST, Linda Hall. **CCC.**
Published by: (Royal Statistical Society), Wiley-Blackwell Publishing Ltd. (Subsidiary of: John Wiley & Sons, Inc.), 9600 Garsington Rd, Oxford, OX4 2DQ, United Kingdom. TEL 44-1865-776868, FAX 44-1865-714591, customerservices@blackwellpublishing.com. Eds. M S Ridout, R Chandler. Adv. contact Craig Pickett TEL 44-1865-476267.

➤ **RUBBER STATISTICAL BULLETIN.** *see* RUBBER—Abstracting, Bibliographies, Statistics

➤ **RUBBER STATISTICAL NEWS.** *see* RUBBER—Abstracting, Bibliographies, Statistics

➤ **RUIMTE IN CIJFERS.** *see* HOUSING AND URBAN PLANNING—Abstracting, Bibliographies, Statistics

314 ROM ISSN 1223-7507
RUMANIA. COMISIA NATIONALA PENTRU STATISTICA. BULETIN STATISTIC LUNAR. Text in Romanian. m. ROL 275,000; USD 110 foreign. **Document type:** *Government.* **Description:** Presents statistical information referring to the main fields of economic and social activity.
Related titles: English ed.: Romania. National Commission for Statistics. Monthly Statistical Bulletin. ISSN 1221-7069.
Published by: Comisia Nationala pentru Statistica/National Commission for Statistics, Bd. Libertatii 16, Sector 5, Bucharest, 70542, Romania. TEL 40-1-3363370, FAX 40-1-3124873.

314 ROM ISSN 1221-7034
HA1641
RUMANIA. COMISIA NATIONALA PENTRU STATISTICA. BULETIN STATISTIC TRIMESTRIAL/ROMANIA. NATIONAL COMMISSION FOR STATISTICS. QUARTERLY STATISTICAL BULLETIN. Text in English, Romanian. q. ROL 250,000; USD 50 foreign. **Document type:** *Government.* **Description:** Presents data on the main fields of economic and social activity, by months and quarters.
Published by: Comisia Nationala pentru Statistica/National Commission for Statistics, Bd. Libertatii 16, Sector 5, Bucharest, 70542, Romania. TEL 40-1-6143371, FAX 40-1-3124873.

RURAL POVERTY AT A GLANCE. *see* SOCIAL SERVICES AND WELFARE—Abstracting, Bibliographies, Statistics

RUSSIA (YEAR). *see* BUSINESS AND ECONOMICS—Abstracting, Bibliographies, Statistics

RUSSIA IN FIGURES (YEAR). *see* BUSINESS AND ECONOMICS—Abstracting, Bibliographies, Statistics

316.7 RWA ISSN 0256-7229
HA4695
RWANDA. DIRECTION GENERALE DE LA STATISTIQUE. BULLETIN DE STATISTIQUE. Text in English. 1964. q. USD 48. Supplement avail. **Document type:** *Government.*
Former titles (until 1976): Rwanda. Direction de la Statistique et de la Documentation. Bulletin de Statistique (0304-9426); (until 1972): Rwanda. Direction de l'Office Generale des Statistiques. Bulletin de Statistique (0557-5583)
Published by: Direction Generale de la Statistique, BP 46, Kigali, Rwanda.

RWANDA. DIRECTION GENERALE DE LA STATISTIQUE. RAPPORT ANNUEL. *see* PUBLIC ADMINISTRATION—Abstracting, Bibliographies, Statistics

RWANDA. MINISTERE DE L'ENSEIGNEMENT PRIMAIRE ET SECONDAIRE. DIRECTION DE LA PLANIFICATION. BULLETIN DES STATISTIQUES DE L'ENSEIGNEMENT. *see* EDUCATION—Abstracting, Bibliographies, Statistics

S A A R F ALL MEDIA & PRODUCT SURVEY. (South Africa Advertising Research Foundation) *see* ADVERTISING AND PUBLIC RELATIONS—Abstracting, Bibliographies, Statistics

S A A R F RADIO AUDIENCE MEASUREMENT SURVEY. (South Africa Advertising Research Foundation) *see* COMMUNICATIONS—Abstracting, Bibliographies, Statistics

S A A R F TELEVISION AUDIENCE MEASUREMENT SURVEY. (South Africa Advertising Research Foundation) *see* ADVERTISING AND PUBLIC RELATIONS—Abstracting, Bibliographies, Statistics

310 ARG ISSN 0329-5583
S A E. REVISTA. (Sociedad Argentina de Estadistica) Text in Multiple languages. 1997. s-a. **Document type:** *Magazine, Trade.*
Published by: Sociedad Argentina de Estadistica, Balcarce 184, 2o Piso, Of 213, Buenos Aires, 1327, Argentina. TEL 54-11-43495774, sae@ccc.uba.ar.

S A R STATISTICS. (Search and Rescue) *see* TRANSPORTATION—Abstracting, Bibliographies, Statistics

314 ARG ISSN 1514-0636
S E C INFORMA. (Sistema Estadistico de la Ciudad) Text in Spanish. 1998. m. back issues avail. **Document type:** *Bulletin, Consumer.*
Related titles: E-mail ed.: ISSN 1852-1703. 2001; Online - full text ed.: ISSN 1852-169X. 2001.
Published by: Ministerio de Hacienda, Direccion General de Estadisticas y Censos, Ave San Juan 1340, Buenos Aires, C1148AAO, Argentina. TEL 54-11-40329147, FAX 54-11-40329148, comunicacion_estadistica@buenosaires.gob.ar, htttp://www.estadisticas.buenosaires.gob.ar/. Ed. Jose M Donati.

310 SWE ISSN 1404-854X
S I K A STATISTIK. (Statens Institut foer Kommunikationsanalys) Text in English, Swedish. 2000. irreg. **Document type:** *Monographic series, Government.*
Related titles: ♦ Series: Bantrafik. ISSN 1652-4373; ♦ Vaegtrafikskador. ISSN 1404-4625; ♦ Postverksamhet. ISSN 1403-5472; ♦ Luftfart. ISSN 1402-1919.
Published by: Statens Institut foer Kommunikationsanalys (SIKA)/Swedish Institute for Transport and Communications Analysis, Maria Skolgata 83, PO Box 17213, Stockholm, 10462, Sweden. TEL 46-8-50620600, FAX 46-8-50620610, sika@sika-institute.se.

310 SWE ISSN 1651-002X
S I K A STATISTISKA MEDDELANDEN. (Statens Institut foer Kommunikationsanalys) Text in English, Swedish. 1969. a. **Document type:** *Government.*
Former titles (until 2002): Statens Institut foer Kommunikationsanalys. Statistiske Meddelanden. Serie Tk, Transport och Kommunikationer (Print) (1404-5877); (until 2000): Statens Institut foer Kommunikationsanalys. Serie T, Transport och Kommunikationer (0082-0334)
Media: Online - full content.
Published by: Statens Institut foer Kommunikationsanalys (SIKA)/Swedish Institute for Transport and Communications Analysis, Maria Skolgata 83, PO Box 17213, Stockholm, 10462, Sweden. TEL 46-8-50620600, FAX 46-8-50620610, sika@sika-institute.se. Ed. Niklas Kristiansson.

S I N E T. (Social Indicators Network News) *see* SOCIOLOGY—Abstracting, Bibliographies, Statistics

S N G V (YEAR). (Sodruzhestvo Nezavisimykh Gosudarst) *see* BUSINESS AND ECONOMICS—Abstracting, Bibliographies, Statistics

570.15195 003 ESP ISSN 1696-2281
➤ **S O R T.** (Statistics and Operations Research Transactions) Variant title: Quaderns d'Estadistica i Investigacio Operativa. Text in English; Abstracts in English, Catalan. 2003 (Jan.). s-a. EUR 22 domestic; EUR 25 foreign (effective 2011). **Document type:** *Journal, Academic/Scholarly.* **Description:** Publishes original articles on official and general statistics, operations research and biometrics.
Former titles (until 2003): Questiio; (until 1992): Quaderns d'Estadistica, Sistemes, Informatica i Investigacio Operativa (0210-8054); (until 1977): Cuadernos de Estadistica Aplicada e Investigacion Operativa
Related titles: Online - full text ed.: ISSN 2013-8830. free (effective 2011).
Indexed: CCMJ, CIS, CPEI, EngInd, IECT, MSN, MathR, SCI, SCOPUS, ST&MA, W07, Z02.
Published by: Generalitat de Catalunya, Institut d'Estadistica de Catalunya, Via Laietana, 58, Barcelona, 08003, Spain. TEL 34-934-120088, FAX 34-934-123145, questiio@iesc.es, http://www.idescat.es/publications/questiio/questiio.shtm. Ed. Montserrat Guillen.

➤ **S R D S INTERNATIONAL MEDIA GUIDE. BUSINESS PUBLICATIONS. ASIA-PACIFIC/MIDDLE EAST/AFRICA.** (Standard Rate & Data Service) *see* ADVERTISING AND PUBLIC RELATIONS—Abstracting, Bibliographies, Statistics

➤ **S R D S OUT-OF-HOME ADVERTISING SOURCE.** (Standard Rate & Data Service) *see* ADVERTISING AND PUBLIC RELATIONS—Abstracting, Bibliographies, Statistics

310 LCA
ST. LUCIA. STATISTICAL DEPARTMENT. ANNUAL STATISTICAL DIGEST. Text in English. 1960. a. XEC 15. **Document type:** *Government.*
Published by: Statistical Department, New Government Bldg, Block C, 2nd Fl, Conway, Castries, St. Lucia. TEL 758-45-22697, FAX 758-45-31648, TELEX 6394 FORAFF. Ed. Bryan Boxill.

310 LCA
ST. LUCIA. STATISTICAL DEPARTMENT. STATISTICAL POCKET DIGEST. Text in English. 1979. a. XEC 2, USD 2. **Document type:** *Government.*
Published by: Statistical Department, New Government Bldg, Block C, 2nd Fl, Conway, Castries, St. Lucia. TEL 758-45-22697, FAX 758-45-31648, TELEX 6394 FORAFF. Ed. Bryan Boxill.

SAMFUNNSSPEILET. *see* SOCIOLOGY—Abstracting, Bibliographies, Statistics

SAN DIEGO REGION. INFO BULLETIN. POPULATION & HOUSING ESTIMATES. *see* HOUSING AND URBAN PLANNING—Abstracting, Bibliographies, Statistics

SAN'EOB SAENGSAN YEONBO/KOREA (REPUBLIC). NATIONAL STATISTICAL OFFICE. ANNUAL REPORT ON MONTHLY INDUSTRIAL PRODUCTION STATISTICS. *see* BUSINESS AND ECONOMICS—Abstracting, Bibliographies, Statistics

SANFORD EVANS GOLD BOOK OF SNOWMOBILE DATA AND USED PRICES. *see* SPORTS AND GAMES—Abstracting, Bibliographies, Statistics

315 IND ISSN 0976-836X
QA276.A1
➤ **SANKHYA. SERIES A**; mathematical statistics and probability. Text in English. 2003. 4/yr. EUR 159, USD 215 combined subscription to institutions (print & online eds.) (effective 2011). stat. **Document type:** *Journal, Academic/Scholarly.* **Description:** Publishes research articles in the broad areas of theoretical statistics, applied statistics, mathematical statistics and probability.
Supersedes in part (in 2007): Sankhya. The Indian Journal of Statistics (0972-7671); Which was formed by the merger of (1961-2003): Sankhya. Series A (0581-572X); (1961-2003): Sankhya. Series B (0581-5738); Both of which superseded in part (in 1961): Sankhya (0036-4452)
Related titles: Online - full text ed.: ISSN 0976-8378.
Indexed: A22, CCMJ, MSN, MathR, SCOPUS.
—BLDSC (8075.005000), IE, INIST, Linda Hall. **CCC.**
Published by: (Indian Statistical Institute), Springer (India) Private Ltd. (Subsidiary of: Springer Science+Business Media), 212, Deen Dayal Upadhyaya Marg, 3rd Fl, Gandharva Mahavidyalaya, New Delhi, 110 002, India. Ed. Pranab K Sen.

310 IND ISSN 0976-8386
CODEN: SANBBV
SANKHYA. SERIES B; applied and interdisciplinary statistics. Text in English. 2003. q. adv. bk.rev. bibl.; stat.; illus. Index. reprints avail. **Document type:** *Journal, Academic/Scholarly.*
Supersedes in part (in 2007): Sankhya. Indian Journal of Statistics (0972-7671); Which was formed by the merger of (1961-2003): Sankhya. Series A (0581-572X); (1961-2003): Sankhya. Series B (0581-5738); Both of which superseded in part (in 1961): Sankhya (0036-4452)
Related titles: Online - full text ed.: ISSN 0976-8394 (from PMC).
Indexed: Biostat, CCMJ, CIS, ChemAb, MSN, MathR, P06, P30, RASB, ST&MA, Z02.
—BLDSC (8075.005000), IE, Infotrieve, Ingenta, INIST, Linda Hall. **CCC.**
Published by: Springer (India) Private Ltd. (Subsidiary of: Springer Science+Business Media), 212, Deen Dayal Upadhyaya Marg, 3rd Fl, Gandharva Mahavidyalaya, New Delhi, 110 002, India. TEL 91-11-45755888, FAX 91-11-45755889. Ed. Pranab K Sen. Circ: 1,400.

314 STP
SAO TOME E PRINCIPE. REPARTICAO PROVINCIAL DOS SERVICOS DE ESTATISTICA. BOLETIN TRIMESTRAL DE ESTATISTICA. Text in Portuguese. 1971. q.
Published by: Reparticao Provincial dos Servicos de Estatistica, Caixa Postal 256, Sao Tome, Sao Tome e Principe.

315 IND
SARVEKSHANA. Text in English, Hindi. 1977. s-a. INR 200 per issue (effective 2011). stat. back issues avail. **Document type:** *Journal, Trade.*
Indexed: RASB.
Published by: National Sample Survey Organisation, Sardar Patel Bhavan, Parliament St, New Delhi, 110 001, India. TEL 91-11-23742026, jdash@nic.in, http://mospi.nic.in/websitensso.htm.
Subscr. to.: Controller of Publications.

SASKATCHEWAN AGRICULTURE AND FOOD. AGRICULTURAL STATISTICS. *see* AGRICULTURE—Abstracting, Bibliographies, Statistics

SASKATCHEWAN CONSUMER PRICE INDEX. *see* BUSINESS AND ECONOMICS—Abstracting, Bibliographies, Statistics

SASKATCHEWAN DRUG PLAN AND EXTENDED BENEFITS BRANCH. ANNUAL STATISTICAL REPORT. *see* PHARMACY AND PHARMACOLOGY—Abstracting, Bibliographies, Statistics

SASKATCHEWAN LABOUR FORCE STATISTICS. *see* BUSINESS AND ECONOMICS—Abstracting, Bibliographies, Statistics

319 SAU ISSN 0581-8605
HA1681
SAUDI ARABIA. CENTRAL DEPARTMENT OF STATISTICS. STATISTICAL YEARBOOK. Text in Arabic, English. 1965. a. **Document type:** *Government.* **Description:** Presents a picture of economic and social development in the kingdom on the basis of scientifically organized studies.
Published by: Central Department of Statistics, P O Box 3735, Riyadh, 11118, Saudi Arabia.

SAUDI ARABIA. MINISTRY OF EDUCATION. ANNUAL STATISTICAL REPORT. *see* EDUCATION—Abstracting, Bibliographies, Statistics

SAUDI ARABIA. MINISTRY OF EDUCATION. EDUCATIONAL STATISTICS. *see* EDUCATION—Abstracting, Bibliographies, Statistics

519.5 GBR ISSN 0303-6898
QA276.A1 CODEN: SJSADG
➤ **SCANDINAVIAN JOURNAL OF STATISTICS**; theory and applications. Abbreviated title: S J S. Text in English. 1974. q. GBP 183 in United Kingdom to institutions; EUR 233 in Europe to institutions; USD 321 in the Americas to institutions; USD 376 elsewhere to institutions; GBP 211 combined subscription in United Kingdom to institutions (print & online eds.); EUR 268 combined subscription in Europe to institutions (print & online eds.); USD 369 combined subscription in the Americas to institutions (print & online eds.); USD 433 combined subscription elsewhere to institutions (print & online eds.) (effective 2012). adv. abstr.; illus. index. Supplement avail.; back issues avail.; reprint service avail. from PSC. **Document type:** *Journal, Academic/Scholarly.* **Description:** Provides significant and innovative original contributions to statistical methodology, both theory and applications.
Related titles: Online - full text ed.: ISSN 1467-9469. GBP 183 in United Kingdom to institutions; EUR 233 in Europe to institutions; USD 321 in the Americas to institutions; USD 376 elsewhere to institutions (effective 2012) (from IngentaConnect).
Indexed: A01, A03, A08, A12, A17, A22, A26, ABIn, ASCA, B01, B06, B07, B09, Biostat, CA, CCMJ, CIS, CMCI, CurCont, E01, H05, IBR, IBZ, ISR, Inspec, JCQM, MSN, MathR, ORMS, P03, P30, P48, P51, P53, P54, PQC, PsycInfo, QC&AS, RefZh, S01, SCI, SCOPUS, ST&MA, T02, W07, Z02.
—BLDSC (8087.549000), IE, Infotrieve, Ingenta, INIST, Linda Hall. **CCC.**
Published by: (Svenska Statistikersamfundet/Swedish Statistical Society SWE, Danish Society for Theoretical Statistics DNK, Suomen Tilastoseura/Finnish Statistical Society FIN), Wiley-Blackwell Publishing Ltd. (Subsidiary of: John Wiley & Sons, Inc.), 9600 Garsington Rd, Oxford, OX4 2DQ, United Kingdom. TEL 44-1865-776868, FAX 44-1865-714591, customerservices@blackwellpublishing.com. Eds. Juha Alho, Paavo Salminen.

➤ **SCHOOL FACTS.** *see* EDUCATION—Abstracting, Bibliographies, Statistics

➤ **SCHOOLS IN WALES: GENERAL STATISTICS.** *see* EDUCATION—Abstracting, Bibliographies, Statistics

➤ **SCHUELERINNEN, SCHUELER UND STUDIERENDE - ELEVES, ETUDIANTES ET ETUDIANTS.** *see* EDUCATION—Abstracting, Bibliographies, Statistics

➤ **SCHWEIZERISCHE STRASSENVERKEHRSZAEHLUNG/COMPTAGE SUISSE DE LA CIRCULATION ROUTIERE.** *see* TRANSPORTATION—Abstracting, Bibliographies, Statistics

➤ **SCHWEIZERISCHE VERKEHRSSTATISTIK/STATISTIQUE SUISSE DES TRANSPORTS.** *see* TRANSPORTATION—Abstracting, Bibliographies, Statistics

➤ **SCHWEIZERISCHE ZEITSCHRIFT FUER VOLKSWIRTSCHAFT UND STATISTIK/REVUE SUISSE D'ECONOMIE POLITIQUE ET DE STATISTIQUE.** *see* BUSINESS AND ECONOMICS

➤ **SCIENCE, TECHNOLOGY AND INNOVATION IN EUROPE.** *see* SCIENCES: COMPREHENSIVE WORKS—Abstracting, Bibliographies, Statistics

➤ **SCOTTISH EDUCATION DEPARTMENT. STATISTICAL BULLETIN.** *see* EDUCATION—Abstracting, Bibliographies, Statistics

310 ITA ISSN 2038-4971
SCRITTI DI STATISTICA ECONOMICA. Text in Italian. 1994. irreg. **Document type:** *Journal, Academic/Scholarly.*
Related titles: CD-ROM ed.: ISSN 2038-498X.
Published by: (Universita degli Studi di Napoli "Parthenope", Istituto Universitario Navale), Liguori Editore, Via Posillipo 394, Naples, 80123, Italy. TEL 39-081-7206111, FAX 39-081-7206244, liguori@liguori.it, http://www.liguori.it.

SECRETARIA PERMANENTE DEL TRATADO GENERAL DE INTEGRACION ECONOMICA CENTROAMERICANA. BOLETIN ESTADISTICO. *see* POLITICAL SCIENCE—Abstracting, Bibliographies, Statistics

SECTOR REVIEW. CATERING AND ALLIED TRADES. *see* HOTELS AND RESTAURANTS—Abstracting, Bibliographies, Statistics

SECTOR REVIEW: MOTOR TRADES. *see* TRANSPORTATION—Abstracting, Bibliographies, Statistics

SECTOR REVIEW. RETAILING. *see* BUSINESS AND ECONOMICS—Abstracting, Bibliographies, Statistics

SECTOR REVIEW. SERVICE TRADES. *see* BUSINESS AND ECONOMICS—Abstracting, Bibliographies, Statistics

SECTOR REVIEW: WHOLESALING AND DEALING. *see* BUSINESS AND ECONOMICS—Abstracting, Bibliographies, Statistics

SECURITE ROUTIERE. *see* TRANSPORTATION—Abstracting, Bibliographies, Statistics

310 JPN ISSN 1344-0446
SEKAI NO TOKEI (YEAR). Variant title: International Statistical Compendia (Year). Text in Japanese. 1951. a. stat. **Document type:** *Report, Government.*
Formerly (until 1993): Kokusai Tokei Yoran (0286-1437)
Related titles: Diskette ed.: JPY 5,250 (effective 2000).
Published by: Japan. Ministry of Internal Affairs and Communications. Statistics Bureau/Somucho. Tokeikyoko, 19-1 Wakamatsu-cho, Shinjyuku-ku, Tokyo, 162-8668, Japan. TEL 81-3-5273-2020.

SELECTED MANPOWER STATISTICS (ONLINE). *see* BUSINESS AND ECONOMICS—Abstracting, Bibliographies, Statistics

S

SELECTED VITAL STATISTICS AND HEALTH STATUS INDICATORS. ANNUAL REPORT. *see* POPULATION STUDIES—Abstracting, Bibliographies, Statistics

SENEGAL. MINISTERE DE L'ECONOMIE, DES FINANCES ET DU PLAN. BANQUE DE DONNEES ECONOMIQUES ET FINANCIERES. *see* BUSINESS AND ECONOMICS—Abstracting, Bibliographies, Statistics

SENEGAL. MINISTERE DE L'ECONOMIE, DES FINANCES ET DU PLAN. BULLETIN ECONOMIQUE ET STATISTIQUE. *see* BUSINESS AND ECONOMICS—Abstracting, Bibliographies, Statistics

SENEGAL. MINISTERE DE L'ECONOMIE, DES FINANCES ET DU PLAN. COMPTES ECONOMIQUES. *see* BUSINESS AND ECONOMICS—Economic Situation And Conditions

SENEGAL. MINISTERE DE L'ECONOMIE, DES FINANCES ET DU PLAN. DOSSIERS DOCUMENTAIRES. *see* BUSINESS AND ECONOMICS—Abstracting, Bibliographies, Statistics

SENEGAL. MINISTERE DE L'ECONOMIE, DES FINANCES ET DU PLAN. ENQUETE DEMOGRAPHIQUE ET SANTE II (YEAR). *see* SOCIAL SERVICES AND WELFARE—Abstracting, Bibliographies, Statistics

SENEGAL. MINISTERE DE L'ECONOMIE, DES FINANCES ET DU PLAN. ENQUETE EMPLOI, SOUS EMPLOI ET CHOMAGE. *see* SOCIAL SERVICES AND WELFARE—Abstracting, Bibliographies, Statistics

SENEGAL. MINISTERE DE L'ECONOMIE, DES FINANCES ET DU PLAN. ENQUETE SUR LA PLANIFICATION FAMILIALE EN MILIEU URBAIN. *see* BIRTH CONTROL—Abstracting, Bibliographies, Statistics

SENEGAL. MINISTERE DE L'ECONOMIE, DES FINANCES ET DU PLAN. ENQUETE SUR LES PRIORITES: DIMENSIONS SOCIALES DE L'AJUSTEMENT (YEAR). *see* SOCIAL SERVICES AND WELFARE—Abstracting, Bibliographies, Statistics

SENEGAL. MINISTERE DE L'ECONOMIE, DES FINANCES ET DU PLAN. INDICE DE LA PRODUCTION INDUSTRIELLE. *see* BUSINESS AND ECONOMICS—Abstracting, Bibliographies, Statistics

SENEGAL. MINISTERE DE L'ECONOMIE, DES FINANCES ET DU PLAN. INDICE DES PRIX A LA CONSOMMATION. *see* BUSINESS AND ECONOMICS—Abstracting, Bibliographies, Statistics

SENEGAL. MINISTERE DE L'ECONOMIE, DES FINANCES ET DU PLAN. NOTE D'ANALYSE DU COMMERCE EXTERIEUR. *see* BUSINESS AND ECONOMICS—Abstracting, Bibliographies, Statistics

SENEGAL. MINISTERE DE L'ECONOMIE, DES FINANCES ET DU PLAN. NOTE DE CONJONCTURE. *see* BUSINESS AND ECONOMICS—Abstracting, Bibliographies, Statistics

SENEGAL. MINISTERE DE L'ECONOMIE, DES FINANCES ET DU PLAN. POPULATION DU SENEGAL. *see* SOCIAL SERVICES AND WELFARE—Abstracting, Bibliographies, Statistics

SENEGAL. MINISTERE DE L'ECONOMIE, DES FINANCES ET DU PLAN. POPULATION DU SENEGAL: STRUCTURE PAR AGE ET SEXE ET PROJECTION. *see* POPULATION STUDIES—Abstracting, Bibliographies, Statistics

SENEGAL. MINISTERE DE L'ECONOMIE, DES FINANCES ET DU PLAN. RAPPORT D'ANALYSE PAR REGION. *see* POPULATION STUDIES—Abstracting, Bibliographies, Statistics

SENEGAL. MINISTERE DE L'ECONOMIE, DES FINANCES ET DU PLAN. RAPPORT NATIONAL. *see* POPULATION STUDIES—Abstracting, Bibliographies, Statistics

SENEGAL. MINISTERE DE L'ECONOMIE, DES FINANCES ET DU PLAN. RAPPORT SUR LES PERSPECTIVES ECONOMIQUES. *see* BUSINESS AND ECONOMICS—Abstracting, Bibliographies, Statistics

SENEGAL. MINISTERE DE L'ECONOMIE, DES FINANCES ET DU PLAN. REPERTOIRE DES VILLAGES PAR REGION. *see* POPULATION STUDIES—Abstracting, Bibliographies, Statistics

SENEGAL. MINISTERE DE L'ECONOMIE, DES FINANCES ET DU PLAN. RESULTATS PROVISOIRES. *see* POPULATION STUDIES—Abstracting, Bibliographies, Statistics

SENEGAL. MINISTERE DE L'ECONOMIE, DES FINANCES ET DU PLAN. SITUATION ECONOMIQUE REGIONALE. *see* BUSINESS AND ECONOMICS—Abstracting, Bibliographies, Statistics

SENEGAL. MINISTERE DE L'ECONOMIE, DES FINANCES ET DU PLAN. TABLEAU DE BORD DE LA SITUATION SOCIALE. *see* SOCIAL SERVICES AND WELFARE—Abstracting, Bibliographies, Statistics

SENEGAL. MINISTERE DE L'ECONOMIE, DES FINANCES ET DU PLAN. TABLEAU DE BORD DE L'ECONOMIE SENEGALAISE. *see* BUSINESS AND ECONOMICS—Abstracting, Bibliographies, Statistics

310 CAN ISSN 1719-4121
SENIORS' STATISTICAL PROFILE. Text in English. 2003. irreg. **Document type:** *Monographic series, Consumer.*
Formerly (until 2004): A Statistical Profile of Nova Scotia Seniors (1711-067X)
Published by: Seniors' Secretariat, PO Box 2065, Halifax, NS B3J 2Z1, Canada. TEL 902-424-0065, 800-670-0065, FAX 902-424-0561, scs@gov.ns.ca, http://www.gov.ns.ca/scs.

SENTENCING SNAPSHOTS. *see* LAW—Judicial Systems

SENTENCING TRENDS & ISSUES; an analysis of New South Wales sentencing statistics. *see* LAW—Abstracting, Bibliographies, Statistics

519.5 USA ISSN 0747-4946
QA279.7 CODEN: SEANEX
SEQUENTIAL ANALYSIS. Text in English. 1982. q. GBP 1,026 combined subscription in United Kingdom to institutions (print & online eds.); EUR 1,358, USD 1,707 combined subscription to institutions (print & online eds.) (effective 2012). adv. abstr. reprint service avail. from PSC. **Document type:** *Journal, Academic/Scholarly.* **Description:** Covers theoretical and applied aspects of sequential methodologies in all areas of statistical science.
Formerly (until 1984): Communications in Statistics. Sequential Analysis (0731-177X)
Related titles: Microform ed.: (from RPI); Online - full text ed.: ISSN 1532-4176. GBP 924 in United Kingdom to institutions; EUR 1,222, USD 1,536 to institutions (effective 2012) (from IngentaConnect).
Indexed: A01, A03, A08, A22, Biostat, CA, CCMJ, CIS, E01, JCQM, MSN, MathR, ORMS, P30, P50, QC&AS, S01, SCOPUS, ST&MA, T02, Z02.
—BLDSC (8242.279500), IE, Infotrieve, Ingenta, INIST, Linda Hall. **CCC.**
Published by: Taylor & Francis Inc. (Subsidiary of: Taylor & Francis Group), 325 Chestnut St, Ste 800, Philadelphia, PA 19106. TEL 215-625-2940, 800-354-1420, orders@taylorandfrancis.com, http://www.taylorandfrancis.com. Ed. Nitis Mukhopadhyay. Adv. contact Linda Hann TEL 44-1344-779945.

SERICULTURE & SILK INDUSTRY STATISTICS (YEAR). *see* TEXTILE INDUSTRIES AND FABRICS—Abstracting, Bibliographies, Statistics

SERVICE ANNUAL SURVEY (ONLINE). *see* BUSINESS AND ECONOMICS—Abstracting, Bibliographies, Statistics

SEYCHELLES. DEPARTMENT OF FINANCE. ECONOMIC INDICATORS. *see* BUSINESS AND ECONOMICS—Abstracting, Bibliographies, Statistics

SEYCHELLES. DEPARTMENT OF FINANCE. NATIONAL ACCOUNTS. *see* BUSINESS AND ECONOMICS—Abstracting, Bibliographies, Statistics

310 SYC
SEYCHELLES. DEPARTMENT OF FINANCE. STATISTICAL BULLETIN. Text in English. 1980. q. SCR 25. stat. back issues avail.
Published by: Department of Finance, Statistics Division, PO Box 206, Victoria, Mahe, Seychelles.

310 SYC
SEYCHELLES. DEPARTMENT OF FINANCE. STATISTICS DIVISION. STATISTICAL ABSTRACT. Text in English. 1977. a. SCR 60. **Document type:** *Abstract/Index.*
Published by: Department of Finance, Statistics Division, PO Box 206, Victoria, Mahe, Seychelles. Circ: 250.

SEYCHELLES. MANAGEMENT AND INFORMATION SYSTEMS DIVISION. TOURISM AND MIGRATION STATISTICS. *see* TRAVEL AND TOURISM—Abstracting, Bibliographies, Statistics

SEYCHELLES. PRESIDENT'S OFFICE. STATISTICS DIVISION. AGRICULTURE SURVEY. *see* AGRICULTURE—Abstracting, Bibliographies, Statistics

SEYCHELLES. PRESIDENT'S OFFICE. STATISTICS DIVISION. CENSUS. *see* POPULATION STUDIES—Abstracting, Bibliographies, Statistics

SEYCHELLES. PRESIDENT'S OFFICE. STATISTICS DIVISION. EMPLOYMENT & EARNINGS. *see* BUSINESS AND ECONOMICS—Abstracting, Bibliographies, Statistics

SEYCHELLES. PRESIDENT'S OFFICE. STATISTICS DIVISION. EXTERNAL TRADE. *see* BUSINESS AND ECONOMICS—Abstracting, Bibliographies, Statistics

SEYCHELLES. PRESIDENT'S OFFICE. STATISTICS DIVISION. POPULATION AND VITAL STATISTICS. *see* POPULATION STUDIES—Abstracting, Bibliographies, Statistics

SEYCHELLES. PRESIDENT'S OFFICE. STATISTICS DIVISION. PRODUCTION INDICATORS. *see* BUSINESS AND ECONOMICS—Abstracting, Bibliographies, Statistics

SEYCHELLES. PRESIDENT'S OFFICE. STATISTICS DIVISION. RETAIL PRICES. *see* BUSINESS AND ECONOMICS—Abstracting, Bibliographies, Statistics

SEYCHELLES. PRESIDENT'S OFFICE. STATISTICS DIVISION. STATISTICAL ABSTRACT. *see* BUSINESS AND ECONOMICS—Abstracting, Bibliographies, Statistics

SEYCHELLES. STATISTICS DIVISION. STATISTICAL BULLETIN. TOURISM. *see* TRAVEL AND TOURISM—Abstracting, Bibliographies, Statistics

SEYCHELLES. STATISTICS DIVISION. STATISTICAL BULLETIN. VISITOR SURVEY. *see* TRAVEL AND TOURISM—Abstracting, Bibliographies, Statistics

SHAKAI SEIKATSU TOKEI SHIHYO/SOCIAL INDICATORS BY PREFECTURE (YEAR). *see* SOCIAL SERVICES AND WELFARE—Abstracting, Bibliographies, Statistics

310 HKG
SHANGHAI STATISTICAL YEARBOOK (YEAR). Text in Chinese, English. 1990. a. HKD 595 in Hong Kong; USD 45 elsewhere. **Description:** Contains the latest comprehensive statistics of Shanghai's social economic development and other important data.
Published by: (Guojia Tongji Ju/State Statistical Bureau CHN), China Phone Book Company Ltd., 24-F Citicorp Centre, 18 Whitfield Rd, GPO Box 11581, Hong Kong, Hong Kong. FAX 852-2503-1526.

310 CHN ISSN 1006-2726
SHANGHAI TONGJI/SHANGHAI STATISTICS. Text in Chinese. 1983. m. USD 3.80 newsstand/cover (effective 2006). **Document type:** *Journal, Academic/Scholarly.*
Related titles: Online - full text ed.
Published by: (Shanghai Shi Tongji-ju/Shanghai Municipal Bureau of Statistics), Shanghai Tongji Zazhishe, 1008 Dong Changzhi Rd, Shanghai, 200082, China. TEL 86-21-65455887, FAX 86-21-65458823.

SHEEP'S BACK TO MILL STATISTICS YEARBOOK. *see* TEXTILE INDUSTRIES AND FABRICS—Abstracting, Bibliographies, Statistics

SHENZHEN TONGJI NIANJIAN (YEAR)/SHENZHEN STATISTICAL YEARBOOK. *see* BUSINESS AND ECONOMICS—Abstracting, Bibliographies, Statistics

SHIPPING STATISTICS AND MARKET REVIEW. *see* TRANSPORTATION—Abstracting, Bibliographies, Statistics

SHIPPING STATISTICS YEARBOOK. *see* TRANSPORTATION—Abstracting, Bibliographies, Statistics

SHOHISHA BUKKA SHISU NENPO/ANNUAL REPORT ON THE CONSUMER PRICE INDEX (YEAR). *see* CONSUMER EDUCATION AND PROTECTION—Abstracting, Bibliographies, Statistics

SHUGYO KOZO KIHON CHOSA HOKOKU. *see* BUSINESS AND ECONOMICS—Abstracting, Bibliographies, Statistics

310 CHN
SHUJU/DATA (BEIJING). Text in Chinese. 1986. m. CNY 120; CNY 10 per issue (effective 2009). **Document type:** *Journal, Academic/Scholarly.*
Formerly (until 2005): Beijing Tongji/Beijing Statistics (1006-5954)
Related titles: Online - full text ed.
Published by: Beijing Shi Tongji Ju, 36, Guanganmen Nan Jie, Beijing, 100054, China. TEL 86-10-63515806, http://www.bjstats.gov.cn/.

310 CHN
SICHUAN TONGJI NIANJIAN/STATISTICAL YEARBOOK OF SICHUAN. Text in Chinese. a. CNY 38. **Document type:** *Government.*
Published by: (Sichuan. Sichuan Tongji Ju), Zhongguo Tongji Chubanshe/China Statistics Press, 6, Xi San Huan Nan Lu Jia, Beijing, 100073, China. TEL 8217162.

316 SLE
SIERRA LEONE. CENTRAL STATISTICS OFFICE. ANNUAL STATISTICAL DIGEST. Text in English. 196?. a. SLL 8.
Related titles: Microfiche ed.: (from PQC).
Published by: Central Statistics Office, Tower Hill, Freetown, Sierra Leone.

314 LUX ISSN 1018-5739
HA1107.5 CODEN: SICMEY
SIGMA. Text in English. 1976. q. free. **Document type:** *Bulletin, Government.* **Description:** Seeks to provide up-to-date information on the progress of measures taken in the run up toward European integration.
Formerly (until 1991): Eurostat News (0378-4207)
Related titles: French ed.: ISSN 1018-5178.
Indexed: IIS, ILD, WBA.
—BLDSC (8275.367000).
Published by: European Commission, Statistical Office of the European Communities (E U R O S T A T), Rue Alcide de Gasperi, Luxembourg, 2920, Luxembourg. TEL 352-4301-34526, FAX 352-4301-34415, eurostat-infodesk@cec.eu.int, http://www.europa.eu.int/comm/eurostat. Ed. J Drappier. **Dist. in U.S. by:** European Commission, Information Service, 2100 M St, NW Ste 707, Washington, DC 20037.

310 GBR ISSN 1740-9705
QA276.A1
SIGNIFICANCE; statistics making sense. Text in English. 2004. q. GBP 128 in United Kingdom to institutions; EUR 162 in Europe to institutions; USD 264 in the Americas to institutions; USD 282 elsewhere to institutions; GBP 148 combined subscription in United Kingdom to institutions (print & online eds.); EUR 187 combined subscription in Europe to institutions (print & online eds.); USD 305 combined subscription in the Americas to institutions (print & online eds.); USD 324 combined subscription elsewhere to institutions (print & online eds.) (effective 2012). adv. back issues avail.; reprint service avail. from PSC. **Document type:** *Journal, Academic/Scholarly.* **Description:** Its aim is to communicate and demonstrate in an entertaining and thought-provoking way the practical use of statistics in all walks of life and to show how statistics benefit society.
Related titles: Online - full text ed.: ISSN 1740-9713. GBP 128 in United Kingdom to institutions; EUR 162 in Europe to institutions; USD 264 in the Americas to institutions; USD 282 elsewhere to institutions (effective 2012) (from IngentaConnect).
Indexed: A01, A22, A26, B21, CA, CCMJ, E01, ESPM, H&SSA, H05, MSN, MathR, RiskAb, SCOPUS, SSciA, T02, Z02.
—BLDSC (8276.280000), IE, Ingenta, INIST, Linda Hall. **CCC.**
Published by: (Royal Statistical Society), Wiley-Blackwell Publishing Ltd. (Subsidiary of: John Wiley & Sons, Inc.), 9600 Garsington Rd, Oxford, OX4 2DQ, United Kingdom. TEL 44-1865-776868, FAX 44-1865-714591, customerservices@blackwellpublishing.com. Ed. Julian Champkin. Adv. contact Jonelle Lewis Chamberlain TEL 44-20-76143947.

SINGAPORE. DEPARTMENT OF STATISTICS. ECONOMIC SURVEYS SERIES. *see* HOTELS AND RESTAURANTS—Abstracting, Bibliographies, Statistics

338 315 SGP ISSN 0037-5640
HA1797.S5
SINGAPORE. DEPARTMENT OF STATISTICS. MONTHLY DIGEST OF STATISTICS. Text in English. 1962. m. SGD 7.70. **Document type:** *Government.* **Description:** Provides current data relating to the demographic, economic and social characteristics of Singapore.
Published by: Department of Statistics, 100 High St #05-01, The Treasury, Singapore, 179434, Singapore. TEL 65-3327686, FAX 65-3327689, info@singstat.gov.sg. **Dist. by:** Myepb Bookstore, 3 Temasek Blvd, #B1-025 Suntec City Mall, Singapore 038983, Singapore. TEL 65-333 9703, FAX 65-333 9236, cr@myepb.com, http://www.myepb.com.

SINGAPORE YEARBOOK OF MANPOWER STATISTICS. *see* BUSINESS AND ECONOMICS—Abstracting, Bibliographies, Statistics

315 SGP ISSN 0583-3655
HA4600.67
SINGAPORE YEARBOOK OF STATISTICS. Text in English. a. SGD 13.40. charts. **Description:** Provides important data on the demographic, economic and social characteristics of Singapore.
Published by: Department of Statistics, 100 High St #05-01, The Treasury, Singapore, 179434, Singapore. TEL 65-3327686, FAX 65-3327689, info@singstat.gov.sg. **Dist. by:** Myepb Bookstore, 3 Temasek Blvd, #B1-025 Suntec City Mall, Singapore 038983, Singapore. TEL 65-333 9703, FAX 65-333 9236, cr@myepb.com, http://www.myepb.com.

318.2 ARG
SINOPSIS ESTADISTICA ARGENTINA. Text in English, Spanish. a. ARS 1.50, USD 10 (effective 1999). **Document type:** *Government.* **Description:** Presents a summary of sociodemographic and economic information from the Anuario Estadistico.
Published by: Instituto Nacional de Estadistica y Censos, Presidente Julio A Roca 615, Buenos Aires, 1067, Argentina. TEL 54-114-3499662, FAX 54-114-3499621.

SINTESIS BASICA DE ESTADISTICA VITINICOLA ARGENTINA. *see* AGRICULTURE—Crop Production And Soil

SISTEMA DE INFORMACION FIANCIERA GRAFICA TRIMESTRAL. *see* INSURANCE—Abstracting, Bibliographies, Statistics

SITUATION ECONOMIQUE ET SOCIALE DU SENEGAL. *see* BUSINESS AND ECONOMICS—Abstracting, Bibliographies, Statistics

314.97 SVN ISSN 1318-3745
SLOVENIA V STEVILKAH/SLOVENIA IN FIGURES. Text in Slovenian, English. 1980. a. EUR 2.60 per issue (effective 2007). stat.
Document type: *Government.*
Related titles: Online - full content ed.
Published by: Statisticni Urad Republike Slovenije/Statistical Office of the Republic of Slovenia, Vozarski pot 12, Ljubjana, 1000, Slovenia. TEL 386-1-2415104, FAX 386-1-2415344, info.stat@gov.si. Eds. Ana Antoncic, Avgustina Kuhar de Domizio. Pub. Tomaz Banovec.

SMALL BUSINESS QUARTERLY. *see* BUSINESS AND ECONOMICS—Abstracting, Bibliographies, Statistics

SOCIAL ASSISTANCE STATISTICAL REPORT. *see* SOCIAL SERVICES AND WELFARE—Abstracting, Bibliographies, Statistics

SOCIAL CARE STATISTICS. ACTUALS (ONLINE). *see* SOCIAL SERVICES AND WELFARE—Abstracting, Bibliographies, Statistics

SOCIAL INDICATORS RESEARCH; an international and interdisciplinary journal for quality-of-life measurement. *see* SOCIOLOGY—Abstracting, Bibliographies, Statistics

SOCIAL SECURITY STATISTICS, CANADA AND PROVINCES. *see* SOCIAL SERVICES AND WELFARE

314 ROM ISSN 1224-8177
SOCIAL SITUATION AND ECONOMY OF ROMANIA. Text in Romanian. 1992. a. ROL 50,000; USD 12 foreign. **Document type:** *Government.*
Description: Contains the main conclusions of statistical data analysis for the year regarding the social situation and by branches of activity.
Formerly (until 1992): Social and Economic Standing of Rumania (Year) (1221-7085)
Published by: Comisia Nationala pentru Statistica/National Commission for Statistics, Bd. Libertatii 16, Sector 5, Bucharest, 70542, Romania. TEL 40-1-3363370, FAX 40-1-3124873.

SOCIAL STATISTICS IN NIGERIA. *see* SOCIAL SCIENCES: COMPREHENSIVE WORKS—Abstracting, Bibliographies, Statistics

314 ROM ISSN 1454-4466
HQ1641
SOCIAL TRENDS. Text in English, Romanian; Summaries in English, Romanian. 1999. a. stat. reprints avail. **Document type:** *Government.* **Description:** Serves as the common bulletin of the CEFTA countries covering social and economic issues with with corresponding statistical analysis.
Published by: Comisia Nationala pentru Statistica/National Commission for Statistics, Bd. Libertatii 16, Sector 5, Bucharest, 70542, Romania. TEL 40-1-3363370, FAX 40-1-3124873. R&P Ivan Ungureanu Clementina.

SOCIETE DE LA BOURSE DES VALEURS DE CASABLANCA. STATISTIQUES MENSUELLES. *see* BUSINESS AND ECONOMICS—Abstracting, Bibliographies, Statistics

310 304.6 BGR ISSN 1311-2422
SOTSIALNI TENDENTSII. Text in Bulgarian. a. BGL 7.03 (effective 2002). 68 p./no.; **Description:** Presents a full statistical picture of the social changes and tendencies in the Bulgarian society.
Published by: Natsionalen Statisticheski Institut/National Statistical Institute, ul P Volov, # 2, Sofia, 1038, Bulgaria. FAX 359-2-9803319, publikacii@nsi.bg, http://www.nsi.bg. **Dist. by:** Sofia Books, ul Silivria 16, Sofia 1404, Bulgaria. TEL 359-2-9586257, info@sofiabooks-bg.com, http://www.sofiabooks-bg.com.

SOTSIAL'NO-EKONOMICHESKOE POLOZHENIE DAL'NEVOSTOCHNOGO FEDERAL'NOGO OKRUGA/SOCIO-ECONOMIC SITUATION OF THE FAR EASTERN FEDERAL REGION. *see* BUSINESS AND ECONOMICS—Abstracting, Bibliographies, Statistics

SOTSIAL'NO-EKONOMICHESKOE POLOZHENIE PRIVOLZHSKOGO FEDERAL'NOGO OKRUGA/SOCIO-ECONOMIC SITUATION OF THE VOLGA FEDERAL REGION. *see* BUSINESS AND ECONOMICS—Abstracting, Bibliographies, Statistics

SOTSIAL'NO-EKONOMICHESKOE POLOZHENIE ROSSII/SOCIAL AND ECONOMIC SITUATION IN RUSSIA; ekonomicheskii obzor. *see* BUSINESS AND ECONOMICS—Abstracting, Bibliographies, Statistics

SOTSIAL'NO-EKONOMICHESKOE POLOZHENIE SEVERO-ZAPADNOGO FEDERAL'NOGO OKRUGA/SOCIO-ECONOMIC SITUATION OF THE NORTH-WESTERN FEDERAL REGION. *see* BUSINESS AND ECONOMICS—Abstracting, Bibliographies, Statistics

SOTSIAL'NO-EKONOMICHESKOE POLOZHENIE SIBIRSKOGO FEDERAL'NOGO OKRUGA/SOCIO-ECONOMIC SITUATION OF THE SIBERIAN FEDERAL REGION. *see* BUSINESS AND ECONOMICS—Abstracting, Bibliographies, Statistics

SOTSIAL'NO-EKONOMICHESKOE POLOZHENIE TSENTRAL'NOGO FEDERAL'NOGO OKRUGA/SOCIO-ECONOMIC SITUATION OF THE CENTRAL FEDERAL REGION. *see* BUSINESS AND ECONOMICS—Abstracting, Bibliographies, Statistics

SOTSIAL'NO-EKONOMICHESKOE POLOZHENIE URAL'SKOGO FEDERAL'NOGO OKRUGA/SOCIO-ECONOMIC SITUATION OF THE URAL FEDERAL REGION. *see* BUSINESS AND ECONOMICS—Abstracting, Bibliographies, Statistics

SOTSIAL'NO-EKONOMICHESKOE POLOZHENIE YUZHNOGO FEDERAL'NOGO OKRUGA/SOCIO-ECONOMIC SITUATION OF THE SOUTHERN FEDERAL REGION. *see* BUSINESS AND ECONOMICS—Abstracting, Bibliographies, Statistics

319.305 NZL ISSN 1178-3265
THE SOURCE. Text in English. 2007. s-a. **Document type:** *Newsletter.*
Description: Reports on statistical news and events from across New Zealand's government sector.
Related titles: Online - full text ed.: ISSN 1178-3273.
Published by: Statistics New Zealand/Te Tari Tatau, Statistics House, The Blvd, Harbour Quays, PO Box 2922, Wellington, 6140, New Zealand. TEL 64-4-9314600, FAX 64-4-9314610, info@stats.govt.nz, http://www.stats.govt.nz.

SOURCE O E C D. MONTHLY INTERNATIONAL TRADE AGGREGATES/SOURCE O C D E STATISTIQUES MENSUELLES DU COMMERCE INTERNATIONAL. *see* BUSINESS AND ECONOMICS—Abstracting, Bibliographies, Statistics

SOURCE O E C D. NATIONAL ACCOUNTS STATISTICS. (Organisation for Economic Cooperation and Development) *see* BUSINESS AND ECONOMICS—Abstracting, Bibliographies, Statistics

SOURCES AND METHODS. LABOUR STATISTICS. *see* BUSINESS AND ECONOMICS—Abstracting, Bibliographies, Statistics

SOUTH AFRICA. COMMISSIONER FOR CUSTOMS AND EXCISE. FOREIGN TRADE STATISTICS. *see* BUSINESS AND ECONOMICS—Abstracting, Bibliographies, Statistics

SOUTH AFRICA. COMMISSIONER FOR CUSTOMS AND EXCISE. MONTHLY ABSTRACT OF TRADE STATISTICS. *see* BUSINESS AND ECONOMICS—Abstracting, Bibliographies, Statistics

SOUTH AFRICA. DEPARTMENT OF AGRICULTURE. DIRECTORATE OF AGRICULTURAL STATISTICS. ABSTRACT OF AGRICULTURAL STATISTICS/KORTBEGRIP VAN LANDBOUSTATISTIEKE. *see* AGRICULTURE—Abstracting, Bibliographies, Statistics

SOUTH AFRICA. STATISTICS SOUTH AFRICA. AGRICULTURAL SURVEY. *see* AGRICULTURE—Abstracting, Bibliographies, Statistics

316.8 ZAF
SOUTH AFRICA. STATISTICS SOUTH AFRICA. ANNUAL REPORT (ONLINE EDITION)/SUID-AFRIKA. STATISTIEKE. JAARVERSLAG. Text in English. a. free. **Document type:** *Government.*
Former titles: South Africa. Statistics South Africa. Annual Report (Print Edition); (until Aug. 1998): South Africa. Central Statistical Service. Annual Report
Media: Online - full text.
Published by: Statistics South Africa/Statistieke Suid-Afrika, Private Bag X44, Pretoria, 0001, South Africa. TEL 27-12-3108911, FAX 27-12-3108500, info@statssa.gov.za, http://www.statssa.gov.za.

SOUTH AFRICA. STATISTICS SOUTH AFRICA. BIRTHS. *see* POPULATION STUDIES—Abstracting, Bibliographies, Statistics

SOUTH AFRICA. STATISTICS SOUTH AFRICA. BUILDING PLANS PASSED AND BUILDINGS COMPLETED. *see* BUILDING AND CONSTRUCTION—Abstracting, Bibliographies, Statistics

316.8 ZAF
HA1991
SOUTH AFRICA. STATISTICS SOUTH AFRICA. BULLETIN OF STATISTICS. Text in Afrikaans, English. 1922. q. ZAR 120 per issue (effective 2008). **Document type:** *Bulletin, Government.*
Former titles (until Aug. 1998): South Africa. Central Statistical Service. Bulletin of Statistics (0034-5024); South Africa. Department of Statistics. Bulletin of Statistics; South Africa. Department of Statistics. Monthly Bulletin of Statistics
Related titles: Online - full text ed.: ISSN 1996-8515.
Indexed: RASB.
Published by: Statistics South Africa/Statistieke Suid-Afrika, Private Bag X44, Pretoria, 0001, South Africa. TEL 27-12-3108911, FAX 27-12-3108500, info@statssa.gov.za. Circ: 1,200.

SOUTH AFRICA. STATISTICS SOUTH AFRICA. CENSUS OF ELECTRICITY, GAS AND STEAM. *see* ENERGY—Abstracting, Bibliographies, Statistics

SOUTH AFRICA. STATISTICS SOUTH AFRICA. CENSUS OF ESTATE AGENCIES, RENT COLLECTORS, APPRAISERS AND VALUERS. *see* REAL ESTATE—Abstracting, Bibliographies, Statistics

SOUTH AFRICA. STATISTICS SOUTH AFRICA. CENSUS OF HOSPITALS, CLINICS AND OTHER HEALTH SERVICE ESTABLISHMENTS. *see* HEALTH FACILITIES AND ADMINISTRATION—Abstracting, Bibliographies, Statistics

SOUTH AFRICA. STATISTICS SOUTH AFRICA. CENSUS OF LETTING OF OWN FIXED PROPERTY. *see* REAL ESTATE—Abstracting, Bibliographies, Statistics

SOUTH AFRICA. STATISTICS SOUTH AFRICA. CENSUS OF LICENSED RESTAURANTS. *see* HOTELS AND RESTAURANTS—Abstracting, Bibliographies, Statistics

SOUTH AFRICA. STATISTICS SOUTH AFRICA. CENSUS OF MANUFACTURING - (YEAR) PRINCIPAL STATISTICS ON A REGIONAL BASIS: WESTERN CAPE. *see* BUSINESS AND ECONOMICS—Abstracting, Bibliographies, Statistics

SOUTH AFRICA. STATISTICS SOUTH AFRICA. CENSUS OF MANUFACTURING - MATERIALS PURCHASED AND MANUFACTURES SOLD. *see* BUSINESS AND ECONOMICS—Abstracting, Bibliographies, Statistics

SOUTH AFRICA. STATISTICS SOUTH AFRICA. CENSUS OF MANUFACTURING - PRINCIPAL STATISTICS ON A REGIONAL BASIS PART-I. *see* BUSINESS AND ECONOMICS—Abstracting, Bibliographies, Statistics

SOUTH AFRICA. STATISTICS SOUTH AFRICA. CENSUS OF MANUFACTURING - STATISTICS ACCORDING TO MAJOR GROUPS AND SUBGROUPS. *see* BUSINESS AND ECONOMICS—Abstracting, Bibliographies, Statistics

SOUTH AFRICA. STATISTICS SOUTH AFRICA. CENSUS OF MEDICAL, DENTAL AND OTHER HEALTH SERVICES - CHIROPRACTORS, HOMEOPATHS, NATUROPATHS, OSTEOPATHS AND HERBALISTS. *see* MEDICAL SCIENCES—Abstracting, Bibliographies, Statistics

SOUTH AFRICA. STATISTICS SOUTH AFRICA. CENSUS OF MEDICAL, DENTAL AND OTHER HEALTH SERVICES - DENTISTS. *see* MEDICAL SCIENCES—Abstracting, Bibliographies, Statistics

SOUTH AFRICA. STATISTICS SOUTH AFRICA. CENSUS OF MEDICAL, DENTAL AND OTHER HEALTH SERVICES - DOCTORS. *see* MEDICAL SCIENCES—Abstracting, Bibliographies, Statistics

SOUTH AFRICA. STATISTICS SOUTH AFRICA. CENSUS OF MEDICAL, DENTAL AND OTHER HEALTH SERVICES - SUPPLEMENTARY HEALTH SERVICES AND DENTAL TECHNICIANS. *see* MEDICAL SCIENCES—Abstracting, Bibliographies, Statistics

SOUTH AFRICA. STATISTICS SOUTH AFRICA. CENSUS OF MINING (YEAR). *see* MINES AND MINING INDUSTRY—Abstracting, Bibliographies, Statistics

SOUTH AFRICA. STATISTICS SOUTH AFRICA. CENSUS OF MOTOR TRADE AND REPAIR SERVICES. *see* BUSINESS AND ECONOMICS—Abstracting, Bibliographies, Statistics

SOUTH AFRICA. STATISTICS SOUTH AFRICA. CENSUS OF PROFESSIONAL AND BUSINESS SERVICES - ACCOUNTING, AUDITING AND BOOK-KEEPING SERVICES. *see* BUSINESS AND ECONOMICS—Abstracting, Bibliographies, Statistics

SOUTH AFRICA. STATISTICS SOUTH AFRICA. CENSUS OF PROFESSIONAL AND BUSINESS SERVICES - ADVERTISING PRACTITIONERS AND ALLIED SERVICES AND MARKETING RESEARCH SERVICES. *see* ADVERTISING AND PUBLIC RELATIONS—Abstracting, Bibliographies, Statistics

SOUTH AFRICA. STATISTICS SOUTH AFRICA. CENSUS OF PROFESSIONAL AND BUSINESS SERVICES - CONSULTING ENGINEERS. *see* BUSINESS AND ECONOMICS—Abstracting, Bibliographies, Statistics

SOUTH AFRICA. STATISTICS SOUTH AFRICA. CENSUS OF PROFESSIONAL AND BUSINESS SERVICES - DATA PROCESSING SERVICES. *see* BUSINESS AND ECONOMICS—Abstracting, Bibliographies, Statistics

SOUTH AFRICA. STATISTICS SOUTH AFRICA. CENSUS OF PROFESSIONAL AND BUSINESS SERVICES - EMPLOYMENT PLACEMENT AGENCIES, RECRUITING ORGANISATIONS AND LABOUR BROKERS SERVICES. *see* BUSINESS AND ECONOMICS—Abstracting, Bibliographies, Statistics

SOUTH AFRICA. STATISTICS SOUTH AFRICA. CENSUS OF PROFESSIONAL AND BUSINESS SERVICES - LEGAL SERVICES. *see* BUSINESS AND ECONOMICS—Abstracting, Bibliographies, Statistics

SOUTH AFRICA. STATISTICS SOUTH AFRICA. CENSUS OF SOCIAL, RECREATIONAL AND PERSONAL SERVICES - HAIRDRESSING AND BEAUTY SERVICES. *see* BEAUTY CULTURE—Abstracting, Bibliographies, Statistics

SOUTH AFRICA. STATISTICS SOUTH AFRICA. CENSUS OF SOCIAL, RECREATIONAL AND PERSONAL SERVICES - LAUNDRY, CLEANING AND DYEING SERVICES. *see* CLEANING AND DYEING—Abstracting, Bibliographies, Statistics

SOUTH AFRICA. STATISTICS SOUTH AFRICA. CENSUS OF SOCIAL, RECREATIONAL AND PERSONAL SERVICES - MOTION PICTURE AND VIDEO PRODUCTION. *see* MOTION PICTURES—Abstracting, Bibliographies, Statistics

SOUTH AFRICA. STATISTICS SOUTH AFRICA. CENSUS OF SOCIAL, RECREATIONAL AND PERSONAL SERVICES - MOTION PICTURE DISTRIBUTION AND PROJECTION AND VIDEO DISTRIBUTION SERVICES. *see* MOTION PICTURES—Abstracting, Bibliographies, Statistics

SOUTH AFRICA. STATISTICS SOUTH AFRICA. CENSUS OF SOCIAL, RECREATIONAL AND PERSONAL SERVICES - PHOTOGRAPHIC STUDIOS. *see* PHOTOGRAPHY—Abstracting, Bibliographies, Statistics

SOUTH AFRICA. STATISTICS SOUTH AFRICA. CENSUS OF SOCIAL, RECREATIONAL AND PERSONAL SERVICES - UNDERTAKERS AND CREMATORIUM SERVICES. *see* FUNERALS—Abstracting, Bibliographies, Statistics

SOUTH AFRICA. STATISTICS SOUTH AFRICA. CENSUS OF SOCIAL, RECREATIONAL AND PERSONAL SERVICES - WELFARE ORGANISATIONS. *see* SOCIAL SERVICES AND WELFARE—Abstracting, Bibliographies, Statistics

SOUTH AFRICA. STATISTICS SOUTH AFRICA. CENSUS OF TRANSPORT AND ALLIED SERVICES. *see* TRANSPORTATION—Abstracting, Bibliographies, Statistics

SOUTH AFRICA. STATISTICS SOUTH AFRICA. CRIMES: PROSECUTIONS AND CONVICTIONS WITH REGARD TO CERTAIN OFFENCES. *see* LAW—Abstracting, Bibliographies, Statistics

SOUTH AFRICA. STATISTICS SOUTH AFRICA. DEMOGRAPHIC STATISTICS. *see* POPULATION STUDIES—Abstracting, Bibliographies, Statistics

SOUTH AFRICA. STATISTICS SOUTH AFRICA. FINAL SOCIAL ACCOUNTING MATRIX FOR SOUTH AFRICA. *see* PUBLIC ADMINISTRATION—Abstracting, Bibliographies, Statistics

SOUTH AFRICA. STATISTICS SOUTH AFRICA. INPUT OUTPUT TABLES. *see* BUSINESS AND ECONOMICS—Abstracting, Bibliographies, Statistics

SOUTH AFRICA. STATISTICS SOUTH AFRICA. LOCAL GOVERNMENT STATISTICS. *see* PUBLIC ADMINISTRATION—Abstracting, Bibliographies, Statistics

SOUTH AFRICA. STATISTICS SOUTH AFRICA. MANPOWER SURVEY (OCCUPATIONAL INFORMATION). *see* BUSINESS AND ECONOMICS—Abstracting, Bibliographies, Statistics

SOUTH AFRICA. STATISTICS SOUTH AFRICA. NEW VEHICLES REGISTERED. *see* TRANSPORTATION—Abstracting, Bibliographies, Statistics

SOUTH AFRICA. STATISTICS SOUTH AFRICA. POPULATION CENSUS, (YEAR). DWELLINGS. *see* POPULATION STUDIES—Abstracting, Bibliographies, Statistics

SOUTH AFRICA. STATISTICS SOUTH AFRICA. POPULATION CENSUS, (YEAR). ECONOMIC CHARACTERISTICS OF POPULATION. *see* POPULATION STUDIES—Abstracting, Bibliographies, Statistics

SOUTH AFRICA. STATISTICS SOUTH AFRICA. POPULATION CENSUS, (YEAR). HOUSEHOLDS. *see* POPULATION STUDIES—Abstracting, Bibliographies, Statistics

SOUTH AFRICA. STATISTICS SOUTH AFRICA. POPULATION CENSUS, (YEAR). SELECTED STATISTICAL REGIONS. *see* POPULATION STUDIES—Abstracting, Bibliographies, Statistics

SOUTH AFRICA. STATISTICS SOUTH AFRICA. POPULATION CENSUS, (YEAR). SOCIAL CHARACTERISTICS OF THE POPULATION. *see* POPULATION STUDIES—Abstracting, Bibliographies, Statistics

S

SOUTH AFRICA. STATISTICS SOUTH AFRICA. POPULATION CENSUS, (YEAR). SUMMARISED RESULTS AFTER ADJUSTMENT FOR UNDERCOUNT. *see* POPULATION STUDIES—Abstracting, Bibliographies, Statistics

316.8 ZAF
SOUTH AFRICA. STATISTICS SOUTH AFRICA. PROVINCIAL PROFILE (YEAR) - EASTERN CAPE (ONLINE EDITION). Text in English. 1994. a. free. **Document type:** *Government.* **Description:** Provides statistical data on demography, housing, education, health, industries, gross geographic product and price indices for the Eastern Cape province.
Former titles: South Africa. Statistics South Africa. Provincial Statistics Part 2 - Eastern Cape (Print Edition); (until 1998): South Africa. Central Statistical Service. Provincial Statistics Part 2 - Eastern Cape
Media: Online - full text.
Published by: Statistics South Africa/Statistieke Suid-Afrika, Private Bag X44, Pretoria, 0001, South Africa. TEL 27-12-3108911, FAX 27-12-3108500, info@statssa.gov.za, http://www.statssa.gov.za.

316.8 ZAF
SOUTH AFRICA. STATISTICS SOUTH AFRICA. PROVINCIAL PROFILE (YEAR) - GAUTENG (ONLINE EDITION). Text in English. 1994. a. ZAR 20 domestic; ZAR 21.90 foreign (effective 2000). **Document type:** *Government.* **Description:** Provides statistics on demography, housing, education, health, industries, gross geographical product and price indices for the PWV province.
Formerly: South Africa. Statistics South Africa. Provincial Profile (Year) - Gauteng (Print Edition)
Published by: Statistics South Africa/Statistieke Suid-Afrika, Private Bag X44, Pretoria, 0001, South Africa. TEL 27-12-3108911, FAX 27-12-3108500, info@statssa.gov.za, http://www.statssa.gov.za.

316.8 ZAF
SOUTH AFRICA. STATISTICS SOUTH AFRICA. PROVINCIAL PROFILE (YEAR) - KWAZULU - NATAL (ONLINE EDITION). Text in English. 1994. a. free. **Document type:** *Government.* **Description:** Provides statistical data on demography, housing, education, health, industries, gross geographic product and price indices for KwaZulu - Natal.
Former titles: South Africa. Statistics South Africa. Provincial Statistics Part 5 - Kwazulu - Natal (Print Edition); (until 1998): South Africa. central Statistical Service. Provincial Statistics Part 5 - Kwazulu - Natal
Media: Online - full text.
Published by: Statistics South Africa/Statistieke Suid-Afrika, Private Bag X44, Pretoria, 0001, South Africa. TEL 27-12-3108911, FAX 27-12-3108500, info@statssa.gov.za, http://www.statssa.gov.za.

316.8 ZAF
SOUTH AFRICA. STATISTICS SOUTH AFRICA. PROVINCIAL PROFILE (YEAR) - LIMPOPO (ONLINE EDITION). Text in English. 1994. a. free. **Document type:** *Government.* **Description:** Provides statistical data on demography, housing, education, health, industries, gross geographic product and price indices for the Northern Transvaal.
Former titles: South Africa. Statistics South Africa. Provincial Statistics Part 9 - Northern Transvaal (Print Edition); (until 1998): South Africa. Central Statistical Service. Provincial Statistics Part 9 - Northern Transvaal
Media: Online - full text.
Published by: Statistics South Africa/Statistieke Suid-Afrika, Private Bag X44, Pretoria, 0001, South Africa. TEL 27-12-3108911, FAX 27-12-3108500, info@statssa.gov.za, http://www.statssa.gov.za.

316.8 ZAF
SOUTH AFRICA. STATISTICS SOUTH AFRICA. PROVINCIAL PROFILE (YEAR) - MPUMALANGA (ONLINE EDITION). Text in English. 1994. a. free. **Document type:** *Government.* **Description:** Provides statistical data on demography, housing, education, health, industries, gross geographic product and price indices for the Eastern Transvaal.
Former titles: South Africa. Statistics South Africa. Provincial Statistics Part 8 - Eastern Transvaal (Print Edition); (until 1998): South Africa. Central Statistical Service. Provincial Statistics Part 8 - Eastern Transvaal
Media: Online - full text.
Published by: Statistics South Africa/Statistieke Suid-Afrika, Private Bag X44, Pretoria, 0001, South Africa. TEL 27-12-3108911, FAX 27-12-3108500, info@statssa.gov.za, http://www.statssa.gov.za.

316.8 ZAF
SOUTH AFRICA. STATISTICS SOUTH AFRICA. PROVINCIAL PROFILE (YEAR) - NORTH WEST (ONLINE EDITION). Text in English. 1994. a. free. **Document type:** *Government.* **Description:** Provides statistical data on demography, housing, education, health, industries, gross geographic product and price industries for the North-West province.
Former titles: South Africa. Statistics South Africa. Provincial Statistics Part 6 - North West (Print Edition); (until 1998): South Africa. Central Statistical Service. Provincial Statistics Part 6 - North-West
Media: Online - full text.
Published by: Statistics South Africa/Statistieke Suid-Afrika, Private Bag X44, Pretoria, 0001, South Africa. TEL 27-12-3108911, FAX 27-12-3108500, info@statssa.gov.za, http://www.statssa.gov.za.

316.8 ZAF
SOUTH AFRICA. STATISTICS SOUTH AFRICA. PROVINCIAL PROFILE (YEAR) - NORTHERN CAPE (ONLINE EDITION). Text in English. 1994. a. free. **Document type:** *Government.* **Description:** Provides statistical data on demography, housing, education, health, industries, gross geographic product and price indices for the Northern Cape province.
Former titles: South Africa. Statistics South Africa. Provincial Statistics Part 3 - Northern Cape (Print Edition); (until 1998): South Africa. Central Statistical Service. Provincial Statistics Part 3 - Northern Cape
Media: Online - full text.
Published by: Statistics South Africa/Statistieke Suid-Afrika, Private Bag X44, Pretoria, 0001, South Africa. TEL 27-12-3108911, FAX 27-12-3108500, info@statssa.gov.za, http://www.statssa.gov.za.

316.8 ZAF
SOUTH AFRICA. STATISTICS SOUTH AFRICA. PROVINCIAL PROFILE (YEAR) - WESTERN CAPE (ONLINE EDITION). Text in English. 1994. a. free. **Document type:** *Government.* **Description:** Provides statistical data on demography, housing, education, health, industries, gross geographical product and price indices for the Western Cape province.
Former titles: South Africa. Statistics South Africa. Provincial Statistics Part 1 - Western Cape (Print Edition); (until 1998): South Africa. Central Statistical Service. Provincial Statistics Part 1 - Western Cape
Media: Online - full text.
Published by: Statistics South Africa/Statistieke Suid-Afrika, Private Bag X44, Pretoria, 0001, South Africa. TEL 27-12-3108911, FAX 27-12-3108500, info@statssa.gov.za, http://www.statssa.gov.za.

316.8 ZAF
SOUTH AFRICA. STATISTICS SOUTH AFRICA. PROVINCIAL STATISTICS PART 10 - REPUBLIC OF SOUTH AFRICA. Text in English. 1994. a. **Document type:** *Government.* **Description:** Provides statistical data on demography, housing, education, health, industries and the gross geographic product for South Africa.
Formerly (until Aug.1998): South Africa. Central Statistical Service. Provincial Statistics Part 10 - Republic of South Africa
Published by: Statistics South Africa/Statistieke Suid-Afrika, Private Bag X44, Pretoria, 0001, South Africa. TEL 27-12-3108911, FAX 27-12-3108500, info@statssa.gov.za, http://www.statssa.gov.za.

316.8 ZAF
SOUTH AFRICA. STATISTICS SOUTH AFRICA. PROVINCIAL STATISTICS PART 4 - FREE STATE. Text in English. 1994. a. **Document type:** *Government.* **Description:** Provides statistical data on demography, housing, education, health, industries, gross geographic product and price indices for the Orange Free State.
Formerly (until Aug.1998): South Africa. Central Statistical Service. Provincial Statistics Part 4 - Orange Free State
Published by: Statistics South Africa/Statistieke Suid-Afrika, Private Bag X44, Pretoria, 0001, South Africa. TEL 27-12-3108911, FAX 27-12-3108500, info@statssa.gov.za, http://www.statssa.gov.za.

SOUTH AFRICA. STATISTICS SOUTH AFRICA. REGISTERED VEHICLES. *see* TRANSPORTATION—Abstracting, Bibliographies, Statistics

SOUTH AFRICA. STATISTICS SOUTH AFRICA. REPORT ON MARRIAGES AND DIVORCES - WHITES, COLOUREDS AND ASIANS - SOUTH AFRICA. *see* POPULATION STUDIES—Abstracting, Bibliographies, Statistics

SOUTH AFRICA. STATISTICS SOUTH AFRICA. ROAD TRAFFIC COLLISIONS. *see* TRANSPORTATION—Abstracting, Bibliographies, Statistics

316.8 ZAF
SOUTH AFRICA. STATISTICS SOUTH AFRICA. SOUTH AFRICAN STATISTICS (YEAR). Text in English. a. ZAR 170 (effective 2007). **Document type:** *Government.* **Description:** Provides summary statistical data on all aspects of South African life for which statistics are collected, including population censuses, vital statistics, business surveys, and government financial statistics.
Former titles (until Aug.1998): South Africa. Central Statistical Service. Statistical Release; South Africa. Department of Statistics. Statistical News Releases
Published by: Statistics South Africa/Statistieke Suid-Afrika, Private Bag X44, Pretoria, 0001, South Africa. TEL 27-12-3108911, FAX 27-12-3108500, info@statssa.gov.za, http://www.statssa.gov.za.

SOUTH AFRICA. STATISTICS SOUTH AFRICA. STANDARD CODE LIST FOR STATISTICAL REGIONS, MAGISTERIAL DISTRICTS, CITIES, TOWNS AND NON-URBAN AREAS. *see* METROLOGY AND STANDARDIZATION—Abstracting, Bibliographies, Statistics

SOUTH AFRICA. STATISTICS SOUTH AFRICA. STANDARD INDUSTRIAL CLASSIFICATION OF ALL ECONOMIC ACTIVITIES. *see* METROLOGY AND STANDARDIZATION—Abstracting, Bibliographies, Statistics

SOUTH AFRICA. STATISTICS SOUTH AFRICA. STATISTICAL RELEASE. ACTUAL AND ANTICIPATED CAPITAL EXPENDITURE OF THE PUBLIC SECTOR. *see* BUSINESS AND ECONOMICS—Abstracting, Bibliographies, Statistics

SOUTH AFRICA. STATISTICS SOUTH AFRICA. STATISTICAL RELEASE. ACTUAL AND ANTICIPATED CONSTRUCTION EXPENDITURE OF THE PUBLIC SECTOR BY REGION. *see* BUSINESS AND ECONOMICS—Abstracting, Bibliographies, Statistics

SOUTH AFRICA. STATISTICS SOUTH AFRICA. STATISTICAL RELEASE. BUILDING INDUSTRY ADVISORY COUNCIL CONTRACT PRICE ADJUSTMENT PROVISIONS - WORKGROUP INDICES (HAYLETT). *see* BUILDING AND CONSTRUCTION—Abstracting, Bibliographies, Statistics

SOUTH AFRICA. STATISTICS SOUTH AFRICA. STATISTICAL RELEASE. BUILDING PLANS PASSED AND BUILDINGS COMPLETED. *see* BUILDING AND CONSTRUCTION—Abstracting, Bibliographies, Statistics

SOUTH AFRICA. STATISTICS SOUTH AFRICA. STATISTICAL RELEASE. CENSUS OF AUXILIARY, HEALTH SERVICES AND DENTAL TECHNICIANS (YEAR). *see* MEDICAL SCIENCES—Abstracting, Bibliographies, Statistics

SOUTH AFRICA. STATISTICS SOUTH AFRICA. STATISTICAL RELEASE. CENSUS OF CHIROPRACTORS AND HOMEOPATHS. *see* MEDICAL SCIENCES—Abstracting, Bibliographies, Statistics

SOUTH AFRICA. STATISTICS SOUTH AFRICA. STATISTICAL RELEASE. CENSUS OF CONSTRUCTION. *see* BUILDING AND CONSTRUCTION—Abstracting, Bibliographies, Statistics

SOUTH AFRICA. STATISTICS SOUTH AFRICA. STATISTICAL RELEASE. CENSUS OF DENTISTS (YEAR). *see* MEDICAL SCIENCES—Abstracting, Bibliographies, Statistics

SOUTH AFRICA. STATISTICS SOUTH AFRICA. STATISTICAL RELEASE. CENSUS OF DOCTORS (YEAR). *see* MEDICAL SCIENCES—Abstracting, Bibliographies, Statistics

SOUTH AFRICA. STATISTICS SOUTH AFRICA. STATISTICAL RELEASE. CENSUS OF ELECTRICITY, GAS AND STEAM. *see* ENERGY—Abstracting, Bibliographies, Statistics

SOUTH AFRICA. STATISTICS SOUTH AFRICA. STATISTICAL RELEASE. CENSUS OF HOSPITALS, CLINICS AND OTHER HEALTH SERVICE ESTABLISHMENTS (YEAR). *see* HEALTH FACILITIES AND ADMINISTRATION—Abstracting, Bibliographies, Statistics

SOUTH AFRICA. STATISTICS SOUTH AFRICA. STATISTICAL RELEASE. CENSUS OF LETTING OF OWN FIXED PROPERTY (YEAR). *see* REAL ESTATE—Abstracting, Bibliographies, Statistics

SOUTH AFRICA. STATISTICS SOUTH AFRICA. STATISTICAL RELEASE. CENSUS OF SOCIAL, RECREATIONAL AND PERSONAL SERVICES (YEAR). *see* SOCIAL SERVICES AND WELFARE—Abstracting, Bibliographies, Statistics

SOUTH AFRICA. STATISTICS SOUTH AFRICA. STATISTICAL RELEASE. CENSUS OF TRANSPORT AND ALLIED SERVICES. *see* TRANSPORTATION—Abstracting, Bibliographies, Statistics

SOUTH AFRICA. STATISTICS SOUTH AFRICA. STATISTICAL RELEASE. CENTRAL GOVERNMENT: REVENUE OF THE STATE REVENUE AND OTHER REVENUE ACCOUNTS. *see* PUBLIC ADMINISTRATION—Abstracting, Bibliographies, Statistics

SOUTH AFRICA. STATISTICS SOUTH AFRICA. STATISTICAL RELEASE. CONSUMER PRICE INDEX. *see* BUSINESS AND ECONOMICS—Abstracting, Bibliographies, Statistics

SOUTH AFRICA. STATISTICS SOUTH AFRICA. STATISTICAL RELEASE. CONSUMER PRICE INDEX BASE. *see* BUSINESS AND ECONOMICS—Abstracting, Bibliographies, Statistics

SOUTH AFRICA. STATISTICS SOUTH AFRICA. STATISTICAL RELEASE. CONSUMER PRICE INDEX WEIGHTS. *see* BUSINESS AND ECONOMICS—Abstracting, Bibliographies, Statistics

SOUTH AFRICA. STATISTICS SOUTH AFRICA. STATISTICAL RELEASE. ELECTRICITY GENERATED AND AVAILABLE FOR DISTRIBUTION. *see* ENERGY—Abstracting, Bibliographies, Statistics

SOUTH AFRICA. STATISTICS SOUTH AFRICA. STATISTICAL RELEASE. FINANCIAL STATISTICS OF COMPANIES. *see* BUSINESS AND ECONOMICS—Abstracting, Bibliographies, Statistics

SOUTH AFRICA. STATISTICS SOUTH AFRICA. STATISTICAL RELEASE. FINANCIAL STATISTICS OF EXTRABUDGETARY ACCOUNTS AND FUNDS. *see* BUSINESS AND ECONOMICS—Abstracting, Bibliographies, Statistics

SOUTH AFRICA. STATISTICS SOUTH AFRICA. STATISTICAL RELEASE. FINANCIAL STATISTICS OF LOCAL AUTHORITIES AND REGIONAL SERVICES COUNCILS AND JOINT SERVICES BOARDS. *see* PUBLIC ADMINISTRATION—Abstracting, Bibliographies, Statistics

SOUTH AFRICA. STATISTICS SOUTH AFRICA. STATISTICAL RELEASE. FINANCIAL STATISTICS OF LOCAL GOVERNMENTS (YEAR). *see* PUBLIC ADMINISTRATION—Abstracting, Bibliographies, Statistics

SOUTH AFRICA. STATISTICS SOUTH AFRICA. STATISTICAL RELEASE. FINANCIAL STATISTICS OF UNIVERSITIES AND TECHNIKONS. *see* EDUCATION—Abstracting, Bibliographies, Statistics

SOUTH AFRICA. STATISTICS SOUTH AFRICA. STATISTICAL RELEASE. GROSS DOMESTIC PRODUCT. *see* BUSINESS AND ECONOMICS—Abstracting, Bibliographies, Statistics

SOUTH AFRICA. STATISTICS SOUTH AFRICA. STATISTICAL RELEASE. GROSS GEOGRAPHIC PRODUCT AT FACTOR INCOMES. *see* BUSINESS AND ECONOMICS—Abstracting, Bibliographies, Statistics

SOUTH AFRICA. STATISTICS SOUTH AFRICA. STATISTICAL RELEASE. INCOME AND EXPENDITURE OF HOUSEHOLDS (YEAR). *see* BUSINESS AND ECONOMICS—Abstracting, Bibliographies, Statistics

SOUTH AFRICA. STATISTICS SOUTH AFRICA. STATISTICAL RELEASE. MANUFACTURING - CAPITAL EXPENDITURE ON NEW ASSETS. *see* BUSINESS AND ECONOMICS—Abstracting, Bibliographies, Statistics

SOUTH AFRICA. STATISTICS SOUTH AFRICA. STATISTICAL RELEASE. MANUFACTURING - FINANCIAL STATISTICS. *see* BUSINESS AND ECONOMICS—Abstracting, Bibliographies, Statistics

SOUTH AFRICA. STATISTICS SOUTH AFRICA. STATISTICAL RELEASE. MANUFACTURING - FINANCIAL STATISTICS (QUARTERLY). *see* BUSINESS AND ECONOMICS—Abstracting, Bibliographies, Statistics

SOUTH AFRICA. STATISTICS SOUTH AFRICA. STATISTICAL RELEASE. MANUFACTURING - PRODUCTION AND SALES. *see* BUSINESS AND ECONOMICS—Abstracting, Bibliographies, Statistics

SOUTH AFRICA. STATISTICS SOUTH AFRICA. STATISTICAL RELEASE. MANUFACTURING STATISTICS: BASIC METAL AND FABRICATED METAL PRODUCTS, MACHINERY AND EQUIPMENT, MOTOR VEHICLES AND PARTS AND MISCELLANEOUS PRODUCTS. *see* BUSINESS AND ECONOMICS—Abstracting, Bibliographies, Statistics

SOUTH AFRICA. STATISTICS SOUTH AFRICA. STATISTICAL RELEASE. MANUFACTURING STATISTICS: CHEMICAL, PETROLEUM, RUBBER, PLASTIC AND NON-METALLIC MINERAL PRODUCTS. *see* BUSINESS AND ECONOMICS—Abstracting, Bibliographies, Statistics

SOUTH AFRICA. STATISTICS SOUTH AFRICA. STATISTICAL RELEASE. MANUFACTURING STATISTICS: PRODUCTS MANUFACTURED: FOODS AND BEVERAGES. *see* BUSINESS AND ECONOMICS—Abstracting, Bibliographies, Statistics

SOUTH AFRICA. STATISTICS SOUTH AFRICA. STATISTICAL RELEASE. MANUFACTURING STATISTICS: PRODUCTS MANUFACTURED: TEXTILES, CLOTHING, LEATHER AND LEATHER PRODUCTS, FOOTWEAR, WOOD AND WOOD PRODUCTS, FURNITURE, PAPER AND PAPER PRODUCTS AND PRINTING. *see* BUSINESS AND ECONOMICS—Abstracting, Bibliographies, Statistics

SOUTH AFRICA. STATISTICS SOUTH AFRICA. STATISTICAL RELEASE. MARRIAGES AND DIVORCES (YEAR). *see* POPULATION STUDIES—Abstracting, Bibliographies, Statistics

SOUTH AFRICA. STATISTICS SOUTH AFRICA. STATISTICAL RELEASE. MID-YEAR POPULATION ESTIMATES (YEAR). *see* POPULATION STUDIES—Abstracting, Bibliographies, Statistics

SOUTH AFRICA. STATISTICS SOUTH AFRICA. STATISTICAL RELEASE. MINING - FINANCIAL STATISTICS. *see* MINES AND MINING INDUSTRY—Abstracting, Bibliographies, Statistics

SOUTH AFRICA. STATISTICS SOUTH AFRICA. STATISTICAL RELEASE. MINING - PRODUCTION AND SALES. *see* MINES AND MINING INDUSTRY—Abstracting, Bibliographies, Statistics

SOUTH AFRICA. STATISTICS SOUTH AFRICA. STATISTICAL RELEASE. MOTOR TRADE - FINANCIAL STATISTICS. *see* BUSINESS AND ECONOMICS—Abstracting, Bibliographies, Statistics

SOUTH AFRICA. STATISTICS SOUTH AFRICA. STATISTICAL RELEASE. NATIONAL GOVERNMENT EXPENDITURE. *see* PUBLIC ADMINISTRATION—Abstracting, Bibliographies, Statistics

SOUTH AFRICA. STATISTICS SOUTH AFRICA. STATISTICAL RELEASE. POPULATION CHARACTERISTICS (YEAR); Boipatong, Bophelong, Evaton, Orange Farm, Sebokeng and Sharpeville. *see* POPULATION STUDIES—Abstracting, Bibliographies, Statistics

SOUTH AFRICA. STATISTICS SOUTH AFRICA. STATISTICAL RELEASE. PRELIMINARY RESULTS POPULATION CENSUS (YEAR). *see* POPULATION STUDIES—Abstracting, Bibliographies, Statistics

SOUTH AFRICA. STATISTICS SOUTH AFRICA. STATISTICAL RELEASE. PRODUCTION PRICE INDEX. *see* BUSINESS AND ECONOMICS—Abstracting, Bibliographies, Statistics

SOUTH AFRICA. STATISTICS SOUTH AFRICA. STATISTICAL RELEASE. PRODUCTION PRICE INDEX BASE (YEAR). *see* BUSINESS AND ECONOMICS—Abstracting, Bibliographies, Statistics

SOUTH AFRICA. STATISTICS SOUTH AFRICA. STATISTICAL RELEASE. PUBLIC ROAD TRANSPORT (NON-GOVERNMENTAL INSTITUTIONS) OF PASSENGERS AND GOODS - FINANCIAL STATISTICS. *see* TRANSPORTATION—Abstracting, Bibliographies, Statistics

SOUTH AFRICA. STATISTICS SOUTH AFRICA. STATISTICAL RELEASE. RECORDED DEATHS. *see* POPULATION STUDIES—Abstracting, Bibliographies, Statistics

SOUTH AFRICA. STATISTICS SOUTH AFRICA. STATISTICAL RELEASE. RECORDED LIVE BIRTHS (YEAR). *see* POPULATION STUDIES—Abstracting, Bibliographies, Statistics

SOUTH AFRICA. STATISTICS SOUTH AFRICA. STATISTICAL RELEASE. REGIONAL MID-YEAR ESTIMATES - REPUBLIC OF SOUTH AFRICA. *see* POPULATION STUDIES—Abstracting, Bibliographies, Statistics

SOUTH AFRICA. STATISTICS SOUTH AFRICA. STATISTICAL RELEASE. REGISTERED HOTELS - FINANCIAL STATISTICS. *see* HOTELS AND RESTAURANTS—Abstracting, Bibliographies, Statistics

SOUTH AFRICA. STATISTICS SOUTH AFRICA. STATISTICAL RELEASE. RETAIL TRADE - FINANCIAL STATISTICS. *see* BUSINESS AND ECONOMICS—Abstracting, Bibliographies, Statistics

SOUTH AFRICA. STATISTICS SOUTH AFRICA. STATISTICAL RELEASE. RETAIL TRADE IN MOTOR VEHICLES AND ACCESSORIES - TRADING REVENUE (FINAL). *see* BUSINESS AND ECONOMICS—Abstracting, Bibliographies, Statistics

SOUTH AFRICA. STATISTICS SOUTH AFRICA. STATISTICAL RELEASE. RETAIL TRADE SALES (FINAL). *see* BUSINESS AND ECONOMICS—Abstracting, Bibliographies, Statistics

SOUTH AFRICA. STATISTICS SOUTH AFRICA. STATISTICAL RELEASE. RETAIL TRADE SALES - PRELIMINARY. *see* BUSINESS AND ECONOMICS—Abstracting, Bibliographies, Statistics

SOUTH AFRICA. STATISTICS SOUTH AFRICA. STATISTICAL RELEASE. ROAD TRAFFIC COLLISIONS. *see* TRANSPORTATION—Abstracting, Bibliographies, Statistics

SOUTH AFRICA. STATISTICS SOUTH AFRICA. STATISTICAL RELEASE. SELECTED BUILDING STATISTICS OF THE PRIVATE SECTOR. *see* BUILDING AND CONSTRUCTION—Abstracting, Bibliographies, Statistics

SOUTH AFRICA. STATISTICS SOUTH AFRICA. STATISTICAL RELEASE. STATISTICS OF CIVIL CASES FOR DEBT. *see* LAW—Abstracting, Bibliographies, Statistics

SOUTH AFRICA. STATISTICS SOUTH AFRICA. STATISTICAL RELEASE. STATISTICS OF LIQUIDATIONS AND INSOLVENCIES. *see* LAW—Abstracting, Bibliographies, Statistics

SOUTH AFRICA. STATISTICS SOUTH AFRICA. STATISTICAL RELEASE. TOTAL VALUE OF WHOLESALE TRADE SALES - EXPECTED SALES. *see* BUSINESS AND ECONOMICS—Abstracting, Bibliographies, Statistics

SOUTH AFRICA. STATISTICS SOUTH AFRICA. STATISTICAL RELEASE. TOURISM - JAN SMUTS, D F MALAN AND LOUIS BOTHA AIRPORTS. *see* TRAVEL AND TOURISM—Abstracting, Bibliographies, Statistics

SOUTH AFRICA. STATISTICS SOUTH AFRICA. STATISTICAL RELEASE. TRANSPORT OF GOODS BY ROAD AND RAIL. *see* TRANSPORTATION—Abstracting, Bibliographies, Statistics

SOUTH AFRICA. STATISTICS SOUTH AFRICA. STATISTICAL RELEASE. UTILIZATION OF PRODUCTION CAPACITY BY LARGE ENTERPRISES. *see* BUSINESS AND ECONOMICS—Abstracting, Bibliographies, Statistics

SOUTH AFRICA. STATISTICS SOUTH AFRICA. STATISTICAL RELEASE. WHOLESALE TRADE SALES. *see* BUSINESS AND ECONOMICS—Abstracting, Bibliographies, Statistics

SOUTH AFRICA. STATISTICS SOUTH AFRICA. THE PEOPLE OF SOUTH AFRICA POPULATION CENSUS (YEAR). *see* POPULATION STUDIES—Abstracting, Bibliographies, Statistics

SOUTH AFRICA. STATISTICS SOUTH AFRICA. TOURISM AND MIGRATION. *see* POPULATION STUDIES—Abstracting, Bibliographies, Statistics

316.8 ZAF
SOUTH AFRICA. STATISTICS SOUTH AFRICA. USER'S GUIDE. Text in English. q. **Document type:** *Catalog, Government.* **Description:** Lists Central Statistical Service publications by subject.
Formerly (until Aug. 1998): South Africa. Central Statistical Service. Statistical Release. User's Guide
Related titles: Afrikaans ed.: Gebruikersgids.
Published by: Statistics South Africa/Statistieke Suid-Afrika, Private Bag X44, Pretoria, 0001, South Africa. TEL 27-12-3108911, FAX 27-12-3108500, info@statssa.gov.za, http://www.statssa.gov.za.

SOUTH AFRICA YEARBOOK (YEAR). *see* HISTORY—Abstracting, Bibliographies, Statistics

SOUTH AFRICAN LABOUR STATISTICS. *see* BUSINESS AND ECONOMICS—Abstracting, Bibliographies, Statistics

519.5 ZAF ISSN 0038-271X
QA276.A1 CODEN: SASSB5
➤ **SOUTH AFRICAN STATISTICAL JOURNAL/SUID-AFRIKAANSE STATISTIESE TYDSKRIF.** Text in Afrikaans, English; Summaries in English. 1967. s-a. ZAR 200 (effective 2007). adv. index. **Document type:** *Journal, Academic/Scholarly.* **Description:** Covers topics in theoretical mathematical statistics and applications.
Related titles: Online - full text ed.: ISSN 1996-8450.
Indexed: A22, ASCA, Biostat, CCMJ, CIS, CMCI, ISAP, JCQM, MSN, MathR, ORMS, QC&AS, SCOPUS, ST&MA, Z02.
—BLDSC (8346.450000), IE, Infotrieve, Ingenta.
Published by: South African Statistical Association/Suid-Afrikaanse Statistiese Vereniging, PO Box 27321, Sunnyside, Pretoria 0132, South Africa. TEL 27-12-8424083, FAX 27-12-8424082. Eds. Dr. Carl Lombard TEL 27-11-9380328, Tim Dunne. Circ: 650.

316.8 ZAF ISSN 0081-2544
HA1991 CODEN: FULAEI
SOUTH AFRICAN STATISTICS. Text in Afrikaans, English. 1968. a., latest 1994. ZAR 170 domestic (effective 2008). **Document type:** *Government.*
Formerly (until 1966): South Africa. Department of Statistics. Statistical Year Book
Related titles: Microfiche ed.: (from PQC).
Published by: Statistics South Africa/Statistieke Suid-Afrika, Private Bag X44, Pretoria, 0001, South Africa. TEL 27-12-3108911, FAX 27-12-3108500, info@statssa.gov.za, http://www.statssa.gov.za.

317.57 USA ISSN 0739-9308
HA621
SOUTH CAROLINA STATISTICAL ABSTRACT. Text in English. 1972. a. USD 35 (effective 2000). bk.rev. stat. **Document type:** *Abstract/Index.* **Description:** Presents data on factors impacting on the state's social and economic development: housing, employment, agriculture, banking and finance, income, education, recreation and tourism, population, transportation, health and public welfare, climate and geography, politics, energy resources, criminal justice, business and industry, and vital statistics.
Related titles: CD-ROM ed.: USD 40 per issue (effective 2007); Diskette ed.; Online - full text ed.: ISSN 1932-4103.
Indexed: SRI.
Published by: Budget and Control Board, Division of Research & Statistics, 1919 Blanding St, Columbia, SC 29201. TEL 803-898-9944, FAX 803-898-9972. Ed. Ashley Pender. R&P Mark Butkus. Circ: 1,400.

SOUTH CAROLINA WEEKLY WEATHER AND CROP PROGRESS REPORT. *see* AGRICULTURE—Abstracting, Bibliographies, Statistics

SOUTH DAKOTA CITIES & COUNTIES GRAPHIC PERFORMANCE ANALYSIS. *see* PUBLIC ADMINISTRATION—Abstracting, Bibliographies, Statistics

SOUTH DAKOTA. DEPARTMENT OF REVENUE. ANNUAL STATISTICAL REPORT. *see* BUSINESS AND ECONOMICS—Abstracting, Bibliographies, Statistics

SOUTH DAKOTA. STATE DEPARTMENT OF SOCIAL SERVICES. ANNUAL STATISTICAL REPORT. *see* SOCIAL SERVICES AND WELFARE—Abstracting, Bibliographies, Statistics

SOUTH DAKOTA WEEKLY CROP-WEATHER REPORT. *see* AGRICULTURE—Abstracting, Bibliographies, Statistics

310 618.202 GBR
SOUTH EAST THAMES PERINATAL MONITORING GROUP. PROVISIONAL STATISTICS. Text in English. a.
Published by: West Kent Health Authority, South East Thames Perinatal Monitoring Unit, Preston Hall, Aylesford, Kent ME20 7NJ, United Kingdom. Ed. Patricia Hanson.

310 NCL ISSN 0377-2039
HA4001
SOUTH PACIFIC COMMISSION. STATISTICAL BULLETIN. Text in English, French. 1973. irreg., latest vol.46, 1995. **Document type:** *Monographic series.*
Published by: Secretariat of the Pacific Community, PO Box D5, Noumea, Cedex 98848, New Caledonia. TEL 687-262000, FAX 687-263818, spc@spc.int, http://www.spc.int.

SOUTH PACIFIC ECONOMIES: STATISTICAL SUMMARY. *see* BUSINESS AND ECONOMICS—Abstracting, Bibliographies, Statistics

SOUTH PACIFIC EPIDEMIOLOGICAL AND HEALTH INFORMATION SERVICE ANNUAL REPORT. *see* PUBLIC HEALTH AND SAFETY—Abstracting, Bibliographies, Statistics

SOUTHERN DISTRICT CRIME STATISTICS. *see* CRIMINOLOGY AND LAW ENFORCEMENT—Abstracting, Bibliographies, Statistics

SOUTIEN AUX ENFANTS. STATISTIQUES. *see* SOCIAL SERVICES AND WELFARE—Abstracting, Bibliographies, Statistics

SPAIN. MINISTERIO DE AGRICULTURA, PESCA Y ALIMENTACION. BOLETIN DE PRECIOS DE PRODUCTOS PESQUEROS. *see* FISH AND FISHERIES—Abstracting, Bibliographies, Statistics

SPAIN. MINISTERIO DE AGRICULTURA PESCA Y ALIMENTACION. SECRETARIA GENERAL TECNICA. ANUARIO DE ESTADISTICA AGROALIMENTARIA. *see* AGRICULTURE—Abstracting, Bibliographies, Statistics

SPAIN. MINISTERIO DE FOMENTO. ANUARIO ESTADISTICO. *see* POPULATION STUDIES—Abstracting, Bibliographies, Statistics

SPAIN. MINISTERIO DEL INTERIOR. DIRECCION GENERAL DE TRAFICO. ANUARIO ESTADISTICO DE ACCIDENTES. *see* TRANSPORTATION—Abstracting, Bibliographies, Statistics

SPAIN. MINISTERIO DEL INTERIOR. DIRECCION GENERAL DE TRAFICO. ANUARIO ESTADISTICO GENERAL. *see* TRANSPORTATION—Abstracting, Bibliographies, Statistics

310 BGR ISSN 1310-7410
SPISANIE STATISTIKA. Text in Bulgarian; Summaries in English, Russian. bi-m. BGL 46.56 (effective 2002). 90 p./no.
Published by: Natsionalen Statisticheski Institut/National Statistical Institute, ul P Volov, # 2, Sofia, 1038, Bulgaria. FAX 359-2-9803319, publikacii@nsi.bg, http://www.nsi.bg.

SPOTREBA PALIV A ENERGIE V C R V ROCE (YEAR). (Ceska Republika) *see* ENERGY—Abstracting, Bibliographies, Statistics

310 USA ISSN 0172-7397
QA276
SPRINGER SERIES IN STATISTICS. Abbreviated title: S S S. Text in English. 1979. irreg., latest 2009. price varies. back issues avail.; reprints avail. **Document type:** *Monographic series.*
Indexed: CCMJ, CIS, Inspec, MathR.
Published by: Springer New York LLC (Subsidiary of: Springer Science+Business Media), 233 Spring St, New York, NY 10013. TEL 212-460-1500, FAX 212-460-1575, service-ny@springer.com.

314 SRB
SRBIJA I CRNA GORA. SAVEZNI ZAVOD ZA STATISTIKU. STATISTICKA REVIJA. Summaries in English, French. 1954. q. bk.rev. bibl. index. **Document type:** *Government.*
Formerly: Yugoslavia. Savezni Zavod za Statistiku. Statisticka Revija (0039-0534)
Indexed: CIS, RASB.
Published by: Srbija i Crna Gora Zavod za Statistiku/Serbia and Montenegro Statistical Office, Kneza Milosa 20, Postanski Fah 203, Belgrade, 11000. TEL 381-11-3617273. Ed. Branislav Ivanovic. Circ: 1,000.

SRBIJA I CRNA GORA ZAVOD ZA STATISTIKU. DEMOGRAFSKA STATISTIKA. *see* POPULATION STUDIES—Abstracting, Bibliographies, Statistics

314.97 SRB
HA1631
SRBIJA I CRNA GORA ZAVOD ZA STATISTIKU. INDEKS; mesecni pregled privredne statistike SFR Jugoslavije. Text in Slavic. 1952. m. mkt.; stat.
Formerly: Yugoslavia. Savezni Zavod za Statistiku. Indeks (0019-3585)
Indexed: RASB.
Published by: Srbija i Crna Gora Zavod za Statistiku/Serbia and Montenegro Statistical Office, Kneza Milosa 20, Postanski Fah 203, Belgrade, 11000. TEL 381-11-3617273. Ed. Ibrahim Latific. Circ: 4,400.

SRBIJA I CRNA GORA ZAVOD ZA STATISTIKU. KOMUNALNI FONDOVI U GRADSKIM NASELJIMA. *see* PUBLIC ADMINISTRATION—Abstracting, Bibliographies, Statistics

310 SRB
SRBIJA I CRNA GORA ZAVOD ZA STATISTIKU. METODOLOSKE STUDIJE, RASPRAVE I DOKUMENTACIJA. Text in Serbo-Croatian. 1973. irreg. **Document type:** *Government.*
Formerly: Yugoslavia. Savezni Zavod za Statistiku. Metodoloske Studije, Rasprave i Dokumentacija (0351-0603)
Published by: Srbija i Crna Gora Zavod za Statistiku/Serbia and Montenegro Statistical Office, Kneza Milosa 20, Postanski Fah 203, Belgrade, 11000. TEL 381-11-3617273.

310 SRB
HA37.Y8
SRBIJA I CRNA GORA ZAVOD ZA STATISTIKU. METODOLOSKI MATERIJALI. Text in Serbo-Croatian. irreg. **Document type:** *Government.*
Formerly: Yugoslavia. Savezni Zavod za Statistiku. Metodoloski Materijali (0513-6547)
Published by: Srbija i Crna Gora Zavod za Statistiku/Serbia and Montenegro Statistical Office, Kneza Milosa 20, Postanski Fah 203, Belgrade, 11000. TEL 381-11-3617273.

SRBIJA I CRNA GORA ZAVOD ZA STATISTIKU. OSNOVNA I SREDNJE. *see* EDUCATION—Abstracting, Bibliographies, Statistics

314 SRB
HD2336.25.Y8
SRBIJA I CRNA GORA. ZAVOD ZA STATISTIKU. STATISTICKI BILTEN. Text in French, Serbian, English, Russian. 1950. w. **Document type:** *Government.*
Formerly: Yugoslavia. Savezni Zavod za Statistiku. Statisticki Bilten (0084-4365)
Related titles: ◆ Series: Srbija i Crna Gora Zavod za Statistiku. Zaposlenost; ◆ Srbija i Crna Gora Zavod za Statistiku. Komunalni Fondovi u Gradskim Naseljima; ◆ Drustveni Proizvod i Narodni Dohodak. ISSN 0300-2527; ◆ Licni Dohoci. ISSN 0300-2535; ◆ Srbija i Crna Gora Zavod za Statistiku. Turizam; ◆ Srbija i Crna Gora Zavod za Statistiku. Anketa o Porodicnim Budzetima Radnickih Domacinstava; ◆ Industrijski Proizvodi; ◆ Investicije. ISSN 0351-4129; ◆ Srbija i Crna Gora Zavod za Statistiku. Samoupravljanje u Privredi; ◆ Srbija i Crna Gora Zavod za Statistiku. Industrijske Organizacije; ◆ Srbija i Crna Gora Zavod za Statistiku. Samoupravljanje u Ustanovama Drustvenih Sluzbi; ◆ Srbija i Crna Gora Zavod za Statistiku. Osnovna i Srednje.
Indexed: RASB.
Published by: Srbija i Crna Gora Zavod za Statistiku/Serbia and Montenegro Statistical Office, Kneza Milosa 20, Postanski Fah 203, Belgrade, 11000. TEL 381-11-3617273, FAX 381-11-3617297, http://www.szs.sv.gov.yu. Ed. Ibragim Catific.

310 SRB
HA37.Y8
SRBIJA I CRNA GORA ZAVOD ZA STATISTIKU. STUDIJE, ANALIZE I PRIKAZI. Text in Serbo-Croatian. 1953; N.S. irreg. **Document type:** *Government.*
Former titles: Yugoslavia. Savezni Zavod za Statistiku. Studije, Analize i Prikazi (0513-6555); (until 1960): Yugoslavia. Savezni Zavod za Statistiku. Studije i Analize

S

Published by: Srbija i Crna Gora Zavod za Statistiku/Serbia and Montenegro Statistical Office, Kneza Milosa 20, Postanski Fah 203, Belgrade, 11000. TEL 381-11-3617273.

SRI LANKA. CENSUS OF POPULATION AND HOUSING. *see* HOUSING AND URBAN PLANNING—Abstracting, Bibliographies, Statistics

314 DEU ISSN 0344-5550
HC287.H4
STAAT UND WIRTSCHAFT IN HESSEN. Text in German. 1946. m. EUR 40.80 (effective 2005). bk.rev. charts. **Document type:** *Government.* **Description:** Government publication, including economic and vital statistics.
Related titles: CD-ROM ed.: ISSN 1616-9867. EUR 44; Diskette ed.; Online - full text ed.
Indexed: PAIS.
Published by: Hessisches Statistisches Landesamt, Rheinstr 35-37, Wiesbaden, 65175, Germany. TEL 49-611-3802950, FAX 49-611-3802992, vertrieb@statistik-hessen.de, http://www.statistik-hessen.de.

310 DEU
STADT AACHEN. FACHBEREICH 01 VERWALTUNGSLEITUNG. WAHLEN, KURZINFORMATION. Text in German. 1971. irreg. charts; stat. 130 p./no.; back issues avail. **Document type:** *Yearbook, Government.* **Description:** Each issue devoted to all important areas of statistics about the city of Aachen.
Formerly (until 1999): Aachen. Statistisches Amt. Statistische Kurzinformation
Published by: Stadt Aachen, Fachbereich 01 Verwaltungsleitung, Rathaus, Markt, Aachen, 52062, Germany. TEL 49-241-4327671, FAX 49-241-4327698, oberbuergermeisterbuero@mail.aachen.de.

STADT BOCHUM. AMT FUER STATISTIK UND STADTFORSCHUNG. BEITRAEGE ZUR STADTENTWICKLUNG. *see* PUBLIC ADMINISTRATION—Abstracting, Bibliographies, Statistics

STADT BOCHUM. AMT FUER STATISTIK UND STADTFORSCHUNG. SONDERBERICHTE. *see* PUBLIC ADMINISTRATION—Abstracting, Bibliographies, Statistics

STADT BOCHUM. AMT FUER STATISTIK UND STADTFORSCHUNG. STATISTISCHES JAHRBUCH. *see* PUBLIC ADMINISTRATION—Abstracting, Bibliographies, Statistics

STADT BOCHUM. AMT FUER STATISTIK UND STADTFORSCHUNG. VERWALTUNGSBERICHT. *see* PUBLIC ADMINISTRATION—Abstracting, Bibliographies, Statistics

STADT BOCHUM. WAHLBUERO. WAHLEN IN BOCHUM. *see* PUBLIC ADMINISTRATION—Abstracting, Bibliographies, Statistics

STADT DUISBURG. MATERIALEN ZUR STADTFORSCHUNG. *see* PUBLIC ADMINISTRATION—Abstracting, Bibliographies, Statistics

STADT DUISBURG. PROGRAMM-INFORMATIONS-DIENST. FOERDERPROGRAMME; Foederprogramme des Bundes, des Landes Nordrhein-Westfalen und der Europaeischen Union in Duisburg. *see* PUBLIC ADMINISTRATION—Abstracting, Bibliographies, Statistics

STADT DUISBURG. WAHLEN (YEAR). *see* PUBLIC ADMINISTRATION—Abstracting, Bibliographies, Statistics

STADT FREIBURG IM BREISGAU. AMT FUER STATISTIK UND EINWOHNERWESEN. JAHRESHEFT. *see* PUBLIC ADMINISTRATION—Abstracting, Bibliographies, Statistics

310 DEU ISSN 0930-2034
STADT REMSCHEID STATISTISCHES JAHRBUCH. Text in German. 1949. a. EUR 15 (effective 2005). bk.rev. back issues avail. **Document type:** *Bulletin, Government.*
Formerly (until 1977): Statistik der Stadt Remscheid (0930-2042)
Published by: Stadt Remscheid, Statistikstelle, Hindenburgstr 52-58, Remscheid, 42853, Germany. TEL 49-2191-163984, FAX 49-2191-163232, einwohneramt@str.de, http://www.remscheid.de/Rathaus/33/33Statistik/33StatistikStandard.htm. Circ: 450.

STADTFORSCHUNG UND STATISTIK; Zeitschrift des Verbandes Deutscher Staedtestatistiker. *see* PUBLIC ADMINISTRATION—Abstracting, Bibliographies, Statistics

STANDARD & POOR'S CURRENT STATISTICS. *see* BUSINESS AND ECONOMICS—Investments

STANDARD TRUCKING AND TRANSPORTATION STATISTICS. *see* TRANSPORTATION—Abstracting, Bibliographies, Statistics

310 USA ISSN 1536-867X
QA276
➤ **THE STATA JOURNAL.** Text in English. 1991. q. USD 69 combined subscription in US & Canada to individuals (print & online eds.); USD 99 combined subscription elsewhere to individuals (print & online eds.); USD 195 combined subscription in US & Canada to institutions (print & online eds.); USD 225 combined subscription elsewhere to institutions (print & online eds.); USD 89 combined subscription in US & Canada to libraries (print & online eds.); USD 119 combined subscription elsewhere to libraries (print & online eds.) (effective 2010). back issues avail. **Document type:** *Journal, Academic/Scholarly.* **Description:** Presents various levels of expertise in statistics, research design, data management, graphics, reporting of results, and of Stata in particular.
Formerly (until 2001): Stata Technical Bulletin (1097-8879)
Related titles: Online - full text ed.: ISSN 1536-8734.
Indexed: CMCI, CurCont, P30, SCI, SCOPUS, SSCI, W07.
—BLDSC (8437.407000), IE, Ingenta.
Published by: Stata Press, 4905 Lakeway Dr, College Station, TX 77845. TEL 979-696-4600, 800-782-8272, FAX 979-696-4601, service@stata-press.com. Eds. H Joseph Newton, Nicholas J Cox.

➤ **STATE AND METROPOLITAN AREA DATA BOOK.** *see* POPULATION STUDIES—Abstracting, Bibliographies, Statistics

➤ **STATE AND METROPOLITAN AREA EMPLOYMENT AND UNEMPLOYMENT.** *see* BUSINESS AND ECONOMICS—Economic Situation And Conditions

➤ **STATE B E A R F A C T S (YEAR) ALABAMA.** (State Bureau of Economic Analysis Regional Fact Sheet) *see* BUSINESS AND ECONOMICS—Abstracting, Bibliographies, Statistics

➤ **STATE B E A R F A C T S (YEAR) ALASKA.** (State Bureau of Economic Analysis Regional Fact Sheet) *see* BUSINESS AND ECONOMICS—Abstracting, Bibliographies, Statistics

➤ **STATE B E A R F A C T S (YEAR) ARIZONA.** (State Bureau of Economic Analysis Regional Fact Sheet) *see* BUSINESS AND ECONOMICS—Abstracting, Bibliographies, Statistics

➤ **STATE B E A R F A C T S (YEAR) ARKANSAS.** (State Bureau of Economic Analysis Regional Fact Sheet) *see* BUSINESS AND ECONOMICS—Abstracting, Bibliographies, Statistics

➤ **STATE B E A R F A C T S (YEAR) CALIFORNIA.** (State Bureau of Economic Analysis Regional Fact Sheet) *see* BUSINESS AND ECONOMICS—Abstracting, Bibliographies, Statistics

➤ **STATE BANK OF PAKISTAN. STATISTICAL BULLETIN (ONLINE).** *see* BUSINESS AND ECONOMICS—Abstracting, Bibliographies, Statistics

➤ **THE STATE OF HAWAII DATA BOOK (ONLINE).** *see* BUSINESS AND ECONOMICS—Abstracting, Bibliographies, Statistics

317.56 USA
STATE PLANNING NEWSLETTER. Text in English. 1979. q. free. **Document type:** *Newsletter, Government.* **Description:** Provides news of the activities and publications of the State Data Center, State Demographer, the Planning Office of the North Carolina Geodetic Survey, and the Center for Geographic Information and Analysis.
Supersedes (in 1994): North Carolina. State Data Center. Newsletter
Published by: Office of State Planning, 116 W Jones St, Raleigh, NC 27603-8003. TEL 919-733-4131, FAX 919-715-3562. Ed. Sheila W Chavis. Circ: 2,700 (controlled).

317.3 510 304.6 USA ISSN 1524-3958
HA203
STATE PROFILES; the population and economy of each U S State. Text in English. 1999. irreg., latest 2009, 4th ed. price varies. back issues avail. **Document type:** *Trade.*
Published by: Bernan Press, 15200 NBN Way, PO Box 191, Blue Ridge Summit, PA 17214. TEL 301-459-7666, 800-865-3457, FAX 301-459-6988, 800-865-3450, customercare@bernan.com.

STATE RANKINGS; a statistical view of America. *see* HOUSING AND URBAN PLANNING—Abstracting, Bibliographies, Statistics

STATE TRANSPORTATION STATISTICS. *see* TRANSPORTATION—Abstracting, Bibliographies, Statistics

THE STATESMAN'S YEAR-BOOK (YEAR); the politics, cultures and economies of the world. *see* POLITICAL SCIENCE—Abstracting, Bibliographies, Statistics

310 ITA ISSN 0390-590X
CODEN: STATDJ
STATISTICA. Text in Multiple languages. 1935. q. bk.rev. bibl. index. **Document type:** *Journal, Academic/Scholarly.*
Formerly (until 1941): Supplemento Statistico ai Nuovi Problemi di Politica, Storia ed Economia (1127-7556)
Related titles: Online - full text ed.: ISSN 1973-2201. 2002 (from PQC).
Indexed: A22, CCMJ, CIS, JCQM, JEL, MSN, MathR, PopulInd, RASB, ST&MA, Z02.
—BLDSC (8447.350000), IE, Infotrieve, Ingenta, INIST.
Published by: Universita degli Studi di Bologna, Dipartimento di Scienze Statistiche "Paolo Fortunati", Via Belle Arti 41, Rome, 40126, Italy. Circ: 2,500.

310 ITA ISSN 1125-1964
STATISTICA APPLICATA; Italian journal of applied statistics. Text in Italian. 1967. q. bk.rev. charts; stat. **Document type:** *Journal, Academic/Scholarly.*
Formerly (until 1988): Rivista di Statistica Applicata (0035-6549)
Related titles: Online - full text ed.: ISSN 2038-5587.
Indexed: CIS, JEL.
—BLDSC (8447.374500).
Published by: (Istituto di Statistica Medica e Biometria), Associazione per la Statistica Applicata, Via Venezian 1, Milan, 20133, Italy. Ed. Luigi Fabbris.

310 ITA ISSN 1824-6672
➤ **STATISTICA & APPLICAZIONI.** Text in Italian. 2003. s-a. EUR 60 domestic to institutions; EUR 100 foreign to institutions (effective 2009). **Document type:** *Journal, Academic/Scholarly.* **Description:** Aims at promoting research in the methodological statistics field.
Related titles: Online - full text ed.
Published by: (Universita degli Studi di Milano, Scienze Statistiche), Vita e Pensiero (Subsidiary of: Universita Cattolica del Sacro Cuore), Largo Gemelli 1, Milan, 20123, Italy. TEL 39-02-72342335, FAX 39-02-72342260, redazione.vp@mi.unicatt.it, http://www.vitaepensiero.it. Ed. A Mazzali.

519.5 GBR ISSN 0039-0402
HA1
➤ **STATISTICA NEERLANDICA.** Text in English. 1946. q. GBP 394 in United Kingdom to institutions; EUR 501 in Europe to institutions; USD 662 in the Americas to institutions; USD 772 elsewhere to institutions; GBP 453 combined subscription in United Kingdom to institutions (print & online eds.); EUR 576 combined subscription in Europe to institutions (print & online eds.); USD 762 combined subscription in the Americas to institutions (print & online eds.); USD 889 combined subscription elsewhere to institutions (print & online eds.) (effective 2012). adv. bk.rev. stat. index. back issues avail.; reprint service avail. from PSC. **Document type:** *Journal, Academic/Scholarly.* **Description:** Publishes research and expository material about new developments in probability, statistics and operations research, and their applications in medical, agricultural, econometric, physical or social sciences and industry, commerce and government.
Formerly (until 1955): Statistica
Related titles: Microform ed.: (from PQC); Online - full text ed.: ISSN 1467-9574. GBP 394 in United Kingdom to institutions; EUR 501 in Europe to institutions; USD 662 in the Americas to institutions; USD 772 elsewhere to institutions (effective 2012) (from IngentaConnect).
Indexed: A01, A03, A08, A12, A17, A22, A26, ABIn, B01, B06, B07, B09, Biostat, CA, CCMJ, CIS, CMCI, E01, H05, IAOP, JCQM, KES, MSN, MathR, ORMS, P06, P30, P48, P51, P53, P54, PQC, QC&AS, S01, S02, S03, SCI, SCOPUS, ST&MA, T02, W07, Z02.
—BLDSC (8447.390000), IE, Infotrieve, Ingenta, INIST. **CCC.**
Published by: (Vereniging voor Statistiek en Operationele Research NLD), Wiley-Blackwell Publishing Ltd. (Subsidiary of: John Wiley & Sons, Inc.), 9600 Garsington Rd, Oxford, OX4 2DQ, United Kingdom. TEL 44-1865-776868, FAX 44-1865-714591, customerservices@blackwellpublishing.com. Ed. P H Franses. Adv. contact Craig Pickett TEL 44-1865-476267. page GBP 445; 138 x 210. Circ: 1,400.

310 TWN ISSN 1017-0405
QA276.A1 CODEN: STSNEO
➤ **STATISTICA SINICA.** Text in English. 1991. q. USD 255 to institutions (effective 2011). stat.; illus. 310 p./no.; back issues avail. **Document type:** *Journal, Academic/Scholarly.* **Description:** Publishes original work in all areas of statistics and probability, including theory, methods and applications.
Related titles: Online - full content ed.; Online - full text ed.
Indexed: A20, A22, CCMJ, CIS, CMCI, CurCont, ISR, MSN, MathR, P30, SCI, SCOPUS, ST&MA, W07, Z02.
—BLDSC (8447.390060), IE, Infotrieve, Ingenta. **CCC.**
Published by: Academia Sinica, Institute of Statistical Science, 128, Sec 2 Yen-chiu-Yuan Rd, Taipei, 115, Taiwan. TEL 886-2-2783-5611, FAX 886-2-2783-1523. Eds. J S Hwang, K-Y Liang, P Hall. **Co-sponsor:** International Chinese Statistical Association.

316.3 ETH ISSN 0425-4279
HA1961
STATISTICAL ABSTRACT (YEAR) OF ETHIOPIA. Text in English. 1968. a. ETB 32, USD 3.20 (effective 1999). back issues avail. **Document type:** *Government.* **Description:** Presents data on land and climate, mining, manufacturing, electrical industry, construction, transport, communication, external trade, national accounts, public finance, banking, insurance, prices, health and education.
Related titles: CD-ROM ed.; Diskette ed.
Published by: Central Statistical Authority, PO Box 1143, Addis Ababa, Ethiopia. TEL 115470, FAX 550334.

STATISTICAL ABSTRACT OF LATIN AMERICA. *see* POLITICAL SCIENCE—Abstracting, Bibliographies, Statistics

315 IND ISSN 0081-4709
STATISTICAL ABSTRACT OF MAHARASHTRA STATE. Text in English. 19??. irreg., latest 2001. **Document type:** *Corporate.*
Related titles: Online - full text ed.
Published by: Directorate of Economics and Statistics, 8th Fl, Administrative Bldg, Government Colony, Bandra (E), Mumbai, 400 051, India. TEL 91-22-26400205, dir_eco_stat@maharashtra.gov.in.

310 IND ISSN 0081-4717
STATISTICAL ABSTRACT OF RAJASTHAN. Text in English. 1958. a. **Document type:** *Report, Government.* **Description:** Provides information on different sectors of the State's economy with break-ups in regard to space, time and important characteristics.
Related titles: Online - full text ed.
Published by: Directorate of Economics and Statistics, Yojana Bhawan, Tilak Marg, C- Scheme, Jaipur, Rajasthan 302 005, India. FAX 91-141-2229756, dir.des@rajasthan.gov.in.

315 LKA ISSN 0259-8086
HA1728
STATISTICAL ABSTRACT OF THE DEMOCRATIC SOCIALIST REPUBLIC OF SRI LANKA. Text in English. 1949. irreg., latest 1995. LKR 187. index. **Document type:** *Government.*
Formerly: Statistical Abstract of Ceylon (0081-4636)
Published by: (Sri Lanka. Ministry of Plan Implementation), Department of Census and Statistics, c/o D.B.P. Suranjana Vidyaratne, 15/12, Maitland Crescent, Colombo, 07, Sri Lanka. suranjana.vidyarathne@statistics.gov.lk, http://www.statistics.gov.lk. Circ: 1,878. **Subscr. to:** Superintendent.

317.3 USA ISSN 1063-1690
STATISTICAL ABSTRACT OF THE UNITED STATES (LARGE PRINT EDITION); the national data book. Variant title: Statistical Abstract of the United States (Library Edition). Text in English. 1992. a. price varies. back issues avail. **Document type:** *Report, Trade.* **Description:** Contains all of the data found in the original abstract in an easier-to-read format.
Media: Large Type (10 pt.). **Related titles:** ◆ Print ed.: Statistical Abstract of the United States (Year). ISSN 0081-4741.
—CCC.
Published by: (U.S. Census Bureau), Bernan Press, 15200 NBN Way, PO Box 191, Blue Ridge Summit, PA 17214. TEL 301-459-7666, 800-865-3457, FAX 301-459-6988, 800-865-3450, customercare@bernan.com.

STATISTICAL ABSTRACT OF THE UNITED STATES (YEAR). *see* POPULATION STUDIES—Abstracting, Bibliographies, Statistics

310 USA ISSN 1932-1864
QA76.9.D343
STATISTICAL ANALYSIS AND DATA MINING. Text in English. 2008. bi-m. GBP 522 in United Kingdom to institutions; EUR 602 in Europe to institutions; USD 740 elsewhere to institutions (effective 2012). adv. back issues avail.; reprint service avail. from PSC. **Document type:** *Journal, Academic/Scholarly.* **Description:** Addresses the broad area of data analysis, including data mining algorithms, statistical approaches, and practical applications.
Related titles: Online - full text ed.: ISSN 1932-1872. 2007 (Jan.). GBP 522 in United Kingdom to institutions; EUR 602 in Europe to institutions; USD 740 elsewhere to institutions (effective 2012).
Indexed: A01, CCMJ, MSN, MathR, P30, Z02.
—IE. **CCC.**
Published by: John Wiley & Sons, Inc., 111 River St, Hoboken, NJ 07030. TEL 201-748-6000, FAX 201-748-6088, info@wiley.com, http://www.wiley.com/WileyCDA/. Ed. Joseph Verducci.

314.15 IRL ISSN 0081-4776
➤ **STATISTICAL AND SOCIAL INQUIRY SOCIETY OF IRELAND. JOURNAL.** Text in English. 1846. a. free membership (effective 2005). cum.index: 1847-1947. 1947-1979. **Document type:** *Journal, Academic/Scholarly.*
Former titles (until 1862): Dublin Statistical Society. Journal (0332-4648); (until 1855): Dublin Statistical Society. Transactions (0332-1606)
Indexed: A01, A26, CA, CREJ, E08, EconLit, I05, JEL, P06, PAIS, PCI, S09, T02.
Published by: Statistical and Social Inquiry Society of Ireland, c/o Robert Watt, Indecon House, 25 Wellington Quay, Dublin, 2, Ireland. info@ssisi.com, http://www.ssisi.ie. Circ: 700.

▼ ➤ **STATISTICAL COMMUNICATIONS IN INFECTIOUS DISEASES.** *see* MEDICAL SCIENCES—Communicable Diseases

➤ **STATISTICAL COMPUTING AND GRAPHICS.** *see* COMPUTERS—Abstracting, Bibliographies, Statistics

310 GBR
A STATISTICAL FOCUS ON WALES: WOMEN. Text in English. 1998. irreg., latest 1998. free (effective 2009). **Document type:** *Government.* **Description:** Contains statistics about women in Wales including comparisons are given with men and with their position ten years ago, wherever possible.
Related titles: Online - full text ed.: free (effective 2009).
Published by: Welsh Assembly Government, Statistical Directorate, Cathays Park, Cardiff, CF10 3NQ, United Kingdom. TEL 44-1443-845500, stats.info.desk@wales.gsi.gov.uk, http://wales.gov.uk/?lang=en.

STATISTICAL HANDBOOK OF JAPAN (YEAR). *see* POPULATION STUDIES—Abstracting, Bibliographies, Statistics

315 IND
STATISTICAL HANDBOOK OF TAMIL NADU. Text in English. 1969. a. **Document type:** *Handbook/Manual/Guide, Government.*
Published by: Department of Economics and Statistics, Central Administrative Bldg, Block II, No 259, Anna Salai, Teynampet, Chennai, Tamilnadu 600 006, India. TEL 91-44-24321189, FAX 91-44-24322871, stats@tn.nic.in, http://www.tnstat.gov.in.

310 PHL
STATISTICAL HANDBOOK OF THE PHILIPPINES. Text in English. a. USD 9. **Description:** Reference book that contains all statistical information possible.
Published by: National Statistics Office, Ramon Magsaysay Blvd, PO Box 779, Manila, Philippines. FAX 63-2-610794.

STATISTICAL HANDBOOK ON AGING AMERICANS. *see* GERONTOLOGY AND GERIATRICS—Abstracting, Bibliographies, Statistics

STATISTICAL INDICATORS FOR ASIA AND THE PACIFIC. *see* BUSINESS AND ECONOMICS—Abstracting, Bibliographies, Statistics

STATISTICAL INSTITUTE OF JAMAICA. DEMOGRAPHIC STATISTICS. *see* POPULATION STUDIES—Abstracting, Bibliographies, Statistics

STATISTICAL INSTITUTE OF JAMAICA. NATIONAL INCOME AND PRODUCT. *see* BUSINESS AND ECONOMICS—Abstracting, Bibliographies, Statistics

319 JAM
STATISTICAL INSTITUTE OF JAMAICA. POCKETBOOK OF STATISTICS. Text in English. 1976. a. USD 15.50.
Formerly (until 1978): Jamaica. Department of Statistics. Pocketbook of Statistics
Published by: Statistical Institute of Jamaica, 9 Swallowfield Rd, Kingston, 5, Jamaica. FAX 809-92-64859. Circ: 573.

317 JAM
STATISTICAL INSTITUTE OF JAMAICA. STATISTICAL ABSTRACT. Text in English. 1972. a. (published 9 months after year to which it relates). USD 31. **Document type:** *Abstract/Index.* **Description:** Presents a wide cross-section of data in both the economic and social fields.
Former titles: Jamaica. Department of Statistics. Statistical Abstract; Jamaica. Department of Statistics. Annual Abstract of Statistics (0075-2983)
Related titles: Microfiche ed.: (from PQC).
Published by: Statistical Institute of Jamaica, 9 Swallowfield Rd, Kingston, 5, Jamaica. FAX 809-92-64859. Circ: 117.

319 JAM
STATISTICAL INSTITUTE OF JAMAICA. STATISTICAL REVIEW. Text in English. q. USD 16 per issue.
Formerly (until 1981): Jamaica. Department of Statistics. Statistical Review
Published by: Statistical Institute of Jamaica, 9 Swallowfield Rd, Kingston, 5, Jamaica. FAX 809-92-64859. Circ: 148.

001.422 DEU ISSN 1618-2510
➤ **STATISTICAL METHODS AND APPLICATIONS.** Text in English. 1992. 3/yr. EUR 367, USD 403 combined subscription to institutions (print & online eds.) (effective 2012). back issues avail.; reprint service avail. from PSC. **Document type:** *Journal, Academic/Scholarly.* **Description:** Promotes the development of statistical methodology and its applications in biological, demographic, economic, health, physical, social and other scientific domains.
Formerly (until 2001): Journal of the Italian Statistical Society (1121-9130)
Related titles: Online - full text ed.: ISSN 1613-981X (from IngentaConnect).
Indexed: A12, A17, A22, A26, ABIn, B01, B06, B07, B09, C23, CA, CCMJ, CIS, E01, EconLit, H05, IBR, IBZ, JEL, MSN, MathR, P03, P10, P26, P30, P48, P50, P51, P52, P53, P54, PQC, PsycInfo, S10, SCI, SCOPUS, T02, W07, Z02.
—BLDSC (4803.130000), IE, Ingenta. **CCC.**
Published by: (Italian Statistical Society ITA), Springer (Subsidiary of: Springer Science+Business Media), Tiergartenstr 17, Heidelberg, 69121, Germany. TEL 49-6221-4870, FAX 49-6221-345229, subscriptions@springer.com. Ed. F Battaglia. **Subscr. in the Americas to:** Springer New York LLC, Journal Fulfillment, PO Box 2485, Secaucus, NJ 07096. TEL 800-777-4643, 201-348-4033, FAX 201-348-4505, journals-ny@springer.com, http://www.springer.com; **Subscr. to:** Springer Distribution Center, Kundenservice Zeitschriften, Haberstr 7, Heidelberg 69126, Germany. TEL 49-6221-3454303, FAX 49-6221-3454229, subscriptions@springer.com.

519.502461 GBR ISSN 0962-2802
R853.S7 CODEN: SMMRFQ
➤ **STATISTICAL METHODS IN MEDICAL RESEARCH.** Text in English. 1992. bi-m. USD 939, GBP 508 combined subscription to institutions (print & online eds.); USD 920, GBP 498 to institutions (effective 2011). illus. back issues avail.; reprint service avail. from PSC. **Document type:** *Journal, Academic/Scholarly.* **Description:** Contains review articles covering all the main areas of medical statistics.
Related titles: Online - full text ed.: ISSN 1477-0334. USD 845, GBP 457 to institutions (effective 2011).
Indexed: A01, A03, A08, A22, A34, A36, ASSIA, C06, C07, CA, CABA, CCMJ, CIS, CMCI, CurCont, E01, E12, EMBASE, ExcerpMed, FamI, GH, H05, H17, ISR, IndMed, IndVet, MEDLINE, MSN, MathR, N02, N03, P20, P22, P26, P30, P32, P33, P39, P48, P50, P52, P54, PQC, SCI, SCOPUS, ST&MA, T02, T05, VS, W07, Z02.
—BLDSC (8448.573050), GNLM, IE, Infotrieve, Ingenta, INIST. **CCC.**
Published by: Sage Publications Ltd. (Subsidiary of: Sage Publications, Inc.), 1 Oliver's Yard, 55 City Rd, London, EC1Y 1SP, United Kingdom. TEL 44-20-73248500, FAX 44-20-73248600, info@sagepub.co.uk, http://www.uk.sagepub.com/home.nav. Eds. Anders Skrondal, Sophia Rabe-Hesketh, Brian Everitt.

➤ **STATISTICAL MODELLING;** an international journal. *see* MATHEMATICS

310 THA
STATISTICAL NEWSLETTER. Text in Thai. 1975. m. free. **Document type:** *Government.* **Description:** Contains monthly statistical news and reports, summary of findings and other movement in statistical field.
Formerly: Statistical News
Published by: (Thailand. Statistical Data Bank and Information Dissemination Division), National Statistical Office, Larn Luang Rd, Bangkok, 10100, Thailand. TEL 66-2-282-1535, FAX 66-2-281-3814, binfodsm@nso.go.th, http://www.nso.go.th/. Circ: 1,500.

STATISTICAL OFFICE OF THE EUROPEAN COMMUNITIES. AGRICULTURAL PRICES; selected series - chronos data bank. *see* AGRICULTURE—Abstracting, Bibliographies, Statistics

STATISTICAL OFFICE OF THE EUROPEAN COMMUNITIES. STATISTICAL YEARBOOK. AGRICULTURE. *see* AGRICULTURE—Abstracting, Bibliographies, Statistics

STATISTICAL OVERVIEW, MIGRATION AND ASYLUM. *see* POPULATION STUDIES—Abstracting, Bibliographies, Statistics

519.5 DEU ISSN 0932-5026
HA15 CODEN: STPAE4
➤ **STATISTICAL PAPERS/STATISTISCHE HEFTE.** Text in English. 1960. q. EUR 687, USD 837 combined subscription to institutions (print & online eds.) (effective 2012). adv. bk.rev. charts; illus. back issues avail.; reprint service avail. from PSC. **Document type:** *Journal, Academic/Scholarly.* **Description:** Forum for the presentation and critical assessment of statistical methods, particularly for discussion of their methodological foundations and potential applications.
Formerly (until 1988): Statistische Hefte (0039-0631)
Related titles: Microform ed.: (from PQC); Online - full text ed.: ISSN 1613-9798 (from IngentaConnect).
Indexed: A12, A17, A22, A26, ABIn, ASCA, B01, B06, B07, B09, CA, CCMJ, CIS, CMCI, E01, EconLit, IBR, IBZ, JCQM, JEL, MSN, MathR, P06, P26, P48, P50, P51, P52, P53, P54, PAIS, PQC, RASB, SCI, SCOPUS, ST&MA, T02, W07, Z02.
—BLDSC (8448.620000), IE, Infotrieve, Ingenta. **CCC.**
Published by: Springer (Subsidiary of: Springer Science+Business Media), Tiergartenstr 17, Heidelberg, 69121, Germany. TEL 49-6221-4870, FAX 49-6221-345229. Eds. Dr. Goetz Trenkler, Sylvia Fruehwirth-Schnatter, Dr. Walter Kraemer. Circ: 800. **Subscr. in the Americas to:** Springer New York LLC, Journal Fulfillment, PO Box 2485, Secaucus, NJ 07096. TEL 800-777-4643, 201-348-4033, FAX 201-348-4505, journals-ny@springer.com, http://www.springer.com; **Subscr. to:** Springer Distribution Center, Kundenservice Zeitschriften, Haberstr 7, Heidelberg 69126, Germany. TEL 49-6221-3454303, FAX 49-6221-3454229, subscriptions@springer.com.

315.8 AFG ISSN 0302-2099
STATISTICAL POCKET-BOOK OF AFGHANISTAN. Text in English. 1972. irreg. illus.
Published by: Department of Statistics, Kabul, Afghanistan.

310 SRB
HA1631
STATISTICAL POCKET-BOOK OF SERBIA AND MONTENEGRO. Text in English. 1955. a.
Formerly (until 2003): Statistical Pocket-Book of Yugoslavia (0585-1815)
Published by: Srbija i Crna Gora Zavod za Statistiku/Serbia and Montenegro Statistical Office, Kneza Milosa 20, Postanski Fah 203, Belgrade, 11000. TEL 381-11-3617273.

315 LKA ISSN 0585-1777
HA1697
STATISTICAL POCKET BOOK OF THE DEMOCRATIC SOCIALIST REPUBLIC OF SRI LANKA. Text in English. 1966. a. LKR 53 English ed.; LKR 189 Sinhalese & Tamil eds. back issues avail. **Document type:** *Government.*
Former titles: Statistical Pocket Book of Sri Lanka; Statistical Pocket Book of Ceylon
Related titles: Tamil ed.; Singhalese ed.
Published by: (Sri Lanka. Ministry of Plan Implementation), Department of Census and Statistics, c/o D.B.P. Suranjana Vidyaratne, 15/12, Maitland Crescent, Colombo, 07, Sri Lanka. Ed. A G W Nanayakkara. Circ: 2,457. **Dist. by:** Superintendent, Government Publications Bureau, Colombo 1, Sri Lanka.

319 IRN
HA4570.2
STATISTICAL POCKET BOOK OF THE ISLAMIC REPUBLIC OF IRAN. Text in English. 1981. a. IRR 4,000 (effective 1999). charts; stat. **Document type:** *Government.*
Formerly (until 1996): Statistical Reflection of the Islamic Republic of Iran (1010-9617)
Related titles: ◆ Persian, Modern ed.: Iran Dar A'inah-i Amar. ISSN 1010-9633.
Published by: Statistical Centre of Iran, Dr. Fatemi Ave., Tehran, 14144, Iran. TEL 98-21-655061, FAX 98-21-653451. Circ: 700.

310 BGD
STATISTICAL POCKETBOOK OF BANGLADESH. Text in English. 1978. a. BDT 100, USD 15. charts; stat. **Description:** Information on Bangladesh's statistics for population, agriculture, industry and banking.
Published by: Bureau of Statistics, Secretariat, Dhaka, 2, Bangladesh. Circ: 5,000.

315.98 IDN ISSN 0126-3595
HA1811
STATISTICAL POCKETBOOK OF INDONESIA/BUKU SAKU STATISTIK INDONESIA. Text in English, Indonesian. 1940. a. IDR 30,000, USD 13.05. **Document type:** *Government.*
Supersedes: Statistik Indonesia
Related titles: Online - full text ed.
Indexed: P14, P52, P53, P54, PQC.
Published by: Central Bureau of Statistics/Biro Pusat Statistik, Jalan Dr. Sutomo No. 8, PO Box 3, Jakarta Pusat, Indonesia. TEL 62-21-372808. Circ: 1,500.

317 USA
STATISTICAL PROFILE OF IOWA. Text in English. biennial. USD 10. index. **Document type:** *Directory.* **Description:** Details on Iowa's business community.
Indexed: SRI.
Published by: Public Interest Institute, Wesleyan College, 600 N. Jackson St., Mt. Pleasant, IA 52641. TEL 319-385-3462. **Co-sponsor:** Iowa Department of Economic Development.

STATISTICAL RECORD OF THE ENVIRONMENT. *see* ENVIRONMENTAL STUDIES—Abstracting, Bibliographies, Statistics

310 011 USA ISSN 0885-6834
Z7554.U5
STATISTICAL REFERENCE INDEX. Text in English. 1980. a. abstr.; stat. index, cum.index: 1980-85, 1986-89; 1990-93. back issues avail. **Document type:** *Abstract/Index.* **Description:** Indexes and abstracts statistics contained in publications from more than 1,000 leading American sources.
Related titles: CD-ROM ed.: Statistical Masterfile.
—Linda Hall.
Published by: Congressional Information Service, Inc. (Subsidiary of: ProQuest), 789 E Eisenhower Pky, PO Box 1346, Ann Arbor, MI 48106. TEL 734-761-4700, academicinfo@proquest.com, http://www.proquest.com.

STATISTICAL REPORT. DISTILLED SPIRITS. *see* BEVERAGES—Abstracting, Bibliographies, Statistics

STATISTICAL REPORT FOR REAL ESTATE AGENTS. SAGUENAY METROPOLITAN AREA. *see* REAL ESTATE—Abstracting, Bibliographies, Statistics

STATISTICAL REPORT FOR REAL ESTATE AGENTS. TROIS-RIVIERES CENSUS METROPOLITAN AREA. SHAWINIGAN CENSUS AGGLOMERATION. *see* REAL ESTATE—Abstracting, Bibliographies, Statistics

STATISTICAL REPORT OF REGION. *see* BUSINESS AND ECONOMICS—Abstracting, Bibliographies, Statistics

STATISTICAL REPORT ON VISITOR ARRIVALS TO INDONESIA. *see* TRAVEL AND TOURISM—Abstracting, Bibliographies, Statistics

310 ESP ISSN 1988-7825
STATISTICAL REPORTS. Text in English. 2008. a.
Media: Online - full text.
Address: C Chile, 5 4o H, Madrid, 28016, Spain. ed@statrep.es. Ed. Mariano Ruiz Espejo.

STATISTICAL REVIEW OF GOVERNMENT IN UTAH. *see* PUBLIC ADMINISTRATION—Abstracting, Bibliographies, Statistics

STATISTICAL REVIEW OF TOURISM IN HONG KONG. *see* TRAVEL AND TOURISM—Abstracting, Bibliographies, Statistics

519.5 USA ISSN 0883-4237
QA276.A1 CODEN: STSCEP
➤ **STATISTICAL SCIENCE;** a review journal. Text in English. 1986. q. USD 225 to institutions (effective 2012). adv. bk.rev. illus. Index. back issues avail.; reprints avail. **Document type:** *Journal, Academic/Scholarly.*
Related titles: Microform ed.: (from PQC); Online - full text ed.
Indexed: A20, A22, ASCA, Biostat, CA, CCMJ, CIS, CMCI, CurCont, IBR, IBZ, ISR, Inspec, MSN, MathR, ORMS, P30, P50, QC&AS, RASB, S02, S03, SCI, SCOPUS, ST&MA, T02, W07, Z02.
—BLDSC (8448.953000), IE, Infotrieve, Ingenta, INIST, Linda Hall. **CCC.**
Published by: Institute of Mathematical Statistics, PO Box 22718, Beachwood, OH 44122. TEL 216-295-2340, 877-557-4674, FAX 216-295-5661, ims@imstat.org. Ed. Jon A. Wellner. **Subscr. to:** 9650 Rockville Pike, Ste L3503A, Bethesda, MD 20814. TEL 301-634-7029, FAX 301-634-7099.

310 SGP ISSN 1793-6195
STATISTICAL SCIENCE AND INTERDISCIPLINARY RESEARCH. Text in English. 2008. irreg., latest vol.11, 2010. price varies. back issues avail. **Document type:** *Monographic series, Academic/Scholarly.* **Description:** Covers various topics such as statistics and mathematics, computer science, machine intelligence, econometrics, other physical sciences, and social and natural sciences.
Indexed: CCMJ, MSN, MathR, Z02.
Published by: World Scientific Publishing Co. Pte. Ltd., 5 Toh Tuck Link, Singapore, 596224, Singapore. TEL 65-6466-5775, FAX 65-6467-7667, wspc@wspc.com.sg, http://www.worldscientific.com. Ed. Sankar K Pal TEL 91-33-25753301. **Dist. by:** World Scientific Publishing Ltd., 57 Shelton St, London WC2H 9HE, United Kingdom. TEL 44-207-8360888, FAX 44-207-8362020, sales@wspc.co.uk; World Scientific Publishing Co., Inc., 27 Warren St, Ste 401-402, Hackensack, NJ 07601. TEL 201-487-9655, 800-227-7562, FAX 201-487-9656, 888-977-2665, wspc@wspc.com.

S

STATISTICAL SERVICE. SECURITY PRICE INDEX RECORD. *see* BUSINESS AND ECONOMICS—Investments

310 AUS ISSN 0314-6820
STATISTICAL SOCIETY OF AUSTRALIA. NEWSLETTER. Text in English. 1977. 4/yr. AUD 30 (effective 2008). adv. **Document type:** *Newsletter.*
Indexed: CIS.
Published by: Statistical Society of Australia, PO Box 5111, Braddon, ACT 2612, Australia. TEL 61-2-62498266, FAX 61-2-62496558, admin@statsoc.org.au. Eds. A Richardson, M Adena.

STATISTICAL TABLES OF PUBLIC NUISANCE, TOKYO. *see* ENVIRONMENTAL STUDIES—Abstracting, Bibliographies, Statistics

317 CUB
STATISTICAL YEARBOOK COMPENDIUM OF THE REPUBLIC OF CUBA. Text in English. a.
Related titles: ◆ Spanish ed.: Anuario Estadistico de Cuba. ISSN 0574-6132.
Published by: Comite Estatal de Estadisticas, Centro de Informacion Cientifico-Tecnica, Almendares No. 156, esq. a Desague, Gaveta Postal 6016, Havana, Cuba.

STATISTICAL YEARBOOK FOR ASIA AND THE PACIFIC/ANNUAIRE STATISTIQUE POUR L'ASIE ET LE PACIFIQUE. *see* BUSINESS AND ECONOMICS—Abstracting, Bibliographies, Statistics

315 BGD ISSN 0302-2374
STATISTICAL YEARBOOK OF BANGLADESH. Text in English. 1964. a. BDT 400, USD 60. **Document type:** *Government.* **Description:** Data on population, agriculture, industry, foreign trade and banking in Bangladesh.
Formerly: Statistical Digest of Bangladesh
Published by: Bureau of Statistics, Secretariat, Dhaka, 2, Bangladesh.

314 GRC ISSN 0081-5071
STATISTICAL YEARBOOK OF GREECE. Text in English, Greek. 1955. irreg., latest 2001. back issues avail. **Document type:** *Government.*
Indexed: RASB.
Published by: National Statistical Service of Greece, Statistical Information and Publications Division/Ethniki Statistiki Yperesia tes Ellados, 14-16 Lykourgou St, Athens, 101 66, Greece. TEL 30-1-3289-397, FAX 30-1-3241-102, http://www.statistics.gr/Main_eng.asp.

STATISTICAL YEARBOOK OF GUANGDONG (YEAR). *see* BUSINESS AND ECONOMICS—Abstracting, Bibliographies, Statistics

314 IRL ISSN 1649-1408
HA1141
STATISTICAL YEARBOOK OF IRELAND. Text in English. 1931. a. EUR 20 (effective 2005). charts; stat. **Document type:** *Government.* **Description:** Comprehensive source of CSO and other statistical data published in Ireland; includes data for Northern Ireland.
Former titles (until 2001): Ireland. Central Statistics Office. Statistical Abstract (0790-8970); (until 1986): Ireland. Central Statistics Office. Statistical Abstract of Ireland (0081-4660); (until 1950): Irish Free State. Department of Industry and Commerce. Statistical Abstract (0790-1976)
Related titles: Online - full text ed.
Published by: Ireland. Central Statistics Office/Eire, An Phriomh-Oifig Staidrimh, Skehard Rd, Cork, Ireland. TEL 353-21-4535000, FAX 353-21-4535555, information@cso.ie. Circ: 2,000.

317.292 JAM ISSN 0304-0992
STATISTICAL YEARBOOK OF JAMAICA. Text in English. 1973. a. illus.
Published by: Statistical Institute of Jamaica, 9 Swallowfield Rd, Kingston, 5, Jamaica. FAX 809-92-64859. Circ: 155.

318.83 SUR
STATISTICAL YEARBOOK OF SURINAME. Text in Dutch, English. 1962. a. **Document type:** *Government.* **Description:** Provides statistical data on area and inhabitants, climate, population, transport, economy, agriculture and animal husbandry, prices and wages, employment, education, social benefits, public health, government finances, justice and police.
Related titles: Series of: Suriname in Cijfers.
Published by: Algemeen Bureau voor de Statistiek/General Bureau of Statistics, PO Box 244, Paramaribo, Suriname. TEL 597-474861, FAX 597-425004.

315 THA ISSN 0857-9067
STATISTICAL YEARBOOK OF THAILAND. Text in English, Thai. 1909. a., latest vol.46, 1999. price varies. **Document type:** *Government.* **Description:** Comprehensive statistics on area and climate, population and labor force, public health and vital statistics, immigration and tourism, education, agriculture, fisheries and forestry, mining, transport and communication, foreign trade, currency and banking, public finance, national income, household income and expenditures, public justice and more.
Published by: (Thailand. Statistical Data Bank and Information Dissemination Division), National Statistical Office, Larn Luang Rd, Bangkok, 10100, Thailand. TEL 66-2-282-1535, FAX 66-2-282-3814, binfodsm@nso.go.th, http://www.nso.go.th/. Circ: 600.

310 NLD ISSN 0303-6448
STATISTICAL YEARBOOK OF THE NETHERLANDS. Text in Dutch. 1942. a. EUR 19.95 (effective 2008). **Document type:** *Yearbook, Government.*
Related titles: Online - full text ed.: ISSN 2211-596X.
Published by: Centraal Bureau voor de Statistiek, Henri Faasdreef 312, The Hague, 2492 JP, Netherlands. TEL 31-70-3373800, infoserv@cbs.nl, http://www.cbs.nl. **Orders to:** Sdu Uitgevers bv, Postbus 20014, The Hague 2500 EA, Netherlands. TEL 31-70-3789880.

STATISTICAL YEARBOOK OF THE REPUBLIC OF CHINA. *see* BUSINESS AND ECONOMICS—Abstracting, Bibliographies, Statistics

STATISTICHE AMBIENTALI. *see* ENVIRONMENTAL STUDIES—Abstracting, Bibliographies, Statistics

STATISTICHE DELLA SANITA. *see* PUBLIC HEALTH AND SAFETY—Abstracting, Bibliographies, Statistics

314 BGR ISSN 1310-7364
HA1621
STATISTICHESKI GODISHNIK NA NARODNA REPUBLIKA BULGARIA. Text in Bulgarian, English. 1909. a. BGL 32.29 (effective 2002). stat. **Description:** Contains detailed statistical information on all spheres of Bulgarian economy and social life.
Related titles: CD-ROM ed.; Microfiche ed.: (from PQC).
Indexed: RASB.
Published by: Natsionalen Statisticheski Institut/National Statistical Institute, ul P Volov, # 2, Sofia, 1038, Bulgaria. TEL 359-2-9857515, FAX 359-2-9857530, publikacii@nsi.bg, http://www.nsi.bg. Circ: 2,000.

314 BGR ISSN 0204-563X
HC407.B9
STATISTICHESKI IZVESTIIA. Text in Bulgarian, English. 1957. q. USD 64 foreign (effective 2002). stat. **Document type:** *Journal, Academic/Scholarly.*
Indexed: RASB.
Published by: Natsionalen Statisticheski Institut/National Statistical Institute, ul P Volov, # 2, Sofia, 1038, Bulgaria. FAX 359-2-9803319, publikacii@nsi.bg, http://www.nsi.bg. Circ: 798.

314 BGR ISSN 0861-0576
HA1621
STATISTICHESKI SPRAVOCHNIK NA REPUBLIKA BULGARIA/ STATISTICAL REFERENCE BOOK OF REPUBLIC OF BULGARIA. Text in English. 1959. a. USD 26 foreign (effective 2002). stat. **Document type:** *Journal, Academic/Scholarly.*
Indexed: RASB.
Published by: Natsionalen Statisticheski Institut/National Statistical Institute, ul P Volov, # 2, Sofia, 1038, Bulgaria. FAX 359-2-9803319, publikacii@nsi.bg, http://www.nsi.bg. Circ: 5,500.

STATISTICHESKII BULLETEN'. *see* BUSINESS AND ECONOMICS—Abstracting, Bibliographies, Statistics

STATISTICHESKOE OBOZRENIE/CURRENT STATISTICAL SURVEY. *see* BUSINESS AND ECONOMICS—Abstracting, Bibliographies, Statistics

310 SRB ISSN 1451-6632
HA1631 CODEN: SGJUEB
STATISTICKI GODISNJAK SRBIJE I CRNE GORE. Text in Serbian, English. 1954. a. **Document type:** *Government.*
Formerly (until 2003): Statisticki Godisnjak Jugoslavije (0585-1920)
Related titles: Microfiche ed.: 1954 (from PQC); English ed.: Socialist Federal Republic of Yugoslavia. Statistical Yearbook. ISSN 0351-1413.
Indexed: RASB.
Published by: Srbija i Crna Gora Zavod za Statistiku/Serbia and Montenegro Statistical Office, Kneza Milosa 20, Postanski Fah 203, Belgrade, 11000. TEL 381-11-3617273, FAX 381-11-3617297, http://www.szs.sv.gov.yu.

310 SRB
STATISTICKI KALENDAR SRBIJE I CRNE GORE. Text in Serbian, English. 1955. a. **Document type:** *Government.*
Formerly (until 2003): Statisticki Kalendar Jugoslavije (0352-3349)
Published by: Srbija i Crna Gora Zavod za Statistiku/Serbia and Montenegro Statistical Office, Kneza Milosa 20, Postanski Fah 203, Belgrade, 11000. TEL 381-11-3617273, FAX 381-11-3617297, http://www.szs.sv.gov.yu.

319.4 HRV ISSN 1333-3305
HA1637
STATISTICKI LJETOPIS REPUBLIKE HRVATSKE. Text in Croatian. 1953. a.
Formerly (until 2000): Statisticki Ljetopis. Drzavni Zavod za Statistiku Republike Hrvatske (1330-0369)
Published by: Drzavni Zavod za Statistiku Republike Hrvatske, Ilica 3, Zagreb, 10000, Croatia. ured@dzs.hr.

314.97 BIH ISSN 0039-0542
STATISTICKI PREGLED SOCIJALISTICKE REPUBLIKE BOSNE I HERCEGOVINE. Text in Serbo-Croatian. 1953. m. USD 10.45.
Indexed: RASB.
Published by: Republicki Zavod za Statistiku, Jugoslavenske Narodne Armije 54, Sarajevo, Bosnia Herzegovina. Ed. Nedjo Kovacevic.

314.97 SVN ISSN 1408-8606
STATISTICNA SPOROCILA/STATISTICAL MESSAGES. Text in Slovenian. 1998. m. free. stat. **Document type:** *Government.* **Description:** Presents activities of the Statistical office, deliberations on statistical methods and critical comparisons of various statistical systems, topical events and other interesting issues from the field of statistics.
Related titles: Online - full content ed.
Published by: Statisticni Urad Republike Slovenije/Statistical Office of the Republic of Slovenia, Vozarski pot 12, Ljubjana, 1000, Slovenia. TEL 386-1-2415104, FAX 386-1-2415344, info.stat@gov.si, http://www.stat.si. Ed. Ana Antoncic. Pub. Tomaz Banovec.

314.97 SVN ISSN 1408-192X
HA1188.S54
STATISTICNE INFORMACIJE/RAPID REPORTS. Text in Slovenian, English. 1957. s-a. price varies. abstr.; stat. **Document type:** *Government.* **Description:** The series are divided into subseries, which are further divided into titles related in terms of contents. They bring the latest statistical data from most fields of statistics. In addition to data and charts, each issue contains the comment, short methodological explanations, basic statistical definitions and the description of the survey.
Related titles: Online - full content ed.
Published by: Statisticni Urad Republike Slovenije/Statistical Office of the Republic of Slovenia, Vozarski pot 12, Ljubjana, 1000, Slovenia. TEL 386-1-2415104, FAX 386-1-2415344, info.stat@gov.si. Eds. Ana Antoncic, Avgustina Kuhar de Domizio. Pub. Tomaz Banovec.

310 SVN
STATISTICNI DNEVI/STATISTICAL DAYS. Text in Slovenian, English. 1987. a. free. abstr.; stat. **Document type:** *Government.* **Description:** Covers the events of the conferences of the Statistical Society of Slovenia.
Published by: Statisticni Urad Republike Slovenije/Statistical Office of the Republic of Slovenia, Vozarski pot 12, Ljubjana, 1000, Slovenia. TEL 386-1-2415104, FAX 386-1-2415344, info.stat@gov.si, http://www.stat.si. Ed. Boris Tkacik. Pub. Tomaz Banovec.

314.97 SVN ISSN 1318-5403
HA1636
STATISTICNI LETOPIS REPUBLIKE SLOVENIJE/STATISTICAL YEARBOOK OF THE REPUBLIC OF SLOVENIA. Text in Slovenian, English. 1953. a. EUR 32.76 per issue (effective 2007). bibl.; charts; maps; stat. **Document type:** *Government.* **Description:** Comprises a rich collection of statistical data from all statistical surveys, methodological explanations, statistical definitions, statistical methodology, charts, review by statistical regions and municipalities, international comparison.
Related titles: Online - full content ed.
Published by: Statisticni Urad Republike Slovenije/Statistical Office of the Republic of Slovenia, Vozarski pot 12, Ljubjana, 1000, Slovenia. TEL 386-1-2415104, FAX 386-1-2415344, info.stat@gov.si. Eds. Ana Antoncic, Avgustina Kuhar de Domizio. Pub. Tomaz Banovec.

314.97 SVN ISSN 1854-5734
STATISTICNI PORTRET SLOVENIJE V E U/STATISTICAL PORTRAIT OF SLOVENIA IN THE E U. (European Union) Text in Slovenian, English. 2004. a. **Document type:** *Government.*
Related titles: Online - full content ed.
Published by: Statisticni Urad Republike Slovenije/Statistical Office of the Republic of Slovenia, Vozarski pot 12, Ljubjana, 1000, Slovenia. TEL 386-1-2415104, FAX 386-1-2415344, info.stat@gov.si.

519.5 GBR ISSN 0233-1888
QA276.A1 CODEN: MOSSD5
➤ **STATISTICS;** a journal of theoretical and applied statistics. Text in English, French, German, Russian. 1970. bi-m. GBP 1,849 combined subscription in United Kingdom to institutions (print & online eds.); EUR 1,948, USD 2,446 combined subscription to institutions (print & online eds.) (effective 2012). adv. illus. back issues avail.; reprint service avail. from PSC. **Document type:** *Journal, Academic/Scholarly.* **Description:** Publishes theoretical and applied papers related to the different fields of statistics such as regression and variance analysis, design of experiments, foundations of statistical inference, statistical decision theory, testing hypotheses, parameter estimation, nonparametric methods, sequential procedures, time series and statistical problems for stochastic processes, and statistical data analysis.
Formerly (until 1985): Series Statistics (0323-3944); Which superseded in part (in 1977): Mathematische Operationsforschung und Statistik (0047-6277)
Related titles: CD-ROM ed.: ISSN 1026-7786; Online - full text ed.: ISSN 1029-4910. GBP 1,664 in United Kingdom to institutions; EUR 1,753, USD 2,202 to institutions (effective 2012) (from IngentaConnect).
Indexed: A01, A03, A08, A22, ASCA, CA, CCMJ, CIS, CMCI, CurCont, E01, IBR, IBZ, ISR, Inspec, JCQM, MSN, MathR, P30, S01, SCI, SCOPUS, ST&MA, T02, W07, Z02.
—IE, Infotrieve, Ingenta, INIST, Linda Hall. **CCC.**
Published by: Taylor & Francis Ltd. (Subsidiary of: Taylor & Francis Group), 4 Park Sq, Milton Park, Abingdon, Oxfordshire OX14 4RN, United Kingdom. TEL 44-20-70176000, FAX 44-20-70176336, subscriptions@tandf.co.uk, http://www.taylorandfrancis.com. Ed. Olaf Bunke. Adv. contact Linda Hann. **Subscr. to:** Journals Customer Service, Sheepen Pl, Colchester, Essex CO3 3LP, United Kingdom. TEL 44-20-70175544, FAX 44-20-70175198, tf.enquiries@tfinforma.com.

➤ **STATISTICS (YEAR) ROAD ACCIDENTS JAPAN.** *see* TRANSPORTATION—Abstracting, Bibliographies, Statistics

➤ **STATISTICS AND COMPUTING.** *see* COMPUTERS—Abstracting, Bibliographies, Statistics

001.422 USA ISSN 1938-7989
QA276.A1
STATISTICS AND ITS INTERFACE. Text in English. 2008 (June). q. USD 353 combined subscription domestic to institutions (print & online eds.); USD 386 combined subscription foreign to institutions (print & online eds.) (effective 2011). **Document type:** *Journal, Academic/Scholarly.* **Description:** Promotes the interface between statistics and other disciplines including, but not limited to, biomedical sciences, geosciences, computer sciences, engineering, and social and behavioral sciences.
Related titles: Online - full text ed.: ISSN 1938-7997. USD 253 to institutions (effective 2012).
Indexed: CCMJ, MSN, MathR, P30, SCI, W07, Z02.
—BLDSC (8453.516660), IE.
Published by: International Press, 387 Somerville Ave, PO Box 43502, Somerville, MA 02143. TEL 617-623-3106, FAX 617-623-3101, journals@intlpress.com. Ed. Heping Zhang.

519.5 NLD ISSN 0167-7152
QA276.A1 CODEN: SPLTDC
➤ **STATISTICS & PROBABILITY LETTERS.** Text in English. 1983. 24/yr. EUR 2,490 in Europe to institutions; JPY 331,000 in Japan to institutions; USD 2,786 elsewhere to institutions (effective 2012). abstr. reprints avail. **Document type:** *Journal, Academic/Scholarly.* **Description:** Covers all fields of statistics and probability, and provides an outlet for rapid publication of short communications in the field.
Related titles: Microform ed.: (from PQC); Online - full text ed.: (from IngentaConnect, ScienceDirect).
Indexed: A01, A03, A08, A22, A26, ASCA, CA, CCMJ, CIS, CMCI, CurCont, FR, I05, JCQM, MSN, MathR, P30, S01, SCI, SCOPUS, ST&MA, T02, W07, Z02.
—BLDSC (8453.518000), IE, Infotrieve, Ingenta, INIST, Linda Hall. **CCC.**
Published by: Elsevier BV, North-Holland (Subsidiary of: Elsevier Science & Technology), Sara Burgerhartstraat 25, Amsterdam, 1055 KV, Netherlands. TEL 31-20-4853911, FAX 31-20-4852457, JournalsCustomerServiceEMEA@elsevier.com. Eds. H Koul, S Datta. **Subscr.:** Elsevier BV, Radarweg 29, PO Box 211, Amsterdam 1000 AE, Netherlands. TEL 31-20-4853757, FAX 31-20-4853432.

310 330 CAN ISSN 0838-4223
Z7554.C2
STATISTICS CANADA CATALOGUE. Text in English. a. USD 18; USD 15 in Canada; USD 21 elsewhere. **Document type:** *Catalog.* **Description:** A guide to the complete collection of facts and figures on Canada's changing business, social and economic environment.
Former titles (until 1988): Statistics Canada. Current Publications Index (0832-8331); (until 1986): Statistics Canada. Catalogue (0317-770X); (until 1972): D B S Catalogue (0590-5699)
Published by: Statistics Canada, Operations and Integration Division (Subsidiary of: Statistics Canada/Statistique Canada), Circulation Management, 120 Parkdale Ave, Ottawa, ON K1A 0T6, Canada. TEL 613-951-7277, 800-267-6677, FAX 613-951-1584.

STATISTICS, COMPUTER SCIENCE AND OPERATION RESEARCH. PART I, MATHEMATICAL STATISTICS. ANNUAL CONFERENCE. *see* COMPUTERS

310 EGY ISSN 2090-1763
STATISTICS, COMPUTER SCIENCE AND OPERATION RESEARCH. PART II, APPLIED STATISTICS & ECONOMETRICS. ANNUAL CONFERENCE. Text in English. 1965. a. **Document type:** *Proceedings, Academic/Scholarly.*
Supersedes in part (in 198?): Statistics, Computer Science and Operations Research. Annual Conference (1110-6778)
Published by: Cairo University, Institute of Statistical Studies and Research, 5 Tharwat St, Orman, Giza, Egypt. TEL 20-2-3358496, FAX 20-2-7482533, dean@issr.cu.edu.eg, http://issr.cu.edu.eg.

310 NLD ISSN 1570-1824
QA276.18
➤ **STATISTICS EDUCATION RESEARCH JOURNAL.** Text in English. 2002. s-a. free (effective 2011). back issues avail. **Document type:** *Journal, Academic/Scholarly.* **Description:** Covers the research in teaching, learning and understanding of statistics of probability at all educational levels.
Media: Online - full content.

Indexed: A39, C27, C29, CA, CIS, D03, D04, E03, E13, ERI, P03, PsycInfo, R14, S14, S15, S18, T02.
Published by: International Association for Statistical Education, PO Box 24070, The Hague, 2490 AB, Netherlands. TEL 31-70-3375737, FAX 31-70-3860025. Eds. Peter Petocz, Tom Short. Co-publisher: International Statistical Institute.

➤ STATISTICS - EUROPE; sources for market research. see BUSINESS AND ECONOMICS—Abstracting, Bibliographies, Statistics

➤ STATISTICS FOR IRON AND STEEL INDUSTRY IN INDIA. see METALLURGY—Abstracting, Bibliographies, Statistics

➤ STATISTICS FOR THE ENVIRONMENT. see ENVIRONMENTAL STUDIES—Abstracting, Bibliographies, Statistics

▼ ➤ STATISTICS IN BIOPHARMACEUTICAL RESEARCH. see PHARMACY AND PHARMACOLOGY

▼ ➤ STATISTICS IN BIOSCIENCES. see BIOLOGY—Abstracting, Bibliographies, Statistics

➤ STATISTICS IN MEDICINE. see MEDICAL SCIENCES—Abstracting, Bibliographies, Statistics

310 POL ISSN 1234-7655
STATISTICS IN TRANSITION. Text in English. 1993. s-a. **Document type:** *Government.* **Description:** Provides a forum for an exchange of ideas and experience in various fields of statistics, especially those relevant to economies undergoing transition from the communist to the market-based system.
Indexed: CIS.
Published by: Glowny Urzad Statystyczny/Polish Statistical Association, Al Niepodleglosci 208, Warsaw, 00925, Poland. TEL 48-22-6083112, FAX 48-22-6083860, dane@stat.gov.pl.

STATISTICS OF JAPANESE NON-LIFE INSURANCE BUSINESS. see INSURANCE—Abstracting, Bibliographies, Statistics

STATISTICS OF LIFE INSURANCE BUSINESS IN JAPAN. see INSURANCE—Abstracting, Bibliographies, Statistics

STATISTICS OF ROAD TRAFFIC ACCIDENTS IN EUROPE AND NORTH AMERICA. see TRANSPORTATION—Abstracting, Bibliographies, Statistics

STATISTICS ON INTERNATIONAL DEVELOPMENT. see BUSINESS AND ECONOMICS—Abstracting, Bibliographies, Statistics

STATISTICS ON SCIENTIFIC AND TECHNOLOGICAL ACTIVITIES/ IHSA'AT AL-ANSHITAH AL-'ILMIYYAH WAL-TEKNOLOJIYYAH FI DAWLAT AL-KUWAYT. see SCIENCES: COMPREHENSIVE WORKS—Abstracting, Bibliographies, Statistics

STATISTICS ON SOCIAL WORK EDUCATION IN THE UNITED STATES. see SOCIAL SERVICES AND WELFARE—Abstracting, Bibliographies, Statistics

▼ **STATISTICS, POLITICS, AND POLICY.** see PUBLIC ADMINISTRATION

▼ **STATISTICS PORTUGAL.** see POPULATION STUDIES—Abstracting, Bibliographies, Statistics

STATISTICS RELATING TO REGIONAL AND MUNICIPAL GOVERNMENTS IN BRITISH COLUMBIA. see PUBLIC ADMINISTRATION—Abstracting, Bibliographies, Statistics

310 SGP ISSN 0218-6810
HA4600.67
STATISTICS SINGAPORE NEWSLETTER. Text in English. 1972. s-a. (Apr. & Oct.). **Document type:** *Newsletter, Government.* **Description:** Covers news of recent research and survey findings as well as the latest statistical activities in the Singapore statistical service.
Former titles (until 1993): Singapore Statistical News (0217-4316); (until 1982): Statistical News (Singapore) (0129-279X); (until 1977): Singapore Statistical Bulletin (0217-8230)
Related titles: Online - full content ed.
Indexed: P30, PAIS.
Published by: Department of Statistics, 100 High St #05-01, The Treasury, Singapore, 179434, Singapore. TEL 65-3327686, FAX 65-3327689, info@singstat.gov.sg.

519.5 USA ISSN 1935-7516
QA276.A1
➤ **STATISTICS SURVEYS.** Text in English. 2007. a. free (effective 2012). back issues avail. **Document type:** *Journal, Academic/Scholarly.*
Media: Online - full text.
Indexed: A39, C27, C29, D03, D04, E13, MSN, P30, R14, S14, S15, S18.
Published by: (American Statistical Association, Statistical Society of Canada CAN), Institute of Mathematical Statistics, PO Box 22718, Beachwood, OH 44122. TEL 216-295-2340, 877-557-4674, FAX 216-295-5661, ims@imstat.org. **Subscr. to:** 9650 Rockville Pike, Ste L3503A, Bethesda, MD 20814. TEL 301-634-7029, FAX 301-634-7099.

314 SWE
STATISTICS SWEDEN. QUARTERLY FOREIGN TRADE STATISTICS S I T C. Abstracts and contents page in English. 1954. q. SEK 250 (effective 1992).
Formerly (until 1990): Sweden. Statistiska Centralbyraan. Utrikeshandel. Maanadsstatistik (0373-2649)
Published by: Statistiska Centralbyraan, Distribution, Orebro, 70189, Sweden. Circ: 1,250.

310 USA ISSN 1040-0672
CODEN: STMOEV
STATISTICS: TEXTBOOKS AND MONOGRAPHS SERIES. Text in English. 1972. irreg., latest 2010. price varies. back issues avail. **Document type:** *Monographic series, Academic/Scholarly.*
Indexed: A22, CCMJ, CIS.
—BLDSC (8453.613000), IE, Ingenta. **CCC.**
Published by: C R C Press, LLC (Subsidiary of: Taylor & Francis Group), 6000 Broken Sound Pky, NW, Ste 300, Boca Raton, FL 33487. TEL 800-272-7737, FAX 800-374-3401, orders@crcpress.com.

STATISTIK AUSTRIA. ERGEBNISSE DER LANDWIRTSCHAFTLICHEN STATISTIK. see AGRICULTURE—Abstracting, Bibliographies, Statistics

STATISTIK AUSTRIA. KRIPPEN, KINDERGAERTEN UND HORTE (KINDERTAGESHEIME). see EDUCATION—Abstracting, Bibliographies, Statistics

STATISTIK AUSTRIA. LANDWIRTSCHAFTLICHE MASCHINENZAEHLUNG. see AGRICULTURE—Abstracting, Bibliographies, Statistics

310 AUT
STATISTIK AUSTRIA. MIKROZENSUS JAHRESERGEBNISSE. Text in German. 1969. a. EUR 40 (effective 2005). stat. **Document type:** *Government.* **Description:** Information on population, employment and stock of dwellings.
Formerly: Austria. Statistisches Zentralamt. Mikrozensus; Jahresergebnisse
Related titles: ◆ Series of: Beitraege zur Oesterreichischen Statistik. ISSN 0067-2319.
Published by: Statistik Austria, Guglgasse 13, Vienna, W 1110, Austria. TEL 43-1-711280, FAX 43-1-711287728, info@statistik.gv.at, http://www.statistik.at.

310 AUT
STATISTIK AUSTRIA. STATISTISCHE NACHRICHTEN. Text in German. 1923. m. EUR 130; EUR 13 per issue (effective 2005). **Document type:** *Government.* **Description:** Data on all censuses in Austria.
Formerly: Austria. Statistisches Zentralamt. Statistische Nachrichten (0029-9960)
Related titles: CD-ROM ed.
Indexed: P30, RASB.
Published by: Statistik Austria, Guglgasse 13, Vienna, W 1110, Austria. TEL 43-1-711280, FAX 43-1-711287728, info@statistik.gv.at, http://www.statistik.at. Ed. Kurt Klein.

STATISTIK AUSTRIA. WOHNEN. see BUILDING AND CONSTRUCTION—Abstracting, Bibliographies, Statistics

▼ **STATISTIK NYT FRA DANSK LANDBRUG.** see AGRICULTURE—Abstracting, Bibliographies, Statistics

STATISTIKA/STATISTICS; ekonomicko-statisticky casopis - journal of economics and statistics. see BUSINESS AND ECONOMICS—Abstracting, Bibliographies, Statistics

310 370 FRA ISSN 2108-6745
▼ ➤ **STATISTIQUE ET ENSEIGNEMENT.** Text in French, English. 2010. s-a. free (effective 2010). **Document type:** *Journal, Academic/ Scholarly.*
Media: Online - full text.
Published by: Societe Francaise de Statistique, 11 rue Pierre et Marie Curie, Paris, 75231, France. TEL 33-1-44276660, FAX 33-1-44070474, http://www.sfds.asso.fr.

➤ **STATISTIQUES DE L'EDITION AU QUEBEC.** see LIBRARY AND INFORMATION SCIENCES—Abstracting, Bibliographies, Statistics

➤ **STATISTIQUES SUR LA SURVIE AU CANCER.** see MEDICAL SCIENCES—Abstracting, Bibliographies, Statistics

➤ **STATISTISCHE BERICHTE - BADEN-WUERTTEMBERG. A: BEVOELKERUNG, GESUNDHEITSWESEN, GEBIET UND ERWERBSTAETIGKEIT.** see PUBLIC ADMINISTRATION—Abstracting, Bibliographies, Statistics

➤ **STATISTISCHE BERICHTE - BADEN-WUERTTEMBERG. B: BILDUNG, RECHTSPFLEGE, WAHLEN.** see PUBLIC ADMINISTRATION—Abstracting, Bibliographies, Statistics

➤ **STATISTISCHE BERICHTE - BADEN-WUERTTEMBERG. C: LAND- UND FORSTWIRTSCHAFT, FISCHEREI.** see FORESTS AND FORESTRY—Abstracting, Bibliographies, Statistics

➤ **STATISTISCHE BERICHTE - BADEN-WUERTTEMBERG. D: GEWERBEANZEIGEN, UNTERNEHMEN UND ARBEITSSTAETTEN, INSOLVENZEN.** see BUSINESS AND ECONOMICS—Abstracting, Bibliographies, Statistics

➤ **STATISTISCHE BERICHTE - BADEN-WUERTTEMBERG. E: PRODUZIERENDES GEWERBE, HANDWERK.** see ENGINEERING—Abstracting, Bibliographies, Statistics

➤ **STATISTISCHE BERICHTE - BADEN-WUERTTEMBERG. F: WOHNUNGSWESEN, BAUTAETIGKEIT.** see HOUSING AND URBAN PLANNING—Abstracting, Bibliographies, Statistics

➤ **STATISTISCHE BERICHTE - BADEN-WUERTTEMBERG. G: HANDEL, TOURISMUS, GASTGEWERBE.** see TRAVEL AND TOURISM—Abstracting, Bibliographies, Statistics

➤ **STATISTISCHE BERICHTE - BADEN-WUERTTEMBERG. H: VERKEHR.** see TRANSPORTATION—Abstracting, Bibliographies, Statistics

➤ **STATISTISCHE BERICHTE - BADEN-WUERTTEMBERG. J: DIENSTLEISTUNGEN, GELD UND KREDIT.** see BUSINESS AND ECONOMICS—Abstracting, Bibliographies, Statistics

➤ **STATISTISCHE BERICHTE - BADEN-WUERTTEMBERG. K: SOZIALLEISTUNGEN.** see SOCIAL SERVICES AND WELFARE—Abstracting, Bibliographies, Statistics

➤ **STATISTISCHE BERICHTE - BADEN-WUERTTEMBERG. L: OEFFENTLICHE FINANZEN, PERSONAL, STEUERN.** see BUSINESS AND ECONOMICS—Abstracting, Bibliographies, Statistics

➤ **STATISTISCHE BERICHTE - BADEN-WUERTTEMBERG. M: PREISE UND PREISINDIZES.** see BUSINESS AND ECONOMICS—Abstracting, Bibliographies, Statistics

➤ **STATISTISCHE BERICHTE - BADEN-WUERTTEMBERG. N: VERDIENSTE UND ARBEITSKOSTEN.** see BUSINESS AND ECONOMICS—Abstracting, Bibliographies, Statistics

➤ **STATISTISCHE BERICHTE - BADEN-WUERTTEMBERG. O: FINANZEN UND VERMOEGEN PRIVATER HAUSHALTE.** see BUSINESS AND ECONOMICS—Abstracting, Bibliographies, Statistics

➤ **STATISTISCHE BERICHTE - BADEN-WUERTTEMBERG. P: GESAMTRECHNUNGEN.** see BUSINESS AND ECONOMICS—Abstracting, Bibliographies, Statistics

➤ **STATISTISCHE BERICHTE - BADEN-WUERTTEMBERG. Q: UMWELT.** see ENVIRONMENTAL STUDIES—Abstracting, Bibliographies, Statistics

➤ **STATISTISCHE BERICHTE - RHEINLAND-PFALZ. A: BEVOELKERUNG, GESUNDHEITSWESEN, GEBIET, ERWERBSTAETIGKEIT.** see POPULATION STUDIES—Abstracting, Bibliographies, Statistics

➤ **STATISTISCHE BERICHTE - RHEINLAND-PFALZ. B: BILDUNG, KULTUR, RECHTSPFLEGE, WAHLEN.** see PUBLIC ADMINISTRATION—Abstracting, Bibliographies, Statistics

➤ **STATISTISCHE BERICHTE - RHEINLAND-PFALZ. C: LAND- UND FORSTWIRTSCHAFT, FISCHEREI.** see FORESTS AND FORESTRY—Abstracting, Bibliographies, Statistics

➤ **STATISTISCHE BERICHTE - RHEINLAND-PFALZ. D: GEWERBEANZEIGEN, UNTERNEHMEN UND ARBEITSSTAETTEN, INSOLVENZEN.** see BUSINESS AND ECONOMICS—Abstracting, Bibliographies, Statistics

➤ **STATISTISCHE BERICHTE - RHEINLAND-PFALZ. E: PRODUZIERENDES GEWERBE, HANDWERK.** see BUSINESS AND ECONOMICS—Abstracting, Bibliographies, Statistics

➤ **STATISTISCHE BERICHTE - RHEINLAND-PFALZ. F: WOHNUNGSWESEN, BAUTAETIGKEIT.** see HOUSING AND URBAN PLANNING—Abstracting, Bibliographies, Statistics

➤ **STATISTISCHE BERICHTE - RHEINLAND-PFALZ. G: HANDEL, TOURISMUS, GASTGEWERBE.** see TRAVEL AND TOURISM—Abstracting, Bibliographies, Statistics

➤ **STATISTISCHE BERICHTE - RHEINLAND-PFALZ. H: VERKEHR.** see TRANSPORTATION—Abstracting, Bibliographies, Statistics

➤ **STATISTISCHE BERICHTE - RHEINLAND-PFALZ. J: DIENSTLEISTUNGEN, GELD UND KREDIT.** see BUSINESS AND ECONOMICS—Abstracting, Bibliographies, Statistics

➤ **STATISTISCHE BERICHTE - RHEINLAND-PFALZ. K: SOZIALLEISTUNGEN.** see SOCIAL SERVICES AND WELFARE—Abstracting, Bibliographies, Statistics

➤ **STATISTISCHE BERICHTE - RHEINLAND-PFALZ. L: OEFFENTLICHE FINANZEN, PERSONAL, STEUERN.** see BUSINESS AND ECONOMICS—Abstracting, Bibliographies, Statistics

➤ **STATISTISCHE BERICHTE - RHEINLAND-PFALZ. M: PREISE UND PREISINDIZES.** see BUSINESS AND ECONOMICS—Abstracting, Bibliographies, Statistics

➤ **STATISTISCHE BERICHTE - RHEINLAND-PFALZ. N: VERDIENSTE, ARBEITSKOSTEN UND -ZEITEN.** see BUSINESS AND ECONOMICS—Abstracting, Bibliographies, Statistics

➤ **STATISTISCHE BERICHTE - RHEINLAND-PFALZ. O: FINANZEN UND VERMOEGEN PRIVATER HAUSHALTE.** see BUSINESS AND ECONOMICS—Abstracting, Bibliographies, Statistics

➤ **STATISTISCHE BERICHTE - RHEINLAND-PFALZ. P: GESAMTRECHNUNGEN (WIRTSCHAFT, UMWELT).** see BUSINESS AND ECONOMICS—Abstracting, Bibliographies, Statistics

➤ **STATISTISCHE BERICHTE - RHEINLAND-PFALZ. Q: UMWELT.** see ENVIRONMENTAL STUDIES—Abstracting, Bibliographies, Statistics

➤ **STATISTISCHE BERICHTE - RHEINLAND-PFALZ. Z.** see PUBLIC ADMINISTRATION—Abstracting, Bibliographies, Statistics

➤ **STATISTISCHE INFORMATION/INFORMATIONS STATISTIQUES;** Katalog der verfuegbaren Publikationen zur Bundestatistik. see PUBLIC ADMINISTRATION—Abstracting, Bibliographies, Statistics

310 AUT
STATISTISCHE MITTEILUNGEN DER STADT WIEN. NEUE FOLGE. Text in German. 1876. q. EUR 14.53; EUR 5.09 newsstand/cover (effective 2003). bk.rev. charts. 50 p./no.; back issues avail. **Document type:** *Journal, Government.* **Description:** Compiles statistical tables and analyses of population, economy, social statistics and education in the city of Vienna.
Former titles (until 1999): Statistische Mitteilungen - Stadt Wien (1028-0677); (until 1985): Mitteilungen aus Statistik und Verwaltung der Stadt Wien (0026-6876)
Published by: Statistisches Amt der Stadt Wien, Volksgartenstrasse 3, Vienna, 1010, Austria. TEL 43-1-4000-88629, FAX 43-1-4000-7166, post@m66.magwien.gv.at, http://www.statistik.wien.at. Ed., R&P Peter Pokay. Circ: 1,150.

STATISTISCHE NACHRICHTEN DER STADT NUERNBERG. see PUBLIC ADMINISTRATION—Abstracting, Bibliographies, Statistics

314 DEU
STATISTISCHER MONATSBERICHT DER STADT AUGSBURG. Text in German. 1998. m. **Document type:** *Government.*
Published by: Stadt Augsburg, Amt fuer Stadtentwicklung und Statistik, Bahnhofstr 18 1-3, Augsburg, 86150, Germany. TEL 49-821-3246850, FAX 49-821-3246877.

STATISTISCHER VIERTELJAHRESBERICHT HANNOVER. see PUBLIC ADMINISTRATION—Abstracting, Bibliographies, Statistics

STATISTISCHES AMT SAARLAND. STATISTISCHE BERICHTE A. see PUBLIC ADMINISTRATION—Abstracting, Bibliographies, Statistics

STATISTISCHES AMT SAARLAND. STATISTISCHE BERICHTE B. see PUBLIC ADMINISTRATION—Abstracting, Bibliographies, Statistics

STATISTISCHES AMT SAARLAND. STATISTISCHE BERICHTE C. see PUBLIC ADMINISTRATION—Abstracting, Bibliographies, Statistics

STATISTISCHES AMT SAARLAND. STATISTISCHE BERICHTE D. see PUBLIC ADMINISTRATION—Abstracting, Bibliographies, Statistics

STATISTISCHES AMT SAARLAND. STATISTISCHE BERICHTE E. see PUBLIC ADMINISTRATION—Abstracting, Bibliographies, Statistics

STATISTISCHES AMT SAARLAND. STATISTISCHE BERICHTE F. see PUBLIC ADMINISTRATION—Abstracting, Bibliographies, Statistics

STATISTISCHES AMT SAARLAND. STATISTISCHE BERICHTE G. see PUBLIC ADMINISTRATION—Abstracting, Bibliographies, Statistics

STATISTISCHES AMT SAARLAND. STATISTISCHE BERICHTE H. see PUBLIC ADMINISTRATION—Abstracting, Bibliographies, Statistics

STATISTISCHES AMT SAARLAND. STATISTISCHE BERICHTE K. see PUBLIC ADMINISTRATION—Abstracting, Bibliographies, Statistics

STATISTISCHES AMT SAARLAND. STATISTISCHE BERICHTE L. see PUBLIC ADMINISTRATION—Abstracting, Bibliographies, Statistics

STATISTISCHES AMT SAARLAND. STATISTISCHE BERICHTE M. see PUBLIC ADMINISTRATION—Abstracting, Bibliographies, Statistics

STATISTISCHES AMT SAARLAND. STATISTISCHE BERICHTE N. see PUBLIC ADMINISTRATION—Abstracting, Bibliographies, Statistics

STATISTISCHES AMT SAARLAND. STATISTISCHE BERICHTE P. see PUBLIC ADMINISTRATION—Abstracting, Bibliographies, Statistics

STATISTISCHES AMT SAARLAND. VEROEFFENTLICHUNGSVERZEICHNIS. see PUBLIC ADMINISTRATION—Abstracting, Bibliographies, Statistics

S

STATISTISCHES BUNDESAMT. AUSGEWAHLTE ZAHLEN ZUR ENERGIEWIRTSCHAFT. *see* ENERGY—Abstracting, Bibliographies, Statistics

STATISTISCHES BUNDESAMT. FACHSERIE 10: RECHTSPFLEGE. REIHE 1: AUSGEWAEHLTE ZAHLEN FUER DIE RECHTSPFLEGE. *see* LAW—Abstracting, Bibliographies, Statistics

STATISTISCHES BUNDESAMT. FACHSERIE 16: VERDIENSTE UND ARBEITSKOSTEN, REIHE 1: VERDIENSTE DER ARBEITER UND ARBEITERINNEN IN DER LANDWIRTSCHAFT IN DEUTSCHLAND. *see* AGRICULTURE—Abstracting, Bibliographies, Statistics

STATISTISCHES BUNDESAMT. FACHSERIE 17: PREISE, REIHE 1: PREISINDIZES FUER DIE LAND- UND FORSTWIRTSCHAFT. *see* AGRICULTURE—Abstracting, Bibliographies, Statistics

STATISTISCHES BUNDESAMT. FACHSERIE 17: PREISE, REIHE 10: INTERNATIONALER VERGLEICH DER PREISE FUER DIE LEBENSHALTUNG. *see* BUSINESS AND ECONOMICS—Abstracting, Bibliographies, Statistics

STATISTISCHES BUNDESAMT. FACHSERIE 17: PREISE, REIHE 2: PREISE UND PREISINDIZES FUER GEWERBLICHE PRODUKTE. ERZEUGERPREISE. *see* BUSINESS AND ECONOMICS—Abstracting, Bibliographies, Statistics

STATISTISCHES BUNDESAMT. FACHSERIE 17: PREISE, REIHE 4: PREISINDIZES FUER DIE BAUWIRTSCHAFT. *see* BUSINESS AND ECONOMICS—Abstracting, Bibliographies, Statistics

STATISTISCHES BUNDESAMT. FACHSERIE 17: PREISE, REIHE 5: KAUFWERTE FUER BAULAND. *see* BUILDING AND CONSTRUCTION—Abstracting, Bibliographies, Statistics

STATISTISCHES BUNDESAMT. FACHSERIE 17: PREISE, REIHE 8: PREISINDIZES FUER DIE EINFUHR. *see* BUSINESS AND ECONOMICS—Abstracting, Bibliographies, Statistics

STATISTISCHES BUNDESAMT. FACHSERIE 17: PREISE, REIHE 9.1: PREISINDIZES FUER NACHRICHTENUEBERMITTLUNG. *see* TRANSPORTATION—Abstracting, Bibliographies, Statistics

STATISTISCHES BUNDESAMT. FACHSERIE 2: UNTERNEHMEN UND ARBEITSSTAETTEN, REIHE 4.1: INSOLVENZVERFAHREN. *see* BUSINESS AND ECONOMICS—Abstracting, Bibliographies, Statistics

STATISTISCHES BUNDESAMT. FACHSERIE 3: LAND- UND FORSTWIRTSCHAFT, FISCHEREI; REIHE 2.1.1: BETRIEBSGROESSENSTRUKTUR. *see* AGRICULTURE—Abstracting, Bibliographies, Statistics

STATISTISCHES BUNDESAMT. FACHSERIE 3: LAND- UND FORSTWIRTSCHAFT, FISCHEREI; REIHE 3: LANDWIRTSCHAFTLICHE BODENNUETZUNG UND PFLANZLICHE ERZEUGUNG. *see* AGRICULTURE—Abstracting, Bibliographies, Statistics

STATISTISCHES BUNDESAMT. FACHSERIE 3: LAND- UND FORSTWIRTSCHAFT, FISCHEREI; REIHE 4: VIEHBESTAND UND TIERISCHE ERZEUGUNG. *see* AGRICULTURE—Abstracting, Bibliographies, Statistics

STATISTISCHES BUNDESAMT. FACHSERIE 4: PRODUZIERENDES GEWERBE, REIHE 3.1: PRODUKTION IM PRODUZIERENDEN GEWERBE. *see* BUSINESS AND ECONOMICS—Abstracting, Bibliographies, Statistics

STATISTISCHES BUNDESAMT. FACHSERIE 4: PRODUZIERENDES GEWERBE, REIHE 5: BAUGEWERBE. *see* BUILDING AND CONSTRUCTION—Abstracting, Bibliographies, Statistics

STATISTISCHES BUNDESAMT. FACHSERIE 5: BAUTAETIGKEIT UND WOHNUNGEN, REIHE 1: BAUTAETIGKEIT. *see* BUILDING AND CONSTRUCTION—Abstracting, Bibliographies, Statistics

STATISTISCHES BUNDESAMT. FACHSERIE 5: BAUTAETIGKEIT UND WOHNUNGEN, REIHE 3: BESTAND AN WOHNUNGEN. *see* BUILDING AND CONSTRUCTION—Abstracting, Bibliographies, Statistics

STATISTISCHES BUNDESAMT. FACHSERIE 6: BINNENHANDEL, GASTGEWERBE, TOURISMUS; REIHE 3: EINZELHANDEL. *see* BUSINESS AND ECONOMICS—Abstracting, Bibliographies, Statistics

STATISTISCHES BUNDESAMT. FACHSERIE 7: AUSSENHANDEL, REIHE 1: ZUSAMMENFASSENDE UEBERSICHTEN FUER DEN AUSSENHANDEL. *see* BUSINESS AND ECONOMICS—Abstracting, Bibliographies, Statistics

STATISTISCHES BUNDESAMT. FACHSERIE 8: VERKEHR, REIHE 2: EISENBAHNVERKEHR. *see* TRANSPORTATION—Abstracting, Bibliographies, Statistics

STATISTISCHES BUNDESAMT. FACHSERIE 8: VERKEHR, REIHE 4: BINNENSCHIFFAHRT. *see* TRANSPORTATION—Abstracting, Bibliographies, Statistics

STATISTISCHES BUNDESAMT. FACHSERIE 8: VERKEHR, REIHE 5: SEESCHIFFFAHRT. *see* TRANSPORTATION—Abstracting, Bibliographies, Statistics

STATISTISCHES BUNDESAMT. FACHSERIE 8: VERKEHR, REIHE 6: LUFTVERKEHR. *see* TRANSPORTATION—Abstracting, Bibliographies, Statistics

STATISTISCHES BUNDESAMT. FACHSERIE 8: VERKEHR, REIHE 7: VERKEHRSUNFAELLE. *see* TRANSPORTATION—Abstracting, Bibliographies, Statistics

314 DEU ISSN 0081-5322
HA1330
STATISTISCHES JAHRBUCH BERLIN. Text in German. 1945. a. EUR 30 (effective 2006). back issues avail. **Document type:** *Government.*
Supersedes: Berlin in Zahlen
Indexed: RASB.
Published by: (Baden-Wuerttemberg. Statistisches Landesamt Baden-Wuerttemberg), Kulturbuch Verlag GmbH, Postfach 470449, Berlin, 12313, Germany. TEL 49-30-6618484, FAX 49-30-6617828, kbvinfo@kulturbuch-verlag.de, http://www.kulturbuch-verlag.de.

314 CHE ISSN 0081-5330
HA1593
STATISTISCHES JAHRBUCH DER SCHWEIZ/ANNUAIRE STATISTIQUE DE LA SUISSE. Text in French, German. 1891. a. CHF 140 (effective 2001). **Document type:** *Bulletin.*
Related titles: Microfiche ed.: (from PQC).
Indexed: RASB.
Published by: (Switzerland. Bundesamt fuer Statistik/Office Federal de la Statistique), Neue Zuercher Zeitung Buchverlag, Postfach, Zuerich, 8021, Switzerland. TEL 41-1-2581505, FAX 41-1-2581399, buch.verlag@nzz.ch, http://www.nzz-buchverlag.ch.

314 DEU ISSN 0931-9239
STATISTISCHES JAHRBUCH DER STADT AUGSBURG. Text in German. 1953. a. EUR 16 (effective 2005). **Document type:** *Yearbook, Government.*
Published by: Stadt Augsburg, Amt fuer Stadtentwicklung und Statistik, Bahnhofstr 18 1-3, Augsburg, 86150, Germany. TEL 49-821-3246850, FAX 49-821-3246877, afste.stadt@augsburg.de, http://www.augsburg.de/Seiten/augsburg_d/frames/stadtentwicklung.shtml. Ed. Werner Mitzscherlich. Circ: 300.

STATISTISCHES JAHRBUCH DER STADT KOELN. *see* PUBLIC ADMINISTRATION—Abstracting, Bibliographies, Statistics

STATISTISCHES JAHRBUCH DER STADT NUERNBERG. *see* PUBLIC ADMINISTRATION—Abstracting, Bibliographies, Statistics

310 AUT ISSN 0259-6083
STATISTISCHES JAHRBUCH DER STADT WIEN; Ausgabe (Year). Text in German. 1883. a. EUR 32.70 (effective 2003). adv. charts; stat. index. 400 p./no.; back issues avail. **Document type:** *Yearbook, Government.* **Description:** Statistical data on the city of Vienna, including statistics of city districts and suburban areas.
Related titles: CD-ROM ed.
Indexed: RASB.
Published by: Statistisches Amt der Stadt Wien, Volksgartenstrasse 3, Vienna, 1010, Austria. TEL 43-1-4000-88629, FAX 43-1-4000-7166, post@m66.magwien.gv.at, http://www.statistik.wien.at. Ed., R&P Peter Pokay. Adv. contact Manfred Hahn. Circ: 1,000.

STATISTISCHES JAHRBUCH DEUTSCHER GEMEINDEN. *see* PUBLIC ADMINISTRATION—Abstracting, Bibliographies, Statistics

STATISTISCHES JAHRBUCH FUER BAYERN. *see* PUBLIC ADMINISTRATION—Abstracting, Bibliographies, Statistics

STATISTISCHES JAHRBUCH FUER DIE BUNDESREPUBLIK DEUTSCHLAND. *see* PUBLIC ADMINISTRATION—Abstracting, Bibliographies, Statistics

314 AUT ISSN 1811-6760
STATISTISCHES JAHRBUCH FUER DIE REPUBLIK OESTERREICH. Text in German. 1883. a. EUR 60 (effective 2005). adv. **Document type:** *Government.*
Formerly (until 1993): Statistisches Handbuch fuer die Republik Oesterreich (0081-5314)
Indexed: RASB.
Published by: Statistik Austria, Guglgasse 13, Vienna, W 1110, Austria. TEL 43-1-711280, FAX 43-1-711287728, info@statistik.gv.at, http://www.statistik.at.

310 LIE ISSN 0259-4676
HA1659.L46
STATISTISCHES JAHRBUCH FUERSTENTUM LIECHTENSTEIN. Text in German. 1977. a. CHF 35 (effective 2007). back issues avail. **Document type:** *Directory, Trade.*
Published by: Amt fuer Volkswirtschaft, Giessenstr 3, Vaduz, 9490, Liechtenstein. TEL 423-2366876, FAX 423-2366931, http://www.llv.li/amtsstellen/llv-avw-home.htm. Circ: 850.

STATISTISCHES JAHRBUCH HAMBURG. *see* PUBLIC ADMINISTRATION—Abstracting, Bibliographies, Statistics

STATISTISCHES JAHRBUCH RHEINLAND-PFALZ. *see* PUBLIC ADMINISTRATION—Abstracting, Bibliographies, Statistics

STATISTISCHES JAHRBUCH SCHLESWIG-HOLSTEIN. *see* PUBLIC ADMINISTRATION—Abstracting, Bibliographies, Statistics

STATISTISCHES JAHRBUCH UEBER ERNAEHRUNG, LANDWIRTSCHAFT UND FORSTEN DER BUNDESREPUBLIK DEUTSCHLAND. *see* AGRICULTURE—Abstracting, Bibliographies, Statistics

STATISTISCHES LANDESAMT HAMBURG. EIN STADTPORTRAET IN ZAHLEN. *see* PUBLIC ADMINISTRATION—Abstracting, Bibliographies, Statistics

STATISTISCHES LANDESAMT RHEINLAND-PFALZ. AMTLICHES GEMEINDEVERZEICHNIS. *see* PUBLIC ADMINISTRATION—Abstracting, Bibliographies, Statistics

STATISTISCHES LANDESAMT RHEINLAND-PFALZ. DIE LANDWIRTSCHAFT. *see* AGRICULTURE—Abstracting, Bibliographies, Statistics

STATISTISCHES LANDESAMT RHEINLAND-PFALZ. STATISTISCHE BAENDE. *see* PUBLIC ADMINISTRATION—Abstracting, Bibliographies, Statistics

STATISTISCHES LANDESAMT RHEINLAND-PFALZ. STATISTISCHE MONATSHEFTE. *see* PUBLIC ADMINISTRATION—Abstracting, Bibliographies, Statistics

314 DEU ISSN 1612-4278
STATISTISCHES MONATSHEFT BADEN-WUERTTEMBERG. Text in German. 1947. m. EUR 54 (effective 2010). bk.rev. **Document type:** *Government.*
Former titles (until 2003): Baden-Wuerttemberg in Wort und Zahl (0721-1821); (until 1970): Statistische Monatshefte Baden-Wuerttemberg (0404-6234); (until 1953): Statistische Monatshefte Wuerttemberg-Baden (0721-1813)
Published by: Statistisches Landesamt Baden-Wuerttemberg, Boeblinger Str 68, Stuttgart, 70199, Germany. TEL 49-711-6410, FAX 49-711-6412440, poststelle@stala.bwl.de, http://www.statistik.baden-wuerttemberg.de. Circ: 1,100.

STATISTISCHES TASCHENBUCH BADEN-WUERTTEMBERG. *see* PUBLIC ADMINISTRATION—Abstracting, Bibliographies, Statistics

310 AUT ISSN 0259-7985
STATISTISCHES TASCHENBUCH DER STADT WIEN; Ausgabe (Year). Text in German. 1884. a. EUR 10 (effective 2003). adv. charts; stat. index. 160 p./no.; back issues avail. **Document type:** *Government.*
Published by: Statistisches Amt der Stadt Wien, Volksgartenstrasse 3, Vienna, 1010, Austria. TEL 43-1-4000-88629, FAX 43-1-4000-7166, post@m66.magwien.gv.at, http://www.statistik.wien.at. Ed., R&P Helga Vimetal. Adv. contact Manfred Hahn. Circ: 1,000.

314.85 SWE ISSN 0081-5381
HA1523
STATISTISK AARSBOK FOER SVERIGE/STATISTICAL YEARBOOK OF SWEDEN. Text in Swedish. 1914. a. SEK 475 (effective 1997).
Related titles: Microfiche ed.: (from PQC).
Indexed: GeoRef, RASB.
Published by: Statistiska Centralbyraan/Statistics Sweden, Karlavaegen 100, PO Box 24300, Stockholm, 10451, Sweden. TEL 46-8-783-48-01, FAX 46-8-783-48-99. Circ: 12,300.

310 658 ZAF ISSN 0379-8836
STATS - MONTHLY STATISTICAL AND MARKETING DIGEST. Text in English. 1965. m. ZAR 237.12; ZAR 260 foreign (effective 1997). **Document type:** *Report, Trade.* **Description:** Market statistical data and economic trend indicators.
Published by: George Warman Publications (Pty.) Ltd., Rondebosch, PO Box 705, Cape Town, 7701, South Africa. info@gwarmanpublications.co.za, http://www.gwarmanpublications.co.za. Ed. R E Pretorius.

STATZING PRIMARY. *see* EDUCATION

314 AUT ISSN 0039-1093
HA1188.S8
STEIRISCHE STATISTIKEN. Text in German. 1957. 12/yr. charts; stat. index. **Document type:** *Government.*
Published by: Amt der Steiermaerkischen Landesregierung, Landesstatistik, Hofgasse 13, Graz, St 8010, Austria. TEL 43-316-8772378, FAX 43-316-8775943, landesstatistik@stmk.gv.at, http://www.statistik.steiermark.at. Ed. Martin Mayer. Circ: 400.

310 389 ITA ISSN 1591-6693
PC1505
STILISTICA E METRICA ITALIANA. Text in Italian. 2001. a. **Document type:** *Journal, Academic/Scholarly.*
Indexed: L&LBA, MLA-IB.
Published by: S I S M E L Edizioni del Galluzzo, Casella Postale 90, Tavarnuzze, FI 50023, Italy. TEL 39-055-2374537, FAX 39-055-2373454, http://www.sismel.it.

519.5 USA ISSN 1532-6349
QA274.A1 CODEN: SMTOBE
➤ **STOCHASTIC MODELS.** Text in English. 1985. q. GBP 1,374 combined subscription in United Kingdom to institutions (print & online eds.); EUR 1,816, USD 2,279 combined subscription to institutions (print & online eds.) (effective 2012). adv. illus. index. back issues avail.; reprint service avail. from PSC. **Document type:** *Journal, Academic/Scholarly.* **Description:** Presents contributions on mathematical methodology ranging from structural, analytic, and algorithmic to experimental approaches.
Formerly (until 2001): Communications in Statistics. Stochastic Models (0882-0287)
Related titles: Microform ed.: (from RPI); Online - full text ed.: ISSN 1532-4214. GBP 1,237 in United Kingdom to institutions; EUR 1,634, USD 2,051 to institutions (effective 2012) (from IngentaConnect).
Indexed: A01, A03, A08, A22, B01, B06, B07, B09, Biostat, CA, CABA, CCMJ, CIS, CMCI, CPEI, E01, EngInd, IAOP, IBR, IBZ, MSN, MathR, P52, R13, S01, SCI, SCOPUS, ST&MA, T02, W07, W11, Z02.
—BLDSC (8465.280000), IE, Ingenta, INIST. **CCC.**
Published by: (Institute for Operations Research and the Management Sciences (I N F O R M S)), Taylor & Francis Inc. (Subsidiary of: Taylor & Francis Group), 325 Chestnut St, Ste 800, Philadelphia, PA 19106. TEL 215-625-8900, 800-354-1420, FAX 215-625-8914, orders@taylorandfrancis.com, http://www.taylorandfrancis.com. Ed. Peter Taylor. **Subscr. to:** Taylor & Francis Ltd., Journals Customer Service, Sheepen Pl, Colchester, Essex CO3 3LP, United Kingdom. TEL 44-20-70175544, FAX 44-20-70175198, subscriptions@tandf.co.uk.

519.23 SGP ISSN 0219-4937
QA274.A1
➤ **STOCHASTICS AND DYNAMICS.** Abbreviated title: S D. Text in English. 2001. q. SGD 878, USD 541, EUR 455 combined subscription to institutions (print & online eds.) (effective 2012). adv. back issues avail. **Document type:** *Journal, Academic/Scholarly.* **Description:** Covers theory, experiments, algorithms, numerical simulation and applications studying the dynamics of stochastic phenomena by means of random or stochastic ordinary, partial or functional differential equations or random mappings.
Related titles: Online - full text ed.: ISSN 1793-6799. SGD 798, USD 492, EUR 414 to institutions (effective 2012).
Indexed: A01, A02, A03, A08, A22, A28, APA, BrCerAb, C&ISA, CA, CA/WCA, CCMJ, CIA, CIS, CMCI, CerAb, CivEngAb, CorrAb, CurCont, E&CAJ, E01, E11, EEA, EMA, ESPM, EnvEAb, H15, M&TEA, M09, MBF, METADEX, MSN, MathR, S01, SCI, SCOPUS, SolStAb, T02, T04, W07, WAA, Z02.
—BLDSC (8465.330500), IE, Linda Hall. **CCC.**
Published by: World Scientific Publishing Co. Pte. Ltd., 5 Toh Tuck Link, Singapore, 596224, Singapore. TEL 65-6466-5775, FAX 65-6467-7667, http://www.worldscientific.com. Ed. Manfred Denker TEL 814-863-9107. **Dist. in the US by:** World Scientific Publishing Co., Inc., 27 Warren St, Ste 401-402, Hackensack, NJ 07601. TEL 201-487-9655, 800-227-7562, FAX 201-487-9656, 888-977-2665, wspc@wspc.com; **Dist. by:** World Scientific Publishing Ltd., 57 Shelton St, London WC2H 9HE, United Kingdom. TEL 44-207-8360888, FAX 44-207-8362020, sales@wspc.co.uk.

310 SWE ISSN 0280-4018
STOCKHOLM STUDIES IN STATISTICS. Text in English. 1981. irreg., latest vol.1, 1981. **Document type:** *Monographic series, Academic/Scholarly.*
Related titles: ◆ Series of: Acta Universitatis Stockholmiensis. ISSN 0346-6418.
Published by: Stockholms Universitet, Acta Universitatis Stockholmiensis, c/o Stockholms Universitetsbibliotek, Universitetsvaegen 10, Stockholm, 10691, Sweden. FAX 46-8-157776. **Dist. by:** Almqvist & Wiksell International, P O Box 7634, Stockholm 10394, Sweden. TEL 46-8-6136100, FAX 46-8-242543, info@akademibokhandeln.se, http://www.akademibokhandeln.se.

STRUCTURAL AND DEMOGRAPHIC BUSINESS STATISTICS (ONLINE). *see* BUSINESS AND ECONOMICS—Abstracting, Bibliographies, Statistics

310 SWE ISSN 1104-1560
STUDIA STATISTICA UPSALIENSIA. Text in English. 1993. irreg., latest vol.5, 2002. price varies. back issues avail. **Document type:** *Monographic series, Academic/Scholarly.*
Related titles: ◆ Series of: Acta Universitatis Upsaliensis. ISSN 0346-5462.
Published by: Uppsala Universitet, Acta Universitatis Upsaliensis/ University Publications from Uppsala, PO Box 256, Uppsala, 75105, Sweden. TEL 46-18-4716804, FAX 46-18-4716804, acta@ub.uu.se, http://www.ub.uu.se/upu/auu/index.html. Ed. Bengt Landgren. **Dist. by:** Almqvist & Wiksell International.

STUDIES IN PROBABILITY, OPTIMIZATION AND STATISTICS. *see* MATHEMATICS—Computer Applications

SUDAN. DEPARTMENT OF STATISTICS. FOREIGN TRADE STATISTICS. *see* BUSINESS AND ECONOMICS—Abstracting, Bibliographies, Statistics

310 SDN
SUDAN. DEPARTMENT OF STATISTICS. STATISTICAL YEARBOOK. Text in English. 1973. a.
Published by: Department of Statistics, P O Box 700, Khartoum, Sudan.

SUDAN YEARBOOK OF AGRICULTURAL STATISTICS. *see* AGRICULTURE—Abstracting, Bibliographies, Statistics

614 USA ISSN 1938-9892
RA407.3
SUMMARY HEALTH STATISTICS FOR THE U.S. POPULATION. Text in English. 1997. a. free (effective 2011). back issues avail. **Document type:** *Report, Government.*
Supersedes in part (in 1997): Current Estimates from the National Health Interview Survey, United States (0891-4591); Which was formerly (until 1979): Current Estimates from the Health Interview Survey, United States (0502-2673)
Related titles: Online - full text ed.: ISSN 1938-9906.
Published by: U.S. National Center for Health Statistics, Metro IV Bldg, 3311 Toledo Rd, Hyattsville, MD 20782. TEL 301-458-4000, cdcinfo@cdc.gov, http://www.cdc.gov/nchs/.

SUMMARY HEALTH STATISTICS FOR U.S. ADULTS. *see* PUBLIC HEALTH AND SAFETY—Abstracting, Bibliographies, Statistics

SUMMARY HEALTH STATISTICS FOR U.S. CHILDREN. *see* PUBLIC HEALTH AND SAFETY—Abstracting, Bibliographies, Statistics

SUMMARY OF INTERNATIONAL TRAVEL TO THE UNITED STATES. *see* TRAVEL AND TOURISM—Abstracting, Bibliographies, Statistics

318.83 SUR
SURINAM. ALGEMEEN BUREAU VOOR DE STATISTIEK. NATIONALE REKENINGEN. Text in Dutch. irreg. (approx. a.).
Related titles: Series of: Suriname in Cijfers.
Published by: Algemeen Bureau voor de Statistiek/General Bureau of Statistics, PO Box 244, Paramaribo, Suriname. TEL 597-474861, FAX 597-425004.

317 CAN ISSN 0714-0045
SURVEY METHODOLOGY. Text in English. 1975. s-a. CAD 58 domestic; CAD 48 in United States; CAD 78 foreign; CAD 30 per issue (effective 2005). **Description:** Presents articles dealing with various aspects of statistical development relevant to a statistical agency and evaluation of specific methodologies as applied to actual data collection or the data themselves.
Indexed: CIS, CurCont, IBSS, ORMS, P30, QC&AS, SCI, SCOPUS, SSCI, ST&MA, W07.
—BLDSC (8550.560000), IE, Infotrieve, Ingenta. **CCC.**
Published by: Statistics Canada, Operations and Integration Division (Subsidiary of: Statistics Canada/Statistique Canada), Circulation Management, 120 Parkdale Ave, Ottawa, ON K1A 0T6, Canada. TEL 613-951-7277, 800-267-6677, FAX 613-951-1584.

SURVEY OF EMPLOYMENT, PAYROLLS AND HOURS. *see* BUSINESS AND ECONOMICS—Abstracting, Bibliographies, Statistics

SURVEY OF HOUSEHOLD ECONOMIC ACTIVITIES (YEAR). *see* BUSINESS AND ECONOMICS—Economic Situation And Conditions

SURVEY OF LABOUR AND INCOME DYNAMICS ELECTRONIC DATA DICTIONARY. *see* BUSINESS AND ECONOMICS—Labor And Industrial Relations

SURVEY OF THE CONSTRUCTION INDUSTRY (YEAR). *see* BUILDING AND CONSTRUCTION—Abstracting, Bibliographies, Statistics

SURVEY ON GRADUATING STUDENTS ABROAD. *see* EDUCATION—Abstracting, Bibliographies, Statistics

▼ **SURVEYS & QUESTIONNAIRES: COLLEGE LITERACY.** *see* EDUCATION—Abstracting, Bibliographies, Statistics

316 SWZ ISSN 0586-1357
SWAZILAND. CENTRAL STATISTICAL OFFICE. ANNUAL STATISTICAL BULLETIN. Text in English. 1966. a. SZL 2. illus. **Document type:** *Bulletin, Government.*
Related titles: Microfiche ed.: (from PQC).
Published by: Central Statistical Office, PO Box 456, Mbabane, Swaziland. TEL 268-43765. Circ: 800.

316 SWZ
SWAZILAND. CENTRAL STATISTICAL OFFICE. ANNUAL SURVEY OF SWAZI NATION LAND. Text in English. 1972. a. free. stat. **Document type:** *Government.*
Published by: Central Statistical Office, PO Box 456, Mbabane, Swaziland. TEL 268-43765. Circ: 500.

SWAZILAND. CENTRAL STATISTICAL OFFICE. CENSUS OF INDIVIDUAL TENURE FARMS. *see* AGRICULTURE—Abstracting, Bibliographies, Statistics

SWAZILAND. CENTRAL STATISTICAL OFFICE. CENSUS OF INDUSTRIES. *see* BUSINESS AND ECONOMICS—Abstracting, Bibliographies, Statistics

SWAZILAND. CENTRAL STATISTICAL OFFICE. EDUCATION STATISTICS. *see* EDUCATION—Abstracting, Bibliographies, Statistics

SWAZILAND. CENTRAL STATISTICAL OFFICE. EMPLOYMENT AND WAGES. *see* BUSINESS AND ECONOMICS—Abstracting, Bibliographies, Statistics

316 SWZ
SWAZILAND. CENTRAL STATISTICAL OFFICE. STATISTICAL NEWS. Text in English. 1967. q. free. **Document type:** *Government.*
Former titles (until 1974): Swaziland. Central Statistical Office. Quarterly Digest of Statistics; Swaziland. Central Statistical Office. Statistical News and Economic Indicators (0302-3907); Swaziland Statistical News (0586-1403)
Media: Duplicated (not offset).
Published by: Central Statistical Office, PO Box 456, Mbabane, Swaziland. TEL 268-268-43765. Circ: 600.

SWAZILAND. CENTRAL STATISTICAL OFFICE. TIMBER STATISTICS. *see* FORESTS AND FORESTRY—Abstracting, Bibliographies, Statistics

SWEDEN. LUFTFARTSVERKET. CHARTERSTATISTIK. *see* TRANSPORTATION—Abstracting, Bibliographies, Statistics

SWEDEN. LUFTFARTSVERKET. FLYGPLATSSTATISTIK. *see* TRANSPORTATION—Abstracting, Bibliographies, Statistics

314.85 SWE ISSN 0039-7253
HA1523
SWEDEN. STATISTISKA CENTRALBYRAAN. ALLMAEN MAANADSSTATISTIK/MONTHLY DIGEST OF SWEDISH STATISTICS. Abstracts and contents page in English. 1963. m. SEK 775; SEK 130 newsstand/cover (effective 1997). Supplement avail. **Document type:** *Government.*
Indexed: RASB.
Published by: Statistiska Centralbyraan/Statistics Sweden, Karlawaegen 100, PO Box 24300, Stockholm, 10451, Sweden. TEL 46-8-483-48-01, FAX 46-8-783-48-99. Circ: 4,000.

SWEDEN. STATISTISKA CENTRALBYRAAN. JORDBRUKSSTATISTISK AARSBOK. *see* AGRICULTURE—Abstracting, Bibliographies, Statistics

339.47021 SWE ISSN 0347-7193
HD7731
SWEDEN. STATISTISKA CENTRALBYRAAN. LEVNADSFOERHAALLANDEN/SWEDEN. STATISTISKA CENTRALBYRAAN. LIVING CONDITIONS. Text in English, Swedish. 1975. irreg. illus.
Related titles: Online - full text ed.: ISSN 1654-1707. 2007.
Published by: Statistiska Centralbyraan/Statistics Sweden, Karlawaegen 100, PO Box 24300, Stockholm, 10451, Sweden. TEL 46-8-50694000, FAX 46-8-6615261, sbc@scb.se.

314 SWE ISSN 0082-0229
SWEDEN. STATISTISKA CENTRALBYRAAN. MEDDELANDEN I SAMORDNINGSFRAAGOR/REPORTS ON STATISTICAL CO-ORDINATION. Variant title: Mis. Text in Swedish. 1966. irreg. (1-4/yr.). price varies. **Document type:** *Monographic series.*
Published by: Statistiska Centralbyraan, Distribution, Stockholm, 11581, Sweden. TEL 46-8-783-40-00, FAX 46-8-783-45-99.

SWEDEN. STATISTISKA CENTRALBYRAAN. STATISTISKA MEDDELANDEN. SERIE BO, BOSTAEDER OCH BYGGNADER. *see* BUILDING AND CONSTRUCTION—Abstracting, Bibliographies, Statistics

SWEDEN. STATISTISKA CENTRALBYRAAN. STATISTISKA MEDDELANDEN. SERIE JO, JORDBRUK, SKOGSBRUK OCH FISKE. *see* AGRICULTURE—Abstracting, Bibliographies, Statistics

SWEDEN. STATISTISKA CENTRALBYRAAN. STATISTISKA MEDDELANDEN. SERIE KU, KULTUR. *see* ANTHROPOLOGY—Abstracting, Bibliographies, Statistics

SWEDEN. STATISTISKA CENTRALBYRAAN. STATISTISKA MEDDELANDEN. SERIE NA, NATURRESURSER OCH MILJOE. *see* ENVIRONMENTAL STUDIES—Abstracting, Bibliographies, Statistics

SWEDEN. STATISTISKA CENTRALBYRAAN. STATISTISKA MEDDELANDEN. SERIE UF, UTBILDNING OCH FORSKNING. *see* EDUCATION—Abstracting, Bibliographies, Statistics

314 SWE ISSN 0082-0350
SWEDEN. STATISTISKA CENTRALBYRAAN. URVAL SKRIFTSERIES - SELECTION SERIES. Text in Swedish; Summaries in English. 1969. irreg. price varies.
Published by: Statistiska Centralbyraan/Statistics Sweden, Publishing Unit, Orebro, 70189, Sweden. Circ: 750.

314 SWE ISSN 0039-727X
SWEDEN. STATISTISKA CENTRALBYRAAN. UTRIKESHANDEL. KVARTALSSTATISTIK. Abstracts and contents page in English. 1961. q. SEK 950.
Indexed: RASB.
Published by: Statistiska Centralbyraan, Distribution, Orebro, 70189, Sweden. Circ: 1,400.

SWITZERLAND. BUNDESAMT FUER STATISTIK. BILANZ DER WOHNBEVOLKERUNG IN DEN GEMEINDEN DER SCHWEIZ - BILAN DEMOGRAPHIQUE DES COMMUNES SUISSES. *see* POPULATION STUDIES—Abstracting, Bibliographies, Statistics

SWITZERLAND. DIRECTORATE GENERAL OF CUSTOMS. ANNUAL REPORT. *see* BUSINESS AND ECONOMICS—Abstracting, Bibliographies, Statistics

SWITZERLAND. DIRECTORATE GENERAL OF CUSTOMS. QUARTERLY STATISTICS. *see* BUSINESS AND ECONOMICS—Abstracting, Bibliographies, Statistics

SWITZERLAND. DIRECTORATE GENERAL OF CUSTOMS. SCHWEIZERISCHE AUSSENHANDELSSTATISTIK. JAHRESSTATISTIK. *see* BUSINESS AND ECONOMICS—Abstracting, Bibliographies, Statistics

510 310 USA ISSN 1938-1743
SYNTHESIS LECTURES ON MATHEMATICS AND STATISTICS. Text in English. 2008. irreg. **Document type:** *Monographic series, Trade.*
Related titles: Online - full text ed.: ISSN 1938-1751.
Published by: Morgan & Claypool Publishers, 40 Oak View Dr, San Rafael, CA 94903. TEL 888-822-9942, FAX 802-864-7626, info@morganclaypool.com. Ed. Steven G Krantz.

315 SYR ISSN 0081-4725
SYRIA. CENTRAL BUREAU OF STATISTICS. STATISTICAL ABSTRACT. Text in Arabic, English. 1948. a., latest 2000. USD 75 in the Middle East; USD 100 elsewhere (effective 2002). **Document type:** *Government.* **Description:** Various current statistics of different sectors.
Published by: Central Bureau of Statistics, Damascus, Syria. TEL 963-11-3335830, FAX 963-11-3322292, TELEX STC 411093 SY.

SYRIA. CENTRAL BUREAU OF STATISTICS. SUMMARY OF FOREIGN TRADE. *see* BUSINESS AND ECONOMICS—Abstracting, Bibliographies, Statistics

T S B STATISTICAL SUMMARY, MARINE OCCURRENCES. *see* TRANSPORTATION—Abstracting, Bibliographies, Statistics

T S B STATISTICAL SUMMARY OF AVIATION OCCURRENCES. *see* PUBLIC HEALTH AND SAFETY—Abstracting, Bibliographies, Statistics

T S B STATISTICAL SUMMARY, RAILWAY OCCURRENCES. (Transportation Safety Board) *see* PUBLIC HEALTH AND SAFETY—Abstracting, Bibliographies, Statistics

TABLEBASE. *see* BUSINESS AND ECONOMICS—Abstracting, Bibliographies, Statistics

315 TWN ISSN 0577-8670
TAIWAN, REPUBLIC OF CHINA. EXECUTIVE YUAN. DIRECTORATE-GENERAL OF BUDGET, ACCOUNTING & STATISTICS. MONTHLY BULLETIN OF STATISTICS. Text in English. 1975. m. TWD 70 (effective 2000). stat.
Published by: Executive Yuan, Directorate-General of Budget, Accounting & Statistics, 2 Kwangchow St, Taipei, Taiwan. TEL 886-2-2381-4910, http://www.stat.gov.tw/main.htm/. Circ: 1,452. **Subscr. to:** Chen Chung Book Co., 3F, 20 Heng-Yang Rd, Taipei, Taiwan. TEL 886-2-2382-1394, FAX 886-2-2382-2805, http://www.ccbc.com.tw.

310 011 TWN ISSN 0257-5736
TAIWAN, REPUBLIC OF CHINA. EXECUTIVE YUAN. DIRECTORATE-GENERAL OF BUDGET, ACCOUNTING & STATISTICS. SOCIAL INDICATORS IN TAIWAN AREA (YEAR). Text in Chinese, English; Summaries in Chinese. 1979. a. TWD 350.
Published by: Executive Yuan, Directorate-General of Budget, Accounting & Statistics, 2 Kwangchow St, Taipei, Taiwan. TEL 886-2-2381-3980, http://www.stat.gov.tw/main.htm/. Circ: 800. **Subscr. to:** Chen Chung Book Co., 3F, 20 Heng-Yang Rd, Taipei, Taiwan. TEL 886-2-2382-1394, FAX 886-2-2382-2805, http://www.ccbc.com.tw.

TAIWAN, REPUBLIC OF CHINA. MINISTRY OF FINANCE. DEPARTMENT OF STATISTICS. MONTHLY STATISTICS OF EXPORTS AND IMPORTS/CHIN CH'U K'OU MAO I T'UNG CHI YUEH PAO. *see* BUSINESS AND ECONOMICS—Abstracting, Bibliographies, Statistics

TAIWAN, REPUBLIC OF CHINA. TOURISM BUREAU. REPORT ON TOURISM STATISTICS (YEAR). *see* TRAVEL AND TOURISM—Abstracting, Bibliographies, Statistics

TAL OG FAKTA PA UDLAENDINGEOMRAADET. *see* POPULATION STUDIES—Abstracting, Bibliographies, Statistics

001.422 378.0021 DNK ISSN 1601-7196
TAL OM FORSKNING; statistik. Text in Danish. 2001. a., latest 2003. stat. back issues avail. **Description:** Statistics on research in Denmark.
Related titles: Online - full text ed.: ISSN 1604-4371. 200?; ◆ English ed.: Figures for Research. ISSN 1901-1830.
Published by: Forsknings- og Innovationsstyrelsen/Danish Agency for Science, Technology and Innovation, Bredgade 40, Copenhagen K, 1260, Denmark. TEL 45-35-446200, FAX 45-35-446201, fi@fi.dk. Ed. Birgitte Ehrhardt.

TAL OM LANDBRUGET. *see* AGRICULTURE—Abstracting, Bibliographies, Statistics

310 IND ISSN 0082-1578
TAMIL NADU. DEPARTMENT OF STATISTICS. ANNUAL STATISTICAL ABSTRACT. Text in English. 1954. a. **Document type:** *Abstract/Index.*
Published by: Department of Economics and Statistics, Central Administrative Bldg, Block II, No 259, Anna Salai, Teynampet, Chennai, Tamilnadu 600 006, India. TEL 91-44-24321189, FAX 91-44-24322871. **Subscr. to:** Government Publication Dpot.

TAMIL NADU. DEPARTMENT OF STATISTICS. SEASON AND CROP REPORT. *see* AGRICULTURE—Abstracting, Bibliographies, Statistics

TAMOZHENNAYA STATISTIKA VNESHNEI TORGOVLI ROSSIISKOI FEDERATSII. *see* BUSINESS AND ECONOMICS—Abstracting, Bibliographies, Statistics

TANZANIA. MINISTRY OF AGRICULTURE AND LIVESTOCK DEVELOPMENT. BULLETIN OF CROP STATISTICS. *see* AGRICULTURE—Abstracting, Bibliographies, Statistics

TANZANIA. NATIONAL BUREAU OF STATISTICS. MIGRATION STATISTICS. *see* POPULATION STUDIES—Abstracting, Bibliographies, Statistics

316.78 TZA ISSN 0039-9469
TANZANIA. NATIONAL BUREAU OF STATISTICS. QUARTERLY STATISTICAL BULLETIN. Text in English. q. mkt. **Document type:** *Government.*
Published by: National Bureau of Statistics, PO Box 796, Dar Es Salaam, Tanzania. **Orders to:** Government Publications Agency, PO Box 1801, Dar Es Salaam, Tanzania.

TANZANIA. NATIONAL BUREAU OF STATISTICS. SURVEY OF EMPLOYMENT. *see* BUSINESS AND ECONOMICS—Abstracting, Bibliographies, Statistics

TANZANIA. NATIONAL BUREAU OF STATISTICS. SURVEY OF INDUSTRIAL PRODUCTION. *see* BUSINESS AND ECONOMICS—Abstracting, Bibliographies, Statistics

314 CHE
TASCHENSTATISTIK DER SCHWEIZ (YEAR)/MEMENTO STATISTIQUE DE LA SUISSE (YEAR). Text in English, French, German, Italian, Romansh. 1985. a. **Document type:** *Government.*
Published by: Bundesamt fuer Statistik, Espace de l'Europe 10, Neuchatel, 2010, Switzerland. TEL 41-32-7136011, FAX 41-32-7136012, information@bfs.admin.ch, http://www.admin.ch/bfs.

TASMAN DISTRICT CRIME STATISTICS. *see* CRIMINOLOGY AND LAW ENFORCEMENT—Abstracting, Bibliographies, Statistics

TEACHING STATISTICS; an international journal for teachers. *see* EDUCATION—Abstracting, Bibliographies, Statistics

310 USA ISSN 1933-4214
QA276.18
TECHNOLOGY INNOVATIONS IN STATISTICS EDUCATION. Notes in English. 2007. s-a. **Document type:** *Journal, Academic/Scholarly.*

S

Related titles: Online - full text ed.: free (effective 2011).
Published by: eScholarship (Subsidiary of: California Digital Library)

TEK I STATISTIKA. *see* ENERGY

310 330.9 BGR ISSN 1311-2449
HA1621
TEKUSHTA STOPANSKA KONIUNKTURA. Text in Bulgarian. m. USD 84 foreign (effective 2002). **Description:** Presents statistical information about the current economic situation in Bulgaria.
Published by: Natsionalen Statisticheski Institut/National Statistical Institute, ul P Volov, # 2, Sofia, 1038, Bulgaria. FAX 359-2-9803319, publikacii@nsi.bg, http://www.nsi.bg. **Dist. by:** Sofia Books, ul Silivria 16, Sofia 1404, Bulgaria. TEL 359-2-9586257, info@sofiabooks-bg.com, http://www.sofiabooks-bg.com.

TELEVISION IN ASIA PACIFIC TO (YEAR). *see* COMMUNICATIONS—Television And Cable

▼ **TEMAS EM METODOS QUANTITATIVOS - QUALIDADE.** *see* MATHEMATICS

TENNESSEE CITIES & COUNTIES GRAPHIC PERFORMANCE ANALYSIS. *see* PUBLIC ADMINISTRATION—Abstracting, Bibliographies, Statistics

TENNESSEE CROP WEATHER. *see* AGRICULTURE—Abstracting, Bibliographies, Statistics

TENNESSEE PUBLIC LIBRARY DIRECTORY AND STATISTICS (YEAR). *see* LIBRARY AND INFORMATION SCIENCES—Abstracting, Bibliographies, Statistics

317 USA ISSN 0082-2760
HA641
TENNESSEE STATISTICAL ABSTRACT. Text in English. 1969. biennial. USD 40 (effective 1997).
Related titles: Microfiche ed.: (from BHP, CIS).
Indexed: SRI.
Published by: University of Tennessee at Knoxville, Center for Business and Economic Research, College of Business Administration, Glocker Building, Ste 100, Knoxville, TN 37996-4170. TEL 423-974-5441, FAX 423-974-3100, TELEX 557461 UTSUPBLST. Ed. Betty B Vickers. Circ: 1,400.

TERRITORIO. REGIAO ALENTEJO. *see* POPULATION STUDIES—Abstracting, Bibliographies, Statistics

TERRITORIO. REGIAO ALGARVE. *see* POPULATION STUDIES—Abstracting, Bibliographies, Statistics

TERRITORIO. REGIAO CENTRO. *see* POPULATION STUDIES—Abstracting, Bibliographies, Statistics

TERRITORIO. REGIAO LISBOA. *see* POPULATION STUDIES—Abstracting, Bibliographies, Statistics

TERRITORIO. REGIAO NORTE. *see* POPULATION STUDIES—Abstracting, Bibliographies, Statistics

314 DEU ISSN 1133-0686
HA1
➤ **TEST.** Text in English. 1950. 3/yr. EUR 312, USD 380 combined subscription to institutions (print & online eds.) (effective 2012). adv. bk.rev. abstr.; bibl.; charts; stat.; illus. index. reprint service avail. from PSC. **Document type:** *Journal, Academic/Scholarly.* **Description:** An international journal of statistics and probability. It focuses on papers that offer original theoretical contributions and that have demonstrated or potential value for applications.
Formerly (until 1992): Trabajos de Estadistica (0213-8190); Which superseded in part (in 1986): Trabajos de Estadistica e Investigacion Operativa (0041-0241); Which was formerly (until 1963): Trabajos de Estadistica (0210-5675)
Related titles: Online - full text ed.: ISSN 1863-8260 (from IngentaConnect).
Indexed: A22, A26, CCMJ, CIS, CMCI, E01, E08, EconLit, IAOP, IECT, MSN, MathR, P30, RASB, S09, SCI, SCOPUS, ST&MA, W07, Z02. —BLDSC (8796.327620), IE, INIST. **CCC.**
Published by: (Sociedad de Estadistica e Investigacion Operativa ESP), Springer (Subsidiary of: Springer Science+Business Media), Tiergartenstr 17, Heidelberg, 69121, Germany. TEL 49-6221-4870, FAX 49-6221-345229, subscriptions@springer.com. Eds. Domingo Morales, Ricardo Cao. Circ: 600.

➤ **TEXAS AGRICULTURAL STATISTICS.** *see* AGRICULTURE—Abstracting, Bibliographies, Statistics

310 976.4 USA ISSN 0363-4248
AY311.D3
(YEARS) TEXAS ALMANAC AND STATE INDUSTRIAL GUIDE. Cover title: Texas Almanac. Text in English. 1857. biennial. USD 19.95 hardbound; USD 13.95 paperbound; USD 9.95 teacher's guide (effective 2002). adv. charts; illus.; stat.; maps. index. 672 p./no.; **Document type:** *Directory, Trade.* **Description:** Covers business, environment, history, state and county demographics, politics and government, education, agriculture, science and health, and more.
Former titles (until 1967): Texas Almanac (0363-423X); (1904-1955): Texas Almanac and State Industrial Guide (0363-4221)
Related titles: Microform ed.
Indexed: SRI.
—**CCC.**
Published by: Dallas Morning News, PO Box 655237, Dallas, TX 75265. TEL 214-977-8261, FAX 214-977-8120. Ed., R&P Mary G Ramos. Adv. contact Pam Lane TEL 214-977-8190. Circ: 50,000.

TEXAS CITIES & COUNTIES GRAPHIC PERFORMANCE ANALYSIS. *see* PUBLIC ADMINISTRATION—Abstracting, Bibliographies, Statistics

TEXAS CROP WEATHER. *see* AGRICULTURE—Abstracting, Bibliographies, Statistics

TEXAS PETROFACTS. *see* PETROLEUM AND GAS—Abstracting, Bibliographies, Statistics

TEXAS PUBLIC LIBRARY STATISTICS. *see* LIBRARY AND INFORMATION SCIENCES—Abstracting, Bibliographies, Statistics

THAILAND. NATIONAL OFFICE OF STATISTICS. REPORT OF BUSINESS TRADE AND SURVEY (YEAR). *see* BUSINESS AND ECONOMICS—Abstracting, Bibliographies, Statistics

THAILAND. NATIONAL STATISTICAL OFFICE. (YEAR) AGRICULTURAL CENSUS. *see* AGRICULTURE—Abstracting, Bibliographies, Statistics

THAILAND. NATIONAL STATISTICAL OFFICE. (YEAR) MARINE FISHERY CENSUS. *see* FISH AND FISHERIES—Abstracting, Bibliographies, Statistics

016 315 THA ISSN 0857-9164
THAILAND. NATIONAL STATISTICAL OFFICE. ANNOTATED STATISTICAL BIBLIOGRAPHY. Text in English. 1961. biennial. price varies. **Document type:** *Bibliography.* **Description:** Lists statistical publications published officially by Thai government agencies, departments and state enterprises with annotation in major fields of study.
Published by: (Thailand. Statistical Data Bank and Information Dissemination Division), National Statistical Office, Larn Luang Rd, Bangkok, 10100, Thailand. TEL 66-2-2810333, FAX 66-2-2813848, onsoadm@nso.go.th, http://www.nso.go.th/. Circ: 700.

310 THA ISSN 0858-2696
THAILAND. NATIONAL STATISTICAL OFFICE. ANNUAL REPORT. Text in Thai. 1963. a. free. **Document type:** *Government.* **Description:** Contains results of work following the program of the National Statistical Office administration in general for the reported year.
Published by: (Thailand. Statistical Data Bank and Information Dissemination Division), National Statistical Office, Larn Luang Rd, Bangkok, 10100, Thailand. TEL 66-2-282-1535, FAX 66-2-281-3814. Circ: 1,200.

315.93 THA ISSN 0857-9482
HA4600.55
THAILAND. NATIONAL STATISTICAL OFFICE. QUARTERLY BULLETIN OF STATISTICS. Text in English, Thai. 1964. q. price varies. charts; stat. **Document type:** *Bulletin, Government.* **Description:** Contains statistical tables on climate, population and vital statistics, social statistics, production, transportation and communication, foreign trade, finance and banking, and prices.
Published by: (Thailand. Statistical Data Bank and Information Dissemination Division), National Statistical Office, Larn Luang Rd, Bangkok, 10100, Thailand. TEL 66-2-282-1535, FAX 66-2-281-3814. Circ: 700.

THAILAND. NATIONAL STATISTICAL OFFICE. REPORT OF HOUSEHOLD SOCIO - ECONOMIC SURVEY (YEAR). *see* BUSINESS AND ECONOMICS—Abstracting, Bibliographies, Statistics

THAILAND. NATIONAL STATISTICAL OFFICE. REPORT OF INDUSTRIAL SURVEY (YEAR). *see* BUSINESS AND ECONOMICS—Abstracting, Bibliographies, Statistics

THAILAND. NATIONAL STATISTICAL OFFICE. REPORT OF THE EDUCATION STATISTICS: ACADEMIC YEAR (YEAR). *see* EDUCATION—Abstracting, Bibliographies, Statistics

THAILAND. NATIONAL STATISTICAL OFFICE. REPORT OF THE HEALTH AND WELFARE SURVEY (YEAR)/RAINGAN KANSAMRUAT KIEOKAP ANAMAI LAE SAWATDIKAN. *see* PUBLIC HEALTH AND SAFETY—Abstracting, Bibliographies, Statistics

THAILAND. NATIONAL STATISTICAL OFFICE. REPORT OF THE LABOR FORCE SURVEY, WHOLE KINGDOM (YEAR). *see* BUSINESS AND ECONOMICS—Abstracting, Bibliographies, Statistics

THAILAND. NATIONAL STATISTICAL OFFICE. REPORT OF THE MIGRATION SURVEY. *see* POPULATION STUDIES—Abstracting, Bibliographies, Statistics

THAILAND. NATIONAL STATISTICAL OFFICE. REPORT ON HOUSING SURVEY (YEAR). *see* HOUSING AND URBAN PLANNING—Abstracting, Bibliographies, Statistics

THEORY AND DECISION LIBRARY. SERIES B: MATHEMATICAL AND STATISTICAL METHODS. *see* MATHEMATICS

314 FIN ISSN 1795-9799
HC240.F5
TIETO&TRENDIT. Text in English, Finnish, Swedish. 2005. 8/yr. EUR 181; EUR 25 per issue (effective 2008). back issues avail. **Document type:** *Magazine, Government.*
Formed by the merger of (1984-2005): Tietoaika (0781-0644); (2001-2005): Economic Trends (1457-6287); Which was formerly (until 2000): Eurooppa-raportti (1455-1438); (1995-1997): E U-Raportti (1238-1993)
Related titles: Online - full text ed.
Published by: Tilastokeskus/Statistics Finland, Tyopajakatu 13, Statistics Finland, Helsinki, 00022, Finland. TEL 358-9-17341, FAX 358-9-17342279. Ed. Maija Metsa-Pauri.

310 658.3 USA
TIMING ANALYSIS PROJECTION. Short title: T A P. Text in English. 1971. s-m. to clients only. index. back issues avail. **Document type:** *Journal, Trade.*
Published by: Covato Research Corporation, Manor Oak II, Ste 333, 1910 Cochran Rd, Pittsburgh, PA 15220. TEL 412-341-3700, FAX 412-341-8922. Ed. Phillip R Covato. Circ: 100.

316.6 TGO
TOGO. DIRECTION DE LA STATISTIQUE. BULLETIN MENSUEL DE STATISTIQUE. Text in French. m. XOF 5,600.
Published by: Direction de la Statistique, BP 118, Lome, Togo.

TOGO. MINISTRY OF ECONOMY AND FINANCE. BULLETIN DE STATISTIQUES. *see* BUSINESS AND ECONOMICS—Abstracting, Bibliographies, Statistics

310 JPN
TOKEI DE MIRU NIPPON (YEAR)/FACTS AND FINDINGS ABOUT JAPAN BY STATISTICAL DATA (YEAR). Text in Japanese. irreg., latest 1999. JPY 1,995 (effective 1999). **Document type:** *Government.*
Published by: Japan. Ministry of Internal Affairs and Communications. Statistics Bureau/Somucho. Tokeikyoko, 19-1 Wakamatsu-cho, Shinjyuku-ku, Tokyo, 162-8668, Japan. TEL 81-3-5273-2020, http://www.stat.go.jp.

310 JPN
TOKEI JOHO INDEKKUSU (YEAR)/INDEX TO STATISTICAL DATA SOURCES (YEAR). Text in Japanese. irreg., latest 1998. JPY 9,240 (effective 2000). **Document type:** *Government.*
Related titles: CD-ROM ed.: JPY 58,800 (effective 2000); Magnetic Tape ed.: JPY 58,800 per issue for cartidge magnetic tape; JPY 60,375 per issue for open-reel magnetic tape (effective 2000).
Published by: Japan. Ministry of Internal Affairs and Communications. Statistics Bureau/Somucho. Tokeikyoko, 19-1 Wakamatsu-cho, Shinjyuku-ku, Tokyo, 162-8668, Japan. TEL 81-3-5273-2020, http://www.stat.go.jp.

310 510 JPN
TOKEI SURI KENKYUJO KENKYUU KYOUIKU KATSUDOU HOUKOKU. Text in Japanese. 1999. s-a. **Document type:** *Academic/Scholarly.*
Published by: Institute of Statistical Mathematics/Tokei Suri Kenkyujo, 4-6-7 Minami-Azabu, Minato-ku, Tokyo, 106-8569, Japan. http://www.ism.ac.jp.

310 510 JPN
TOKEI SURI KENKYUJO KENKYUU RIPOOTO/INSTITUTE OF STATISTICAL MATHEMATICS. RESEARCH REPORT. GENERAL SERIES. Text in Japanese. irreg., latest no.93, 2004. **Document type:** *Academic/Scholarly.*
Published by: Institute of Statistical Mathematics/Tokei Suri Kenkyujo, 4-6-7 Minami-Azabu, Minato-ku, Tokyo, 106-8569, Japan.

310 510 JPN
TOKEI SURI KENKYUJO NYUUSU/I S M NEWS. Text in Japanese. q. back issues avail. **Document type:** *Academic/Scholarly.*
Related titles: Online - full content ed.
Published by: Institute of Statistical Mathematics/Tokei Suri Kenkyujo, 4-6-7 Minami-Azabu, Minato-ku, Tokyo, 106-8569, Japan.

TOKEI SURI KENKYUZYO KENKYU RIPOTO/INSTITUTE OF STATISTICAL MATHEMATICS. RESEARCH REPORT. GENERAL SERIES. *see* MATHEMATICS

310 CHN ISSN 0496-4225
TONGJI YANJIU/STATISTICS RESEARCH. Text in Chinese. bi-m.
Published by: Zhongguo Tongji Chubanshe/China Statistics Press, 6, Xi San Huan Nan Lu Jia, Beijing, 100073, China. TEL 217162. Ed. Mo Rida.

310 330 CHN ISSN 1674-537X
TONGJI YU GUANLI/STATISTICS AND MANAGEMENT. Text in Chinese. 1986. bi-m. **Document type:** *Journal, Academic/Scholarly.*
Former titles (until 2008): Hebei Tongji Xinxi (1009-8801); (until 1992): Hebei Tongji
Related titles: Online - full text ed.
Published by: Tongji yu Guanli Zazhishe, 312, Hezou Lu, Shijiazhuang, 050051, China. TEL 86-311-87045971ext 6402, FAX 86-311-87046614.

519.5 330 CHN ISSN 1009-7651
TONGJI YU JINGSUAN/STATISTICS AND ACCURATE CALCULATION. Text in Chinese. 1980. bi-m. USD 32.50 (effective 2009). 72 p./no.; **Document type:** *Journal, Academic/Scholarly.* **Description:** Covers statistical mathematics and its application in economics.
Former titles (until 2000): Tongjixue; (until 1999): Tongjixue, Jingji Shuxue Fangfa (1001-3369)
Published by: Zhongguo Renmin Daxue Shubao Ziliao Zhongxin/Renmin University of China, Information Center for Social Sciences, Dongcheng-qu, 3, Zhangzizhong Lu, Beijing, 100007, China. TEL 86-10-64039458, FAX 86-10-64015080, center@zlzx.org, http://www.zlzx.org/. **Dist. in US by:** China Publications Service, PO Box 49614, Chicago, IL 60649. TEL 312-288-3291, FAX 312-288-8570; **Dist. by:** China International Book Trading Corp, 35 Chegongzhuang Xilu, Haidian District, PO Box 399, Beijing 100044, China. TEL 86-10-68412045, FAX 86-10-68412023, cibtc@mail.cibtc.com.cn, http://www.cibtc.com.cn/.

TORGOVLYA V ROSSII (YEAR). *see* BUSINESS AND ECONOMICS—Abstracting, Bibliographies, Statistics

315.2 JPN ISSN 1880-1358
HA4621
TOUKEI DE MIRU TODOUFUKEN NO SUGATA/STATISTICAL OBSERVATIONS OF PREFECTURES. Text in Japanese. 1981. a. **Document type:** *Government.*
Formerly (until 2004): Tokei de Miru Ken No Sugata (Year)/Statistical Observations of Prefectures (0289-131X)
Related titles: Diskette ed.: JPY 2,000 (effective 2000).
Published by: Japan. Ministry of Internal Affairs and Communications. Statistics Bureau/Somucho. Tokeikyoko, 19-1 Wakamatsu-cho, Shinjyuku-ku, Tokyo, 162-8668, Japan. TEL 81-3-5273-2020. **Subscr. to:** Japan Statistical Association, Meito Shinjuku Bldg, 6th Fl, 2-4-6 Shinjuku-ku, Tokyo 169-0073, Japan. TEL 81-3-53323151, http://www.jstat.or.jp/.

TOUKEI KENKYUU IHOU/RESEARCH MEMOIR OF OFFICIAL STATISTICS. *see* PUBLIC ADMINISTRATION—Abstracting, Bibliographies, Statistics

TOURISM RESEARCH AUSTRALIA. OCCASIONAL PAPER. *see* TRAVEL AND TOURISM—Abstracting, Bibliographies, Statistics

TOURISM SECTOR MONITOR. *see* TRAVEL AND TOURISM—Abstracting, Bibliographies, Statistics

TOURISM STATISTICAL DIGEST/CANADA. STATISTIQUE CANADA. VOYAGES, TOURISME ET LOISIRS DE PLEIN AIR-RESUME STATISTIQUE. *see* TRAVEL AND TOURISM

TOURISM TRENDS IN DEVON. *see* TRAVEL AND TOURISM—Abstracting, Bibliographies, Statistics

310 JPN
TOYO KEIZAI. STATISTICS MONTHLY. Text in Japanese. 1939. m.
Published by: Toyo Keizai Inc., 1-2-1 Nihonbashihongoku-cho, Chuo-ku, Tokyo, 1030021, Japan. TEL 81-3-3246-5575, FAX 81-3-3242-4068. Ed. Jun Ishibashi. Circ: 15,000.

TRADE TOPICS; quarterly statistics. *see* BUSINESS AND ECONOMICS—International Commerce

TRANSFORMACNI PROCESY V ENERGETICE V C R C ROCE (YEAR). (Ceska Republika) *see* ENERGY—Abstracting, Bibliographies, Statistics

TRANSFORMATION PROCESSES IN THE ENERGY SECTOR OF THE CZECH REPUBLIC (YEAR). *see* ENERGY—Abstracting, Bibliographies, Statistics

TRANSPORT AND COMMUNICATIONS (SINGAPORE). *see* TRANSPORTATION—Abstracting, Bibliographies, Statistics

310 388 BGR
TRANSPORT I SUOBSHCHENIA. Text in Bulgarian. a. BGL 12.81 (effective 2002). 110 p./no.

Published by: Natsionalen Statisticheski Institut/National Statistical Institute, ul P Volov, # 2, Sofia, 1038, Bulgaria. FAX 359-2-9803319, publikacii@nsi.bg, http://www.nsi.bg.

TRANSPORT IN CIJFERS. *see* TRANSPORTATION—Abstracting, Bibliographies, Statistics

TRANSPORT STATISTICS BULLETIN. ROAD FREIGHT STATISTICS. *see* TRANSPORTATION—Abstracting, Bibliographies, Statistics

TRANSPORT STATISTICS GREAT BRITAIN. *see* TRANSPORTATION—Abstracting, Bibliographies, Statistics

TRANSPORT V ROSSII (YEAR). *see* TRANSPORTATION—Abstracting, Bibliographies, Statistics

TRAVEL IN AUSTRALIA. *see* TRAVEL AND TOURISM

TRAVEL TRENDS; data from international passenger survey (year). *see* TRAVEL AND TOURISM—Abstracting, Bibliographies, Statistics

TRENDINFO. *see* PUBLIC ADMINISTRATION—Abstracting, Bibliographies, Statistics

TRENDS. *see* EDUCATION—Abstracting, Bibliographies, Statistics

TRENDS IN STATISTICAL PHYSICS. *see* PHYSICS

TRINIDAD AND TOBAGO. CENTRAL STATISTICAL OFFICE. AGRICULTURAL REPORT. *see* AGRICULTURE—Abstracting, Bibliographies, Statistics

317.2983 TTO ISSN 0082-6502

TRINIDAD AND TOBAGO. CENTRAL STATISTICAL OFFICE. ANNUAL STATISTICAL DIGEST. Text in English. 1951. a. TTD 20, USD 10 (effective 2000). **Document type:** *Government.*

Related titles: Microfiche ed.: (from PQC).

Published by: Central Statistical Office, 35-41 Queen St, PO Box 98, Port-of-Spain, Trinidad, Trinidad & Tobago. TEL 868-623-6495, FAX 868-625-3802.

TRINIDAD AND TOBAGO. CENTRAL STATISTICAL OFFICE. BUSINESS SURVEYS. *see* BUSINESS AND ECONOMICS—Abstracting, Bibliographies, Statistics

TRINIDAD AND TOBAGO. CENTRAL STATISTICAL OFFICE. ECONOMIC INDICATORS. *see* BUSINESS AND ECONOMICS—Abstracting, Bibliographies, Statistics

TRINIDAD AND TOBAGO. CENTRAL STATISTICAL OFFICE. ESTIMATED INTERNAL MIGRATION. BULLETIN. *see* POPULATION STUDIES—Abstracting, Bibliographies, Statistics

TRINIDAD AND TOBAGO. CENTRAL STATISTICAL OFFICE. INTERNATIONAL TRAVEL REPORT. *see* TRAVEL AND TOURISM—Abstracting, Bibliographies, Statistics

TRINIDAD AND TOBAGO. CENTRAL STATISTICAL OFFICE. LABOUR FORCE BY SEX. *see* BUSINESS AND ECONOMICS—Abstracting, Bibliographies, Statistics

TRINIDAD AND TOBAGO. CENTRAL STATISTICAL OFFICE. OVERSEAS TRADE. ANNUAL REPORT. *see* BUSINESS AND ECONOMICS—Abstracting, Bibliographies, Statistics

TRINIDAD AND TOBAGO. CENTRAL STATISTICAL OFFICE. OVERSEAS TRADE. BI-MONTHLY REPORT. *see* BUSINESS AND ECONOMICS—Abstracting, Bibliographies, Statistics

317 TTO

TRINIDAD AND TOBAGO. CENTRAL STATISTICAL OFFICE. POCKET DIGEST. Text in English. 1973. a. TTD 100 (effective 2000). **Document type:** *Government.*

Published by: Central Statistical Office, 35-41 Queen St, PO Box 98, Port-of-Spain, Trinidad, Trinidad & Tobago. TEL 868-623-6495, FAX 868-625-3802.

TRINIDAD AND TOBAGO. CENTRAL STATISTICAL OFFICE. POPULATION AND VITAL STATISTICS; REPORT. *see* POPULATION STUDIES—Abstracting, Bibliographies, Statistics

TRINIDAD AND TOBAGO. CENTRAL STATISTICAL OFFICE. QUARTERLY ECONOMIC REPORT. *see* BUSINESS AND ECONOMICS—Abstracting, Bibliographies, Statistics

310 TTO

TRINIDAD AND TOBAGO. CENTRAL STATISTICAL OFFICE. STAFF PAPERS. Text in English. 1967. irreg. free. **Document type:** *Monographic series, Government.*

Published by: Central Statistical Office, 35-41 Queen St, PO Box 98, Port-of-Spain, Trinidad, Trinidad & Tobago. TEL 868-623-6495, FAX 868-625-3802.

TRUCKING ACTIVITY REPORT. *see* TRANSPORTATION—Abstracting, Bibliographies, Statistics

TRUD I ZANYATOST' V ROSSII (YEAR). *see* BUSINESS AND ECONOMICS—Abstracting, Bibliographies, Statistics

TRUST IN FOCUS. *see* HOUSING AND URBAN PLANNING—Abstracting, Bibliographies, Statistics

TSENA DAIDZHEST. *see* BUSINESS AND ECONOMICS—Abstracting, Bibliographies, Statistics

TSENTRAL'NYI BANK ROSSIISKOI FEDERATSII. BYULLETEN' BANKOVSKOI STATISTIKI. *see* BUSINESS AND ECONOMICS—Abstracting, Bibliographies, Statistics

TUNGSTEN STATISTICS. *see* METALLURGY—Abstracting, Bibliographies, Statistics

316.11 TUN ISSN 0041-4115
HC820.A1+

TUNISIA. INSTITUT NATIONAL DE LA STATISTIQUE. BULLETIN MENSUEL DE STATISTIQUE. Text in Arabic, French. 1954. m. TND 25,000 (effective 2000). **Document type:** *Government.*

Published by: Institut National de la Statistique, 70 Rue Ech-Cham, B P 260, Tunis, Tunisia. TEL 216-1-891002, FAX 216-1-792559.

TUNISIA. OFFICE DES PORTS NATIONAUX. BULLETIN ANNUEL DES STATISTIQUES. *see* TRANSPORTATION—Abstracting, Bibliographies, Statistics

TURISMUL IN ROMANIA/TOURISM IN ROMANIA. *see* TRAVEL AND TOURISM—Abstracting, Bibliographies, Statistics

310 338.4791 BGR

TURIZUM/TOURISM. Text in Bulgarian, English. 1967. a. BGL 29.70 (effective 2002). stat.

Published by: Natsionalen Statisticheski Institut/National Statistical Institute, ul P Volov, # 2, Sofia, 1038, Bulgaria. FAX 359-2-9803319, publikacii@nsi.bg, http://www.nsi.bg. Circ: 690.

315.61 TUR ISSN 1300-4328
HA4556.5

TURKEY IN STATISTICS (YEAR). Text in English. 1938. a. free (effective 2009). **Document type:** *Government.*

Formerly (until 1991): Statistical Pocket Book of Turkey

Related titles: ◆ Turkish ed.: Istatistiklerle Turkiye (Year). ISSN 1300-431X.

Published by: T.C. Basbakanlik, Turkiye Istatistik Kurumu/Prime Ministry Republic of Turkey, Turkish Statistical Institute, Yucetepe Mah. Necatibey Cad No.114, Cankaya, Ankara, 06100, Turkey. TEL 90-312-4100410, FAX 90-312-4175886, ulka.unsal@tuik.gov.tr, bilgi@tuik.gov.tr, http://www.tuik.gov.tr. Circ: 900.

TURKEY. TURKISH STATISTICAL INSTITUTE. METHODOLOGY EXPLANATION OF TRADE PRICE AND QUANTITY INDEXES. *see* BUSINESS AND ECONOMICS—Abstracting, Bibliographies, Statistics

TURKEY. TURKIYE ISTATISTIK KURUMU. ADALET ISTATISTIKLERI/ TURKEY. TURKISH STATISTICAL INSTITUTE. JUDICIAL STATISTICS. *see* LAW—Abstracting, Bibliographies, Statistics

TURKEY. TURKIYE ISTATISTIK KURUMU. AYLIK EKONOMIK GOSTERGELER/TURKEY. TURKISH STATISTICAL INSTITUTE. MONTHLY ECONOMIC INDICATORS. *see* BUSINESS AND ECONOMICS—Abstracting, Bibliographies, Statistics

TURKEY. TURKIYE ISTATISTIK KURUMU. BOSANMA ISTATISTIKLERI/TURKEY. TURKISH STATISTICAL INSTITUTE. DIVORCE STATISTICS. *see* MATRIMONY—Abstracting, Bibliographies, Statistics

TURKEY. TURKIYE ISTATISTIK KURUMU. BUTCELER - BELEDIYELER, IL OZEL IDARLER VE KOYLER (YEAR)/TURKEY. TURKISH STATISTICAL INSTITUTE. BUDGETS - MUNICIPAL AND SPECIAL PROVINCIAL ADMINISTRATIONS AND VILLAGES (YEAR). *see* PUBLIC ADMINISTRATION—Abstracting, Bibliographies, Statistics

TURKEY. TURKIYE ISTATISTIK KURUMU. DENIZ TASITLARI ISTATISTIKLERI (18 VE DAHA YUKARI GROS TONILATOLUK)/ TURKEY. TURKISH STATISTICAL INSTITUTE. STATISTICS OF SEA VESSELS (18 GROSS TONNAGES AND OVER). *see* TRANSPORTATION—Abstracting, Bibliographies, Statistics

TURKEY. TURKIYE ISTATISTIK KURUMU. DIS TICARET ISTATISTIKLERI YILLIGI/TURKEY. TURKISH STATISTICAL INSTITUTE. FOREIGN TRADE STATISTICS YEARBOOK. *see* BUSINESS AND ECONOMICS—Abstracting, Bibliographies, Statistics

TURKEY. TURKIYE ISTATISTIK KURUMU. DONEMLERE GORE BINA INSAATI MALIYET ENDEKSI (YEAR)/TURKEY. TURKISH STATISTICAL INSTITUTE. QUARTERLY BUILDING CONSTRUCTION COST INDEX (YEAR). *see* BUILDING AND CONSTRUCTION—Abstracting, Bibliographies, Statistics

TURKEY. TURKIYE ISTATISTIK KURUMU. EVLENME ISTATISTIKLERI (YEAR)/TURKEY. TURKISH STATISTICAL INSTITUTE. MARRIAGE STATISTICS (YEAR). *see* MATRIMONY—Abstracting, Bibliographies, Statistics

TURKEY. TURKIYE ISTATISTIK KURUMU. GAYRI SAFI MILLI HASILA, HABER BULTENI/TURKEY. TURKISH STATISTICAL INSTITUTE. GROSS NATIONAL PRODUCT RESULTS, NEWS BULLETIN. *see* BUSINESS AND ECONOMICS—Abstracting, Bibliographies, Statistics

TURKEY. TURKIYE ISTATISTIK KURUMU. GENEL NUFUS SAYIMI. GECICI SONUCLAR/TURKEY. TURKISH STATISTICAL INSTITUTE. CENSUS OF POPULATION. PRELIMINARY RESULTS. *see* POPULATION STUDIES—Abstracting, Bibliographies, Statistics

TURKEY. TURKIYE ISTATISTIK KURUMU. GENEL NUFUS SAYIMI; GOC ISTATISTIKLERI (YEAR)/TURKEY. TURKISH STATISTICAL INSTITUTE. CENSUS OF POPULATION; MIGRATION STATISTICS (YEAR). *see* POPULATION STUDIES—Abstracting, Bibliographies, Statistics

TURKEY. TURKIYE ISTATISTIK KURUMU. GENEL NUFUS SAYIMI. IDARI BOLUNUS/TURKEY. TURKISH STATISTICAL INSTITUTE. CENSUS OF POPULATION. ADMINISTRATIVE DIVISION. *see* POPULATION STUDIES—Abstracting, Bibliographies, Statistics

TURKEY. TURKIYE ISTATISTIK KURUMU. GENEL NUFUS SAYIMI. NUFUSAN SOSYAL VE EKONOMIK NITELIKLERI/TURKEY. TURKISH STATISTICAL INSTITUTE. CENSUS OF POPULATION. SOCIAL AND ECONOMIC CHARACTERISTICS OF POPULATION. *see* POPULATION STUDIES—Abstracting, Bibliographies, Statistics

TURKEY. TURKIYE ISTATISTIK KURUMU. GENEL TARIM SAYIMI. TARIMSAL ISLETMELER (HANEHALKI)/TURKEY. TURKISH STATISTICAL INSTITUTE. CENSUS OF AGRICULTURE. AGRICULTURAL HOLDINGS (HOUSEHOLDS). *see* AGRICULTURE—Abstracting, Bibliographies, Statistics

TURKEY. TURKIYE ISTATISTIK KURUMU. HANEHALKI BUTCE ARASTIRMASI GELIR DAGILIMI (YEAR)/TURKEY. TURKISH STATISTICAL INSTITUTE. HOUSEHOLD INCOME DISTRIBUTION (YEAR). *see* BUSINESS AND ECONOMICS—Abstracting, Bibliographies, Statistics

TURKEY. TURKIYE ISTATISTIK KURUMU. HANEHALKI BUTCE ARASTIRMASI TURKETIM HARCAMALARI (YEAR)/TURKEY. TURKISH STATISTICAL INSTITUTE. HOUSEHOLD BUDGET SURVEY CONSUMPTION EXPENDITURES (YEAR). *see* BUSINESS AND ECONOMICS—Abstracting, Bibliographies, Statistics

TURKEY. TURKIYE ISTATISTIK KURUMU. HANEHALKI ISGUCU ISTATISTIKLERI (YEAR)/TURKEY. TURKISH STATISTICAL INSTITUTE. HOUSEHOLD LABOR FORCE STATISTICAL (YEAR). *see* BUSINESS AND ECONOMICS—Abstracting, Bibliographies, Statistics

315.61 TUR ISSN 1304-6292

TURKEY. TURKIYE ISTATISTIK KURUMU. IL GOSTERGELERI (YEAR)/TURKEY. TURKISH STATISTICAL INSTITUTE. PROVINCIAL INDICATORS (YEAR). Text in English, Turkish. irreg., latest 1980. **Document type:** *Government.* **Description:** In order to demostrate the diversities in the development of provinces, selected indicators have been calculated under the topics of population, education, health, national accounts, labour, manufacturing industry, energy, agriculture, mining, building construction, banking, finance, foreign trade, transportation, communication and infrastructure.

Related titles: CD-ROM ed.: TRY 5 per issue domestic; USD 10 per issue foreign (effective 2009).

Published by: T.C. Basbakanlik, Turkiye Istatistik Kurumu/Prime Ministry Republic of Turkey, Turkish Statistical Institute, Yucetepe Mah. Necatibey Cad No.114, Cankaya, Ankara, 06100, Turkey. TEL 90-312-4100410, FAX 90-312-4175886, bilgi@tuik.gov.tr, ulka.unsal@tuik.gov.tr, http://www.tuik.gov.tr.

TURKEY. TURKIYE ISTATISTIK KURUMU. INTIHAR ISTATISTIKLERI (YEAR)/TURKEY. TURKISH STATISTICAL INSTITUTE. SUICIDE STATISTICS (YEAR). *see* POPULATION STUDIES—Abstracting, Bibliographies, Statistics

315.61 TUR ISSN 1300-0535
HA1911

TURKEY. TURKIYE ISTATISTIK KURUMU. ISTATISTIK GOSTERGELER (YEAR)/TURKEY. TURKISH STATISTICAL INSTITUTE. STATISTICAL INDICATORS (YEAR). Text in English, Turkish. 1991. a., latest 1923. **Document type:** *Government.* **Description:** Provides statistical tables and data from the earliest years of the Turkish Republic, from 1923 to the present.

Related titles: CD-ROM ed.: TRY 7 per issue domestic; USD 10 per issue foreign (effective 2009).

Published by: T.C. Basbakanlik, Turkiye Istatistik Kurumu/Prime Ministry Republic of Turkey, Turkish Statistical Institute, Yucetepe Mah. Necatibey Cad No.114, Cankaya, Ankara, 06100, Turkey. TEL 90-312-4100410, FAX 90-312-4175886, bilgi@tuik.gov.tr, ulka.unsal@tuik.gov.tr, http://www.tuik.gov.tr. Circ: 1,500.

TURKEY. TURKIYE ISTATISTIK KURUMU. KESIN HESAPLAR - BELEDIYELER VE IL OZEL IDARELERI (YEAR)/TURKEY. TURKISH STATISTICAL INSTITUTE. FINAL ACCOUNTS - MUNICIPALITIES AND SPECIAL PROVINCIAL ADMINISTRATIONS (YEAR). *see* PUBLIC ADMINISTRATION—Abstracting, Bibliographies, Statistics

306.021 TUR ISSN 1300-1167
HA1911

TURKEY. TURKIYE ISTATISTIK KURUMU. KULTUR ISTATISTIKLERI (YEAR)/TURKEY. TURKISH STATISTICAL INSTITUTE. CULTURAL STATISTICS (YEAR). Key Title: Kultur Istatistikleri. Text in English, Turkish. 1936. a., latest 2007. TRY 10 per issue domestic; USD 20 per issue foreign (effective 2009). **Document type:** *Government.* **Description:** Provides information on number of museums and works of art in the museums, number of visitors of museums and ruins, number of personnel and acquisitions belonging to foundations in the context of cultural heritage.

Related titles: CD-ROM ed.: TRY 5 per issue domestic; USD 10 per issue foreign (effective 2009).

Published by: T.C. Basbakanlik, Turkiye Istatistik Kurumu/Prime Ministry Republic of Turkey, Turkish Statistical Institute, Yucetepe Mah. Necatibey Cad No.114, Cankaya, Ankara, 06100, Turkey. TEL 90-312-4100410, FAX 90-312-4175886, bilgi@tuik.gov.tr, ulka.unsal@tuik.gov.tr, http://www.tuik.gov.tr. Circ: 1,130.

TURKEY. TURKIYE ISTATISTIK KURUMU. MAHALLI IDARELER SECIMI/TURKEY. TURKISH STATISTICAL INSTITUTE. ELECTIONS OF LOCAL ADMINISTRATIONS. *see* PUBLIC ADMINISTRATION—Abstracting, Bibliographies, Statistics

TURKEY. TURKIYE ISTATISTIK KURUMU. MILLETVEKILI GENEL SECIMI IL VE ILCE SONUCLARI (YEAR)/TURKEY. TURKISH STATISTICAL INSTITUTE. GENERAL ELECTION OF REPRESENTATIVES; PROVINCE AND DISTRICT RESULTS (YEAR). *see* POLITICAL SCIENCE—Abstracting, Bibliographies, Statistics

TURKEY. TURKIYE ISTATISTIK KURUMU. MILLETVEKILI GENERL SECIMLERI (YEAR)/TURKEY. TURKISH STATISTICAL INSTITUTE. THE GENERAL ELECTIONS (YEAR). *see* POLITICAL SCIENCE—Abstracting, Bibliographies, Statistics

TURKEY. TURKIYE ISTATISTIK KURUMU. MILLI EGITIM ISTATISTIKLERI ORGUN EGITIM/TURKEY. TURKISH STATISTICAL INSTITUTE. NATIONAL EDUCATIONAL STATISTICS FORMAL EDUCATION. *see* EDUCATION—Abstracting, Bibliographies, Statistics

TURKEY. TURKIYE ISTATISTIK KURUMU. MILLI EGITIM ISTATISTIKLERI; YAYGIN EGITIM (YEAR)/TURKEY. TURKISH STATISTICAL INSTITUTE. NATIONAL EDUCATION STATISTICS; ADULT EDUCATION (YEAR). *see* EDUCATION—Abstracting, Bibliographies, Statistics

TURKEY. TURKIYE ISTATISTIK KURUMU. MOTORLU KARA TASITLARI ISTATISTIKLERI (YEAR)/TURKEY. TURKISH STATISTICAL INSTITUTE. ROAD MOTOR VEHICLE STATISTICS (YEAR). *see* TRANSPORTATION—Abstracting, Bibliographies, Statistics

TURKEY. TURKIYE ISTATISTIK KURUMU. OLUM ISTATISTIKLERI; IL VE ILCE MERKEZLERINDE (YEAR)/TURKEY. TURKISH STATISTICAL INSTITUTE. DEATH STATISTICS; PROVINCIAL AND DISTRICT CENTERS (YEAR). *see* POPULATION STUDIES—Abstracting, Bibliographies, Statistics

TURKEY. TURKIYE ISTATISTIK KURUMU. SIRKET KOOPERATIFL VE TICARET UNVANLI ISYERI ISTATISTIKLERI (2007)/TURKEY. TURKISH STATISTICAL INSTITUTE. STATISTICS ON COMPANIES, COOPERATIVES AND TRADE NAME ESTABLISHMENT (2007). *see* BUSINESS AND ECONOMICS—Abstracting, Bibliographies, Statistics

TURKEY. TURKIYE ISTATISTIK KURUMU. SU URUNLERI ISTATISTIKLERI (YEAR)/TURKEY. TURKISH STATISTICAL INSTITUTE. FISHERY STATISTICS (YEAR). *see* FISH AND FISHERIES—Abstracting, Bibliographies, Statistics

S

TURKEY. TURKIYE ISTATISTIK KURUMU. TARIM ISTATISTIKLERI OZETI (YEAR)/TURKEY. TURKISH STATISTICAL INSTITUTE. SUMMARY OF AGRICULTURAL STATISTICS (YEAR). *see* AGRICULTURE—Abstracting, Bibliographies, Statistics

TURKEY. TURKIYE ISTATISTIK KURUMU. TARIMSAL YAPI; URETIM, FIYAT, DEGER (YEAR)/TURKEY. TURKISH STATISTICAL INSTITUTE. AGRICULTURAL STRUCTURE; PRODUCTION, PRICE, VALUE (YEAR). *see* AGRICULTURE—Abstracting, Bibliographies, Statistics

TURKEY. TURKIYE ISTATISTIK KURUMU. TOPTAN FIYAT ISTATISTIKLERI/TURKEY. TURKISH STATISTICAL INSTITUTE. WHOLESALE PRICE STATISTICS. *see* BUSINESS AND ECONOMICS—Abstracting, Bibliographies, Statistics

TURKEY. TURKIYE ISTATISTIK KURUMU. TRAFIK KAZA ISTATISTIKLERI; KARAYOLU (YEAR)/TURKEY. TURKISH STATISTICAL INSTITUTE. TRAFFIC ACCIDENT STATISTICS; ROAD (YEAR). *see* TRANSPORTATION—Abstracting, Bibliographies, Statistics

TURKEY. TURKIYE ISTATISTIK KURUMU. TURIZM ISTATISTIKLERI (YEAR)/TURKEY. TURKISH STATISTICAL INSTITUTE. TOURISM STATISTICS (YEAR). *see* TRAVEL AND TOURISM—Abstracting, Bibliographies, Statistics

315.61 TUR ISSN 0259-3491
TURKEY. TURKIYE ISTATISTIK KURUMU. TURKIYE ISTATISTIK YILLIGI (YEAR)/TURKEY. TURKISH STATISTICAL INSTITUTE. TURKEY'S STATISTICAL YEARBOOK (YEAR). Text in Turkish, English. 1929. a., latest 2007. TRY 20 per issue domestic; USD 20 per issue foreign (effective 2009). **Document type:** *Government.*
Description: Covers data on land and climate, environment, population and migration, demography, health, education and culture, tourism, justice, elections, social security, labour, agriculture, industry, construction, energy, transportation and communication, foreign trade, prices, and indexes, purchasing power parity, money, banking and finance, national accounts, income, consumption and poverty, science, technology and information communication, life satisfaction, and also some international statistics in five years period.
Formerly (until 1972): Turkiye Istatistik Yilligi (0082-691X)
Related titles: CD-ROM ed.: TRY 10 per issue domestic; USD 10 per issue foreign (effective 2009).
Published by: T.C. Basbakanlik, Turkiye Istatistik Kurumu/Prime Ministry Republic of Turkey, Turkish Statistical Institute, Yucetepe Mah. Necatibey Cad No.114, Cankaya, Ankara, 06100, Turkey. TEL 90-312-4100410, FAX 90-312-4175886, bilgi@tuik.gov.tr, ulka.unsal@tuik.gov.tr, http://www.tuik.gov.tr. Circ: 2,500.

TURKEY. TURKIYE ISTATISTIK KURUMU. ULASTIRMA ISTATISTIKLERI OZETI/TURKEY. TURKISH STATISTICAL INSTITUTE. SUMMARY STATISTICS ON TRANSPORTATION (YEAR). *see* TRANSPORTATION—Abstracting, Bibliographies, Statistics

TURKEY. TURKIYE ISTATISTIK KURUMU. YAYINLAY VE ELEKTRONIK HIZMETLER KATALOGU/TURKEY. TURKISH STATISTICAL INSTITUTE. PUBLICATIONS AND ELECTRONIC SERVICES CATALOGUE. *see* BUSINESS AND ECONOMICS—Abstracting, Bibliographies, Statistics

310 TUR ISSN 1300-4077
TURKIYE ISTATISTIK DERNEGI ISTATISTIK DERGISI. Text in Turkish. 1994. q. **Document type:** *Journal, Government.*
Indexed: CCMJ, CIS, MSN, MathR.
Published by: (Turk Istatistik Dernegi/Turkish Statistical Association), T.C. Basbakanlik, Turkiye Istatistik Kurumu/Prime Ministry Republic of Turkey, Turkish Statistical Institute, Yucetepe Mah. Necatibey Cad No.114, Cankaya, Ankara, 06100, Turkey. TEL 90-312-4100410, FAX 90-312-4175886, ulka.unsal@tuik.gov.tr, bilgi@tuik.gov.tr, http://www.tuik.gov.tr.

U I DATA SUMMARY. (Unemployment Insurance) *see* INSURANCE—Abstracting, Bibliographies, Statistics

U K ECONOMIC ACCOUNTS. *see* BUSINESS AND ECONOMICS—Abstracting, Bibliographies, Statistics

U K IRON AND STEEL INDUSTRY. ANNUAL STATISTICS. *see* METALLURGY—Abstracting, Bibliographies, Statistics

U K MEDIA YEARBOOK. *see* COMMUNICATIONS

U K STANDARD INDUSTRIAL CLASSIFICATION OF ECONOMIC ACTIVITIES (ONLINE). (United Kingdom) *see* BUSINESS AND ECONOMICS—Abstracting, Bibliographies, Statistics

U K STEEL EXPORTS. *see* METALLURGY

U K STEEL IMPORTS. *see* METALLURGY

U K TELEVISION FORECASTS. *see* COMMUNICATIONS—Television And Cable

U N C T A D COMMODITY YEARBOOK. (United Nations Conference on Trade and Development) *see* BUSINESS AND ECONOMICS—Abstracting, Bibliographies, Statistics

U.S.A. STATISTICS IN BRIEF (ONLINE). *see* POPULATION STUDIES—Abstracting, Bibliographies, Statistics

U.S. BUREAU OF LABOR STATISTICS. BULLETIN. *see* BUSINESS AND ECONOMICS—Abstracting, Bibliographies, Statistics

U.S. BUREAU OF LABOR STATISTICS. C P I DETAILED REPORT (ONLINE). (Consumer Price Index) *see* BUSINESS AND ECONOMICS—Economic Situation And Conditions

U.S. BUREAU OF LABOR STATISTICS. NATIONAL COMPENSATION SURVEY. *see* BUSINESS AND ECONOMICS—Abstracting, Bibliographies, Statistics

U.S. BUREAU OF LABOR STATISTICS. NATIONAL OFFICE NEWS RELEASES. *see* BUSINESS AND ECONOMICS—Abstracting, Bibliographies, Statistics

U.S. BUREAU OF LABOR STATISTICS. REPORTS. *see* BUSINESS AND ECONOMICS—Abstracting, Bibliographies, Statistics

U.S. BUREAU OF LABOR STATISTICS. REPRINT SERIES. *see* BUSINESS AND ECONOMICS—Abstracting, Bibliographies, Statistics

U.S. BUREAU OF LABOR STATISTICS. SOUTHWEST STATISTICAL SUMMARY. *see* BUSINESS AND ECONOMICS—Abstracting, Bibliographies, Statistics

U.S. BUREAU OF LAND MANAGEMENT. PUBLIC LAND STATISTICS. *see* HOUSING AND URBAN PLANNING—Abstracting, Bibliographies, Statistics

U.S. BUREAU OF THE CENSUS. (YEAR) ECONOMIC CENSUS. CONSTRUCTION (ONLINE). *see* BUILDING AND CONSTRUCTION—Abstracting, Bibliographies, Statistics

U.S. BUREAU OF THE CENSUS. (YEAR) ECONOMIC CENSUS. INFORMATION (ONLINE). *see* BUSINESS AND ECONOMICS—Abstracting, Bibliographies, Statistics

U.S. BUREAU OF THE CENSUS. (YEAR) ECONOMIC CENSUS. MANUFACTURING (ONLINE). *see* BUSINESS AND ECONOMICS—Abstracting, Bibliographies, Statistics

U.S. BUREAU OF THE CENSUS. (YEAR) ECONOMIC CENSUS. RETAIL TRADE (ONLINE). *see* BUSINESS AND ECONOMICS—Abstracting, Bibliographies, Statistics

U.S. BUREAU OF THE CENSUS. (YEAR) ECONOMIC CENSUS. TRANSPORTATION AND WAREHOUSING (ONLINE). *see* BUSINESS AND ECONOMICS—Abstracting, Bibliographies, Statistics

U.S. BUREAU OF THE CENSUS. (YEAR) ECONOMIC CENSUS. WHOLESALE TRADE (ONLINE). *see* BUSINESS AND ECONOMICS—Abstracting, Bibliographies, Statistics

U.S. BUREAU OF THE CENSUS. CENSUS OF POPULATION AND HOUSING (ONLINE). *see* POPULATION STUDIES—Abstracting, Bibliographies, Statistics

U.S. BUREAU OF THE CENSUS. GOVERNMENTS DIVISION. LOCAL GOVERNMENT EMPLOYMENT AND PAYROLL DATA. *see* BUSINESS AND ECONOMICS—Abstracting, Bibliographies, Statistics

U.S. BUREAU OF THE CENSUS. GOVERNMENTS DIVISION. PUBLIC EDUCATION FINANCES. *see* EDUCATION—Abstracting, Bibliographies, Statistics

U.S. CENSUS BUREAU. ANNUAL REVISION OF MONTHLY WHOLESALE DISTRIBUTORS: SALES AND INVENTORIES. *see* BUSINESS AND ECONOMICS—Abstracting, Bibliographies, Statistics

U.S. CENSUS BUREAU. ECONOMIC CENSUS. *see* BUSINESS AND ECONOMICS—Abstracting, Bibliographies, Statistics

U.S. CENSUS BUREAU. NONEMPLOYER STATISTICS. *see* BUSINESS AND ECONOMICS—Abstracting, Bibliographies, Statistics

U.S. CENTERS FOR DISEASE CONTROL. REPORTED TUBERCULOSIS IN THE UNITED STATES. *see* MEDICAL SCIENCES—Respiratory Diseases

U S CHEMICAL INDUSTRY STATISTICAL HANDBOOK. *see* CHEMISTRY—Abstracting, Bibliographies, Statistics

U.S. DEPARTMENT OF AGRICULTURE. NATIONAL AGRICULTURAL STATISTICS SERVICE. AGRICULTURAL PRICES. *see* AGRICULTURE—Abstracting, Bibliographies, Statistics

U.S. DEPARTMENT OF AGRICULTURE. NATIONAL AGRICULTURAL STATISTICS SERVICE. AGRICULTURAL STATISTICS. *see* AGRICULTURE—Abstracting, Bibliographies, Statistics

U.S. DEPARTMENT OF AGRICULTURE. NATIONAL AGRICULTURAL STATISTICS SERVICE. CATFISH PROCESSING. *see* FISH AND FISHERIES—Abstracting, Bibliographies, Statistics

U.S. DEPARTMENT OF AGRICULTURE. NATIONAL AGRICULTURAL STATISTICS SERVICE. CATFISH PRODUCTION (ONLINE). *see* FISH AND FISHERIES—Abstracting, Bibliographies, Statistics

U.S. DEPARTMENT OF AGRICULTURE. NATIONAL AGRICULTURAL STATISTICS SERVICE. CATTLE (ONLINE). *see* AGRICULTURE—Abstracting, Bibliographies, Statistics

U.S. DEPARTMENT OF AGRICULTURE. NATIONAL AGRICULTURAL STATISTICS SERVICE. CATTLE ON FEED. *see* AGRICULTURE—Abstracting, Bibliographies, Statistics

U.S. DEPARTMENT OF AGRICULTURE. NATIONAL AGRICULTURAL STATISTICS SERVICE. CHICKENS AND EGGS. *see* AGRICULTURE—Abstracting, Bibliographies, Statistics

U.S. DEPARTMENT OF AGRICULTURE. NATIONAL AGRICULTURAL STATISTICS SERVICE. COLD STORAGE. *see* AGRICULTURE—Abstracting, Bibliographies, Statistics

U.S. DEPARTMENT OF AGRICULTURE. NATIONAL AGRICULTURAL STATISTICS SERVICE. CROP PRODUCTION. *see* AGRICULTURE—Abstracting, Bibliographies, Statistics

U.S. DEPARTMENT OF AGRICULTURE. NATIONAL AGRICULTURAL STATISTICS SERVICE. DAIRY PRODUCTS (ONLINE). *see* AGRICULTURE—Abstracting, Bibliographies, Statistics

U.S. DEPARTMENT OF AGRICULTURE. NATIONAL AGRICULTURAL STATISTICS SERVICE. DAIRY PRODUCTS PRICES. *see* AGRICULTURE—Abstracting, Bibliographies, Statistics

U.S. DEPARTMENT OF AGRICULTURE. NATIONAL AGRICULTURAL STATISTICS SERVICE. EGG PRODUCTS. *see* AGRICULTURE—Abstracting, Bibliographies, Statistics

U.S. DEPARTMENT OF AGRICULTURE. NATIONAL AGRICULTURAL STATISTICS SERVICE. FARM LABOR (ONLINE). *see* AGRICULTURE—Abstracting, Bibliographies, Statistics

U.S. DEPARTMENT OF AGRICULTURE. NATIONAL AGRICULTURAL STATISTICS SERVICE. LIVESTOCK SLAUGHTER. (United States) *see* AGRICULTURE—Abstracting, Bibliographies, Statistics

U.S. DEPARTMENT OF AGRICULTURE. NATIONAL AGRICULTURAL STATISTICS SERVICE. MARYLAND & DELAWARE WEEKLY CROP AND WEATHER REPORT. *see* AGRICULTURE—Abstracting, Bibliographies, Statistics

U.S. DEPARTMENT OF AGRICULTURE. NATIONAL AGRICULTURAL STATISTICS SERVICE. MILK PRODUCTION. *see* AGRICULTURE—Abstracting, Bibliographies, Statistics

U.S. DEPARTMENT OF AGRICULTURE. NATIONAL AGRICULTURAL STATISTICS SERVICE. NONCITRUS FRUITS AND NUTS. *see* AGRICULTURE—Abstracting, Bibliographies, Statistics

U.S. DEPARTMENT OF AGRICULTURE. NATIONAL AGRICULTURAL STATISTICS SERVICE. PEANUT STOCKS AND PROCESSING (ONLINE). *see* AGRICULTURE—Abstracting, Bibliographies, Statistics

U.S. DEPARTMENT OF AGRICULTURE. NATIONAL AGRICULTURAL STATISTICS SERVICE. POTATO STOCKS. *see* AGRICULTURE—Abstracting, Bibliographies, Statistics

U.S. DEPARTMENT OF AGRICULTURE. NATIONAL AGRICULTURAL STATISTICS SERVICE. POULTRY SLAUGHTER (ONLINE). *see* AGRICULTURE—Abstracting, Bibliographies, Statistics

U.S. DEPARTMENT OF AGRICULTURE. NATIONAL AGRICULTURAL STATISTICS SERVICE. QUARTERLY HOGS AND PIGS. *see* AGRICULTURE—Abstracting, Bibliographies, Statistics

U.S. DEPARTMENT OF AGRICULTURE. NATIONAL AGRICULTURAL STATISTICS SERVICE. RICE STOCKS (ONLINE). *see* AGRICULTURE—Abstracting, Bibliographies, Statistics

U.S. DEPARTMENT OF AGRICULTURE. NATIONAL AGRICULTURAL STATISTICS SERVICE. UNITED STATES AND CANADIAN CATTLE. *see* AGRICULTURE—Abstracting, Bibliographies, Statistics

U.S. DEPARTMENT OF AGRICULTURE. NATIONAL AGRICULTURAL STATISTICS SERVICE. VEGETABLES. *see* AGRICULTURE—Abstracting, Bibliographies, Statistics

U.S. DEPARTMENT OF AGRICULTURE. RURAL BUSINESS - COOPERATIVE SERVICE. COOPERATIVE STATISTICS. *see* AGRICULTURE—Abstracting, Bibliographies, Statistics

U.S. DEPARTMENT OF EDUCATION. NATIONAL CENTER FOR EDUCATION STATISTICS. DIGEST OF EDUCATION STATISTICS. *see* EDUCATION—Abstracting, Bibliographies, Statistics

U.S. DEPARTMENT OF EDUCATION. NATIONAL CENTER FOR EDUCATION STATISTICS. POSTSECONDARY INSTITUTIONS IN THE UNITED STATES: FALL (YEAR) AND DEGREES AND OTHER AWARDS CONFERRED. *see* EDUCATION—Abstracting, Bibliographies, Statistics

U.S. DEPARTMENT OF EDUCATION. NATIONAL CENTER FOR EDUCATION STATISTICS. PROJECTIONS OF EDUCATION STATISTICS. *see* EDUCATION—Abstracting, Bibliographies, Statistics

U.S. DEPARTMENT OF ENERGY. ENERGY INFORMATION ADMINISTRATION. ELECTRIC SALES, REVENUE, AND AVERAGE PRICE. *see* ENERGY—Abstracting, Bibliographies, Statistics

U.S. DEPARTMENT OF ENERGY. ENERGY INFORMATION ADMINISTRATION. QUARTERLY COAL REPORT (ONLINE). *see* MINES AND MINING INDUSTRY—Abstracting, Bibliographies, Statistics

U.S. DEPARTMENT OF HEALTH AND HUMAN SERVICES. NATIONAL CENTER FOR HEALTH STATISTICS. NATIONAL VITAL STATISTICS REPORTS. *see* POPULATION STUDIES—Abstracting, Bibliographies, Statistics

U.S. DEPARTMENT OF HOUSING AND URBAN DEVELOPMENT. CHARACTERISTICS OF F H A SINGLE-FAMILY MORTGAGES: SELECTED SECTIONS ON NATIONAL HOUSING ACT. *see* HOUSING AND URBAN PLANNING

U.S. DEPARTMENT OF HOUSING AND URBAN DEVELOPMENT. F H A HOME MORTGAGE INSURANCE OPERATIONS: STATE, COUNTY AND M S A - P M S A. *see* HOUSING AND URBAN PLANNING—Abstracting, Bibliographies, Statistics

U.S. DEPARTMENT OF HOUSING AND URBAN DEVELOPMENT. F H A TRENDS OF HOME MORTGAGE CHARACTERISTICS. *see* HOUSING AND URBAN PLANNING—Abstracting, Bibliographies, Statistics

U.S. DEPARTMENT OF JUSTICE. BUREAU OF JUSTICE STATISTICS. CRIME AND JUSTICE DATA. *see* CRIMINOLOGY AND LAW ENFORCEMENT—Abstracting, Bibliographies, Statistics

U.S. DEPARTMENT OF JUSTICE. BUREAU OF JUSTICE STATISTICS. CRIMINAL VICTIMIZATION. *see* CRIMINOLOGY AND LAW ENFORCEMENT—Abstracting, Bibliographies, Statistics

U.S. DEPARTMENT OF LABOR. BUREAU OF LABOR STATISTICS. NEWS. MULTIFACTOR PRODUCTIVITY TRENDS. *see* BUSINESS AND ECONOMICS—Abstracting, Bibliographies, Statistics

U.S. DEPARTMENT OF STATE INDEXES OF LIVING COSTS ABROAD, QUARTERS ALLOWANCES, AND HARDSHIP DIFFERENTIALS. *see* BUSINESS AND ECONOMICS—Abstracting, Bibliographies, Statistics

U.S. DEPARTMENT OF TRANSPORTATION. FEDERAL RAILROAD ADMINISTRATION. OFFICE OF SAFETY ANALYSIS. RAILROAD SAFETY STATISTICS. ANNUAL REPORT (YEAR). *see* TRANSPORTATION—Abstracting, Bibliographies, Statistics

U.S. DEPARTMENT OF TRANSPORTATION. NATIONAL TRANSPORTATION STATISTICS. ANNUAL; a supplement to the summary of national transportation statistics. *see* TRANSPORTATION—Abstracting, Bibliographies, Statistics

U.S. EQUAL EMPLOYMENT OPPORTUNITY COMMISSION. EQUAL OPPORTUNITY REPORT. JOB PATTERNS FOR MINORITIES AND WOMEN IN PRIVATE INDUSTRY. *see* OCCUPATIONS AND CAREERS—Abstracting, Bibliographies, Statistics

U.S. EXPORTS OF MERCHANDISE (DVD-ROM). *see* BUSINESS AND ECONOMICS—Abstracting, Bibliographies, Statistics

U.S. FEDERAL HIGHWAY ADMINISTRATION. HIGHWAY STATISTICS. *see* TRANSPORTATION—Abstracting, Bibliographies, Statistics

U.S. FEDERAL HIGHWAY ADMINISTRATION. MONTHLY MOTOR FUEL REPORTED BY STATES (ONLINE). *see* PETROLEUM AND GAS—Abstracting, Bibliographies, Statistics

U.S. FISH AND WILDLIFE SERVICE. NATIONAL SURVEY OF FISHING, HUNTING AND WILDLIFE - ASSOCIATED RECREATION. *see* SPORTS AND GAMES—Abstracting, Bibliographies, Statistics

U.S. GEOLOGICAL SURVEY. MINERAL RESOURCES PROGRAM. MINERAL COMMODITY SUMMARIES. BARITE. *see* BUSINESS AND ECONOMICS—Production Of Goods And Services

U.S. GEOLOGICAL SURVEY. MINERAL RESOURCES PROGRAM. MINERAL COMMODITY SUMMARIES. BORON. *see* BUSINESS AND ECONOMICS—Production Of Goods And Services

U.S. GEOLOGICAL SURVEY. MINERAL RESOURCES PROGRAM. MINERAL COMMODITY SUMMARIES. BROMINE. *see* BUSINESS AND ECONOMICS—Production Of Goods And Services

S

UNITED KINGDOM NATIONAL ACCOUNTS. *see* BUSINESS AND ECONOMICS—Abstracting, Bibliographies, Statistics

310 314 CHE ISSN 0069-8458
JX1977
UNITED NATIONS CONFERENCE OF EUROPEAN STATISTICIANS. STATISTICAL STANDARDS AND STUDIES. Text in English. 1963. irreg.
Indexed: GeoRef.
Published by: (United Nations Economic Commission for Europe, Conference of European Statisticians SWZ), United Nations, Economic Commission for Europe (ECE), Palais des Nations, Geneva 10, 1211, Switzerland. TEL 41-22-9174444, FAX 41-22-9170505, info.ece@unece.org, http://www.unece.org.

UNITED NATIONS. INTERNATIONAL TRADE STATISTICS YEARBOOK. *see* BUSINESS AND ECONOMICS—Abstracting, Bibliographies, Statistics

UNITED NATIONS. NATIONAL ACCOUNTS STATISTICS. ANALYSIS OF MAIN AGGREGATES. *see* BUSINESS AND ECONOMICS—Abstracting, Bibliographies, Statistics

UNITED NATIONS. NATIONAL ACCOUNTS STATISTICS. MAIN AGGREGATES AND DETAILED TABLES. *see* BUSINESS AND ECONOMICS—Abstracting, Bibliographies, Statistics

310 USA ISSN 0041-7432
HC57
UNITED NATIONS STATISTICAL OFFICE. MONTHLY BULLETIN OF STATISTICS. Text in English, French. 1920. m. USD 225 in Africa to institutions; USD 755 to institutions in Australia, New Zealand & Japan; USD 750 in Europe to institutions in Europe & Asia; USD 735 in North America to institutions; USD 465 elsewhere to institutions (effective 2011). charts; mkt. back issues avail. **Document type:** *Bulletin, Government.* **Description:** Provides monthly statistics on 74 subjects from over 200 countries and territories, including special tables that graphically portray important economic developments.
Formerly (until 1946): Societe des Nations. Bulletin Mensuel de Statistique (1014-8450)
Related titles: Online - full text ed.: ISSN 1564-3794. 1996; ◆ Supplement to: United Nations. Statistical Yearbook. ISSN 0082-8459.
Indexed: IIS, INIS AtomInd, P06, P30.
—**CCC.**
Published by: United Nations Publications, 2 United Nations Plaza, Rm DC2-853, New York, NY 10017. TEL 212-963-8302, 800-253-9646, FAX 212-963-3489, publications@un.org, https://unp.un.org. **Subscr. to:** EBSCO Information Services, PO Box 361, Birmingham, AL 35201. TEL 205-995-1567, 800-633-4931, FAX 205-995-1588

310 USA ISSN 0082-8459
HA12.5 CODEN: STYBDH
UNITED NATIONS. STATISTICAL YEARBOOK. Text in English, French. 1949. a. USD 150 per issue (effective 2008). back issues avail.; reprints avail. **Document type:** *Yearbook, Consumer.* **Description:** Covers a wide range of international economic, social and environmental statistics on over 200 countries and areas, compiled from sources including UN agencies and other international, national and specialized organizations.
Related titles: CD-ROM ed.; Online - full text ed.: USD 120 per issue (effective 2008); ◆ Supplement(s): United Nations Statistical Office. Monthly Bulletin of Statistics. ISSN 0041-7432; United Nations. Supplement to the Statistical Yearbook and the Monthly Bulletin of Statistics. ISSN 0503-4019.
Indexed: IIS, RASB.
—BLDSC (8452.800000), CASDDS. **CCC.**
Published by: (United Nations Statistical Office), United Nations Publications, 2 United Nations Plaza, Rm DC2-853, New York, NY 10017. TEL 212-963-8302, 800-253-9646, FAX 212-963-3489, publications@un.org, https://unp.un.org.

310 USA ISSN 1020-1114
HA12.5
UNITED NATIONS STATISTICS ON CD-ROM. Text in English. 1993. a.
Media: CD-ROM.
Published by: (United Nations Statistical Office), United Nations Publications, 2 United Nations Plaza, Rm DC2-853, New York, NY 10017. TEL 212-963-8302, 800-253-9646, FAX 212-963-3489, publications@un.org, https://unp.un.org.

UNITED STATES ATTORNEYS ANNUAL STATISTICAL REPORT. *see* LAW—Abstracting, Bibliographies, Statistics

UNITED STATES POPULATION PROJECTIONS BY AGE, SEX, RACE, AND HISPANIC ORIGIN. *see* POPULATION STUDIES—Abstracting, Bibliographies, Statistics

310 URY ISSN 1510-8031
UNIVERSIDAD DE LA REPUBLICA. ESTADISTICAS BASICAS. Text in Spanish. 2000. a. back issues avail. **Document type:** *Bulletin, Academic/Scholarly.*
Related titles: Online - full text ed.: ISSN 1510-804X. 2000.
Published by: Universidad de la Republica, Direccion General de Planeamiento, Ave 18 de Julio 1968, Montevideo, Uruguay. TEL 598-2-4009201, dgplan@once.edu.uy, http://www.universidad.edu.uy/index.php.

339 URY ISSN 0041-8439
UNIVERSIDAD DE LA REPUBLICA. FACULTAD DE CIENCIAS ECONOMICAS Y DE ADMINISTRACION. INSTITUTO DE ESTADISTICA. INDICE DE PRECIOS AL CONSUMIDOR. Text in Spanish. 1962. m. UYP 3.40. stat.
Media: Duplicated (not offset).
Published by: (Instituto de Estadistica), Universidad de la Republica, Facultad de Ciencias Economicas y de Administracion, Montevideo, Uruguay.

UNIVERSIDAD DE TOLIMA. BOLETIN ESTADISTICO. *see* EDUCATION—Abstracting, Bibliographies, Statistics

UNIVERSIDADE FEDERAL DE PERNAMBUCO. ANUARIO ESTATISTICO. *see* EDUCATION—Abstracting, Bibliographies, Statistics

UNIVERSIDADE FEDERAL DO RIO DE JANEIRO. INSTITUTO DE MATEMATICA. MEMORIAS DE MATEMATICA. *see* MATHEMATICS—Abstracting, Bibliographies, Statistics

UNIVERSITA DEGLI STUDI DI PERUGIA. DIPARTIMENTO DI ECONOMIA, FINANZA E STATISTICA. QUADERNI. *see* BUSINESS AND ECONOMICS

UNIVERSITY OF BERGEN. DEPARTMENT OF MATHEMATICS. STATISTICAL REPORT. *see* MATHEMATICS

UNIVERSITY OF GHANA. INSTITUTE OF STATISTICAL, SOCIAL AND ECONOMIC RESEARCH. DISCUSSION PAPERS. *see* SOCIAL SCIENCES: COMPREHENSIVE WORKS

UNIVERSITY OF JOENSUU. DEPARTMENT OF COMPUTER SCIENCE AND STATISTICS. DISSERTATIONS. *see* COMPUTERS

330 AUS ISSN 1449-0633
UNIVERSITY OF NEW ENGLAND. SCHOOL OF ECONOMIC STUDIES, ECONOMETRICS DISCIPLINE. WORKING PAPERS IN ECONOMETRICS AND APPLIED STATISTICS (ONLINE). Text in English. 1979. irreg. looseleaf. free (effective 2008). cum.index. back issues avail. **Document type:** *Monographic series, Academic/Scholarly.* **Description:** Provides research results in econometric theory and applied statistics.
Formerly (untill 1998): University of New England. School of Economic Studies, Econometrics Discipline. Working Papers in Econometrics and Applied Statistics (0157-0188)
Media: Online - full text.
Published by: University Of New England, School of Economic Studies, Econometrics Discipline, Faculty of The Professions, Trevenna Rd., EBL Bldg., Armidale, NSW 2351, Australia. bepp@une.edu.au, http://www.une.edu.au/bepp/. Circ: 100.

310 USA ISSN 0078-1495
UNIVERSITY OF NORTH CAROLINA, CHAPEL HILL. INSTITUTE OF STATISTICS. MIMEO SERIES. Text in English. 1947. irreg. (approx. 3/mo.). price varies. cum.index.
Published by: University of North Carolina at Chapel Hill, Department of Statistics, 117 New West, CB 3260, Cameron Ave, Chapel Hill, NC 27599-3260. TEL 919-962-2307.

URNER BARRY'S NATIONAL WEEKLY HATCH REPORT. *see* AGRICULTURE—Abstracting, Bibliographies, Statistics

URUGUAY. DIRECCION GENERAL DE ESTADISTICA Y CENSOS. INDICE MEDIO DE SALARIOS. *see* BUSINESS AND ECONOMICS—Abstracting, Bibliographies, Statistics

310 URY ISSN 0797-3594
URUGUAY EN CIFRAS. Text in Spanish. 1975. a. back issues avail.
Related titles: Online - full text ed.
Published by: Instituto Nacional de Estadistica, Rio Negro 1520, Montevideo, 11100, Uruguay. TEL 598-2-9027303.

USUAL WEEKLY EARNINGS OF WAGE AND SALARY WORKERS. *see* BUSINESS AND ECONOMICS—Economic Situation And Conditions

UTAH AGRICULTURAL STATISTICS. *see* AGRICULTURE—Abstracting, Bibliographies, Statistics

UTAH CROP PROGRESS & CONDITIONS. *see* AGRICULTURE—Abstracting, Bibliographies, Statistics

VAELFAERD; SCB's tidskrift om arbetsliv, demografi och vaelfaerd. *see* PUBLIC ADMINISTRATION—Abstracting, Bibliographies, Statistics

VAND I TAL. *see* WATER RESOURCES—Abstracting, Bibliographies, Statistics

VANUATU. STATISTICS OFFICE. MONETARY AND BANKING STATISTICS. *see* BUSINESS AND ECONOMICS—Abstracting, Bibliographies, Statistics

VANUATU. STATISTICS OFFICE. REPORT OF THE AGRICULTURAL CENSUS. *see* AGRICULTURE—Abstracting, Bibliographies, Statistics

VANUATU. STATISTICS OFFICE. REPORT ON SMALL HOLDER AGRICULTURE SURVEY. *see* AGRICULTURE—Abstracting, Bibliographies, Statistics

VANUATU. STATISTICS OFFICE. STATISTICAL INDICATORS. *see* BUSINESS AND ECONOMICS—Abstracting, Bibliographies, Statistics

VENEZUELA. MINISTERIO DE AGRICULTURA Y CRIA. BOLETIN DE PRECIOS DE PRODUCTOS AGROPECUARIOS. *see* AGRICULTURE—Abstracting, Bibliographies, Statistics

VENEZUELA. MINISTERIO DE AGRICULTURA Y CRIA. DIRECCION DE ECONOMICA Y ESTADISTICA AGROPECUARIA. ANUARIO ESTADISTICO AGROPECUARIO. *see* AGRICULTURE—Abstracting, Bibliographies, Statistics

VENEZUELA. MINISTERIO DE AGRICULTURA Y CRIA. DIRECCION DE PLANIFICACION Y ESTADISTICA. ESTADISTICAS AGROPECUARIAS DE LAS ENTIDADES FEDERALES. *see* AGRICULTURE—Abstracting, Bibliographies, Statistics

VENEZUELA. MINISTERIO DE ENERGIA Y MINAS. ANUARIO ESTADISTICO MINERO. *see* MINES AND MINING INDUSTRY—Abstracting, Bibliographies, Statistics

VENEZUELA. MINISTERIO DE ENERGIA Y MINAS. APENDICE ESTADISTICO. *see* ENERGY—Abstracting, Bibliographies, Statistics

VENEZUELA. MINISTERIO DE ENERGIA Y MINAS. COMPENDIO ESTADISTICO DEL SECTOR ELECTRICO. *see* ENERGY—Abstracting, Bibliographies, Statistics

VENEZUELA. MINISTERIO DE ENERGIA Y MINAS. PETROLEO Y OTROS DATOS ESTADISTICOS. *see* PETROLEUM AND GAS—Abstracting, Bibliographies, Statistics

VENEZUELAN PETROLEUM INDUSTRY. STATISTICAL DATA. *see* PETROLEUM AND GAS—Abstracting, Bibliographies, Statistics

VERKEERSVEILIGHEID. *see* TRANSPORTATION—Abstracting, Bibliographies, Statistics

VERMONT CITIES & COUNTIES GRAPHIC PERFORMANCE ANALYSIS. *see* PUBLIC ADMINISTRATION—Abstracting, Bibliographies, Statistics

VEROEFFENTLICHUNGEN DER LANDESFACHSTELLE FUER ARCHIVE UND OEFFENTLICHE BIBLIOTHEKEN IM BRANDENBURGISCHEN LANDESHAUPTARCHIV. *see* HISTORY—Abstracting, Bibliographies, Statistics

VERZEICHNIS BERATUNGSSTELLEN DER OEFFENTLICHEN UND FREIEN WOHLFAHRTSPFLEGE IN BAYERN. *see* SOCIAL SERVICES AND WELFARE—Abstracting, Bibliographies, Statistics

VINNUMARKADUR/LABOR MARKET STATISTICS. *see* BUSINESS AND ECONOMICS—Abstracting, Bibliographies, Statistics

VIRGIN ISLANDS (U.S.). DEPARTMENT OF LABOR. BUREAU OF LABOR STATISTICS. LABOR MARKET REVIEW. *see* BUSINESS AND ECONOMICS—Abstracting, Bibliographies, Statistics

VIRGINIA CITIES & COUNTIES GRAPHIC PERFORMANCE ANALYSIS. *see* PUBLIC ADMINISTRATION—Abstracting, Bibliographies, Statistics

VITAL STATISTICS OF IOWA. *see* POPULATION STUDIES—Abstracting, Bibliographies, Statistics

VITAL STATISTICS OF THE UNITED STATES. *see* PUBLIC HEALTH AND SAFETY—Abstracting, Bibliographies, Statistics

VITAL STATISTICS ON CONGRESS. *see* PUBLIC ADMINISTRATION—Abstracting, Bibliographies, Statistics

VOLKSWIRTSCHAFTLICHE GESAMTRECHUNGEN FUER BAYERN. *see* PUBLIC ADMINISTRATION—Abstracting, Bibliographies, Statistics

VOPROSY STATISTIKI/STATISTICAL STUDIES. *see* BUSINESS AND ECONOMICS—Abstracting, Bibliographies, Statistics

310 382 BGR ISSN 1311-2260
HF227
VUNSHNA TURGOVIA NA REPUBLIKA BULGARIA/FOREIGN TRADE IN THE REPUBLIC OF BULGARIA. Text in Bulgarian, English. a. BGL 18.37 (effective 2002). 300 p./no.
Published by: Natsionalen Statisticheski Institut/National Statistical Institute, ul P Volov, # 2, Sofia, 1038, Bulgaria. FAX 359-2-9803319, publikacii@nsi.bg, http://www.nsi.bg. **Dist. by:** Sofia Books, ul Silivria 16, Sofia 1404, Bulgaria. TEL 359-2-9586257, info@sofiabooks-bg.com, http://www.sofiabooks-bg.com.

VYBRANE EKONOMICKE VYSLEDKY MALYCH A STREDNICH SUBJEKTU C R V LETECH (YEARS). *see* BUSINESS AND ECONOMICS—Abstracting, Bibliographies, Statistics

VYROBA VYBRANYCH VYROBKU V PRUMYSLU C R ZA ROK (YEAR). (Ceska Republika) *see* BUSINESS AND ECONOMICS—Abstracting, Bibliographies, Statistics

W T O WORLD TOURISM BAROMETER. *see* TRAVEL AND TOURISM—Abstracting, Bibliographies, Statistics

WAHL ZUM BAYERISCHEN LANDTAG. *see* PUBLIC ADMINISTRATION—Abstracting, Bibliographies, Statistics

WAIKATO DISTRICT CRIME STATISTICS. *see* CRIMINOLOGY AND LAW ENFORCEMENT—Abstracting, Bibliographies, Statistics

WAITEMATA DISTRICT CRIME STATISTICS. *see* CRIMINOLOGY AND LAW ENFORCEMENT—Abstracting, Bibliographies, Statistics

WASHINGTON (STATE). DEPARTMENT OF REVENUE. RESEARCH DIVISION. PROPERTY TAX STATISTICS. *see* BUSINESS AND ECONOMICS—Abstracting, Bibliographies, Statistics

WASHINGTON (STATE). DEPARTMENT OF REVENUE. RESEARCH DIVISION. TAX STATISTICS. *see* BUSINESS AND ECONOMICS—Abstracting, Bibliographies, Statistics

WASHINGTON (STATE). EMPLOYMENT SECURITY DEPARTMENT. AFFIRMATIVE ACTION INFORMATION. *see* BUSINESS AND ECONOMICS—Abstracting, Bibliographies, Statistics

WASHINGTON AGRICULTURAL STATISTICS. *see* AGRICULTURE—Abstracting, Bibliographies, Statistics

WASHINGTON CITIES & COUNTIES GRAPHIC PERFORMANCE ANALYSIS. *see* PUBLIC ADMINISTRATION—Abstracting, Bibliographies, Statistics

WASHINGTON CROP WEATHER. *see* AGRICULTURE—Abstracting, Bibliographies, Statistics

WATER TREATMENT IN CHINA. *see* CHEMISTRY—Abstracting, Bibliographies, Statistics

WEATHER AND CROPS. NEW YORK STATE. *see* AGRICULTURE—Abstracting, Bibliographies, Statistics

WEATHER & CROPS. VIRGINIA. *see* AGRICULTURE—Abstracting, Bibliographies, Statistics

WEATHER AND FORECASTING. *see* METEOROLOGY

WEATHER CROP. *see* AGRICULTURE—Abstracting, Bibliographies, Statistics

WEEKLY CROP & WEATHER. *see* AGRICULTURE—Abstracting, Bibliographies, Statistics

WEEKLY CROP & WEATHER ROUNDUP. *see* AGRICULTURE—Abstracting, Bibliographies, Statistics

WEEKLY WEATHER CROP REPORT. *see* AGRICULTURE—Abstracting, Bibliographies, Statistics

WELLINGTON DISTRICT CRIME STATISTICS. *see* CRIMINOLOGY AND LAW ENFORCEMENT—Abstracting, Bibliographies, Statistics

WELSH AGRICULTURAL STATISTICS. *see* AGRICULTURE—Abstracting, Bibliographies, Statistics

WELSH HOUSE CONDITION SURVEY. *see* HOUSING AND URBAN PLANNING—Abstracting, Bibliographies, Statistics

WELSH HOUSING STATISTICS. *see* HOUSING AND URBAN PLANNING—Abstracting, Bibliographies, Statistics

WELSH LOCAL GOVERNMENT FINANCIAL STATISTICS. *see* PUBLIC ADMINISTRATION—Abstracting, Bibliographies, Statistics

WEST BENGAL. ANNUAL FINANCIAL STATEMENT (BUDGET). *see* BUSINESS AND ECONOMICS—Abstracting, Bibliographies, Statistics

THE WEST CITIES & COUNTIES GRAPHIC PERFORMANCE ANALYSIS. *see* PUBLIC ADMINISTRATION—Abstracting, Bibliographies, Statistics

WEST VIRGINIA CITIES & COUNTIES GRAPHIC PERFORMANCE ANALYSIS. *see* PUBLIC ADMINISTRATION—Abstracting, Bibliographies, Statistics

WEST VIRGINIA COAL FACTS. *see* MINES AND MINING INDUSTRY—Abstracting, Bibliographies, Statistics

WEST VIRGINIA RESEARCH LEAGUE. STATISTICAL HANDBOOK; a digest of selected data on state and local government in West Virginia. *see* PUBLIC ADMINISTRATION—Abstracting, Bibliographies, Statistics

WESTERN EUROPEAN MARKET & MEDIA FACT. *see* COMMUNICATIONS—Abstracting, Bibliographies, Statistics

WHO'S MINDING THE KIDS? (PRINT); child care arrangements. *see* CHILDREN AND YOUTH—Abstracting, Bibliographies, Statistics

WIEN IN ZAHLEN; Ausgabe (Year). *see* BUSINESS AND ECONOMICS—Abstracting, Bibliographies, Statistics

WILEY INTERDISCIPLINARY REVIEWS. COMPUTATIONAL STATISTICS. *see* MATHEMATICS—Computer Applications

001.422 USA ISSN 1942-9088
WILEY SERIES IN SURVEY METHODOLOGY. Text in English. 200?. irreg., latest 2010, May. price varies. back issues avail. **Document type:** *Monographic series, Academic/Scholarly.*
Published by: John Wiley & Sons, Inc., 111 River St, Hoboken, NJ 07030. TEL 201-748-6000, FAX 201-748-6088, info@wiley.com.

WIRTSCHAFT UND STATISTIK. *see* BUSINESS AND ECONOMICS

WISCONSIN CITIES & COUNTIES GRAPHIC PERFORMANCE ANALYSIS. *see* PUBLIC ADMINISTRATION—Abstracting, Bibliographies, Statistics

WISCONSIN. DIVISION OF CORRECTIONS. OFFICE OF INFORMATION MANAGEMENT. ADMISSIONS TO JUVENILE INSTITUTIONS. *see* CRIMINOLOGY AND LAW ENFORCEMENT—Abstracting, Bibliographies, Statistics

WOMEN IN AUSTRALIA. *see* WOMEN'S STUDIES—Abstracting, Bibliographies, Statistics

WOMEN IN THE PROFESSIONS SURVEY REPORT. *see* OCCUPATIONS AND CAREERS—Abstracting, Bibliographies, Statistics

WORK EXPERIENCE OF THE POPULATION. *see* OCCUPATIONS AND CAREERS—Abstracting, Bibliographies, Statistics

WORKING PAPERS IN ECONOMICS AND STATISTICS. *see* BUSINESS AND ECONOMICS

WORKING PAPERS IN ECONOMICS, MATHEMATICS & STATISTICS. *see* BUSINESS AND ECONOMICS

WORKING RESULTS. *see* AGRICULTURE—Abstracting, Bibliographies, Statistics

WORKPLACE INJURIES AND ILLNESSES IN (YEAR). *see* OCCUPATIONAL HEALTH AND SAFETY—Abstracting, Bibliographies, Statistics

WORLD COUNCIL OF CREDIT UNIONS. ANNUAL AND STATISTICAL REPORT. *see* BUSINESS AND ECONOMICS—Banking And Finance

WORLD DRYWALL & BUILDING PLASTERS. *see* BUILDING AND CONSTRUCTION—Abstracting, Bibliographies, Statistics

WORLD FLEET STATISTICS. *see* TRANSPORTATION—Abstracting, Bibliographies, Statistics

WORLD METAL STATISTICS. *see* METALLURGY—Abstracting, Bibliographies, Statistics

WORLD METAL STATISTICS. YEARBOOK. *see* METALLURGY—Abstracting, Bibliographies, Statistics

WORLD MINERAL PRODUCTION. *see* MINES AND MINING INDUSTRY—Abstracting, Bibliographies, Statistics

WORLD NICKEL STATISTICS (ONLINE). *see* METALLURGY—Abstracting, Bibliographies, Statistics

WORLD RUBBER STATISTICS HANDBOOK. *see* RUBBER—Abstracting, Bibliographies, Statistics

WORLD SHIPPING STATISTICS (YEAR). *see* TRANSPORTATION—Abstracting, Bibliographies, Statistics

WORLD STEEL EXPORTS. *see* METALLURGY—Abstracting, Bibliographies, Statistics

WORLD STEEL EXPORTS - STAINLESS, HIGH SPEED & OTHER ALLOY. *see* METALLURGY—Abstracting, Bibliographies, Statistics

310 CHN
XINJIANG PRODUCTION AND CONSTRUCTION CORP. STATISTICAL YEARBOOK/XINJIANG SHENGCHAN JIANSHE BINGTUAN TONGJI NIANJIAN. Text in Chinese. a. CNY 50.
Published by: (Xinjian Production and Construction Corp.), Zhongguo Tongji Chubanshe/China Statistics Press, 6, Xi San Huan Nan Lu Jia, Beijing, 100073, China. TEL 86-10-8217162.

YEAR BOOK OF LABOUR STATISTICS/ANNUAIRE DES STATISTIQUES DU TRAVAIL/ANUARIO DE ESTADISTICAS DEL TRABAJO. *see* BUSINESS AND ECONOMICS—Abstracting, Bibliographies, Statistics

YEARBOOK OF AGRICULTURAL STATISTICS OF BANGLADESH. *see* AGRICULTURE—Abstracting, Bibliographies, Statistics

YINGYONG GAILU TONGJI/CHINESE JOURNAL OF APPLIED PROBABILITY AND STATISTICS. *see* MATHEMATICS

317.17 CAN ISSN 0832-669X
YUKON FACT SHEET. Text in English. 1986. a.
Published by: (Yukon Government, Bureau of Statistics), Yukon Government, Executive Council Office, Box 2703, Whitehorse, YT Y1A 2C6, Canada. TEL 867-667-5393, 800-661-0408, FAX 867-393-6202, ecoinfo@gov.yk.ca.

310 CAN ISSN 1195-812X
YUKON MONTHLY STATISTICAL REVIEW. Text in English. 199?. m.
Indexed: C05.
Published by: Yukon Government, Bureau of Statistics, P O Box 2703, Whitehorse, YT, Canada. TEL 867-667-5640, 800-661-0408, FAX 867-393-6203, ybsinfo@gov.yk.ca, http://www.gov.yk.ca/depts/eco/stats/index.html.

310 BGR ISSN 1311-2309
ZAETOST I BEZRABOTITSA/EMPLOYMENT AND UNEMPLOYMENT. Text in Bulgarian, English. q. BGL 35.28 (effective 2002). 120 p./no.; **Document type:** *Bulletin.*
Published by: Natsionalen Statisticheski Institut/National Statistical Institute, ul P Volov, # 2, Sofia, 1038, Bulgaria. FAX 359-2-9803319, publikacii@nsi.bg, http://www.nsi.bg.

ZAMBIA. CENTRAL STATISTICAL OFFICE. AGRICULTURAL AND PASTORAL PRODUCTION (COMMERCIAL AND NON-COMMERCIAL). *see* AGRICULTURE—Abstracting, Bibliographies, Statistics

ZAMBIA. CENTRAL STATISTICAL OFFICE. AGRICULTURAL AND PASTORAL PRODUCTION (COMMERCIAL FARMS). *see* AGRICULTURE—Abstracting, Bibliographies, Statistics

ZAMBIA. CENTRAL STATISTICAL OFFICE. AGRICULTURAL AND PASTORAL PRODUCTION (NON-COMMERCIAL). *see* AGRICULTURE—Abstracting, Bibliographies, Statistics

ZAMBIA. CENTRAL STATISTICAL OFFICE. BALANCE OF PAYMENTS STATISTICS. *see* BUSINESS AND ECONOMICS—Abstracting, Bibliographies, Statistics

ZAMBIA. CENTRAL STATISTICAL OFFICE. CONSUMER PRICE STATISTICS. *see* BUSINESS AND ECONOMICS—Abstracting, Bibliographies, Statistics

ZAMBIA. CENTRAL STATISTICAL OFFICE. FINANCIAL STATISTICS OF GOVERNMENT SECTOR (ECONOMIC AND FUNCTIONAL ANALYSIS). *see* PUBLIC ADMINISTRATION—Abstracting, Bibliographies, Statistics

ZAMBIA. CENTRAL STATISTICAL OFFICE. FISHERIES STATISTICS (NATURAL WATERS). *see* FISH AND FISHERIES—Abstracting, Bibliographies, Statistics

ZAMBIA. CENTRAL STATISTICAL OFFICE. INDUSTRY MONOGRAPHS. *see* BUSINESS AND ECONOMICS—Abstracting, Bibliographies, Statistics

316 ZMB ISSN 0027-0377
HC517.R42
ZAMBIA. CENTRAL STATISTICAL OFFICE. MONTHLY DIGEST OF STATISTICS. Text in English. 1964. m. USD 32. stat. **Document type:** *Government.* **Description:** For the study of social and economic conditions in Zambia.
Published by: Central Statistical Office, PO Box 31908, Lusaka, Zambia. TEL 260-1-211231.

ZAMBIA. CENTRAL STATISTICAL OFFICE. NATIONAL ACCOUNTS. *see* PUBLIC ADMINISTRATION—Abstracting, Bibliographies, Statistics

ZAMBIA. CENTRAL STATISTICAL OFFICE. QUARTERLY AGRICULTURAL STATISTICAL BULLETIN. *see* AGRICULTURE—Abstracting, Bibliographies, Statistics

316 ZMB ISSN 0084-4551
HA1977.R48
ZAMBIA. CENTRAL STATISTICAL OFFICE. STATISTICAL YEAR BOOK. Text in English. 1967. a. ZMK 3. **Document type:** *Government.*
Related titles: Microfiche ed.: (from PQC).
Published by: Central Statistical Office, PO Box 31908, Lusaka, Zambia. TEL 260-1-211231.

ZAMBIA. CENTRAL STATISTICAL OFFICE. TRANSPORT STATISTICS. *see* TRANSPORTATION—Abstracting, Bibliographies, Statistics

ZAMBIA. CENTRAL STATISTICAL OFFICE. VITAL STATISTICS. *see* POPULATION STUDIES—Abstracting, Bibliographies, Statistics

ZAMBIA. MINISTRY OF AGRICULTURE, FOOD AND FISHERIES. ANNUAL AGRICULTURAL STATISTICAL BULLETIN. *see* AGRICULTURE—Abstracting, Bibliographies, Statistics

310 304.63 304.64 BGR ISSN 0324-1920
RA407.5.B8
ZDRAVEOPAZVANE. Text in Bulgarian. a. BGL 8.88 (effective 2002). 170 p./no.; **Description:** Contains information on the following demographic factors: reasons of death and disease of the population as well as the information about the health network and medical personnel in health facilities in Bulgaria.
Published by: Natsionalen Statisticheski Institut/National Statistical Institute, ul P Volov, # 2, Sofia, 1038, Bulgaria. FAX 359-2-9803319, publikacii@nsi.bg, http://www.nsi.bg. **Dist. by:** Sofia Books, ul Silvria 16, Sofia 1404, Bulgaria. TEL 359-2-9586257, info@sofiabooks-bg.com, http://www.sofiabooks-bg.com.

ZDRAVOOKHRANENIE V ROSSII (YEAR). *see* PUBLIC HEALTH AND SAFETY—Abstracting, Bibliographies, Statistics

310 BGR
ZHILISHCHEN FOND. Text in Bulgarian. a. BGL 4.56 (effective 2002).
Related titles: Diskette ed.
Published by: Natsionalen Statisticheski Institut/National Statistical Institute, ul P Volov, # 2, Sofia, 1038, Bulgaria. FAX 359-2-9803319, publikacii@nsi.bg, http://www.nsi.bg. **Dist. by:** Sofia Books, ul Silivria 16, Sofia 1404, Bulgaria. TEL 359-2-9586257, info@sofiabooks-bg.com, http://www.sofiabooks-bg.com.

ZHONGGUO KEJI TONGJI NIANJIAN/CHINA STATISTICAL YEARBOOK ON SCIENCE AND TECHNOLOGY. *see* SCIENCES: COMPREHENSIVE WORKS—Abstracting, Bibliographies, Statistics

315 CHN ISSN 1002-4557
HA1
ZHONGGUO TONGJI/CHINA STATISTICS. Text in Chinese. 1951. m. USD 49.20 (effective 2009). back issues avail. **Document type:** *Journal, Academic/Scholarly.* **Description:** Covers government statistical organization, practice and research on statistics.
Related titles: Online - full text ed.
—East View.
Published by: (Guojia Tongji Ju/State Statistical Bureau), Zhongguo Tongji Chubanshe/China Statistics Press, 6, Xi San Huan Nan Lu Jia, Beijing, 100073, China. TEL 86-10-63262285. Circ: 150,000.

310 TWN ISSN 0529-6528
ZHONGGUO TONGJI XUEBAO. Text in Chinese. 1963. bi-m. **Document type:** *Journal, Academic/Scholarly.*
Related titles: English ed.: Chinese Statistical Association. Journal. ISSN 1560-9154.
Indexed: CIS, EconLit, JEL.
Published by: Zhongguo Tongji Xueshe/Chinese Statistical Association, Institute of Statistical Science, Academia Sinica, 128, Academia Rd. Sec. 2, Taipei, 115, Taiwan. TEL 886-2-27835611 ext 429.

ZHUHAI TONGJI NIANJIAN (YEAR)/ZHUHAI STATISTICAL YEARBOOK. *see* BUSINESS AND ECONOMICS—Abstracting, Bibliographies, Statistics

ZIMBABWE. CENTRAL STATISTICAL OFFICE. CENSUS OF PRODUCTION. *see* BUSINESS AND ECONOMICS—Abstracting, Bibliographies, Statistics

ZIMBABWE. CENTRAL STATISTICAL OFFICE. FACTS AND FIGURES. *see* BUSINESS AND ECONOMICS—Abstracting, Bibliographies, Statistics

ZIMBABWE. CENTRAL STATISTICAL OFFICE. NATIONAL ACCOUNTS. *see* BUSINESS AND ECONOMICS—Abstracting, Bibliographies, Statistics

316 ZWE ISSN 1012-649X
ZIMBABWE. CENTRAL STATISTICAL OFFICE. QUARTERLY DIGEST OF STATISTICS. Key Title: Quarterly Digest of Statistics - Central Statistical Office. Text in English. 1964. q. ZWD 189.50 in Africa; ZWD 250.20 in Europe; ZWD 316 elsewhere. **Document type:** *Government.*
Supersedes: Zimbabwe. Central Statistical Office. Monthly Digest of Statistics (0556-8706)
Published by: Central Statistical Office, Causeway, PO Box 8063, Harare, Zimbabwe. TEL 263-4-706681, FAX 263-4-728529. Circ: 1,100.

ZIMBABWE. CENTRAL STATISTICAL OFFICE. QUARTERLY MIGRATION AND TOURIST STATISTICS. *see* TRAVEL AND TOURISM—Abstracting, Bibliographies, Statistics

ZIMBABWE. CENTRAL STATISTICAL OFFICE. QUARTERLY POULTRY CENSUS. *see* AGRICULTURE—Abstracting, Bibliographies, Statistics

ZIMBABWE. CENTRAL STATISTICAL OFFICE. STATISTICAL YEARBOOK. *see* BUSINESS AND ECONOMICS—Abstracting, Bibliographies, Statistics

ZIMBABWE. REGISTRAR OF INSURANCE. REPORT. *see* INSURANCE—Abstracting, Bibliographies, Statistics

ZOOM SANTE. *see* PUBLIC HEALTH AND SAFETY—Abstracting, Bibliographies, Statistics

SURGERY

see MEDICAL SCIENCES—Surgery

S

TAXATION

see BUSINESS AND ECONOMICS—Public Finance, Taxation

TEACHING METHODS AND CURRICULUM

see EDUCATION—Teaching Methods And Curriculum

TECHNOLOGY: COMPREHENSIVE WORKS

600 USA ISSN 1066-3878
A B Q CORRESPONDENT. Text in English. 1985. bi-m. USD 30 (effective 2001). 2 p./no.; back issues avail. **Document type:** *Newsletter, Consumer.* **Description:** Emphasizes technology and its social impact.
Related titles: Online - full text ed.: ISSN 1087-2302. 1985.
Published by: A B Q Communications Corporation, PO Box 1432, Corrales, NM 87048. TEL 505-897-0822, FAX 505-898-6525. Ed. Nelson B Winkless III. Pub. Nelson B. Winkless III. Circ: 120 (controlled).

A F P SCIENCES; bulletin information scientifique, technique, medicale. *see* MEDICAL SCIENCES

600 DEU
A I R MAIL. Text in German. q. **Document type:** *Journal, Trade.*
Media: Online - full content.
Published by: Aachener Institute fuer Rohstofftechnik, Wuellnerstr 2, Aachen, 52056, Germany. TEL 49-241-8094948, FAX 49-241-8092227. Ed. Sabine Backus.

600 IND ISSN 0975-9514
▼ **A K G E C JOURNAL OF TECHNOLOGY.** Text in English. 2010. s-a. **Document type:** *Journal, Academic/Scholarly.*
Related titles: Online - full text ed.: free (effective 2011).
Published by: Ajay Kumar Garg Engineering College, 27th KM Stone, Delhi-Hapur Bypass Rd, Post Adhyatmik Nagar, Ghaziabad, Uttar Pradesh 201 009, India. TEL 91-120-3251275, akrecor@akgec.org.

600 USA ISSN 1935-2298
A M M T I A C QUARTERLY. (Advanced Materials, Manufacturing and Testing Information Analysis Center) Text in English. 1997. q. free to qualified personnel (effective 2007). **Document type:** *Newsletter, Trade.* **Description:** Provides for the rapid dissemination of information in the following categories: ceramic and ceramic composites, organic structural materials and organic matrix composites, monolithic metal alloys and metal matrix composites, electronic/optical/photonic materials.
Formerly (until 2006): A M P T I A C Quarterly
Related titles: Online - full text ed.: ISSN 1945-5437.
Indexed: APA, C&ISA, CorrAb, E&CAJ, EEA, ESPM, EnvEAb, SolStAb, WAA.
—Linda Hall.
Published by: Advanced Materials, Manufacturing, and Testing Information Analysis Center, 201 Mill St, Rome, NY 13440. TEL 315-339-7019, FAX 315-339-7107. Ed. Benjamin Craig. Circ: 15,000 (controlled).

▼ **A N U JOURNAL OF ENGINEERING AND TECHNOLOGY.** *see* ENGINEERING

600 AUT
A P A - JOURNAL. INNOVATION. Text in German. w. EUR 380 combined subscription for print & online eds. (effective 2003). **Document type:** *Journal, Trade.*
Related titles: Online - full text ed.
Published by: Austria Presse Agentur, Gunoldstr 14, Vienna, W 1190, Austria. TEL 43-1-360600, FAX 43-1-360603099, kundenservice@apa.at, http://www.apa.at.

A S E A N JOURNAL ON SCIENCE AND TECHNOLOGY FOR DEVELOPMENT. *see* SCIENCES: COMPREHENSIVE WORKS

600 USA ISSN 0257-5973
A T A S BULLETIN. (Advance Technology Alert System) Text in English. 1984. s-a.
Published by: United Nations, Centre for Science and Technology for Development, One United Nations Plaza, New York, NY 10017. TEL 212-963-8600, FAX 212-963-4116.

A T A S INFORMATION TECHNOLOGY FOR DEVELOPMENT. *see* BUSINESS AND ECONOMICS—International Development And Assistance

600 ESP ISSN 1132-9327
A T. ACTUALIDAD TECNOLOGICA; periodico de equipos y tecnologia. Text in Spanish. 1988. 11/yr. adv. bk.rev. illus.; tr.lit. back issues avail. **Document type:** *Newspaper, Trade.* **Description:** Reviews products and news in many technological areas, along with professional publications and conferences.
Formerly (until 1992): Actualidad Tecnologica (1132-6492)
Related titles: Online - full text ed.
Published by: Reed Business Information SA (Subsidiary of: Reed Business Information International), C Albarracin 34, Madrid, 28037, Spain. TEL 34-91-4402920, FAX 34-91-4402931, info@mad@rbi.es, http://www.alcion.es/. Ed. Mar Canas Asanza. adv.: color page EUR 2,335. Circ: 30,000.

A T E A JOURNAL. (American Technical Education Association) *see* EDUCATION

600 620 AUS ISSN 1326-8708
A T S E FOCUS. Text in English. 1978. bi-m. **Document type:** *Journal, Academic/Scholarly.* **Description:** Promotes the application of scientific and engineering knowledge for practical purposes.
Formerly (until 1995): A T S Focus (0727-3096)
Indexed: INIS AtomInd.
—Linda Hall.
Published by: Australian Academy of Technological Sciences and Engineering, Ian McLennan House, 197 Royal Parade, Parkville, Melbourne, VIC 3052, Australia. TEL 61-3-93401200, FAX 61-3-93478237. Ed. Bill Mackey.

600 620 AUS ISSN 1838-0921
▼ **A T S E FOCUS (INTERNATIONAL EDITION).** Text in English. 2009. irreg. (2-3/yr). **Document type:** *Journal, Trade.* **Description:** Aims to highlight Australia's relationship with the international community in the areas of science and technology and the Academy's role in engaging with partner countries.
Related titles: Online - full text ed.: free (effective 2011).
Published by: Australian Academy of Technological Sciences and Engineering, GPO Box 4055, Melbourne, VIC 3001, Australia. TEL 61-3-98640900, FAX 61-3-98640930, info@atse.org.au. Ed. Bill Mackey.

500 LSO
A T S NEWSLETTER. Text in English. 1987. 2/yr. **Document type:** *Newsletter.*
Indexed: PLESA.
Published by: Appropriate Technology Section, PO Box 686, Maseru, 100, Lesotho.

606.0489 DNK ISSN 1603-3078
A T V NYT (ONLINE). (Akademiet for de Tekniske Videnskaber) Variant title: Akademiet for de Tekniske Videnskaber. Nyt (Online). Text in Danish. 2001. 5/yr. free (effective 2004). back issues avail. **Document type:** *Newsletter, Trade.*
Media: Online - full content.
Published by: Akademiet for de Tekniske Videnskaber/Danish Academy of Technical Sciences, Lundtoftevej 266, Lyngby, 2800, Denmark. TEL 45-45-881311, FAX 45-45-881351, atvmail@atv.dk. Ed. Lasse Skovby Rasmussen.

A T Z ELEKTRONIK. (Automobiltechnische Zeitschrift) *see* TRANSPORTATION—Automobiles

AACHENER BEITRAEGE ZUR WISSENSCHAFTS- UND TECHNIKGESCHICHTE DES 20. JAHRHUNDERTS. *see* SCIENCES: COMPREHENSIVE WORKS

ACADEMIA DE STIINTE A REPUBLICII MOLDOVA. BULETINUL. FIZICA SI TEHNICA. *see* PHYSICS

ACADEMIC OPEN INTERNET JOURNAL. *see* SCIENCES: COMPREHENSIVE WORKS

600 SRB ISSN 0374-0781
ACADEMIE SERBE DES SCIENCES ET DES ARTS. CLASSE DES SCIENCES TECHNIQUES.BULLETIN. Text in French. 1963. irreg.
Related titles: ♦ Serbo-Croatian ed.: Srpska Akademija Nauka i Umetnosti. Odeljenje Tehnickih Nauka. Glas. ISSN 0081-3974.
Indexed: A28, APA, BrCerAb, C&ISA, CA/WCA, CIA, CerAb, CivEngAb, CorrAb, E&CAJ, E11, EEA, EMA, ESPM, EnvEAb, GeoRef, H15, Inspec, M&TEA, M09, MBF, METADEX, RefZh, SolStAb, T04, WAA.
—INIST, Linda Hall.
Published by: Srpska Akademija Nauka i Umetnosti/Serbian Academy of Arts and Sciences, Knez Mihailova 35, Belgrade, 11000. TEL 381-11-2027154, FAX 381-11-2027178, izdavacka@sanu.ac.rs, http://www.sanu.ac.rs.

620 DEU ISSN 1862-4200
ACATECH BERICHTET UND EMPFIEHLT. Text in German. 2006. irreg. price varies. **Document type:** *Monographic series, Academic/Scholarly.*
Published by: acatech - Konvent fuer Technikwissenschaften der Union der Deutschen Akademien der Wissenschaften e.V., Hofgartenstr 2, Munich, 80539, Germany. TEL 49-89-5203090, FAX 49-89-5203099, info@acatech.de, http://www.acatech.de.

ACCESSWORLD (ONLINE EDITION); technology and people who are blind or visually impaired. *see* HANDICAPPED—Visually Impaired

686.22 HRV ISSN 0353-4707
CODEN: AGGRER
ACTA GRAPHICA; journal of printing science and graphic communications. Text in English. 1989. q. **Document type:** *Journal, Academic/Scholarly.* **Description:** Covers entire field of printing and graphic design, especially all aspects of research and development.
Related titles: Online - full text ed.: free (effective 2011).
Indexed: A26, ABIPC, Inspec.
—AskIEEE.
Published by: Acta Graphica Publishers, Getaldiceva 2, PO Box 225, Zagreb, 41001, Croatia. TEL 385-1-2371080, FAX 385-1-2371077, acta.graphica@grf.hr.

600 SRB ISSN 1450-7188
CODEN: APTEFF
➤ **ACTA PERIODICA TECHNOLOGICA.** Text in English; Summaries in Serbian, English. 1967. a. bibl. **Document type:** *Journal, Academic/Scholarly.* **Description:** Publishes articles from all branches of technology.
Formerly (until 1999): Univerzitet u Novom Sadu. Tehnoloski Fakultet. Zbornik Radova (0550-2187)
Related titles: Online - full text ed.: free (effective 2011).
Indexed: CIN, ChemAb, ChemTitl, RefZh, SCOPUS.
—BLDSC (0644.420000), CASDDS.
Published by: Univerzitet u Novom Sadu, Tehnoloski Fakultet, Zavod za Tehnologiju Zita i Brasna/University in Novy Sad, Institut for Cereal and Flour Technology, Bul Cara Lazara 1, Novi Sad, 21000. TEL 381-21-350133, FAX 381-21-450413, nscereal@eunet.yu. Ed., R&P Sonja Dilas.

600 HUN ISSN 1785-8860
T1
ACTA POLYTECHNICA HUNGARICA. Text in English. 2004. s-a. **Document type:** *Journal, Academic/Scholarly.*
Related titles: Online - full text ed.: free (effective 2011).
Indexed: SCI, W07.
Published by: Obudai Egyetem/Obuda University http://www.uni-obuda.hu.

600 BRA ISSN 1806-2563
T1
➤ **ACTA SCIENTIARUM. TECHNOLOGY.** Text in Portuguese. 1974. q. **Document type:** *Journal, Academic/Scholarly.*
Supersedes in part (in 2003): Acta Scientiarum (1415-6814); Which was formerly (until 1998): Revista U N I M A R (0100-9354)
Related titles: Online - full text ed.: ISSN 1807-8664. free (effective 2011).
Indexed: A26, A34, A36, A37, A38, AgrForAb, B25, BA, BIOSIS Prev, C01, C25, C30, CA, CABA, D01, E12, F08, F11, F12, FCA, GH, H16, I04, I05, I11, LT, MaizeAb, MycolAb, N02, N03, N04, O01, OR, P32, P37, PGegResA, PHN&I, PN&I, R07, R11, R12, RRTA, RefZh, S12, S13, S16, S17, SCI, SCOPUS, SoyAb, T02, T05, TAR, VS, W07, W11, Z02.
Published by: Universidade Estadual de Maringa, Editora da Universidade - Eduem, Av Colombo, 5790 - Zona 7, Maringa, Parana 87020-900, Brazil. TEL 55-44-2614253, FAX 55-44-2222754, http://www.uem.br. Ed., R&P Alessandro de Lucca e Braccini.

600 FIN ISSN 0355-3213
CODEN: AUOTDY
➤ **ACTA UNIVERSITATIS OULUENSIS. SERIES C. TECHNICA.** Text in Multiple languages. 1971. irreg. price varies. back issues avail. **Document type:** *Monographic series, Academic/Scholarly.*
Related titles: Online - full text ed.: ISSN 1796-2226.
Indexed: GeoRef, INIS AtomInd.
Published by: Oulun Yliopisto, Julkaisupalvelut/University of Oulu. Publications Committee, Pentti Kaiteran Katu 1, PO Box 8000, Oulu, 90014, Finland. TEL 358-8-5531011, FAX 358-8-5534112, university.of.oulu@oulu.fi, http://www.oulu.fi. Eds. Hannu Heusala, Olli Vuolteenaho TEL 358-8-5375302.

➤ **ACTV8.** *see* CHILDREN AND YOUTH—For

▼ ➤ **ADVANCE JOURNAL OF FOOD SCIENCE AND TECHNOLOGY.** *see* NUTRITION AND DIETETICS

600 THA
ADVANCED TECHNOLOGY NEWSLETTER. Text in English. 1997. s-a. free. **Document type:** *Newsletter.*
Published by: (School of Advanced Technologies), Asian Institute of Technology, Klong Luang, PO Box 4, Pathum Thani, 12120, Thailand. TEL 66-2-524-5731, FAX 66-2-5745, deansat@ait.ac.th, http://www.sat.ait.ac.th.

ADVANCES IN COMPLEX SYSTEMS. *see* SCIENCES: COMPREHENSIVE WORKS

ADVANCES IN MATERIALS SCIENCE & TECHNOLOGY. *see* SCIENCES: COMPREHENSIVE WORKS

551.5 600 NLD ISSN 1878-9897
➤ **ADVANCES IN NATURAL AND TECHNOLOGICAL HAZARDS RESEARCH.** Text in English. 1993. irreg., latest vol.27, 2007. price varies. back issues avail. **Document type:** *Monographic series, Academic/Scholarly.*
Indexed: SpeleolAb.
—BLDSC (0709.460500), IE.
Published by: Springer Netherlands (Subsidiary of: Springer Science+Business Media), Van Godewijckstraat 30, Dordrecht, 3311 GX, Netherlands. TEL 31-78-6576050, FAX 31-78-6576474.

➤ **ADVANCES IN UNDERWATER TECHNOLOGY, OCEAN SCIENCE AND OFFSHORE ENGINEERING.** *see* EARTH SCIENCES—Oceanography

➤ **AERONAUTICS AND SPACE REPORT OF THE PRESIDENT. ACTIVITIES.** *see* SCIENCES: COMPREHENSIVE WORKS

➤ **AEROSPACE TESTING SEMINAR. PROCEEDINGS.** *see* AERONAUTICS AND SPACE FLIGHT

600 KEN ISSN 0958-6105
AFRICAN CENTRE FOR TECHNOLOGY STUDIES. RESEARCH SERIES. Text in English. 1989. irreg. **Document type:** *Monographic series, Academic/Scholarly.*
—CCC.
Published by: African Centre for Technology Studies, ICRAF Campus, United Nations Ave, Gigiri, PO Box 45917, Nairobi, Kenya. TEL 254-20-7224700, FAX 254-20-7224701, acts@cgiar.org, http://www.acts.or.ke.

AFRICAN JOURNAL OF MATHEMATICS, SCIENCE AND TECHNOLOGY EDUCATION. *see* MATHEMATICS

AFRICAN JOURNAL OF SCIENCE AND TECHNOLOGY/JOURNAL AFRICAIN DE SCIENCE ET TECHNOLOGIE. *see* SCIENCES: COMPREHENSIVE WORKS

600 330 GBR ISSN 0954-6782
AFRICAN REVIEW OF BUSINESS AND TECHNOLOGY. Text in English. 1964. 11/yr. GBP 73, USD 140, EUR 107 (effective 2010). adv. Supplement avail.; back issues avail. **Document type:** *Magazine, Trade.* **Description:** Designed for personnel in executive and managerial capacities in government, industry and commerce operating in Africa.
Former titles (until 1988): African Technical Review (0266-6677); (until 1983): West African Technical Review (0043-3039)
Related titles: Online - full text ed.
Indexed: B02, B15, B17, B18, G04, G08, I05, RICS.
—CIS. **CCC.**
Published by: Alain Charles Publishing Ltd., University House, 11-13 Lower Grosvenor Pl, London, SW1W 0EX, United Kingdom. TEL 44-20-78347676, FAX 44-20-79730076, post@alaincharles.com. Circ: 14,227.

AGHAM MINDANAW. *see* SCIENCES: COMPREHENSIVE WORKS

607.21 DNK ISSN 1901-8444
AKADEMIET FOR DE TEKNISKE VIDENSKABER. AARSRAPPORT. Text in Danish. 1955. a. back issues avail. **Document type:** *Yearbook, Trade.*
Former titles (until 2006): Akademiet for de Tekniske Videnskaber. Aarsberetning (1398-5043); (until 1997): Akademiet for de Tekniske Videnskaber. Beretning (0901-0564); (until 1979): A T V-Beretning (0105-9955); (until 1974): Virksomheden inden for ATV (0400-9428)
Related titles: Online - full text ed.; English ed.: ISSN 0908-3839.
Published by: Akademiet for de Tekniske Videnskaber/Danish Academy of Technical Sciences, Lundtoftevej 266, Lyngby, 2800, Denmark. TEL 45-45-881311, FAX 45-45-881351, atvmail@atv.dk.

620 ARM
TA4.A35 CODEN: IATNAK
AKADEMIYA NAUK ARMENII. IZVESTIYA. SERIYA TEKHNICHESKIKH NAUK/HAYASTANI HANRAPETUTIAN GITUTSUNNERI AZGAIN ACADEMIAY TEKHNIKAKAN GITUTSUNNERY HANDES. Text in Armenian, English, Russian. 1948. q. AMD 4,000 domestic; USD 7 foreign (effective 2004). charts. index. **Document type:** *Journal, Academic/Scholarly.*
Formerly: Akademiya Nauk Armyanskoi S.S.R. Izvestiya. Seriya Tekhnicheskikh Nauk (0002-306X)

Indexed: INIS AtomInd, Inspec, MathR, RefZh.
—CASDDS. **CCC.**
Published by: (State Engineering University of Armenia), Hayastany Guitoutyunnery Azgayin Academia/National Academy of Sciences of the Republic of Armenia, Marshal Bagramyan Ave 24b, Erevan, 375019, Armenia. TEL 374-1-524802, FAX 374-1-569281, http://www.sci.am. Ed. R M Martirossyan TEL 374-1-554629. Circ: 200 (paid); 200 (controlled).

600 CHE
AKTUELLE TECHNIK. Text in German. 1977. m. CHF 29; CHF 4 newsstand/cover (effective 2001). adv. **Document type:** *Magazine, Trade.*
Published by: B & L Verlags AG, Steinwiesenstr 3, Schlieren, 8952, Switzerland. TEL 41-1-7333999, FAX 41-1-7333989, info@blverlag.ch, http://www.blverlag.ch. Eds. Heinz Radde, Volker Richert. Circ: 16,000.

ALBANY LAW JOURNAL OF SCIENCE AND TECHNOLOGY. *see* LAW—Civil Law

600 CAN CODEN: RCAIAN
ALBERTA GEOLOGICAL SURVEY. INFORMATION SERIES. Text in English. 1947. irreg., latest vol.125, 2002. price varies. **Document type:** *Monographic series, Academic/Scholarly.* **Description:** Covers indices, symposia proceedings and reports of applied studies.
Incorporates: Alberta Research Council. Information Series (0701-5178)
Indexed: ChemAb, SpeleolAb.
Published by: Alberta Geological Survey, 4999 - 98th Ave, 4th Fl, Twin Atria, Edmonton T6B 2X3, AB T6B 2X3, Canada. TEL 780-422-3767, FAX 780-422-1918, EUB.AGS-Infosales@gov.ab.ca, http://www.ags.gov.ab.ca.

600 CAN
ALBERTA GEOLOGICAL SURVEY. REPORTS. Text in English. 1919. irreg. price varies.
Former titles: Alberta Research Council. Reports; Research Council of Alberta. Report (0080-1607)
Indexed: SpeleolAb.
—Linda Hall.
Published by: Alberta Geological Survey, 4999 - 98th Ave, 4th Fl, Twin Atria, Edmonton T6B 2X3, AB T6B 2X3, Canada. TEL 780-422-3767, FAX 780-422-1918, EUB.AGS-Infosales@gov.ab.ca, http://www.ags.gov.ab.ca.

600 CAN ISSN 0701-5151
ALBERTA RESEARCH COUNCIL. ANNUAL REPORT. Text in English. 1921. a., latest 2003. free (effective 2003). **Description:** Current programs research of the Alberta Research Council.
Formerly (until 1971): Research Council of Alberta. Annual Report (0080-1526)
Related titles: Online - full content ed.
Indexed: SpeleolAb.
—BLDSC (1104.175000), Linda Hall.
Published by: Alberta Research Council, 250 Karl Clark Rd, Edmonton, AB T6N 1E4, Canada. TEL 780-450-5111, FAX 780-450-5333, referral@arc.ab.ca, http://www.arc.ab.ca.

600 970 500 USA ISSN 8756-7296
T1 CODEN: AHETEU
AMERICAN HERITAGE OF INVENTION & TECHNOLOGY. Text in English. 1985. 4/yr. illus.
Indexed: A22, A28, APA, AmH&L, BiolDig, BrCerAb, C&ISA, CA/WCA, CIA, CerAb, CivEngAb, CorrAb, E&CAJ, E11, EEA, EMA, FR, H15, HistAb, M&TEA, M09, MBF, P30, RILM, SCOPUS, SolStAb, T04, WAA.
—BLDSC (0817.734000), IE, Infotrieve, Ingenta, INIST, Linda Hall. **CCC.**
Published by: (General Motors), American Heritage (Subsidiary of: Forbes, Inc.), 90 Fifth Ave, New York, NY 10011. Ed. Frederick Allen. Adv. contact Susan Cooney TEL 212-367-3104. Circ: 162,000.

AMERICAN SOCIETY OF MECHANICAL ENGINEERS. TECHNOLOGY & SOCIETY DIVISION. NEWSLETTER. *see* ENGINEERING—Mechanical Engineering

338 USA
AMERON NEWS. Text in English. 1970. q. charts; illus. **Document type:** *Newsletter.*
Published by: Ameron, 245 S Los Robles Ave, Pasadena, CA 91101. FAX 818-683-4060. Ed. S D Stracner. Circ: 10,000 (controlled).

AN-FANG KEJI/SECURITY AND SAFETY TECHNOLOGY MAGAZINE. *see* CRIMINOLOGY AND LAW ENFORCEMENT—Security

ANADOLU UNIVERSITESI BILIM VE TEKNOLOJI DERGISI/ANADOLU UNIVERSITY JOURNAL OF SCIENCES AND TECHNOLOGY. *see* SCIENCES: COMPREHENSIVE WORKS

ANALYTIC SEPARATIONS NEWS. *see* CHEMISTRY—Analytical Chemistry

600 CHN ISSN 1006-4613
ANGANG JISHU/ANGANG TECHNOLOGY. Text in Chinese; Abstracts in Chinese, English. 1964. bi-m. CNY 36, USD 36; CNY 6 per issue (effective 2011 & 2012). back issues avail. **Document type:** *Journal, Academic/Scholarly.*
Related titles: Online - full text ed.
Address: 63 Wuyi Rd., Anshan, 114009, China. TEL 86-412-6723728, FAX 86-412-6729276. Ed. Gui-hua Chang. Circ: 4,000.

ANHUI KEJI/ANHUI SCIENCE & TECHNOLOGY. *see* SCIENCES: COMPREHENSIVE WORKS

330 600 CHN ISSN 1007-3981
ANHUI KEJI YU QIYE/ANHUI TECHNOLOGY AND ENTERPRISES. Text in English. 1994. m. **Document type:** *Magazine, Trade.*
Published by: Anhui Keji yu Qiye Zazhishe, 1, Wangjiang Dong Lu, Hefei, 230053, China.

ANHUI SHANG-MAO ZHIYE JISHU XUEYUAN XUEBAO/ANHUI BUSINESS COLLEGE OF VOCATIONAL TECHNOLOGY. JOURNAL. *see* BUSINESS AND ECONOMICS

891.7 POL ISSN 2081-5468
ANNALES UNIVERSITATIS PAEDAGOGICAE CRACOVIENSIS. STUDIA TECHNICA. Text in Polish. 1973. irreg., latest vol.3, 2010. price varies. **Document type:** *Monographic series, Academic/Scholarly.*
Former titles (until 2009): Annales Academiae Paedagogicae Cracoviensis. Studia Technica (1896-1223); (until 2005): Wyzsza Szkola Pedagogiczna im. Komisji Edukacji Narodowej w Krakowie. Rocznik Naukowe-Dydaktyczny. Prace Techniczne (0860-276X)
Published by: (Uniwersytet Pedagogiczny im. Komisji Edukacji Narodowej w Krakowie), Wydawnictwo Naukowe Uniwersytetu Pedagogicznego im. Komisji Edukacji Narodowej w Krakowie, ul Podchorazych 2, Krakow, 30084, Poland. TEL 48-12-6626383, redakcja@wydawnictwoup.pl, http://www.wydawnictwoap.pl. Ed. Kazimierz Jaracz. **Co-sponsor:** Ministerstwo Edukacji Narodowej.

600 USA
ANNUAL MEMBRANE TECHNOLOGY - PLANNING CONFERENCE PROCEEDINGS (YEAR). Text in English. a. USD 375 (effective 2005). **Document type:** *Proceedings.*
Published by: Business Communications Co., Inc., 40 Washington St, Ste 110, Wellesley, MA 02481. TEL 781-489-7301, FAX 781-489-7308, sales@bccresearch.com, http://www.bccresearch.com.

ANTILIA; revista espanola de historia de las ciencias de la naturaleza y de la tecnologia. *see* BIOLOGY

600 CHN ISSN 1673-2928
ANYANG GONGXUEYUAN XUEBAO/ANYANG INSTITUTE OF TECHNOLOGY. JOURNAL. Text in Chinese. 2002. bi-m. CNY 10 newsstand/cover (effective 2006).
Formerly: Anyang Daxue Xuebao/Anyang University. Journal (1671-928X)
Related titles: Online - full text ed.
Published by: Anyang Gongxueyuan, Huanhe Dadao, Anyang, 455000, China. TEL 86-372-2909894.

APORTES PEDAGOGICOS PARA CARRERAS DE DISCIPLINAS TECNOLOGICAS. *see* EDUCATION

APPLIED ERGONOMICS; human factors in technology and society. *see* ENGINEERING

600 CZE ISSN 1804-1191
▼ ➤ **APPLIED TECHNOLOGIES AND INNOVATIONS.** Text in English. 2010 (Jan.). q. CZK 500 (effective 2010). adv. **Document type:** *Journal, Academic/Scholarly.* **Description:** Contains articles related to technologies, mathematics, IT/ICT and other non-social areas of knowledge.
Related titles: Online - full text ed.: free (effective 2011).
Indexed: C10.
Published by: Prague Development Center, Nam. Winstona Churchilla 2, Prague 3, 13000, Czech Republic. TEL 42-2-34462023, study@pradec.info, http://www.pradec.info. Eds. Arif Namozov, Petr Hajek. Circ: 200.

600 BRA ISSN 1676-501X
ARAUCARIA C&T. (Araucaria Ciencia e Tecnologia) Text in Portuguese. 2001. bi-w. back issues avail. **Document type:** *Journal, Academic/Scholarly.*
Published by: Fundacao Araucaria de Apoio ao Desenvolvimento Cientifico Tecnologico do Parana, Ave Comnedador Franco, 1341, Jardim Botanico, Curitiba, 80215-090, Brazil. TEL 55-41-32717803, FAX 55-41-32717421, rogele@fundacaoaraucaria.org.br, http://www.fundacaoaraucaria.org.br/.

ARBEIT UND TECHNIK. *see* BUSINESS AND ECONOMICS

ARCHITECTURE - TECHNOLOGY - CULTURE. *see* LITERATURE

600 ARG ISSN 0326-8101
ARGENTINA TECNOLOGICA. Text in Spanish. 1986. bi-m. free.
Indexed: C01.
Published by: Banco de la Provincia de Buenos Aires, San Martin 137, Buenos Aires, 1004, Argentina. TEL 54-114-3318375. Circ: 20,000.

ARMY A L & T. (Acquisition, Logistics and Technology) *see* MILITARY

ARMY R D & A; professional publication of the R D & A community. (Research, Development and Acquisition) *see* MILITARY

ARQUEOLOGIA INDUSTRIAL. *see* ARCHAEOLOGY

ARTNODES; revista d'art, ciencia i tecnologia. *see* ART

ARTS AND SCIENCES NEWSLETTER. *see* SCIENCES: COMPREHENSIVE WORKS

338.926 IND
T27.A1
ASIA PACIFIC TECH MONITOR (ONLINE). Text in English. 1984. bi-m. free (effective 2011). adv. bibl.; charts; illus.; mkt.; pat.; stat.; tr.lit. index. back issues avail. **Document type:** *Journal, Trade.* **Description:** Presents up-to-date information on trends in technology transfer and development, technology policies, new products and processes, technology offers, requests and events.
Formerly (until 2008): Asia Pacific Tech Monitor (Print) (0256-9957)
Media: Online - full text.
Indexed: CRIA.
—Ingenta.
Published by: Asian and Pacific Centre for Transfer of Technology, APCTT Bldg, C-2 Qutab Institutional Area, PO Box 4575, New Delhi, 110 016, India. TEL 91-11-26966509, FAX 91-11-26856274, sahu@apctt.org, http://www.apctt.org. Circ: 2,000.

ASIAN DEFENCE AND DIPLOMACY. *see* MILITARY

600 THA
T173.A7
ASIAN INSTITUTE OF TECHNOLOGY. ANNUAL RESEARCH AND ACTIVITIES REPORT. Text in Thai. 1962. a. free. **Document type:** *Bulletin, Academic/Scholarly.*
Formerly: Asian Institute of Technology. Research Summary (0572-4198)
Media: Microfiche.
Indexed: SpeleolAb.
Published by: Asian Institute of Technology, Klong Luang, PO Box 4, Pathum Thani, 12120, Thailand. TEL 66-2-524-5731, FAX 66-2-524-5745, TELEX 84276 AIT TH, deansat@ait.ac.th, http://www.sat.ait.ac.th. Ed. Roger A Hawkey. Circ: 1,000.

600 THA
ASIAN INSTITUTE OF TECHNOLOGY. SCHOOL OF ADVANCED TECHNOLOGIES. CATALOGUE. Text in English. 1995. s-a. free. **Document type:** *Catalog.*
Published by: (School of Advanced Technologies), Asian Institute of Technology, Klong Luang, PO Box 4, Pathum Thani, 12120, Thailand. TEL 66-2-524-5731, FAX 66-2-524-5745, deansat@ait.ac.th, http://www.sat.ait.ac.th.

ASIAN JOURNAL OF INFORMATION TECHNOLOGY. *see* COMPUTERS

600 GBR ISSN 1976-1597
➤ **ASIAN JOURNAL OF TECHNOLOGY INNOVATION.** Abbreviated title: A J T I. Text in English. 1993. s-a. GBP 259 combined subscription in United Kingdom to institutions (print & online eds.); EUR 376, USD 414 combined subscription to institutions (print & online eds.) (effective 2012). adv. **Document type:** *Journal, Academic/Scholarly.* **Description:** Devoted to the exploration of the innovation policy and management problems posed by players and their interaction with economic, social and political processes.
Supersedes in part (in 2004): Gi'sul Hyeogsin Yeon'gu (1598-1347)
Related titles: Online - full text ed.: ISSN 2158-6721. GBP 233 in United Kingdom to institutions; EUR 339, USD 372 to institutions (effective 2012).
Indexed: SSCI, W07.
—CCC.
Published by: (Korean Society for Technology Management and Economics KOR), Taylor & Francis Ltd. (Subsidiary of: Taylor & Francis Group), 4 Park Sq, Milton Park, Abingdon, Oxfordshire OX14 4RN, United Kingdom. TEL 44-20-70176000, FAX 44-20-70176336, info@tandf.co.uk, http://www.tandf.co.uk. Ed. Kong-Rae Lee. Pub. Eunhea Lee TEL 822-3284-1839. Adv. contact Linda Hann.

▼ ➤ **ASIAN TRANSACTIONS ON SCIENCE & TECHNOLOGY.** *see* SCIENCES: COMPREHENSIVE WORKS

➤ **ASSISTIVE TECHNOLOGY OUTCOMES AND BENEFITS.** *see* HANDICAPPED

➤ **ASSOCIATED SCIENTIFIC AND TECHNICAL SOCIETIES OF SOUTH AFRICA. ANNUAL PROCEEDINGS.** *see* SCIENCES: COMPREHENSIVE WORKS

600 500 FRA ISSN 1770-9547
ASSOCIATION NATIONALE DE LA RECHERCHE TECHNIQUE. LETTRE EUROPEENNE. Variant title: La Lettre Europeenne de l'A N R T. Text in French. 1984. m. EUR 419 to members; EUR 449 to non-members (effective 2008). **Document type:** *Newsletter, Trade.*
Formerly (until 2004): La Lettre Europeenne du Progres Technique (0765-0094)
Published by: Association Nationale de la Recherche Technique, 41 Boulevard des Capucines, Paris, 75002, France. TEL 33-01-55352550, FAX 33-01-55352555, info@anrt.asso.fr.

ASSOCIATION OF COLLEGE AND RESEARCH LIBRARIES. SCIENCE AND TECHNOLOGY SECTION SIGNAL. *see* LIBRARY AND INFORMATION SCIENCES

AUGUST MAN. *see* MEN'S INTERESTS

600 AUS ISSN 1445-2901
AUSTRALIAN T3. Text in English. 2001. m. AUD 75; AUD 8.95 newsstand/cover (effective 2008). **Document type:** *Magazine, Consumer.* **Description:** Presents the latest and greatest technology from all over the world.
Published by: Derwent Howard Media Pty Ltd., PO Box 1037, Bondi Junction, NSW 1355, Australia. TEL 61-2-83056900, 800-007-820, FAX 61-2-83056999, enquiries@derwenthoward.com.au. Ed. Nic Healey TEL 61-2-83056900. Adv. contact Richard Sossen TEL 61-2-83056943.

600 AUT ISSN 1022-9124
AUSTRIA INNOVATIV. Text in German. 1986. 6/yr. EUR 43.90 domestic; EUR 59.60 foreign (effective 2005). adv. bk.rev. back issues avail. **Document type:** *Journal, Academic/Scholarly.* **Description:** Covers new technological research and experiments in industry and universities.
Related titles: English ed.
Indexed: INIS AtomInd.
Published by: Bohmann Druck und Verlag GmbH & Co. KG, Leberstr 122, Vienna, W 1110, Austria. TEL 43-1-740950, FAX 43-1-74095183, http://www.bohmann.at. Ed. Christian Klobucsar. Adv. contact Christoph Jenschke TEL 43-1-74095476. B&W page EUR 3,469, color page EUR 4,949; trim 185 x 250. Circ: 12,500.

AUTOMATA. *see* SCIENCES: COMPREHENSIVE WORKS

AUTOMATIK & PROCES; teknisk udvikling. *see* COMPUTERS—Automation

AVANCES DE LA CIENCIA Y LA TECNOLOGIA. *see* SCIENCES: COMPREHENSIVE WORKS

AVANZADA CIENTIFICA. *see* SCIENCES: COMPREHENSIVE WORKS

AWISHKARA. *see* SCIENCES: COMPREHENSIVE WORKS

B B R; Fachmagazin fuer Brunnen- und Leitungsbau. *see* WATER RESOURCES

607 CAN
B C I T ANNUAL REPORT. (British Columbia Institute of Technology) Text in English. 1975. a. illus.
Former titles: B C I T: The Career Campus (0707-3291); British Columbia Institute of Technology. Annual Report (0381-260X)
Published by: British Columbia Institute of Technology, Marketing & Development, Information & Community Relations, 3700 Willingdon Ave, Burnaby, BC V5G 3H2, Canada. TEL 604-434-5734. Ed. Carol Dion.

607.11 CAN
B C I T UPDATE. (British Columbia Institute of Technology) Text in English. w. free.
Published by: British Columbia Institute of Technology, Marketing & Development, Information & Community Relations, 3700 Willingdon Ave, Burnaby, BC V5G 3H2, Canada. TEL 604-434-5734. Ed. Carol Dion.

600 CAN ISSN 1911-0553
B C INNOVATION COUNCIL. ANNUAL SERVICE PLAN REPORT. Text in English. 1979. a. **Document type:** *Report, Trade.*
Former titles (until 2005): Innovation and Science Council of British Columbia. Annual Service Plan Report (1711-2869); (until 2003): Science Council of British Columbia. Annual Report (1704-8478); (until 2002): Science Council of British Columbia. Annual Review (1190-8505); (until 1994): Science Council of British Columbia. Annual Report (0710-8419)
Published by: B C Innovation Council, 9th Flr 1188 W Georgia St, Vancouver, BC V6E 4A2, Canada. TEL 604-438-2752, 800-665-7222, FAX 604-438-6564, info@bcinnovationcouncil.com, http://www.bcinnovationcouncil.com.

B I T. DESIGN. (Boletim de Informacao Tecnologica. Design) *see* ARCHITECTURE

TU

600 DEU
B T B MAGAZIN. (Bund der Technischen Beamten, Angestellten und Arbeiter) Text in German. 1963. 10/yr. adv. **Document type:** *Magazine, Trade.*
Published by: Vereinigte Verlagsanstalten GmbH, Hoeherweg 278, Duesseldorf, 40231, Germany. TEL 49-211-73570, FAX 49-211-7357123, info@vva.de, http://www.vva.de. Ed. Bernd Niesen. Adv. contact Panagiotis Chrissovergis. B&W page EUR 1,410, color page EUR 2,350. Circ: 12,500 (controlled).

600 340 DEU
BAUNORMEN-KATALOG (YEAR). Text in English, French, German, Spanish. 1975. a. EUR 75 for single user; EUR 259 for network version (effective 2009). **Document type:** *Catalog, Trade.*
Former titles: Fuehrer Durch die Baunormung (0178-8639); (until 1986): Normen und Norm-Entwurfe ueber das Bauwesen (0723-0281)
Media: CD-ROM.
Published by: (Deutsches Institut fuer Normung e.V.), Beuth Verlag GmbH, Burggrafenstr 6, Berlin, 10787, Germany. TEL 49-30-26012260, FAX 49-30-26011260, postmaster@beuth.de, http://www.beuth.de. Circ: 1,000. **Dist. in U.S. by:** Global Engineering Documents, 2805 McGaw Ave, PO Box 19539, Irvine, CA 92714.

BEESCENE. *see* AGRICULTURE

BEIJING KEJIE BAO/BEIJING SCIENCE TECHNOLOGY REPORT. *see* SCIENCES: COMPREHENSIVE WORKS

BERKELEY TECHNOLOGY LAW JOURNAL. *see* LAW

BERUFS- UND KARRIERE-PLANER. TECHNIK. *see* OCCUPATIONS AND CAREERS

BESSATSU SAIENSU. *see* SCIENCES: COMPREHENSIVE WORKS

303.483 USA
BETA ONLINE; technology - culture. Text in English. 1998. m. bk.rev. back issues avail. **Document type:** *Newsletter.* **Description:** Covers technology and its impact on culture.
Media: Online - full text. Ed. David Tomere.

600 RUS
BEZOPASNOST'. Text in Russian. m. USD 165 in United States.
Indexed: RASB.
Published by: Fond Natsional'noi i Mezhdunarodnoi Bezopasnosti, Ul Butlerova 40, kom 805, Moscow, 117342, Russian Federation. TEL 7-095-1648547. **Dist. by:** East View Information Services, 10601 Wayzata Blvd, Minneapolis, MN 55305. TEL 952-252-1201, 800-477-1005, FAX 952-252-1202, info@eastview.com, http://www.eastview.com.

600 RUS
BEZOPASNOST' INFORMATSIONNYKH TEKHNOLOGII. Text in Russian. s-a. USD 89.95 in United States.
Published by: Moskovskii Inzhenerno-Fizicheskii Institut, Kashirskoe shosse 31, Moscow, 115409, Russian Federation. TEL 7-095-3239085, FAX 7-095-3239435. **Dist. by:** East View Information Services, 10601 Wayzata Blvd, Minneapolis, MN 55305. TEL 952-252-1201, 800-477-1005, FAX 952-252-1202, info@eastview.com, http://www.eastview.com.

600 SWE ISSN 1653-2090
BLEKINGE INSTITUTE OF TECHNOLOGY. DOCTORAL DISSERTATION SERIES. Text in English; Summaries in Swedish. 2001. irreg. **Document type:** *Monographic series, Academic/Scholarly.*
Formerly (until 2005): Blekinge Institute of Technology. Dissertation Series (1650-2159)
Published by: Blekinge Tekniska Hoegskola/Blekinge Institute of Technology, Karlskrona, 37179, Sweden. TEL 46-455-385000, FAX 46-455-385057.

BOLETIN DE NOVEDADES CIENTIFICO-TECNICAS. *see* SCIENCES: COMPREHENSIVE WORKS

BOMBAY TECHNOLOGIST. *see* CHEMISTRY

600 BWA ISSN 1019-1593
T28.B55 CODEN: BJTOA9
BOTSWANA JOURNAL OF TECHNOLOGY. Text in English. 1993. s-a. back issues avail. **Document type:** *Journal, Academic/Scholarly.*
Related titles: Online - full text ed.
Indexed: Inspec.
Published by: University of Botswana, PB 0061, Gaborone, Botswana. TEL 267-3554210, FAX 267-352309, ngowiab@mopipi.ub.bw, http://www.ub.bw. Ed. M. Oladiran.

600 NLD ISSN 1574-3306
BRIGHT. Text in Dutch. 2005. 6/yr. EUR 27.50 domestic; EUR 42.10 in Europe; EUR 48.10 elsewhere (effective 2010). adv.
—IE.
Published by: TechMedia BV, Postbus 256, Diemen, 1110 AG, Netherlands. TEL 31-20-5310959, FAX 31-20-5310950. Eds. Corrie Gerritsma, Erwin van der Zande. adv.: color page EUR 9,995. Circ: 25,000.

BROADCAST TECHNOLOGY; N H K Science and Technical Research Laboratories bulletin. *see* COMMUNICATIONS

BROADCASTING EQUIPMENT AND TECHNOLOGY. *see* COMMUNICATIONS

BUILDING SERVICES ENGINEERING RESEARCH & TECHNOLOGY; an international journal. *see* BUILDING AND CONSTRUCTION

BULLETIN OF SCIENCE, TECHNOLOGY & SOCIETY. *see* SCIENCES: COMPREHENSIVE WORKS

BUNSEOG GWAHAG/ANALYTICAL SCIENCE AND TECHNOLOGY. *see* SCIENCES: COMPREHENSIVE WORKS

BUSIDATE. *see* BUSINESS AND ECONOMICS—Personnel Management

BUSINESS VIEW; the H P magazine of business and technology. (Hewlett-Packard) *see* BUSINESS AND ECONOMICS—Investments

600 POL ISSN 0068-4597
BYDGOSKIE TOWARZYSTWO NAUKOWE. WYDZIAL NAUK TECHNICZNYCH. PRACE. SERIA Z (PRACE ZBIOROWE). Text in Polish. 1966. irreg. price varies.
Published by: Bydgoskie Towarzystwo Naukowe, Jezuicka 4, Bydgoszcz, Poland. **Dist. by:** Ars Polona, Obroncow 25, Warsaw 03933, Poland.

600 DEU
C A E S A R NEWSLETTER. Text in German. q. **Document type:** *Newsletter, Trade.*
Published by: Center of Advanced European Studies and Research, Ludwig-Erhard-Allee 2, Bonn, 53175, Germany. TEL 49-228-96560, FAX 49-228-9656111, office@please-remove-everything.tv@between-at-signs@caesar.de, http://www.caesar.de. Circ: 5,000 (controlled).

C A P S T JOURNAL. (Chinese Association of Professionals in Science and Technology) *see* ETHNIC INTERESTS

C E A ANNUAL REPORT (YEAR). (Commissariat a l'Energie Atomique) *see* SCIENCES: COMPREHENSIVE WORKS

600 BRA ISSN 1518-8744
C E N D O T E C DOSSIER. (Centro Franco-Brasileiro de Documentacao Tecnica e Cientifica Dossier) Text in Portuguese, French. 2000. irreg. free (effective 2006). back issues avail. **Document type:** *Bulletin, Government.*
Media: Online - full text.
Published by: Centro Franco-Brasileiro de Documentacao Tecnica e Cientifica, Ave Prof. Dr. Lineu Prestes, 2242, IPEN Cidade Universitaria, Sao Paulo, SP 05505-000, Brazil. TEL 55-11-30321214, FAX 55-11-30321552.

C E T. REVISTA DE CIENCIAS EXACTAS E INGENIERIA. (Ciencias Exactas y Tecnologia) *see* SCIENCES: COMPREHENSIVE WORKS

600 500 620 USA
C I R A S NEWS. (Center for Industrial Research and Service) Text in English. 1966. q. back issues avail. **Document type:** *Newsletter, Trade.* **Description:** Provides Iowa manufacturing executives with information about methods for improving their management techniques and manufacturing and processing operations. Also describes services available to them from the CIRAS and other service agencies.
Published by: Iowa State University, Center for Industrial Research and Service, 2272 Howe Hall, No 2620, Ames, IA 50011-0001. TEL 515-294-3420, FAX 515-294-4925, ciras.info@iastate.edu. Circ: 6,306 (controlled).

C I S T I NEWS (ONLINE). *see* SCIENCES: COMPREHENSIVE WORKS—Computer Applications

C L S U SCIENTIFIC JOURNAL. *see* AGRICULTURE

C N K I WEB. (China National Knowledge Infrastructure) *see* SCIENCES: COMPREHENSIVE WORKS

600 362.1 GBR
➤ **C O M A D E M INTERNATIONAL. PROCEEDINGS.** (Condition Monitoring and Diagnostic Engineering Management) Text in English. 19??. a. GBP 150 per issue (effective 2009). 581 p./no.; back issues avail. **Document type:** *Proceedings, Academic/Scholarly.* **Description:** Contains the latest information on innovative topics related to competitive world-class manufacturing covering a wide variety of industrial sectors.
Published by: C O M A D E M International, 307 Tiverton Rd, Selly Oak, Birmingham, B29 6DA, United Kingdom. TEL 44-121-4722338. Pub. Raj B K N Rao.

600 BEL ISSN 1025-4013
C O R D I S FOCUS R T D RESULTS. (Community Research and Development Information Service Focus Research and Development Technology) Text in English. 1994. irreg. free. **Document type:** *Monographic series, Academic/Scholarly.*
Related titles: Online - full text ed.; ◆ Supplement to: C O R D I S Focus (English Edition). ISSN 1022-6559.
—BLDSC (3470.504760).
Published by: European Commission, Directorate General - Research, PO Box 2201, Luxembourg, 1022, Belgium. FAX 32-2-2958220.

C S I R ANNUAL REPORT - TECHNOLOGY IMPACT. (Council for Scientific and Industrial Research) *see* SCIENCES: COMPREHENSIVE WORKS

600 AUS ISSN 1030-4215
Q180.A8 CODEN: ASIRAF
C S I R O ANNUAL REPORT. (Commonwealth Scientific and Industrial Research Organization) Text in English. 1948. a. back issues avail. **Document type:** *Corporate.*
Formerly (until 1995): Commonwealth Scientific and Industrial Research Organization. Annual Report (0069-7184)
Related titles: Online - full text ed.: free (effective 2008).
Indexed: AESIS, GeoRef, SpeleolAb.
—Linda Hall. **CCC.**
Published by: C S I R O, 150 Oxford St, PO Box 1139, Collingwood, VIC 3066, Australia. TEL 61-3-96627500, FAX 61-3-96627555, publishing@csiro.au, http://www.publish.csiro.au/.

C T S. CIENCIA, TECNOLOGIA Y SOCIEDAD. *see* SCIENCES: COMPREHENSIVE WORKS

CADERNOS DE CIENCIA E TECNOLOGIA. *see* SCIENCES: COMPREHENSIVE WORKS

600 340 FRA ISSN 1967-0311
CAHIERS DROIT, SCIENCES, & TECHNOLOGIES. Text in French. 2008. a. EUR 33.25 newsstand/cover (effective 2011). back issues avail. **Document type:** *Journal, Academic/Scholarly.*
Published by: Centre National de la Recherche Scientifique, 15 Rue Malebranche, Paris, 75005, France. TEL 33-1-53102700, FAX 33-1-53102727.

300 USA
CALIFORNIA TECHNOLOGY. Text in English. m. USD 39 (effective 2002). adv. back issues avail.; reprints avail. **Document type:** *Magazine, Consumer.*
Related titles: Online - full content ed.
Published by: Power Media Group, 13490 TI Blvd Ste 100, Dallas, TX 75243. TEL 972-690-6222, 800-687-3256, FAX 972-690-6333, 800-687-3290, editor@ttechnology.com, http://www.ttechnology.com. Ed. Laurie Kline TEL 972-690-6222 ext 16. Pub. Roger Powers TEL 972-690-6222 ext 20.

CAMEROON ACADEMY OF SCIENCES. JOURNAL. *see* SCIENCES: COMPREHENSIVE WORKS

CANADA SCHOLARS IN TECHNOLOGY. TERMS AND CONDITIONS FOR CANADA SCHOLARS. *see* EDUCATION—Higher Education

600 CAN
CANADIAN CORPORATE R & D DIRECTORY. Text in English. 1992. a. (plus updates 10/yr.). CAD 975 (effective 1999). **Document type:** *Directory.* **Description:** Overviews about 370 Canadian R and D intensive companies and organizations.
Media: Diskette.
Published by: Evert Communications Ltd., 1296 Carling Ave, 2nd Fl, Ottawa, ON K1Z 7K8, Canada. TEL 613-728-4621, FAX 613-728-0385. Ed. Natalie Gallimore. Pub. Gordon Hutchison.

CANADIAN JOURNAL OF LAW AND TECHNOLOGY. *see* LAW

CANADIAN JOURNAL OF SCIENCE, MATHEMATICS AND TECHNOLOGY EDUCATION/REVUE CANADIENNE DE L'ENSEIGNEMENT DES SCIENCES, DES MATHEMATIQUES ET DES TECHNOLOGIES. *see* SCIENCES: COMPREHENSIVE WORKS

CANADIAN R & D DIRECTORY. *see* BUSINESS AND ECONOMICS—Trade And Industrial Directories

600 001.3 DEU ISSN 1434-4645
CAROLO-WILHELMINA. Text in German. 1966. s-a. bibl.; charts; illus. **Document type:** *Journal, Academic/Scholarly.*
Former titles (until 1997): Carolo-Wilhelmina-Mitteilungen (0934-6708); (until 1987): Mitteilungen der Technische Universitat Carolo-Wilhelmina zu Braunschweig (0176-0629); (until 1968): Mitteilungen der Technischen Hochschule Carolo-Wilhelmina Braunschweig (0176-0610)
Related titles: E-mail ed.; Fax ed.
Indexed: GeoRef, SpeleolAb.
—Linda Hall.
Published by: Technische Universitaet Braunschweig, Presse- und Oeffentlichkeitsarbeit, Pockelsstr 14, Braunschweig, 38106, Germany. TEL 49-531-3914124, FAX 49-531-3914120, presse@tu-braunschweig.de. Ed. Dr. Hergen Manns. R&P Agentur Alpha.

CATALYST (FAIRFAX). *see* BUSINESS AND ECONOMICS—Management

CEHUI JISHU ZHUANGBEI/GEOMATICS TECHNOLOGY AND EQUIPMENT. *see* GEOGRAPHY

CENTAURUS; an international journal of the history of science and its cultural aspects. *see* SCIENCES: COMPREHENSIVE WORKS

CENTER FOR RURAL POLICY AND DEVELOPMENT. RESEARCH REPORTS. *see* POPULATION STUDIES

CENTRALE VIDENSKABSETISKE KOMITE. AARSBERETNING/ CENTRAL SCIENTIFIC - ETHICAL COMMITTEE OF DENMARK. REPORT. *see* PHILOSOPHY

658.5 FRA ISSN 1156-7104
T2
CENTRALIENS. Variant title: Arts et Manufactures Centraliens. Text in French. 10/yr.
Formerly (until 1990): Arts et Manufactures (0004-3990)
—INIST.
Published by: Association des Anciens Eleves de l'Ecole Centrale des Arts et Manufactures, 8 rue Jean Goujon, Paris, 75008, France. TEL 33-1-42-25-02-37, FAX 33-1-49-53-08-21. Ed. Pierre Chappaz. Circ: 11,477.

600 MDG
CENTRE D'INFORMATION ET DE DOCUMENTATION SCIENTIFIQUE ET TECHNIQUE. RECHERCHES POUR LE DEVELOPPEMENT. SERIE SCIENCES TECHNOLOGIQUES. Text in French. 2/yr. MGF 60, USD 10.
Published by: Centre d'Information et de Documentation Scientifique et Technique, BP 6224, Antananarivo, 101, Madagascar. TEL 261-2-33288.

600 ITA ISSN 1123-816X
LA CERAMICA MODERNA ED ANTICA; mensile di informazione tecnica. Text in Italian. 1979. m. (8/yr.). **Document type:** *Magazine, Consumer.* **Description:** Presents all the information that cermist must know.
Formerly (until 1995): Ceramica Moderna (0392-8225)
Published by: Il Sole 24 Ore Business Media, Via Monte Rosa 91, Milan, 20149, Italy. TEL 39-02-30221, FAX 39-02-312055, info@ilsole24ore.com, http://www.gruppo24ore.com.

CEYLON INSTITUTE OF SCIENTIFIC & INDUSTRIAL RESEARCH. ANNUAL REPORT. *see* SCIENCES: COMPREHENSIVE WORKS

CEYLON INSTITUTE OF SCIENTIFIC & INDUSTRIAL RESEARCH. NEWS BULLETIN. *see* SCIENCES: COMPREHENSIVE WORKS

600 SWE ISSN 0366-8746
CODEN: DCTHAT
CHALMERS TEKNISKA HOEGSKOLA. DOKTORSAVHANDLINGAR. Text in Swedish, English. 1942. irreg. price varies. back issues avail. **Document type:** *Monographic series, Academic/Scholarly.* **Description:** Publishes Ph.D. dissertations defended at Chalmers Technical University.
Related titles: Online - full text ed.
Indexed: C&ISA, E&CAJ, ISMEC, SCOPUS, SolStAb.
—BLDSC (3615.280000), IE, Ingenta.
Published by: Chalmers Tekniska Hoegskola/Chalmers University of Technology, Goeteborg, 41296, Sweden. TEL 46-31-7721000, FAX 46-31-7723872.

600 SWE ISSN 1652-8913
CHALMERS TEKNISKA HOEGSKOLA. INSTITUTIONEN FOER MATERIAL- OCH TELLVERKNINGSTEKNIK. EXAMENSARBETE/ CHALMERS UNIVERSITY OF TECHNOLOGY. DEPARTMENT OF MATERIALS AND MANUFACTURING TECHNOLOGY. MASTER'S THESIS. Text in English. 2001. irreg. **Document type:** *Monographic series, Academic/Scholarly.*
Formerly (until 2005): Chalmers Tekniska Hoegskola. Department of Materials Science and Engineering. Diploma Work (1651-0003); Which was formed by the merger of (1997-2001): Chalmers Tekniska Hoegskola. Institutionen foer Polymera Material. Examensarbete (1402-7399); (1967-2001): Chalmers Tekniska Hoegskola. Institutionen foer Metalliska Konstruktionsmaterial. R (1102-5867)
Published by: Chalmers Tekniska Hoegskola, Institutionen foer Material- och Tellverkningsteknik/Chalmers University of Technology. Department of Materials and Manufacturing Technology, Goeteborg, 41296, Sweden. TEL 46-31-7721000, http://www.chalmers.se/mmt.

600 CHN
CHANGCHUN GONGYE DAXUE XUEBAO (ZIRAN KEXUE BAN)/ CHANGCHUN UNIVERISTY OF TECHNOLOGY. JOURNAL (NATURAL SCIENCE EDITION). Text in Chinese. 1980. bi-m. **Document type:** *Journal, Academic/Scholarly.*
Former titles (until 2003): Jilin Gongxueyuan Xuebao (Ziran Kexue Ban); (until 1999): Jilin Gongxueyuan Xuebao/Jilin Institute of Technology. Journal (1006-2939)
Related titles: Online - full text ed.
Published by: Changchun Gongye Daxue/Changchun Univeristy of Technology, 2055, Yanan Dajie, Changchun, 130012, China. TEL 86-431-85716257, http://www.jlit.edu.cn/.

600 CHN
CHANGSHU LIGONG XUEYUAN XUEBAO/CHANGSHU INSTITUTE OF TECHNOLOGY. JOURNAL. Text in Chinese. 1988. bi-m. CNY 8 newsstand/cover (effective 2006). **Document type:** *Journal, Academic/Scholarly.*
Former titles (until 20004): Changshu Gao-Zhuan Xuebao (1008-2794); Which was formed by the merger of: Wuzhong Xuekan (Renwen Shehui Kexue Leikanwu); Changshu Gao-Zhuan Xuebao (Ziran Kexueban); Changshu Gao-Zhuan Xuebao (Wenli Zongheban)
Related titles: Online - full text ed.
Published by: Changshu Ligong Xueyuan, 98, Yuanhe Lu, Changshu, 215500, China. TEL 86-512-52251276.

CHEMICAL ENGINEERING WORLD. *see* ENGINEERING—Chemical Engineering

600 CHN ISSN 1671-9727
QE294
CHENGDU LIGONG DAXUE XUEBAO (ZIRAN KEXUE BAN)/ CHENGDU UNIVERSITY OF TECHNOLOGY. JOURNAL (SCIENCE & TECHNOLOGY EDITION). Text in Chinese. 1960. q. USD 18 (effective 2009). **Document type:** *Academic/Scholarly.*
Former titles (until 2002): Chengdu Ligong Xueyuan Xuebao/Chengdu Institute of Technology. Journal (1005-9539); (until 1993): Chengdu Dizhi Xueyuan Xuebao/Chengdu College of Geology. Journal (0256-2197)
Related titles: Online - full content ed.; Online - full text ed.
Indexed: A22, GEOBASE, GeoRef, INIS AtomInd, MinerAb, PetrolAb, RefZh, SCOPUS, SpeleolAb, Z01.
—BLDSC (4729.140000), East View, IE, Ingenta, PADDS.
Published by: Chengdu Ligong Daxue/Chengdu University of Technology, 1, Erxianquiao Dongsan Lu, Chengdu, 610059, China. TEL 86-28-84078973, FAX 86-28-84077066.

CHENGSHI GUANLI YU KEJI/MUNICIPAL ADMINISTRATION & TECHOLOGY. *see* PUBLIC ADMINISTRATION—Municipal Government

500 JPN ISSN 0385-7026
T4 CODEN: RPCTAL
CHIBA KOGYO DAIGAKU KENKYU HOKOKU. RIKO-HEN/CHIBA INSTITUTE OF TECHNOLOGY. REPORT. RIKO-HEN. Text in Japanese. 1962. a. **Document type:** *Academic/Scholarly.*
Supersedes in part (in 1965): Chiba Kogyo Daigaku Kenkyu Hokoku (0388-4627)
Indexed: Inspec, MLA-IB, RefZh.
—BLDSC (7396.900000).
Published by: Chiba Kogyo Daigaku/Chiba Institute of Technology, 2-17-1 Tsudanuma, Narashino, Chiba 275-0016, Japan. http://www.it-chiba.ac.jp/.

CHILDREN'S TECHNOLOGY AND ENGINEERING. *see* EDUCATION—Teaching Methods And Curriculum

CHONGQING KEJI/CHONGQING SCIENCE AND TECHNOLOGY. *see* SCIENCES: COMPREHENSIVE WORKS

600 CHN ISSN 1004-1699
CHUAN'GAN JISHU XUEBAO/CHINESE JOURNAL OF SENSORS AND ACTUATORS/JOURNAL OF TRANSDUCTION TECHNOLOGY. Text in Chinese; Contents page in English. 1988. q. USD 186 (effective 2009). **Document type:** *Journal, Academic/Scholarly.*
Related titles: Online - full text ed.
Indexed: EngInd, Inspec, SCOPUS.
—East View.
Published by: Guojia Jiaowei Quanguo Gaoxiao Chuangan Jishu Yanjiuhui, Sipai Building, no.2, Dongnan University, Nanjing, 210096, China. TEL 86-25-3792242, FAX 86-25-3793261.

600 CHN
CHUANGANQI YU WEIXITONG/TRANSDUCER AND MICROSYSTEM TECHNOLOGIES. Text in Chinese. 1982. m. USD 62.40 (effective 2009). **Document type:** *Journal, Academic/Scholarly.*
Formerly: Chuanganqi Jishu/Sensor Technology (1000-9787)
—East View.
Published by: Xinxi Chanyebu, Dianzi Di-49 Yanjiusuo, 29, Yiman Jie, Ha'erbin, 150001, China. TEL 86-451-82514848, FAX 86-451-82516128.

CHUANGYI SHIJIE/CREATIVITY. *see* SCIENCES: COMPREHENSIVE WORKS

CHUBU UNIVERSITY. COLLEGE OF ENGINEERING. MEMOIRS/ CHUBU DAIGAKU KOGAKUBU KIYO. *see* ENGINEERING

600 TWN ISSN 0255-6030
CHUNG CHENG LING HSUEH PAO/CHUNG CHENG INSTITUTE OF TECHNOLOGY. JOURNAL. Key Title: Zhongzhengling Xuebao. Text in Chinese. 1970. a. **Document type:** *Journal, Academic/Scholarly.*
Indexed: CPEI, EngInd, SCOPUS.
Published by: Chung Cheng Institute of Technology, No. 190, Sanyuan 1st St., Tashi, Taoyuan, Taiwan. TEL 886-3-3800647.

CHURCH & WORSHIP TECHNOLOGY. *see* RELIGIONS AND THEOLOGY

CIENCIA; revista de difusion cientifica y tecnologica universitaria autonoma de nuevo leon. *see* SCIENCES: COMPREHENSIVE WORKS

CIENCIA AL DIA INTERNACIONAL. *see* SCIENCES: COMPREHENSIVE WORKS

CIENCIA, DOCENCIA Y TECNOLOGIA. *see* SCIENCES: COMPREHENSIVE WORKS

600 PRT ISSN 0870-8312
CIENCIA E TECNOLOGIA DOS MATERIAIS. Text in Portuguese. 1989. q. **Document type:** *Journal, Academic/Scholarly.*
Related titles: Online - full text ed.: free (effective 2011).
Published by: Sociedade Portuguesa de Materiais, Apartado 4538, EC Carnide, Lisbon, 1511-601, Portugal. TEL 351-21-0924653, FAX 351-21-7166568.

CIENCIA PARA TODOS. *see* SCIENCES: COMPREHENSIVE WORKS

▼ **CIENCIA TECNOLOGIA E INNOVACION PARA EL DESARROLLO DE MEXICO.** *see* SCIENCES: COMPREHENSIVE WORKS

CIENCIA Y DESARROLLO. *see* SCIENCES: COMPREHENSIVE WORKS

CIENCIA Y TECNOLOGIA EN (YEAR). *see* SCIENCES: COMPREHENSIVE WORKS

600 500 CUB ISSN 0253-7397
CODEN: CTFMDH
CIENCIAS TECNICAS FISICAS Y MATEMATICAS. Text in Spanish. 1981. s-a. USD 26 in South America; USD 30 in North America; USD 36 elsewhere.
Indexed: C01, INIS AtomInd, Inspec.
—AskIEEE, CASDDS.
Published by: Academia de Ciencias de Cuba, Capitolio, Havana, 12400, Cuba. Ed. Jose Altshuler. Circ: 1,500. **Dist. by:** Ediciones Cubanas.

600 GBR ISSN 0305-6120
TK7800 CODEN: CIWODV
➤ **CIRCUIT WORLD.** Abbreviated title: C W. Text in English. 1973. q. EUR 2,859 combined subscription in Europe (print & online eds.); USD 3,259 combined subscription in the Americas (print & online eds.); GBP 2,059 combined subscription in the UK & elsewhere (print & online eds.); AUD 3,849 combined subscription in Australasia (print & online eds.) (effective 2012). adv. bk.rev. back issues avail.; reprint service avail. from PSC. **Document type:** *Journal, Academic/Scholarly.* **Description:** Provides up-to-date coverage of international activities related to printed circuit board and interconnect technology. Discusses standards, design, analysis, materials, processing, reliability and equipment relevant to the manufacturing of circuit boards, multichip modules and semiconductor packaging substrates.
Related titles: Online - full text ed.: ISSN 1758-602X (from IngentaConnect).
Indexed: A01, A03, A05, A08, A12, A17, A22, A28, ABIn, APA, AS&TA, AS&TI, B04, BrCerAb, BrTechI, C&ISA, C10, CA, CA/WCA, CIA, CPEI, CerAb, CivEngAb, CoppAb, CorrAb, CurCont, E&CAJ, E01, E11, EEA, EMA, ESPM, EmerIntel, EngInd, EnvEAb, H15, ISMEC, Inspec, M&TEA, M09, MBF, METADEX, MSCI, P26, P48, P51, P52, P53, P54, PQC, RefZh, SCI, SCOPUS, SolStAb, T02, T04, W07, WAA.
—BLDSC (3198.839000), AskIEEE, CASDDS, IE, Infotrieve, Ingenta, Linda Hall. **CCC.**
Published by: (Printed Circuit & Interconnection Federation, Institute of Ciruit Technology), Emerald Group Publishing Ltd., Howard House, Wagon Ln, Bingley, W Yorks BD16 1WA, United Kingdom. TEL 44-1274-777700, FAX 44-1274-785201, information@emeraldinsight.com. Ed. Martin Goosey. Pub. Harry Colson. **Subscr. addr. in N America:** Emerald Group Publishing Limited, One Mifflin Pl, Ste 400, Harvard Sq, Cambridge, MA 02138. TEL 617-576-5782, 888-309-7810, FAX 617-576-5883.

➤ **CLASS N K TECHNICAL BULLETIN.** *see* SCIENCES: COMPREHENSIVE WORKS

➤ **CLEFS C E A.** (Commissariat a l'Energie Atomique) *see* SCIENCES: COMPREHENSIVE WORKS

600 USA
CLOVERVIEW. Text in English. q.
Published by: Virginia Polytechnic Institute and State University, 202 Media Bldg, Blacksburg, VA 24061. TEL 703-961-7370.

600 NLD ISSN 0165-232X
GB641 CODEN: CRSTDL
➤ **COLD REGIONS SCIENCE AND TECHNOLOGY.** Text in Dutch. 1979. 15/yr. EUR 1,505 in Europe to institutions; JPY 200,300 in Japan to institutions; USD 1,686 elsewhere to institutions (effective 2012). abstr. back issues avail. **Document type:** *Journal, Academic/Scholarly.* **Description:** Deals with the scientific and technical problems of cold environments, including both natural and artificial environments.
Related titles: Microform ed.: (from PQC); Online - full text ed.: ISSN 1872-7441 (from IngentaConnect, ScienceDirect).
Indexed: A01, A03, A08, A20, A22, A26, A28, A33, APA, ASCA, ASFA, ApMecR, BrCerAb, C&ISA, C10, CA, CA/WCA, CIA, CPEI, CerAb, ChemAb, CivEngAb, CorrAb, CurCont, E&CAJ, E&PHSE, E11, EEA, EMA, ESPM, EngInd, EnvEAb, GEOBASE, GP&P, GeoRef, GeotechAb, H15, I05, ISMEC, ISR, Inspec, M&GPA, M&TEA, M09, MBF, METADEX, OffTech, PetrolAb, PollutAb, S01, SCI, SCOPUS, SWRA, SolStAb, SpeleolAb, T02, T04, W07, WAA.
—BLDSC (3295.760000), CASDDS, IE, Infotrieve, Ingenta, INIST, Linda Hall, PADDS. **CCC.**
Published by: Elsevier BV (Subsidiary of: Elsevier Science & Technology), Radarweg 29, PO Box 211, Amsterdam, 1000 AE, Netherlands. TEL 31-20-4853911, FAX 31-20-4852457, JournalsCustomerServiceEMEA@elsevier.com, http://www.elsevier.nl. Ed. G W Timco.

600 070.5 USA ISSN 1062-6727
COLE PAPERS; technology, journalism, publishing. Text in English. 1989. m. USD 167 domestic; USD 177 in Canada & Mexico; USD 187 elsewhere (effective 2005). bk.rev. charts; illus. 12 p./no.; back issues avail.; reprints avail. **Document type:** *Newsletter, Trade.* **Description:** Discusses technologies publishers can use to put out newspapers and magazines.
Related titles: Online - full content ed.: USD 99 (effective 2005); Online - full text ed.
Published by: The Cole Group, PO Box 719, Pacifica, CA 94044-0719. TEL 650-557-9595, FAX 650-557-96961, info@colegroup.com. Ed., Pub., R&P David M Cole.

COLLEGE & UNIVERSITY MEDIA REVIEW; a look at practices, trends & research. *see* EDUCATION—Higher Education

COLLIDE MAGAZINE; where the media and the church converge. *see* RELIGIONS AND THEOLOGY—Protestant

300 USA
COLORADO TECHNOLOGY. Text in English. m. USD 39 (effective 2002). adv. back issues avail.; reprints avail. **Document type:** *Magazine, Consumer.*
Related titles: Online - full content ed.
Published by: Power Media Group, 13490 TI Blvd Ste 100, Dallas, TX 75243. TEL 972-690-6222, 800-687-3256, FAX 972-690-6333, 800-687-3290, editor@ttechnology.com, http://www.ttechnology.com. Ed. Laurie Kline TEL 972-690-6222 ext 16. Pub. Roger Powers TEL 972-690-6222 ext 20.

THE COLUMBIA SCIENCE AND TECHNOLOGY LAW REVIEW. *see* LAW

COMISION ECONOMICA PARA AMERICA LATINA Y EL CARIBE. SERIE DESARROLLO PRODUCTIVO. *see* BUSINESS AND ECONOMICS—International Development And Assistance

600 USA
COMP MEDIA; exploring art and technology in today's world!. Text in English. m. free.
Media: Online - full text.

600 USA ISSN 1542-0132
T174.3
➤ **COMPARATIVE TECHNOLOGY TRANSFER AND SOCIETY.** Abbreviated title: C T T S. Text in English. 2003 (Win.). 3/yr. USD 95 to institutions (print or online ed.); USD 133 combined subscription to institutions (print & online eds); USD 38 per issue to institutions (effective 2010). adv. back issues avail.; reprint service avail. from PSC. **Document type:** *Journal, Academic/Scholarly.* **Description:** Provides links between researchers and scholars who share an interest in the process, nature, significance, and implications of technology transfer.
Related titles: Online - full text ed.: ISSN 1543-3404.
Indexed: A12, A22, ABIn, E01, E09, EconLit, JEL, P02, P10, P16, P48, P51, P52, P53, P54, PQC.
—BLDSC (3363.875500), IE, Ingenta. **CCC.**
Published by: The Johns Hopkins University Press, 2715 N Charles St, Baltimore, MD 21218. TEL 410-516-6900, FAX 410-516-6968, psmith@press.jhu.edu. Eds. Bruce E Seely, Donald E Klingner, Gary Klein. Circ: 27. **Subscr. to:** PO Box 19966, Baltimore, MD 21211. TEL 410-516-6987, 800-548-1784, FAX 410-516-3866, jrnlcirc@press.jhu.edu.

600 GBR
COMPETE!. Text in English. q. **Document type:** *Journal, Trade.*
Formerly (until 1995): Technology Transfer Supplement (1357-7999)
Published by: Technology Transfer Team, Government Office for the South West, The Pithay, Bristol, Glos BS1 2PB, United Kingdom. TEL 44-117-9308448, FAX 44-117-9299494.

660 677 GBR ISSN 0266-3538
TA418.9.C6 CODEN: CSTCEH
➤ **COMPOSITES SCIENCE AND TECHNOLOGY.** Text in English. 1968. 16/yr. EUR 4,934 in Europe to institutions; JPY 655,100 in Japan to institutions; USD 5,515 elsewhere to institutions (effective 2012). adv. bk.rev. illus. index. back issues avail. **Document type:** *Journal, Academic/Scholarly.* **Description:** Contains original articles, occasional review papers, and letters on all aspects of the fundamental and applied science of engineering composites.
Formerly (until 1985): Fibre Science and Technology (0015-0568)
Related titles: Microform ed.: (from PQC); Online - full text ed.: (from IngentaConnect, ScienceDirect).
Indexed: A01, A03, A08, A22, A26, A28, ABIPC, APA, ASCA, ApMecR, B21, BrCerAb, C&ISA, C10, C24, CA, CA/WCA, CIA, CIN, CMCI, CPEI, CerAb, ChemAb, ChemTitl, CivEngAb, CorrAb, CurCont, E&CAJ, E11, EEA, EMA, ESPM, EngInd, EnvEAb, H&SSA, H15, I05, IBR, IBZ, ISMEC, ISR, Inspec, JOF, M&TEA, M09, MBF, METADEX, MSCI, P30, R18, RefZh, S01, SCI, SCOPUS, SolStAb, T01, T02, T04, TM, TTI, W07, WAA, WTA.
—BLDSC (3365.650000), AskIEEE, CASDDS, IE, Infotrieve, Ingenta, INIST, Linda Hall. **CCC.**
Published by: Pergamon (Subsidiary of: Elsevier Science & Technology), The Blvd, Langford Ln, East Park, Kidlington, Oxford OX5 1GB, United Kingdom. TEL 44-1865-843000, FAX 44-1865-843010, JournalsCustomerServiceEMEA@elsevier.com. Ed. T W Chou. **Subscr. to:** Elsevier BV, Radarweg 29, PO Box 211, Amsterdam 1000 AE, Netherlands. http://www.elsevier.nl.

600 RUS ISSN 1608-2753
COMPUPRINT. Text in Russian. 1999. bi-m. RUR 720 (effective 2004). adv. **Document type:** *Magazine, Trade.*
Published by: S K Press, Marksistkaya 34, str 10, Moscow, 109147, Russian Federation. deliver@skpress.ru, http://www.skpress.ru. Ed. V Pogorely. Pub. E Adlerov.

COMUNICACIONES CIENTIFICAS TECNOLOGICAS ANUALES. *see* ARCHITECTURE

600 PHL
CON - SCIENCE. Text in English, Tagalog; Summaries in English. 1979. bi-m. PHP 1. bk.rev.
Formerly: N I S T Newsletter
Published by: Industrial Technology Development Institute, P. Gil, Taft Ave, P.O. Box 744, Manila, Philippines. FAX 632-592275, TELEX ITT 40404. Ed. Ronand Henson. Circ: 750.

CONECTA/CONECTA: BULLETIN OF NEWS IN THE HISTORY OF SCIENCE AND TECHNOLOGY; Boletin de Noticias sobre Historia de la Ciencia, la Medicina y la Tecnologia. *see* SCIENCES: COMPREHENSIVE WORKS

CONFIGURATIONS; a journal of literature, science and technology. *see* LITERATURE

600 USA ISSN 2152-940X
▼ **CONNECTED WORLD.** Variant title: Connected World Magazine. Text in English. 2010 (July). 8/yr. USD 24.95 (effective 2011). **Document type:** *Magazine, Trade.* **Description:** Features news and information on the latest trends, advances, and innovations in technology.
Related titles: Online - full text ed.: ISSN 2152-9418. 2010 (July).
Published by: Specialty Publishing Co., 135 E Saint Charles Rd, Carol Stream, IL 60188. TEL 630-933-0844, FAX 630-933-0845, http://www.specialtypub.com. Ed. Mike Carrozzo TEL 630-933-0844 ext 256. Pub. Peggy Smedley TEL 630-933-0844 ext 226.

CONOZCA MAS. *see* SCIENCES: COMPREHENSIVE WORKS

600 CRI ISSN 0253-2492
Q180.C75
CONSEJO NACIONAL PARA INVESTIGACIONES CIENTIFICAS Y TECNOLOGICAS, COSTA RICA. INFORME ANUAL. Text in Spanish. 1975. a. free.

Published by: Consejo Nacional para Investigaciones Cientificas y Tecnologicas, Apdo. 10318-1000, Zapote, San Jose, Costa Rica. TEL 506-224-4172, FAX 506-225-7041, info@www.conicit.go.cr, http://www.conicit.go.cr. Circ: 1,000.

CONSTRUCTECH. *see* BUILDING AND CONSTRUCTION

CONSUMER GOODS TECHNOLOGY; improving business performance. *see* BUSINESS AND ECONOMICS—Management

▼ **CONTEMPORARY EDUCATIONAL TECHNOLOGY.** *see* EDUCATION

[CONTEXT]; where strategy and technology meet. *see* BUSINESS AND ECONOMICS—Computer Applications

600 USA
CORPTECH EXPLORE DATABASE. Text in English. a. (plus q. updates). USD 5,500 (effective 2008). **Document type:** *Trade.* **Description:** Presents data on 50,000 emerging manufacturers and developers of technology products that can be searched by over 30 different criteria.
Media: Online - full text.
Published by: CorpTech Information Services, Inc., 5711 South 86th Circle, Omaha, NE 68127. TEL 866-313-6367, editorial@corptech.com, corptech@infousa.com, http://www.corptech.com. R&P Steven Parker.

COSMILE UPDATE. (Competence Network Small & Micro Learning Enterprises) *see* BUSINESS AND ECONOMICS

COTTBUSER STUDIEN ZUR GESCHICHTE VON TECHNIK, ARBEIT UND UMWELT. *see* HISTORY—History Of Europe

CROSSINGS (DUBLIN); electronic journal of art and technology. *see* ART

CRYO-LETTERS. *see* BIOLOGY—Physiology

CUADERNOS DE CIENCIA Y TECNICA. *see* SCIENCES: COMPREHENSIVE WORKS

600 ESP ISSN 1133-9365
CUADERNOS I N T E M A C. (Instituto Tecnico de Materiales y Construcciones) Text in Spanish. 1991. q. EUR 35 domestic (effective 2009). **Document type:** *Journal, Trade.*
Indexed: IECT.
Published by: Intemac Ediciones, C. Monte Esquinza, 28, Madrid, 28010, Spain. FAX 34-91-3083609, 34-91-3083609, intemac@intemac.es.

600 620 363.7 ESP ISSN 1697-820X
CUADERNOS INTERNACIONALES DE TECNOLOGIA PARA EL DESARROLLO HUMANO. Text in Catalan, Spanish. 1992. s-a. **Document type:** *Journal, Academic/Scholarly.*
Former titles (until 2003): Revista de Cooperacion (1139-5532); (until 1995): Ingenieria sin Fronteras. Boletin Informativo (1139-5524); (until 1993): Ingenieros sin Fronteras. Boletin Informativo (1139-5516)
Related titles: Online - full text ed.: ISSN 1885-8104. 2004. free (effective 2011).
—CCC.
Published by: Federacion Espanola de Ingenieria sin Fronteras, C Cristobal Bordie, 19-21 4o. D., Madrid, 28003, Spain. TEL 34-91-5900190, http://www.isf.es/home/index.php.

CULTURA CIENTIFICA Y TECNOLOGICA. *see* SCIENCES: COMPREHENSIVE WORKS

600 NLD ISSN 0929-7006
➤ **CURRENT ISSUES IN PRODUCTION ECOLOGY.** Text in English. 1993. irreg., latest vol.5, 1999. price varies. **Document type:** *Monographic series, Academic/Scholarly.*
—BLDSC (3499.075450). **CCC.**
Published by: Springer Netherlands (Subsidiary of: Springer Science+Business Media), Van Godewijckstraat 30, Dordrecht, 3311 GX, Netherlands. TEL 31-78-6576050, FAX 31-78-6576474.

600 340 DEU ISSN 0722-9313
D I N - KATALOG FUER TECHNISCHE REGELN. BAND 1: DEUTSCHE NORMEN UND TECHNISCHE REGELN. (Deutsches Institut fuer Normung) Text in German. 1926. a. EUR 281 (effective 2009). bibl. **Document type:** *Catalog, Trade.*
Supersedes in part (in 1993): D I N - Catalogue of Technical Rules
Related titles: English ed.: D I N - Catalogue of Technical Rules. Vol. 1: German Standards and Technical Rules.
Published by: (Deutsches Institut fuer Normung e.V.), Beuth Verlag GmbH, Burggrafenstr 6, Berlin, 10787, Germany. TEL 49-30-26012260, FAX 49-30-26011260, postmaster@beuth.de, http://www.beuth.de.

600 340 DEU ISSN 0945-1080
TA368
D I N - KATALOG FUER TECHNISCHE REGELN. BAND 2: INTERNATIONALE NORMEN UND AUSGEWAEHLTE AUSLAENDISCHE NORMEN. (Deutsches Institut fuer Normung) Text in English. 1926. a. EUR 169 (effective 2009). **Document type:** *Catalog, Trade.*
Formerly (until 1993): D I N - Katalog fuer Technische Regeln. Band 3: Internationale Normen und Ausgewaehlte Auslaendische Normen (0942-6264)
Related titles: English ed.: D I N - Catalogue of Technical Rules. Vol. 2: International Standards and Technical Rules.
Published by: (Deutsches Institut fuer Normung e.V.), Beuth Verlag GmbH, Burggrafenstr 6, Berlin, 10787, Germany. TEL 49-30-26012260, FAX 49-30-26011260, postmaster@beuth.de, http://www.beuth.de. Circ: 4,000.

607.1 DNK ISSN 1604-1232
D T U AVISEN. (Danmarks Tekniske Universitet) Text in Danish. 1971. 10/yr. adv. back issues avail. **Document type:** *Newsletter, Consumer.*
Formerly (until 2004): Sletten (0108-6073)
Related titles: Online - full text ed.
Published by: Danmarks Tekniske Universitet/Technical University of Denmark, Anker Engelundsvej 1, Bygning 101 A, Lyngby, 2800, Denmark. TEL 45-45-252525, FAX 45-45-881799, dtu@dtu.dk. Ed. Dan Jensen TEL 45-45-251020. Adv. contact Ida Bangert. B&W page DKK 10,500, color page DKK 13,500; 260 x 373. Circ: 10,000.

700 USA
PN1992.93
D V D - LASER DISC NEWSLETTER. (Digital Video Disc) Text in English. 1984. m. USD 35 domestic; USD 50 foreign (effective 2000). adv. **Document type:** *Newsletter.* **Description:** Covers consumer news on movie, cultural, and educational laser discs available in both the American and Japanese markets.
Formerly (until 199?): Laser Disc Newsletter (0749-5250)
Indexed: MRD.
Published by: Douglas Pratt, Ed. & Pub., PO Box 420, East Rockaway, NY 11518. TEL 516-594-9304. Circ: 4,000.

DAEDALUS (STOCKHOLM); tekniska museets aarsbok. *see* MUSEUMS AND ART GALLERIES

607.48913 DNK ISSN 1603-1784
DANMARKS TEKNISKE UNIVERSITET. AARSRAPPORT. Text in Danish. 1998. a. back issues avail. **Document type:** *Yearbook, Consumer.*
Formerly (until 2004): Danmarks Tekniske Universitet. Virksomhedsregnskab (1600-3578)
Related titles: Online - full text ed.: ISSN 1604-7117.
Published by: Danmarks Tekniske Universitet/Technical University of Denmark, Anker Engelundsvej 1, Bygning 101 A, Lyngby, 2800, Denmark. TEL 45-45-252525, FAX 45-45-881799, dtu@dtu.dk. Ed. Morten Lund. Circ: 300.

600 658 300 TWN ISSN 1992-4534
DAOJIANG XUEBAO. Text in Chinese. 2006. s-a. **Document type:** *Journal, Academic/Scholarly.*
Published by: Daojiang Keji ji Guanli Xueyuan/T O K O University, no.51, sec.2, University Rd, Pu-tzu, Chia Yi 613, Taiwan. http://www.toko.edu.tw.

DATA LINK (ONLINE). *see* ENGINEERING—Computer Applications

600 ZAF ISSN 0256-8934
DATAWEEK; electronics & Networking technology. Text in English. 1979. bi-w. ZAR 210 (effective 2001). adv. back issues avail. **Document type:** *Journal, Trade.* **Description:** Covers electronic technology: components, design, manufacture, testing and maintenance.
Related titles: Online - full text ed.
Published by: Technews (Pty.) Ltd., PO Box 626, Kloof, 3640, South Africa. TEL 27-31-764-0593, FAX 27-31-764-0386, technews@iafrica.com.za, http://www.technews.co.za. Ed. James Williamson. Adv. contact Jane Fortmann TEL 27-31-764-5316. B&W page ZAR 8,480, color page ZAR 10,175; 260 x 385. Circ: 3,631 (controlled).

600 CHN ISSN 1008-1151
DAZHONG KEJI. Text in Chinese. 1999. m. CNY 120 (effective 2009). **Document type:** *Magazine, Consumer.*
Related titles: Online - full text ed.
Published by: Zhongguo Keji Kaifayuan Guangxi Fenyuan, 20, Xinzhu Lu, 3/F, Nanning, 530022, China. TEL 86-771-5710391, FAX 86-771-5710392.

DEFENCE SCIENCE JOURNAL. *see* MILITARY

DEFENSE SYSTEMS; information technology and net-centric warfare. *see* MILITARY

500 USA
DEFENSE TECH BRIEFS. Text in English. 6/yr. USD 75 domestic includes Puerto Rico; USD 195 elsewhere; free to qualified personnel (effective 2009). adv. back issues avail. **Document type:** *Magazine, Trade.* **Description:** Features articles on major technology development initiatives, tech briefs describing new inventions and their applications, special reports spotlighting spin-offs of military R&D, and announcements of cutting-edge products.
Formerly (until 2007): Technology Horizons
Related titles: Online - full text ed.: USD 36 (effective 2009).
Indexed: C&ISA, E&CAJ.
Published by: (Air Force Research Laboratory), Associated Business Publications International, 1466 Broadway, Ste 910, New York, NY 10036. TEL 212-490-3999, 800-944-6272, FAX 212-986-7864, info@abpi.net, http://www.abpi.net. Ed., Pub. Linda Bell. adv.: B&W page USD 6,260, color page USD 7,530. Circ: 90,643. **Subscr. to:** PO Box 3525, Northbrook, IL 60065. TEL 847-291-5220, FAX 847-291-4816, nasa@omeda.com.

LES DEFIS DU C E A; mensuel d'informations generales et scientifiques. (Commissariat a l'Energie Atomique) *see* SCIENCES: COMPREHENSIVE WORKS

DEJINY VED A TECHNIKY/HISTORY OF SCIENCES AND TECHNOLOGY. *see* SCIENCES: COMPREHENSIVE WORKS

DELEGATION REGIONALE DE COOPERATION DANS LE CONE SUD ET LE BRESIL. BULLETIN ELETRONIQUE. *see* SCIENCES: COMPREHENSIVE WORKS

600 NLD ISSN 0920-508X
DELFT INTEGRAAL. Text in Dutch. 1984. q. free (effective 2010). adv. back issues avail. **Document type:** *Magazine, Academic/Scholarly.* **Description:** Deals with technological research at the university.
Published by: Technische Universiteit Delft/Delft University of Technology, PO Box 5, Delft, 2600 AA, Netherlands. TEL 31-15-2789111, info@tudelft.nl, http://www.tudelft.nl. Ed. Frank Nuijens. Circ: 45,000.

600 NLD ISSN 0926-7212
T26.N4
DELFT OUTLOOK. Text in English. 1985. q. free (effective 2010). back issues avail. **Document type:** *Magazine, Academic/Scholarly.* **Description:** Contains articles about the research carried out at the university.
Published by: Technische Universiteit Delft/Delft University of Technology, PO Box 5, Delft, 2600 AA, Netherlands. TEL 31-15-2789111, info@tudelft.nl, http://www.tudelft.nl. Ed. Frank Nuijens.

600 USA ISSN 1753-3198
DENTAL PRODUCTS REPORT EUROPE. Text in English. 1980. 7/yr. USD 40 domestic; USD 75 in Canada & Mexico; USD 60 elsewhere; USD 8 per issue domestic; USD 11 per issue foreign (effective 2007). adv. **Document type:** *Magazine, Trade.* **Description:** Introduces dental materials, equipment, and service available to dentists and their laboratory technicians.
Formerly: Dental Products Report International
Related titles: Microform ed.: (from PQC); Online - full text ed.
Indexed: A15, ABIn, P20, P48, P51, P52, P54, PQC.
—CCC.
Published by: Advanstar Dental Communications (Subsidiary of: Advanstar Communications, Inc.), 2 Northfield Plaza, Ste 300, Northfield, IL 60093-1219. TEL 847-441-3700, FAX 847-441-3702, http://www.dentalproducts.net. Ed. Pam Johnson TEL 847-441-3716. Circ: 40,000.

600 MEX
➤ **DESARROLLO TECNOLOGICO.** Text in Spanish; Summaries in English, Spanish. 1992. irreg. (2-3/yr.). MXN 8 per issue. bibl.; charts. **Document type:** *Academic/Scholarly.* **Description:** Specializes in electronics and computer sciences.
Published by: Universidad Nacional Autonoma de Mexico, Instituto de Investigaciones en Matematicas Aplicadas y en Sistemas, Apdo. Postal 20-726, Del. V.A. Obregon, Mexico City, DF 01000, Mexico. TEL 622-35-62, FAX 550-00-47. Ed. Maria Ochoa Macedo. Circ: 500.

745.2 USA ISSN 0011-9407
TA175 CODEN: DIGNAO
DESIGN NEWS; news for OEM design engineers. Text in English. 1946. 18/m. free to qualified personnel (effective 2008); includes Design News OEM Directory issue. adv. software rev. abstr.; charts; illus.; pat.; tr.lit. index. Supplement avail.; back issues avail.; reprints avail. **Document type:** *Magazine, Trade.* **Description:** Provides information on power transmission, fastening, computers and CAD-CAM, fluid power, electrical and electronic design, new materials, new processes and new patents. Emphasis is on both mechanical and electrical-electronic design.
Incorporates (in 200?): Global Design News
Related titles: Online - full text ed.: Design News Online. free to qualified personnel (effective 2008); Chinese ed.: Design News China; Polish ed.: Design News Poland; Japanese ed.: Design News Japan; ◆ International ed.: Global Design News; ◆ Supplement(s): Design News O E M Supplier Search.
Indexed: A01, A02, A03, A05, A08, A09, A10, A15, A20, A22, A23, A24, A25, A26, A28, ABIn, AIA, APA, AS&TA, AS&TI, AcoustA, B01, B02, B03, B04, B06, B07, B09, B11, B13, B15, B17, B18, B21, BRD, BrCerAb, BusI, C&ISA, C10, CA/WCA, CADCAM, CIA, CerAb, ChemAb, CivEngAb, CorrAb, DM&T, E&CAJ, E08, E11, EEA, EIA, EMA, ESPM, EnvAb, EnvEAb, G04, G05, G06, G07, G08, H&SSA, H15, HlthInd, I05, I07, ISMEC, ISR, Inspec, M&TEA, M09, MBF, METADEX, MagInd, P02, P10, P26, P34, P48, P51, P52, P53, P54, PMR, PQC, RoboAb, S&VD, S04, S08, S09, S10, S23, SCOPUS, SolStAb, T&II, T01, T02, T04, TTI, TelAb, V02, V03, V04, W03, W05, WAA.
—BLDSC (3560.000000), CIS, IE, Infotrieve, Ingenta, INIST, Linda Hall. **CCC.**
Published by: Canon Communications LLC (Subsidiary of: Apprise Media LLC), 33 Hayden Ave., Lexington, MA 02421. TEL 800-869-6882, FAX 866-658-6156, info@cancom.com, http://www.cancom.com. adv.: B&W page USD 13,362, color page USD 15,904; trim 7.875 x 10.5. Circ: 170,000.

DESIGN NEWS O E M SUPPLIER SEARCH. (Original Equipment Manufacturer) *see* MACHINERY

745.2 SWE ISSN 1653-6886
DESIGN PAA CHALMERS/DESIGN AT CHALMERS. Text in English, Swedish. 2004. a. **Document type:** *Journal, Academic/Scholarly.*
Formerly (until 2006): Teknisk Design (1653-9044)
Published by: Chalmers Tekniska Hoegskola, Institutionen foer Produkt- och Produktionsutveckling/Chalmers University of Technology, Department of Product and Production Development, Goeteborg, 41296, Sweden. TEL 46-31-7721000, http://www.chalmers.se/ppd/sv.

DESIGN PRODUCTS AND APPLICATION; the engineer's guide to new products and design ideas. *see* ENGINEERING

DESIGN STUDIES. *see* ARCHITECTURE

745.209489 DNK ISSN 1603-1059
DESIGNMATTERS. Text in Danish, English. 2003. 4/yr. DKK 320; DKK 80 per issue (effective 2008). bk.rev. illus. **Document type:** *Journal, Trade.* **Description:** Gives an up-to-date review of the developments taking place in Danish and international industrial design and graphic communication.
Formed by the merger of (1979-2003): Rum og Form (0107-6035); (1991-2003): Design DK (0906-9194); Which was formerly (until 1991): Design (0900-3517); (until 1988): D D Bulletin (0107-0908)
Indexed: ABM, SCOPUS.
Published by: (Danske Designere), Dansk Design Center/Danish Design Centre, HC Andersens Boulevard 27, Copenhagen V, 1553, Denmark. TEL 45-33-693369, FAX 45-33-693300, design@ddc.dk. Ed. Anne-Marie Gregersen.

600 COL ISSN 0123-2592
DIALECTICA. Text in Spanish. 1996. s-a. **Document type:** *Journal, Academic/Scholarly.*
Published by: Fundacion Universitaria Panamericana, Ave 32 No. 17-62, Bogota, Colombia. TEL 57-2-3402373, FAX 57-2-3380666, unipanamericana@unipanamericana.edu.co, http://www.unipanamericana.edu.co/. Ed. Sara Teresa Aldana. Circ: 1,000.

600 CHN ISSN 1001-0548
TK7800 CODEN: DKDAEM
DIANZI KEJI DAXUE XUEBAO/UNIVERSITY OF ELECTRONIC SCIENCE AND TECHNOLOGY OF CHINA. JOURNAL. Text in Chinese. 1959. bi-m. USD 31.20 (effective 2009). **Document type:** *Journal, Academic/Scholarly.*
Formerly (until 1989): Chengdu Dianxun Gongcheng Xueyuan Xuebao (1000-2626)
Related titles: Online - full text ed.
Indexed: A22, A28, APA, BrCerAb, C&ISA, CA/WCA, CCMJ, CIA, CPEI, CerAb, CivEngAb, CorrAb, E&CAJ, E11, EEA, EMA, ESPM, EngInd, EnvEAb, H15, Inspec, M&TEA, M09, MBF, METADEX, MSN, MathR, RefZh, RiskAb, SCOPUS, SolStAb, T04, WAA, Z02.
—BLDSC (4912.248000), East View, IE, Ingenta, Linda Hall.
Published by: Dianzi Keji Daxue/University of Electronic Science and Technology of China, Main Bldg., Rm.219, No.4, Section 2, N. Jianshe Rd., Chengdu, Sichuan 610054, China. http://www.uestc.edu.cn.

DIANZI SHANGWU YANJIU/ELECTRONIC COMMERCE STUDIES. *see* BUSINESS AND ECONOMICS

600 FRA ISSN 1142-2580
Q2 CODEN: ORSIAF
DIDACTIQUES. Text in French. 1962. irreg., latest 2008. price varies. **Document type:** *Monographic series.*
Formerly (until 1989): O.R.S.T.O.M. Initiations Documentations Techniques (0071-9021)
Indexed: GeoRef, SpeleolAb.
—INIST.

Published by: O R S T O M Editions - Diffusion, 32 av. Henri Varagnat, Bondy, Cedex 93143, France. TEL 33-1-48037777, FAX 33-1-48030829, editions@paris.ird.fr, http://www.bondy.ird.fr/editions/ . **Co-publisher:** Institut de Recherche pour le Developpement (IRD).

DIGITAL MARKETING (TORONTO, 2000). *see* BUSINESS AND ECONOMICS—Marketing And Purchasing

600 OMN ISSN 1815-753X
DIGITAL OMAN/DIGITAL 'UMAN. Text in Arabic, English. 2005. q. **Document type:** *Magazine, Consumer.*
Published by: Oman Establishment for Press News Publications and Advertising/Mu'assasat 'uman al-Sihafat wa-al-Anba' wa-al-Nashr wa-al-I'lan, PO Box 200, Rusayl, 124, Oman. TEL 968-2415-5118, FAX 968-2444-9094. Ed. Ibrahim Al-Hamdani. Pub. Abdullah bin Nassir ar-Rahbi.

DIME; trend magazine for business people. *see* BUSINESS AND ECONOMICS

600 SWE ISSN 1654-031X
DIN TEKNIK. Text in Swedish. 1986. m. SEK 449 (effective 2007). adv. back issues avail. **Document type:** *Magazine, Consumer.* **Description:** Modern technology in everyday life.
Former titles (until 2007): P C Hemma (1400-4828); (until 1994): Svenska Hemdatornytt (1100-5467); (until 1988): Svenska Hemdator Hacking (0283-3115)
Related titles: Online - full text ed.; Includes: PC Hemma Special.
Published by: Hjemmet Mortensen AB (Subsidiary of: Hjemmet-Mortensen AS), Gaevlegatan 22, Stockholm, 11378, Sweden. TEL 46-8-6920100, FAX 46-8-6509705, info@hjemmetmortensen.se, http://www.hjemmetmortensen.se. Ed. Robert Laangstroem. Adv. contact Magnus Aahlund TEL 46-8-6926611. color page SEK 38,900; trim 190 x 285.

600 IND
DIRECTORY OF EXTRAMURAL RESEARCH AND DEVELOPMENT PROJECTS APPROVED FOR FUNDING BY CENTRAL GOVERNMENT. Text in English. 1991. a. **Document type:** *Directory, Government.*
Published by: Department of Science and Technology, Technology Bhavan, New Mehrauli Rd, New Delhi, 110 016, India. TEL 91-11-26567373, FAX 91-11-26864570, dstinfo@nic.in, http://www.dst.gov.in.

600 USA
DIRECTORY OF MEMBRANE & HIGH TECH SEPARATIONS (YEAR). Text in English. a. USD 395 (effective 2005). **Document type:** *Directory.*
Formerly: Yearbook and Directory of Members and Separation Technology
Published by: Business Communications Co., Inc., 40 Washington St, Ste 110, Wellesley, MA 02481. TEL 781-489-7301, FAX 781-489-7308, sales@bccresearch.com, http://www.bccresearch.com.

600 IND
DIRECTORY OF RESEARCH AND DEVELOPMENT INSTITUTIONS. Text in English. 1980. irreg., latest 2006. **Document type:** *Directory, Government.*
Published by: Department of Science and Technology, Technology Bhavan, New Mehrauli Rd, New Delhi, 110 016, India. TEL 91-11-26567373, FAX 91-11-26864570, dstinfo@nic.in, http://www.dst.gov.in.

DIRECTORY OF THE SCIENTISTS, TECHNOLOGISTS, AND ENGINEERS OF THE P C S I R. *see* SCIENCES: COMPREHENSIVE WORKS

DISCOVER; science, technology and the future. *see* SCIENCES: COMPREHENSIVE WORKS

DOMINI. TECNOLOGIA E PROGETTO DI ARCHITETTURA. *see* ARCHITECTURE

600 500 CHN ISSN 1005-3026
T4 CODEN: THYPDK
DONGBEI DAXUE XUEBAO (ZIRAN KEXUE BAN)/NORTHEASTERN UNIVERSITY. JOURNAL (NATURAL SCIENCES). Text in Chinese; Abstracts and contents page in English. 1955. m. USD 62.40 (effective 2009). 104 p./no.; **Document type:** *Journal, Academic/Scholarly.*
Formerly (until 1993): Dongbei Gongxueyuan Xuebao - Northeast Institute of Technology. Journal (0253-4258)
Related titles: Online - full content ed.; Online - full text ed.
Indexed: A22, A28, APA, BrCerAb, C&ISA, CA/WCA, CCMJ, CIA, CIN, CPEI, CerAb, ChemAb, ChemTitl, CivEngAb, CorrAb, E&CAJ, E11, EEA, EMA, ESPM, EngInd, EnvEAb, H15, Inspec, M&TEA, M09, MBF, METADEX, MSN, MathR, RefZh, SCOPUS, SolStAb, T04, TM, WAA, Z02.
—BLDSC (4834.180000), CASDDS, East View, IE, Ingenta, Linda Hall.
Published by: Dongbei Daxue, Xuebao Bianjibu, PO Box 269, Shenyang, Liaoning 110004, China. TEL 86-24-83687378, FAX 86-24-23891072. Eds. Dr. Tao Gu, Dr. Yongji Xu, Dr. Liang Zuo. R&P Dr. Tao Gu. **Dist. overseas by:** China International Book Trading Corp, 35 Chegongzhuang Xilu, Haidian District, PO Box 399, Beijing 100044, China. TEL 86-10-68412045, FAX 86-10-68412023, cibtc@mail.cibtc.com.cn, http://www.cibtc.com.cn.

▼ **DOW JONES E-MOBILITY.** *see* BUSINESS AND ECONOMICS—Economic Situation And Conditions

600 POL ISSN 0209-1763
DOZOR TECHNICZNY. Text in Polish. 1979. bi-m. PLZ 154.35 domestic; EUR 97 foreign (effective 2011). adv. 28 p./no.; **Document type:** *Journal, Trade.*
Supersedes in part (in 1982): Eksploatacja i Dozor (0208-5097); Which was formed by the merger of (1972-1979): Eksploatacja Maszyn (0137-3684); (1968-1979): Dozor Techniczny (0137-3781)
Related titles: Online - full text ed.
—BLDSC (3620.165000).
Published by: (Federacja Stowarzyszen' Naukowo-Technicznych NOT), Wydawnictwo SIGMA - N O T Sp. z o.o., ul Ratuszowa 11, PO Box 1004, Warsaw, 00950, Poland. TEL 48-22-8180918, FAX 48-22-6192187, sekretariat@sigma-not.pl. Ed. Waclaw Plewko TEL 48-22-5722115. adv.: B&W page PLZ 1,650, color page PLZ 3,630. **Dist. by:** Ars Polona, Obroncow 25, Warsaw 03933, Poland. TEL 48-22-5098609, FAX 48-22-5098610, arspolona@arspolona.com.pl, http://www.arspolona.com.pl.

DRESDEN PHILOSOPHY OF TECHNOLOGY STUDIES/DRESDNER STUDIEN ZUR PHILOSOPHIE DER TECHNOLOGIE. *see* PHILOSOPHY

600 DEU ISSN 0232-5349
T15
DRESDENER BEITRAEGE ZUR GESCHICHTE DER TECHNIKWISSENSCHAFT. Text in German. 1980. irreg., latest vol.27, 2001. EUR 3.33 per vol. (effective 2003). **Document type:** *Monographic series, Academic/Scholarly.*
Indexed: FR.
—BLDSC (3623.380000), INIST.
Published by: Technische Universitaet Dresden, Institut fuer Geschichte der Technik und der Technikwissenschaften, Mommsenstr. 13, Dresden, 01069, Germany. TEL 49-351-46334723, FAX 49-351-46337265, technikgeschichte@mailbox.tu-dresden.de, http://www.tu-dresden.de/phfigtt/.

DZALUU DZOHION BUTEEGCH/YOUNG INVENTOR. *see* SCIENCES: COMPREHENSIVE WORKS

E A S S T ELECTRONIC COMMUNICATIONS. (European Association of Software Science and Technology) *see* SCIENCES: COMPREHENSIVE WORKS—Computer Applications

E-GNOSIS. *see* SCIENCES: COMPREHENSIVE WORKS

E-JOURNAL OF SCIENCE & TECHNOLOGY. *see* SCIENCES: COMPREHENSIVE WORKS

E-NEWSLETTER FOR SCIENCE AND TECHNOLOGY. *see* SCIENCES: COMPREHENSIVE WORKS

600 USA
E O S - E S D TECHNOLOGY; the magazine for ESD-control professionals in the electronics industry. (Electrical Overstress - Electrostatic Discharge) Text in English. 1989. bi-m. USD 65. adv. **Document type:** *Magazine, Trade.*
Related titles: Microfiche ed.; Microfilm ed.
Published by: Brinton Group Inc., 49 Eaton Rd, Ste 100, Framingham, MA 01701. TEL 508-877-7958, FAX 508-877-3457, TELEX 6503201857 MCIUW. Ed. Lisa Gillette. Circ: 30,000.

600 GBR ISSN 0306-6215
E R A REPORT. (Electrical Research Association) Text in English. 19??. irreg., latest 2009. price varies. back issues avail. **Document type:** *Monographic series, Trade.* **Description:** Provides information to readers to develop their businesses in an increasingly competitive commercial environment.
Formerly (until 1963): British Electrical and Allied Industries Research Association. Technical Report
Related titles: Online - full text ed.
Indexed: Inspec.
—**CCC.**
Published by: E R A Technology Ltd., Cleeve Rd, Leatherhead, Surrey KT22 7SA, United Kingdom. TEL 44-1372-367000, FAX 44-1372-367099, era.info@cobham.com, http://www.era.co.uk.

E X S. (Experientia Supplementum) *see* BIOLOGY

EAST ASIAN SCIENCE, TECHNOLOGY, AND MEDICINE. *see* ASIAN STUDIES

EAST ASIAN SCIENCE, TECHNOLOGY AND SOCIETY; an international journal. *see* SCIENCES: COMPREHENSIVE WORKS

EASY TECH. *see* ELECTRONICS

001.891 CZE ISSN 1214-7982
T26.C9
ECHO; informace o evropskem vyzkumu, vyvoji a inovacich. Text in Czech. 2004. bi-m. **Document type:** *Journal, Academic/Scholarly.*
Related titles: Online - full text ed.: ISSN 1214-8229.
Published by: Technologicke Centrum AV CR, Rozvojova 135, Prague 6, 16502, Czech Republic. TEL 420-2-34006100, FAX 420-2-20922689, techno@tc.cz. Ed. Vladimir Albrecht.

620 FRA
ECOLE NATIONALE SUPERIEURE DE TECHNIQUES AVANCEES. RAPPORT D'ACTIVITE SUR LES RECHERCHES. Text in French. 1972. biennial. free. bk.rev.
Published by: Ecole Nationale Superieure de Techniques Avancees, Centre de Documentation, 32 bd. Victor, Paris, Cedex 15 75739, France. TEL 33-1-45525411, FAX 33-1-45525587. Circ: 1,200.

600 GBR ISSN 1043-8599
HC79.T4 CODEN: EINTEO
➤ **ECONOMICS OF INNOVATION AND NEW TECHNOLOGY.** Text in English. 1990. 8/yr. GBP 1,085 combined subscription in United Kingdom to institutions (print & online eds.); EUR 1,114, USD 1,400 combined subscription to institutions (print & online eds.) (effective 2012). adv. back issues avail.; reprint service avail. from PSC. **Document type:** *Journal, Academic/Scholarly.* **Description:** Devoted to theoretical and empirical analysis of innovation and new technology, this ournal acts as a bridge between the contributions of economic theory and empirical economics in this field.
Related titles: Microform ed.; Online - full text ed.: ISSN 1476-8364. 2002. GBP 977 in United Kingdom to institutions; EUR 1,002, USD 1,260 to institutions (effective 2012) (from IngentaConnect).
Indexed: A12, A17, A22, ABIn, B01, B06, B07, B08, B09, BAS, C23, CA, E01, EconLit, IBSS, JEL, P41, P48, P51, P52, P53, P54, PQC, SCOPUS, T02.
—IE, Infotrieve, Ingenta. **CCC.**
Published by: Routledge (Subsidiary of: Taylor & Francis Group), 4 Park Square, Milton Park, Abingdon, Oxon OX14 4RN, United Kingdom. subscriptions@tandf.co.uk, http://www.routledge.com. Adv. contact Linda Hann TEL 44-1344-779945. **Subscr. to:** Taylor & Francis Ltd., Journals Customer Service, Sheepen Pl, Colchester, Essex CO3 3LP, United Kingdom. TEL 44-20-70175544, FAX 44-20-70175198.

600 338 NLD ISSN 1381-0480
ECONOMICS OF SCIENCE, TECHNOLOGY AND INNOVATION. Key Title: Economy of Science, Technology and Innovation. Text in English. 1994. irreg., latest vol.31, 2006. price varies. back issues avail. **Document type:** *Monographic series, Academic/Scholarly.*
—BLDSC (3657.160000), IE, Ingenta.
Published by: Springer Netherlands (Subsidiary of: Springer Science+Business Media), Van Godewijckstraat 30, Dordrecht, 3311 GX, Netherlands. TEL 31-78-6576050, FAX 31-78-6576474. Eds. Bo Carlsson, Cristiano Antonelli.

600 USA ISSN 1537-1344
QA76.76.I59
EDESIGN; the magazine of interactive design and commerce. Text in English. 2002. bi-m. USD 39 domestic; USD 59 foreign (effective 2003). adv. bk.rev. illus.; stat. back issues avail.; reprints avail. **Document type:** *Magazine, Trade.*
Published by: eDesign Communications, 3200 Tower Oaks Blvd, Rockville, MD 20852. TEL 301-770-2900, FAX 301-984-3203, circ@edesignmag.com. Ed. Katherine Nelson. Circ: 15,000 (paid).

EDINBURGH ARCHITECTURE RESEARCH. *see* ARCHITECTURE

EDUCACAO, FORMACAO & TECNOLOGIAS. *see* EDUCATION

600 JPN ISSN 0387-7434
EDUCATIONAL TECHNOLOGY RESEARCH. Text in Japanese. s-a. USD 22.
Published by: Educational Technology Journal Association of Japan, 4-1-1 Nukui-Kita-Machi, Koganei-shi, Tokyo-to 184-0015, Japan. **Dist. by:** Business Center for Academic Societies Japan, 5-16-19 Honkomagome, Bunkyo-ku, Tokyo 113-0021, Japan. TEL 81-3-58145811.

600 CAN ISSN 1914-0681
EDUCATORS OF BUSINESS AND INFORMATION TECHNOLOGY IN MANITOBA. NEWSLETTER. Text in English. 1975. irreg. **Document type:** *Newsletter, Trade.*
Former titles (until 2006): Business Buzz (1491-2503); (until 199?): Manitoba Business and Computer Technology Educators' Association. Newsletter (1207-2826); (until 1995): M B E T A Newsletter (0381-6788)
Published by: Educators of Business and Information Technology in Manitoba (E B I T), 191 Harcourt St, Winnipeg, MB R3J 3H2, Canada. http://www.ebitmb.ca.

600 370 POL ISSN 1425-1566
EDUKACJA OGOLNOTECHNICZNA. Text in Polish. 1995. s-a. EUR 18 foreign (effective 2006).
Published by: Uniwersytet Rzeszowski, Instytut Techniki, Zaklad Dydaktyki Techniki i Informatyki, ul Rejtana 16A, Rzeszow, 35959, Poland. TEL 48-17-8625628. **Dist. by:** Ars Polona, Obroncow 25, Warsaw 03933, Poland. TEL 48-22-5098609, FAX 48-22-5098610, arspolona@arspolona.com.pl, http://www.arspolona.com.pl.

EDUPAGE. *see* EDUCATION

EKOLOGIA I TECHNIKA/ECOLOGY AND TECHNOLOGY. *see* ENVIRONMENTAL STUDIES

EKOLOGICHESKIE SISTEMY I PRIBORY; nauchno-tekhnicheskii i proizvodsvennyi zhurnal. *see* ENVIRONMENTAL STUDIES

363.7 POL ISSN 1428-2852
EKOTECHNIKA. Text in Polish. 1997. q. EUR 28 foreign (effective 2006). **Document type:** *Magazine, Trade.*
Indexed: B22.
Published by: Wydawnictwo Lektorium, ul Robotnicza 72, Wroclaw, 53608, Poland. TEL 48-71-7985900, FAX 48-71-7985947, info@lektorium.pl, http://www.lektorium.com. **Dist. by:** Ars Polona, Obroncow 25, Warsaw 03933, Poland. TEL 48-22-5098609, FAX 48-22-5098610, arspolona@arspolona.com.pl, http://www.arspolona.com.pl.

ELECTRICAL + AUTOMATION TECHNOLOGY. *see* COMPUTERS—Automation

THE ELECTRONIC JOURNAL OF MATHEMATICS & TECHNOLOGY. *see* MATHEMATICS

ELHUYAR: ZIENTZIA ETA TEKNIKA. *see* SCIENCES: COMPREHENSIVE WORKS

EMERGING COMMUNICATIONS: STUDIES IN NEW TECHNOLOGIES AND PRACTICES IN COMMUNICATION. *see* COMMUNICATIONS

600 USA ISSN 1040-2802
U393
EMERGING TECHNOLOGIES. Text in English. 1989. a. USD 1,495. charts; illus. **Description:** Examines the U.S. Department of Defense funding of research into weapon systems of the 21st century, such as submarine detection, computers and software, propulsion, optics, direct energy, robotics and machine intelligence, sensors, and signal processing.
Formerly (until 1989): Emerging Technologies Market Study (1042-1017)
Published by: Forecast International Inc., 22 Commerce Rd, Newtown, CT 06470. TEL 203-426-0800, 800-451-4975, FAX 203-426-0233, info@forecast1.com, http://www.forecast1.com.

ENERGIA AMBIENTE E INNOVAZIONE; bimestrale di informazione sulle nuove tecnologie, l'energia, e l'ambiente. *see* ENERGY

ENERGIAS. *see* ENERGY

604.2 USA ISSN 1949-9167
➤ **ENGINEERING DESIGN GRAPHICS JOURNAL (ONLINE).** Text in English. 1936. 3/yr. USD 40 (effective 2012). adv. bk.rev. charts; illus. cum.index: 1936-1978. back issues avail.; reprints avail. **Document type:** *Journal, Academic/Scholarly.* **Description:** Articles devoted to the fundamentals of engineering graphics education and graphics technology. Topics include engineering graphics, computer graphics, descriptive geometry, geometric modeling, computer-aided drafting and design, graphic data processing, visualization techniques, and graphics instruction.
Former titles (until 2009): Engineering Design Graphics Journal (Print) (0046-2012); (until vol.33, no.3, 1969): Journal of Engineering Graphics; (until vol.22, no.2, 1958): Journal of Engineering Drawing
Media: Online - full text. **Related titles:** CD-ROM ed.: (from PQC).
Indexed: A22, CPEI, EngInd, Inspec, RefZh, SCOPUS.
—BLDSC (3758.960000), IE, Ingenta, Linda Hall. **CCC.**
Published by: American Society for Engineering Education, Engineering Design Graphics Division, c/o Kathryn Holliday-Darr, Penn State Behrend, REDC, Rm. 234, 5101 Jordan Rd, Erie, PA 16563-1701. TEL 814-898-6271, FAX 814-898-6125, chinr@ecu.edu. Ed. Robert A Chin TEL 252-328-9648. Circ: 800 (paid).

➤ **ENVIRONMENTAL SCIENCE AND TECHNOLOGY.** *see* ENVIRONMENTAL STUDIES

600 CUB
EQUIPOS Y PRODUCTOS. TECNOLOGIA. Text in Spanish. m.
Published by: Academia de Ciencias de Cuba, Instituto de Documentacion e Informacion Cientifico-Tecnica (I D I C T), Capitolio Nacional, Prado y San Jose, Habana, 2, Cuba.

609 NLD ISSN 0927-3026
ERFGOED VAN INDUSTRIE EN TECHNIEK. Text in Dutch. 1992. q. EUR 25 domestic to individuals; EUR 30 foreign to individuals; EUR 50 domestic to institutions; EUR 60 foreign to institutions; EUR 20 domestic to students; EUR 25 foreign to students (effective 2010). **Document type:** *Journal, Academic/Scholarly.* **Description:** Covers industrial and technical heritage.
Formed by the merger of (1981-1991): Industriele Archeologie (0167-9619); Histechnicon (0923-3482); Which was formerly titled (until 1989): Histechnica Nieuws (0922-1018); (1975-1986): H Nieuws (0922-100X)
Indexed: B24.
Published by: Stichting Erfgoed, Brilduikerhof 12, Delft, 2623 NT, Netherlands. TEL 31-15-2622499. **Co-publisher:** Vlaamse Vereniging voor Industriele Archeologie.

001.891 CZE ISSN 1802-2006
➤ **ERGO.** Text in Czech; Text and summaries in Czech, English. 2006. 2/yr. free (effective 2009). abstr.; charts. back issues avail. **Document type:** *Journal, Academic/Scholarly.*
Related titles: Online - full text ed.: ISSN 1802-2170.
Published by: Technologicke Centrum AV CR, Rozvojova 135, Prague 6, 16502, Czech Republic. TEL 420-2-34006100, FAX 420-2-20922689, techno@tc.cz, http://www.tc.cz. Ed. Martin Fatun. Pub. Karel Klusacek. Circ: 1,200 (controlled).

607 DNK ISSN 0902-0152
ERHVERVLIVETS FORSKNING OG UDVIKLINGSARBEJDE. Text in Danish. 1975. biennial. charts; stat. back issues avail. **Document type:** *Academic/Scholarly.*
Related titles: Online - full text ed.: ISSN 1399-5146.
Published by: Dansk Center for Forskningsanalyse/Danish Centre for Studies in Research and Research Policy, Aarhus Universitet, Finlandsgade 4, Aarhus N, 8200, Denmark. TEL 45-89-422394, FAX 45-89-422399, cfa@cfa.au.dk, http://www.cfs.au.dk.

ESPACIOS. *see* SCIENCES: COMPREHENSIVE WORKS

ESPIRAL; revista electronica. *see* SCIENCES: COMPREHENSIVE WORKS

ESTACAO CIENTIFICA. *see* SCIENCES: COMPREHENSIVE WORKS

ESTRATEGIA GLOBAL; revista bimestral de relaciones internacionales, economia, seguridad y defensa y tecnologia. *see* POLITICAL SCIENCE—International Relations

600 330.9 MEX
ESTRATEGICA SOBRE NUEVO LEON EN UNA EPOCA DE CAMBIO. Text in Spanish. 1993. q. MXN 15 newsstand/cover.
Published by: Instituto Tecnologico y de Estudios Superiores de Monterrey, Centro de Estudios Estrategicos, Ave. EUGENIO GARZA SADA 2501 Sur, Monterrey, NL 64849, Mexico. TEL 52-81-83582000. Ed. Hector Moreira Rodriguez. Circ: 1,300.

600 370 ETH
ETHIOPIAN JOURNAL OF TECHNOLOGY, EDUCATION AND SUSTAINABLE DEVELOPMENT. Text in English. 2005. s-a. **Document type:** *Journal, Academic/Scholarly.*
Formed by the merger of (2005-2005): Bahir Dar Journal of Education (1816-336X); Which was formerly (1993-2005): Bahir Dar University. Education Faculty. Research Bulletin (1816-3351); (2002-2005): The Ethiopian Journal of Science and Technology (1816-3378)
Published by: Bahir Dar University, Research and Publications Office, PO Box 79, Bahir Dar, Ethiopia. TEL 251-8-200143, FAX 251-8-202025, bdtc@ethionet.et, http://www.telecom.net.et/~bdu/. Ed. Dr. Simie Tola TEL 251-8-205926.

EURASIA; journal of mathematics, science & technology education. *see* EDUCATION—Teaching Methods And Curriculum

600 NLD ISSN 0927-4057
CODEN: ECATEJ
EURO COURSES. ADVANCED SCIENTIFIC TECHNIQUES. Text in English. 1991. irreg., latest vol.2, 1992. price varies. **Document type:** *Monographic series, Trade.* **Description:** A series devoted to the publication of courses and educational seminars organized by the European Commission's Joint Research Centre Ispra, as part of its education and training program.
Indexed: CIN, ChemAb, ChemTitl.
—CASDDS. **CCC.**
Published by: Springer Netherlands (Subsidiary of: Springer Science+Business Media), Van Godewijckstraat 30, Dordrecht, 3311 GX, Netherlands. TEL 31-78-6576050, FAX 31-78-6576474.

EURO COURSES. CHEMICAL AND ENVIRONMENTAL SCIENCE. *see* ENVIRONMENTAL STUDIES

EURO COURSES. COMPUTER AND INFORMATION SCIENCE. *see* COMPUTERS

EURO COURSES. ENVIRONMENTAL IMPACT ASSESSMENT. *see* ENVIRONMENTAL STUDIES

EURO COURSES. ENVIRONMENTAL MANAGEMENT. *see* ENVIRONMENTAL STUDIES

EURO COURSES. HEALTH PHYSICS AND RADIATION PROTECTION. *see* ENERGY—Nuclear Energy

EURO COURSES. MECHANICAL AND MATERIALS SCIENCE. *see* ENGINEERING—Engineering Mechanics And Materials

EURO COURSES. NUCLEAR SCIENCE AND TECHNOLOGY. *see* ENERGY—Nuclear Energy

620 NLD ISSN 0926-9789
CODEN: EUCOE4
EURO COURSES. RELIABILITY AND RISK ANALYSIS. Text in English. 1991. irreg., latest vol.3, 1992. price varies. **Document type:** *Monographic series, Trade.* **Description:** A series devoted to the publication of courses and educational seminars organized by the European Commission's Joint Research Centre Ispra, as part of its education and training program.
Indexed: CIN, ChemAb, ChemTitl.
—CASDDS. **CCC.**
Published by: Springer Netherlands (Subsidiary of: Springer Science+Business Media), Van Godewijckstraat 30, Dordrecht, 3311 GX, Netherlands. TEL 31-78-6576050, FAX 31-78-6576474.

621.36 NLD ISSN 0926-9797
EURO COURSES. REMOTE SENSING. Text in English. 1991. irreg., latest vol.5, 1996. price varies. back issues avail. **Document type:** *Monographic series, Trade.* **Description:** A series devoted to the publication of courses and educational seminars organized by the European Commission's Joint Research Centre Ispra, as part of its education and training program.
Indexed: GeoRef, SpeleolAb.
Published by: Springer Netherlands (Subsidiary of: Springer Science+Business Media), Van Godewijckstraat 30, Dordrecht, 3311 GX, Netherlands. TEL 31-78-6576050, FAX 31-78-6576474.

600 NLD ISSN 0927-1007
CODEN: EUCTEJ
EURO COURSES. TECHNOLOGICAL INNOVATION. Text in English. 1991. irreg., latest vol.2, 1994. price varies. **Document type:** *Monographic series, Trade.* **Description:** A series devoted to the publication of courses and educational seminars organized by the European Commission's Joint Research Centre Ispra, as part of its education and training program.
Indexed: CIN, ChemAb, ChemTitl.
—CASDDS.
Published by: Springer Netherlands (Subsidiary of: Springer Science+Business Media), Van Godewijckstraat 30, Dordrecht, 3311 GX, Netherlands. TEL 31-78-6576050, FAX 31-78-6576474.

600 GBR
EURO TECHNOLOGY. Text in English. 1995. bi-m. free (effective 2010). adv. bk.rev. 96 p./no.; reprints avail. **Document type:** *Journal, Trade.* **Description:** Provides information on latest and broadest of industrial, scientific, and manufacturing technological developments.
Related titles: CD-ROM ed.; Online - full text ed.
Indexed: BMT.
Published by: Industrial and Technological Publications, 8 Matthew Wren Close, Little Downham, Ely, Cambs CB6 2UL, United Kingdom. TEL 44-1353-699916. Ed. William R Digby-Hammerton. Pub. Trevor Bennet. adv.: page GBP 500; 184 x 269.

600 DEU ISSN 0721-359X
EUROPAEISCHE HOCHSCHULSCHRIFTEN. REIHE 26: TECHNISCHE WISSENSCHAFTEN. Text in German. 1972. irreg., latest vol.3, 1981. price varies. **Document type:** *Monographic series, Academic/Scholarly.*
Published by: Peter Lang GmbH (Subsidiary of: Peter Lang Publishing Group), Eschborner Landstr 42-50, Frankfurt Am Main, 60489, Germany. TEL 49-69-7807050, FAX 49-69-78070550, zentrale.frankfurt@peterlang.com, http://www.peterlang.com.

EUROPEAN JOURNAL OF LAW AND TECHNOLOGY. *see* LAW

600 620 GBR ISSN 1450-202X
➤ **THE EUROPEAN JOURNAL OF TECHNOLOGY AND ADVANCED ENGINEERING RESEARCH.** Text in English. 2005. q. **Document type:** *Journal, Academic/Scholarly.* **Description:** The scope of the journal encompasses scientific articles, original research reports, reviews, short communication and scientific commentaries on technology and engineering.
Media: Online - full text.
Indexed: SCOPUS.
Published by: EuroJournals, 115 Ashby Rd., Leicestershire, LE153AB, United Kingdom. editor@eurojournals.com. Ed. Oliver H Fowinkel.

745.2 NLD ISSN 1567-7141
HE242
EUROPEAN JOURNAL OF TRANSPORT AND INFRASTRUCTURE RESEARCH (ONLINE). Text in English. q. free (effective 2011). **Document type:** *Journal, Academic/Scholarly.*
Media: Online - full text.
Indexed: A39, C27, C29, D03, D04, E13, ESPM, R14, RiskAb, S14, S15, S18, SCOPUS, SSciA.
Published by: Technische Universiteit Delft/Delft University of Technology, PO Box 5, Delft, 2600 AA, Netherlands. TEL 31-15-2789111, info@tudelft.nl, http://www.tudelft.nl. Eds. B van Wee, C G Chorus.

600 CHE
EUROPEAN ORGANIZATION FOR QUALITY. CONFERENCE PROCEEDINGS. Text in English. 1970. a. price varies. **Document type:** *Proceedings.*
Formerly: European Organization for Quality Control. Conference Proceedings (0071-2981)
Published by: European Organization for Quality/Organisation Europeenne pour la Qualite, PO Box 5032, Bern, 3001, Switzerland. TEL 41-31-3206166, FAX 41-31-3206828.

658.5 GBR ISSN 0969-059X
CODEN: EOQUDF
EUROPEAN QUALITY. Text in English; Summaries in French, German, Italian, Russian. 1958. bi-m. EUR 90 (effective 2009). bk.rev. abstr.; bibl.; charts; illus.; stat. back issues avail. **Document type:** *Magazine, Trade.*
Formerly (until 1994): E O Q Quality (0033-5169)
Indexed: CIS, Inspec, ORMS, P06, PAIS, QC&AS, RoboAb.
—BLDSC (3829.843280), IE, Infotrieve, Ingenta. **CCC.**
Published by: European Quality Publications Ltd., 29 Romilly Rd, London, N4 2QY, United Kingdom. TEL 4420-7503-8426, FAX 4420-7690-6860, mbe@european-quality.co.uk. Circ: 6,000 (paid).

658.5 CHE ISSN 0014-3243
EUROTEC; European technical news. Text in English, French, German. 1942. bi-m. adv. bk.rev. bibl.; charts; illus.; mkt.; pat.; stat.; tr.lit. **Document type:** *Journal, Trade.*
Related titles: Online - full text ed.
Indexed: G08, I05.
Published by: Nielsen Business Publications, Route des Acacias 25, PO Box 30, Geneva 24, 1211, Switzerland. TEL 41-22- 3077837, FAX 41-22- 3003748, http://www.nielsenbusinessmedia.com. Pub., Adv. contact Karl Wurzburger TEL 41-22-3077858. Circ: 11,000.

EVERYMAN'S SCIENCE. *see* SCIENCES: COMPREHENSIVE WORKS

600 USA ISSN 1934-7413
T49.5
EXTRAORDINARY TECHNOLOGY. Text in English. 2003. q. back issues avail. **Document type:** *Magazine, Academic/Scholarly.*
Related titles: Online - full text ed.
Published by: TeslaTech, Inc, 296 E Donna Dr, Queen Valley, AZ 85218. TEL 520-463-1994, teslatech@teslatech.info.

658.7 621 AUS ISSN 0728-9413
F E N. Text in English. 1966. m. AUD 140; AUD 9.90 per issue; free domestic to qualified personnel (effective 2008). adv. illus.; tr.lit. back issues avail. **Document type:** *Magazine, Trade.* **Description:** Provides information of new equipment and technology information for key buyers in manufacturing.
Former titles: F E N: Australian Factory Equipment News (0014-5807); (until 2001): Metalworking Australia (1444-4771); (until 2000): Metalworking (1440-2327); (until 1997): Metalworking Australia (1326-3951); (until 1995): Thomson's Metalworking Australia (1039-9917); (until 1993): Sheet Metal Australia (0818-1764)
Related titles: Online - full text ed.
Indexed: A10, B01, B02, B15, B17, B18, C10, G04, G08, I05, M01, M02, P48, P52, PQC, T02, V03.
Published by: Reed Business Information Pty Ltd. (Subsidiary of: Reed Business Information International), Tower 2, 475 Victoria Ave, Locked Bag 2999, Chatswood, NSW 2067, Australia. TEL 61-2-94222999, FAX 61-2-94222922, customerservice@reedbusiness.com.au, http://www.reedbusiness.com.au. Ed. Daniel Hall TEL 61-2-94222478. Pub. Chris Williams TEL 61-2-94222957. Adv. contact Hayden Reed TEL 61-2-94222110. B&W page AUD 4,630, color page AUD 6,051; trim 248 x 345. Circ: 15,238.

530 JPN
F G M NEWS. (Functionally Gradient Materials) Text in Japanese. q. JPY 5,000 to non-members; JPY 2,500 to members.
Published by: Society of Non-Traditional Technology/Mito Kagaku Gijutsu Kyokai, Toranomon Kotohira Kaikan, 1-2-8 Toranomon, Minato-ku, Tokyo, 105-0001, Japan. TEL 81-3-3503-4681, FAX 81-3-3597-0535.

FABRIKART; arte, tecnologia, industria, sociedad. *see* ART

FACHHOCHSCHULE-BOCHUM-JOURNAL. *see* COLLEGE AND ALUMNI

FACTA UNIVERSITATIS. SERIES PHYSICS, CHEMISTRY AND TECHNOLOGY. *see* PHYSICS

600 CHN ISSN 1672-0954
FAMING YU CHUANGXIN. (Publishes 2 editions: Combined Edition (Zhonghe Ban) and Student Edition (Xuesheng Ban)) Text in Chinese. 1984. m. CNY 60 (effective 2009).
Formerly (until 2003): Faming yu Gexin (1005-1317)
Related titles: Online - full text ed.
Published by: (Hu'nan Sheng Faming Xiehui), Faming yu Chuangxin Zazhishe, 59, Ba-Yi Lu, Changsha, 410001, China. TEL 86-731-4461871, FAX 86-731-4461178. **Co-sponsor:** Xianggang Faming Xiehui/Hong Kong Invention Association Ltd.

FEDERAL SCIENTIFIC ACTIVITIES. *see* SCIENCES: COMPREHENSIVE WORKS

600 USA ISSN 0886-7836
T1
FEDERAL TECHNOLOGY CATALOG. Text in English. 1981. a. back issues avail. **Document type:** *Catalog, Government.*
Formerly (until 1982): Tech Notes .. Annual Index
—Linda Hall.
Published by: U.S. Department of Commerce, National Technical Information Service, 5301 Shawnee Rd, Alexandria, VA 22312. TEL 703-605-6000, 800-553-6847, info@ntis.gov, http://www.ntis.gov.

FERRUM; Nachrichten aus der Eisenbibliothek. *see* METALLURGY

FIBEROPTIC PRODUCT NEWS TECHNOLOGY REFERENCE MANUAL. *see* COMMUNICATIONS—Telephone And Telegraph

FIBRECULTURE JOURNAL; internet theory criticism research. *see* COMMUNICATIONS

600 USA ISSN 2159-7065
FIELD TECHNOLOGIES. Text in English. 1997. m. free (effective 2011). adv. back issues avail. **Document type:** *Magazine, Trade.* **Description:** Provides in-depth feature articles, exemplary case histories and application stories, technology-specific trends and outlooks, practical insights to emerging technologies, topical and insightful columns, new product releases and developments.
Former titles (until 2011): Integrated Solutions for Wireless, Mobility & R F I D (1934-3191); (until 200?): Integrated Solutions for Retailers (1553-5894); (until 200?): Integrated Solutions (1096-3553)
Related titles: Online - full text ed.: ISSN 2159-709X.
Published by: Jameson Publishing, Inc., Knowledge Park, 5340 Fryling Rd, Ste 300, Erie, PA 16510. TEL 814-897-9000, FAX 814-899-5582, http://www.jamesonpublishing.com. Ed. Sarah Howland TEL 814-897-9000 ext 325. Adv. contact Tracy Tasker TEL 814-897-9000 ext 297. Circ: 28,000.

FILTER. *see* ART

FISH TECHNOLOGY NEWSLETTER. *see* FISH AND FISHERIES

600 GBR
FLAMES. Text in English. 1995. m. free. **Description:** Covers topics that relate to the way in which the development of new forms of technology impact on the way we live and the way society is organized.
Media: Online - full text.
Published by: Steinkrug Publications Ltd., 20 Leaden Hill, Orwell, Royston, Herts SG8 5QH, United Kingdom. TEL 44-1223-208926, FAX 44-1223-208098, pkruger@steinkrug.co.uk, http://www.steinkrug.co.uk/. Ed. Peter Kruger.

600 150 IND
FOCUS GROUP KIT. Text in English. 1997. irreg. USD 251 per issue (effective 2011). **Document type:** *Monographic series, Trade.* **Description:** Provides the reader with a systematic and readable approach to the design, implementation and analysis of focus group data.
Published by: Sage Publications India Pvt. Ltd. (Subsidiary of: Sage Publications, Inc.), B-1/I-1 Mohan Cooperative Industrial Area, Mathura Rd, PO Box 7, New Delhi, 110 044, India. TEL 91-11-40539222, FAX 91-11-40539234, info@sagepub.in, http://www.sagepub.in.

FOCUS ON SCIENCE AND TECHNOLOGY. *see* SCIENCES: COMPREHENSIVE WORKS

600 300 GBR ISSN 1463-6689
➤ **FORESIGHT (CAMBRIDGE)**; the journal for future studies, strategic thinking and policy. Text in English. 1999. bi-m. EUR 1,799 combined subscription in Europe (print & online eds.); USD 1,989 combined subscription in the Americas (print & online eds.); GBP 1,289 combined subscription in the UK & elsewhere (print & online eds.); AUD 3,829 combined subscription in Australasia (print & online eds.) (effective 2012). bk.rev. 96 p./no.; back issues avail.; reprint service avail. from PSC. **Document type:** *Journal, Academic/Scholarly.*
Description: Covers future studies, strategic thinking and policy.
Related titles: Online - full text ed.: ISSN 1465-9832. GBP 55, USD 95 to individuals; GBP 224, USD 389 to institutions (effective 2001) (from IngentaConnect).
Indexed: A01, A03, A08, A12, A22, ABIn, ASFA, B21, CA, E01, ESPM, EconLit, Emerald, Inspec, JEL, P02, P10, P42, P48, P51, P53, P54, PQC, RiskAb, S02, S03, S11, SCOPUS, SSciA, SociolAb, T02.
—BLDSC (3987.779200), IE, Infotrieve, Ingenta. **CCC.**
Published by: Emerald Group Publishing Ltd., Howard House, Wagon Ln, Bingley, W Yorks BD16 1WA, United Kingdom. TEL 44-1274-777700, FAX 44-1274-785201, information@emeraldinsight.com. Ed. Colin Blackman. Pub. Nicola Codner. **Subscr. in N America:** Emerald Group Publishing Limited, One Mifflin Pl, Ste 400, Harvard Sq, Cambridge, MA 02138. TEL 617-576-5782, 888-309-7810, FAX 617-576-5883.

➤ **FORMA.** *see* SCIENCES: COMPREHENSIVE WORKS

658.5 DEU ISSN 0944-8977
FORSCHUNGSBEITRAEGE ZU HANDWERK UND TECHNIK. Text in German. 1989. irreg., latest vol.17, 2007. price varies. **Document type:** *Monographic series, Academic/Scholarly.*
Published by: L W L - Freilichtmuseum Hagen, Maeckingerbach, Hagen, 58091, Germany. TEL 49-2331-78070, FAX 49-2331-7807120, freilichtmuseum-hagen@lwl.org, http://www.lwl.org/LWL/Kultur/LWL-Freilichtmuseum_Hagen/.

▼ **FORSCHUNGSBERICHTE KUNST UND TECHNIK.** *see* ART

607.489 DNK ISSN 1604-990X
FORSKERHISTORIER. Variant title: 8 Forskerhistorier. Text in Danish. 1970. a. free. illus. back issues avail. **Document type:** *Monographic series, Academic/Scholarly.*
Former titles (until 2005): Teknisk Videnskabelig Forskning (0105-192X); (until 1970): Denmark. Statens Teknisk-Videnskabelige Forskningsraad. Beretning
Related titles: Online - full text ed.: ISSN 1902-0023.
Published by: Det Frie Forskningsraad, Teknologi og Produktion/The Danish Council for Technology and Innovation, Bredgade 40, Copenhagen K, 1260, Denmark. TEL 45-35-446200, FAX 45-35-446201, fi@fi.dk. Ed. Pia Joernoe.

FORSKNING & FRAMSTEG. *see* SCIENCES: COMPREHENSIVE WORKS

FORTSCHRITT-BERICHTE V D I. REIHE 16: TECHNIK UND WIRTSCHAFT. *see* ENGINEERING

FORUM PRAXISFUEHRER. *see* OCCUPATIONS AND CAREERS

FORUM WISSENSCHAFT; das kritische Wissenschaftsmagazine. *see* SCIENCES: COMPREHENSIVE WORKS

FOUNDATION FOR RESEARCH, SCIENCE AND TECHNOLOGY. STATEMENT OF INVESTMENT OUTCOMES. *see* SCIENCES: COMPREHENSIVE WORKS

600.21 DNK ISSN 1600-2105
FRA RAADET TIL TINGET/FROM BOARD TO PARLIAMENT; teknologiraadets nyhedsbrev til folketinget. Text in Danish; Text occasionally in English. 199?. irreg. free. **Document type:** *Newsletter, Consumer.*
Formerly (until 1996): Fra Naevnet til Tinget (1600-2091)
Related titles: Online - full text ed.: ISSN 1602-4311. 199?.
Published by: Teknologiraadet/Danish Board of Technology, Antoniogade 4, Copenhagen K, 1106, Denmark. TEL 45-33-320503, FAX 45-33-910509, tekno@tekno.dk.

FROM NOW ON; the educational technology journal. *see* EDUCATION—Teaching Methods And Curriculum

600 JPN
FUKUI UNIVERSITY. FACULTY OF EDUCATION. MEMOIRS. SERIES 5: APPLIED SCIENCE AND TECHNOLOGY. Text in Japanese; Summaries in English, Japanese. 1964. a. free. **Document type:** *Academic/Scholarly.*
Published by: Fukui University, Faculty of Education/Fukui Daigaku Kyoikugakubu, 9-1 Bunkyo 3-chome, Fukui-shi, 910-0017, Japan.

600 JPN ISSN 0285-2799
FUKUOKA DAIGAKU KOGAKU SHUHO/FUKUOKA UNIVERSITY. REVIEW OF TECHNOLOGICAL SCIENCES. Text in English, Japanese. 1967. s-a. **Document type:** *Journal, Academic/Scholarly.*
Indexed: A22, Inspec, RefZh.
—BLDSC (4054.899810), IE, Ingenta, Linda Hall. **CCC.**
Published by: Fukuoka Daigaku, Kenkyujo/Fukuoka University, Central Research Institute, 8-19-1 Nanakuma, Jonan-ku, Fukuoka, 814-0180, Japan. TEL 86-92-8716631 ext 2813, sien@adm.fukuoka-u.ac.jp, http://www.adm.fukuoka-u.ac.jp/fu844/home2/Ronso/Ronso-top/Ronso-top.htm.

FUKUOKA KYOIKU DAIGAKU KIYO. DAI-3-BUNSATSU. SUGAKU, RIKA, GIJUTSUKA HEN/FUKUOKA UNIVERSITY OF EDUCATION. BULLETIN. PART 3: MATHEMATICS, NATURAL SCIENCES AND TECHNOLOGY. *see* SCIENCES: COMPREHENSIVE WORKS

FUTURES; the journal of policy, planning and futures studies. *see* BUSINESS AND ECONOMICS—Economic Situation And Conditions

600 USA ISSN 1056-8107
FUTURETECH. Text in English. 1971. 18/yr. looseleaf. bibl.; pat. back issues avail. **Document type:** *Newsletter, Trade.* **Description:** Presents strategic technologies judged capable of having an impact on broad industrial fronts.
Related titles: Online - full text ed.
Indexed: A26, B02, B15, B17, B18, E08, G04, G06, G07, G08, I05, I07, S06, S09, S23.
Published by: Technical Insights (Subsidiary of: Frost & Sullivan), 7550 IH 10 W, Ste 400, San Antonio, TX 78229. TEL 210-348-1000, 877-463-7678, FAX 888-690-3329, myfrost@frost.com, http://www.frost.com/prod/servlet/ti-home.pag.

THE FUTURIST; a journal of forecasts, trends, and ideas about the future. *see* SCIENCES: COMPREHENSIVE WORKS

500 CHE
FUTUROLOGY. Text in English. q. CHF 60. adv.
Published by: International Creative Center/Rencontres Creatives Internationales, 20 Ch Colladon, Geneva 28, 1211, Switzerland. Ed. Dali Schindler.

G I S T GLOBAL INFORMATION ON SCIENCE AND TECHNOLOGY. *see* SCIENCES: COMPREHENSIVE WORKS

G M S. HEALTH TECHNOLOGY ASSESSMENT. (German Medical Science) *see* MEDICAL SCIENCES

600 CHN ISSN 1002-0470
T4 CODEN: GTONE8
➤ **GAOJISHU TONGXUN/CHINESE HIGH TECHNOLOGY LETTERS.** Text in Chinese. 1991. m. USD 80.40 (effective 2009). **Document type:** *Journal, Academic/Scholarly.* **Description:** Covers China's latest high-tech research achievements in the areas of biotechnology, information science, automation, energy and advanced materials.
Related titles: Online - full text ed.; ◆ English ed.: High Technology Letters. ISSN 1006-6748.
Indexed: CIN, CPEI, ChemAb, ChemTitl, EngInd, INIS AtomInd, Inspec, SCOPUS.
—BLDSC (4307.363600), CASDDS, East View, Linda Hall.
Address: 54, Sanlihe Lu, PO Box 2143, Beijing, 100045, China. TEL 86-10-68598272, FAX 86-10-68514060. Circ: 3,000. **Dist. by:** China International Book Trading Corp, 35 Chegongzhuang Xilu, Haidian District, PO Box 399, Beijing 100044, China. TEL 86-10-68412045, FAX 86-10-68412023, cibtc@mail.cibtc.com.cn, http://www.cibtc.com.cn.

600 CHN ISSN 1006-222X
GAOKEJI YU CHANYEHUA/HIGH-TECH AND INDUSTRIALIZATION. Text in Chinese. 1994. bi-m. USD 159.60 (effective 2009). **Document type:** *Academic/Scholarly.* **Description:** Reports on the developments in the field of high-tech and its industrialization all over the world.
Related titles: Online - full text ed.
—East View.
Published by: Zhongguo Kexueyuan Wenxian Qingbao Zhongxin/Chinese Academy of Sciences, Documentation and Information Center, 8 Kexueyuan Nanlu, Zhongguancun, Beijing, 100080, China. TEL 86-1-6256-5310, FAX 86-1-6256-6846, hitech@las.ac.cn. Ed. Yue Xiaozhu. Circ: 10,000.

605 CHN
GAOXIN JISHU CHANYEHUA/HIGH-TECH INDUSTRIALIZATION. Text in Chinese. 1986. bi-m. CNY 34.80 (effective 2004). 80 p./no.; **Document type:** *Journal, Academic/Scholarly.* **Description:** Covers the trends, development and influence of both Chinese and foreign, new and high technologies.
Former titles (until 2000): Xin Jishu Geming ji Gao Jishu Chanye (1001-9987); (until 1991): Xin Jishu Geming Wenti ji Duice Yanjiu (1001-3113)
Published by: Zhongguo Renmin Daxue Shubao Ziliao Zhongxin/Renmin University of China, Information Center for Social Sciences, Dongcheng-qu, 3, Zhangzizhong Lu, Beijing, 100007, China. TEL 86-10-84043003, FAX 86-10-64015080, center@zlzx.org, http://www.zlzx.org/. **Dist. in US by:** China Publications Service, PO Box 49614, Chicago, IL 60649. TEL 312-288-3291, FAX 312-288-8570; **Dist. by:** China International Book Trading Corp, 35 Chegongzhuang Xilu, Haidian District, PO Box 399, Beijing 100044, China. TEL 86-10-68412045, FAX 86-10-68412023, cibtc@mail.cibtc.com.cn, http://www.cibtc.com.cn.

GEAR. *see* ELECTRONICS

GENDER, TECHNOLOGY & DEVELOPMENT. *see* WOMEN'S STUDIES

GENRYU. *see* SCIENCES: COMPREHENSIVE WORKS

GEORGIAN INTERNATIONAL JOURNAL OF SCIENCE, TECHNOLOGY AND MEDICINE. *see* MEDICAL SCIENCES

GHANA SCIENCE ASSOCIATION. JOURNAL. *see* SCIENCES: COMPREHENSIVE WORKS

600 JPN ISSN 0285-6301
T4
GIEN/INNOVATIVE TECHNOLOGY WORLD. Text in Japanese. 1966. s-a. **Document type:** *Journal, Academic/Scholarly.*
Indexed: A28, APA, BrCerAb, C&ISA, CA/WCA, CIA, CerAb, CivEngAb, CorrAb, E&CAJ, E11, EEA, EMA, ESPM, EnvEAb, H15, M&TEA, M09, MBF, METADEX, RefZh, SolStAb, T04, WAA.
—Linda Hall.
Published by: Kansai Daigaku, Kogyo Gijutsu Kenkyujo/Kansai University, Research Institute of Industrial Technology, 3-35 Yamate-cho 3-chome, Suita-shi, Osaka-fu 564-0073, Japan.

GIJUTSU MANEJIMENTO KENKYUU/YOKOHAMA JOURNAL OF TECHNOLOGY MANAGEMENT STUDIES. *see* BUSINESS AND ECONOMICS—Management

600 USA
GILDER TECHNOLOGY REPORT. Text in English. 1996. m. USD 295 domestic; USD 350 foreign (effective 2001). 8 p./no.; back issues avail. **Document type:** *Newsletter.* **Description:** Focuses on emerging trends in technology.
Related titles: Online - full content ed.
Published by: Gilder Publishing, 291A Main St, Great Barrington, MA 01230. TEL 888-484-2727, FAX 413-644-2123. Adv. contact Brian Cole TEL 413-644-2127.

GLOBAL BIOGEOCHEMICAL CYCLES; an international journal of global change. *see* SCIENCES: COMPREHENSIVE WORKS

▼ **GLOBAL JOURNAL OF TECHNOLOGY AND OPTIMIZATION.** *see* SCIENCES: COMPREHENSIVE WORKS

GLOBAL LINK. *see* AGRICULTURE—Agricultural Economics

600 USA ISSN 0882-3766
Q179.98
GOVERNMENT RESEARCH DIRECTORY. Text in English. 1980. irreg., latest 2009, 24th ed. USD 775 per issue (print & online eds.) (effective 2009). back issues avail. **Document type:** *Directory, Trade.* **Description:** Features information on the facilities and programs of the U.S. and Canadian federal governments.
Formerly (until 1985): Government Research Centers Directory (0270-4811)
Related titles: Online - full text ed.
Indexed: GeoRef, SpeleolAb.
—BLDSC (4206.060300).
Published by: Gale (Subsidiary of: Cengage Learning), 27500 Drake Rd, Farmington Hills, MI 48331. TEL 248-699-4253, 800-877-4253, FAX 877-363-4253, gale.customerservice@cengage.com, http://gale.cengage.com. Ed. Annette Piccirelli.

600 CUB ISSN 1027-975X
GRANMA CIENCIA. Text in Spanish. 1995. q. back issues avail.
Media: Online - full text.
Indexed: CA, F04, T02.
Published by: Centro de Informacion y Gestion Tecnologica de Granma, Carr. Central Via de Santiago de Cuba, km. 3 1/2, Bayamo, Granma, Cuba. TEL 53-7-481217, http://www.granma.inf.cu/ciget/. Ed. Teresa Dumenigo Jimenez.

600 USA ISSN 1549-7321
GREENWOOD TECHNOGRAPHIES. Variant title: Technographies. Text in English. 2004. irreg., latest 2007. price varies. back issues avail. **Document type:** *Monographic series.*
Related titles: Online - full text ed.
Published by: Greenwood Publishing Group Inc. (Subsidiary of: A B C - C L I O), 88 Post Rd W, PO Box 5007, Westport, CT 06881. TEL 203-226-3571, 800-225-5800, FAX 877-231-6980, sales@greenwood.com, http://www.greenwood.com.

600 BEL
GROWTH IN ACTION; the competitive and sustainable growth programme magazine. Text in English. 2000. s-a. **Document type:** *Journal, Academic/Scholarly.* **Description:** Presents the tangible results of research projects and other activities funded by the Growth programme.
Published by: European Commission, Directorate General - Research, PO Box 2201, Luxembourg, 1022, Belgium. FAX 32-2-296-5987.

GUANGDONG SHUILI DIANLI ZHIYE JISHU XUEYUAN XUEBAO/GUANGDONG TECHNICAL COLLEGE OF WATER RESOURCES AND ELECTRIC ENGINEERING. JOURNAL. *see* EDUCATION

600 CHN ISSN 1004-6410
GUANGXI GONGXUEYUAN XUEBAO/GUANGXI UNIVERSITY OF TECHNOLOGY. JOURNAL. Text in Chinese. 1990. q. CNY 8 newsstand/cover (effective 2006). **Document type:** *Journal, Academic/Scholarly.*
Related titles: Online - full text ed.
Indexed: A28, APA, BrCerAb, C&ISA, CA/WCA, CIA, CerAb, CivEngAb, CorrAb, E&CAJ, E11, EEA, EMA, H15, M&TEA, M09, MBF, METADEX, SolStAb, T04, WAA.
Published by: Guangxi Gongxueyuan/Guangxi University of Technology, 268, Donghuan Lu, Liuzhou, 545006, China. TEL 86-772-2685373.

600 ESP ISSN 1988-7493
GUIAS PARA ENSENANZAS MEDIAS. TECNOLOGIA. Text in Spanish. 2007. m. **Document type:** *Monographic series, Academic/Scholarly.*
Media: Online - full text.
Published by: Wolters Kluwer Espana - Educacion (Subsidiary of: Wolters Kluwer N.V.), C Collado Mediano 9, Las Rozas, Madrid, 28230, Spain. TEL 34-902-250510, FAX 34-902-250515, cleintes@wkeducacion.es, http://www.wkeducacion.es/index.asp. Ed. Joaquin Gairin.

600 FRA ISSN 1958-7104
LE GUIDE IPROFESSIONNEL. Text in French. 2007. irreg.
Published by: 18 Productions, 18 Rue du Sentier, Paris, 75002, France. http://www.idistribution.fr.

600 608.7 USA
GUIDE TO AVAILABLE TECHNOLOGIES; an annual guide to business opportunities in technology. Text in English. 1985. a. USD 165. **Document type:** *Newsletter.*
Published by: Louis Schiffman, Pub, PO Box 1036, Willow Grove, PA 19090-0736. TEL 215-887-5980, FAX 215-576-7924. Pub. Louis F Schiffman.

600 CHN ISSN 1674-9057
GUILIN LIGONG DAXUE XUEBAO/GUILIN UNIVERSITY OF TECHNOLOGY. JOURNAL. Text in English. 1981. q. **Document type:** *Journal, Academic/Scholarly.*
Former titles (until 2010): Guilin Gongxueyuan Xuebao/Guilin Institute of Technology. Journal (1006-544X); (until 1994): Guilin Yejin Dizhi Xueyuan Xuebao/Guilin College of Geology. Journal (1000-2545)
Related titles: Online - full text ed.
Indexed: A28, APA, BrCerAb, C&ISA, CA/WCA, CIA, CerAb, CivEngAb, CorrAb, E&CAJ, E11, EEA, EMA, ESPM, EnvEAb, GeoRef, H15, M&TEA, M09, MBF, METADEX, PollutAb, RefZh, RiskAb, SSciA, SolStAb, T04, WAA.
—BLDSC (4757.742100).
Published by: Guilin Gongxueyuan/Guilin University of Technology, 12, Jiankan Lu, Guilin, 541004, China. TEL 86-773-5896423, FAX 86-773-5812796.

GUNMA UNIVERSITY, FACULTY OF EDUCATION. ANNUAL REPORT: ART, TECHNOLOGY, HEALTH & PHYSICAL EDUCATION, AND SCIENCE OF HUMAN LIVING SERIES. *see* EDUCATION—Higher Education

GUOFANG KEJI/NATIONAL DEFENSE SCIENCE & TECHNOLOGY. *see* MILITARY

GUOFANG KEJI DAXUE XUEBAO/NATIONAL UNIVERSITY OF DEFENSE TECHNOLOGY. JOURNAL. *see* MILITARY

GUOLI BINGDONG KEJI DAXUE XUEBAO. *see* SCIENCES: COMPREHENSIVE WORKS

HAERBIN LIGONG DAXUE XUEBAO/HARBIN UNIVERSITY OF SCIENCE AND TECHNOLOGY. JOURNAL. *see* SCIENCES: COMPREHENSIVE WORKS

600 JPN ISSN 0286-5491
T4 CODEN: HKSKDY
HAKODATE TECHNICAL COLLEGE. RESEARCH REPORTS/HAKODATE KOGYO KOTO SENMON GAKKO KIYO. Text in Japanese; Summaries in English. 1967. a. illus.
Indexed: CIN, ChemAb, ChemTitl.
—CASDDS.
Published by: Hakodate Technical College/Hakodate Kogyo Koto Senmon Gakko, 226 Tokura-cho, Hakodate, 2-042, Japan.

600 CHE ISSN 1420-4878
HANDBUCH DER AUTOMATISIERUNGSTECHNIK. Text in German. 1992. a.
Related titles: ◆ Supplement to: T R Transfer. ISSN 1023-0823.
Published by: Hallwag AG, Nordring 4, Bern, 3001, Switzerland. TEL 41-31-3355555, FAX 41-31-3355784.

TU

658.5 DEU ISSN 0942-8976
HANDWERK MAGAZIN. Text in German. 1947. m. EUR 72 (effective 2010). adv. bk.rev. **Document type:** *Magazine, Trade.* **Description:** For all craft trades. Includes news and information, features, reports of events and exhibitions.
Former titles: Handwerk; Neue Handwerk (0028-3193)
Published by: Holzmann Medien GmbH & Co. KG, Gewerbestr 2, Bad Woerishofen, 86825, Germany. TEL 49-8247-35401, FAX 49-8247-354127, info@holzmannverlag.de, http://www.holzmannverlag.de. Ed. Holger Externbrink. Adv. contact Eva-Maria Hammer. Circ: 80,339 (paid and controlled).

600 CHN ISSN 1005-9113
T4 CODEN: JHITED
➤ **HARBIN INSTITUTE OF TECHNOLOGY. JOURNAL.** Text and summaries in English. 1994. q. USD 79.80 (effective 2009). **Document type:** *Journal, Academic/Scholarly.* **Description:** Covers mechano-electronics, material science and technology, civil administration and engineering, precision instruments and mechanics, structure engineering, communication and information system, navigation guidance and control, fundamental mechanics, computer applications, environmental engineering, management science and engineering, aircraft design, machine building and automation, electronic motors and appliances, power plant and engineering, physicoelectronics and optics.
Related titles: Online - full text ed.; ◆ Chinese ed.: Harbin Gongye Daxue Xuebao. ISSN 0367-6234.
Indexed: A28, APA, BrCerAb, C&ISA, CA/WCA, CIA, CIN, CPEI, CerAb, ChemAb, CivEngAb, CorrAb, E&CAJ, E11, EEA, EMA, EngInd, H15, Inspec, M&TEA, M09, MBF, METADEX, SCOPUS, SolStAb, T04, WAA, Z02.
—BLDSC (4757.878200), CASDDS, East View, IE, Ingenta, Linda Hall.
Published by: Harbin Gongye Daxue/Harbin Institute of Technology, 92 Xidazhi St, Harbin, Heilongjiang 150001, China. TEL 86-451-6414435, FAX 86-451-6418376, pan@hopc.hit.edu.cn. Ed. Qishu Pan. R&P Xianfang Wen. Circ: 1,000.

➤ **HARVARD JOURNAL OF LAW AND TECHNOLOGY.** *see* LAW

➤ **HEALTH FUTURES DIGEST.** *see* HEALTH FACILITIES AND ADMINISTRATION

600 CHN ISSN 1008-1534
HEBEI GONGYE KEJI/HEBEI JOURNAL OF INDUSTRIAL SCIENCE AND TECHNOLOGY. Text in Chinese. 1997. bi-m.
Related titles: Online - full content ed.; Online - full text ed.
Indexed: ASFA, ESPM, Inspec, RefZh, SWRA.
—BLDSC (4282.215734), IE, Ingenta.
Published by: Hebei Keji Daxue, 186 Yuhua Dong Lu, Shijiazhuang, Hebei 050018, China. TEL 86-311-8632141. **Dist. by:** China International Book Trading Corp, 35 Chegongzhuang Xilu, Haidian District, PO Box 399, Beijing 100044, China. TEL 86-10-68412045, FAX 86-10-68412023, cibtc@mail.cibtc.com.cn, http://www.cibtc.com.cn.

HEBEI KEJI DAXUE XUEBAO/HEBEI UNIVERSITY OF SCIENCE AND TECHNOLOGY. JOURNAL. *see* SCIENCES: COMPREHENSIVE WORKS

600 CHN ISSN 1674-0262
HEBEI LIGONG DAXUE XUEBAO (ZIRAN KEXUE BAN)/HEBEI POLYTECHNIC UNIVERSITY. JOURNAL. Text in Chinese. 1979. q. **Document type:** *Journal, Academic/Scholarly.*
Former titles (until 2007): Hebei Ligong Xueyuan Xuebao/Hebei Institute of Technology. Journal (1007-2829); (until 1995): Tangshan Gongcheng Jishu Xueyuan Xuebao (1005-9199)
Related titles: Online - full text ed.
—BLDSC (4996.910000), IE, Ingenta.
Published by: Hebei Ligong Daxue/Hebei Institute of Technology, 46 Xinhua-dao, Tangshan, 063009, China. TEL 86-315-2592093, http://www.heut.edu.cn/. **Dist. by:** China International Book Trading Corp, 35 Chegongzhuang Xilu, Haidian District, PO Box 399, Beijing 100044, China. TEL 86-10-68412045, FAX 86-10-68412023, cibtc@mail.cibtc.com.cn, http://www.cibtc.com.cn.

600 CHN ISSN 1006-334X
HECHENG JISHU JI YINGYONG/SYNTHETIC TECHNOLOGY AND APPLICATION. Text in Chinese. 1986. q. **Document type:** *Journal, Academic/Scholarly.*
Related titles: Online - full text ed.
—BLDSC (4282.765000), IE.
Published by: Zhongguo Shi-hua Yizheng Huaxian Gufen Youxian Gongsi/Sinopec Yizheng Chemical Fibre Company Limited, Xupu, 211900, China. TEL 86-514-3233547, FAX 86-514-3233325.

HEIDELBERGER JAHRBUECHER. *see* SCIENCES: COMPREHENSIVE WORKS

600 CHN ISSN 1672-6871
HENAN KEJI DAXUE XUEBAO (ZIRAN KEXUE BAN)/HENAN UNIVERSITY OF SCIENCE & TECHNOLOGY. JOURNAL (NATURAL SCIENCE). Text in Chinese. 1964. bi-m. CNY 8 newsstand/cover (effective 2007). abstr.; charts; bibl.; illus. 96 p./no.; back issues avail. **Document type:** *Journal, Academic/Scholarly.*
Formerly: Luoyang Gongxueyuan Xuebao/Luoyang Institute of Technology. Journal (1000-5080)
Related titles: Online - full text ed.
Indexed: A28, APA, B21, BrCerAb, C&ISA, CA/WCA, CIA, CerAb, CivEngAb, CorrAb, E&CAJ, E11, EEA, EMA, ESPM, EnvEAb, H15, Inspec, M&TEA, M09, MBF, METADEX, RefZh, RiskAb, SWRA, SolStAb, T04, WAA, Z02.
—Linda Hall.
Published by: Henan Keji Daxue, 48, Xiyuan Jie, PO Box 54, Luoyang, 471003, China. TEL 86-379-64231476, FAX 86-379-64231476.

600 JPN ISSN 0910-3848
HIGH-TECH NEWS. Text in Japanese. 1984. w. **Document type:** *Newsletter, Trade.*
Published by: Jukagaku Kogyo Tsushinsha/Heavy & Chemical Industry News Agency, 2-36 Jinbo-cho, Kanda, Chiyoda-ku, Tokyo, 101-0051, Japan. TEL 81-3-3230-3531, FAX 81-3-3264-0728, fcnews@jkn.co.jp, http://www.jkn.co.jp/.

600 CHN ISSN 1006-6748
T1 CODEN: HTLEFC
➤ **HIGH TECHNOLOGY LETTERS.** Text in English. 1994. q. USD 44.40 (effective 2009). **Document type:** *Journal, Academic/Scholarly.* **Description:** Covers China's latest high-tech research achievements in the areas of biotechnology, information science, automation, energy, and advanced materials.
Related titles: Online - full content ed.; Online - full text ed.; ◆ Chinese ed.: Gaojishu Tongxun. ISSN 1002-0470.
Indexed: CPEI, EngInd, Inspec, RefZh, SCOPUS, Z02.
—BLDSC (4307.363620), CASDDS, East View, IE, Ingenta, INIST, Linda Hall.
Published by: (Zhongguo Kexue Jishu Xinxi Yanjiusuo/Institute of Scientific and Technical Information of China), Kexue Chubanshe/Science Press, 16 Donghuang Cheng Genbei Jie, Beijing, 100717, China. TEL 86-10-64000246, FAX 86-10-64030255, http://www.sciencep.com/. Ed. Zhang Shuqing. Circ: 1,000. **Dist. by:** China International Book Trading Corp, 35 Chegongzhuang Xilu, Haidian District, PO Box 399, Beijing 100044, China. TEL 86-10-68412045, FAX 86-10-68412023, cibtc@mail.cibtc.com.cn, http://www.cibtc.com.cn.

600 AUT ISSN 1020-2994
HIGH TECHNOLOGY SPIN-OFFS: MONITOR. Text in German. 1994. s-a. free.
Published by: (Statistical and Industrial Networking Section), United Nations Industrial Development Organization, Wagramerstr 5, Vienna International Ctr, PO Box 300, Vienna, W 1400, Austria. TEL 43-1-26026-3736, FAX 43-1-26026-6843. Ed. V Kojarnovitch. Circ: 1,500.

600 JPN ISSN 1346-9975
T4 CODEN: HKDKCQ
HIROSHIMA KOUGYOU DAIGAKU KIYOU. KENKYUU HEN/HIROSHIMA INSTITUTE OF TECHNOLOGY. BULLETIN. RESEARCH VOLUME. Text in English, Japanese. 1966. a. **Document type:** *Bulletin, Academic/Scholarly.*
Supersedes in part (in 2002): Hiroshima Kogyo Daigaku Kenkyu Kiyo (0385-1672)
Indexed: A22, A28, APA, BrCerAb, C&ISA, CA/WCA, CIA, CerAb, CivEngAb, CorrAb, E&CAJ, E11, EEA, EMA, ESPM, EnvEAb, H15, Inspec, M&TEA, M09, MBF, METADEX, SolStAb, T04, WAA.
—BLDSC (2555.071420), IE, Ingenta, INIST, Linda Hall.
Published by: Hiroshima Kogyo Daigaku/Hiroshima Institute of Technology, 2-1-1 Miyake, Saeki, Hiroshima, 731-5193, Japan. TEL 81-82-921-3121, FAX 81-82-923-4551, http://www.cc.it-hiroshima.ac.jp.

600 JPN ISSN 1346-9983
T61
HIROSHIMA KOUGYOU DAIGAKU KIYOU. KYOUIKU HEN/HIROSHIMA INSTITUTE OF TECHNOLOGY. BULLETIN. EDUCATION VOLUME. Text in English, Japanese. 1966. a.
Supersedes in part (in 2002): Hiroshima Kogyo Daigaku Kenkyu Kiyo (0385-1672)
Indexed: A22, A28, APA, BrCerAb, C&ISA, CA/WCA, CIA, CerAb, CivEngAb, CorrAb, E&CAJ, E11, EEA, EMA, ESPM, EnvEAb, H15, M&TEA, M09, MBF, METADEX, SolStAb, T04, WAA.
—BLDSC (2555.071400), IE, Ingenta, INIST, Linda Hall.
Published by: Hiroshima Kogyo Daigaku/Hiroshima Institute of Technology, 2-1-1 Miyake, Saeki, Hiroshima, 731-5193, Japan. TEL 81-82-921-3121, FAX 81-82-923-4551, http://www.cc.it-hiroshima.ac.jp.

HISTORICAL STUDIES IN IRISH SCIENCE AND TECHNOLOGY. *see* SCIENCES: COMPREHENSIVE WORKS

HISTORY AND TECHNOLOGY. *see* HISTORY

600 GBR ISSN 0307-5451
T14.7
HISTORY OF TECHNOLOGY. Text in English. 1976. s-a. USD 180 (effective 2010). back issues avail. **Document type:** *Journal, Academic/Scholarly.* **Description:** Contains essays on the technical problems of various periods and societies, as well as the measures taken to solve them.
Related titles: Online - full text ed.
Indexed: A22, AmH&L, BrArAb, CA, FR, HistAb, IBR, IBZ, RASB, SCOPUS, T02.
—BLDSC (4318.560000), IE, Ingenta, INIST, Linda Hall. **CCC.**
Published by: Continuum International Publishing Group, The Tower Bldg, 11 York Rd, London, SE1 7NX, United Kingdom. TEL 44-20-79220880, FAX 44-20-79287894, info@continuumbooks.com. Ed. Ian Inkster.

600 GBR ISSN 0266-1721
HISTORY OF TECHNOLOGY SERIES. Text in English. 1979. irreg., latest 2009. price varies. back issues avail. **Document type:** *Monographic series, Academic/Scholarly.* **Description:** Provides information on latest technologies.
Indexed: A22, Inspec.
—BLDSC (4362.727500), IE, Ingenta.
Published by: The Institution of Engineering and Technology, Michael Faraday House, Stevenage, Herts SG1 2AY, United Kingdom. TEL 44-1438-313311, FAX 44-1438-765526, books@theiet.org. **Subscr. to:** Publication Sales Dept, PO Box 96, Stevenage SG1 2SD, United Kingdom. TEL 44-1438-767328, FAX 44-1438-767375.

600 330 DEU ISSN 1433-4135
HOCHSCHULE FUER TECHNIK UND WIRTSCHAFT DRESDEN. BERICHTE UND INFORMATIONEN. Text in German. 1993. 2/yr. EUR 10 per issue (effective 2007). adv. **Document type:** *Journal, Academic/Scholarly.*
Formerly (until 1996): Hochschule fuer Technik und Wirtschaft. Berichte und Informationen aus Forschung, Lehre und Praxis (0942-8240)
Published by: Hochschule fuer Technik und Wirtschaft Dresden, Friedrich-List-Platz 1, Dresden, 01069, Germany. TEL 49-351-4622312, FAX 49-351-4622185, http://www.htw-dresden.de. Ed. Dieter Preuss. adv.: B&W page EUR 485. Circ: 1,000 (controlled).

600 JPN ISSN 0385-0862
T4 CODEN: HODKDL
HOKKAIDO KOGYO DAIGAKU KENKYU KIYO/HOKKAIDO INSTITUTE OF TECHNOLOGY. MEMOIRS. Text in Japanese. 1970. irreg. **Document type:** *Academic/Scholarly.*
Indexed: A22, Inspec.
—BLDSC (5617.430000), IE, Ingenta.
Published by: Hokkaido Kogyo Daigaku/Hokkaido Institute of Technology, 7-15-4, Maeda, Teine-ku, Sapporo, 006-8585, Japan. TEL 81-11-681-2161, FAX 81-11-681-3622, http://www.hit.ac.jp/.

600 JPN
HOKKAIDO NATIONAL INDUSTRIAL RESEARCH INSTITUTE. TECHNICAL DATA/HOKKAIDO KOGYO GIJUTSU KENKYUJO SHIRYOH. Text in Japanese. 1961. irreg. free.
Formerly: Government Industrial Development Laboratory, Hokkaido. Technical Data - Hokkaido Kogyo Kaihatsu Shikenjo Gijutsu
Published by: Hokkaido National Industrial Research Institute, 2-17 Tsukisamu-Higashi, Toyohira-ku, Sapporo-shi, Hokkaido 062-0000, Japan. FAX 81-11-857-8901.

600 COL ISSN 0121-0777
AS82.A1
EL HOMBRE Y LA MAQUINA. Text in Spanish. 1988. s-a. **Document type:** *Journal, Academic/Scholarly.*
Related titles: Online - full text ed.: free (effective 2011).
Published by: Universidad Autonoma de Occidente, Calle 25 No.115 85 Km. 2 Via Cali, Jamundi, Cali, Colombia. maquina@uao.edu.co, http://www.uao.edu.co/. Ed. Omar Diaz Saldana.

HOME HEALTH CARE TECHNOLOGY REPORT. *see* MEDICAL SCIENCES

HORIZON/SHIYU. *see* SCIENCES: COMPREHENSIVE WORKS

HOW STUFF WORKS EXPRESS. *see* CHILDREN AND YOUTH—For

HUABEI KEJI XUEYUAN XUEBAO/NORTH CHINA INSTITUTE OF SCIENCE AND TECHNOLOGY. JOURNAL. *see* SCIENCES: COMPREHENSIVE WORKS

HUANAN LIGONG DAXUE XUEBAO (ZIRAN KEXUE BAN)/SOUTH CHINA UNIVERSITY OF SCIENCE AND ENGINEERING. JOURNAL (NATURAL SCIENCE EDITION). *see* SCIENCES: COMPREHENSIVE WORKS

600 CHN
HUANGSHI LIGONG XUEYUAN XUEBAO/HUANGSHI INSTITUTE OF TECHNOLOGY. JOURNAL. Text in Chinese. 1985. bi-m. CNY 10 newsstand/cover (effective 2007). **Document type:** *Journal, Academic/Scholarly.*
Formerly: Huangshi Gaodeng Zhuanke Xuexiao Xuebao/Huangshi Polytechnic College. Journal (1008-8245)
Related titles: Online - full text ed.
Published by: Huangshi Ligong Xueyuan, 16, Guilin Bei Lu, Huangshi, 435003, China. TEL 86-714-6350127, FAX 86-714-6368326.

HUAZHONG KEJI DAXUE XUEBAO (ZIRAN KEXUE BAN)/HUAZHONG UNIVERSITY OF SCIENCE AND TECHNOLOGY. JOURNAL (NATURE SCIENCE). *see* SCIENCES: COMPREHENSIVE WORKS

600 CHN ISSN 1003-4684
HUBEI GONGXUEYUAN XUEBAO/HUBEI INSTITUTE OF TECHNOLOGY. JOURNAL. Text in Chinese. 1986. bi-m. USD 24.60 (effective 2009). **Document type:** *Journal, Academic/Scholarly.*
Related titles: Online - full text ed.
—East View.
Published by: Hubei Gongxueyuan, Nanhu Lijiadun, Wuchang, 430068, China. TEL 86-27-88032247.

745.2 AUT ISSN 0018-7224
HUMAN INDUSTRIAL DESIGN. Text in German. 1968. irreg. adv. bk.rev. **Document type:** *Monographic series, Trade.*
Published by: Verlag Dr. Herta Ranner, Zeismannsbrunngasse 1, Vienna, W 1070, Austria. TEL 43-1-5235387, FAX 43-1-52353874. Ed. H Ranner.

HUOGONGPIN/INITIATORS & PYROTECHNICS. *see* MILITARY

HUOLI YU ZHIHUI KONGZHI/FIRE CONTROL & COMMAND CONTROL. *see* MILITARY

600 JPN
HYOGO PREFECTURAL INSTITUTE OF TECHNOLOGY. REPORT. Text in Japanese. 1991. a. **Document type:** *Academic/Scholarly.*
Formerly: Hyogo Kenritsu Kogyo Gijutsu Senta Hokokusho/Hyogo Prefectural Institute of Industrial Research. Report (0918-0192)
Published by: Hyogo Prefectural Institute of Technology, 3-1-12 Yukihiracho, Suma-ku, Kobe-shi, Hyogo 654-0037, Japan. TEL 81-78-731-4481, FAX 81-78-735-7845, http://www.hyogo-kg.go.jp/.

600 USA ISSN 0160-1040
T37
➤ **I A.** (Industrial Archeology) Text in English. 1975. s-a. adv. bk.rev. illus. back issues avail. **Document type:** *Journal, Academic/Scholarly.* **Description:** Contains scholarly articles, essays and book reviews.
Indexed: AIAP, AmH&L, CA, HistAb, RILM, T02.
—Linda Hall.
Published by: Society for Industrial Archeology, Department of Social Sciences, 1400 Townsend Dr, Houghton, MI 49931. TEL 906-487-1889, sia@mtu.edu. Ed. Patrick E Martin TEL 906-487-2070.

➤ **THE I A L L T JOURNAL OF LANGUAGE LEARNING TECHNOLOGIES.** *see* LINGUISTICS

600 USA
TJ217
I E E E CONFERENCE ON DECISION AND CONTROL. PROCEEDINGS. (Institute of Electrical and Electronics Engineers) Text in English. 19??. a. back issues avail. **Document type:** *Proceedings, Trade.*
Former titles (until 2004): I E E E Conference on Decision and Control. Proceedings (0743-1546); (until 1982): I E E E Conference on Decision and Control, including the Symposium on Adaptive Processes. Proceedings (0191-2216); (until 1972): I E E E Conference on Decision and Control, including the Symposium on Adaptive Processes (0888-3610)
Related titles: CD-ROM ed.; Microfiche ed.; Online - full text ed.
Indexed: A28, APA, BrCerAb, C&ISA, CA/WCA, CIA, CIS, CerAb, CivEngAb, CompC, CorrAb, E&CAJ, E11, EEA, EMA, EngInd, H15, ISMEC, M&TEA, M09, MBF, METADEX, SCOPUS, SolStAb, T04, WAA.
—IE, Ingenta. **CCC.**
Published by: (I E E E Control Systems Society), I E E E, 445 Hoes Ln, Piscataway, NJ 08855. contactcenter@ieee.org, http://www.ieee.org.

I E E E PULSE. (Institute of Electrical and Electronics Engineers) *see* BIOLOGY—Bioengineering

600 621.3 USA ISSN 0278-0097
T14.5
I E E E TECHNOLOGY AND SOCIETY MAGAZINE. (Institute of Electrical and Electronics Engineers) Text in English. 19??. q. USD 370; USD 465 combined subscription (print & online eds.) (effective 2012). adv. back issues avail.; reprints avail. **Document type:** *Magazine, Academic/Scholarly.* **Description:** Examines the impact of technology on society, and the impact of society on the engineering profession.
Former titles (until 1982): Technology and Society (0194-3359); (until 197?): I E E E. C S I T Newsletter (0364-7188)
Related titles: CD-ROM ed.; Microfiche ed.; Online - full text ed.: ISSN 1937-416X. USD 335 (effective 2012).
Indexed: A01, A02, A03, A05, A08, A20, A22, A25, A26, A28, APA, AS&TA, AS&TI, ASCA, B01, B04, B06, B07, B09, BrCerAb, C&ISA, C10, CA, CA/WCA, CIA, CMCI, CPEI, CerAb, CivEngAb, CorrAb, CurCont, E&CAJ, E08, E11, EEA, EMA, ESPM, EngInd, EnvEAb, FR, G01, G08, H15, I05, Inspec, M&TEA, M05, M06, M09, MBF, METADEX, P34, PAIS, PRA, RASB, RI-1, RI-2, RefZh, RiskAb, S01, S02, S03, S08, S09, SCI, SCOPUS, SolStAb, T02, T04, TM, W07, WAA.
—BLDSC (4363.095000), AskIEEE, IE, Infotrieve, Ingenta, INIST, Linda Hall. **CCC.**
Published by: I E E E, 445 Hoes Ln, Piscataway, NJ 08854. TEL 732-981-0060, 800-678-4333, FAX 732-562-6380, contactcenter@ieee.org, http://www.ieee.org. Ed. Keith W Miller TEL 217-206-7327. **Co-sponsor:** Society on Social Implications of Technology.

I E E E TRANSACTIONS ON INDUSTRY APPLICATIONS. (Institute of Electrical and Electronics Engineers) *see* ENGINEERING—Electrical Engineering

600 GBR
THE I E T MANAGEMENT OF TECHNOLOGY SERIES. Text in English. 19??. irreg., latest 2010. price varies. adv. back issues avail.; reprints avail. **Document type:** *Monographic series, Academic/Scholarly.* **Description:** Covers information about management of technology.
Formerly (until 2007): I E E Management of Technology Series (0268-6171)
Related titles: Online - full text ed.
Indexed: Inspec.
—BLDSC (4363.252730), IE.
Published by: The Institution of Engineering and Technology, Michael Faraday House, Stevenage, Herts SG1 2AY, United Kingdom. TEL 44-1438-313311, FAX 44-1438-765526, books@theiet.org. Ed. Mrs. J Lorriman. Adv. contact Louise Hall TEL 44-1438-767351. **Subscr. to:** Publication Sales Dept, PO Box 96, Stevenage SG1 2SD, United Kingdom. TEL 44-1438-767328, FAX 44-1438-767375, sales@theiet.org.

600 USA
I N: INSIDE INNOVATION. Text in English. 2006. q. free with subscr. to Business Week. **Document type:** *Magazine, Trade.*
Related titles: ◆ Issued with: BusinessWeek. ISSN 0007-7135.
Published by: McGraw-Hill Companies, Inc., 1221 Ave of the Americas, 43rd fl, New York, NY 10020. TEL 212-512-2000, FAX 212-426-7087, customer.service@mcgraw-hill.com, http://www.mcgraw-hill.com. Ed. Bruce Nussbaum.

THE I P T S REPORT (ENGLISH EDITION). *see* POLITICAL SCIENCE—International Relations

THE I P T S REPORT (FRENCH EDITION). *see* POLITICAL SCIENCE—International Relations

THE I P T S REPORT (GEMAN EDITION). *see* POLITICAL SCIENCE—International Relations

THE I P T S REPORT (SPANISH EDITION). *see* POLITICAL SCIENCE—International Relations

600 AUT ISSN 1818-6556
I T A - BERICHTE. Text in English, German. 1998. irreg. **Document type:** *Monographic series, Academic/Scholarly.*
Media: Online - full content.
Published by: Institut fuer Technikfolgen-Abschaetzung, Strohgasse 45, Vienna, 1030, Austria. TEL 43-1-515816582, FAX 43-1-7109883, tamail@oeaw.ac.at, http://www.oeaw.ac.at/ita/index.htm.

600 378 IRL ISSN 1649-5969
I T B JOURNAL. Text in English. 2000. s-a. **Document type:** *Journal, Academic/Scholarly.*
Published by: Institute of Technology Blanchardstown, Blanchardstown Rd N, Blanchardstown, Dublin, 15, Ireland. TEL 353-1-8851000, FAX 353-1-8851001. Ed. Brian Nolan.

600 USA ISSN 1054-0229
I T E A JOURNAL OF TEST AND EVALUATION. Text in English. 1983. q. USD 60 to institutions; USD 20 per issue; free to members (effective 2011). adv. back issues avail. **Document type:** *Journal, Academic/Scholarly.* **Description:** Publishes articles on test and evaluation procedures, methods and philosophies used in testing both software and hardware.
Related titles: Online - full text ed.
Indexed: A09, A10, V03, V04.
—Linda Hall.
Published by: International Test & Evaluation Association, 4400 Fair Lakes Ct, Ste 104, Fairfax, VA 22033. TEL 703-631-6220, FAX 703-631-6221. Adv. contact Bill Dallas TEL 703-631-6226.

I T E S T BULLETIN. *see* RELIGIONS AND THEOLOGY

I T E S T CONFERENCE PROCEEDINGS. *see* RELIGIONS AND THEOLOGY

600 016 BEL ISSN 0019-0810
➤ **I T L/INTERNATIONAL TECHNICAL LITERATURE GUIDE;** international journal of applied linguistics. (Internationaler Technischer Literaturanzeiger) Text in English, French, German, Spanish. 1933. s-a. EUR 50 combined subscription (print & online eds.) (effective 2011). adv. bk.rev. bibl.; illus.; tr.lit. **Document type:** *Journal, Academic/Scholarly.*
Related titles: Online - full text ed.: ISSN 1783-1490.
Indexed: BibLing, FR, L&LBA, L11, MLA-IB, SCOPUS, SOPODA, SocioIAb.
—IE, Infotrieve.
Published by: Peeters Publishers, Bondgenotenlaan 153, Leuven, 3000, Belgium. TEL 32-16-235170, FAX 32-16-228500, peeters@peeters-leuven.be, http://www.peeters-leuven.be. Ed. L Sercu. Circ: 22,000.

➤ **I T REVIEW.** (Information Technology) *see* LIBRARY AND INFORMATION SCIENCES

➤ **I T S QUARTERLY.** *see* TRANSPORTATION

➤ **THE I U P JOURNAL OF SCIENCE AND TECHNOLOGY.** *see* SCIENCES: COMPREHENSIVE WORKS

620 SWE ISSN 1102-8254
I V A - M. Text in Swedish. 1920. irreg., latest vol.416, 2010. charts; illus. back issues avail. **Document type:** *Monographic series, Academic/Scholarly.*
Former titles (until 1990): I V A - Meddelande (1100-3022); (until 1983): Ingenjoersvetenskapsakademien. Meddelanden (0020-1278)
Indexed: ApMecR, ChemAb.
—Linda Hall.
Published by: Kungliga Ingenjoersvetenskapsakademien/Royal Swedish Academy of Engineering Sciences, Grev Turegatan 14, PO Box 5073, Stockholm, 10243, Sweden. TEL 46-8-7912900, FAX 46-8-6115623, info@iva.se, http://www.iva.se.

609 DEU ISSN 1361-8113
T14.7
➤ **ICON.** Text in English. 1996. a. EUR 36 per vol. in Europe; EUR 39 per vol. elsewhere (effective 2009). adv. bk.rev. back issues avail. **Document type:** *Journal, Academic/Scholarly.* **Description:** Covers all aspects and periods in the history of technology, devoting special attention to the discussion of contemporary problems of technology within various socio-economic and cultural settings.
Indexed: AmH&L, CA, FR, HistAb, P30, T02.
—BLDSC (4362.060855), INIST. **CCC.**
Published by: International Committee for the History of Technology, c/o Prof. Wolfhard Weber, Treasurer, Historisches Institut Ruhr-Universitaet Bochum, Rm GA 4-55, Bochum, 44780, Germany. wolfhard.weber@rub.de. Ed. Alexander Keller. adv.: page GBP 195. Circ: 150,000.

600 ETH ISSN 2074-1480
▼ **ICONCEPT.** Text in English. 2009. q. **Document type:** *Magazine, Consumer.*
Published by: iConcept Publishing PLC, Kirkos Sub City - Bole Rd, Aberus Building Complex, 4th Flr. Rm. No. 404/C, PO Box, Addis Ababa, Ethiopia. TEL 251-118-500303, http://www.iconceptmagazine.com/blue/homepage.html.

ICYT. (Informacion Cientifica y Tecnologica) *see* SCIENCES: COMPREHENSIVE WORKS

600 ARG ISSN 0326-3878
N7
IDEAS EN ARTE Y TECNOLOGIA. Text in Spanish. 1984. 3/yr. USD 48. bk.rev. bibl. back issues avail. **Description:** Covers architecture, engineering and computer science.
Indexed: AIAP.
Published by: Universidad de Belgrano, Teodoro Garcia, 2090, Buenos Aires, 1426, Argentina. TEL 54-114-7742133. Ed. Avelino J Porto. Circ: 1,000.

IHOMES & BUILDINGS. *see* ENGINEERING—Electrical Engineering

600 371.3 USA ISSN 1545-6684
ILLINOIS JOURNAL OF TECHNOLOGY EDUCATION. Text in English. 3/yr. **Document type:** *Journal, Trade.*
Formerly (until 1988): Illinois Industrial Educator
Published by: Illinois Industrial Education Association, Illinois State University, Dept. of Technology, Campus Box 5100, Normal, IL 61790. TEL 309-438-7862, FAX 309-438-8626, http://www.teai.net. Ed. Chris Merrill.

300 USA
ILLINOIS TECHNOLOGY. Text in English. m. USD 39 (effective 2002). adv.
Related titles: Online - full content ed.
Published by: Power Media Group, 13490 TI Blvd Ste 100, Dallas, TX 75243. TEL 972-690-6222, 800-687-3256, FAX 972-690-6333, 800-687-3290, editor@ttechnology.com, http://www.ttechnology.com. Ed. Laurie Kline TEL 972-690-6222 ext 16. Pub. Roger Powers TEL 972-690-6222 ext 20.

ILLUSTRERAD VETENSKAP. *see* SCIENCES: COMPREHENSIVE WORKS

IMPACT ASSESSMENT AND PROJECT APPRAISAL. *see* ENVIRONMENTAL STUDIES

338 658.5 USA ISSN 1554-8848
IN M F G; innovation solutions trends. (Manufacturing) Text in English. 1942. 9/yr. adv. illus.; tr.lit. back issues avail.; reprints avail. **Document type:** *Magazine, Trade.* **Description:** Serves the general US industrial field, primarily manufacturing industries classified in SIC 20-39, encompassing the processing and metalworking industries.
Former titles (until 2005): Industrial Product Bulletin (0199-2074); (until 197?): Industrial Bulletin (0019-8021)
Related titles: Microform ed.: (from PQC); Online - full text ed.
Indexed: A15, ABIn, B02, B15, B17, B18, G04, G06, G07, G08, I05, P48, P51, P52, PQC.
—**CCC.**
Published by: Reed Business Information (Subsidiary of: Reed Business), 360 Park Ave S, New York, NY 10010. TEL 646-746-6400, FAX 646-746-7131, corporatecommunications@reedbusiness.com, http://www.reedbusiness.com. Ed. Anita LaFond TEL 973-292-5100 ext 269. Pub. Scott Sward TEL 973-292-5100 ext 236. adv.: B&W page USD 17,795; trim 8.8125 x 11. Circ: 174,000 (controlled). **Subscr. to:** Reed Business Information, PO Box 9020, Maple Shade, NJ 08052. TEL 303-470-4466, FAX 303-470-4691.

IN TECHNOLOGY. *see* BUSINESS AND ECONOMICS

INCITES; Australian science and technology online's innovations citations. *see* SCIENCES: COMPREHENSIVE WORKS

INDIA. DEPARTMENT OF SCIENCE & TECHNOLOGY. ANNUAL REPORT. *see* SCIENCES: COMPREHENSIVE WORKS

INDIAN JOURNAL OF HISTORY OF SCIENCE. *see* SCIENCES: COMPREHENSIVE WORKS

INDIAN JOURNAL OF SCIENCE AND TECHNOLOGY. *see* SCIENCES: COMPREHENSIVE WORKS

607 IND ISSN 0971-3034
T61
➤ **INDIAN JOURNAL OF TECHNICAL EDUCATION.** Text in English. 1971. q. INR 800 to non-members; INR 600 to institutional members; INR 500 to members (effective 2011). adv. bk.rev. illus. **Document type:** *Journal, Academic/Scholarly.*
Published by: Indian Society for Technical Education, Shaheed Jeet Singh Marg, Near Katwaria Sarai, New Delhi, 110016, India. TEL 91-11-26513542, FAX 91-11-26852421, istedhq@vsnl.net.

➤ **INDICADORES DE ACTIVIDADES CIENTIFICAS Y TECNOLOGICAS.** *see* BUSINESS AND ECONOMICS

600 GBR
INDUSTRIAL ANALYTICAL INSTRUMENTATION. Text in English. 1986. bi-m. free (effective 2010). adv. **Document type:** *Journal, Academic/Scholarly.* **Description:** Dedicated to industrial analytical instrumentation, science and research, keeping readers abreast of the latest and broadest of industrial developments.
Related titles: CD-ROM ed.; Online - full text ed.
Published by: Industrial and Technological Publications, 8 Matthew Wren Close, Little Downham, Ely, Cambs CB6 2UL, United Kingdom. TEL 44-1353-699916, FAX 44-1353-699054. Ed. William R Digby-Hammerton. Pubs. Trevor Bennet, William R Digby-Hammerton. adv.: page GBP 500; 184 x 269.

621.9 GBR ISSN 0019-8145
TJ1193 CODEN: INDRA9
INDUSTRIAL DIAMOND REVIEW. Abbreviated title: I D R. Variant title: I D R. Industrial Diamond Review. Text in English. 1940. q. adv. bk.rev. illus. index. reprints avail. **Document type:** *Journal, Trade.* **Description:** Contains reviews developments in the design and manufacture of diamond, CBN, PCD, and PCBN tooling; also provides applications in industry and science.
Formerly (until 1971): Industrial Diamond Review (0959-8294); Incorporates (1958-1961): Industrial Diamond Abstracts (0446-043X); Which was formerly (until 1958): Bibliography of Industrial Diamond Applications; (until 1947): Bibliography of Diamond Tools and Related Subjects
Related titles: Microfilm ed.: (from PQC); Online - full text ed.: IDR-online.com. free (effective 2009).
Indexed: A22, A28, APA, ASCA, BrCerAb, BrTechI, C&ISA, CA/WCA, CIA, CPEI, CerAb, ChemAb, CivEngAb, CorrAb, CurCont, E&CAJ, E11, EEA, EMA, EngInd, H15, IMMAb, ISMEC, M&TEA, M09, MBF, METADEX, MSCI, MinerAb, SCI, SCOPUS, SolStAb, T04, TM, W07, WAA.
—BLDSC (4450.000000), CASDDS, IE, Infotrieve, Ingenta, INIST, Linda Hall.
Published by: De Beers Industrial Diamond Division, Odeon House, 146 College Rd, Harrow, Middlesex HA1 1BH, United Kingdom. TEL 44-20-88632767, FAX 44-20-88633917. adv.: page EUR 2,705, page USD 3,565; trim 210 x 297.

INDUSTRIAL PRODUCTS FINDER. *see* BUSINESS AND ECONOMICS—Trade And Industrial Directories

607.11 USA
INDUSTRIAL TEACHER EDUCATION DIRECTORY. Text in English. 1958. a., latest 2006. **Document type:** *Directory, Trade.*
Published by: National Association of Industrial and Technical Teacher Educators, c/o Karen R Juneau, University of Southern Mississippi, Department of Technology Education, 118 College Dr 5036, Hattiesburg, MS 3906. TEL 601-266-5588, FAX 601-266-5957, karen.juneau@usm.edu. Ed. Klaus Schmidt TEL 309-438-3502. Circ: 3,800 (controlled). **Co-sponsor:** Council on Technology Teacher Education.

600 TWN
INDUSTRIAL TECHNOLOGY RESEARCH INSTITUTE. ANNUAL REPORT. Text in English. a.
Published by: Industrial Technology Research Institute, 195 Chung Hsing Rd, Sec 4, Chu Tung, Hsin Chu, 310, Taiwan.

600 THA ISSN 0859-0095
INDUSTRIAL TECHNOLOGY REVIEW; for keeping abreast of industrial technology. Text and summaries in Thai, English. 1994. m. THB 540; THB 50 newsstand/cover. adv. bk.rev.; software rev. charts; illus.; mkt.; maps; stat.; tr.lit. Index. back issues avail. **Document type:** *Academic/Scholarly.*
Published by: Se - Education Public Company Ltd., Asok-Dindang Rd, Dindang, 800-43-45 Soi Trakulsuk, Bangkok, 10320, Thailand. TEL 66-2-6429800, FAX 66-2-6429866. Ed. Suparkit Ampas. Adv. contact Nujchanart Kongvisaisuk.

INDUSTRIAS PESQUERAS; revista maritima quincenal. *see* BUSINESS AND ECONOMICS

338 671 DEU ISSN 0019-9036
TJ3 CODEN: IANZAQ
INDUSTRIE-ANZEIGER; polytechnische Zeitschrift fuer die technische Industrie. Text in German. 1879. 33/yr. EUR 196.50 domestic; EUR 220.50 foreign (effective 2011). adv. bk.rev. charts; illus.; mkt.; stat. **Document type:** *Magazine, Trade.* **Description:** For the machine industry. Provides news and information on manufacturing, technological research and new products.
Incorporates (1958-1974): Berichtsheft zum Aachener Werkzeugmaschinen-Kolloquium (0567-4476); (1949-1949): Eisen- und Metall-Verarbeitung (0930-214X)
Related titles: ◆ Supplement(s): Industrie-Anzeiger Produkt Report.
Indexed: A22, AcoustA, CEABA, CIN, CISA, ChemAb, ChemTitl, CybAb, INIS AtomInd, Inspec, KES, PST, TM.
—BLDSC (4474.620000), AskIEEE, CASDDS, IE, Infotrieve, INIST, Linda Hall. **CCC.**
Published by: (Wirtschaftsverband Eisen, Blech und Metall Verarbeitende Industrie), Konradin Verlag Robert Kohlhammer GmbH, Ernst Mey Str 8, Leinfelden-Echterdingen, 70771, Germany. TEL 49-711-75940, FAX 49-711-7594390, info@konradin.de, http://www.konradin.de. Ed. Werner Goetz. Adv. contact Klaus-Dieter Mehnert. Circ: 40,038 (controlled).

338 DEU
INDUSTRIE-ANZEIGER PRODUKT REPORT. Text in German. 1879. s-a. EUR 4 newsstand/cover (effective 2007). adv. **Document type:** *Magazine, Trade.*
Related titles: ◆ Supplement to: Industrie-Anzeiger. ISSN 0019-9036.

Published by: Konradin Verlag Robert Kohlhammer GmbH, Ernst Mey Str 8, Leinfelden-Echterdingen, 70771, Germany. TEL 49-711-75940, FAX 49-711-7594390, info@konradin.de, http://www.konradin.de. Ed. Rolf Langbein. Adv. contact Burkhardt Lemke. color page EUR 7,390, B&W page EUR 5,880; trim 190 x 270. Circ: 44,844 (paid and controlled).

600 FRA ISSN 1633-7107
INDUSTRIE ET TECHNOLOGIES. Text in French. 1960. m. (11/yr). EUR 98 (effective 2009). adv. illus.; mkt.; tr.lit. **Document type:** *Magazine, Trade.*
Former titles (until 2002): Industries et Techniques (0150-6617); (until 1960): Industries et Techniques Francaises (0150-6625); Which was formed by the merger of (1959-1960): Industries et Techniques. Documents (0537-5800); (1958-1960): Industries et Techniques. Informations (0150-6633); Which was formerly (until 1959): Industries et Techniques Francaises (0537-5819); (until 1958): Industries et Techniques (0019-9354)
Indexed: A22, CISA.
—BLDSC (4468.180000), IE, INIST.
Published by: Groupe Industrie Services Info, Antony Parc II, 10 Av. du General de Gaulle, Antony, 92160, France. TEL 33-1-77929775, http://www.librairie-gisi.fr. Circ: 35,000.

INDUSTRIEARCHAEOLOGIE; Zeitschrift fuer industrielle Kulturgueter, Kunst und Reisen. *see* HISTORY

600 310 CAN ISSN 1913-0236
INDUSTRY CANADA. CANADIAN I C T SECTOR. QUARTERLY MONITOR. (Information and Communications Technologies) Text in English. 2002. q. free (effective 2011). **Document type:** *Report, Government.*
Media: Online - full text.
Published by: Industry Canada/Industrie Canada, Industry Canada Web Service Ctr, C D Howe Bldg, 235 Queen St, Ottawa, ON K1A 0H5, Canada. TEL 613-954-5031, 800-328-6189, FAX 613-954-2340, info@ic.gc.ca.

INDUSTRY, TRADE, AND TECHNOLOGY REVIEW. *see* BUSINESS AND ECONOMICS—International Commerce

INFO R U V I D. (Red de Universidades Valencianas para el Fomento de la Investigacion, el Desarrollo y la Innovacion) *see* SCIENCES: COMPREHENSIVE WORKS

INFORMACION TECNOLOGICA. *see* SCIENCES: COMPREHENSIVE WORKS

600 PRT ISSN 1647-1407
▼ **INFORMATION AND COMMUNICATION TECHNOLOGIES FOR THE ADVANCED ENTERPRISE.** Text in Portuguese, English. 2009. s-a. **Document type:** *Journal, Academic/Scholarly.*
Published by: Instituto Politecnico do Cavado e do Ave, Escola Superior de Tecnologia, Campus do IPCA, Lugar do Aldao, Vila Fresc, 4750-810, Portugal. TEL 351-253-802260, FAX 351-253-823127, est@ipca.pt, http://www.est.ipca.pt.

600 BRA ISSN 1679-3838
INFORMATIVO TECNICO. Text in Portuguese. 2003. s-a. BRL 5 newsstand/cover (effective 2006). back issues avail. **Document type:** *Monographic series, Academic/Scholarly.*
Published by: Editora da Universidade de Santa Cruz do Sul, Av Independencia 2293, Barrio Universitario, Santa Cruz do Sul, RS 96815-900, Brazil. TEL 55-51-37177461, FAX 55-51-37177402, editora@unisc.br.

INGENIERIAS. *see* SCIENCES: COMPREHENSIVE WORKS

600 CHL ISSN 0716-6311
TN4 CODEN: INNOBH
INNOVACION. Text in Spanish. 1986. irreg. **Document type:** *Journal, Academic/Scholarly.*
Formerly (until 1988): Desarrollo (0716-3665)
Related titles: Online - full text ed.: ISSN 0718-5545. 2008.
Indexed: A28, APA, BrCerAb, C&ISA, C01, CA/WCA, CIA, CerAb, CivEngAb, CorrAb, E&CAJ, E11, EEA, EMA, H15, M&TEA, M09, MBF, METADEX, SolStAb, T04, WAA.
—Linda Hall.
Published by: (Universidad de Antofagasta, Facultad de Ingenieria), Universidad de Antofagasta, Av Angamos 601, Antofagasta, Chile. TEL 56-55-637194, FAX 56-55-637102, rectoria@uantof.cl, http://www.uantof.cl.

600 CUB ISSN 1025-6504
INNOVACION TECNOLOGICA. Text in Spanish. 1995. q.
Media: Online - full text.
Indexed: CA, F04, T02.
Published by: Polo Cientifico-Productivo de la Provincia las Tunas, Maceo No. 31 Esq. Cucas Ortiz y Lico Cruz, Las Tunas, 75100, Cuba. TEL 537-3143345, FAX 537-3145360, cmictlt@ltunas.inf.cu.

600 CAN ISSN 1205-9331
INNOVACORP. ANNUAL REPORT. Text in English. 1947. q. adv. **Document type:** *Newsletter.*
Former titles (until 1996): Nova Scotia Research Foundation Corporation. Annual Report (0706-7739); (until 1976): Nova Scotia Research Foundation. Annual Report (0078-2475)
—Linda Hall.
Published by: InNOVAcorp, 101 Research Dr, Woodside Industrial Park, P O Box 790, Dartmouth, NS B2Y 3Z7, Canada. TEL 902-424-8670, FAX 902-424-4679. Ed. Kimberly MacDonald-Vibert. Adv. contact R. F. (Bob) MacNeill. Circ: 1,600.

INNOVATION (ABINGDON); the European journal of social sciences. *see* SOCIAL SCIENCES: COMPREHENSIVE WORKS

INNOVATION (ALBUQUERQUE); America's journal of technology communication. *see* BUSINESS AND ECONOMICS—Production Of Goods And Services

INNOVATIONS. *see* SCIENCES: COMPREHENSIVE WORKS

INNOVATIONS (PRINCETON); news on research, products and solutions for learning and education. *see* EDUCATION

600 RUS
INNOVATSII; zhurnal ob innovatsionnoi deyatel'nosti. Text in Russian. 1996. bi-m.
Related titles: Online - full text ed.
Published by: Izdatelstvo Transfer Sankt-Peterburgskii Gosudarstvennyi Elektrotekhnicheskii Universitet, ul. Prof. Popova 5, Sankt-Peterburg, 197376, Russian Federation. TEL 7-812-2346658, FAX 7-812-2340918, transfer@eltech.ru. Ed. B. Salov.

600 USA ISSN 0300-757X
T173.8
INSIDE R & D. Text in English. 1971. w. charts; pat.; stat.; tr.lit. Supplement avail.; back issues avail. **Document type:** *Newsletter, Trade.* **Description:** Covers new and significant developments in technology.
Incorporates (in 1994): Technology Transfer Week (1074-4363)
Related titles: Online - full text ed.
Indexed: B02, B15, B17, B18, G04, G06, G07, G08, I05, P29, P47, P48, P52, P53, P54, PQC.
—CIS.
Published by: Technical Insights (Subsidiary of: Frost & Sullivan), 7550 IH 10 W, Ste 400, San Antonio, TX 78229. TEL 210-348-1000, 877-463-7678, FAX 888-690-3329, myfrost@frost.com, http://www.frost.com/prod/servlet/ti-home.pag.

600 DEU ISSN 1616-5284
INSPECT. Text in German. 2000. 10/yr. EUR 54; EUR 14 newsstand/cover (effective 2010). adv. **Document type:** *Magazine, Trade.*
Published by: G I T Verlag GmbH (Subsidiary of: Wiley - V C H Verlag GmbH & Co. KGaA), Roesslerstr 90, Darmstadt, 64293, Germany. TEL 49-6151-80900, FAX 49-6151-8090146, info@gitverlag.com. Ed. Dr. Peter Ebert TEL 49-6151-8090-162. Adv. contact Claudia Vogel. Circ: 15,000 (paid and controlled).

L'INSTALLATORE ITALIANO; la rivista mensile degli impianti tecnici. *see* HEATING, PLUMBING AND REFRIGERATION

INSTANTANES TECHNIQUES. *see* ENGINEERING

INSTITUT FRANCAIS DE RECHERCHE SCIENTIFIQUE POUR LE DEVELOPPEMENT EN COOPERATION. COLLOQUES ET SEMINAIRES. *see* SCIENCES: COMPREHENSIVE WORKS

600 GBR ISSN 1369-7919
INSTITUTE FOR JAPANESE - EUROPEAN TECHNOLOGY STUDIES. PAPERS. Variant title: J E T S Paper. Text in English. 1990. irreg., latest vol.19, 2000. GBP 7.50 per issue (effective 2009). back issues avail. **Document type:** *Monographic series, Academic/Scholarly.* **Description:** Covers information about European technology studies.
—BLDSC (4668.132500), Ingenta.
Published by: University of Edinburgh, Institute for Japanese - European Technology Studies, Old Surgeons Hall, High School Yards, Edinburgh, EH1 1LZ, United Kingdom. TEL 44-131-6502450, FAX 44-131-6502450, ian.duff@ed.ac.uk.

INSTITUTE OF FOOD TECHNOLOGISTS MEETING. BOOK OF ABSTRACTS. *see* FOOD AND FOOD INDUSTRIES

INSTITUTION OF MECHANICAL ENGINEERS. PROCEEDINGS. PART P: JOURNAL OF SPORTS, ENGINEERING AND TECHNOLOGY/ JOURNAL OF SPORTS, ENGINEERING AND TECHNOLOGY. *see* SPORTS AND GAMES

600 DOM
INSTITUTO TECNOLOGICO DE SANTO DOMINGO. BIBLIOTECA. BOLETIN DE ANALITICAS. Text in Spanish. 1983. s-a.
Published by: (Biblioteca), Instituto Tecnologico de Santo Domingo, Apdo Postal 342-9, Santo Domingo, Dominican Republic. Ed. Lucero Arboleda de Roa. Circ: 600.

600 SRB ISSN 1451-3749
INTEGRITET I VEK KONSTRUKCIJA/STRUCTURAL INTEGRITY AND LIFE. Text in Serbian. 1975. s-a. **Document type:** *Journal, Academic/Scholarly.*
Formerly (until 1991): Gosa. Strucni Bilten (0352-017X)
Related titles: Online - full text ed.: ISSN 1820-7863. free (effective 2011).
Published by: Drustvo za Integritet i Vek Knonstrukcija, Institut za Ispitvanje Materijala, Bulevar Vojvode Misica 43, Belgrade.

600 370 GBR ISSN 1741-5659
➤ **INTERACTIVE TECHNOLOGY AND SMART EDUCATION**; promoting innovation and a human touch. Abbreviated title: I T S E. Spine title: International Journal of Interactive Technology and Smart Education. Text in English. 2004 (Feb.). q. EUR 479 combined subscription in Europe (print & online eds.); USD 589 combined subscription in the Americas (print & online eds.); GBP 339 combined subscription in the UK & elsewhere (print & online eds.); AUD 729 combined subscription in Australasia (print & online eds.) (effective 2012). reprint service avail. from PSC. **Document type:** *Journal, Academic/Scholarly.* **Description:** Provides a distinct forum to specially promote innovation and human-/user-centered approaches.
Related titles: Online - full text ed.: ISSN 1758-8510 (from IngentaConnect).
—BLDSC (4531.872358), IE. **CCC.**
Published by: Emerald Group Publishing Ltd., Howard House, Wagon Ln, Bingley, W Yorks BD16 1WA, United Kingdom. TEL 44-1274-777700, FAX 44-1274-785201, information@emeraldinsight.com. Eds. Claude Ghaoui, Dr. Philip Tsang. Pub. Lizzie Scott.

➤ **INTERFACE FOCUS.** *see* SCIENCES: COMPREHENSIVE WORKS

600 ZAF ISSN 1684-498X
➤ **INTERIM.** Text in English. 2002. s-a. **Document type:** *Journal, Academic/Scholarly.*
Published by: Central University of Technology, Free State, Private Bag X20539, Bloemfontein, 9300, South Africa. TEL 27-51-5073911, FAX 27-51-5073199. Ed. Laetus Lategan.

▼ ➤ **INTERNATIONAL ARCHIVE OF APPLIED SCIENCES AND TECHNOLOGY.** *see* SCIENCES: COMPREHENSIVE WORKS

▼ ➤ **INTERNATIONAL BUSINESS & TECHNOLOGY REVIEW.** *see* BUSINESS AND ECONOMICS

➤ **INTERNATIONAL CONFERENCE ON BUSINESS AND TECHNOLOGY. PROCEEDINGS.** *see* BUSINESS AND ECONOMICS

➤ **INTERNATIONAL CONFERENCE ON DUBLIN CORE AND METADATA APPLICATIONS. PROCEEDINGS (ONLINE).** *see* COMPUTERS—Data Communications And Data Transmission Systems

600 KWT ISSN 1997-7697
INTERNATIONAL CONFERENCE ON TECHNOLOGY, COMMUNICATION AND EDUCATION. PROCEEDINGS. Text in English. 2008. a. **Document type:** *Proceedings, Academic/Scholarly.*
Related titles: CD-ROM ed.: ISSN 1997-9576.
Published by: Kuwait University, Computer Engineering Department, i-TCE Secretariat, PO Box 5969, Safat, 13060, Kuwait. TEL 96549-87412, FAX 96548-39461, info@i-tce.org, http://www.i-tce.org.

INTERNATIONAL CONGRESS ON TECHNOLOGY AND TECHNOLOGY EXCHANGE. PROCEEDINGS. *see* ENGINEERING

INTERNATIONAL FIBER SCIENCE AND TECHNOLOGY SERIES. *see* CHEMISTRY—Organic Chemistry

600 SGP ISSN 0219-1989
QA269
➤ **INTERNATIONAL GAME THEORY REVIEW.** Abbreviated title: I G T R. Text in English. 1999. q. SGD 853, USD 536, EUR 431 combined subscription to institutions (print & online eds.) (effective 2012). adv. back issues avail. **Document type:** *Journal, Academic/Scholarly.* **Description:** Addresses and reviews designs, problems, solutions, and applications pertaining to the game theoretic analysis of strategic decisions.
Related titles: Online - full text ed.: ISSN 1793-6675. SGD 775, USD 487, EUR 392 to institutions (effective 2012).
Indexed: A22, B01, B06, B07, B09, CA, CCMJ, E01, EconLit, IBSS, JEL, M05, MSN, MathR, SCOPUS, T02, Z02.
—BLDSC (4540.458500), IE, Ingenta. **CCC.**
Published by: World Scientific Publishing Co. Pte. Ltd., 5 Toh Tuck Link, Singapore, 596224, Singapore. TEL 65-6466-5775, FAX 65-6467-7667, wspc@wspc.com.sg, http://www.worldscientific.com. Eds. Leon A Petrosjan, Steffen Jorgensen. **Dist. in Europe by:** World Scientific Publishing Ltd., 57 Shelton St, London WC2H 9HE, United Kingdom. TEL 44-207-8360888, FAX 44-207-8362020, sales@wspc.co.uk; **Dist. in the US by:** World Scientific Publishing Co., Inc., 27 Warren St, Ste 401-402, Hackensack, NJ 07601. TEL 201-487-9655, 800-227-7562, FAX 201-487-9656, 888-977-2665, wspc@wspc.com.

➤ **THE INTERNATIONAL JOURNAL FOR THE HISTORY OF ENGINEERING & TECHNOLOGY.** *see* ENGINEERING

▼ ➤ **INTERNATIONAL JOURNAL OF ADULT VOCATIONAL EDUCATION AND TECHNOLOGY.** *see* EDUCATION—Adult Education

➤ **INTERNATIONAL JOURNAL OF ADVANCED SCIENCE AND TECHNOLOGY.** *see* SCIENCES: COMPREHENSIVE WORKS

600 IND ISSN 0976-4860
▼ ➤ **INTERNATIONAL JOURNAL OF ADVANCEMENTS IN TECHNOLOGY.** Text in English. 2010. s-a. free (effective 2011). Index. back issues avail. **Document type:** *Journal, Academic/Scholarly.* **Description:** Covers the latest outstanding developments in the field of engineering science and technology, including: Machine vision, modeling, simulation and visualization, robotics, tribology, communication systems, computational fluid dynamics and heat transfer, fluid engineering, bioinformatics, bioengineering and biotechnology, virtual reality, image processing, computer networks, brain mapping, genomics, manufacturing, information theory, soft computing, data engineering and architecture, search engine design, and other innovative and interesting works from other fields.
Media: Online - full text.
Published by: I J o A T Foundation TEL 91-99912-76724. Ed. Dimple Juneja.

➤ **INTERNATIONAL JOURNAL OF AGRICULTURE, ENVIRONMENT AND BIOTECHNOLOGY.** *see* AGRICULTURE

▼ ➤ **INTERNATIONAL JOURNAL OF APPLIED SCIENCE AND TECHNOLOGY.** *see* SCIENCES: COMPREHENSIVE WORKS

➤ **INTERNATIONAL JOURNAL OF BUSINESS AND SYSTEMS RESEARCH.** *see* BUSINESS AND ECONOMICS

▼ ➤ **INTERNATIONAL JOURNAL OF BUSINESS, HUMANITIES AND TECHNOLOGY.** *see* BUSINESS AND ECONOMICS

362.1 600 GBR ISSN 1363-7681
➤ **INTERNATIONAL JOURNAL OF C O M A D E M.** (Condition Monitoring and Diagnostic Engineering Management) Text in English. 1997. q. GBP 100 domestic to individuals; GBP 120 foreign to individuals; GBP 200 domestic to institutions; GBP 220 foreign to institutions; GBP 50 per issue domestic; GBP 55 per issue foreign (effective 2009). adv. bk.rev. back issues avail. **Document type:** *Journal, Academic/Scholarly.* **Description:** Dedicated to advanced sensor technology, intelligent manufacturing, risk management, technology management, industrial logistics and tribology, biomedical engineering, advanced signal processing, and environmental management.
Indexed: A28, APA, BrCerAb, C&ISA, CA, CA/WCA, CIA, CPEI, CerAb, CivEngAb, CorrAb, E&CAJ, E11, EEA, EMA, ESPM, EngInd, EnvEAb, H15, Inspec, M&TEA, M09, MBF, METADEX, S&VD, SCOPUS, SolStAb, T02, T04, WAA.
—BLDSC (4542.172420), IE, Ingenta, Linda Hall.
Published by: C O M A D E M International, 307 Tiverton Rd, Selly Oak, Birmingham, B29 6DA, United Kingdom. TEL 44-121-4722338. Ed., Adv. contact Raj B K N Rao. B&W page GBP 1,050, color page GBP 1,700.

600 GBR ISSN 1740-0546
▼ ➤ **INTERNATIONAL JOURNAL OF COMPLEXITY IN APPLIED SCIENCE AND ENGINEERING.** Text in English. forthcoming 2011. 4/yr. EUR 494 to institutions (print or online ed.); EUR 672 combined subscription to institutions (print & online eds.) (effective 2011). **Document type:** *Journal, Academic/Scholarly.* **Description:** Aims to develop, integrate and promote the study of complexity and complex systems in industry.
Formerly announced as (until Sep.2008): International Journal of Complexity
Related titles: Online - full text ed.: ISSN 1740-0554. forthcoming.
—**CCC.**
Published by: Inderscience Publishers, PO Box 735, Olney, Bucks MK46 5WB, United Kingdom. TEL 44-1234-240519, FAX 44-1234-240515, editorial@inderscience.com. Ed. Waguih H ElMaraghy. **Subscr. to:** World Trade Centre Bldg, 29 Rte de Pre-Bois, Case Postale 856, Geneva 15 1215, Switzerland. FAX 41-22-7910885, subs@inderscience.com.

▼ ➤ **INTERNATIONAL JOURNAL OF COMPUTER SCIENCE ENGINEERING AND TECHNOLOGY.** *see* COMPUTERS

745.2 FRA ISSN 1630-7267
INTERNATIONAL JOURNAL OF DESIGN SCIENCES & TECHNOLOGY/REVUE DES SCIENCES ET TECHNIQUES DE LA CONCEPTION. Text in Multiple languages. 1992. s-a. EUR 110 domestic; EUR 130 foreign (effective 2009). **Document type:** *Journal, Academic/Scholarly.* **Description:** Multidisciplinary forum dealing with all facets and fields of design.

Former titles (until 2000): Revue des Sciences et Techniques de la Conception (1270-0517); (until 1994): Revue Sciences et Techniques de la Conception (1257-8703)
Indexed: A22, SCOPUS.
—BLDSC (4542.185010), IE, Ingenta.
Published by: Europia Productions, 15 Avenue de Segur, Paris, 75007, France. TEL 33-1-45512607, FAX 33-1-45512632, ijdst@europia.org, http://europia.org.

THE INTERNATIONAL JOURNAL OF EMERGING TECHNOLOGIES AND SOCIETY. *see* SCIENCES: COMPREHENSIVE WORKS

INTERNATIONAL JOURNAL OF EMERGING TECHNOLOGIES IN LEARNING. *see* EDUCATION

INTERNATIONAL JOURNAL OF ENERGY TECHNOLOGY AND POLICY. *see* ENERGY

▼ **INTERNATIONAL JOURNAL OF ENGINEERING AND TECHNOLOGY.** *see* ENGINEERING

▼ **INTERNATIONAL JOURNAL OF ENGINEERING AND TECHNOLOGY.** *see* ENGINEERING

▼ **INTERNATIONAL JOURNAL OF ENGINEERING SCIENCE AND TECHNOLOGY.** *see* SCIENCES: COMPREHENSIVE WORKS

▼ **INTERNATIONAL JOURNAL OF ENGINEERING, SCIENCE AND TECHNOLOGY.** *see* ENGINEERING

INTERNATIONAL JOURNAL OF ENVIRONMENTAL SCIENCE AND TECHNOLOGY. *see* ENVIRONMENTAL STUDIES

INTERNATIONAL JOURNAL OF FASHION DESIGN, TECHNOLOGY AND EDUCATION. *see* CLOTHING TRADE—Fashions

▼ **INTERNATIONAL JOURNAL OF GENDER, SCIENCE AND TECHNOLOGY.** *see* SOCIOLOGY

INTERNATIONAL JOURNAL OF GEOINFORMATICS. *see* GEOGRAPHY

600 SGP ISSN 2010-0248
▼ ➤ **INTERNATIONAL JOURNAL OF INNOVATION, MANAGEMENT AND TECHNOLOGY.** Text in English. 2010. bi-m. USD 150 per issue (effective 2011). abstr. back issues avail. **Document type:** *Journal, Academic/Scholarly.*
Related titles: Online - full text ed.: free.
Published by: International Association of Computer Science and Information Technology, 9 Jurong Town Hall Rd. iHUB, Singapore, 609431, Singapore. iacsit@gmail.com, http://www.iacsit.org/.

600 GBR ISSN 2045-869X
▼ ➤ **INTERNATIONAL JOURNAL OF INNOVATIVE TECHNOLOGY AND CREATIVE ENGINEERING.** Abbreviated title: I J I T C E. Text in English. 2011. m. back issues avail. **Document type:** *Journal, Academic/Scholarly.* **Description:** Provides a platform for publishing novel ideas, prototypes, research results and innovative solutions in all aspects of engineering and technology.
Related titles: Online - full text ed.: ISSN 2045-8711. free (effective 2011).
Published by: I J A E T Journal, 1a park Ln, Cranford, London, TW5 9WA, United Kingdom. TEL 44-773-0430249.

➤ **INTERNATIONAL JOURNAL OF INSTRUCTIONAL MEDIA.** *see* EDUCATION—Teaching Methods And Curriculum

➤ **INTERNATIONAL JOURNAL OF INTELLECTUAL PROPERTY MANAGEMENT.** *see* PATENTS, TRADEMARKS AND COPYRIGHTS

➤ **INTERNATIONAL JOURNAL OF INTERACTIVE MOBILE TECHNOLOGIES.** *see* COMMUNICATIONS

➤ **INTERNATIONAL JOURNAL OF LAW AND INFORMATION TECHNOLOGY.** *see* LAW

600 GBR ISSN 1477-8386
➤ **INTERNATIONAL JOURNAL OF LEARNING TECHNOLOGY.** Abbreviated title: I J L T. Text in English. 2003. 4/yr. EUR 494 to institutions (print or online ed.); EUR 672 combined subscription to institutions (print & online eds.) (effective 2012). abstr.; bibl.; illus.; charts. back issues avail. **Document type:** *Journal, Academic/Scholarly.* **Description:** Provides an interdisciplinary forum for the presentation and discussion of important ideas, concepts, and exemplars that can deeply influence the role of learning technologies in learning and instruction.
Related titles: Online - full text ed.: ISSN 1741-8119 (from IngentaConnect).
Indexed: A26, A28, APA, B29, BrCerAb, C&ISA, C23, CA, CA/WCA, CIA, CPE, CerAb, CivEngAb, CorrAb, E&CAJ, E03, E07, E08, E11, EEA, EMA, ERI, ESPM, EnvEAb, ErgAb, G08, H15, I05, Inspec, M&TEA, M09, MBF, METADEX, S09, SolStAb, T02, T04, WAA.
—BLDSC (4542.314750), IE, Ingenta, Linda Hall. **CCC.**
Published by: Inderscience Publishers, PO Box 735, Olney, Bucks MK46 5WB, United Kingdom. TEL 44-1234-240519, FAX 44-1234-240515, editorial@inderscience.com. Ed. Dr. M A Dorgham. **Subscr. to:** World Trade Centre Bldg, 29 Rte de Pre-Bois, Case Postale 856, Geneva 15 1215, Switzerland. FAX 41-22-7910885, subs@inderscience.com.

▼ ➤ **INTERNATIONAL JOURNAL OF MANAGEMENT ENTREPRENEURSHIP & TECHNOLOGY.** *see* BUSINESS AND ECONOMICS

▼ ➤ **INTERNATIONAL JOURNAL OF MANAGING PUBLIC SECTOR INFORMATION AND COMMUNICATION TECHNOLOGIES.** *see* COMMUNICATIONS

➤ **INTERNATIONAL JOURNAL OF MOBILE LEARNING AND ORGANISATION.** *see* BUSINESS AND ECONOMICS—Management

➤ **INTERNATIONAL JOURNAL OF NANO AND BIOMATERIALS.** *see* SCIENCES: COMPREHENSIVE WORKS

600 MYS ISSN 2229-9114
▼ **INTERNATIONAL JOURNAL OF NETWORK AND MOBILE TECHNOLOGIES.** Abbreviated title: I J N M T. Text in English. 2010. s-a. free (effective 2011). **Document type:** *Journal, Academic/Scholarly.*
Media: Online - full text.
Published by: INTI International University, Persiaran Perdana BBN, Putra Milai, Nilai, N Sembilan 71800, Malaysia. TEL 60-6-7982000, FAX 60-6-7997536, http://www.newinti.edu.my. Ed. Alain Yee-Loong Chong.

620 600 DEU ISSN 1861-2121
T55.4
➤ **INTERNATIONAL JOURNAL OF ONLINE ENGINEERING.** Text in English. 2005. q. free (effective 2011). **Document type:** *Journal, Academic/Scholarly.* **Description:** Aims to bridge the gap between pure academic research journals and more practical publications and covers the full range from research and application development to experience reports and product descriptions.
Media: Online - full text.
Indexed: C10, CA, T02.
—IE.
Published by: Kassel University Press GmbH, Diagonale 10, Kassel, 34127, Germany. TEL 49-561-8042159, FAX 49-561-8043429, geschaeftsfuehrung@upress.uni-kassel.de, http://www.upress.uni-kassel.de. Ed. Michael E Auer TEL 43-664-895353.

▼ ➤ **INTERNATIONAL JOURNAL OF PHARMACY AND TECHNOLOGY.** *see* PHARMACY AND PHARMACOLOGY

➤ **INTERNATIONAL JOURNAL OF POWER AND ENERGY SYSTEMS.** *see* ENERGY

▼ ➤ **INTERNATIONAL JOURNAL OF PURE AND APPLIED SCIENCES AND TECHNOLOGY.** *see* SCIENCES: COMPREHENSIVE WORKS

▼ ➤ **INTERNATIONAL JOURNAL OF RESEARCH STUDIES IN EDUCATIONAL TECHNOLOGY.** *see* EDUCATION

▼ ➤ **INTERNATIONAL JOURNAL OF SOCIOTECHNOLOGY AND KNOWLEDGE DEVELOPMENT.** *see* SOCIOLOGY

▼ ➤ **INTERNATIONAL JOURNAL OF SUDAN RESEARCH, POLICY AND SUSTAINABLE DEVELOPMENT.** *see* SCIENCES: COMPREHENSIVE WORKS

➤ **INTERNATIONAL JOURNAL OF SYSTEM OF SYSTEMS ENGINEERING.** *see* ENGINEERING

➤ **INTERNATIONAL JOURNAL OF TECHNOENTREPRENEURSHIP.** *see* BUSINESS AND ECONOMICS—Management

600 GBR ISSN 1753-1942
➤ **INTERNATIONAL JOURNAL OF TECHNOLOGICAL LEARNING, INNOVATION AND DEVELOPMENT.** Text in English. 2007. 4/yr. EUR 494 to institutions (print or online ed.); EUR 672 combined subscription to institutions (print & online eds.) (effective 2012). stat.; abstr.; bibl.; charts. **Document type:** *Journal, Academic/Scholarly.* **Description:** Aims to bridge the communication gap between government policymakers, corporate executives, development agencies and investors on the one hand, and scholars/academics and research institutions concerned with the impact of technological progress on industrial, economic, and social development in latecomer economies.
Related titles: Online - full text ed.: ISSN 1753-1950 (from IngentaConnect).
Indexed: A26, A28, APA, BrCerAb, C&ISA, CA/WCA, CIA, CerAb, CivEngAb, CorrAb, E&CAJ, E08, E11, EEA, EMA, ESPM, EconLit, EnvEAb, H15, M&TEA, M09, MBF, METADEX, SolStAb, T04, WAA.
—BLDSC (4542.693165), IE, Linda Hall. **CCC.**
Published by: Inderscience Publishers, PO Box 735, Olney, Bucks MK46 5WB, United Kingdom. TEL 44-1234-240519, FAX 44-1234-240515, editorial@inderscience.com. Ed. Paulo N Figueiredo. **Subscr. to:** World Trade Centre Bldg, 29 Rte de Pre-Bois, Case Postale 856, Geneva 15 1215, Switzerland. FAX 41-22-7910885, subs@inderscience.com.

➤ **INTERNATIONAL JOURNAL OF TECHNOLOGICAL MANAGEMENT.** *see* BUSINESS AND ECONOMICS—Management

600 CAN ISSN 1192-2575
CODEN: TIJAFB
INTERNATIONAL JOURNAL OF TECHNOLOGY ADVANCES. Text in Arabic, English. 1993. 4/yr. CAD 400 (effective 2006). adv. bk.rev. **Document type:** *Magazine, Trade.* **Description:** Designed for concise, cooperative publication of simple and creative ideas.
Related titles: Microform ed.: (from MML).
Indexed: ChemAb.
—CASDDS. **CCC.**
Published by: M.I. Ismail, Ed. & Pub., 9 Finsh DDO, Montreal, PQ H9A 3G9, Canada. TEL 514-626-9800, ismail.csc@usa.net. Ed., Pub. M I Ismail TEL 965-918-9996.

INTERNATIONAL JOURNAL OF TECHNOLOGY AND DESIGN EDUCATION. *see* EDUCATION—Teaching Methods And Curriculum

600 370 USA ISSN 2155-5605
▼ ➤ **INTERNATIONAL JOURNAL OF TECHNOLOGY AND EDUCATIONAL MARKETING.** Text in English. 2011. s-a. USD 210 to individuals; USD 595 to institutions; USD 275 combined subscription to individuals (print & online eds.); USD 860 combined subscription to institutions (print & online eds.) (effective 2012). **Document type:** *Journal, Academic/Scholarly.* **Description:** Features research on marketing management and technological innovations in all segments of education.
Related titles: Online - full text ed.: ISSN 2155-5613. 2011. USD 140 to individuals; USD 595 to institutions (effective 2012).
Published by: I G I Global, 701 E Chocolate Ave, Ste 200, Hershey, PA 17033. TEL 717-533-8845 ext 100, FAX 717-533-8661, cust@igi-global.com, http://www.igi-pub.com. Eds. Purnendu Tripathi, Siran Mukerji.

600 GBR ISSN 1476-5667
T1
➤ **INTERNATIONAL JOURNAL OF TECHNOLOGY AND GLOBALISATION.** Abbreviated title: I J T G. Text in English. 2004. 4/yr. EUR 494 to institutions (print or online ed.); EUR 672 combined subscription to institutions (print & online eds.) (effective 2012). abstr.; bibl.; charts; illus. back issues avail. **Document type:** *Journal, Trade.* **Description:** Provides a forum for the exchange of ideas and views on the global implications of technology for economic growth, sustainable development and international security.
Related titles: Online - full text ed.: ISSN 1741-8194 (from IngentaConnect).
Indexed: A26, A28, A35, A37, APA, AgBio, B01, B02, B06, B07, B09, B15, B17, B18, BrCerAb, C&ISA, C25, CA, CA/WCA, CABA, CIA, CerAb, CivEngAb, CorrAb, E&CAJ, E11, E12, EEA, EMA, ESPM, EconLit, EnvEAb, G04, G08, GH, H15, H16, I05, Inspec, LT, M&TEA, M09, MBF, METADEX, MaizeAb, N02, P32, P40, PGegResA, R12, RRTA, RiskAb, SCOPUS, SSciA, SolStAb, SoyAb, T02, T04, T05, TAR, W11, WAA.
—BLDSC (4542.693270), IE, Ingenta, Linda Hall. **CCC.**
Published by: Inderscience Publishers, PO Box 735, Olney, Bucks MK46 5WB, United Kingdom. TEL 44-1234-240519, FAX 44-1234-240515, editorial@inderscience.com. Ed. Dr. M A Dorgham. **Subscr. to:** World Trade Centre Bldg, 29 Rte de Pre-Bois, Case Postale 856, Geneva 15 1215, Switzerland. FAX 41-22-7910885, subs@inderscience.com.

600 301 USA ISSN 1548-3908
TA167
➤ **INTERNATIONAL JOURNAL OF TECHNOLOGY AND HUMAN INTERACTION.** Text in English. 2005. q. USD 210 to individuals; USD 595 to institutions; USD 275 combined subscription to individuals (print & online eds.); USD 860 combined subscription to institutions (print & online eds.) (effective 2012). **Document type:** *Journal, Academic/Scholarly.* **Description:** Aims to provide a platform for leading research that addresses issues of human and technology interaction.
Related titles: Online - full text ed.: ISSN 1548-3916. USD 140 to individuals; USD 595 to institutions (effective 2012).
Indexed: A26, A28, APA, BrCerAb, C&ISA, CA/WCA, CIA, CPEI, CerAb, CivEngAb, CompD, CorrAb, E&CAJ, E11, EEA, EMA, ESPM, EnvEAb, H15, I05, Inspec, L13, M&TEA, M09, MBF, METADEX, P03, P17, P27, P48, P52, P53, P54, PQC, PsycInfo, SCOPUS, SolStAb, T04, WAA.
—BLDSC (4542.693285), IE, Ingenta, Linda Hall. **CCC.**
Published by: (Information Resources Management Association), I G I Global, 701 E Chocolate Ave, Ste 200, Hershey, PA 17033. TEL 717-533-8845 ext 100, 866-342-6657, FAX 717-533-8661, cust@igi-global.com. Ed. Bernd Carsten Stahl.

➤ **INTERNATIONAL JOURNAL OF TECHNOLOGY IN TEACHING AND LEARNING.** *see* EDUCATION

600 GBR ISSN 1740-2832
➤ **INTERNATIONAL JOURNAL OF TECHNOLOGY INTELLIGENCE AND PLANNING.** Text in English. 2004. 4/yr. EUR 494 to institutions (print or online ed.); EUR 672 combined subscription to institutions (print & online eds.) (effective 2012). charts; illus.; bibl.; abstr. back issues avail. **Document type:** *Journal, Academic/Scholarly.* **Description:** Provides a source of information in the field of technology intelligence, technology planning, R&D resource allocation, technology controlling, technology decision-making processes and related disciplines.
Related titles: Online - full text ed.: ISSN 1740-2840 (from IngentaConnect).
Indexed: A26, A28, APA, B02, B15, B17, B18, BrCerAb, C&ISA, CA, CA/WCA, CIA, CPEI, CerAb, CivEngAb, CompD, CorrAb, E&CAJ, E08, E11, EEA, EMA, ESPM, EnvEAb, G04, G08, H15, I05, Inspec, M&TEA, M09, MBF, METADEX, S09, SCOPUS, SolStAb, T02, T04, WAA.
—BLDSC (4542.693500), IE, Ingenta, Linda Hall. **CCC.**
Published by: Inderscience Publishers, PO Box 735, Olney, Bucks MK46 5WB, United Kingdom. TEL 44-1234-240519, FAX 44-1234-240515, editorial@inderscience.com. Ed. Dr. M A Dorgham. **Subscr. to:** World Trade Centre Bldg, 29 Rte de Pre-Bois, Case Postale 856, Geneva 15 1215, Switzerland. FAX 41-22-7910885, subs@inderscience.com.

➤ **INTERNATIONAL JOURNAL OF TECHNOLOGY, KNOWLEDGE AND SOCIETY.** *see* LIBRARY AND INFORMATION SCIENCES

600 658 GBR ISSN 0267-5730
T1 CODEN: IJTMEG
➤ **INTERNATIONAL JOURNAL OF TECHNOLOGY MANAGEMENT/ INTERNATIONALE ZEITSCHRIFT FUR TECHNOLOGIEMANAGEMENT/JOURNAL INTERNATIONAL DE LA GESTION TECHNOLOGIQUE.** Text in English. 1986. 16/yr. (in 4 vols., 4 nos./vol.). EUR 1,386 to institutions (print or online ed.); EUR 1,917 combined subscription to institutions (print & online eds.) (effective 2012). bk.rev. abstr.; charts; illus.; bibl. index. back issues avail.; reprints avail. **Document type:** *Journal, Academic/Scholarly.* **Description:** Aims to provide a source of information in the field of managing with technology, and the management of engineering, science and technology.
Related titles: Online - full text ed.: ISSN 1741-5276 (from IngentaConnect).
Indexed: A01, A02, A03, A08, A12, A13, A14, A17, A20, A22, A26, A28, ABIn, AIA, APA, ASCA, Agr, B01, B02, B06, B07, B08, B09, B11, B15, B17, B18, BPI, BRD, BrCerAb, BrTechI, C&ISA, C10, C12, C23, CA, CA/WCA, CADCAM, CIA, CLOSS, CPEI, CerAb, CivEngAb, CompLI, CorrAb, CurCont, E&CAJ, E08, E11, EEA, EIA, EMA, ESPM, Emerald, EngInd, EnvAb, EnvEAb, EnvInd, G04, G06, G07, G08, H15, I05, IBSS, ISTA, Inspec, M&MA, M&TEA, M09, MBF, METADEX, P30, P34, P41, P48, P51, P53, P54, PQC, RASB, RoboAb, S09, SCI, SCOPUS, SSCI, SSciA, SolStAb, T02, T04, TM, Telegen, W01, W02, W03, W07, WAA.
—BLDSC (4542.693700), AskIEEE, IE, Infotrieve, Ingenta, Linda Hall. **CCC.**
Published by: Inderscience Publishers, PO Box 735, Olney, Bucks MK46 5WB, United Kingdom. TEL 44-1234-240519, FAX 44-1234-240515, editorial@inderscience.com. Ed. Dr. M A Dorgham. **Subscr. to:** World Trade Centre Bldg, 29 Rte de Pre-Bois, Case Postale 856, Geneva 15 1215, Switzerland. FAX 41-22-7910885, subs@inderscience.com.

600 GBR ISSN 1474-2748
➤ **INTERNATIONAL JOURNAL OF TECHNOLOGY MANAGEMENT & SUSTAINABLE DEVELOPMENT.** Abbreviated title: I J T M S D. Variant title: Technology Management & Sustainable Development. Text in English. 2002. 3/yr. GBP 210 domestic to institutions; GBP 219 in the European Union to institutions; USD 330 in US & Canada to institutions; GBP 222 elsewhere to institutions (effective 2011). adv. back issues avail. **Document type:** *Journal, Academic/Scholarly.* **Description:** Seeks to provide expert and interdisciplinary insight into the technology dimension of international development, and aims to advance contemporary knowledge about the empirical and theoretical aspects of technology management and sustainable development from the vantage point of developing countries.
Related titles: Online - full text ed.: ISSN 2040-0551. USD 265 in US & Canada to institutions; GBP 177 elsewhere to institutions (effective 2011).
Indexed: A01, A02, A03, A08, A12, A17, A22, ABIn, B01, B06, B07, B08, B09, CA, CompLI, E01, Inspec, P34, P41, P48, P51, P52, P53, P54, P56, PQC, S01, T02.
—BLDSC (4542.693750), IE, Ingenta. **CCC.**

Published by: Intellect Ltd., The Mill, Parnall Rd, Fishponds, Bristol, BS16 3JG, United Kingdom. TEL 44-117-9589910, FAX 44-117-9589911, info@intellectbooks.com. Eds. Girma Zawdie, Mohammed Saad. Pub. Masoud Yazdani. **Subscr. to:** Turpin Distribution Services Ltd., Pegasus Dr, Stratton Business Park, Biggleswade, Bedfordshire SG18 8QB, United Kingdom. TEL 44-1767-604951, FAX 44-1767-601640, custserv@turpin-distribution.com, http://www.turpin-distribution.com/.

600 GBR ISSN 1468-4322
T1

➤ **INTERNATIONAL JOURNAL OF TECHNOLOGY, POLICY AND MANAGEMENT.** Abbreviated title: I J T P M. Text in English. 2001. 4/yr. EUR 494 to institutions (print or online ed.); EUR 672 combined subscription to institutions (print & online eds.) (effective 2012). abstr.; bibl.; stat.; charts; illus. back issues avail. **Document type:** *Journal, Academic/Scholarly.* **Description:** Provides a professional and scholarly forum in the emerging field of decision making and problem solving in the integrated area of technology policy and management at the operational, organizational and public policy levels.

Related titles: Online - full text ed.: ISSN 1741-5292 (from IngentaConnect).

Indexed: A12, A17, A26, A28, ABIn, APA, B01, B02, B06, B07, B09, B15, B17, B18, BrCerAb, C&ISA, C23, CA, CA/WCA, CIA, CPEI, CerAb, CivEngAb, CorrAb, E&CAJ, E08, E11, EEA, EMA, ESPM, EngInd, EnvEAb, G04, G08, H15, I05, Inspec, M&TEA, M09, MBF, METADEX, P34, P41, P48, P51, P53, P54, PQC, RiskAb, S09, SCOPUS, SolStAb, T02, T04, WAA.

—BLDSC (4542.693800), IE, Ingenta, Linda Hall. **CCC.**

Published by: Inderscience Publishers, PO Box 735, Olney, Bucks MK46 5WB, United Kingdom. TEL 44-1234-240519, FAX 44-1234-240515, editorial@inderscience.com. Ed. Kurt J Engemann. **Subscr. to:** World Trade Centre Bldg, 29 Rte de Pre-Bois, Case Postale 856, Geneva 15 1215, Switzerland. FAX 41-22-7910885, subs@inderscience.com.

600 GBR ISSN 1470-6075
T174.3

➤ **INTERNATIONAL JOURNAL OF TECHNOLOGY TRANSFER AND COMMERCIALISATION.** Abbreviated title: I J T T C. Text in English. 2002. 4/yr. EUR 494 to institutions (print or online ed.); EUR 672 combined subscription to institutions (print & online eds.) (effective 2012). bk.rev. charts; illus.; abstr.; bibl. **Document type:** *Journal, Academic/Scholarly.* **Description:** Provides an authoritative source of information in the field of knowledge and technology transfer and diffusion, as well as commercialization and related disciplines objectives.

Related titles: Online - full text ed.: ISSN 1741-5284 (from IngentaConnect).

Indexed: A12, A17, A26, A28, ABIn, APA, B01, B02, B06, B07, B09, B15, B17, B18, BrCerAb, C&ISA, C23, CA, CA/WCA, CIA, CerAb, CivEngAb, CorrAb, E&CAJ, E08, E11, EEA, EMA, ESPM, EnvEAb, G04, G08, H15, I05, M&TEA, M09, MBF, METADEX, P41, P48, P51, P53, P54, PQC, PollutAb, RiskAb, S09, SSciA, SolStAb, T02, T04, WAA.

—BLDSC (4542.693850), IE, Ingenta, INIST, Linda Hall. **CCC.**

Published by: Inderscience Publishers, PO Box 735, Olney, Bucks MK46 5WB, United Kingdom. TEL 44-1234-240519, FAX 44-1234-240515, editorial@inderscience.com. Ed. Dr. M A Dorgham. **Subscr. to:** World Trade Centre Bldg, 29 Rte de Pre-Bois, Case Postale 856, Geneva 15 1215, Switzerland. FAX 41-22-7910885, subs@inderscience.com.

600 GBR ISSN 2046-3375

▼➤ **INTERNATIONAL JOURNAL OF THE DIGITAL HUMAN.** Text in English. forthcoming 2011. 4/yr. EUR 494 to institutions (print or online ed.); EUR 672 combined subscription to institutions (print & online eds.) (effective 2011). abstr.; bibl. **Document type:** *Journal, Academic/Scholarly.* **Description:** Aims to create a platform where researchers, scientist, practitioners and industrialists can communicate, promote and coordinate the developments of digital humans in society. It provides a channel for people from multiple disciplines to have a common goal to advance the development of digital human research.

Related titles: Online - full text ed.: ISSN 2046-3383. forthcoming.

Published by: Inderscience Publishers, PO Box 735, Olney, Bucks MK46 5WB, United Kingdom. TEL 44-1234-240519, FAX 44-1234-240515, editorial@inderscience.com. Ed. Dr. Ameersing Luximon. **Subscr. to:** World Trade Centre Bldg, 29 Rte de Pre-Bois, Case Postale 856, Geneva 15 1215, Switzerland. FAX 41-22-7910885, subs@inderscience.com.

➤ **INTERNATIONAL JOURNAL OF VEHICLE AUTONOMOUS SYSTEMS.** *see* TRANSPORTATION

➤ **INTERNATIONAL JOURNAL OF VEHICLE DESIGN**; the journal of vehicle engineering and components. *see* TRANSPORTATION

➤ **THE INTERNATIONAL LIBRARY OF ETHICS, LAW AND TECHNOLOGY.** *see* PHILOSOPHY

➤ **INTERNATIONAL NAVIGATION ASSOCIATION. TECHNICAL BRIEFS.** *see* TRANSPORTATION—Ships And Shipping

➤ **INTERNATIONAL OCEAN SYSTEMS.** *see* EARTH SCIENCES—Oceanography

➤ **INTERNATIONAL SERIES ON MATERIALS SCIENCE AND TECHNOLOGY.** *see* ENGINEERING—Engineering Mechanics And Materials

➤ **INTERNATIONAL TECHNOLOGY EDUCATION STUDIES.** *see* EDUCATION

600 610 USA ISSN 1559-4610

➤ **THE INTERNET JOURNAL OF MEDICAL TECHNOLOGY.** Text in English. 2002. s-a. free (effective 2011). **Document type:** *Journal, Academic/Scholarly.*

Supersedes in part (in 2003): The Internet Journal of Medical Simulation and Technology (1540-2657)

Media: Online - full text.

Indexed: A01, A02, A03, A08, A26, A39, C06, C07, C11, C27, C29, CA, D03, D04, E13, G08, H11, H12, I05, R14, S14, S15, S18, T02.

Published by: Internet Scientific Publications, Llc., 23 Rippling Creek Dr, Sugar Land, TX 77479. TEL 832-443-1193, FAX 281-240-1533, wenker@ispub.com. Ed. Claudio Zanon.

600 610 USA ISSN 1937-8262

➤ **THE INTERNET JOURNAL OF NANOTECHNOLOGY.** Text in English. 2004. s-a. free (effective 2011). **Document type:** *Journal, Academic/Scholarly.*

Media: Online - full text.

Indexed: A01, A26, A39, C27, C29, CA, D03, D04, E08, E13, G08, H11, H12, I05, R14, S06, S09, S14, S15, S18, T02.

Published by: Internet Scientific Publications, Llc., 23 Rippling Creek Dr, Sugar Land, TX 77479. TEL 832-443-1193, FAX 281-240-1533, wenker@ispub.com.

➤ **INTERNET MAGAZINE**; Thailand's leading Internet magazine. *see* COMPUTERS—Internet

➤ **INTERVIR**; online journal of education, technology and politics. *see* EDUCATION

600 IND ISSN 2229-7782

▼➤ **INVENTI RAPID TECH RESEARCH & REVIEWS.** Text and summaries in English. 2010. q. INR 1,000 domestic; USD 20 foreign (effective 2011). adv. abstr. Index. back issues avail.; reprints avail. **Document type:** *Journal, Academic/Scholarly.* **Description:** Publishes research reports, review articles and scientific commentaries on technology research.

Media: Online - full text.

Published by: Inventi Journals Pvt. Ltd., SDX 33, Minal Residency, JK Rd, Bhopal, Madhya Pradesh 462 023, India. TEL 91-9425536487, FAX 91-11-66173705, info@inventi.in, editor@inventi.in, http://www.inventi.in. Ed. Dr. Tarun Kant. Pub. V B Gupta. R&P Emmanuel Toppo. Circ: 50.

600 IND

▼➤ **INVENTI RAPID V L S I.** (Very Large Scale Integration) Text and summaries in English. 2010. q. INR 1,000 domestic; USD 20 foreign (effective 2011). adv. abstr. a. index. back issues avail.; reprints avail. **Document type:** *Journal, Academic/Scholarly.* **Description:** Publishes research reports, review articles and scientific commentaries on microprocessor technology.

Media: Online - full text.

Published by: Inventi Journals Pvt. Ltd., SDX 33, Minal Residency, JK Rd, Bhopal, Madhya Pradesh 462 023, India. TEL 91-9425536487, FAX 91-11-66173705, info@inventi.in, editor@inventi.in, http://www.inventi.in. Ed. Dr. Tarun Kant. Pub. V B Gupta. R&P Emmanuel Toppo. Circ: 50.

600 PRT ISSN 1647-1148

INVESTIGACAO E DESENVOLVIMENTO TECNOLOGICO. Text in Portuguese. 2007. a. **Document type:** *Journal, Academic/Scholarly.*

Published by: Fundacao Luis de Molina, Largo dos Colegiais 2, Evora, 7000-803, Portugal. http://www.flmolina.uevora.pt.

INVESTIGACION Y CIENCIA. *see* SCIENCES: COMPREHENSIVE WORKS

600 IRN ISSN 1028-6284

➤ **IRANIAN JOURNAL OF SCIENCE AND TECHNOLOGY. TRANSACTION B: TECHNOLOGY.** Text in English; Abstracts in Persian, Modern. 1971. d. IRR 180,000, USD 200 (effective 2005). **Document type:** *Journal, Academic/Scholarly.*

Supersedes in part (in 1995): Iranian Journal of Science and Technology (0360-1307)

Indexed: A28, APA, BrCerAb, C&ISA, CA/WCA, CIA, CerAb, CivEngAb, CorrAb, E&CAJ, E11, EEA, EMA, ESPM, EnvEAb, FLUIDEX, GEOBASE, H15, INIS AtomInd, M&TEA, M09, MBF, METADEX, MSN, SCI, SCOPUS, SWRA, SolStAb, T04, W07, WAA, Z02.

—BLDSC (4567.529500), IE, Ingenta, Linda Hall.

Published by: Shiraz University, School of Engineering, Iranian Journal of Science & Technology, Shiraz, Iran. TEL 98-711-6272060, FAX 98-711-6272060, ijst_trans_a@susc.ac.ir, http://hafez.shirazu.ac.ir. Ed. M. Yaghoubi. Pub. H. Sharif.

➤ **THE IRISH SCIENTIST.** *see* SCIENCES: COMPREHENSIVE WORKS

➤ **ISRAEL ACADEMY OF SCIENCES AND HUMANITIES. PROCEEDINGS.** *see* HUMANITIES: COMPREHENSIVE WORKS

338 600 ISR ISSN 0334-6307

ISRAEL HIGH-TECH & INVESTMENT REPORT. Text in English. 1985. m. USD 95 (effective 2008). **Document type:** *Newsletter, Trade.* **Description:** Covers current business and technology issues and trends, including research and development, investment prospects, international cooperation, and regional issues.

Formerly: Israel High-Tech Report

Address: P O Box 33633, Tel Aviv, 61336, Israel. TEL 972-3-5235279, FAX 972-3-5227799. Ed., Pub. Joseph Morgenstern.

600 USA ISSN 1547-5840
T58.5

➤ **ISSUES IN INFORMING SCIENCE & INFORMATION TECHNOLOGY.** Variant title: Journal of Issues in Informing Science & Information Technology. Text in English. 2004. a. USD 49.99 to members; USD 79.99 to non-members (effective 2009). **Document type:** *Journal, Academic/Scholarly.* **Description:** Encourage the sharing of knowledge and collaboration among the wide variety of fields that use information technology to inform clients.

Related titles: CD-ROM ed.: ISSN 1547-5859; Online - full text ed.: ISSN 1547-5867. free (effective 2011).

Indexed: A01, A09, A10, A26, A39, C10, C27, C29, CA, D03, D04, E07, E08, E11, E13, ESPM, EnvEAb, H15, I05, M09, R14, S09, S14, S15, S18, T02, T04, V03, V04.

Published by: Informing Science Institute, 131 Brookhill Ct, Santa Rosa, CA 95409. TEL 707-531-4925, FAX 480-247-5724, http://informingscience.org. Ed. Dr. Eli B Cohen.

➤ **ISSUES IN SCIENCE AND TECHNOLOGY.** *see* SCIENCES: COMPREHENSIVE WORKS

600 ITA ISSN 0391-738X

ITALIAN TECHNOLOGY; the journal of machine tools. Variant title: Italian Technology Machine Tools. Text in English. 1975. 3/yr. EUR 14 domestic; EUR 23 foreign (effective 2009). adv. bk.rev. **Document type:** *Magazine, Trade.*

Indexed: R18.

Published by: Reed Business Information Spa (Subsidiary of: Reed Business Information International), Viale Giulio Richard 1, Milan, 20143, Italy. TEL 39-02-818301, FAX 39-02-81830406, info@reedbusiness.it, http://www.reedbusiness.it. Circ: 14,200.

600 RUS ISSN 1560-3644

IZVESTIYA VYSSHIKH UCHEBNYKH ZAVEDENII. SEVERO-KAVKAZSKII REGION. SERIYA TEKHNICHESKIE NAUKI/ BULLETIN OF THE HIGHER EDUCATIONAL INSTITUTIONS. NORTH CAUCASES REGION. SERIES OF TECHNICAL SCIENCES. Text in Russian. 1997. q. USD 110 in United States. **Description:** Covers all aspects of theoretical and experimental researches in technical sciences in the North Caucuses region of the Russian Federation. Generalizes experience in civil engineering and construction materials, mining and petroleum engineering, fuel technology, mechanical and metallurgical engineering, power engineering, etc.

Indexed: GeoRef.

Published by: Rostovskii Gosudarstvennyi Universitet, B Sadovaya 105, Rostov-on-Don, 344006, Russian Federation. TEL 7-8632-640500. Ed. Yu. Zhdanov. **Dist. by:** East View Information Services, 10601 Wayzata Blvd, Minneapolis, MN 55305. TEL 952-252-1201, 800-477-1005, FAX 952-252-1202, info@eastview.com, http://www.eastview.com.

J A I I O. A S T. ANALES. (Jornadas Argentinas de Informatica e Investigacion Operativa. Simposio Argentino de Tecnologia. Anal) *see* COMPUTERS

J O L T DIGEST. (Journal of Law & Technology) *see* LAW

600 DEU ISSN 0935-0292

JAHRBUCH SCHWEISSTECHNIK. Text in German. 1986. a. EUR 44.80 (effective 2011). adv. bk.rev. **Document type:** *Journal, Trade.*

Published by: (Deutscher Verband fuer Schweissen und verwandte Verfahren e.V.), D V S Verlag GmbH, Aachener Str 172, Duesseldorf, 40223, Germany. TEL 49-211-15910, FAX 49-211-1591150, verlag@dvs-hg.de, http://www.dvs-verlag.de. Circ: 7,000.

600 JPN ISSN 0385-5236

JAPAN JOURNAL OF EDUCATIONAL TECHNOLOGY. Text in Japanese. q. JPY 3,600.

Published by: Educational Technology Journal Association of Japan, 4-1-1 Nukui-Kita-Machi, Koganei-shi, Tokyo-to 184-0015, Japan. **Dist. by:** Business Center for Academic Societies Japan, 5-16-19 Honkomagome, Bunkyo-ku, Tokyo 113-0021, Japan. TEL 81-3-58145811.

600 FRA ISSN 0021-5554

LA JAUNE ET LA ROUGE. Text in French. 1948. 10/yr. EUR 40 (effective 2009). adv. bk.rev. **Document type:** *Magazine, Consumer.* **Description:** Publications of the former students of Ecole Polytechnique Association.

Published by: Societe Amicale des Anciens Eleves de l'Ecole Polytechnique, 5 rue Descartes, Paris, 75005, France. TEL 33-1-56811113, FAX 33-1-56811102. Ed. Jean Duquesne. Circ: 13,000.

JIANCAI SHIJIE/WORLD OF BUILDING MATERIALS. *see* BUILDING AND CONSTRUCTION

500 CHN ISSN 1004-7530

JIANGSU KEJI XINXI/JIANGSU SCIENCE & TECHNOLOGY INFORMATION. Text in Chinese. 1984. m. CNY 180 domestic; USD 45.60 in Hong Kong, Macau & Taiwan; USD 67.20 elsewhere (effective 2007). **Document type:** *Journal, Academic/Scholarly.*

Related titles: Online - full text ed.

Published by: Jiangsu-sheng Keji Qingbaosuo, 77, Suojin-Cun, Nanjing, 210042, China. TEL 86-25-85410349. **Dist. by:** China International Book Trading Corp, 35 Chegongzhuang Xilu, Haidian District, PO Box 399, Beijing 100044, China. TEL 86-10-68412045, FAX 86-10-68412023, cibtc@mail.cibtc.com.cn, http://www.cibtc.com.cn.

JIANZHU JIYI/ARCHITECTURE TECHNIQUE. *see* ARCHITECTURE

JIAOTONG KEJI YU JINGJI/TECHNOLOGY & ECONOMY IN AREAS OF COMMUNICATIONS. *see* COMMUNICATIONS

600 CHN

JIATING KEXUE. Text in Chinese. d. CNY 45.60; CNY 3.80 newsstand/cover (effective 2004). **Document type:** *Consumer.*

Related titles: Online - full content ed.

Published by: Liaoning Ribao Baoye Jituan/Liaoning Daily Newspaper Group, Heping-qu, 47, Nanjiuma Lu, Chenyang, Liaoning 110005, China. TEL 86-24-23381900, FAX 86-24-23397062. **Dist. by:** China International Book Trading Corp, 35 Chegongzhuang Xilu, Haidian District, PO Box 399, Beijing 100044, China. TEL 86-10-68412045, FAX 86-10-68412023, cibtc@mail.cibtc.com.cn, http://www.cibtc.com.cn.

600 CHN ISSN 1672-4801

JIDIAN JISHU/MECHANICAL & ELECTRICAL TECHNOLOGY. Text in Chinese. 1977. q. CNY 5 newsstand/cover (effective 2006). **Document type:** *Journal, Academic/Scholarly.*

Formerly: Shuilunbeng

Related titles: Online - full text ed.

Published by: Fujian Sheng Jixie Kexue Yanjiuyuan, 115, Liu-Yi Zhong Lu, Fuzhou, 350005, China.

JIEFANGJUN LIGONG DAXUE XUEBAO (ZIRAN KEXUE BAN)/P L A UNIVERSITY OF SCIENCE AND TECHNOLOGY (NATURAL SCIENCE EDITION). JOURNAL. *see* SCIENCES: COMPREHENSIVE WORKS

JILIN DAXUE XUEBAO (GONGXUE BAN). *see* ENGINEERING

JINGCHA JISHU/POLICE TECHNOLOGY. *see* CRIMINOLOGY AND LAW ENFORCEMENT

JINHUA ZHIYE JISHU XUEYUAN XUEBAO/JINHUA COLLEGE OF PROFESSION AND TECHNOLOGY. JOURNAL. *see* OCCUPATIONS AND CAREERS

JINRI KEJI/TODAY SCIENCE AND TECHNOLOGY. *see* SCIENCES: COMPREHENSIVE WORKS

J'INTEGRE. *see* SCIENCES: COMPREHENSIVE WORKS

JINZHAN: GUOJI MAOYI YU KEJI JIAOLIU/PROGRESS: INTERNATIONAL EXCHANGE IN TRADE, SCIENCE AND TECHNOLOGY. *see* BUSINESS AND ECONOMICS—International Commerce

600 USA

➤ **JOHNS HOPKINS STUDIES IN THE HISTORY OF TECHNOLOGY.** Text in English. 1967; N.S. 1978. irreg., latest 2008. price varies. back issues avail.; reprints avail. **Document type:** *Monographic series, Academic/Scholarly.*

Published by: The Johns Hopkins University Press, 2715 N Charles St, Baltimore, MD 21218. TEL 410-516-6900, FAX 410-516-6968, psmith@press.jhu.edu, http://www.press.jhu.edu. Ed. Merritt Roe Smith.

600 NZL ISSN 2230-2115
▼ ➤ **JOURNAL. CREATIVE TECHNOLOGIES.** Text in English. 2011. s-a. free. bk.rev.; dance rev.; film rev.; rec.rev.; music rev.; software rev.; video rev. abstr.; bibl.; charts; illus. back issues avail. **Document type:** *Journal, Academic/Scholarly.* **Description:** Covers creative technologies, transmedia, design and technology, art and technology, convergence, interdiciplinarity.
Media: Online - full text.
Published by: CoLab, AUT University, WT Bldg., Rm. WT033, C-41, Private Bag 92006, Auckland, 1142, New Zealand. TEL 64-9-9219566, dawn.hutchesson@aut.ac.nz, http://www.colab.org.nz. Ed., R&P Jennie Watts.

600 003.3 FRA ISSN 1952-3645
LE JOURNAL DU VRAC. Variant title: Manutention et Systemes Special VRAC. Text in French. 1998. bi-m. EUR 75 domestic (effective 2009).
Former titles (until 2006): Process Manutention (1632-4242); (until 2003): Manutention et Systemes (1291-696X)
Published by: Worldex Media, 2 Rue Du Nouveau Bercy, Charenton Le Pont (Val-de-Marne), 94220, France. TEL 33-1-58731150, FAX 33-1-58731168, http://http://www.worldex.fr.

JOURNAL FOR NEW GENERATION SCIENCE. *see* SCIENCES: COMPREHENSIVE WORKS

JOURNAL OF ADVANCED CONCRETE TECHNOLOGY. *see* BUILDING AND CONSTRUCTION

JOURNAL OF AGRICULTURAL EDUCATION AND TECHNOLOGY. *see* AGRICULTURE

JOURNAL OF AGRICULTURAL SCIENCES AND TECHNOLOGY. *see* AGRICULTURE

JOURNAL OF AGRICULTURE, SCIENCE AND TECHNOLOGY. *see* AGRICULTURE

JOURNAL OF ALGORITHMS & COMPUTATIONAL TECHNOLOGY. *see* MATHEMATICS

▼ **JOURNAL OF ANALYTICAL SCIENCE AND TECHNOLOGY.** *see* SCIENCES: COMPREHENSIVE WORKS

▼ **JOURNAL OF ANIMAL RESEARCH & TECHNOLOGY.** *see* BIOLOGY—Zoology

600 MEX ISSN 1665-6423
JOURNAL OF APPLIED RESEARCH AND TECHNOLOGY. Text in English. 2003. s-a. back issues avail. **Document type:** *Journal, Academic/Scholarly.*
Related titles: Online - full text ed.
Indexed: C01, SCI, W07.
Published by: Universidad Nacional Autonoma de Mexico, Centro de Ciencias Aplicadas y Desarrollo Tecnologico, Circuito Exterior s-n, Ciudad Universitaria, Mexico, D.F., 04510, Mexico. TEL 52-55-56228625, jart@cibernetica.ccadet.unam.mx, http://www.cinstrum.unam.mx/. Ed. Felipe Lara Rosano.

600 GHA ISSN 0855-2215
T1 CODEN: JASTGG
➤ **JOURNAL OF APPLIED SCIENCE AND TECHNOLOGY.** Text in English. 1996. s-a. USD 40 foreign (effective 2007). back issues avail. **Document type:** *Journal, Academic/Scholarly.* **Description:** Seeks to promote and disseminate knowledge in the applied sciences, specifically addressing issues that relate to technological developments in the Tropics.
Related titles: Online - full text ed.
Indexed: AgrForAb, BA, C25, C30, CABA, CIS, E12, F08, F11, F12, GH, H16, I11, INIS AtomInd, MaizeAb, N02, PGrRegA, PHN&I, R12, S13, S16, S17, SoyAb, T05, TAR, W11.
Published by: Council for Scientific and Industrial Research, Industry, Natural and Social Sciences Sector, PO Box M32, Accra, Ghana. TEL 233-21-776991, FAX 233-21-777655. Ed. A Ayensu.

➤ **JOURNAL OF APPLIED SCIENCE, ENGINEERING AND TECHNOLOGY.** *see* ENGINEERING

➤ **JOURNAL OF BIOCHEMICAL TECHNOLOGY.** *see* BIOLOGY—Biochemistry

➤ **JOURNAL OF COMPUTER SCIENCE AND TECHNOLOGY.** *see* COMPUTERS

600 CHN ISSN 1672-6340
➤ **JOURNAL OF CONTROL THEORY AND APPLICATIONS.** Text in English. 2003. q. EUR 556, USD 673 combined subscription to institutions (print & online eds.) (effective 2012). back issues avail.; reprint service avail. from PSC. **Document type:** *Journal, Academic/Scholarly.* **Description:** Publishes original survey papers, regular papers, and brief papers on the theory, design and applications in the systems and control field.
Related titles: Online - full text ed.: ISSN 1993-0623; ◆ Chinese ed.: Kongzhi Lilun yu Yingyong. ISSN 1000-8152.
Indexed: A22, A26, A28, APA, BrCerAb, C&ISA, CA/WCA, CCMJ, CIA, CPEI, CerAb, CivEngAb, CorrAb, E&CAJ, E01, E11, EEA, EMA, ESPM, EnvEAb, H15, Inspec, M&TEA, M09, MBF, METADEX, MSN, MathR, SCOPUS, SolStAb, T04, WAA, Z02.
—BLDSC (4965.258000), IE, Ingenta, Linda Hall. **CCC.**
Published by: (Zhongguo Kexueyuan Shuxue yu Xitong Kexue Yanjiuyuan/Chinese Academy of Sciences, Academy of Mathematics and Systems Science), Huanan Ligong Daxue/South China University of Technology, 381Wushan Lu, Guangzhou, 510640, China. TEL 86-20-87111464, FAX 86-20-87111464, http://www.scut.edu.cn/. Ed. Daizhan Cheng. **Co-publisher:** Springer.

745.2 GBR ISSN 1748-3050
➤ **JOURNAL OF DESIGN RESEARCH.** Text in English. 2001. 4/yr. EUR 494 to institutions (print or online ed.); EUR 672 combined subscription to institutions (print & online eds.) (effective 2012). bk.rev. abstr.; bibl.; charts; illus. **Document type:** *Journal, Academic/Scholarly.* **Description:** Emphasizes human aspects as a central issue of design through integrative studies of social sciences and design disciplines.
Related titles: Online - full text ed.: ISSN 1569-1551 (from IngentaConnect).
Indexed: A28, APA, BrCerAb, C&ISA, CA/WCA, CIA, CerAb, CivEngAb, CorrAb, D05, E&CAJ, E11, EEA, EMA, ESPM, EnvEAb, H15, Inspec, M&TEA, M09, MBF, METADEX, SolStAb, T04, WAA.
—BLDSC (4968.820000), IE, Ingenta. **CCC.**
Published by: Inderscience Publishers, PO Box 735, Olney, Bucks MK46 5WB, United Kingdom. TEL 44-1234-240519, FAX 44-1234-240515, editorial@inderscience.com. Eds. Dr. Henri Christiaans, Dr. Ina T Klaasen, Dr. Paulien M Herder. **Subscr. to:** World Trade Centre Bldg, 29 Rte de Pre-Bois, Case Postale 856, Geneva 15 1215, Switzerland. FAX 41-22-7910885, subs@inderscience.com.

➤ **JOURNAL OF DIABETES SCIENCE AND TECHNOLOGY.** *see* MEDICAL SCIENCES—Endocrinology

600 USA ISSN 1948-5859
▼ ➤ **JOURNAL OF DISRUPTIVE TECHNOLOGY.** Text in English. 2009. q. **Document type:** *Journal, Academic/Scholarly.* **Description:** Features new work on disruptive technologies and innovations.
Media: Online - full text.
Published by: Joseph Aluya, Ed. & Pub., 200 N Bradford Ave, Placentia, CA 92870. TEL 714-528-1063, jparadigm@aol.com.

600 370 USA ISSN 1941-8027
LB1028.3
➤ **JOURNAL OF EDUCATIONAL TECHNOLOGY DEVELOPMENT AND EXCHANGE.** Abbreviated title: J E T D E. Text in English. 2008 (Oct.). a. free (effective 2010). back issues avail. **Document type:** *Journal, Academic/Scholarly.* **Description:** Aims to provide a platform for international Chinese scholars and experts in the field of education technology and encourages academic cooperation, communication, and support among professionals.
Related titles: Online - full text ed.: ISSN 1941-8035.
Indexed: E03, T02.
Published by: Society of International Chinese in Educational Technology Ed. Dr. Harrison Hao Yang.

➤ **JOURNAL OF ENGINEERING AND APPLIED SCIENCES (ISLAMABAD).** *see* ENGINEERING

➤ **JOURNAL OF ENGINEERING AND APPLIED SCIENCES (PESHAWAR).** *see* ENGINEERING

▼ ➤ **JOURNAL OF ENGINEERING AND TECHNOLOGY.** *see* ENGINEERING

➤ **JOURNAL OF EVOLUTION AND TECHNOLOGY.** *see* PHILOSOPHY

607.2 MYS ISSN 1394-5629
CODEN: JITEFV
JOURNAL OF INDUSTRIAL TECHNOLOGY. Text in English. s-a.
Indexed: INIS AtomInd.
Published by: SIRIM Berhad/Standards and Industrial Research Institute of Malaysia, PO Box 7035, Shah Alam, 40911, Malaysia. TEL 60-3-55446000, FAX 60-3-55103535, http://www.sirim.my/.

629 USA ISSN 1537-0429
➤ **JOURNAL OF INDUSTRIAL TECHNOLOGY (ONLINE).** Abbreviated title: J I T. Text in English. 1984. q. free (effective 2011). adv. bk.rev. charts; illus.; stat. back issues avail. **Document type:** *Journal, Academic/Scholarly.* **Description:** Publishes articles on industrial technology subjects, research, and practical applications for professionals and scholars.
Formerly (until 1999): Journal of Industrial Technology (Print) (0882-6404)
Media: Online - full text.
Indexed: A22, A39, C10, C27, C29, CA, CPEI, D03, D04, E13, R14, S14, S15, S18, SCOPUS, T02.
—Ingenta.
Published by: The Association of Technology, Management, and Applied Engineering, 1390 Eisenhower Pl, Ann Arbor, MI 48108. TEL 734-677-0720, FAX 734-677-0046, atmae@atmae.org, http://atmae.org. Ed. Dennis Field TEL 859-622-6781. Adv. contact Dave Monforton.

600 GBR
JOURNAL OF INDUSTRY AND TECHNOLOGY. Text in English. 1978. bi-m. free (effective 2010). adv. bk.rev. **Document type:** *Journal, Trade.* **Description:** Dedicated to industry and technology, keeping readers abreast of the latest and broadest of industrial developments.
Related titles: CD-ROM ed.; Online - full text ed.
Published by: Industrial and Technological Publications, 8 Matthew Wren Close, Little Downham, Ely, Cambs CB6 2UL, United Kingdom. TEL 44-1353-699916. Ed. William R Digby-Hammerton. Pubs. Trevor Bennet, William R Digby-Hammerton. adv.: page GBP 500; 184 x 269.

JOURNAL OF INFORMATION, LAW AND TECHNOLOGY. *see* LAW

JOURNAL OF INTERNATIONAL COMMUNICATION. *see* SOCIOLOGY

600 BGR ISSN 1313-8014
TA404.2
JOURNAL OF INTERNATIONAL RESEARCH PUBLICATIONS: MATERIALS, METHODS & TECHNOLOGIES. Text in English. 2006. irreg. free (effective 2011). **Document type:** *Journal, Academic/Scholarly.*
Media: Online - full text.
Indexed: A01.
Published by: Science & Education Foundation, PO Box 309, Burgas, 8000, Bulgaria. TEL 359-56-950077, publishing@ejournalnet.com, http://www.science-edu.eu.

THE JOURNAL OF LITERACY AND TECHNOLOGY; an international online academic journal. *see* EDUCATION

JOURNAL OF MANAGEMENT AND SOCIAL SCIENCES. *see* BUSINESS AND ECONOMICS

JOURNAL OF MANUFACTURING TECHNOLOGY MANAGEMENT. *see* ENGINEERING—Computer Applications

600 USA ISSN 1943-8095
T183
JOURNAL OF MANUFACTURING TECHNOLOGY RESEARCH. Text in English. 2008. q. USD 275 to institutions; USD 412 combined subscription to institutions (print & online eds.) (effective 2012). **Document type:** *Journal, Academic/Scholarly.*
Related titles: Online - full text ed.: USD 275 to institutions (effective 2012).
Published by: Nova Science Publishers, Inc., 400 Oser Ave, Ste 1600, Hauppauge, NY 11788. TEL 631-231-7269, FAX 631-231-8175, main@novapublishers.com. Eds. J P Davim, Mark J Jackson.

▼ **JOURNAL OF MATHEMATICS AND TECHNOLOGY.** *see* MATHEMATICS

▼ **JOURNAL OF MECHANICAL ENGINEERING AND TECHNOLOGY.** *see* ENGINEERING—Mechanical Engineering

JOURNAL OF MUSIC, TECHNOLOGY AND EDUCATION. *see* MUSIC

JOURNAL OF NANOBIOTECHNOLOGY. *see* BIOLOGY—Biotechnology

600 001.3 DEU ISSN 1868-6648
T14.5
▼ **JOURNAL OF NEW FRONTIERS IN SPATIAL CONCEPTS**; sociohistorical, sociotechnical and transcultural analysis. Text in Multiple languages. 2009. bi-m. free (effective 2011). **Document type:** *Journal, Academic/Scholarly.*
Media: Online - full text.
Published by: (Universitaet Karlsruhe), K I T Scientific Publishing, Kaiserstr 12, Karlsruhe, 76131, Germany. TEL 49-721-6080, FAX 49-721-6084290, info@kit.edu, http://uvka.ubka.uni-karlsruhe.de/shop/.

JOURNAL OF RECENT ADVANCES IN APPLIED SCIENCES. *see* SCIENCES: COMPREHENSIVE WORKS

JOURNAL OF RESIDUALS SCIENCE & TECHNOLOGY. *see* SCIENCES: COMPREHENSIVE WORKS

JOURNAL OF S T E M EDUCATION (ONLINE); innovations and research. (Science Technology Engineering Math) *see* SCIENCES: COMPREHENSIVE WORKS

JOURNAL OF S T E M TEACHER EDUCATION. (Science, Engineering, Technology, and Mathematics) *see* EDUCATION

JOURNAL OF SCIENCE AND TECHNOLOGY. *see* SCIENCES: COMPREHENSIVE WORKS

JOURNAL OF SCIENCE AND TECHNOLOGY. *see* SCIENCES: COMPREHENSIVE WORKS

JOURNAL OF SCIENCE AND TECHNOLOGY. *see* SCIENCES: COMPREHENSIVE WORKS

THE JOURNAL OF SCIENCE & TECHNOLOGY LAW. *see* LAW

▼ **JOURNAL OF SCIENCE AND TECHNOLOGY OF THE ARTS/ REVISTA DE CIENCIA E TECNOLOGIA DAS ARTES.** *see* ART

▼ **JOURNAL OF SCIENCE AND TECHNOLOGY POLICY IN CHINA.** *see* SCIENCES: COMPREHENSIVE WORKS

502.8 USA ISSN 1936-5020
JOURNAL OF SCIENTIFIC AND PRACTICAL COMPUTING. Text in English. 2007. bi-m. back issues avail. **Document type:** *Journal, Academic/Scholarly.*
Related titles: Online - full text ed.: ISSN 1558-2752.
Published by: Scientific and Practical Computing, PO Box 238, Ashburn, VA 20146. TEL 571-223-5733, FAX 703-726-2558, publisher@spclab.com.

600 CHL ISSN 0718-2724
T173.8
➤ **JOURNAL OF TECHNOLOGY MANAGEMENT & INNOVATION.** Text in English, Portuguese, Spanish. 2005. q. free (effective 2011). **Document type:** *Journal, Academic/Scholarly.* **Description:** Aims to develop, promote and coordinate the science and practice of technology management and innovation.
Media: Online - full text.
Indexed: B01, B07, CA, SCOPUS, T02.
Published by: Universidad de Talca, 2 Norte 685, Talca, Chile. TEL 56-71-200200, FAX 56-71-200410, http://www.utalca.cl. Ed. Luis Alejandro Jimenez.

➤ **JOURNAL OF TECHNOLOGY MANAGEMENT AND STRATEGY IN CHINA.** *see* BUSINESS AND ECONOMICS—Management

▼ ➤ **JOURNAL OF TECHNOLOGY MANAGEMENT FOR GROWING ECONOMIES.** *see* BUSINESS AND ECONOMICS—Management

600.951 658 GBR ISSN 1746-8779
➤ **JOURNAL OF TECHNOLOGY MANAGEMENT IN CHINA.** Abbreviated title: J T M C. Text in English. 2006. 3/yr. EUR 459 combined subscription in Europe (print & online eds.); USD 619 combined subscription in the Americas (print & online eds.); GBP 319 combined subscription in the UK & elsewhere (print & online eds.); AUD 829 combined subscription in Australasia (print & online eds.) (effective 2012). back issues avail.; reprint service avail. from PSC. **Document type:** *Journal, Academic/Scholarly.* **Description:** Committed to encouraging and publishing work from researchers and practitioners within the technology and knowledge transfer, technology and business strategy and technology management fields in China.
Related titles: Online - full text ed.: ISSN 1746-8787 (from IngentaConnect).
Indexed: A12, A17, A22, ABIn, E01, Inspec, P26, P41, P48, P51, P52, P53, P54, PQC.
—BLDSC (5068.565400), IE, Ingenta. **CCC.**
Published by: Emerald Group Publishing Ltd., Howard House, Wagon Ln, Bingley, W Yorks BD16 1WA, United Kingdom. TEL 44-1274-777700, FAX 44-1274-785201, information@emeraldinsight.com. Ed. Dr. Richard Li-Hua. Pub. Lucy Sootheran.

600 USA ISSN 1071-6084
T61
➤ **THE JOURNAL OF TECHNOLOGY STUDIES**; promoting excellence in preparation and excellence in practice. Abbreviated title: J O T S. Text in English. 1974. s-a. free to members (effective 2010). bk.rev. 64 p./no.; back issues avail. **Document type:** *Journal, Academic/Scholarly.*
Formerly (until 1993): The Journal of Epsilon Pi Tau (0887-9532)
Related titles: Microfilm ed.; Online - full text ed.: ISSN 1541-9258. free (effective 2010).
Indexed: A01, A03, A08, A09, A10, CA, E02, E03, ERI, EdA, EdI, P04, P18, P48, P53, P54, PQC, T02, V03, V04, W03, W05.
—BLDSC (5068.568000).
Published by: Epsilon Pi Tau, Technology Bldg, Bowling Green State University, Bowling Green, OH 43403. ept@bgsu.edu, http://www.epsilonpitau.org. Ed. Dominick E Fazarro TEL 903-565-5911.

600 USA ISSN 0892-9912
T174.3 CODEN: JTTREA
➤ **JOURNAL OF TECHNOLOGY TRANSFER.** Text in English. 1976. bi-m. EUR 646, USD 676 combined subscription to institutions (print & online eds.) (effective 2012). adv. bk.rev. back issues avail.; reprint service avail. from PSC. **Document type:** *Journal, Academic/Scholarly.* **Description:** Contains articles describing methods, mechanisms, case studies and theories of technology transfer in international public, private, and non-profit sectors. For business consultants, product development engineers, scientists, and technology managers.

Related titles: CD-ROM ed.; Online - full text ed.: ISSN 1573-7047 (from IngentaConnect).
Indexed: A12, A13, A17, A22, A26, A28, ABIn, APA, ASCA, Agr, B02, B17, B18, BibLing, BrCerAb, C&ISA, CA, CA/WCA, CIA, CerAb, CivEngAb, CorrAb, CurCont, E&CAJ, E01, E08, E11, EEA, EMA, ESPM, EconLit, EnvEAb, G04, G08, H15, I05, JEL, M&TEA, M09, MBF, METADEX, P11, P26, P30, P41, P48, P51, P52, P53, P54, PAIS, PQC, S09, SCOPUS, SSCI, SociolAb, SolStAb, T02, T04, W07, WAA.
—BLDSC (5068.570000), IE, Infotrieve, Ingenta, Linda Hall. **CCC.**
Published by: (Technology Transfer Society), Springer New York LLC (Subsidiary of: Springer Science+Business Media), 233 Spring St, New York, NY 10013. TEL 212-460-1500, FAX 212-460-1575, service-ny@springer.com, http://www.springer.com/. Ed. Albert N Link. **Subscr. to:** Journal Fulfillment, PO Box 2485, Secaucus, NJ 07096. TEL 201-348-4033, FAX 201-348-4505, journals-ny@springer.com.

➤ **JOURNAL OF THE ROYAL SOCIETY. INTERFACE.** *see* SCIENCES: COMPREHENSIVE WORKS

711.4 GBR ISSN 1063-0732
HT101
➤ **JOURNAL OF URBAN TECHNOLOGY.** Text in English. 1992. 3/yr. GBP 419 combined subscription in United Kingdom to institutions (print & online eds.); EUR 553, USD 694 combined subscription to institutions (print & online eds.) (effective 2012). adv. bk.rev. illus. Index. back issues avail.; reprint service avail. from PSC. **Document type:** *Journal, Academic/Scholarly.* **Description:** Examines the interaction between cities and technologies for a general audience whose businesses, occupations, or studies require their understanding of what technologies do to cities and cities do to technologies.
Related titles: Online - full text ed.: ISSN 1466-1853. GBP 378 in United Kingdom to institutions; EUR 498, USD 624 to institutions (effective 2012) (from IngentaConnect).
Indexed: A01, A03, A08, A22, AIAP, ASCA, BibInd, C23, CA, CurCont, E01, ERIC, FamI, GEOBASE, HRIS, IBR, IBZ, P34, P52, S01, S02, S03, SCOPUS, SSCI, SUSA, T02, UAA, W07.
—IE, Infotrieve, Ingenta. **CCC.**
Published by: (Society of Urban Technology), Routledge (Subsidiary of: Taylor & Francis Group), 4 Park Sq, Milton Park, Abingdon, Oxon OX14 4RN, United Kingdom. TEL 44-20-70176000, FAX 44-20-70176336, subscriptions@tandf.co.uk, http://www.routledge.com. Ed. Richard E Hanley TEL 718-260-5130. Adv. contact Linda Hann TEL 44-1344-779945. **Subscr. to:** Taylor & Francis Ltd., Journals Customer Service, Sheepen Pl, Colchester, Essex CO3 3LP, United Kingdom. TEL 44-20-70175544, FAX 44-20-70175198.

➤ **JOURNAL ON BUSINESS AND TECHNOLOGY.** *see* BUSINESS AND ECONOMICS

600 MYS ISSN 0127-9696
CODEN: JUTEFD
JURNAL TEKNOLOGI. Text in Multiple languages. 1977. s-a. **Document type:** *Journal, Academic/Scholarly.*
Indexed: INIS AtomInd.
Published by: Penerbit Universiti Teknologi Malaysia, No 34-38, Jalan Kebudayaan 1, Taman Universiti, Skudai, Johor Darul Takzim 81300, Malaysia. TEL 60-7-5218135, FAX 60-7-5218174.

600 MYS ISSN 1979-3405
JURNAL TEKNOLOGI (YOGYAKARTA). Variant title: Jurnal Teknologi Ist Akprind. Text in Indonesian. 2008. s-a. **Document type:** *Journal, Academic/Scholarly.*
Related titles: Online - full text ed.: free (effective 2011).
Published by: Institut Sains & Teknologi Akprind, Fakultas Teknologi Industri, Jl Kalisahak 28, Yogyakarta, 55222, Malaysia. TEL 60-0274-563029, FAX 60-0274-563847.

600 CUB ISSN 0449-4555
T4
JUVENTUD TECNICA. Text in Spanish. 1965. m. bibl.; illus. **Document type:** *Magazine, Consumer.* **Description:** Reflects the Technical Youth Brigades' participation in the multifaced economic development of the country. Covers articles, commentaries, photo features, and national and international sports events.
Related titles: Online - full text ed.: ISSN 1605-9131. 1999.
Published by: (Union de Jovenes Comunistas, Movimiento de Brigadas Tecnicas), Casa Editora Abril, Prado 535 esq a Tte Rey, Havan, 10200, Cuba. http://www.editoraabril.cu. Circ: 100,000.

600 500 JPN
KAGAKU GIJUTSU HAKUSHO/WHITE PAPER OF SCIENCE AND TECHNOLOGY IN JAPAN. Text in Japanese. 1958. a. JPY 3,400 (effective 2000). bk.rev. stat. **Document type:** *Government.*
Published by: Okura-sho, Insatsu-kyoku/Ministry of Finance, Printing Bureau, 2-4 Toranomon 2-chome, Minato-ku, Tokyo, 105-0001, Japan.

600 JPN
KAGAKU GIJUTSU HAKUSHO NO ARAMASHI. Text in Japanese. 1987. a. JPY 320 (effective 2000). **Document type:** *Government.* **Description:** Summary of Kagaku Gijutsu Hakusho.
Published by: Okura-sho, Insatsu-kyoku/Ministry of Finance, Printing Bureau, 2-4 Toranomon 2-chome, Minato-ku, Tokyo, 105-0001, Japan.

600 JPN
KAGAKU GIJUTSU SHINKO CHOSEIHI NYUSU. Text in Japanese. 1983. irreg. **Document type:** *Government.* **Description:** Contains news of special coordination funds for promoting science and technology.
Published by: Kagaku Gijutsucho/Science and Technology Agency, Planning Bureau, 2-1 Kasumigaseki 2-chome, Chiyoda-ku, Tokyo, 100-0013, Japan.

600 JPN
KAGAKU GIJUTSU SHINKO CHOSEIHI SHIKEN KENKYU JISSHI KEIKAKU. Text in Japanese. a. **Description:** Contains planning papers of experimental studies by special coordination funds for promoting science and technology.
Published by: Kagaku Shinbunsha, 8-1 Hamamatsu-cho 1-chome, Minato-ku, Tokyo, 105-0013, Japan.

600 JPN
KAGAKU GIJUTSUCHO NENPO. Text in Japanese. 1957. a., latest 1997. JPY 4,500. **Document type:** *Government.* **Description:** The annual report of the agency.
Published by: (Japan. Kagaku Gijutsucho/Science and Technology Agency, Planning Bureau), Ministry of Finance, Printing Bureau, 2-2-4 Toranomon, Minato-ku, Tokyo, 105-0001, Japan. **Subscr. to:** Government Publications Service Center, 2-1 Kasumigaseki 1-chome, Chiyoda-ku, Tokyo 100-0013, Japan. TEL 81-3-3504-3885, FAX 81-3-3504-3889.

600 JPN ISSN 0368-5918
T177.J3 CODEN: KKGOAG
KAGAKU TO KOGYO (OSAKA)/SCIENCE AND INDUSTRY. Text and summaries in Japanese, English. 1926. m. abstr. **Description:** Contains original papers, reviews, commentary, and news.
Indexed: CIN, ChemAb, ChemTitl, RefZh.
—BLDSC (5081.110000), CASDDS, INIST, Linda Hall.
Published by: Oosaka Koken Kyokai/Osaka Society of Industrial Research, Osaka-shiritsu Kogyo Kenkyujo, 6-50 Morinomiya 1-chome, Joto-ku, Osaka-shi, 536-0025, Japan.

600 500 JPN ISSN 0916-1902
CODEN: KKDREE
KANAGAWA KOKA DAIGAKU KENKYU HOKOKU. B RIKOGAKU HEN/KANAGAWA INSTITUTE OF TECHNOLOGY. RESEARCH REPORTS. PART B. SCIENCE AND TECHNOLOGY. Text in English, Japanese; Summaries in English. 1976. a. **Document type:** *Journal, Academic/Scholarly.*
Formerly (until 1988): Ikutoku Kogyo Daigaku Kenkyu Hokoku. B Rikogaku Hen (0386-1163)
Indexed: A28, APA, BrCerAb, C&ISA, CA/WCA, CIA, CerAb, ChemAb, ChemTitl, CivEngAb, CorrAb, E&CAJ, E11, EEA, EMA, H15, JPI, M&TEA, M09, MBF, METADEX, SolStAb, T04, WAA.
—CASDDS, Linda Hall.
Published by: Kanaguwa Koka Daigaku/Kanagawa Institute of Technology, c/o Library, 1030 Simo-Ogino, Atsugi-shi, Kanagawa-ken 243-0203, Japan. TEL 81-46-2416221, FAX 81-46-2426111, tosho@kait.jp, http://www.kanagawa-it.ac.jp/.

620 JPN ISSN 0453-2198
TA7 CODEN: TRKUAW
KANSAI UNIVERSITY TECHNOLOGY REPORTS/KANSAI DAIGAKU KOGAKU KENKYU HOKOKU. Text in English. 1959. a. per issue exchange basis. bk.rev.
Indexed: A28, APA, BrCerAb, C&ISA, CA/WCA, CIA, CIN, CIS, CPEI, CerAb, ChemAb, ChemTitl, CivEngAb, CorrAb, E&CAJ, E11, EEA, EMA, ESPM, EngInd, EnvEAb, GeoRef, H15, INIS AtomInd, Inspec, JCT, JTA, M&TEA, M09, MBF, METADEX, MathR, RefZh, SCOPUS, SolStAb, SpeleolAb, T04, WAA, Z02.
—BLDSC (8759.600000), AskIEEE, CASDDS, IE, Ingenta, Linda Hall.
Published by: Kansai University, Faculty of Engineering/Kansai Daigaku Kogakubu, 3-3-35 Yamate-cho, Suite 564, Osaka-shi, Japan. Ed. Katsutaro Katsuta.

KATHMANDU UNIVERSITY JOURNAL OF SCIENCE, ENGINEERING AND TECHNOLOGY. *see* SCIENCES: COMPREHENSIVE WORKS

KE XUE. *see* SCIENCES: COMPREHENSIVE WORKS

KECHE JISHU/COACH TECHNOLOGY. *see* TRANSPORTATION—Automobiles

600 500 JPN
KEIO GIJUKU DAIGAKU RIKOGAKUBUHO. Text in Japanese. 1962. a. **Document type:** *Newsletter.* **Description:** Contains news of the faculty.
Formerly (until 1981): Keio Gijuku Daigaku Kogakubuho
Published by: Keio Gijuku Daigaku, Rikogakubu/Keio University, Faculty of Science and Technology, Matsushita Memorial Library, 14-1 Hiyoshi 3-chome, Kohoku-ku, Yokohama-shi, Kanagawa-ken 223-0061, Japan.

600 530 JPN
KEISHA KINO ZAIRYO SHINPOJUMU KOENSHU/SYMPOSIUM OF FUNCTIONALLY GRADIENT MATERIALS FORUM. PROCEEDINGS. Text in English, Japanese. a. JPY 8,000 to non-members; JPY 5,000 to members. **Document type:** *Proceedings.*
Published by: Mito Kagaku Gijutsu Kyokai, Keisha Kino Zairyo/Society of Non-Traditional Technology, Functionally Gradient Materials Forum, 2-8 Toranomon 1-chome, Minato-ku, Tokyo, 105-0001, Japan. TEL 81-3-3503-4681, FAX 81-3-3597-0535.

600 CHN ISSN 2095-1043
▼ **KEJI CHUANGYEJIA/TECHNOLOGICAL PIONEERS.** Text in Chinese. 2010. m.
Related titles: Online - full text ed.
Address: Yuanyang Tandi 62-Lou, 1001-shi, Beijing, 100025, China. TEL 86-10-85861170.

KEJI DAOBAO/SCIENCE & TECHNOLOGY REVIEW. *see* SCIENCES: COMPREHENSIVE WORKS

KEJI FAZHAN BIAOGAN/BENCHMARKING SCI-TECH DEVELOPMENT. *see* SCIENCES: COMPREHENSIVE WORKS

KEJI GUANLI/MANAGEMENT OF SCIENCE AND TECHNOLOGY. *see* BUSINESS AND ECONOMICS—Management

KEJI JINBU YU DUICE/SCIENCE & TECHNOLOGY PROGRESS AND POLICY. *see* SCIENCES: COMPREHENSIVE WORKS

KEJI RIBAO/SCIENCE & TECHNOLOGY DAILY. *see* SCIENCES: COMPREHENSIVE WORKS

KEJI YU GUANLI/SCIENCE-TECHNOLOGY AND MANAGEMENT. *see* BUSINESS AND ECONOMICS—Management

600 CHN ISSN 1673-9671
KEJI YU SHENGHUO/FORTUNE LIFE. Text in Chinese. 2007. m. **Document type:** *Magazine, Consumer.*
Related titles: Online - full text ed.
Published by: (Zhongguo Keji Xinwen Xuehui/Chinese Society for Science and Technology Journalism), Keji yu Shenghuo Zazhishe, 8, Dongtucheng Lu, Beijing, 100013, China. TEL 86-10-81869993.

KENKYU GIJUTSU KEIKAKU/JOURNAL OF SCIENCE POLICY AND RESEARCH MANAGEMENT. *see* BUSINESS AND ECONOMICS—Management

600 NLD ISSN 1384-6973
Q180.N35
KENNIS EN ECONOMIE/KNOWLEDGE-BASED ECONOMY. Text in Dutch, English. 1959. a. EUR 32.65 (effective 2008). **Document type:** *Government.*
Formerly (until 1996): Speur- en Ontwikkelingswerk in Nederland (0168-468X)
Published by: Centraal Bureau voor de Statistiek, Henri Faasdreef 312, The Hague, 2492 JP, Netherlands. TEL 31-70-3373800, infoserv@cbs.nl, http://www.cbs.nl.

KENYA JOURNAL OF SCIENCES. SERIES A: PHYSICAL AND CHEMICAL SCIENCES. *see* SCIENCES: COMPREHENSIVE WORKS

KENYA NATIONAL ACADEMY FOR ADVANCEMENT OF ARTS AND SCIENCES. NEWSLETTER. *see* SCIENCES: COMPREHENSIVE WORKS

KEXUE GUANCHA/SCIENCE FOCUS. *see* SCIENCES: COMPREHENSIVE WORKS

KEXUE JISHU YU BIANZHENGFA/SCIENCE, TECHNOLOGY, AND DIALECTICS. *see* SCIENCES: COMPREHENSIVE WORKS

KEXUE JISHU YU GONGCHENG. *see* SCIENCES: COMPREHENSIVE WORKS

KEXUE JISHU ZHEXUE/PHILOSOPHY OF SCIENCE AND TECHNOLOGY. *see* PHILOSOPHY

KHIMICHESKAYA TEKHNOLOGIYA/CHEMICAL TECHNOLOGY. *see* CHEMISTRY

KHOA HOC KY THUAT KINH TE THE GIOI/WORLD SCIENCE, TECHNOLOGY AND ECONOMY. *see* SCIENCES: COMPREHENSIVE WORKS

KINKI DAIGAKU RIKOGAKUBU KENKYU HOKOKU/KINKI UNIVERSITY. FACULTY OF SCIENCE AND TECHNOLOGY. JOURNAL. *see* SCIENCES: COMPREHENSIVE WORKS

600 JPN ISSN 0387-7035
CODEN: KKDHDH
KITAMI KOGYO DAIGAKU KENKYU HOKOKU/KITAMI INSTITUTE OF TECHNOLOGY. MEMOIRS. Text in English, Japanese. 1963. s-a.
Formerly (until 1967): Kitami Kogyo Tanki Daigaku. Kenkyu Hokoku (0368-6035)
Indexed: Inspec.
—IE, Ingenta.
Published by: Kitami Kogyo Daigaku/Kitami Institute of Technology, 165 Koen-cho Kitami, Hokkaido, 090-8507, Japan. TEL 81-157-26-9189, http://www.kitami-it.ac.jp.

KNOWLEDGE AND SPACE. *see* SOCIAL SCIENCES: COMPREHENSIVE WORKS

KOBE DAIGAKU DAIGAKUIN SHIZEN KAGAKU KENKYUKA KIYO B/KOBE UNIVERSITY. GRADUATE SCHOOL OF SCIENCE AND TECHNOLOGY. MEMOIRS. SERIES B. *see* SCIENCES: COMPREHENSIVE WORKS

600 JPN ISSN 0287-6507
Q1
KOBE UNIVERSITY. GRADUATE SCHOOL OF SCIENCE AND TECHNOLOGY. MEMOIRS. SERIES A/KOBE DAIGAKU DAIGAKUIN SHIZEN KAGAKU KENKYUKA KIYO. A. Text and summaries in English. 1983. a. abstr.
—Ingenta.
Published by: Kobe Daigaku, Daigakuin Shizen Kagaku Kenkyuka/Kobe University, Graduate School of Science and Technology, 1-1 Rokko-Dai-cho, Nada-ku, Kobe-shi, Hyogo-ken 657-0013, Japan.

620 DEU ISSN 1435-893X
KONSTRUKTION & ENTWICKLUNG; Maschinenbau - Anlagenbau - Elektrotechnik - Fahrzeugbau. Text in German. 1994. 10/yr. EUR 45 domestic; EUR 63 foreign; EUR 15 newsstand/cover (effective 2010). adv. **Document type:** *Magazine, Trade.*
Published by: Schluetersche Verlagsgesellschaft mbH und Co. KG, Hans-Boeckler-Allee 7, Hannover, 30173, Germany. TEL 49-511-85500, FAX 49-511-85501100, info@schluetersche.de, http://www.schluetersche.de. Ed. Harald Klieber. Adv. contact Gabriele Maier. B&W page EUR 4,330, color page EUR 5,560; trim 188 x 272. Circ: 23,910 (paid and controlled).

KONVERSIYA/CONVERSION. *see* BUSINESS AND ECONOMICS

600 620 KOR
KOREAN AGENCY FORTECHNOLOGY AND STANDARDS. ANNUAL REPORT. Text in English. 1948. a. free. illus. **Document type:** *Corporate.*
Former titles: Gug-rib Gisul Pumjil-weon. Yeon-gu Bogo/National Industrial Technology Institute. Annual Report (1226-2331); (until 1966): Gug-rib Gong-eob Yeon-guso Bogo/National Industrial Research Institute. Report (0368-606X)
Related titles: Online - full text ed.
Indexed: FS&TA.
Published by: Korean Agency forTechnology and Standards, Technology & Standards Information Service Division, 96, Gyoyukwongil, Gwacheon-Si, Gyonggi-Do 427-723, Korea, S. TEL 82-2-5097234, FAX 82-2-5097415, info@kats.go.kr.

658.5 DEU ISSN 0023-4435
KRAFTHAND. Text in German. 1927. 24/yr. EUR 99; EUR 7 newsstand/cover (effective 2007). adv. bk.rev. charts; illus.; mkt.; tr.lit. index. **Document type:** *Magazine, Trade.*
Indexed: TM.
—IE. **CCC.**
Published by: Krafthand Verlag Walter Schulz, Walter-Schulz-Str 1, Bad Woerishofen, 86825, Germany. TEL 49-8247-30070, FAX 49-8247-300770, info@krafthand.de. Ed. W Schweizer. adv.: B&W page EUR 4,944, color page EUR 6,591. Circ: 22,970 (paid and controlled).

KULTUR UND TECHNIK; Das Magazin aus dem Deutschen Museum. *see* MUSEUMS AND ART GALLERIES

KUNMING LIGONG DAXUE XUEBAO (LIGONG BAN)/KUNMING UNIVERSITY OF SCIENCE AND TECHNOLOGY. JOURNAL (SCIENCE AND TECHNOLOGY). *see* SCIENCES: COMPREHENSIVE WORKS

▼ **KUNST UND TECHNIK.** *see* ART

KURIN TEKUNOROJI/CLEAN TECHNOLOGY. *see* ENVIRONMENTAL STUDIES

600 JPN ISSN 0389-6897
CODEN: KHKDEK
KURUME KOGYO DAIGAKU KENKYU HOKOKU/KURUME INSTITUTE OF TECHNOLOGY. BULLETIN. Text in English, Japanese. 1977. a. **Document type:** *Bulletin, Academic/Scholarly.*
Indexed: Inspec.

Published by: Kurume Kogyo Daigaku/Kurume Institute of Technology, 2228, Kamitsu-machi, Kurume, Fukuoka 830-0052, Japan. TEL 81-942-22-2345, http://www.kurume-it.ac.jp/.

600 JPN ISSN 1598-7264
KUSHIRO KOGYO KOTO SENMON GAKKO KIYO/KUSHIRO NATIONAL COLLEGE OF TECHNOLOGY. RESEARCH REPORTS. Text in Japanese. 1967. a. **Document type:** *Journal, Academic/Scholarly.*
Indexed: CCMJ, MSN, MathR, RefZh, SCOPUS, Z02.
Published by: Kushiro Kogyo Koto Senmon Gakko/Kushiro National College of Technology, Otanoshike-nishi 2-32-1, Kushiro, Hokkaido 084-0916, Japan. TEL 81-154-577203, FAX 81-154-575360.

KWARTALNIK HISTORII NAUKI I TECHNIKI/QUARTERLY JOURNAL OF THE HISTORY OF SCIENCE AND TECHNOLOGY. *see* SCIENCES: COMPREHENSIVE WORKS

KYOTO INSTITUTE OF TECHNOLOGY. FACULTY OF ENGINEERING AND DESIGN. MEMOIRS. *see* SCIENCES: COMPREHENSIVE WORKS

500 600 JPN ISSN 0453-0357
T4 CODEN: KKDKAN
KYUSHU INSTITUTE OF TECHNOLOGY. BULLETIN: SCIENCE AND TECHNOLOGY/KYUSHU KOGYO DAIGAKU KENKYU HOKOKU: KOGAKU. Text in Japanese; Abstracts in English. 1951. s-a. per issue exchange basis. abstr.
Incorporates: Kyushu Institute of Technology. Memoirs: Engineering (0369-0512)
Indexed: ChemAb, GeoRef, Inspec, JTA, SpeleolAb.
—AskIEEE, CASDDS, Ingenta, Linda Hall.
Published by: Kyushu Institute of Technology/Kyushu Kogyo Daigaku, 1-1 Sensui-cho, Tobata-ku, Kitakyushu-shi, Fukuoka-ken 804-0015, Japan.

364.048 342.648 USA ISSN 0270-174X
K12
L E S NOUVELLES. (Licensing Executives Society) Text in English. 1966. q. free to members. bk.rev. pat. Index. **Document type:** *Journal, Trade.*
Formerly: Nouvelles
—Infotrieve. **CCC.**
Published by: Licensing Executives Society (USA and Canada), Inc., 1800 Diagonal Rd Ste 280, Alexandria, VA 22314. info@les.org, http://www.usa-canada.les.org/. Circ: 8,000.

LAINGYOU SHIPIN KEJI/SCIENCE AND TECHNOLOGY OF CEREALS, OILS AND FOODS. *see* AGRICULTURE

LAMY DROIT DE L'INFORMATIQUE ET DES RESEAUX. *see* LAW

LANGFANG SHIFAN XUEYUAN XUEBAO (ZIRAN KEXUE BAN)/LANGFANG TEACHERS COLLEGE. JOURNAL (NATURAL SCIENCE EDITION). *see* SOCIAL SCIENCES: COMPREHENSIVE WORKS

LATVIJAS FIZIKAS UN TEHNISKO ZINATNU ZURNALS/LATVIAN JOURNAL OF PHYSICS AND TECHNICAL SCIENCES. *see* PHYSICS

▼ **LAW, INNOVATION AND TECHNOLOGY.** *see* LAW

LAW TECHNOLOGY NEWS. *see* LAW

LAWRENCE LIVERMORE NATIONAL LABORATORY. REPORT. *see* SCIENCES: COMPREHENSIVE WORKS

600 ROM ISSN 1583-1078
LEONARDO JOURNAL OF PRACTICES AND TECHNOLOGY. Text in Romanian. 2002. s-a. free (effective 2011). **Document type:** *Journal, Academic/Scholarly.*
Media: Online - full text.
Indexed: A34, A37, AgrForAb, BA, C10, C25, CA, CABA, D01, E12, F08, F12, FCA, GH, H16, MaizeAb, N02, P32, P40, PHN&I, R11, S12, S13, S16, SCOPUS, SoyAb, T02, TAR, W11.
Published by: AcademicDirect, 103-105 Muncii Bvd, Cluj-Napoca, Romania. TEL 40-766-239997. Ed. Lorentz Jantschi.

LIAONING KEJI XUEYUAN XUEBAO/LIAONING INSTITUTE OF SCIENCE AND TECHNOLOGY. JOURNAL. *see* SCIENCES: COMPREHENSIVE WORKS

LICENSING LAW HANDBOOK; the new companion to licensing negotiations. *see* LAW

600 500 USA
THE LIGHTBULB - INVENT!; for the professional inventor/entrepreneur. Text in English. 1972. bi-m. USD 24.95 domestic; USD 34.95 in Canada; USD 50 elsewhere (effective 2005). adv. bk.rev.; software rev.; Website rev. pat. **Document type:** *Magazine, Trade.* **Description:** Covers a broad range of the latest developments in practically all fields of human enterprise and technological advancement.
Former titles (until 1992): Invent! (1040-3485); (until 1988): Lightbulb (0883-6914)
Published by: Inventors Workshop International, 1029 Castillo St, Santa Barbara, CA 93101-3736. TEL 805-962-5722, FAX 805-899-4927. Ed. Maggie Weisberg. Pub., Adv. contact Alan Tratner. B&W page USD 600. Circ: 15,000 (paid and free).

LIGONG GAOJIAO YANJIU/JOURNAL OF TECHNOLOGY COLLEGE EDUCATION. *see* EDUCATION

LIGONG YANJIU XUEBAO/JOURNAL OF SCIENTIFIC AND TECHNOLOGICAL STUDIES. *see* SCIENCES: COMPREHENSIVE WORKS

LINDE TECHNOLOGY (GERMAN EDITION). *see* SCIENCES: COMPREHENSIVE WORKS

LINKOEPING STUDIES IN SCIENCE AND TECHNOLOGY; dissertations. *see* SCIENCES: COMPREHENSIVE WORKS

600 GBR ISSN 1478-484X
T1
LINKS; the bulletin of the Newcomen Society. Text in English. 1939. q. free membership (effective 2005). bk.rev. bibl. **Document type:** *Bulletin, Academic/Scholarly.*
Formerly: Newcomen Bulletin (0266-7533)
Indexed: BrArAb, NumL.
Published by: Newcomen Society for the Study of the History of Engineering and Technology, Science Museum, Exhibition Rd, South Kensington, London, SW7 2DD, United Kingdom. Ed. L R Day.

600 USA ISSN 0024-5852
U168
LOGISTICS SPECTRUM. Text in English. 1967. m. USD 95; USD 105 foreign. adv. bk.rev. reprints avail. **Document type:** *Proceedings, Trade.*
Related titles: Online - full text ed.
Indexed: AMB, AUNI, CLT&T, DM&T, HRIS, M07, P02, P10, P47, P48, P52, P53, P54, PQC, TM.
—BLDSC (5292.350000), Ingenta, Linda Hall. **CCC.**
Published by: The S O L E - International Society of Logistics, 8100 Professional Pl, Suite 211, Hyattsville, MD 20785-2225. TEL 301-459-8446, FAX 301-459-1522, solehq@sole.org, http://www.sole.org. Ed., R&P Paul D Wisniewski. Adv. contact Michael C Fink. Circ: 5,000.

600 340 USA ISSN 1930-9422
K12
LOYOLA LAW AND TECHNOLOGY ANNUAL. Variant title: Loyola University New Orleans School of Law: Law & Technology Annual. Text in English. 1997. a. **Document type:** *Journal, Academic/Scholarly.* **Description:** Presents articles and comments on topics in patents, copyrights, trademarks, and related areas of law affected by new technological developments.
Former titles (until 2004): Loyola University New Orleans School of Law Intellectual Property & High Technology Journal; (until 2000): Loyola Intellectual Property & High Technology Law Quarterly
Indexed: A26, E08, G08, I05, LRI.
Published by: Loyola University New Orleans, College of Law, 7214 St Charles Ave, PO Box 901, New Orleans, LA 70118. TEL 504-861-5550. Eds. Chris Kaul, Tracy Tran.

600 USA ISSN 1555-5135
HD9696.M493
M E M S: MICRO-ELECTROMECHANICAL SYSTEMS. Variant title: M E M S. Text in English. 19??. irreg., latest 2004. USD 4,100 per issue (print or online ed.) (effective 2008). **Document type:** *Report, Trade.* **Description:** Analyzes the US MEMS industry, presents historical demand data for the years 1993, 1998 and 2003, and forecasts to 2008 and 2013 by product and by application.
Related titles: Online - full text ed.
Published by: The Freedonia Group, Inc., 767 Beta Dr, Cleveland, OH 44143. TEL 440-684-9600, 800-927-5900, FAX 440-646-0484, info@freedoniagroup.com.

M O - METALLOBERFLAECHE; Beschichten von Kunststoff und Metall. *see* METALLURGY

M T D - MEDIZIN-TECHNISCHER DIALOG UND DER SANITAETSFACHHANDEL. *see* MEDICAL SCIENCES

MACHINE VISION & APPLICATIONS; an international journal. *see* COMPUTERS—Cybernetics

MAEJO INTERNATIONAL JOURNAL OF SCIENCE AND TECHNOLOGY. *see* SCIENCES: COMPREHENSIVE WORKS

MAGAZIN DER FACHHOCHSCHULE KARLSRUHE HOCHSCHULE FUER TECHNIK. *see* COLLEGE AND ALUMNI

600 USA ISSN 0899-5729
TJ153
MAINTENANCE TECHNOLOGY. Text in English. 1988. m. USD 100 domestic; USD 180 foreign; free to qualified personnel (effective 2005). adv. bk.rev. **Document type:** *Magazine, Trade.* **Description:** Provides practical technical and business information to maintenance professionals (engineers, managers, and supervisors) in four broad subject areas: Maintenance of electrical systems and instrumentation, maintenance of mechanical systems, maintenance of plant facilities, and management of maintenance operations.
Related titles: Online - full content ed.
Indexed: S&VD.
—BLDSC (5352.631000), IE, Ingenta, Linda Hall.
Published by: Applied Technology Publications, Inc., 1300 S. Grove Ave. Ste. 105, Barrington, IL 60010. TEL 847-382-8100, FAX 847-304-8603, editors@mt-online.com. Ed., R&P Robert C Baldwin. Pub. Tom Madding. adv.: B&W page USD 6,270, color page USD 7,570. Circ: 54,000 (controlled).

600 IDN ISSN 0541-7406
CODEN: MJPGAI
MAJALAH PERUSAHAAN GULA. Text in Indonesian; Summaries in English. q. USD 25.
—CASDDS.
Published by: Pusat Penelitian Perkebunan Gula Indonesia, Jl Pahlawan 25, Pasuruan, 67126, Indonesia. TEL 0343-21086, FAX 0343-21178, TELEX 31008 SUGEXS IA.

MAJALLAT AL-ULUM. *see* SCIENCES: COMPREHENSIVE WORKS

600 GBR ISSN 1468-2184
MAJOR INFORMATION TECHNOLOGY COMPANIES OF THE WORLD (YEAR). Text in English. 1999. a. USD 1,200 per issue (effective 2010). back issues avail. **Document type:** *Directory, Trade.* **Description:** Covers 2,700 of the world's largest IT companies including nearly 13,000 names of board members and senior executives.
Published by: Graham & Whiteside Ltd. (Subsidiary of: Gale), Cengage Learning, Cheriton House, N Way, Andover, Hampshire SP10 5BE, United Kingdom. TEL 44-1264-332424, FAX 44-800-0664750, emea.enquiries@cengage.com. **Dist. by:** Current Pacific Ltd., 7 La Roche Pl, Northcote, PO Box 36-536, Auckland 0627, New Zealand. TEL 64-9-4801388, FAX 64-9-4801387, info@cplnz.com, http://www.cplnz.com.

600 IDN ISSN 1693-6698
MAKARA SERI TEKNOLOGI. Text in English, Indonesian. 1997. 3/yr. **Document type:** *Monographic series, Academic/Scholarly.*
Related titles: Online - full text ed.: free (effective 2011).
Published by: Universitas Indonesia, Kamous Universitas Indonesia, Depok, 16424, Indonesia. http://www.ui.ac.id. Ed. Misri Gozan.

600 MYS ISSN 0127-6441
MALAYSIAN TECHNOLOGIST. Text in English. 1974 (vol.24). bi-m. MYR 7 per issue. adv. abstr.; charts; illus.; stat.; tr.lit. index.
Formerly: Technical Association of Malaysia. Journal (0040-0882)
Published by: Technological Association of Malaysia, 46 Jalan 52-4, New Town Centre, Petaling Jaya, Selangor 46200, Malaysia. FAX 03-756-9637. Ed. Ir Chang Choong Kong. Circ: 1,500.

600 658 SGP ISSN 2010-2135
MANAGEMENT OF TECHNOLOGY. Text in English. 2007 (Fall). irreg., latest vol.3, 2010. price varies. back issues avail. **Document type:** *Monographic series, Academic/Scholarly.* **Description:** Covers new developments in bio- and nanotechnologies and also in information and communication technologies.
Published by: World Scientific Publishing Co. Pte. Ltd., 5 Toh Tuck Link, Singapore, 596224, Singapore. TEL 65-6466-5775, FAX 65-6467-7667, wspc@wspc.com.sg, http://www.worldscientific.com. **Dist. by:** World Scientific Publishing Co., Inc., 27 Warren St, Ste 401-402, Hackensack, NJ 07601. TEL 201-487-9655, 800-227-7562, FAX 201-487-9656, 888-977-2665, wspc@wspc.com; World Scientific Publishing Ltd., 57 Shelton St, London WC2H 9HE, United Kingdom. TEL 44-207-8360888, FAX 44-207-8362020, sales@wspc.co.uk.

MANAGEMENT OF TECHNOLOGY. *see* BUSINESS AND ECONOMICS—Management

MANAGING TECHNOLOGY. *see* BUSINESS AND ECONOMICS—Banking And Finance

MANTRAM. *see* BUSINESS AND ECONOMICS

MARINE TECHNOLOGY DIRECTIONS. *see* EARTH SCIENCES—Oceanography

MASARYK UNIVERSITY JOURNAL OF LAW AND TECHNOLOGY. *see* LAW

600 USA ISSN 8750-2100
HC107.M43
MASS HIGH TECH. Text in English. 1982. w. free. adv. bk.rev. illus. back issues avail. **Document type:** *Newspaper.*
Related titles: Microfiche ed.: (from PQC); Online - full text ed.
Indexed: A16, ABIn, B12, EIA, P48, P51, P52, P53, PQC, PROMT, TelAb, Telegen.
—**CCC.**
Published by: Mass Tech Communications, 200 High St, 4th Fl, Boston, MA 02110-3036. TEL 617-242-1224, FAX 617-478-0638, http://www.masshightech.com. Ed. Mark Pillsbury. Pub. Mike Olivieri. Adv. contact Jill Cohen. B&W page USD 25. Circ: 22,000.

MASSACHUSETTS DIRECTORY OF TECHNOLOGY COMPANIES. *see* BUSINESS AND ECONOMICS—Trade And Industrial Directories

600 DEU ISSN 1613-8279
MATERIALFLUSS. MARKT. Text in German. 197?. a. adv. **Document type:** *Journal, Trade.*
Former titles (until 2004): Europaeischer Materialfluss-Markt (0938-9180); (until 198?): Materialfluss-Markt (0938-9199)
Related titles: ♦ Supplement to: Materialfluss. ISSN 0170-334X.
Published by: Verlag Moderne Industrie AG & Co. KG, Justus-von-Liebig-Str 1, Landsberg, 86899, Germany. TEL 08191-125-1, 49-8191-1250, FAX 08191-125-211, 49-8191-125211, info@mi-verlag.de, http://www.mi-verlag.de. Ed. Reinhard Irrgang.

600 TWN ISSN 1010-2744
TA404.2 CODEN: MBRDEZ
MATERIALS RESEARCH LABORATORIES. BULLETIN OF RESEARCH AND DEVELOPMENT. Text in English. 1987. s-a.
Indexed: Inspec.
—Linda Hall.
Published by: Industrial Technology Research Institute, 195 Chung Hsing Rd, Sec 4, Chu Tung, Hsin Chu, 310, Taiwan.

MATERIALS SCIENCE AND ENGINEERING B: ADVANCED FUNCTIONAL SOLID-STATE MATERIALS. *see* ENGINEERING—Engineering Mechanics And Materials

600 620 BLR ISSN 1607-9922
➤ **MATERIALY, TEKHNOLOGII, INSTRUMENTY/MATERIALS, TECHNOLOGIES, TOOLS**; international scientific and engineering journal. Text in Russian; Summaries in English. 1996. q. USD 227 in United States (effective 2008). **Document type:** *Journal, Academic/Scholarly.* **Description:** Focuses on the state of scientific research in areas of material science, resource-saving technologies, designing of the tools of various assignments and practical applications of this research.
Related titles: Online - full text ed.
Indexed: RefZh.
—BLDSC (0102.877000), East View, IE.
Published by: Natsiyanal'naya Akademiya Navuk Belarusi, Institut Mekhaniki Metallopolimernykh Sistem im. V. A. Belogo/National Academy of Sciences of Belarus, V. A. Belyi Metal-Polymer Research Institute, ul Kirova, 32a, Gomel, 246050, Belarus. TEL 375-232-774640, FAX 375-232-775211, mpri@mail.ru. Ed. Yurii M Pleskachevskii. **Dist. by:** East View Information Services, 10601 Wayzata Blvd, Minneapolis, MN 55305. TEL 952-252-1201, 800-477-1005, FAX 952-252-1202, info@eastview.com, http://www.eastview.com.

➤ **MAXPLANCKFORSCHUNG.** *see* SCIENCES: COMPREHENSIVE WORKS

➤ **MCGRAW-HILL YEARBOOK OF SCIENCE AND TECHNOLOGY.** *see* SCIENCES: COMPREHENSIVE WORKS

620 ARG
MECANICA POPULAR. Text in Spanish. m. adv. **Document type:** *Magazine, Consumer.*
Published by: Editorial Televisa Argentina, Av Paseo Colon 275, Piso 10, Buenos Aires, Buenos Aires 1063, Argentina. TEL 54-11-4343-2225, FAX 54-11-4345-0955, http://www.televisa.com.ar.

MEDICAL DESIGN TECHNOLOGY (ONLINE). *see* MEDICAL SCIENCES

MEDIZIN, TECHNIK UND GESELLSCHAFT/MEDICINE, TECHNOLOGY AND SOCIETY. *see* MEDICAL SCIENCES

600 500 JPN ISSN 0285-8258
Q4
MEIJI DAIGAKU KAGAKU GIJUTSU KENKYUJO HOKOKU. SOGO KENKYU/MEIJI UNIVERSITY. INSTITUTE OF SCIENCE AND TECHNOLOGY. REPORT. SPECIAL PROJECT. Text and summaries in English, Japanese. 1981. a.
Published by: Meiji Daigaku, Kagaku Gijutsu Kenkyujo/Meiji University, Institute of Science and Technology, 1-1-1 Higashi-Mita, Tama-ku, Kawasaki-shi, Kanagawa-ken 214-0033, Japan.

600 500 JPN ISSN 0386-4944
Q4 CODEN: MDKKDY
MEIJI DAIGAKU KAGAKU GIJUTSU KENKYUJO KIYO/MEIJI UNIVERSITY. INSTITUTE OF SCIENCE AND TECHNOLOGY. MEMOIRS. Text in English, Japanese; Summaries in English. 1962. a. (number of issues in each volume varies), latest vol.45, 2006. **Document type:** *Journal, Academic/Scholarly.*
Indexed: ChemAb, JPI.
Published by: Meiji Daigaku, Kagaku Gijutsu Kenkyujo/Meiji University, Institute of Science and Technology, 1-1-1 Higashi-Mita, Tama-ku, Kawasaki-shi, Kanagawa-ken 214-0033, Japan. TEL 81-44-9347613, FAX 81-44-9347917, gi_ken@mics.meiji.ac.jp.

600 500 JPN ISSN 0543-3916
Q4 CODEN: MDKGBK
MEIJI DAIGAKU KAGAKU GIJUTSU KENKYUJO NENPO/MEIJI UNIVERSITY. INSTITUTE OF SCIENCE AND TECHNOLOGY. ANNUAL REPORT. Text in Japanese. 1959. a., latest 2006. abstr. **Document type:** *Academic/Scholarly.*
Indexed: ChemAb.
—CASDDS.
Published by: Meiji Daigaku, Kagaku Gijutsu Kenkyujo/Meiji University, Institute of Science and Technology, 1-1-1 Higashi-Mita, Tama-ku, Kawasaki-shi, Kanagawa-ken 214-0033, Japan. TEL 81-44-9347613, FAX 81-44-9347917, gi_ken@mics.meiji.ac.jp.

600 JPN
Q179.9 CODEN: MDRKAW
➤ **MEIJO DAIGAKU RIKOGAKUBU KENKYU HOKOKU (CD-ROM)/ MEIJO UNIVERSITY. FACULTY OF SCIENCE AND TECHNOLOGY. RESEARCH REPORTS.** Text in Japanese; Abstracts and contents page in English. 1957. a., latest vol.41. abstr.; bibl.; charts; illus. 130 p./no.; back issues avail. **Document type:** *Journal, Academic/ Scholarly.*
Formerly (until 2007): Meijo Daigaku Rikogakubu Kenkyu Hokoku (Print) (0386-4952)
Media: CD-ROM. **Related titles:** Online - full text ed.
Indexed: A22, A28, APA, BrCerAb, C&ISA, CA/WCA, CCMJ, CIA, CIN, CerAb, ChemAb, ChemTitl, CivEngAb, CorrAb, E&CAJ, E11, EEA, EMA, ESPM, EnvEAb, H15, Inspec, JPI, M&TEA, M09, MBF, METADEX, MSN, MathR, SolStAb, T04, WAA, Z02.
—BLDSC (7467.085000), AskIEEE, CASDDS, IE, Ingenta, Linda Hall.
Published by: Meijo Daigaku, Rikogakubu/Meijo University, Faculty of Science and Technology, 1-501 Shiogama-guchi, Tenpaku-ku, Nagoya-shi, Aichi-ken 468-8502, Japan. TEL 81-52-8382053, http://wwwrr.meijo-u.ac.jp/. Circ: 1,000.

➤ **MEITAN JISHU/COAL TECHNOLOGY.** *see* ENERGY

➤ **MEITAN KEXUE JISHU/COAL SCIENCE AND TECHNOLOGY.** *see* ENGINEERING—Chemical Engineering

➤ **MICROCOMPUTER**; for general P C user. *see* COMPUTERS—Microcomputers

➤ **MICROCOMPUTER USER**; for PC buyers and general public. *see* COMPUTERS—Microcomputers

➤ **MICROGRAVITY - SCIENCE AND TECHNOLOGY**; international journal for microgravity research and applications. *see* AERONAUTICS AND SPACE FLIGHT

➤ **MILITARY TRAINING TECHNOLOGY.** *see* MILITARY

➤ **MIND: THE MEETINGS INDEX (ONLINE).** *see* MEETINGS AND CONGRESSES

600 USA
MINDJACK MAGAZINE. Text in English. m. free. **Description:** Covers technology, culture and technosocial issues with a bit of technorealist and critical bent.
Media: Online - full text. Ed., Pub. Donald Melanson.

600 USA ISSN 1060-8281
MINNESOTA TECHNOLOGY; inside technology and manufacturing business. Text in English. 1991. bi-m. **Document type:** *Magazine, Trade.*
Published by: Minnesota Technology, Incorporated, 111 Third Ave. S., Suite 400, Minneapolis, MN 55401. TEL 612-672-3412, FAX 612-339-5214, lball@mntech.org, http://www.mntechnologymag.com. Ed. Linda Ball. Circ: 20,000.

600 HUN ISSN 1215-0851
TA4
MISKOLCI EGYETEM. KOZLEMENYEI. 3 SOROZAT, GEPESZET. Text in Hungarian. 1975. irreg.
Formerly (until 1989): Nehezipari Muszaki Egyetem. Kozlemenyei. 3 Sorozat, Gepeszet (0324-6728)
Indexed: SpeleolAb.
—Linda Hall.
Published by: Miskolci Egyetem/University of Miskolc, Miskolc, 3515, Hungary.

600 JPN ISSN 0914-627X
MITO KAGAKU GIJUTSU/SOCIETY OF NON-TRADITIONAL TECHNOLOGY. JOURNAL. Text in Japanese. 1973. m. JPY 500 per issue. **Description:** Contains reviews, commentary, and news of the organization.
Published by: Mito Kagaku Gijutsu Kyokai/Society of Non-Traditional Technology, Toranomon Kotohira Kaikan, 2-8 Toranomon 1-chome, Minato-ku, Tokyo, 105, Japan. TEL 81-3-3503-4681, FAX 81-3-3597-0535.

MITSUBISHI ELECTRIC ADVANCE; a quarterly survey of new products, systems and technology. *see* ENGINEERING—Electrical Engineering

600 JPN
MITSUBISHI HEAVY INDUSTRIES TECHNICAL REVIEW (ONLINE). Text in Japanese. bi-m. back issues avail. **Document type:** *Corporate.*
Media: Online - full content.
Published by: Mitsubishi Heavy Industries, Ltd., Technology Planning Department, 3-1, Minatomirai 3-chome, Nishi-ku, Yokohama, 220-8401, Japan. TEL 81-45-224-9050, FAX 81-45-224-9906, http://www.mhi.co.jp/indexj.html.

600 JPN ISSN 0387-2432
T4 CODEN: MIJGAF
MITSUBISHI JUKO GIHO. Text in Japanese. 1964. 6/yr. **Document type:** *Academic/Scholarly.* **Description:** Introduces new technologies and products of the company. Aims to contribute to improvements in technology, and to advertise the company.
Indexed: A28, APA, BMT, BrCerAb, C&ISA, CA/WCA, CIA, CIN, CerAb, ChemAb, ChemTitl, CivEngAb, CorrAb, E&CAJ, E11, EEA, EMA, H15, INIS AtomInd, JCT, M&TEA, M09, MBF, METADEX, SolStAb, T04, WAA.
—CASDDS, IE, Ingenta, Linda Hall.
Published by: Mitsubishi Heavy Industries, Ltd., Technology Planning Department, 3-1, Minatomirai 3-chome, Nishi-ku, Yokohama, 220-8401, Japan. TEL 81-45-224-9050, FAX 81-45-224-9906, http://www.mhi.co.jp/indexj.html. Circ: 10,000. **Subscr. to:** The Ohm-Sha Ltd., 1 Kanda-Nishiki-cho 3-chome, Chiyoda-ku, Tokyo 101-0054, Japan. **Dist. overseas by:** Japan Publications Trading Co., Ltd., Book Export II Dept, PO Box 5030, Tokyo International, Tokyo 101-3191, Japan. TEL 81-3-32923753, FAX 81-3-32920410, infoserials@jptco.co.jp, http://www.jptco.co.jp.

600 JPN ISSN 0286-3707
MIYAGI KOGYO KOTO SENMON GAKKO KENKYU KIYO/MIYAGI NATIONAL COLLEGE OF TECHNOLOGY. RESEARCH REPORTS. Text in Japanese. 1965. a.
Indexed: CCMJ, MSN, MathR, RILM, RefZh.
Published by: Miyagi Kogyo Koto Senmon Gakko/Miyagi National College of Technology, 48 Nodayama, Medeshima-Shiote, Natori, Miyagi 981-1239, Japan. http://www.miyagi-ct.ac.jp/.

604.24 USA
MODERN DRAFTING PRACTICES AND STANDARDS MANUAL. Text in English. base vol. plus s-a. updates. looseleaf. USD 129 domestic; USD 155 foreign (effective 2000). **Document type:** *Handbook/ Manual/Guide, Trade.*
Related titles: CD-ROM ed.
Published by: Genium Publishing Corp., 1171 Riverfront Ctr, Amsterdam, NY 12010-4600. TEL 518-377-8854, 800-243-6486, FAX 518-377-1891. Ed. Robert A Roy.

600 500 IRN
MOKHTAREIN VA MOBTAKERIN. Text in Persian, Modern. q.
Published by: Soroush Press, 228 Mottahhari Ave., P O Box 15875-1163, Teheran, Iran. TEL 021-830771.

MOKSLO IR TECHNIKOS RAIDA/EVOLUTION OF SCIENCE AND TECHNOLOGY. *see* SCIENCES: COMPREHENSIVE WORKS

MONOGRAFIE Z DZIEJOW NAUKI I TECHNIKI. *see* SCIENCES: COMPREHENSIVE WORKS

MOSAICO CIENTIFICO. *see* SCIENCES: COMPREHENSIVE WORKS

600 LTU ISSN 0134-3165
MOSKLAS IR TEKNIKA. Text in Lithuanian. m. USD 149 in North America (effective 2000).
Address: Laisves pr 60, Vilnius, 2056, Lithuania. TEL 3702-624493. Ed. A Zverzdinas. **Dist. by:** East View Information Services, 10601 Wayzata Blvd, Minneapolis, MN 55305. TEL 952-252-1201, 800-477-1005, FAX 952-252-1202, info@eastview.com, http://www.eastview.com.

600 DEU ISSN 0932-5395
MOTORIST; Technik fuer Garten und Landschaft. Text in German. 1986. bi-m. EUR 102 domestic; EUR 112 foreign; EUR 19.50 newsstand/ cover (effective 2011). adv. **Document type:** *Magazine, Trade.*
Formerly (until 1987): Motoristen Markt und Technik (0931-9824)
Indexed: RefZh.
Published by: Verlag Siegfried Rohn GmbH & Co. KG, Stolberger Str 84, Cologne, 50933, Germany. TEL 49-221-54974, FAX 49-221-5497278, rohn@rudolf-mueller.de, http://www.rohn.de. Ed. Juergen Krieger. Adv. contact Verena Thiele. Circ: 6,911 (paid).

MULTICULTURAL EDUCATIONAL & TECHNOLOGY JOURNAL. *see* EDUCATION

MUNDO. *see* SCIENCES: COMPREHENSIVE WORKS

600 LBY
AL-MUNTIJUN. Text in Arabic. m.
Published by: Muntijun, P O Box 734, Tripoli, Libya.

MUSEU DE CIENCIAS E TECNOLOGIA. DIVULGACOES. *see* SCIENCES: COMPREHENSIVE WORKS

MUSICA TECNOLOGIA. *see* MUSIC

600 USA
▼ **MY TEKLIFE.** Text in English. 2009. q. USD 19.95 (effective 2010). adv. illus. **Document type:** *Magazine, Consumer.* **Description:** Covers intriguing stories about people who have been impacted by technology in unique ways. The articles not only explore technological innovation, It highlights experiences and achievements in film, music, aviation, automotive, science, history and discovery, and the latest in green innovation. It's mission is to educate, entertain and inspire by sharing the humanity behind technology. Every issue also contains news on exciting products and consumer tips to help audience enhance their technology experience.
Related titles: Online - full text ed.
Published by: MyTekLife Magazine, Llc., 60 E. Rio Salado Pkwy, Ste 9090, Tempe, AZ 85281. TEL 480-366-5957. Ed. Ed Martinez.

303.48 USA ISSN 1947-0894
N A S A TECHNOLOGY INNOVATION. (National Aeronautics and Space Administration) Text in English. 1992. s-a. back issues avail. **Document type:** *Magazine, Trade.* **Description:** Provides information about NASA's technology needs and opportunities, as well as interesting facts and feature articles about NASA's successes.
Former titles (until 2004): Aerospace Technology Innovation; (until 1996): Space Technology Innovation; (until 1993): Commercial Space Opportunities
Related titles: Online - full text ed.: ISSN 1947-0886. free (effective 2009).
Published by: N A S A, Exploration Systems Mission Directorate, 300 E St, S W, Washington, DC 20546. http://www.nasa.gov/exploration/ home/index.html. Ed. Janelle Turner TEL 202-358-0704.

N A T A NEWS. *see* SCIENCES: COMPREHENSIVE WORKS

N A T O ADVANCED SCIENCE INSTITUTES SERIES. PARTNERSHIP SUB-SERIES 4: SCIENCE AND TECHNOLOGY POLICY. (North Atlantic Treaty Organization) *see* SCIENCES: COMPREHENSIVE WORKS

N A T O SCIENCE SERIES. SERIES V: SCIENCE AND TECHNOLOGY POLICY. (North Atlantic Treaty Organization) *see* SCIENCES: COMPREHENSIVE WORKS

N D T & E INTERNATIONAL. (Non Destructive Testing and Evaluation) *see* ENGINEERING—Engineering Mechanics And Materials

600 JPN ISSN 1880-5884
TK1
N E C TECHNICAL JOURNAL. (Nippon Electric Company) Text in English. 2004; N.S. 2006. q. USD 58 (effective 2005). **Document type:** *Journal, Academic/Scholarly.* **Description:** Covers NEC's research & development, technologies used for newly developed products, new systems and services.
Formerly (until 2006): N E C Journal of Advanced Technology (1348-8341)
Indexed: CPEI, EngInd, Inspec, SCOPUS, TM.
—BLDSC (6068.443000), IE, INIST, Linda Hall.
Published by: (N E C Media Products Ltd.), N E C Corp., External Relations Division, 7-1, Shiba 5-Chome, Minato-ku, Tokyo, 108-8001, Japan. **Dist. by:** Japan Publications Trading Co., Ltd., Book Export II Dept, PO Box 5030, Tokyo International, Tokyo 101-3191, Japan. TEL 81-3-32923753, FAX 81-3-32920410, infoserials@jptco.co.jp, http://www.jptco.co.jp.

600 USA ISSN 0742-2652
KF2138
N R C REGULATORY AGENDA. (Nuclear Regulatory Commission) Text in English. 1982. s-a. free (effective 2011). back issues avail. **Document type:** *Report, Government.*
Related titles: Online - full text ed.
Published by: U.S. Nuclear Regulatory Commission, Washington, DC 20555. TEL 301-415-7000, 800-368-5642.

600 USA ISSN 1062-130X
V394.W2
N R L REVIEW. (Naval Research Laboratory) Text in English. 1988. a. **Document type:** *Magazine, Government.*
Indexed: P30.
—Linda Hall.
Published by: Naval Research Laboratory, 4555 Overlook Ave, SW, Washington, DC 20375. http://www.nrl.navy.mil.

600 JPN
CODEN: NSMNEY
N S M F NEWS. (New Superconducting Materials Forum) Text in Japanese. bi-m. JPY 10,000 to individuals; JPY 20,000 to institutions.
Indexed: CIN, ChemAb, ChemTitl.
Published by: Society of Non-Traditional Technology/Mito Kagaku Gijutsu Kyokai, Toranomon Kotohira Kaikan, 1-2-8 Toranomon, Minato-ku, Tokyo, 105-0001, Japan. TEL 81-3-3503-4681, FAX 81-3-3597-0535.

600 UKR ISSN 0548-1414
NAFTOVA I HAZOVA PROMYSLOVIST'. Text in Ukrainian, Russian, English. 1960. bi-m. USD 148 foreign (effective 2004).
Indexed: GeoRef, PetrolAb, RefZh, SpeleolAb.
—East View, INIST, Linda Hall, PADDS. **CCC.**
Published by: Ukrgazprom, vul B Khmel'nitskogo 6, Kyiv, Ukraine. **Dist. by:** East View Information Services, 10601 Wayzata Blvd, Minneapolis, MN 55305. TEL 952-252-1201, 800-477-1005, FAX 952-252-1202, info@eastview.com, http://www.eastview.com.

600 JPN ISSN 1340-3729
TA4 CODEN: NKGSAR
NAGOYA KOGYO GIJUTSU KENKYUJO HOKOKU/NATIONAL INDUSTRIAL RESEARCH INSTITUTE OF NAGOYA. REPORTS. Text in Japanese. 1952. m. abstr.; bibl. index, cum.index.
Formerly (until 1993): Japan. Government Industrial Research Institute, Nagoya. Technical News (0027-7614)
Indexed: INIS AtomInd, Inspec.
—AskIEEE, CASDDS, Linda Hall.
Published by: National Industrial Research Institute of Nagoya/Nagoya Kogyo Gijutsu Kenkyujo, Kogyo Gijutsuin, 1 Hirate-cho, Kita-ku, Nagoya-shi, Aichi-ken 462-0057, Japan. TEL 81-52-911-2111, gyoumu-ka@nirin.go.jp. Ed. S Suzuki.

600 CHN ISSN 1006-0456
➤ **NANCHANG DAXUE XUEBAO (GONGKE BAN)/NANCHANG UNIVERSITY. JOURNAL (ENGINEERING TECHNOLOGY).** Text in Chinese. 1964. q. CNY 32; CNY 8 newsstand/cover (effective 2009). **Document type:** *Journal, Academic/Scholarly.* **Description:** Covers the latest developments of theoretical and applied research in the fields of science and engineering.
Formerly (until 1994): Jiangxi Gongye Daxue Xuebao/Jiangxi Polytechnic University. Journal (1000-5803)
Related titles: Online - full text ed.
Indexed: A28, APA, BrCerAb, C&ISA, CA/WCA, CIA, CerAb, CivEngAb, CorrAb, E&CAJ, E11, EEA, EMA, ESPM, EnvEAb, H15, M&TEA, M09, MBF, METADEX, SolStAb, T04, WAA.
Published by: Nanchang Daxue/Nanchang University, 235, Nanjing Dong Lu, Bei-qu, Nanchang, 330047, China. TEL 86-791-8305805, FAX 86-791-8305820. Ed. Dong-rong Xu. Circ: 1,000 (paid).

➤ **NANJING DAXUE XUEBAO (ZHEXUE RENWEN SHEHUI KEXUE)/ NANJING UNIVERSITY. JOURNAL (PHILOSOPHY, HUMANITIES AND SOCIAL SCIENCES).** *see* SCIENCES: COMPREHENSIVE WORKS

➤ **NANJING SHIFAN DAXUE XUEBAO (GONGCHENG JISHU BAN)/NANJING NORMAL UNIVERSITY. JOURNAL (ENGINEERING AND TECHNOLOGY).** *see* ENGINEERING

531.16 170 NLD ISSN 1871-4757
➤ **NANOETHICS**; ethics for technologies that converge at the nanoscale. Text in English. 2007. 3/yr. EUR 265, USD 294 combined subscription to institutions (print & online eds.) (effective 2012). reprint service avail. from PSC. **Document type:** *Journal, Academic/Scholarly.* **Description:** Examines both the ethical and societal considerations as well as the public and policy concerns inherent in nanotechnology research and development.
Related titles: Online - full text ed.: ISSN 1871-4765 (from IngentaConnect).
Indexed: A01, A12, A22, A26, ABIn, Agr, AmHI, BRD, CA, E01, E08, ESPM, H07, H08, HAb, HumInd, P20, P22, P26, P30, P48, P51, P53, P54, PQC, RiskAb, S09, SCOPUS, SSciA, T02, W03, W05.
—IE. **CCC.**
Published by: Springer Netherlands (Subsidiary of: Springer Science+Business Media), Van Godewijckstraat 30, Dordrecht, 3311 GX, Netherlands. TEL 31-78-6576050, FAX 31-78-6576474. Ed. John Weckert.

620.5 USA ISSN 1931-6941
T174.7
NANORISK. Text in English. 2006. bi-m. USD 49 (effective 2006). **Document type:** *Newsletter.*

Related titles: Online - full content ed.
Published by: Nanowerk LLC., 157 Poipu Dr., Honolulu, HI 96825. TEL 800-942-5414, FAX 808-396-0493.

600 USA ISSN 1524-3613
NANOTECH ALERT. Text in English. 19??. w. back issues avail. **Document type:** *Newsletter, Trade.*
Media: Online - full text.
Published by: Technical Insights (Subsidiary of: Frost & Sullivan), 7550 IH 10 W, Ste 400, San Antonio, TX 78229. TEL 210-348-1000, 877-463-7678, FAX 888-690-3329, myfrost@frost.com, http://www.frost.com/prod/servlet/ti-home.pag. **Subscr. to:** John Wiley & Sons Ltd.

▼ **NANOTECHNOLOGY LAW.** *see* LAW

600 JPN ISSN 0387-1150 CODEN: NKKOB2
NARA KOGYO KOTO SENMON GAKKO KENKYU KIYO/NARA NATIONAL COLLEGE OF TECHNOLOGY. RESEARCH REPORTS. Text in Japanese. 1965. a. **Document type:** *Academic/Scholarly.*
Indexed: INIS AtomInd.
Published by: Nara Kogyo Koto Senmon Gakko/Nara National College of Technology, 22 Yata-cho, Yamatokoriyama, Nara 639-1080, Japan. TEL 81-743-556000, FAX 81-743-556019, http://www.nara-k.ac.jp/.

NARODNI TECHNICKE MUZEUM. KATALOG. *see* MUSEUMS AND ART GALLERIES

NATIONAL CAPITAL SCAN. *see* BUSINESS AND ECONOMICS

NATIONAL DEFENSE ACADEMY. MEMOIRS. MATHEMATICS, PHYSICS, CHEMISTRY AND ENGINEERING/BOEI DAIGAKKO KIYO RIKOGAKU-HEN. *see* SCIENCES: COMPREHENSIVE WORKS

NATIONAL RESEARCH CENTRE. BULLETIN. *see* SCIENCES: COMPREHENSIVE WORKS

600 UKR ISSN 2079-0074
NATSIONAL'NYI TEKHNICHESKII UNIVERSITET "KHAR'KOVSKII POLITEKHNICHESKII INSTITUT". VESTNIK. ISTORIYA NAUKI I TEKHNIKI/NATSIONAL'NYI TEKHNICHNYI UNIVERSYTET "KHARKIVS'KYI POLITEKHNICHNYI INSTYTUT". VISNYK. ISTORIYA NAUKY TA TEKHNIKY. Text in Russian, Ukrainian; Summaries in Russian, Ukrainian, English. 2008. s-a. bk.rev. abstr.; bibl.; charts; illus. **Document type:** *Journal, Academic/Scholarly.* **Description:** Intended for the research workers and specialists in the field of ICE, it covers the topics of construction, production technology and calculation of the ICE.
Published by: Natsional'nyi Tekhnicheskii Universitet "Kharkovskii Politekhnicheskii Institut"/National Technical University "Kharkiv Polytechnical Institute", vul Frunze 21, Kharkiv, 310002, Ukraine. TEL 380-572-7076212, FAX 380-572-7076601, omsroot@kpi.kharkov.ua, http://www.kpi.kharkov.ua. Ed. Leonid Besov. Pub. Natalia Annenkova.

NATSIYANAL'NAYA AKADEMIYA NAVUK BELARUSI. VESTSI. SERYYA FIZIKA-TECHNICHNYKH NAVUK/NATIONAL ACADEMY OF SCIENCES OF BELARUS. PROCEEDINGS. SERIES OF PHYSICAL AND TECHNICAL SCIENCES/NATSIONAL'NAYA AKADEMIYA NAUK BELARUSI. IZVESTIYA. SERIYA FIZIKO-TEKHNICHESKIKH NAUK. *see* PHYSICS

NATURE BIOTECHNOLOGY. *see* BIOLOGY—Biotechnology

NATUURWETENSCHAP & TECHNIEK. *see* SCIENCES: COMPREHENSIVE WORKS

NAUKA I ZHIZN'; nauchno-populyarnyi zhurnal. *see* SCIENCES: COMPREHENSIVE WORKS

600 RUS
NAUKOEMKIE TEKHNOLOGII/HIGH TECHNOLOGIES. Text in Russian. bi-m. RUR 330 per issue domestic (effective 2004). **Document type:** *Journal, Academic/Scholarly.*
Published by: Izdatel'stvo Radiotekhnika, Kuznetskii Most 20/6, Moscow, 103031, Russian Federation. iprzhr@online.ru, http://webcenter.ru/~iprzhr/.

NEDERLANDSE ORGANISATIE VOOR TOEGEPAST NATUURWETENSCHAPPELIJK ONDERZOEK. JAARVERSLAG. *see* SCIENCES: COMPREHENSIVE WORKS

600 NZL ISSN 1177-1852
NELSON MARLBOROUGH INSTITUTE OF TECHNOLOGY. OCCASIONAL PAPER SERIES. Text in English. 2005. irreg. **Document type:** *Monographic series, Academic/Scholarly.*
Related titles: Online - full text ed.: ISSN 1178-8836.
Published by: Nelson Marlborough Institute of Technology, Private Bag 19, Nelson, New Zealand. TEL 64-3-5469175, FAX 64-3-5463325, info@nmit.ac.nz.

600 NZL ISSN 1178-8437
NELSON MARLBOROUGH INSTITUTE OF TECHNOLOGY. WORKING PAPER SERIES. Text in English. 2001. irreg. **Document type:** *Monographic series, Academic/Scholarly.*
Media: Online - full text.
Published by: Nelson Marlborough Institute of Technology, Private Bag 19, Nelson, New Zealand. TEL 64-3-5469175, info@nmit.ac.nz.

NEPAL JOURNAL OF SCIENCE AND TECHNOLOGY. *see* SCIENCES: COMPREHENSIVE WORKS

NETSU SHORI/JAPAN SOCIETY FOR HEAT TREATMENT. JOURNAL. *see* METALLURGY

▼ **NEUE TECHNOLOGIEN IM SPORT.** *see* SPORTS AND GAMES

THE NEW ATLANTIS; a journal of technology & society. *see* POLITICAL SCIENCE

745.2 688.8 GBR ISSN 1472-2674
NEW DESIGN. Text in English. 2000. 10/yr. GBP 65 domestic; GBP 90 in Europe; GBP 105 elsewhere; GBP 39 domestic to students; GBP 54 in Europe to students; GBP 63 elsewhere to students (effective 2009). back issues avail. **Document type:** *Magazine, Trade.* **Description:** Covers the products and processes of design in all its forms.
Indexed: D05, SCOPUS.
Published by: New Design Magazine, 6A New St, Warwick, Warks CV34 4RX, United Kingdom. TEL 44-1926-408207, FAX 44-1926-408206.

658.7 USA ISSN 0028-4963
TJ1
NEW EQUIPMENT DIGEST. Text in English. 1936. m. USD 59 domestic; USD 67 in Canada; USD 84 elsewhere; free domestic to qualified personnel (effective 2011). adv. bk.rev. illus.; tr.lit. reprints avail. **Document type:** *Magazine, Trade.* **Description:** Descriptions of new or significantly improved industrial products.
Related titles: Microform ed.: (from PQC); Online - full text ed.
Indexed: A09, A10, A15, A22, A28, ABIn, APA, B01, B02, B06, B07, B09, B15, B17, B18, BrCerAb, C&ISA, CA/WCA, CIA, CerAb, CivEngAb, CorrAb, E&CAJ, E11, EEA, EMA, ESPM, EnvEAb, G04, G06, G07, G08, H15, I05, I07, M&TEA, M09, MBF, METADEX, P52, PQC, S23, SolStAb, T02, T04, V03, V04, WAA.
—Linda Hall. **CCC.**
Published by: Penton Media, Inc., 1300 E 9th St, Cleveland, OH 44114. TEL 216-696-7000, FAX 216-696-3432, information@penton.com, http://www.penton.com. Ed. Robert F King TEL 216-931-9269. Pub. John Di Paola TEL 216-931-9709. adv.: B&W page USD 9,695, color page USD 13,085. Circ: 210,069 (controlled).

658.7 ZAF ISSN 0028-498X
NEW EQUIPMENT NEWS. Abbreviated title: N E N. Text in English. 1963. m. ZAR 96 domestic; ZAR 204 foreign (effective 2000). adv. abstr.; illus.; tr.lit. **Document type:** *Magazine, Trade.*
Related titles: Supplement(s): New Equipment News. Natal Supplement. ISSN 0379-9263; New Equipment News Western Cape. ISSN 0379-9271.
Published by: T M L Business Publishing (Subsidiary of: Times Media Ltd.), PO Box 182, Pinegowrie, Gauteng 2123, South Africa. TEL 27-11-789-2144, FAX 27-11-789-3196. Ed. Andronica Motlhabane. Adv. contact Samantha Smith. Circ: 9,036.

NEW SCIENTIST (CHATSWOOD). *see* SCIENCES: COMPREHENSIVE WORKS

NEW TECHNOLOGIES / NEW CULTURES. *see* SOCIAL SCIENCES: COMPREHENSIVE WORKS

NEW TECHNOLOGY-BASED FIRMS IN THE NEW MILLENNIUM. *see* BUSINESS AND ECONOMICS

NEWTON/NYUTON; graphic science magazine. *see* SCIENCES: COMPREHENSIVE WORKS

NICKLE'S NEW TECHNOLOGY MAGAZINE. *see* PETROLEUM AND GAS

600 500 JPN ISSN 0369-4313
Q1 CODEN: NDRSD2
NIHON DAIGAKU RIKOGAKU KENKYUJO SHOHO/NIHON UNIVERSITY. RESEARCH INSTITUTE OF SCIENCE AND TECHNOLOGY. JOURNAL. Text in Japanese. 1950. s-a. per issue exchange basis. abstr.
Indexed: A28, APA, BrCerAb, C&ISA, CA/WCA, CCMJ, CIA, CerAb, ChemAb, CivEngAb, CorrAb, E&CAJ, E11, EEA, EMA, H15, Inspec, JCT, JTA, M&TEA, M09, MBF, METADEX, MathR, SolStAb, T04, WAA.
—BLDSC (4847.900000), AskIEEE, CASDDS, Linda Hall.
Published by: Nihon Daigaku, Rikogaku Kenkyujo/Nihon University, Research Institute of Science and Technology, 1-8 Kanda-Surugadai, Chiyoda-ku, Tokyo, 101-0062, Japan. Circ: (controlled).

600 JPN
NIHON DAIGAKU RIKOGAKUBU GAKUJUTSU KOENKAI KOEN RONBUNSHU/NIHON UNIVERSITY. RESEARCH INSTITUTE OF SCIENCE AND TECHNOLOGY. PROCEEDINGS OF MEETING. Text in English, Japanese. a. **Document type:** *Proceedings.* **Description:** Contains proceedings from the meetings of the institute.
Published by: Nihon Daigaku, Rikogaku Kenkyujo/Nihon University, Research Institute of Science and Technology, 1-8 Kanda-Surugadai, Chiyoda-ku, Tokyo, 101-0062, Japan. Circ: (controlled).

600 JPN ISSN 0385-4442 CODEN: NDSADL
NIHON DAIGAKU SEISAN KOGAKUBU KENKYU HOKOKU. A, RIKOKEI/NIHON UNIVERSITY. COLLEGE OF INDUSTRIAL TECHNOLOGY. JOURNAL. A. Text in Japanese. 1967. s-a. **Document type:** *Journal, Academic/Scholarly.*
Supersedes in part (in 1975): Nihon Daigaku Seisan Kogakubu Hokoku
Indexed: RILM.
—Linda Hall. **CCC.**
Published by: Nihon Daigaku, Seisan Kogakubu/Nihon University, College of Industrial Technology, 1-2-1 Izumicho, Narashino, Chiba 275-8575, Japan. TEL 81-47-4742201.

600 JPN ISSN 0385-4450
AS552.N376
NIHON DAIGAKU SEISAN KOGAKUBU KENKYU HOKOKU. B, BUNKEI/NIHON UNIVERSITY. COLLEGE OF INDUSTRIAL TECHNOLOGY. JOURNAL. B. Text in Japanese. 1967. a. **Document type:** *Journal, Academic/Scholarly.*
Supersedes in part (in 1975): Nihon Daigaku Seisan Kogakubu Hokoku (0385-9800)
—Linda Hall. **CCC.**
Published by: Nihon Daigaku, Seisan Kogakubu/Nihon University, College of Industrial Technology, 1-2-1 Izumicho, Narashino, Chiba 275-8575, Japan. TEL 81-47-4742201.

NIHON KAGAKU GIJUTSU KANKEI CHIKUJI KANKOBUTSU SORAN (ONLINE)/DIRECTORY OF JAPANESE SCIENTIFIC PERIODICALS (ONLINE). *see* PUBLISHING AND BOOK TRADE—Abstracting, Bibliographies, Statistics

NIHON SEKIGAISEN GAKKAISHI/JAPAN SOCIETY OF INFRARED SCIENCE AND TECHNOLOGY. JOURNAL. *see* PHYSICS—Heat

NIHON UNIVERSITY. RESEARCH INSTITUTE OF SCIENCE AND TECHNOLOGY. REPORT. *see* SCIENCES: COMPREHENSIVE WORKS

600 JPN ISSN 0913-7912
NIIGATA KOGYO TANKI DAIGAKU KENKYU KIYO/NIIGATA TECHNICAL JUNIOR COLLEGE. JOURNAL. Text in Japanese; Summaries in English. 1971. irreg. **Description:** Contains original papers.
Published by: Niigata Kogyo Tanki Daigaku/Niigata Technical Junior College, 5827 Kami-Shinei-cho, Niigata-shi, 950-2076, Japan.

600 620 500 JPN ISSN 0286-2743
Q4 CODEN: NKHEDR
NIIHAMA KOGYO KOTO SENMON GAKKO KIYO. RIKOGAKU HEN/NIIHAMA NATIONAL COLLEGE OF TECHNOLOGY. MEMOIRS. SCIENCE AND ENGINEERING. Text in English, Japanese; Summaries in English. 1965. a.
Indexed: CIN, ChemAb, ChemTitl, JPI.
—CASDDS.
Published by: Niihama Kogyo Koto Senmon Gakko/Niihama National College of Technology, 7-1 Yagumo-cho, Niihama-shi, Ehime-ken 792-0805, Japan.

NIKKEI SAIENSU. *see* SCIENCES: COMPREHENSIVE WORKS

600 JPN
NIKKEI TECHNO FRONTIER. Text in Japanese. s-m. **Document type:** *Newsletter.* **Description:** Covers a wide range of high-tech topics, and new products and services.
Published by: Nihon Keizai Shimbun Inc., 1-9-5 Ote-Machi, Chiyoda-ku, Tokyo, 100-0004, Japan. TEL 81-3-32700251, FAX 81-3-52552661.

600 CHN
NINGBO GONGCHENG XUEYUAN XUEBAO/NINGBO UNIVERSITY OF TECHNOLOGY. JOURNAL. Text in Chinese. 1983. q. CNY 10 newsstand/cover (effective 2006). **Document type:** *Journal, Academic/Scholarly.*
Formerly: Ningbo Gaodeng Zhuanke Xuexiao Xuebao/Ningbo College. Journal (1008-7109)
Related titles: Online - full text ed.
Published by: Ningbo Gongcheng Xueyuan, Wenhua Lu Houhe Xiang 20, Ningbo, 315016, China. TEL 86-574-87081207.

600 JPN ISSN 0910-6227
NISHINIPPON KOGYO DAIGAKU KIYO. RIKOGAKU HEN/NISHINIPPON INSTITUTE OF TECHNOLOGY. MEMOIRS. SCIENCE AND TECHNOLOGY. Text in English, Japanese; Summaries in English. 1969. a.
Published by: Nishinippon Kogyo Daigaku/Nishinippon Institute of Technology, 1633 Aratsu, Miyako-gun, Kanda-machi, Fukuoka-ken 800-0344, Japan.

NONGCUN SHIYONG JISHU YU XINXI. *see* AGRICULTURE

NONGYE KEJI GUANLI/MANAGEMENT OF AGRICULTURE SCIENCE AND TECHNOLOGY. *see* AGRICULTURE

NONGYE KEJI YU ZHUANGBEI/AGRICULTURAL SCIENCE & TECHNOLOGY AND EQUIPMENT. *see* AGRICULTURE—Agricultural Equipment

NORDRHEIN-WESTFAELISCHE AKADEMIE DER WISSENSCHAFTEN UND DER KUENSTE. VORTRAEGE. N - NATURWISSENSCHAFTEN UND MEDIZIN. *see* SCIENCES: COMPREHENSIVE WORKS

NORTHWEST SCIENCE & TECHNOLOGY (ONLINE). *see* SOCIAL SCIENCES: COMPREHENSIVE WORKS

NORTHWESTERN JOURNAL OF TECHNOLOGY AND INTELLECTUAL PROPERTY. *see* LAW—Corporate Law

600 CUB
NOTICIERO CIENTIFICO. SERIE: TECNOLOGIA. Text in Spanish. fortn.
Published by: Academia de Ciencias de Cuba, Instituto de Documentacion e Informacion Cientifico-Tecnica (I D I C T), Capitolio Nacional, Prado y San Jose, Habana, 2, Cuba.

NOTRE DAME TECHNICAL REVIEW. *see* ENGINEERING

NOVA SCIENTIA; revista de investigacion de la Universidad De La Salle Bajio. *see* SCIENCES: COMPREHENSIVE WORKS

600 RUS ISSN 1606-1470
NOVYE TEKHNOLOGII. Text in Russian. 1999. w. free (effective 2004). **Document type:** *Consumer.*
Media: Online - full text.
Published by: Al'yans Midiya, Bolotnaya ul 12, str 3, Moscow, 115035, Russian Federation. TEL 7-095-2345380, FAX 7-095-2345363, allmedia@allmedia.ru, http://allmedia.ru, http://www.businesspress.ru.

NUTS & VOLTS; exploring everything for electronics. *see* ELECTRONICS

607.2 NOR ISSN 1504-8276
NYTT FRA EUREKA. Text in Norwegian. 1995. q. free. back issues avail. **Document type:** *Newsletter, Consumer.*
Former titles (until 2007): Eureka-Nytt (1502-3583); (until 1999): Eureka. Nyhetsbrev (0806-1424)
Related titles: Online - full text ed.: Nytt fra Eureka. ISSN 1504-8284. 2004.
Published by: Norges Forskningsraad, Eureka-Kontoret/The Research Council of Norway, Stensberggata 26, PO Box 2700, Oslo, 0131, Norway. TEL 47-22-037011, FAX 47-22-037001, post@forskningsradet.no. Circ: 2,500.

600 USA
O C D DIAMOND. (Organic Chemical Division) Text in English. 1935. m.
Formerly (until 1976): Bound Brook Diamond
Published by: American Cyanamid Co., Organic Chemical Division, Bound Brook, NJ 08805. TEL 908-831-2000. Ed. Robert G Meyer. Circ: 6,500 (controlled).

600 FRA ISSN 1011-792X
Q172.5.S34 CODEN: MSTIE9
O E C D MAIN SCIENCE AND TECHNOLOGY INDICATORS/O C D E PRINCIPAUX INDICATEURS DE LA SCIENCE ET DE LA TECHNOLOGIE. (Organisation for Economic Cooperation and Development) Text in French. 1988. s-a. EUR 116, USD 150, GBP 92, JPY 16,500 combined subscription (print & online eds.) (effective 2011). **Document type:** *Journal, Trade.*
Related titles: Diskette ed.; Online - full text ed.: ISSN 1609-7327. EUR 74, USD 97, GBP 60, JPY 10,600 (effective 2010) (from IngentaConnect).
Indexed: A01, A03, A08, A22, CA, E01, IIS.
—CASDDS, IE, Infotrieve, Ingenta. **CCC.**
Published by: Organisation for Economic Cooperation and Development (O E C D), Nuclear Energy Agency/Organisation de Cooperation et de Developpement Economiques, Agence pour l'Energie Nucleaire, 2 rue Andre Pascal, Paris, Cedex 16 75775, France. **Subscr. to:** O E C D Washington Center, 2001 L St., N.W., Ste. 700, Washington, DC 20036-4095.

OAK RIDGE NATIONAL LABORATORY. REVIEW; the laboratory's research and development magazine. *see* ENERGY

TU

600 USA ISSN 1934-1490
T174.7
OATUBE NANOTECHNOLOGY. Text in English. 2008. irreg. free (effective 2011). back issues avail. **Document type:** *Journal, Academic/Scholarly.* **Description:** Provides an open-access approach for conference presentations to reach the widest possible audience through the Internet.
Media: Online - full text.
Indexed: A01, T02.
Published by: Open Access House of Science and Technology http://oahost.org. Eds. Emmanouil E Lioudakis, Zongwen Liu, Zhiming M Wang.

OCCASIONAL PAPERS IN IRISH SCIENCE AND TECHNOLOGY. *see* SCIENCES: COMPREHENSIVE WORKS

600 SWE ISSN 1650-8580
OEREBRO STUDIES IN TECHNOLOGY. Text in English. 2001. irreg., latest vol.22, 2006. price varies. back issues avail. **Document type:** *Monographic series, Academic/Scholarly.*
Published by: Oerebro Universitet, Universitetsbiblioteket/University of Oerebro. University Library, Fakultetsgatan 1, Oerebro, 70182, Sweden. TEL 46-19-303240, FAX 46-19-331217, biblioteket@ub.oru.se. Ed. Joanna Jansdotter.

600 CAN ISSN 0380-1969
ONTARIO TECHNOLOGIST. Text in English. 1958. 6/yr. CAD 24 to individuals; CAD 48 in United States to individuals; CAD 96 elsewhere to individuals (effective 1999). adv. bk.rev. **Document type:** *Journal, Trade.*
Published by: Ontario Association of Certified Engineering Technicians & Technologists, 209 3228 South Service Rd, Burlington, ON L7N 3H8, Canada. TEL 905-634-2100, FAX 905-634-2238. Ed. Colleen Mellor. Adv. contact Clifford Elliot. Circ: 19,499.

600 JPN ISSN 0387-365X
OOSAKA FURITSU KOGYO KOTO SENMON GAKKO KENKYU KIYO/OSAKA PREFECTURAL TECHNICAL COLLEGE. BULLETIN. Text in Japanese. 1968. a. **Document type:** *Journal, Academic/Scholarly.*
Indexed: CCMJ, MSN, MathR.
Published by: Oosaka Kogyo Koto Senmon Gakko/Osaka Prefectural College of Technology, Saiwai 26-12, Neyagawa, Osaka 572-8572, Japan. http://www.osaka-pct.ac.jp/.

600 500 JPN ISSN 0375-0191
T4 CODEN: OKDRAK
OOSAKA KOGYO DAIGAKU KIYO. RIKO HEN/OSAKA INSTITUTE OF TECHNOLOGY. MEMOIRS. SERIES A. SCIENCE & TECHNOLOGY. Text in English, Japanese; Summaries in English. 1951. s-a. charts; illus. **Document type:** *Bulletin, Academic/Scholarly.*
Indexed: B25, BIOSIS Prev, CCMJ, ChemAb, INIS AtomInd, JCT, JPI, MSN, MathR, MycolAb.
—CASDDS.
Published by: Oosaka Kogyo Daigaku/Osaka Institute of Technology, 16-1 Omiya 5-chome, Asahi-ku, Osaka-shi, 535-0002, Japan.

OOSAKA KYOIKU DAIGAKU KIYO. DAI 3-BUMON, SHIZEN KAGAKU, OYO KAGAKU/OSAKA KYOIKU UNIVERSITY. MEMOIRS. SERIES 3: NATURAL SCIENCE AND APPLIED SCIENCE. *see* SCIENCES: COMPREHENSIVE WORKS

600 BRA
OPEMA EM RITMO DE BRASIL JOVEM. Text in Portuguese. 1968. irreg. free. adv. illus.; stat.
Published by: (Brazil. Operacao Maua), Assessoria de Relacoes Publicas, Editora, Promocoes e Publicidade Ltda., Av. Beira Mar 406, Grupo 906, Rio De Janeiro, RJ, Brazil. Circ: 60,000.

▼ **OPEN CONFERENCE PROCEEDINGS JOURNAL.** *see* MEDICAL SCIENCES

660 600 NLD ISSN 1874-1401
T174.7
➤ **THE OPEN NANOSCIENCE JOURNAL.** Text in English. 2007. irreg. free (effective 2011). **Document type:** *Journal, Academic/Scholarly.*
Media: Online - full text.
Indexed: A01, A28, A39, APA, B19, BrCerAb, C&ISA, C27, C29, CA, CA/WCA, CIA, CerAb, CivEngAb, CorrAb, D03, D04, E&CAJ, E11, E13, EEA, EMA, ESPM, H15, M&TEA, M09, MBF, METADEX, R14, S14, S15, S18, SolStAb, T02, T04, WAA.
—CCC.
Published by: Bentham Open (Subsidiary of: Bentham Science Publishers Ltd.), PO Box 294, Bussum, AG 1400, Netherlands. TEL 31-35-6923800, FAX 31-35-6980150, subscriptions@bentham.org. Ed. Pu-Chun Ke.

➤ **ORGANIZATION OF AFRICAN UNITY. SCIENTIFIC TECHNICAL AND RESEARCH COMMISSION. PUBLICATION.** *see* SCIENCES: COMPREHENSIVE WORKS

➤ **ORIENTAL JOURNAL OF COMPUTER SCIENCE AND TECHNOLOGY**; an international research journal. *see* COMPUTERS

620 RUS
ORUZHIE; nauchno-populyarnyi illyustrirovannyi zhurnal. Text in Russian. 1994 (May). 10/yr.
Published by: Vostochnyi Gorizont, Novodmitrovskaya ul 5-a, Moscow, 125015, Russian Federation. TEL 7-095-2341678, FAX 7-095-2851687, tiangong@mtu-net.ru. Ed. A N Perevozchikov. Circ: 50,000 (paid).

607 JPN ISSN 0369-0369
Q180.J3 CODEN: MISIAW
OSAKA UNIVERSITY. INSTITUTE OF SCIENTIFIC AND INDUSTRIAL RESEARCH. MEMOIRS/OOSAKA DAIGAKU SANGYO KAGAKU KENKYUJO KIYO. Text in Multiple languages. 1941. a. per issue exchange basis. **Document type:** *Academic/Scholarly.*
Indexed: APA, C&ISA, CIN, ChemAb, ChemTitl, CorrAb, E&CAJ, EEA, EIA, INIS AtomInd, SolStAb, WAA.
—BLDSC (5620.000000), CASDDS, INIST, Linda Hall.
Published by: Oosaka Daigaku, Sangyo Kagaku Kenkyujo/Osaka University, Institute of Science and Industrial Research, Radiation Laboratory, 8-1 Mihogaoka, Ibaraki-shi, Osaka-fu 567-0047, Japan. TEL 81-6-877-5111, FAX 81-6-879-8509. Circ: 750.

OTTAWA R & D REPORT. *see* ENGINEERING

600 DEU ISSN 0936-0492
CODEN: PBNTES
P T B BERICHTE. NEUTRONENPHYSIK. Variant title: P T B-Bericht. N. Text in German. 1968. irreg. **Document type:** *Monographic series.*
Formed by the merger of (1968-1988): P T B-Bericht. Forschungs- und Messreaktor Braunschweig (0341-6666); (1970-1988): P T B-Bericht. Neutronendosimetrie (0572-7170)
Indexed: GeoRef, Inspec.
—CASDDS.
Published by: Physikalisch-Technische Bundesanstalt, Bundesallee 100, Braunschweig, 38116, Germany. TEL 49-531-5920, FAX 49-531-5929292, info@ptb.de. **Dist. by:** Wirtschaftsverlag Neue Wissenschaft GmbH, Postfach 101110, Bremerhaven 27511, Germany. TEL 49-471-9454488, 49-471-94544-0.

PACIFIC JOURNAL OF SCIENCE AND TECHNOLOGY (HILO). *see* SCIENCES: COMPREHENSIVE WORKS

PAKISTAN COUNCIL OF SCIENTIFIC AND INDUSTRIAL RESEARCH. ANNUAL REPORT. *see* SCIENCES: COMPREHENSIVE WORKS

PAKISTAN JOURNAL OF SCIENTIFIC AND INDUSTRIAL RESEARCH. *see* SCIENCES: COMPREHENSIVE WORKS

PAP; form function Finland. *see* ARCHITECTURE

PAPUA NEW GUINEA UNIVERSITY OF TECHNOLOGY. REPORTER. *see* COLLEGE AND ALUMNI

600 338.91 IND ISSN 0970-3691
PEOPLE'S ACTION (NEW DELHI). Text in English. 1987. bi-m. **Document type:** *Journal, Academic/Scholarly.*
Published by: Council for Advancement of People's Action and Rural Technology (C A P A R T), India Habitat Centre, Zone-V-A, 2nd Fl, Lodhi Rd, New Delhi, 110 003, India. TEL 91-11-24642391, FAX 91-11-24648607, capart@caparthq.delhi.nic.in.

338 ITA ISSN 0031-5435
IL PERITO INDUSTRIALE. Text in Italian. 1932. bi-m. EUR 44 (effective 2008). adv. bk.rev. **Document type:** *Magazine, Trade.*
Published by: Associazione Periti Industriali di Milano, Via del Carroccio 6, Milan, MI 20123, Italy. TEL 39-02-89408444, FAX 39-02-89408424, rivista@periti-industriali.milano.it, http://www.periti-industriali.milano.it. adv.: page EUR 1,300. Circ: 11,000 (paid).

PERSPECTIVES ON GLOBAL DEVELOPMENT AND TECHNOLOGY. *see* SOCIAL SCIENCES: COMPREHENSIVE WORKS

PERTANIKA JOURNAL OF SCIENCE AND TECHNOLOGY. *see* SCIENCES: COMPREHENSIVE WORKS

PHARMA TECHNOLOGIE JOURNAL. *see* PHARMACY AND PHARMACOLOGY

PHILICA; where ideas are free. *see* SCIENCES: COMPREHENSIVE WORKS

600 PHL ISSN 0116-7294
T1 CODEN: PTEJEB
PHILIPPINE TECHNOLOGY JOURNAL; a quarterly organ for Philippine technological researchers. Text in English. 1976. q. PHP 260, USD 60. adv. bk.rev. cum.index every 5 yrs. back issues avail.
Former titles: D O S T Technology Journal (0115-2777); National Science and Technology Journal; N S D B Technology Journal
Indexed: ChemAb, FS&TA, INIS AtomInd, IPP, PhilipAb.
—CASDDS, Ingenta, INIST, Linda Hall.
Published by: (Department of Science and Technology), Science and Technology Information Institute, P.O. Box 3596, Manila, Philippines. TEL 8220961. Ed. Ricardo M Lantican. Circ: 2,000.

PHILOSOPHY & TECHNOLOGY. *see* SOCIAL SCIENCES: COMPREHENSIVE WORKS

600 NLD ISSN 0923-0106
➤ **PHILOSOPHY AND TECHNOLOGY.** Text in English. 1983. irreg., latest vol.11, 1995. price varies. **Document type:** *Monographic series, Academic/Scholarly.*
Related titles: Online - full text ed.
—CCC.
Published by: (Society for Philosophy and Technology USA), Springer Netherlands (Subsidiary of: Springer Science+Business Media), Van Godewijckstraat 30, Dordrecht, 3311 GX, Netherlands. TEL 31-78-6576050, FAX 31-78-6576474. Ed. P E Vermaas.

▼ ➤ **PHILOSOPHY OF ENGINEERING AND TECHNOLOGY.** *see* ENGINEERING

600 DEU ISSN 0340-4366
QC47.G33
PHYSIKALISCH-TECHNISCHE BUNDESANSTALT. JAHRESBERICHT. Text in German. 1971. a. free. **Document type:** *Corporate.* **Description:** Describes activities of all laboratories of the PTB; includes a list of publications.
Indexed: GeoRef, SpeleolAb.
—BLDSC (4636.360000).
Published by: Physikalisch-Technische Bundesanstalt, Bundesallee 100, Braunschweig, 38116, Germany. TEL 49-531-5920, FAX 49-531-5929292, TELEX 952822-PTB-D, info@ptb.de. Circ: 1,800.

600 DEU ISSN 0341-7964
PHYSIKALISCH-TECHNISCHE BUNDESANSTALT. PRUEFREGELN. Text in German. 1967. irreg. **Document type:** *Bulletin.* **Description:** Instructions for testing measuring instruments and working equipment, including descriptions of testing procedures, necessary standard instruments and other appliances.
Published by: Physikalisch-Technische Bundesanstalt, Bundesallee 100, Braunschweig, 38116, Germany. TEL 49-531-5920, FAX 49-531-5929292, TELEX 592822-PTB-D, info@ptb.de. Ed. Helmut Klages.

THE PLAN; architecture & technologies in detail. *see* ARCHITECTURE

053.1 DEU
PLUGGED; technik & lifestyle. Text in German. bi-m. EUR 21 (effective 2007). adv. **Document type:** *Magazine, Consumer.* **Description:** Contains reviews and features on all aspects of consumer technologies and electronics.
Published by: Plugged Media GmbH, Franz-Haniel-Str 20, Moers, 47443, Germany. TEL 49-2841-887760, FAX 49-2841-8877629, info@plugged-media.de, http://www.pluggedmedia.de. Adv. contact Dirk Stachowski. B&W page EUR 4,619, color page EUR 7,118; trim 210 x 297. Circ: 42,000 (paid and controlled).

▼ **POIESIS ACADEMICA.** *see* SCIENCES: COMPREHENSIVE WORKS

600 300 DEU ISSN 1615-6609
➤ **POIESIS & PRAXIS**; international journal of ethics of science and technology assessment. Text in German. 2002. q. free (effective 2011). adv. back issues avail.; reprint service avail. from PSC. **Document type:** *Journal, Academic/Scholarly.* **Description:** Provides an interdisciplinary forum for reflection and deliberation on the scientific and technological future of our civilization.
Related titles: Online - full text ed.: ISSN 1615-6617 (from IngentaConnect).
Indexed: A01, A03, A08, A22, A26, CA, E01, P30, P52, SCOPUS, T02.
—BLDSC (6541.840600), IE, Ingenta. **CCC.**
Published by: SpringerOpen (Subsidiary of: Springer Science+Business Media), Tiergartenstr 17, Heidelberg, 69121, Germany. info@springeropen.com, http://www.springeropen.com. Ed. Carl Gethmann.

609 SWE ISSN 1653-4964
T14.7
➤ **POLHEM/JOURNAL FOR THE HISTORY OF TECHNOLOGY**; tidskrift foer teknikhistoria. Text in Danish, English, Norwegian, Swedish. 1983-2000; resumed 2002. a., latest 2004. SEK 150 per issue (effective 2007). back issues avail. **Document type:** *Monographic series, Academic/Scholarly.* **Description:** Covers the history of technology.
Formerly (until 2004): Polhem (0281-2142)
Published by: Svenska Nationalkommitten foer Teknik- och Vetenskabshistoria/Swedish National Committee for History of Technology and Science, c/o Kungliga Vetenskalbsakademien, Stockholm, 10405, Sweden. sntv@kva.se, http://www.sntv.kva.se. Ed. Anders Lundgren.

620 POL ISSN 0239-7528
CODEN: BASSEP
➤ **POLISH ACADEMY OF SCIENCES. BULLETIN. TECHNICAL SCIENCES.** Text in English. 1953. q. price varies. adv. bibl.; charts; illus. index. **Document type:** *Journal, Academic/Scholarly.*
Formerly (until 1983): Academie Polonaise des Sciences. Bulletin. Serie des Sciences Techniques (0001-4125)
Related titles: Online - full text ed.: free (effective 2011).
Indexed: ApMecR, CIN, CPEI, ChemAb, ChemTitl, EngInd, GeoRef, GeotechAb, IBR, IBZ, Inspec, KWIWR, MathR, SCI, SCOPUS, SpeleolAb, W07, Z02.
—AskIEEE, CASDDS, INIST, Linda Hall.
Published by: Polska Akademia Nauk, Centrum Upowszechniania Nauki/Polish Academy of Sciences, Center for the Advancement of Science, Palac Kultury i Nauki, PO Box 20, Warsaw, 00901, Poland. TEL 48-22-6204900, FAX 48-22-8272768, ceunpan@pan.pl, http://www.pan.pl. Ed. Tadeusz Kaczorek. R&P Andrzej Kostkowski. adv.: page USD 1,000. Circ: 150. **Dist. by:** Ars Polona, Obroncow 25, Warsaw 03933, Poland. TEL 48-22-5098609, FAX 48-22-5098610, arspolona@arspolona.com.pl, http://www.arspolona.com.pl.

509 POL ISSN 1232-9568
POLITECHNIKA KRAKOWSKA. MONOGRAFIE. SERIA: HISTORYCZNO-TECHNICZNA. Text in Polish. 1993. irreg. price varies. **Document type:** *Monographic series, Academic/Scholarly.*
Related titles: ◆ Series of: Politechnika Krakowska. Monografie. ISSN 0860-097X.
Published by: Politechnika Krakowska im. Tadeusza Kosciuszki/Tadeusz Kosciuszko Cracow University of Technology, ul Warszawska 24, Krakow, 31155, Poland. TEL 48-12-6374289, FAX 48-12-6374289. Ed. Elzbieta Nachlik. Adv. contact Ewa Malochleb.

600 POL
POLITECHNIKA KRAKOWSKA. MONOGRAFIE. SERIA: PODSTAWOWE NAUKI TECHNICZNE. Text in Polish; Summaries in English, German, French, Russian. 1985. irreg. price varies. bibl.; charts; illus. **Document type:** *Monographic series, Academic/Scholarly.*
Related titles: ◆ Series of: Politechnika Krakowska. Monografie. ISSN 0860-097X.
Published by: Politechnika Krakowska im. Tadeusza Kosciuszki/Tadeusz Kosciuszko Cracow University of Technology, ul Warszawska 24, Krakow, 31155, Poland. TEL 48-12-6374289, FAX 48-12-6374289. Circ: 200.

600 POL ISSN 0137-138X
POLITECHNIKA KRAKOWSKA. ZESZYTY NAUKOWE. PODSTAWOWE NAUKI TECHNICZNE. Text in Polish; Summaries in English, French, German, Russian. 1968. irreg. price varies. bibl.; charts; illus. **Document type:** *Monographic series, Academic/Scholarly.*
Indexed: Z02.
Published by: Politechnika Krakowska im. Tadeusza Kosciuszki/Tadeusz Kosciuszko Cracow University of Technology, ul Warszawska 24, Krakow, 31155, Poland. TEL 48-12-6374289, FAX 48-12-6374289. Ed. Elzbieta Nachlik. Adv. contact Ewa Malochleb. Circ: 200.

600 PRT ISSN 1645-006X
POLITECNIA. Text in Portuguese. 2000. q. **Document type:** *Journal, Academic/Scholarly.*
Published by: Instituto Politecnico de Lisboa, Estrada de Benfica, Lisbon, 1549-020, Portugal. TEL 351-217-101200, FAX 351-217-101235, http://www.ipl.pt.

600 PRT ISSN 0874-8799
POLITECNICA. Text in Portuguese. 2000. q. **Document type:** *Journal, Academic/Scholarly.*
Published by: Instituto Politecnico de Leiria, Rua Gen Norton de Matos, Leiria, 2411, Portugal. TEL 351-244-830010, http://www.ipleiria.pt.

POLITEKNIK DERGISI/GAZI UNIVERSITY. FACULTY OF TECHNICAL EDUCATION. JOURNAL OF POLYTECHNIC/JOURNAL OF POLYTECHNIC. *see* SCIENCES: COMPREHENSIVE WORKS

POLYMER. *see* CHEMISTRY

620 USA ISSN 0032-4558
T1
POPULAR MECHANICS. Text in English. 1902. m. USD 12 domestic (effective 2010). adv. illus. Index. 158 p./no.; back issues avail.; reprints avail. **Document type:** *Magazine, Consumer.* **Description:** Features information on the latest innovations in science and technology, and educates with informative 'how-to' stories on automotive, the home and digital technology.
Former titles (until 1959): Popular Mechanics Magazine (0736-993X); Which incorporated (in 1923): Illustrated World; (in 1931): Science and Invention; (until 1913): Popular Mechanics (0736-9913)

Related titles: Braille ed.; CD-ROM ed.; Microfiche ed.: (from NBI, PQC); Online - full text ed.: Popular Mechanics PMZone; ♦ Russian ed.: Populyarnaya Mekhanika; ♦ Spanish ed.: Popular Mechanics en Espanol. ISSN 1544-5216.
Indexed: A&ATA, A01, A02, A03, A06, A08, A09, A10, A11, A22, A23, A24, A25, A26, ARG, AcaI, B04, B07, B13, BRD, C03, C05, C12, CBCARef, CBPI, CPerI, ConsI, E08, G01, G05, G06, G07, G08, G09, GdIns, GeoRef, HRIS, I05, I06, I07, IHTDI, JHMA, M01, M02, M04, M05, M06, MASUSE, MELSA, MagInd, P02, P10, P13, P16, P47, P48, P52, P53, P54, PMR, PQC, R03, R04, R06, RGAb, RGPR, S01, S06, S08, S09, S23, SD, SpeleolAb, T02, TOM, U01, V02, V03, V04, W03, WBA, WMB.
—CIS, IE, Infotrieve, Ingenta, Linda Hall.
Published by: Hearst Magazines (Subsidiary of: Hearst Corporation), 300 W 57th St, 12th Fl, New York, NY 10019. TEL 212-649-4468, FAX 646-280-1069, HearstMagazines@hearst.com, http://www.hearst.com. Ed. James B Meigs. Adv. contact Wladar Jane. B&W page USD 88,635, color page USD 125,770; trim 7.875 x 10.5. Circ: 1,234,277 (paid).

620 ZAF ISSN 1682-5136
POPULAR MECHANICS (SOUTH AFRICA EDITION). Text in English. 2002. m. ZAR 225 domestic; ZAR 296 neighboring countries; ZAR 382 elsewhere (effective 2007). adv. **Document type:** *Magazine, Consumer.*
Published by: Ramsay, Son & Parker (Pty) Ltd., PO Box 180, Howard Place, Cape Town 7450, South Africa. TEL 27-21-5303100, FAX 27-21-5319495. Adv. contact Kim Black. color page ZAR 22,100; bleed 215 x 285.

620 MEX ISSN 1544-5216
POPULAR MECHANICS EN ESPANOL. (Editions avail. for Central America, Argentina, Brazil, Colombia, Educador, Mexico, Peru, Puerto Rico, US, Venezuela.) Text in Spanish. 1947. m. adv. illus. **Document type:** *Magazine, Consumer.* **Description:** Instructs readers about everything from automobiles to airplanes, electronics, cameras, audio and video equipment.
Formerly (until 2003): Mecanica Popular (0025-6420)
Related titles: Online - full text ed.; ♦ Russian ed.: Populyarnaya Mekhanika; ♦ English ed.: Popular Mechanics. ISSN 0032-4558.
Published by: Editorial Televisa, Vasco de Quiroga 2000, Edificio E, Colonia Santa Fe, Mexico City, DF 01210, Mexico. TEL 52-55-52612761, FAX 52-55-52612704, info@editorialtelevisa.com, http://www.esmas.com/editorialtelevisa/. Circ: 173,000.

620 USA ISSN 0161-7370
AP2 CODEN: PSCIEP
POPULAR SCIENCE. Text in English. 1872. m. USD 12; USD 4.99 newsstand/cover (effective 2011). adv. bk.rev. charts; illus.; pat.; tr.lit. index. back issues avail.; reprints avail. **Document type:** *Magazine, Consumer.* **Description:** Provides comprehensive coverage of a broad range of scientific and technological topics such as computers and electronics, energy, tools and techniques, and new products and inventions, as well as horticulture.
Formerly: Popular Science Monthly (0032-4647)
Related titles: CD-ROM ed.; Microfiche ed.: (from NBI, PMC, PQC); Online - full text ed.: PopSci.com.
Indexed: A01, A02, A03, A08, A09, A10, A11, A22, A25, A26, ABS&EES, AIA, ARG, AcaI, B04, B07, BIOSIS Prev, BRD, BiolDig, C03, C05, C11, C12, CADCAM, CBCARef, CBPI, CPerI, ConsI, E08, EIA, EnvAb, EnvInd, G01, G03, G05, G06, G07, G08, G09, GSA, GSI, GdIns, GeoRef, H03, I05, I06, I07, IHTDI, JHMA, M01, M02, M04, M05, M06, MASUSE, MELSA, MLA-IB, MagInd, MycolAb, P02, P10, P13, P15, P16, P26, P34, P47, P48, P52, P53, P54, PMR, PQC, R03, R04, R06, RGAb, RGPR, RGYP, RoboAb, S06, S08, S09, S10, S23, SpeleolAb, T02, TOM, TelAb, U01, V02, V03, V04, W03, W05, WBA, WMB.
—BLDSC (6550.990000), IE, Infotrieve, Ingenta, Linda Hall. **CCC.**
Published by: Bonnier Corp. (Subsidiary of: Bonnier Group), 2 Park Ave, 9th Fl, New York, NY 10016. TEL 212-779-5000, http://www.bonniercorp.com. Ed. Mark Jannot.

600 RUS
POPULYARNAYA MEKHANIKA/POPULAR MECHANICS. Text in Russian. 2002. m. USD 20.25 domestic; USD 119 foreign (effective 2005). **Document type:** *Magazine, Consumer.*
Related titles: ♦ English ed.: Popular Mechanics. ISSN 0032-4558; ♦ Spanish ed.: Popular Mechanics en Espanol. ISSN 1544-5216.
Published by: Independent Media (Moscow), 3 Polkovaya Ul, Bldg 1, Moscow, 127018, Russian Federation. TEL 7-095-2323200, FAX 7-095-2321761, podpiska@imedia.ru, http://www.independent-media.ru. Ed. Alexander Grek. Circ: 80,000.

POSITIVE ALTERNATIVES. *see* POLITICAL SCIENCE

POST; a magazine for the promotion of science and technology. *see* SCIENCES: COMPREHENSIVE WORKS

POUR LA SCIENCE. *see* SCIENCES: COMPREHENSIVE WORKS

PRACE Z DEJIN TECHNIKY A PRIRODNICH VED. *see* SCIENCES: COMPREHENSIVE WORKS

PRISMA (KASSEL). *see* SCIENCES: COMPREHENSIVE WORKS

600 DEU ISSN 1864-2802
PRO-4-PRO SICHERHEIT. Text in German. 1998. a. EUR 24 (effective 2010). **Document type:** *Directory, Trade.* **Description:** Focuses on market overviews, company portraits and text advertisements, and is a guide to purchasing and as a reference work. The major topics covered are automation, fire protection, information technology, instrument technology, safety, security, inspection procedures and environmental and process technology.
Formerly (until 2006): PRO-4-PRO Industrie (1610-3939)
Published by: G I T Verlag GmbH (Subsidiary of: Wiley - V C H Verlag GmbH & Co. KGaA), Roesslerstr 90, Darmstadt, 64293, Germany. TEL 49-6151-80900, FAX 49-6151-8090146, info@gitverlag.com. Ed. Steffen Ebert. Circ: 30,000.

PRO ZUKUNFT. *see* ENVIRONMENTAL STUDIES

600 UZB
CODEN: IUZTA4
PROBLEMY INFORMATIKI I ENERGETIKI. Text in Russian, Uzbek. 1957. bi-m.
Supersedes in part (in 1992): Akademiya Nauk Uzbekistana. Izvestiya. Seriya Tekhnicheskikh Nauk (1027-9792); Which was formerly (until 1991): Akademiya Nauk Uzbekskoi S.S.R. Izvestiya. Seriya Tekhnicheskikh Nauk (0516-2629)
Indexed: ChemAb, Inspec, SpeleolAb.
—CASDDS, INIST, Linda Hall.
Published by: (O'zbekiston Respublikasi Fanlar Akademiyasi/Academy of Sciences of Uzbekistan), Izdatel'stvo Fan, Ya Gulyamov ul 70, k 105, Tashkent, 700047, Uzbekistan.

600 UZB
CODEN: IUZTA4
PROBLEMY MEKHANIKI. Text in Russian, Uzbek. 1957. bi-m.
Supersedes in part (in 1992): Akademiya Nauk Uzbekistana. Izvestiya. Seriya Tekhnicheskikh Nauk (1027-9792); Which was formerly (until 1991): Akademiya Nauk Uzbekskoi S.S.R. Izvestiya. Seriya Tekhnicheskikh Nauk (0516-2629)
Indexed: ChemAb, Inspec, SpeleolAb.
—CASDDS, INIST, Linda Hall.
Published by: (O'zbekiston Respublikasi Fanlar Akademiyasi/Academy of Sciences of Uzbekistan), Izdatel'stvo Fan, Ya Gulyamov ul 70, k 105, Tashkent, 700047, Uzbekistan.

660 SWE ISSN 1652-0114
PROCESS NORDIC. Text in Swedish. 2003. m. SEK 408 domestic print ed.; SEK 510 domestic print & online eds.; SEK 608 foreign print ed.; SEK 710 foreign print & online eds.; SEK 306 online ed. (effective 2007). adv. back issues avail. **Document type:** *Magazine, Trade.*
Related titles: Online - full text ed.
Published by: Mentor Online AB, Tryffelslingan 10, PO Box 72001, Lidingoe, 18172, Sweden. TEL 46-8-6704100, FAX 46-8-6616455, info@mentoronline.se, http://www.mentoronline.se. Ed. Marie Granmar TEL 46-9-6704134. Adv. contact Stephan Martins TEL 46-8-6704185. Circ: 19,900.

PRODUCTS FINISHING. *see* PAINTS AND PROTECTIVE COATINGS

PRODUCTS FINISHING DIRECTORY. *see* PAINTS AND PROTECTIVE COATINGS

600 NLD
PRODUCTS4ENGINEERS.NL. Text in Dutch. 1972. irreg. adv. illus.; tr.lit. **Document type:** *Trade.* **Description:** For management in commercial enterprises.
Former titles (until 2009): Products4engineer (Print) (1879-0488); (until 2008): Technische Revue (0165-3202); Which superseded in part (1963-2004): Metaal & Kunststof (0026-0460)
Media: Online - full text. **Related titles:** ♦ Supplement(s): Elektronica Revue.
—IE.
Published by: Reed Business bv (Subsidiary of: Reed Business), Postbus 4, Doetinchem, 7000 BA, Netherlands. TEL 31-314-349911, FAX 31-314-343991, info@reedbusiness.nl, http://www.reedbusiness.nl. Ed. Maurice Matser. Pub. Rex Bierlaagh.

600 CAN ISSN 0701-1687
TS191P56
PRODUITS POUR L'INDUSTRIE QUEBECOISE. Abbreviated title: P I Q. Text in French. 1976. 6/yr. free domestic to qualified personnel (effective 2008). adv. back issues avail. **Document type:** *Magazine, Trade.*
Published by: C L B Media, Inc. (Subsidiary of: Canada Law Book Inc.), 240 Edward St, Aurora, ON L4G 3S9, Canada. TEL 905-727-0077, FAX 905-727-0017, http://www.clbmedia.ca. Ed. Tim Gouldson TEL 905-727-0077 ext 4390. Circ: 15,035 (controlled).

600 CHE
➤ **PROGRESS IN NUMERICAL SIMULATION FOR MICROELECTRONICS.** Text in English. 1991. irreg., latest vol.3, 1995. price varies. **Document type:** *Monographic series, Academic/Scholarly.*
Published by: Birkhaeuser Verlag AG (Subsidiary of: Springer Science+Business Media), Viaduktstr 42, Postfach 133, Basel, 4051, Switzerland. TEL 41-61-2050707, FAX 41-61-2050792, birkhauser@springer.de, http://www.birkhauser.ch. Eds. A Gilg, K Merten.

600 POL ISSN 0239-3174
PROJEKTOWANIE I SYSTEMY. Text in Polish; Summaries in English, Russian. a., latest vol.17, 2003. price varies. **Document type:** *Monographic series, Academic/Scholarly.* **Description:** Papers on designing process and system science.
Indexed: RASB.
Published by: Polska Akademia Nauk, Komitet Naukoznawstwa, Uniwersytet Warszawski, Centrum Badan Polityki Naukowej i Szkolnictwa Wyzszego, ul Nowy Swiat 69, Warsaw, 00046, Poland. TEL 48-22-6200381, ext 155.

PROSPECTIVA UNIVERSITARIA. *see* SCIENCES: COMPREHENSIVE WORKS

600 POL ISSN 0137-8783
HD8536
PRZEGLAD TECHNICZNY. Text in Polish. 1974. w. PLZ 270.27 domestic; EUR 164 foreign (effective 2011). adv. 32 p./no.; **Document type:** *Journal, Trade.*
Former titles (until 1982): Przeglad Techniczny, Innowacje (1230-8374); (until 1977): Innowacje (0208-5615); Which was formed by the merger of (1866-1974): Przeglad Techniczny (0033-2380); (1971-1974): Wektory (1230-8358); Which was formerly: Zeszyty Problemowe Przegladu Technicznego (1230-8382); (1960-1966): Przeglad Techniczny. Zeszyty Problemowe (1230-8366)
Related titles: Online - full text ed.
Indexed: AgrLib, CISA.
Published by: (Federacja Stowarzyszen' Naukowo-Technicznych NOT, Naczelna Organizacja Techniczna), Wydawnictwo SIGMA - N O T Sp. z o.o., ul Ratuszowa 11, PO Box 1004, Warsaw, 00950, Poland. TEL 48-22-8180918, FAX 48-22-6192187, sekretariat@sigma-not.pl. Ed. Ewa Mankiewicz-Cudny TEL 48-22-6510068. adv.: B&W page PLZ 3,300, color page PLZ 3,950. Circ: 12,000. **Dist. by:** Ars Polona, Obroncow 25, Warsaw 03933, Poland. TEL 48-22-5098609, FAX 48-22-5098610, arspolona@arspolona.com.pl, http://www.arspolona.com.pl. **Co-sponsor:** Polskie Towarzystwo Ekonomiczne.

PSYCHOLOGY. *see* PSYCHOLOGY

600 DEU ISSN 2191-7299
▼ **PUBLIC DISCLOSURE.** Text in German. 2011. irreg. **Document type:** *Monographic series, Trade.*
Published by: Prior Art Publishing GmbH, Dieffenbachstr 33, Berlin, 10967, Germany. TEL 49-30-26304025, FAX 49-30-32896808, office@priorartpublishing.com.

QINGDAO DAXUE XUEBAO (GONGCHENG JISHU BAN)/QINGDAO UNIVERSITY. JOURNAL (ENGINEERING & TECHNOLOGY EDITION). *see* SCIENCES: COMPREHENSIVE WORKS

QINGHAI KEJI/QINGHAI SCIENCE AND TECHNOLOGY. *see* SCIENCES: COMPREHENSIVE WORKS

QIYE JISHU JINBU/TECHNOLOGICAL DEVELOPMENT OF ENTERPRISE. *see* BUSINESS AND ECONOMICS

600 ESP ISSN 1133-2417
QUALITAS HODIE. Text in Spanish. 1996. m. EUR 135 domestic; EUR 177 in Europe; EUR 312 elsewhere (effective 2009). **Document type:** *Magazine, Trade.*
Published by: Ediciones Tecnicas Izaro S.A., Mazustegui, 21, 3a planta, Bilbao, Vizcaya 48006, Spain. TEL 34-94-4487110, FAX 34-94-4162743, izaro@izaro.com, http://www.izaro.com/izaro_2005/index.php.

QUANQIU KEJI JINGJI LIAOWANG/OUTLOOK ON GLOBAL SCIENCE, TECHNOLOGY AND ECONOMY. *see* SCIENCES: COMPREHENSIVE WORKS

QUARK. *see* SCIENCES: COMPREHENSIVE WORKS

QUEBEC SCIENCE. *see* SCIENCES: COMPREHENSIVE WORKS

600 USA
T175 CODEN: REDEEA
R & D MAGAZINE; where innovation begins. (Research & Development) Text in English. 1978. m. USD 63 domestic; USD 83 in Canada; USD 133 elsewhere; USD 11 per issue domestic; USD 20 per issue foreign; free domestic to qualified personnel (effective 2009). adv. bk.rev. charts; illus.; stat.; tr.lit. Index. back issues avail.; reprints avail. **Document type:** *Magazine, Trade.* **Description:** Designed for the lab, research and development and project managers across all industries, government and universities.
Former titles (until Jul. 1995): Research & Development (0746-9179); (until 1984): Industrial Research and Development (0160-4074); Which was formed by the merger of (1959-1978): Industrial Research (0019-8722); (1950-1978): Research - Development (0034-5199); Which was formerly (until 1960): Industrial Laboratories (0096-1671)
Related titles: Microfiche ed.: (from CIS); Microform ed.; Online - full text ed.: free (effective 2009); ♦ Supplement(s): R & D Product Source Telephone Directory.
Indexed: A09, A10, A12, A13, A14, A15, A17, A20, A22, A23, A24, A26, ABIPC, ABIn, ASCA, Agr, B01, B02, B03, B04, B06, B07, B08, B09, B11, B13, B15, B17, B18, BMT, BPI, BRD, BusI, C10, C12, C13, CA, CIN, CWI, Cadscan, ChemAb, ChemTitl, CompD, CurCont, CurPA, E08, E14, EIA, EnerInd, EngInd, G04, G05, G06, G07, G08, GALA, I05, ISR, Inspec, L09, LeadAb, MagInd, P02, P10, P26, P48, P51, P53, P54, PQC, RASB, S06, S09, S10, SCI, SCOPUS, SRI, SoftBase, T&II, T02, V03, V04, W01, W02, W03, W07, Zincscan.
—BLDSC (7218.301500), CASDDS, CIS, IE, Ingenta, INIST, Linda Hall. **CCC.**
Published by: Advantage Business Media, 100 Enterprise Dr, Ste 600, PO Box 912, Rockaway, NJ 07886. TEL 973-920-7000, FAX 973-920-7531, AdvantageCommunications@advantagemedia.com, http://www.advantagebusinessmedia.com. Eds. Paul Livingstone TEL 973-920-7032, Martha Walz TEL 973-920-7063. Pub. George Fox TEL 973-920-7035. adv.: B&W page USD 9,480, color page USD 11,535; trim 9 x 10.875. Circ: 80,000 (controlled).

338.0029 USA
T175
R & D PRODUCT SOURCE TELEPHONE DIRECTORY. (Research & Development) Text in English. 19??. a. adv. back issues avail. **Document type:** *Directory.* **Description:** Lists companies and individuals in the industrial research and development industry.
Former titles: Research and Development Product Source Guide; Research and Development Product Source Telephone Directory; (until 1992): Research and Development Telephone Directory
Related titles: ♦ Supplement to: R & D Magazine.
Published by: Advantage Business Media, 100 Enterprise Dr, Ste 600, PO Box 912, Rockaway, NJ 07886. TEL 973-920-7000, FAX 973-920-7531, AdvantageCommunications@advantagemedia.com, http://www.advantagebusinessmedia.com. Circ: 100,000 (controlled).

600 CUB ISSN 1684-6826
R E C I D T. (Revista Electronica del Centro de Investigacion y Desarrollo Tecnico) Variant title: Centro de Investigacion y Desarrollo Tecnico. Revista Electronica. Text in Spanish. 1999. q.
Media: Online - full text.
Published by: Centro de Investigacion y Desarrollo Tecnico, Calle E. Esq. 1 y Alday, Havana, Cuba.

500 600 USA
AS36.R344
RAND CORPORATION. ANNUAL REPORT. Text in English. a.
Former titles (until 1996): Rand (0162-8704); (until 1974): Rand Corporation. Annual Report (0485-9804)
—BLDSC (7254.270000). **CCC.**
Published by: Rand Corporation, 1700 Main St, Box 2138, Santa Monica, CA 90406-2138. TEL 310-393-0411, FAX 310-393-4818, http://www.rand.org.

RAND PUBLICATIONS SERIES. *see* SCIENCES: COMPREHENSIVE WORKS

RAPPORTO ENERGIA E AMBIENTE. *see* ENERGY

REAL ESTATE TECHNOLOGY. *see* REAL ESTATE

LA RECHERCHE. *see* SCIENCES: COMPREHENSIVE WORKS

679.9 DEU ISSN 1433-4399
RECYCLING MAGAZIN; Trends, Analysen, Meinungen und Fakten zur Kreislaufwirtschaft. Text in German. 1938. fortn. EUR 198.50; EUR 97.90 to students; EUR 10 newsstand/cover (effective 2011). adv. illus.; stat. index. **Document type:** *Magazine, Trade.*
Formerly (until 1996): Rohstoff Rundschau (0035-7863)
Related titles: Online - full text ed.
Indexed: TM.
—CCC.
Published by: ATEC Business Information GmbH, Hackerbruecke 6, Munich, 80335, Germany. TEL 49-89-89817364, FAX 49-89-89817350, stephan.krafzik@atec-bi.de. Ed. Stephan Peter Krafzik.

600 330 USA ISSN 1080-076X
HD9999.I49
THE RED HERRING (SAN FRANCISCO); the business of technology. Text in English. 1993 (Apr., no.20)-2003 (Mar.); N.S. 2005 (Jan.). m. illus. back issues avail.; reprints avail. **Document type:** *Magazine, Trade.* **Description:** Designed for anyone interested in the emerging technologies, trends, investments, companies and executives who build, finance and drive the global technology economy.
Related titles: Online - full text ed.: Redherring.com.
Indexed: A01, A02, A03, A08, A11, A26, B01, B02, B03, B06, B07, B08, B09, B11, B15, B17, B18, C05, C10, C23, CPerI, CWI, CompD, G04, G06, G07, G08, I05, I07, M02, MicrocompInd, SoftBase, T02, U01.
Published by: Red Herring, Inc., 1900 Alameda de Las Pulgas, Ste 112, San Mateo, CA 94403. TEL 650-428-2900, FAX 650-428-2901, Info@RedHerring.com. Pub. Alex Vieux.

600 CAN ISSN 1718-0627
RED RIVER COLLEGE FORUM: APPLIED RESEARCH AND INNOVATION. Text in English. 2004. irreg. **Document type:** *Monographic series, Academic/Scholarly.*
Formerly (until 2005): Red River College Journal of Applied Research (1710-985X)
Published by: Red River College, 2055 Notre Dame Ave, Winnipeg, MB R3H 0J9, Canada. TEL 204-632-3960, 888-515-7722.

RELIABILITY ENGINEERING & SYSTEM SAFETY. *see* ENGINEERING

620 USA ISSN 0034-4508
RENSSELAER ENGINEER. Text in English. 1947. irreg. (2-3/yr.). USD 10. adv. bk.rev. charts; illus. **Document type:** *Magazine, Trade.* **Description:** Engineering, science and technology journal of the students of Rensselaer Polytechnic Institute.
Published by: Rensselaer Polytechnic Institute, Rensselaer Union, 110 8th St, Troy, NY 12180-3590. TEL 518-266-6515. Ed. Paul Singh. Circ: 4,000.

600 JPN ISSN 2185-3525
Q180.J3
REPORT ON THE SURVEY OF RESEARCH AND DEVELOPMENT. Text in English, Japanese. 1954. a. stat. **Document type:** *Government.*
Superseded in part (in 2010): Kagaku Gijutsu Kenkyu Chosa Hokoku/ Report on the Survey of Research and Development (Year) (0447-5089); Which was formerly (until 1959): Kenkyu Kikan Kihon Tokei Chosa Kekka Hokoku (0286-1496); Incorporated (1978-1995): Kagaku Gijutsu Kenkyu Chosa Ni Futaisuru Energi Kenkyu Chosa Hokoku (0289-1328); (1983-1995): Kagaku Gijutsu Kenkyu Chosa Ni Futai Suru Raifu Saiensu Kenkyu Chosa Hokoku (0289-2626)
Published by: Japan. Ministry of Internal Affairs and Communications. Statistics Bureau/Somucho. Tokeikyoko, 19-1 Wakamatsu-cho, Shinjyuku-ku, Tokyo, 162-8668, Japan. TEL 81-3-5273-2020, http://www.stat.go.jp. **Subscr. to:** Japan Statistical Association, Meito Shinjuku Bldg, 6th Fl, 2-4-6 Shinjuku-ku, Tokyo 169-0073, Japan. TEL 81-3-53323151, http://www.jstat.or.jp/.

REPORTERO INDUSTRIAL; new equipment, machinery and techniques for industry. *see* MACHINERY

600 IND
RESEARCH & DEVELOPMENT IN INDUSTRY. Text in English. 1977. biennial. **Document type:** *Government.*
Published by: Department of Science and Technology, Technology Bhavan, New Mehrauli Rd, New Delhi, 110 016, India. TEL 91-11-26567373, FAX 91-11-26864570, dstinfo@nic.in.

600 500 JPN ISSN 0289-9329
RESEARCH AND DEVELOPMENT IN JAPAN AWARDED THE OKOCHI MEMORIAL PRIZE. Text in English. 1970. a.
—INIST.
Published by: Okochi Kinenkai/Okochi Memorial Foundation, 17-1 Toranomon 1-chome, Minato-ku, Tokyo, 105-0001, Japan.

RESEARCH & TECHNOLOGY TRANSPORTER. *see* TRANSPORTATION

RESEARCH COUNCIL OF ZIMBABWE. SYMPOSIUM ON SCIENCE AND TECHNOLOGY. PROCEEDINGS. *see* SCIENCES: COMPREHENSIVE WORKS

RESEARCH DEVELOPMENT AND TECHNOLOGICAL INNOVATION. *see* STATISTICS

600 BEL ISSN 1830-7361
RESEARCH*EU (ENGLISH EDITION); magazine for European research. (European Union) Text in English. 1993. 10/yr. free (effective 2010). **Document type:** *Magazine, Consumer.* **Description:** Provides information updates about European research programs including dates of calls for proposals, events, conferences, and publications.
Formerly (until 2007): R D T Info (1024-0802); Incorporates (1994-2007): C O R D I S Focus (English Edition) (1022-6559)
Related titles: French ed.: Research E U (French Edition). ISSN 1830-737X; German ed.: Research E U (German Edition). ISSN 1830-7388; Spanish ed.: Research E U (Spanish Edition). ISSN 1830-7396; ◆ Supplement(s): Research E U. Special Issue. ISSN 1830-7981.
Indexed: PAIS.
—BLDSC (8037.167000).
Published by: European Commission, Directorate General - Research, PO Box 2201, Luxembourg, 1022, Belgium. FAX 32-2-2958220. Ed. Michel Claessens TEL 32-2-2959971. Circ: 126,000.

001.891 BEL ISSN 1830-7981
RESEARCH E U. SPECIAL ISSUE; magazine of the European research area. (European Union) Text in English. 2007. q. free. **Document type:** *Magazine, Academic/Scholarly.*
Related titles: Online - full text ed.; ◆ Supplement to: Research*eu (English Edition). ISSN 1830-7361.
—BLDSC (7739.911000).
Published by: European Commission, Directorate General - Research, PO Box 2201, Luxembourg, 1022, Belgium. FAX 32-2-296-5987, ecsc-steel@cec.eu.int, http://www.cordis.lu/ecsc/home.html. Ed. Michel Claessens TEL 32-2-2959971.

RESEARCH HORIZONS. *see* ENGINEERING

RESEARCH INFORMATION. *see* SCIENCES: COMPREHENSIVE WORKS

▼ **RESEARCH JOURNAL OF APPLIED SCIENCE, ENGINEERING AND TECHNOLOGY.** *see* SCIENCES: COMPREHENSIVE WORKS

▼ **RESEARCH JOURNAL OF SCIENCE AND TECHNOLOGY.** *see* SCIENCES: COMPREHENSIVE WORKS

RESEARCH JOURNAL TELECOMMUNICATION AND INFORMATION TECHNOLOGY. *see* COMMUNICATIONS

600 GBR ISSN 0737-1071
HD45
➤ **RESEARCH ON TECHNOLOGICAL INNOVATION, MANAGEMENT AND POLICY.** Abbreviated title: R T I M P. Text in English. 1983. irreg., latest vol.9, 2005. price varies. back issues avail. **Document type:** *Monographic series, Academic/Scholarly.* **Description:** Provides valuable information to thoughtful managers, who increasingly source ideas from the world of science and technology, and compete to commercialize them in global markets.
Related titles: Online - full text ed.
Indexed: SCOPUS.
—BLDSC (7773.714000). **CCC.**
Published by: Emerald Group Publishing Ltd., Howard House, Wagon Ln, Bingley, W Yorks BD16 1WA, United Kingdom. TEL 44-1274-777700, FAX 44-1274-785201, emerald@emeraldinsight.com. Eds. Henry Chesbrough, Robert A Burgelman.

➤ **RESURSY. TEKHNOLOGII. EKONOMIKA.** *see* ENERGY

➤ **RETAIL TECHNOLOGY JOURNAL**; information, communication and security technologies within the trade. *see* BUSINESS AND ECONOMICS—Marketing And Purchasing

➤ **REVIEW OF SCIENCE AND TECNOLOGY IN ECONOMIC AND SOCIAL COMMISSION FOR WESTERN ASIA MEMBER COUNTRIES.** *see* SCIENCES: COMPREHENSIVE WORKS

600 500 BRA ISSN 1677-2504
HC79.T4
➤ **REVISTA BRASILEIRA DE INOVACAO.** Text in English, Portuguese, Spanish. 2002. s-a. bibl. back issues avail. **Document type:** *Journal, Academic/Scholarly.* **Description:** Publishes original articles in the fields of technology and innovation, including: Industrial economics; economics of technology; changes in organizational technology; economics and sociology of innovation; the working relationship between science and technology; innovation management; policies for science, technology and innovation; and the history of science and technology.
Related titles: Online - full text ed.: ISSN 2178-2822. free (effective 2011).
Published by: Universidade Estadual de Campinas, Instituto de Geociencias, Departamento de Politica Cientifica e Tecnologica, A/C Revista Brasileira de Inovacao, Caixa Postal 6152, Campinas, Sao Paulo 13083-870, Brazil. TEL 55-19-35215167, FAX 55-19-35214555. Ed., Pub. Wilson Suzigan. R&P, Adv. contact Monica Frigeri. **Co-publisher:** Ministerio da Ciencia e Tecnologia, Financiadora de Estudos e Projetos (F I N E P).

➤ **REVISTA C & T.** (Ciencia y Tecnologia) *see* SCIENCES: COMPREHENSIVE WORKS

➤ **REVISTA CIENTIFICA.** *see* SCIENCES: COMPREHENSIVE WORKS

600 COL ISSN 1692-7257
REVISTA COLOMBIANA DE TECNOLOGIAS DE AVANZADA. Text in Spanish. 2002. s-a. **Document type:** *Journal, Academic/Scholarly.*
Published by: Universidad de Pamplona, Facultad de Ciencias Basicas, Km. 1 Via Bucaramanga, Bucaramanga, Santander, Colombia. informacion@unipamplona.edu.co, http://www.unipamplona.edu.co/.

REVISTA DE CIENCIA & TECNOLOGIA. *see* SCIENCES: COMPREHENSIVE WORKS

REVISTA DE DERECHO Y NUEVAS TECNOLOGIAS. *see* LAW

REVISTA DE EGRESADOS. *see* COLLEGE AND ALUMNI

▼ **REVISTA DE ENGENHARIA E TECNOLOGIA.** *see* ENGINEERING

621.9 ESP ISSN 1132-7200
HC381
REVISTA DE HISTORIA INDUSTRIAL. Text in Spanish, Catalan. 1992. s-a. **Document type:** *Journal, Academic/Scholarly.*
Related titles: Online - full text ed.
Indexed: A20, ArtHuCI, CA, CurCont, EconLit, HistAb, JEL, SSCI, T02, W07.
Published by: (Universitat de Barcelona, Departament de Historia e Instituciones Economicas), Universitat de Barcelona, Servei de Publicacions, Gran Via Corts Catalanes 585, Barcelona, 08007, Spain. TEL 34-93-4021100, http://www.publicacions.ub.es. Ed. Alex Sanchez.

▼ **REVISTA DE HUMANIDADES MEDICAS & ESTUDIOS SOCIALES DE LA CIENCIA Y LA TECNOLOGIA/JOURNAL OF MEDICAL HUMANITIES & SOCIAL STUDIES OF SCIENCE AND TECHNOLOGY.** *see* SOCIOLOGY

REVISTA DE INVESTIGACIONES. *see* SCIENCES: COMPREHENSIVE WORKS

REVISTA DE LA SECYT. *see* SOCIAL SCIENCES: COMPREHENSIVE WORKS

600 ROM ISSN 1454-3087
➤ **REVISTA DE TEHNOLOGII NECONVENTIONALE/ NONCONVENTIONAL TECHNOLOGIES REVIEW.** Text in Romanian. q. free to qualified personnel (effective 2010). bk.rev. back issues avail. **Document type:** *Journal, Academic/Scholarly.* **Description:** Publishes original scientific papers about machining by means of nonconventional technologies, such as EDM (electrical discharge machining), ultrasonic, chemical and electro-chemical erosion, rapid prototyping, selective laser sintering etc. It reflects mainly the fundamental and experimental research activity concerning nonconventional technologies in Romania, papers presented at international conferences held in Romania, as well as the contributions of some specialists from abroad.
Related titles: Online - full text ed.
Indexed: P16, P48, P52, P53, P54, PQC.
Published by: Asociatia Romana de Tehnologii Neconventionale (ARTN)/Romanian Association for Nonconventional Technologies, University "Lucian Blaga" of Sibiu, str.Emil Cioran nr.4, sala IM, Sibiu, Romania. TEL 40-26-9231320, FAX 40-26-9231320, http:// www.artn.ro/. Ed., R&P Dan Nanu. Adv. contact Bungau Constantin TEL 40-25-9408136. **Co-sponsor:** Editurii "Politehnica".

600 370 BRA ISSN 1516-280X
REVISTA EDUCACAO & TECNOLOGIA. Text in Portuguese. 1997. s-a. **Document type:** *Magazine, Trade.*
Published by: (Centro Federal de Educacao Tecnologica do Parana (C E F E T - P R)), Associacao Brasileira de Engenharia de Producao (A B E P R O), Av Prof Almeida Prado 531, 1o Andar, Sala 102, Sao Paulo, 05508-900, Brazil. TEL 55-11-30915363, FAX 55-11-30915399, http://abepro.locaweb.com.br.

▼ **REVISTA ELECTRONICA IBEROAMERICANA DE EDUCACION EN CIENCIAS Y TECNOLOGIA.** *see* SCIENCES: COMPREHENSIVE WORKS

REVISTA INTERAMERICANA DE NUEVAS TECNOLOGIAS. *see* HUMANITIES: COMPREHENSIVE WORKS

600 COL
REVISTA T E D. (Tecne Episteme y Didaxis) Text in Spanish. 1991. s-a. **Document type:** *Journal, Academic/Scholarly.*
Formerly: Universidad Pedagogica Nacional. Facultad de Ciencia y Tecnologia. Revista (0121-3814)
Published by: Universidad Pedagogica Nacional, Facultad de Ciencia y Tecnologia, Edif. B Ofic. 222, Calle 72 No. 11-86, Bogota, Colombia. TEL 57-1-5941894, upn@uni.pedagogica.edu.co, http:// w3.pedagogica.edu.co/index.php?inf=1055&=.

600 BRA ISSN 1518-5540
REVISTA TECNOLOGIA. Text in Portuguese. 2000. s-a. **Document type:** *Journal, Academic/Scholarly.*
Published by: Universidade Luterana do Brasil, Centro de Tecnologia, Ave Farroupilha No. 8001, Bairro San Jose, Canoas, RS 92425-900, Brazil. TEL 55-51-3474000, FAX 55-51-34771313, ultra@ultra.br, http://www.ulbra.br/.

600 BRA ISSN 0101-8191
REVISTA TECNOLOGIA. Text in Portuguese. 1980. s-a. **Document type:** *Journal, Academic/Scholarly.*
Published by: (Universidade de Fortaleza, Centro de Ciencias Tecnologicas), Associacao Brasileira de Engenharia de Producao (A B E P R O), Av Prof Almeida Prado 531, 1o Andar, Sala 102, Sao Paulo, 05508-900, Brazil. TEL 55-11-30915363, FAX 55-11-30915399, http://abepro.locaweb.com.br.

600 BRA ISSN 1517-8048
REVISTA TECNOLOGICA. Text in Portuguese. 1992. a.
Indexed: A28, APA, BrCerAb, C&ISA, CA/WCA, CIA, CerAb, CivEngAb, CorrAb, E&CAJ, E11, EEA, EMA, H15, M&TEA, M09, MBF, METADEX, SolStAb, T04, WAA.
—Linda Hall.
Published by: Universidade Estadual de Maringa, Centro de Tecnologia, Av Colombo, 5790, Bloco C-67, Maringa, PR 87020-900, Brazil. TEL 55-44-2614321, FAX 55-44-2677368, sec-ctc@uem.br.

600 CUB ISSN 0864-1897
➤ **REVISTA TECNOLOGICA**; series: petroleo, electroenergetics, mineria-geologie, quimica. Text in Spanish. 1962-1975; resumed. s-a. USD 55 in the Americas; USD 65 elsewhere (effective 1999). adv. abstr.; bibl.; illus.; maps. back issues avail. **Document type:** *Monographic series, Academic/Scholarly.* **Description:** Publishes original articles that contribute to the development of the fields of electricity, chemistry, geology and mining.
Formerly: Nuestra Industria. Revista Tecnologia (0029-5736)
Related titles: E-mail ed.; Fax ed.
Indexed: C01, GeoRef, SpeleolAb.
Published by: (Cuba. Ministerio de Industria Basica), Divulgacion-Editorial, Calle San JOSE, 857, Havana, 10300, Cuba. TEL 537-702540, FAX 537-335345. Ed. Mario Chapottin Barco. Pub. Adis Suero Enriquez. Adv. contact Alba Iris Macias. Circ: 2,000. **Dist. by:** San Jose 857, Oquende y Soledad, Centro Habana CP-10300, Cuba.

➤ **REVUE D'HISTOIRE DES SCIENCES**; la revue pluridisciplinaire de l'histoire des sciences. *see* SCIENCES: COMPREHENSIVE WORKS

➤ **LA REVUE DU MANAGEMENT TECHNOLOGIQUE.** *see* BUSINESS AND ECONOMICS—Management

600 620 CHE ISSN 0374-4256
LA REVUE POLYTECHNIQUE. Text in French. 1898. m. CHF 81.85 domestic; CHF 61.40 domestic to libraries; CHF 90 in Europe; CHF 67.50 in Europe to libraries; CHF 180 elsewhere; CHF 135 elsewhere to libraries (effective 2001). adv. bk.rev. bibl.; charts; illus.; tr.lit. **Document type:** *Journal, Trade.* **Description:** Provides technical information of relevance to Swiss machine, electronics and information technology industries.
Indexed: CybAb, Inspec.
—BLDSC (7942.560000), IE, Ingenta, INIST, Linda Hall.
Published by: Polymedia Meichtry SA, Chemin de la Caroline 26, Petit-Lancy, 1213, Switzerland. TEL 41-22-8798820, FAX 41-22-8798825, info@polymedia.ch, http://www.polymedia.ch. Eds. Michel Giannoni, Pierre-Henri Bolle. R&P Michel Giannoni. Circ: 9,800.

620 LUX ISSN 0035-4260
CODEN: RTLXA4
REVUE TECHNIQUE LUXEMBOURGEOISE. Text in English, French, German. 1908. q. adv. bk.rev. bibl. index. **Document type:** *Journal, Trade.*
Indexed: ChemAb.
—CASDDS, Linda Hall.
Published by: Association Luxembourgeoise des Ingenieurs Architectes et Industriels, 4 bd Grande-Duchesse Charlotte, Luxembourg, 1330, Luxembourg. TEL 352-45-1354, FAX 352-45-0932. Ed. Michel Pundel. Circ: 3,000.

507.1 JPN ISSN 1346-1206
RIDAI KAGAKU FORAMU. Text and summaries in Japanese. 1984. m. **Description:** Contains reviews and commentary.
Formerly (until 2000): S U T Bulletin (0289-7016)
Published by: Tokyo Rika Daigaku/Tokyo University of Science, 1-3, Kagurazaka, Shinjuku Ku, Tokyo, 162-8601, Japan.

RIKOUGAKU TO GIJUTSU/ENGINEERING & TECHNOLOGY. *see* ENGINEERING

RIVISTA DEL CONSULENTE TECNICO. *see* BUILDING AND CONSTRUCTION

ROAD GEAR. *see* TRANSPORTATION—Automobiles

ROZPRAWY Z DZIEJOW NAUKI I TECHNIKI. *see* SCIENCES: COMPREHENSIVE WORKS

600 ARG ISSN 1852-7698
▼ ➤ **RUMBOS TECNOLOGICOS.** Text in Spanish. 2009. a. back issues avail. **Document type:** *Journal, Academic/Scholarly.*
Related titles: Online - full text ed.: ISSN 1852-7701.

Published by: Universidad Tecnologica Nacional, Facultad Regional Avellaneda, Ave Mitre 750, Avellaneda, 1870, Argentina. TEL 54-1776-42014133, infomacion@fra.utn.edu.ar, http://www.fra.utn.edu.ar/.

➤ **RUSSIA AND WORLD: SCIENCE AND TECHNOLOGY/ROSSIYA I MIR: NAUKA I TECHNOLOGIYA.** *see* SCIENCES: COMPREHENSIVE WORKS

➤ **THE RUTHERFORD JOURNAL**; the New Zealand journal for the history and philosophy of science and technology. *see* PHILOSOPHY

600 ZAF ISSN 1025-272X
S A INSTRUMENT & CONTROL BUYER'S GUIDE. (South Africa) Text in English. 1994. a. free (effective 2001). adv. **Document type:** *Handbook/Manual/Guide, Trade.*
Published by: Technews (Pty.) Ltd., PO Box 626, Kloof, 3640, South Africa. TEL 27-31-764-0593, FAX 27-31-764-0386, technews@iafrica.com.za. Ed. R K Beaumont. Pub. Kevin Beaumont. Adv. contact Jane Fortmann TEL 27-31-764-5316. Circ: 5,774.

S A T I JOURNAL OF SCIENCE AND TECHNOLOGY. *see* SCIENCES: COMPREHENSIVE WORKS

S & T POST. (Science and Technology) *see* SCIENCES: COMPREHENSIVE WORKS

300 600 USA
S H O T NEWSLETTER. Text in English. 1969. q. USD 10 to members. adv. back issues avail. **Document type:** *Newsletter.* **Description:** Circulates news among members of the society.
Published by: Society for the History of Technology, c/o Lindy Biggs, Sec, History Dept, 310 Thach Hall, Auburn University, Auburn, AL 36849-5259. TEL 334-844-6645, FAX 334-844-6673. Ed., Adv. contact Lindy Biggs. Circ: 2,100.

600 GBR
S I G S: MANAGING OBJECT TECHNOLOGY SERIES. (Special Interest Groups) Variant title: Managing Object Technology Series. Text in English. 1998. irreg., latest vol.23, 2003. price varies. back issues avail.; reprints avail. **Document type:** *Monographic series, Academic/Scholarly.* **Description:** Focuses on the managerial aspects of object orientation. Provides readers with information dealing with a wide range of issues related to managing object-oriented software projects.
Published by: Cambridge University Press, The Edinburgh Bldg, Shaftesbury Rd, Cambridge, CB2 8RU, United Kingdom. TEL 44-1223-312393, FAX 44-1223-315052, journals@cambridge.org, http://www.cambridge.org/uk. Ed. Barry McGibbon. R&P Linda Nicol TEL 44-1223-325702.

607.2 NOR ISSN 0802-3700
S I N T E F. AARSBERETNING. (Stiftelsen for Industriell og Teknisk Forskning) Text in Norwegian. 1950. a. back issues avail. **Document type:** *Report, Consumer.*
Related titles: Online - full text ed.: 2001.
Published by: S I N T E F Group/Foundation for Scientific and Industrial Research, Strindveien 4, Trondheim, 7465, Norway. TEL 47-73-593000, FAX 47-73-593350, info@sintef.no.

600 USA ISSN 0893-3499
S O L E - INTERNATIONAL SOCIETY OF LOGISTICS. PROCEEDINGS. Key Title: Proceedings of the Annual International Logistics Symposium. Text in English. 1966. a. price varies. adv. reprints avail. **Document type:** *Proceedings.* **Description:** Aims to assist attendees of symposium in their analytical work.
Formerly (until 198?): Society of Logistics Engineers. International Symposium Proceedings (0734-5461)
—CCC.
Published by: The S O L E - International Society of Logistics, 8100 Professional Pl, Suite 211, Hyattsville, MD 20785-2225. TEL 301-459-8446, FAX 301-459-1522, solehq@sole.org, http://www.sole.org.

600 500 JPN
S T A: ITS ROLES AND ACTIVITIES. (Science and Technology Agency) Text in English. a. free. **Document type:** *Government.*
Published by: Kagaku Gijutsu-cho/Science and Technology Agency, 2-1 Kasumigaseki 2-chome, Chiyoda-ku, Tokyo, 100-0013, Japan. FAX 81-3-3593-1370.

S T E MTRENDS; science, technology, engineering, mathematics. (Science, Technology, Engineering, Mathematics) *see* OCCUPATIONS AND CAREERS

600 DEU
SAECHSISCHE AKADEMIE DER WISSENSCHAFTEN, LEIPZIG. TECHNIKWISSENSCHAFTLICHE KLASSE. ABHANDLUNGEN. Text in German. 1998. irreg. price varies. **Document type:** *Monographic series, Academic/Scholarly.*
Published by: S. Hirzel Verlag, Postfach 101061, Stuttgart, 70009, Germany. TEL 49-711-25820, FAX 49-711-2582290, service@hirzel.de, http://www.hirzel.de.

600 DEU ISSN 1437-9716
SAECHSISCHE AKADEMIE DER WISSENSCHAFTEN, LEIPZIG. TECHNIKWISSENSCHAFTLICHE KLASSE. SITZUNGSBERICHTE. Text in German. 1999. irreg., latest vol.2, no.4, 2007. price varies. **Document type:** *Monographic series, Academic/Scholarly.*
Indexed: GeoRef.
—Linda Hall.
Published by: S. Hirzel Verlag, Postfach 101061, Stuttgart, 70009, Germany. TEL 49-711-25820, FAX 49-711-2582290, service@hirzel.de, http://www.hirzel.de.

500 JPN ISSN 0918-8177
SAITAMA KOGYO DAIGAKU KIYO/SAITAMA INSTITUTE OF TECHNOLOGY. Text in Japanese. 1992. a. **Document type:** *Journal, Academic/Scholarly.*
—BLDSC (4869.033000).
Published by: Saitama Kogyo Daigaku/Saitama Institute of Technology, 1690 Fusaiji, Okabe-machi, Osatogun, Saitama 369-0293, Japan. TEL 81-8-5852521, http://www.sit.ac.jp/.

SALARIES OF SCIENTISTS, ENGINEERS AND TECHNICIANS; a summary of salary surveys. *see* OCCUPATIONS AND CAREERS

600 KOR ISSN 1738-7752
TK1
SAMSUNG JOURNAL OF INNOVATIVE TECHNOLOGY. Text in English. 2005. s-a. **Document type:** *Journal, Academic/Scholarly.* **Description:** Covers all aspects of science, technology, and the commercialization of the technology fields in Samsung: Multimedia, communications & network, material, device, and analysis & simulation.
—BLDSC (8072.560500), IE.
Published by: Samsung Advanced Institute of Technology, Samsung Tech. Conference Administration office, PO Box 111, Suwon, 440-600, Korea, S. TEL 82-31-2809261.

SANG TAO/CREATIVITY. *see* BUSINESS AND ECONOMICS

658.5 JPN ISSN 0036-4371
SANGYO GIJUTSU JOHO YOKKAICHI/INDUSTRIAL AND TECHNOLOGICAL INFORMATION OF YOKKAICHI CITY. Text in Japanese. 1961. m. free. bk.rev. charts; illus.; pat.
Media: Duplicated (not offset).
Published by: Yokkaichi-shiritsu Toshokan/Yokkaichi City Library, 2-42 Kubota 1-chome, Yokkaichi-shi, Mie-ken 510-0821, Japan. Circ: (controlled).

SANTA CLARA COMPUTER AND HIGH TECHNOLOGY LAW JOURNAL. *see* LAW

SASKATCHEWAN RESEARCH COUNCIL. ANNUAL REPORT. *see* SCIENCES: COMPREHENSIVE WORKS

600 SAU ISSN 1319-2388
TN860
SAUDI ARAMCO JOURNAL OF TECHNOLOGY. Text in English. 1993. q. **Document type:** *Journal, Academic/Scholarly.*
Indexed: APIAb, PetrolAb, SCOPUS.
—Ingenta, Linda Hall, PADDS.
Published by: Saudi Aramco, R-2220 East Administration Bldg, P O Box 5000, Dhahran, 31311, Saudi Arabia. TEL 966-3-8720115, FAX 966-3-8738190, TELEX 801220 A SAO SJ, david.kaiser@aramco.com, webmaster@aramco.com.

SCANFILE. *see* BUSINESS AND ECONOMICS—Management

SCHOLARLY RESEARCH EXCHANGE. *see* SCIENCES: COMPREHENSIVE WORKS

600 DEU ISSN 0946-7939
CODEN: SCHUF8
SCHUETTGUT. Text in German. 1995. bi-m. EUR 156; EUR 66 to students; EUR 36 newsstand/cover (effective 2005). adv. **Document type:** *Journal, Trade.* **Description:** Interdisciplinary journal for the powder and bulk handling industries.
Indexed: TM.
—CASDDS. **CCC.**
Published by: Vogel TransTech Publications (Subsidiary of: Vogel Business Media GmbH & Co.KG), Max-Planck-Str 7/9, Wuerzburg, 97064, Germany. TEL 49-931-4182345, FAX 49-931-4182090, gerd.kielburger@vogel.de, http://www.vogel-media.de. Ed. Enno Mueller. Pub. Reiner Grochowski. Adv. contact Karl-Heinz Maisold. B&W page EUR 1,914, color page EUR 2,724; trim 180 x 270. Circ: 4,738 (paid and controlled).

600 CHE ISSN 1420-4827
SCHWEIZERISCHE MARKTSTATISTIK FUR TECHNISCHE SOFTWARE. Text in German. 1990. irreg.
Related titles: ♦ Supplement to: T R Transfer. ISSN 1023-0823.
Published by: Hallwag AG, Nordring 4, Bern, 3001, Switzerland. TEL 41-31-3355555, FAX 41-31-3355784.

SCI-TECH FOCUS. *see* SCIENCES: COMPREHENSIVE WORKS

SCIENCA REVUO. *see* SCIENCES: COMPREHENSIVE WORKS

SCIENCE & SOCIETY. *see* SCIENCES: COMPREHENSIVE WORKS

SCIENCE AND TECHNOLOGY DESK REFERENCE. *see* SCIENCES: COMPREHENSIVE WORKS

600 GBR
SCIENCE AND TECHNOLOGY FACILITIES COUNCIL. ANNUAL REPORT. Text in English. 1995. a. free (effective 2009). **Document type:** *Government.* **Description:** Outlines a year of significant scientific and technological achievement and selected highlights of the many economic and societal benefits resulting from STFC's wide array of research disciplines.
Former titles (until 2007): C C L R C. Annual Report and Accounts; (until 2002): Council for the Central Laboratory of the Research Councils. Annual Report (1366-235X); (until 1996): Daresbury and Rutherford Appleton Laboratories. Annual Report (1359-5865); (until 1995): Daresbury Laboratory
Related titles: Online - full text ed.
—Linda Hall.
Published by: Great Britain. Department for Business, Innovation and Skills. Science and Technology Facilities Council, Polaris House, North Star Ave, Swindon, SN2 1SZ, United Kingdom. TEL 44-1793-442000, FAX 44-1793-442002, enquiries@stfc.ac.uk.

SCIENCE AND TECHNOLOGY FOR CULTURAL HERITAGE. *see* SOCIAL SCIENCES: COMPREHENSIVE WORKS

SCIENCE AND TECHNOLOGY IN CONGRESS (ONLINE). *see* PUBLIC ADMINISTRATION

600 CHN ISSN 1674-7321
T1 CODEN: SCETFO
➤ **SCIENCE CHINA TECHNOLOGICAL SCIENCES.** Text in English. 1952. m. EUR 1,277, USD 1,576 combined subscription to institutions (print & online eds.) (effective 2012). reprint service avail. from PSC. **Document type:** *Journal, Academic/Scholarly.* **Description:** Contains academic papers on scientific work in the field of technological sciences.
Former titles (until 2010): Science in China. Series E: Technological Sciences; (until 2005): Science in China. Series E: Engineering & Materials Science; (until 2004): Science in China. Series E: Technological Sciences (1006-9321); Which superseded in part (in 1996): Science in China. Series A: Mathematics, Physics, Astronomy and Technological Sciences (1001-6511); Which was formerly (until 1989): Scientia Sinica. Series A: Mathematics, Physics, Astronomy and Technological Sciences (0253-5831); Which superseded in part (in 1981): Zhongguo Kexue (English Edition)/Scientia Sinica (0250-7870); Which was formerly (until 1954): Acta Scientia Sinica (0365-7183)
Related titles: Online - full text ed.: ISSN 1869-1900; ♦ Chinese ed.: Zhongguo Kexue. E Ji: Jishu Kexue. ISSN 1006-9275.
Indexed: A20, A22, A26, A28, APA, BrCerAb, C&ISA, CA/WCA, CCMJ, CIA, CPEI, CerAb, CivEngAb, CorrAb, CurCont, E&CAJ, E01, E11, EEA, EMA, ESPM, EngInd, EnvEAb, H15, I05, ISR, M&TEA, M09, MBF, METADEX, MSN, MathR, SCI, SCOPUS, SolStAb, T04, W07, WAA, Z02.
—BLDSC (8141.785000), AskIEEE, CASDDS, IE, Ingenta, INIST, Linda Hall. **CCC.**
Published by: Zhongguo Kexue Zazhishe/Science in China Press, 16 Donghuangchenggen North Street, Beijing, 100717, China. TEL 86-10-64010631, sale@scichina.com, http://www.scichina.com/. Ed. Luguang Yan. **Dist. in the Americas by:** Springer New York LLC, Journal Fulfillment, PO Box 2485, Secaucus, NJ 07096. TEL 212-460-1500, FAX 201-348-4505, journals-ny@springer.com; **Dist. outside the Americas by:** Springer, Haber Str 7, Heidelberg 69126, Germany. service@springer.de, http://www.springer.de. **Co-sponsors:** National Natural Science Foundation of China; Chinese Academy of Sciences/Zhongguo Kexueyuan.

➤ **SCIENCE STUDIES**; an interdisciplinary journal for science and technology studies. *see* SCIENCES: COMPREHENSIVE WORKS

600 300 DEU ISSN 1861-3675
Q175.4
➤ **SCIENCE, TECHNOLOGY AND INNOVATION STUDIES.** Abbreviated title: S T I Studies. Text in English. 2005. s-a. free (effective 2011). **Document type:** *Journal, Academic/Scholarly.* **Description:** Publishes analytical, theoretical and methodological studies on the creation and use of scientific knowledge and its relation to society, on the development of technology and its social impact and control and on innovation in industry and in the public sector.
Media: Online - full text.
Published by: Universitaet Dortmund, Wirtschafts- und Sozialwissenschaftliche Fakultaet, Dortmund, 44221, Germany. TEL 49-231-7553281, FAX 49-231-7553293, http://www.wiso.tu-dortmund.de/wiso/de/fakultaet. Eds. Ingo Schulz-Schaeffer, Johannes Weyer, Raymund Werle.

➤ **SCIENCE, TECHNOLOGY AND SOCIETY**; curriculum newsletter. *see* EDUCATION—Higher Education

620 GBR ISSN 0141-9099
➤ **SCIENCE TECHNOLOGY JOURNAL.** Cover title: Science Technology. Text in English. 1955. q. membership. adv. bk.rev. abstr. **Document type:** *Journal, Academic/Scholarly.*
Formerly (until 1989): Institute of Science Technology. Bulletin (0020-3130)
Indexed: A&ATA.
Published by: Institute of Science Technology, Stowe House, Netherstowe, Lichfield, Staffs WS13 6TJ, United Kingdom. TEL 44-1543-251346, FAX 44-1543-415804. Ed. Ian Gray. Circ: 1,500 (controlled).

➤ **SCIENCES ET TECHNIQUES EN PERSPECTIVE/SCIENCES AND TECHNOLOGY IN PERSPECTIVE.** *see* HISTORY

➤ **SCIENCES ET TECHNIQUES EN PERSPECTIVES.** *see* SCIENCES: COMPREHENSIVE WORKS

➤ **SCIENTIFIC AND TECHNICAL INFORMATION IN FOREIGN COUNTRIES/KAIGAKI KAGAKU GIJUTSU JOHO SHIRYO.** *see* SCIENCES: COMPREHENSIVE WORKS

➤ **THE SCITECH LAWYER.** *see* LAW

621.9 GBR ISSN 2040-5421
➤ **SCOTTISH BUSINESS AND INDUSTRIAL HISTORY.** Abbreviated title: S I H. Text in English. 1969. s-a. free to members (effective 2009). bk.rev. illus. 1977-2000 included in vol 21 (2000). back issues avail. **Document type:** *Journal, Academic/Scholarly.* **Description:** Contains articles by professional and amateur historians, covering a wide range of topics on Scotland's industrial past.
Former titles (until 2008): Scottish Industrial History (0266-7428); (until 1976): Scottish Society for Industrial Archaeology. Newsletter
Indexed: FR.
—INIST.
Published by: University of Glasgow, Business Archives Council of Scotland, Archive Services, University of Glasgow, 77-87 Dumbarton Rd, Glasgow, Scotland G11 6PW, United Kingdom. TEL 44-141-3304159, FAX 44-141-3304158, bacs@archives.gla.ac.uk, http://www.gla.ac.uk/archives/bacs.

600 607 USA ISSN 0080-830X
SCRIPPS CLINIC AND RESEARCH FOUNDATION. ANNUAL REPORT. Text in English. 1924. a. free.
Published by: Scripps Clinic and Research Foundation, 10666 N Torrey Pines Rd, La Jolla, CA 92037. TEL 619-455-9100, FAX 619-554-8841. Circ: 5,000.

SCRIPT-ED. *see* LAW

600 ITA ISSN 1723-168X
SCUOLA OFFICINA; periodico di cultura tecnica. Text in Italian. 1992 (vol.11). s-a. EUR 10.33 (effective 2005). **Document type:** *Magazine, Consumer.*
Published by: Museo del Patrimonio Industriale, Via della Beverara, Bologna, BO 40131, Italy. TEL 39-051-635661, FAX 39-051-6346053, museopat@comune.bologna.it, http://www.comune.bologna.it/patrimonioindustriale/sito/it/home.htm. Ed. Roberto Curti.

SECURITY PRODUCTS & TECHNOLOGY NEWS. *see* CRIMINOLOGY AND LAW ENFORCEMENT—Security

SEE-SCIENCE.EU. *see* SCIENCES: COMPREHENSIVE WORKS

600 JPN ISSN 0037-105X
TS183 CODEN: SEKEAI
SEISAN KENKYU/PRODUCTION RESEARCH. Text in English, Japanese. 1949. m. free. charts; illus. **Document type:** *Journal, Academic/Scholarly.*
Related titles: Online - full text ed.: ISSN 1881-2058.
Indexed: A28, AJEE, APA, ApMecR, BrCerAb, C&ISA, CA/WCA, CIA, CerAb, ChemAb, ChemTitl, CivEngAb, CorrAb, E&CAJ, E11, EEA, EMA, H15, INIS AtomInd, Inspec, M&TEA, M09, MBF, METADEX, RefZh, RoboAb, SolStAb, T04, WAA.
—BLDSC (8219.800000), AskIEEE, CASDDS, INIST, Linda Hall.

TU

Published by: University of Tokyo, Institute of Industrial Science/Tokyo Daigaku Seisan Gijutsu Kenkyujo, Komaba Research Campus, 4-6-1 Komaba Meguro-ku, Tokyo, 153-8505, Japan. TEL 81-3-54526024, FAX 81-3-54526094, kokusai@iis.u-tokyo.ac.jp, http://www.iis.u-tokyo.ac.jp/. Circ: 1,980.

SELSKOSTOPANSKA TEKHNIKA. *see* AGRICULTURE—Agricultural Equipment

600 370 AUS ISSN 1832-4827
SENIOR SECONDARY ASSESSMENT BOARD OF SOUTH AUSTRALIA TECHNOLOGY SHOW. Text in English. 200?. a., latest 2006. back issues avail. **Document type:** *Journal, Consumer.* **Description:** Provides information about Senior Secondary Assessment Board of South Australia technology show.
Related titles: Online - full text ed.
Published by: Senior Secondary Assessment Board of South Australia, 60 Greenhill Rd, Wayville, SA 5034, Australia. TEL 61-8-83727400, FAX 61-8-83727590, info@ssabsa.sa.gov.au, http://www.ssabsa.sa.edu.au.

SERIES ON INFORMATION DISPLAY. *see* ELECTRONICS

600 GBR ISSN 0219-9823
SERIES ON TECHNOLOGY MANAGEMENT. Text in English. 1998. irreg., latest vol.17, 2010. price varies. 300 p./no.; back issues avail. **Document type:** *Monographic series, Academic/Scholarly.* **Description:** Provides information for practicing managers, consultants and academics interested or responsible for measuring and improving the management of technology and innovation.
—BLDSC (8250.202490).
Published by: Imperial College Press (Subsidiary of: World Scientific Publishing Co. Pte. Ltd.), 57 Shelton St, Covent Garden, London, WC2H 9HE, United Kingdom. TEL 44-20-78360888, FAX 44-20-78362020, edit@icpress.co.uk, http://www.icpress.co.uk/. **Subscr. addr. in the US:** World Scientific Publishing Co., Inc., 27 Warren St, Ste 401-402, Hackensack, NJ 07601. TEL 201-487-9655, 800-227-7562, FAX 201-487-9656, 888-977-2665, wspc@wspc.com; **Dist. by:** World Scientific Publishing Ltd.

SERIES ON THE FOUNDATIONS OF NATURAL SCIENCE AND TECHNOLOGY. *see* SCIENCES: COMPREHENSIVE WORKS

600 500 BEL
T10.65.B4 CODEN: CDORBV
SERVICE D'INFORMATION SCIENTIFIQUE ET TECHNIQUE. RAPPORT D'ACTIVITE. Text in Dutch. 1964. biennial. free. index. **Document type:** *Directory.* **Description:** Offers a concise evaluation of activities and accomplishments of the year. Also reports on results of the previous years, to illuminate long-term projects.
Formerly: Centre National de Documentation Scientifique et Technique. Rapport d'Activite (0069-1968)
Indexed: GeoRef, SpeleolAb.
—INIST, Linda Hall.
Published by: Service d'Information Scientifique et Technique, Bd de l'Empereur 4, Brussels, 1000, Belgium. TEL 32-2-519-5640, FAX 32-2-519-5645. Circ: 1,000 (controlled).

SERVO. *see* COMPUTERS—Robotics

600 RUS ISSN 0321-2653
T4 CODEN: ISSND8
SEVERO-KAVKAZSKII NAUCHNYI TSENTR VYSSHEI SHKOLY. TEKHNICHESKIE NAUKI. IZVESTIYA/NORTH-CAUCASUS SCIENTIFIC CENTER OF HIGH SCHOOL. TECHNICAL SCIENCE. NEWS. Text in Russian. 4/yr.
Indexed: RefZh, Z02.
—CASDDS.
Published by: Rostovskii Universitet, Pushkinskaya ul 160, Rostov-on-Don, 344700, Russian Federation. TEL 8-8630536411, TELEX 123520.

SHANDONG GONGSHANG XUEYUAN XUEBAO/SHANDONG INSTITUTE OF BUSINESS AND TECHNOLOGY. JOURNAL. *see* BUSINESS AND ECONOMICS

SHANDONG LIGONG DAXUE XUEBAO (ZIRAN KEXUE BAN)/ SHANDONG UNIVERSITY OF TECHNOLOGY. JOURNAL (SCIENCE AND TECHNOLOGY). *see* SCIENCES: COMPREHENSIVE WORKS

600 500 CHN ISSN 1006-2467
Q4 CODEN: SCTPDH
SHANGHAI JIAOTONG DAXUE XUEBAO. Text in Chinese; Summaries in Chinese, English. 1956. m. **Document type:** *Journal, Academic/Scholarly.* **Description:** Covers education, research and alumni affairs in the university.
Formerly: Shanghai Jiaotong Daxue Xuebao/Shanghai Jiaotong University. Bulletin (0253-9942)
Related titles: Online - full text ed.; ◆ English ed.: Shanghai Jiaotong University. Journal. ISSN 1007-1172.
Indexed: A22, A28, APA, ASFA, ApMecR, BrCerAb, C&ISA, CA/WCA, CCMJ, CIA, CPEI, CerAb, ChemAb, ChemTitl, CivEngAb, CorrAb, E&CAJ, E11, EEA, EMA, ESPM, EngInd, EnvEAb, H15, Inspec, M&TEA, M09, MBF, METADEX, MSN, MathR, SCOPUS, SolStAb, T04, WAA, Z02.
—BLDSC (4874.780000), AskIEEE, CASDDS, East View, IE, Ingenta, Linda Hall.
Published by: Shanghai Jiaotong Daxue/Shanghai Jiaotong University, 1954 Huasha Lu, Shanghai, 200030, China. TEL 86-21-62933373, FAX 86-21-62933373, http://www.sjtu.edu.cn/. Circ: 3,000.

600 500 CHN ISSN 1007-1172
Q4
➤ **SHANGHAI JIAOTONG UNIVERSITY. JOURNAL.** Text in English. 1996. bi-m. EUR 900, USD 1,198 combined subscription to institutions (print & online eds.) (effective 2012). reprint service avail. from PSC. **Document type:** *Journal, Academic/Scholarly.* **Description:** Covers the scientific research achievements at the University.
Related titles: Online - full text ed.: ISSN 1995-8188; ◆ Chinese ed.: Shanghai Jiaotong Daxue Xuebao. ISSN 1006-2467.
Indexed: A22, A26, A28, APA, ASFA, ApMecR, B21, BrCerAb, C&ISA, CA/WCA, CIA, CPEI, CerAb, CivEngAb, CorrAb, E&CAJ, E01, E08, E11, EEA, EMA, ESPM, EngInd, EnvEAb, H15, Inspec, M&TEA, M09, MBF, METADEX, NSA, R10, Reac, S09, SCOPUS, SolStAb, T04, WAA, Z02.
—BLDSC (4874.782000), East View, IE, Ingenta, Linda Hall. **CCC.**
Published by: Shanghai Jiaotong Daxue/Shanghai Jiaotong University, 1954 Huasha Lu, Shanghai, 200030, China. TEL 86-21-62933373, FAX 86-21-62933373, http://www.sjtu.edu.cn/. Circ: 1,000. **Co-publisher:** Springer.

600 CHN ISSN 1007-6735
T4 CODEN: SLDXFQ
SHANGHAI LIGONG DAXUE XUEBAO. Text in Chinese. 1979. bi-m. USD 31.20 (effective 2009). **Document type:** *Journal, Academic/Scholarly.*
Former titles (until 1997): Huadong Gongye Daxue Xuebao (1007-0761); (until 1996): Shanghai Jixie Xueyuan Xuebao (1000-1921)
Related titles: Online - full text ed.
Indexed: A28, APA, BrCerAb, C&ISA, CA/WCA, CIA, CerAb, CivEngAb, CorrAb, E&CAJ, E11, EEA, EMA, ESPM, EngInd, EnvEAb, H15, M&TEA, M09, MBF, METADEX, RefZh, SCOPUS, SolStAb, T04, WAA.
—BLDSC (8254.589799), East View, Linda Hall.
Published by: Shanghai Ligong Daxue/University of Shanghai for Science and Technology, 516, Jungong Lu, Shanghai, 200093, China. TEL 86-21-65687251. **Dist. by:** China International Book Trading Corp, 35 Chegongzhuang Xilu, Haidian District, PO Box 399, Beijing 100044, China. TEL 86-10-68412045, FAX 86-10-68412023, cibtc@mail.cibtc.com.cn, http://www.cibtc.com.cn.

SHANXI DIANZI JISHU/SHANXI ELECTRONIC TECHNOLOGY. *see* ELECTRONICS

SHIJIE KEXUE JISHU/WORLD SCIENCE AND TECHNOLOGY. *see* SCIENCES: COMPREHENSIVE WORKS

607 JPN ISSN 0919-9403
T7 CODEN: SGKEE2
SHIKOKU KOGYO GIJUTSU KENKYUJO HOKOKU/SHIKOKU NATIONAL INDUSTRIAL RESEARCH INSTITUTE. REPORTS. Text in Japanese. 1968. s-a.
Formerly (until 1993): Shikoku Kogyo Gijutsu Shikenjo Hokoku - Government Industrial Research Institute, Sikoku. Reports (0389-3375)
—CASDDS.
Published by: Shikoku Kogyo Gijutsu Kenkyujo, 2217-14 Hayashi-cho, Takamatsu-shi, Kagawa-ken 761-0301, Japan.

502.8 CHN ISSN 1002-4956
CODEN: SJYGAR
SHIYAN JISHU YU GUANLI/EXPERIMENTAL TECHNOLOGY AND MANAGEMENT. Text in Chinese; Summaries in English, Chinese. 1963. m. USD 64.80 (effective 2009). **Document type:** *Journal, Academic/Scholarly.* **Description:** Covers theoretical research and innovation involving experimental technology.
Indexed: A28, APA, BrCerAb, C&ISA, CA/WCA, CIA, CerAb, CivEngAb, CorrAb, E&CAJ, E11, EEA, EMA, ESPM, EnvEAb, H15, M&TEA, M09, MBF, METADEX, SolStAb, T04, WAA.
—East View.
Address: Equipment Department Courtyard, Tsinghua University, Beijing, 100084, China. TEL 86-10-62783005, FAX 86-10-62783005, bjbzhou@tsiinghua.edu.cn. Ed. De-hua Li. Circ: 6,000 (controlled).

600 CHN ISSN 1006-7167
SHIYANSHI YANJIU YU TANSUO/RESEARCH AND EXPLORATION IN LABORATORY. Text in Chinese. 1982. m. CNY 960 (effective 2008 & 2009). **Document type:** *Journal, Academic/Scholarly.* **Description:** Covers theoretical foundation and application in Physics,Chemistry,Biologic,Electrical and Electhronic Engineering, Computer,Mechanical,Automatic Control Technique and others.
Related titles: Online - full text ed.
Indexed: A28, APA, BrCerAb, C&ISA, CA/WCA, CIA, CerAb, CivEngAb, CorrAb, E&CAJ, E11, EEA, EMA, ESPM, EnvEAb, H15, M&TEA, M09, MBF, METADEX, RefZh, SolStAb, T04, WAA.
—BLDSC (8267.297590).
Published by: Shanghai Jiaotong Daxue/Shanghai Jiaotong University, Rm1501, Baozhaolong Library, 1954 Huasha Lu, Shanghai, 200030, China. TEL 86-21-62932952, FAX 86-21-62932952. Ed. You-wei Xia. Circ: 7,000.

600 JPN ISSN 0387-0014
CODEN: SHIZAO
SHIZEN/NATURE. Text in Japanese. 1946. m. JPY 8,450.
Indexed: ChemAb, ISR.
—CASDDS.
Published by: Chuokoron-Sha Inc., 2-8-7 Kyobashi, Chuo-ku, Tokyo, 104-0031, Japan. Ed. Akihiko Okabe.

SHOKUBUTSU KANKYOU KOUGAKU/SOCIETY OF HIGH TECHNOLOGY IN AGRICULTURE. JOURNAL. *see* AGRICULTURE

600 CHN
SHUZI JISHU YU YINGYONG/DIGITAL TECHNOLOGY AND APPLICATION. Text in Chinese. 1982. m. CNY 15 per issue (effective 2009).
Former titles: Dianzi yu Jin Xilie Gongcheng Xinxi/Electronics & Golden Projects Collection (1007-9416); (until 1998): Xinxi-Dianzi yu Zidonghua Yibiao (1007-6379); Which was formed by the 1981 merger of: Guowai Yidian Dongtai; (1980-1981): Yidian Jishu; Which was formerly: Keji Qingbao
Published by: (Tianjin Shi Dianzi Yibiao Xinxi Yanjiusuo USA), Digital Technology and Application Editorial Office, Chaoyang-qu, Yixian Guoji, Beijing, 100025, China. TEL 86-10-86175100. Ed. Changji Wei.

600 DEU ISSN 0934-9391
SIEG TECH. Text in German. 1985. 20/yr. EUR 310 (effective 2001). adv. bk.rev. back issues avail. **Document type:** *Journal, Trade.*
Published by: Sieg Tech Verlags GmbH, Gottfried-Claren-Str 21, Bonn, 53225, Germany. TEL 49-228-466034, FAX 49-228-477418, sieg.tech@t-online.de. Ed. Manfred Sieg. Circ: 15,000.

600 USA ISSN 2159-0060
▼ **SIGNAGE SOLUTIONS MAGAZINE.** Text in English. 2010. bi-m. free to qualified personnel (effective 2011). **Document type:** *Magazine, Trade.*
Related titles: Online - full text ed.
Published by: Partners Publishers, 306 S Tennessee, McKinney, TX 75069. TEL 972-587-9064, info@partnerspr.com, http://www.partnerspr.com/. Pub. Ben Skidmore TEL 972-587-9064.

SILICONEER. *see* ETHNIC INTERESTS

SILICONINDIA; technology and business magazine. *see* COMPUTERS—Computer Industry

SILPAKORN UNIVERSITY. SCIENCE AND TECHNOLOGY JOURNAL. *see* SCIENCES: COMPREHENSIVE WORKS

500 600 NLD ISSN 2210-3864
SIMON STEVIN GEZEL. Variant title: Technologisch Toptalent. Text in Dutch. 2007. a.
Published by: Technologiestichting S T W, Postbus 3021, Utrecht, 3502 GA, Netherlands. TEL 31-30-6001211, FAX 31-30-6014408, info@stw.nl, http://www.stw.nl.

SIMON STEVIN SERIES IN THE PHILOSOPHY OF TECHNOLOGY. *see* PHILOSOPHY

SINGAPORE TECHNOLOGY & COMPUTING. *see* BUSINESS AND ECONOMICS—Trade And Industrial Directories

SISTEMA NACIONAL DE INFORMACION CIENTIFICA Y TECNOLOGIA. BOLETIN. *see* SCIENCES: COMPREHENSIVE WORKS

SMITHSONIAN. *see* SOCIAL SCIENCES: COMPREHENSIVE WORKS

SOCIEDAD LATINOAMERICANA DE HISTORIA DE LA CIENCIA Y LA TECNOLOGIA. BOLETIN INFORMATIVO. *see* SCIENCES: COMPREHENSIVE WORKS

600 USA ISSN 0160-1067
T37
SOCIETY FOR INDUSTRIAL ARCHEOLOGY. NEWSLETTER. Abbreviated title: S I A N. Text in English. 1972. q. free to members (effective 2010). bk.rev. bibl. **Document type:** *Newsletter, Academic/Scholarly.* **Description:** Examines current activity in the preservation of post-18th century technologies and industries.
Related titles: Online - full text ed.: free (effective 2010).
Indexed: AIAP.
Published by: Society for Industrial Archeology, Department of Social Sciences, 1400 Townsend Dr, Houghton, MI 49931. TEL 906-487-1889, sia@mtu.edu. Ed. Patrick Harshbarger.

SOCIETY FOR UNDERWATER TECHNOLOGY. NEWS. *see* EARTH SCIENCES—Oceanography

SOGO GAKUJUTSU KENKYU SHUKAI. *see* SCIENCES: COMPREHENSIVE WORKS

600 500 JPN ISSN 0289-5560
SOGO KENKYUJO HOKOKU. Text in Japanese. 1984. a. **Description:** Provides news of the institute.
Published by: Tokyo Rika Daigaku, Sogo Kenkyujo/Science University of Tokyo, Research Institute for Science and Technology, 2641 Yamazaki, Noda-shi, Chiba-ken 278-0022, Japan.

IL SOLE 24 ORE. BIBLIOTECA DEL SAPERE. *see* HUMANITIES: COMPREHENSIVE WORKS

600 AUS ISSN 1832-651X
SOLVE; a CSIRO review of scientific innovations for Australian industry. Text in English. 2004. q. free (effective 2008). back issues avail. **Document type:** *Magazine, Trade.* **Description:** Provides information on business and industry of the emerging science and technology that is coming through the pipeline from CSIRO.
Formerly: Innovations
Related titles: Online - full text ed.: free (effective 2008).
Published by: C S I R O, 150 Oxford St, PO Box 1139, Collingwood, VIC 3066, Australia. TEL 61-3-96627500, FAX 61-3-96627611, publishing@csiro.au, http://www.publish.csiro.au/. Ed. Kelly Claudius TEL 61-2-94908275.

SONGKLANAKARIN JOURNAL OF SCIENCE AND TECHNOLOGY. *see* SCIENCES: COMPREHENSIVE WORKS

620.1 JPN ISSN 0038-1586
TS200 CODEN: SOKAB9
SOSEI TO KAKO/JAPAN SOCIETY FOR TECHNOLOGY OF PLASTICITY. JOURNAL. Text in Japanese; Summaries in English. 1960. m. free to members. adv. bk.rev. abstr.; charts; bibl. cum.index. back issues avail. **Document type:** *Journal, Academic/Scholarly.* **Description:** Contains original research papers, explanations and reviews which describe the present state and future tendencies in the field of plasticity and related technologies.
Indexed: A22, CIN, ChemAb, ChemTitl, INIS AtomInd, JTA.
—BLDSC (4808.150000), CASDDS, IE, Ingenta, Linda Hall. **CCC.**
Published by: Nihon Sosei Kako Gakkai/Japan Society for Technology of Plasticity, Y.S.K Bldg.4F, 1-3-11 Shibadaimon, Minato-ku, Tokyo, 105-0012, Japan. TEL 81-3-34358301, FAX 81-3-57333730, jstp@jstp.or.jp. Circ: 5,000.

600 ZAF ISSN 1025-1812
SOUTH AFRICA INSTRUMENTATION & CONTROL. Text in English. 1985. m. ZAR 216 (effective 2001). adv. bk.rev. back issues avail. **Document type:** *Magazine, Trade.* **Description:** Covers advanced industrial technology: automation, computation, instrumentation.
Formerly (until 1995): Computech
Related titles: Online - full text ed.
Published by: Technews (Pty.) Ltd., PO Box 626, Kloof, 3640, South Africa. TEL 27-31-764-0593, FAX 27-31-764-0386, technews@iafrica.com.za, http://www.technews.co.za. Ed. Graeme Bell. Pub. Kevin Beaumont. Adv. contacts Jane Fortmann TEL 27-31-764-5316, Vivian Dorrington TEL 27-11-886-3640. B&W page ZAR 6,350, color page ZAR 8,060; 180 x 260. Circ: 5,679 (controlled).

604.24 ZAF ISSN 0036-0643
SOUTH AFRICAN DRAUGHTSMAN/S A TEKENAAR. Variant title: S A Draughtsman. Text in Afrikaans, English. 1970 (vol.5). a. membership. adv. bk.rev. charts; illus.; stat. **Document type:** *Bulletin.* **Description:** News of interest to members of the institute.
Published by: South African Institute of Draughtsmen/Suid Afrikaanse Instituut van Tekenaars, PO Box 30, Bergvliet, 7864, South Africa. TEL 27-21-750156, FAX 27-21-750156. Ed., R&P William H Young TEL 27-21-4123938. Circ: 3,000 (controlled).

600 NCL ISSN 0081-2862
DU1 CODEN: SPCTAW
SOUTH PACIFIC COMMISSION. TECHNICAL PAPER. Text in English. 1949. irreg., latest vol.211, 1997. **Document type:** *Monographic series.*
Related titles: French ed.: Commission de Pacifique Sud. Document Technique. ISSN 0489-958X.
Published by: Secretariat of the Pacific Community, PO Box D5, Noumea, Cedex 98848, New Caledonia. TEL 687-262000, FAX 687-263818, spc@spc.int, http://www.spc.int.

SPACE SIMULATION CONFERENCE. PROCEEDINGS. *see* AERONAUTICS AND SPACE FLIGHT

SPACE TECHNOLOGY (LONDON). *see* AERONAUTICS AND SPACE FLIGHT

SPECIAL EDUCATION TECHNOLOGY PRACTICE. *see* EDUCATION—Special Education And Rehabilitation

SPECIAL OPERATIONS TECHNOLOGY. *see* MILITARY

600 USA ISSN 0148-2203
T1
SPINOFF. Text in English. a. illus.
Indexed: IHTDI.
Published by: U.S. National Aeronautics and Space Administration, Code RW, c/o Janelle Turner, Washington, DC 20546. TEL 202-358-2000. R&P Danielle Israel TEL 301-621-0242. **Subscr. to:** U.S. Government Printing Office, Superintendent of Documents, PO Box 371954, Pittsburgh, PA 15250. TEL 202-512-1800, FAX 202-512-2250, orders@gpo.gov, http://www.access.gpo.gov.

SPORTS TECHNOLOGY. *see* SPORTS AND GAMES

600 SRB ISSN 0351-9171
P323.4.Y8
SRPSKA ADAMEMIJA NAUKA I UMETNOSTI. ONOMATOLOSKI PRILOZI/ACADEMIE SERBE DES SCIENCES ET DES ARTS. CONTRIBUTIONS ONOMATOLOGIQUES. Text in Serbo-Croatian. 1979. a.
Indexed: IBR, IBZ, L&LBA.
Published by: Srpska Akademija Nauka i Umetnosti/Serbian Academy of Arts and Sciences, Knez Mihailova 35, Belgrade, 11000. TEL 381-11-2027154, FAX 381-11-2027178, izdavacka@sanu.ac.rs, http://www.sanu.ac.rs.

600 SRB ISSN 0081-3974
SRPSKA AKADEMIJA NAUKA I UMETNOSTI. ODELJENJE TEHNICKIH NAUKA. GLAS. Text in Serbo-Croatian; Summaries in English, French, German, Russian. N.S. 1949. irreg. Price varies.
Related titles: ◆ French ed.: Academie Serbe des Sciences et des Arts. Classe des Sciences Techniques.Bulletin. ISSN 0374-0781.
Indexed: A&ATA, CIN, ChemAb, ChemTitl, IBR, IBZ, Inspec, RefZh.
—AskIEEE, INIST, Linda Hall.
Published by: Srpska Akademija Nauka i Umetnosti/Serbian Academy of Arts and Sciences, Knez Mihailova 35, Belgrade, 11000. TEL 381-11-2027154, FAX 381-11-2027178, izdavacka@sanu.ac.rs, http://www.sanu.ac.rs. Circ: 500. **Dist. by:** Prosveta, Terazije 16, Belgrade, Serbia, Yugoslavia.

600 SRB ISSN 0081-4040
SRPSKA AKADEMIJA NAUKA I UMETNOSTI. ODELJENJE TEHNICKIH NAUKA. POSEBNA IZDANJA. Text in Serbo-Croatian; Summaries in English, French, German, Russian. 1950. irreg. Price varies.
Indexed: APA, C&ISA, CorrAb, E&CAJ, EEA, IBR, IBZ, Inspec, SolStAb, WAA.
—AskIEEE.
Published by: Srpska Akademija Nauka i Umetnosti/Serbian Academy of Arts and Sciences, Knez Mihailova 35, Belgrade, 11000. TEL 381-11-2027154, FAX 381-11-2027178, izdavacka@sanu.ac.rs, http://www.sanu.ac.rs. Circ: 600. **Dist. by:** Prosveta, Terazije 16, Belgrade, Serbia, Yugoslavia.

600 ITA ISSN 1121-063X
STAMPI; progettazione e costruzione. Text in Italian. 1991. m. (11/yr.). EUR 40 domestic; EUR 80 in Europe; EUR 100 elsewhere (effective 2011). adv. **Document type:** *Magazine, Trade.*
Related titles: Online - full text ed.
Published by: Tecniche Nuove SpA, Via Eritrea 21, Milan, MI 201, Italy. TEL 39-02-390901, FAX 39-02-7570364, info@tecnichenuove.com. Ed. Cinzia Galimberti.

STAR TECH JOURNAL. *see* BUSINESS AND ECONOMICS—Production Of Goods And Services

STATE EXPEDITURE ON SCIENCE & TECHNOLOGY. *see* SCIENCES: COMPREHENSIVE WORKS

STATE INVESTMENT IN SCIENCE & TECHNOLOGY (YEAR). *see* SCIENCES: COMPREHENSIVE WORKS

STIINTA SI TEHNICA. *see* SCIENCES: COMPREHENSIVE WORKS

STORAGE & ENTERTAINMENT; the storage magazine for entertainment and broadcast technologies. *see* COMMUNICATIONS

STROM MAGAZIN; Stromanbieter & Strompreise Infos. *see* ENERGY—Electrical Energy

600 620 GBR ISSN 1475-9217
➤ **STRUCTURAL HEALTH MONITORING**; an international journal. Abbreviated title: S H M. Text in English. 2002 (July). bi-m. USD 984, GBP 579 combined subscription to institutions (print & online eds.); USD 964, GBP 567 to institutions (effective 2011). adv. back issues avail.; reprint service avail. from PSC. **Document type:** *Journal, Academic/Scholarly.* **Description:** Publishes papers that contain theoretical, analytical, and experimental investigations that will advance the body of knowledge and its application in the discipline of structural health monitoring.
Related titles: Online - full text ed.: ISSN 1741-3168. USD 886, GBP 521 to institutions (effective 2011).
Indexed: A20, A22, A28, APA, B21, BrCerAb, C&ISA, CA, CA/WCA, CIA, CerAb, CivEngAb, CorrAb, CurCont, E&CAJ, E01, E11, EEA, EMA, ESPM, EnvEAb, H&SSA, H15, M&TEA, M09, MBF, METADEX, S&VD, SCI, SCOPUS, SolStAb, T02, T04, W07, WAA.
—BLDSC (8477.350000), IE, Ingenta, Linda Hall. **CCC.**
Published by: Sage Publications Ltd. (Subsidiary of: Sage Publications, Inc.), 1 Oliver's Yard, 55 City Rd, London, EC1Y 1SP, United Kingdom. TEL 44-20-73248500, FAX 44-20-73248600, info@sagepub.co.uk, http://www.uk.sagepub.com/home.nav. Ed. Fu-Kuo Chang. adv.: B&W page GBP 400; 180 x 265. **Subscr. in the Americas to:** Sage Publications, Inc., 2455 Teller Rd, Thousand Oaks, CA 91320. TEL 805-499-9774, FAX 805-499-0871, journals@sagepub.com.

➤ **STUDIEN ZU SPRACHE UND TECHNIK.** *see* LINGUISTICS

➤ **STUDIES IN ETHICS, LAW, AND TECHNOLOGY.** *see* LAW

620 ROM ISSN 0039-4017
TA350 CODEN: SCMAA2
STUDII SI CERCETARI DE MECANICA APLICATA. Text in Romanian. 1950. 6/yr. bk.rev. charts; illus. index.
Indexed: ApMecR, CCMJ, ChemAb, MathR.
—CASDDS, Linda Hall.
Published by: (Academia Romana/Romanian Academy, Institutul de Mecanica Aplicata), Editura Academiei Romane/Publishing House of the Romanian Academy, Calea 13 Septembrie 13, Sector 5, Bucharest, 050711, Romania. Ed. Ioan Anton. Circ: 1,000. **Dist. by:** Rodipet S.A., Piata Presei Libere 1, sector 1, PO Box 33-57, Bucharest 3, Romania. TEL 40-21-2226407, 40-21-2224126, rodipet@rodipet.ro.

600 ESP ISSN 0214-3046
SU FUTURO. Text in Spanish. 1988. m. adv. **Document type:** *Magazine, Consumer.*
Published by: Editorial Andina S.A., Caridad, 24, Pozuelo Estacion, Madrid, 28007, Spain. TEL 34-1-352-09-18, FAX 34-1-352-63-30. Ed. Pedro Bucher. Adv. contact Angelines Lagos. Circ: 40,000.

600 500 TUR ISSN 2146-2119
▼ ➤ **SULEYMAN DEMIREL UNIVERSITESI. TEKNIK BILIMLER DERGISI/S D U JOURNAL OF TECHNICAL SCIENCES.** Text in Turkish. 2011. s-a. free (effective 2011). **Document type:** *Journal, Academic/Scholarly.* **Description:** Publishes research articles about radio and television, textiles, electrical and electronics, biomedical, crafts, construction, machinery, computer, and other disciplines.
Media: Online - full text.
Published by: Suleyman Demirel University, Technical Sciences Vocational School/Suleyman Demirel Universitesi, Teknik Bilimler Meslek Yuksekokulu, West Campus, Isparta, Turkey. TEL 90-246-2111517, tbmyo@sdu.edu.tr. Ed. Hakan Ceylan.

600 500 TUR ISSN 1309-1220
SULEYMAN DEMIREL UNIVERSITESI. ULUSLARARASI TEKNOLOJIK BILIMLER DERGISI/S D U INTERNATIONAL JOURNAL OF TECHNOLOGICAL SCIENCES. Text in Turkish. 3/yr. free (effective 2011). **Document type:** *Journal, Academic/Scholarly.* **Description:** Publishes articles in the area of building technology and mechanical technology, electronics and computer technology, electrical technology, mechatronics technologies and educational technologies.
Media: Online - full text.
Indexed: A01.
Published by: Suleyman Demirel University, Faculty of Technical Education/Suleyman Demirel Universitesi, Teknik Egitim Fakultesi, West Campus, Isparta, 32200, Turkey. TEL 90-246-2111451, FAX 90-246-2371283, sterzi@sdu.edu.tr.

SWAZILAND JOURNAL OF SCIENCE AND TECHNOLOGY. *see* SCIENCES: COMPREHENSIVE WORKS

SWIAT NAUKI. *see* SCIENCES: COMPREHENSIVE WORKS

600 DEU
SYNERGIE JOURNAL; Magazin fuer innovative Unternehmen. Text in German. 4/yr. adv. **Document type:** *Magazine, Trade.* **Description:** Contains articles and research on technological innovations and products.
Published by: Technologie- und Gruenderzentren Nordrhein-Westfalen e.V., Mendelstr 11, Muenster, 48149, Germany. TEL 49-251-9801112, FAX 49-251-9801106, info@tgz-nrw.de. Circ: 10,000.

SYNTHESIS LECTURES ON ENGINEERS, TECHNOLOGY AND SOCIETY. *see* ENGINEERING

600 USA ISSN 1559-8136
SYNTHESIS LECTURES ON IMAGE, VIDEO, AND MULTIMEDIA PROCESSING. Text in English. 2005. irreg., latest vol.3, 2007. USD 40 per issue (effective 2008). **Document type:** *Monographic series, Academic/Scholarly.* **Description:** Provide a groundbreaking forum for the world's experts in the field of image, video and multimedia processing to express their knowledge in unique and effective ways.
Related titles: Online - full text ed.: ISSN 1559-8144. USD 30 per issue (effective 2008).
Indexed: SCOPUS.
Published by: Morgan & Claypool Publishers, 1537 4th St, Ste 228, San Rafael, CA 94901. TEL 415-785-8003, info@morganclaypool.com. Ed. Dr. Alan C Bovik.

600 USA ISSN 1932-4367
SYRACUSE UNIVERSITY. CENTER FOR TECHNOLOGY AND INFORMATION POLICY. WORKING PAPERS. Text in English. 19??. irreg., latest 2007. back issues avail. **Document type:** *Monographic series, Academic/Scholarly.*
Former titles (until 2001): C T I P Working Paper Series; (until 199?): Maxwell School of Citizenship and Public Affairs. Technology and Information Policy Program. Working Paper
Published by: Syracuse University, The Maxwell School of Citizenship and Public Affairs. Center for Technology and Information Policy, 419 Crouse-Hinds Hall, Syracuse University, 900 S Crouse Ave, Syracuse, NY 13244. TEL 315-443-1890, FAX 315-443-1075, ctip@maxwell.syr.edu.

600 UKR ISSN 1681-6048
SYSTEMNI DOSLIDZHENNYA TA INFORMATSIINI TEKHNOLOGII/ SYSTEM RESEARCHES & INFORMATION TECHNOLOGIES. Text in Ukrainian, Russian, English. 2001. bi-m. **Document type:** *Journal, Academic/Scholarly.*
Indexed: RefZh.
Published by: (Natsional'na Akademiya Nauk Ukrainy, Instytut Prykladnoho Systemnoho Analiza), Natsional'nyi Tekhnichnyi Universytet Ukrainy "Kyivs'kyi Politekhnichnyi Instytut", pr-kt Peremohy 37, Kyiv, 03056, Ukraine. TEL 380-44-2367989, post@ntu-kpi.kiev.ua, http://www.ntu-kpi.kiev.ua. **Co-sponsor:** Ministerstvo Osvity i Nauky Ukrainy/Ministry of Education and Science of Ukraine.

384 388.3 600 004 FRA ISSN 1968-7168
T 3. Variant title: Tendances, Technologies, Tentations. Text in French. 2008. m. EUR 30 (effective 2009). **Document type:** *Magazine, Consumer.* **Description:** Presents innovative products and new technologies in various areas including computers, telephones, cars, stereos, etc.
Published by: Yellow Media, 101-109 Rue Jean Jaures, Levallois Perret, 92300, France. TEL 33-1-41273838, http://www.mesmagazinesfavoris.fr.

005.5 USA
HC107.P43
T E Q. (Technology, Entrepreneurship, Quality) Variant title: Pittsburgh T E Q. Text in English. 1990. 7/yr. USD 29.95 (effective 2005); free to members (effective 2008). **Document type:** *Magazine, Trade.* **Description:** For all levels of management, and professionals in engineering, computers, marketing and sales.
Former titles (until 1994): Pennsylvania Business and Technology (1065-0261); (until 1991): Pennsylvania Technology
Related titles: Online - full text ed.: 1990.
Indexed: P23, P48, P52, P53, PQC.
Published by: Pittsburgh Technology Council, 2000 Technology Dr., Pittsburgh, PA 15219-3109. TEL 412-687-2700, FAX 412-687-5232, http://www.pghtech.org. Ed. Jonathan Kersting. Adv. contact Matthew Holjes. Circ: 18,000 (paid and free).

600 230 CAN
T F W M NEWSLETTER. Text in English. bi-w. free. **Document type:** *Newsletter.* **Description:** Covers everything related to technology. Includes educational columns on various technical topics, new product announcements, church install updates on upcoming events relevant to tech users in the worship environment.
Media: Online - full text.
Published by: T W M Media Inc., 3891 Holburn Rd, Queensville, ON L0G 1R0, Canada. TEL 905-473-9822, FAX 905-473-9928, info@tfwm.com. Ed. Kevin R Cobus.

607.1 USA
T I E S (ONLINE); the magazine of design and technology education. (Technology, Innovation and Entrepreneurship for Students) Text in English. 1988. s-a. adv. bk.rev.; software rev.; tel.rev.; video rev. bibl.; charts; illus.; stat.; tr.lit. **Document type:** *Magazine, Trade.* **Description:** Supports design and technology education from middle school through high school, with articles addressing the problem-solving nature, systems, impacts and history of technology.
Formerly (until 2001): T I E S (Print) (1041-6587)
Media: Online - full content.
Published by: College of New Jersey, School of Engineering, 103 Armstrong Hall, PO Box 7718, Ewing, NJ 08628-0718. TEL 609-771-2295, FAX 609-771-3330, maskell@tcnj.edu, http://www.tcnj.edu. Ed. Ken Maskell. Pub. Ronald Todd. adv.: color page USD 1,400. Circ: 25,000.

T I M; revija za tehnicno in znanstveno dejavnost mladine. *see* CHILDREN AND YOUTH—For

T I S T R RESEARCH NEWS. *see* SCIENCES: COMPREHENSIVE WORKS

330 338.4 384 SGP ISSN 1793-6020
➤ **T M C ACADEMIC JOURNAL.** (Technology, Management and Communications) Text in English. 2006. s-a. free (effective 2011). bk.rev.; film rev. abstr.; bibl. back issues avail. **Document type:** *Journal, Academic/Scholarly.* **Description:** published original and unpublished research articles, and reflections in any fields of business, mass communications, hospitality, tourism, and IT. The target audience is academia in different fields, researchers, students at tertiary institutes, and those who are interested in the above fields.
Media: Online - full text.
Published by: T M C Educational Group, 111 N Bridge Rd, #06-15 Peninsula Plaza, Singapore, 179098, Singapore. http://www.tmc.com.sg/index.html. Ed. Huong Ha.

➤ **T M. TEKNIIKAN MAAILMA.** *see* CONSUMER EDUCATION AND PROTECTION

➤ **T N O MAGAZINE (INTERNATIONAL EDITION)**; a quarterly technology update. (Toegepast Natuurwetenschappelijk Onderzoek) *see* SCIENCES: COMPREHENSIVE WORKS

600 CHE ISSN 1023-0823
T3
T R TRANSFER; Europaeische Industrie- und Handelszeitung. Text in German. 1908. w. CHF 138; CHF 202 foreign (effective 1997). adv. bk.rev. bibl.; charts; illus.; tr.lit. index. **Document type:** *Newspaper.*
Formerly: Technische Rundschau (0040-148X)
Related titles: ◆ Supplement(s): Schweizerische Marktstatistik fur Technische Software. ISSN 1420-4827; ◆ T R - Wissen. ISSN 1023-3377; ◆ Handbuch der Automatisierungstechnik. ISSN 1420-4878.
Indexed: C&ISA, CISA, ChemAb, CorrAb, CybAb, E&CAJ, Inspec, SolStAb, WAA.
—IE, Infotrieve, INIST, Linda Hall.
Published by: Hallwag AG, Nordring 4, Bern, 3001, Switzerland. TEL 41-31-3323131, FAX 41-31-3314133. Ed. Alois Altenweger. Circ: 15,000.

600 CHE ISSN 1023-3377
T R - WISSEN. Text in German. 1994. irreg.
Related titles: ◆ Supplement to: T R Transfer. ISSN 1023-0823.
Published by: Hallwag AG, Nordring 4, Bern, 3001, Switzerland. TEL 41-31-3355555, FAX 41-31-3355784.

371.3 DEU ISSN 0342-6254
T U - ZEITSCHRIFT FUER TECHNIK IM UNTERRICHT. Text in German. 1973. q. EUR 24; EUR 6.80 newsstand/cover (effective 2011). adv. **Document type:** *Journal, Academic/Scholarly.*
Formerly (until 1976): T W U - Technik und Wirtschaft im Unterricht (0170-7094)
Indexed: IBR, IBZ.
Published by: Neckar Verlag GmbH, Postfach 1820, Villingen-Schwenningen, 78008, Germany. TEL 49-7721-89870, FAX 49-7721-898750, service@neckar-verlag.de, http://www.neckar-verlag.de. Adv. contact Uwe Stockburger. Circ: 2,406 (paid and controlled).

600 DEU ISSN 1863-8198
T UE V SUED JOURNAL. Text in German, English. 1962. 4/yr. free (effective 2009). **Document type:** *Magazine, Trade.*
Former titles (until 2006): T Ue V Journal (0178-322X); (until 1983): Technischer Ueberwachungs-Verein Bayern. Mitteilungen fuer die Mitglieder (0341-2415)
Published by: T Ue V Sued AG, Westendstr 199, Munich, 80686, Germany. TEL 49-89-57910, FAX 49-89-57911551, info@tuev-sued.de. Circ: 43,000 (controlled).

600 NLD ISSN 2211-1271
T W A NIEUWSBRIEF. (Technisch Wetenschappelijk Attaches) Text in Dutch. 1995. q. adv.

Supersedes in part (in 2010): T W A Nieuws (1572-6045); Which was formerly (until 2003): Technieuws (1381-3730)
Published by: Agentschap NL, Technisch Wetenschappelijk Attaches, Postbus 20105, The Hague, 2500 EC, Netherlands. TEL 31-88-6021990, twanetwerk@agenschapnl.nl, http://www.twanetwerk.nl.

600 NLD ISSN 2211-128X
T W A SPECIAL. (Technisch Wetenschappelijke Attaches) Text in Dutch. 1995. q. adv.
Supersedes in part (in 2010): T W A Nieuws (1572-6045); Which was formerly (until 2003): Technieuws (1381-3730)
Published by: Agentschap NL, Technisch Wetenschappelijk Attaches, Postbus 20105, The Hague, 2500 EC, Netherlands. TEL 31-88-6021990, twanetwerk@agenschapnl.nl, http://www.twanetwerk.nl.

600 DNK ISSN 1603-595X
T3. (Tomorrow's Technology Today) Text in Danish. 2004. m. DKK 549 (effective 2008). adv. **Document type:** *Magazine, Consumer.* **Description:** News about gadgets and luxury "toys".
Published by: Audio Media A-S, Sejroegade 7-9, Copenhagen OE, 2100, Denmark. TEL 45-33-912833, FAX 45-33-747191, forlaget@audio.dk, http://www.audio.dk. Eds. Mette Eklund TEL 45-33-747157, Jeppe Christensen TEL 45-33-747154. adv.: color page DKK 29,900; 210 x 297. Circ: 20,000.

T3; toys for the boys. (Tomorrow's Technology Today) *see* ELECTRONICS

T3. (Tomorrow's Technology Today) *see* ELECTRONICS

T3. (Tomorrow's Technology Today) *see* ELECTRONICS

600 CHN ISSN 1007-9432
T4
TAIYUAN LIGONG DAXUE XUEBAO/TAIYUAN UNIVERSITY OF TECHNOLOGY. JOURNAL. Text in Chinese. 1998. bi-m. USD 37.20 (effective 2009). **Document type:** *Journal, Academic/Scholarly.*
Formed by the merger of (1984-1998): Taiyuan Gongye Daxue Xuebao/Taiyuan University of Technology. Journal (1000-1611); Which was formerly (1981-1983): Taiyuan Gongxueyuan Xuebao/Taiyuan Institute of Technology. Journal (0253-2387); (1983-1998): Shanxi Kuangye Xueyuan Xuebao/Shanxi Mining College Learned Journal (1000-1603)
Related titles: Online - full content ed.
Indexed: A22.
—BLDSC (4905.370000), East View, IE, Ingenta.
Published by: Taiyuan Ligong Daxue, Yingze Xi Dajie Xinkuangyuan Lu #18, Taiyuan, 030024, China. **Dist. outside of China by:** China International Book Trading Corp, 35 Chegongzhuang Xilu, Haidian District, PO Box 399, Beijing 100044, China. TEL 86-10-68412045, FAX 86-10-68412023, cibtc@mail.cibtc.com.cn, http://www.cibtc.com.cn.

600 TWN ISSN 1560-6686
TAMKANG JOURNAL OF SCIENCE AND ENGINEERING. Text in Multiple languages. 1998. q. **Document type:** *Academic/Scholarly.*
Indexed: A22, CPEI, EngInd, SCOPUS.
—BLDSC (8601.615000), IE, Ingenta, Linda Hall.
Published by: Tamkang University, 151 Ying Chuan Rd Tamsui, Taipei, 25137, Taiwan. TEL 886-2-26220781, FAX 886-2-26223204, http://www.tku.edu.tw/.

600 500 BRA ISSN 0104-3285
T25.B82 CODEN: TCBAEU
TECBAHIA; revista baiana de tecnologia. Text in English, French, Italian, Portuguese, Spanish; Summaries in English. 3/yr. BRL 17 (effective 2006). adv. bk.rev. bibl.; charts; illus. index. **Document type:** *Bulletin.* **Description:** Covers various themes such as: agriculture, chemistry, environment, energy, mining, metallurgy, materials and petrochemistry.
Former titles (until 1993): Bahia, Brazil (State). Centro de Pesquisas e Desenvolvimento. Boletim Tecnico (0100-1949); (until 1975, vol.2): C E P E D. Boletim Tecnico. Serie Tecnologia de Alimentos
Related titles: Online - full text ed.
Indexed: CPEI, ChemAb, EngInd, FS&TA, INIS AtomInd, SCOPUS.
—CASDDS, Linda Hall.
Published by: Centro de Pesquisas e Desenvolvimento, Rodovia BA, 512 Km 0, Caixa Postal 09, Camacari, BA 42800-000, Brazil. TEL 55-71-8347300, FAX 55-71-8322095. Ed., R&P, Adv. contact Ricardo Baroud. Circ: 500; 700 (controlled).

TECH COAST. *see* BUSINESS AND ECONOMICS

362.4 600 USA
TECH - N J. Text in English. bi-m. free. **Document type:** *Newsletter, Trade.*
Indexed: V03, V04.
Published by: The College of New Jersey, Dept of Special Education, Ewing, NJ 08628-0718. TEL 609-771-2268, FAX 609-637-5183. Ed. Amy G. Dell.

600 PHL ISSN 0116-4333
TECH TIPS. Text in English. 1986. bi-m. PHP 200; USD 45 foreign. **Description:** Profiles the current technological breakthroughs.
Published by: (Department of Science and Technology), Science and Technology Information Institute, P.O. Box 3596, Manila, Philippines. TEL 822-0954.

TECHCONNECT. *see* BUSINESS AND ECONOMICS—Economic Situation And Conditions

600 371.42 USA ISSN 1537-288X
TECHLINKS. Text in English. 2000. bi-m. USD 15 domestic; USD 50 foreign; free to Georgia residents (effective 2001). adv.
Published by: Techlinks Media Inc, 3630 Stonewall Dr, Atlanta, GA 30339. TEL 770-436-6789. Ed., Pub. Mike Adkinson.

600 DEU
TECHMAX; Neugierig auf Wissenschaft. Text in German. 2003. 2/yr. free. **Document type:** *Newsletter, Academic/Scholarly.*
Published by: Max-Planck-Institut fuer Gesellschaft zur Foerderung der Wissenschaften, Hofgartenstr 8, Munich, 80539, Germany. TEL 49-89-21081232, FAX 49-89-21081405, presse@gv.mpg.de. Ed., R&P Christina Beck.

▼ **TECHNAI.** *see* ARCHAEOLOGY

TECHNE: RESEARCH IN PHILOSOPHY AND TECHNOLOGY. *see* PHILOSOPHY

600 CHE ISSN 0040-0866
T4 CODEN: TCHNAR
TECHNICA; die Fachzeitschrift fuer die Industrie. Text in German. 1951. 26/yr. CHF 95 domestic; CHF 135 in Europe; CHF 159 elsewhere (effective 2005). adv. bk.rev. illus. index. 84 p./no.; **Document type:** *Magazine, Trade.* **Description:** Devoted to research in all fields of technology in the machine industry. Covers mechanization, automation, controls, manufacturing, instruments and materials. Includes reports of events, new products, industry news, and positions available.
Indexed: A22, BMT, CEABA, CISA, ChemAb, Inspec, M09, T04, TM, Weldasearch.
—BLDSC (8614.850000), AskIEEE, CASDDS, IE, Infotrieve, Ingenta, INIST. **CCC.**
Published by: Technica Verlags AG, Hoehenweg 1, Rupperswil, 5102, Switzerland. TEL 41-62-8893000, FAX 41-62-8893003, verkauf@technica-verlag.ch. Ed. Bernhard Herzog. Pub. Martin Gysi. adv.: B&W page CHF 2,990; trim 185 x 268. Circ: 15,785 (paid).

TECHNICAL AND VOCATIONAL EDUCATION AND TRAINING; issues, concerns and prospects. *see* EDUCATION—Higher Education

600 CHE ISSN 1012-294X
TC1 CODEN: TBVEEX
TECHNICAL BULLETIN VEVEY. Text in French. 1985. a. **Document type:** *Bulletin.*
Formerly: Bulletin Technique Vevey
Indexed: Inspec.
—AskIEEE, Linda Hall.
Published by: Bombardier Transportation, Case Postale 32, Villeneuve Vd, 1844, Switzerland. TEL 41-21-9670505, FAX 41-21-9670500.

TECHNICAL COMMUNICATION QUARTERLY. *see* EDUCATION—Teaching Methods And Curriculum

600 GBR ISSN 0267-5307
TECHNICAL REVIEW MIDDLE EAST/AL-NASHRAH AL-TIQNIYYAH AL-SHARQ AL-AWSAT. Text in Arabic, English, Persian, Modern. 1984. bi-m. GBP 63, USD 124, EUR 93 (effective 2010). adv. **Document type:** *Newsletter, Trade.* **Description:** Aims to serve the requirements of management and technical readership across business and industry in the Middle East.
Related titles: Online - full text ed.; ◆ Supplement to: Oil Review Middle East. ISSN 1464-9314.
Indexed: B02, B15, B17, B18, G04, G06, G07, G08, I05.
—**CCC.**
Published by: Alain Charles Publishing Ltd., University House, 11-13 Lower Grosvenor Pl, London, SW1W 0EX, United Kingdom. TEL 44-20-78347676, FAX 44-20-79730076, post@alaincharles.com, http://www.alaincharles.com. Ed. David Clancy. Adv. contact Stephen Thomas. Circ: 18,204.

600 500 POL ISSN 1505-4675
TECHNICAL SCIENCES. Text in English, Polish. 1985. irreg. **Document type:** *Monographic series, Academic/Scholarly.*
Supersedes in part (in 1998): Acta Academiae Agriculturae ac Technicae Olstenensis (1509-3727)
Indexed: B22.
Published by: (Uniwersytet Warminsko-Mazurski), Wydawnictwo Uniwersytetu Warminsko-Mazurskiego, ul J Heweliusza 14, Olsztyn, 10724, Poland. TEL 48-89-5233661, FAX 48-89-5233438, wydawca@uwm.edu.pl, http://www.uwm.edu.pl/wydawnictwo.

600 CZE ISSN 1210-616X
TECHNIK. Text in Czech. 1993. m. CZK 950 (effective 2010). adv. **Document type:** *Magazine, Trade.*
Published by: Economia a.s., Dobrovskeho 25, Prague 7, 170 55, Czech Republic. TEL 420-233-071111, FAX 420-233-072003, economia@economia.cz, http://www.economia.cz. Ed. Josef Valiska. Adv. contact Zuzana Nikolovova. Circ: 5,500 (paid and controlled).

600 DEU ISSN 1024-5340
TECHNIK INTERDISZIPLINAR. Text in German. 1995. irreg., latest vol.5, 2008. prices varies. **Document type:** *Monographic series, Academic/Scholarly.*
Indexed: SCOPUS.
—**CCC.**
Published by: (Technical University of Berlin, The Centre of Technology and Society), Peter Lang GmbH (Subsidiary of: Peter Lang Publishing Group), Eschborner Landstr 42-50, Frankfurt Am Main, 60489, Germany. TEL 49-69-7807050, FAX 49-69-78070550, zentrale.frankfurt@peterlang.com, http://www.peterlang.com. Eds. Meinolf Dierkes, Wolfgang Konig.

600 DEU ISSN 2190-2399
TECHNIK UP2DATE; neue Ideen aus Industrie und Forschung. Text in German. 2008. fortn. **Document type:** *Journal, Trade.*
Formerly (until 2010): Technisches Journal (1867-8106)
Published by: Prior Art Publishing GmbH, Dieffenbachstr 33, Berlin, 10967, Germany. TEL 49-30-26304025, FAX 49-30-32896808, office@priorartpublishing.com.

TECHNIKA CHRONIKA/ANNALES TECHNIQUES. *see* SCIENCES: COMPREHENSIVE WORKS

600 DEU
TECHNIKDIALOG. Text in German. 1997. irreg., latest vol.20, 2000. EUR 7 per issue (effective 2011). **Document type:** *Monographic series, Academic/Scholarly.* **Description:** Provides a forum for discussions on applications of technology and innovations in science and business.
Published by: Lemmens Verlags- und Mediengesellschaft mbH, Matthias-Gruenewald-Str 1-3, Bonn, 53175, Germany. TEL 49-228-421370, FAX 49-228-4213729, info@lemmens.de, http://www.lemmens.de.

600 DEU ISSN 1619-7623
TECHNIKFOLGENABSCHAETZUNG; Theorie und Praxis. Text in German. 1992. 3/yr. **Document type:** *Journal, Academic/Scholarly.*
Formerly (until 2001): T A Datenbank Nachrichten (0943-8246)
Related titles: Online - full text ed.: free (effective 2011).
—**CCC.**
Published by: Forschungszentrum Karlsruhe, Institut fuer Technikfolgenabschaetzung und Systemanalyse, Hermann-von-Helmholtz-Platz 1, Eggenstein-Leopoldshafen, 76344, Germany. TEL 49-7247-822513, FAX 49-7247-824806, TATuP-Redaktion@itas.fzk.de. Eds. Armin Grunwald, Brigitte Hoffmann, Peter Hocke-Bergler.

620 DEU ISSN 0040-117X
T5 CODEN: TECHDZ
TECHNIKGESCHICHTE. Text in German. 1909. q. EUR 84.20 domestic; EUR 91.66 in Europe; EUR 86.20 elsewhere; EUR 53 domestic to students; EUR 55 elsewhere to students; EUR 21.50 newsstand/cover (effective 2002). bk.rev. bibl.; charts; illus. index. **Document type:** *Magazine, Trade.*
Indexed: A22, AmH&L, DIP, HistAb, IBR, IBZ, MathR, RASB, SCOPUS.
—BLDSC (8736.835000), IE, Infotrieve, Ingenta, Linda Hall. **CCC.**
Published by: (Verein Deutscher Ingenieure e.V.), Kiepert GmbH und Co. KG, Hardenbergstr 4-5, Berlin, 10623, Germany. TEL 49-30-31188261, FAX 49-30-31188530, ahippe@kiepert.de, http://www.kiepert.de, http://www-philosophie.kgw.tu-berlin.de/w3/philosophie/phzstechnikg/phtechnikgeschichte.htm. Ed., R&P Reinhold Reith. Pub. Robert Kiepert.

TECHNIKPHILOSOPHIE. *see* PHILOSOPHY

600 NLD
TECHNISCH INFO MAGAZINE; vakblad voor hoofden technische dienst onderhoud en productie. Variant title: T I M. Text in Dutch. 1995. 8/yr. EUR 78.80 domestic; EUR 118.80 foreign; EUR 13.50 newsstand/cover (effective 2009). adv. **Document type:** *Magazine, Trade.*
Formerly: Technisch Inkoop Magazine (1382-5178)
Published by: Uitgeverij Industriele Pers, PO Box 1297, Amersfoort, 3800 BG, Netherlands. TEL 31-33-4637977, FAX 31-33-4637976, info@indpers.nl, http://www.indpers.nl/. Ed. Marieke Moraal. Pub. Peter van Nierop. adv.: B&W page EUR 2,035, color page EUR 3,030; bleed 210 x 297. Circ: 5,500.

600 DEU ISSN 1435-6856
TECHNISCHE FORSCHUNGSERGEBNISSE. Variant title: Schriftenreihe Technische Forschungsergebnisse. Text in German. 1997. irreg., latest vol.10, 2010. price varies. **Document type:** *Monographic series, Academic/Scholarly.*
Published by: Verlag Dr. Kovac, Leverkusenstr 13, Hamburg, 22761, Germany. TEL 49-40-3988800, FAX 49-40-39888055, info@verlagdrkovac.de.

600 DEU ISSN 0724-1593
TECHNISCHE REVUE; Magazin fuer Konstrukteure. Text in German. 1981. 10/yr. free to qualified personnel (effective 2006). bk.rev. **Document type:** *Magazine, Trade.*
Indexed: TM.
Published by: Thomas Industrial Media GmbH, Friedrichstr 5, Hattingen, 45525, Germany. TEL 49-2324-919504, FAX 49-2324-919506. Ed. Juergen Wirtz. Pub. Marketta Laehde. Circ: 37,199 (controlled).

620 DEU ISSN 0043-6925
Q3 CODEN: WZTUAU
TECHNISCHE UNIVERSITAET DRESDEN. WISSENSCHAFTLICHE ZEITSCHRIFT. Text in German; Summaries in English, German. 1952. bi-m. EUR 7.50 newsstand/cover (effective 2004). adv. bk.rev. bibl.; charts; illus. index. back issues avail. **Document type:** *Journal, Academic/Scholarly.*
Indexed: A22, A37, BA, BibCart, C25, C30, CABA, CEABA, CIN, CIS, ChemAb, ChemTitl, DokStr, E12, F08, F11, F12, FR, G11, GH, GeoRef, GeotechAb, I11, IBR, IBZ, INIS AtomInd, Inspec, LT, MathR, P33, R08, RASB, RRTA, S13, S16, SCOPUS, SpeleolAb, TM, VITIS, W11, Z02.
—BLDSC (9339.110000), AskIEEE, CASDDS, IE, Ingenta, INIST, Linda Hall. **CCC.**
Published by: Technische Universitaet Dresden, Pressestelle, Noethnitzer Str. 43, Dresden, 01187, Germany. TEL 49-351-4632773, FAX 49-351-4637768, pressestelle@mailbox.tu-dresden.de. Ed. Ute Hendlmeier. Circ: 1,400.

500 AUT ISSN 1682-5675
TECHNISCHE UNIVERSITAET GRAZ. FOSCHUNGSJOURNAL. Text in German. 2002. s-a. **Document type:** *Journal, Academic/Scholarly.*
Published by: Technische Universitaet Graz, Rechbauerstr 12, Graz, 8010, Austria. TEL 43-316-8730, FAX 43-316-8736562, info@tugraz.at, http://www.tugraz.at. Circ: 3,500 (controlled).

500 AUT ISSN 1990-357X
TECHNISCHE UNIVERSITAET GRAZ. MONOGRAPHIC SERIES. Text in German. 2006. irreg., latest vol.3, 2006. price varies. **Document type:** *Monographic series, Academic/Scholarly.*
Published by: (Technische Universitaet Graz), Verlag der Technischen Universitaet Graz, Technikerstr 4, Graz, 8010, Austria. TEL 43-316-8736157, FAX 43-316-8736671, verlag@tugraz.at, http://www.ub.tugraz.at/Verlag/index.htm.

600 DEU ISSN 1868-7105
TECHNISCHE UNIVERSITAET HAMBURG-HARBURG. INSTITUT FUER WERKZEUGMASCHINEN, ROBOTER UND MONTAGEANLAGEN. A W A - FORTSCHRITTSBERICHTE. (Arbeitsbereich Werkzeugmaschinen und Automatisierungstechnik) Text in German. 1991. irreg., latest vol.20, 2010. price varies. **Document type:** *Monographic series, Academic/Scholarly.*
Formerly (until 2009): Technische Universitaet Hamburg-Harburg. Arbeitsbereich Werkzeugmaschinen und Automatisierungstechnik. Schriftenreihe (1438-8529)
Published by: (Technische Universitaet Hamburg-Harburg, Institut fuer Werkzeugmaschinen, Roboter und Montageanlagen), Cuvillier Verlag, Nonnenstieg 8, Goettingen, 37075, Germany. TEL 49-551-547240, FAX 49-551-5472421, info@cuvillier.de, http://www.cuvillier.de.

607.11 DEU ISSN 0077-2089
Q9
TECHNISCHE UNIVERSITAET MUENCHEN. JAHRBUCH. Text in German. 1952. a. **Document type:** *Bibliography.*
Related titles: CD-ROM ed.
Indexed: GeoRef, SpeleolAb.
Published by: Technische Universitaet Muenchen, Arcisstr 21, Munich, 80290, Germany. TEL 49-89-28928601, FAX 49-89-28928622. Ed. Elfriede Maier. Circ: 1,100.

658.5 DEU ISSN 0040-1552
TECHNISCHER HANDEL; Menschen, Maerkte, Management. Text in German. 1914. m. EUR 88 domestic; EUR 114.49 foreign (effective 2010). adv. bk.rev. abstr. **Document type:** *Magazine, Trade.*
—**CCC.**

Published by: (Verband der Technischen Haendler), Vincentz Verlag, Plathnerstr 4c, Hannover, 30175, Germany. TEL 49-511-9910000, FAX 49-511-9910099, info@vincentz.de, http://www.vincentz.de. Ed. Bernhard Flacke TEL 49-511-9910331. Adv. contact Henning Lothar Litka TEL 49-511-9910350. B&W page EUR 1,360, color page EUR 2,539; trim 175 x 250. Circ: 1,130 (paid and controlled).

TECHNO ONLINE. *see* MUSIC

600 GBR
TECHNOCRAT. Text in English. 1997. q.
Published by: Central Telecom UK Ltd, 3 The Maltings, Wetmore Rd, Burton on Trent, Staffs, DE14 1SF, United Kingdom. TEL 44-128-356-0661, FAX 44-128-356-0631, marking@central-telecom.co.uk. Ed. Julie White. Circ: 15,000.

600 001.3 USA ISSN 1938-0526
▼ ➤ **TECHNOCULTURE**; a journal of technology studies. Text in English. 2010 (Fall). a. free (effective 2011). **Document type:** *Journal, Academic/Scholarly.* **Description:** Features research from a broad range of disciplines on technology, society and culture.
Media: Online - full content.
Published by: Keith Dorwick, Ed. & Pub., PO Box 44691, Lafayette, LA 70504-4691. TEL 337-962-1991, kdorwick@yahoo.com.

700 600 GBR ISSN 1477-965X
B105.I28
➤ **TECHNOETIC ARTS**; a journal of speculative research. Abbreviated title: T A. Text in English. 2003. 3/yr. GBP 36, USD 68 to individuals; GBP 235, GBP 368 to institutions (effective 2012). adv. back issues avail. **Document type:** *Journal, Academic/Scholarly.* **Description:** Presents the cutting edge of ideas, projects and practices as they arise from the confluence of art, science, technology and consciousness research.
Related titles: Online - full text ed.: ISSN 1758-9533. GBP 192, USD 290 (effective 2012).
Indexed: A01, A02, A03, A07, A08, A22, A30, A31, AA, ABM, ArtInd, B04, BRD, BrHumI, CA, E01, MLA-IB, T02, W03, W05.
—BLDSC (8755.463000), IE. **CCC.**
Published by: Intellect Ltd., The Mill, Parnall Rd, Fishponds, Bristol, BS16 3JG, United Kingdom. TEL 44-117-9589910, FAX 44-117-9589911, info@intellectbooks.com. Ed. Roy Ascott. Pub. Masoud Yazdani. **Subscr. to:** Turpin Distribution Services Ltd., Pegasus Dr, Stratton Business Park, Biggleswade, Bedfordshire SG18 8QB, United Kingdom. TEL 44-1767-604951, FAX 44-1767-601640, custserv@turpin-distribution.com, http://www.turpin-distribution.com/.

600 500 BEL ISSN 0771-6826
TECHNOLOGIA; historical and social studies in science, technology and industry. Text in French. 1978. q. bk.rev. **Document type:** *Journal, Academic/Scholarly.*
Incorporates (in 1983): Comite Belge d'Histoire des Sciences. Notes Bibliographiques - Belgisch Komitee voor de Geschiedeis der Wetenschappen. Bibliografische Notas (0010-2415); Formerly (until 1981): Technologia Bruxellensis (0771-7415)
Indexed: FR, P30.
Published by: Association des Ingenieurs Industriels de Bruxelles (AIIBr), Rue des Goujons, 28, Bruxelles, 1070, Belgium. secretariat@aiibr.be, http://www.aiibr.be. Ed. Jean C Baudet. Circ: 1,000.

303.4 USA ISSN 0040-1625
T174 CODEN: TFSCB3
➤ **TECHNOLOGICAL FORECASTING AND SOCIAL CHANGE.** Text in English. 1969. 9/yr. EUR 1,113 in Europe to institutions; JPY 147,600 in Japan to institutions; USD 1,243 elsewhere to institutions (effective 2012). adv. bk.rev. illus. back issues avail.; reprints avail. **Document type:** *Journal, Academic/Scholarly.* **Description:** Deals directly with the methodology and practice of technological forecasting and future studies as planning tools as they interrelate social, environmental and technological factors.
Formerly (until 1970): Technological Forecasting (0099-3964)
Related titles: Microform ed.: (from PQC); Online - full text ed.: ISSN 1873-5509 (from IngentaConnect, ScienceDirect).
Indexed: A20, A22, A26, ABS&EES, ASCA, ASFA, Agr, B02, B03, B04, B17, B18, B21, BAS, BPI, BPIA, BRD, BibAg, BusI, C&ISA, CA, CIS, CLOSS, CPEI, CPM, CurCont, E&CAJ, E08, EAA, ESPM, Emerald, EngInd, FR, FutSurv, G04, G06, G07, G08, GEOBASE, GeoRef, HPNRM, HRIS, I05, IAOP, ISMEC, Inspec, JCQM, JEL, KES, MEA&I, ManagAb, P30, P41, P42, PAIS, PSA, RASB, S02, S03, S09, SCIMP, SCOPUS, SOPODA, SSA, SSCI, SSciA, SociolAb, SolStAb, T&II, T02, W01, W02, W03, W07.
—BLDSC (8757.351000), AskIEEE, IE, Infotrieve, Ingenta, INIST, Linda Hall. **CCC.**
Published by: Elsevier Inc. (Subsidiary of: Elsevier Science & Technology), 360 Park Ave S, New York, NY 10010. TEL 212-989-5800, FAX 212-633-3990, usinfo-f@elsevier.com. Ed. Harold A Linstone.

600 FRA ISSN 1145-5217
➤ **TECHNOLOGIE & SANTE.** Text in French. 1990. q. adv. back issues avail. **Document type:** *Journal, Academic/Scholarly.* **Description:** Covers hospital organization, medical technology, and information systems.
Indexed: FR.
Published by: Centre National de l'Equipement Hospitalier, 3 Rue Danton, Malakoff, 92240, France. TEL 33-1-41171515, FAX 33-1-41171516, communication@cneh.fr. Circ: 1,000.

➤ **TECHNOLOGIE-NACHRICHTEN - MANAGEMENT-INFORMATIONEN.** *see* BUSINESS AND ECONOMICS—Management

600 DEU ISSN 0344-9750
TECHNOLOGIE-NACHRICHTEN - PROGRAMM-INFORMATIONEN. Text in German. 1970. s-m.
Published by: T N V GmbH, An den Eichen, Hennef, 53773, Germany. TEL 02248-1881, FAX 02248-1796. Ed. Nicola Gasterstaedt. Circ: 500.

600 DEU ISSN 0932-2558
TECHNOLOGIE UND MANAGEMENT. Text in German. 1951. bi-m. EUR 58.80 domestic; EUR 69 foreign; EUR 9.90 newsstand/cover (effective 2011). adv. index. back issues avail. **Document type:** *Magazine, Trade.*
Former titles (until 1987): Technologie Manager (0178-4463); (until 1985): Verband Deutscher Wirtschaftsingenieure. Zeitschrift (0178-4846); (until 1967): Verband Deutscher Wirtschaftsingenieure. Mitteilungsblatt (0178-4854)
Indexed: B01, DIP, IBR, IBZ, TM.
Published by: (Verband Deutscher Wirtschaftsingenieure e.V.), Fachverlag Schiele und Schoen GmbH, Markgrafenstr 11, Berlin, 10969, Germany. TEL 49-30-2537520, FAX 49-30-2517248, service@schiele-schoen.de, http://www.schiele-schoen.de.

600 NLD ISSN 1872-0773
DE TECHNOLOGIEKRANT. Text in Dutch. 2004. 27/yr. EUR 32.50; EUR 2.50 newsstand/cover (effective 2009). adv.
Incorporates (2004-2006): Technology Review (Nederlandse Editie) (1573-4269)
Published by: Veen Magazines, Postbus 256, Diemen, 1110 AG, Netherlands. TEL 31-20-5310900, FAX 31-20-5310950, http://www.veenmagazines.nl. Ed. Ton van Doorn. Pub. Erno Eskens. adv.: B&W page EUR 4,900, color page EUR 6,755; trim 280 x 410. Circ: 38,408.

600 ISR ISSN 0333-9521
T4
TECHNOLOGIES/TEKHNOLOGIYOT; Israel's magazine of high technology. Text in English. 1983. m. USD 100 (effective 1992). adv. **Description:** Information on high-tech applicable to the Israeli market, both local and imported. Covers electronics, industry oriented computers, control and automation as well as tests.
Published by: Shukit Publishing Ltd., P O Box 39244, Tel Aviv, 61392, Israel. TEL 052-581054, FAX 052-573628. Ed. Haim Amit. Circ: 15,000.

600 CAN
TECHNOLOGIES DE L'INFORMATION ET SOCIETE. Abbreviated title: T.I.S. Text in French. 1988. 3/yr.
Indexed: PdeR.
Published by: Universite du Quebec a Montreal, Service des Publications, Succ Centre Ville, C P 8888, Montreal, PQ H3C 3P8, Canada. TEL 514-282-4511.

600 230 CAN ISSN 1498-3184
TECHNOLOGIES FOR WORSHIP. Text in English. 1992. 10/yr. USD 14.95 in US & Canada; USD 65.95 elsewhere (effective 2007). adv. back issues avail. **Document type:** *Magazine, Trade.* **Description:** Aimed at church technical teams, pastors, music and youth ministers. Intended to educate houses of worship about technology and how to incorporate technology into services and special events.
Former titles (until 2000): Technologies For Worship Magazine (1482-7859); (until 1996): Religion - Technologies for Communications and Worship (1188-9381)
Related titles: Online - full text ed.
Published by: T W M Media Inc., 3891 Holburn Rd, Queensville, ON L0G 1R0, Canada. TEL 905-473-9822, FAX 905-473-9928, info@tfwm.com, http://www.tfwm.com. Ed. Kevin R Cobus. Pub., R&P Shelagh Rogers. Adv. contact Barry Cobus. page USD 1,200; trim 10.88 x 8.38. Circ: 30,000 (controlled).

600 FRA ISSN 1165-8568
TECHNOLOGIES INTERNATIONALES. Text in French. 198?. m.
Former titles (until 1992): Veillet Technologique et Strategique (1154-2853); (until 1990): Centre de Prospective et d'Evaluation. Bulletin (0766-6462)
Related titles: Online - full text ed.
Indexed: B01, B07, FR, V01.
—INIST.
Published by: Agence pour la Diffusion de l'Information Technologique, 2, rue Brulee, Strasbourg, 67000, France. TEL 33-3-88214242, FAX 33-3-88214240, info@adit.fr, http://www.adit.fr/.

600 USA ISSN 1050-043X
T174.3
TECHNOLOGY ACCESS REPORT; newsletter for technology transfer, commercialization, defense conversion, technology policy and management. Text in English. 1988. m. USD 497. bk.rev. back issues avail. **Document type:** *Newsletter.* **Description:** Covers technology transfer and commercialization of research from universities, government, and independent laboratories and medical centers; defense-conversion, manufacturing modernization, technology management, industrial policy, licensing, venture capital, and cooperative research and developments for all companies in all industries.
Formerly: Technology Access
Related titles: Diskette ed.; Online - full text ed.
Indexed: B02, B15, B17, B18, G04, G06, G07, G08, I05, P17, P48, P52, P53, P54, PQC.
—CCC.
Published by: University R & D Opportunities, Inc., 64 Shattuck Sq., # 220, Berkeley, CA 94704-1135. TEL 415-883-7600, 800-733-1556, FAX 415-883-6421. Ed., Pub. Michael Odza. Circ: 1,000 (paid).

600 GBR ISSN 0953-7325
HD45
➤ **TECHNOLOGY ANALYSIS & STRATEGIC MANAGEMENT.** Text in English. 1989. 8/yr. GBP 1,787 combined subscription in United Kingdom to institutions (print & online eds.); EUR 2,566, USD 3,206 combined subscription to institutions (print & online eds.) (effective 2012). adv. bk.rev. back issues avail.; reprint service avail. from PSC. **Document type:** *Journal, Academic/Scholarly.* **Description:** Presents international research linking the analysis of science and technology with the strategic needs of policymakers and management.
Related titles: Microfiche ed.; Online - full text ed.: ISSN 1465-3990. GBP 1,608 in United Kingdom to institutions; EUR 2,309, USD 2,886 to institutions (effective 2012) (from IngentaConnect).
Indexed: A01, A03, A08, A12, A17, A20, A22, ABIn, ASCA, B01, B06, B07, B08, B09, C12, C23, CA, CPE, CurCont, DIP, E01, ESPM, EconLit, Emerald, GEOBASE, HPNRM, IBR, IBSS, IBZ, JEL, M&MA, P34, P41, P48, P51, P52, P53, P54, PQC, RASB, RiskAb, S01, SCOPUS, SSCI, SSciA, T02, W07.
—IE, Infotrieve, Ingenta. **CCC.**
Published by: Routledge (Subsidiary of: Taylor & Francis Group), 4 Park Sq, Milton Park, Abingdon, Oxon OX14 4RN, United Kingdom. TEL 44-20-70176000, FAX 44-20-70176336, subscriptions@tandf.co.uk, http://www.routledge.com. Ed. Harry Rothman. Adv. contact Linda Hann TEL 44-1344-779945. **Subscr. to:** Taylor & Francis Ltd., Journals Customer Service, Sheepen Pl, Colchester, Essex CO3 3LP, United Kingdom. TEL 44-20-70175544, FAX 44-20-70175198.

609 NLD ISSN 1385-920X
➤ **TECHNOLOGY AND CHANGE IN HISTORY.** Text in English. 1997. irreg., latest vol.10, 2008. price varies. **Document type:** *Monographic series, Academic/Scholarly.*
Indexed: IZBG.
—BLDSC (8758.548000), IE, Ingenta.
Published by: Brill, PO Box 9000, Leiden, 2300 PA, Netherlands. TEL 31-71-5353500, FAX 31-71-5317532, cs@brill.nl, http://www.brill.nl. **Dist. in N. America by:** Brill, PO Box 605, Herndon, VA 20172-0605. TEL 703-661-1585, 800-337-9255, FAX 703-661-1501, cs@brillusa.com; **Dist. by:** Turpin Distribution Services Ltd., Pegasus Dr, Stratton Business Park, Biggleswade, Bedfordshire SG18 8QB, United Kingdom. TEL 44-1767-604954, FAX 44-1767-601640, custserv@turpin-distribution.com, http://www.turpin-distribution.com/.

300 600 USA ISSN 0040-165X
➤ **TECHNOLOGY AND CULTURE.** Abbreviated title: T & C. Text in English. 1960. q. USD 173 to institutions (print or online ed.); USD 242.20 combined subscription to institutions (print & online eds.); USD 52 per issue to institutions (effective 2011). bk.rev. bibl.; charts; illus. cum.index: vols.1-10 (1959-1969). 256 p./no.; back issues avail.; reprint service avail. from PSC. **Document type:** *Journal, Academic/Scholarly.* **Description:** Explores the history of technology from antiquity to the present day over all geographical and cultural boundaries.
Related titles: Microform ed.: (from PQC); Online - full text ed.: ISSN 1097-3729. 1959; Supplement(s): Technology and Culture. Current Bibliography in the History of Technology. ISSN 1080-1979.
Indexed: A&ATA, A01, A02, A03, A05, A08, A12, A20, A21, A22, A25, A26, ABIn, ABS&EES, AS&TA, AS&TI, ASCA, AcaI, AmH&L, ArtHuCI, B04, B14, B24, BAS, BRD, BRI, BrArAb, C10, CA, CBRI, CommAb, CompLI, CurCont, DIP, E01, E08, EMBASE, ExcerpMed, FR, G08, H09, HistAb, I05, IBR, IBSS, IBZ, JEL, M01, M02, MEA&I, MEDLINE, MLA-IB, NumL, P02, P10, P13, P26, P27, P30, P34, P48, P51, P53, P54, PCI, PQC, RASB, RI-1, RI-2, RILM, S02, S03, S05, S08, S09, S11, SCI, SCOPUS, SOPODA, SSA, SSAI, SSAb, SSCI, SSI, SociolAb, T02, W03, W07, W09.
—BLDSC (8758.600000), IE, Infotrieve, Ingenta, INIST, Linda Hall. **CCC.**
Published by: (Society for the History of Technology), The Johns Hopkins University Press, 2715 N Charles St, Baltimore, MD 21218. TEL 410-516-6900, FAX 410-516-6968, bjs@press.jhu.edu. Ed. Suzanne Moon. Pub. William M Breichner. Circ: 1,949. **Subscr. to:** PO Box 19966, Baltimore, MD 21211. TEL 410-516-6987, 800-548-1784, FAX 410-516-3866, jrnlcirc@press.jhu.edu.

➤ **TECHNOLOGY AND ENGINEERING TEACHER.** *see* EDUCATION—Teaching Methods And Curriculum

600 USA ISSN 1949-8241
T1 CODEN: TJFIFM
TECHNOLOGY AND INNOVATION; proceedings of the National Academy of Inventors. Text in English. 199?. bi-m. USD 280 combined subscription to institutions (print & online eds.) (effective 2011). adv. back issues avail. **Document type:** *Proceedings, Academic/Scholarly.* **Description:** Encompasses all fields of applied sciences and advanced technology. Reports scientific findings, reviews developments in science, engineering and technology, including laws, regulations, judicial decisions and government actions. Also covers the economics, and environmental and health aspects of technology, as well as historical, social and ethical aspects.
Formerly (until 2010): Technology (1072-9240)
Related titles: Online - full text ed.: ISSN 1949-825X. USD 240 (effective 2011) (from IngentaConnect).
Indexed: EngInd, P30, SCOPUS.
—IE, Ingenta. **CCC.**
Published by: (National Academy of Inventors), Cognizant Communication Corp., 18 Peeksill Hollow Rd, P O Box 37, Putnam Valley, NY 10579. http://www.cognizantcommunication.com. Ed. Paul R Sanberg. Circ: 320 (paid).

600 332.6 USA ISSN 2150-4059
▼ **TECHNOLOGY AND INVESTMENT/JISHU YU TOUZI.** Text in English. 2009. q. **Document type:** *Journal, Academic/Scholarly.*
Related titles: Online - full text ed.: ISSN 2150-4067. free (effective 2011).
Published by: Scientific Research Publishing, Inc., PO Box 54821, Irvine, CA 92619. TEL 408-329-4591, srp@srpublishing.org, http://www.srpublishing.org.

500 ESP ISSN 2172-0436
▼ **TECHNOLOGY AND KNOWLEDGE TRANSFER.** Text in Spanish. 2010. q. back issues avail. **Document type:** *Bulletin, Academic/Scholarly.*
Media: Online - full text.
Published by: Universidad Politecnica de Cartagena, Servicio de Documentacion, Plaza del Cronista Isicho Valverde, Edif. La Milagrosa, Cartagena, 30202, Spain. TEL 34-968-325400, http://www.upct.es/. Ed. Maria Jose Vicente.

TECHNOLOGY & PRODUCTIVITY WEEKLY. *see* BUSINESS AND ECONOMICS

TECHNOLOGY BUSINESS JOURNAL. *see* BUSINESS AND ECONOMICS

600 346.04 GBR ISSN 0965-0326
TECHNOLOGY COMMERCIALIZATION - EUROPE EDITION. Text in English. 1991. m.
Published by: Neil MacDonald Publisher, Enterprise House, Ocean Village, Southampton, SO14 3XB, United Kingdom. TEL 01703-331666, FAX 01703-332050. Ed. Neil MacDonald.

600 346.04 GBR ISSN 1059-292X
TECHNOLOGY COMMERCIALIZATION - NORTH AMERICA EDITION. Text in English. 1991. m. **Document type:** *Newsletter.*
Published by: Neil MacDonald Publisher, Enterprise House, Ocean Village, Southampton, SO14 3XB, United Kingdom. TEL 01703-331666, FAX 01703-332050. Ed. Neil MacDonald.

TECHNOLOGY EDUCATION. *see* EDUCATION

TECHNOLOGY FOCUS. *see* MILITARY

600 USA ISSN 0886-0890
TECHNOLOGY FORECASTS & TECHNOLOGY SURVEYS. Text in English. 1969. m. USD 192 domestic; USD 196 in Canada & Mexico; USD 202 elsewhere (effective 2005). bk.rev. back issues avail. **Document type:** *Newsletter, Trade.* **Description:** Discusses important trends or advances in science and technology likely to have a great effect in the future.
Published by: Technology Forecasts, 205 S Beverly Dr, Ste 208, Beverly Hills, CA 90212. TEL 310-273-3486, FAX 310-858-8272. Ed. Irwin Stambler.

TECHNOLOGY GRANT NEWS. *see* SOCIAL SERVICES AND WELFARE

TECHNOLOGY IN EDUCATION; devoted to the teaching of science and design technology including art & design, business studies, craft design technology, home economics, and information technology. *see* EDUCATION

658.2 600 GBR ISSN 1365-7062
TECHNOLOGY IN PRACTICE. Text in English. 1996. m. **Document type:** *Magazine, Trade.*
Related titles: Online - full text ed.
Indexed: B02, B15, B17, B18, G04, G06, G07, G08, I05.
Published by: Gillard Welch Ltd., 355 Station Rd, Dorridge, Solihull, W Mids B93 8EY, United Kingdom. TEL 44-1564-771772, FAX 44-1564-774776.

TECHNOLOGY INTERFACE; the electronic journal for engineering technology. *see* ENGINEERING

TECHNOLOGY INVESTOR (ONLINE). *see* BUSINESS AND ECONOMICS—Investments

620 IRL ISSN 0040-1676
T1 CODEN: TEIRDR
TECHNOLOGY IRELAND. Text in English. 1969. 10/yr. EUR 49 (effective 2005). adv. bk.rev. abstr.; illus. index. **Document type:** *Magazine, Trade.* **Description:** Covers aspects of technology in engineering, construction, chemicals, electronics, plastics, energy, food, packaging, and textiles.
Indexed: A22, BrArAb, F&EA, FS&TA, ICEA, INIS AtomInd, IPackAb, M&MA, NumL, P&BA, SoftAbEng.
—BLDSC (8758.900000), IE, Ingenta, Linda Hall.
Published by: Enterprise Ireland, Merrion Hall, Strand Rd, Dublin, 4, Ireland. TEL 353-1-2066337, FAX 353-1-2066342, http://www.enterprise-ireland.com. Ed. Sean Duke. R&P Duncan Black. Adv. contact Barry Bradshaw TEL 353-1-2066378. color page EUR 1,740; 210 x 297. Circ: 5,500 (paid).

TECHNOLOGY MANAGEMENT ACTION. *see* BUSINESS AND ECONOMICS—International Commerce

600 004 USA ISSN 1521-5202
TECHNOLOGY MEETINGS; meeting and incentive solutions for the high-tech industry. Text in English. 1998. bi-m. **Description:** Serves manufacturers of computer and office equipment, communications equipment, electronic components and accessories, computer and data processing services, communication companies, and other corporations in the technology industry.
Related titles: Online - full text ed.
Indexed: A10, B01, B06, B07, B09, BPI, BRD, S04, V03, W01, W02, W03, W05.
—CCC.
Published by: Adams Business Media, 2101 S Arlington Heights Rd, 150, Arlington, IL 60005. http://www.abm.net.

600 USA ISSN 1944-2734
TECHNOLOGY NEWS FOCUS. Text in English. 2008. w. USD 2,295 in US & Canada; USD 2,495 elsewhere; USD 2,525 combined subscription in US & Canada (print & online eds.); USD 2,755 combined subscription elsewhere (print & online eds.) (effective 2011). back issues avail. **Document type:** *Newsletter, Trade.* **Description:** Provides a broad range of technology news, including chemical, electrical, manufacturing, optical, solid state, fiber and nanotechnology research and developments.
Related titles: E-mail ed.; Online - full text ed.: ISSN 1944-2742. USD 2,295 combined subscription (online & e-mail eds.) (effective 2011).
Indexed: I05, P10, P16, P26, P48, P52, P53, P54, PQC.
Published by: NewsRx, 2727 Paces Ferry Rd SE, Ste 2-440, Atlanta, GA 30339. TEL 770-435-8286, 800-726-4550, FAX 770-435-6800, pressrelease@newsrx.com, http://www.newsrx.com. Pub., Adv. contact Susan Hasty TEL 770-507-7777.

600 AUS
TECHNOLOGY PARK TENANT DIRECTORY. Text in English. 2004. a. free (effective 2009). **Document type:** *Directory, Trade.* **Description:** Contains information the source of each user waives and releases the department and the State of Western Australia.
Formerly (until 2007): Technology Park, Bentley Directory (1832-0406)
Published by: Western Australia, Department of Commerce, The Forrest Ctr, 221 St. Georges Terrace, Perth, W.A. 6000, Australia. TEL 300-136-237, http://www.commerce.wa.gov.au.

600 USA ISSN 1528-4263
TECHNOLOGY RESEARCH NEWS. Text in English. 2000. bi-w. USD 29 (effective 2004). **Document type:** *Magazine, Consumer.*
Media: Online - full content. **Related titles:** Online - full text ed.
Indexed: P17, P48, P52, P53, P54, PQC.
Published by: Technology Research News LLC, 22 Conway St, Boston, MA 02131. TEL 617-325-4940. Eds. Eric Smalley, Kimberly Patch.

TECHNOLOGY REVIEW; das M.I.T. Magazin fuer Innovation. *see* SCIENCES: COMPREHENSIVE WORKS

TECHNOLOGY REVIEW. *see* SCIENCES: COMPREHENSIVE WORKS

600 613.62 USA ISSN 1093-7137
TECHNOLOGY SPECIAL INTEREST SECTION QUARTERLY. Text in English. 1991. q. free to members (effective 2010). adv. **Document type:** *Newsletter, Trade.* **Description:** Provides a forum for learning about technologies specific to individuals with disabilities and focuses on the role of the occupational therapy professionals in technology service delivery.
Formerly (until 1997): Technology Special Interest Section Newsletter (1059-0609)
Related titles: Online - full text ed.; ◆ Series: Developmental Disabilities Special Interest Section Quarterly. ISSN 1093-7196; ◆ Gerontology Special Interest Section Quarterly. ISSN 1093-717X; ◆ Physical Disabilities Special Interest Section Quarterly. ISSN 1093-7234; ◆ Sensory Integration Special Interest Section Quarterly. ISSN 1093-7250; ◆ Work & Industry Special Interest Section Quarterly; ◆ Education Special Interest Section Quarterly. ISSN 1093-7188; ◆ Administration & Management Special Interest Section Quarterly. ISSN 1093-720X; ◆ Mental Health Special Interest Section Quarterly. ISSN 1093-7226.
Indexed: C06, C07, C08, CINAHL, P24, P48, PQC.
—CCC.
Published by: American Occupational Therapy Association, Inc., 4720 Montgomery Ln, PO Box 31220, Bethesda, MD 20824. TEL 301-652-2682, 800-377-8555, FAX 301-652-7711, members@aota.org. Ed. Katherine M Post.

TECHNOLOGY TRANSFERS AND LICENSING. *see* PATENTS, TRADEMARKS AND COPYRIGHTS

600 USA ISSN 1949-4254
TECHNOLOGYPROFESSIONAL.ORG; advance the profession. advance your career. Text in English. 2008. m. free (effective 2009). **Document type:** *Magazine, Trade.* **Description:** Provides a forum to share insights and best practices with other technology leaders.
Media: Online - full content.
Published by: Philip Stevens, Ed. & Pub, 1595 Peachtree Pky, Cumming, GA 30041. TEL 888-267-7833.

600 USA ISSN 1087-965X
TECHNOTRENDS NEWSLETTER; the big ideas that are changing everything. Text in English. 1985. m. USD 39.95 domestic; USD 47 in Canada; USD 51.95 elsewhere (effective 2007). 2 cols./p.; back issues avail. **Document type:** *Newsletter, Trade.* **Description:** Features short, easy-reading news articles describing breakthrough innovations in technology and science.
Formerly (until 1993): Technology Futures Newsletter (0896-744X)
Indexed: A10, V03.
Published by: Burrus Research Associates, Inc., P O Box 47, Hartland, WI 53029-0047. TEL 262-367-0949, FAX 262-367-7163, office@burrus.com, http://www.burrus.com. Ed. Patti A Thomsen. Pub. Daniel Burrus. R&P Rosey Teays. Circ: 2,000.

600 GBR ISSN 0166-4972
HD45
➤ **TECHNOVATION.** Text in English. 1981. 12/yr. EUR 1,787 in Europe to institutions; JPY 237,200 in Japan to institutions; USD 1,998 elsewhere to institutions (effective 2012). adv. illus. back issues avail.; reprints avail. **Document type:** *Journal, Academic/Scholarly.* **Description:** Covers all facets of the technical innovation process, from the development of a new product or process through commercial utilization.
Related titles: Online - full text ed.: ISSN 1879-2383 (from IngentaConnect, ScienceDirect).
Indexed: A12, A13, A17, A20, A22, A26, A28, ABIn, APA, ASCA, B01, B02, B06, B07, B08, B09, B11, B15, B17, B18, B21, Biostat, BrCerAb, C&ISA, CA, CA/WCA, CIA, CPEI, CPM, CerAb, CivEngAb, CorrAb, CurCont, E&CAJ, E08, E11, EEA, EMA, ESPM, Emerald, EngInd, EnvEAb, G04, G06, G07, G08, H15, I05, IBSS, M&TEA, M09, MBF, METADEX, ManagCont, P34, P41, P48, P51, P53, P54, PQC, RASB, RiskAb, S09, SCI, SCOPUS, SSCI, SolStAb, T02, T04, TM, VITIS, W07, WAA.
—BLDSC (8761.150000), IE, Infotrieve, Ingenta, INIST, Linda Hall. **CCC.**
Published by: Pergamon (Subsidiary of: Elsevier Science & Technology), The Blvd, Langford Ln, East Park, Kidlington, Oxford OX5 1GB, United Kingdom. TEL 44-1865-843000, FAX 44-1865-843010, JournalsCustomerServiceEMEA@elsevier.com. Ed. J Linton. **Subscr. to:** Elsevier BV, Radarweg 29, PO Box 211, Amsterdam 1000 AE, Netherlands. TEL 31-20-4853757, FAX 31-20-4853432, http://www.elsevier.nl.

600 AUS ISSN 1838-2754
▼ **TECHSTATE**; news from South Australia's technology industry. Text in English. 2011. m. free (effective 2011). **Document type:** *Magazine, Trade.* **Description:** Contains trends in the sector in South Australia, recent developments and people making news.
Related titles: Online - full text ed.
Published by: Solstice Media Pty. Ltd., 4 Cinema Pl, Adelaide, SA 5000, Australia. TEL 61-8-82241614, FAX 61-8-82241650, editorial@solsticemedia.com.au.

600 PAN ISSN 1609-8102
TECNOCIENCIA. Text in Spanish. 1995. s-a. back issues avail. **Document type:** *Journal, Academic/Scholarly.*
Indexed: C01.
Published by: Universidad de Panama, Facultad de Ciencias Naturales, Exactas y Tecnologia, Campus Octavio Mendez Pereira, Panama, Panama. TEL 507-223-9280, FAX 507-263-7636, decacnet@ancon.up.ac.pa, http://www.up.ac.pa/PortalUp/index.aspx.

600 338 MEX ISSN 0188-6452
HD45 CODEN: MSCEEE
TECNOINDUSTRIA. Text in Spanish. MXN 90; USD 45 foreign. adv. **Document type:** *Trade.*
Published by: Consejo Nacional de Ciencia y Tecnologia, Ave Insurgentes Sur 1582, Col Credito Constructor, Mexico, D.F., 03940, Mexico. TEL 52-5-627-7400. Ed. Concepcion Garrido Barriga. Adv. contact Jose Luis Miranda Salgado.

TECNOINTELECTO. *see* SCIENCES: COMPREHENSIVE WORKS

600 BRA ISSN 0103-7064
TECNOLOGIA & HUMANISMO. Text in Portuguese. 1986. s-a. **Document type:** *Journal, Academic/Scholarly.*
Published by: Centro Federal de Educacao Tecnologica do Parana (C E F E T - P R), Av Sete de Setembro 3165 Reboucas, Curitiba, PR 80230-901, Brazil. TEL 55-41-33104545, http://www.cefetpr.br/instituicao/apresent.htm.

TECNOLOGIA, CIENCIA, EDUCACION. *see* SCIENCES: COMPREHENSIVE WORKS

623 355 ITA ISSN 1724-594X
TECNOLOGIA & DIFESA. Text in Italian. 2004. m. EUR 40 (effective 2008). **Document type:** *Magazine, Consumer.*
Published by: Gruppo Editoriale Olimpia SpA, Via E Fermi 24, Loc Osmannoro, Sesto Fiorentino, FI 50129, Italy. TEL 39-055-30321, FAX 39-055-3032280, info@edolimpia.it, http://www.edolimpia.it.

600 CRI ISSN 0379-3982
T4
TECNOLOGIA EN MARCHA. Text in Spanish. 1978. q. USD 20. adv. bk.rev. bibl.; charts. **Document type:** *Academic/Scholarly.*
Indexed: IBR, IBZ, INIS AtomInd.
Published by: Instituto Tecnologico de Costa Rica, Apdo 159, Cartago, 7050, Costa Rica. TEL 506-552-5333, FAX 506-551-5348, TELEX 8013-ITCR-CR. Ed. Mario Castillo. Circ: 1,500.

600 384 MEX ISSN 0187-0785
TECNOLOGIA Y COMUNICACION EDUCATIVAS. Text in Spanish. irreg. **Document type:** *Magazine, Trade.*
Indexed: C01.
Published by: Instituto Latinoamericano de la Comunicacion Educativa (I L C E), Calle del Puente 45, Col Ejidos de Huipulco, Delegacion Tlalpan, Mexico City, 14380, Mexico. TEL 52-57-286500, contacto@ilce.edu.mx, http://www.ilce.edu.mx.

600 PRT ISSN 1646-8856
TECNOLOGICA. Text in Portuguese. 2007. irreg. **Document type:** *Monographic series, Academic/Scholarly.*
Published by: Universidade Tecnica de Lisboa, Instituto Superior Tecnico (I S T), Av Rovisco Pais 1, Lisbon, 1049-001, Portugal. TEL 351-218-417000, FAX 351-218-499242, http://www.ist.utl.pt.

600 ECU ISSN 0257-1749
T4
TECNOLOGICA. Text in Spanish. 1976. q. USD 30.
Media: Microform.
Published by: Escuela Superior Politecnica del Litoral, Apdo 5863, Guayaquil, Guayas, Ecuador. Ed. Homero Ortiz. Circ: 500.

600 ITA ISSN 2035-5157
TECNOLOGIE & SOLUZIONI PER L'AMBIENTE. Text in Italian. 2007. bi-m.
Formerly (until 2007): Tecnologie e Soluzioni (2035-5165)
Published by: Il Sole 24 Ore Business Media, Via Monte Rosa 91, Milan, 20149, Italy. TEL 39-02-30221, FAX 39-02-312055, info@ilsole24ore.com, http://www.gruppo24ore.com.

TECNURA. *see* ENGINEERING

600 PRT ISSN 1645-9911
TEKHNE; revista de estudos politecnicos. Text in Portuguese. 2004. s-a. back issues avail. **Document type:** *Journal, Academic/Scholarly.*
Related titles: Online - full text ed.
Published by: Instituto Politecnico do Cavado e do Ave, Ave Dr. Sidonio Pais 222, Barcelos, 4750-333, Portugal. TEL 351-253-802190, FAX 351-253-812281, mjfernandes@ipca.pt, http://www.ipca.pt/tekhne/index.htm. Ed. Joao Carvalho.

620 RUS ISSN 0320-331X
TEKHNIKA MOLODEZHI. Text in Russian. 1933. m. USD 72 foreign (effective 2005). adv. bk.rev. illus. index. **Document type:** *Magazine, Trade.*
Indexed: ChemAb, RASB.
—East View.
Published by: Redaktsiya Tekhnika Molodezhi, Novodmitrovskaya ul 5-a, Moscow, 125015, Russian Federation. TEL 7-095-2852018, FAX 7-095-2851687. Ed. Aleksander N Perevozchikov. adv.: color page USD 2,300. Circ: 50,000. **Dist. by:** M K - Periodica, ul Gilyarovskogo 39, Moscow 129110, Russian Federation. TEL 7-095-2845008, FAX 7-095-2813798, info@periodicals.ru, http://www.mkniga.ru.

600 BGR ISSN 1312-6806
TEKHNOLOGICHEN DOM. Text in Bulgarian. 2005. 9/yr. free. **Document type:** *Journal, Trade.*
Related titles: Online - full text ed.
Published by: TLL Media Ltd., Akad Ivan Ev Geshov 104, ofis 9, Sofia, 1612, Bulgaria. TEL 359-2-8183838, FAX 359-2-8183800, office@tllmedia.bg, http://www.tllmedia.bg. Eds. Petya Nakova, Amelia Stoimenova.

605 SWE ISSN 1653-2139
TEKLA. Text in Swedish. 2005. bi-m. SEK 199 (effective 2006). adv. **Document type:** *Magazine, Consumer.* **Description:** Science and technology magazine aimed at teen-age girls.
Published by: M. U. C. S. Media AB, PO Box 7285, Goeteborg, 40235, Sweden. Ed. Camilla Sjoestedt TEL 46-706-783789. Adv. contact Malin Ulfvarson TEL 46-709586377. page SEK 15,000; 215 x 277.

620 NOR ISSN 0040-2354
T4 CODEN: TEKKBE
TEKNISK UKEBLAD/TECHNOLOGY REVIEW WEEKLY; Norges fremste paa teknologi. Short title: T U. Variant title: Teknisk Ukeblad. Teknikk. Text in Norwegian. 1883. 42/yr. NOK 2,079; NOK 1,089 to students (effective 2011). adv. bk.rev. charts; illus.; tr.lit. index. 64 p./no.; back issues avail. **Document type:** *Magazine, Trade.* **Description:** Covers every aspect of technology as well as the political and financial impact of these technologies in society.
Incorporates (2007-2009): Forbrukerteknologi (1890-4785); Former titles (until 1977): Teknisk Ugeblad. Teknikk (0806-4024); (until 1969): Teknisk Ukeblad (0806-4016); Incorporates (1930-1967): Teknikk (0371-6341); Incorporates (1883-1896): Norsk Teknisk Tidsskrift (0806-4083); Which was formed by the merger of (1878-1882): Den Norske Ingenioer- og Arkitektforenings Organ (0806-4091); (1854-1882): Polyteknisk Tidsskrift (0806-4105)
Related titles: Online - full text ed.: ISSN 1501-6633. 1995.
Indexed: CISA, ChemAb, GeoRef, INIS AtomInd, Inspec, SCIMP, SpeleolAb.
—CASDDS, Linda Hall.
Published by: Teknisk Ukeblad Media AS, PO Box 5844, Majorstuen, Oslo, 0308, Norway. TEL 47-23-199300, FAX 47-23-199301. Ed. Tormod Haugstad. Adv. contact Lizzie Nilsen. Circ: 117,000.
Co-sponsors: Norske Sivilingenioerers Forening/Norwegian Society of Chartered Engineers; Norges Ingenioerorganisasjon/Association of Norwegian Engineers; Polytekniske Forening - Polytechnical Society.

600 DNK ISSN 0905-5681
TEKNOLOGIDEBAT. Text in Danish. 1986. q. free (effective 2004). **Document type:** *Magazine, Consumer.*
Formerly (until 1990): Tit (0902-2317); Incorporates (1975-1999): Teknologiraadet. Aarsberetning (0105-8967)
Related titles: Online - full text ed.: 2000.
Published by: Teknologiraadet/Danish Board of Technology, Antoniogade 4, Copenhagen K, 1106, Denmark. TEL 45-33-320503, FAX 45-33-910509, tekno@tekno.dk. Ed. Joergen Madsen.

600 DNK ISSN 1904-3066
▼ **TEKNOLOGIHISTORIER.** Text in Danish. 2010. irreg. **Document type:** *Monographic series, Consumer.*
Media: Online - full text.
Published by: Dansk Teknologihistorisk Selskab, c/o Frank Allen Rasmussen, Industrimuseet Frederiks Vaerk, Jernbanegade 4, Frederiksvaerk, 3200, Denmark. TEL 45-47-720605, far@indmus.dk. Ed. Soeren B Andersen.

600 DNK ISSN 1395-7392
TEKNOLOGIRAADET. RAPPORTER/DANISH BOARD OF TECHNOLOGY. REPORT. Text in Danish; Text occasionally in English. 1987. irreg. Price varies. **Document type:** *Monographic series, Consumer.*
Formerly (until 1995): Teknologinaevnet. Rapporter (0903-2789)
Related titles: Online - full text ed.: ISSN 1601-1910. 199?.
Published by: Teknologiraadet/Danish Board of Technology, Antoniogade 4, Copenhagen K, 1106, Denmark. TEL 45-33-320503, FAX 45-33-910509, tekno@tekno.dk.

TELEVISION SERVICING. *see* ELECTRONICS

TENSOR. *see* MATHEMATICS

TEORIE VEDY/THEORY OF SCIENCE. *see* SCIENCES: COMPREHENSIVE WORKS

600 USA
TETRA TECH INCORPORATED. TECHNICAL REPORT. Text in English. irreg.
Published by: Tetra Tech, Incorporated, 670 N Rosemead Blvd, Pasadena, CA 91107. TEL 626-351-4664, FAX 626-351-5291, info@tetratech.com, http://www.tetratech.com.

300 USA
TEXAS TECHNOLOGY; innovation for government and education. Text in English. 1997. q. free (effective 2008). adv. back issues avail.; reprints avail. **Document type:** *Magazine, Trade.* **Description:** Enables state and local government and education officials to share technology information specific to the State of Texas.
Related titles: Online - full content ed.
Published by: e.Republic, Inc., 100 Blue Ravine Rd, Folsom, CA 95630. TEL 916-932-1300, FAX 916-932-1470, getinfo@govtech.net, http://www.govtech.net/. Ed. Steve Towns TEL 916-932-1333. Pub. Jon Fyffe TEL 916-932-1300. adv.: page USD 7,350; trim 8 x 10.5. Circ: 30,000.

TEZHONG SHEBEI ANQUAN JISHU/SAFETY TECHNOLOGY OF SPECIAL EQUIPMENT. *see* OCCUPATIONAL HEALTH AND SAFETY

THAMMASAT INTERNATIONAL JOURNAL OF SCIENCE AND TECHNOLOGY. *see* SCIENCES: COMPREHENSIVE WORKS

THEAETETO ATHENIENSI MATHEMATICA; revista latinoamericana de ciencias e ingenieria. *see* SCIENCES: COMPREHENSIVE WORKS

600 DEU ISSN 1612-2771
TS300
THYSSENKRUPP TECHFORUM (ENGLISH EDITION). Text in English. 1986. s-a. **Document type:** *Journal, Trade.*
Former titles (until 2003): Forum Technische Mitteilungen ThyssenKrupp (English Edition) (1438-9754); (until 1999): Technische Mitteilungen Krupp (English Edition) (0930-9284)
Related titles: ◆ German ed.: ThyssenKrupp Techforum (Germany Edition). ISSN 1612-2763.
Indexed: A28, APA, BrCerAb, C&ISA, CA/WCA, CIA, CPEI, CerAb, CivEngAb, CorrAb, E&CAJ, E11, EEA, EMA, EngInd, H15, Inspec, M&TEA, M09, MBF, METADEX, SCOPUS, SolStAb, T04, WAA.
—BLDSC (8820.392000), IE, INIST, Linda Hall. **CCC.**
Published by: ThyssenKrupp AG, August-Thyssen-Str 1, PO Box 101010, Duesseldorf, 40211, Germany. TEL 49-211-8240, FAX 49-211-82436000, info@thyssenkrupp.com, http://www.thyssenkrupp.com.

600 DEU ISSN 1612-2763
THYSSENKRUPP TECHFORUM (GERMANY EDITION). Text in German. 1920-1943; resumed 1954. 2/yr. free. charts; illus. index. **Document type:** *Journal, Trade.*
Former titles (until 2003): Forum Technische Mitteilungen ThyssenKrupp (Germany Edition) (1438-5635); (until 1999): Technische Mitteilungen Krupp (Germany Edition) (0930-9276); Incorporates (1986-1992): Berichte aus Forschung und Entwicklung Unserer Gesellschaften (0931-0207); Formed by the 1985 merger of: Technische Mitteilungen Krupp. Werksberichte (0494-9390); Technische Mitteilungen Krupp. Forschungsberichte (0494-9382); Both of which superseded (in 1961): Technische Mitteilungen Krupp (0931-0924); Which was formed by the merger of (1938-1943): Technische Mitteilungen Krupp. Ausgabe A, Forschungsberichte (0276-0812); (1938-1943): Technische Mitteilungen Krupp. Ausgabe B, Technische Berichte (0371-9707); Both of which superseded in part (in 1938): Technische Mitteilungen Krupp (0371-9731); Which was formerly (until 1933): Kruppsche Montatshefte (0368-6779)
Related titles: ◆ English ed.: ThyssenKrupp Techforum (English Edition). ISSN 1612-2771.
Indexed: CEABA, CIN, ChemAb, ChemTitl, IMMAb, Inspec, SCOPUS, TM.
—CASDDS, Ingenta, INIST, Linda Hall. **CCC.**
Published by: ThyssenKrupp AG, August-Thyssen-Str 1, PO Box 101010, Duesseldorf, 40211, Germany. info@thyssenkrupp.com, http://www.thyssenkrupp.com. Circ: 8,000.

600 CHN ISSN 1673-095X
TIANJIN LIGONG DAXUE XUEBAO/TIANJIN UNIVERSITY OF TECHNOLOGY. JOURNAL. Text in Chinese. 1985. bi-m. CNY 6 newsstand/cover (effective 2007). **Document type:** *Journal, Academic/Scholarly.*
Formerly: Tianjin Ligong Xueyuan Xuebao/Tianjin Institute of Technology. Journal (1004-2261)
Related titles: Online - full text ed.
—BLDSC (8820.509750).
Published by: Tianjin Ligong Daxue, 263, Hongqi Nan Lu, Tianjin, 300191, China. TEL 86-22-23679427, FAX 86-22-23362948.

600 FRA ISSN 1961-9510
T14.5T43 CODEN: TINSEG
TICETSOCIETE. Text in French. 1988-1997; resumed 2007. s-a. free (effective 2011). **Document type:** *Journal, Academic/Scholarly.* **Description:** Covers economics, sociology, law, philosophy, ergonomics, psychology and the sciences of management, communication and education.
Formerly (until 2006): Technologies de l'Information et Societe (0840-4836)
Media: Online - full text.
Indexed: FR, IBR, IBZ, Inspec, PdeR, SCOPUS, SOPODA, SociolAb.
Published by: Association de Recherche en Technologies de l'Information et de la Communication ticetsociete@revues.org, http://www.ticetsociete.org. Eds. Dominique Carre, Eric George.

TIERRA Y TECNOLOGIA. *see* EARTH SCIENCES—Geology

600 630 LBN
AL-TIKNULUJIA AL-MULA'IMAH/MIDDLE EAST APPROPRIATE TECHNOLOGY NEWS. Text in Arabic; Summaries in English. 1984. irreg. (2-4/yr.). looseleaf. free. **Document type:** *Newsletter.* **Description:** Publishes review articles on aspects of appropriate technology of interest to scientists, engineers, agricultural technicians and planners, introducing new ideas and defining a technical vocabulary in Arabic in the various fields.
Published by: Markaz al-Sharq al-Awsat lil-Tiknulujia al-Mula'imah/ Middle East Center for the Transfer of Appropriate Technology, P O Box 113 5474, Beirut, Lebanon. TEL 346465, TELEX 41224 MEEA LE. Circ: 3,000.

600 NLD ISSN 1877-5721
▼ **TILBURG CENTRE FOR CREATIVE COMPUTING. TECHNICAL REPORT SERIES.** Key Title: TiCC Technical Report Series. Text in English. 2009. irreg. **Document type:** *Monographic series, Academic/Scholarly.*
Media: Online - full text.
Published by: Tilburg Centre for Creative Computing, Tilburg University, School of Humanities, PO Box 90153, Tilburg, 5000 LE, Netherlands. TEL 31-13-4668118, ticc@uvt.nl.

TNOTIME. *see* SCIENCES: COMPREHENSIVE WORKS

600 JPN ISSN 0919-8881
T177.J3 CODEN: TKKEE7
TOHOKU NATIONAL INDUSTRIAL RESEARCH INSTITUTE. REPORTS/TOHOKU KOGYO GIJUTSU KENKYUJO HOKOKU. Text in English. 1972. a.
Formerly (until 1994): Government Industrial Research Institute, Tohoku. Reports - Tohoku Kogyo Gijutsu Shikenjo Hokoku (0389-939X)
—CASDDS.
Published by: Tohoku National Industrial Research Institute, 4-2-1 Nigatake, Miyagino-ku, Sendai-shi, Miyagi-ken 983-0036, Japan.

605 JPN ISSN 0495-8055
TOKYO INSTITUTE OF TECHNOLOGY. RESEARCH LABORATORY OF RESOURCES UTILIZATION. REPORT/SHIGEN KAGAKU KENKYUJO. Text in English. a.
Indexed: Inspec.
Published by: Tokyo Kogyo Daigaku, Shigen Kagaku Kenkyujo/Tokyo Institute of Technology, Research Laboratory of Resources Utilization, 2-1 Okayama 2-chome, Meguro-ku, Tokyo, 152-0033, Japan.

TOKYO METROPOLITAN UNIVERSITY. GRADUATE SCHOOL OF ENGINEERING. MEMOIRS. *see* ENGINEERING

600 JPN ISSN 0913-8897
CODEN: TTKKBH
TOKYO TORITSU KAGAKU GIJUTSU DAIGAKU KENKYU HOKOKU/ TOKYO METROPOLITAN INSTITUTE OF TECHNOLOGY. MEMOIRS. Text in English, Japanese. 1987. a. **Document type:** *Journal, Academic/Scholarly.*
Formed by the merger of (1962-1987): Kenkyu Kiyo - Tokyo Toritsu Koku Kogyo Tanki Daigaku (0387-1363); (1973-1987): Tokyo Toritsu Koka Tanki Daigaku Kenkyu Hokoku (0387-1371)
—CASDDS.
Published by: Tokyo Toritsu Kagaku Gijutsu Daigaku/Tokyo Metropolitan Institute of Technology, 6-6 Asahigaoka, Hino-shi, Tokyo-to 191-0065, Japan. TEL 81-425-83-5111, FAX 81-425-83-5119. Circ: 500.

500 JPN ISSN 1344-4867
T178.T65 CODEN: KHGKFM
TOKYO TORITSU SANGYO GIJUTSU KENKYUJO KENKYU HOKOKU/ TOKYO METROPOLITAN INDUSTRIAL TECHNOLOGY RESEARCH INSTITUTE. BULLETIN. Text in Multiple languages. 1998. a.
Indexed: A28, APA, BrCerAb, C&ISA, CA/WCA, CIA, CerAb, CivEngAb, CorrAb, E&CAJ, E11, EEA, EMA, H15, M&TEA, M09, MBF, METADEX, SolStAb, T04, WAA.
—Linda Hall.
Published by: Tokyo Toritsu Sangyo Gijutsu Kenkyujo/Tokyo Metropolitan Industrial Technology Research Institute, 3-13-10 Nishigaoka, Kita-ku, Tokyo, 115-8586, Japan.

TONE (AUCKLAND); technology to change your life. *see* ELECTRONICS

TOYODA GOSEI GIHO/TOYODA GOSEI TECHNICAL REPORTS. *see* TRANSPORTATION—Automobiles

600 388.31 DEU ISSN 1433-0334
TRAFFIC TECH. Text in German. 1991. 6/yr. EUR 98 (effective 2001). adv. bk.rev. **Document type:** *Journal, Trade.*
Published by: Sieg Tech Verlags GmbH, Gottfried-Claren-Str 21, Bonn, 53225, Germany. TEL 49-228-466034, FAX 49-228-477418, sieg.tech@t-online.de. Ed. Manfred Sieg.

TRAFODION Y GYMDEITHAS WYDDONOL GENEDLAETHOL. *see* SCIENCES: COMPREHENSIVE WORKS

654 DEU ISSN 1862-1635
TRANSFER. Text in German. 2006. q. **Document type:** *Newsletter, Trade.*
Published by: acatech - Konvent fuer Technikwissenschaften der Union der Deutschen Akademien der Wissenschaften e.V., Hofgartenstr 2, Munich, 80539, Germany. TEL 49-89-5203090, FAX 49-89-5203099, info@acatech.de, http://www.acatech.de. Ed. Jann Gerrit Ohlendorf.

600 GBR ISSN 2045-4813
▼ ➤ **TRANSFERS**; interdisciplinary journal of mobility studies. Text in English. 2011. 3/yr. GBP 103 combined subscription domestic to institutions (print & online eds.); EUR 125 combined subscription in Europe to institutions (print & online eds.); USD 162 combined subscription elsewhere to institutions (print & online eds.) (effective 2011). adv. **Document type:** *Journal, Academic/Scholarly.* **Description:** Contains cutting-edge research on the processes, structures and consequences of the movement of people, resources, and commodities.
Related titles: Online - full text ed.: ISSN 2045-4821. GBP 89 domestic to institutions; EUR 108 in Europe to institutions; USD 140 elsewhere to institutions (effective 2011).
Published by: Berghahn Books Ltd, 3 Newtec Pl, Magdalen Rd, Oxford, OX4 1RE, United Kingdom. TEL 44-1865-250011, FAX 44-1865-250056, journals@berghahnbooks.com, http://www.berghahnbooks.com. Ed. Gijs Mom.

600 GBR ISSN 0308-2644
TREVITHICK SOCIETY. JOURNAL. Text in English. 1973. a. free to members (effective 2009). back issues avail. **Document type:** *Journal, Academic/Scholarly.*
Related titles: Online - full text ed.
—BLDSC (4910.300000).
Published by: Trevithick Society, PO Box 62, CAMBORNE, Cornwall TR14 7ZN, United Kingdom. info@trevithick-society.org.uk. Ed. Owen Baker.

600 GBR
TREVITHICK SOCIETY. QUARTERLY NEWSLETTER. Text in English. 1974. q. free to members (effective 2009). back issues avail. **Document type:** *Newsletter, Trade.* **Description:** Contains information on the industrial archaeology of Cornwall.
Indexed: IMMAb.
Published by: Trevithick Society, PO Box 62, CAMBORNE, Cornwall TR14 7ZN, United Kingdom. info@trevithick-society.org.uk. Ed. Colin French.

600 JPN ISSN 0287-8585
TRIGGER. Text in Japanese. 1982. m. **Document type:** *Trade.* **Description:** Offers general information on all industrial technology.
Published by: Nikkan Kogyo Shimbun, Ltd., 14-1 Nihonbashikoamicho, Chuo-ku, Tokyo, 103-8548, Japan. TEL 81-3-3222-7095, FAX 81-3-3262-4603. Ed. Mitsuo Lijima. Circ: 100,000.

TSINGHUA SCIENCE & TECHNOLOGY. *see* SCIENCES: COMPREHENSIVE WORKS

TUDOMANY. *see* SCIENCES: COMPREHENSIVE WORKS

TWO THIRDS. *see* AGRICULTURE—Agricultural Economics

U C L A BULLETIN OF LAW AND TECHNOLOGY. (University of California at Los Angeles) *see* LAW

U C L A JOURNAL OF LAW AND TECHNOLOGY. (University of California at Los Angeles) *see* LAW

600 COL ISSN 0123-4226
U D C A. REVISTA; actualidad y divulgacion cientifica. Text in Spanish. 1998. s-a. back issues avail. **Document type:** *Journal, Academic/ Scholarly.*
Indexed: A34, A35, A36, A38, AgBio, AgrForAb, B23, BA, BP, C01, C25, C30, CABA, D01, E12, F08, F12, FCA, G11, GH, H16, H17, I11, IndVet, LT, MaizeAb, N02, N03, N04, O01, OR, P32, P33, P37, P38, P39, P40, PGegResA, PHN&I, PN&I, R07, R08, R11, R12, R13, RA&MP, RRTA, S13, S16, S17, T05, TAR, VS, W11.
Published by: Universidad de Ciencias Aplicadas y Ambientales, Campus Universitario, Calle 222 No. 55-30, Bogota, Colombia. TEL 57-1-6684700 ext. 168. Ed. Ingeborg Zenner de Palania.

U D T FORUM. *see* MILITARY

U.S. AIR FORCE INSTITUTE OF TECHNOLOGY. REPORT. *see* MILITARY

600 359 USA
U.S. NAVAL POSTGRADUATE SCHOOL. TECHNICAL REPORT. Text in English. irreg.
Published by: U.S. Naval Postgraduate School, Code 91, 699 Dyer Rd., Monterey, CA 93943-5001. TEL 831-656-3164, research@nps.navy.mil, http://www.nps.navy.mil.

600 USA ISSN 1530-2180
T58.5
UBIQUITY. Text in English. 2000. w. free (effective 2010). bk.rev. back issues avail. **Document type:** *Journal, Academic/Scholarly.* **Description:** Aims to foster critical analysis and in-depth commentary on issues relating to the nature, constitution, structure of technology and engineering.
Media: Online - full text.
Indexed: A28, APA, BrCerAb, C&ISA, CA/WCA, CIA, CerAb, CivEngAb, CorrAb, E&CAJ, E11, EEA, EMA, H15, M&TEA, M09, MBF, METADEX, SolStAb, T04, WAA.
—Linda Hall.
Published by: Association for Computing Machinery, Inc., 2 Penn Plz, Ste 701, New York, NY 10121. TEL 212-626-0500, FAX 212-944-1318, acmhelp@acm.org. Eds. Lauren Weinstein, Peter J Denning.

UKIO TECHNOLOGINIS IR EKONOMINIS VYSTYMAS/ TECHNOLOGICAL AND ECONOMIC DEVELOPMENT OF ECONOMY. *see* BUSINESS AND ECONOMICS

UMBRAL UNIVERSITARIO. *see* SCIENCES: COMPREHENSIVE WORKS

UNDERWATER TECHNOLOGY. *see* EARTH SCIENCES—Oceanography

600 URY
UNESCO REGIONAL OFFICE FOR SCIENCE AND TECHNOLOGY FOR LATIN AMERICA AND THE CARIBBEAN. BOLETIN. (United Nations Educational, Scientific and Cultural Organization) Text in Spanish. 1952. 2/yr. free. bk.rev. abstr.; bibl.
Formerly: UNESCO. Field Science Office for Latin America. Boletin
Indexed: RASB.
Published by: UNESCO, Regional Office of Science and Technology for Latin America and the Caribbean, 1320 Bulevar Artigas, Casilla de Correo 859, Montevideo, Uruguay. Circ: 2,000.

600 DEU ISSN 1616-4075
T3 CODEN: HUNMEI
➤ **UNIMAGAZIN HANNOVER.** Text in German. 1974. 2/yr. EUR 6 (effective 2003). adv. **Document type:** *Magazine, Academic/ Scholarly.*
Former titles (until 2000): Hannover Uni Magazin (0943-5107); (until 1993): Uni Hannover (0171-2268); (until 1978): T U Hannover (0340-8981)
Indexed: GeoRef, SpeleolAb.
—BLDSC (9090.696500), Linda Hall.
Published by: Universitaet Hannover, Pressestelle, Postfach 6009, Hannover, 30060, Germany. TEL 49-511-7620, FAX 49-511-7623456, info@pressestelle.uni-hannover.de, http://www.uni-hannover.de. Ed. Stefanie Beier. Circ: 8,000.

➤ **UNION LIST OF SCIENTIFIC AND TECHNICAL PERIODICALS IN ZAMBIA.** *see* BIBLIOGRAPHIES

➤ **UNISERVE SCIENCE. ANNUAL REPORT.** *see* SCIENCES: COMPREHENSIVE WORKS

➤ **UNISERVE SCIENCE NEWS (ONLINE).** *see* SCIENCES: COMPREHENSIVE WORKS

➤ **UNISERVE SCIENCE. SYMPOSIUM PROCEEDINGS.** *see* SCIENCES: COMPREHENSIVE WORKS

➤ **UNIVERSIDAD NACIONAL AUTONOMA DE MEXICO. INSTITUTO DE INVESTIGACIONES HISTORICAS. SERIE HISTORIA DE LA CIENCIA Y LA TECNOLOGIA.** *see* SCIENCES: COMPREHENSIVE WORKS

607.11 COL ISSN 1657-3498
UNIVERSIDAD TECNOLOGICA DEL CHOCO. REVISTA. Text in Spanish. 1976. irreg.
Published by: Universidad Tecnologica del Choco, Difusion Cultural, Carrera 2, 25-22, Quibdo, CHOCO, Colombia. http://200.26.134.109:8091/unichoco/hermesoft/portal/home_1/htm/cont.jsp?rec=not_251.jsp. Ed. Giorgio M Manzini.

600 BRA
UNIVERSIDADE FEDERAL DO CEARA. CENTRO DE TECNOLOGIA. BOLETIM TRIMESTRAL. Text in Portuguese. q.
Published by: Universidade Federal do Ceara, Centro de Tecnologia, Campus Universitario do Pici, Bl. 713, C.P. 2574, Fortaleza, CEARA, Brazil.

▼ **UNIVERSIDADE PORTUCALENSE. DEPARTAMENTO DE INOVACAO. CIENCIA E TECNOLGIA. REVISTA.** *see* SCIENCES: COMPREHENSIVE WORKS

UNIVERSITAET KIEL. FORSCHUNGS- UND TECHNOLOGIEZENTRUM WESTKUESTE. BERICHTE. *see* SCIENCES: COMPREHENSIVE WORKS

600 BEL ISSN 0075-9333
T2
UNIVERSITE DE LIEGE. FACULTE DES SCIENCES APPLIQUEES. COLLECTION DES PUBLICATIONS. Text in French; Summaries in English, German. 1966. bi-m.
Indexed: GeoRef, SpeleolAb.
—INIST.
Published by: Universite de Liege, Faculte des Sciences Appliquees, Rue du Val Benoit 75, Liege, 4000, Belgium.

UNIVERSITE DE LOME. JOURNAL DE LA RECHERCHE SCIENTIFIQUE. *see* SCIENCES: COMPREHENSIVE WORKS

UNIVERSITY OF ILLINOIS JOURNAL OF LAW, TECHNOLOGY AND POLICY. *see* LAW

UNIVERSITY OF MAURITIUS RESEARCH JOURNAL. SCIENCE & TECHNOLOGY. *see* SCIENCES: COMPREHENSIVE WORKS

UNIVERSITY OF OTTAWA LAW & TECHNOLOGY JOURNAL/DROIT & TECHNOLOGIE DE L'UNIVERSITE D'OTTAWA. REVUE. *see* LAW

600 GBR
UNIVERSITY OF TEESSIDE. SCHOOL OF SCIENCE AND TECHNOLOGY. TECHNICAL REPORT. Text in English. irreg. **Document type:** *Report, Academic/Scholarly.*
Formerly: University of Teesside. School of Science and Technology. Construction Research Unit. Technical Report
Published by: University of Teesside, School of Science and Technology, University Of Teesside, Borough Rd, Middlesbrough, TS1 3BA, United Kingdom.

UNIVERSITY OF THE PUNJAB. FACULTY OF ENGINEERING & TECHNOLOGY. JOURNAL. *see* ENGINEERING

UNTERSUCHUNGEN ZUR WIRTSCHAFTS-, SOZIAL- UND TECHNIKGESCHICHTE. *see* SOCIAL SCIENCES: COMPREHENSIVE WORKS

600 ESP ISSN 1684-5285
Z699
UPGRADE (ENGLISH EDITION); the European journal for the informatics professional. Text in English. 2000 (Oct.). bi-m. free (effective 2011). back issues avail. **Document type:** *Journal, Academic/Scholarly.*
Media: Online - full text.
Indexed: Inspec.
Published by: (Council of European Professional Informatics Societies DEU), Asociacion de Tecnicos de Informatica, Via Laietana 46, Barcelona, 08003, Spain. TEL 34-93-4125235, FAX 34-93-4127713, http://www.ati.es. Ed. Rafael Fernandez Calvo.

658.2 FRA ISSN 0042-126X
HC271
L'USINE NOUVELLE. Text in French. 1896. w. (46/yr.). EUR 161 combined subscription domestic print & online eds. (effective 2009). adv. charts; illus.; mkt.; pat.; stat.; tr.lit. **Document type:** *Magazine, Trade.*
Formerly (until 1945): Usine (0372-4786)
Related titles: Online - full text ed.
Indexed: A22, CISA, ChemAb, ELLIS, FR, GeoRef, ILD, INIS AtomInd, KES, PROMT, RASB, SpeleolAb.
—BLDSC (9134.000000), CIS, IE, Infotrieve, Ingenta, INIST. **CCC.**
Published by: Groupe Industrie Services Info, Antony Parc II, 10 Av. du General de Gaulle, Antony, 92160, France. TEL 33-1-77929775, http://www.librairie-gisi.fr. Ed. Jean-Louis Marrou. Circ: 60,000.

600 SLV
UTEC. Text in Spanish. 1989. q. **Document type:** *Academic/Scholarly.*
Published by: Universidad Tecnologica San Salvador, Extension Cultural, Calle Arce, 1020, Apdo. Postal 1770, San Salvador, El Salvador. TEL 71-5990.

600 FIN ISSN 1235-0605
CODEN: VTIEEE
V T T TIEDOTTEITA/MEDDELANDEN/RESEARCH NOTES. (Valtion Teknillinen Tutkimuskeskus) Text in English, Finnish, Swedish. 1981. irreg. price varies. reprints avail. **Document type:** *Monographic series, Trade.*
Formerly (until 1992): Valtion Teknillinen Tutkimuskeskus. Tiedotteita (0358-5085)
Related titles: Online - full text ed.
Indexed: A22, A28, A35, A37, AIAP, APA, AgBio, BA, BrCerAb, C&ISA, CA/WCA, CABA, CIA, CIN, CerAb, ChemAb, CivEngAb, CorrAb, E&CAJ, E11, E12, EEA, EMA, EngInd, F08, F11, FS&TA, GH, GeoRef, H15, I11, M&TEA, M09, MBF, METADEX, N02, S13, S16, SCOPUS, SolStAb, SpeleolAb, T04, TM, W11, WAA.
—BLDSC (9258.909000), CASDDS, IE, Ingenta, Linda Hall.
Published by: Valtion Teknillinen Tutkimuskeskus/Technical Research Centre of Finland, Vuorimiehentie 5, PO Box 2000, Espoo, 02044, Finland. TEL 358-9-4561, FAX 358-9-4564374, inf@vtt.fi, http://www.vtt.fi. R&P Pirjo Sutela.

VADEMECUM DEUTSCHER LEHR- UND FORSCHUNGSSTAETTEN. STAETTEN DER FORSCHUNG. *see* SCIENCES: COMPREHENSIVE WORKS

VALAHIA UNIVERSITY OF TARGOVISTE. ANNALS. FOOD SCIENCE AND TECHNOLOGY. *see* SCIENCES: COMPREHENSIVE WORKS

VALTION TEKNILLINEN TUTKIMUSKESKUS. V T T PUBLICATIONS. *see* SCIENCES: COMPREHENSIVE WORKS

600 FIN ISSN 0357-9387
CODEN: VTTSE9
VALTION TEKNILLINEN TUTKIMUSKESKUS. V T T SYMPOSIUM. Text in English, Finnish. 1974. irreg. price varies. **Document type:** *Proceedings, Academic/Scholarly.*
Related titles: Online - full text ed.: Valtion Teknillinen Tutkimuskeskus. V T T Symposium (Online). ISSN 1455-0873.
Indexed: A22, A35, A36, A37, AgBio, CABA, CIN, CPEI, ChemAb, ChemTitl, E12, EngInd, F08, FS&TA, GH, GeoRef, Inspec, N02, N03, P32, P33, R13, RA&MP, RM&VM, S13, S16, SCOPUS, SpeleolAb, VS, W11.
—BLDSC (9258.907000), CASDDS, IE, Ingenta.
Published by: Valtion Teknillinen Tutkimuskeskus/Technical Research Centre of Finland, Vuorimiehentie 5, PO Box 2000, Espoo, 02044, Finland. TEL 358-2-722111, FAX 358-2-7227001, inf@vtt.fi, http://www.vtt.fi. R&P Pirjo Sutela.

VAULT GUIDE TO THE TOP 25 TECH CONSULTING FIRMS. *see* BUSINESS AND ECONOMICS

600 RUS ISSN 1561-7408
VESTNIK MOLODYCH UCHENYCH. TEKHNICHESKIYE NAUKI. Text in Russian. 1998. s-a. **Document type:** *Journal, Academic/Scholarly.*
Related titles: Online - full text ed.: ISSN 1609-5413. 2000.
Published by: Redaktsiya Zhurnala Vestnik Molodych Uchenych, 1-ya Krasnoarmeiskaya Ul., dom 1, Sankt-Peterburg, 198005, Russian Federation. vmu@peterlink.ru. Ed. R Yevdokimov TEL 7-812-5976301. **Co-sponsors:** Ministerstvo Obrazovaniya i Nauki Rossiiskoi Federatsii/Ministry of Education and Science of the Russian Federation; Rossiiskaya Akademiya Nauk, Sankt-Peterburgskii Nauchnyi Tsentr; Sovet Rektorov Vuzov Sankt-Peterburga.

600 USA ISSN 0745-7200
VIRGINIA EXTENSION. Text in English. q. **Description:** Magazine concerning Virginia's extension activities.
Published by: Virginia Polytechnic Institute and State University, 202 Media Bldg, Blacksburg, VA 24061. TEL 703-961-7370.

VIRGINIA JOURNAL OF LAW AND TECHNOLOGY. *see* LAW

658.5 DEU ISSN 1436-5006
TJ3
W T WERKSTATTSTECHNIK; Forschung und Entwicklung fur die Produktion. Text in German. 1907. 9/yr. EUR 205 (effective 2010). adv. bk.rev.; Website rev. reprints avail. **Document type:** *Magazine, Trade.*
Former titles: W T Produktion und Management (0941-2360); (until 1991): W T - Werkstattstechnik (0340-4544); Werkstattstechnik (0043-2806)
Related titles: Microform ed.: (from PQC); Online - full text ed.: ISSN 1436-4980.
Indexed: ApMecR, CISA, Inspec.
—IE, INIST, Linda Hall. **CCC.**
Published by: (Verein Deutscher Ingenieure e.V.), Springer V D I Verlag GmbH & Co. KG, VDI-Platz 1, Duesseldorf, 40468, Germany. TEL 49-211-61030, FAX 49-211-6103300, info@technikwissen.de. Ed., Adv. contact Dag Heidecker TEL 49-211-6103509. Circ: 3,000.

W Z B DISCUSSION PAPERS. *see* SOCIAL SCIENCES: COMPREHENSIVE WORKS

WARASAN WITTHAYASAT LAE THEKNOLOYI MAHAWITTHAYALAI MAHASARAKHAM. *see* SCIENCES: COMPREHENSIVE WORKS

600 USA ISSN 1537-3088
HD9971.5.E54
WARREN'S CONSUMER ELECTRONICS DAILY. Variant title: Consumer Electronics Daily. Text in English. 2001. d. **Document type:** *Journal, Trade.* **Description:** Provides information on complex and rapidly changing business sector, from the people who in 1945 literally gave the consumer electronics industry its name.
Related titles: Online - full text ed.
Published by: Warren Communications News, Inc., 2115 Ward Ct, NW, Washington, DC 20037. TEL 202-872-9200, 800-771-9202, FAX 202-318-8350, info@warren-news.com. Ed. Daniel Warren. Pub. Paul Warren.

WEI-NA DIANZI JISHU/MICRONANOELECTRONIC TECHNOLOGY. *see* ELECTRONICS

WEIZMANN INSTITUTE OF SCIENCE, REHOVOT, ISRAEL. SCIENTIFIC ACTIVITIES. *see* SCIENCES: COMPREHENSIVE WORKS

600 CHE
WERKMEISTER/CONTREMAITRE. Text in French, German. 1894. fortn. CHF 43. adv. illus. index.
Formerly: Werkmeister und Techniche Arbeitsleiter - Contremaitre et Agent de Maitrise (0043-2776)
Indexed: CISA.
Published by: Schweizerischer Verband Technischer Betriebskader, Schaffhauserstr 2-4, Zuerich, 8006, Switzerland. Ed. Roger Erb.

WERKSTATT UND BETRIEB; Zeitschrift fuer spanende Fertigung. *see* MACHINERY

600 DEU ISSN 0939-2629
WERKSTOFFE - IN DER FERTIGUNG; Die Fachzeitschrift fuer technische Fuehrungskraefte. Text in German. 1963. 6/yr. EUR 64.20 (effective 2010). adv. bk.rev. illus.; pat.; tr.lit. index. **Document type:** *Magazine, Trade.*
Former titles (until 1990): Werkstoffe - Betriebsleitung Technik (0176-6058); Werkstoffe und Technik; Werkstoffe (0043-2814)
Indexed: RefZh, TM.
Published by: H W - Verlag, Sonnenblumenring 35, Mering, 86415, Germany. TEL 49-8233-32761, FAX 49-8233-32762. Ed. Manfred Kittel. Adv. contact Tea Malik.

600 500 JPN
WHITE PAPER ON SCIENCE AND TECHNOLOGY (YEAR). Text in English. a. USD 83. **Document type:** *Journal, Academic/Scholarly.* **Description:** Covers science and technology trends, activities, developments and policies of Japan.
Published by: Japan Science and Technology Agency/Kagaku Gijutsu Shinko Jigyodan, 5-3, Yonbancho, Chiyoda-ku, Tokyo, Saitama 102-8666, Japan. TEL 81-3-52148401, FAX 81-3-52148400, http://www.jst.go.jp/.

WINAY YACHAY. *see* SCIENCES: COMPREHENSIVE WORKS

WORCESTER POLYTECHNIC INSTITUTE - STUDIES IN SCIENCE, TECHNOLOGY AND CULTURE. *see* SCIENCES: COMPREHENSIVE WORKS

▼ **WORLD JOURNAL ON EDUCATIONAL TECHNOLOGY.** *see* EDUCATION

600 CHN
WORLD PRODUCTS AND TECHNOLOGY. Text in Chinese. 1980. bi-m. CNY 30 (effective 1998). adv. **Description:** Contains electronics, machinery, medical instrument, materials, light industry, environmental protection, automobile, modern communications, market, world business information, and world science and technology.
Published by: China Chamber of International Commerce, China Council for the Promotion of International Trade, 1 Fuxingmenwai St, Beijing, 100860, China. TEL 86-10-6851-3344, FAX 86-10-6851-0201. Circ: 50,000.

WORLD REVIEW OF SCIENCE, TECHNOLOGY AND SUSTAINABLE DEVELOPMENT. *see* SCIENCES: COMPREHENSIVE WORKS

WORLD TRANSACTIONS ON ENGINEERING AND TECHNOLOGY EDUCATION. *see* EDUCATION

WUHAN GONGCHENG DAXUE XUEBAO/WUHAN INSTITUTE OF TECHNOLOGY. JOURNAL. *see* ENGINEERING—Chemical Engineering

620.11 CHN ISSN 1000-2413
TA401 CODEN: JWUTE8
➤ **WUHAN UNIVERSITY OF TECHNOLOGY. JOURNAL (MATERIAL SCIENCE EDITION).** Text in English. 1986. bi-m. EUR 545, USD 661 combined subscription to institutions (print & online eds.) (effective 2012). back issues avail.; reprint service avail. from PSC. **Document type:** *Journal, Academic/Scholarly.*
Related titles: CD-ROM ed.; Online - full text ed.: ISSN 1993-0437.
Indexed: A22, A26, A28, APA, BrCerAb, C&ISA, CA/WCA, CIA, CPEI, CerAb, CivEngAb, CorrAb, E&CAJ, E01, E08, E11, EEA, EMA, ESPM, EngInd, EnvEAb, H15, M&TEA, M09, MBF, METADEX, MSCI, RefZh, S09, SCI, SCOPUS, SolStAb, T04, W07, WAA.
—BLDSC (4917.469420), East View, IE, Ingenta, Linda Hall. **CCC.**
Published by: Wuhan Ligong Daxue/Wuhan University of Technology, 122, Luoshi Road, Wuhan, Hubei 430070, China. TEL 86-27-87651870, FAX 86-27-87384113. **Co-publisher:** Springer.

600 CHN ISSN 1671-4806
WUXI SHANGYE ZHIYE JISHU XUEYUAN XUEBAO/WUXI VOCATIONAL INSTITUTE OF COMMERCIAL TECHNOLOGY. JOURNAL. Text in Chinese. 2001. bi-m. CNY 12 newsstand/cover (effective 2006). **Document type:** *Journal, Academic/Scholarly.*
Related titles: Online - full text ed.
Published by: Wuxi Shangye Zhiye Jishu Xueyuan, 90, Rongxiang Zhengxiang, Wuxi, 214063, China. TEL 86-510-5517477, FAX 86-510-5515696.

600 USA
X-OLOGY. Text in English. 2006. q. **Document type:** *Magazine, Trade.* **Description:** Covers southeastern Michigan industries, companies, people, technologies, and ideas.
Published by: Automation Alley, 29200 Northwestern Hwy., Ste. 110, Southfield, MI 48034. TEL 866-284-0038, FAX 248-304-8885. Ed. Jane Gleeson. Circ: 20,000 (controlled).

XI'AN JIANZHU KEJI DAXUE XUEBAO (ZIRAN KEXUE BAN)/XI'AN UNIVERSITY OF ARCHITECTURE AND TECHNOLOGY. JOURNAL (NATURAL SCIENCE EDITION). *see* ARCHITECTURE

600 CHN ISSN 1006-4710
XI'AN LIGONG DAXUE XUEBAO/XI'AN UNIVERSITY OF TECHNOLOGY. JOURNAL. Text in Chinese. 1978. q. CNY 6 newsstand/cover (effective 2007). **Document type:** *Journal, Academic/Scholarly.*
Formerly (until 1993): Shaanxi Jixie Xueyuan Xuebao (1000-2766)
Related titles: Online - full text ed.
Indexed: Inspec, RefZh.
—BLDSC (9367.036310).
Published by: Xi'an Ligong Daxue/Xi'an University of Technology, No.5 of Jinhua South Road, Tablet Forset District, Xi'an, 710048, China. TEL 86-29-2312403, FAX 86-29-3238731, http://www.xaut.edu.cn/. **Dist. by:** China International Book Trading Corp, 35 Chegongzhuang Xilu, Haidian District, PO Box 399, Beijing 100044, China. TEL 86-10-68412045, FAX 86-10-68412023, cibtc@mail.cibtc.com.cn, http://www.cibtc.com.cn.

XIANDAI FANGYU JISHU/MODERN DEFENCE TECHNOLOGY. *see* MILITARY

600 CHN ISSN 1000-2758
XIBEI GONGYE DAXUE XUEBAO/NORTHWESTERN POLYTECHNICAL UNIVERSITY. JOURNAL. Text in Chinese. 1957. bi-m. USD 31.20 (effective 2009). **Document type:** *Journal, Academic/Scholarly.*
Related titles: Online - full text ed.
Indexed: A28, APA, BrCerAb, C&ISA, CA/WCA, CIA, CPEI, CerAb, CivEngAb, CorrAb, E&CAJ, E11, EEA, EMA, ESPM, EngInd, EnvEAb, H15, M&TEA, M09, MBF, METADEX, SCOPUS, SolStAb, T04, WAA.
—BLDSC (4834.411500), East View, IE, Ingenta, Linda Hall.

Published by: Xibei Gongye Daxue/Northwestern Polytechnical University, 127, Youyi Xilu, 647 Xinxiang, Xi'an, Shaanxi 710072, China. TEL 86-29-8495455, FAX 86-29-8494000, http://www.nwpu.edu.cn/. **Dist. by:** China International Book Trading Corp, 35 Chegongzhuang Xilu, Haidian District, PO Box 399, Beijing 100044, China. TEL 86-10-68412045, FAX 86-10-68412023, cibtc@mail.cibtc.com.cn, http://www.cibtc.com.cn.

XIBEI LINXUEYUAN XUEBAO/NORTHWESTERN FORESTRY UNIVERSITY. JOURNAL. *see* FORESTS AND FORESTRY

600 CHN ISSN 1673-7563
XIN TANSUO/QUO CHINA. Text in Chinese. 2004. m. **Document type:** *Magazine, Consumer.*
Formerly (until 2006): Dadi Zongheng/Overview of the Earth (1673-0100)
Related titles: Online - full text ed.
Published by: Beijing Bierde Guanggao Youxian Gongsi/Beijing Hachette Advertising Co., Ltd. (Subsidiary of: Hachette Filipacchi Medias S.A.), Rm. 1601, Capital Tower, No.6 Jia, Jianguomenwai Ave., Chaoyang District, Beijing, 100022, China. TEL 86-10-85676767, FAX 86-10-85679606.

XINHUA SHUMUBAO. KEJI XINSHU MUBAN/XINHUA CATALOGUE, SCIENCE & TECHNOLOGY. *see* ABSTRACTING AND INDEXING SERVICES

605 JPN ISSN 0386-3433
T1 CODEN: TRYUAY
YAMAGUCHI UNIVERSITY. FACULTY OF ENGINEERING. TECHNOLOGY REPORTS. Text in English. 1972. a. per issue exchange basis.
Indexed: CIN, ChemAb, ChemTitl, GeoRef, Inspec, JCT, JTA, SpeleolAb. —AskIEEE, CASDDS, Ingenta, Linda Hall.
Published by: Yamaguchi Daigaku, Kogakubu/Yamaguchi University, Faculty of Engineering, 16-1 Tokiwadai 2-chome, Ube, 755-8611, Japan.

600 CHN ISSN 1671-9131
YANGLING ZHIYE JISHU XUEYUAN XUEBAO. Text in Chinese. 2002. q. CNY 6 newsstand/cover (effective 2006). **Document type:** *Journal, Academic/Scholarly.*
Published by: Yangling Zhiye Jishu Xueyuan, 24, Weihui Lu, Yangling, 712100, China. TEL 86-29-87087156.

600 CHN ISSN 1009-671X
YINGYONG KEJI/APPLIED SCIENCE AND TECHNOLOGY. Text in Chinese. 1974. m. **Document type:** *Journal, Academic/Scholarly.*
Formerly (until 1988): Chuangong Keji
Related titles: Online - full text ed.: (from WanFang Data Corp.).
Indexed: A28, APA, BrCerAb, C&ISA, CA/WCA, CIA, CerAb, CivEngAb, CorrAb, E&CAJ, E11, EEA, EMA, ESPM, EnvEAb, H15, M&TEA, M09, MBF, METADEX, SolStAb, T04, WAA. —BLDSC (9418.470700), East View, Linda Hall.
Published by: Ha'erbin Gongcheng Daxue/Ha'erbin Engineering University, 1F, 145 Nantong Dajie, Nangang-qu, Ha'erbin, Heilongjiang 150001, China. TEL 86-451-82518135, http://www.hrbeu.edu.cn/.

600 500 JPN ISSN 0388-8738
YOSHIDA KAGAKU GIJUTSU ZAIDAN NYUSU/YOSHIDA FOUNDATION FOR SCIENCE AND TECHNOLOGY. NEWS. Text in Japanese. 1975. q.
Published by: Yoshida Kagaku Gijutsu Zaidan/Yoshida Foundation for Science and Technology, Rm 502 Maison Yonbancho, 6 Yonban-cho, Chiyoda-ku, Tokyo, 102-0081, Japan.

YULEI JISHU/TORPEDO TECHNOLOGY. *see* MILITARY

YUNCHOUXUE XUEBAO/OPERATIONS RESEARCH TRANSACTIONS. *see* SCIENCES: COMPREHENSIVE WORKS

YUNYI TEKHNIK. *see* CHILDREN AND YOUTH—For

Z D NET ANCHORDESK. *see* COMPUTERS

Z W F. (Zeitschrift fuer Wirtschaftlichen Fabrikbetrieb) *see* MACHINERY

ZENIT. *see* SCIENCES: COMPREHENSIVE WORKS

600 CHN ISSN 1008-8156
ZHANGJIAKOU ZHIYE JISHU XUEYUAN XUEBAO. Text in Chinese. 1999. q. CNY 3 newsstand/cover (effective 2006). **Document type:** *Journal, Academic/Scholarly.*
Related titles: Online - full text ed.
Published by: Zhangjiakou Zhiye Jishu Xueyuan, 59, Ma Lu Dong, Zhangjiakou, 075051, China.

600 CHN ISSN 1006-4303
T4
ZHEJIANG GONGYE DAXUE XUEBAO/ZHEJIANG UNIVERSITY OF TECHNOLOGY. JOURNAL. Text in Chinese. 1973. bi-m. USD 37.20 (effective 2009). **Document type:** *Journal, Academic/Scholarly.*
Formerly (until 1995): Zhejiang Gongxueyuan Xuebao/Zhejiang Engineering Institute. Journal (1000-209X)
Related titles: Online - full text ed.
Indexed: A22, Inspec, RefZh. —BLDSC (4918.150530), East View, IE, Ingenta.
Published by: Zhejiang Gongye Daxue/Zhejiang University of Technology, Zhaohuiliu-qu, Hangzhou, 310032, China. TEL 86-571-88320516, http://www.zjut.edu.cn/. **Dist. by:** China International Book Trading Corp, 35 Chegongzhuang Xilu, Haidian District, PO Box 399, Beijing 100044, China. TEL 86-10-68412045, FAX 86-10-68412023, cibtc@mail.cibtc.com.cn, http://www.cibtc.com.cn.

ZHENKONG KEXUE YU JISHU/VACUUM SCIENCE AND TECHNOLOGY. *see* ENGINEERING—Mechanical Engineering

ZHENZHI GONGYE/TIANJIN TEXTILE SCIENCE & TECHNOLOGY. *see* TEXTILE INDUSTRIES AND FABRICS

600 CHN ISSN 1672-0601
ZHIYE JISHU. Text in Chinese. 2002. m. CNY 6 newsstand/cover (effective 2006). **Document type:** *Journal, Academic/Scholarly.*
Related titles: Online - full text ed.
Published by: Daqing Zhiye Xueyuan, 105, Haicheng Jie, Ha'erbing, 150006, China. TEL 86-451-3630411, FAX 86-451-3602790.

600 CHN ISSN 1673-3193
ZHONGBEI DAXUE XUEBAO (ZIRAN KEXUE BAN)/NORTH UNIVERSITY OF CHINA. JOURNAL (NATURAL SCIENCE EDITION). Text in Chinese; Abstracts in Chinese, English. 1979. bi-m. USD 31.20 (effective 2009). **Document type:** *Journal, Academic/Scholarly.*
Former titles (until 2004): Huabei Gongxueyuan Xuebao/Huabei North China Institute of Technology. Journal (1006-5431); (until 1994): Taiyuan Jixie Xueyuan Xuebao/Taiyuan Institute of Machinery. Journal (1001-5833)
Related titles: Online - full text ed.
Indexed: CCMJ, MSN, MathR, RefZh, SCOPUS, Z02. —BLDSC (9512.726130), East View, IE, Ingenta.
Published by: Zhongbei Daxue Chubanbu/Press of North University of China, Xueyuan Lu, Taiyuan, 030051, China. TEL 86-351-3925798, FAX 86-351-3922085, http://xuebao.nuc.edu.cn/. Ed. Han-chang Zhou TEL 86-351-3922287. **Dist. by:** China International Book Trading Corp, 35 Chegongzhuang Xilu, Haidian District, PO Box 399, Beijing 100044, China. TEL 86-10-68412045, FAX 86-10-68412023, cibtc@mail.cibtc.com.cn, http://www.cibtc.com.cn.

ZHONGGUO CHUANMEI DAXUE (ZIRAN KEXUE BAN)/ COMMUNICATION UNIVERSITY OF CHINA. JOURNAL (SCIENCE AND TECHNOLOGY). *see* SCIENCES: COMPREHENSIVE WORKS

600 CHN ISSN 1671-8615
ZHONGGUO GAOXIAO KEJI YU CHANYEHUA/CHINESE UNIVERSITY TECHNOLOGY TRANSFER. Text in Chinese. 1988. m. USD 80.40 (effective 2009). **Document type:** *Journal, Academic/Scholarly.*
Related titles: Online - full text ed.
Address: 35, Zhongguancun Dajie, Rm. 805, Beijing, 100080, China. TEL 86-10-62510206, FAX 86-10-62510209.

ZHONGGUO KEJI LUNTAN/FORUM ON SCIENCE AND TECHNOLOGY IN CHINA. *see* SCIENCES: COMPREHENSIVE WORKS

ZHONGGUO KEJI SHILIAO/CHINA HISTORICAL MATERIALS OF SCIENCE AND TECHNOLOGY. *see* SCIENCES: COMPREHENSIVE WORKS

ZHONGGUO KEJISHI ZAZHI/HISTORICAL MATERIAL OF CHINESE SCIENCE AND TECHNOLOGY. *see* SCIENCES: COMPREHENSIVE WORKS

ZHONGGUO KEXUE JISHU DAXUE XUEBAO/UNIVERSITY OF SCIENCE AND TECHNOLOGY OF CHINA. JOURNAL. *see* SCIENCES: COMPREHENSIVE WORKS

ZHONGGUO NONGYE KEJI DAOBAO/REVIEW OF CHINA AGRICULTURAL SCIENCE AND TECHNOLOGY. *see* AGRICULTURE

ZHONGGUO RENMIN JINGGUAN DAXUE XUEBAO (ZIRAN KEXUE BAN)/CHINESE PEOPLE'S PUBLIC SECURITY UNIVERSITY. JOURNAL (SCIENCE AND TECHNOLOGY). *see* SCIENCES: COMPREHENSIVE WORKS

ZHONGGUO ZIXINGCHE/CHINA BICYCLE. *see* SPORTS AND GAMES—Bicycles And Motorcycles

ZHUANGBEI ZHIHUI JISHU XUEYUAN XUEBAO/ACADEMY OF EQUIPMENT COMMAND & TECHNOLOGY. JOURNAL. *see* MACHINERY

ZIVE. *see* COMPUTERS

600 SVN ISSN 0514-017X
ZIVLJENJE IN TEHNIKA. Text in Slovenian. 1950. m. EUR 34.85 (effective 2007). **Document type:** *Magazine, Consumer.*
Formerly (until 1952): Ljudska Tehnika (1318-136X)
Published by: Tehniska Zalozba Slovenije, Lepi pot 6, p p 541, Ljubljana, 1000, Slovenia. TEL 386-1-4790211, FAX 386-1-4790230, info@tzs.si. Ed. Matej Pavlic.

745.2 AUS ISSN 1838-7047
▼ **ZOONTECHNICA**; the journal of redirective design. Text in English. forthcoming 2011. irreg. AUD 20 for 2 yrs.; free to qualified personnel (effective 2011). **Document type:** *Journal, Academic/Scholarly.*
Description: Provides a forum that supports career starters and innovatory research.
Media: Online - full text.
Published by: Queensland College of Art, S Bank Campus, Griffith University, 226 Grey St, PO Box 3370, South Bank, QLD 4101, Australia. TEL 61-7-37353157, FAX 61-7-37353159, http://www.griffith.edu.au/visual-creative-arts/queensland-college-art. Pub. Philip Whiting.

600 NLD ISSN 1386-4076
ZORGINSTELLINGEN. Text in Dutch. 1976. 8/yr. EUR 107.50 domestic; EUR 15 newsstand/cover (effective 2011). adv. **Document type:** *Magazine, Trade.*
Incorporates (2008-2009): Z I Facilitair (1876-7346); Which was formerly (1985-2008): Ziekenhuis en Instelling (1381-9291); Formerly (until 1997): Instellingen (0165-2990); Which incorporated (1956-1975): Economisch Beheer (0304-4947); (1955-1981): Technische Gids voor Ziekenhuis en Instelling (0040-1404); (1950-1975): Christelijk Instellingswezen (0922-3908); (1978-1979): Onderhoud Management (1385-6812)
Indexed: KES. —IE, Infotrieve.
Published by: B + B Vakmedianet, Postbus 219, Bussum, 1400 AE, Netherlands. TEL 31-35-6940740, FAX 31-35-6940743, info@vakmedianet.nl, http://www.vakmedianet.nl. Ed. Annet van den Berg. Pub. Ruud Bakker. Circ: 3,700.

600 300 DEU ISSN 0942-0436
ZUKUENFTE. Text in German. 1991. 4/yr. EUR 30 (effective 2006). adv. bk.rev. abstr.; bibl.; illus. back issues avail. **Document type:** *Consumer.*
Published by: (Sekretariat fuer Zukunftsforschung), Netwerk Zukunft eV, Erkelenzdamm 47, Berlin, 10999, Germany. netwerk-zukunft@gmx.de. Circ: 2,000 (controlled).

21ST CENTURY SCIENCE & TECHNOLOGY (ONLINE). *see* SCIENCES: COMPREHENSIVE WORKS

TECHNOLOGY: COMPREHENSIVE WORKS— Abstracting, Bibliographies, Statistics

016.6 USA ISSN 1367-9899
Z7913
ABSTRACTS IN NEW TECHNOLOGIES AND ENGINEERING. Abbreviated title: A N T E. Text in English. 1962. bi-m. (a. cum.index on CD). USD 2,485 combined subscription (includes a. cum. index on CD-ROM & in print) (effective 2011). illus. Index. reprints avail. **Document type:** *Abstract/Index.* **Description:** Indexes British and American periodicals in all branches of engineering, chemical technology, instrumentation, building, transport, and information technology.
Former titles (until 1997): Current Technology Index (0260-6593); British Technology Index (0007-1889)
Indexed: RASB. —BLDSC (0565.437000), Linda Hall. **CCC.**
Published by: ProQuest LLC (Bethesda) (Subsidiary of: Cambridge Information Group), 7200 Wisconsin Ave, Ste 715, Bethesda, MD 20814. TEL 301-961-6798, 800-843-7751, FAX 301-961-6799, service@csa.com.

600 500 JPN ISSN 0914-4897
ABSTRACTS OF SCIENTIFIC AND TECHNOLOGICAL PUBLICATIONS. Text in English. 1965. a. **Document type:** *Abstract/Index.*
Published by: Ajinomoto K.K., Chuo Kenkyujo/Ajinomoto Co., Inc., Central Research Laboratories, 1-1 Suzuki-cho, Kawasaki-ku, Kawasaki-shi, Kanagawa-ken 210-0801, Japan.

APPLIED SCIENCE & BUSINESS PERIODICALS RETROSPECTIVE: 1913-1983. *see* SCIENCES: COMPREHENSIVE WORKS—Abstracting, Bibliographies, Statistics

APPLIED SCIENCE & TECHNOLOGY FULL TEXT. *see* SCIENCES: COMPREHENSIVE WORKS—Abstracting, Bibliographies, Statistics

APPLIED SCIENCE & TECHNOLOGY INDEX. *see* SCIENCES: COMPREHENSIVE WORKS

APPLIED SCIENCE & TECHNOLOGY INDEX RETROSPECTIVE: 1913-1983. *see* SCIENCES: COMPREHENSIVE WORKS—Abstracting, Bibliographies, Statistics

600 016 AUS ISSN 1030-4495
APPROPRIATE TECHNOLOGY INDEX. Short title: A T Index. Text in English. 1980. q. back issues avail. **Document type:** *Abstract/Index.* **Description:** Bibliographical indexing service to literature on appropriate technology and related fields.
Formerly (until 1986): Atindex (0143-3938)
Published by: Noyce Publishing, GPO Box 2222 T, Melbourne, VIC 3001, Australia. noycepublishing@hotmail.com.

600 318 ARG
ARGENTINA. INSTITUTO DE ASUNTOS TECNICOS. ESTADISTICAS. Text in Spanish. 1974. irreg. charts.
Published by: Instituto de Asuntos Tecnicos, Direccion de Estadistica, Palacio Municipal, Cordoba, Argentina.

658 THA ISSN 0857-9253
ASIAN INSTITUTE OF TECHNOLOGY. ABSTRACTS ON MANAGEMENT OF TECHNOLOGY AND INTERNATIONAL BUSINESS. Text in English. 1988. q. USD 56. **Document type:** *Journal, Academic/Scholarly.*
Published by: (Management of Technology Information Center), Asian Institute of Technology, School of Management, Klong Luang, PO Box 4, Pathum Thani, 12120, Thailand. TEL 66-2-516-0110, FAX 66-2-516-2126. Circ: 500.

016.6 016.5 POL
BAZTECH. Text in Polish. 1998. base vol. plus irreg. updates. free (effective 2011). **Document type:** *Database, Abstract/Index.*
Media: Online - full text.
Published by: Konsorcjum BazTech/Consortium BazTech, c/o Uniwersytet Technologiczno-Przyrodniczy w Bydgoszczy, Biblioteka Glowna, ul. Kalinskiego 7, Bydgoszcz, 85796, Poland. TEL 48-52-3408043, FAX 48-52-3408043, http://www.biblos.pk.edu.pl/konsorcjum/. Eds. Elzbieta Tomczak, Lidia Derfert-Wolf.

BIBLIOGRAFIA ESPANOLA DE REVISTAS CIENTIFICAS DE CIENCIA Y TECNOLOGIA. *see* SCIENCES: COMPREHENSIVE WORKS—Abstracting, Bibliographies, Statistics

600 900 DEU ISSN 0323-4355
BIBLIOGRAPHIE GESCHICHTE DER TECHNIK. Text in German. 1971. a. EUR 46 (effective 2001). bk.rev. **Document type:** *Bibliography.*
Indexed: FR.
Published by: Saechsische Landesbibliothek, Staats- und Universitaetsbibliothek Dresden, Dresden, 01054, Germany. TEL 49-351-8130-0, FAX 49-351-8130200. Eds. Michael Letocha, Peter Hesse.

016.6 USA
C S A TECHNOLOGY RESEARCH DATABASE. Text in English. base vol. plus m. updates. **Document type:** *Database, Abstract/Index.* **Description:** A single mega-file of all the unique records available through its 3 components: the CSA Materials Research Database with METADEX, CSA High Technology Research Database with Aerospace, and the CSA Engineering Research Database.
Media: Online - full text.
Published by: ProQuest LLC (Bethesda) (Subsidiary of: Cambridge Information Group), 7200 Wisconsin Ave, Ste 715, Bethesda, MD 20814. TEL 301-961-6798, 800-843-7751, FAX 301-961-6799.

CARINDEX: SCIENCE & TECHNOLOGY. *see* SCIENCES: COMPREHENSIVE WORKS—Abstracting, Bibliographies, Statistics

600 JPN ISSN 0577-9774
Q4
CHOSEN GAKUJUTSU TSUHO/KOREAN SCIENTIFIC INFORMATION. Text in English, Japanese. 1964. s-a.
Published by: Korean Association of Science and Technology in Japan/Zainihon Chosenjin Kagaku Gijutsu Kyokai, 33-14 Hakusan 4-chome, Bunkyo-ku, Tokyo, 112-0000, Japan.

CLASE AND PERIODICA. *see* SOCIAL SCIENCES: COMPREHENSIVE WORKS—Abstracting, Bibliographies, Statistics

DEPONIROVANNYE NAUCHNYE RABOTY. BIBLIOGRAFICHESKII UKAZATEL'; estestvennye i tochnye nauki, tekhnika. *see* SCIENCES: COMPREHENSIVE WORKS—Abstracting, Bibliographies, Statistics

DIRECTORIO DE REVISTAS ESPANOLAS DE CIENCIA Y TECNOLOGIA (ONLINE EDITION). *see* SCIENCES: COMPREHENSIVE WORKS—Abstracting, Bibliographies, Statistics

DISSERTATION ABSTRACTS INTERNATIONAL. SECTION B: THE SCIENCES AND ENGINEERING. *see* SCIENCES: COMPREHENSIVE WORKS—Abstracting, Bibliographies, Statistics

016.6 BEL ISSN 1606-6340
TP325
EUROABSTRACTS. Text in English. 1989. bi-m. free (effective 2005). adv. index. **Document type:** *Magazine, Abstract/Index.* **Description:** Reports on selected new publications relevant to European research and innovation.
Formed by the 1989 merger of: Euro Abstracts. Section 1: Euratom and E E C Research (0379-8771); Euro Abstracts. Section 2: Coal and Steel (0378-3472); Which both superseded (in 1975): Euro Abstracts (0014-2352); Which was formerly (until 1969): Euratom Information (0376-9437)
Related titles: Microform ed.: (from PQC); Online - full text ed.; ◆ Supplement(s): Progress in Coal Steel and Related Social Research. ISSN 1015-6275.
Indexed: ErgAb, GeoRef, SpeleolAb.
—BLDSC (3829.155000), INIST, Linda Hall.
Published by: European Commission, Directorate General - Information Society, Rue de la Loi 200, Brussels, 1049, Belgium. TEL 32-2-2968800, FAX 32-2-2994170, http://europa.eu.int/information_society/. Circ: 13,000.

FINLAND. TILASTOKESKUS. SCIENCE AND TECHNOLOGY IN FINLAND. *see* SCIENCES: COMPREHENSIVE WORKS

FINLAND. TILASTOKESKUS. TIEDE JA TEKNOLOGIA. *see* SCIENCES: COMPREHENSIVE WORKS

FINLAND. TILASTOKESKUS. TIEDE, TEKNOLOGIA JA TIETOYHTEISKUNTA/FINLAND. STATISTICS FINLAND. SCIENCE, TECHNOLOGY, AND INFORMATION SOCIETY/ FINLAND. STATISTIKCENTRALEN. VETENSKAP, TEKNOLOGI OCH INFORMATIONSSAMHAELLE. *see* SCIENCES: COMPREHENSIVE WORKS

FOOD INDUSTRY UPDATES. SCIENCE. *see* SCIENCES: COMPREHENSIVE WORKS—Abstracting, Bibliographies, Statistics

HUNGARIAN R AND D ABSTRACTS. SCIENCE AND TECHNOLOGY. *see* SCIENCES: COMPREHENSIVE WORKS—Abstracting, Bibliographies, Statistics

INDEX TO SCIENTIFIC & TECHNICAL PROCEEDINGS. *see* SCIENCES: COMPREHENSIVE WORKS—Abstracting, Bibliographies, Statistics

INDIA. DEPARTMENT OF SCIENCE AND TECHNOLOGY. RESEARCH AND DEVELOPMENT STATISTICS. *see* SCIENCES: COMPREHENSIVE WORKS—Abstracting, Bibliographies, Statistics

600 016 IND
INDIAN INSTITUTE OF TECHNOLOGY, MADRAS. ABSTRACTS OF PH. D. THESES. Text in English. 1968. a. **Document type:** *Abstract/Index.*
Former titles (until 1980): Indian Institute of Technology, Madras. M.S., Ph. D. Dissertation Abstracts; (until 1972): Indian Institute of Technology, Madras. Ph.D. Dissertation Abstracts
Published by: Indian Institute of Technology Madras, I.I.T. Post Office, Chennai, 600 036, India. TEL 91-44-22570509, http://www.iitm.ac.in.

600 016 TZA ISSN 0856-0404
INDUSTRIAL ABSTRACTS FOR TANZANIA. Text in English. 1981. s-a. USD 28. **Document type:** *Abstract/Index.*
Published by: Library Services Board, National Documentation Centre, P O Box 9283, Dar es Salaam, Tanzania. TEL 255-51-150048-9. Ed. D A Sekimang'a. Circ: 200.

IPARI FORMATERVEZESI SZAKIRODALMI TAJEKOZTATO/ INDUSTRIAL DESIGN ABSTRACTS. *see* ENGINEERING—Abstracting, Bibliographies, Statistics

600 500 JPN
KAGAKU GIJUTSU FORAMU HOKOKUSHO. Text in English, Japanese. a. abstr. **Description:** Annual report of the forum on science and technology.
Published by: (Japan. Kagaku Gijutsu Seisaku-kyoku), Kagaku Gijutsucho/Science and Technology Agency, Planning Bureau, 2-1 Kasumigaseki 2-chome, Chiyoda-ku, Tokyo, 100-0013, Japan.

KATAB: INDEX ANALYTIQUE BIBLIOGRAPHIQUE. *see* BUSINESS AND ECONOMICS—Abstracting, Bibliographies, Statistics

600 500 JPN
KUNI NO SHIKEN KENKYU GYOMU KEIKAKU. Text in Japanese. 1979. a. abstr. **Document type:** *Government.* **Description:** Contains information on national research projects.
Published by: (Japan. Kagaku Gijutsu Seisaku-kyoku), Kagaku Gijutsucho/Science and Technology Agency, Planning Bureau, 2-1 Kasumigaseki 2-chome, Chiyoda-ku, Tokyo, 100-0013, Japan.

MALAWI JOURNAL OF SCIENCE AND TECHNOLOGY. *see* SCIENCES: COMPREHENSIVE WORKS—Abstracting, Bibliographies, Statistics

600 016 USA
N T I S ALERTS: GOVERNMENT INVENTIONS FOR LICENSING. (National Technical Information Service) Text in English. 19??. s-m. USD 325 in North America; USD 465 elsewhere (effective 2011). index. back issues avail. **Document type:** *Newsletter, Government.* **Description:** Identifies government R&D inventions available for licensing. Summarizes inventions from all government agencies.
Former titles: Abstract Newsletter: Government Inventions for Licensing; Weekly Abstract Newsletter: Government Inventions for Licensing; Weekly Government Abstracts. Government Inventions for Licensing (0364-6491)
Related titles: Microform ed.
Published by: U.S. Department of Commerce, National Technical Information Service, 5301 Shawnee Rd, Alexandria, VA 22312. TEL 703-605-6000, 800-553-6847, info@ntis.gov.

629.8 USA ISSN 1043-9897
N T I S ALERTS: MANUFACTURING TECHNOLOGY. (National Technical Information Service) Text in English. 1983. s-m. USD 320 in North America; USD 399 elsewhere (effective 2011). index. back issues avail. **Document type:** *Newsletter, Government.* **Description:** Reports on computer-aided design, computer-aided manufacturing, technology transfer and other matters related manufacturing technology. Also covers subjects on planning, marketing and economics and research program administration.
Formerly (until 1992): Abstract Newsletter: Manufacturing Technology
Related titles: Microform ed.: (from NTI).
Published by: U.S. Department of Commerce, National Technical Information Service, 5301 Shawnee Rd, Alexandria, VA 22312. TEL 703-605-6000, 800-553-6847, info@ntis.gov.

NEW TECHNICAL BOOKS; a selective list with descriptive annotations. *see* SCIENCES: COMPREHENSIVE WORKS—Abstracting, Bibliographies, Statistics

NIHON KAGAKUSHI GAKKAI NENKAI KENKYU HAPPYO KOEN YOSHISHU. *see* SCIENCES: COMPREHENSIVE WORKS

600 JPN
NIHON SANGYO GIJUTSUSHI GAKKAI NENKAI KOEN GAIYOSHU/ JAPAN SOCIETY FOR THE HISTORY OF INDUSTRIAL TECHNOLOGY. ANNUAL CONFERENCE. PROCEEDINGS. Text in Japanese. 1985. a. abstr. **Document type:** *Proceedings.*
Published by: Nihon Sangyo Gijutsushi Gakkai/Japan Society for the History of Industrial Technology, Osaka Kogyokai Osaka Shoko Kaigisho Bldg 5F, 58-7 Uchihon-machi, Hashizume-cho, Higashi-ku, Osaka-shi, Osaka-fu 540, Japan.

PROQUEST SCITECH JOURNALS. *see* SCIENCES: COMPREHENSIVE WORKS—Abstracting, Bibliographies, Statistics

600 PHL ISSN 0115-9984
Q76
R & D PHILIPPINES. (Research and Development) Text in English. s-a. PHP 250; USD 45 foreign. **Document type:** *Bibliography.* **Description:** Contains completed, on-going and pipeline R & Ds with complete bibliographic information.
Published by: (Department of Science and Technology), Science and Technology Information Institute, P.O. Box 3596, Manila, Philippines. TEL 822-0954. **Subscr. to:** Dept. of Science and Technology, Bicutan, Taguig, P.O. Box 2131, Manila, Philippines.

REFERATIVNYI ZHURNAL. LEGKAYA PROMYSHLENNOST'. TEKHNOLOGIYA I OBORUDOVANIYE. OTDEL'NYI VYPUSK. *see* BUSINESS AND ECONOMICS—Abstracting, Bibliographies, Statistics

016.6 RUS ISSN 0235-8824
REFERATIVNYI ZHURNAL. NAUCHNO-TEKHNICHESKII PROGRESS. INTEGRATSIYA NAUKI S PROIZVODSTVOM. ORGANIZATSIYA I FINANSIROVANIE; vypusk svodnogo toma. Text in Russian. 1960. m. USD 172.80 foreign (effective 2011). **Document type:** *Journal, Abstract/Index.*
Related titles: CD-ROM ed.; Online - full text ed.
—East View.
Published by: VINITI RAN, ul Usievicha 20, Moscow, 125190, Russian Federation. TEL 7-499-1526113, FAX 7-499-9430060, dir@viniti.ru, http://www.viniti.ru. **Dist. by:** Informnauka Ltd., Ul Usievicha 20, Moscow 125190, Russian Federation. alfimov@viniti.ru.

S B & F; your guide to science resources for all ages. (Science Books & Films) *see* SCIENCES: COMPREHENSIVE WORKS—Abstracting, Bibliographies, Statistics

S E A ABSTRACTS. *see* SCIENCES: COMPREHENSIVE WORKS—Abstracting, Bibliographies, Statistics

S R D S TECHNOLOGY MEDIA SOURCE. (Standard Rate & Data Service) *see* ADVERTISING AND PUBLIC RELATIONS—Abstracting, Bibliographies, Statistics

SCI-TECH NEWS. *see* SCIENCES: COMPREHENSIVE WORKS—Abstracting, Bibliographies, Statistics

SCIENCE AND TECHNOLOGY. *see* SCIENCES: COMPREHENSIVE WORKS—Abstracting, Bibliographies, Statistics

SCIENCE, TECHNOLOGY AND INNOVATION IN EUROPE. *see* SCIENCES: COMPREHENSIVE WORKS—Abstracting, Bibliographies, Statistics

SCIENTIFIC AND TECHNICAL PUBLICATIONS IN BULGARIA. *see* SCIENCES: COMPREHENSIVE WORKS—Abstracting, Bibliographies, Statistics

SCIENTIFIC SERIALS IN THAI LIBRARIES. *see* SCIENCES: COMPREHENSIVE WORKS—Abstracting, Bibliographies, Statistics

SCITECH BOOK NEWS; an annotated bibliography of new books in science, technology, & medicine. *see* BIBLIOGRAPHIES

SCOPUS. *see* SCIENCES: COMPREHENSIVE WORKS—Abstracting, Bibliographies, Statistics

SELECTED RAND ABSTRACTS; a semiannual guide to publications of the Rand Corporation. *see* SCIENCES: COMPREHENSIVE WORKS—Abstracting, Bibliographies, Statistics

SHINKU TANKU NENPO/ALMANAC OF THINK TANKS IN JAPAN. *see* SCIENCES: COMPREHENSIVE WORKS—Abstracting, Bibliographies, Statistics

600 DEU ISSN 0340-0859
Z802.U5764
TECHNISCHE INFORMATIONSBIBLIOTHEK UND UNIVERSIATETSBIBLIOTHEK HANNOVER. JAHRESBERICHT. Text in German. 1968. a. **Document type:** *Monographic series, Academic/Scholarly.*
—BLDSC (4638.680000).
Published by: Technische Informationsbibliothek und Universiatetsbibliothek Hannover, Welfengarten 1B, Hannover, 30167, Germany. TEL 49-511-7622268, FAX 49-511-715936, ubtib@tib.uni-hannover.de, http://www.tib.uni-hannover.de.

016.6 DEU
TEMA - TECHNOLOGY AND MANAGEMENT. Text in English, German. base vol. plus w. updates. **Document type:** *Database, Abstract/Index.*
Media: Online - full text.
Published by: FIZ Technik e.V., Hanauer Landstr. 151-153, Frankfurt a.M., D-60314, Germany. TEL 49-69-4308111, FAX 49-69-4308200, customer-service@fiz-technik.de.

THAI ABSTRACTS, SERIES A. SCIENCE AND TECHNOLOGY. *see* SCIENCES: COMPREHENSIVE WORKS—Abstracting, Bibliographies, Statistics

338 600 USA
T176
U.S. NATIONAL SCIENCE FOUNDATION. RESEARCH AND DEVELOPMENT IN INDUSTRY. Text in English. 1954. a. back issues avail. **Document type:** *Government.* **Description:** Provides national estimates of the expenditures on R&D performed within the US by industrial firms, whether US or foreign owned. Includes all for-profit, non-farm R&D-performing companies, either publicly or privately held.
Former titles (until 1966): Basic Research, Applied Research, and Development in Industry (0083-2383); (until 1962): National Science Foundation. Research and Development in Industry; (until 1960): Funds for Research and Development in Industry; (until 1957): Science and Engineering in American Industry
Related titles: Online - full text ed.; ◆ Series of: U.S. National Science Foundation. Surveys of Science Resources Series. ISSN 0083-2405.
—Linda Hall.
Published by: U.S. Department of Commerce, National Science Foundation, 4201 Wilson Blvd, Ste 245, Arlington, VA 22230. TEL 703-292-8774, FAX 703-292-9092, info@nsf.gov.

WASEDA DAIGAKU DAIGAKUIN RIKOGAKU KENKYU IHO/WASEDA UNIVERSITY. GRADUATE SCHOOL OF SCIENCE AND ENGINEERING. SYNOPSES OF SCIENCE AND ENGINEERING PAPERS. *see* ENGINEERING—Abstracting, Bibliographies, Statistics

ZHONGGUO KEJI TONGJI NIANJIAN/CHINA STATISTICAL YEARBOOK ON SCIENCE AND TECHNOLOGY. *see* SCIENCES: COMPREHENSIVE WORKS—Abstracting, Bibliographies, Statistics

TELEPHONE AND TELEGRAPH

see COMMUNICATIONS—Telephone And Telegraph

TELEVISION AND CABLE

see COMMUNICATIONS—Television And Cable

TEXTILE INDUSTRIES AND FABRICS

see also CLEANING AND DYEING ; CLOTHING TRADE

677 667 USA ISSN 1532-8813
TP890 CODEN: ARAEBW
A A T C C REVIEW. Text in English. 1999. bi-m. USD 200 to non-members; free to members (effective 2011). adv. 48 p./no. 3 cols./p.; back issues avail.; reprints avail. **Document type:** *Journal, Trade.*
Formerly (until Jan. 2001): Textile Chemist and Colorist & American Dyestuff Reporter (1526-2847); Which was formed by the merger of (1969-1999): Textile Chemist and Colorist (0040-490X); (1917-1999): American Dyestuff Reporter (0002-8266); Which incorporated (1879-1948): Textile Colorist & Converter (0096-591X); Which was formerly (until 1944): Textile Colorist (0096-5901)
Related titles: Online - full text ed.
Indexed: A05, A20, A22, AS&TA, AS&TI, B04, C10, CA, CCI, CurCont, Englnd, MSCI, SCI, SCOPUS, T01, T02, TM, TTI, W07, WTA.
—BLDSC (0537.694370), IE, Infotrieve, Ingenta, INIST, Linda Hall. **CCC.**
Published by: American Association of Textile Chemists and Colorists, PO Box 12215, Research Triangle Park, NC 27709. TEL 919-549-8141, FAX 919-549-8933, orders@aatcc.org. Pub. Jack Daniels. Circ: 3,000.

677 667 USA ISSN 0734-8894
TP890
A A T C C TECHNICAL MANUAL. Text in English. 1923. a. USD 285 per issue to non-members (print or CD-ROM eds.); USD 195 per issue to members (print or CD-ROM eds.) (effective 2011). **Document type:** *Handbook/Manual/Guide, Trade.*
Former titles (until 1963): American Association of Textile Chemists and Colorists. Technical Manual (0883-4539); (until 1958): American Association of Textile Chemists and Colorists. Technical Manual and Year Book; (until 1948): American Association of Textile Chemists and Colorists. Year Book
Related titles: CD-ROM ed.
Indexed: T01, T02, TTI, WTA.
—BLDSC (0537.694500). **CCC.**
Published by: American Association of Textile Chemists and Colorists, PO Box 12215, Research Triangle Park, NC 27709. TEL 919-549-8141, FAX 919-549-8933, orders@aatcc.org.

677 IND ISSN 0971-0833
CODEN: ATTDD4
A C T. Abbreviated title: A T I R A Communication on Textiles. Text in English. 1966. q. **Document type:** *Magazine, Academic/Scholarly.*
Formerly: A T I R A Technical Digest (0378-8148)
Indexed: ChemAb, SCOPUS, T01, TTI, WTA.
—BLDSC (1765.886800), CASDDS.
Published by: Ahmedabad Textile Industry's Research Association, Ambawadi Vistar P.O., Ahmedabad, Gujarat 380 015, India. TEL 91-79-26307921, FAX 91-79- 26304677, atiraad1@sancharnet.in, http://www.atira.in.

677 HKG ISSN 1015-8138
A T A JOURNAL; journal for Asia on textile & apparel. Text in English; Summaries in English. 1990. bi-m. HKD 455 domestic; USD 75 in Asia; USD 85 elsewhere (effective 2003). adv. abstr.; charts; illus.; stat. Index. 80 p./no.; back issues avail. **Document type:** *Journal, Trade.* **Description:** Provides up-to-date trade information, as well as useful market analysis, to assist decision makers in the textile and garment industry in Asia when devising business strategies and making daily production or operation decisions.
Formerly: Asia Textile and Apparel
Indexed: R&TA, SCOPUS, WTA.
—BLDSC (1765.425000), IE, Ingenta.

Published by: Yashi Chuban Gongsi/Adsale Publishing Ltd., 4-F, Stanhope House, 734 King's Rd, North Point, Hong Kong. TEL 852-2811-8897, FAX 852-2516-5119, circulation@adsalepub.com.hk, http://www.adsalepub.com.hk. Ed. Naomi Lee. Pub. Annie Chu. Adv. contact Anthony Ling. B&W page USD 2,951, color page USD 4,540; trim 280 x 215. Circ: 15,432.

677 USA
TS1312
A T I OFFICIAL NORTH AMERICAN TEXTILE RED BOOK. (American Textile International) Variant title: Textile Red Book. Text in English. a. USD 145. **Document type:** *Directory.*
Former titles (until 1999): Textile Red Book (1083-3420); (until 1995): A T I Directory (American Textile International) (1047-692X); (until 1988): Clark's Directory of Southern Textile Mills
Published by: Billian Publishing, Inc., 2100 Powers Ferry Rd, Ste 300, Atlanta, GA 30339. TEL 770-955-5656, 800-533-8484, FAX 770-952-0669, info@billian.com, http://www.billian.com.

338.4 DEU ISSN 0170-4060
A V R. (Allgemeiner Vliestoff-Report) Text in English, German. 1972. bi-m. EUR 95 domestic; EUR 110 foreign (effective 2009). adv. bk.rev. abstr.; bibl.; illus.; pat.; stat. **Document type:** *Magazine, Trade.*
Indexed: A22, ABIPC, Englnd, P&BA, SCOPUS, T01, TM, TTI, WTA.
—BLDSC (0792.380000), IE, Ingenta. **CCC.**
Published by: D P W Verlagsgesellschaft mbH, Industriestr 2, Heusenstamm, 63150, Germany. TEL 49-6104-6060, FAX 49-6104-606317, info@kepplermediengruppe.de, http://www.kepplermediengruppe.de. Ed. Angelika Hoerschelmann. Adv. contact Jean-Pierre Ferreira. B&W page EUR 2,745, color page EUR 4,095; trim 216 x 303. Circ: 6,800 (paid and controlled).

ADVANCED COMPOSITES BULLETIN. *see* PLASTICS

677 GBR ISSN 1472-0256
ADVANCES IN TEXTILES TECHNOLOGY. Text in English. 1980. m. GBP 457, USD 829 combined subscription (effective 2010). adv. bk.rev. stat. back issues avail. **Document type:** *Newsletter, Trade.* **Description:** Features articles for directors and senior managers responsible for technology, research, development, design, new ventures and overall corporate strategy.
Formerly (until 2000): High Performance Textiles (0144-5871)
Related titles: E-mail ed.; Online - full text ed.
Indexed: A22, A28, APA, BrCerAb, C&ISA, CA/WCA, CIA, CerAb, CivEngAb, CorrAb, E&CAJ, E11, EEA, EMA, ESPM, EnvEAb, H15, I05, M&TEA, M09, MBF, METADEX, R18, SCOPUS, SolStAb, T01, T02, T04, TM, TTI, WAA, WTA.
—BLDSC (0711.602000), IE, Infotrieve, Ingenta, Linda Hall. **CCC.**
Published by: International Newsletters Ltd., 9A Victoria Sq, Droitwich, Worcs WR9 8DE, United Kingdom. TEL 44-870-1657210, FAX 44-870-1657212, in@intnews.com, http://www.intnews.com. Ed. Nick Butler. Adv. contact David Kay TEL 44-1273-423512.

677 GBR ISSN 1744-6767
AFRICAN AND MIDDLE EAST TEXTILES/TEXTILES AFRICAINS; serving the textile and clothing industries. Text in English, French. 1980. q. GBP 34, USD 72, EUR 56 (effective 2010). adv. back issues avail. **Document type:** *Magazine, Trade.* **Description:** Reviews new industry developments in textile machinery and materials throughout the world in order to provide comprehensive coverage of the apparel and textile industries to a pan-African and Middle East readership.
Formerly (until 2004): African Textiles (0144-7521)
Indexed: A22, CTFA, SCOPUS, T01, T02, TTI, WTA.
—BLDSC (0734.931000). **CCC.**
Published by: Alain Charles Publishing Ltd., University House, 11-13 Lower Grosvenor Pl, London, SW1W 0EX, United Kingdom. TEL 44-20-78347676, FAX 44-20-79730076, post@alaincharles.com. Circ: 10,705.

677.7 USA
AGENT. Text in English. 1940. a. adv. **Document type:** *Directory, Trade.* **Description:** Contains more than 1,000 resources covering over 150 product and service classifications aimed at apparel and sewn products manufacturers.
Published by: Halper Publishing Company, 830 Moseley Rd., Highland Park, IL 60035-4636. TEL 847-433-1114, FAX 847-433-6602, info@halper.com, http://www.halper.com. Ed. Brian Ness. Pub., Adv. contact Rick Levine.

667 ESP ISSN 2173-1012
AITEX. Text in Spanish. 2001. q. **Document type:** *Magazine, Consumer.*
Published by: Instituto de Educacion Secundaria Los Alcores (San Miguel de Salinas), C San Rafael, 17, Los Alcores, San Miguel de Salinas, 03193, Spain. TEL 34-96-6723342, FAX 34-96-6723348, http://ieslosalcores.edu.gva.es/.

ALL PAKISTAN TEXTILE MILLS ASSOCIATION. CHAIRMAN'S REVIEW (ONLINE). *see* BUSINESS AND ECONOMICS—Production Of Goods And Services

AMERICAN FLOCK ASSOCIATION DIRECTORY. *see* BUSINESS AND ECONOMICS—Trade And Industrial Directories

677 621.9 USA
AMERICAN SOCIETY OF MECHANICAL ENGINEERS. TEXTILE ENGINEERING DIVISION. NEWSLETTER. Text in English. irreg. free to members (effective 2009).
Related titles: Online - full text ed.
Indexed: APA, C&ISA, CorrAb, E&CAJ, EEA, SolStAb, WAA.
Published by: A S M E International, Three Park Ave, New York, NY 10016. TEL 212-591-7158, 800-843-2763, FAX 212-591-7739, infocentral@asme.org, http://www.asme.org.

ANNUAL BOOK OF A S T M STANDARDS. VOLUME 06.04. PAINT-SOLVENTS; AROMATIC HYDROCARBONS. (American Society for Testing and Materials) *see* ENGINEERING—Engineering Mechanics And Materials

ANNUAL BOOK OF A S T M STANDARDS. VOLUME 07.01. TEXTILES (I): D76 - D4391. (American Society for Testing and Materials) *see* ENGINEERING—Engineering Mechanics And Materials

ANNUAL BOOK OF A S T M STANDARDS. VOLUME 07.02. TEXTILES (II): D4393 - LATEST. (American Society for Testing and Materials) *see* ENGINEERING—Engineering Mechanics And Materials

677 IND
APPAREL. Text in English. 1974. m. INR 1,000 to non-members; free to members (effective 2011). bk.rev. back issues avail. **Document type:** *Magazine, Trade.* **Description:** Serves with rich content supplemented with thorough analysis, round the globe surveys, fashion and trend forecasts by analysts, experts, top-end decision makers and veterans of the industry, from India and abroad.
Related titles: Online - full text ed.: free (effective 2011).
Published by: Clothing Manufacturers' Association of India, 902 Mahalaxmi Chambers, 22 Bhulabhai Desai Rd., Mumbai, Maharashtra 400 026, India. TEL 91-22-23538245, FAX 91-22-23515908, info@cmai.in.

THE APPAREL ANALYST. *see* CLOTHING TRADE

APPAREL MANUFACTURER. *see* CLOTHING TRADE

338.47687 USA ISSN 0275-8873
HD4966.C62
APPAREL PLANT WAGES SURVEY. Text in English. a. USD 60 to non-members; USD 25 to members. **Document type:** *Journal, Trade.*
Supersedes in part: Apparel Plant Wages and Personnel Policies (0084-6678)
Indexed: SRI.
Published by: American Apparel & Footwear Association, 1601 N Kent St, Ste. 1200, Arlington, VA 22209. TEL 703-524-1864, FAX 703-522-6741.

APPAREL TRADE DIRECTORY. *see* BUSINESS AND ECONOMICS—Trade And Industrial Directories

ARCHAEOLOGICAL TEXTILES NEWSLETTER. *see* ARCHAEOLOGY

677 PAK ISSN 1819-3358
ASIAN JOURNAL OF TEXTILE. Text in English. 2006. q. **Document type:** *Journal, Academic/Scholarly.* **Description:** Devoted to dissemination of fundamental and applied scientific information in the physical, chemical, and engineering sciences related to the textile and allied industries.
Related titles: Online - full text ed.: free (effective 2011).
Indexed: CA, T01, T02, TTI.
Published by: A N S I Network, 308 Lasani Town, Sargodha Rd, Faisalabad, 38090, Pakistan. TEL 92-41-8787087, FAX 92-41-8815544, ansinet@ansimail.org, http://ansinet.com, http://www.ansijournals.com.

677 JPN ISSN 1346-3276
CODEN: JTENAL
ASIAN TEXTILE BUSINESS. Variant title: J T N Monthly. Text in English. 1954. m. JPY 19,573 domestic; USD 180 foreign (effective 2002). adv. charts; stat. **Document type:** *Newspaper, Trade.*
Formerly (until 2001): Japan Textile News (0021-4752)
Related titles: Online - full text ed.
Indexed: A22, ChemAb, KES, P14, P48, P52, P53, P54, PQC, SCOPUS, T01, T02, TM, TTI, WTA.
—BLDSC (1742.750490), IE, Ingenta.
Published by: Oosaka Senken Ltd., 3-4-9 Bingomachi, Chuo-ku, Osaka-shi, 541-0051, Japan. TEL 81-6-202-7891, FAX 81-6-226-0106, http://www.sen-i-news.co.jp.

677 IND ISSN 0971-3425
ASIAN TEXTILE JOURNAL. Text in English. 1992. m. INR 1,000 (effective 2011). **Document type:** *Journal, Trade.*
Indexed: SCOPUS, T01, T02, TM, TTI, WTA.
—BLDSC (1742.750530), IE, Ingenta.
Published by: Kwatra/G.P.S, Ed. & Pub, 201, New Sonal Link Industrial Estate, Bldg No 2, Link Rd, Malad W, Mumbai, Maharastra 400 064, India. TEL 91-22-28812709, FAX 91-22-28898573, textile@ATjournal.com.

677 JPN
ASIAN TEXTILE RECORD. Text in Japanese. 51/yr. USD 980 (effective 1999).
Published by: Intercontinental Marketing Corp., I.P.O. Box 5056, Tokyo, 100-3191, Japan. TEL 81-3-3661-7458.

677 JPN ISSN 1346-3284
ASIAN TEXTILE WEEKLY. Variant title: J T N's Asian Textile Weekly. Text in English. 1975. w. USD 360; USD 570 for 2 yrs.; USD 780 for 3 yrs. (effective 2000). **Document type:** *Newspaper, Trade.*
Formerly (until 2001): J T N Weekly (1346-0358)
Related titles: Online - full text ed.
Indexed: A15, ABIn, P14, P48, P51, P52, P53, P54, PQC, SCOPUS, WTA.
Published by: Oosaka Senken Ltd., 3-4-9 Bingomachi, Chuo-ku, Osaka-shi, 541-0051, Japan. TEL 81-6-202-7891, FAX 81-6-226-0106.

677 746.9 AUS ISSN 1327-4414
AUSTRALASIAN TEXTILES & FASHION. Text in English. 1981. bi-m. AUD 55; AUD 120 foreign. adv. bk.rev. **Document type:** *Journal, Trade.*
Formerly (until 1996): Australasian Textiles (0725-086X)
Indexed: A22, SCOPUS, T01, T02, TTI, WTA.
—BLDSC (1796.375500). **CCC.**
Published by: (Society of Dyers & Colourists of Australia and New Zealand, Southern Australia Section of the Textile Institute), Australasian Textiles Publishers, PO Box 286, Belmont, VIC 3216, Australia. TEL 61-3-555500, FAX 61-3-52561668. Ed. S Boston. Circ: 2,800.

677 NZL ISSN 1176-337X
AUSTRALIAN & NEW ZEALAND APPAREL. Text in English. 1969. 11/yr. NZD 88 (effective 2008). adv. bk.rev. back issues avail. **Document type:** *Magazine, Trade.* **Description:** Content covers production, marketing and distribution of apparel and textiles within New Zealand. Audience is primarily manufacturers and retailers of clothing.
Formerly (until 2003): Apparel (1175-1673)
Related titles: Online - full text ed.
Indexed: A11, ABIX, B01, B02, B07, B15, B17, B18, G04.
—**CCC.**
Published by: 3 Media Group, Wellesley St, PO Box 5544, Auckland, 1141, New Zealand. TEL 64-9-9098400, FAX 64-9-9098401, http://www.admedia.co.nz. Ed. Tracey Strange TEL 64-9-9098449. Adv. contact Fiona Anderson. page NZD 2,277; bleed 210 x 297. Circ: 16,200.

677.3 AUS
AUSTRALIAN WOOL COMPENDIUM. Text in English. 1974. m. looseleaf. AUD 35 domestic; AUD 40 foreign (effective 2002).
Published by: Australian Wool Innovation Ltd., G P O Box 4177, Sydney, NSW 2001, Australia. TEL 1-800-070-099, FAX 1-800-899-515, info@woolinnovation.com.au, http://www.woolinnovation.com.au, http://www.woolinnovation.com.au. Ed. Mark Gabrys.

667.31 AUS
AUSTRALIAN WOOL PRODUCTION FORECAST REPORT. Text in English. q. **Document type:** *Report, Trade.* **Description:** Provides estimates of wool production and micron profile, both nationally and by state. It gives detailed forecasts, historical data and commentary on the key drivers of the forecasts.
Related titles: Online - full text ed.
Published by: Australian Wool Innovation Ltd., G P O Box 4177, Sydney, NSW 2001, Australia. TEL 1-800-070-099, FAX 1-800-899-515, info@woolinnovation.com.au.

687 DEU
B T E TASCHENBUCH. Text in German. 1951. a. adv. **Document type:** *Yearbook, Trade.*
Published by: (Bundesverband des Deutschen Textileinzelhandels e.V.), Deutscher Fachverlag GmbH, Mainzer Landstr 251, Frankfurt Am Main, 60326, Germany. TEL 49-69-75952052, FAX 49-69-75952999, info@dfv.de, http://www.dfv.de. adv.: page EUR 3,130; trim 105 x 148. Circ: 10,500 (controlled).

677 IND ISSN 0972-8341
B T R A SCAN. Text in English. 1970. q. back issues avail. **Document type:** *Journal, Academic/Scholarly.*
Indexed: CA, SCOPUS, T01, T02, TM, TTI, WTA.
—BLDSC (2354.760000), IE, Ingenta.
Published by: Bombay Textile Research Association, c/o Dr. A.N. Desai, Director, Lal Bahadur Shastri Marg, Ghatkopar W, Mumbai, Maharastra 400 086, India. TEL 91-22-25003651, FAX 91-22-25000459, btra@vsnl.com.

677 BGD ISSN 0253-5424
CODEN: BJJRD5
BANGLADESH JOURNAL OF JUTE & FIBRE RESEARCH. Text in Bengali. 1976. s-a. USD 5 per issue.
—CASDDS.
Published by: Bangladesh Jute Research Institute, Sher-e-Banglanagar, Dhaka, 7, Bangladesh. Ed. Harun Ur Rashid.

677 667 POL ISSN 0867-7824
BARWNIKI, SRODKI POMOCNICZE. Text in Polish. 1970. m.
Former titles (until 1992): Biuletyn Informacyjny Barwniki i Srodki Pomocnicze (0209-1259); (until 1973): Barwniki i Srodki Pomocnicze (1230-1027)
—BLDSC (1863.835200), IE, Ingenta.
Published by: Instytut Barwnikow i Produktow Organicznych, Ul A. Struga 29, Zgierz, 95100, Poland. TEL 48-42-7162034, FAX 48-42-7161319, ibpo_eh@priv3.onet.pl.

BELTWIDE COTTON CONFERENCES. PROCEEDINGS. *see* AGRICULTURE—Crop Production And Soil

BLACK SHEEP NEWSLETTER; a magazine for shepherds and fiber enthusiasts. *see* AGRICULTURE—Poultry And Livestock

677 ZAF
BLER; wolproduksie-inligtingsjoernaal - wool production information journal. Text in Afrikaans, English. 1995. 3/yr. **Document type:** *Newspaper.*
Indexed: ISAP.
Published by: S.A. Wool Board, PO Box 2191, Port Elizabeth, 6056, South Africa. TEL 27-41-544301, FAX 27-41-546760.

677 JPN ISSN 0385-7352
BOKEN REPORT. Text in Japanese. 1951. a. JPY 2,000. adv. back issues avail.
Formerly (until vol.49, 1970): J S I F Report
Published by: Japan Spinners Inspecting Foundation, 18-15 Ue-Machi 1-chome, Chuo-ku, Osaka-shi, 540-0005, Japan. TEL 06-762-5881, FAX 06-762-5889. Ed. Tadanori Inoko. Circ: 1,000.

677 DEU
BRUECKE; Informationen fuer Arbeitssicherheit und Gesundheitsschutz. Text in German. bi-m. **Document type:** *Magazine, Trade.*
Former titles (until 2006): Der Sicherheitsschirm (0944-7776); (until 1993): Der Unfallschirm
Indexed: TM.
Published by: Textil- und Bekleidungs-Berufsgenossenschaft, Oblatterwallstr 18, Augsburg, 86153, Germany. TEL 49-821-31590, FAX 49-821-3159201, direktion@textil-bg.de.

677 658.8 GBR ISSN 1358-3662
BUSINESS RATIO PLUS: COTTON & MAN - MADE FIBRE PROCESSORS. Text in English. 1974. a. charts; stat. **Document type:** *Journal, Trade.*
Formerly (until 1994): Business Ratio Report. Cotton and Man - Made Fibre Processes (0261-7773)
Published by: I C C Business Ratios Ltd. (Subsidiary of: Bonnier Business Information), Freepost, Field House, Hampton, Middx TW12 2HC, United Kingdom. TEL 44-181-783-0922, FAX 44-181-783-1940.

677 USA
C L A GUIDELINES; management guidelines for C L A members. Text in English. 1972. 3/yr. membership. back issues avail. **Document type:** *Newsletter.*
Published by: Coin Laundry Association, 1315 Butterfield Rd, Ste 212, Downers Grove, IL 60515. TEL 630-963-5547, FAX 630-963-5864. Ed. Brian Wallace. R&P John Vassiliades. Circ: 3,000.

677.39 IND
C S R & T I (MYSORE); bulletins on improved practices of sericulture. Text in English. 200?. 3/yr. INR 9 per set of 3 bulletins (effective 2011). **Document type:** *Bulletin, Trade.* **Description:** It is a kind of description literature available on Mulberry cultivation in South India, new technology of silkworm rearing & improved methods of rearing young-age (chawki) silkworm.
Related titles: Telugu ed.; Hindi ed.
Published by: Central Silk Board, c/o Ministry of Textiles, Government of India, C S B Complex, B T M Layout, Madanala Hosur Rd, Bangalore, Karnataka 560 068, India. TEL 91-80-26282699, FAX 91-80-26681511, csb@silkboard.org.

CANADIAN TEXTILE DIRECTORY. *see* BUSINESS AND ECONOMICS—Trade And Industrial Directories

TU

677 USA
HD9937.U5
CARPET AND RUG INSTITUTE. DIRECTORY. Text in English. 1950. a. USD 20. **Document type:** *Directory.*
Formerly: Carpet and Rug Institute. Directory and Report (0069-0740)
Published by: Carpet and Rug Institute, 310 Holiday Ave S, Box 2048, Dalton, GA 30720-2048. TEL 404-278-3176, FAX 404-278-8835. Ed. Truett Lomax.

677 USA ISSN 0095-6457
TS1772
CARPET SPECIFIER'S HANDBOOK. Text in English. 1974. irreg., latest vol.4, 1987. USD 10.25. illus.
Published by: Carpet and Rug Institute, 310 Holiday Ave S, Box 2048, Dalton, GA 30720-2048. TEL 404-278-3176, FAX 404-278-8835.

677 FRA ISSN 1016-8982
NK8806 CODEN: CGIMEA
CENTRE INTERNATIONAL D'ETUDE DES TEXTILES ANCIENS. BULLETIN. Short title: Bulletin du C I E T A. Text and summaries in English, French. 1955. a. bk.rev. bibl.; illus. back issues avail. **Document type:** *Bulletin.*
Former titles (until 1989): Textiles Anciens (0995-6638); (until 1987): Centre International d'Etude des Textiles Anciens. Bulletin de Liaison (0008-980X)
Media: Duplicated (not offset).
Indexed: B24, BAS.
Published by: Centre International d'Etude des Textiles Anciens, 34 rue de la Charite, Lyon, 69002, France. TEL 33-1-78384200, FAX 33-1-72402512, cieta@lyon.cci.fr, http://www.cieta-textiles.org.

677 CHN ISSN 1004-7093
CHANYEYONG FANGZHIPIN. Text in Chinese. 1983. m. USD 49.20 (effective 2009). **Document type:** *Journal, Academic/Scholarly.*
Related titles: Online - full text ed.
—East View.
Address: 1882, Yan'an Lu, Shanghai, 200051, China. TEL 86-21-62752920, FAX 86-21-62754501.

677 DEU ISSN 1434-3584
TS1300 CODEN: CFTXAJ
CHEMICAL FIBERS INTERNATIONAL; magazine for fiber polymers, fibers, texturing and spunbonds. Text in English. 1919. q. EUR 166.40 domestic; EUR 170.40 in Europe; EUR 176.60 elsewhere; EUR 29 newsstand/cover (effective 2009). adv. bk.rev. abstr.; charts; illus. index. **Document type:** *Magazine, Trade.*
Former titles (until 1995): Chemiefasern - Textil-Industrie (0340-3343); (until 1973): Chemiefasern + Textile Anwendungstechnik (0009-2878); (until 1968): Chemiefasern (0340-3327); (until 1960): Reyon, Zellwolle und Andere Chemie-Fasern (0370-8055)
Related titles: Online - full text ed.
Indexed: A&ATA, A22, ABIPC, C24, CBNB, CIN, CISA, CPEI, CTFA, ChemAb, ChemTitl, EngInd, KES, P&BA, P31, RefZh, SCOPUS, T01, T02, TM, TTI, WTA.
—BLDSC (3146.450000), CASDDS, IE, Ingenta, INIST, Linda Hall. **CCC.**
Published by: Deutscher Fachverlag GmbH, Mainzer Landstr 251, Frankfurt Am Main, 60326, Germany. TEL 49-69-75952052, FAX 49-69-75952999, info@dfv.de, http://www.dfv.de. Ed. Claudia van Bonn. Adv. contact Dagmar Henning. B&W page EUR 2,980, color page EUR 4,490; trim 182 x 260. Circ: 4,867 (paid and controlled).

677 CHN ISSN 1008-5580
CHENGDU FANGZHI GAODENG ZHUANKE XUEXIAO XUEBAO/ CHENGDU TEXTILE COLLEGE. JOURNAL. Text in Chinese. 1982. q. CNY 5 newsstand/cover (effective 2006). **Document type:** *Journal, Academic/Scholarly.*
Related titles: Online - full text ed.
Published by: Chengdu Fangzhi Gaodeng Zhuanke Xuexiao, Sanwaoyao, Chengdu, 610063, China. TEL 86-28-85353423, FAX 86-28-85354840.

677 CHN ISSN 1000-1484
CODEN: JCTUE2
CHINA TEXTILE UNIVERSITY. JOURNAL. Text in English. 1956. 4/yr. USD 60. adv. **Document type:** *Journal, Academic/Scholarly.* **Description:** Covers textile science and technology, fiber science, man-made fibers, mechanical engineering, applied chemistry and textile management engineering, clothing, automation & computer.
Related titles: Online - full text ed.; ◆ Chinese ed.: Zhongguo Fangzhi Daxue Xuebao. ISSN 1000-1476.
Indexed: SCOPUS.
—CASDDS, Ingenta.
Published by: Zhongguo Fangzhi Daxue/China Textile University, 1882 Yan an Xilu, Shanghai, 200051, China. TEL 86-21-6219-3-57, FAX 86-21-6208-9144.

CLEANING & RESTORATION. *see* CLEANING AND DYEING

CLEO EN LA MODA. *see* LEATHER AND FUR INDUSTRIES

677 GBR ISSN 2044-7833
▼ **CLOTH.** Text in English. 2009. q. GBP 12 domestic; GBP 20 foreign; GBP 3.50 per issue (effective 2010). **Document type:** *Magazine, Trade.* **Description:** Offers inspiring, practical and easy-to-follow advice on clothes making and homeware, embellishing and updating your existing wardrobe.
Published by: Real Design & Media, Tower House, Fairfax St, Bristol, BS1 3BN, United Kingdom. TEL 44-117-3148341, hello@therealdesigncompany.co.uk, http://www.therealdesigncompany.co.uk. Ed. Scott Purnell.

CLOTHING & TEXTILES RESEARCH JOURNAL. *see* CLOTHING TRADE

677 FRA ISSN 2107-0148
▼ **C!MAG.** Text in French. 2010. q. **Document type:** *Magazine, Trade.*
Formed by the merger of (2005-2010): Prom'objet (1778-1841); (2002-2010): Marquage Textile (1633-6151)
Published by: 656 Editions, 21 Rue Longue, BP 1072, Lyon Cedex 01, 69202, France. TEL 33-4-78304173, FAX 33-4-78304179, http://www.656editions.net.

677.1 IND ISSN 0530-0495
COIR NEWS. Text in English. 1956. m. INR 600; INR 60 per issue (effective 2011). adv. **Document type:** *Magazine, Trade.* **Description:** Articles on India's coir industry.
Published by: Coir Board, M.G. Rd, Ernakulam, Kochi, Kerala 682 016, India. TEL 91-484-2351807, FAX 91-484-2370034, coirboard@vsnl.com.

677 667 GBR
COLOUR INDEX INTERNATIONAL. Text in English. 1971. irreg., latest 4th ed. GBP 495 (effective 2010). adv. back issues avail. **Document type:** *Guide, Trade.* **Description:** Covers international classification system for dyes and pigments including information on their nomenclature, constitution, main applications and suppliers.
Formerly: Colour Index (Print)
Media: Online - full text. **Related titles:** CD-ROM ed.: GBP 450.
Published by: Society of Dyers and Colourists, Perkin House, 82 Grattan Rd, PO Box 244, Bradford, Yorks BD1 2JB, United Kingdom. TEL 44-1274-725138, FAX 44-1274-392888, http://www.sdc.org.uk. **Co-sponsor:** American Association of Textile Chemists and Colorists.

COLOURAGE. *see* CLEANING AND DYEING

COMPOSITES SCIENCE AND TECHNOLOGY. *see* TECHNOLOGY: COMPREHENSIVE WORKS

CONFECCION INDUSTRIAL. *see* CLOTHING TRADE

677.2 PAK
COTISTICS BI-ANNUAL COTTON STATISTICAL BULLETIN. Text in English. 1972. q. free. charts; stat. **Document type:** *Bulletin.*
Formerly: Cotistics Quarterly Cotton Statistical Bulletin
Published by: (Pakistan. Marketing and Economic Research Section), Pakistan Central Cotton Committee, c/o Secretary, Moulvi Tamizuddin Khan Rd., Karachi 1, Pakistan. TEL 524104-6.

COTTON DIRECTORY OF THE WORLD. *see* BUSINESS AND ECONOMICS—Trade And Industrial Directories

677.21 USA ISSN 0010-9800
SB245
COTTON GIN AND OIL MILL PRESS; the magazine of the cotton ginning and oilseed processing industries. Text in English. 1889. bi-w. (Sat.). USD 10 (effective 2005). adv. charts; illus.; stat. **Document type:** *Magazine, Trade.*
Related titles: Microfilm ed.: (from PQC).
Indexed: A22, ChemAb, T01, T02, TTI.
Published by: Haughton Publishing Co. of Texas, PO Box 180218, Dallas, TX 75218-0218. TEL 972-288-7511, FAX 972-285-4881. Adv. contact Susan Heston. color page USD 1,256.25. Circ: 2,000.

677.21 USA
COTTON INCORPORATED TECHNICAL BULLETIN. Text in English. a. **Document type:** *Bulletin.*
Published by: Cotton Board, 871 Ridgeway Loop, Ste 100, Memphis, TN 38120. TEL 901-683-2500, FAX 901-685-1401, info@cottonboard.org.

677.21 USA ISSN 0070-0673
TS1550
COTTON INTERNATIONAL. Variant title: Cotton International Annual. Text in English. 1914. a. free to qualified personnel (effective 2008). adv. reprints avail. **Document type:** *Magazine, Trade.* **Description:** Features information on the world cotton and textile industry.
Former titles (until 1969): Cotton (International Edition) (1059-1850); (until 1966): The Cotton Trade Journal (International Edition) (1059-1842); (until 1964): The Cotton Trade Journal & Agricultural Reporter (International Edition) (1059-1834); (until 1961): The Cotton Trade Journal (International Edition) (1059-1826)
Related titles: Online - full text ed.
Indexed: Agr, P06, T01, T02, TTI.
—BLDSC (3477.940000), IE, Ingenta. **CCC.**
Published by: Meister Media Worldwide, 37733 Euclid Ave, Willoughby, OH 44094. TEL 440-942-2000, 800-572-7740, FAX 440-975-3447, info@meistermedia.com, http://www.meistermedia.com. Eds. Anna Mullins, Frank Giles, Paul Schrimpf TEL 440-602-9142. Pub. Mike Gonitzke TEL 901-756-8822. Adv. contact Mary Shepard. Circ: 10,000.

677.21 USA ISSN 2154-9338
COTTON INTERNATIONAL E-NEWS. Text in English. 2007. w. free (effective 2010). **Document type:** *Newsletter, Consumer.* **Description:** Features information on the world cotton and textile industry.
Media: Online - full text.
Published by: Meister Media Worldwide, 37733 Euclid Ave, Willoughby, OH 44094. TEL 440-942-2000, 800-572-7740, FAX 440-975-3447, info@meistermedia.com, http://www.meistermedia.com.

677.21 USA ISSN 1934-3566
HD9070.1
COTTON INTERNATIONAL MAGAZINE. Text in English. 2002 (Fall). m. free to qualified personnel (effective 2008). adv. reprints avail. **Document type:** *Magazine, Trade.* **Description:** Features industry information about cotton markets, conferences, and major business figures worldwide.
Formerly (until 2006): C I World Report (1543-2084)
Related titles: Online - full text ed.
Indexed: A15, ABIn, P48, P51, P52, PQC.
—CCC.
Published by: Meister Media Worldwide, 37733 Euclid Ave, Willoughby, OH 44094. TEL 440-942-2000, 800-572-7740, FAX 440-975-3447, info@meistermedia.com, http://www.meistermedia.com. Ed. Paul Schrimpf TEL 440-602-9142. Pub. Mike Gonitzke TEL 901-756-8822. Adv. contact Mary Shepard.

677.21 GBR
COTTON OUTLOOK. Text in English. 1923. w. USD 715.82. adv. charts; mkt.; stat.
Formerly: Cotton and General Economic Review (0010-9789)
Media: Duplicated (not offset).
Published by: Cotlook Ltd., Cotlook House, Rock Ferry, 458 New Chester Rd, Birkenhead, Merseyside L42 2AE, United Kingdom. Ed. Ray Butler. **Dist. in U.S. by:** Cotlook Ltd., 5100 Poplar, Ste 2520, Memphis, TN 38137.

677.21 USA ISSN 0008-9729
COTTON: REVIEW OF THE WORLD SITUATION. Text in English. 1947. bi-m. USD 230 (effective 2011). charts; stat. back issues avail.
Formerly (until 1984): Cotton Monthly Review of the World Situation (0010-9754)
Related titles: CD-ROM ed.; E-mail ed.: USD 185 (effective 2011); Fax ed.; Microfiche ed.: (from CIS); Online - full text ed.: USD 125 (effective 2000); Spanish ed.; French ed.
Indexed: IIS, KES.
Published by: International Cotton Advisory Committee, 1629 K St N W, Ste 702, Washington, DC 20006. publications@icac.org. Ed. Armelle Gruere.

677.002294489 DNK
DANISH TEXTILE AND CLOTHING INDUSTRIES. GUIDE (ONLINE). Variant title: Guide to Danish Textile and Clothing Industries. Guide to the Textile and Clothing Industries in Denmark. Text in Danish, English, German. 1983. a. free. adv. **Document type:** *Directory, Trade.*
Former titles (until 1998): Danish Textile and Clothing Industries. Guide (Print) (0908-8296); (until 1991): Dansk Textil- og Beklaedningsguide (0907-0931); (until 1989): Dansk Textil Exportguide (0109-8586)
Media: Online - full text.
Published by: Dansk Textil og Beklaedningsindustri/Federation of Danish Textile and Clothing, Birk Centerpark 38, PO Box 507, Herning, 7400, Denmark. TEL 45-97-117200, FAX 45-97-117215, info@textile.dk.

677.0029 USA ISSN 0070-2951
DAVISON'S TEXTILE BLUE BOOK. Variant title: Textile Blue Book. Text in English. 1866. a. USD 165 (print or online ed.) (effective 2008). adv. illus. 800 p./no. 3 cols./p.; back issues avail. **Document type:** *Directory, Trade.* **Description:** Provides information about mills, dyers, finishers, converters and jobbers in the U.S., Canada, Mexico and Central America. It also includes various suppliers to the textile industry including machinery, chemicals, supplies and services.
Related titles: CD-ROM ed.; Diskette ed.; Online - full text ed.: USD 165 (effective 2001).
Published by: Davison Publishing Co., LLC (Subsidiary of: Simmons-Boardman Publishing Corp.), 3452 Lake Lynda Dr, Ste 363, Orlando, FL 32817. TEL 407-380-8900, 800-328-4766, FAX 407-380-5222, info@davisonpublishing.com, http://www.davisonpublishing.com. adv.: B&W page USD 1,520; 6 x 9.

DIRECTORY OF EUROPEAN TEXTILES. *see* BUSINESS AND ECONOMICS—Trade And Industrial Directories

DOW JONES AGRAR UND ERNAEHRUNG. *see* BUSINESS AND ECONOMICS—Investments

677 TUR ISSN 1301-2320
DUNYA TEKSTIL. Text in Turkish. 1997. m. **Document type:** *Magazine, Trade.*
Published by: Dunya Yayincilik A.S., Balamir Sokak No 7, Kavacik-Beykoz, Istanbul, 34830, Turkey. TEL 90-216-6811814, FAX 90-216-6803971. Circ: 12,000 (controlled).

E M B MAGAZINE. (Embroidery Monogram Business) *see* CLOTHING TRADE

677 FRA ISSN 0181-8120
E.T.N. REVUE DE L'ENTRETIEN DES TEXTILES ET NETTOYAGE. Key Title: E.T.N. Text in French. 1969. bi-m. EUR 61 (effective 2008). adv. bk.rev. **Document type:** *Magazine, Trade.*
Former titles (until 1978): Entretien des Textiles, Cuirs et Tapis (0181-8112); (until 1971): Entretien des Textiles (1250-1204); (until 1968): Techniques de la Teinture et du Nettoyage (1250-1190)
Indexed: TM.
Published by: Centre Technique de la Teinture et du Nettoyage (CTTN), Av. Guy de Collongue, BP 41, Ecully, Cedex 69131, France. TEL 33-4-78330861, FAX 33-4-78433412, http://www.cttn-iren.fr. Ed. Joelle Josserand. Circ: 3,000 (controlled).

677.028 GBR ISSN 1752-7422
TD195.T48
ECOTEXTILE NEWS. Text in English. 2007. 10/yr. GBP 199 (effective 2009). adv. back issues avail. **Document type:** *Magazine, Trade.* **Description:** Dedicated to the production of sustainable and ethical textiles and apparel.
Related titles: Online - full text ed.: ISSN 1752-7430.
Published by: Mowbray Communications Ltd., 80 Featherstone Ln, Featherstone, Pontefract, W Yorks WF7 6LR, United Kingdom. TEL 44-1977-708488, FAX 44-870-4862498, info@mowbray.uk.com, http://www.mowbray.uk.com. Ed. John Mowbray.

677.21 EGY ISSN 0367-0392
EGYPTIAN COTTON GAZETTE. Text in Arabic. 1947. 2/yr. adv. illus.; mkt.; stat. **Description:** Covers the Egyptian cotton exporting industry.
Incorporates: Egyptian Cotton Statistics; Formerly: Egyptian Cotton Year Book
Indexed: ChemAb.
Published by: Alexandria Cotton Exporters Association, P O Box 1772, Alexandria, Egypt. TEL 20-3-4808377, FAX 20-3-4833002, info@alcotexa.org, http://www.alcotexa.org/pages/home.aspx. Ed. Mr. Galal Er-Rifaii. Adv. contact Mrs. Hanaa Badar.

677 668.9 EGY ISSN 1110-600X
TS1300 CODEN: EJTPAB
EGYPTIAN JOURNAL OF TEXTILE & POLYMER SCIENCE & TECHNOLOGY. Text in Arabic. 1997. a. USD 42 (effective 2002). **Document type:** *Journal, Academic/Scholarly.*
Published by: National Information and Documentation Centre (NIDOC), Tahrir St., Dokki, Awqaf P.O., Giza, Egypt. TEL 20-2-3371696, FAX 20-2-3371746. Ed. Dr. Aly A Hebeish.

677 USA ISSN 1097-9255
EMBROIDERY NEWS. Text in English. 1955. bi-m. free to qualified personnel; USD 10 to individuals (effective 2004). adv. bk.rev. 8 p./no.; **Document type:** *Newsletter, Trade.*
Published by: Schiffli Lace and Embroidery Manufacturers Association, Inc., 20 Industrial Ave., # 26, Fairview, NJ 07022-1614. TEL 201-943-7757, FAX 201-943-7793. Ed., Adv. contact I Leonard Seiler. Circ: 250 (controlled).

677 GRC ISSN 1105-4069
EPITHEORESIS KLOSTOUFANTOURGIAS/EPITHEORISIS KLOSTOUFANTOURGIAS. Text in Greek. 1961. bi-m. (Greek edition; q., Arabic edition). adv. Supplement avail. **Document type:** *Trade.*
Related titles: Arabic ed.
Published by: Textile Review, 9 Irinis St, 18547 N. Faliron, Athens, Greece. TEL 30-1-4813-515, TELEX 213379 TEXR.

677 BEL ISSN 1028-5954
EURATEX. BULLETIN. Text in English, French. 5/yr. EUR 140 domestic; EUR 165 foreign; EUR 40 newsstand/cover (effective 2000).
Formerly (until 1996): ComiTextil. Bulletin (1028-5946)
Indexed: GEOBASE, SCOPUS, T01, T02, TTI, WTA.

Published by: European Apparel and Textile Organisation (Euratex), Rue Montoyer 24, Brussels, 1000, Belgium. TEL 32-2-2309580, FAX 32-2-2306054.

EURODECOR. *see* BUSINESS AND ECONOMICS

677.76 DEU ISSN 0945-1943
EUROSEIL. Text in German. 1993. 2/yr. adv. bk.rev. illus. **Document type:** *Magazine, Trade.* **Description:** Publishes information to the textile industry and fabrics trade.
Formerly (until 1994): Corderie d'Europe (0945-1595); Which was formed by the merger of (1879-1993): Deutsche Seiler-Zeitung (0012-0758); (1???-1993): Corderie Francaise
Indexed: SCOPUS, TM, WTA.
—CCC.
Published by: (Bundesverband des Deutschen Seiler-, Segel- und Netzmacherhandwerks e.V. CHE), Deutscher Fachverlag GmbH, Mainzer Landstr 251, Frankfurt Am Main, 60326, Germany. TEL 49-69-75952052, FAX 49-69-75952999, info@dfv.de, http://www.dfv.de. Ed. Petra Gottwald. Adv. contact Dagmar Henning. Circ: 2,000 (controlled).

EXPORTS HOME TEXTILE; monthly textile magazine. *see* BUSINESS AND ECONOMICS—International Commerce

FABRIC ARCHITECTURE; design for sustainability. *see* ARCHITECTURE

677 380.1029 GBR ISSN 1472-0523
TS1312
FABRIC BUYER'S DIRECTORY; the global sourcing guide for fashion fabrics, trimmings and garment accessories. Text in English; Summaries in English, French. 1999. a., latest 2002, 3rd Ed. GBP 75 per issue (effective 2002). adv. back issues avail. **Document type:** *Directory, Trade.* **Description:** Global sourcing for fashion designers and buyers of fabrics, trimmings, fur, leather and garment accessories. 3000 companies profiled in-depth. 22,000 product references under 500 catagory headings.
Related titles: E-mail ed.
Published by: (Textile Institute), Publishing Events Media Ltd., 40 Bowling Green Ln, London, EC1R 0NE, United Kingdom. TEL 44-20-7713-8200, FAX 44-20-7713-0202. Ed. Alexa Michael. Pub., R&P Rupert Darrington. adv.: color page GBP 950; trim 16.5 x 25.5.

677.028 USA ISSN 1938-9132
FABRIC GRAPHICS. Text in English. 2007. bi-m. USD 39 domestic; USD 49 in Canada & Mexico; USD 69 elsewhere (effective 2008). adv. back issues avail.; reprints avail. **Document type:** *Magazine, Trade.* **Description:** Contains information about textile printing and design, as well as the latest in technology and industry information to improve product quality and profit.
Related titles: Online - full text ed.
Published by: Industrial Fabrics Association International, 1801 W County Rd B W, Ste B, Roseville, MN 55113. TEL 651-222-2508, 800-255-4324, FAX 651-631-9334, generalinfo@ifai.com. Eds. Janet L Preus TEL 651-225-6980, Lou Dzierzak, Susan Nieme. Pub. Mary Hennessy. Adv. contacts Jane Anthone TEL 651-225-6911, Sarah C Hyland TEL 651-225-6950. page USD 3,985.

677 USA ISSN 1555-2756
FABRIC TRENDS; for quilters. Text in English. 2003. q. USD 19.97 domestic; USD 27.97 in Canada; USD 31.97 elsewhere; USD 6.99 per issue (effective 2008). adv. back issues avail. **Document type:** *Magazine, Consumer.*
Published by: All American Crafts, Inc., 7 Waterloo Rd, Stanhope, NJ 07874-2621. dcohen@allamericancrafts.com, http://www.allamericancrafts.com. Ed. Lisa Swenson Ruble. Pub. Jerry Cohen. Adv. contact Carol Newman TEL 570-395-3196.

677.028 CAN ISSN 1196-9318
FABRICARE CANADA. Text in English. 1955. bi-m. free. adv. bk.rev. tr.lit. back issues avail. **Document type:** *Magazine, Trade.*
Formerly (until 1995): Canadian Cleaner and Launderer (0008-3224)
Indexed: A09, A10, T01, T02, TTI, V03, V04.
Published by: Todd's Your Answer Ltd., P O Box 968, Oakville, ON L6J 5E8, Canada. TEL 905-337-0516, FAX 905-337-0525. Ed., Pub., Adv. contact Marcia Todd. B&W page USD 1,531, color page USD 2,307; trim 10.88 x 8.13. Circ: 6,000 (controlled).

677 CHN ISSN 1003-0611
FANGZHI BIAOZHUN YU ZHILIANG. Text in Chinese. 1979. bi-m. CNY 120 (effective 2009). **Document type:** *Journal, Academic/Scholarly.*
Formerly (until 1989): Fangzhi Biaozhun Jiance
Published by: Fangzhi Gongyebu Biaozhunhua Yanjiusuo/Standardization Institute of Textile Industry, 3, Yanjingli Zhong Lu, Beijing, 100025, China. TEL 86-10-65003779.

677 CHN ISSN 1003-3025
FANGZHI DAOBAO/CHINA TEXTILE LEADER. Text in Chinese. 1982. m. **Document type:** *Magazine, Trade.*
Formerly: Fangzhi Xiaoxin
Related titles: Online - full text ed.
Indexed: T01, TTI.
—BLDSC (3865.579600).
Published by: Zhongguo Fangzhi Xinxi Zhongxin/China Textile Information Center, 12, Dongchangan Lu, Beijing, 100742, China. TEL 86-10-85229746, FAX 86-10-85229747, http://www.ctic.org.cn/. Ed. Ruizhe Sun.

677 CHN ISSN 1674-196X
FANGZHI FUZHUANG ZHOUKAN/TEXTILE CLOTHING WEEKLY. Text in Chinese. 2000. w. CNY 780 domestic; USD 197.60 in Hong Kong, Macau & Taiwan; USD 291.20 elsewhere (effective 2007). **Document type:** *Magazine, Trade.*
Former titles (until 2006): Fangzhi Xinxi Zhoukan/Textile Information Weekly (1009-0770); Which was formed by the merger of: Zhongguo Fangzhi Xinxi Wangluo Kuaixun; Fangzhi Jingji Xinxi
Related titles: Online - full text ed.
—East View.
Published by: Fangzhi Fuzhuang Zhoukan Zazhishe, 12, Dongchangan Jie, Beijing, 100742, China. TEL 86-10-85229553, FAX 86-10-65135947. **Dist. by:** China International Book Trading Corp, 35 Chegongzhuang Xilu, Haidian District, PO Box 399, Beijing 100044, China. TEL 86-10-68412045, FAX 86-10-68412023, cibtc@mail.cibtc.com.cn, http://www.cibtc.com.cn.

677 CHN ISSN 1003-1308
FANGZHI KEXUE YANJIU/TEXTILE SCIENCE RESEARCH. Text in Chinese. 1990. q. CNY 30 (effective 2008). **Document type:** *Journal, Academic/Scholarly.*
—BLDSC (3865.580500).
Published by: Zhongguo Fangzhi Kexue Yanjiuyuan/Chinese Textile Academy, Zhaoyang-qu, Yinjiafen, Beijing, 100025, China. TEL 86-10-65014466 ext 3450.

677 CHN ISSN 1001-9634
FANGZHI QICAI/TEXTILE ACCESSORIES. Text in Chinese. 1972. bi-m. **Document type:** *Magazine, Trade.*
Formerly (until 1974): Fangzhi Qicai Tongxun
Related titles: Online - full text ed.
Published by: Quanguo Fangzhi Qicaike Keji Xinxi Zhongxin/China Textile Accessories Info, 37, Weiyang Xi Lu, Xianyang, 712000, China. TEL 86-29-33579905, FAX 86-29-33579903, ctainfo@ctainfo.cn. **Co-sponsors:** Shaanxi Fangzhi Qicai Yanjiuso; Zhongguo Fangzhi Jixie Qicaike Gongye Xiehui.

677 CHN ISSN 0253-9721
TS1300 CODEN: FCHPDI
FANGZHI XUEBAO/JOURNAL OF TEXTILE RESEARCH. Text in Chinese. 1979. bi-m. USD 133.20 (effective 2009). **Document type:** *Journal, Academic/Scholarly.*
Related titles: Online - full text ed.
Indexed: A22, CIN, ChemAb, ChemTitl, T01, TTI, WTA.
—BLDSC (5069.048000), East View, IE, Ingenta.
Published by: Zhongguo Fangzhi Gongcheng Xuehui/China Textile Engineering Association, 3, Chaowai Yanjing Li Zhongjie, 6/F, Zhulou, Beijing, 100025, China. TEL 86-10-65017772 ext 8001, 8003, 8005, FAX 86-10-65016538.

677 TWN ISSN 1019-0473
FANGZHI ZHONGXIN QIKAN/CHINA TEXTILE INSTITUTE. JOURNAL. Text in Chinese. 1991. bi-m. USD 30 domestic; USD 41 in Asia; USD 50 elsewhere. **Description:** Contains research papers on textile industry. Covers fibers, yarn, fabric, dyeing and finishing, apparel manufacturing, textile testing and more.
Indexed: SCOPUS, WTA.
Published by: Zhongguo Fangzhi Gongye Yanjiu Zhongxin/China Textile Institute, No 6, Chen-Tian Rd, Tu-Chen City, Taipei, Taiwan. TEL 886-2-2644720, FAX 886-2-2675110. Eds. C L Liu, J L Ting. Pub. S C Yao. R&P M H Yan. Circ: 500 (paid).

FASHION THEORY; the journal of dress, body and culture. *see* ART

677 CHN ISSN 1005-2054
FEIZHI ZAOBU/NONWOVENS. Text in Chinese. 1993. bi-m. CNY 90 (effective 2009). **Document type:** *Magazine, Trade.*
Related titles: Online - full text ed.
Published by: Fangzhi Gongye Feizhi Zaobu Jishu Kaifa Zhongxin, 124, Nanta Jie, Shenyang, 110016, China. TEL 86-24-23916067, FAX 86-24-23894580.

677 USA
HD9929.5.U6
FIBER ORGANON; featuring manufactured fibers. Text in English. 1930. m. USD 300 domestic; USD 400 foreign (effective 2000). bk.rev. charts; mkt.; stat. index. **Document type:** *Report, Trade.* **Description:** Covers statistics of production, shipments, stocks on manufactured fibers and contains features such as global production and capacities of fibers, end use and per capita consumption and other to provide an on-going statistical profile of trends in the U.S. and global fiber industries.
Formerly: Textile Organon (0040-5132)
Indexed: P06, PAIS, RASB, SCOPUS, SRI, T01, T02, TTI, WTA.
—Linda Hall.
Published by: Fiber Economics Bureau, Inc., 1530 Wilson Blvd., Ste. 690, Arlington, VA 22209-2418. TEL 202-467-0916, FAX 202-467-0917. Ed., Pub., R&P Frank J Horn. Circ: 2,500.

677.4 CHE ISSN 2079-6439
▼ ➤ **FIBERS.** Text in English. forthcoming 2011. q. free (effective 2011). **Document type:** *Journal, Academic/Scholarly.*
Media: Online - full text.
Published by: M D P I AG, Postfach, Basel, 4005, Switzerland. TEL 41-61-6837734, FAX 41-61-3028918, http://www.mdpi.org/.

547.85 USA ISSN 0015-0541
TS1548.5 CODEN: FICYAP
➤ **FIBRE CHEMISTRY.** Text in English. 1969. bi-m. EUR 3,813, USD 3,940 combined subscription to institutions (print & online eds.) (effective 2012). adv. back issues avail.; reprint service avail. from PSC. **Document type:** *Journal, Academic/Scholarly.* **Description:** Contains original research and review articles of Russian-speaking authors in the field of man-made fibre production and application.
Related titles: Microfilm ed.: (from PQC); Online - full text ed.: ISSN 1573-8493 (from IngentaConnect); ◆ Translation of: Khimicheskie Volokna. ISSN 0023-1118.
Indexed: A01, A03, A08, A22, A26, A28, APA, ASCA, Agr, ApMecR, BibLing, BrCerAb, C&ISA, C33, CA, CA/WCA, CCI, CIA, CerAb, ChemAb, ChemTitl, CivEngAb, CorrAb, E&CAJ, E01, E11, EEA, EMA, ESPM, EnvEAb, H15, M&TEA, M09, MBF, METADEX, MSCI, P52, S01, SCI, SCOPUS, SolStAb, T01, T02, T04, TTI, W07, WAA, WTA.
—BLDSC (0411.752000), CASDDS, East View, IE, Infotrieve, Ingenta, INIST, Linda Hall. **CCC.**
Published by: (Rossiiskaya Akademiya Nauk/Russian Academy of Sciences RUS), Springer New York LLC (Subsidiary of: Springer Science+Business Media), 233 Spring St, New York, NY 10013. TEL 212-460-1500, FAX 212-460-1575, service-ny@springer.com. Ed. N N Machalaba.

677 POL ISSN 1230-3666
FIBRES & TEXTILES IN EASTERN EUROPE. Text in English. 1993. bi-m. EUR 147 foreign (effective 2006). **Description:** Publishes articles associated with investigation into the production and application of fibres and textiles.
Related titles: Online - full text ed.: free (effective 2011).
Indexed: A20, A28, APA, BrCerAb, C&ISA, CA, CA/WCA, CIA, CerAb, CivEngAb, CorrAb, CurCont, E&CAJ, E11, EEA, EMA, H15, Inspec, M&TEA, M09, MBF, METADEX, MSCI, R18, RefZh, SCI, SCOPUS, SolStAb, T01, T02, T04, TM, TTI, W07, WAA, WTA.
—BLDSC (3917.810000), IE, Ingenta, Linda Hall.
Published by: Instytut Wlokien Chemicznych/Institute of Chemical Fibres, ul Sklodowskiej-Curie 19-27, Lodz, 90570, Poland. TEL 48-42-6380300, FAX 48-42-6376214, http://www.iwch.lodz.pl. Ed. Bogdan Mac TEL 48-42-6380314. **Dist. by:** Ars Polona, Obroncow 25, Warsaw 03933, Poland. TEL 48-22-5098609, FAX 48-22-5098610, arspolona@arspolona.com.pl, http://www.arspolona.com.pl.

677 660 USA
FILTRATION CONFERENCE PAPERS. Text in English. 1993. a. USD 100 per issue to non-members; USD 75 per issue to members (effective 2010). back issues avail. **Document type:** *Proceedings.*
Related titles: CD-ROM ed.; Online - full text ed.
Published by: Association of the Nonwoven Fabrics Industry (I N D A), PO Box 1288, Cary, NC 27512. TEL 919-233-1210, FAX 919-233-1282, info@inda.org.

677 USA
FILTRATION TECHNOLOGY HANDBOOK. Text in English. 2000. irreg. USD 75 to non-members; USD 55 to members (effective 2010). **Document type:** *Handbook/Manual/Guide, Trade.*
Published by: Association of the Nonwoven Fabrics Industry (I N D A), PO Box 1288, Cary, NC 27512. TEL 919-233-1210, FAX 919-233-1282, info@inda.org.

677 GBR
FINANCIAL SURVEY. COMPANY DATA FOR SUCCESS: COTTON & MAN MADE FIBRE MANUFACTURERS & DISTRIBUTORS. Text in English. a. charts; stat. **Document type:** *Report, Trade.*
Formerly (until 1991): Financial Survey Company Directory. Cotton and Man Made Fibre Manufacturers and Distributors
Published by: I C C Financial Surveys Ltd, Field House, 72 Oldfield Rd, Hampton, Mddx TW12 2HQ, United Kingdom. TEL 081-783-0977, FAX 081-783-1940.

677 DEU
FORWARD TEXTILE TECHNOLOGIES; das Fachmagazin fuer die Textil- und Bekleidungsindustrie. Text in German. 1992. 12/yr. EUR 120; EUR 10 newsstand/cover (effective 2009). adv. bk.rev. bibl.; charts; illus.; tr.lit. index. **Document type:** *Magazine, Trade.* **Description:** Constitutes a trade publication for the clothing industry, featuring manufacturing, trade, latest styles and fashions, industrial technology, industry news, reports and announcements of events.
Former titles: B W Fashion Technics; Bekleidung Wear (0944-7067); Which was formed by the merger of (1962-1992): Bekleidung und Maschenware (0005-8270); (1949-1992): Bekleidung und Waesche (0005-8289)
Indexed: SCOPUS, T01, TTI, WTA.
—CCC.
Published by: F I S - Fashion Innovation Service, Franz-Haniel-Str 79, Moers, 47443, Germany. TEL 49-841-1426380, FAX 49-841-1426896, info@fisgmbh.com, http://www.fisgmbh.com. Ed. Iris Schlomski. Adv. contact Viola Konrad. B&W page EUR 2,850; trim 210 x 280.

677 JPN
FRATERNITY MONTHLY MAGAZINE. Text in Japanese. m. JPY 250 newsstand/cover. **Document type:** *Newsletter.*
Published by: Zensen the Japanese Federation of Textile Garment Chemical Commercial and Allied Industries Workers' Unions, 8-16 Kudan-Minami 4-chome, Chiyoda-ku, Tokyo, 102-0074, Japan. TEL 81-3-3288-3723, TELEX ZENSEN TOKYO. Ed. Tadanobu Abe. Pub. Kiyoshi Ochiai.

677.028 GBR ISSN 1740-4126
FUTURE MATERIALS. Text in English. 2002. bi-m. GBP 275; EUR 350 (print or online ed.) (effective 2009). adv. **Document type:** *Magazine, Trade.* **Description:** Reports on fusion of disciplines in technical textiles, nonwovens, paper, resins, films, composites, coatings and lamites.
Related titles: Online - full text ed.
Indexed: T01, T02, TM, TTI.
—CCC.
Published by: World Textile Publications Ltd., Perkin House, 1 Longlands St, Bradford, W Yorks BD1 2TP, United Kingdom. TEL 44-1274-378800, FAX 44-1274-378811, info@world-textile.net, http://www.world-textile.net/. Ed. Andrew Thornton TEL 44-1274-378839. Adv. contact James Wilson TEL 44-1274-378800. color page GBP 2,723, B&W page GBP 1,736; bleed 216 x 303.

GAAF GOED; vakblad voor de interieur-textiel-branche. *see* INTERIOR DESIGN AND DECORATION—Furniture And House Furnishings

677 ARG ISSN 0046-5364
GACETA TEXTIL. Text in Spanish. 1934. m. adv. abstr.; bibl.; illus.; stat.
Published by: Gaceta Editora Coop Ltda., 25 de Mayo, 786, Buenos Aires, 1002, Argentina. Ed. Emma P Zappettini. Circ: 15,000.

677 ARG ISSN 0016-3996
CODEN: GALAAL
➤ **GALAXIA.** Text in Spanish. 1963. q. USD 60 (effective 1996 & 1997). adv. bk.rev. abstr.; bibl.; charts; illus.; stat. **Document type:** *Academic/Scholarly.* **Description:** Provides information on the society's activities.
Indexed: C01, ChemAb.
—CASDDS.
Published by: Asociacion Argentina de Quimicos y Coloristas Textiles, Bulnes 1425, Buenos Aires, 1176, Argentina. TEL 54-114-9630394. Ed. Silvio Roldan. R&P, Adv. contact Nivea Surian. B&W page ARS 700. Circ: 1,500.

677.028 USA ISSN 1931-8189
GEOSYNTHETICS. Text in English. 1983. bi-m. USD 59 domestic to non-members; USD 69 in Canada & Mexico to non-members; USD 99 elsewhere to non-members; USD 55 to members (effective 2009). adv. tr.lit. cum.index: 1983-1993. back issues avail.; reprints avail. **Document type:** *Magazine, Trade.* **Description:** Provides a forum for consistent and accurate information to increase the acceptance and to promote the correct use of geosynthetics.
Formerly (until Mar.2006): Geotechnical Fabrics Report (0882-4983)
Related titles: Online - full text ed.: free (effective 2009).
Indexed: A22, GEOBASE, GeoRef, GeotechAb, HRIS, SCOPUS, SpeleolAb, T01, T02, TM, TTI, WTA.
—BLDSC (4158.897812), IE, Infotrieve, Ingenta, Linda Hall.
Published by: (Geosynthetics Materials Association), Industrial Fabrics Association International, 1801 W County Rd B W, Ste B, Roseville, MN 55113. TEL 651-222-2508, 800-255-4324, FAX 651-631-9334, generalinfo@ifai.com. Ed. Ron Bygness TEL 651-225-6988. Pub. Mary Hennessy. Adv. contact Jane Anthone TEL 651-225-6911. page USD 5,045. Circ: 16,000 (paid).

TU

677.028 GBR ISSN 1751-7613
➤ **GEOSYNTHETICS INTERNATIONAL (ONLINE).** Text in English. 2003. bi-m. GBP 525 (effective 2011). back issues avail. **Document type:** *Journal, Academic/Scholarly.* **Description:** Features technical papers, technical notes, and discussions on all topics relevant to geosynthetic materials research, behaviour, performance analysis, testing, design, construction methods, case histories, and field experience.
Media: Online - full text.
Published by: (Institution of Civil Engineers (I C E), International Geosynthetics Society USA), I C E Publishing, 2nd Fl, 40 Marsh Wall, London, E14 9TP, United Kingdom. TEL 44-20-76652460, info@icepublishing.com, http://www.icepublishing.com. Ed. Dr. R J Bathurst TEL 613-541-6000 ext 6479. Pub. Leon Heward-Mills TEL 44-20-76652450.

677.028 GBR ISSN 0266-1144
TA418
➤ **GEOTEXTILES AND GEOMEMBRANES.** Text in English. 1984. 6/yr. EUR 1,136 in Europe to institutions; JPY 151,000 in Japan to institutions; USD 1,272 elsewhere to institutions (effective 2012). adv. bk.rev. back issues avail. **Document type:** *Journal, Academic/Scholarly.* **Description:** Covers current technology available to research workers, designers, users and manufacturers of geotextiles and geomembranes.
Related titles: Online - full text ed.: ISSN 1879-3584 (from IngentaConnect, ScienceDirect).
Indexed: A01, A03, A08, A22, A26, ASCA, ApMecR, CA, CPEI, CurCont, ESPM, EngInd, GEOBASE, GeotechAb, HRIS, I05, ICEA, MSCI, R18, RefZh, S01, SCI, SCOPUS, SWRA, T01, T02, TM, TTI, W07, WTA.
—BLDSC (4161.010000), IE, Infotrieve, Ingenta, INIST, Linda Hall. **CCC.**
Published by: (International Geotextile Society USA), Elsevier Ltd (Subsidiary of: Elsevier Science & Technology), The Blvd, Langford Ln, Kidlington, Oxford, OX5 1GB, United Kingdom. TEL 44-1865-843000, FAX 44-1865-843010, journalscustomerserviceemea@elsevier.com. Ed. R Kerry Rowe. **Subscr. to:** Elsevier BV, Radarweg 29, PO Box 211, Amsterdam 1000 AE, Netherlands. http://www.elsevier.nl.

667 USA
(YEAR) GLOBAL COMPARISON OF TEST METHODS. Text in English. 2000. irreg., latest 2000. **Document type:** *Trade.*
Published by: Association of the Nonwoven Fabrics Industry (I N D A), PO Box 1288, Cary, NC 27512. TEL 919-233-1210, FAX 919-233-1282, info@inda.org, http://www.inda.org.

677 SGP ISSN 1747-6690
GLOBAL SOURCES. GARMENTS & TEXTILES. Short title: Garments & Textiles. Text in English. 2005. m. USD 75; USD 6.25 per issue (effective 2010). adv. back issues avail. **Document type:** *Magazine, Trade.* **Description:** Provides information about new garment and textile products and suppliers worldwide, with a focus on manufacturers in China and India.
Formerly: Asian Sources Garments & Textiles
Related titles: Online - full text ed.: ISSN 2045-6018. free (effective 2010).
Published by: Global Sources, c/o Media Data Systems Pte Ltd, PO Box 0203, Raffles City, 911707, Singapore. TEL 65-6547-2800, FAX 65-6547-2888, service@globalsources.com, http://www.globalsources.com/.

667 677 NLD ISSN 1877-9980
GOED GOED NIEUWS. Text in Dutch. 2003. s-a. free membership (effective 2011).
Incorporates (200?-2007): Protest! (1875-7200); Formerly (until 2009): Schoon Genoeg (1574-9800)
Related titles: Online - full text ed.: ISSN 1877-9999.
Published by: Schone Kleren Kampagne, Postbus 11584, Amsterdam, 1001 GN, Netherlands. TEL 31-20-4122785, FAX 31-20-4122786, info@schonekleren.nl, http://www.schonekleren.nl. Ed. Miriam van Ommeren.

677 CHN ISSN 1674-2400
GUANGXI FANGZHI KEJI. Text in Chinese. 1972. bi-m. **Document type:** *Magazine, Trade.*
Former titles (until 1982): Guangxi Fangzhi; (until 1979): Guangxi Fangzhi Jianxun
Related titles: Online - full text ed.
Published by: Guangxi Juanma Fangzhi Kexue Yanjiusuo, 43, Tinghong Lu, Nanning, 530031, China. TEL 86-771-4813746.

677 CHN ISSN 1007-6867
GUOJI FANGZHI DAOBAO/MELLIAND - CHINA. Text in Chinese. 1973. m. adv.
Related titles: Online - full text ed.
Published by: Donghua Daxue/Donghua University, 1882, Yanan Xilu, Shanghai, 200051, China. TEL 86-21-62752920, FAX 86-21-62754501. adv.: B&W page EUR 1,640, color page EUR 2,490. Circ: 7,000 (controlled).

677.39 CHN
GUOWAI SICHOU/FOREIGN SILK. Text in Chinese. bi-m.
Published by: Suzhou Sichou Gongxueyuan/Suzhou Institute of Silk Engineering, 14 Xiangmen Lu, Suzhou, Jiangsu 215005, China. TEL 225614. Ed. Wu Rongru.

677 HKG ISSN 1024-4638
H K P C TEXTILE AND CLOTHING BULLETIN. Text in Chinese. 1989. bi-m. HKD 30; HKD 170 newsstand/cover. adv. **Document type:** *Bulletin.* **Description:** Provides up-to-date information to designers, engineers, technical management and approved authorities in industrial and scientific establishments concerned with the textile and clothing industry.
Published by: Hong Kong Productivity Council, HKPC Bldg, 78 Tat Chee Ave, Kowloon, Hong Kong. TEL 852-2788-5961, FAX 852-2788-5959. Ed. Mansien Liu. adv.: B&W page HKD 3,400, color page HKD 58,000. Circ: 5,000.

HABIT; mode og affaerer. *see* CLOTHING TRADE—Fashions

THE HALI ANNUAL (YEAR). *see* ARTS AND HANDICRAFTS

338.4 IND ISSN 0436-7316
HD9886.I42
HANDBOOK OF THE INDIAN COTTON TEXTILE INDUSTRY. Text in English. 19??. a. INR 15 (effective 2011).
Published by: Cotton Textiles Export Promotion Council, Engineering Centre 9, 4 Mathew Rd, Mumbai, Maharashtra, India.

677 IND
HISTORIC TEXTILES OF INDIA. Text in English. 1972. irreg., latest 2009. INR 2,650 per issue (effective 2011). adv. **Document type:** *Catalog, Trade.*
Published by: Calico Museum of Textiles, Sarabhai Foundation, Opp Underbridge, Shahibag, Ahmedabad, Gujarat 380 004, India. TEL 91-79-22868172, FAX 91-79-22865759.

677 USA ISSN 0195-3184
HD9969.H833 CODEN: HTTOFE
HOME TEXTILES TODAY; the business and fashion newspaper of the home textiles industry. Abbreviated title: H T T. Text in English. 1979. 30/yr. USD 127.50 in US & Canada; USD 244.50 elsewhere (effective 2010). adv. bk.rev. charts; illus.; stat.; tr.lit. back issues avail.; reprints avail. **Document type:** *Magazine, Trade.* **Description:** Covers all aspects of business in the home textiles industry from product announcements and personnel changes to financial and fashion trend news.
Related titles: Online - full text ed.; Supplement(s): Business Annual Supplement. USD 149 in North America; USD 295 elsewhere; USD 10 newsstand/cover domestic; USD 15 newsstand/cover foreign (effective 2001).
Indexed: A09, A10, A12, A13, A15, A17, A22, ABIn, B01, B02, B03, B06, B07, B08, B09, B11, B15, B17, B18, C12, G04, G06, G07, G08, I05, P48, P51, P53, P54, PQC, SCOPUS, T01, T02, TTI, V03, V04, WTA.
—CIS. **CCC.**
Published by: Sandow Media Corp., 360 Park Ave. S., 17th Fl., New York, NY 10010. sandowinfo@sandowmedia.com, http://www.sandowmedia.com. Ed. Jennifer Marks TEL 212-945-9151. Pub. Joseph V. Carena Jr. TEL 203-321-0232. Circ: 7,200.

677 HKG ISSN 1025-7802
HONG KONG FABRICS & ACCESSORIES. Text in English. 1995. s-a. adv. back issues avail. **Document type:** *Magazine, Trade.* **Description:** Provides complete guide to Hong Kong fabrics and accessories industry. Covers textiles, labels, badges, zippers, buttons, threads and more.
Related titles: Online - full content ed.
Published by: Hong Kong Trade Development Council, 38th Fl Office Tower, Convention Plaza, 1 Harbour Rd, Wanchai, Hong Kong. TEL 852-1830668, FAX 852-28240249, publications@tdc.org.hk, http://www.tdc.org.hk. adv.: color page HKD 130; 213 x 280.

677 JPN
HYOGO PREFECTURAL INSTITUTE OF TECHNOLOGY. TECHNICAL SUPPORT CENTER FOR TEXTILES INDUSTRIES. REPORTS. Text in Japanese. a.
Former titles: Hyogo Kenritsu Kogyo Gijutsu Senta. Sen'i Kogyo Shidosho. Kenkyu hokoku/Technical Center for Textiles, Hyogo Prefectural Institute of Industrial Research. Reports (1342-7709); (until 1990): Hyogo Kenritsu Sen'i Kogyo Shidosho Kenkyu Hokoku/Textile Research Institute of Hyogo Prefecture. Reports (0289-9493); Hyogo-ken Kogyo Shidosho Kenkyu Hokoku
Published by: Hyogo Prefectural Institute of Technology, Technical Support Center for Textiles Industries, 1790-496 Uenodan, Nomuracho, Nishiwaki-shi, Hyogo 677-0054, Japan. TEL 81-795-22-2041, FAX 81-795-22-3671.

677.21 USA ISSN 1022-6303
CODEN: ICRCET
I C A C RECORDER. Text in English, French, Spanish. 1983. q. USD 205 (effective 2011). back issues avail.
Related titles: CD-ROM ed.; E-mail ed.: USD 165 (effective 2011); Online - full text ed.
Indexed: IIS, T01, T02, TTI.
Published by: International Cotton Advisory Committee, 1629 K St N W, Ste 702, Washington, DC 20006. publications@icac.org.

677 USA
I D E A CONFERENCE PAPERS. Text in English. 1971. triennial. USD 140 per issue to non-members; USD 100 per issue to members (effective 2010); price varies. **Document type:** *Proceedings, Trade.* **Description:** Covers all areas of the nonwovens industry.
Related titles: Online - full text ed.
Published by: Association of the Nonwoven Fabrics Industry (I N D A), PO Box 1288, Cary, NC 27512. TEL 919-233-1210, FAX 919-233-1282, info@inda.org.

677 USA ISSN 1049-3328
TK4035.T4 CODEN: ITFCFL
I E E E TEXTILE, FIBER AND FILM INDUSTRY TECHNICAL CONFERENCE. PROCEEDINGS. (Institute of Electrical and Electronics Engineers) Text in English. 1970. a., latest 1999. adv. back issues avail. **Document type:** *Proceedings, Trade.*
Former titles (until 1990): I E E E Annual Textile Industry Technical Conference (0094-9884); (until 19??): I E E E Textile Industry Technical Conference. Record (0082-3651)
Related titles: CD-ROM ed.; Microfiche ed.; Online - full text ed.
Indexed: EngInd, Inspec.
—IE, Ingenta. **CCC.**
Published by: I E E E, 445 Hoes Ln, Piscataway, NJ 08855. contactcenter@ieee.org, http://www.ieee.org.

677 USA
I F I BULLETIN: FABRICS, FASHIONS. Text in English. irreg. looseleaf.
Formerly: I F I Bulletin: Textile Notes
Indexed: A&ATA.
Published by: International Fabricare Institute, 14700 Sweitzer Ln, Laurel, MD 20707. TEL 301-622-1900.

677 USA
I N D A ASSOCIATION OF THE NONWOVEN FABRICS INDUSTRY. I N T C PAPERS. (International Nonwovens Technical Conference) Text in English. 1973. a. USD 175 per issue to non-members; USD 130 per issue to members (effective 2010); price varies. back issues avail. **Document type:** *Proceedings, Trade.*
Formerly: I N D A Association of the Nonwoven Fabrics Industry. I N D A - Tec Symposium Papers
Related titles: CD-ROM ed.
Published by: Association of the Nonwoven Fabrics Industry (I N D A), PO Box 1288, Cary, NC 27512. TEL 919-233-1210, FAX 919-233-1282, info@inda.org.

677 CHE
I T M F COUNTRY STATEMENTS. Text in English. 1977. a. CHF 100 (effective 2001). charts; illus.; stat. **Document type:** *Journal, Trade.* **Description:** Provides information on the current state of the textile industry in each member country. Data relates general economic situation, textile manufacturing capacities, activities, and trade in textiles.
Published by: International Textile Manufacturers Federation, Am Schanzengraben 29, Postfach, Zurich, 8039, Switzerland. TEL 41-1-2017080, FAX 41-1-2017134, secretariat@itmf.org, http://www.itmf.org.

677 CHE
I T M F DIRECTORY. Text in English. biennial. free. **Document type:** *Directory, Trade.*
Formerly: I F C A T I Directory (0445-0698)
Published by: International Textile Manufacturers Federation, Am Schanzengraben 29, Postfach, Zurich, 8039, Switzerland. TEL 41-1-2017080, FAX 41-1-2017134, secretariat@itmf.org, http://www.itmf.org. Ed. Herwig M Strolz.

677 CHE
I T M F STATE OF TRADE REPORT. Text in English. 1989. 4/yr. CHF 100 per issue (effective 2001). **Document type:** *Journal, Trade.* **Description:** Shows country-by-country changes in the spinning and weaving sectors for production, outstanding orders and stocks.
Published by: International Textile Manufacturers Federation, Am Schanzengraben 29, Postfach, Zurich, 8039, Switzerland. TEL 41-1-2017080, FAX 41-1-2017134, secretariat@itmf.org, http://www.itmf.org.

IDAHO WOOL GROWERS BULLETIN. *see* AGRICULTURE—Poultry And Livestock

677 GBR ISSN 0073-604X
INDEX TO TEXTILE AUXILIARIES. Text in English. 1967. biennial, latest 2008. GBP 210 per issue (effective 2009). **Document type:** *Directory, Trade.* **Description:** Lists textile chemicals and auxiliaries from suppliers around the world.
Related titles: CD-ROM ed.: GBP 95 (effective 2000).
—**CCC.**
Published by: World Textile Publications Ltd., Perkin House, 1 Longlands St, Bradford, W Yorks BD1 2TP, United Kingdom. TEL 44-1274-378800, FAX 44-1274-378811, info@world-textile.net, http://www.world-textile.net/.

677 IND ISSN 0971-0426
TS1540 CODEN: IJFRET
➤ **INDIAN JOURNAL OF FIBRE & TEXTILE RESEARCH.** Abbreviated title: I J F T R. Text in English. 1976. q. USD 240 (effective 2009). bk.rev. **Document type:** *Journal, Academic/Scholarly.* **Description:** Devoted to the publication of communications embodying the results of original work in different branches of fibre & textile research/technology and in allied areas, such as Production and properties of natural and synthetic fibres (including industrial fibres); Production and properties of yarns; Production and properties of fabrics; Chemical and finishing processes; Physics and chemistry of fibre-forming polymers; Fibre-reinforced composites; Analysis testing and quality control; Application of microprocessors; Instrumentation; and Industrial engineering.
Formerly (until 1990): Indian Journal of Textile Research (0377-8436)
Related titles: Online - full text ed.: ISSN 0975-1025. free (effective 2011).
Indexed: A&ATA, ABIPC, ASCA, C33, CA, CIN, CTFA, ChemAb, ChemTitl, ISA, RefZh, SCI, SCOPUS, T01, T02, TM, TTI, W07, WTA.
—BLDSC (4412.470000), CASDDS, IE, Ingenta, INIST, Linda Hall.
Published by: National Institute of Science Communication and Information Resources (N I S C A I R), Dr. K.S. Krishnan Marg, New Delhi, 110 012, India. TEL 91-11-25841647, FAX 91-11-25847062, http://www.niscair.res.in/. Ed. Neelu Srivastav.

677.39 638 IND ISSN 0445-7722
SF541 CODEN: IJSEAH
INDIAN JOURNAL OF SERICULTURE. Text in English. 1962. s-a. USD 100 (effective 2011). **Document type:** *Journal, Academic/Scholarly.* **Description:** Documents research findings on recent innovations in sericulture and the silk industry.
Indexed: A34, A35, A37, A38, AgBio, AgrForAb, B23, B25, BIOSIS Prev, BP, C25, C30, CABA, E12, F08, F11, F12, FCA, GEOBASE, H16, I11, IndVet, LT, MycolAb, N04, OR, P32, P33, P39, P40, PGegResA, PGrRegA, R07, R08, R12, R13, RA&MP, RM&VM, RRTA, S13, S16, S17, SCOPUS, TAR, TOSA, VS, W10, W11, WTA, Z01.
—CASDDS.
Published by: Central Sericultural Research & Training Institute, Central Silk Board, Manandawadi Rd, Srirampura, Mysore, Karnataka 570 008, India. TEL 91-821-2362406, FAX 91-821-2362845, director@csrtimys.res.in.

677.39 IND ISSN 0019-6355
INDIAN SILK. Text in English, Hindi. 1960. m. INR 360 domestic; USD 30 for Bangladesh, Bhutan, Nepal, Pakistan; USD 65 elsewhere (effective 2011). adv. bk.rev. charts; illus.; mkt.; stat.; tr.lit. 48 p./no. 3 cols./p.; back issues avail. **Document type:** *Magazine, Government.* **Description:** Devoted to sericulture and industry of the Country. It publishes articles on R&D, extension, socio-economic studies, current affairs, success stories, monthly reviews of exports and imports and vital statistics.
Formerly (until 1961): Indian Silk Journal (0445-8125)
Indexed: SCOPUS, TM, WTA.
Published by: Central Silk Board, c/o Ministry of Textiles, Government of India, C S B Complex, B T M Layout, Madanala Hosur Rd, Bangalore, Karnataka 560 068, India. TEL 91-80-26282699, FAX 91-80-26681511, csb@silkboard.org. Eds. M N Ramesha, M Sathiyavathy.

677 IND ISSN 0537-2666
TS1312
INDIAN TEXTILE ANNUAL & DIRECTORY. Text in English. 1965. a., latest no.37. INR 525 per issue (effective 2011). bk.rev. charts; illus.; pat. **Document type:** *Directory, Trade.*
Published by: Eastland Publications (Pvt.) Ltd., 44 Chittaranjan Ave, Kolkata, West Bengal 700 012, India. TEL 91-33-22122233, text_223308@bsnl.in.

677 IND ISSN 0019-6436
TS1300 CODEN: INTJAV
THE INDIAN TEXTILE JOURNAL. Abbreviated title: I T J. Text in English. 1890. m. INR 300 domestic; USD 115, EUR 85 foreign (effective 2011). bk.rev. abstr.; charts; illus. index. **Document type:** *Magazine, Trade.* **Description:** Covers new products and news briefs.
Indexed: A22, B02, CTFA, ChemAb, G04, G08, I05, T01, T02, TM, TTI, WTA.
—BLDSC (4430.000000), CASDDS, IE, Ingenta, Linda Hall.
Published by: IPFonline Ltd., 2nd Fl, Shafika Bldg, 17/7 Kodambakkam High Rd, Nungambakkam, Chennai, 600 034, India. TEL 91-44-42991234, FAX 91-44-28262737, admin@ipfonline.com, http://www.ipfonline.com. Adv. contact G Balu.

677 ARG ISSN 0019-7742
INDUSTRIA TEXTIL SUD AMERICANA. Text in Spanish. 1941. bi-m. ARS 18, USD 5. adv. charts; illus.; mkt.
Indexed: ChemAb.
Published by: EDITESA S.A., Avda Pena Roque Saenz 825, Buenos Aires, 1035, Argentina. Ed. Dr. Elio Gabellini. Circ: 2,000.

677 ROM ISSN 1222-5347
TS1300 CODEN: IDTEFJ
INDUSTRIA TEXTILA; textiles, knitting, textile garments. Text in Romanian; Summaries in English, French. 1950. q. EUR 100 (effective 2005). adv. bk.rev. abstr.; bibl.; charts; illus. index. 72 p./no.; **Document type:** *Magazine, Trade.* **Description:** Contains scientific articles, general information about textile sector.
Former titles (until 1994): Industria Usoara - Textile, Tricotaje, Confectii Textile (1017-2254); (until 1974): Industria Textila (0019-7750)
Indexed: CIN, CISA, CLL, CTFA, ChemAb, ChemTitl, MSCI, RASB, RefZh, SCI, SCOPUS, T01, TTI, W07, WTA.
—BLDSC (4442.500000), CASDDS, INIST.
Published by: Certex. Institutul National de Cercetare-Dezvoltare pentru Textile si Pielarie/Research Development National Institute for Textile and Leather, Str. Lucretiu Patrascanu 16, Sector 3, Bucharest, 030508, Romania. TEL 040-21-3404928, FAX 040-21-3405515, http://www.certex.ro. Eds. Mrs. Emilia Visileanu, Ms. Maria Nazarenco. R&P, Adv. contact Mrs. Emilia Visileanu. B&W page EUR 300, color page EUR 1,200; 205 x 295.

677 GBR ISSN 0968-0861
INDUSTRIAL TEXTILES. Text in English. 1993. q. GBP 33 in United Kingdom; GBP 40 rest of Europe; GBP 50 rest of world (effective 2001). adv. bk.rev. back issues avail. **Document type:** *Journal, Trade.* **Description:** Covers the following industrial textile topics: marques, structures, and suppliers, coated fabrics for industrial and leisure applications, sewing and welding machinery, and tarpaulin manufacture.
Indexed: SCOPUS, T01, TTI, WTA.
Published by: (Made Up Textiles Association), Impact!, Media House, 55 Old Rd, Linslade, Leighton Buzzard, Beds LU7 7RB, United Kingdom. TEL 44-1525-370013, FAX 44-1525-382487. Ed. Colin Bryer. Adv. contact Victoria Gardner. B&W page GBP 635, color page GBP 795; trim 210 x 297. Circ: 3,000.

677 FRA ISSN 0019-9176
TS1300 CODEN: INTPAF
L'INDUSTRIE TEXTILE. Text in French. 1883. 9/yr. EUR 160 domestic includes Filiere Maille; EUR 205 foreign includes Filiere Maille (effective 2005). adv. bk.rev. abstr.; bibl.; charts; illus.; mkt.; pat.; stat. index. **Document type:** *Magazine, Trade.*
Incorporates (1936-1982): Teintex (0040-2192)
Related titles: Online - full text ed.
Indexed: A22, CISA, ChemAb, KES, SCOPUS, T01, TM, TTI, WTA.
—BLDSC (4474.000000), CASDDS, IE, Infotrieve, Ingenta, INIST, Linda Hall. **CCC.**
Published by: Editions de l' Industrie Textile, 16 rue Ballu, Paris, 75311 Cedex 9, France. TEL 33-1-48741596, FAX 33-1-48740189, LL@industrietextile.com. Ed. Claude Levy Rueff. Adv. contact Evelyne Merigot. Circ: 6,000.

677 DEU ISSN 1869-1773
TS1300
INSTITUT FUER TEXTILTECHNIK DER RHEINISCH-WESTFAELISCHEN TECHNISCHEN HOCHSCHULE AACHEN. MITTEILUNGEN. Text in English, German. 1953. a. **Document type:** *Proceedings, Academic/Scholarly.*
Formerly (until 2001): Institut fuer Textiltechnik der Rheinisch-Westfaelischen Technischen Hochschule Aachen. Mitteilungen (Print) (0515-0582)
Media: CD-ROM.
Published by: Institut fuer Textiltechnik der Rheinisch-Westfaelischen Technischen Hochschule Aachen, Otto-Blumenthal-Str 1, Aachen, 52074, Germany. TEL 49-241-8023400, FAX 49-241-8022422, ita@ita.rwth-aachen.de, http://www.ita.rwth-aachen.de/. Circ: 250.

677 IND ISSN 0257-4438
TS1300 CODEN: JIENFH
➤ **INSTITUTION OF ENGINEERS (INDIA). TEXTILE ENGINEERING DIVISION. JOURNAL.** Text in English. 1982. s-a. INR 600 (effective 2011). adv. charts; illus. index. **Document type:** *Journal, Academic/Scholarly.*
Related titles: Online - full text ed.
Indexed: CA, CPEI, EngInd, SCOPUS, T01, T02, TTI.
—Linda Hall.
Published by: (Textile Engineering Division), The Institution of Engineers (India), 8 Gokhale Rd, Kolkata, West Bengal 700 020, India. TEL 91-33-40155400, technical@ieindia.org.

677 ESP ISSN 1131-6756
TS1300 CODEN: BIIIEZ
INSTITUTO DE INVESTIGACION TEXTIL Y DE COOPERACION INDUSTRIAL. BOLETIN INTEXTER. Text in Spanish; Abstracts in English, French. 1956. 2/yr. adv. bk.rev. illus. **Document type:** *Bulletin, Trade.*
Former titles (until 1989): Instituto de Investigacion Textil y de Cooperacion Industrial. Boletin Intextar (0212-6699); (until 1982): Instituto de Investigacion Textil y de Cooperacion Industrial. Boletin (0210-251X); (until 1964): Centro de Investigacion Textil y de Cooperacio Industrial (0211-3651); (until 1963): Laboratorio de Investigacion Textil y de Cooperacion Industrial (0211-366X)
Related titles: Online - full text ed.: ISSN 1886-4856.
Indexed: CA, CIN, ChemAb, ChemTitl, IECT, SCOPUS, T01, T02, TTI, WTA.
—CASDDS. **CCC.**
Published by: Universitat de Catalunya, Instituto de Investigacion Textil y de Cooperacion Industrial, Colon, 15, Terrassa, Barcelona 08222, Spain. TEL 34-93-7398270, FAX 34-93-7398272, boletin@intexter.ups.es, http://www.ct.upc.es/intexter. Circ: 1,000 (controlled).

675 ROM
CODEN: BPTPAK
INSTITUTUL POLITEHNIC DIN IASI. BULETINUL. SECTIA TEXTILE, PIELARIE/POLYTECHNIC INSTITUTE OF IASI. BULLETIN. TEXTILE, LEATHERSHIP. Text in English, French, German, Italian, Russian, Spanish. 1946. q. free to qualified personnel. adv. bk.rev. bibl.
Former titles: Institutul Politehnic din Iasi. Buletinul. Sectia 8: Textile, Pielarie (1454-3265); (until 1990): Institutul Politehnic din Iasi. Buletinul. Sectia 7: Textile, Pielarie (0253-1119); Which superseded in part (in 1970): Institutului Politehnic din Iasi. Buletinul (0032-6100)
Related titles: ◆ Series of: Institutul Politehnic din Iasi. Buletinul.
Indexed: ApMecR, ChemAb, MathR, T01, TTI.
—CASDDS, INIST, Linda Hall.
Published by: Universitatea Tehnica "Gheorghe Asachi" Iasi. Editura Politehnium/"Gheorghe Asachi" Technical University of Iasi. Politehnium Publishing House, Strada Prof.dr.doc. D, Mangeron nr.67, Iasi, 700050, Romania. TEL 40-232-231343, FAX 40-232-231343, simonasimionescu@yahoo.uk.co, http://www.tuiasi.ro. Circ: 450. **Dist. by:** Universitatea Tehnica "Gheorghe Asachi" Iasi Biblioteca, B-dul Carol I, nr.11, Iasi 700506, Romania. diatan@library.tuiasi.ro, http://www.tuiasi.ro/index.php?page=1145.

677.028 USA ISSN 1090-8366
INTENTS. Text in English. 1994. bi-m. USD 39 domestic; USD 49 in Canada & Mexico; USD 69 elsewhere (effective 2009). adv. back issues avail.; reprints avail. **Document type:** *Magazine, Trade.* **Description:** Features the latest innovations in fabric structures and event products, showcases the world's best tent installations, profiles leading figures and firms, offers tips from experienced professionals, covers new trends and reports on the activities and services of trade support groups.
Related titles: Online - full text ed.: free (effective 2009).
Indexed: SCOPUS, WTA.
Published by: Industrial Fabrics Association International, 1801 W County Rd B W, Ste B, Roseville, MN 55113. TEL 651-222-2508, 800-255-4324, FAX 651-631-9334, generalinfo@ifai.com. Ed. Sigrid A Tornquist TEL 651-222-2508. Pub. Mary Hennessy. Adv. contact Jane Anthone TEL 651-225-6911. page USD 5,285. Circ: 36,887.

677 GBR ISSN 1357-5201
INTERNATIONAL CARPET YEARBOOK. Text in English. 1970. a. GBP 105 per issue (effective 2009). adv. charts; illus.; stat.; tr.lit. back issues avail. **Document type:** *Yearbook, Trade.* **Description:** Reviews key developments in the carpet industry. Includes "World-Wide-Carpet Index".
Indexed: SCOPUS, TM, WTA.
—**CCC.**
Published by: World Textile Publications Ltd., Perkin House, 1 Longlands St, Bradford, W Yorks BD1 2TP, United Kingdom. TEL 44-1274-378800, FAX 44-1274-378811, info@world-textile.net, http://www.world-textile.net/. Ed. Philip Owen. Adv. contact James Wilson TEL 44-1274-378800. color page GBP 2,700, B&W page GBP 1,700; bleed 216 x 303. Circ: 2,000.

677.21 USA ISSN 1022-629X
HD9070.1
INTERNATIONAL COTTON ADVISORY COMMITTEE. PROCEEDINGS. Text in English, French, Spanish. 1993. a. USD 65 (effective 2000). back issues avail. **Document type:** *Proceedings.*
Related titles: Online - full text ed.: USD 35 (effective 2011).
Published by: International Cotton Advisory Committee, 1629 K St N W, Ste 702, Washington, DC 20006. publications@icac.org.

INTERNATIONAL DIRECTORY OF DESIGN. *see* ART

THE INTERNATIONAL DIRECTORY OF TEXTILES AND FABRICS IMPORTERS. *see* BUSINESS AND ECONOMICS—Trade And Industrial Directories

677 667 GBR ISSN 0020-658X
TP890 CODEN: INDYFZ
INTERNATIONAL DYER. Variant title: International Dyer, Textile Printer, Bleacher and Finisher. Text in English. 1879. m. (11/yr.). GBP 195 domestic; GBP 245 in Europe; GBP 265 elsewhere; EUR 364 (print or online ed.) (effective 2009). adv. bk.rev. abstr.; illus.; pat.; tr.lit. reprints avail. **Document type:** *Magazine, Trade.* **Description:** Covers textile dyeing, printing and finishing industry world-wide.
Former titles (until 1963): Dyer (0366-9831); (until 1934): Dyer and Calico Printer, Bleacher, Finisher and Textile Review
Related titles: Online - full text ed.
Indexed: ChemAb, SCOPUS, T01, T02, TM, TTI, WTA.
—BLDSC (4539.753000), CASDDS, IE, Infotrieve, Ingenta, INIST, Linda Hall. **CCC.**
Published by: World Textile Publications Ltd., Perkin House, 1 Longlands St, Bradford, W Yorks BD1 2TP, United Kingdom. TEL 44-1274-378800, FAX 44-1274-378811, info@world-textile.net, http://www.world-textile.net/. Ed. John Scrimshaw TEL 44-1274-378819. Adv. contact David Jagger TEL 44-1274-378840. color page GBP 2,953, B&W page GBP 1,778; bleed 303 x 216. Circ: 6,000.

677 546 USA ISSN 1049-801X
HD9929.2.A1
INTERNATIONAL FIBER JOURNAL. Text in English. 1986. bi-m. USD 36 in North America; USD 80 elsewhere (effective 2008). adv. bk.rev. 80 p./no. 3 cols./p.; back issues avail.; reprints avail. **Document type:** *Journal, Trade.* **Description:** Designed for corporate and site managers, scientists, engineers and technical personnel at synthetic fiber plants, fiber-grade polymer plants, texturing plants, spunbound nonwovens plant, textile mills, yarn manufacturing and spi ning facilities and polyster film plants worldwide.
Related titles: CD-ROM ed.; ◆ Supplement(s): T3 - Technical Textile Technology. ISSN 1553-944X.
Indexed: SCOPUS, T01, T02, TM, TTI, WTA.
—BLDSC (4540.186450), IE, Ingenta. **CCC.**
Published by: International Media Group, Inc., 6000 Fairview Rd, Ste 1200, Charlotte, NC 28210. TEL 704-552-3708, FAX 704-552-3705. Ed. Ken Norberg. Pub. Klaas De Waal. adv.: B&W page USD 2,750, color page USD 3,785. Circ: 8,800 (paid and controlled).

677 747.5 USA
INTERNATIONAL HAJJI BABA SOCIETY. NEWSLETTER. Text in English. m. **Document type:** *Newsletter.* **Description:** Promotes interest in oriental rugs and textiles.
Published by: International Hajji Baba Society, c/o Virginia Day, 6500 Pinecrest Ct, Annandale, VA 22063. TEL 703-354-4880.

INTERNATIONAL JOURNAL OF SHEEP AND WOOL SCIENCE. *see* AGRICULTURE—Poultry And Livestock

667 338.4 USA
HD9869.N64
INTERNATIONAL NONWOVENS DIRECTORY. Text in English. 1970. a. USD 200 per issue to non-members; free to members (effective 2010). **Document type:** *Directory, Trade.* **Description:** Contains lists thousands of nonwovens companies from over 60 countries, alphabetically and by each product/service.
Former titles (until 1989): International Directory of the Nonwoven Fabrics Industry (Print) (0095-683X); (until 197?): Directory for the Nonwoven Fabrics and Disposable Soft Goods Industries (0070-5020)
Media: Online - full text.
Published by: Association of the Nonwoven Fabrics Industry (I N D A), PO Box 1288, Cary, NC 27512. TEL 919-233-1210, FAX 919-233-1282, info@inda.org.

677 CHE ISSN 1017-270X
HD9850.1 CODEN: IPCWE3
INTERNATIONAL PRODUCTION COST COMPARISON. Text in English. 1979. biennial. CHF 200 (effective 2001). **Document type:** *Handbook/Manual/Guide, Trade.* **Description:** Focuses on costs of producing yarns and fabrics in spinning, texturing, weaving and knitting in Brazil, India, Indonesia, Italy, Korea, Turkey and the U.S.
Published by: International Textile Manufacturers Federation, Am Schanzengraben 29, Postfach, Zurich, 8039, Switzerland. TEL 41-1-2017080, FAX 41-1-2017134, secretariat@itmf.org, http://www.itmf.org.

677 CHE ISSN 1029-8525
INTERNATIONAL TEXTILE BULLETIN. Text in English. 1998. bi-m. **Document type:** *Magazine, Trade.* **Description:** Global information coverage in the field of yarn and fabric formation and related machinery and technology.
Formed by the merger of (1983-1998): International Textile Bulletin: Dyeing, Printing, Finishing (1012-8417); (1994-1998): International Textile Bulletin: Yarn and Fabric Forming (1024-6541); Which was formed by the merger of (1983-1994): International Textile Bulletin. Yarn Forming (1012-8433); (1983-1994): International Textile Bulletin. Fabric Forming (1012-8425)
Related titles: Chinese ed.; French ed.; Spanish ed.; Italian ed.; German ed.
Indexed: Inspec, SCOPUS, T01, TTI, WTA.
—Linda Hall.
Published by: I T S Publishing, International Textile Service, Kesslerstr 9, Schlieren, 8952, Switzerland. TEL 41-1-7384800, FAX 41-1-7384832, circulation-management@its-publishing.com, http://www.its-publishing.com. Eds. Eugene Dempsey, Juerg Rupp. Circ: 40,000.

677 CHE ISSN 1024-6592
INTERNATIONAL TEXTILE BULLETIN: NONWOVENS - INDUSTRIAL TEXTILES. Text in English. 1954. q. **Document type:** *Magazine, Trade.* **Description:** Global information coverage in the fields of nonwovens and industrial textiles, related machinery, and converting.
Formerly: International Nonwoven Bulletin (1026-1222)
Related titles: Chinese ed.; French ed.; Spanish ed.; Italian ed.; German ed.
Indexed: SCOPUS, T01, TTI, WTA.
Published by: I T S Publishing, International Textile Service, Kesslerstr 9, Schlieren, 8952, Switzerland. TEL 41-1-7384800, FAX 41-1-7384830. Ed. Juerg Rupp. Pub. Rosmarie Keller. Adv. contact Peter Frei.

677 GBR ISSN 0263-5879
TS1300 CODEN: ITCLEW
INTERNATIONAL TEXTILE CALENDAR. Abbreviated title: I T C. Text in English. 1993. bi-m. GBP 95 combined subscription to non-members (print & online eds.); GBP 59 combined subscription to members (print & online eds.) (effective 2009). **Document type:** *Journal, Trade.* **Description:** Lists forthcoming conferences, exhibitions, seminars, short courses and textile events.
Related titles: Online - full text ed.
Published by: Textile Institute, 1st Fl, St James Bldg, Oxford St, Manchester, Lancs M1 6FQ, United Kingdom. TEL 44-161-2371188, FAX 44-161-2361991, tiihq@textileinst.org.uk.

677 CHE ISSN 1727-4761
INTERNATIONAL TEXTILE MANUFACTURERS FEDERATION. ANNUAL CONFERENCE REPORT (YEAR). Text in English. 1960. a. CHF 100 (effective 2001). **Document type:** *Proceedings, Trade.* **Description:** Contains full text of papers presented at annual conference.
Formerly (until 1997): International Textile Manufacturing (1012-9545); Which supersedes: Cotton and Allied Textile Industries (0574-2315)
Indexed: SCOPUS, T01, T02, TTI, WTA.
Published by: International Textile Manufacturers Federation, Am Schanzengraben 29, Postfach, Zurich, 8039, Switzerland. TEL 41-1-2017080, FAX 41-1-2017134, secretariat@itmf.org, http://www.itmf.org.

677 RUS ISSN 0021-3497
TS1300 CODEN: IVTTAF
IZVESTIYA VYSSHIKH UCHEBNYKH ZAVEDENII. TEKHNOLOGIYA TEKSTIL'NOI PROMYSHLENNOSTI. Text in Russian. 1957. bi-m. USD 97 (effective 1998). charts. index.
Indexed: A22, ABIPC, CIN, CTFA, ChemAb, ChemTitl, RefZh, SCOPUS, T01, TM, TTI, WTA.
—BLDSC (0077.860000), CASDDS, East View, IE, Ingenta, INIST, Linda Hall.
Published by: Ivanovskaya Gosudarstvennaya Tekstil'naya Akademiya, F Engels 21, Ivanovo, 153000, Russian Federation. TEL 7-0932-377887, FAX 7-0932-415088, root@igta.asinet.ivanovo.su. Ed. V Zryukin.

687 USA
JEANSFLASH. Text in English. s-a. **Description:** Covers industry and association developments.
Published by: Jeanswear Communication, 475 Park Ave S, 9th Fl, New York, NY 10016-6901. TEL 212-689-3462, FAX 212-545-1709.

TU

667 IND
JOINT TECHNOLOGICAL CONFERENCE: RESUME OF PAPERS. Text in English. 19??. irreg. **Document type:** *Proceedings, Trade.*
—BLDSC (4673.206500).
Published by: South India Textile Research Association, 13/37, Avinashi Rd, Coimbatore Aerodrome Post, Coimbatore, Tamil Nadu 641 014, India. TEL 91-422-2574367, FAX 91-422-2571896, sitraindia@dataone.in, http://www.sitra.org.in.

677 FRA ISSN 0021-8197
JOURNAL DU TEXTILE. Abbreviated title: J T. Text in French. 1964. w. EUR 175 (effective 2009). adv. bk.rev. illus. **Document type:** *Magazine, Trade.* **Description:** Contains news and features about textile and apparel goods and markets, including home textiles. Also includes information on economics, manufacturing, retailing, marketing, fashion (including accessories), careers and schools.
Indexed: B03, KES.
Published by: Editions Hennessen, 61 rue de Malte, Paris, Cedex 11 75541, France. TEL 33-1-43572189, FAX 33-1-47000835, contact@journaldutextile.com. Ed. Catherine Guyot. Pub., R&P Lucien Abra. Adv. contact Nathalie Guillery. color page EUR 6,155, B&W page EUR 3,955. Circ: 20,000 (controlled); 16,538 (paid).

667.3 672.028 746.14 GBR ISSN 0267-7806
THE JOURNAL FOR WEAVERS, SPINNERS & DYERS. Text in English. 1952. q. GBP 18 domestic; GBP 22 foreign; GBP 5 per issue (effective 2010). adv. bk.rev. charts; illus.; mkt.; pat.; tr.mk. back issues avail.; reprints avail. **Document type:** *Magazine, Trade.* **Description:** Covers a wide range of textile subjects, including articles on historic textile techniques and cutting edge modern design.
Former titles (until 1984): Weavers Journal (0308-9207); (until 1976): Guilds of Weavers, Spinners and Dyers. Quarterly Journal (0017-5439)
Indexed: A07, A30, A31, AA, ArtInd, B04, IHTDI, SCOPUS, WTA.
—IE, Ingenta.
Published by: Association of Guilds of Weavers Spinners & Dyers, c/o Belinda Rose, East Steading, Banchory, AB31 5QT, United Kingdom. sec@thejournalforwsd.org.uk, http://www.wsd.org.uk/.

677.028 USA ISSN 1558-9250
TS1828
➤ **JOURNAL OF ENGINEERED FABRICS AND FIBERS.** Text in English. 2006 (Sum.). q. free (effective 2011). reprints avail. **Document type:** *Journal, Academic/Scholarly.*
Media: Online - full text.
Indexed: A39, C27, C29, CA, D03, D04, E13, MSCI, R14, S14, S15, S18, SCI, SCOPUS, T01, T02, TTI, W07.
Published by: Association of the Nonwoven Fabrics Industry (I N D A), PO Box 1288, Cary, NC 27512. TEL 919-233-1210, FAX 919-233-1282, info@inda.org, http://www.inda.org. Eds. Michael Jaffe, Norman Lifshutz.

677 698 GBR ISSN 1528-0837
TS1512 CODEN: JINTFC
➤ **JOURNAL OF INDUSTRIAL TEXTILES.** Abbreviated title: J I T. Text in English. 1971. q. USD 1,179, GBP 693 combined subscription to institutions (print & online eds.); USD 1,155, GBP 679 to institutions (effective 2011). adv. bk.rev. charts; illus. index. back issues avail.; reprint service avail. from PSC. **Document type:** *Journal, Academic/ Scholarly.* **Description:** Reports on the chemistry, processing, applications and performance of coated and laminated fabrics.
Former titles (until 2000): Journal of Coated Fabrics (0093-4658); (until 1973): Journal of Coated Fibrous Materials (0047-2298)
Related titles: E-mail ed.; Microform ed.: (from PQC); Online - full text ed.: ISSN 1530-8057. USD 1,061, GBP 624 to institutions (effective 2011).
Indexed: A&ATA, A22, A28, ABIPC, APA, ApMecR, B01, B06, B07, B09, BrCerAb, C&ISA, CA, CA/WCA, CIA, CIN, CPEI, CerAb, ChemAb, ChemTitl, CivEngAb, CorrAb, CurCont, E&CAJ, E01, E11, EEA, EMA, ESPM, EngInd, EnvEAb, H04, H15, M&TEA, M09, MBF, METADEX, MSCI, P31, R18, SCI, SCOPUS, SolStAb, T01, T02, T04, TM, TTI, V02, W07, WAA, WTA.
—BLDSC (5006.425000), CASDDS, IE, Infotrieve, Ingenta, INIST, Linda Hall. **CCC.**
Published by: Sage Publications Ltd. (Subsidiary of: Sage Publications, Inc.), 1 Oliver's Yard, 55 City Rd, London, EC1Y 1SP, United Kingdom. TEL 44-20-73248500, FAX 44-20-73248600, info@sagepub.co.uk, http://www.uk.sagepub.com/home.nav. Eds. Dong Zhang, William C Smith. adv.: B&W page GBP 550; 130 x 205. **Subscr. in the Americas to:** Sage Publications, Inc., 2455 Teller Rd, Thousand Oaks, CA 91320. TEL 805-499-9774, FAX 805-499-0871, journals@sagepub.com.

677 JPN ISSN 1346-8235
TS1300 CODEN: JTMJAF
JOURNAL OF TEXTILE ENGINEERING. Text in English. 1955. bi-m. JPY 7,320 to non-members; free to members (effective 2006). adv. bk.rev. charts; illus. 40 p./no.; back issues avail. **Document type:** *Journal, Academic/Scholarly.*
Formerly (until vol.45, no.4, 1999): Textile Machinery Society of Japan. Journal (0040-5043)
Related titles: Online - full text ed.; ◆ Japanese ed.: Sen'i Kikai Gakkaishi. ISSN 0371-0580.
Indexed: A&ATA, CA, ChemAb, ISMEC, JTA, RefZh, SCOPUS, T01, T02, TM, TTI, WTA.
—INIST, Linda Hall. **CCC.**
Published by: Nihon Sen'i Kikai Gakkai/Textile Machinery Society of Japan, Osaka Science and Technology Center Bldg., 8-4, Utsubo-Honmachi 1 chome, Nishi-ku, Osaka-shi, 550-0004, Japan. TEL 81-6-64434691, FAX 81-6-64434694, i-love-tmsJ@nifty.com. Ed. T Nishimura. Pub., R&P, Adv. contact K Nakajima. Circ: 4,000.

677 POL ISSN 1426-7411
JOURNAL TEKSTYLNY. Text in Polish. 1996. bi-m. PLZ 70; PLZ 9 newsstand/cover. adv. **Document type:** *Magazine, Trade.* **Description:** Contains current news on fashion trends for the coming season, and detailed characteristics of new fabrics and clothing accessories.
Published by: Polskie Wydawnictwo Fachowe Sp. Z o.o. (Subsidiary of: Deutscher Fachverlag GmbH), Jadzwingow 14, Warsaw, 02-692, Poland. FAX 48-22-8536702, pwf@pwf.com.pl, http://www.pwf.com.pl.

677.13 BGD ISSN 1010-3791
HD9156.J8
JUTE AND JUTE FABRICS - BANGLADESH. Text in English. 1975. m. BDT 30, USD 5. adv. charts; stat.
Formerly (until Jan. 1975): Jute and Jute Fabrics - Pakistan (0022-7099)
Indexed: A&ATA, ChemAb, T01, TTI.
Published by: Bangladesh Jute Research Institute, Sher-e-Banglanagar, Dhaka, 7, Bangladesh. Ed. Harun Ur Rashid. Circ: 500.

677 DEU ISSN 0047-3405
KETTENWIRK-PRAXIS. Text in German; Summaries in English, French, Japanese. 1967. q. EUR 43.50 domestic; EUR 53.50 foreign; EUR 10.50 newsstand/cover (effective 2003). adv. bk.rev.; film rev. abstr.; bibl.; illus.; pat. cum.index. **Document type:** *Journal, Trade.*
Related titles: Supplement(s): ISSN 0170-401X.
Indexed: A22, SCOPUS, T01, TM, TTI, WTA.
—BLDSC (5090.610000), IE, Ingenta. **CCC.**
Published by: Karl Mayer GmbH, Postfach 1120, Obertshausen, 63166, Germany. TEL 49-6104-402-0, FAX 49-6104-43574. Ed., R&P, Adv. contact Ulrike Schlenker. Circ: 2,300.

677 BEL ISSN 1781-2534
KHIL'A; journal of dress and textiles in the Islamic world. Text in English. 2003. a., latest vol.1, 2005. EUR 60 combined subscription (print & online eds.) (effective 2011). **Document type:** *Journal, Academic/ Scholarly.* **Description:** Dedicated to the study of dress and textiles in the Islamic world.
Related titles: Online - full text ed.: ISSN 1783-1571.
Published by: Peeters Publishers, Bondgenotenlaan 153, Leuven, 3000, Belgium. TEL 32-16-235170, FAX 32-16-228500, peeters@peeters-leuven.be, http://www.peeters-leuven.be. Ed. W Vogelsang.

677 JPN
KNIT DESIGN. Text in Japanese. 1968. m. JPY 200. adv. abstr.; stat.
Published by: Nihon Nitto Uea, Dezain Kyokai/Japan Knitwear Designer's Association, 3-1-8 Ebisu-Minami, Shibuya-ku, Tokyo, 150-0022, Japan. TEL 81-3-57213773, FAX 81-3-37109837, info@jakda.or.jp, http://www.jakda.or.jp/.

677 GBR ISSN 0266-8394
KNITTING INTERNATIONAL. Text in English. 1984. 11/yr. GBP 299; EUR 364 (print or online ed.) (effective 2009). adv. **Document type:** *Magazine, Trade.* **Description:** Provides coverage of all aspects of the knitting sector from fibres and yarns through fabrics and garments, hosiery, dyeing, printing and finishing to machine and product developments.
Incorporates (2001-2005): Knit Americas (1476-1696); Formerly (until 1974): Hosiery Trade Journal (0018-5434)
Related titles: Online - full text ed.
Indexed: A22, A28, APA, BrCerAb, BrTechI, C&ISA, CA/WCA, CIA, CerAb, CivEngAb, CorrAb, E&CAJ, E11, EEA, EMA, H15, Inspec, M&TEA, M09, MBF, METADEX, RefZh, SCOPUS, SolStAb, T01, T02, T04, TM, TTI, WAA, WTA.
—BLDSC (5100.364000), IE, Ingenta, Linda Hall. **CCC.**
Published by: World Textile Publications Ltd., Perkin House, 1 Longlands St, Bradford, W Yorks BD1 2TP, United Kingdom. TEL 44-1274-378800, FAX 44-1274-378811, info@world-textile.net, http://www.world-textile.net/. Ed. Jonathan Dyson. Adv. contact Richard Hutchinson TEL 44-1274-378821. color page GBP 2,702, B&W page GBP 1,949; bleed 216 x 303.

KONFEKSIYON TEKNIK/CLOTHING TECHNOLOGY MAGAZINE. *see* CLOTHING TRADE

677 GBR ISSN 0308-3039
LACE. Text in English. 1976. q. free to members (effective 2010). bk.rev. illus. 64 p./no.; back issues avail. **Document type:** *Magazine, Academic/Scholarly.* **Description:** Features information on quilting.
Indexed: SCOPUS, WTA.
Published by: Lace Guild, The Hollies, 53 Audnam, Stourbridge, W Mids DY8 4AE, United Kingdom. TEL 44-1384-390739, FAX 44-1384-444415, hollies@laceguild.org, http://www.laceguild.demon.co.uk/.

677.0029 USA ISSN 1097-9220
TS1783
LACES & EMBROIDERY DIRECTORY ANNUAL. Variant title: Schiffli Lace and Embroidery Manufacturers Association. Annual Directory. Text in English. 1947. a. free to qualified personnel; USD 5 (effective 2004). adv. 96 p./no.; back issues avail. **Document type:** *Directory, Trade.*
Former titles: Embroidery Directory (0080-6811); Schiffli Digest and Directory; Schiffli Directory
Published by: Schiffli Lace and Embroidery Manufacturers Association, Inc., 20 Industrial Ave., # 26, Fairview, NJ 07022-1614. TEL 201-943-7757, FAX 201-943-7793. Ed., Adv. contact I Leonard Seiler. page USD 350. Circ: 1,000 (paid and controlled).

746.432 ESP ISSN 1888-4717
LANAS STOP. Text in Spanish. 1978. q.
Published by: Industrias de Fibras Textiles, S.A., Pol. Industrial Lardero, Logrono, La Rioja 26080, Spain. http://www.lanasstop.com/portada/.

338 677 UKR ISSN 0135-230X
LEHKA PROMYSLOVIST'; naukovo-vyrobnychyi zhurnal. Text in Ukrainian. 1960. q. **Document type:** *Journal, Trade.* **Description:** Journal is intended for specialists in textile industry. Covers different aspects of economics and technology in this area.
Indexed: RefZh.
Published by: Vydavnytstvo Tekhnika, Vul Observatorna 25, Kyiv, Ukraine. TEL 380-44-2721080. Ed. Yu V Chernii. **Co-sponsor:** Derzhavnyi Komitet Ukrainy z Lehkoyi i Tekstyl'noyi Promyslovosti.

LIVESTOCK, MEAT AND WOOL MARKET NEWS. *see* AGRICULTURE—Poultry And Livestock

677 HUN ISSN 1788-1722
TS1300 CODEN: MGTXAY
MAGYAR TEXTILTECHNIKA. Text in Hungarian. 1947. bi-m. adv. bk.rev. charts; illus. **Document type:** *Magazine, Trade.* **Description:** Informs professionals of the textile and clothing as well as of the textile cleaning industry on technical and technological novelties, current issues of these sectors, on the state of domestic and foreign markets.
Formerly (until 2006): Magyar Textiltechnika. Textiltisztitas (1787-1395); Which was formed by the merger of (1947-2005): Magyar Textiltechnika (0025-0309); (1968-2005): Textiltisztitas (0133-4867)
Indexed: A&ATA, ABIPC, CIN, CTFA, ChemAb, ChemTitl, T01, TTI, WTA.
—CASDDS, Ingenta, INIST.
Published by: Textilipari Muszaki es Tudomanyos Egyesulet/Hungarian Society of Textile Technology and Science, Fo utca 68, Budapest, 1027, Hungary. info.tmte@mtesz.hu, http://www.tmte.hu. Eds. Pal Fusti, Sandor Gonci. Circ: 1,000.

338.4 DEU ISSN 0932-5522
MAN-MADE FIBER YEAR BOOK. Text in English. 1986. a. EUR 25 per issue (effective 2009). **Document type:** *Yearbook, Trade.*
—BLDSC (5360.930000).
Published by: Deutscher Fachverlag GmbH, Mainzer Landstr 251, Frankfurt Am Main, 60326, Germany. TEL 49-69-75952052, FAX 49-69-75952999, info@dfv.de, http://www.dfv.de. Adv. contact Dagmar Henning. Circ: 5,000 (controlled).

677.39 IND ISSN 0377-7537
TS1640 CODEN: MMTIBW
➤ **MAN-MADE TEXTILES IN INDIA.** Text in English. 1958. m. INR 600 domestic; USD 100 foreign (effective 2011). bk.rev. abstr.; charts; illus.; stat. index. **Document type:** *Journal, Academic/Scholarly.* **Description:** Technical magazine dealing with all aspects of technology, R & D, testing and marketing of textile fibres, yarns, fabrics and technical textiles.
Formerly (until 1973): Silk and Rayon Industries of India (0037-525X)
Indexed: A22, CA, ChemAb, ChemTitl, RefZh, SCOPUS, T01, T02, TM, TTI, WTA.
—BLDSC (5361.032000), CASDDS, IE, Ingenta.
Published by: Synthetic and Art Silk Mills' Research Association (S A S M I R A), Sasmira Marg, Worli, Mumbai, Maharashtra 4000030, India. TEL 91-22-24935351, FAX 91-22-24930225, sasmira@vsnl.com, http://www.sasmira.org/. Ed. R K Sarkar. Pub. L Simon. R&P R.K. Sarkar. Adv. contact L. Simon.

677.31 CHN ISSN 1003-1456
MAOFANG KEJI/WOOL TEXTILE JOURNAL. Text in Chinese. 1973. m. CNY 120 (effective 2009). back issues avail. **Document type:** *Journal, Academic/Scholarly.*
Related titles: Online - full text ed.
Indexed: RefZh, SCOPUS, WTA.
—BLDSC (5369.196400), East View.
Published by: Quanguo Maofangzhi Keji Xinxi Zhongxin, 3, Chaowai Yanjing Lizhong Jie, Zhu Lou 6/F-603, Beijing, 100025, China. TEL 86-10-65071871, FAX 86-10-65913844, http://www.ctic.org.cn/. **Co-sponsors:** Quanguo Maofang Xinxi Zhongxin/China Textile Information Center; Beijing Maofangzhi Kexue Yanjiusuo.

677.028 USA ISSN 1079-8250
MARINE FABRICATOR; dedicated to the arts of marine craftsmanship. Variant title: I F A I's Marine Fabricator. Industrial Fabrics Association International's Marine Fabricator. Text in English. 1995. bi-m. USD 34 domestic; USD 44 in Canada & Mexico; USD 54 elsewhere (effective 2009). adv. back issues avail.; reprints avail. **Document type:** *Magazine, Trade.* **Description:** Educates and informs marine shop professionals, and provides reportage that reflects the innovations and trends of the industry.
Related titles: Online - full text ed.: free (effective 2009).
Indexed: SCOPUS, WTA.
Published by: Industrial Fabrics Association International, 1801 W County Rd B W, Ste B, Roseville, MN 55113. TEL 651-222-2508, 800-255-4324, FAX 651-225-6966, generalinfo@ifai.com. Ed. Chris Tschida TEL 651-225-6970. Pub. Mary Hennessy. Adv. contact Jane Anthone TEL 651-225-6911. color page USD 4,395. Circ: 5,000.

MEDICAL TEXTILES. *see* MEDICAL SCIENCES

677 DEU ISSN 0947-9163
TS1300 CODEN: MEINF8
MELLIAND INTERNATIONAL. Text in German. 1995. bi-m. EUR 149.90 in the European Union; EUR 154.90 elsewhere; EUR 29 newsstand/ cover (effective 2009). adv. **Document type:** *Journal, Trade.*
Indexed: CA, CIN, ChemAb, ChemTitl, SCOPUS, T01, T02, TTI, WTA.
—BLDSC (5544.989500), CASDDS, IE, Ingenta, Linda Hall. **CCC.**
Published by: Deutscher Fachverlag GmbH, Mainzer Landstr 251, Frankfurt Am Main, 60326, Germany. TEL 49-69-75952052, FAX 49-69-75952999, info@dfv.de, http://www.dfv.de. Eds. Claudia van Bonn, Petra Gottwald. Adv. contact Dagmar Henning. color page EUR 4,630, B&W page EUR 3,190; trim 210 x 297. Circ: 10,400 (paid and controlled).

677 DEU ISSN 0341-0781
TS1300 CODEN: MTIRDL
MELLIAND TEXTILBERICHTE/INTERNATIONAL TEXTILE REPORTS. Text in German. 1920. q. EUR 169.60 domestic; EUR 175.40 in the European Union; EUR 186 elsewhere; EUR 25 per issue (effective 2009). adv. bk.rev. abstr.; bibl.; mkt.; pat.; stat. **Document type:** *Journal, Trade.* **Description:** Provides information on all aspects of the textile industry, including spinning, twisting, weaving, knitting, nonwovens production, washing, bleaching, dyeing, printing, finishing and textile machinery.
Incorporates (in 2009): Band- und Flechtindustrie (1432-3745); Which was formerly (1964-1994): Band- und Flechtindustrie/Narrow Fabric and Braiding Industry (0005-4925); Incorporates (in 1990): Textiltechnik (0323-3804); Which was formerly (until 1973): Deutsche Textiltechnik (0012-0839); (1951-1957): Textil- und Faserstofftechnik (0372-3402); Incorporates (in 1986): Textilbetrieb (0340-4188); Which was formerly (until 1971): Spinner, Weber, Textilveredlung (0038-7541); (1883-1958): Spinner und Weber (0371-2427); Former titles (until 1976): Melliand Textilberichte International (0375-9350); (until 1969): Melliand Textilberichte (0025-8989); (until 1923): Textil uber Wissenschaft (0936-5575)
Related titles: Multiple languages ed.: ISSN 0931-9735. 1986; English ed.: ISSN 0198-7275.
Indexed: A&ATA, A22, ABIPC, CTFA, ChemAb, ChemTitl, IBR, IBZ, SCOPUS, T01, T02, TM, TTI.
—BLDSC (5546.020050), CASDDS, IE, Infotrieve, Ingenta, INIST, Linda Hall. **CCC.**
Published by: Deutscher Fachverlag GmbH, Mainzer Landstr 251, Frankfurt Am Main, 60326, Germany. TEL 49-69-75952052, FAX 49-69-75952999, info@dfv.de, http://www.dfv.de. Ed. Petra Gottwald. Adv. contact Dagmar Henning. B&W page EUR 3,190, color page EUR 4,630; trim 210 x 297. Circ: 5,945 (controlled).

677.21 CHN ISSN 1000-7415
MIAN FANGZHI JISHU/COTTON TEXTILE TECHNOLOGY. Text in Chinese. 1973. m. CNY 96; CNY 8 per issue (effective 2011). back issues avail. **Document type:** *Academic/Scholarly.*
Related titles: Online - full text ed.
Indexed: Inspec.
Published by: Quanquo Fangzhi Keji Xinxi Zhongxin/China Cotton Textile Information Centre, 138, Fangzhicheng Xi Jie, Xi'an, 710038, China. TEL 86-29-83553538, FAX 86-29-83553519, sf-ctsti@ctsti.cn, http://www.ctsti.cn/. Ed. Lei e Yan.

677 USA
MILL REPORT. Text in English. 1976. irreg. charts; illus.
Published by: Platt Saco Lowell, Drawer 2327, Greenville, SC 29602. TEL 803-859-3211.

677 CHE ISSN 1015-5910
MITTEX: MITTEILUNGEN UEBER TEXTILINDUSTRIE; Schweizerische Fachschrift fuer die gesamte Textilindustrie. Text in German. 1973 (vol.80). m. CHF 62. adv. bk.rev. charts; illus.; mkt.; pat.; tr.lit. index. **Document type:** *Trade.*
Formerly (until 1971): Mitteilungen ueber Textilindustrie (0026-6949)
Indexed: ChemAb, T01, TM, TTI.
Published by: Schweizerische Vereinigung von Textilfachleuten, Lindenweg 7, Pfaffhausen-Zurich, 8122, Switzerland. Ed. Anthony U Trinkler. Circ: 3,000.

MOBILIA INTERIEURTEXTIEL; vakblad voor de interieurtextielbranche. *see* INTERIOR DESIGN AND DECORATION—Furniture And House Furnishings

677 ITA ISSN 1825-1668
MODA E INDUSTRIA. Text in Italian. 1967. 6/yr. EUR 55 domestic; EUR 80 in Europe; EUR 110 elsewhere (effective 2009). adv. bk.rev. abstr.; bibl.; illus.; pat.; stat.; tr.lit. index. **Document type:** *Magazine, Trade.* **Description:** Technical and economic news for the knitting industry.
Former titles (until 1999): Maglie Calze Moda Industria Abbigliamento (1825-165X); (until 1996): Maglie Calze Industria (0024-9947)
Indexed: SCOPUS, T01, TTI.
Published by: Gesto Editore Srl, Via Mercato 28, Milan, MI 20121, Italy. Ed. Eugenio Faiella.

677 746.92 FIN ISSN 1457-554X
MODIN. Text in Finnish. 2000. 6/yr. EUR 80 domestic; EUR 100 in Scandinavia; EUR 111 elsewhere (effective 2002). adv. **Document type:** *Trade.* **Description:** Covers the the clothing and textile retail business, wholesale trade and textile industry in Finland.
Formed by the merger of (1972-2000): Teksi (0355-7898); Which was formerly: Tekstiilikauppias; (1962-2000): Kenkalusikka (0355-6999)
Published by: Association of Fashion Retailers in Finland, Mariankatu 26 B 14, Helsinki, 00170, Finland. TEL 358-9-6844-7300, FAX 358-9-6844-7344. Eds. Kaisa Virtanen TEL 358-9-6844 7337, Marittae Lahikari TEL 358-9-6844 7336, Yrjo Gorski TEL 358-9-6844-7333. R&P Yrjo Gorski. adv.: color page EUR 2,500; 210 x 297. Circ: 5,000.

677 BEL ISSN 0773-4468
MODIS. Text in French. 1978. 6/yr. USD 24. adv. charts; illus.; stat. **Document type:** *Trade.*
Formed by the merger of (1949-1978): Navetex (French Edition) (0028-1514); (1949-1978): Navetex (Dutch Edition) (0773-400X)
Related titles: Dutch ed.
Published by: (Nationaal Verbond der Textieldetaillisten/National Association of Tailors and Retailers), Danny Huysmans Ed. & Pub., 8 Spastraat, Brussels, 1000, Belgium. TEL 32-2-2380651, FAX 32-2-2306444. Adv. contact Caroline Bels. Circ: 10,000 (paid).

MONTHLY COTTON LINTERS REVIEW. *see* AGRICULTURE—Agricultural Economics

677 ARG ISSN 0027-3376
MUNDO TEXTIL ARGENTINO. Text in Spanish. 1962. m. adv.
Address: 25 de Mayo, 267-218, Buenos Aires, 1002, Argentina. Ed. Leonor F Breitman. Circ: 2,800.

NATIONAL COTTONSEED PRODUCTS ASSOCIATION. TRADING RULES. *see* AGRICULTURE—Feed, Flour And Grain

677 USA
NATIONAL TEXTILE CENTER - RESEARCH BRIEFS. Text in English. a.
Published by: National Textile Center, 1121 N. Bethlehem Pike, Ste 60 #317, Spring House, PA 19477-1102. TEL 215-540-0760, FAX 215-689-4835.

NATIONAL WOOL MARKET REVIEW. *see* AGRICULTURE—Poultry And Livestock

677 USA
NATSTAT; the natural fibers statistical database. Text in English. a. **Description:** Contains a compilation of marketing and economic statistics on the natural fibers, oilseeds, textile, apparel, and related industries.
Media: Online - full content.
Published by: Natural Fibers Information Center (Subsidiary of: Bureau of Business Research), P.O. Box 7459, Austin, TX 78713-7459. TEL 512-475-7817, FAX 512-471-1063, natfiber@uts.cc.utexas.edu, http://www.utexas.edu/depts/bbr/natfiber/. **Co-sponsor:** Texas Food and Fibers Commission.

677 POL ISSN 1230-4476
CODEN: NAFIFT
➤ **NATURAL FIBRES/WLOKNA NATURALNE.** Text in English, Polish. 1953. a. USD 75 (effective 2002). abstr.; bibl.; charts; illus.; maps; stat. **Document type:** *Journal, Academic/Scholarly.* **Description:** Contains scientific publications regarding complex research on obtaining and processing of natural textile raw materials; research on breeding and agrotechnology of fibre crops, retting biotechnology and spinning technology, agricultural and retting machinery construction and natural environment protection.
Former titles (until 1992): Instytut Krajowych Wlokien Naturalnych. Prace (0208-7685); (until 1973): Instytut Przemyslu Wlokien Lykowatych. Prace (0551-648X)
Related titles: Special ed(s).: 1993. price varies.
Indexed: AgrLib, T01, TTI.
—CASDDS.
Published by: Instytut Wlokien Naturalnych/Institute of Natural Fibres, Ul Wojska Polskiego 71 b, Poznan, 60630, Poland. TEL 48-61-8455800, FAX 48-61-8417830, sekretar@inf.poznan.pl, http://iwn.inf.poznan.pl. Ed., R&P Ryszard Kozlowski TEL 48-61-8480061. Adv. contact Jolanta Kraus. Circ: 400.

677 USA
NEEDLEPUNCH CONFERENCE PAPERS. Text in English. 1990. biennial. USD 120 per issue to non-members; USD 95 per issue to members (effective 2010). back issues avail. **Document type:** *Proceedings, Trade.* **Description:** Covers the applications, technology, raw materials and machinery of the needlepunch industry.
Published by: Association of the Nonwoven Fabrics Industry (I N D A), PO Box 1288, Cary, NC 27512. TEL 919-233-1210, FAX 919-233-1282, info@inda.org.

677 USA ISSN 1065-5247
THE NEW NONWOVENS WORLD; a journal for management. Text in English. 1986. bi-m. free. adv. reprints avail. **Document type:** *Magazine, Trade.*
Formerly (until 1993): Nonwovens World (0888-1979)
Related titles: Microform ed.: (from PQC).
Indexed: A22, SCOPUS, T01, T02, TM, TTI, WTA.
—IE, Ingenta. **CCC.**
Published by: Marketing - Technology Service, Inc., 4100 S 7th St, Kalamazoo, MI 49009-8461. TEL 269-375-1236, FAX 269-375-6710, http://www.marketingtechnologyservice.com/index.html. Ed. James P Hanson. adv.: B&W page USD 1,850; trim 10.88 x 8.13. Circ: 10,100.

338.4 JPN ISSN 0910-8505
NIHON BOSEKI GEPPO/JAPAN SPINNERS' ASSOCIATION. MONTHLY REPORT. Text in Japanese. 1947. bi-m. JPY 6,000 (effective 2001). adv. 80 p./no.; back issues avail. **Document type:** *Journal, Trade.*
Published by: Nihon Mengyo Gijyutsu-Keizai Kenkyusho/Japan Institute of Cotton Textile Technology and Economy, Mengyo Kaikan, 5-8 Bingo-Machi 2-chome, Chuo-ku, Osaka-shi, 541-0051, Japan. TEL 81-6-62035161, FAX 81-6-62291590, TELEX 81-6-6522-2230-SPINAS-J. Ed. Kiyonori Mayumi. Adv. contact Ms. Yuko Kamachi. Circ: 5,000.

677.39 JPN ISSN 1880-8204
NIHON SHIRUKU GAKKAISHI. Text in Japanese. 1992. a. **Document type:** *Journal, Academic/Scholarly.*
Formerly (until 2000): Seishi Kinu Kenkyuukaishi Seishi Kinu Kenkyuu Happyou Youshi Shuuroku
Related titles: Online - full text ed.: ISSN 1881-1698.
Indexed: A34, A37, AgrForAb, C30, CABA, E12, F08, F11, F12, GH, H16, P33, R07, R08, R12, RA&MP, TAR, W11.
—BLDSC (6113.071200).
Published by: Nihon Shiruku Gakkai/Japanese Society of Silk Science and Technology, The Silk Science Research Institute, 3-25-1 Hyakunincho Shinjyuku-ku, Tokyo, 169-0073, Japan. TEL 81-3-33684891, silk@silk.or.jp, http://www.silk.or.jp/ssstj/.

667 USA
NONWOVEN FABRICS HANDBOOK. Text in English. 1999. irreg. USD 85 to non-members; USD 65 to members (effective 2010). **Document type:** *Handbook/Manual/Guide, Trade.*
Published by: Association of the Nonwoven Fabrics Industry (I N D A), PO Box 1288, Cary, NC 27512. TEL 919-233-1210, FAX 919-233-1282, info@inda.org.

667 USA
NONWOVEN FABRICS SAMPLER AND TECHNOLOGY REFERENCE. Text in English. 1998. irreg. USD 65 to non-members; USD 50 to members (effective 2010). **Document type:** *Handbook/Manual/Guide, Trade.*
Published by: Association of the Nonwoven Fabrics Industry (I N D A), PO Box 1288, Cary, NC 27512. TEL 919-233-1210, FAX 919-233-1282, info@inda.org.

677 SGP
NONWOVENS ASIA. Text in Chinese, English. 3/yr. adv. **Document type:** *Magazine, Trade.*
Published by: C M P Asia Trade Fairs Ptd Ltd. (Subsidiary of: C M P Asia Ltd.), 111 Somerset Rd, #09-07, Singapore Power Bldg, Singapore, 238164, Singapore. TEL 65-6735-3366, FAX 65-6738-9057. adv.: page USD 2,300; trim 210 x 285.

677 676 USA ISSN 0163-4429
HD9869.N64 CODEN: NOINDJ
NONWOVENS INDUSTRY; the international magazine for the nonwoven fabrics and disposable soft goods industry. Text in English. 1970. m. USD 75; free to qualified personnel (effective 2008). adv. bk.rev. charts; illus.; pat.; stat.; tr.lit. index. back issues avail. **Document type:** *Magazine, Trade.* **Description:** Provides news, markets and analysis for and of the nonwovens industry.
Former titles (until 1977): Formed Fabrics Industry (0163-4399); Nonwovens and Disposable Soft Goods; Disposable Soft Goods (0046-0362)
Related titles: Online - full text ed.: free to qualified personnel (effective 2008).
Indexed: A22, ABIPC, B03, B11, ChemAb, EngInd, G06, G07, G08, I05, P&BA, S22, SCOPUS, T01, T02, TM, TTI, WTA.
—BLDSC (6117.343000), CASDDS, IE, Infotrieve, Ingenta. **CCC.**
Published by: Rodman Publishing, Corp., 70 Hilltop Rd, 3rd Fl, Ramsey, NJ 07446. TEL 201-825-2552, FAX 201-825-0553, info@rodpub.com, http://www.rodmanpublishing .com. Ed. Karen Bitz McIntyre. Pub. Matt Carey. Adv. contact Kathleen Scully. B&W page USD 2,830, color page USD 4,030; trim 178 x 253. Circ: 10,111.

677 USA
NONWOVENS MARKETS. Text in English. 19??. s-m. USD 867; USD 897 combined subscription (online and E-mail eds.) (effective 2008). adv. Index. back issues avail. **Document type:** *Newsletter, Trade.* **Description:** Covers developments in the nonwovens industry around the world. Analyzes complex industry issues, offers insight into company strategies, market growth, and technology trends.
Related titles: Online - full text ed.: USD 677 (effective 2005).
Published by: R I S I, Inc., 4 Alfred Cir, Bedford, MA 01730. TEL 781-734-8900, FAX 781-271-0337, info@risiinfo.com, http://www.risiinfo.com. Ed. Steve Chaikin TEL 908-484-7272. adv.: B&W page USD 1,500.

677 608.7 USA ISSN 1062-2780
NONWOVENS PATENT NEWS. Text in English. 1990. m. USD 935 (effective 1999). bibl. **Document type:** *Newsletter.* **Description:** Contains articles, patent abstracts, and diagrams of U.S., European and Japanese patents that affect the nonwoven textile industry. Includes polymers, films, tissues, processes, equipment, converted products, and related items.
Published by: D.K. Smith, Ed.& Pub., 3112 E Hampton Ave, Mesa, AZ 85204. TEL 602-924-0813, FAX 602-924-6966. R&P D K Smith. Circ: 100 (paid).

677 GBR ISSN 0953-1092
TS1828
NONWOVENS REPORT INTERNATIONAL. Text in English. 1971. bi-m. (plus 12 PDF newsletters & 2 directories). GBP 299 (effective 2009). adv. bk.rev. charts; pat.; stat. **Document type:** *Magazine, Trade.* **Description:** Covers technical articles, conference reports and comprehensive news, product and machinery reviews, that is indispensable to all decision-makers within this competitive industry.
Formerly (until 1978): Nonwovens Report
Indexed: ABIPC, EngInd, SCOPUS, T01, T02, TTI, WTA.
—BLDSC (6117.346000), IE. **CCC.**
Published by: World Textile Publications Ltd., Perkin House, 1 Longlands St, Bradford, W Yorks BD1 2TP, United Kingdom. TEL 44-1274-378800, FAX 44-1274-378811, info@world-textile.net, http://www.world-textile.net/.

NONWOVENS REPORT YEARBOOK. *see* BUSINESS AND ECONOMICS—Trade And Industrial Directories

677 676 JPN ISSN 1341-5697
NONWOVENS REVIEW. Text in Japanese. 1990. q. JPY 10,500 (effective 2008). **Document type:** *Trade.*
Published by: Tekku Taimusu/Tec Times Co. Ltd., 3-13-7 Kanda-Nishikicho, Chiyoda-ku, Tokyo, 101-0054, Japan. TEL 81-3-32332580, FAX 81-3-32332523, http://www.st-times.co.jp/.

677 SWE ISSN 1404-2487
➤ **THE NORDIC TEXTILE JOURNAL.** Text in Multiple languages. 1999. s-a. free. back issues avail. **Document type:** *Journal, Academic/Scholarly.*
Related titles: Online - full text ed.
Published by: Hoegskolan i Boraas, Centrum foer Textilforskning/University College of Boraas. Textile Research Centre, c/o Institutionen Textilhoegskolan, Bryggaregatan 7, Boraas, 50190, Sweden. TEL 46-33-4354000. Ed. Kenneth Tingsvik.

677 ESP ISSN 1137-084X
NOTICIERO TEXTIL. Text in Spanish. 1984. 11/yr. adv. back issues avail. **Document type:** *Magazine, Trade.*
Formerly (until 1987): Moda Pronta (1137-0998)
Published by: Astoria Ediciones S.L., Calle Girona 148 4o-2o, Barcelona, 08037, Spain. TEL 34-93-4581900, FAX 34-93-4592513, info@astoriaediciones.com, http://www.astoriaediciones.com/. Circ: 6,400.

677 ESP
NUEVAS TECNICAS DE MODA. Text in Spanish. 1970. s-a. adv. illus. **Document type:** *Monographic series, Academic/Scholarly.* **Description:** Includes issues on textile industry and fabrics.
Published by: Arte y Tecnica del Vestir, S.L., Guillermo Tell 47, Barcelona, 08006, Spain. TEL 34-93-237-2740, FAX 34-93-237-2789, http://www.institutofeli.com. Ed. Mercedes Freixas. Circ: 1,000.

677 AUT ISSN 1817-1168
OESTERREICHISCHE TEXTIL ZEITUNG. Text in German. 1947. m. EUR 50 domestic; EUR 65 foreign (effective 2005). adv. **Document type:** *Magazine, Trade.*
Published by: Manstein Zeitschriften Verlagsgesellschaft mbH, Brunner Feldstr 45, Perchtoldsdorf, N 2380, Austria. TEL 43-1-866480, FAX 43-1-86648100, office@manstein.at. Ed. Brigitte Medlin. Adv. contact Andrea Dite. color page EUR 5,960, B&W page EUR 4,995; trim 208 x 294. Circ: 10,000 (paid and controlled).

677 AUT ISSN 1817-1176
OESTERREICHISCHE TEXTIL ZEITUNG WOHNEN. Variant title: Oe T Z Wohnen. Text in German. 1997. q. EUR 15.50 domestic; EUR 20 foreign (effective 2005). adv. **Document type:** *Magazine, Trade.*
Published by: Manstein Zeitschriften Verlagsgesellschaft mbH, Brunner Feldstr 45, Perchtoldsdorf, N 2380, Austria. TEL 43-1-866480, FAX 43-1-86648100, office@manstein.at. Ed. Brigitte Medlin. Adv. contact Andrea Dite. B&W page EUR 4,995, color page EUR 5,960; trim 208 x 294. Circ: 10,000 (paid and controlled).

677 NLD ISSN 1876-5203
TS1300
➤ **THE OPEN TEXTILE JOURNAL.** Text in English. 2008. irreg. free (effective 2011). **Document type:** *Journal, Academic/Scholarly.*
Media: Online - full text.
Indexed: T01, TTI.
Published by: Bentham Open (Subsidiary of: Bentham Science Publishers Ltd.), PO Box 294, Bussum, AG 1400, Netherlands. TEL 31-35-6923800, FAX 31-35-6980150, subscriptions@bentham.org. Ed. Gang Sun.

➤ **PAKISTAN CENTRAL COTTON COMMITTEE. AGRICULTURAL SURVEY REPORT.** *see* AGRICULTURE—Crop Production And Soil

➤ **PAKISTAN CENTRAL COTTON COMMITTEE. TECHNOLOGICAL BULLETIN. SERIES A.** *see* AGRICULTURE—Crop Production And Soil

➤ **PAKISTAN CENTRAL COTTON COMMITTEE. TECHNOLOGICAL BULLETIN. SERIES B.** *see* AGRICULTURE—Crop Production And Soil

677 PAK
PAKISTAN TEXTILE. Text in English. 1977. q. PKR 40.
Published by: All Pakistan Textile Mills Association, APTMA House, 44-A,Lalazar, Moulvi Tamizuddin Khan Rd, Karachi, 74000, Pakistan.

677 PAK ISSN 0048-2757
PAKISTAN TEXTILE JOURNAL; the journal for textile industry of Pakistan. Text in English. 1950. m. PKR 975 domestic; USD 100 foreign; PKR 100 newsstand/cover (effective 2002). adv. bk.rev. charts; illus.; mkt.; stat.; tr.lit.; abstr. back issues avail.; reprints avail. **Document type:** *Journal, Trade.* **Description:** Reports on the practical experiences and innovations in spinning, weaving, threading, knitting, non-wovens, embroidery, dyeing, fabrics and garments. Also includes technology, equipment machinery and plants for energy, environment and economy.
Media: Diskette. **Related titles:** E-mail ed.; Fax ed.; Online - full text ed.
Indexed: A&ATA, A26, ChemAb, G08, I05, SCOPUS, T01, TTI, WTA.
Published by: National Technical Press, D-16, KDA Scheme No. 1, Karachi, Pakistan. TEL 92-21-4311674, FAX 92-21-4533911. Ed., Pub. Mazhar Yusuf. R&P Amina Baqai TEL 92-21-4311675. Adv. contact Subine Dussey. B&W page USD 550, color page USD 805; trim 175 x 225. Circ: 2,500 (controlled).

PERFORMANCE APPAREL MARKETS; business and market analysis for the world's fibre, textile and apparel industries. *see* CLOTHING TRADE

PERSONAL PROTECTION AND FASHION. *see* OCCUPATIONAL HEALTH AND SAFETY

PHILADELPHIA COLLEGE OF TEXTILES & SCIENCE. PORTFOLIO. *see* COLLEGE AND ALUMNI

TU

677 746.92 ESP ISSN 1576-1452
PINKER MODA. Text in Spanish. 1960. 7/yr. EUR 125 domestic; EUR 210 in Europe; EUR 280 elsewhere (effective 2009). adv. bk.rev. bibl.; illus.; stat.; tr.lit. **Document type:** *Magazine, Trade.*
Related titles: Online - full text ed.
Published by: E T D Prensa Profesional, SA, Sicilia 95, Atico, Barcelona, 08013, Spain. TEL 34-93-5569500, FAX 34-93-5569560, http://www.etd.es. Ed. Javier Gomex. Circ: 6,900 (controlled).

677.21 GRC ISSN 0032-0234
PIRAIKI-PATRAIKI. Text in Greek. 1955. q. free. adv. bk.rev. charts; illus.
Published by: Piraiki-Patraiki Cotton Manufacturing Co. Inc., 8 Dragatsaniou St, Athens, 105 59, Greece. Ed. Haris Makrykostas. Circ: 10,000.

PLANET LAUNDRY. *see* CLEANING AND DYEING

677 POL ISSN 0076-0331
CODEN: ZNLWAD
➤ **POLITECHNIKA LODZKA. ZESZYTY NAUKOWE. WLOKIENNICTWO.** Text in English; Summaries in Polish. 1954. irreg. price varies. **Document type:** *Monographic series, Academic/ Scholarly.* **Description:** Spinning technology, synthetic fibers technology, weaving technology and fiber science.
Indexed: B22, ChemAb.
—CASDDS.
Published by: (Politechnika Lodzka/Technical University of Lodz), Wydawnictwo Politechniki Lodzkiej, ul Wolczanska 223, Lodz, 93005, Poland. TEL 48-42-6840793. Ed., R&P Wlodzimierz Wiezlak TEL 48-42-313311. Circ: 186. **Dist. by:** Ars Polona, Obroncow 25, Warsaw 03933, Poland. TEL 48-22-5098609, FAX 48-22-5098610, arspolona@arspolona.com.pl, http://www.arspolona.com.pl.

677 USA
PRINCIPLES OF NONWOVENS; a CD for technical and manufacturing professionals. Text in English. irreg. USD 210 to non-members; USD 150 to members (effective 2005). **Description:** Covers information on non-woven fabrics manufacturing.
Media: CD-ROM.
Published by: I N D A - Assocation of the Nonwoven Fabrics Industry, PO Box 1288, Cary, NC 27512-1288. TEL 919-233-1210, FAX 919-233-1282, http://www.inda.org.

677 IND
➤ **PROGRESS IN TEXTILES: SCIENCE & TECHNOLOGY.** Text in English. 1999. irreg., latest vol.4. back issues avail. **Document type:** *Monographic series, Academic/Scholarly.* **Description:** Covering the entire gamut of textiles, this series aims at all professionals in the field of textiles and its apparels. Covers various aspects of textile materials and their properties, state-of-the-art technology for textile and apparel manufacture, testing and quality mangement and last but not the least, new developments in this area.
Published by: I A F L Publications, HS 27 FF, Kailash Colony Market, New Delhi, 110048, India. TEL 91-11-41730976, FAX 91-11-29235557, info@iaflpublications.com.

677 POL ISSN 1731-8645
PRZEGLAD WLOKIENNICZY - WLOKNO, ODZIEZ, SKORA. Text in Polish. 2004. m. PLZ 315 domestic; EUR 195 foreign (effective 2011). 36 p./no.; **Document type:** *Journal, Trade.*
Formed by the merger of (1972-2004): Wiadomosci - Wlokno, Odziez, Skora (1429-0359); Which was formerly (until 1993): Wiadomosci Produkcyjne (0137-8120); (1992-2004): Przeglad Wlokienniczy i Technik Wlokienniczy (1230-0381); Which was formed by the merger of (1947-1992(: Przeglad Wlokienniczy (0033-2410); Which was formerly (until 1958): Przemysl Wlokienniczy (0370-1700); (1929-1992): Technik Wlokienniczy (Warszawa) (0492-4851); Which was formerly (until 1958): Wlokiennictwo (0510-713X); (until 1952): Technik Wlokienniczy (Lodz) (1230-0438)
Related titles: Online - full text ed.
Indexed: B22, EngInd, SCOPUS, T01, T02, TM, TTI, WTA.
—BLDSC (6944.910000), INIST.
Published by: (Federacja Stowarzyszen' Naukowo-Technicznych NOT), Wydawnictwo SIGMA - N O T Sp. z o.o., ul Ratuszowa 11, PO Box 1004, Warsaw, 00950, Poland. TEL 48-22-8180918, FAX 48-22-6192187, sekretariat@sigma-not.pl. Ed. Zdzislaw Marzec TEL 48-42-6322315. **Dist. by:** Ars Polona, Obroncow 25, Warsaw 03933, Poland. TEL 48-22-5098609, FAX 48-22-5098610, arspolona@arspolona.com.pl, http://www.arspolona.com.pl.

677.13 BGD
QUARTERLY SUMMARY OF JUTE GOODS STATISTICS. Text in English. 1955. q. BDT 72. **Document type:** *Report, Trade.*
Formerly: Pakistan Jute Association. Monthly Summary of Jute Goods Statistics (0027-0601)
Published by: (Bangladesh Jute Industries Corp.), Bangladesh Jute Association, BJA Bhaban, 77, Motijheel Commercial Area, P.O. Box 59, Dhaka, 1000, Bangladesh. TEL 88-2-9552916, FAX 88-2-9560137.

677 HKG ISSN 1560-6074
RESEARCH JOURNAL OF TEXTILE AND APPAREL. Text in English. 1997. 4/yr. HKD 460 domestic; HKD 520 in China; USD 80 in Asia; USD 90 elsewhere (effective 2008). **Document type:** *Journal, Academic/Scholarly.* **Description:** Aims to cover current developments in scientific research results that introduce new concepts, innovative technologies, and improved understanding of materials and processing, management, design and retailing related to fiber, yarn, fabric, dyeing and finishing.
Indexed: T01, T02, TTI.
Published by: Hong Kong Polytechnic University, Hong Kong Institution of Textile and Apparel, Hung Hom, Hong Kong, Hong Kong. TEL 852-2766-6554, FAX 852-2773-1432, info@hkita.org, http://www.hkita.org. Ed. Jin-lian Hu.

677 ESP ISSN 0210-0800
TS1300 CODEN: IITTCS
REVISTA DE LA INDUSTRIA TEXTIL. Text in Spanish. 1959. m. (10/yr.). EUR 60 domestic; EUR 90 foreign. adv. bk.rev. bibl.; illus.; stat. **Document type:** *Magazine, Trade.* **Description:** For personnel involved in the spinning, weaving, knitting, chemical, printing, dyeing, and finishing of man-made fibers.
Incorporates (1958-1992): Investigacion e Informacion Textil y de Tensioactivos (0302-5268)
Indexed: IECT, SCOPUS, T01, TTI, WTA.
—CASDDS. **CCC.**
Published by: (Camara de Directivos, Tecnicos y Administrativos del Arte Textil), Revitextil, S.L., Cerdena 269, entlo. 2a, Barcelona, 08013, Spain. TEL 34-3-4571220, FAX 34-3-2075568. Ed. Carlos Schneegluth Cugat. Pub. Carlos Schneegluth. adv.: B&W page EUR 730, color page EUR 790. Circ: 3,400.

677 ESP ISSN 0300-3418
CODEN: RQTED3
REVISTA DE QUIMICA TEXTIL. Text in Spanish. 1966. 5/yr. adv. bk.rev. charts; illus. **Document type:** *Bulletin, Trade.* **Description:** Covers fabric dyeing, printing and finishing technologies.
Indexed: A22, ChemAb, ChemTitl, IECT, SCOPUS, T01, TTI, WTA.
—BLDSC (7870.300000), GNLM, IE, Ingenta. **CCC.**
Published by: Asociacion Espanola de Quimicos y Coloristas Textiles, Gran Via de Les Corts Catalanes, 670 Planta 6, Barcelona, 08010, Spain. TEL 34-93-317728, FAX 34-93-3174526, aeqet@aeqct.org, http://www.arqct.org. Ed. Carlos Schneegluth. Circ: 1,200.

677 BRA ISSN 0035-0524
REVISTA TEXTIL. Text in Portuguese. 1930. 6/yr. USD 200. bk.rev. **Document type:** *Directory, Trade.* **Description:** Covers all sections of the textile industry, including machinery and equipment for spinning, weaving, knitting, printing, dyeing, and finishing processes.
Published by: (Primeira Escola de Tecelagem), R. da Silva Haydu & Cia. Ltda., Rua Parana, 136, Bras, Sao Paulo, SP 03041-010, Brazil. TEL 55-11-2709066, FAX 55-11-2792409, TELEX 1124187. Ed. Ricardo da Silva Haydu. Pub. Beatriz Seinprini. adv.: B&W page USD 1,750, color page USD 2,950; trim 300 x 220. Circ: 10,000.

338.642 746 645.1 USA ISSN 0278-9795
HD9937
RUG NEWS. Text in English. 1978. m. USD 78 domestic; USD 100 in Canada; USD 142 elsewhere (effective 2000). adv. **Document type:** *Magazine, Trade.*
Related titles: Online - full text ed.: 2001.
—**CCC.**
Published by: Museum Books, Inc., 26 Broadway., Ste. 776, New York, NY 10004-1748. Adv. contact Kathleen Bingham. color page USD 2,100; trim 11 x 5.5. Circ: 4,500 (paid).

SANSHI KONCHUU BAIOTEKKU. *see* BIOLOGY—Entomology

677 ITA ISSN 1125-5579
CODEN: NUSTES
SELEZIONE TESSILE (MILAN). Text in Italian. 1963; N.S. 1989. bi-m. (5/yr.). EUR 50 domestic; EUR 100 in Europe; EUR 120 elsewhere (effective 2009). adv. bk.rev. bibl.; charts; illus. index. back issues avail. **Document type:** *Magazine, Trade.* **Description:** Features articles on the textile industry. Includes textile texture, color, machinery and production.
Former titles (until 1997): Nuova Selezione Tessile (1125-5188); (until 1988): Selezione Tessile (0392-9809); (until 1983): Nuova Selezione Tessile (0391-6448); (until 1965): Selezione Tessile (0037-1513)
Related titles: Online - full text ed.
Indexed: SCOPUS, T01, TM, TTI, WTA.
—BLDSC (8235.320000), CASDDS, IE, Ingenta.
Published by: Tecniche Nuove SpA, Via Eritrea 21, Milan, MI 201, Italy. TEL 39-02-390901, FAX 39-02-7570364, info@tecnichenuove.com. Ed. Stefania Parisi. Circ: 8,000.

677 JPN ISSN 0037-9875
TS1300 CODEN: SENGA5
➤ **SEN'I GAKKAISHI/SOCIETY OF FIBER SCIENCE AND TECHNOLOGY, JAPAN. JOURNAL.** Text in Japanese; Summaries in English. 1944. m. free to members. adv. abstr.; bibl.; illus. **Document type:** *Journal, Academic/Scholarly.* **Description:** Publishes original research articles on the science and technology of fibers and other related materials including pulps, papers, plastic films, membranes, composite materials, and optical fibers.
Incorporates (1968-1972): Sen'i to Kogyo / Fiber Science and Industry, Japan (0037-2188); Formed by the merger of (1935-1943): Sen'i Kogyo Gakkaish / Society of Textile Industry, Japan. Journal (0911-8780); (1925-1943): Sen'iso Kogyo / Cellulose Institute, Tokyo. Journal (0371-070X)
Related titles: Online - full text ed.
Indexed: A&ATA, A20, A22, ABIPC, ASCA, CA, CCI, CEABA, CPEI, ChemAb, ChemTitl, EngInd, INIS AtomInd, JTA, MSCI, P31, RefZh, SCI, SCOPUS, T01, T02, TM, TTI, W07, WTA.
—BLDSC (4887.400000), CASDDS, IE, Ingenta, INIST, Linda Hall. **CCC.**
Published by: Sen'i Gakkai/Society of Fiber Science and Technology, 3-3-9-208 Kami-Osaki, Shinagawa-ku, Tokyo, 141-0021, Japan. TEL 81-3-34415627, FAX 81-3-34413260, fiber@jd5.so-net.ne.jp. Ed. Takeshi Kikutani. Circ: 5,000.

677 JPN ISSN 0371-0580
TS1300
SEN'I KIKAI GAKKAISHI/TEXTILE MACHINERY SOCIETY OF JAPAN. JOURNAL. Text in Japanese. 1972. m. JPY 8,000 membership (effective 2005). adv. bk.rev. abstr.; charts; illus. 70 p./no.; **Document type:** *Journal, Academic/Scholarly.*
Formed by the merger of (1965-1972): Sen'i Kikai Gakkai Ronbunshu (0040-5051); (1965-1972): Sen'i kogaku (0040-506X); Both titles superseded (1948-1965): Sen'i Kikai Gakkaishi (0285-905X)
Related titles: Online - full text ed.: ISSN 1880-1986; ◆ English ed.: Journal of Textile Engineering. ISSN 1346-8235.
Indexed: JTA, SCOPUS, T01, TTI, WTA.
—BLDSC (4908.499000), Linda Hall. **CCC.**
Published by: Nihon Sen'i Kikai Gakkai/Textile Machinery Society of Japan, Osaka Science and Technology Center Bldg., 8-4, Utsubo-Honmachi 1 chome, Nishi-ku, Osaka-shi, 550-0004, Japan. TEL 81-6-64434691, FAX 81-6-64434694. Circ: 8,000.

677 JPN ISSN 0037-2072
TS1300 CODEN: SESKB9
SEN'I SEIHIN SHOHI KAGAKU/JAPAN RESEARCH ASSOCIATION FOR TEXTILE END-USES. JOURNAL. Text in Japanese; Summaries in English. 1960. m. free to members. adv. bk.rev. charts; illus.; tr.lit. Index. 60 p./no.; back issues avail. **Document type:** *Journal, Trade.*
Indexed: A&ATA, A22, CA, ChemAb, ChemTitl, JTA, SCOPUS, T01, T02, TTI, WTA.
—BLDSC (4805.800000), CASDDS, IE, Ingenta. **CCC.**
Published by: Nihon Sen'i Seihin Shohi Kagakkai/Japan Research Association for Textile End-Uses, Rm No 201 Yoshin Ogimachi City Heights, 2-11-5 Doshin, Kita-ku, Osaka, 530-0035, Japan. TEL 81-6-63581441, FAX 81-6-63581442. Ed. Yoh Masuda. Pub. S Tajimi. R&P, Adv. contact S. Tajimi. Circ: 6,000.

677 JPN ISSN 0370-9574
CODEN: SEKOBF
SENSHOKU KOGYO/DYEING INDUSTRY. Text in Japanese. 1953. m. Subscr. incld. with membership. **Document type:** *Journal, Trade.*
Indexed: CIN, ChemAb, ChemTitl, WTA.
—CASDDS.
Published by: Shikisensha Co., Ltd., Tenrokuhankiyu Bldg 5F, 7-1-10, Tenjinbashi, Kita-ku, Osaka, 531, Japan. TEL 81-6-63516915, FAX 81-6-63516920, http://www.shikisensha.com/. **Dist. by:** International Marketing Corp., I.P.O. Box 5056, Tokyo 100-30, Japan. TEL 81-3-3661-7458, FAX 81-3-3667-9646.

677.39 GBR ISSN 0266-0822
SERICA. Text in English. 1970. q. free to members (effective 2009). **Document type:** *Newsletter, Trade.* **Description:** Covers all aspects of silk and silk production.
Formerly (until 1974): Silk Association. Newsletter
Published by: Silk Association of Great Britain, 5 Portland Pl, London, W1N 3AA, United Kingdom. TEL 44-171-6367788, FAX 44-171-6367515, sagb@dial.pipex.com, http://www.silk.org.uk/.

SERICULTURE & SILK INDUSTRY STATISTICS (YEAR). *see* TEXTILE INDUSTRIES AND FABRICS—Abstracting, Bibliographies, Statistics

677 ITA
LA SETA; bollettino ufficiale della Stazione Sperimentale per la Seta. Text in English, Italian; Summaries in English, French, Italian. 1931. 3/yr. free to qualified personnel. adv. bk.rev. abstr.; bibl.; charts; illus.; stat. back issues avail. **Document type:** *Journal, Trade.* **Description:** Includes scientific and technological reports concerned with silk, protein, synthetic fibers and textiles.
Published by: Stazione Sperimentale per la Seta, Via Giuseppe Colombo 83, Milan, MI 20133, Italy. TEL 39-02-2665990, FAX 39-02-2362788, http://www.ssiseta.it. Circ: 1,500.

SEWING TODAY. *see* CLOTHING TRADE—Fashions

677 CHN ISSN 1001-2044
SHANGHAI FANGZHI KEJI/SHANGHAI TEXTILE SCIENCE AND TECHNOLOGY. Text in Chinese. 1973. bi-m. CNY 30. adv. **Document type:** *Academic/Scholarly.*
Related titles: Online - full text ed.
Published by: Shanghai Fangzhi Kexue Yanjiuyuan/Shanghai Textile Research Institute, 545 Lanzhou Lu, Shanghai, 200082, China. TEL 86-21-6546-1341, FAX 86-21-6545-8418. Ed. Yang Zhangfang. Circ: 7,000.

SHEEP MAGAZINE; the magazine for entrepreneurial flockmasters. *see* AGRICULTURE—Poultry And Livestock

667.3 AUS ISSN 1449-1532
SHEEP'S BACK TO MILL. Text in English. 1900. irreg. free (effective 2008). back issues avail. **Document type:** *Yearbook, Trade.* **Description:** Covers the Australian wool industry of harvesting, marketing and distribution of raw wool from the sheep's back in Australia to overseas mills.
Formerly (until 1997): Harvesting, Marketing and Distribution Costs for Australian Wool - Sheep's Back to Overseas Mill
Related titles: Online - full text ed.: free (effective 2009).
Published by: Australian Wool Innovation Ltd., Level 5, 16-20 Barrack St, Sydney, NSW 2000, Australia. TEL 61-2-82953100, FAX 61-2-82954100, info@woolinnovation.com.au, http://www.woolinnovation.com.au. Ed. Mark Gabrys.

677 CHN
SHISHANG NEIYI/MODE UNDERWEAR. Text in English. 1985. q. CNY 12.80 newsstand/cover (effective 2005). **Document type:** *Journal, Academic/Scholarly.*
Formerly (until 2003): Zhongguo Fangzhi Meishu/China Textiles Design (1006-2262)
Published by: Zhongwai Fuzhuang Zazhishe, 889, Changjiang Lu, Dalian, 116021, China. **Dist. by:** China International Book Trading Corp, 35 Chegongzhuang Xilu, Haidian District, PO Box 399, Beijing 100044, China. TEL 86-10-68412045, FAX 86-10-68412023, cibtc@mail.cibtc.com.cn, http://www.cibtc.com.cn.

677 667 USA ISSN 0049-0423
TT848
SHUTTLE, SPINDLE & DYEPOT. Text in English. 1969. q. USD 35 (effective 2006). adv. bk.rev. illus. Index. 66 p./no.; reprints avail. **Document type:** *Magazine, Consumer.*
Related titles: Microform ed.: 1969 (from PQC).
Indexed: A&ATA, A06, A07, A22, A30, A31, AA, ArtInd, B04, IHTDI, MELSA, Pinpoint, T01, TTI.
—BLDSC (8271.000000), IE, Ingenta.
Published by: Handweavers Guild of America, 1255 Buford Highway, Ste 211, Suwanee, GA 30024. TEL 678-730-0010, FAX 678-730-0836. Ed. Sandra Bowles. Adv. contact Dorothy Holt. Circ: 75,000.

677.39 CHN ISSN 1001-7003
➤ **SICHOU/SILK MONTHLY.** Text in Chinese; Abstracts in Chinese, English. 1956. m. CNY 240, USD 180; CNY 20 per issue (effective 2011 & 2012). adv. **Document type:** *Journal, Academic/Scholarly.* **Description:** Contains contribution to the development of the silk, including special columns: "Research and Technology," "Design and Production," and "History and Culture.".
Former titles (until 1959): Zhejiang Sichou/Zhejiang Silk (0528-9025); (until 1956): Zhejiang Sichou Gongye Tongxun/Zhejiang Silk Industry Communication
Related titles: Online - full text ed.
—East View.
Published by: (Zhongguo Sichou Xuehui, Zhejiang Ligong Daxue/ Zhejiang Sci-Tech University), Sichou Zazhishe, No.5, 2nd St., Gaojiaoyuan Dist., Xiasha, Hangzhou 310018, China. TEL 86-571-88081769, FAX 86-571-88839613. Ed. You-mu Xuan. Circ: 4,000. **Dist. over seas by:** China International Book Trading Corp, 35 Chegongzhuang Xilu, Haidian District, PO Box 399, Beijing 100044, China. TEL 86-10-68412045, FAX 86-10-68412023, cibtc@mail.cibtc.com.cn, http://www.cibtc.com.cn.

677.39 CHN ISSN 1004-1265
SICHUAN SICHOU/SICHUAN SILK. Text in Chinese. 1979. q. USD 20. adv. **Document type:** *Academic/Scholarly.*
Related titles: Online - full text ed.
Published by: (Sichuansheng Sichou Gongye Yanjiusuo/Sichuan Silk Manufacturing Research Institute), Sichuan Sichou Bianjibu, 33 Jinxianqiao Jie, Chengdu, Sichuan 610031, China. TEL 86-28-7747284. Ed. Zhao Lian. Adv. contact Wang Yuede.

677 USA ISSN 0038-4607
SOUTHERN TEXTILE NEWS. Text in English. 1945. bi-w. (Mon.). USD 25; USD 35 in Canada & Mexico; USD 50 elsewhere (effective 2005). adv. illus.; mkt.; stat. **Document type:** *Newspaper.*
Related titles: Microfilm ed.
Indexed: A09, A10, T01, T02, TTI, V03, V04.
Published by: Mullen Publications, Inc. (Charlotte), 9629 Old Nations Ford Rd., Charlotte, Mecklenberg, NC 28273. TEL 704-527-5111, 800-738-5111, FAX 704-527-5114. Ed. Devin Steele. Pub., Adv. contact Chip Smith. B&W page USD 2,215, color page USD 2,665. Circ: 20,000.

677 USA
SPECIALTY FABRIC REVIEW BUYER'S GUIDE. Text in English. 1915. a. USD 50 per issue (effective 2009); included with subscr. to Specialty Fabric Review. adv. back issues avail. **Document type:** *Directory, Trade.* **Description:** Provides current news, trends and technology related to specific markets in the specialty fabrics industry.
Former titles (until 2008): Industrial Fabric Products Review Buyer's Guide; (until 1966): Canvas Products Review; (until 1956): National Canvas Goods Manufacturers Review; (until 1924): National Tent and Awning Maufacturers Review
Related titles: Online - full text ed.
Published by: Industrial Fabrics Association International, 1801 W County Rd B W, Ste B, Roseville, MN 55113. TEL 651-222-2508, 800-225-4324, FAX 651-225-6966, generalinfo@ifai.com, http://www.ifai.com. Ed. Galynn D Nordstrom TEL 651-225-6928. Pub. Mary Hennessy. Adv. contact Sarah C Hyland TEL 651-225-6950. Circ: 10,000.

677 USA ISSN 2155-5095
HD9938
SPECIALTY FABRICS REVIEW. Text in English. 1915. m. USD 69 domestic; USD 79 in Canada & Mexico; USD 169 elsewhere (effective 2010). adv. bk.rev. illus.; tr.lit. index. 84 p./no.; back issues avail. **Document type:** *Magazine, Trade.* **Description:** Profiles, product news, how-to, industry news and other information of industrial and technical fabric and product manufacturers.
Former titles (until 2008): Industrial Fabric Products Review (0019-8307); (until 1966): Canvas Products Review
Indexed: A22, SCOPUS, T01, T02, TTI, WTA.
—BLDSC (8404.904300), IE, Ingenta.
Published by: Industrial Fabrics Association International, 1801 W County Rd B W, Ste B, Roseville, MN 55113. TEL 651-222-2508, FAX 651-225-6966, generalinfo@ifai.com, http://www.ifai.com. Pub. Mary Hennessy. adv.: color page USD 4,505; trim 8.25 x 11. Circ: 15,000 (controlled).

677 POL
SPEKTRUM. Text in Polish. bi-m. PLZ 48 domestic; PLZ 96 foreign (effective 2005). **Document type:** *Magazine, Trade.*
Published by: Wydawnictwo Elamed, Al Rozdzienskiego 188, Katowice, 40203, Poland. TEL 48-32-2580361, FAX 48-32-2039356, elamed@elamed.com.pl, http://www.elamed.com.pl. Ed. Robert Cholewa.

SPUNBONDED AND MELTBLOWN TECHNOLOGY HANDBOOK. *see* ENGINEERING—Chemical Engineering

677 USA
STANDARD TEST METHODS. Text in English. 2001. biennial. USD 1,275 combined subscription per issue to non-members (print & CD-ROM eds.); USD 945 combined subscription per issue to members (print & CD-ROM eds.) (effective 2010). **Document type:** *Handbook/Manual/Guide, Trade.*
Related titles: CD-ROM ed.: USD 1,125 per issue to non-members; USD 795 per issue to members (effective 2010).
Published by: Association of the Nonwoven Fabrics Industry (I N D A), PO Box 1288, Cary, NC 27512. TEL 919-233-1210, FAX 919-233-1282, info@inda.org.

677 GBR ISSN 2046-7338
THE STOCKLISTS. Variant title: The Stocklists with Flooring News. Text in English. 1973. m. GBP 21 domestic; GBP 39 foreign (effective 2011). adv. back issues avail. **Document type:** *Magazine, Trade.* **Description:** Designed for the carpet and floor market buyers.
Formerly (until 200?): Stocklists and News Service for Carpet and Floor Covering Buyers (0950-5024)
Related titles: Online - full text ed.: free (effective 2011).
Published by: Mayville Publishing Co., Ltd., 219 W Ella Rd, W Ella, Hull, HU10 7SD, United Kingdom. TEL 44-1482-659396, FAX 44-1482-659397, info@mayvillepublishing.co.uk.

STUDIES IN TEXTILE AND COSTUME HISTORY. *see* HISTORY

677.2 SDN ISSN 0562-5033
SUDAN COTTON BULLETIN. Text in English. 1960. m. charts; stat. **Document type:** *Bulletin.*
Published by: (Department of Research and Statistics), Cotton Public Corporation, P O Box 1672, Khartoum, Sudan.

SURFACE DESIGN. *see* ART

677 CHE
SURVEY ON COTTON CONTAMINATION, FOREIGN MATTER & STICKINESS. Text in English. 1989. biennial. free. **Document type:** *Report, Trade.* **Description:** Survey on the perception of cotton spinning mills concerning problems of cotton contamination, foreign matter and stickiness.
Published by: International Textile Manufacturers Federation, Am Schanzengraben 29, Postfach, Zurich, 8039, Switzerland. TEL 41-1-2017080, FAX 41-1-2017134, secretariat@itmf.org, http://www.itmf.org.

677.39 CHN ISSN 1673-047X
CODEN: SSGXEL
SUZHOU DAXUE XUEBAO (GONGKE BAN)/SUZHOU UNIVERSITY. JOURNAL (ENGINEERING SCIENCE EDITION). Text in Chinese. 1981. bi-m. (formerly q.). **Document type:** *Journal, Academic/Scholarly.*
Formerly (until 2002): Suzhou Sichou Gongxueyuan Xuebao/Suzhou Institute of Silk Textile Technology. Journal (1000-1999)
Related titles: Online - full text ed.
Indexed: SCOPUS, WTA.
—BLDSC (4899.770000).
Published by: Suzhou Daxue Chubanshe/Suzhou University Press, 200, Ganjian Dong Rd, 5th Fl, Rm 515, Suzhou, 215021, China. TEL 86-512-67480098, FAX 86-512-67258875, sdcbs@suda.edu.cn, http://sudapress.com/.

677 USA
SWATCHES. Text in English. 1984. s-a. adv.
Published by: National Association of Decorative Fabric Distributors, 1 Windsor Cv., Ste. 305, Columbia, SC 29223-1833. TEL 803-252-5646. Circ: 17,000 (controlled).

677 FRA ISSN 1161-9317
TS1300
T U T; la revue des utilisateurs. (Textiles a Usages Techniques) Text in English, French. 1991. q. EUR 85 domestic; EUR 95 foreign (effective 2005). adv. illus. **Document type:** *Magazine, Trade.* **Description:** Directed to the end-users of technical material.
Indexed: A22, A28, APA, BrCerAb, C&ISA, CA/WCA, CIA, CerAb, CivEngAb, CorrAb, E&CAJ, E11, EEA, EMA, H15, M&TEA, M09, MBF, METADEX, SCOPUS, SolStAb, T01, T02, T04, TM, TTI, WAA, WTA.
—BLDSC (9076.170500), IE, Ingenta, Linda Hall. **CCC.**
Published by: Editions de l' Industrie Textile, 16 rue Ballu, Paris, 75311 Cedex 9, France. TEL 33-1-48741596, FAX 33-1-48740189, LL@industrietextile.com. Ed. Pierre S Robin. Adv. contact Evelyne Merigot.

677 DEU ISSN 1613-2505
T V P - FACHZEITSCHRIFT FUER TEXTILVEREDLUNG UND PROMOTION. Text in German. 1999. bi-m. EUR 38; EUR 8 newsstand/cover (effective 2011). adv. **Document type:** *Magazine, Trade.*
Formerly (until 2004): S I P Textil (1615-7117)
Indexed: TM.
Published by: Verlagshaus Gruber GmbH, Max-Planck-Str 2, Eppertshausen, 64859, Germany. TEL 49-6071-39410, FAX 49-6071-394111, info@verlagshaus-gruber.de, http://www.verlagshaus-gruber.de. Ed. Moritz Matthes. adv.: B&W page EUR 1,540, color page EUR 2,240. Circ: 6,000 (paid and controlled).

677 JPN
T W A R O NEWS. Text in Japanese. m.
Published by: Asian Regional Organisation of the International Textile Garment and Leather Workers' Federation, Zeusen Kaikan Bldg 8-16, kudan-Minami 4-chome, Chiyoda-ku, Tokyo, 102-0074, Japan. TEL 03-2655465.

677 USA ISSN 1553-944X
TS1770.I53
T3 - TECHNICAL TEXTILE TECHNOLOGY; the forum for performance textiles and nonwovens. Text in English. 2004. q. free to qualified personnel (effective 2007). adv. **Document type:** *Journal, Trade.* **Description:** Dedicated to spotlighting innovation and market successes in technical textiles and engineered nonwoven fabrics.
Related titles: ♦ Supplement to: International Fiber Journal. ISSN 1049-801X.
Published by: International Media Group, Inc., 6000 Fairview Rd, Ste 1200, Charlotte, NC 28210. TEL 704-552-3708, FAX 704-552-3705, ifj@ifj.com, http://www.fiberjournal.com. adv.: B&W page USD 2,240, color page USD 3,225.

677 TWN
TAIWAN TEXTILE INDUSTRY GUIDE. Text in English. a. USD 50 in America, Europe & Africa; USD 40 in Middle East, Asia & Oceania (effective 2000). **Document type:** *Directory, Trade.* **Description:** Contains of companies from upstream to downstream: fiber to fabric to apparel.
Published by: China Economic News Service, 561 Chunghsiao E. Rd Sec 4, Taipei, 10516, Taiwan. TEL 886-2-642-2629, FAX 886-2-2642-7422, TELEX 27710-CENSPC, webmaster@www.cens.com, http://www.cens.com.

677 DEU ISSN 1864-7189
TASCHENBUCH DES TEXTILEINZELHANDELS. Text in German. 1962. a. adv. **Document type:** *Journal, Trade.*
Former titles (until 2007): Taschenbuch des Textil- und Lederwareneinzelhandels (0171-4902); (until 1972): Taschenbuch des Textileinzelhandels (0082-1837)
Published by: Deutscher Fachverlag GmbH, Mainzer Landstr 251, Frankfurt Am Main, 60326, Germany. TEL 49-69-75952052, FAX 49-69-75952999, info@dfv.de, http://www.dfv.de. adv.: page EUR 3,130; trim 105 x 148. Circ: 13,000 (controlled).

677 GBR ISSN 0959-9185
HD9869.I53 CODEN: TTEMEU
TECHNICAL TEXTILE MARKETS. Text in English. 1990. q. USD 2,065; USD 3,098 combined subscription to individuals (print & online eds.); USD 18,585 combined subscription to institutions (print & online eds.); USD 774 per issue; USD 1,162 combined subscription per issue to individuals (print & online eds.); USD 6,969 combined subscription per issue to institutions (print & online eds.) (effective 2009). charts; mkt.; maps; stat.; tr.lit. 150 p./no.; back issues avail. **Document type:** *Journal, Trade.* **Description:** Aimed at senior textile executives in man-made fibres and technical and industrial textile manufacturing industries, provides industry and market analysis, corporate strategy and company profiles, forecasts trends and developments.
Related titles: E-mail ed.; Online - full text ed.
Indexed: A09, A10, T01, T02, TM, TTI, V03, V04.
—BLDSC (8731.156000), IE, Ingenta. **CCC.**
Published by: Textiles Intelligence Ltd., Alderley House, Alderley Rd, Wilmslow, SK9 1AT, United Kingdom. TEL 44-1625-536136, FAX 44-1625-536137, info@textilesintelligence.com.

677 668.4 GBR ISSN 0964-5993
TS1300
TECHNICAL TEXTILES INTERNATIONAL. Text in English. 1992. 8/yr. GBP 220, USD 397 combined subscription (effective 2010). adv. back issues avail. **Document type:** *Newsletter, Trade.* **Description:** Covers the latest developments in technical textiles and fiber-reinforced materials, from design to end-products, with analyses of industry trends and reports from major exhibitions and conferences.
Related titles: Online - full text ed.: ISSN 1878-6677.
Indexed: A15, ABIn, EngInd, Inspec, P48, P51, P52, PQC, SCOPUS, T01, T02, TM, TTI, WTA.
—BLDSC (8731.158000), IE, Infotrieve, Ingenta. **CCC.**
Published by: International Newsletters Ltd., 9A Victoria Sq, Droitwich, Worcs WR9 8DE, United Kingdom. TEL 44-870-1657210, FAX 44-870-1657212, in@intnews.com, http://www.intnews.com. Ed. Nick Butler. Adv. contact David Kay TEL 44-1273-423512.

677 DEU ISSN 0323-3243
TECHNISCHE TEXTILIEN/TECHNICAL TEXTILES. Text in English, German. 1958. bi-m. EUR 114 domestic; EUR 114.80 in Europe; EUR 119 elsewhere; EUR 25 per issue (effective 2009). adv. **Document type:** *Magazine, Trade.*
Formerly (until 1965): Mitteilungen fuer die Bastfaserindustrie (0323-8121)
Indexed: CA, IBR, IBZ, RefZh, SCOPUS, T01, T02, TM, TTI, WTA.
—BLDSC (8753.450000), IE, Ingenta. **CCC.**
Published by: Deutscher Fachverlag GmbH, Mainzer Landstr 251, Frankfurt Am Main, 60326, Germany. TEL 49-69-75952052, FAX 49-69-75952999, info@dfv.de, http://www.dfv.de. Eds. Claudia van Bonn, Petra Gottwald. Adv. contact Dagmar Henning. B&W page EUR 2,850, color page EUR 4,420; trim 182 x 260. Circ: 5,000 (paid and controlled).

677 DEU
TECHTEX EUROPE. Text in German. 1990. bi-m. adv. **Document type:** *Magazine, Trade.*
Published by: Usa-Verlag GmbH, Usinger Str 115, Ober-Moerlen, 61239, Germany. TEL 49-6002-930073, FAX 49-6002-930075, info@usa-verlag.de, http://www.usa-verlag.de. adv.: B&W page EUR 515, color page EUR 1,415. Circ: 2,000 (controlled).

677 DEU ISSN 0933-8128
TECHTEX FORUM. Text in German. 1988. bi-m. adv. **Document type:** *Magazine, Trade.*
Published by: Usa-Verlag GmbH, Usinger Str 115, Ober-Moerlen, 61239, Germany. TEL 49-6002-930073, FAX 49-6002-930075, info@usa-verlag.de, http://www.usa-verlag.de. adv.: B&W page EUR 1,145, color page EUR 2,045. Circ: 2,000 (controlled).

677 ESP
TECNOFABRICS. Text in Spanish. 1991. q. adv. **Document type:** *Magazine, Trade.*
Published by: Difusion Ediciones S.L., Rosellon 102, Entlo. 1a, Barcelona, 08029, Spain. TEL 34-93-235702, FAX 34-93-236080, mail@diffusionsport.com, http://www.diffusionsport.com. Ed. Jordi Mullor. Circ: 4,000.

677 ITA ISSN 0394-5413
TECNOLOGIE TESSILI. Text in Italian. 1987. 8/yr. EUR 70 domestic; EUR 105 foreign (effective 2009). adv. **Document type:** *Magazine, Trade.*
Indexed: A22, SCOPUS, T01, T02, TTI, WTA.
—BLDSC (7993.451500), IE, Ingenta.
Published by: Reed Business Information Spa (Subsidiary of: Reed Business Information International), Viale Giulio Richard 1, Milan, 20143, Italy. TEL 39-02-818301, FAX 39-02-81830406, info@reedbusiness.it, http://www.reedbusiness.it. Circ: 15,000.

677 FIN ISSN 0040-2370
TEKSTIILILEHTI. Text in Finnish. 1937. 6/yr. EUR 51 (effective 2005). adv. bk.rev. charts; illus. **Document type:** *Magazine, Trade.*
Published by: Suomen Tekstiiliteknillinen Liitto r. y./Finnisgh Textile Technical Society, Pyynikintie 25, Tampere, 33230, Finland. Ed. Irma Boncamper. adv.: B&W page EUR 925, color page EUR 1,430; 180 x 270. Circ: 1,300.

677 374 640 FIN ISSN 0355-8991
TEKSTIILIOPETTAJA/TEXTILLAREN. Text in Finnish, Swedish. 1957. q. EUR 25 (effective 2004). adv. bk.rev.
Published by: Tekstiiliopettajaliitto/Trade Union of Finnish Textile Teachers, Rautatielaeisenkatu 6, Helsinki, 00520, Finland. TEL 358-9-1502295, FAX 358-9-7262015. Ed. Kaiju Kangas. adv.: B&W page EUR 450, color page EUR 800; 186 x 260. Circ: 1,500 (controlled).

677 HRV ISSN 0492-5882
CODEN: TEKTA6
TEKSTIL; casopis za tekstilnu tehnologiju i konfekciju/journal of textile and clothing technology. Text in Croatian, English. 1952. m. HRK 600 domestic to institutions; EUR 110 foreign to institutions (effective 2011). adv. 60 p./no. 3 cols./p.; **Document type:** *Journal, Academic/Scholarly.* **Description:** Covers important technical and technological developments in the field of textiles and clothing, featuring production, properties and application of natural and man-made fibres, dystaffs and agents, energy, ecology, and economic and commercial developments relevant to the industry, both locally and worldwide.
Indexed: A&ATA, A20, A22, ASCA, CA, CIN, CTFA, ChemAb, ChemTitl, MSCI, RefZh, SCI, SCOPUS, T01, T02, TM, TTI, W07, WTA.
—BLDSC (8779.000000), CASDDS, IE, Ingenta, INIST.
Published by: Hrvatski Inzenjerski Savez Tekstilaca/Croatian Association of Textile Engineers, Novakova 8/II, pp 829, PO Box 829, Zagreb, 10001, Croatia. TEL 385-1-4818252, FAX 385-1-4818242, hist@zg.t-com.hr. Eds. Agata Vincic, Zvonko Dragcevic. adv.: B&W page EUR 500, color page EUR 850; 205 x 290. Circ: 800.

677 TUR ISSN 1300-9982
TEKSTIL & TEKNIK/INTERNATIONAL TEXTILE MAGAZINE; spinning, weaving, knitting, dyeing, printing, finishing, nonwoven. Text in Turkish; Summaries in Arabic, English, Russian. 1985. m. EUR 100, USD 130 (effective 2009). adv. illus. **Document type:** *Magazine, Trade.* **Description:** Reports on technical and commercial developments affecting the textile industry in Turkey, with special emphasis on exports of textiles.
Published by: Iletisim Magazin Gazetecilik San. ve Tic. A.S., Ihlas Holding Merkez Binasi, 29 Ekim Cad. 23, P.K. 34197, Yenibosna - Istanbul, 34197, Turkey. TEL 90-212-4542520, FAX 90-212-4542555, info@img.com.tr, turkey@ihlas.net.tr, http://www.img.com.tr. Ed. Mehmet Soztutan. Pub. Ferruh Isik. R&P Muhsin Yilmaz. Circ: 15,750.

677 TUR ISSN 1300-3356
TEKSTIL VE KONFEKSIYON DERGISI/JOURNAL OF TEXTILE AND APPAREL. Text in Turkish. 1991. bi-m. EUR 15 (effective 2010). **Document type:** *Journal, Academic/Scholarly.* **Description:** Publishes papers on both fundamental and applied research in various branches of apparel and textile technology and allied areas such as production and properties of natural and synthetic fibres, yarns and fabrics, finising applications, garment technology, analysis, testing and quality control and textile marketing.
Related titles: Online - full text ed.: free (effective 2010).
Indexed: CA, SCI, T01, T02, TTI, W07.
Published by: Textile and Apparel Research & Application Center, Ege University, Bornova - Izmir, 35100, Turkey. TEL 90-232-3742868, FAX 90-232-3887859, cetin.erdogan@tekstilvekonfeksiyon.com, m.cetin.erdogan@ege.edu.tr. Ed. Dr. M Cetin Erdogan.

T U

677 500 SVN ISSN 0351-3386
CODEN: TEKSF8
TEKSTILEC; glasilo Slovenskih tekstilcev. Text mainly in Slovenian; Abstracts in English; Text occasionally in English. 1957. 4/yr. EUR 90 domestic to institutions; EUR 110 foreign to institutions (effective 2011). adv. bk.rev.; Website rev. abstr.; bibl.; charts; illus.; pat.; stat. index. back issues avail.; reprints avail. **Document type:** *Journal, Trade.* **Description:** Publishes original reports on textile development and research; news from all textile, mechanical and chemical technologies; trade in ready-made clothes and design; and information on the Slovenian textile industry.
Related titles: Online - full text ed.
Indexed: CA, CPEI, EngInd, SCOPUS, T01, T02, TM, TTI, WTA.
—BLDSC (8779.050000), CASDDS, IE, Ingenta.
Published by: (Zveza Inzenirjev in Tehnikov Tekstilcev Slovenije/ Association of Slovene Textile Engineers and Technicians, Univerza v Ljubljani, Naravoslovnotehniska Fakulteta, Oddelek za Tekstilstvo/ University of Ljubljana, Faculty of Natural Sciences and Engineering, Department of Textiles), Urednistvo Tekstilec, Snezniska 5, pp 312, Ljubljana, 1000, Slovenia. TEL 386-1-2003200, FAX 386-1-2003270. Ed. Diana G Svetec. Adv. contact Anica Levin. page MRK 900; 170 x 234. Circ: 600 (paid and controlled).

677 659.152 NOR ISSN 0809-2230
TEKSTILFORUM; mote, miljoe, velvaere. Text in Norwegian. 1997. m. NOK 695 domestic; NOK 795 foreign (effective 2002). adv. bk.rev. charts; illus. **Document type:** *Trade.*
Superseded in part (in 1997): Tekstilforum med Parfymeriet (0807-2280); Which was formed by the merger of (1956-1996): Parfymeriet (0803-7167); (1973-1996): Tekstilforum (0332-5520); Which was formerly (until 1973): Manufaktur (0025-259X)
Published by: Norges Tekstilforbund/Norwegian Textile Retailers Association, Sjoelyst Plass 3, Oslo, 0278, Norway. TEL 47-23-00-15-15, FAX 47-23-00-15-16. Ed. Live Nordby. Adv. contact Pia Jensen. B&W page NOK 13,300, color page NOK 18,500; 263 x 185.

677 SRB ISSN 0040-2389
CODEN: TKIDBP
TEKSTILNA INDUSTRIJA/TEXTILE INDUSTRY. Text in Serbo-Croatian. 1953. 6/yr. adv. bk.rev. index. **Document type:** *Journal, Academic/ Scholarly.* **Description:** Covers latest achievements in textile industry, development of new technologies and modern processes in clothing manufacture.
Indexed: ChemAb, SCOPUS, T01, TTI, WTA.
—CASDDS.
Published by: Savez Inzenjera i Tehnicara Tekstilaca Srbije, Kneza Milosa 7, Belgrade, Serbia 11000. TEL 381-11-3230065, FAX 381-11-3230067, sittstekstil@eunet.yu, http://www.sits.org.yu. Ed. Branko Ilic. Circ: 2,600.

677 RUS ISSN 0040-2397
TS1300 CODEN: TTLPA2
TEKSTIL'NAYA PROMYSHLENNOST'. Text in Russian. 1941. bi-m. USD 249 foreign (effective 2005). adv. bk.rev. bibl.; charts; illus.; pat.; tr.lit. **Document type:** *Magazine, Trade.* **Description:** Contains latest textile and sewn goods industry information, advance research into treatment of raw materials and textiles.
Indexed: ABIPC, CIN, CTFA, ChemAb, ChemTitl, RASB, RefZh, T01, TTI, WTA.
—BLDSC (0177.000000), CASDDS, East View, INIST, Linda Hall. **CCC.**
Published by: Informatsionno-izdatel'skaya Firma LEGO, ul Timura Frunze 11, Moscow, 119021, Russian Federation. TEL 7-095-2450615, FAX 7-095-2460157. Ed. I A Dimitrieva. Circ: 11,500. **Dist. by:** East View Information Services, 10601 Wayzata Blvd, Minneapolis, MN 55305. TEL 952-252-1201, 800-477-1005, FAX 952-252-1202, info@eastview.com, http://www.eastview.com.

677 746 BEL ISSN 1375-7814
TEXBEL INTERNATIONAL. Text in Dutch. 1999. 8/yr. EUR 37.50 (effective 2005). adv. **Document type:** *Trade.*
Formed by the merger of (1968-1999): Texbel (Nederlandse Editie) (0770-6995); (1975-1999): Texbel (Edition Francaise) (0770-7045)
Related titles: ◆ French ed.: Texbel (Edition Francaise). ISSN 0770-7045.
Published by: Nielsen Business Publications, Jean Monnetlaan z.n., Vilvoorde, 1804, Belgium. TEL 32-2-6781611, FAX 32-2-6603600, http://www.vnunet.be. Ed. Chris Vermuyten TEL 32-2-678-1603. Adv. contact Annika Lens TEL 32-2-678-1602.

677 NLD ISSN 0040-4772
TEXPRESS; economic and technical weekly for the textile and clothing industry and trade in the Benelux countries. Text in Dutch. 1957. m. EUR 172.50 domestic; EUR 183 in Europe; EUR 225 elsewhere (effective 2010). adv. bk.rev. charts; illus.; mkt.; tr.lit. **Document type:** *Trade.*
Indexed: KES.
Published by: Nedem Business Publications, Postbus 7839, Amsterdam, 1008 AA, Netherlands. TEL 31-20-6449030, FAX 31-20-6449035. Ed. Brigitta van der Lelie. Pub. Hans Huitenga. Adv. contact Patrick Harder. B&W page EUR 1,845, color page EUR 2,310; trim 320 x 240. Circ: 5,000.

677.3 ZAF
TEXREPORT. Text in English. 1952. irreg. USD 16 per issue (effective 2000). back issues avail.; reprints avail. **Document type:** *Report, Academic/Scholarly.* **Description:** Publishes fundamental applied research findings and reports on technology development affecting textiles and clothing.
Formerly (until 1989): S A W T R I Technical Report (0081-2560)
Published by: Council for Scientific and Industrial Research (C S I R), PO Box 395, Pretoria, 0001, South Africa. TEL 27-12-8412911, FAX 27-12-3491153, http://www.csir.co.za. Circ: 250.

338.4 USA ISSN 0092-3540
HD9853
TEXSCOPE: U S A TEXTILE INDUSTRY OVERVIEW. Key Title: Texscope. Text in English. 1974. irreg., latest 1983. stat.
Published by: Werner Management Consultants, Inc., 55 E 52nd St, 29th Fl, New York, NY 10055-0002. TEL 212-730-1280. Ed. Raoul Verret. Circ: (controlled).

677 NLD ISSN 1384-0398
TEXTIELHISTORISCHE BIJDRAGEN. Text in Dutch. 1959. a. EUR 18.50 (effective 2009). bk.rev. **Document type:** *Journal, Academic/ Scholarly.*
Published by: (Stichting Textielgeschiedenis), Uitgeverij Verloren, Torenlaan 25, Hilversum, 1211 JA, Netherlands. TEL 31-35-6859856, FAX 31-35-6836557, info@verloren.nl, http://www.verloren.nl.

677 746.9 NLD ISSN 2210-9781
▼ **TEXTIELLAB YEARBOOK.** Variant title: Yearbook TextielLab. Text in Dutch. 2010. a. EUR 14.95 (effective 2010).
Published by: (TextielLab), Audax Textielmuseum Tilburg, Goirkestraat 96, Tilburg, 5046 GN, Netherlands. TEL 31-13-5367475, FAX 31-13-5363240, info@textielmuseum.nl, http:// www.textielmuseum.nl.

381.456 677 DNK ISSN 0040-4837
TEXTIL. Variant title: Tekstil. Text in Danish. 1935. 10/yr. adv. **Document type:** *Magazine, Trade.*
Incorporates (1955-1971): Klaeder Skaber Folk (0023-2009)
Indexed: SCOPUS.
Published by: (Dansk Textil og Beklaedningsindustri/Federation of Danish Textile and Clothing), Dansk Detail, Svanemoellevej 41, PO Box 34, Hellerup, 2900, Denmark. TEL 45-33-121708, FAX 45-33-931708, mail@dansk-detail.dk, http://www.dansk-detail.dk. Ed. Pia Finne TEL 45-35-824551. Circ: 4,100.

677 VEN
TEXTIL. Text in Spanish. 1976. q.
Published by: Instituto de Capacitacion Textil, Ave. Urdaneta Ibarra a Pilota,, Edificio Karam, Piso 4, 403-406, Apdo 2173, Caracas, DF 1010-A, Venezuela.

677 DEU ISSN 0492-9934
TEXTIL-BEKLEIDUNG. Text in German. 1950. m. **Document type:** *Trade.*
Published by: Gewerkschaft Textile-Bekleidung, Rossstr 94, Duesseldorf, 40476, Germany. TEL 43091, TELEX 584365.

677 ESP
TEXTIL EXPRES NOTICIAS. Text in Spanish. 1983. 20/yr. adv. **Document type:** *Newsletter.* **Description:** Contains economic and professional news in the textile industry. Includes information for the professional and trade personnel in the textile and garment industries.
Published by: Aramo Editorial S.A., Muntaner, 50, Atico 3a, Barcelona, 08011, Spain. TEL 34-93-4537938, aramo@docupress.es, http://www.aramo-editorial.com/. Ed. Humberto Martinez. Circ: 2,000.

677 ESP
TEXTIL EXPRES SUPLEMENTOS. Text in Spanish. 1985. 9/yr. adv. **Document type:** *Trade.*
Published by: Aramo Editorial S.A., Muntaner, 50, Atico 3a, Barcelona, 08011, Spain. TEL 34-93-4537938, aramo@docupress.es, http://www.aramo-editorial.com/. Ed. Humberto Martinez. Circ: 4,500 (controlled).

677 DEU ISSN 0082-3627
DIE TEXTIL-INDUSTRIE UND IHRE HELFER. Text in German. 1957. a. USD 51 (effective 2000). **Document type:** *Directory.*
Related titles: CD-ROM ed.; Online - full text ed.
Published by: Industrieschau-Verlagsgesellschaft mbH, Postfach 100262, Darmstadt, 64202, Germany. TEL 49-6151-3892-0, FAX 49-6151-33164. Ed. Margit Selka. Circ: 3,500. **U.S. subscr. to:** Western Hemisphere Publishing Corp. TEL 503-640-3736, FAX 503-640-2748.

677 DEU ISSN 0342-2224
TEXTIL MITTEILUNGEN; mit dem Wirtschaftsblatt Branche und Business. Text in German. 1946. 20/yr. looseleaf. EUR 191 domestic; EUR 244 in Europe; EUR 322 elsewhere (effective 2009). adv. **Document type:** *Magazine, Trade.*
Published by: Branche und Business Fachverlag, Koenigsallee 70, Duesseldorf, 40212, Germany. TEL 49-211-83030, FAX 49-211-324862. adv.: B&W page EUR 9,100, color page EUR 10,500; trim 232 x 299. Circ: 29,263 (paid and controlled).

677 CHE ISSN 0040-4861
TEXTIL-REVUE. Text in German. 1921. 41/yr. CHF 196 domestic; CHF 241 foreign (effective 2002). adv. illus. **Document type:** *Journal, Trade.*
Incorporates (1921-1965): Schweizerische Textildetaillisten-Zeitung (1421-5381); (1934-1968): Schweizer Textil-Zeitung (1421-539X); Which was formed by the merger of (1932-1934): Allgemeine Textil-Zeitung (1421-542X); Which was formerly (until 1933): Strickerei und Wirkerei (1421-5438); (1921-1934): Schweizer Textil Die Blaue (1421-5446); Which was formerly (until 1929): Schweizer Textil-Journal (1421-5403); (until 1927): Schweizerische Textil-Industrie-Konfektions- und Waesche-Zeitung (1421-5411)
Indexed: KES, RefZh, SCOPUS, WTA.
Published by: St. Galler Tagblatt AG, Fuerstenlandstr 122, St Gallen, 9001, Switzerland. TEL 41-71-2727439, FAX 41-71-2727449. Ed. Sybille Frei. Adv. contact Roselyne Maria Schwarz. Circ: 7,500.

677 DEU ISSN 0040-487X
TEXTIL-WIRTSCHAFT. Text in German. 1946. w. EUR 267 domestic; EUR 346 in Europe; EUR 449 elsewhere (effective 2009). adv. bk.rev. charts; illus.; mkt.; pat.; tr.lit.; tr.mk. index. **Document type:** *Magazine, Trade.*
Related titles: Online - full text ed.
Indexed: B01, B03, CBNB, PROMT, SCOPUS, TM, WTA.
—CCC.
Published by: Deutscher Fachverlag GmbH, Mainzer Landstr 251, Frankfurt Am Main, 60326, Germany. TEL 49-69-75952052, FAX 49-69-75952999, info@dfv.de, http://www.dfv.de. Ed. Juergen Mueller. adv.: page EUR 10,780; trim 230 x 300. Circ: 27,604 (paid and controlled).

TEXTIL ZURNAL. *see* CLOTHING TRADE

677 CAN ISSN 1490-8530
TS1300 CODEN: CTJOA6
TEXTILE/REVUE CANADIENNE DU TEXTILE. Text in English, French. 1883. 6/yr. CAD 38 domestic; USD 45 in United States; USD 55 elsewhere (effective 2008). adv. bk.rev. charts; illus.; tr.lit. index. **Document type:** *Journal, Trade.*
Formerly (until 1993): Canadian Textile Journal (0008-5170); Which incorporated (1928-1984): Textile Manual (0381-551X); Which was formerly (until 1969): Manual of the Textile Industry of Canada (0076-4183)
Indexed: A&ATA, A22, C03, CBCABus, CBPI, CIN, ChemAb, ChemTitl, KES, P48, P52, PQC, SCOPUS, T01, T02, TM, TTI, WTA.
—BLDSC (8802.902000), CASDDS, IE, Ingenta, INIST, Linda Hall. **CCC.**
Published by: Groupe C T T Group, 3000 Boulle, St-Hyacinthe, PQ J2S 1H9, Canada. TEL 450-778-1870, FAX 450-778-9016, rleclerc@ctt.ca. Ed. Roger Leclerc. Adv. contact Lumina Fillion. B&W page CAD 1,860, color page CAD 2,850; trim 206 x 276. Circ: 3,500.

677 GBR ISSN 1475-9756
NK8800
➤ **TEXTILE**; the journal of cloth and culture. Text in English. 2003 (Mar.). 3/yr. USD 331 combined subscription in US & Canada to institutions (print & online eds.); GBP 170 combined subscription elsewhere to institutions (print & online eds.) (effective 2011). adv. bk.rev. back issues avail.; reprint service avail. from PSC. **Document type:** *Journal, Academic/Scholarly.* **Description:** Brings together research in textiles in an innovative and distinctive academic forum, and will be of interest to all those who share a multifaceted view of textiles within an expanded field.
Related titles: Online - full text ed.: ISSN 1751-8350. 2003. USD 282 in US & Canada to institutions; GBP 144 elsewhere to institutions (effective 2011) (from IngentaConnect).
Indexed: A01, A02, A03, A07, A08, A20, A26, A30, A31, AA, ABM, AICP, ArtHuCI, ArtInd, B04, BRD, BrHumI, CA, CurCont, D05, I05, IBR, IBSS, IBZ, SCOPUS, SociolAb, T01, T02, TTI, W03, W05, W07, WTA.
—BLDSC (8801.395000), IE, Ingenta. **CCC.**
Published by: Berg Publishers (Subsidiary of: Oxford International Publishers Ltd.), 1st Fl Angel Ct, 81 St Clements St, Oxford, Berks OX4 1AW, United Kingdom. TEL 44-1865-245104, FAX 44-1865-791165, enquiry@bergpublishers.com. Eds. Catherine Harper, Doran Ross. Pub. Ms. Kathryn Earle. **Subscr. addr.:** Turpin Distribution Services Ltd., Pegasus Dr, Stratton Business Park, Biggleswade, Bedfordshire SG18 8QB, United Kingdom. TEL 44-1767-604800, FAX 44-1767-601640, custserv@turpin-distribution.com, http:// www.turpin-distribution.com/.

677 667 USA ISSN 0894-8267
TEXTILE ANALYSIS BULLETIN SERVICE. Text in English. irreg. **Document type:** *Bulletin, Consumer.* **Description:** Technical information on problem garments, cleaning process and technology.
Related titles: ◆ Supplement to: Fabricare. ISSN 1084-6778.
Indexed: T01, TTI.
Published by: International Fabricare Institute, 14700 Sweitzer Ln, Laurel, MD 20707. TEL 301-622-1900, 800-638-2627, FAX 240-295-0685, communications@ifi.org, http://www.ifi.org.

677 HKG ISSN 0049-3554
TS1399 CODEN: TASIDM
TEXTILE ASIA; The Asian Textile & Apparel Monthly. Text in Chinese. 1970. m. HKD 506 in Hong Kong; HKD 639 China & Macau; USD 121 in Asia except Japan; USD 133 elsewhere (effective 2005). bk.rev. charts; illus.; stat. Index. back issues avail. **Document type:** *Magazine, Trade.* **Description:** Covers news and comment on the current state of cotton, wool, silk and manmade fibre textile trade and industry, including finishing and garments, throughout Asia.
Indexed: A22, CTFA, HongKongiana, Inspec, SCOPUS, T01, T02, TM, TTI, WTA.
—BLDSC (8801.730000), CASDDS, Ingenta.
Published by: Business Press Ltd., 11/F, California Tower, 30-32 D'Aguilar St., GPO Box 185, Hong Kong, Hong Kong. TEL 852-25233744, FAX 852-28106966. Circ: 17,000.

677 IND ISSN 0368-4636
TS1300 CODEN: JTXAA9
TEXTILE ASSOCIATION (INDIA). JOURNAL. Text in English. 1940. bi-m. bk.rev. **Document type:** *Journal, Academic/Scholarly.*
Formerly (until 1972): Textile Digest (0970-4108)
Indexed: CA, CTFA, ChemAb, ISA, SCOPUS, T01, T02, TM, TTI, WTA.
—CASDDS.
Published by: Textile Association (India), Amar Villa, Behind Villa Diana, Flat No 3, 3rd Fl, 86 College Ln, Off Gokhale Rd, Near Portuguese Church / Maher Hall, Dadar (W), Mumbai, Maharashtra 400 028, India. TEL 91-22-24328044, FAX 91-22-24307708, taimu@mtnl.net.in, http://www.textileassociationindia.com/.

677 570.285 HKG ISSN 1942-3438
TA164
➤ **TEXTILE BIOENGINEERING AND INFORMATICS SYMPOSIUM PROCEEDINGS.** Text in English. 2008. a. USD 250 (effective 2011 & 2012). **Document type:** *Proceedings, Academic/Scholarly.*
Related titles: CD-ROM ed.: USD 100 per issue (effective 2011 & 2012).
Published by: Textile Bioengineering and Informatics Society Limited, c/o Institute of Textiles & Clothing, The Hong Kong Polytechnic University, Hung Hom, Kowloon, Hong Kong. TEL 852-2766-4206, FAX 852-2764-5489, admin@tbisociety.org, http://www.tbisociety.org. Ed. Yi Li. Circ: 1,000. **Co-publisher:** Binary Information Press.

677 700 AUS ISSN 0818-6308
TT1
TEXTILE FIBRE FORUM; the fibre magazine of the Australian region. Text in English. 1981. q. looseleaf. AUD 38.50 domestic; NZD 52 in New Zealand; USD 40 in United States; GBP 20 in Europe (effective 2008). adv. bk.rev. Index. 56 p./no.; back issues avail. **Document type:** *Magazine, Trade.* **Description:** Covers all aspects of contemporary textile arts and crafts.
Formerly (until 1986): Fibre Forum (0725-9565)
Indexed: A07, A30, A31, AA, ABM, ArtInd, B04, D05, SCOPUS.
—Ingenta.
Published by: Australian Forum for Textile Arts, Ltd., PO Box 38, The Gap, QLD 4061, Australia. TEL 61-7-33006491, FAX 61-7-33002148. Ed., R&P, Adv. contact Janet De Boer. color page AUD 1,235, B&W page AUD 880. Circ: 7,500.

677 DEU ISSN 1431-3510
TEXTILE FORUM (DEUTSCHE AUSGABE). Text in German. 1982. q. EUR 46; EUR 11 newsstand/cover (effective 2006). adv. bk.rev. **Document type:** *Magazine, Trade.* **Description:** Contains information on important international events and developments occurring in the field of textile culture.
Former titles (until 1994): Textilforum (0937-9797); (until 1990): Deutsches Textilforum (0722-1258)
Related titles: English ed.: Textile forum (English edition). ISSN 1431-3529.
Indexed: IBR, IBZ, RASB, SCOPUS, TM, WTA.
Published by: (European Textile Network), Textil-Forum-Service, Friedenstr 5, Hannover, 30175, Germany. TEL 49-511-817006, FAX 49-511-813108, tfs@etn-net.org. Ed. Dietmar Laue. Pub., R&P, Adv. contact Beatrijs Sterk. B&W page EUR 1,270, color page EUR 1,885; trim 184 x 272. Circ: 5,500 (paid and controlled).

677 GBR ISSN 0040-4969
HD9850.1

➤ **TEXTILE HISTORY.** Text in English. 1968. s-a. GBP 134 combined subscription to institutions (print & online eds.); USD 255 combined subscription in United States to institutions (print & online eds.) (effective 2012). adv. bk.rev. bibl.; charts; illus.; stat. index. back issues avail.; reprint service avail. from PSC. **Document type:** *Journal, Academic/Scholarly.* **Description:** Covers a wide cross-section of books from all parts of the world, dealing with any aspect of textile and clothing history.
Related titles: Online - full text ed.: ISSN 1743-2952. GBP 123 to institutions; USD 218 in United States to institutions (effective 2012) (from IngentaConnect).
Indexed: A&ATA, A01, A02, A03, A07, A08, A20, A22, A30, A31, AA, ABM, AIAP, AICP, AmH&L, AmHI, ArtHuCI, ArtInd, B04, B24, BAS, BrArAb, BrHumI, CA, CurCont, D05, DIP, FR, H05, H07, HistAb, I14, IBR, IBZ, MLA-IB, NumL, P30, PCI, SCOPUS, T01, T02, TTI, W07, WTA.
—BLDSC (8801.990000), IE, Infotrieve, Ingenta, INIST. **CCC.**
Published by: (Pasold Research Fund), Maney Publishing, Ste 1C, Joseph's Well, Hanover Walk, Leeds, W Yorks LS3 1AB, United Kingdom. TEL 44-113-2432800, FAX 44-113-3868178, maney@maney.co.uk. Eds. Dr. Katrina Honeyman, Mary M Brooks. **Subscr. in N. America to:** Maney Publishing, 875 Massachusetts Ave, 7th Fl, Cambridge, MA 02139. TEL 866-297-5154, FAX 617-354-6875, maney@maneyusa.com.

677 660 GBR ISSN 1353-6184
HD9850.1

TEXTILE HORIZONS; providing essential reading for all present and future decision makers in textiles and fashion worldwide. Text in English. 1963. bi-m. GBP 235 (effective 2009). adv. bk.rev. bibl.; charts; illus.; stat. index. **Document type:** *Magazine, Trade.* **Description:** Caters to the professional needs of persons concerned with the management, economics, design, research, and production aspects of the textiles industry.
Former titles (until 1994): Textile Horizons International (1351-0266); (until 1992): Textile Horizons (0260-6518); (until 1981): Textile Institute and Industry (0039-8357); (until 1963): Journal of the Textile Institute. Proceedings (0368-4482); (until 1956): Journal of the Textile Institute. Proceedings and Abstracts (0368-4504)
Indexed: A&ATA, ABIPC, ApMecR, ChemAb, EngInd, Inspec, RefZh, SCOPUS, T01, T02, TM, TTI, WTA.
—BLDSC (8801.992000), IE, Ingenta, INIST, Linda Hall. **CCC.**
Published by: (Textile Institute), World Textile Publications Ltd., Perkin House, 1 Longlands St, Bradford, W Yorks BD1 2TP, United Kingdom. TEL 44-1274-378800, FAX 44-1274-378811, info@world-textile.net, http://www.world-textile.net/. Ed. Andrew Thornton TEL 44-1274-378839. Adv. contact James Wilson TEL 44-1274-378800.

677 ZAF

TEXTILE INDUSTRIES BUYERS GUIDE FOR SOUTHERN AFRICA. Text in English. 1985. a. ZAR 100. **Document type:** *Directory.* **Description:** Guide for buyers of textiles, yarns, textile machinery, and consumables.
Published by: George Warman Publications (Pty.) Ltd., Rondebosch, PO Box 705, Cape Town, 7701, South Africa. info@gwarmanpublications.co.za, http://www.gwarmanpublications.co.za. Ed. Karen Kuehlcke.

677 ZAF ISSN 0254-0533
CODEN: TIDADD

TEXTILE INDUSTRIES DYEGEST SOUTHERN AFRICA. Text in English. 1982. m. ZAR 98.04; ZAR 124 in Africa; ZAR 140 elsewhere. adv. **Document type:** *Journal, Trade.* **Description:** Technical journal of spinning, weaving, knitting and yarn preparation, dyeing and textile finishing.
Formed by the merger of (1972-1981): Dyers Dyegest (0250-0019); (1978-1981): Textile Industries Southern Africa (1013-8587)
Indexed: ISAP, SCOPUS, T01, TTI, WTA.
—CASDDS.
Published by: (Textile Institute - South Africa), George Warman Publications (Pty.) Ltd., Rondebosch, PO Box 705, Cape Town, 7701, South Africa. info@gwarmanpublications.co.za, http://www.gwarmanpublications.co.za. Ed. Karen Kuelcke. Circ: 1,300.

677 IND ISSN 0040-4993
TS1300

TEXTILE INDUSTRY & TRADE JOURNAL. Text in English. 1962. bi-m. USD 75 (effective 2011). bk.rev. bibl.; illus. **Document type:** *Journal, Trade.*
Indexed: A&ATA, CTFA, T01, TTI.
Published by: Synthetic and Art Silk Mills' Research Association (S A S M I R A), Sasmira Marg, Worli, Mumbai, Maharashtra 4000030, India. TEL 91-22-24935351, FAX 91-22-24930225, sasmira@vsnl.com, http://www.sasmira.org/.

677 USA

TEXTILE INSIGHT; trends and analysis on textile design and innovation. Text in English. 2005. bi-m. USD 24 domestic; USD 54 foreign (effective 2011). adv. back issues avail. **Document type:** *Magazine, Trade.* **Description:** Provides trends, insight and analysis on textile design, innovations and its exciting product applications.
Related titles: Online - full text ed.
Published by: Formula4 Media, LLC, PO Box 231318, Great Neck, NY 11023. TEL 518-305-4710, FAX 518-305-4712, http://www.formula4media.com. Pub. Jeff Nott TEL 516-305-4711.

677 GBR ISSN 0040-5000
TS1300 CODEN: JTINA7

➤ **TEXTILE INSTITUTE. JOURNAL.** Text in English. 1910. 8/yr. GBP 672 combined subscription in United Kingdom to institutions (print & online eds.); EUR 1,020, USD 1,278 combined subscription to institutions (print & online eds.) (effective 2012). adv. abstr.; bibl.; illus. index, cum.index. back issues avail.; reprint service avail. from PSC. **Document type:** *Journal, Academic/Scholarly.* **Description:** Publishes papers for textile institute in science, engineering, economics, management and design related to the textile industry and the use of fibres in consumer and engineering applications.
Supersedes in part (in 1981): Textile Institute and Industry (0039-8357); Which was formerly (until 1965): Textile Institute. Journal. Proceedings (0368-4482); (until 1956): Textile Institute. Journal. Proceedings and Abstracts (0368-4504)
Related titles: Online - full text ed.: ISSN 1754-2340. GBP 605 in United Kingdom to institutions; EUR 918, USD 1,150 to institutions (effective 2012) (from IngentaConnect).
Indexed: A&ATA, A20, A22, A23, A24, ABIPC, ASCA, ApMecR, B13, C&ISA, CA, CIN, CLL, CMCI, CPEI, ChemAb, ChemTitl, E&CAJ, E01, ISR, Inspec, MSCI, P&BA, P52, SCI, SCOPUS, SolStAb, T01, T02, TM, TTI, W07, WTA.
—BLDSC (4908.000000), CASDDS, IE, Ingenta, INIST, Linda Hall. **CCC.**
Published by: (Textile Institute), Routledge (Subsidiary of: Taylor & Francis Group), 4 Park Sq, Milton Park, Abingdon, Oxon OX14 4RN, United Kingdom. TEL 44-20-70176000, FAX 44-20-70176336, subscriptions@tandf.co.uk, http://www.routledge.com. Ed. David R Buchanan. Adv. contact Linda Hann TEL 44-1344-779945. **Subscr. to:** Taylor & Francis Ltd., Journals Customer Service, Sheepen Pl, Colchester, Essex CO3 3LP, United Kingdom. TEL 44-20-70175544, FAX 44-20-70175198, tf.enquiries@tfinforma.com.

677 GBR

TEXTILE INSTITUTE. WORLD CONFERENCE. Text in English. 19??. a. bibl.; charts; illus.; stat. **Document type:** *Proceedings.* **Description:** Covers papers and posters presented at the conference.
Formerly: Textile Institute. Annual Conference
Related titles: CD-ROM ed.: GBP 60, USD 99 per issue (effective 2009).
Published by: Textile Institute, 1st Fl, St James Bldg, Oxford St, Manchester, Lancs M1 6FQ, United Kingdom. TEL 44-161-2371188, FAX 44-161-2361991, tiihq@textileinst.org.uk, http://www.texi.org.

677 USA

TEXTILE LABOUR COST COMPARISON - INTERNATIONAL. Text in English. 1950. a. stat. **Document type:** *Bulletin.* **Description:** Covers the annual textile industry spinning and weaving labor costs. Includes international comparisons of hourly wages, shift premiums, holidays, and social changes.
Published by: Werner International, 53 E 52nd St, 29th Fl, New York, NY 10055-0002. TEL 212-909-1260, FAX 212-909-1273. Ed. Richard Downing.

677 CHE ISSN 1016-7536

TEXTILE LEADER. Key Title: I T S Textile Leader. Text in English. 3/yr. **Document type:** *Magazine, Trade.* **Description:** Covers management in the global textile mill industry and textile machinery manufacturing.
Indexed: SCOPUS, T01, TTI, WTA.
Published by: I T S Publishing, International Textile Service, Kesslerstr 9, Schlieren, 8952, Switzerland. TEL 41-1-7384800, FAX 41-1-7384832. Ed. Eugene Dempsey. Pub. Rosmarie Keller. Adv. contact Peter Frei. Circ: 33,000.

677 IND ISSN 0040-5078

TEXTILE MAGAZINE. Text in English. 1959. m. INR 400 domestic; USD 100 foreign (effective 2011). bk.rev. **Document type:** *Magazine, Trade.*
Indexed: KES, SCOPUS, T01, T02, TTI, WTA.
—BLDSC (8803.790100), IE, Ingenta.
Published by: (Textile Mills and Manufacturing Association), Gopali & Co., Quanta Zen Bldg, No.38, (Old No.2), Thomas Rd, 2nd St, Off. S Boag Rd, T.Nagar, Chennai, 600 017, India. TEL 91-44-42024951, FAX 91-44-24332413.

677 GBR ISSN 2040-5162
TS1300 CODEN: TXMOAW

TEXTILE MONTH INTERNATIONAL. Text in English. 1968. bi-m. GBP 299 (effective 2009). adv. bk.rev. illus.; mkt.; tr.lit. index. **Document type:** *Magazine, Trade.* **Description:** Contains comprehensive news coverage, features and analysis on all aspects of international textile manufacturing.
Formerly (until 2009): Textile Month (0040-5116); Which was formed by the merger of (1883-1967): Textile Recorder (0372-1094); (1962-1967): Skinner's Record of the Manmade Fibres Industry (0371-2648); Which was formerly: Skinner's Silk and Rayon Record (0371-313X); (until 1950): Silk and Rayon (0371-0386); (until 1933): Rayon Record (0370-7008); (1928-1929): Artificial Silk World (0365-6349); and (1955-1967): Man-Made Textiles (0369-0989); Which was formerly (1948-1955): British Rayon & Silk Journal (0366-2993); Silk Journal and Rayon World (0371-0483); (1924-1928): Silk Journal (0371-0262)
Related titles: Online - full text ed.
Indexed: A&ATA, A22, B02, B03, B15, B17, B18, C&ISA, CTFA, ChemAb, E&CAJ, EngInd, G04, G08, I05, Inspec, KES, RefZh, SCOPUS, SolStAb, T01, T02, TM, TTI, WTA.
—BLDSC (8805.050000), CASDDS, IE, Infotrieve, Ingenta, Linda Hall. **CCC.**
Published by: World Textile Publications Ltd., Perkin House, 1 Longlands St, Bradford, W Yorks BD1 2TP, United Kingdom. TEL 44-1274-378800, FAX 44-1274-378811, info@world-textile.net, http://www.world-textile.net/. Ed. Adrian Wilson. Adv. contact James Wilson TEL 44-1274-378800. Circ: 10,000.

THE TEXTILE MUSEUM MEMBERS' MAGAZINE. *see* MUSEUMS AND ART GALLERIES

677 DEU ISSN 1612-5096

TEXTILE NETWORK; Das Magazin fuer die Herstellung textiler Produkte. Text in English, German. 2004. bi-m. EUR 128 domestic; EUR 149 foreign (effective 2011). adv. **Document type:** *Magazine, Trade.*
Formed by the merger of (1996-2004): TexDecor (1430-7774); (1995-2004): Maschen-Industrie (0946-7718); Which was formerly (1951-1995): Wirkerei- und Strickerei-Technik (0043-6097); (1995-2004): Knitting Technology (0947-0972); Which was formerly (1985-1995): Knitting Technique (0177-4875); (1979-1985): W S T Knitting Technic (0173-4415)
Indexed: RefZh, SCOPUS, T01, T02, TTI, WTA.
—INIST. **CCC.**
Published by: Meisenbach GmbH, Franz-Ludwig-Str 7a, Bamberg, 96047, Germany. TEL 49-951-8610, FAX 49-951-861158, info@meisenbach.de, http://www.meisenbach.de. Ed. Iris Schlomski. Adv. contact Matthias Fichtel. Circ: 2,571 (paid and controlled).

677 GBR ISSN 0268-4764
HD9850.1 CODEN: TOINEI

TEXTILE OUTLOOK INTERNATIONAL. Text in English. 1985. bi-m. USD 2,000; USD 3,000 combined subscription to individuals (print & online eds.); USD 18,000 combined subscription to institutions (print & online eds.); USD 500 per issue; USD 750 combined subscription per issue to individuals (print & online eds.); USD 4,500 combined subscription per issue to institutions (print & online eds.) (effective 2009). back issues avail. **Document type:** *Journal, Trade.* **Description:** Aimed at senior textile executives, provides industry and market analysis and company profiles. Forecasts trends and developments.
Related titles: E-mail ed.; Online - full text ed.
Indexed: A09, A10, A22, B02, B15, B17, B18, G04, G08, I05, SCOPUS, T01, T02, TM, TTI, V03, V04, WTA.
—BLDSC (8805.605000), IE, Ingenta. **CCC.**
Published by: Textiles Intelligence Ltd., Alderley House, Alderley Rd, Wilmslow, SK9 1AT, United Kingdom. TEL 44-1625-536136, FAX 44-1625-536137, info@textilesintelligence.com.

677 GBR ISSN 0040-5167
TS1300 CODEN: TXPRAM

TEXTILE PROGRESS. Text in English. 1969. q. GBP 244 combined subscription in United Kingdom to institutions (print & online eds.); EUR 370, USD 464 combined subscription to institutions (print & online eds.) (effective 2012). adv. bibl.; charts; illus. index. back issues avail.; reprint service avail. from PSC. **Document type:** *Journal, Trade.* **Description:** Series of monographs, each devoted to a particular subject, examines the origination and application of developments in the international fibre, textile and apparel industry in a critical and comprehensive manner.
Related titles: Online - full text ed.: ISSN 1754-2278. GBP 219 in United Kingdom to institutions; EUR 333, USD 417 to institutions (effective 2012).
Indexed: A22, ABIPC, CA, ChemAb, E01, EngInd, Inspec, P52, SCOPUS, T01, T02, TTI, WTA.
—BLDSC (8805.700000), IE, Infotrieve, Ingenta, INIST, Linda Hall. **CCC.**
Published by: (Textile Institute), Routledge (Subsidiary of: Taylor & Francis Group), 4 Park Sq, Milton Park, Abingdon, Oxon OX14 4RN, United Kingdom. TEL 44-20-70176000, FAX 44-20-70176336, subscriptions@tandf.co.uk, http://www.routledge.com. Ed. Xiaoming Tao. Adv. contact Linda Hann TEL 44-1344-779945. **Subscr. to:** Taylor & Francis Ltd., Journals Customer Service, Sheepen Pl, Colchester, Essex CO3 3LP, United Kingdom. TEL 44-20-70175544, FAX 44-20-70175198.

TEXTILE RENTAL. *see* CLOTHING TRADE

677 GBR ISSN 0040-5175
TS1300 CODEN: TRJOA9

➤ **TEXTILE RESEARCH JOURNAL.** Abbreviated title: T R J. Text in English. 1930. 20/yr. USD 2,132, GBP 1,254 combined subscription to institutions (print & online eds.); USD 2,089, GBP 1,229 to institutions (effective 2011). adv. bk.rev. bibl.; charts; illus.; abstr. index. 100 p./no.; back issues avail.; reprint service avail. from PSC. **Document type:** *Journal, Academic/Scholarly.* **Description:** Devoted to disseminating fundamental and applied scientific information in the physical, chemical, and engineering sciences related to the textiles and allied industries.
Former titles (until 1945): Textile Research (0096-5928); (until 1932): United States. Institute for Textile Research. Bulletin (0096-7882)
Related titles: Microform ed.: (from PQC); Online - full text ed.: ISSN 1746-7748. USD 1,919, GBP 1,129 to institutions (effective 2011).
Indexed: A&ATA, A05, A20, A22, A23, A24, A26, ABIPC, AS&TA, AS&TI, ASCA, Agr, ApMecR, B04, B13, BRD, BibAg, C&ISA, C10, C33, CA, CIN, CMCI, CPEI, CTFA, ChemAb, ChemTitl, CurCont, E&CAJ, E01, EngInd, IBR, IBZ, ISMEC, ISR, Inspec, MSCI, P&BA, P06, P11, P26, P31, P48, P52, P54, P56, PQC, PROMT, S04, SCI, SCOPUS, SolStAb, T01, T02, TM, TTI, W03, W05, W07, WTA.
—BLDSC (8809.000000), CASDDS, IE, Infotrieve, Ingenta, INIST, Linda Hall. **CCC.**
Published by: (TRI/Princeton USA), Sage Publications Ltd. (Subsidiary of: Sage Publications, Inc.), 1 Oliver's Yard, 55 City Rd, London, EC1Y 1SP, United Kingdom. TEL 44-20-73248500, FAX 44-20-73248600, info@sagepub.co.uk, http://www.uk.sagepub.com/home.nav. Ed. Dong Zhang. adv.: B&W page GBP 450; 180 x 265. **Subscr. to:** Sage Publications, Inc., 2455 Teller Rd, Thousand Oaks, CA 91320. TEL 805-499-9774, FAX 805-499-0871, journals@sagepub.com.

677 NLD ISSN 0920-4083
CODEN: TSTEE6

➤ **TEXTILE SCIENCE AND TECHNOLOGY.** Text in English. 1975. irreg., latest vol.13, 2002. price varies. **Document type:** *Monographic series, Academic/Scholarly.* **Description:** Reports on developments and research in the textile sciences.
Related titles: Online - full text ed.
Indexed: CIN, ChemAb, ChemTitl, SCOPUS.
—CASDDS. **CCC.**
Published by: Elsevier BV (Subsidiary of: Elsevier Science & Technology), Radarweg 29, PO Box 211, Amsterdam, 1000 AE, Netherlands. TEL 31-20-4853911, FAX 31-20-4852457, JournalsCustomerServiceEMEA@elsevier.com, http://www.elsevier.nl.

677 IND ISSN 0040-5205

➤ **TEXTILE TRENDS.** Text in English. 1958. m. INR 300 (effective 2011). bk.rev. charts; illus.; mkt.; pat.; tr.lit.; tr.mk. 2 cols./p.; **Document type:** *Magazine, Trade.* **Description:** Addresses loyal readers who are either the decision makers or influencers in the spinning industry.
Indexed: A&ATA, SCOPUS, T01, T02, TM, TTI, WTA.
Published by: Eastland Publications (Pvt.) Ltd., 44 Chittaranjan Ave, Kolkata, West Bengal 700 012, India. TEL 91-33-22122233, text_223308@bsnl.in.

677 NLD ISSN 1384-5306

TEXTILE VIEW. Text in English. 1988. 4/yr. EUR 201.87 in Europe; EUR 290 elsewhere (effective 2009). **Document type:** *Magazine, Trade.*
Indexed: SCOPUS, WTA.
—IE.
Published by: Metropolitan Publishing BV, Saxen Weimarlaan 6, Amsterdam, 1075 CA, Netherlands. TEL 31-20-6177624, FAX 31-20-6179357, office@view-publications.com, http://www.view-publications.com. Pub. David R Shah.

677 USA ISSN 0040-5213
CODEN: TEWOAH

TEXTILE WORLD. Text in English. 1915. m. free domestic; USD 95 foreign (effective 2009). adv. bk.rev. charts; illus.; tr.lit. back issues avail.; reprints avail. **Document type:** *Magazine, Trade.* **Description:** For executives, specialists and managers. Covers yarn manufacturing, knitting, weaving, nonwovens, dyeing, chemical treatment, and fibers.
Incorporates (2001-2001): Textile Industries (1542-054X); Which was formerly (until 2001): America's Textiles International (0890-9970); (until 1986): America's Textile (0737-0040); Which was formed by the merger of (19??-1983): America's Textiles. Knitter - Apparel (0194-4428); (1971-1983): America's Textiles. Reporter - Bulletin (0095-8921); Which was formed by the merger of (1908-1971):

America's Textile Reporter (0003-1607); (1933-1971): Textile Bulletin (0040-4896); Which was formerly (1911- 1933): Southern Textile Bulletin (0099-3735); Incorporated: Fiber World (0748-0733); (1973-1984): Fiber Producer (0361-4921); Which superseded: Fiber Producer Buyer's Guide (0091-6617); (1947-1984): Textile Industries (0040-4985); Former titles (until 1931): Textile Advance News; (until 1924): Textiles; (until 1923): Posselt's Textile Journal (0096-8358); (until 1921): Textile World Journal (0096-5936); Which was formed by the merger of (1903-1915): Textile World Record (0096-5944); (1894-1915): Textile Manufacturers Journal (0096-5766)
Related titles: Microform ed.: (from PMC, PQC); Online - full text ed.; Ed.: Textile World Latina; Supplement(s): Textile World - Textile Maintenance & Engineering; Textile World - Carpet & Rug.
Indexed: A05, A10, A12, A13, A14, A15, A17, A22, A23, A24, ABIn, AS&ATA, AS&TI, ASCA, B01, B02, B03, B04, B06, B07, B08, B09, B13, B15, B17, B18, BPI, BRD, BusI, C10, C12, CIN, CISA, CTFA, ChemAb, ChemTitl, EngInd, G04, G06, G07, G08, I05, Inspec, M01, M02, P06, P26, P34, P48, P51, P52, P53, P54, PQC, R18, SCOPUS, SRI, T&II, T01, T02, TM, TTI, V03, W01, W02, W03, W05, WTA.
—CASDDS, IE, Infotrieve, Ingenta, Linda Hall. **CCC.**
Published by: Billian Publishing, Inc., 2100 Powers Ferry Rd, Ste 300, Atlanta, GA 30339. TEL 770-955-5656, FAX 770-952-0669, info@billian.com, http://www.billian.com. Ed. Jim Borneman. adv.: B&W page USD 5,555, color page USD 7,625. Circ: 32,340 (paid and controlled).

677 USA ISSN 1546-4598
HD9866.A1
TEXTILE WORLD ASIA/YAZHOU FANGZHI SHIJIE. Text in Chinese. 2003. q. free in Asia to qualified personnel. **Document type:** *Magazine, Trade.*
Published by: Billian Publishing, Inc., 2100 Powers Ferry Rd, Ste 300, Atlanta, GA 30339. TEL 770-955-5656, FAX 770-952-0669, info@billian.com, http://www.billian.com.

677 GBR ISSN 1367-1308
TS1300 CODEN: TEXSBZ
TEXTILES MAGAZINE. Text in English. 1965. q. GBP 50, USD 82.50 to non-members; free to members (effective 2009). adv. bk.rev. charts; illus. index. reprints avail. **Document type:** *Magazine, Trade.* **Description:** Aims to provide topical material that updates the standard texts, opens-up new subjects and perspectives, and contributes to professional development.
Former titles (until 1994): Textiles (0306-0748); (until 1972): Shirley Link (0037-3974)
Indexed: A&ATA, A22, ABIPC, CTFA, EngInd, SCOPUS, T01, T02, TM, TTI, WTA.
—BLDSC (8813.737000), IE, Infotrieve, Ingenta, Linda Hall. **CCC.**
Published by: Textile Institute, 1st Fl, St James Bldg, Oxford St, Manchester, Lancs M1 6FQ, United Kingdom. TEL 44-161-2371188, FAX 44-161-2361991, tiihq@textileinst.org.uk. Ed. Vanessa Knowles TEL 44-1942-886402. Adv. contact Emma Scott. color page USD 3,500, B&W page USD 2,200; trim 210 x 297.

677 USA ISSN 0049-3570
TS1300
TEXTILES PANAMERICANOS; revista para la industria textil. Text in Spanish, English. 1941. bi-m. USD 50 domestic; USD 80 in Canada; USD 125 elsewhere; free to qualified personnel (effective 2009). adv. bk.rev. charts; illus.; stat.; tr.lit. back issues avail.; reprints avail. **Document type:** *Magazine, Trade.* **Description:** For the textile and apparel industry; offers current information on new technology, manufacturing processes, and modern management methods as well as Latin American and worldwide news.
Related titles: Online - full text ed.
Indexed: A&ATA, A01, A22, F03, F04, SCOPUS, T01, T02, TTI, WTA.
—Infotrieve.
Published by: Billian Publishing, Inc., 2100 Powers Ferry Rd, Ste 300, Atlanta, GA 30339. TEL 770-955-5656, FAX 770-952-0669, info@billian.com, http://www.billian.com. Ed. German Garcia. Pub. Jim Borneman. Adv. contact Marcella Nacmias. Circ: 15,000 (controlled).

677 ESP ISSN 0211-7975
TEXTILES PARA EL HOGAR. Text in Spanish. 1967. 6/yr. EUR 76; EUR 95 combined subscription print & online eds. (effective 2010). adv. illus. **Document type:** *Magazine, Trade.*
Related titles: Online - full text ed.: EUR 38 (effective 2010).
Published by: Publica S.A., Calle Ecuador 75, Barcelona, 08029, Spain. TEL 34-933-215045, FAX 34-933-221972, publica@publica.es, http://www.publica.es. Circ: 4,000.

677 GBR ISSN 1743-3231
TEXTILES SOUTH EAST ASIA. Text in English. 2004. m. GBP 345 (effective 2009). back issues avail. **Document type:** *Newsletter, Trade.* **Description:** Provides hard-to-find commercial news, information and business opportunities of the textile and clothing industries in the emerging markets of Southeast Asia.
Indexed: SCOPUS, WTA.
Published by: Textile Media Services Ltd., 2A Bridge St, Silsden, Keighley, BD20 9NB, United Kingdom. TEL 44-1535-656489, FAX 44-8700-940868, info@textilemedia.com. Ed. Geoff Fisher. Pub. Judy Holland.

677 GBR ISSN 1477-6294
➤ **TEXTILES THAT CHANGED THE WORLD.** Text in English. 2006. irreg., latest 2009. price varies. back issues avail. **Document type:** *Monographic series, Academic/Scholarly.* **Description:** Chronicles the cultural life of individual textiles through sustained, book-length examinations.
Published by: Berg Publishers (Subsidiary of: Oxford International Publishers Ltd.), 1st Fl Angel Ct, 81 St Clements St, Oxford, Berks OX4 1AW, United Kingdom. TEL 44-1865-245104, FAX 44-1865-791165, enquiry@bergpublishers.com. Eds. Linda Welters, Ruth Barnes.

677 NLD ISSN 0040-5264
TEXTILIA. Text in Dutch. 1921. 41/yr. EUR 119; EUR 59.50 to students (effective 2010). adv. bk.rev. abstr.; bibl.; charts; illus.; mkt.; pat.; stat.; tr.lit. **Document type:** *Trade.* **Description:** Trade publication for the business in textiles, fashions, and home textiles. Features trade news and information, fashion news and trends, and international news. Includes list of events, positions available.
Incorporates (in 1999): Mode Nieuws (1381-9321)
Indexed: KES.
—**CCC.**
Published by: MYbusinessmedia b.v., Joan Muyskensweg 22, Amsterdam, 1096 CJ, Netherlands. TEL 31-20-4602200, FAX 31-20-4602244, info@mybusinessmedia.nl, http://www.mybusinessmedia.nl. Ed. Rosanne Loffeld. Pub. Hein Bronk. adv.: page EUR 5,080; trim 202 x 268. Circ: 24,000.

677 DEU ISSN 0934-3342
TEXTILKUNST INTERNATIONAL. Text in German. 1973. 4/yr. EUR 46; EUR 12.50 per issue (effective 2011). adv. bk.rev. illus. **Document type:** *Magazine, Trade.*
Formerly (until 1986): Textilkinst (0341-5724)
Indexed: A&ATA, DIP, IBR, IBZ, SCOPUS, T01, TM, TTI, WTA.
—**CCC.**
Published by: PresseDienstleistungsGesellschaft, Borsigstr 5, Alfeld, 31061, Germany. TEL 49-5181-800921, FAX 49-5181-800933, info@p-d-g.de. adv.: B&W page EUR 1,212, color page EUR 1,932. Circ: 5,200 (paid).

677 CHE ISSN 0040-5310
TS1510 CODEN: TXLVAE
TEXTILVEREDLUNG. Text in German. 1965. 6/yr. CHF 90 domestic; CHF 107 foreign (effective 2004). adv. bk.rev. **Document type:** *Journal, Trade.*
Formed by merger of (1946-1965): S V F Fachorgan Textilveredlung (0371-4292); (1946-1965): Textil-Rundschau (0371-6465)
Indexed: A22, ABIPC, CIN, ChemAb, ChemTitl, EngInd, RefZh, SCOPUS, T01, TM, TTI, WTA.
—BLDSC (8813.762000), CASDDS, IE, Infotrieve, Ingenta, INIST, Linda Hall.
Published by: Schweizerische Vereinigung Textil und Chemie, Kesslerstr 9, Schlieren, 8952, Switzerland. TEL 41-1-7384828, FAX 41-1-7384829, texver@swissonline.ch. Ed. Juergen Lamsfuss. Adv. contact Rene Iseli. B&W page CHF 2,200; trim 180 x 264. Circ: 3,000 (paid and controlled).

TEXTUUR. *see* MUSEUMS AND ART GALLERIES

677.028 CHN ISSN 1671-024X
➤ **TIANJIN GONGYE DAXUE XUEBAO/TIANJIN POLYTECHNIC UNIVERSITY. JOURNAL.** Text in Chinese. 1982. bi-m. adv. **Document type:** *Journal, Academic/Scholarly.* **Description:** Covers textile industry, textile machinery, materials science, clothing engineering, industrial automation, and dyeing and finishing.
Formerly (until 2000): Tianjin Fangzhi Gongxueyuan Xuebao/Tianjin College of Textile Technology. Journal (1000-1557)
Related titles: Online - full text ed.: (from WanFang Data Corp.).
Indexed: A28, APA, BrCerAb, C&ISA, CA/WCA, CIA, CerAb, CivEngAb, CorrAb, E&CAJ, E11, EEA, EMA, ESPM, EnvEAb, H15, M&TEA, M09, MBF, METADEX, RefZh, SCOPUS, SolStAb, T04, WAA, WTA.
—BLDSC (8820.509400), Linda Hall.
Published by: Tianjin Gongye Daxue/Tianjin Polytechnic University, 63, Changlinzhuang Dao, Tianjin, 300160, China. TEL 86-22-24528151, FAX 86-22-24528151, http://www.tjpu.edu.cn/index.shtml. Circ: 2,000.

677 JPN
TORAY INDUSTRIES. ANNUAL REPORT. Text in Japanese. a.
Published by: Toray Industries Inc., Zaimubu Kokusai Zaimuka, 2-2-1 Muro-Machi-Nihonbashi, Chuo-ku, Tokyo, 103-0000, Japan. TEL 03-3245-5222, FAX 03-3245-5818.

667 ITA ISSN 1124-2957
TRENDS COLLEZIONI. Text in English, Italian. s-a. EUR 100 domestic; EUR 160 in Europe; EUR 172 elsewhere (effective 2009). illus. **Document type:** *Magazine, Consumer.* **Description:** Covers trends in the textile sector, the latest fabrics, colors and patterns.
Formerly: Tessuto Collezioni
Published by: Logos Publishing, Via Curtatona 5/2, Modena, MO 41100, Italy. TEL 39-059-412603, FAX 39-059-412567, it.market@logos.net, http://www.logos.net.

677.31 GBR ISSN 1759-0418
TS1600
TWIST; the international magazine for luxury fabrics, yarns and fibres. Text in English. 1909. m. GBP 299 (effective 2009). bk.rev. mkt. **Document type:** *Magazine, Trade.* **Description:** Provides information for luxury textiles, and is designed to meet the rapidly growing demand from retailers, fashion brands and designers for information on the fabrics, yarns and fibres used in today's luxury clothing and interiors.
Former titles (until 2008): Wool Record (0263-6131); (until 1982): Wool Record and Textile World (0043-7832); (until 194?): Wool Record
Related titles: Online - full text ed.; ◆ Chinese ed.: Yangmao Hangye Jiyao. ISSN 1752-7643.
Indexed: A&ATA, ChemAb, KES, SCOPUS, T01, T02, TM, TTI, WTA.
—BLDSC (9076.958200), IE, Infotrieve, Ingenta. **CCC.**
Published by: World Textile Publications Ltd., Perkin House, 1 Longlands St, Bradford, W Yorks BD1 2TP, United Kingdom. TEL 44-1274-378800, FAX 44-1274-378811, info@world-textile.net, http://www.world-textile.net/. Ed. Jonathan Dyson. Adv. contact Liz Pollard.

U.S. DEPARTMENT OF AGRICULTURE. AGRICULTURAL MARKETING SERVICE. COTTON PROGRAM. COTTON QUALITY CROP. *see* AGRICULTURE—Agricultural Economics

U.S. DEPARTMENT OF AGRICULTURE. AGRICULTURAL MARKETING SERVICE. COTTON PROGRAM. COTTON QUALITY CROP (MONTHLY). *see* AGRICULTURE—Agricultural Economics

UNITE HERE!. *see* LABOR UNIONS

677 685 ROM ISSN 1843-813X
UNIVERSITY OF ORADEA. ANNALS. FASCICLE OF TEXTILE, LEATHERWORK. Text in English. 2001 (May). s-a. bk.rev. abstr. back issues avail. **Document type:** *Journal, Academic/Scholarly.* **Description:** Publishes contributions in original experimental, methodological or theoretical research to disseminate scientifically information and ideas among researchers from the fields of textile, leather, management and quality and environment.
Related titles: CD-ROM ed.: ISSN 2068-1070; Online - full text ed.: free (effective 2011).
Published by: Editura Universitatii din Oradea/University of Oradea Publishing House, Str Universitatii 1, Geotermal Bldg., 2nd Fl., Oradea, Jud.Bihor 410087, Romania. TEL 40-259-408642, editura@uoradea.ro, http://webhost.uoradea.ro/editura/. Ed. Indrie Liliana.

677 USA ISSN 1072-5628
TS840
UPHOLSTERY JOURNAL. Text in English. 1993. bi-m. USD 39 domestic; USD 49 in Canada & Mexico; USD 69 elsewhere (effective 2009). adv. back issues avail.; reprints avail. **Document type:** *Magazine, Trade.* **Description:** Designed for those interested in upholstery and reupholstery work.
Incorporates (1986-1998): Marine Textiles Buyers' Guide; Marine Textiles (0885-9949)
Related titles: Online - full text ed.: free (effective 2009); ◆ Supplement(s): Marine Textiles. ISSN 0885-9949.
Published by: Industrial Fabrics Association International, 1801 W County Rd B W, Ste B, Roseville, MN 55113. TEL 651-222-2508, 800-255-4324, FAX 651-631-9334, generalinfo@ifai.com. Ed. Chris Tschida TEL 651-225-6970. Pub. Mary Hennessy. Adv. contact Jane Anthone TEL 651-225-6911. page USD 3,785. Circ: 12,000 (paid and controlled).

UTSUKUSHII KIMONO/BEAUTIFUL KIMONO. *see* CLOTHING TRADE—Fashions

VAEVMAGASINET; Scandinavian weaving magazine. *see* NEEDLEWORK

677.39 IND
VANYA; wild silks of India in English. Text in English. a. INR 500 domestic; USD 50 foreign (effective 2011). **Document type:** *Journal, Trade.*
Published by: Central Silk Board, c/o Ministry of Textiles, Government of India, C S B Complex, B T M Layout, Madanala Hosur Rd, Bangalore, Karnataka 560 068, India. TEL 91-80-26282699, FAX 91-80-26681511, csb@silkboard.org.

VICTORIAN JOURNAL OF HOME ECONOMICS. *see* HOME ECONOMICS

677 646.4 NLD ISSN 1872-6127
VIEW2. Cover title: Textile View2 Magazine. Text in Dutch. 2006. 4/yr. EUR 140.19 per issue in Europe; EUR 198 per issue elsewhere (effective 2009).
Indexed: SCOPUS, WTA.
Published by: Metropolitan Publishing BV, Saxen Weimarlaan 6, Amsterdam, 1075 CA, Netherlands. TEL 31-20-6177624, FAX 31-20-6179357, office@view-publications.com, http://www.view-publications.com. Pub. David R Shah.

677.4 SVK ISSN 1335-0617
TS1760 CODEN: VLTEED
VLAKNA A TEXTIL/FIBRES AND TEXTILES. Text in English, Slovak. 1994. q. USD 40. adv. **Document type:** *Journal, Academic/Scholarly.*
Formed by the merger of (1951-1994): Chemicke Vlakna (0528-9432); (1971-1994): Textil a Chemia (0139-7656)
Indexed: ABIPC, CIN, ChemAb, SCOPUS, WTA.
—BLDSC (9246.014850), CASDDS, INIST, Linda Hall.
Published by: Vyskumny Ustav Chemickych Vlaken/Research Institute for Man-Made Fibres, Okr Poprad, Svit, 059 21, Slovakia. TEL 421-92-756225, FAX 421-92-755663. Ed. Dusan Budzak. R&P, Adv. contact Daniel Kello. Circ: 500.

677.028 CHE ISSN 1424-5752
WEAVER'S DIGEST (ENGLISH EDITION). Text in English. 1977. q.
Former titles (until 1999): Sulzer Rueti. Bulletin (English Edition) (1422-6839); (until 1991): Weaving Machine Bulletin (1422-7053)
Related titles: ◆ German ed.: Weaver's Digest (German Edition). ISSN 1424-5728; ◆ French ed.: Weaver's Digest (French Edition). ISSN 1424-5736; ◆ Italian ed.: Weaver's Digest (Italian Edition). ISSN 1424-5744; ◆ Spanish ed.: Weaver's Digest (Spanish Edition). ISSN 1424-5760.
Indexed: SCOPUS, WTA.
Published by: Sultex Limited, Rueti, 8630, Switzerland. TEL 41-55-2502121, FAX 41-55-2502101, http://www.sultex.com.

677.028 CHE ISSN 1424-5736
WEAVER'S DIGEST (FRENCH EDITION). Text in French. q. **Document type:** *Magazine, Trade.*
Former titles (until 1999): Sulzer Rueti. Bulletin (Ed. Francaise) (1422-6847); (until 1991): Bulletin des Machines a Tisser (1013-879X)
Related titles: ◆ German ed.: Weaver's Digest (German Edition). ISSN 1424-5728; ◆ Italian ed.: Weaver's Digest (Italian Edition). ISSN 1424-5744; ◆ Spanish ed.: Weaver's Digest (Spanish Edition). ISSN 1424-5760; ◆ English ed.: Weaver's Digest (English Edition). ISSN 1424-5752.
Published by: Sultex Limited, Rueti, 8630, Switzerland. TEL 41-55-2502121, FAX 41-55-2502101, http://www.sultex.com.

677.028 CHE ISSN 1424-5728
WEAVER'S DIGEST (GERMAN EDITION). Text in German. 195?. q. **Document type:** *Magazine, Trade.*
Former titles (until 1999): Sulzer Rueti. Bulletin (Deutsche Ausgabe) (1422-6855); (until 1991): Webmaschinen Bulletin (1422-7045)
Related titles: ◆ English ed.: Weaver's Digest (English Edition). ISSN 1424-5752; ◆ French ed.: Weaver's Digest (French Edition). ISSN 1424-5736; ◆ Italian ed.: Weaver's Digest (Italian Edition). ISSN 1424-5744; ◆ Spanish ed.: Weaver's Digest (Spanish Edition). ISSN 1424-5760.
Indexed: TM.
Published by: Sultex Limited, Rueti, 8630, Switzerland. TEL 41-55-2502121, FAX 41-55-2502101, http://www.sultex.com.

677.028 CHE ISSN 1424-5744
WEAVER'S DIGEST (ITALIAN EDITION). Text in Italian. 1977. q. **Document type:** *Magazine, Trade.*
Former titles (until 1999): Sulzer Rueti. Bulletin (Ed. Italiana) (1422-6871); (until 1995): Sulzer Rueti. Bollettino (1422-7061); (until 1991): Bollettino delle Macchine da Tessere (1422-7088)
Related titles: ◆ German ed.: Weaver's Digest (German Edition). ISSN 1424-5728; ◆ French ed.: Weaver's Digest (French Edition). ISSN 1424-5736; ◆ Spanish ed.: Weaver's Digest (Spanish Edition). ISSN 1424-5760; ◆ English ed.: Weaver's Digest (English Edition). ISSN 1424-5752.
Published by: Sultex Limited, Rueti, 8630, Switzerland. TEL 41-55-2502121, FAX 41-55-2502101, http://www.sultex.com.

677.028 CHE ISSN 1424-5760
WEAVER'S DIGEST (SPANISH EDITION). Text in Spanish. 1977. q. **Document type:** *Magazine, Trade.*
Former titles (until 1999): Sulzer Rueti. Bulletin (Ed. Espanola) (1422-6863); (until 1995): Sulzer Rueti. Boletin (1422-710X); (until 1991): Boletin de Maquinas de Tejer (1422-7096)

Related titles: ◆ German ed.: Weaver's Digest (German Edition). ISSN 1424-5728; ◆ French ed.: Weaver's Digest (French Edition). ISSN 1424-5736; ◆ Italian ed.: Weaver's Digest (Italian Edition). ISSN 1424-5744; ◆ English ed.: Weaver's Digest (English Edition). ISSN 1424-5752.
Published by: Sultex Limited, Rueti, 8630, Switzerland. TEL 41-55-2502121, FAX 41-55-2502101, http://www.sultex.com.

677 DEU ISSN 0947-3386
WEBEN. Text in German. 1956. 2/yr. EUR 16.40 domestic; EUR 20 foreign; EUR 9 newsstand/cover (effective 2011). adv. bk.rev.
Document type: *Magazine, Consumer.*
Formerly (until 1994): Webe Mit (0043-1699)
Indexed: TM.
Published by: Verlag Inge Seelig, c/o Werkhof Kukate, Waddeweitz, 29496, Germany. TEL 49-5849468, FAX 49-58491202, info@werkhof-kukate.de. Ed. Inge Seelig. adv.: page EUR 520. Circ: 1,500 (paid and controlled).

WEEKLY COTTON MARKET REVIEW. *see* AGRICULTURE—Agricultural Economics

677 USA ISSN 1931-1443
WILD FIBERS. Text in English. 200?. q. USD 28 (effective 2007).
Document type: *Magazine, Consumer.*
Indexed: H20.
Address: P.O. Box 1752, Rockland, ME 04841. TEL 207-594-9455, http://www.wildfibersmagazine.com/index.php.

677.3 ZAF ISSN 0259-0182
WOLNUUS/WOOL NEWS. Text in Afrikaans, English. 1980. w. free.
Document type: *Newsletter, Trade.*
Incorporates: Cape Wools Market Report; Formed by the merger of: Wool News Service; Wolnuusdiens
Published by: S.A. Wool Board, PO Box 2191, Port Elizabeth, 6056, South Africa. TEL 27-41-544301, FAX 27-41-546760. Ed., R&P Ona Viljoen. Circ: 150.

673.3 AUS ISSN 1441-9440
WOOL MARKET REVIEW. Variant title: Australian Wool Market Review. Text in English, French, German. 199?. w. back issues avail.
Document type: *Magazine, Trade.*
Related titles: Online - full text ed.
Published by: The Woolmark Company, PO Box 4867, Melbourne, VIC 3001, Australia. TEL 61-3-93419111, FAX 61-3-93419273, wbi@wool.com.au, http://www.wool.com.

677.31 IND ISSN 0043-7824
WOOL NEWS. Text in English. 1965. q. **Document type:** *Magazine, Trade.*
Published by: Wool & Woollens Export Promotion Council, Flat No 614, Indra Prakash Bldg, 21, Barakhamba Rd, New Delhi, 110 001, India. TEL 91-11-23315512, FAX 91-11-23730182, wwepc@bol.net.in, http://www.wwepcindia.com/.

677.31 GBR
WOOL RECORD WEEKLY MARKET REPORT (EMAIL). Text in English. 1907. w. (51/yr.). GBP 199 (effective 2009). adv. charts; mkt. index.
Document type: *Newsletter, Trade.* **Description:** Contains wool and specialty fibre prices, news and analysis from around the world.
Formerly (until 19??): Wool Record Weekly Market Report (Print) (1470-823X); Which incorporated (in Dec.1977): Weekly Wool Chart (0043-2008)
Media: E-mail.
Published by: World Textile Publications Ltd., Perkin House, 1 Longlands St, Bradford, W Yorks BD1 2TP, United Kingdom. TEL 44-1274-378800, FAX 44-1274-378811, info@world-textile.net, http://www.world-textile.net/. Ed. John Liddle TEL 44-1274-378800. Adv. contact Joan Rowbotham.

677.3 NZL ISSN 0112-2754
WOOL RESEARCH ORGANISATION OF NEW ZEALAND SPECIAL PUBLICATIONS. Text in English. 1976. irreg. price varies. adv.
Document type: *Monographic series.* **Description:** Proceedings of meetings on New Zealand wool, including cellular, chemical and physical properties, appraisal, sale, scouring, processing, end-use performance and marketing.
Published by: Wool Research Organisation of New Zealand Inc., Private Bag 4749, Christchurch, New Zealand. TEL 64-3-3256622, boa@woolresearch.com, http://www.woolresearch.com/. Adv. contact Barbara H Vaile.

WOOL TRADE DIRECTORY OF THE WORLD. *see* BUSINESS AND ECONOMICS—Trade And Industrial Directories

677.31 IND
WOOLLEN EXPORTERS DIRECTORY. Text in English. 1970 (vol.4). s-a. free to members (effective 2011). illus.; mkt.; stat. **Document type:** *Directory, Trade.*
Formerly: Woollens and Worsteds of India (0043-7883)
Published by: Wool & Woollens Export Promotion Council, Flat No 614, Indra Prakash Bldg, 21, Barakhamba Rd, New Delhi, 110 001, India. TEL 91-11-23315512, FAX 91-11-23730182, wwepc@bol.net.in, http://www.wwepcindia.com/.

677.31 USA
THE WOOLLY TIMES. Text in English. 2000. q. USD 12 (effective 2001). bk.rev. **Description:** Published with the aim of connecting wool growers with those who enjoy working with fibers: spinners, weavers, dyers, felters and knitters. It covers the full range of sheep, wool processing and textile topics. At the same time, it reaches out to smaller and home-based businesses while maintaining a hands-on approach. Each issue contains an interview of a person active in wool growing, articles, reviews, patterns and columns. It also contains a directory of mills across the country with specialties outlined.
Published by: Presson - North and Co., P O Box 123, Pecos, NM 87552. twt@cybermesa.com, http://www.thewoollytimes.com. Ed. Anne Hillerman. Circ: 1,000.

677.2 PAK
WORLD COTTON MARKETS REVIEW. Text in English. 1972. m. charts; stat.
Published by: (Pakistan. Marketing and Economic Research Section), Pakistan Central Cotton Committee, c/o Secretary, Moulvi Tamizuddin Khan Rd., Karachi 1, Pakistan. TEL 524104-6.

WORLD INDEX OF YARNS AND FIBRES. *see* BUSINESS AND ECONOMICS—Trade And Industrial Directories

WORLD TEXTILE ABSTRACTS (ONLINE). *see* TEXTILE INDUSTRIES AND FABRICS—Abstracting, Bibliographies, Statistics

677.028 CHN ISSN 1671-850X
CODEN: XFGXEJ
➤ **XI'AN GONGCHENG KEJI XUEYUAN XUEBAO/XI'AN UNIVERSITY OF ENGINEERING SCIENCE AND TECHNOLOGY. JOURNAL.** Text in Chinese. 1986. q. CNY 5 newsstand/cover (effective 2006). bk.rev. back issues avail. **Document type:** *Journal, Academic/Scholarly.* **Description:** Discusses experimental and applied research in textile science and technology.
Formerly (until 2001): Xibei Fangzhi Gongxueyuan Xuebao/Northwest Institute of Textile Science and Technology. Journal (1001-7305)
Related titles: Online - full text ed.
Indexed: SCOPUS, WTA.
—BLDSC (4917.477100), IE, Ingenta.
Published by: Xi'an Gongcheng Daxue/Xi'an Polytechnic University, 19, Jinhua Nan Lu, 179 Xinxiang, Xi'an, 710048, China. TEL 86-29-82330694, FAX 86-29-83235130.

677 CHN ISSN 1009-265X
XIANDAI FANGZHI JISHU/ADVANCED TEXTILE TECHNOLOGY. Text in Chinese. 1992. bi-m. USD 24.60 (effective 2009). **Document type:** *Journal, Academic/Scholarly.*
Related titles: Online - full text ed.
—BLDSC (0696.935550).
Published by: Zhejiang Ligong Daxue/Zhejiang Sci-Tech University, Xiasha Gaojiaoyuan Qu, Hangzhou, 310018, China. http://www.zist.edu.cn.

677.31 GBR ISSN 1752-7643
YANGMAO HANGYE JIYAO. Text in Chinese. 200?. m. adv. **Document type:** *Magazine, Trade.*
Related titles: ◆ English ed.: Twist. ISSN 1759-0418.
Published by: World Textile Publications Ltd., Perkin House, 1 Longlands St, Bradford, W Yorks BD1 2TP, United Kingdom. TEL 44-1274-378800, FAX 44-1274-378811, info@world-textile.net, http://www.world-textile.net/. Ed. John Liddle TEL 44-1274-378800. Adv. contact James Wilson TEL 44-1274-378800. B&W page GBP 984, color page GBP 1,808.

677 CHN ISSN 1000-4017
YIN RAN/DYEING AND FINISHING. Text in Chinese; Abstracts in English. 1975. s-a. USD 148.80 (effective 2009). adv. **Document type:** *Magazine, Trade.*
Related titles: Online - full text ed.
Published by: Shanghai Shi Fanzhi Kexue Yanjiuyuan/Shanghai Textile Research Institute, 988 Ping Liang Rd, Shanghai, 200082, China. TEL 86-21-51670288, FAX 86-21-55213681. adv.: page CNY 800. Circ: 12,000. **Dist. by:** China International Book Trading Corp, 35 Chegongzhuang Xilu, Haidian District, PO Box 399, Beijing 100044, China. TEL 86-10-68412045, FAX 86-10-68412023, cibtc@mail.cibtc.com.cn, http://www.cibtc.com.cn. **Co-sponsor:** Quanguo Yinran Gongye Keji Qingbao Zhan.

677 CHN ISSN 1004-0439
YINRAN ZHUJI/TEXTILE AUXILIARIES. Text in Chinese. 1984. m. USD 62.40 (effective 2009). **Document type:** *Magazine, Trade.*
Related titles: Online - full text ed.
—BLDSC (9418.485700), East View.
Published by: Changzhou Huagong Yanjiusuo Youxian Gongsi/Changzhou Chemical Research Institute Co., Ltd., 102, Qingliang Lu, Changzhou, 213001, China. TEL 86-519-6646602, FAX 86-519-6646602, http://www.crichem.com/. **Dist. by:** China International Book Trading Corp, 35 Chegongzhuang Xilu, Haidian District, PO Box 399, Beijing 100044, China. TEL 86-10-68412045, FAX 86-10-68412023, cibtc@mail.cibtc.com.cn, http://www.cibtc.com.cn.

677 JPN
ZENSEN NEWSPAPER. Text in Japanese. w. **Document type:** *Newspaper.*
Published by: Japanese Federation of Textile Garment Chemical Mercantile and Allied Industry Workers' Union, 8-16 Kudan-Minami 4-chome, Chiyoda-ku, Tokyo, 102-0074, Japan. TEL 03-3265-5465, TELEX ZENSEN TOKYO.

677 JPN
ZENZEN COMPASS. Text in Japanese. bi-m. JPY 3,000 (effective 1999).
Document type: *Newsletter.*
Former title: Zenzen Monthly Journal
Published by: Zensen Japanese Federation of Textile, Garment, Chemical, Commercial and Allied Industries Workers' Unions, 8-16 Kudan Minami 4-chome, Chiyoda-ku, Tokyo, Japan. TEL 81-3-3288-3723, TELEX ZENSEN TOKYO. Ed. Naoti Ohmi. Pub. Kiyoshi Ochiai.

ZHEJIANG FANGZHI FUZHUANG ZHIYE JISHU XUEYUAN XUEBAO/ZHEJIANG TEXTILE & FASHION VOCATIONAL COLLEGE. JOURNAL. *see* CLOTHING TRADE—Fashions

677.39 CHN ISSN 1673-3851
CODEN: ZSGXEU
ZHEJIANG LIGONG DAXUE XUEBAO/ZHEJIANG SCI-TECH UNIVERSITY. JOURNAL. Text in Chinese; Summaries in English. 1979. q. CNY 40 (effective 2006). **Document type:** *Journal, Academic/Scholarly.*
Former titles (until 2005): Zhejiang Gongcheng Xueyuan Xuebao/Zhejiang Institute of Science and Technology. Journal (1009-4741); (until 1998): Zhejiang Sichou Gongxueyuan Xuebao/Zhejiang Institute of Silk Textiles. Journal (1000-2103); (until 1984): Zhesi Keji
Related titles: Online - full text ed.
Indexed: CIN, ChemAb, ChemTitl.
—BLDSC (9512.663010), CASDDS.
Published by: Zhejiang Ligong Daxue/Zhejiang Sci-Tech University, Xiasha Gaojiaoyuan Qu, Hangzhou, 310018, China. Circ: 2,000.

677 600 CHN ISSN 1000-4033
ZHENZHI GONGYE/TIANJIN TEXTILE SCIENCE & TECHNOLOGY. Text in Chinese. 1962. q. **Document type:** *Journal, Academic/Scholarly.*
Related titles: Online - full text ed.
Published by: Tianjin Fangzhi Gongcheng Yanjiuyuan Youxian Gongsi/Tianjin Textile Engineering Research Institute, 111, Zhonghuan Nan Lu, Tianjin Free Trade Zone, Tianjin, 300308, China. TEL 86-22-60406581, FAX 86-22-60406582, http://www.tteri.com/. **Co-sponsor:** Tianjin Fangzhi Fuzhuang Yanjiuyuan.

677 CHN ISSN 0529-6013
HD9866.C5
ZHONGGUO FANGZHI. Text in Chinese. 1950-1966; resumed 1979. m. CNY 336; CNY 28 newsstand/cover (effective 2009). adv. back issues avail. **Document type:** *Magazine, Trade.* **Description:** Covers business management, international trade, marketing and economic development in the field of textile.
Related titles: Online - full text ed.; English ed.: China Textile. ISSN 1673-1468.
—East View.
Published by: Zhongguo Fangzhi Gongye Xiehui/China National Textile Council General Office, no.12, Changan Jie, Rm.515, Beijing, 100742, China. TEL 86-10-85229088, FAX 86-10-85229180. Ed. Wang Zhifu. adv.: page USD 2,000. Circ: 20,000 (controlled).

677 CHN
ZHONGGUO FANGZHI BAO/CHINA TEXTILES NEWS. Text in Chinese. 1985. d. (Mon.-Fri.). CNY 126, USD 52.80 (effective 2005).
Document type: *Newspaper, Trade.*
Related titles: Online - full content ed.
Published by: Jingji Ribao Baoye Jituan/Economic Daily Newspaper Group, Zhaoyang-qu, Dongsanhuan Zhong Lu #12, 2/F, Beijing, 100022, China. TEL 86-10-87751055. **Dist. by:** China International Book Trading Corp, 35 Chegongzhuang Xilu, Haidian District, PO Box 399, Beijing 100044, China. TEL 86-10-68412045, FAX 86-10-68412023, cibtc@mail.cibtc.com.cn, http://www.cibtc.com.cn.

677 CHN ISSN 1000-1476
TS1300 CODEN: ZFDXEQ
ZHONGGUO FANGZHI DAXUE XUEBAO. Text in Chinese. 1956. 6/yr. USD 30. adv. **Document type:** *Academic/Scholarly.* **Description:** Academic journal of natural science and engineering, focusing on textile science and technology.
Former titles (until 1986): Shanghai College of Textile Technology. Journal; East China Institute of Textile Science and Technology. Journal
Related titles: ◆ English ed.: China Textile University. Journal. ISSN 1000-1484.
Indexed: CIN, ChemAb, ChemTitl, T01, TTI.
—CASDDS, Ingenta.
Published by: Zhongguo Fangzhi Daxue/China Textile University, 1882 Yan an Xilu, Shanghai, 200051, China. TEL 86-21-6219-3057, FAX 86-21-6208-9144.

677 HKG ISSN 1021-5824
ZHONGGUO FANGZHI JI CHENGYI/CHINA TEXTILE & APPAREL. Variant title: C T A. Text in Chinese; Contents page in Chinese, English. 1983. bi-m. HKD 455 domestic; USD 90 in Asia; USD 100 elsewhere (effective 2003); includes annual Buyers' Guide. adv. abstr.; charts; illus.; stat. 80 p./no.; back issues avail.; reprints avail.
Document type: *Magazine, Trade.* **Description:** Introduces to China advanced foreign technology, machinery and processing materials in the textile industry.
Formerly: Zhongguo Fangzhi/China Textile (1021-1349)
Indexed: SCOPUS, WTA.
—BLDSC (3180.234897).
Published by: (China National Textile Economic Research Centre), Yashi Chuban Gongsi/Adsale Publishing Ltd., 6th Fl., 321 Java Rd, North Point, Hong Kong. TEL 852-28118897, FAX 852-25165119, http://www.adsalepub.com.hk. Eds. Joany Hao, Michelle Phong. Adv. contact Janet Tong TEL 852-2516-3380. B&W page USD 3,227, color page USD 4,965; trim 280 x 215. Circ: 36,200. **Co-sponsor:** China National Machinery Import & Export Corp.

TEXTILE INDUSTRIES AND FABRICS—
Abstracting, Bibliographies, Statistics

677 310 AUS
A W E X WOOL STATISTICS YEARBOOK. (Australian Wool Exchange) Variant title: Australian Wool Statistics. Text in English. 1972. a. AUD 85 domestic; AUD 105 foreign (effective 2002).
Former titles (until 2002): Australian Wool Statistics Yearbook; (until 1997): Australian Wool Sale Statistics. Statistical Analysis. Part A & B & C & D (0311-9882); Australian Wool (0067-222X); Australian Wool Corporation. Statistical Analysis (0084-764X)
Related titles: Diskette ed.
Published by: Australian Wool Innovation Ltd., G P O Box 4177, Sydney, NSW 2001, Australia. Ed. W Watkins. Circ: 200.

677 CAN ISSN 0319-891X
CANADA. STATISTICS CANADA. TEXTILE PRODUCTS INDUSTRIES/ CANADA. STATISTIQUE CANADA. INDUSTRIE DE PRODUITS TEXTILES. Text in English, French. 1960. a. CAD 40 domestic; USD 40 foreign (effective 1999). **Document type:** *Government.*
Formerly (until 1985): Canada. Statistics Canada. Carpet, Mat and Rug Industry (0527-4893)
Related titles: Microform ed.: (from MML); Online - full text ed.
Published by: Statistics Canada, Operations and Integration Division (Subsidiary of: Statistics Canada/Statistique Canada), Circulation Management, 120 Parkdale Ave, Ottawa, ON K1A 0T6, Canada. TEL 613-951-7277, 800-267-6677, FAX 613-951-1584.

677 USA ISSN 1530-6542
HD9850.3
DAVISON'S GOLD BOOK. Text in English. 1934. a. USD 75 (effective 2001). illus. **Document type:** *Directory, Trade.* **Description:** Directory with separate classifications for suppliers of chemicals, equipment, machinery, services and supplies used in the textile industry.
Former titles (until 1998): Davison's Textile Buyers Guide (0734-4708); (until 1980): Davison's Textile Buyers and Buyers' Guide (0730-5990)
Related titles: Online - full text ed.
Published by: Davison Publishing Co., LLC (Subsidiary of: Simmons-Boardman Publishing Corp.), 3452 Lake Lynda Dr, Ste 363, Orlando, FL 32817. TEL 407-380-8900, 800-328-4766, FAX 407-380-5222, info@davisonpublishing.com, http://www.davisonpublishing.com.

677 CHN ISSN 1000-3916
FANGZHI WENZHAI/TEXTILE ABSTRACT. Text in Chinese. 1979. bi-m. USD 74.40 (effective 2009). adv. **Document type:** *Abstract/Index.*
Published by: Shanghai Fangzhi Kexue Yanjiuyuan/Shanghai Textile Research Institute, 545 Lanzhou Lu, Shanghai, 200082, China. TEL 86-21-6546-1341, FAX 86-21-6545-8418, TELEX 33365 STRI CN. Ed. Gao Dequan. Circ: 3,000.

TU

677.0021 HKG
HONG KONG SPECIAL ADMINISTRATIVE REGION OF CHINA. CENSUS AND STATISTICS DEPARTMENT. QUARTERLY TEXTILE PRODUCTION STATISTICS. Text in Chinese, English. 1996. q. HKD 8; HKD 2 newsstand/cover (effective 2001). stat. **Document type:** *Government.* **Description:** Covers the textile production and statistics on employment and imports of raw materials in the textile industry.
Published by: Census and Statistics Department/Zhengfu Tongjichu, Industrial Production Statistics Section, 16/F Chuang's Hung Hom Plaza, 83 Wuhu St, Hung Hom, Kowloon, Hong Kong. TEL 852-2805-6167, FAX 852-2805-6105, ips_1@censtatd.gov.hk, http://www.statisticalbookstore.gov.hk. **Subscr. to:** Information Services Department, Publications Sales Unit, Rm 402, 4th Fl, Murray Bldg, Garden Rd, Hong Kong, Hong Kong. TEL 852-2842-8844, FAX 852-2598-7482, puborder@isd.gcn.gov.hk, http://www.info.gov.hk/isd/book_e.htm. **Dist. by:** Government Publications Centre, Low Block, Ground Fl, Queensway Government Offices, 66 Queensway, Hong Kong, Hong Kong. TEL 852-2537-1910, FAX 852-2523-7195.

677.2 CHE ISSN 0538-6829
HD9870.4
INTERNATIONAL COTTON INDUSTRY STATISTICS. Text in English. 1958. a. CHF 100 (effective 2001). charts; stat. **Document type:** *Yearbook, Trade.* **Description:** Covers productive capacity, machinery utilization and raw material consumption in the short-staple sector.
Indexed: T01, T02, TTI.
Published by: International Textile Manufacturers Federation, Am Schanzengraben 29, Postfach, Zurich, 8039, Switzerland. TEL 41-1-2017080, FAX 41-1-2017134, secretariat@itmf.org, http://www.itmf.org.

677 BEL ISSN 0074-7599
INTERNATIONAL RAYON AND SYNTHETIC FIBRES COMMITTEE. STATISTICAL YEARBOOK. Text in English. 1965. a. EUR 200 (effective 2000). adv.
Published by: International Rayon and Synthetic Fibres Committee - C.I.R.F.S./Comite International de la Rayonne et des Fibres Synthetiques, Av Van Nieuwenhuyse 4, Brussels, 1160, Belgium. info@cirfs.org. Ed. Colin M Purvis. Pub. B Bruyere. Adv. contact D Morris.

677.2 CHE
INTERNATIONAL TEXTILE MACHINERY SHIPMENT STATISTICS. Text in English. 1974. a. CHF 250 (effective 2001). charts; stat. **Document type:** *Report, Trade.* **Description:** Provides information on spinning and weaving capacities installed in almost the entire world and effectively identifies investment trends.
Formerly: International Cotton Industry Statistics. Supplement
Published by: International Textile Manufacturers Federation, Am Schanzengraben 29, Postfach, Zurich, 8039, Switzerland. TEL 41-1-2017080, FAX 41-1-2017134, secretariat@itmf.org, http://www.itmf.org.

677 338.1 JPN ISSN 0447-5321
HD9086.J3
JAPAN COTTON STATISTICS AND RELATED DATA. Text in Japanese. 1953. a. USD 60 (effective 2006). **Document type:** *Academic/Scholarly.*
Published by: Nihon Menka Kyokai/Japan Cotton Traders' Association, Cotton Nissei Bldg.10F, 1-8-2, Utsubo Hon-machi, Nishi-ku, Osaka, 550-0004, Japan. TEL 81-6-64458839, FAX 81-6-64458893, menkyo@jcta.co.jp, http://www.jcta.co.jp/.

677.3 310 GBR ISSN 0260-8855
KNITSTATS; yearly statistical bulletin for the hosiery and knitwear industry. Text in English. 1976. a. GBP 50 (effective 2000). bk.rev. index. back issues avail. **Document type:** *Bulletin.*
—BLDSC (5100.335000).
Published by: Knitting Industries' Federation, Leicester City Museums Service, 12th Fl, A Block, New Walk Centre, Welford Pl, Leicester, LE1 6ZG, United Kingdom. knittingtogether.museums@leicester.gov.uk, http://www.knittingtogether.co.uk/. Ed., R&P J A Smirfitt. Circ: 500 (paid).

677 JPN
SEN-I KOUGYO YORAN/JAPAN TEXTILE INDUSTRY. DIRECTORY. Text in Japanese. 1910. a. JPY 19,500. adv. **Document type:** *Directory.* **Description:** Covers Japanese textile manufacturers, institutes and universities. Also lists inspection and testing institutes, textile associations, and textile machinery traders and dealers in Japan.
Published by: Boshoku Zasshisha/Textile Journal and Book Pub. Co., 7-9 Ono-Dai 1-chome, Osakasayama-shi, Osaka-fu 589-0023, Japan. TEL 81-06-633-7734. Ed. Ken Ichi Uno. Adv. contact Yoji Uno. Circ: 3,000.

677.0021 677.39 IND
SERICULTURE & SILK INDUSTRY STATISTICS (YEAR). Text in English. 200?. irreg., latest 2003. INR 100 combined subscription domestic (print & CD-ROM eds.); USD 50 combined subscription foreign (print & CD-ROM eds.) (effective 2011). **Document type:** *Journal, Trade.* **Description:** Provides the latest information on the vital statistics of the world and Indian sericulture and silk industry.
Related titles: CD-ROM ed.
Published by: Central Silk Board, c/o Ministry of Textiles, Government of India, C S B Complex, B T M Layout, Madanala Hosur Rd, Bangalore, Karnataka 560 068, India. TEL 91-80-26282699, FAX 91-80-26681511, csb@silkboard.org.

677.0021 AUS
SHEEP'S BACK TO MILL STATISTICS YEARBOOK. Text in English. a. **Document type:** *Yearbook, Trade.* **Description:** Provides information on a costs for the Australian wool industry of producing, harvesting and marketing wool from the farm gate to the early stage processor.
Related titles: Online - full text ed.: free (effective 2009).
Published by: Australian Wool Innovation Ltd., G P O Box 4177, Sydney, NSW 2001, Australia. TEL 1-800-070-099, FAX 1-800-899-515, info@woolinnovation.com.au, http://www.woolinnovation.com.au.

016.677 DEU
TECSCAN JOURNAL. BEKLEIDUNGSTECHNIK, MANAGEMENT, WIRTSCHAFT. Variant title: Bekleidungstechnik, Management, Wirtschaft. Text in German. m. EUR 240 (effective 2010). **Document type:** *Journal, Abstract/Index.*
Formerly (until 2009): Informationsdienst F I Z Technik. Bekleidungstechnik, Management, Wirtschaft
Published by: Fachinformationszentrum Technik e.V., Hanauer Landstr 151-153, Frankfurt Am Main, 60314, Germany. TEL 49-69-4308213, FAX 49-69-4308200, kundenberatung@fiz-technik.de, http://www.fiz-technik.de.

016.677 DEU
TECSCAN JOURNAL. TECHNISCHE TEXTILIEN. Variant title: Technische Textilien. Text in German. m. EUR 240 (effective 2010). **Document type:** *Journal, Abstract/Index.*
Formerly (until 2009): Informationsdienst F I Z Technik. Technische Textilien
Published by: Fachinformationszentrum Technik e.V., Hanauer Landstr 151-153, Frankfurt Am Main, 60314, Germany. TEL 49-69-4308213, FAX 49-69-4308200, kundenberatung@fiz-technik.de, http://www.fiz-technik.de.

016.677 DEU
TECSCAN JOURNAL. TEXTIL- UND BEKLEIDUNGSTECHNIK, TEXTILVEREDLUNG, TEXTILMASCHINENBAU. Variant title: Textil- und Bekleidungstechnik, Textilveredlung, Textilmaschinenbau. Text in German. m. EUR 420 (effective 2010). **Document type:** *Journal, Abstract/Index.*
Formerly (until 2009): Informationsdienst F I Z Technik. Textil- und Bekleidungstechnik, Textilveredlung, Textilmaschinenbau
Published by: Fachinformationszentrum Technik e.V., Hanauer Landstr 151-153, Frankfurt Am Main, 60314, Germany. TEL 49-69-4308213, FAX 49-69-4308200, kundenberatung@fiz-technik.de, http://www.fiz-technik.de.

016.677 DEU
TECSCAN JOURNAL. TEXTILVEREDLUNG. Variant title: Textilveredlung. Text in German. m. EUR 240 (effective 2010). **Document type:** *Journal, Abstract/Index.*
Formerly (until 2009): Informationsdienst F I Z Technik. Textilveredlung
Published by: Fachinformationszentrum Technik e.V., Hanauer Landstr 151-153, Frankfurt Am Main, 60314, Germany. TEL 49-69-4308213, FAX 49-69-4308200, kundenberatung@fiz-technik.de, http://www.fiz-technik.de.

677 AUS ISSN 1323-661X
TEXTILE AND APPAREL OF AUSTRALASIA; the comprehensive reference of the textile, footwear and apparel industry. Text in English. 1962. irreg. illus. **Description:** Comprehensive listings of all companies associated with textile, clothing and apparel industries in Australia and New Zealand.
Former titles (until 1996): Textile and Apparel Index of Australasia (1036-112X); (until 1990): Textile and Apparel Index of Australia (0159-0014); (until 1979): Textile Index of Australia (0495-3630)
Published by: Morescope Publishing Pty. Ltd., 50 Carter Rd, Port Huon, TAS 7116, Australia. TEL 61-3-98829922, FAX 61-3-98829239. Ed. B Pesanaley.

677 HKG
TEXTILE ASIA INDEX. Text in Chinese. 1982. a. HKD 145 in Hong Kong & Macau; USD 24 elsewhere in Hong Kong & Macau (effective 2000). adv. **Document type:** *Abstract/Index.*
Published by: Business Press Ltd., 11/F, California Tower, 30-32 D'Aguilar St., GPO Box 185, Hong Kong, Hong Kong. TEL 852-25233744, FAX 852-28106966. Ed., Pub., R&P Kayser Sung. Adv. contact Vicky Sung.

016.677 USA
TEXTILE TECHNOLOGY COMPLETE. Text in English. base vol. plus s-m. updates. **Document type:** *Database, Abstract/Index.*
Media: Online - full text.
Published by: EBSCO Publishing (Subsidiary of: EBSCO Industries, Inc.), 10 Estes St, PO Box 682, Ipswich, MA 01938. TEL 978-356-6500, 800-653-2726, FAX 978-356-6565, information@ebscohost.com.

016.677 USA
TEXTILE TECHNOLOGY INDEX. Text in English. base vol. plus s-m. updates. **Document type:** *Database, Abstract/Index.*
Formerly (until 2002): Textile Technology Digest (Online)
Media: Online - full text.
Published by: EBSCO Publishing (Subsidiary of: EBSCO Industries, Inc.), 10 Estes St, PO Box 682, Ipswich, MA 01938. TEL 978-356-6500, 800-653-2726, FAX 978-356-6565, information@ebscohost.com.

677 011 USA
VITAL TEXTILE LITERATURE (YEAR). Text in English. 1989. s-m. (except once in Dec., plus a. cumulation). USD 110 (effective 2000). **Document type:** *Abstract/Index.* **Description:** Publishes abstracts selected from the parent publication Textile Technology Digest for their importance in alerting the industry to vital information.
Formerly (until 1993): Textile Technology Digest: Abstract Alert
Published by: Institute of Textile Technology, 2551 Ivy Rd, Charlottesville, VA 22903-4614. TEL 804-296-5511, FAX 804-977-5400. Ed. Dennis Loy. R&P Adrienne D Granitz.

677.0021 BEL ISSN 0260-2016
WOOL STATISTICS. Text in English. a. GBP 60 domestic; GBP 85 foreign (effective 2001). **Document type:** *Report, Trade.* **Description:** Contains information on raw wool production, external trade, and employment and machinery capacities. The interim version, published in August, focuses on major wool producing and consuming nations and the complete version, published in December, extends this information to cover almost all nations with a wool industry of any significance.
Formerly (until 1960): Research of the Wool Questionnaire Prepared by the Commonwealth Economic Commissioner
Published by: International Wool Textile Organisation, Rue de l'Industrie 4, Brussels, 1000, Belgium. TEL 32 2 5054010, FAX 32 2 5034785, z.dimitrova@iwto.org, http://www.iwto.org.

016.677 USA
WORLD TEXTILE ABSTRACTS (ONLINE). Variant title: World Textiles. Text in English. 1969. base vol. plus m. updates. **Document type:** *Database, Abstract/Index.* **Description:** Provides researchers with international coverage of scientific, trade, technical and economic publications.
Media: Online - full text. **Related titles:** CD-ROM ed.
Published by: EBSCO Publishing (Subsidiary of: EBSCO Industries, Inc.), 10 Estes St, PO Box 682, Ipswich, MA 01938. TEL 212-678-3774, FAX 212-678-6619, information@ebscohost.com.

TEXTILE INDUSTRIES AND FABRICS—Computer Applications

677.00285 GBR ISSN 1742-1128
DIGITAL TEXTILE. Text in English. 2003. bi-m. GBP 199; EUR 248 (print or online ed.) (effective 2009). adv. **Document type:** *Newsletter, Trade.* **Description:** Dedicated to textile applications in the rapidly developing field of digital inkjet printing.
Media: Online - full content. **Related titles:** Print ed.
Indexed: SCOPUS, WTA.
Published by: World Textile Publications Ltd., Perkin House, 1 Longlands St, Bradford, W Yorks BD1 2TP, United Kingdom. TEL 44-1274-378800, FAX 44-1274-378811, info@world-textile.net, http://www.world-textile.net/. Ed. John Scrimshaw TEL 44-1274-378819. Adv. contact David Jagger TEL 44-1274-378840. color page GBP 2,953, B&W page GBP 1,778; bleed 216 x 303.

THEATER

see also DANCE

A B C D E FOCUS. *see* EDUCATION—Teaching Methods And Curriculum

792 ESP ISSN 1133-8792
PN2780
A D E - TEATRO. Text in Spanish. 1985. 4/yr. EUR 47.50 domestic; EUR 80 foreign (effective 2008). adv. bk.rev. 200 p./no.; back issues avail. **Document type:** *Magazine, Consumer.* **Description:** Covers study, analysis, news and debates about matters related to Spanish and international theater.
Formerly (until 1989): Associacion de Directores de Escena. Boletin (1133-8784)
Indexed: MLA-IB, RILM.
Published by: Asociacion de Directores de Escena de Espana, C Costanilla de los Angeles 13, bajo Izq, Madrid, 28013, Spain. TEL 34-91-5591246, FAX 34-91-5483012. Ed. Juan A Hormigon. **Dist. by:** Asociacion de Revistas Culturales de Espana, C Covarruvias 9 2o. Derecha, Madrid 28010, Spain. TEL 34-91-3086066, FAX 34-91-3199267, info@arce.es, http://www.arce.es/.

792 DEU
A K T. (Aktuelles Theater) Text in German. 1969. 11/yr. adv. bk.rev. **Document type:** *Magazine, Consumer.*
Published by: Frankfurter Bund fuer Volksbildung e.V., Frankenallee 111, Frankfurt Am Main, 60326, Germany. TEL 49-69-56030106, info@fbfv.de, http://www.fbfv.de. Eds. G Holzapfel, J Kessler. Adv. contact Ursula Pigge. Circ: 15,000.

A M S STUDIES IN THE RENAISSANCE. (Abrahams Magazine Service) *see* LITERATURE

792 FRA ISSN 0986-1351
A S - ACTUALITE DE LA SCENOGRAPHIE. Text in French. 6/yr. EUR 76 domestic; EUR 100 in Europe; EUR 120 elsewhere (effective 2009). **Document type:** *Journal.* **Description:** Covers the news concerning the theater industry.
Published by: Editions A.S., 14 Rue Crucy, Nantes, 44000, France. TEL 33-2-40486424, FAX 33-2-40486432, as-editions@as-editions.fr, http://www.as-editions.com. Ed. Michel Gladyrewsky. Adv. contact Isabelle Girault. Circ: 10,000 (controlled).

792 USA ISSN 0044-7927
PN2016
A S T R NEWSLETTER. Text in English. 1972. 2/yr. membership. adv. **Document type:** *Newsletter.*
Media: Duplicated (not offset).
Indexed: IBT&D, MLA-IB.
Published by: American Society for Theatre Research, c/o P T Dircks, Ed, C W Post College, Dept of English, Greenvale, NY 11548. TEL 516-299-2391. Circ: 600 (controlled).

791.53 NOR ISSN 0800-2479
AAND I HANSKE; tidsskrift for norsk dukketeaterfofrening. Text in Norwegian. 1983. s-a. **Description:** Puppetry in Norway.
Indexed: MLA-IB.
Published by: U N I M A Norge, c/o Norsk Dukketeater Forening, Hovinveien 1, Oslo, 0576, Norway. TEL 47-22-677356, post@unima.no, http://www.unima.no.

792 ESP ISSN 1889-5131
▼ **ABIERTO AL PUBLICO.** Text in Spanish. 2009. a. **Document type:** *Magazine, Consumer.*
Published by: Red Espanola de Teatros, Auditorios, Circuitos y Festivales de Titularidad Publica, C Hileras, 4 5a. Planta, Oficina 7, Madrid, 28013, Spain. TEL 34-915-489560, FAX 34-915-487754, redteatros@redescena.net, http://www.redescena.net/.

ACADEMY PLAYERS DIRECTORY. *see* MOTION PICTURES

792 ESP ISSN 1130-7269
PQ6115
ACOTACIONES; revista de investigacion teatral. Text in Spanish; Abstracts in English. 1990. s-a. price varies. **Document type:** *Monographic series, Academic/Scholarly.*
Published by: Real Escuela Superior de Arte Dramatico, Ave. de Nazaret No. 2, Madrid, 28009, Spain. TEL 34-9-5042151.

▼ **ACT;** zeitschrift fuer musik & performance. *see* MUSIC

792.09 POL ISSN 0860-7443
ACTA UNIVERSITATIS LODZIENSIS: FOLIA SCIENTIAE ARTIUM ET LITTERARUM. Text in Polish; Summaries in Multiple languages. irreg., latest vol.10, 2001. price varies. **Document type:** *Monographic series, Academic/Scholarly.* **Description:** Presents articles about history of theatre, drama and film.
Supersedes in part (in 1989): Acta Universitatis Lodziensis: Folia Scientiarum Artium et Librorum
Published by: Wydawnictwo Uniwersytetu Lodzkiego/Lodz University Press, ul Lindleya 8, Lodz, 90-131, Poland. TEL 48-42-6655861, FAX 48-42-6655861, wdwul@uni.lodz.pl, http://www.wydawnictwo.uni.lodz.pl.

792 USA
ACTORS THEATRE. Text in English. 2003. m. adv. **Document type:** *Magazine, Consumer.* **Description:** Program for Actors Theatre of Lousiville productions.

Published by: Fearless Designs, Inc, 622 E Main St, Ste 206, Louisville, KY 40202. TEL 502-582-9713, FAX 502-584-1332, fearlessdesigns@bellsouth.net, http://www.theaudiencegroup.com/fearless.html. adv.: color page USD 1,750; trim 5.5 x 8.5. Circ: 20,000 (free).

800 FRA ISSN 1952-5516
ADAPTATIONS THEATRALES. Text in French. 2006. irreg. back issues avail. **Document type:** *Monographic series, Consumer.*
Published by: Editions Les Solitaires Intempestifs, 1 Rue Gay Lussac, Besancon, 25000, France. TEL 33-3-81810022, FAX 33-3-81833215, http://www.solitairesintempestifs.com/.

AFRICALIA THE NEWSLETTER. *see* ART

AFRICAN ARTS. *see* ART

792 GBR ISSN 1750-4848
➤ **AFRICAN PERFORMANCE REVIEW.** Text in English. 2007. 3/yr. free to members (effective 2009). back issues avail. **Document type:** *Journal, Academic/Scholarly.* **Description:** Features articles and reviews on all aspects of African performance and theatre.
Related titles: Online - full text ed.: ISSN 1753-5964.
Published by: (African Theatre Association), Adonis & Abbey Publishers Ltd., PO Box 43418, London, SE11 4XZ, United Kingdom. TEL 44-845-3887248, editor@adonis-abbey.com. Ed. Dr. Osita Okagbue.

792 305.896 USA ISSN 1941-4781
▼ **AFRICAN THEATRE.** Text in English. 2009. s-a. USD 24.95 per issue (effective 2010). adv. back issues avail. **Document type:** *Journal, Academic/Scholarly.* **Description:** Topics include the remarkable collaboration between Horse and Bamboo, a puppet theatre company based in the United Kingdom, and Nigerian playwright Sam Ukala that was inspired by the infamous execution of Nigerian playwright Ken Saro-Wiwa and other Ogoni activists; the plays of Femi Osofisan; and plays by Ghanaian playwrights Joe de Graft and Mohammed Ben-Abdallah.
Related titles: Online - full text ed.: ISSN 1941-479X.
Published by: Indiana University Press, 601 N Morton St, Bloomington, IN 47404. TEL 812-855-8817, 800-842-6796, journals@indiana.edu, http://iupress.indiana.edu. Eds. Femi Osofisan, James Gibbs, Martin Banham.

AGENCIES: WHAT THE ACTOR NEEDS TO KNOW (HOLLYWOOD EDITION). *see* MOTION PICTURES

AGENTS, MANAGERS & CASTING DIRECTORS 411. *see* MOTION PICTURES

792 USA
AISLESAY; the internet magazine of stage reviews and opinion. Text in English. 1995. bi-w. **Document type:** *Magazine, Consumer.* **Description:** Provides professional theatre criticism online.
Media: Online - full text.
Indexed: IBT&D.
Published by: TheatreNet Enterprizes, 41-02 42nd St, Ste 4B, Long Island City, NY 11014. TEL 718-786-2084. Ed. John Chatterton.

792 SWE
AKT-NYTT FRAAN TEATERFOERBUNDET. Text in Swedish. 1961. 9/yr. SEK 350 (effective 2004). adv. **Document type:** *Magazine, Trade.*
Formerly (until 1996): Nytt fraan Teaterfoerbundet (0283-8176)
Published by: Svenska Teaterfoerbundet/Swedish Union for Theatre, Artists, and Media, Kaplansbacken 2A, PO Box 12710, Stockholm, 11294, Sweden. TEL 46-8-4411300, FAX 46-8-6539507, info@teaterforbundet.se, http://www.teaterforbundet.se. Ed. Magdalena Boman. Adv. contact Kurt Alm TEL 46-8-54130510. B&W page SEK 9,000, color page SEK 11,200; trim 195 x 265. Circ: 9,000.

792 CAN ISSN 1922-1436
ALL STAGES MAGAZINE. Text in English. 3/yr. free to members (effective 2010). adv. back issues avail. **Document type:** *Magazine, Consumer.* **Description:** Features articles about the Alberta theatre community.
Formerly (until 2009): Theatre Alberta News (1204-4156)
Published by: Theatre Alberta, 3rd Fl Percy Page Ctr, 11759 Groat Rd, Edmonton, AB T5M 3K6, Canada. TEL 780-422-8162, 888-422-8160, FAX 780-422-2663, theatreab@theatrealberta.com. Ed. David van Belle. adv.: page USD 225; 7 x 9.5.

791 POL ISSN 0065-6526
ALMANACH SCENY POLSKIEJ. Text in Polish. 1961. a. price varies. play rev. stat.; illus. index. back issues avail. **Document type:** *Yearbook, Academic/Scholarly.* **Description:** Contains annual repertory of Polish theatres.
Published by: Polska Akademia Nauk, Instytut Sztuki/Polish Academy of Science, Institute of Art, ul Dluga 28, Warsaw, 00950, Poland. TEL 48-22-5048200, FAX 48-22-8313149, ispan@ispan.pl. Ed. Anna Chojnacka. Circ: 300 (paid).

792 USA
ALPHA PSI OMEGA: PLAYBILL. Text in English. 1927. a. free (effective 2011). bk.rev.; play rev. illus.; stat. back issues avail. **Document type:** *Newsletter, Trade.*
Related titles: Online - full text ed.: free (effective 2010).
Published by: Alpha Psi Omega National Theatre Honorary, Wichita State University, 1845 Fairmount St, PO Box 153, Wichita, KS 67260. president@alphapsiomega.org. Ed. Bret Jones TEL 316-978-3646. Circ: 7,000 (controlled). **Co-sponsor:** Delta Psi Omega.

780 790 USA
ALTERNATE ROOTS NEWSLETTER. Text in English. 1977. q. USD 20; USD 30 foreign (effective 2000 & 2001). adv. dance rev.; music rev.; play rev. back issues avail. **Document type:** *Newsletter.*
Published by: Alternate Roots, Little Five Points Community Center, 1083 Austin Ave, Atlanta, GA 30307. TEL 404-577-1079, FAX 404-577-7991, http://www.home.earthlink.net/~altroots/. Ed., R&P, Adv. contact Alice Lovelace. B&W page USD 400, color page USD 950; trim 10 x 8. Circ: 6,500.

792.0222 CZE ISSN 0002-6786
AMATERSKA SCENA; dvoumesicnik pro otazky amaterskeho divadla a umeleckeho prednesu. Text in Czech. 1965 (vol.2). bi-m. CZK 240 domestic; USD 69 foreign; CZK 40 newsstand/cover (effective 2009). play rev. abstr. **Document type:** *Magazine, Trade.*
Indexed: RASB.
Published by: Narodni Informacni a Poradenske Stredisko pro Kulturu (N I P O S), Blanicka 4, Prague 2, 120 21, Czech Republic. TEL 420-2-21507900, FAX 420-2-21507929, nipos@nipos-mk.cz, http://www.nipos-mk.cz. Circ: 1,600.

792.022 GBR ISSN 0002-6867
AMATEUR STAGE. Text in English. 1946. m. GBP 24; GBP 2.40 newsstand/cover (effective 2000). adv. bk.rev.; music rev.; play rev. illus. index. **Document type:** *Magazine, Consumer.* **Description:** Provides practical, up-top-date news, information and opinion for all those involved in community and amateur theater.
Related titles: Microform ed.: (from PQC).
Published by: Platform Publications Ltd., Hampden House, 2 Weymouth St, London, W1N 3FD, United Kingdom. TEL 44-20-7636-4343, FAX 44-20-7636-2323. Ed. Charles Vance. Adv. contact Dawn Kellogg. Circ: 7,000.

792 GBR ISSN 0964-5470
AMATEUR THEATRE YEARBOOK. Text in English. 1989. a. GBP 16 (effective 2000). adv. back issues avail. **Document type:** *Directory, Trade.*
Published by: Platform Publications Ltd., Hampden House, 2 Weymouth St, London, W1N 3FD, United Kingdom. TEL 44-20-7636-4343, FAX 44-20-7636-2323. Ed. Charles Vance. Adv. contact Dawn Kellogg. page GBP 350; trim 190 x 120. Circ: 2,000 (controlled).

792 USA ISSN 8750-3255
PN2000
AMERICAN THEATRE; the monthly forum for news, features and opinion about the American theatre. Text in English. 1973. 10/yr. free to members (effective 2010). adv. bk.rev.; play rev. illus. 96 p./no.; back issues avail.; reprints avail. **Document type:** *Magazine, Consumer.* **Description:** Each issue features reports on plays in print, performances, and theater season schedules in the US and abroad. Includes full-length play scripts five times per year.
Former titles (until 1984): Theatre Communications (0275-5971); (until 1979): Theatre Communications Group Newsletter (0163-9137)
Related titles: Microform ed.: (from PQC); Online - full text ed.
Indexed: A01, A02, A03, A08, A10, A21, A22, A25, A26, A27, ASIP, AmHI, B04, B14, BRD, BRI, C05, C12, CBRI, CPerI, ChPerI, Chicano, E08, G05, G06, G07, G08, H07, H08, HAb, HumInd, I05, I07, IBT&D, IIPA, L05, L06, M01, M02, MASUSE, MLA-IB, P02, P10, P13, P48, P53, P54, PCI, PQC, RASB, RI-1, RI-2, S07, S08, S09, S23, SRI, T02, V03, W03.
—BLDSC (0857.860000), IE, Infotrieve, Ingenta.
Published by: Theatre Communications Group, Inc., 520 Eighth Ave, 24th Fl, New York, NY 10018. TEL 212-609-5900, FAX 212-609-5901, tcg@tcg.org. Ed. Jim O'Quinn TEL 212-609-5900 ext 220. adv.: color page USD 2,335, B&W page USD 1,900; 7 x 10. Circ: 18,000.

792 USA ISSN 0899-9880
AMERICAN UNIVERSITY STUDIES. SERIES 26. THEATER ARTS. Text in English. 1989. irreg., latest vol.31, 2003. price varies. **Document type:** *Monographic series, Academic/Scholarly.* **Description:** Studies all areas and aspects of the theatre, both art and history.
Indexed: IIPA.
Published by: Peter Lang Publishing, Inc. (Subsidiary of: Peter Lang Publishing Group), 29 Broadway, New York, NY 10006. TEL 212-647-7700, 212-647-7706, 800-770-5264, FAX 212-647-7707, customerservice@plang.com.

792 CHN
ANHUI XIN XI. Text in Chinese. bi-m. CNY 1.20 per issue. adv.
Published by: Anhui Yishu Yanjiusuo/Anhui Art Institute, Hefei, Anhui 230001, China. TEL 255920.

791 GBR ISSN 1754-3053
ANIMATIONS IN PRINT; a review of puppets and related theatre. Text in English. 19??. q. USD 15 (effective 2009). adv. bk.rev. back issues avail. **Document type:** *Magazine, Consumer.* **Description:** Features reviews on animation in theater, film and television.
Former titles (until 2007): Animations (0140-7740); (until 1977): Puppet Centre Trust. Bulletin
Related titles: Online - full text ed.
Indexed: IBT&D.
Published by: Puppet Centre Trust, Battersea Arts Centre, Lavender Hill, London, SW11 5TN, United Kingdom. TEL 44-20-72285335, pct@puppetcentre.org.uk. Ed. Dorothy Max Prior.

ANIMEFANTASTIQUE. *see* MOTION PICTURES

792 301 ITA ISSN 2039-2281
▼ **ANTROPOLOGIA E TEATRO.** Text in Multiple languages. 2010. a. **Document type:** *Journal, Academic/Scholarly.*
Media: Online - full text.
Published by: Universita degli Studi di Bologna, Dipartimento di Musica e Spettacolo, Via Galliera 3-40121, Bologna, Italy. http://www.muspe.unibo.it.

792 780 DEU ISSN 0936-7446
APPLAUS; Kultur-Magazin. Text in German. 1977. m. EUR 39 domestic; EUR 62 foreign; EUR 30 to students; EUR 3.95 newsstand/cover (effective 2009). adv. **Document type:** *Magazine, Consumer.* **Description:** Contains articles on items of cultural interest, including theater, music, cinema, arts and comics.
Published by: Christian Hartmann Verlag GmbH, Agnes-Bernauer-Str 129, Munich, 80687, Germany. TEL 49-89-6936560, FAX 49-89-69365656. Ed. Angela Pillatzki. Pub. Christian Hartmann. Adv. contact Cornelia Handel. color page EUR 3,590, B&W page EUR 2,300; trim 210 x 297. Circ: 11,900 (paid).

800 USA
APPLAUSE FIRST FOLIO EDITIONS. Text in English. 19??. irreg. USD 12.95 per vol. (effective 2011). back issues avail. **Document type:** *Monographic series, Trade.*
Published by: Applause Theatre & Cinema Books, 118 E 30th St, New York, NY 10016. TEL 800-637-2852, info@halleonardbooks.com, http://www.halleonardbooks.com. Ed. Neil Freeman.

800 USA
THE APPLAUSE SHAKESPEARE LIBRARY. Text in English. 19??. irreg. USD 9.95 per vol. (effective 2011). **Document type:** *Monographic series, Trade.*
Published by: Applause Theatre & Cinema Books, 118 E 30th St, New York, NY 10016. TEL 212-532-5525, 800-637-2852, FAX 646-562-5852, info@halleonardbooks.com.

792.02 AUS ISSN 1443-1726
➤ **APPLIED THEATRE RESEARCHER.** Text in English. 1999. a. free (effective 2011). back issues avail. **Document type:** *Journal, Academic/Scholarly.* **Description:** Covers theatre and drama in non-traditional contexts - theatre in the community, theatre in business and industry, theatre in political debate and action, theatre in lifelong education and learning.
Media: Online - full content.
Indexed: A39, C27, C29, CA, D03, D04, E13, IBT&D, R14, S14, S15, S18, T02.
Published by: (International Drama/Theatre and Education Association), The Center for Applied Theatre Researcher, Rm 1.58, Macrossen Bldg (N16), Griffith University, Nathan Campus, 170 Kessels Rd, Nathan, QLD 4111, Australia. TEL 61-7-37357338, FAX 61-7-37354132, j.jones@griffith.edu.au. Eds. John O'Toole, Penny Bundy.

792 CHL ISSN 0716-4440
PN2491
➤ **APUNTES.** Text in Spanish. 1960. s-a. CLP 6,400 domestic; USD 30 in United States; USD 36 in Europe (effective 2003). adv. bk.rev. bibl.; illus. 124 p./no.; back issues avail. **Document type:** *Academic/Scholarly.* **Description:** Presents the founding philosophy and supporting methods for theater activities. Contains a modern drama in its entirety and news of the theater in Chile and in the world.
Indexed: MLA-IB, RI-1.
Published by: Pontificia Universidad Catolica de Chile, Escuela de Teatro, Jaime Guzman Errazuriz, 3300, Santiago, Chile. TEL 56-2-6865214, FAX 56-2-6865249. Ed. Maria de la Luz Hurtado Merino. Circ: 1,200.

792 ITA ISSN 0066-6661
ARCHIVIO DEL TEATRO ITALIANO. Text in Italian. 1968. irreg., latest 1982. price varies. **Document type:** *Monographic series, Academic/Scholarly.*
Published by: Edizioni Il Polifilo, Via Borgonuovo, 2, Milan, MI 20121, Italy. http://www.ilpolifilo.it.

792 ITA ISSN 1125-3967
PN2005
ARIEL. Text in Italian. 1986. 3/yr. EUR 40 domestic; EUR 60 foreign (effective 2010). **Document type:** *Journal, Academic/Scholarly.*
Related titles: Online - full text ed.: ISSN 2037-6626.
Indexed: MLA-IB.
Published by: (Istituto di Studi Pirandelliani), Bulzoni Editore, Via dei Liburni 14, Rome, 00185, Italy. bulzoni@bulzoni.it, http://www.bulzoni.it. Ed. Alfredo Barbina.

ART LAW & ACCOUNTING REPORTER. *see* LAW

792 IRL ISSN 0790-746X
ART MATTERS. Text in English. 1986. q. free (effective 2004). **Document type:** *Bulletin, Consumer.* **Description:** Contains information and schedules for arts activities throughout Ireland.
Related titles: Online - full content ed.
Published by: Arts Council/An Chomhairle Ealaion, 70 Merrion Sq, Dublin, 2, Ireland. TEL 353-1-6180200, FAX 353-1-6610349, http://www.artscouncil.ie.

ARTISTEN. *see* LABOR UNIONS

792 GBR ISSN 0143-8131
PN2598.5
ARTISTES & AGENTS. Key Title: Artistes and Their Agents. Text in English. 1981. a. GBP 46.95; GBP 96 combined subscription (print & online eds.); GBP 8 combined subscription per issue (print & online eds.) (effective 2009). adv. 503 p./no.; **Document type:** *Directory, Trade.* **Description:** Lists all the agents and personal managers in the UK along with the artistes they represent such as, actors, actresses, musicians, bands, chefs, presenters, public/guest/after dinner speakers, comedians, magicians and illusionists, sports personalities, politicians, and so on.
Related titles: Online - full content ed.
Published by: Richmond House Publishing Company Ltd., 70-76 Bell St, Marylebone, London, NW1 6SP, United Kingdom. TEL 44-20-72249666, FAX 44-20-72249688, sales@rhpco.co.uk.

792 USA ISSN 1051-9718
ARTISTS AND ISSUES IN THE THEATRE. Text in English. 1990. irreg., latest vol.16, 2008. price varies. **Document type:** *Monographic series, Academic/Scholarly.* **Description:** Discusses the theatre from all standpoints: art, society, and politics.
—BLDSC (1735.283660).
Published by: Peter Lang Publishing, Inc. (Subsidiary of: Peter Lang Publishing Group), 29 Broadway, New York, NY 10006. TEL 212-647-7700, 212-647-7706, 800-770-5264, FAX 212-647-7707, customerservice@plang.com. Ed. August W Staub.

792 CAN ISSN 1719-7864
ARTISTS' WORKSHOPS AND PERFORMANCES. Text in English. a. **Document type:** *Journal, Consumer.*
Former titles (until 2005): Artists for Schools and Community (1711-6538); (until 2001): Artists Workshop & Performances (1711-652X); (until 2000): Artists Workshops & Performances for Schools & Communities (1711-6511)
Related titles: French ed.: Spectacles et Ateliers d'Artistes. ISSN 1719-7872.
Published by: M A S C, 250 Holland Ave., Ottawa, ON K1Y 0Y6, Canada. TEL 613-725-9119, FAX 613-728-3872, masc@masconline.ca, http://www.masconline.ca.

▼ **ARTS.** *see* ART

792 USA
ARTS ALIVE!; a magazine promoting the arts. Text in English. 1977. m. USD 18 (effective 1998). adv. **Document type:** *Magazine, Consumer.*
Formerly (until 1986): Theatrical Faces
Published by: Admar Associates - Theatrical Faces Inc., 3140 B Tilghman St, Box 204, Allentown, PA 18104. TEL 610-398-5660, FAX 610-398-5663. Pub. Adeline S Burt. Adv. contact Adeline Burt. Circ: 18,000 (controlled).

792 CAN
ARTS CLUB THEATRE ENCORE. Text in English. 1984. bi-m. adv.
Published by: Arts Club Theatre, 1585 Johnston St, Vancouver, BC V6H 3R9, Canada. TEL 604-687-5315, FAX 604-687-3306. Ed. Lin Bennett.

ARTS COUNCIL. ANNUAL REPORT/AN CHOMHAIRLE EALAION. TUARASCAIL BHILANTUIL. *see* ART

792 FRA ISSN 0296-2292
ARTS DU SPECTACLE. Variant title: Collection Arts du Spectacle. Text in French. 1954. irreg. price varies. **Document type:** *Monographic series, Academic/Scholarly.*
Formerly (until 1983): Le Choeur des Muses (0768-150X)
Related titles: ◆ Series: Recherches et Editions Musicales. ISSN 1284-7119; ◆ Les Voies de la Creation Theatrale. ISSN 1140-5309.

Published by: Centre National de la Recherche Scientifique, Campus Gerard-Megie, 3 Rue Michel-Ange, Paris, 75794, France. TEL 33-1-44964000, FAX 33-1-44965390, http://www.cnrseditions.fr.

792 USA ISSN 0004-4067
N1
ARTS MANAGEMENT. Text in English. 1962. 5/yr. USD 22 in United States; USD 23 in Canada; USD 25 elsewhere. adv. bk.rev. stat. index. reprints avail. **Document type:** *Newsletter.* **Description:** National news service for those who finance, manage and communicate the arts.
Related titles: Microform ed.: (from PQC).
Published by: Radius Group Inc., 110 Riverside Dr, No 4E, New York, NY 10024. TEL 212-579-2039, FAX 212-579-2049. Ed., Pub., R&P, Adv. contact Alvin H Reiss. Circ: 12,000 (paid).

792 791.43 700 GBR ISSN 1748-9628
ARTS NEWS. Text in English. 1980. bi-m. **Document type:** *Magazine, Consumer.*
Related titles: Online - full text ed.
Published by: Canadian High Commission, Canada House, London, SW1Y 5BJ, United Kingdom. TEL 44-20-72586600, FAX 44-20-72586533, http://www.international.gc.ca./canadaeuropa/united_kingdom/.

700 USA
ARTSEARCH (ONLINE). Text in English. 19??. s-m. USD 60 to individuals; USD 150 to institutions (effective 2010). **Document type:** *Consumer.* **Description:** Lists jobs in theater, dance, opera companies, symphony orchestras, universities, arts councils, performing arts centers, and more.
Media: Online - full text.
Published by: Theatre Communications Group, Inc., 520 Eighth Ave, 24th Fl, New York, NY 10018. TEL 212-609-5900, FAX 212-609-5901, tcg@tmn.com.

792 950 USA ISSN 0742-5457
PN2860
➤ **ASIAN THEATRE JOURNAL.** Abbreviated title: A T J. Text in English. 1984. s-a. USD 30 domestic to individuals; USD 54 foreign to individuals; USD 80 domestic to institutions; USD 104 foreign to institutions; USD 20 per issue domestic to individuals; USD 32 per issue foreign to individuals; USD 40 per issue domestic to institutions; USD 52 per issue foreign to institutions (effective 2009). adv. bk.rev.; play rev. illus. 160 p./no.; back issues avail.; reprint service avail. from PSC. **Document type:** *Journal, Academic/Scholarly.* **Description:** Focuses on the performing arts of Asia.
Supersedes: Asian Theatre Reports (0161-4908)
Related titles: Online - full text ed.: ISSN 1527-2109. 2000.
Indexed: A01, A03, A08, A20, A22, A26, A27, ASCA, AmHI, ArtHuCI, BAS, BibInd, CA, CurCont, DIP, E01, E08, G08, H07, I05, I07, I08, IBR, IBT&D, IBZ, IDP, IIPA, MLA-IB, P10, P48, P53, P54, PCI, PQC, RASB, RILM, S07, S09, S23, SCOPUS, T02, W07.
—BLDSC (1742.752300), IE, Infotrieve, Ingenta. **CCC.**
Published by: (Association for Asian Performance), University of Hawaii Press, Journals Department, 2840 Kolowalu St, Honolulu, HI 96822. TEL 808-956-8255, FAX 808-988-6052. Ed. Kathy Foley TEL 831-459-4189. R&P Joel Bradshaw TEL 808-956-6790. Adv. contact Norman Kaneshiro TEL 808-956-8833. page USD 200; 4.75 x 8. Circ: 450.

➤ **ASOCIACION ARGENTINA DE ACTORES. MEMORIA Y BALANCE.** *see* LABOR UNIONS

792 ESP ISSN 1134-7643
PN1608
ASSAIG DE TEATRE. Text in Catalan. 1994. s-a. back issues avail. **Document type:** *Monographic series, Academic/Scholarly.*
Indexed: MLA-IB.
Published by: Associacio d'Investigacio i Experimentacio Teatral, C Torre d'En Damians, 40 Baixos, Barcelona, 08014, Spain. TEL 34-93-2892481, aiet@ub.edu.

792 ISR ISSN 0334-5963
PN2001
➤ **ASSAPH. SECTION C: STUDIES IN THE THEATRE.** Text in English. 1984. a. USD 7 to individuals; USD 12 to institutions; USD 12 per issue (effective 2003). back issues avail. **Document type:** *Journal, Academic/Scholarly.*
Indexed: CA, IBT&D, MLA-IB, T02.
Published by: Tel Aviv University, Faculty of Visual and Performing Arts (Subsidiary of: Tel Aviv University), Department of Theatre Arts, Ramat Aviv, Tel Aviv, 69978, Israel. TEL 972-3-6409487, FAX 972-3-6409482. Ed. Linda Ben-Zvi. Circ: 500.

792 CAN ISSN 1193-7564
PN2009
ASSOCIATION FOR CANADIAN THEATRE RESEARCH. NEWSLETTER/ASSOCIATION DE LA RECHERCHE THEATRALE AU CANADA. BULLETIN DE LIAISON. Text mainly in English; Text in French. 1975. s-a. looseleaf. CAD 75; CAD 30 to students (effective 2006). adv. back issues avail. **Document type:** *Newsletter.* **Description:** Contains a range of news items of interest to members, including reports of association business, conferences in related disciplines, calls for papers, annual bibliography, progress reports on research projects, abstracts from annual conference.
Formerly (until 1991): Association for Canadian Theatre History. Newsletter (0705-7989)
Related titles: Online - full content ed.
Published by: Association for Canadian Theatre Research, Departement d'Anglais, Universite de Moncton, Moncton, NB E1A 3E9, Canada. TEL 506-858-4244, FAX 506-858-4144, nicholgs@umoncton.ca. Ed. Susan Knutson. R&P Kathy Chung. Circ: 250.

792 USA
ASSOCIATION OF TALENT AGENTS. NEWSLETTER. Text in English. m. membership. **Document type:** *Newsletter.*
Formerly: Association of Talent Agents. Bulletin
Published by: Association of Talent Agents, 9255 Sunset Blvd, Ste 930, Los Angeles, CA 90069. TEL 310-274-0628, FAX 310-274-5063, shellie@agentassociation.com, http://www.agentassociation.com. Ed. Karen Stuart.

ATOKA; Yoruba photoplay series. *see* LITERATURE

792 USA
AUDITION NEWS. Text in English. m. USD 24.95 (effective 1998). adv. illus. **Document type:** *Magazine, Consumer.*
Published by: Chicago Entertainment Co., 360 23 W Schick Rd, 126, PO Box 250, Bloomingdale, IL 60108.

792 USA
AUDITIONS U S A. Text in English. bi-w. USD 69 (effective 2000).
Published by: The John King Network, 244 Madison Ave, Ste 393, New York, NY 10016. TEL 212-969-8715, 212-969-8715.

792 AUS ISSN 0810-4123
PN3010
➤ **AUSTRALASIAN DRAMA STUDIES.** Text in English. 1982. s-a. AUD 75 domestic to individuals; AUD 100 domestic to institutions; AUD 110 foreign (effective 2008). adv. bk.rev. back issues avail. **Document type:** *Journal, Academic/Scholarly.* **Description:** Theatre studies with an emphasis on Australian and New Zealand drama.
Related titles: Online - full text ed.
Indexed: A11, A20, ArtHuCI, AusPAIS, BEL&L, CA, IBT&D, IIPA, INZP, L05, L06, MLA-IB, PCI, RASB, RILM, SCOPUS, T02, W07.
—Ingenta.
Published by: La Trobe University, Theatre & Drama Program, Bundoora, VIC 3086, Australia. Ed. Geoffrey Milne. Circ: 350.

➤ **AUSTRALIAN DRAMA EDUCATION MAGAZINE.** *see* EDUCATION

792 FRA ISSN 0045-1169
PN6113
L'AVANT-SCENE. THEATRE. Variant title: L' Avant-Scene du Theatre. Text in French. 1949. 20/yr. EUR 163 domestic to individuals; EUR 191 foreign to individuals; EUR 132 domestic to students (effective 2009). adv. illus. reprints avail. **Document type:** *Magazine, Consumer.*
Former titles (until 1961): L' Avant-Scene (1144-1380); (until 1953): Radiopera (1144-1372); (until 1952): Opera. Supplement Theatral (1144-1364)
Indexed: A20, A22, DIP, IBR, IBT&D, IBZ, IIPA, MLA-IB, RASB.
—IE, Infotrieve.
Published by: Editions de l' Avant Scene, 6 rue Git-le-Coeur, Paris, 75006, France. TEL 33-01-46342820, FAX 33-01-43545014, astheatre@aol.com.

792 USA ISSN 1946-5440
BACK STAGE. Text in English. 2008. w. USD 79; USD 195 combined subscription (print & online eds.) (effective 2011). adv. **Document type:** *Newspaper, Trade.* **Description:** Provides updated production listings or reading our periodic spotlights on photography, college programs, acting schools and coaches informations for actors, singers and dancers they need to succeed in the entertainment business.
Formed by the merger of (2000-2008): Back Stage West (1531-572X); Which was formerly (1998-2000): Back Stage West, Drama-Logue (1520-2917); Which was formed by the merger of (19??-1998): Drama-Logue (0272-2720); (1993-1998): Back Stage West (1076-5379); (2005-2008): Back Stage East (1930-5966); Which was formerly (1960-2005): Back Stage (0005-3635)
Related titles: Online - full text ed.: USD 79 (effective 2011).
Indexed: A10, A26, B02, B07, B15, B17, B18, F01, F02, G04, G06, G07, G08, I05, IBT&D, P34, P48, PQC, T02, V03.
—CCC.
Published by: Prometheus Global Media, 5700 Wilshire Blvd, 5th Fl, Los Angeles, CA 90036. TEL 323-525-2270, http://www.prometheusgm.com.

800 USA ISSN 1931-0528
PS627.O53
THE BACK STAGE BOOK OF NEW AMERICAN SHORT PLAYS. Text in English. 2005. a. **Document type:** *Journal, Consumer.*
Published by: Watson-Guptill Publications, 770 Broadway, New York, NY 10003-9522. TEL 646-654-5500, http://www.watsonguptill.com.

BACKSTAGE; la rivista dello show business. *see* MUSIC

792 DEU
BADISCHES STAATSTHEATER KARLSRUHE. SPIELPLAN. Text in German. a. free (effective 2008). adv. **Document type:** *Directory, Consumer.* **Description:** Provides information on events and performances at the Badisches Staatstheater.
Published by: Badisches Staatstheater Karlsruhe, Baumeisterstr 11, Karlsruhe, 76137, Germany. TEL 49-721-35570, FAX 49-721-373223, pressestelle@badisches-staatstheater.de.

792 DEU
BADISCHES STAATSTHEATER KARLSRUHE. THEATERSPIEGEL. Text in German. 1987. m. adv. play rev. illus. **Document type:** *Newspaper, Consumer.* **Description:** Contains information on the productions and personnel of the Badische Staatstheater.
Former titles (until 2002): Badisches Staatstheater Karlsruhe. Theaterzeitung; (until 1998): Thema - Das Theatermagazin; (until 1989): Musengaul
Published by: Badisches Staatstheater Karlsruhe, Baumeisterstr 11, Karlsruhe, 76137, Germany. TEL 49-721-35570, FAX 49-721-373223, pressestelle@badisches-staatstheater.de, http://www.staatstheater.karlsruhe.de. Circ: 20,000.

BALLET-HOO. *see* DANCE

792 ISR ISSN 0045-138X
BAMAH (JERUSALEM); educational theatre review. Text in Hebrew. 1933. q. USD 40. adv. bk.rev. index, cum.index. **Document type:** *Academic/Scholarly.*
Indexed: IBT&D, IHP, MLA-IB.
Published by: Bamah Association, P O Box 7311, Jerusalem, 91072, Israel. TEL 972-2-5661815, FAX 972-2-5631022. Eds. Amos Yovel, Dwora Gilula.

791.3 USA ISSN 0005-4968
GV1800
BANDWAGON; the journal of the Circus Historical Society. Text in English. 1956. bi-m. USD 40 domestic; USD 42 in Canada; USD 44 elsewhere (effective 2007). adv. bk.rev. illus. back issues avail.; reprints avail. **Document type:** *Magazine, Consumer.*
Related titles: Microform ed.; Online - full text ed.
Indexed: IBT&D, IIPA, RASB, T02.
Published by: Circus Historical Society, 1075 W Fifth Ave, Columbus, OH 43212. TEL 614-294-5361. Circ: 1,400.

792 821 GBR ISSN 0264-6137
BARE NIBS. Text in English. 1983. q. GBP 2.60, USD 5. adv. back issues avail.
Published by: Ware Arts Centre, 31 Richmond Close, Ware, Herts SG12 0EN, United Kingdom. Ed. Steve Woollard. Circ: 150. **Subscr. to:** 24 The Ridgeway, Ware, Herts SG12 0RT, United Kingdom.

BEAMER; Kulturzeitschrift junger Menschen. *see* CHILDREN AND YOUTH—For

792 DEU ISSN 1863-2106
BERLINER SCHRIFTEN ZUM THEATER DER UNTERDRUECKTEN. Text in German. 2006. irreg., latest vol.4, 2009. price varies. **Document type:** *Monographic series, Academic/Scholarly.*
Published by: Ibidem Verlag, Melchiorstr 15, Stuttgart, 70439, Germany. TEL 49-711-9807954, FAX 49-711-9807952, ibidem@ibidem-verlag.de, http://www.ibidem-verlag.de.

792 DEU ISSN 0948-7646
BERLINER THEATERWISSENSCHAFT. Text in German. 1995. irreg., latest vol.12, 2006. price varies. **Document type:** *Monographic series, Academic/Scholarly.*
Published by: Vistas Verlag GmbH, Goltzstr 11, Berlin, 10781, Germany. TEL 49-30-32707446, FAX 49-30-32707455, medienverlag@vistas.de.

792 USA ISSN 1067-134X
PN2080
THE BEST MEN'S STAGE MONOLOGUES. Text in English. 1990. a. USD 11.95 per issue (effective 2004).
Published by: Smith and Kraus Publishers, Inc., 6 Lower Mill Rd, North Stratford, NH 03590. TEL 603-669-7032, 800-895-4331, FAX 603-669-7945, sandk@sover.net, http://www.smithkraus.com.

792 USA ISSN 1942-339X
THE BEST PLAYS THEATER YEARBOOK. Text in English. 1899. a. USD 49.99 (effective 2011). **Document type:** *Monographic series, Trade.*
Former titles (until 2004): The Best Plays of .. (1071-6971); until 1993): The Applause - Best Plays Theatre Yearbook (1063-620X); (until 1991): The Burns Mantle Theater Yearbook of .. Featuring the Ten Best Plays of the Season; (until 1980): Best Plays (0276-2625); (until 1953): Best Plays and the Year Book of the Drama in America (0276-6183); (until 1951): Burns Mantle Best Plays and the Year Book of the Drama in America (0197-6427); (until 1948): Best Plays and the Year Book of the Drama in America (0197-6435); (until 1909): Best Plays (0197-6443)
—BLDSC (1942.327600).
Published by: Applause Theatre & Cinema Books, 118 E 30th St, New York, NY 10016. TEL 212-532-5525, 800-637-2852, FAX 646-562-5852, info@halleonardbooks.com. Ed. Jeffrey Eric Jenkins. Circ: 20,000.

792 USA ISSN 1067-3253
PN2080
THE BEST STAGE SCENES. Text in English. 1992. a.
Published by: Smith and Kraus Publishers, Inc., 6 Lower Mill Rd, North Stratford, NH 03590. TEL 603-669-7032, FAX 603-669-7945, office@smithkraus.com, http://www.smithkraus.com.

792 ARG ISSN 1851-2275
BIBLIOTECA DE HISTORIA DEL TEATRO OCCIDENTAL. Text in Spanish. 2003. a. **Document type:** *Monographic series, Academic/Scholarly.*
Published by: Editorial Atuel, Pichincha 1901 4o. A, Buenos Aires, C1249ABO, Argentina. TEL 54-11-43051141, info@editorialatuel.com.ar, http://www.editorialatuel.com.ar/.

792 ITA ISSN 2036-0533
BIBLIOTECA DELLA RICERCA. STUDI SUL TEATRO. Variant title: Biblicteca della Ricerca. Studi sul Teatro in Onore di Paolo Grassi. Text in Italian. 2005. irreg. **Document type:** *Monographic series, Academic/Scholarly.*
Published by: Schena Editore, Viale Stazione 177, Fasano, BR 72015, Italy. TEL 39-080-4414681, FAX 39-080-4426690, info@schenaeditore.com, http://www.schenaeditore.com. Ed. Franco Punzi.

792 ITA ISSN 1828-8723
BIBLIOTECA DI DRAMMATURGIA. Text in Italian. 2006. a. price varies. **Document type:** *Monographic series, Academic/Scholarly.*
Published by: Fabrizio Serra Editore (Subsidiary of: Accademia Editoriale), c/o Accademia Editoriale, Via Santa Bibbiana 28, Pisa, 56127, Italy. TEL 39-050-542332, FAX 39-050-574888, accademiaeditoriale@accademiaeditoriale.it, http://www.libraweb.net.

BIBLIOTECA FENIANOS. *see* DANCE

792 ITA ISSN 0045-1959
PN2005
BIBLIOTECA TEATRALE; rivista di studi e ricerche sullo spettacolo. Text in Italian. 1971-1979 (no.23-24); resumed 1987. q. EUR 55 domestic; EUR 85 foreign (effective 2010). adv. bk.rev. abstr.; bibl. index, cum.index. back issues avail. **Document type:** *Journal, Academic/Scholarly.*
Related titles: Online - full text ed.: ISSN 2037-6561.
Indexed: DIP, IBR, IBZ, MLA-IB.
Published by: (Istituto Internazionale per la Ricerca Teatrale), Bulzoni Editore, Via dei Liburni 14, Rome, 00185, Italy. TEL 39-06-4455207, FAX 39-06-4450355, bulzoni@bulzoni.it, http://www.bulzoni.it. Eds. Cesare Molinari, Ferruccio Marotti.

792.029 USA ISSN 1551-7942
BILLBOARD AUDARENA INTERNATIONAL GUIDE. Text in English. 1959. a. (Oct.). USD 129 per issue (effective 2011). adv. **Document type:** *Directory, Trade.* **Description:** Directory of over 4,400 arenas, auditoriums, stadiums, exhibit halls and amphitheatres worldwide. Complete data on facilities, including contacts, seating capacities, floor size and services offered. Also, companies supplying and servicing the industry.
Former titles (until 2003): AudArena Stadium International Guide (1521-1312); (until 1996): AudArena Stadium International Guide & Facility Buyers Guide (1082-0795); AudArena Stadium International Guide; Audarena Stadium Guide and International Directory (0067-0537); Arena, Auditorium, Stadium Guide (0518-3979)
Indexed: SD, SportS.
—CCC.
Published by: Billboard Directories (Subsidiary of: Nielsen Business Publications), PO Box 15158, North Hollywood, CA 91606. TEL 818-487-4582, 800-562-2706, info@billboard.com, http://www.billboard.com. Circ: 5,000.

792 305.896 USA ISSN 0887-7580
PN2270.A35
BLACK MASKS. Text in English. 1984. bi-m. USD 25; USD 4 per issue (effective 2010). adv. illus. back issues avail.; reprints avail. **Document type:** *Magazine, Consumer.* **Description:** Devoted to information about Black performing, literary and visual arts and artists of African descent throughout the U.S. and abroad.
Related titles: Online - full text ed.
Indexed: CA, DYW, ENW, IBT&D, IIBP, T02.
Address: PO Box 7334, Athens, GA 30604. TEL 706-552-3431. Ed., Pub. Beth Turner. Adv. contact Rod Ivey.

792 USA ISSN 1062-3825
BLACK TALENT NEWS; the entertainment trade publication. Text in English. 1994-2000; resumed 2001 (Dec.). 12/yr. USD 23.97 domestic; USD 33.97 in Canada & Mexico; USD 38.97 elsewhere; USD 2.95, GBP 3.95 newsstand/cover (effective 2001). adv. bk.rev.; film rev.; music rev.; play rev.; tel.rev.; video rev. illus. back issues avail.; reprints avail. **Document type:** *Magazine, Trade.* **Description:** Delivers the latest news for and about Blacks in the entertainment industry from casting to production and box office charts, including interviews with industry executives and insightful how-to articles.
Related titles: Alternate Frequency ed(s).: B T N Weekly.
Address: PO Box 34858, Los Angeles, CA 90034-0858. TEL 310-348-3944, FAX 310-348-3949. Ed. Tanya Kersey-Henley. Pub. Tanya Kersey Henley. R&P Darrell D Miller. Adv. contact Ron Henley. B&W page USD 1,875, color page USD 2,400; trim 10.25 x 7.75. Circ: 25,000.

792 NLD ISSN 1879-9752
BLICK. Text in Dutch. 2006. bi-m. free (effective 2010). **Document type:** *Magazine, Consumer.*
Published by: Theaterwerkplaats De Prins van Groningen, Noorderbuitensingel 11, Groningen, 9717 KK, Netherlands. TEL 31-50-8507150, info@theaterwerkplaatsgroningen.nl, http://www.theaterwerkplaatsgroningen.nl. Ed. Nynke Oele. Circ: 2,500.

792 AUT ISSN 1814-5663
BLICKPUNKTE. Text in German. 1978. irreg., latest vol.12, 2007. price varies. index. **Document type:** *Monographic series, Academic/Scholarly.*
Former titles: Wiener Forschungen zur Theater und Medienwissenschaft; Vienna. Universitaet. Institut fuer Theaterwissenschaft. Wissenschaftliche Reihe (0083-6176)
Published by: (Universitaet Wien, Universitaet Wien, Institut fuer Theaterwissenschaft DEU), Wilhelm Braumueller Universitaets-Verlagsbuchhandlung GmbH, Servitengasse 5, Vienna, 1090, Austria. TEL 43-1-3191159, FAX 43-1-3102805, office@braumueller.at, http://www.braumueller.at. Ed. Hilde Haider-Pregler. Circ: 1,000.

792.08854 DNK ISSN 1904-0725
BOERNETEATERAVISEN (ONLINE). Text in Danish. 2003. q. adv. **Document type:** *Magazine, Consumer.*
Media: Online - full text.
Published by: Teatercentrum i Danmark, Farvergade 10, Copenhagen K, 1463, Denmark. TEL 45-35-304400, FAX 45-35-304401, info@teatercentrum.dk, http://www.teatercentrum.dk. Ed. Carsten Jensen.

BOMB; interviews with artists, writers, musicians, directors and actors. *see* ART

BORDER CROSSINGS; a magazine of the arts. *see* ART

BORROWERS AND LENDERS; the journal of Shakespeare and appropriation. *see* LITERATURE

BRITISH JOURNAL OF PLAY THERAPY. *see* PSYCHOLOGY

792 GBR ISSN 0951-5208
PN2001
BRITISH PERFORMING ARTS YEARBOOK. Text in English. 1987. a. GBP 35, AUD 105, EUR 57.80, DKK 38,840, JPY 6,800, USD 57.80 per issue (effective 2009). **Document type:** *Directory, Trade.* **Description:** Provides a complete guide to venues, performers, arts centers, festivals, education, support organizations, and services for the arts professional.
Indexed: RILM.
—BLDSC (2334.400000). **CCC.**
Published by: Rhinegold Publishing Ltd., 239-241 Shaftesbury Ave, London, WC2H 8TF, United Kingdom. TEL 44-20-73331720, FAX 44-20-73331765, enquiries@rhinegold.co.uk.

791.53 GBR
BRITISH PUPPET AND MODEL THEATRE GUILD. NEWSLETTER. Text in English. 1956. m. free to members (effective 2009). bk.rev. **Document type:** *Newsletter, Trade.* **Description:** Features for amateur and professional puppeteers thoughout the U K and the world.
Published by: British Puppet & Model Theatre Guild, c/o Peter Charlton, 65 Kinglsey Ave, Ealing, London, W13 OEH, United Kingdom. TEL 44-20-89978236. Circ: 400.

792 USA ISSN 0068-2748
BROADSIDE (NEW YORK, 1940). Text in English. 1940. q. free to members (effective 2010). bk.rev. back issues avail. **Document type:** *Newsletter, Consumer.* **Description:** Contains information regarding TLA sponsored events, articles about exhibits and collections related to the performing arts, and other items of interest in the fields of theatre, film and dance worldwide.
Related titles: ◆ Supplement(s): Performing Arts Resources. ISSN 0360-3814.
Published by: Theatre Library Association, c/o The New York Public Library for the Performing Arts, 40 Lincoln Ctr Plz, New York, NY 10023. info@tla-online.org. Ed. Angela Weaver.

792 USA
BROADWAY MAGAZINE. Text in English. 2007 (Mar.). bi-m. free (effective 2009). adv. **Document type:** *Magazine, Consumer.*
Address: 244 5th Ave, Ste 2006, New York, NY 10001-7604. TEL 212-252-4111. Eds. Brian Bellmont, Jen Bellmont. Pubs. Christopher Moore, Ellen Anthony. Adv. contact Michael Hasselt. color page USD 8,900; trim 6.75 x 9.125. Circ: 150,000 (free).

BROT & SPIELE; das Kulturmagazin fuer die Region Aschaffenburg. *see* MUSIC

792 AUT ISSN 0007-3075
PN2004
BUEHNE. Text in German. 1923. 11/yr. EUR 39.90; EUR 3.10 newsstand/cover (effective 2006). adv. bk.rev.; play rev.; rec.rev. illus. **Document type:** *Magazine, Consumer.*
Indexed: IBR, IBZ, IIMP, IIPA, M11, MusicInd, RASB, RILM.
Published by: Verlagsgruppe News Gesellschaft mbH (Subsidiary of: Gruner + Jahr AG & Co), Taborstr 1-3, Vienna, W 1020, Austria. TEL 43-1-213129011, FAX 43-1-213121650, redaktion@news.at, http://www.news.at. Ed. Peter Blaha. adv.: page EUR 4,900; trim 210 x 280. Circ: 57,734 (paid and controlled).

792 DEU ISSN 0007-3083
BUEHNENGENOSSENSCHAFT. Text in German. 1949. 10/yr. EUR 27 domestic; EUR 32 foreign; EUR 3.20 newsstand/cover (effective 2009). adv. bk.rev. illus. **Document type:** *Journal, Trade.*
Indexed: RASB.
Published by: (Genossenschaft Deutscher Buehnen-Angehoeriger), Buehnenschriften-Vertriebs-Gesellschaft, Feldbrunnenstr 74, Hamburg, 20148, Germany. TEL 49-40-445185, FAX 49-40-456002, gdba@buehnengenossenschaft.de, http://www.gdba.info. Ed. Michael Kuehn. Adv. contact Gerhard Draeger. Circ: 7,500 (controlled).

792 DEU ISSN 0007-3091
BUEHNENTECHNISCHE RUNDSCHAU; Zeitschrift fuer Veranstaltungstechnik, Ausstattung, Management. Abbreviated title: B T R. Text in German. 1907. bi-m. EUR 75; EUR 49 to students; EUR 9.90 newsstand/cover (effective 2010). adv. bk.rev. abstr.; bibl.; charts; illus. cum.index every 2 yrs. **Document type:** *Journal, Trade.*
Indexed: RASB, RILM.
—Linda Hall.
Published by: (Deutsche Theatertechnische Gesellschaft), Friedrich Berlin Verlagsgesellschaft mbH, Knesebeckstr 59-61, Berlin, 10719, Germany. TEL 49-30-25449520, FAX 49-30-25449512, verlag@friedrichberlin.de, http://www.friedrich-berlin.de. Ed. Karin Winkelsesser. Adv. contact Monika Kusche TEL 49-2154-429051. Circ: 1,600.

820 DEU
C D E STUDIES. (Contemporary Drama in English) Text in English, German. 1996. irreg., latest vol.18, 2009. price varies. **Document type:** *Monographic series, Academic/Scholarly.*
Published by: (German Society for Contemporary Theater and Drama in English), Wissenschaftlicher Verlag Trier, Bergstr 27, Trier, 54295, Germany. TEL 49-651-41503, FAX 49-651-41504, wvt@wvttrier.de, http://www.wvttrier.de. Ed. Martin Middeke.

792 GBR
CAMBRIDGE STUDIES IN AMERICAN THEATRE AND DRAMA. Text in English. 1994. irreg. price varies. adv. back issues avail.; reprints avail. **Document type:** *Monographic series, Trade.* **Description:** Explores various aspects of theater and drama in a cultural and social context, with a general emphasis on the American stage.
Published by: Cambridge University Press, The Edinburgh Bldg, Shaftesbury Rd, Cambridge, CB2 8RU, United Kingdom. TEL 44-1223-312393, FAX 44-1223-315052, journals@cambridge.org, http://www.cambridge.org/uk. Ed. Don B Wilmeth. Adv. contact Rebecca Roberts TEL 44-1223-325083.

CAMPUS ACTIVITIES PROGRAMMING. *see* EDUCATION—Higher Education

CANADIAN COUNCIL FOR THE ARTS. ANNUAL REPORT/CONSEIL DES ARTS DU CANADA. RAPPORT ANNUEL. *see* ART

800 CAN ISSN 1917-5086
CANADIAN PLAYS. Text in English. 2008. irreg., latest vol.2, 2010. price varies. **Document type:** *Monographic series, Academic/Scholarly.* **Description:** Features a broad range of new Canadian plays, with at least one professional production, and with a particular emphasis on Alberta works.
Related titles: Online - full text ed.: ISSN 1917-5094.
Published by: Athabasca University, 1 University Dr, Athabasca, AB T9S 3A3, Canada. TEL 780-675-6111, FAX 780-675-6437, http://www.athabascau.ca. Ed. Anne Nothof.

792.971 CAN ISSN 0315-0836
PN2009
➤ **CANADIAN THEATRE REVIEW.** Abbreviated title: C T R. Text in English. 1974. q. USD 125 in North America to institutions; USD 145 elsewhere to institutions; USD 145 combined subscription in North America to institutions (print & online eds.); USD 165 combined subscription elsewhere to institutions (print & online eds.) (effective 2011). bk.rev.; play rev. illus. cum.index: nos.1-16. back issues avail.; reprint service avail. from PSC. **Document type:** *Journal, Academic/Scholarly.*
Related titles: Microfiche ed.: (from MML); Microform ed.: (from MML); Online - full text ed.: USD 120 to institutions (effective 2011).
Indexed: A01, A03, A08, A20, A22, A25, A26, AmHI, B04, BAS, BRD, C03, C05, CA, CBCARef, CBPI, CPerI, CWPI, E01, E08, G08, H07, H08, HAb, HumInd, I05, IBR, IBRH, IBT&D, IBZ, IIPA, MEA&I, MLA, MLA-IB, P48, PCI, PQC, RASB, RILM, S07, S08, S09, SCOPUS, T02, W03.
—CIS, Ingenta. **CCC.**
Published by: (York University, Faculty of Fine Arts), University of Toronto Press, Journals Division, 5201 Dufferin St, Toronto, ON M3H 5T8, Canada. TEL 416-667-7810, FAX 416-667-7881, journals@utpress.utoronto.ca. Ed. Ric Knowles. R&P Jessica Shulist TEL 416-667-7777 ext 7849. Adv. contact Audrey Greenwood TEL 416-667-7777 ext 7766. Circ: 565.

792 CAN ISSN 0829-3627
CANPLAY. Text in English. bi-m. CAD 26; USD 26 foreign. back issues avail. **Document type:** *Newsletter.*
Former titles (until 1984): Playwrights Union of Canada. Newsletter (0827-3073); (until 1983): Guild of Canadian Playwrights. Newsletter (0824-5460)
Published by: Playwrights Union of Canada, 54 Wolseley St, 2nd Fl, Toronto, ON M5T 1A5, Canada. TEL 416-703-0201, 800-561-3318, FAX 416-703-0059. Ed. Jodi Armstrong. Circ: 700.

792 ITA ISSN 1828-8650
I CANTI DEL TEATRO GRECO. Text in Italian. 2002. a. price varies. **Document type:** *Monographic series, Academic/Scholarly.*
Published by: Fabrizio Serra Editore (Subsidiary of: Accademia Editoriale), c/o Accademia Editoriale, Via Santa Bibbiana 28, Pisa, 56127, Italy. TEL 39-050-542332, FAX 39-050-574888, accademiaeditoriale@accademiaeditoriale.it, http://www.libraweb.net.

CARNETS DE RUE. *see* ART

792 FRA ISSN 1268-0478
CASSANDRE; l'art principe actif. Text in French. 1995. bi-m. EUR 35 (effective 2005 - 2006). bk.rev.; dance rev.; play rev. illus. **Document type:** *Monographic series.* **Description:** Concerns art and society, dance, literature, music, sociology and theater.
Related titles: Online - full text ed.
Published by: (Paroles de Theatre), Paroles de Theatre-Casandre, 49 A av. de la Resistance, Montreuil, 93100, France. TEL 33-1-42874320, FAX 33-1-42874399. Ed. Nicolas Romeas. R&P Lydia Garrido. Adv. contact Leonor Delaunay. **Dist. by:** DIF-POP, 21 terrace, rue Voltaire, Paris 75011, France. TEL 33-1-40242131, FAX 33-1-40241588.

CASSIDY FOCUS. *see* CLUBS

792 ITA ISSN 0394-9389
PN2005
IL CASTELLO DI ELSINORE. Text in Italian. 1988. 3/yr. **Document type:** *Journal, Academic/Scholarly.*
Indexed: CA, IBT&D, T02.
Published by: (Universita degli Studi di Torino, Discipline Arti Musica e Spettacolo (DA M S)), Edizioni di Pagina, Via dei Mille 205, Bari, 70126, Italy. info@paginasc.it, http://www.paginasc.it. Ed. Paolo Bertinetti.

792 USA
CASTING DIRECTORS. Text in English. bi-w. USD 69 (effective 2000).
Published by: The John King Network, 244 Madison Ave, Ste 393, New York, NY 10016. TEL 212-969-8715, 212-969-8715.

792 ZAF ISSN 0250-2011
CASTING DIRECTORY/LIMELIGHT ROLVERDELINGSGIDS. Key Title: Limelight Casting Directory. Text in English. 1973. a. adv. **Document type:** *Directory, Trade.*
Published by: Limelight Publications CC, PO Box 760, Randpark Ridge, Johannesburg 2156, South Africa. TEL 27-11-793-7231, FAX 27-11-793-7231. Ed., R&P Barbara Entressangle. Circ: 800.

792 USA
CASTING NEWS. Text in English. bi-w. USD 69 (effective 2000).
Published by: The John King Network, 244 Madison Ave, Ste 393, New York, NY 10016. TEL 212-969-8715, 212-969-8715.

792 USA ISSN 2154-2538
Z5785.Z9
CATALOGUE OF NEW PLAYS. Text in English. 1936. a. free. adv. bk.rev. **Document type:** *Catalog.* **Description:** Lists all plays leased by the Dramatists Play Service, including title, author, quotes from reviews, cast and scenic requirements, and a description of the play.
Former titles (2008): Complete Catalog of Plays (1547-7460); (until 2001): Complete Catalog of Plays and Musicals (1534-7540); (until 1991): Complete Catalogue of Plays (Year)
Published by: Dramatists Play Service, Inc., 440 Park Ave S, New York, NY 10016. TEL 212-683-8960, FAX 212-213-1539. Ed. Eleanore Speert. Pub., R&P Stephen Sultan. Circ: 45,000.

792 306.766 USA
CENTER STAGE (NEW YORK). Text in English. 1987. m. free. adv. **Document type:** *Newsletter.*
Published by: Lesbian & Gay Community Services Center, Inc., 208 W. 13th St., New York, NY 10011-7702. TEL 212-620-7310, http://www.gaycenter.org. Ed. Daniel Willson. Adv. contact Paul Fricken. Circ: 75,000.

CENTRE CULTUREL FRANCAIS DE YAOUNDE. PROGRAMME SAISON. *see* ART

792 FRA ISSN 1635-6306
CHAMP THEATRAL. Text in French. 2002. irreg. back issues avail. **Document type:** *Monographic series, Consumer.*
Published by: Editions L' Entretemps, Domaine de Lafeuillade, 264 Rue du Capitaine Pierre Pontal, Montpellier, 34000, France. TEL 33-4-99530975, FAX 33-4-99533198, info.entretemps@wanadoo.fr, http://www.lekti-ecriture.com/editeurs/-L-Entretemps-.html.

CHIRICU. *see* LITERATURE

792 ESP ISSN 1989-8916
▼ **CICLORAMA.** Text in Spanish. 2010. q. **Document type:** *Bulletin, Consumer.*
Media: Online - full text.
Published by: Escuela Superior de Arte Dramatico de Cordoba, C Blanco Belmonte, 14, Cordoba, 14003, Spain. TEL 34-957-379605, FAX 34-957-379609, http://www.esad.cordoba.ms.

CINEGUIA; anuario espanol del espectaculo y audiovisuales. *see* MOTION PICTURES

791.3 USA ISSN 1056-1463
ML1354
CIRCUS FANFARE. Text in English. 1974. bi-m. USD 20 domestic membership; USD 27 in Canada membership (effective 2007). adv. **Document type:** *Newsletter, Consumer.* **Description:** Dedicated to preserving traditional circus music. Features articles about circus bands, musicians, circuses and society information.
Published by: Windjammers Unlimited, 1204 Hobson Oaks Ct, Naperville, IL 60540. TEL 630-428-1747, mike.montgomery@circusmusic.org, http://www.circusmusic.org. Ed. April Zink. adv.: page USD 35.

791.3 USA ISSN 0889-5996
CIRCUS REPORT. Text in English. 1972. w. USD 40 domestic; USD 80 in Canada & Mexico; USD 110 foreign Air Mail (effective 2001). adv. bk.rev. 20 p./no. 4 cols./p.; **Document type:** *Report, Trade.*
Indexed: RASB.
Address: 525 Oak St, El Cerrito, CA 94530-3699. TEL 510-525-3332. Ed. Don Marcks. adv.: page USD 200. Circ: 2,000 (paid).

791.3 DEU ISSN 0941-2867
CIRCUS-ZEITUNG/CIRCUS MAGAZINE. Text in German. 1955. m. EUR 52; EUR 5 newsstand/cover (effective 2009). adv. illus. **Document type:** *Magazine, Trade.*
Former titles (until 1992): Circus (0172-2557); (until 1977): Die Circus-Zeitung (0172-2646); (until 1971): Deutsche Circus-Zeitung (0012-0022)
Indexed: RASB.

TU

Published by: (Gesellschaft der Circusfreunde in Deutschland e.V.), Circus Verlag, Am Latourshof 6, Dormagen, 41542, Germany. TEL 49-2133-91555, FAX 49-2133-91553, circus.verlag@t-online.de, http://www.circus-verlag.de.

791.3 FRA ISSN 1140-6178
CIRQUE DANS L'UNIVERS. Text in French. 1949. q. adv. bk.rev. illus. back issues avail. **Document type:** *Magazine, Consumer.*
Formerly (until 1951): Club du Cirque (1140-6127)
Indexed: RASB.
Published by: Club du Cirque, 116 rue Damremont, Paris, 75018, France. FAX 33-1-64880364. Ed., R&P Alain Chevillard. Circ: 2,000.

CITYSLICKER ENTERTAINMENT MAGAZINE. *see* MUSIC

792 BRA
COLECCAO TEATRO. Text in Portuguese. 1974 (no.2). irreg. bibl. **Document type:** *Monographic series.*
Published by: Universidade Federal do Rio Grande do Sul, Porto Alegre, RGS, Brazil.

792 ITA
COLLANA DEL TEATRO DI ROMA. Text in Italian. 1977. irreg. **Document type:** *Monographic series, Academic/Scholarly.*
Published by: Officina Edizioni, Via Agnelli Virginia 58, Rome, 00151, Italy. TEL 39-06-56740514, http://www.officinaedizioni.it.

800 100 FRA ISSN 1779-7861
COLLECTION THEATRE ET CONNAISSANCES. Variant title: Theatre et Connaissances. Text in French. 2005. irreg. **Document type:** *Monographic series.*
Published by: Cap Bear Editions, 302 av. Joffre, Perpignan, 66000, France. TEL 33-4-68512556, FAX 33-4-68513996, contact@cap-bear-editions.com, http://www.cap-bear-editions.com/. **Dist. by:** Square Partners S. A., 4 rue Pierre Talrich, Perpignan 66000, France. TEL 33-4-68346095, FAX 33-4-68346068, contact@squarepartners.com, http://www.little-france.com.

800 CHE ISSN 0946-2457
COLLECTION THETA; Etudes de semiologie theatrale - essays on semiotics of the theatre. Text in French, English. 1994. irreg., latest vol.6, 2002. price varies. **Document type:** *Monographic series, Academic/Scholarly.*
Published by: Peter Lang AG (Subsidiary of: Peter Lang Publishing Group), Hochfeldstr 32, Postfach 746, Bern 9, 3000, Switzerland. TEL 41-31-3061717, FAX 41-31-3061727, info@peterlang.com.

792 USA ISSN 1553-6505
PN2780
COMEDIA PERFORMANCE. Text in English. 2004. a. USD 15 per vol. (effective 2006).
Indexed: MLA-IB.
Published by: Association for Hispanic Classical Theater, Inc., PO Box 206, Cabin John, MD 20818-0206. lvidler@comedias.org, http://www.comedias.org.

792 USA
COMIC NEWS. Text in English. bi-w. USD 69 (effective 2000).
Published by: The John King Network, 244 Madison Ave, Ste 393, New York, NY 10016. TEL 212-969-8715, 212-969-8715.

792 ITA ISSN 1974-1294
PQ4155
COMMEDIA DELL'ARTE; annuario internazionale. Text in Multiple languages. 2008. a. EUR 80 combined subscription foreign to institutions (print & online eds.) (effective 2012). **Document type:** *Journal, Academic/Scholarly.*
Related titles: Online - full text ed.: ISSN 2035-6285.
Published by: Casa Editrice Leo S. Olschki, Viuzzo del Pozzetto 8, Florence, 50126, Italy. TEL 39-055-6530684, FAX 39-055-6530214, celso@olschki.it, http://www.olschki.it. Eds. Anna Maria Testaverde, Siro Ferrone.

792.12 USA
➤ **COMMUNICATION, SPEECH & THEATRE ASSOCIATION OF NORTH DAKOTA. JOURNAL.** Text in English. 1987. a. **Document type:** *Journal, Academic/Scholarly.* **Description:** Provides a forum for cross-disciplinary research in communication.
Formerly (until 2007): North Dakota Journal of Speech and Theatre (1081-8057)
Related titles: Online - full text ed.: free (effective 2011).
Indexed: CA, CMM, IBT&D, T02.
Published by: Communication, Speech & Theatre Association of North Dakota, c/o Jeannine Saabye, University of Mary Communication Departmen, 7500 University Dr, Bismarck, ND 58504. TEL 701-355-8184, jlsaabye@umary.edu. Ed. Shannon C VanHorn.

➤ **COMMUNICATIONS FROM THE INTERNATIONAL BRECHT SOCIETY.** *see* LITERATURE

➤ **COMUNICAZIONE E SPETTACOLO.** *see* COMMUNICATIONS

792 CUB ISSN 0010-5937
PN1608
CONJUNTO. Text in Spanish. 1964. q. USD 10 in North America; USD 12 in South America; USD 17 in Europe. abstr.; bibl.; illus.
Indexed: C01, H21, IBR, IBT&D, IBZ, IIPA, MLA-IB, P08, P09, PCI, RILM.
Published by: (Casa de las Americas, Departamento de Teatro), Ediciones Cubanas, Obispo 527, Havana, Cuba. Ed. Manuel Galich. Circ: 3,000.

CONSCIOUSNESS, LITERATURE AND THE ARTS. *see* LITERATURE

070.5 ZAF ISSN 0250-2003
CONTACTS. Key Title: Limelight Contacts. Text in English. 1978. a. ZAR 30 (effective 2000). adv. **Document type:** *Directory, Trade.*
Published by: Limelight Publications CC, PO Box 760, Randpark Ridge, Johannesburg 2156, South Africa. TEL 27-11-793-7231, FAX 27-11-793-7231. Ed., R&P Barbara Entressangle. Circ: 3,000.

792 GBR ISSN 1366-4646
CONTACTS (YEAR); the essential handbook for the entertainment industry. Text in English. 1947. a. (Nov.). GBP 12.50 per issue (effective 2010). adv. back issues avail. **Document type:** *Directory, Trade.* **Description:** Essential handbook for anyone working or looking to get started in the UK entertainment industry.
Formerly (199?): Spotlight Contacts (0010-7344)
—CCC.
Published by: The Spotlight, 7 Leicester Pl, London, WC2H 7RJ, United Kingdom. TEL 44-20-74377631, questions@spotlight.com, http://www.spotlight.com/. Ed. Kate Poynton. adv.: B&W page GBP 1,079, color page GBP 1,336.

792 CHE ISSN 0176-2931
CONTACTS. SERIE 1: THEATRICA. Text in French. 1984. irreg., latest vol.26, 2007. price varies. **Document type:** *Monographic series, Academic/Scholarly.*
Published by: Peter Lang AG (Subsidiary of: Peter Lang Publishing Group), Hochfeldstr 32, Postfach 746, Bern 9, 3000, Switzerland. TEL 41-31-3061717, FAX 41-31-3061727, info@peterlang.com, http://www.peterlang.com. Ed. Jean-Marie Valentin.

820 DEU
CONTEMPORARY DRAMA IN ENGLISH. Abbreviated title: C D E. Text in English. 1994. irreg., latest vol.17, 2010. price varies. **Document type:** *Monographic series, Academic/Scholarly.*
Published by: (German Society for Contemporary Theater and Drama in English), Wissenschaftlicher Verlag Trier, Bergstr 27, Trier, 54295, Germany. TEL 49-651-41503, FAX 49-651-41504, wvt@wvttrier.de, http://www.wvttrier.de. Ed. Martin Middeke.

792 USA ISSN 1050-3919
PR737
CONTEMPORARY DRAMATISTS. Text in English. 1973. irreg.
—CCC.
Published by: St. Martin's Press, LLC (Subsidiary of: Holtzbrink Publishers), 175 Fifth Ave, New York, NY 10010. TEL 646-307-5151, press.inquiries@macmillanusa.com, http://us.macmillan.com/SMP.aspx.

CONTEMPORARY THEATRE, FILM & TELEVISION. *see* BIOGRAPHY

792 GBR ISSN 1048-6801
PN2001 CODEN: CTHRE9
➤ **CONTEMPORARY THEATRE REVIEW.** Abbreviated title: C T R. Text in English. 1992. q. GBP 586 combined subscription in United Kingdom to institutions (print & online eds.); EUR 641, USD 804 combined subscription to institutions (print & online eds.) (effective 2012). adv. back issues avail.; reprint service avail. from PSC. **Document type:** *Journal, Academic/Scholarly.* **Description:** Covers research in the field of performance, including all aspects of the theatre event.
Related titles: Microform ed.; Online - full text ed.: ISSN 1477-2264. GBP 527 in United Kingdom to institutions; EUR 576, USD 724 to institutions (effective 2012) (from IngentaConnect); Print ed.: Contemporary Theatre Review (Hardback). ISSN 1026-7166.
Indexed: A01, A03, A08, A20, A22, ASCA, AmHI, ArtHuCI, CA, CurCont, E01, H07, IBR, IBT&D, IBZ, IIPA, L06, MLA-IB, SCOPUS, T02, W07.
—IE, Ingenta. **CCC.**
Published by: Routledge (Subsidiary of: Taylor & Francis Group), 4 Park Square, Milton Park, Abingdon, Oxon OX14 4RN, United Kingdom. subscriptions@tandf.co.uk, http://www.routledge.com. Eds. David Bradby, Maria M Delgado. Adv. contact Linda Hann TEL 44-1344-779945. **Subscr. to:** Taylor & Francis Ltd., Journals Customer Service, Sheepen Pl, Colchester, Essex CO3 3LP, United Kingdom. TEL 44-20-70175544, FAX 44-20-70175198, tf.enquiries@tfinforma.com.

792 370 FRA ISSN 2107-4739
CONTINU(UM). Text in French. 2002. s-a. EUR 5 per issue (effective 2011).
Formerly (until 2010): Trait d'Union (1957-1518)
Published by: L' Association Nationale de Recherche et d'Action Theatrale, 38 Rue du Faubourg Saint-Jacques, Paris, 75014, France. TEL 33-1-45262222, FAX 33-1-45261620, contact@anrat.asso.fr, http://www.anrat.asso.fr.

792 USA ISSN 0163-3821
CONTRIBUTIONS IN DRAMA AND THEATRE STUDIES. Text in English. 1979. irreg., latest vol.105, 2004. price varies. back issues avail. **Document type:** *Monographic series, Academic/Scholarly.*
—BLDSC (3458.310000), IE, Ingenta. **CCC.**
Published by: Greenwood Publishing Group Inc. (Subsidiary of: A B C - C L I O), 88 Post Rd W, PO Box 5007, Westport, CT 06881. TEL 203-226-3571, 800-225-5800, FAX 877-231-6980, sales@greenwood.com, http://www.greenwood.com. Ed. Joseph Donohue.

792.028 USA
THE COSTUMER. Text in English. 1923. 6/yr. USD 30. adv. bk.rev. **Document type:** *Journal, Trade.*
Formerly: National Costumers Magazine
Published by: National Costumers Association, Inc., c/o Mary Lou Landes Schultz, Ed, 811 N Capitol Ave, Indianapolis, IN 46204. TEL 317-635-3655, FAX 317-267-8978. Circ: 500.

792 USA
COUNCIL OF JEWISH THEATRES NEWSLETTER. Text in English. 1991. s-a. free. play rev. back issues avail. **Document type:** *Newsletter.* **Description:** Dedicated to promoting the interests of non-profit theaters in North America whose primary mission is the development and production of plays relevant to Jewish life and values.
Published by: National Foundation for Jewish Culture, 330 Seventh Ave, 21st Fl, New York, NY 10001. TEL 212-629-0500, FAX 212-629-0508. Circ: 350 (controlled).

792 FRA ISSN 1254-745X
CREATION ET ARTS DU SPECTACLE. Variant title: Collection les Arts du Spectacle. Text in French. 1994. irreg.
Published by: Honore Champion, 3 Rue Corneille, Paris, 75006, France. TEL 33-1-46340729, FAX 33-1-46346406, champion@honorechampion.com, http://www.honorechampion.com.

792 USA ISSN 1098-6103
CREATIVE DRAMA MAGAZINE. Text in English. 1998. q.
Published by: Dramatata Editions, 850-a Hwy 14, Winona, MN 55987. TEL 507-452-4693.

792 ESP ISSN 2172-170X
CUADERNOS PEDAGOGICOS. Text in Spanish. 2008. a. **Document type:** *Monographic series, Academic/Scholarly.*
Published by: Compania Nacional de Teatro Clasico, Principe, 14, Madrid, 28012, Spain. TEL 34-91-5327927, FAX 34-91-5214932.

CULTURAL EVENTS OF NEW JERSEY. *see* MUSEUMS AND ART GALLERIES

792 ITA ISSN 1825-8220
CULTURE TEATRALI. Text in Italian. 1999. s-a. **Document type:** *Journal, Academic/Scholarly.*
Related titles: Online - full text ed.: ISSN 2035-1585. 2008.
Published by: Universita degli Studi di Bologna, Dipartimento di Musica e Spettacolo, Via Galliera 3-40121, Bologna, Italy. http://www.muspe.unibo.it.

CULTUREVULTURE.NET; choices for the cognoscenti. *see* MOTION PICTURES

792 USA
CURTAINUP; the Internet magazine of theater news, reviews and features. Text in English. 1996. 3/w. free (effective 2010). play rev.; bk.rev. **Document type:** *Magazine, Consumer.* **Description:** New York-based magazine about the theater.
Media: Online - full text.
Address: PO Box 751133, Forest Hills, NY 11375. TEL 718-263-2668, FAX 718-263-2668, esommer@pipeline.com. Ed., Pub. Elyse Sommer.

CYFRWNG. *see* COMMUNICATIONS

792 CZE ISSN 0862-9390
CZECH THEATRE/THEATRE TCHEQUE. Text in Czech, English. 1994. s-a. CZK 150 per issue (effective 2011). **Document type:** *Journal, Academic/Scholarly.*
Related titles: Online - full text ed.
Published by: Institut Umeni, Divadelni Ustav/Arts and Theatre Institute, Celetna 17, Prague 1, 110 00, Czech Republic. TEL 420-2-24809111, info@idu.cz.

792 DEU
DA CAPO (EYSTRUP); Das Magazin Musical - Cabaret - Show. Text in German. 2003 (Sep.). 8/yr. EUR 23; EUR 3 newsstand/cover (effective 2008). **Document type:** *Magazine, Consumer.*
Published by: Da Capo, Am Vehrenkamp 54, Eystrup, 27324, Germany. TEL 49-4254-802863, FAX 49-4254-802864. Ed., Pub. Joerg Beese. Circ: 20,000 (controlled).

DAILY VARIETY (LOS ANGELES); news of the entertainment industry. *see* COMMUNICATIONS—Television And Cable

792 CHN ISSN 1002-171X
PN2870
DANGDAI XIJU/CONTEMPORARY THEATRE. Text in Chinese. 1985. bi-m. USD 18 (effective 2009). illus. 64 p./no.; **Document type:** *Journal, Academic/Scholarly.* **Description:** Covers Chinese opera, drama, TV and broadcasting plays as well as outstanding theatrical artists.
Formerly (until 1985): Shaanxi Xiju
Related titles: Online - full text ed.
—East View.
Published by: Shaanxi Sheng Xijujia Xiehui, 200, Dongmutou Shi, Xi'an, 710001, China. TEL 86-29-87210330. Ed. Luo Sheyang. R&P, Adv. contact SheYang Luo. Circ: 8,000. **Dist. by:** China International Book Trading Corp, 35 Chegongzhuang Xilu, Haidian District, PO Box 399, Beijing 100044, China. TEL 86-10-68412045, FAX 86-10-68412023, cibtc@mail.cibtc.com.cn, http://www.cibtc.com.cn.

DARMSTAEDTER KULTURNACHRICHTEN. *see* MUSIC

792 CHN ISSN 1003-1200
PL2603
DAWUTAI. Text in Chinese. bi-m. USD 24.60 (effective 2009).
Related titles: Online - full text ed.
Published by: Hebei Sheng Yishu Yanjiusuo/Hebei Art Research Institute, 41 Tiyu Middle St, Shijiazhuang, Hebei 050021, China. Ed. Feng Feng. **Dist. by:** China International Book Trading Corp, 35 Chegongzhuang Xilu, Haidian District, PO Box 399, Beijing 100044, China. TEL 86-10-68412045, FAX 86-10-68412023, cibtc@mail.cibtc.com.cn, http://www.cibtc.com.cn.

792 792.8 780 TWN
DAXITAI. Text in Chinese. 2007. q. **Document type:** *Journal, Academic/Scholarly.*
Published by: Guoli Taiwan Xiqu Xueyuan/National Taiwan College of Performing Arts, 177, Sec. 2, Neihu Rd., Taipei, Taiwan. TEL 886-2-27962666, FAX 886-2-27909127, http://www.tcpa.edu.tw/.

700 USA
DENVER ARTS CENTER PROGRAMS. Text in English. m.
Published by: Publishing House, Inc., 1101 13th St, Denver, CO 80204. TEL 303-893-4100, 800-641-1222, feedback@dcpa.org, http://www.denvercenter.org.

792 DEU ISSN 0011-975X
DIE DEUTSCHE BUEHNE; Theatermagazin. Text in German. 1909. m. EUR 51.60; EUR 42 to students; EUR 6 newsstand/cover (effective 2008). adv. bk.rev.; play rev. charts; illus. index. reprints avail. **Document type:** *Magazine, Trade.* **Description:** Covers German and international performing arts.
Indexed: RASB.
Published by: Deutscher Buehnenverein, 17-21 St Apern Str, Cologne, 50667, Germany. TEL 49-221-208120, FAX 49-221-2081228, debue@buehnenverein.de, http://www.buehnenverein.de. Ed. Detlef Brandenburg. adv.: B&W page EUR 1,650, color page EUR 2,490; trim 192 x 245. Circ: 6,000 (paid and controlled).

792 DEU ISSN 0070-4431
PN2640
DEUTSCHES BUEHNEN-JAHRBUCH. Text in German. 1889. a. EUR 32 to members; EUR 39 to non-members (effective 2009). adv. **Document type:** *Directory, Trade.*
Published by: (Genossenschaft Deutscher Buehnen-Angehoeriger), Buehnenschriften-Vertriebs-Gesellschaft, Feldbrunnenstr 74, Hamburg, 20148, Germany. TEL 49-40-445185, FAX 49-40-456002, gdba@buehnengenossenschaft.de, http://www.gdba.info. adv.: page EUR 698; trim 146 x 206. Circ: 9,000 (controlled).

792 700 USA
DIABLO MAGAZINE. Text in English. 1979. m. USD 18 (effective 2008). adv. back issues avail. **Document type:** *Magazine, Consumer.* **Description:** Covers art galleries and visual and performing arts, focusing on the East Bay.
Formerly (until 2005): Diablo Arts Magazine
Published by: Diablo Publications, 2520 Camino Diablo, Walnut Creek, CA 94597. TEL 925-943-1111, FAX 925-943-1045, info@cdpubs.com, http://www.dcpubs.com/. Ed. Susan Dowdney Safipour. Pub. Barney Fonzi TEL 925-943-1199 ext 204. Circ: 45,000 (paid).

792 POL ISSN 0012-2041
PN1607
DIALOG; miesiecznik poswiecony dramaturgii wspolczesnej teatralnej, filmowej, radiowej i telewizyjnej. Text in Polish. 1956. m. USD 60. bk.rev. **Description:** Devoted to contemporary drama and theatre.
Indexed: MLA, MLA-IB, RASB, RILM.
Address: Ul Pulawska 61, Warsaw, 02595, Poland. TEL 48-22-455475, FAX 48-22-453935. Ed. Jacek Sieradzki. Circ: 3,000. **Dist. by:** Ars Polona, Obroncow 25, Warsaw 03933, Poland. TEL 48-22-267622.

792 808.8026 SWE ISSN 0283-5207
DIALOGER. Text in Swedish. 1986. q. price varies. back issues avail. **Document type:** *Monographic series, Academic/Scholarly.* **Description:** Contains material and reflections related to the Dialogue Seminar at the Royal Dramatic Theatre. Each issue is devoted to a special theme on the relationship between science and art.
Published by: (Foereningen Dialoger), Dialoger Foerlag och Metod AB, c/o Santerus Foerlag, Suerbrunnsgate 56, Stockholm, 11348, Sweden. TEL 46-8-303462, FAX 46-8-343707, info@dialoger.se, http://www.dialoger.se. Ed. Bo Goeranzon. **Co-sponsors:** Kungliga Tekniska Hoegskolan/Royal Institute of Technology; Kungliga Dramatiska Teatern/Royal Dramatic Theater.

842 944 FRA ISSN 1951-5294
DICTIONNAIRES & REFERENCES. SERIE HISTOIRE DU THEATRE FRANCAIS. Text in French. 2006. irreg. back issues avail. **Document type:** *Monographic series, Consumer.*
Related titles: ◆ Series of: Dictionnaires et References. ISSN 1275-0387.
Published by: Honore Champion, 3 Rue Corneille, Paris, 75006, France. TEL 33-1-46340729, FAX 33-1-46346406, champion@honorechampion.com, http://www.champion.ch.

DIDASKALIA; ancient theater today. *see* CLASSICAL STUDIES

792 POL ISSN 1233-0477
PN2859.P6
DIDASKALIA; gazeta teatralna. Text in Polish. 1993. bi-m. EUR 47 foreign (effective 2006). adv. bk.rev.; play rev. illus. back issues avail. **Document type:** *Newspaper, Consumer.* **Description:** Presents reviews of Polish and international theatrical events.
Published by: Krakowskie Stowarzyszenie Teatralne, ul Golebia 18, Krakow, 31007, Poland. Eds. Anna Burzynska, Tadeusz Kornas. Adv. contact Olga Katafiasz. page PLZ 610. Circ: 1,200 (paid). **Dist. by:** Ars Polona, Obroncow 25, Warsaw 03933, Poland. TEL 48-22-5098609, FAX 48-22-5098610, arspolona@arspolona.com.pl, http://www.arspolona.com.pl. **Co-sponsor:** Uniwersytet Jagiellonski.

792 ITA ISSN 2038-5137
▼ **DIONYSUS EX MACHINA.** Text in Italian. 2010. a. EUR 48 (effective 2011). **Document type:** *Journal, Academic/Scholarly.*
Media: Online - full text.
Published by: G.B. Palumbo & C. Editore SpA, Via Ricasoli 59, Palermo, 90139, Italy. TEL 39-091-588850, FAX 39-091-6111848, http://www.palumboeditore.it.

791.53 GBR ISSN 0142-3681
DIRECTORY OF PROFESSIONAL PUPPETEERS. Text in English. 1976. biennial. GBP 8.50 (effective 2000). adv. illus. back issues avail. **Document type:** *Directory.* **Description:** Information on and about the wide variety of puppetry available.
Published by: Puppet Centre Trust, Battersea Arts Centre, Lavender Hill, London, SW11 5TN, United Kingdom. TEL 44-20-7228-5335, FAX 44-20-7228-8863, pct@puppetcentre.org.uk. Ed. Keith Allen. Adv. contact Allyson Kirk. Circ: 2,000.

DIRECTORY OF THE ARTS. *see* ART

792 USA ISSN 1041-5211
PN2078.U6
DIRECTORY OF THEATRE TRAINING PROGRAMS. Text in English. 1987. irreg. ((Nov.- odd years)), latest vol.7. USD 28.95 (effective 2001). **Document type:** *Directory, Trade.* **Description:** Lists over 430 colleges, universities, and conservatories with both undergraduate and graduate programs in all areas.
Published by: American Theatre Works, Inc., Theatre Directories, PO Box 510, Dorset, VT 05251. TEL 802-867-2223, FAX 802-867-0144. Ed., Pub. Jill Charles. Adv. contact Barbara Ax.

792 CZE ISSN 1210-471X
DIVADELNI NOVINY. Text in Czech. 1957. s-m. CZK 506; CZK 25 per issue (effective 2011). adv. **Document type:** *Newspaper.*
Formerly (until 1992): Divadelni a Filmove Noviny (0012-4141)
Related titles: Online - full text ed.
Published by: Institut Umeni, Divadelni Ustav/Arts and Theatre Institute, Celetna 17, Prague 1, 110 00, Czech Republic. TEL 420-2-24809111, info@idu.cz, http://www.idu.cz. Ed. Jan Kolar.

792 CZE ISSN 0862-5409
➤ **DIVADELNI REVUE.** Text in Czech. 1990. 3/yr. CZK 270 (effective 2011). bk.rev.; film rev.; play rev. 112 p./no. 2 cols./p.; **Document type:** *Journal, Academic/Scholarly.* **Description:** Covers theater history and theory.
Indexed: RASB, RILM.
Published by: Institut Umeni, Divadelni Ustav/Arts and Theatre Institute, Celetna 17, Prague 1, 110 00, Czech Republic. TEL 420-2-24809111, info@idu.cz, http://www.idu.cz. Ed. Honza Petruzela. Circ: 150 (controlled); 150 (paid).

792 CZE
DIVADELNI USTAV. INFORMACNI SERVIS (ONLINE). Text in Czech. 10/yr. free. tr.lit. 56 p./no. 1 cols./p.; back issues avail. **Document type:** *Magazine, Consumer.*
Former titles (until 2004): Divadelni Ustav. Informacni Servis (Print) (1211-9660); Premery Divadel v Ceske Republice
Media: Online - full text.
Published by: Institut Umeni, Divadelni Ustav/Arts and Theatre Institute, Celetna 17, Prague 1, 110 00, Czech Republic. TEL 420-2-24809111, info@idu.cz. Ed. Ondrej Cerny.

DOCTOR WHO MAGAZINE. *see* COMMUNICATIONS—Television And Cable

792 BEL ISSN 0771-8640
PN2002 CODEN: VIOEF2
➤ **DOCUMENTA**; tijdschrift voor theater. Text in Dutch. 1983. q. EUR 15 domestic; EUR 18 foreign (effective 2003). adv. bk.rev.; play rev. abstr.; bibl.; illus. back issues avail. **Document type:** *Journal, Academic/Scholarly.*
Indexed: MLA-IB.
Published by: Documentatiecentrum voor Dramatische Kunst v.z.w., Rozier 44, Ghent, 9000, Belgium. TEL 32-9-2643696, FAX 32-9-2644184. Ed., R&P, Adv. contact Jozef de Vos. Circ: 600.

792 SRB ISSN 0351-5494
DOKUMENTI - INFORMACIJE. Text in Macedonian, Serbo-Croatian, Slovenian. 1978. s-a.
Published by: Sterijino Pozorje, Zmaj Jovina 22, Novi Sad, 21000. TEL 381-21-27255, FAX 381-21-615976, sterija@neobee.net.

792 DEU
DOUBLE; Magazin fuer Puppen-, Figuren- und Objekttheater. Text in German. 2004. 3/yr. EUR 16 (effective 2010). adv. **Document type:** *Magazine, Trade.*
Published by: I.G. Theater der Zeit e.V., Klosterstr 68-70, Berlin, 10179, Germany. TEL 49-30-24722414, FAX 49-30-24722415.

792 USA ISSN 1077-8233
HQ77
DRAGAZINE; the magazine for Halloweeners and inbetweeners. Text in English. 1991. s-a. USD 10.95; USD 5.95 newsstand/cover. adv. bk.rev. **Description:** A witty look at the subject of drag or crossdressing as a tool in performance art.
Address: PO Box 461795, W. Hollywood, CA 90046. Ed., R&P, Adv. contact Lois Commondenominator. Circ: 17,000.

792 GBR ISSN 0967-4454
DRAMA; one forum many voices. Text in English. 1973. s-a. GBP 18 domestic to non-members; GBP 19.50 foreign to non-members; free to members (effective 2009). adv. bk.rev. illus. back issues avail. **Document type:** *Magazine, Trade.* **Description:** Provides a forum for all drama practitioners to: share theory and practice, debate key issues, publish research, engage in critical analysis, and express opinion.
Formerly (until 1992): Drama Magazine (0964-5780); Incorporates (in 1990): London Drama Magazine
Related titles: Online - full text ed.
Published by: National Drama Publications, 6 Cornwell Ct, Castle Dene, S. Gosforth, Newcastle-Upon-Tyne NE3 1TT, United Kingdom. http://www.nationaldrama.co.uk. Ed. Marie-Jeanne McNaughton. Adv. contact Peter Wild. color page GBP 250. Circ: 1,500.

792 USA
DRAMA BEAT. Text in English. 1998 (Jun.). q. USD 20 domestic; USD 30 foreign (effective 2000). adv. **Document type:** *Newspaper.* **Description:** Publishes news on theater, film, acting, singing, dancing, commercial, modeling, voice over, theater reviews, film reviews, audition and casting information and general information fro the state of Arizona.
Published by: Drama Beat Newspaper, 18409 N Cave Creek Rd #310 S-2, Phoenix, AZ 85032. TEL 602-385-9228, 602-593-9150, FAX 602-385-9228. Ed., Pub., R&P, Adv. contact Faith Hibbs-Clark. page USD 500; trim 10 x 16. Circ: 1,000.

792 800 USA ISSN 1056-4349
PN1601
DRAMA CRITICISM. Text in English. 1991. irreg., latest vol.27, 2006. USD 180 per issue (effective 2008). back issues avail. **Document type:** *Monographic series, Consumer.* **Description:** Provides excerpts from significant commentary on 12-15 of the most widely studied dramatists from antiquity to contemporary times in each volume.
Published by: Gale (Subsidiary of: Cengage Learning), 27500 Drake Rd, Farmington Hills, MI 48331. TEL 248-699-4253, 800-877-4253, FAX 877-363-4253, gale.galeord@cengage.com. Ed. Lawrence J Trudeau.

792 810 USA ISSN 1094-9232
PN1601
DRAMA FOR STUDENTS. Text in English. 1998. irreg., latest vol.26, 2007. USD 105 vols.1-26 (effective 2009). back issues avail. **Document type:** *Monographic series, Academic/Scholarly.* **Description:** Analyzes important English-language plays for high school students.
Related titles: Online - full text ed.
Published by: Gale (Subsidiary of: Cengage Learning), 27500 Drake Rd, Farmington Hills, MI 48331. TEL 248-699-4253, 800-877-4253, FAX 877-363-4253, gale.customerservice@cengage.com, http://gale.cengage.com.

647.968 USA ISSN 1559-193X
DRAMABIZ MAGAZINE. Text in English. 2006. bi-m. USD 49; USD 12 per issue (effective 2006). adv. **Document type:** *Magazine, Trade.* **Description:** Provides the theatre industry with well-tested business tools and management perspectives to help them succeed in running their organization.
Published by: Enlighten Entertainment LLC, PO Box 722581, San Diego, CA 92172-2581. TEL 858-484-3936, FAX 858-484-6653. Pub., Adv. contact Julie Peterson. color page USD 2,940; trim 8.375 x 10.875. Circ: 12,200 (controlled).

DRAMAFORUM. *see* EDUCATION—Teaching Methods And Curriculum

DRAMASCOPE. *see* PSYCHOLOGY

792.071 USA ISSN 0012-5989
PN3175.A1
DRAMATICS; the magazine for students and teachers of theatre. Text in English. 1929. m. (9/yr.). USD 27 to non-members; free to members (effective 2010). adv. bk.rev. charts; illus. index. back issues avail.; reprints avail. **Document type:** *Magazine, Consumer.* **Description:** Publishes articles on acting, directing, playwriting, tech theatre and other performing art skills. Also contains college and career information, playscripts, and features on theatre and theatre people.
Formerly (until 1944): Dramatics-Dramatic Curtain
Related titles: Microform ed.: (from PQC).
Indexed: A22, AmHI, H07, IBT&D, IIPA, PCI.
—IE, Infotrieve, Ingenta.
Published by: Educational Theatre Association, 2343 Auburn Ave, Cincinnati, OH 45219. TEL 513-421-3900, FAX 513-421-7077, info@edta.org. Ed. Donald A Corathers. Adv. contact Sarah O'Bryan. Circ: 32,000.

792 USA ISSN 1551-7683
THE DRAMATIST; the voice of American theater. Text in English. 1960. bi-m. USD 25 to non-members; free to members (effective 2010). adv. bk.rev. illus. back issues avail.; reprints avail. **Document type:** *Magazine, Trade.* **Description:** Covers all aspects of theatre.
Incorporates (1982-1998): Dramatists Guild. Newsletter; Former titles (until 1998): Dramatists Guild Quarterly (0012-6004); (until 1964): Dramatists Bulletin
Related titles: Online - full text ed.; ◆ Supplement(s): Guildworks.
Indexed: A10, AmHI, B04, H07, H08, HAb, HumInd, IBT&D, IIPA, T02, V03, W03, W05.
—Ingenta.
Published by: Dramatists Guild, Inc., 1501 Broadway, Ste 701, New York, NY 10036. TEL 212-398-9366, FAX 212-944-0420. Adv. contact Larry Pontius TEL 212-398-9366 ext 22. B&W page USD 500, color page USD 675; 8.375 x 10.875. Circ: 5,752.

792 USA
DRAMATISTS GUILD RESOURCE DIRECTORY. Text in English. biennial. **Document type:** *Directory, Trade.* **Description:** Contains up-to-date information on agents, attorneys, grants, producers, playwriting contests, conferences and workshops.
Published by: Dramatists Guild, Inc., 1501 Broadway, Ste 701, New York, NY 10036. FAX 212-944-0420, http://www.dramatistsguild.com.

800 USA ISSN 0733-1606
PN2289
DRAMATISTS SOURCEBOOK. Text in English. 1982. a. USD 19.95 (effective 2001). index. 384 p./no.; **Document type:** *Handbook/Manual/Guide, Trade.* **Description:** Lists opportunities for playwrights, translations, composers, lyricists, and librettists, in addition to screen, radio, and television writers.
Indexed: IBT&D, T02.
Published by: Theatre Communications Group, Inc., 355 Lexington Ave, New York, NY 10017. TEL 212-697-5230, FAX 212-983-4847, tcg@tcg.org, http://www.tcg.org. Ed., R&P Kathy Sova. Pub. Terence Nemeth. Circ: 7,000.

792 RUS ISSN 1029-7227
DRAMATURG. Text in Russian. 1993. q.
Indexed: RASB.
Published by: Tovarishchestvo Rezhisserov, Strastnoi b-r, d 12, str 1, Moscow, 103031, Russian Federation. TEL 7-095-2006644, FAX 7-095-2002171. **Dist. by:** East View Information Services, 10601 Wayzata Blvd, Minneapolis, MN 55305. TEL 952-252-1201, 800-477-1005, FAX 952-252-1202, info@eastview.com, http://www.eastview.com.

DRAMATURGIES FRANCOPHONES. ETUDES. *see* LITERATURE

E B LIVE. (Entertainment Business) *see* MUSIC

700 800 USA
EARLY DRAMA, ART, AND MUSIC MONOGRAPH SERIES. Variant title: E D A M Monograph Series. Text in English. 1977. irreg., latest vol.30, 2003. price varies. back issues avail. **Document type:** *Monographic series, Academic/Scholarly.* **Description:** Focuses on an important aspect of iconography, staging, music (including music aesthetics and musical iconography), etc.
Published by: Medieval Institute Press, Western Michigan University, Walwood Hall, 1903 W Michigan, Kalamazoo, MI 49008. TEL 269-387-8755, FAX 269-387-8750.

792 800 CAN ISSN 1206-9078
PR641
➤ **EARLY THEATRE**; a journal associated with the Records of Early English Drama. Text in English. 1976. 2/yr. CAD 59 domestic to institutions; USD 59 foreign to institutions; CAD 69 combined subscription domestic to institutions (print & online eds.); USD 69 combined subscription foreign to institutions (print & online eds.) (effective 2009). bk.rev. bibl. cum.index every 5 yrs. back issues avail. **Document type:** *Journal, Academic/Scholarly.* **Description:** Articles and notes on the performance history of art, entertainment and festive occasions of the medieval era.
Formerly (until 1997): Records of Early English Drama Newsletter (0700-9283)
Related titles: Online - full text ed.
Indexed: A26, BibInd, C03, CA, CBCARef, E08, I05, IBT&D, IIPA, MLA, MLA-IB, P48, PCI, PQC, RILM, S23, T02.
—BLDSC (3642.999745), IE. **CCC.**
Published by: University of Toronto, Victoria College, Centre for Reformation and Renaissance Studies, 71 Queen's Park Cresc East, Toronto, ON M5S 1K7, Canada. TEL 416-585-4465, FAX 416-585-4430, crss.publications@utoronto.ca, http://www.crrs.ca. Ed., R&P Helen Ostovich. Circ: 200 (paid and controlled).

791.3 FRA ISSN 1771-8910
ECRITS SUR LE SABLE. Text in French. 2004. irreg. back issues avail. **Document type:** *Monographic series, Consumer.*
Published by: Editions L' Entretemps, Domaine de Lafeuillade, 264 Rue du Capitaine Pierre Pontal, Montpellier, 34000, France. TEL 33-4-99530975, FAX 33-4-99533198, info.entretemps@wanadoo.fr, http://www.lekti-ecriture.com/editeurs/-L-Entretemps-.html.

792 USA ISSN 1942-4558
PN2000
ECUMENICA. Text in English. 2004. s-a. **Document type:** *Journal, Academic/Scholarly.* **Description:** Discusses about the performing arts and the relationship between performance and society and variety of topics and approaches to criticism, including theatrical performance and theatre history, dramatic literary criticism, social, political and cultural studies of theatre and performance.
Formerly (until 2007): Baylor Journal of Theatre and Performance (1553-0469)
Indexed: A21, CA, IBT&D, MLA-IB, T02.
Published by: Baylor Journal of Theatre & Performance, c/o Carolyn Roark, Editor, Hooper Schafer Fine Arts, Rm 203, One Bear Place, TX 97262. TEL 254-710-6452, FAX 524-710-1785, carolyn_roark@baylor.edu, http://www.baylor.edu. Ed. Carolyn Roark.

792 USA
EDICIONES DE GESTOS: COLECCION HISTORIA DEL TEATRO. Text in Spanish. irreg., latest vol.6. USD 22.50 per vol. (effective 2004). **Document type:** *Monographic series.* **Description:** Publishes works contributing to the history of theater.
Related titles: ◆ Series of: Gestos. ISSN 1040-483X.
Published by: University of California, Irvine, Department of Spanish and Portuguese, Humanities Hall, Irvine, CA 92697. TEL 949-824-7171, FAX 949-552-4820, gestos@uci.edu.

T
U

800 USA
EDICIONES DE GESTOS: COLECCION TEORIA. Text in Spanish. irreg., latest vol.2. USD 22.50 per vol. (effective 2004). **Document type:** *Monographic series.*
Related titles: ◆ Series of: Gestos. ISSN 1040-483X.
Published by: University of California, Irvine, Department of Spanish and Portuguese, Humanities Hall, Irvine, CA 92697. TEL 949-824-7171, FAX 949-552-4820, gestos@uci.edu.

792 RUS ISSN 0868-9024
PN1993
EKRAN. Text in Russian. 1957. bi-m. USD 40. illus. index.
Formerly (until no.1, 1991): Sovetskii Ekran (0038-5123)
Related titles: Microform ed.: (from EVP).
Published by: (Soyuz Kinematografistov), Ekran, Chasovaya ul 5-b, Moscow, 125319, Russian Federation. TEL 7-095-1527937, FAX 7-095-1529791. Ed. B V Pinskii. Circ: 50,000. **Dist. by:** East View Information Services, 10601 Wayzata Blvd, Minneapolis, MN 55305. TEL 952-252-1201, 800-477-1005, FAX 952-252-1202, info@eastview.com, http://www.eastview.com.

822.3 CAN ISSN 0317-4964
ELIZABETHAN THEATRE. Text in English. 1968. irreg., latest vol.15, 2002. price varies. **Document type:** *Monographic series, Academic/Scholarly.*
—**CCC.**
Published by: P.D. Meany Publishers, 71 Fermanagh Ave, Toronto, ON M6R 1M1, Canada. TEL 416-516-2903, FAX 416-516-7632, info@pdmeany.com, http://www.pdmeany.com.

792 USA
ENCORE (NEW YORK); the off-Broadway theater magazine. Text in English. 9/yr. adv.
Published by: Encore Entertainment Productions Inc., 160 W. 75th St., Apt. 2A, New York, NY 10023-1915. TEL 212-447-0018, FAX 212-447-8709. Ed., Pub. Tom Holmes.

792 791.43 JPN ISSN 1345-4315
PN2009
ENGEKI EIZO/STUDIES ON THEATRE AND FILM ARTS. Text in Japanese. 1959. a. **Document type:** *Journal, Academic/Scholarly.*
Formerly (until 1999): Engekigaku/Studies on Theatre Arts (0387-2750)
Indexed: RILM.
Published by: Waseda Daigaku, Dai-ichi Bungakubu, 1-24-1, Toyama, Shinjuku-ku, Tokyo, 162-8644, Japan.

792 JPN ISSN 0913-039X
PN2921
ENGEKI KENKYU/STUDIES IN DRAMATIC ART. Text in Japanese. 1965. a. JPY 500 newsstand/cover (effective 2006). **Document type:** *Journal, Academic/Scholarly.*
Indexed: RILM.
Published by: Waseda Daigaku, Tsubouchi Hakushi Kinen Engeki Hakubutsukan/Waseda University, Tsubouchi Memorial Theatre Museum, 1-6-1 Nishiwaseda, Shinjuku-ku, Tokyo, 169-8050, Japan. TEL 86-3-52861829, FAX 86-3-52734398.

791.4 GBR
ENGLISH NATIONAL OPERA PROGRAMME. Text in English. m. GBP 1 per issue. adv. **Description:** Each opera has separate program.
Published by: English National Opera, London Coliseum, St Martin's Ln, London, WC2N 4ES, United Kingdom. TEL 44-20-78360111, mediaenquiries@eno.org, http://www.eno.org/. Ed., R&P Philip Reed TEL 44-20-78459429. Circ: 25,000.

ENTERTAINMENT LAW & FINANCE. *see* LAW

ENTERTAINMENT, PUBLISHING AND THE ARTS HANDBOOK. *see* COMMUNICATIONS—Television And Cable

792 ESP ISSN 1575-9490
ENTRECAJAS. Text in Spanish. 1999. bi-m. back issues avail. **Document type:** *Bulletin, Academic/Scholarly.*
Published by: Asociacion de Autores de Teatro, Benito Gutierrez, 27 1a. Izq., Madrid, 28008, Spain. TEL 34-91-5430271, FAX 34-91-5496292, aat@aat.es, http://www.aat.es/.

792 CAN ISSN 0319-8650
ENVERS DU DECOR; la vie du theatre. Text in French. 1973 (vol.5). bi-m. free. adv. illus.
Related titles: Microfilm ed.: (from BNQ).
Published by: Theatre du Nouveau Monde, 84 Ouest, rue Ste Catherine, Montreal, PQ H2X 1Z6, Canada. TEL 514-861-0563. Ed. Roch Carrier.

792 378 FIN ISSN 1459-7349
EPISODI - TEATTERIKORKEAKOULU. Text in Finnish. 2003. irreg. EUR 13 per issue (effective 2005). **Document type:** *Monographic series.*
Published by: Teatterikorkeakoulu/Theatre Academy, PO Box 163, Helsinki, 00531, Finland. TEL 358-9-431361, FAX 358-9-43136200, international@teak.fi.

792.028 GBR ISSN 1749-4184
EQUITY (LONDON); performing for you. Text in English. 1931. q. free to members (effective 2009). adv. back issues avail. **Document type:** *Magazine, Trade.*
Formerly (until 2004): Equity Journal (0141-3147)
Published by: British Actors' Equity Association, Guild House, Upper St Martin's Ln, London, WC2H 9EG, United Kingdom. TEL 44-20-73796000, FAX 44-20-73797001, info@equity.org.uk. Circ: 45,000.

792 ARG ISSN 1515-8349
LA ESCALERA. ANUARIO DE LA ESCUELA SUPERIOR DE TEATRO. Text in Spanish. 1991. a. back issues avail. **Document type:** *Monographic series, Academic/Scholarly.*
Published by: Universidad Nacional del Centro de la Provincia de Buenos Aires, Escuela Superior de Teatro, Pinto 399, Piso 3o., Tandil, Buenos Aires, B7000GHG, Argentina. Ed. Pablo M. Moro Rodriguez.

792 ESP ISSN 2172-2757
ESCRITS TEORICS. Text in Catalan. 1991. a. **Document type:** *Monographic series, Academic/Scholarly.*
Published by: Diputacio de Barcelona, Institut del Teatre, Pl Margarida Xirgu, s-n, Barcelona, 08004, Spain. TEL 34-932-273900, FAX 34-932-273939, http://www.diba.cal/.

792 ARG
ESPACIO DE CRITICA E INVESTIGACION TEATRAL. Text in Spanish. 1986. s-a. ARS 60, USD 30. bk.rev. back issues avail. **Description:** Critical reviews of theatre.
Published by: Fundacion de la Rancheria, Mexico, 1152, Buenos Aires, 1097, Argentina. TEL 54-114-3837887, FAX 54-114-9611504. Ed. Eduardo Rovner. Circ: 3,000.

792 CAN ISSN 0821-4425
PN2009
➤ **ESSAYS IN THEATRE/ETUDES THEATRALES.** Text in English. 1982. s-a. CAD 18 to individuals; CAD 24 to libraries (effective 1999). adv. bk.rev. illus. reprints avail. **Document type:** *Journal, Academic/Scholarly.*
Indexed: A20, A22, ASCA, AmHI, ArtHuCI, CurCont, IBT&D, IIPA, MLA, MLA-IB, PCI, W07.
—BLDSC (3811.789000), IE, Ingenta. **CCC.**
Published by: University of Guelph, Department of Drama, Guelph, ON N1G 2W1, Canada. TEL 519-824-4120, FAX 519-766-0844, http://www.drama.uoguelph.ca/. Ed. Ann Wilson. R&P Harry Lane. Circ: 300.

792 BGR ISSN 0204-8329
ESTRADA. Text in Bulgarian. 1973. 10/yr. BGL 20; BGL 2 newsstand/cover (effective 2002). **Document type:** *Magazine, Consumer.* **Description:** Features alphabet of theater play (for use by theater workshops in schools and culture centers), contemporary poets, poems for children, plays for puppet and drama theaters, and sketches for pop concerts and social events, all involving fun without borders.
Published by: Estrada Folk ST, PO Box 49, Sofia, 1172, Bulgaria. TEL 359-2-620627. Ed. Valentin Tkachov.

860 USA
ESTRENO; contemporary spanish plays. Text in Spanish. irreg., latest vol.26, 2004. price varies. **Document type:** *Monographic series.*
Published by: Rutgers University, Department of Spanish and Portuguese, 105 George St, New Brunswick, NJ 08901-1414. TEL 732-932-9412 ext 25, FAX 732-932-9837. Ed. Phyllis Zatlin.

792 ESP ISSN 1988-6233
ESTUDIOS SOBRE TEORIA Y CRITICA TEATRAL. Text in Spanish. 200?. a. **Document type:** *Monographic series, Academic/Scholarly.*
Published by: Universidad de Alcala de Henares, Aula de Estudios Escenicos y Medios Audiovisuales, Colegio Caracciolos, C. Trinidad, 5, Alcala de Henares, Madrid 28801, Spain. TEL 34-91-8832869, FAX 34-91-8832869, contacta@teatrostudio.com, http://www.uah.es/.

792 BEL ISSN 0778-8738
PN2003
ETUDES THEATRALES. Text in French. 1992. 3/yr. EUR 48 domestic; EUR 72 foreign (effective 2009). adv. bk.rev. bibl. 150 p./no.; back issues avail. **Document type:** *Journal, Academic/Scholarly.* **Description:** Dedicated to theatrical contemporary research.
Former titles (until 1992): Cahiers Theatre Louvain (0771-4653); Cahiers - Theatre (0068-5232)
Indexed: DIP, IBR, IBZ, MLA-IB, RASB.
Published by: Universite Catholique de Louvain, Centre d'Etudes Theatrales, Place de l'Hocaille 4, Louvain-la-Neuve, 1348, Belgium. TEL 32-10-472272, FAX 32-10-472237, http://www.uclouvain.be/thea/. Ed. Anne Wibo. Circ: 1,000.

EUGENE O'NEILL REVIEW. *see* LITERATURE

792 791.43 DEU ISSN 0721-3662
EUROPAEISCHE HOCHSCHULSCHRIFTEN. REIHE 30: THEATER-, FILM- UND FERNSEHWISSENSCHAFTEN/EUROPEAN UNIVERSITY PAPERS. SERIES 30: THEATRE, FILM AND TELEVISION. Text in Multiple languages. 1973. irreg., latest vol.93, 2008. price varies. **Document type:** *Monographic series, Academic/Scholarly.*
Formerly (until 1979): Europaeische Hochschulschriften. Reihe 30: Film- und Theaterwissenschaftliche Studien (0721-3689)
Published by: Peter Lang GmbH (Subsidiary of: Peter Lang Publishing Group), Eschborner Landstr 42-50, Frankfurt Am Main, 60489, Germany. TEL 49-69-7807050, FAX 49-69-78070550, zentrale.frankfurt@peterlang.com, http://www.peterlang.com.

792 CAN ISSN 1911-1495
EVENING OUT. Text in English. 2006. 3/yr. CAD 16 (effective 2007). adv. **Document type:** *Directory, Consumer.*
Published by: Evening Out Inc., 44 Clancy Drive, Toronto, ON M2J 2V8, Canada. TEL 905-839-1968, info@eveningout.ca, http://www.eveningout.ca/index.htm.

792 CAN ISSN 1922-8740
EVENTS CALENDAR/CALENDRIER D'EVENEMENTS. Text in English, French. 200?. q. free to members (effective 2010). **Document type:** *Journal, Consumer.* **Description:** Contains events for its members as well as for the community at large each year.
Former titles (until 2009): Calendar of Events (1719-7929); (until 2006): Arts Calendar (1716-6950)
Related titles: Online - full text ed.: free (effective 2010).
Published by: Arts Ottawa East/Arts Ottawa Est, Shenkman Arts Centre, 245 Centrum Blvd, Ste 260, Ottawa, ON K1E 0A1, Canada. TEL 613-580-2767, FAX 613-580-2768, info@artsoe.ca.

792 USA
EXPERIMENT THEATRE; "one minute" poetic drama. Text in English. irreg. USD 5.50.
Published by: Experiment Press, 6565 N E Windermere Rd, Seattle, WA 98105-2057. Ed. Carol Ely Harper.

792 USA ISSN 1010-2817
F I R T - I F T R - S I B M A S BULLETIN. Text in English. 1977. 4/yr. membership. **Document type:** *Bulletin.*
Related titles: French ed.
Published by: Federation Internationale pour la Recherche Theatrale/International Federation for Theatre Research, PO Box 1028, Boulder, CO 80306-1028. TEL 31-20-6766964, FAX 31-20-6731495, nericksn@aol.com. **Co-sponsor:** Societe Internationale des Bibliotheques et Musees des Arts du Spectacle - International Association of Libraries and Museums of the Performing Arts.

FACE TO FACE WITH TALENT. *see* COMMUNICATIONS—Television And Cable

FACILITY MANAGER. *see* BUSINESS AND ECONOMICS—Management

792.2 USA
FADE TO BLACK COMEDY MAGAZINE. Text in English. w.
Media: Online - full text.
Published by: Fade to Black, PO Box 826, Ramsey, NJ 07446. Ed. Michael Page.

792 CAN ISSN 0046-3256
PN2306.S77
FANFARES. Text in English. 1967. q. membership. **Document type:** *Newsletter.*
Published by: Stratford Shakespearean Festival Foundation of Canada, P O Box 520, Stratford, ON N5A 6V2, Canada. TEL 519-271-4040. Circ: 20,000.

792 USA ISSN 1074-0880
PN2071.F5
THE FIGHT MASTER. Text in English. s-a. USD 35 domestic; USD 40 foreign (effective 2006). **Document type:** *Journal, Consumer.*
Indexed: IBT&D, T02.
Published by: Society of American Fight Directors, 1350 East Flamingo Rd, #25, Las Vegas, NV 89119. http://www.safd.org.

791.53 CHE ISSN 1021-3244
PN1970
FIGURA; zeitschrift fuer theater und spiel mit figuren. Text in French, German. 1960. 4/yr. CHF 36 domestic; CHF 40 foreign (effective 2003). adv. bk.rev. illus. reprints avail. **Document type:** *Magazine, Consumer.*
Formerly (until 1992): Puppenspiel und Puppenspieler (0033-4405)
Indexed: MLA-IB, RASB.
Published by: U N I M A Suisse, Postfach 2328, Winterthur, 8401, Switzerland. TEL 41-52-2136991, FAX 41-52-2136991. Ed. Elke Krafka. Circ: 1,150.

792 DEU ISSN 0930-5874
FORUM MODERNES THEATER. Text in English, German. 1986. 2/yr. EUR 54; EUR 64 combined subscription (print & online eds.) (effective 2011). **Document type:** *Journal, Academic/Scholarly.* **Description:** Publishes studies in modern theater.
Related titles: Online - full text ed.
Indexed: A20, A22, ASCA, ArtHuCI, CA, CurCont, DIP, IBR, IBT&D, IBZ, IIPA, MLA-IB, PCI, RASB, SCOPUS, T02, W07.
—IE, Infotrieve. **CCC.**
Published by: (Theaterforschung), Gunter Narr Verlag, Postfach 2567, Tuebingen, 72015, Germany. TEL 49-7071-97970, FAX 49-7071-75288, info@narr.de, http://www.narr.de. Ed. Guenter Ahrends. Circ: 600 (paid and controlled).

792 DEU ISSN 0935-0012
FORUM MODERNES THEATER. SCHRIFTENREIHE. Text in German. 1988. irreg., latest vol.35, 2006. price varies. **Document type:** *Monographic series, Academic/Scholarly.* **Description:** Studies a particular topic pertaining to modern theatre.
Published by: Gunter Narr Verlag, Postfach 2567, Tuebingen, 72015, Germany. TEL 49-7071-9797-0, FAX 49-7071-75288, http://www.narr.de. Ed. Guenter Ahrends.

FOTNOTEN; tidningen foer dig som arbetar pedagogiskt med musik, dans eller drama. *see* EDUCATION

FRAMING FILM; the history and art of cinema. *see* MOTION PICTURES

792 GBR ISSN 2045-8533
▼ **THE FRENCHMAG.** Text in English, French. 2010. w. free (effective 2010). back issues avail. **Document type:** *Magazine, Consumer.* **Description:** Focuses on the history of French theatre, drama and performance from 1600 to 1914.
Media: Online - full text.
Published by: Sabine Chaouche

FRONT OF HOUSE; the news magazine for live sound. *see* SOUND RECORDING AND REPRODUCTION

791.43 CHL ISSN 0718-5316
LA FUGA. Key Title: laFuga. Text in Spanish. 2005. w.
Media: Online - full text.
Published by: LaFuga contacto@lafuga.cl, http://lafuga.cl/. Ed. Carolina Urrutia.

792 CHN ISSN 1004-2075
FUJIAN YISHU/FUJIAN ARTS. Text in Chinese. 1979. bi-m. USD 18 (effective 2009). **Document type:** *Journal, Academic/Scholarly.* **Description:** Focuses on local drama and theater in Fujian Province.
Formerly (until 1991): Fujian Xiju/Fujian Theater (0257-0211)
Related titles: Online - full text ed.
—East View.
Published by: Fujiang Sheng Yishu Yanjiusuo, 183, Yangqiao Dong Lu, Fuzhou, Fujian 350001, China. Ed. Yuan Rongsheng. **Dist. by:** China International Book Trading Corp, 35 Chegongzhuang Xilu, Haidian District, PO Box 399, Beijing 100044, China. TEL 86-10-68412045, FAX 86-10-68412023, cibtc@mail.cibtc.com.cn, http://www.cibtc.com.cn.

792 ARG ISSN 1851-5991
G E T E A. CUADERNOS. Text in Spanish. 1990. a.
Published by: Grupo de Estudios de Teatro Argentino e Iberoamericano, 25 de Mayo, 221 4o. Piso, Buenos Aires, Argentina. TEL 54-11-43347512, getea@comnet.com.ar, http://www.getea-uba.com.ar/.

G I AKTUELL. (Goethe-Institut) *see* ART

792 JPN ISSN 0919-0600
PN2920
GEINO NO KAGAKU/TOKYO NATIONAL RESEARCH INSTITUTE OF CULTURAL PROPERTIES. DEPARTMENT OF PERFORMING ARTS. JOURNAL. Text in Japanese. 1967. a. **Document type:** *Journal, Academic/Scholarly.*
Indexed: RILM.
Published by: Tokyo Kokuritsu Bunkazai Kenkyujo Bunkazai, Kenkyuujo Toukyou Bunkazai Kenkyuujo/National Research Institute of Cultural Properties, Tokyo, Department of Performing Arts, 13-43 Ueno-Park, Taito-ku, Tokyo, 110-8713, Japan. TEL 81-3-38232241, FAX 81-3-38282434.

GENII; the conjurors' magazine. *see* HOBBIES

792 DEU ISSN 0176-8905
PN2640
GESELLSCHAFT FUER THEATERGESCHICHTE. KLEINE SCHRIFTEN. Text in German. 1906. irreg., latest vol.43, 2005. price varies. **Document type:** *Monographic series, Academic/Scholarly.*
Indexed: MLA-IB.
Published by: Gesellschaft fuer Theatergeschichte e.V., c/o Andrea Heinz, Friedrich-Schiller-Universitaet Jena, Institut fuer Germanistische Literaturwissenschaft, Jena, 07737, Germany. webmaster@theatergeschichte.org, http://www.theatergeschichte.org.

792 DEU ISSN 0176-8891
PN2640
GESELLSCHAFT FUER THEATERGESCHICHTE. SCHRIFTEN. Text in German. 1902. irreg., latest vol.77, 2003. price varies. **Document type:** *Monographic series, Academic/Scholarly.*
Published by: Gesellschaft fuer Theatergeschichte e.V., c/o Andrea Heinz, Friedrich-Schiller-Universitaet Jena, Institut fuer Germanistische Literaturwissenschaft, Jena, 07737, Germany. webmaster@theatergeschichte.org, http://www.theatergeschichte.org.

792 DEU
GESELLSCHAFT FUER UNTERHALTENDE BUEHNENKUNST. KLEINE SCHRIFTEN. Text in German. 1996. irreg., latest vol.8, 2002. price varies. **Document type:** *Monographic series, Academic/Scholarly.*
Published by: (Gesellschaft fuer Unterhaltende Buehnenkunst), Weidler Buchverlag Berlin, Luebecker Str 8, Berlin, 10559, Germany. TEL 49-30-3948668, FAX 49-30-3948698, weidler_verlag@yahoo.de.

792 917.306 USA ISSN 1040-483X
PQ6098.7
➤ **GESTOS**; revista de teoria y practica del teatro hispanico. Text in English, Spanish, Portuguese. 1986. s-a. bk.rev.; play rev. illus. index. 208 p./no.; back issues avail.; reprints avail. **Document type:** *Journal, Academic/Scholarly.* **Description:** Features articles devoted to critical studies of Spanish, Latin American and US Latin theater.
Related titles: Online - full text ed.; ◆ Series: Ediciones de Gestos: Coleccion Teoria; ◆ Ediciones de Gestos: Coleccion Historia del Teatro.
Indexed: A22, BibInd, CA, F04, IBR, IBT&D, IBZ, MLA, MLA-IB, P09, PCI, RASB, T02.
—IE, Infotrieve, Ingenta.
Published by: University of California, Irvine, Department of Spanish and Portuguese, Humanities Hall, Irvine, CA 92697. TEL 949-824-7171, FAX 949-552-4820.

792 VNM
GIAO VIEN NHAN DAN/PEOPLE'S THEATRE. Text in Vietnamese. 1959. w.
Published by: Ministry of Education and Training, Le Truc, Hanoi, Viet Nam. TEL 52849. Ed. Nguyen Truong Thuy.

GIORNALE DELLO SPETTACOLO. *see* DANCE

GLENDORA REVIEW; an African quarterly on the arts. *see* LITERATURE

800 GBR
GLOBE QUARTOS. Text in English. 2002. irreg. GBP 7.50 per issue (effective 2009). **Description:** Features Shakespeare's plays.
Published by: Shakespeare's Globe, 21 New Globe Walk, Bankside, London, SE1 9DT, United Kingdom. TEL 44-20-79021400, FAX 44-20-79021401, info@shakespearesglobe.com.

792 SRB ISSN 1820-2977
PN2850
GODISNJAK POZORISTA SRBIJE I CRNE GORE/YEARBOOK OF SERBIA AND MONTENEGRO THEATRES. Text in Albanian, Hungarian, Serbian. 1978. a. USD 20 (effective 1999).
Formerly (until 2002): Godisnjak Jugoslovenskih Pozorista (0351-9120)
Published by: Sterijino Pozorje, Zmaj Jovina 22, Novi Sad, 21000. TEL 381-21-451273, FAX 381-21-6615976, sterija@neobee.net, http://www.pozorje.org.yu. Ed. Svetko Borovcanin.

800 USA
GREENWOOD GUIDES TO SHAKESPEARE. Text in English. 1997. irreg., latest 2005. price varies. back issues avail. **Document type:** *Monographic series, Academic/Scholarly.*
Related titles: Online - full text ed.
Published by: Greenwood Publishing Group Inc. (Subsidiary of: A B C - C L I O), 88 Post Rd W, PO Box 5007, Westport, CT 06881. TEL 203-226-3571, 800-225-5800, FAX 877-231-6980, sales@greenwood.com.

792 FRA ISSN 0295-9909
PA3133
GROUPE INTERDISCIPLINAIRE DU THEATRE ANTIQUE. CAHIERS. Key Title: Cahiers du G I T A. Text in French. 1982. irreg., latest vol.16, 2008. price varies. bk.rev. **Document type:** *Academic/Scholarly.*
Published by: Universite de Montpellier III (Paul Valery), Groupe Interdisciplinaire du Theatre Antique, Route de Mende, Montpellier, Cedex 5 34199, France. TEL 33-4-67142006, FAX 33-4-67142332, publications.recherche@univ-montp3.fr. Ed. P Sauzeau.

792 USA
GUILDWORKS. Text in English. 1977. 6/yr. free to members (effective 2007). 16 p./no. 2 cols./p.; back issues avail. **Document type:** *Newsletter, Trade.* **Description:** Contains announcements of all Guild activities, news and information of interest to dramatists.
Formerly: Dramatists Guild Newsletter
Related titles: ◆ Supplement to: The Dramatist. ISSN 1551-7683.
Published by: Dramatists Guild, Inc., 1501 Broadway, Ste 701, New York, NY 10036. TEL 212-398-9366, FAX 212-944-0420, http://www.dramatistsguild.com. Ed. Gregory Bossler. Circ: 7,000 (controlled).

792 USA
GUTHRIE THEATER PROGRAM. Text in English. 1963. 10/yr. free (effective 2006). adv. **Document type:** *Magazine, Consumer.* **Description:** Contains information about mainstage productions, including background on the play, playwright, production, actors, and other theater events.
Formerly: Guthrie Theater Program Magazine
Published by: Guthrie Theater, 818 South 2nd St, Minneapolis, MI 55415. TEL 612-225-6000, FAX 612-347-1188. Ed. Michael Lupu. Circ: 40,000 (free).

H D K MAGAZIN. (Hochschule der Kuenste Berlin) *see* ART

HALF MASK. *see* EDUCATION

792 791 791.45 USA ISSN 1098-948X
HENDERSON'S CASTING DIRECTORS GUIDE. Text in English. 1998. m. USD 14 (effective 2008). **Document type:** *Directory, Trade.* **Description:** Provides contact information and updates for casting directors and producers in theatre, television and motion picture industries in the New York area.
Published by: Henderson Enterprises, Inc, 360 E 65th St, Ste 15E, New York, NY 10065. TEL 212-472-2292, FAX 212-472-5999, info@hendersonenterprises.com, http://www.hendersonenterprises.com. Ed. Porter Henderson Sue.

▼ **HOCHSCHULE FUER MUSIK UND THEATER FELIX MENDELSSOHN BARTHOLDY LEIPZIG. SCHRIFTEN.** *see* MUSIC

HOCHSCHULE FUER MUSIK UND THEATER HANNOVER. PUBLIKATIONEN. *see* MUSIC

HOLA PAGES; national directory of Hispanic talent. *see* MOTION PICTURES

HOLLYWOOD ACTING COACHES AND TEACHERS DIRECTORY. *see* EDUCATION—Teaching Methods And Curriculum

THE HOLLYWOOD REPORTER. INTERNATIONAL EDITION. *see* MOTION PICTURES

HORISONT. *see* LITERATURE

HORIZONT; veszprem megyei kozmuvelodesi tajekoztato. *see* CLUBS

700 CHN ISSN 1003-5826
M1805.4.A5
HUANGMEIXI YISHU/ART OF HUANGMEI OPERA. Text in Chinese. 1981. q. USD 9.60 (effective 2009). **Document type:** *Journal, Academic/Scholarly.*
Related titles: Online - full content ed.; Online - full text ed.
Address: 4, Xixiao Nanlu Bei 3-xiang, Anqing, 246001, China. TEL 86-556-5574135.

I C A MONTHLY BULLETIN. *see* ART

791.53 ITA ISSN 1123-0517
I LOVE PUPPETS. Text in Italian. 1994. bi-w. **Document type:** *Magazine, Consumer.*
Published by: De Agostini Editore, Via G da Verrazzano 15, Novara, 28100, Italy. TEL 39-0321-4241, FAX 39-0321-424305, info@deagostini.it, http://www.deagostini.it.

792 946 USA ISSN 1056-5000
IBERICA. Text in English. 1991. irreg., latest vol.40, 2009. price varies. **Document type:** *Monographic series, Academic/Scholarly.* **Description:** Focuses on theater in 16th and 17th century Spain.
Indexed: RASB.
Published by: Peter Lang Publishing, Inc. (Subsidiary of: Peter Lang Publishing Group), 29 Broadway, New York, NY 10006. TEL 212-647-7700, 212-647-7706, 800-770-5264, FAX 212-647-7707, customerservice@plang.com. Ed. Robert Lauer.

ILLINOIS SPEECH AND THEATRE ASSOCIATION. JOURNAL. *see* COMMUNICATIONS

792 700 ITA ISSN 2038-5536
PN1993.5.A1
▼ **IMAGO (ROME).** Text in Italian. 2010. s-a. **Document type:** *Journal, Academic/Scholarly.*
Published by: (Universita degli Studi di Roma "La Sapienza", Dipartimento di Storia dell'Arte e dello Spettacolo, Universita degli Studi di Roma Tre, Dipartimento Comunicazione e Spettacolo), Bulzoni Editore, Via dei Liburni 14, Rome, 00185, Italy. TEL 39-06-4455207, FAX 39-06-4450355, bulzoni@bulzoni.it, http://www.bulzoni.it.

792 USA ISSN 1949-2650
▼ **INCITEINSIGHT.** Text in English. 2009. bi-m. free to members (effective 2009). **Document type:** *Magazine, Trade.*
Indexed: B04, E02, E03, EdA, EdI, W03, W05.
Published by: American Alliance for Theatre & Education, 4811 Saint Elmo Ave, Unit B, Bethesda, MD 20814. TEL 301-951-7977, FAX 515-474-1720, info@aate.com.

792 ITA ISSN 1825-2885
INSCENA. Text in Italian. 2005. m. EUR 90 domestic; EUR 180 foreign (effective 2009). **Document type:** *Magazine, Consumer.*
Published by: Gangemi Editore, Piazza San Pantaleo 4, Rome, Italy. TEL 39-06-6872774, FAX 39-06-68806189, info@gangemieditore.it, http://www.gangemi.com. Ed. Valentina Venturini.

700 780.65 792.8 USA ISSN 1069-2029
PN1561
INSIDE ARTS. Text in English. 1989. bi-m. USD 42 to non-members (effective 2004). adv. bk.rev. **Document type:** *Magazine, Trade.* **Description:** Performing arts; feature stories on artists, facilities, events and projects of significance; first-person essays by artists; profiles of performers.
Formerly (until Dec. 1989): Inside Performance (1050-7973)
Published by: Association of Performing Arts Presenters, 1112 16th St, N W, Ste 400, Washington, DC 20036. TEL 202-833-2787, 888-820-2787, FAX 202-833-1543, info@artspresenters.org. Ed. Alicia Anstead. adv.: B&W page USD 2,040; trim 8.5 x 10.875. Circ: 3,500.

INSIDER. *see* ART

INSTITUTO BRASIL - ESTADOS UNIDOS. BOLETIM. *see* EDUCATION

792 ARG ISSN 1851-6017
INSTITUTO NACIONAL DEL TEATRO. COLECCION. Text in Spanish. 2003. irreg. **Document type:** *Monographic series, Academic/Scholarly.*
Published by: Instituto Nacional del Teatro, Ave Santa Fe 1243 7o Piso, Buenos Aires, Argentina. TEL 54-11-48156661.

792 USA
INTERMISSION (ALEXANDRIA). Text in English. 1988. m. USD 12 (effective 2000). adv. bk.rev. **Document type:** *Newspaper.* **Description:** Covers theatre and related performing arts. Also reviews films and occasionally restaurants in the area.
Formerly (until 1989): Review (Alexandria)
Published by: K Communications, 6205 Redwood Lane, Alexandria, VA 22310. TEL 703-971-7530. Ed., Adv. contact Verna A Kerans. B&W page USD 300; trim 14 x 9.5. Circ: 20,000. **Subscr. to:** 135 W. Rose, Webster Grove, MO 63119.

792 GBR ISSN 1479-4713
NX456.5.P38
➤ **INTERNATIONAL JOURNAL OF PERFORMANCE ARTS AND DIGITAL MEDIA.** Abbreviated title: I J P A D M. Text in English. 2005. s-a. GBP 36, USD 68 to individuals; GBP 215, USD 330 to institutions (effective 2012). adv. back issues avail. **Document type:** *Journal, Academic/Scholarly.* **Description:** Draws on research from the rapidly developing interface between new technologies and performance arts. Topics include cultural mediatization, live performance with interactive systems, and motion capture technologies, among many others.
Related titles: Online - full text ed.: ISSN 2040-0934. GBP 177, USD 265 (effective 2012).
Indexed: A10, CA, IBT&D, MLA-IB, T02, V03.
—BLDSC (4542.452150), IE. **CCC.**
Published by: Intellect Ltd., The Mill, Parnall Rd, Fishponds, Bristol, BS16 3JG, United Kingdom. TEL 44-117-9589910, FAX 44-117-9589911, info@intellectbooks.com. Ed. Dr. David Collins TEL 44-1302-553909. Pub. Masoud Yazdani. **Subscr. to:** Turpin Distribution Services Ltd., Pegasus Dr, Stratton Business Park, Biggleswade, Bedfordshire SG18 8QB, United Kingdom. TEL 44-1767-604951, FAX 44-1767-601640, custserv@turpin-distribution.com, http://www.turpin-distribution.com/.

792 GBR ISSN 1471-5198
PN2604
➤ **INTERNATIONAL JOURNAL OF SCOTTISH THEATRE.** Abbreviated title: I J O S T. Text in English. 2000. s-a. **Document type:** *Journal, Academic/Scholarly.* **Description:** Presents papers on all aspects of theater in Scotland and on the (re) presentation of Scotland and Scottish theatre on the international stage.
Media: Online - full content.
Published by: Queen Margaret University College, Department of Drama, Corstorphine Campus, Clerwood Terrace, Edinburgh, EH12 8TS, United Kingdom. TEL 44-131-317-3000, FAX 44-131-317-3256, http://www.qmuc.ac.uk.

▼ ➤ **INTERNATIONAL STUDIES FOR NON-TRADITIONAL STUDENTS: PEDAGOGY OF PERFORMING ARTS AND MUSIC.** *see* MUSIC

792 USA
INTERNATIONAL THEATRE INSTITUTE OF THE UNITED STATES. NEWSLETTER. Text in English. 1989. q. bk.rev. back issues avail. **Document type:** *Newsletter.* **Description:** Reports on the activities of ITI worldwide, ITI US and the theatre professionals who are served by ITI's international programs.
Published by: International Theatre Institute of the United States, Inc., 355 Lexington Ave, New York, NY 10017-6603. TEL 212-697-5230, FAX 212-983-4847, 1rachow@tcg.org, http://www.tcg.org. Ed. Louis A Rachow. Circ: 1,500 (controlled).

792 CAN
INTERVAL. Text in English. 1994. q. CAD 10 to non-members; CAD 20 foreign to non-members. adv. **Document type:** *Newsletter.*
Published by: Theatre Nova Scotia, 1113 Marginal Rd, Halifax, NS B3H 4P7, Canada. TEL 902-425-3876, FAX 902-422-0881, nsdl@nsdl.org. Adv. contact Jackie Burke. Circ: 300.

800 AUS ISSN 1833-3362
INVERESK PLAY SERIES. Text in English. 2006. irreg., latest 2008. back issues avail. **Document type:** *Monographic series, Trade.*
Published by: University of Tasmania, School of Visual and Performing Arts, Locked Bag 1362, Launceston, TAS 7250, Australia. TEL 61-3-63244400, FAX 61-3-63244401, Academy.Admin@utas.edu.au, http://www.acadarts.utas.edu.au/.

792 ITA ISSN 1824-6699
INVITO ALL'OPERA. Text in Italian. 2004. w. **Document type:** *Magazine, Consumer.*
Related titles: Optical Disk - DVD ed.: ISSN 1827-6881. 2006.
Published by: De Agostini Editore, Via G da Verrazzano 15, Novara, 28100, Italy. TEL 39-0321-4241, FAX 39-0321-424305, info@deagostini.it, http://www.deagostini.it.

800 792 GBR ISSN 0260-7964
IRISH DRAMA SELECTIONS. Abbreviated title: I D S. Text in English. 1982. irreg., latest vol.15. price varies. back issues avail.; reprints avail. **Document type:** *Monographic series, Academic/Scholarly.* **Description:** Contains volumes of selected plays by Irish dramatists.
Published by: (Catholic University of America Press USA), Colin Smythe Ltd., PO Box 6, Gerrards Cross, Bucks SL9 8XA, United Kingdom. TEL 44-1753-886000, FAX 44-1753-886469, cpsmythe@aol.com, http://www.colinsmythe.co.uk. **Dist. by:** Oxford University Press.

792 IRL ISSN 2009-0870
➤ **IRISH THEATRE INTERNATIONAL.** Text in English. 2008. a. **Document type:** *Journal, Academic/Scholarly.* **Description:** Publishes interdisciplinary research between theater studies in Ireland and the wider community of theater and performance studies in its international contexts.
Published by: (Irish Society for Theatre Research), Carysfort Press Ltd, 58 Woodfield, Scholarstown Rd, Rathfarnham, Dublin, 16, Ireland. TEL 353-1-4937383, FAX 353-1-4069815, info@carysfortpress.com, http://www.carysfortpress.com. Ed. Paul Murphy.

792 IRL ISSN 1393-7855
PN2601
IRISH THEATRE MAGAZINE. Text in English. 1998. q. EUR 32 (effective 2007). **Document type:** *Journal, Academic/Scholarly.*
Address: 74 Dame St, Dublin 2, Ireland. Ed. Helen Meany.

792 DEU
IXYPSILONZETT; Das Magazin fuer Kinder- und Jugendtheater. Text in German. 2005. 3/yr. EUR 16 domestic; EUR 22 foreign (effective 2010). adv. **Document type:** *Magazine, Trade.*
Published by: I.G. Theater der Zeit e.V., Klosterstr 68-70, Berlin, 10179, Germany. TEL 49-30-24722414, FAX 49-30-24722415.

792 SVK ISSN 0323-2883
JAVISKO. Text in Slovak. 1968. q. EUR 7; EUR 2 newsstand/cover (effective 2009). bk.rev.; dance rev.; film rev. 40 p./no.; **Document type:** *Magazine, Consumer.*
Indexed: RASB.
Published by: Narodne Osvetove Centrum, Nam. SNP 12, Bratislava, 81234, Slovakia. TEL 421-918-716018, nocka@nocka.sk. Ed. Jaroslava Cajkova.

T U

792 CAN ISSN 0382-0335
PN2305.Q4
JEU; cahiers de theatre. Text in English. 1976. q. CAD 40 to individuals; USD 50 foreign to individuals; CAD 50 to institutions; USD 61 foreign to institutions (effective 1999). adv. bk.rev.; play rev. illus. back issues avail. **Description:** Informs about various tendencies of contemporary theatre in Quebec and other countries.
Indexed: IBT&D, MLA-IB, PdeR, RASB.
Published by: Cahiers de Theatre Jeu Inc., 460 rue St Catherine Ouest, Bur 838, Montreal, PQ H3B 1A7, Canada. TEL 514-875-2549, FAX 514-875-8827. Ed. Louise Vigeant. R&P, Adv. contact Michele Vincelette. Circ: 1,200.

792 USA ISSN 1076-4802
PN2016
JOURNAL FOR STAGE DIRECTORS & CHOREOGRAPHERS. Text in English. 1979. s-a. USD 18 domestic; USD 28 foreign (effective 2000). adv. bk.rev. illus. **Document type:** *Journal, Trade.* **Description:** Provides insight into the world of directing and choreography, including craft and career information, written by professionals in the field.
Former titles: Stage Directors and Choreographers Foundation. Journal (1055-6974); (until 1988): Society of Stage Directors and Choreographers. Journal (0735-1577)
Published by: Stage Directors and Choreographers Foundation, 1501 Broadway, Ste 1701, New York, NY 10036. TEL 212-302-5359, FAX 212-302-6195, http://www.ssdc.org/foundation. Ed. Jim O'Quinn. R&P David Diamond. Adv. contact Bob Johnson. Circ: 1,800.

792 GBR ISSN 1753-6421
➤ **JOURNAL OF ADAPTATION IN FILM AND PERFORMANCE.** Abbreviated title: J A F P. Text in English. 2008. 3/yr. GBP 36, USD 68 to individuals; GBP 235, USD 368 to institutions (effective 2012). adv. back issues avail. **Document type:** *Journal, Academic/Scholarly.* **Description:** Designed to engage with specific issues relating to performance on stage, film, television, radio and other media.
Related titles: Online - full text ed.: ISSN 1753-643X. GBP 192, USD 290 (effective 2012).
Indexed: CA, F01, F02, MLA-IB, T02.
—BLDSC (4918.933850).
Published by: Intellect Ltd., The Mill, Parnall Rd, Fishponds, Bristol, BS16 3JG, United Kingdom. TEL 44-117-9589910, FAX 44-117-9589911, info@intellectbooks.com. Eds. Katja Krebs, Richard Hand. Pub. Masoud Yazdani. **Subscr. to:** Turpin Distribution Services Ltd., Pegasus Dr, Stratton Business Park, Biggleswade, Bedfordshire SG18 8QB, United Kingdom. TEL 44-1767-604951, FAX 44-1767-601640, custserv@turpin-distribution.com, http://www.turpin-distribution.com/.

792 USA ISSN 1044-937X
PS332
➤ **JOURNAL OF AMERICAN DRAMA AND THEATRE.** Text in English. 1989. 3/yr. USD 20 domestic; USD 30 foreign (effective 2010). adv. illus. back issues avail.; reprints avail. **Document type:** *Journal, Academic/Scholarly.*
Related titles: Online - full text ed.
Indexed: CA, IBT&D, IIPA, MLA-IB, T02.
—BLDSC (4927.236000), Ingenta.
Published by: Martin E. Segal Theatre Center, The CUNY Graduate Center, 365 Fifth Ave, New York, NY 10016. TEL 212-817-1860, mestc@gc.cuny.edu. Ed. David Savran. Circ: 3,400 (paid).

➤ **THE JOURNAL OF BECKETT STUDIES.** *see* LITERATURE

792 USA ISSN 0888-3203
PN1601
➤ **JOURNAL OF DRAMATIC THEORY AND CRITICISM.** Text in English. 1986. s-a. USD 30 in US & Canada to individuals; USD 40 elsewhere to individuals; USD 40 in US & Canada to institutions; USD 45 elsewhere to institutions (effective 2010). adv. bk.rev. illus. back issues avail.; reprints avail. **Document type:** *Journal, Academic/Scholarly.* **Description:** Brings out articles that contribute to the varied conversations in dramatic theory and criticism, and explores the relationship between theory and theatre practice, and/or examine recent scholarship by a single author.
Indexed: A22, ABS&EES, CA, IBT&D, IIPA, MLA-IB, T02.
—BLDSC (4970.200000), IE, Infotrieve, Ingenta.
Address: 356 Murphy Hall, Lawrence, KS 66045. TEL 785-864-3511. Ed. Scott Magelssen. **Subscr. to:** Allen Press Inc., PO Box 1897, Lawrence, KS 66044.

792 AUS ISSN 1994-1250
➤ **JOURNAL OF INTERACTIVE DRAMA**; a multi-discipline peer-reviewed journal of scenario-based theatre-style interactive drama freeform live action roleplaying games. Text in English. 2006. q. free (effective 2008). bk.rev. back issues avail. **Document type:** *Journal, Academic/Scholarly.* **Description:** Provides a forum for serious discussion on the theory, design and practice of live roleplaying games, freeforms, and interactive dramas.
Media: Online - full content.
Address: PO Box 14428, Melbourne, VIC 8001, Australia. TEL 61-3-99194784, FAX 61-3-99195066. Ed., Pub. Scott Beattie.

792 792.8 780 GHA ISSN 0855-2606
JOURNAL OF PERFORMING ARTS. Text in English. 1996. s-a. **Document type:** *Journal, Academic/Scholarly.*
Indexed: RILM.
Published by: University of Ghana, School of Performing Arts, PO Box 201, Legon, Accra, Ghana. kanyidoho@ug.gn.apc.org.

▼ **JOURNAL OF PERFORMING ARTS LEADERSHIP IN HIGHER EDUCATION.** *see* EDUCATION—Higher Education

THE JOURNAL OF RELIGION AND THEATRE. *see* RELIGIONS AND THEOLOGY

JOURNAL OF ROMANCE STUDIES. *see* LINGUISTICS

792 CHN ISSN 0578-0659
PL2603
JUBEN/PLAY MONTHLY. Text in Chinese. 1953. m. USD 46.80 (effective 2009). **Document type:** *Journal, Academic/Scholarly.*
Related titles: Online - full text ed.
—East View.
Published by: (Zhongguo Xijujia Xiehui/Chinese Theater Artists' Association), Zhongguo Xiju Chubanshe, 52, Dong Siba Tiao, Beijing, 100700, China. Ed. Wei Min. **Dist. by:** China International Book Trading Corp, 35 Chegongzhuang Xilu, Haidian District, PO Box 399, Beijing 100044, China. TEL 86-10-68412045, FAX 86-10-68412023, cibtc@mail.cibtc.com.cn, http://www.cibtc.com.cn.

792 808 BHS
JUNKANOO. Text in English. m. USD 18.
Published by: Junkanoo Publications, PO Box N 4923, Nassau, Bahamas. Eds. John Munnings, Melanie Pintard.

792 CHN ISSN 1004-5864
PN2870
JUYING YUEBAO/DRAMA & MOVIES MONTHLY. Text in Chinese. 1959-1961; resumed 1980. bi-m. USD 31.20 (effective 2009). **Document type:** *Journal, Academic/Scholarly.* **Description:** Contains film, drama and TV play scripts, and review articles.
Formerly: Jiangsu Xiju
Related titles: Online - full text ed.
—East View.
Published by: Jiangsu Sheng Wenhua Ting, 2, Huaihai Lu, Nanjing, Jiangsu 210005, China. TEL 86-25-84522126, FAX 86-25-84500126. Ed. Wang Hong. Circ: 5,000. **Dist. by:** China International Book Trading Corp, 35 Chegongzhuang Xilu, Haidian District, PO Box 399, Beijing 100044, China. TEL 86-10-68412045, FAX 86-10-68412023, cibtc@mail.cibtc.com.cn, http://www.cibtc.com.cn.

792 CHN ISSN 1001-3768
PL2603
JUZUOJIA/PLAYWRIGHT. Text in Chinese. 1979. bi-m. USD 18 (effective 2009). **Document type:** *Journal, Academic/Scholarly.*
Related titles: Online - full text ed.
Published by: Heilongjiang Sheng Wenhuating/Heilongjiang Provincial Bureau of Culture, 197, Zhongshan Lu, Ha'erbin, Heilongjiang 150001, China. TEL 86-451-82617334, FAX 86-451-82640437. **Dist. by:** China International Book Trading Corp, 35 Chegongzhuang Xilu, Haidian District, PO Box 399, Beijing 100044, China. TEL 86-10-68412045, FAX 86-10-68412023, cibtc@mail.cibtc.com.cn, http://www.cibtc.com.cn.

K C STUDIO. (Kansas City) *see* MOTION PICTURES

792.1 USA ISSN 1937-8572
PN2309
➤ **KARPA**; journal of theatricalities and visual culture. Text in English. 2008. s-a. free (effective 2009). back issues avail. **Document type:** *Journal, Academic/Scholarly.*
Media: Online - full content.
Indexed: MLA-IB.
Published by: Gaston A. Alzate, Ed., c/o Department of Modern Language and Literatures, Cal State University, 5151 State University Dr, Los Angeles, CA 90032. TEL 323-343-2267, FAX 323-434-4234, galzate@calstatela.edu. Ed. Paola Marin.

792 HRV
KAZALISTE; revija za scensku glazbu i kulturu. Text in Croatian. 1965. fortn. USD 5.20. illus.
Published by: Hrvatsko Narodno Kazaliste u Osijeku, Prolaz Radoslava Bacica 1, Osijek, Croatia. Ed. Ljubomir Standjevic.

KEY NOTE MARKET REPORT: ARTS & MEDIA SPONSORSHIP. *see* BUSINESS AND ECONOMICS—Marketing And Purchasing

KEY NOTE MARKET REPORT: CINEMAS & THEATRES. *see* BUSINESS AND ECONOMICS—Production Of Goods And Services

KIDS' ACTING FOR BRAIN SURGEONS; the insiders guide for kids in the industry. *see* CHILDREN AND YOUTH—For

792 DEU ISSN 0723-8312
KINDER-, SCHUL- UND JUGENDTHEATER; Beitraege zu Theorie und Praxis. Text in German. 1983. irreg., latest vol.13, 2009. price varies. **Document type:** *Monographic series, Academic/Scholarly.*
Published by: Peter Lang GmbH (Subsidiary of: Peter Lang Publishing Group), Eschborner Landstr 42-50, Frankfurt Am Main, 60489, Germany. TEL 49-69-7807050, FAX 49-69-78070550, zentrale.frankfurt@peterlang.com. Ed. Wolfgang Schneider.

792 GBR ISSN 0451-9566
KING POLE CIRCUS MAGAZINE. Text in English. 194?. q. free to members (effective 2009). adv. bk.rev. illus.; stat. 42 p./no.; back issues avail. **Document type:** *Magazine, Consumer.* **Description:** Contains articles and reviews on circus productions and personalities of past and present.
Related titles: Supplement(s): Circus Directory of the British Isles.
Indexed: RASB.
Published by: Circus Friends' Association of Great Britain, c/o Membership Secretary, 49 Lake View, North Holmwood, Dorking, Surrey RH5 4TH, United Kingdom. joditimmscfa@aol.com. Ed. David Jamieson.

KINO-TEATR. *see* MOTION PICTURES

792 DEU ISSN 1867-7568
KLEINE MAINZER SCHRIFTEN ZUR THEATERWISSENSCHAFT. Text in German. 2005. irreg., latest vol.19, 2010. price varies. **Document type:** *Monographic series, Academic/Scholarly.*
Published by: Tectum Wissenschaftsverlag Marburg, Biegenstr 4, Marburg, 35037, Germany. TEL 49-6421-481523, FAX 49-6421-43470, email@tectum-verlag.de. Eds. Friedemann Kreuter, Kati Roettger, Peter Marx.

792 DEU ISSN 0941-2107
KORRESPONDENZEN. Text in German. 1986. s-a. EUR 13 (effective 2006). **Document type:** *Journal, Academic/Scholarly.*
Indexed: MLA-IB.
Published by: Gesellschaft fuer Theaterpaedagogik, c/o Florian Vassen, Koenigsworther Platz 1, Hannover, 30167, Germany. TEL 49-511-7624210, FAX 49-511-7624060, vassen@fbls.uni-hannover.de.

792 BGR
KRATKI STRANITSI/BRIEF PAGES. Text in Bulgarian. 1997. m. BGL 0.50 newsstand/cover (effective 2002). **Document type:** *Magazine, Consumer.* **Description:** Includes monthly schedules of Sofia theater halls, the Music Hall, Sofia Opera Hall, National Palace of Culture, etc. Presents theater, musicals and other festivals and events of Sofia's cultural life.
Published by: Konstantin Zarev ET, 12 Serdika St., Sofia, 1000, Bulgaria. TEL 359-2-834712, FAX 359-2-9800157. Ed. Konstantin Zarev.

KULTUR LIFE; Veranstaltungsvorschau. *see* MUSEUMS AND ART GALLERIES

KULTURA-EXTRA; das online-magazin. *see* ART

KUNST-, MUSIK- UND THEATERWISSENSCHAFT. *see* ART

792 AUT
KURSBUCH KULTUR. Text in German. a. adv. **Document type:** *Magazine, Consumer.*
Formerly: Spielplan
Published by: Verlagsgruppe News Gesellschaft mbH (Subsidiary of: Gruner + Jahr AG & Co), Alfred-Feierfeil-Str. 3, Perchtoldsdorf, N 2380, Austria. TEL 43-1-86331-0, FAX 43-1-86331-590. adv.: color page EUR 1,850; trim 100 x 145. Circ: 57,000 (controlled).

647.968 USA ISSN 2157-1007
L M D A REVIEW. Text in English. 19??. s-a. free (effective 2010). back issues avail. **Document type:** *Trade.* **Description:** Features essays, articles and announcements of interest to LMDA members, news of the organization and the profession, and other communications between LMDA members.
Media: Online - full text.
Indexed: MLA-IB.
Published by: Literary Managers and Dramaturgs of the Americas, PO Box 36, New York, NY 10129. TEL 800-680-2148, lmdanyc@gmail.com. Ed. D J Hopkins.

792 ESP ISSN 1575-9504
LAS PUERTAS DEL DRAMA. Text in Spanish. 1999. q. EUR 9 domestic; EUR 12 foreign (effective 2010). back issues avail. **Document type:** *Journal, Academic/Scholarly.*
Published by: Asociacion de Autores de Teatro, Benito Gutierrez, 27 1a. Izq., Madrid, 28008, Spain. TEL 34-91-5430271, FAX 34-91-5496292, aat@aat.es.

782.81 ITA ISSN 1827-4080
LASCALAINFORMA. Text in Italian. 2003. q. **Document type:** *Newsletter, Consumer.*
Published by: Fondazione Teatro alla Scala, Via Filodrammatici 2, Milan, 20121, Italy. TEL 39-02-88791, http://www.teatroallascala.org.

792 USA ISSN 0023-8813
PN2309
➤ **LATIN AMERICAN THEATRE REVIEW.** Abbreviated title: L A T R. Text in English, Portuguese, Spanish; Summaries in English. 1967. s-a. USD 25 to individuals; USD 65 to institutions (effective 2011). adv. bk.rev.; play rev. bibl.; illus. cum.index. back issues avail.; reprints avail. **Document type:** *Journal, Academic/Scholarly.* **Description:** Presents interviews, theatre history, international stories, profiles, news, and articles about leading theatre companies and innovators in the field.
Related titles: Online - full text ed.: ISSN 2161-0576.
Indexed: A20, A22, ASCA, AmHI, ArtHuCI, ChPerI, Chicano, CurCont, DIP, FR, H21, IBR, IBRH, IBT&D, IBZ, IIPA, MLA, MLA-IB, P08, P09, PCI, RASB, RILM, SCOPUS, W07.
—Ingenta.
Published by: Center of Latin American Studies, 107 Lippincott Hall, University of Kansas, Lawrence, KS 66045. TEL 785-864-2700, http://www.ku.edu. Ed. Stuart A Day.

➤ **LAUGH-MAKERS**; variety arts for family entertainment. *see* HOBBIES

792 DEU ISSN 1869-3520
▼ **LEIPZIGER BEITRAEGE ZUR THEATERGESCHICHTSFORSCHUNG.** Text in German. 2009. irreg., latest vol.2, 2010. price varies. **Document type:** *Monographic series, Academic/Scholarly.*
Published by: Leipziger Universitaetsverlag GmbH, Oststr 41, Leipzig, 04317, Germany. TEL 49-341-9900440, FAX 49-341-9900440, info@univerlag-leipzig.de.

LIAISON (VANIER); la revue des arts en Ontario Francais. *see* ART

792.02 621.32 GBR ISSN 0268-7429
LIGHTING & SOUND INTERNATIONAL. Abbreviated title: L & S I. Text in English. 1985. m. GBP 30 domestic; GBP 50 in Europe; GBP 60 elsewhere; GBP 3.50 per issue; free to qualified personnel (effective 2009). adv. bk.rev.; music rev.; play rev.; software rev.; tel.rev.; video rev. pat.; stat.; tr.lit. back issues avail. **Document type:** *Magazine, Trade.*
Related titles: Online - full text ed.: ISSN 1759-6343. free.
—CCC.
Published by: Professional Lighting and Sound Association, Redoubt House, 1 Edward Rd, Eastbourne, E Sussex BN23 8AS, United Kingdom. TEL 44-1323-524120, FAX 44-1323-524121, news@plasa.org, http://www.plasa.org. Ed. Lee Baldock TEL 44-1323-524133. Adv. contact Barry Howse TEL 44-1323-524135. page GBP 1,860; trim 297 x 210. Circ: 10,250.

792 USA
LINCOLN CENTER CALENDAR. Text in English. 19??. m. free to members. adv. **Document type:** *Guide, Consumer.* **Description:** Covers events at Lincoln Center.
Formerly: Lincoln Center Calendar of Events
Published by: Lincoln Center for the Performing Arts, Inc., 70 Lincoln Center Plaza, 9th Fl, New York, NY 10023. TEL 212-875-5456, customerservice@lincolncenter.org, http://www.lincolncenter.org. adv.: B&W page USD 6,000, color page USD 7,060; trim 5.375 x 8.375. Circ: 100,000.

792 USA ISSN 1524-0940
PN2000
LINCOLN CENTER THEATER REVIEW. Text in English. 1985. 3/yr. USD 10 (effective 2009). **Document type:** *Magazine, Consumer.*
Formerly (until 1998): New Theater Review (0898-8013)
Related titles: Online - full text ed.
Published by: Lincoln Center Theater, 150 W 65th St, New York, NY 10023. TEL 212-362-7600 212-362-7600 Administrative Offices:, FAX 212-873-0761, info@lct.org, http://www.lct.org. Ed. Alexis Gargagliano.

792 AUT ISSN 0024-4139
LINZER THEATERZEITUNG. Text in German. 1955. 9/yr. EUR 13.50 (effective 2005). adv. bk.rev. **Document type:** *Magazine, Trade.*
Published by: Landestheater Linz, Promenade 39, Linz, O 4020, Austria. TEL 43-70-76110, FAX 43-70-7611539, office@landestheater-linz.at, http://www.landestheater-linz.at. Circ: 10,000.

LITTERATUR TEATER FILM; nya serien. *see* LITERATURE

792 USA ISSN 1559-2359
PN2053
LIVE DESIGN. Text in English. 2005. m. free to qualified personnel (effective 2011). adv. bk.rev. charts; illus. back issues avail.; reprints avail. **Document type:** *Magazine, Trade.* **Description:** Presents a new view of the art and technology of show business. Features the latest in lighting design and technology, sound design and reinforcement, set design and construction. Includes Annual Source Book.
Incorporates: Live Design's T Q; Formed by the merger of (2002-2005): S R O (1541-1834); (1977-2005): Lighting Dimensions (0191-541X); (1999-2005): Entertainment Design (1520-5150); Which superseded (in 1999): T C I (Theatre Crafts International) (1063-9497); Which was formed by the merger of (1967-1992): Theatre Crafts (0040-5469); (1991-1992): Theatre Crafts International (1060-3042); Which incorporated: Cue International; Which was formerly: Cue Technical Theatre Review (0144-6088)
Related titles: Microform ed.: (from PQC); Online - full text ed.
Indexed: A01, A02, A03, A07, A08, A09, A10, A20, A22, A26, A27, A30, A31, AA, ArtInd, B01, B03, B04, B06, B07, B09, BRD, BRI, C12, CA, CBRI, D05, E06, E08, F01, F02, G05, G06, G07, G08, I05, I07, IBT&D, IIPA, M01, M02, MASUSE, MLA-IB, MagInd, P02, P10, P13, P53, P54, PMR, PQC, R03, R04, R06, RASB, RGAb, RGPR, RILM, S09, SCOPUS, T02, TOM, V03, V04, W03, W05.
—BLDSC (5279.385000), CIS, IE, Infotrieve, Ingenta. **CCC.**
Published by: Penton Media, Inc., 249 W 17th St, New York, NY 10011. TEL 212-204-4200, FAX 212-206-3622, information@penton.com, http://www.pentonmedia.com. Ed. Marian Sandberg TEL 212-204-4266. Pub., Adv. contact David Johnson TEL 212-204-4272.

792 GBR
LONDON THEATRE GUIDE; all hit musicals currently on London stage explained. Text in Japanese. 1987. a., latest vol.9. GBP 6.95 newsstand/cover; JPY 1,500 newsstand/cover in Japan (effective 2001). adv. maps. 64 p./no. 2 cols./p.; back issues avail. **Document type:** *Handbook/Manual/Guide, Consumer.* **Description:** Provides detailed storylines of musicals.
Published by: (Japan Airlines), Eikoku Communications, Ste. 1, 1 Ave Elmers, Surbiton, Surrey KT6 4SP, United Kingdom. emilondon@mac.com. Ed., Pub., R&P, Adv. contact Emi Kazuko. page GBP 1,800; trim 105 x 215. Circ: 30,000.

792 USA
LONDON THEATRE GUIDE. Text in English. 1995. w. **Document type:** *Newsletter, Consumer.*
Media: Online - full text.
Address: 12 East 86th St, New York, NY 10028. Ed. Darren Dalglish.

792 USA ISSN 1064-0312
LONDON THEATRE NEWS. Text in English. 1988. 10/yr. USD 51 domestic; USD 70 foreign (effective 2000). adv. bk.rev.; rec.rev. **Document type:** *Newsletter.* **Description:** Provides critical reviews of shows, new and old, recommendations, interviews, restaurant reviews and current show listings for London.
Media: Online - full text.
Address: 12 E 86th St, New York, NY 10028. TEL 212-517-8608, FAX 212-585-4173. Ed., R&P Roger B Harris. Adv. contact Ellen Harris. Circ: 2,100 (paid).

791.53 CZE ISSN 1211-4065
LOUTKAR/PUPPETEER. Text in Czech; Summaries in English. 1951. 6/yr. CZK 300 domestic; EUR 52, USD 65 foreign (effective 2011). 48 p./no.; **Document type:** *Magazine, Consumer.* **Description:** Aims to promote Czech puppet theatre.
Formerly (until 1994): Ceskoslovensky Loutkar (0323-1178)
Related titles: Online - full text ed.
Indexed: RASB.
Published by: Institut Umeni, Divadelni Ustav/Arts and Theatre Institute, Celetna 17, Prague 1, 110 00, Czech Republic. TEL 420-2-24809111, info@idu.cz, http://www.idu.cz. Ed. Nina Malikova.

800 NLD ISSN 1385-0393
➤ **LUDUS**; medieval and early Renaissance theatre and drama. Text in English. 1996. irreg., latest vol.10, 2007. price varies. adv. illus. back issues avail. **Document type:** *Monographic series, Academic/Scholarly.* **Description:** Introduces those interested in literature, in the performing arts, or in history to the various aspects of theatre and drama from the Middle Ages to the early Renaissance.
Related titles: Online - full text ed.: ISSN 1875-743X (from IngentaConnect).
Indexed: IBT&D, T02.
—IE, Ingenta.
Published by: Editions Rodopi B.V., Tijnmuiden 7, Amsterdam, 1046 AK, Netherlands. TEL 31-20-6114821, FAX 31-20-4472979, orders-queries@rodopi.nl. Ed. Wim Huesken. Adv. contact Mr. Eric van Broekhuizen. page USD 250. Circ: 500. **Dist in France by:** Nordeal, 30 rue de Verlinghem, BP 139, Lambersart 59832, France. TEL 33-3-20099060, FAX 33-3-20929495; **Dist in N America by:** Rodopi - USA, 295 North Michigan Avenue, Suite 1B, Kenilworth, NJ 07033. TEL 908-298-9071, 800-225-3998, FAX 908-298-9075.

➤ **M A R G I N**; life and letters in early Australia. (Monash Australian Research Group Informal Notes) *see* LITERATURE

▼ ➤ **M D W GENDER WISSEN.** *see* WOMEN'S STUDIES

➤ **M M NIEUWS.** (Marketing Management) *see* ART

➤ **M T - JOURNAL.** (Musik Theater) *see* MUSIC

792 DEU
DAS MAGAZIN - THEATER BONN. Text in German. 1987. 10/yr. EUR 21; EUR 1 newsstand/cover (effective 2010). adv. **Document type:** *Magazine, Consumer.*
Formerly: Theatermagazin der Bundesstadt Bonn
Published by: (Theater der Bundesstadt Bonn), Ideal Werbeagentur, Junkerstr 21, Bonn, 53177, Germany. TEL 49-228-559020, FAX 49-228-5590222, info@idealbonn.de, http://www.bonnzept.de.

791.3 FRA ISSN 1959-4658
LE MAGAZINE DU CIRQUE ET DE L'ILLUSION. Text in French. 2006. bi-m. EUR 36 (effective 2008). back issues avail. **Document type:** *Magazine, Consumer.*
Formerly (until 2007): Cirque Magazine (1953-6038)
Published by: Mediacirquemag, La Lande du Resto, Moustoir-Ac, 56500, France. TEL 33-2-97441236, http://www.mediacirquemag.fr.

MAGISCHE WELT; Zeitschrift fuer angewandte Tricktechnik und Wahrnehmungstaeuschung. *see* HOBBIES

MAILOUT; arts work with people. *see* ART

792 DEU ISSN 0940-4767
MAINZER FORSCHUNGEN ZU DRAMA UND THEATER. Text in German. 1987. irreg., latest vol.42, 2010. price varies. **Document type:** *Monographic series, Academic/Scholarly.* **Description:** Publishes research in theatre studies and other forms of drama.
Published by: A. Francke Verlag GmbH, Dischinger Weg 5, Tuebingen, 72070, Germany. TEL 49-7071-97970, FAX 49-7071-979711, info@francke.de, http://www.francke.de.

MAJOR ATTRACTIONS. ANNUAL DIARY. *see* MUSIC

791.53 FRA ISSN 1772-2950
MANIP; le journal de la marionnette. Text in French. 1993. q. EUR 10 (effective 2008). **Document type:** *Magazine, Consumer.*
Former titles (until 2005): T H E M A A. Lettre d'Information (1634-2763); (until 2002): T H E M A A. Theatre Marionnettes Arts Associes (1247-5270)
Published by: Association Nationale des Theatres de Marionnettes et des Arts Associes (T H E M A A), 24 Rue Saint Lazare, Paris, 75009, France.

792 CAN
MANITOBA THEATRE CENTRE. OVATION HOUSE PROGRAMME. Text in English. 1958. 6/yr. free. adv. illus. **Document type:** *Journal, Trade.*
Formerly: Stage Center
Published by: Manitoba Theatre Centre, 174 Market Ave, Winnipeg, MB R3B 0P8, Canada. TEL 204-956-1340, FAX 204-947-3741. Ed. Marnie Grona. Circ: 22,000.

792 ARG ISSN 1852-4257
MAPA DEL TEATRO. Text in Spanish. 2004. bi-m. **Document type:** *Magazine, Consumer.*
Published by: Temarte Srl, Ave Figueroa Alcorta, Buenos Aires, 3415, Argentina. TEL 54-155-8457475.

792 NLD ISSN 1876-2034
MARGREET DVD. Text in Dutch. 1988. bi-m. EUR 49.50 (effective 2008).
Formerly (until 2006): Mens en Gevoelens (0923-0866)
Published by: Betty Asfalt Productions, Nieuwezijds Voorburgwal 282, Amsterdam, 1012 RT, Netherlands. TEL 31-20-6204748, postmaster@bettyasfalt.nl, http://www.bettyasfalt.nl.

792 CAN ISSN 0700-5008
PN1993
MARQUEE. Text in English. 1976. 8/yr. CAD 19.26 domestic to individuals; CAD 27 foreign to individuals (effective 2000). adv. illus. **Document type:** *Newspaper, Consumer.*
Published by: Marquee Media Inc., 1325 Burnhamthorpe Rd E, Mississauga, ON L4Y 3V8, Canada. TEL 905-274-7174, FAX 905-274-9799. Ed. Alexandra Lenhoff. Pub. David Haslam. R&P Alexander Lenhoff. Adv. contact Fred Hussey. B&W page CAD 11,000, color page CAD 13,850; trim 10 x 7.88. Circ: 299,000.

MARQUEE (ELMHURST). *see* ARCHITECTURE

792 ITA ISSN 1970-3511
MASCHERE DELL'IMMAGINARIO. Text in Italian. 1996. irreg. **Document type:** *Magazine, Consumer.*
Published by: Maria Pacini Fazzi Editore, Via dell'Angelo Custode 33, Lucca, 55100, Italy. TEL 39-538-440188, FAX 39-538-464656, mpf@pacinifazzi.it, http://www.pacinifazzi.it.

MASK. *see* EDUCATION—Teaching Methods And Curriculum

792 AUT ISSN 0025-4606
PN2004
MASKE UND KOTHURN; Internationale Beitrage zur Theater-, Film und Medienwissenschaft. Text in English, French, German, Italian. 1955. q. EUR 78.30; EUR 39.90 to students (effective 2011). adv. bk.rev. bibl.; illus. index. **Document type:** *Journal, Academic/Scholarly.*
Indexed: A20, A22, BAS, BibInd, BrHumI, DIP, FR, IBR, IBT&D, IBZ, MLA, MLA-IB.
—IE, Infotrieve.
Published by: (Universitaet Wien, Universitaet Wien, Institut fuer Theaterwissenschaft DEU), Boehlau Verlag GmbH & Co.KG., Wiesingerstr 1, Vienna, W 1010, Austria. TEL 43-1-3302427, FAX 43-1-3302432, boehlau@boehlau.at. Ed. Wolfgang Greisenegger.

MEDIASCAPE. *see* SOCIOLOGY

792 DEU ISSN 0944-7970
MEDIEN UND THEATER. Variant title: MuTh. Text in German. 1993. irreg., latest vol.11, 2009. price varies. **Document type:** *Monographic series, Academic/Scholarly.*
Published by: Georg Olms Verlag, Hagentorwall 7, Hildesheim, 31134, Germany. TEL 49-5121-15010, FAX 49-5121-150150, info@olms.de.

792.02 USA ISSN 0731-3403
PR621
MEDIEVAL AND RENAISSANCE DRAMA IN ENGLAND; an annual gathering of research, criticism, and reviews. Text in English. 1984. a., latest vol.16. USD 72.50 per issue domestic; USD 82 per issue in Canada; USD 90 per issue elsewhere (effective 2011). bk.rev. index. back issues avail. **Document type:** *Journal, Academic/Scholarly.* **Description:** Contains essays and studies by critics and cultural historians from both hemispheres as well as substantial reviews of books and essays dealing with medieval and early modern English drama.
Related titles: Online - full text ed.
Indexed: A01, A03, A08, A22, A26, CA, E08, G08, I05, IBT&D, IIPA, L05, L06, LIFT, MLA-IB, S07, S09, T02, U01.
—BLDSC (5534.262600), Ingenta. **CCC.**
Published by: Associated University Presses, 2010 Eastpark Blvd, Cranbury, NJ 08512. TEL 609-655-4770, FAX 609-655-8366, AUP440@aol.com, http://www.aupresses.com. Ed. S P Cerasano. **Subscr. to:** Eurospan Group, 3 Henrietta St, Covent Garden, London WC2E 8LU, United Kingdom. TEL 44-20-7240-0856, FAX 44-20-7379-0609, http://www.eurospanonline.com. **Co-publisher:** Fairleigh Dickinson University Press.

792 GBR ISSN 0143-3784
PN2587
➤ **MEDIEVAL ENGLISH THEATRE.** Text in English. 1979. a. GBP 12 domestic; GBP 15 foreign (effective 2009). bk.rev. back issues avail. **Document type:** *Journal, Academic/Scholarly.* **Description:** Articles on all aspects of medieval and Tudor English and continental theatres.
Indexed: CA, IBT&D, IIPA, MLA, MLA-IB, PCI, T02.
—Ingenta.
Address: c/o Sue Niebrzydowski, School of English, Bangor University, Gwynedd, LL57 2DG, United Kingdom. s.niebrzydowski@bangor.ac.uk. Eds. Gordon L Kipling TEL 310-825-2274, Meg Twycross TEL 44-1524-594247, Sarah Carpenter.

792 GBR ISSN 0264-2786
MEDIEVAL ENGLISH THEATRE MODERN SPELLING TEXTS. Text in English. 1983. irreg. **Document type:** *Monographic series, Consumer.*
Published by: Medieval English Theatre, c/o Dept. of English, University of Lancaster, Lancaster, LA1 4YT, United Kingdom. TEL 44-1524-65201, FAX 44-1524-63806, meth-ed@lancaster.ac.uk.

792 USA ISSN 0145-787X
PN1985
MIME JOURNAL. Text in English. 1974. irreg. price varies. back issues avail. **Document type:** *Monographic series, Academic/Scholarly.*
Indexed: A27, CA, IBT&D, IIPA, P10, P48, P53, P54, PQC, RASB, T02.
—Ingenta.
Published by: Pomona College, Department of Theatre and Dance, 300 E Bonita Ave, Claremont, CA 91711. TEL 909-621-8186, FAX 909-621-8780, mtr04747@pomona.edu, http://theatre.pomona.edu. Ed. Thomas Leabhart.

792 CHE ISSN 0026-4385
MIMOS. Text in French, German. q. CHF 30 to non-members (effective 2000). **Document type:** *Academic/Scholarly.*
Published by: Schweizerische Gesellschaft fuer Theaterkultur/Swiss Association for Theatre Research, Postfach 1940, Basel, 4001, Switzerland. TEL 41-61-3211060, FAX 41-61-3211075.

CAITUAN FAREN SHI HEZHENG MINSU WENHUA JIJINHUI/ JOURNAL OF CHINESE RITUAL, THEATRE AND FOLKLORE. *see* ASIAN STUDIES

MINZU YILIN/WORLD OF NATIONAL ART. *see* ART

792 CZE ISSN 1803-2818
MISTNI KULTURA (ONLINE). Text in Czech. 1991. d. free. **Document type:** *Magazine, Consumer.*
Formerly (until 2008): Mistni Kultura (Print) (1211-7994)
Media: Online - full text.
Published by: Narodni Informacni a Poradenske Stredisko pro Kulturu (N I P O S), Blanicka 4, Prague 2, 120 21, Czech Republic. TEL 420-2-21507900, FAX 420-2-21507929, nipos@nipos-mk.cz, http://www.nipos-mk.cz.

792 USA
MODELS & TALENT CONTRACTS. Text in English. bi-w. USD 69 (effective 2000). adv.
Published by: The John King Network, 244 Madison Ave, Ste 393, New York, NY 10016. TEL 212-969-8715, 212-969-8715.

MODERN DRAMA; world drama from 1850 to the present. *see* LITERATURE

792 780 792.8 ISR ISSN 1565-8473
➤ **MOFA**; magazine of performing arts. Variant title: Magazine of Performing Arts. Text in English. 2007 (Winter). q. free. **Document type:** *Journal, Academic/Scholarly.* **Description:** Covers all areas of the performing arts from around the world with special interest in articles that build bridges between artists and researchers of art and culture in the region of Israel.
Media: Online - full content.
Indexed: CA, IBT&D, J01, T02.
Published by: The Israeli Association for Theatre Research Ed. Avraham Oz.

➤ **MOLODEZHNAYA ESTRADA.** *see* CHILDREN AND YOUTH—For

➤ **MOVEMENT RESEARCH PERFORMANCE JOURNAL.** *see* DANCE

792 USA ISSN 1065-1519
PN2071.G4
MOVEMENT THEATRE QUARTERLY. Text in English. 1983. q. USD 20. adv. bk.rev. illus. **Document type:** *Newsletter.*
Formerly: Mime News (0892-4910)
Published by: National Movement Theatre Association, PO Box 1437, Portsmouth, NH 03802-1437. TEL 603-436-6660. Ed. William Fisher. Circ: 300.

MUSICA CINEMA IMMAGINE TEATRO. *see* MUSIC

792 NLD ISSN 1574-924X
MUSICAL MAGAZINE. Text in Dutch. 2003. s-a. EUR 3.45 newsstand/cover (effective 2009). **Document type:** *Magazine, Consumer.*
Published by: Ende Theaterproducties B.V., Museumplein 9, Postbus 75177, Amsterdam, 1070 AD, Netherlands. TEL 31-20-3052299, FAX 31-20-3052610.

792.022 USA ISSN 0027-4658
MUSICAL SHOW; devoted to the amateur presentation of Broadway musical shows on the stage. Text in English. 1962. q. free to producers of musical shows. bk.rev.
Published by: Tams-Witmark Music Library, Inc., 560 Lexington Ave, New York, NY 10022. TEL 212-688-2525, FAX 212-688-3232. Ed. Robert A Hut. Circ: 175,000.

792 GBR ISSN 1361-3693
ML1699
MUSICAL STAGES; the world of musical theatre. Text in English. 1995. q. GBP 20 domestic; GBP 25 foreign; GBP 4 newsstand/cover (effective 2009). adv. back issues avail. **Document type:** *Magazine, Consumer.* **Description:** Provides regular updates and extensive coverage of musical theater in the United Kingdom.
Related titles: Online - full text ed.
Published by: Musical Stages Ltd., PO Box 8365, London, W14 0GL, United Kingdom. Ed. Lynda Trapnell. Adv. contact Michael Tornay.

792 782.1 DEU ISSN 0932-7118
MUSICALS; das Musicalmagazin. Text in German. 1986. bi-m. adv. bk.rev.; play rev. back issues avail. **Document type:** *Magazine, Consumer.* **Description:** Provides reports and reviews on musicals and musical comedies from all over the world.
Published by: Musicalverlag, Dohnenstiege 18, Meppen, 49716, Germany. TEL 49-5931-590102. Eds. Felix Rothermundt, Michael Potthast. Circ: 8,000.

MUSIK & THEATER; die aktuelle Kulturzeitschrift. *see* MUSIC

MUSIKTHEATER; Beitraege zur Didaktik und Methodik. *see* MUSIC

N A D I E RESEARCH MONOGRAPH SERIES. (National Association for Drama in Education) *see* EDUCATION

792 USA
N A P A M A NEWS. Text in English. q. USD 200 to members (effective 2000). **Document type:** *Newsletter.*
Formerly: National Association of Performing Arts Managers and Agents. Newsletter
Published by: National Association of Performing Arts Managers and Agents, c/o Mainstage Management Internat, Inc, P O Box 1270, Los Alamitos, CA 90720. TEL 714-220-6707, FAX 714-220-6747. Ed. Luisa Cariaga.

N C A NEWS. *see* ART

792 AUS ISSN 1445-2294
N J DRAMA AUSTRALIA JOURNAL. Text in English. 1976. s-a. (May & Oct.). AUD 25 domestic to members; AUD 30 domestic to non-members; AUD 40 foreign (effective 2007). **Document type:** *Journal, Academic/Scholarly.*
Former titles (until 1999): N A D I E Journal (1326-5490); (until 1994): N A D I E Journal Australia (1037-700X); (until 1986): N A D I E Journal (0159-6659); (until 1981): Drama in Education (0727-873X)
Indexed: AEI, CA, IBT&D, T02.
Published by: Drama Australia: National Association for Drama in Education, PO Box 15163, City East, QLD 4002, Australia. TEL 61-7-30090664, FAX 61-7-30090668, admin@dramaaustralia.org.au, http://www.dramaaustralia.org.au/.

792 GBR ISSN 0266-464X
PN2001
N T Q. NEW THEATRE QUARTERLY. Text in English. 1971. q. GBP 140, USD 233 to institutions; GBP 150, USD 248 combined subscription to institutions (print & online eds.) (effective 2012). adv. bk.rev. illus. back issues avail.; reprint service avail. from PSC. **Document type:** *Journal, Academic/Scholarly.* **Description:** Subjects prevailing dramatic assumptions to scrutiny.
Formerly (until 1985): T Q. Theatre Quarterly (0049-3600)
Related titles: Microform ed.: (from PQC); Online - full text ed.: ISSN 1474-0613. GBP 135, USD 223 to institutions (effective 2012).
Indexed: A01, A02, A03, A08, A20, A22, A25, A26, A27, ASCA, AmH&L, AmHI, ArtHuCI, B04, BRD, C12, CA, CurCont, E01, E08, G08, H07, H08, H09, H10, HAb, HumInd, I05, IBT&D, IIPA, M01, M02, MLA-IB, P02, P10, P30, P48, P53, P54, PCI, PQC, RASB, RILM, S07, S08, S09, SCOPUS, T02, W03, W07.
—BLDSC (6088.870500), IE, Infotrieve, Ingenta. **CCC.**
Published by: Cambridge University Press, The Edinburgh Bldg, Shaftesbury Rd, Cambridge, CB2 8RU, United Kingdom. TEL 44-1223-312393, FAX 44-1223-315052, journals@cambridge.org, http://www.cambridge.org/uk. Eds. Maria Shevtsova, Simon Trussler. R&P Linda Nicol TEL 44-1223-325702. Circ: 1,000. **Subscr. to:** Cambridge University Press, 32 Ave of the Americas, New York, NY 10013. TEL 212-337-5000, FAX 212-691-3239, journals_subscriptions@cup.org.

792 680 USA
N Y C - ON STAGE. (New York City) Text in English. a. **Document type:** *Directory.* **Description:** Contains listings of Broadway, off-Broadway, and off-off-Broadway theaters, and dance and music companies.
Formerly: New York on Stage
Address: c/o Theatre Development Fund, 1501 Broadway, Rm 2110, New York, NY 10036. TEL 212-221-0885, FAX 212-768-1563. Ed. Eve Rodriguez. Circ: (controlled).

NACHTFLUG. *see* HOTELS AND RESTAURANTS

NACHTLICHTER. *see* HOTELS AND RESTAURANTS

NASHVILLE SCENE. *see* MUSIC

792 JPN ISSN 0388-0648
NATIONAL THEATRE OF JAPAN. Text in Japanese. 6/yr.
Address: 4-1 Hayabusa-cho, Chiyoda-ku, Tokyo, 102-0092, Japan. TEL 03-3265-7411, FAX 03-3265-7402.

NEUES RHEINLAND; Zeitschrift fuer Landschaft und Kultur. *see* LITERATURE

791.33 USA ISSN 1072-1045
NEW CALLIOPE. Text in English. 1984. bi-m. free to members. adv. bk.rev. illus. **Document type:** *Magazine, Trade.* **Description:** Provides articles on clowning. Photos and illustrations include ideas for costuming, makeup design, props, skits and magic.
Published by: Clowns of America International, PO Box C, Richeyville, PA 15358-0532. TEL 724-938-8765, 888-522-5696. Circ: 5,750.

NEW CULTURE; a review of contemporary African arts. *see* ART

792 USA ISSN 1050-9720
PN2000
➤ **NEW ENGLAND THEATRE JOURNAL.** Text in English. 1990. a. USD 95 membership (effective 2009). adv. bk.rev. **Document type:** *Journal, Academic/Scholarly.* **Description:** Covers a broad range of subjects, including traditional scholarship, performance theory, and pedagogy, as well as theatre performance, design, and technology.
Related titles: Online - full text ed.
Indexed: CA, IBT&D, IIPA, MLA-IB, T02.
—BLDSC (6084.033100).
Published by: New England Theatre Conference, Inc., 215 Knob Hill Dr, Hamden, CT 06518. TEL 617-851-8535, mail@netconline.org, http://www.netconline.org. Ed. Stuart Hecht. R&P, Adv. contact Clinton Campbell. Circ: 1,000.

800 GBR ISSN 1750-6581
PA1
NEW VOICES IN CLASSICAL RECEPTION STUDIES. Text in English. 2006. a. free (effective 2011). back issues avail. **Document type:** *Journal, Academic/Scholarly.* **Description:** Provides showcase for scholars who have reached the stage where they wish to publish the results of their research.
Media: Online - full content.
Indexed: A39, C27, C29, D03, D04, E13, R14, S14, S15, S18.
—CCC.
Published by: Open University, Faculty of Arts, Department of Classical Studies, Faculty of Arts, The Open University, Walton Hall, Milton Keynes, MK7 6AA, United Kingdom. TEL 44-1908-655141, FAX 44-1908-653750, arts-faculty-enquiries@open.ac.uk, http://www.open.ac.uk/Arts/. Ed. Lorna Hardwick.

792 USA
NEW YORK THEATRE GUIDE. Text in English. 2003. d. free (effective 2010). adv. **Document type:** *Guide, Consumer.* **Description:** Provides up to date information essential to find what's new on Broadway theatre.
Media: Online - full text.
Address: 12 E 86th St, New York, NY 10028. Ed. Alan Bird.

NEW ZEALAND JOURNAL OF RESEARCH IN PERFORMING ARTS AND EDUCATION/MAHI A REHIA NO AOTEAROA. *see* DANCE

792 820 GBR ISSN 1748-3727
PN1851
NINETEENTH CENTURY THEATRE AND FILM. Text in English. 1973. s-a. GBP 96, EUR 125, USD 173 combined subscription to institutions (print & online eds.) (effective 2010). adv. bk.rev. bibl.; illus. back issues avail.; reprints avail. **Document type:** *Journal, Academic/Scholarly.*
Former titles (until 2000): Nineteenth Century Theatre (0893-3766); (until 1987): Nineteenth Century Theatre Research (0316-5329); Which incorporates (1976-1979): N C T R Newsletter (0710-5576)
Related titles: Microform ed.: (from PQC); Online - full content ed.: 2002; Online - full text ed.: (from IngentaConnect).
Indexed: A07, A20, A22, AA, AES, AmH&L, AmHI, ArtInd, BibInd, CA, F01, F02, H07, HistAb, IBR, IBT&D, IBZ, IIPA, L06, LCR, MLA, MLA-IB, PCI, T02, W03, W05.
—IE, Ingenta. **CCC.**
Published by: Manchester University Press, Oxford Rd, Manchester, Lancs M13 9NR, United Kingdom. TEL 44-161-2752310, FAX 44-161-2743346, mup@manchester.ac.uk. Eds. David Mayer, Kate Newey, Viv Gardner. Circ: 400.

792 NOR ISSN 0904-6380
PN2730
➤ **NORDIC THEATRE STUDIES**; yearbook for theatre research in Scandinavia. Text in English. 1988. a. EUR 34; EUR 12 to students (effective 2011). back issues avail. **Document type:** *Monographic series, Academic/Scholarly.* **Description:** Contributions on all aspects of Nordic theatre, including the Baltic countries, Estonia, Latvia and Lithuania.
Indexed: A20, ArtHuCI, CA, CurCont, IBT&D, MLA-IB, RILM, T02, W07.
Published by: Foereningen Nordiska Teaterforskare/The association of Nordic Theatre Scholars, c/o Rikard Hoogland, Institut for Musik och Teatervetenskap, Stockholm Universitet, Stockholm, 10691, Norway. teaterforskare@gmail.com, http://www.helsinki.fi/teatervetenskap/ntf. Eds. Magnus Tessing Schneider, Rikard Hoogland.

➤ **NORSK SHAKESPEARE OG TEATER-TIDSSKRIFT.** *see* LITERATURE

➤ **NORTH - WEST PASSAGE.** *see* MOTION PICTURES

792 POL ISSN 0867-2598
PN2859.P6
NOTATNIK TEATRALNY. Text in Polish. 1991. q. PLZ 48 domestic; PLZ 144 foreign (effective 2002).
Published by: Osrodek Badan Tworczosci Jerzego Grotowskiego i Poszukiwan Teatralno-Kulturowych, Rynek-Ratusz 27, Wroclaw, 50101, Poland. grotcenter@mikrozet.wroc.pl. Ed. Krzysztof Mieszkowski. Circ: 1,000.

792 FRA ISSN 1760-2602
NOUVELLES SCENES. Text in Multiple languages. 1998. irreg. **Document type:** *Monographic series, Academic/Scholarly.*
Formerly (until 2002): Collection Hesperides. Theatre (1291-9047)
Published by: (Theatre de la Digue), Presses Universitaires du Mirail, Universite de Toulouse II (Le Mirail), 5, Allee Antonio Machado, Toulouse, 31058, France. TEL 33-5-6150-4250, FAX 33-5-6150-4209, pum@univ-tlse2.fr, http://www.univ-tlse2.fr.

792 FRA ISSN 1712-8242
NOUVELLES "VUES" SUR LE CINEMA QUEBECOIS. Text in English, French. 2004. s-a. free (effective 2011). **Document type:** *Journal, Academic/Scholarly.*
Media: Online - full text.
—CCC.
Published by: Cadrage, 3 Rue Agathoise, Toulouse, 31000, France. http://www.cadrage.net.

NOW PLAYING MAGAZINE. *see* TRAVEL AND TOURISM

647.968 USA
NUMBER ONE AGENTS & CONTACTS. Text in English. bi-w. USD 69 (effective 2000).
Published by: The John King Network, 244 Madison Ave, Ste 393, New York, NY 10016. TEL 212-969-8715, 212-969-8715.

NUOVA RASSEGNA; attualita, lettere, storia, scienze, cinema, teatro. *see* LITERARY AND POLITICAL REVIEWS

792 USA
O O B R. (Off-Off-Broadway Review) Text in English. m. free (effective 2007). **Document type:** *Journal, Consumer.*
Media: Online - full text.
Address: c/o Cynthia Leathers, Mng. Ed., 341 W 24th St, Ste 20F, New York, NY 10011. FAX 646-207-2926. Ed., Pub. John Chatterton.

790.2 USA ISSN 1087-9617
PN1583
OBITUARIES IN THE PERFORMING ARTS. Text in English. 1994. a. USD 49.95 per issue (effective 2010). back issues avail. **Document type:** *Trade.*
Published by: McFarland & Company, Inc., PO Box 611, Jefferson, NC 28640. TEL 336-246-4460, FAX 336-246-5018, info@mcfarlandpub.com.

791 DEU ISSN 1861-129X
OESTERREICHISCHES THEATERMUSEUM. SCHRIFTENREIHE. Variant title: Schriftenreihe des Oesterreichischen Theatermuseums. Text in German. 2006. irreg., latest vol.3, 2008. price varies. **Document type:** *Monographic series, Academic/Scholarly.*
Published by: (Oesterreichisches Theatermuseum AUT), Peter Lang GmbH (Subsidiary of: Peter Lang Publishing Group), Eschborner Landstr 42-50, Frankfurt Am Main, 60489, Germany. TEL 49-69-7807050, FAX 49-69-78070550, zentrale.frankfurt@peterlang.com, http://www.peterlang.com. Ed. Thomas Trabitsch.

OFFICIAL CITY GUIDE. *see* TRAVEL AND TOURISM

792 GBR ISSN 1358-7412
THE OFFICIAL LONDON SEATING PLAN GUIDE. Text in English. 1992. irreg. GBP 14.95 (effective 2009). **Document type:** *Directory, Trade.* **Description:** Provides any theatregoer with information on A4 seating plans of all the major London theatre and concert venues including box office numbers, ticket and theatre break information, disabled access, and transport details.
Published by: Richmond House Publishing Company Ltd., 70-76 Bell St, Marylebone, London, NW1 6SP, United Kingdom. TEL 44-20-72249666, FAX 44-20-72249686, sales@rhpco.co.uk.

792 USA ISSN 1065-805X
PN2270.H57
OLLANTAY THEATER MAGAZINE. Text in Multiple languages. 1993. s-a.
Indexed: MLA-IB.
Published by: Ollantay Press, PO Box 720636, Jackson Heights, NY 11372-0636. TEL 718-565-6499, FAX 718-446-7206.

792 USA
ON AND OFF OFF BROADWAY. Text in English. bi-w. USD 69 (effective 2000).
Published by: The John King Network, 244 Madison Ave, Ste 393, New York, NY 10016. TEL 212-969-8715, 212-969-8715.

OPER AKTUELL. *see* MUSIC

OPERA AMERICA. *see* MUSIC

OPERA AMERICA. ANNUAL FIELD REPORT. *see* MUSIC

OPERA AMERICA. SEASON SCHEDULE OF PERFORMANCES. *see* MUSIC

OPERANET. *see* MUSIC

792.029 GBR
PN2595
THE ORIGIONAL BRITISH THEATRE DIRECTORY. Text in English. 1971. a. GBP 54.95; GBP 96 combined subscription (print & online eds.); GBP 8 combined subscription per issue (print & online eds.) (effective 2009). 699 p./no.; **Document type:** *Directory, Trade.* **Description:** Details all the theatre and concert venues in the UK, with administration and technical details, contact names and numbers.
Formerly (until 1988): British Theatre Directory (0306-4107)
Related titles: Online - full text ed.
—BLDSC (6291.237800). **CCC.**
Published by: Richmond House Publishing Company Ltd., 70-76 Bell St, Marylebone, London, NW1 6SP, United Kingdom. TEL 44-20-72249666, FAX 44-20-72249688, sales@rhpco.co.uk.

792 910.03 USA
OVERTURE (NEW YORK); a Black theatre annual. Text in English. 1981. a. USD 5.
Published by: Audience Development Committee, PO Box 30, Manhattanville, New York, NY 10027. Ed. A Peter Bailey.

THE OXFORDIAN. *see* LITERATURE—Poetry

790 ZAF
P A C O F S NEWS/S U K O V S NUUS. Text in Afrikaans, English. 1972. q. free. illus.
Published by: Performing Arts Council Orange Free State, PO Box 1292, Bloemfontein, 9300, South Africa. FAX 51-305523, TELEX 267145 SA. Ed. Charmaine Ferreira. Circ: 6,000.

792 USA ISSN 1520-281X
PN1561
➤ **P A J**; a journal of performance and art. (Performing Arts Journal) Text in English. 1976. 3/yr. USD 140 combined subscription in US & Canada to institutions (print & online eds.); USD 47 per issue in US & Canada to institutions (effective 2012). adv. bk.rev.; play rev. illus. back issues avail. **Document type:** *Journal, Academic/Scholarly.* **Description:** Integrates theater and the visual arts in charting the directions of new work in performance, video, film, and music. Featured in the issues are artists' writings, critical commentary, interviews and dialogues, historical documents, critical commentary, performance texts and plays.
Formerly (until 1998): Performing Arts Journal (0735-8393)
Related titles: Online - full text ed.: ISSN 1537-9477. 1996. USD 121 in US & Canada to institutions (effective 2012).
Indexed: A01, A02, A03, A08, A20, A22, A25, A26, A27, ABM, ABS&EES, ASCA, AmHI, ArtHuCI, B04, B14, BRD, BRI, BrHumI, CA, CBRI, CurCont, DIP, E01, E08, F01, F02, G08, H07, H08, H09, H10, HAb, HumInd, I05, IBR, IBT&D, IBZ, IIPA, M01, M02, MLA-IB, P02, P07, P10, P48, P53, P54, PCI, PQC, RILM, S08, S09, SCOPUS, T02, W03, W07.
—BLDSC (6340.433800), IE.
Published by: (P A J Publications), M I T Press, 55 Hayward St, Cambridge, MA 02142. TEL 617-253-2889, FAX 617-577-1545, journals-cs@mit.edu, http://mitpress.mit.edu. Ed. Bonnie Marranca.

792 784 USA
PALACE PEEPER. Text in English. 1937. 10/yr. USD 35 membership (effective 2008). **Document type:** *Newsletter, Consumer.* **Description:** Contains history, criticism, humor, and membership news.
Published by: Gilbert and Sullivan Society of New York, 1770 E 14th St, Ste 2B, Brooklyn, NY 11229-2031. editor@g-and-s.org, http://www.g-and-s.org. Ed. Dan Kravetz. Circ: 350.

792 ITA ISSN 2035-3685
IL PALCOSCENICO. Text in Italian. 2008. m. **Document type:** *Magazine, Consumer.*
Published by: Associazione Culturale EducArte, Podere Noceto, Str Grotti Bagnaia 1216 C, Ville di Corsano, SI, Italy. http://www.educarte.it.

792 POL ISSN 0031-0522
PN2859.P6
➤ **PAMIETNIK TEATRALNY**; kwartalnik poswiecony historii i krytyce teatru. Text in Polish. 1951. q. EUR 42 foreign (effective 2005). adv. bk.rev. bibl.; illus.; abstr. index. back issues avail. **Document type:** *Journal, Academic/Scholarly.* **Description:** Devoted to the history of Polish theatre and theatrical criticism.
Indexed: IBR, IBT&D, IBZ, RASB.
Published by: Polska Akademia Nauk, Instytut Sztuki/Polish Academy of Science, Institute of Art, ul Dluga 28, Warsaw, 00950, Poland. TEL 48-22-5048200, FAX 48-22-8313149, ispan@ispan.pl. Eds. Edward Krasinski TEL 48-22-8313271 ext 242, Marek Waszkiel, Piotr Paszkiewicz. Circ: 500 (paid). **Dist. by:** Ars Polona, Obroncow 25, Warsaw 03933, Poland. TEL 48-22-5098609, FAX 48-22-5098610, arspolona@arspolona.com.pl, http://www.arspolona.com.pl.

792 900 USA ISSN 1061-8112
THE PASSING SHOW. Text in English. 1977. a. free (effective 2011). illus. back issues avail. **Document type:** *Newsletter, Consumer.* **Description:** Serves archivists, historians, and others interested in the history of theatrical productions on Broadway, particularly the history of the Shubert Theatrical Organization and its producing activities.
Related titles: Online - full text ed.
Indexed: IBT&D, RILM, T02.
Published by: (Shubert Foundation), Shubert Archive, 149 W 45th St, New York, NY 10036. TEL 212-944-3895, FAX 212-944-4139, information@shubertarchive.org, http://www.shubertarchive.org. Ed. Mark E Swartz.

792 ITA
IL PATALOGO; annuario dello spettacolo teatro. Text in Italian. 1979. a. price varies. adv. bk.rev. **Document type:** *Magazine, Consumer.* **Description:** Presents all the spectacles staged in Italy, includes reviews by theatrical critics.
Published by: Edizioni Ubulibri, Via Bernardino Ramazzini 8, Milan, MI 20129, Italy. TEL 39-02-20241604, FAX 39-02-29510265, edizioni@ubulibri.it.

PEAKE STUDIES; dedicated to the life and work of Mervyn Peake (1911-1968). *see* LITERARY AND POLITICAL REVIEWS

792 BRA ISSN 0104-7671
➤ **O PERCEVEJO**; revista de teatro, critica e estetica. Text in Portuguese. 1993. irreg., latest vol.6. USD 10. **Document type:** *Monographic series, Academic/Scholarly.* **Description:** Covers aspects of Brazilian theatre.
Published by: Universidade do Rio de Janeiro, Departamento de Teoria do Teatro, Av Pasteur, 436 Andar 4, Rio De Janeiro, RJ 22290-240, Brazil. TEL 55-21-2956096, FAX 55-21-2753090. Eds. Ana Marie de Bulhoe-Carvalho, Angela Materno.

792 780 USA ISSN 2157-4049
▼ **PERFORMANCE AND SPIRITUALITY.** Text in English. 2009. s-a. back issues avail. **Document type:** *Journal, Academic/Scholarly.* **Description:** Explores intersections between new/alternaitve modes of religion and spirituality and innovative forms of live performance, multimedia performance, and media events.
Media: Online - full text.
Published by: University of Toledo, Institute for the Study of Performance and Spirituality, 2801 W Bancroft St, Toledo, OH 43606. TEL 419-530-4636, 800-586-5336, http://www.utoledo.edu. Eds. Deborah Kathleen Middleton, Edmund B Lingan, Franc Chamberlain.

PERFORMANCE MAGAZINE. *see* MUSIC

792 793.3 GBR ISSN 1352-8165
PN1561
➤ **PERFORMANCE RESEARCH**; a journal of the performing arts. Text in English. 1996. q. GBP 419 combined subscription in United Kingdom to institutions (print & online eds.); EUR 569, USD 717 combined subscription to institutions (print & online eds.) (effective 2012). adv. illus. back issues avail.; reprint service avail. from PSC. **Document type:** *Journal, Academic/Scholarly.* **Description:** Covers contemporary and historical performance and promotes a cross-disciplinary exchange of ideas, images and analysis.
Related titles: Online - full text ed.: ISSN 1469-9990. GBP 377 in United Kingdom to institutions; EUR 512, USD 645 to institutions (effective 2012).
Indexed: A01, A03, A08, A20, A22, ABM, AmHI, ArtHuCI, BrHumI, CA, CurCont, E01, H07, IBT&D, IIPA, M11, MLA-IB, P10, P48, P53, P54, PQC, RILM, SCOPUS, T02, W07.
—BLDSC (6423.832100), IE, Ingenta. **CCC.**
Published by: (Centre for Performance Research), Routledge (Subsidiary of: Taylor & Francis Group), 4 Park Sq, Milton Park, Abingdon, Oxon OX14 4RN, United Kingdom. TEL 44-20-70176000, FAX 44-20-70176336, info@routledge.co.uk, http://www.tandf.co.uk/journals, http://www.routledge.com. Eds. Ric Allsopp, Richard Gough. **Subscr. to:** Taylor & Francis Ltd., Journals Customer Service, Sheepen Pl, Colchester, Essex CO3 3LP, United Kingdom. TEL 44-20-70175544, FAX 44-20-70175198, tf.enquiries@tfinforma.com.

792 USA
PN1560
PERFORMANCES; theatre program and lifestyle. Text in English. 1967. m. free (effective 2007). adv. bk.rev.; film rev.; play rev. 72 p./no.; **Document type:** *Magazine, Trade.* **Description:** Covers music, film, theatre, audio-video, travel and real estate. Provides synopses, cast biographies and background information on plays and concerts.
Formerly: Performing Arts (0031-5222)
Indexed: AmHI, RASB, RILM.
—Ingenta.
Published by: (Performing Arts Network), Southern California Magazine Group, 3679 Motor Ave, Ste 300, Los Angeles, CA 90034. TEL 310-280-2880, FAX 310-280-2890. Ed. Benjamin Epstein. Pub. Jeff Levy. Adv. contacts David Bronow, Susan Holloway. B&W page USD 15,525, color page USD 23,288; trim 8.125 x 10.875. Circ: 260,000 (controlled).

792 CAN ISSN 1185-3433
PN1582.C3
PERFORMING ARTS AND ENTERTAINMENT IN CANADA. Text in English. 1961. q. CAD 8.56 domestic to individuals; CAD 15 foreign to individuals; CAD 5.34 domestic to institutions; CAD 12.34 foreign to institutions; CAD 3 newsstand/cover (effective 2000). adv. bk.rev.; dance rev.; music rev.; play rev. illus. index. reprints avail. **Document type:** *Journal, Academic/Scholarly.* **Description:** Covers performing arts in Canada: music, dance, theater and film.
Formerly (until 1990): Performing Arts in Canada (0031-5230)
Related titles: Microfiche ed.: (from MML, PQC); Microform ed.: (from MML); Online - full text ed.
Indexed: A01, A02, A03, A08, A20, A22, A26, A27, ASCA, AmHI, C03, C05, C12, CA, CBCARef, CBPI, CMPI, CPerI, E08, G05, G06, G07, G08, H07, I05, I07, IBT&D, IIMP, IIPA, M01, M02, M11, MASUSE, MagInd, MusicInd, P02, P10, P48, P53, P54, PQC, RASB, S07, S09, TOM.
—CIS, Ingenta.
Published by: Canadian Stage and Art Publications, 104 Glenrose Ave, Toronto, ON M4T 1K8, Canada. TEL 416-484-4534, FAX 416-484-6214, kbell@interlog.ca. Ed. Sarah Hood. Pub., R&P, Adv. contact George Hencz. B&W page CAD 1,593, color page CAD 2,293; trim 10.88 x 8.13. Circ: 44,630 (paid).

PERFORMING ARTS BUYERS GUIDE. *see* DANCE

792 USA
PERFORMING ARTS INSIDER; the journal for entertainment professionals. Text in English. 1944. w. USD 165 (effective 2008). **Document type:** *Journal, Trade.* **Description:** A source of information about the performing arts in New York City and around the country.
Former titles (until 1998): Performing Arts Bulletin; (until 1997): Theatre Information Bulletin (0040-5515)
Published by: TotalTheater, PO Box 62, Hewlett, NY 11557-0062. TEL 516-295-1511, totalpost@totaltheater.com. Ed. David Lefkowitz.

792 016 USA ISSN 0360-3814
Z6935
PERFORMING ARTS RESOURCES. Abbreviated title: P A R. Text in English. 1974. irreg., latest 2010. free to members (effective 2010). back issues avail. **Document type:** *Monographic series, Academic/Scholarly.* **Description:** Covers articles on resources relating to theatre, popular entertainment, film, television and radio, descriptions of collections, and essays on conservation and management.
Related titles: Online - full text ed.; ◆ Supplement to: Broadside (New York, 1940). ISSN 0068-2748.
Indexed: A10, BibInd, IBT&D, IDP, IIPA, MLA, MLA-IB, RASB, T02, V03.
Published by: Theatre Library Association, c/o The New York Public Library for the Performing Arts, 40 Lincoln Ctr Plz, New York, NY 10023. info@tla-online.org.

792 GBR
▼ **PERFORMING ARTS YEARBOOK.** Text in English. 2009. a. EUR 145 per issue in Europe; USD 187 per issue in United States; GBP 135 per issue in UK & elsewhere (effective 2009). adv. **Document type:** *Directory, Trade.* **Description:** Designed to be the annual directories for the performing arts sector.
Formed by the merger of (1991-2009): Performing Arts Yearbook for Europe (0969-0603); (1993-2009): M O D - Music, Opera, Dance & Drama in Asia, the Pacific and North America (1357-8871)
Related titles: Online - full text ed.: free (effective 2009).
Published by: Impromptu Publishing Ltd., Century House, 2nd Fl, St Peter's Sq, Manchester, M2 3DN, United Kingdom. TEL 44-161-2369526, FAX 44-161-2477978, info@impromptupublishing.com, http://www.impromptupublishing.com. Ed. Christian Lloyd TEL 44-161-2369526 ext 29. Adv. contact Sabrina Abdelhak TEL 44-161-2369526 ext 23. B&W page GBP 2,050, color page GBP 3,150; trim 210 x 297.

792 GBR ISSN 1757-1979
▼ ➤ **PERFORMING ETHOS**; an international journal of ethics in theatre & performance. Abbreviated title: P E E T. Text in English. 2010. s-a. GBP 36, USD 68 to individuals; GBP 150, USD 240 to institutions (effective 2012). adv. back issues avail. **Document type:** *Journal, Academic/Scholarly.* **Description:** Considers ethical questions relating to contemporary theatre and live performance. It provides a unique forum for rigorous scholarship and serious reflection on the ethical dimensions of a wide range of performance practices from the politically and aesthetically radical to the mainstream.
Related titles: Online - full text ed.: ISSN 1757-1987. GBP 117, USD 175 (effective 2012).
Indexed: CA, IBT&D, T02.
Published by: Intellect Ltd., The Mill, Parnall Rd, Fishponds, Bristol, BS16 3JG, United Kingdom. TEL 44-117-9589910, FAX 44-117-9589911, info@intellectbooks.com. Pub. Masoud Yazdani. **Subscr. to:** Turpin Distribution Services Ltd., Pegasus Dr, Stratton Business Park, Biggleswade, Bedfordshire SG18 8QB, United Kingdom. TEL 44-1767-604951, FAX 44-1767-601640, custserv@turpin-distribution.com, http://www.turpin-distribution.com/.

792 DEU ISSN 1868-4815
▼ **PERIPETEIA**; Studien zu Drama und Theater. Text in German. 2009. irreg. price varies. **Document type:** *Monographic series, Academic/Scholarly.*
Published by: Verlag Dr. Kovac, Leverkusenstr 13, Hamburg, 22761, Germany. TEL 49-40-3988800, FAX 49-40-39888055, info@verlagdrkovac.de.

792 CAN ISSN 1911-9313
LE PERISKOPEIN. Text in French. 2004. q. **Document type:** *Magazine, Consumer.*
Published by: Theatre Periscope, 939, rue de Salaberry, Quebec, PQ G1R 2v2, Canada. TEL 418-648-9989, FAX 418-648-6569, info@theatreperiscope.qc.ca, http://www.theatreperiscope.qc.ca/fr/default.asp.

792 FRA ISSN 1952-0492
LES PETITS CAHIERS DE THEATRE. Text in French. 2006. irreg. back issues avail. **Document type:** *Monographic series, Consumer.*
Published by: Editions du Petit Vehicule, 20 rue du Coudray, Nantes, 44300, France. TEL 33-2-40521494, FAX 33-2-40521508.

792 RUS
PETRUSHKA. Text in Russian. 1997. bi-m. USD 60 in North America (effective 2000).
Published by: Firma Era, Ul. Tverskaya, 12, str.7, Moscow, 103009, Russian Federation. TEL 7-095-2096635. **Dist. by:** East View Information Services, 10601 Wayzata Blvd, Minneapolis, MN 55305. TEL 952-252-1201, 800-477-1005, FAX 952-252-1202, info@eastview.com, http://www.eastview.com.

792 USA
PHILADELPHIA THEATRE COMPANY PROGRAM. Text in English. 2007. 4/yr. free (effective 2008). adv. **Document type:** *Guide, Consumer.* **Description:** Provides information to help understand and enjoy Philadelphia Theatre Company's theatrical productions.
Published by: Philadelphia Theatre Company, 230 S. Broad St, Ste 1105, Philadelphia, PA 19102. TEL 215-985-1400, FAX 215-985-5800, http://www.philadelphiatheatrecompany.org/. Ed. Janette Amadio. adv.: color page USD 1,575; trim 5.375 x 8.5. Circ: 8,000 (free).

PIA KANSAI EDITION. *see* LEISURE AND RECREATION

792 USA
PR6066.I53
➤ **THE PINTER REVIEW**; prize for drama. Text in English. 1987. a. bk.rev. **Document type:** *Journal, Academic/Scholarly.* **Description:** Publishes critical essays, notes, production reviews and commentaries on the plays, screenplays and other writings of Harold Pinter.
Indexed: AmHI, H07, IBT&D, MLA-IB, T02.
Published by: University of Tampa, 401 W Kennedy Blvd, Tampa, Hillsborgh, FL 33606. TEL 813-253-3333, http://www.ut.edu/.

➤ **PIRANDELLIANA**; rivista internazionale di studi e documenti. *see* LITERATURE

792 USA ISSN 1075-2757
CODEN: AJTHFG
PITTSBURGH STUDIES IN THEATRE AND CULTURE. Text in English. 1995. irreg., latest vol.2, 1999. price varies. **Description:** Connects the study of theatre practice with larger issues in history, politics, art, social institutions, popular entertainment, or performance theory.
Published by: Peter Lang Publishing, Inc. (Subsidiary of: Peter Lang Publishing Group), 29 Broadway, New York, NY 10006. TEL 212-647-7700, 800-770-5264, FAX 212-647-7707. Ed. Dennis Kennedy.

708 CAN ISSN 0847-3366
PLACE DES ARTS. MAGAZINE. Text in English, French. 1989. bi-m. CAD 14 (effective 2000). adv. bk.rev.
Indexed: CMPI.
Published by: Societe de la Place des Arts, 260 bd de Maisonneuve Ouest, Montreal, PQ H2X 1Y9, Canada. TEL 514-285-4270, FAX 514-285-4272. Ed. Savienne Couturier. adv.: B&W page CAD 6,090, color page CAD 7,350; trim 6.75 x 4.88. Circ: 200,000. **Subscr. to:** Agence Periodica, C P 444, Outremont, PQ H2V 4R6, Canada.

791.3 DEU ISSN 1434-5137
PLANET CIRCUS. Text in German, English. 1997. q. EUR 28; EUR 8 newsstand/cover (effective 2009). adv. **Document type:** *Magazine, Trade.*
Published by: Circus Verlag, Am Latourshof 6, Dormagen, 41542, Germany. TEL 49-2133-91555, FAX 49-2133-91553, circus.verlag@t-online.de, http://www.circus-verlag.de.

DAS PLATEAU. *see* ART

792 GBR ISSN 1751-0171
PN2001
PLATFORM; postgraduate e-journal of theatre and performing arts. Text in English. 2006. s-a. free (effective 2011). back issues avail. **Document type:** *Journal, Academic/Scholarly.* **Description:** Provides a space for postgraduate researchers and entry-level academics to have their work disseminated through online publication.
Media: Online - full content.
Indexed: A39, C27, C29, D03, D04, E13, R14, S14, S15, S18.
—CCC.
Published by: University of London, Royal Holloway, Department of Drama & Theatre, Department of Drama & Theatre, Royal Holloway, University of London, Egham, Surrey TW20 0EX, United Kingdom. TEL 44-1784-443922, FAX 44-1784-431018, drama@rhul.ac.uk, http://www.rhul.ac.uk/Drama/. Eds. Jim Ellison, Rachel Clements.

792 AUS ISSN 1449-583X
PLATFORM PAPERS. Text in English. 2004. q. AUD 60; free to members (effective 2008). back issues avail. **Document type:** *Journal, Consumer.* **Description:** Covers issues affecting the health of the performing arts.
Published by: Currency House Inc., PO Box 2270, Strawberry Hills, NSW 2011, Australia. TEL 61-2-93194953, FAX 61-2-93193649, info@currencyhouse.org.au. Ed. John Golder.

792.13 USA ISSN 1545-3235
PS634.2
PLAY (BROOKLYN). Text in English. 2003. a. USD 22 (effective 2005). **Document type:** *Journal, Consumer.*
Published by: Play a Journal of Plays, 185 Rogers Ave #2, Brooklyn, NY 11216. Eds. Jordan Harrison, Sally Oswald.

792 USA ISSN 0032-146X
PLAYBILL (THEATRE EDITION); the national magazine of the theatre. Text in English. 1884; N.S. 1982. m. adv. illus. reprints avail. **Document type:** *Magazine, Consumer.* **Description:** Contain information for many plays, general articles on the theater, backstage topics, fashion, food ads and program inserts.
Related titles: Microform ed.: N.S.; ◆ Online - full text ed.: Playbill On-Line; Special ed(s).: Playbill (Newstand Edition). ISSN 0745-9076. USD 2.50 newsstand/cover (effective 2004).
Indexed: IIPA, RASB.
Published by: TotalTheater, PO Box 62, Hewlett, NY 11557-0062. Ed. Judy Samelson. Pub., R&P Philip S Birsh.

794 USA
PLAYBILL ON-LINE. Text in English. 1994. d. free (effective 2009). adv. **Document type:** *Magazine, Consumer.*
Media: Online - full text. **Related titles:** Microform ed.: N.S.; ◆ Print ed.: Playbill (Theatre Edition). ISSN 0032-146X.
Published by: TotalTheater, PO Box 62, Hewlett, NY 11557-0062. TEL 212-557-5757, FAX 212-682-2932, http://www.playbill.com.

791.53 USA
PLAYBOARD. Text in English. bi-m. free to members. **Document type:** *Newsletter, Trade.* **Description:** Contains current information on puppeteers, puppet festivals, guilds, membership news and technical advice.
Published by: Puppeteers of America, 330, West Liberty, IA 52776-0330. TEL 888-568-6235, PofAjoin@aol.com, http://www.puppeteers.org. Ed. Fred Thompson.

792 CAN ISSN 0048-4415
PLAYBOARD; professional stage magazine. Text in English. 1965. m. free (effective 2009). adv. **Document type:** *Magazine, Consumer.* **Description:** Distributed free in all of the Vancouver Civic theatres, the Arts Club Theatres, the Richmond Gateway Theatre and all the other major theatres in Vancouver and surrounding areas, the Vancouver International Airport, Tourism Vancouver Offices, selected hotels and restaurants.
Indexed: CMPI.
Published by: Arch-Way Publishers Ltd., 311720 Voyager Way, Richmond, BC V6X 3G9, Canada. TEL 604-278-5881, FAX 604-278-5813, aslater@direct.ca. Circ: 260,000.

PLAYER'S GUIDE. *see* MOTION PICTURES

792.071 USA ISSN 0032-1540
PN1601
PLAYS; the drama magazine for young people. Text in English. 1940. m. (Oct-May; except Jan.-Feb. combined). USD 44 (effective 2010). bk.rev. illus. index. back issues avail.; reprints avail. **Document type:** *Magazine, Consumer.* **Description:** Provides a complete supply of royalty-free one-act plays and programs, skits and choral readings for schools, young people's clubs and libraries.

Incorporates (1937-1942): One Act Play Magazine and Radio-Drama Review
Related titles: Microform ed.: (from PQC); Online - full text ed.
Indexed: A01, A02, A03, A08, A10, A22, A26, C05, C22, CPerl, E07, E08, G05, G06, G07, G08, I05, I06, I07, I09, IBT&D, ICM, L05, L06, M01, M02, M04, MASUSE, MagInd, P01, P07, P10, P48, P53, P54, PQC, R04, RASB, S09, S23, T02, V03.
Published by: Plays Magazine, PO Box 600160, Newton, MA 02460. TEL 617-630-9100, 800-630-5755, FAX 617-630-9101, customerservice@playsmagazine.com, http://www.playsmag.com/. Ed. Liz Preston.

822 GBR ISSN 0554-3045
PLAYS. A CLASSIFIED GUIDE TO PLAY SELECTION. Text in English. 1951. a. GBP 2.20, USD 6. adv. bibl.
Published by: Stacey Publications, 1 Hawthorndene Rd, Hayes, Bromley, Kent BR2 7DZ, United Kingdom. Ed. Roy Stacey.

792 GBR ISSN 0268-2028
PN2001
PLAYS INTERNATIONAL. Text in English. m. GBP 28; GBP 63 foreign. adv. bk.rev. back issues avail. **Document type:** *Bulletin.*
Indexed: IBT&D, IIPA, T02.
—BLDSC (6539.233000), Ingenta.
Published by: Plays International Ltd., F6 Greenwood Ct, Harlescott, Shrewsbury, Shrops SY1 3TB, United Kingdom. TEL 44-1743-462303, FAX 44-1743-446177. Ed., R&P Peter Roberts. Adv. contact Ken Vine.

800 NLD ISSN 1386-0712
PLOT; over scenarioschrijven. Text in Dutch. 1992. q. EUR 29.95; EUR 8.25 newsstand/cover (effective 2010). adv. bk.rev. bibl.; illus. back issues avail. **Document type:** *Journal, Trade.* **Description:** Includes everything the professional script writer needs to know, through interviews, discussions, and general information on the state of the art.
Published by: Netwerk Scenarioschrijvers, De Lairessestraat 125, Amsterdam, 1075 HH, Netherlands. TEL 31-20-6234296, FAX 31-20-6247755, scenario@vsenv.nl, http://www.netwerkscenario.nl.

POEMS & PLAYS. *see* LITERATURE—Poetry

792 DEU ISSN 0232-3303
POINTE. Text in German. 1968. irreg., latest vol.72, 2008. **Document type:** *Magazine, Trade.*
—CCC.
Published by: Bundesvereinigung Kabarett e.V., c/o Baerbel Kuzak, An der Rennbahn 16, Panitzsch, 04451, Germany. TEL 49-34291-21084, post@bundesvereinigung-kabarett.de.

PREMIERE. *see* MOTION PICTURES

792 USA
PREVIEW THEATER BROCHURE. Text in English. m. USD 20. film rev.
Formerly: American Film Institute Theater Brochure
Published by: American Film Institute, 2021 N Western Ave, Los Angeles, CA 90027-1657. TEL 323-856-7600, 800-774-4243, FAX 323-467-4578, http://www.afi.com. Circ: (controlled).

792 ESP ISSN 0032-8367
PN2008
PRIMER ACTO. Text in Spanish. 1957. 5/yr. EUR 29.90 domestic; EUR 52.44 foreign (effective 2003). adv. bk.rev.; film rev.; play rev.; rec.rev. 170 p./no.; **Document type:** *Magazine, Consumer.* **Description:** Presents a critical view of international theater. Includes an unpublished play in each issue with commentaries.
Indexed: BibInd, IBR, IBZ, MLA-IB.
—CCC.
Published by: Primer Acto S.A., Ricardo de la Vega 18, Madrid, 28028, Spain. TEL 34-91-7258085, FAX 34-91-7263711, primer-acto@dat.es. Ed. Jose Monleon. Circ: 2,500. **Dist. by:** Asociacion de Revistas Culturales de Espana, C Covarruvias 9 2o. Derecha, Madrid 28010, Spain. TEL 34-91-3086066, FAX 34-91-3199267, info@arce.es, http://www.arce.es/.

PRO LIGHTS & STAGING NEWS. *see* ENGINEERING—Electrical Engineering

PRODUCTION AND CASTING REPORT. *see* MOTION PICTURES

PRODUCTION PARTNER; Das Fachmagazin fuer Beschallung, Licht, Buhne, Event-Technik und Projektion. *see* SOUND RECORDING AND REPRODUCTION

792 CAN ISSN 1719-6973
PROFESSIONAL ASSOCIATION OF CANADIAN THEATRES. ANNUAL REPORT. Text in English. 2004. a. **Document type:** *Report, Trade.*
Media: Online - full text.
Published by: Professional Association of Canadian Theatres, 215 Spadina Ave., Ste. 210, Toronto, ON M5T 2C7, Canada. TEL 416-595-6455, FAX 416-595-6450, info@pact.ca, http://www.pact.ca.

792 AUS ISSN 1834-6316
PROLOGUE. Text in English. 2004. bi-m. **Document type:** *Newsletter, Consumer.*
Media: Online - full text. **Related titles:** Print ed.: ISSN 1834-6308. 19??.
Published by: Queanbeyan Players Inc., PO Box 390, Queanbeyan, NSW 2620, Australia. http://www.qp.org.au.

792 USA ISSN 0033-1007
PROLOGUE (MEDFORD). Text in English. 1945. irreg. (3-4/yr.). free. play rev. **Document type:** *Newsletter.*
Indexed: ABS&EES.
Published by: Tufts University, Department of Drama & Dance, Medford, MA 02155. TEL 617-627-3524. Pub., R&P Joanne Barnett. Circ: 5,000.

792 USA
PROLOGUE (MILWAUKEE). Text in English. every 6 wks. free to qualified personnel. **Document type:** *Newsletter.* **Description:** Articles on theater pieces produced by the Milwaukee Repertory Theater.
Published by: Milwaukee Repertory Theater, 108 E Wells St, Milwaukee, WI 53202. TEL 414-224-1761, FAX 414-224-9790. Ed. Cindy Moran. Circ: 11,000.

792 DEU
PROSPEKTE; Studien zum Theater. Text in German. 1997. irreg., latest vol.11, 2008. price varies. **Document type:** *Monographic series, Academic/Scholarly.*
Published by: Wissenschaftlicher Verlag Trier, Bergstr 27, Trier, 54295, Germany. TEL 49-651-41503, FAX 49-651-41504, wvt@wvttrier.de, http://www.wvttrier.de.

791.53 GBR ISSN 0033-4413
THE PUPPET MASTER; the journal of the B P M T G. Text in English. 19??. a., latest vol.15, no.8. free to members (effective 2009). bk.rev. back issues avail. **Document type:** *Newsletter, Consumer.* **Description:** Deals with various aspects of professional and amateur puppetry.
Formerly (until 1946): British Puppet and Model Theatre Guild. Wartime Bulletin
Published by: British Puppet & Model Theatre Guild, c/o Peter Charlton, 65 Kinglsey Ave, Ealing, London, W13 OEH, United Kingdom. TEL 44-20-89978236, peter@peterpuppet.co.uk. Ed. Brian Hibbitt.

791.53 USA ISSN 0033-443X
PN1970
PUPPETRY JOURNAL. Text in English. 1949. q. USD 40 to individual members; USD 50 in Canada & Mexico to individual members; USD 60 elsewhere to individual members; USD 35 to libraries; USD 45 in Canada & Mexico to libraries; USD 50 elsewhere to libraries (effective 1999). adv. bk.rev.; play rev. charts; illus. reprints avail. **Document type:** *Newsletter.* **Description:** Explores all aspects of puppetry, professional and amateur.
Related titles: Microform ed.: (from PQC); Online - full text ed.
Indexed: A10, A22, CA, H20, IBT&D, IIPA, MLA-IB, T02, V03.
—Ingenta.
Published by: Puppeteers of America, 330, West Liberty, IA 52776-0330. PofAjoin@aol.com, http://www.puppeteers.org. Ed. Paul Eide. Circ: 2,200 (controlled).

791.53 USA ISSN 1070-3624
PN1972
PUPPETRY YEARBOOK. Text in English. 1995. a. USD 109.95 per vol. domestic; GBP 69.95 per vol. in United Kingdom (effective 2010). back issues avail. **Document type:** *Yearbook, Academic/Scholarly.* **Description:** Examines the artistry of the puppet stage, past and present.
Published by: Edwin Mellen Press, 415 Ridge St, PO Box 450, Lewiston, NY 14092. TEL 716-754-2266, FAX 716-754-4056, cservice@mellenpress.com. Ed. James Fisher TEL 317-364-4394.

791.43 ESP ISSN 1888-4571
QUADERNS DE CINE. Text in Multiple languages. 2007. a. **Document type:** *Monographic series, Academic/Scholarly.*
Published by: Universidad de Alicante, Vicerrectorado de Extension Universitaria, Carretera San Vicente del Raspeig s-n, Alicante, 03690, Spain. TEL 34-96-5903400, FAX 34-96-5903464, investigacion.hemeroteca@cervantesvirtual.com, http://www.ua.es/es/index.html.

792 USA
QUARTO (HIGH POINT). Text in English. 1989. 3/yr. free. **Document type:** *Newsletter, Consumer.*
Published by: North Carolina Shakespeare Festival, PO Box 6066, High Point, NC 27262. TEL 336-841-2273, FAX 336-841-8627, http://www.ncshakes.org.

781.546 CHN ISSN 0578-0608
PL2567
QUYI/VARIETY SHOW. Text in Chinese. 1957. m. USD 48 (effective 2009). **Document type:** *Magazine, Consumer.* **Description:** Covers Chinese folk arts including ballad singing, story telling, comic dialogues, clapper talks and cross talks.
—East View.
Published by: Zhongguo Quyijia Xiehui, 10 Nongzhanguan Nanli, Beijing, 100026, China. Ed. Luo Yang. **Dist. outside China by:** China International Book Trading Corp, 35 Chegongzhuang Xilu, Haidian District, PO Box 399, Beijing 100044, China. TEL 86-10-68412045, FAX 86-10-68412023, cibtc@mail.cibtc.com.cn, http://www.cibtc.com.cn.

792.0222 DNK ISSN 0107-1882
RAMPELYSET. Text in Danish. 1948. 2/yr. DKK 225, DKK 325 to institutional members; DKK 125 to students (effective 2008). bk.rev.; play rev. cum index: 1996-2004. back issues avail. **Document type:** *Magazine, Trade.* **Description:** Articles and reviews about amateur theater activities.
Published by: D A T S - Landsforeningen for Dramatisk Virksomhed/The Danish Amateur Theatre Association, Nygade 15, Graasten, 6300, Denmark. TEL 45-74-651103, FAX 45-74-652093, dats@dats.dk, http://www.dats.dk.

792 AUS ISSN 1321-4799
REALTIME; +onscreen. Variant title: OnScreen. Text in English. 1994. bi-m. AUD 40 domestic to individuals; AUD 65 foreign to individuals; AUD 65 domestic to institutions; AUD 85 foreign to institutions (effective 2009). adv. dance rev.; music rev.; play rev.; tel.rev.; film rev.; video rev.; rec.rev.; Website rev. 44 p./no.; back issues avail. **Document type:** *Magazine, Consumer.* **Description:** Focuses on innovation in performance photomedia, film, video, interactive media and hybrid arts.
Related titles: Online - full text ed.: free to members (effective 2008); Supplement(s): Working the Screen.
—IE.
Published by: Open City Inc., 84 Womerah Ave, Rushcutlers BAy, NSW 2011, Australia. TEL 61-2-92832723, FAX 61-2-92832724, opencity@ozemail.com.au. Adv. contact Gail Priest. B&W page AUD 1,000, color page AUD 1,500. Circ: 27,000 (controlled). **Subscr. to:** PO Box A2246, Sydney South, NSW 1235, Australia. **Co-sponsors:** Screen Australia; N.S.W. Government Ministry for the Arts.

792 FRA ISSN 2107-6820
▼ **REGARDS CROISES SUR LA SCENE EUROPEENNE.** Text in French. 2010. irreg. **Document type:** *Monographic series, Academic/Scholarly.*
Media: Online - full text.
Published by: Universite de Tours (Francois-Rabelais), Centre d'Etudes Superieures de la Renaissance, BP 11328, Tours Cedex 1, 37013, France. TEL 33-2-47367760, FAX 33-2-47367762, cesr@univ-tours.fr, http://cesr.univ-tours.fr.

792 USA ISSN 1041-9411
PN2289
REGIONAL THEATRE DIRECTORY (YEAR). Text in English. 1986. a. USD 19.95 (effective 2001). **Document type:** *Directory, Trade.* **Description:** Hiring, casting, and internships at 438 regional and dinner theatres.
Published by: American Theatre Works, Inc., Theatre Directories, PO Box 510, Dorset, VT 05251. TEL 802-867-2223, FAX 802-867-0144. Ed., Pub. Jill Charles. Adv. contact Barbara Ax.

800 FRA ISSN 1274-2414
PN2003
REGISTRES. Text in French. 1996. irreg., latest 2009. price varies.
Indexed: FR, MLA-IB.
—INIST.
Published by: (Universite de Paris III (Sorbonne-Nouvelle), Institut d'Etudes Theatrales), Presses de la Sorbonne Nouvelle, 8 Rue de la Sorbonne, Paris, 75005, France. TEL 33-1-40464802, FAX 33-1-40464804, psn@univ-paris3.fr, http://www.univ-paris3.fr/recherche/psn.

792 809 USA ISSN 0486-3739
PN1785
RENAISSANCE DRAMA. Text in English. 19??. a., latest vol.38, 2010. price varies. back issues avail. **Document type:** *Monographic series, Academic/Scholarly.* **Description:** Provides the collection of essays on topics in Renaissance drama.
Supersedes in part (in 1964): Renaissance Drama, a Report on Research Opportunities
Related titles: Online - full text ed.
Indexed: A22, BEL&L, CA, IBR, IBT&D, IBZ, IIPA, MLA, MLA-IB, PCI, SCOPUS, T02.
—BLDSC (7356.865200), IE, Ingenta. **CCC.**
Published by: Northwestern University Press, 629 Noyes St, Evanston, IL 60208. TEL 847-491-2046, FAX 847-491-8150, nupress@northwestern.edu.

RENTAL AND STAGING SYSTEMS. *see* BUSINESS AND ECONOMICS—Trade And Industrial Directories

792 USA
THE REP REPORT. Text in English. m. **Document type:** *Newsletter, Consumer.* **Description:** Offers insight and information on current and upcoming productions at the Tennessee Repertory Theatre.
Published by: Hammock Publishing, Inc., 3322 W End Ave, Ste 700, Nashville, TN 37203. TEL 615-690-3400, FAX 615-690-3401, info@hammock.com, http://www.hammock.com.

792 778.5 GBR ISSN 0142-6303
REPERTORY REPORT. Text in English. 1972. m. GBP 35 (effective 2000). **Document type:** *Report, Trade.* **Description:** Covers the regional repertory theatre scene, including specific companies, casting, and audition plans.
Address: PO Box 11, London, N1 7JZ, United Kingdom. TEL 44-171-566-8282, FAX 44-171-566-8284. Ed. Lainey Alexander.

792.07 GBR ISSN 1356-9783
PN3171
➤ **RESEARCH IN DRAMA EDUCATION**; the journal of applied theatre and performance. Text in English. 1996. q. GBP 458 combined subscription in United Kingdom to institutions (print & online eds.); EUR 584, USD 732 combined subscription to institutions (print & online eds.) (effective 2012). adv. bk.rev. illus. back issues avail.; reprint service avail. from PSC. **Document type:** *Journal, Academic/Scholarly.* **Description:** Provides an international forum for research into drama and theatre conducted in community, educational, developmental and therapeutic contexts.
Related titles: Online - full text ed.: ISSN 1470-112X. GBP 412 in United Kingdom to institutions; EUR 526, USD 659 to institutions (effective 2012) (from IngentaConnect).
Indexed: A01, A02, A03, A08, A20, A22, A27, AEI, ArtHuCI, B29, CA, CPE, CurCont, E01, E03, E09, ERI, ERIC, FR, IBT&D, MLA-IB, P02, P04, P10, P18, P48, P53, P54, P55, PQC, SSCI, T02, W07.
—IE, Infotrieve, Ingenta, INIST. **CCC.**
Published by: Routledge (Subsidiary of: Taylor & Francis Group), 4 Park Sq, Milton Park, Abingdon, Oxon OX14 4RN, United Kingdom. TEL 44-20-70176000, FAX 44-20-70176336, subscriptions@tandf.co.uk, http://www.routledge.com. Eds. Helen Nicholson, Joe A Winston. Adv. contact Linda Hann TEL 44-1344-779945. **Subscr. in N America to:** Taylor & Francis Inc., Customer Services Dept, 325 Chestnut St, 8th Fl, Philadelphia, PA 19106. TEL 215-625-8900, 800-354-1420, FAX 215-625-2940, customerservice@taylorandfrancis.com; **Subscr. to:** Taylor & Francis Ltd., Journals Customer Service, Sheepen Pl, Colchester, Essex CO3 3LP, United Kingdom. TEL 44-20-70175544, FAX 44-20-70175198, tf.enquiries@tfinforma.com.

➤ **RESEARCH OPPORTUNITIES IN MEDIEVAL AND RENAISSANCE DRAMA.** *see* LITERATURE

792 USA ISSN 1931-8820
RESOURCE DIRECTORY. Text in English. a. **Document type:** *Directory, Trade.*
Published by: New England Theatre Conference, Inc., 215 Knob Hill Dr, Hamden, CT 06518. TEL 617-851-8535, mail@netconline.org, http://www.netconline.org.

THE REVELS PLAYS. *see* LITERATURE

REVELS STUDENT EDITIONS. *see* LITERATURE

THE REVIEW; a monthly arts and entertainment e-zine. *see* ART

792 BRA ISSN 0102-7336
REVISTA DE TEATRO. Text in Portuguese. 1920. q. adv. bk.rev. back issues avail. **Document type:** *Magazine, Consumer.*
Indexed: H21, MLA-IB, P08, RASB.
Published by: Sociedade Brasileira de Autores Teatrais, Rua da Quitanda, 194 Salas 1008-1010, Centro, Rio De Janeiro, RJ 20091-000, Brazil. TEL 5521-263-7856, FAX 5521-240-7431. Ed. Maria Helena Kuhner. Circ: 5,000.

792 FRA ISSN 1291-2530
PN2003
➤ **REVUE D'HISTOIRE DU THEATRE.** Text in French. 1948. q. EUR 57 domestic; EUR 60 in Europe; EUR 63 elsewhere (effective 2009). adv. bk.rev. charts; illus.; abstr. index, cum.index. reprints avail. **Document type:** *Journal, Academic/Scholarly.*
Formerly (until 1997): Revue de la Societe d'Histoire du Theatre (0035-2373)
Indexed: A20, A22, ASCA, ArtHuCI, BibInd, CA, CurCont, DIP, FR, HistAb, IBR, IBT&D, IBZ, IIPA, MLA, MLA-IB, P30, PCI, RASB, RILM, SCOPUS, T02, W07.
—BLDSC (7920.450000), IE, Ingenta, INIST.
Published by: Societe d'Histoire du Theatre, BnF - 58 rue de Richelieu, Paris, 75084 Cedex 02, France. TEL 33-1-42602705, FAX 33-1-42602765, info@sht.asso.fr. R&P Rose-Marie Moudoues. Adv. contact Maryline Romain.

792 FRA ISSN 1770-510X
LA REVUE MARSEILLAISE DU THEATRE. Text in French. 2004. m. **Document type:** *Magazine, Consumer.*

Published by: La Revue Marseillaise du Theatre, 7 Rue Pierre Lalou, Marseille, 13006, France. TEL 33-4-91421507, FAX 33-4-62341507.

792 ITA ISSN 0035-5186
PQ4231.A9
RIDOTTO; rassegna mensile di teatro. Text in Italian. 1951. m. adv. bk.rev. bibl.; charts; illus. index.
Indexed: MLA, MLA-IB, RASB.
Published by: Societa Italiana Autori Drammatici (S I A D), Viale della Letteratura 30, Rome, 00144, Italy. TEL 39-06-5990692. Ed. Maricla Boggio. Circ: 5,000.

792 800 ITA ISSN 1973-7602
PN2005
➤ **RIVISTA DI LETTERATURA TEATRALE.** Text in Multiple languages. 2008. a. **Document type:** *Journal, Academic/Scholarly.*
Related titles: Online - full text ed.: ISSN 2035-3553.
Published by: Fabrizio Serra Editore (Subsidiary of: Accademia Editoriale), c/o Accademia Editoriale, Via Santa Bibbiana 28, Pisa, 56127, Italy. TEL 39-050-542332, FAX 39-050-574888, accademiaeditoriale@accademiaeditoriale.it, http://www.libraweb.net.

➤ **RODMAN HALL BULLETIN.** *see* ART

792 CZE ISSN 1803-7100
ROZRAZIL - SOUCASNA CESKA HRA. Text in Czech. 2002. irreg., latest vol.93, 2011. CZK 49 per issue (effective 2011). **Document type:** *Monographic series, Academic/Scholarly.*
Formerly (until 2007): Soucasna Ceska Hra (1213-7022)
Published by: Vetrne Mlyny, Radlas 5, Brno, 602 00, Czech Republic. TEL 420-545-212487, FAX 420-545-212487, redakce@vetrnemlyny.cz.

RUCH MUZYCZNY; a musical review. *see* MUSIC

792.927 UAE
AL-RUWALAH. Text in Arabic. 1963. q. **Description:** Discusses the development and status of Arab theater in the Gulf region, and provides a forum for exchange of information and experience among persons connected with the theater.
Published by: Sharjah National Theater, PO Box 5373, Sharjah, United Arab Emirates. TEL 354522. Ed. Ahmed Bin Muhammad Al Qasimi. Circ: 1,000.

792 POL ISSN 1509-412X
RZECZY TEATRALNE. Text in Polish. 1999. irreg., latest vol.6, 2001. bk.rev. bibl. back issues avail. **Document type:** *Journal, Academic/Scholarly.* **Description:** Provides information on academic conferences, scholarly publications, academic work in progress on theatre in Poland.
Published by: Polska Akademia Nauk, Instytut Sztuki/Polish Academy of Science, Institute of Art, ul Dluga 28, Warsaw, 00950, Poland. TEL 48-22-5048200, FAX 48-22-8313149, ispan@ispan.pl. Circ: 300.
Co-sponsor: Polska Akademia Nauk, Komitet Badan Naukowych/Polish Academy of Sciences, Committee for Scientific Research.

791.437 800 FRA ISSN 1769-4450
S A C D. JOURNAL DES AUTEURS. (Societe des Auteurs et Compositeurs Dramatiques) Text in French. 2004. bi-m. back issues avail. **Document type:** *Magazine, Trade.*
Published by: Societe des Auteurs et Compositeurs Dramatiques (S A C D), 9 rue Ballu, Paris, Cedex 9 75009, France. http://www.sacd.fr. Ed. Catherine Walrafen.

792.071 CAN
S D A JOURNAL. Text in English. a. CAD 35 (effective 2000). adv. **Document type:** *Newsletter.*
Published by: (Saskatchewan Drama Association), Saskatchewan Teachers' Federation, 2317 Arlington Ave., Saskatoon, SK S7J 2H8, Canada. stf@stf.sk.ca.

808 USA ISSN 1073-8460
S T A M JOURNAL. (Speech and Theatre Association of Missouri) Text in English. 1970. a. free to members (effective 2010). bk.rev. **Document type:** *Journal, Academic/Scholarly.*
Former titles (until 1991): Missouri Speech & Theatre Journal; (until 19??): Missouri Speech Journal
Published by: Webster University, 470 E Lockwood Ave, St Louis, MO 63119. marketing@webster.edu, http://www.webster.edu/.

792 GBR
SADLER'S WELLS THEATRE PROGRAMME. Text in English. 1931. irreg. (approx. m.). GBP 1. adv. bk.rev. bibl.; illus. back issues avail. **Description:** Details of performances, casts, synopsis, biographies and credits.
Published by: Sadler's Wells Trust Ltd., Rosebery Ave, London, EC1R 4TN, United Kingdom. TEL 44-20-78638198, FAX 44-20-78638199, reception@sadlerswells.com, http://www.sadlerswells.com/. Circ: 9,000.

SAMUEL BECKETT TODAY - AUJOURD'HUI; annual bilingual review - revue annuelle bilingue. *see* LITERATURE

792 USA ISSN 0361-6495
SAMUEL FRENCH BASIC CATALOGUE OF PLAYS AND MUSICALS. Text in English. a. USD 3.50. adv. **Document type:** *Catalog.*
Published by: Samuel French, Inc., 45 W 25th St, New York, NY 10010. TEL 212-206-8990, FAX 212-206-1429. Ed. Lawrence Harbison. Pub. Charles R Van Nostrand. R&P Linda Kirland. Adv. contact Karen Kari.

792 VNM
SAN KHAU/THEATRE. Text in Vietnamese. 1976. m.
Address: 51 Tran Hung Dao St, Hanoi, Viet Nam. TEL 64423. Ed. Xuan Trinh.

SANDBOX MAGAZINE. *see* ART

SANDBOX WEB-ZINE. *see* ART

SANGEET NATAK. *see* MUSIC

SASKATCHEWAN DRAMA ASSOCIATION. NEWSLETTER. *see* EDUCATION—Teaching Methods And Curriculum

SCANDINAVICA. *see* LITERATURE

792 SRB ISSN 0036-5734
PN2007
SCENA; casopis za pozorisnu umetnost. Text in Serbo-Croatian. 1965. bi-m. EUR 20 domestic; EUR 30 foreign; EUR 3 newsstand/cover (effective 2006). bk.rev. **Document type:** *Magazine, Trade.*
Indexed: MLA-IB, RILM.
Published by: Sterijino Pozorje, Zmaj Jovina 22, Novi Sad, 21000. TEL 381-21-451273, FAX 381-21-6615976, sterija@neobee.net. Ed. Darinka Nikolic. Circ: 500 (paid and controlled).

792 780 ZAF ISSN 0256-002X
SCENARIA. Text in English. 1977. m. ZAR 102; ZAR 150 foreign (effective 1998). adv. bk.rev.; film rev.; play rev. illus. back issues avail. **Document type:** *Magazine, Consumer.* **Description:** Discusses the performing arts in South Africa and worldwide.
Incorporates: Arabesque
Indexed: ISAP, MLA-IB.
Published by: Encore Publications (Pty) Ltd., PO Box 72161, Park View, Johannesburg 2122, South Africa. TEL 27-11-4471173, FAX 27-11-7886313. Ed., Pub., R&P, Adv. contact Julius F Eichbaum. Circ: 9,000 (paid).

SCENARIO; journal for drama and theatre in foreign and second language education. *see* LINGUISTICS

792.028 DNK ISSN 1902-5076
SCENELIV; sang, dans, teater, film. Text in Danish. 1947. m. DKK 375 (effective 2007). adv. bk.rev. back issues avail. **Document type:** *Magazine, Trade.* **Description:** Publishes articles and essays on theater, film and television, focusing on the actor.
Former titles (until 2007): Spektakel (1399-1701); (until 1997): Teaterbladet (0900-0119); (until 1984): Teater, Film og T V (0108-6251)
Related titles: Online - full text ed.
Published by: Dansk Skuespillerforbund/The Danish Actors Association, Sankt Knuds Vej 26, Frederiksberg C, 1903, Denmark. TEL 45-33-242200, FAX 45-33-248159, dsf@skuespillerforbundet.dk. Ed. Gerz Feigenberg. adv.: page DKK 9,000; 170 x 270.

SCENES MAGAZINE; mensuel suisse d'information culturelle. *see* ART

792 FRA ISSN 1778-5499
SCENOGRAMMES. Text in French. 2005. irreg. back issues avail. **Document type:** *Monographic series, Consumer.*
Published by: Editions L' Entretemps, Domaine de Lafeuillade, 264 Rue du Capitaine Pierre Pontal, Montpellier, 34000, France. TEL 33-4-99530975, FAX 33-4-99533198, info.entretemps@wanadoo.fr, http://www.lekti-ecriture.com/editeurs/-L-Entretemps-.html.

729 DEU ISSN 0342-4553
SCHAUSPIELFUEHRER; der Inhalt der wichtigsten Theaterstuecke aus aller Welt. Text in German. 1953. triennial, latest vol.20, 2007. price varies. **Document type:** *Monographic series, Abstract/Index.*
Published by: (Universitaet Wien, Institut fuer Theaterwissenschaft), Anton Hiersemann Verlag, Haldenstr 30, Stuttgart, 70376, Germany. TEL 49-711-5499710, FAX 49-711-54997121, info@hiersemann.de, http://www.hiersemann.de.

792 CHE ISSN 1664-7130
▼ **SCHAUSPIELHAUS ZUERICH ZEITUNG.** Text in German. 2011. q. adv. **Document type:** *Journal, Trade.*
Published by: Schauspielhaus Zuerich, Zeltweg 5, Zuerich, 8032, Switzerland. TEL 41-44-2587070, FAX 41-44-2597070, http://www.schauspielhaus.ch. Circ: 30,000 (controlled).

792 DEU ISSN 1869-9758
▼ **SCHULTHEATER.** Text in German. 2010. 4/yr. EUR 48; EUR 16 newsstand/cover (effective 2011). adv. **Document type:** *Journal, Academic/Scholarly.*
Published by: Erhard Friedrich Verlag GmbH, Im Brande 17, Seelze, 30926, Germany. TEL 49-511-400040, FAX 49-511-40004170, info@friedrich-verlag.de. Adv. contact Bianca Kraft.

SCHWARZER FADEN; Vierteljahresschrift fuer Lust und Freiheit. *see* POLITICAL SCIENCE

792 CHE
SCHWEIZERISCHE GESELLSCHAFT FUER THEATERKULTUR. JAHRBUECHER. Text in German. 1928. a. price varies. **Document type:** *Academic/Scholarly.*
Published by: Schweizerische Gesellschaft fuer Theaterkultur/Swiss Association for Theatre Research, Postfach 1940, Basel, 4001, Switzerland. TEL 41-61-3211060, FAX 41-61-3211075.

792 CHE
SCHWEIZERISCHE GESELLSCHAFT FUER THEATERKULTUR. SCHRIFTEN. Text in German. 1928. irreg. **Document type:** *Monographic series.*
Published by: Schweizerische Gesellschaft fuer Theaterkultur/Swiss Association for Theatre Research, Postfach 1940, Basel, 4001, Switzerland. TEL 41-61-3211060, FAX 41-61-3211075.

SEVERNIAK. *see* LITERATURE

800 USA ISSN 0748-2558
PR3091
➤ **SHAKESPEARE BULLETIN**; a journal of performance, criticism, and scholarship . Abbreviated title: S B. Text in English. 1982. q. USD 100 to institutions (print or online ed.); USD 140 combined subscription to institutions (print & online eds.); USD 30 per issue to institutions (effective 2011). adv. bk.rev.; play rev. illus. back issues avail.; reprint service avail. from PSC. **Document type:** *Journal, Academic/Scholarly.* **Description:** Provides commentary on Shakespeare and Renaissance drama through feature articles, theatre and film reviews, and book reviews.
Incorporates (1976-1992): Shakespeare on Film Newsletter (0739-6570); Formerly (until 1983): New York Shakespeare Society. Bulletin (1075-1661)
Related titles: Online - full text ed.: ISSN 1931-1427.
Indexed: A22, A26, AmHI, BEL&L, CA, E01, E08, G08, H07, I05, IBT&D, IIPA, L05, L06, MLA, MLA-IB, S07, S09, T02.
—BLDSC (8254.582600), IE, Ingenta.
Published by: The Johns Hopkins University Press, 2715 N Charles St, Baltimore, MD 21218. TEL 410-516-6900, FAX 410-516-6968, bjs@press.jhu.edu, http://www.press.jhu.edu. Ed. Andrew James Hartley. Pub. William M Breichner. Circ: 280. **Subscr. to:** PO Box 19966, Baltimore, MD 21211. TEL 410-516-6987, 800-548-1784, FAX 410-516-3866, jrnlcirc@press.jhu.edu.

➤ **SHAKESPEARE IN PERFORMANCE.** *see* LITERATURE

➤ **SHAKESPEARE IN SOUTHERN AFRICA.** *see* LITERATURE

➤ **SHAKESPEARE INTERNATIONAL YEARBOOK.** *see* LITERATURE

➤ **SHAKESPEARE NEWSLETTER.** *see* LITERATURE

➤ **THE SHAKESPEARE OXFORD NEWSLETTER.** *see* LITERATURE

➤ **SHAKESPEARE QUARTERLY.** *see* LITERATURE

➤ **SHAKESPEARE SURVEY.** *see* LITERATURE

792 CHN ISSN 0559-7277
PN2009
SHANGHAI XIJU/SHANGHAI DRAMA. Text in Chinese. 1959. m. USD 36 (effective 2009). play rev. 56 p./no.; **Document type:** *Magazine.*
Indexed: RASB.
—East View.
Published by: (Shanghai Xijujia Xiehui), Shanghai Xiju Zazhishe, 105, Hunan Lu, Shanghai, 200031, China. TEL 86-21-64332735, FAX 86-21-64311727. Ed. Zhao Laijing. **Dist. by:** China International Book Trading Corp, 35 Chegongzhuang Xilu, Haidian District, PO Box 399, Beijing 100044, China. TEL 86-10-68412045, FAX 86-10-68412023, cibtc@mail.cibtc.com.cn, http://www.cibtc.com.cn.

792 CHN
SHANGHAI YISHUJIA/SHANGHAI ARTISTS. Text in Chinese. 1976. bi-m. USD 48 (effective 2009). adv. **Document type:** *Journal, Academic/Scholarly.*
Formerly (until 1979): Xinju Zuo (0257-5639)
Related titles: Online - full text ed.
Indexed: RILM.
Published by: Shanghai Yishu Yanjiusuo/Shanghai Art Institute, no.2, Alley112, Fengyang Lu, Shanghai, 200031, China. **Dist. by:** China International Book Trading Corp, 35 Chegongzhuang Xilu, Haidian District, PO Box 399, Beijing 100044, China. TEL 86-10-68412045, FAX 86-10-68412023, cibtc@mail.cibtc.com.cn, http://www.cibtc.com.cn.

SHAVIAN. *see* LITERATURE

792 USA ISSN 1522-0370
SHOW BIZ NEWS AND MODEL NEWS. Variant title: John King's Show Biz News and Model News. Text in English. 1970. bi-w. USD 39 domestic; USD 79.35 in Canada; USD 86.25 foreign; USD 3 newsstand/cover (effective 2003). adv. tel.rev.; rec.rev.; bk.rev.; dance rev.; film rev.; music rev.; play rev.; software rev.; video rev. bibl.; tr.lit. 4 cols./p.; back issues avail. **Document type:** *Newspaper, Trade.* **Description:** Covers the entertainment world. Aimed at show people, models, producers, agents, directors, photographers, fashion VIPs and celebrities.
Formerly: Model News and Talent; Which was formed by the merger of: Model News; Model and Talent
Related titles: Microfiche ed.; Online - full text ed.
Published by: The John King Network, 244 Madison Ave, Ste 393, New York, NY 10016. TEL 212-969-8715, 631-289-2338. Eds., Pubs. John King, Laura Fleming. Adv. contact John King. B&W page USD 1,500, color page USD 1,650; trim 10 x 16. Circ: 100,000 (controlled).

792 USA ISSN 0037-4318
PN2000
SHOW BUSINESS; the original casting weekly for the performing artist. Text in English. 1941-199?; N.S. 1999. w. (50/yr). USD 75; USD 2 newsstand/cover in New York; USD 2.50 newsstand/cover elsewhere (effective 2000). adv. film rev.; play rev.; tel.rev.; music rev.; dance rev. charts; illus. back issues avail. **Document type:** *Newspaper, Trade.* **Description:** Compiles casting news and listings for performers and all artists in theatre, film, TV, cabaret, summer theatre and other forms of entertainment.
Related titles: Microfilm ed.: N.S. (from PQC); Online - full text ed.: N.S.
Indexed: RASB.
Published by: Show Business, Inc, 141 E 45th St, 3rd Fl, New York, NY 10017. TEL 212-986-4100, FAX 212-972-5107, editor@showbusinessweekly.com. Ed. Jay Baik. Pub., Adv. contact David Pearlstein. B&W page USD 1,184; trim 11 x 14. Circ: 15,000 (paid).

792 USA ISSN 1544-9831
SHOW PEOPLE; from the stage door to your door. Text in English. 2002 (Sep.). q. USD 15; USD 3.95 newsstand/cover (effective 2006). adv. **Document type:** *Magazine, Consumer.* **Description:** Aims to inform and entertain the lifestyle of the theatergoer.
Address: 220 W 42nd St., 14th Fl, New York, NY 10036. TEL 877-783-4847, subservice@clearchannel.com. Ed. Erik Jackson. adv.: B&W page USD 8,750, color page USD 12,500; trim 8.5 x 10.5.

790 780 GBR ISSN 0264-4150
SHOWCALL. Text in English. 1973. a. GBP 35 (effective 2002). adv. index. back issues avail. **Document type:** *Directory, Trade.* **Description:** Directory of light entertainment, artists.
Related titles: Online - full content ed.
—CCC.
Published by: Stage Newspaper Ltd., Stage House, 47 Bermondsey St, London, SE1 3XT, United Kingdom. TEL 44-20-74031818, FAX 44-20-7403-1418, admin@thestage.co.uk. Pub. Catherine Comerford. Adv. contact Marcus Collingbourne. page GBP 135.

792 647.968 GBR ISSN 0265-9808
NA6840.G7
SIGHTLINE; journal of theatre technology and design. Text in English. 1990 (vol.24, no.4). q. free membership (effective 2009). adv. bk.rev. **Document type:** *Magazine, Trade.* **Description:** Covers all technical aspects of theatrical production, including design, technology, lighting, sound, training, planning, safety and regulations, and serves as a forum for issues of concern to technicians.
Formerly: Association of British Theatre Technicians. Newsletter
Indexed: IBT&D.
—BLDSC (8275.295000), Ingenta.
Published by: Association of British Theatre Technicians, 55 Farringdon Rd, London, EC1M 3JB, United Kingdom. TEL 44-20-72429200, FAX 44-20-72429303, office@abtt.org.uk, http://www.abtt.org.uk/.

792 USA ISSN 1048-955X
PN2053
SIGHTLINES (NEW YORK). Text in English. 1965. m. membership. adv. 40 p./no. 3 cols./p.; **Document type:** *Newsletter, Trade.*
Formerly (until 1988): U S I T T Newsletter (0565-6311)
Indexed: IBT&D, RASB.
Published by: U S Institute for Theatre Technology, Inc., 6443 Ridings Rd, Syracuse, NY 13206-1111. Ed. Tom Scharff. Adv. contact Michelle L Smith TEL 800-93 US ITT. Circ: 3,600.

792 MEX ISSN 1605-4105
SKENE; revista teatral especializada. Text in Spanish. w.
Media: Online - full text.
Address: MIGUEL E SHULTZ 135-A, Col San Rafael, Mexico City, DF 06470, Mexico. TEL 52-5-5350141, FAX 52-5-5460609. Ed. Alejandro Laborie.

T U

792 USA ISSN 1069-2800
SLAVIC AND EAST EUROPEAN PERFORMANCE. Abbreviated title: S E E P. Text in English. 1981. 3/yr. USD 20 domestic; USD 30 foreign (effective 2010). back issues avail. **Document type:** *Journal, Academic/Scholarly.* **Description:** Features on important new plays in performance, archival documents, innovative productions, significant revivals, emerging artists, and the latest in film.
Former titles (until 1992): Soviet and East European Performance (1047-0018); (until 1989): Soviet and East-European Drama, Theatre, and Film; (until 1985): Newsnotes on Soviet and East European Drama and Theatre
Related titles: Online - full text ed.
Indexed: ABS&EES, IBT&D, IIPA, MLA-IB, T02.
Published by: Martin E. Segal Theatre Center, The CUNY Graduate Center, 365 Fifth Ave, New York, NY 10016. TEL 212-817-1860, mestc@gc.cuny.edu. Ed. Daniel Gerould.

792 SVK ISSN 0037-699X
PN2859.C93
➤ **SLOVENSKE DIVADLO/SLOVAK THEATER.** Text in Slovak; Summaries in English. 1952. q. USD 20 (effective 2002). bk.rev.; film rev.; play rev. illus. 120 p./no.; **Document type:** *Academic/Scholarly.* **Description:** Deals with the history of film, theater, radio and television art.
Indexed: MLA, MLA-IB, RASB, RILM.
Published by: Slovenska Akademia Vied, Kabinet Divadla a Filmu, Dubravska cesta 9, Bratislava, 813 64, Slovakia. TEL 421-7-54777193, FAX 421-7-54773567, kadfdapo@savba.savba.sk. Ed., Adv. contact Dagmar Podmakova. **Dist. in Western countries by:** John Benjamins Publishing Co.

792 USA
SOCIETY FOR THE PERFORMING ARTS. Text in English. m.
Published by: Walker Media, 1805 Haver, Houston, TX 77006. TEL 713-524-3560, FAX 713-524-3549, marlenewal@aol.com.

SONDHEIM NEWS. *see* MUSIC

792.2 782.42 USA ISSN 1076-450X
ML410.S6872
THE SONDHEIM REVIEW; dedicated to the work of the musical theater's foremost composer and lyricist. Text in English. 1994. q. USD 19.95 domestic; USD 24.95 in Canada; USD 29.95 elsewhere (effective 2000); USD 5.95 newsstand/cover. adv. bk.rev.; music rev.; play rev.; video rev. illus. back issues avail. **Document type:** *Newsletter, Consumer.* **Description:** Covers productions of the musical plays by Stephen Sondheim.
Related titles: Online - full text ed.
Indexed: IBT&D, IIPA, M11, MLA-IB, T02.
Published by: Sondheim Review, 2230 E Bradford Ave, Unit G, Milwaukee, WI 53211-4059. TEL 414-964-1719. Ed., R&P Paul Salsini. Pub., Adv. contact Ray Birks. B&W page USD 500. Circ: 4,100 (paid). **Subscr. to:** Department S 2, The Sondheim Review, Box 11213, Chicago, IL 60611-0213.

792 GBR ISSN 1013-7548
PN2001
➤ **SOUTH AFRICAN THEATRE JOURNAL.** Text in English. 1987. 3/yr. GBP 250 combined subscription in United Kingdom to institutions (print & online eds.); EUR 319, USD 399 combined subscription to institutions (print & online eds.) (effective 2012). adv. bk.rev. **Document type:** *Journal, Academic/Scholarly.* **Description:** Provides a forum for the discussion of theatre, performance studies, and the performing arts in Southern Africa.
Related titles: Online - full text ed.: GBP 225 in United Kingdom to institutions; EUR 287, USD 360 to institutions (effective 2012).
Indexed: BibInd, CA, I05, IBT&D, ISAP, MLA-IB, T02.
Published by: Taylor & Francis Ltd. (Subsidiary of: Taylor & Francis Group), 4 Park Sq, Milton Park, Abingdon, Oxfordshire OX14 4RN, United Kingdom. TEL 44-20-70176000, FAX 44-20-70176336, info@tandf.co.uk, http://www.tandf.co.uk.

792 USA ISSN 0584-4738
PN2000
SOUTHERN THEATRE. Text in English. 1964. q. USD 17.50 (effective 2001 - 2002). adv. bk.rev.; play rev. index. back issues avail. **Document type:** *Magazine, Consumer.* **Description:** Provides current articles on the theatre.
Related titles: Online - full text ed.
Indexed: CA, IBT&D, MLA-IB, T02.
—Ingenta.
Published by: (Southeastern Theatre Conference, Inc.), Clinton Press, PO Box 9868, Greensboro, NC 27429-0868. TEL 336-272-3645, FAX 336-272-8810, setc@mindspring.com, http://www.setc.org. Ed. Deanna Thompson. Adv. contact Regina Cialone. B&W page USD 450; trim 10.88 x 8.5. Circ: 3,600.

792 RUS ISSN 0207-7698
PG3242
SOVREMENNAYA DRAMATURGIYA. Text in Russian. q. USD 109.95 in United States.
Related titles: Microform ed.: (from EVP).
Indexed: RASB.
—East View. **CCC.**
Published by: Ministerstvo Kul'tury Rossiiskoi Federatsii, Fond Razvitiya i Pooshchreniya Dramaturgii, Dmitrovskii per 4, Moscow, 103031, Russian Federation. TEL 7-095-9254648, FAX 7-095-9234595. Ed. N I Miroshnichenko. **Dist. by:** East View Information Services, 10601 Wayzata Blvd, Minneapolis, MN 55305. TEL 952-252-1201, 800-477-1005, FAX 952-252-1202, info@eastview.com, http://www.eastview.com.

792 USA
SPARKS (GRAND RAPIDS); the magazine of creative audio. Text in English. 1989. irreg., latest vol.1, no.3. USD 3.50 per issue. back issues avail. **Description:** Designed for the radio - audio and theatre arts aficionado. Covers the activities of radio theatre producers, including profiles, current releases, technology, sources and history. Also covers activities of the Fireside Theatre.
Address: PO Box 3540, Grand Rapids, MI 49501-3540. TEL 616-363-8231. Eds. Jim Middleton, Michael Packer.

SPETTACOLO E COMUNICAZIONE. *see* COMMUNICATIONS

792.02 DEU ISSN 1616-6809
SPIEL & BUEHNE. Text in German. 1974. 4/yr. EUR 18; EUR 5 newsstand/cover (effective 2009). adv. bk.rev.; play rev. **Document type:** *Journal, Trade.*
Published by: Bund Deutscher Amateurtheater e.V., Steinheimer Str 7-1, Heidenheim, 89518, Germany. TEL 49-7321-9469900, FAX 49-7321-48341, bdat-@t-online.de. Eds. Andreas Salemi, Norbert Radermacher. adv.: page EUR 500; trim 173 x 255. Circ: 3,500 (paid).

792 DEU ISSN 0038-7509
SPIEL UND THEATER; Die Zeitschrift fuer Theater von und mit Jugendlichen. Text in German. 1949. 2/yr. EUR 12; EUR 6.50 newsstand/cover (effective 2009). adv. bk.rev.; play rev. **Document type:** *Journal, Trade.*
Formerly (until 1970): Laienspieler
Indexed: DIP, IBR, IBZ.
Published by: Deutscher Theaterverlag GmbH, Postfach 200263, Weinheim, 69459, Germany. TEL 49-6201-879070, FAX 49-6201-507082, theater@dtver.de, http://www.dtver.de.

792 DEU ISSN 0038-7517
DER SPIELPLAN; die monatliche Theatervorschau. Text in German. 1896. m. EUR 68 (effective 2011). adv. illus. **Document type:** *Magazine, Consumer.*
Former titles (until 1964): Der Spielplan der Deutschen Buehnen; (until 1954): Deutscher Buehnenspielplan
Published by: Loewendruck Bertram GmbH, Rebhuhnweg 3, Braunschweig, 38108, Germany. TEL 49-531-352246, FAX 49-531-352266, info@loewendruck.de, http://www.loewendruck.de.

792 GBR ISSN 0309-0183
SPOTLIGHT ACTORS. Text in English. 1927. a. **Document type:** *Directory, Trade.* **Description:** Contains over 13,000 entries, each comprising a photograph of the actor, a brief summary of his physical characteristics, and his agent contact details.
Supersedes in part (in 1979): Spotlight (0038-836X)
Related titles: Online - full text ed.
—CCC.
Published by: The Spotlight, 7 Leicester Pl, London, WC2H 7RJ, United Kingdom. TEL 44-20-74377631, questions@spotlight.com.

792 GBR ISSN 0308-9827
SPOTLIGHT ACTRESSES. Text in English. 1927. a. (Oct.). **Document type:** *Directory, Trade.* **Description:** Contains over 13,500 entries, each comprising a photograph of the actress, a brief summary of her physical characteristics, and her agent contact details.
Supersedes in part (in 1979): Spotlight (0038-836X)
—CCC.
Published by: The Spotlight, 7 Leicester Pl, London, WC2H 7RJ, United Kingdom. TEL 44-20-74377631, questions@spotlight.com, http://www.spotlight.com/.

792 GBR
SPOTLIGHT CHILDREN & YOUNG PERFORMERS. Text in English. 1980. a. free to qualified personnel (effective 2010). **Document type:** *Directory, Trade.* **Description:** Features child artists from leading theatre schools and agencies. It provides the casting professional with photographs, brief descriptions, agent / school contact details, and credits.
Formerly (until 1999): Spotlight Children (0142-8926)
Published by: The Spotlight, 7 Leicester Pl, London, WC2H 7RJ, United Kingdom. TEL 44-20-74377631, questions@spotlight.com.

792 GBR ISSN 1743-2448
THE SPOTLIGHT. GRADUATES. Text in English. 1980. a. (Feb.). free to qualified personnel (effective 2009). **Document type:** *Directory, Trade.* **Description:** Lists almost 1200 students, all final-year students of the member schools and colleges that form the Conference of Drama Schools (CDS), plus additional, selected NCDT accredited courses.
Formerly (until 2002): Spotlight. New Actors and Actresses (0142-8918)
Published by: (Conference of Drama Schools), The Spotlight, 7 Leicester Pl, London, WC2H 7RJ, United Kingdom. TEL 44-20-74377631, questions@spotlight.com.

792 GBR ISSN 1351-7597
SPOTLIGHT ON PRESENTERS. Variant title: Spotlight Presenters. Text in English. 1994. a. (Jan.). GBP 20 per issue (effective 2009). **Document type:** *Directory, Trade.* **Description:** Features over 750 famous faces, Spotlight Presenters is the definitive reference tool for sourcing dynamic and professional radio and television presenters across areas including news, entertainment, comedy, celebrity, documentaries and sport.
Published by: The Spotlight, 7 Leicester Pl, London, WC2H 7RJ, United Kingdom. TEL 44-20-74377631, questions@spotlight.com.

792 DEU
STAATSTHEATER STUTTGART. SPIELPLAN. Text in German. m. adv. **Document type:** *Bulletin, Consumer.*
Formerly: Staatstheater Stuttgart. Monatsvorschau
Published by: Staatstheater Stuttgart, Postfach 104345, Stuttgart, 70038, Germany. TEL 49-711-2032220, FAX 49-711-2032300, abo@staatstheater-stuttgart.de, http://www.staatstheater-stuttgart.de.

STAD ANTWERPEN. CULTUREEL JAARBOEK. *see* MUSEUMS AND ART GALLERIES

792 ZMB
STAGE. Text in English. 1956. irreg. price varies. adv. bk.rev.; play rev.
Published by: Lusaka Theatre Club (Co-Op) Ltd., PO Box 30615, Lusaka, Zambia. Ed. Mase Mulondiwa. Circ: 300 (controlled).

791.43 GBR ISSN 1660-2560
STAGE AND SCREEN STUDIES. Text in English. 2002. irreg., latest vol.12, 2008. price varies. back issues avail. **Document type:** *Monographic series, Academic/Scholarly.*
—BLDSC (8426.469420).
Published by: Peter Lang Ltd. (Subsidiary of: Peter Lang Publishing Group), Evenlode Ct, Main Rd, Long Hanborough, Oxfordshire OX29 8SZ, United Kingdom. TEL 44-1993-880088, FAX 44-1993-882040, info@peterlang.com. Ed. Kenneth Richards.

792 USA ISSN 1047-1901
PN2267
STAGE DIRECTIONS. Abbreviated title: S D. Text in English. 1988. m. free (effective 2009). adv. bk.rev. illus. reprints avail. **Document type:** *Magazine, Trade.*
Related titles: Online - full text ed.: free (effective 2009).
Indexed: A10, A27, IBT&D, IIPA, M02, MASUSE, P02, P10, P48, P53, P54, PQC, T02, V03.
—Ingenta.
Published by: Macfadden Performing Arts Media, LLC., 6000 S Eastern Ave. Ste 14-J, Las Vegas, NV 89119. TEL 702-932-5585, FAX 702-932-5584, http://dancemedia.com/. Ed. Jacob Coakley TEL 702-932-5585. Pub. Terry Lowe TEL 702-932-5585. Adv. contact Greg Gallardo TEL 702-454-8550. color page USD 3,843, B&W page USD 2,720; trim 8 x 10.875.

792 NLD ISSN 2211-7865
▼ **STAGE & THEATRE.** Text in Dutch. 2009. bi-m. EUR 29 (effective 2011). **Document type:** *Magazine, Trade.*
Published by: Buzzfacts Publishers & Mediagroup, Postbus 155, Nijmegen, 6500 AD, Netherlands. TEL 31-24-3722900, FAX 31-24-3886017, info@bp-m.nl, http://www.brinkmanpublishers.nl. Ed. Marieke van Dam. Circ: 3,800.

792 AUS ISSN 1321-5965
STAGE WHISPERS; performing arts magazine. Text in English. 1991. bi-m. AUD 39.50 domestic; AUD 49 in New Zealand; AUD 6.95 per issue (effective 2009). adv. back issues avail. **Document type:** *Magazine, Trade.* **Description:** Provides a platform for all people from all areas of the industry to speak out and learn more about the world of performing arts.
Related titles: Online - full text ed.: free (effective 2009).
Address: PO Box 2274, Rose Bay North, NSW 2030, Australia. Adv. contact Angela . TEL 61-3-97584522. B&W page AUD 1,125, color page AUD 1,575; 25 x 17.8.

792 782.81 USA
STAGEBILL. (Separate regional editions avail.) Text in English. 1924. m. bk.rev.; music rev. charts; illus. **Document type:** *Magazine, Consumer.* **Description:** Presents readers with essential information on a wide range of performing arts.
Related titles: Large type ed.
Published by: Stagebill, Inc., 520 Madison Ave., New York, NY 10022-4213. TEL 212-476-0640, FAX 212-949-0518. Ed. John Istel. Pub. Shira Kalish.

791.43 IRL
STAGECAST - IRISH STAGE AND SCREEN DIRECTORY. Text in English. 1962. biennial. USD 15. adv. illus.; stat. back issues avail. **Document type:** *Directory.*
Published by: Stagecast Publications, 15 Eaton Sq., Monkstown, Co. Dublin, Ireland. TEL 01-2808968. Ed. Derek Young. Circ: 500.

STAGEREPORT; Informationen ueber Buehnen- und Showproduktionen. *see* BUSINESS AND ECONOMICS—Marketing And Purchasing

792 USA ISSN 1041-6048
STAGES; the national theatre magazine. Text in English. 1984. q. USD 15. adv. bk.rev.; play rev. illus. back issues avail. **Document type:** *Magazine, Consumer.*
Published by: Curtains, Inc., 301 W 45th St 5A, New York, NY 10036. TEL 212-245-9186, FAX 201-836-4107. Ed. Frank Scheck. Circ: 10,000.

647.968 CAN
STAGEWORKS. Text in English. q.
Published by: Canadian Institute for Theatre, 2500 University Dr NW, Calgary, AB T2N 1NR, Canada.

STATE OF THE ARTS. *see* MUSEUMS AND ART GALLERIES

STERZ; Zeitschrift fuer Literatur, Kunst und Kulturpolitik. *see* LITERATURE

792 SWE ISSN 1400-2132
STOCKHOLM THEATRE STUDIES. Text in Multiple languages. 1967. irreg., latest vol.3, 1997. price varies. **Document type:** *Monographic series, Academic/Scholarly.*
Formerly (until 1977): Stockholm Studies in Theatrical History (0585-3605)
Related titles: ◆ Series of: Acta Universitatis Stockholmiensis. ISSN 0346-6418.
Published by: Stockholms Universitet, Acta Universitatis Stockholmiensis, c/o Stockholms Universitetsbibliotek, Universitetsvaegen 10, Stockholm, 10691, Sweden. TEL 46-8-162800, FAX 46-8-157776, http://www.sub.su.se. Ed. Margaretha Fathli. **Dist. by:** Eddy.se AB, Norra Kyrkogatan 3, Visby 62155, Sweden. TEL 46-498-253900, FAX 46-498-249789, info@eddy.se, order@eddy.se, http://www.eddy.se, http://acta.bokorder.se.

STRANDGUT; Stadtmagazin Frankfurt am Main. *see* MOTION PICTURES

792 CAN ISSN 0085-6770
PN2306.S77
STRATFORD FESTIVAL; souvenir book. Text in English. 1953. a. CAD 10 (effective 1999). Supplement avail. **Document type:** *Handbook/Manual/Guide, Consumer.*
Published by: Stratford Shakespearean Festival Foundation of Canada, P O Box 520, Stratford, ON N5A 6V2, Canada. TEL 519-271-4040.

STRINDBERGIANA. *see* LITERATURE

792 USA ISSN 0081-6051
PN2277.N5
STUBS (METRO NY); the seating plan guide for New York theatres, music halls, sports stadia. Text in English. 1967. irreg. USD 15.25 domestic; USD 12.95 newsstand/cover; USD 18.25 foreign (effective 2000). adv. charts; illus.; maps. **Document type:** *Magazine, Consumer.* **Description:** Features the seating plan guide for New York theatres, music halls and sports stadia.
Published by: Stubs Communications Co., 226 W 47th St, New York, NY 10036. TEL 212-398-8370, FAX 212-398-1726. Ed., Pub., R&P, Adv. contact Ronald S Lee. Circ: 30,000.

792 POL ISSN 0208-404X
STUDIA I MATERIALY DO DZIEJOW TEATRU POLSKIEGO. Text in Polish. 1957. irreg., latest vol.24, 1994. price varies. **Document type:** *Monographic series.* **Description:** Polish theatre life in Poland.
Formerly: Studia i Materialy z Dziejow Teatru Polskiego (0081-6647)
Published by: Polska Akademia Nauk, Instytut Sztuki/Polish Academy of Science, Institute of Art, ul Dluga 28, Warsaw, 00950, Poland. TEL 48-22-5048200, FAX 48-22-8313149, ispan@ispan.pl, http://www.ispan.pl.

792 ROM ISSN 1842-2799
➤ **STUDIA UNIVERSITATIS BABES-BOLYAI. DRAMATICA.** Text in English, Romanian. 2006. s-a. exchange basis. bk.rev. abstr.; bibl.; illus. **Document type:** *Journal, Academic/Scholarly.*
Related titles: Online - full text ed.: ISSN 2065-9539.
Indexed: CA, T02.

Published by: Universitatea "Babes-Bolyai", Studia/Babes-Bolyai University, Studia, 51 Hasdeu Str, Cluj-Napoca, 400371, Romania. TEL 40-264-405352, FAX 40-264-591906, office@studia.ubbcluj.ro. Ed. Liviu Malita. **Dist by:** "Lucian Blaga" Central University Library, International Exchange Department, Clinicilor st no 2, Cluj-Napoca 400371, Romania. TEL 40-264-597092, FAX 40-264-597633, iancu@bcucluj.ro.

792 DEU ISSN 0721-4162
STUDIEN ZUM THEATER, FILM UND FERNSEHEN. Text in German. 1982. irreg., latest vol.45, 2009. price varies. **Document type:** *Monographic series, Academic/Scholarly.*
Published by: Peter Lang GmbH (Subsidiary of: Peter Lang Publishing Group), Eschborner Landstr 42-50, Frankfurt Am Main, 60489, Germany. TEL 49-69-7807050, FAX 49-69-78070550, zentrale.frankfurt@peterlang.com. Eds. Dieter Ahlert, Renate Moehrmann.

792 DEU
STUDIEN ZUR MUENCHNER THEATERGESCHICHTE. Text in German. 2000. irreg., latest vol.3, 2008. price varies. **Document type:** *Monographic series, Academic/Scholarly.*
Published by: Herbert Utz Verlag GmbH, Adalbertstr 57, Munich, 80799, Germany. TEL 49-89-27779100, FAX 49-89-27779101, utz@utzverlag.com. Eds. Hans-Michael Koerner, Juergen Schlaeder.

800 GBR
STUDIES IN MODERN DRAMA. Text in English. 19??. irreg., latest 2005. price varies. back issues avail. **Document type:** *Monographic series, Academic/Scholarly.* **Description:** Contains the studies about modern drama.
Published by: Routledge (Subsidiary of: Taylor & Francis Group), 4 Park Sq, Milton Park, Abingdon, Oxon OX14 4RN, United Kingdom. TEL 44-20-70176000, FAX 44-20-70176336, subscriptions@tandf.co.uk.

792 780 GBR ISSN 1750-3159
➤ **STUDIES IN MUSICAL THEATRE.** Abbreviated title: S M T. Text in English. 2007. 3/yr. GBP 36, USD 68 to individuals; GBP 235, USD 368 to institutions (effective 2012). adv. back issues avail. **Document type:** *Journal, Academic/Scholarly.* **Description:** Covers areas of live performance that use vocal and instrumental music in conjunction with theatrical performance as a principal part of their expressive language.
Related titles: Online - full text ed.: ISSN 1750-3167. GBP 192, USD 290 (effective 2012).
Indexed: AmHI, BRD, CA, H07, H08, HAb, HumInd, IBT&D, M11, MLA-IB, T02, W03, W05.
—BLDSC (8491.141950), IE.
Published by: Intellect Ltd., The Mill, Parnall Rd, Fishponds, Bristol, BS16 3JG, United Kingdom. TEL 44-117-9589910, FAX 44-117-9589911, info@intellectbooks.com. Eds. Dominic Symonds TEL 44-2392-845126, George Burrows TEL 44-2392-845132. Pub. Masoud Yazdani. **Dist. by:** Turpin Distribution Services Ltd., Pegasus Dr, Stratton Business Park, Biggleswade, Bedfordshire SG18 8QB, United Kingdom. TEL 44-1767-604951, FAX 44-1767-601640, custserv@turpin-distribution.com, http://www.turpin-distribution.com/.

792 GBR
STUDIES IN PERFORMANCE AND EARLY MODERN DRAMA. Text in English. 2002. irreg. price varies. back issues avail. **Document type:** *Monographic series, Academic/Scholarly.* **Description:** Presents research on theatre histories and performance histories from 1500 to the early eighteenth century.
Related titles: Online - full text ed.
Published by: Ashgate Publishing Ltd (Subsidiary of: Gower Publishing Co. Ltd.), Wey Ct E, Union Rd, Farnham, Surrey GU9 7PT, United Kingdom. TEL 44-1252-736600, FAX 44-1252-736736, ashgate.online@ashgate.com. Ed. Helen Ostovich. **Dist. by:** Ashgate Publishing Co, PO Box 2225, Williston, VT 05495. TEL 800-535-9544, FAX 802-864-7626, orders@ashgate.com.

792 GBR ISSN 1468-2761
PN2001
➤ **STUDIES IN THEATRE AND PERFORMANCE.** Abbreviated title: S T P. Text in English. 1990. 3/yr. GBP 36, USD 68 to individuals; GBP 235, USD 368 to institutions (effective 2012). adv. back issues avail. **Document type:** *Journal, Academic/Scholarly.* **Description:** Provides a forum for scholars, teachers and practitioners to share the methods and results of practical research, to debate issues related to theater practice and to examine experiments in teaching and performance.
Formerly (until 2000): Studies in Theatre Production (1357-5341)
Related titles: Online - full text ed.: ISSN 2040-0616. GBP 192, USD 290 (effective 2012).
Indexed: A01, A02, A03, A08, A22, AmHI, BrHumI, CA, E01, H07, IBT&D, MLA-IB, T02.
—IE. **CCC.**
Published by: Intellect Ltd., The Mill, Parnall Rd, Fishponds, Bristol, BS16 3JG, United Kingdom. TEL 44-117-9589910, FAX 44-117-9589911, info@intellectbooks.com. Eds. Andrew Wyllie, Kate Dorney, Peter Thomson TEL 44-1392-264580. Pub. Masoud Yazdani. **Subscr. to:** Turpin Distribution Services Ltd., Pegasus Dr, Stratton Business Park, Biggleswade, Bedfordshire SG18 8QB, United Kingdom. TEL 44-1767-604951, FAX 44-1767-601640, custserv@turpin-distribution.com, http://www.turpin-distribution.com/.

800 USA
STUDIES IN THEATRE HISTORY & CULTURE. Text in English. 1991. irreg. price varies. **Document type:** *Monographic series, Academic/Scholarly.* **Description:** Publishes on the history of theater, including Chakespearean performance, American theater and cultural history, European theater, and theater historiography.
Published by: University of Iowa Press, 119 W Park Rd, 100 Kuhl House, Iowa City, IA 52242-1000. TEL 319-335-2000, FAX 319-335-2055, uipress@uiowa.edu, http://www.uiowapress.org/.

791.43 ROM ISSN 0039-3991
PN1609.R6
STUDII SI CERCETARI DE ISTORIA ARTEI. SERIA TEATRU, MUZICA, CINEMATOGRAFIE/STUDIES AND RESEARCH IN ART HISTORY. SERIES: THEATRE, MUSIC, CINEMATOGRAPHY. Text in Romanian, French, English. 1954. a. bk.rev. illus. index. **Document type:** *Journal, Academic/Scholarly.*
Related titles: Online - full text ed.: free (effective 2011).
Indexed: RASB.
Published by: (Academia Romana/Romanian Academy, Institutul de Istoria Artei George Oprescu), Editura Academiei Romane/Publishing House of the Romanian Academy, Calea 13 Septembrie 13, Sector 5, Bucharest, 050711, Romania. Ed. Silviu Angelescu.

791.43028 GBR ISSN 1742-3651
STUNT PERFORMERS. Text in English. 1985. biennial. free to qualified personnel (effective 2009). **Document type:** *Directory, Trade.* **Description:** Features professionally trained and experienced stunt artists, with full credits and contact details, plus head, body and action shots.
Formerly (until 2002): Register of Stunt Performers and Arrangers (0967-7127)
Published by: The Spotlight, 7 Leicester Pl, London, WC2H 7RJ, United Kingdom. TEL 44-20-74377631, questions@spotlight.com.

SUB CULTURE FREIBURG; Trendmagazin fuer Popkultur & Freizeitgestaltung. *see* MUSIC

SUB CULTURE KOELN - FRANKFURT. *see* MUSIC

SUB CULTURE RHEIN-NECKAR. *see* MUSIC

SUB CULTURE STUTTGART. *see* MUSIC

SUB CULTURE ULM. *see* MUSIC

792 USA ISSN 0884-5840
PN2289
SUMMER THEATRE DIRECTORY (YEAR). Text in English. 1984. a. USD 19.95 (effective 2001). **Document type:** *Directory, Trade.* **Description:** Opportunities at over 450 Summer theatres, theme parks, and Summer training programs.
Published by: American Theatre Works, Inc., Theatre Directories, PO Box 510, Dorset, VT 05251. TEL 802-867-2223, FAX 802-867-0144. Ed., Pub. Jill Charles. Adv. contact Barbara Ax.

SUN BELT JOURNAL. *see* BUSINESS AND ECONOMICS

SYDNEY OPERA HOUSE. EVENTS. *see* MUSIC

SZENE KOELN/BONN. *see* MUSIC

SZENE KULTUR. *see* MUSIC

SZENE LUEBECK. *see* MUSIC

SZENE ROSTOCK. *see* MUSIC

792 CHE
SZENE SCHWEIZ/SCENA SVIZZERA/SCENE SUISSE. Text in German. 1973. a. CHF 30 (effective 2000). **Document type:** *Bulletin.*
Published by: Schweizerische Gesellschaft fuer Theaterkultur/Swiss Association for Theatre Research, Postfach 1940, Basel, 4001, Switzerland. TEL 41-61-3211060, FAX 41-61-3211075.

SZENE SCHWERIN. *see* MUSIC

SZENE WISMAR. *see* MUSIC

792 DEU
▼ **SZENOGRAFIE UND SZENOLOGIE.** Text in German. 2009. irreg., latest vol.4, 2011. price varies. **Document type:** *Monographic series, Academic/Scholarly.*
Published by: Transcript, Muehlenstr 47, Bielefeld, 33607, Germany. TEL 49-521-63454, FAX 49-521-61040, live@transcript-verlag.de.

792 USA ISSN 1052-6765
NA1
T D & T. (Theatre Design & Technology) Text in English. 1965. q. USD 60 domestic membership; USD 90 foreign membership (effective 2006). adv. bk.rev.; play rev. bibl.; charts; illus.; pat. reprints avail. **Document type:** *Magazine, Trade.*
Formerly: Theatre Design and Technology (0040-5477)
Related titles: Microform ed.: (from PQC); Online - full text ed.
Indexed: A07, A22, A30, A31, AA, ABS&EES, AIAP, API, ArtInd, B04, BRD, CA, IBT&D, IDP, IIPA, RASB, T02, W03, W05.
—BLDSC (8814.343000), IE, Infotrieve, Ingenta.
Published by: U S Institute for Theatre Technology, Inc., 6443 Ridings Rd, Syracuse, NY 13206-1111. Ed. David Rodger. Adv. contact Michelle L Smith TEL 800-93 US ITT. Circ: 4,500.

792 USA
T D F SIGHTLINES. Text in English. 1986. q. free to qualified personnel. **Description:** Covers matters of general theater interest. Includes news of the fund.
Published by: Theatre Development Fund, 1501 Broadway, New York, NY 10036. TEL 212-221-0885, FAX 212-768-1563. Ed. Stuart W Little. Circ: 1,800.

792.9 USA ISSN 1054-2043
PN2000
T D R. (The Drama Review) Text in English. 1955. q. USD 213 combined subscription in US & Canada to institutions (print & online eds.); USD 53 per issue in US & Canada to institutions (effective 2012). adv. bk.rev. illus. Index. 200 p./no.; back issues avail.; reprints avail. **Document type:** *Magazine, Consumer.* **Description:** Provides a forum for writing about performances and their social, economic, and political contexts, emphasizing the experimental, avant-garden, intercultural, and interdisciplinary.
Former titles (until 1988): The Drama Review (0012-5962); (until 1968): T D R (0273-4354); (until 1967): Tulane Drama Review (0886-800X); (until 1957): The Carleton Drama Review (0161-3936); (until 1956): Carleton Drama Bulletin
Related titles: Microform ed.: (from PQC); Online - full text ed.: ISSN 1531-4715. 199?. USD 187 in US & Canada to institutions (effective 2012).
Indexed: A01, A02, A03, A08, A20, A22, A25, A26, A27, ABS&EES, AES, ASCA, Acal, AmHI, ArtHuCI, B04, B14, BAS, BRD, BRI, CA, CBRI, CurCont, DIP, E01, E08, G05, G06, G07, G08, H07, H08, H09, H10, HAb, HumInd, I05, I07, IBR, IBT&D, IBZ, IDP, IIPA, L05, L06, M01, M02, MEA&I, MLA, MLA-IB, MagInd, P02, P10, P13, P48, P53, P54, PCI, PQC, RASB, RILM, S05, S08, S09, SCOPUS, T02, TOM, W03, W05, W07.
—BLDSC (3623.197000), IE, Infotrieve. **CCC.**
Published by: (New York University, Tisch School of the Arts), M I T Press, 55 Hayward St, Cambridge, MA 02142. TEL 617-253-2889, FAX 617-577-1545, journals-cs@mit.edu, http://mitpress.mit.edu. Ed. Richard Schechner.

792 USA ISSN 1948-0253
T H S NEWS. (Theatre Historical Society) Text in English. 1979. q. free to members (effective 2009). **Document type:** *Newsletter, Trade.* **Description:** Contains current news items of interest on members, theaters, and theater-related activities and events nationwide.
Formerly (until 2001): T H S Newsletter (0735-5734)
Indexed: IBT&D, T02, V03.
Published by: Theatre Historical Society of America, c/o Richard J. Sklenar, York Theatre Bldg, 152 N York St, 2nd Fl, Elmhurst, IL 60126. TEL 630-782-1800, FAX 630-782-1802, thrhistsoc@aol.com, http://www.historictheatres.org.

792 NLD ISSN 1567-8628
PN2002
T M (AMSTERDAM); tijdschrift over theater, muziek en dans. (Theatermaker) Text in Dutch. 1997. 10/yr. EUR 65; EUR 42 to students (effective 2010). adv. bk.rev.; play rev. charts; illus. **Document type:** *Magazine, Consumer.*
Formerly (until 1999): Theatermaker (1385-7754); Which was formed by the 1997 merger of: Nederlands Instituut voor de Dans. Notes (0920-2897); Toneel Teatraal (0928-5059); Which was formerly (until 1990): T T (0923-246X); (until 1981): Toneel Teatraal (0040-9170); (until 1974): Mickery Mouth en Toneel Teaatral (0301-9292); Which was formed by the 1973 merger of: Toneel Teatraal (1380-4383); Mickery Mouth (1380-4375)
Indexed: RASB.
Published by: Stichting Vakblad voor de Podiumkunst, Sarphatistraat 47-b, Amsterdam, 1018 EW, Netherlands. TEL 31-20-6249057, FAX 31-20-4218250. Ed. Constant Meijers. adv.: color page EUR 1,275, B&W page EUR 815; trim 240 x 297. Circ: 3,350.

792 028.5 USA
T Y A TODAY. (Theatre for Young Audiences) Text in English. 1985. s-a. USD 75 to individuals; USD 60 to libraries; USD 35 to students (effective 2008). adv. bk.rev.; play rev. illus. back issues avail. **Document type:** *Magazine, Trade.* **Description:** Concerned with promotion and development of the professional theatre for young audiences in America and with the international inter-change of theatre artistry and research.
Published by: International Association of Theatre for Children and Young People, United States Center, 1602 Belle View Blvd, Ste 810, Alexandria, VA 22307. FAX 703-671-0640, info@tyausa.org. Ed. Megan Alrutz. Adv. contact David Kilpatrick. page USD 450; trim 8.5 x 11. Circ: 1,000.

TACOMA REPORTER. *see* MUSIC

792 305.868 USA
TAFT AND THE UNIVERSITY OF CINCINNATI SERIES IN LATIN AMERICAN AND HISPANIC AMERICAN THEATRE. Text in English. 1992. irreg., latest vol.5, 1996. price varies. **Document type:** *Monographic series, Academic/Scholarly.*
Former titles: Taft Memorial Fund and University of Cincinnati Series in Latin American and Hispanic Theatre; Taft Memorial Fund and University of Cincinnati Series in Latin American and U S Latino Theatre (1062-5453)
Published by: Peter Lang Publishing, Inc. (Subsidiary of: Peter Lang Publishing Group), 29 Broadway, New York, NY 10006. TEL 212-647-7706, 212-647-7700, 800-770-5264, FAX 212-647-7707, customerservice@plang.com, http://www.peterlang.com. Ed. Kirsten F Nigro.

TANZ-JOURNAL. *see* DANCE

TANZSCRIPTE. *see* DANCE

TAPROOT REVIEWS. *see* LITERATURE

372.66 792 USA ISSN 1077-2561
TEACHING THEATRE. Text in English. 1989. q. USD 34 to libraries; free to members (effective 2005). back issues avail. **Document type:** *Magazine, Consumer.* **Description:** Focuses on K-12 theater education in the U.S.
Related titles: Microfilm ed.: 1989.
Indexed: E03, ERI, IBT&D, T02.
Published by: Educational Theatre Association, 2343 Auburn Ave, Cincinnati, OH 45219-2815. TEL 513-421-3900. Ed., R&P James Palmarini. Circ: 3,500 (paid).

792 BGR
TEATAR/THEATRE. Text in Bulgarian. 1946. bi-m. BGL 1.20 newsstand/cover (effective 2002). **Description:** Documents the developments in theatre arts in Bulgaria and abroad; aims to provide a kaleidoscopic view of everything in theatre through reviews, studies, comments, problem articles, thematic discussions and round tables, interviews, portraits, translations, information, and plays.
Published by: Ministerstvo na Kulturata i Turizma na Republika Bulgaria/Ministry of Culture and Tourism of the Republic of Bulgaria, Bul Al Stamboliiski, 17, Sofia, 1000, Bulgaria. TEL 359-2-881763, FAX 359-2-880347. Ed. Keva Apostolova.

792 DNK ISSN 0905-3026
PN1566
TEATER 1. Text in Danish. 1986. 5/yr. DKK 225 (effective 2010). adv. **Document type:** *Magazine, Consumer.*
Formerly (until 1989): Teater (0902-1957)
Related titles: Online - full text ed.: 2008.
Published by: Teaterforeningen Teater 1, PO Box 191, Copenhagen K, 1006, Denmark. TEL 45-33-324050, teater1@teater1.dk, http://www.teater1.dk. Ed. Rikke Rottensten. adv.: page DKK 4,000.

792 EST ISSN 0207-6535
PN2725.E8
TEATER. MUUSIKA. KINO. Text in Estonian. 1982. m. EUR 19.81 (effective 2011). **Document type:** *Magazine, Consumer.*
Related titles: Online - full text ed.
Indexed: RASB, RILM.
Published by: SA Kultuurileht, Voorimehe St 9, Tallinn, 10146, Estonia. TEL 372-6833110, FAX 372-6833111, info@kl.ee, http://www.kl.ee. Ed. Madis Kolk.

792 SWE ISSN 0347-8890
TEATERFORUM; tidskrift foer amatoerteater. Text in Swedish. 1968. 8/yr. SEK 150 (effective 1999).
Formerly (until 1974): Informationsblad fraan Teaterforum
Indexed: IBT&D.
Published by: Amatoerteaterns Riksfoerbund (ATR), Von Rosens vaeg 1 A, Fagersta, 73740, Sweden. TEL 46-223-170-10, FAX 46-223-172-66. Ed. Lena Lindstedt.

792 SWE ISSN 1101-9107
TEATERTIDNINGEN. Text in Swedish. 1977. 5/yr. SEK 215 in Scandinavia; SEK 260 in Europe; SEK 300 elsewhere (effective 2004). adv. bk.rev. back issues avail. **Document type:** *Magazine, Consumer.*
Formerly (until 1990): Nya Teatertidningen (0348-0119)
Related titles: Online - full text ed.

Address: PO Box 4066, Stockholm, 10273, Sweden. TEL 46-8-849287. Ed. Rikard Hoogland. adv.: B&W page SEK 3,800, color page SEK 4,050; 196 x 298. Circ: 1,500. **Subscr. to:** Naetverkstan Ekonomitjaenst, Fack 12034, Goeteborg 40241, Sweden. ekonomitjanst@natverkstan.net, http://www.natverkstan.net.

792 POL ISSN 0040-0769
PN2007
TEATR. Text in Polish. 1946. m. PLZ 84 domestic; PLZ 168 foreign (effective 2001). adv. bk.rev. illus. index.
Indexed: MLA-IB, RASB.
Published by: Art-Program Sp. z o.o., ul. Grochowska 170 m. 83, Warsaw, 04-357, Poland. TEL 48-22-6103461, FAX 48-22-6103461. Ed. Janusz Majcherek. Circ: 6,800.

792 RUS ISSN 0131-6885
PN2007
TEATR; zhurnal dramaturgii i teatra. Text in Russian. 1937. 10/yr. USD 128 (effective 1998). bk.rev.; dance rev.; play rev. illus.
Indexed: CDSP, RASB.
Published by: (Teatral'nyi Soyuz Rabochikh), Izdatel'stvo Izvestiya, Pushkinskaya pl 5, Moscow, 103798, Russian Federation. TEL 7-095-2099100. Ed. A Salinskii. Circ: 32,600. **Co-sponsor:** Soyuz Pisatelei.

792 USA ISSN 1535-6159
PN2720
➤ **TEATR**; Russian theatre past and present. Text in English, French, German, Russian. 2000. a. bk.rev.; play rev. 250 p./no.; reprints avail. **Document type:** *Journal, Academic/Scholarly.* **Description:** Contains articles, reviews, texts of plays and documents.
Published by: Charles Schlacks, Jr., PO Box 1256, Idyllwild, CA 92512. TEL 951-659-4641, info@schlacks.com.

792.97 POL ISSN 0239-667X
TEATR LALEK. Text in Polish. 1950. q. 48 p./no.; **Document type:** *Magazine, Consumer.*
Published by: Polski Osrodek Lalkarski Polunima, ul 1 Maja 2, Lodz, 90718, Poland. TEL 48-42-6327385, teatrlalek@wp.pl, http://polunima.republika.pl. Ed. Lucyna Kozien. Circ: 700.

792 RUS ISSN 0131-6915
PN2007
TEATRAL'NAYA ZHIZN'. Text in Russian. 1958. m. USD 84 foreign (effective 2004). adv. bk.rev. illus. index. reprints avail.
Indexed: RASB.
—East View.
Published by: (Teatral'noe Obschestvo/Theatrical Workers' Union), Izdatel'stvo Russkaya Kniga, Kisel'nyi tup 1, Moscow, 103031, Russian Federation. Ed. Oleg Pivovarov. Adv. contact Galina Homatova. Circ: 10,000. **Dist. by:** M K - Periodica, ul Gilyarovskogo 39, Moscow 129110, Russian Federation. TEL 7-095-2845008, FAX 7-095-2813798, info@periodicals.ru, http://www.mkniga.ru. **Co-sponsors:** Soyuz Pisatelei; Ministerstvo Kul'tury Rossiiskoi Federatsii.

792 ESP ISSN 2013-4444
TEATRE NACIONAL DE CATALUNYA. BUTLETI. Text in Catalan. 2000. s-a. **Document type:** *Bulletin, Consumer.*
Media: Online - full text.
Published by: Generalitat de Catalunya, Teatre Nacional de Catalunya, Placa de les Arts, 1, Barcelona, 08013, Spain. TEL 34-933-065700, FAX 34-933-065701, info@tnc.cat.

792 ESP ISSN 1132-2233
PN2008
TEATRO; revista de estudios teatrales. Text in Spanish. 1992. q. **Document type:** *Journal, Academic/Scholarly.*
Related titles: Online - full text ed.: Revista Teatro.
Indexed: A01, F03, F04, R15.
Published by: Universidad de Alcala de Henares, Aula de Estudios Escenicos y Medios Audiovisuales, Colegio Caracciolos, C. Trinidad, 5, Alcala de Henares, Madrid 28801, Spain. TEL 34-91-8832869, FAX 34-91-8832869, contacta@teatrostudio.com, http://www.uah.es/.

792 NIC
TEATRO. Text in Spanish. 1993. irreg. NIC 20.
Published by: Comedia Nacional Ediciones, CIUDAD JARDIN F, 18, Managua, Nicaragua. TEL 41268. Ed. Socorro Bonilla Castellon.

792 ARG ISSN 1514-7916
PN2309
TEATRO AL SUR. Text in Spanish. 1994. s-a. ARS 26 domestic; USD 26 Mercosur members; USD 35 elsewhere (effective 2005). **Document type:** *Journal, Academic/Scholarly.*
Address: Casilla de Correo 5238, Correo Central, Buenos Aires, 1000, Argentina. revista@teatroalsur.com.at. Ed. Halima Tahan.

792 PRT ISSN 1647-385X
▼ **TEATRO AVEIRENSE.** Text in Portuguese. 2009. q. **Document type:** *Magazine, Consumer.*
Address: Rua Belem do Para, Aveiro, 3810-066, Portugal. TEL 351-234-400920, FAX 351-234-400921.

792 ARG
TEATRO C E L C I T; revista de teatrologia, tecnicas y reflexion sobre la practica teatral iberoamericana. Text in Spanish. 1987. 2/yr. USD 50 in the Americas; USD 65 in Europe; USD 80 elsewhere. adv. bk.rev. back issues avail.
Supersedes: Teatro: Teoria y Practica
Published by: Centro Latinoamericano de Creacion e Investigacion Teatral, Bolivar 827, Buenos Aires, 1066, Argentina. TEL 54-114-3618358, FAX 54-114-3317353. Ed. Carlos A Ianni. Circ: 1,000.

792 ESP ISSN 2172-1025
TEATRO COMPLETO ESCOGIDO. Text in Spanish. 1998. irreg. **Document type:** *Monographic series, Academic/Scholarly.*
Published by: Asociacion de Autores de Teatro, Benito Gutierrez, 27 1a. Izq., Madrid, 28008, Spain. TEL 34-91-5430271, FAX 34-91-5496292, aat@aat.es, http://www.aat.es/.

792 791.43 ITA ISSN 2036-6418
TEATRO CONTEMPORANEO E CINEMA. Text in Italian. 2008. 3/yr. **Document type:** *Magazine, Consumer.*
Published by: Pagine, Via Gualtiero Serafino 8, Rome, 00136, Italy. http://www.pagine.net.

792 ARG ISSN 1851-6378
TEATRO DEL MUNDO. Text in Spanish. 1990. s-a.
Published by: Editorial Leviatan, Salta 259, Buenos Aires, 1074, Argentina. TEL 54-11-43817947, http://www.e-leviatan.com.ar/#.

IL TEATRO DI SHAKESPEARE. *see* LITERATURE

792 780 945 ITA ISSN 0394-6932
TEATRO E STORIA. Text in Italian. 1984. a. EUR 25 (effective 2010). index. back issues avail. **Document type:** *Journal, Academic/Scholarly.*
Indexed: IBR, IBT&D, IBZ, PCI.
Published by: Bulzoni Editore, Via dei Liburni 14, Rome, 00185, Italy. TEL 39-06-4455207, FAX 39-06-4450355, bulzoni@bulzoni.it, http://www.bulzoni.it. Ed. Mirella Schino.

792 DEU
TEATRO EN LATINOAMERICA/THEATER IN LATEINAMERIKA. Text in Multiple languages. 1998. irreg., latest vol.14, 2004. price varies. **Document type:** *Monographic series, Academic/Scholarly.*
Published by: Vervuert Verlag, Elisabethenstr 3-9, Frankfurt Am Main, 60594, Germany. TEL 49-69-5974617, FAX 49-69-5978743, info@iberoamericanalibros.com.

792 ITA ISSN 1122-0678
TEATRO. STUDI E TESTI. Text in Italian. 1985. irreg., latest vol.11, 2001. price varies. **Document type:** *Monographic series, Academic/Scholarly.*
Published by: Casa Editrice Leo S. Olschki, Viuzzo del Pozzetto 8, Florence, 50126, Italy. TEL 39-055-6530684, FAX 39-055-6530214, celso@olschki.it, http://www.olschki.it.

792 ARG ISSN 0328-9230
PN2451
TEATRO XXI. Text in Spanish. 1994. s-a. **Document type:** *Journal, Academic/Scholarly.*
Indexed: MLA-IB.
Published by: Grupo de Estudios de Teatro Argentino e Iberoamericano, 25 de Mayo, 221 4o. Piso, Buenos Aires, Argentina. TEL 54-11-43347512, getea@comnet.com.ar, http://www.getea-uba.com.ar/. Ed. Osvaldo Pellettieri. Circ: 600.

800 ITA ISSN 1128-7500
TEATROMESE. Text in Italian. 1977. 5/yr. free. adv. bk.rev. **Document type:** *Newsletter, Consumer.*
Formerly (until 1978): Piccolo Teatro di Milano (1128-711X)
Related titles: Online - full text ed.
Published by: Piccolo Teatro di Milano, Via Rovello, 2, Milan, MI 20121, Italy. TEL 39-2-723331, FAX 2-874836, TELEX 316279. Circ: 60,000.

792 ARG
LOS TEATROS. Text in Spanish. 1992. q. ARS 16.
Published by: Ediciones del Valle, Pasco 615, 3o B, Buenos Aires, 1219, Argentina. TEL 941-0353. Ed. Andres O Valle.

792 ROM ISSN 1220-4676
PN2844
TEATRULAZI. Text in Romanian. 1956. m. ROL 300, USD 64. adv. bk.rev.; play rev. illus.
Formerly: Teatrul (0040-0815)
Indexed: MLA-IB, RASB.
Published by: Ministerul Culturii, Piata Presi Libere 1, Sector 1, Bucharest, Romania. Ed. Dumitro Solomon.

792 FIN ISSN 1238-5913
TEATTERIKORKEAKOULU. ACTA SCENICA. Text in English, Finnish. 1995. irreg., latest vol.17, 2004. price varies. back issues avail. **Document type:** *Monographic series, Academic/Scholarly.* **Description:** Research, essays and reports on different areas of theatre, dance and performing arts.
Published by: Teatterikorkeakoulu/Theatre Academy, PO Box 163, Helsinki, 00531, Finland. TEL 358-9-431361, FAX 358-9-43136200, international@teak.fi.

792 FIN ISSN 0783-3385
TEATTERIKORKEAKOULU. JULKAISUSARJA. Text in Finnish. 1986. irreg., latest vol.37, 2001. price varies. back issues avail. **Document type:** *Monographic series.*
Formerly (until 1987): Teatterikorkeakoulun. Julkaisusarja. B (0783-2702)
Published by: Teatterikorkeakoulu/Theatre Academy, PO Box 163, Helsinki, 00531, Finland. TEL 358-9-431361, FAX 358-9-43136200, international@teak.fi.

792 BGR ISSN 0204-6253
TEATUR/THEATER. Text in Bulgarian. 1946. m. USD 65 foreign (effective 2002). play rev.
Indexed: RASB.
Published by: Ministerstvo na Kulturata, Foreign Trade Co "Hemus", 1-B Raiko Daskalov pl, Sofia, 1000, Bulgaria. TEL 359-2-871686, FAX 359-2-9803319. Ed. K Apostolova. Circ: 4,046. **Dist. by:** Sofia Books, ul Silivria 16, Sofia 1404, Bulgaria. TEL 359-2-9586257, info@sofiabooks-bg.com, http://www.sofiabooks-bg.com. **Co-sponsor:** Suiuz na Artistite.

792 USA ISSN 1053-8860
PN2091.S8
TECHNICAL BRIEF. Text in English. 1982. 3/yr. looseleaf. USD 12 to individuals; USD 18 to institutions (effective 2000). illus.; tr.lit. index. back issues avail. **Document type:** *Newsletter.* **Description:** Publishes articles by and for technical theater practitioners complete with mechanical drawings representing solutions to technical theater problems.
Indexed: IBT&D, IPP, T02.
Published by: Yale University, School of Drama, PO Box 208325, New Haven, CT 06520. TEL 203-432-9664, FAX 203-432-8336, technicalbrief@yale.edu, http://www.yale.edu/drama/publications/technicalbrief. Eds. Bronislaw Sammler, Don Harvey. R&P Laraine Sammler. Circ: 1,000 (paid).

792 ARG ISSN 1669-6301
➤ **TELONDEFONDO**; revista de teoria y critica teatral. Text in Spanish. 2005. s-a. free (effective 2011). back issues avail. **Document type:** *Journal, Academic/Scholarly.* **Description:** Intended for readers interested and/or specializing in theatrical subjects.
Media: Online - full text.
Indexed: MLA-IB.
Address: 25 de Mayo 221, Buenos Aires, 1002, Argentina. TEL 54-11-43435981, FAX 54-11-43431196, secretaria@telondefondo.org, http://www.telondefondo.org/home.php. Ed. Beatriz Trastoy.

792 ARG ISSN 1851-619X
TEMAS TEATRO. Text in Spanish. 1996. s-a.
Published by: Temas Grupo Editorial, Bernardo de Irigoyen 972 Piso 9, Buenos Aires, C1072AAT, Argentina. TEL 54-11-43074531, http://www.editorialtemas.com.ar/.

792 PRT ISSN 1647-614X
TEMPO (PORTIMAO). Text in Portuguese. 2008. 3/yr. **Document type:** *Magazine, Consumer.*
Published by: Teatro Municipal de Portimao (T E M P O), Largo 1o de Dezembro, Portimao, 8500-538, Portugal. TEL 351-282-402470, http://www.teatromunicipaldeportimao.pt.

792 ESP ISSN 1698-6369
TEORIA Y PRACTICA DEL TEATRO. Variant title: Serie Teoria y Practica del Teatro. Text in Spanish. 1991. irreg. back issues avail. **Document type:** *Monographic series, Academic/Scholarly.*
Published by: Asociacion de Directores de Escena de Espana, C Costanilla de los Angeles 13, bajo Izq, Madrid, 28013, Spain. TEL 34-91-5591246, FAX 34-91-5483012, redaccion@adeteatro.com.

792 DEU ISSN 1866-9514
TEORIA Y PRACTICA DEL TEATRO/THEORIE UND PRAXIS DES THEATERS. Text in Multiple languages. 1993. irreg., latest vol.22, 2010. price varies. **Document type:** *Monographic series, Academic/Scholarly.*
Published by: Georg Olms Verlag, Hagentorwall 7, Hildesheim, 31134, Germany. TEL 49-5121-15010, FAX 49-5121-150150, info@olms.de.

792 USA ISSN 1555-6832
PN2000
TEXAS THEATRE JOURNAL. Abbreviated title: T T J. Text in English. 2005. a. USD 10 per issue to individuals (effective 2008). back issues avail. **Document type:** *Journal, Academic/Scholarly.* **Description:** Features articles, documents and book reviews relating to theatre and performing arts, with an emphasis on theatre and performance in Texas.
Indexed: MLA-IB.
Published by: Texas Educational Theatre Association, Inc., NE Station, PO Box 15990, Austin, TX 78761.

792 USA ISSN 1054-724X
➤ **TEXT & PRESENTATION.** Text in English. 1980. a. USD 59.95 per issue (effective 2010). bk.rev. back issues avail. **Document type:** *Proceedings, Academic/Scholarly.* **Description:** Covers international drama, including emerging trends, discourse and views.
Indexed: CA, IBT&D, MLA-IB, T02.
—CCC.
Published by: (Comparative Drama Conference), McFarland & Company, Inc., PO Box 611, Jefferson, NC 28640. TEL 336-246-4460, FAX 336-246-5018, info@mcfarlandpub.com. Ed. Kiki Gounaridou.

800 830 DEU ISSN 1433-7592
THALIA GERMANICA. Text in German. 1997. irreg., latest vol.2, 2000. price varies. **Document type:** *Monographic series, Academic/Scholarly.*
Published by: Peter Lang GmbH (Subsidiary of: Peter Lang Publishing Group), Eschborner Landstr 42-50, Frankfurt Am Main, 60489, Germany. TEL 49-69-7807050, FAX 49-69-78070550, zentrale.frankfurt@peterlang.com, http://www.peterlang.com. Ed. Laurence Kitching.

792 DEU ISSN 1436-1981
THEAOMAI; Studien zu den performativen Kuensten. Text in German. 1999. irreg., latest vol.2, 2008. price varies. **Document type:** *Monographic series, Academic/Scholarly.*
Published by: Peter Lang GmbH (Subsidiary of: Peter Lang Publishing Group), Eschborner Landstr 42-50, Frankfurt Am Main, 60489, Germany. TEL 49-69-7807050, FAX 49-69-78070550, zentrale.frankfurt@peterlang.com, http://www.peterlang.com. Ed. Helga Finter.

792 DEU
THEATER. Text in German. 2008. irreg., latest vol.30, 2011. price varies. **Document type:** *Monographic series, Academic/Scholarly.*
Published by: Transcript, Muehlenstr 47, Bielefeld, 33607, Germany. TEL 49-521-63454, FAX 49-521-61040, live@transcript-verlag.de.

792 NLD ISSN 2210-5816
THEATER!. Text in Dutch. 1968. q. EUR 20; EUR 6.50 newsstand/cover (effective 2011). adv. bk.rev.; play rev. abstr.; bibl.; illus. back issues avail. **Document type:** *Magazine, Consumer.*
Former titles (until 2010): Cue (1878-9668); (until 2009): De Theater N V (1571-9286); (until 2002): N V Amateurtheater (1389-7640); (until 1998): Skript (0166-4344); Which incorporated (1976-1991): Spieltribune (0166-1884)
Published by: (Nederlandse Vereniging voor Amateurtheater), Virtumedia, Postbus 595, Zeist, 3700 AN, Netherlands. TEL 31-30-6920677, FAX 31-30-6913312, info@virtumedia.nl, http://www.virtumedia.nl. Circ: 5,000.

800 USA
THEATER (ANN ARBOR); theory/text/performance. Text in English. 1992. irreg., latest 2010. price varies. back issues avail. **Document type:** *Monographic series, Academic/Scholarly.* **Description:** Focuses on playwrights and other theater practitioners who have made their mark on the twentieth-century stage.
Published by: University of Michigan Press, 839 Greene St, Ann Arbor, MI 48104. TEL 734-764-4388, FAX 734-615-1540, umpress.title.info@umich.edu. Eds. David Krasner, Rebecca Schneider.

792 USA ISSN 0161-0775
PN2000
➤ **THEATER (DURHAM).** Text in English. 1968. 3/yr. USD 30 to individuals; USD 147 to institutions; USD 153 combined subscription to institutions (print & online eds.); USD 49 per issue to institutions (effective 2012). bk.rev.; play rev. illus. index. back issues avail.; reprint service avail. from PSC. **Document type:** *Journal, Academic/Scholarly.* **Description:** Focuses on modern and contemporary theater with an emphasis on what's new, experimental, and even radical.
Formerly (until 1977): Yale - Theatre (0044-0167)
Related titles: Microfilm ed.: (from PQC); Online - full text ed.: ISSN 1527-196X. 2000. USD 128 to institutions (effective 2012).
Indexed: A01, A02, A03, A08, A10, A20, A22, A26, A27, AmHI, ArtHuCI, CA, CurCont, E01, E08, G08, H07, H09, H10, I05, IBRH, IBT&D, IIPA, MEA&I, MLA, MLA-IB, P02, P10, P48, P53, P54, PCI, PQC, RASB, RILM, S09, SCOPUS, T02, V03, W07.
—BLDSC (8814.306000), IE, Infotrieve, Ingenta. **CCC.**

Published by: (Yale University, School of Drama), Duke University Press, 905 W Main St, Ste 18 B, Durham, NC 27701. TEL 919-688-5134, 888-651-0122, FAX 919-688-2615, 888-651-0124, subscriptions@dukeupress.edu, http://www.dukeupress.edu. Ed. Tom Sellar.

792 DEU ISSN 0040-5418
PN2004
THEATER DER ZEIT. Text in German. 1946. m. EUR 60 domestic; EUR 85 foreign; EUR 6 newsstand/cover (effective 2010). adv. bk.rev.; dance rev.; play rev. bibl.; illus. index. **Document type:** *Magazine, Consumer.* **Description:** Covers all areas of theater in Germany: dramatic art, opera, children's theater, musicals, ballet and puppet theater.
Incorporates: Theaterdienst (0323-6390)
Indexed: A20, DIP, IBR, IBZ, MLA-IB, PCI, RASB, RILM.
—BLDSC (8814.310000). **CCC.**
Published by: I.G. Theater der Zeit e.V., Klosterstr 68-70, Berlin, 10179, Germany. TEL 49-30-24722414, FAX 49-30-24722415. Adv. contact Harald Muller TEL 49-30-2423626. Circ: 5,500 (paid).

792 DEU ISSN 0040-5507
PN2004
THEATER HEUTE. Text in German. 1960. m. EUR 135 domestic; EUR 155 foreign; EUR 95 to students; EUR 9.80 newsstand/cover (effective 2010). adv. bk.rev.; dance rev.; film rev.; music rev.; play rev. illus. reprints avail. **Document type:** *Magazine, Consumer.*
Related titles: Supplement(s): Theater. ISSN 0343-527X. 196?. EUR 19.90 newsstand/cover (effective 2006).
Indexed: A20, A22, ASCA, ArtHuCI, CurCont, DIP, IBR, IBT&D, IBZ, IIPA, MLA-IB, PCI, RASB, RILM, SCOPUS, W07.
—IE, Infotrieve. **CCC.**
Published by: Friedrich Berlin Verlagsgesellschaft mbH, Knesebeckstr 59-61, Berlin, 10719, Germany. TEL 49-30-25449520, FAX 49-30-25449512, verlag@friedrichberlin.de, http://www.friedrich-berlin.de. Ed. Franz Wille. Adv. contact Marion Schamuthe TEL 49-30-25449510. Circ: 14,500 (controlled).

792 AUT
THEATER IN DER JOSEFSTADT. SPIELPLAN. Text in German. 1953. m. adv. illus. 14 p./no.; **Document type:** *Journal, Consumer.*
Formerly: Neue Blaetter des Theaters in der Josefstadt (0028-3096)
Published by: Theater in der Josefstadt, Direktion, Josefstaedterstrasse 26, Vienna, W 1082, Austria. TEL 43-1-42700212, FAX 43-1-4270060, office@josefstadt.org, http://www.josefstadt.org. Ed. Petra Gruber. Adv. contact Christiane Huemer-Strobele. Circ: 20,000.

792 AUT
THEATER IN GRAZ. Text in German. 1952. w. adv. bk.rev.; play rev. illus. **Document type:** *Journal, Consumer.*
Formerly: Theaternachrichten (0040-5450)
Published by: Vereinigte Buehnen Graz, Kaiser-Josef-Platz 10, Graz, St 8010, Austria. TEL 43-316-8008, info@buehnen-graz.com, http://www.buehnen-graz.com. Ed. Gernot Schoeppl. Circ: 6,000.

792 CHE
THEATER-KURIER. Text in German. m. membership. **Document type:** *Bulletin.*
Published by: (Theatergemeinde Baden), Buchdruckerei AG Baden, Baden, 5401, Switzerland. TEL 056-225504. Circ: 3,000.

792 DEU ISSN 0040-5442
THEATER-RUNDSCHAU. Text in German. 1955. m. EUR 3.85 newsstand/cover (effective 2002). adv. bk.rev. bibl.; illus. **Document type:** *Magazine, Consumer.*
Published by: (Bund der Theatergemeinden e.V.), Theater Rundschau Verlag GmbH, Bonner Talweg 10, Bonn, 53113, Germany. TEL 49-228-915031, FAX 49-228-9150345. Ed., Adv. contact Roswitha Kleinwaechter. page EUR 3,950. Circ: 46,000 (paid and controlled).

792 NLD ISSN 1871-3009
THEATER TOPICS. Text in Dutch, English. 2005. irreg., latest vol.3, 2007. price varies. **Document type:** *Monographic series, Academic/Scholarly.*
Published by: Amsterdam University Press, Herengracht 221, Amsterdam, 1016 BG, Netherlands. TEL 31-20-4200050, FAX 31-20-4203214, info@aup.nl, http://www.aup.nl.

792 CHE ISSN 0378-6935
THEATER-ZYTIG; Magazin fuer das Volkstheater in der Schweiz. Text in French. 1972. 11/yr. CHF 55; CHF 65 in Europe; CHF 70 overseas (effective 1999). adv. bk.rev. bibl.; illus. **Document type:** *Trade.* **Description:** Information and calendar of Swiss amateur and national theatre.
Former titles (until 1981): Dialog; (until 1973): Laientheater
—CCC.
Published by: (Zentralverband Schweizer Volkstheater), Sauerlaender AG, Laurenzenvorstadt 89, Aarau, 5001, Switzerland. FAX 41-62-8245780. Ed. Hannes Zaugg Graf. adv.: B&W page CHF 615; trim 250 x 192. Circ: 5,000.

792 DEU
DER THEATERBESUCHER. Text in German. 5/yr. adv. **Document type:** *Magazine, Consumer.*
Published by: (Volksbuehne Karlsruhe e.V.), Druck und Verlagsgesellschaft Suedwest mbH Druckhaus Karlsruhe, Ostring 6, Karlsruhe, 76131, Germany. TEL 49-721-62830, FAX 49-721-628310, dhk@druckhaus-karlsruhe.de, http://www.druckhaus-karlsruhe.de. Ed. Michael Bender. Adv. contact Silke Klass. Circ: 2,400 (controlled).

792 AUT
THEATERMAGAZIN. Text in German. 1990. m. **Document type:** *Magazine, Trade.* **Description:** Contains short essays on opera and theater productions.
Published by: Vereinigte Buehnen Graz, Kaiser-Josef-Platz 10, Graz, St 8010, Austria. TEL 43-316-80081115, FAX 43-316-8008585, info@buehnen-graz.com, http://www.buehnen-graz.com. Pub. Gerhard Brunner. R&P Johannes Frankfurter. Adv. contact Zoltan Galamb. Circ: 10,000 (paid).

792 DEU
THEATERPAEDAGOGISCHE BIBLIOTHEK. Text in German. 1983. irreg., latest vol.8, 1993. **Document type:** *Monographic series.*
Published by: Florian Noetzel Verlag, Heinrichshofen Buecher, Holtermannstr 32, Wilhelmshaven, 26384, Germany. Eds. Georg Immelmann, Rudolf Liechtenhan. **Dist. in U.S. by:** C. F. Peters Corporation, 373 Park Ave S, New York, NY 10016.

800 DEU ISSN 1863-8406
THEATERTEXTE. Text in German. 1998. irreg., latest vol.24, 2010. price varies. **Document type:** *Monographic series, Academic/Scholarly.*
Published by: Wehrhahn Verlag, Am Mittelfelde 1, Hannover, 30519, Germany. TEL 49-511-8988906, FAX 49-511-8988245, info@wehrhahn-verlag.de.

792 DEU
THEATERWISSENSCHAFT. Text in German. 2003. irreg., latest vol.17, 2010. price varies. **Document type:** *Monographic series, Academic/Scholarly.*
Published by: Herbert Utz Verlag GmbH, Adalbertstr 57, Munich, 80799, Germany. TEL 49-89-27779100, FAX 49-89-27779101, utz@utzverlag.com. Eds. Juergen Schlaeder, Michael Gissenwehrer.

792 GBR
THEATERWORLD INTERNET MAGAZINE. Text in English. 1996. w. free (effective 2009). back issues avail. **Document type:** *Magazine, Consumer.*
Media: Online - full content.
Published by: Graham Powner gpowner@aol.com. Ed., Pub. Graham Powner.

792 DEU
THEATERZEITUNG. Text in German. 1988. m. adv. play rev. illus. back issues avail. **Document type:** *Newsletter.*
Formerly (until 1992): Thema
Published by: Theater und Philharmonie Essen GmbH, Opernplatz 10, Essen, 45128, Germany. TEL 49-201-8122-0, FAX 49-201-8122-211. Ed. Andreas Wendholz. Adv. contact Blumentrat. Circ: 185,000.

792 FRA ISSN 1772-6662
THEATRAL. Text in French. 2003. bi-m. EUR 24.90 domestic to individuals; EUR 31.80 in the European Union to individuals; EUR 32.40 in Africa to individuals; EUR 34.80 elsewhere to individuals; EUR 22.90 domestic Theater Professionals; EUR 18.90 domestic to students (effective 2009). back issues avail. **Document type:** *Magazine, Consumer.*
Published by: Coulisses Editions, 4 Rue Armand Moisant, Paris, 75015, France.

792 CZE ISSN 1803-845X
PN2859.C9
➤ **THEATRALIA.** Text in Czech, Slovak, English, German. 1998. s-a. price varies. **Document type:** *Journal, Academic/Scholarly.* **Description:** Specializes is in theater history and theory.
Former titles (until 2009): Masarykova Univerzita. Filozoficka Fakulta. Sbornik Praci. Q: Rada Teatrologicka (1214-0406); (until 2002): Masarykova Univerzita. Filozoficka Fakulta. Sbornik Praci. Q: Rada Teatrologicka a Filmologicka (1212-3358)
Published by: Masarykova Univerzita, Filozoficka Fakulta/Masaryk University, Faculty of Arts, Arna Novaka 1, Brno, 60200, Czech Republic. TEL 420-549-491111, FAX 420-549-491520, podatelna@phil.muni.cz. Ed. Jitka Sotkovska.

792 DEU ISSN 1617-2604
THEATRALITAET. Text in German. 2000. irreg., latest vol.11, 2010. price varies. **Document type:** *Monographic series, Academic/Scholarly.* **Description:** Provides research and insight into the cultural and social aspects of theater.
Published by: A. Francke Verlag GmbH, Dischinger Weg 5, Tuebingen, 72070, Germany. TEL 49-7071-97970, FAX 49-7071-979711, info@francke.de, http://www.francke.de.

792 USA
THEATRE; theory-practice-performance. Text in English. 2002. irreg., latest 2009. price varies. back issues avail. **Document type:** *Monographic series.*
Published by: Palgrave Macmillan (Subsidiary of: Macmillan Publishers Ltd.), 175 Fifth Ave, New York, NY 10010. TEL 212-982-3900, 800-221-7945, FAX 212-982-5562, subscriptions@palgrave.com, http://us.macmillan.com/palgrave.aspx.

792 CAN ISSN 0705-0453
THEATRE. Text in English. 1976. bi-m.
Formerly: Theatre du Trident (0705-0445)
Published by: Theatre du Trident, 269 Bd Rene-Levesques Est, Quebec, PQ G1R 2B3, Canada. TEL 418-643-5873, FAX 418- 646-5451, info@letrident.com, http://www.letrident.com.

792 USA
THEATRE. Text in English. 1977. 8/yr. USD 12.
Indexed: RASB.
Address: 41 W 72nd St, Apt 14G, New York, NY 10023. TEL 212-221-6078. Eds. Debbi Wasserman, Ira J Bilowit. Circ: 10,000.

842.008 FRA ISSN 2104-6840
THEATRE (PARIS, 2005). Text in French. 2005. irreg. **Document type:** *Monographic series, Consumer.*
Formerly (until 2008): Collection L'Oeil du Souffleur (1775-1152)
Published by: L' Oeil du Souffleur, 12 Rue Lamartine, Paris, 75009, France. TEL 33-6-16011092, oeildusouffleur@hotmail.com, http://www.oeildusouffleur.com.

792 GBR ISSN 1753-3058
THEATRE AND CONSCIOUSNESS. Text in English. 2007. irreg., latest 2008. price varies. back issues avail. **Document type:** *Monographic series, Trade.*
Related titles: Online - full text ed.: ISSN 2043-7773.
Published by: Intellect Ltd., The Mill, Parnall Rd, Fishponds, Bristol, BS16 3JG, United Kingdom. TEL 44-117-9589910, FAX 44-117-9589911, info@intellectbooks.com.

792 AUS ISSN 1837-8390
▼ **THEATRE & Z'ARTS.** Text in English. 2010. m. AUD 72 (effective 2011). back issues avail. **Document type:** *Magazine, Consumer.*
Published by: T A Z Entertainment, PO Box 4072, Swan View, W.A. 6056, Australia. TEL 61-8-92553336, FAX 61-8-92553395, taz@tazentertainment.com.au.

792 USA ISSN 0082-3821
PN2012
➤ **THEATRE ANNUAL;** a journal of performance studies. Text in English. 1942. a. USD 10 per issue domestic to institutions; USD 12 per issue foreign to institutions (effective 2011). back issues avail. **Document type:** *Journal, Academic/Scholarly.* **Description:** Publishes articles on the history and ethnography of performance, drawing from such areas as theatre studies, popular culture, music, anthropology, communication, dance, philosophy, folklore, history, and performance studies across disciplinary lines.
Related titles: Online - full text ed.
Indexed: A22, AES, AIAP, CA, IBT&D, IIPA, MLA, MLA-IB, PCI, T02.
—BLDSC (8814.335000), IE, Ingenta.
Published by: College of William and Mary, Department of Theatre, Speech & Dance, PO Box 8795, Williamsburg, VA 23187. TEL 757-221-4000, http://www.wm.edu/as/tsd/index.php. Ed. Dorothy Chansky.

792 ISR ISSN 2076-667X
▼ ➤ **THEATRE ARTS JOURNAL;** studies in scenography and performance. Short title: T A J. Text in English. 2009. s-a. **Document type:** *Journal, Academic/Scholarly.*
Media: Online - full text.
Indexed: MLA-IB.
Published by: Tel Aviv University, Morris E. Curiel Institute for European Studies, PO Box 1157, Ramat-Hasharon, 47111, Israel. Ed. Irene Eynat-Confino.

792 USA ISSN 1547-4607
PN2275.C3 CODEN: AICNE9
THEATRE BAY AREA. Text in English. 1976. m. USD 65 to individual members (effective 2008). adv. bk.rev. back issues avail. **Document type:** *Directory, Trade.* **Description:** Provides news, audition notices, job opportunities and additional trade information for theatre professionals in the Bay Area. Includes playbills and essays.
Formerly (until 2004): Callboard (San Francisco) (1064-0703)
Related titles: Online - full text ed.
Indexed: IBT&D.
Address: 870 Market St, Ste 375, San Francisco, CA 94102. TEL 415-430-1140, tba@theatrebayarea.org. Ed., R&P Belinda Taylor. Adv. contact Russell Blackwood. Circ: 5,000 (paid).

792 GBR ISSN 2042-6089
THEATRE BUSINESS. Text in English. 1935. q. GBP 14 to non-members; free to members (effective 2010). adv. bk.rev.; play rev. illus. back issues avail. **Document type:** *Magazine, Trade.* **Description:** Provides a range of useful advice and information for amateur societies and enthusiasts, as well as free listings of performances in the National Theatre Diary, and details of shows released or restricted for amateurs.
Former titles (until 2009): N O D A National News (1475-3812); (until 1993): N O D A News; (until 19??): N O D A Bulletin (0027-6863)
Published by: National Operatic and Dramatic Association, 58-60 Lincoln Rd, Peterborough, PE1 2RZ, United Kingdom. TEL 44-1733-865790, FAX 44-1733-319506, info@noda.org.uk, http://www.noda.org.uk.

792 GBR ISSN 1944-3927
PN1580
▼ ➤ **THEATRE, DANCE AND PERFORMANCE TRAINING.** Text in English. 2010. 2/yr. GBP 147 combined subscription in United Kingdom to institutions (print & online eds.); EUR 195, USD 244 combined subscription to institutions (print & online eds.) (effective 2012). **Document type:** *Journal, Academic/Scholarly.* **Description:** Dedicated to revealing the vital and diverse processes of training and their relationship to performance making both past and present, a diversity reflected in the journal's international scope and interdisciplinary form and focus.
Related titles: Online - full text ed.: ISSN 1944-3919. GBP 133 in United Kingdom to institutions; EUR 176, USD 220 to institutions (effective 2012).
Indexed: IBT&D, T02.
—CCC.
Published by: Routledge (Subsidiary of: Taylor & Francis Group), 4 Park Sq, Milton Park, Abingdon, Oxon OX14 4RN, United Kingdom. TEL 44-20-7017-6000, FAX 44-20-7017-6336, info@routledge.co.uk. Eds. Jonathan Pitches, Simon Murray.

842 FRA ISSN 0151-5713
THEATRE D'AUJOURD'HUI. Text in French. 1976. irreg. price varies.
Published by: Editions Klincksieck, 95 Bd Raspail, Paris, 75006, France. TEL 33-1-43544757, FAX 33-1-43544562.

792 USA ISSN 0271-3136
PN2289
THEATRE DIRECTORY; the annual contact resource of theatres and related organizations. Text in English. 1972. a. USD 11.95 (effective 2001). **Document type:** *Directory, Trade.*
Published by: Theatre Communications Group, Inc., 355 Lexington Ave, New York, NY 10017. TEL 212-697-5230, FAX 212-983-4847, tcg@tcg.org, http://www.tcg.org. Ed., R&P Kathy Sova. Pub. Terence Nemeth. Circ: 5,000.

792 POL ISSN 0040-5493
PN2859.P6
THEATRE EN POLOGNE/THEATRE IN POLAND; revue trimestrielle de centre polonais de l'Institut International du Theatre. Text in English, French. 1958. q. PLZ 42 domestic; USD 30 foreign (effective 2002). adv. bk.rev.; play rev. abstr.; bibl.; illus.; tr.lit. index. 60 p./no. 3 cols./p.; back issues avail. **Document type:** *Bulletin, Consumer.*
Indexed: A20, IBT&D, RASB.
Published by: Miedzynarodowy Instytut Teatralny, Polski Osrodek/International Theatre Institute, Polish Center, Pl Pilsudskiego 9, Warsaw, 00078, Poland. TEL 48-22-8261771. Ed., Adv. contact Elzbieta Wysinska. page USD 500. Circ: 1,050.

792.02 FRA ISSN 0398-0049
THEATRE ET ANIMATION; revue trimestrielle des spectacles non-professionnels et des techniques d'expression et d'animation. Text in French. 1976. q. play rev. 24 p./no.; **Document type:** *Magazine.* **Description:** Presents articles reviewing non-professional theater and shows, techniques of self-expression, animation and playwriting.
Incorporating: Nos Spectacles (0398-0057); Theatre Amateur (0029-3741); Theatre et Spectacles Non Professionnels, Techniques d'Expression et d'Animation
Published by: Federation Nationale des Compagnies de Theatre et d'Animation, 12 rue de la Chaussee d'Antin, Paris, 75009, France. FAX 33-1-47701700. Ed. Patrick Schoenstein.

792 791.43 FRA ISSN 1952-0905
THEATRE ET CINEMA. Text in French. 2006. irreg. back issues avail. **Document type:** *Monographic series, Consumer.*
Published by: Editions L' Entretemps, Domaine de Lafeuillade, 264 Rue du Capitaine Pierre Pontal, Montpellier, 34000, France. TEL 33-4-99530975, FAX 33-4-99533198, info.entretemps@wanadoo.fr, http://www.lekti-ecriture.com/editeurs/-L-Entretemps-.html.

840 ITA ISSN 1122-066X
THEATRE FRANCAIS DE LA RENAISSANCE; deuxieme serie. Text in French. 1986; N.S. 1999 (2nd). irreg., latest vol.2, 2000. price varies. **Document type:** *Monographic series, Academic/Scholarly.*

Published by: Casa Editrice Leo S. Olschki, Viuzzo del Pozzetto 8, Florence, 50126, Italy. TEL 39-055-6530684, FAX 39-055-6530214, celso@olschki.it, http://www.olschki.it.

THEATRE HISTORICAL SOCIETY. ANNUAL. *see* ARCHITECTURE

792 GBR ISSN 0967-019X
PN2596.L6
THEATRE INDEX (YEAR). Text in English. 1981. a. free with subscr. to Theatre Record. adv. **Document type:** *Directory.* **Description:** Annual critical review, with name index to who did what in the year's London productions.
Formerly (until 1992): London Theatre Index (0263-2322)
Related titles: CD-ROM ed.: GBP 1,000, USD 2,000 (effective 2000).
Published by: Theatre Index, 131 Sherringham Ave, London, N17 9RU, United Kingdom. TEL 44-20-88083656, FAX 44-20-83500211, editor@theatrerecord.demon.uk, http://www.theatrerecord.org.

792 USA ISSN 0192-2882
PN3171
➤ **THEATRE JOURNAL (BALTIMORE).** Text in English. 1949. q. USD 148 to institutions (print or online ed.); USD 207.20 combined subscription to institutions (print & online eds.); USD 44 per issue to institutions (effective 2011). adv. bk.rev.; play rev. bibl.; illus. 152 p./no.; back issues avail.; reprint service avail. from PSC. **Document type:** *Journal, Academic/Scholarly.* **Description:** Features social and historical studies, production reviews, and theoretical inquiries that analyze dramatic texts and production.
Formerly (until 1979): Educational Theatre Journal (0013-1989)
Related titles: Microfiche ed.: (from PQC); Online - full text ed.: ISSN 1086-332X. 1979.
Indexed: A01, A02, A03, A08, A20, A22, A25, A26, A27, ABS&EES, AES, AIAP, ASCA, AmHI, ArtHuCI, B04, B14, BAS, BRD, BRI, CA, CBRI, ChPerI, CurCont, DIP, E01, E06, E08, G08, G10, H07, H08, H09, H10, HAb, HumInd, I05, IBR, IBT&D, IBZ, IIPA, M01, M02, MLA-IB, P02, P10, P13, P48, P53, P54, PCI, PQC, RASB, RILM, S07, S08, S09, SCOPUS, T02, W03, W07, W09.
—BLDSC (8814.347500), IE, Infotrieve, Ingenta. **CCC.**
Published by: (Association for Theatre in Higher Education), The Johns Hopkins University Press, 2715 N Charles St, Baltimore, MD 21218. TEL 410-516-6900, FAX 410-516-6968, bjs@press.jhu.edu. Ed. Catherine A Schuler. Pub. William M Breichner. Circ: 1,919. **Subscr. to:** PO Box 19966, Baltimore, MD 21211. TEL 410-516-6987, 800-548-1784, FAX 410-516-3866, jrnlcirc@press.jhu.edu.

792 GBR ISSN 0040-5523
PN2001
➤ **THEATRE NOTEBOOK**; a journal of the history and technique of the British theatre. Text in English. 1946. 3/yr. GBP 20 domestic to non-members; GBP 25 foreign to non-members; free to members (effective 2009). adv. bk.rev. illus. index, cum.index: vols. 1-25, 26-40. back issues avail.; reprints avail. **Document type:** *Journal, Academic/Scholarly.*
Related titles: Online - full text ed.
Indexed: A01, A02, A03, A08, A20, A22, A25, A26, AES, ASCA, AmHI, ArtHuCI, B04, BRD, BrHumI, CA, CurCont, DIP, E08, G08, H07, H08, H09, H10, H14, HAb, HumInd, I05, IBR, IBT&D, IBZ, IIPA, L05, L06, MLA, MLA-IB, P10, P48, P53, P54, PCI, PQC, RASB, S07, S08, S09, SCOPUS, T02, W03, W05, W07.
—BLDSC (8814.350000), IE, Infotrieve, Ingenta. **CCC.**
Published by: Society for Theatre Research, The Secretary, PO Box 53971, London, SW15 6UL, United Kingdom. contact@str.org.uk. Ed. Gabriel Egan.

792 USA
THEATRE PUBLICATIONS (LAS VEGAS); program for the performing arts since 1932. Text in English. 2007. m. free. adv. **Document type:** *Magazine, Consumer.* **Description:** Provides the primary program distributed at Stomp Out Loud at the Planet Hollywood in Las Vegas. Serves the audience with all show information to educate and enhance their experience, complete with performer bios and performace highlights.
Published by: Theatre Publications, Inc., 3485 Victor St, Santa Clara, CA 95054. TEL 408-748-1600, FAX 408-748-1122, info@theatrepublications.com, http://www.theatrepublications.com/. Adv. contact Gail Pisani. color page USD 3,600; trim 5.375 x 8.25. Circ: 48,000 (free).

792 070 GBR ISSN 0962-1792
PN2596.L6
THEATRE RECORD. Text in English. 1981. bi-w. GBP 150 domestic; GBP 180 foreign (effective 2009). adv. bk.rev.; play rev. illus. index. back issues avail.; reprints avail. **Document type:** *Magazine, Consumer.* **Description:** Provides unabridged critical reviews and cast lists of all London and most new British theatre.
Formerly (until 1991): London Theatre Record (0261-5282)
Related titles: CD-ROM ed.
Indexed: A22, IBT&D, IIPA, RASB, T02.
—IE, Infotrieve.
Address: 131 Sherringham Ave, London, N17 9RU, United Kingdom. TEL 44-20-88083656, FAX 44-20-83500211. Ed., Pub. Ian Shuttleworth.

792 CAN ISSN 1196-1198
PN2009
➤ **THEATRE RESEARCH IN CANADA/RECHERCHES THEATRALES AU CANADA.** Text in English, French. 1980. s-a. CAD 25 domestic to individuals; CAD 32 in United States to individuals; CAD 35 elsewhere to individuals; CAD 32 domestic to institutions; CAD 39 in United States to institutions; CAD 42 elsewhere to institutions (effective 2007). bk.rev. illus. reprints avail. **Document type:** *Journal, Academic/Scholarly.*
Formerly (until vol.13): Theatre History in Canada (0226-5761)
Related titles: Microfiche ed.: (from MML); Microform ed.: (from MML); Online - full text ed.
Indexed: A01, A02, A03, A08, A20, A26, ASCA, ArtHuCI, C03, CA, CBCARef, CBPI, CLitI, CPerI, CurCont, E08, G08, I05, IBT&D, IIPA, MLA-IB, P48, PQC, RASB, S09, SCOPUS, T02, W07.
—CCC.
Published by: University of Toronto, Graduate Centre for Study of Drama, 214 College St, Toronto, ON M5T 2Z9, Canada. TEL 416-978-7984, FAX 416-971-1378, trican@chass.utoronto.ca. Ed. Bruce Barton. R&P Richard Plant. Circ: 490.

792 GBR ISSN 0307-8833
PN2001
➤ **THEATRE RESEARCH INTERNATIONAL.** Text in English; Summaries in French. 1975. 3/yr. GBP 158, USD 265 to institutions; GBP 163, USD 276 combined subscription to institutions (print & online eds.) (effective 2012). adv. bk.rev. bibl.; illus. index. back issues avail.; reprints avail. **Document type:** *Journal, Academic/Scholarly.* **Description:** Presents history and criticism of drama conceived and the art of the theatre, providing both a medium of communication for scholars and a service to students of art, architecture, design, music and drama literature.
Formed by the merger of: Theatre Research (0040-5566); New Theatre Magazine (0028-6893)
Related titles: Microform ed.: (from PQC); Online - full text ed.: ISSN 1474-0672. GBP 147, USD 249 to institutions (effective 2012).
Indexed: A01, A02, A03, A08, A20, A22, A25, A26, A27, ASCA, AmH&L, AmHI, ArtHuCI, B04, BRD, BrHumI, CA, CurCont, DIP, E01, E08, G08, H07, H08, H09, H10, HAb, HistAb, HumInd, I05, IBR, IBRH, IBT&D, IBZ, IDP, IIPA, LIFT, M01, M02, MEA&I, MLA, MLA-IB, P02, P10, P48, P53, P54, PCI, PQC, RASB, RILM, S07, S08, S09, SCOPUS, T02, W03, W07.
—BLDSC (8814.370300), IE, Infotrieve, Ingenta. **CCC.**
Published by: (International Federation for Theatre Research), Cambridge University Press, The Edinburgh Bldg, Shaftesbury Rd, Cambridge, CB2 8RU, United Kingdom. TEL 44-1223-312393, FAX 44-1223-315052, journals@cambridge.org, http://www.cambridge.org/uk. Ed. Freddie Rokem. Adv. contact Rebecca Roberts TEL 44-1223-325083. page GBP 440, page USD 835. Circ: 1,100. **Subscr. addr. in N America:** Cambridge University Press, 32 Ave of the Americas, New York, NY 10013. TEL 212-337-5000, FAX 212-691-3239, journals_subscriptions@cup.org

792 GBR ISSN 0040-5574
PN2000
➤ **THEATRE SURVEY.** Text in English. 1956. s-a. GBP 104, USD 172 to institutions; GBP 114, USD 187 combined subscription to institutions (print & online eds.) (effective 2012). adv. bk.rev. illus. back issues avail.; reprint service avail. from PSC. **Document type:** *Journal, Academic/Scholarly.* **Description:** Provides rigorous historical and theoretical studies of performance across all periods.
Related titles: Microform ed.: (from PQC); Online - full text ed.: ISSN 1475-4533. GBP 97, USD 161 to institutions (effective 2012).
Indexed: A01, A02, A03, A08, A20, A22, A26, A27, ABS&EES, AES, ASCA, AmH&L, AmHI, ArtHuCI, B04, BRD, CA, ChPerI, CurCont, E01, E08, G08, H07, H08, H09, H10, HAb, HistAb, HumInd, I05, IBT&D, IDP, IIPA, M01, M02, MLA, MLA-IB, P02, P10, P30, P48, P53, P54, PCI, PQC, RASB, RILM, S07, S09, SCOPUS, T02, W03, W05, W07.
—IE, Infotrieve, Ingenta. **CCC.**
Published by: (American Society for Theatre Research USA), Cambridge University Press, The Edinburgh Bldg, Shaftesbury Rd, Cambridge, CB2 8RU, United Kingdom. TEL 44-1223-312393, FAX 44-1223-315052, journals@cambridge.org, http://www.cambridge.org/uk. Ed. Rosemarie K Bank. R&P Linda Nicol TEL 44-1223-325702. Adv. contact Rebecca Roberts TEL 44-1223-325083. page GBP 440, page USD 835. Circ: 1,200. **Subscr. addr. in N America:** Cambridge University Press, 32 Ave of the Americas, New York, NY 10013. TEL 212-337-5000, FAX 212-691-3239, journals_subscriptions@cup.org

792 USA ISSN 1065-4917
PN2018
THEATRE SYMPOSIUM. Text in English. 1993. a. USD 15 per issue to individuals; USD 30 per issue to institutions; free to members (effective 2010). back issues avail.; reprint service avail. from PSC. **Document type:** *Journal, Academic/Scholarly.* **Description:** Publishes scholarly work in theatre studies resulting from a single-topic meeting held on a southeastern university campus each spring.
Indexed: A26, AmHI, B04, BRD, CA, DIP, E08, H07, H08, HAb, HumInd, I05, IBR, IBT&D, IBZ, IIPA, MLA-IB, S09, T02, W03, W05.
—CCC.
Published by: (Southeastern Theatre Conference, Inc.), University of Alabama Press, PO Box 870380, Tuscaloosa, AL 35487. TEL 205-348-6010, FAX 205-348-9201, Help.Desk@ua.edu. Eds. J K Curry TEL 336-758-3941, Daniel Waterman TEL 205-348-5538.

792 USA ISSN 1054-8378
PN2000
➤ **THEATRE TOPICS.** Text in English. 1991. s-a. USD 78 to institutions (print or online ed.); USD 109.20 combined subscription to institutions (print & online eds.); USD 47 per issue to institutions (effective 2011). adv. illus. 116 p./no.; back issues avail.; reprint service avail. from PSC. **Document type:** *Journal, Academic/Scholarly.* **Description:** Addresses the concerns of scholars and artists in the areas of performance studies, dramaturgy, and theatre pedagogy.
Related titles: Online - full text ed.: ISSN 1086-3346. 1996.
Indexed: A01, A03, A08, A22, A27, AmHI, B04, BEL&L, BRD, CA, DIP, E01, E02, E03, ERI, EdA, EdI, H07, IBR, IBT&D, IBZ, IIPA, MLA-IB, P10, P18, P48, P53, P54, PCI, PQC, T02, W03.
—BLDSC (8814.376800), IE, Infotrieve, Ingenta. **CCC.**
Published by: (Association for Theatre in Higher Education), The Johns Hopkins University Press, 2715 N Charles St, Baltimore, MD 21218. TEL 410-516-6900, FAX 410-516-6968, bjs@press.jhu.edu. Ed. Kanta Kochhar-Lindgren. Pub. William M Breichner. Circ: 1,405. **Subscr. to:** PO Box 19966, Baltimore, MD 21211. TEL 410-516-6987, 800-548-1784, FAX 410-516-3866, jrnlcirc@press.jhu.edu.

792.0973 USA ISSN 1088-4564
PN2277.N5
THEATRE WORLD. Variant title: John Willis Theatre World. Text in English. 1945. a. USD 49.99 per issue (effective 2011). **Document type:** *Monographic series, Trade.* **Description:** Provides cast lists and production information for professional theatre in the US and Canada. Includes over 1000 pictures.
Former titles (until 1981): John Willis' Theatre World (1088-4556); (until 1972): Theatre World; (until 1966): Daniel Blum's Theatre World; (until 1951): Theatre World (0082-3856)
Indexed: IBT&D, T02.
Published by: Applause Theatre & Cinema Books, 118 E 30th St, New York, NY 10016. TEL 212-532-5525, FAX 646-562-5852, info@halleonardbooks.com. Ed. Ben Hodges.

792 USA ISSN 1060-5320
PN2000
THEATREFORUM; an international journal of innovative performance. Text in English. 1992. s-a. USD 25, GBP 16 domestic to individuals; USD 31 foreign to individuals; USD 50 domestic to institutions; USD 56 foreign to institutions (effective 2010). adv. illus. back issues avail.; reprints avail. **Document type:** *Journal, Academic/Scholarly.* **Description:** Documents and discusses the work of innovative theatre artists in Africa, Asia, Australia, Europe, and the Americas with a focus on new performance works that reflect contemporary sensibilities and articulate new concepts and forms.
Related titles: Online - full text ed.
Indexed: A01, A03, A08, A10, A27, AmHI, CA, H07, IBT&D, IIPA, MLA-IB, P10, P48, P53, P54, PQC, T02, V03.
—IE, Ingenta. **CCC.**
Published by: University of California, San Diego, Theatre Department, 9500 Gilman Dr, La Jolla, CA 92093. TEL 858-822-2179, FAX 858-534-1080, tfbiz@ucsd.edu, http://theatre.ucsd.edu/.

792 CAN
THEATRES; New York, London, Toronto & International. Text in English. q. **Document type:** *Journal, Consumer.*
Media: Online - full content.
Published by: Dear Friends, 811-85 The Esplanade, Toronto, ON M5E 1Y8, Canada. Ed. Clair Sedore.

792 DEU ISSN 0934-6252
THEATRON; Studien zur Geschichte und Theorie der dramatischen Kuenste. Text in German. 1983. irreg., latest vol.57, 2010. price varies. **Document type:** *Monographic series, Academic/Scholarly.*
Indexed: CMCI.
Published by: Max Niemeyer Verlag GmbH (Subsidiary of: Walter de Gruyter GmbH & Co. KG), Pfrondorfer Str 6, Tuebingen, 72074, Germany. TEL 49-7071-98940, FAX 49-7071-989450, info@niemeyer.de, http://www.niemeyer.de. Eds. Andreas Hoefele, Christopher B Balme, Dieter Borchmeyer, Hans-Peter Bayerdoerfer.

792 NLD ISSN 1871-8736
THEMES IN THEATRE; collective approaches to theatre and performance. Text in English. 2004. irreg., latest vol.3, 2007. price varies. **Document type:** *Monographic series, Academic/Scholarly.*
Related titles: Online - full text ed.: ISSN 1879-6060.
Indexed: IBT&D, T02.
Published by: Editions Rodopi B.V., Tijnmuiden 7, Amsterdam, 1046 AK, Netherlands. TEL 31-20-6114821, FAX 31-20-4472979, info@rodopi.nl. Ed. Dr. Peter G F Eversmann.

792 BOL ISSN 1609-6819
EL TONTO DEL PUEBLO; revista de artes escenicas de teatro de los Andes. Text in Spanish. 1995. s-a. back issues avail.
Media: Online - full text.
Published by: Teatro de los Andes, Casilla No. 685, Sucre, Bolivia. TEL 591-464-80232, FAX 591-464-60121, losandes@pelicano.cnb.net. Ed. Jose Antonio Quiroga.

792 USA
TOP PRODUCERS & DIRECTORS. Text in English. bi-w. USD 69 (effective 2000).
Published by: The John King Network, 244 Madison Ave, Ste 393, New York, NY 10016. TEL 212-969-8715, 212-969-8715.

792.3 GBR ISSN 0960-6106
TOTAL THEATRE. Text in English. 1989. q. GBP 250 combined subscription domestic to institutions (print & online eds.); GBP 300 combined subscription foreign to institutions (print & online eds.); free to members (effective 2009). adv. back issues avail. **Document type:** *Magazine, Consumer.* **Description:** Promotes innovative contemporary theatre and physical/visual performance.
Related titles: Online - full text ed.: (from IngentaConnect).
—Ingenta.
Address: c/o The World Famous Fireworkers Ltd, Boundary Farm, Maidstone Rd, Hadlow, Kent TN11 0JH, United Kingdom. TEL 44-7813-936362, info@totaltheatre.org.uk%20. Ed. Dorothy Max Prior. adv.: page GBP 450; 215 x 310.

792 MEX ISSN 0187-4160
TRAMOYA; cuaderno de teatro. Text in Spanish. 1975. q. USD 75 (effective 1999). cum.index: 1975-1992. **Document type:** *Academic/Scholarly.*
Indexed: MLA-IB.
Published by: Universidad Veracruzana, Direccion Editorial, Apdo. Postal 97, Xalapa, Ver. 91001, Mexico. TEL 52-28-174435. Circ: 1,000.

TRANSATLANTIC AESTHETICS AND CULTURE. *see* LITERATURE

792 745.5 636 USA ISSN 1524-6132
THE TRUMPETER (WESTBROOK). Text in English. 1990. bi-w. USD 20; free newsstand/cover (effective 2000). adv. dance rev.; music rev.; play rev.; bk.rev. 20 p./no.; back issues avail. **Document type:** *Newspaper.* **Description:** Covers positive news and upcoming events for arts, theartre, nature, crafts, dining.
Published by: M E A A Publishing, 30 Orchard Rd, East Haddam, CT 06423-0119. Ed. Emil Trabor. Pub., R&P, Adv. contact Leland W Morgan. Circ: 16,000.

TUITION, ENTERTAINMENT, NEWS, VIEWS. *see* ART

792 CZE ISSN 1211-8001
TVORIVA DRAMATIKA. Text in Czech. 1990. 3/yr. CZK 120; CZK 40 newsstand/cover (effective 2009). **Document type:** *Journal, Academic/Scholarly.*
Published by: Narodni Informacni a Poradenske Stredisko pro Kulturu (N I P O S), Blanicka 4, Prague 2, 120 21, Czech Republic. TEL 420-2-21507900, FAX 420-2-21507929, nipos@nipos-mk.cz, http://www.nipos-mk.cz. Ed. Jaroslav Provaznik.

U K WRITER. (United Kingdom) *see* LITERATURE

792.2 USA
U - LAFF SEATTLE COMEDY. Text in English. 1995. m. free. **Description:** Contains original comedies from Seattle.
Media: Online - full text. Ed. Scott Schaefer.

792 USA
U S OUTDOOR DRAMA. Text in English. 1964. 12/yr. looseleaf. USD 12 (effective 2000). bk.rev. **Document type:** *Newsletter.* **Description:** Covers news, announcements, theatre literature citations, and information on all aspects of outdoor historical drama planning and production such as writing, directing, designing, staging, promotion, auditions, and management.

Formerly (until 1990): Institute of Outdoor Drama Newsletter (0020-3017)
Published by: Institute of Outdoor Drama, University of North Carolina at Chapel Hill, CB 3240, Chapel Hill, NC 27599-3240. TEL 919-962-1328, FAX 919-962-4212, outdoor@unc.edu, http://www.unc.edu/depts/outdoor/. Eds. Cindy Biles, Scott Parker. R&P Cindy Biles. Circ: 1,500 (paid and controlled).

792 FRA ISSN 1255-7196
PN2003
UBU; scenes d'Europe - European stages. Text in English, French. 1996. q. EUR 36 (effective 2008). bk.rev. **Document type:** *Magazine, Consumer.* **Description:** Reports on contemporary theatre in Europe.
Indexed: MLA-IB.
Published by: A P I T E Editions, c/o L'Odeon Theatre de l'Europe, 1 Place Paul Claudel, Paris, 75006, France. TEL 33-1-45747396, FAX 33-1-45747596, ubu.apite@freesbee.fr. Eds. Chantal Boiron, Gilles Costaz.

792 UKR ISSN 0207-7159
UKRAINS'KYI TEATR. Text in Ukrainian. 1936. bi-m. USD 159 in United States (effective 2008). **Document type:** *Magazine.*
Indexed: RASB.
—East View.
Published by: Ministerstvo Kul'tury i Turyzmu Ukrainy/Ministry of Culture and Tourism of Ukraine, vul I Franka, 19, Kyiv, 01601, Ukraine. http://www.mincult.gov.ua. **Dist. by:** East View Information Services, 10601 Wayzata Blvd, Minneapolis, MN 55305. TEL 952-252-1201, 800-477-1005, FAX 952-252-1202, info@eastview.com, http://www.eastview.com.

792.07 TZA
UNIVERSITY OF DAR ES SALAAM. THEATRE ARTS DEPARTMENT. ANNUAL REPORT. Text in English. a.
Published by: University of Dar es Salaam, Theatre Arts Department, PO Box 35091, Dar Es Salaam, Tanzania.

792 ITA ISSN 1828-4663
L'UOMO NERO. Text in Italian. 2003. s-a. **Document type:** *Magazine, Consumer.*
Published by: Universita degli Studi di Milano, Dipartimento di Storia delle Arti, della Musica e dello Spettacolo, Via Noto 6-8, Milan, 20141, Italy. TEL 39-02-50322000, FAX 39-02-50322012, http://users.unimi.it/starte/.

792 USA ISSN 1946-5947
VALLEY THEATRE ARTS. Text in English. 2008. q. USD 20 per issue; free to qualified personnel (effective 2009). back issues avail. **Document type:** *Magazine, Consumer.* **Description:** Aims to showcase the work of youth theatre productions in the Valley of the Sun, Arizona.
Published by: Zphotos.net, PO Box 12226, Tempe, AZ 85284. TEL 602-427-7113.

791.3 DEU
VARIETE SPECIAL. Text in German. a. EUR 7.50 newsstand/cover (effective 2009). **Document type:** *Magazine, Trade.*
Published by: Circus Verlag, Am Latourshof 6, Dormagen, 41542, Germany. TEL 49-2133-91555, FAX 49-2133-91553, circus.verlag@t-online.de, http://www.circus-verlag.de.

791.43 USA ISSN 0042-2738
PN2000
VARIETY; the international entertainment weekly. Text in English. 1905. w. USD 299.99 domestic; USD 359.99 in Canada & Mexico; USD 399.99 in Europe; USD 599.99 elsewhere (effective 2009); includes 10 issues of VLife. adv. bk.rev.; film rev.; music rev.; play rev.; rec.rev.; tel.rev. illus. back issues avail.; reprints avail. **Document type:** *Newspaper, Consumer.* **Description:** Provides an insider's perspective on the latest developments and trends in film, television and music with concise, provocative insight.
Related titles: Microform ed.: (from BHP, PQC); Online - full text ed.: USD 329.99 (effective 2009); Japanese ed.
Indexed: A09, A10, A25, A26, A27, B02, B03, B04, B07, B15, B17, B18, BPI, BRD, BusI, C12, Chicano, E07, E08, F01, F02, G04, G05, G06, G07, G08, I05, I06, I07, IBT&D, IIFP, IIPA, IITV, M01, M02, M06, M11, MASUSE, MRD, MagInd, MusicInd, P02, P07, P10, P34, P48, P53, P54, PMR, PQC, R06, RASB, S08, S09, S23, SRI, T&II, T02, V02, V03, V04, W01, W02, W03, W05.
—CIS. **CCC.**
Published by: Reed Business Information (Subsidiary of: Reed Business), 5900 Wilshire Blvd, Ste 3100, Los Angeles, CA 90036. TEL 323-857-6600, FAX 323-965-2475, corporatecommunications@reedbusiness.com, http://www.reedbusiness.com. Eds. Rachel Wimberly TEL 323-617-9349, Michael Hart TEL 323-965-5305. adv.: B&W page USD 10,740, color page USD 16,640; bleed 276 x 371. Circ: 28,956 (paid). **Subscr. to:** Reed Business Information.

791.43 USA
VARIETY.COM. Text in English. 1999. d. USD 329 (effective 2009). adv. film rev.; music rev.; play rev.; rec.rev.; tel.rev. charts. reprints avail. **Document type:** *Magazine, Consumer.* **Description:** Provides box office figures, breaking news, insider coverage of awards, in-depth film festival coverage, a calendar of industry events plus film, theatre and music reviews.
Media: Online - full text. **Related titles:** Alternate Frequency ed(s).: w.
Published by: Reed Business Information (Subsidiary of: Reed Business), 5900 Wilshire Blvd, Ste 3100, Los Angeles, CA 90036. TEL 323-857-6600, FAX 323-857-0494, corporatecommunications@reedbusiness.com, http://www.reedbusiness.com. Eds. Dana Harris, Peter Bart TEL 323-965-4434. Adv. contact Dru Montgomery TEL 323-617-9242.

VEGAS REPORT. *see* MUSIC

VLAANDEREN; tijdschrift voor kunst en cultuur. *see* ART

792 ITA ISSN 1970-3570
VOCI DI REPERTORIO. Text in Italian. 1988. irreg. **Document type:** *Monographic series, Academic/Scholarly.*
Published by: Maria Pacini Fazzi Editore, Via dell'Angelo Custode 33, Lucca, 55100, Italy. TEL 39-538-440188, FAX 39-538-464656, mpf@pacinifazzi.it, http://www.pacinifazzi.it.

792 FRA ISSN 1140-5309
LES VOIES DE LA CREATION THEATRALE. Text in French. 1970. a. price varies. adv. bk.rev. index.
Related titles: ◆ Series of: Arts du Spectacle. ISSN 0296-2292.
Published by: Centre National de la Recherche Scientifique, Campus Gerard-Megie, 3 Rue Michel-Ange, Paris, 75794, France. TEL 33-1-44964000, FAX 33-1-44965390, http://www.cnrseditions.fr. Circ: 1,500 (controlled).

792 FRA ISSN 1296-0969
LES VOIES DE L'ACTEUR. Text in French. 1999. irreg. back issues avail. **Document type:** *Monographic series, Consumer.*
Published by: Editions L' Entretemps, Domaine de Lafeuillade, 264 Rue du Capitaine Pierre Pontal, Montpellier, 34000, France. TEL 33-4-99530975, FAX 33-4-99533198, info.entretemps@wanadoo.fr, http://www.lekti-ecriture.com/editeurs/-L-Entretemps-.html.

792 RUS ISSN 0507-3952
PN2007
VOPROSY TEATRA; sbornik statei i materialov. Text in Russian. 1965. a. bibl.; illus.
Indexed: RASB.
Published by: Teatral'noe Obshchestvo/Theatrical Workers' Union, Kisel'nyi tup 1, Moscow, 103031, Russian Federation. **Co-sponsor:** Institut Istorii Iskusstv.

W A S I. *see* ART

791.53 NLD ISSN 1871-4161
W P. (Wij Poppenspelers) Text in Dutch. 1955. 6/yr. free membership (effective 2009).
Formerly (until 2003): Wij Poppenspelers (1380-4596); Which was formed by the merger of (1990-1993): N V P - U N I M A Nieuws (0927-8281); (1955-1993): Poppenpodium (0167-9996); Which was formerly (until 1983): Wij Poppenspelers (1380-4391)
Published by: Nederlandse Vereniging voor het Poppenspel - Unima Centrum Nederland, c/o Trudy Kuyper, Sec., Hoocamp 10, Akersloot, 1921 WD, Netherlands. TEL 31-251-313447, secretaris@poppenspelers.nl, http://www.poppenspelers.nl.

WASHINGTON OPERA MAGAZINE. *see* MUSIC

WEEKLY PIA. *see* LEISURE AND RECREATION

DIE WERKSTATT. *see* DANCE

792 USA ISSN 1050-1991
PN2570
WESTERN EUROPEAN STAGES. Abbreviated title: W E S. Text in English. 1989. 3/yr. USD 20 domestic; USD 30 foreign (effective 2010). adv. music rev.; dance rev.; film rev.; play rev. illus. index. back issues avail.; reprints avail. **Document type:** *Journal, Academic/Scholarly.* **Description:** Covers the contemporary West European theatrical performances. Includes information about recent European festivals and productions, reviews, interviews, and reports.
Related titles: Online - full text ed.
Indexed: CA, IBT&D, IIPA, MLA-IB, T02.
—Ingenta.
Published by: Martin E. Segal Theatre Center, The CUNY Graduate Center, 365 Fifth Ave, New York, NY 10016. TEL 212-817-1860, mestc@gc.cuny.edu. Ed. Marvin Carlson.

WESTERN JOURNAL OF COMMUNICATION. *see* LINGUISTICS

791 ZAF
WHAT'S ON AT THE STATE THEATRE. Text in Afrikaans, English. 1968. q. free. **Document type:** *Handbook/Manual/Guide, Consumer.* **Description:** Informs theatre enthusiasts of forthcoming productions and gives general theatre news.
Former titles (until 1997): T R U K P A C T Info; (until 1991): Theatre Guide - Theatre Gids; (until 1990): T R U K - P A C T (0085-7416)
Published by: State Theatre, PO Box 566, Pretoria, 0001, South Africa. FAX 27-12-322-3913, TELEX 3-20753 PACT SA. Ed. Robert Perry. adv.: color page ZAR 7,000. Circ: 40,000.

WHAT'S ON IN LONDON. *see* TRAVEL AND TOURISM

791.3 USA ISSN 0043-499X
GV1800
WHITE TOPS; devoted exclusively to the circus. Text in English. 1927. bi-m. USD 30 to non-members. adv. bk.rev. illus.
Related titles: Online - full text ed.
Indexed: A10, IBT&D, IIPA, RASB, T02, V03.
Published by: Circus Fans Association of America, 2380 Mosquito Point Rd, White Stone, VA 22578. TEL 804-435-2951, FAX 804-435-6662. Ed., R&P James E Foster. Adv. contact Maxine House. Circ: 2,500 (paid).

796 USA ISSN 0740-770X
PN1590.W64
➤ **WOMEN & PERFORMANCE**; a journal of feminist theory. Text in English. 1983. 3/yr. GBP 119 combined subscription in United Kingdom to institutions (print & online eds.); EUR 174, USD 217 combined subscription to institutions (print & online eds.) (effective 2012). adv. bk.rev. illus. back issues avail.; reprint service avail. from PSC. **Document type:** *Journal, Academic/Scholarly.* **Description:** Features scholarly essays on performance, dance, film, new media, and the performance of everyday life from interdisciplinary feminist perspectives.
Related titles: Online - full text ed.: ISSN 1748-5819. GBP 107 in United Kingdom to institutions; EUR 156, USD 196 to institutions (effective 2012) (from IngentaConnect).
Indexed: A22, BibInd, BrHumI, CA, E01, F01, F02, FemPer, G10, IBT&D, IDP, IIPA, LeftInd, MLA-IB, PCI, RILM, T02, W09, WSI.
—BLDSC (9343.273000), IE, Ingenta. **CCC.**
Published by: Routledge (Subsidiary of: Taylor & Francis Group), 325 Chestnut St, Ste 800, Philadelphia, PA 19106. TEL 800-354-1420, FAX 215-625-2940, journals@routledge.com, http://www.routledge.com. Adv. contact Linda Hann TEL 44-1344-779945. Circ: 1,300 (paid).

800 USA ISSN 1539-5758
PR2976
THE WOODEN O SYMPOSIUM. JOURNAL. Text in English. a. USD 15 (effective 2004). **Document type:** *Journal, Academic/Scholarly.* **Description:** Publishes selected papers from the annual conference, which explores Medieval and Renaissance studies through the texts and performance of Shakespeare's plays.
Indexed: A01, A03, A08, AmHI, CA, H07, IBT&D, MLA-IB, T02.
Published by: (Utah Shakespearean Festival), Southern Utah University Press, Gerald R Sherratt Library, 351 W Center St, Cedar City, UT 84720. TEL 435-586-7947, http://www.li.suu.edu/library/suupress/.

792 GBR ISSN 1757-9384
PN4071
➤ **WORD MATTERS.** Text in English. 1951. s-a. GBP 10 domestic to non-members; GBP 16 foreign to non-members; free to members (effective 2009). adv. bk.rev.; play rev. illus. index. back issues avail. **Document type:** *Journal, Academic/Scholarly.* **Description:** Contains articles on the inter-relationship of communication, theater, drama and speech at all levels of education.
Formerly (until 2008): Speech and Drama (0038-7142)
Related titles: Microform ed.: (from PQC).
Indexed: B29, MLA-IB, RASB.
—BLDSC (9347.850500), IE, Ingenta.
Published by: Society of Teachers of Speech and Drama, 73 Berry Hill Rd, Mansfield, Notts NG18 4RU, United Kingdom. stsd@stsd.org.uk. Ed. Salli Felling. Adv. contact David Felling. **Subscr. to:** Penny Charteris, 8 Colebrook Rd, Southwick, Brighton, W Sussex BN42 4AL, United Kingdom. TEL 44-1273-591324.

➤ **WORLD SHAKESPEARE BIBLIOGRAPHY (ONLINE).** *see* LITERATURE

➤ **WUTAI YISHU/STAGECRAFT.** *see* MUSIC

792 791.43 CHN
WUTAI YU YINMU. Text in Chinese. 1934. m. CNY 78 (effective 2004). **Document type:** *Consumer.*
Related titles: Online - full content ed.
Published by: Guangzhou Ribao Baoye Jituan/Guangzhou Daily Newspaper Group, 10, Renmin Zhonglu Tongle Lu, Guangzhou, 510121, China. TEL 86-20-81883088. **Dist. by:** China International Book Trading Corp, 35 Chegongzhuang Xilu, Haidian District, PO Box 399, Beijing 100044, China. TEL 86-10-68412045, FAX 86-10-68412023, cibtc@mail.cibtc.com.cn, http://www.cibtc.com.cn.

792.02 CHN ISSN 1003-0549
PN2009
XIJU/DRAMA. Variant title: Zhongyang Xiju Xueyuan Xuebao. Text in Chinese. 1986. q. USD 30 (effective 2009). bk.rev. **Document type:** *Journal, Academic/Scholarly.*
Related titles: Online - full text ed.
—East View.
Published by: Zhongyang Xiju Xueyuan/Central Academy of Drama, 39 Dong Mianhua Hutong, Beijing, China. TEL 86-10-64056580. **Dist. by:** China International Book Trading Corp, 35 Chegongzhuang Xilu, Haidian District, PO Box 399, Beijing 100044, China. TEL 86-10-68412045, FAX 86-10-68412023, cibtc@mail.cibtc.com.cn, http://www.cibtc.com.cn.

792 CHN
XIJU CHUNQIU/WORLD OF DRAMAS. Text in Chinese. 1990. bi-m. CNY 18 (effective 2004). **Document type:** *Academic/Scholarly.*
Related titles: Online - full text ed.
Address: 261, Bashiyi Lu, Changsha, Hunan 410001, China. TEL 86-731-4464600. **Dist. by:** China International Book Trading Corp, 35 Chegongzhuang Xilu, Haidian District, PO Box 399, Beijing 100044, China. TEL 86-10-68412045, FAX 86-10-68412023, cibtc@mail.cibtc.com.cn, http://www.cibtc.com.cn.

792.2 CHN ISSN 1003-4676
XIJU SHIJIE/COMEDY WORLD. Text in Chinese. 1988. m. USD 28.80 (effective 2009). **Document type:** *Magazine, Consumer.*
Address: 83, Dongliu Lu, Xi'an, 710005, China. TEL 86-29-7541004. **Dist. by:** China International Book Trading Corp, 35 Chegongzhuang Xilu, Haidian District, PO Box 399, Beijing 100044, China. TEL 86-10-68412045, FAX 86-10-68412023, cibtc@mail.cibtc.com.cn, http://www.cibtc.com.cn.

XIJU WENXUE/DRAMA LITERATURE. *see* LITERATURE

792 CHN ISSN 0257-943X
PN2009
XIJU YISHU (SHANGHAI)/THEATRE ARTS. Text in Chinese. 1978. bi-m. USD 31.20 (effective 2009). **Document type:** *Journal, Academic/Scholarly.*
Indexed: IIPA, RASB.
—East View.
Published by: Shanghai Xiju Xueyuan/Shanghai Theatre Academy, 630 Huashan Lu, Shanghai, 200040, China. TEL 86-21-62482920, FAX 86-21-62482646. Circ: 5,000. **Dist. by:** China International Book Trading Corp, 35 Chegongzhuang Xilu, Haidian District, PO Box 399, Beijing 100044, China. TEL 86-10-68412045, FAX 86-10-68412023, cibtc@mail.cibtc.com.cn, http://www.cibtc.com.cn.

792 CHN ISSN 1003-2681
XIJU YU DIANYING/THEATRE AND CINEMA. Text in Chinese. 1980. m. CNY 12. adv. bk.rev.
Published by: Zhongguo Xijujia Xiehui, Sichuan Fenhui/China Dramatists Association, Sichuan Chapter, 85, Hongxing Zhonglu 2 Duan, Chengdu, Sichuan 610012, China. TEL 663834. Circ: 5,000.

792 CHN ISSN 1007-0125
XIJU ZHIJIA/HOME OF DRAMAS. Text in Chinese. 1990. bi-m. USD 14.40 (effective 2009). **Document type:** *Academic/Scholarly.*
Related titles: Online - full text ed.
—East View.
Address: 417, Donghu Lu, Wuhan, Hubei 430077, China. TEL 86-27-86781967. **Dist. by:** China International Book Trading Corp, 35 Chegongzhuang Xilu, Haidian District, PO Box 399, Beijing 100044, China. TEL 86-10-68412045, FAX 86-10-68412023, cibtc@mail.cibtc.com.cn, http://www.cibtc.com.cn.

792.071 USA ISSN 0892-9092
PN3157
➤ **YOUTH THEATRE JOURNAL.** Text in English. 1986. s-a. GBP 64 combined subscription in United Kingdom to institutions (print & online eds.); EUR 94, USD 115 combined subscription to institutions (print & online eds.) (effective 2012). adv. bk.rev. reprint service avail. from PSC. **Document type:** *Journal, Academic/Scholarly.* **Description:** Includes articles covering theater and drama education for young audiences.
Formerly (until 1986): Children's Theatre Review (0009-4196)
Related titles: Microfilm ed.: (from PQC); Online - full text ed.: ISSN 1948-4798. GBP 58 in United Kingdom to institutions; EUR 84, USD 104 to institutions (effective 2012).
Indexed: A10, A22, CA, E03, ERI, IBT&D, MLA-IB, T02, V03.
—BLDSC (9421.582200), IE, Ingenta. **CCC.**

Published by: (American Alliance for Theatre & Education), Routledge (Subsidiary of: Taylor & Francis Group), 325 Chestnut St, Ste 800, Philadelphia, PA 19106. TEL 800-354-1420, FAX 215-625-2940, 215-625-8914, orders@taylorandfrancis.com, http://www.routledge.com. Ed. Stephani Etheridge Woodson. Adv. contact Christy M Taylor. Circ: 1,200.

792 780 SRB ISSN 0352-9738
PN2851
➤ **ZBORNIK MATICE SRPSKE ZA SCENSKE UMETNOSTI I MUZIKU/ MATICA SRPSKA REVIEW OF STAGE ART AND MUSIC.** Text in Serbian. 1987. s-a. EUR 10 per issue (effective 2007). **Document type:** *Journal, Academic/Scholarly.*
Indexed: RILM.
Published by: Matica Srpska, Matice Srpske 1, Novi Sad, 21000. TEL 381-21-527622, FAX 381-21- 528901, ms@maticasrpska.org.yu. Ed. Bozhidar Kovacek.

792 CHN ISSN 1001-8018
PN2870
ZHONGGUO XIJU/CHINESE THEATRE. Text in Chinese. 1976. m. USD 36 (effective 2009). **Document type:** *Journal, Academic/Scholarly.*
Former title (until 1988): Xijubao (Beijing) (0258-803X); (until 1982): Renmin Xiju (1001-800X)
Related titles: Online - full text ed.
Published by: (Zhongguo Xijujia Xiehui/Chinese Theater Artists' Association), Zhongguo Xiju Chubanshe, 52, Dong Siba Tiao, Beijing, 100700, China. TEL 86-10-64040706. Ed. Huo Dashou. **Dist. by:** China International Book Trading Corp, 35 Chegongzhuang Xilu, Haidian District, PO Box 399, Beijing 100044, China. TEL 86-10-68412045, FAX 86-10-68412023, cibtc@mail.cibtc.com.cn, http://www.cibtc.com.cn.

792 CHN
ZHONGGUO YANYUAN BAO/CHINA ACTING NEWS. Text in Chinese. 1995. w. CNY 246 (effective 2004). **Document type:** *Newspaper, Trade.*
Address: Zhaoyang-qu, 16, Ganyangshujia, Zhongheluo 1-men 3-ceng, Beijing, 100101, China. TEL 86-10-64913703, FAX 86-10-64915653. **Dist. by:** China International Book Trading Corp, 35 Chegongzhuang Xilu, Haidian District, PO Box 399, Beijing 100044, China. TEL 86-10-68412045, FAX 86-10-68412023, cibtc@mail.cibtc.com.cn, http://www.cibtc.com.cn.

ZOOM (LUBLIN). *see* MUSIC

792 AUT
ZUGABE. Text in German. 1957. m. adv. bk.rev.; rec.rev. illus. **Document type:** *Bulletin, Consumer.*
Former titles (until 1992): Publicum (0020-1642); Innsbrucker Konzertspiegel
Published by: Tiroler Landestheater, Rennweg 2, Innsbruck, T 6020, Austria. TEL 43-512-52074, FAX 43-512-52074333, tiroler@landestheater.at, http://www.landestheater.at. Ed. Jutta Hoepfel. Circ: 10,000.

792 DNK ISSN 1902-7354
1. RAEKKE; Koebenhavns teatermagasin. Variant title: Foerste Raekke. Text in Danish. 2007. s-a. **Document type:** *Magazine, Consumer.*
Description: Focus on the current theater life in Copenhagen.
Related titles: Online - full text ed.: ISSN 1902-7362.
Published by: Koebenhavns Teater, Nr. Voldgade 2,5, Copenhagen K, 1358, Denmark. TEL 45-33-366766, FAX 45-33-366769, kbht@kbht.dk. Ed. Mettemalou Eden. Circ: 125,000.

792 NOR ISSN 0807-6316
3 T; tidsskrift for teori og teater. Text in Norwegian; Text occasionally in English. 1996. q. NOK 250 (effective 2004). adv.
Published by: 3 t, PO Box 1287, Sentrum, Bergen, 5811, Norway. TEL 47-97-005448, FAX 47-91-111309, 3t@trete.no. Ed. Melanie Fieldseth. Adv. contact Aasne Dahl Torp.

THEATER—Abstracting, Bibliographies, Statistics

792.021 AUS
AUSTRALIA. BUREAU OF STATISTICS. PERFORMING ARTS, AUSTRALIA (ONLINE). Text in English. 1998. irreg., latest 2007. free (effective 2009). back issues avail. **Document type:** *Government.*
Description: Presents results for the reference year from surveys conducted by the Australian Bureau of Statistics (ABS) of businesses or organisations primarily involved in performing arts operation or performing arts venue operation.
Formerly: Australia. Bureau of Statistics. Performing Arts Industry, Australia (Print)
Media: Online - full text.
Published by: Australian Bureau of Statistics, Locked Bag 10, Belconnen, ACT 2616, Australia. TEL 61-2-92684909, 61-2-62527037, 300-135-070, FAX 61-2-62528103, client.services@abs.gov.au.

016.79143 USA ISSN 0892-5550
BIO-BIBLIOGRAPHIES IN THE PERFORMING ARTS. Text in English. 1987. irreg., latest 1999. price varies. back issues avail. **Document type:** *Monographic series, Bibliography.*
Published by: Greenwood Publishing Group Inc. (Subsidiary of: A B C - C L I O), 88 Post Rd W, PO Box 5007, Westport, CT 06881. TEL 203-226-3571, 800-225-5800, FAX 877-231-6980, sales@greenwood.com. Ed. James Parish Robert.

016.792 USA
INTERNATIONAL BIBLIOGRAPHY OF THEATRE & DANCE WITH FULL TEXT. Abbreviated title: I B T D. Text in English. 1984-2003; resumed 2005. base vol. plus m. updates. **Document type:** *Database, Abstract/Index.* **Description:** Indexes over 60,000 journal articles, books, dissertations, and ephemeral publications on all aspects of theatre and performance in 126 countries.
Formerly (until 1999): International Bibliography of Theatre (Print) (0882-9446)
Media: Online - full text.
Published by: (Columbia University), EBSCO Publishing (Subsidiary of: EBSCO Industries, Inc.), 10 Estes St, PO Box 682, Ipswich, MA 01938. TEL 978-356-6500, 800-653-2726, FAX 978-356-6565, information@ebscohost.com.

016.792 016.78 USA ISSN 1528-3119
INTERNATIONAL INDEX TO THE PERFORMING ARTS. Abbreviated title: I I P A. Text in English. 1998. base vol. plus m. updates. back issues avail. **Document type:** *Database, Abstract/Index.*
Description: Provides bibliographic resource for the performing arts information and research community.
Media: Online - full text. **Related titles:** CD-ROM ed.: ISSN 1463-0109; Online - full content ed.: ISSN 1528-3127.
Published by: ProQuest (Subsidiary of: Cambridge Information Group), 789 E Eisenhower Pky, PO Box 1346, Ann Arbor, MI 48106. TEL 734-761-4700, 800-521-0600, FAX 734-997-4040, 888-241-5612, info@proquest.com.

792 016 CAN
PLAYWRIGHTS UNION OF CANADA CATALOGUE OF CANADIAN PLAYS. Text in English. 1977. a. free. illus.
Formerly: Directory of Canadian Plays and Playwrights (0707-5456)
Published by: Playwrights Union of Canada, 54 Wolseley St, 2nd Fl, Toronto, ON M5T 1A5, Canada. TEL 416-703-0201, 800-561-3318, FAX 416-703-0059. Ed. Jodi Armstrong. Circ: 10,000.

THEORY OF COMPUTING

see COMPUTERS—Theory Of Computing

TOBACCO

see also AGRICULTURE—Crop Production And Soil

ANDREW'S LITIGATION REPORTER: TOBACCO INDUSTRY. *see* LAW

658.8 679.7 AUS ISSN 0727-078X
AUSTRALIAN RETAIL TOBACCONIST. Text in English. 1940. m.
Former titles (until 1966): Retail Tobacconist; (until 1949): Retail Tobacconist of N S W
Published by: New South Wales Retail Tobacco Traders Association, Alexander House, 1st Fl, 107 Alexander St, Crows Nest, NSW 2065, Australia.

679.73 DEU ISSN 0173-783X
TS2220 CODEN: BTAID3
➤ **BEITRAEGE ZUR TABAKFORSCHUNG INTERNATIONAL**; contributions to tobacco research. Text in English; Summaries in English, French, German. 1961. irreg., latest vol.23, no.2, 2008. free (effective 2009). bk.rev. charts; illus.; stat. back issues avail.; reprints avail. **Document type:** *Monographic series, Academic/Scholarly.*
Description: Publishes original contributions and review articles relating to the various aspects of tobacco science including physical and chemical analysis of tobacco and tobacco smoke, pertinent matters to the manufacture of tobacco products, research into tobacco plants including biotechnology, plant treatment substances, protecting agents, leaf tobacco, statistical data processing, and human smoking behavior including biomonitoring.
Formerly (until 1978): Beitraege zur Tabakforschung (0005-819X)
Related titles: Microfilm ed.: (from PQC); Online - full content ed.: ISSN 1612-9237.
Indexed: A22, A35, A36, A37, AgBio, Agr, B25, BA, BIOBASE, BIOSIS Prev, C25, C30, CABA, CIN, ChemAb, ChemTitl, E12, FCA, GH, H16, I11, IABS, MycolAb, P32, P33, P40, PGegResA, PHN&I, R07, R13, RM&VM, S12, S13, S16, S17, SCOPUS, T05.
—BLDSC (1887.451000), CASDDS, IE, Ingenta, INIST. **CCC.**
Address: Unter den Linden 42, Berlin, 10117, Germany. TEL 49-30-886636140, FAX 49-30-886636111, tietzela@beitraege-bti.de. Eds. Dr. Gerhard Scherer, Dr. Wolf-Dieter Heller. R&Ps Angela Tietzel, Brigitte Mueller. Circ: 1,000.

➤ **BRANDSTAND**; viewing the world of cigarette collecting. *see* HOBBIES

679.7 FRA ISSN 1639-2140
BURALISTES; le mensuel d'information des buralistes de Paris-Ile-de-France. Text in French. 1904. 11/yr. bk.rev. **Document type:** *Magazine, Trade.*
Formerly (until 2002): Debitant de Tabac (0994-8589)
Published by: Federation des Gerants de Debits de Tabac de l'Ile de France, 5 Rue de Vienne, Paris, 75008, France. TEL 33-1-45224344, FAX 33-1-45227606, contact@buralistesidf.fr, http://www.buralistesidf.fr. Ed., Adv. contact Patricia Lefeuvre. R&P Michel Arnaud TEL 45-22-43-44. Circ: 6,000.

C T N; the voice of the local newsagent. (Confectioner, Tobacconist, Newsagent) *see* FOOD AND FOOD INDUSTRIES—Bakers And Confectioners

679.7 CAN ISSN 1492-1448
C T U M S. (Canadian Tobacco Use Monitoring Survey) Text in English. 1999. a.
Published by: Health Canada, Tobacco Control Programme, P.L. 3507A1, Ottawa, ON K1A 0K9, Canada.

633.71 IND
CENTRAL TOBACCO RESEARCH INSTITUTE AND ITS REGIONAL RESEARCH STATIONS. ANNUAL REPORT. Text in English. 1967. a. charts; stat. **Document type:** *Report, Trade.*
Incorporates: Tobacco Research Institute. Annual Report; Tobacco Research Station, Hunsur. Report; Wrapper and Hookah Tobacco Research Station. Report
Published by: Indian Council of Agricultural Research, Central Tobacco Research Institute, Bhaskar Nagar, Rajahmundry, Andhra Pradesh 533 105, India. TEL 91-883-2448995, ctri@sify.com.

658.8 051 910.202 BRA ISSN 1517-4840
CHARUTO ET CIA; pecadilhos e prazeres. Text in Portuguese. 1999. bi-m. **Description:** Contains tips and stories about well made cigars, reviews on the best restaurants and cigar clubs and the latest on international travel for business and pleasure.
Published by: Market Press Editora Ltda, Rua Hugo Carotini 445, Parque Previdencia, Sao Paulo, 05532-020, Brazil. TEL 55-11-37211950, http://www.marketpress.com.br.

CHINA FOOD & DRINK REPORT. *see* BUSINESS AND ECONOMICS

633.71 CUB ISSN 0138-8185
CIENCIA Y TECNICA EN LA AGRICULTURA. SERIE: TABACO. Abstracts and contents page in English. 2/yr. USD 14 in the Americas; USD 16 in Europe; USD 17 elsewhere.
Former titles (until 1978): Cuba. Centro de Informacion y Documentacion Agropecuario. Boletin de Resenas. Serie: Tabaco; Cuba. Centro de Informacion y Divulgacion Agropecuario. Boletin de Resenas. Serie: Tobacco
Indexed: Agrind.
Published by: Centro de Informacion y Documentacion Agropecuario, Gaveta Postal 4149, Havana, 4, Cuba. **Dist. by:** Ediciones Cubanas, Obispo 527, Havana, Cuba.

394.14 CHE
CIGAR. Text in German. q. CHF 36 domestic; CHF 42 in Europe; CHF 46 elsewhere; CHF 9.50 newsstand/cover (effective 2000). adv. **Document type:** *Magazine, Consumer.* **Description:** Contains articles and features on the finer points of cigars.
Published by: Salz & Pfeffer, Postfach 351, Winterthur, 8401, Switzerland. TEL 41-52-2240136, FAX 41-52-2240132. Ed. Bruno Botschi. adv.: B&W page CHF 6,900, color page CHF 7,900; trim 177 x 264. Circ: 35,000 (paid).

394.14 USA ISSN 1063-7885
TS2260
CIGAR AFICIONADO; the good life magazine for men. Text in English. 1991. bi-m. USD 19.95 domestic; USD 38 in Canada; USD 56 elsewhere (effective 2008). adv. illus. back issues avail.; reprints avail. **Document type:** *Magazine, Consumer.* **Description:** Provides information on fine cigars and other pleasures of life, such as travel, dining, the arts, collecting and hobbies. Includes personality profiles, restaurants that permit cigar smoking, and pastime activities from golf and fishing to music and literature.
Related titles: Online - full text ed.
Indexed: B01, B06, B07, B09, M01, M02.
Published by: Marvin R. Shanken Communications, Inc., 387 Park Ave S, New York, NY 10016. FAX 212-481-1540, mmorgenstern@mshanken.com, http://www.mshanken.com/. Ed., Pub. Marvin R Shanken. Adv. contact Barry Abrams TEL 212-481-8610 ext 388. B&W page USD 21,510, color page USD 25,300. Circ: 290,000 (paid). **Subscr. to:** PO Box 51091, Boulder, CO 80323-1091. **Dist in UK by:** Comag, Tavistock Rd, W Drayton, Middlesex UB7 7QE, United Kingdom.

658.8 GBR ISSN 1742-5948
CIGAR BUYER. Text in English. 2005. s-a. adv. **Document type:** *Magazine, Consumer.* **Description:** Celebrates the cigars of the world, with a range if in-depth articles and extensive tastings.
Related titles: Online - full text ed.
Published by: Paragraph Publishing, St Faiths House, Mountergate, Norwich, NR1 1PY, United Kingdom. TEL 44-1603-633808, FAX 44-1603-632808, office@paragraphpublishing.com, http://www.paragraphpublishing.com. Ed. Rob Allanson. Adv. contact Joanne Morley.

394.14 USA
CIGAR INSIDER (ONLINE). Text in English. s-m. free to members (effective 2008). **Document type:** *Newsletter, Trade.*
Formerly (until 2005): Cigar Insider (Print)
Media: Online - full text.
Published by: Marvin R. Shanken Communications, Inc., 387 Park Ave, S, 8th Fl, New York, NY 10016-8810. TEL 212-684-4224, mmorgenstern@mshanken.com, http://www.mshanken.com/. Ed., Pub. Marvin R Shanken.

679.7 USA ISSN 1937-9269
TS2260
CIGAR MAGAZINE (WHIPPANY). Text in English. 2004. q. USD 19.80 (effective 2008). adv. **Document type:** *Magazine, Consumer.*
Description: Provides information about the cigar industry, tobacco and cigar-related topics and products for tobacco consumers.
Published by: Cigar Magazine, Inc, 301 Rte 10 E, Whippany, NJ 07981. TEL 877-777-6926, customerservice@cigar-magazine.com, http://www.cigar-magazine.com. Ed. Marni Wolff. adv.: color page USD 16,000;.

394.14 USA
CIGARLIFE. Text in English. m. **Description:** Information on the latest cigar products and news.
Media: Online - full text. Ed. Ray Sola. Pub. Stephen Petri.

CLEAN AIR UPDATE. *see* PUBLIC HEALTH AND SAFETY

633.71 CUB ISSN 0138-7456
CUBATABACO. Text in English, Spanish. 1972. s-a. adv. bk.rev. **Document type:** *Magazine, Trade.*
Indexed: C01.
Published by: (Cuba. Ministerio de la Agricultura), Ediciones Cubanas, Obispo 527, Havana, Cuba. TEL 53-7-631942, FAX 53-7-338943. Ed. Zoila Couceyro. Circ: 8,000.

679.7 DEU
D T Z SHOP. (Die Tabak Zeitung) Text in German. 2000. q. adv. **Document type:** *Magazine, Trade.*
Published by: Konradin Selection GmbH (Subsidiary of: Konradin Verlag Robert Kohlhammer GmbH), Erich-Dombrowski-Str 2, Mainz, 55127, Germany. TEL 49-6131-484505, FAX 49-6131-484533. Ed. Folker Kling. Adv. contact Michael Guenther. Circ: 12,000 (controlled).

679.7 DEU ISSN 0932-4534
D T Z TABAKJAHRBUCH. (Die Tabak Zeitung) Text in German. 1986. a. EUR 27 (effective 2007). adv. **Document type:** *Magazine, Trade.*
Published by: Konradin Selection GmbH (Subsidiary of: Konradin Verlag Robert Kohlhammer GmbH), Erich-Dombrowski-Str 2, Mainz, 55127, Germany. TEL 49-6131-484505, FAX 49-6131-484533. adv.: B&W page EUR 875, color page EUR 1,524. Circ: 3,300 (paid and controlled).

679.7 DEU ISSN 0012-0820
DER DEUTSCHE TABAKBAU. Text in German. 1916. 4/yr. adv. bk.rev. charts; illus.; stat. **Document type:** *Magazine, Trade.*
Indexed: ChemAb.
Published by: Konradin Selection GmbH (Subsidiary of: Konradin Verlag Robert Kohlhammer GmbH), Erich-Dombrowski-Str 2, Mainz, 55127, Germany. TEL 49-6131-484505, FAX 49-6131-484533. Ed. Herbert Steins. Adv. contact Peter Schmidtmann. B&W page EUR 1,674, color page EUR 2,484. Circ: 2,200 (paid and controlled).

394.14 AUT ISSN 1728-3574
EUROPEAN CIGAR CULT JOURNAL; das Magazin fuer savoir vivre. Text in German. q. EUR 21 (effective 2005). **Document type:** *Magazine, Consumer.*

Published by: Falstaff Verlag, Bueropark Donau, Inkustr 1-7, Stg 4, Klosterneuburg, N 3400, Austria. TEL 43-2243-34798, FAX 43-2243-25840, redaktion@falstaff.at, http://www.falstaff.at.

658.8 USA
FEDERAL TRADE COMMISSION. CIGARETTE REPORT FOR (YEAR). Text in English. 19??. irreg., latest 2009. free (effective 2011). back issues avail. **Document type:** *Report, Government.*
Formerly (until 1999): Federal Trade Commission Report to Congress for (Year). Pursuant to the Federal Cigarette Labeling and Advertising Act (Online)
Media: Online - full text.
Published by: U.S. Federal Trade Commission, 600 Pennsylvania Ave, NW, Washington, DC 20580. TEL 202-326-2222, HSRhelp@hsr.gov.

394.14 DEU
FINE TOBACCO. Text in German. 2005. q. EUR 20; EUR 5 newsstand/cover (effective 2009). adv. **Document type:** *Magazine, Consumer.*
Published by: Medienmarketing Meinsen, Chiemseering 11, Munich, 85551, Germany. TEL 49-89-90529072, FAX 49-89-90529073, petra@medien-marketing-meinsen.de, http://www.genussverlag.de. Ed. Peter Nitz. Pub. Bodo Meinsen. adv.: page EUR 4,600. Circ: 23,000 (paid and controlled).

FOODPRESS. *see* FOOD AND FOOD INDUSTRIES

FRANCE FOOD & DRINK REPORT. *see* BUSINESS AND ECONOMICS

630 FRA ISSN 0296-3361
FRANCE TABAC. Text in French. 1946. 11/yr. adv. illus. **Document type:** *Magazine, Trade.* **Description:** Contains informations about tobacco growing trade, first processing and consumption.
Formerly (until 1984): Voix des Cultures (0296-337X)
Address: 19 rue Ballu, Paris, 75009, France. TEL 33-1-44534800, FAX 33-1-42811686, ft-spet@wanadoo.fr. Ed., Pub., R&P, Adv. contact Francois Vedel. Circ: 9,000.

FREEDOM ORGANISATION FOR THE RIGHT TO ENJOY SMOKING TOBACCO. *see* POLITICAL SCIENCE—Civil Rights

GERMANY FOOD & DRINK REPORT. *see* BUSINESS AND ECONOMICS

338.17371 USA
GLOBAL TOBACCO INDUSTRY GUIDE. Abbreviated title: G T I G. Text in English. 199?. a. (Sep.). USD 78 per issue domestic; USD 96 per issue foreign (effective 2011). adv. charts; stat. reprints avail. **Document type:** *Handbook/Manual/Guide, Trade.*
Related titles: Online - full text ed.
Published by: SpecComm International, Inc., 5808 Faringdon Pl, Ste 200, Raleigh, NC 27609. TEL 919-872-5040, 800-346-7469, FAX 919-876-6531, http://www.speccomm.com. Ed. Taco Tuinstra TEL 919-875-9964. Pub. Noel Morris TEL 919-872-4213. Adv. contact Elise Rasmussen TEL 44-1252-878619.

679.7 ESP
GOURMETABACO. Text in Spanish. 1997. q. **Document type:** *Trade.* **Description:** Covers everything related to tobacco, cigarettes and cigars.
Related titles: ◆ Supplement to: Club de Gourmets. ISSN 0210-170X.
Published by: Club G. S.A., Aniceto Marinas 92, Madrid, 28008, Spain. TEL 34-91-577-0418, FAX 34-91-5487133, reyes@gourmets.net, http://www.gourmets.net. Ed. Francisco Lopez Canis.

HONG KONG FOOD & DRINK REPORT. *see* BUSINESS AND ECONOMICS

HUNGARY FOOD & DRINK REPORT. *see* BUSINESS AND ECONOMICS

INDIA FOOD & DRINK REPORT. *see* BUSINESS AND ECONOMICS

679.7 IND
INDIA. TOBACCO BOARD. ANNUAL REPORT. Text in English. 1975. a. free to members (effective 2011). **Document type:** *Report, Trade.*
Published by: Tobacco Board, G T Rd, Srinivasarao Thota, Guntur, Andhra Pradesh 522 004, India. TEL 91-863-2358399, FAX 91-863-2354232, info@indiantobacco.com, http://tobaccoboard.com.

INDONESIA FOOD & DRINK REPORT. *see* BUSINESS AND ECONOMICS

ISRAEL FOOD & DRINK REPORT. *see* BUSINESS AND ECONOMICS

ITALY FOOD & DRINK REPORT. *see* BUSINESS AND ECONOMICS

JAPAN FOOD & DRINK REPORT. *see* BUSINESS AND ECONOMICS

679.7 338 GBR
KEY NOTE MARKET REPORT: CIGARETTES & TOBACCO. Variant title: Cigarettes & Tobacco Market Report. Text in English. 1989. irreg., latest 2008, Oct. GBP 460 per issue (effective 2010). **Document type:** *Report, Trade.* **Description:** Provides an overview of a specific UK market segment and includes executive summary, market definition, market size, industry background, competitor analysis, current issues, forecasts, company profiles, and more.
Formerly (until 1995): Key Note Report: Cigarettes and Tobacco (0961-1673)
Related titles: CD-ROM ed.; Online - full text ed.
Published by: Key Note Ltd. (Subsidiary of: Bonnier Business Information), Harlequin House, 5th Fl, 7 High St, Teddington, Richmond upon Thames, TW11 8EE, United Kingdom. TEL 44-845-5040452, FAX 44-845-5040453, info@keynote.co.uk.

KUWAIT FOOD & DRINK REPORT. *see* BUSINESS AND ECONOMICS

LATVIA FOOD & DRINK REPORT. *see* BUSINESS AND ECONOMICS

658.8 FRA ISSN 0755-4680
LOSANGE; le magazine des buralistes de France. Text in French. 1983. 11/yr. EUR 27.45 domestic; EUR 30.50 foreign (effective 2007). **Document type:** *Magazine, Trade.*
Address: 75 Rue d'Amsterdam, Paris, 75008, France. TEL 33-1-53211010, FAX 33-1-53211019, accueil.losange@buralistes.fr, http://www.buralistes.fr/losange.php. Ed. Bertrand Blin. Circ: 45,000.

679.7 658.8 MUS ISSN 1694-0318
MAURITIUS. TOBACCO BOARD. ANNUAL REPORT AND ACCOUNTS. Text in English. 1932. a. free (effective 2006). charts. **Document type:** *Corporate.* **Description:** Covers the operations and activities of the board.
Formerly: Mauritius. Tobacco Board. Annual Report
Indexed: TobAb.
Published by: Tobacco Board, Plaine Lauzun, Port Louis, Mauritius. TEL 230-212-2323, FAX 230-208-6426, tobaco@intnet.mu, http://www.gov.mu/portal/site/tobacco/. Circ: 325.

MEALEY'S LITIGATION REPORT: TOBACCO. *see* LAW—Civil Law

679.72 USA
METRO CIGAR NEWS; serving metropolitan New York & New Jersey. Text in English. 1998. q. free per issue in the better tobacconists; USD 10 subscr - mailed (effective 2006). adv. back issues avail. **Document type:** *Newspaper, Consumer.* **Description:** Devoted to cigar smokers and their interests.
Related titles: Online - full text ed.
Published by: Metro Publishing Group, Inc., 626 McCarthy Dr., New Milford, NJ 07646. TEL 201-385-2000, FAX 201-385-2092. Ed., Pub. Barbara Thorson. Adv. contact Joseph Colombo. color page USD 1,500. Circ: 30,000 (paid and free).

NEW ZEALAND. STATISTICS NEW ZEALAND. ALCOHOL AND TOBACCO AVAILABLE FOR CONSUMPTION. *see* BEVERAGES

616 GBR ISSN 1462-2203
RC567 CODEN: NTREF6
➤ **NICOTINE & TOBACCO RESEARCH.** Text in English. 1999. m. GBP 957 in United Kingdom to institutions; EUR 1,437 in Europe to institutions; USD 1,437 in US & Canada to institutions; GBP 957 elsewhere to institutions; GBP 1,044 combined subscription in United Kingdom to institutions (print & online eds.); EUR 1,567 combined subscription in Europe to institutions (print & online eds.); USD 1,567 combined subscription in US & Canada to institutions (print & online eds.); GBP 1,044 combined subscription elsewhere to institutions (print & online eds.) (effective 2012). adv. back issues avail.; reprint service avail. from PSC. **Document type:** *Journal, Academic/Scholarly.* **Description:** Aims to provide a forum for empirical findings on the many aspects of nicotine and tobacco, including research from a variety of arenas.
Related titles: Online - full text ed.: ISSN 1469-994X. GBP 870 in United Kingdom to institutions; EUR 1,306 in Europe to institutions; USD 1,306 in US & Canada to institutions; GBP 870 elsewhere to institutions (effective 2012) (from IngentaConnect).
Indexed: A01, A02, A03, A08, A20, A22, A34, A36, AddicA, B21, C06, C07, C11, C25, CA, CABA, CurCont, D01, E01, E12, EMBASE, ESPM, ExcerpMed, GH, H&SSA, H04, IndMed, IndVet, LT, MEDLINE, N02, N03, NSA, P03, P30, P34, PHN&I, PsycInfo, PsycholAb, R10, R12, RRTA, Reac, RiskAb, S02, S03, SCI, SCOPUS, SSCI, T02, T05, TAR, ToxAb, VS, W07, W11.
—BLDSC (6110.106500), IE, Infotrieve, Ingenta, INIST. **CCC.**
Published by: (Society for Research on Nicotine and Tobacco USA), Oxford University Press, Great Clarendon St, Oxford, OX2 6DP, United Kingdom. TEL 44-1865-556767, FAX 44-1865-556646, enquiry@oup.co.uk, http://www.oxfordjournals.org. Ed. David J K Balfour.

633.71 NGA ISSN 0331-443X
NIGERIAN TOBACCO COMPANY. ANNUAL REPORT AND ACCOUNTS. Text in English. 1961. a. free. **Document type:** *Corporate.*
Formerly: Nigerian Tobacco Company. Report (0078-0820)
Published by: Nigerian Tobacco Company plc., Corporate Affairs Department, 18 Temple Rd, Lagos, Ikoyi, Nigeria. TEL 234-1-269471-8, FAX 234-1-2690470. Ed. Irene Ubah. Circ: 50,000.

679.7 USA ISSN 0897-9626
NONSMOKERS' VOICE. Text in English. 1977. biennial. USD 35 domestic; USD 50 foreign (effective 2000 - 2001). adv. **Document type:** *Newsletter.* **Description:** Contains new research on effects of secondhand smoke, smoke-free actions, local and state legislation, tactics of the tobacco industry.
Published by: Group to Alleviate Smoking Pollution (GASP), 2885 Aurora Ave, 37, Boulder, CO 80303-2252. TEL 303-444-9799, FAX 303-444-2399, gaspco@gaspforair.org, http://www.gaspforair.org. Ed. Peter Bialick. Pub., R&P, Adv. contact Pete Bialick. Circ: 1,000.

633.71 USA
NORTH CAROLINA TOBACCO REPORT. Text in English. 1950. a. free. charts; stat. back issues avail. **Document type:** *Government.* **Description:** Record of former sales, warehouse sales and quotas of tobacco growing in North Carolina.
Published by: Department of Agriculture, PO Box 27647, Raleigh, NC 27611. TEL 919-733-7887. Ed., R&P William Upchurch. Circ: 6,000.

679.7 AUT ISSN 0029-9561
OESTERREICHISCHE TRAFIKANTEN-ZEITUNG. Text in German. m. EUR 50 domestic; EUR 71 foreign (effective 2005). adv. illus. **Document type:** *Newspaper, Trade.*
Published by: Oesterreichischer Wirtschaftsverlag GmbH (Subsidiary of: Sueddeutscher Verlag GmbH), Wiedner Hauptstr 120-124, Vienna, W 1051, Austria. TEL 43-1-546640, FAX 43-1-54664406, office@wirtschaftsverlag.at, http://www.wirtschaftsverlag.at. Ed. Peter Hauer. Adv. contact Christine Fasching. color page EUR 3,000; trim 183 x 257. Circ: 4,800 (paid and controlled).

OFFICE OF TOBACCO CONTROL. ANNUAL REPORT/OIFIG UM RIALU TOBAC. TUARASCAIL BHLIANTUIL. *see* PUBLIC HEALTH AND SAFETY

679.7 668.4 DNK ISSN 0106-3235
PIBER & TOBAK. Text in Danish. 1978. q. DKK 250 membership (effective 2009). bk.rev. back issues avail. **Document type:** *Magazine, Consumer.*
Related titles: Online - full text ed.
Published by: Nordisk Tobakskollegium, c/o Leif Slot, Myggenaesgade 11, Copenhagen S, 2300, Denmark. TEL 45-35-365010. Eds. Ib Fagerlund, Leif Slot. Adv. contact Leif Slot.

679.7 394.14 NLD ISSN 0924-4158
PIJPELOGISCHE KRING NEDERLAND. Text in Dutch. 1978. q. EUR 18.50 domestic membership; EUR 26 foreign membership (effective 2009 - 2010). adv. illus. back issues avail. **Document type:** *Magazine, Consumer.* **Description:** For collectors of clay pipes.
Address: Utrechtse Jaagpad 115, Leiden, 2314 AT, Netherlands. info@tabakspijp.nl, http://www.tabakspijp.nl/.

658.8 LBN ISSN 1995-0438
PIPE CLUB OF LEBANON. JOURNAL. Text in English. 2006. s-a. **Document type:** *Magazine, Consumer.*
Media: Online - full text.
Published by: The Pipe Club of Lebanon http://www.pipecluboflebanon.org/Index1.htm. Ed. Paul Jahshan.

658.8 679.7 USA ISSN 0032-0161
THE PIPE SMOKER'S EPHEMERIS. Text in English. 1964. s-a. free. adv. bk.rev.; film rev.; tel.rev.; video rev. abstr.; bibl.; illus.; tr.lit.; charts; mkt.; pat.; stat.; tr.mk. Index. 100 p./no. 2 cols./p.; back issues avail. **Document type:** *Journal, Consumer.* **Description:** Carries original short stories, artwork, poetry, pipe, cigar and tobacco club news and convention information.
Published by: The Universal Coterie of Pipe Smokers, 20-37 120th St., College Point, NY 11356-2128. Ed., Pub. Tom Dunn. Circ: 7,500 (controlled).

688.42 USA ISSN 1095-2667
PIPES AND TOBACCOS. Abbreviated title: P & T. Text in English. 1996. q. USD 28 (effective 2011). adv. illus. back issues avail. **Document type:** *Magazine, Consumer.*
Published by: SpecComm International, Inc., 5808 Fairingdon Pl, Ste 200, Raleigh, NC 27609. TEL 919-872-5083, FAX 919-876-6531, http://www.speccomm.com. Ed. Chuck Stanion. Pub. Phil Bowling. Adv. contact Rich Perkins TEL 919-327-1598.

658.8 DEU
RADFORD'S MAGAZIN. Text in German. 2/yr. adv. **Document type:** *Magazine, Consumer.*
Published by: Poeschl Tabak GmbH, Dieselstr. 1, Geisenhausen, 84144, Germany. TEL 49-8743-971-0, FAX 49-8743-971110, poeschl@poeschl-tobacco.com, http://www.poeschl-tobacco.com. adv.: B&W page EUR 3,070, color page EUR 4,990. Circ: 95,000 (controlled).

RETAIL NEWSAGENT. *see* BUSINESS AND ECONOMICS—Small Business

679.7 FRA ISSN 0753-1605
HD9130.1
REVUE DES TABACS. Text in French. 1925. m. adv. charts; illus.; mkt.; pat.; tr.mk. **Document type:** *Magazine, Trade.*
Published by: Michel Burton Communication (M B C), 16 Rue Saint Fiacre, Paris, 75002, France. TEL 33-1-42365102, FAX 33-1-42338324, diffusion@groupembc.com, http://www.pnpapetier.com/. Circ: 30,000.

338.17371 FRA ISSN 1964-4108
REVUE DES TABACS. ANNUAIRE. Text in French. 1993. a. adv. **Document type:** *Magazine.*
Formerly (until 2005): Annuaire du Tabac (1258-8075)
Published by: Michel Burton Communication (M B C), 16 Rue Saint Fiacre, Paris, 75002, France. TEL 33-1-42365102, FAX 33-1-42338324, diffusion@groupembc.com, http://www.pnpapetier.com/. Circ: 20,000.

SERBIA FOOD & DRINK REPORT. *see* BUSINESS AND ECONOMICS

SINGAPORE FOOD & DRINK REPORT. *see* BUSINESS AND ECONOMICS

SLOVAKIA FOOD & DRINK REPORT. *see* BUSINESS AND ECONOMICS

SLOVENIA FOOD & DRINK REPORT. *see* BUSINESS AND ECONOMICS

051 394.14 679.7 USA
SMOKE; cigars, pipes and life's other burning desires. Text in English. 1996. q. USD 11.98 domestic; USD 17.97 in Canada; USD 23.98 elsewhere; USD 4.99 newsstand/cover domestic (effective 2004). adv. illus. **Document type:** *Magazine, Consumer.* **Description:** Lifestyle magazine for the cigar and pipe enthusiast.
Published by: Lockwood Publications, 26 Broadway, Fl. 9M, New York, NY 10004. TEL 212-391-2060, FAX 212-827-0945. Eds. Robert M Lockwood, Alyson Boxman Levine. Adv. contact Robert Olesen. color page USD 7,900; trim 8.75 x 10.875. Circ: 175,000 (paid).

658.8 DEU ISSN 1435-9987
SMOKERS CLUB. Text in German. 1974. q. EUR 18.80 domestic; EUR 20.20 foreign (effective 2011). adv. bk.rev. back issues avail. **Document type:** *Magazine, Consumer.* **Description:** Contains articles and features on items of interest for pipe smokers.
Formerly (until 1997): Pipe Club (0935-0675)
Published by: Konradin Selection GmbH (Subsidiary of: Konradin Verlag Robert Kohlhammer GmbH), Erich-Dombrowski-Str 2, Mainz, 55127, Germany. TEL 49-6131-484505, FAX 49-6131-484533. Ed. Folker Kling. Adv. contact Michael Guenther. Circ: 31,800 (paid and controlled).

658.8 USA
SMOKERS PIPELINE; the journal of kapnismology. Text in English. 1983. bi-m. adv. bk.rev. **Description:** Contains articles on pipes, tobacco, events, history, and people; promotes pipe collecting as a hobby and for profit.
Former titles: Pipe Smoker and Tobacciana Trader; Pipe Smoker (0746-1380)
Published by: Pipe Collectors Club of America, PO Box 5179, Woodbridge, VA 22194-5179. FAX 703-670-9701. Circ: 4,500.

338.17371 USA ISSN 0146-9266
SMOKESHOP. Text in English. 1970. bi-m. USD 24 (effective 2005). adv. **Document type:** *Magazine, Trade.*
Related titles: Online - full text ed.
Published by: Lockwood Publications, 26 Broadway, Fl. 9M, New York, NY 10004. TEL 212-391-2060. Ed. E Edward Hoyt III. Circ: 4,500.

SOUTH AFRICA FOOD & DRINK REPORT. *see* BUSINESS AND ECONOMICS

SOUTH KOREA FOOD & DRINK REPORT. *see* BUSINESS AND ECONOMICS

SPAIN FOOD & DRINK REPORT. *see* BUSINESS AND ECONOMICS

663.71 NLD ISSN 2211-4211
STICHTING NEDERLANDSE TABAKSHISTORIE. JAARBOEK. Variant title: S N T Jaarboek. Text in Dutch. 2004. a. EUR 27.76 (effective 2011).
Published by: Stichting Nederlandse Tabakshistorie, c/o Bert Bohnen, Sec., Onder de Bompjes 2, Gouda, 2801 AV, Netherlands. TEL 31-182-520564, tabakshistorie@telfort.nl, http://www.tabakshistorie.nl.

679.72029 USA
T M A DIRECTORY OF CIGARETTE BRANDS. Text in English. 1977. base vol. plus a. updates. looseleaf. **Document type:** *Directory.*
Related titles: CD-ROM ed.

Published by: Tobacco Merchants Association of the United States, Inc., PO Box 8019, Princeton, NJ 08543. TEL 609-275-4900, FAX 609-275-8379, tma@tma.org, http://www.tma.org.

658.8 USA
T M A EXECUTIVE SUMMARY. (Tobacco Merchants Association) Variant title: Executive Summary. Text in English. w. free to members (effective 2008). **Document type:** *Newsletter, Trade.* **Description:** Provides a high level summary of the principal industry developments occurring over the past week around the world and serves as an index to other TMA publications issued that week.
Media: Online - full content. **Related titles:** E-mail ed.: free (effective 2008); Fax ed.
Published by: Tobacco Merchants Association of the United States, Inc., PO Box 8019, Princeton, NJ 08543. TEL 609-275-4900, FAX 609-275-8379, tma@tma.org, http://www.tma.org.

658.8 USA
T M A INTERNATIONAL TOBACCO GUIDE. (Tobacco Merchants Association) Text in English. 1990. 2 base vols. plus a. updates. illus. **Document type:** *Handbook/Manual/Guide, Trade.*
Media: Online - full content. **Related titles:** CD-ROM ed.
Published by: Tobacco Merchants Association of the United States, Inc., PO Box 8019, Princeton, NJ 08543. TEL 609-275-4900, FAX 609-275-8379, tma@tma.org, http://www.tma.org.

658.8 USA
T M A ISSUES MONITOR. (Tobacco Merchants Association) Text in English. s-a. free to members (effective 2008). **Document type:** *Journal, Trade.* **Description:** Tracks the principal tobacco issues in the U.S. and worldwide and summarizes the principal economic, legislative, and regulatory developments.
Media: Online - full content. **Related titles:** E-mail ed.; Fax ed.
Published by: Tobacco Merchants Association of the United States, Inc., PO Box 8019, Princeton, NJ 08543. TEL 609-275-4900, FAX 609-275-8379, tma@tma.org, http://www.tma.org.

679.7 USA
T M A LEAF BULLETIN. (Tobacco Merchants Association) Variant title: Leaf Bulletin. Text in English. 1950. w. free to members (effective 2008). **Document type:** *Bulletin, Trade.* **Description:** Furnishes tobacco auction market statistics, for all leaf types, including stabilization inventories, and provides a brief legislative and regulatory rundown on matters impacting the leaf sector.
Media: Online - full text. **Related titles:** E-mail ed.; Fax ed.
Published by: Tobacco Merchants Association of the United States, Inc., PO Box 8019, Princeton, NJ 08543. TEL 609-275-4900, FAX 609-275-8379, tma@tma.org, http://www.tma.org.

679.7 340 USA
T M A LEGISLATIVE BULLETIN. (Tobacco Merchants Association) Variant title: Legislative Bulletin. Text in English. w. free to members (effective 2008). stat. back issues avail. **Document type:** *Bulletin, Trade.* **Description:** Analyzes congressional and state legislative activity on all issues affecting all tobacco products and summarizes key provisions of these bills and laws.
Incorporates (1924-198?): T M A State Bulletin; (1924-198?): T M A National Bulletin
Media: Online - full content. **Related titles:** E-mail ed.; Fax ed.; Print ed.
Published by: Tobacco Merchants Association of the United States, Inc., PO Box 8019, Princeton, NJ 08543. TEL 609-275-4900, FAX 609-275-8379, tma@tma.org, http://www.tma.org.

679.7 USA
T M A TOBACCO BAROMETER. (Tobacco Merchants Association) Variant title: Tobacco Barometer. Text in English. 1923. m. free to members (effective 2008). **Document type:** *Handbook/Manual/Guide, Trade.* **Description:** Domestic industry guide to manufactured production, taxable removals, and tax-exempt removals for cigarettes, large cigars, little cigars, chewing tobacco, snuff, and pipe tobacco.
Media: Online - full content. **Related titles:** E-mail ed.; Fax ed.
Published by: Tobacco Merchants Association of the United States, Inc., PO Box 8019, Princeton, NJ 08543. TEL 609-275-4900, FAX 609-275-8379, tma@tma.org, http://www.tma.org.

679.7 USA
T M A TOBACCO BAROMETER: SMOKING, CHEWING, SNUFF. (Tobacco Merchants Association) Variant title: Tobacco Barometer (S C S). Text in English. 1923. q. free to members (effective 2008). **Document type:** *Handbook/Manual/Guide, Trade.* **Description:** Domestic industry guide to manufactured production, invoiced domestic sales, imports, and exports for chewing tobacco, snuff, and all forms of smoking tobacco, including roll-your-own tobacco. Provides seasonal adjustments.
Media: Online - full text. **Related titles:** E-mail ed.; Fax ed.
Published by: Tobacco Merchants Association of the United States, Inc., PO Box 8019, Princeton, NJ 08543. TEL 609-275-4900, FAX 609-275-8379, tma@tma.org, http://www.tma.org.

679.7 USA
T M A TOBACCO TAX GUIDE. (Tobacco Merchants Association) Abbreviated title: T T G. Variant title: U S Tobacco Tax Guide. Text in English. 1962. base vol. plus q. updates. USD 2,400 to non-members; USD 800 to members (effective 2008). **Document type:** *Database, Trade.* **Description:** Compendium of federal and state tobacco tax law showing comparisons between states on all key tax variables such as excise tax rates, discount rates, sales prohibitions to minors, and other marketing related information.
Formerly: T M A Guide to Tobacco Taxes
Media: Online - full content. **Related titles:** CD-ROM ed.
Published by: Tobacco Merchants Association of the United States, Inc., PO Box 8019, Princeton, NJ 08543. TEL 609-275-4900, FAX 609-275-8379, tma@tma.org, http://www.tma.org.

679.7 USA ISSN 0495-6753
T M A TOBACCO TRADE BAROMETER. (Tobacco Merchants Association) Variant title: U S Tobacco Trade Barometer. (In 6 parts: Part 1: Balance of Trade Summary - all imports and all exports; Part 2: Exports of Leaf Tobacco - US exports by product & country; Part 3: Exports of Tobacco Products - US exports by product & country; Part 4: Imports of Leaf Tobacco - US imports by product & country; Part 5: Imports of Tobacco Products - US imports by products & country; Part 6: Imports of Smokers' Accessories - US imports by products & country) Text in English. 1967. m. looseleaf. free to members (effective 2008). **Document type:** *Report, Trade.* **Description:** Details all imports and all exports of all tobacco leaf and products, including tobacco sundries, by product and country providing values and quantities. Compares current data to the previous year.
Related titles: E-mail ed.; Online - full text ed.
Published by: Tobacco Merchants Association of the United States, Inc., PO Box 8019, Princeton, NJ 08543. TEL 609-275-4900, FAX 609-275-8379, tma@tma.org, http://www.tma.org.

658.8 336 USA
T M A TOBACCO WEEKLY. (Tobacco Merchants Association) Text in English. w. free to members (effective 2008). **Document type:** *Magazine, Trade.* **Description:** Covers excise taxes, marketing and distribution issues, corporate finance, leaf and trade, health campaigns, and product liability.
Media: Online - full content. **Related titles:** E-mail ed.: free to members (effective 2008); Fax ed.
Published by: Tobacco Merchants Association of the United States, Inc., PO Box 8019, Princeton, NJ 08543. TEL 609-275-4900, FAX 609-275-8379, tma@tma.org, http://www.tma.org.

658.8 602.7 USA
T M A TRADEMARK REPORT. (Tobacco Merchants Association) Variant title: Trademark Report. Text in English. m. free to members (effective 2008). **Document type:** *Report, Trade.* **Description:** Follows all the trademarks for tobacco products and tobacco accessory products in the United States from test market through registration and covers all renewals and cancellations.
Media: Online - full content. **Related titles:** E-mail ed.: free to members (effective 2008); Fax ed.
Published by: Tobacco Merchants Association of the United States, Inc., PO Box 8019, Princeton, NJ 08543. TEL 609-275-4900, FAX 609-275-8379, tma@tma.org, http://www.tma.org.

679.7 USA
T M A WORLD ALERT. (Tobacco Merchants Association) Variant title: World Alert. Text in English. w. free to members. back issues avail. **Document type:** *Bulletin.* **Description:** Provides news-flash country by country description of key industry and corporate developments around the world including corporate finance, excise taxes, marketing and distribution issues, leaf and trade, and health campaigns.
Formerly: International Executive Summary
Media: Online - full text. **Related titles:** E-mail ed.; Fax ed.
Published by: Tobacco Merchants Association of the United States, Inc., PO Box 8019, Princeton, NJ 08543. TEL 609-275-4900, FAX 609-275-8379, tma@tma.org, http://www.tma.org. Circ: 375.

658.8 USA
T M A WORLD CONSUMPTION & PRODUCTION. (Tobacco Merchants Association) Text in English. 19??. a. stat. **Document type:** *Report, Trade.* **Description:** Details country-by-country consumption and production of tobacco products over the previous 10 years.
Media: Online - full content. **Related titles:** E-mail ed.; Fax ed.
Published by: Tobacco Merchants Association of the United States, Inc., PO Box 8019, Princeton, NJ 08543. TEL 609-275-4900, FAX 609-275-8379, tma@tma.org, http://www.tma.org.

633.71 ITA ISSN 1970-1187
TABACCOLOGIA. Text in Multiple languages. 2000. q. **Document type:** *Magazine, Consumer.*
Related titles: Online - full text ed.: ISSN 1970-1195.
Published by: Societa Italiana di Tabaccologia (S I T A B), Via Giorgio Scalia 39, Rome, 00136, Italy.

679.7 CHE ISSN 0039-8721
TABAK/TABAC. Text in French, German. 1903. 10/yr. CHF 40 (effective 2000). adv. illus.; stat. **Document type:** *Magazine, Trade.*
Published by: (Verband Schweizerischer Tabakhaendler/Federation Suisse des Marchands de Tabacs), Druckerei Leo Fuerer AG, Davidstr 9, Postfach 634, St. Gallen, 9001, Switzerland. TEL 41-71-2285810, FAX 41-71-2285828. Pub. Peter Fuerer. adv.: B&W page CHF 1,190. Circ: 1,000.

658.8 338 NLD ISSN 1566-8142
TABAK PLUS GEMAK; vakblad voor de tabaksdetailhandel. Text in Dutch. 1939. 10/yr. EUR 27.50 (effective 2009). adv. bk.rev. charts; illus.; stat.; tr.lit. **Document type:** *Trade.*
Former titles (until l999): Tabak Plus Benelux (0925-7543); (until l990): Tabak Plus (0169-460X)
Published by: (N S O, Branche Organisatie Tabaksdetailhandel, Stichting Promotie Tabaksdetailhandel), Uitgeverij van Vlaardingen BV, Dorpsweg 198, Maartensdijk, 3738 CL, Netherlands. TEL 31-346-213690, FAX 31-346-216584, info@vanvlaardingen.nl, http://www.tabaksdetailhandel.nl. Ed., Adv. contact Dick van Vlaardingen. B&W page EUR 1,290, color page EUR 1,810; bleed 16.5 x 23. Circ: 4,000.

633.71 DEU ISSN 0049-2825
DIE TABAK ZEITUNG. Text in German. 1891. w. EUR 163.80 domestic; EUR 202.80 foreign (effective 2011). adv. bk.rev. **Document type:** *Newspaper, Trade.*
Published by: Konradin Selection GmbH (Subsidiary of: Konradin Verlag Robert Kohlhammer GmbH), Erich-Dombrowski-Str 2, Mainz, 55127, Germany. TEL 49-6131-484505, FAX 49-6131-484533. Ed. Folker Kling. Adv. contact Michael Guenther. Circ: 10,231 (paid and controlled).

658.8 NLD ISSN 1876-7435
TABAKMAG. Text in Dutch. 2008. 6/yr. **Document type:** *Magazine, Trade.*
Related titles: ◆ Supplement to: Pompshop. ISSN 0922-8896.
Published by: Uitgeverij Lakerveld BV, Postbus 160, Wateringen, 2290 AD, Netherlands. TEL 31-174-315000, FAX 31-174-315001, uitgeverij@lakerveld.nl.

658.8 DEU
DER TABAKWAREN-GROSSHANDEL. Text in German. 1951. bi-m. adv. **Document type:** *Magazine, Trade.*
Published by: Bundesverband Deutscher Tabakwaren - Grosshaendler und Automatenaufsteller e.V., Stadtwaldguertel 44, Cologne, 50931, Germany. TEL 49-221-400700, FAX 49-221-4007020, zenner@bdta.de, http://www.bdta.de. adv.: B&W page EUR 850, color page EUR 2,170. Circ: 550 (controlled).

TAIWAN FOOD & DRINK REPORT. *see* BUSINESS AND ECONOMICS

THAILAND FOOD & DRINK REPORT. *see* BUSINESS AND ECONOMICS

679.7 USA ISSN 0082-4593
TOBACCO ASSOCIATES. ANNUAL REPORT. Text in English. 1948. a. free. charts; stat. cum.index: 1948-2000. **Document type:** *Corporate.* **Description:** Provides a summary of the association's activities and industry news.
Published by: Tobacco Associates, Inc., 1306 Annapolis Dr, Ste 102, Raleigh, NC 27608. TEL 919-821-7670, FAX 919-821-7674. Ed. Charlie King. Circ: 7,500 (controlled).

679.7 610 GBR ISSN 0964-4563
HV5725
➤ **TOBACCO CONTROL**; an international peer-reviewed journal for health professionals and others in tobacco control. Abbreviated title: T C. Text in English; Summaries in Chinese, French, Spanish. 1992. bi-m. GBP 344 to institutions; GBP 426 combined subscription to institutions small FTE (print & online eds.) (effective 2011). adv. bk.rev. charts; illus.; stat. index. back issues avail.; reprints avail. **Document type:** *Journal, Academic/Scholarly.* **Description:** Covers the nature and consequences of tobacco use worldwide; tobacco's effects on population health, the economy, the environment, and society; efforts to prevent and control the global tobacco epidemic through population level education and policy changes; the ethical dimensions of tobacco control policies; and the activities of the tobacco industry and its allies.
Related titles: Online - full text ed.: e T C. ISSN 1468-3318. GBP 352 to institutions small FTE (effective 2011).
Indexed: A01, A03, A08, A20, A22, A26, A36, AddicA, B21, BP, C06, C07, C08, CA, CABA, CINAHL, CurCont, E08, E12, EMBASE, ESPM, ExcerpMed, FR, G08, GH, H&SSA, H11, H12, H16, H17, HospAb, I05, INI, ISR, IndMed, Inpharma, LT, MEDLINE, N02, N03, P03, P11, P20, P22, P24, P30, P33, P34, P48, P50, P52, P54, P56, PHN&I, PQC, PsycInfo, R10, R12, RA&MP, RRTA, Reac, S02, S03, S09, S13, S16, S21, SCI, SCOPUS, SSCI, T02, T05, TAR, W07, W11.
—BLDSC (8859.576550), GNLM, IE, Infotrieve, Ingenta, INIST. **CCC.**
Published by: (Department of Public Health & Community Medicine AUS), B M J Group, BMA House, Tavistock Sq, London, WC1H 9JR, United Kingdom. TEL 44-20-73836373, FAX 44-20-73836668, http://group.bmj.com. Ed. Ruth Malone. Pub. Christiane Notarmarco TEL 44-20-78747096. Adv. contact Nick Gray TEL 44-20-73836386. Circ: 1,080. **Subscr. to:** PO Box 299, London WC1H 9TD, United Kingdom. TEL 44-20-73836270, FAX 44-20-73836402.

633.71 USA
SB273
THE TOBACCO FARM QUARTERLY. Abbreviated title: T F Q. Text in English. 1964. q. USD 24.95 (effective 2011). adv. charts; illus.; mkt.; pat.; tr.mk. back issues avail. **Document type:** *Magazine, Trade.* **Description:** For commercial growers of flue-cured tobacco and related agribusiness.
Incorporates (in 2005): Burely Tobacco Farmer; Formerly (until 2005): The Flue Cured Tobacco Farmer (0015-4512)
Published by: SpecComm International, Inc., 5808 Fairingdon Pl, Ste 200, Raleigh, NC 27609. TEL 919-872-4780, FAX 919-876-6531, http://www.speccomm.com. Ed. Taco Tunistra TEL 919-875-9964. Pub. Noel Morris TEL 919-872-4213. Adv. contact Kay O'Neill.

362.1 DEU ISSN 1617-9625
QP801.T57
➤ **TOBACCO INDUCED DISEASES (ONLINE).** Text in English. 2002. q. free (effective 2011). **Document type:** *Journal, Academic/Scholarly.* **Description:** Aims to publish original scientific papers that advance the understanding of the mechanisms underlying tobacco induced diseases and of tobacco addiction prevention.
Formerly (until 2002): Tobacco Induced Diseases (Print) (2070-7266)
Media: Online - full text.
Indexed: A01, A26, B21, C06, C07, CA, E08, EMBASE, ESPM, ExcerpMed, H&SSA, H12, I05, P30, RiskAb, S09, SCOPUS, T02, ToxAb.
—CCC.
Published by: International Society for the Prevention of Tobacco Induced Diseases, PO Box 185431, Essen, 45204, Germany. FAX 49-360-376-5845, PTIDsociety@aol.com, http://members.aol.com/ptidsociety/home/. Ed. J Elliot Scott.

338.476797 USA ISSN 0049-3945
HD9130.1 CODEN: TBCIAE
TOBACCO INTERNATIONAL. Text in English. 1886. m. USD 40 (effective 2005). adv. bk.rev. charts; illus.; mkt.; stat.; tr.lit. reprints avail. **Document type:** *Magazine, Trade.*
Formerly (until 1971): Tobacco (0040-828X)
Related titles: Online - full text ed.
Indexed: A22, ChemAb, G08.
—CASDDS, Linda Hall.
Published by: Lockwood Publications, 26 Broadway, Fl. 9M, New York, NY 10004. TEL 212-391-2060, FAX 212-827-0945. Pub. Robert M Lockwood. Circ: 5,000 (controlled).

658.8 AUS
TOBACCO JOURNAL. Text in English. 1931. m.
Indexed: IPackAb.
Published by: Retail Tobacco Sellers Association of Victoria, PO Box 1780, Melbourne, VIC 3001, Australia. **Co-sponsor:** Retail Tobacco Traders' Association of Tasmania.

679.7 DEU ISSN 0939-8627
HD9130.1
TOBACCO JOURNAL INTERNATIONAL. Text in English. 1963. bi-m. EUR 110.39 in Europe; EUR 116.39 elsewhere (effective 2011). adv. bk.rev. charts; illus.; stat. cum.index. **Document type:** *Magazine, Trade.*
Former titles (until 1990): T J I - Tobacco, Tabac, Tabaco, Tabacco, Tabak Journal International (0721-5185); (until 1981): Tabak Journal International (0039-8748)
Related titles: Online - full text ed.
Indexed: IPackAb.
—CCC.

Published by: Konradin Selection GmbH (Subsidiary of: Konradin Verlag Robert Kohlhammer GmbH), Erich-Dombrowski-Str 2, Mainz, 55127, Germany. TEL 49-6131-484505, FAX 49-6131-484533. Ed. Stefanie Rossel. Adv. contact Stefanie Scherrer. Circ: 6,100 (paid and controlled).

679.7 USA ISSN 0272-2771
HD9134
TOBACCO MARKET REVIEW. FIRE-CURED AND DARK AIR-CURED. Text in English. 19??. a. back issues avail. **Document type:** *Government.*
Formerly (until 1974): Fire-Cured and Dark Air-Cured Tobacco Market Review (0498-2150); Which was formed by the merger of (1945-1956): Fire-Cured Tobacco Market Review (0887-0454); Which was formerly: Tobacco Market Review. Class 2, Fire-Cured; (1945-1956): Dark Air-Cured Tobacco Market Review (0500-3016); Which was formerly: Tobacco Market Review. Class 3(b), Dark Air-Cured
Related titles: Online - full text ed.
—Linda Hall.
Published by: U.S. Department of Agriculture, Agricultural Marketing Service, Tobacco Programs, Stop 0280, Cotton Annex Rm. 502, 1400 Independence Ave., S.W., Washington, DC 20250-0280. http://www.ams.usda.gov/tob/.

679.7 ZWE
TOBACCO NEWS. Text in English. 1977. m. ZWD 200.40; ZWD 284.40 foreign (effective 1999). adv. illus. **Document type:** *Magazine, Trade.* **Description:** Provides independent coverage of the tobacco industry in Zimbabwe.
Former titles (until 1992): Zimbabwe Tobacco Today; (until 1980): Rhodesia Tobacco Today; Rhodesian Tobacco Journal (0035-4880); Incorporating: Tobacco Today; Stock and Crops (0039-1557)
Published by: Thomson Publications Zimbabwe (Pvt) Ltd., Thomson House, PO Box 1683, Harare, Zimbabwe. TEL 263-4-736835, FAX 263-4-752390.

679.7 USA ISSN 0361-5693
HD9130.1
TOBACCO REPORTER. Text in English. 1874. m. USD 60 (effective 2011). adv. bk.rev. charts; illus.; mkt.; pat.; tr.lit. Supplement avail.; back issues avail. **Document type:** *Magazine, Trade.* **Description:** Devoted to all segments of the international tobacco industry: processing, trading, manufacturing.
Former titles: T R; Tobacco Reporter (0040-8328); Supersedes: Western Tobacco Journal
Related titles: Online - full text ed.
Indexed: G08.
—BLDSC (8859.578500), IE, Ingenta.
Published by: SpecComm International, Inc., 5808 Fairingdon Pl, Ste 200, Raleigh, NC 27609. TEL 919-872-5040, FAX 919-876-6531, http://www.speccomm.com. Ed. Taco Tunistra TEL 919-875-9964. Pub. Noel LeGette Morris TEL 919-872-4213. Adv. contact Kay O'Neill.

658.8 USA ISSN 1521-8236
HD9131
TOBACCO RETAILER. Abstracts and contents page in English. 1998. bi-m. USD 29 domestic; USD 50 in Canada & Mexico; USD 130 elsewhere; USD 39 combined subscription domestic (print & onine eds.); USD 60 combined subscription in Canada & Mexico (print & onine eds.); USD 140 combined subscription elsewhere (print & onine eds.); free to qualified personnel (effective 2011). adv. 48 p./no.; back issues avail.; reprints avail. **Document type:** *Magazine, Trade.* **Description:** Features sales, marketing and operations articles, news and new products, personnel advice, cigar reviews, updates on the National Association of Tobacco Outlets and profiles of leading retailers.
Related titles: Online - full text ed.: USD 10 (effective 2011).
Indexed: B02, B03, B11, B15, B17, B18, G04, G06, G07, G08, I05.
—CIS.
Published by: M2Media360, 1030 W Higgins Rd, Ste 230, Park Ridge, IL 60068. TEL 847-720-5600, FAX 847-720-5601, http://www.m2media360.com/. Ed. Richard Brandes. Pub., Adv. contact Charles Forman TEL 845-426-6072. Circ: 15,000.

633.71 USA
TOBACCO SCIENCE. Text in English. 1957. q. charts; stat. **Document type:** *Magazine, Trade.*
Published by: SpecComm International, Inc., 5808 Faringdon Pl, Ste 200, Raleigh, NC 27609. TEL 919-872-5040, 800-346-7469, FAX 919-876-6531, http://www.speccomm.com.

658.8 USA ISSN 1071-815X
HD9131
TOBACCONIST. Text in English. 1990. bi-m. USD 28 (effective 2011). adv. illus. back issues avail. **Document type:** *Magazine, Consumer.*
Formerly (until 1993): Retail Tobacconist
Published by: (Retail Tobacco Dealers of America), SpecComm International, Inc., 5808 Fairingdon Pl, Ste 200, Raleigh, NC 27609. TEL 919-872-5040, FAX 919-876-6531, http://www.speccomm.com. Ed. Phil Bowling. Adv. contact Rich Perkins TEL 919-327-1598.

TURKEY FOOD & DRINK REPORT. *see* BUSINESS AND ECONOMICS

U.S. BUREAU OF ALCOHOL, TOBACCO AND FIREARMS. QUARTERLY BULLETIN. *see* CRIMINOLOGY AND LAW ENFORCEMENT

UKRAINE FOOD & DRINK REPORT. *see* BUSINESS AND ECONOMICS

UNITED ARAB EMIRATES FOOD & DRINK REPORT. *see* BUSINESS AND ECONOMICS

UNITED KINGDOM FOOD & DRINK REPORT. *see* BUSINESS AND ECONOMICS

VENEZUELA FOOD & DRINK REPORT. *see* BUSINESS AND ECONOMICS

VIETNAM FOOD AND DRINK REPORT. *see* BUSINESS AND ECONOMICS

679.7 ITA ISSN 0042-7829
LA VOCE DEL TABACCAIO. Text in Italian. 1927. w. membership. adv. illus. **Document type:** *Magazine, Trade.*
Published by: Federazione Italiana Tabaccai, Via Leopoldo Serra 32, Rome, 00153, Italy. http://www.tabaccai.it. Circ: 48,000.

679.7 GBR ISSN 0043-9126
SB273
WORLD TOBACCO. Text in English. 1963. bi-m. GBP 106.80 in Europe; GBP 112.80 elsewhere (effective 2009). adv. bk.rev. charts; illus.; mkt.; pat.; tr.lit.; tr.mk. back issues avail. **Document type:** *Magazine, Trade.* **Description:** Provides tobacco industry reports from around the world, along with information about other world tobacco products.
Related titles: Online - full text ed.; Chinese ed.; Russian ed.; ◆ Supplement(s): World Tobacco Directory. ISSN 0084-2273.
Indexed: B01, B02, B03, B06, B07, B08, B09, B15, B17, B18, C12, G04, G06, G07, G08, I05, IPackAb, M01, M02, P30, P34, T02, WBA, WMB.
—BLDSC (9360.100000), IE, Infotrieve, Ingenta. **CCC.**
Published by: Quartz Business Media Ltd., Westgate House, 120/130 Station Rd, Redhill, Surrey RH1 1ET, United Kingdom. TEL 44-1737-855000, FAX 44-1737-855475, http://www.quartzltd.co.uk/business. Eds. Anja Helk TEL 49-6131-484514, William McEwen TEL 49-6131-484511, Stefanie Rossel TEL 49-6131-484513. adv.: page GBP 4,230; bleed 214 x 292.

679.7029 GBR ISSN 0084-2273
WORLD TOBACCO DIRECTORY. Text in English. 1938. a. (Jul.). GBP 149 per issue domestic; GBP 155, EUR 195, USD 307 per issue foreign (effective 2009). adv. **Document type:** *Directory, Trade.* **Description:** Provides the essential, comprehensive guide to the companies, organisations and associations that make up the worldwide tobacco industry.
Formerly (until 1972): Costa's World Tobacco Directory
Related titles: Online - full text ed.; ◆ Supplement to: World Tobacco. ISSN 0043-9126.
Indexed: G08, I05.
—**CCC.**
Published by: Quartz Business Media Ltd., Westgate House, 120/130 Station Rd, Redhill, Surrey RH1 1ET, United Kingdom. TEL 44-1737-855000, FAX 44-1737-855475, http://www.quartzltd.co.uk/business.

633.71 CHN ISSN 1007-5119
ZHONGGUO YANCAO KEXUE/CHINESE TOBACCO SCIENCE. Text in Chinese. 1979. bi-m. CNY 30; CNY 5 per issue (effective 2009). **Document type:** *Magazine, Trade.*
Formerly (until 1996): Zhongguo Yancao (1002-6398)
Related titles: Online - full text ed.
Indexed: A35, A37, AgBio, B23, C25, C30, CABA, E12, F08, FCA, GH, H16, I11, N02, N05, OR, P32, P33, P40, PGegResA, PGrRegA, PHN&I, R07, R08, R11, R12, R13, RA&MP, S12, S13, S16, S17, SoyAb, TAR, VS, W10, W11.
Published by: (Zhongguo Nongye Kexueyuan Caoyuan Yanjiusuo/Chinese Academy of Agricultural Sciences, Tobacco Research Institute), Zhongguo Yancao Zonggongsi Qingzhou Yancao Yanjiusuo, 11, Keyuanjing Si Lu, Qingdao, 266101, China. TEL 86-532-88703238, FAX 86-532-88702056.

ZIMBABWE FOOD & DRINK REPORT. *see* BUSINESS AND ECONOMICS

679.7 ZWE ISSN 0375-4065
ZIMBABWE. TOBACCO RESEARCH BOARD. ANNUAL REPORT AND ACCOUNTS. Text in English. 1954. a. free. charts. **Document type:** *Corporate.*
Formerly: Rhodesia. Tobacco Research Board. Annual Report and Accounts (0080-2875)
Published by: Zimbabwe. Tobacco Research Board, PO Box 1909, Kutsaga Stationt, Harare, Zimbabwe. TEL 263-4-575289, FAX 263-4-575288. Ed., R&P B W Blair. Circ: 660.

TOBACCO—Abstracting, Bibliographies, Statistics

679.7 016 FRA ISSN 0525-6240
C O R E S T A; bulletin d'information. Text in English, French. 1957. q. membership. bk.rev. abstr.; charts; illus. **Document type:** *Bulletin.*
—INIST. **CCC.**
Published by: Centre de Cooperation pour les Recherches Scientifiques Relatives au Tabac, 11 Rue du Quatre Septembre, Paris, 75002, France. TEL 33-1-58625870, FAX 33-1-58625879, emarignac@coresta.org, http://www.coresta.org. Ed. Francois Jacob. Circ: 1,000.

338.4 CAN ISSN 0835-0019
CANADA. STATISTICS CANADA. BEVERAGE AND TOBACCO PRODUCTS INDUSTRIES/INDUSTRIES DES BOISSONS ET DU TABAC. Text in English, French. 1985. a. CAD 40 domestic; USD 40 foreign (effective 1999). **Document type:** *Government.*
Formed by the merger of (19??-1985): Canada. Statistics Canada. Tobacco Products Industries (0300-0249); Which was formerly (until 1960): Canada. Dominion Bureau of Statistics. Tobacco and Tobacco Products Industries (0384-4390); (until 1950): Canada. Dominion Bureau of Statistics. Tobacco Industries (0829-9234); (19??-1985): Canada. Statistics Canada. Soft Drink Industry (0833-7497); Which was formerly (until 1984): Soft Drink Manufacturers (0527-6217); (until 1960): Carbonated Beverages Industry (0384-4919); (until 1951): Aerated Waters Industry (0825-9348); (until 1948): Aerated Waters Industry in Canada (0825-933X); (until 1927): Advance Report on the Aerated and Mineral Water Industry; (1981-1985): Canada. Statistics Canada. Alcoholic Beverage Industries (0319-8871); Which was formed by the merger of (19??-1981): Canada. Statistics Canada. Breweries (0527-4869); Which was formerly (until 1960): Canada. Bureau of Statistics. Brewing Industry (0384-2827); (until 1948): Canada. Dominion Bureau of Statistics. Report on the Brewing Industry in Canada (0825-4486); (until 192?): Canada. Dominion Bureau of Statistics. Advance Report on the Malt Liquor Industry in Canada; (19??-1981): Canada. Statistics Canada. Wineries (0384-4854); Which was formerly (until 1960): Canada. Bureau of Statistics. Wine Industry (0384-4862); (until 1949): Canada. Dominion Bureau of Statistics. Report on the Wine Industry in Canada (0825-4478); (until 192?): Canada. Dominion Bureau of Statistics. Preliminary Report on the Wine Industry; (19??-1981): Canada. Statistics Canada. Distilleries (0527-5024); Which was formerly (until 1960): Canada. Bureau of Statistics. Distilling Industry (0384-3009); (until 1951): Canada. Dominion Bureau of Statistics. Distilled Liquor Industry
Related titles: Microform ed.: (from MML); Online - full text ed.
Published by: Statistics Canada/Statistique Canada, Circulation Management, Jean Talon Bldg, 2 C12, Tunney's Pasture, Ottawa, ON K1A 0T6, Canada. TEL 613-951-7277, 800-267-6677, FAX 613-951-1584, http://www.statcan.gc.ca.

633.71 338 679.7 658.8 CAN ISSN 0708-336X
CANADA. STATISTICS CANADA. PRODUCTION AND DISPOSITION OF TOBACCO PRODUCTS/CANADA. STATISTIQUE CANDA. PRODUCTION ET DISPOSITION DES PRODUITS DU TABAC. Text in English, French. 1979. m. looseleaf. CAD 62; USD 62 foreign. 4 p./no.; back issues avail. **Document type:** *Government.* **Description:** Shows monthly and cumulative production, sales and inventory of cigarettes, cigars and cut tobacco in Canada.
Related titles: Diskette ed.; Microform ed.: (from MML); Online - full text ed.
Published by: Statistics Canada, Operations and Integration Division (Subsidiary of: Statistics Canada/Statistique Canada), Circulation Management, 120 Parkdale Ave, Ottawa, ON K1A 0T6, Canada. TEL 613-951-7277, 800-267-6677, FAX 613-951-1584.

633.71 016 USA ISSN 1555-5119
SB273
TOBACCO ABSTRACTS; world literature on Nicotiana. Text in English. 2002. q. index. **Document type:** *Abstract/Index.* **Description:** Covers tobacco culture, economics, genetics, chemistry, manufacture and distribution.
Media: CD-ROM.
Published by: Tobacco Literature Service, 3210 Faucette Dr, Rm 204-206 Budler Bldg, Campus Box 7603, NC State University, Raleigh, NC 27695-7603. TEL 919-513-3045, FAX 919-515-8602, pam_puryear@ncsu.edu, http://www.cals.ncsu.edu/agcomm/tobacco.htm. Ed. Pamela E Puryear.

TOXICOLOGY AND ENVIRONMENTAL SAFETY

see ENVIRONMENTAL STUDIES—Toxicology And Environmental Safety

TRADE AND INDUSTRIAL DIRECTORIES

see BUSINESS AND ECONOMICS—Trade And Industrial Directories

TRANSPORTATION

see also TRANSPORTATION—Air Transport ; TRANSPORTATION—Automobiles ; TRANSPORTATION—Computer Applications ; TRANSPORTATION—Railroads ; TRANSPORTATION—Roads And Traffic ; TRANSPORTATION—Ships And Shipping ; TRANSPORTATION—Trucks And Trucking

A A A TOUCH. *see* TRAVEL AND TOURISM

A A P E X TODAY. (Automotive Aftermarket Products Expo) *see* MEETINGS AND CONGRESSES

388 AUT
A P A - JOURNAL. MOTOR - MOBILITAET. Text in German. w. EUR 380 combined subscription for print & online eds. (effective 2003). **Document type:** *Journal, Trade.*
Related titles: Online - full text ed.
Published by: Austria Presse Agentur, Gunoldstr 14, Vienna, W 1190, Austria. TEL 43-1-360600, FAX 43-1-360603099, kundenservice@apa.at, http://www.apa.at.

388 388.322 385.37 GBR ISSN 1460-0587
A TO B. Text in English. 1993. bi-m. GBP 13.80 domestic; GBP 19, USD 31 foreign (effective 2009). adv. bk.rev.; video rev. mkt. 56 p./no.; back issues avail. **Document type:** *Magazine, Consumer.* **Description:** Features news on folding bikes, electric bikes, trailers, trikes, trains and alternative transport.
Formerly (until 1997): The Folder
Related titles: Online - full text ed.: GBP 11 (effective 2009).
Published by: A to B Magazine, 40 Manor Rd, Dorchester, DT1 2AX, United Kingdom. TEL 44-1305-259998. Eds. David Henshaw, Jane Henshaw.

ACCESS CURRENTS. *see* HANDICAPPED—Physically Impaired

388 FRA ISSN 0769-0266
ACTES. Text in French. 1986. irreg. **Document type:** *Monographic series, Academic/Scholarly.*
—INIST.
Published by: Institut National de Recherche sur les Transports et leur Securite, 25 Av. Francois Mitterrand, Bron, Cedex 69675, France. TEL 33-4-72142300, FAX 33-4-72376837. **Subscr. to:** Lavoisier, Lavoisier - Dept Abonnements, 14 rue de Provigny, Cachan 94236, France. TEL 33-1-47406700, FAX 33-1-47406702, abo@lavoisier.fr.

383 BEL ISSN 0774-613X
AD REM. Text in Dutch. 1987. q. EUR 42 (effective 2008). **Document type:** *Journal, Trade.*
Published by: Die Keure NV, Kleine Pathoekeweg 3, Bruges, 8000, Belgium. TEL 32-50-471272, FAX 32-50-335154, juridische.uitgaven@diekeure.be, http://www.diekeure.be.

388 GBR ISSN 1462-608X
➤ **ADVANCES IN TRANSPORT.** Text in English. 1998. irreg., latest vol.17, 2006. price varies. back issues avail. **Document type:** *Monographic series, Academic/Scholarly.* **Description:** Covers advances in the field of transportation. Each volume contains papers from leading researchers in the field of transportation and covers areas of current interest or active research.
Indexed: EngInd, SCOPUS.
—BLDSC (0711.634000).
Published by: W I T Press, Ashurst Lodge, Ashurst, Southampton, Hants SO40 7AA, United Kingdom. TEL 44-238-0293223, FAX 44-238-0292853, marketing@witpress.com.

388 ITA ISSN 1824-5463
ADVANCES IN TRANSPORTATION STUDIES. Text in Italian. 2003. q. **Document type:** *Magazine, Trade.*

Indexed: A01, CPEI, HRIS.
Published by: Aracne Editrice, Via Raffaele Garofalo 133 A/B, Rome, 00173, Italy. info@aracneeditrice.it, http://store.aracneeditrice.com.

AIR TRANSPORT WORLD. *see* AERONAUTICS AND SPACE FLIGHT

AIRPORT BUSINESS; connecting airports, businesses, their people and suppliers. *see* AERONAUTICS AND SPACE FLIGHT

AIRPORTS INTERNATIONAL MAGAZINE. *see* AERONAUTICS AND SPACE FLIGHT

AIRSTREAM LIFE; the official Airstream lifestyle magazine. *see* SPORTS AND GAMES—Outdoor Life

ALABAMA CRIMINAL, VEHICLES AND TRAFFIC AND RELATED STATUTES. *see* LAW—Criminal Law

ALASKA CRIMINAL AND TRAFFIC LAW MANUAL. *see* LAW—Criminal Law

388 351 CAN ISSN 1715-5029
HC117.A6
ALBERTA. ALBERTA INFRASTRUCTURE AND TRANSPORTATION. ANNUAL REPORT. Text in English. 2000. a. **Document type:** *Government.*
Formed by the merger of (2002-2004): Alberta Transportation. Annual Report (Year) (1703-8510); (2000-2004): Alberta Infrastructure. Annual Report (1497-0694); Which was formed by the merger of (1983-2000): Alberta. Public Works, Supply and Services. Annual Report (0834-4043); Which was formed by the merger of (1???-1983): Alberta Housing and Public Works. Annual Report (0702-3111); Which was formerly (until 1976): Alberta Public Works. Annual Report (0702-309X); (until 1972): Department of Public Works of the Province of Alberta (0702-3081); Which superseded in part (in 1906): Department of Public Works of the North-West Territories; (1976-1983): Alberta Government Services (0702-9640); (1987-2000): Alberta Transportation and Utilities (0836-1509); Which was formed by the merger of (1952-1987): Alberta Transportation. Annual Report (0702-7702); Which was formerly (until 1976): Alberta Highways and Transport. Annual Report (0318-4757); (until 1972): Department of Highways and Transport. Province of Alberta (0318-4749); (until 1969): Department of Highways of the Province of Alberta. Annual Report (0516-5164); (1974-1987): Alberta Utilities (0839-573X); Which superseded in part (until 1986): Alberta Utilities and Telecommunications. Annual Report (0826-323X); Which was formerly (until 1983): Alberta Utilities and Telephones. Annual report (0707-8870); (until 1976): Telephone and Utilities. Utilities Division (0381-2294)
Published by: Canada, Alberta Transportation, Twin Atria Building, 4999-98 Ave, Edmonton, AB T6B 2X3, Canada. TEL 780-427-2731, 310-0000, FAX 780-466-3166, http://www.tu.gov.ab.ca/home/index.asp.

388 NLD
ALLE BESTEL- EN VRACHTAUTO'S. Text in Dutch. 2003. a. EUR 14.95 (effective 2009).
Formerly (until 2008): Alle Bestelauto's (1574-4264)
Published by: Uitgeverij de Alk bv, Postbus 9006, Alkmaar, 1800 GA, Netherlands. TEL 31-72-5113965, FAX 31-72-5129989, info@alk.nl, http://www.alk.nl.

388.342 GBR ISSN 2046-4584
AMERICAN CAR. Variant title: American Car Magazine. Text in English. 2002. m. adv. **Document type:** *Magazine, Consumer.* **Description:** Contains reports on news and trends about American high-performance cars.
Formerly (until 2010): American Car World (0969-3726); Which superseded in part (in 2004): Street Machine & American Car World (1744-7720); Which was formed by the merger of (1979-2002): Street Machine (0143-5949); (1993-2002): American Car World (1745-1582)
Related titles: Online - full text ed.
Published by: Shut Up and Drive Publishing Ltd., 321 Broadstone Mill, Broadstone Ln, Stockport, Cheshire SK5 7DL, United Kingdom. andy.craig@shutupanddrivepublishing.com. Adv. contact Emma Taylor.

380 USA ISSN 1529-1820
THE AMERICAN JOURNAL OF TRANSPORTATION. Text in English. 1918. w. (Mon.). USD 98 domestic; CAD 139 in Canada (effective 2005). adv. bk.rev. maps; stat.; tr.lit. back issues avail. **Document type:** *Newspaper, Trade.* **Description:** Covers all modes of cargo transportation and relevant developments in international and domestic trade for businesses in North America.
Former titles: The Atlantic Journal of Transportation (1089-0327); (until 1996): Northeast Journal of Transportation (1061-8090); (until 1991): New England Journal of Transportation (1062-4309); (until 1989): Boston Marine Guide (0162-0797)
Published by: American Journal of Transportation, Inc., 1354 Hancock St, Ste 300, Quincy, MA 02169. TEL 617-328-5005, FAX 617-328-5999. Ed. George Lauriat. Pub. William Bourbon. R&P Ann Radwan TEL 617-328-5005. Adv. contact Mathew Weidner. B&W page USD 3,200, color page USD 3,725; trim 10 x 15. Circ: 7,500 (paid and controlled).

380.5 USA ISSN 1546-2595
HF5487
AMERICAN PUBLIC WAREHOUSE REGISTER. Text in English. a. **Document type:** *Directory, Trade.* **Description:** Designed to be comprehensive reference source for buyers of logistics-related services.
Related titles: Online - full text ed.
Published by: Reed Business Information (Subsidiary of: Reed Business), 2 Brandywine Way, Sicklerville, NJ 08081. TEL 856-728-9745, FAX 856-728-5788, corporatecommunications@reedbusiness.com, http://www.reedbusiness.com.

388 ARG ISSN 1851-362X
ANDANTE. Text in Spanish. 2007. q.
Published by: Asociacion Argentina de Empresarios del Transporte Automotor, Bernardo de irigoyen No. 330, 6o. Piso, Buenos Aires, 1072, Argentina. TEL 54-11-43343254, FAX 54-11-43346513, info@aaeta.org.ar, http://www.aaeta.org.ar/.

388 CHN
ANHUI JIAOTONGBAO/ANHUI COMMUNICATIONS NEWS. Text in Chinese. 1955. 3/w. **Document type:** *Newspaper, Trade.*
Published by: Anhui Ribao Baoye Jituan, 206, Jinzhai Lu, Hefei, 230061, China. TEL 86-551-4291416, FAX 86-551-2832587.

380.5 USA ISSN 1054-0288
ANIMAL TRANSPORTATION ASSOCIATION. INTERNATIONAL CONFERENCE. PROCEEDINGS. Text in English. 1978. a. price varies. adv. bk.rev. **Document type:** *Proceedings.* **Description:** Covers all areas involved in the transport of animals worldwide.
Formerly: Animal Air Transportation Association. International Conference. Proceedings (8755-9447)
Published by: Animal Transportation Association, Inc., 111 East Loop North, Houston, TX 77029. TEL 713-532-2177, FAX 713-532-2166. Circ: 400.

ANNALES DE LA VOIRIE. *see* LAW

380.5 FRA ISSN 1965-2321
ANNUAIRE FRANCE TRANSPORTS. Text in French. 1948. a. EUR 203.32 newsstand/cover (effective 2009). adv. **Document type:** *Directory, Trade.*
Formerly (until 2006): Annuaire National des Transports (0066-3549)
Published by: Wolters Kluwer France (Subsidiary of: Wolters Kluwer N.V.), 1 Rue Eugene et Armand Peugeot, Rueil-Malmaison, Cedex 92856, France. TEL 33-8-25080800, FAX 33-1-76733040, www.wkf.fr.

388 CAN ISSN 1914-1270
ANNUAL SUPPLY CHAIN CONNECTIONS CONFERENCE PROCEEDINGS. Text in English. 2005. a. **Document type:** *Proceedings, Academic/Scholarly.*
Published by: University of Manitoba, Transport Institute, 631 Drake Centre Bldg, 181 Freedman Cres., Winnipeg, MB R3T 5V4, Canada. TEL 204-474-9842, FAX 204-474-7530, transport_institute@umanitoba.ca, umanitoba.ca/faculties/management/ti.

380.52 BRA ISSN 0102-4671
HE48
ANUARIO ESTATISTICO DOS TRANSPORTES. Text in Portuguese. 1970. a. free. **Document type:** *Government.* **Description:** Presents statistics on all modes of transport (air, pipeline, road, rail, shipping,and urban) in Brazil and in other countries.
Related titles: Diskette ed.; Online - full text ed.
Published by: Empresa Brasileira de Planejamento de Transportes, G E I P O T, SAN Quadra 3 Blocos N-O, Brasilia, DF 70040902, Brazil. TEL 55-61-3154890, FAX 55-61-315-4895. Ed. Joao Luiz Correa Samy. Circ: 1,500.

ARBEIT UND GESUNDHEIT. SONDERAUSGABE VERKEHR. *see* PUBLIC HEALTH AND SAFETY

388 POL ISSN 0866-9546
ARCHIVES OF TRANSPORT/ARCHIWUM TRANSPORTU. Text in English. 1989. q. **Document type:** *Journal, Academic/Scholarly.*
Related titles: Online - full text ed.: free (effective 2011).
Indexed: B22.
Published by: Polska Akademia Nauk, Komitet Transportu, Wydzial Transportu PW, ul Koszykowa 75, Warsaw, 00662, Poland. TEL 48-22-6288681, FAX 48-22-6280366, dziekan@it.pw.edu.pl. **Dist. by:** Ars Polona, Obroncow 25, Warsaw 03933, Poland. TEL 48-22-5098609, FAX 48-22-5098610, arspolona@arspolona.com.pl, http://www.arspolona.com.pl.

388.0440982 GBR ISSN 1752-5225
ARGENTINA FREIGHT TRANSPORT REPORT. Text in English. 2006. q. EUR 820, USD 1,030 combined subscription (print & email eds.) (effective 2010). **Document type:** *Report, Trade.* **Description:** Provides industry professionals and strategists, sector analysts, investors, trade associations and regulatory bodies with independent forecasts and competitive intelligence on the Argentinian freight transport and logistics industry.
Related titles: E-mail ed.
Published by: Business Monitor International Ltd., Senator House, 85 Queen Victoria St, London, EC4V 4AB, United Kingdom. TEL 44-20-72480468, FAX 44-20-72480467, subs@businessmonitor.com.

ARIZONA CRIMINAL AND TRAFFIC LAW MANUAL. *see* LAW—Criminal Law

ARKANSAS CRIMINAL AND TRAFFIC LAW MANUAL. *see* LAW—Criminal Law

ARKANSAS CRIMINAL, TRANSPORTATION & RELATED STATUTES. *see* LAW—Criminal Law

343.093 USA
ARKANSAS MOTOR VEHICLE AND TRAFFIC LAWS AND STATE HIGHWAY COMMISSION REGULATIONS. Text in English. biennial, latest 2007. USD 33 per issue (effective 2008). 348 p./no.; **Document type:** *Handbook/Manual/Guide, Trade.* **Description:** Contains statutes and official regulations governing use of public highways, roads and streets in Arkansas as well as the control of motor vehicles and their operators.
Related titles: Online - full text ed.
Published by: Michie Company (Subsidiary of: LexisNexis North America), 701 E Water St, Charlottesville, VA 22902. TEL 434-972-7600, 800-446-3410, FAX 434-972-7677, customer.support@lexisnexis.com, http://www.michie.com.

388 AUS ISSN 1322-1337
ASIA PACIFIC JOURNAL OF TRANSPORT. Text in English. 1996. **Document type:** *Journal, Academic/Scholarly.* **Description:** Discusses transportation issues.
Related titles: Online - full text ed.
Published by: University of Queensland, School of Tourism, CNR of Blair & Campbell St, St Lucia Campus, Brisbane, QLD 4072, Australia. TEL 61-7-33468717, FAX 61-7-33468716, tourism@uq.edu.au, http://tourism.uq.edu.au/.

ASSOCIATIONS SECTORIELLES PARITAIRES, LESIONS PROFESSIONNELLES, STATISTIQUES. TOME 3. ASSOCIATION PARITAIRE POUR LA SANTE ET LA SECURITE DU TRAVAIL DU SECTEUR TRANSPORT ET ENTREPOSAGE. *see* OCCUPATIONAL HEALTH AND SAFETY—Abstracting, Bibliographies, Statistics

388 ITA
ASSOCIAZIONE NAZIONALE AUTOTRASPORTO VIAGGIATORI. NEWSLETTER. Short title: A N A V Newsletter. Text in Italian. 19??. w.
Formerly (until 2001): Associazione Nazionale Servizi Autotrasporti. Informa
Published by: Associazione Nazionale Autotrasporto Viaggiatori (A N A V), Piazza dell'Esquilino 29, Rome, 00185, Italy. TEL 39-06-4879301, FAX 39-06-4821204, http://www.anav.it.

380.5 USA
ASTRALOG. Text in English. 1964. bi-m. USD 25 (effective 1999). adv. **Document type:** *Newsletter.* **Description:** News and information on the activities of the society.
Formerly (until 1983): A S T L Newsletter
Indexed: LogistBibl.
Published by: American Society of Transportation and Logistics, Inc., 1700 N Moore St., Ste 1900, Arlington, VA 22209-1904. TEL 703-524-5011, info@astl.org, http://www.astl.org. Adv. contact Sherri L Walker. Circ: 2,000.

385.284 CAN ISSN 0381-9345
ATLANTIC PROVINCES TRANSPORTATION COMMISSION. TIPS & TOPICS. Variant title: Tips & Topics. Text in English. 1961. m. back issues avail. **Document type:** *Newsletter.*
—CCC.
Published by: Atlantic Provinces Transportation Commission, 1133 St George Blvd, Ste 330, Moncton, NB E1E 4E1, Canada. TEL 506-857-2820, FAX 506-857-2835. Ed. Mona Savoie. R&P Peter Vuillemot. Circ: 2,000.

380.5 CAN ISSN 0842-9596
ATLANTIC TRANSPORTATION JOURNAL. Text in English. 1988. q. CAD 20.70 domestic; CAD 25.68 foreign (effective 2003). adv. **Document type:** *Journal, Trade.*
Indexed: A10, C05, V03.
Published by: Transcontinental Specialty Publications (Subsidiary of: Transcontinental Media, Inc.), 11 Thornhill Dr, Dartmouth, NS B3B 1R9, Canada. TEL 902-468-8027, 800-565-2601, FAX 902-468-2322. Pub. Don Brander TEL 902-468-8027 ext 116. Adv. contact Peter Coleman TEL 902-468-8027 ext 108. page CAD 3,050. Circ: 12,500.

380.5 AUS ISSN 1324-8634
AUSTRALASIAN BUS AND COACH; the management magazine for bus and coach operators. Variant title: A B C. Text in English. 1988. m. AUD 69 domestic; AUD 79.35 in New Zealand; AUD 89.70 elsewhere (effective 2008); AUD 5 newsstand/cover (effective 2001). adv. back issues avail. **Document type:** *Magazine, Trade.* **Description:** Provides information on new and used buses, coach and equipment catering to tourism and private school sectors.
Related titles: Supplement(s): Manufacturers and Suppliers Directory (Year).
Published by: A C P Trader International Group (Subsidiary of: P B L Media Pty Ltd.), 73 Atherton Rd, Oakleigh, VIC 3166, Australia. TEL 61-3-95674200, FAX 61-3-95634554, http://www.tradergroup.com.au/. Eds. Chris Smith TEL 61-7-38541286, Greg Leech TEL 61-3-95674194. Adv. contact Michael Brazier TEL 61-7-31662308. B&W page AUD 2,320, color page AUD 3,400; trim 205 x 275. Circ: 5,440.

388 AUS ISSN 1832-9497
➤ **AUSTRALASIAN COLLEGE OF ROAD SAFETY. JOURNAL.** Text in English. 1988. q. AUD 52 domestic; AUD 63 foreign; free to members (effective 2008). back issues avail. **Document type:** *Journal, Academic/Scholarly.* **Description:** Aims to promote and implement improved road safety practices for individuals and organizations working in or interested in promoting road safety.
Formerly (until 2005): Roadwise (1030-7168)
Related titles: Online - full content ed.
Published by: Australasian College of Road Safety, PO Box 198, Mawson, ACT 2607, Australia. TEL 61-2-62902509, FAX 61-2-62900914, eo@acrs.org.au.

388.0440994 GBR ISSN 1752-5233
AUSTRALIA FREIGHT TRANSPORT REPORT. Text in English. 2006. q. EUR 820, USD 1,030 combined subscription (print & email eds.) (effective 2010). **Document type:** *Report, Trade.* **Description:** Provides industry professionals and strategists, sector analysts, investors, trade associations and regulatory bodies with independent forecasts and competitive intelligence on the Australian freight transport and logistics industry.
Related titles: E-mail ed.
Indexed: A15, ABIn, B02, B15, B17, B18, G04, I05, P48, P51, P52, PQC.
Published by: Business Monitor International Ltd., Senator House, 85 Queen Victoria St, London, EC4V 4AB, United Kingdom. TEL 44-20-72480468, FAX 44-20-72480467, subs@businessmonitor.com.

380.5 629.288 AUS ISSN 1449-1613
AUSTRALIAN BUS & COMMERCIAL VEHICLE HERITAGE. Abbreviated title: A B C V H. Text in English. 19??. bi-m. AUD 56 domestic to non-members; AUD 75 in New Zealand to non-members; AUD 85 elsewhere to non-members; AUD 9.90 per issue to non-members; free to members (effective 2009). adv. bk.rev. 36 p./no.; back issues avail. **Document type:** *Magazine, Consumer.* **Description:** Provides current news regarding buses in Australia as well as historical articles.
Former titles (until 2004): Fleetline (0312-4681); (until 1975): H C V A. Newsheet
Published by: (The Sydney Bus and Truck Museum Ltd.), Historic Commercial Vehicle Association Co-Op Ltd., PO Box 623, Rockdale, NSW 2216, Australia. TEL 61-2-95673103. Ed. John Clifton.

796.77 IDN
AUTO BILD. Text in Indonesian. 2003 (May). fortn. adv. **Document type:** *Magazine, Consumer.*
Published by: P T Gramedia, Jalan Palmerah Selatan 22-26, Jakarta, 10270, Indonesia. TEL 62-21-5483008, FAX 62-21-5494035, ulj@gramedia-majalah.com, http://www.gramedia.com. Ed. Hendra Noor Saleh.

388.322 ITA ISSN 1825-6716
AUTOBUS. Text in Italian. 1977. m. EUR 35 (effective 2009). bk.rev. charts; illus. **Document type:** *Magazine, Trade.*
Formerly (until 1990): Trans. Autocarri & Autobus (0393-8239)
Published by: Vado e Torno Edizioni S.r.l., Via Cassano d'Adda 20, Milan, 20139, Italy. TEL 39-02-55230950, FAX 39-02-55230592, abbonamenti@vadoetorno.com. Ed. Marino Ginanneschi. Pub. Gianni Sacedotti. Adv. contact Ornella Cavalli. Circ: 11,000.

388.322 ESP ISSN 1888-1823
AUTOBUSES Y AUTOCARES. Text in Spanish. 1989. m. EUR 135.34 combined subscription domestic (print, online & email eds.); EUR 195 combined subscription foreign (print, online & email eds.) (effective 2009). adv. **Document type:** *Magazine, Trade.* **Description:** Covers passenger transport and public transportation by bus.
Related titles: E-mail ed.: ISSN 1988-5482; Online - full text ed.: Autobuses & Autocares Digital. ISSN 1988-8759. 2000.
Published by: Tecnipublicaciones Espana, S.L., Avda de Manoteras 44, 3a Planta, Madrid, 28050, Spain. TEL 34-91-2972000, FAX 34-91-2972154, tp@tecnipublicaciones.com. Ed. Miguel Saez. Circ: 7,000.

388.322 NLD ISSN 1384-0436
AUTOBUSKRONIEK. Text in Dutch. 1963. 8/yr. EUR 38.50 domestic; EUR 50 foreign (effective 2009). adv. bk.rev.
Published by: Autobus Documentatie Vereniging, c/o A H G Hermes, Nijenrodeweg 64, Rotterdam, 3077 ES, Netherlands. ledenadmin@autobusdoc.nl, http://www.audobusdoc.nl. Circ: 1,200.

388 NLD ISSN 1386-5544
AUTOMOTIVE; het vakblad voor managers in de autobranche. Text in Dutch. 1997. bi-w. EUR 119 (effective 2010). adv. **Document type:** *Magazine, Trade.*
Published by: RAI Langfords bv, Postbus 10099, Amsterdam, 1001 EB, Netherlands. TEL 31-20-5042800, FAX 31-20-5042888, http://www.railangfords.nl. Ed. Jelle Heidstra. Pub. Ron Brokking. Adv. contact Marc Krijnen. B&W page EUR 2,250, color page EUR 2,975; trim 210 x 285. Circ: 13,109.

388 GBR ISSN 1471-6003
HD9710.A1
AUTOMOTIVE LOGISTICS. Text in English. 1998. q. free (effective 2009). adv. back issues avail. **Document type:** *Magazine, Trade.* **Description:** Covers all aspects of logistics and supply chain management, from purchasing, production planning, materials management and handling, air/sea/land transport, marketing and with a special concern for information systems.
Related titles: Online - full text ed.
Indexed: A10, A28, APA, B01, B07, BrCerAb, C&ISA, CA/WCA, CIA, CerAb, CivEngAb, CorrAb, E&CAJ, E11, EEA, EMA, H15, M&TEA, M09, MBF, METADEX, SolStAb, T02, T04, V03, WAA.
—Linda Hall. **CCC.**
Published by: Ultima Media Ltd., Lamb House, Church St, London, W4 2PD, United Kingdom. TEL 44-20-89870900, FAX 44-20-89870948, info@ultimamedia.com, http://www.ultimamedia.org/. Ed. Christopher Ludwig TEL 44-20-89870968. Pub. Louis Yiakoumi TEL 44-20-89870944. Adv. contact Kim Man TEL 44-20-89870905.

388.3 AUT ISSN 0005-0830
AUTOREVUE. Text in German. 1965. m. EUR 33; EUR 3.40 newsstand/cover (effective 2006). adv. illus. back issues avail. **Document type:** *Magazine, Consumer.*
Related titles: Online - full text ed.
—CCC.
Published by: Verlagsgruppe News Gesellschaft mbH (Subsidiary of: Gruner + Jahr AG & Co), Taborstr 1-3, Vienna, W 1020, Austria. TEL 43-1-213129011, FAX 43-1-213121650, redaktion@news.at, http://www.news.at. Ed. Christian Kornherr. Adv. contact Klaus Edelhofer. page EUR 9,700; trim 210 x 280. Circ: 48,294 (paid).

388 RUS ISSN 1608-8174
AVTOPEREVOZCHIK. Text in Russian. 2000. m. **Document type:** *Magazine, Trade.*
Published by: Izdatel'stvo MaksMedia, Bogoyavlennskii per., dom 3, str 4, Moscow, 103012, Russian Federation. TEL 7-095-2061103, FAX 7-095-9214929, red@apmedia.ru.

388 TWN ISSN 1684-4432
B A M ASIA. (Bicycle - Auto - Motor) Text in English. 2002. s-a.
Published by: Interface Global Taiwan Co., Ltd., 8F, No.3, Lane 235, Paochiao Road, Hsintien, Taipei Hsien, 231, Taiwan. TEL 886-2-29180500 886 2 29180500, FAX 886-2-89119401, service@asiatrademart.com, http://www.asiatrademart.com.

B I C - CODE. *see* PACKAGING

BAHRAIN FREIGHT TRANSPORT REPORT. *see* BUSINESS AND ECONOMICS—Production Of Goods And Services

343.093 NZL
BECROFT AND HALL'S TRANSPORT LAW. Text in English. 1976. 4 base vols. plus updates 6/yr. looseleaf. **Document type:** *Handbook/ Manual/Guide, Trade.* **Description:** Contains the Land Transport Act 1998, the Traffic Regulations 1976, and the Land Transport Rules.
Related titles: CD-ROM ed.; Online - full text ed.
Published by: Butterworths of New Zealand Ltd. (Subsidiary of: LexisNexis Asia Pacific), PO Box 472, Wellington, 6140, New Zealand. TEL 64-4-3851479, FAX 64-4-3851598, Customer.Service@lexisnexis.co.nz. Eds. Andrew J Becroft, Geoff Hall.

380.5 DEU ISSN 0722-9399
BERLINER VERKEHRSBLAETTER. Text in German. 1954. m. EUR 23.40; EUR 1.95 newsstand/cover (effective 2009). adv. bk.rev. charts; illus. index. back issues avail. **Document type:** *Magazine, Consumer.* **Description:** Information magazine on public transportation in Berlin. Focuses on traffic situation, roads, bus system and railroads.
Published by: Arbeitskreis Berliner Nahverkehr e.V., Binger Str 88, Berlin, 14197, Germany. TEL 49-30-8223245, FAX 49-30-3424855. Ed. Uwe Kerl. Circ: 4,000.

380.5 NLD ISSN 1381-8848
BESTELAUTO; Misset select. Text in Dutch. 1985. s-a. free (effective 2008). adv. illus. **Document type:** *Magazine, Trade.* **Description:** Publishes road tests of vans and light trucks for entrepreneurs and business and industrial fleet managers.
Published by: Reed Business bv (Subsidiary of: Reed Business), Hanzestraat 1, Doetinchem, 7006 RH, Netherlands. TEL 31-314-349911, FAX 31-314-343839, info@reedbusiness.nl, http://www.reedbusiness.nl. Ed. Pieter Wieman. Pub. Gijs Gjaltema.

386 DEU ISSN 0939-1916
HE669
BINNENSCHIFFAHRT. Text in German. 1991. 12/yr. EUR 81.60 domestic; EUR 86 foreign (effective 2007). adv. bk.rev. bibl.; charts; illus.; stat. **Document type:** *Magazine, Trade.*
Formed by the merger of (1970-1991): B W - Zeitschrift fuer Binnenschiffahrt und Wasserstrassen (0930-7370); Which was formerly (until 1985): Zeitschrift fuer Binnenschiffahrt und Wasserstrassen (0340-3963); (1946-1991): Binnenschiffahrts-Nachrichten (0179-7743); Which was formerly (until 1983): Binnenschiffahrts-Nachrichten. Ausgabe B (0172-2069); Which supersedes in part (in 1952): Binnenschiffahrts-Nachrichten (0006-2847)
Indexed: A22, IBR, IBZ, RefZh.
—IE, Infotrieve. **CCC.**
Published by: (Bundesverband der Deutschen Binnenschiffahrt e.V.), Schiffahrts Verlag Hansa, Striepenweg 31, Hamburg, 21147, Germany. TEL 49-40-79713225, FAX 49-40-79713208. Ed. Friedbert Barg. Adv. contact Monika Lamottke. B&W page EUR 1,500, color page EUR 2,262. Circ: 3,651 (paid and controlled). **Co-sponsor:** C.Schroedter & Co. (GmbH & Co. KG).

388 FRA ISSN 2106-9913
LES BIOGRAPHIES.COM. MINISTERE DE L'ECOLOGIE, DE L'ENERGIE, DU DEVELOPPEMENT DURABLE ET DE L'AMENAGEMENT DU TERRITOIRE. TOME II: TRANSPORTS, EQUIPEMENT. Text in French. 200?. irreg. EUR 240 (effective 2011).
Supersedes in part (in 2007): Les Biographies.com. Ministere de l'Ecologie et du Developpement Durable (1954-409X)
Published by: Societe Generale de Presse, 13 Avenue de l'Opera, Paris Cedex 01, 75001, France. TEL 33-1-40151789, FAX 33-1-40151715, contact@sna.asso.fr, http://www.lesbiographies.com, http://www.sgpresse.fr.

BLACK BOOK. OFFICIAL DOLLAR RESIDUAL VALUE GUIDE. *see* BUSINESS AND ECONOMICS—Trade And Industrial Directories

380.5 DEU ISSN 0173-0290
BLICKPUNKT STRASSENBAHN; Berichte aus dem Nahverkehr. Text in German. 1979. bi-m. EUR 21 domestic; EUR 24 in Europe; EUR 39 elsewhere; EUR 4.50 newsstand/cover (effective 2008). adv. bk.rev. cum.index: 1979-1992. **Document type:** *Magazine, Trade.*
Formerly (until 1979): Strassenbahn Aktuell (0170-5466)
Published by: Arbeitsgemeinschaft Blickpunkt Strassenbahn e.V., Burgherrenstr 2, Berlin, 12101, Germany. TEL 49-721-151495015, FAX 49-30-7859208, bs@tramway.com, http://www.blickpunktstrassenbahn.de. Ed., R&P Thomas E Fischer. Adv. contact Dieter Kaddoura. Circ: 4,000.

380.5 PAN
BOLETIN. Text and summaries in English, Spanish. 1981. w. PAB 30 domestic; USD 50 foreign (effective 2000); USD 0.50 newsstand/ cover. adv. bk.rev. back issues avail. **Document type:** *Trade.* **Description:** For importers and exporters in Panama and nearby countries. Provides ship and air schedules connecting through Panama.
Published by: El Boletin S.A., Calle 55, El Congrejo, Ed Deveaux, Of. 1, Panama City, Panama. TEL 507-2236967, FAX 507-2692789. Ed., Pub. Theodore J James. adv.: B&W page USD 570, color page USD 858; 10 x 16. Circ: 855 (paid); 300 (controlled).

380.5021 330.9021 BWA ISSN 1013-5731
BOTSWANA. CENTRAL STATISTICS OFFICE. TRANSPORT STATISTICS. Text in English. a. back issues avail. **Document type:** *Government.*
Related titles: E-mail ed.; Fax ed.
Published by: Central Statistics Office, c/o Government Statistician, Private Bag 0024, Gaborone, Botswana. TEL 267-31-352200, FAX 267-31-352201. Ed. G M Charumbira. Pub. J G Segwe. **Subscr. to:** Government Printer, Private Bag 0081, Gaborone, Botswana. TEL 267-353202, FAX 267-312001, http://www.gov.bw.

388 352 NLD ISSN 2212-0351
BRABANTS MEERJARENPROGRAMMA INFRASTRUCTUUR EN TRANSPORT. Text in Dutch. 1973. a.
Former titles (until 2006): Meerjarenprogramma Verkeer, Vervoer en Infrastructuur (1871-5796); (until 1996): Uitvoeringsprogramma Verkeer en Vervoer (0924-8390); (until 1989): Uitvoeringsprogramma Provinciale Planwegen (0924-8382)
Published by: Provincie Noord-Brabant, Postbus 90151, 's-Hertogenbosch, 5200 MC, Netherlands. TEL 31-73-6812812, FAX 31-73-6141115, info@brabant.nl, http://www.brabant.nl.

388.0440981 GBR ISSN 1752-5241
BRAZIL FREIGHT TRANSPORT REPORT. Text in English. 2006. q. EUR 820, USD 1,030 combined subscription (print & email eds.) (effective 2010). **Document type:** *Report, Trade.* **Description:** Provides industry professionals and strategists, sector analysts, investors, trade associations and regulatory bodies with independent forecasts and competitive intelligence on the Brazilian freight transport and logistics industry.
Related titles: E-mail ed.
Indexed: A15, ABIn, P48, P51, P52, PQC.
Published by: Business Monitor International Ltd., Senator House, 85 Queen Victoria St, London, EC4V 4AB, United Kingdom. TEL 44-20-72480468, FAX 44-20-72480467, subs@businessmonitor.com.

BRITISH COLUMBIA. MINISTRY OF TRANSPORTATION. ANNUAL SERVICE PLAN. *see* PUBLIC ADMINISTRATION

380.5 GBR ISSN 1472-4286
BROOKLANDS SOCIETY GAZETTE. Text in English. 1976. q. free to members (effective 2009). adv. bk.rev. back issues avail. **Document type:** *Bulletin.* **Description:** Discusses historic racing cars, motorcycles, and aircraft related to the Brooklands Motor Course and airfield.
Published by: The Brooklands Society, Copse House, Coxheath Rd, Fleet, GU52 6QG, United Kingdom. TEL 44-1252-408877, FAX 44-1252-408878, graham.skillen@brooklands.org.uk. Ed. Chris Bass TEL 44-1483-481836.

388.04409499 GBR ISSN 1752-5489
BULGARIA FREIGHT TRANSPORT REPORT. Text in English. 2006. a. EUR 820, USD 1,030 combined subscription per issue (print & email eds.) (effective 2010). **Document type:** *Report, Trade.* **Description:** Provides industry professionals and strategists, sector analysts, investors, trade associations and regulatory bodies with independent forecasts and competitive intelligence on the Bulgarian freight transport and logistics industry.
Related titles: E-mail ed.
Indexed: A15, ABIn, B02, B15, B17, B18, G04, I05, P48, P51, P52, PQC.
Published by: Business Monitor International Ltd., Senator House, 85 Queen Victoria St, London, EC4V 4AB, United Kingdom. TEL 44-20-72480468, FAX 44-20-72480467, subs@businessmonitor.com.

380 628.5 NLD ISSN 1380-569X
BULK; magazine voor stortgoedtechnologie. Variant title: Bulk Benelux. Text in Dutch. 8/yr. EUR 110; EUR 88 to students (effective 2009). adv. illus. **Document type:** *Journal, Trade.* **Description:** Covers bulk goods handling technology, including storage and processing.
Indexed: IMMAb.
—IE, Infotrieve.
Published by: Eisma Businessmedia bv, Celsiusweg 41, Postbus 340, Leeuwarden, 8901 BC, Netherlands. TEL 31-58-2954854, FAX 31-58-2954875, businessmedia@eisma.nl, http://www.eisma.nl/businessmedia/index.asp. Ed. Jos Verleg. Pub. Minne Hovenga. Adv. contact Ed Rothuis. B&W page EUR 2,086, color page EUR 3,518; trim 230 x 300. Circ: 5,000.

380.5 COG
BULLETIN ANNUEL DES TRANSPORTS ET PARC AUTO. Text in French. 1984. a. XAF 3,000 per issue.
Published by: Centre National de la Statistique et des Etudes Economiques, BP 2031, Brazzaville, Congo, Republic. TEL 242-83-43-24.

388.322 ZAF
BUS & COACH. Text in English. 1996. bi-m. ZAR 3.50 newsstand/cover; included with FleetWatch. adv.
Published by: Newslink C C, PO Box 3097, Honeydew, 2040, South Africa. TEL 27-11-7942490, FAX 27-11-7941474. Ed. Andrew Parker. Pub., R&P Patrick O'Leary. Adv. contact Lorinda Stoltz. B&W page ZAR 4,600, color page ZAR 5,900. Circ: 6,400.

338.322 GBR
BUS & COACH BUYER. Text in English. 1989. w. GBP 35 in United Kingdom. adv. **Document type:** *Journal, Trade.* **Description:** For operators, manufacturers, and suppliers of buses and coaches. Covers the operation, design, manufacture, and supply of buses, coaches, and minibuses.
Published by: Bus & Coach Buyer Ltd., The Publishing Centre, Bus & Coach Uk, 1 Woolram Wygate, Spalding, Lincs PE11 1NU, United Kingdom. TEL 44-1775-711777, FAX 44-1775-711737. Ed., R&P Stuart Jones. Pub. Steve Cole. Adv. contact Martin Laverton. B&W page GBP 594, color page GBP 995; trim 298 x 210. Circ: 6,405 (controlled).

388.3 BEL ISSN 0779-1267
BUS & COACH MAGAZINE (DUTCH EDITION). Text in Dutch. 1992. 5/yr. **Document type:** *Trade.* **Description:** Covers the management and operation of bus and coach fleets.
Related titles: French ed.: Bus & Coach Magazine (French Edition). ISSN 0779-1305.
Published by: Multi Media Management, Parc Artisanal 11-13, Blegny-Barchon, 4670, Belgium. TEL 32-4-387-8787, FAX 32-4-387-9087, mmmg@mmm.be, http://www.mmm.be. Ed. Jean-Marie Becker. R&P Jean Marie Becker.

388.322 GBR ISSN 1471-1060
BUS & COACH PRESERVATION. Text in English. 1998. m. GBP 45 domestic; GBP 53.80 in Europe; GBP 58.80 elsewhere; GBP 3.75 per issue (effective 2009). adv. 64 p./no.; back issues avail. **Document type:** *Magazine, Consumer.* **Description:** Provides complete up-to-date coverage of all that is happening in the world of bus preservation.
Incorporates: Preserved Bus (1461-5584); Which was formerly (until 1999): Bus & Coach Preservation Monthly (1462-1886)
—CCC.
Published by: Ian Allan Publishing Ltd., Riverdene Business Park, Riverdene Industrial Estate, Molesey Rd, Walton-on-Thames, Surrey KT12 4RG, United Kingdom. TEL 44-1932-266622, FAX 44-1932-266633, magazines@ianallanpublishing.co.uk, http://www.ianallanpublishing.com. Ed. Philip Lamb TEL 44-23-92655224. Adv. contact Nigel Appleford. **Dist. by:** MarketForce UK Ltd, The Blue Fin Bldg, 3rd Fl, 110 Southwark St, London SE1 0SU, United Kingdom. TEL 44-20-31483333, FAX 44-20-31488105, salesinnovation@marketforce.co.uk, http://www.marketforce.co.uk/.

388.322 DEU ISSN 1613-3331
BUS BLICKPUNKT; Informationen fuer Busunternehmer. Text in German. 1985. m. EUR 48; EUR 4.50 newsstand/cover (effective 2009). adv. **Document type:** *Magazine, Trade.*
Published by: Verlag Michaela Rothe, Darmstaedter Str 121, Bensheim, 64625, Germany. TEL 49-6251-93490, FAX 49-6251-934949. Ed. Juergen Weidlich. Pub. Michaela Rothe. Adv. contact Katja Dehn. B&W page EUR 4,248, color page EUR 4,930; trim 265 x 378. Circ: 11,094 (controlled).

388.322 USA ISSN 1070-6526
BUS CONVERSIONS. Text in English. 1992. m. USD 36; USD 4.45 newsstand/cover (effective 2001). adv. **Document type:** *Magazine, Consumer.* **Description:** Covers bus conversions.
Published by: M A K Publishing, Inc., 6196 Garden Grove Blvd, Westminster, CA 92683. TEL 714-799-0062, FAX 714-799-0042. Ed., Adv. contact Ricky Gee. Pub. Michael Kadletz. R&P Theresa Hagen. Circ: 8,000.

388.322 338.4791 FRA ISSN 0399-2535
BUS ET CAR MAGAZINE. Text in French. 1976. 23/yr. EUR 166; EUR 314 combined subscription print & online eds. (effective 2009). **Document type:** *Magazine, Trade.*
Related titles: Online - full text ed.
Published by: Wolters Kluwer France (Subsidiary of: Wolters Kluwer N.V.), 1 Rue Eugene et Armand Peugeot, Rueil-Malmaison, Cedex 92856, France. FAX 33-1-76733040, www.wk-transport-logistique.fr. Circ: 7,500.

BUS-FAHRT; Das Magazin fuer Technik und Touristik. *see* TRAVEL AND TOURISM

380.1 USA ISSN 0739-7194
BUS INDUSTRY MAGAZINE. Text in English. 1963. q. free to members (effective 2011). adv. bk.rev. illus. 2 cols./p.; back issues avail. **Document type:** *Magazine, Trade.* **Description:** News and articles pertaining to city and intercity historical and contemporary bus operations.
Former titles: Bus Review; Bus History

Published by: Bus History Association, Inc., Loring M Lawrence, Ed, 195 Lancelot Dr, Manchester, NH 03104. http://www.bus-history.org. Ed. Loring M Lawrence.

338.7629222330 GBR ISSN 0962-791X
BUS INDUSTRY MONITOR. Text in English. 1991. a. **Document type:** *Journal, Trade.* **Description:** Covers information on analysis of the market and financial performance of the UK bus industry.
Related titles: CD-ROM ed.: ISSN 1752-5012. 2002. GBP 330 (effective 2008); Online - full text ed.: ISSN 1752-6507. 2006. GBP 330 (effective 2008).
—CCC.
Published by: T A S Publications & Events Ltd., Ross Holme, West End, Long Preston, Skipton, N Yorks BD23 4QL, United Kingdom. TEL 44-1729-840756, FAX 44-1729-840705, info@taspublications.co.uk.

388.322 USA ISSN 1083-5849
HD9710.34.U5
THE BUS PAGES. Text in English. 1992. a. USD 19.95 (effective 2001). adv. back issues avail. **Document type:** *Directory, Trade.* **Description:** Covers the North American bus, coach and limousine industry.
Related titles: Online - full content ed.
Published by: Bus Book Publishing, Inc., PO Box 9, Mcminnville, OR 97128-0009. TEL 503-472-3536, FAX 503-472-3293, geninfo@busbook.com, http://www.busbook.com. Ed., Pub. Dave Mendenhall. Circ: 50,000.

388.322 USA ISSN 0192-8902
BUS RIDE. Variant title: BusRide. Text in English. 1965. m. USD 39 domestic; USD 42 in Canada; USD 75 elsewhere (effective 2010). adv. bk.rev. illus. back issues avail.; reprints avail. **Document type:** *Magazine, Trade.* **Description:** Covers the bus transit and motorcoach industry.
Indexed: HRIS.
Published by: Power Trade Media, LLC, 4742 N 24th St, Ste 340, Phoenix, AZ 85016. TEL 602-265-7600, 800-541-2670, FAX 602-265-4300. Eds. David Hubbard TEL 602-265-7600 ext 213, Steve Kane TEL 602-265-7600 ext 205. Adv. contact John Adel TEL 602-265-7600 ext 214. Circ: 16,000.

388.322 USA ISSN 0199-6096
BUS TOURS MAGAZINE. Text in English. 1979. bi-m. USD 15 (effective 2007). adv. 40 p./no.; **Document type:** *Magazine, Trade.*
Published by: National Bus Trader, Inc., 9698 W Judson Rd., Polo, IL 61064. TEL 815-946-2341, FAX 815-946-2347. Ed., Pub. Larry Plachno. Circ: 7,200 (paid and controlled).

385 388 DEU ISSN 0341-5228
BUS UND BAHN; Personenverkehr - Gueterverkehr - Verkehrspolitik. Text in German. 1967. 11/yr. EUR 16.50; EUR 1.50 newsstand/cover (effective 2010). bk.rev. back issues avail. **Document type:** *Magazine, Trade.*
Indexed: DokStr, IBR, IBZ.
—CCC.
Published by: (Verband Deutscher Verkehrsunternehmen), Alba Fachverlag GmbH und Co., Willstaetterstr 9, Duesseldorf, 40549, Germany. TEL 49-211-520130, FAX 49-211-5201328, braun@alba-verlag.de, http://www.alba-verlag.de. Circ: 5,850.

388.3 GBR ISSN 0007-6392
BUSES. Text in English. 1949. m. GBP 45.60 domestic; GBP 54.40 in Europe; GBP 59.40 elsewhere; GBP 3.95 per issue (effective 2009). adv. bk.rev. charts; illus. index. 64 p./no.; back issues avail.; reprints avail. **Document type:** *Magazine, Consumer.* **Description:** Publishes articles relating to the road passenger transport industry primarily in the U.K.
Formed by the merger of (1949-1968): Buses Illustrated; (1947-1968): Passenger Transport; Which was formerly (until 1947): Passenger Transport Journal; (until 1937): The Electric Railway, Bus and Tram Journal; (until 1928): Electric Railway and Tramway Journal; (until 1914): Light Railway and Tramway Journal
Indexed: HRIS.
—CCC.
Published by: Ian Allan Publishing Ltd., Riverdene Business Park, Riverdene Industrial Estate, Molesey Rd, Walton-on-Thames, Surrey KT12 4RG, United Kingdom. magazines@ianallanpublishing.co.uk, http://www.ianallanpublishing.com. Ed. Alan Miller TEL 44-1333-340637. Adv. contact David Lane TEL 44-1780-484633. **Dist. by:** MarketForce UK Ltd, The Blue Fin Bldg, 3rd Fl, 110 Southwark St, London SE1 0SU, United Kingdom. TEL 44-20-31483333, FAX 44-20-31488105, salesinnovation@marketforce.co.uk, http://www.marketforce.co.uk/.

388.322 USA
BUSES INTERNATIONAL. Text in English. 1980. q. USD 30 to members (effective 2000). back issues avail. **Document type:** *Newspaper.* **Description:** Focuses on bus transportation.
Indexed: CLT&T.
Published by: Buses International Association, PO Box 9337, Spokane, WA 99209. Ed. William A Luke. Circ: 100.

388.322 GBR
HE5601
BUSES YEARBOOK (YEAR). Text in English. 19??. a. GBP 14.99 per issue (effective 2010). illus. back issues avail.; reprints avail. **Document type:** *Yearbook, Consumer.* **Description:** Contains historic and contemporary articles illustrating aspects of passenger road transport.
Formerly (until 1989): Buses Annual (0068-4376)
—BLDSC (2933.136000).
Published by: Ian Allan Publishing Ltd., Riverdene Business Park, Riverdene Industrial Estate, Molesey Rd, Walton-on-Thames, Surrey KT12 4RG, United Kingdom. TEL 44-1932-266622, FAX 44-1932-266633, magazines@ianallanpublishing.co.uk. Ed. Stewart J Brown.

388.322 DEU ISSN 1614-0656
BUSFAHRER. Text in German. 2004. q. EUR 76.80; EUR 14 per issue (effective 2010). adv. **Document type:** *Magazine, Trade.*
Published by: Verlag Heinrich Vogel (Subsidiary of: Springer Science+Business Media), Neumarkterstr 18, Munich, 81664, Germany. TEL 49-89-43722878, FAX 49-89-2030432100, kontakt@verlag-heinrich-vogel.de, http://www.springerfachmedien-muenchen.de. Ed. Anne K Peters. Adv. contact Marisa d'Arbonneau. B&W page EUR 2,705, color page EUR 3,865. Circ: 30,000 (paid and controlled).

388.322 330.9 GBR ISSN 1473-7310
BUSINESS RATIO REPORT. BUS AND COACH OPERATORS. Text in English. 1986. a., latest no.23, 2008, Apr. GBP 365 per issue (effective 2010). charts; stat. back issues avail. **Document type:** *Report, Trade.* **Description:** Covers companies active as bus and coach operators.
Former titles (until 2001): Business Ratio. Bus and Coach Operators (1470-6806); (until 2000): Business Ratio Plus: Bus and Coach Operators (1357-5228); (until 1994): Business Ratio Report: Bus and Coach Operators (0269-6401)
Related titles: CD-ROM ed.; Online - full text ed.
Published by: Key Note Ltd. (Subsidiary of: Bonnier Business Information), Harlequin House, 5th Fl, 7 High St, Teddington, Richmond upon Thames, TW11 8EE, United Kingdom. TEL 44-845-5040452, FAX 44-845-5040453, sales@keynote.co.uk.

380.52 658.8 GBR ISSN 1472-751X
BUSINESS RATIO REPORT. FREIGHT FORWARDERS. Text in English. 1978. a. GBP 365 per issue (effective 2010). charts; stat. back issues avail. **Document type:** *Report, Trade.*
Former titles (until 2000): Business Ratio. Freight Forwarders (1468-8883); (until 1999): Business Ratio Plus. Freight Forwarders (1357-0447); (until 1994): Business Ratio Report: Freight Forwarders (0261-8168)
Published by: Key Note Ltd. (Subsidiary of: Bonnier Business Information), Harlequin House, 5th Fl, 7 High St, Teddington, Richmond upon Thames, TW11 8EE, United Kingdom. TEL 44-845-5040452, FAX 44-845-5040453, sales@keynote.co.uk.

388.322 USA
BUSLINE; serving the tour and transit industries. Text in English. 19??. bi-m. USD 25 domestic; USD 60 foreign; USD 10 per issue; free to qualified personnel (effective 2011). adv. back issues avail. **Document type:** *Magazine, Trade.*
Related titles: Online - full text ed.: free (effective 2011).
Indexed: HRIS.
Published by: Rankin Publishing, 204 E Main St, PO Box 130, Arcola, IL 61910. TEL 217-268-4959, FAX 217-268-4815, drankin126@aol.com, http://www.rankinpublishing.com. Ed. Harrell Kerkhoff. Pub. Don Rankin. Adv. contact Kevin Kennedy.

380.5 DEU ISSN 0942-346X
BUSMAGAZIN; Die Fachzeitschrift fuer Busunternehmer und Gruppenreiseveranstalter. Text in German. 1981. 10/yr. EUR 76.50; EUR 7.65 newsstand/cover (effective 2011). bk.rev. bibl.; charts; illus. index. **Document type:** *Magazine, Trade.*
Formerly (until 1992): Busverkehr (0720-4507)
—CCC.
Published by: Kirschbaum Verlag GmbH, Siegfriedstr 28, Bonn, 53179, Germany. TEL 49-228-954530, FAX 49-228-9545327, info@kirschbaum.de, http://www.kirschbaum.de. Ed. Dirk Sanne. Pub. Bernhard Kirschbaum. Adv. contact Volker Rutkowski. Circ: 8,068 (paid and controlled).

388.322 CHE
BUSOLDTIMER KALENDER. Text in German. 1986. a. CHF 38.20 (effective 1999). back issues avail. **Document type:** *Monographic series.*
Published by: Verlag Verkehrs Fotoarchiv, Wuehrestr 43, Uster, 8610, Switzerland. TEL 41-1-9410085, FAX 41-1-9410085. Ed., Pub. Juerg Biegger.

BUSPLANER INTERNATIONAL. *see* TRAVEL AND TOURISM

▼ **BUTTERWORTHS INTERNATIONAL TRADE AND TRANSPORT LAW NEWSLETTER.** *see* LAW—International Law

388 RUS
➤ **BYULLETEN' TRANSPORTNOI INFORMATSII.** Text in Russian. 1994. m. USD 580 in North America (effective 2011). **Document type:** *Journal, Academic/Scholarly.*
Published by: Natsional'naya Assotsyatsiya Transportnikov/National Association of Transportation Workers, Kulakov per. 17, str.1, ofis 45, Moscow, 129626, Russian Federation. TEL 7-495-6879649, bti@natrans.ru. Ed. G E Davydov. **Dist. by:** East View Information Services, 10601 Wayzata Blvd, Minneapolis, MN 55305. TEL 952-252-1201, 800-477-1005, FAX 952-252-1202, info@eastview.com, http://www.eastview.com.

658.5005 GBR
C I L T WORLD. Text in English. 2000 (Spr.). m. free to members (effective 2009). adv. back issues avail. **Document type:** *Journal, Trade.* **Description:** Contains news about the logistics and transport sector, as well as news and releases from the institute.
Formerly (until 2001): C I T World
Related titles: Online - full text ed.: free (effective 2009).
Indexed: B06, CA.
Published by: Chartered Institute of Logistics and Transport in the UK, Earlstrees Ct, Earlstrees Rd, Corby, Northants NN17 4AX, United Kingdom. TEL 44-1536-740100, FAX 44-1536-740101, enquiry@ciltuk.org.uk, http://www.ciltuk.org.uk/. Ed., Pub. David Jinks TEL 44-1536-740117. Adv. contact Kevin Shoemake.

380.5 362.4 GBR ISSN 1750-3671
C T A JOURNAL. Text in English. 19??. bi-m. free to members (effective 2009). bk.rev. **Document type:** *Journal, Trade.* **Description:** Features on working in community transport and the voluntary sector.
Former titles (until 2006): Community Transport Magazine; (until 1986): Community Transport Quarterly (0263-9378); (until 1982): Roadrunner
Published by: Community Transport Association, Highbank, Halton St, Hyde, Cheshire SK14 2NY, United Kingdom. TEL 44-161-3511475, FAX 44-161-3517221, info@ctauk.org.

354.8 USA
C T A P PUBLICATION. Text in English. irreg. **Document type:** *Monographic series, Government.* **Description:** Discusses programs and technologies to make public transportation vehicles more accessible to disabled persons, in compliance with the Americans with Disabilities Act of 1990.
Published by: (U.S. Department of Health and Human Services, Community Transportation Assistance Project), Community Transportation Association of America, 1341 G St, NW, 10th Fl, Washington, DC 20005. TEL 800-527-8279, bogren@ctaa.org, http://web1.ctaa.org/webmodules/webarticles/anmviewer.asp?a=23&z=2. **Co-sponsor:** Easter Seals Project Action.

354.7 USA ISSN 1082-345X
CALIFORNIA CORRIDORS. Text in English. 1995. m. looseleaf. USD 125 (effective 2000). index. back issues avail. **Document type:** *Newsletter.* **Description:** Covers the politics of California transportation issues. Covers the Legislature and Commissions and matters relating to all modes of transportation in the state.
Published by: York Family Publishing, 926 J St, Ste 1214, Sacramento, CA 95814. TEL 916-446-3956, FAX 916-498-3195. Ed. Anthony York. Pub. Bud Lembke. Circ: 200 (paid).

388.346 FRA ISSN 0769-3249
CAMPING-CAR MAGAZINE. Text in French. 1985. 10/yr. (includes one special issue). EUR 39 (effective 2010). adv. illus. **Document type:** *Magazine, Consumer.*
Formed by the merger of (1978-1985): Camping-Cars and Motor-Homes (0183-4002); (1978-1985): Van le Camping-Car (0292-6857); Which was formerly (until 1980): Camping Car et le Van (0183-0139)
Published by: Motor Presse France, 12 rue Rouget de Lisle, Issy-les-Moulineaux, 92442, France. http://www.motorpresse.fr. Circ: 75,450 (paid).

388 354 CAN ISSN 1912-1342
HE215.A15
CANADA. PARLIAMENT. HOUSE OF COMMONS. STANDING COMMITTEE ON TRANSPORT, INFRASTRUCTURE AND COMMUNITIES. MINUTES OF PROCEEDINGS. Text in English. 2001. irreg. **Document type:** *Government.*
Formerly (until 2006): Canada. Parliament. House of Commons. Standing Committee on Transport. Minutes of Proceedings (1707-8342); Which superseded in part (in 2002): Canada. Parliament. House of Commons. Standing Committee on Transport and Government Operations. Minutes of Proceedings (1706-3302); Which was formed by the merger of (1965-2001): Canada. Parliament. House of Commons. Standing Committee on Transport. Minutes of Proceedings (1204-5187); Which was formerly (until 1995): Canada. Parliament. House of Commons. Standing Committee on Transport. Minutes of Proceedings and Evidence (0826-3531); (until 1979): Canada. Parliament. House of Commons. Standing Committee on Transport and Communications. Minutes of Proceedings and Evidence (0576-3665); (1988-2001): Canada. Parliament. House of Commons. Standing Committee on Government Operations. Minutes of Proceedings (1196-9474); Which was formerly (until 1995): Canada. Parliament. House of Commons. Standing Committee on Government Operations. Minutes of Proceedings and Evidence (1200-0086); (until 1994): Canada. Parliament. House of Commons. Standing Committee on Consumer and Corporate Affairs and Government Operations. Minutes of Proceedings and Evidence (0844-8590); Which was formed by the merger of (1986-1988): Canada. Parliament. House of Commons. Standing Committee on Consumer and Corporate Affairs. Minutes of Proceedings and Evidence (0834-9878); (1986-1988): Canada. Parliament. House of Commons. Standing Committee on Government Operations. Minutes of Proceedings and Evidence (0840-2299)
Related titles: Online - full text ed.: ISSN 1706-3825.
Published by: (House of Commons, Standing Committee on Transport), Canada, House of Commons (Subsidiary of: Parliament), Information Service, Ottawa, ON K1A 0A9, Canada. TEL 613-992-4793, info@parl.gc.ca, http://www.parl.gc.ca.

380.5 CAN ISSN 0824-8265
HE2801
CANADIAN NATIONAL. ANNUAL REPORT. Text in English. 1922. a.
Formerly (until 1979): Canadian National Railways. Annual Report (0225-1868)
Related titles: French ed.
Published by: Canadian National, 935 de La Gauchetiere St W, Montreal, PQ H3B 2M9, Canada. TEL 888-888-5909, cn@wpq.faneuil.com. Circ: 25,000.

CANADIAN RAIL/RAIL CANADIEN. *see* TRANSPORTATION—Railroads

388 CAN ISSN 1487-6671
CANADIAN TRANSPORTATION AGENCY. ANNUAL REPORT. Text in English, French. 1977. a.
Former titles (until 1994): National Transportation Agency of Canada. Annual Review (0845-1109); (until 1985): Transport Review (0711-3218)
Related titles: Online - full content ed.: ISSN 1494-7927. 1996.
Published by: Canadian Transportation Agency/Office des Transports du Canada, 15 Eddy St, Ottawa, ON K1A 0N9, Canada. TEL 819-953-8353, 888-222-2592, FAX 819-953-5686, cta.comment@cta-otc.gc.ca.

388 354.76 CAN ISSN 1483-6912
CA1BT31-4 31
CANADIAN TRANSPORTATION AGENCY. PERFORMANCE REPORT. Text in English, French. 1997. a.
Related titles: Online - full text ed.: ISSN 1490-4802.
Published by: (Canadian Transportation Agency/Office des Transports du Canada), Treasury Board of Canada Secretariat, Corporate Communications/Secretariat du Conseil du Tresor du Canada, West Tower, Rm P-135, 300 Laurier Ave W, Ottawa, ON K1A 0R5, Canada. TEL 613-995-2855, FAX 613-996-0518, services-publications@tbs-sct.gc.ca, http://www.tbs-sct.gc.ca.

340 380.5 CAN
CANADIAN TRANSPORTATION LAW REPORTER. Text in English. 1990. bi-m. looseleaf. CAD 530 (effective 2008). **Document type:** *Newsletter, Trade.* **Description:** Covers the Canadian Transportation Regulations environment, including transportation by rail, road, water, air and pipeline.
Published by: C C H Canadian Ltd. (Subsidiary of: Wolters Kluwer N.V.), 90 Sheppard Ave E, Ste 300, North York, ON M2N 6X1, Canada. TEL 416-224-2248, 800-268-4522, FAX 416-224-2243, 800-461-4131, cservice@cch.ca.

380.5 658.7 CAN ISSN 1187-4295
HE1
CANADIAN TRANSPORTATION LOGISTICS. Text in English. 1898. 11/yr. CAD 60.95 domestic; USD 99.95 foreign (effective 2007). adv. illus.; stat. Supplement avail. **Document type:** *Magazine, Trade.* **Description:** For those in charge of transportation, distribution, warehousing, inventory control and all functions of logistics including customs services and freight forwarding.

Former titles (until 1991): Canadian Transportation (1184-1052); (until 1989): Canadian Transportation and Distribution (0008-5200); (until 1968): Canadian Transportation (0319-4388); Which incorporates: Traffic and Distribution Management
Related titles: Microfiche ed.: (from MML); Microform ed.: (from MML); Online - full text ed.
Indexed: A09, A10, A15, ABIn, B01, B06, B07, B08, B09, BPIA, C03, C05, CA, CBCABus, CBPI, LogistBibl, P48, P51, P52, PQC, S22, T02, V03, V04.
—BLDSC (3046.031000), Linda Hall. **CCC.**
Published by: Business Information Group, 12 Concorde Pl, Ste 800, Toronto, ON M3C 4J2, Canada. TEL 416-442-2122, 800-668-2374, FAX 416-442-2191, orders@businessinformationgroup.ca, http://www.businessinformationgroup.ca. Pub. Nick Krukowski TEL 416-510-5108. Circ: 14,000.

388 CAN ISSN 1915-7274
CANADIAN TRANSPORTATION RESEARCH FORUM. PROCEEDINGS OF THE ANNUAL CONFERENCE. Text in English. 196?. a. **Document type:** *Proceedings, Trade.*
Formerly (until 199?): Canadian Transportation Research Forum. Proceedings of the Annual Meeting (1183-2770)
—CCC.
Published by: Canadian Transportation Research Forum, PO Box 23033, Woodstock, ON N4T 1R9, Canada. TEL 519-421-9701, FAX 519-421-9319, cawoudsma@ctrf.ca, http://www.ctrf.ca.

CAR & BUS MAGAZINE (NEDERLANDSE EDITIE). *see* TRAVEL AND TOURISM

388 PRT ISSN 1645-4111
CARACTERIZACAO DA REDE NACIONAL DE TRANSPORTES EM (YEAR). Text in Portuguese. 2000. a. **Document type:** *Report, Government.*
Published by: Redes Energeticas Nacionais, Avenida dos Estados Unidos da America 55, Lisbon, 1749-061, Portugal. TEL 351-210-013500, FAX 351-210-013310, http://www.ren.pt.

388 AUS
CARAVAN PARKS NEWS. Text in English. 1992. q. **Document type:** *Newsletter, Trade.*
Published by: Caravan Parks Association of Queensland Inc., PO Box 5542, Stafford Heights, QLD 4053, Australia. TEL 61-7-38621833, FAX 61-7-32629890, admin@caravanqld.com.au, http://www.caravanqld.com.au. Circ: 550 (controlled).

CARAVAN WORLD. *see* TRAVEL AND TOURISM

388.346 DEU ISSN 0008-6185
CARAVANING; Europas grosses Camping-Magazin. Text in German. 1959. m. EUR 33.50; EUR 3 newsstand/cover (effective 2010). adv. bk.rev. bibl.; charts; illus.; mkt.; stat.; tr.lit. index. **Document type:** *Magazine, Consumer.*
—CCC.
Published by: Motor Presse Stuttgart GmbH & Co. KG (Subsidiary of: Gruner + Jahr AG & Co), Leuschnerstr 1, Stuttgart, 70174, Germany. TEL 49-711-18201, FAX 49-711-1821779, internet-redaktion@motor-presse-stuttgart.de, http://www.motorpresse.de. Ed. Kai Feyerabend. Adv. contact Peter Steinbach. Circ: 28,867 (paid and controlled).

388 AUS
CARAVANS & CAMPERVANS GUIDE. Text in English. 1977. 3/yr. AUD 333.30 (effective 2008). adv. **Document type:** *Handbook/Manual/Guide, Consumer.* **Description:** Provides information about new and used boats, motors and trailers and new personal water craft.
Former titles (until 1992): Glass's Caravan and Campervan Guide; (until 1989): Glass's Dealers Guide. Caravan & Campervan Values; (until 1984): Glass's Dealers Guide. Caravan Values
Published by: Glass' Guide Pty. Ltd., 48 La Trobe St, Melbourne, VIC 3000, Australia. TEL 61-3-96633009, FAX 61-3-96633049, customers@glassguide.com.au, http://www.glassguide.com.au. adv.: color page USD 100; trim 80 x 125.

387 GBR ISSN 1362-766X
TA1215 CODEN: CSYIBN
CARGO SYSTEMS. Text in English. 1973. bi-m. GBP 795 combined subscription domestic (print & online eds.); EUR 1,105 combined subscription in Europe (print & online eds.); USD 1,640, GBP 995 combined subscription elsewhere (print & online eds.) (effective 2010); subscr. includes (Containerisation International). adv. bk.rev. illus. back issues avail.; reprints avail. **Document type:** *Magazine, Trade.* **Description:** Provides international coverage of the container, ports, and cargo-handling industries.
Former titles (until 1994): Cargo Systems International (0306-0985); (until 1973): I C H C A Monthly Journal; Which was formed by the merger of: International Cargo Handling Coordination Association. Monthly Bulletin; I C H C A Quarterly Journal
Related titles: Online - full text ed.
Indexed: A22, BMT, BrRB, CLT&T, EngInd, HRIS, SCOPUS.
—BLDSC (3052.150000), IE, Infotrieve, Ingenta, Linda Hall. **CCC.**
Published by: Informa Trade & Energy (Subsidiary of: Informa U K Ltd.), Informa House, 30-32 Mortimer St, London, W1W 7RE, United Kingdom. TEL 44-20-70175000, http://www.informa.com/divisions/commercial/informa_Informa_Trade_and_Energy. Ed. Benedict Young TEL 44-20-70174695. Adv. contact Ed Andrews TEL 44-20-70174294. Circ: 5,283.

CARGOVISION. *see* TRANSPORTATION—Air Transport

380.5 NGA
CHARTERED INSTITUTE OF TRANSPORT. ANNUAL. Text in English. 1959. a. adv.
Published by: Chartered Institute of Transport, Nigerian Ports Authority, Ebuke-Metta, 51 Herbert Macauley St, Lagos, Nigeria.

343.09322 USA ISSN 1942-5155
CHEMICAL REGULATION REPORTER: HAZARDOUS MATERIALS TRANSPORTATION. Text in English. 1977 (Apr). m. looseleaf. USD 421 (effective 2010 - 2011). **Document type:** *Handbook/Manual/Guide, Trade.* **Description:** Contains rules and regulations governing shipment of hazardous material by rail, air, ship, highway and pipeline, including DOT's Harzardous Materials Tables and EPA's rules for it's hazardous waste tracking system.
Published by: The Bureau of National Affairs, Inc., 1801 S Bell St, Arlington, VA 22202. TEL 703-341-3000, 800-372-1033, FAX 703-341-4634, bnaplus@bna.com.

388 CHN ISSN 1009-6760
CHENGSHI CHELIANG/URBAN VEHICLES. Text in Chinese. 1983. bi-m. USD 39.60 (effective 2009). **Document type:** *Journal, Academic/Scholarly.*
Related titles: Online - full text ed.
—East View.
Published by: Zhongguo Chengshi Gonggong Jiaotong Xiehui, 9, San-Lihe Lu, Beijing, 100835, China. TEL 86-10-68459870, FAX 86-10-68414610.

388 307.1 CHN ISSN 1009-1467
CHENGSHI GONGGONG JIAOTONG/URBAN PUBLIC TRANSPORT. Text in Chinese. 1989. m. CNY 150; CNY 12.50 per issue (effective 2010). **Document type:** *Journal, Academic/Scholarly.*
Formerly (until 1999): Chengshi Gonggong Jiaotong Jianshe
Related titles: Online - full text ed.: (from WanFang Data Corp.).
Published by: (Zhongguo Tumu Gongcheng Xuehui/China Civil Engineering Society), Chengshi Gonggong Jiaotong Zazhishe, 38, Chegongzhuang Xi Lu, Beijing, 100044, China. TEL 86-10-68729968, FAX 86-10-68729968.

388 CHN ISSN 1007-869X
CHENGSHI GUIDAO JIAOTONG YANJIU/URBAN MASS TRANSIT. Text in Chinese. 1998. bi-m. USD 106.80 (effective 2009). **Document type:** *Journal, Academic/Scholarly.*
Related titles: Online - full text ed.
—East View.
Published by: Tongji Daxue/Tongji University, 500, Zhennan Lu, Huxixiao-qu, Shanghai, 200331, China.

388 CHN ISSN 1672-5328
CHENGSHI JIAOTONG/URBAN TRANSPORT OF CHINA. Text in Chinese. 2003. bi-m. CNY 18 per issue (effective 2010). **Document type:** *Journal, Academic/Scholarly.*
Related titles: Online - full text ed.: CNY 120; CNY 20 per issue (effective 2010).
—BLDSC (3172.396730), East View.
Published by: Zhongguo Chengshi Guihua Sheji Yanjiuyuan/China Academy of Urban Planning Design, 9, Sanlihe Lu, Beijing, 100037, China.

388.094 FRA ISSN 1775-2906
LES CHIFFRES CLES DU TRANSPORT EN ALSACE. Text in French. 199?. a., latest 2008. **Document type:** *Bulletin, Trade.*
Published by: Observatoire Regional des Transports d'Alsace, 42 rue Jacques Kable, Strasbourg, 67070 Cedex, France. TEL 33-3-90238352, FAX 33-3-90238350.

388.0440983 GBR ISSN 1752-5497
CHILE FREIGHT TRANSPORT REPORT. Text in English. 2006. q. EUR 820, USD 1,030 combined subscription (print & email eds.) (effective 2010). **Document type:** *Report, Trade.* **Description:** Provides industry professionals and strategists, sector analysts, investors, trade associations and regulatory bodies with independent forecasts and competitive intelligence on the Chilean freight transport and logistics industry.
Related titles: E-mail ed.
Indexed: A15, ABIn, P48, P51, P52, PQC.
Published by: Business Monitor International Ltd., Senator House, 85 Queen Victoria St, London, EC4V 4AB, United Kingdom. TEL 44-20-72480468, FAX 44-20-72480467, subs@businessmonitor.com.

388.0440951 GBR ISSN 1752-5756
CHINA FREIGHT TRANSPORT REPORT. Text in English. 2006. q. EUR 820, USD 1,030 combined subscription (print & email eds.) (effective 2010). **Document type:** *Report, Trade.* **Description:** Provides industry professionals and strategists, sector analysts, investors, trade associations and regulatory bodies with independent forecasts and competitive intelligence on the Chinese freight transport and logistics industry.
Related titles: E-mail ed.
Indexed: A15, ABIn, B02, B15, B17, B18, G04, I05, P48, P51, P52, PQC.
Published by: Business Monitor International Ltd., Senator House, 85 Queen Victoria St, London, EC4V 4AB, United Kingdom. TEL 44-20-72480468, FAX 44-20-72480467, subs@businessmonitor.com.

388 CHN ISSN 1674-0696
CODEN: CJDXAZ
CHONGQING JIAOTONG DAXUE XUEBAO (ZIRAN KEXUE BAN)/ CHONGQING JIAOTONG UNIVERSITY. JOURNAL (NATURAL SCIENCES). Text in Chinese. 1982. bi-m. **Document type:** *Journal, Academic/Scholarly.* **Description:** Covers the latest developments of theoretical and applied researches in the fields of Transit Science and Engineering.
Formerly (until 2006): Chongqing Jiaotong Xueyuan Xuebao/Chongqing Jiaotong Institute. Journal (1001-716X)
Related titles: Online - full text ed.
Indexed: A28, APA, BrCerAb, C&ISA, CA/WCA, CIA, CerAb, CivEngAb, CorrAb, E&CAJ, E11, EEA, EMA, ESPM, EnvEAb, H15, M&TEA, M09, MBF, METADEX, SolStAb, T04, WAA.
—East View.
Published by: Chongqing Jiaotong Daxue/Chongqing Jiaotong University, 66, Xuefu Ave., Nan'an District, Chongqing, 400074, China. TEL 86-23-62652428, FAX 86-23-62652104, http://www.cqjtu.edu.cn/index.html. Ed. Chang-xian Wang. Circ: 500.

CHUANDONG JISHU/DRIVE SYSTEM TECHNIQUE. *see* ENGINEERING

380.5 FRA ISSN 1956-9629
CIRCULER AUTREMENT. Text in French. 1984. q. EUR 24 (effective 2009). adv. bk.rev.
Formerly (until 2001): Circuler (0765-3522)
Indexed: FR.
Published by: Prevention Routiere, 6 av. Hoche, Paris, 75008, France. TEL 44-15-27-00, FAX 44-15-27-40. Ed. J Yves Salaun. Circ: 8,000.

CITY CYCLIST. *see* SPORTS AND GAMES—Bicycles And Motorcycles

388.322 GBR ISSN 0966-8438
CLASSIC BUS. Text in English. 1992. bi-m. GBP 22.20 domestic; GBP 29.20 in Europe; GBP 34.70 elsewhere; GBP 3.70 per issue (effective 2009). adv. bk.rev. back issues avail. **Document type:** *Magazine, Consumer.* **Description:** Contains articles that gives perspective and understanding to how we got to where we are today.
Former titles (until 1992): Buses Extra (0141-9927); (until 1977): Buses Special
—CCC.
Published by: Classic Bus Publishing Ltd., 15 Starfield Rd, London, W12 9SN, United Kingdom. TEL 44-844-7365693. Ed. Ray Stenning. **Subscr. to:** 18 Brunstane Rd, Edinburgh EH15 2QJ, United Kingdom. subs@classicbusmag.co.uk. **Dist. by:** MarketForce UK Ltd.

CLASSIC MILITARY VEHICLE. *see* MILITARY

388.322 GBR ISSN 1351-3877
COACH & BUS WEEK. Abbreviated title: C B W. Text in English. 1978. w. GBP 85 domestic; GBP 140 in Europe; GBP 180 elsewhere; GBP 2.95 newsstand/cover (effective 2009). adv. bk.rev. back issues avail. **Document type:** *Magazine, Trade.* **Description:** Contains national and regional industry news, coach operator and big company profiles, vehicle launches, technical up-dates, test reports, road tests, legal up-dates including employment, safety and road traffic legislation, business news, job hunters, local authority tenders and the like.
Formed by the merger of (1987-1992): Coachmart & Bus Operator (0953-8240); Which was formerly (until 1987): Coachmart; (1986-1992): Bus Business (0957-8951)
Related titles: Online - full text ed.
Published by: Rouncy Media, Ltd., 3 The Office Village, Forder Way, Cygnet Park, Hampton, Peterborough, PE7 8GX, United Kingdom. TEL 44-1733-293240, FAX 44-845-2802927. Ed. Andrew Sutcliffe TEL 44-1733-293242. Adv. contact Dan Warren TEL 44-1733-293487. **Subscr. to:** Tower House, Sovereign Park, Market Harborough, Leicestershire LE16 9EF, United Kingdom. TEL 44-1733-293247.

388.322 GBR
COACH OPERATORS HANDBOOK. Text in English. 1986. a. GBP 30 (effective 2010). adv. **Document type:** *Directory, Trade.* **Description:** Read by the entire UK coach industry. Contains listings of attractions targeting group bookings and provides details of associated services.
—BLDSC (3287.726000).
Published by: Rouncy Media, Ltd., 3 The Office Village, Forder Way, Cygnet Park, Hampton, Peterborough, PE7 8GX, United Kingdom. TEL 44-1733-293240, FAX 44-845-2802927. adv.: B&W page GBP 1,995, color page GBP 2,350; trim 210 x 297. Circ: 5,000 (controlled).

388.346 USA ISSN 1093-3581
COAST TO COAST. Text in English. 1982. 8/yr. free to members (effective 2009). adv. illus. **Document type:** *Magazine, Consumer.* **Description:** Covers 500 private camping and resort clubs in N. America. Focuses on vacation, travel, recreation and the coast to coast system.
Formerly (until 1997): Coast to Coast Magazine (1062-2349)
Related titles: Online - full text ed.: free (effective 2005).
Published by: (Coast to Coast Resorts), Affinity Group Inc., 2575 Vista Del Mar, Ventura, CA 93001. TEL 805-667-4100, FAX 805-667-4419, info@affinitygroup.com, http://www.affinitygroup.com. Ed. Valerie Law TEL 805-667-4217. Pub. Bob Helms. Adv. contact Terry Thompson TEL 206-283-9545. B&W page USD 7,045, color page USD 9,415; trim 10.5 x 7.88. Circ: 230,000.

388 343.093 ITA ISSN 1121-6840
IL CODICE DELLA STRADA. Text in Italian. 1992. bi-w. **Document type:** *Magazine, Consumer.*
Related titles: CD-ROM ed.: ISSN 1824-5439. 2002; Online - full text ed.: ISSN 1826-8749. 2006.
Published by: Edizioni Giuridico Amministrative e Formazione (E G A F), Via Filippo Guarini 2, Forli, 47100, Italy. TEL 39-0543-473347, FAX 39-0543-474133, gruppo@egaf.it, http://www.egaf.it.

COLLANA DI DIRITTO DEI TRASPORTI. *see* LAW

388.04409861 GBR ISSN 1752-5764
COLOMBIA FREIGHT TRANSPORT REPORT. Text in English. 2006. a. EUR 820, USD 1,030 combined subscription per issue (print & email eds.) (effective 2010). **Document type:** *Report, Trade.* **Description:** Provides industry professionals and strategists, sector analysts, investors, trade associations and regulatory bodies with independent forecasts and competitive intelligence on the Colombian freight transport and logistics industry.
Related titles: E-mail ed.
Published by: Business Monitor International Ltd., Senator House, 85 Queen Victoria St, London, EC4V 4AB, United Kingdom. TEL 44-20-72480468, FAX 44-20-72480467, subs@businessmonitor.com.

COMLINE: TRANSPORTATION INDUSTRY OF JAPAN. *see* BUSINESS AND ECONOMICS

388 USA
COMMUNITY TRANSPORTATION. Abbreviated title: C T. Text in English. 1983. bi-m. free to members (effective 2010). adv. bk.rev. illus. index, cum.index: 1983-1992. back issues avail.; reprints avail. **Document type:** *Magazine, Consumer.* **Description:** Provides funding, legislation, trends, accessibility, coordination, environmental issues, vehicles and components, and surveys in community transportation.
Former titles (until 1997): Community Transportation Reporter (0895-4437); (until 1987): Rural Transportation Reporter
Indexed: HRIS.
Published by: Community Transportation Association of America, 1341 G St, NW, 10th Fl, Washington, DC 20005. TEL 202-628-1480, 800-891-0590, FAX 202-737-9197, http://web1.ctaa.org/webmodules/webarticles/anmviewer.asp?a=23&z=2. Ed. Scott Bogren TEL 202-247-1921. Adv. contact Bill Shoemaker TEL 302-436-4375. B&W page USD 1,562; 7 x 10. Circ: 15,000.

388 FRA ISSN 2108-2588
LES COMPTES DES TRANSPORTS EN (YEAR). Text in French. 2008. a., latest 2009. **Document type:** *Government.*
Published by: France. Ministere de l'Ecologie, du Developpement Durable, des Transports et du Logement, 20 av. de Segur, Paris, Cedex 7 75302, France. http://www.developpement-durable.gouv.fr.

388 GBR ISSN 1367-6059
CONCESSIONARY FARES. Text in English. 1992. irreg., latest vol.5, 2006. **Document type:** *Monographic series, Trade.* **Description:** Provides essential background, information and analysis for authorities, operators and their advisers.
Related titles: Online - full text ed.: ISSN 1752-6531.
—CCC.
Published by: T A S Publications & Events Ltd., Ross Holme, West End, Long Preston, Skipton, N Yorks BD23 4QL, United Kingdom. TEL 44-1729-840756, FAX 44-1729-840705, info@taspublications.co.uk.

TU

CONFIDENTIAL A-I-R LETTER. (Air Incident Research) *see* CRIMINOLOGY AND LAW ENFORCEMENT

388 USA ISSN 0069-9039
HE28.C8
CONNECTICUT MASTER TRANSPORTATION PLAN. Text in English. 1971. biennial. **Document type:** *Government.* **Description:** It consists of two parts: a narrative section and appendices. The narrative section of the plan identifies major issues and challenges for the State of Connecticut, discusses the Department's approaches and concerns in addressing them and explains the transportation planning process and the impact of the federal requirements for fiscally constrained plans on the transportation programs. The appendices of this plan list the programs and projects that are expected to be implemented during the next ten-year period, 2000-2009, and describe the TEA-21 federal funding programs and the federal/state funding ratios.
Incorporates (in 1973): Connecticut Highway Needs Report
Published by: Department of Transportation (Conndot), 2800 Berlin Turnpike, PO Box 317546, Newington, CT 06131-7546. TEL 860-594-2038. Ed. Roxane Framson. Circ: 1,000.

380.5 JPN ISSN 0289-8322
CONTAINER AGE; the authoritative voice of intermodal transportation and distribution. Text in Japanese. 1967. m. JPY 9,000. adv. bk.rev. **Document type:** *Trade.* **Description:** Serves intermodal transportation industry, specifically shippers, manufacturers, carriers, and freight forwarders.
Published by: Container Age Ltd., 601 NS Iwamotocho Bldg, 1-4-5 Iwamoto-cho, Chiyoda-ku, Tokyo, 101-0032, Japan. TEL 81-3-3851-1211, FAX 81-3-3851-1212. Ed. Eiji Niimoto. Circ: 21,600.

380.1029 DEU ISSN 0174-2701
CONTAINER CONTACTS. Text in German. 1971. a. EUR 22 (effective 2006). adv. **Document type:** *Directory, Trade.*
Formerly: Container, Wo? (0174-2698)
Published by: K.O. Storck Verlag, Striepenweg 31, Hamburg, 21147, Germany. TEL 49-40-7971301, FAX 49-40-79713101, webmaster@storck-verlag.de, http://www.storck-verlag.de. adv.: B&W page EUR 1,050, color page EUR 1,830; 105 x 210. Circ: 7,000.

388 DEU
CONTAKT; aktuelle Informationen fuer unsere Fahrgaeste im MVV. Text in German. 4/yr. **Document type:** *Magazine, Consumer.*
Published by: Muenchner Verkehrs- und Tarifverbund GmbH, Thierschstr 2, Munich, 80538, Germany. TEL 49-89-210330, FAX 49-89-21033282, info@mvv-muenchen.de, http://www.mvv-muenchen.de. Circ: 150,000 (controlled).

388 ITA ISSN 1974-2088
CONTO NAZIONALE DELLE INFRASTRUTTURE E DEI TRASPORTI. Text in Italian. 1966. a. **Document type:** *Directory, Government.*
Formerly (until 2000): Conto Nazionale dei Trasporti (0391-5220); Which incorporated (1975-1977): Compendio di Statistiche sui Trasporti (1974-2096)
Published by: Istituto Poligrafico e Zecca dello Stato, Piazza Verdi 10, Rome, 00198, Italy. TEL 39-06-85082147, editoriale@ipzs.it, http://www.ipzs.it.

388 352 GBR
CORNWALL LOCAL TRANSPORT PLAN (YEAR). Text in English. 2001. quinquennial. back issues avail. **Document type:** *Handbook/Manual/ Guide, Trade.* **Description:** Contains plan for all types of transport in Cornwall.
Related titles: Online - full text ed.: free (effective 2009).
Published by: Cornwall County Council, County Hall, Treyev Rd, Truro, TR 3AY, United Kingdom. TEL 44-1872-322000, 44-300-1234100, enquiries@cornwall.ac.uk, http://www.cornwall.gov.uk.

380.5 USA ISSN 1075-3621
COURIER MAGAZINE; newsmagazine of the messenger, courier, & expedited delivery industry. Text in English. 1992. bi-m. USD 35 domestic; USD 45 in Canada; USD 55 elsewhere (effective 2005). adv. back issues avail. **Document type:** *Magazine, Trade.*
Published by: Courier Magazine, Inc., 1236, Staunton, VA 24402-1236. TEL 703-330-5600, FAX 703-330-5357. Ed. Mary Deluca. Pub., R&P Bruce H Joffe. Adv. contact Russ Warren. Circ: 4,000.

388 USA
THE COURIER TIMES. Text in English. 1993. m. USD 36. adv. bk.rev. back issues avail. **Document type:** *Magazine, Trade.* **Description:** Includes information on the delivery industry in the northeast U.S. Contains legal advice, tax advice, financial advice, and operational advice.
Published by: Courier Times, Inc., 27 16 168th St, Flushing, NY 11358. TEL 800-495-9400, FAX 718-359-1959. Ed., Adv. contact William Goodman. Pub. Janet Goodman. Circ: 1,000.

344.044094972 GBR ISSN 1752-7880
CROATIA FREIGHT TRANSPORT REPORT. Text in English. 2007. a. EUR 820, USD 1,030 combined subscription per issue (print & email eds.) (effective 2010). **Document type:** *Report, Trade.* **Description:** Provides industry professionals and strategists, sector analysts, investors, trade associations and regulatory bodies with independent forecasts and competitive intelligence on the Croatian freight transport and logistics industry.
Related titles: E-mail ed.
Indexed: A15, ABIn, B02, B15, B17, B18, G04, I05, P48, P51, P52, PQC.
Published by: Business Monitor International Ltd., Senator House, 85 Queen Victoria St, London, EC4V 4AB, United Kingdom. TEL 44-20-72480468, FAX 44-20-72480467, subs@businessmonitor.com.

388.322 GBR ISSN 0969-2568
CRONER'S COACH AND BUS OPERATIONS. Variant title: Coach and Bus Bulletin. Text in English. 1983. base vol. plus q. updates. looseleaf. GBP 385; GBP 620 combined subscription (print & CD-ROM eds.) (effective 2010). **Document type:** *Bulletin, Trade.* **Description:** Covers the rules and regulations governing coach and bus operations in the U.K.
Related titles: CD-ROM ed.; Online - full text ed.
Published by: Croner C C H Group Ltd. (Subsidiary of: Wolters Kluwer UK Ltd.), 145 London Rd, Kingston upon Thames, Surrey KT2 6SR, United Kingdom. TEL 44-20-85473333, FAX 44-20-85472638, info@croner.co.uk.

388.3 USA
CULTURE CHANGE. Text in English. 1989. s-a. USD 20 (effective 2002). adv. bk.rev. back issues avail. **Document type:** *Newsletter.* **Description:** Contains articles, interviews and photos advocating and chronicling the road-fighting and auto-free movements internationally.
Former titles (until 2001): Auto-Free Times; Paving Moratorium Update - Auto-Free Times (1078-7747); Fossil Fuels Action Update; Ecodemocracy
Related titles: Online - full text ed.
Indexed: APW, AltPI.
Published by: Sustainable Energy Institute, PO Box 4347, Arcata, CA 95518. TEL 707-826-7775, FAX 707-822-7007. Ed. Jan Lundberg. R&P, Adv. contact Randy Ghent. Circ: 15,000. **Co-sponsor:** Alliance for a Paving Moratorium.

388.0440943710 GBR ISSN 1752-5772
CZECH REPUBLIC FREIGHT TRANSPORT REPORT. Text in English. 2006. q. EUR 820, USD 1,030 combined subscription (print & email eds.) (effective 2010). **Document type:** *Report, Trade.* **Description:** Provides industry professionals and strategists, sector analysts, investors, trade associations and regulatory bodies with independent forecasts and competitive intelligence on the Czech freight transport and logistics industry.
Related titles: E-mail ed.
Indexed: A15, ABIn, B02, B15, B17, B18, G04, I05, P48, P51, P52, PQC.
Published by: Business Monitor International Ltd., Senator House, 85 Queen Victoria St, London, EC4V 4AB, United Kingdom. TEL 44-20-72480468, FAX 44-20-72480467, subs@businessmonitor.com.

388 NLD ISSN 1877-7465
D N. (Dag Nacht) Variant title: Dag en Nacht Mobiliteit. Text in Dutch. 3/yr. **Document type:** *Magazine, Trade.*
Former titles (until 2009): Matrix (1567-1968); (until 2000): Van Kruispunt tot Kruispunt (1384-0029)
Related titles: Online - full text ed.: ISSN 1877-7473; ◆ English ed.: D N (English Edition). ISSN 1877-7481.
Published by: Vialis, Postbus 665, Haarlem, 2003 RR, Netherlands. TEL 31-23-5189191, FAX 31-23-5189111, info@vialis.nl, http:// www.vialis.nl.

388 NLD ISSN 1877-7481
▼ **D N (ENGLISH EDITION).** (Day Night) Variant title: Day and Night. Text in English. 2009. 3/yr.
Related titles: Online - full text ed.: ISSN 1877-749X; ◆ Dutch ed.: D N. ISSN 1877-7465.
Published by: Vialis, Postbus 665, Haarlem, 2003 RR, Netherlands. TEL 31-23-5189191, FAX 31-23-5189111, info@vialis.nl, http:// www.vialis.nl.

388.1 DNK ISSN 1397-9418
D S B I DAG; ugeavis for medarbejdere i dsb. (De danske Statsbaner) Text in Danish. 1997. w. bk.rev. **Document type:** *Newsletter, Corporate.*
Published by: D S B Kommunikation/The Danish State Railways, Soelvgade 40, Copenhagen K, 1349, Denmark. TEL 45-33-544222, FAX 45-33-544276, http://www.dsb.dk. Ed. Keld Soegaard.

380.5 DEU
D V Z BRIEF. (Deutsche Verkehrs - Zeitung) Text in German. 1981. w. EUR 402 (effective 2009). **Document type:** *Newspaper, Trade.*
Published by: Deutscher Verkehrs Verlag GmbH, Nordkanalstr 36, Hamburg, 20097, Germany. TEL 49-40-2371401, FAX 49-40-23714205, info@dvv-gruppe.de, http://www.dvv-gruppe.de.

380.5 DNK ISSN 0106-0724
DANMARKS TRANSPORT-TIDENDE; uafhaengigt nyhedsmagasin for danske transporterhverv. Variant title: Transport-Tidende. Text in Danish. 1978. 23/yr. DKK 616 (effective 2009). adv. **Document type:** *Newspaper, Trade.*
Related titles: Online - full text ed.
Published by: Danmarks Transport Forlag A/S, Jernbanegade 18, PO Box 352, Padborg, 6330, Denmark. TEL 45-70-100506, FAX 45-74-674047, http://www.transinform.com. Ed. Gwyn Nissen. Adv. contact Trine Philipsen. color page DKK 18,995; 365 x 254. Circ: 5,000.

DATA WAREHOUSING CAREER NEWSLETTER. *see* BUSINESS AND ECONOMICS—Management

796.7 CHN
DAZHONG QICHE (MOTUOCHE). Text in Chinese. 2001. m. **Document type:** *Magazine, Consumer.*
Published by: Dazhong Qiche Zazhishe (Subsidiary of: Jilin Chuban Jituan/Jilin Publishing Group), Jike Zhongda Chuanmei Guanggao, 16-17, A225, Chunshuyuan Xiao-qu, Beijing, 100052, China. TEL 86-10-63109491.

388 FRA ISSN 2107-4887
▼ **DECISION ATELIER P L.** (Poids Lourds) Text in French. 2010. bi-m. **Document type:** *Magazine.*
Published by: Editions Techniques pour l'Automobile et l'Industrie (E T A I), ETAI-GISI, Immeuble Parc II, 10 Pl. du General de Gaulle, Antony, 92160, France. TEL 33-1-77929292, http://www.etai.fr.

DEFENSE TRANSPORTATION JOURNAL; magazine of international defense transportation and logistics. *see* MILITARY

DELAWARE CRIMES, VEHICLES, TRANSPORTATION & RELATED STATUTES. *see* LAW

DELAWARE CRIMINAL AND TRAFFIC LAW MANUAL. *see* LAW—Criminal Law

380.5 USA
DELAWARE VALLEY PLANNING NEWS. Text in English. 1980. 3/yr. free. Supplement avail.; back issues avail. **Document type:** *Newsletter.*
Published by: Delaware Valley Regional Planning Commission, Bourse Bldg, 21 S Fifth St, Philadelphia, PA 19103. TEL 215-592-1800, FAX 215-592-9125. Ed., R&P Candace B Snyder. Circ: 2,500.

380.5 USA ISSN 0896-0747
HT393.P42
DELAWARE VALLEY REGIONAL PLANNING COMMISSION. ANNUAL REPORT. Cover title: D.V.R.P.C. Annual Report. Text in English. a. free. illus. **Document type:** *Corporate.* **Description:** Overview of activities of the Delaware Valley Regional Planning Commission in areas of transportation, strategic planning and regional information services.
Formerly: Delaware Valley Regional Planning Commission. Biennial Report (0098-6232)
Published by: Delaware Valley Regional Planning Commission, Bourse Bldg, 21 S Fifth St, Philadelphia, PA 19103. TEL 215-592-1800, FAX 215-592-9125. R&P Candace B Snyder.

DEVELOPMENT HANDBOOK. *see* BUSINESS AND ECONOMICS—Domestic Commerce

380.5 NLD ISSN 0924-5324
DEVELOPMENTS IN TRANSPORT STUDIES. Text in English. 1980. irreg., latest vol.4, 1982. price varies. **Document type:** *Monographic series, Trade.*
Published by: Springer Netherlands (Subsidiary of: Springer Science+Business Media), Van Godewijckstraat 30, Dordrecht, 3311 GX, Netherlands. TEL 31-78-6576050, FAX 31-78-6576474.

796.6 CHN ISSN 1672-6936
DIANDONG ZIXINGCHE. Text in Chinese. 2003. m. **Document type:** *Journal, Academic/Scholarly.*
Published by: Diandong Zixingche Zazhishe, 171, Longpan Lu, Nanjing, 210042, China. TEL 86-25-85426389, FAX 86-25-85426389.

DIESEL; mensile di cultura, attualita, tecnica che tratta di tutte le motorizzazioni diesel per usi industriali, agricoli, nautici. *see* ENGINEERING—Mechanical Engineering

DIRITTO DEI TRASPORTI. *see* LAW

DISTRICT OF COLUMBIA CRIMINAL LAW AND MOTOR VEHICLE HANDBOOK. *see* LAW—Criminal Law

380.5 CZE ISSN 0012-5520
DOPRAVA/TRANSPORT; ctvrtletni ekonomicko-technicka revue. Text in Czech; Contents page in English, French, German; Summaries in English. 1959. bi-m. EUR 53.50 (effective 2009). adv. bibl.; illus. **Document type:** *Magazine, Trade.* **Description:** Focuses on transport development and policy in Czech Republic.
Indexed: RASB.
—INIST.
Published by: Ministerstvo Dopravy Ceske Republiky, Nabrezi Ludvika Svobody 1222/12, Prague 1, 11000, Czech Republic. TEL 420-2-25131111, FAX 420-2-25131184, posta@mdcr.cz, http:// www.ministerstvodopravy.cz. Circ: 3,000. **Dist. by:** Kubon & Sagner Buchexport - Import GmbH, Hessstr 39-41, Munich 80798, Germany. TEL 49-89-542180, FAX 49-89-54218218, postmaster@kubon-sagner.de, http://www.kubon-sagner.de.

629 CZE ISSN 1210-1141
DOPRAVNI NOVINY. Text in Czech. 1992. w. CZK 1,300 (effective 2008). adv. **Document type:** *Magazine, Trade.* **Description:** Contains the latest information on all aspects of transportation and related businesses.
Published by: Ceske Dopravni Vydavatelstvi, s. r. o., Krkonosska 14, Prague 2, 120 00, Czech Republic. TEL 420-2-22723881, FAX 420-2-22729228. adv.: B&W page CZK 56,800, color page CZK 89,000; trim 275 x 380.

629 USA
DRIVER LETTER. Text in English. bi-m. **Document type:** *Newsletter.* **Description:** Professional driver letter for defensive driving course instructors.
Published by: (Periodicals Department), National Safety Council, 1121 Spring Lake Dr, Itasca, IL 60143. TEL 630-775-2056, 800-621-7619, FAX 630-285-0797, customerservice@nsc.org, http://www.nsc.org.

388 330 AUS ISSN 1449-4299
E B C BUSINESS BENCHMARKING GUIDE UPDATE FOR TYRE DEALERS. (Entrepreneur Business Centre) Text in English. 2004. a. AUD 295 (effective 2008). back issues avail. **Document type:** *Handbook/Manual/Guide, Trade.* **Description:** Presents the survey results on tire dealers.
Related titles: Online - full text ed.: AUD 195 (effective 2008).
Published by: MAUS Business Systems (Subsidiary of: CorpRat Pty Ltd), Level 1, 39 E Esplanade, Manly, NSW 2095, Australia. TEL 1300-300-586, FAX 61-2-99762137, sbsales@maus.com.au, http://www.maus.com.au/.

E-DRIVE MAGAZINE. *see* ENGINEERING—Mechanical Engineering

656 CZE ISSN 1214-3073
E-MAIL NOVINY PRO LOGISTIKU A DOPRAVU. Text in Czech. 2003. fortn. free. **Document type:** *Newsletter, Trade.*
Media: E-mail.
Published by: Verlag Dashoefer s.r.o., Na Prikope 18, PO Box 756, Prague 1, 11121, Czech Republic. TEL 420-224-197333, FAX 420-224-197555, info@dashofer.cz, http://www.dashofer.cz.

388 382 KEN
EAST AFRICAN FREIGHT FORWARDING. Text in English. a. KES 600, TZS 8,000, UGX 14,000, USD 20. adv. **Document type:** *Journal, Trade.*
Published by: Kenya School of Exports and Imports, IBEA Bldg. 2 fl., Moi Avenue, PO Box 21832, Nairobi, Kenya. TEL 254-2-340509. Ed. Makomboti Wambakaya. adv.: B&W page KES 30,000, color page KES 50,000.

380.5 ECU
ECUADOR. INSTITUTO NACIONAL DE ESTADISTICA Y CENSOS. ENCUESTA ANUAL DE TRANSPORTE. Text in Spanish. 1965. a. USD 8.28 per issue (effective 2001).
Formerly: Ecuador. Instituto Nacional de Estadistica y Censos. Anuario de Estadisticas de Transporte
Related titles: Diskette ed.
Published by: Instituto Nacional de Estadistica y Censos, Juan Larrea N15-36 y Jose Riofrio, Quito, Ecuador. TEL 593-2-529858, FAX 593-2-509836. Circ: 500.

388 BRA ISSN 1517-8854
EDUTRAN 2000. (Educacao para o Transito Dois Mil) Text in Portuguese. 2000. m. **Document type:** *Magazine, Consumer.*
Media: Online - full text.
Published by: Instituto de Pesquisas Avancadas em Educacao, Ave Nilo Pecanha 12 Conj 807, Caixa Postal 21123, Rio de Janeiro, 20020-100, Brazil. TEL 55-21-39050963, FAX 55-21-39050964, ipae@ipae.com.br.

388.0440962 GBR ISSN 1752-5780
EGYPT FREIGHT TRANSPORT REPORT. Text in English. 2006. q. EUR 820, USD 1,030 combined subscription (print & email eds.) (effective 2010). **Document type:** *Report, Trade.* **Description:** Provides industry professionals and strategists, sector analysts, investors, trade associations and regulatory bodies with independent forecasts and competitive intelligence on the Egyptian freight transport and logistics industry.
Related titles: E-mail ed.
Indexed: A15, ABIn, B02, B15, B17, B18, G04, I05, P48, P51, P52, PQC.
Published by: Business Monitor International Ltd., Senator House, 85 Queen Victoria St, London, EC4V 4AB, United Kingdom. TEL 44-20-72480468, FAX 44-20-72480467, subs@businessmonitor.com.

388 ITA ISSN 1121-7995
ELEVATORI; the European elevator magazine. Text in Italian. 1972. bi-m. EUR 40 (effective 2009). adv. bk.rev. **Document type:** *Magazine, Trade.*
Former titles (until 1992): Elevatori Moderni (1120-2289); (until 1973): Elevatori (0391-450X)
Published by: Volpe Editore, Via di Vittorio 21 A, Vignate, MI 20060, Italy. TEL 39-02-95360416, FAX 39-02-95360418. Ed. Giovanni Varisco. Circ: 2,800.

380.5 GBR
ENGINE REPAIR AND REMANUFACTURE. Text in English. 1982. q. GBP 14 (effective 1995). adv. bk.rev. tr.lit. back issues avail. **Document type:** *Magazine, Trade.* **Description:** Covers all aspects of this emerging industry and discusses related environmental issues.
Published by: R G O Exhibitions and Publications Ltd., Oakapple Cottage, Furnace Ln, Broad Oak Brede, Rye, E Sussex TN31 6ES, United Kingdom. TEL 44-1424-882702, FAX 44-1424-882702. Ed. Chris Hancock. Adv. contact Pam Bourne. B&W page GBP 270, color page GBP 450; trim 150 x 212. Circ: 1,400 (controlled).

ENVIRONMENTAL PERFORMANCE REPORT. *see* ENVIRONMENTAL STUDIES

380.5 GRC
EPITHEORESIS SYNKOINONIAKOU DIKAIOU. Text in Greek. 1973. m. bk.rev.
Address: c/o Onoufrios Onouphriades, Ed., Metamorphoseos 3, Kalamaki, Athens 174 55, Greece. TEL 30-1-9820-336. Circ: 5,000.

354.7 FRA ISSN 1263-5618
EQUIPEMENT, TRANSPORT ET SERVICES INFOS. Text in French. 1995. bi-m. adv. bk.rev. charts; illus.; stat. **Document type:** *Newsletter, Trade.*
Formed by the merger of (1990-1995): Equipement - Transport - Services Magazine (1145-3869); (1984-1995): Infos Federales (0763-9236); Which was formerly: Federation des Travaux Publics et des Transports. Revue (0046-3523)
Related titles: Online - full text ed.: free.
—CCC.
Published by: Federation de l'Equipement des Transports et des Services, 46 rue des Petites Ecuries, Paris, 75010, France. TEL 33-1-44838620, contact@fets-fo.fr. Ed., Adv. contact Yves Veyrier.

388.347 FRA ISSN 2102-4111
▼ **L'ESSENTIEL DU SCOOTER.** Text in French. 2009. q. **Document type:** *Magazine, Consumer.*
Published by: Lafont Presse, 53 Rue du Chemin Vert, Boulogne-Billancourt, 92100, France. TEL 33-1-46102121, FAX 33-1-45792211.

380.5 001.5 PAN ISSN 1012-3555
HE222.A1
ESTADISTICA PANAMENA. SITUACION ECONOMICA. SECCION 333. TRANSPORTE. Text in Spanish. 1958. a. PAB 0.75 domestic (effective 2000). **Document type:** *Bulletin, Government.* **Description:** Offers data on land transportation: cars, passengers, cargo transported, and railroads. Includes transportation by air and sea.
Supersedes in part (in 1985): Estadistica Panamena. Situacion Economica. Seccion 333-334. Transporte y Comunicaciones (0378-7389)
Published by: Direccion de Estadistica y Censo, Contraloria General, Apdo. 5213, Panama City, 5, Panama. FAX 507-210-4801. Circ: 800.

388.044094798 GBR ISSN 1752-5799
ESTONIA FREIGHT TRANSPORT REPORT. Text in English. 2006. a. EUR 820, USD 1,030 combined subscription per issue (print & email eds.) (effective 2010). **Document type:** *Report, Trade.* **Description:** Provides industry professionals and strategists, sector analysts, investors, trade associations and regulatory bodies with independent forecasts and competitive intelligence on the Estonian freight transport and logistics industry.
Related titles: E-mail ed.
Indexed: A15, ABIn, B02, B15, B17, B18, G04, I05, P48, P51, P52, PQC.
Published by: Business Monitor International Ltd., Senator House, 85 Queen Victoria St, London, EC4V 4AB, United Kingdom. TEL 44-20-72480468, FAX 44-20-72480467, subs@businessmonitor.com.

380 ESP ISSN 1576-7108
HE261.A15
ESTUDIOS DE CONSTRUCCION Y TRANSPORTES. Text in Spanish. 1982. q. **Document type:** *Government.*
Former title (until 1999): Estudios de Construccion, Transportes y Comunicaciones (1138-0586); (until 1996): Estudios de Transportes y Comunicaciones (1133-2832); (until 1992): Estudios de Transportes (1132-9599); (until 1992): T T C (0213-7380); (until 1986): Spain. Ministerio de Transportes, Turismo y Comunicaciones. Revista (0213-7372); (until 1985): Spain. Ministerio de Transportes, Turismo y Comunicaciones. Boletin de Informacion (0212-1506)
Indexed: GeoRef, HRIS, IECT, RefZh, SpeleolAb.
Published by: Ministerio de Fomento, Centro de Publicaciones, Paseo de la Castellana 67, Madrid, 28029, Spain. http://www.fomento.es.

388.322 DEU
EUROBUS. Text in German. m. EUR 46 domestic; EUR 54 in Europe (effective 2011). adv. **Document type:** *Magazine, Trade.*
Published by: Verlag EuroBus GmbH, Kanzlerweg 3, Saulheim, 55291, Germany. TEL 49-6732-4588, FAX 49-6732-4587, info@eurobus.de. Ed. Heinz Lopuszansky. Adv. contact Irene Kleefeld. color page EUR 4,980; trim 265 x 378. Circ: 8,394 (paid).

380.5 LUX
EUROPA TRANSPORT. Text in English, French, German. irreg., latest 1989. USD 65.
Published by: European Commission, Office for Official Publications of the European Union, 2 Rue Mercier, Luxembourg, L-2985, Luxembourg. **Dist. in the U.S. by:** Bernan Associates, Bernan, 4611-F Assembly Dr., Lanham, MD 20706-4391. TEL 301-459-0056, 800-274-4447.

385.2 387.54 GBR ISSN 1748-0817
HE3004 CODEN: TCETEY
EUROPEAN RAIL TIMETABLE. Text in English; Summaries in French, German, Spanish. 1873. m. GBP 150 domestic; GBP 174 in Europe; GBP 192 elsewhere (effective 2009). adv. index. **Document type:** *Directory, Trade.* **Description:** Supplies a comprehensive timetable for railway and shipping services throughout Europe, with maps, town plans, and passport and travel information.
Former titles (until 2005): Thomas Cook European Timetable (0952-620X); (until 1980): Thomas Cook Continental Timetable (0144-7467); Supersedes in part (in 1980): Thomas Cook International Timetable (0141-2701); Thomas Cook Continental Timetable; Cooks Continental Timetable (0010-8286)
—CASDDS. **CCC.**
Published by: Thomas Cook Publishing, PO Box 227, Peterborough, Cambs PE3 8SB, United Kingdom. TEL 44-1733-416477, FAX 44-1733-416688, publishing-sales@thomascook.com. Circ: 150,000.

347.7 385.1 BEL ISSN 0014-3154
K5
EUROPEAN TRANSPORT LAW/DERECHO EUROPEO DE TRANSPORTES/DIRITTO EUROPEO DEI TRASPORTI/DROIT EUROPEEN DES TRANSPORTS/EUROPAEISCHES TRANSPORTRECHT/EUROPEES VERVOERRECHT. Text in Dutch, English, French, German, Italian, Spanish. 1966. bi-m. EUR 134.25 domestic; EUR 135.15 in Europe; EUR 154.70 elsewhere (effective 2004). bk.rev. charts; illus.; stat. back issues avail. **Document type:** *Journal, Academic/Scholarly.*
Indexed: A22, ELLIS, FLP, IBR, IBZ, RefZh.
—BLDSC (3830.320000), IE, Ingenta. **CCC.**
Address: Maria Henriettalei 1, Antwerp, 2018, Belgium. TEL 32-3-2035858, FAX 32-3-2342380. Ed. Robert Wijffels. Circ: 1,000.

388 DEU ISSN 1867-0717
▼ **EUROPEAN TRANSPORT RESEARCH REVIEW.** Text in English. 2009. 4/yr. EUR 422, USD 632 combined subscription to institutions (print & online eds.) (effective 2010). reprint service avail. from PSC. **Document type:** *Journal, Academic/Scholarly.* **Description:** Provides a forum for ideas and developments that originate in, or are of interest to, the European transport research community.
Related titles: Online - full text ed.: ISSN 1866-8887. 2009. free (effective 2011).
Indexed: A22, CPEI, E01, SCOPUS.
—IE. **CCC.**
Published by: Springer (Subsidiary of: Springer Science+Business Media), Tiergartenstr 17, Heidelberg, 69121, Germany. TEL 49-6221-4870, FAX 49-6221-345229, orders-hd-individuals@springer.com. Ed. Evangelos Bekiaris.

388 ITA ISSN 1825-3997
➤ **EUROPEAN TRANSPORT - TRASPORTI EUROPEI.** Text in English. 1995. 3/yr. **Document type:** *Journal, Academic/Scholarly.* **Description:** Focuses on the role of transport in promoting and facilitating European economic integration.
Formerly (until 2003): Trasporti Europei (1129-5627)
Related titles: Supplement(s): I Quaderni di Trasporti Europei. ISSN 1825-3989. 1997.
Indexed: EconLit, JEL.
Published by: Universita degli Studi di Trieste, Istituto per lo Studio dei Trasporti nell'Integrazione Economica Europea (I S T I E E), Via del Lazzaretto Vecchio 13, Trieste, 34123, Italy. TEL 39-040-311464, FAX 39-040-311465, istiee@univ.trieste.it, http://www.istiee.org.

➤ **EUROPEAN TRUCK + BUS TECHNOLOGY.** *see* ENGINEERING

388 GBR ISSN 1478-8217
EUROTRANSPORT. Text in English. 2003. bi-m. GBP 90 combined subscription (print & online eds.) (effective 2009). adv. back issues avail. **Document type:** *Magazine, Trade.* **Description:** Features articles on ticketing, real-time passenger information, intelligent transport systems, bus and coach, metro, security, trams and trolleybuses, communications, light railways, financing and legislation.
Related titles: Online - full text ed.: free to qualified personnel (effective 2009).
—CCC.
Published by: Russell Publishing Ltd., Court Lodge, Hogtrough Hill, Brasted, Kent TN16 1NU, United Kingdom. TEL 44-1959-563311, FAX 44-1959-563123, info@russellpublishing.com, http://www.russellpublishing.com/. Adv. contact Tim Dean TEL 44-1959-563311. page GBP 4,397; trim 210 x 297. Circ: 11,794.

388 AUS ISSN 1838-3068
▼ **EXECUTIVE COMPLIANCE NEWS. INDEPENDENT NEWS FOR TRANSPORT & LOGISTICS.** Text in English. 2010. w. AUD 1,200 combined subscription (online & email eds.) (effective 2011). **Document type:** *Newsletter, Trade.* **Description:** Provides news and analysis impacting on the transport and logistics industry sector.
Media: Online - full text. **Related titles:** E-mail ed.
Published by: Thomson Reuters (Professional) Australia Limited (Subsidiary of: Thomson Reuters Corp.), PO Box 3502, Rozelle, NSW 2039, Australia. TEL 61-2-85877980, FAX 61-2-85877981, LTA.Service@thomsonreuters.com.

(YEAR) EXPEDITED CARRIERS NETWORK GUIDE. *see* BUSINESS AND ECONOMICS—Trade And Industrial Directories

388 GBR ISSN 2041-7802
EXPORT & FREIGHT. Text in English. 1978. 7/yr. GBP 37 domestic; GBP 44 foreign; GBP 2.75, EUR 5.75 newsstand/cover (effective 2009). adv. back issues avail. **Document type:** *Magazine, Trade.* **Description:** Examines market trends and the key players in the Northern Ireland export and freight industries.
Related titles: Online - full text ed.: ISSN 2041-7810. free (effective 2009).
Published by: 4 Square Media NI Ltd., The Old Coach House, 12 Main St, Hillsborough, Co. Down BT23 6AE, United Kingdom. TEL 44-28-92688888, FAX 44-28-92688866, info@4squaremedia.net. Ed. David Stokes. Pub. Garfield Harrison.

388 CHE
F I A T A REVIEW. Text in English. 1995. bi-m. **Document type:** *Newsletter, Trade.* **Description:** Offers valuable advertising access to an important segment of the freight forwarding industry in 150 countries on all continents. Serves as an important sales promotion tool for airlines, airports, shipping lines, port authorities, railways, insurance companies, etc.
Published by: Federation Internationale des Associations de Transitaires et Assimiles/International Federation of Freight Forwarders Associations, Baumackerstrasse 24, Zurich, 8050, Switzerland. TEL 41-1-3116511, FAX 41-1-3119044, http://www.fiata.com. Adv. contact Patricia Widmer. Circ: 4,000 (paid).

380 DEU ISSN 1610-5613
F M - DAS LOGISTIK-MAGAZIN. Abbreviated title: F M. Text in German. 1969. 10/yr. EUR 79; EUR 8.10 newsstand/cover (effective 2007). adv. bk.rev. 60 p./no. 4 cols./p.; back issues avail. **Document type:** *Magazine, Trade.* **Description:** Focuses on in-company and external transport, distribution, storage, transport packaging, materials handling, transhipment and logistics.
Former titles (until 2002): Fracht und Materialfluss (1430-9807); (until 1993): F M - Fracht Management (0342-3042); (until 1972): Frachtmanagement (0342-3050)
Related titles: Online - full text ed.
Indexed: TM.
Published by: Konradin Verlag Robert Kohlhammer GmbH, Ernst Mey Str 8, Leinfelden-Echterdingen, 70771, Germany. TEL 49-711-75940, FAX 49-711-7594390, info@konradin.de, http://www.konradin.de. Ed. Hans Martin Piazza. Adv. contact Annedore Rupp. B&W page EUR 4,540, color page EUR 5,560; trim 188 x 270. Circ: 15,983 (controlled).

388.3 340 GBR ISSN 1359-091X
F T A YEARBOOK OF ROAD TRANSPORT LAW. Text in English. 1963. a. GBP 78 to non-members; free to members (effective 2009). adv. back issues avail. **Document type:** *Yearbook, Trade.* **Description:** Provides information on all aspects of road transport legislation and other relevant areas, such as health and safety.
Formerly (until 1992): F T A Yearbook (0306-1523)
—CCC.
Published by: Freight Transport Association, Hermes House, St John's Rd, Tunbridge Wells, Kent TN4 9UZ, United Kingdom. TEL 44-1892-526171, FAX 44-1892-534989, info@fta.co.uk. Adv. contact Naomi Queree TEL 44-1892-552211. B&W page GBP 1,610, color page GBP 2,810; trim 156 x 234. Circ: 14,000 (controlled).

320 CAN
F Y I. (For Your Information) Text in English. 1967. bi-m. free to qualified personnel. stat. back issues avail. **Document type:** *Newsletter.*
Published by: Trans Mountain Pipe Line Company Ltd., 1333 W Broadway, Ste 900, Vancouver, BC V6H 4C2, Canada. TEL 604-739-5000, FAX 604-739-5004. Ed. E Fitz Morris. Circ: 500.

FACILITACION DEL COMERCIO Y EL TRASNPORTE EN AMERICA LATINA Y EL CARIBE. BOLETIN. *see* BUSINESS AND ECONOMICS—Domestic Commerce

388.346 USA ISSN 0360-3024
TL298
FAMILY MOTOR COACHING. Text in English. 1963. m. USD 30 domestic to non-members; USD 42 in Canada to non-members; USD 48 elsewhere to non-members; free to members (effective 2009). adv. bk.rev. index. back issues avail.; reprints avail. **Document type:** *Magazine, Consumer.* **Description:** Contains information about all facets of motor home ownership and travel.
Related titles: Online - full text ed.: free (effective 2009).
Published by: (Family Motor Coach Association), Family Motor Coaching, Inc., 8291 Clough Pike, Cincinnati, OH 45244. TEL 513-474-3622, 800-543-3622, FAX 513-474-2332. Ed. Robbin Gould. Adv. contact Ranita Jones.

380.5 USA
FEDERAL CARRIERS REPORTER. Text in English. 4 base vols. plus s-m. updates. USD 1,638 base vol(s). (effective 2004). **Description:** Enables to keep up with the rapid changes following the demise of the Interstate Commerce Commission and dispersement of its regulatory authority.
Formerly: Federal Carriers Reports (0162-1106)
—CCC.
Published by: C C H Inc. (Subsidiary of: Wolters Kluwer N.V.), 2700 Lake Cook Rd, Riverwoods, IL 60015. TEL 847-267-7000, 800-449-6439, cust_serv@cch.com, http://www.cch.com. Pub. Stacey Caywood.

FEMNET. *see* WOMEN'S INTERESTS

388.322 ESP
FENEBUS. REVISTA. (Federacion Nacional Empresarial de Transporte en Autobus) Text in Spanish. 1979. 6/yr. free. adv. **Document type:** *Bulletin, Consumer.*
Published by: Fenebus, Orense, 20, 2o planta, Madrid, 28020, Spain. TEL 34-91-5552095, FAX 34-915552995, info@fenebus.es, http://www.fenebus.es/. Ed. J Pertierra Rodriguez. Circ: 5,000.

FIETS; het race & mtb magazine. *see* SPORTS AND GAMES—Bicycles And Motorcycles

380.5 BEL
FLEET EUROPE. Text in English, French, German, Dutch, Spanish, Italian. 4/yr. EUR 45 (effective 2000). adv. **Document type:** *Magazine, Trade.* **Description:** Provides European fleet owners with useful fleet management information.
Published by: Multi Media Management, Parc Artisanal 11-13, Blegny-Barchon, 4670, Belgium. TEL 32-4-3878787, FAX 32-4-3879087, ymathieu@mmm.be. Ed. Yannick Mathieu. Pub. Jean-Marie Becker. Adv. contact Philippe Penasse. Circ: 11,500.

388 USA ISSN 2150-4911
FLEET MAINTENANCE; best practices for maintenance management. Text in English. 1997. 10/yr. USD 59 domestic; USD 85 in Canada & Mexico; USD 120 elsewhere; free to qualified personnel (effective 2009). adv. back issues avail.; reprints avail. **Document type:** *Magazine, Trade.* **Description:** Provides a curriculum of managerial, technical and regulatory information that enables maintenance managers to better perform their roles in purchasing and maintaining a safe, efficient and profitable fleet.
Related titles: Online - full text ed.: ISSN 2150-492X. free (effective 2009).
Indexed: A15, ABIn, P48, P51, P52, PQC.

T U

Published by: Cygnus Business Media, Inc., 1233 Janesville Ave, PO Box 803, Fort Atkinson, WI 53538. TEL 920-563-6388, 800-547-7377, FAX 920-563-1699, http://www.cygnusb2b.com. Ed. Mark Gehred-O'Connell TEL 920-563-1611. Pub. Larry M Greenberger TEL 847-454-2722. Adv. contact Joel Franke TEL 920-563-1775. color page USD 10,880; trim 9 x 10.875. Circ: 65,000.

388 USA ISSN 1528-7610
FLEET MAINTENANCE SUPERVISOR. Text in English. 199?. bi-m. USD 32 domestic; USD 64 foreign (effective 2000). tr.lit.
Formerly: Fleet Maintenace Tool and Equipment News
Related titles: Online - full text ed.
Indexed: A09, A10, B02, B15, B17, B18, G04, G08, I05, T02, V03, V04. **—CCC.**
Published by: Cygnus Business Media, Inc., 1233 Janesville Ave, PO Box 803, Fort Atkinson, WI 53538. TEL 920-563-6388, FAX 920-563-1702, http://www.cygnusb2b.com.

380.5 GBR ISSN 0953-8526
FLEET NEWS. Text in English. 1978. w. free to qualified personnel (effective 2009). bk.rev. **Document type:** *Magazine, Trade.* **Description:** Provides for decision makers within the D40 billion company car and van industry with in-depth news coverage, unrivalled vehicle launch reports, extensive features, supplements, and live events.
Formerly (until 1986): Fleet News (Car Edition) (0950-3943); Which superseded in part (in 1983): Fleet News (0143-0351)
Published by: H. Bauer Publishing Ltd. (Subsidiary of: Bauer Media Group), Media House, Lynchwood, Peterborough, Cambridgeshire PE2 6EA, United Kingdom. TEL 44-1733-468000, http://www.bauer.co.uk. Ed. Stephen Briers TEL 44-1733-468024. Adv. contact Dan Atkin TEL 44-1733-468800.

388 GBR ISSN 2046-6471
▼ **FLEET NEWS. SMALL FLEET REVIEW**; practical advice for buying and running company vehicles. Text in English. 2009. q. GBP 2.25 per issue (effective 2011). adv. back issues avail. **Document type:** *Magazine, Trade.*
Related titles: Online - full text ed.: free (effective 2011).
Published by: Bauer Media, Media House, Lynch Wood, Peterborough, PE2 6EA, United Kingdom. TEL 44-1733-468000, http://www.bauermedia.co.uk/. Ed. Stephen Briers TEL 44-1733-468024. Adv. contact Sarah Wilson TEL 44-1733-468320.

380.5 IRL ISSN 1649-9433
FLEET TRANSPORT. Text in English. 1989. m. EUR 65 in Ireland; EUR 85 in UK & Europe; EUR 120 elsewhere (effective 2007). adv. bk.rev. **Document type:** *Magazine, Trade.* **Description:** Transportation information for Ireland, circulated to fleet managers, distribution managers, and haulers.
Formerly (until 2007): Fleet Management Magazine (0957-7998) **—CCC.**
Published by: J J D S Publications, D'Alton St, Claremorris, Co. Mayo, Ireland. TEL 353-94-9372819, FAX 353-94-9373571, enquiries@fleet.ie. Ed. Jariath Sweeney. Adv. contact Orla Sweeney. Circ: 5,300.

388 NLD ISSN 1879-8586
FLEETMOTIVE. Text in Dutch. 200?. q. EUR 29 (effective 2010). adv. **Document type:** *Magazine, Trade.*
Published by: RAI Langfords bv, Postbus 10099, Amsterdam, 1001 EB, Netherlands. TEL 31-20-5042800, FAX 31-20-5042888, http://www.railangfords.nl. Ed. Jelle Heidstra. Pub. Ron Brokking. Adv. contact Marc Krijnen.

388 ZAF
FLEETWATCH. Text in English. 1993. m. ZAR 150; ZAR 12.50 newsstand/cover. adv. illus. **Document type:** *Magazine, Trade.* **Description:** Covers all aspects of commercial transport and trucking.
Published by: (South African Transport Security Association), Newslink C C, PO Box 3097, Honeydew, 2040, South Africa. TEL 27-11-7942490, FAX 27-11-7941474. Ed., Pub., R&P Patrick O'Leary. Adv. contact Lorinda Stoltz. B&W page ZAR 4,600, color page ZAR 5,900. Circ: 6,400.

388.3 USA ISSN 0092-0177
HE5633.F6
FLORIDA. DIVISION OF MOTOR VEHICLES. TAGS AND REVENUE. Text in English. 1928. a. free.
Published by: Department of Highway Safety and Motor Vehicles, Division of Administrative Services, Neil Kirkman Bldg, Tallahassee, FL 32304. TEL 904-488-6084. Circ: 1,000.

FLORIDA MOTOR VEHICLE LAWS. *see* LAW

388.322 DEU
FLOTTENMANAGEMENT. Text in German. bi-m. EUR 20; EUR 4 newsstand/cover (effective 2007). adv. **Document type:** *Magazine, Trade.*
Published by: Flottenmanagement Verlag GmbH, Rudolf-Diesel-Str 14, Niederkassel, 53859, Germany. TEL 49-228-4595470, FAX 49-228-4595479, info@flottenmanagement-verlag.de. Ed. Ralph Wuttke. Adv. contact Bernd Franke. B&W page EUR 4,400, color page EUR 4,790. Circ: 24,692 (paid and controlled).

FRACHT-DIENST; Fachzeitschrift fuer Lager, Logistik, Transport und Verkehr. *see* TRANSPORTATION—Ships And Shipping

FRANCE FREIGHT TRANSPORT REPORT. *see* BUSINESS AND ECONOMICS—Production Of Goods And Services

354.44 FRA ISSN 2105-245X
FRANCE. MINISTERE DE L'ECOLOGIE, DU DEVELOPPEMENT ET DE L'AMENAGEMENT DURABLES. BULLETIN OFFICIEL (ONLINE). Text in French. 1956. 3/m. **Document type:** *Bulletin, Government.*
Former titles (until 2009): France. Ministere de l'Ecologie, du Developpement et de l'Amenagement Durables. Bulletin Officiel (Print) (1959-5557); (until 2007): France. Ministere de l'Equipement, des Transports, du Logement, du Tourisme et de la Mer. Bulletin Officiel (1635-897X); (until 2002): France. Ministere de l'Equipement, des Transports et du Logement. Bulletin Officiel (1635-8961); (until 1997): France. Ministere de l'Equipement, du Logement, des Transports et du Tourisme. Bulletin Officiel (1268-8134); (until 1995): France. Ministere de l'Amenagement du Territoire, de l'Equipement et des Transports. Bulletin Officiel (1266-2623); (until 1995): France. Ministere de l'Equipement, des Transports et du Tourisme. Bulletin Officiel (1245-4699); (until 1994): France. Ministere de l'Equipement, du Logement, des Transports et de l'Espace. Bulletin Officiel (1158-2404); (until 1991): France. Ministere de l'Equipement et du Logement. Bulletin Officiel (0990-5405); (until 1988): France. Ministere de l'Equipement, du Logement, de l'Amenagement du Territoire et des Transports. Bulletin Officiel (0298-8224); (until 1986): France. Ministere de l'Urbanisme et du Logement et Ministere des Transports et Ministere de l'Environnement. Bulletin Officiel (0292-1766)
Media: Online - full text.
Indexed: FR.
Published by: France. Ministere de l'Ecologie, du Developpement Durable, des Transports et du Logement, 20 av. de Segur, Paris, Cedex 7 75302, France. http://www.developpement-durable.gouv.fr.

380.5 FRA ISSN 0993-1953
FRANCE ROUTES. Text in French. 1980. m. EUR 46 (effective 2008). **Document type:** *Magazine, Trade.*
Formerly (until 1988): France Routiers (0248-174X)
Published by: Wolters Kluwer France (Subsidiary of: Wolters Kluwer N.V.), 1 Rue Eugene et Armand Peugeot, Rueil-Malmaison, Cedex 92856, France. Circ: 79,588.

380.5 GBR ISSN 0964-1513
FREIGHT. Text in English. 19??. m. free to members. adv. bk.rev. **Document type:** *Magazine, Trade.* **Description:** Features key legislative issues that are on the transport agenda; knowledge of the latest developments in the industry; an update on the work FTA is undertaking.
Former titles (until 1990): Freight Transport (0955-4696); (until 1988): Freight (0016-0849); (until 1945): Industrial Road Transport
Indexed: BMT, HRIS.
—BLDSC (4033.460000). **CCC.**
Published by: Freight Transport Association, Hermes House, St John's Rd, Tunbridge Wells, Kent TN4 9UZ, United Kingdom. TEL 44-1892-526171, FAX 44-1892-534989, info@fta.co.uk. Circ: 14,989 (controlled).

388 GBR ISSN 0071-9471
FREIGHT INDUSTRY YEARBOOK; classified reference guide for transport vehicle manufacturers, operators and users. Text in English. 1950. a. adv. **Document type:** *Directory, Trade.* **Description:** British guide to the U.K. freight industry, the yearbook contains over 20 specialist sections, and covers the spectrum of freighting services.
Formerly: Goods Vehicle Year Book
Published by: Ten Alps Publishing (Subsidiary of: Ten Alps Group), Bridgewater House, Whitworth St, Manchester, M1 6LT, United Kingdom. TEL 44-161-8326000, FAX 44-161-8324176, info@tenalpspublishing.com.

380.5 IRL
THE FREIGHT OBSERVER. Text in English. 10/yr.
Published by: Freight Observer, Strand House, Strand St., Malahide, Co. Dublin, Ireland. TEL 450928. Ed. Colin Walsh.

388 NLD ISSN 1573-8051
FREIGHT TRANSPORT IN THE NETHERLANDS. KEY FIGURES. Text in English. 2004. a.
Published by: Ministerie van Verkeer en Waterstaat Rijkswaterstaat, Dienst Verkeer en Scheepvaart, Postbus 5044, Delft, 2600 GA, Netherlands. TEL 31-88-7982222, FAX 31-88-7982999, dvsloket@rws.nl, http://www.rijkswaterstaat.nl/dvs.

380.5 DEU ISSN 0016-5808
T55.3.H3
GEFAEHRLICHE LADUNG; Das Magazin fuer die Gefahrgut-Logistik. Text in German. 1956. m. EUR 134; EUR 11.80 newsstand/cover (effective 2011). adv. bk.rev. bibl.; charts; illus. index. **Document type:** *Magazine, Trade.*
Formerly (until 1971): Gefaehrliche Fracht (0172-987X)
Indexed: A22, CEABA.
—IE, Infotrieve. **CCC.**
Published by: K.O. Storck Verlag, Striepenweg 31, Hamburg, 21147, Germany. TEL 49-40-7971301, FAX 49-40-79713101, webmaster@storck-verlag.de. Ed. Uwe Heins. Circ: 5,056 (paid and controlled).

363.17 DEU ISSN 0944-6117
GEFAHR-GUT. Text in German. 1993. m. EUR 189 domestic; EUR 201 foreign (effective 2010). adv. bk.rev. charts; illus. **Document type:** *Magazine, Trade.* **Description:** Covers the handling and transportation of hazardous materials and cargo.
Published by: Verlag Heinrich Vogel (Subsidiary of: Springer Science+Business Media), Neumarkterstr 18, Munich, 81664, Germany. TEL 49-89-2030431100, FAX 49-89-2030432100, vertriebsservice@springer.com, http://www.springerfachmedien-muenchen.de. Ed. Birgit Bauer. Adv. contact Melanie Heinrich. B&W page EUR 2,085, color page EUR 3,000; trim 185 x 253. Circ: 6,817 (paid and controlled).

388 DEU ISSN 1434-2170
GEFAHRGUT AKTUELL. Text in German. 1992. fortn. EUR 169 (effective 2011). **Document type:** *Newsletter, Trade.*
Published by: Ecomed Verlagsgesellschaft AG & Co. KG (Subsidiary of: Verlagsgruppe Huethig Jehle Rehm GmbH), Justus-von-Liebig-Str 1, Landsberg, 86899, Germany. TEL 49-8191-1250, FAX 49-8191-125492, info@ecomed.de, http://www.ecomed.de.

380.5 DEU ISSN 1439-5770
DER GEFAHRGUT-BEAUFTRAGTE. Text in German. 1990. m. adv. **Document type:** *Magazine, Trade.* **Description:** Provides a source of reliable information and a discussion forum for all dangerous goods safety advisers.
Published by: K.O. Storck Verlag, Striepenweg 31, Hamburg, 21147, Germany. TEL 49-40-7971301, FAX 49-40-79713101, webmaster@storck-verlag.de, http://www.storck-verlag.de. Circ: 3,936 (paid and controlled).

GEORGIA CRIMINAL AND TRAFFIC LAW MANUAL. *see* LAW—Criminal Law

GEORGIA CRIMINAL LAW AND MOTOR VEHICLE HANDBOOK. *see* LAW—Criminal Law

388.0440943 GBR ISSN 1752-5810
GERMANY FREIGHT TRANSPORT REPORT. Text in English. 2006. a. EUR 820, USD 1,030 combined subscription per issue (print & email eds.) (effective 2010). **Document type:** *Report, Trade.* **Description:** Provides industry professionals and strategists, corporate analysts, freight transport associations, government departments and regulatory bodies with independent forecasts and competitive intelligence on the freight transport industry in Germany.
Related titles: E-mail ed.
Indexed: A15, ABIn, B02, B15, B17, B18, G04, I05, P48, P51, P52, PQC.
Published by: Business Monitor International Ltd., Senator House, 85 Queen Victoria St, London, EC4V 4AB, United Kingdom. TEL 44-20-72480468, FAX 44-20-72480467, subs@businessmonitor.com.

380.52 DEU
GESAMTFAHRPLAN. Text in English, French, German. 1972. a. EUR 3 per issue (effective 2009). adv. back issues avail. **Document type:** *Directory.*
Formerly: Verbundfahrplan
Related titles: CD-ROM ed.: 1996.
Published by: Muenchner Verkehrs- und Tarifverbund GmbH, Thierschstr 2, Munich, 80538, Germany. TEL 49-89-210330, FAX 49-89-21033282, info@mvv-muenchen.de, http://www.mvv-muenchen.de. Circ: 110,000.

380.5 CAN ISSN 0779-2492
GESTION LOGISTIQUE. Text in English. 1988. 10/yr. CAD 25, USD 45 (effective 1999). **Document type:** *Journal, Trade.* **Description:** Covers the latest developments on the shipping scene, profiling their technical, economical or social dimensions.
Formerly: Expediteur (0838-5416)
Published by: Editions Bomart Ltee., 7493 TransCanada Hwy, Ste 103, St Laurent, PQ H4T 1T3, Canada. TEL 514-337-9043, FAX 514-337-1862. Ed. Alexandre Daudelin. Pub. Pierre Gravel. Circ: 11,123 (controlled).

388 331 FRA ISSN 1290-371X
GESTION SOCIALE DU PERSONNEL DE CONDUITE. Text in French. 1998. q. EUR 270.08 print & CD-ROM eds. (effective 2004).
Media: CD-ROM. **Related titles:** Online - full text ed.; Print ed.: EUR 341 base vol(s). print & CD-ROM eds. (effective 2010).
Published by: Lamy S.A. (Subsidiary of: Wolters Kluwer France), 1 Rue Eugene et Armand Peugeot, Rueil-Malmaison, 92856 Cedex, France. TEL 33-1-76733000, FAX 33-1-76734809, lamy@lamy.fr.

GEVAARLIJKE LADING. *see* OCCUPATIONAL HEALTH AND SAFETY

380.5 VNM ISSN 0866-8345
GIAO THONG-VAN TAI/TRANSPORT. Text in Vietnamese. 1962. w. VND 1,000 (effective Jan. 1998). **Document type:** *Newspaper, Trade.*
Formerly: Giao Thong-Van Tai and Buu Dien
Published by: Ministry of Communications Transport Posts and Telegraphs, 1 Nha Tho, Hanoi, Viet Nam. Ed. Bui Cong Phieu. Pub. Ngo Duc Nguyen.

380.5 DEU ISSN 0931-8852
GIESSENER STUDIEN ZUR TRANSPORTWIRTSCHAFT UND KOMMUNIKATION. Text in German. 1987. irreg., latest vol.20, 2004. price varies. **Document type:** *Monographic series, Trade.*
Published by: Deutscher Verkehrs Verlag GmbH, Nordkanalstr 36, Hamburg, 20097, Germany. TEL 49-40-2371401, FAX 49-40-23714205, info@dvv-gruppe.de, http://www.dvv-gruppe.de. Ed. Gerd Aberle.

380.5 FRA ISSN 1775-965X
LA GIRAFE; ponts et ouvrages d'art a hauteurs et charges limitees. Text in French. base vol. plus updates 3/yr. looseleaf. EUR 301 base vol(s). print & CD-ROM eds. (effective 2010). **Description:** Lists, by department, limitations of bridges.
Related titles: CD-ROM ed.; Online - full text ed.
Published by: Lamy S.A. (Subsidiary of: Wolters Kluwer France), 1 Rue Eugene et Armand Peugeot, Rueil-Malmaison, 92856 Cedex, France. TEL 33-1-76733000, FAX 33-1-76734809, lamy@lamy.fr. Ed. Bernadette Kerguelen Neyrolles.

388 GBR
GLASS'S COMMERCIAL VEHICLE CHECKBOOK. Text in English. a. adv. **Document type:** *Handbook/Manual/Guide, Trade.*
Published by: Glass's Information Services Ltd., 1 Princes Rd, Weybridge, Surrey KT13 9TU, United Kingdom. TEL 44-1932-823823, FAX 44-1932-849299, customer@glass.co.uk, http://www.glass.co.uk.

GLOBAL; comercio exterior e transporte. *see* BUSINESS AND ECONOMICS—Domestic Commerce

GOODS IN TRANSIT. *see* LAW—Corporate Law

388 NLD ISSN 1877-8429
▼ **GOVERA MAGAZINE.** (GoederenVervoer Randstad) Text in Dutch. 2009. irreg.
Published by: Projectbureau GOVERA, c/o Provincie Utrecht, Postbus 80300, Utrecht, 3508 TH, Netherlands. TEL 31-30-2582680, FAX 31-30-2522564, info@govera.nl, http://www.govera.nl.

380.5 633 USA
GRAIN TRANSPORTATION SITUATION. Text in English. 1981. w. free. reprints avail. **Document type:** *Government.* **Description:** Features current happenings within the university community.
Related titles: Microfiche ed.: (from CIS).
Indexed: AmStI.
Published by: U.S. Department of Agriculture, AMS-T&M Division, 1217 South Bldg, Washington, DC 20250. TEL 202-447-6793. Ed. William L Dunton.

GREAT BRITAIN. DEPARTMENT OF TRANSPORT. ANNUAL REPORT. *see* ENVIRONMENTAL STUDIES

388 GBR
GREAT BRITAIN. DEPARTMENT OF TRANSPORT, LOCAL GOVERNMENT, AND THE REGIONS. PLANNING POLICY GUIDANCE NOTES. Text in English. irreg.
Published by: Department of the Environment, Transport and Regions, c/o Brian Freeland, 4/B2 Eland House, Bressenden Pl, London, SW1E 5DU, United Kingdom. TEL 44-20-7944-3856, http://www.dtlr.gov.uk/consult.htm.

388 CAN ISSN 1496-0710
GREATER TORONTO TRANSIT AUTHORITY. YEAR IN REVIEW. Text in English. 1976. a.

Former titles (until 1998): G O Transit Annual Report (1188-3782); (until 1990): Toronto Area Transit Operating Authority. Annual Report (0225-7858)
Published by: Greater Toronto Transit Authority, 20 Bay St Ste 600, Toronto, ON M5J 2W3, Canada. TEL 416-869-3200, FAX 416-869-3525, http://www.gotransit.com/.

380.5 GRC
GREECE AND INTERNATIONAL TRANSPORT/ELLAS KAI DIEDNIS METAPHORES; monthly financial magazine. Text in Greek; Summaries in English. 1974. m. EUR 60 (effective 2005). adv. back issues avail. **Document type:** *Trade.* **Description:** Covers all forms of transportation in Greece.
Published by: Athens Publicity Center, 3 Peanon St, Nea Kypseli, Athens, 113 63, Greece. TEL 30-210-823-0631, FAX 30-210-821-2838. Ed. Yiannis E Papadimitropoulos. Pub. Aspa I Papadimitropoulos. adv.: B&W page USD 2,400, color page USD 3,400. Circ: 5,000.

388.0440938 GBR ISSN 1752-5829
GREECE FREIGHT TRANSPORT REPORT. Text in English. 2006. a. EUR 820, USD 1,030 combined subscription per issue (print & email eds.) (effective 2010). **Document type:** *Report, Trade.* **Description:** Provides industry professionals and strategists, sector analysts, investors, trade associations and regulatory bodies with independent forecasts and competitive intelligence on the Greek freight transport and logistics industry.
Related titles: E-mail ed.
Indexed: A15, ABIn, B02, B15, B17, B18, G04, I05, P48, P51, P52, PQC.
Published by: Business Monitor International Ltd., Senator House, 85 Queen Victoria St, London, EC4V 4AB, United Kingdom. TEL 44-20-72480468, FAX 44-20-72480467, subs@businessmonitor.com.

363.12 USA ISSN 1931-6208
HE194.5.U6
THE GREY HOUSE TRANSPORTATION SECURITY DIRECTORY & HANDBOOK. Text in English. 2005. irreg., latest 1st ed. USD 195 1st ed. (effective 2008). **Document type:** *Directory, Trade.* **Description:** Covers information necessary for creating and maintaining a security plan for a wide range of transportation facilities.
Related titles: Online - full text ed.: USD 385 (effective 2007).
Published by: Grey House Publishing, 4919 Rte 22, PO Box 56, Amenia, NY 12501. TEL 518-789-8700, 800-562-2139, FAX 518-789-0556, customerservice@greyhouse.com. Ed. Kathleen M Sweet.

387 GBR ISSN 1364-8330
GROUND HANDLING INTERNATIONAL. Abbreviated title: G H I. Text in English. 1996. bi-m. GBP 63, EUR 73, USD 108 to qualified personnel; GBP 175, EUR 208, USD 299 (effective 2011). adv. back issues avail. **Document type:** *Magazine, Trade.* **Description:** Covers the business of passenger, ramp and cargo handling.
Related titles: Online - full text ed.: ISSN 2047-2005. free (effective 2011); Supplement(s): G H I Green.
Indexed: B02, B03, B11, B15, B17, B18, G04, G06, G07, G08, I05.
Published by: Airports Publishing Network, The Stables, Willow Ln, Paddock Wood, Kent TN12 6PF, United Kingdom. TEL 44-1892-839202, FAX 44-1892-839210. Ed., Pub. Tim Ornellas TEL 44-1892-839209.

388 RUS ISSN 1684-1298
GRUZOVIK &/TRUCK &; proizvodstvennyi i nauchno-tekhnicheskii zhurnal. Text in Russian. 1996. m. USD 951 foreign (effective 2006). **Document type:** *Journal, Trade.*
Indexed: RefZh.
—East View.
Published by: Izdatel'stvo Mashinostroenie, Stromynskii per 4, Moscow, 107076, Russian Federation. TEL 7-095-2683858, mashpubl@mashin.ru. **Dist. by:** East View Information Services, 10601 Wayzata Blvd, Minneapolis, MN 55305. TEL 952-252-1201, 800-477-1005, FAX 952-252-1202, info@eastview.com, http://www.eastview.com.

GUIA AEREA. *see* TRAVEL AND TOURISM

380.5 VEN
GUIA AEREA Y MARITIMA DE VENEZUELA C.A.; Aruba, Curacao y Bonaire. Text in Spanish. 1968. m. USD 90. adv.
Published by: Ministerio de Fomento, Apdo 68121, Caracas, DF 1062-A, Venezuela. Ed. Gregorio Burgana. Circ: 5,400. **Dist. by:** Target Group Communications Inc., 7225 N W 12th St, 2nd Fl, Miami, FL 33126.

629.28 MEX
GUIA AUTOMOTRIZ. Text in Spanish. 1954. m. adv.
Published by: J. Rodriguez & Cia, S.A., Sur 51 No. 118, Col. Ermita, Mexico City 13, DF, Mexico. Ed. Juan Rodriguez. Circ: 15,000.

387 ESP
GUIA ESPANOLA DEL TRANSPORTE. Abbreviated title: G E T. Text in Spanish. 1971. s-a. adv. tr.lit. back issues avail.
Published by: Aeroguia S.A., Monteleon, 18, Madrid, Spain. TEL 34-91-4465377, FAX 34-91-5944867. Ed. Fernando Margareto. Circ: 8,000.

388.044 FRA ISSN 1775-9587
GUIDE D'APPLICATION DE L'A D R. (Accord Europeen Relatif au Transport International des Marchandises Dangereuses par Route) Text in French. 2001. a. **Document type:** *Bulletin, Trade.*
Published by: Form-Edit, 5 rue Janssen, Paris, 75921 Cedex 19, France.

382 337 FRA ISSN 1290-3736
GUIDE DES PROCEDURES DOUANIERES. Text in French. base vol. plus updates 3/yr. looseleaf. EUR 550 base vol(s). print & CD-ROM eds. (effective 2010). **Document type:** *Trade.* **Description:** Covers duties still existing within the EC and between EC countries and the US, Japan, Eastern Europe and developing countries.
Related titles: CD-ROM ed.; Online - full text ed.: EUR 82 (effective 2003).
Published by: Lamy S.A. (Subsidiary of: Wolters Kluwer France), 1 Rue Eugene et Armand Peugeot, Rueil-Malmaison, 92856 Cedex, France. TEL 33-1-76733000, FAX 33-1-76734809, lamy@lamy.fr. Ed. Cyrille Chatail.

380.5 CAN ISSN 0706-9995
GUIDE DU TRANSPORT PAR CAMION. Text in English, French. 1938. a. CAD 75, USD 85 (effective 1999). **Document type:** *Handbook/Manual/Guide, Trade.* **Description:** For the person who wants to receive or ship material between Montreal and most Canadian, American and foreign cities. Lists companies offering products or services related to the transportation industry.
Formerly: Guide du Transport
Published by: Editions Bomart Ltee., 7493 TransCanada Hwy, Ste 103, St Laurent, PQ H4T 1T3, Canada. TEL 514-337-9043, FAX 514-337-1862. Pub. Pierre Gravel. Circ: 3,000.

388 NLD ISSN 2211-9574
HANDBOEK A D N+. Cover title: Vervoer Gevaarlijke Stoffen over de Binnenwateren. Spine title: A D N Vervoer Gevaarlijke Stoffen over de Binnenwateren. Text in Dutch. 2002. biennial. EUR 80 (effective 2011).
Formerly (until 2011): Handboek Accord Europeen Relatif au Transport International des Marchandises Dangereuses par voie de Navigation du Rhin (1872-3969)
Published by: (Centraal Bureau voor de Rijn- en Binnenvaart), GDS Europe BV, Postbus 3111, Hoofddorp, 2130 KC, Netherlands. TEL 31-23-5542970, FAX 31-23-5542971, info@gdseurope.nl, http://www.gds-europe.com.

388 NLD ISSN 1872-3748
HANDBOEK VERVOER GEVAARLIJKE STOFFEN OVER DE BINNENWATEREN. Text in Dutch. 2002. biennial. EUR 65 (effective 2009).
Published by: Nederlandsche Uitgeversmaatschappij, Postbus 4, Leiden, 2300 AA, Netherlands. TEL 31-71-5143747, FAX 31-71-5133629, info@numij.nl, http://www.numij.nl.

388 GBR ISSN 1472-7889
HANDBOOKS IN TRANSPORT. Text in English. 2001. irreg., latest vol.6. price varies. back issues avail. **Document type:** *Monographic series, Academic/Scholarly.* **Description:** Covers the essential knowledge of a major area within transportation. To practitioners, researchers and students alike, this set will be authoritative, accessible, and invaluable.
Published by: Emerald Group Publishing Ltd., Howard House, Wagon Ln, Bingley, W Yorks BD16 1WA, United Kingdom. TEL 44-1274-777700, FAX 44-1274-785201, books@emeraldinsight.com, http://www.emeraldinsight.com. Eds. David A Hensher, Kenneth J Button.

380.5 DEU ISSN 0946-7432
HANDBUCH DER VERKEHRSUNTERNEHMEN IM V D V. (Verband Deutscher Verkehrsunternehmen) Text in German. 1992. irreg., latest 2009. price varies. adv. **Document type:** *Monographic series, Academic/Scholarly.*
Formed by the merger of (1928-1992): Handbuch Oeffentlicher Verkehrsbetriebe (0073-019X); (1952-1992): B D E Mitgliederhandbuch (0946-7424)
Published by: (Verband Deutscher Verkehrsunternehmen), Erich Schmidt Verlag GmbH & Co. (Berlin), Genthiner Str 30 G, Berlin, 10785, Germany. TEL 49-30-2500850, FAX 49-30-250085305, esv@esvmedien.de, http://www.esv.info.

HAWAII CRIMINAL AND TRAFFIC LAW MANUAL. *see* LAW—Criminal Law

HAWAII PENAL CODE, MOTOR VEHICLES & RELATED STATUTES. *see* LAW

380.5 GBR ISSN 0143-6864
HAZARDOUS CARGO BULLETIN. Text in English. 1980. m. free to qualified personnel (effective 2010). adv. bk.rev. bibl.; charts; illus.; stat.; tr.lit. back issues avail. **Document type:** *Bulletin, Trade.* **Description:** Designed to keep readers up-to-date with safety-critical information on regulatory compliance issues by providing timely news on transport regulations, safety issues, market developments, new products and services of relevance to all those involved in the dangerous goods supply chain.
Related titles: Online - full text ed.
Indexed: CurPA, IPackAb, PST.
—BLDSC (4274.396000), IE, Infotrieve, Ingenta. **CCC.**
Published by: Informa Trade & Energy (Subsidiary of: Informa U K Ltd.), Informa House, 30-32 Mortimer St, London, W1W 7RE, United Kingdom. TEL 44-20-70175000, http://www.informa.com/divisions/commercial/informa_Informa_Trade_and_Energy. Adv. contact Greg Emmenis TEL 44-20-76816125. page GBP 2,500; trim 208 x 273.

HAZMAT TRANSPORT NEWS; policy - technology - research. *see* ENVIRONMENTAL STUDIES—Waste Management

363.17 388.044 USA ISSN 1539-7661
HAZMAT TRANSPORTATION NEWS. Text in English. 2001. d. USD 220 to individuals (effective 2005 - 2006). back issues avail. **Document type:** *Newsletter, Trade.* **Description:** Contains latest laws, rules, and policies affecting the packaging, labeling, and transportation of hazardous materials in the U.S.
Formerly (until 2002): HazMat Transport News (1539-3968)
Media: Online - full text.
—CCC.
Published by: The Bureau of National Affairs, Inc., 1801 S Bell St, Arlington, VA 22202. TEL 703-341-3000, 800-372-1033, FAX 703-341-4634, 800-253-0332, bnaplus@bna.com. Ed. Gregory C McCaffery.

388 GBR ISSN 1476-2110
HERITAGE COMMERCIALS. Text in English. 1986. m. GBP 35 domestic; GBP 46 in Europe; GBP 56 elsewhere (effective 2009). adv. back issues avail. **Document type:** *Magazine, Consumer.* **Description:** Aims to provide authoritative historical and present day coverage of vintage commercial vehicles.
Former titles (until 2001): Vintage Commercial Vehicles (1469-7114); (until 1996): Vintage Commercial Vehicle Magazine (0958-3718)
Published by: Mortons Heritage Media (Subsidiary of: Mortons Media Group Ltd.), PO Box 43, Horncastle, LN9 6JR, United Kingdom. TEL 44-1507-529300, FAX 44-1507-529490. Ed. Stephen Pullen. Circ: 10,000.

380.5 USA ISSN 0161-0325
HE5614.2
HIGHWAY & VEHICLE - SAFETY REPORT; the nation's only independent traffic safety publication. Abbreviated title: H & V S R. Text in English. 1974. s-m. USD 395 (effective 2011). bk.rev. abstr.; bibl.; stat.; tr.lit. back issues avail.; reprints avail. **Document type:** *Newsletter, Trade.* **Description:** Covers developments in highway and vehicle safety.
Related titles: Online - full text ed.: USD 345 (effective 2011).
Published by: Stamler Publishing Co., PO Box 3367, Branford, CT 06405. TEL 203-488-9808, 800-422-4121, FAX 203-488-3129, newsgroup@trafficsafetynews.com.

351 388 USA ISSN 0732-8230
HE355.A3
HIGHWAY TAXES AND FEES (YEAR). Text in English. 19??. irreg. **Document type:** *Government.*
Published by: U.S. Department of Transportation, 400 Seventh St, SW, Washington, DC 20590. TEL 202-366-4000.

388.044095125 GBR ISSN 1752-5837
HONG KONG FREIGHT TRANSPORT REPORT. Text in English. 2006. q. EUR 820, USD 1,030 combined subscription (print & email eds.) (effective 2010). **Document type:** *Report, Trade.* **Description:** Provides industry professionals and strategists, sector analysts, investors, trade associations and regulatory bodies with independent forecasts and competitive intelligence on the Hong Kong freight transport and logistics industry.
Related titles: E-mail ed.
Indexed: A15, ABIn, B02, B15, B17, B18, G04, I05, P48, P51, PQC.
Published by: Business Monitor International Ltd., Senator House, 85 Queen Victoria St, London, EC4V 4AB, United Kingdom. TEL 44-20-72480468, FAX 44-20-72480467, subs@businessmonitor.com.

388.04409439 GBR ISSN 1752-5845
HUNGARY FREIGHT TRANSPORT REPORT. Text in English. 2006. q. EUR 820, USD 1,030 combined subscription (print & email eds.) (effective 2010). **Document type:** *Report, Trade.*
Related titles: E-mail ed.
Indexed: A15, ABIn, B02, B15, B17, B18, G04, I05, P48, P51, P52, PQC.
Published by: Business Monitor International Ltd., Senator House, 85 Queen Victoria St, London, EC4V 4AB, United Kingdom. TEL 44-20-72480468, FAX 44-20-72480467, subs@businessmonitor.com.

388 333.79 USA ISSN 1946-1011
THE HYBRID VEHICLE AND ALTERNATIVE FUEL REPORT. Text in English. bi-m. free (effective 2009). back issues avail. **Document type:** *Government.* **Description:** Contains a summary of articles appearing in business and technical media referring to the impact of fuel costs and fuel efficiency on vehicle technology, development, and markets.
Formerly: Hybrid, Fuel and Vehicle Report
Media: Online - full content.
Published by: (Washington Secretary of State), Washington State Department of Transportation, 310 Maple Park Ave, SE, PO Box 47300, Olympia, WA 98504. TEL 360-705-7000, FAX 360-705-6800, hammonp@wsdot.wa.gov, http://www.wsdot.wa.gov. Ed. Thomas L. R Smith TEL 360-705-7941.

I C A D T S REPORTER. (International Council on Alcohol, Drugs and Traffic Safety) *see* DRUG ABUSE AND ALCOHOLISM

388 USA
I E E E INTELLIGENT TRANSPORTATION SYSTEMS CONFERENCE. PROCEEDINGS. (Institute of Electrical and Electronics Engineers) Text in English. 2000. a. adv. back issues avail. **Document type:** *Proceedings, Trade.*
Related titles: Online - full text ed.
Published by: I E E E, 445 Hoes Ln, Piscataway, NJ 08855. contactcenter@ieee.org, http://www.ieee.org.

388 624 USA ISSN 1939-1390
➤ **I E E E INTELLIGENT TRANSPORTATION SYSTEMS MAGAZINE.** (Institute of Electrical and Electronics Engineers) Text in English. 2008. q. USD 395; USD 495 combined subscription (print & online eds.) (effective 2012). back issues avail.; reprints avail. **Document type:** *Magazine, Trade.* **Description:** Provides innovative research ideas, report significant application case studies, and raise awareness of pressing research and application challenges in all areas of intelligent transportation systems.
Related titles: Online - full text ed.: ISSN 1941-1197. USD 360 (effective 2012).
Indexed: HRIS, RefZh, SCOPUS.
—BLDSC (4362.935755), IE. **CCC.**
Published by: (Intelligent Transportation Systems Society), I E E E, 445 Hoes Ln, Piscataway, NJ 08854. TEL 732-981-0060, 800-678-4333, FAX 732-562-6380, contactcenter@ieee.org, http://www.ieee.org. Ed. Dr. Christoph Stiller.

388 006.3 USA ISSN 1931-0587
TL152.8
I E E E INTELLIGENT VEHICLES SYMPOSIUM. (Institute of Electrical and Electronics Engineers) Text in English. 1992. a. adv. back issues avail. **Document type:** *Proceedings, Academic/Scholarly.*
Formerly (until 2004): I E E E Intelligent Vehicles Symposium. Proceedings
Related titles: Online - full text ed.
Published by: I E E E, 445 Hoes Ln, Piscataway, NJ 08854. TEL 732-981-0060, 800-678-4333, FAX 732-562-6380, contactcenter@ieee.org, http://www.ieee.org.

388 USA
I E E E INTERNATIONAL VEHICLE ELECTRONICS CONFERENCE. PROCEEDINGS. (Institute of Electrical and Electronics Engineers) Text in English. 2000. a. adv. back issues avail. **Document type:** *Proceedings, Trade.*
Related titles: Online - full text ed.
Published by: I E E E, 445 Hoes Ln, Piscataway, NJ 08855. contactcenter@ieee.org, http://www.ieee.org. **Co-sponsor:** I E E E Industry Applications Society.

380.5 621 USA ISSN 1524-9050
TA1235
➤ **I E E E TRANSACTIONS ON INTELLIGENT TRANSPORTATION SYSTEMS.** (Institute of Electrical and Electronics Engineers) Text in English. 2000. q. USD 580; USD 725 combined subscription (print & online eds.) (effective 2012). adv. back issues avail.; reprints avail. **Document type:** *Journal, Academic/Scholarly.* **Description:** Contains articles and research on the application of information technology to transportation.
Related titles: Online - full text ed.: ISSN 1558-0016. USD 525 (effective 2012).
Indexed: A22, A28, APA, B21, BrCerAb, C&ISA, CA/WCA, CIA, CPEI, CerAb, CivEngAb, CorrAb, CurCont, E&CAJ, E11, EEA, EMA, ESPM, EngInd, EnvEAb, H&SSA, H15, HRIS, Inspec, M&TEA, M09, MBF, METADEX, RefZh, SCI, SCOPUS, SolStAb, T04, W07, WAA.
—BLDSC (4363.199300), IE, Infotrieve, Ingenta, INIST, Linda Hall. **CCC.**
Published by: I E E E, 445 Hoes Ln, Piscataway, NJ 08854. TEL 732-981-0060, 800-678-4333, FAX 732-562-6380, contactcenter@ieee.org, http://www.ieee.org. Eds. Fei-Yue Wang TEL 520-621-6558, Dawn Melley. **Co-sponsor:** Intelligent Transportation Systems Society.

➤ **I E E E TRANSACTIONS ON VEHICULAR TECHNOLOGY.** (Institute of Electrical and Electronics Engineers) *see* ENGINEERING—Electrical Engineering

➤ **I E E E VEHICULAR TECHNOLOGY MAGAZINE**; connecting the mobile world. (Institute of Electrical & Electronics Engineers) *see* ENGINEERING

388 GBR ISSN 1751-956X
TE228.3
➤ **I E T INTELLIGENT TRANSPORT SYSTEMS.** Abbreviated title: I T S. Text in English. 2006 (Mar.). q. GBP 397, USD 764; GBP 476, USD 916 combined subscription (print & online eds.) (effective 2011). adv. back issues avail. **Document type:** *Journal, Academic/Scholarly.* **Description:** Features research on the practical applications of intelligent transport systems and infrastructures.
Formerly (until 2007): I E E Proceedings - Intelligent Transport Systems (1748-0248)
Related titles: Online - full text ed.: ISSN 1751-9578. GBP 385, USD 756 (effective 2011).
Indexed: A28, APA, BrCerAb, C&ISA, C10, CA, CA/WCA, CIA, CPEI, CerAb, CivEngAb, CorrAb, CurCont, E&CAJ, E11, EEA, EMA, EngInd, H15, Inspec, M&TEA, M09, MBF, METADEX, RefZh, SCI, SCOPUS, SolStAb, T02, T04, W07, WAA.
—BLDSC (4363.252700), IE, Linda Hall. **CCC.**
Published by: The Institution of Engineering and Technology, Michael Faraday House, Stevenage, Herts SG1 2AY, United Kingdom. TEL 44-1438-313311, FAX 44-1438-765526, journals@theiet.org, http://www.theiet.org/. Ed. Alan Stevens. Adv. contact Louise Hall TEL 44-1438-767351. **Subscr. to:** Publication Sales Dept, PO Box 96, Stevenage SG1 2SD, United Kingdom. TEL 44-1438-767328, FAX 44-1438-767375, sales@theiet.org.

380.5 DEU ISSN 0170-5652
I F O STUDIEN ZUR VERKEHRSWIRTSCHAFT. (Information und Forschung) Text in German. 1972. irreg., latest vol.31, 1998. price varies. **Document type:** *Monographic series, Academic/Scholarly.*
Published by: I F O Institut fuer Wirtschaftsforschung, Poschingerstr 5, Munich, 81679, Germany. TEL 49-89-92241410, FAX 49-89-92241409, ifo@ifo.de, http://www.ifo.de. Circ: 400.

388 634.9 USA
I F P T A JOURNAL. Text in English. 1984. q. free to members (effective 2008). adv. back issues avail.; reprints avail. **Document type:** *Journal, Trade.* **Description:** Covers information for the forest products logistics industry.
Published by: (International Forest Products Transportation Association), R I S I, Inc., 4 Alfred Cir, Bedford, MA 01730. TEL 781-734-8900, FAX 781-271-0337, info@risiinfo.com, http://www.risiinfo.com. Ed. Graeme Rodden TEL 322-536-0738. Adv. contact Mary Anne Cauthen TEL 770-373-3003. B&W page USD 1,260, color page USD 1,800; trim 210 x 297.

I S T A RESOURCE BOOK. *see* PACKAGING

I T F NEWS. *see* LABOR UNIONS

388 GBR ISSN 1463-6344
I T S INTERNATIONAL; advanced technology for traffic management and urban mobility. (Intelligent Transport Systems) Text in English. 1995. bi-m. GBP 57, EUR 90, USD 101 combined subscription (print & online eds.) (effective 2009). adv. illus. back issues avail.; reprints avail. **Document type:** *Magazine, Trade.* **Description:** Covers advanced transportation for traffic management and urban mobility worldwide. Each issues delivers comprehensive and exclusive international reports on the latest news, developments, product launches and major deployments with the ITS industry.
Formerly (until 1996): I T S - Intelligent Transport Systems (1357-6542)
Related titles: Online - full text ed.
Indexed: HRIS.
Published by: Route One Publishing Ltd., Horizon House, Azalea Dr, Swanley, Kent BR8 8JR, United Kingdom. TEL 44-1322-612055, FAX 44-161-6030891, media@ropl.com, http://www.routeonepub.com. Ed. Jason Barnes. Pub. Andrew Barriball TEL 44-1322-612057. Circ: 22,147.

388 330 USA
I T S QUARTERLY. Text in English. q.
Published by: Intelligent Transportation Society of America, 1100 17th St NW, Washington, DC 20036-4601. Ed. Don Knight.

IDAHO CRIMINAL AND TRAFFIC LAW MANUAL. *see* LAW—Criminal Law

ILLINOIS CRIMINAL AND TRAFFIC LAW MANUAL. *see* LAW—Criminal Law

ILLINOIS CRIMINAL LAW AND MOTOR VEHICLE HANDBOOK. *see* LAW—Criminal Law

ILLINOIS VEHICLE CODE. *see* LAW

IN TRANSIT. *see* LABOR UNIONS

380.5 USA
INBOUND LOGISTICS; the magazine for demand-driven logistic. Text in English. 1981. m. USD 95 in North America; USD 129 elsewhere; USD 10 per issue in North America; USD 12 per issue elsewhere; free to qualified personnel (effective 2009). adv. illus. back issues avail.; reprints avail. **Document type:** *Magazine, Trade.* **Description:** Contains informative articles on managing logistics and the supply chain.
Former titles (until 1990): Thomas Register's Inbound Logistics (0888-8493); (until 1985): Inbound Traffic Guide (0736-9751); (until 1983): Thomas Register's Inbound Traffic Guide for Industrial Buyers & Specifiers (0732-2828)
Related titles: Online - full text ed.
Indexed: A28, APA, BrCerAb, C&ISA, CA/WCA, CIA, CLT&T, CerAb, CivEngAb, CorrAb, E&CAJ, E11, EEA, EMA, H15, HRIS, LogistBibl, M&TEA, M09, MBF, METADEX, SolStAb, T04, WAA.
—Linda Hall. **CCC.**
Published by: Thomas Publishing Company (New York), Five Penn Plz, New York, NY 10001. TEL 212-629-1560, FAX 212-629-1565, contact@thomaspublishing.com, http://www.thomaspublishing.com. Ed. Felecia J Stratton. Pub. Keith G Blondo. Circ: 60,000.

388.0440934 GBR ISSN 1752-5853
INDIA FREIGHT TRANSPORT REPORT. Text in English. 2006. q. EUR 820, USD 1,030 combined subscription (print & email eds.) (effective 2010). **Document type:** *Report, Trade.* **Description:** Provides industry professionals and strategists, sector analysts, investors, trade associations and regulatory bodies with independent forecasts and competitive intelligence on the Indian freight transport and logistics industry.
Related titles: E-mail ed.
Indexed: A15, ABIn, B02, B15, B17, B18, G04, I05, P48, P51, P52, PQC.
Published by: Business Monitor International Ltd., Senator House, 85 Queen Victoria St, London, EC4V 4AB, United Kingdom. TEL 44-20-72480468, FAX 44-20-72480467, subs@businessmonitor.com.

380.5 IND ISSN 0972-5695
➤ **INDIAN JOURNAL OF TRANSPORT MANAGEMENT.** Text in English. 1966. q. INR 400 domestic; USD 100 foreign (effective 2011). adv. bk.rev. abstr.; charts; illus.; stat. **Document type:** *Journal, Academic/Scholarly.* **Description:** Publishes research articles and papers pertaining to all modes of transportation management with special reference to bus transport.
Formerly: Journal of Transport Management (0970-4736); Supersedes (in Aug. 1977): State Transport News (0039-016X)
—CCC.
Published by: Association of State Road Transport Undertakings, Pune-Nashik Rd, PO Box 1897, Pune, maharastra 411 026, India. TEL 91-20-27125292, FAX 91-20-27125426, library@cirtindia.com. **Subscr. to:** I N S I O Scientific Books & Periodicals, PO Box 7234, Indraprastha HPO, New Delhi 110 002, India.

➤ **INDIANA CRIMINAL AND TRAFFIC LAW MANUAL.** *see* LAW—Criminal Law

➤ **INDIANA CRIMINAL LAW AND MOTOR VEHICLE HANDBOOK.** *see* LAW—Criminal Law

388.04409598 GBR ISSN 1752-5861
INDONESIA FREIGHT TRANSPORT REPORT. Text in English. 2006. q. EUR 820, USD 1,030 combined subscription (print & email eds.) (effective 2010). **Document type:** *Report, Trade.* **Description:** Provides industry professionals and strategists, sector analysts, investors, trade associations and regulatory bodies with independent forecasts and competitive intelligence on the Indonesian freight transport and logistics industry.
Related titles: E-mail ed.
Indexed: A15, ABIn, B02, B15, B17, B18, G04, I05, P48, P51, P52, PQC.
Published by: Business Monitor International Ltd., Senator House, 85 Queen Victoria St, London, EC4V 4AB, United Kingdom. TEL 44-20-72480468, FAX 44-20-72480467, subs@businessmonitor.com.

INDUSTRIAL-UTILITY VEHICLE & MOBILE EQUIPMENT MAGAZINE. *see* ENGINEERING—Mechanical Engineering

388 DEU ISSN 1863-8031
INFORM. Text in German. 1948. 9/yr. adv. **Document type:** *Bulletin, Trade.*
Former titles (until 2000): G d E D Inform (0949-314X); (until 1995): Der Deutsche Eisenbahner (0343-7108)
Published by: Transnet Gerwerkschaft GdED, Chausseestr 84, Berlin, 10115, Germany. TEL 49-30-42439072, FAX 49-30-42439071, presse@transnet.org, http://www.transnet.org. adv.: B&W page EUR 10,900, color page EUR 19,600. Circ: 260,000 (controlled).

INFORMATION ON HANDLING & STORAGE IN .. *see* MACHINERY

INFRASTRUCTUUR, TRANSPORT EN LOGISTIEK. *see* HOUSING AND URBAN PLANNING

388 POL ISSN 1899-0622
INFRASTRUKTURA TRANSPORTU. Text in Polish. 2008. bi-m. PLZ 96 domestic (effective 2011). **Document type:** *Magazine, Trade.* **Description:** Covers development of transport infrastructure in Poland, including articles on technology, comments and statements of best professionals in the industry, legal topics, events, the image of companies operating in Poland.
Related titles: Online - full text ed.
Published by: Wydawnictwo Elamed, Al Rozdzienskiego 188, Katowice, 40203, Poland. TEL 48-32-2580361, FAX 48-32-2039356, elamed@elamed.com.pl, http://www.elamed.com.pl. Ed. Dorota Bartoszek.

INFRASTRUKTURRECHT; Energie - Verkehr - Abfall - Wasser. *see* LAW

388 GBR
INSIGHT REPORTS. Text in English. irreg. GBP 97.50 per issue (effective 2010). **Document type:** *Monographic series, Academic/Scholarly.* **Description:** Covers research on a particular topic with each issue, including many aspects of transport research.
Related titles: Online - full text ed.: GBP 87.50 per issue (effective 2010).
Published by: Transport Research Laboratory, Crowthorne House, Nine Mile Ride, Wokingham, Berks RG40 3GA, United Kingdom. TEL 44-1344-773131, FAX 44-1344-770356, enquiries@trl.co.uk.

380.5 AUT
INSTITUT FUER VERKEHRSWESEN. SCHRIFTENREIHE. Text in German. 1970. irreg. index. back issues avail. **Document type:** *Monographic series, Academic/Scholarly.*
Former titles: Institut fuer Verkehrswesen. Mitteilungen (1017-2750); (until 1989): Institut fuer Geotechnik und Verkehrsbau. Mitteilungen (0379-1483)
Published by: Universitaet fuer Bodenkultur, Institut fuer Verkehrswesen, Peter-Jordan-Strasse 82, Vienna, W 1190, Austria. TEL 43-1-476545300, FAX 43-1-476545344, verkehr@mail.boku.ac.at, http://www.boku.ac.at/verkehr/. Ed. Dr. G Sammer. Circ: 400 (controlled).

388 USA ISSN 2162-1608
▼ ➤ **INSTITUTE OF TRANSPORTATION ENGINEERS. JOURNAL OF TRANSPORTATION.** Text in English. 2011. s-a. USD 25 per issue to non-members; free to members (effective 2011). **Document type:** *Journal, Academic/Scholarly.* **Description:** Publishes basic and applied transportation research findings aimed at advancing transportation knowledge and practices for the benefit of society.
Related titles: Online - full text ed.: ISSN 2162-1616.
Published by: Institute of Transportation Engineers, 1627 Eye St, NW, Ste 600, Washington, DC 20006. TEL 202-785-0060, FAX 202-785-0609, ite_staff@ite.org.

➤ **INSTITUTION OF CIVIL ENGINEERS. PROCEEDINGS. TRANSPORT.** *see* ENGINEERING—Civil Engineering

388 POL ISSN 0239-4855
INSTYTUT TRANSPORTU SAMOCHODOWEGO. ZESZYTY NAUKOWE. Text in Polish; Summaries in English, German, Russian. 1962. irreg. (approx. 2-3/yr.). free. bk.rev. illus.; stat.; pat. **Document type:** *Journal, Trade.*
Published by: Instytut Transportu Samochodowego, Ul. Jagiellonska 80, Warsaw, Poland. TEL 48-22-8113231, FAX 48-22-8110906. Ed., R&P Andrzej Damm TEL 48-22-8110297. Circ: (controlled).

796.77 IDN ISSN 0215-7713
INTAN MOTOR. Text in Indonesian. 1987. fortn. adv. **Document type:** *Magazine, Consumer.*
Published by: P T Gramedia, Jalan Palmerah Selatan 22-26, Jakarta, 10270, Indonesia. TEL 62-21-5483008, FAX 62-21-5494035, ulj@gramedia-majalah.com, http://www.gramedia.com.

380.5 ESP ISSN 0213-3091
INTER-TRANSPORT; semanario de transporte internacional. Text in Spanish. 1965. w. EUR 185.50 domestic; EUR 238 foreign (effective 2009). adv. illus.; stat. back issues avail. **Document type:** *Magazine, Trade.*
Formerly (until 1983): Men-Car, Guia de Medios de Transporte Internacional (0213-3083)
Published by: Grupo Editorial Men-Car, Passeig de Colom, 24, Barcelona, 08002, Spain. TEL 34-93-301-5749, FAX 34-93-302-1779, men-car@men-car.com, http://www.men-car.com. Eds. Juan Cardona, Manuel Cardona. Circ: 13,500.

INTERCHANGE (ROCKVILLE). *see* LABOR UNIONS

388 USA
INTERCITY RAIL PASSENGER SYSTEMS UPDATE. Text in English. 19??. irreg. back issues avail. **Document type:** *Monographic series, Trade.* **Description:** Provides information on current research and development about Intercity Rail Passenger Systems.
Related titles: Online - full text ed.: free (effective 2010).
Indexed: HRIS.
Published by: U.S. National Research Council, Transportation Research Board, The National Academies, 500 Fifth St, NW, Washington, DC 20001. TEL 202-334-3213, FAX 202-334-2519, TRBsales@nas.edu, http://www.trb.org.

658.7 USA
INTERMODAL BUSINESS. Text in English. 1996. w. **Document type:** *Newsletter, Trade.* **Description:** Dedicated to covering the container shipment industry from all angles.
Formerly: Intermodal Week (1087-741X)
—CCC.
Published by: Energy Argus, Inc. (Subsidiary of: Argus Media Inc.), 129 Washington St, Ste 400, Hoboken, NJ 07030. TEL 201-659-4400, FAX 201-659-6006, info@energyargus.com, http://www.energyargus.com.

343.09 341.7 NLD
INTERNATIONAL ENCYCLOPAEDIA OF LAWS. TRANSPORT LAW. Text in English. 1994. updates 1/2 yr.), 3 base vols. plus irreg. updates. looseleaf. USD 748 (effective 2009). **Document type:** *Monographic series.* **Description:** Discusses all aspects of transport law at the international level and for individual countries, including maritime law, inland navigation, transport by air, rail, and road, and multimodal transport.
Published by: Kluwer Law International (Subsidiary of: Aspen Publishers, Inc.), PO Box 316, Alphen aan den Rijn, 2400 AH, Netherlands. TEL 31-172-641562, FAX 31-172-641555, sales@kluwerlaw.com, http://www.kluwerlaw.com. Ed. Marc A Huybrechts.

388 363.7392 GBR ISSN 1758-8480
INTERNATIONAL GREENFLEET. Abbreviated title: G F. Text in English. 2000. m. back issues avail. **Document type:** *Magazine, Trade.* **Description:** Aimed at fleet managers and heads of transport in both public and private sector organisations.
Formerly (until 2008): GreenFleet Magazine (1471-3713)
Related titles: Online - full text ed.: free (effective 2009).
Published by: Public Sector Publishing Ltd., 226 High Rd, Loughton, Essex IG10 1ET, United Kingdom. TEL 44-20-85320055, FAX 44-20-85320066, info@psp-media.co.uk, http://www.psp-media.co.uk. Ed. Sofie Lidefjard TEL 44-20-85325707. Pub. Martin Freedman TEL 44-20-85325723.

629 GBR ISSN 1358-8265
TL242
➤ **INTERNATIONAL JOURNAL OF CRASHWORTHINESS.** Text in English. 1996. bi-m. GBP 616 combined subscription in United Kingdom to institutions (print & online eds.); EUR 939, USD 1,178 combined subscription to institutions (print & online eds.) (effective 2012). adv. back issues avail.; reprint service avail. from PSC. **Document type:** *Journal, Academic/Scholarly.* **Description:** Covers all matters relating to crashworthiness of road and rail vehicles, air- and spacecraft, ships and submarines, on- and offshore installations.
Related titles: Online - full text ed.: ISSN 1754-2111. GBP 554 in United Kingdom to institutions; EUR 846, USD 1,061 to institutions (effective 2012).

Indexed: A22, A26, A28, APA, ApMecR, B21, BrCerAb, C&ISA, C10, CA, CA/WCA, CIA, CPEI, CerAb, CivEngAb, CorrAb, CurCont, E&CAJ, E01, E11, EEA, EMA, ESPM, EngInd, EnvEAb, ErgAb, H&SSA, H15, HRIS, Inspec, M&TEA, M09, MBF, METADEX, P10, P16, P26, P48, P52, P53, P54, PQC, RiskAb, S10, SCI, SCOPUS, SolStAb, T02, T04, W07, WAA.
—BLDSC (4542.178700), IE, Infotrieve, Ingenta, Linda Hall. **CCC.**
Published by: Taylor & Francis Ltd. (Subsidiary of: Taylor & Francis Group), 4 Park Sq, Milton Park, Abingdon, Oxfordshire OX14 4RN, United Kingdom. TEL 44-20-70176000, FAX 44-20-70176336, subscriptions@tandf.co.uk, http://www.taylorandfrancis.com. Ed. E Clive Chirwa. Adv. contact Linda Hann. **Subscr. to:** Journals Customer Service, Sheepen Pl, Colchester, Essex CO3 3LP, United Kingdom. TEL 44-20-70175544, FAX 44-20-70175198, tf.enquiries@tfinforma.com.

388 GBR ISSN 1742-6952
▼➤ **INTERNATIONAL JOURNAL OF ELECTRONIC TRANSPORT.** Text in English. forthcoming 2011. 4/yr. EUR 494 to institutions (print or online ed.); EUR 672 combined subscription to institutions (print & online eds.) (effective 2012). **Document type:** *Journal, Academic/Scholarly.*
Related titles: Online - full text ed.: ISSN 1742-6960. forthcoming.
—CCC.
Published by: Inderscience Publishers, PO Box 735, Olney, Bucks MK46 5WB, United Kingdom. TEL 44-1234-240519, FAX 44-1234-240515, editorial@inderscience.com. **Subscr. to:** World Trade Centre Bldg, 29 Rte de Pre-Bois, Case Postale 856, Geneva 15 1215, Switzerland. FAX 41-22-7910885, subs@inderscience.com.

➤ **INTERNATIONAL JOURNAL OF ENGINE RESEARCH.** *see* ENGINEERING—Mechanical Engineering

380.5 GBR ISSN 1744-232X
➤ **INTERNATIONAL JOURNAL OF HEAVY VEHICLE SYSTEMS.** Abbreviated title: I J H V S. Text in English. 1993. 4/yr. EUR 494 to institutions (print or online ed.); EUR 672 combined subscription to institutions (print & online eds.) (effective 2012). bk.rev. charts; illus.; abstr.; bibl. index. back issues avail. **Document type:** *Journal, Academic/Scholarly.* **Description:** Provides information on the field of on-off road heavy vehicle systems.
Formerly (until 2004): International Journal of Vehicle Design. Heavy Vehicle Systems (1351-7848)
Related titles: Online - full text ed.: ISSN 1741-5152 (from IngentaConnect).
Indexed: A26, A28, A37, APA, ApMecR, B01, B02, B06, B07, B09, B15, B17, B18, B21, BrCerAb, BrTechI, C&ISA, CA, CA/WCA, CABA, CIA, CPEI, CerAb, CivEngAb, CorrAb, CurCont, D01, E&CAJ, E08, E11, EEA, EMA, ESPM, EngInd, EnvAb, EnvEAb, ErgAb, F08, F11, G04, G08, GH, H&SSA, H15, HRIS, I05, ISMEC, Inspec, M&TEA, M09, MBF, METADEX, N02, S&VD, S09, S13, S16, SCI, SCOPUS, SolStAb, T02, T04, W07, WAA.
—BLDSC (4542.280360), AskIEEE, IE, Infotrieve, Ingenta, INIST, Linda Hall. **CCC.**
Published by: (International Association for Vehicle Design CHE), Inderscience Publishers, PO Box 735, Olney, Bucks MK46 5WB, United Kingdom. TEL 44-1234-240519, FAX 44-1234-240515, editorial@inderscience.com. **Subscr. to:** World Trade Centre Bldg, 29 Rte de Pre-Bois, Case Postale 856, Geneva 15 1215, Switzerland. FAX 41-22-7910885, subs@inderscience.com.

➤ **INTERNATIONAL JOURNAL OF INTELLIGENT TRANSPORTATION SYSTEMS RESEARCH.** *see* ENGINEERING—Mechanical Engineering

388 USA ISSN 1948-0024
▼➤ **INTERNATIONAL JOURNAL OF LOGISTICS AND TRANSPORTATION RESEARCH.** Text in English. 2010 (Jan.). s-a. free (effective 2011). **Document type:** *Journal, Academic/Scholarly.* **Description:** Covers research on fundamental theories, analytical models, advanced methodologies and applications in logistics transportation and supply chain systems analysis, planning and design.
Media: Online - full text.
Published by: University of Southern Mississippi, 2701 Hardy St, Hattiesburg, MS 39406. mohd.shiratuddin@usm.edu, http://www.usm.edu.

388 330 GBR ISSN 1741-5373
➤ **INTERNATIONAL JOURNAL OF LOGISTICS ECONOMICS AND GLOBALISATION.** Abbreviated title: I J L E G. Text in English. 2007. 4/yr. EUR 494 to institutions (print or online ed.); EUR 672 combined subscription to institutions (print & online eds.) (effective 2012). abstr.; bibl.; charts; illus.; stat. back issues avail. **Document type:** *Journal, Academic/Scholarly.* **Description:** Proposes and fosters discussion on the development and application of logistics in the world economy and globalized arena.
Related titles: Online - full text ed.: ISSN 1741-5381 (from IngentaConnect).
Indexed: A26, A28, APA, B02, B15, B17, B18, BrCerAb, C&ISA, CA/WCA, CIA, CerAb, CivEngAb, CorrAb, E&CAJ, E11, EEA, EMA, ESPM, EnvEAb, G04, H15, I05, M&TEA, M09, MBF, METADEX, RiskAb, SolStAb, T04, WAA.
—BLDSC (4542.321750), IE. **CCC.**
Published by: Inderscience Publishers, PO Box 735, Olney, Bucks MK46 5WB, United Kingdom. TEL 44-1234-240519, FAX 44-1234-240515, editorial@inderscience.com. Ed. Siau Ching Lenny Koh. **Subscr. to:** World Trade Centre Bldg, 29 Rte de Pre-Bois, Case Postale 856, Geneva 15 1215, Switzerland. FAX 41-22-7910885, subs@inderscience.com.

388 GBR ISSN 1556-8318
INTERNATIONAL JOURNAL OF SUSTAINABLE TRANSPORTATION. Text in English. 2007. bi-m. GBP 275 combined subscription in United Kingdom to institutions (print & online eds.); EUR 364, USD 456 combined subscription to institutions (print & online eds.) (effective 2012). adv. back issues avail.; reprint service avail. from PSC. **Document type:** *Journal, Academic/Scholarly.* **Description:** Provides a discussion forum for the exchange of new and innovative ideas on sustainable transportation research in the context of environmental, economical, social, and engineering aspects, as well as current and future interactions of transportation systems and other urban subsystems.
Related titles: Online - full text ed.: ISSN 1556-8334. 2007. GBP 248 in United Kingdom to institutions; EUR 328, USD 410 to institutions (effective 2012) (from IngentaConnect).
Indexed: A01, A22, A28, APA, BrCerAb, C&ISA, CA, CA/WCA, CIA, CerAb, CivEngAb, CorrAb, CurCont, E&CAJ, E01, E11, EEA, EMA, ESPM, EnvEAb, GEOBASE, H15, HRIS, M&TEA, M09, MBF, METADEX, SCOPUS, SSCI, SSciA, SolStAb, T02, T04, W07, WAA.
—IE. **CCC.**
Published by: Taylor & Francis Ltd. (Subsidiary of: Taylor & Francis Group), 4 Park Sq, Milton Park, Abingdon, Oxfordshire OX14 4RN, United Kingdom. TEL 44-20-70176000, FAX 44-20-70176336, subscriptions@tandf.co.uk, http://www.taylorandfrancis.com. Eds. Chang-Ho Park, S C Wong. **Subscr. to:** Journals Customer Service, Sheepen Pl, Colchester, Essex CO3 3LP, United Kingdom. TEL 44-20-70175544, FAX 44-20-70175198, tf.enquiries@tfinforma.com.

380.5 ITA ISSN 0303-5247
➤ **INTERNATIONAL JOURNAL OF TRANSPORT ECONOMICS/ RIVISTA INTERNAZIONALE DI ECONOMIA DEI TRASPORTI.** Text and summaries in English. 1974. 3/yr. EUR 695 combined subscription domestic to institutions (print & online eds.); EUR 795 combined subscription foreign to institutions (print & online eds.) (effective 2009). adv. bk.rev. illus. index. back issues avail.; reprints avail. **Document type:** *Journal, Academic/Scholarly.* **Description:** Intends to bring together research in transport economics and arrange it organically in the form of a synthesis theory and fact.
Related titles: Online - full text ed.: ISSN 1724-2185. 2002.
Indexed: A22, BPIA, CREJ, HRIS, JEL, PCI, RASB.
—Infotrieve.
Published by: Fabrizio Serra Editore (Subsidiary of: Accademia Editoriale), c/o Accademia Editoriale, Via Santa Bibbiana 28, Pisa, 56127, Italy. TEL 39-050-542332, FAX 39-050-574888, accademiaeditoriale@accademiaeditoriale.it, http://www.libraweb.net. Circ: 1,000.

388 JOR ISSN 1682-2587
➤ **INTERNATIONAL JOURNAL OF TRANSPORTATION, PRIVATIZATION & PUBLIC POLICY.** Text in English. 2001. s-a. JOD 30 domestic; USD 40 foreign to individuals; USD 60 foreign to institutions (effective 2003). adv. bk.rev. stat. Index. 120 p./no.; back issues avail.; reprints avail. **Document type:** *Journal, Academic/Scholarly.*
Indexed: ESPM, HRIS, RiskAb.
Published by: International Journal of Transportation, Privatization & Public Policy (IJTPPP), PO Box 7631, Amman, 11180, Jordan. TEL 962-079-661830, FAX 962-6-4610793, info@ijtppp.org, mhamed@go.com.jo, http://www.ijtppp.org. Ed., R&P Mohammad M Hamed. Pub. Miss R Tahtamoni. adv.: B&W page USD 250.

388 GBR ISSN 2046-0430
▼➤ **INTERNATIONAL JOURNAL OF TRANSPORTATION SCIENCE AND TECHNOLOGY.** Text in English. forthcoming 2012. q. GBP 115, USD 185 to individuals (print or online ed.); GBP 225, USD 360 to institutions (print or online ed.); GBP 135, USD 220 combined subscription to individuals (print & online eds.); GBP 250, USD 400 combined subscription to institutions (print & online eds.) (effective 2012). **Document type:** *Journal, Academic/Scholarly.*
Related titles: Online - full text ed.: ISSN 2046-0449. forthcoming.
Published by: Multi-Science Publishing Co. Ltd., 5 Wates Way, Brentwood, Essex CM15 9TB, United Kingdom. TEL 44-1277-244632, FAX 44-1277-223453, info@multi-science.co.uk. Eds. Chiu Liu, Zhongyin Guo.

380.5 621 GBR ISSN 1471-0226
TL1
➤ **INTERNATIONAL JOURNAL OF VEHICLE AUTONOMOUS SYSTEMS.** Abbreviated title: I J V A S. Text in English. 2002. 4/yr. EUR 494 to institutions (print or online ed.); EUR 672 combined subscription to institutions (print & online eds.) (effective 2012). abstr.; bibl.; charts; illus. back issues avail. **Document type:** *Journal, Academic/Scholarly.* **Description:** Provides an international forum in the field of vehicle autonomous systems that investigates how these systems contribute to the reliability and cost effectiveness of vehicles in an ecologically friendly environment, to driver comfort and reducing working load during driving, and to the design and acceptance of the systems by the driver.
Related titles: Online - full text ed.: ISSN 1741-5306 (from IngentaConnect).
Indexed: A26, A28, APA, B01, B02, B06, B07, B09, B15, B17, B18, BrCerAb, C&ISA, CA, CA/WCA, CIA, CPEI, CerAb, CivEngAb, CorrAb, E&CAJ, E08, E11, EEA, EMA, ESPM, EngInd, EnvEAb, ErgAb, G04, G08, H15, HRIS, I05, Inspec, M&TEA, M09, MBF, METADEX, S09, SCOPUS, SolStAb, T02, T04, WAA.
—BLDSC (4542.697400), IE, Ingenta, INIST, Linda Hall. **CCC.**
Published by: Inderscience Publishers, PO Box 735, Olney, Bucks MK46 5WB, United Kingdom. TEL 44-1234-240519, FAX 44-1234-240515, editorial@inderscience.com. Ed. Kevin Deng. **Subscr. to:** World Trade Centre Bldg, 29 Rte de Pre-Bois, Case Postale 856, Geneva 15 1215, Switzerland. FAX 41-22-7910885, subs@inderscience.com.

380.5 621 GBR ISSN 0143-3369
TL1 CODEN: IJVDDW
➤ **INTERNATIONAL JOURNAL OF VEHICLE DESIGN;** the journal of vehicle engineering and components. Abbreviated title: I J V D. Text in English. 1979. m. (in 3 vols., 4 nos./vol.). EUR 1,025 to institutions (print or online ed.); EUR 1,434 combined subscription to institutions (print & online eds.) (effective 2012). bk.rev. abstr.; charts; illus.; bibl.; stat. keyword index. back issues avail. **Document type:** *Journal, Academic/Scholarly.* **Description:** Contains articles on the engineering design, research into and development of all types of self-propelled vehicles and their components. Includes reports of events, technical notes, and readers' letters.
Related titles: Online - full text ed.: ISSN 1741-5314 (from IngentaConnect).
Indexed: A22, A28, AIA, APA, ASCA, AcoustA, ApMecR, B01, B06, B07, B09, B21, BiolDig, BrCerAb, BrTechI, C&ISA, CA, CA/WCA, CADCAM, CIA, CPEI, Cadscan, CerAb, CivEngAb, CorrAb, CurCont, E&CAJ, E11, EEA, EIA, EMA, ESPM, EngInd, EnvAb, EnvEAb, EnvInd, ErgAb, H&SSA, H15, HRIS, ISMEC, ISR, Inspec, LeadAb, M&TEA, M09, MBF, METADEX, PollutAb, RiskAb, RoboAb, S&VD, SCI, SCOPUS, SSciA, SolStAb, T02, T04, TM, W07, WAA, Zincscan.
—BLDSC (4542.697500), AskIEEE, IE, Infotrieve, Ingenta, INIST, Linda Hall. **CCC.**
Published by: (International Association for Vehicle Design CHE), Inderscience Publishers, PO Box 735, Olney, Bucks MK46 5WB, United Kingdom. TEL 44-1234-240519, FAX 44-1234-240515, editorial@inderscience.com. Ed. Dr. M A Dorgham. **Subscr. to:** World Trade Centre Bldg, 29 Rte de Pre-Bois, Case Postale 856, Geneva 15 1215, Switzerland. FAX 41-22-7910885, subs@inderscience.com.

380.5 GBR ISSN 1471-0242
➤ **INTERNATIONAL JOURNAL OF VEHICLE INFORMATION AND COMMUNICATION SYSTEMS.** Abbreviated title: I J V I C S. Text in English. 2005. 4/yr. EUR 494 to institutions (print or online ed.); EUR 672 combined subscription to institutions (print & online eds.) (effective 2012). back issues avail. **Document type:** *Journal, Academic/Scholarly.* **Description:** Provides a forum on how information flow and communication takes place, as well as their interaction, effects and implications between systems and subsystems within the vehicle itself, between the vehicle and other vehicles and between the vehicle and the surrounding environment.
Related titles: Online - full text ed.: ISSN 1741-8208 (from IngentaConnect).
Indexed: A26, B02, B15, B17, B18, B21, CPEI, E08, ESPM, ErgAb, G04, G08, H&SSA, I05, Inspec, S09, SCOPUS.
—BLDSC (4542.697702), IE, Ingenta, INIST, Linda Hall. **CCC.**
Published by: Inderscience Publishers, PO Box 735, Olney, Bucks MK46 5WB, United Kingdom. TEL 44-1234-240519, FAX 44-1234-240515, editorial@inderscience.com. Ed. Dr. M A Dorgham. **Subscr. to:** World Trade Centre Bldg, 29 Rte de Pre-Bois, Case Postale 856, Geneva 15 1215, Switzerland. subs@inderscience.com.

380.5 GBR ISSN 1479-1471
➤ **INTERNATIONAL JOURNAL OF VEHICLE NOISE AND VIBRATION.** Text in English. 2004. 4/yr. EUR 494 to institutions (print or online ed.); EUR 672 combined subscription to institutions (print & online eds.) (effective 2012). abstr.; bibl.; charts; illus.; stat. **Document type:** *Journal, Academic/Scholarly.* **Description:** Addresses vehicle noise and vibration from the perspectives of customers, engineers and manufacturing.
Related titles: Online - full text ed.: ISSN 1479-148X (from IngentaConnect).
Indexed: A26, A28, APA, B02, B15, B17, B18, B21, BrCerAb, C&ISA, CA, CA/WCA, CIA, CPEI, CerAb, CivEngAb, CorrAb, E&CAJ, E04, E05, E08, E11, EEA, EMA, ESPM, EnvEAb, G04, G08, H&SSA, H15, I05, Inspec, M&TEA, M09, MBF, METADEX, S09, SCOPUS, SolStAb, T02, T04, TM, WAA.
—BLDSC (4542.697703), IE, Ingenta, INIST, Linda Hall. **CCC.**
Published by: Inderscience Publishers, PO Box 735, Olney, Bucks MK46 5WB, United Kingdom. TEL 44-1234-240519, FAX 44-1234-240515, editorial@inderscience.com. Eds. Dr. M K Abdelhamid, Dr. Mohamad Qatu. **Subscr. to:** World Trade Centre Bldg, 29 Rte de Pre-Bois, Case Postale 856, Geneva 15 1215, Switzerland. FAX 41-22-7910885, subs@inderscience.com.

380.5 GBR ISSN 1479-3105
TL242
➤ **INTERNATIONAL JOURNAL OF VEHICLE SAFETY.** Abbreviated title: I J V S. Text in English. 2005. 4/yr. EUR 494 to institutions (print or online ed.); EUR 672 combined subscription to institutions (print & online eds.) (effective 2012). abstr.; bibl.; charts; illus. back issues avail. **Document type:** *Journal, Academic/Scholarly.* **Description:** Aims to provide a source of information in the field of vehicle safety design, research and development.
Related titles: Online - full text ed.: ISSN 1479-3113 (from IngentaConnect).
Indexed: A26, A28, APA, B02, B15, B17, B18, B21, BrCerAb, C&ISA, CA/WCA, CIA, CPEI, CerAb, CivEngAb, CorrAb, E&CAJ, E08, E11, EEA, EMA, ESPM, EnvEAb, G04, G08, H&SSA, H15, HRIS, I05, M&TEA, M09, MBF, METADEX, S09, SCOPUS, SolStAb, T04, WAA.
—BLDSC (4542.697705), IE, Ingenta, INIST. **CCC.**
Published by: (International Association for Vehicle Design CHE), Inderscience Publishers, PO Box 735, Olney, Bucks MK46 5WB, United Kingdom. TEL 44-1234-240519, FAX 44-1234-240515, editorial@inderscience.com. Ed. Dr. Jesse Ruan. **Subscr. to:** World Trade Centre Bldg, 29 Rte de Pre-Bois, Case Postale 856, Geneva 15 1215, Switzerland. FAX 41-22-7910885, subs@inderscience.com.

➤ **INTERNATIONAL SYMPOSIUM ON THE AERODYNAMICS AND VENTILATION OF VEHICLE TUNNELS. PAPERS PRESENTED.** *see* ENGINEERING—Civil Engineering

380.5 CHE ISSN 1420-5688
INTERNATIONAL TRANSPORT JOURNAL. Text in English. 1939. w. CHF 220 (effective 2000). adv. **Document type:** *Magazine, Trade.*
Related titles: ◆ German ed.: Internationale Transport Zeitschrift. ISSN 0020-9341; French ed.: Journal pour le Transport International. ISSN 1022-7334.
Published by: Swiss Professional Meda AG - Rittmann (Subsidiary of: Sueddeutscher Verlag GmbH), Hochbergerstr 15, Postfach, Basel, 4002, Switzerland. TEL 41-61-2618830, FAX 41-61-2610878, info@s-p-m.ch, http://www.swissprofessionalmedia.ch. Ed. Ursula Schmeling. Pub. Severin Schlegel. R&P Eric Derrer. Adv. contact Marcus Alder. B&W page CHF 4,200, color page CHF 6,300; 185 x 268. Circ: 29,800.

INTERNATIONAL TRANSPORT WORKERS' FEDERATION REPORT ON ACTIVITIES. *see* LABOR UNIONS

388 IRN ISSN 1728-2179
INTERNATIONAL TRANSPORTATION MAGAZINE. Text in English. 2003. m. **Document type:** *Magazine, Trade.*
Published by: Trabar Publication Institute, PO Box 15875-1618, Tehran, Iran. TEL 98-21-8735705, FAX 98-21-8762488, info@itm.ir, http://www.itm.ir. Ed. Homayoun Zarghany.

388 BEL
INTERNATIONAL UNION OF PUBLIC TRANSPORT. CONGRESS REPORTS. Text in English. 1885. biennial. back issues avail. **Document type:** *Proceedings, Trade.* **Description:** Deals with all problems of the urban and regional public transport.
Formerly: International Union of Public Transport. Technical Reports of the Congresses
Media: CD-ROM. **Related titles:** ◆ German ed.: Internationaler Verband fuer Oeffentliches Verkehrswesen. Berichte zu den Kongressen; ◆ French ed.: Union Internationale des Transports Publics. Rapports des Congres.

Published by: International Union of Public Transport/Union Internationale des Transports Publics, Rue Sainte-Marie 6, Brussels, 1080, Belgium. FAX 32-2-6601072, http://www.uitp.org. Ed. H Rat.

625.5 AUT
INTERNATIONALE SEILBAHN-RUNDSCHAU/INTERNATIONAL AERIAL LIFT REVIEW. Text in French, German, English, Chinese. 8/yr. EUR 100.70 domestic; EUR 134.40 foreign (effective 2004). adv. abstr.; charts; illus. **Document type:** *Magazine, Trade.*
Formerly: Internationale Berg- und Seilbahn-Rundschau (0253-3715)
Published by: (Organizzazione Internationale dei Trasporti a Fune), Bohmann Druck und Verlag GmbH & Co. KG, Leberstr 122, Vienna, W 1110, Austria. TEL 43-1-74095-0, FAX 43-1-74095-183, http://www.bohmann.at. Ed. Josef Nejez. Adv. contact Josef Schiessbuhl TEL 43-1-7409548. B&W page EUR 2,460, color page EUR 3,800; trim 185 x 270. Circ: 7,650.

380.5 CHE ISSN 0020-9341
INTERNATIONALE TRANSPORT ZEITSCHRIFT. Text in German. 1939. w. CHF 220 (effective 2000). adv. bk.rev. illus. **Document type:** *Newspaper, Trade.*
Related titles: Online - full text ed.; ◆ English ed.: International Transport Journal. ISSN 1420-5688; French ed.: Journal pour le Transport International. ISSN 1022-7334.
Indexed: RASB.
Published by: Swiss Professional Meda AG - Rittmann (Subsidiary of: Sueddeutscher Verlag GmbH), Hochbergerstr 15, Postfach, Basel, 4002, Switzerland. TEL 41-61-2618830, FAX 41-61-2610878, info@s-p-m.ch, http://www.swissprofessionalmedia.ch. Ed. Ursula Schmeling. Pub. Severin Schlegel. R&P Eric Derrer. adv.: B&W page CHF 4,200, color page CHF 6,300; trim 185 x 268. Circ: 10,900.

388.0440955 GBR ISSN 1752-587X
IRAN FREIGHT TRANSPORT REPORT. Text in English. 2006. q. EUR 820, USD 1,030 combined subscription (print & email eds.) (effective 2010). **Document type:** *Report, Trade.* **Description:** Provides industry professionals and strategists, sector analysts, investors, trade associations and regulatory bodies with independent forecasts and competitive intelligence on the Iranian freight transport and logistics industry.
Related titles: E-mail ed.
Published by: Business Monitor International Ltd., Senator House, 85 Queen Victoria St, London, EC4V 4AB, United Kingdom. TEL 44-20-72480468, FAX 44-20-72480467, subs@businessmonitor.com.

388.044095694 GBR ISSN 1752-5888
ISRAEL FREIGHT TRANSPORT REPORT. Text in English. 2006. q. EUR 820, USD 1,030 combined subscription (print & email eds.) (effective 2010). **Document type:** *Report, Trade.* **Description:** Provides industry professionals and strategists, sector analysts, investors, trade associations and regulatory bodies with independent forecasts and competitive intelligence on the Israeli freight transport and logistics industry.
Related titles: E-mail ed.
Indexed: A15, ABIn, B02, B15, B17, B18, G04, I05, P48, P51, P52, PQC.
Published by: Business Monitor International Ltd., Senator House, 85 Queen Victoria St, London, EC4V 4AB, United Kingdom. TEL 44-20-72480468, FAX 44-20-72480467, subs@businessmonitor.com.

ISTITUTO ITALIANO DI NAVIGAZIONE. ATTI. *see* AERONAUTICS AND SPACE FLIGHT

388.0440945 GBR ISSN 1752-5896
ITALY FREIGHT TRANSPORT REPORT. Text in English. 2006. a. EUR 820, USD 1,030 combined subscription per issue (print & email eds.) (effective 2010). **Document type:** *Report, Trade.* **Description:** Provides industry professionals and strategists, sector analysts, investors, trade associations and regulatory bodies with independent forecasts and competitive intelligence on the Italian freight transport and logistics industry.
Related titles: E-mail ed.
Indexed: A15, ABIn, B02, B15, B17, B18, G04, I05, P48, P51, P52, PQC.
Published by: Business Monitor International Ltd., Senator House, 85 Queen Victoria St, London, EC4V 4AB, United Kingdom. TEL 44-20-72480468, FAX 44-20-72480467, subs@businessmonitor.com.

JANE'S TRANSPORT FINANCE. *see* BUSINESS AND ECONOMICS—Banking And Finance

388 355.27 GBR
JANE'S TRANSPORT LIBRARY. Text in English. 19??. q. USD 45,805 (effective 2010). **Document type:** *Journal, Trade.* **Description:** Provides a comprehensive portfolio of information bringing together 18 Janes products as well as provides transport-related reference, news and analysis covering air, land and sea.
Media: CD-ROM. **Related titles:** Online - full text ed.: GBP 17,615, USD 29,050, AUD 49,450 (effective 2008).
Published by: I H S Jane's (Subsidiary of: I H S), Sentinel House, 163 Brighton Rd, Coulsdon, Surrey CR5 2YH, United Kingdom. TEL 44-20-87003700, FAX 44-20-87003751, info@janes.co.uk, http://www.janes.com.

380.5 GBR ISSN 0263-8460
JANE'S URBAN TRANSPORT SYSTEMS. Text in English. 1982. a. GBP 565 per issue (2010-2011 ed.) (effective 2010). adv. illus. index. **Document type:** *Yearbook, Trade.* **Description:** Comprehensive survey of urban transport systems and equipment manufacturers. Gives details of public transport of over 155 cities around the world. Identifies more than 1,000 manufacturers and their products and services.
Related titles: CD-ROM ed.: GBP 1,275 (effective 2010); Online - full text ed.: GBP 1,755 (effective 2010).
—BLDSC (4647.120000), IE, Ingenta. **CCC.**
Published by: I H S Jane's (Subsidiary of: I H S), Sentinel House, 163 Brighton Rd, Coulsdon, Surrey CR5 2YH, United Kingdom. TEL 44-20-87003700, FAX 44-20-87003751, info@janes.co.uk, http://www.janes.com. Ed. Mary Webb. Adv. contact Janine Boxall TEL 44-20-87003852. **Dist. in Asia by:** Jane's Information Group Asia, 60 Albert St, #15-01 Albert Complex, Singapore 189969, Singapore. TEL 65-331-6280, FAX 65-336-9921, info@janes.com.sg; **Dist. in Australia by:** Jane's Information Group Australia, PO Box 3502, Rozelle, NSW 2039, Australia. TEL 61-2-8587-7900, FAX 61-2-8587-7901, info@janes.thomson.com.au; **Dist. in the Americas by:** 1340 Braddock Pl, Ste 300, Alexandria, VA 22314-1651. TEL 703-683-3700, 800-824-0768, FAX 703-836-0297, 800-836-0297, info@janes.com.

388.044095205 GBR ISSN 1752-590X
JAPAN FREIGHT TRANSPORT REPORT. Text in English. 2006. q. EUR 820, USD 1,030 combined subscription (print & email eds.) (effective 2010). **Document type:** *Report, Trade.* **Description:** Provides industry professionals and strategists, sector analysts, investors, trade associations and regulatory bodies with independent forecasts and competitive intelligence on the Japanese freight transport and logistics industry.
Related titles: E-mail ed.
Indexed: A15, ABIn, B02, B15, B17, B18, G04, I05, P48, P51, P52, PQC.
Published by: Business Monitor International Ltd., Senator House, 85 Queen Victoria St, London, EC4V 4AB, United Kingdom. TEL 44-20-72480468, FAX 44-20-72480467, subs@businessmonitor.com.

JARMUVEK/VEHICLES; motorok, vasuti jarmuvek, kozuti jarmuvek, hajok, mezogazdasagi gepek, epitoipari gepek, repulogepek. *see* ENGINEERING—Mechanical Engineering

388 620 CHN ISSN 1674-599X
JIAOTONG KEXUE YU GONGCHENG/JOURNAL OF TRANSPORT SCIENCE AND ENGINEERING. Text in Chinese. q. **Document type:** *Journal, Academic/Scholarly.*
Formerly (until 2009): Changsha Jiaotong Xueyuan Xuebao/Changsha Communications College. Transactions (1000-9779)
Related titles: Online - full text ed.
Indexed: Z02.
Published by: Changsha Ligong Daxue/Changsha University of Science and Technology, Yuhua-qu, Yiwanjia Li 2-duan #960, 1-Bangong Lou, 840, Changsha, 410004, China. TEL 86-731-85258187, http://www.cscu.edu.cn/.

380.5 383.4 CHN ISSN 1001-9979
JIAOTONG YUNSHU JINGJI, YOUDIAN JINGJI/ECONOMY IN COMMUNICATIONS AND TRANSPORTATION & IN POST AND TELECOMMUNICATION. Text in Chinese. 1978. bi-m. USD 27.25. 80 p./no.; **Description:** Covers transportation and postal services.
Formerly (until 1988): Jiaotong Yunshu Jingji (1001-2575)
Indexed: RASB.
Published by: Zhongguo Renmin Daxue Shubao Ziliao Zhongxin/Renmin University of China, Information Center for Social Sciences, Dongcheng-qu, 3, Zhangzizhong Lu, Beijing, 100007, China. TEL 86-10-64039458, center@zlzx.org, http://www.zlzx.org/. **Dist. in US by:** China Publications Service, PO Box 49614, Chicago, IL 60649. FAX 312-288-8570, 312-288-8570.

388 629.04 USA ISSN 0197-6729
TF1300 CODEN: JATRDC
➤ **JOURNAL OF ADVANCED TRANSPORTATION.** Text in English. 1967. 3/yr. GBP 340 in United Kingdom to institutions; EUR 400 in Europe to institutions; USD 556 elsewhere to institutions; GBP 393 combined subscription in United Kingdom to institutions (print & online eds.); EUR 460 combined subscription in Europe to institutions (print & online eds.); USD 640 combined subscription elsewhere to institutions (print & online eds.) (effective 2012). bk.rev. abstr.; bibl.; charts; illus.; stat. Index. back issues avail.; reprints avail. **Document type:** *Journal, Academic/Scholarly.* **Description:** Includes articles for practitioners and scholars principally on advances in planning, engineering, design, operations and economics of transportation systems.
Formerly (until vol.12, 1979): High Speed Ground Transportation Journal (0018-1501)
Related titles: Microform ed.: (from MIM, PQC); Online - full text ed.: ISSN 2042-3195. GBP 340 in United Kingdom to institutions; EUR 400 in Europe to institutions; USD 556 elsewhere to institutions (effective 2012).
Indexed: A01, A22, A26, A28, APA, ASCA, ApMecR, B02, B15, B17, B18, B21, BrCerAb, BrRB, C&ISA, CA/WCA, CIA, CPEI, CerAb, CivEngAb, CorrAb, E&CAJ, E11, EEA, EMA, ESPM, EngInd, EnvEAb, G04, G08, H&SSA, H15, HRIS, I05, IBR, IBZ, ICEA, ISMEC, M&TEA, M09, MBF, METADEX, RefZh, S06, SCI, SCOPUS, SUSA, SolStAb, T02, T04, TRA, W07, WAA.
—IE, Infotrieve, Ingenta, INIST, Linda Hall. **CCC.**
Published by: (Institute for Transportation, Inc. CAN), John Wiley & Sons, Inc., 111 River St, Hoboken, NJ 07030. TEL 201-748-6000, FAX 201-748-5915, info@wiley.com, http://www.wiley.com/WileyCDA/. Eds. S Chan Wirasinghe TEL 403-220-7180, William H K Lam TEL 852-27666045. Circ: 300 (paid).

387.7 USA ISSN 1544-6980
➤ **JOURNAL OF AIR TRANSPORTATION.** Text in English. 1996. s-a. USD 35 domestic to individuals; USD 55 foreign to individuals; USD 99 domestic to institutions; USD 119 foreign to institutions (effective 2009). bk.rev. **Document type:** *Journal, Academic/Scholarly.* **Description:** Covers both technical and non-technical topics relating to air transportation.
Formerly: Journal of Air Transportation World Wide (1093-8826)
Related titles: Online - full text ed.: ISSN 1093-863X.
Indexed: A01, A02, A03, A08, A10, A12, A13, A17, ABIn, B01, B06, B07, B09, CA, HRIS, P26, P48, P51, P52, P53, P54, PQC, S01, T02, V03.
Published by: University of Nebraska at Omaha, Aviation Institute, 6001 Dodge St, Omaha, NE 68182. TEL 800-335-9886. Ed. Brent Bowen. R&P Fred Hanson TEL 402-554-3095. Circ: 300.

➤ **JOURNAL OF FACILITIES MANAGEMENT.** *see* BUSINESS AND ECONOMICS—Management

388 USA ISSN 1077-291X
HE305
JOURNAL OF PUBLIC TRANSPORTATION. Text in English. 1997. q. back issues avail. **Document type:** *Journal, Academic/Scholarly.*
Related titles: Online - full text ed.: free (effective 2011).
Indexed: B21, CA, ESPM, H&SSA, HRIS, RiskAb, S02, S03, SSciA, T02.
—BLDSC (5043.648800), IE, Ingenta. **CCC.**
Published by: University of South Florida, Center for Urban Transportation Research, College of Engineering, 4202 E Fowler Ave, CUT100, Tampa, FL 33620-5375. TEL 813-974-3120, FAX 813-974-5168, http://www.cutr.usf.edu/. Ed. Gary L Brosch.

JOURNAL OF SAFETY RESEARCH. *see* OCCUPATIONAL HEALTH AND SAFETY

621.9 GBR ISSN 0022-4898
TE208.5 CODEN: JTRMAF
➤ **JOURNAL OF TERRAMECHANICS**; application to terrain-vehicle systems. Text in English. 1964. 6/yr. EUR 970 in Europe to institutions; JPY 128,800 in Japan to institutions; USD 1,086 elsewhere to institutions (effective 2012). adv. bk.rev. abstr.; charts; illus.; pat.; tr.lit. cum.index. back issues avail.; reprints avail. **Document type:** *Journal, Academic/Scholarly.* **Description:** Covers recent research and developments in off-road locomotion, soil excavation, and related engineering aspects, including vehicle design, construction, maintenance and operation.
Related titles: Microfilm ed.: (from PQC); Online - full text ed.: ISSN 1879-1204 (from IngentaConnect, ScienceDirect).
Indexed: A01, A03, A08, A22, A26, A33, A34, A37, ASCA, ApMecR, B21, C&ISA, C25, CA, CABA, CPEI, E&CAJ, E12, ESPM, EngInd, F08, F11, F12, FCA, GH, GeoRef, GeotechAb, H&SSA, H16, I05, I11, ISMEC, IndVet, MaizeAb, N02, P33, PHN&I, R08, R11, S01, S13, S16, SCI, SCOPUS, SSciA, SolStAb, SpeleolAb, T02, TAR, TM, TriticAb, VS, W07, W10.
—BLDSC (5069.030000), IE, Infotrieve, Ingenta, INIST, Linda Hall. **CCC.**
Published by: (International Society for Terrain Vehicle Systems), Pergamon (Subsidiary of: Elsevier Science & Technology), The Blvd, Langford Ln, East Park, Kidlington, Oxford OX5 1GB, United Kingdom. TEL 44-1865-843000, FAX 44-1865-843010, JournalsCustomerServiceEMEA@elsevier.com. Ed. R Lal Kushwaha. **Subscr. to:** Elsevier BV, Radarweg 29, PO Box 211, Amsterdam 1000 AE, Netherlands. TEL 31-20-4853757, FAX 31-20-4853432, http://www.elsevier.nl.

➤ **JOURNAL OF TRANSPORT AND LAND USE.** *see* HOUSING AND URBAN PLANNING

658.7 388 ZAF ISSN 1995-5235
JOURNAL OF TRANSPORT AND SUPPLY CHAIN MANAGEMENT. Text in English. 2007. a. **Document type:** *Journal, Academic/Scholarly.* **Description:** Covers research in the areas of traffic and transportation, customer service, warehousing, inventory management, procurement, packaging, materials handling, reverse logistics, demand forecasting, distribution communications, and information technology.
Media: Online - full text.
Published by: (University of Johannesburg, Department of Transport and Supply Chain Management), Sabinet Online Ltd., PO Box 9785, Centurion, 0046, South Africa. TEL 27-12-6439500, FAX 27-12-6632543, info@sabinet.co.za, http://www.sabinet.co.za. Ed. Beverley Kujawa TEL 27-11-5592918.

380.5 330 GBR ISSN 0022-5258
HE1 CODEN: JTEPEV
➤ **JOURNAL OF TRANSPORT ECONOMICS AND POLICY.** Abbreviated title: J T E P. Text in English. 1967. 3/yr. USD 267 combined subscription in North America to institutions (print & online eds.); GBP 137 combined subscription elsewhere to institutions (print & online eds.) (effective 2009). bk.rev. abstr.; illus. index. back issues avail.; reprint service avail. from PSC. **Document type:** *Journal, Academic/Scholarly.* **Description:** Contains research on all aspects of transport economics and transport policies.
Related titles: Online - full text ed.: ISSN 1754-5951. 2001 (from IngentaConnect).
Indexed: A12, A13, A17, A22, A26, ABIn, ASCA, AmHI, B01, B02, B06, B07, B08, B09, B11, B15, B16, B17, B18, BAS, BMT, BPIA, BrHumI, BrRB, C12, CA, CMM, CREJ, CurCont, DIP, E08, EIP, EconLit, G04, G06, G07, G08, GEOBASE, H07, HRIS, I05, IBR, IBSS, IBZ, ICEA, JEL, P06, P10, P34, P48, P51, P53, P54, PAIS, PCI, PQC, RASB, RefZh, S09, SCOPUS, SSCI, SUSA, T02, W07.
—BLDSC (5069.900000), IE, Infotrieve, Ingenta, INIST. **CCC.**
Published by: University of Bath, Claverton Down, Bath, Avon BA2 7AY, United Kingdom. FAX 44-1225-386767, education@bath.ac.uk. Eds. D N Starkie, T H Oum, Steven A Morrison. **Dist. addr. in the UK:** Turpin Distribution Services Ltd. **Co-sponsor:** London School of Economics and Political Science.

380.5 900 GBR ISSN 0022-5266
HE1
➤ **THE JOURNAL OF TRANSPORT HISTORY.** Text in English. 1953; N.S. 1971. s-a. GBP 125, EUR 163, USD 225 combined subscription to institutions (print & online eds.) (effective 2010). adv. bk.rev. bibl.; illus. back issues avail. **Document type:** *Journal, Academic/Scholarly.* **Description:** Covers the history of transportation from a social and economic perspective.
Related titles: Online - full text ed.: N.S. (from IngentaConnect).
Indexed: A01, A02, A03, A08, A22, AmH&L, AmHI, B04, BRD, BrHumI, CA, FR, GEOBASE, H07, H08, HAb, HRIS, HistAb, HumInd, IBR, IBZ, MEA&I, P10, P48, P52, P53, P54, PCI, PQC, RASB, SCOPUS, T02, W03, W05.
—BLDSC (5070.000000), IE, Infotrieve, Ingenta, INIST. **CCC.**
Published by: Manchester University Press, Oxford Rd, Manchester, Lancs M13 9NR, United Kingdom. TEL 44-161-2752310, FAX 44-161-2743346, mup@manchester.ac.uk. Ed. Lena Andersson-Skog. Pub. David Rodgers. R&P Alison Sparkes. Adv. contact Mr. Ben Stebbing TEL 44-161-2752310. B&W page GBP 165; 120 x 195. Circ: 600.

388 387.7 385 USA ISSN 1944-1916
JOURNAL OF TRANSPORTATION. Text in English. 2008. w. USD 2,295 in US & Canada; USD 2,495 elsewhere; USD 2,525 combined subscription in US & Canada (print & online eds.); USD 2,755 combined subscription elsewhere (print & online eds.) (effective 2011). adv. back issues avail. **Document type:** *Newsletter, Trade.* **Description:** Provides information and news on the latest state and federal transportation projects, common carriers and shippers in trucking, airline, train, and trans-oceanic shipping, as well as important transportation company and industry developments.
Related titles: E-mail ed.; Online - full text ed.: ISSN 1944-1924. USD 2,295 combined subscription (online & e-mail eds.) (effective 2011).
Indexed: A15, ABIn, I05, P10, P26, P47, P48, P51, P52, P53, P54, PQC.
Published by: NewsRx, 2727 Paces Ferry Rd SE, Ste 2-440, Atlanta, GA 30339. TEL 770-435-8286, 800-726-4550, FAX 770-435-6800, pressrelease@newsrx.com, http://www.newsrx.com. Pub., Adv. contact Susan Hasty TEL 770-507-7777.

629.04 USA ISSN 0733-947X
TA1001 CODEN: JTPEDI
➤ **JOURNAL OF TRANSPORTATION ENGINEERING.** Text in English. 1969. m. USD 887 domestic to institutions; USD 947 foreign to institutions; USD 1,011 combined subscription domestic to institutions (print & online eds.); USD 1,071 combined subscription foreign to institutions (print & online eds.) (effective 2012). adv. bk.rev. illus. index. back issues avail.; reprints avail. **Document type:** *Journal, Academic/Scholarly.* **Description:** Contains technical and professional articles on the planning, design, construction, maintenance and operation of air, highway, rail, and urban transportation, as well as pipeline facilities for water, oil and gas.
Formerly (until 1983): American Society of Civil Engineers. Transportation Engineering Journal (0569-7891); Which was formed by the merger of (1962-1969): American Society of Civil Engineers. Aero-Space Transport Division. Journal (0193-3078); Which was formerly (until 1962): American Society of Civil Engineers. Air Transport Division. Journal (0272-4375); (1956-1969): American Society of Civil Engineers. Highway Division. Journal (0569-7972); (1957-1969): American Society of Civil Engineers. Pipeline Division. Journal (0569-8014); All of which superseded in part (1873-1956): American Society of Civil Engineers. Proceedings (0097-417X)
Related titles: CD-ROM ed.: USD 62 to members for CD-ROM and online eds.; USD 93 to individuals for CD-ROM and online eds.; USD 279 to institutions for CD-ROM and online eds. (effective 2001); Microform ed.: (from PQC); Online - full text ed.: ISSN 1943-5436. USD 778 to institutions (effective 2011).
Indexed: A01, A02, A03, A05, A08, A22, A23, A24, A25, A26, A28, APA, AS&TA, AS&TI, ASCA, ASFA, B04, B10, B13, B21, BMT, BrCerAb, C&ISA, C10, CA, CA/WCA, CADCAM, CIA, CPEI, CerAb, CivEngAb, CorrAb, CurCont, DokStr, E&CAJ, E&PHSE, E04, E05, E08, E11, EEA, EIA, EMA, ESPM, EngInd, EnvAb, EnvEAb, EnvInd, G01, G08, GEOBASE, GP&P, GasAb, GeoRef, H&SSA, H15, HRIS, I05, ICEA, ISMEC, ISR, Inspec, M&TEA, M09, MBF, METADEX, OffTech, P02, P10, P26, P47, P48, P53, P54, PQC, PetrolAb, RefZh, RiskAb, S01, S08, S09, S10, SCI, SCOPUS, SoftAbEng, SolStAb, SpeleolAb, T02, T04, W07, WAA.
—BLDSC (5070.350000), IE, Infotrieve, Ingenta, INIST, Linda Hall, PADDS. **CCC.**
Published by: (Air Transport, Highway, Pipeline, Urban Transportation Divisions), American Society of Civil Engineers, 1801 Alexander Bell Dr, Reston, VA 20191. TEL 703-295-6300, FAX 703-295-6333. Ed. Chris T Hendrickson. Adv. contact Dianne Vance TEL 703-295-6234.

➤ **JOURNAL OF TRANSPORTATION LAW, LOGISTICS AND POLICY.** *see* LAW

388 USA ISSN 1058-6199
HE1
➤ **JOURNAL OF TRANSPORTATION MANAGEMENT.** Text in English. 1989. s-a. USD 50 domestic; USD 75 foreign (effective 2010). adv. back issues avail.; reprints avail. **Document type:** *Journal, Academic/Scholarly.* **Description:** Contains policy and managerial articles which cover the subjects of: logistics and transportation management, purpose: advance management of logistics and transportation. The audience includes: academics, management and policymakers.
Related titles: Online - full text ed.
Indexed: A01, A26, B02, B15, B17, B18, E08, G04, I05, T02.
—IE.
Published by: Delta Nu Alpha Transportation Fraternity, Inc., 265 N. Chicago Ave., #2, South Milwaukee, WI 53172. TEL 414-764-3063, admin@deltanualpha.org, http://www.deltanualpha.org/. Ed., R&P, Adv. contact John C. Taylor. Pub. Don Adams. Circ: 275 (paid); 25 (controlled). **Co-publisher:** Georgia Southern University.

363.12 USA ISSN 1943-9962
HE194.5 U6
▼ ➤ **JOURNAL OF TRANSPORTATION SAFETY & SECURITY.** Text in English. 2009 (Mar.). q. GBP 193 combined subscription in United Kingdom to institutions (print & online eds.); EUR 279, USD 347 combined subscription to institutions (print & online eds.) (effective 2012). **Document type:** *Journal, Academic/Scholarly.* **Description:** Provides a discussion forum for the exchange of academic ideas, data, and integrated transportation safety solutions developed through engineering research in multimodal transportation safety arenas, which encompass the highway, transit, ridesharing, pedestrian, and bicycle modes, as well as rail, water, and aviation safety issues.
Related titles: Online - full text ed.: ISSN 1943-9970. 2009 (Mar.). GBP 174 in United Kingdom to institutions; EUR 251, USD 313 to institutions (effective 2012).
Indexed: A01, B21, CA, ESPM, H&SSA, T02.
—CCC.
Published by: Taylor & Francis Inc. (Subsidiary of: Taylor & Francis Group), 325 Chestnut St, Ste 800, Philadelphia, PA 19106. TEL 215-625-8900, 800-354-1420, FAX 215-625- 8914, http://www.taylorandfrancis.com. Ed. Dr. Stephen H Richards.

363.12 USA ISSN 1938-7741
HE194
JOURNAL OF TRANSPORTATION SECURITY. Text in English. 2008 (Jan.). q. USD 436 combined subscription to institutions (print & online eds.) (effective 2011). adv. back issues avail.; reprint service avail. from PSC. **Document type:** *Journal, Academic/Scholarly.*
Related titles: Online - full text ed.: ISSN 1938-775X. 2008 (Jan.) (from IngentaConnect).
Indexed: A12, A17, A22, A26, ABIn, B21, E01, E08, ESPM, H&SSA, P26, P47, P48, P51, P53, P54, PAIS, PQC, S09, SCOPUS.
—IE. **CCC.**
Published by: Springer New York LLC (Subsidiary of: Springer Science+Business Media), 233 Spring St, New York, NY 10013. TEL 212—460-1500, FAX 212-460-1575, service-ny@springer.com, http://www.springer.com. Ed. Andrew R Thomas.

388 USA ISSN 2160-0473
▼ ➤ **JOURNAL OF TRANSPORTATION TECHNOLOGIES.** Abbreviated title: J T T. Text in English. 2011. q. USD 156 (effective 2011). **Document type:** *Journal, Academic/Scholarly.* **Description:** Dedicated to the latest advancement of transportation technologies.
Related titles: Online - full text ed.: ISSN 2160-0481. free (effective 2011).
Published by: Scientific Research Publishing, Inc., PO Box 54821, Irvine, CA 92619. service@scirp.org. Ed. Tschangho Kim.

388 CHN ISSN 1674-2192
JUNSHI JIAOTONG XUEYUAN XUEBAO/ACADEMY OF MILITARY TRANSPORTATION. JOURNAL. Text in Chinese. 1999. bi-m. **Document type:** *Journal, Academic/Scholarly.*
Related titles: Online - full text ed.
Published by: Zhongguo Renmin Jiefangjun Junshi Jiaotong Xueyuan, 1, Dongjuzi, Hedong-qu, Tianjin, 300161, China. TEL 86-22-84656381, FAX 86-22-84657548, http://www.jjxy.cn/.

380.5 DEU
K E P AKTUELL. (Kurier Express Paketdienste) Text in German. 1994. fortn. EUR 75.40 (effective 2011). adv. **Document type:** *Magazine, Trade.*
Published by: EuroTransportMedia Verlags- und Veranstaltungs-GmbH, Handwerkstr 15, Stuttgart, 70565, Germany. TEL 49-711-784980, FAX 49-711-7849888, info@etm-verlag.de, http://www.etm-verlag.de. Ed. Nicole de Jong. Adv. contact Werner Faas. Circ: 61,559 (paid).

380.5 PAK ISSN 0075-5109
HE560.K3
KARACHI PORT TRUST. YEAR BOOK OF INFORMATION, PORT OF KARACHI, PAKISTAN. Text in English. 1961. a. PKR 50.
Published by: Karachi Port Trust, P O Box 4725, Karachi, Pakistan. TEL 201305, FAX 2415567, TELEX 2739 KPT PK. Ed. Kafil Ahmed Khan.

388.044095845 GBR ISSN 1752-7899
KAZAKHSTAN FREIGHT TRANSPORT REPORT. Text in English. 2006. a. EUR 820, USD 1,030 combined subscription per issue (print & email eds.) (effective 2010). **Document type:** *Report, Trade.* **Description:** Provides industry professionals and strategists, sector analysts, investors, trade associations and regulatory bodies with independent forecasts and competitive intelligence on the Kazakhstani freight transport and logistics industry.
Related titles: E-mail ed.
Indexed: A15, ABIn, B02, B15, B17, B18, G04, I05, P48, P51, PQC.
Published by: Business Monitor International Ltd., Senator House, 85 Queen Victoria St, London, EC4V 4AB, United Kingdom. TEL 44-20-72480468, FAX 44-20-72480467, subs@businessmonitor.com.

363.12 USA ISSN 1082-104X
KELLER'S TRANSPORTATION SAFETY TRAINING NEWSLETTER. Variant title: Transportation Safety Training Newsletter. Text in English. 1995. m. USD 189 (effective 2008). **Document type:** *Newsletter, Trade.* **Description:** Provides information on current training methods, DOT regulations, and other transportation related topics.
—CCC.
Published by: J.J. Keller & Associates, Inc., 3003 W Breezewood Ln, PO Box 368, Neenah, WI 54957. TEL 877-564-2333, FAX 800-727-7516, kellersoft@jjkeller.com. Ed. Jill M Schultz.

KENTUCKY CRIMINAL LAW AND PROCEDURE. *see* LAW—Criminal Law

343.093 USA
KFK1469.A29
KENTUCKY MOTOR VEHICLE LAWS AND REGULATIONS ANNOTATED. Text in English. a. USD 44 combined subscription (print & CD-ROM eds.) (effective 2008). **Document type:** *Handbook/ Manual/Guide, Trade.* **Description:** Contains the complete spectrum of statutes and regulations affecting motor vehicle ownership and operation in Kentucky.
Former titles (until 2004): Kentucky Motor Vehicle Laws Annotated (1549-4284); Commonwealth of Kentucky Motor Vehicle Laws
Related titles: CD-ROM ed.
Published by: Michie Company (Subsidiary of: LexisNexis North America), 701 E Water St, Charlottesville, VA 22902. TEL 434-972-7600, 800-446-3410, FAX 434-972-7677, customer.support@lexisnexis.com, http://www.michie.com.

388.044096762 GBR ISSN 1752-5918
KENYA FREIGHT TRANSPORT REPORT. Text in English. 2006. a. EUR 820, USD 1,030 combined subscription per issue (print & email eds.) (effective 2010). **Document type:** *Report, Trade.* **Description:** Provides industry professionals and strategists, sector analysts, investors, trade associations and regulatory bodies with independent forecasts and competitive intelligence on the Kenyan freight transport and logistics industry.
Related titles: E-mail ed.
Indexed: A15, ABIn, B02, B15, B17, B18, G04, I05, P48, P51, P52, PQC.
Published by: Business Monitor International Ltd., Senator House, 85 Queen Victoria St, London, EC4V 4AB, United Kingdom. TEL 44-20-72480468, FAX 44-20-72480467, subs@businessmonitor.com.

385 387 KEN ISSN 1015-0986
HE3419
KENYA RAILWAYS. ANNUAL REPORT. Text in English. 1900. a. **Document type:** *Corporate.*
Formerly (until 1979): East African Railways. Annual Report (0070-8003)
Published by: Kenya Railways Corporation, PO Box 30121, Nairobi, Kenya. TEL 254-2-221211, FAX 254-2-340049. Circ: 2,500.

363.12 NLD ISSN 1573-2541
KERNCIJFERS VERKEERSVEILIGHEID. Text in Dutch. 2004. a.
Related titles: ◆ English ed.: Road Safety in the Netherlands, Key Figures. ISSN 1573-255X.
Published by: Ministerie van Verkeer en Waterstaat Rijkswaterstaat, Dienst Verkeer en Scheepvaart, Postbus 5044, Delft, 2600 GA, Netherlands. TEL 31-88-7982222, FAX 31-88-7982999, dvsloket@rws.nl, http://www.rijkswaterstaat.nl/dvs.

388 GBR ISSN 1474-7103
KEY NOTE MARKET ASSESSMENT. PUBLIC TRANSPORT. Variant title: Public Transport Market Assessment. Text in English. 2001. irreg., latest 2001, Mar. GBP 599 per issue (effective 2010). **Document type:** *Report, Trade.* **Description:** Provides an in-depth strategic analysis across a broad range of industries and contains an examination on the scope, dynamics and shape of key UK markets in the consumer, financial, lifestyle and business to business sectors.
Published by: Key Note Ltd. (Subsidiary of: Bonnier Business Information), Harlequin House, 5th Fl, 7 High St, Teddington, Richmond upon Thames, TW11 8EE, United Kingdom. TEL 44-845-5040452, FAX 44-845-5040453, info@keynote.co.uk.

388.22 658.8 GBR ISSN 1369-491X
KEY NOTE MARKET REPORT: BUS & COACH OPERATORS. Variant title: Bus & Coach Operators Market Report. Text in English. 1989. irreg., latest 2008, Dec. GBP 460 per issue (effective 2010). charts; stat. **Document type:** *Report, Trade.* **Description:** Provides an overview of a specific UK market segment and includes executive summary, market definition, market size, industry background, competitor analysis, current issues, forecasts, company profiles, and more.
Formerly (until 1997): Key Note Report. Bus & Coach Operators (0963-4401)
Related titles: CD-ROM ed.; Online - full text ed.
Published by: Key Note Ltd. (Subsidiary of: Bonnier Business Information), Harlequin House, 5th Fl, 7 High St, Teddington, Richmond upon Thames, TW11 8EE, United Kingdom. TEL 44-845-5040452, FAX 44-845-5040453, info@keynote.co.uk.

388 GBR
KEY NOTE MARKET REPORT: FREIGHT FORWARDING. Variant title: Freight Forwarding Market Report. Text in English. 19??. irreg., latest 2009, Oct. GBP 460 per issue (effective 2010). **Document type:** *Report, Trade.* **Description:** Provides an overview of a specific UK market segment and includes executive summary, market definition, market size, industry background, competitor analysis, current issues, forecasts, company profiles, and more.
Former titles (until 1995): Key Note Report: Freight Forwarding (1352-6952); (until 1988): Key Note Report. Freight Forwarding (0954-4593)
Related titles: CD-ROM ed.; Online - full text ed.
Published by: Key Note Ltd. (Subsidiary of: Bonnier Business Information), Harlequin House, 5th Fl, 7 High St, Teddington, Richmond upon Thames, TW11 8EE, United Kingdom. TEL 44-845-5040452, FAX 44-845-5040453, info@keynote.co.uk.

388.3 NLD ISSN 1574-3322
KING OF THE ROAD. Text in Dutch. 2004. 3/yr. **Document type:** *Magazine, Trade.*
Published by: Scania Beers BV, Stadionstr 18, Postbus 9598, Breda, 1801 LN, Netherlands. TEL 31-76-7511600, FAX 31-76-7511610.

380.5 HUN ISSN 0023-4362
TA1001 CODEN: KOSZAZ
KOZLEKEDESTUDOMANYI SZEMLE/SCIENTIFIC REVIEW OF COMMUNICATIONS. Summaries in English, French, German; Text in Hungarian. 1951. m. charts; illus. **Document type:** *Journal, Academic/Scholarly.*
Indexed: Inspec, RASB.
Published by: Kozlekedestudomanyi Egyesulet/Hungarian Scientific Association for Transport, Pf. 451, Budapest 5, 1372, Hungary. info.kte@mtesz.hu, http://www.kte.mtesz.hu. Ed. Bela Czere.

341.756 DEU
KRAFTVERKEHRSKONTROLLE. Text in German. 2 base vols. plus updates 4/yr. EUR 479 base vol(s).; EUR 156 updates (effective 2007). adv. **Document type:** *Trade.*
Published by: Walhalla Fachverlag, Haus an der Eisernen Bruecke, Regensburg, 93042, Germany. TEL 49-941-56840, FAX 49-941-5684111, walhalla@walhalla.de, http://www.walhalla.de. adv.: B&W page EUR 350. Circ: 550 (controlled).

388.04095367 GBR ISSN 1752-5926
KUWAIT FREIGHT TRANSPORT REPORT. Text in English. 2006. q. EUR 820, USD 1,030 combined subscription (print & email eds.) (effective 2010). **Document type:** *Report, Trade.* **Description:** Provides industry professionals and strategists, sector analysts, investors, trade associations and regulatory bodies with independent forecasts and competitive intelligence on the Kuwaiti freight transport and logistics industry.
Related titles: E-mail ed.
Indexed: A15, ABIn, B02, B15, B17, B18, G04, I05, P48, P51, P52, PQC.
Published by: Business Monitor International Ltd., Senator House, 85 Queen Victoria St, London, EC4V 4AB, United Kingdom. TEL 44-20-72480468, FAX 44-20-72480467, subs@businessmonitor.com.

388 USA ISSN 0162-8429
L R T NEWS (ONLINE). (Light Rail Transit) Text in English. 1978. irreg. free (effective 2010). back issues avail. **Document type:** *Newsletter, Trade.* **Description:** Provides information about new developments in light rail transit planning, technology, operations and also reports on new studies, completed research, and current literature.
Formerly (until 1999): L R T News (Print)
Media: Online - full text.
Indexed: HRIS.
—Linda Hall.
Published by: U.S. National Research Council, Transportation Research Board, The National Academies, 500 Fifth St, NW, Washington, DC 20001. TEL 202-334-3213, FAX 202-334-2519, TRBsales@nas.edu, http://www.trb.org.

LAMY TRANSPORT. TOME 1; route. *see* LAW—International Law

LAMY TRANSPORT. TOME 2; mer, fer, air. *see* LAW—International Law

LAMY TRANSPORT. TOME 3; marchandises dangereuses. *see* LAW—International Law

388 NLD ISSN 1389-434X
LANDENDOCUMENTATIE. Text in Dutch. 1979. a. EUR 76 to non-members; EUR 27 to members; EUR 49 to students (effective 2010).
Formerly (until 1992): N I W O - Landendocumentatie (1389-4358)
Published by: Transport en Logistiek Nederland, Postbus 3008, Zoetermeer, 2700 KS, Netherlands. TEL 31-79-3636111, FAX 31-79-3636200, info@tln.nl, http://www.tln.nl.

388.044094796 GBR ISSN 1752-5934
LATVIA FREIGHT TRANSPORT REPORT. Text in English. 2006. a. EUR 820, USD 1,030 combined subscription per issue (print & email eds.) (effective 2010). **Document type:** *Report, Trade.* **Description:** Provides industry professionals and strategists, sector analysts, investors, trade associations and regulatory bodies with independent forecasts and competitive intelligence on the Latvian freight transport and logistics industry.
Related titles: E-mail ed.
Indexed: A15, ABIn, B02, B15, B17, B18, G04, I05, P48, P51, P52, PQC.
Published by: Business Monitor International Ltd., Senator House, 85 Queen Victoria St, London, EC4V 4AB, United Kingdom. TEL 44-20-72480468, FAX 44-20-72480467, subs@businessmonitor.com.

LAZYDAYS R V SHOWCASE. (Recreational Vehicle) *see* SPORTS AND GAMES—Outdoor Life

380.5 CHE
LEONARDO; VCS Magazin. Text in French, German. 1979. 6/yr. adv.
Document type: *Magazine, Consumer.*
Formerly: V C S Zeitung
Published by: Verkehrs Club der Schweiz, Aarbergergasse 61, Postfach, Bern 2, 3000, Switzerland. TEL 41-31-328-8200, FAX 41-31-3288201, red@vcs-ate.ch. Eds. Anne Lise Hilty, Claire Houriet Rime. Adv. contact Myriam Vetsch. Circ: 95,000.

LEONARD'S GUIDE. NATIONAL THIRD PARTY LOGISTICS DIRECTORY. *see* BUSINESS AND ECONOMICS—Trade And Industrial Directories

LEONARD'S GUIDE. NATIONAL WAREHOUSE AND DISTRIBUTION DIRECTORY. *see* BUSINESS AND ECONOMICS—Trade And Industrial Directories

388 FRA ISSN 2107-674X
▼ **LETTRE D'INFORMATION DE L'OBSERVATOIRE DES DEPLACEMENTS DE LA REGION GRENOBLOISE.** Text in French. 2009. q. **Document type:** *Newsletter, Consumer.*
Media: Online - full text.
Published by: Agence d'Urbanisme de la Region Grenobloise, 21, Rue Lesdiguieres, Grenoble, 38000, France. TEL 33-4-76288600, FAX 33-4-76288612.

380.5 FRA ISSN 0180-7811
LIAISONS TRANSPORTS EQUIPEMENT. Text in French. 1977. m.
Published by: Confederation Francaise Democratique du Travail, Federation Generale des Transports et de l'Equipement, 47-49 av. Simon Bolivar, Paris, Cedex 19 75950, France. TEL 33-1-56415600, federation@fgte-cfdt.org, http://www.fgte-cfdt.org.

388.044094793 GBR ISSN 1752-5942
LITHUANIA FREIGHT TRANSPORT REPORT. Text in English. 2006. a. EUR 820, USD 1,030 combined subscription per issue (print & email eds.) (effective 2010). **Document type:** *Report, Trade.* **Description:** Provides industry professionals and strategists, sector analysts, investors, trade associations and regulatory bodies with independent forecasts and competitive intelligence on the Lithuanian freight transport and logistics industry.
Related titles: E-mail ed.
Indexed: A15, ABIn, B02, B15, B17, B18, G04, I05, P48, P51, P52, PQC.
Published by: Business Monitor International Ltd., Senator House, 85 Queen Victoria St, London, EC4V 4AB, United Kingdom. TEL 44-20-72480468, FAX 44-20-72480467, subs@businessmonitor.com.

388.322 GBR ISSN 0076-0013
THE LITTLE RED BOOK (YEAR). Text in English. 1899. a. GBP 35 per issue (effective 2010). adv. back issues avail.; reprints avail.
Document type: *Directory, Trade.* **Description:** Trade directory for the road passenger transport industry.
Formerly (until 1970): Passenger Transport Year Book
—BLDSC (5278.600000). **CCC.**
Published by: Ian Allan Publishing Ltd., Riverdene Business Park, Riverdene Industrial Estate, Molesey Rd, Walton-on-Thames, Surrey KT12 4RG, United Kingdom. TEL 44-1932-266622, FAX 44-1932-266633, magazines@ianallanpublishing.co.uk. Ed. Ian Barlex.

287 GBR ISSN 1561-7823
LLOYD'S FREIGHT TRANSPORT BUYER ASIA. Text in English. 1999. bi-m. **Document type:** *Magazine, Trade.* **Description:** Covers financial briefings, logistics and shipping profiles. Useful for all freighting and logistics managers within Asia's import-export, manufacturing, freight forwarding and transport sectors.
Published by: Informa Maritime & Transport (Subsidiary of: T & F Informa plc), Mortimer House, 37-41 Mortimer St, London, W1T 3JH, United Kingdom. TEL 44-20-70175000. Ed. Turloch Mooney. Pub. Emma Murray TEL 44-207-5531681. Adv. contact Frank Paul TEL 852-2854-3222.

380.5 GBR ISSN 0962-6220
LOCAL TRANSPORT TODAY. Abbreviated title: L T T. Text in English. 1989. fortn. GBP 96 (effective 2009). bk.rev. illus. 28 p./no. 5 cols./p.; back issues avail. **Document type:** *Newspaper, Trade.* **Description:** Provides information on urban and regional transportation from the viewpoint of planners, policy makers, traffic engineers, and economic and environmental analysts.
Related titles: Online - full text ed.
—BLDSC (5290.048910). **CCC.**
Published by: (Local Transport Today Ltd.), Landor Publishing Ltd, Apollo House, 359 Kennington Ln, London, SE11 5QY, United Kingdom. TEL 44-845-2707950, business@landor.co.uk, http://www.landor.co.uk. Ed. Andrew Forster TEL 44-845-2707875. Adv. contact Daniel Simpson TEL 44-845-2707861.

380.5 GBR ISSN 0305-5493
LOCOMOTION PAPERS. Abbreviated title: L P. Text in English. 1947. irreg. **Document type:** *Monographic series, Trade.*
—BLDSC (5290.950000), IE, Ingenta.
Published by: Oakwood Press, PO Box 13, Usk, Mon NP15 1YS, United Kingdom. TEL 44-1291-650444, FAX 44-1291-650484, sales@oakwoodpress.co.uk.

LOG TRUCKER. *see* FORESTS AND FORESTRY—Lumber And Wood

380.5 658 BEL
LOGISTIC. Text in Dutch, French. 1969. m. adv. **Document type:** *Trade.*
Former titles (until 1986): Transport, Handling and Packaging (0770-6332); (until 1981): Manutention Emballages - Behandeling Verpakking (0770-6383); (until 1974): Industrie Manutention (0537-5630)
Related titles: ◆ Supplement(s): Logistic Digest.
Published by: Technipress nv, Stationsstraat 30, Bus 1, Groot-Bijgaarden, 1702, Belgium. TEL 32-2-4218100, FAX 32-2-4818182. Ed., R&P, Adv. contact Maurice Florquin.

380.5 ITA
LOGISTICA. Text in Italian. 1970. m. (10/yr.). EUR 60 domestic; EUR 120 in Europe; EUR 140 elsewhere (effective 2011). adv. **Document type:** *Magazine, Trade.*
Former titles (until 2005): Logistica News (1593-795X); (until 2004): Logistica (0394-4867); (until 1970): Magazzini e Trasporti (0024-9874)
Related titles: Online - full text ed.
Published by: Tecniche Nuove SpA, Via Eritrea 21, Milan, MI 201, Italy. TEL 39-02-390901, FAX 39-02-7570364, info@tecnichenuove.com. Ed. Paola Pagani.

388 ESP ISSN 1888-1815
LOGISTICA PROFESIONAL. Text in Spanish. 1997. m. EUR 144.83 combined subscription domestic (print, online & email eds.); EUR 189 combined subscription foreign (print, online & email eds.) (effective 2009). adv. **Document type:** *Magazine, Trade.* **Description:** Covers all aspects of the distribution of goods, strategies, equipment, automation, software and programs.
Related titles: E-mail ed.: ISSN 1988-5210; Online - full text ed.: Logistica Profesional Digital. ISSN 1988-8627.
Published by: Tecnipublicaciones Espana, S.L., Avda de Manoteras 44, 3a Planta, Madrid, 28050, Spain. TEL 34-91-2972000, FAX 34-91-2972154, tp@tecnipublicaciones.com.

658.5 388 ESP ISSN 1695-8772
LOGISTICA, TRANSPORTE, PAQUETERIA Y ALMACENAJE. Text in Spanish. 1998. m. adv. **Document type:** *Magazine, Trade.*
Formerly (until 1999): Logistica, Transporte y Almacenaje (1576-0626); Which superseded in part (in 1999): Logistica & Transporte (1133-7117)
Published by: Medios de Distribucion 2000 S.L., El Algabeno 53, Madrid, 28043, Spain. TEL 34-91-721895, FAX 34-91-721902, correo@logisticaytransporte.es, http://www.logisticaytransporte.es.

658.500 BEL ISSN 1368-9037
LOGISTICS EUROPE YEARBOOK. Text in English. 1995. a. **Document type:** *Directory, Trade.*
Formerly (until 1997): Official European Logistics Association Yearbook (1357-6305)
—**CCC.**
Published by: European Logistics Association, Kunstlaan 19 Ave des Arts, Brussels, 1210, Belgium. TEL 32-2-2300211, FAX 32-2-2308123, ela@elalog.org, http://www.elalog.org.

388 DEU ISSN 1860-5923
HD38.5
LOGISTICS JOURNAL. NICHT-REFERIERTE VEROEFFENTLICHUNGEN. Text in English, German. 2004. irreg. free (effective 2011). **Document type:** *Journal, Academic/Scholarly.*
Media: Online - full text.
Indexed: TM.
Published by: Wissenschaftliche Gesellschaft fuer Technische Logistik (W G T L), Holzgartenstrasse 15B, Stuttgart, 70174, Germany. TEL 49-0711-1213770, http://www.wgtl.de. Ed. Christoph Vornholt.

388.31 USA ISSN 1540-3890
HE1
LOGISTICS MANAGEMENT. Abbreviated title: L M(Logistics Management). (Includes 2 bound-in bimonthlies: International Shipping; Warehousing and Distribution) Text in English. 1997. m. (Plus annual directory). free to qualified personnel. adv. illus.; tr.lit. back issues avail. **Document type:** *Magazine, Trade.* **Description:** Covers supply chain management, transportation, logistics and distribution of materials, products and equipment.
Formerly (until Jun.2002): Logistics Management & Distribution Report (1098-7355); Which was formed by the merger (1996-1997): Logistics Management (1089-537X); Which was formerly (until 1996): Traffic Management (0041-0691); (1992-1997): Distribution (1066-8489); Which was formerly (until 1992): Chilton's Distribution (1057-9710); (until 1986): Chilton's Distribution for Traffic and Transportation Decision Makers (0273-6721); (until 1980): Chilton's Distribution (0195-7244); (until 1979): Chilton's Distribution Worldwide (0193-3248); (until 1977): Distribution Worldwide (0886-3512); (until 1972): Chilton's Distribution Worldwide (0886-3237); (until 1970): Distribution Worldwide (0012-3951); (until 1969): Distribution Manager (0196-7290); (until 1967): Physical Distribution Manager; (until 1966): Distribution Age (0734-256X); (until 1945): D and W (0734-2586); (until 1937): Distribution & Warehousing (0734-4562); (until 1920): Transfer & Storage (0734-2527); (until 1915): Team Owners Review
Related titles: Microform ed.: (from PQC); Online - full text ed.
Indexed: A09, A10, A12, A13, A14, A15, A17, A22, A26, ABIn, ASFA, B01, B02, B03, B04, B06, B07, B08, B09, B11, B15, B17, B18, BPI, BPIA, BRD, BusI, C12, CA, CLT&T, CWI, DPD, E08, ESPM, G04, G06, G07, G08, HRIS, I05, Inspec, LogistBibl, ManagCont, P48, P51, P52, P53, P54, PQC, S09, SRI, T&II, T02, V02, V03, V04, W01, W02, W03, W05.
—BLDSC (5292.317700), CIS, IE, Ingenta, Linda Hall. **CCC.**
Published by: E H Publishing, Inc., 111 Speen St, Ste 200, PO Box 989, Framingham, MA 01701. TEL 508-663-1500, 800-375-8015, FAX 508-663-1599, info@ehpub.com, http://www.ehpub.com. adv.: B&W page USD 11,685, color page USD 13,985; trim 8.125 x 10.75. Circ: 74,060.

380.5 658 ZAF ISSN 1025-0492
LOGISTICS NEWS. Text in English. 1981. m. adv. illus. **Document type:** *Journal, Trade.* **Description:** Covers logistics, distribution & materials handling, for industry professionals and logistics executives.
Published by: Bolton Publications (Pty) Ltd., PO Box 966, Parklands, Johannesburg 2121, South Africa. TEL 27-11-8803520, FAX 27-11-8806574. Ed. Richard Proctor Sims. Adv. contact Kamal H Saad.

LOGISTIEK. *see* BUSINESS AND ECONOMICS—Management

LOGISTIEK TOTAAL. *see* BUSINESS AND ECONOMICS—Marketing And Purchasing

658.5 388.324 FIN ISSN 1238-6022
LOGISTIIKKA/LOGISTICS. Text in Finnish. 1996. 9/m. EUR 67 (effective 2005). adv. **Document type:** *Journal, Trade.* **Description:** Promotes the development of logistics by functioning as a link between all professionals in the field. Covers purchase, transport, equipment, production, forwarding and customs, storage, packing, marking, and labelling, contracting and legislative practice, environmental logistics, new products, and industry news.
Formed by the merger of (1991-1996): Materiaalitalous (1235-6204); Which was formerly (1984-1991): Suomen Materiaalitalous (0780-7368); (1993-1996): Kuljetus - Logistiikka (1237-2358); Which was formerly (1959-1993): Kuljetus (0023-5091)
Indexed: Inspec.
Published by: Suomen Logistiikkayhdistys/Finnish Association of Logistics, Saerkiniementie 3, Helsinki, 00210, Finland. TEL 358-9-6963743, FAX 358-9-177675, logy@logy.fi. Ed. Kari Litja. Adv. contact Juhani Piipponen. B&W page EUR 1,680, color page EUR 1,630; trim 297 x 210. Circ: 6,200.

LOGISTIK-JOURNAL. *see* MACHINERY

LOGISTIK UND FOERDERTECHNIK. *see* BUSINESS AND ECONOMICS—Production Of Goods And Services

388 RUS ISSN 2219-7222
LOGISTIKA. Text in Russian. 1997. q. RUR 2,400 domestic (effective 2011). **Document type:** *Magazine, Trade.*
Related titles: Online - full text ed.
Indexed: RefZh.
Published by: Agenstvo Market Gaid, ul Ibragimova, dom 31, korpus 47, Moscow, 105318, Russian Federation. TEL 7-499-3902093, FAX 7-495-6518255, info@mg-agency.com, http://www.mg-agency.com. Ed. Mikhail Vasil'yev. Circ: 6,000.

LOGISTIKMANAGER; Praxis-Werkzeuge und Know-how fuer Logistik-Profis. *see* BUSINESS AND ECONOMICS—Production Of Goods And Services

LOGISTIKUNTERNEHMEN AKTUELL. *see* BUSINESS AND ECONOMICS—Production Of Goods And Services

388 DEU ISSN 1862-7250
LOGISTRA. Text in German. 1989. 10/yr. EUR 98; EUR 49 to students; EUR 12 newsstand/cover (effective 2010). adv. **Document type:** *Magazine, Trade.*
Formerly (until 2004): Eurocargo (0936-3033)
Published by: Huss-Verlag GmbH, Joseph-Dollinger-Bogen 5, Munich, 80807, Germany. TEL 49-89-323910, FAX 49-89-32391416, management@huss-verlag.de, http://www.huss-verlag.de. Ed. Tobias Schweikl. Adv. contact Michaela Pech. Circ: 14,300 (paid).

388 GBR ISSN 1756-025X
LONDON ANALYTICS RESEARCH JOURNAL. Text in English. 2005. s-a. free. **Document type:** *Journal, Trade.*
Published by: London Analytics Ltd., 3 Queens House, 175 S Lambeth Rd, London, SW8 1QS, United Kingdom. enquiries@londonanalytics.info.

914.210025 GBR ISSN 1468-9855
THE LONDON TAXI DRIVER'S HANDBOOK. Text in English. 1999. s-a. GBP 7.99 per issue (effective 2007). **Document type:** *Handbook/Manual/Guide, Trade.* **Description:** Designed to be a working tool for the London cab driver. Helps to find a small hotel or a city livery company, etc.
Published by: Fever Publishing Co., 43 Silk Mill Rd, Watford, Herts WD19 4TW, United Kingdom. TEL 44-1923-445242.

LONDON TRAVELWATCH. ANNUAL REVIEW. *see* TRAVEL AND TOURISM

363.12514 362.88 USA
MADDVOCATE; a magazine for victims and their advocates. Text in English. 1988. s-a. free. **Description:** Provides a forum where bereaved and injured victims of crime and those who advocate for them can share ideas, insights and incentives for emotional, physical and justice-oriented healing.
Published by: Mothers Against Drunk Driving, 511 E John Carpenter Fwy, Ste 700, Irving, TX 75062. TEL 214-744-6233, FAX 972-869-2206. Ed. Stephanie Foagge. R&P Stephanie Frogge. Circ: 40,000.

MAINE CRIMES, CRIMINAL CODE, MOTOR VEHICLES AND RELATED STATUTES. *see* LAW—Criminal Law

388.04409595 GBR ISSN 1752-5950
MALAYSIA FREIGHT TRANSPORT REPORT. Text in English. 2006. q. EUR 820, USD 1,030 combined subscription (print & email eds.) (effective 2010). **Document type:** *Report, Trade.* **Description:** Provides industry professionals and strategists, sector analysts, investors, trade associations and regulatory bodies with independent forecasts and competitive intelligence on the Malaysian freight transport and logistics industry.
Related titles: E-mail ed.
Indexed: A15, ABIn, B02, B15, B17, B18, G04, I05, P48, P51, P52, PQC.
Published by: Business Monitor International Ltd., Senator House, 85 Queen Victoria St, London, EC4V 4AB, United Kingdom. TEL 44-20-72480468, FAX 44-20-72480467, subs@businessmonitor.com.

388 MYS
MALAYSIA LOGISTICS DIRECTORY. Text in English. a. USD 30 per issue (effective 2008). **Document type:** *Directory, Trade.*
Published by: Marshall Cavendish (Malaysia) Sdn Bhd (Subsidiary of: Times Publishing Group), Bangunan Times Publishing, Lot 46 Subang Hi-Tech Industrial Park, Batu Tiga, 40000 Shah Alam, Selangor Darul Ehsan, Malaysia. TEL 603-5628-6888, FAX 603-5636-9688, bizinfo@my.marshallcavendish.com, http://www.marshallcavendish.com/.

388.041 USA
MANUAL ON UNIFORM TRAFFIC CONTROL DEVICES. Abbreviated title: M U T C D. Text in English. 1971. irreg., latest 2009. **Document type:** *Handbook/Manual/Guide, Government.* **Description:** Defines the standards used by road managers nationwide to install and maintain traffic control devices on all public streets, highways, bikeways, and private roads open to public traffic.
Related titles: Online - full text ed.: free (effective 2011).
Published by: U.S. Federal Highway Administration (Subsidiary of: U.S. Department of Transportation), 1200 New Jersey Ave, SE, Washington, DC 20590. TEL 202-366-4000, execsecretariat.fhwa@fhwa.dot.gov, http://www.fhwa.dot.gov.

388 ESP ISSN 0025-2646
MANUTENCION Y ALMACENAJE; revista de logistica. Text in Spanish. 1962. m. EUR 203.45 domestic; EUR 275 foreign (effective 2009). adv. bk.rev. illus.; tr.lit. Supplement avail.; back issues avail.
Document type: *Magazine, Trade.* **Description:** Covers new products, technology and solutions for the logistics of production and distribution.
Formerly (until 1964): Manejo de Materiales (0211-3821)
Related titles: ◆ Supplement(s): Anuario Manutencion y Almacenaje.
Published by: (Federation Europeenne de la Manutention, Comite Nacional Espanol), Tecnipublicaciones Espana, S.L., Avda de Manoteras 44, 3a Planta, Madrid, 28050, Spain. TEL 34-91-2972000, FAX 34-91-2972154, tp@tecnipublicaciones.com.

343.093 USA
MARYLAND MOTOR VEHICLE LAWS ANNOTATED. Text in English. a. (w/ CD), latest 2002. USD 75 (effective 2003). **Description:** Provides access to comprehensive coverage of Maryland criminal and motor vehicle law.
Related titles: Diskette ed.: USD 49.95.
Published by: Michie Company (Subsidiary of: LexisNexis North America), 701 E Water St, Charlottesville, VA 22902. TEL 434-972-7600, 800-446-3410, FAX 434-972-7677, customer.support@lexisnexis.com, http://www.michie.com.

343.093 USA
THE MARYLAND VEHICLE LAW. Text in English. irreg. (in 1 vol.), latest 2007. USD 38 combined subscription per issue (print & CD-ROM eds.) (effective 2008). 783 p./no.; **Document type:** *Monographic series, Trade.* **Description:** Contains statutes dealing with the Motor Vehicle Administration, accidents and accident reports, and rules of the road.
Related titles: CD-ROM ed.; Diskette ed.
Published by: Michie Company (Subsidiary of: LexisNexis North America), 701 E Water St, Charlottesville, VA 22902. TEL 434-972-7600, 800-446-3410, FAX 434-972-7677, customer.support@lexisnexis.com, http://www.michie.com.

380.5 MEX
MAS CAMINOS; por un sistema integral de transportes. Text in Spanish. 1970. q. free. adv. charts; illus. **Document type:** *Bulletin.*
Formerly (until Dec. 1990): Caminos (0008-2236)
Indexed: DokStr.
Published by: Asociacion Mexicana de Caminos, Tiber 103, 3o piso, Mexico City, DF 06500, Mexico. TEL 207-46-60. Ed. Hector Arvizu Hernandez.

380.5 USA ISSN 0364-3484
HE4201
MASS TRANSIT; better transit through better management. Abbreviated title: M T. Text in English. 1974. 8/yr. USD 59 domestic; USD 85 in Canada & Mexico; USD 120 elsewhere; free to qualified personnel (effective 2009). adv. bk.rev. illus. Supplement avail.; back issues avail.; reprints avail. **Document type:** *Magazine, Trade.* **Description:** Focuses on the people who manage the business and their successful management practices.
Related titles: Online - full text ed.: ISSN 2150-413X. free (effective 2009).
Indexed: A05, A09, A10, A15, A22, A26, ABIn, AIAP, AS&TA, AS&TI, B02, B03, B04, B10, B11, B15, B17, B18, BPI, BRD, BrRB, C10, DokStr, E08, EIP, G04, G06, G07, G08, HRIS, I05, ISR, P26, P48, P51, P52, P54, PQC, S09, S22, T&II, T02, T03, V03, V04, W01, W02, W03, W05.
—CIS, IE, Infotrieve, Ingenta. **CCC.**
Published by: Cygnus Business Media, Inc., 1233 Janesville Ave, PO Box 803, Fort Atkinson, WI 53538. TEL 920-563-6388, 800-547-7377, FAX 920-563-1702, http://www.cygnusb2b.com. Ed. Fred Jandt TEL 920-563-1688. Pub. John Hollenhorst TEL 920-563-1650. Adv. contact Sara-Emily Steadman. B&W page USD 5,955, color page USD 7,230; trim 7.875 x 10.75. Circ: 21,206.

MASSACHUSETTS MOTOR VEHICLE AND TRAFFIC LAWS. *see* LAW

MATERIAL FLOW. *see* MACHINERY

380.5 USA ISSN 2155-1685
MATERIAL HANDLING NETWORK; the magazine for international material handling. Text in English. 1982. m. USD 73 in North America; USD 165 elsewhere (effective 2010). adv. 160 p./no.; **Document type:** *Magazine, Trade.* **Description:** Covers news, manufacturers, new products, feature stories and people profiles.
Formerly: Network
Published by: WoodwardBizMedia (Subsidiary of: Woodward Communications Inc.), 2407 Washington Rd, Washington, IL 61571. TEL 309-699-4431, 800-447-6901, FAX 309-698-0801, sales@woodwardbizmedia.com, http://www.wcinet.com/.

621.86 DEU ISSN 0170-334X
MATERIALFLUSS; das Fachmagazin fuer den Logistikleiter. Text in German. 1970. 9/yr. EUR 108 domestic; EUR 128 foreign; EUR 15 newsstand/cover (effective 2011). adv. bk.rev. illus. **Document type:** *Magazine, Trade.* **Description:** Aimed at managers and decision makers in the industry and trade who have responsibility for the planning, organization and implementation of logistical processes, and the management of the whole logistic chain.
Related titles: ◆ Supplement(s): Materialfluss. Markt. ISSN 1613-8279.
Indexed: TM.
—IE, Infotrieve. **CCC.**
Published by: Verlag Moderne Industrie AG & Co. KG, Justus-von-Liebig-Str 1, Landsberg, 86899, Germany. TEL 49-8191-1250, FAX 49-8191-125211, info@mi-verlag.de, http://www.mi-verlag.de. Ed. Leo Breu. Adv. contact Hedwig Michl. B&W page EUR 4,580, color page EUR 5,880; trim 178 x 257. Circ: 19,773 (paid and controlled).

658.7 380.5 CAN ISSN 0025-5343
MATERIALS MANAGEMENT & DISTRIBUTION; Canada's supply chain magazine. Abbreviated title: M M & D. Variant title: Bar Code Quarterly. Text in English. 1956. m. adv. bk.rev. charts; illus.; stat.; tr.lit. index. **Document type:** *Magazine, Trade.* **Description:** Provides a solution oriented editorial approach to the movement, storage and control of materials, products and information.
Former titles (until 1970): Materials Handling in Canada (0315-7377); (until 1959): Materials Handling in Canadian Industry (0380-0113)
Related titles: Microfiche ed.: (from MML); Microform ed.: (from MML); Online - full text ed.
Indexed: A15, ABIn, C03, CBCABus, CBPI, Inspec, P10, P49, P52, P53, P54, PQC.
—CIS. **CCC.**
Published by: Business Information Group, 80 Valleybrook Dr., Toronto, ON M3B 2S9, Canada. TEL 416-442-5600, FAX 416-510-5140, orders@businessinformationgroup.ca, http://www.businessinformationgroup.ca. Ed. Michael Power TEL 416-442-5600 ext 3259. Pub. Emily Atkins TEL 416-510-5130. Adv. contact Dorothy Jakovina TEL 416-442-5600 ext 6899. Circ: 19,500.

388 USA
MCTRANS; moving technology. Text in English. 19??. s-a. free (effective 2010). **Document type:** *Newsletter, Academic/Scholarly.* **Description:** Updates and lists new and improved U.S. government highway transportation and transit software.
Related titles: Online - full text ed.
Published by: University of Florida, Department of Civil and Coastal Engineering, PO Box 116580, Gainesville, FL 32611. TEL 352-392-9537, khh@ce.ufl.edu, http://www.ce.ufl.edu/.

MERGENT PUBLIC UTILITY & TRANSPORTATION MANUAL. *see* PUBLIC ADMINISTRATION

388 RUS
METRO. GAZETA. Text in Russian. 3/w. USD 75 in United States.
Published by: Gazeta Metro, Ul. Krasnaya Presnya 1, Moscow, 123242, Russian Federation. TEL 7-095-2524405, FAX 7-095-2524425. Ed. Vladimir Yevstaf'ev. Circ: 500,000. **Dist. by:** East View Information Services, 10601 Wayzata Blvd, Minneapolis, MN 55305. TEL 952-252-1201, 800-477-1005, FAX 952-252-1202, info@eastview.com, http://www.eastview.com.

380.5 USA
HE5601
METRO MAGAZINE. Text in English. 1904. 10/yr. USD 40 domestic; USD 60 in Canada & Mexico; USD 100 elsewhere (effective 2008). adv. charts; illus.; stat. back issues avail.; reprints avail. **Document type:** *Magazine, Trade.* **Description:** Covers both public transit systems and private bus operators, addresses topics such as funding mechanisms, procurement, rolling stock maintenance, privatization, risk management and sustainability.
Former titles: Metro (Torrance) (1098-0083); (until 1994): Metro Magazine (1057-8196); (until 1985): Metro (0162-6221); (until 1974): Metropolitan (0026-1467)
Related titles: Online - full text ed.
Indexed: AIAP, B02, B12, B15, B17, B18, F01, F02, G04, G06, G07, G08, HRIS, I05, P16, P48, P53, P54, PQC, SRI.
—Ingenta.
Published by: Bobit Business Media, 3520 Challenger St, Torrance, CA 90503. TEL 310-533-2400, FAX 310-533-2500, order@bobit.com, http://www.bobit.com. Eds. Alex Roman, Janna Starcic. Pub. Frank DiGiacomo TEL 856-596-0999. adv.: color page USD 6,780, B&W page USD 5,585; trim 7.875 x 10.75. Circ: 20,616 (controlled).

388 FRA ISSN 1955-9003
METRO TRAMWAY MAGAZINE. Text in French. 2005. q. **Document type:** *Magazine, Consumer.*
Published by: Metro-Tramway Magazine, Palais du Pharo, 58 Bd. Charles Livon, Marseille, 13007, France.

388.0440972 GBR ISSN 1752-5969
MEXICO FREIGHT TRANSPORT REPORT. Text in English. 2006. q. EUR 820, USD 1,030 combined subscription (print & email eds.) (effective 2010). **Document type:** *Report, Trade.* **Description:** Provides industry professionals and strategists, sector analysts, investors, trade associations and regulatory bodies with independent forecasts and competitive intelligence on the Mexican freight transport and logistics industry.
Related titles: E-mail ed.
Published by: Business Monitor International Ltd., Senator House, 85 Queen Victoria St, London, EC4V 4AB, United Kingdom. TEL 44-20-72480468, FAX 44-20-72480467, subs@businessmonitor.com.

343.093 USA ISSN 1536-5786
KFA297.A29
MICHIE'S ALABAMA MOTOR VEHICLE LAWS ANNOTATED WITH COMMENTARIES. Text in English. a., latest 2007. USD 43 combined subscription (print & CD-ROM eds.) (effective 2008). 300 p./no.; **Document type:** *Handbook/Manual/Guide, Trade.* **Description:** Provides access to motor vehicle law, and many related statutes that law enforcement professionals and trial attorneys need most often.
Formerly: Michie's Alabama Motor Vehicle Laws Annotated
Related titles: CD-ROM ed.; Diskette ed.: USD 49.95.
Published by: Michie Company (Subsidiary of: LexisNexis North America), 701 E Water St, Charlottesville, VA 22902. TEL 434-972-7600, 800-446-3410, FAX 434-972-7677, customer.support@lexisnexis.com, http://www.michie.com.

MICHIGAN MOTOR VEHICLE LAWS; with uniform traffic code. *see* LAW

MINI AUTO. *see* HOBBIES

MINI-STORAGE MESSENGER; the original voice of the self storage industry. *see* BUSINESS AND ECONOMICS—Domestic Commerce

MINNESOTA CRIMES, VEHICLES AND RELATED STATUTES. *see* LAW—Criminal Law

MISSISSIPPI CRIMES, VEHICLES, TRAFFIC REGULATIONS AND RELATED STATUTES. *see* LAW

MISSOURI CRIME AND PUNISHMENT, VEHICLES & RELATED STATUTES. *see* LAW

380.5 DEU
MOBILOGISCH!; Oekologie - Politik - Bewegung. Text in German. 1980. q. EUR 18; EUR 4.50 newsstand/cover (effective 2008). adv. bk.rev. bibl.; illus.; stat. back issues avail. **Document type:** *Magazine, Consumer.*
Former titles (until 2003): Informationdienst Verkehr (0931-1688); (until 1986): Informationsdienst Verkehr des Arbeitskreises Verkehr und Umwelt (0930-5599); (until 1985): Informationsdienst Verkehr des Arbeitskreises Verkehr (0174-3198)
Published by: Arbeitskreis Verkehr und Umwelt e.V. (Umkehr), Exerzierstr 20, Berlin, 13357, Germany. TEL 49-30-4927473, FAX 49-30-4927972, info@umkehr.de, http://www.umkehr.de. Circ: 1,400.

380.52 NOR ISSN 0802-5193
MODERNE TRANSPORT; logistikk i praksis. Text in Norwegian. 1989. 10/yr. NOK 280. adv. **Document type:** *Magazine, Trade.* **Description:** Covers logistics and transport. Also focuses on forwarding, warehousing, materials handling and packaging.
Formed by the merger of (1987-1989): Moderne Materialhaandtering (0801-5228); (1987-1989): Moderne Biltransport (0801-5384); Both superseded in part (1968-1986): Moderne Transport (0332-6128); Which was formerly (until 1970): Transport og Lager (0801-5678)
—**CCC.**
Published by: Bjoergu AS, Sofiemyrveien 6 E, PO Box 11, Kolbotn, 1411, Norway. TEL 47-66-822121, FAX 47-66-822120, bjorgu@bjorgu.no, http://www.bjorgu.no. Ed. Bjoern Eilert Eriksen. Adv. contact Finn Egen Mobaek TEL 47-66-822126. Circ: 9,164.

645 DEU ISSN 0047-780X
DER MOEBELSPEDITEUR. Text in German. 1946. fortn. EUR 177.50 (effective 2010). adv. **Document type:** *Magazine, Trade.*
—**CCC.**
Published by: (Arbeitsgemeinschaft Moebeltransport Bundesverband e.V.), Brandeis Verlag und Medien GmbH & Co. KG, Schulstr 53, Hattersheim, 65795, Germany. TEL 49-6190-800900, FAX 49-6190-800910, info@brandeisweb.de, http://www.brandeisweb.de. Pub. Eckhard Weber. adv.: color page EUR 1,380, B&W page EUR 840; trim 185 x 260. Circ: 1,094 (paid and controlled).

LE MONDE DU CAMPING CAR. *see* TRAVEL AND TOURISM

MONTANA CRIMES, CRIMINAL PROCEDURE, MOTOR VEHICLES & RELATED STATUTES. *see* LAW—Criminal Law

341 NLD
MONTREAL CONVENTION. Text in English. 1992. 2-3/yr.), base vol. plus irreg. updates. looseleaf. USD 297 (effective 2009). **Description:** Detailed article by article commentary of the Warsaw Convention as amended by the Hague Protocol (1955) and successor instruments. Includes historical material, international case law and significant journal articles relating to transport law.
Formerly (until 2006): Warsaw Convention
Published by: Kluwer Law International (Subsidiary of: Aspen Publishers, Inc.), PO Box 316, Alphen aan den Rijn, 2400 AH, Netherlands. TEL 31-172-641562, FAX 31-172-641555, sales@kluwerlaw.com, http://www.kluwerlaw.com. Eds. Elmar Giemulla, Ronald Schmid.

388 NZL ISSN 1177-1569
MOTIVATE; New Zealand's leading transportation newsletter. Text in English. 2005. q. free (effective 2009). **Document type:** *Newsletter, Trade.* **Description:** Covers the development of transport policy and the Ministry activities.
Related titles: Online - full text ed.: ISSN 1178-6884.
Published by: Ministry of Transport, PO Box 3175, Wellington, New Zealand. TEL 64-4-4721253, FAX 64-4-4733697, info@transport.govt.nz.

MOTOR CARAVAN. *see* SPORTS AND GAMES—Outdoor Life

MOTOR CARAVANNER. *see* SPORTS AND GAMES—Outdoor Life

363.12 658.31244 USA ISSN 1092-3101
MOTOR CARRIER SAFETY REPORT. Text in English. 1974. m. looseleaf. USD 189; USD 249 combined subscription (print & online eds.) (effective 2008). back issues avail. **Document type:** *Newsletter, Trade.* **Description:** Contains articles on transport-related topics like alcohol and drug testing, driver training, enforcement, and more.
Related titles: Online - full text ed.: USD 239 (effective 2008).
—**CCC.**
Published by: J.J. Keller & Associates, Inc., 3003 W Breezewood Ln, PO Box 368, Neenah, WI 54957. TEL 877-564-2333, FAX 800-727-7516, kellersoft@jjkeller.com. Ed. Daren B Hansen.

388.322 USA ISSN 0739-117X
HE5601
MOTOR COACH AGE. Abbreviated title: M C A. Text in English. 1948. q. free to members (effective 2010). illus. 30 p./no.; back issues avail.; reprints avail. **Document type:** *Magazine, Consumer.* **Description:** Features information on classic and contemporary motor coaches.
Indexed: HRIS.
Published by: Motor Bus Society, Inc, PO Box 261, Paramus, NJ 07653. info@motorbussociety.org. Ed. Eli Bail.

MOTOR INDUSTRY BARGAINING COUNCIL CONSOLIDATED AGREEMENTS. *see* LAW

343.093 USA
MOTOR VEHICLE ACCIDENT RECONSTRUCTION AND CAUSE ANALYSIS. Text in English. irreg. (in 1 vol.), latest 1999, 5th ed. USD 146 per vol. (effective 2008). Supplement avail. **Document type:** *Monographic series, Trade.* **Description:** Translates engineering principles and equations used by experts into physical concepts easily understood by lawyers, jurors, claims adjusters, and investigating officers.
Related titles: Online - full text ed.
Published by: Michie Company (Subsidiary of: LexisNexis North America), 701 E Water St, Charlottesville, VA 22902. TEL 434-972-7600, 800-446-3410, FAX 434-972-7677, customer.support@lexisnexis.com, http://www.michie.com. Ed. Rudolf Limpert.

343.093 USA ISSN 1537-1549
MOTOR VEHICLE LAWS OF NORTH CAROLINA. Text in English. a., latest 2007. USD 40 combined subscription (print & CD-ROM eds.) (effective 2008). 1004 p./no.; Supplement avail. **Document type:** *Handbook/Manual/Guide, Trade.* **Description:** Contains information about current North Carolina motor vehicle law.
Related titles: CD-ROM ed.
Published by: Michie Company (Subsidiary of: LexisNexis North America), 701 E Water St, Charlottesville, VA 22902. TEL 434-972-7600, 800-446-3410, FAX 434-972-7677, customer.support@lexisnexis.com, http://www.michie.com.

MOTOR VEHICLE LAWS OF VERMONT. *see* LAW

388 AUS ISSN 1833-0347
MOTOR VEHICLE REPAIR INDUSTRY AUTHORITY. ANNUAL REPORT. Text in English. 1982. a. free (effective 2009). back issues avail. **Document type:** *Report, Trade.*
Formerly (until 2003): Motor Vehicle Repair Industry Council. Annual Report
Media: Online - full text.
Published by: New South Wales. Motor Vehicle Repair Industry Authority, PO Box 972, Parramatta, NSW 2124, Australia. TEL 61-2-98950111, FAX 61-2-98950222, http://www.fairtrading.nsw.gov.au.

380.5 340 CAN ISSN 0709-5341
KE2112.A45
MOTOR VEHICLE REPORTS (4TH SERIES). Text in English. 1979. 8/yr. CAD 235 domestic; USD 199.15 foreign (effective 2005). adv. **Description:** Features decisions in motor vehicle law from all Canadian jurisdictions. Covers cases on Criminal Code motor vehicle offences including alcohol-related offences and Charter of Rights defences, Highway Traffic Act offences, civil actions relating to motor vehicles and registration and licensing issues.
Indexed: ICLPL.
—**CCC.**
Published by: Carswell (Subsidiary of: Thomson Reuters Corp.), One Corporate Plz, 2075 Kennedy Rd, Toronto, ON M1T 3V4, Canada. TEL 416-609-8000, 800-387-5164, FAX 416-298-5094, carswell.customerrelations@thomson.com, http://www.carswell.com. Ed. Murray D Segal. Adv. contact Mariam Lalani TEL 416-298-5050.

388.322 USA
MOTORCOACH MARKETER. Text in English. 1985. a. adv. **Document type:** *Directory, Trade.* **Description:** Lists bus and tour operators and suppliers of bus products and services.
Published by: (American Bus Association), Tom Jackson & Associates, Inc., 223 8th Ave N, Nashville, TN 37203-3513. TEL 615-242-7747, FAX 615-259-2042. Circ: 5,500.

388 AUS
MOTORCYCLE GUIDE. Text in English. 1973. q. AUD 275 (effective 2008). adv. **Document type:** *Handbook/Manual/Guide, Consumer.* **Description:** Provides information about motorcycles.
Former titles (until 1991): Glass's Motorcycle Guide; (until 1989): Glass's Dealers Guide. Motor Cycle Values
Published by: Glass' Guide Pty. Ltd., 48 La Trobe St, Melbourne, VIC 3000, Australia. TEL 61-3-96633009, FAX 61-3-96633049, customers@glassguide.com.au, http://www.glassguide.com.au. adv.: color page USD 100; trim 80 x 125.

380.5 296.7 JPN
MOTORCYCLE JAPAN; annual guide to Japan's motorcycle industry. Text in English. 1983. a. JPY 3,150 domestic; JPY 5,940 in Asia; JPY 6,080 elsewhere (effective 2000). adv. **Document type:** *Handbook/ Manual/Guide, Trade.* **Description:** Provides a print showcase of the current lineup of Japanese motorcycles built and sold worldwide. Includes a technical section, as well as a features section which discusses trends among the top 4 motorcycle companies, with related data and figures.
Published by: J A N Corporation, DIK Shinbashi Bldg, 415, 5-4 Shinbashi 6-chome, Minato-ku, Tokyo, 105-0004, Japan. TEL 81-3-3438-0361, FAX 81-3-3438-0362. Ed. Makio Sakurazawa. R&P, Adv. contact Hijiri Ito. B&W page JPY 150,000, color page JPY 350,000; trim 257 x 182. Circ: 3,880.

MOTORCYCLE SAFETY FOUNDATION. *see* SPORTS AND GAMES—Bicycles And Motorcycles

MOTORHOME; travel tech lifestyle for the RV enthusiast. *see* SPORTS AND GAMES—Outdoor Life

388.346 GBR ISSN 1363-8971
MOTORHOME MONTHLY. Text in English. 1996. m. GBP 15 (effective 2010). adv. illus. back issues avail. **Document type:** *Magazine, Consumer.* **Description:** Magazine covering all aspects of motorized recreational vehicles in Europe.
Former titles: Motor Caravan World (0142-0011); Motor Caravan Monthly
Related titles: Online - full text ed.: free (effective 2010).
Published by: Stone Leisure Ltd., Andrew House, Granville Rd, Sidcup, Kent DA14 4BN, United Kingdom. TEL 44-20-83026150, FAX 44-20-83002315, http://www.stoneleisure.com/. Ed. Robert C Griffiths. Adv. contact Stephanie Walker TEL 44-1332-874731.

388 AUS ISSN 1323-4595
MOTORING DIRECTIONS. Text in English. 1995. q. free. **Document type:** *Magazine, Consumer.* **Description:** Provides reports and articles on motoring. Includes related issues intended to generate debate among authorities in transportation.
Related titles: Online - full text ed.
Published by: Australian Automobile Association, 216 Northbourne Ave, Canberra, ACT 2601, Australia. TEL 61-2-62477311, FAX 61-2-62575320, aaa@aa.asn.au, http://www.aaa.asn.au/aaa.htm. Ed. Allan Yates. Circ: 2,000.

388 ITA ISSN 1120-415X
LA MOTORIZZAZIONE. Text in Italian. 1981. bi-w. **Document type:** *Magazine, Trade.*
Related titles: CD-ROM ed.: ISSN 1824-5471. 2002; Online - full text ed.: ISSN 1826-8757. 2006.
Published by: Edizioni Giuridico Amministrative e Formazione (E G A F), Via Filippo Guarini 2, Forli, 47100, Italy. TEL 39-0543-473347, FAX 39-0543-474133, gruppo@egaf.it, http://www.egaf.it.

388 ESP
MOTOTALLER. Text in Spanish. 1992. m. adv. back issues avail. **Document type:** *Magazine, Trade.*
Published by: BCV Reto, S.L., C. Consejo de Ciento No. 217, Entlo. 3a., Barcelona, 08011, Spain. TEL 34-93-4538162, FAX 34-93-4512836, barreto@intercom.es. Ed. Antonio Conde.

363.12 USA
MOVE MAGAZINE. Text in English. q. USD 26 (effective 1999).
Published by: American Association of Motor Vehicle Administrators, 4301 Wilson Blvd, Ste 400, Arlington, VA 22203. TEL 703-522-4200, FAX 703-522-1553. Pub. Kenneth Beam. R&P Melissa D Clague. Circ: 4,500.

388 USA ISSN 1932-4766
MOVING THROUGH HISTORY: TRANSPORTATION AND SOCIETY. Text in English. 2006. irreg., latest 2008. USD 49.95, GBP 34.95 per issue (effective 2010). back issues avail. **Document type:** *Monographic series, Academic/Scholarly.*
Published by: Praeger Publishers (Subsidiary of: Greenwood Publishing Group Inc.), 88 Post Rd W, Westport, CT 06881. TEL 800-368-6868, tech.support@greenwood.com, http://www.greenwood.com. Ed. Guillaume de Syon.

380.5 USA ISSN 1053-1203
N A F A FLEET EXECUTIVE; the magazine for vehicle management. Variant title: Fleet Executive. Text in English. 1957. bi-m. USD 48 to non-members (effective 2007). adv. bk.rev. illus.; stat. index. back issues avail. **Document type:** *Magazine, Trade.* **Description:** Focus is paid to cars, van and light-duty truck management in U.S. and Canadaian corporations, government agencies and utilities. Editorial emphasis is on improving job skills, productivity and professionalism; legislation and regulation; alternative fuels; safety; interviews with prominent industry personalities; technology; Association news; public service fleet management; and light-duty truck fleet management.
Formerly: N A F A Bulletin
Related titles: Microfiche ed.: (from CIS); Online - full text ed.
Indexed: CLT&T, HRIS, SRI.
Published by: National Association of Fleet Administrators, Inc., 100 Wood Ave S, Ste 310, Iselin, NJ 08830-2716. TEL 732-494-8100, FAX 732-494-6789, info@nafa.org, http://www.nafa.org. Ed. Carolann McLoughlin. Circ: 4,000 (paid and controlled).

380.5 USA
N A F A FLEETFOCUS. Text in English. 1974. bi-w. **Document type:** *Newsletter.* **Description:** Features timely legislative and association news, meeting and conference information and technological updates.
Formerly: N A F A Newsletter
Indexed: CLT&T, HRIS.
Published by: National Association of Fleet Administrators, Inc., 100 Wood Ave S, Ste 310, Iselin, NJ 08830-2716. TEL 732-494-8100, FAX 732-494-6789. Ed. Jessica Sypniewski. Pub. David Lefever.

380.5 USA
N F T A ANNUAL REPORT. Text in English. 1967. a. free. **Description:** Defines aims and goals of the NFTA, which are to maintain a transportation network for the benefit of the people of Western New York State. Reports on the NFTA's financial position.
Published by: Niagara Frontier Transportation Authority, 181 Ellicott St, Buffalo, NY 14205. TEL 716-855-7300, FAX 716-855-7657. Circ: 500.

363.72 USA
N O A C A NEWS; news about transportation and environmental planning. Text in English. 1969. q. free. back issues avail. **Document type:** *Newsletter.* **Description:** Contains news about current studies NOACA is involved withplans produced, new transportation or environmental policies, board actions, calender of events, board member biograaphies.
Related titles: Fax ed.
Published by: Northeast Ohio Areawide Coordinating Agency, 1299 Superior Avenue, Cleveland, OH 44114. TEL 216-241-2414, FAX 216-621-3024. Ed., R&P Cheryl Onesky TEL 216-241-2414 ext 221. Circ: 2,500.

380.5 DEU ISSN 0722-8287
DER NAHVERKEHR; Personen- und Gueterverkehr in Stadt und Region. Text in German. 1983. 10/yr. EUR 110; EUR 12 newsstand/cover (effective 2008). adv. bk.rev. **Document type:** *Magazine, Trade.*
Indexed: DokStr, IBR, IBZ, Inspec.
—BLDSC (6015.300960), IE, Infotrieve, Ingenta. **CCC.**
Published by: Alba Fachverlag GmbH und Co., Willstaetterstr 9, Duesseldorf, 40549, Germany. TEL 49-211-520130, FAX 49-211-5201328, braun@alba-verlag.de, http://www.alba-verlag.de. Ed. Lothar Kuttig. Adv. contact Beatrice van Dijk. B&W page EUR 2,145, color page EUR 2,985. Circ: 1,774 (paid and controlled).

380.5 DEU ISSN 0179-504X
NAHVERKEHRS NACHRICHTEN. Cover title: NaNa. Text in German. 1956. 3/m. EUR 276 (effective 2009). adv. bk.rev. **Document type:** *Bulletin, Trade.* **Description:** Provides information on all aspects of public transportation.
Published by: Alba Fachverlag GmbH und Co., Willstaetterstr 9, Duesseldorf, 40549, Germany. TEL 49-211-520130, FAX 49-211-5201328, braun@alba-verlag.de, http://www.alba-verlag.de. Ed. Wolfgang Bauchhenss. Adv. contact Beatrice van Dijk. B&W page EUR 2,755, color page EUR 3,995; trim 266 x 421. Circ: 1,604 (paid and controlled).

656 DEU ISSN 0342-9849
NAHVERKEHRS-PRAXIS. Text in German. 1953. 10/yr. EUR 50; EUR 37.50 to students; EUR 5.30 newsstand/cover (effective 2010). adv. **Document type:** *Magazine, Trade.*
Indexed: IBR, IBZ, RefZh.
Published by: Fachverlag Dr. H. Arnold GmbH, Siegburgstr 5-7, Dortmund, 44359, Germany. TEL 49-231-33690, FAX 49-231-336920. Ed. Gudrun Arnold-Schoenen. Adv. contact Martina Kaczmarek. Circ: 5,385 (paid).

388 DEU ISSN 1436-3739
NAHVERKEHRS-TASCHENBUCH. BERATER, INDUSTRIE, LIEFERANTEN. Variant title: NaTaBu - Berater, Industrie, Lieferanten. Text in German. 1960. a. (in 3 vols.). EUR 76.50 (effective 2008). adv. **Document type:** *Directory, Trade.*
Supersedes in part (in 1995): Nahverkehrs-Taschenbuch. Personenverkehr (0941-8865); Which was formerly (until 1991): Nahverkehrs-Taschenbuch (0171-824X)
Published by: Alba Fachverlag GmbH und Co., Willstaetterstr 9, Duesseldorf, 40549, Germany. TEL 49-211-520130, FAX 49-211-5201328, braun@alba-verlag.de, http://www.alba-verlag.de. adv.: B&W page EUR 1,130, color page EUR 1,880.

388 DEU ISSN 1436-3720
NAHVERKEHRS-TASCHENBUCH. VERKEHRSUNTERNEHMEN, VERKEHRSORGANISATION, VERBAENDE, BEHOERDEN, WISSENSCHAFT. Variant title: NaTaBu - Verkehrsunternehmen, Verkehrsorganisation, Verbaende, Behoerden, Wissenschaft. Text in German. 1960. a. EUR 82 (effective 2009). adv. **Document type:** *Directory, Trade.*
Supersedes in part (in 1995): Nahverkehrs-Taschenbuch. Personenverkehr (0941-8865); Which was formerly (until 1991): Nahverkehrs-Taschenbuch (0171-824X)
Published by: Alba Fachverlag GmbH und Co., Willstaetterstr 9, Duesseldorf, 40549, Germany. TEL 49-211-520130, FAX 49-211-5201328, braun@alba-verlag.de, http://www.alba-verlag.de. adv.: B&W page EUR 1,130, color page EUR 1,880. Circ: 2,641 (controlled).

388 DEU ISSN 1436-3747
NAHVERKEHRS-TASCHENBUCH. WER, WAS, WO IM NAHVERKEHR. Variant title: NaTaBu - Wer, Was, Wo im Nahverkehr. Text in German. 1960. a. adv. **Document type:** *Directory, Trade.*
Supersedes in part (in 1995): Nahverkehrs-Taschenbuch. Personenverkehr (0941-8865); Which was formerly (until 1991): Nahverkehrs-Taschenbuch (0171-824X)
Published by: Alba Fachverlag GmbH und Co., Willstaetterstr 9, Duesseldorf, 40549, Germany. TEL 49-211-520130, FAX 49-211-5201328, braun@alba-verlag.de, http://www.alba-verlag.de. adv.: B&W page EUR 1,130, color page EUR 1,880.

388.322 USA ISSN 0194-939X
TL232
NATIONAL BUS TRADER; the magazine of bus equipment for the United States and Canada. Text in English. 1977. m. USD 25 domestic; USD 30 foreign (effective 2007). adv. bk.rev. back issues avail. **Document type:** *Magazine, Trade.* **Description:** Covers integral design bus vehicles, primarily inter-city coaches.
Published by: National Bus Trader, Inc., 9698 W Judson Rd., Polo, IL 61064. TEL 815-946-2341, FAX 815-946-2347. Ed., Pub., R&P Larry Plachno. adv.: B&W page USD 990, color page USD 1,440. Circ: 5,800.

388 USA ISSN 1946-9705
TA1001
▼ **NATIONAL COOPERATIVE FREIGHT RESEARCH PROGRAM. RESEARCH RESULTS DIGEST.** Text in English. 2009. irreg., latest vol.1. USD 19 per issue (effective 2009). back issues avail. **Document type:** *Report, Trade.*
Related titles: Online - full text ed.: free (effective 2009).
—Linda Hall.
Published by: Transportation Research Board, 500 Fifth St, NW, Washington, DC 20001. TEL 202-334-3213, FAX 202-334-2519, TRBSales@nas.edu.

388 340 USA ISSN 1080-4781
KF5524
NATIONAL COOPERATIVE HIGHWAY RESEARCH PROGRAM. LEGAL RESEARCH DIGEST. Text in English. 1988. irreg. price varies. back issues avail. **Document type:** *Monographic series, Trade.*
Related titles: Online - full text ed.: free (effective 2011).
Indexed: HRIS.
—Linda Hall.
Published by: Transportation Research Board, National Cooperative Highway Research Program, 500 Fifth St, NW, Washington, DC 20001. TEL 202-334-2934, http://www.trb.org/NCHRP/Public/NCHRP.aspx.

388 USA
NATIONAL COOPERATIVE HIGHWAY RESEARCH PROGRAM. PROJECT REPORTS. Text in English. 19??. irreg. price varies. back issues avail. **Document type:** *Monographic series, Trade.*
Related titles: Online - full text ed.: free (effective 2011).
Published by: Transportation Research Board, National Cooperative Highway Research Program, 500 Fifth St, NW, Washington, DC 20001. TEL 202-334-2934, http://www.trb.org/NCHRP/Public/NCHRP.aspx.

388 USA
NATIONAL COOPERATIVE HIGHWAY RESEARCH PROGRAM. RESEARCH RESULTS DIGEST. Text in English. 19??. irreg. price varies. back issues avail. **Document type:** *Monographic series, Trade.*
Related titles: Online - full text ed.: free (effective 2011).
Published by: Transportation Research Board, National Cooperative Highway Research Program, 500 Fifth St, NW, Washington, DC 20001. TEL 202-334-2934, http://www.trb.org/NCHRP/Public/NCHRP.aspx.

388 USA ISSN 0547-5562
TE153
NATIONAL COOPERATIVE HIGHWAY RESEARCH PROGRAM. SUMMARY OF PROGRESS. Text in English. 1966. a., latest 2008. free (effective 2011). back issues avail. **Document type:** *Report, Government.*
Related titles: Online - full text ed.
Indexed: HRIS.
—Linda Hall.
Published by: Transportation Research Board, National Cooperative Highway Research Program, 500 Fifth St NW, Washington, DC 20001. TEL 202-334-2934, http://www.trb.org/NCHRP/Public/NCHRP.aspx.

388 USA
NATIONAL COOPERATIVE HIGHWAY RESEARCH PROGRAM. SYNTHESIS REPORTS. Text in English. 19??. irreg. price varies. back issues avail. **Document type:** *Monographic series, Trade.*
Related titles: Online - full text ed.: free (effective 2011).
Published by: Transportation Research Board, National Cooperative Highway Research Program, 500 Fifth St, NW, Washington, DC 20001. TEL 202-334-2934, http://www.trb.org/NCHRP/Public/NCHRP.aspx.

388 USA
NATIONAL COOPERATIVE HIGHWAY RESEARCH PROGRAM. WEB DOCUMENTS. Variant title: National Cooperative Highway Research Program. Web-Only Documents. Text in English. 19??. irreg. free (effective 2011). back issues avail. **Document type:** *Monographic series, Trade.*
Media: Online - full text.
Indexed: HRIS.
Published by: Transportation Research Board, National Cooperative Highway Research Program, 500 Fifth St, NW, Washington, DC 20001. TEL 202-334-2934, http://www.trb.org/NCHRP/Public/NCHRP.aspx.

NATIONAL CUSTOMS BROKERS & FORWARDERS ASSOCIATION OF AMERICA. MEMBERSHIP DIRECTORY. *see* BUSINESS AND ECONOMICS—Trade And Industrial Directories

THE NATIONAL CYCLE NETWORK ROUTE USER MONITORING REPORT TO THE END OF (YEAR). *see* SPORTS AND GAMES—Bicycles And Motorcycles

380.5 USA ISSN 0275-3286
HE5623.A45
NATIONAL HIGHWAY & AIRWAY CARRIERS & ROUTES. Text in English. 1941. s-a. USD 275 domestic; USD 315 foreign (effective 2000). adv. **Document type:** *Directory.* **Description:** Provides comprehensive information on carrier routes throughout North America, including company listings for LTL motor freight carriers, intermodal trucking, airline cargo companies, contract carriers, warehousing companies, refrigerated carriers, Canadian carriers, transportation brokers and freight forwarders, and truckload carriers.
Published by: National Highway Carriers Directory, Inc., PO Box 6099, Buffalo, IL 60089. TEL 847-634-0606, FAX 847-634-1026. Ed., Pub., R&P William J Ferreira. Adv. contact P Ferreira. B&W page USD 2,295, color page USD 5,000; trim 10.88 x 9.38. Circ: 5,000 (paid).

388 USA
NATIONAL INDUSTRIAL TRANSPORTATION LEAGUE. NOTICE. Text in English. 1936. w. membership only. adv. **Document type:** *Newsletter.* **Description:** Comprehensive information on domestic and international transportation issues.
Published by: National Industrial Transportation League, 1700 N Moore St, Ste 1900, Arlington, VA 22209-1904. TEL 703-524-5011, FAX 703-524-5017. Ed., R&P, Adv. contact Bill Clapper. Circ: 2,000 (controlled).

388 USA ISSN 1073-1652
TE220
NATIONAL RESEARCH COUNCIL. TRANSPORTATION RESEARCH BOARD. CONFERENCE PROCEEDINGS. Text in English. 1994. irreg., latest vol.47, 2010. back issues avail. **Document type:** *Proceedings, Government.*
Related titles: Online - full text ed.: free (effective 2010).
Indexed: HRIS.
—BLDSC (3409.770960), Linda Hall. **CCC.**
Published by: U.S. National Research Council, Transportation Research Board, The National Academies, 500 Fifth St, NW, Washington, DC 20001. TEL 202-334-3213, FAX 202-334-2519, TRBsales@nas.edu.

388 USA
NATIONAL RESEARCH COUNCIL. TRANSPORTATION RESEARCH BOARD. MILLENNIUM PAPERS. Text in English. 19??. irreg. back issues avail. **Document type:** *Monographic series, Trade.*
Related titles: Online - full text ed.: free (effective 2010).
Published by: U.S. National Research Council, Transportation Research Board, The National Academies, 500 Fifth St, NW, Washington, DC 20001. TEL 202-334-3213, FAX 202-334-2519, TRBsales@nas.edu.

388 USA
NATIONAL RESEARCH COUNCIL. TRANSPORTATION RESEARCH BOARD. RESEARCH PAYS OFF. Text in English. 19??. irreg., latest no.268, 2010. price varies. back issues avail. **Document type:** *Monographic series, Government.*
Related titles: Online - full text ed.: free (effective 2010).
Published by: U.S. National Research Council, Transportation Research Board, The National Academies, 500 Fifth St, NW, Washington, DC 20001. TEL 202-334-3213, FAX 202-334-2519, TRBsales@nas.edu.

363.12 USA
NATIONAL TRANSPORTATION SAFETY BOARD. REPORT. Text in English. 19??. irreg. free (effective 2011). back issues avail. **Document type:** *Report, Government.*
Related titles: Online - full text ed.
Published by: (U.S. National Transportation Safety Board), U.S. Department of Commerce, National Technical Information Service, 5301 Shawnee Rd, Alexandria, VA 22312. TEL 703-605-6000, info@ntis.gov, http://www.ntis.gov.

665.7 USA
TP350
NATURAL GAS FUELS. Text in English. 1992. bi-m. free to qualified personnel. adv. **Document type:** *Bulletin, Trade.* **Description:** Focuses on natural gas as a transportation fuel.
Published by: R P Publishing, Inc., 2696 S Colorado Blvd, Ste 595, Denver, CO 80222-5944. TEL 303-863-0521, FAX 303-863-1722, info@rppublishing.com. Ed. David Port. Pub. Frank Rowe. Adv. contact Todd Allen.

380.5 RUS
NAUCHNO-ISSLEDOVATEL'SKII INSTITUT TRANSPORTNOGO STROITEL'STVA. TRUDY. Variant title: Trudy O A O Ts N I I S. Text in Russian. 1977 (vol.106). q. **Document type:** *Journal, Academic/Scholarly.*
Formerly (until 199?): Vsesoyuznyi Nauchno-Issledovatel'skii Institut Transportnogo Stroitel'stva. Trudy
Indexed: ChemAb.
Published by: Nauchno-Isseldovatel'skii Institut Transportnogo Stroitel'stva/Research Insitute of Transport Construction, ul Kol'skaya, dom 1, Moscow, 129323, Russian Federation. TEL 7-095-1809386, FAX 7-095-1897261, mail@tsniis.com. Circ: 1,000.

388 RUS
NAUKA I TEKHNIKA V DOROZHNOI OTRASLI. Text in Russian. q. USD 65 in United States.
Published by: Izdatel'stvo Dorogi, Ul Shchepkina 11, Moscow, 129090, Russian Federation. TEL 7-095-2843189, FAX 7-095-2843838. Ed. V F Polyakov. **Dist. by:** East View Information Services, 10601 Wayzata Blvd, Minneapolis, MN 55305. TEL 952-252-1201, 800-477-1005, FAX 952-252-1202, info@eastview.com, http://www.eastview.com.

388 ITA
NAVIGAZIONE. MONOGRAFIE. Text in English, Italian. irreg. **Document type:** *Monographic series, Trade.*
Published by: Istituto Italiano di Navigazione, Via Cremona 15B, Rome, 00161, Italy. http://www.istitutoitalianonavigazione.org.

388 NLD ISSN 1875-421X
NEA NIEUWS. Text in Dutch. 1986. q.
Former titles (until 2006): NEA News (Nederlandse Editie) (1568-2129); (until 2000): NEA-Info (Nederlandse Editie) (1386-9426)
Published by: NEA Transportonderzoek en -Opleiding B.V., Postbus 276, Zoetermeer, 2700 AG, Netherlands. TEL 31-79-3222221, FAX 31-79-3222211, email@nea.nl, http://www.nea.nl.

NEBRASKA CRIMINAL AND TRAFFIC LAW MANUAL. *see* LAW—Criminal Law

388 NLD ISSN 0924-6584
NEDERLANDS VERVOER. Text in Dutch. 1990. 10/yr. EUR 68.75 domestic; EUR 96.90 foreign (effective 2009). adv. index. **Document type:** *Magazine, Trade.* **Description:** Covers the transport of persons, including public transportation, buses, coaches and taxicabs.
Formed by the merger of (1972-1990): Personenvervoer (0376-6772); (1959-1990): Nederlands Transport (0028-2219); Which was formerly (1950-1959): Transport (1570-6915)
Related titles: ♦ Supplement(s): TransportVisie. ISSN 1381-690X.
Indexed: KES.
—IE, Infotrieve.
Published by: Koninklijke Nederlands Vervoer, Postbus 19365, The Hague, 2500 CJ, Netherlands. TEL 31-70-3751751, FAX 31-70-3455853, knvmedia@knv.nl, postbus@knv.nl, http://www.knv.nl. Ed. Jos Haas. adv.: B&W page EUR 1,337, color page EUR 2,117; trim 210 x 297. Circ: 3,500.

796.60941 GBR ISSN 1750-1733
THE NETWORK. Text in English. 1996. q. **Document type:** *Magazine, Trade.*
Formerly (until 2005): Network News (1366-3828)
Related titles: Online - full text ed.: ISSN 1755-3652. 2005.
—CCC.
Published by: (National Cycle Network), Sustrans, 2 Cathedral Sq, College Green, Bristol, Avon BS1 5DD, United Kingdom. TEL 44-117-9268893, FAX 44-117-9294173, info@sustrans.org.uk.

380.15 DEU ISSN 0934-1307
NEUE ZEITSCHRIFT FUER VERKEHRSRECHT; Haftungs- und Versicherungsrecht, Straf- und Ordnungswidrigkeitenrecht, Verwaltungsrecht. Abbreviated title: NZV. Text in German. 1988. m. EUR 172; EUR 136 to students; EUR 16.40 newsstand/cover (effective 2011). adv. bk.rev. back issues avail. **Document type:** *Journal, Trade.*
Indexed: DIP, IBR, IBZ, RASB.
Published by: Verlag C.H. Beck oHG, Wilhelmstr 9, Munich, 80801, Germany. TEL 49-89-381890, FAX 49-89-38189398, abo.service@beck.de, http://www.beck.de. Circ: 2,600 (paid and controlled).

388 ESP
NEUMATICO Y TALLER. Text in Spanish. 1999. biennial. free (effective 2009). adv. **Document type:** *Trade.*
Formerly (until 2003): Fenacor Pneu
Published by: BCV Reto, S.L., C. Consejo de Ciento No. 217, Entlo. 3a., Barcelona, 08011, Spain. TEL 34-93-4538162, FAX 34-93-4512836, barreto@intercom.es, http://www.edicionesbcv.com/. Ed. Antonio Conde.

NEVADA CRIMES AND PUNISHMENTS, VEHICLES AND RELATED STATUTES. *see* LAW—Criminal Law

NEVADA CRIMINAL AND TRAFFIC LAW MANUAL. *see* LAW—Criminal Law

NEW JERSEY ADMINISTRATIVE CODE. TRANSPORTATION. *see* LAW

NEW JERSEY MOTOR VEHICLE AND TRAFFIC LAWS. *see* LAW

NEW MEXICO CRIMINAL AND TRAFFIC LAW MANUAL. *see* LAW—Criminal Law

NEW MEXICO CRIMINAL, VEHICLES AND RELATED STATUTES. *see* LAW

788.3 NZL ISSN 1175-1827
NEW ZEALAND 4 W D MAGAZINE. Text in English. 1996. m. NZD 89 domestic; NZD 140 in Australia; NZD 150 elsewhere (effective 2008). adv. **Document type:** *Magazine, Consumer.* **Description:** Aims to provide a wide range of information covering vehicle selection, accessories and upgrading, 4WD clubs and sport, lifestyle activites associated with 4WD, adventure and track stories and technical articles.
Indexed: A09, A10, A11, T02, V03, V04.
Published by: Adrenalin Publishing Ltd, 14C Vega Pl, North Shore City, 0754, New Zealand. TEL 64-9-4784771, FAX 64-9-4784779, http://www.adrenalin.co.nz/. Ed. John Oxley. Pubs. Cathy Parker, Yvonne Carter. Adv. contact Dan Prestige. B&W page NZD 1,070, color page NZD 2,370; 18.5 x 26.5.

363.12 NZL
NEW ZEALAND. LAND TRANSPORT NZ. ROAD SAFETY ISSUES. Text in English. 2001. a. **Document type:** *Journal, Trade.*
Formerly: New Zealand. Land Transport Safety Authority. Road Safety Issues (1175-897X)
Published by: New Zealand Transport Agency, Lambton Quay, PO Box 5084, Wellington, 6145, New Zealand. TEL 64-4-8945200, FAX 64-4-8943305, info@nzta.govt.nz, http://www.nzta.govt.nz/.

328 363.12 NZL ISSN 1173-1559
NEW ZEALAND. LAND TRANSPORT SAFETY AUTHORITY. RULES. Text in English. 1997. irreg. **Document type:** *Government.* **Description:** Includes the official rules and advisory updates of the Authority.
Published by: New Zealand Transport Agency, Lambton Quay, PO Box 5084, Wellington, 6145, New Zealand. TEL 64-4-8945200, FAX 64-4-8943305, info@nzta.govt.nz.

363.12 NZL ISSN 1174-6017
NEW ZEALAND ROAD SAFETY RESEARCH. Text in English. a. **Document type:** *Report, Trade.* **Description:** Includes all reported road safety research with a New Zealand component being undertaken or completed during the year under review.
Former titles (until 1997): Traffic Safety Research (1174-3301); (until 1995): Road Traffic Safety Research Council. Annual Report
Related titles: Online - full text ed.: ISSN 1178-4245.
Published by: Ministry of Transport, PO Box 3175, Wellington, New Zealand. TEL 64-4-4721253, FAX 64-4-4733697, info@transport.govt.nz.

388 NZL
NEW ZEALAND TRANSPORT AGENCY. FACTSHEET. Text in English. 200?. irreg. **Document type:** *Handbook/Manual/Guide, Trade.* **Description:** Provides information on transport safety, standards and processes.
Former titles (until Jul.2008): New Zealand. Land Transport NZ. Factsheet (1177-0759); (until 2005): N L T P Fact Sheet; (until 2002): N R P Factsheet
Published by: New Zealand Transport Agency, Lambton Quay, PO Box 5084, Wellington, 6145, New Zealand. TEL 64-4-8945200, FAX 64-4-8943305, info@nzta.govt.nz, http://www.nzta.govt.nz/.

388 NZL ISSN 1173-3756
NEW ZEALAND TRANSPORT AGENCY RESEARCH REPORT. Text in English. 1991. irreg., latest vol.301, 2006. price varies. **Document type:** *Monographic series.*
Former titles (until no.350, 2008): Land Transport New Zealand Research Report (1177-0600); (until 2005): Transfund New Zealand Research Report (1174-0574); (until 1997): Transit New Zealand Research Report (1170-9405)
Published by: New Zealand Transport Agency, Lambton Quay, PO Box 5084, Wellington, 6145, New Zealand. TEL 64-4-8945200, FAX 64-4-8943305, info@nzta.govt.nz, http://www.nzta.govt.nz/.

380.5 USA
NEWSLINE (EVANSTON). Text in English. s-a. **Document type:** *Newsletter.* **Description:** Newsletter covering Transportation Center research, executive education, graduate education, alumni news and placement, industry updates.
Indexed: CLT&T, HRIS.
Published by: Northwestern University, Transportation Center, 1936 Sheridan Rd, Evanston, IL 60208. TEL 847-491-7287, FAX 847-491-3090. Ed. Georgiana Johnson. Circ: 10,000.

388 AUS ISSN 0310-7477
TF122.V5
NEWSRAIL. Text in English. 1973. m. AUD 95 include membership; AUD 8.50 newsstand/cover (effective 2008). adv. back issues avail. **Document type:** *Magazine, Consumer.*
Formerly (until 1972): Divisional Diary
Related titles: Supplement(s): Members Newsletter.
Published by: Australian Railway Historical Society, Victoria Division, GPO Box 5177, Melbourne, VIC 3001, Australia. TEL 61-3-97645011, 300-220-220, FAX 61-3-97645056, sales@arhsvic.org.au. Ed., Adv. contact Geoff Peterson. Circ: 2,100.

380.52 658.788 NLD ISSN 0921-4593
NIEUWSBLAD TRANSPORT. Text in Dutch. 1987. w. EUR 418 (effective 2009). adv. bk.rev. back issues avail. **Document type:** *Newspaper, Trade.* **Description:** Covers transportation, distribution, export, and logistics.
Formed by the merger of (1980-1987): Vervoerskrant (0921-4607); Which incorporated (1977-1980): Aircargo Magazine (0016-6596); (1945-1987): Dagblad Scheepvaart (0169-099X)
Published by: NT Publishers B.V., Postbus 200, Rotterdam, 3000 AE, Netherlands. TEL 31-10-2801000, FAX 31-10-2801005, informatie@ntpublishers.nl, http://www.ntpublishers.nl. Ed. Donald Suidman. Circ: 6,000.

388.0440966905 GBR ISSN 1752-5977
NIGERIA FREIGHT TRANSPORT REPORT. Text in English. 2006. a. EUR 820, USD 1,030 combined subscription per issue (print & email eds.) (effective 2010). **Document type:** *Report, Trade.* **Description:** Provides industry professionals and strategists, sector analysts, investors, trade associations and regulatory bodies with independent forecasts and competitive intelligence on the Nigerian freight transport and logistics industry.
Related titles: E-mail ed.
Indexed: A15, ABIn, B02, B15, B17, B18, G04, I05, P48, P51, P52, PQC.
Published by: Business Monitor International Ltd., Senator House, 85 Queen Victoria St, London, EC4V 4AB, United Kingdom. TEL 44-20-72480468, FAX 44-20-72480467, subs@businessmonitor.com.

388 ITA
NONSOLOBUS; mensile di informazione. Text in Italian. 1990. irreg. free. illus. back issues avail. **Document type:** *Newsletter, Consumer.*
Media: Online - full text.
Published by: Azienda Trasporti Area Fiorentina (A T A F), Viale dei Mille 115, Florence, 50131, Italy. TEL 39-055-56501, http://www.ataf.net.

338 624 SWE ISSN 1401-8772
NORDISK INFRASTRUKTUR. Text in Swedish. 1996. bi-m. SEK 699 (effective 2007). adv. **Document type:** *Magazine, Trade.*
Incorporates (1998-2003): Nordisk Geometrik (1403-9796); Which incorporated (1987-2000): U L I Information (0284-1401)
Published by: Conventus Communication AB, PO Box 24053, Stockholm, 10450, Sweden. TEL 46-8-50624400, FAX 46-8-50624499, http://www.branschnyheter.se. Ed. Christer Wiik TEL 46-8-50624402.

NORTH CAROLINA CRIMINAL AND TRAFFIC LAW MANUAL. *see* LAW—Criminal Law

NORTH CAROLINA CRIMINAL LAW AND MOTOR VEHICLE HANDBOOK. *see* LAW—Criminal Law

388 GBR
NORTH SOMERSET COUNCIL. LOCAL TRANSPORT PLAN. Text in English. a.
Formerly: North Somerset Council. Provisional Local Transport Plan
Published by: North Somerset Council, Planning & Environment, Somerset House, Oxford St, P O Box 141, Weston-super-Mare, Somerset BS23 1TG, United Kingdom. TEL 44-1934-888-888, comments@n-somerset.gov.uk.

380.5 USA
NORTHWESTERN UNIVERSITY. TRANSPORTATION CENTER. PUBLICATIONS LIST. Text in English. 1978. a. free. **Document type:** *Catalog.*
Published by: Northwestern University, Transportation Center, 1936 Sheridan Rd, Evanston, IL 60208. TEL 708-492-7287. Circ: 2,500.

388 RUS
NOVYE PROMYSHLENNYE KATALOGI. TRANSPORT. POD'EMNO-TRANSPORTNOE I SKLADSKOE OBORUDOVANIE. Text in Russian. m. USD 365 in United States.
Published by: Rossiiskii N.I.I. Problem Transporta, Lubyanskii pr 5, Moscow, 101820, Russian Federation. TEL 7-095-9254609, FAX 7-095-2002203. **Dist. by:** East View Information Services, 10601 Wayzata Blvd, Minneapolis, MN 55305. TEL 952-252-1201, 800-477-1005, FAX 952-252-1202, info@eastview.com, http://www.eastview.com.

380.5 CHE
NUTZVERKEHR MAGAZIN T I R; Transport Werkverkehr Logistik Bus Touristik. Text in German. 1970. m. CHF 82 domestic; CHF 98 foreign (effective 2000). **Document type:** *Journal, Trade.*
Published by: Huber und Co. AG, Promenadenstr 16, Frauenfeld, 8501, Switzerland. TEL 41-54-271111. Circ: 12,000.

388 NLD ISSN 1872-6674
O P C NIEUWS. Text in Dutch. 2003. bi-m. free (effective 2010).
Formerly (until 2006): Nieuwsbrief O P C (1572-2864)
Published by: Stichting O P C, Postbus 2797, Utrecht, 3500 GT, Netherlands. TEL 31-30-2916790, FAX 31-30-2916798, info@stichting-opc.nl, http://www.stichting-opc.nl. Ed. Wytze Schouten. Circ: 1,320.

388 CAN ISSN 1914-8259
O T MAGAZINE. (Ontario Traffic) Text in English. q. adv. **Document type:** *Magazine, Trade.*
Formerly (until 2007): Ontario Traffic (0842-0394)
Published by: Ontario Traffic Conference, 6355 Kennedy Rd., Unit 2, Mississauga, ON L5T 2L5, Canada. traffic@otc.org. Ed. Leighton A Peach. Adv. contact Judith A Woodley.

385 NLD ISSN 1382-3884
HE7
O V MAGAZINE; vakblad over openbaar vervoer. (Openbaar Vervoer) Text in Dutch. 1928; N.S. 1995. 9/yr. EUR 65 to individuals; EUR 110 to institutions; EUR 55 to students (effective 2008). adv. bk.rev. illus. index. **Document type:** *Magazine, Consumer.* **Description:** Covers all aspects of public transport in the Netherlands and abroad.
Former titles (until 1995): Openbaar Vervoer (Amsterdam, 1928) (0030-3461); Rail en Weg
—IE, Infotrieve.

Published by: Constant Stroecken Ed. & Pub., Generaal Foulkesweg 72, Wageningen, 6703 BW, Netherlands. TEL 31-317-425880, FAX 31-317-425886, administratie@ovmagazine.nl. adv.: color page EUR 1,875; 225 x 290.

388 FRA ISSN 1763-590X
OBSERVATOIRE DES DEPLACEMENTS A PARIS. BULLETIN. Text in French. 1989. q. free. back issues avail. **Document type:** *Bulletin, Consumer.*
Published by: Mairie de Paris, Observatoire des Deplacements, 40 rue du Louvre, Paris, 75001, France.

380.5 MNG
ODTEY BICHIG/SPECIAL DELIVERY. Text in Mongol. 1990. q.
Description: Published for transport and communication workers.
Published by: Ulan Bator Railway Administration, Ulan Bator, Mongolia. Circ: 35,603.

380.5 AUT ISSN 0029-9790
OESTERREICHISCHER PERSONENVERKEHR. Text in German. 1970 (vol.10). m. EUR 60 domestic; EUR 75 foreign (effective 2005). adv. bk.rev. stat. **Document type:** *Magazine, Trade.*
—CCC.
Published by: (Fachverband und Fachgruppe fuer die Befoerderungsgewerbe mit Personenkraftwagen sowie Autobusunternehmungen Oesterreichs), Oesterreichischer Wirtschaftsverlag GmbH (Subsidiary of: Sueddeutscher Verlag GmbH), Wiedner Hauptstr 120-124, Vienna, W 1051, Austria. TEL 43-1-546640, FAX 43-1-54664406, office@wirtschaftsverlag.at, http://www.wirtschaftsverlag.at. Ed. Marco Dittrich. Adv. contact Bernhard Geyer. color page EUR 4,672; trim 168 x 245. Circ: 12,458 (paid and controlled).

388.322 USA ISSN 1046-3372
HD9710.34.A1
OFFICIAL BUS BOOK MARKET REPORT. Text in English. 1987. s-a. USD 214 (effective 2001). **Document type:** *Report, Trade.*
Description: Wholesale and retail bus values and replacement values for over 4,500 different makes, models and years.
Published by: Bus Book Publishing, Inc., PO Box 9, Mcminnville, OR 97128-0009. TEL 503-472-3536, FAX 503-472-3293, geninfo@busbook.com, http://www.busbook.com. Ed., Pub. Dave Mendenhall. Circ: 1,000.

380.5 USA ISSN 0190-6690
HE8.9
OFFICIAL INTERMODAL EQUIPMENT REGISTER. Text in English. 1969. q. adv. **Document type:** *Directory, Trade.* **Description:** Contains dimensions and capacities for 3,000,000 containers, trailers, bogies and chassis used by the companies listed.
Incorporates: Official Intermodal Guide
Related titles: Magnetic Tape ed.
—CCC.
Published by: Commonwealth Business Media, Inc. (Subsidiary of: United Business Media Limited), 400 Windsor Corporate Park, 50 Millstone Rd, Ste 200, East Windsor, NJ 08520. TEL 800-221-5488, FAX 609-371-7883, cbizservices@sunbeltfs.com, http://www.cbizmedia.com. Ed. Teri Schneider. Pub., Adv. contact Kathy Keeney TEL 410-788-0376. Circ: 2,500.

388.322 USA ISSN 1083-5857
HD9710.34.U5
OFFICIAL SCHOOL BUS RESALE GUIDE. Text in English. 1995. a., latest vol.7. USD 109 (effective 2001). **Document type:** *Handbook/Manual/Guide, Trade.* **Description:** Lists wholesale and resale used school bus values.
Published by: Bus Book Publishing, Inc., PO Box 9, Mcminnville, OR 97128-0009. TEL 503-472-3536, FAX 503-472-3293, geninfo@busbook.com, http://www.busbook.com. Ed., Pub. Dave Mendenhall. Circ: 200.

OHIO MOTOR VEHICLE LAWS. *see* LAW

388 343.094 USA ISSN 1551-3424
KFO297.A29
OHIO TRAFFIC LAW HANDBOOK. Variant title: Anderson's (Year) Ohio Traffic Law Handbook. Text in English. 1997. a. USD 45 (effective 2008). 951 p./no.; **Document type:** *Handbook/Manual/Guide, Trade.* **Description:** Features the full text of title 45, the Ohio motor vehicles law (as amended through september 30, 2007), as well as hundreds of other related statutes, rules, and administrative code provisions related to motor vehicles and traffic enforcement.
Related titles: Online - full text ed.
Published by: Anderson Publishing Co. (Subsidiary of: LexisNexis North America), 9443 Springboro Pike, Miamisburg, OH 45342. TEL 877-374-2919, 800-533-1637, FAX 513-562-8116, mail@andersonpublishing.com, http://www.andersonpublishing.com.

OKLAHOMA CRIMES AND PUNISHMENTS, VEHICLES AND RELATED STATUTES. *see* LAW—Criminal Law

388 GBR ISSN 0956-5922
OLD GLORY MAGAZINE. Text in English. 1988. m. GBP 36 domestic; GBP 49 in Europe; GBP 59 elsewhere (effective 2009). adv. bk.rev. back issues avail. **Document type:** *Magazine, Consumer.*
Description: Road, steam and vintage transport magazine. Contains historical features, news, restoration stories, product reviews, and regular event guides.
Published by: Mortons Heritage Media (Subsidiary of: Mortons Media Group Ltd.), PO Box 43, Horncastle, LN9 6JR, United Kingdom. TEL 44-1507-529300, FAX 44-1507-529490, http://www.mortonsmediagroup.com. Ed. Colin Tyson TEL 44-1507-529306. Adv. contact Andrew Bruce TEL 44-1507-529443. Circ: 24,250 (paid).

338.044095353 GBR ISSN 1752-7902
OMAN FREIGHT TRANSPORT REPORT. Text in English. 2007. a. EUR 820, USD 1,030 combined subscription per issue (print & email eds.) (effective 2010). **Document type:** *Report, Trade.* **Description:** Provides industry professionals and strategists, sector analysts, investors, trade associations and regulatory bodies with independent forecasts and competitive intelligence on the Omani freight transport and logistics industry.
Related titles: E-mail ed.
Indexed: A15, ABIn, B02, B15, B17, B18, G04, I05, P48, P51, P52, PQC.
Published by: Business Monitor International Ltd., Senator House, 85 Queen Victoria St, London, EC4V 4AB, United Kingdom. TEL 44-20-72480468, FAX 44-20-72480467, subs@businessmonitor.com.

388.322 GBR ISSN 0305-9243
OMNIBUS MAGAZINE. Text in English. 1931. bi-m. free to members (effective 2009). adv. bk.rev. bibl. back issues avail. **Document type:** *Magazine, Consumer.* **Description:** Contains historical and topical articles and records route development across the UK.
Published by: The Omnibus Society, c/o PR Wallis, Willow Cottage, The St, Bramley, Tadley, RG26 5DD, United Kingdom. Ed. Cyril Macintyre.

388.322 DEU ISSN 1432-3923
OMNIBUSNACHRICHTEN. Text in German. 1996. bi-m. EUR 44 domestic; EUR 53 foreign (effective 2010). adv. **Document type:** *Magazine, Consumer.*
Published by: Omnibusspiegel-Verlag, Am Weitgarten 37, Bonn, 53227, Germany. TEL 49-228-9442853, FAX 49-228-445280, info@omnibusspiegel.de, http://www.omnibusspiegel.de. Ed., R&P Dieter Hanke.

388.322 DEU ISSN 0724-7664
OMNIBUSSPIEGEL. Text in German. 1979. 9/yr. EUR 59 domestic; EUR 68 foreign (effective 2010). adv. bk.rev. **Document type:** *Magazine.*
Published by: Omnibusspiegel-Verlag, Am Weitgarten 37, Bonn, 53227, Germany. TEL 49-228-9442853, FAX 49-228-445280, info@omnibusspiegel.de, http://www.omnibusspiegel.de. Pub., R&P Dieter Hanke. Circ: 1,200.

388 NLD ISSN 1874-4478
HE1
➤ **THE OPEN TRANSPORTATION JOURNAL.** Text in English. 2007. irreg. free (effective 2011). **Document type:** *Journal, Academic/Scholarly.* **Description:** Covers all areas of transportation science and analysis including transportation practice, planning, policy, technology and methodology.
Media: Online - full text.
Indexed: A01, A28, APA, BrCerAb, C&ISA, C27, C29, CA/WCA, CIA, CerAb, CivEngAb, CorrAb, E&CAJ, E11, EEA, EMA, ESPM, H15, M&TEA, M09, MBF, METADEX, R14, S14, S15, SolStAb, T04, WAA.
—Linda Hall.
Published by: Bentham Open (Subsidiary of: Bentham Science Publishers Ltd.), PO Box 294, Bussum, AG 1400, Netherlands. TEL 31-35-6923800, FAX 31-35-6980150, subscriptions@bentham.org. Eds. Karel Martens, Lyudmila S Mihaylova.

388 RUS ISSN 0236-2414
OPYT MORSKIKH UCHEBNYKH ZAVEDENII. Text in Russian. q. USD 85 in United States.
Published by: Ministerstvo Transporta Rossiiskoi Federatsii, Volokolamskoe shosse 14, Moscow, 125080, Russian Federation. TEL 7-095-1581234. **Dist. by:** East View Information Services, 10601 Wayzata Blvd, Minneapolis, MN 55305. TEL 952-252-1201, 800-477-1005, FAX 952-252-1202, info@eastview.com, http://www.eastview.com.

796.77 IDN
OTOMOTIF. Text in Indonesian. m. adv. **Document type:** *Magazine, Consumer.*
Published by: P T Gramedia, Jalan Palmerah Selatan 22-26, Jakarta, 10270, Indonesia. TEL 62-21-5483008, FAX 62-21-5494035, ulj@gramedia-majalah.com, http://www.gramedia.com.

796.77 IDN
OTOSPORT. Text in Indonesian. m. adv. **Document type:** *Magazine, Consumer.*
Published by: P T Gramedia, Jalan Palmerah Selatan 22-26, Jakarta, 10270, Indonesia. TEL 62-21-5483008, FAX 62-21-5494035, ulj@gramedia-majalah.com, http://www.gramedia.com.

388 CAN ISSN 1925-8380
▼ **OWNING YOUR SUCCESS. TRANSPORT VERSION.** Text in English. 2011. bi-m. free (effective 2011). **Document type:** *Newsletter, Trade.*
Media: Online - full text.
Published by: Outridge Enterprises Inc. consulting@outridge.ca, http://www.outridgeenterprises.ca/.

388 USA
P I P DIRECTORY. (People in Parking) Text in English. a. **Document type:** *Directory.*
Published by: Bricepac, Inc., 12228 Venice Blvd, 541, PO Box 66515, Los Angeles, CA 90066. TEL 310-390-5277, FAX 310-390-4777, http://www.bricepac.com.

363.12 658.788 GBR ISSN 1746-5095
TK9001 CODEN: IJRTER
➤ **PACKAGING, TRANSPORT, STORAGE & SECURITY OF RADIOACTIVE MATERIAL.** Text in English. 1990. q. GBP 392 combined subscription to institutions (print & online eds.); USD 740 combined subscription in United States to institutions (print & online eds.) (effective 2012). adv. bk.rev. 80 p./no. 2 cols./p.; back issues avail.; reprint service avail. from PSC. **Document type:** *Journal, Academic/Scholarly.* **Description:** Covers all aspects of the transport of radioactive materials, including regulations, package design, safety analysis, package testing, routine operations and experiences, storage and security, and accidents and emergency planning.
Formerly (until 2004): International Journal of Radioactive Materials Transport (0957-476X)
Related titles: Online - full text ed.: ISSN 1746-5109. GBP 369 to institutions; USD 690 in United States to institutions (effective 2012) (from IngentaConnect).
Indexed: A22, ASFA, B21, CA, CIN, ChemAb, ChemTitl, E04, E05, E11, EIA, ESPM, EnvAb, H&SSA, IBR, IBZ, INIS AtomInd, Inspec, PollutAb, T02, T04.
—BLDSC (6333.019660), AskIEEE, CASDDS, IE, Ingenta. **CCC.**
Published by: Maney Publishing, Ste 1C, Joseph's Well, Hanover Walk, Leeds, W Yorks LS3 1AB, United Kingdom. TEL 44-113-2432800, FAX 44-113-3868178, maney@maney.co.uk. Ed. R B Pope. **Subscr. in N. America to:** Maney Publishing, 875 Massachusetts Ave, 7th Fl, Cambridge, MA 02139. TEL 866-297-5154, FAX 617-354-6875, maney@maneyusa.com.

388.044095491 GBR ISSN 1752-606X
PAKISTAN FREIGHT TRANSPORT REPORT. Text in English. 2006. a. EUR 820, USD 1,030 combined subscription per issue (print & email eds.) (effective 2010). **Document type:** *Report, Trade.* **Description:** Provides industry professionals and strategists, sector analysts, investors, trade associations and regulatory bodies with independent forecasts and competitive intelligence on the Pakistani freight transport and logistics industry.
Related titles: E-mail ed.
Indexed: A15, ABIn, B02, B15, B17, B18, G04, I05, P48, P51, P52, PQC.
Published by: Business Monitor International Ltd., Senator House, 85 Queen Victoria St, London, EC4V 4AB, United Kingdom. TEL 44-20-72480468, FAX 44-20-72480467, subs@businessmonitor.com.

PAR ONERI. *see* MILITARY

383.125 USA
PARCEL; small shipment logistics management. Text in English. 1994. 9/yr. USD 12 domestic; USD 35 in Canada & Mexico; USD 55 elsewhere; free to qualified personnel (print or online ed.) (effective 2009). back issues avail.; reprints avail. **Document type:** *Magazine, Trade.* **Description:** Covers all aspects of parcel shipment logistics, including import-export systems, EDI technology and barcoding, management, warehousing, and business issues.
Formerly: Parcel Shipping & Distribution (1081-4035)
Related titles: Online - full text ed.
Indexed: LogistBibl.
Published by: R B Publishing, Inc., 2901 International Ln, Ste 200, Madison, WI 53704. TEL 608-241-8777, 800-536-1992, FAX 608-241-8666, rbpub@rbpub.com, http://www.rbpub.com. Ed. Daniel O'Rourke TEL 608-442-5079. Pub. Ron Brent TEL 608-442-5062. **Subscr. to:** PO Box 259098, Madison, WI 53725.

388.322 GBR ISSN 1740-7818
PARK & RIDE GREAT BRITAIN. Text in English. 1997. triennial. **Document type:** *Report, Trade.* **Description:** Contains survey and report analysing the latest trends in the development of bus-based park and ride systems in the UK.
Related titles: Online - full text ed.: ISSN 1752-654X.
—CCC.
Published by: T A S Publications & Events Ltd., Ross Holme, West End, Long Preston, Skipton, N Yorks BD23 4QL, United Kingdom. TEL 44-1729-840756, FAX 44-1729-840705, info@taspublications.co.uk.

388.3 USA ISSN 1095-5062
PARKING TODAY. Text in English. m.
Indexed: HRIS.
Published by: Bricepac, Inc., 12228 Venice Blvd, 541, PO Box 66515, Los Angeles, CA 90066. TEL 310-390-5277, FAX 310-390-4777, http://www.bricepac.com.

380.5 USA ISSN 0364-345X
HE4441
PASSENGER TRANSPORT; the source for public transportation news and analysis. Text in English. 1943. bi-w. USD 75 in North America; USD 87 elsewhere (effective 2010). adv. stat.; illus. index. back issues avail.; reprints avail. **Document type:** *Magazine, Trade.*
Description: Covers full range of news affecting mass transit, from congressional and federal developments to local public transportation developments.
Related titles: Online - full text ed.
Indexed: CLT&T, HRIS.
Published by: American Public Transportation Association, 1666 K St, NW Ste 1100, Washington, DC 20006. TEL 202-496-4800, FAX 202-496-4321, sberlin@apta.com. adv.: B&W page USD 2,360, color page USD 3,375; trim 10.625 x 14.

388 GBR ISSN 2046-3278
▼ **PASSENGER TRANSPORT.** Text in English. 2011. fortn. GBP 140 domestic; GBP 220 in Europe; GBP 280 elsewhere (effective 2011). adv. back issues avail. **Document type:** *Magazine, Trade.*
Published by: Passenger Transport Publishing Ltd., Industry Adelaide Wharf, 21 Whiston Rd, London, E2 8EX, United Kingdom. TEL 44-20-77496909. Ed., Pub. Robert Jack. Adv. contact David Crawford TEL 44-20-86434948.

PC-TRANS; the resource for personal computing in transportation. *see* COMPUTERS—Electronic Data Processing

PERIODICA POLYTECHNICA. TRANSPORT ENGINEERING. *see* ENGINEERING—Civil Engineering

388 CZE ISSN 1801-674X
➤ **PERNER'S CONTACTS.** Text in Czech, English. 2006. q. free (effective 2011). **Document type:** *Journal, Academic/Scholarly.*
Media: Online - full text.
Published by: Univerzita Pardubice, Dopravni Fakulta Jana Pernera/ Pardubice University, Faculty of Transportation Jana Pernera, Studentska 95, Pardubice, 532 10, Czech Republic. TEL 420-466-036111, FAX 420-466-036361.

380.5 DEU ISSN 0937-8715
PERSONENBEFOERDERUNGSRECHT. Text in German. 1961. 2 base vols. plus updates 2/yr. looseleaf. EUR 98 base vol(s).; EUR 39.95 updates per issue (effective 2009). **Document type:** *Monographic series, Trade.*
Published by: Erich Schmidt Verlag GmbH & Co. (Berlin), Genthiner Str 30 G, Berlin, 10785, Germany. TEL 49-30-2500850, FAX 49-30-250085305, vertrieb@esvmedien.de, http://www.erich-schmidt-verlag.de.

388 NLD ISSN 1384-4407
PERSONENVERVOER (HEEMSKERK). Text in Dutch. 1991. 7/yr. EUR 33 (effective 2010). adv. **Document type:** *Magazine, Trade.*
Published by: Pressofoon Uitgeverij bv, Postbus 2093, Heemskerk, 1960 GB, Netherlands. TEL 31-251-207400, FAX 31-251-207401, info@pressofoon.nl, http://www.pressofoon.nl. Ed. Wim Faber. Adv. contact Frans van der Werf. B&W page EUR 1,430, color page EUR 1,930. Circ: 5,500 (paid).

388.0440985 GBR ISSN 1752-5985
PERU FREIGHT TRANSPORT REPORT. Text in English. 2006. q. EUR 820, USD 1,030 combined subscription (print & email eds.) (effective 2010). **Document type:** *Report, Trade.* **Description:** Provides industry professionals and strategists, sector analysts, investors, trade associations and regulatory bodies with independent forecasts and competitive intelligence on the Peruvian freight transport and logistics industry.
Related titles: E-mail ed.
Indexed: A15, ABIn, P48, P51, P52, PQC.
Published by: Business Monitor International Ltd., Senator House, 85 Queen Victoria St, London, EC4V 4AB, United Kingdom. TEL 44-20-72480468, FAX 44-20-72480467, subs@businessmonitor.com.

388.04409599 GBR ISSN 1750-5186
PHILIPPINES FREIGHT TRANSPORT REPORT. Text in English. 2005. q. EUR 820, USD 1,030 combined subscription (print & email eds.) (effective 2010). **Document type:** *Report, Trade.* **Description:** Provides industry professionals and strategists, sector analysts, investors, trade associations and regulatory bodies with independent forecasts and competitive intelligence on the Philippine freight transport and logistics industry.
Related titles: E-mail ed.
Indexed: A15, ABIn, B02, B15, B17, B18, G04, I05, P48, P51, P52, PQC.
Published by: Business Monitor International Ltd., Senator House, 85 Queen Victoria St, London, EC4V 4AB, United Kingdom. TEL 44-20-72480468, FAX 44-20-72480467, subs@businessmonitor.com.

388.04409438 GBR ISSN 1750-5194
POLAND FREIGHT TRANSPORT REPORT. Text in English. 2006. q. EUR 820, USD 1,030 combined subscription (print & email eds.) (effective 2010). **Document type:** *Report, Trade.* **Description:** Provides industry professionals and strategists, sector analysts, investors, trade associations and regulatory bodies with independent forecasts and competitive intelligence on the Polish freight transport and logistics industry.
Related titles: E-mail ed.
Indexed: A15, ABIn, B02, B15, B17, B18, G04, I05, P48, P51, P52, PQC.
Published by: Business Monitor International Ltd., Senator House, 85 Queen Victoria St, London, EC4V 4AB, United Kingdom. TEL 44-20-72480468, FAX 44-20-72480467, subs@businessmonitor.com.

380.5 POL ISSN 0209-3324
HE7 CODEN: ZNPTES
POLITECHNIKA SLASKA. ZESZYTY NAUKOWE. TRANSPORT. Text in Polish. 1983. irreg.
Indexed: B22.
—Linda Hall.
Published by: Politechnika Slaska, ul Akademicka 5, Gliwice, 44100, Poland. wydawnictwo_mark@polsl.pl. Ed. Barbara Maciejna. Circ: 205. **Dist. by:** Ars Polona, Obroncow 25, Warsaw 03933, Poland.

388 POL ISSN 1230-9265
POLITECHNIKA WARSZAWSKA. PRACE NAUKOWE. TRANSPORT. Text in Polish. 1972. irreg., latest 1999, 42. **Document type:** *Academic/Scholarly.*
Formerly (until 1992): Politechnika Warszawska. Instytut Transportu. Prace (0137-2289)
Indexed: B22.
—Linda Hall.
Published by: Oficyna Wydawnicza Politechniki Warszawskiej/Publishing House of the Warsaw University of Technology, ul Polna 50, Warsaw, 00644, Poland. http://www.wpw.pw.edu.pl.

380.5 POL ISSN 1230-7599
POLSKA GAZETA TRANSPORTOWA. Text in Polish. 1993. w. PLZ 247; PLZ 5.50 newsstand/cover (effective 2005). adv. back issues avail. **Document type:** *Newspaper, Trade.* **Description:** Covers all aspects of transport in Poland and Europe.
Published by: Polskie Wydawnictwo Transportowe, Ul Koniczynowa 11, Warsaw, 03612, Poland. TEL 48-22-6783592, FAX 48-22-6795203. Ed. Krzysztof Koprowski. Adv. contact Marcin Marczuk. color page PLZ 15,960, B&W page PLZ 9,120; trim 266 x 380. Circ: 4,000. **Co-publisher:** Deutscher Verkehrs Verlag, GW.

POLYTECHNICAL UNIVERSITY OF BUCHAREST. SCIENTIFIC BULLETIN. SERIES D: MECHANICAL ENGINEERING. *see* ENGINEERING—Mechanical Engineering

387 USA ISSN 0085-5030
HE554.N4
PORT OF NEW ORLEANS ANNUAL DIRECTORY. Text in English. 1969. a. free to qualified personnel. adv. bk.rev. charts; illus.; stat. 164 p./no. 2 cols./p.; **Document type:** *Directory.* **Description:** Covers port administration, planned improvements, computer capabilities, intermodal connections, facilities and tariffs. Includes a listing of maritime businesses in the New Orleans area by services.
Published by: New Orleans Publishing Group, 111 Veterans Memorial Blvd., Ste. 1440, Metairie, LA 70005-3050. TEL 504-834-9292, FAX 504-837-2258. Ed. Kathy Finn. Pub. Carolyn McCellan. R&P Paul Dauphin. Circ: 10,300 (controlled).

380.5 ESP ISSN 1695-5838
PORTNEWSPAPER. Text in English, Spanish. 1985. m. EUR 68.50 domestic; EUR 159 foreign (effective 2009). adv. **Document type:** *Newspaper, Trade.*
Formerly (until 2002): Spanish International Transport Newspaper (0213-3377)
Published by: Grupo Editorial Men-Car, Passeig de Colom, 24, Barcelona, 08002, Spain. TEL 34-93-301-5749, FAX 34-93-302-1779, men-car@men-car.com, http://www.men-car.com. Ed. J Cardona Delclos. Circ: 32,000.

POWDER / BULK SOLIDS; the magazine for the processing, handling, packaging and storing of dry particulates. *see* ENGINEERING—Chemical Engineering

POWDER / BULK SOLIDS INDUSTRY MASTER; the source for dry processing and bulk handling technology. *see* ENGINEERING—Chemical Engineering

380.52 FRA ISSN 0765-6386
PRACTIC EXPORT. Text in French. 1986. 10/yr. EUR 120 (effective 2009). adv. **Document type:** *Magazine, Trade.*
Published by: Societe Meridionale des Editions du Commerce International (S M E C I), 32 Av. Andre Roussin, B.P. 36, Marseille, Cedex 16 13321, France. TEL 33-4-91924720, FAX 33-4-91924030, redaction@pratic-export.fr. Ed. Claude Mezzana. Circ: 5,800.

PRACTICAL PEDAL; the journal of practical bicycling. *see* SPORTS AND GAMES—Bicycles And Motorcycles

380.5 CZE ISSN 0032-7514
PREPRAVNI A TARIFNI VESTNIK/TRANSPORTATION AND TARIFF NEWS. Text in Czech. 1945. s-m. bk.rev. **Document type:** *Journal, Government.*
Published by: Ministerstvo Dopravy Ceske Republiky, Nabrezi Ludvika Svobody 1222/12, Prague 1, 11000, Czech Republic. TEL 420-2-25131111, FAX 420-2-25131184, posta@mdcr.cz, http://www.ministerstvodopravy.cz. Circ: 9,760.

PRESHIPMENT TESTING. *see* PACKAGING

380.5 USA
PRESIDENT TRANSPORT WORLD. Variant title: Transport World. Text in English. 1979. q. USD 25 domestic; USD 35 foreign (effective 2001). adv. bk.rev.; video rev. back issues avail.; reprints avail. **Document type:** *Bulletin.* **Description:** Covers post cards showing various types of transportation. Includes checklists on various transportation subjects.
Published by: International Transportation Postcard Collectors Club, PO Box 6782, Providence, RI 02940. Ed., R&P, Adv. contact Robert J Andrews. page USD 3,000. Circ: 500.

PROCLAIM (FORT WASHINGTON). *see* INSURANCE

388.3 SWE ISSN 1103-3614
PROFFS. Text in Swedish. 1990. 10/yr. SEK 289 (effective 2001). adv. 32 p./no. 5 cols./p.; **Document type:** *Magazine, Consumer.*
Formerly (until 1991): Proffs i Trafik (1101-4997)
Published by: Vaegpress Foerlag AB, Box 304, Aakersberga, 18424, Sweden. TEL 46-8-540-888-00, FAX 46-8-540-205-31. Ed., Pub. Bobby Hommerberg. Adv. contact Pekka Tikkanen. B&W page SEK 26,300, color page SEK 31,900; trim 255 x 365. Circ: 16,900 (paid).

388 NZL ISSN 1177-9187
PROFITABLE TRANSPORT & LOGISTICS. Text in English. 2005. 46/yr. NZD 297 (effective 2008). **Document type:** *Newsletter, Trade.*
Formerly (until 2007): New Zealand Transport & Logistics Business Week (1176-4929)
Related titles: Online - full text ed.: New Zealand Transport & Logistics Business Week (Online). ISSN 1177-9209.
Published by: Media Information Ltd., PO Box 2197, Christchurch, 8015, New Zealand. TEL 64-3-3653891, FAX 64-3-3653894.

388 CAN ISSN 1910-4103
PROGRAMME DE DEMONSTRATION EN TRANSPORT URBAIN. REVUE ANNUELLE. Short title: P D T U Revue Annuelle. Text in French. 2005. a. **Document type:** *Government.*
Media: Online - full text. **Related titles:** Print ed.: ISSN 1912-1040; ◆ English ed.: Urban Transportation Showcase Program. Annual Review. ISSN 1910-409X.
Published by: Transport Canada/Transports Canada, 300 Sparks St, Ottawa, ON K1A 0N5, Canada. TEL 613-990-2309, FAX 613-954-4731, http://www.tc.gc.ca.

665.7 USA
PROPANE VEHICLE. Text in English. 1996. bi-m. free to qualified personnel. adv. **Document type:** *Magazine, Trade.* **Description:** Focuses on the use of propane as a transportation fuel.
Published by: R P Publishing, Inc., 2696 S Colorado Blvd, Ste 595, Denver, CO 80222-5944. TEL 303-863-0521, FAX 303-863-1722. Ed. Joy Keller. Pub. Frank Rowe. Adv. contact Mark Hahn. B&W page USD 2,400. Circ: 5,000 (controlled).

380.5 POL ISSN 0033-2232
PRZEGLAD KOMUNIKACYJNY; miesiecznik ekonomiczno-techniczny. Text in Polish. 1945. m. PLZ 180 domestic; PLZ 15 per issue domestic; USD 6 per issue foreign (effective 2004). bk.rev. bibl.; charts; illus.; stat. index, cum.index. **Document type:** *Magazine, Trade.*
Indexed: B22.
Published by: Stowarzyszenie Inzynierow i Technikow Komunikacji (SITK)/Polish Association of Engineers & Technicians of Transportation, Ul Czackiego 3-5, Warsaw, 00043, Poland. TEL 48-22-8270259, FAX 48-22-8270258, redakcja@sitk.org.pl, http://www.sitk.org.pl. Ed. Tadeusz Basiewicz. Circ: 3,600.

363.12 NZL ISSN 1176-9017
PUBLIC ATTITUDES TO ROAD SAFETY. Text in English. 1974. a. **Document type:** *Journal, Consumer.* **Description:** Evaluates attitudes to road safety issues, primarily alcohol-impaired driving and speed.
Published by: Ministry of Transport, PO Box 3175, Wellington, New Zealand. TEL 64-4-4721253, FAX 64-4-4733697.

388 DEU ISSN 1866-749X
▼ **PUBLIC TRANSPORT.** Text in English. 2009. 4/yr. EUR 263, USD 395 combined subscription to institutions (print & online eds.) (effective 2010). reprint service avail. from PSC. **Document type:** *Journal, Academic/Scholarly.*
Related titles: Online - full text ed.: ISSN 1613-7159. 2009.
Indexed: A22, E01.
—IE. **CCC.**
Published by: Springer (Subsidiary of: Springer Science+Business Media), Tiergartenstr 17, Heidelberg, 69121, Germany. TEL 49-6221-4870, FAX 49-6221-345229, orders-hd-individuals@springer.com, http://www.springer.com.

388 BEL ISSN 1029-1261
PUBLIC TRANSPORT INTERNATIONAL (FRENCH EDITION). Text in French. 1952. bi-m. EUR 74 to non-members; TPE 56 to members (effective 2000). adv. bk.rev. illus. index, cum.index: 1952-1984. back issues avail.; reprints avail. **Document type:** *Journal, Trade.* **Description:** Discusses issues in public and mass transit: buses, trains, and ferry boats.
Supersedes in part (in 1997): Public Transport International (Multilingual Edition) (1016-796X); Which was formerly (until 1990): U I T P Revue (0041-5154); International Union of Tramways, Light Railways and Motor Omnibuses. Review
Related titles: English ed.: Public Transport International (English Edition). ISSN 1029-127X; German ed.: Public Transport International (Deutsche Ausgabe). ISSN 1029-1288.
Indexed: A28, APA, BrCerAb, C&ISA, CA/WCA, CIA, CerAb, CivEngAb, CorrAb, DokStr, E&CAJ, E11, EEA, EMA, ESPM, EngInd, EnvEAb, H15, HRIS, M&TEA, M09, MBF, METADEX, SCOPUS, SolStAb, T04, WAA.
—IE, Ingenta, INIST, Linda Hall. **CCC.**
Published by: International Union of Public Transport/Union Internationale des Transports Publics, Rue Sainte-Marie 6, Brussels, 1080, Belgium. FAX 32-2-6601072, http://www.uitp.org. Ed. Heather Allen. Adv. contact Sylvie Cappaert. B&W page EUR 1,753.16, color page EUR 2,927.02. Circ: 3,000.

388.322 USA ISSN 0730-5443
PUPIL TRANSPORTATION NEWS. Text in English. 1982. m. USD 72. adv. stat.; tr.lit. back issues avail. **Document type:** *Newsletter, Trade.* **Description:** Contains facts and information on the operation and management of school bus fleets.
Address: PO Box 191, Fords, NJ 08863. TEL 732-750-2561, FAX 732-750-2561. Ed., Pub., R&P, Adv. contact Donna Simeone. B&W page USD 125; trim 10.5 x 7.5. Circ: 1,565 (paid).

PUTNOTRANSPORTNI PROIZSHESTVIA V REPUBLIKA BULGARIA. *see* STATISTICS

388.044095363 GBR ISSN 1752-7910
QATAR FREIGHT TRANSPORT REPORT. Text in English. 2007. a. EUR 820, USD 1,030 combined subscription per issue (print & email eds.) (effective 2010). **Document type:** *Report, Trade.*
Related titles: E-mail ed.
Indexed: A15, ABIn, B02, B15, B17, B18, G04, I05, P48, P51, P52, PQC.
Published by: Business Monitor International Ltd., Senator House, 85 Queen Victoria St, London, EC4V 4AB, United Kingdom. TEL 44-20-72480468, FAX 44-20-72480467, subs@businessmonitor.com.

388 AUS
QUEENSLAND TAXI MAGAZINE. Text in English. 1948. bi-m. AUD 55 domestic to non-members; AUD 95 foreign to non-members; free to members (effective 2008). adv. **Document type:** *Magazine, Trade.* **Description:** Provides comprehensive information on developments within the taxi industry including technology updates, TCQ initiatives and changes in government policy which affect the industry.
Formerly (until 1986): Taxi News
Published by: (Taxi Council of Queensland), The Magazine Publishing Company Pty. Ltd., 34 Station St, PO Box 406, Nundah, QLD 4012, Australia. TEL 61-7-38660000, FAX 61-7-38660066, info@tmpc.com.au. adv.: color page AUD 2,340; trim 210 x 275. Circ: 4,800.

380.5 DEU ISSN 1614-4554
QUER DURCH HAMBURG/SCHLESWIG-HOLSTEIN. SPEDITION UND TRANSPORT. Text in German. a. EUR 23.80 (effective 2006). adv. **Document type:** *Trade.*
Former titles (until 2002): Quer Durch Hamburg. Spedition und Transport (0934-196X); (until 1983): Quer Durch Spedition und Transportwesen Hamburg (0173-6043); (until 1979): Quer Durch Hamburgs Spedition und Transportwesen (0170-1118)
Published by: Seehafen Verlag GmbH, Nordkanalstr 36, Hamburg, 20097, Germany. TEL 49-40-23714228, FAX 49-40-23714259, info@seehafen-verlag.de, http://www.schiffundhafen.de. Ed. Sabine Radzuweit. adv.: page EUR 1,180; trim 82 x 122. Circ: 4,500.

380.5 ITA
QUOTA NEVE. Text in Italian. 5/yr. free to qualified personnel; EUR 20 (effective 2009). **Document type:** *Magazine, Trade.*
Address: Via Bartolomeo Panizza 12, Milan, 20144, Italy. red@quotaneve.it, quotaneve@tin.it. Circ: 8,000.

387.0074 USA
R.E. OLDS TRANSPORTATION MUSEUM NEWSLETTER. Text in English. 1980. q. looseleaf. membership. adv. bk.rev. back issues avail. **Document type:** *Newsletter.* **Description:** Covers topics of interest to museum members, including Lansing-built transportation (cars, airplanes, bicycles and trucks).
Published by: R.E. Olds Transportation Museum Association, Inc., 240 Museum Dr, Lansing, MI 48933. TEL 517-372-4150. Circ: 1,200.

380.5 DEU ISSN 0935-901X
R K W HANDBUCH LOGISTIK. (Rationalisierungs-Kuratorium der Deutschen Wirtschaft) Text in German. 1981. irreg. price varies. **Document type:** *Monographic series, Trade.*
Published by: (R K W - Rationalisierungs- und Innovationszentrum der Deutschen Wirtschaft e.V.), Erich Schmidt Verlag GmbH & Co. (Berlin), Genthiner Str 30 G, Berlin, 10785, Germany. TEL 49-30-2500850, FAX 49-30-250085305, esv@esvmedien.de, http://www.esv.info.

380.5 DEU ISSN 0935-9265
R K W HANDBUCH TRANSPORT. (Rationalisierungs-Kuratorium der Deutschen Wirtschaft) Text in German. 1982. irreg. looseleaf. price varies. **Document type:** *Monographic series, Trade.*
Published by: (R K W - Rationalisierungs- und Innovationszentrum der Deutschen Wirtschaft e.V.), Erich Schmidt Verlag GmbH & Co. (Berlin), Genthiner Str 30 G, Berlin, 10785, Germany. TEL 49-30-2500850, FAX 49-30-250085305, esv@esvmedien.de, http://www.esv.info.

R M F. (Rail Miniature Flash) *see* HOBBIES

R V AMERICA; the rvers guide to the open road. (Recreational Vehicle) *see* SPORTS AND GAMES—Outdoor Life

796.5 USA ISSN 0742-6208
TL298
R V BUYERS GUIDE. (Recreational Vehicle) Variant title: Trailer Life R V Buyers Guide. Text in English. 1982. a. USD 6.99 per issue to non-members; USD 6.29 per issue to members (effective 2009). adv. back issues avail. **Document type:** *Directory, Consumer.* **Description:** Contains indispensable tips and information designed to help seasoned RVers and novices make the right choices.
Published by: Affinity Group Inc., PO Box 10204, Des Moines, IA 50381. TEL 800-309-0311, info@affinitygroup.com, http://www.affinitygroup.com. Pub. Bill Estes. Adv. contact Terry Thompson TEL 206-283-9545. B&W page USD 9,325, color page USD 13,400; trim 7.875 x 10.5. Circ: 115,000.

388 USA
R V ENTHUSIAST. (Recreational Vehicle) Text in English. bi-m. USD 14.95 (effective 2006). **Document type:** *Magazine, Consumer.*
Published by: Roundabout Publications, PO Box 19235, Lenexa, KS 66285. TEL 800-455-2207, http://www.travelbooksusa.com.

388.346 USA ISSN 1934-4309
R V EXTREME MAGAZINE. (Recreational Vehicle) Text in English. 2006 (Dec.). m. USD 18.95 domestic; USD 29.95 foreign (effective 2007). adv. **Document type:** *Magazine, Consumer.* **Description:** Showcases detailed reviews of cutting-edge new-model RVs and related products.
Published by: Xtreme Publishing Group, Inc., 1541-D Parkway Loop, Tustin, CA 92780. TEL 714-566-1200, FAX 714-566-0120. Ed. Jeff Dusing. adv.: B&W page USD 3,095, color page USD 4,455; trim 8.75 x 10.875.

388.346 USA
R V NEWS (ONLINE); the voice of the R V industry. (Recreational Vehicle) Text in English. 1975. m. free (effective 2007). adv. 40 p./no. 3 cols./p.; reprints avail. **Document type:** *Magazine, Trade.* **Description:** Reports all news affecting the recreational vehicle industry. Feature articles include spotlights on RV manufacturers, suppliers, distributors, associations.
Formerly (until 2004): R V News (Print) (0193-2888)
Media: Online - full text.

Published by: D & S Media Enterprises, Inc., 3116 S Mill Ave, Ste 610, Tempe, AZ 85282-3657. TEL 480-784-4060, FAX 480-784-4420. Pub. Don Magary. adv.: B&W page USD 2,950, color page USD 3,550. Circ: 11,971 (paid and controlled).

388.346 384.5 USA ISSN 1941-9228
R V PRO; products & profits for R V professionals. (Recreational Vehicle) Text in English. 2005. m. free domestic to qualified personnel; USD 85 combined subscription in Canada & Mexico (print & online eds.); USD 110 combined subscription elsewhere (print & online eds.) (effective 2008). adv. reprints avail. **Document type:** *Magazine, Trade.* **Description:** Features articles showcasing up-to-date industry trends and the latest in RV-related technologies.
Related titles: Online - full text ed.: free to qualified personnel (effective 2008).
Published by: National Business Media, Inc., PO Box 1416, Broomfield, CO 80038. TEL 303-469-0424, 800-669-0424, FAX 303-469-5730. Ed. Bradley Worrel TEL 303-469-0424 ext 299. Pub. Mike Wieber TEL 303-469-0424 ext 239. Adv. contact Kristina Anderson TEL 303-469-0424 ext 220. B&W page USD 3,405, color page USD 4,405; trim 8.125 x 10.875. Circ: 15,000.

388.346 796.79 USA
R V VIEW. (Recreational Vehicle) Text in English. 2004. 5/yr. USD 3.99 newsstand/cover (effective 2009). adv. back issues avail. **Document type:** *Magazine, Consumer.* **Description:** Offers informative tips on travel, maintenance, RV events and new product features.
Related titles: Online - full text ed.
Published by: Affinity Group Inc., 2575 Vista Del Mar, Ventura, CA 93001. TEL 805-667-4100, FAX 805-667-4419, info@affinitygroup.com, http://www.affinitygroup.com. Adv. contact Justin Hurst TEL 888-772-1235. B&W page USD 16,670, color page USD 18,505; trim 8 x 10.5. Circ: 578,681.

RACE, POVERTY AND THE ENVIRONMENT. *see* ENVIRONMENTAL STUDIES

388.4094 GBR ISSN 1367-6040
RAPID TRANSIT MONITOR. Text in English. 1991. a. looseleaf. **Document type:** *Report, Trade.* **Description:** Contains three volumes on light rail, underground and bus-based systems, plus separate planning and finance guide. Includes market statistics, supply structure, financial reports and network diagrams for light rail schemes.
Former titles (until 1991): Rapid Transit UK (0962-6239); (until 1989): Rapid Transit Update (0964-9611)
Related titles: CD-ROM ed.: ISSN 1752-4741. 2002. GBP 195 (effective 2006); Online - full text ed.: ISSN 1752-6515. 2006. GBP 190 (effective 2006).
—CCC.
Published by: T A S Publications & Events Ltd., Ross Holme, West End, Long Preston, Skipton, N Yorks BD23 4QL, United Kingdom. TEL 44-1729-840756, FAX 44-1729-840705, info@taspublications.co.uk, http://www.taspublications.co.uk.

388 FRA ISSN 0768-9756
RAPPORT. Text in French. 1986. irreg. **Document type:** *Monographic series, Academic/Scholarly.*
—INIST.
Published by: Institut National de Recherche sur les Transports et leur Securite, 25 Av. Francois Mitterrand, Bron, Cedex 69675, France. TEL 33-4-72142300, FAX 33-4-72376837. **Subscr. to:** Lavoisier, Lavoisier - Dept Abonnements, 14 rue de Provigny, Cachan 94236, France. TEL 33-1-47406700, FAX 33-1-47406702, abo@lavoisier.fr.

380.5 MEX
REALIDADES. Text in Spanish. 1955. m. MXN 4 per issue. adv.
Published by: Direccion General de Transito, Palma Norte 413-105, Mexico City 1, DF, Mexico. Circ: 10,000.

380.5 363.22 FRA ISSN 0761-8980
➤ **RECHERCHE - TRANSPORTS - SECURITE.** Short title: R T S. Text in French. 1972. q. EUR 150, USD 184 combined subscription to institutions (print & online eds.) (effective 2012). back issues avail. **Document type:** *Journal, Academic/Scholarly.* **Description:** Includes articles that assess, organize, and execute research and development in the enhancement of the means and systems of transportation and traffic, from technical, social, and economic perspectives.
Formerly (until 1983): Recherche Transports (0291-8439)
Related titles: Online - full text ed.: ISSN 1951-6614. 2000 (from IngentaConnect).
Indexed: A22, B01, B06, B07, B09, CA, FR, HRIS, SCOPUS.
—IE, Infotrieve, Ingenta, INIST. **CCC.**
Published by: (French Institute for Transport and Safety Research), Springer France (Subsidiary of: Springer Science+Business Media), 22 Rue de Palestro, Paris, 75002, France. TEL 33-1-53009860, FAX 33-1-53009861, sylvie.kamara@springer.com. Ed. Catherine Berthelon.

388.322 370 NLD ISSN 1879-8977
▼ **REGELINGEN LEERLINGENVERVOER.** Text in Dutch. 2009. a. EUR 37.74 (effective 2010).
Published by: Sdu Uitgevers bv, Postbus 20025, The Hague, 2500 EA, Netherlands. TEL 31-70-3789911, FAX 31-70-3854321, sdu@sdu.nl, http://www.sdu.nl/.

656 DEU ISSN 1438-6763
REGIO-TRANS. Text in German. 1999. a. EUR 12 (effective 2008). adv. **Document type:** *Directory, Trade.*
Published by: Kuhn Fachverlag GmbH & Co. KG, Bert-Brecht-Str 15-19, Villingen-Schwenningen, 78054, Germany. TEL 49-7720-3940, FAX 49-7720-394175, kataloge@kuhnverlag.de. Ed. Axel Bethge. Adv. contact Siegfried Girrbach. B&W page EUR 2,330, color page EUR 2,945. Circ: 5,690 (paid and controlled).

380.5 USA
REGIONAL TRANSIT ADVOCATE. Text in English. 1998. q. USD 25 domestic; USD 25 foreign (effective 2000). bk.rev.; video rev. bibl. reprints avail. **Document type:** *Newsletter.* **Description:** Offers news and views on mass transit and related areas, with emphasis on the New York-New Jersey metropolitan area.
Formed by the 1998 merger of: New York Streetcar News; (1970-1998): Notes from Underground (0029-4039); Which incorporated: Better Transit Bulletin (0006-0240)
Related titles: Microform ed.: (from PQC).
Published by: Committee for Better Transit, Inc., PO Box 3106, Long Island City, NY 11103. TEL 718-728-0091. Ed. George Haikalis. Pub., R&P Stephen Dobrow. Circ: 2,500.

RELIANT LOGISTIC NEWS; magazin pro vyrobu, obchod a 3PL. *see* BUSINESS AND ECONOMICS—Production Of Goods And Services

380.5 658 GBR ISSN 0034-4265
REMOVALS AND STORAGE. Text in English. 1924. m. membership. adv. bk.rev. **Document type:** *Magazine, Trade.*
Published by: (British Association of Removers), Quarrington-Curtis Ltd., 15-17 Canute Rd, Southampton, Hants SO14 3FJ, United Kingdom. TEL 44-1703-635438, FAX 44-1703-632198. Ed. Stephen J Webb. Circ: 1,800 (controlled).

RESALE WEEKLY. *see* BUILDING AND CONSTRUCTION

388.1 600 USA
RESEARCH & TECHNOLOGY TRANSPORTER. Text in English. 1996. m.
Indexed: APA, C&ISA, CorrAb, E&CAJ, EEA, SolStAb, WAA.
Published by: Turner-Fairbank Highway Research Center (Subsidiary of: U.S. Department of Transportation, Federal Highway Administration), 6300 Georgetown Pike, McLean, VA 22101. TEL 202-493-3423.

380.5 NLD ISSN 0739-8859
HE1
RESEARCH IN TRANSPORTATION ECONOMICS. Text in English. 1983. 3/yr. EUR 423 in Europe to institutions; JPY 71,600 in Japan to institutions; USD 600 elsewhere to institutions (effective 2012). back issues avail. **Document type:** *Journal, Academic/Scholarly.* **Description:** Devoted to the dissemination of high quality economics research in the field of transportation.
Related titles: Online - full text ed.: ISSN 1875-7979 (from ScienceDirect).
Indexed: EconLit, SCOPUS.
—BLDSC (7773.785000), IE. **CCC.**
Published by: Elsevier BV (Subsidiary of: Elsevier Science & Technology), Radarweg 29, PO Box 211, Amsterdam, 1000 AE, Netherlands. TEL 31-20-4853911, FAX 31-20-4852457, JournalsCustomerServiceEMEA@elsevier.com. Ed. M Dresner.

388 ITA ISSN 1824-5617
LE REVISIONI DEI VEICOLI. Text in Italian. 1998. m. **Document type:** *Magazine, Consumer.*
Related titles: CD-ROM ed.: ISSN 1824-5625. 2002; Online - full text ed.: ISSN 1826-8773. 2006.
Published by: Edizioni Giuridico Amministrative e Formazione (E G A F), Via Filippo Guarini 2, Forli, 47100, Italy. TEL 39-0543-473347, FAX 39-0543-474133, gruppo@egaf.it, http://www.egaf.it.

388 BRA ISSN 2177-1065
REVISTA DE LITERATURA DOS TRANSPORTES. Text in Portuguese. 2007. s-a. free (effective 2011). **Document type:** *Journal, Academic/Scholarly.*
Media: Online - full text.
Published by: Rede de Pesquisas em Transportes (R P T) Eds. Alessandro Vinicius Marques de Oliveira, Maria Cristina Barbot.

REVISTA DE TRANSPORTE Y SEGUROS. *see* INSURANCE

380.5 BRA
REVISTA O CARRETEIRO. Text in Portuguese. m. free. **Document type:** *Magazine, Trade.*
Address: Rua Palacete das Aguias 395 - VI, Alexandria, SP 04635-021, Brazil. Ed. Jose A de Castro. Circ: 160,000.

380.5 ARG ISSN 1852-7175
▼ **REVISTA TRANSPORTE Y TERRITORIO.** Text in Spanish. 2009. s-a. back issues avail. **Document type:** *Journal, Academic/Scholarly.*
Media: Online - full text.
Published by: Universidad de Buenos Aires, Instituto de Geografia, Puan 480 Piso 4, Buenos Aires, 1406, Argentina. rtt@filo.uba.ar, http://www.filo.uba.ar/contenidos/investigacion/institutos/geo/homepage.html. Ed. Susan Kralich.

388 BRA ISSN 1415-7713
➤ **REVISTA TRANSPORTES.** Text in Portuguese. 1993. 2/yr. **Document type:** *Journal, Academic/Scholarly.* **Description:** Aims to improve research and teaching on transportation by promoting the diffusion of technical and scientific articles on transportation and related issues.
Published by: Associacao Nacional de Ensino e Pesquisa em Transportes, Caixa Postal 68512, Rio de Janeiro, 21945-970, Brazil. TEL 55-21-25628727, FAX 55-21-25628727. Ed. Yaeko Yamashita. Circ: 4,500 (controlled).

388.3 CHE ISSN 0035-0761
REVUE AUTOMOBILE; journal suisse de l'automobile. Text in French. 1906. w. CHF 127 (effective 2007). adv. bk.rev. charts; illus.; mkt.; stat. **Document type:** *Magazine, Consumer.*
Related titles: German ed.: Automobil - Revue. ISSN 0005-1314. CHF 155 (effective 2007).
Published by: Buechler Grafino AG, Dammweg 9, Bern, 3001, Switzerland. TEL 41-31-3303555, FAX 41-31-3303377, redaktion@espace.ch, http://www.espace.ch. Circ: 15,937 (paid).

RIVISTA DI DIRITTO DEI TRASPORTI. *see* LAW

RIVISTA DI DIRITTO DELL'ECONOMIA, DEI TRASPORTI E DELL'AMBIENTE. *see* LAW

RIVISTA GIURIDICA DELLA CIRCOLAZIONE E DEI TRASPORTI (ONLINE). *see* LAW

RIVISTA GIURIDICA DELLA CIRCOLAZIONE E DEI TRASPORTI. ANTOLOGIA (YEAR). *see* LAW

ROAD AND TRANSPORT RESEARCH; a journal of Australian and New Zealand research and practice. *see* ENGINEERING—Civil Engineering

363.12 FRA ISSN 1960-9655
ROAD SAFETY IN FRANCE. Text in English. 2002. a. free. **Document type:** *Government.*
Published by: (France. Observatoire National Interministeriel de Securite Routiere), Documentation Francaise, 29-31 Quai Voltaire, Paris, Cedex 7 75344, France. TEL 33-1-40157000, FAX 33-1-40157230, http://www.ladocumentationfrancaise.fr.

363.12 NLD ISSN 1573-255X
ROAD SAFETY IN THE NETHERLANDS, KEY FIGURES. Text in English. 2004. a.
Related titles: ◆ Dutch ed.: Kerncijfers Verkeersveiligheid. ISSN 1573-2541.
Published by: Ministerie van Verkeer en Waterstaat Rijkswaterstaat, Dienst Verkeer en Scheepvaart, Postbus 5044, Delft, 2600 GA, Netherlands. TEL 31-88-7982222, FAX 31-88-7982999, dvsloket@rws.nl, http://www.rijkswaterstaat.nl/dvs.

388.346 USA ISSN 1098-2051
ROADS TO ADVENTURE. Text in English. 199?. q. **Document type:** *Magazine, Consumer.* **Description:** Provides information on trips, trip planning, road travel, RVs, RVing and travel arrangements.
Published by: Affinity Group Inc., 2575 Vista Del Mar, Ventura, CA 93001. TEL 805-667-4100, FAX 805-667-4419, info@affinitygroup.com, http://www.affinitygroup.com.

388 USA ISSN 0035-7898
ROLL SIGN; the magazine of New England transit news. Text in English. 1964. bi-m. USD 12 domestic; USD 16 foreign (effective 2000). bk.rev. illus. index. reprints avail. **Document type:** *Newsletter.* **Description:** News and historical feautures about public transportation in greater Boston, New England, and elsewhere.
Published by: Boston Street Railway Association, Inc., PO Box 181037, Boston, MA 02118-1037. Ed. Daniel T Lenihan. Pub. Bradley H Clarke. R&P Charles Bahne. Circ: 1,200 (paid).

388 USA ISSN 0048-8542
ROLLING ALONG. Text in English. 1949. q. free. adv. **Document type:** *Journal, Trade.*
Published by: North Dakota Motor Carriers Association, PO Box 874, Bismarck, ND 58502. Ed. Leroy H Ernst. Circ: 3,000.

388.04409498 GBR ISSN 1750-5208
ROMANIA FREIGHT TRANSPORT REPORT. Text in English. 2005. q. EUR 820, USD 1,030 combined subscription (print & email eds.) (effective 2010). **Document type:** *Report, Trade.* **Description:** Provides industry professionals and strategists, sector analysts, investors, trade associations and regulatory bodies with independent forecasts and competitive intelligence on the Romanian freight transport and logistics industry.
Related titles: E-mail ed.
Indexed: A15, ABIn, B02, B15, B17, B18, G04, I05, P48, P51, P52, PQC.
Published by: Business Monitor International Ltd., Senator House, 85 Queen Victoria St, London, EC4V 4AB, United Kingdom. TEL 44-20-72480468, FAX 44-20-72480467, subs@businessmonitor.com.

629.34 388.322 NLD ISSN 1874-5407
ROMEO NIEUWS. Text in Dutch. 200?. q.
Published by: Stichting Rotterdams Openbaar Vervoer Museum en Exploitatie van Oldtimers, Postbus 156, Rotterdam, 3000 AD, Netherlands. TEL 31-6-36144083, info@stichtingromeo.nl, http://www.stichtingromeo.nl.

388 NLD ISSN 1383-7095
ROTTERDAM TRANSPORT HANDBOOK. Text in Dutch. 1995. a. EUR 69.50 (effective 2011). **Document type:** *Directory, Trade.*
Published by: (Federatie van Nederlandse Expediteursorganisaties, Vereniging van Rotterdamse Cargadoors), Uitgeverij Logistiek, Postbus 3064, Ridderkerk, 2980 DB, Netherlands. TEL 31-180-490122, FAX 31-180-424835, info@rotterdamtransport.nl, http://www.rotterdamtransport.nl, http://www.uitgeverijlogistiek.nl.

388.3 USA ISSN 1522-7448
ROUTE DRIVER AND SERVICE TECHNICIAN. Text in English. 1998. s-a.
Published by: Cygnus Business Media, Inc., 1233 Janesville Ave, PO Box 803, Fort Atkinson, WI 53538. TEL 920-563-6388, FAX 920-563-1702, http://www.cygnusb2b.com.

388.3 NLD ISSN 1877-7228
ROUTIERS. Text in Dutch. 1967. bi-m. EUR 45 membership (effective 2011). **Document type:** *Magazine, Trade.*
Former titles (until 2007): Routierswereld (0166-8870); (until 1976): Chauffeurswereld (1381-8619)
Published by: Stichting Les Routiers Europeens, Pieter Zeemanstraat 3, Wijchen, 6603 AV, Netherlands. TEL 31-24-6421144, berns@routiers.nl, http://www.routiers.nl.

388.0440947 GBR ISSN 1750-5216
RUSSIA FREIGHT TRANSPORT REPORT. Text in English. 2005. q. EUR 820, USD 1,030 combined subscription (print & email eds.) (effective 2010). **Document type:** *Report, Trade.* **Description:** Provides industry professionals and strategists, sector analysts, investors, trade associations and regulatory bodies with independent forecasts and competitive intelligence on the Russian freight transport and logistics industry.
Related titles: E-mail ed.
Indexed: A15, ABIn, B02, B15, B17, B18, G04, I05, P48, P51, P52, PQC.
Published by: Business Monitor International Ltd., Senator House, 85 Queen Victoria St, London, EC4V 4AB, United Kingdom. TEL 44-20-72480468, FAX 44-20-72480467, subs@businessmonitor.com.

629.106273 USA ISSN 1946-391X
TL230.A1
➤ **S A E INTERNATIONAL JOURNAL OF COMMERCIAL VEHICLES.** (Society of Automotive Engineers) Text in English. 1906. a. USD 232 per issue to non-members; USD 185.40 per issue to members (effective 2009). back issues avail. **Document type:** *Journal, Academic/Scholarly.* **Description:** Contains technical papers pertaining to both on-road vehicles and off-road vehicles.
Supersedes in part (in 2009): S A E Transactions (0096-736X); Which was formerly (until 1927): Society of Automotive Engineers. Transactions
Related titles: Online - full text ed.: ISSN 1946-3928. USD 342.37 per issue to non-members; USD 273.90 per issue to members (effective 2009).
Indexed: SCOPUS.
—BLDSC (8062.950000), IE, Linda Hall.
Published by: S A E Inc., 400 Commonwealth Dr, Warrendale, PA 15096. TEL 724-776-4970, 877-606-7323, FAX 724-776-0790, CustomerService@sae.org, http://www.sae.org.

➤ **S A E VEHICLE ENGINEERING.** (Society of Automotive Engineers) *see* ENGINEERING

388 GBR
S A P T NEWSLETTER. Text in English. 1972. q. free to members (effective 2009). bk.rev. back issues avail. **Document type:** *Newsletter.* **Description:** Reviews developments in public transportation in Scotland.
Published by: Scottish Association for Public Transport, 11 Queens Crescent, Glasgow, Scotland G4 9BL, United Kingdom. TEL 44-7760-381729, mail@sapt.org.uk.

S C & R A NEWSLETTER. *see* TRANSPORTATION—Trucks And Trucking

388 690 RUS ISSN 2071-7296
➤ **S I B A D I. VESTNIK.** Text in Russian; Summaries in English, Russian. 2004. q. free to qualified personnel. Index. **Document type:** *Journal, Academic/Scholarly.*
Indexed: RefZh.
Published by: Sibirskaya Gosudarstvennaya Avtomobil'no-Doroznaya Akademiya/Siberian State Automobile And Highway Academy, pr-kt Mira, 5, Rm 108, Omsk, 644080, Russian Federation. zavyalov_ma@sibadi.org. Ed. Victor Salnikov. Pub. Mikhail Zavyalov.

338 SWE ISSN 1402-6651
S I K A RAPPORT. (Statens Institut foer Kommunikationsanalys) Text in English, Swedish. 1995. irreg. back issues avail. **Document type:** *Monographic series, Government.*
Related titles: Online - full text ed.
Published by: Statens Institut foer Kommunikationsanalys (SIKA)/ Swedish Institute for Transport and Communications Analysis, Maria Skolgata 83, PO Box 17213, Stockholm, 10462, Sweden. TEL 46-8-50620600, FAX 46-8-50620610, sika@sika-institute.se.

380.5 USA ISSN 0898-8749
SAFE DRIVER. Text in English. 1954. m. USD 15 to members; USD 19.50 to non-members (effective 2003). illus. **Description:** Practical advice about safe driving for the professional bus, truck or passenger car driver.
Published by: (Periodicals Department), National Safety Council, 1121 Spring Lake Dr, Itasca, IL 60143. TEL 630-775-2056, 800-621-7619, FAX 630-285-0797, customerservice@nsc.org, http://www.nsc.org.

SAFE RIDE NEWS. *see* CHILDREN AND YOUTH—For

SAFE ROUTES TO SCHOOL. NORTHERN IRELAND. *see* SPORTS AND GAMES—Bicycles And Motorcycles

SAFE ROUTES TO SCHOOL. SCOTLAND. *see* SPORTS AND GAMES—Bicycles And Motorcycles

SAFETY, INDUSTRIAL RELATIONS, AND GOVERNMENT AFFAIRS SPECIAL REPORT. *see* TRANSPORTATION—Trucks And Trucking

SAMFERDSEL. *see* TRANSPORTATION—Roads And Traffic

380.5 USA ISSN 0362-2800
SAN FRANCISCO BAY AREA RAPID TRANSIT DISTRICT. ANNUAL REPORT. Text in English. 1958. a. illus.
Published by: San Francisco Bay Area Rapid Transit District, 800 Madison St, Oakland, CA 94607. TEL 415-464-6000. Ed. Michael Healy. Circ: 5,000.

380.5 630 CAN ISSN 0822-241X
HE2321.G7
SASKATCHEWAN GRAIN CAR CORPORATION. ANNUAL REPORT. Text in English. 1979. a. free. stat. **Document type:** *Government.*
Related titles: Microfiche ed.
Published by: Saskatchewan Grain Car Corporation, P O Box 2498, Melville, SK S0A 2P0, Canada. TEL 306-728-7444, FAX 306-728-7446. Circ: 500.

388.04409538 GBR ISSN 1750-5224
SAUDI ARABIA FREIGHT TRANSPORT REPORT. Text in English. 2005. q. EUR 820, USD 1,030 combined subscription (print & email eds.) (effective 2010). **Document type:** *Report, Trade.* **Description:** Provides industry professionals and strategists, sector analysts, investors, trade associations and regulatory bodies with independent forecasts and competitive intelligence on the Saudi Arabian freight transport and logistics industry.
Related titles: E-mail ed.
Indexed: A15, ABIn, B02, B15, B17, B18, G04, I05, P48, P51, P52, PQC.
Published by: Business Monitor International Ltd., Senator House, 85 Queen Victoria St, London, EC4V 4AB, United Kingdom. TEL 44-20-72480468, FAX 44-20-72480467, subs@businessmonitor.com.

SCHIP EN SCHADE; beslissingen op het gebied van zee- en binnenvaartrecht, transport en brandverzekeringsrecht. *see* TRANSPORTATION—Ships And Shipping

388.3 USA ISSN 0036-6501
LB2864
SCHOOL BUS FLEET. Text in English. 1956. 10/yr. USD 25 domestic; USD 30 in Canada & Mexico; USD 75 elsewhere; free (effective 2008). adv. charts; illus.; stat. back issues avail. **Document type:** *Magazine, Trade.* **Description:** Provides information on the management and maintenance of school bus fleets operated by public school districts, private schools, head start agencies and childcare centers.
Related titles: Online - full text ed.
Indexed: HRIS, SRI.
Published by: Bobit Business Media, 3520 Challenger St, Torrance, CA 90503. TEL 310-533-2400, FAX 310-533-2500, order@bobit.com, http://www.bobit.com. Ed. John Lacasale. Pub. Frank DiGiacomo TEL 856-596-0999. adv.: color page USD 7,250, B&W page USD 6,080; trim 7.875 x 10.75. Circ: 24,460 (controlled).

SCHOOL TRANSPORTATION NEWS. *see* EDUCATION

388 DEU ISSN 0720-6747
SCHRIFTEN ZUR BETRIEBSWIRTSCHAFTSLEHRE DES VERKEHRS. Text in German. 1979. irreg., latest 1997. price varies. **Document type:** *Monographic series, Academic/Scholarly.*
Published by: Duncker und Humblot GmbH, Carl-Heinrich-Becker-Weg 9, Berlin, 12165, Germany. TEL 49-30-7900060, FAX 49-30-79000631, info@duncker-humblot.de.

SCHUETTGUT. *see* TECHNOLOGY: COMPREHENSIVE WORKS

SCIENTIFIC AUTO ACCIDENT RECONSTRUCTION. *see* INSURANCE

388 GBR ISSN 1351-3869
SCOTTISH OFFICE. TRANSPORT SERIES. STATISTICAL BULLETIN. Text in English. 1993. irreg. **Document type:** *Trade.*
Related titles: Online - full text ed.: ISSN 1759-7056.
—CCC.
Published by: The Scottish Government, St. Andrew's House, Regent Rd, Edinburgh, EH1 3DG, United Kingdom. TEL 44-8457-741741, FAX 44-1397-795001, ceu@scotland.gsi.gov.uk, http://www.scotland.gov.uk/.

388 GBR ISSN 0048-9808
SCOTTISH TRANSPORT. Text in English. 1964. a. GBP 6.50 per issue to non-members; free to members (effective 2009). adv. bk.rev. back issues avail.; reprints avail. **Document type:** *Magazine, Consumer.*
Formerly (until 1970): Scottish Tramlines
Published by: Scottish Tramway and Transport Society, PO Box 7342, Glasgow, Lanarkshire G51 4YQ, United Kingdom. Sales@scottishtransport.org, http://www.scottishtransport.org/. Ed. Ian Stewart.

388 GBR ISSN 1462-8708
SCOTTISH TRANSPORT REVIEW. Abbreviated title: S T R. Text in English. 1998. q. free to members (effective 2009). bk.rev.; Website rev. abstr.; bibl. 24 p./no.; back issues avail. **Document type:** *Newsletter, Trade.* **Description:** Provides review of transport and land use developments affecting Scotland.
Related titles: Online - full text ed.: free (effective 2009).
Published by: Scottish Transport Studies Group, 26 Palmerston Pl, Edinburgh, Scotland EH12 5AL, United Kingdom. TEL 44-131-6653326, enquiries@stsg.org, http://www.stsg,org. Ed. Derek Halden.

SELF-STORAGE ALMANAC. *see* BUSINESS AND ECONOMICS—Domestic Commerce

SELF-STORAGE NOW; a management tool for self-storage professionals. *see* BUSINESS AND ECONOMICS—Domestic Commerce

380.5 CAN ISSN 1209-563X
SENATE OF CANADA. SUBCOMMITTEE ON TRANSPORTATION SAFETY. PROCEEDINGS. Text in English. 1996. irreg.
Published by: Senate of Canada, Subcommittee on Transportation Safety, Parliament of Canada, Ottawa, ON K1A 0A9, Canada. TEL 613-992-4793, 866-599-4999.

388.0440949771 GBR ISSN 1752-7929
SERBIA FREIGHT TRANSPORT REPORT. Text in English. 2007. a. EUR 820, USD 1,030 combined subscription per issue (print & email eds.) (effective 2010). **Document type:** *Report, Trade.* **Description:** Provides industry professionals and strategists, corporate analysts, freight transport associations, government departments and regulatory bodies with independent forecasts and competitive intelligence on the freight transport industry in Serbia.
Related titles: E-mail ed.
Indexed: A15, ABIn, B02, B15, B17, B18, G04, I05, P48, P51, P52, PQC.
Published by: Business Monitor International Ltd., Senator House, 85 Queen Victoria St, London, EC4V 4AB, United Kingdom. TEL 44-20-72480468, FAX 44-20-72480467, subs@businessmonitor.com.

388 CHN ISSN 1006-3226
SHIJIAZHUANG TIEDAO XUEYUAN XUEBAO/SHIJIAZHUANG RAILWAY INSTITUTE. JOURNAL. Text in Chinese. 1982. q. USD 20.80 (effective 2009). **Document type:** *Journal, Academic/Scholarly.*
Formerly (until 1987): Jiaoxue yu Keji
Related titles: Online - full text ed.
Published by: Shijiazhuang Tiedao Xueyuan, 17, Beierhua Dong Lu, Shijiazhuang, 050043, China. TEL 86-311-7935146.

380.5 GBR
SHROPSHIRE COUNTY COUNCIL. LOCAL TRANSPORT PLAN. Abbreviated title: L T P. Text in English. 1977. a. free (effective 2009). back issues avail. **Document type:** *Government.* **Description:** Provides the strategy and action plan for improving local transport facilities and services in Shropshire.
Former titles (until 199?): Shropshire County Council. Transport Policies and Programme; Shropshire County Council and Wrekin Council. Transport Policies and Programme; Shropshire County Council. Transport Policies and Programme
Related titles: Online - full text ed.
Published by: Shropshire County Council, Development Services, Shirehall, Abbey Foregate, Shrewsbury, Shrops SY2 6ND, United Kingdom. TEL 44-1743-253008, FAX 44-1743-253003, transport@shropshire.gov.uk.

388 UKR
SIGNAL. Text in Ukrainian. m. USD 130 in United States. **Document type:** *Government.*
Published by: Ministerstvo Transporta, Ul Artema 22, Kiev, Ukraine. TEL 380-44-216-8684, FAX 380-44-215-2522. **Dist. by:** East View Information Services, 10601 Wayzata Blvd, Minneapolis, MN 55305. TEL 952-252-1201, 800-477-1005, FAX 952-252-1202, info@eastview.com, http://www.eastview.com.

388.044095957 GBR ISSN 1750-5232
SINGAPORE FREIGHT TRANSPORT REPORT. Text in English. 2005. q. EUR 820, USD 1,030 combined subscription (print & email eds.) (effective 2010). **Document type:** *Report, Trade.* **Description:** Covers independent forecasts and competitive intelligence on the Singaporean freight transport and logistics industry.
Related titles: E-mail ed.
Indexed: A15, ABIn, B02, B15, B17, B18, G04, I05, P48, P51, P52, PQC.
Published by: Business Monitor International Ltd., Senator House, 85 Queen Victoria St, London, EC4V 4AB, United Kingdom. TEL 44-20-72480468, FAX 44-20-72480467, subs@businessmonitor.com.

388 ITA ISSN 0394-8471
SISTEMI DI TRASPORTO. Text in Italian. 1976. 3/yr. **Document type:** *Journal, Trade.*
Indexed: HRIS.
Published by: Centro Studi sui Sistemi di Trasporto, Strada Torino 50, Orbassano, TO 10042, Italy. TEL 39-011-9080701, FAX 39-011-9080711, info@csst.it, http://www.csstspa.it.

388.044094373 GBR ISSN 1750-5240
SLOVAKIA FREIGHT TRANSPORT REPORT. Text in English. 2005. a. EUR 820, USD 1,030 combined subscription per issue (print & email eds.) (effective 2010). **Document type:** *Report, Trade.* **Description:** Covers independent forecasts and competitive intelligence on the Slovak freight transport and logistics industry.
Related titles: E-mail ed.
Indexed: A15, ABIn, B02, B15, B17, B18, G04, I05, P48, P51, P52, PQC.
Published by: Business Monitor International Ltd., Senator House, 85 Queen Victoria St, London, EC4V 4AB, United Kingdom. TEL 44-20-72480468, FAX 44-20-72480467, subs@businessmonitor.com.

388.044094973 GBR ISSN 1750-5259
SLOVENIA FREIGHT TRANSPORT REPORT. Text in English. 2005. a. EUR 820, USD 1,030 combined subscription per issue (print & email eds.) (effective 2010). **Document type:** *Report, Trade.* **Description:** Covers independent forecasts and competitive intelligence on the Slovenian freight transport and logistics industry.
Related titles: E-mail ed.
Indexed: A15, ABIn, B02, B15, B17, B18, G04, I05, P48, P51, P52, PQC.
Published by: Business Monitor International Ltd., Senator House, 85 Queen Victoria St, London, EC4V 4AB, United Kingdom. TEL 44-20-72480468, FAX 44-20-72480467, subs@businessmonitor.com.

388 ITA ISSN 1590-0274
IL SOLE 24 ORE. TRASPORTI. Text in Italian. 2001. fortn. **Document type:** *Magazine, Trade.*
Published by: Il Sole 24 Ore Business Media, Via Monte Rosa 91, Milan, 20149, Italy. TEL 39-02-30221, FAX 39-02-312055, info@ilsole24ore.com, http://www.gruppo24ore.com.

SOLIDS & BULK HANDLING. *see* MACHINERY

388 FRA ISSN 2108-2103
▼ **SOLUTION SCOOTERS.** Text in French. 2009. bi-m. **Document type:** *Magazine, Consumer.*
Published by: B'Art Editions, 131 Bd de Creteil, Saint-Maur-des-Fosses, 94100, France. TEL 33-1-77018303, FAX 33-1-77018318.

388.0440968 GBR ISSN 1750-5267
SOUTH AFRICA FREIGHT TRANSPORT REPORT. Text in English. 2005. q. EUR 820, USD 1,030 combined subscription (print & email eds.) (effective 2010). **Document type:** *Report, Trade.* **Description:** Covers independent forecasts and competitive intelligence on the South African freight transport and logistics industry.
Related titles: E-mail ed.
Indexed: A15, ABIn, B02, B15, B17, B18, G04, I05, P48, P51, P52, PQC.
Published by: Business Monitor International Ltd., Senator House, 85 Queen Victoria St, London, EC4V 4AB, United Kingdom. TEL 44-20-72480468, FAX 44-20-72480467, subs@businessmonitor.com.

SOUTH AFRICA. STATISTICS SOUTH AFRICA. ROAD TRAFFIC COLLISIONS. *see* TRANSPORTATION—Abstracting, Bibliographies, Statistics

380.5 ZAF ISSN 0038-2760
SOUTH AFRICAN TRANSPORT; the independent transport journal. Text in English. 1969. m. ZAR 110, USD 50. adv. bk.rev. charts; illus. index. reprints avail. **Document type:** *Journal, Trade.* **Description:** Covers multi-modal transport (air, road, rail and sea), for industry professionals and executives.
Related titles: Microform ed.: (from PQC).
Indexed: CLT&T, HRIS, ISAP.
Published by: Bolton Publications (Pty) Ltd., PO Box 966, Parklands, Johannesburg 2121, South Africa. TEL 27-11-8803520, FAX 27-11-8806574. Ed. Richard Proctor Sims. Adv. contact Michele Nicholson. color page ZAR 5,000; trim 297 x 210. Circ: 608 (paid); 5,039 (controlled).

SOUTH CAROLINA CRIMINAL LAW AND MOTOR VEHICLE HANDBOOK. *see* LAW—Criminal Law

SOUTH DAKOTA CRIMES, CRIMINAL PROCEDURE, MOTOR VEHICLES AND RELATED STATUTES. *see* LAW—Criminal Law

388.044095195 GBR ISSN 1750-5275
SOUTH KOREA FREIGHT TRANSPORTATION REPORT. Text in English. 2005. q. EUR 820, USD 1,030 combined subscription (print & email eds.) (effective 2010). **Document type:** *Report, Trade.* **Description:** Provides industry professionals and strategists, sector analysts, investors, trade associations and regulatory bodies with independent forecasts and competitive intelligence on the South Korean freight transport and logistics industry.
Related titles: E-mail ed.
Indexed: A15, ABIn, B02, B15, B17, B18, G04, I05, P48, P51, P52, PQC.
Published by: Business Monitor International Ltd., Senator House, 85 Queen Victoria St, London, EC4V 4AB, United Kingdom. TEL 44-20-72480468, FAX 44-20-72480467, subs@businessmonitor.com.

388.0440946 GBR ISSN 1750-5283
SPAIN FREIGHT TRANSPORT REPORT. Text in English. 2005. a. EUR 820, USD 1,030 combined subscription per issue (print & email eds.) (effective 2010). **Document type:** *Report, Trade.* **Description:** Provides industry professionals and strategists, corporate analysts, freight transport associations, government departments and regulatory bodies with independent forecasts and competitive intelligence on the freight transport industry in Spain.
Related titles: E-mail ed.
Indexed: B02, B15, B17, B18, G04, I05.
Published by: Business Monitor International Ltd., Senator House, 85 Queen Victoria St, London, EC4V 4AB, United Kingdom. TEL 44-20-72480468, FAX 44-20-72480467, subs@businessmonitor.com.

SPEDITEUR ADRESSBUCH. *see* BUSINESS AND ECONOMICS—Trade And Industrial Directories

380.5 340 DEU
SPEDITIONS-, FRACHT- UND LAGERRECHT. Text in German. 1975. base vol. plus a. updates. looseleaf. EUR 49.80 base vol(s).; EUR 26.80 updates per issue (effective 2009). **Document type:** *Monographic series, Trade.*
Formerly (until 2008): Speditions- und Lagerrecht (0941-0651)
Published by: Erich Schmidt Verlag GmbH & Co. (Berlin), Genthiner Str 30 G, Berlin, 10785, Germany. TEL 49-30-2500850, FAX 49-30-250085305, vertrieb@esvmedien.de, http://www.erich-schmidt-verlag.de.

380.5 USA
SPEEDVISION.COM. Text in English. 1996. m.
Media: Online - full content.
Published by: Sporting News (Subsidiary of: American City Business Journals, Inc.), Box 18449, Anaheim, CA 92817.

388 RUS
SPETSTEKHNIKA. Text in Russian. 2001. bi-m. **Document type:** *Magazine, Trade.*
Published by: Izdatel'stvo MaksMedia, Bogoyavlenskii per., dom 3, str 4, Moscow, 103012, Russian Federation. TEL 7-095-2061103, FAX 7-095-9214929, red@apmedia.ru, http://perevozchik.com.

388.322 DEU ISSN 1860-6067
STADT, BAHN, BUS; Stuttgarter Nahverkehr gestern, heute, morgen. Text in German. 2004. 4/yr. EUR 15.20 (effective 2010). adv. **Document type:** *Magazine, Consumer.*

T
U

Published by: Stuttgarter Historische Strassenbahnen e.V., Veielbrunnenweg 3, Stuttgart, 70372, Germany. TEL 49-711-822210, FAX 49-711-8266490, info@shb-ev.info.

380.5 DEU ISSN 0038-9013
STADTVERKEHR. Text in German. 1956. 10/yr. EUR 48; EUR 5.20 newsstand/cover (effective 2009). adv. bk.rev. charts; illus. index. **Document type:** *Magazine, Trade.* **Description:** Discusses public transport facilities.
Indexed: HRIS, RefZh.
—IE, Infotrieve. **CCC.**
Published by: E K Verlag GmbH, Loerracher Str 16, Freiburg, 79115, Germany. TEL 49-761-703100, FAX 49-761-7031050, vertrieb@eisenbahn-kurier.de, http://www.eisenbahn-kurier.de. Ed. Stefan Goebel. Adv. contact Waltraud Gaenssmantel. B&W page EUR 1,350, color page EUR 2,150; trim 210 x 297. Circ: 5,465 (paid and controlled).

380.5 GBR
STEAM HERITAGE GUIDE (YEAR). Variant title: The Heritage Guide. Text in English. 1968. a. GBP 4.80 per issue domestic; GBP 5.60 per issue in Europe; GBP 6.60 per issue elsewhere (effective 2009). adv. **Document type:** *Directory.* **Description:** Covers information on museums and other venues.
Former titles: Steam Heritage Museums & Rally Guide (Year) (0269-2368); (until 1992): Steam Heritage Yearbook, Preserved Transport and Industrial Archaeology Guide; Steam Year Book, Preserved Transport and Industrial Archaeology Guide; Steam and Organ Year Book and Preserved Transport Guide
Published by: T E E Publishing, The Fosse, Fosse Way, Leamington Spa, Warks CV31 1XN, United Kingdom. TEL 44-1926-614101, FAX 44-1926-614293, info@teepublishing.com. Ed., R&P Christopher Deith. Adv. contact Jane Deciyannis. Circ: 20,000.

363.12 NLD ISSN 0929-2713
STICHTING WETENSCHAPPELIJK ONDERZOEK VERKEERSVEILIGHEID S W O V. JAARVERSLAG. Text in Dutch. 1968. a.
Formerly (until 1987): Stichting Wetenschappelijk Onderzoek Verkeersveiligheid S W O V. Jaaroverzicht (0929-2705)
Published by: Stichting Wetenschappelijk Onderzoek Verkeersveiligheid, Postbus 1090, Leidschendam, 2260 BB, Netherlands. TEL 31-70-3173333, FAX 31-70-3201261, info@swov.nl.

380.5 AUT ISSN 0029-9073
STRASSENGUETERVERKEHR. Text in German. m. EUR 60 domestic; EUR 75 foreign (effective 2005). adv. **Document type:** *Magazine, Trade.*
Formerly: Oesterreichische Fuhrwerker-Zeitung
Indexed: Inspec, RASB.
—**CCC.**
Published by: (Gewerbliches Gueterbefoerderungswesen Oesterreichs), Oesterreichischer Wirtschaftsverlag GmbH (Subsidiary of: Sueddeutscher Verlag GmbH), Wiedner Hauptstr 120-124, Vienna, W 1051, Austria. TEL 43-1-546640, FAX 43-1-54664406, 43-1-54664284, office@wirtschaftsverlag.at, http://www.wirtschaftsverlag.at. Ed. Marco Dittrich. Adv. contact Bernhard Geyer. color page EUR 4,672; trim 168 x 245. Circ: 12,456 (paid and controlled).

STRASSENVERKEHRSRECHT; Zeitschrift fuer die Praxis des Verkehrsjuristen. *see* LAW

380.5 AUS ISSN 0810-0187
STREET MACHINE. Text in English. 1977. m. AUD 79.95 domestic; AUD 102.85 in New Zealand; AUD 120.95 elsewhere; AUD 8.60 newsstand/cover (effective 2008). adv. **Document type:** *Magazine, Consumer.* **Description:** Provides coverage of the Aussie muscle car and modified car scenes.
Former titles (until 1982): Street Machine & Van Wheels (0810-0195); (until 19??): Van Wheels (0155-5391)
Related titles: Online - full text ed.
Indexed: A11, T02.
Published by: A C P Magazines Ltd. (Subsidiary of: P B L Media Pty Ltd.), 54-58 Park St, Sydney, NSW 2000, Australia. TEL 61-2-92828000, FAX 61-2-91263769, research@acpaction.com.au. Ed. Geoff Seddon. Pub. Paul Franks TEL 61-2-82686258. Adv. contact Chris West TEL 61-2-92639706. color page AUD 6,751; trim 225 x 297. Circ: 58,202. **Subscr. to:** Magshop, Reply Paid 4967, Sydney, NSW 2001, Australia. TEL 61-2-136116, subs@magstore.com.au, http://shop.magstore.com.au.

STRUCTURAL MOVER. *see* ENGINEERING—Civil Engineering

380.5 340 DEU ISSN 1860-8876
STUDIEN ZUM PLANUNGS- UND VERKEHRSRECHT. Text in German. 2006. irreg., latest vol.6, 2009. price varies. **Document type:** *Monographic series, Academic/Scholarly.*
Published by: Verlag Dr. Kovac, Leverkusenstr 13, Hamburg, 22761, Germany. TEL 49-40-3988800, FAX 49-40-39888055, info@verlagdrkovac.de.

380.5 CAN ISSN 1199-1755
HE4501
SUMMARY OF CANADIAN TRANSIT STATISTICS. Text in English. 1969. a. CAD 20 to non-members; CAD 10 to members (effective 2006). adv.
Former titles (until 1991): Urban Transit Facts in Canada. Membership Directory (0821-2996); (until 1983): Transit Fact Book & Membership Directory (0706-7658); (until 1978): Transit Fact Book (0082-5913)
Published by: Canadian Urban Transit Association, 55 York St, Ste 1401, Toronto, ON M5J 1R7, Canada. Ed. A Cormier. Circ: 500.

388 658 FRA ISSN 1625-8312
➤ **SUPPLY CHAIN FORUM.** Text in English. 2000. s-a. EUR 55 combined subscription to individuals print & online eds.; EUR 300 combined subscription to institutions print & online eds. (effective 2010). **Document type:** *Journal, Academic/Scholarly.* **Description:** Interactive supply chain management periodical for supply chain researchers and professionals.
Related titles: Online - full text ed.: ISSN 1624-6039 (from IngentaConnect).
Indexed: A09, A10, B01, LogistBibl, T02, V01, V03, V04.
—BLDSC (8547.630580), IE, Ingenta.
Published by: Institut Superieur de Logistique Industrielle, Domaine de Raba, 680 Cours de la Liberation, Talence, 33405, France. TEL 33-5-56845570, FAX 33-5-56845580, isli@bordeaux-bs.edu, http://www.isli.bordeaux-bs.edu. Ed. Dominique Estampe.

➤ **SUPPLY CHAIN MAGASINET.** *see* BUSINESS AND ECONOMICS—Management

➤ **SURFACE TRANSPORTATION.** *see* ENGINEERING—Civil Engineering

➤ **THE SUSTAINABLE WORLD.** *see* ENVIRONMENTAL STUDIES

388 UKR
SYHNAL. Text in Ukrainian. 1991. m. USD 130 in United States (effective 2000).
Published by: Redaktsiya Syhnal, Ul Artema 22, Kiev, Ukraine. TEL 216-86-84. **Dist. by:** East View Information Services, 10601 Wayzata Blvd, Minneapolis, MN 55305. TEL 952-252-1201, 800-477-1005, FAX 952-252-1202, info@eastview.com, http://www.eastview.com.

388 FRA ISSN 0769-0274
SYNTHESE. Text in French. 1986. irreg. **Document type:** *Monographic series, Academic/Scholarly.*
—INIST.
Published by: Institut National de Recherche sur les Transports et leur Securite, 25 Av. Francois Mitterrand, Bron, Cedex 69675, France. TEL 33-4-72142300, FAX 33-4-72376837. **Subscr. to:** Lavoisier, Lavoisier - Dept Abonnements, 14 rue de Provigny, Cachan 94236, France. TEL 33-1-47406700, FAX 33-1-47406702, abo@lavoisier.fr.

380.5 CAN
T A C NEWS; executive digest - focus. Text in English. 1975. q. CAD 60 to non-members (effective 1999). back issues avail. **Document type:** *Newsletter.* **Description:** Reviews association activities and general developments and trends in transportation in Canada and abroad.
Formerly: R T A C News (0317-1280)
Related titles: French ed.: A T C. Nouvelles.
Indexed: A28, APA, BrCerAb, C&ISA, CA/WCA, CIA, CerAb, CivEngAb, ConcrAb, CorrAb, E&CAJ, E11, EEA, EMA, H15, M&TEA, M09, MBF, METADEX, SolStAb, T04, WAA.
Published by: Transportation Association of Canada, 2323 St Laurent Blvd, Ottawa, ON K1G 4J8, Canada. TEL 613-736-1350, FAX 613-736-1395. Ed. Marc Comeau. Circ: 2,000.

380.5 CAN ISSN 1206-7342
T A C SEARCH. Text in English. 1963. a. CAD 45 to non-members; CAD 30 to members. index. **Document type:** *Monographic series, Academic/Scholarly.* **Description:** Searchable database of surface transportation research projects carried out by Canadian transportation research organizations and agencies, universities, private firms, municipalities and associations.
Former titles (until 1995): Surface Transportation R & D in Canada (0834-3594); (until 1986): Inventory of Road and Highway Research and Development Activities in Canada (0833-949X); (until 1984): Surface Transportation R and D in Canada (0828-9042); (until 1983): Transportation R and D in Canada (0709-5538); Transportation Research in Canada (0381-8284); Road Research in Canada (0381-8292)
Media: Online - full text.
Published by: Transportation Association of Canada, 2323 St Laurent Blvd, Ottawa, ON K1G 4J8, Canada. TEL 613-736-1350, FAX 613-736-1395. Ed. C J Hedges.

388 621 USA ISSN 1553-1988
HE4401
T C R P SYNTHESIS. (Transit Cooperative Research Program) Text in English. 1993. m. **Document type:** *Bulletin, Government.* **Description:** Compiles the best-practice use of alternative fuels in public buses.
Formerly (until 200?): Synthesis of Transit Practice (1073-4880)
Indexed: HRIS.
—Linda Hall.
Published by: Advanced Public Transportation Systems Division (Subsidiary of: Office of Research, Demonstration and Innovation), 400 7th St, SW, RM 9409, Washington, DC 20590. TEL 202-366-0195, FAX 202-366-3765.

T - COMM; telecommunications and transport. *see* COMMUNICATIONS

380.5 USA
T I A UPDATE. Text in English. m. adv. **Document type:** *Newsletter.*
Former titles: T I Update; T C B A Update
Published by: Transportation Intermediaries Association, 1625 Prince St., Ste. 200, Alexandria, VA 22314-2883. TEL 703-329-1894, FAX 703-329-1898. Ed. Christopher Falaguerra. Adv. contact Melanie Wilson.

388 USA
T P PLUS. (TransitPulse) Text in English. bi-w. USD 745 (effective 2001).
Media: Fax.
Published by: Trans.21, PO Box 220249, Fields Corner Sta, Boston, MA 02122. TEL 617-825-2318, FAX 617-482-7417, lfabian@airfront.uf.

T Q. (Transportation Quarterly) *see* LAW

388 658.8 NLD ISSN 1566-6336
T R A I L CONFERENCE PROCEEDINGS. (Transport, Infrastructure and Logistics) Text in English. 1998. irreg., latest 2004. price varies.
Published by: (Netherlands TRAIL Research School), Delft University Press (Subsidiary of: I O S Press), Nieuwe Hemweg 6B, Amsterdam, 1013 BG, Netherlands. TEL 31-20-6883355, FAX 31-20-6870039, info.dupress@iospress.nl.

388 NLD
T R A I L REPORTS IN TRANSPORTATION PLANNING. (Transportation, Infrastructure and Logistics) Text in English. irreg., latest 2002. price varies. **Document type:** *Monographic series, Academic/Scholarly.*
Published by: (Netherlands TRAIL Research School), Delft University Press (Subsidiary of: I O S Press), Nieuwe Hemweg 6B, Amsterdam, 1013 BG, Netherlands. TEL 31-20-6883355, FAX 31-20-6870039, info.dupress@iospress.nl.

388 NLD
T R A I L STUDIES IN TRANSPORTATION SCIENCE. (Transport, Infrastructure and Logistics) Text in English. 2000. irreg., latest 2006. price varies. **Document type:** *Monographic series, Academic/Scholarly.*
Published by: (Netherlands TRAIL Research School), Delft University Press (Subsidiary of: I O S Press), Nieuwe Hemweg 6B, Amsterdam, 1013 BG, Netherlands. TEL 31-20-6883355, FAX 31-20-6870039, info.dupress@iospress.nl.

T R A I L THESIS SERIES. (Transportation, Infrastructure and Logistics) *see* BUSINESS AND ECONOMICS—Marketing And Purchasing

380.5 USA ISSN 0738-6826
TE1
T R NEWS. (Transportation Research) Text in English. 1963. bi-m. USD 55 domestic; USD 75 foreign (effective 2010). bk.rev. charts; illus. back issues avail.; reprints avail. **Document type:** *Magazine, Government.* **Description:** Features articles on innovative practices and current research in all modes of transportation.
Former titles (until 1983): Transportation Research News (0095-2656); (until 1974): Highway Research News (0018-1749)
Related titles: Online - full text ed.: free (effective 2010).
Indexed: A22, A28, APA, BrCerAb, BrRB, C&ISA, CA/WCA, CIA, CPEI, CerAb, CivEngAb, ConcrAb, CorrAb, DokStr, E&CAJ, E11, EEA, EMA, ESPM, EngInd, EnvEAb, GeoRef, GeotechAb, H15, HRIS, ICEA, M&TEA, M09, MBF, METADEX, NPPA, SCOPUS, SoftAbEng, SolStAb, T04, WAA.
—BLDSC (8873.791000), IE, Infotrieve, Ingenta, Linda Hall. **CCC.**
Published by: U.S. National Research Council, Transportation Research Board, The National Academies, 500 Fifth St, NW, Washington, DC 20001. TEL 202-334-2934. Ed. Javy Awan. Circ: 10,000.

388 384 ESP ISSN 1578-5777
T S T. TRANSPORTES, SERVICIOS Y TELECOMUNICACIONES. Text in Spanish. 2001. s-a. EUR 25 (effective 2009). **Document type:** *Magazine, Trade.*
Published by: Fundacion de los Ferrocarriles Espanoles, Santa Isabel 44, Madrid, 28012, Spain. TEL 34-91-1511071, FAX 34-915-281003, vlibre@ffe.es, http://www.ffe.es. Eds. Javier Vidal Olivares, Miguel Munoz Rubio.

T W U EXPRESS. *see* LABOR UNIONS

388 USA
T3 - TRANSPORT TECHNOLOGY TODAY. Text in English. 1996. 12/yr. USD 82 (effective 2001). adv. software rev. **Description:** Covers information technology utilized in the transportation market and focuses on management solutions through information technology.
Related titles: Online - full text ed.
Published by: Maple Communications, 134 W Slade St, Palatine, IL 60067. TEL 847-359-6100, FAX 847-359-6420. Ed. Lawson Marshall. Pub., R&P, Adv. contact Robert Dorn. B&W page USD 3,835, color page USD 5,095; trim 10.75 x 8. Circ: 46,000.

388 CZE ISSN 1211-5827
TACHOGRAF. Text in Czech. 1994. fortn. **Document type:** *Magazine, Trade.*
Published by: Bohemia Press s.r.o., Turkmenska 1418-6, Prague 10, 101 00, Czech Republic. TEL 42-2-67312603, FAX 42-2-67312708.

388.0440951249 GBR ISSN 1750-5291
TAIWAN FREIGHT TRANSPORT REPORT. Text in English. 2005. q. EUR 820, USD 1,030 combined subscription (print & email eds.) (effective 2010). **Document type:** *Report, Trade.* **Description:** Provides industry professionals and strategists, sector analysts, investors, trade associations and regulatory bodies with independent forecasts and competitive intelligence on the Taiwanese freight transport and logistics industry.
Related titles: E-mail ed.
Indexed: A15, ABIn, B02, B15, B17, B18, G04, I05, P48, P51, P52, PQC.
Published by: Business Monitor International Ltd., Senator House, 85 Queen Victoria St, London, EC4V 4AB, United Kingdom. TEL 44-20-72480468, FAX 44-20-72480467, subs@businessmonitor.com.

380.5 TWN
TAIWAN TRANSPORTATION EQUIPMENT GUIDE. Text in Chinese. 3/yr. USD 80 in Americas, Europe & Africa; USD 70 in Middle East & Asia; USD 50 elsewhere (effective 2000). adv. **Description:** Provides detailed listings of Taiwan's best suppliers of auto parts and accessories.
Published by: China Economic News Service, 555 Chunghsiao E. Rd Sec 4, Taipei, 110, Taiwan. TEL 886-2-2642-2629, FAX 886-2-2642-7422. adv.: B&W page TWD 40,000, color page TWD 45,000. **Dist. by:** Current Pacific Ltd., 7 La Roche Pl, Northcote, PO Box 36-536, Auckland 0627, New Zealand. TEL 64-9-4801388, FAX 64-9-4801387, info@cplnz.com, http://www.cplnz.com.

380 ESP
TALLERES EN COMUNICACION; revista tecnica de automocion, equipos y componentes. Text in Spanish. 1990. m. adv. **Document type:** *Magazine, Trade.*
Published by: BCV Reto, S.L., C. Consejo de Ciento No. 217, Entlo. 3a., Barcelona, 08011, Spain. TEL 34-93-4538162, FAX 34-93-4512836, barreto@intercom.es. Ed. Antonio Conde.

TANKE ZHUANGJIA CHELIANG/TANK & ARMOURED VEHICLE. *see* MILITARY

380.5 FRA ISSN 0153-9205
TARIF PIECES DETACHEES. Text in French. 1969. q. **Description:** Covers 120 domestic and import cars. Indicates prices of car parts (body as well as engine).
Related titles: ◆ Supplement to: Auto Expertise. ISSN 0150-7230.
Published by: Editions Techniques pour l'Automobile et l'Industrie (E T A I), 20-22 rue de la Saussiere, Boulogne Billancourt, 92100, France. FAX 33-1-48255692, TELEX ETAIRTA 204850F, http://www.groupe-etai.com. Ed. Daniel Thallinger.

338.321 ESP ISSN 1888-4520
EL TAXI. Text in Spanish. 2007. m.
Related titles: Online - full text ed.
Published by: Confederacion del Taxi en Espana, C Otero, s-n, Centro Comercial Parcela 4J, Oviedo, Asturias 33008, Spain. eltaxi@etrasa.com, http://www.confetaxi.org/index.php.

388.346 DNK ISSN 1903-1300
TAXI; officiel brancheblad for dansk taxi raad. Text in Danish. 1924. 11/yr. DKK 80 (effective 2009). adv. charts; illus. back issues avail. **Document type:** *Magazine, Trade.*
Former titles (until 2008): Dansk Taxi Tidende (0108-0709); (until 1975): Droske Tidende (0040-0130)
Published by: Dansk Taxi Raad, Klingseyvej 15 A, Vanloese, 2720, Denmark. TEL 45-38-777890, FAX 45-38-717891, dtr@taxi.dk, http://www.taxi.dk. Adv. contact Rasmus Brylle. color page DKK 13,565; 175 x 267. Circ: 5,400. **Dist. by:** Horisont Gruppen A/S, Center Boulevard 5, Copenhagen S 2300, Denmark. TEL 45-32-473230, FAX 45-32-473239, info@horisontgruppen.dk, http://www.horisontgruppen.dk.

388.413 NOR ISSN 0332-5881
TAXI. Text in Norwegian. 1923. m. (10/yr.). NOK 250 (effective 2000). adv. **Document type:** *Journal, Trade.*
Former titles (until 1977): Norsk Drosjeeirblad (0048-0584); (until 1929): Auto-Droschen (0332-6985)
Published by: (Norges Taxiforbund), Media Markedskommunikasjon AS, Trondheimsvn 100, Postboks 6538 R, Oslo, 0501, Norway. nortaxi@nortaxi.no, http://www.nortaxi.no. Ed. Viggo Korsnes. Adv. contact Orjan Tvedt.

388.321 USA
TAXI & LIVERY MANAGEMENT. Text in English. 1982. q. USD 16 in North America; USD 26 elsewhere. adv. **Document type:** *Magazine, Trade.* **Description:** For for-hire fleet operators - the people who own and manage limousine, livery, taxicab, van, and minibus fleets.
Formerly: Taxicab Management
Indexed: HRIS.
Published by: International Taxicab and Livery Association, 3849 Farragut Ave, Kensington, MD 20895-2004. TEL 301-946-5701, FAX 301-946-4641. Ed., R&P Alfred Lagasse TEL 301-946-5700. Pub., Adv. contact Nancy Murphy. B&W page USD 1,050, color page USD 1,650; trim 11 x 8.5. Circ: 5,800.

388.346 GBR ISSN 1468-6643
TAXI GLOBE. Text in English. 1982. fortn. GBP 20; free to qualified personnel (effective 2009). adv. bk.rev.; play rev. illus.; mkt.; maps; stat.; tr.lit. 28 p./no. 5 cols./p.; back issues avail. **Document type:** *Newspaper, Trade.* **Description:** Provides drivers, proprietors and those involved in the running of London's taxi service with articles on every aspect of the trade, together with competitions and product reviews.
Related titles: E-mail ed.; Fax ed.
Published by: Warners Group Publications Plc., The Maltings, Manor Ln, Bourne, Lincs PE10 9PH, United Kingdom. wgpsubs@warnersgroup.co.uk, http://www.warnersgroup.co.uk. Ed. Sandie Goodwin TEL 44-1707-885439. Adv. contact Jayne Notley TEL 44-1778-391189. page GBP 550; 264 x 340.

388.413 SWE ISSN 0283-5576
TAXI IDAG. Text in Swedish. 1986. 8/yr. SEK 415 (effective 2001). adv. 40 p./no. 4 cols./p.; **Document type:** *Magazine, Trade.* **Description:** Publishes news and articles of interest to taxi drivers and others in the industry.
Incorporates (1966-1989): Taxitrafiken (0040-022X); Which was formerly (until 1966): Drosktrafiken
Published by: (Svenska Taxiforbundet), Wiksten & Iger Information AB, Box 11119, Stockholm, 10061, Sweden. TEL 46-8-702-09-14, FAX 46-8-643-09-12. Ed., Pub. Dan Wiksten. Adv. contact Turid Korsvold. B&W page SEK 15,300, color page SEK 23,900; trim 185 x 270. Circ: 8,700.

388.321 GBR ISSN 0965-836X
TAXI MAGAZINE. Text in English. 1968. fortn. free to members (effective 2009). adv. bk.rev. illus.; tr.lit. back issues avail. **Document type:** *Magazine, Trade.*
Formerly (until 1991): Taxi (0049-304X)
Related titles: Online - full text ed.: free (effective 2009).
Published by: Licensed Taxi Drivers Association, Taxi House, 9-11 Woodfield Rd, London, W9 2BA, United Kingdom. TEL 44-20-72861046, http://www.ltda.co.uk. Adv. contact Keygan Cyrus TEL 44-1727-739183. Circ: 14,000.

388.321 CAN ISSN 0834-3489
TAXI NEWS. Text in English. 1985. m. CAD 15, USD 25 (effective 2000). adv. bk.rev. back issues avail. **Document type:** *Newspaper, Trade.* **Description:** News and events affecting Toronto's taxi industry.
Published by: Chedmount Investment Ltd., 38 Fairmount Cres, Toronto, ON M4L 2H4, Canada. TEL 416-468-2328, FAX 416-466-4220. Ed. Bill McOuat. Pub. John Q Duffy. Adv. contact John Duffy. Circ: 10,100.

388.346 USA
TAXI TALK. Text in English. m. free (effective 2005). **Document type:** *Newspaper.*
Published by: Taxi Talk, Inc., 101 W. 23rd. St., # 2402, New York, NY 10011. TEL 212-765-3232, FAX 212-765-3184. Ed. Jack Ponomarev. Pub. Michael Higgins.

388.346 GBR ISSN 2044-9674
TAXI-TODAY. Text in English. 2005. m. adv. back issues avail. **Document type:** *Magazine, Trade.*
Former titles (until 2010): Taxi Today Monthly (1758-132X); (until 2008): Taxi-Today (1751-3111)
Address: The Advertising Specialists Ltd, 19 Fountain St, Morley, Leeds, LS27 9AE, United Kingdom. TEL 44-1133-202727, FAX 44-1133-202828.

380.54 USA ISSN 1062-5240
TECH TRANSFER. Text in English. q. **Document type:** *Newsletter.*
Indexed: HRIS.
Published by: University of California, Berkeley, Institute of Transportation Studies, 109 McLaughlin Hall, Berkeley, CA 94720-1720. TEL 510-231-5675, FAX 510-642-1246. Ed., R&P Donna Reid TEL 510-642-3585.

388 DEU ISSN 1432-2560
TECHNISCHE UNIVERSITAET BERLIN. FACHGEBIET REGELUNGSTECHNIK UND SYSTEMDYNAMIK. BERICHTE. Text in German. 1996. irreg., latest vol.2, 1997. price varies. **Document type:** *Monographic series, Academic/Scholarly.*
Published by: (Technische Universitaet Berlin, Fachgebiet Regelungstechnik und Systemdynamik), Shaker Verlag GmbH, Kaiserstr 100, Herzogenrath, 52134, Germany. TEL 49-2407-95960, FAX 49-2407-95969, info@shaker.de, http://www.shaker.de.

380.5 620 USA
TECHNOLOGY FOR ALASKAN TRANSPORTATION; improving Alaska's quality of transportation through technology application, traning and information exchange. Text in English. 1986. q. free (effective 2011). bk.rev. bibl.; charts; illus.; stat. index. **Document type:** *Newsletter, Trade.* **Description:** Seeks to dessseminate innovative technology regarding transportation to transportation professionals throughout the state of Alaska, Canada, and also to share and work with T2 Centers throughout the US and Puerto Rico.
Published by: (F H W A), Alaska Transportation Technology Transfer Center Library, Department of Transportation and Public Facilities, 2301 Peger Rd., M/S 2550, Fairbanks, AK 99709-5399. TEL 907-451-5320, FAX 907-451-5340, http://www.dot.state.ak.us/. Ed. Dave Waldo TEL 907-451-5323. Circ: 2,400 (controlled).

TENNESSEE CRIMINAL OFFENSES, VEHICLES AND RELATED STATUTES. see LAW—Criminal Law

343.093 USA
TENNESSEE MOTOR VEHICLE LAWS ANNOTATED. Text in English. irreg. USD 43 combined subscription per issue (print & CD-ROM eds.) (effective 2008). 425 p./no.; **Document type:** *Monographic series, Trade.* **Description:** Contains statutes dealing with motor carriers, the highway patrol, ride-sharing, criminal offenses and petroleum products taxes.
Related titles: CD-ROM ed.
Published by: Michie Company (Subsidiary of: LexisNexis North America), 701 E Water St, Charlottesville, VA 22902. TEL 434-972-7600, 800-446-3410, FAX 434-972-7677, customer.support@lexisnexis.com, http://www.michie.com.

TEXAS CRIMINAL LAW & MOTOR VEHICLE HANDBOOK. see LAW

380.5 USA ISSN 0040-4748
TE1 CODEN: TXTRA8
TEXAS TRANSPORTATION RESEARCHER. Text in English. 1965. q. free (effective 2005). illus. index. **Document type:** *Newsletter.* **Description:** Showcases transportation research and professional activities of the institute.
Related titles: Microform ed.: (from PQC); Online - full text ed.
Indexed: CPEI, Englnd, HRIS, SCOPUS.
—Linda Hall.
Published by: Texas Transportation Institute, Texas A & M Univ System, College Station, TX 77843-3135. TEL 409-845-1734, FAX 409-845-7575. Ed. Kelly West. Pub. Herbert Richardson. Circ: 6,000.

388.04409593 GBR ISSN 1750-5305
THAILAND FREIGHT TRANSPORT REPORT. Text in English. 2005. q. EUR 820, USD 1,030 combined subscription (print & email eds.) (effective 2010). **Document type:** *Report, Trade.* **Description:** Provides industry professionals and strategists, sector analysts, investors, trade associations and regulatory bodies with independent forecasts and competitive intelligence on the Thai freight transport and logistics industry.
Related titles: E-mail ed.
Indexed: A15, ABIn, B02, B15, B17, B18, G04, I05, P48, P51, P52, PQC.
Published by: Business Monitor International Ltd., Senator House, 85 Queen Victoria St, London, EC4V 4AB, United Kingdom. TEL 44-20-72480468, FAX 44-20-72480467, subs@businessmonitor.com.

385.2 387.54 GBR ISSN 0144-7475
HE1805 CODEN: TCOTDF
THOMAS COOK OVERSEAS TIMETABLE. Text in English; Summaries in French, German, Italian, Spanish. 1981. bi-m. GBP 75 domestic; GBP 87 in Europe; GBP 96 elsewhere (effective 2009). adv. index. **Document type:** *Directory, Trade.* **Description:** Provides comprehensive timetables for rail, bus and shipping services for virtually all countries outside Europe, with maps and town plans. Includes a useful Travel Information section and index of over 7000 places.
Supersedes in part (in 1980): Thomas Cook International Timetable (0141-2701)
—BLDSC (8820.230300), CASDDS. **CCC.**
Published by: Thomas Cook Publishing, PO Box 227, Peterborough, Cambs PE3 8SB, United Kingdom. TEL 44-1733-416477, FAX 44-1733-416688, publishing-sales@thomascook.com. Circ: 24,000.

TIJDSCHRIFT VERVOER EN RECHT. see LAW

388 NLD ISSN 1571-9227
TIJDSCHRIFT VERVOERSWETENSCHAP. Text in Dutch. 1999. q. **Document type:** *Journal, Trade.*
Formerly (until 2002): Connektie (1389-4773); Which incorporated (1965-1999): Tijdschrift voor Vervoerswetenschap (0040-7623)
Published by: Connekt, Postbus 48, Delft, 2600 AA, Netherlands. TEL 31-15-2516565, FAX 31-15-2516599, info@connekt.nl, http://www.connekt.nl.

380.5 ESP ISSN 0212-8357
TODOTRANSPORTE; revista mensual del transporte. Text in Spanish. 1984. m. EUR 135.34 combined subscription domestic (print, online and email eds.); EUR 195 combined subscription foreign (print, online and email eds.) (effective 2009). adv. **Document type:** *Magazine, Trade.* **Description:** Covers the transportation industry, including travel, cargo, air, railroad, ship and highway.
Related titles: E-mail ed.: ISSN 1988-8937. EUR 348.59 (effective 2002); Online - full text ed.: Todotransporte Digital. ISSN 1988-8929. 2001.
Published by: Tecnipublicaciones Espana, S.L., Avda de Manoteras 44, 3a Planta, Madrid, 28050, Spain. TEL 34-91-2972000, FAX 34-91-2972154, tp@tecnipublicaciones.com. Circ: 15,600.

388 658.8 NLD ISSN 1871-1790
TON; magazine voor mensen die werken in transport en logistiek. Text in Dutch. 2005. bi-m. EUR 22.50 (effective 2008). adv. **Document type:** *Magazine, Trade.*
Published by: Boss en Wijnhoven b.v., Maliebaan 9, Utrecht, 3581 CA, Netherlands. TEL 31-30-2322517, FAX 31-30-2302560, info@boss-wijnhoven.nl, http://www.boss-wijnhoven.nl. adv.: color page EUR 5,408; trim 200 x 240. Circ: 140,000.

388 NLD ISSN 0928-1576
TOPICS IN TRANSPORTATION. Text in English. 1987. irreg., latest vol.5, 1994. price varies. stat. back issues avail. **Document type:** *Monographic series, Academic/Scholarly.* **Description:** Examines issues in trapnsportation theory and applications in specific contexts, including transport analysis, planning operations, and transport policy studies.
Indexed: IZBG.
Published by: V S P (Subsidiary of: Brill), Brill Academic Publishers, PO Box 9000, Leiden, 2300 PA, Netherlands. TEL 31-71-5353500, FAX 31-71-5317532, marketing@brill.nl.

388 CAN ISSN 1199-2352
TORONTO TRANSPORTATION COMMISSION. ANNUAL REPORT. Text in English. a. **Document type:** *Report, Trade.*
Former titles (until 1954): Toronto Transportation Commission. Annual Statement (1910-2984); (until 192?): Toronto Transportation Commission. Annual Report (1910-2976); (until 1923): Toronto Transportation Commission. Financial Statement (1910-2968)
Published by: Toronto Transit Commission, 1900 Yonge St, Toronto, ON M4S 1Z2, Canada. TEL 416-393-4000, http://www.toronto.ca/ttc.

388.322 338.4791 NLD ISSN 1388-6088
TOUR MAGAZINE. Text in Dutch. 1995. q. EUR 15 domestic; EUR 25 foreign (effective 2010). adv. **Document type:** *Magazine, Trade.*
Published by: Stichting Bus, Postbus 19365, The Hague, 2500 CJ, Netherlands. TEL 31-70-3751776. Ed. Jos Haas TEL 31-70-3751728. Adv. contact Danielle van Essen. B&W page EUR 1,132, color page EUR 1,932; trim 210 x 297. Circ: 8,000.

380.5 MWI
TRAFFIC. Text in English. q.
Published by: Centraf Associates Ltd., Chichiri, PO Box 30462, Blantyre, Malawi.

388.31 SWE ISSN 1403-2988
TRAFIK FORUM. Variant title: Res och Trafik Forum. Trafikforum. Text in Swedish. 1998. 10/yr. SEK 564 domestic; SEK 695 foreign (effective 2007). adv. **Document type:** *Magazine, Trade.*
Supersedes in part (in 1998): Resor och Trafik (1104-4594); Which was formed by the merger of (1954-1993): Svensk Lokaltrafik (0039-6648); (1992-1993): Busstidningen (1102-6693); Which was formerly (until 1991): Buss, Svensk Omnibustidning (0282-7654); (1929-1982): Svensk Omnibustidning (0039-6672)
Published by: Res och Trafik Media i Stockholm AB (Subsidiary of: Mentor Online AB), Observatoriegatan 17, Stockholm, 11329, Sweden. TEL 46-8-315940, FAX 46-8-6601272, http://www.rt-forum.se. Ed., Pub. Ulo Maasing. Adv. contact Gunilla Hagberg. color page SEK 22,300; trim 245 x 339. Circ: 2,500.

TRAIL ZONE; trail, enduro & adventure riding magazine. see SPORTS AND GAMES—Outdoor Life

TRAILER LIFE; follow the road to adventure. see SPORTS AND GAMES—Outdoor Life

388.4 GBR ISSN 0049-4372
TRAMWAY MUSEUM SOCIETY. JOURNAL. Text in English. 19?? (vol.2). q. free to members (effective 2010). adv. bk.rev.; video rev. charts; illus. 40 p./no. 1 cols./p.; back issues avail. **Document type:** *Journal, Trade.* **Description:** Provides historians, scholars and students with information on trams.
Formerly (until 1961): Tramway Museum Society. Newsletter
Published by: Tramway Museum Society, Crich Tramway Village, nr Matlock, Derbyshire, DE4 5DP, United Kingdom. TEL 44-1773-854321, FAX 44-1773-854320, enquiries@tramway.co.uk, http://www.tramway.co.uk/.

380.5 DEU ISSN 0947-7268
TRANS AKTUELL; die Zeitung fuer Transport, Verkehr und Management. Text in German. 1992. fortn. EUR 75.40; EUR 2.90 newsstand/cover (effective 2011). adv. bk.rev. 24 p./no. 6 cols./p.; back issues avail. **Document type:** *Newspaper, Trade.*
Incorporates (1970-2007): Distribution (0342-1635); Which incorporated (1979-1983): Cargo-Journal (0720-7328)
Published by: EuroTransportMedia Verlags- und Veranstaltungs-GmbH, Handwerkstr 15, Stuttgart, 70565, Germany. TEL 49-711-784980, FAX 49-711-7849888, info@etm-verlag.de, http://www.etm-verlag.de. Circ: 61,559 (paid).

380.5 DEU
TRANS AKTUELL SPEZIAL. Text in German. 1994. a. EUR 14.90 newsstand/cover (effective 2011). adv. **Document type:** *Magazine, Trade.*
Published by: EuroTransportMedia Verlags- und Veranstaltungs-GmbH, Handwerkstr 15, Stuttgart, 70565, Germany. TEL 49-711-784980, FAX 49-711-7849888, info@etm-verlag.de, http://www.etm-verlag.de. Circ: 40,000 (paid and controlled).

388 DNK ISSN 0904-6534
TRANS-INFORM. Text in Danish. 1987. m. DKK 350 (effective 2009). adv. **Document type:** *Magazine, Trade.*
Related titles: Online - full text ed.
Published by: Danmarks Transport Forlag A/S, Jernbanegade 18, PO Box 352, Padborg, 6330, Denmark. TEL 45-70-100506, FAX 45-74-674047. Ed. Gwyn Nissen. Adv. contact Trine Philipsen. color page DKK 16,945; 176 x 265. Circ: 4,800.

388 POL ISSN 1802-971X
TRANSACTIONS ON TRANSPORT SCIENCES. Text in English. 2008. q. **Document type:** *Journal, Academic/Scholarly.*
Related titles: Online - full text ed.: ISSN 1802-9876. free (effective 2011).
Published by: Ministerstwo Infrastruktury, ul Chalubinskiego 4/6, Warsaw, 00-928, Poland. http://www.mi.gov.pl.

▼ **TRANSFERS**; interdisciplinary journal of mobility studies. see TECHNOLOGY: COMPREHENSIVE WORKS

388 USA ISSN 2156-3594
TRANSFORUM. Text in English. 1998. s-a. back issues avail. **Document type:** *Newsletter, Consumer.* **Description:** Provides reports on accomplishments in Argonne's transportation research.
Related titles: Online - full text ed.: ISSN 2156-373X. free (effective 2010).
Published by: Transportation Technology R & D Center, Argonne National Laboratory, 9700 S Cass Ave, Bldg - 362, Argonne, IL 60439. TEL 630-252-8170, ttrdc@anl.gov. Ed. Else Tennessen.

380.5 USA ISSN 1067-0297
HE4487.C2
TRANSIT CALIFORNIA. Text in English. 1990. 10/yr. USD 18 (effective 2009). adv. bk.rev. charts; illus.; stat.; tr.lit. **Document type:** *Report, Trade.* **Description:** Covers transit funding and transit-related legislation, public transit system profiles, federal and state transit issues, Americans with Disabilities Act, Clean Air Acts, transit financing issues, air quality, alternate fuels, drug and alcohol testing requirements, and more.
Indexed: HRIS.
Published by: California Transit Association, 1414 K St, Ste 320, Sacramento, CA 95814-3967. TEL 916-446-4656, FAX 916-446-4318, info@transitassociation.org. Ed. Joshua W Shaw. Circ: 6,000.

388 340 USA ISSN 1078-4403
KF2391.A15
TRANSIT COOPERATIVE RESEARCH PROGRAM. LEGAL RESEARCH DIGEST. Text in English. 1994. irreg., latest 2011. price varies. back issues avail. **Document type:** *Monographic series, Trade.*
Related titles: Online - full text ed.: free (effective 2011).
Indexed: HRIS.
—Linda Hall.

Published by: Transportation Research Board, Transit Cooperative Research Program, The National Academies, 500 Fifth St, NW, Washington, DC 20001. TEL 202-334-2934, TRBSales@nas.edu.

388 USA
TRANSIT COOPERATIVE RESEARCH PROGRAM. PROJECT REPORTS. Text in English. 19??. irreg. price varies. back issues avail. **Document type:** *Report, Trade.*
Related titles: Online - full text ed.
Published by: Transportation Research Board, Transit Cooperative Research Program, The National Academies, 500 Fifth St, NW, Washington, DC 20001. TEL 202-334-2934, TRBSales@nas.edu.

388 628.53 USA ISSN 1075-8186
HE4401
TRANSIT COOPERATIVE RESEARCH PROGRAM. RESEARCH RESULTS DIGEST. Text in English. 1994. bi-m. price varies. back issues avail. **Document type:** *Monographic series, Government.* **Description:** Updates on the results of TCRP research into safer and more efficient public transport.
Related titles: Online - full text ed.
Indexed: HRIS.
—BLDSC (7769.587700), Linda Hall.
Published by: Transportation Research Board, Transit Cooperative Research Program, The National Academies, 500 Fifth St, NW, Washington, DC 20001. TEL 202-334-2934, TRBSales@nas.edu.

388 USA
TRANSIT COOPERATIVE RESEARCH PROGRAM. SYNTHESIS REPORTS. Text in English. irreg. price varies. back issues avail. **Document type:** *Report, Trade.*
Related titles: Online - full text ed.
Published by: Transportation Research Board, Transit Cooperative Research Program, The National Academies, 500 Fifth St, NW, Washington, DC 20001. TEL 202-334-2934, TRBSales@nas.edu.

388 USA
TRANSIT COOPERATIVE RESEARCH PROGRAM. WEB DOCUMENTS. Text in English. 19??. irreg. free (effective 2011). back issues avail. **Document type:** *Monographic series, Trade.*
Media: Online - full text.
Indexed: HRIS.
Published by: Transportation Research Board, Transit Cooperative Research Program, The National Academies, 500 Fifth St, NW, Washington, DC 20001. TEL 202-334-2934, TRBSales@nas.edu.

388 USA ISSN 0149-0656
K24
TRANSIT LAW REVIEW. Text in English. 1977. irreg.
Indexed: G08.
Published by: American Public Transportation Association, 1666 K St, NW Ste 1100, Washington, DC 20006. TEL 202-496-4800, FAX 202-496-4321, http://www.apta.com.

388 USA
TRANSIT RESEARCH & TECHNOLOGY 5-YEAR PLAN. EXCUTIVE SUMMARY. Text in English. every 5 yrs. **Document type:** *Government.*
Published by: U.S. Federal Transit Administration (Subsidiary of: U.S. Department of Transportation), 400 7th Street, SW, Washington, DC 20590. TEL 202-366-4043, FAX 202-366-3472, http://www.fta.dot.gov/index.html.

TRANSIT TIMES. *see* TRANSPORTATION—Railroads

388 USA
TRANSITPULSE. Text in English. 1983. bi-m. USD 95 (effective 2007). 12 p./no.; **Document type:** *Newsletter, Trade.* **Description:** Covers new ways to overcome congestion, as well as urban, suburban and airport travel.
Media: E-mail.
Published by: Trans.21, PO Box 220249, Fields Corner Sta, Boston, MA 02122. TEL 617-825-2318, FAX 617-482-7417, lfabian@airfront.uf, http://www.airfront.uf. Circ: 4,050 (paid and free).

380.5 ZAF
TRANSNET ANNUAL REPORT (YEAR). Text in Afrikaans, English. a. free. charts; illus.; stat. index. **Document type:** *Corporate.* **Description:** Reports on the activities of all Transnet divisions, including the railways, ports, petroleum pipelines, container services, and South African Airways, rail commuter transport and road transport.
Formerly (until 1990): S A Transport Services Annual Report (Year)
Related titles: English ed.
Published by: Group Corporate Communications, PO Box 72501, Parkview, Johannesburg 2122, South Africa. TEL 27-11-488-7116, FAX 27-11-488-8009, http://www.tnet.co.za. Circ: 7,000.

380.5 MEX
TRANSPOR. Text in Spanish. 1978. m. adv.
Address: San FRANCISCO 224 Piso 5, Col Del Valle, Apartado Postal 12879, Mexico City, DF 12879, Mexico. Ed. Enrique Landgrave Villanueva. Circ: 5,000.

388.3 BEL ISSN 0778-6964
TRANSPORAMA (DUTCH EDITION); truck & bus maagzine. Text in Dutch. 1982. 11/yr. EUR 45 domestic; EUR 82 in the European Union; EUR 88 elsewhere (effective 2005). adv. software rev. illus. back issues avail. **Document type:** *Magazine, Trade.* **Description:** Covers the transportation of goods and people via truck, van, bus, and motorcoach.
Related titles: French ed.: Transporama (French Edition). ISSN 0778-6972.
—Infotrieve.
Published by: Transporama Publishing, Mechelsesteenweg 326/4, Edegem, 2650, Belgium. TEL 32-3-4558795, FAX 32-3-4551087, info@ transporama.be, http://www.transporama.be. Ed., Pub. Leo Nuyens. Circ: 22,500. **Subscr. to:** PO Box 72, Edegem 2650, Belgium.

380.5 910.09 ECU ISSN 1018-2179
TRANSPORT; guia ecuatoriana de transporte y turismo. Text in Spanish. 1963. m. USD 119 (effective 1993). adv. back issues avail. **Document type:** *Trade.* **Description:** Airline and shipline guide for travel agents and others in the Ecuadorian travel industry.
Address: SUCRE, 2204, Apartado de Correos 09 01 5603, Guayaquil, Guayas, Ecuador. TEL 593-4-363848, FAX 593-4-454717. Ed. Pablo Cevallos Estarellas. Pub. Nelson Cevallos Aviles. Adv. contact Roberto Wagner. Circ: 4,100 (paid).

380.5 LUX
TRANSPORT. Text in French. fortn.
Address: 5 rue C.M. Spoo, Luxembourg, 2546, Luxembourg.

388 DEU ISSN 0946-7416
TRANSPORT; die Zeitung fuer den Gueterverkehr. Text in German. 1991. fortn. EUR 88; EUR 5 newsstand/cover (effective 2010). adv. **Document type:** *Newspaper, Trade.*
Published by: Huss-Verlag GmbH, Joseph-Dollinger-Bogen 5, Munich, 80807, Germany. TEL 49-89-323910, FAX 49-89-32391416, management@huss-verlag.de, http://www.huss-verlag.de. Ed. Torsten Buchholz. Adv. contact Frank Hochhaeusler. Circ: 21,272 (paid).

388 LTU ISSN 1648-4142
HE255.9.A15
➤ **TRANSPORT.** Text in English; Abstracts in Lithuanian, Russian. 1986. q. GBP 333 combined subscription in United Kingdom to institutions (print & online eds.); EUR 439, USD 549 combined subscription to institutions (print & online eds.) (effective 2012). back issues avail. **Document type:** *Journal, Academic/Scholarly.* **Description:** Publishes research papers, short reports and notes, reviews, reports about conferences and workshops. Topics include: transport policy, fundamentals of the transport system, transportation technology of passengers and freight, multimodal transportation technology and logistics, loading technology, roads, railways, airports, ports, pipeline transport, production and technological transport, agricultural motor vehicles, traffic safety and environment protection, motor vehicles, transport power engineering, fuels, lubricants and maintenance materials, common work of customs and transport, insurance, information technology of transport, transport economics and management, transport standards, transport educilogy, and transport history.
Former titles (until 2001): Transportas (1392-1533); (until 1995): Vilniaus Technikos Universiteto Mokslo Darbai. Transportas (1392-1711); Both of which superseded (in 1991): Automobiliu Transportas (0136-1589)
Related titles: Online - full text ed.: ISSN 1648-3480. GBP 300 in United Kingdom to institutions; EUR 395, USD 494 to institutions (effective 2012).
Indexed: A01, A26, A28, APA, B21, BrCerAb, C&ISA, CA, CA/WCA, CIA, CPEI, CerAb, CivEngAb, CorrAb, E&CAJ, E08, E11, EEA, EMA, ESPM, EngInd, EnvEAb, H&SSA, H15, HRIS, I05, M&TEA, M09, MBF, METADEX, PollutAb, RefZh, SCI, SCOPUS, SSciA, SolStAb, T02, T04, W07, WAA.
—BLDSC (9025.440000), IE, Linda Hall. **CCC.**
Published by: (Vilniaus Gedimino Technikos Universitetas, Publishing House "Technika"/Vilnius Gediminas Technical University), Vilniaus Gedimino Technikos Universitetas, Leidykla Technika, Sauletekio aleja 11, Vilnius, 10223, Lithuania. TEL 370-5-2745038, FAX 370-5-2370602, books@vgtu.lt, http://leidykla.vgtu.lt. Ed. Adolfas Baublys TEL 370-5-2745070. **Co-sponsor:** Republic of Lithuania. Ministry of Education and Science.

380.52 USA ISSN 0733-0197
TRANSPORT (DE) REGULATION REPORT. Text in English. 1981. m. USD 167. adv. **Document type:** *Newsletter.*
Published by: I C C Logistics Services, Inc., 960 S Broadway, Hicksville, NY 11801. TEL 516-822-1183, FAX 516-822-1126. Ed., Pub., R&P, Adv. contact Anthony N Nuzio. Circ: 600 (paid).

388 UKR
TRANSPORT (KIEV). Text in Russian. 1998. w. 40 p./no.; **Document type:** *Journal.* **Description:** Focuses on economic issues in the Ukrainian transportation sector. Covers worldwide events affecting the industry. Includes analysis and commentary, and news on related taxation, tariffs, legislation and regulation.
Media: Online - full content.
Published by: Ekspressinform, Ul Bozhenko 15, korp 7, k 309, Kiev, Ukraine. TEL 380-44-2615406, FAX 380-44-2278952.

380.5 CAN ISSN 0227-3020
TRANSPORT - ACTION; the newsletter of public transport consumers. Text in English, French. 1975. bi-m. CAD 20. adv. bk.rev. **Document type:** *Newsletter.* **Description:** News and opinion on urban transit, passenger rail, airlines and intercity busses for users of public transport services in Canada.
Formerly: Transport 2000 Canada. Bulletin
Indexed: HRIS.
—CCC.
Published by: Transport 2000 Canada, P O Box CP 858, Sta B, Ottawa, ON K1P 5P9, Canada. TEL 613-594-3290, FAX 613-594-3271. Ed. J Goss. Circ: 1,850.

388 SAU
TRANSPORT & COMMUNICATIONS. Text in Arabic. m. SAR 200; SAR 5 newsstand/cover (effective 1999). adv. charts; illus.; maps; stat. back issues avail. **Document type:** *Magazine, Trade.* **Description:** Covers the transport and communication industries in Saudi Arabia by addressing related economic, technological, social and financial issues. Highlights the status of the industry and its future worldwide.
Published by: Makkah Advertising, Al Khaleej Plaza III Fl., Flat 314, P O Box 53502, Jeddah, 21593, Saudi Arabia. TEL 966-2-669-0932, FAX 966-2653-0693. Ed. Mohammed Omar Al Amoudi. adv.: color page SAR 15,000; 210 x 280. Circ: 50,000. **Dist. by:** Saudi Distribution Co., P O Box 13195, Jeddah 21493, Saudi Arabia. TEL 966-2-653-0909, FAX 966-2-653-3191.

TRANSPORT AND COMMUNICATIONS (SINGAPORE). *see* TRANSPORTATION—Abstracting, Bibliographies, Statistics

380 THA ISSN 0252-4392
HE269
TRANSPORT & COMMUNICATIONS BULLETIN FOR ASIA & THE PACIFIC. Text in English. 1957. a., latest no.71, 2001. USD 20 (effective 2003). bk.rev. charts; illus.; stat. back issues avail.
Formerly: Transport and Communications Bulletin for Asia and the Far East (0041-1396)
Indexed: HRIS, IIS, P06, PAIS, RASB.
Published by: United Nations Economic and Social Commission for Asia and the Pacific, United Nations Bldg., Rajadamnern Ave., Bangkok, 10200, Thailand. TEL 662-2881174, FAX 662-2883022, unescap@unescap.org, http://www.unescap.org. **Dist. by:** United Nations Publications, Sales Office and Bookshop, Bureau E4, Geneva 10 1211, Switzerland; United Nations Publications, 2 United Nations Plaza, Rm DC2-853, New York, NY 10017; Conference Services Unit, Conference Services Unit, ESCAP, Bangkok 10200, Thailand.

388 CAN ISSN 1912-8134
TRANSPORT CANADA. ENTRY SUSTAINABLE DEVELOPMENT STRATEGY. Text in English. 1997. triennial. **Document type:** *Government.*
Media: Online - full text. **Related titles:** Print ed.: ISSN 1711-3962; ◆ English ed.: Transports Canada. Strategie de Developpement Durable. ISSN 1912-8142.
Published by: Transport Canada/Transports Canada, 300 Sparks St, Ottawa, ON K1A 0N5, Canada. TEL 613-990-2309, FAX 613-954-4731, http://www.tc.gc.ca.

388 BEL ISSN 0775-0552
TRANSPORT ECHO (DUTCH EDITION). Text in Dutch. 1945. m. adv. bk.rev. illus.; stat. **Document type:** *Magazine, Trade.* **Description:** Covers issues and technical advances affecting transport management.
Supersedes in part (in 1987): Transport Echo (Bilingual Edition) (0009-6083); Which was formerly (until 1970): Transportkroniek (0770-2418)
Related titles: French ed.: Transport Echo (French Edition). ISSN 0775-0544. 1945.
Indexed: KES.
Published by: De Lloyd N.V./Le Lloyd S.A., Vleminckstraat 18, Antwerpen, 2000, Belgium. TEL 32-3-234-0550, FAX 32-3-234-0850, info@lloyd.be, http://www.anlloyd.be. adv.: B&W page EUR 2,200, color page EUR 3,000; bleed 307 x 215. Circ: 15,000 (paid).

380.5 GBR ISSN 1368-2229
TRANSPORT ECONOMIST. Text in English. 1973. 3/yr. free to members (effective 2009). back issues avail. **Document type:** *Journal, Abstract/Index.* **Description:** Contains reports on papers given at meetings and items discussed. It reviews recent publications of interest and contains papers or short articles from members.
Published by: Transport Economist Group, TEG Treasurer & Membership Secretary, 4 Seymour Sq, Brighton, BN2 1DP, United Kingdom. gregorymarchant.teg@btinternet.com, 44-1273-621522. Ed. Peter Gordon.

388.3 NLD ISSN 0929-0508
TRANSPORT EN LOGISTIEK; weekblad voor het goedenvervoer. Text in Dutch. 1940; N.S. 1992. fortn. EUR 168.50; EUR 260 in Europe; EUR 341 elsewhere (effective 2009). adv. bk.rev. illus.; stat. index. **Document type:** *Trade.* **Description:** Covers transport logistics, trucks and trucking, roads and traffic in the Netherlands and Europe, as well as related issues and developments in management, automation and communications.
Formed by the 1992 merger of: Beroepsvervoer (0005-9447); Wegvervoer (0043-2083); Incorporates: Vervoer en Transport Techniek; Formerly: Vrije Vervoerder
Indexed: KES.
—IE, Infotrieve.
Published by: Transport en Logistiek Nederland, Postbus 726, Zoetermeer, 2700 AS, Netherlands. TEL 31-79-3636138, FAX 31-79-3636262, info@tln.nl, http://www.tln.nl. Circ: 9,548 (paid). **Subscr. to:** Postbus 3008, Zoetermeer 2700 KS, Netherlands. TEL 31-79-3636244, FAX 31-79-3636263.

380.52 NLD ISSN 0165-330X
TRANSPORT & OPSLAG; maandblad voor managers in de interne logistiek. Text in Dutch. 1977. 9/yr. EUR 229 (effective 2009). adv. bk.rev. charts; illus. index. **Document type:** *Trade.* **Description:** Information on materials handling, storage, distribution and warehousing.
Incorporates (1991-1994): Logistiek Signaal (0927-0590)
Indexed: KES.
—CIS, IE, Infotrieve.
Published by: Reed Business bv (Subsidiary of: Reed Business), Postbus 4, Doetinchem, 7000 BA, Netherlands. TEL 31-314-349911, FAX 31-314-343991, info@reedbusiness.nl, http://www.reedbusiness.nl. Ed. Heres Stad. Pub. Geert van de Bosch.

380.5 GBR ISSN 0020-3122
TL230.A1
TRANSPORT ENGINEER. Text in English. 1945. m. GBP 64 in Europe to non-members; GBP 66 elsewhere to non-members; GBP 25 to members (effective 2009). adv. bk.rev. **Document type:** *Magazine, Trade.* **Description:** Contains vehicle and maintenance developments and legal updates. Includes progress reports on oils, fuels, tires, repairs equipment, workshops, training and management.
Formerly (until 1970): Institute of Road Transport Engineers. Journal and Proceedings
Indexed: A22, A28, APA, BrCerAb, BrTechI, C&ISA, CA/WCA, CIA, CerAb, CivEngAb, CorrAb, E&CAJ, E11, EEA, EMA, ESPM, EngInd, EnvEAb, H15, HRIS, Inspec, M&TEA, M09, MBF, METADEX, RefZh, SCOPUS, SolStAb, T04, WAA.
—BLDSC (9025.590000), IE, Infotrieve, Ingenta, Linda Hall. **CCC.**
Published by: Society of Operations Engineers, 22 Greencoat Pl, London, SW1P 1PR, United Kingdom. TEL 44-20-76301111, FAX 44-20-76306677, soe@soe.org.uk. Adv. contact Debbie Trout TEL 44-1883-382591. Circ: 11,106.

388 BEL ISSN 1021-4127
TRANSPORT EUROPE. Text in English. 1991. 11/yr. EUR 625 (effective 2000). **Document type:** *Bulletin.* **Description:** Covers all transport types: air, road, inland waterways, ports and rail. Presents information on infrastructure, environment, competition, taxation, company law and transeuropean activity.
Related titles: CD-ROM ed.: EUR 635 (effective 2000); Online - full text ed.; French ed.: Europe Transports. ISSN 1021-4135.
Indexed: A15, ABIn, G08, I05, P48, P51, P52, P53, P54, PQC.
—CIS. **CCC.**
Published by: Europe Information Service SA (E I S), Av Adolphe Lacomble 66-68, Brussels, 1030, Belgium. TEL 32-2-737-7709, FAX 32-2-732-6757, eis@eis.be, http://www.eis.be. Pub. Eric Damiens.

TRANSPORT FINANCE REVIEW. *see* BUSINESS AND ECONOMICS—Banking And Finance

380.5 900 GBR ISSN 0041-1469
HE151
TRANSPORT HISTORY. Text in English. 1968. a. GBP 24, USD 48; GBP 26, USD 52 foreign. adv. bk.rev. illus. index. back issues avail. **Document type:** *Journal, Academic/Scholarly.*
Indexed: AIAP, HistAb, P30.
—Linda Hall.
Published by: Graphmitre Ltd., 1 West St, Tavistock, Devon PL19 8DS, United Kingdom. Circ: 600.

TRANSPORT I KHRANENIE NEFTEPRODUKTOV/TRANSPORTATION AND STORAGE OF PETROLEUM PRODUCTS; nauchnyi informatsionnyi sbornik. *see* PETROLEUM AND GAS

TRANSPORT I SUOBSHCHENIA. *see* STATISTICS

388 FRA ISSN 1774-8917
TRANSPORT INFO HEBDO. Text in French. 2004. w. (45/yr). EUR 179 (effective 2009). **Document type:** *Magazine, Consumer.*
Published by: Editions Lariviere, 6 Rue Olof Palme, Clichy, 92587, France. TEL 33-1-47565400, http://www.editions-lariviere.fr.

388 NOR ISSN 1503-5921
TRANSPORT INSIDE. Text in Norwegian. 1990. 23/yr. NOK 1,280 (effective 2005). adv. **Document type:** *Newsletter, Trade.*
Former titles (until 2003): Moderne Transport Inside (1502-1270); (until 2000): Transport Inside (0804-5836)
Published by: Bjoergu AS, Sofiemyrveien 6 E, PO Box 11, Kolbotn, 1411, Norway. TEL 47-66-822121, FAX 47-66-822120, bjorgu@bjorgu.no, http://www.bjorgu.no. Ed. Bjoern Eilert Eriksen. Adv. contact Finn Egen Mobaek TEL 47-66-822126.

341 NLD
TRANSPORT: INTERNATIONAL TRANSPORT TREATIES. Text in English, French. 1974. base vol. plus a. updates. looseleaf. USD 549 (effective 2009). **Description:** Provides a clear synopsis of global air, seal, rail, inland waterway and overland transport treaties currently in force, and those not yet ratified.
Published by: Kluwer Law International (Subsidiary of: Aspen Publishers, Inc.), PO Box 316, Alphen aan den Rijn, 2400 AH, Netherlands. TEL 31-172-641562, FAX 31-172-641555, sales@kluwerlaw.com, http://www.kluwerlaw.com.

388 SWE ISSN 2000-6497
TRANSPORT, LOGISTIK IDAG; transport och logistik, landsvaeg, sjoefart, flygfrakt, jaernvaeg, materialhantering. Variant title: Transport och Logistik Idag. Text in Swedish. 2001. 10/yr. SEK 1,290 domestic print ed.; SEK 1,613 combined subscription domestic print & online eds.; SEK 1,960 foreign print ed.; SEK 2,283 combined subscription foreign print & online eds.; SEK 969 online ed. (effective 2010). adv. back issues avail. **Document type:** *Magazine, Trade.* **Description:** Magazine for the Swedish haulage and logistics industry.
Formerly (until 2010): Transport iDag (1654-2118); Which superseded in part (in 2007): Transport iDag och i Trafik (1650-9730); Which was formed by the merger of (1992-2001): Transport iDag (1103-0755); (1985-2001): I Trafik (0282-7123)
Related titles: Online - full text ed.
Published by: Mentor Online AB, Tryffelslingan 10, PO Box 72001, Lidingoe, 18172, Sweden. TEL 46-8-6704100, FAX 46-8-6616455, info@mentoronline.se, http://www.mentoronline.se. Ed. Lars Kjellberg TEL 46-42-4901933. Adv. contact Jacob Albertson TEL 46-8-6704152. color page SEK 27,700; 225 x 315. Circ: 8,400 (controlled).

388.324 621.86 DNK ISSN 0908-0570
TRANSPORT-MAGASINET; the periodical rallying all transport interests. Text in Danish. 1960. 19/yr. DKK 299 domestic; DKK 539 in Europe; DKK 659 elsewhere (effective 2010). adv. bk.rev. **Document type:** *Magazine, Trade.*
Formerly (until 1991): Transport (0041-1361); Incorporates (in 1980): Emballage (0013-6549)
Related titles: Online - full text ed.; Supplement(s): Intern Transport.
Indexed: CREJ.
—CCC.
Published by: Danske Fagmedier, Marielundvej 46 E, Herlev, 2730, Denmark. TEL 45-44-858899, FAX 45-44-858887, info@danskefagmedier.dk, http://www.danskefagmedier.dk. Ed. Jesper B Nielsen TEL 45-44-857315. Adv. contact Jan Hansen TEL 45-44-857313. color page DKK 25,200; 266 x 360. Circ: 8,737.

380.5 658.8 ZAF
TRANSPORT MANAGEMENT. Text in English. 1980. m. ZAR 96.80 domestic; ZAR 204.80 foreign (effective 2000). adv. bk.rev. illus. **Document type:** *Magazine, Trade.*
Indexed: ISAP.
Published by: T M L Business Publishing (Subsidiary of: Times Media Ltd.), PO Box 182, Pinegowrie, Gauteng 2123, South Africa. TEL 27-11-789-2144, FAX 27-11-789-3196. Ed. Elvira Whitmore. Adv. contact Reardon Sandderson. Circ: 4,857.

380.5 GBR
TRANSPORT MANAGEMENT. Text in English. 1944. q. free to members (effective 2009). adv. **Document type:** *Journal, Trade.* **Description:** Aim to broaden, and improve, the knowledge, skills and experience of its members in the practice of efficient transport management, having regard of all spheres of transport, covering road, rail, air and sea.
Published by: Institute of Transport Administration, The Old Studio, 25 Greenfield Rd, Westoning, Bedfordshire MK45 5JD, United Kingdom. TEL 44-1525-634940, FAX 44-1525-750016, info@iota.org.uk.

388 GBR ISSN 0958-1561
TRANSPORT MANAGER'S AND OPERATOR'S HANDBOOK. Text in English. 1970. a. GBP 55 per issue (effective 2010). charts; illus. back issues avail. **Document type:** *Handbook/Manual/Guide, Trade.* **Description:** Covers UK and EU transport legislation, major technical developments and significant changes within the transport industry.
Formerly (until 1989): Transport Manager's Handbook (0306-9435)
Related titles: Online - full text ed.
—CCC.
Published by: Kogan Page Ltd., 120 Pentonville Rd, London, N1 9JN, United Kingdom. TEL 44-20-72780433, FAX 44-20-78376348, KPinfo@koganpage.com, http://www.koganpage.com.

380.5 POL ISSN 0137-4435
TRANSPORT MUSEUMS. Variant title: Yearbook of the International Association of Transport Museums. Text in English. irreg., latest vol.10, 1986.
Published by: Centralne Muzeum Morskie Gdansk/Central Maritime Museum, Gdansk, Ul Szeroka 67-68, Gdansk, 80835, Poland. Ed. Przemyslaw Smolarek. **Subscr. to:** International Association of Transport Museums, Zeughaus Str 1-5, Cologne, Germany.
Co-sponsor: International Association of Transport Museums.

380.5 GBR ISSN 0969-1022
TRANSPORT NEWS. Text in English. 1977. m. GBP 22 (effective 2009). adv. 64 p./no. 4 cols./p.; back issues avail. **Document type:** *Magazine, Trade.* **Description:** Contains news about the broad spectrum of road transportation in the north with particular emphasis on new vehicle developments within companies, plus the people involved in all aspects of the transport industry, both sides of the border.
Formerly (until 1991): Scotland's Transport News (0958-6385); Incorporates (1981-1997): Freight Handler
Indexed: ASCA.
—CCC.
Published by: K A V Publicity (Glasgow) Ltd., Wheatsheaf House, Montgomery St, The Village, E Kilbride, G74 4JS, United Kingdom. TEL 44-1355-279077, FAX 44-1355-279088. Ed. Alistair M Vallance. Adv. contact Mary Connelly. B&W page GBP 675, color page GBP 990; trim 210 x 297. **Dist. by:** Warners Group Publications Plc., The Maltings, Manor Ln, Bourne, Lincs PE10 9PH, United Kingdom. TEL 44-1778-393652, FAX 44-1778-393668.

380.5 GBR ISSN 0967-070X
HE193 CODEN: TRPOE9
➤ **TRANSPORT POLICY.** Text in English. 1993. 6/yr. EUR 637 in Europe to institutions; JPY 84,600 in Japan to institutions; USD 713 elsewhere to institutions (effective 2012). adv. illus. Index. back issues avail.; reprints avail. **Document type:** *Journal, Academic/Scholarly.* **Description:** Aimed at bridging the gap between theory and practice in transport.
Related titles: Microform ed.: (from PQC); Online - full text ed.: ISSN 1879-310X (from IngentaConnect, ScienceDirect).
Indexed: A01, A03, A08, A22, A26, APEL, ASFA, B01, B06, B07, B09, B21, CA, CurCont, E11, ESPM, EnvAb, GEOBASE, H&SSA, HRIS, I05, ICEA, P34, PAIS, PollutAb, SCOPUS, SSCI, SSciA, SUSA, T02, T04, W07.
—BLDSC (9025.857730), IE, Infotrieve, Ingenta. **CCC.**
Published by: (World Conference on Transport Research Society FRA), Pergamon (Subsidiary of: Elsevier Science & Technology), The Blvd, Langford Ln, East Park, Kidlington, Oxford OX5 1GB, United Kingdom. TEL 44-1865-843000, FAX 44-1865-843010, JournalsCustomerServiceEMEA@elsevier.com. Ed. M Ben-Akiva TEL 617-253-5324. **Subscr. to:** Elsevier BV, Radarweg 29, PO Box 211, Amsterdam 1000 AE, Netherlands. TEL 31-20-4853757, FAX 31-20-4853432, http://www.elsevier.nl.

388 POL ISSN 1896-0596
HE7
TRANSPORT PROBLEMS/PROBLEMY TRANSPORTU; an international scientific journal. Text in English, Polish. 2007. q. EUR 48 (effective 2008). **Document type:** *Journal, Academic/Scholarly.*
Related titles: Online - full text ed.: free (effective 2011).
Indexed: A28, APA, B22, BrCerAb, C&ISA, CA/WCA, CIA, CerAb, CivEngAb, CorrAb, E&CAJ, E11, EEA, EMA, H15, M&TEA, M09, MBF, METADEX, RefZh, SolStAb, T04, WAA.
Published by: Politechnika Slaska, Wydzial Transportu/Silesian University of Technology, Faculty of Transport, ul. Krasinkiego 8, Katowice, 40-019, Poland. Ed. Aleksander Sladkowski.

TRANSPORT PROCESSES IN ENGINEERING. *see* ENGINEERING—Mechanical Engineering

388 POL ISSN 1640-5455
TRANSPORT PRZEMYSLOWY. Text in Polish. 2000. q. **Document type:** *Magazine, Trade.*
Indexed: B22.
Published by: Wydawnictwo Lektorium, ul Robotnicza 72, Wroclaw, 53608, Poland. TEL 48-71-7985900, FAX 48-71-7985947, info@lektorium.pl, http://www.lektorium.pl. **Dist. by:** Ars Polona, Obroncow 25, Warsaw 03933, Poland. TEL 48-22-5098609, FAX 48-22-5098610, arspolona@arspolona.com.pl, http://www.arspolona.com.pl.

380.5 FRA ISSN 0249-5643
TRANSPORT PUBLIC. Text in French. 1907. 11/yr. (plus supplement). EUR 90 domestic; EUR 110 foreign (effective 2010). adv. bk.rev. **Document type:** *Magazine, Trade.* **Description:** Covers news, facts, events and analyses of public transportation.
Former titles (until 1981): Revue des Transports Publics Urbain et Regionaux (0397-474X); (until 1970): L' Industrie des Tramways de France (0996-1399)
Indexed: CLT&T, FR, HRIS.
—CCC.
Published by: Union des Transports Publics (UTP), 5-7 rue d'Aumale, Paris, 75009, France. TEL 33-1-48746351, FAX 33-1-44919460. Ed. Robert Viennet. Circ: 3,000.

380.5 GBR ISSN 0144-1647
➤ **TRANSPORT REVIEWS**; a transnational, transdisciplinary journal. Text in English. 1981. bi-m. GBP 852 combined subscription in United Kingdom to institutions (print & online eds.); EUR 1,123, USD 1,410 combined subscription to institutions (print & online eds.) (effective 2012). adv. bk.rev. illus. Index. back issues avail.; reprint service avail. from PSC. **Document type:** *Journal, Academic/Scholarly.* **Description:** Covers all modes of transport. Describes transport organizations and policies in individual countries.
Related titles: Online - full text ed.: ISSN 1464-5327. GBP 766 in United Kingdom to institutions; EUR 1,011, USD 1,269 to institutions (effective 2012) (from IngentaConnect).
Indexed: A01, A03, A08, A20, A22, A28, APA, APEL, B01, B06, B07, B09, BrCerAb, C&ISA, CA, CA/WCA, CIA, CerAb, CivEngAb, CorrAb, CurCont, DIP, E&CAJ, E01, E11, EEA, EMA, ESPM, EnvEAb, ErgAb, GEOBASE, H15, HRIS, IBR, IBZ, ICEA, M&TEA, M09, MBF, METADEX, P26, P34, P54, PQC, RASB, SCOPUS, SSCI, SolStAb, T02, T04, W07, WAA.
—IE, Infotrieve, Ingenta, Linda Hall. **CCC.**
Published by: Routledge (Subsidiary of: Taylor & Francis Group), 4 Park Sq, Milton Park, Abingdon, Oxon OX14 4RN, United Kingdom. TEL 44-20-70176000, FAX 44-20-70176336, journals@routledge.com, http://www.routledge.com. Ed. David Banister TEL 44-1865-285070. Adv. contact Linda Hann TEL 44-1344-779945. **Subscr. in N. America to:** Taylor & Francis Inc., Customer Services Dept, 325 Chestnut St, 8th Fl, Philadelphia, PA 19106. TEL 800-354-1420, FAX 215-625-2940, customerservice@taylorandfrancis.com; **Subscr. to:** Taylor & Francis Ltd., Journals Customer Service, Sheepen Pl, Colchester, Essex CO3 3LP, United Kingdom. TEL 44-20-70175544, FAX 44-20-70175198, tf.enquiries@tfinforma.com.

363.12 USA ISSN 1550-2074
TRANSPORT SAFETY PRO ADVISOR. Text in English. 2004. m. USD 189; USD 249 combined subscription (print & online eds.) (effective 2008). back issues avail. **Document type:** *Newsletter, Trade.* **Description:** Covers the latest regulatory and non-regulatory issues and best practices.
Related titles: Online - full text ed.: ISSN 1939-2842. USD 239 (effective 2008).
—CCC.
Published by: J.J. Keller & Associates, Inc., 3003 W Breezewood Ln, PO Box 368, Neenah, WI 54957. TEL 877-564-2333, FAX 800-727-7516, kellersoft@jjkeller.com. Ed. Thomas Bray.

TRANSPORT SALARIED STAFF JOURNAL. *see* BUSINESS AND ECONOMICS—Labor And Industrial Relations

363.12 USA ISSN 1539-3232
TRANSPORT SECURITY ADVISOR. Text in English. 2002. m. USD 189 combined subscription (effective 2008). **Document type:** *Newsletter, Trade.*
Related titles: Online - full text ed.
—CCC.
Published by: J.J. Keller & Associates, Inc., 3003 W Breezewood Ln, PO Box 368, Neenah, WI 54957. TEL 877-564-2333, FAX 800-727-7516, kellersoft@jjkeller.com. Ed. Kathy L Close.

380.5 GBR ISSN 0144-347X
TRANSPORT TICKET SOCIETY. JOURNAL. Text in English. 1964. m. free to members (effective 2009). adv. bk.rev. illus. index. **Document type:** *Journal, Academic/Scholarly.* **Description:** Contains news and features on transport, tickets, transfers, tokens and fare collection systems worldwide.
Published by: Transport Ticket Society, 81 Pilgrims Way, Kemsing, Sevenoaks, TN15 6TD, United Kingdom. transport.ticket@btinternet.com.

388 GBR
TRANSPORT TRENDS. Text in English. a. free (effective 2009). back issues avail. **Document type:** *Government.* **Description:** Presents an overview and analysis of trends in transport and travel in Great Britain.
Related titles: Online - full text ed.: free (effective 2009).
Published by: Great Britain. Department for Transport, Great Minster House, 76 Marsham St, London, SW1P 4DR, United Kingdom. TEL 44-20-79443078, FAX 44-20-79449643, publications@communities.gsi.gov.uk. Ed. Dorothy Anderson.

388 UKR
TRANSPORT UKRAYINY. NORMATYVNE REHULIUVANNIA. Text in Ukrainian. bi-w. **Document type:** *Bulletin.* **Description:** Contains information on the tariff and duties regulations as well as the official informative news of the Ministry of Transportation of Ukraine.
Related titles: Russian ed.: Transport Ukrainy. Normativnoye Regulirovaniye.
Published by: (Ministerstvo Transportu Ukrainy/Ministry of Transport of Ukraine), Izdatel'stvo Yunikon Press, a/ya 648, Kyiv, 03035, Ukraine. TEL 380-44-2440153, FAX 380-44-2237680, info@u-press.com.ua, http://www.1520mm.com/. Circ: 3,000.

331.88 MYS
TRANSPORT WORKERS UNION. TRIENNIAL REPORT. Text in English. triennial.
Published by: Transport Workers Union, Transport Workers House, 21 Jalan Barat, Petaling Jaya, Malaysia. TEL 03-7566115. Ed. V David.

388 GBR
TRANSPORT YEARBOOK (YEAR); information sources and contacts. Text in English. 19??. biennial. GBP 50 per issue to non-members; free to members (effective 2010). back issues avail. **Document type:** *Government.* **Description:** Provides an easy-to-use reference guide to major UK transport organisations, sources of transport statistics and other important UK and international contacts.
Published by: (Transport Statistics Users Group), The Stationery Office, St Crispins, Duke St, Norwich, NR3 1PD, United Kingdom. TEL 44-1603-622211, FAX 44-870-6005533, customer.services@tso.co.uk, http://www.tso.co.uk. **Subscr. to:** PO Box 29, Norwich NR3 1GN, United Kingdom. TEL 44-870-6005522, FAX 44-870-6005533, subscriptions@tso.co.uk.

388.092 SWE ISSN 0492-004X
TRANSPORTARBETAREN/TRANSPORTWORKER. Text in Swedish. 1897. m. (11/yr.). SEK 100 (effective 2002). adv. bk.rev. abstr.; illus. index. back issues avail. **Document type:** *Bulletin, Trade.* **Description:** Directed to the transport market; articles on politics, economy, working conditions, the environment and other current issues.
Published by: Svenska Transportarbetarefoerbundet/Swedish Transport Workers' Union, Olof Palmes Gata 6, PO Box 714, Stockholm, 10133, Sweden. TEL 46-8-7237700, FAX 46-8-7237776, transportfk@transport.se. Ed. Jan Lindkvist. adv.: B&W page SEK 17,500, color page SEK 24,300; trim 370 x 254. Circ: 73,500 (controlled).

388 USA ISSN 0049-4488
HE7 CODEN: TRPOB6
➤ **TRANSPORTATION.** Text in English. 1972. 5/yr. EUR 994, USD 1,069 combined subscription to institutions (print & online eds.) (effective 2012). adv. bk.rev. illus. index. back issues avail.; reprint service avail. from PSC. **Document type:** *Journal, Academic/Scholarly.* **Description:** Covers issues related to the formulation of transportation policy, preparation and evaluation of transportation plans, as well as the management of transport systems in all parts of the world.
Related titles: Microform ed.: (from PQC); Online - full text ed.: ISSN 1572-9435 (from IngentaConnect).
Indexed: A05, A12, A13, A18, A22, A26, A28, A36, ABIn, AIAP, APA, AS&TA, AS&TI, ASCA, B04, B16, B21, BMT, BRD, BibLing, BrCerAb, C&ISA, C10, CA, CA/WCA, CABA, CIA, CPEI, CerAb, CivEngAb, CorrAb, CurCont, DokStr, E&CAJ, E01, E11, E12, EEA, EMA, ESPM, EconLit, EngInd, EnvAb, EnvEAb, EnvInd, FamI, GEOBASE, GH, H&SSA, H15, HRIS, IBSS, ICEA, ISR, JEL, LT, M&TEA, M09, MBF, METADEX, N02, N03, P10, P13, P26, P30, P48, P51, P52, P53, P54, PQC, PollutAb, R12, RRTA, RefZh, S04, S13, S16, SCI, SCOPUS, SSCI, SSciA, SUSA, SoftAbEng, SolStAb, T02, T04, TRA, W03, W05, W07, W11, WAA.
—BLDSC (9026.050000), IE, Infotrieve, Ingenta, INIST, Linda Hall. **CCC.**

TU

Published by: Springer New York LLC (Subsidiary of: Springer Science+Business Media), 233 Spring St, New York, NY 10013. TEL 212-460-1500, FAX 212-460-1575, service-ny@springer.com. Eds. David T Hartgen, Kay Axhausen, Martin G Richards. **Subscr. to:** Journal Fulfillment, PO Box 2485, Secaucus, NJ 07096. TEL 201-348-4033, FAX 201-348-4505, journals-ny@springer.com.

388 343.71 CAN ISSN 1714-129X
TRANSPORTATION APPEAL TRIBUNAL OF CANADA. PERFORMANCE REPORT. Text in English, French. 1997. a.
Formerly (until 2004): Canada. Civil Aviation Tribunal. Performance Report (1483-7277)
Published by: (Transportation Appeal Tribunal of Canada), Treasury Board of Canada Secretariat, Corporate Communications/Secretariat du Conseil du Tresor du Canada, West Tower, Rm P-135, 300 Laurier Ave W, Ottawa, ON K1A 0R5, Canada. TEL 613-995-2855, FAX 613-996-0518, services-publications@tbs-sct.gc.ca.

388 330 USA ISSN 1945-8436
TRANSPORTATION BUSINESS JOURNAL. Text in English. 2008. w. USD 2,295 in US & Canada; USD 2,495 elsewhere; USD 2,525 combined subscription in US & Canada (print & online eds.); USD 2,755 combined subscription elsewhere (print & online eds.) (effective 2011). back issues avail. **Document type:** *Newsletter, Trade.* **Description:** Covers the financial health of shippers and transportation companies, including financials, business trends, mergers and acquisitions, management changes and contract awards.
Related titles: E-mail ed.; Online - full text ed.: ISSN 1945-8444. USD 2,295 combined subscription (online & e-mail eds.) (effective 2011).
Indexed: P10, P26, P47, P48, P53, P54, PQC.
Published by: NewsRx, 2727 Paces Ferry Rd SE, Ste 2-440, Atlanta, GA 30339. TEL 770-435-8286, 800-726-4550, FAX 770-435-6800, pressrelease@newsrx.com, http://www.newsrx.com. Pub., Adv. contact Susan Hasty TEL 770-507-7777.

388 CAN ISSN 0840-9854
CA1T47-1
TRANSPORTATION DEVELOPMENT CENTRE. ANNUAL REVIEW. Text in Multiple languages. 1981. a.
Formerly (until 1984): T D C Annual Report (0715-6340)
Related titles: Online - full text ed.: T D C Annual Review. ISSN 1493-6356.
Published by: Canada. Minister of Transport, Transportation Development Centre, 800 Renelevesque Blvd. W Ste 600, Montreal, PQ H3B 1X9, Canada. TEL 514-283-0000, FAX 514-283-7158, tdccdt@tc.qc.ca.

380.5 USA ISSN 0889-0889
HE203
TRANSPORTATION IN AMERICA; a statistical analysis of transportation in the United States. Text in English. 1983. irreg. USD 55 to individuals; USD 44 university libraries & bookstores (effective 2005). adv. back issues avail. **Document type:** *Monographic series, Trade.* **Description:** Analysis of traffic and costs of commercial and private freight and passenger transport in US by all modes.
Indexed: SRI.
Published by: Eno Transportation Foundation, 1634 I St, N W Ste 500, Washington, DC 20006-4003. TEL 202-879-4700, FAX 202-879-4719. Ed. Rosalyn A Wilson. R&P Tracy Dunleavy. Adv. contact Charleen Blankenship. Circ: 1,000.

380.5 CAN ISSN 1484-2351
HE215.A15
TRANSPORTATION IN CANADA. ANNUAL REPORT. Text in English. 1996. a.
Published by: Transport Canada/Transports Canada, 300 Sparks St, Ottawa, ON K1A 0N5, Canada. TEL 613-990-2309, FAX 613-954-4731.

388.0971 CAN ISSN 1483-2496
CA1T1-10
TRANSPORTATION IN CANADA. REPORT HIGHLIGHTS/ TRANSPORTS AU CANADA. POINTS SAILLANTS DU RAPPORT. Text in English, French. 1996. a.
Published by: Transport Canada/Transports Canada, 300 Sparks St, Ottawa, ON K1A 0N5, Canada. TEL 613-990-2309, FAX 613-954-4731, http://www.tc.gc.ca.

380.5 USA ISSN 0041-1612
HE1 CODEN: TRNJA
➤ **TRANSPORTATION JOURNAL.** Text in English. 1961. q. USD 330 combined subscription to institutions (print & online eds.) (effective 2012). adv. bk.rev. charts; illus.; pat.; stat. Index. back issues avail.; reprint service avail. from PSC. **Document type:** *Journal, Academic/Scholarly.* **Description:** Covers research findings and original writings on transportation and logistics.
Related titles: Microform ed.: (from PQC); Online - full text ed.: ISSN 2157-328X. USD 236 to institutions (effective 2012).
Indexed: A01, A02, A03, A08, A10, A12, A13, A14, A15, A17, A22, A23, A25, A26, ABIn, ASCA, B01, B02, B04, B06, B07, B08, B09, B13, B15, B16, B17, B18, BPI, BRD, BusI, C12, CA, CLI, CurCont, E04, E05, E08, EnerRev, EnvAb, EnvInd, G04, G06, G07, G08, GEOBASE, HRIS, I02, I05, IBR, IBZ, JEL, LogistBibl, M01, M02, M05, M06, MAB, MEA&I, P02, P06, P10, P13, P26, P34, P47, P48, P51, P52, P53, P54, PAIS, PQC, S08, S09, SCOPUS, SSCI, T&II, T02, V02, V03, W01, W02, W03, W07.
—BLDSC (9026.250000), IE, Infotrieve, Ingenta, INIST, Linda Hall. **CCC.**
Published by: (American Society of Transportation and Logistics, Inc.), Pennsylvania State University Press, 820 N University Dr, University Support Bldg 1, Ste C, University Park, PA 16802. TEL 814-865-1327, FAX 814-863-1408, info@psupress.org. Eds. Evelyn Thomchick, Kendra Boileau. Adv. contact Brian Beer TEL 814-863-5992. **Dist. by:** The Johns Hopkins University Press, PO Box 19966, Baltimore, MD 21211. TEL 410-516-6987, 800-548-1784, FAX 410-516-3866, jrnlcirc@press.jhu.edu, https://www.press.jhu.edu/.

➤ **TRANSPORTATION LAW JOURNAL**; industry leader in multi-modal law, economics & policy. *see* LAW

388 USA ISSN 1942-7867
HE192.5
TRANSPORTATION LETTERS; the international journal of transportation research. Text in English. 2008. q. USD 325 combined subscription to individuals (print & online eds.); USD 650 combined subscription domestic to institutions (print & online eds.); USD 695 combined subscription foreign to institutions (print & online eds.); USD 200 combined subscription per issue (print & online eds.) (effective 2009). bk.rev. back issues avail. **Document type:** *Journal, Academic/ Scholarly.* **Description:** Contains technical notes on the state of the art in transportation research.
Related titles: Online - full text ed.: ISSN 1942-7875. USD 275 to individuals; USD 595 to institutions (effective 2009).
—IE.
Published by: J Ross Publishing, Inc, 5765 N Andrews Way, Fort Lauderdale, FL 33309. TEL 954-727-9333, FAX 561-892-0700, customerservice@jrosspub.com, http://www.jrosspub.com. Eds. Kostas Goulias, Kouros Mohammadian.

380.5 USA ISSN 1537-0259
TRANSPORTATION MANAGEMENT & ENGINEERING. Abbreviated title: T M & E. Text in English. 1996. q. free domestic to qualified personnel; USD 95 foreign (effective 2007). adv. illus. Index. back issues avail.; reprints avail. **Document type:** *Magazine, Trade.* **Description:** Provides information on ITS news, technologies, products and issues and developments.
Formerly (until 2001): I T S World (1086-2145)
Related titles: Online - full text ed.; ◆ Supplement to: Roads & Bridges. ISSN 8750-9229.
Indexed: A15, ABIn, B03, B11, HRIS, P48, P51, PQC.
—**CCC.**
Published by: Scranton Gillette Communications, Inc., 380 E Northwest Hwy, Ste 200, Des Plaines, IL 60016-2282. TEL 847-391-1000, FAX 847-390-0408, hgillette@sgcmail.com, http:// www.scrantongillette.com.

363.12 CAN ISSN 1719-7848
TRANSPORTATION OF DANGEROUS GOODS ACT. ANNUAL REPORT. Text in English. a., latest 2005. **Document type:** *Government.*
Formerly (until 2005): Northwest Territories. Minister of Transportation's Report to the Legislative Assembly for (Year) Transportation of Dangerous Goods Act (1498-3877)
Published by: Northwest Territories, Department of Transportation, PO Box 1320, Yellowknife, NT X1A 2L9, Canada. TEL 867-873-7500, http://www.gov.nt.ca/Transportation/documents/index.html.

380.5 GBR ISSN 0308-1060
HE1 CODEN: TPLTAK
➤ **TRANSPORTATION PLANNING AND TECHNOLOGY.** Text in English. 1972. bi-m. GBP 2,489 combined subscription in United Kingdom to institutions (print & online eds.); EUR 2,414, USD 3,031 combined subscription to institutions (print & online eds.) (effective 2012). adv. bk.rev. back issues avail.; reprint service avail. from PSC. **Document type:** *Journal, Academic/Scholarly.* **Description:** Presents papers covering transport demand models, land use forecasting models, economic evaluation and its relationship to policy in both developed and developing countries, conventional and possibly unconventional future systems technology, urban and interurban transport terminals and interchanges and environmental aspects associated with transport.
Formerly: Transportation Technology (0041-1671)
Related titles: CD-ROM ed.: ISSN 1026-7840. 1995; Microform ed.; Online - full text ed.: ISSN 1029-0354. GBP 2,240 in United Kingdom to institutions; EUR 2,173, USD 2,728 to institutions (effective 2012) (from IngentaConnect).
Indexed: A01, A03, A08, A22, A28, APA, ASCA, B01, B06, B07, B09, BrCerAb, BrRB, C&ISA, CA, CA/WCA, CIA, CPEI, CerAb, CivEngAb, CorrAb, CurCont, E&CAJ, E01, E11, EEA, EMA, ESPM, EngInd, EnvEAb, GEOBASE, H15, HRIS, ICEA, Inspec, M&TEA, M09, MBF, METADEX, P26, P54, PQC, SCI, SCOPUS, SolStAb, T02, T04, W07, WAA.
—IE, Infotrieve, Ingenta, INIST, Linda Hall. **CCC.**
Published by: Taylor & Francis Ltd. (Subsidiary of: Taylor & Francis Group), 4 Park Sq, Milton Park, Abingdon, Oxfordshire OX14 4RN, United Kingdom. TEL 44-1235-828600, FAX 44-1235-829000, info@tandf.co.uk. Ed. David Gillingwater. **Subscr. to:** Journals Customer Service, Sheepen Pl, Colchester, Essex CO3 3LP, United Kingdom. TEL 44-20-70175544, FAX 44-20-70175198, tf.enquiries@tfinforma.com.

388 NZL ISSN 1175-8538
TRANSPORTATION PUBLICATION. Text in English. 1991. irreg. back issues avail. **Document type:** *Monographic series, Government.* **Description:** Provides comments and suggestions about public transport and also helps to make more sustainable modes of transport to home, business or school.
Supersedes in part (in 2002): Bay of Plenty Regional Council. Resource Planning Publication (1170-9022)
Related titles: CD-ROM ed.: free (effective 2011); Online - full text ed.: ISSN 1179-9552. free (effective 2011).
Published by: Environment Bay of Plenty, Bay of Plenty Regional Council, PO Box 364, Whakatane, 3158, New Zealand. TEL 64-7-9223390, 800-884-881, FAX 64-7-9223323, 800-884-882, info@envbop.govt.nz.

380.5 USA ISSN 0278-9434
HE331 CODEN: TRQUDV
TRANSPORTATION QUARTERLY. Text in English. 1947. q. USD 55 domestic; USD 75 foreign (effective 2000). adv. illus. Index. reprints avail. **Document type:** *Journal, Trade.* **Description:** Features research analyses and public policy issues. Addresses transportation issues such as planning, design, operation, and regulation.
Formerly (until 1982): Traffic Quarterly (0041-0713)
Related titles: Microfilm ed.: 1947; Online - full text ed.
Indexed: A01, A02, A03, A05, A08, A09, A10, A22, A23, A24, A25, A26, A28, AIAP, APA, AS&TA, AS&TI, ASCA, B01, B02, B04, B06, B07, B08, B09, B11, B13, B15, B16, B17, B18, BAS, BRD, BrCerAb, C&ISA, C10, C12, CA, CA/WCA, CIA, CPEI, CerAb, CivEngAb, CorrAb, DokStr, E&CAJ, E08, E11, EEA, EMA, EngInd, EnvAb, FutSurv, G04, G08, H15, HRIS, I05, IBR, IBZ, ICEA, ISMEC, M&TEA, M09, MBF, MEA&I, METADEX, P02, P06, P10, P13, P26, P34, P48, P53, P54, PAIS, PCI, PQC, S04, S08, S09, SCOPUS, SUSA, SoftAbEng, SolStAb, T04, V02, V03, V04, W03, W05, WAA.
—IE, Infotrieve, Ingenta, Linda Hall.

Published by: Eno Transportation Foundation, 1634 I St, N W Ste 500, Washington, DC 20006-4003. TEL 202-879-4700, FAX 202-879-4719. Ed. Sandra Selva. R&P, Adv. contact Charleen Blankenship. Circ: 1,500.

388 USA ISSN 0892-6891
TA1001.5
TRANSPORTATION RESEARCH BOARD. STATE-OF-THE-ART REPORT. Text in English. 1984. irreg., latest vol.9, 2004. price varies. back issues avail. **Document type:** *Monographic series, Government.*
Related titles: Online - full text ed.: free (effective 2010).
—Linda Hall.
Published by: U.S. National Research Council, Transportation Research Board, The National Academies, 500 Fifth St, NW, Washington, DC 20001. TEL 202-334-3213, FAX 202-334-2519, TRBsales@nas.edu.

380.5 USA
TE1 CODEN: HWRCAI
TRANSPORTATION RESEARCH CIRCULAR (ONLINE). Text in English. 19??. irreg., latest no.145, 2010. free (effective 2010). back issues avail. **Document type:** *Monographic series, Trade.* **Description:** Presents interim research findings and research problem statements.
Former titles (until 2001): Transportation Research Circular (Print) (0097-8515); (until 1974): Highway Research Circular (0547-860X); Which superseded (in 1965): National Research Council. Highway Research Board. Highway Research Correlation Service. Circular
Related titles: Microfiche ed.
Indexed: DokStr, HRIS.
—CASDDS, Ingenta, Linda Hall.
Published by: U.S. National Research Council, Transportation Research Board, The National Academies, 500 Fifth St, NW, Washington, DC 20001. TEL 202-334-3213, FAX 202-334-2519, TRBsales@nas.edu. **Co-sponsor:** National Highway Traffic Safety Administration, Federal Highway Administration.

388 NLD ISSN 1572-4387
➤ **TRANSPORTATION RESEARCH, ECONOMICS AND POLICY.** Text in English. 1993. irreg., latest vol.10, 2004. price varies. back issues avail. **Document type:** *Monographic series, Academic/Scholarly.* **Description:** Aims to develop practical solutions, assist in policy formulation and inform debate on transportation issues and questions.
—BLDSC (9026.274300).
Published by: Springer Netherlands (Subsidiary of: Springer Science+Business Media), Van Godewijckstraat 30, Dordrecht, 3311 GX, Netherlands. TEL 31-78-6576050, FAX 31-78-6576474. Eds. David Gillen, Werner Rothengatter.

380.5 USA ISSN 1046-1469
HE11
➤ **TRANSPORTATION RESEARCH FORUM. JOURNAL.** Text in English. 1971. 3/yr. USD 150 to non-members; free membership (effective 2011). bk.rev. illus.; stat. reprints avail. **Document type:** *Journal, Academic/Scholarly.*
Supersedes in part (in 1987): Transportation Research Forum. Annual Meeting. Proceedings (0091-2468)
Related titles: Online - full text ed.: USD 50 (effective 2011).
Indexed: C&ISA, CLT&T, CorrAb, E&CAJ, EconLit, HRIS, JEL, PAIS, SolStAb, WAA.
—BLDSC (4910.135000), IE, Ingenta.
Published by: North Dakota University, Upper Great Plains Transportation Institute, NDSU Department 2880, PO Box 6050, Fargo, ND 58108. TEL 701-231-7767, info@ugpti.org, http:// www.ugpti.org/.

388 GBR ISSN 0965-8564
HE192.5 CODEN: TRPPEC
➤ **TRANSPORTATION RESEARCH. PART A: POLICY & PRACTICE.** Text in English. 1967. 10/yr. EUR 1,746 in Europe to institutions; JPY 231,900 in Japan to institutions; USD 1,953 elsewhere to institutions (effective 2012). adv. bk.rev. back issues avail.; reprints avail. **Document type:** *Journal, Academic/Scholarly.* **Description:** Covers the management, political and socio-economic aspects of transportation. Publishes case studies, surveys and reviews, and pure and applied research into the movement of passengers and freight.
Formerly (until 1992): Transportation Research. Part A: General (0191-2607); Which superseded in part (in 1978): Transportation Research (0041-1647)
Related titles: Microfilm ed.: (from PQC); Online - full text ed.: ISSN 1879-2375. 200? (from IngentaConnect, ScienceDirect).
Indexed: A01, A03, A05, A08, A20, A22, A23, A24, A26, A28, APA, AS&TA, AS&TI, B01, B02, B06, B07, B09, B13, B15, B17, B18, B21, BPIA, BrCerAb, BusI, C&ISA, C10, CA, CA/WCA, CIA, CIS, CMCI, CPEI, CPM, CerAb, CivEngAb, CorrAb, CurCont, DokStr, E&CAJ, E04, E05, E11, EEA, EMA, ESPM, EconLit, EnerRev, EngInd, EnvAb, EnvEAb, EnvInd, ErgAb, FR, G04, G06, G07, G08, GEOBASE, H&SSA, H15, HRIS, I05, IAOP, ICEA, ISR, Inspec, JEL, M&TEA, M09, MBF, METADEX, ManagCont, OceAb, P34, RefZh, SCI, SCOPUS, SSCI, SUSA, SolStAb, T02, T04, W07, WAA.
—BLDSC (9026.274604), AskIEEE, IE, Infotrieve, Ingenta, INIST, Linda Hall. **CCC.**
Published by: Pergamon (Subsidiary of: Elsevier Science & Technology), The Blvd, Langford Ln, East Park, Kidlington, Oxford OX5 1GB, United Kingdom. TEL 44-1865-843000, FAX 44-1865-843010, JournalsCustomerServiceEMEA@elsevier.com. Ed. D A Niemeier. **Subscr. to:** Elsevier BV, Radarweg 29, PO Box 211, Amsterdam 1000 AE, Netherlands. TEL 31-20-4853757, FAX 31-20-4853432, http://www.elsevier.nl.

388 GBR ISSN 0191-2615
HE192.5 CODEN: TRBMDY
➤ **TRANSPORTATION RESEARCH. PART B: METHODOLOGICAL.** Text in English. 1979. 10/yr. EUR 1,741 in Europe to institutions; JPY 231,400 in Japan to institutions; USD 1,948 elsewhere to institutions (effective 2012). adv. bk.rev. abstr. back issues avail.; reprints avail. **Document type:** *Journal, Academic/Scholarly.* **Description:** Features papers on all methodological aspects of transportation, with a particular focus on mathematical analysis.
Supersedes in part (in 1987): Transportation Research (0041-1647)
Related titles: Microfilm ed.: (from PQC); Online - full text ed.: ISSN 1879-2367 (from IngentaConnect, ScienceDirect).

Indexed: A01, A03, A05, A08, A22, A23, A24, A26, A28, APA, AS&TA, AS&TI, ASCA, B01, B06, B07, B09, B13, B21, BPIA, BrCerAb, BrRB, C&ISA, C10, CA, CA/WCA, CIA, CIS, CMCI, CPEI, CerAb, CivEngAb, CorrAb, CurCont, E&CAJ, E04, E05, E11, EEA, EMA, ESPM, EconLit, EnerRev, EngInd, EnvAb, EnvEAb, EnvInd, ErgAb, FR, G06, G07, GEOBASE, H&SSA, H15, HRIS, IAOP, ICEA, ISR, Inspec, JEL, M&TEA, M09, MBF, METADEX, MathR, PollutAb, RefZh, SCI, SCOPUS, SSCI, SUSA, SolStAb, T02, T04, W07, WAA.
—BLDSC (9026.274610), AskIEEE, IE, Infotrieve, Ingenta, INIST, Linda Hall. **CCC.**
Published by: Pergamon (Subsidiary of: Elsevier Science & Technology), The Blvd, Langford Ln, East Park, Kidlington, Oxford OX5 1GB, United Kingdom. TEL 44-1865-843000, FAX 44-1865-843010, JournalsCustomerServiceEMEA@elsevier.com. Ed. Fred Mannering. **Subscr. to:** Elsevier BV, Radarweg 29, PO Box 211, Amsterdam 1000 AE, Netherlands. TEL 31-20-4853757, FAX 31-20-4853432, http://www.elsevier.nl.

388 GBR ISSN 0968-090X
HE1 CODEN: TRCEFH
➤ **TRANSPORTATION RESEARCH. PART C: EMERGING TECHNOLOGIES.** Text in English. 1993. 6/yr. EUR 1,143 in Europe to institutions; JPY 152,000 in Japan to institutions; USD 1,279 elsewhere to institutions (effective 2012). back issues avail.; reprints avail. **Document type:** *Journal, Academic/Scholarly.* **Description:** Addresses development, applications, and implications, in the field of transportation, of emerging technologies from such fields as operations research, computer science, electronics, control systems, artificial intelligence, and telecommunications, among others.
Related titles: Microfiche ed.: (from MIM); Microfilm ed.: (from PQC); Online - full text ed.: ISSN 1879-2359 (from IngentaConnect, ScienceDirect).
Indexed: A01, A03, A05, A08, A22, A26, A28, APA, AS&TA, AS&TI, ASCA, B01, B06, B07, B09, B21, BrCerAb, C&ISA, C10, CA, CA/WCA, CIA, CIS, CPEI, CerAb, CivEngAb, CorrAb, CurCont, E&CAJ, E04, E05, E11, EEA, EMA, ESPM, EngInd, EnvAb, EnvEAb, EnvInd, ErgAb, GEOBASE, H&SSA, H15, HRIS, I05, IAOP, ICEA, Inspec, M&TEA, M09, MBF, METADEX, SCI, SCOPUS, SUSA, SolStAb, T02, T04, W07, WAA.
—BLDSC (9026.274620), AskIEEE, IE, Infotrieve, Ingenta, INIST. **CCC.**
Published by: Pergamon (Subsidiary of: Elsevier Science & Technology), The Blvd, Langford Ln, East Park, Kidlington, Oxford OX5 1GB, United Kingdom. TEL 44-1865-843000, FAX 44-1865-843010, JournalsCustomerServiceEMEA@elsevier.com. Ed. M Papageorgiou. **Subscr. to:** Elsevier BV, Radarweg 29, PO Box 211, Amsterdam 1000 AE, Netherlands. TEL 31-20-4853757, FAX 31-20-4853432, http://www.elsevier.nl.

388 GBR ISSN 1361-9209
HE192.5 CODEN: TRDTFX
➤ **TRANSPORTATION RESEARCH. PART D: TRANSPORT & ENVIRONMENT.** Text in English. 1996. 8/yr. EUR 1,191 in Europe to institutions; JPY 158,300 in Japan to institutions; USD 1,333 elsewhere to institutions (effective 2012). back issues avail.; reprints avail. **Document type:** *Journal, Academic/Scholarly.* **Description:** Features original research on the environmental impacts of transportation, policy responses to those impacts, and their implications for the design, planning and management of transportation systems.
Related titles: Online - full text ed.: ISSN 1879-2340 (from IngentaConnect, ScienceDirect).
Indexed: A01, A03, A05, A08, A22, A26, A28, APA, AS&TA, AS&TI, ASFA, B01, B06, B07, B09, B21, BrCerAb, C&ISA, C10, CA, CA/WCA, CIA, CIS, CPEI, CerAb, CivEngAb, CorrAb, CurCont, E&CAJ, E04, E05, E11, EEA, EMA, ESPM, EconLit, EngInd, EnvAb, EnvEAb, ErgAb, GEOBASE, H&SSA, H15, HRIS, I05, IAOP, ICEA, Inspec, JEL, M&TEA, M09, MBF, METADEX, P34, PollutAb, SCI, SCOPUS, SSCI, SSciA, SolStAb, T02, T04, W07, WAA.
—BLDSC (9026.274630), IE, Infotrieve, Ingenta, INIST. **CCC.**
Published by: Pergamon (Subsidiary of: Elsevier Science & Technology), The Blvd, Langford Ln, East Park, Kidlington, Oxford OX5 1GB, United Kingdom. TEL 44-1865-843000, FAX 44-1865-843010, JournalsCustomerServiceEMEA@elsevier.com. Ed. Kenneth Button TEL 703-993-4647. **Subscr. to:** Elsevier BV, Radarweg 29, PO Box 211, Amsterdam 1000 AE, Netherlands. TEL 31-20-4853757, FAX 31-20-4853432, http://www.elsevier.nl.

355.4 GBR ISSN 1366-5545
U168 CODEN: TRERFW
➤ **TRANSPORTATION RESEARCH. PART E: LOGISTICS AND TRANSPORTATION REVIEW.** Text in English. 1965. 6/yr. EUR 1,179 in Europe to institutions; JPY 156,700 in Japan to institutions; USD 1,321 elsewhere to institutions (effective 2012). adv. bk.rev. charts; illus.; pat.; tr.mk.; abstr. index. back issues avail.; reprints avail. **Document type:** *Journal, Academic/Scholarly.* **Description:** Contains informative articles drawn from across the spectrum of logistics and transportation research.
Former titles (until 1997): Logistics and Transportation Review (0047-4991); (until 1972): Logistics Review (0024-5844); (until 1967): Logistics Review and Military Logistics Journal
Related titles: Microform ed.; Online - full text ed.: ISSN 1878-5794 (from IngentaConnect, ScienceDirect).
Indexed: A01, A02, A03, A08, A12, A13, A17, A22, A26, A28, ABIn, APA, ASCA, B01, B02, B06, B07, B08, B09, B15, B17, B18, B21, BPIA, BrCerAb, BusI, C&ISA, C03, CA, CA/WCA, CBCABus, CIA, CIS, CPM, CPerI, CerAb, CivEngAb, CorrAb, CurCont, E&CAJ, E08, E11, EEA, EMA, ESPM, EconLit, EnvEAb, G04, G06, G07, G08, GEOBASE, H&SSA, H15, HRIS, I05, ICEA, Inspec, JEL, LogistBibl, M&TEA, M05, M09, MBF, METADEX, ManagCont, P06, P47, P48, P51, P52, P53, P54, PQC, RiskAb, S09, SCI, SCOPUS, SSCI, SSciA, SolStAb, T&II, T02, T04, W07, WAA.
—BLDSC (9026.274640), IE, Infotrieve, Ingenta, Linda Hall. **CCC.**
Published by: Pergamon (Subsidiary of: Elsevier Science & Technology), The Blvd, Langford Ln, East Park, Kidlington, Oxford OX5 1GB, United Kingdom. TEL 44-1865-843000, FAX 44-1865-843010, JournalsCustomerServiceEMEA@elsevier.com. Ed. W K Talley. **Subscr. to:** Elsevier BV, Radarweg 29, PO Box 211, Amsterdam 1000 AE, Netherlands. TEL 31-20-4853757, FAX 31-20-4853432, http://www.elsevier.nl.

388 GBR ISSN 1369-8478
TL152.35
➤ **TRANSPORTATION RESEARCH. PART F: TRAFFIC PSYCHOLOGY AND BEHAVIOUR.** Text in English. 1998. 6/yr. EUR 855 in Europe to institutions; JPY 113,700 in Japan to institutions; USD 957 elsewhere to institutions (effective 2012). back issues avail. **Document type:** *Journal, Academic/Scholarly.* **Description:** Focuses on behavioral and psychological aspects of traffic and transport.
Related titles: Online - full text ed.: ISSN 1873-5517 (from IngentaConnect, ScienceDirect).
Indexed: A01, A03, A08, A26, A28, APA, B01, B06, B07, B09, B21, BrCerAb, C&ISA, CA, CA/WCA, CIA, CIS, CPEI, CerAb, CivEngAb, CorrAb, CurCont, DIP, E&CAJ, E-psyche, E11, EEA, EMA, ESPM, EngInd, EnvEAb, ErgAb, H&SSA, H15, HRIS, IBR, IBZ, M&TEA, M09, MBF, METADEX, P03, P30, PsycInfo, PsycholAb, RiskAb, S02, S03, SCOPUS, SSCI, SolStAb, T02, T04, W07, WAA.
—BLDSC (9026.274650), IE, Infotrieve, Ingenta. **CCC.**
Published by: Pergamon (Subsidiary of: Elsevier Science & Technology), The Blvd, Langford Ln, East Park, Kidlington, Oxford OX5 1GB, United Kingdom. TEL 44-1865-843000, FAX 44-1865-843010, JournalsCustomerServiceEMEA@elsevier.com. Ed. J A Groeger. **Subscr. to:** Elsevier BV, Radarweg 29, PO Box 211, Amsterdam 1000 AE, Netherlands. TEL 31-20-4853757, FAX 31-20-4853432, http://www.elsevier.nl.

388 CAN ISSN 1910-2682
TRANSPORTATION SAFETY BOARD OF CANADA. BUSINESS PLAN. Text in English. 2003. a., latest 2007. **Document type:** *Handbook/ Manual/Guide, Trade.*
Media: Online - full text. **Related titles:** Print ed.: ISSN 1910-9180. 200?; French ed.: Bureau de la Securite des Transports du Canada. Plan d'Activites. ISSN 1910-2690.
Published by: Transportation Safety Board of Canada, 200 Promenade de Portage, Place du Centre 4th Fl, Gatineau, PQ KIA 1K8, Canada. TEL 819-994-3741, FAX 819-997-2239.

TRANSPORTATION SAFETY BOARD OF CANADA. PERFORMANCE REPORT. *see* PUBLIC ADMINISTRATION

363.12 USA ISSN 0276-8852
HE5614.2
TRANSPORTATION SAFETY INFORMATION REPORT. Text in English. 1974. q. **Document type:** *Government.*
Published by: U.S. Department of Transportation, Office of the Secretary, 400 Seventh St., S.W., Rm. 10200, Washington, DC 20590. TEL 202-366-1111. **Co-sponsor:** Transportation Systems Center.

TRANSPORTATION SAFETY RECOMMENDATIONS. *see* PUBLIC HEALTH AND SAFETY

363.12 CAN ISSN 1499-2442
TL553.5
TRANSPORTATION SAFETY REFLEXIONS. AIR. Text in English. 1993. a. free (effective 2006). **Description:** Provides feedback to the transportation community on safety lessons learned.
Formerly (until 2002): Aviation Safety Reflexions (1192-8832)
Indexed: HRIS.
Published by: Transportation Safety Board of Canada, 200 Promenade de Portage, Place du Centre 4th Fl, Gatineau, PQ KIA 1K8, Canada. TEL 819-994-3741, FAX 819-997-2239.

338.324 CAN ISSN 1498-9980
TRANSPORTATION SAFETY REFLEXIONS. RAIL. Text in English. 1994. q.
Formerly (until 2000): Rail Safety Reflexions (1198-1318)
Published by: Transportation Safety Board of Canada, 200 Promenade de Portage, Place du Centre 4th Fl, Gatineau, PQ KIA 1K8, Canada. TEL 819-994-3741, FAX 819-997-2239, http://www.tsb.gc.ca.

388 USA ISSN 0041-1655
TA1001 CODEN: TRSCBJ
➤ **TRANSPORTATION SCIENCE.** Text in English. 1967. q. USD 428 combined subscription domestic to institutions (print & online eds.); USD 462 combined subscription foreign to institutions (print & online eds.) (effective 2012). bk.rev. charts; illus.; bibl. index. back issues avail. **Document type:** *Journal, Academic/Scholarly.* **Description:** Features comprehensive, timely articles and surveys that cover all levels of planning and all modes of transportation.
Related titles: Microform ed.: (from PQC); Online - full text ed.: ISSN 1526-5447. USD 373 to institutions (effective 2012).
Indexed: A01, A03, A05, A08, A12, A13, A14, A17, A22, A23, A24, A26, A28, ABIn, APA, AS&TA, AS&TI, ASCA, B01, B02, B04, B06, B07, B09, B13, B15, B17, B18, BMT, BrCerAb, C&ISA, C10, CA, CA/WCA, CIA, CIS, CMCI, CPEI, CerAb, CivEngAb, CorrAb, CurCont, DokStr, E&CAJ, E08, E11, EEA, EMA, ESPM, EngInd, EnvEAb, G04, G08, H15, HRIS, I05, IAOP, IBSS, ICEA, ISMEC, ISR, Inspec, M&TEA, M09, MBF, METADEX, MathR, ORMS, P06, P26, P48, P51, P52, P53, P54, PQC, QC&AS, RASB, S01, S06, S09, SCI, SCOPUS, SSCI, SoftAbEng, SolStAb, T02, T04, W07, WAA, Z02.
—BLDSC (9026.280000), AskIEEE, IE, Infotrieve, Ingenta, INIST, Linda Hall. **CCC.**
Published by: Institute for Operations Research and the Management Sciences (I N F O R M S), 7240 Pky Dr, Ste 300, Hanover, MD 21076. TEL 443-757-3500, 800-446-3676, FAX 443-757-3515, informs@informs.org, http://www.informs.org. Ed. Michel Gendreau TEL 514-343-7435. Pub. Patricia Shaffer.

➤ **TRANSPORTATION TELEPHONE TICKLER.** *see* BUSINESS AND ECONOMICS—Trade And Industrial Directories

388 USA ISSN 1542-6122
TRANSPORTATION WATCH (ONLINE). Text in English. 1998. d. USD 1,763 (effective 2010 - 2011). back issues avail. **Document type:** *Newsletter, Trade.*
Media: Online - full text. **Related titles:** E-mail ed.
Published by: The Bureau of National Affairs, Inc., 1801 S Bell St, Arlington, VA 22202. TEL 703-341-3000, 800-372-1033, FAX 703-341-4634, bnaplus@bna.com.

380.5 ESP ISSN 0210-5047
TRANSPORTE 3; revista mensual de automocion y transporte. Text in Spanish. 1977. 11/yr. EUR 65.49 domestic; EUR 100 foreign (effective 2009). **Document type:** *Magazine, Trade.* **Description:** Covers new technology, interviews, legal matters. Presents articles dedicated to the subject of trucks and cars.
Related titles: E-mail ed.; Fax ed.; Online - full content ed.
Indexed: IECT.
Address: Padilla, 72, Madrid, 28006, Spain. TEL 34-1-4016921, FAX 34-1-4010315. Circ: 20,000.

388 USA
TRANSPORTE MAGAZINE/TRANSPORT MAGAZINE. Text in English, Spanish. 1997. m. adv. back issues avail. **Document type:** *Magazine, Trade.*
Media: Online - full text.
Address: 721 Michigan Ave, Miami, FL 33139.

380.5 ESP
TRANSPORTE PROFESIONAL. Text in Chinese. m. EUR 75 domestic; EUR 135 in Europe; EUR 245 elsewhere (effective 2008). adv. back issues avail. **Document type:** *Magazine, Consumer.*
Published by: Confederacion Espanola de Transporte de Mercancias, C Lopez de Hoyos, 322, Madrid, 28043, Spain. TEL 34-91-7444700, FAX 34-91-7444730, informacion@cetm.es, http://www.cetm.es/. Ed. Javier Baranda. Circ: 40,000.

338 ESP ISSN 1576-0642
TRANSPORTE Y LOGISTICA TERRESTRE. Text in Spanish. 1999. m. adv. bk.rev. **Document type:** *Magazine, Trade.* **Description:** Covers transport, logistics, vehicles and handling equipment.
Formerly (until 1999): Logistica y Transporte por Carretera (1576-0634); Which supersedes in part (1993-1999): Logistica & Transporte (1133-7117)
Indexed: LogistBibl.
Published by: Medios de Distribucion 2000 S.L., El Algabeno 53, Madrid, 28043, Spain. TEL 34-91-721895, FAX 34-91-721902, correo@logisticaytransporte.es, http://www.logisticaytransporte.es. Circ: 11,000 (paid).

380.5 CUB ISSN 0258-6029
TRANSPORTE Y VIAS DE COMUNICACION. Text in Spanish. 1977. q. USD 25 in North America; USD 26 in South America; USD 28 elsewhere.
Indexed: C01.
Published by: (Cuba. Ministerio de Educacion Superior), Ediciones Cubanas, Obispo 527, Havana, Cuba.

388 384 SWE ISSN 1403-7912
TRANSPORTER OCH KOMMUNIKATIONER/TRANSPORT AND COMMUNICATIONS. Text in English, Swedish. 1998. biennial. **Document type:** *Government.*
Related titles: Online - full text ed.
Published by: Statens Institut foer Kommunikationsanalys (SIKA)/ Swedish Institute for Transport and Communications Analysis, Maria Skolgata 83, PO Box 17213, Stockholm, 10462, Sweden. TEL 46-8-50620600, FAX 46-8-50620610, sika@sika-institute.se.

383.42 ESP ISSN 1577-1377
HE261.A15
LOS TRANSPORTES Y LOS SERVICIOS POSTALES. Text in Spanish. 1981. a. **Document type:** *Government.*
Former titles (until 1999): Los Transportes y la Comunicacion (1132-0680); (until 1990): Informe Anual sobre los Transportes, el Turismo y la Comunicacion (1131-5504); (until 1983): Los Transportes, el Turismo y la Comunicacion (0212-579X)
Published by: Ministerio de Fomento, Centro de Publicaciones, Paseo de la Castellana 67, Madrid, 28029, Spain. http://www.fomento.es.

380.5 MEX ISSN 0188-8013
TRANSPORTES Y TURISMO. Text in Spanish. 1935. m. USD 100. adv. **Document type:** *Consumer.*
Related titles: Online - full text ed.: ISSN 1607-1255. 1998.
Address: Insurgentes Norte No. 696, Mexico City 4, DF, Mexico. TEL 782-21-40, FAX 583-33-18. Ed. Dolores Marquez V de Mejia. Circ: 4,000.

TRANSPORTEUR; au service du personnel dans le transport et les industries connexes. *see* RELIGIONS AND THEOLOGY—Protestant

380.5 SWE ISSN 0347-0970
TRANSPORTFORSKNINGKOMMISSIONEN. RAPPORT. Text in Swedish. 1976. irreg. (12-15/yr.). price varies. back issues avail.
Formed by the merger of (1952-1976): Transportforskningskommissionen. Ingenjoersvetenskapsakademien. Utredningsrapport (0081-5667); (1959-1976): Transportforskningskommissionen. Ingenjoersvetenskapsakademien. Meddelande (0081-5659)
Published by: (Ingenjoersvetenskapsakademien, Transportforskningskommissionen), T F K - Institutet foer Transportforskning/T F K - Transport Research Institute, Pipersgatan 29, PO Box 12667, Stockholm, 11293, Sweden. TEL 46-08-652 41 30, FAX 46-08-652 54 98. Circ: 2,000.

388.3 NOR ISSN 0803-6640
TRANSPORTFORUM. Text in English, Norwegian. 1929. m. NOK 310 to individuals; NOK 170 to students; NOK 400 foreign; NOK 30 newsstand/cover (effective 2001). adv. bk.rev. **Document type:** *Journal, Trade.* **Description:** Directed to managers, employees in coach service, bus line service and city transit, transport of goods, ferry boat service and coastal liners.
Former titles (until 1991): Transportforum, Kollektivtraffikk og Transportservice (0803-1916); (until 1990): Transportforum (0802-2917); (until 1989): Rutebiltidende (0048-8836)
—CCC.
Published by: Transportbedriftenes Landsforening, Postboks 5477, Majorstua, Oslo, 0305, Norway. TEL 47-23-08-86-06, FAX 47-23-08-86-01. Ed. Einar Spurkeland. adv.: B&W page NOK 10,000, color page NOK 15,000; trim 185 x 260. Circ: 5,600.

656 GBR ISSN 1812-8602
HE1
➤ **TRANSPORTMETRICA.** Text in English. 2005. q. GBP 356 combined subscription in United Kingdom to institutions (print & online eds.); EUR 571, USD 713 combined subscription to institutions (print & online eds.) (effective 2012). reprint service avail. from PSC. **Document type:** *Journal, Academic/Scholarly.*
Related titles: Online - full text ed.: ISSN 1944-0987. GBP 320 in United Kingdom to institutions; EUR 514, USD 642 to institutions (effective 2012) (from IngentaConnect).
Indexed: A01, CA, CurCont, HRIS, P52, SCI, SCOPUS, SSCI, T02, W07.
—IE. **CCC.**
Published by: (Hong Kong Society for Transportation Studies Limited HKG), Taylor & Francis Ltd. (Subsidiary of: Taylor & Francis Group), 4 Park Sq, Milton Park, Abingdon, Oxfordshire OX14 4RN, United Kingdom. TEL 44-20-70176000, FAX 44-20-70176336, info@tandf.co.uk. Eds. S.C. Wong, William Lam.

TU

380.52 DEU ISSN 0174-559X
K24 CODEN: TRSPER
TRANSPORTRECHT; Zeitschrift fuer das gesamte Recht der Gueterbefoerderung, der Spedition, der Versicherungen des Transports, der Personenbefoerderung und der Reiseverstaltung. Text in German. 1979. 10/yr. EUR 218; EUR 30 newsstand/cover (effective 2011). adv. bk.rev. index. back issues avail. **Document type:** *Journal, Trade.*
Formerly: Transportation Law and Legislation
Indexed: A22, DIP, IBR, IBZ.
—IE, Infotrieve.
Published by: Hermann Luchterhand Verlag GmbH (Subsidiary of: Wolters Kluwer Deutschland GmbH), Heddesdorfer Str 31, Neuwied, 56564, Germany. TEL 49-2631-8012222, FAX 49-2631-8012223, info@luchterhand.de, http://www.luchterhand.de. Adv. contact Marcus Kipp. Circ: 1,200 (controlled).

380.5 FRA ISSN 0564-1373
HE3
TRANSPORTS. Text in French. 1956. bi-m. adv. bk.rev. bibl.; illus.; stat. index. back issues avail. **Document type:** *Journal, Trade.*
Description: Covers the economies of all methods of transport.
Related titles: Supplement(s): Les Cahiers Scientifiques du Transport. ISSN 1150-8809. 1979.
Indexed: A22, ELLIS, FR, HRIS, P48, P51, P53, P54, PAIS, PQC, RASB, RefZh.
—IE, Infotrieve, INIST. **CCC.**
Published by: (Association Francaise des Instituts de Transport et de Logistique), Editions Techniques et Economiques, 19 Rue du Banquier, Paris, 75013, France. TEL 33-1-55426130, FAX 33-1-55426139, contact-editecom@orange.fr. Ed. Genevieve Epstein. Circ: 4,000.

380.5 FRA ISSN 0151-5861
TRANSPORTS ACTUALITES. Text in French. 1976. 39/yr. **Document type:** *Magazine, Trade.*
Published by: Wolters Kluwer France (Subsidiary of: Wolters Kluwer N.V.), 1 Rue Eugene et Armand Peugeot, Rueil-Malmaison, Cedex 92856, France. TEL 33-1-76734809, FAX 33-1-76733040. Circ: 10,336.

388 CAN ISSN 1912-8142
TRANSPORTS CANADA. STRATEGIE DE DEVELOPPEMENT DURABLE. Text in English. 1997. triennial. **Document type:** *Government.*
Media: Online - full text. **Related titles:** ◆ English ed.: Transport Canada. Entry Sustainable Development Strategy. ISSN 1912-8134.
Published by: Transport Canada/Transports Canada, 300 Sparks St, Ottawa, ON K1A 0N5, Canada. TEL 613-990-2309, FAX 613-954-4731.

388 FRA ISSN 1766-8255
TRANSPORTS INTERNATIONAUX & LOGISTIQUE; le magazine des professionnels de la logistique. Text in French. 2003. 11/yr. EUR 110; EUR 10 per issue (effective 2010). **Document type:** *Magazine, Trade.*
Formerly (until 2004): Logistique Portuaire (1766-8247)
Published by: Transports Internationaux et Logistique, 163 Rue de Charenton, Paris, 75012, France. TEL 33-1-43434949, t-i-l@wanadoo.fr.

380.5 FRA ISSN 0397-6521
➤ **TRANSPORTS URBAINS**; forum des transports publics. Text in French. 1964. q. EUR 33 domestic to individuals; EUR 37 foreign to individuals; EUR 45 domestic to institutions; EUR 52 foreign to institutions (effective 2009). adv. bk.rev. **Document type:** *Journal, Academic/Scholarly.* **Description:** Looks at urban and suburban transportation issues.
Formerly (until 1974): Forum des Transports Publics (0071-8033)
Indexed: HRIS.
—**CCC.**
Published by: Groupement pour l'Etude des Transports Urbains Modernes, 5 Rue Danes de Montardat, Saint-Germain en Laye, 78100, France. zembri@latts.enpc.fr. Ed. Francis Beaucire. R&P, Adv. contact Alain Sutter TEL 33-1-43334454. Circ: 1,800.

363.12 SWE ISSN 2000-1975
▼ **TRANSPORTSTYRELSENS FOERFATTNINGSSAMLING.** Variant title: T S F S. Text in Swedish. 2009. irreg. back issues avail. **Document type:** *Monographic series, Government.*
Formed by the merger of (2005-2008): Sweden. Luftfartsstyrelsen. Foerfattningssamling (1652-8956); Which was formerly (1977-2005): Sweden. Luftfartsverket. Foerfattningssamling (0280-0233); (2005-2008): Sweden. Jaernvaegsstyrelsen Foerfattningssamling (1653-2074)
Related titles: Online - full text ed.
Published by: Transportstyrelsen/Swedish Transport Agency, Vikboplan 7, Norrkoeping, 60173, Sweden. TEL 46-11-4152100, FAX 46-11-4152250, kontakt@transportstyrelsen.se.

388 341.756 BEL
TRANSPORTZAKBOEKJE. Text in Dutch. a. EUR 72 (effective 2003). **Document type:** *Trade.* **Description:** Covers national and international transportation law.
Published by: Kluwer Uitgevers (Subsidiary of: Wolters Kluwer Belgique), Ragheno Business Park, Motstraat 30, Mechelen, B-2800, Belgium. TEL 32-15-800-94571, info@kluwer.be, http://www.kluwer.be. Ed. Frans Ponet.

380.5 ZAF
TRANSTALK. Text in English. 1991. q. free. illus. **Document type:** *Newspaper.* **Description:** General interest magazine for Transnet employees, with health, education, sports, and environmental news.
Published by: Transnet Limited, PO Box 72501, Parkview, Johannesburg 2122, South Africa. TEL 27-11-4887116, FAX 27-11-4888009. Eds. Carelo Mulder, Tami Didiza.

380.5 340 ITA ISSN 0390-4520
TRASPORTI; diritto, economia, politica. Text in Italian. 1973. 3/yr. **Document type:** *Journal, Academic/Scholarly.*
Published by: Universita degli Studi di Trieste, Edizioni Universita di Trieste (E U T), Piazzale Europa 1, Trieste, 34127, Italy. TEL 39-040-5587111, http://www.eut.units.it.

388 ITA ISSN 1971-6524
TRASPORTI & CULTURA. Text in Italian. 2001. q. ptice varies. **Document type:** *Magazine, Trade.*
Published by: Campanotto Editore, Via Marano 46, Pasian di Prato, UD 33037, Italy. TEL 39-0432-699390, FAX 39-0432-644728, edizioni@campanottoeditore.it, http://www.campanottoeditore.it.

380.5 ITA
TRASPORTI NEWS. Text in Italian. m. (11/yr.). EUR 75 domestic (effective 2009). **Document type:** *Magazine, Trade.* **Description:** Publishes export formalities, practical advises for the forwarders, new regulations concerning economy, trading and finance. Shows all the shipments by sea, by air and by land, as well as the names of the direct carrier for each country.
Related titles: Online - full text ed.
Published by: Editrice Trasporti s.r.l., Piazza Duca D'Aosta, 6, Milan, MI 20124, Italy. TEL 39-02-6690427, FAX 39-02-6694185, editrice.trasporti@galactica.it, http://www.cargonet.it. Ed. Anna Maria Boidi. R&P Annamaria Boidi. Circ: 11,500.

388 ITA ISSN 1971-1603
TRASPORTO COMMERCIALE. Text in Italian. 2007. q. **Document type:** *Magazine, Trade.*
Published by: Nuovi Periodici Milanesi, Via Molise 3, Locate Triulzi, MI 20085, Italy. http://www.nuoviperiodicimilanesi.com.

388.4 AUS ISSN 0155-1264
TROLLEY WIRE. Text in English. 1952. q. bk.rev. stat. **Document type:** *Magazine, Trade.*
Former titles (until 1959): Trolley Wire Review; (until 1956): The Trolley Wire
Indexed: ARI.
Published by: South Pacific Electric Railway Co-Operative Society Ltd., PO Box 103, Sutherland, NSW 1499, Australia. TEL 61-2-95423646, FAX 61-2-95453390, http://www.sydneytramwaymuseum.com.au.

388.413 GBR ISSN 0266-7452
TROLLEYBUS MAGAZINE. Text in English. 1963. bi-m. free to members (effective 2009). adv. bk.rev.; video rev. illus.; maps. 24 p./no.; back issues avail. **Document type:** *Magazine, Trade.* **Description:** Features descriptions of present-day operations around the world (often with route and wiring maps), new vehicle developments, historical articles, preservation developments, and comprehensive worldwide news.
Formerly (until 1966): National Trolleybus Association. Newsletter
Indexed: CLT&T, HRIS.
Published by: National Trolleybus Association (Subsidiary of: Trolleybus Museum Company Ltd), c/o Ian Martin, 2 St Johns Close, Claines, Worcester, WR3 7PT, United Kingdom. Ed. Carl Isgar.

380.5 AZE
TURAN-TRANSPORT. Text in English. s-w. **Document type:** *Bulletin.*
Related titles: Russian ed.
Published by: Turan Information Agency/Turna Informasiya Agentilyi, Khagani ul 33, Baku, 370000, Azerbaijan. TEL 994-12-984226, 994-12-935967, FAX 994-12-983817, root@turan.baku.az, http://www.turaninfo.com.

388.04409561 GBR ISSN 1750-5313
TURKEY FREIGHT TRANSPORT REPORT. Text in English. 2005. q. EUR 820, USD 1,030 combined subscription (print & email eds.) (effective 2010). **Document type:** *Report, Trade.* **Description:** Provides industry professionals and strategists, sector analysts, investors, trade associations and regulatory bodies with independent forecasts and competitive intelligence on the Turkish freight transport and logistics industry.
Related titles: E-mail ed.
Indexed: A15, ABIn, B02, B15, B17, B18, G04, I05, P48, P51, P52, PQC.
Published by: Business Monitor International Ltd., Senator House, 85 Queen Victoria St, London, EC4V 4AB, United Kingdom. TEL 44-20-72480468, FAX 44-20-72480467, subs@businessmonitor.com.

388 GBR
TYNE AND WEAR PASSENGER TRANSPORT AUTHORITY. ANNUAL ACCOUNTS. Text in English. a. **Document type:** *Corporate.*
Supersedes in part: Tyne and Wear Passenger Transport Authority. Annual Report and Accounts
Published by: Tyne and Wear Passenger Transport Authority, Civic Centre, Newcastle upon Tyne, Tyne and Wear NE99 2BN, United Kingdom.

388 GBR
TYNE AND WEAR PASSENGER TRANSPORT AUTHORITY. ANNUAL REPORT. Text in English. a. **Document type:** *Corporate.*
Supersedes in part: Tyne and Wear Passenger Transport Authority. Annual Report and Accounts
Published by: Tyne and Wear Passenger Transport Authority, Civic Centre, Newcastle upon Tyne, Tyne and Wear NE99 2BN, United Kingdom.

380.5 USA ISSN 0739-7100
U M T R I RESEARCH REVIEW. Text in English. 1970. q. charts; illus. back issues avail. **Document type:** *Newsletter, Academic/Scholarly.*
Former titles (until 1982): H S R I Research Review (0146-8545); (until 1977): H S R I Research (0364-3476); (until 197?): Hit Lab Reports (0146-8421)
Related titles: Microfilm ed.; Online - full text ed.: free (effective 2010).
Indexed: A15, ABIn, B01, B07, CA, E-psyche, HRIS, P25, P26, P34, P48, P51, P52, P54, PAIS, PQC, PsycholAb, T02.
—BLDSC (9083.200000), IE, Ingenta, Linda Hall.
Published by: University of Michigan, Transportation Research Institute, 2901 Baxter Rd, Ann Arbor, MI 48109. TEL 734-764-6504, FAX 734-936-1081, umtri@umich.edu, http://www.umtri.umich.edu/news.php.

354.8 USA
U.S. FEDERAL TRANSIT ADMINISTRATION. ANNUAL REPORT ON NEW STARTS. Text in English. a. free. **Document type:** *Government.* **Description:** Provides U.S. Department of Transportation recommendations to Congress for the following fiscal year funds to be made available to build new fixed guideway systems and extensions.
Formerly: U.S. Federal Transit Administration. Report on Funding Levels and Allocation of Funds
Published by: U.S. Federal Transit Administration, Office of Policy Development, U S Department of Transportation, TBP 10, 400 Seventh St, S W, Rm 9310, Washington, DC 20590. TEL 202-366-4060, FAX 202-366-7116, http://www.fta.dot.gov.

388.3 USA
U.S. FEDERAL TRANSIT ADMINISTRATION. TECHNOLOGY SHARING PROGRAM. REPORT. Text in English. irreg. **Document type:** *Monographic series, Government.* **Description:** Publishes technical reports concerning all aspects of public transportation.
Published by: U.S. Department of Transportation, Technology Sharing Program, 400 Seventh St., S.W., (Rm. 8417), Washington, DC 20590. TEL 703-487-4650, FAX 703-321-5847. **Orders to:** U.S. Department of Commerce, National Technical Information Service, 5301 Shawnee Rd, Alexandria, VA 22312. TEL 800-363-2068, subscriptions@ntis.gov.

U.S. HOUSE OF REPRESENTATIVES. COMMITTEE ON TRANSPORTATION AND INFRASTRUCTURE. LEGISLATIVE CALENDAR. *see* PUBLIC ADMINISTRATION

U S TOY COLLECTOR MAGAZINE. *see* ANTIQUES

388.04409477 GBR ISSN 1750-5321
UKRAINE FREIGHT TRANSPORT REPORT. Text in English. 2005. a. EUR 820, USD 1,030 combined subscription per issue (print & email eds.) (effective 2010). **Document type:** *Report, Trade.* **Description:** Covers independent forecasts and competitive intelligence on the Ukrainian freight transport and logistics industry.
Related titles: E-mail ed.; Online - full text ed.
Indexed: A15, ABIn, B02, B15, B17, B18, G04, I05, P48, P51, P52, PQC.
Published by: Business Monitor International Ltd., Senator House, 85 Queen Victoria St, London, EC4V 4AB, United Kingdom. TEL 44-20-72480468, FAX 44-20-72480467, subs@businessmonitor.com.

388.0440953572 GBR ISSN 1750-533X
UNITED ARAB EMIRATES FREIGHT TRANSPORT REPORT. Text in English. 2005. q. EUR 820, USD 1,030 combined subscription (print & email eds.) (effective 2010). **Document type:** *Report, Trade.*
Description: Covers independent forecasts and competitive intelligence on the UAE freight transport and logistics industry.
Related titles: E-mail ed.
Indexed: A15, ABIn, B02, B15, B17, B18, G04, I05, P48, P51, P52, PQC.
Published by: Business Monitor International Ltd., Senator House, 85 Queen Victoria St, London, EC4V 4AB, United Kingdom. TEL 44-20-72480468, FAX 44-20-72480467, subs@businessmonitor.com.

388.0440941 GBR ISSN 1750-5348
UNITED KINGDOM FREIGHT TRANSPORT REPORT. Text in English. 2005. a. EUR 820, USD 1,030 combined subscription per issue (print & email eds.) (effective 2010). **Document type:** *Report, Trade.*
Description: Covers independent forecasts and competitive intelligence on the freight transport industry in UK.
Related titles: E-mail ed.
Indexed: A15, ABIn, B02, B15, B17, B18, G04, I05, P48, P51, P52, PQC.
Published by: Business Monitor International Ltd., Senator House, 85 Queen Victoria St, London, EC4V 4AB, United Kingdom. TEL 44-20-72480468, FAX 44-20-72480467, subs@businessmonitor.com.

388 LBN ISSN 1020-5772
HE281.5.A15
UNITED NATIONS. ECONOMIC AND SOCIAL COMMISSION FOR WESTERN ASIA. REVIEW OF TRANSPORT IN E S C W A MEMBER COUNTRIES. Text in Arabic, English. a. USD 35 (effective 2004).
Published by: United Nations, Economic and Social Commission for Western Asia, PO Box 11-8575, Beirut, Lebanon. TEL 961-1-981301, FAX 961-1-981510, webmaster-eswa@un.org.

388 351 USA ISSN 8755-4836
HE206.3
UNITED STATES DEPARTMENT OF TRANSPORTATION. OFFICE OF INSPECTOR GENERAL. SEMIANNUAL REPORT TO THE CONGRESS. Text in English. s-a.
Former titles (until 1981): United States Department of Transportation. Office of Inspector General. Semiannual Report (8755-4488); (until 1980): United States Department of Transportation. Office of Inspector General (8755-447X)
Published by: (U.S. Department of Transportation, Office of Inspector General), U.S. Department of Transportation, 400 Seventh St, SW, Washington, DC 20590. TEL 202-366-4000.

UNIVERSITATEA POLITEHNICA DIN TIMISOARA. BULETINUL STIINTIFIC. SERIA MANAGEMENT INGINERIE, ECONOMICA, INGINERIA, TRANSPORTURILOR. *see* ENGINEERING

625.7 USA ISSN 0192-3994
HE192.5
UNIVERSITY OF CALIFORNIA AT BERKELEY. INSTITUTE OF TRANSPORTATION STUDIES. REVIEW. Text in English. 1977. irreg. free. illus. back issues avail. **Document type:** *Newsletter.*
Supersedes: I T S Bulletin
Related titles: Online - full text ed.: 2002.
Indexed: HRIS.
Published by: University of California, Berkeley, Institute of Transportation Studies, 109 McLaughlin Hall, Berkeley, CA 94720-1720. TEL 510-642-3585, FAX 510-642-1246, its@its.berkeley.edu. Ed. Phyllis Orrick TEL 510-643-2591. Circ: 5,000.

385.1 CAN ISSN 0841-8659
UNIVERSITY OF MANITOBA. TRANSPORT INSTITUTE. OCCASIONAL PAPER. Text in English. 1968. irreg., latest 1995. price varies. back issues avail. **Document type:** *Monographic series, Trade.*
Formerly: University of Manitoba. Center for Transportation Studies. Occasional Paper. (0076-3977)
Published by: University of Manitoba, Transport Institute, 631 Drake Centre Bldg, 181 Freedman Cres., Winnipeg, MB R3T 5V4, Canada. TEL 204-474-9842, FAX 204-474-7530, transport_institute@umanitoba.ca, umanitoba.ca/faculties/management/ti.

385.1 CAN
UNIVERSITY OF MANITOBA. TRANSPORT INSTITUTE. QUADRENNIAL REPORT. Text in English. quadrennial. free. **Document type:** *Monographic series, Trade.*
Published by: University of Manitoba, Tier Bldg, Rm 208, Winnipeg, MB R3T 2N2, Canada. TEL 204-474-9763, FAX 204-474-7584, mosaic_journal@umanitoba.ca, http://www.umanitoba.ca.

385.1 CAN ISSN 0845-762X
UNIVERSITY OF MANITOBA. TRANSPORT INSTITUTE. RESEARCH BULLETIN. Text in English. 1986. irreg. back issues avail. **Document type:** *Monographic series, Trade.*
Published by: University of Manitoba, Transport Institute, 631 Drake Centre Bldg, 181 Freedman Cres., Winnipeg, MB R3T 5V4, Canada. TEL 204-474-9842, FAX 204-474-7530, transport_institute@umanitoba.ca, umanitoba.ca/faculties/management/ti.

385.1 CAN
UNIVERSITY OF MANITOBA. TRANSPORT INSTITUTE. STUDY REPORT. Text in English. 1998. irreg. CAD 26.75 (effective 2000). **Document type:** *Monographic series, Trade.*
Published by: University of Manitoba, Transport Institute, 631 Drake Centre Bldg, 181 Freedman Cres., Winnipeg, MB R3T 5V4, Canada. TEL 204-474-9842, FAX 204-474-7530, transport_institute@umanitoba.ca, umanitoba.ca/faculties/management/ti.

388 AUS ISSN 1832-570X
UNIVERSITY OF SYDNEY. INSTITUTE OF TRANSPORT AND LOGISTICS STUDIES. WORKING PAPER. Text in English. 1980. irreg., latest 2008. back issues avail. **Document type:** *Monographic series, Academic/Scholarly.*
Former titles (until 2005): Institute of Transport and Logistics Studies. Working Paper (1440-3501); (until 1996): University of Sydney. Institute of Transport Studies. Working Paper; (until 1991): Macquarie University. Transport Research Group. Working Paper
Related titles: Online - full text ed.: free (effective 2009).
—CCC.
Published by: University of Sydney, Institute of Transport and Logistics Studies, School of Business, Faculty of Economics and Business, Sydney, NSW 2006, Australia. TEL 61-2-93510071, FAX 61-2-93510088, info@itls.usyd.edu.au.

380.50 JPN ISSN 0287-8305
UN'YU TO KEIZAI/TRANSPORTATION AND ECONOMY. Text in Japanese. 1948. m. JPY 11,904 (effective 1997 & 1998). **Document type:** *Academic/Scholarly.*
Published by: Un'yu Chosa Kyoku/Institute of Transportation Economics, 1-1 Ueno 7-chome, Taito-ku, Tokyo, 110-0005, Japan. TEL 81-3-3841-4101, FAX 81-3-3841-4859. Ed. Tunetake Ohta.

380.5 ITA ISSN 1592-0534
UOMINI E TRASPORTI. Text in Italian. 1983. 10/yr. EUR 25 (effective 2009). adv. **Document type:** *Magazine, Trade.*
Published by: Gruppo Federtrasporti, Via G di Vittorio 21/B1, Castelmaggiore, BO 40013, Italy. Circ: 20,000.

388.322 USA ISSN 1040-4880
THE URBAN TRANSPORTATION MONITOR. Text in English. 1987. bi-w. USD 295 (effective 2005). adv. bk.rev.; software rev. abstr.; charts; stat.; tr.lit. back issues avail.; reprints avail. **Document type:** *Newsletter, Trade.* **Description:** Up-to-date news, new technologies, exclusive nationwide surveys on transportation issues, statistics, information on new reports, books, RFP notices, comprehensive conference list.
Indexed: CLT&T, HRIS.
Published by: Lawley Publications, PO Box 12300, Burke, VA 22009-2300. TEL 703-764-0512, FAX 703-764-0516. Ed., Pub., R&P, Adv. contact Daniel B Rathbone. page USD 425. Circ: 1,000 (paid).

388 CAN ISSN 1910-409X
URBAN TRANSPORTATION SHOWCASE PROGRAM. ANNUAL REVIEW. Text in English. 2005. a. **Document type:** *Government.*
Media: Online - full text. **Related titles:** Print ed.: ISSN 1912-1032; ♦ French ed.: Programme de Demonstration en Transport Urbain. Revue Annuelle. ISSN 1910-4103.
Published by: Transport Canada/Transports Canada, 300 Sparks St, Ottawa, ON K1A 0N5, Canada. TEL 613-990-2309, FAX 613-954-4731.

388 GBR ISSN 2042-8804
▼ **USED CARS NI.COM MAGAZINE.** Text in English. 2010. bi-w. adv. **Document type:** *Magazine, Trade.*
Published by: Used Cars NI, 30 University St, Belfast, BT7 1FZ, United Kingdom. TEL 44-28-90324065, FAX 44-28-90324029, info@usedcarsni.com, http://www.usedcarsni.com.

UTAH CRIMINAL AND TRAFFIC CODE. *see* LAW—Criminal Law

UTAH CRIMINAL, MOTOR VEHICLE, AND RELATED STATUTES. *see* LAW—Criminal Law

380.5 AUT
V C OE MAGAZIN. Text in German. 1988. 6/yr. EUR 20 (effective 2001). adv. bk.rev. 12 p./no. 6 cols./p.; back issues avail. **Document type:** *Newspaper, Consumer.* **Description:** Promotes means of transportation which are environmentally friendly and economically efficient.
Formerly (until 2000): V C Oe Zeitung
Published by: Verkehrsclub Oesterreich, Brauhausgasse 7-9, Vienna, 1050, Austria. TEL 43-1-8932697, FAX 43-1-8932431, vcoe@vcoe.at, http://www.vcoe.at. Ed., Adv. contact Christian Hoeller. page EUR 3,500; trim 284 x 405. Circ: 20,000 (controlled).

▼ **VAK M. SECTOR VERVOER.** *see* LABOR UNIONS

380.5 GBR
VEHICLE ELECTRICS & ELECTRONICS. Text in English. 1993. q. GBP 18 (effective 1995). adv. bk.rev. tr.lit. back issues avail. **Document type:** *Journal, Trade.* **Description:** Discusses the design and maintenance of automotive electrical and electronic systems.
Incorporates: Fuel Injection News
Published by: R G O Exhibitions and Publications Ltd., Oakapple Cottage, Furnace Ln, Broad Oak Brede, Rye, E Sussex TN31 6ES, United Kingdom. TEL 44-1424-882702, FAX 44-1424-882702. Ed. Chris Hancock. Adv. contact Pam Bourne. B&W page GBP 320, color page GBP 495; trim 150 x 212. Circ: 2,400.

VEHICLE SYSTEM DYNAMICS; international journal of vehicle mechanics and mobility. *see* ENGINEERING—Mechanical Engineering

388 ISR ISSN 0792-9951
VEHICLES & TRANSPORTATION/REKHEV W'TAHBURA. Text in Hebrew. 1991. m. ILS 300; USD 75 foreign (effective 2000). adv. charts; illus.; tr.lit. **Document type:** *Trade.*
Related titles: Online - full text ed.
Published by: Taler Communication Ltd., Derekh Ben-Zvi 84, Tel Aviv, 68104, Israel. TEL 972-3-6839666, FAX 972-3-6839626. Ed. Ofer Taler. adv.: B&W page USD 1,131, color page USD 1,797; trim 360 x 240. Circ: 11,000 (controlled).

388.0440987 GBR ISSN 1750-5356
VENEZUELA FREIGHT TRANSPORT REPORT. Text in English. 2005. a. EUR 820, USD 1,030 combined subscription per issue (print & email eds.) (effective 2010). **Document type:** *Report, Trade.* **Description:** Covers independent forecasts and competitive intelligence on the Venezuelan freight transport and logistics industry.
Related titles: E-mail ed.
Indexed: A15, ABIn, P48, P51, P52, PQC.
Published by: Business Monitor International Ltd., Senator House, 85 Queen Victoria St, London, EC4V 4AB, United Kingdom. TEL 44-20-72480468, FAX 44-20-72480467, subs@businessmonitor.com.

388 340 BEL ISSN 0773-171X
VERKEERSRECHT - JURISPRUDENTIE/DROIT DE LA CIRCULATION - JURISPRUDENCE. Text in Dutch, French. 1985. 10/yr. EUR 144 (effective 2003). index. back issues avail. **Document type:** *Trade.* **Description:** Publishes commentary on developments in transportation law.
Published by: Kluwer Uitgevers (Subsidiary of: Wolters Kluwer Belgique), Ragheno Business Park, Motstraat 30, Mechelen, B-2800, Belgium. TEL 32-15-800-94571, info@kluwer.be, http://www.kluwer.be.

380.5 AUT ISSN 1019-7346
VERKEHR UND UMWELT. Text in German. 6/yr. **Document type:** *Trade.*
Published by: Erwin Schwaiger Verlag GmbH, Jenullgasse 4, Vienna, W 1140, Austria. TEL 43-1-894644910, FAX 43-1-8946449160. Ed. Reinherd Fleckl. Circ: 10,000.

380.5 388.31 DEU ISSN 0341-2148
VERKEHRS RUNDSCHAU. Variant title: Verkehrs Rundschau. Ausgabe A. Text in German. 1944. w. EUR 165.90 domestic; EUR 217.90 foreign (effective 2010). adv. charts; stat. **Document type:** *Magazine, Trade.* **Description:** Contains information on all sectors of the transportation industry, including local and long-distance road haulers.
—CCC.
Published by: Verlag Heinrich Vogel (Subsidiary of: Springer Science+Business Media), Neumarkterstr 18, Munich, 81664, Germany. TEL 49-89-2030431100, FAX 49-89-2030432100, vertriebsservice@springer.com, http://www.springerfachmedien-muenchen.de. Ed. Birgit Bauer. adv.: B&W page EUR 3,235, color page EUR 5,395; trim 185 x 253. Circ: 15,842 (paid and controlled).

380.5 CHE
VERKEHRS UND STAATSPERSONAL. Text in German. w.
Address: Hopfenweg 21, Bern, 3007, Switzerland. TEL 031-455562. Ed. Robert Andenmatten. Circ: 18,529.

556 DEU ISSN 0938-7803
DAS VERKEHRSGEWERBE. Text in German. 1950. 10/yr. adv. **Document type:** *Magazine, Trade.*
Published by: (Fachvereinigung Gueterfernverkehr im Gesamtverband Verkehrsgewerbe Niedersachsen), Winkler & Stenzel GmbH, Schulze-Delitzsch-Str. 35, Burgwedel, 30938, Germany. TEL 49-5139-89990, FAX 49-5139-899950, info@winkler-stenzel.de, http://www.winkler-stenzel.de. Adv. contact Kerstin Cordes. B&W page EUR 1,700, color page EUR 2,240; trim 184 x 270. Circ: 5,200 (paid and controlled).

380.5 340 DEU ISSN 1615-3995
VERKEHRSRECHT AKTUELL. Text in English. 2000. m. EUR 73.50 for 6 mos. (effective 2010). **Document type:** *Journal, Trade.*
Published by: I W W - Institut fuer Wirtschaftspublizistik, Aspastr 24, Nordkirchen, 59394, Germany. TEL 49-2596-9220, FAX 49-2596-92299, info@iww.de. Ed. Christian Stake.

380.5 340 DEU ISSN 0342-6734
VERKEHRSRECHTLICHE MITTEILUNGEN. Text in German. 1954. m. EUR 26.50; EUR 3.50 newsstand/cover (effective 2011). adv. **Document type:** *Magazine, Trade.*
Indexed: DokStr.
—CCC.
Published by: Kirschbaum Verlag GmbH, Siegfriedstr 28, Bonn, 53179, Germany. TEL 49-228-954530, FAX 49-228-9545327, info@kirschbaum.de, http://www.kirschbaum.de. Ed. Bernhard Kirschbaum. Adv. contact Volker Rutkowski.

380.5 DEU
VERKEHRSWIRTSCHAFT UND LOGISTIK N R W. (Nordrhein-Westfalen) Text in German. 1952. m. back issues avail. **Document type:** *Magazine, Trade.*
Former titles (until 2008): Das Verkehrsgewerbe Nordrhein-Westfalen (1866-2536); (until 2007): Das Verkehrsgewerbe Westfalen-Lippe (1866-2528); (until 1973): Das Verkehrsgewerbe (0938-779X)
Published by: Verband Verkehrswirtschaft und Logistik Nordrhein-Westfalen e.V., Haferlandweg 8, Muenster, 48155, Germany. TEL 49-251-6061401, info@vvwl.spediteure.de, http://www.vvwl.spediteure.de. Circ: 2,200 (controlled).

VERMONT CRIMINAL, MOTOR VEHICLES & RELATED STATUTES. *see* LAW

388 UKR
VES' TRANSPORT; informatsionno-analiticheskii zhurnal. Text in Russian. m. **Document type:** *Journal, Trade.* **Description:** Contains information about the current situation and tendencies of development of Ukrainian transportation system.
Published by: Izdatel'stvo Yunikon Press, a/ya 648, Kyiv, 03035, Ukraine. TEL 380-44-2440153, FAX 380-44-2237680, info@u-press.com.ua, editor@u-press.com.ua, http://www.1520mm.com/. Circ: 8,000 (paid).

388 UKR
VES' TRANSPORT ONLAIN. Text in Russian. 5/w. **Document type:** *Bulletin.* **Description:** Contains news on all kinds of transportation in Ukraine. Includes official information of the Ministry of Transport of Ukraine.
Media: Online - full content.
Published by: Izdatel'stvo Yunikon Press, a/ya 648, Kyiv, 03035, Ukraine. TEL 380-44-2440153, FAX 380-44-2237680, info@u-press.com.ua, editor@u-press.com.ua, http://www.1520mm.com/.

388 UKR
VES' TRANSPORT ZA NEDELIU. Text in Russian. w. free. **Document type:** *Bulletin.* **Description:** Contains news and announcements of the publishing house Yunikon Press as well as transport advertisements.
Media: Online - full content.
Published by: Izdatel'stvo Yunikon Press, a/ya 648, Kyiv, 03035, Ukraine. TEL 380-44-2440153, FAX 380-44-2237680, info@u-press.com.ua, editor@u-press.com.ua, http://www.1520mm.com/.

380.5 AUS
VICTORIAN ROAD TRANSPORT ASSOCIATION. ANNUAL REPORT. Text in English. 1975. a.
Published by: Victorian Road Transport Association, PO Box 5, South Melbourne, VIC 3205, Australia. TEL 61-3-96468590, FAX 61-3-96453598, reception@vta.com.au, http://www.vta.com.au.

380.5 ITA ISSN 0393-8077
TE4
VIE E TRASPORTI; rassegna di tecnica ed economia dei trasporti. Text in Italian. 1929. 10/yr. EUR 80 domestic; EUR 180 foreign (effective 2008). adv. abstr.; charts; illus.; stat. index. back issues avail. **Document type:** *Magazine, Trade.*
Former titles: Rivista della Strada (0035-5992); Asfalti, Bitumi, Catrami
Indexed: ChemAb.
—INIST, Linda Hall.
Published by: Casa Editrice la Fiaccola, Via Conca del Naviglio 37, Milan, MI 20123, Italy. TEL 39-02-89421350, FAX 39-02-89421484, http://www.fiaccola.it. Ed. Giuseppe Saronni. Circ: 50,300.

VIETMAN FREIGHT TRANSPORT REPORT. *see* BUSINESS AND ECONOMICS—Production Of Goods And Services

VINTAGE SPIRIT. *see* HISTORY—History Of Europe

VIRGINIA CRIMINAL AND TRAFFIC LAW MANUAL. *see* LAW—Criminal Law

VIRGINIA CRIMINAL LAW AND MOTOR VEHICLE HANDBOOK. *see* LAW—Criminal Law

387 RUS
VODNYI TRANSPORT. Text in Russian. w.
Related titles: Microfilm ed.
Indexed: RASB.
Address: Zemlyanoi Val ul 64, Moscow, 109004, Russian Federation. TEL 7-095-9155965. Ed. V S Gordeichik. **Dist. by:** East View Information Services, 10601 Wayzata Blvd, Minneapolis, MN 55305. TEL 952-252-1201, 800-477-1005, FAX 952-252-1202, info@eastview.com, http://www.eastview.com.

388 796.6 NLD ISSN 0166-0276
VOGELVRIJE FIETSER. Text in Dutch. 1975. bi-m. EUR 26 (effective 2009). adv. bk.rev. index. back issues avail. **Document type:** *Magazine, Consumer.* **Description:** Covers issues relating to the use of the bicycle as a means of transportation.
—IE, Infotrieve.
Published by: Fietsersbond E N F B, Postbus 2828, Utrecht, 3500 GV, Netherlands. TEL 31-30-2918171, FAX 31-30-2918188, info@fietsersbond.nl, http://www.fietsersbond.nl. Circ: 27,000.

W S S A GRAPEVINE. *see* BEVERAGES

DAS WARNKREUZ; Zeitschrift fuer Sicherheit und Gesundheit in Verkehrsunternehmen. *see* OCCUPATIONAL HEALTH AND SAFETY

WEST VIRGINIA CRIMINAL AND TRAFFIC LAW MANUAL. *see* LAW—Criminal Law

343.093 USA
WEST VIRGINIA MOTOR VEHICLE LAWS. Text in English. irreg., latest 2005. USD 32 (effective 2008). 635 p./no.; Supplement avail. **Document type:** *Monographic series, Trade.* **Description:** Contains information about motor vehicle administration, registration, certificate of title and anti-theft provisions, motor vehicle licenses, traffic regulations and laws of the road and motor vehicle responsibility act.
Related titles: CD-ROM ed.: ISSN 1558-8076. USD 59.95 (effective 2003).
Published by: Michie Company (Subsidiary of: LexisNexis North America), 701 E Water St, Charlottesville, VA 22902. TEL 434-972-7600, 800-446-3410, FAX 434-972-7677, customer.support@lexisnexis.com, http://www.michie.com.

354 AUS ISSN 1035-1671
HE289.Z7
WESTERN AUSTRALIA. DEPARTMENT OF TRANSPORT. ANNUAL REPORT. Text in English. 1934. a. **Document type:** *Corporate.*
Formerly (until 1986): Western Australia. Transport Commission. Annual Report of the Commissioner of Transport
Related titles: E-mail ed.
Published by: Department of Transport, 441 Murray St, Perth, W.A. 6000, Australia. http://www.transport.wa.gov.au.

WETBOEK WEGVERKEER. *see* LAW—Criminal Law

388 AUS ISSN 1832-4452
WHEELS & DEALS MAGAZINE. Text in English. 2002. 3/w. **Document type:** *Magazine, Consumer.*
Published by: Wheels and Deals Magazine, PO Box 3428, Robina, QLD 4230, Australia. TEL 617-5519-3663, FAX 617-5519-4663.

WHO IS WHO IN N F Z - FLOTTENMARKT. *see* BUSINESS AND ECONOMICS—Trade And Industrial Directories

WHO'S BUYING TRANSPORTATION. *see* BUSINESS AND ECONOMICS—Marketing And Purchasing

388.322 GBR ISSN 1369-961X
WHO'S WHO IN THE BUS AND COACH INDUSTRY. Text in English. 19??. a. GBP 37.50 per issue (effective 2010). adv. **Document type:** *Directory.* **Description:** Provides in depth information on the leading businesses serving the PSV sector.
Formerly (until 1992): Who's Who in the Bus Industry
—CCC.
Published by: Yandell Publishing, Ltd., PO Box 5122, Milton Keynes, Buckinghamshire MK15 8ZP, United Kingdom. TEL 44-1908-613323, FAX 44-1908-210656. Pub. Rob Yandell.

380.5 ZAF ISSN 0257-5426
WIEL. Text in Afrikaans. 1978. m. ZAR 287 domestic; ZAR 438 foreign (effective 2008). adv. bk.rev. back issues avail. **Document type:** *Trade.*
Published by: Ramsay, Son & Parker (Pty) Ltd., PO Box 180, Howard Place, Cape Town 7450, South Africa. TEL 27-21-5303311. Circ: 21,925.

WINGMAN; The United States Air Force journal of occupational, operational and off-duty safety. *see* MILITARY

388.346 USA ISSN 0162-7368
TL298
WOODALL'S R V BUYER'S GUIDE. Text in English. 1978. a. USD 6.99 per issue (effective 2009). illus.; tr.lit. **Document type:** *Directory, Consumer.* **Description:** Features over 400 recreation vehicles profiled with complete information about construction features, dimensions and popular options.
Published by: Woodall Publications Corp. (Subsidiary of: Affinity Group Inc.), 2575 Vista Del Mar Dr, Ventura, CA 93001. TEL 877-680-6155, FAX 805-667-4122, 805-667-4100, info@woodallpub.com.

387.7 USA
WORLD AIRLINE REPORT. Text in English. 1964. a. (July), latest 2001. USD 40 per issue (effective 2008). charts; illus.; mkt.; stat. back issues avail. **Document type:** *Report, Trade.* **Description:** Reviews the activities of 700 airlines worldwide, providing detailed statistical information on fleet operation and maintenance.
Related titles: ◆ Supplement to: Air Transport World. ISSN 0002-2543.
Published by: A T W Media Group (Subsidiary of: Penton Media, Inc.), 8380 Colesville Rd, Ste 700, Silver Spring, MD 20910. TEL 301-650-2420, FAX 301-650-2434. Ed. J A Donoghue. Pub. William A Freeman III.

388 GBR ISSN 1749-4729
➤ **WORLD REVIEW OF INTERMODAL TRANSPORTATION RESEARCH.** Abbreviated title: W R I T R. Text in English. 2006. 4/yr. EUR 494 to institutions (print or online ed.); EUR 672 combined subscription to institutions (print & online eds.) (effective 2012). bk.rev. abstr.; bibl.; illus.; charts; stat. back issues avail. **Document type:** *Journal, Academic/Scholarly.* **Description:** Forum for practitioners, academics, and policymakers from around the world to exchange concepts, research, and best practices in the field of intermodal transportation.
Related titles: Online - full text ed.: ISSN 1749-4737 (from IngentaConnect).
Indexed: A26, A28, APA, B21, BrCerAb, C&ISA, CA/WCA, CIA, CerAb, CivEngAb, CorrAb, E&CAJ, E11, EEA, EMA, ESPM, EnvEAb, H&SSA, H15, HRIS, I05, Inspec, M&TEA, M09, MBF, METADEX, RiskAb, SCOPUS, SSciA, SolStAb, T04, WAA.
—BLDSC (9359.175555), Ingenta. **CCC.**
Published by: Inderscience Publishers, PO Box 735, Olney, Bucks MK46 5WB, United Kingdom. TEL 44-1234-240519, FAX 44-1234-240515, editorial@inderscience.com. Ed. Dr. Dawna L Rhoades. **Subscr. to:** World Trade Centre Bldg, 29 Rte de Pre-Bois, Case Postale 856, Geneva 15 1215, Switzerland. FAX 41-22-7910885, subs@inderscience.com.

➤ **WYOMING CRIMINAL AND TRAFFIC LAW MANUAL.** *see* LAW—Criminal Law

➤ **YOUQI CHUYUN/OIL & GAS STORAGE AND TRANSPORTATION.** *see* PETROLEUM AND GAS

388.322 NOR ISSN 1501-3235
YRKESTRAFIKK. Text in Norwegian. 1956. bi-m. NOK 150 (effective 2002). adv.
Formerly (until 1998): Bussen (0800-5389)
Published by: Yrkestrafikkforbundet, Brugata 19, PO Box 9175, Groenland, Oslo, 0134, Norway. TEL 47-21-01-36-00, FAX 47-21-01-38-51. Ed. Anne Ulven. Adv. contact Jan Erik Kalgaard TEL 47-62-94-64-00. B&W page NOK 5,300, color page NOK 10,100; 185 x 260. Circ: 10,000.

388 RUS
ZHELEZNODOROZHNOE DELO. Text in Russian. 1994. bi-m. USD 89 in United States (effective 2000).
Published by: Tsentral'nyi Muzei Zheleznodorozhnogo Transporta, Kutuzovskii pr 39 komn 531, Moscow, 127521, Russian Federation. TEL 7-095-2842346. Ed. A G Myasnikov. **Dist. by:** East View Information Services, 10601 Wayzata Blvd, Minneapolis, MN 55305. TEL 952-252-1201, 800-477-1005, FAX 952-252-1202, info@eastview.com, http://www.eastview.com.

388 RUS
ZHELEZNODOROZHNYI KUR'ER. Text in Russian. 1995. m. USD 165 in United States (effective 2000).
Published by: Izdatel'stvo Transport, Aviamotornaya ul, dom 34/2, Moscow, 107174, Russian Federation. TEL 7-095-2627661. **Dist. by:** East View Information Services, 10601 Wayzata Blvd, Minneapolis, MN 55305. TEL 952-252-1201, 800-477-1005, FAX 952-252-1202, info@eastview.com, http://www.eastview.com.

ZHONGGUO JIAOTONG NIANJIAN/CHINA COMMUNICATIONS AND TRANSPORTATION YEARBOOK. *see* COMMUNICATIONS

380.5 CHE ISSN 1421-4342
ZUERICH NEWS; Offizielles Informationsbulletin. Text in English, German. 1941. fortn. CHF 58 (effective 2001). adv. **Document type:** *Bulletin, Consumer.*
Published by: Axel Springer Schweiz AG (Subsidiary of: Axel Springer Verlag AG), Postfach 3374, Zuerich, 8021, Switzerland. TEL 41-1-4488721, FAX 41-1-4488938, http://www.axelspringer.ch. Ed. Rudolf Brosi. Adv. contact Adrienne Rothen. B&W page CHF 1,770; trim 97 x 175. Circ: 30,000.

TRANSPORTATION—Abstracting, Bibliographies, Statistics

629.13 DEU ISSN 0001-0987
A D V - INFORMATIONSDIENST. Text in German. 1949. bi-m. bk.rev. stat. index. **Document type:** *Abstract/Index.* **Description:** Summary of press publications on airports, air transportation and the aerospace industry.
—CCC.
Published by: Arbeitsgemeinschaft Deutscher Verkehrsflughaefen/German Airports Association, Gertraudenstr 20, Berlin, 10178, Germany. TEL 49-30-3101180, FAX 49-30-31011890, erichsen@adv.aero, http://www.adv.aero. Ed., R&P Sabine Rohlff. Circ: 400.

629.2 ITA ISSN 2039-1234
A N F I A NOTIZIARIO STATISTICO. (Associazione Nazionale fra le Industrie Automobilistiche) Text in Italian. 1959. m. (11/yr.). stat. back issues avail. **Document type:** *Bulletin, Trade.* **Description:** Contains Italian statistics for production and exports by brand, car registrations by brand; deliveries of commercial vehicles up to 3.5 t by brand, fuel prices and taxation. Monthly international production, export and registration statistics, Western European car registrations by brand, and commercial vehicle registrations by individual markets and category.
Formerly (until 1976): A N F I A Bollettino Statistico (0001-2033)
Related titles: Online - full text ed.: EUR 260 domestic; EUR 550 in the European Union; EUR 650 elsewhere (effective 2006).
Published by: Associazione Nazionale fra le Industrie Automobilistiche (A N F I A), Corso Galileo Ferraris 61, Turin, TO 10128, Italy. TEL 39-011-5613661, FAX 39-011-545986, anfia@anfia.it, http://www.anfia.it. Ed. Paola Viggiani. Circ: 500.

363.12 CAN ISSN 1014-4498
ACCIDENT - INCIDENT REPORTING A D R E P. Text in English. 1981. a. price varies. back issues avail.
Related titles: Spanish ed.: Notificacion de Accidentes - Incidentes A D R E P. ISSN 1014-451X; French ed.: Compte Rendus d'Accident - Incident A D R E P. ISSN 1014-4501.
Indexed: IIS.
Published by: International Civil Aviation Organization (I C A O), External Relations and Public Information Office, 999 University St, Montreal, PQ H3C 5H7, Canada. TEL 514-954-8022, FAX 514-954-6769, icaohq@icao.int.

388.3 621.382 USA
ADVANCED PUBLIC TRANSPORTATION SYSTEMS: STATE OF THE ART UPDATE (YEAR). Text in English. a. **Document type:** *Bulletin, Government.* **Description:** Focuses on improving information, communications, and control strategies for transit and ridesharing. Contains the results of a limited investigation of the extent of the adoption of advanced technology in public transportation in the U.S. and Canada.
Published by: U.S. Federal Transit Administration, Technology Sharing Program, U S Department of Transportation, 400 Seventh St, S W M 433 2, Washington, DC 20590. **Co-sponsor:** John A Volpe National Transportation Systems Center.

387.7 FRA ISSN 1240-8255
AEROPORTS DE PARIS. RAPPORT ANNUEL. Text in French. 1985. a.
Formerly (until 1989): A D P en.. (0767-5178)
Published by: Aeroports de Paris, Orly sud 103, Paris, Cedex 94396, France.

387.7 FRA ISSN 0078-947X
AEROPORTS DE PARIS. SERVICE STATISTIQUE. STATISTIQUE DE TRAFIC; resultats generaux. Text in French. 1951. a.
Published by: Aeroports de Paris, Orly sud 103, Paris, Cedex 94396, France.

387.74 317 USA ISSN 0002-2225
HE9803.A1
AIR CARRIER FINANCIAL STATISTICS. Text in English. 1970. q. USD 16. reprints avail. **Document type:** *Government.*
Related titles: Microfiche ed.: (from CIS).
Indexed: AmStI.
Published by: (Office of Aviation Information Management), U.S. Department of Transportation, Research & Special Programs Administration, 400 Seventh St, S W, Rm 8410, Washington, DC 20590. TEL 202-366-4000. Circ: 500.

387.7 USA
AIR CARRIER INDUSTRY SCHEDULE SERVICE TRAFFIC STATISTICS. MEDIUM REGIONAL CARRIERS. Text in English. 1970. q. USD 12. stat. reprints avail. **Document type:** *Government.*
Former titles: Air Carrier Industry Scheduled Service Traffic Statistics Quarterly (0896-0577); (until 1981): Commuter Air Carrier Traffic Statistics (0270-448X)
Media: Duplicated (not offset). **Related titles:** Microfiche ed.: (from CIS).
Indexed: AmStI.
Published by: (Office of Aviation), U.S. Department of Transportation, Research & Special Programs Administration, 400 Seventh St, S W, Rm 8410, Washington, DC 20590. TEL 202-366-4000. Circ: 700.

387.7 CAN ISSN 1483-2399
AIR CARRIER TRAFFIC AT CANADIAN AIRPORTS. Text in English, French. 1976. a. CAD 31 domestic; USD 31 foreign (effective 1999). **Description:** Provides enplaned and deplaned passenger data by airport, by sector for scheduled and charter services.
Formerly (until 1995): Air Carrier Traffic at Canadian Airports (0701-7928); Which incorporated (1971-1983): Air Carrier Traffic at Canadian Airports (0705-5781); Both of which superseded (in 1976): Airport Activity Statistics (0576-0208)
Related titles: Online - full text ed.
—CCC.
Published by: Statistics Canada, Operations and Integration Division (Subsidiary of: Statistics Canada/Statistique Canada), Circulation Management, 120 Parkdale Ave, Ottawa, ON K1A 0T6, Canada. TEL 613-951-7277, 800-267-6677, FAX 613-951-1584.

387.7021 CAN ISSN 1193-9087
AIRCRAFT MOVEMENT STATISTICS. MONTHLY REPORT. Text in English, French. 197?. m. free (effective 2006).
Formerly (until 1979): Transport Canada, Air. Monthly Report, Aircraft Movement Statistics (0844-7896)
Published by: (Transport Canada/Transports Canada), Statistics Canada/Statistique Canada, Communications Division, 3rd Fl, R H Coats Bldg, Ottawa, ON K1A 0A6, Canada. TEL 800-263-1136, infostats@statcan.ca, http://www.statcan.gc.ca.

338 AGO
ANGOLA. DIRECCAO DOS SERVICOS DE ESTATISTICA. ESTATISTICA DOS VEICULOS MOTORISADOS. Text in Portuguese. 1967. a.
Published by: Direccao dos Servicos de Estatistica, Luanda, 1215, Angola. Circ: 750.

380.5 CHE ISSN 1027-3093
HE242 CODEN: ABTSEQ
ANNUAL BULLETIN OF TRANSPORT STATISTICS FOR EUROPE AND NORTH AMERICA. Text in English, French, Russian. 1950. a. USD 60 (effective 2001). **Document type:** *Bulletin, Government.* **Description:** Outlines trends in the European and North American transportation sectors.
Formerly (until 1995): Annual Bulletin of Transport Statistics for Europe (0250-9911)
Related titles: Microfiche ed.: (from CIS).
Indexed: IIS.
Published by: United Nations, Economic Commission for Europe (ECE), Palais des Nations, Geneva 10, 1211, Switzerland. TEL 41-22-9174444, FAX 41-22-9170505, info.ece@unece.org, http://www.unece.org. **Orders in N. America to:** United Nations Publications, 2 United Nations Plaza, Rm DC2-853, New York, NY 10017. **Dist. by:** Unipub, 4611-F Assembly Dr., Lanham, MD 20706-4391.

387.7021 ESP ISSN 0213-0009
ANUARIO ESTADISTICO DEL TRANSPORTE AEREO ESPANA - (YEAR). Text in Spanish. 1970. a. **Document type:** *Directory, Government.*
Formerly (until 1980): Estadisticas de la Aviacion Civil en Espana (0421-4986)
Published by: (Spain. Ministerio de Fomento, Direccion General de Aviacion Civil), Ministerio de Fomento, Centro de Publicaciones, Paseo de la Castellana 67, Madrid, 28029, Spain. http://www.fomento.es.

621.86 016 HUN ISSN 0230-5348
ANYAGMOZGATASI ES CSOMAGOLASI SZAKIRODALMI TAJEKOZTATO/ABSTRACT JOURNAL FOR MATERIALS HANDLING AND PACKAGING. Text in Hungarian. 1982. m. HUF 7,000. abstr. index. **Document type:** *Abstract/Index.*
Supersedes (1967-1982): Muszaki Lapszemle. Anyagmozgatas, Csomagolas - Technical Abstracts. Materials Handling, Packaging (0027-3023)
Published by: Orszagos Muszaki Informacios Kozpont es Konyvtar/National Technical Information Centre and Library, Muzeum utca 17, PO Box 12, Budapest, 1428, Hungary. Eds. Bela Kertesz, Felenc Hervai. Circ: 350. **Subscr. to:** Kultura, PO Box 149, Budapest 1389, Hungary.

388 JPN
ASIAN AUTO ABSTRACTS. Text in English. w. JPY 240,000. **Document type:** *Abstract/Index.* **Description:** Abstracts of press articles related to the Asian auto industry.
Published by: (P.D.S. International), Dodwell Marketing Consultants, Kowa no 35 Bldg, 14-14 Akasaka 1-chome, Minato-ku, Tokyo, 107-0052, Japan. TEL 03-3589-0207, FAX 03-5570-7132.

387.7 AUS ISSN 0729-6096
AUSTRALIA. AIR TRANSPORT STATISTICS. AIRPORT TRAFFIC DATA. Text in English. 1980. a. free (effective 2009). **Description:** Provides time series financial year data on passenger, freight and mail traffic; aircraft movements by airline sectors; and analysis of traffic trends at major airports.
Related titles: Diskette ed.: AUD 65 (effective 2000).
Published by: (Australia. Aviation Statistics and Analysis), Bureau of Infrastructure, Transport and Regional Economics, GPO Box 501, Canberra City, ACT 2600, Australia. TEL 61-2-62747818, FAX 61-2-62746816, publicaffairs@infrastructure.gov.au.

387.7 AUS ISSN 0727-6672
AUSTRALIA. AIR TRANSPORT STATISTICS. AUSTRALIAN AIR DISTANCES. Text in English. 1982. irreg. charts. back issues avail. **Document type:** *Government.* **Description:** Reports air distances of routes used in commercial services.
Related titles: Diskette ed.: AUD 65 (effective 2000).
Published by: (Australia. Aviation Statistics and Analysis), Bureau of Infrastructure, Transport and Regional Economics, GPO Box 501, Canberra City, ACT 2600, Australia. TEL 61-2-62747818, FAX 61-2-62746816, publicaffairs@infrastructure.gov.au.

387.7 AUS ISSN 1832-1968
AUSTRALIA. AIR TRANSPORT STATISTICS. DOMESTIC AIRLINE ACTIVITY (MAJOR AUSTRALIAN AIRLINES) MONTHLY STATUS REPORT. Text in English. 1967. m. free (effective 2009). back issues avail. **Document type:** *Government.* **Description:** Covers traffic carried by the major Australian airlines over the top twenty routes as well as industry totals. Includes commentary on the industry and events.
Formerly (until 1994): Australia. Air Transport Statistics. Provisional Statistics of Domestic Airlines (0727-2782)
Related titles: Online - full text ed.
Published by: (Australia. Aviation Statistics and Analysis), Bureau of Infrastructure, Transport and Regional Economics, GPO Box 501, Canberra City, ACT 2600, Australia. TEL 61-2-62747818, FAX 61-2-62746816, avstats@dotrs.gov.au, http://www.btre.gov.au.

387.7 AUS ISSN 1320-3274
AUSTRALIA. AIR TRANSPORT STATISTICS. GENERAL AVIATION. Text in English. 1964. a. free (effective 2009). back issues avail. **Document type:** *Government.* **Description:** Compiles statistics on hours flown and the number of aircraft by category of operation and aircraft type and total landings by aircraft type.
Formerly: Australia. Air Transport Statistics. Survey of Hours Flown (0727-2766)
Related titles: Diskette ed.: AUD 65 (effective 2000); Online - full text ed.
Published by: (Australia. Aviation Statistics and Analysis), Bureau of Infrastructure, Transport and Regional Economics, GPO Box 501, Canberra City, ACT 2600, Australia. TEL 61-2-62747818, FAX 61-2-62746816, publicaffairs@infrastructure.gov.au, http://www.btre.gov.au.

387.7 AUS
AUSTRALIA. AIR TRANSPORT STATISTICS. MONTHLY PROVISIONAL STATISTICS OF INTERNATIONAL SCHEDULED AIR TRANSPORT (ONLINE). Text in English. 1981. m. free (effective 2009). back issues avail. **Document type:** *Government.* **Description:** Covers passenger, freight and mail data collected from airlines performing international operation to and from Australia. Includes a comparison of data for the equivalent month in previous years.
Formerly: Australia. Air Transport Statistics. Monthly Provisional Statistics of International Scheduled Air Transport (print) (0727-2790)
Media: Online - full text.
Published by: (Australia. Aviation Statistics and Analysis), Bureau of Infrastructure, Transport and Regional Economics, GPO Box 501, Canberra City, ACT 2600, Australia. TEL 61-2-62747818, FAX 61-2-62746816, publicaffairs@infrastructure.gov.au, http://www.btre.gov.au. Ed. I M Hunter.

388.021 AUS
AUSTRALIA. BUREAU OF STATISTICS. AUSTRALIAN TRANSPORT FREIGHT COMMODITY CLASSIFICATION AND AUSTRALIAN PACK CLASSIFICATION (ONLINE). Text in English. 1982. irreg., latest 1994. free (effective 2009). **Document type:** *Government.* **Description:** Classifies goods transported by sea, rail, road or pipeline by type of commodity and pack characteristics.
Formerly: Australia. Bureau of Statistics. Australian Transport Freight Commodity Classification and Australian Pack Classification (Print)
Media: Online - full text.
Published by: Australian Bureau of Statistics, Locked Bag 10, Belconnen, ACT 2616, Australia. TEL 61-2-62527037, 61-2-92684909, 300-135-070, FAX 61-2-62528103, client.services@abs.gov.au.

388.021 AUS
AUSTRALIA. BUREAU OF STATISTICS. AUSTRALIAN TRANSPORT FREIGHT COMMODITY CLASSIFICATION ON FLOPPY DISK. Text in English. 1990. irreg., latest 1993. **Document type:** *Government.*
Media: Diskette.
Published by: Australian Bureau of Statistics, Locked Bag 10, Belconnen, ACT 2616, Australia. TEL 61-2-92684909, 61-2-62527037, 300-135-070, FAX 61-2-62528103, client.services@abs.gov.au.

388.021 AUS
AUSTRALIA. BUREAU OF STATISTICS. DIRECTORY OF TRANSPORT STATISTICS (ONLINE). Text in English. 2000. irreg., latest 2000. free (effective 2009). back issues avail. **Document type:** *Government.* **Description:** Contains comprehensive information on sources of transport statistics in the public and private sectors.
Media: Online - full text.
Published by: Australian Bureau of Statistics, Locked Bag 10, Belconnen, ACT 2616, Australia. TEL 61-2-92684909, 61-2-62527037, 300-135-070, FAX 61-2-62528103, client.services@abs.gov.au.

385.264021 AUS
AUSTRALIA. BUREAU OF STATISTICS. FREIGHT MOVEMENTS, AUSTRALIA, SUMMARY (ONLINE). Text in English. 2000. irreg., latest 2001. free (effective 2009). **Document type:** *Government.* **Description:** Provides statistics on tonnes and tonne-kilometres of freight moved in Australia between selected statistical divisions by mode (rail, sea, air and selected road).
Formerly: Australia. Bureau of Statistics. Freight Movements, Australia, Summary (Print)
Media: Online - full text.
Published by: Australian Bureau of Statistics, Locked Bag 10, Belconnen, ACT 2616, Australia. TEL 61-2-92684909, 300-135-070, FAX 61-2-92684654, client.services@abs.gov.au.

387.021 AUS
AUSTRALIA. BUREAU OF STATISTICS. INFORMATION PAPER: FREIGHT MOVEMENTS, AUSTRALIA. Text in English. 1994. irreg., latest 1994. back issues avail. **Document type:** *Government.* **Description:** Provides statistics on tonnes of freight moved in Australia between selected statistical divisions by mode (road, rail, sea and air).
Formerly: Australia. Bureau of Statistics. Freight Movements, Australia (1322-8773)
Related titles: Online - full text ed.
Published by: Australian Bureau of Statistics, Locked Bag 10, Belconnen, ACT 2616, Australia. TEL 61-2-92684909, 61-2-62527037, 300-135-070, FAX 61-2-62528103, client.services@abs.gov.au.

388.021 AUS
AUSTRALIA. BUREAU OF STATISTICS. MOTOR VEHICLE CENSUS, AUSTRALIA (ONLINE). Text in English. 1995. a. free (effective 2009). back issues avail. **Document type:** *Government.* **Description:** Presents statistics relating to vehicles which were registered with a motor vehicle registration authority. Motor vehicle registration statistics are compiled from data made available by various state and territory motor vehicle registration authorities and reflect the information as recorded in registration documents.
Formerly: Australia. Bureau of Statistics. Motor Vehicle Census, Australia (Print) (0728-2923)
Media: Online - full text.
Published by: Australian Bureau of Statistics, Locked Bag 10, Belconnen, ACT 2616, Australia. TEL 61-2-92684909, 300-135-070, FAX 61-2-92684654, client.services@abs.gov.au.

380.5021 AUS
AUSTRALIA. BUREAU OF STATISTICS. MOTOR VEHICLE HIRE INDUSTRY, AUSTRALIA (ONLINE). Text in English. 1986. irreg., latest 1992. free (effective 2009). **Document type:** *Government.* **Description:** Contains details of employment, wages and salaries, components of income and expenses, assets and liabilities, and details of motor vehicle rentals such as total vehicle rental days and number of motor vehicles in rental fleet.
Formerly: Australia. Bureau of Statistics. Motor Vehicle Hire Industry, Australia (Print)
Media: Online - full text.
Published by: Australian Bureau of Statistics, Locked Bag 10, Belconnen, ACT 2616, Australia. TEL 61-2-92684909, 61-2-62527037, 300-135-070, FAX 61-2-62528103, client.services@abs.gov.au.

388.021 AUS
AUSTRALIA. BUREAU OF STATISTICS. SOUTH AUSTRALIAN OFFICE. TRAVEL TO WORK AND PLACE OF EDUCATION, ADELAIDE STATISTICAL DIVISION (ONLINE). Text in English. 1991. irreg., latest 1997. free (effective 2009). back issues avail. **Document type:** *Government.* **Description:** Provides information about modes of travel to and from work and to place of education.
Formerly: Australia. Bureau of Statistics. South Australian Office. Travel to Work and Place of Education, Adelaide Statistical Division (Print)
Media: Online - full text.
Published by: Australian Bureau of Statistics, South Australian Office, GPO Box 2272, Adelaide, SA 5001, Australia. TEL 61-2-92684909, 300-135-070, client.services@abs.gov.au.

388.3021 AUS
AUSTRALIA. BUREAU OF STATISTICS. SURVEY OF MOTOR VEHICLE USE, AUSTRALIA TWELVE MONTHS ENDED (ONLINE). Text in English. 1971. a., latest 2007. free (effective 2009). back issues avail. **Document type:** *Government.* **Description:** Contains estimates for private and commercial vehicles registered for road use with a motor vehicle registration authority; by state/territory of registration, area of operation, number of vehicles, total and average kilometres travelled, vehicle usage, fuel consumption and load carried.
Former titles (until 2007): Australia. Bureau of Statistics. Survey of Motor Vehicle Use, Australia, Twelve Months Ended (Print); (until 2003): Australia. Bureau of Statistics. Survey of Motor Vehicle Use, Australia (1444-5670); (until 1988): Australia. Bureau of Statistics. Survey of Motor Vehicle Use, Twelve Months Ended (Date)
Media: Online - full text.
Published by: Australian Bureau of Statistics, Locked Bag 10, Belconnen, ACT 2616, Australia. TEL 61-2-92684909, 300-135-070, FAX 61-2-92684654, client.services@abs.gov.au.

380.521 AUS
AUSTRALIAN SEA FREIGHT. Text in English. 1983. a. free (effective 2008). back issues avail. **Document type:** *Directory, Trade.* **Description:** Provides information on Australian sea freight movements.
Former titles (until 1999): Coastal Freight in Australia; (until 1995): Sea Transport Statistics (0815-5577)
Related titles: Online - full text ed.
Published by: Bureau of Infrastructure, Transport and Regional Economics, GPO Box 501, Canberra, ACT 2600, Australia. TEL 61-2-62747210, FAX 61-2-62746816, bitre@infrastructure.gov.au, http://www.bitre.gov.au.

629.283 FIN ISSN 0567-1795
AUTO JA TIE/AUTOMOBILES AND HIGHWAYS IN FINLAND (YEAR). STATISTICS; tilastoa. Text in English, Finnish. 1960. a., latest 2000. price varies. charts; illus.; stat. index. back issues avail. **Document type:** *Yearbook.*
Published by: Suomen Tieyhdistys/Finnish Road Association, Malminkari 5, PO Box 131, Helsinki, 00701, Finland. TEL 358-9-70010882, FAX 358-9-3511181, http://www.tieyhdistys.fi. Ed. Jouko Perkkio. Circ: 1,700.

388.3021 ITA
AUTOMOBILE IN CIFRE (YEAR)/MOTOR INDUSTRY IN FIGURES (YEAR). Text in Italian, English. a. EUR 65 domestic to members; EUR 75 domestic to non-members; EUR 100 in Europe to non-members; EUR 120 elsewhere to non-members (effective 2008). **Document type:** *Yearbook, Trade.* **Description:** Interactive CD-ROM containing statistics of the Italian car industry. Covers, among other things, the production by model, exports by brand and country of destination, imports by country of origin, registrations and total cars in use by brand, province and region, as well as fuel consumption and prices. Also contains a review of the international economy.
Media: CD-ROM.
Published by: Anfia Service Srl, Corso Galileo Ferraris 61, Turin, 10128, Italy. TEL 39-011-545160, FAX 39-011-545464, http://www.anfia.it/anfiaservice/service.htm.

AUTOMOTIVE INDUSTRY DATA NEWSLETTER. *see* TRANSPORTATION—Automobiles

385.21 USA
AVERAGE DAILY TRAFFIC VOLUMES WITH VEHICLE CLASSIFICATION DATA ON INTERSTATE, ARTERIAL AND PRIMARY ROUTES. Text in English. a.
Formerly: Average Daily Traffic Volumes on Interstate, Arterial and Primary Routes (0094-7415)
Published by: Virginia Department of Transportation, Mobility Management Division, 1221 E Broad St, Richmond, VA 23219. TEL 804-786-2801. **Co-sponsor:** U.S. Federal Highway Administration.

016.387 GBR ISSN 0268-9650
VM1 CODEN: BMABE2
B M T ABSTRACTS; international maritime technology. Text in English. 1946. m. GBP 220 domestic; GBP 240 foreign (effective 2010). bk.rev. abstr. index. **Document type:** *Abstract/Index.* **Description:** Contains bibliographic information providing a reference and description for technical articles, reports, conference and transaction papers and other material on all aspects of maritime technology published worldwide, in at least 10 languages.
Former titles (until 1986): B S R A. Journal of Abstracts (0141-9048); (until 1970): British Ship Research Association. Journal of Abstracts (0141-903X); (until 1968): British Ship Research Association. Journal (0007-1765); (until 1962): British Shipbuilding Research Association. Journal (0141-9021)
Related titles: ◆ Online - full text ed.: Marine Technology Abstracts. —Linda Hall.
Published by: British Maritime Technology Ltd., Goodrich House, 1 Waldegrave Rd, Teddington, Middx TW11 8LZ, United Kingdom. TEL 44-20-89435544, FAX 44-20-89435347, enquiries@bmtmail.com, http://www.bmt.org/. Circ: 400.

387.2 SWE ISSN 0346-9387
BAATOLOGEN. Text in Swedish. 1963. bi-m. SEK 210 domestic; SEK 230 foreign (effective 2001). adv. bk.rev. 1984-2000. 56 p./no. 2 cols./p.; back issues avail. **Document type:** *Magazine.* **Description:** Features articles about merchant ships and shipping of today and the past, particularly in the Scandinavian countries.
Published by: Klubb Maritim, c/o T. Johanneson, Maloertsv 11, Viken, 26040, Sweden. TEL 46-42-23-72-76. Ed., Adv. contact Tomas Johannesson TEL 46-42-23-66-29. Circ: 4,000.

387.7021 SWE ISSN 1652-4373
BANTRAFIK/RAIL TRAFFIC. Text in Swedish, English. 1955. a., latest 2000. free. **Document type:** *Government.*
Former titles (until 2003): Jaernvaegar (1402-7003); (until 1996): Sveriges Jaernvaeger (0081-9964); Which was formed by the 1955 merger of: Allmaen Jaernvaegsstatistik; Statens Jaernvaegar
Related titles: Online - full content ed.; ◆ Series of: S I K A Statistik. ISSN 1404-854X.
Published by: Statens Institut foer Kommunikationsanalys (SIKA)/Swedish Institute for Transport and Communications Analysis, Maria Skolgata 83, PO Box 17213, Stockholm, 10462, Sweden. TEL 46-8-50620600, FAX 46-8-50620610, sika@sika-institute.se. **Co-sponsor:** Banverket/National Rail Administration.

388 IND ISSN 0067-6462
BASIC ROAD STATISTICS OF INDIA. Text in English. 1948. a. back issues avail. **Document type:** *Report, Government.*
Related titles: Online - full text ed.: free (effective 2011); Hindi ed.: Mool Sarak Ankrey.
Published by: Ministry of Road Transport & Highways, Transport Bhavan, 1, Parliament St, New Delhi, 110 011, India. dirrt@nic.in. **Orders to:** Controller of Publications.

385.21 DEU ISSN 1430-3248
BAYERISCHES LANDESAMT FUER STATISTIK UND DATENVERARBEITUNG. STATISTISCHE BERICHTE H: VERKEHR. Text in German. 195?. irreg. **Document type:** *Government.*
Formerly (until 1982): Bayerisches Statistisches Landesamt. Statistische Berichte H (1430-3078)
Published by: Bayerisches Landesamt fuer Statistik und Datenverarbeitung, Neuhauser Str 8, Munich, 80331, Germany. TEL 49-89-2119205, FAX 49-89-2119410, poststelle@statistik.bayern.de, http://www.statistik.bayern.de.

614.86021 BEL ISSN 1378-1227
HE5614.5.B4
BELGIUM. INSTITUT NATIONAL DE STATISTIQUE. SANTE. ACCIDENTS DE LA CIRCULATION SUR LA VOIE PUBLIQUE AVEC TUES ET BLESSES EN (ANNEE). Key Title: Accidents de la Circulation sur la Voie Publique avec Tues et Blesses. Text in French. 1954. a. EUR 41; EUR 10 per issue (effective 2001). charts. back issues avail. **Document type:** *Government.* **Description:** Provides a statistical overview of deaths and injuries in traffic accidents on public highways.
Former titles (until 2000): Belgium. Institut National de Statistique. Accidents de la Circulation sur la Voie Publique avec Tues et Blesses (0770-237X); (until 1973): Belgium. Institut National de Statistique. Statistique des Accidents de la Circulation sur la Voie Publique (0067-5504); (until 1962): Belgium. Institut National de Statistique. Statistique des Accidents de Roulage (0067-5512)
Related titles: ◆ Dutch ed.: Belgium. Nationaal Instituut voor de Statistiek. Gezondheid. Verkeersongevallen op de Openbare Weg met Doden en Gewonden in (Year). ISSN 1378-1219.
Published by: Institut National de Statistique/Nationaal Instituut voor de Statistiek (Subsidiary of: Ministere des Affaires Economiques), Rue de Louvain 44, Brussels, 1000, Belgium. TEL 32-2-548-6211, FAX 32-2-548-6367.

387.1021 BEL ISSN 0772-7739
BELGIUM. INSTITUT NATIONAL DE STATISTIQUE. STATISTIQUE DU TRAFIC INTERNATIONAL DES PORTS (U E B L). Variant title: Statistique du Trafic International des Ports (Union Economique Belgo-Luxembourgeoise). Text in French. 1952. a. charts. back issues avail. **Document type:** *Government.*
Formerly (until 1977): Belgium. Institut National de Statistique. Statistique Annuelle du Trafic International des Ports (0067-5482)
Related titles: ◆ Dutch ed.: Belgium. Nationaal Instituut voor de Statistiek. Statistiek over de Internationale Trafiek (B.L.E.U.) in de Havens. ISSN 0772-800X.
Published by: Institut National de Statistique/Nationaal Instituut voor de Statistiek (Subsidiary of: Ministere des Affaires Economiques), Rue de Louvain 44, Brussels, 1000, Belgium. TEL 32-2-548-6211, FAX 32-2-548-6367.

388.3021 BEL ISSN 1379-3780
BELGIUM. INSTITUT NATIONAL DE STATISTIQUE. STATISTIQUES DU TRANSPORT. PARC DES VEHICULES A MOTEUR AU (YEAR). Key Title: Statistiques du Transport. Parc des Vehicules a Moteur - Institut National de Statistique. Text in French. 195?. a. EUR 7 (effective 2002). charts. back issues avail. **Document type:** *Government.*
Formerly (until 2000): Belgium. Institut National de Statistique. Parc de Vehicules a Moteur (1370-1738)
Related titles: ◆ Dutch ed.: Belgium. Nationaal Instituut voor de Statistiek. Vervoerstatistieken. Motorvoertuigenpark op (Year). ISSN 1379-3772.
Published by: Institut National de Statistique/Nationaal Instituut voor de Statistiek (Subsidiary of: Ministere des Affaires Economiques), Rue de Louvain 44, Brussels, 1000, Belgium. TEL 32-2-548-6211, FAX 32-2-548-6367.

386.021 BEL ISSN 1379-3888
BELGIUM. INSTITUT NATIONAL DE STATISTIQUE. TRANSPORT. NAVIGATION INTERIEURE. Key Title: Transport. Navigation Interieure. Text in French. 19??. a. EUR 10 (effective 2002). charts. back issues avail. **Document type:** *Government.* **Description:** Examines economic domestic shipping activity.
Former titles (until 1998): Belgium. Institut National de Statistique. Navigation Interieure (Annee) (0773-2805); Which incorporated (1949-1982): Belgium. Institut National de Statistique. Statistique de la Navigation du Rhin (0067-5520); (until 1981): Belgium. Institut National de Statistique. Statistique de la Navigation Interieure (0067-5539); (until 1968): Belgium. Institut National de Statistique. Statistiques du Commerce et des Transports (0773-3038)
Related titles: ◆ Dutch ed.: Belgium. Nationaal Instituut voor de Statistiek. Vervoer. Binnenscheepvaart (Jaar). ISSN 1379-387X.
Published by: Institut National de Statistique/Nationaal Instituut voor de Statistiek (Subsidiary of: Ministere des Affaires Economiques), Rue de Louvain 44, Brussels, 1000, Belgium. TEL 32-2-548-6211, FAX 32-2-548-6367, http://www.statbel.fgov.be.

338.4021 BEL ISSN 1377-4271
HE5673
BELGIUM. INSTITUT NATIONAL DE STATISTIQUE. TRANSPORT. VEHICULES A MOTEUR NEUFS ET D'OCCASION MIS EN CIRCULATION EN (ANNEE). Text in French. 1955. a. charts. back issues avail. **Document type:** *Government.* **Description:** Provides a statistical overview of motor vehicles and traffic trends in Belgium.
Formerly (until 2001): Belgium. Institut National de Statistique. Vehicules a Moteur Neufs Mis en Circulation (0773-3070); Which superseded in part (in 1971): Belgium. Institut National de Statistique. Statistique des Vehicules a Moteurs Neufs Mis en Circulation (0067-5555)
Related titles: ◆ Dutch ed.: Belgium. Nationaal Instituut voor de Statistiek. Vervoer. In het Verkeer Gebrachte Nieuwe en Tweedehands Motorvoertuigen in (Year). ISSN 1377-4263.
Published by: Institut National de Statistique/Nationaal Instituut voor de Statistiek (Subsidiary of: Ministere des Affaires Economiques), Rue de Louvain 44, Brussels, 1000, Belgium. TEL 32-2-548-6211, FAX 32-2-548-6367.

BELGIUM. NATIONAAL INSTITUUT VOOR DE STATISTIEK. GEZONDHEID. VERKEERSONGEVALLEN OP DE OPENBARE WEG MET DODEN EN GEWONDEN IN (YEAR). *see* PUBLIC HEALTH AND SAFETY—Abstracting, Bibliographies, Statistics

387.1021 BEL ISSN 0772-800X
BELGIUM. NATIONAAL INSTITUUT VOOR DE STATISTIEK. STATISTIEK OVER DE INTERNATIONALE TRAFIEK (B.L.E.U.) IN DE HAVENS. Key Title: Statistiek over de Internationale Trafiek (B.L.E.U.) in de Havens. Text in Dutch. 1952. a. charts. **Document type:** *Government.*
Formerly (until 1974): Belgium. Institut National de Statistique. Statistique Annuelle du Trafic International des Ports (0067-5482)
Related titles: ◆ French ed.: Belgium. Institut National de Statistique. Statistique du Trafic International des Ports (U E B L). ISSN 0772-7739.
Published by: Institut National de Statistique/Nationaal Instituut voor de Statistiek (Subsidiary of: Ministere des Affaires Economiques), Rue de Louvain 44, Brussels, 1000, Belgium. TEL 32-2-548-6211, FAX 32-2-548-6367.

386.021 BEL ISSN 1379-387X
BELGIUM. NATIONAAL INSTITUUT VOOR DE STATISTIEK. VERVOER. BINNENSCHEEPVAART (JAAR). Key Title: Vervoer. Binnenscheepvaart Jaar .. Text in Dutch. 1971. a. charts. back issues avail. **Document type:** *Government.* **Description:** Examines economic domestic shipping activity.
Former titles (until 1998): Belgium. Nationaal Instituut voor de Statistiek. Binnenscheepvaart (0773-2813); (until 1982): Belgium. Nationaal Instituut voor de Statistiek. Statistiek van de Binnenscheepvaart (0773-302X); (until 1968): Belgium. Nationaal Instituut voor de Statistiek. Binnenscheepvaart (0773-3011)
Related titles: ◆ French ed.: Belgium. Institut National de Statistique. Transport. Navigation Interieure. ISSN 1379-3888.
Published by: Institut National de Statistique/Nationaal Instituut voor de Statistiek (Subsidiary of: Ministere des Affaires Economiques), Rue de Louvain 44, Brussels, 1000, Belgium. TEL 32-2-548-6211, FAX 32-2-548-6367.

388.1021 BEL ISSN 1377-4263
BELGIUM. NATIONAAL INSTITUUT VOOR DE STATISTIEK. VERVOER. IN HET VERKEER GEBRACHTE NIEUWE EN TWEEDEHANDS MOTORVOERTUIGEN IN (YEAR). Key Title: Vervoer, Verkeer Gebrachte Nieuwe Tweedehands Motorvoert - Nationaal Instituut voor de Statistiek. Text in Dutch. 1955. a. charts. **Document type:** *Government.* **Description:** Provides a statistical overview of motor vehicles and traffic trends in Belgium.
Former titles (until 2000): Belgium. Nationaal Instituut voor de Statistiek. Nieuwe to het Verkeer Toegelaten Motorvoergtuigen (0773-3089); (until 1970): Belgium. Nationaal Instituut voor de Statistiek. Statistique des Vehicules a Moteurs Neufs Mis en Circulation (0067-5555)
Related titles: ◆ French ed.: Belgium. Institut National de Statistique. Transport. Vehicules a Moteur Neufs et d'Occasion Mis en Circulation en (Annee). ISSN 1377-4271.
Published by: Institut National de Statistique/Nationaal Instituut voor de Statistiek (Subsidiary of: Ministere des Affaires Economiques), Rue de Louvain 44, Brussels, 1000, Belgium. TEL 32-2-548-6211, FAX 32-2-548-6367.

388.3021 BEL ISSN 1379-3772
BELGIUM. NATIONAAL INSTITUUT VOOR DE STATISTIEK. VERVOERSTATISTIEKEN. MOTORVOERTUIGENPARK OP (YEAR). Key Title: Vervoerstatistieken. Motorvoertuigenpark - Nationaal Instituut voor de Statistiek. Text in Dutch. 195?. a. charts. back issues avail. **Document type:** *Government.*
Formerly (until 2000): Belgium. Nationaal Instituut voor de Statistiek. Motorvoertuigenpark (1370-1746)
Related titles: ◆ French ed.: Belgium. Institut National de Statistique. Statistiques du Transport. Parc des Vehicules a Moteur au (Year). ISSN 1379-3780.
Published by: Institut National de Statistique/Nationaal Instituut voor de Statistiek (Subsidiary of: Ministere des Affaires Economiques), Rue de Louvain 44, Brussels, 1000, Belgium. TEL 32-2-548-6211, FAX 32-2-548-6367.

387 ECU
BOLETIN ESTADISTICO DE TRAFICO AEREO INTERNACIONAL. Text in Spanish. 1976. a. free. stat.
Formerly: Ecuador. Direccion de Aviacion Civil. Estadisticas de Trafico Aereo
Published by: Direccion General de Aviacion Civil, Buenos Aires 149 y Avda. 10 de Agosto, Quito, Ecuador. TEL 552288, TELEX 22710 DACUIO ED.

388 BDI
BURUNDI. INSTITUT DE STATISTIQUES ET D'ETUDES ECONOMIQUES. PARC AUTOMOBILE. Text in French. biennial. USD 23. **Document type:** *Monographic series.*
Published by: Institut de Statistiques et d'Etudes Economiques, BP 1156, Bujumbura, Burundi.

387.74 USA ISSN 0731-3411
TL521
C A B AIR CARRIER TRAFFIC STATISTICS. (Civil Aeronautics Board) Text in English. 1970. m. USD 52. reprints avail. **Document type:** *Government.*
Formerly (until 1980): Air Carrier Traffic Statistics (0098-0404)
Related titles: Microfiche ed.: (from CIS).
Indexed: AmStI.
Published by: (Office of Aviation Information Management), U.S. Department of Transportation, Research & Special Programs Administration, 400 Seventh St, S W, Rm 8410, Washington, DC 20590. TEL 202-366-4000. Circ: 500.

387.5 FRA
CAHIER STATISTIQUE MARITIME. Text in French. 1956. a. EUR 65.
Former titles: Transport Maritime: Etudes et Statistiques; Marine Marchand: Etudes et Statistiques (0069-6439)
Published by: Comite Central des Armateurs de France, 47 rue de Monceau, Paris, 75008, France. FAX 33-1-53895253, ccaf@ccaf.asso.fr. Circ: 4,500.

387.7 CAN ISSN 0828-8208
CANADA. STATISTICS CANADA. AIR CHARTER STATISTICS. Text in English. 1970. q. CAD 41 domestic; USD 41 foreign (effective 1999). **Description:** Examines the domestic and international air charter operations of more than 80 Canadian and foreign carriers. Covers passenger and cargo charter traffic.
Formerly: Canada. Statistics Canada. International Air Charter Statistics (0705-4297)
Related titles: Online - full text ed.
—CCC.
Published by: Statistics Canada, Operations and Integration Division (Subsidiary of: Statistics Canada/Statistique Canada), Circulation Management, 120 Parkdale Ave, Ottawa, ON K1A 0T6, Canada. TEL 613-951-7277, 800-267-6677, FAX 613-951-1584.

387.7 CAN ISSN 0705-4343
CANADA. STATISTICS CANADA. AIR PASSENGER ORIGIN AND DESTINATION. CANADA - UNITED STATES REPORT. Text in English, French. 1968. a. CAD 47 domestic; USD 47 foreign (effective 1999). **Description:** Presents information on the volume of air passenger traffic between points in Canada and the US.
Related titles: Microform ed.: -suspended (from MML); Online - full text ed.
Published by: Statistics Canada, Transportation Division (Subsidiary of: Statistics Canada/Statistique Canada), Aviation Statistics Centre, 1506 Main Building, Ottawa, ON K1A 0T6, Canada. TEL 613-951-0151, FAX 613-951-0010. Ed. Kathie Davidson.

387.7 CAN ISSN 0703-2692
CANADA. STATISTICS CANADA. AIR PASSENGER ORIGIN AND DESTINATION. DOMESTIC REPORT. Text in English. a. CAD 43 (effective 1999). **Description:** Includes information on the volume of domestic air passenger traffic at Canadian cities and carried between Canadian city-pairs.
Related titles: Online - full text ed.
Published by: Statistics Canada, Operations and Integration Division (Subsidiary of: Statistics Canada/Statistique Canada), Circulation Management, 120 Parkdale Ave, Ottawa, ON K1A 0T6, Canada. TEL 613-951-7277, 800-267-6677, FAX 613-951-1584. Circ: 530.

387.7 CAN ISSN 0068-7057
CANADA. STATISTICS CANADA. AVIATION STATISTICS CENTRE. SERVICE BULLETIN/CANADA. CENTRE DES STATISTIQUES DE L'AVIATION. BULLETIN DE SERVICE. Text in English, French. 1968. m. CAD 82 (effective 1999). **Description:** Includes financial and operational advance statistics for Level I carriers. Covers the air transport industry, airports, fare basis statistics, passenger and cargo traffic.
Related titles: Microform ed.: (from MML); Online - full text ed.: ISSN 1480-7483.
Published by: Statistics Canada, Operations and Integration Division (Subsidiary of: Statistics Canada/Statistique Canada), Circulation Management, 120 Parkdale Ave, Ottawa, ON K1A 0T6, Canada. TEL 613-951-7277, FAX 613-951-1584.

388.3 CAN ISSN 0705-5595
CANADA. STATISTICS CANADA. NEW MOTOR VEHICLE SALES. Text in English, French. 1932. m. CAD 124 domestic (effective 1999); USD 124 foreign. **Document type:** *Government.* **Description:** Presents data on new motor vehicles: number and value of new passenger cars, trucks and buses sold, by month, as well as cumulatively, for both current and previous years.
Related titles: Online - full text ed.
Published by: Statistics Canada, Operations and Integration Division (Subsidiary of: Statistics Canada/Statistique Canada), Circulation Management, 120 Parkdale Ave, Ottawa, ON K1A 0T6, Canada. TEL 613-951-7277, 800-267-6677, FAX 613-951-1584.

388 CAN ISSN 0383-5766
CANADA. STATISTICS CANADA. PASSENGER BUS AND URBAN TRANSIT STATISTICS/CANADA. STATISTIQUE CANDA. STATISTIQUE DU TRANSPORT DES VOYAGEURS PAR AUTOBUS ET DU TRANSPORT URBAIN. Text in English, French. 1956. a. CAD 40 domestic; USD 40 foreign (effective 1999). **Document type:** *Government.* **Description:** Shows investment, operating revenues, expenses on intercity and rural bus companies and urban transit systems.
Related titles: Microform ed.: (from MML); Online - full text ed.
Published by: Statistics Canada, Operations and Integration Division (Subsidiary of: Statistics Canada/Statistique Canada), Circulation Management, 120 Parkdale Ave, Ottawa, ON K1A 0T6, Canada. TEL 613-951-7277, 800-267-6677, FAX 613-951-1584.

387.7021 CAN ISSN 1209-1316
CANADA. STATISTICS CANADA. RAIL IN CANADA. Text in English, French. 1987. a. CAD 39 (effective 2004). **Document type:** *Government.*
Formerly (until 1995): Canada. Statistics Canada. Rail in Canada (Print) (0843-4530); Which was formed by the merger of (1979-1987): Canada. Statistics Canada. Railway Transport. Railway Commodity Origin and Destination Statistics (0229-883X); (1982-1987): Canada. Statistics Canada. Railway Transport in Canada. General Statistics (0823-3950); (1952-1987): Canada. Statistics Canada. Railway Transport in Canada. Commodity Statistics (0823-3969); Which was formerly (until 1981): Canada. Statistics Canada. Railway Transport. Part 5. Freight Carried by Principal Commodity Classes (0706-2087)
Media: Online - full content.
Published by: Statistics Canada/Statistique Canada, Publications Sales and Services, Ottawa, ON K1A 0T6, Canada. TEL 800-267-6677, infostats@statcan.ca, http://www.statcan.gc.ca.

385 CAN ISSN 0380-6308
CANADA. STATISTICS CANADA. RAILWAY CARLOADINGS/ CANADA. STATISTIQUE CANADA. CHARGEMENTS FERROVIAIRES. Text in English, French. 1924. m. CAD 103; USD 103 foreign (effective 1999). **Document type:** *Government.* **Description:** Outlines 69 commodities by cars loaded and tonnes of revenue freight carried in eastern and western Canada by class I and II railways.
Formerly (until 1948): Canada. Statistics Canada. Carloadings
Related titles: Microform ed.: (from MML).
—CCC.
Published by: Statistics Canada, Operations and Integration Division (Subsidiary of: Statistics Canada/Statistique Canada), Circulation Management, 120 Parkdale Ave, Ottawa, ON K1A 0T6, Canada. TEL 613-951-7277, 800-267-6677, FAX 613-951-1584.

388.3 CAN ISSN 0703-654X
CANADA. STATISTICS CANADA. ROAD MOTOR VEHICLES, FUEL SALES/CANADA. STATISTIQUE CANADA. VEHICULES AUTOMOBILES, VENTES DE CARBURANTS. Text in English, French. 1960. a. CAD 28 domestic; USD 28 foreign (effective 1999). **Document type:** *Government.* **Description:** Presents gross and net sales of gasolines and net fuel sales of diesel oil and liquefied petroleum gas used for automotive purposes by year and month, province and territory.
Formerly: Canada. Statistics Canada. Motor Vehicle. Part 2. Motive Fuel Sales (0527-5830)
Related titles: Microform ed.: (from MML).
Published by: Statistics Canada, Operations and Integration Division (Subsidiary of: Statistics Canada/Statistique Canada), Circulation Management, 120 Parkdale Ave, Ottawa, ON K1A 0T6, Canada. TEL 613-951-7277, 800-267-6677, FAX 613-951-1584.

388.3 CAN ISSN 0706-067X
HE5635
CANADA. STATISTICS CANADA. ROAD MOTOR VEHICLES, REGISTRATIONS/CANADA. STATISTIQUE CANADA. VEHICULES AUTOMOBILES, IMMATRICULATIONS. Text in English, French. 1960. a. CAD 28 domestic; USD 28 foreign (effective 1999). **Document type:** *Government.* **Description:** Presents data on registrations of motor vehicles by type including passenger automobiles, trucks, motorcycles, buses and trailers.
Related titles: Microform ed.: (from MML); Online - full text ed.
Published by: Statistics Canada, Operations and Integration Division (Subsidiary of: Statistics Canada/Statistique Canada), Circulation Management, 120 Parkdale Ave, Ottawa, ON K1A 0T6, Canada. TEL 613-951-7277, 800-267-6677, FAX 603-951-1584.

387 CAN ISSN 0835-5533
CANADA. STATISTICS CANADA. SHIPPING IN CANADA/CANADA. STATISTIQUES CANADA. TRANSPORT MARITIME AU CANADA. Text in English, French. 1946. a. CAD 52 domestic; USD 52 foreign (effective 1999). **Document type:** *Government.* **Description:** Presents domestic and international shipping activities at Canadian ports.
Formed by the merger of: Canada. Statistics Canada. International Seaborne Shipping Statistics; Canada. Statistics Canada. Coastwise Shipping Statistics; Canada. Statistics Canada. Water Transportation (0380-0342)
Related titles: Microform ed.: (from MML); Online - full text ed.
Published by: Statistics Canada, Operations and Integration Division (Subsidiary of: Statistics Canada/Statistique Canada), Circulation Management, 120 Parkdale Ave, Ottawa, ON K1A 0T6, Canada. TEL 613-951-7277, FAX 613-951-1584.

385 CAN ISSN 0828-2897
CANADA. STATISTICS CANADA. SURFACE AND MARINE TRANSPORT/CANADA. STATISTIQUE CANADA. TRANSPORTS TERRESTRE ET MARITIME. Text in English, French. 1971. irreg. CAD 83 domestic; USD 83 foreign (effective 1999). **Document type:** *Government.* **Description:** Presents analytical data, time series analysis and special tabulations covering trucking, rail, bus, urban, and marine transportation, and highway infrastructure.
Formerly (until 1984): Canada. Statistics Canada. Railway Transport. Service Bulletin (0700-2211)
—CCC.
Published by: Statistics Canada, Operations and Integration Division (Subsidiary of: Statistics Canada/Statistique Canada), Circulation Management, 120 Parkdale Ave, Ottawa, ON K1A 0T6, Canada. TEL 613-951-7277, 800-267-6677, FAX 613-951-1584.

380.5 CAN ISSN 0826-6026
CANADIAN CIVIL AVIATION. Text in English, French. 1934. a. CAD 31 (effective 1999). **Document type:** *Journal, Trade.* **Description:** Reports on activities of over 250 air Canadian carriers operating in Canada. Includes operational and financial statistics on number of passengers carried, kilometers and hours flown, income statements and balance sheets as well as fare basis information.
Formerly (until 1981): Air Carrier Financial Statements (0380-5174); Which superseded in part (in 1970): Civil Aviation (0380-5247); Which was formerly (until 1948): Civil Aviation in Canada (0380-5239); (until 1936): Statistical Summary of Civil Aviation (0844-6865)
Related titles: Online - full text ed.
Published by: Statistics Canada, Operations and Integration Division (Subsidiary of: Statistics Canada/Statistique Canada), Circulation Management, 120 Parkdale Ave, Ottawa, ON K1A 0T6, Canada. TEL 613-951-7277, 800-267-6677, FAX 613-951-1584. Circ: 390.

380.5 BRA ISSN 0103-6610
CENSO DOS TRANSPORTES. Text in Portuguese. 1985. quinquennial. USD 40 (effective 1998). **Document type:** *Government.*
Published by: Fundacao Instituto Brasileiro de Geografia e Estatistica, Centro de Documentacao e Disseminacao de Informacoes, Rua General Canabarro, 706 Andar 2, Maracana, Rio de Janeiro, RJ 20271-201, Brazil. TEL 55-21-2645424, FAX 55-21-2841959, http://www.ibge.gov.br.

380.5 GBR ISSN 1472-2151
HE243.A15
CHARTERED INSTITUTE OF PUBLIC FINANCE AND ACCOUNTANCY. HIGHWAYS AND TRANSPORTATION STATISTICS. ESTIMATES. Text in English. 1991. a. GBP 120 per issue (effective 2010). back issues avail. **Document type:** *Report, Trade.* **Description:** Provides details of authorities' estimated revenue and capital expenditure, including information on the cost of structural maintenance, routine maintenance, street lighting, winter maintenance, road safety, public transport.
Supersedes in part (in 2000): Chartered Institute of Public Finance and Accountancy. Highways and Transportation Statistics. Estimates & Actuals (0964-5624); Which was formed by the merger of (1981-1991): Chartered Institute of Public Finance and Accountancy. Highways and Transportation Statistics. Actuals (0260-9886); (1981-1991): Chartered Institute of Public Finance and Accountancy. Highways and Transportation Statistics. Estimates (0260-9894); Which was formerly (until 1981): County Surveyors' Society. Highways & Transportation Statistics. Based on Estimates (0307-8310); (until 1975): County Surveyors' Society. Highways Statistics. Estimates
—CCC.

Published by: (Statistical Information Service), Chartered Institute of Public Finance and Accountancy, 3 Robert St, London, WC2N 6RL, United Kingdom. TEL 44-20-75435600, FAX 44-20-75435700, info@cipfa.org.uk, http://www.cipfa.org.uk.

388.021 FRA ISSN 2107-3627
▼ **CHIFFRES CLES DU TRANSPORT.** Text in French. 2010. a. **Document type:** *Report, Government.*
Related titles: Online - full text ed.
Published by: France. Commissariat General au Developpement Durable, Service de l'Observation et des Statistiques, Tour Voltaire, La Defense, Cedex 92055, France.

380.021 CHL
CHILE. INSTITUTO NACIONAL DE ESTADISTICAS. ANUARIO DE TRANSPORTE Y COMUNICACIONES. Text in Spanish. 1977. a. CLP 2,000; USD 13.50 in United States; USD 15.90 elsewhere.
Published by: Instituto Nacional de Estadisticas, Casilla 498, Correo 3, Ave. Bulnes, 418, Santiago, Chile. TEL 56-2-6991441, FAX 56-2-6712169.

380.021 CHL
CHILE. INSTITUTO NACIONAL DE ESTADISTICAS. TRANSPORTE, COMUNICACIONES, TURISMO. Text in Spanish. 1989. q. CLP 750; USD 4.80 in United States; USD 5.30 elsewhere.
Published by: Instituto Nacional de Estadisticas, Casilla 498, Correo 3, Ave. Bulnes, 418, Santiago, Chile. TEL 56-2-6991441, FAX 56-2-6712169.

388.476 CHN ISSN 1002-0918
CHINA AUTO/ZHONGGUO QICHE. Text in English. 1991. bi-m. USD 150. adv. **Document type:** *Journal, Trade.* **Description:** Provides comprehensive analysis of the automotive industry in China.
Related titles: Online - full text ed.
Published by: China Automotive Technology and Research Center, PO Box 59, Tianjin, 300162, China. TEL 86-22-84771318, FAX 86-22-24370843, arc@catarc.ac.cn, http://www.catarc.ac.cn/index_english.htm.

387.7 629.1 CAN
CIVIL AVIATION STATISTICS OF THE WORLD (YEAR). Text in English, French, Russian, Spanish. irreg., latest 1995. USD 40.
Indexed: IIS, RASB.
Published by: International Civil Aviation Organization (I C A O), External Relations and Public Information Office, 999 University St, Montreal, PQ H3C 5H7, Canada. TEL 514-954-8022, FAX 514-954-6769, icaohq@icao.int.

385 016 DEU
D B - SELECT. (Deutsche Bahn) Text in German. 1956. m. adv. bk.rev. abstr.; stat.; tr.lit. **Document type:** *Bibliography.* **Description:** Documentation of specialized railway publications, including abstracts.
Former titles (until 1999): Fachinformation Bahn (0946-0438); (until 1993): Information Eisenbahn (0170-2947); (until 1978): Kurzauszuege aus dem Schrifttum fuer das Eisenbahnwesen (0023-5695)
—CCC.
Published by: Deutsche Bahn AG, Information und Dokumentation Bahn, Potsdamer Platz 2, Berlin, 10785, Germany. TEL 49-6131-325131, FAX 49-6131-325136, http://www.bahn.de. Circ: 2,300.

387 GBR ISSN 1751-3944
HE561
DREWRY SHIPPING INSIGHT. Text in English. 1970. m. GBP 840 combined subscription in Europe (print & online eds.); GBP 895 combined subscription elsewhere (print & online eds.) (effective 2009). **Document type:** *Journal, Trade.* **Description:** Provides the shipping professional with numerous tables and charts supported by commentary on worldwide trends.
Former titles (until 2006): The Drewry Monthly (1364-4912); (until 1996): Shipping Statistics and Economics (0306-1817)
Related titles: Online - full text ed.
Indexed: PAIS.
—CCC.
Published by: Drewry Shipping Consultants Ltd., Drewry House, Meridian Gate - S Quay, 213 Marsh Wall, London, E14 9FJ, United Kingdom. TEL 44-20-75380191, FAX 44-20-79879396, info@drewry.co.uk.

016.388 RUS
▼ **EKSPRESS INFORMATSIYA. UPRAVLENIE PEREVOZOCHNYM PROTSESSOM. LOGISTIKA. KONTEINERY.** Text in Russian. 2011. s-m. USD 330 foreign (effective 2011). **Document type:** *Journal, Abstract/Index.*
Formed by the merger of (1962-2011): Ekspress Informatsiya. Upravlenie, Logistika i Informatika na Transporte; (1962-2011): Ekspress Informatsiya. Tara i Upakovka. Konteinery
Published by: VINITI RAN, ul Usievicha 20, Moscow, 125190, Russian Federation. TEL 7-499-1526113, FAX 7-499-9430060, dir@viniti.ru, http://www.viniti.ru. **Dist. by:** Informnauka Ltd., Ul Usievicha 20, Moscow 125190, Russian Federation. alfimov@viniti.ru.

ENERGY, TRANSPORT AND ENVIRONMENT INDICATORS. *see* ENERGY—Abstracting, Bibliographies, Statistics

388.41 PAN ISSN 0378-6765
HE5614.5.P33
ESTADISTICA PANAMENA. SITUACION SOCIAL. SECCION 451. ACCIDENTES DE TRANSITO. Text in Spanish. 1958. a. PAB 1 domestic (effective 2000). **Document type:** *Bulletin, Government.* **Description:** Offers detailed information on transportation accidents in the country.
Published by: Direccion de Estadistica y Censo, Contraloria General, Apdo. 5213, Panama City, 5, Panama. FAX 507-210-4801. Circ: 700.

380.5 GTM
ESTADISTICAS DE TRANSPORTE DE GUATEMALA. Text in Spanish. irreg., latest 1988-89. USD 15. **Document type:** *Government.*
Published by: Instituto Nacional de Estadistica, Ministerio de Economia, 8A Calle no. 9-55, Guatemala City Zona, Guatemala. TEL 502-26136. **Co-sponsor:** Ministerio de Comunicaciones, Transportes y Obras Publicas.

380.021 PRT ISSN 0870-0451
HE77
ESTATISTICAS DOS TRANSPORTES E COMUNICACOES. Text in Portuguese. 1970. a. EUR 20 (effective 2005). **Document type:** *Government.* **Description:** Provides statistical data on different aspects of transport, such as road accidents, fuel consumption, automobile sales.
Formerly (until 1976): Estatisticas dos Trnasportes (0377-2292)
Published by: Instituto Nacional de Estatistica, Av Antonio Jose de Almeida 2, Lisbon, 1000-043, Portugal. TEL 351-21-8426100, FAX 351-21-8426380, http://www.ine.pt.

388.021 PRT ISSN 0872-5969
HE5682
ESTATISTICAS DOS TRANSPORTES RODOVIARIOS DE PASSAGEIROS E DE MERCADORIAS. Text in Portuguese. 1975. a. EUR 20 (effective 2005). **Description:** Provides statistical data on transportation of goods by roads.
Formerly (until 1992): Inquerito ao Transporte Rodoviario de Mercadorias (0870-2586)
Published by: Instituto Nacional de Estatistica, Av Antonio Jose de Almeida 2, Lisbon, 1000-043, Portugal. TEL 351-21-8426100, FAX 351-21-8426380, ine@ine.pt, http://www.ine.pt.

016.385 DEU ISSN 0173-0037
EUROPAEISCHES UEBEREINKOMMEN UEBER DIE INTERNATIONALE BEFOERDERUNG GEFAEHRLICHER GUETER AUF DER STRASSE (A D R). Text in German. 1974. irreg. **Document type:** *Trade.*
—IE.
Published by: Bundesministerium fuer Verkehr, Bau und Stadtentwicklung/Federal Ministry of Transport, Building and Urban Affairs, Krausenstr 17-20, Berlin, 10117, Germany. TEL 49-30-183000, FAX 49-30-183001942, buergerinfo@bmvbs.bund.de, http://www.bmvbs.de.

388 LUX ISSN 1562-1324
HE242.A15
EUROSTAT STATISTICS IN FOCUS. TRANSPORT. Text in English. 1991. m. charts. **Document type:** *Journal, Trade.*
Former titles (until 1999): Statistics in Focus. Distributive Trades, Services and Transport; Eurostat. Statistics in Focus. Distributive Trades, Services and Transport (1560-3652); (until 1996): Eurostat. Rapid Reports. Services and Transports (1017-589X)
Related titles: German ed.; French ed.
Indexed: IIS.
Published by: (European Commission, Statistical Office of the European Communities (E U R O S T A T)), European Commission, Office for Official Publications of the European Union, 2 Rue Mercier, Luxembourg, L-2985, Luxembourg. TEL 352-29291, FAX 352-29291, info@publications.europa.eu, http://publications.europa.eu. **Dist. in the U.S. by:** Bernan Associates, Bernan, 4611-F Assembly Dr., Lanham, MD 20706-4391. TEL 301-459-7666, 800-274-4888.

387.7021 USA ISSN 0566-9618
TL521
F A A STATISTICAL HANDBOOK OF AVIATION. Text in English. a.
Published by: (Federal Aviation Administration, Office of Aviation Policy and Plans), U.S. Department of Transportation, Federal Aviation Administration (Subsidiary of: Department of Transportation, National Transportation and S.A.), 800 Independence Ave, SW, Washington, DC 20591.

380.5 FJI ISSN 0256-8063
FIJI. BUREAU OF STATISTICS. SHIPPING STATISTICS. Text in English. 1971. a., latest 1994. USD 5 per issue (effective 2000 & 2001). **Document type:** *Government.*
Published by: Bureau of Statistics, c/o Librarian, Govt. Bldg. 5, PO Box 2221, Suva, Fiji. TEL 679-315-822, FAX 679-303-656.

330 FIN ISSN 0786-0366
FINLAND. TILASTOKESKUS. KUORMA-AUTOLIIKENTEEN KUSTANNUSINDEKSI/FINLAND. STATISTICS FINLAND. COST INDEX FOR ROAD TRANSPORT OF GOODS/FINLAND. STATISTIKCENTRALEN. KOSTNADSINDEX FOER LASTBILTRAFIK. Text in English, Finnish, Swedish. 1978. m. EUR 34 (effective 2008). stat. **Document type:** *Government.*
Formerly (until 1988): Finland Tilastokeskus. Ammattimaisen Kuorma-Autoliikenteen Kustannustekijoiden Hintaindeksi (0357-1661)
Related titles: Online - full text ed.: ISSN 1796-3745. 2006; ◆ Series of: Finland. Tilastokeskus. Suomen Virallinen Tilasto. ISSN 1795-5165.
Published by: Tilastokeskus/Statistics Finland, Tyopajakatu 13, Statistics Finland, Helsinki, 00022, Finland. TEL 358-9-17341, FAX 358-9-17342279.

385.1 FIN ISSN 0785-6172
FINLAND. TILASTOKESKUS. LIIKENNETILASTOLLINEN VUOSIKIRJA/FINLAND. STATISTICS FINLAND. TRANSPORT AND COMMUNICATIONS STATISTICAL YEARBOOK FOR FINLAND/FINLAND. STATISTIKCENTRALEN. SAMFAERDSELSTATISTISKAARSBOK. Text in English, Finnish, Swedish. 1958. a. EUR 62 (effective 2008). **Document type:** *Yearbook, Government.*
Formerly (until 1987): Finland. Tilastokeskus. Suomen Virallinen Tilasto. 36, Liikennetilastollinen (0430-5272)
Related titles: Online - full text ed.: ISSN 1796-1246; ◆ Series of: Finland. Tilastokeskus. Suomen Virallinen Tilasto. ISSN 1795-5165.
Published by: Tilastokeskus/Statistics Finland, Tyopajakatu 13, Statistics Finland, Helsinki, 00022, Finland. TEL 358-9-17341, FAX 358-9-17342279.

388.31 FIN ISSN 0785-613X
HE255.3.A15
FINLAND. TILASTOKESKUS. MOOTTORIAJONEUVOT/FINLAND. STATISTICS FINLAND. MOTOR VEHICLES/FINLAND. STATISTIKCENTRALEN. MOTORFORDON. Text in English, Finnish, Swedish. 1969. a. EUR 37 (effective 2008). back issues avail. **Document type:** *Government.*
Formerly: Finland. Tilastokeskus. Tieliikenneonnettomuudet (0355-2284)
Related titles: Online - full text ed.: ISSN 1796-4040. 2006; ◆ Series of: Finland. Tilastokeskus. Suomen Virallinen Tilasto. ISSN 1795-5165.
Indexed: RASB.
Published by: Tilastokeskus/Statistics Finland, Tyopajakatu 13, Statistics Finland, Helsinki, 00022, Finland. TEL 358-9-17341, FAX 358-9-17342279, http://www.stat.fi.

338.4021 388.021 FIN ISSN 0785-6245
FINLAND. TILASTOKESKUS. TIELIIKENNEONNETTOMUUDET/FINLAND. STATISTICS FINLAND. ROAD ACCIDENTS IN FINLAND/FINLAND. STATISTIKCENTRALEN. VAEGTRAFIKOLYKOR. Text in English, Finnish, Swedish. 1988. a. EUR 37 (effective 2008). **Document type:** *Government.*
Supersedes in part (1988-1989): Finland. Tilastokeskus. Tieliikenneonnettomuudet, Tiietoja Henkilovahingoista (0785-6261); (1968-1988): Finland. Tilastokeskus. Tilastotiedotus - Tilastokeskus. LI, Liikenne (0355-2284)
Related titles: Online - full text ed.: ISSN 1796-5195. 2006; ◆ Series of: Finland. Tilastokeskus. Suomen Virallinen Tilasto. ISSN 1795-5165.
Published by: Tilastokeskus/Statistics Finland, Tyopajakatu 13, Statistics Finland, Helsinki, 00022, Finland. TEL 358-9-17341, FAX 358-9-17342279, http://www.stat.fi.

388.021 USA ISSN 1944-8791
HE199.U5
FREIGHT FACTS AND FIGURES. Text in English. 2004. a. **Document type:** *Government.*
Related titles: Online - full text ed.: ISSN 1944-8805.
Published by: U.S. Department of Transportation, Office of Freight Management and Operations, Mail Stop E84-403, 1200 New Jersey Ave, SE, Washington, DC 20590. TEL 202-366-9210, FAX 202-366-3225.

387.7 USA
GENERAL AVIATION STATISTICAL DATABOOK. Text in English. 1980. a. USD 3 (effective 2005). stat. **Document type:** *Handbook/Manual/Guide, Trade.*
Related titles: Microfiche ed.: (from CIS).
Indexed: SRI.
Published by: General Aviation Manufacturers Association, 1400 K St, N W, Ste 801, Washington, DC 20005. TEL 202-393-1500, FAX 202-842-4063, webmaster@GAMA.aero, http://www.gama.aero. R&P Elizabeth Davis.

629 GHA
GHANA. STATISTICAL SERVICE. MOTOR VEHICLE REGISTRATION. Text in English. q. USD 20. **Document type:** *Government.*
Formerly: Ghana. Central Bureau of Statistics. Motor Vehicle Registration
Published by: Statistical Service, Information Section, PO Box 1098, Accra, Ghana. TEL 233-21-663578, FAX 233-21-667069.

388 USA
GRANT ASSISTANCE PROGRAM. FISCAL YEAR STATISTICAL SUMMARIES. Text in English. a. free. **Document type:** *Government.* **Description:** Presents selected analyzed data on the distribution of various Grant Assistance Program Funds administered by the Federal Transit Administration.
Published by: U.S. Federal Transit Administration, Office of Program Management (TGM-10), U S Department of Transportation, TPM 10, 400 Seventh St, S W, Rm 9311, Washington, DC 20590. TEL 202-366-2053, FAX 202-366-7951.

387.742 GBR
GREAT BRITAIN. CIVIL AVIATION AUTHORITY. ANNUAL PUNCTUALITY STATISTICS - FULL AND SUMMARY ANALYSIS (YEAR). Text in English. 19??. a. back issues avail. **Document type:** *Government.* **Description:** Features analyzes the on-time performance of charter and scheduled air services for each airline and route.
Formed by the merger of: Great Britain. Civil Aviation Authority. Annual Punctuality Statistics - Summary Analysis (Year); Great Britain. Civil Aviation Authority. Annual Punctuality Statistics - Full Analysis (Year)
Related titles: Online - full text ed.: free (effective 2010); ◆ Series: Air Traffic Control Licensing; ◆ Air Navigation - The Order and the Regulations; ◆ Great Britain. Civil Aviation Authority. Airport Surveys; ◆ Manual of Air Traffic Services - Part 1; ◆ Great Britain. Civil Aviation Authority. Mandatory Requirements for Airworthiness; ◆ Great Britain. Civil Aviation Authority. Approved Aerial Positions; ◆ Mandatory Aircraft Modifications and Inspections Summary; ◆ Civil Aircraft Airworthiness Information and Procedures; ◆ A A I B Recommendations - C A A Progress Report (Year); ◆ Air Traffic Services Engineering Requirements; ◆ Great Britain. Civil Aviation Authority. Annual Punctuality Statistics - Full Analysis (Year); ◆ United Kingdom Aeronautical Information Publication; ◆ Overseas Non-scheduled Flight Clearances Guide.
Published by: Civil Aviation Authority, Printing and Publication Services, C A A House, 45-59 Kingsway, London, WCB2 6TE, United Kingdom. TEL 44-20-73797311, FAX 44-20-74536097, infoservices@caa.co.uk.

387.742 GBR ISSN 0957-5154
GREAT BRITAIN. CIVIL AVIATION AUTHORITY. PUNCTUALITY STATISTICS HEATHROW, GATWICK, MANCHESTER, BIRMINGHAM, LUTON AND STANSTEAD - FULL ANALYSIS. Text in English. m. back issues avail. **Document type:** *Government.* **Description:** Provides a full analysis of on-time performance by route and airline (both scheduled and charter) for major U.K. airports.
Published by: Civil Aviation Authority, Printing and Publication Services, C A A House, 45-59 Kingsway, London, WCB2 6TE, United Kingdom. TEL 44-20-73797311, FAX 44-20-74536097, infoservices@caa.co.uk.

387.742 GBR ISSN 0957-5162
GREAT BRITAIN. CIVIL AVIATION AUTHORITY. PUNCTUALITY STATISTICS HEATHROW, GATWICK, MANCHESTER, BIRMINGHAM, LUTON AND STANSTEAD - SUMMARY ANALYSIS. Variant title: Punctuality Statistics - Summary Analysis. Text in English. 1989. m. back issues avail. **Document type:** *Government.* **Description:** Features reports analyzing the on-time performance of each route to and from the major U.K. airports.
Published by: Civil Aviation Authority, Printing and Publication Services, C A A House, 45-59 Kingsway, London, WCB2 6TE, United Kingdom. TEL 44-20-73797311, FAX 44-20-74536097, infoservices@caa.co.uk.

387.71 GBR
GREAT BRITAIN. CIVIL AVIATION AUTHORITY. U.K. AIRLINES ANNUAL OPERATING, TRAFFIC & FINANCIAL STATISTICS. Text in English. 1973. a. **Document type:** *Government.* **Description:** Features reports analyzing the operation of U.K. airlines in various measures such as passengers, passenger-kilometers, cargo-tonnage kilometers, and load factors.

TU

Supersedes in part (in 1983): Great Britain. Civil Aviation Authority. Annual Statistics
Published by: Civil Aviation Authority, Printing and Publication Services, C A A House, 45-59 Kingsway, London, WCB2 6TE, United Kingdom. TEL 44-20-73797311, FAX 44-20-74536097, infoservices@caa.co.uk, http://www.caa.co.uk/. **Dist. by:** Westward Documedia Limited.

387.74 310 GBR
GREAT BRITAIN. CIVIL AVIATION AUTHORITY. U.K. AIRLINES MONTHLY OPERATING & TRAFFIC STATISTICS. Text in English. 1973. m. **Document type:** *Government.* **Description:** Features analyzes the operation of U.K. airlines for number of passengers flown, passenger-kilometers, cargo tonnage-kilometers, and load factors.
Supersedes in part (in 1983): Great Britain. Civil Aviation Authority. C A A Monthly Operating and Traffic Statistics (0265-0266); Former titles (until 1983): Great Britain. Civil Aviation Board. C A A Monthly Statistics (0306-3577); (until 19??): Business Monitor Civil Aviation Series
—CCC.
Published by: Civil Aviation Authority, Printing and Publication Services, C A A House, 45-59 Kingsway, London, WCB2 6TE, United Kingdom. FAX 44-20-74536097, infoservices@caa.co.uk, http://www.caa.co.uk/. **Dist. by:** Westward Documedia Limited.

387.74 GBR
GREAT BRITAIN. CIVIL AVIATION AUTHORITY. U.K. AIRPORTS ANNUAL STATEMENTS OF MOVEMENTS, PASSENGERS AND CARGO (YEAR). Text in English. 1973. a. **Document type:** *Government.* **Description:** Features reports analyzing the number of movements, passengers, and cargo tonnage handled at nearly 50 U.K. airports.
Supersedes in part (in 1983): Great Britain. Civil Aviation Authority. Annual Statistics
Published by: Civil Aviation Authority, Printing and Publication Services, C A A House, 45-59 Kingsway, London, WCB2 6TE, United Kingdom. TEL 44-20-73797311, FAX 44-20-74536097, infoservices@caa.co.uk, http://www.caa.co.uk/. **Dist. by:** Westward Documedia Limited.

387.74 620.3 GBR
GREAT BRITAIN. CIVIL AVIATION AUTHORITY. U.K. AIRPORTS MONTHLY STATEMENTS OF MOVEMENTS, PASSENGERS AND CARGO. Text in English. 1973. m. charts. **Document type:** *Government.* **Description:** Features reports analyzing the number of movements, passengers, and cargo tonnage handled at 50 U.K. airports.
Supersedes in part (in 1983): Great Britain. Civil Aviation Authority. C A A Monthly Operating and Traffic Statistics (0265-0266)
Published by: Civil Aviation Authority, Printing and Publication Services, C A A House, 45-59 Kingsway, London, WCB2 6TE, United Kingdom. TEL 44-20-73797311, FAX 44-20-74536097, infoservices@caa.co.uk, http://www.caa.co.uk/. **Dist. by:** Westward Documedia Limited.

387 GRC ISSN 0072-7423
GREECE. NATIONAL STATISTICAL SERVICE. SHIPPING STATISTICS. Text in English, Greek. 1967. a., latest 1995. back issues avail. **Document type:** *Government.*
Formerly (until 1974): Greece. National Statistical Service. Bulletin of Shipping Statistics
Published by: National Statistical Service of Greece, Statistical Information and Publications Division/Ethniki Statistiki Ypersia tes Ellados, 14-16 Lykourgou St, Athens, 101 66, Greece. TEL 30-1-3289-397, FAX 30-1-3241-102.

380.021 GRC ISSN 0256-3657
HE250
GREECE. NATIONAL STATISTICAL SERVICE. TRANSPORT AND COMMUNICATION STATISTICS. Text in Greek. 1967. a., latest 1992-94. back issues avail. **Document type:** *Government.*
Published by: National Statistical Service of Greece, Statistical Information and Publications Division/Ethniki Statistiki Ypersia tes Ellados, 14-16 Lykourgou St, Athens, 101 66, Greece. TEL 30-1-3289-397, FAX 30-1-3241-102, http://www.statistics.gr, http://www.statistics.gr/Main_eng.asp.

388 016 HUN ISSN 0231-1941
HAJOZASI SZAKIRODALMI TAJEKOZTATO/SHIPPING ABSTRACTS. Text in Hungarian. 1949. bi-m. HUF 2,700. abstr. index. **Document type:** *Abstract/Index.*
Supersedes in part (in 1982): Muszaki Lapszemle. Kozlekedes - Technical Abstracts. Transportation (0027-5042)
Published by: Orszagos Muszaki Informacios Kozpont es Konyvtar/ National Technical Information Centre and Library, Muzeum utca 17, PO Box 12, Budapest, 1428, Hungary. Ed. Nandorne Raics. Circ: 350. **Subscr. to:** Kultura, PO Box 149, Budapest 1389, Hungary.

388.021 HKG
HONG KONG SPECIAL ADMINISTRATIVE REGION OF CHINA. CENSUS AND STATISTICS DEPARTMENT. REPORT ON ANNUAL SURVEY OF TRANSPORT AND RELATED SERVICES. Text in Chinese, English. 1980. a., latest 1999. HKD 30 newsstand/cover (effective 2001). stat. back issues avail. **Document type:** *Government.* **Description:** Covers the statistics on the structure and operating characteristics of the transport industry.
Related titles: Online - full content ed.
Published by: Census and Statistics Department/Zhengfu Tongjichu, Distribution and Services Statistics Section 2(B), 20/F Chuang's Hung Hom Plaza, 83 Wuhu St, Hung Hom, Kowloon, Hong Kong. TEL 852-2802-1273, FAX 852-2123-1048, ds2b_1@censtatd.gov.hk, http://www.statisticalbookstore.gov.hk. **Subscr. to:** Information Services Department, Publications Sales Unit, Rm 402, 4th Fl, Murray Bldg, Garden Rd, Hong Kong, Hong Kong. TEL 852-2842-8844, FAX 852-2598-7482, puborder@isd.gcn.gov.hk, http://www.info.gov.hk/isd/book_e.htm. **Dist. by:** Government Publications Centre, Low Block, Ground Fl, Queensway Government Offices, 66 Queensway, Hong Kong, Hong Kong. TEL 852-2537-1910, FAX 852-2523-7195.

388.31 HUN ISSN 0237-8280
HE247.5.A15
HUNGARY. KOZPONTI STATISZTIKAI HIVATAL. KOZLEKEDESI EVKONYV. Text in Hungarian. a. HUF 310. stat. **Document type:** *Government.*
Former titles: Hungary. Kozponti Statisztikai Hivatal. Kozlekedesi Posta es Tavkozlesi; Hungary. Kozponti Statisztikai Hivatal. Kozlekedesi es Hirkozlesi Evkonyv (0133-9133)
Indexed: RASB.
Published by: Kozponti Statisztikai Hivatal, Marketing Oszta'ly, Keleti Karoly utca 5-7, Budapest, 1024, Hungary. TEL 36-1-345-6000, FAX 36-1-345-6699. Circ: 650.

387.74 CAN
I A T A MONTHLY INTERNATIONAL STATISTICS. Text in English. 1980. m. **Document type:** *Journal, Trade.* **Description:** Report showing traffic, capacity and passenger load factor trends of international scheduled services.
Related titles: Diskette ed.
Published by: International Air Transport Association, 800 Place Victoria, PO Box 113, Montreal, PQ H4Z 1M1, Canada. TEL 514-390-6726, 800-716-6326, FAX 514-874-9659, sales@iata.org. Circ: 300.

387 CAN ISSN 1014-5834
I C A O PUBLICATIONS AND AUDIO VISUAL TRAINING AIDS CATALOGUE. Key Title: Catalogue of I C A O Publications and Audio Visual Training Aids. Text in English. a. (plus m. updates). free. **Document type:** *Catalog.* **Description:** Lists all I.C.A.O. publications, current and back issues, available. Includes list of discontinued titles.
Related titles: Online - full text ed.; Russian ed.; Spanish ed.; French ed.
Published by: International Civil Aviation Organization (I C A O), External Relations and Public Information Office, 999 University St, Montreal, PQ H3C 5H7, Canada. TEL 514-954-8022, FAX 514-954-6769, icaohq@icao.int.

387 016 GBR ISSN 1029-1768
I C H C A NEWS AND CARGO TODAY. Text in English. 1978. bi-m. adv. bk.rev. **Document type:** *Abstract/Index.* **Description:** Contains information bulletins and a comprehensive listing of upcoming international industry conferences, exhibitions and seminars, along with articles and news.
Former titles (until 1997): Cargo Today (1359-2378); (until 1995): I C H C A Quarterly Bulletin (1367-8167); Cargo Handling Abstracts (0141-0687)
Related titles: ◆ Supplement(s): I C H C A News and Cargo Management. ISSN 1028-8821.
Indexed: CLT&T, HRIS.
—IE, Infotrieve.
Published by: International Cargo Handling Co-ordination Association, Ste 2, 85 Western Rd, Romford, Essex RM1 3LS, United Kingdom. TEL 44-1708-735295, FAX 44-1708-735225, info@ichcainternational.co.uk, http://www.ichcainternational.co.uk. Circ: 2,000.

388 USA
INDEX OF AVAILABLE RESOURCES. Text in English. 1992. base vol. plus s-m. updates. free. **Document type:** *Abstract/Index.* **Description:** Lists reference materials in the Transportation Library (all available for loan).
Published by: Council of State Governments, Midwestern Office, 641 E Butterfield Rd, 401, Lombard, IL 60148-5651. TEL 630-810-0210, 800-800-1910.

385 IND ISSN 0376-9909
HE3291
INDIAN RAILWAYS YEARBOOK. Text in English. 1973. a. free (effective 2011). **Document type:** *Yearbook, Government.*
Related titles: Online - full text ed.
Published by: (India. Directorate of Statistics and Economics), Railway Board, Director Statistics & Economics, Public Relations, New Delhi, 110 001, India. secyrb@rb.railnet.gov.in, http://www.indianrailways.gov.in.

387.7021 PRT ISSN 1647-1687
▼ **INQUERITO AO TRANSPORTE RODOVIARIO TRANSFRONTERICO.** Text in Portuguese. 2009. irreg. **Document type:** *Report, Government.*
Published by: Instituto Nacional de Estatistica, Av Antonio Jose de Almeida 2, Lisbon, 1000-043, Portugal. TEL 351-21-8426100, FAX 351-21-8426380, ine@ine.pt, http://www.ine.pt.

016.388 RUS
INTEGRIROVANNAYA LOGISTIKA. NAUCHNYI INFORMATSIONNYI ZHURNAL. Text in Russian. 2001. bi-m. USD 237.60 foreign (effective 2011). **Document type:** *Journal, Abstract/Index.*
Former titles (until 2007): Informatsionnyi Sbornik. Integrirovannaya Logistika; (until 2004): Informatsionnyi Zhurnal. Transport. Ekspedirovanie i Logistika
Related titles: CD-ROM ed.; Online - full text ed.
Published by: VINITI RAN, ul Usievicha 20, Moscow, 125190, Russian Federation. TEL 7-499-1526113, FAX 7-499-9430060, dir@viniti.ru, http://www.viniti.ru. Ed. Semen Rezer. **Dist. by:** Informnauka Ltd., Ul Usievicha 20, Moscow 125190, Russian Federation. alfimov@viniti.ru.

629.2 DEU ISSN 0946-9230
HD9710.A1
INTERNATIONAL AUTO STATISTICS. Text in English. 1981. a. EUR 113 to non-members; EUR 67 to members (effective 2006). back issues avail. **Document type:** *Report, Trade.*
Formerly (until 1994): Auto-International in Zahlen (0175-9531)
Published by: Verband der Automobilindustrie e.V., Westendstr 61, Frankfurt Am Main, 60325, Germany. TEL 49-69-975070, FAX 49-69-97507261, info@vda.de, http://www.vda.de.

387.71 CAN ISSN 1010-1500
INTERNATIONAL CIVIL AVIATION ORGANIZATION. DIGESTS OF STATISTICS. SERIES AF. AIRPORT AND ROUTE FACILITIES. FINANCIAL DATA AND SUMMARY TRAFFIC DATA/ MEZHDUNARODNAYA ORGANIZATSIYA GRAZHDANSKOI AVIATSII. STATISTICHESKII SBORNIK. SERIYA AF. AEROPORTNOE I MARSHRUTNOE OBORUDOVANIE. FINANSOVYE IZLOZHENIYA DANNYKH PO PEREVOZKAM/ ORGANISATION DE L'AVIATION CIVILE. RECUEIL DE STATISTIQUES. SERIE AF. INSTALLATIONS ET SERVICES D'AEROPORT ET DE ROUTE. DONNES FINANCIERES ET STATISTIQUES DE TRAFFIC SOMMAIRES/ORGANIZACION DE AVIACION CIVIL INTERNACIONAL. COMPENDIO ESTADISTICO. SERIE AF. INSTALACIONES Y SERVICIOS DE AEROPUERTO Y EN RUTA. DATOS FINANCIEROS Y RESUMEN DE DATOS DE TRAFICO. Text in English, French, Russian, Spanish. 1985 (no.3). irreg., latest 1999. USD 98 (effective 2002). back issues avail. **Description:** Contains the financial data and summary traffic data for international airports and route facilities.
Related titles: Diskette ed.: USD 200; E-mail ed.
Indexed: IIS.
Published by: International Civil Aviation Organization (I C A O), External Relations and Public Information Office, 999 University St, Montreal, PQ H3C 5H7, Canada. TEL 514-954-8022, FAX 514-954-6769, icaohq@icao.int.

387 CAN ISSN 0074-2422
INTERNATIONAL CIVIL AVIATION ORGANIZATION. DIGESTS OF STATISTICS. SERIES AT. AIRPORT TRAFFIC. Text in English, French, Spanish, Russian. 1960. irreg., latest 1997. USD 76. back issues avail. **Description:** Presents statistics on airports open to international traffic.
Related titles: Diskette ed.: USD 200; E-mail ed.; Magnetic Tape ed.
Indexed: IIS.
Published by: International Civil Aviation Organization (I C A O), External Relations and Public Information Office, 999 University St, Montreal, PQ H3C 5H7, Canada. TEL 514-954-8022, FAX 514-954-6769, icaohq@icao.int.

387 CAN ISSN 0074-2430
INTERNATIONAL CIVIL AVIATION ORGANIZATION. DIGESTS OF STATISTICS. SERIES F. FINANCIAL DATA - COMMERCIAL AIR CARRIERS. Text in English. irreg., latest vol.50, 1996. USD 123. back issues avail. **Description:** Supplies the balance sheets of commercial air carriers, along with profit-and-loss statements.
Related titles: Diskette ed.: USD 200; E-mail ed.; Magnetic Tape ed.; Spanish ed.; French ed.; Russian ed.
Indexed: IIS.
Published by: International Civil Aviation Organization (I C A O), External Relations and Public Information Office, 999 University St, Montreal, PQ H3C 5H7, Canada. TEL 514-954-8022, FAX 514-954-6769.

387 CAN
INTERNATIONAL CIVIL AVIATION ORGANIZATION. DIGESTS OF STATISTICS. SERIES FP. FLEET - PERSONNEL - COMMERCIAL AIR CARRIERS. Text in English. irreg., latest vol.50, 1996. USD 54. back issues avail. **Description:** Provides statistical material on the number and types of aircraft, along with figures on employees.
Formerly: International Civil Aviation Organization. Digests of Statistics. Series FP. Fleet, Personnel (0074-2449)
Related titles: Diskette ed.: USD 200; E-mail ed.; Magnetic Tape ed.; Spanish ed.; French ed.; Russian ed.
Indexed: IIS.
Published by: International Civil Aviation Organization (I C A O), External Relations and Public Information Office, 999 University St, Montreal, PQ H3C 5H7, Canada. TEL 514-954-8022, FAX 514-954-6769, icaohq@icao.int.

387.71 CAN ISSN 0251-267X
INTERNATIONAL CIVIL AVIATION ORGANIZATION. DIGESTS OF STATISTICS. SERIES OFOD. ON-FLIGHT ORIGIN AND DESTINATION/MEZHDUNARODNAYA ORGANIZATSIYA GRAZHDANSKOI AVIATSII. STATISTICHESKII SBORNIK. SERIYA OFOD. NACHALNYI I KONECHNYI PUNKTY POLETA/ ORGANISATION DE L'AVIATION CIVILE INTERNATIONALE. RECUEIL DE STATISTIQUES. SERIE OFOD. ORIGINE ET DESTINATION PAR VOL/ORGANIZACION DE AVIACION CIVIL INTERNACIONAL. COMPENDIO ESTADISTICO. SERIE OFOD. ORIGEN Y DESTINO POR VUELO. (series OFOD, no.77 out of print) Text in English, French, Russian, Spanish. 1979. q. (plus a. series). CAD 60 (effective 2000). back issues avail. **Description:** Contains the revenue traffic performed for various city pairs.
Related titles: Diskette ed.: USD 200; E-mail ed.
Indexed: IIS.
Published by: International Civil Aviation Organization (I C A O), External Relations and Public Information Office, 999 University St, Montreal, PQ H3C 5H7, Canada. TEL 514-954-8022, FAX 514-954-6769, icaohq@icao.int.

387 CAN ISSN 0074-2457
INTERNATIONAL CIVIL AVIATION ORGANIZATION. DIGESTS OF STATISTICS. SERIES R. CIVIL AIRCRAFT ON REGISTER. Text in English. 1961. irreg., latest vol.35, 1995. USD 35. back issues avail. **Description:** Compiles statistical data on registered civil aircraft heavier than 9,000 kg.
Related titles: Diskette ed.: USD 200; E-mail ed.; Magnetic Tape ed.; Spanish ed.; French ed.; Russian ed.
Indexed: IIS.
Published by: International Civil Aviation Organization (I C A O), External Relations and Public Information Office, 999 University St, Montreal, PQ H3C 5H7, Canada. TEL 514-954-8022, FAX 514-954-6769, icaohq@icao.int.

387 CAN ISSN 1014-0077
INTERNATIONAL CIVIL AVIATION ORGANIZATION. DIGESTS OF STATISTICS. SERIES T. TRAFFIC, COMMERCIAL AIR TRAFFIC. Text in English. 1947. irreg., latest vol.56, 1996. USD 92. **Description:** Presents commercial air traffic statistics for scheduled airlines provided by country.
Former titles (until 1977): International Civil Aviation Organization. Digests of Statistics. Series T. Airline Traffic (1014-0085); (until 1975): International Civil Aviation Organization. Digests of Statistics. Series T. Traffic (0074-2465)
Related titles: Diskette ed.: USD 200; Magnetic Tape ed.; Russian ed.; Spanish ed.; French ed.
Indexed: IIS.

Published by: International Civil Aviation Organization (I C A O), External Relations and Public Information Office, 999 University St, Montreal, PQ H3C 5H7, Canada. TEL 514-954-8022, FAX 514-954-6769, icaohq@icao.int.

387 CAN ISSN 1014-0093
INTERNATIONAL CIVIL AVIATION ORGANIZATION. DIGESTS OF STATISTICS. SERIES TF. TRAFFIC BY FLIGHT STAGE. Text in English, French, Russian, Spanish. irreg., latest vol.111, 1996. USD 149. back issues avail. **Description:** Provides statistics on the flow of commercial air traffic from point to point.
Formerly: International Civil Aviation Organization. Digests of Statistics. Series TF. Traffic Flow (0074-2473)
Related titles: Diskette ed.: USD 200; E-mail ed.; Microfiche ed.: (from CIS).
Indexed: IIS.
—CCC.
Published by: International Civil Aviation Organization (I C A O), External Relations and Public Information Office, 999 University St, Montreal, PQ H3C 5H7, Canada. TEL 514-954-8022, FAX 514-954-6769, icaohq@icao.int.

016.388 GBR ISSN 1362-3230
INTERNATIONAL LOGISTICS ABSTRACTS. Text in English. 1971. bi-m. GBP 205 domestic; GBP 252 foreign (effective 2005). bk.rev. index. back issues avail. **Document type:** *Journal, Abstract/Index.* **Description:** Offers information and abstracts relating to storage, handling, distribution and logistics.
Formerly (until 1996): International Distribution and Handling Review (0141-9501)
Related titles: Online - full content ed.
Published by: Supply Chain Knowledge Centre, Cranfield Centre for Logistics & Transportation, Cranfield School for Management, Cranfield, Beds MK43 0AL, United Kingdom. TEL 44-1234-754931, FAX 44-1234-754930, http://www.logistics.co.uk. Ed., R&P Hilary Keeble.

385 FRA ISSN 0074-7580
INTERNATIONAL RAILWAY STATISTICS (YEAR). Text in English, French, German. 1927. a., latest 2008. EUR 260 per issue (effective 2009). adv. **Document type:** *Corporate.* **Description:** Collection of statistics on lines, traction, rolling stock, personnel, traffic and finances.
Published by: Union Internationale des Chemins de Fer, Service Publications/International Union of Railways, 16 rue Jean Rey, Paris, 75015, France. TEL 33-1-44492181, FAX 33-1-44492189. Ed., R&P Alain Jehan TEL 33-1-44492281. Adv. contact Cecile Leroy.

385.1021 BEL ISSN 0378-1968
INTERNATIONAL STATISTICAL HANDBOOK OF URBAN PUBLIC TRANSPORT/INTERNATIONALES STATISTIK-HANDBUCH FUER DEN OEFFENTLICHEN STADTVERKEHR/RECUEIL INTERNATIONAL DE STATISTIQUES DES TRANSPORTS PUBLICS URBAINS. Text in English, French, German. 1964. irreg. EUR 112 per vol. to non-members; EUR 74 per vol. to members. charts. **Document type:** *Monographic series, Trade.* **Description:** Contains statistical information on more than 1100 urban public transport networks in the five continents.
Formerly (until 1968): International Union of Public Transport. Transports Publics dans les Principales Villes du Monde (0539-113X)
Published by: International Union of Public Transport/Union Internationale des Transports Publics, Rue Sainte-Marie 6, Brussels, 1080, Belgium. FAX 32-2-6601072, http://www.uitp.org.

IRELAND. CENTRAL STATISTICS OFFICE. ROAD FREIGHT TRANSPORT SURVEY. *see* BUSINESS AND ECONOMICS—Abstracting, Bibliographies, Statistics

387.1021 IRL ISSN 0791-346X
IRELAND. CENTRAL STATISTICS OFFICE. STATISTICS OF PORT TRAFFIC. Text in English. 1985. a. charts; stat. **Document type:** *Government.* **Description:** Presents information for each harbour authority on the number of arrivals and net register tonnage of trading and passenger vessels. Includes the weight of goods and number of livestock handled and details on the type of traffic.
Media: Duplicated (not offset). **Related titles:** Online - full text ed.
Published by: Ireland. Central Statistics Office/Eire, An Phriomh-Oifig Staidrimh, Skehard Rd, Cork, Ireland. TEL 353-21-4535000, FAX 353-21-4535555, information@cso.ie.

330.9021 IRL ISSN 1393-7081
IRELAND. CENTRAL STATISTICS OFFICE. VEHICLES LICENSED FOR THE FIRST TIME (YEAR). Text in English. 1985. a. charts; stat. **Document type:** *Government.* **Description:** Compiles statistical data regarding sales and purchases of new motor vehicles, classified by make and type, for the year.
Former titles (until 1998): Ireland. Central Statistics Office. Particulars of Vehicles Licensed for the First Time During the Year (1393-0117); (until 1994): Ireland. Central Statistics Office. Particulars of Vehicles Registered and Licensed for the First Time (0444-5147)
Media: Duplicated (not offset). **Related titles:** Online - full text ed.
Published by: Ireland. Central Statistics Office/Eire, An Phriomh-Oifig Staidrimh, Skehard Rd, Cork, Ireland. TEL 353-21-4535000, FAX 353-21-4535555, information@cso.ie.

388.3 310 ISR ISSN 0333-6050
ISRAEL. CENTRAL BUREAU OF STATISTICS. ROAD ACCIDENTS WITH CASUALTIES. PART 1. Text in English, Hebrew. 1950. a., latest 2006. ILS 18.50. **Document type:** *Government.*
Published by: Central Bureau of Statistics/Ha-Lishka Ha-Merkazit L'Statistiqa, PO Box 13015, Jerusalem, 91130, Israel. TEL 972-2-6553364, FAX 972-2-6521340.

388 ISR ISSN 0333-6107
ISRAEL. CENTRAL BUREAU OF STATISTICS. ROAD ACCIDENTS WITH CASUALTIES. PART 2/T'UNOT D'RAKHIM 'IM NIFGA'IM. Text in Hebrew. a., latest 2006. ILS 36. **Document type:** *Government.*
Published by: Central Bureau of Statistics/Ha-Lishka Ha-Merkazit L'Statistiqa, PO Box 13015, Jerusalem, 91130, Israel. TEL 972-2-6553364, FAX 972-2-6521340.

388 ISR ISSN 0333-8266
ISRAEL. CENTRAL BUREAU OF STATISTICS. SURVEY OF TRUCKS/ SEQER MASA'IYOT. Text in English, Hebrew. 1961. irreg., latest 1990. ILS 75 (effective 2008). **Document type:** *Government.*
Published by: Central Bureau of Statistics/Ha-Lishka Ha-Merkazit L'Statistiqa, PO Box 13015, Jerusalem, 91130, Israel. TEL 972-2-6553364, FAX 972-2-6521340.

388 ISR ISSN 0334-2220
ISRAEL. CENTRAL BUREAU OF STATISTICS. TRANSPORT STATISTICS QUARTERLY/RIV'ON L'STATISTIQA SHEL HA-TAHBURA. Key Title: Quarterly Transport Statistics. Text in English, Hebrew. 1974. q. ILS 125 (effective 1999). **Document type:** *Government.*
Published by: Central Bureau of Statistics/Ha-Lishka Ha-Merkazit L'Statistiqa, PO Box 13015, Jerusalem, 91130, Israel. TEL 972-2-6553364, FAX 972-2-6521340, http://www1.cbs.gov.il/reader/cw_usr_view_Folder?ID=141.

614.86021 ITA ISSN 0075-188X
ITALY. ISTITUTO NAZIONALE DI STATISTICA. STATISTICA DEGLI INCIDENTI STRADALI. Text in Italian. 1953. a. **Document type:** *Government.*
Published by: Istituto Nazionale di Statistica (I S T A T), Via Cesare Balbo 16, Rome, 00184, Italy. TEL 39-06-46731, http://www.istat.it.

387 314 ITA ISSN 1126-3210
HE839
ITALY. ISTITUTO NAZIONALE DI STATISTICA. STATISTICHE DEI TRASPORTI MARITTIMI. Text in Italian. 1863. a. **Document type:** *Government.*
Former titles (until 1991): Italy. Istituto Nazionale di Statistica. Statistiche della Navigazione Marittima (1126-3202); (until 1983): Italy. Istituto Centrale di Statistica. Annuario Statistico della Navigazione Marittima (0075-1898); (until 1969): Italy. Istituto Centrale di Statistica. Statistica della Navigazione Marittima (1126-3199); (until 1938): Italy. Istituto Centrale di Statistica. Statistica del Movimento della Navigazione (1126-3180); (until 1932): Regno d'Italia. Movimento della Navigazione nel (Year) (1126-3172); (until 1901): Regno d'Italia. Movimento della Navigazione (1126-3164); (until 1894): Movimento della Navigazione nei Porti del Regno (1126-3156); (until 1877): Navigazione nei Porti del Regno (1126-3148); (until 1867): Movimento della Navigazione nei Porti del Regno (1126-313X)
Published by: Istituto Nazionale di Statistica (I S T A T), Via Cesare Balbo 16, Rome, 00184, Italy. TEL 39-06-46731, http://www.istat.it.

629.286 JPN
JAPAN AUTO ABSTRACTS; real time database. Text in English. w. JPY 840,000. **Document type:** *Abstract/Index.* **Description:** English abstracts of Japanese-press articles related to the Japanese auto industry.
Published by: Dodwell Marketing Consultants, Kowa no 35 Bldg, 14-14 Akasaka 1-chome, Minato-ku, Tokyo, 107-0052, Japan. TEL 03-3589-0207, FAX 03-5570-7132, TELEX J22274 DODWELL.

388.41 NGA
KANO (STATE). MOTOR VEHICLE STATISTICS. Text in English. 1978. biennial. USD 30 (effective 1996). stat. **Document type:** *Government.*
Published by: Budget & Economic Planning Directorate, Ministry of Finance, Audu Bako Secretariat, PMB 3291, Kano, Kano State, Nigeria.

388 HUN ISSN 0231-0724
KOZUTI KOZLEKEDESI SZAKIRODALMI TAJEKOZTATO/ROAD TRANSPORT ABSTRACTS. Text in Hungarian. 1949. m. HUF 3,200. **Document type:** *Abstract/Index.*
Supersedes in part (in 1982): Muszaki Lapszemle. Kozlekedes - Technical Abstracts. Transportation (0027-5042)
Published by: Orszagos Muszaki Informacios Kozpont es Konyvtar/ National Technical Information Centre and Library, Muzeum utca 17, PO Box 12, Budapest, 1428, Hungary. Ed. E Vajda. Circ: 510.

388.413 DEU ISSN 2190-5002
HE5669
KRAFTFAHRT-BUNDESAMT. FAHRZEUGUNTERSUCHUNGEN. 1: HAUPTUNTERSUCHUNGEN UND EINZELABNAHMEN NACH UEBERWACHUNGSINSTITUTIONEN. Text in German. 1955. s-a. **Document type:** *Government.*
Former titles (until 2008): Germany. Kraftfahrt-Bundesamt. Fahrzeuguntersuchungen (1868-4076); (until 2007): Germany. Kraftfahrt-Bundesamt. Fahrzeugmaengelstatistik (0943-1535); Which superseded in part (in 1993): Statistische Mitteilungen des Kraftfahrt-Bundesamtes und der Bundesanstalt fuer den Gueterfernverkehr (0341-468X); Which was formerly (until 1958): Kraftfahrt-Bundesamt. Statistische Mitteilungen (0431-6452)
Published by: Kraftfahrt-Bundesamt, Foerdestr 16, Flensburg, 24944, Germany. TEL 49-461-3160, FAX 49-461-3161495, Pressestelle@kba.de, http://www.kba.de.

384.021 KWT
KUWAIT. CENTRAL STATISTICAL OFFICE. ANNUAL STATISTICAL BULLETIN FOR TRANSPORT AND COMMUNICATION/KUWAIT. AL-IDARAH AL-MARKAZIYYAH LIL-IHSA'. AL-NASHRAH AL-IHSA'IYYAH AL-SANAWIYYAH LIL-NAQL WAL-MUWASALAT. Text in Arabic, English. 1972. a., latest 1995. **Document type:** *Government.*
Supersedes in part (in 1981): Kuwait. Al-Idarah al-Markaziyyah lil-Ihsa'. Nashrah Sanawiyyah li-Ihsa'at al-Khadamat al-Aamah
Published by: Central Statistical Office/Al-Idarah al-Markaziyyah lil-Ihsa', P O Box 26188, Safat, 13122, Kuwait. TEL 965-2428200, FAX 965-2430464.

387.7 SWE ISSN 1402-1919
LUFTFART/CIVIL AVIATION. Text in English, Swedish. 1961. a. stat.
Former titles (until 2000): Luftfartsverket (0348-2251); (until 1976): Luftfartsverket. Aarsbok (0586-1632)
Related titles: Online - full text ed.; ◆ Series of: S I K A Statistik. ISSN 1404-854X.
Published by: (Sweden. Luftfartsverket/Swedish Civil Aviation Administration), Statens Institut foer Kommunikationsanalys (SIKA)/Swedish Institute for Transport and Communications Analysis, Maria Skolgata 83, PO Box 17213, Stockholm, 10462, Sweden. TEL 46-8-50620600, FAX 46-8-50620610, sika@sika-institute.se.

388 LUX ISSN 1012-6635
LUXEMBOURG. SERVICE CENTRAL DE LA STATISTIQUE ET DES ETUDES ECONOMIQUES. INDICATEURS RAPIDES. SERIE D. IMMATRICULATIONS DE VEHICULES AUTOMOTEURS. Text in French. m. looseleaf. **Document type:** *Government.*
Published by: Service Central de la Statistique et des Etudes Economiques, 13, rue Erasme, Luxembourg, L-1468, Luxembourg. TEL 352-478-4233, FAX 352-464-289, statec.post@statec.etat.lu, http://www.statec.public.lu.

629.2 GBR
M I R A VIRTUAL AUTOMOTIVE INFORMATION CENTRE. (Motor Industry Research Association) Text in English. 1997. d. free to members (effective 2010).
Formerly (until 1998): M I R A AutoInfo CD-ROM
Media: Online - full text.
Published by: M I R A Ltd., Watling St, Nuneaton, Warks CV10 0TU, United Kingdom. TEL 44-24-76355000, FAX 44-24-76355355, enquiries@mira.co.uk.

380.5 MWI
MALAWI. NATIONAL STATISTICAL OFFICE. TRANSPORT STATISTICS. Text in English. 1980. a. MWK 70. **Document type:** *Government.*
Published by: (Malawi. Commissioner for Census and Statistics), National Statistical Office, PO Box 333, Zomba, Malawi. TEL 265-50-5223777, FAX 265-50-523130.

387.7 MLT ISSN 0377-791X
MALTA. CENTRAL OFFICE OF STATISTICS. SHIPPING AND AVIATION STATISTICS. Text in English. 1936. a. **Document type:** *Government.*
Formerly: Shipping and Aviation Statistics of the Maltese Islands (0080-9268)
Published by: Central Office of Statistics, Auberge d'Italie, Merchants' St., Valletta, Malta. FAX 356-248483. **Subscr. to:** Publications Bookshop, Castille Place, Valletta, Malta.

388.314 MUS
MAURITIUS. CENTRAL STATISTICAL OFFICE. DIGEST OF ROAD TRANSPORT & ROAD ACCIDENTS STATISTICS. Text in English. 1984. a., latest 1999. MUR 75 per issue (effective 2001). charts. **Document type:** *Government.* **Description:** Provides a statistical overview of the economic situation in Mauritius as reflected by all forms of road transportation.
Formerly (until 1994): Mauritius. Central Statistical Office. Digest of Road Transport Statistics
Published by: Mauritius. Central Statistical Office, L.I.C. Centre, President John Kennedy St, Port Louis, Mauritius. TEL 230-212-2316, FAX 230-212-4150, cso@intnet.mu, http://statsmauritius.gov.mu. **Subscr. to:** Mauritius. Government Printing Office, Ramtoolah Bldg, Sir S Ramgoolam St, Port Louis, Mauritius. TEL 230-234-5294, 230-242-0234, FAX 230-234-5322.

318 BRA
MINAS GERAIS, BRAZIL. DEPARTAMENTO DE ESTRADAS DE RODAGEM. SERVICO DE TRANSITO. ESTATISTICA DE TRAFEGO E ACIDENTES. Text in Portuguese. 1969. a. free. stat.
Formerly: Minas Gerais, Brazil. Departamento de Estradas de Rodagem. Servico de Transito. Estatistica de Trafego
Published by: Departamento de Estradas de Rodagem, Servico de Transito, Av dos Andradas, 1120, Centro, Belo Horizonte, MG 30120-010, Brazil. Circ: 1,000.

385 IND ISSN 0027-0504
MONTHLY RAILWAY STATISTICS. Text in English, Hindi. 1967 (vol.16). m. charts; stat. **Document type:** *Report, Government.*
Published by: Railway Board, Director Statistics & Economics, Public Relations, New Delhi, 110 001, India. secyrb@rb.railnet.gov.in, http://www.indianrailways.gov.in.

388.3 USA
HE5623.A1
MOTOR CARRIER ANNUAL REPORTS. Text in English. a. USD 199 to non-members; USD 149.25 to members (effective 2007). illus. **Document type:** *Bulletin, Trade.*
Former titles: F & O S Motor Carrier Annual Report (0160-4570); F and O S (0098-2245)
Published by: American Trucking Associations, 2200 Mill Rd, Alexandria, VA 22314-4677. TEL 703-838-1700, media@trucking.org, http://www.truckline.com.

388.3021 363.12 NZL ISSN 1176-3949
MOTOR VEHICLE CRASHES IN NEW ZEALAND. Text in English. 19??. a. **Document type:** *Report, Trade.* **Description:** Contains detailed information about crash circumstances and causes.
Formerly (until 2002): Motor Accidents in New Zealand (0550-5089)
Related titles: Online - full text ed.: ISSN 1178-4253.
Published by: Ministry of Transport, PO Box 3175, Wellington, New Zealand. TEL 64-4-4721253, FAX 64-4-4733697, info@transport.govt.nz.

388.3 310 CHE
MOTORFAHRZEUGE IN DER SCHWEIZ. BESTAND AM 30. SEPTEMBER (YEAR)/VEHICULES A MOTEUR EN SUISSE. EFFECTIF AU 30 SEPTEMBRE (YEAR). Text in French, German. 1951. a. CHF 18 (effective 2001). **Document type:** *Government.*
Former titles: Motorfahrzeuge in der Schweiz. Motorfahrzeugbestand in der Schweiz am 30. September (Year) (1423-3932); (until 1993): Motorfahrzeugbestand in der Schweiz am 30. September (Year) (0258-7904)
Published by: Bundesamt fuer Statistik, Espace de l'Europe 10, Neuchatel, 2010, Switzerland. TEL 41-32-7136011, FAX 41-32-7136012, information@bfs.admin.ch, http://www.admin.ch/bfs.

388.3 310 CHE ISSN 1422-5107
HD9710.S9
MOTORFAHRZEUGE IN DER SCHWEIZ. EINGEFUEHRTE MOTORFAHRZEUGE/VEHICULES A MOTEUR EN SUISSE. VEHICULES A MOTEUR IMPORTES. Text in French, German. 1929. a. CHF 5 (effective 2001). **Document type:** *Government.*
Former titles (until 1993): Eingefuehrte Fahrzeuge (1422-5093); (until 1990): Eingefuehrte Motorfahrzeuge (0258-7858)
Published by: Bundesamt fuer Statistik, Espace de l'Europe 10, Neuchatel, 2010, Switzerland. TEL 41-32-7136011, FAX 41-32-7136012, information@bfs.admin.ch, http://www.admin.ch/bfs.

388.324 USA
MOVING INDUSTRY TRANSPORTATION STATISTICS (YEAR); demographic, economic and financial data of the moving industry. Text in English. a. **Document type:** *Report, Trade.* **Description:** Covers moving industry statistics, including financial data, demographics, and wage information. For persons involved with this industry.
Former titles (until 1997): Movers Statistical Profile; Which incorporated (in 1996): Transportation Fact Book; (until 1994): Moving Industry Financial and Economic Statistics

TU

Published by: American Moving and Storage Association, 1611 Duke St, Alexandria, VA 22314. TEL 703-683-7410, 888-849-2672, FAX 703-683-7527, info@moving.org, http://www.moving.org.

380.5 016 USA
N T I S ALERTS: TRANSPORTATION. (National Technical Information Service) Text in English. 19??. s-m. USD 255 in North America; USD 332 elsewhere (effective 2011). index. back issues avail. **Document type:** *Newsletter, Government.* **Description:** Provides summaries of titles received by NTIS - results of research and studies sponsored by the U.S. government and international sources. Covers air and marine transportation, railroad, and road transportation.
Former titles: Abstract Newsletter: Transportation; Weekly Abstract Newsletter: Transportation; Weekly Government Abstracts. Transportation (0163-1527)
Related titles: Microform ed.: (from NTI).
Indexed: HRIS.
Published by: U.S. Department of Commerce, National Technical Information Service, 5301 Shawnee Rd, Alexandria, VA 22312. TEL 703-605-6000, 800-553-6847, info@ntis.gov.

387 JPN ISSN 0469-4783
NAGOYA PORT STATISTICS ANNUAL/NAGOYAKO TOKEI NENPO. Text in Japanese. 1914. a. free. stat. **Document type:** *Government.*
Published by: Nagoya Port Authority/Nagoyako Kanri Kumiai, 8-21 Irifune 1-chome, Minato-ku, Nagoya-shi, Aichi-ken 455-0032, Japan. TEL 81-52-654-7840, FAX 81-52-654-7995. Circ: 1,000.

387 JPN
NAGOYAKO TOKEI SOKUHO/NAGOYA PORT STATISTICS MONTHLY. Text in Japanese. 1949. m. free. bk.rev. stat. **Document type:** *Government.*
Formerly (until Jan. 1994): Nagoyako Tokei Geppo (0027-7592)
Published by: Nagoya Port Authority/Nagoyako Kanri Kumiai, 8-21 Irifune 1-chome, Minato-ku, Nagoya-shi, Aichi-ken 455-0032, Japan. TEL 81-52-654-7840, FAX 81-52-654-7995. Circ: 400.

363.125021 USA
NATIONAL AUTOMOTIVE SAMPLING SYSTEM. Text in English. 1979. a.
Formerly: National Accident Sampling System (0741-1723)
Published by: National Center for Statistics and Analysis (Subsidiary of: U.S. Department of Transportation, National Highway Traffic Safety Administration), NPO-100, 400 Seventh St., S.W., Washington, DC 20590g. TEL 202-366-4198, 800-934-8517, FAX 202-366-7078, ncsaweb@nhtsa.dot.gov, http://www.nrd.nhtsa.dot.gov.

016.388 USA
NATIONAL RESEARCH COUNCIL. TRANSPORTATION RESEARCH BOARD. PUBLICATIONS INDEX. Text in English. 19??. base vol. plus irreg. updates. free (effective 2010). **Document type:** *Database, Abstract/Index.* **Description:** Contains over 20,000 annotated citations for all TRB and Strategic Highway Research Program (SHRP) publications from the mid-1970s until present. All NCHRP and TCRP publications, Special reports, Circulars, TR News, Conference Proceedings, and Records are included.
Media: Online - full text.
Published by: U.S. National Research Council, Transportation Research Board, The National Academies, 500 Fifth St. NW, Washington, DC 20001. TEL 202-334-3213, FAX 202-334-2519, TRBsales@nas.edu, http://www.trb.org.

385 BEL ISSN 0777-4931
NATIONALE MAATSCHAPPIJ VAN BELGISCHE SPOORWEGEN. INFORMATIE EN AANWINSTEN. Text in Dutch. 1947. m. bk.rev. abstr.; bibl.; charts. **Document type:** *Bulletin, Academic/Scholarly.* **Description:** Catalog of articles of periodicals and books especially on railway transport.
Former titles (until 1990): Nationale Maatschappij van Belgische Spoorwegen. Documentatiebulletin (0771-517X); (until 1978): Societe Nationale des Chemins de Fer Belges. Documentaire (0012-4567); (until 1965): Nationale Maatschappij van Belgische Spoorwegen. Maandelijks Documentatiebulletin (0773-1191)
Related titles: French ed.: Societe Nationale des Chemins de Fer Belges. Bulletin des Acquisitions. ISSN 1377-2945.
Published by: Nationale Maatschappij der Belgische Spoorwegen, Co 047, Sec 80-1/Societe Nationale des Chemins de Fer Belges, Rue de France 85, Brussels, 1060, Belgium. TEL 32-2-525-3011, FAX 32-2-525-4012, doccenter@b-rail.be. Circ: 345.

388.1 USA
NEBRASKA. DEPARTMENT OF ROADS. NEBRASKA SELECTED TRANSPORTATION STATISTICS. Text in English. a. free. illus. **Document type:** *Government.*
Former titles (until 1994): Nebraska. Department of Roads. Nebraska Selected Highway Statistics; (until 1993): Nebraska. Department of Roads. Selected Nebraska Statistics; (until 1983): Nebraska. Department of Roads. Highway Statistics: State and Local Road and Street Data for (Year); Nebraska Highway Statistics: State and Local Construction Mileage (0099-0442)
Published by: (Nebraska. Transportation Planning Division), Nebraska Department of Roads, 1500 NE Hwy 2, Box 94759, Lincoln, NE 68509-4759. TEL 402-479-4519, FAX 402-479-4325. Circ: 160.

388.1 NLD ISSN 1574-5473
NETHERLANDS. MINISTERIE VAN VERKEER EN WATERSTAAT. DIRECTORAAT-GENERAAL RIJKSWATERSTAAT. ADVIESDIENST VERKEER EN VERVOER. VERKEERSONGEVALLEN IN NEDERLAND/NETHERLANDS. CENTRAL BUREAU OF STATISTICS. STATISTICS OF ROAD-TRAFFIC ACCIDENTS. Key Title: Verkeersongevallen in Nederland. Text in Dutch, English. 1937. a. free (effective 2009). **Document type:** *Government.*
Former titles (until 2002): Netherlands. Centraal Bureau voor de Statistiek. Verkeersongevallen (1387-7089); (until 1997): Netherlands. Centraal Bureau voor de Statistiek. Statistiek van de Verkeersongevallen op de Openbare Weg (0168-5023); (until 1943): Netherlands. Centraal Bureau voor de Statistiek. Statistiek van de Verkeersongevallen (0077-7234)
Published by: Ministerie van Verkeer en Waterstaat Rijkswaterstaat, Dienst Verkeer en Scheepvaart, Postbus 5044, Delft, 2600 GA, Netherlands. TEL 31-88-7982222, FAX 31-88-7982999, dvsloket@rws.nl, http://www.rijkswaterstaat.nl/dvs. Ed. Marien de Wit.

388.3 SWE
NEW CAR PRICE-LIST. Text in Swedish. bi-m. SEK 172 (effective 1993).
Published by: AB Bilstatistik, Fack 5514, Stockholm, 11485, Sweden. TEL 46-8-701-63-60, FAX 46-8-791-23-11, TELEX 119-23-BIL S.

388.3 SWE
NEW REGISTRATIONS. Text in Swedish. m. SEK 1,024.
Published by: AB Bilstatistik, Fack 5514, Stockholm, 11485, Sweden. TEL 46-8-701-63-60, FAX 46-8-791-23-11, TELEX 119-23 BIL S.

387.5 JPN
NIHON SHOSEN SENPUKU TOKEI. Text in Japanese. 1972. a. free. stat. **Description:** Statistical summary of the Japanese merchant fleet.
Published by: (Research and Public Relations Division), Japanese Shipowners' Association/Nihon Senshu Kyokai, c/o Kaiun Bldg, 6-4 Hirakawa-cho 2-chome, Chiyoda-ku, Tokyo, 102-0093, Japan. FAX 03-262-4760, TELEX J2322148. Circ: 2,800.

388.021 NOR ISSN 1503-4445
NORWAY. STATISTISK SENTRALBYRAA. INNENLANDSKE TRANSPORTYTELSER. Text in English, Norwegian. 2003. irreg.
Supersedes in part (in 2003): Norway. Statistisk Sentralbyraa. Samferdselsstatistikk (0468-8147); Which incorporated (1963-1987): Rutebilstatistik (0550-0524)
Related titles: Online - full text ed.; ◆ Series of: Norges Offisielle Statistikk. ISSN 0300-5585.
Published by: Statistisk Sentralbyraa/Statistics Norway, Kongensgate 6, P O Box 8131, Dep, Oslo, 0033, Norway. TEL 47-21-090000, FAX 47-21-094973, ssb@ssb.no.

388.021 NOR ISSN 1503-9447
NORWAY. STATISTISK SENTRALBYRAA. LASTEBILSTATISTIKK. Text in Norwegian. 1998. m. **Document type:** *Government.*
Formerly (until 2004): Norway. Statistisk Sentralbyraa. Aktuelll Lastebilstatistikk (1500-8398)
Related titles: Online - full text ed.
Published by: (Norges Lastebileier-Forbund/Norwegian Haulier's Association), Statistisk Sentralbyraa/Statistics Norway, Kongensgate 6, P O Box 8131, Dep, Oslo, 0033, Norway. TEL 47-21-090000, FAX 47-21-094973, ssb@ssb.no.

388.021 NOR ISSN 1503-4364
HA1501
NORWAY. STATISTISK SENTRALBYRAA. STRUKTURSTATISTIKK FOR SAMFERSEL OG REISELIV/STATISTICS NORWAY. STRUCTURAL TRANSPORT AND TOURISM STATISTICS. Text in English, Norwegian. 1958. irreg. **Document type:** *Government.*
Supersedes in part (in 2003): Norway. Statistisk Sentralbyraa. Samferdselsstatistikk (0468-8147); Which incorporated (1963-1987): Rutebilstatistikk (0550-0524)
Related titles: Online - full text ed.: ISSN 0809-8891. 2003; ◆ Series of: Norges Offisielle Statistikk. ISSN 0300-5585.
Published by: Statistisk Sentralbyraa/Statistics Norway, Kongensgate 6, P O Box 8131, Dep, Oslo, 0033, Norway. TEL 47-21-090000, FAX 47-21-094973, ssb@ssb.no.

388.3021 ITA
NOTIZIARIO STATISTICO (YEAR)/STATISTICAL BULLETIN (YEAR). Text in Italian, English. m. EUR 280 domestic to members; EUR 340 domestic to non-members (effective 2008). **Document type:** *Bulletin, Trade.* **Description:** Contains Italian statistics for production and exports by brand, car registrations by brand, deliveries of commercial vehicles up to 3.5 t by brand, fuel prices and taxation. Also includes monthly international production, export and registration.
Published by: Anfia Service Srl, Corso Galileo Ferraris 61, Turin, 10128, Italy. TEL 39-011-545160, FAX 39-011-545464, http://www.anfia.it/anfiaservice/service.htm.

016.388 RUS ISSN 0236-1914
OBZORNAYA INFORMATSIYA. TRANSPORT: NAUKA, TEKHNIKA, UPRAVLENIE. Text in Russian. 1990. m. USD 290.40 foreign (effective 2011). **Document type:** *Journal, Abstract/Index.*
Indexed: RefZh.
—East View. **CCC.**
Published by: VINITI RAN, ul Usievicha 20, Moscow, 125190, Russian Federation. TEL 7-499-1526113, FAX 7-499-9430060, dir@viniti.ru, http://www.viniti.ru. **Dist. by:** Informnauka Ltd., Ul Usievicha 20, Moscow 125190, Russian Federation. alfimov@viniti.ru.

388.021 LUX ISSN 1725-275X
PANORAMA OF TRANSPORT; statistical overview of road, rail and inland waterway transport in the European Union. Text in English. 1990. irreg., latest 2009. **Document type:** *Directory, Trade.*
Published by: European Commission, Statistical Office of the European Communities (E U R O S T A T), Rue Alcide de Gasperi, Luxembourg, 2920, Luxembourg. TEL 352-4301-34526, FAX 352-4301-32600, eurostat-infodesk@cec.eu.int, http://www.europa.eu.int/comm/eurostat.

388 310 PNG
PAPUA NEW GUINEA. NATIONAL STATISTICAL OFFICE. STATISTICAL BULLETIN: REGISTERED MOTOR VEHICLES. Text in English. 1962. a. PGK 1.50. **Document type:** *Government.* **Description:** Provides statistics on the total stock of motor vehicles in Papua New Guinea that have been registered or reregistered during the year. Registrations are broken down by vehicle type, ownership, province, make, and capacity of vehicle.
Published by: National Statistical Office, Waigani, National Capital District, PO Box 337, Port Moresby, Papua New Guinea. Circ: 100.

318 BRA ISSN 0103-6653
HE5653.A1
PESQUISA ANUAL DO TRANSPORTE RODOVIARIO. Text in Portuguese. 1968. a. USD 40 (effective 1998). back issues avail. **Document type:** *Government.*
Formerly (until 1986): Empresas de Transporte Rodoviario (0100-154X)
Published by: Fundacao Instituto Brasileiro de Geografia e Estatistica, Centro de Documentacao e Disseminacao de Informacoes, Rua General Canabarro, 706 Andar 2, Maracana, Rio de Janeiro, RJ 20271-201, Brazil. TEL 55-21-2645424, FAX 55-21-2841959.

315.2 JPN
PORT OF YOKOHAMA. ANNUAL STATISTICS. Text in Japanese. 1969 (Nov., no. 212). a. free.
Formerly: Port of Yokohama. Monthly Statistics. (0032-4876)
Media: Duplicated (not offset).
Published by: Port and Harbor Bureau, Industry and Trade Center Bldg, 2 Yamashita-cho, Naka-ku, Yokohama-shi, Kanagawa-ken 231-0023, Japan. TEL 81-45-671-7190, FAX 81-45-671-7310.

388.3 362.4 USA
PROJECT ACTION PRODUCTS AND PUBLICATIONS RESOURCE GUIDE. Text in English. 1991. a. free. **Document type:** *Abstract/Index.* **Description:** Lists products and publications related to making public transportation ADA accessible to persons with disabilities.
Published by: Easter Seals Project Action, 700 13th St, NW, Ste 200, Washington, DC 20005. TEL 202-347-3066, 800-659-6428, FAX 202-737-7914, http://projectaction.easterseals.com. Ed., R&P Sharon Ransome Smith. Circ: 10,000.

388.021 USA
HE4451
PUBLIC TRANSPORTATION FACT BOOK. Text in English. a. free (effective 2004).
Formerly (until 2000): Transit Fact Book (0149-3132)
Published by: American Public Transportation Association, 1666 K St, NW Ste 1100, Washington, DC 20006. TEL 202-496-4800, FAX 202-496-4321, http://www.apta.com.

338.324 USA
QUARTERLY OPERATING STATISTICS; of major household goods carriers. Text in English. q. **Document type:** *Report, Trade.* **Description:** Earnings of major household goods carriers. For anyone dealing with the moving business.
Published by: American Moving and Storage Association, 1611 Duke St, Alexandria, VA 22314. TEL 703-683-7410, 888-849-2672, FAX 703-683-7527, info@moving.org, http://www.moving.org.

016.62913 016.3877 RUS ISSN 0202-9790
REFERATIVNYI ZHURNAL. AVIASTROENIE; vypusk svodnogo toma. Text in Russian. 1964. m. USD 346.80 foreign (effective 2011). **Document type:** *Journal, Abstract/Index.*
Related titles: CD-ROM ed.; Online - full text ed.
—East View.
Published by: VINITI RAN, ul Usievicha 20, Moscow, 125190, Russian Federation. TEL 7-499-1526113, FAX 7-499-9430060, dir@viniti.ru, http://www.viniti.ru. **Dist. by:** Informnauka Ltd., Ul Usievicha 20, Moscow 125190, Russian Federation. alfimov@viniti.ru.

016.621382 016.385 RUS ISSN 0202-9847
REFERATIVNYI ZHURNAL. AVTOMATIKA, TELEMEKHANIKA I SVIAZ' NA ZHELEZNYKH DOROGAKH; vypusk svodnogo toma. Text in Russian. 1962. m. USD 169.20 foreign (effective 2011). **Document type:** *Journal, Abstract/Index.*
Related titles: CD-ROM ed.; Online - full text ed.
—East View.
Published by: VINITI RAN, ul Usievicha 20, Moscow, 125190, Russian Federation. TEL 7-499-1526113, FAX 7-499-9430060, dir@viniti.ru, http://www.viniti.ru. **Dist. by:** Informnauka Ltd., Ul Usievicha 20, Moscow 125190, Russian Federation. alfimov@viniti.ru.

016.3883 RUS ISSN 0202-974X
REFERATIVNYI ZHURNAL. AVTOMOBILESTROENIE; vypusk svodnogo toma. Text in Russian. 1963. m. USD 346.80 foreign (effective 2011). **Document type:** *Journal, Abstract/Index.*
Related titles: CD-ROM ed.; Online - full text ed.
—East View.
Published by: VINITI RAN, ul Usievicha 20, Moscow, 125190, Russian Federation. TEL 7-499-1526113, FAX 7-499-9430060, dir@viniti.ru, http://www.viniti.ru. **Dist. by:** Informnauka Ltd., Ul Usievicha 20, Moscow 125190, Russian Federation. alfimov@viniti.ru.

016.3881 RUS ISSN 0486-2252
REFERATIVNYI ZHURNAL. AVTOMOBIL'NYE DOROGI. OTDEL'NYI VYPUSK. Text in Russian. 1963. m. USD 290.40 foreign (effective 2011). **Document type:** *Journal, Abstract/Index.*
Formerly (until 2006): Referativnyi Zhurnal. Avtomobil'nye Dorogi. Svodnyi Tom; Incorporates (1963-2006): Referativnyi Zhurnal. Iskusstvennye Sooruzheniya na Avtomobil'nykh Dorogakh. Vypusk Svodnogo Toma (0202-9723); (1963-2006): Referativnyi Zhurnal. Stroitel'stvo i Ekspluatatsiya Avtomobilnykh Dorog. Vypusk Svodnogo Toma (0202-9731)
Related titles: CD-ROM ed.; Online - full text ed.
—East View. **CCC.**
Published by: VINITI RAN, ul Usievicha 20, Moscow, 125190, Russian Federation. TEL 7-499-1526113, FAX 7-499-9430060, dir@viniti.ru, http://www.viniti.ru. Ed. Valentin Lukanin. **Dist. by:** Informnauka Ltd., Ul Usievicha 20, Moscow 125190, Russian Federation. alfimov@viniti.ru.

016.388 RUS ISSN 0034-2297
REFERATIVNYI ZHURNAL. AVTOMOBIL'NYI I GORODSKOI TRANSPORT; svodnyi tom. Text in Russian. 1963. m. USD 530.40 foreign (effective 2011). **Document type:** *Journal, Abstract/Index.*
Related titles: CD-ROM ed.; Online - full text ed.
—**CCC.**
Published by: VINITI RAN, ul Usievicha 20, Moscow, 125190, Russian Federation. TEL 7-499-1526113, FAX 7-499-9430060, dir@viniti.ru, http://www.viniti.ru. Ed. Valentin Lukanin. **Dist. by:** Informnauka Ltd., Ul Usievicha 20, Moscow 125190, Russian Federation. alfimov@viniti.ru.

016.3883 RUS ISSN 0202-9758
REFERATIVNYI ZHURNAL. AVTOMOBIL'NYI TRANSPORT; vypusk svodnogo toma. Text in Russian. 1962. m. USD 246 foreign (effective 2011). **Document type:** *Journal, Abstract/Index.*
Related titles: CD-ROM ed.; Online - full text ed.
—East View.
Published by: VINITI RAN, ul Usievicha 20, Moscow, 125190, Russian Federation. TEL 7-499-1526113, FAX 7-499-9430060, dir@viniti.ru, http://www.viniti.ru. **Dist. by:** Informnauka Ltd., Ul Usievicha 20, Moscow 125190, Russian Federation. alfimov@viniti.ru.

REFERATIVNYI ZHURNAL. EKONOMIKA TRANSPORTA, SVYAZI I TELEKOMMUNIKATSII; vypusk svodnogo toma. *see* BUSINESS AND ECONOMICS—Abstracting, Bibliographies, Statistics

REFERATIVNYI ZHURNAL. ELEKTROOBORUDOVANIE TRANSPORTA; vypusk svodnogo toma. *see* ENGINEERING—Abstracting, Bibliographies, Statistics

016.3884 RUS ISSN 0202-9766
REFERATIVNYI ZHURNAL. GORODSKOI TRANSPORT; vypusk svodnogo toma. Text in Russian. 1962. m. USD 202.80 foreign (effective 2011). **Document type:** *Journal, Abstract/Index.*
Related titles: CD-ROM ed.; Online - full text ed.
—East View.

Published by: VINITI RAN, ul Usievicha 20, Moscow, 125190, Russian Federation. TEL 7-499-1526113, FAX 7-499-9430060, dir@viniti.ru, http://www.viniti.ru. **Dist. by:** Informnauka Ltd., Ul Usievicha 20, Moscow 125190, Russian Federation. alfimov@viniti.ru.

016.6252 RUS ISSN 0202-9855
REFERATIVNYI ZHURNAL. LOKOMOTIVOSTROENIE I VAGONOSTROENIE; vypusk svodnogo toma. Text in Russian. 1963. m. USD 274.80 foreign (effective 2011). **Document type:** *Journal, Abstract/Index.*
Related titles: CD-ROM ed.; Online - full text ed.
—East View.
Published by: VINITI RAN, ul Usievicha 20, Moscow, 125190, Russian Federation. TEL 7-499-1526113, FAX 7-499-9430060, dir@viniti.ru, http://www.viniti.ru. **Dist. by:** Informnauka Ltd., Ul Usievicha 20, Moscow 125190, Russian Federation. alfimov@viniti.ru.

016.3883 016.3621 RUS ISSN 0202-9952
REFERATIVNYI ZHURNAL. ORGANIZATSIYA I BEZOPASNOST' DOROZHNOGO DVIZHENIYA; otdel'nyi vypusk. Text in Russian. 1973. m. USD 259.20 foreign (effective 2011). **Document type:** *Journal, Abstract/Index.*
Related titles: CD-ROM ed.; Online - full text ed.
—East View. **CCC.**
Published by: VINITI RAN, ul Usievicha 20, Moscow, 125190, Russian Federation. TEL 7-499-1526113, FAX 7-499-9430060, dir@viniti.ru, http://www.viniti.ru. Ed. Valentin Lukanin. **Dist. by:** Informnauka Ltd., Ul Usievicha 20, Moscow 125190, Russian Federation. alfimov@viniti.ru.

REFERATIVNYI ZHURNAL. POD'EMNO-TRANSPORTNOE MASHINOSTROENIE; vypusk svodnogo toma. *see* ENGINEERING—Abstracting, Bibliographies, Statistics

016.388 RUS ISSN 0034-2556
REFERATIVNYI ZHURNAL. PROMYSHLENNYI TRANSPORT; svodnyi tom. Text in Russian. 1963. m. USD 500.40 foreign (effective 2011). **Document type:** *Journal, Abstract/Index.*
Related titles: CD-ROM ed.; Online - full text ed.
—East View.
Published by: VINITI RAN, ul Usievicha 20, Moscow, 125190, Russian Federation. TEL 7-499-1526113, FAX 7-499-9430060, dir@viniti.ru, http://www.viniti.ru. **Dist. by:** Informnauka Ltd., Ul Usievicha 20, Moscow 125190, Russian Federation. alfimov@viniti.ru.

REFERATIVNYI ZHURNAL. STROITEL'NYE I DOROZHNYE MASHINY; otdel'nyi vypusk. *see* ENGINEERING—Abstracting, Bibliographies, Statistics

016.6251 016.625 RUS ISSN 0202-9863
REFERATIVNYI ZHURNAL. STROITELSTVO ZHELEZNYKH DOROG. PUT' I PUTEVOE KHOZYAISTVO; vypusk svodnogo toma. Text in Russian. 1962. m. USD 169.20 foreign (effective 2011). **Document type:** *Journal, Abstract/Index.*
Related titles: CD-ROM ed.; Online - full text ed.
—East View.
Published by: VINITI RAN, ul Usievicha 20, Moscow, 125190, Russian Federation. TEL 7-499-1526113, FAX 7-499-9430060, dir@viniti.ru, http://www.viniti.ru. **Dist. by:** Informnauka Ltd., Ul Usievicha 20, Moscow 125190, Russian Federation. alfimov@viniti.ru.

016.3872 RUS ISSN 0132-2931
REFERATIVNYI ZHURNAL. SUDOSTROENIE; vypusk svodnogo toma. Text in Russian. 1963. m. USD 315.60 foreign (effective 2011). **Document type:** *Journal, Abstract/Index.*
Related titles: CD-ROM ed.; Online - full text ed.
—East View.
Published by: VINITI RAN, ul Usievicha 20, Moscow, 125190, Russian Federation. TEL 7-499-1526113, FAX 7-499-9430060, dir@viniti.ru, http://www.viniti.ru. **Dist. by:** Informnauka Ltd., Ul Usievicha 20, Moscow 125190, Russian Federation. alfimov@viniti.ru.

016.6251 RUS ISSN 0202-9871
REFERATIVNYI ZHURNAL. TEKHNICHESKAYA EKSPLUATATSIYA PODVIZHNOGO SOSTAVA I TYAGA POEZDOV; vypusk svodnogo toma. Text in Russian. 1963. m. USD 169.20 foreign (effective 2011). **Document type:** *Journal, Abstract/Index.*
Related titles: CD-ROM ed.; Online - full text ed.
—East View.
Published by: VINITI RAN, ul Usievicha 20, Moscow, 125190, Russian Federation. TEL 7-499-1526113, FAX 7-499-9430060, dir@viniti.ru, http://www.viniti.ru. **Dist. by:** Informnauka Ltd., Ul Usievicha 20, Moscow 125190, Russian Federation. alfimov@viniti.ru.

016.38833 RUS
REFERATIVNYI ZHURNAL. TRANSPORT PROMYSHLENNYKH PREDPRIYATII. LOGISTIKA. SKLADY. AVTOMATIZATSIYA POGRUZOCHNO-RAZGRUZOCHNYKH RABOT; vypusk svodnogo toma. Text in Russian. 1962. m. USD 337.20 foreign (effective 2011). **Document type:** *Journal, Abstract/Index.*
formerly (until 1999): Referativnyi Zhurnal. Mekhanizatsiya i Avtomatizatsiya Pogruzochno-Razgruzochnykh Rabot na Promyshlennom Transporte (0202-9928)
Related titles: CD-ROM ed.; Online - full text ed.
Published by: VINITI RAN, ul Usievicha 20, Moscow, 125190, Russian Federation. TEL 7-499-1526113, FAX 7-499-9430060, dir@viniti.ru, http://www.viniti.ru. **Dist. by:** Informnauka Ltd., Ul Usievicha 20, Moscow 125190, Russian Federation. alfimov@viniti.ru.

REFERATIVNYI ZHURNAL. TRUBOPROVODNYI TRANSPORT; otdel'nyi vypusk. *see* ENGINEERING—Abstracting, Bibliographies, Statistics

016.385264 RUS ISSN 0202-988X
REFERATIVNYI ZHURNAL. UPRAVLENIE PEREVOZOCHNYM PROTSESSOM NA ZHELEZNYKH DOROGAKH; vypusk svodnogo toma. Text in Russian. 1963. m. USD 169.20 foreign (effective 2011). **Document type:** *Journal, Abstract/Index.*
Related titles: CD-ROM ed.; Online - full text ed.
—East View.
Published by: VINITI RAN, ul Usievicha 20, Moscow, 125190, Russian Federation. TEL 7-499-1526113, FAX 7-499-9430060, dir@viniti.ru, http://www.viniti.ru. **Dist. by:** Informnauka Ltd., Ul Usievicha 20, Moscow 125190, Russian Federation. alfimov@viniti.ru.

016.387 RUS ISSN 0869-4001
REFERATIVNYI ZHURNAL. VODNYE PEREVOZKI. TEKHNICHESKAYA EKSPLUATATSIYA I REMONT FLOTA; vypusk svodnogo toma. Text in Russian. 1962. m. USD 315.60 foreign (effective 2011). **Document type:** *Journal, Abstract/Index.*
Related titles: CD-ROM ed.; Online - full text ed.
—East View.
Published by: VINITI RAN, ul Usievicha 20, Moscow, 125190, Russian Federation. TEL 7-499-1526113, FAX 7-499-9430060, dir@viniti.ru, http://www.viniti.ru. **Dist. by:** Informnauka Ltd., Ul Usievicha 20, Moscow 125190, Russian Federation. alfimov@viniti.ru.

016.387 RUS ISSN 0484-2545
REFERATIVNYI ZHURNAL. VODNYI TRANSPORT; svodnyi tom. Text in Russian. 1962. m. USD 436.80 foreign (effective 2011). **Document type:** *Journal, Abstract/Index.*
Related titles: CD-ROM ed.; Online - full text ed.
—East View. **CCC.**
Published by: VINITI RAN, ul Usievicha 20, Moscow, 125190, Russian Federation. TEL 7-499-1526113, FAX 7-499-9430060, dir@viniti.ru, http://www.viniti.ru. **Dist. by:** Informnauka Ltd., Ul Usievicha 20, Moscow 125190, Russian Federation. alfimov@viniti.ru.

016.3877 RUS ISSN 0484-2561
REFERATIVNYI ZHURNAL. VOZDUSHNYI TRANSPORT; svodnyi tom. Text in Russian. 1962. m. USD 440.40 foreign (effective 2011). **Document type:** *Journal, Abstract/Index.*
Related titles: CD-ROM ed.; Online - full text ed.
—CCC.
Published by: VINITI RAN, ul Usievicha 20, Moscow, 125190, Russian Federation. TEL 7-499-1526113, FAX 7-499-9430060, dir@viniti.ru, http://www.viniti.ru. Ed. Konstantin Frolov. **Dist. by:** Informnauka Ltd., Ul Usievicha 20, Moscow 125190, Russian Federation. alfimov@viniti.ru.

016.3877 RUS
REFERATIVNYI ZHURNAL. VOZDUSHNYI TRANSPORT. AEROPORTY; vypusk svodnogo toma. Text in Russian. 2008. m. USD 324 foreign (effective 2011). **Document type:** *Journal, Abstract/Index.*
Formed by the merger of (1962-2008): Referativnyi Zhurnal. Upravlenie Vozdushnym Dvizheniem. Organizatsiya Perevozok (0869-401X); (1964-2008): Referativnyi Zhurnal. Ekspluatatsiya i Remont Samoletov i Drugikh Letatel'nykh Apparatov. Aeroporty (0869-4028)
Related titles: CD-ROM ed.; Online - full text ed.
Published by: VINITI RAN, ul Usievicha 20, Moscow, 125190, Russian Federation. TEL 7-499-1526113, FAX 7-499-9430060, dir@viniti.ru, http://www.viniti.ru. Ed. Yurii Arskii. **Dist. by:** Informnauka Ltd., Ul Usievicha 20, Moscow 125190, Russian Federation. alfimov@viniti.ru.

016.38833 RUS ISSN 0034-2645
REFERATIVNYI ZHURNAL. VZAIMODEISTVIE RAZNYKH VIDOV TRANSPORTA I KONTEINERNYE PEREVOZKI; otdel'nyi vypusk. Text in Russian. 1961. m. USD 249.60 foreign (effective 2011). **Document type:** *Journal, Abstract/Index.*
Related titles: CD-ROM ed.; Online - full text ed.
—East View. **CCC.**
Published by: VINITI RAN, ul Usievicha 20, Moscow, 125190, Russian Federation. TEL 7-499-1526113, FAX 7-499-9430060, dir@viniti.ru, http://www.viniti.ru. **Dist. by:** Informnauka Ltd., Ul Usievicha 20, Moscow 125190, Russian Federation. alfimov@viniti.ru.

016.385 RUS ISSN 0484-2596
REFERATIVNYI ZHURNAL. ZHELEZNODOROZHNYI TRANSPORT; svodnyi tom. Text in Russian. 1960. m. USD 603.60 foreign (effective 2011). **Document type:** *Journal, Abstract/Index.*
Related titles: CD-ROM ed.; Online - full text ed.
—East View. **CCC.**
Published by: VINITI RAN, ul Usievicha 20, Moscow, 125190, Russian Federation. TEL 7-499-1526113, FAX 7-499-9430060, dir@viniti.ru, http://www.viniti.ru. Ed. Semen Rezer. **Dist. by:** Informnauka Ltd., Ul Usievicha 20, Moscow 125190, Russian Federation. alfimov@viniti.ru.

388.1 ZMB
REPORT ON PASSENGER ROAD TRANSPORT IN ZAMBIA. Text in English. 1968. a. USD 4.
Published by: Central Statistical Office, PO Box 31908, Lusaka, Zambia. TEL 211-231.

388 HUN ISSN 0231-3928
REPULESI SZAKIRODALMI TAJEKOZTATO/AVIATION AND AIR TRANSPORT ABSTRACTS. Text in Hungarian. bi-m. HUF 3,000. **Document type:** *Abstract/Index.*
Supersedes in part (in 1982): Muszaki Lapszemle. Kozlekedes - Technical Abstracts. Transportation (0027-5042)
Published by: Orszagos Muszaki Informacios Kozpont es Konyvtar/ National Technical Information Centre and Library, Muzeum utca 17, PO Box 12, Budapest, 1428, Hungary. Ed. Ferenc Bardosi. Circ: 200. **Subscr. to:** Kultura, PO Box 149, Budapest 1389, Hungary.

388.31 GBR ISSN 1749-7280
ROAD CASUALTIES: WALES. Text in English. 1979. irreg., latest vol.26, 2006. free (effective 2009). **Document type:** *Government.* **Description:** Provides analyses of the centrally held road accident statistics database for Wales.
Formerly (until 2004): Road Accidents: Wales (0263-9653)
Related titles: Online - full text ed.
Published by: Welsh Assembly Government, Statistical Directorate, Cathays Park, Cardiff, CF10 3NQ, United Kingdom. TEL 44-1443-845500, stats.info.desk@wales.gsi.gov.uk, http://wales.gov.uk/?lang=en.

388.324094021 GBR ISSN 1751-679X
ROAD GOODS VEHICLES TRAVELLING TO MAINLAND EUROPE (ONLINE). Text in English. 19??. q. free (effective 2009). stat. back issues avail. **Document type:** *Magazine, Trade.*
Former titles (until 2006): Road Goods Vehicles Tavelling to Mainland Europe (Print) (1367-5095); (until 1994): Road Goods Vehicles on Roll-on Roll-off Ferries to Mainland Europe (0951-1156)
Media: Online - full text.
Published by: Great Britain. Department for Transport, Great Minster House, 76 Marsham St, London, SW1P 4DR, United Kingdom. publications@communities.gsi.gov.uk.

388.021 GBR
ROADS GOODS VEHICLES TRAVELLING TO MAINLAND EUROPE (QUARTERLY). Text in English. q. free. back issues avail. **Document type:** *Government.*
Media: Online - full text.
Published by: Great Britain. Department for Transport, Great Minster House, 76 Marsham St, London, SW1P 4DR, United Kingdom. TEL 44-20-79443078, FAX 44-20-79449643, publications@communities.gsi.gov.uk.

359.97 USA ISSN 0163-2833
TL553.8
S A R STATISTICS. (Search and Rescue) Text in English. 19??. a. back issues avail. **Document type:** *Trade.* **Description:** Compiles statistics on U.S. Coast Guard maritime search and rescue activities.
Published by: (Office of Navigation Safety and Waterway Services), U.S. Coast Guard, 2100 Second St, SW, Washington, DC 20593. TEL 202-267-1061, FAX 202-267-4402, gchappell@comdt.uscg.mil, http://www.uscg.mil/default.asp.

388.021 SWE ISSN 1400-9528
S I K A KOMMUNIKATIONER. (Statens Institut foer Kommunikationsanalys) Text in Swedish. 1993. 3/yr. stat. back issues avail. **Document type:** *Magazine, Government.*
Formerly (until 1995): V T I Transportstatistik (1103-5528)
Related titles: Online - full text ed.
Published by: Statens Institut foer Kommunikationsanalys (SIKA)/ Swedish Institute for Transport and Communications Analysis, Maria Skolgata 83, PO Box 17213, Stockholm, 10462, Sweden. TEL 46-8-50620600, FAX 46-8-50620610, sika@sika-institute.se. Ed. Niklas Kristiansson.

388.31 310 CHE ISSN 1013-5804
SCHWEIZERISCHE STRASSENVERKEHRSZAEHLUNG/COMPTAGE SUISSE DE LA CIRCULATION ROUTIERE. Text in French, German. 1985. every 5 yrs. CHF 40 (effective 2001). **Document type:** *Government.*
Published by: Bundesamt fuer Statistik, Espace de l'Europe 10, Neuchatel, 2010, Switzerland. TEL 41-32-7136011, FAX 41-32-7136012, information@bfs.admin.ch, http://www.admin.ch/bfs.

388.31 310 CHE ISSN 0258-7874
SCHWEIZERISCHE VERKEHRSSTATISTIK/STATISTIQUE SUISSE DES TRANSPORTS. Text in French, German. 1985. a. CHF 18 (effective 2001). **Document type:** *Government.*
Published by: Bundesamt fuer Statistik, Espace de l'Europe 10, Neuchatel, 2010, Switzerland. TEL 41-32-7136011, FAX 41-32-7136012, information@bfs.admin.ch, http://www.admin.ch/bfs.

380.5 GBR
SECTOR REVIEW: MOTOR TRADES. Text in English. a. GBP 39.50 (effective 2010). charts; stat. back issues avail. **Document type:** *Government.*
Formerly (until 1998): Business Monitor. SDA27. Motor Trades
Related titles: ♦ Series: Retail Sales (Online). ISSN 2042-1753; ♦ Sector Review. Service Trades. ISSN 1464-7567; ♦ Sector Review. Catering and Allied Trades. ISSN 1465-4229; ♦ Sector Review. Retailing; ♦ Sector Review: Wholesaling and Dealing.
Published by: Office for National Statistics, Rm 1.101, Government Bldgs, Cardiff Rd, Newport, S Wales NP10 8XG, United Kingdom. TEL 44-845-6013034, FAX 44-1633-652747, info@statistics.gsi.gov.uk, http://www.statistics.gov.uk/default.asp.

388 BEL ISSN 0776-9636
SECURITE ROUTIERE. Text in French. 1967. a. **Document type:** *Corporate.* **Description:** Provides detailed statistical information on traffic safety in Belgium.
Supersedes (in 1986): Conseil Superieur de la Securite Routiere. Rapport (0776-961X)
Related titles: ♦ Dutch ed.: Verkeersveiligheid. ISSN 0776-9628.
Published by: Institut Belge pour la Securite Routiere/Belgisch Instituut voor de Verkeersveiligheid, Ch de Haecht 1405, Brussels, 1130, Belgium. TEL 32-2-2441511, FAX 32-2-2164342, info@bivv.be, http://www.bivv.be. Ed. Christian van den Meersschaut.

623.81 JPN
SEIBU ZOSENKAI RONBUN KOGAI/WEST JAPAN SOCIETY OF NAVAL ARCHITECTS. ABSTRACTS FROM RESEARCH REPORT. Text in English, Japanese. s-a.
Published by: Seibu Zosenkai, c/o Kyushu Daigaku Kogakubu Zosengaku Kyoshitsu, 10-1 Hakozaki 6-chome, Higashi-ku, Fukuoka-shi, 812-0053, Japan.

387.5 DEU ISSN 0947-0220
HE561
SHIPPING STATISTICS AND MARKET REVIEW. Text in English. 1957. m. (9/yr.). EUR 480 (effective 2009). **Document type:** *Report, Trade.* **Description:** Contains worldwide information on merchant fleet figures, freight rate indices, statistical information on trading, shipbuilding markets, and port traffic development.
Former titles: Shipping Statistics (0721-3751); Institut fuer Seeverkehrswirtschaft Bremen
Related titles: Online - full text ed.: EUR 420 (effective 2009).
Indexed: BMT, PAIS, RASB.
Published by: Institut fuer Seeverkehrswirtschaft und Logistik/Institute of Shipping Economics and Logistics, Universitaetsallee 11-13, Bremen, 28359, Germany. TEL 49-421-2209673, FAX 49-421-2209655, infoline@isl.org, http://www.isl.org. Eds. Christel Heideloff, Manfred Zachcial.

387.5021 DEU ISSN 0721-3220
SHIPPING STATISTICS YEARBOOK. Text in English. 1973. a. EUR 325 (effective 2009). stat. back issues avail. **Document type:** *Yearbook, Trade.* **Description:** Reference source for merchant fleet developments, seaborne trade, commodity markets, freight rate indices, and world port traffic patterns.
Related titles: Online - full text ed.: EUR 295 (effective 2009).
—BLDSC (8262.930000).
Published by: Institut fuer Seeverkehrswirtschaft und Logistik/Institute of Shipping Economics and Logistics, Universitaetsallee 11-13, Bremen, 28359, Germany. TEL 49-421-2209673, FAX 49-421-2209655, infoline@isl.org, http://www.isl.org.

629.222 388.324 GBR
SOCIETY OF MOTOR MANUFACTURERS AND TRADERS. QUARTERLY STATISTICAL REVIEW. Text in English. 19??. q. free to members (effective 2010). stat. **Document type:** *Report, Trade.* **Description:** Provides a monthly review of the latest statistics relating to the motor industry; including commentaries and data on production, new registrations and vehicles in use in the UK and abroad.
Formerly (until 2009): Society of Motor Manufacturers and Traders. Monthly Statistical Review
Related titles: Online - full text ed.

Published by: Society of Motor Manufacturers and Traders Ltd., Forbes House, Halkin St, London, SW1X 7DS, United Kingdom. TEL 44-20-72357000, FAX 44-20-2357112, memberservices@smmt.co.uk.

388.314 ZAF
SOUTH AFRICA. DIVISION OF ROADS AND TRANSPORT TECHNOLOGY. TRANSPORT STATISTICS. Text in Afrikaans, English. 1969. a. ZAR 45. charts; illus. **Document type:** *Government.*
Former titles: National Institute for Transport and Road Research. Transport Statistics; National Institute for Transport and Road Research. Road Statistics
Published by: Division of Roads and Transport Technology, PO Box 395, Pretoria, 0001, South Africa. FAX 841-32-32, TELEX 3-21312SA. Ed. C C Hamilton. Circ: 1,000. **Co-sponsor:** Great Britain. Department for Transport.

SOUTH AFRICA. STATISTICS SOUTH AFRICA. CENSUS OF MOTOR TRADE AND REPAIR SERVICES. *see* BUSINESS AND ECONOMICS—Abstracting, Bibliographies, Statistics

380.5 ZAF
SOUTH AFRICA. STATISTICS SOUTH AFRICA. CENSUS OF TRANSPORT AND ALLIED SERVICES. Text in English. irreg., latest 1998. **Document type:** *Government.*
Formerly (until Aug.1998): South Africa. Central Statistical Service. Census of Transport and Allied Services
Published by: Statistics South Africa/Statistieke Suid-Afrika, Private Bag X44, Pretoria, 0001, South Africa. TEL 27-12-3108911, FAX 27-12-3108500, info@statssa.gov.za, http://www.statssa.gov.za.

388 ZAF
SOUTH AFRICA. STATISTICS SOUTH AFRICA. NEW VEHICLES REGISTERED. Key Title: Nuwe Voertuie Geregistreer. Text in English. a., latest 1993. ZAR 8 domestic; ZAR 10 foreign (effective 2000). **Document type:** *Government.*
Former titles (until Aug.1998): South Africa. Central Statistical Service. New Vehicles Registered (0259-0409); South Africa. Central Statistical Service. Statistics of New Vehicles Registered; South Africa. Department of Statistics. Statistics of New Vehicles Registered; South Africa. Department of Statistics. Statistics of New Vehicles Licensed
Published by: Statistics South Africa/Statistieke Suid-Afrika, Private Bag X44, Pretoria, 0001, South Africa. TEL 27-12-3108911, FAX 27-12-3108500, info@statssa.gov.za, http://www.statssa.gov.za.

388.3 310 ZAF
SOUTH AFRICA. STATISTICS SOUTH AFRICA. REGISTERED VEHICLES. Text in English. 1972. a., latest 1994. **Document type:** *Government.*
Former titles (until Aug.1998): South Africa. Central Statistical Service. Registered Vehicles; South Africa. Central Statistical Service. Statistics of Motor and Other Vehicles; South Africa. Department of Statistics. Statistics of Motor and Other Vehicles
Published by: Statistics South Africa/Statistieke Suid-Afrika, Private Bag X44, Pretoria, 0001, South Africa. TEL 27-12-3108911, FAX 27-12-3108500, info@statssa.gov.za, http://www.statssa.gov.za.

388.021 ZAF
SOUTH AFRICA. STATISTICS SOUTH AFRICA. ROAD TRAFFIC COLLISIONS. Text in English. a., latest 1999. ZAR 30 domestic; ZAR 33 foreign (effective 2000). **Document type:** *Government.*
Former titles (until Aug.1998): South Africa. Central Statistical Service. Road Traffic Collisions (0258-7793); South Africa. Department of Statistics. Road Traffic Accidents (0584-195X)
Published by: Statistics South Africa/Statistieke Suid-Afrika, Private Bag X44, Pretoria, 0001, South Africa. TEL 27-12-3108911, FAX 27-12-3108500, info@statssa.gov.za, http://www.statssa.gov.za.

380.5 316.8 ZAF
SOUTH AFRICA. STATISTICS SOUTH AFRICA. STATISTICAL RELEASE. CENSUS OF TRANSPORT AND ALLIED SERVICES. Text in English. irreg., latest 1997. **Document type:** *Government.*
Formerly (until Aug. 1998): South Africa. Central Statistical Service. Statistical Release. Census of Transport and Allied Services
Published by: Statistics South Africa/Statistieke Suid-Afrika, Private Bag X44, Pretoria, 0001, South Africa. TEL 27-12-3108911, FAX 27-12-3108500, info@statssa.gov.za, http://www.statssa.gov.za.

SOUTH AFRICA. STATISTICS SOUTH AFRICA. STATISTICAL RELEASE. MOTOR TRADE - FINANCIAL STATISTICS. *see* BUSINESS AND ECONOMICS—Abstracting, Bibliographies, Statistics

380.5 316.8 ZAF
SOUTH AFRICA. STATISTICS SOUTH AFRICA. STATISTICAL RELEASE. PUBLIC ROAD TRANSPORT (NON-GOVERNMENTAL INSTITUTIONS) OF PASSENGERS AND GOODS - FINANCIAL STATISTICS. Text in English. q. **Document type:** *Government.*
Formerly (until Aug. 1998): South Africa. Central Statistical Service. Statistical Release. Public Road Transport (Non-governmental Institutions) of Passengers and Goods - Financial Statistics
Published by: Statistics South Africa/Statistieke Suid-Afrika, Private Bag X44, Pretoria, 0001, South Africa. TEL 27-12-3108911, FAX 27-12-3108500, info@statssa.gov.za, http://www.statssa.gov.za.

SOUTH AFRICA. STATISTICS SOUTH AFRICA. STATISTICAL RELEASE. RETAIL TRADE IN MOTOR VEHICLES AND ACCESSORIES - TRADING REVENUE (FINAL). *see* BUSINESS AND ECONOMICS—Abstracting, Bibliographies, Statistics

388 316.8 ZAF
SOUTH AFRICA. STATISTICS SOUTH AFRICA. STATISTICAL RELEASE. ROAD TRAFFIC COLLISIONS. Text in English. m. **Document type:** *Government.*
Formerly (until Aug. 1998): South Africa. Central Statistical Service. Statistical Release. Road Traffic Collisions
Published by: Statistics South Africa/Statistieke Suid-Afrika, Private Bag X44, Pretoria, 0001, South Africa. TEL 27-12-3108911, FAX 27-12-3108500, info@statssa.gov.za, http://www.statssa.gov.za.

388 316.8 ZAF
SOUTH AFRICA. STATISTICS SOUTH AFRICA. STATISTICAL RELEASE. TRANSPORT OF GOODS BY ROAD AND RAIL. Text in English. m. **Document type:** *Government.*
Formerly (until Aug. 1998): South Africa. Central Statistical Service. Statistical Release. Transport of Goods by Road and Rail
Published by: Statistics South Africa/Statistieke Suid-Afrika, Private Bag X44, Pretoria, 0001, South Africa. TEL 27-12-3108911, FAX 27-12-3108500, info@statssa.gov.za, http://www.statssa.gov.za.

614.8621 ESP ISSN 1575-3298
SPAIN. MINISTERIO DEL INTERIOR. DIRECCION GENERAL DE TRAFICO. ANUARIO ESTADISTICO DE ACCIDENTES. Text in Spanish. 1962. a. back issues avail. **Document type:** *Bulletin, Government.* **Description:** Presents official data on traffic accidents in Spain.
Former titles (until 1999): Spain. Ministerio del Interior. Direccion General de Trafico. Boletin Informativo: Accidentes (0085-655X); (until 1972): Spain. Direccion General de la Jefatura Central de Trafico. Boletin Informativo. Accidentes (0210-9190); (until 1968): Spain. Jefatura Central de Trafico. Boletin Informativo. Accidentes (0210-9204)
Related titles: Diskette ed.
Published by: Ministerio del Interior, Direccion General de Trafico, Calle J. Valcarcel, 28, Madrid, 28071, Spain. TEL 34-91-3018100, FAX 34-91-3018533, inspeccion@dgtrafico.org, http://www.dgt.es.

388.3121 ESP ISSN 1575-3395
HE5081
SPAIN. MINISTERIO DEL INTERIOR. DIRECCION GENERAL DE TRAFICO. ANUARIO ESTADISTICO GENERAL. Text in Spanish. 1960. a. back issues avail. **Document type:** *Bulletin, Government.* **Description:** Presents statistics on driving licenses, transfers, and permits, and on national auto parks and traffic fines.
Formerly (until 1999): Spain. Ministerio del Interior. Direccion General de Trafico. Boletin Informativo: Anuario Estadistico General (0304-9191)
Related titles: Diskette ed.
Published by: Ministerio del Interior, Direccion General de Trafico, Calle J. Valcarcel, 28, Madrid, 28071, Spain. TEL 34-91-3018374, 34-91-3018100, inspeccion@dgtrafico.org, http://www.dgt.es.

388.324021 USA ISSN 1942-2687
STANDARD TRUCKING AND TRANSPORTATION STATISTICS. Abbreviated title: S T A T S. Text in English. 1995. q. USD 105 to non-members; USD 78.75 to members (effective 2011). back issues avail. **Document type:** *Report, Trade.* **Description:** Features quarterly data on everything from state fuel taxes to stock performance. Gives quick answers to common questions about the state of the industry.
Related titles: Online - full text ed.: ISSN 1942-2695.
Published by: American Trucking Associations, Inc., 950 N Glebe Rd, Ste 210, Alexandria, VA 22203. TEL 703-838-1700, orders@trucking.org.

388.021 USA
STATE TRANSPORTATION STATISTICS. Text in English. 2003. a. **Document type:** *Government.*
Formerly (until 2004): Summary: State Transportation Profile
Related titles: Online - full content ed.
Published by: U.S. Department of Transportation, Research and Innovative Technology Administration. Bureau of Transportation Statistics, 1200 New Jersey Ave. SE, Washington, DC 20590. TEL 202-366-3492, 800-853-1351, FAX 202-366-3759, http://www.rita.dot.gov.

380.5 LUX ISSN 0257-2419
STATISTICAL OFFICE OF THE EUROPEAN COMMUNITIES. TRANSPORT, COMMUNICATIONS, TOURISME - ANNUAIRE STATISTIQUE. Text in Dutch, French, German, Italian. irreg., latest 1994. USD 50.
Formerly: Statistical Office of the European Communities. Statistiques des Transports. Annuaire (0081-4962)
Published by: (European Commission, Statistical Office of the European Communities (E U R O S T A T)), European Commission, Office for Official Publications of the European Union, 2 Rue Mercier, Luxembourg, L-2985, Luxembourg. **Dist. in the U.S. by:** Bernan Associates, Bernan, 4611-F Assembly Dr., Lanham, MD 20706-4391. TEL 301-459-0056, 800-274-4447.

388.31 310 JPN ISSN 1012-6430
STATISTICS (YEAR) ROAD ACCIDENTS JAPAN. Text in English. a. USD 25 (effective 2003). back issues avail. **Document type:** *Government.*
Formerly (until 1983): Statistics of Road Traffic Accidents in Japan (0386-1708)
Published by: International Association of Traffic and Safety Sciences, 6-20 Yaesu 2-chome, Chuo-ku, Tokyo, 104-0028, Japan. TEL 81-3-3273-7884, FAX 81-3-3272-7054, iatss@db3.so-net.ne.jp, http://wwwsoc.nii.ac.jp/iatss/.

388.1 CHE ISSN 1026-9134
STATISTICS OF ROAD TRAFFIC ACCIDENTS IN EUROPE AND NORTH AMERICA. Text in English, French, Russian. 1956. a. USD 40 (effective 2001). **Document type:** *Government.* **Description:** Summarizes statistics on traffic accidents in Europe and North America, along with data on their causes, number of crashes involving intoxicated drivers, and casualties in nonfatal accidents.
Formerly: Statistics of Road Traffic Accidents in Europe (0497-9575)
Related titles: Microfiche ed.: (from CIS).
Indexed: IIS.
Published by: United Nations, Economic Commission for Europe (ECE), Palais des Nations, Geneva 10, 1211, Switzerland. TEL 41-22-9174444, FAX 41-22-9170505, info.ece@unece.org, http://www.unece.org.

387.736 FRA ISSN 0245-8756
STATISTIQUES DE TRAFIC. Text in French. 1966. m.
Former titles (until 1980): Bulletin Mensuel de Statistiques de Trafic (0396-5481); (until 1974): Statistiques de Trafic (0396-5473)
Published by: Aeroports de Paris, Orly sud 103, Paris, Cedex 94396, France.

385.21 DEU ISSN 1433-2507
STATISTISCHE BERICHTE - BADEN-WUERTTEMBERG. H: VERKEHR. Text in German. 1956. irreg. **Document type:** *Government.*
Formerly (until 1992): Statistisches Landesamt Baden-Wuerttemberg. Statistische Berichte H (1433-2329)
Published by: Statistisches Landesamt Baden-Wuerttemberg, Boeblinger Str 68, Stuttgart, 70199, Germany. TEL 49-711-6410, FAX 49-711-6412440, poststelle@stala.bwl.de.

385.21 DEU ISSN 1430-5127
STATISTISCHE BERICHTE - RHEINLAND-PFALZ. H: VERKEHR. Text in German. 1951. irreg. **Document type:** *Government.*
Formerly (until 1976): Statistisches Landesamt Rheinland-Pfalz. Statistische Berichte H (1430-497X); Which superseded in part (in 1956): Statistisches Landesamt Rheinland-Pfalz. Mitteilungen (0482-8887)
Published by: Statistisches Landesamt Rheinland-Pfalz, Mainzerstr 14-16, Bad Ems, 56130, Germany. TEL 49-2603-713240, FAX 49-2603-71193240, pressestelle@statistik.rlp.de.

380.5 314 DEU
STATISTISCHES BUNDESAMT. FACHSERIE 17: PREISE, REIHE 9.1: PREISINDIZES FUER NACHRICHTENUEBERMITTLUNG. Text in German. 1955. m. **Document type:** *Government.*
Supersedes in part (in 2003): Germany. Statistisches Bundesamt. Fachserie 17, Preise, Reihe 9: Preise und Preisindizes fuer Verkehr und Nachrichtenuebermittlung (1431-8725); Which was formerly (until 1995): Germany. Statistisches Bundesamt. Fachserie 17, Preise, Reihe 9: Preise und Preisindizes fuer Verkehrsleistungen (0179-7956); (until 1985): Statistisches Bundesamt. Fachserie 17: Preise. Reihe 9: Preise fuer Verkehrsleistungen (0179-7964); (until 1977): Statistisches Bundesamt. Fachserie 17: Preise, Loehne, Wirtschaftsrechnungen. Reihe 7: Preise fuer Verkehrsleistungen (0072-3924)
Published by: Statistisches Bundesamt, Gustav-Stresemann-Ring 11, Wiesbaden, 65180, Germany. TEL 49-611-752405, FAX 49-611-753330, info@destatis.de, http://www.destatis.de.

385.1 314 DEU ISSN 0932-1861
STATISTISCHES BUNDESAMT. FACHSERIE 8: VERKEHR, REIHE 2: EISENBAHNVERKEHR. Text in German. 1960. m. **Document type:** *Government.*
Former titles (until 1977): Statistisches Bundesamt. Fachserie 8: Verkehr. Reihe 4: Eisenbahnverkehr (0932-1888); (until 1962): Der Verkehr in der Bundesrepublik Deutschland. Reihe 4: Eisenbahnverkehr (0932-187X)
Published by: Statistisches Bundesamt, Gustav-Stresemann-Ring 11, Wiesbaden, 65180, Germany. TEL 49-611-752405, FAX 49-611-753330, info@destatis.de, http://www.destatis.de.

388 314 DEU
STATISTISCHES BUNDESAMT. FACHSERIE 8: VERKEHR, REIHE 3: PERSONENVERKEHR MIT BUSSEN UND BAHNEN. Text in German. 196?. q. **Document type:** *Government.*
Former titles (until 2004): Statistisches Bundesamt. Fachserie 8: Verkehr, Reihe 3: Strassenpersonenverkehr (0935-7726); (until 1988): Germany. Statistisches Bundesamt. Fachserie 8: Verkehr, Reihe 3.2: Personenverkehr der Strassenverkehrsunternehmen (0170-7744); (until 1977): Germany. Statistisches Bundesamt. Fachserie 8: Verkehr. Reihe 5: Strassenverkehr. 2 - Personenverkehr (0341-4655)
Published by: Statistisches Bundesamt, Gustav-Stresemann-Ring 11, Wiesbaden, 65180, Germany. TEL 49-611-752405, FAX 49-611-753330, info@destatis.de, http://www.destatis.de.

387 314 DEU ISSN 0932-4259
CODEN: ASTTA8
STATISTISCHES BUNDESAMT. FACHSERIE 8: VERKEHR, REIHE 4: BINNENSCHIFFAHRT. Text in German. 1949. a. **Document type:** *Government.*
Former titles (until 1977): Statistisches Bundesamt. Fachserie 8: Verkehr, Reihe 1: Binnenschiffahrt (0932-4267); (until 1962): Der Verkehr in der Bundesrepublik Deutschland. Reihe 1: Binnenschiffahrt (0932-4275); (until 1958): Die Binnenschiffahrt (0932-4283)
Published by: Statistisches Bundesamt, Gustav-Stresemann-Ring 11, Wiesbaden, 65180, Germany. TEL 49-611-752405, FAX 49-611-753330, info@destatis.de, http://www.destatis.de.

387 314 DEU ISSN 0175-6036
STATISTISCHES BUNDESAMT. FACHSERIE 8: VERKEHR, REIHE 5: SEESCHIFFFAHRT. Text in German. 1958. m. **Document type:** *Government.*
Former titles (until 1977): Statistisches Bundesamt. Fachserie 8: Verkehr, Reihe 2: Seeschifffahrt (0175-6052); (until 1962): Der Verkehr in der Bundesrepublik Deutschland. Reihe 2: Seeschifffahrt (0175-6044)
Published by: Statistisches Bundesamt, Gustav-Stresemann-Ring 11, Wiesbaden, 65180, Germany. TEL 49-611-752405, FAX 49-611-753330, info@destatis.de, http://www.destatis.de.

387.7 314 DEU ISSN 0932-2183
STATISTISCHES BUNDESAMT. FACHSERIE 8: VERKEHR, REIHE 6: LUFTVERKEHR. Text in German. 1958. m. **Document type:** *Government.*
Former titles (until 1977): Statistisches Bundesamt. Fachserie 8: Verkehr. Reihe 3: Luftverkehr (0932-2175); (until 1962): Der Verkehr in der Bundesrepublik Deutschland. Reihe 3: Luftverkehr (0932-2167)
Published by: Statistisches Bundesamt, Gustav-Stresemann-Ring 11, Wiesbaden, 65180, Germany. TEL 49-611-752405, FAX 49-611-753330, info@destatis.de, http://www.destatis.de.

614 DEU ISSN 0937-8294
STATISTISCHES BUNDESAMT. FACHSERIE 8: VERKEHR, REIHE 7: VERKEHRSUNFAELLE. Text in German. 196?. m. (plus a. cumulation). **Document type:** *Government.*
Former titles (until 1989): Germany. (Federal Republic, 1949-). Statistisches Bundesamt. Fachserie 8, Verkehr, Reihe 3.3: Strassenverkehrsunfaelle (0170-7752); (until 1977): Germany. (Federal Republic, 1949-). Statistisches Bundesamt. Fachserie 8: Verkehr. Reihe 6: Strassenverkehrsunfaelle (0341-213X)
Published by: Statistisches Bundesamt, Gustav-Stresemann-Ring 11, Wiesbaden, 65180, Germany. TEL 49-611-752405, FAX 49-611-753330, info@destatis.de, http://www.destatis.de.

387.7 SWE
SWEDEN. LUFTFARTSVERKET. CHARTERSTATISTIK. Text in Swedish. 1970. s-a. SEK 84.
Published by: Luftfartsverket/Swedish Civil Aviation Administration, Vikboplan 11, Norrkoping, 60173, Sweden.

387.7 SWE
SWEDEN. LUFTFARTSVERKET. FLYGPLATSSTATISTIK. Text in Swedish. m. SEK 180.
Published by: Luftfartsverket/Swedish Civil Aviation Administration, Vikboplan 11, Norrkoping, 60173, Sweden.

388 CHE
SWITZERLAND. BUNDESAMT FUER STATISTIK. MOTORFAHRZEUGE IN DER SCHWEIZ. INVERKEHRSETZUNG NEUE FAHRZEUGE - VEHICULES A MOTEUR EN SUISSE. MISES EN CIRCULATION DE VEHICULES NEUFS. Text in French, German. 1929. a. CHF 16 (effective 2001). **Document type:** *Government.*
Former titles (until 1999): Switzerland. Bundesamt fuer Statistik. Motorfahrzeuge in der Schweiz. In Verkehr Gesetzte Neue Motorfahrzeuge - Vehicules a Moteur en Suisse. Vehicules a Moteur Neufs Mis en Circulation; Switzerland. Bundesamt fuer Statistik. In Verkehr Gesetzte Neue Motorfahrzeuge - Vehicules a Moteur Neufs Mis en Circulation; Which superseded in part: Switzerland. Statistisches Amt. Eingefuehrte Motorfahrzeuge: In Verkehr Gesetzte Neue Motorfahrzeuge
Published by: Bundesamt fuer Statistik, Espace de l'Europe 10, Neuchatel, 2010, Switzerland. TEL 41-32-7136011, FAX 41-32-7136012, information@bfs.admin.ch, http://www.admin.ch/bfs.

363.12021 CAN ISSN 1191-7245
CA1TU1-1
T S B STATISTICAL SUMMARY, MARINE OCCURRENCES. Variant title: Sommaire Statistique du B S T, Evenements Maritimes. Text in English, French. 1977. a.
Formerly (until 1990): Canadian Coast Guard. Marine Casualty Investigations. Statistical Summary of Marine Accidents (0844-8779)
Related titles: Online - full text ed.: ISSN 1701-6517.
Published by: Transportation Safety Board of Canada, 200 Promenade de Portage, Place du Centre 4th Fl, Gatineau, PQ KIA 1K8, Canada. TEL 819-994-3741, FAX 819-997-2239.

387.7 AUT
TAETIGKEITSBERICHT DES VERKEHRS ARBEITSINSPEKTORATES FUER DAS JAHR (YEAR). Text in German. 1952. a. free. **Document type:** *Government.*
Published by: Bundesministerium fuer Wissenschaft und Verkehr, Gruppe Verkehrs - Arbeitsinspektorat, Radetzkystrasse 2, Vienna, W 1031, Austria. TEL 43-1-71162-4400, FAX 43-1-711624499. Circ: 450.

380.5 315 TWN
TAIWAN ANNUAL STATISTICAL REPORT OF TRANSPORTATION/TAI-WAN SHENG CHIAO T'UNG T'UNG CHI NIEN PAO. Text in Chinese, English. 1946. a. stat.
Published by: Taiwan Provincial Government, Department of Transportation/Tai-wan Sheng Cheng Fu Chiao T'ung Chu, Nantou Hsien, Taiwan.

016 629.2 620 USA
TECHNICAL LITERATURE ABSTRACTS (WARRENDALE). Text in English. 1975. q. back issues avail. **Document type:** *Abstract/Index.*
Supersedes (in 1985): S A E Quarterly Abstracts; Former titles (until 19??): S A E Technical Literature Abstracts (0741-2029); (until 1981): Society of Automotive Engineers. Technical Literature Abstracts
Related titles: Online - full text ed.
—CCC.
Published by: S A E Inc., 400 Commonwealth Dr, Warrendale, PA 15096. TEL 724-776-4841, 877-606-7323, FAX 724-776-0790, CustomerService@sae.org, http://www.sae.org.

016.3883 DEU
TECSCAN JOURNAL. AUTOELEKTRIK UND -ELEKTRONIK. Text in German. m. EUR 295 (effective 2010). **Document type:** *Journal, Abstract/Index.*
Published by: Fachinformationszentrum Technik e.V., Hanauer Landstr 151-153, Frankfurt Am Main, 60314, Germany. TEL 49-69-4308213, FAX 49-69-4308200, kundenberatung@fiz-technik.de, http://www.fiz-technik.de.

016.3883 DEU
TECSCAN JOURNAL. SOLAR-, ELEKTRO- UND HYBRIDFAHRZEUGE. Text in German. m. EUR 295 (effective 2010). **Document type:** *Journal, Abstract/Index.*
Published by: Fachinformationszentrum Technik e.V., Hanauer Landstr 151-153, Frankfurt Am Main, 60314, Germany. TEL 49-69-4308213, FAX 49-69-4308200, kundenberatung@fiz-technik.de, http://www.fiz-technik.de.

315.2 JPN
TETSUDO SHARYOTO SEISAN DOTAI TOKEI GEPPO/MONTHLY SURVEY ON CURRENT ROLLING STOCK PRODUCTION. Text in Japanese. 1954. m. free.
Formerly: Monthly Statistics of Actual Production of Railway Cars (0040-4055)
Published by: Ministry of Transport, Transport Policy Bureau/Un'Yu-sho Un'Yu-seisaku-kyoku, Information and Research Department, 2-1-3 Kasumigaseki, Chiyoda-ku, Tokyo, 100-0013, Japan.

315.2 JPN
TETSUDO SHARYOTO SEISAN DOTAI TOKEI NENPO/ANNUAL SURVEY ON CURRENT ROLLING STOCK PRODUCTION. Text in Japanese. 1954. a. free.
Formerly: Annual Statistics of Actual Production of Railway Cars
Published by: Ministry of Transport, Transport Policy Bureau/Un'Yu-sho Un'Yu-seisaku-kyoku, Information and Research Department, 2-1-3 Kasumigaseki, Chiyoda-ku, Tokyo, 100-0013, Japan.

388.021 384.021 SGP
HD9987.S57
TRANSPORT AND COMMUNICATIONS (SINGAPORE). Text in English. 1972. a. SGD 20.40. **Document type:** *Government.*
Formerly (until 1989): Singapore. Department of Statistics. Report on the Survey of Services (Year) (0129-9786)
Related titles: ◆ Series of: Singapore. Department of Statistics. Economic Surveys Series.
Published by: Department of Statistics, 100 High St #05-01, The Treasury, Singapore, 179434, Singapore. TEL 65-3327686, FAX 65-3327689, info@singstat.gov.sg.

388.021 NLD ISSN 1388-6983
TRANSPORT IN CIJFERS. Text in Dutch. 1970. a. EUR 37.50 (effective 2010).
Formerly (until 1995): Wegvervoer in Cijfers (1388-6975)
Published by: Transport en Logistiek Nederland, Postbus 3008, Zoetermeer, 2700 KS, Netherlands. TEL 31-79-3636111, FAX 31-79-3636200, info@tln.nl, http://www.tln.nl.

388.021 GBR
TRANSPORT STATISTICS BULLETIN. ROAD FREIGHT STATISTICS. Text in English. 2005. a. free. **Document type:** *Government.* **Description:** Covers the activity of heavy goods vehicles (over 3.5 tons gross weight), including domestic activity of GB-registered goods vehicles, the international activity of UK-registered goods vehicles and the activity of foreign-registered goods vehicles in great Britain, the van sector, goods vehicle licensing and operators, and environment and safety.
Formed by the merger of (1975-2004): Transport of Goods by Road in Great Britain (0954-2647); International Road Haulage Statistics; Survey of Company Van Activity; Review of Road Freight Statistics
Related titles: Online - full text ed.
Published by: Great Britain. Department for Transport, Great Minster House, 76 Marsham St, London, SW1P 4DR, United Kingdom. TEL 44-20-79443078, FAX 44-20-79449643, publications@communities.gsi.gov.uk, http://www.dft.gov.uk.

388.121 GBR ISSN 0144-8021
TRANSPORT STATISTICS GREAT BRITAIN. Abbreviated title: T S G B. Text in English. 1974. a. GBP 36 per issue (effective 2009). charts. back issues avail. **Document type:** *Government.* **Description:** Provides an accurate coverage of the transport patronage in Great Britain.
Formed by the merger of (1963-1974): Great Britain. Department of the Environment. Highway Statistics (0072-6893); Which incorporated: Road Motor Vehicles; (1962-1974): Passenger Transport in Great Britain (0079-0133)
Related titles: Microfiche ed.: (from PQC); Online - full text ed.: free (effective 2009).
—BLDSC (9025.952000).
Published by: Great Britain. Department for Transport, Great Minster House, 76 Marsham St, London, SW1P 4DR, United Kingdom. TEL 44-20-79443078, FAX 44-20-79449643, publications@communities.gsi.gov.uk.

388.021 RUS
TRANSPORT V ROSSII (YEAR). Text in Russian. a., latest 2005. RUR 187 per issue (effective 2005). **Document type:** *Yearbook, Government.*
Published by: Gosudarstvennyi Komitet Rossiiskoi Federatsii po Statistike/Federal State Statistics Office, ul Myasnitskaya 39, Moscow, 107450, Russian Federation. TEL 7-095-2074902, FAX 7-095-2074087, stat@gks.ru, http://www.gks.ru.

TRANSPORTATION ACCIDENT BRIEFS. PIPELINE. *see* PETROLEUM AND GAS—Abstracting, Bibliographies, Statistics

385 USA
TRANSPORTATION ACCIDENT BRIEFS. RAILROADS. Text in English. 19??. irreg. back issues avail. **Document type:** *Report, Government.*
Related titles: Microform ed.: (from NTI); ◆ Series of: Transportation Accident Briefs.
Published by: (U.S. Department of Transportation, National Transportation Safety Board), U.S. Department of Commerce, National Technical Information Service, 5301 Shawnee Rd, Alexandria, VA 22312. TEL 703-605-6000, info@ntis.gov.

380.5 USA
TRANSPORTATION ACCIDENT REPORTS. HIGHWAY. Text in English. 19??. irreg. **Document type:** *Report, Government.*
Related titles: Microform ed.: (from NTI); ◆ Series of: Transportation Accident Reports.
Published by: (U.S. Department of Transportation, National Transportation Safety Board), U.S. Department of Commerce, National Technical Information Service, 5301 Shawnee Rd, Alexandria, VA 22312. TEL 703-605-6000, 800-553-6847, info@ntis.gov, http://www.ntis.gov.

387 USA
TRANSPORTATION ACCIDENT REPORTS. MARINE. Text in English. 19??. irreg., latest 2011. **Document type:** *Report, Government.*
Related titles: Microform ed.: (from NTI); ◆ Series of: Transportation Accident Reports.
Published by: (U.S. Department of Transportation, National Transportation Safety Board), U.S. Department of Commerce, National Technical Information Service, 5301 Shawnee Rd, Alexandria, VA 22312. TEL 703-605-6000, 800-553-6847, info@ntis.gov.

TRANSPORTATION ACCIDENT REPORTS. PIPELINE. *see* PETROLEUM AND GAS—Abstracting, Bibliographies, Statistics

TRANSPORTATION ENERGY RESEARCH. *see* ENERGY—Abstracting, Bibliographies, Statistics

388.324021 USA ISSN 1942-2784
TRUCKING ACTIVITY REPORT. Text in English. 1993. m. USD 525 to non-members; USD 393 to members (effective 2011). back issues avail. **Document type:** *Report, Trade.* **Description:** Features timely information on changes in mileage, revenue, and traffic.
Related titles: Online - full text ed.: ISSN 1942-2792.
Published by: American Trucking Associations, Inc., 950 N Glebe Rd, Ste 210, Alexandria, VA 22203. TEL 703-838-1700, orders@trucking.org.

387.1 TUN
TUNISIA. OFFICE DES PORTS NATIONAUX. BULLETIN ANNUEL DES STATISTIQUES. Cover title: Tunisia. Office des Ports Nationaux. Trafic Maritime. Text in French. a. **Document type:** *Bulletin, Government.*
Published by: Office des Ports Nationaux, Tunis, Tunisia.

387.2021 TUR ISSN 1300-1698
HA1911
TURKEY. TURKIYE ISTATISTIK KURUMU. DENIZ TASITLARI ISTATISTIKLERI (18 VE DAHA YUKARI GROS TONILATOLUK)/ TURKEY. TURKISH STATISTICAL INSTITUTE. STATISTICS OF SEA VESSELS (18 GROSS TONNAGES AND OVER). Key Title: Deniz Tasitlari Istatistikleri. Text in English, Turkish. 1960. a., latest 2001. **Document type:** *Government.*
Related titles: Diskette ed.
Published by: T.C. Basbakanlik, Turkiye Istatistik Kurumu/Prime Ministry Republic of Turkey, Turkish Statistical Institute, Yucetepe Mah. Necatibey Cad No.114, Cankaya, Ankara, 06100, Turkey. TEL 90-312-4100410, FAX 90-312-4175886, bilgi@tuik.gov.tr, ulka.unsal@tuik.gov.tr, http://www.tuik.gov.tr. Circ: 1,100.

388.3021 TUR ISSN 1300-106X
HA1911
TURKEY. TURKIYE ISTATISTIK KURUMU. MOTORLU KARA TASITLARI ISTATISTIKLERI (YEAR)/TURKEY. TURKISH STATISTICAL INSTITUTE. ROAD MOTOR VEHICLE STATISTICS (YEAR). Key Title: Motorlu Kara Tasitlari Istatistikleri. Text in English, Turkish. 1947. a., latest 1995. TRY 10 per issue domestic; USD 20 per issue foreign (effective 2009). **Document type:** *Government.* **Description:** Comprehensive statistics of road motor vehicles is provided according to province, vehicle type, trademark, use, fuel type and model year.
Related titles: CD-ROM ed.: TRY 5 per issue domestic; USD 10 per issue foreign (effective 2009).
Published by: T.C. Basbakanlik, Turkiye Istatistik Kurumu/Prime Ministry Republic of Turkey, Turkish Statistical Institute, Yucetepe Mah. Necatibey Cad No.114, Cankaya, Ankara, 06100, Turkey. TEL 90-312-4100410, FAX 90-312-4175886, ulka.unsal@tuik.gov.tr, bilgi@tuik.gov.tr, http://www.tuik.gov.tr. Circ: 1,100.

363.125021 TUR ISSN 1300-1175
TURKEY. TURKIYE ISTATISTIK KURUMU. TRAFIK KAZA ISTATISTIKLERI; KARAYOLU (YEAR)/TURKEY. TURKISH STATISTICAL INSTITUTE. TRAFFIC ACCIDENT STATISTICS; ROAD (YEAR). Key Title: Trafik Kaza Istatistikleri. Text in English, Turkish. 1976. a., latest 2007. TRY 10 per issue domestic; USD 20 per issue foreign (effective 2009). **Document type:** *Government.* **Description:** Provides data on road traffic accidents by time of day, month, and year of occurrence; type of vehicle; place and type of accident; and persons killed or injured by age group, sex, and type of vehicle.
Related titles: CD-ROM ed.: TRY 5 per issue domestic; USD 10 per issue foreign (effective 2009).
Published by: T.C. Basbakanlik, Turkiye Istatistik Kurumu/Prime Ministry Republic of Turkey, Turkish Statistical Institute, Yucetepe Mah. Necatibey Cad No.114, Cankaya, Ankara, 06100, Turkey. TEL 90-312-4100410, FAX 90-312-4175886, ulka.unsal@tuik.gov.tr, bilgi@tuik.gov.tr, http://www.tuik.gov.tr. Circ: 920.

388.021 TUR ISSN 1300-1019
HE268.25.A15
TURKEY. TURKIYE ISTATISTIK KURUMU. ULASTIRMA ISTATISTIKLERI OZETI/TURKEY. TURKISH STATISTICAL INSTITUTE. SUMMARY STATISTICS ON TRANSPORTATION (YEAR). Key Title: Ulastirma Istatistikleri Ozeti. Text in English, Turkish. 1982. a., latest 2007. TRY 10 per issue domestic; USD 20 per issue foreign (effective 2009). **Document type:** *Government.* **Description:** Includes statistics on the transport of freight and passengers by mode of transport, length of pipeline for petroleum and natural gas and transport volume of them, circulation and traffic volume on state and provincial roads, number of road motor vehicles by usage and kinds of fuel, number of road motor vehicles registrated and withdrawn, number of road traffic accidents and results by responsibility area, length of railways, frieght and passengers carried in railroads, number of maritime accidents in domestic and international airlines by airports, and postal and telephone communications.
Formerly (until 1991): Turkey. State Institute of Statistics. Transportation and Road Traffic Accidents Statistics Summary
Related titles: CD-ROM ed.: TRY 5 per issue domestic; USD 10 per issue foreign (effective 2009).
Published by: T.C. Basbakanlik, Turkiye Istatistik Kurumu/Prime Ministry Republic of Turkey, Turkish Statistical Institute, Yucetepe Mah. Necatibey Cad No.114, Cankaya, Ankara, 06100, Turkey. TEL 90-312-4100410, FAX 90-312-4175886, ulka.unsal@tuik.gov.tr, bilgi@tuik.gov.tr, http://www.tuik.gov.tr. Circ: 975.

U.S. BUREAU OF THE CENSUS. (YEAR) ECONOMIC CENSUS. TRANSPORTATION AND WAREHOUSING (ONLINE). *see* BUSINESS AND ECONOMICS—Abstracting, Bibliographies, Statistics

363.122021 USA ISSN 1931-860X
HE1780
U.S. DEPARTMENT OF TRANSPORTATION. FEDERAL RAILROAD ADMINISTRATION. OFFICE OF SAFETY ANALYSIS. RAILROAD SAFETY STATISTICS. ANNUAL REPORT (YEAR). Variant title: Railroad Safety Statistics. Annual Report (Year). Text in English. 1997. a. USD 33.50. **Document type:** *Government.*
Formed by the merger of (19??-1997): Trespasser Bulletin; (19??-1997): Highway-Rail Crossing Accident - Incident and Inventory Bulletin; (1971-1997): Accident - Incident Bulletin (0163-4674); Which was formerly (until 1975): Accident Bulletin (0092-1645)
Related titles: Online - full text ed.: ISSN 1931-8618.
Published by: U.S. Department of Transportation, Federal Railroad Administration, Office of Safety, 1120 Vermont Ave, N W, Mail Stop 25, Washington, DC 20590. TEL 202-493-6211. **Orders to:** Bernan Associates, Bernan, 4611-F Assembly Dr., Lanham, MD 20706-4391. TEL 301-459-0056.

310 380.5 USA ISSN 0161-8628
HE203
U.S. DEPARTMENT OF TRANSPORTATION. NATIONAL TRANSPORTATION STATISTICS. ANNUAL; a supplement to the summary of national transportation statistics. Text in English. 1977. a. USD 13. illus. **Document type:** *Government.*
Formed by the 1977 merger of: U.S. Department of Transportation. Energy Statistics (0360-8980); U.S. Department of Transportation. Summary of National Transportation Statistics (0145-2541)
—Linda Hall.
Published by: (U.S. Department of Transportation, Research and Innovative Technology Administration. Bureau of Transportation Statistics), U.S. Department of Transportation, Office of the Assistant Secretary for Policy, Plans, and International Affairs, Washington, DC 20590. TEL 202-655-4000. **Orders to:** U.S. Government Printing Office, Superintendent of Documents.

388.3 USA ISSN 0095-344X
HE355.A3
U.S. FEDERAL HIGHWAY ADMINISTRATION. HIGHWAY STATISTICS. Key Title: Highway Statistics. Text in English. 1945. a. stat. **Document type:** *Government.*
Related titles: Online - full text ed.: ISSN 1936-6507.
Published by: U.S. Federal Highway Administration, Office of Highway Information Management (Subsidiary of: U.S. Department of Transportation), 400 7th St, SW, Washington, DC 20590. http://www.fhwa.dot.gov/.

387.7 USA
U.S. INTERNATIONAL AIR TRAVEL STATISTICS. Text in English. 19??. m. USD 1,635; USD 2,450 combined subscription (print & online eds.); USD 140 per issue; USD 210 combined subscription per issue (print & online eds.) (effective 2011). back issues avail. **Document type:** *Report, Government.* **Description:** Provides air travel flow data for international arrival and departure flights to and from the U.S.
Related titles: Online - full text ed.
Published by: International Trade Administration, Tourism Industries, U S Department of Commerce, Main Commerce Bldg, Rm 1868, Washington, DC 20230. http://www.tinet.ita.doc.gov.

387.7 USA
U S INTERNATIONAL AIR TRAVEL STATISTICS REPORT. Text in English. 1975. a. (plus m. & q. updates). USD 2,340 for 2000 Report; price varies by year. stat. back issues avail. **Document type:** *Government.* **Description:** Provides international air traffic data on arrival and departure flights for approximately 120 countries, 90 US airports and almost 280 non-US airports.
Indexed: AmStI.
Published by: (US. U.S. Department of Commerce, International Trade Administration), Tourism Industries (Subsidiary of: U.S. Department of Commerce, International Trade Administration), Main Commerce Bldg., Rm. 2073, 14th and Constitution Ave., N.W., Washington, DC 20230. TEL 202-482-4028, FAX 202-482-2887, http://tinet.ita.doc.gov. Ed. Ron Erdmann.

625.7 016 USA ISSN 0068-6115
UNIVERSITY OF CALIFORNIA. INSTITUTE OF TRANSPORTATION STUDIES. LIBRARY REFERENCES. Text in English. 1955. irreg., latest vol.78, 1978. price varies. **Document type:** *Bibliography.*
Published by: University of California, Berkeley, Institute of Transportation Studies, 109 McLaughlin Hall, Berkeley, CA 94720-1720. TEL 510-642-3593, FAX 510-642-1246.

388.021 KOR ISSN 1599-063X
UNSU'EOB TONG'GYE JO'SA BO'GO'SEO/KOREA (REPUBLIC). NATIONAL STATISTICAL OFFICE. REPORT ON THE TRANSPORT SURVEY. Text in English, Korean. 1978. a. USD 14 newsstand/cover (effective 2008). stat. **Document type:** *Government.*
Related titles: CD-ROM ed.: ISSN 1599-1229. 2000.
Published by: Tong'gyecheong/Korea National Statistical Office, Government Complex Daejeon, 139 Seonsaro (920 Dunsan 2-dong), Seo-gu, Daejeon, 302-701, Korea, S. TEL 82-42-4814114. **Subscr. to:** The Korean Statistical Association, Rm. 103, Seoul Statistical Branch Office Bldg. 71, Nonhyun-Dong, Kangnam-Ku, Seoul 135701, Korea, S. TEL 82-2-34437954, FAX 82-2-34437957, kosa@nso.go.kr.

V R S. (Verkehrsrechts-Sammlung) *see* LAW—Abstracting, Bibliographies, Statistics

385.21 SWE ISSN 1404-4625
HE5614.5.S8
VAEGTRAFIKSKADOR/ROAD TRAFFIC INJURIES. Text in English, Swedish. 1968. a. **Document type:** *Government.*
Former titles (until 1999): Trafikskador (0283-8540); (until 1987): Vaegtrafikolyckor med Personskade (0347-6359); Vaegtrafikolyckor
Related titles: Online - full text ed.; ◆ Series of: S I K A Statistik. ISSN 1404-854X.
Published by: Statens Institut foer Kommunikationsanalys (SIKA)/ Swedish Institute for Transport and Communications Analysis, Maria Skolgata 83, PO Box 17213, Stockholm, 10462, Sweden. TEL 46-8-50620600, FAX 46-8-50620610, sika@sika-institute.se.

388 HUN ISSN 0231-0767
VASUTI KOZLEKEDESI SZAKIRODALMI TAJEKOZTATO/RAILWAY TRANSPORTATION ABSTRACTS. Text in Hungarian. m. HUF 4,000. **Document type:** *Abstract/Index.*
Supersedes in part (in 1982): Muszaki Lapszemle. Kozlekedes - Technical Abstracts. Transportation (0027-5042)
Published by: Orszagos Muszaki Informacios Kozpont es Konyvtar/ National Technical Information Centre and Library, Muzeum utca 17, PO Box 12, Budapest, 1428, Hungary. Ed. Raczne Agnes Kovacs. Circ: 400. **Subscr. to:** Kultura, PO Box 149, Budapest 1389, Hungary.

387.7 FRA ISSN 0291-9508
VENTILATION DU TRAFIC COMMERCIAL. Text in French. m.
Published by: Aeroports de Paris, Orly sud 103, Paris, Cedex 94396, France.

388 BEL ISSN 0776-9628
VERKEERSVEILIGHEID. Text in Dutch. 1967. a. **Document type:** *Corporate.*
Supersedes (in 1986): Hoger Raad voor de Verkeersveiligheid. Verslag (0776-9601)
Related titles: ◆ French ed.: Securite Routiere. ISSN 0776-9636.
Published by: Institut Belge pour la Securite Routiere/Belgisch Instituut voor de Verkeersveiligheid, Ch de Haecht 1405, Brussels, 1130, Belgium. TEL 32-2-2441511, FAX 32-2-2164342, info@bivv.be, http://www.bivv.be. Ed. Christian van den Meersschaut.

380.5 DEU ISSN 1863-527X
HE249
VERKEHR IN ZAHLEN. Text in German. 1971. a. **Document type:** *Journal, Trade.*
Published by: Bundesministerium fuer Verkehr, Bau und Stadtentwicklung/Federal Ministry of Transport, Building and Urban Affairs, Krausenstr 17-20, Berlin, 10117, Germany. TEL 49-30-183000, FAX 49-30-183001942, buergerinfo@bmvbs.bund.de, http://www.bmvbs.de. Circ: 3,000 (paid).

012 380.5 CHE
VERKEHRSTECHNIK IN DER SCHWEIZ; Lieferantenkatalog der schweizerischer oeffentlicher Verkehrsbetriebe. Text in German. 1965. a. CHF 28. adv. **Document type:** *Catalog.*
Published by: Cicero Verlag AG, Spindelstr 2, Zuerich, 8021, Switzerland. TEL 41-1-4888400, FAX 41-1-4888300, TELEX 812648-CH. Ed. Renato Oliva. Circ: 5,000.

629.2 USA ISSN 0083-7229
HD9710.U5
WARD'S AUTOMOTIVE YEARBOOK. Text in English. 1938. a. USD 580 per issue; USD 910 combined subscription per issue (print & CD-ROM eds.) (effective 2011). bk.rev. charts; illus.; stat. index. **Document type:** *Yearbook, Trade.* **Description:** Comprehensive reference for vital industry statistics: U.S. and worldwide auto and truck production; sales by market segment, engine size, and model year; factory-installed equipment tables; vehicle registrations; supplier directory.
Related titles: CD-ROM ed.
—CCC.
Published by: Ward's Automotive Group (Subsidiary of: Penton Media, Inc.), 3000 Town Ctr, Ste 2750, Southfield, MI 48075. TEL 248-357-0800, FAX 248-357-0810, wards@wardsauto.com, http://www.wardsauto.com.

388.31 GBR ISSN 0267-8160
HE244.A15
WELSH TRANSPORT STATISTICS. Text in English. 1985. a. free (effective 2009). **Document type:** *Government.* **Description:** Designed to bring together the available information on transport in Wales from a number of sources and to cover a range of years in a single volume.
Related titles: Online - full text ed.
—BLDSC (9294.704200).
Published by: Welsh Assembly Government, Statistical Directorate, Cathays Park, Cardiff, CF10 3NQ, United Kingdom. TEL 44-1443-845500, stats.info.desk@wales.gsi.gov.uk, http://wales.gov.uk/?lang=en.

388 USA ISSN 0084-0572
WISCONSIN. DEPARTMENT OF TRANSPORTATION. DIVISION OF PLANNING AND BUDGET. HIGHWAY MILEAGE DATA. Text in English. 1946. a. **Document type:** *Government.*
Published by: Department of Transportation, Division of Planning, 4802 Sheboygan Ave, Rm 901, Madison, WI 53702-7913. TEL 608-266-3661. Circ: 200.

387.7 CAN ISSN 0084-1366
TL720.A1
WORLD AIR TRANSPORT STATISTICS. Text in English. 1956. a., latest 45th ed. USD 599 per issue includes CD-ROM (effective 2008). charts. back issues avail. **Document type:** *Report, Trade.* **Description:** Contains the latest figures on the world's airlines' traffic, capacity, financial results and operating fleet, provides a review of air transport development, gives detailed global statistics and lists individual IATA Member airlines' results and rankings.
Related titles: Online - full content ed.: USD 749 (effective 2008).
Published by: International Air Transport Association, 800 Place Victoria, PO Box 113, Montreal, PQ H4Z 1M1, Canada. TEL 514-390-6726, 800-716-6326, FAX 514-874-9659, sales@iata.org.

387 GBR ISSN 1364-9876
HE565.A3
WORLD CASUALTY STATISTICS. Text in English. 1891. a. **Document type:** *Report, Trade.* **Description:** Presents an annual statistical summary and listing of all merchant ships lost or reported broken.
Former titles (until 1995): Casualty Returns (0268-0815); (until 1985): Casualty Return Statistical Summary of Merchant Ships Totally Lost, Broken Up, Etc. (0261-2712); (until 1967): Casualty Return Statistical Summary (0008-7572); Merchant Ships Totally Lost, Broken Up, Etc.
—CCC.
Published by: Lloyd's Register - Fairplay Ltd., Lombard House, 3 Princess Way, Redhill, Surrey RH1 1UP, United Kingdom. TEL 44-1737-379000, FAX 44-1737-379001, info@lrfairplay.com.

387 GBR
HE563.A3
WORLD FLEET STATISTICS. Text in English. 1878. a., latest 2009. USD 590 per issue (effective 2010). charts. **Document type:** *Report, Trade.* **Description:** Contains tables and notes about vessels completed within the year, together with losses and disposals.
Formerly: Lloyd's Register of Shipping. Statistical Tables (0076-0234)
Related titles: Microfiche ed.: (from BHP).
Indexed: BMT.
—CCC.
Published by: Lloyd's Register - Fairplay Ltd., Lombard House, 3 Princess Way, Redhill, Surrey RH1 1UP, United Kingdom. TEL 44-1737-379000, FAX 44-1737-379001, info@lrfairplay.com.

388.411 CHE ISSN 0444-1419
WORLD ROAD STATISTICS. Text in English, French, German. 1964. a. CHF 320, EUR 200, USD 270 (effective 2008). **Document type:** *Bulletin, Trade.* **Description:** Presents statistical data on transport, road networks, traffic, accidents, taxation, production, imports and exports of motor vehicles, etc.
—BLDSC (9359.700000).
Published by: International Road Federation/Federation Routiere Internationale, Chemin de Blandonnet 2, Vernier, 1214, Switzerland. TEL 41-22-3060260, FAX 41-22-3060270, info@irfnet.org, http://www.irfnews.org.

387 GBR ISSN 1361-4665
WORLD SHIPBUILDING STATISTICS. Text in English. 1888. q. USD 815 per issue (effective 2009). **Document type:** *Journal, Trade.* **Description:** Provides statistical summaries of all self-propelled ships of 100 gross tonnage and above under construction or on order, including analyses by country of build, size, type and registration.
Former titles (until 1995): Merchant Shipbuilding Return (0261-1848); (until 1967): Merchant Shipbuilding
—CCC.
Published by: Lloyd's Register - Fairplay Ltd., Lombard House, 3 Princess Way, Redhill, Surrey RH1 1UP, United Kingdom. TEL 44-1737-379000, FAX 44-1737-379001, info@lrfairplay.com.

387 GBR ISSN 0959-7719
WORLD SHIPPING STATISTICS (YEAR). Text in English. 19??. a. USD 770 per issue (effective 2009). **Document type:** *Directory, Trade.* **Description:** Analyzes supply and demand and market prices in the shipping industry.
Formerly (until 1989): Fairplay World Shipping Statistics
—CCC.
Published by: Fairplay Publications Ltd., Lombard House, 3 Princess Way, Redhill, Surrey RH1 1UP, United Kingdom. TEL 44-1737-379000, FAX 44-1737-379001, sales@fairplay.co.uk, http://www.fairplay.co.uk.

380.5 ZMB ISSN 0514-5392
ZAMBIA. CENTRAL STATISTICAL OFFICE. TRANSPORT STATISTICS. Text in English. q. USD 4. **Document type:** *Government.*
Published by: Central Statistical Office, PO Box 31908, Lusaka, Zambia. TEL 260-1-211231.

TRANSPORTATION—Air Transport

387.7 GBR
A A I B RECOMMENDATIONS - C A A PROGRESS REPORT (YEAR). Text in English. 1990. a. free (effective 2010). back issues avail. **Document type:** *Government.* **Description:** Contains lists the year's AAIB recommendations and reports on CAA action taken.
Related titles: Online - full text ed.: free (effective 2010); ◆ Series: Air Traffic Control Licensing; ◆ Air Navigation - The Order and the Regulations; ◆ Great Britain. Civil Aviation Authority. Airport Surveys; ◆ Manual of Air Traffic Services - Part 1; ◆ Great Britain. Civil Aviation Authority. Mandatory Requirements for Airworthiness; ◆ Great Britain. Civil Aviation Authority. Approved Aerial Positions; ◆ Mandatory Aircraft Modifications and Inspections Summary; ◆ Civil Aircraft Airworthiness Information and Procedures; ◆ Air Traffic Services Engineering Requirements; ◆ Great Britain. Civil Aviation Authority. Annual Punctuality Statistics - Full Analysis (Year); ◆ Great Britain. Civil Aviation Authority. Annual Punctuality Statistics - Full and Summary Analysis (Year); ◆ United Kingdom Aeronautical Information Publication; ◆ Overseas Non-scheduled Flight Clearances Guide.
Published by: (Air Accidents Investigation Branch), Civil Aviation Authority, Printing and Publication Services, C A A House, 45-59 Kingsway, London, WCB2 6TE, United Kingdom. TEL 44-20-73797311, infoservices@caa.co.uk, http://www.caa.co.uk/. **Dist. by:** Westward Documedia Limited.

A D V - INFORMATIONSDIENST. *see* TRANSPORTATION—Abstracting, Bibliographies, Statistics

658 USA
HE9781
A G I F O R S ANNUAL SYMPOSIUM PROCEEDINGS. Text in English. 1961. a. back issues avail. **Document type:** *Proceedings, Academic/ Scholarly.*
Former titles (until 1979): A G I F O R S Proceedings; (until 1962): International Federation of Operational Research Societies. Airline Group. Proceedings (0538-7442)
Related titles: CD-ROM ed.: USD 100 per issue (effective 2011).
Published by: International Federation of Operational Research Societies, Airline Group, 270 Ferst Dr NW, Atlanta, GA 30332. TEL 404-385-7206, FAX 404-894-2760, johnpaul@gatech.edu, http://www.agifors.org. Circ: 300.

387.70971 CAN
A I P CANADA. (Aeronautical Information Products) Text in English. 1981. 7/yr. CAD 250 (effective 2006).
Supersedes in part: A I P Canada (English Edition) (0825-5229)
Published by: NAV Canada, PO Box 9840, Sta T, Ottawa, ON K1G 6S8, Canada. TEL 866-731-7827, FAX 866-740-9992, aeropubs@navcanada.ca.

629.1333430216 GBR
A I R. (Aerospace Information Redefined) Text in English. 1995. d. GBP 2,650 (effective 2010). **Document type:** *Journal, Trade.* **Description:** Provides a guide to the world's western-built commercial turboprop airliner fleets which are currently inactive.
Formed by the 200? merger of: Blue Print; Airliner Orders Backlog on Disk; Airclaims Space Intelligencer Newsletter; International Aircraft Price Guide; Turbine Airliner Fleet Survey; Airline Finance and Traffic; Jet Storage Update; Turboprop Storage Update (1366-6797)
Media: Online - full text.
Published by: Ascend Worldwide Ltd., Cardinal Point, Newall Rd, Heathrow Airport, London, TW6 2AS, United Kingdom. TEL 44-20-85646700, FAX 44-20-88970300, uk@ascendworldwide.com, http://www.ascendworldwide.com.

387.4 CAN ISSN 0256-3290
JX5763 .I57
A I R I M P - PASSENGER. (Air Reservations Interline Message Procedures) Text in English. 1977. a., latest 25th ed. USD 140 per issue includes CD-ROM (effective 2008). **Document type:** *Journal, Trade.* **Description:** The official source of passenger reservations interline message procedures used worldwide.
Published by: International Air Transport Association, 800 Place Victoria, PO Box 113, Montreal, PQ H4Z 1M1, Canada. TEL 514-390-6726, 800-716-6326, FAX 514-874-9659, sales@iata.org. Adv. contact Sandra Davies.

629.13 USA ISSN 1072-3145
A M T; the source for the professional maintenance team. (Aircraft Maintenance Technology) Text in English. 1989. 11/yr. USD 58 domestic; USD 74 in Canada & Mexico; USD 114 elsewhere; free to qualified personnel (effective 2009). adv. illus. Supplement avail.; back issues avail.; reprints avail. **Document type:** *Magazine, Trade.* **Description:** Provides in-depth coverage of the critical technical and professional issues facing today's technicians.
Formerly (until 1993): Aircraft Technician (1044-8012)
Related titles: Online - full text ed.: ISSN 2150-2064. free (effective 2009).
Indexed: A09, A10, A15, ABIn, B02, B15, B17, B18, G04, G08, I05, P16, P48, P51, P52, P53, P54, PQC, T02, V03, V04.
—CIS. **CCC.**
Published by: Cygnus Business Media, Inc., 1233 Janesville Ave, PO Box 803, Fort Atkinson, WI 53538. TEL 920-563-6388, 800-547-7377, FAX 920-563-1702, http://www.cygnusb2b.com. Pub. Jon Jezo TEL 920-568-8338. Adv. contact Denise Rimmer. B&W page USD 12,159, color page USD 13,484; trim 7.875 x 10.75. Circ: 42,165.

629.13 USA
A M T NEWSLETTER. (Aircraft Maintenance Technology) Text in English. m. free (effective 2005). **Document type:** *Newsletter.*
Media: E-mail.
Published by: Cygnus Business Media, Inc., 1233 Janesville Ave, PO Box 803, Fort Atkinson, WI 53538. TEL 920-563-6388, FAX 920-563-1702, http://www.cygnusb2b.com.

387.7 NLD ISSN 1872-5554
A O P A PILOTS & PLANES. Text in Dutch. 1979. 10/yr. EUR 60 (effective 2008). adv. **Document type:** *Magazine, Trade.*

Formerly (until 2005): A O P A Netherlands Bulletin (1385-0210)
Published by: Aircraft Owners and Pilots Association (A O P A) - Netherlands, Leidsevaart 594, Unit 121, Haarlem, 2014 HT, Netherlands. TEL 31-23-7114467, FAX 31-84-2296569, secretary@aopa.nl, http://www.aopa.nl. adv.: page EUR 615; bleed 240 x 340. Circ: 2,000.

A S U TRAVEL GUIDE; the airline employee's discount directory. (Airline Services Unlimited) *see* TRAVEL AND TOURISM

387.7 USA ISSN 1933-9933
HE9788.5.U5
A T A ECONOMIC REPORT. Text in English. 1937. a. USD 105 per issue to members; USD 150 per issue to non-members (effective 2011). back issues avail. **Document type:** *Report, Corporate.*
Former titles (until 2003): A T A Annual Report; (until 199?): Air Transport (0190-552X); (until 1971): Air Transport Facts & Figures; (until 196?): Facts & Figures. Air Transportation; (until 1963): Facts and Figures About Air Transport; (until 1960): Air Transport Facts and Figures; (until 1946): Air Transportation; (until 1945): Little Known Facts About the Scheduled Air Transport Industry
Related titles: Microfiche ed.: (from CIS); Online - full text ed.: free (effective 2011).
Indexed: SRI.
Published by: Air Transport Association of America, 1301 Pennsylvania Ave, N W, Ste 1100, Washington, DC 20004. ata@airlines.org. **Subscr. to:** ATA Distribution Center, PO Box 511, Annapolis, MD 20701.

ACCIDENT - INCIDENT REPORTING A D R E P. *see* TRANSPORTATION—Abstracting, Bibliographies, Statistics

AERO. *see* AERONAUTICS AND SPACE FLIGHT

387.742 DEU ISSN 0946-0802
AERO INTERNATIONAL; das Magazin der Zivilluftfahrt. Text in German. 1993. m. EUR 68.40; EUR 5.20 newsstand/cover (effective 2011). adv. **Document type:** *Magazine, Consumer.* **Description:** Contains information and features on civilian air transportation.
Published by: Jahr Top Special Verlag, Troplowitzstr 5, Hamburg, 22529, Germany. TEL 49-40-389060, FAX 49-40-38906300, info@jahr-tsv.de, http://www.jahr-tsv.de. Ed. Dietmar Plath. Adv. contact Klaus Macholz. Circ: 27,232 (paid).

387.7 USA
AERO TRADER. Text in English. 1978. m. **Document type:** *Magazine, Trade.*
Formerly: Aero Trader - Chopper Shopper
Related titles: Online - full text ed.
Published by: Trader Publishing Co., 150 Granby St, Norfolk, VA 23510. TEL 757-640-4020, http://www.traderonline.com/.

387.81 DEU
AEROMARKT. Text in German. 1988. m. EUR 12 domestic; EUR 33 foreign (effective 2008). adv. **Document type:** *Magazine, Trade.* **Description:** Provides an up-to-the-minute picture of the European aviation market.
Published by: Aeromarkt Verlag GmbH, Airport Center, 2 OG, Greven, 48268, Germany. TEL 49-2571-944610, FAX 49-2571-944614. Pub. Dieter Stricker. Adv. contact Horst Brinkmann. B&W page EUR 2,142, color page EUR 3,966; trim 192 x 267. Circ: 50,000 (paid and controlled).

387.7 056.1 MEX
AEROMEXICO ESCALA. Text in English, Spanish. 1989. m. USD 25 domestic; USD 60 in United States; USD 75 elsewhere. adv. illus. **Document type:** *Magazine, Consumer.* **Description:** Provides short, practical articles on a wide range of themes for passengers aboard AeroMexico flights.
Related titles: Online - full text ed.
Published by: (AeroMexico), Impresiones Aereas S.A. de C.V., Arquimides 5, Col Polanco, Mexico City, DF 11560, Mexico. TEL 52-5-7269060, FAX 52-5-7268968. Ed. Patricia Segura Barragan. Pub. Guillermo Perez Vargas. adv. contact Tato Sandoval Gutierrez. color page USD 13,200. Circ: 110,000.

387.7 056.1 MEX
AEROMEXICO PREMIER. Text in English, Spanish. 3/yr. illus. **Document type:** *Magazine, Consumer.*
Published by: Impresiones Aereas S.A. de C.V., Arquimides 5, Col Polanco, Mexico City, DF 11580, Mexico. TEL 52-5-7269060, FAX 52-5-7268968. adv.: color page USD 6,100; trim 10.81 x 8.81. Circ: 32,000 (controlled).

387.74 GBR
AERONAUTICAL INFORMATION CIRCULARS. Abbreviated title: A I C. Text in English. 19??. m. (13/yr.). looseleaf. **Document type:** *Government.* **Description:** Provides advanced warnings of impending operational changes and to add explanation or emphasis on matters of safety or operational significance.
Related titles: ◆ Issued with: United Kingdom Aeronautical Information Publication.
Published by: Civil Aviation Authority, Printing and Publication Services, C A A House, 45-59 Kingsway, London, WCB2 6TE, United Kingdom. TEL 44-20-73797311, FAX 44-20-74536097, infoservices@caa.co.uk. **Dist. by:** Westward Documedia Limited.

387.7 CAN ISSN 0443-7918
AERONAUTICAL INFORMATION SERVICES PROVIDED BY STATES/ AERONAVIGATSIONNOE OBSLUZHIVANIE, PREDOSTAVLYAEMOE GOSUDARSTVAMI/SERVICES D'INFORMATION AERONAUTIQUE ASSURES PAR LES ETATS/SERVICIOS DE INFORMACION AERONAUTICA SUMINISTRADOS POR LOS ESTADOS. Text in English, French, Russian, Spanish. 1960. irreg., latest 2000, 88th ed. USD 34 (effective 2000).
Published by: International Civil Aviation Organization (I C A O), External Relations and Public Information Office, 999 University St, Montreal, PQ H3C 5H7, Canada. TEL 514-954-8022, FAX 514-954-6769, icaohq@icao.int.

387.7 USA
AERONAUTICAL NEWSLETTER; New Jersey Aviation News. Text in English. 1989. m. free. bk.rev. 6 p./no. 3 cols./p.; Supplement avail. **Document type:** *Newsletter, Government.* **Description:** News of New Jersey events.
Published by: Department of Transportation, 1035 Parkway Ave, PO Box 610, Trenton, NJ 08625-0610. TEL 609-530-2915. Circ: 13,000 (paid).

387.7 FRA ISSN 0065-3721
AEROPORTS DE PARIS. RAPPORT DU CONSEIL D'ADMINISTRATION. Text in French. a. free.
Related titles: English ed.
Published by: Aeroports de Paris, Orly sud 103, Paris, Cedex 94396, France.

AEROPORTS DE PARIS. SERVICE STATISTIQUE. STATISTIQUE DE TRAFIC; resultats generaux. *see* TRANSPORTATION—Abstracting, Bibliographies, Statistics

387.736 FRA ISSN 1240-6309
AEROPORTS DE PARIS. TRAFIC DES PRINCIPAUX AEROPORTS MONDIAUX. Text in English, French. a.
Published by: Aeroports de Paris, Orly sud 103, Paris, Cedex 94396, France.

387.736 624 RUS
AEROPORTY. PROGRESSIVNYE TEKHNOLOGII/AIRPORTS. PROGRESSIVE TECHNOLOGIES. Text in Russian. q. **Document type:** *Magazine, Trade.* **Description:** Designed for the airport technology experts, it covers various aspects of airport construction technologies.
Published by: N P O Progresstekh, Mikrorayon im Y A Gagarina, korpus 124, Moscow, 105179, Russian Federation. mail@progresstech.ru, http://www.progresstech.ru. Ed. Nikolai Vasiliev. Circ: 1,000.

387.7 USA ISSN 1934-4015
TL553.5
AEROSAFETY WORLD. Text in English. 2006 (Jul.). m. free to members (effective 2010). adv. back issues avail.; reprints avail. **Document type:** *Magazine, Trade.* **Description:** Offers in-depth analysis of important safety issues facing the airline industry.
Formerly (until 2007): Aviation Safety World (1931-6135); Formed by the merger of (1987-2006): Accident Prevention (1057-5561); Which was formerly (until 1987): F S F Accident Prevention Bulletin (0898-5774); (1987-2006): Airport Operations (1057-5537); Which was formerly (until 1987): F S F Airport Operations Safety Bulletin (0898-574X); (1954-2006): Aviation Mechanics Bulletin (0005-2140); (1987-2006): Cabin Crew Safety (1057-5553); Which was formerly (until 1987): F S F Cabin Crew Safety Bulletin (0898-5758); (until 1975): Cabin Crew Safety Exchange; (1988-2006): Flight Safety Digest (1057-5588); Which was formerly (until 1988): F S F Flight Safety Digest (0898-5715); (until 1984): Flight Safety Digest (0736-7554); (until 1982): Flight Safety Facts and Reports (0098-7182); (until 1974): Flight Safety Facts and Analysis (0894-4571); (1987-2006): Helicopter Safety (1042-2048); Which was formerly (until 1987): F S F Helicopter Safety Bulletin (0898-8145); (until 1985): Helicopter Safety Bulletin (0361-5405); (1988-2006): Human Factors & Aviation Medicine (1057-5545); Which was formerly (until 1988): F S F Human Factors Bulletin & Aviation Medicine (0898-5723)
Related titles: Online - full text ed.: ISSN 1937-0830. free (effective 2010).
Indexed: HRIS, RefZh.
—BLDSC (0721.055000), IE, Ingenta.
Published by: Flight Safety Foundation, Inc., 601 Madison St, Ste 300, Alexandria, VA 22314. TEL 703-739-6700, FAX 703-739-6708, http://www.flightsafety.org. Pub. William R Voss. Adv. contact Arlene Braithwaite TEL 410-772-0820. page USD 2,835.

AIR AFFAIRS. *see* INSURANCE

387.7 GBR ISSN 0963-9993
AIR & BUSINESS TRAVEL NEWS. Text in English. 1965. w. free (effective 2009). adv. bk.rev. **Document type:** *Newsletter, Trade.* **Description:** Aimed at the professional traveler and travel market, mainly airlines and hotels.
Former titles: Air and Business Travel; Air Travel; Air Travel and Interline News (0262-4249); Interline and Air Travel News; Interline News
Related titles: Online - full text ed.: 1998.
Published by: Panacea Publishing International, 2nd Fl, Cardinal House, 39-40 Albemarle St, London, W1S 4TE, United Kingdom. TEL 44-20-76476363, enquiries@panaceapublishing.co.uk, http://www.panaceapublishing.com/. Circ: 13,000.

341.46 NLD ISSN 0927-3379
K1
➤ **AIR & SPACE LAW.** Text in English. 1974. bi-m. USD 671 to institutions; USD 823 combined subscription to institutions (print & online eds.) (effective 2011). bk.rev. illus. Index. back issues avail.; reprint service avail. from PSC. **Document type:** *Journal, Academic/Scholarly.* **Description:** Presents topical information on aviation policy, along with the civil, commercial, administrative and penal aspects of the study of air and space law.
Formerly (until 1992): Air Law (0165-2079)
Related titles: Online - full text ed.: ISSN 1875-8339. USD 621 to institutions (effective 2011).
Indexed: A01, A02, A03, A08, A22, A26, ABRCLP, AC&P, CA, CLI, E01, E08, ELJI, G01, G08, I05, L03, LRI, PAIS, RASB, S01, S09, T02.
—BLDSC (0774.131000), IE, Infotrieve, Ingenta, Linda Hall. **CCC.**
Published by: Kluwer Law International (Subsidiary of: Aspen Publishers, Inc.), PO Box 316, Alphen aan den Rijn, 2400 AH, Netherlands. TEL 31-172-641500, FAX 31-172-641555, sales@kluwerlaw.com, http://www.kluwerlaw.com.

387.7 GBR
AIR-BRITAIN AIRLINE FLEETS. Text in English. 19??. a. GBP 25 per issue to non-members; GBP 19.95 per issue to members (effective 2009). **Document type:** *Report, Trade.* **Description:** Contains airline fleet data worldwide on over 1500 operators in 166 countries.
Former titles (until 19??): Airline Fleets (0262-1657); (until 1980): World Airline Fleets Handbook
Published by: Air-Britain (Historians) Ltd., Victoria House, Stanbridge Park, Staplefield Ln, Staplefield, W Sussex RH17 6AS, United Kingdom. membership@air-britain.co.uk, http://www.air-britain.com. Ed. Pete Webber. **Subscr. to:** 41 Penshurst Rd, Leigh, Tonbridge, Kent TN11 8HL, United Kingdom. TEL 44-1732-835637, FAX 44-1732-835637, sales@air-britain.co.uk.

387.744 USA
AIR CARGO NEWS. Text in English. 1975. 12/yr. USD 39.95 (effective 2003). adv.
Published by: Air Cargo News, Inc., 343, Kew Gardens, NY 11415-0343. Ed., Pub. Geoffrey Arend TEL 718-479-0716. Circ: 42,000.

387.7 USA ISSN 0745-5100
HE9788
AIR CARGO WORLD; international trends and analysis. Text in English. 1910. m. USD 58 domestic; USD 78 foreign (effective 2007). adv. bk.rev. illus.; tr.lit. index. 64 p./no./3 cols./p.; reprints avail. **Document type:** *Magazine, Trade.* **Description:** International magazine devoted to the expeditious movement of goods and information. Serves the fields of transportation, physical distribution, courier and small package shipping, import-export and bulk freight traffic in industries utilizing air as a distribution vehicle.
Former titles (until 1983): Air Cargo Magazine (0148-7469); (until 1976): Cargo Airlift; Air Transportation (0002-2551)
Related titles: Microform ed.: (from PQC); Online - full text ed.: ISSN 1542-8591; International ed.: ISSN 1933-1614.
Indexed: A09, A10, A15, ABIn, B01, B02, B06, B07, B09, B15, B17, B18, BPI, BRD, C12, CA, CLT&T, G04, G06, G07, G08, HRIS, I02, I05, LogistBibl, M06, P48, P51, P52, PQC, T02, V03, V04, W01, W02, W03, W05.
—CIS. **CCC.**
Published by: U B M Aviation (Subsidiary of: United Business Media Limited), 3025 Highland Pkwy, Ste 200, Downer's Grove, IL 60515. TEL 630-515-5300, FAX 630-515-5301, http://www.ubmaviation.com. Ed. Simon Keeble. Circ: 41,000 (controlled).

388.044 387.744 GBR ISSN 1476-2684
AIR CARGO YEARBOOK (YEAR). Text in English. 2002. a. GBP 140 per issue (effective 2009). adv. **Document type:** *Directory, Trade.* **Description:** Contains information covering global air cargo developments, as well as directory listings, with contact details, of airports, airlines, cargo handling agents, general sales agents, plus manufacturers and suppliers of air cargo related equipment, systems and services.
Related titles: Online - full text ed.: GBP 100 (effective 2009).
—**CCC.**
Published by: Air Transport Publications Ltd., 16 Hampden Gurney St, London, W1H 5AL, United Kingdom. TEL 44-20-77243456, FAX 44-20-77242632. Adv. contact Rosa Bellanca. page GBP 3,250, page EUR 5,700, page USD 6,470; trim 203 x 280. Circ: 3,500.

AIR CARRIER INDUSTRY SCHEDULE SERVICE TRAFFIC STATISTICS. MEDIUM REGIONAL CARRIERS. *see* TRANSPORTATION—Abstracting, Bibliographies, Statistics

387.7 USA ISSN 0890-2925
HE9768
THE AIR CHARTER GUIDE. Text in English. 1987. s-a. USD 195 domestic; USD 205 foreign (effective 2011). **Document type:** *Handbook/Manual/Guide, Trade.* **Description:** Covers charter air industry, including plan, booking, catering, amenities, special needs, brokers, ambulance and cargo.
Related titles: Online - full content ed.
Published by: Penton Media, Inc., 10 Fawcett St, Ste 500, Cambridge, MA 02138. TEL 617-547-5811, FAX 617-868-5335.

AIR FRANCE MAGAZINE. *see* TRAVEL AND TOURISM

387.7029 USA ISSN 0092-2870
HE9788.5.U5
AIR FREIGHT DIRECTORY. Text in English. 1961. bi-m. USD 84 domestic; USD 106.50 foreign (effective 2000). adv. **Document type:** *Directory.* **Description:** Features comprehensive listing of ground transportation service points and rates.
Superseded: Air Freight Directory of Points in the United States Served Directly by Air and by Pick-up and Delivery Service and by Connecting Motor Carriers (0515-8125)
Published by: Air Cargo, Inc., 1819 Bay Ridge Ave, Annapolis, MD 21403. TEL 410-280-8911, FAX 410-268-3154. Ed., Pub., R&P, Adv. contact Valere A Zorn. Circ: 7,500.

AIR LINE PILOT; the magazine of professional flight deck crews. *see* AERONAUTICS AND SPACE FLIGHT

AIR MODELLER. *see* HOBBIES

387.74 341. GBR
AIR NAVIGATION - THE ORDER AND THE REGULATIONS. Text in English. 19??. base vol. plus irreg. updates. looseleaf. GBP 38.50 per issue (effective 2010). **Document type:** *Government.* **Description:** Publishes the provisions of the CAA regulations, the CAA schemes of charges, air navigation (Noise Certification) order, investigations of accidents regulations, and dangerous goods regulations.
Related titles: ◆ Series: United Kingdom Aeronautical Information Publication; ◆ Air Traffic Control Licensing; ◆ Great Britain. Civil Aviation Authority. Airport Surveys; ◆ Manual of Air Traffic Services - Part 1; ◆ Overseas Non-scheduled Flight Clearances Guide; ◆ Great Britain. Civil Aviation Authority. Approved Aerial Positions; ◆ Great Britain. Civil Aviation Authority. Mandatory Requirements for Airworthiness; ◆ Civil Aircraft Airworthiness Information and Procedures; ◆ A A I B Recommendations - C A A Progress Report (Year); ◆ Air Traffic Services Engineering Requirements; ◆ Great Britain. Civil Aviation Authority. Annual Punctuality Statistics - Full Analysis (Year); ◆ Great Britain. Civil Aviation Authority. Annual Punctuality Statistics - Full and Summary Analysis (Year); ◆ Mandatory Aircraft Modifications and Inspections Summary.
Published by: Civil Aviation Authority, Printing and Publication Services, C A A House, 45-59 Kingsway, London, WCB2 6TE, United Kingdom. TEL 44-20-7453-6088, FAX 44-20-74536097, infoservices@caa.co.uk. **Dist. by:** Westward Documedia Limited.

387.7 NZL ISSN 0065-4817
AIR NEW ZEALAND. ANNUAL REPORT. Text in English. 1965. a. free. charts; illus. 75 p./no.; back issues avail. **Document type:** *Corporate.*
Published by: Air New Zealand Ltd, Investor Relations, Private Bag 92007, Auckland, 1142, New Zealand. TEL 64-9-3362287, FAX 64-9-3362664, http://www.airnz.co.nz. Circ: 30,000.

341.46 USA
AIR SERVICE RIGHTS IN U S INTERNATIONAL AIR TRANSPORT AGREEMENTS. Text in English. a. USD 100 per issue to non-members; free to members (effective 2011). **Document type:** *Handbook/Manual/Guide, Corporate.* **Description:** Provides a compilation of air service rights provided by US international bilateral air transport agreements. The rights include both scheduled and charter air services.
Published by: Air Transport Association of America, 1301 Pennsylvania Ave, N W, Ste 1100, Washington, DC 20004. TEL 202-626-4260, http://www.airlines.org.

387.7 USA
AIR TRAFFIC CONTROL. Text in English. 19??. base vol. plus q. updates. looseleaf. back issues avail. **Document type:** *Handbook/ Manual/Guide, Government.* **Description:** Prescribes air traffic control procedures and phrases for air traffic controllers.
Related titles: Online - full text ed.: free (effective 2011).
Published by: U.S. Federal Aviation Administration, 800 Independence Ave, SW, Washington, DC 20591. TEL 202-267-8212, 866-835-5322, FAX 202-267-9463.

341.46 USA ISSN 0400-1915
AIR TRAFFIC CONTROL ASSOCIATION. BULLETIN. Text in English. 19??. m. free to members (effective 2010). **Document type:** *Bulletin, Trade.* **Description:** Provides information on activities of the association, its members, and important developments in the air traffic control industry.
Indexed: A28, APA, BrCerAb, C&ISA, CA/WCA, CIA, CerAb, CivEngAb, CorrAb, E&CAJ, E11, EEA, EMA, H15, M&TEA, M09, MBF, METADEX, SolStAb, T04, WAA.
—Linda Hall.
Published by: Air Traffic Control Association, Inc., 1101 King St, Ste 300, Arlington, VA 22314. TEL 703-299-2430, FAX 703-299-2437, info@atca.org.

387.74 GBR
AIR TRAFFIC CONTROL LICENSING. Variant title: Air Traffic Controllers - Licensing. Text in English. 1982. irreg., latest 2009. **Document type:** *Government.* **Description:** Contains requirements and guidance associated with the harmonised air traffic controller licence.
Related titles: Online - full text ed.: free (effective 2010); ◆ Series: Air Navigation - The Order and the Regulations; ◆ Great Britain. Civil Aviation Authority. Airport Surveys; ◆ Manual of Air Traffic Services - Part 1; ◆ Overseas Non-scheduled Flight Clearances Guide; ◆ Great Britain. Civil Aviation Authority. Mandatory Requirements for Airworthiness; ◆ Mandatory Aircraft Modifications and Inspections Summary; ◆ Civil Aircraft Airworthiness Information and Procedures; ◆ A A I B Recommendations - C A A Progress Report (Year); ◆ Air Traffic Services Engineering Requirements; ◆ Great Britain. Civil Aviation Authority. Annual Punctuality Statistics - Full Analysis (Year); ◆ Great Britain. Civil Aviation Authority. Annual Punctuality Statistics - Full and Summary Analysis (Year); ◆ United Kingdom Aeronautical Information Publication; ◆ Great Britain. Civil Aviation Authority. Approved Aerial Positions.
Published by: Civil Aviation Authority, Printing and Publication Services, C A A House, 45-59 Kingsway, London, WCB2 6TE, United Kingdom. TEL 44-20-73797311, FAX 44-20-74536097, infoservices@caa.co.uk. **Dist. by:** Westward Documedia Limited.

387.74 USA ISSN 1064-3818
TL725.3.T7 CODEN: ATCQER
➤ **AIR TRAFFIC CONTROL QUARTERLY**; an international journal of engineering and operations. Text in English. 1993. q. USD 220 in US & Canada to non-members; USD 270 elsewhere to non-members; USD 120 to members (effective 2010). back issues avail. **Document type:** *Journal, Academic/Scholarly.* **Description:** Focuses on combining rigorous scholarship with effective practical applications, both national and international in scope.
Related titles: Microform ed.: (from PQC).
Indexed: A28, APA, BrCerAb, C&ISA, CA/WCA, CIA, CerAb, CivEngAb, CorrAb, E&CAJ, E11, EEA, EMA, ESPM, EnvEAb, ErgAb, H15, HRIS, M&TEA, M09, MBF, METADEX, RefZh, SolStAb, T04, WAA.
—IE, Infotrieve, Ingenta, Linda Hall.
Published by: Air Traffic Control Association, Inc., 1101 King St, Ste 300, Arlington, VA 22314. TEL 703-299-2430, FAX 703-299-2437, info@atca.org.

387.74 629.136 GBR ISSN 0969-6725
AIR TRAFFIC MANAGEMENT. Text in English. 1993. q. GBP 349, EUR 520, USD 700 combined subscription (print & online eds.) (effective 2010). bk.rev. back issues avail. **Document type:** *Magazine, Trade.* **Description:** Provides the key decision makers and strategy advisers with the in-depth analysis and business information necessary for the global development of a modern ATC environment.
Related titles: Online - full text ed.
Indexed: A09, A10, A15, ABIn, B01, B02, B03, B04, B06, B07, B09, B11, B15, B17, B18, BPI, BRD, CA, G04, G06, G07, G08, I05, P34, P48, P51, P52, PQC, T02, T03, V03, V04, W01, W02, W03, W05.
—CIS, IE. **CCC.**
Published by: Key Publishing Ltd., PO Box 100, Stamford, PE9 1XQ, United Kingdom. TEL 44-1780-755131, FAX 44-1780-751323, info@keypublishing.com, http://www.keypublishing.com. Ed. Paul Hamblin. Pub. Adrian Cox. Adv. contact Chris Cope. Circ: 3,000.

629.1366025 GBR ISSN 1742-8378
AIR TRAFFIC MANAGEMENT DIRECTORY. Text in English. 199?. a. **Document type:** *Directory, Trade.*
Related titles: Online - full text ed.: free (effective 2010).
—CCC.
Published by: Key Publishing Ltd., PO Box 100, Stamford, PE9 1XQ, United Kingdom. TEL 44-1780-755131, FAX 44-1780-751323, info@keypublishing.com, http://www.keypublishing.com. Pub. Adrian Cox. Adv. contact Chris Cope.

387.74 GBR ISSN 1366-7041
AIR TRAFFIC TECHNOLOGY INTERNATIONAL. Text in English. 1997. a. (Sep.). free (effective 2010). **Document type:** *Magazine, Trade.* **Description:** Covers the latest and most innovative ATC technologies, products, services, simulation and training.
Related titles: Online - full text ed.
Indexed: HRIS.
—CCC.
Published by: U K & International Press (Subsidiary of: AutoIntermediates Ltd.), Abinger House, Church St, Dorking, Surrey RH4 1DF, United Kingdom. TEL 44-1306-743744, FAX 44-1306-887546, info@ukintpress.com, http://www.ukipme.com.

343.0978 GBR ISSN 1751-9098
AIR TRANSPORT. Variant title: Getting the Deal Through. Air Transport. Text in English. 2006. a. GBP 200 per issue (effective 2011). adv. back issues avail.; reprints avail. **Document type:** *Handbook/Manual/ Guide, Trade.* **Description:** Addresses the key issues of concern to corporations and their counsel regarding international air transport regulations.
Published by: (Global Arbitration Review), Law Business Research Ltd., 87 Lancaster Rd, London, W11 1QQ, United Kingdom. TEL 44-20-79081188, FAX 44-20-72296910, http://www.lbresearch.com/. Ed. Callum Campbell. Pub. Richard Davey.

387.7 CAN ISSN 0065-485X
AIR TRANSPORT ASSOCIATION OF CANADA. ANNUAL REPORT. Text in English. 1960. a. adv. **Document type:** *Corporate.*
Published by: Air Transport Association of Canada, 255 Albert St, Ste 1100, Ottawa, ON K1P 6A9, Canada. TEL 613-233-7727. Ed. Ian Anderson. R&P Michael Skrobica. Adv. contact Deborah Simpson. Circ: 2,000.

387.7 CAN ISSN 1719-9379
AIR TRAVEL COMPLAINTS REPORT (ONLINE). Text in English. 2000. s-a.
Formerly (until 2004): Air Travel Complaints Commissioner. Report (Online) (1498-1122)
Media: Online - full text. **Related titles:** ◆ Print ed.: Air Travel Complaints Report (Print). ISSN 1719-9352; French ed.: Plaintes Relatives au Transport Aerien. Rapport. ISSN 1719-9387.
Published by: Canadian Transportation Agency/Office des Transports du Canada, 15 Eddy St, Ottawa, ON K1A 0N9, Canada. TEL 819-953-8353, 888-222-2592, FAX 819-953-5686, cta.comment@cta-otc.gc.ca, http://www.cta-otc.gc.ca.

387.7 CAN ISSN 1719-9352
AIR TRAVEL COMPLAINTS REPORT (PRINT)/RAPPORT SUR LES PLAINTES RELATIVES AU TRANSPORT AERIEN. Text in English. 2000. s-a. **Document type:** *Report, Trade.*
Former titles (until 2004): The Air Travel Complaints Commissioner's Report (1910-1198); (until 2000): Report of the Air Travel Complaints Commissioner (1498-0975)
Related titles: ◆ Online - full text ed.: Air Travel Complaints Report (Online). ISSN 1719-9379.
Published by: Canadian Transportation Agency/Office des Transports du Canada, 15 Eddy St, Ottawa, ON K1A 0N9, Canada. TEL 819-953-8353, 888-222-2592, FAX 819-953-5686, cta.comment@cta-otc.gc.ca.

387.7 ZWE
AIR ZIMBABWE ANNUAL REPORT. Text in English. 1968. a. free. **Document type:** *Corporate.*
Formerly: Air Rhodesia Annual Report
Published by: Air Zimbabwe Corporation, Harare Airport, PO Box AP 1, Harare, Zimbabwe. TEL 263-4-575111, FAX 263-4-575068, TELEX 40008 ZW. Circ: 2,000.

387.7 AUS ISSN 1328-7192
AIRCARGO ASIA - PACIFIC. Text in English. 1990. 10/yr. AUD 82.50 domestic; USD 85 including Asia & New Zealand; USD 110 elsewhere (effective 2009). adv. back issues avail. **Document type:** *Magazine, Trade.* **Description:** Presents news, information and insights into current and potential sales opportunities throughout the world's airfreight and aviation industry.
Formerly (until 1992): Aircargo
Related titles: Online - full text ed.
Published by: Impact Publications, PO Box 1035, West Perth, W.A. 6872, Australia. TEL 61-8-93828388, FAX 61-8-93809974, info@impactpub.com.au. Ed. Chris Hurd. Adv. contact Sofia Hurd. color page AUD 3,850; trim 210 x 297. Circ: 3,000.

363.12 GBR ISSN 1367-5117
AIRCRAFT ACCIDENT REPORT. Text in English. irreg. back issues avail. **Document type:** *Government.*
Formerly: Civil Aircraft Accident Report
Related titles: Online - full text ed.
—BLDSC (0779.030000), IE, Ingenta.
Published by: Great Britain. Department for Transport. Air Accidents Investigation Branch, Berkshire Copse Rd., Aldershot, Hampshire GU11 2HH, United Kingdom. TEL 44-1252-510300, FAX 44-1252-376999, enquiries@aaib.gov.uk.

629.133 330 GBR
AIRCRAFT FINANCE; registration, security and enforcement. Variant title: Hames Aircraft Finance. Text in English. 1989. 3 base vols. plus updates 3/yr. looseleaf. GBP 1,785 base vol(s). domestic; EUR 2,357 base vol(s). in Europe; USD 3,068 base vol(s). elsewhere (effective 2011). **Document type:** *Journal, Trade.* **Description:** Provides country-by-country coverage of virtually every aspect of the relevant law.
Published by: Sweet & Maxwell Ltd. (Subsidiary of: Thomson Reuters Corp.), 100 Avenue Rd, London, NW3 3PF, United Kingdom. TEL 44-20-73937000, FAX 44-20-74491144, sweetandmaxwell.customer.services@thomson.com. Ed. Graham McBain. **Subscr. to:** PO Box 1000, Andover SP10 9AF, United Kingdom. TEL 44-20-73938051, sweetandmaxwell.international.queries@thomson.com.

387.7 GBR ISSN 2044-8015
AIRCRAFT FINANCE GUIDE. Abbreviated title: A F G. Text in English. 200?. a. GBP 55 per issue domestic; USD 110 per issue foreign (effective 2011). back issues avail. **Document type:** *Handbook/ Manual/Guide, Trade.* **Description:** Covers all areas of finance and leasing within the aviation market.
Formerly (until 2010): Guide to Financing & Investing in Aircraft, Engines & Airlines
Related titles: Online - full text ed.: ISSN 2044-8023. free (effective 2011).
Published by: U B M Aviation Publication Ltd., The OAG Bldg, Church St, Dunstable, Bedfordshire LU5 4HB, United Kingdom. TEL 44-1582-600111, FAX 44-1582-695230, http://www.ubmaviation.com. Ed. Jason Holland TEL 44-20-75794849. Pub. Simon Barker TEL 44-207-5794845.

346 629.133 330 GBR
AIRCRAFT LIENS AND DETENTION RIGHTS. Text in English. 1998. 2 base vols. plus updates 2/yr. looseleaf. GBP 1,250 base vol(s). domestic; EUR 1,651 base vol(s). in Europe; USD 2,148 base vol(s). elsewhere (effective 2011). **Document type:** *Handbook/Manual/ Guide, Trade.* **Description:** Covers the rights of third parties to seize and detain aircraft until unpaid debts are met or if aviation law has been infringed.
Published by: Sweet & Maxwell Ltd. (Subsidiary of: Thomson Reuters Corp.), 100 Avenue Rd, London, NW3 3PF, United Kingdom. TEL 44-20-73937000, FAX 44-20-74491144, sweetandmaxwell.customer.services@thomson.com. Ed. Graham McBain. **Subscr. to:** PO Box 1000, Andover SP10 9AF, United Kingdom. TEL 44-20-73938051, sweetandmaxwell.international.queries@thomson.com.

387.744065 GBR ISSN 1369-1031
AIRCRAFT MAINTENANCE & ENGINEERING DIRECTORY (YEAR). Text in English. 1997. a. GBP 140 per issue (effective 2009). adv. **Document type:** *Directory, Trade.* **Description:** Contains articles on worldwide MRO (maintenance, repair and overhaul) developments and industry reference information, together with data on the major players in the industry.
Related titles: Online - full text ed.: GBP 100 (effective 2009).
—CCC.
Published by: Air Transport Publications Ltd., 16 Hampden Gurney St, London, W1H 5AL, United Kingdom. TEL 44-20-77243456, FAX 44-20-77242632, info@airtransportpubs.com. Ed. Ian Harbison TEL 44-20-83542679. Adv. contact Jina Lawrence TEL 44-20-84056006. page GBP 3,250, page EUR 5,700, page USD 6,350; trim 203 x 280. Circ: 3,500.

387.7 CAN ISSN 1911-6314
AIRCRAFT MOVEMENT STATISTICS : N A V CANADA TOWERS AND FLIGHT SERVICE STATIONS. Text in English. 2007. m. free (effective 2010). back issues avail. **Document type:** *Report, Trade.*
Media: Online - full text.
Published by: Statistics Canada/Statistique Canada, 150 Tunney's Pasture Driveway, Ottawa, ON K1A 0T6, Canada. TEL 613-951-8116, 800-263-1136, FAX 613-951-0581, 877-287-4369, infostats@statcan.ca.

387.7 659.1 USA
AIRCRAFT OWNER; the monthly buyers guide for aviation products and services. Text in English. 2005 (Apr.). m. adv. **Document type:** *Magazine, Trade.* **Description:** Designed to be a complete buyer's guide for all aviation products and services, including new and used aircraft.
Address: 121 Fifth Ave, NW, New Brighton, MN 55112-3220. TEL 651-633-1045, FAX 651-636-6415. Pub. Greg Herrick TEL 651-638-8400. Adv. contacts Chris Jenks TEL 651-638-8432, Scott Plum TEL 651-638-8431. page USD 4,754; trim 10.875 x 16.75. Circ: 127,000.

AIRCRAFT TECHNOLOGY, ENGINEERING & MAINTENANCE. *see* AERONAUTICS AND SPACE FLIGHT

AIRCRAFT TYPE DESIGNATORS/DESIGNADORES DE TIPOS DE AERONAVE/INDICATIFS DE TYPE D'AERONEF. *see* AERONAUTICS AND SPACE FLIGHT

387.7 USA ISSN 1071-0655
TL501
AIRCRAFT VALUE NEWS. Text in English. 1989. bi-w. USD 1,573 (effective 2011). back issues avail. **Document type:** *Newsletter, Trade.*
Incorporates (in Aug.2005): Airline Business Report; Which was formerly (until 2004): Airline Financial News (1040-5410); Which incorporated (1991-2001): World Airline News (1059-4183); Former titles (until 1993): Aircraft Value Newsletter (1065-8688); (until 1992): Slipstream (0961-7388)
Related titles: Online - full text ed.
Indexed: A09, A10, A15, ABIn, B01, B03, B07, B11, I05, P16, P48, P51, P52, P53, P54, PQC, PROMT, V03, V04.
—CCC.
Published by: Access Intelligence, LLC (Subsidiary of: Veronis, Suhler & Associates Inc.), 4 Choke Cherry Rd, 2nd Fl, Rockville, MD 20850. TEL 301-354-2000, 800-777-5006, FAX 301-340-3819, clientservices@accessintel.com, http://www.accessintel.com. Ed. Paul Leighton TEL 44-1789-730498. Adv. contact Sarah Garwood TEL 301-354-1705.

AIRFINANCE ANNUAL; reference book on the aircraft financing markets. *see* BUSINESS AND ECONOMICS—Banking And Finance

387.7 332 GBR ISSN 0143-2257
HE9782
AIRFINANCE JOURNAL. Text in English. 1980. 10/yr. GBP 895 combined subscription domestic (print & online eds.); EUR 1,175 combined subscription in Europe (print & online eds.); USD 1,575 combined subscription elsewhere (print & online eds.) (effective 2010). adv. back issues avail. **Document type:** *Journal, Trade.* **Description:** Provides commercial airline industry investors, lessors, lawyers, and insurance firms with news and analysis.
Related titles: Online - full text ed.; Supplement(s): Airfinance Journal Business Handbook. ISSN 1351-4407. 1993.
Indexed: A09, A10, A12, A15, A17, A22, ABIn, B01, B02, B03, B04, B06, B07, B09, B11, B15, B17, B18, BPI, BRD, CLT&T, G04, G06, G07, G08, HRIS, I05, P34, P48, P51, P53, P54, PQC, RASB, T02, T03, V03, V04, W01, W02, W03, W05.
—IE, Infotrieve. **CCC.**
Published by: Euromoney Institutional Investor Plc., Nestor House, Playhouse Yard, London, EC4V 5EX, United Kingdom. TEL 44-20-77798673, information@euromoneyplc.com, http://www.euromoneyplc.com/. Ed. Sophie Segal TEL 44-20-77798853. Adv. contact Andrew Leggatt TEL 44-20-77798231. Circ: 2,920 (paid); 900 (controlled).

AIRFRAMER. *see* AERONAUTICS AND SPACE FLIGHT

387.742 USA ISSN 1542-4707
AIRGUIDE FOR THE FREQUENT FLYER; the best source for air travel. Text in English. 2002. q. free to qualified personnel (effective 2011). adv. back issues avail. **Document type:** *Magazine, Trade.* **Description:** Provides comprehensive information on all aspects of air travel for the business and corporate traveler.
Related titles: CD-ROM ed.: USD 59.95 (effective 2002); Online - full text ed.
Indexed: B01, B07.
Published by: Pyramid Media Group, One Penn Plz, Ste 6166, New York, NY 10119. TEL 212-626-9070, info@pyramid.ch, http://www.pyramid.ch.

387.7 USA
▼ **AIRINTEL MONTHLY.** Text in English. 2009. m. USD 260 (effective 2009). **Document type:** *Directory, Consumer.* **Description:** A listing of commercial aircraft available for private use.
Related titles: E-mail ed.: ISSN 2151-9811.
Published by: Commercial Aircraft Intelligence, Inc., 395 Taylor Blvd, Ste 101, Pleasant Hill, CA 94523. TEL 925-689-2402, tiernan@airintel.aero.

387.7 USA ISSN 1949-0674
▼ **AIRINTEL WEEKLY.** Text in English. 2009. w. free (effective 2009). **Document type:** *Newsletter, Trade.* **Description:** The week's top headlines, new aircraft listings, new engine listings, and upcoming events.
Media: Online - full content.
Published by: Commercial Aircraft Intelligence, Inc., 395 Taylor Blvd, Ste 101, Pleasant Hill, CA 94523. TEL 925-689-2402, tiernan@airintel.aero.

387.7 658 GBR ISSN 0268-7615
HE9781
AIRLINE BUSINESS; the voice of airline managements. Text in English. 1985. m. free to qualified personnel (effective 2010). adv. illus. back issues avail.; reprints avail. **Document type:** *Magazine, Trade.* **Description:** Dedicated to keeping senior airline executives updated with the latest industry trends and strategic thinking. Includes hard-edged profiles, interviews with key players worldwide, and comprehensive market analysis.
Related titles: Online - full text ed.
Indexed: A09, A10, A15, A22, A26, A28, ABIn, APA, B01, B02, B03, B06, B07, B09, B11, B15, B17, B18, BPI, BRD, BrCerAb, C&ISA, CA, CA/WCA, CIA, CLT&T, CerAb, CivEngAb, CorrAb, CurCont, E&CAJ, E08, E11, EEA, EMA, ESPM, EnvEAb, G04, G06, G07, G08, H&TI, H06, H15, HRIS, Hospl, I05, M&TEA, M09, MBF, METADEX, P10, P34, P48, P51, P52, P53, P54, PQC, S09, SCOPUS, SolStAb, T02, T03, T04, V03, V04, W01, W02, W03, W05, WAA.
—BLDSC (0784.505000), CIS, IE, Infotrieve, Ingenta, Linda Hall. **CCC.**
Published by: Reed Business Information Ltd. (Subsidiary of: Reed Business), Quadrant House, The Quadrant, Sutton, Surrey SM2 5AS, United Kingdom. TEL 44-20-86523500, FAX 44-20-86528932, rbi.subscriptions@qss-uk.com, http://www.reedbusiness.co.uk/. Ed. Mark Pilling TEL 44-20-86524993. adv.: page GBP 7,055; bleed 200 x 273. Circ: 22,999. **Subscr. to:** Quadrant Subscription Services, Rockwood House, 9-17 Perrymount Rd, Haywards Heath, W. Sussex RH16 3DH, United Kingdom. TEL 44-845-0777744, FAX 44-845-6760030, qss.customer.services@quadrantsubs.com, http://www.quadrantsubs.com.

388.044658 387.744658 GBR ISSN 1478-5358
AIRLINE CARGO MANAGEMENT. Text in English. 2002 (Oct.). q. free to qualified personnel (effective 2009). adv. **Document type:** *Magazine, Trade.* **Description:** Examines the relationship between airlines and their customers, as well as the on-airport business relationship between airports and specialist cargo handlers that serve them.
Related titles: Online - full text ed.: free to qualified personnel (effective 2009).
—CCC.
Published by: Air Transport Publications Ltd., 16 Hampden Gurney St, London, W1H 5AL, United Kingdom. TEL 44-20-77243456, FAX 44-20-77242632, info@airtransportpubs.com, http://www.airtransportpubs.com/. Ed. Alex Lennane. Adv. contact Rosa Bellanca. page GBP 2,950, page EUR 5,160, page USD 5,750; trim 203 x 280. Circ: 7,000.

387.7 CAN ISSN 1013-4050
TL512
AIRLINE CODING DIRECTORY. Text in English. 1988. 2/yr. (in June & Dec.). USD 330 (effective 2008). **Document type:** *Directory, Trade.* **Description:** The official industry source for airline designators, location identifiers and three-digit airline numeric codes. Includes ISO currency and country codes.
Related titles: Diskette ed.; Magnetic Tape ed.
Published by: International Air Transport Association, 800 Place Victoria, PO Box 113, Montreal, PQ H4Z 1M1, Canada. TEL 514-390-6726, 800-716-6326, FAX 514-874-9659, sales@iata.org. Adv. contact Sandra Davies.

387.7 330.9 CAN
AIRLINE ECONOMIC RESULTS AND PROSPECTS. Text in English. a. **Description:** Offers an overview of the economic performance of the industry with a detailed analysis of cost trends by route area for specified periods.
Related titles: Online - full content ed.
Published by: International Air Transport Association, 800 Place Victoria, PO Box 113, Montreal, PQ H4Z 1M1, Canada. TEL 514-390-6726, 800-716-6326, FAX 514-874-9659, sales@iata.org.

387.74 658 GBR ISSN 1757-8833
AIRLINE FLEET MANAGEMENT; independent analysis for operators of, and investors in, aircraft & airlines. Text in English. 1998. bi-m. GBP 150 domestic; USD 300 in United States; GBP 170 elsewhere (effective 2009). back issues avail. **Document type:** *Magazine, Trade.* **Description:** Designed for aircraft owners, operators and lessors and everything that may affect the day-to-day running of their businesses.
Former titles (until 2008): Airline Fleet & Network Management (1753-8106); (until 2004): Airline Fleet & Asset Management (1466-3767); (until 1999): Airline Fleet Management (1464-6846)
Related titles: Online - full text ed.: ISSN 1757-8841. free (effective 2009); Supplement(s): The Operators' Guide; Financing & Investing in Aircraft & Engines; The M R O Yearbook.
Indexed: APA, C&ISA, CorrAb, E&CAJ, EEA, SolStAb, WAA.
—Linda Hall.
Published by: U B M Aviation Publication Ltd., The OAG Bldg, Church St, Dunstable, Bedfordshire LU5 4HB, United Kingdom. TEL 44-1582-600111, FAX 44-1582-695230, http://www.ubmaviation.com. Ed. Daniella Horwitz TEL 44-20-75794847. Pub. Simon Barker TEL 44-207-5794845. Circ: 10,000.

387.74 USA
AIRLINE FLEETS WORLD REVIEW. Text in English. 19??. a. USD 59.95 combined subscription (print, online & CD-ROM eds.) (effective 2011). adv. **Document type:** *Magazine, Trade.* **Description:** Provides comprehensive information on all major international airlines.
Former titles (until 1999): Airline Fleets; World Airline Fleets Handbook
Related titles: CD-ROM ed.; Online - full text ed.
Published by: Pyramid Media Group, One Penn Plz, Ste 6166, New York, NY 10119. TEL 646-808-9057, 212-626-9070, info@pyramid.ch.

387.74 GBR ISSN 2040-476X
AIRLINE GROUND SERVICES. Text in English. 2007. q. GBP 30 domestic; EUR 48 in Europe; USD 60 in United States (effective 2009). adv. back issues avail. **Document type:** *Magazine, Trade.* **Description:** Aimed at airline ground handling procurement departments and focuses on the business aspects of handling passengers and freight, with particular emphasis on growth strategies and managing the pressures on the handling industry.
Formerly (until 2009): Airline Handling International (1754-1174)
Published by: E V A International, Chestnut, PO Box 632, Waltham Cross, EN8 1EG, United Kingdom. TEL 44-1992-424193, FAX 44-1992-313002, advertising@evaint.com, http://evaint.com. Ed. Jo Murray. Pub. Steve Murray.

387.7 USA ISSN 0095-4683
HE9768
AIRLINE HANDBOOK. Text in English. 1972. a. USD 16. illus.
Published by: AeroTravel Research Publications, PO Box 3694, Cranston, RI 02910. TEL 401-941-6140. Ed. Paul K Martin.

387.7 USA
AIRLINE INDUSTRIAL RELATIONS CONFERENCE. NEWSLETTER. Text in English. bi-m.
Published by: Airline Industrial Relations Conference, 1300 19th St NW, Ste. 750, Washington, DC 20036-1651. TEL 202-861-7550.

387.7 332 USA
THE AIRLINE INDUSTRY: AN INDUSTRY OVERVIEW. Text in English. 1990. a. **Description:** Features an analysis of the top 25 airlines including an overview of financial conditions.
Published by: Dun & Bradstreet Information Services (Subsidiary of: Dun & Bradstreet, Inc.), 103 JFK Pkwy, Short Hills, NJ 07078. TEL 973-921-5500, 800-234-3867, SMSinfo@dnb.com, http://www.dnb.com.

387.7 GBR
AIRLINE INDUSTRY INFORMATION. Abbreviated title: A I I. Text in English. 19??. d. GBP 200 (effective 2010). back issues avail. **Document type:** *Journal, Trade.* **Description:** Provides a timely overview into the worldwide airlines and its related industries.
Media: Online - full text. **Related titles:** Fax ed.
Indexed: A15, G07.
Published by: M2 Communications Ltd., PO Box 4030, Bath, BA1 0EE, United Kingdom. TEL 44-20-70470200, FAX 44-20-70570200, info@M2.com.

387.74 USA
AIRLINE MONITOR; a review of trends in the airline and commercial jet aircraft industries. Text in English. 1988. m. USD 1,100; USD 1,300 combined subscription (print & online eds.) (effective 2010). back issues avail. **Document type:** *Magazine, Trade.* **Description:** Serves as a source for forecasting airline and commercial aircraft market trends.
Related titles: Online - full text ed.
Indexed: HRIS.
Published by: E S G Aviation Services, PO Box 1781, Ponte Vedra Beach, FL 32004. TEL 904-249-4215, FAX 904-249-5893. Ed., Pub. Edmund S Greanslet.

387.7 ESP
AIRLINE NINETY TWO; revista de aviacion comercial y aeropuertos. Text in Spanish. 1989. m. adv. bk.rev. illus.; bibl.; charts; maps; stat. 84 p./no.; back issues avail. **Document type:** *Magazine, Trade.* **Description:** Concerns commercial aviation and airsport for the Spanish and Latin American markets.
Published by: Grupo Edefa S.A., C Puerto Principe No. 3-B 1o.-A, Madrid, 28043, Spain. TEL 34-91-38219445, edefa@edefa.com, http://www.edefa.es. Ed. Javier Taibo. Pub. Vicente Talon. Adv. contact Eva Cervera. B&W page USD 1,850, color page USD 3,225; trim 210 x 310. Circ: 15,000.

338 USA ISSN 1945-1822
HE9780
AIRLINE PROCUREMENT; global supply issues, logistics and technology for the airline industry. Text in English. 2007. bi-m. USD 34 domestic; USD 45 in Canada; USD 49 elsewhere (effective 2009). adv. **Document type:** *Magazine, Trade.* **Description:** Focuses on the issues of supplier relationship management, supply chain management, alliance purchasing, parts and materials, vendor relationships, procurement at the OEM, technology integration, new purchasing technology software and more.
Indexed: APA, C&ISA, CorrAb, E&CAJ, EEA, SolStAb, WAA.
Published by: A T W Media Group (Subsidiary of: Penton Media, Inc.), 8380 Colesville Rd, Ste 700, Silver Spring, MD 20910. TEL 301-650-2420, FAX 301-650-2434. Pub. William A Freeman III. adv.: B&W page USD 4,300, color page USD 3,813; trim 7.75 x 10.75.

387.7 USA
AIRLINE REVIEW; the world's fastest growing airline magazine. Text in English. 2002. m. USD 39.99 domestic; USD 54.99 in Canada; USD 69.99 elsewhere (effective 2004). adv. **Document type:** *Magazine, Trade.* **Description:** Provides insight, reviews and in-depth analysis for airline professionals and avid enthusiasts worldwide.
Published by: Airline Press, Inc., 1900 Van Buren St, Ste 321, Hollywood, FL 33020. Pub. Phil Bertasevic. adv.: color page USD 1,150; trim 9 x 12. Circ: 8,500 (paid and controlled).

387.7 GBR ISSN 1745-6355
AIRLINE YEARBOOK (YEAR). Text in English. 2004. a. GBP 140 per issue (effective 2009). adv. **Document type:** *Yearbook, Trade.* **Description:** Contains information covering global airline developments, as well as directory listings, with contact details, of airlines, ground handling agents and manufacturers and suppliers of airline-related equipment, systems and services.
—CCC.
Published by: Air Transport Publications Ltd., 16 Hampden Gurney St, London, W1H 5AL, United Kingdom. TEL 44-20-77243456, FAX 44-20-77242632, info@airtransportpubs.com. Adv. contact Rosa Bellanca. page GBP 3,250, page EUR 5,700, page USD 6,470; trim 203 x 280.

363.124105 GBR
AIRLINER LOSS RATES (CD-ROM). Abbreviated title: A L R. Text in English. 200?. a. GBP 630 per issue (effective 2009). **Document type:** *Report, Trade.*
Media: CD-ROM.
Published by: Ascend Worldwide Ltd., Cardinal Point, Newall Rd, Heathrow Airport, London, TW6 2AS, United Kingdom. TEL 44-20-85646700, FAX 44-20-88970300, uk@ascendworldwide.com.

387.7 629.133 GBR
AIRLINER WORLD; the global airline scene. Text in English. 1999. m. GBP 41 includes domestic & USA; GBP 51 elsewhere; GBP 4.20 per issue (effective 2010). adv. charts; illus.; stat. back issues avail.; reprints avail. **Document type:** *Magazine, Consumer.* **Description:** Offers insight into all aspects of commercial aviation worldwide.
Published by: Key Publishing Ltd., PO Box 300, Stamford, Lincs PE9 1NA, United Kingdom. info@keypublishing.com, http://www.keypublishing.com. Ed. Tony Dixon. Adv. contact Andrew Mason.

387.7 629.13 USA ISSN 0896-6575
AIRLINERS; the world's airline magazine. Text in English. 1988. bi-m. USD 26.95 domestic; CAD 40.95 in Canada (effective 2009). adv. bk.rev. illus. back issues avail.; reprints avail. **Document type:** *Magazine, Trade.* **Description:** Presents news, air transport trends, articles, and photography for commercial aviation enthusiasts.
Indexed: CLT&T, HRIS.
Published by: Airliners Publications LLC, PO Box 668336, Miami, FL 33166. TEL 305-871-4561. Ed. Dwayne Darnell. Circ: 45,000 (paid).

AIRLINERS IN SERVICE AROUND THE WORLD SERIES. *see* AERONAUTICS AND SPACE FLIGHT

AIRLINERTECH SERIES. *see* AERONAUTICS AND SPACE FLIGHT

387 CAN
AIRLINES INTERNATIONAL. Text in English. 1966. bi-m. free. **Document type:** *Magazine, Trade.* **Description:** Designed to inform airline management, industry associates and government officials on key air transport priorities and IATA projects and services.
Former titles (until 1994): I A T A Review (0376-642X); I A T A News Review (0085-199X)
Published by: International Air Transport Association, 800 Place Victoria, PO Box 113, Montreal, PQ H4Z 1M1, Canada. TEL 514-390-6726, FAX 514-874-9659, sales@iata.org. Circ: 8,000.

387.71 CAN
AIRPORT AND AIR NAVIGATION CHARGES MANUAL. Text in English. 6-8/yr), base vol. plus irreg. updates. looseleaf. USD 640 per issue to non-members; USD 350 per issue to members (effective 2008). **Document type:** *Handbook/Manual/Guide, Trade.* **Description:** Details the airport and navigation charges made by over 200 national and supra-national authorities world-wide: landing fees, passenger services charges, parking, terminal navigation, noise, security and en route navigation charges.
Related titles: CD-ROM ed.; Online - full content ed.
Published by: International Air Transport Association, 800 Place Victoria, PO Box 113, Montreal, PQ H4Z 1M1, Canada. TEL 514-390-6726, 800-716-6326, FAX 514-874-9659, sales@iata.org. Ed. Johanna Ruttner.

387.736 CAN
AIRPORT CHARACTERISTICS DATA BANK. VOLUME 1 - SUMMARY AND EXPLANATION. Text in English, French, Spanish, Russian. a. USD 19; USD 436 for vols. 1-6. **Description:** Contains all the information users need to understand the I.C.A.O. Airport Data Bank.
Related titles: Diskette ed.
Published by: International Civil Aviation Organization (I C A O), External Relations and Public Information Office, 999 University St, Montreal, PQ H3C 5H7, Canada. TEL 514-954-8022, FAX 514-954-6769, icaohq@icao.int.

387.736 CAN
AIRPORT CHARACTERISTICS DATA BANK. VOLUME 2 - INDIAN OCEAN REGION. Text in English, French, Spanish, Russian. a. USD 50; USD 436 for vols. 1-6. **Description:** Provides information on airport facilities in and off the coast of Africa.
Related titles: Diskette ed.
Published by: International Civil Aviation Organization (I C A O), External Relations and Public Information Office, 999 University St, Montreal, PQ H3C 5H7, Canada. TEL 514-954-8022, FAX 514-954-6769, icaohq@icao.int.

387.736 CAN
AIRPORT CHARACTERISTICS DATA BANK. VOLUME 3 - CARIBBEAN AND SOUTH AMERICAN REGIONS. Text in English, French, Spanish, Russian. a. USD 56; USD 436 for vols. 1-6. **Description:** Provides information on the main airports in South America and the Caribbean.
Related titles: Diskette ed.
Published by: International Civil Aviation Organization (I C A O), External Relations and Public Information Office, 999 University St, Montreal, PQ H3C 5H7, Canada. TEL 514-954-8022, FAX 514-954-6769, icaohq@icao.int.

387.736 CAN
AIRPORT CHARACTERISTICS DATA BANK. VOLUME 4 - EUROPEAN REGION. Text in English, French, Russian, Spanish. a. USD 168; USD 436 for vols. 1-6. **Description:** Provides information on the facilities of the main European airports.
Related titles: Diskette ed.
Published by: International Civil Aviation Organization (I C A O), External Relations and Public Information Office, 999 University St, Montreal, PQ H3C 5H7, Canada. TEL 514-954-8022, FAX 514-954-6769, icaohq@icao.int.

387.736 CAN
AIRPORT CHARACTERISTICS DATA BANK. VOLUME 5 - MIDDLE EAST AND ASIA REGIONS. Text in English, French, Russian, Spanish. a. USD 77; USD 436 for vols. 1-6. **Description:** Provides information on facilities of the main airports in Asia and the Middle East.
Related titles: Diskette ed.
Published by: International Civil Aviation Organization (I C A O), External Relations and Public Information Office, 999 University St, Montreal, PQ H3C 5H7, Canada. TEL 514-954-8022, FAX 514-954-6769, icaohq@icao.int.

387.736 CAN
AIRPORT CHARACTERISTICS DATA BANK. VOLUME 6 - NORTH ATLANTIC, NORTH AMERICAN AND PACIFIC REGIONS. Text in English, French, Russian, Spanish. a. USD 66; USD 436 for vols. 1-6. **Description:** Provides information on facilities at the main airports in North America, as well as the North Atlantic and Pacific regions.
Related titles: Diskette ed.

TU

Published by: International Civil Aviation Organization (I C A O), External Relations and Public Information Office, 999 University St, Montreal, PQ H3C 5H7, Canada. TEL 514-954-8022, FAX 514-954-6769, icaohq@icao.int.

387.74 CAN ISSN 0256-3193
AIRPORT HANDLING MANUAL. Text in English. a. USD 310 per issue (effective 2008). **Document type:** *Handbook/Manual/Guide, Trade.* **Description:** Contains recommended industry procedures covering load control, aircraft handling messages, standard delay codes, aircraft loading and departure control systems.
—CCC.
Published by: International Air Transport Association, 800 Place Victoria, PO Box 113, Montreal, PQ H4Z 1M1, Canada. TEL 514-390-6726, 800-716-6326, FAX 514-874-9659, sales@iata.org. Adv. contact Sandra Davies.

387.7 USA
AIRPORT HIGHLIGHTS. Text in English. 1964. 12/yr. USD 495 to individuals; USD 125 to libraries. adv. bk.rev. **Document type:** *Newsletter.* **Description:** Contains the latest airport news, regulatory and Congressional developments, domestic and international aviation news, industry issues, and employment and business opportunities.
Published by: Airports Council International - North America, 1775 K St, N W, Ste 500, Washington, DC 20006. TEL 202-293-8500, FAX 202-331-1362. Ed., R&P Juliet C Wright. Adv. contact Evangeline Premdas. Circ: 2,000.

387.736 USA
AIRPORT IMPROVEMENT. Text in English. 2008. bi-m. free in North America to qualified personnel (effective 2009). **Document type:** *Magazine, Trade.* **Description:** Focuses on airport construction. Targets airport management, consultants, architects, engineers, planners and government officials.
Published by: Chapel Road Communications, LLC, 3780 Chapel Rd, Brookfield, WI 53045. TEL 262-510-7832, FAX 262-439-2978. Ed. Rebecca Douglas. Pub. Paul Bowers. Circ: 5,200 (controlled).

387.736 USA
AIRPORT JOURNAL. Text in English. m. USD 17. adv.
Address: PO Box 273, Clarendon Hills, IL 60514-0273. TEL 630-986-8132. Ed. John S Andrews. Circ: 26,500.

387.7 USA ISSN 1048-2091
TL725.A1
AIRPORT MAGAZINE. Text in English. 1989. 7/yr. USD 50 domestic; USD 100 elsewhere (effective 2010). adv. illus. index. back issues avail.; reprints avail. **Document type:** *Magazine, Trade.*
Related titles: Online - full text ed.: free (effective 2010).
Indexed: HRIS.
Published by: American Association of Airport Executives, 601 Madison St, Ste 400, Alexandria, VA 22314. TEL 703-824-0504, FAX 703-820-1395, http://www.aaae.org/. Ed. Barbara Cook TEL 703-824-0500 ext.133. Adv. contact Greg Mihelic. page USD 6,400; trim 8.375 x 10.875.

387 USA ISSN 1041-8318
AIRPORT NOISE REPORT. Text in English. 1989. w. USD 624 (effective 2004). **Document type:** *Newsletter, Trade.* **Description:** Contains valuable insight into noise problems at airports throughout the country and finds effective ways to deal with noise problems through in-depth coverage, timely reporting of federal, state, local, and international developments, and incisive analysis of events.
—CCC.
Address: 43978 Urbancrest Ct, Ashburn, VA 20147. TEL 703-729-4867, FAX 703-729-4528.

387.7 USA
AIRPORT PRESS. Text in English. 1978. m. USD 32 domestic; USD 48 foreign (effective 2002). adv. 24 p./no. 4 cols./p.; back issues avail. **Document type:** *Newspaper, Trade.* **Description:** Provides news and information of interest to the US and overseas airport community.
Indexed: CLT&T, HRIS.
Address: PO BOX 300879, J F K STA, Jamaica, NY 11430. TEL 718-244-6788, 800-982-5832, FAX 718-995-3432, airprtpres@aol.com, http://www.airportpress.com. Ed. Dick Eisley. Pub., R&P William Puckhaber. Adv. contact Thomas Middlemiss. B&W page USD 2,450, color page USD 3,200; trim 10.75 x 15. Circ: 18,000 (controlled).

387.7 USA ISSN 0044-7021
AIRPORT REPORT. Text in English. 1954. s-m. looseleaf. USD 100 (effective 2001). adv. bk.rev. illus. **Document type:** *Report, Trade.*
Published by: American Association of Airport Executives, 601 Madison St, Ste 400, Alexandria, VA 22314. TEL 703-824-0504, FAX 703-820-1395, http://www.aaae.org/. Ed. Holly Ackerman. Adv. contact Michelle McCatty. Circ: (controlled).

AIRPORT REVENUE NEWS. *see* BUSINESS AND ECONOMICS—Production Of Goods And Services

387.736 NZL ISSN 1176-9432
AIRPORT TIMES; keeping the Auckland Airport community informed. Text in English. 2001. m.
Related titles: Online - full text ed.: free.
Published by: Auckland International Airport Ltd., PO Box 73020, Auckland Airport, New Zealand. TEL 64-9-2568899, FAX 64-9-2755835, admin@akl-airport.co.nz.

AIRPORT WILDLIFE MANAGEMENT. *see* ENVIRONMENTAL STUDIES

387.7 GBR ISSN 1360-4341
HE9791.A1
AIRPORT WORLD. Text in English. 1995. bi-m. EUR 80, USD 119.50; free to qualified personnel (effective 2009). adv. illus. back issues avail. **Document type:** *Magazine, Trade.* **Description:** Contains interviews with airport executives and general features on safety, technology, business management.
Formerly (until 1996): Airlines International (1360-6387)
Related titles: Online - full text ed.: free (effective 2009).
Indexed: CLT&T, HRIS.
—CCC.
Published by: (Airports Council International CHE), Insight Media Ltd., 26-30 London Rd, Twickenham, Mddx TW1 3RW, United Kingdom. TEL 44-20-88910123. Eds. Joe Bates TEL 44-208-8317507, Joe Bates TEL 44-208-8317507. Adv. contact Sev Fevzi TEL 44-208-8317508.

387.736 GBR ISSN 2045-9181
AIRPORT YEARBOOK (YEAR). Text in English. 1996. a. GBP 140 per issue (effective 2011). adv. back issues avail. **Document type:** *Directory, Trade.* **Description:** Contains information covering airport developments around the world as well as directory listings, with contact details, of airports, manufacturers and suppliers of equipment, systems and services, organisations and associations, and airport authorities.
Former titles (until 2010): Airport Equipment & Services Buyers' Guide (1750-693X); (until 2006): Airport Yearbook (1369-1023)
—CCC.
Published by: Air Transport Publications Ltd., 16 Hampden Gurney St, London, W1H 5AL, United Kingdom. TEL 44-20-77243456, FAX 44-20-77242632, info@airtransportpubs.com. Adv. contact Rosa Bellanca.

387.7 USA ISSN 1044-9469
AIRPORTS. Text in English. 1985. w. 4 p./no.; **Document type:** *Newsletter, Trade.* **Description:** Aimed at airport managers, users, and suppliers. Subjects covered include noise abatement, landing rights, curfews, franchise and rental fees, regulation, funding, FAA grants.
Related titles: Online - full text ed.: ISSN 1930-9430.
Indexed: B16, P10, P13, P48, P53, P54, PQC.
—CIS. **CCC.**
Published by: Aviation Week Group (Subsidiary of: McGraw-Hill Companies, Inc.), 2 Penn Plz, 25th Fl, New York, NY 10121. TEL 800-525-5003, FAX 888-385-1428, buccustserv@cdsfulfillment.com, http://www.aviationweek.com. Eds. Benet Wilson, Jim Matthews. Circ: 6,000 (paid).

387.7 NLD ISSN 1877-2196
AIRSPACE. Text in English. 2008. q. adv. **Document type:** *Journal, Trade.*
Related titles: Online - full text ed.: ISSN 1877-220X.
Published by: CANSO, The Civil Air Navigation Services Organisation, Transpolis Schipol Airport, Polaris Ave 85e, Hoofddorp, 2132 JH, Netherlands. TEL 31-23-5685380, FAX 31-23-5685389, info@canso.org. Eds. Robert Hutchison, Tim Hoy.

387.7 JAM
AIRTEAM CIRCLE. Text in English. s-a. adv.
Published by: Airports Authority of Jamaica, 64 Knutsford Blvd, Kingston, 5, Jamaica. TEL 809-92-61622. Ed. Trevor Spence.

387.7 629.133 USA ISSN 1074-4320
HE9761.1
AIRWAYS; a global review of commercial flight. Text in English. 1994. m. USD 39.95 domestic; USD 69 foreign; USD 5.99 newsstand/cover domestic; USD 6.99 newsstand/cover in Canada (effective 2007). adv. charts; illus. 80 p./no.; back issues avail. **Document type:** *Magazine, Consumer.* **Description:** Contains information for people interested in commercial air transport, concerning airlines, aircraft, personalities and airports.
Published by: Airways International, Inc., PO Box 1109, Sandpoint, ID 83864-0872. TEL 208-263-2098, FAX 208-263-5906, airways@nidlink.com. Ed. John Wegg. R&P, Adv. contact Seija Wegg TEL 208-683-6009. color page USD 3,995. Circ: 40,000 (paid). **Dist. by:** Eastern News Distributors Inc., 3360 Industrial Rd., Harrisburg, PA 17110-2933. TEL 800-221-3148; **Dist. in UK by:** Comag, Tavistock Rd, W Drayton, Middlesex UB7 7QE, United Kingdom. TEL 44-1895-444055, FAX 44-1895-433602.

387.7 GBR ISSN 2045-1105
▼ **AIRWAYS**; real pilots read. Text in English. 2009. bi-m. free (effective 2010). back issues avail. **Document type:** *Magazine, Consumer.*
Media: Online - full text.
Published by: British Airways Virtual, c/o British Airways Plc, Waterside, PO Box 365, Harmondsworth, UB7 0GB, United Kingdom. Ed. Christopher Elliot.

387.7 USA ISSN 1547-8785
AIRWAYS CLASSICS. Text in English. 2003. a. USD 6.95 newsstand/cover (effective 2003).
Published by: Airways International, Inc., PO Box 1109, Sandpoint, ID 83864-0872. TEL 208-263-2098, FAX 208-263-5906. Ed. John Wegg.

387.7 USA
ALL AMERICAN AVIATION ASSOCIATION NEWS. Text in English. 1992. q. USD 50 to members (effective 1998). **Document type:** *Newsletter.* **Description:** Addresses aviation employment issues of interest to African Americans, including historical topics.
Published by: All American Aviation Association, PO Box 5793, Englewood, NJ 07631. TEL 201-568-8145. Ed., Pub. Eddie R Hadden.

387.7 USA
AMERICA'S FLYWAYS. Text in English. 1992. m. USD 17.95 to non-members; free to members (effective 2005). **Document type:** *Newsletter, Trade.*
Formerly: Aviators Journal
Published by: U.S. Pilots Association, 2637 East Air Lane, Phoenix, AZ 85034. TEL 602-275-1016, FAX 602-275-2152. Pub. Arvin C Schultz. Circ: 100,000 (paid).

387.7 GBR ISSN 1479-2729
ANALYSIS & AIRPROX IN U K AIRSPACE. (United Kingdom) Text in English. 1998. s-a. back issues avail. **Document type:** *Government.*
Formed by the merger of (1996-1998): U K Airprox (P) Involving Commercial Air Transport (1365-7453); Which was formerly (until 1996): U K Airmisses Involving Commercial Air Transport (1460-8928); (until 1988): U K Airmiss Statistics (0951-6301); (1996-1998): Aircraft Proximity Reports. A I R P R O X (C) - Controller Reported (1365-6260); Which was formerly (until 1996): Aircraft Proximity Hazards (0960-9261)
Related titles: CD-ROM ed.: ISSN 1479-2737; Online - full text ed.: free (effective 2010).
Published by: Civil Aviation Authority, Printing and Publication Services, C A A House, 45-59 Kingsway, London, WCB2 6TE, United Kingdom. TEL 44-20-73797311, FAX 44-20-74536097, infoservices@caa.co.uk, http://www.caa.co.uk/. **Dist. by:** Westward Documedia Limited.

ANDREWS LITIGATION REPORTER: AVIATION. *see* LAW

387.7 ESP
ANUARIO DE LA AVIACION COMERCIAL ESPANOLA. Text in Spanish. 1996. a. EUR 5 per issue (effective 2009). adv. **Document type:** *Catalog, Consumer.*
Related titles: ◆ Supplement to: Avion Revue Internacional. ISSN 1887-8997.
Published by: Motorpress Iberica (Subsidiary of: Gruner + Jahr AG & Co), Ancora 40, Madrid, 28045, Spain. TEL 34-91-3470100, FAX 34-91-3470152, http://www.motorpress-iberica.es. Circ: 7,000 (paid).

387.742 051 CYP
APOLLO EXECUTIVE REVIEW. Text in English. 1982. q. adv. bk.rev. illus. back issues avail. **Document type:** *Magazine, Consumer.* **Description:** Functions as Cyprus Airways's business-class in-flight magazine.
Formerly: Executive Review (Nicosia) (1016-1147)
Published by: Action Publications Ltd, PO Box 24676, Nicosia, 1302, Cyprus. TEL 357-2-590555, FAX 357-2-590048. Ed. Dina Wilde TEL 357-2-590555. R&P Tony Christodoulou. Adv. contact Oriana Patala. Circ: 12,000 (controlled).

ARAB AVIATION REVIEW; an air transport and aerospace quarterly magazine. *see* AERONAUTICS AND SPACE FLIGHT

387.7 TWN ISSN 1021-3740
ASIAN AIR TRANSPORT. Text in Chinese, English. 1988. m. USD 80. adv. **Document type:** *Magazine, Trade.*
Indexed: CLT&T.
Published by: Tzeng Brothers Information Group, P.O. Box 43-345, 7G-09 World Trade Ctr., Taipei, 105, Taiwan. TEL 886-2-725-1904, FAX 723-8898. Ed. Robert Tzeng. Adv. contact Jack Lee. B&W page USD 2,500, color page USD 4,000; trim 248 x 180. Circ: 11,750.

387.7 629.1 MYS
ASIAN AIRLINES & AEROSPACE. Text in English. m. adv.
Published by: A D P R Consult (M) Sdn. Bhd., 10-F, Bangunan Koperasi Polis, No. 1, Jln. Sulaiman, Kuala Lumpur, 50000, Malaysia. TEL 3-273-1355, FAX 3-2735318. Ed. R Sachi Thananthan. Adv. contact R Vellayutham. B&W page USD 2,600, color page USD 3,500; trim 285 x 210. Circ: 7,225.

387.7 MYS
ASIAN COMMERCIAL AVIATION. Text in English. q. **Document type:** *Magazine, Trade.*
Published by: S H P Media Sdn Bhd., C-17-1, 17th Fl., Block C, Megan Phileo Ave., 12, Jalan Yap Kwan Seng, PO Box 10836, Kuala Lumpur, 50726, Malaysia. TEL 60-3-21660852 ext 5175, FAX 60-3-2161-0541, info@shpmedia.com, http://www.shpmedia.com/. Ed. Adlan Lufti Abas.

387.7 USA
ATLANTIC FLYER. Text in English. m. USD 16.50; USD 75 foreign. adv. **Document type:** *Newspaper, Trade.* **Description:** Features aviation news and history of interest to general-aviation pilots, historians, and restorers of antique aircraft; lists aviation events.
Related titles: Online - full text ed.
Address: PO Box 668, Litchfield, CT 06759-0668. TEL 203-266-7947, FAX 203-266-7946. Ed., R&P, Adv. contact Jacquelyn Lanpher. Circ: 84,000.

387.71 CAN ISSN 0708-9058
ATLANTIC PILOTAGE AUTHORITY. ANNUAL REPORT. Text in English. 1973. a.
Published by: Atlantic Pilotage Authority, Cogswell Tower, Suite 910, 2000 Barrington St, Halifax, NS B3J 3K1, Canada. TEL 902-426-2550, FAX 902-426-4004.

AUDITS OF AIRLINES, WITH CONFORMING CHANGES. *see* INSURANCE

387.7 AUS ISSN 0727-338X
AUSTRALIAN AIR PILOT. Variant title: Air Pilot. Text in English. 1952. s-a. free to members (effective 2008). adv. bk.rev. illus. **Document type:** *Magazine, Trade.* **Description:** Focuses on improvement of employment conditions for members, to protect the entitlements that pilots already possess, and provides a forum for pilots to meet and discuss aviation and industrial matters.
Published by: Australian Federation of Air Pilots, 6th Fl, 132-136 Albert Rd, South Melbourne, VIC 3205, Australia. TEL 61-3-99285737, FAX 61-3-96998199, admin@afap.org.au, http://www.afap.org.au. Ed. Terry O'Connell. Circ: 5,000 (controlled).

AUSTRALIAN PILOT. *see* AERONAUTICS AND SPACE FLIGHT

AVIACION GENERAL Y DEPORTIVA. *see* SPORTS AND GAMES

387.7 910.09 IND ISSN 0970-3578
HE9761.1
AVIATION & SPACE JOURNAL. Text in English. 1977. q. charts; illus.; stat. reprints avail. **Document type:** *Journal, Trade.* **Description:** Devoted to air transport, travel and tourism, as well as the trade fair and hotel industries.
Related titles: Online - full text ed.: free (effective 2011).
Published by: V.J. Joseph Ed. & Pub., 2nd Fl., Orange House, 41 Hamam St, Mumbai, Maharashtra 400 001, India. TEL 91-22-22653187, FAX 91-22-22655691.

387.7 USA
AVIATION BUSINESS JOURNAL. Text in English. 1969. m. USD 20 to non-members; free to members (effective 2005). adv. charts; illus.; stat.; tr.lit. 56 p./no.; reprints avail. **Document type:** *Newsletter, Trade.*
Former titles: N A T A News (1060-4340); (until 1988): AirTran News
Published by: National Air Transportation Association, 4226 King St, Alexandria, VA 22302-1507. TEL 703-845-9000, FAX 703-845-8176. Ed., R&P Clifton Stroud. Circ: 3,000 (paid).

387.7 FRA ISSN 1248-9980
AVIATION CIVILE. Text in French. 1993. bi-m. EUR 26 (effective 2009). **Document type:** *Magazine.*
Published by: Direction Generale de l'Aviation Civile, Bureau des Publications, 50 Rue Henry Farman, Paris, 75720 Cedex 15, France. TEL 33-1-58094616, FAX 33-1-58094280.

THE AVIATION CONSUMER. *see* AERONAUTICS AND SPACE FLIGHT

387.7 USA ISSN 0193-4597
TL501
AVIATION DAILY; the business daily of the airline industry since 1939. Text in English. 1973 (vol.205). d. (excluding saturday). looseleaf. USD 1,985 domestic; USD 2,185 foreign (effective 2009); includes Airports. charts; stat. 8 p./no.; reprints avail. **Document type:** *Newsletter, Trade.* **Description:** Contains news, data and analytics on the global commercial airline industry.
Incorporates: Regional Aviation Weekly; Formerly: American Aviation Daily
Related titles: E-mail ed.: USD 1,785 (effective 2009); Online - full text ed.: USD 1,785 (effective 2009).
Indexed: A15, ABIn, G08, I05, M06, P02, P27, P47, P48, P51, P54, PQC. —CIS. **CCC.**
Published by: Aviation Week Group (Subsidiary of: McGraw-Hill Companies, Inc.), 1200 G St, NW, Ste 900, Washington, DC 20005. TEL 202-383-2374, FAX 202-383-2438, buccustserv@cdsfulfillment.com. Eds. Darren Shannon, Jim Matthews. Circ: 20,000 (paid).

629.132 FRA ISSN 1252-6096
AVIATION & PILOTE. Text in French. 1973. m. EUR 75 domestic; EUR 97 foreign (effective 2009). adv. bk.rev. **Description:** Addresses business and general aviation. Deals with transportation, schooling, flight test report, travel, technology and safety.
Former titles: Aviation et Pilote Prive; Pilote Prive; Aero-Club et le Pilote Prive
Published by: Societe d'Edition et d'Exploitation de Supports, Aerodrome de Lognes-Emerainville, Lognes, 77185, France. TEL 1-64-62-05-06, FAX 1-64-62-11-09. Ed. Philippe De Segovia. Pub., R&P Jacques Callies. Adv. contact Laurent Galili. Circ: 15,000.

387.7 USA ISSN 0887-9877
HD9711.A1
AVIATION INTERNATIONAL NEWS; the newsmagazine of corporate, business and regional aviation. Text in English. 1972. m. (14/yr.). USD 74.99 domestic; USD 79.99 in Canada & Mexico; USD 149.99 elsewhere (effective 2005). adv. bk.rev. illus. back issues avail. **Document type:** *Magazine, Trade.* **Description:** Reports on news and developments in the world of business and regional commercial aviation. Includes news of new aircraft.
Formerly: Aviation Convention News (0164-9906)
Related titles: Online - full text ed.
Indexed: CLT&T, HRIS.
Published by: Convention News Co., Inc., 214 Franklin Ave, PO Box 277, Midland Park, NJ 07432. TEL 201-444-5075, FAX 201-444-4647, http://www.aionline.com. Ed. R Randall Padfield. Pub. Wilson Leach. R&P Mary Ann Albert. Adv. contact John McCarthy. Circ: 35,000 (controlled). **Subscr. to:** Circulation Dept., 81 Kenosia Ave, Danbury, CT 06810. TEL 203-798-2400, FAX 203-798-2104.

341.46 USA
AVIATION LAW REPORTER. Text in English. 5 base vols. plus bi-w. updates. looseleaf. USD 2,425 base vol(s).; USD 3,996 combined subscription print, online & CD-ROM eds. (effective 2004). **Description:** Authoritative source for aviation-related court cases, laws and regulations since 1947, and is a must-have for aviation corporate executives, legal counsel, airlines and aircraft manufacturers.
Formerly: Aviation Law Reports (0273-7310)
Related titles: CD-ROM ed.: USD 2,380 (effective 2004); Online - full content ed.: USD 2,590 (effective 2004).
—CCC.
Published by: C C H Inc. (Subsidiary of: Wolters Kluwer N.V.), 2700 Lake Cook Rd, Riverwoods, IL 60015. TEL 847-267-7000, 800-449-6439, cust_serv@cch.com, http://www.cch.com. Pub. Stacey Caywood.

341.756 USA ISSN 1938-7032
AVIATION LITIGATION QUARTERLY. Text in English. 2000. q. free to members (effective 2007). back issues avail. **Document type:** *Newsletter, Trade.*
Formerly (until 2000): Committee on Aviation Litigation. Newsletter
Related titles: Online - full text ed.: ISSN 1938-7040.
Indexed: A01, L03.
Published by: American Bar Association, Section of Litigation, 321 N Clark St, Chicago, IL 60610. TEL 312-988-5000. Eds. Frederick Alimonti, Jonathan Stern.

AVIATION MEDICINE. *see* MEDICAL SCIENCES

341.46 CAN
AVIATION REGULATORY WATCH GROUP REPORTS. Text in English. 1988. a. **Description:** Reports on regulatory changes in the US, Europe, Latin America, Asia, Africa and the Middle East and the effects those changes have on the global aviation system.
Formerly: Aviation Regulatory Watch Reports
Published by: International Air Transport Association, 800 Place Victoria, PO Box 113, Montreal, PQ H4Z 1M1, Canada. TEL 514-390-6726, 800-716-6326, FAX 514-874-9659, sales@iata.org, http://www.iata.org.

AVIATION SAFETY. *see* AERONAUTICS AND SPACE FLIGHT

387.736 GBR ISSN 1352-0148
AVIATION SECURITY INTERNATIONAL. Short title: A S I. Text in English. 1995. bi-m. GBP 45; GBP 60 foreign. adv. bk.rev. back issues avail. **Document type:** *Magazine, Trade.* **Description:** Focuses on security arrangements followed by major airlines and airports, including various technologies and products in use.
Related titles: Online - full text ed.
—IE, Infotrieve. **CCC.**
Published by: Halldale Publishing & Media Ltd., 84 Alexandra Rd, Farnborough, Hants GU14 6DD, United Kingdom. TEL 44-1252-517974, FAX 44-1252-512714, http://www.halldale.com/. Ed. Phillip Baum. Pub., R&P, Adv. contact Andrew Smith. B&W page GBP 1,595, color page GBP 2,190; trim 278 x 209. Circ: 9,500 (controlled).

387.7 GBR ISSN 1463-9254
AVIATION STRATEGY. Text in English. 1997. m. GBP 420, EUR 600, USD 650 (effective 2009). 24 p./no. 2 cols./p.; back issues avail. **Document type:** *Newsletter, Corporate.* **Description:** Designed for high level executives within airline industry.
Related titles: Online - full content ed.
Indexed: CLT&T, HRIS.
—CCC.
Published by: Aviation Economics, First Fl, James House, 22-24 Corsham St, London, N1 6DR, United Kingdom. TEL 44-20-74905215, FAX 44-20-74905218, info@aviationeconomics.com, http://www.aviationeconomics.com.

387.7 USA ISSN 1075-1378
HE9804.A2
AVIATION TELEPHONE DIRECTORY. EASTERN, WESTERN, SOUTHWESTERN AND NORTH CENTRAL STATES. Text in English. 1949. a. USD 18.95 (effective 2000). adv. **Document type:** *Directory.*
Former titles: Aviation Telephone Directory: Pacific and Western States; (until 1979): Pacific Coast Aviation Directory
Published by: Aviation Telephone Directory, 6619 Tumbleweed Ridge Ln., Unit 102, Henderson, NV 89015-1464. TEL 714-816-1040. Ed. Nancy Wettlin. Pub., R&P, Adv. contact Jodi Sacco. Circ: 7,500.

387.7 USA ISSN 1075-136X
HE9812.A2
AVIATION TELEPHONE DIRECTORY. WESTERN & NORTHCENTRAL STATES. Text in English. 1949. a. USD 29.95 (effective 2000). adv. **Document type:** *Directory.*
Published by: Aviation Telephone Directory, 6619 Tumbleweed Ridge Ln., Unit 102, Henderson, NV 89015-1464. TEL 714-816-1040. Ed. Nancy Wettlin. Pub., R&P, Adv. contact Jodi Sacco. Circ: 7,500.

AVIATOR'S GUIDE. *see* TRAVEL AND TOURISM

387.7 RUS
AVIATRANSPORTNOE OBOZRENIE/AIR TRANSPORT OBSERVER. Text in Russian. 1996. bi-m. USD 24 domestic; USD 36 foreign (effective 2004). **Document type:** *Journal, Trade.*
Published by: Redaktsiya Zhurnala Aviatransportnoe Obozrenie, ul Usacheva, dom 35, ofis 709, PO Box 127, Moscow, 119048, Russian Federation. TEL 7-095-9265356, FAX 7-095-9330297.

387.7 ESP ISSN 1887-8997
AVION REVUE INTERNACIONAL. Text in Spanish. 1982. m. illus. **Document type:** *Magazine, Consumer.*
Former titles (until 2000): Avion Revue (1887-9004); (until 1999): Avion Revue Internacional (1887-9055)
Related titles: ◆ Supplement(s): Anuario de la Aviacion Comercial Espanola.
Published by: Motorpress Iberica (Subsidiary of: Gruner + Jahr AG & Co), Ancora 40, Madrid, 28045, Spain. TEL 34-91-3470100, FAX 34-91-3470152, http://www.motorpress-iberica.es. Circ: 27,500 (paid and controlled).

387.7 358.4 FRA ISSN 1243-8650
AVIONS. Text in French. 1993. bi-m. back issues avail. **Document type:** *Magazine, Consumer.*
Published by: Lela Presse, 29 Rue Paul Bert, Outreau, 62230, France. TEL 33-3-21338896, FAX 33-3-21320039, lela.presse@wanadoo.fr. Ed. Christophe Cony.

387.7 GBR
B A A ANNUAL REPORT. Text in English. 1966. a., latest 2007. free (effective 2009). illus. **Document type:** *Corporate.*
Former titles: B A A Reports and Accounts (1351-4849); Great Britain. British Airports Authority. Annual Report and Accounts (0068-1229)
Related titles: Online - full text ed.
Published by: B A A plc., 130 Wilton Rd, London, SW1V 1LQ, United Kingdom. baamediacentre@baa.com, http://www.baa.com.

387.71 629.132 BEL
B A R T INTERNATIONAL. (Business Aviation & Regional Transport) Short title: B A R T. Text in English. 1989. bi-m. USD 80 for 2 yrs. (effective 2005). adv. bk.rev.; video rev. bibl.; illus.; mkt.; stat. back issues avail. **Document type:** *Magazine, Trade.* **Description:** Promotes business and corporate aviation. Covers the top 200 European aircraft companies and operations.
Formerly: Business Aviation and Regional Transport (0776-7595); Which incorporates: European Avianews (0778-7502); Which was formerly (until 1991): Avianews International (0772-876X); (1972-1982): Avianews
Published by: Aerospace Resource Group, Rue Ste Gertrude 12b, Nivelles, 1400, Belgium. TEL 326-784-3299, FAX 326-784-3599. Ed. Didier Daoust. Pub., R&P, Adv. contact Fernand M Francois TEL 326-484-9450. B&W page USD 2,864, color page USD 5,516; trim 210 x 285. Circ: 4,686 (paid); 5,858 (controlled).

387.7 658.3 DNK ISSN 1604-9020
B L 8-10 AARSRAPPORT/DANISH MANDATORY OCCURRANCE REPORTING. Variant title: B L Otte-ti Aarsrapport. Text in Danish, English. 2003. a. **Document type:** *Yearbook, Government.*
Formerly (until 2005): Flyvesikkerhedsmaessige Begivenheder Indrapporteret til SLV (1604-1089)
Related titles: Online - full text ed.
Published by: Statens Luftfartsvaesen/Danish Civil Aviation Administration, Ellebergvej 50, Copenhagen SV, 2450, Denmark. TEL 45-36-186000, FAX 45-36-186001, dcaa@slv.dk. Circ: 500.

B S P DATA INTERCHANGE SPECIFICATIONS HANDBOOK. (Billing and Settlement Plans) *see* BUSINESS AND ECONOMICS—Banking And Finance

387.74 DEU
BERLINER FLUGHAEFEN. Text in German. 1952. 4/yr. free (effective 2009). bk.rev. abstr.; mkt. **Document type:** *Bulletin, Consumer.* **Description:** Contains schedules of flights of the Berlin-Tegel, Berlin-Schoenefeld and Berlin Tempelhof airports. Also includes airport information.
Former titles (until 1999): Berlin-Flugplan (0005-9242); (until 1967): Berliner Gesamt-Flugplan
Published by: Berliner Flughafen Gesellschaft mbH, Pressestelle, Flughafen Schoenefeld, Berlin, 12521, Germany. TEL 49-1805-000186, FAX 49-30-60911643, pressestelle@berlin-airport.de, http://www.berlin-airport.de. Circ: 50,000 (controlled).

387.7 FRA ISSN 1761-9238
BLEU CIEL. Text in French. 2003. s-a. EUR 39 for 2 yrs. (effective 2007). **Document type:** *Magazine, Consumer.*
Published by: Bleu Ciel Editions, Espace Aff Air, Aeroport Angers-Marce, Marce, 49140, France. TEL 33-2-41605592, FAX 33-2-41605621, http://www.bleu-ciel-editions.com.

BOLETIN ESTADISTICO DE TRAFICO AEREO INTERNACIONAL. *see* TRANSPORTATION—Abstracting, Bibliographies, Statistics

387.7 GBR
BRITISH AIRWAYS NEWS. Text in English. 1940. w. free to qualified personnel. adv. bk.rev. illus. **Document type:** *Newsletter.*
Former titles (until 197?): B O A C News; B O A C Review (0005-3252)
Published by: British Airways plc., Waterside, PO Box 365, Harmondsworth, UB7 0GB, United Kingdom. http://www.britishairways.com/. Circ: 57,000.

BUILD THE RED BARON'S FIGHTER PLANE. *see* HOBBIES

387.7 GBR ISSN 2042-7212
▼ **BUSINESS AIRPORT INTERNATIONAL.** Text in English. 2009. q. free to qualified personnel (effective 2010). adv. back issues avail. **Document type:** *Magazine, Trade.* **Description:** Contains reviews of selected FBOs and general and business aviation airports.
Related titles: Online - full text ed.: free (effective 2010).
Published by: U K I P Media & Events Ltd. (Subsidiary of: AutoIntermediates Ltd.), Abinger House, Church St, Dorking, Surrey RH4 1DF, United Kingdom. TEL 44-1306-743744, FAX 44-1306-887546, info@ukintpress.com. Eds. Lzzy Kington, Anthony James. Adv. contact Simon Hughes.

BUSINESS AVIATION INSIDER. *see* AERONAUTICS AND SPACE FLIGHT

387.7 330 USA ISSN 1554-1339
BUSINESS JET TRAVELER. Text in English. 2003. bi-m. USD 37.50 in US & Canada; USD 49.50 elsewhere (effective 2005). adv. **Document type:** *Magazine, Trade.*
Published by: Convention News Co., Inc., 214 Franklin Ave, PO Box 277, Midland Park, NJ 07432. TEL 201-444-5075, FAX 201-444-4647. Ed. R Randall Padfield. Adv. contact Anthony Romano. B&W page USD 6,975, color page USD 8,275; trim 10.875 x 14.5.

338.6 GBR ISSN 1350-1623
BUSINESS LIFE; your essential executive toolkit. Text in English. 1986 (Feb.). m. GBP 26 domestic; GBP 67 in Australia & New Zealand; GBP 36 elsewhere (effective 2010). adv. **Document type:** *Magazine, Consumer.* **Description:** Aims to entertain and inform the BA business passenger by putting a business twist on lifestyle subjects (film, music, sport etc) and by adding a lifestyle twist to business subjects.
Published by: (British Airways), Cedar Communications, 85 Strand, London, WC2R 0WD, United Kingdom. TEL 44-20-75508019, 44-20-75508000, info@cedarcom.co.uk, http://www.cedarcom.co.uk/. adv.: page GBP 7,300; trim 210 x 289. Circ: 95,697.

BYWAYS (FAIRFAX). *see* TRAVEL AND TOURISM

387 GBR
C A A SPECIFICATIONS. Text in English. 19??. irreg., latest vol.22, 2005. price varies. back issues avail. **Document type:** *Bulletin, Government.* **Description:** Covers detailed specifications on aircraft safety devices.
Published by: Civil Aviation Authority, Printing and Publication Services, C A A House, 45-59 Kingsway, London, WCB2 6TE, United Kingdom. TEL 44-20-73797311, FAX 44-20-74536097, infoservices@caa.co.uk. **Dist. by:** Westward Documedia Limited.

387.7 USA ISSN 1947-4547
▼ **C J.** (Citation Jet) Text in English. 2009. 3/yr. USD 19.95; USD 4.50 per issue (effective 2011). adv. **Document type:** *Magazine, Trade.* **Description:** Features all aspects of citation ownership and operation.
Published by: Village Press, Inc., 2779 Aero Park Dr, PO Box 968, Traverse City, MI 49685. TEL 231-946-3712, 800-327-7377, FAX 231-946-3289, info@villagepress.com, http://www.villagepress.com. Adv. contact John Shoemaker TEL 231-946-3712.

387.7 USA
C N S FOCUS. Text in English. 1986. 4/yr. membership. adv. **Document type:** *Newsletter, Trade.*
Indexed: CLT&T, HRIS.
Published by: Cargo Network Services, 300 Garden City Plaza, Ste 312, Garden City, NY 11530-3325. TEL 516-747-3312, FAX 516-747-3331. Ed. Tony Calabrese. Adv. contact Eugene Whalen. B&W page USD 2,350. Circ: 7,000 (controlled).

C O P A FLIGHT. *see* AERONAUTICS AND SPACE FLIGHT

CANADIAN CIVIL AIRCRAFT REGISTER (CD-ROM EDITION). *see* AERONAUTICS AND SPACE FLIGHT

CANADIAN CIVIL AVIATION. *see* TRANSPORTATION—Abstracting, Bibliographies, Statistics

387.7 USA ISSN 1541-7131
TL720
THE CAPTAIN'S LOG. Text in English. q.
Published by: World Airline Historical Society, 489, Ocoee, FL 34761-0489. information@wahsonline.com, http://www.wahsonline.com. Eds. Philip Glatt, William M. Demarest.

387.744 HKG
CARGO CLAN (WANCHAI). Text in English, Chinese. 2002. q. adv. **Description:** Covers air-cargo related topics and news, lifestyle, travel, health, sports and other general interest stories, Freight Mate cover and centerfold.
Published by: Cathay Pacific Airways Ltd, 10/F Chung Nam Bldg 1, Lockhart Rd, Wanchai, Hong Kong. TEL 852-2527-3822, FAX 852-2861-3621. adv.: color page HKD 1,300; trim 210 x 280. Circ: 8,850 (free).

387.444 USA ISSN 0278-0801
HE9788
CARGO FACTS; the airfreight and express industry newsletter of record. Text in English. 1981. m. USD 345 domestic; USD 425 foreign (effective 2000); includes Cargo Facts Update. adv. back issues avail. **Document type:** *Newsletter, Trade.* **Description:** Reviews the air cargo market and industry worldwide.
Related titles: Supplement(s): Cargo Facts Update.
Published by: Air Cargo Management Group, 520 Pike St, Ste 1010, Seattle, WA 98101-4058. TEL 206-587-6537, FAX 206-587-6540. Ed. John Vair. Pub. Edwin Laird. R&P Robert Dahl. Adv. contact Lee Hibbets. Circ: 1,000.

387.7 NLD ISSN 0925-7748
CARGOVISION. Text in English. 1986. q. free (effective 2009). charts; illus.; stat. back issues avail. **Document type:** *Magazine, Trade.* **Description:** Provides information across the spectrum of worldwide cargo news and information, logistics, business activities, international trade and freight market, airports, and profiles of cities served by KLM Cargo.

Related titles: Online - full text ed.
Published by: K L M Royal Dutch Airlines, K L M Cargo/Koninklijke Luchtvaart Maatschappij, Box 7700, 4003135510, 1117, Netherlands. arwert@cargovision.org. Ed. Mark W Lyon.

CESTE I MOSTOVI/ROADS AND BRIDGES. *see* ENGINEERING—Civil Engineering

387.742 GBR ISSN 2041-9279
▼ **CHARTER BROKER.** Text in English. 2009. bi-m. GBP 35; free to qualified personnel (effective 2011). adv. **Document type:** *Magazine, Trade.*
—CCC.
Published by: Stansted News Ltd., 134 South St, Bishop's Stortford, Herts CM23 3BQ, United Kingdom. TEL 44-1279-714511, FAX 44-1279-714519, http://www.stanstednews.com/. Ed. Rod Smith TEL 44-1279-714506. Adv. contact Mark Ranger TEL 44-1279-714509.

387.7 HKG
CIVIL AIRCRAFT ACCIDENT REPORTS. Text in English. irreg., latest 1979. price varies.
Published by: (Hong Kong. Civil Aviation Department), Government Publications Centre, G.P.O. Bldg, Ground Fl, Connaught Pl, Hong Kong, Hong Kong. TEL 5-8428801. **Subscr. to:** Director of Information Services, Information Services Dept., 1 Battery Path G-F, Central, Hong Kong, Hong Kong.

629.13 GBR
CIVIL AIRCRAFT AIRWORTHINESS INFORMATION AND PROCEDURES. Abbreviated title: C A A I P. Text in English. 19??. base vol. plus irreg. updates. looseleaf. GBP 87 base vol(s). (effective 2010). **Document type:** *Government.* **Description:** Provides general information on various matters regarding civil aircraft manufacture, overhaul, repair, maintenance, operation and policies.
Related titles: Online - full text ed.: free (effective 2010); ◆ Series: Air Traffic Control Licensing; ◆ Air Navigation - The Order and the Regulations; ◆ Great Britain. Civil Aviation Authority. Airport Surveys; ◆ Manual of Air Traffic Services - Part 1; ◆ Great Britain. Civil Aviation Authority. Mandatory Requirements for Airworthiness; ◆ Great Britain. Civil Aviation Authority. Approved Aerial Positions; ◆ Mandatory Aircraft Modifications and Inspections Summary; ◆ A A I B Recommendations - C A A Progress Report (Year); ◆ Air Traffic Services Engineering Requirements; ◆ Great Britain. Civil Aviation Authority. Annual Punctuality Statistics - Full Analysis (Year); ◆ Great Britain. Civil Aviation Authority. Annual Punctuality Statistics - Full and Summary Analysis (Year); ◆ United Kingdom Aeronautical Information Publication; ◆ Overseas Non-scheduled Flight Clearances Guide.
Published by: Civil Aviation Authority, Printing and Publication Services, C A A House, 45-59 Kingsway, London, WCB2 6TE, United Kingdom. TEL 44-20-73797311, FAX 44-20-74536097, infoservices@caa.co.uk. **Dist. by:** Westward Documedia Limited.

CIVIL AVIATION AUTHORITY OF NEW ZEALAND. ANNUAL REPORT. *see* PUBLIC ADMINISTRATION

387.7 351.93 NZL ISSN 1177-9411
CIVIL AVIATION AUTHORITY OF NEW ZEALAND. STATEMENT OF INTENT. Text in English. 199?. a.
Related titles: Online - full text ed.: ISSN 1177-942X.
Published by: Civil Aviation Authority of New Zealand, PO Box 31-441, Lower Hutt, 5040, New Zealand. TEL 64-4-5699400, FAX 64-4-5692024, info@caa.govt.nz.

387.7 331.88 GBR
CIVIL AVIATION NEWS; the paper that unites all aviation workers. Text in English. 1978. bi-m. GBP 2, USD 5. adv. bk.rev.
Address: Community Centre, F.C.A., Hanworth Rd, Feltham, Mddx, United Kingdom. Circ: 10,000.

CIVIL AVIATION STATISTICS OF THE WORLD (YEAR). *see* TRANSPORTATION—Abstracting, Bibliographies, Statistics

387.7 GBR ISSN 0960-9024
CIVIL AVIATION TRAINING. Abbreviated title: C A T. Text in English. 1990. bi-m. GBP 65 domestic; EUR 85 in Europe; GBP 85 elsewhere (effective 2009). adv. bk.rev. back issues avail. **Document type:** *Magazine, Trade.* **Description:** Provides reports on training within air carriers for airlines, training centers, pilot schools, and trade bodies.
Related titles: Online - full text ed.
—CCC.
Published by: Halldale Publishing & Media Ltd., Pembroke House, 8 St Christopher's Place, Farnborough, Hampshire GU14 0NH, United Kingdom. TEL 44-1252-532000, FAX 44-1252-512714, janet@halldale.com. Ed. Chris Lehman. Pub. Andrew Smith. Circ: 14,000.

387.71 330 HKG
THE CLUB. Text in English, Chinese. 2002. bi-m. adv. **Document type:** *Magazine, Consumer.* **Description:** Contains travel and lifestyle features that inform and entertain. It also provides a guide to good living for people on the move.
Published by: Cathay Pacific Airways Ltd, 10/F Chung Nam Bldg 1, Lockhart Rd, Wanchai, Hong Kong. TEL 852-2527-3822, FAX 852-2861-3621. adv.: color page HKD 10,000; trim 205 x 273. Circ: 120,000 (free).

COMMERCIAL AIRCRAFT. *see* AERONAUTICS AND SPACE FLIGHT

387.71 GBR
COMMERCIAL AVIATION ONLINE. Text in English. 2007 (Oct.). d.
Formed by the merger of (1989-2007): Commercial Aviation Report (Print) (1474-1105); (1996-2007): Commercial Aviation Value Report (Print) (1474-1113)
Published by: Reed Business Information Ltd. (Subsidiary of: Reed Business), Lacon House, 84 Theobald's Rd, London, WC1X 8NS, United Kingdom. TEL 44-20-76111200, FAX 44-20-76111250, http://www.reedbusiness.co.uk/.

CONCISE B2B AEROSPACE (ONLINE); aerospace news from the commonwealth of independent states. *see* AERONAUTICS AND SPACE FLIGHT

387.7 USA
CONTRACTIONS HANDBOOK. Text in English. 19??. base vol. plus irreg. updates. looseleaf. **Document type:** *Handbook/Manual/Guide, Government.* **Description:** Lists all the approved word and phrase contractions used by F.A.A. personnel and by other organizations providing air traffic control, communications, weather, and other air navigation services.
Published by: U.S. Federal Aviation Administration, 800 Independence Ave, SW, Washington, DC 20591. TEL 202-267-8212, 866-835-5322, FAX 202-267-9463, http://www.faa.gov.

387.7 USA
CONTROLLER. Text in English. 1980. w. USD 59; free to qualified personnel (effective 2008). adv. **Document type:** *Magazine, Trade.* **Description:** Provides information linking buyers and sellers of general aviation aircraft.
Related titles: Online - full text ed.
Indexed: CLT&T.
Published by: Sandhills Publishing Co., PO Box 82545, Lincoln, NE 68501. TEL 402-479-2181, 800-331-1978, FAX 402-479-2195, feedback@sandhills.com, http://www.sandhills.com.

387.7 332.6 CAN
CORPORATE AIR TRAVEL SURVEY. Abbreviated title: C A T S. Text in English. 1989. a. **Document type:** *Report, Trade.* **Description:** Surveys international business travellers for opinions and attitudes toward air travel.
Published by: International Air Transport Association, 800 Place Victoria, PO Box 113, Montreal, PQ H4Z 1M1, Canada. TEL 514-390-6726, 800-716-6326, FAX 514-874-9659, sales@iata.org. Ed. Lynn Allard.

CORPORATE AVIATION SAFETY SEMINAR. PROCEEDINGS. *see* AERONAUTICS AND SPACE FLIGHT

D O M; the business of aircraft maintenance. (Director of Maintenance) *see* AERONAUTICS AND SPACE FLIGHT

387.7 NOR ISSN 1504-4181
DAKOTA NORWAY. Text in Norwegian. 199?. s-a. NOK 200 membership (effective 2005). **Document type:** *Magazine, Consumer.*
Address: c/o Sandefjord Lufthavn, Vatakerveien 30, Sandefjord, 3241, Norway. TEL 47-33-470300, thl@ossnor.no, http://www.dakotanorway.no.

387.7 CAN ISSN 0256-3223
K4121.D3
DANGEROUS GOODS REGULATIONS. Text in English. 1957. a. USD 153 per issue (effective 2008). **Document type:** *Handbook/Manual/Guide, Trade.* **Description:** Contains all provisions mandated by ICAO and all rules universally agreed by airlines to correctly package and safely transport dangerous goods by air.
Related titles: CD-ROM ed.: USD 130 (effective 2005); Spanish ed.; German ed.; Chinese ed.; French ed.
—BLDSC (3518.810000). CCC.
Published by: International Air Transport Association, 800 Place Victoria, PO Box 113, Montreal, PQ H4Z 1M1, Canada. TEL 514-390-6726, 800-716-6326, FAX 514-874-9659, sales@iata.org. Adv. contact Sandra Davies. Circ: 55,000.

387.74 USA
DELTA AIR LINES. WORLDWIDE TIMETABLE (ONLINE). Text in English. 1947. q. free (effective 2009). charts; illus.; maps. **Document type:** *Directory, Trade.* **Description:** Provides travelers and travel planners with important information on Delta Air Lines and Delta connection flights, both domestic and international, Includes office locations worldwide, airport codes, flight itineraries, services, and general information.
Formerly (until 2004): Delta Air Lines. Worldwide Timetable (Print Edition)
Media: Online - full text. **Related titles:** Print ed.
Published by: Delta Air Lines, Inc., PO Box 20706, Atlanta, GA 30320. TEL 404-715-2600, FAX 404-715-5042, InvestorRelations@delta.com.

DESIGNATORS FOR AIRCRAFT OPERATING AGENCIES, AERONAUTICAL AUTHORITIES AND SERVICES. *see* AERONAUTICS AND SPACE FLIGHT

387.7 910.22 USA
DETROIT NEWSPAPER AGENCY. TRAVEL DIRECTORY. Text in English. biennial. free. **Document type:** *Directory.*
Formerly: Detroit News Travel Directory
Published by: Detroit Newspaper Agency, Market Development - Promotion, 615 W Lafayette, Detroit, MI 48226. TEL 313-223-4367, FAX 313-222-2190, TELEX 810-221-7448. Circ: 6,000.

341.46 ITA ISSN 0391-2434
DIRITTO E PRATICA DELL'AVIAZIONE CIVILE. Text in Italian. 1987. s-a. EUR 26 domestic to individuals; EUR 30 domestic to institutions; EUR 45 foreign (effective 2009). **Document type:** *Journal, Trade.*
Indexed: IBR, IBZ.
Published by: Edizioni Scientifiche Italiane SpA, Via Chiatamone 7, Naples, NA 80121, Italy. TEL 39-081-7645443, FAX 39-081-7646477, info@edizioniesi.it, http://www.edizioniesi.it. Ed. Guido Rinaldi Baccelli.

DRIVING RADIO CONTROL CANADA. *see* HOBBIES

E A A SPORT PILOT & LIGHT SPORT AIRCRAFT. (Experimental Aircraft Association) *see* AERONAUTICS AND SPACE FLIGHT

387 510 ECU
ECUADOR. DIRECCION DE AVIACION CIVIL. MATHEMATICS. Text in Spanish. m.
Published by: Direccion General de Aviacion Civil, Buenos Aires 149 y Avda. 10 de Agosto, Quito, Ecuador.

EINSATZ (STUTTGART). *see* MEDICAL SCIENCES—Orthopedics And Traumatology

363.7 CAN
EMERGENCY RESPONSE GUIDANCE FOR AIRCRAFT INCIDENTS INVOLVING DANGEROUS GOODS. Text in English. biennial. USD 22 (effective 2002).
Related titles: French ed.; Spanish ed.; Russian ed.
Published by: International Civil Aviation Organization (I C A O), External Relations and Public Information Office, 999 University St, Montreal, PQ H3C 5H7, Canada. TEL 514-954-8022, FAX 514-954-6769, icaohq@icao.int.

ENROUTE; your complimentary in-flight magazine. *see* TRAVEL AND TOURISM

341 NLD
EUROPEAN AIR LAW; texts and documents. Text in English. 1992. 2-3/yr.), base vol. plus irreg. updates. looseleaf. USD 875 base vol(s). (effective 2009). **Description:** Compilation of EC legislation and case law of the European Court of Justice pertaining to aviation law, including all important European treaties and references to relevant literature.
Published by: Kluwer Law International (Subsidiary of: Aspen Publishers, Inc.), PO Box 316, Alphen aan den Rijn, 2400 AH, Netherlands. TEL 31-172-641562, FAX 31-172-641555, sales@kluwerlaw.com, http://www.kluwerlaw.com. Eds. Elmar Giemulla, Ronald Schmid.

341 NLD
EUROPEAN AIR LAW ASSOCIATION CONFERENCE PAPERS. Text in English. 1991. a., latest vol.18, 2003. price varies. back issues avail. **Document type:** *Proceedings, Academic/Scholarly.* **Description:** Presents an overview of topics discussed at association conferences, covering a variety of legal, economic and regulatory issues in European air law.
Published by: (European Air Law Association), Kluwer Law International (Subsidiary of: Aspen Publishers, Inc.), PO Box 316, Alphen aan den Rijn, 2400 AH, Netherlands. TEL 31-172-641562, FAX 31-172-641555, sales@kluwerlaw.com, http://www.kluwerlaw.com. Ed. P Dagtoglou. **Co-publisher:** Sakkoulas, GR.

EUROPEAN AVIATION SAFETY SEMINAR. PROCEEDINGS. *see* AERONAUTICS AND SPACE FLIGHT

387.7 GBR ISSN 0959-1311
EUROPEAN BUSINESS AIR NEWS. Abbreviated title: E B A N. Text in English. 1989. m. GBP 40 in Europe; GBP 70 elsewhere; free to qualified personnel (effective 2010). adv. back issues avail. **Document type:** *Magazine, Trade.* **Description:** Designed for all business aviation professionals throughout the European continent.
—CCC.
Published by: Stansted News Ltd., 134 South St, Bishop's Stortford, Herts CM23 3BQ, United Kingdom. TEL 44-1279-714511, FAX 44-1279-714519, http://www.stanstednews.com/. Pub. David Wright TEL 44-1279-714502. Adv. contact Mark Ranger TEL 44-1279-714509. color page USD 9,988; trim 420 x 297.

387.7 FRA ISSN 0071-2558
EUROPEAN CIVIL AVIATION CONFERENCE (REPORT OF SESSION). Text in English. 1955. triennial (since 1961 with intermediate sessions; trennial 15th, 1993; intermediate 22nd 1993). free. reprints avail. **Document type:** *Proceedings.*
Related titles: French ed.
Published by: European Civil Aviation Conference, 3 bis Villa Emile Bergerat, Neuilly-sur-Seine, Cedex 92522, France. TEL 33-1-46418544, FAX 33-1-46241818.

387.7 LUX ISSN 1028-348X
EUROSTAT INTERNATIONAL TRANSPORT BY AIR. INTRA - AND EXTRA - EU. Text in English. 199?. a.
Related titles: CD-ROM ed.: ISSN 1606-3465; Diskette ed.: ISSN 1028-3498.
Published by: European Commission, Statistical Office of the European Communities (E U R O S T A T), Rue Alcide de Gasperi, Luxembourg, 2920, Luxembourg. TEL 352-4301-34526, FAX 352-4301-32600, eurostat-infodesk@cec.eu.int, http://www.europa.eu.int/comm/eurostat.

387.428068 GBR ISSN 1754-1166
EXECUTIVE & V I P AVIATION INTERNATIONAL. (Very Important Person) Text in English. 2007 (Jun.). q. GBP 30 domestic; EUR 48 in Europe; USD 60 in United States (effective 2009). adv. back issues avail. **Document type:** *Journal, Trade.* **Description:** Provides owners and operators of private aircraft with information on new aircraft orders, advances in technology and services to the private aviation industry.
Published by: E V A International, Chestnut, PO Box 632, Waltham Cross, EN8 1EG, United Kingdom. TEL 44-1992-424193, FAX 44-1992-313002, advertising@evaint.com, http://evaint.com. Ed. Jo Murray. Pub. Steve Murray.

629.13 USA
EXECUTIVE CONTROLLER; the marketplace for corporate aircraft. Text in English. 1991. w. USD 42 in US & Canada; free (effective 2008). adv. illus. **Document type:** *Magazine, Trade.* **Description:** For buyers and sellers of executive aircraft.
Related titles: Online - full text ed.
Published by: Sandhills Publishing Co., PO Box 82545, Lincoln, NE 68501. TEL 402-479-2181, 800-331-1978, FAX 402-479-2195, feedback@sandhills.com, http://www.sandhills.com.

F A A AVIATION FORECASTS. (Federal Aviation Administration) *see* AERONAUTICS AND SPACE FLIGHT

387.7 USA
HE9761.1
F A A SAFETY BRIEFING; your source for general aviation news and information. Text in English. 1961. bi-m. USD 21 domestic; USD 29.40 foreign; USD 8 per issue domestic; USD 11.20 per issue foreign (effective 2010). charts; illus.; stat. back issues avail.; reprints avail. **Document type:** *Newsletter, Government.* **Description:** Covers FAA regulations and directives to enhance aviation safety as well as provides updates for student and professional pilots on rule changes and information on aircraft maintenance, avionics, and accident analysis and prevention.
Former titles (until 2010): F A A Aviation News (1057-9648); (until 1987): F A A General Aviation News (0362-7942); (until 1976): F A A Aviation News (0014-553X); (until 196?): United States. Federal Aviation Agency. Aviation News
Related titles: Microform ed.: (from MIM, PQC); Online - full text ed.: ISSN 2157-2453. free (effective 2010).
Indexed: A10, HRIS, IUSGP, MEA&I, V03.
—IE, Ingenta, Linda Hall.
Published by: U.S. Federal Aviation Administration, 800 Independence Ave, SW, Washington, DC 20591. TEL 202-267-8212, 866-835-5322, FAX 202-267-9463. Ed. Susan Parson. **Subscr. to:** U.S. Government Printing Office, Superintendent of Documents.

387.74 614.86 USA
FACTS AND ADVICE FOR AIRLINE PASSENGERS. Text in English. 1979. biennial. USD 5 (effective 2000). **Document type:** *Guide, Consumer.* **Description:** Shows how to avoid or minimize the inconvenience of airline service problems.
Published by: Aviation Consumer Action Project, PO Box 19029, Washington, DC 20036. TEL 202-638-4000. R&P Paul Hudson.

387.73 USA
FEDERAL AVIATION ADMINISTRATION: HIGH ALTITUDE POLLUTION PROGRAM. Text in English. biennial.
Published by: Federal Aviation Administration, Office of Environment and Energy, 800 Independence Ave, S W, Washington, DC 20591.

FEDERAL AVIATION REGULATIONS. PART 119, CERTIFICATION: AIR CARRIERS AND COMMERCIAL OPERATORS. *see* AERONAUTICS AND SPACE FLIGHT

FEDERAL AVIATION REGULATIONS. PART 125, CERTIFICATION AND OPERATIONS: AIRPLANES HAVING A SEATING CAPACITY OF 20 OR MORE PASSENGERS OR A MAXIMUM PAYLOAD CAPACITY OF 6,000 POUNDS OR MORE. *see* AERONAUTICS AND SPACE FLIGHT

FEDERAL AVIATION REGULATIONS. PART 129, OPERATIONS: FOREIGN AIR CARRIERS AND FOREIGN OPERATORS OF UNITED STATES-REGISTERED AIRCRAFT ENGAGED IN COMMON CARRIAGE. *see* AERONAUTICS AND SPACE FLIGHT

FEDERAL AVIATION REGULATIONS. PART 135, OPERATING REQUIREMENTS: COMMUTER AND ON-DEMAND OPERATIONS AND RULES GOVERNING PERSONS ON BOARD SUCH AIRCRAFT. *see* AERONAUTICS AND SPACE FLIGHT

FEDERAL AVIATION REGULATIONS. PART 25, AIRWORTHINESS STANDARDS: TRANSPORT CATEGORY AIRPLANES. *see* AERONAUTICS AND SPACE FLIGHT

FEDERAL AVIATION REGULATIONS. PART 29, AIRWORTHINESS STANDARDS: TRANSPORT CATEGORY ROTORCRAFT. *see* AERONAUTICS AND SPACE FLIGHT

387.7 FIN
FINNAIR LENTO. Text in Finnish. 2002. 5/yr. adv. **Document type:** *Magazine.* **Description:** Inflight magazine for the national airline of Finland.
Published by: Finnair, PO Box 2, Helsinki, 00040, Finland. TEL 358-9120-5965, http://www.finnair.com/. Ed. Pirjo Pyysianen.

FLAP INTERNACIONAL; revista latinoamericana de aviacao. *see* AERONAUTICS AND SPACE FLIGHT

387.7 AUS ISSN 1325-5002
FLIGHT SAFETY AUSTRALIA. Text in English. 1996. q. free. **Document type:** *Magazine, Trade.*
Related titles: Online - full content ed.
Published by: Civil Aviation Safety Authority, PO Box 2005, Canberra, ACT 2601, Australia. FAX 61-2-62171209, publicenquiries@casa.gov.au.

387.7 USA
FLIGHTLINE (MINNEAPOLIS). Text in English. 1965. q. USD 21.50. back issues avail. **Description:** Covers general aviation topics. Provides membership information, safety tips.
Published by: Allied Pilots Association, O'Connell Bldg, 14600 Trinity Blvd, Ste 500, Fort Worth, TX 76155-2512. TEL 817-302-2272, PUBLIC-COMMENT@alliedpilots.org, http://www.alliedpilots.org/index.asp. Circ: 6,000.

387.742 331.8 USA ISSN 0164-8691
HD6515.A43
FLIGHTLOG. Text in English. 1962. 4/yr. USD 14 (effective 2008). adv. bk.rev. back issues avail. **Document type:** *Magazine, Trade.* **Description:** Covers labor union issues pertaining to member flight attendants; includes air safety and health issues, aviation industry news and trends.
Indexed: CLT&T, HRIS.
Published by: A F L - C I O, Association of Flight Attendants, 501 Third St NW, Washington, DC 20001. TEL 202-434-1300, http://www.afa.net. Circ: 33,000.

387.7 DEU
FLUGBLATT; der aktuelle Report. Text in German. 1969. 4/yr. adv. bk.rev. reprints avail. **Document type:** *Magazine, Trade.*
Published by: Flughafen Stuttgart GmbH, Postfach 230461, Stuttgart, 70624, Germany. Ed. Volkmar Kramer. adv.: B&W page EUR 2,150, color page EUR 2,560. Circ: 70,000 (controlled).

387.736 CHE ISSN 0015-4555
FLUGHAFEN-REVUE ZURICH AIRPORT MAGAZIN. Text in English, German. 1957. 2/yr. adv. back issues avail. **Document type:** *Magazine, Consumer.* **Description:** Contains information for passengers at the Zurich airport.
Formerly (until 1962): Was Sie in Kloten Sehen (1421-7147)
Published by: Verlag B. Cohn, Postfach 1161, Zurich Flughafen, CH-8058, Switzerland. TEL 41-1-8140140, FAX 41-1-8142441. Ed., Pub., R&P, Adv. contact Bruno Cohn. B&W page CHF 2,740, color page CHF 3,550; trim 176 x 121. Circ: 10,000 (paid).

387.7 DEU ISSN 0015-4563
TL503 CODEN: FLGLAR
DER FLUGLEITER. Text in German. 1954. q. looseleaf. adv. bk.rev. bibl.; illus.; pat.; stat. 86 p./no.; back issues avail. **Document type:** *Newsletter, Trade.*
Published by: Gewerkschaft der Flugsicherung e.V., Herzogstr 41, Neu-isenburg, 63263, Germany. TEL 49-6102-372606, FAX 49-6102-3726070, geschaeftsstelle@gdf.de, http://www.vdf-online.de. Adv. contact Ursula Kromert. page EUR 800; 183 x 266. Circ: 3,700.

387.7 DEU
FLUGPLAN FLUGHAFEN STUTTGART. Text in German. 4/yr. adv. **Document type:** *Magazine, Consumer.*
Published by: Flughafen Stuttgart GmbH, Postfach 230461, Stuttgart, 70624, Germany. http://www.stuttgart-airport.de. adv.: B&W page EUR 1,435, color page EUR 1,864. Circ: 40,000 (controlled).

387.7 DEU
FLUGPLAN KOELN-BONN. Text in German. 1952. 7/yr. free (effective 2006). adv. **Document type:** *Bulletin, Consumer.*
Published by: Flughafen Koeln-Bonn GmbH, Postfach 980120, Cologne, 51129, Germany. TEL 49-2203-404001, FAX 49-2203-404044, info@koeln-bonn-airport.de, http://www.koeln-bonn-airport.de. Ed. Cornelia Krahforst. adv.: page EUR 1,980. Circ: 150,000 (controlled).

387.7 DEU ISSN 0932-8238
FLUGUNFALL JAHRESBERICHT. Text in German. 1964. a. **Document type:** *Bulletin.*
Former titles (until 1986): Ergebnisse der Fachlichen Untersuchung von Unfaellen bei dem Betrieb Deutscher Luftfahrzeuge im In- und Ausland sowie Auslaendische Luftfahrzeuge im Inland (0178-8094); (until 1983): Ergebnisse der Fachlichen Untersuchung von Unfaellen bei dem Betrieb von Luftfahrzeugen (0343-6594)
Published by: Luftfahrt-Bundesamt, Flugunfalluntersuchungsstelle, Postfach 3054, Braunschweig, 38020, Germany. TEL 0531-2355-0, FAX 0531-2355246.

666 USA
FLY DENVER. Text in English. q. **Document type:** *Magazine, Consumer.* **Description:** Information guide and news source for Denver International Airport.
Published by: Indelible Inc., 391 Emerson Street, Denver, CO 80218. TEL 303-722-4779, info@iidesign.com, http://www.iidesign.com/.

387.7 CAN ISSN 1912-0656
FLY SMART. Text in English. 200?. irreg. (4th ed.). **Document type:** *Monographic series, Consumer.*
Media: Online - full text. **Related titles:** French ed.: Prenez l'Air Averti. ISSN 1912-0664.
Published by: Canadian Transportation Agency/Office des Transports du Canada, 15 Eddy St, Ottawa, ON K1A 0N9, Canada. TEL 819-953-8353, 888-222-2592, FAX 819-953-5686, cta.comment@cta-otc.gc.ca.

387.7 GBR
FLYER. Text in English. 1990. m. (13/yr.). GBP 32.45; GBP 3.60 newsstand/cover (effective 2009). adv. illus. back issues avail. **Document type:** *Magazine, Consumer.* **Description:** Covers all aspects of noncommercial aviation, particularly light aircraft.
Published by: Seager Publishing Ltd., 9 Riverside Ct, Lower Bristol Rd, Bath, Avon BA2 3DZ, United Kingdom. TEL 44-1225-481440, FAX 44-1225-481262, katem@flyermag.co.uk. Ed. Ian Waller. Pub. Ian Seager. Adv. contact Darren Ward. B&W page GBP 1,100, color page GBP 1,650; trim 222 x 300.

387.7 PAK ISSN 0046-4236
FLYER INTERNATIONAL; aviation and tourism. Text in English. 1964. m. USD 75. adv. bk.rev. charts; illus.; tr.lit.
Published by: (Azam Ali), Manhattan International Ltd., 187-3B-2 P.E.C.H. Society, Karachi 29, Pakistan. Ed. Ms. Semeen Jaffery. Circ: 15,000.

387.72 SWE ISSN 0015-4776
FLYGPOSTEN. Variant title: Nya Flygposten. Text in Swedish. 1954. q. adv. illus.
Formerly (until vol.6, 1955): Skandinavisk Flygpersonalfoerening
Published by: Svensk Pilotfoerening/Swedish Air Line Pilots Association, Wallingatan 33, PO Box 1139, Stockholm, 11181, Sweden. TEL 46-8-103311, FAX 46-8-208940, spf@swealpa.se, http://www.swealpa.se. Circ: 3,000.

387.7 NOR ISSN 1891-1048
TL526.N6
FLYHISTORIE. Text in Norwegian. 2005. q. NOK 320 (effective 2011). adv. back issues avail. **Document type:** *Magazine, Consumer.*
Formerly (until 2009): Norsk Luftfatshistorisk Magasin (0809-8409)
Published by: Norsk Luftfartsmuseum/The National Norwegian Aviation Museum, PO Box 1124, Bodoe, 8001, Norway. TEL 47-75-507850, FAX 47-75-507851, flymuseum@luftfart.museum.no, http://www.luftfart.museum.no. Ed. Ulf Larsstuvold.

FLYING DOCTOR QUEENSLAND. *see* HEALTH FACILITIES AND ADMINISTRATION

387.7 IRL ISSN 1649-6329
FLYING IN IRELAND. Text in English. 2005. m. EUR 60 domestic; EUR 66 in Europe; EUR 72 elsewhere (effective 2006). adv. **Document type:** *Magazine, Consumer.*
Address: PO Box 10004, Churchtown, Dublin, 14, Ireland. Ed. Laurence Dwyer.

FLYING RADIO CONTROL CANADA. *see* HOBBIES

387.7 GBR ISSN 1355-1523
FOCUS ON COMMERCIAL AVIATION SAFETY. Text in English. 1990. q. GBP 14 to non-members; free to members (effective 2009). adv. **Document type:** *Bulletin, Trade.* **Description:** Designed for commercial pilots, flight engineers and air traffic control officers, holding current licences.
—IE, Infotrieve.
Published by: (U K Flight Safety Committee), J M H Publishing, 7 Stafford Rd, Cornford Ln, Tunbridge Wells, Kent TN2 4QZ, United Kingdom. Ed. Rich Jones.

387.7 CAN
FREIGHT FORECAST (ONLINE). Text in English. quinquennial. USD 2,499 (effective 2008). **Document type:** *Report, Trade.* **Description:** Shows global and regional forecasts of air freight tonnage and highlights major historical and projected trends.
Former titles (until 200?): Freight Forecast (Print); (until 1998): International Scheduled and Charter Freight Forecast; Freight Traffic Forecast
Media: Online - full content. **Related titles:** CD-ROM ed.: USD 1,099 per issue (effective 2008).
Published by: International Air Transport Association, 800 Place Victoria, PO Box 113, Montreal, PQ H4Z 1M1, Canada. TEL 514-390-6726, 800-716-6326, FAX 514-874-9659, sales@iata.org.

387.736 GBR ISSN 1748-6394
FUTURE AIRPORT; investing in the future of airports. Text in English. 1987. s-a. GBP 5.95 per issue domestic; EUR 8 per issue in Europe; USD 8.95 per issue in United States; free to qualified personnel (effective 2010). back issues avail. **Document type:** *Magazine, Trade.* **Description:** Focuses on the most important issues facing the Airport industry.
Formerly (until 2005): Airport Technology International (0952-7141)
Related titles: Online - full text ed.
—**CCC.**
Published by: S P G Media Ltd. (Subsidiary of: Sterling Publishing Group Plc.), Brunel House, 55-57 N Wharf Rd, London, W2 1LA, United Kingdom. TEL 44-20-79159660, FAX 44-20-77242089, info@spgmedia.com, http://www.spgmedia.com/. Eds. Lucy Schwerdtfeger TEL 44-20-79159714, John Lawrence. Pub. William Crocker.

387.7 ARG
G A T A REPORT. (Guia Argentina de Trafico Aereo) Text in Spanish. 1993. w. ARS 65, USD 65 (effective 2001). adv. Website rev. **Document type:** *Trade.* **Description:** Presents news on airlines services, tourism, leisure and recreation.
Published by: Impresiones Newgate S.A., Viamonte, 723-9od, Buenos Aires, 1053, Argentina. TEL 54-114-3228301, FAX 54-114-3220242. Ed. Raul Feldman. Adv. contact Monique Larrain. color page USD 1,650; trim 250 x 170. Circ: 6,500.

GAY AIRLINE & TRAVEL CLUB NEWSLETTER. *see* HOMOSEXUALITY

387.7 USA
GENERAL AVIATION AIRCRAFT SHIPMENT REPORT. Text in English. 1946. a. USD 3 (effective 2005). stat. back issues avail. **Document type:** *Report, Trade.*
Formerly: General Aviation Airplane Shipment Report
Related titles: Microfiche ed.: (from CIS).
Indexed: SRI.
Published by: General Aviation Manufacturers Association, 1400 K St, N W, Ste 801, Washington, DC 20005. TEL 202-393-1500, FAX 202-842-4063, webmaster@GAMA.aero, http://www.gama.aero. R&P Elizabeth Davis. Circ: 1,500.

387.71 USA ISSN 1529-8841
GENERAL AVIATION BUSINESS REPORT. Text in English. 1999. bi-w. USD 298 domestic; USD 389 foreign (effective 2001). charts; mkt.; stat. back issues avail. **Document type:** *Newsletter, Trade.* **Description:** Covers the people, companies, products, marketing campaigns that impact general aviation business.
Formerly (until 2000): General Aviation Market Report
Published by: Maracom, PO Box 274, Warner, NH 03278-0274. maracom1@sprynet.com, http://www.ga-business.com/. Ed. Frank Marafiote.

GENERAL AVIATION STATISTICAL DATABOOK. *see* TRANSPORTATION—Abstracting, Bibliographies, Statistics

387.7 598 CAN ISSN 1910-4510
GESTION DE LA FAUNE DANS LES AEROPORTS. Text in French. 1994. irreg. **Document type:** *Bulletin, Trade.*
Media: Online - full text. **Related titles:** English ed.: Airport Wildlife Management Bulletins.
Published by: Transport Canada/Transports Canada, 300 Sparks St, Ottawa, ON K1A 0N5, Canada. TEL 613-990-2309, FAX 613-954-4731.

387.74 NLD ISSN 1574-6518
GILDEBRIEF. Text in Dutch. 1982. q.
Published by: Vereniging het Nederlandse Luchtverkeersleidersgilde/ Netherlands Guild of Air Traffic Controllers, Postbus 75109, Schiphol, 1117 ZR, Netherlands. TEL 31-20-4063243, FAX 31-20-4062159, office@atc-gilde.nl.

387.742 GBR ISSN 1466-6510
GLOBAL BUSINESS JET. Text in English. 1999. a. GBP 28.50; free to qualified personnel (effective 2010). adv. **Document type:** *Yearbook, Trade.* **Description:** Contains news and information for long-range business jet operators worldwide.
—**CCC.**
Published by: Stansted News Ltd., 134 South St, Bishop's Stortford, Herts CM23 3BQ, United Kingdom. TEL 44-1279-714511, FAX 44-1279-714519, http://www.stanstednews.com/. Pub. David Wright TEL 44-1279-714502. Adv. contact Mark Ranger TEL 44-1279-714509. color page GBP 1,197; trim 137 x 137.

341.46 NLD ISSN 1386-4823
GLOBAL JOURNAL ON AIR & SPACE LAW. Text in English. 1992. s-a. USD 140 (effective 2009). back issues avail. **Document type:** *Journal, Academic/Scholarly.* **Description:** Reports on the aviation policy, along with the penal and administrative aspects of the study and practice of air and space law.
Formerly: Dutch Journal on Air and Space Law
Published by: Global Law Association, PO Box 9001, Tilburg, 5000 HA, Netherlands. TEL 31-13-5821366, FAX 31-13-5821367, info@wolfpublishers.nl, http://www.globallaw.org. Ed. C Tofan. **Dist. in N. America by:** Gaunt, Inc., Gaunt Bldg, 3011 Gulf Dr, Holmes Beach, FL 34217. TEL 941-778-5211, FAX 941-778-5252, info@gaunt.com, http://www.gaunt.com.

387.7 USA
THE GRAPEVINE (AURORA). Text in English. m. **Document type:** *Magazine, Trade.*
Published by: Aircraft Mechanics Fraternal Association (A M F A), 14001 E Iliff Ave, Ste 217, Aurora, CO 80014. TEL 303-752-2632, FAX 303-362-7736, http://amfanational.org.

629.13 RUS ISSN 0017-3606
CODEN: GRAVAC
GRAZHDANSKAYA AVIATSIYA. Text in Russian. 1930. m. USD 139.95. bk.rev. illus. index.
Indexed: ChemAb.
—East View, Linda Hall. **CCC.**
Address: Staropanskii per 1-5, Moscow, 103012, Russian Federation. TEL 7-095-2983417, FAX 7-095-9284156. Ed. A M Troshin. **Dist. by:** East View Information Services, 10601 Wayzata Blvd, Minneapolis, MN 55305. TEL 952-252-1201, 800-477-1005, FAX 952-252-1202, info@eastview.com, http://www.eastview.com.

GREAT AIRLINERS SERIES. *see* AERONAUTICS AND SPACE FLIGHT

387.7 GBR
GREAT BRITAIN. AIR TRANSPORT USERS COUNCIL ANNUAL REPORT. Text in English. 1975. a. free (effective 2009). back issues avail. **Document type:** *Corporate.*
Formerly (until 2000): Great Britain. Air Transport Users Committee. Annual Report for the Year Ended 30 September ..
Related titles: Online - full text ed.: free (effective 2009).
Published by: Air Transport Users Council, C A A House, 45-59 Kingsway, London, WC2B 6TE, United Kingdom. TEL 44-20-72406061, FAX 44-20-72407071, complaints@auc.org.uk.

387.742 GBR
GREAT BRITAIN. CIVIL AVIATION AUTHORITY. AIR TRAVEL INSOLVENCY PROTECTION ADVISORY COMMITTEE. ANNUAL REPORT. Text in English. 1987. a. back issues avail. **Document type:** *Government.*
Formerly (until 2001): Great Britain. Civil Aviation Authority. Air Travel Trust Committee. Annual Report
Related titles: Online - full text ed.: free (effective 2010).
Published by: (Great Britain. Air Travel Trust Committee), Civil Aviation Authority, Printing and Publication Services, C A A House, 45-59 Kingsway, London, WCB2 6TE, United Kingdom. TEL 44-20-73797311, FAX 44-20-74536097, infoservices@caa.co.uk.

387.742 GBR
GREAT BRITAIN. CIVIL AVIATION AUTHORITY. AIR TRAVEL TRUST. ANNUAL REPORT AND ACCOUNTS. Text in English. 19??. a. GBP 20 per issue (effective 2010). **Document type:** *Government.* **Description:** Provides financial protection to air passengers through informative reports.
Related titles: Online - full text ed.: free (effective 2010).

TU

Published by: (Great Britain. Air Travel Trust), Civil Aviation Authority, Printing and Publication Services, C A A House, 45-59 Kingsway, London, WCB2 6TE, United Kingdom. TEL 44-20-73797311, FAX 44-20-74536097, infoservices@caa.co.uk.

387.71 GBR ISSN 0306-3569
HE9843.A1
GREAT BRITAIN. CIVIL AVIATION AUTHORITY. ANNUAL REPORT AND ACCOUNTS. Text in English. 1949. a. free (effective 2010). back issues avail. **Document type:** *Government.*
Formerly (until 19??): Great Britain. Air Transport Licensing Board. Report (0072-5617)
Related titles: Online - full text ed.: free (effective 2010).
Published by: Civil Aviation Authority, Printing and Publication Services, C A A House, 45-59 Kingsway, London, WCB2 6TE, United Kingdom. TEL 44-20-73797311, FAX 44-20-74536097, infoservices@caa.co.uk. **Dist. by:** Westward Documedia Limited.

621.13 GBR
GREAT BRITAIN. CIVIL AVIATION AUTHORITY. APPROVED AERIAL POSITIONS. Text in English. 19??. base vol. plus irreg. updates. looseleaf. **Document type:** *Government.* **Description:** Contains lists of approved antenna locations for B.CAR compliance.
Related titles: Online - full text ed.: free (effective 2010); ◆ Series: Air Traffic Control Licensing; ◆ Air Navigation - The Order and the Regulations; ◆ Great Britain. Civil Aviation Authority. Airport Surveys; ◆ Manual of Air Traffic Services - Part 1; ◆ Great Britain. Civil Aviation Authority. Mandatory Requirements for Airworthiness; ◆ Mandatory Aircraft Modifications and Inspections Summary; ◆ Civil Aircraft Airworthiness Information and Procedures; ◆ A A I B Recommendations - C A A Progress Report (Year); ◆ Air Traffic Services Engineering Requirements; ◆ Great Britain. Civil Aviation Authority. Annual Punctuality Statistics - Full Analysis (Year); ◆ Great Britain. Civil Aviation Authority. Annual Punctuality Statistics - Full and Summary Analysis (Year); ◆ United Kingdom Aeronautical Information Publication; ◆ Overseas Non-scheduled Flight Clearances Guide.
Published by: Civil Aviation Authority, Printing and Publication Services, C A A House, 45-59 Kingsway, London, WCB2 6TE, United Kingdom. TEL 44-20-73797311, FAX 44-20-74536097, infoservices@caa.co.uk. **Dist. by:** Westward Documedia Limited.

363.74 GBR
GREAT BRITAIN. CIVIL AVIATION AUTHORITY. D O R A COMMUNICATION. Text in English. 19??. irreg. back issues avail. **Document type:** *Monographic series, Government.* **Description:** Covers various aspects of disturbances caused by aircraft noise.
Published by: Civil Aviation Authority, Printing and Publication Services, C A A House, 45-59 Kingsway, London, WCB2 6TE, United Kingdom. TEL 44-20-73797311, FAX 44-20-74536097, infoservices@caa.co.uk.

363.74 GBR
GREAT BRITAIN. CIVIL AVIATION AUTHORITY. D O R A REPORT. Text in English. 19??. irreg. back issues avail.; reprints avail. **Document type:** *Monographic series, Government.* **Description:** Covers noise disturbance caused by aircraft.
Related titles: Online - full text ed.: free (effective 2010).
Published by: Civil Aviation Authority, Printing and Publication Services, C A A House, 45-59 Kingsway, London, WCB2 6TE, United Kingdom. TEL 44-20-73797311, FAX 44-20-74536097, infoservices@caa.co.uk. **Dist. by:** Westward Documedia Limited.

363.74 GBR
GREAT BRITAIN. CIVIL AVIATION AUTHORITY. D R REPORT. Text in English. 19??. irreg. back issues avail. **Document type:** *Monographic series, Government.* **Description:** Publishes studies on the effects of aircraft noise.
Published by: Civil Aviation Authority, Printing and Publication Services, C A A House, 45-59 Kingsway, London, WCB2 6TE, United Kingdom. TEL 44-20-73797311, FAX 44-20-74536097, infoservices@caa.co.uk.

387.42 GBR
GREAT BRITAIN. CIVIL AVIATION AUTHORITY. DOCUMENT. Variant title: C A A Document. Text in English. irreg., latest 2010. free (effective 2010). back issues avail. **Document type:** *Monographic series, Government.*
Related titles: Online - full text ed.: free (effective 2010).
Published by: Civil Aviation Authority, Printing and Publication Services, C A A House, 45-59 Kingsway, London, WCB2 6TE, United Kingdom. TEL 44-20-73797311, FAX 44-20-74536097, infoservices@caa.co.uk. **Dist. by:** Westward Documedia Limited.

387.7 GBR ISSN 0309-667X
GREAT BRITAIN. CIVIL AVIATION AUTHORITY. GENERAL AVIATION SAFETY INFORMATION LEAFLETS. Abbreviated title: G A S I L. Text in English. 1977. m. looseleaf. back issues avail. **Document type:** *Government.* **Description:** Features reports on occurrences and selected aviation accidents and contains safety information for owners and operators of small private aircraft.
Related titles: Online - full text ed.: free (effective 2010).
—CCC.
Published by: Civil Aviation Authority, Printing and Publication Services, C A A House, 45-59 Kingsway, London, WCB2 6TE, United Kingdom. TEL 44-20-73797311, FAX 44-20-74536097, infoservices@caa.co.uk. Ed. David Cockburn TEL 44-1293-573225. **Dist. by:** Westward Documedia Limited.

387.7 GBR
GREAT BRITAIN. CIVIL AVIATION AUTHORITY. INTERNATIONAL REGISTER OF CIVIL AIRCRAFT. Abbreviated title: I R C A. Text in English, French. 1961. 4 base vols. plus q. updates. GBP 172 for base vols.; GBP 65 updates only. Supplement avail. **Document type:** *Government.* **Description:** Provides public and private aeronautical entities with an international database comprising of harmonized and substantial information on national aircraft fleets.
Related titles: CD-ROM ed.; Microfiche ed.: GBP 114 for base vols.; GBP 40 updates only; Online - full text ed.: EUR 1,320 (effective 2010).
Published by: Civil Aviation Authority, Printing and Publication Services, C A A House, 45-59 Kingsway, London, WCB2 6TE, United Kingdom. TEL 44-20-73797311, FAX 44-20-74536097, infoservices@caa.co.uk, http://www.caa.co.uk/. **Dist. by:** Westward Documedia Limited.

629.13 GBR
GREAT BRITAIN. CIVIL AVIATION AUTHORITY. MANDATORY REQUIREMENTS FOR AIRWORTHINESS. Text in English. 19??. base vol. plus irreg. updates. looseleaf. GBP 41.50 per issue (effective 2010). back issues avail. **Document type:** *Government.* **Description:** Provides a single source of mandatory information for continuing airworthiness.
Supersedes in part (in 2009): Great Britain. Civil Aviation Authority. Airworthiness Notices
Related titles: Online - full text ed.: free (effective 2010); ◆ Series: Air Traffic Control Licensing; ◆ Air Navigation - The Order and the Regulations; ◆ Great Britain. Civil Aviation Authority. Airport Surveys; ◆ Manual of Air Traffic Services - Part 1; ◆ Great Britain. Civil Aviation Authority. Annual Punctuality Statistics - Full and Summary Analysis (Year); ◆ Great Britain. Civil Aviation Authority. Approved Aerial Positions; ◆ Mandatory Aircraft Modifications and Inspections Summary; ◆ Civil Aircraft Airworthiness Information and Procedures; ◆ A A I B Recommendations - C A A Progress Report (Year); ◆ Air Traffic Services Engineering Requirements; ◆ Great Britain. Civil Aviation Authority. Annual Punctuality Statistics - Full Analysis (Year); ◆ United Kingdom Aeronautical Information Publication; ◆ Overseas Non-scheduled Flight Clearances Guide.
Published by: Civil Aviation Authority, Printing and Publication Services, C A A House, 45-59 Kingsway, London, WCB2 6TE, United Kingdom. TEL 44-20-73797311, FAX 44-20-74536097, infoservices@caa.co.uk.

387.7 GBR
GREAT BRITAIN. CIVIL AVIATION AUTHORITY. NEW REPORTABLE OCCURRENCES. Text in English. 19??. m. stat. **Document type:** *Government.*
Published by: Civil Aviation Authority, Safety Data Analysis Unit, CAA House, 45-59 Kingsway, London, WC2B 6TE, United Kingdom. TEL 44-20-73797311, infoservices@caa.co.uk, http://www.caa.co.uk.

387.744 GBR
GREAT BRITAIN. CIVIL AVIATION AUTHORITY. NOTICES TO A O C HOLDERS. (Air Operator's Certificate) Text in English. 19??. base vol. plus irreg. updates. looseleaf. **Document type:** *Bulletin, Government.*
Published by: Civil Aviation Authority, Printing and Publication Services, C A A House, 45-59 Kingsway, London, WCB2 6TE, United Kingdom. TEL 44-20-73797311, FAX 44-20-74536097, infoservices@caa.co.uk, http://www.caa.co.uk/. **Dist. by:** Westward Documedia Limited.

387.7 GBR
GREAT BRITAIN. CIVIL AVIATION AUTHORITY. OCCURRENCE DIGEST. Text in English. 19??. m. stat. **Document type:** *Government.*
Published by: Civil Aviation Authority, Safety Data Analysis Unit, CAA House, 45-59 Kingsway, London, WC2B 6TE, United Kingdom. TEL 44-20-73797311, infoservices@caa.co.uk, http://www.caa.co.uk.

387.7 GBR ISSN 0306-4646
GREAT BRITAIN. CIVIL AVIATION AUTHORITY. OFFICIAL RECORD SERIES 2: LICENSING NOTICES. Text in English. 19??. base vol. plus w. updates. looseleaf. back issues avail. **Document type:** *Government.* **Description:** Contains details of licence applications made to and decisions made by the CAA.
Published by: Civil Aviation Authority, Printing and Publication Services, C A A House, 45-59 Kingsway, London, WCB2 6TE, United Kingdom. TEL 44-20-73797311, FAX 44-20-74536097, infoservices@caa.co.uk. **Dist. by:** Westward Documedia Limited.

387.7 GBR ISSN 0306-4654
GREAT BRITAIN. CIVIL AVIATION AUTHORITY. OFFICIAL RECORD SERIES 2: NOTICES RELATING TO AIR TRANSPORT LICENSES, ROUTE LICENSES AND OPERATING LICENSES. Variant title: Notices About Air Transport Licenses, Route Licenses, Operating Licenses and Scarce Capacity Allocation. Text in English. 19??. base vol. plus irreg. updates. looseleaf. **Document type:** *Government.* **Description:** Contains notices about applications for and decisions on licences.
Published by: Civil Aviation Authority, Printing and Publication Services, C A A House, 45-59 Kingsway, London, WCB2 6TE, United Kingdom. TEL 44-20-7453-6330, FAX 44-20-7453-6322, infoservices@caa.co.uk. **Dist. by:** Westward Documedia Limited, 37 Windsor St, Cheltemham, Glou GL52 2DG, United Kingdom.

387.7 GBR ISSN 0951-0036
GREAT BRITAIN. CIVIL AVIATION AUTHORITY. OFFICIAL RECORD SERIES 3: AIR TRAVEL ORGANISER LICENSING, PART 1. Text in English. 19??. base vol. plus irreg. updates. looseleaf. GBP 26.75 base vol(s). per issue (effective 2010). **Document type:** *Government.* **Description:** Highlights A.T.O.L. requirements and procedures.
Supersedes in part (in 19??): Great Britain. Civil Aviation Authority. Official Record Series 3: Air Travel Organiser Licensing (0306-4662)
Related titles: Online - full text ed.: free (effective 2009).
Published by: Civil Aviation Authority, Printing and Publication Services, C A A House, 45-59 Kingsway, London, WCB2 6TE, United Kingdom. TEL 44-20-73797311, FAX 44-20-74536097, infoservices@caa.co.uk. **Dist. by:** Westward Documedia Limited.

387.7 GBR ISSN 0306-4670
GREAT BRITAIN. CIVIL AVIATION AUTHORITY. OFFICIAL RECORD SERIES 4: MISCELLANEOUS. Text in English. 1974. base vol. plus irreg. updates. looseleaf. GBP 2 per issue (effective 2010). back issues avail. **Document type:** *Monographic series, Government.*
Related titles: Online - full text ed.: free (effective 2010).
Published by: Civil Aviation Authority, Printing and Publication Services, C A A House, 45-59 Kingsway, London, WCB2 6TE, United Kingdom. TEL 44-20-73797311, FAX 44-20-74536097, infoservices@caa.co.uk. **Dist. by:** Westward Documedia Limited.

387.7 GBR ISSN 0306-4689
GREAT BRITAIN. CIVIL AVIATION AUTHORITY. OFFICIAL RECORD SERIES 5: SCHEMES OF CHANGES. Text in English. 1974. base vol. plus a. updates. looseleaf. GBP 2 per issue (effective 2010). back issues avail. **Document type:** *Monographic series, Government.* **Description:** Contains schemes to be paid to CAA in connection with the performance by C.A.A. of specified functions.
Related titles: Online - full text ed.: free (effective 2010).
Published by: Civil Aviation Authority, Printing and Publication Services, C A A House, 45-59 Kingsway, London, WCB2 6TE, United Kingdom. TEL 44-20-73797311, FAX 44-20-74536097, infoservices@caa.co.uk. **Dist. by:** Westward Documedia Limited.

387.7 GBR ISSN 0951-0052
GREAT BRITAIN. CIVIL AVIATION AUTHORITY. OFFICIAL RECORD SERIES 6: AIRPORTS - ECONOMIC REGULATION, PART 1. Text in English. 19??. base vol. plus irreg. updates. looseleaf. **Document type:** *Government.* **Description:** Details what must be included in an application from an airport operator to levy fees.
Supersedes in part: Great Britain. Civil Aviation Authority. Official Record Series 6: Airports - Economic Regulation
Related titles: Online - full text ed.: free (effective 2010).
Published by: Civil Aviation Authority, Printing and Publication Services, C A A House, 45-59 Kingsway, London, WCB2 6TE, United Kingdom. TEL 44-20-73797311, FAX 44-20-74536097, infoservices@caa.co.uk. **Dist. by:** Westward Documedia Limited.

387.7 GBR ISSN 0951-0060
GREAT BRITAIN. CIVIL AVIATION AUTHORITY. OFFICIAL RECORD SERIES 6: AIRPORTS - ECONOMIC REGULATION, PART 2. Text in English. 19??. base vol. plus irreg. updates. looseleaf. back issues avail. **Document type:** *Monographic series, Government.* **Description:** Features decisions regarding applications by airport operators to levy fees.
Supersedes in part: Great Britain. Civil Aviation Authority. Official Record Series 6: Airports - Economic Regulation
Related titles: Online - full text ed.: free (effective 2010).
Published by: Civil Aviation Authority, Printing and Publication Services, C A A House, 45-59 Kingsway, London, WCB2 6TE, United Kingdom. TEL 44-20-73797311, FAX 44-20-74536097, infoservices@caa.co.uk. **Dist. by:** Westward Documedia Limited.

387.74 GBR
GREAT BRITAIN. CIVIL AVIATION AUTHORITY. PAPERS. Variant title: C A A Paper. C A A Safety Research Papers. Text in English. 19??. irreg., latest 2009. price varies. back issues avail. **Document type:** *Monographic series, Government.*
Related titles: Online - full text ed.: free (effective 2010).
Published by: Civil Aviation Authority, Printing and Publication Services, C A A House, 45-59 Kingsway, London, WCB2 6TE, United Kingdom. TEL 44-20-73797311, FAX 44-20-74536097, infoservices@caa.co.uk. **Dist. by:** Westward Documedia Limited.

387.7 GBR
GREAT BRITAIN. CIVIL AVIATION AUTHORITY. REPORTABLE A T C OCCURRENCES. (Air Traffic Control) Text in English. 19??. m. stat. **Document type:** *Government.*
Published by: Civil Aviation Authority, Safety Data Analysis Unit, CAA House, 45-59 Kingsway, London, WC2B 6TE, United Kingdom. TEL 44-20-73797311, infoservices@caa.co.uk, http://www.caa.co.uk.

387.7 GBR
GREAT BRITAIN. CIVIL AVIATION AUTHORITY. REPORTABLE OCCURRENCES. Text in English. 19??. m. stat. **Document type:** *Government.*
Published by: Civil Aviation Authority, Safety Data Analysis Unit, CAA House, 45-59 Kingsway, London, WC2B 6TE, United Kingdom. TEL 44-20-73797311, infoservices@caa.co.uk, http://www.caa.co.uk.

387.742 CHN
GUANGZHOU MINHANG/GUANGZHOU CIVIL AVIATION. Text in Chinese. bi-m.
Published by: Guangzhou Minhang Baoshe, Baiyun Jichang (Airport), Guangzhou, Guangdong 510406, China. TEL 678901. Ed. Ma Tingwei.

387.72 MEX
GUIA AEREA DE MEXICO. Text in Spanish. 1968. m. MXN 220, USD 65 (effective 1996). adv. illus. **Document type:** *Trade.* **Description:** Reference tool for travel professionals.
Formerly: Guia Aerea de Mexico y Centro-America
Published by: E G Ediciones Especializadas S.A. de C.V., HDA DE ZACATEPEC 373, Hacienda de Echegaray, Naucalpan, MEX 53300, Mexico. TEL 525-3734149, FAX 525-3734147. Ed. Horacio Echeverria German. Adv. contact Carolina Echeverria. B&W page USD 1,551, color page USD 2,200. Circ: 5,500.

387.7 338 CHL
GUIA AEREA OFICIAL - CHILE. Text in Spanish. 1977. m. CLP 36,100, USD 80. adv. illus.; mkt.; maps. **Document type:** *Trade.* **Description:** Contains airline schedules, tour, car rental, and hotel information.
Published by: Travel Industry Experts Ltda., Antonio Varas, 175, Of. 908-909, Providencia, Santiago, Chile. TEL 56-2-3630354, FAX 56-2-3650142. adv.: page USD 1,050; trim 250 x 170. Circ: 3,500.

629.13 BRA ISSN 0017-5145
GUIA AERONAUTICO. Text in Portuguese. 1947. m. USD 120. adv. charts.
Published by: Editora Guia Aeronautico Ltda., Rua Joao Alvares, 27, Gamboa, Rio De Janeiro, RJ 20220-330, Brazil. Ed. Ruy Costa Barros. Circ: 15,000.

387.74 ARG ISSN 0326-1050
GUIA ARGENTINA DE TRAFICO AEREO. Text in Spanish. 1947. m. ARS 200, USD 200 (effective 2001). adv. back issues avail. **Document type:** *Trade.*
Published by: Impresiones Newgate S.A., Viamonte, 723-9od, Buenos Aires, 1053, Argentina. TEL 54-114-3228301, FAX 54-114-3220242. Ed., Pub., R&P Raul Feldman. Adv. contact Monique Larrain. Circ: 8,000.

387.744 BRA ISSN 1415-3971
HE9788.5.B6
GUIA DA CARGA AEREA/AIR CARGO GUIDE. Text in Portuguese; Summaries in English. 1995. bi-m. USD 12 per issue (effective 2000). adv. **Document type:** *Trade.* **Description:** Covers cargo aviation activities in Brazil, import and export market news and global trends in air freight.
Formerly (until 1997): Aviacao Cargo (1414-0608)
Published by: Aviacao em Revista Editora Ltda., Rua da Consolacao, 1992 Andar 10, Consolacao, Sao Paulo, SP 01302-001, Brazil. aviacaoemrevista@uol.com.br. Ed., Pub., R&P Helcio Estrella. Adv. contact Francisco Carlos Alves. B&W page USD 5,700, color page USD 6,750; trim 280 x 210. Circ: 10,000.

629.133 BRA ISSN 0104-7949
GUIA DO HELICOPTERO/HELICOPTER GUIDE. Text in Portuguese; Summaries in English. a. adv. **Document type:** *Directory.* **Description:** Provides a review of the helicopter industry in Brazil. Lists products and services available on the Brazilian market.

Published by: Aviacao em Revista Editora Ltda., Rua da Consolacao, 1992 Andar 10, Consolacao, Sao Paulo, SP 01302-001, Brazil. aviacaoemrevista@uol.com.br. Ed., Pub., R&P Helcio Estrella. Adv. contact Francisco Carlos Alves. B&W page USD 4,500, color page USD 4,950; trim 280 x 210. Circ: 10,000.

387.7 BRA ISSN 0104-4966
GUIA DO TAXI AEREO/AIR TAXI GUIDE. Text in Portuguese. 1991. a. adv. **Document type:** *Directory.* **Description:** Provides information on air taxi operation in Brazil.
Published by: Aviacao em Revista Editora Ltda., Rua da Consolacao, 1992 Andar 10, Consolacao, Sao Paulo, SP 01302-001, Brazil. aviacaoemrevista@uol.com.br. Ed., Pub., R&P Helcio Estrella. Adv. contact Francisco Carlos Alves. B&W page USD 4,500, color page USD 4,950; trim 280 x 210. Circ: 10,000.

387.736 BRA
GUIA DOS TERMINAIS AEREOS/AIRPORTS GUIDE. Text in Portuguese; Summaries in English. 1992. a. adv. **Description:** Presents a view of airport activities in Brazil, from operations to management and service providers.
Published by: Aviacao em Revista Editora Ltda., Rua da Consolacao, 1992 Andar 10, Consolacao, Sao Paulo, SP 01302-001, Brazil. aviacaoemrevista@uol.com.br. Ed., Pub., R&P Helcio Estrella. Adv. contact Francisco Carlos Alves. B&W page USD 12,000, color page USD 18,000; trim 280 x 210. Circ: 10,000.

GUILD OF AIR PILOTS AND AIR NAVIGATORS. GUILD NEWS. *see* AERONAUTICS AND SPACE FLIGHT

GUOJI HANGKONG/INTERNATIONAL AVIATION. *see* AERONAUTICS AND SPACE FLIGHT

HADSHOT SAPPANUT UTEUFAH - YIDION; shipping and aviation news. *see* TRANSPORTATION—Ships And Shipping

387.736 DEU
HAM.AIRPORT MAGAZINE. Text in German, English. 1998. 2/yr. adv. **Document type:** *Magazine, Consumer.*
Former titles (until 2007): Hamburg-Airport-Journal; (until 2004): Airport Life
Published by: Flughafen Hamburg GmbH, Flughafenstr 1-3, Hamburg, 22335, Germany. TEL 49-40-50750, FAX 49-40-50751234, fhg@ham.airport.de, http://www.hamburg-airport.de. Ed. CLaudia Luersen. adv.: page EUR 4,700; trim 210 x 280. Circ: 100,000 (controlled).

387.7 NLD ISSN 1872-3985
HANDBOEK I C A O. Cover title: Vervoer Gevaarlijke Stoffen door de Lucht. Variant title: International Civil Aviation Organization Handboek. Text in Dutch. 2002. biennial. EUR 100 (effective 2009).
Published by: GDS Europe BV, Postbus 3111, Hoofddorp, 2130 KC, Netherlands. TEL 31-23-5542970, FAX 31-23-5542971, info@gdscrossmediagroup.nl, http://www.gds-europe.com.

HANDBOEK VERRE REIZEN. *see* TRAVEL AND TOURISM

HANGKONG ZHISHI/AEROSPACE KNOWLEDGE. *see* AERONAUTICS AND SPACE FLIGHT

387.736 CHN ISSN 1006-7310
HANGKONGGANG/AIRPORT JOURNAL. Text in Chinese. 1988. bi-m. **Document type:** *Journal, Academic/Scholarly.*
Published by: Shanghai Jichang (Jituan) Youxian Gongsi/Shanghai Airport Authority, 18, Xinjinqiao Lu, Shanghai, 201206, China. http://www.shanghaiairport.com/.

387.7 CHN ISSN 1006-3242
TL787
HANGTIAN KONGZHI/AEROSPACE CONTROL. Text in Chinese. 1983. bi-m. USD 31.20 (effective 2009). **Document type:** *Journal, Academic/Scholarly.*
Related titles: Online - full text ed.
Indexed: A28, APA, BrCerAb, C&ISA, CA/WCA, CIA, CerAb, CivEngAb, CorrAb, E&CAJ, E11, EEA, EMA, ESPM, EnvEAb, H15, M&TEA, M09, MBF, METADEX, SolStAb, T04, WAA.
—BLDSC (0729.855660), East View, Linda Hall.
Published by: Beijing Hangtian Zidong Kongzhi Yanjiusuo, 142 Xinxiang 402 fenxian, Beijing, 100854, China. TEL 86-1-68388585. Ed. Yongping Wang. **Dist. by:** China International Book Trading Corp, 35 Chegongzhuang Xilu, Haidian District, PO Box 399, Beijing 100044, China. TEL 86-10-68412045, FAX 86-10-68412023, cibtc@mail.cibtc.com.cn, http://www.cibtc.com.cn.

387.7 USA ISSN 0739-5728
HD9711.25.A1
HELICOPTER ANNUAL. Text in English. 1983. a. free to members (effective 2011). adv. **Document type:** *Directory, Trade.* **Description:** A comprehensive reference guide for the civil helicopter industry. Includes helicopter specifications, industry statistics, membership directories, listings of international civil aviation contacts, aviation periodicals, and more.
Related titles: Online - full text ed.: free (effective 2011) (from CIS).
Indexed: SRI.
Published by: Helicopter Association International, 1635 Prince St, Alexandria, VA 22314. TEL 703-683-4646, FAX 703-683-4745, marilyn.mckinnis@rotor.com. Adv. contact Lisa Henderson.

387.7 USA
HELICOPTER ASSOCIATION INTERNATIONAL. MAINTENANCE UPDATE. Text in English. 19??. q. free to members (effective 2011). **Document type:** *Newsletter, Trade.* **Description:** Provides a forum for mechanics and technicians to exchange information. Includes regulatory issues, airworthiness directives, and aircraft alerts.
Related titles: Online - full text ed.
Published by: Helicopter Association International, 1635 Prince St, Alexandria, VA 22314. TEL 703-683-4646, FAX 703-683-4745, marilyn.mckinnis@rotor.com.

387.7 USA
HELICOPTER ASSOCIATION INTERNATIONAL. OPERATIONS UPDATE. Text in English. 1987. m. looseleaf. free to members (effective 2011). **Document type:** *Newsletter, Trade.* **Description:** Reports related to government and industry activities that effect helicopter operators.
Published by: Helicopter Association International, 1635 Prince St, Alexandria, VA 22314. TEL 703-683-4646, FAX 703-683-4745, marilyn.mckinnis@rotor.com, http://www.rotor.com.

HELICOPTER ASSOCIATION INTERNATIONAL. PRELIMINARY ACCIDENT REPORTS. *see* AERONAUTICS AND SPACE FLIGHT

359 CAN ISSN 0227-3160
HELICOPTERS. Text in English. 1980. q. CAD 28 domestic; CAD 31 in United States; CAD 45 elsewhere (effective 2007). adv. bk.rev. **Document type:** *Magazine, Trade.* **Description:** Domestic and international coverage of corporate, commercial and military rotary-wing aviation.
Formerly: Helicopters in Canada (0826-1237)
—CCC.
Published by: Annex Publishing & Printing, Inc., 105 Donly Dr S, PO Box 530, Simcoe, ON N3Y 4N5, Canada. TEL 519-429-3966, 800-265-2827, FAX 519-429-3112, 888-404-1129, mfredericks@annexweb.com, http://www.annexweb.com. Ed. Drew McCarthy TEL 888-599-2228 ext 265. Pub. Diane Kleer TEL 888-599-2228 ext 231. Circ: 7,500.

387.7 629.1 USA ISSN 0882-6633
HELIPORT DEVELOPMENT GUIDE. Variant title: The H A I Heliport Development Planning Guide. Text in English. 19??. irreg. **Document type:** *Handbook/Manual/Guide, Trade.* **Description:** Includes copies of selected FAA publications and lists consultants.
Related titles: Online - full text ed.: free (effective 2011).
Published by: Helicopter Association International, 1635 Prince St, Alexandria, VA 22314. TEL 703-683-4646, FAX 703-683-4745, marilyn.mckinnis@rotor.com.

387.7 GBR ISSN 1758-8391
▼ **HELIVATOR.** Text in English. 2009. q. GBP 23.95; GBP 4.99 per issue (effective 2010). back issues avail. **Document type:** *Magazine, Trade.*
Published by: Helivator Ltd., Ashland House, Manchester Rd, Ince, Wigan, WN2 2DX, United Kingdom. TEL 44-845-0743300, FAX 44-845-0743301. Ed. Mark Smith.

387.74 HKG
HONG KONG & MACAU AIRLINE TIMETABLE. Text in English. 1978. m. HKD 260, USD 65. adv. back issues avail. **Document type:** *Handbook/Manual/Guide, Consumer.* **Description:** Contains airline flight schedules and information on hotels, consulates, holidays, events, currency conversion rates, airline codes, and airport taxes.
Formerly: Hong Kong Airline Timetable
Published by: Thomson Press Hong Kong Ltd., 202-203 Hollywood Centre, 233 Hollywood Rd, Hong Kong, Hong Kong. TEL 852-2815-9111, FAX 852-2851-1933. Ed. Doonam Malik. Pub. J S Uberoi. R&P Rajesh Malik. Adv. contact Megan Chan. B&W page HKD 13,000, color page HKD 16,500; trim 210 x 108. Circ: 19,490.

387.74 HKG
HONG KONG. CIVIL AVIATION DEPARTMENT. DIRECTOR'S ANNUAL REPORT. Text in English. 1984. a. HKD 25.
Published by: (Hong Kong. Civil Aviation Department), Government Publications Centre, G.P.O. Bldg, Ground Fl, Connaught Pl, Hong Kong, Hong Kong. TEL 5-8428801. **Subscr. to:** Director of Information Services, Information Services Dept., 1 Battery Path G-F, Central, Hong Kong, Hong Kong.

387.7 CAN
I A T A ANNUAL REPORT. Text in English, French, Spanish. 1945. a. free. **Document type:** *Proceedings.*
Formerly: State of the Air Transport Industry (0081-4571)
Published by: International Air Transport Association, 800 Place Victoria, PO Box 113, Montreal, PQ H4Z 1M1, Canada. TEL 514-390-6726, 800-716-6326, FAX 514-874-9659, sales@iata.org, http://www.iata.org. Circ: (controlled).

387.7 CAN
I A T A CITY CODE DIRECTORY. Text in English. a. USD 480 per issue (effective 2008). **Document type:** *Directory, Trade.* **Description:** World-wide list of city, country numerical and alphabetical codes, state, province or territory codes as well as currency alphabetical codes for use by the airline industry when computing tariffs and mileage.
Related titles: CD-ROM ed.: USD 7,750 per issue (effective 2008); Online - full content ed.: USD 7,750 (effective 2008).
Published by: International Air Transport Association, 800 Place Victoria, PO Box 113, Montreal, PQ H4Z 1M1, Canada. TEL 514-390-6726, 800-716-6326, FAX 514-874-9659, sales@iata.org. Ed. Karin Bengtsson.

I A T A ENVIRONMENTAL REVIEW (ONLINE). *see* ENVIRONMENTAL STUDIES

387.71 CAN
I A T A LIST OF TICKET AND AIRPORT TAXES AND FEES (ONLINE). Text in English. 2 base vols. plus q. updates. looseleaf. USD 710 (effective 2008). **Document type:** *Report, Trade.* **Description:** Lists more than 900 information records for over 580 different ticket and airport taxes and fees imposed in some 230 countries.
Formerly: I A T A List of Ticket and Airport Taxes and Fees (Print)
Related titles: CD-ROM ed.: USD 890 (effective 2008).
Published by: International Air Transport Association, 800 Place Victoria, PO Box 113, Montreal, PQ H4Z 1M1, Canada. TEL 514-390-6726, 800-716-6326, FAX 514-874-9659, sales@iata.org.

387.74 CAN ISSN 0256-4459
JX5763
I A T A TICKETING HANDBOOK. Text in English. 1968. a., latest 33d ed. USD 115 includes CD-ROM (effective 2008). **Document type:** *Handbook/Manual/Guide, Trade.* **Description:** Explains in detail what entries are to be made on tickets, MCOs, MPDs and PTAs.
Related titles: French ed.: Manuel de Billeterie. ISSN 0256-4440. USD 55 (effective 2000); Chinese ed.: USD 43 (effective 2000); Spanish ed.: Guia para la Emision de Billetes. ISSN 0256-4432. USD 55 (effective 2000).
Published by: International Air Transport Association, 800 Place Victoria, PO Box 113, Montreal, PQ H4Z 1M1, Canada. TEL 514-390-6726, 800-716-6326, FAX 514-874-9659, sales@iata.org. Adv. contact Sandra Davies.

387.74 341 CAN
I C A O ABBREVIATIONS AND CODES. (Incorporates Amendments 1-20) Text in English. irreg., latest vol.4, 1989. USD 21.
Related titles: French ed.; Spanish ed.; Russian ed.
Published by: International Civil Aviation Organization (I C A O), External Relations and Public Information Office, 999 University St, Montreal, PQ H3C 5H7, Canada. TEL 514-954-8022, FAX 514-954-6769, icaohq@icao.int.

387 CAN ISSN 1014-4412
I C A O CIRCULARS. Text in English. 1968. irreg. price varies. **Document type:** *Monographic series, Consumer.*
Related titles: Spanish ed.: Circular O A C I. ISSN 1014-4420; French ed.: Circulaire O A C I. ISSN 1014-4439; Russian ed.: Tsirkulyar I K A O. ISSN 1014-4447; ◆ Series: Aircraft Accident Digest. ISSN 0443-7926; ◆ Regional Differences in Fares, Rates and Costs for International Air Transport (Year). ISSN 1012-6538; ◆ Surveys of International Air Transport Fares and Rates.
Published by: International Civil Aviation Organization (I C A O), External Relations and Public Information Office, 999 University St, Montreal, PQ H3C 5H7, Canada. TEL 514-954-8022, FAX 514-954-6769, icaohq@icao.int.

387 341 CAN
THE I C A O FINANCIAL REGULATIONS. Text in English. irreg., latest vol.10, 1999. USD 5.
Published by: International Civil Aviation Organization (I C A O), External Relations and Public Information Office, 999 University St, Montreal, PQ H3C 5H7, Canada. TEL 514-954-8022, FAX 514-954-6769, icaohq@icao.int.

I C A O PUBLICATIONS AND AUDIO VISUAL TRAINING AIDS CATALOGUE. *see* TRANSPORTATION—Abstracting, Bibliographies, Statistics

378 341 CAN
I C A O PUBLICATIONS REGULATIONS. Text in English. irreg., latest vol.8, 1998. USD 6.
Published by: International Civil Aviation Organization (I C A O), External Relations and Public Information Office, 999 University St, Montreal, PQ H3C 5H7, Canada. TEL 514-954-8022, FAX 514-954-6769, icaohq@icao.int.

387.7 USA ISSN 0276-640X
TL501
ILLINOIS AVIATION. Text in English. 1950. bi-m. USD 5. **Document type:** *Government.*
Indexed: CLT&T, HRIS.
Published by: Department of Transportation, Division of Aeronautics, Capital Airport, Springfield, IL 62707. TEL 217-785-8516. Ed. Jan Draper. Circ: 25,000.

IN-FLIGHT SURVEY OF INTERNATIONAL AIR TRAVELERS: INBOUND NATIONAL REPORT. *see* TRAVEL AND TOURISM

387.7 629.1 USA
IN FLIGHT U S A. Text in English. m. **Document type:** *Magazine, Trade.* **Description:** Features a variety of aviation-related articles and photos, including special sections on various aviation topics.
Media: Online - full text.

387.7 GBR ISSN 2045-385X
INFLIGHT (ONLINE). Text in English. 1994. q. free (effective 2011). adv. back issues avail. **Document type:** *Magazine, Trade.* **Description:** Provides information on the most dynamic business growth opportunities in the airline industry.
Formerly (until 2003): Inflight (Print) (1356-1715)
Media: Online - full text. **Related titles:** ◆ Supplement(s): Shephard's Inflight Handbook. ISSN 1461-619X.
—CCC.
Published by: H M G Aerospace Ltd., Ste 2, 7 Alexandra Rd, Farnborough, Hampshire GU14 6BU, United Kingdom. TEL 44-1252-501055, FAX 44-1252-408674, info@hmgaerospace.com. Pub., Adv. contact Mark Howells.

387.742 GBR ISSN 2045-9904
▼ **INFLIGHT HANDBOOK.** Text in English. 2010. a. adv. **Document type:** *Handbook/Manual/Guide, Trade.* **Description:** Provides a global guide to the inflight entertainment and passenger communications industry.
Supersedes in part (in 2011): Commercial Aviation and Inflight Handbook (2041-9333); Which was formed by the merger of (1998-2010): Shephard's Inflight Handbook (1461-619X); (2007-2010): Low-Fare and Regional Aviation (1753-1845); Which was formerly (until 2007): Shephard's Regional Aviation Handbook (1365-6589); (until 1996): Commuter World. World Operators' Handbook (1356-6334)
Published by: H M G Aerospace Ltd., Ste 2, 7 Alexandra Rd, Farnborough, Hampshire GU14 6BU, United Kingdom. TEL 44-1252-501055, FAX 44-1252-408674, info@hmgaerospace.com. Circ: 5,500.

INITIAL ATTACK; wildfire management technology. *see* FORESTS AND FORESTRY

387.7 USA
INSIDE F A A. (Federal Aviation Administration) Text in English. 1995. bi-w. USD 595 in US & Canada; USD 645 elsewhere (effective 2004). **Document type:** *Newsletter, Trade.*
Related titles: E-mail ed.
Published by: Inside Washington Publishers, 1919 South Eads St, Ste 201, Arlington, VA 22202. TEL 703-416-8500, 800-424-9068, custsvc@iwpnews.com, http://www.iwpnews.com.

387.742 USA ISSN 1061-4494
INSIDE FLYER (AMERICAS EDITION). Text in English. 1986. m. USD 36 domestic; USD 41 foreign (effective 2001). adv. charts; mkt.; maps; stat.; tr.lit. back issues avail. **Document type:** *Magazine, Consumer.* **Description:** Provides in-depth information on frequent travel programs, including those of airlines, hotels and affinity cards.
Related titles: Online - full text ed.
Published by: FlightPlan, Inc., 1930 Frequent Flyer Point, Colorado Springs, CO 80915. TEL 719-597-8880, FAX 719-597-6855, randy@insideflyer.com. Ed. Pam Lewis. Pub. Randy Peterson. R&P Roseanne Ward TEL 719-572-2750. Adv. contact John Toler. B&W page USD 5,735, color page USD 7,570; trim 11 x 8.25. Circ: 79,000 (paid). **Co-sponsor:** Inside Flyer.

387.742 USA ISSN 1359-768X
INSIDE FLYER (INTERNATIONAL EDITION). Text in English. 1995. bi-m. USD 36 domestic; USD 41 foreign (effective 2001). adv. charts; illus.; maps; stat.; tr.lit. back issues avail. **Document type:** *Magazine, Consumer.* **Description:** Offers airline, hotel, car rental and affinity credit card programme membership information.
Related titles: Online - full text ed.

Published by: FlightPlan, Inc., 1930 Frequent Flyer Point, Colorado Springs, CO 80915. TEL 719-597-8880, FAX 719-597-6855, randy@insideflyer.com. Pub. Randy Peterson. Adv. contact John Toler. B&W page USD 6,309, color page USD 8,327; trim 10.88 x 8.38. Circ: 38,000 (paid). **Co-sponsor:** Inside Flyer.

629.133 GBR ISSN 1747-0382
INSTRUMENT PILOT. Text in English. 1993. bi-m. free to members (effective 2009). back issues avail. **Document type:** *Magazine, Trade.* **Description:** Announces and reviews meetings, reports on PPL/IR Europe activities, and publishes articles written by members on subjects touching upon every aspect of instrument flying.
Formerly (until 2002): Network
Related titles: Online - full text ed.: ISSN 1747-0390.
Published by: P P L / I R Europe, The Business Centre, Llangarron, Ross-on-Wye, Herefordshire HR9 6PG, United Kingdom. TEL 44-1644-440232, FAX 44-1644-440263, memsec@pplir.org. Ed. David Earle TEL 44-7802-685642.

387.7 USA ISSN 2155-4943
TL725.3.T7
INTEGRATED COMMUNICATIONS, NAVIGATION, AND SURVEILLANCE CONFERENCE. PROCEEDINGS. Text in English. 200?. a. **Document type:** *Proceedings, Trade.*
Related titles: Online - full text ed.: ISSN 2155-4951.
Published by: I E E E, 445 Hoes Ln, Piscataway, NJ 08854. TEL 732-981-0060, FAX 732-981-1721, customer.service@ieee.org, http://www.ieee.org.

INTER - CANADIAN. *see* CONSUMER EDUCATION AND PROTECTION

INTERNATIONAL AIR POWER REVIEW. *see* MILITARY

INTERNATIONAL AIR SAFETY SEMINAR. PROCEEDINGS. *see* AERONAUTICS AND SPACE FLIGHT

387.7029 GBR
INTERNATIONAL AIRLINE GUIDE. Variant title: IntAG. Text in Dutch. a. GBP 21.95 (effective 2005). **Document type:** *Directory, Trade.* **Description:** Lists for every airline each aircraft by type, registration, construction number, and various technical data. Also provides addresses and telephone and fax numbers for each airline and, when applicable, lists previous owners and registrations for individual airframes.
Related titles: CD-ROM ed.
Published by: E P S Aviation Publishers, PO Box 4751, Early, Berks RG5 3HU, United Kingdom. TEL 44-1189-694626, FAX 44-1189-691417, http://www.eps-aviation.com.

387.7 GBR ISSN 1366-6339
INTERNATIONAL AIRPORT REVIEW. Text in English. 1997. bi-m. GBP 90 combined subscription (print & online eds.) (effective 2009). adv. back issues avail.; reprints avail. **Document type:** *Magazine, Trade.* **Description:** Addresses the latest technologies and developments within the aviation industry.
Related titles: Online - full text ed.: free to qualified personnel (effective 2009).
Indexed: ESPM, EnvEAb, HRIS.
—CCC.
Published by: Russell Publishing Ltd., Court Lodge, Hogtrough Hill, Brasted, Kent TN16 1NU, United Kingdom. TEL 44-1959-563311, FAX 44-1959-563123, info@russellpublishing.com, http://www.russellpublishing.com/. Adv. contact Daren Quinn TEL 44-1959-563311. page GBP 4,755; trim 210 x 297. Circ: 10,994.

387 CAN ISSN 0074-221X
K4093
INTERNATIONAL CIVIL AVIATION ORGANIZATION. AERONAUTICAL AGREEMENTS AND ARRANGEMENTS. ANNUAL SUPPLEMENT. Text in English, French. 1965. a. USD 5.
Published by: International Civil Aviation Organization (I C A O), External Relations and Public Information Office, 999 University St, Montreal, PQ H3C 5H7, Canada. TEL 514-954-8022, FAX 514-954-6769, icaohq@icao.int.

387.7 CAN
INTERNATIONAL CIVIL AVIATION ORGANIZATION. AERONAUTICAL CHART CATALOGUE. Text in English, French, Russian, Spanish. irreg., latest vol.28, 1993. USD 44. **Document type:** *Catalog.*
Published by: International Civil Aviation Organization (I C A O), External Relations and Public Information Office, 999 University St, Montreal, PQ H3C 5H7, Canada. TEL 514-954-8022, FAX 514-954-6769, icaohq@icao.int.

387.74 341 CAN
INTERNATIONAL CIVIL AVIATION ORGANIZATION. AIRCRAFT OPERATIONS. Text in English. irreg. (in 2 vols.), latest vol.4, 1993. USD 24.
Related titles: French ed.; Spanish ed.; Russian ed.
Published by: International Civil Aviation Organization (I C A O), External Relations and Public Information Office, 999 University St, Montreal, PQ H3C 5H7, Canada. TEL 514-954-8022, FAX 514-954-6769, icaohq@icao.int.

387 341 CAN
INTERNATIONAL CIVIL AVIATION ORGANIZATION. ANNEXES TO THE CONVENTION ON CIVIL AVIATION. Text in English. irreg. price varies. back issues avail.
Related titles: French ed.; Spanish ed.; Russian ed.
Published by: International Civil Aviation Organization (I C A O), External Relations and Public Information Office, 999 University St, Montreal, PQ H3C 5H7, Canada. TEL 514-954-8022, FAX 514-954-6769, icaohq@icao.int.

387 629.1 CAN ISSN 1014-0646
INTERNATIONAL CIVIL AVIATION ORGANIZATION. ASSEMBLY. MINUTES OF THE PLENARY MEETINGS. Text in English. 1947. irreg., latest 1995, 31st, Montreal. USD 39. **Document type:** *Proceedings.*
Related titles: Arabic ed.: At-Taqrir - Munazzamat at-Tayaran al-Madani ad-Duwali. Al-Qararat at-Taqrir al Wataiq. Al-Gamiyyat al-Umumiyyat. ISSN 1014-076X; Spanish ed.: Organizacion de Aviacion Civil Internacional. Asamblea. Actas de las Sesiones Plenarias. ISSN 1014-0670; Russian ed.: Mezhdunarodnaya Organizatsiya Grazhdanskoi Aviatsii. Assambleya. Rezolyutsii i Protokoly Plenarnogo Zasedaniya. ISSN 1014-0654; French ed.: Organisation de l'Aviation Civile. Assemble. Procedes Verbaux des Seances Plenieres. ISSN 1014-0662.
Published by: International Civil Aviation Organization (I C A O), External Relations and Public Information Office, 999 University St, Montreal, PQ H3C 5H7, Canada. TEL 514-954-8022, FAX 514-954-6769, icaohq@icao.int.

387 CAN ISSN 1014-0603
INTERNATIONAL CIVIL AVIATION ORGANIZATION. ASSEMBLY. REPORT AND MINUTES OF THE ADMINISTRATIVE COMMISSION. Text in English. 1947. irreg., latest 1995, 31st, Montreal. USD 11. **Document type:** *Proceedings.*
Related titles: Arabic ed.: At-Taqrir - Munazzamant at-Tayaran al Madani ad-Duwali. Al-Gammiyat al-Umumiyyat ad-Dawarat. Al-Lagnat al-Idarriyyat. ISSN 1014-0751; Spanish ed.: Organizacion de Aviacion Civil Internacional. Asamblea. Informe y Actas de la Comision Administrativa. ISSN 1014-062X; Russian ed.: Mezhdunarodnaya Organizatsiya Grazhdanskoi Aviatsii. Assambleya. Doklady i Protokoly Administrativnoi Komissii. ISSN 1014-0611; French ed.: Organisation de l'Aviation Civile Internationale. Assemble. Rapport et Procedes Verbaux de la Commission Administrative. ISSN 1014-0638.
Published by: International Civil Aviation Organization (I C A O), External Relations and Public Information Office, 999 University St, Montreal, PQ H3C 5H7, Canada. TEL 514-954-8022, FAX 514-954-6769, icaohq@icao.int.

387.7 CAN ISSN 0074-2376
INTERNATIONAL CIVIL AVIATION ORGANIZATION. ASSEMBLY. REPORT AND MINUTES OF THE ECONOMIC COMMISSION. Text in English. 1947. irreg., latest vol.31, 1995. USD 5. **Document type:** *Proceedings.*
Related titles: Arabic ed.; Spanish ed.; Russian ed.; French ed.
Published by: International Civil Aviation Organization (I C A O), External Relations and Public Information Office, 999 University St, Montreal, PQ H3C 5H7, Canada. TEL 514-954-8022, FAX 514-954-3769, icaohq@icao.int.

387.7 CAN ISSN 0074-2368
INTERNATIONAL CIVIL AVIATION ORGANIZATION. ASSEMBLY. REPORT AND MINUTES OF THE LEGAL COMMISSION. Text in English. 1947. irreg. **Document type:** *Proceedings.*
Related titles: Arabic ed.: At-Taqrir - Munazzamat at-Tayaran al-Umumiyyat ad-Dawrat. Al Langnat al-Qanumiyyat. ISSN 1014-045X; Spanish ed.: Organizacion de Aviacion Civil Internacional. Asamblea. Informe y Actas de la Comision Juridica. ISSN 1014-0409; Russian ed.: Mezhdunarodnaya Organizatsiya Grazhdanskoi Aviatsii. Assambleya. Doklady i Protokoly Yuridicheskoi Komissii. ISSN 1014-0425; French ed.: Organisation de l'Aviation Civile Internationale. Assemble. Rapport et Procedes de la Commission Juridique. ISSN 1014-0417.
Published by: International Civil Aviation Organization (I C A O), Legal Affairs and External Relations Bureau, 999 University St, Montreal, PQ H3C 5H7, Canada. TEL 514-954-8022, FAX 514-954-6769, TELEX 05-24513, icaohq@icao.int.

387 CAN ISSN 1014-0565
INTERNATIONAL CIVIL AVIATION ORGANIZATION. ASSEMBLY. REPORTS AND MINUTES OF THE EXECUTIVE COMMITTEE. Text in English. 1947. irreg., latest 1995, 31st, Montreal. USD 44. back issues avail.
Related titles: Arabic ed.: At-Taqrir - Munazzamat at-Tayaran al-Madani ad-Duwali. Al-Gamiyyat al-Umumiyyat ad-Dawarat. Al-Lagnat at-Tanfidyyat. ISSN 1014-0727; Russian ed.: Mezhdunarodanaya Organizatsiya Grazhdanskoi Aviatsii. Assambleya. Doklady i Protokoly Ispolnitel'nogo Komiteta. ISSN 1014-0581; French ed.: Organisation de l'Aviation Civile Internationale. Assemble. Rapport et Procedes Verbaux du Comite Executif.
Published by: International Civil Aviation Organization (I C A O), External Relations and Public Information Office, 999 University St, Montreal, PQ H3C 5H7, Canada. TEL 514-954-8022, FAX 514-954-6769, icaohq@icao.int.

387.7 CAN ISSN 0074-235X
INTERNATIONAL CIVIL AVIATION ORGANIZATION. ASSEMBLY. RESOLUTIONS. Text in English. 1965 (15th ed.). irreg., latest 1982, 29th, Montreal. USD 21.
Related titles: Arabic ed.; Spanish ed.; Russian ed.; French ed.
Published by: International Civil Aviation Organization (I C A O), External Relations and Public Information Office, 999 University St, Montreal, PQ H3C 5H7, Canada. TEL 514-954-8022, FAX 514-954-3769, icaohq@icao.int.

387 341 CAN
INTERNATIONAL CIVIL AVIATION ORGANIZATION. CONVENTIONS. Text in English, French, Russian, Spanish. 1948. irreg. price varies. back issues avail.
Published by: International Civil Aviation Organization (I C A O), External Relations and Public Information Office, 999 University St, Montreal, PQ H3C 5H7, Canada. TEL 514-954-8022, FAX 514-954-6769, icaohq@icao.int.

387 CAN
INTERNATIONAL CIVIL AVIATION ORGANIZATION. COUNCIL. ANNUAL REPORT. Text in English. a. USD 39. back issues avail. **Document type:** *Corporate.*
Related titles: Microfiche ed.: (from CIS); Spanish ed.; Russian ed.; Arabic ed.; French ed.
Indexed: IIS.
Published by: International Civil Aviation Organization (I C A O), External Relations and Public Information Office, 999 University St, Montreal, PQ H3C 5H7, Canada. TEL 514-954-8022, FAX 514-954-6769, icaohq@icao.int.

INTERNATIONAL CIVIL AVIATION ORGANIZATION. COUNCIL TO CONTRACTING STATES ON CHARGES FOR AIRPORTS AND AIR NAVIGATION SYSTEMS. STATEMENTS. *see* AERONAUTICS AND SPACE FLIGHT

INTERNATIONAL CIVIL AVIATION ORGANIZATION. DIGESTS OF STATISTICS. SERIE AF. AIRPORT AND ROUTE FACILITIES. FINANCIAL DATA AND SUMMARY TRAFFIC DATA/ MEZHDUNARODNAYA ORGANIZATSIYA GRAZHDANSKOI AVIATSII. STATISTICHESKII SBORNIK. SERIYA AF. AEROPORTNOE I MARSHRUTNOE OBORUDOVANIE. FINANSOVYE IZLOZHENIYA DANNYKH PO PEREVOZKAM/ ORGANISATION DE L'AVIATION CIVILE. RECUEIL DE STATISTIQUES. SERIE AF. INSTALLATIONS ET SERVICES D'AEROPORT ET DE ROUTE. DONNES FINANCIERES ET STATISTIQUES DE TRAFFIC SOMMAIRES/ORGANIZACION DE AVIACION CIVIL INTERNACIONAL. COMPENDIO ESTADISTICO. SERIE AF. INSTALACIONES Y SERVICIOS DE AEROPUERTO Y EN RUTA. DATOS FINANCIEROS Y RESUMEN DE DATOS DE TRAFICO. *see* TRANSPORTATION—Abstracting, Bibliographies, Statistics

INTERNATIONAL CIVIL AVIATION ORGANIZATION. DIGESTS OF STATISTICS. SERIES AT. AIRPORT TRAFFIC. *see* TRANSPORTATION—Abstracting, Bibliographies, Statistics

INTERNATIONAL CIVIL AVIATION ORGANIZATION. DIGESTS OF STATISTICS. SERIES F. FINANCIAL DATA - COMMERCIAL AIR CARRIERS. *see* TRANSPORTATION—Abstracting, Bibliographies, Statistics

INTERNATIONAL CIVIL AVIATION ORGANIZATION. DIGESTS OF STATISTICS. SERIES FP. FLEET - PERSONNEL - COMMERCIAL AIR CARRIERS. *see* TRANSPORTATION—Abstracting, Bibliographies, Statistics

INTERNATIONAL CIVIL AVIATION ORGANIZATION. DIGESTS OF STATISTICS. SERIES OFOD. ON-FLIGHT ORIGIN AND DESTINATION/MEZHDUNARODNAYA ORGANIZATSIYA GRAZHDANSKOI AVIATSII. STATISTICHESKII SBORNIK. SERIYA OFOD. NACHALNYI I KONECHNYI PUNKTY POLETA/ ORGANISATION DE L'AVIATION CIVILE INTERNATIONALE. RECUEIL DE STATISTIQUES. SERIE OFOD. ORIGINE ET DESTINATION PAR VOL/ORGANIZACION DE AVIACION CIVIL INTERNACIONAL. COMPENDIO ESTADISTICO. SERIE OFOD. ORIGEN Y DESTINO POR VUELO. *see* TRANSPORTATION—Abstracting, Bibliographies, Statistics

INTERNATIONAL CIVIL AVIATION ORGANIZATION. DIGESTS OF STATISTICS. SERIES R. CIVIL AIRCRAFT ON REGISTER. *see* TRANSPORTATION—Abstracting, Bibliographies, Statistics

INTERNATIONAL CIVIL AVIATION ORGANIZATION. DIGESTS OF STATISTICS. SERIES T. TRAFFIC, COMMERCIAL AIR TRAFFIC. *see* TRANSPORTATION—Abstracting, Bibliographies, Statistics

INTERNATIONAL CIVIL AVIATION ORGANIZATION. DIGESTS OF STATISTICS. SERIES TF. TRAFFIC BY FLIGHT STAGE. *see* TRANSPORTATION—Abstracting, Bibliographies, Statistics

629.13 CAN
INTERNATIONAL CIVIL AVIATION ORGANIZATION. GENERAL CONCEPT OF SEPARATION PANEL. REPORT OF THE MEETING. Text in English. irreg., latest vol.7, 1990. price varies. **Document type:** *Proceedings.*
Related titles: French ed.; Spanish ed.; Russian ed.
Published by: International Civil Aviation Organization (I C A O), External Relations and Public Information Office, 999 University St, Montreal, PQ H3C 5H7, Canada. TEL 514-954-8022, FAX 514-954-6769, icaohq@icao.int.

387.7 CAN ISSN 0074-2503
INTERNATIONAL CIVIL AVIATION ORGANIZATION. LEGAL COMMITTEE. MINUTES AND DOCUMENTS (OF SESSIONS). Text in English. 1948. triennial. USD 59 Supplement and corrigenda free on request. (effective Nov. 2000). back issues avail. **Document type:** *Proceedings.*
Related titles: French ed.; Spanish ed.; Russian ed.
Published by: International Civil Aviation Organization (I C A O), External Relations and Public Information Office, 999 University St, Montreal, PQ H3C 5H7, Canada. TEL 514-954-8022, FAX 514-954-6769, icaohq@icao.int.

INTERNATIONAL CIVIL AVIATION ORGANIZATION. LOCATION INDICATORS. *see* AERONAUTICS AND SPACE FLIGHT

387 341 CAN
INTERNATIONAL CIVIL AVIATION ORGANIZATION. PROCEEDINGS AND ACTION. Text in English. irreg. (122nd session). USD 12. back issues avail. **Document type:** *Proceedings.*
Related titles: French ed.; Spanish ed.; Russian ed.
Published by: International Civil Aviation Organization (I C A O), External Relations and Public Information Office, 999 University St, Montreal, PQ H3C 5H7, Canada. TEL 514-954-8022, FAX 514-954-6769, icaohq@icao.int.

387 341 CAN
INTERNATIONAL CIVIL AVIATION ORGANIZATION. PROTOCOLS. Text in English. irreg. price varies. back issues avail.
Published by: International Civil Aviation Organization (I C A O), External Relations and Public Information Office, 999 University St, Montreal, PQ H3C 5H7, Canada. TEL 514-954-8022, FAX 514-954-6769, icaohq@icao.int.

629.1 CAN ISSN 0074-2546
INTERNATIONAL CIVIL AVIATION ORGANIZATION. REPORT OF THE AIR NAVIGATION CONFERENCE. Text in English. 1953. irreg., latest vol.10, 1991. USD 37.
Related titles: French ed.; Spanish ed.; Russian ed.
Published by: International Civil Aviation Organization (I C A O), External Relations and Public Information Office, 999 University St, Montreal, PQ H3C 5H7, Canada. TEL 514-954-8022, FAX 514-954-6769, icaohq@icao.int.

387 341 CAN
INTERNATIONAL CIVIL AVIATION ORGANIZATION. RULES OF THE AIR AND AIR TRAFFIC SERVICES. (Incorporates Amendments 1-4) Text in English. irreg., latest vol.13, 1996. USD 47.
Related titles: French ed.; Spanish ed.; Russian ed.
Published by: International Civil Aviation Organization (I C A O), External Relations and Public Information Office, 999 University St, Montreal, PQ H3C 5H7, Canada. TEL 514-954-8022, FAX 514-954-6769, icaohq@icao.int.

INTERNATIONAL CIVIL AVIATION ORGANIZATION. SPECIAL COMMITTEE FOR THE MONITORING AND CO-ORDINATION OF DEVELOPMENT AND TRANSITION PLANNING FOR THE FUTURE AIR NAVIGATION SYSTEM (FANS - PHASE II). REPORT OF THE MEETING. *see* AERONAUTICS AND SPACE FLIGHT

387.744 USA ISSN 1522-2136

INTERNATIONAL CONNECTION; FedEx worldwide customer service. Text in English, French. 1997. bi-m. **Document type:** *Newsletter, Corporate.* **Description:** Contains FedEX news and international call center developments within FedEx.

Published by: Federal Express Corporation, 3003 Airways Blvd, Ste 1102, Memphis, TN 38194-1712. TEL 901-922-1447, FAX 901-922-4691. Ed., R&P David Yawn. Circ: 2,700 (controlled).

629.13 AUS

INTERNATIONAL DIRECTORY OF CIVIL AIRCRAFT (YEAR). Text in English. 1995. biennial. AUD 22.95 domestic; AUD 35 foreign (effective 2000). illus. **Document type:** *Directory.* **Description:** Lists all civil aircraft in production and revenue service, giving performance specifications, dimensions, weight, production runs, and a brief history for each type. Notes news and trends in civil aviation.

Published by: Aerospace Publications Pty. Ltd., PO Box 1777, Fyshwick, ACT 2609, Australia. TEL 61-2-62800111, FAX 61-2-62800007. Ed. Gerard Frawley. R&P Jim Thorn. Adv. contact Lee-Anne Simm.

387.7 USA

INTERNATIONAL FLIGHT ATTENDANTS ASSOCIATION NEWSLETTER. Text in English. 3/yr. **Document type:** *Newsletter.*

Published by: International Flight Attendants Association, c/o P R Miller, 2314 Old New Windsor Pike, New Windsor, MD 21776.

387.7 658 GBR ISSN 1755-9901
HE9761.1

▼ ➤ **INTERNATIONAL JOURNAL OF AVIATION MANAGEMENT.** Text in English. 2011. 4/yr. EUR 494 to institutions (print or online ed.); EUR 672 combined subscription to institutions (print & online eds.) (effective 2012). abstr.; bibl. **Document type:** *Journal, Academic/Scholarly.* **Description:** Offers practitioners and academics a forum for analysis and discussion in the field of aviation management covering all the major sectors of the industry: airlines, airports, air traffic control and related organizations.

Related titles: Online - full text ed.: ISSN 1755-991X (from IngentaConnect).

—CCC.

Published by: Inderscience Publishers, PO Box 735, Olney, Bucks MK46 5WB, United Kingdom. TEL 44-1234-240519, FAX 44-1234-240515, editorial@inderscience.com. Eds. Dr. Andreas Wald, Jaideep Motwani. **Subscr. to:** World Trade Centre Bldg, 29 Rte de Pre-Bois, Case Postale 856, Geneva 15 1215, Switzerland. FAX 41-22-7910885, subs@inderscience.com.

387.72 GBR ISSN 1744-2796

▼ ➤ **INTERNATIONAL JOURNAL OF AVIATION MANAGEMENT AND LOGISTICS.** Text in English. forthcoming 2011. 4/yr. EUR 494 to institutions (print or online ed.); EUR 672 combined subscription to institutions (print & online eds.) (effective 2009). **Document type:** *Journal, Academic/Scholarly.*

Related titles: Online - full text ed.: ISSN 1744-280X. forthcoming 2011. USD 450 to institutions (effective 2005).

—CCC.

Published by: Inderscience Publishers, PO Box 735, Olney, Bucks MK46 5WB, United Kingdom. TEL 44-1234-240519, FAX 44-1234-240515, editorial@inderscience.com, http://www.inderscience.com. Ed. Dr. Yahaya Yusuf. **Subscr. to:** World Trade Centre Bldg, 29 Rte de Pre-Bois, Case Postale 856, Geneva 15 1215, Switzerland. FAX 41-22-7910885, subs@inderscience.com.

370.19 USA ISSN 1050-8414
TL553.6

➤ **THE INTERNATIONAL JOURNAL OF AVIATION PSYCHOLOGY.** Text in English. 1991. q. GBP 476 combined subscription in United Kingdom to institutions (print & online eds.); EUR 634, USD 798 combined subscription to institutions (print & online eds.) (effective 2012). adv. bk.rev. back issues avail.; reprint service avail. from PSC. **Document type:** *Journal, Academic/Scholarly.* **Description:** Publishes scholarly papers developed within this increasingly important field of study—the development and management of safe, effective aviation systems from the standpoint of the human operators.

Related titles: Online - full text ed.: ISSN 1532-7108. GBP 428 in United Kingdom to institutions; EUR 571, USD 718 to institutions (effective 2012).

Indexed: A01, A03, A08, A22, A28, APA, ASCA, B07, B21, BrCerAb, C&ISA, C23, CA, CA/WCA, CIA, CerAb, CivEngAb, CorrAb, CurCont, E&CAJ, E-psyche, E01, E11, EEA, EMA, ESPM, EnvEAb, ErgAb, H&SSA, H15, HRIS, M&GPA, M&TEA, M09, MBF, METADEX, P02, P03, P10, P12, P26, P30, P43, P47, P48, P53, P54, PQC, PsycInfo, PsycholAb, SCOPUS, SSCI, SolStAb, T02, T04, W07, WAA.

—BLDSC (4542.125500), IE, Infotrieve, Ingenta, Linda Hall. **CCC.**

Published by: (Association for Aviation Psychology), Taylor & Francis Inc. (Subsidiary of: Taylor & Francis Group), 325 Chestnut St, Ste 800, Philadelphia, PA 19106. TEL 215-625-2940, 800-354-1420, orders@taylorandfrancis.com, http://www.taylorandfrancis.com. Ed. Richard S Jensen. Adv. contact Linda Hann TEL 44-1344-779945.

387.7 USA ISSN 2155-6962

▼ ➤ **INTERNATIONAL JOURNAL OF AVIATION TECHNOLOGY, ENGINEERING AND MANAGEMENT.** Text in English. 2011. q. USD 210 to individuals; USD 595 to institutions; USD 275 combined subscription to individuals (print & online eds.); USD 860 combined subscription to institutions (print & online eds.) (effective 2012). **Document type:** *Journal, Trade.* **Description:** Features current developments in aviation information technology, aeronautics and computing.

Related titles: Online - full text ed.: ISSN 2155-6970. 2011. USD 140 to individuals; USD 595 to institutions (effective 2012).

Published by: I G I Global, 701 E Chocolate Ave, Ste 200, Hershey, PA 17033. TEL 717-533-8845 ext 100, FAX 717-533-8661, cust@igi-global.com, http://www.igi-pub.com. Ed. Evon Abu-Taieh.

➤ **INTERNATIONAL JOURNAL OF CIVIL AVIATION.** *see* AERONAUTICS AND SPACE FLIGHT

▼ ➤ **INTERNATIONAL JOURNAL OF MICRO AIR VEHICLES.** *see* AERONAUTICS AND SPACE FLIGHT

➤ **INTERNATIONAL OPERATIONS BULLETIN.** *see* AERONAUTICS AND SPACE FLIGHT

387.7 USA ISSN 2151-8122
TL527.I7

▼ **IRANIAN AVIATION REVIEW.** Text in English. 2010. m. USD 120 (effective 2011). **Document type:** *Magazine, Consumer.* **Description:** Features history, data and photographs of Iranian military and commercial aviation.

Published by: Top Kit Publishing, 237 N Central Ave, Ste 208, Glendale, CA 91207. TEL 818-389-5220.

ISSUES IN AVIATION LAW AND POLICY. *see* LAW

387.7 CHE

J P AIRLINE FLEETS INTERNATIONAL. Text in English. 1966. a. CHF 75; CHF 85 in Europe; CHF 110 elsewhere. adv. illus. **Document type:** *Directory.* **Description:** Lists for each airline each aircraft, along with serial number, year built, and airframe history.

Related titles: CD-ROM ed.

Published by: Bucher & Co., Publikationen, PO Box 44, Zurich - Airport, 8058, Switzerland. TEL 41-1-8741747, FAX 41-1-8741757. Ed. Ulrich Klee. R&P, Adv. contact Frank E Bucher. Circ: 13,000 (paid). **Dist. in UK by:** BuchAir (UK) Ltd., PO Box 89, Reigate, Surrey RH2 7FG, United Kingdom. TEL 44-1737-224747, FAX 44-1737-226777; **Dist. in US by:** BuchAir (USA) Inc., PO Box 750515, Forest Hills, NY 11375-0515. TEL 718-263-8748, 718-275-6190.

387.7 GBR ISSN 1357-339X

JANE'S AIR TRAFFIC CONTROL. Text in English. 1982. a. GBP 430 per vol. (effective Dec. 2009). adv. illus. Index. **Document type:** *Yearbook, Trade.* **Description:** International coverage of ATC manufacturers and their systems. Provides information on over 600 manufacturers and more than 1,100 ATC systems worldwide.

Formerly (until 1993): Jane's Airport and A T C Equipment (0264-0953)

Related titles: CD-ROM ed.: GBP 1,085 (effective 2010); Online - full text ed.: GBP 1,500 (effective 2010).

—CCC.

Published by: I H S Jane's (Subsidiary of: I H S), Sentinel House, 163 Brighton Rd, Coulsdon, Surrey CR5 2YH, United Kingdom. TEL 44-20-87003700, FAX 44-20-87003751, info@janes.co.uk, http://www.janes.com. Ed. Jenny Beechener. Pub. Janine Boxall TEL 44-20-87003852. Adv. contact Catherine Sneath. **Dist. in Asia by:** Jane's Information Group Asia, 60 Albert St, #15-01 Albert Complex, Singapore 189969, Singapore. TEL 65-331-6280, FAX 65-336-9921, info@janes.com.sg; **Dist. in Australia by:** Jane's Information Group Australia, PO Box 3502, Rozelle, NSW 2039, Australia. TEL 61-2-8587-7900, FAX 61-2-8587-7901, info@janes.thomson.com.au; **Dist. in the Americas by:** 1340 Braddock Pl, Ste 300, Alexandria, VA 22314-1651. TEL 703-683-3700, 800-824-0768, FAX 703-836-0297, 800-836-0297, info@janes.com.

JANE'S AIRCRAFT COMPONENT MANUFACTURERS. *see* AERONAUTICS AND SPACE FLIGHT

387.736 GBR ISSN 0954-7649
HE9797.A1

JANE'S AIRPORT REVIEW; the global airport business magazine. Text in English. 1989. 10/yr. GBP 180 domestic; GBP 185 in Europe; GBP 195 elsewhere (effective 2010). illus. reprints avail. **Document type:** *Magazine, Trade.* **Description:** For senior executives in airport management, airlines and air traffic control, and national and international regulatory authorities. Covers new products and services.

Related titles: CD-ROM ed.: GBP 645 (effective 2010); Online - full text ed.: GBP 870 (effective 2010).

Indexed: A28, APA, B21, BrCerAb, C&ISA, CA/WCA, CIA, CLT&T, CerAb, CivEngAb, CorrAb, E&CAJ, E11, EEA, EMA, ESPM, EngInd, EnvEAb, H&SSA, H15, HRIS, M&TEA, M09, MBF, METADEX, P16, P48, P53, P54, PQC, SCOPUS, SolStAb, T04, WAA.

—BLDSC (4645.975000), IE, Infotrieve. **CCC.**

Published by: I H S Jane's (Subsidiary of: I H S), Sentinel House, 163 Brighton Rd, Coulsdon, Surrey CR5 2YH, United Kingdom. TEL 44-20-87003700, FAX 44-20-87003751, info@janes.co.uk, http://www.janes.com. **Dist. in Asia by:** Jane's Information Group Asia, 60 Albert St, #15-01 Albert Complex, Singapore 189969, Singapore. TEL 65-331-6280, FAX 65-336-9921, info@janes.com.sg; **Dist. in Australia by:** Jane's Information Group Australia, PO Box 3502, Rozelle, NSW 2039, Australia. TEL 61-2-8587-7900, FAX 61-2-8587-7901, info@janes.thomson.com.au; **Dist. in the Americas by:** 1340 Braddock Pl, Ste 300, Alexandria, VA 22314-1651. TEL 703-683-3700, 800-824-0768, FAX 703-836-0297, 800-836-0297, info@janes.com.

387.74 GBR ISSN 0969-1243

JANE'S AIRPORTS AND HANDLING AGENTS. CENTRAL LATIN AMERICA INCLUDING THE CARIBBEAN. Text in English. 1988. a. GBP 480 per issue (2010-2011 ed.) (effective 2010). adv. **Document type:** *Yearbook, Trade.* **Description:** Contains in-depth planning guides containing extensive information on airports around the world and their service suppliers.

Related titles: CD-ROM ed.: GBP 565 (effective 2010); Online - full text ed.: GBP 810 (effective 2010).

—CCC.

Published by: I H S Jane's (Subsidiary of: I H S), Sentinel House, 163 Brighton Rd, Coulsdon, Surrey CR5 2YH, United Kingdom. TEL 44-20-87003700, FAX 44-20-87003751, info@janes.co.uk, http://www.janes.com. Ed. Jacqui Bowell. Pub. Janine Boxall TEL 44-20-87003852. Adv. contact Catherine Sneath. **Dist. in Asia by:** Jane's Information Group Asia, 60 Albert St, #15-01 Albert Complex, Singapore 189969, Singapore. TEL 65-331-6280, FAX 65-336-9921, info@janes.com.sg; **Dist. in Australia by:** Jane's Information Group Australia, PO Box 3502, Rozelle, NSW 2039, Australia. TEL 61-2-8587-7900, FAX 61-2-8587-7901, info@janes.thomson.com.au; **Dist. in the Americas by:** 1340 Braddock Pl, Ste 300, Alexandria, VA 22314-1651. TEL 703-683-3700, 800-824-0768, FAX 703-836-0297, 800-836-0297, info@janes.com.

387.74 GBR ISSN 0952-4673

JANE'S AIRPORTS AND HANDLING AGENTS. EUROPE. Text in English. 1984. a. GBP 480 per issue (2010-2011 ed.) (effective 2010). **Document type:** *Yearbook, Trade.*

Formerly (until 1987): World Handling Agents Manual. Europe (0266-6987)

Related titles: CD-ROM ed.: GBP 565 (effective 2010); Online - full text ed.: GBP 810 (effective 2010).

—BLDSC (4645.981000). **CCC.**

Published by: I H S Jane's (Subsidiary of: I H S), Sentinel House, 163 Brighton Rd, Coulsdon, Surrey CR5 2YH, United Kingdom. TEL 44-20-87003700, FAX 44-20-87003751, info@janes.co.uk, http://www.janes.com. Ed. Jacqui Bowell. **Dist. in Asia by:** Jane's Information Group Asia, 60 Albert St, #15-01 Albert Complex, Singapore 189969, Singapore. TEL 65-331-6280, FAX 65-336-9921, info@janes.com.sg; **Dist. in Australia by:** Jane's Information Group Australia, PO Box 3502, Rozelle, NSW 2039, Australia. TEL 61-2-8587-7900, FAX 61-2-8587-7901, info@janes.thomson.com.au; **Dist. in the Americas by:** 1340 Braddock Pl, Ste 300, Alexandria, VA 22314-1651. TEL 703-683-3700, 800-824-0768, FAX 703-836-0297, 800-836-0297, info@janes.com.

387.74 GBR ISSN 0952-469X

JANE'S AIRPORTS AND HANDLING AGENTS. FAR EAST, ASIA AND AUSTRALASIA. Text in English. 1987. a. GBP 480 per issue (2010-2011 ed.) (effective 2010). adv. **Document type:** *Yearbook, Trade.* **Description:** Contains in-depth planning guides containing extensive information on airports around the world and their service suppliers.

Related titles: CD-ROM ed.: GBP 565 (effective 2010); Online - full text ed.: GBP 810 (effective 2010).

—CCC.

Published by: I H S Jane's (Subsidiary of: I H S), Sentinel House, 163 Brighton Rd, Coulsdon, Surrey CR5 2YH, United Kingdom. TEL 44-20-87003700, FAX 44-20-87003751, info@janes.co.uk, http://www.janes.com. Ed. Jacqui Bowell. Pub. Janine Boxall TEL 44-20-87003852. Adv. contact Catherine Sneath. **Dist. in Asia by:** Jane's Information Group Asia, 60 Albert St, #15-01 Albert Complex, Singapore 189969, Singapore. TEL 65-331-6280, FAX 65-336-9921, info@janes.com.sg; **Dist. in Australia by:** Jane's Information Group Australia, PO Box 3502, Rozelle, NSW 2039, Australia. TEL 61-2-8587-7900, FAX 61-2-8587-7901, info@janes.thomson.com.au; **Dist. in the Americas by:** 1340 Braddock Pl, Ste 300, Alexandria, VA 22314-1651. TEL 703-683-3700, 800-824-0768, FAX 703-836-0297, 800-836-0297, info@janes.com.

387.74 GBR ISSN 0952-4665

JANE'S AIRPORTS AND HANDLING AGENTS. MIDDLE EAST AND AFRICA. Text in English. 1985. a. GBP 480 per issue (2010-2011 ed.) (effective 2010). adv. **Document type:** *Yearbook, Trade.* **Description:** Covers in-depth planning guides containing extensive information on airports around the world and their service suppliers.

Formerly (until 1986): World Handling Agents Manual. Middle East & Africa (0267-4408)

Related titles: CD-ROM ed.: GBP 565 (effective 2010); Online - full text ed.: GBP 810 (effective 2010).

—CCC.

Published by: I H S Jane's (Subsidiary of: I H S), Sentinel House, 163 Brighton Rd, Coulsdon, Surrey CR5 2YH, United Kingdom. TEL 44-20-87003700, FAX 44-20-87003751, info@janes.co.uk, http://www.janes.com. Ed. Jacqui Bowell. Adv. contact Janine Boxall TEL 44-20-87003852. **Dist. in Asia by:** Jane's Information Group Asia, 60 Albert St, #15-01 Albert Complex, Singapore 189969, Singapore. TEL 65-331-6280, FAX 65-336-9921, info@janes.com.sg; **Dist. in Australia by:** Jane's Information Group Australia, PO Box 3502, Rozelle, NSW 2039, Australia. TEL 61-2-8587-7900, FAX 61-2-8587-7901, info@janes.thomson.com.au; **Dist. in the Americas by:** 1340 Braddock Pl, Ste 300, Alexandria, VA 22314-1651. TEL 703-683-3700, 800-824-0768, FAX 703-836-0297, 800-836-0297, info@janes.com.

387.74 GBR ISSN 1365-7836

JANE'S AIRPORTS AND HANDLING AGENTS. UNITED STATES AND CANADA. Text in English. 1988. a. GBP 480 per issue (2010-2011 ed.) (effective 2010). adv. **Document type:** *Yearbook, Trade.* **Description:** Contains in-depth planning guides containing extensive information on airports around the world and their service suppliers.

Formerly (until 1992): Jane's Airports and Handling Agents. U S A and Canada (0952-4681)

Related titles: CD-ROM ed.: GBP 565 (effective 2010); Online - full text ed.: GBP 810 (effective 2010).

—CCC.

Published by: I H S Jane's (Subsidiary of: I H S), Sentinel House, 163 Brighton Rd, Coulsdon, Surrey CR5 2YH, United Kingdom. TEL 44-20-87003700, FAX 44-20-87003751, info@janes.co.uk, http://www.janes.com. Ed. Jacqui Bowell. Pub. Janine Boxall TEL 44-20-87003852. Adv. contact Catherine Sneath. **Dist. in Asia by:** Jane's Information Group Asia, 60 Albert St, #15-01 Albert Complex, Singapore 189969, Singapore. TEL 65-331-6280, FAX 65-336-9921, info@janes.com.sg; **Dist. in Australia by:** Jane's Information Group Australia, PO Box 3502, Rozelle, NSW 2039, Australia. TEL 61-2-8587-7900, FAX 61-2-8587-7901, info@janes.thomson.com.au; **Dist. in the Americas by:** 1340 Braddock Pl, Ste 300, Alexandria, VA 22314-1651. TEL 703-683-3700, 800-824-0768, FAX 703-836-0297, 800-836-0297, info@janes.com.

387.7 GBR

JANE'S AIRPORTS, EQUIPMENT AND SERVICE. Text in English. a. GBP 475 per issue (2010-2011 ed.) (effective 2010). illus. **Document type:** *Yearbook, Trade.* **Description:** Contains information to the world's airport suppliers and their products.

Related titles: CD-ROM ed.: GBP 1,145 (effective 2010); Online - full text ed.: GBP 1,575 (effective 2010).

Published by: I H S Jane's (Subsidiary of: I H S), Sentinel House, 163 Brighton Rd, Coulsdon, Surrey CR5 2YH, United Kingdom. TEL 44-20-87003700, FAX 44-20-87003751, info@janes.co.uk, http://www.janes.com. Ed. Kylie Bull. **Dist. in Asia by:** Jane's Information Group Asia, 60 Albert St, #15-01 Albert Complex, Singapore 189969, Singapore. TEL 65-331-6280, FAX 65-336-9921, info@janes.com.sg; **Dist. in Australia by:** Jane's Information Group Australia, PO Box 3502, Rozelle, NSW 2039, Australia. TEL 61-2-8587-7900, FAX 61-2-8587-7901, info@janes.thomson.com.au; **Dist. in the Americas by:** 1340 Braddock Pl, Ste 300, Alexandria, VA 22314-1651. TEL 703-683-3700, 800-824-0768, FAX 703-836-0297, 800-836-0297, info@janes.com.

JANE'S HELICOPTER MARKETS AND SYSTEMS. *see* AERONAUTICS AND SPACE FLIGHT

387.7 GBR ISSN 1748-2518

JANE'S WORLD AIRLINES. Text in English. 1991. s-a. **Document type:** *Report, Trade.* **Description:** Features airline-wise reports covering airline structure and operations including fleet structure, routes operated, traffic statistics and financial data.

TU

Related titles: CD-ROM ed.: GBP 1,235, USD 2,070, AUD 3,215 (effective 2008); Online - full text ed.: GBP 1,335, USD 2,235, AUD 3,460 (effective 2008).
Published by: I H S Jane's (Subsidiary of: I H S), Sentinel House, 163 Brighton Rd, Coulsdon, Surrey CR5 2YH, United Kingdom. TEL 44-20-87003700, FAX 44-20-87003751, info@janes.co.uk, http://www.janes.com. Ed. Danny Pratt.

387.7 333 USA ISSN 1528-1183
JET FUEL INTELLIGENCE. Abbreviated title: J F I. Text in English. 1991. w. adv. back issues avail. **Document type:** *Newsletter, Trade.* **Description:** Analyzes the growing international aviation fuels business. Includes airport by airport jet fuel and spot cargo pricing, regional trends, and other factors influencing the market.
Related titles: E-mail ed.: USD 3,110 (effective 2009); Fax ed.; Online - full text ed.: USD 2,980 (effective 2009).
Indexed: A15, ABIn, P48, P51, P52, PQC.
—CCC.
Published by: Energy Intelligence Group, Inc., 5 E 37th St, 5th Fl, New York, NY 10016. TEL 212-532-1112, FAX 212-532-4479, info@energyintel.com. Ed. Cristina Haus. Adv. contact Mark Hoff TEL 212-532-1112 ext 1130.

387.71 GBR
JET OPERATOR STATISTICS (CD-ROM). Text in English. 200?. s-a. GBP 630 (effective 2010). **Document type:** *Journal, Trade.*
Media: CD-ROM.
Published by: Ascend Worldwide Ltd., Cardinal Point, Newall Rd, Heathrow Airport, London, TW6 2AS, United Kingdom. TEL 44-20-85646700, FAX 44-20-88970300, uk@ascendworldwide.com, http://www.ascendworldwide.com.

387.7 USA
JETRADER. Text in English. bi-m. adv. **Document type:** *Magazine, Trade.*
Published by: (International Society of Transport Aircraft Traders), Naylor LLC, 5950 NW 1st Pl, Gainesville, FL 32607. TEL 800-369-6220, FAX 352-331-3525, http://www.naylor.com.

387.7 910.09 CHE
JETSTREAM AIR NEWS; Swiss aviation magazine. Text in English. 1961. m. CHF 42. adv. back issues avail.
Address: Postfach 1130, Zurich-Airport, CH-8058, Switzerland. Ed. Martin Hirzel. Circ: 5,000.

387.736 FRA ISSN 1250-8500
LE JOURNAL D'A D P. (Aeroports de Paris) Text in French. 1956. 11/yr. free. adv. bk.rev. illus.; stat.
Former titles (until 1994): A D P a la Une (0761-9286); (until 1984): Propos en l'Air (0033-1384)
—CCC.
Published by: Aeroports de Paris, Direction Marketing et Communication, 291 bd. Raspail, Paris, Cedex 14 75675, France. Ed. Anatole Rojinski. Circ: 6,000.

JOURNAL OF AIR TRANSPORT MANAGEMENT. *see* BUSINESS AND ECONOMICS—Management

387.7 658 GBR ISSN 1750-1938
➤ **JOURNAL OF AIRPORT MANAGEMENT.** Abbreviated title: J A M. Text in English. 2006. q. GBP 235 combined subscription per vol. in the UK & Europe (print & online eds.) (effective 2012). adv. **Document type:** *Journal, Academic/Scholarly.* **Description:** Contains detailed, authoritative briefings, analysis, case studies, research and reviews by leading experts and practitioners in the field, to keep subscribers up to date with the latest developments and thinking in airport management.
Related titles: Online - full text ed.: ISSN 1750-1946.
Indexed: A01, CA, T02.
—BLDSC (4926.710000). **CCC.**
Published by: (Airports Council International CHE), Henry Stewart Publications LLP, c/o Gwen Yates, Russell House, 28-30 Little Russell St, London, WC1A 2HN, United Kingdom. TEL 44-20-70923496, FAX 44-20-70742081, qweny@henrystewart.co.uk, http://www.henrystewart.com/default.aspx. Ed., Pub. Daryn Moody TEL 44-20-74043040. **Subscr. to:** Henry Stewart Publications, PO Box 361, Birmingham, AL 35201. TEL 205-995-1588, 800-633-4931, hsp@ebsco.com.

387.7 SGP
JOURNAL OF AVIATION MANAGEMENT. Text in English. a. SGD 36 (effective 2009). **Document type:** *Journal, Academic/Scholarly.* **Description:** Covers a wide range of aviation issues such as: Aviation safety, security, accident investigation, technology, crisis management, airport management, and sustainable aviation.
—BLDSC (4949.990000).
Published by: Singapore Aviation Academy, 1 Aviation Dr., Singapore, 499867, Singapore. TEL 65-65-430433, FAX 65-65-429890, saa@caas.gov.sg, http://www.saa.com.sg/.

K L M AGENT. (Koninklijke Luchtvaart Maatschappij) *see* TRAVEL AND TOURISM

387.744 GBR ISSN 1476-7481
KEY NOTE MARKET REPORT: AIR FREIGHT. Variant title: Air Freight Market Report. Text in English. 2001. irreg., latest 2005, Jun. GBP 399 per issue (effective 2010). **Document type:** *Report, Trade.* **Description:** Provides an overview of a specific UK market segment and includes executive summary, market definition, market size, industry background, competitor analysis, current issues, forecasts, company profiles, and more.
Published by: Key Note Ltd. (Subsidiary of: Bonnier Business Information), Harlequin House, 5th Fl, 7 High St, Teddington, Richmond upon Thames, TW11 8EE, United Kingdom. TEL 44-845-5040452, FAX 44-845-5040453, info@keynote.co.uk.

387.7 GBR ISSN 1367-5362
KEY NOTE MARKET REPORT: AIRLINES. Variant title: Airlines Market Report. Text in English. 1981. irreg., latest 2008, Jul. GBP 460 per issue (effective 2010). **Document type:** *Report, Trade.* **Description:** Provides an overview of a specific UK market segment and includes executive summary, market definition, market size, industry background, competitor analysis, current issues, forecasts, company profiles, and more.
Formerly (until 1997): Key Note Report: Airlines (0951-6735); Which superseded in part: Key Note Market Report: Airports and Airlines
Related titles: CD-ROM ed.; Online - full text ed.
—CCC.
Published by: Key Note Ltd. (Subsidiary of: Bonnier Business Information), Harlequin House, 5th Fl, 7 High St, Teddington, Richmond upon Thames, TW11 8EE, United Kingdom. TEL 44-845-5040452, FAX 44-845-5040453, info@keynote.co.uk.

387.7 GBR ISSN 1460-8308
KEY NOTE MARKET REPORT: AIRPORTS. Variant title: Airports Market Report. Text in English. 19??. irreg., latest 2009, Jun. GBP 460 per issue (effective 2010). **Document type:** *Report, Trade.* **Description:** Provides an overview of a specific UK market segment and includes executive summary, market definition, market size, industry background, competitor analysis, current issues, forecasts, company profiles, and more.
Formerly (until 1997): Key Note Report: Airports; Which superseded in part: Key Note Market Report: Airports and Airlines
Related titles: CD-ROM ed.; Online - full text ed.
Published by: Key Note Ltd. (Subsidiary of: Bonnier Business Information), Harlequin House, 5th Fl, 7 High St, Teddington, Richmond upon Thames, TW11 8EE, United Kingdom. TEL 44-845-5040452, FAX 44-845-5040453, info@keynote.co.uk.

387.736 NZL ISSN 1170-8018
KIWIFLYER. Text in English. 2008. bi-m. NZD 25; NZD 5.90 per issue; free to qualified personnel (effective 2011). adv. back issues avail. **Document type:** *Magazine, Trade.*
Related titles: Online - full text ed.: ISSN 2230-3545. free (effective 2011).
Published by: Kiwi Flyer Ltd., Papakura, PO Box 72-841, Auckland, 2244, New Zealand. TEL 800-535-937, FAX 64-9-9293079. Ed. Michael Norton.

387.7 330 CHN ISSN 1671-3095
KONGYUN SHANGWU/AIR TRANSPORT & BUSINESS. Text in Chinese. 2001. s-m. USD 98.40 (effective 2009). **Document type:** *Magazine, Trade.*
—East View.
Published by: Minhang Guanli Zazhishe, 3, Huajiadi Dong, Beijing, 100102, China. TEL 86-10-64720474, FAX 86-10-58250408, http://www.cacs.net.cn/qikan/zazhishe.asp. **Dist. by:** China International Book Trading Corp, 35 Chegongzhuang Xilu, Haidian District, PO Box 399, Beijing 100044, China. TEL 86-10-68412045, FAX 86-10-68412023, cibtc@mail.cibtc.com.cn, http://www.cibtc.com.cn.

387.7 USA ISSN 2154-3763
L S A NEWS. (Light Sport Aircraft) Text in English. 2007. d. free (effective 2010). **Document type:** *Magazine, Trade.* **Description:** Provides news and information for the light sport aircraft industry and manufacturers.
Media: Online - full text.
Published by: K R D Corporation

387.7 USA
LIGHT AIRCRAFT MANUFACTURERS ASSOCIATION. NEWSLETTER. Text in English. 1984. irreg. free. **Document type:** *Newsletter.*
Published by: Light Aircraft Manufacturers Association, c/o TEAM, 10790 Ivy Bluff Rd, Bradyville, TN 37026. TEL 615-765-5397, FAX 615-765-7234. Circ: 400.

LIGHT PLANE MAINTENANCE; practical maintenance advice for owners and pilots. *see* AERONAUTICS AND SPACE FLIGHT

341.46 CAN ISSN 0256-4742
HE9788.4.A55
LIVE ANIMALS REGULATIONS. Text in English. 1975. a. **Document type:** *Handbook/Manual/Guide, Trade.* **Description:** Describes the container to be used for carriage for each kind of animal and the precautionary measures to be taken during ground and air transportation.
Related titles: French ed.: Reglementation du Transport des Animaux Vivants. ISSN 1012-8271; Chinese ed.; Spanish ed.
—CCC.
Published by: International Air Transport Association, 800 Place Victoria, PO Box 113, Montreal, PQ H4Z 1M1, Canada. TEL 514-390-6726, 800-716-6326, FAX 514-874-9659, sales@iata.org. Adv. contact Sandra Davies.

THE LOG. *see* AERONAUTICS AND SPACE FLIGHT

LOST BIRDS; discover aviation archaeology. *see* AERONAUTICS AND SPACE FLIGHT

387.796 GBR ISSN 1755-1242
LOW COST & REGIONAL AIRLINE BUSINESS. Text in English. 2006 (Apr.). q. free to qualified personnel (effective 2009). adv. **Document type:** *Magazine, Trade.* **Description:** Provides a detailed insight into the airlines, aircraft, airports, routes, maintenance, onboard services, airline handling, finance, IT and e-commerce applications.
Formerly (until 2007): Low Cost Airline Business (1750-6921)
—CCC.
Published by: Air Transport Publications Ltd., 16 Hampden Gurney St, London, W1H 5AL, United Kingdom. TEL 44-20-77243456, FAX 44-20-77242632, info@airtransportpubs.com. Ed. Martin Roebuck. Adv. contact Nimita Patel. page GBP 3,250, page USD 6,350, page EUR 5,700; trim 203 x 280. Circ: 7,000 (controlled).

387.7 GBR ISSN 1753-0598
LOW-FARE & REGIONAL AIRLINES. Abbreviated title: L A R A. Text in English. 1984. 10/yr. USD 160 to institutions; free to qualified personnel (effective 2010). adv. back issues avail. **Document type:** *Magazine, Trade.* **Description:** Contains articles and news of the worldwide regional aviation industry.
Former titles (until 2006): Regional Airline World (1465-6817); (until 1998): Commuter World (0265-4504); Which incorporated (1993-199?): Regional Air International (1070-065X); Which was formerly (until 1993): Commuter Air International (1054-7436); (1979-1990): Commuter Air (0199-2686)
Related titles: Online - full text ed.: free (effective 2010).
Indexed: CLT&T, HRIS.
—Ingenta. **CCC.**
Published by: Shephard Press Ltd., 268 Bath Rd, Slough, Berkshire SL1 4DX, United Kingdom. TEL 44-1753-727001, FAX 44-1753-727002, info@shephard.co.uk. Ed. Bernie Baldwin TEL 44-1753-727021. Adv. contact Mike Wild TEL 44-1753-727007. color page GBP 10,160; 205 x 273. **Subscr. to:** CDS Global, Tower House, Sovereign Park, Market Harborough, Leics LE16 9EF, United Kingdom. TEL 44-1858-438879, FAX 44-1858-461739, shephardgroup@subscription.co.uk.

387.7 GBR ISSN 2045-9890
▼ **LOW-FARE & REGIONAL AVIATION HANDBOOK.** Text in English. 2011. a. adv. **Document type:** *Handbook/Manual/Guide, Trade.* **Description:** Provides reference source for aviation professionals.
Supersedes in part (in 2011): Commercial Aviation and Inflight Handbook (2041-9333); Which was formed by the merger of (1998-2010): Shephard's Inflight Handbook (1461-619X); (2007-2010): Low-Fare and Regional Aviation (1753-1845); Which was formerly (until 2007): Shephard's Regional Aviation Handbook (1365-6589); (until 1996): Commuter World. World Operators' Handbook (1356-6334)
Related titles: Online - full text ed.
Published by: H M G Aerospace Ltd., Ste 2, 7 Alexandra Rd, Farnborough, Hampshire GU14 6BU, United Kingdom. TEL 44-1252-501055, FAX 44-1252-408674, info@hmgaerospace.com. Circ: 5,500.

387.7 NLD ISSN 1381-7078
LUCHTVRACHT; Air cargo magazine for the benelux. Text in Dutch. 1969. 10/yr. EUR 35 (effective 2009). adv. **Document type:** *Journal, Trade.* **Description:** Covers news and issues affecting the air cargo sector.
Published by: Disque '67 B.V., Minervaplein 22-3, Amsterdam, 1077 TR, Netherlands. TEL 33-20-6711142, FAX 33-20-6721899. Circ: 4,500 (paid).

387.74 629.13 DEU
LUFTFAHRT JOURNAL. Text in German. m. illus. back issues avail. **Document type:** *Magazine, Trade.* **Description:** Reports news and developments in commercial passenger and freight air transportation. Discusses topics in aircraft orders, construction, modifications, and business.
Published by: Coincat e.V., Postfach 510143, Hamburg, 22501, Germany. coincat-luftfahrt@gmx.de. Ed. Ulf Boie.

387.7 DEU ISSN 0949-5487
LUFTHANSEAT; Zeitung fuer die Mitarbeiter in Lufthansa Konzern. Text in English, German. 1955. w. free to members (effective 2008). adv. bk.rev. **Document type:** *Newspaper, Trade.*
Published by: Deutsche Lufthansa AG, FRA EC-A, Flughafen, Frankfurt Am Main, 60546, Germany. TEL 49-69-6960, FAX 49-69-69633022, http://konzern.lufthansa.com. adv.: color page EUR 4,578.75. Circ: 74,000 (controlled).

387.7 620.004 GBR ISSN 1466-6448
M R O MANAGEMENT. (Maintenance, Repair and Overhaul) Text in English. 1999. q. free to qualified personnel (effective 2009). adv. **Document type:** *Magazine, Trade.* **Description:** Contains in-depth articles covering the management of airframes, engines and components; manpower and resources; facilities; IT and e-commerce application; mergers and acquisitions; and regional reports from around the world.
—CCC.
Published by: Air Transport Publications Ltd., 16 Hampden Gurney St, London, W1H 5AL, United Kingdom. TEL 44-20-77243456, FAX 44-20-77242632, info@airtransportpubs.com, http://www.airtransportpubs.com/. Ed. Ian Harbison TEL 44-20-83542679. Adv. contact Nimita Patel. page GBP 3,250, page EUR 5,700, page USD 6,350; trim 203 x 280. Circ: 8,000 (controlled).

387.7 620.004 629.134 GBR
M R O NEWS FOCUS. (Maintenance, Repair and Overhaul) Text in English. 19??. m. free to qualified personnel (effective 2009). **Document type:** *Newsletter, Trade.* **Description:** Features headline news, news digest, contracts, products and services, financial results, appointments and industry events.
Related titles: Online - full text ed.: free (effective 2009).
Published by: Air Transport Publications Ltd., 16 Hampden Gurney St, London, W1H 5AL, United Kingdom. TEL 44-20-77243456, FAX 44-20-77242632, info@airtransportpubs.com, http://www.airtransportpubs.com/. Ed. Ian Harbison TEL 44-20-83542679. Adv. contact Nimita Patel.

387.736 DEU
DAS MAGAZIN (DUESSELDORF). Text in German. 2000. 4/yr. free (effective 2009). adv. **Document type:** *Magazine, Consumer.*
Published by: Flughafen Duesseldorf GmbH, Postfach 300363, Duesseldorf, 40403, Germany. TEL 49-211-4210, FAX 49-211-4216666, mediencenter@dus-int.de. Ed. Karl-Heinz Morawietz. Adv. contact Christophe Brandenburger. page EUR 4,800; trim 220 x 305. Circ: 60,000 (controlled).

363.12465 GBR
MAJOR LOSS RECORD (CD-ROM). Abbreviated title: M L R. Text in English. 19??. a. GBP 500 per issue for pdf; GBP 1,250 per issue for Access database (effective 2009).
Media: CD-ROM.
Published by: Ascend Worldwide Ltd., Cardinal Point, Newall Rd, Heathrow Airport, London, TW6 2AS, United Kingdom. TEL 44-20-85646700, FAX 44-20-88970300, uk@ascendworldwide.com.

387.7 MWI ISSN 0076-3055
MALAWI. DEPARTMENT OF CIVIL AVIATION. ANNUAL REPORT. Text in English. a. **Document type:** *Government.*
Published by: (Malawi. Department of Civil Aviation), Government Printer, PO Box 37, Zomba, Malawi.

MALTA. CENTRAL OFFICE OF STATISTICS. SHIPPING AND AVIATION STATISTICS. *see* TRANSPORTATION—Abstracting, Bibliographies, Statistics

629.13 GBR
MANDATORY AIRCRAFT MODIFICATIONS AND INSPECTIONS SUMMARY. Text in English. 1970. base vol. plus irreg. updates. looseleaf. **Document type:** *Government.* **Description:** Contains associated Airworthiness directive numbers modifications, inspections and service bulletins declared mandatory by the CAA for aircraft, engines, propellers and equipment of UK design.
Related titles: Online - full text ed.: free (effective 2010); ◆ Series: Air Traffic Control Licensing; ◆ Air Navigation - The Order and the Regulations; ◆ Great Britain. Civil Aviation Authority. Airport Surveys; ◆ Manual of Air Traffic Services - Part 1; ◆ Great Britain. Civil Aviation Authority. Mandatory Requirements for Airworthiness; ◆ Great Britain. Civil Aviation Authority. Approved Aerial Positions; ◆ Civil Aircraft Airworthiness Information and Procedures; ◆ A A I B

Recommendations - C A A Progress Report (Year); ◆ Air Traffic Services Engineering Requirements; ◆ Great Britain. Civil Aviation Authority. Annual Punctuality Statistics - Full Analysis (Year); ◆ Great Britain. Civil Aviation Authority. Annual Punctuality Statistics - Full and Summary Analysis (Year); ◆ United Kingdom Aeronautical Information Publication; ◆ Overseas Non-scheduled Flight Clearances Guide.
Published by: Civil Aviation Authority, Printing and Publication Services, C A A House, 45-59 Kingsway, London, WCB2 6TE, United Kingdom. TEL 44-20-73797311, FAX 44-20-74536097, infoservices@caa.co.uk. **Dist. by:** Westward Documedia Limited.

387.74 GBR
MANUAL OF AIR TRAFFIC SERVICES - PART 1. Text in English. 19??. base vol. plus irreg. updates. looseleaf. GBP 60.50 per issue (effective 2010). **Document type:** *Government.* **Description:** Contains procedures, instructions and information which are intended to form the basis of air traffic services within the United Kingdom.
Related titles: Online - full text ed.: free (effective 2010); ◆ Series: Air Traffic Control Licensing; ◆ Air Navigation - The Order and the Regulations; ◆ Great Britain. Civil Aviation Authority. Airport Surveys; ◆ Overseas Non-scheduled Flight Clearances Guide; ◆ Great Britain. Civil Aviation Authority. Mandatory Requirements for Airworthiness; ◆ Mandatory Aircraft Modifications and Inspections Summary; ◆ Civil Aircraft Airworthiness Information and Procedures; ◆ A A I B Recommendations - C A A Progress Report (Year); ◆ Air Traffic Services Engineering Requirements; ◆ Great Britain. Civil Aviation Authority. Annual Punctuality Statistics - Full Analysis (Year); ◆ Great Britain. Civil Aviation Authority. Annual Punctuality Statistics - Full and Summary Analysis (Year); ◆ United Kingdom Aeronautical Information Publication; ◆ Great Britain. Civil Aviation Authority. Approved Aerial Positions.
Published by: Civil Aviation Authority, Printing and Publication Services, C A A House, 45-59 Kingsway, London, WCB2 6TE, United Kingdom. TEL 44-20-73797311, FAX 44-20-74536097, infoservices@caa.co.uk. **Dist. by:** Westward Documedia Limited.

387.71 GBR
MARKET INTELLIGENCE (ONLINE). Text in English. 200?. m. GBP 500 (effective 2009).
Media: Online - full text.
Published by: Ascend Worldwide Ltd., Cardinal Point, Newall Rd, Heathrow Airport, London, TW6 2AS, United Kingdom. TEL 44-20-85646700, FAX 44-20-88970300, uk@ascendworldwide.com, http://www.ascendworldwide.com.

MASSACHUSETTS INSTITUTE OF TECHNOLOGY. FLIGHT TRANSPORTATION LABORATORY. F T L REPORTS AND MEMORANDA. *see* AERONAUTICS AND SPACE FLIGHT

387.736 USA
MICHIGAN AIRPORT DIRECTORY. Text in English. 1922. a. USD 8.
Published by: Aeronautics Commission, 2700 E Airport Service Dr, Capital City Airport, Lansing, MI 48906. TEL 517-335-8521, FAX 517-321-6422. Ed. John L Wagner. Circ: 8,000 (controlled).

387.7 USA ISSN 0194-5068
MIDWEST FLYER MAGAZINE; serving the Upper Midwest. Text in English. 1978. m. USD 15 (effective 2007). adv. bk.rev. 60 p./no.; **Document type:** *Magazine, Consumer.* **Description:** General aviation magazine serving aircraft owners and pilots in the Upper Midwest.
Formerly (until 1980): Wisconsin Flyer Magazine
Related titles: Alternate Frequency ed(s).: bi-m.
Published by: Flyer Publications, Inc., PO Box 199, Oregon, WI 53575-0199. TEL 608-835-7063, FAX 608-835-3323, weiman@mailbag.com. Ed., Pub. Dave Weiman. adv.: color page USD 1,824; trim 7.5 x 10. Circ: 10,000.

387.7 CAN
MILEAGE MANUAL. Text in English. a. USD 3,200 per issue (effective 2008). **Document type:** *Handbook/Manual/Guide, Trade.* **Description:** Compilation of the shortest operated mileage and maximum permitted mileage between more than 700,000 specified city pairs on the world airline map.
Related titles: CD-ROM ed.: USD 66,250 (effective 2008); Online - full content ed.: USD 66,250 (effective 2008).
Published by: International Air Transport Association, 800 Place Victoria, PO Box 113, Montreal, PQ H4Z 1M1, Canada. TEL 514-390-6726, 800-716-6326, FAX 514-874-9659, sales@iata.org. Ed. Karin Bengtsson.

387.7 658 CHN ISSN 1005-491X
MINHANG GUANLI/CIVIL AVIATION MANAGEMENT. Text in Chinese. 1993. m. USD 56.40 (effective 2009). **Document type:** *Magazine, Trade.*
—East View.
Published by: Minhang Guanli Zazhishe, 3, Huajiadi Dong, Beijing, 100102, China. TEL 86-10-64720474, FAX 86-10-58250408, http://www.cacs.net.cn/qikan/zazhishe.asp.

387.7 CHN
MINHANG ZHENGGONG. Text in Chinese. 1995. bi-m. CNY 36; CNY 6 newsstand/cover (effective 2007). **Document type:** *Magazine, Trade.*
Published by: Minhang Guanli Zazhishe, 3, Huajiadi Dong, Beijing, 100102, China. TEL 86-10-64720474, FAX 86-10-58250408, http://www.cacs.net.cn/qikan/zazhishe.asp.

387.71 DEU
MOMBERGER AIRPORT INFORMATION (ONLINE). Text in English. 1973. bi-w. EUR 360 in Europe; USD 490 elsewhere (effective 2009). bk.rev. **Document type:** *Newsletter, Consumer.* **Description:** Serves as a research tool for airport professionals. This is an information service on worldwide airport development.
Former titles (until 200?): Momberger Airport Information (Print) (0942-3478); (until 1992): Airport Forum News (0174-3279); (until 1979): Airport Forum Report (0341-0579)
Media: Online - full text.
Indexed: KES.
—CCC.
Published by: Momberger Airport Information, Postfach 1127, Rutesheim, 71273, Germany. TEL 49-7152-997760, FAX 49-7152-55005, info@momberger.com, http://www.momberger.com. Ed. Manfred Momberger. Pub. Karin Momberger.

387.7 USA
MONTANA AND THE SKY. Text in English. 1961. m. USD 5 (effective 1997). **Document type:** *Government.*
Published by: Department of Transportation, Aeronautics Division, PO Box 5178, Helena, MT 59604. TEL 406-444-2506, FAX 406-444-2519. Ed. Debbie Alke. Circ: 3,000.

388.3 ITA ISSN 1591-240X
HE7
MOTOR. Text in Italian. 1942. m. EUR 30 domestic; EUR 45 foreign (effective 2009). adv. bk.rev.
Published by: Societa Edizioni Tecniche, Piazza Antonio Mancini 4-G, Rome, RM 00196, Italy. TEL 39-06-3220209, FAX 39-06-3233309. Ed. Sergio Favia del Core. Circ: 112,250.

387.1 USA
MOUNTAIN PILOT; the mountains aviation magazine. Text in English. 1985. q. USD 19 domestic; USD 28 in Canada; USD 42 elsewhere (effective 2001). adv. bk.rev. back issues avail. **Document type:** *Magazine, Consumer.* **Description:** Presents news and information for mountain aircraft owners, pilots and their families.
Formerly: Wings West (1049-7781)
Published by: Frostbite Publications, LLC, PO Box 220168, Anchorage, AK 99522-0168 . http://www.mountainpilot.com/. Pub. Peter M Diemer. Circ: 14,571 (paid).

387.71 CAN ISSN 1013-4344
MULTILATERAL INTERLINE TRAFFIC AGREEMENTS MANUAL. Text in English. 3/yr. USD 315 includes CD-ROM (effective 2008). **Document type:** *Handbook/Manual/Guide, Trade.* **Description:** Contains the passenger and cargo Interline Agreements, which spell out the basic rules airlines follow when collecting money and issuing documents for carriage on each other's services.
Published by: International Air Transport Association, 800 Place Victoria, PO Box 113, Montreal, PQ H4Z 1M1, Canada. TEL 514-390-6726, 800-716-6326, FAX 514-874-9659, sales@iata.org. Adv. contact Sandra Davies.

387.7 USA
N A T C A VOICE. Text in English. 1995. irreg. **Document type:** *Newsletter, Trade.*
Formerly (19??): N A T C A Newsletter (1055-5994)
Published by: National Air Traffic Controllers Association, 2833 Overbeck Ln, West Chicago, IL 60185. TEL 630-513-8728, FAX 630-513-8782, Staff@NATCAVoice.org, http://www.natca.org/.

387.7 USA ISSN 0745-9874
N T S B REPORTER. (National Transportation Safety Board) Text in English. 1983. m. USD 48 domestic; USD 58 in Canada; USD 68 elsewhere (effective 2000). back issues avail. **Description:** Reports on aviation accident investigations.
Published by: Peter Katz Productions, Inc., PO Box 831, White Plains, NY 10602-0831. TEL 914-949-7443. Ed. Peter Katz.

387.736 310 CAN ISSN 1719-3656
N W T AIRPORT STATISTICS REPORT. (Northwest Territories) Text in English. 2003. a., latest 2004. **Document type:** *Government.*
Published by: Northwest Territories, Department of Transportation, PO Box 1320, Yellowknife, NT X1A 2L9, Canada. TEL 867-873-7500, http://www.gov.nt.ca/Transportation/documents/index.html.

387.7 USA
NATIONAL AIR TRANSPORTATION ASSOCIATION. ANNUAL REPORT. Text in English. a. **Document type:** *Corporate.*
Published by: National Air Transportation Association, 4226 King St, Alexandria, VA 22302-1507. TEL 703-845-9000, FAX 703-845-8176. Ed., R&P Clifton Stroud.

387.7 USA
HD4966.A482
NATIONAL AIR TRANSPORTATION ASSOCIATION. INDUSTRY COMPENSATION GUIDE. Text in English. 1978. a. USD 50 (effective 2000). **Document type:** *Handbook/Manual/Guide, Trade.*
Formerly: National Air Transportation Association. Wage and Salary Handbook (0191-3433)
Published by: National Air Transportation Association, 4226 King St, Alexandria, VA 22302-1507. TEL 703-845-9000, FAX 703-845-8176. Ed., R&P Clifton Stroud.

629.133 USA
NATIONAL BUSINESS AIRCRAFT ASSOCIATION. MAINTENANCE AND OPERATIONS BULLETIN. Text in English. irreg.
Published by: National Business Aviation Association, 1200 18th St, NW, Ste 400, Washington, DC 20036. TEL 202-783-9000, FAX 202-331-8364. Ed. Fred W Kirby.

387.7 USA ISSN 0091-6978
TL726.3.N5
NEW JERSEY AIRPORT DIRECTORY. Text in English. 1968. irreg., latest 1998. free. illus. **Document type:** *Directory, Government.*
Published by: New Jersey Department of Transportation, 1035 Parkway Ave, Box 600, Trenton, NJ 08625. TEL 609-530-2900.

629.130099305 NZL ISSN 1172-0522
NEW ZEALAND AVIATION NEWS. Variant title: Aviation News. Text in English. 1978. m. NZD 45 domestic; NZD 70 in Australia and Pacific Islands; NZD 80 elsewhere (effective 2008). adv. back issues avail. **Document type:** *Newspaper, Consumer.* **Description:** Focuses on activities within the professional and recreational aviation industries in New Zealand and the Pacific region.
Formerly (until Oct.1992): Aviation News
Related titles: Online - full text ed.
Published by: New Zealand Aviation News Ltd., PO Box 9711, Newmarket, 1149, New Zealand. Ed. John King TEL 64-9-3077849.

629.1 JPN
NIPPON KOKU SHIMBUN/JAPAN AVIATION NEWS. Text in Japanese. 1953. bi-w. JPY 8,800 (effective 2008). adv. **Document type:** *Newspaper, Trade.*
Published by: Nippon Koku Shimbunsha/Japan Aviation News Co., Ltd., Tokyo ST Bldg, 3F, 4-9-4, Hatchobori, Chuo-ku, Tokyo, 104-0032, Japan. TEL 81-3-35551491, FAX 81-3-35527580, Info@aviation-news.co.jp. Pub. Takashi Satoh. adv.: B&W page USD 5,437, color page USD 10,506. Circ: 30,000.

387.7 USA
NORTHWEST PASSAGES. Text in English. s-m. USD 25 to non-employees. adv. **Document type:** *Newspaper.* **Description:** Employee newspaper with articles on the aviation industry and specifically Northwest Airlines, covering corporate developments, employee news and concerns.
Published by: Northwest Airlines, Inc., 5101 Northwest Dr., St. Paul, MN 55111-3034. TEL 612-726-7357, FAX 612-726-3942. Ed. John F Heenehan. Circ: 56,000 (controlled).

341.46 GBR
NOTICES TO AERODROME LICENSE HOLDERS. Text in English. 19??. base vol. plus irreg. updates. back issues avail. **Document type:** *Monographic series, Government.*
Related titles: Online - full text ed.: free (effective 2010).
Published by: Civil Aviation Authority, Printing and Publication Services, C A A House, 45-59 Kingsway, London, WCB2 6TE, United Kingdom. TEL 44-20-73797311, FAX 44-20-74536097, infoservices@caa.co.uk. **Dist. by:** Westward Documedia Limited.

387.744 GBR
O A G CARGO GUIDE. (Official Airline Guide) Text in English. 1969. m. GBP 399; GBP 39.99 per issue (effective 2009). adv. charts. **Document type:** *Directory, Trade.* **Description:** Contains compilation of cargo schedules worldwide on both dedicated cargo and passenger flights.
Former titles (until 1999): O A G Air Cargo Guide with Rates (1365-9774); (until 1996): A B C Air Cargo Guide (0141-6529)
Related titles: CD-ROM ed.: O A G Air CargoDisk. GBP 399; Diskette ed.; ◆ Supplement to: O A G Cargo Rules.
—CCC.
Published by: O A G Worldwide, Church St, Dunstable, Bedfordshire LU5 4HB, United Kingdom. TEL 44-1582-600111, FAX 44-1582-695230, customers@oag.com. Adv. contact Sue Davidson TEL 44-1582-695470.

387.744 GBR
O A G CARGO RULES. (Official Airline Guide) Text in English. 19??. s-a. includes subscr. with O A G Cargo Guide. adv. charts. **Document type:** *Directory, Trade.* **Description:** Contains compilation of airfreight regulations-listed by country, documentary requirements, and aircraft loading restrictions.
Former titles (until 1999): O A G Air Cargo Rules (1367-9414); (until 1996): A B C Air Cargo Rules
Related titles: CD-ROM ed.; Diskette ed.; ◆ Supplement(s): O A G Cargo Guide.
—CCC.
Published by: O A G Worldwide, Church St, Dunstable, Bedfordshire LU5 4HB, United Kingdom. TEL 44-1582-600111, FAX 44-1582-695230, customers@oag.com, http://www.oag.com. Adv. contact Sue Davidson TEL 44-1582-695470.

387.744 GBR
THE O A G EXECUTIVE FLIGHT GUIDE ASIA PACIFIC. (Official Airline Guide) Text in English. 1983. m. GBP 149, EUR 229, USD 290 (effective 2010). adv. **Document type:** *Directory, Consumer.* **Description:** Provides a regionalized guide to air schedules.
Former titles (until 200?): O A G Executive Flight Planner: Asia, Pacific (1365-9782); (until 1996): A B C Executive Flight Planner: Asia, Pacific (0959-2911); A B C Air Asia (0265-4024)
—CCC.
Published by: O A G Worldwide, Church St, Dunstable, Bedfordshire LU5 4HB, United Kingdom. TEL 44-1582-600111, FAX 44-1582-695230, customers@oag.com.

387.74 USA ISSN 1541-373X
O A G EXECUTIVE FLIGHT GUIDE. LATIN AMERICAN - CARIBBEAN. (Official Airline Guide) Text in English. 2002. m. USD 149; USD 12.42 per issue (effective 2011). **Document type:** *Handbook/Manual/Guide, Trade.* **Description:** Guide to direct and connecting air services for travel to and from Latin America and within the region.
—CCC.
Published by: O A G Worldwide, 3025 Highland Pky, Ste 200, Downer's Grove, IL 60515. TEL 630-515-5300, 800-342-5624, FAX 630-515-5301, contactus@oag.com.

387.74 USA ISSN 1528-7556
HE9802.A2 CODEN: ODFEEE
O A G FLIGHT GUIDE. NORTH AMERICA; the complete guide to flight schedules within North America. (Official Airline Guide) Text in English. 1948. s-m. USD 569; USD 56.99 per issue (effective 2011). adv. illus. reprints avail. **Document type:** *Handbook/Manual/Guide, Trade.* **Description:** Reference guide to direct and connecting air services within the US, Canada, Mexico and the Caribbean.
Former titles (until 2000): O A G Desktop Guide (North American Edition) (1528-6622); (until 1995): O A G Desktop Flight Guide (North American Edition) (1057-0918); (until 1991): O A G. Official Airline Guide. North American Edition (0191-1619); (until 1974): Official Airline Guide (North American Edition)
—CASDDS. **CCC.**
Published by: O A G Worldwide, 3025 Highland Pky, Ste 200, Downer's Grove, IL 60515. TEL 630-515-5300, 800-342-5624, FAX 630-515-5301, contactus@oag.com, http://www.oag.com.

387.7 GBR ISSN 1466-8718
HE9768 CODEN: ODGEEJ
O A G FLIGHT GUIDE - WORLDWIDE. (Official Airline Guide) Text in English. 1999. m. GBP 769 domestic; USD 739 in United Kingdom; EUR 1,144 in Europe; AUD 1,665 in Australia; SGD 1,799 in Singapore; GBP 76.99 per issue domestic; USD 73.99 per issue in United Kingdom; EUR 114.99 per issue in Europe (effective 2009). adv. **Document type:** *Directory, Trade.* **Description:** Designed to be a guide to international direct and connecting air services for all scheduled airlines worldwide.
Formed by the 1999 merger of: O A G World Airways Guide (1464-7958); Which superseded (in 1998): O A G World Airways Guide - Corporate Edition (1355-4972); (1992-1994): A B C World Airways Guide - Corporate Edition (0966-1832); And: O A G Desktop Flight Guide - Worldwide Edition (1057-0454); Which was formerly (until 1991): Official Airline Guide. World Wide Edition (0364-3875); (until 1976): Official Airline Guide. International Edition (0097-5192); Official Airline Guide. Quick Reference International Edition. Part 1
Related titles: Online - full text ed.
Indexed: RehabLit.
—BLDSC (6196.390300), CASDDS. **CCC.**
Published by: O A G Worldwide, Church St, Dunstable, Bedfordshire LU5 4HB, United Kingdom. TEL 44-1582-600111, FAX 44-1582-695230, customers@oag.com. Adv. contact Sue Davidson TEL 44-1582-695470.

387.74 GBR
O A G FLIGHTDISK. (Official Airline Guide) Text in English. m. GBP 330. **Document type:** *Directory.* **Description:** Contains worldwide flight schedules, car rental and ground transportation contact numbers, details on frequent-flyer and lodge programs, and travel related destination data for more than 200 countries.
Media: Diskette. **Related titles:** CD-ROM ed.; Spanish ed.

Published by: Reed Travel Group, Church St, Dunstable, Beds LU5 4HB, United Kingdom. TEL 44-1582-600111, FAX 44-1582-695230. Ed. Janet Mathews.

387.7 USA ISSN 2151-2892
O A G OFFICIAL AIRPORT GUIDE. (Official Airline Guides) Text in English. 200?. q. **Document type:** *Handbook/Manual/Guide, Trade.*
Published by: O A G Worldwide, 3025 Highland Pky, Ste 200, Downer's Grove, IL 60515. TEL 630-515-5300, 800-342-5624, FAX 630-515-5301, contactus@oag.com.

O A G OFFICIAL TRAVELER. TRAVEL GUIDE. (Official Airline Guide) *see* TRAVEL AND TOURISM

387.74 USA ISSN 1756-557X
CODEN: OPPEEC
O A G POCKET FLIGHT GUIDE. ASIA PACIFIC. (Official Airline Guide) Text in English. 1982. m. GBP 149; GBP 14.99 per issue (effective 2011). **Document type:** *Handbook/Manual/Guide, Trade.* **Description:** Pocket-size guide to direct and connecting air service for travel to and within all countries of the Pacific geographical region.
Former titles (until 2008): O A G Executive Flight Guide. Asia Pacific (1478-453X); (until 2002): O A G Pocket Flight Guide. Asia Pacific (1526-0437); (until 198?): O A G Pocket Flight Guide. Pacific Area Edition (0745-5275)
—BLDSC (6196.390100). **CCC.**
Published by: O A G Worldwide, 3025 Highland Pky, Ste 200, Downer's Grove, IL 60515. TEL 630-515-5300, 800-342-5624, FAX 630-515-5301, contactus@oag.com, http://www.oag.com.

387.74 USA ISSN 1756-5588
O A G POCKET FLIGHT GUIDE. EUROPE, AFRICA, MIDDLE EAST. (Official Airline Guide) Text in English. 1978. m. GBP 149; GBP 14.99 per issue (effective 2011). charts. **Document type:** *Handbook/Manual/Guide, Trade.* **Description:** Pocket-size guide to direct and connecting air services to and from Europe, the Middle East, and Africa, including travel within these regions.
Former titles (until 2007): O A G Executive Flight Guide. Europe, Africa, Middle East (1478-4416); (until 2002): O A G Pocket Flight Guide. Europe, Africa, Middle East (1469-1264); Which superseded in part (in 1999): O A G Pocket Flight Guide. Europe and Middle East Edition (8750-0310); Which was formerly (until 19??): O A G Europe and Middle East Pocket Flight Guide (0191-1546)
—BLDSC (6196.392801). **CCC.**
Published by: O A G Worldwide, 3025 Highland Pky, Ste 200, Downer's Grove, IL 60515. TEL 630-515-5300, 800-342-5624, FAX 630-515-5301, contactus@oag.com, http://www.oag.com.

387.74 USA
HE9803.A2 CODEN: ONAGDU
O A G POCKET FLIGHT GUIDE. NORTH AMERICA EDITION. (Official Airline Guide) Text in English. 1970. m. USD 149; USD 14.99 per issue (effective 2011). **Document type:** *Handbook/Manual/Guide, Trade.* **Description:** Pocket-size guide to direct and connecting air services for travel among the US, Canada, Mexico and the Caribbean.
Former titles (until 2007): North America Executive Flight Guide (1541-3233); (until 2002): O A G Pocket Flight Guide. North American Edition (0743-8249); (until 19??): O A G North American Pocket Flight Guide (0191-1538)
—CASDDS. **CCC.**
Published by: O A G Worldwide, 3025 Highland Pky, Ste 200, Downer's Grove, IL 60515. TEL 630-515-5300, 800-342-5624, FAX 630-515-5301, contactus@oag.com.

387.7 USA
OFFSHORE DESIGN GUIDE: HELIPORTS. Text in English. 1984. s-a. free. **Document type:** *Handbook/Manual/Guide, Trade.*
Published by: Helicopter Safety Advisory Conference, PO Box 60220, Houston, TX 77205. TEL 713-960-7654.

OKECIE; airport magazine. *see* TRAVEL AND TOURISM

387.7 NLD ISSN 1383-1178
OP DE BOK; monthly magazine of Dutch Airline Pilots Association. Text in Dutch. 1959. m. membership only. adv. bk.rev.; Website rev. illus. back issues avail. **Document type:** *Magazine, Trade.* **Description:** Magazine for Dutch airline pilots, including union news and general aviation information.
Published by: Vereniging van Nederlandse Verkeersvliegers, Dellaertlaan 61, PO Box 192, Badhoevedorp, 1170 AD, Netherlands. TEL 31-20-4498585, FAX 31-20-4498588, http://www.vnv-dalpa.nl. Ed. Herma Flipsen TEL 31-2004490517.

OVERHAUL & MAINTENANCE; the magazine for m & o management. *see* AERONAUTICS AND SPACE FLIGHT

387.74 341.46 GBR
OVERSEAS NON-SCHEDULED FLIGHT CLEARANCES GUIDE. Text in English. 19??. base vol. plus irreg. updates. looseleaf. **Document type:** *Government.* **Description:** Provides charter and general-aviation operators with details of U.K. foreign entry and overflight requirements of U.S. airspace, together with useful associated information on U.K. airports, refueling, and various limitations or restrictions.
Related titles: Online - full text ed.: free (effective 2010); ◆ Series: Air Traffic Control Licensing; ◆ Air Navigation - The Order and the Regulations; ◆ Great Britain. Civil Aviation Authority. Airport Surveys; ◆ Manual of Air Traffic Services - Part 1; ◆ Great Britain. Civil Aviation Authority. Mandatory Requirements for Airworthiness; ◆ Mandatory Aircraft Modifications and Inspections Summary; ◆ Civil Aircraft Airworthiness Information and Procedures; ◆ A A I B Recommendations - C A A Progress Report (Year); ◆ Air Traffic Services Engineering Requirements; ◆ Great Britain. Civil Aviation Authority. Annual Punctuality Statistics - Full Analysis (Year); ◆ Great Britain. Civil Aviation Authority. Annual Punctuality Statistics - Full and Summary Analysis (Year); ◆ United Kingdom Aeronautical Information Publication; ◆ Great Britain. Civil Aviation Authority. Approved Aerial Positions.
Published by: Civil Aviation Authority, Aeronautical Information Service, NATS Ltd, 1st Fl, N Wing, Heathrow House, Bath Rd, Hounslow, Middlesex TW5 9AT, United Kingdom. TEL 44-20-87503777, FAX 44-20-87503771, ais.supervisor@nats.co.uk, http://www.nats-uk.ead-it.com/public/index.php%3Foption=com_content&task=blogcategory&id=1&Itemid=2.html. **Dist. by:** Westward Documedia Limited.

387.7 USA
PACIFIC FLYER. Text in English. 1977. m. USD 21.95 domestic; USD 30 in Canada; USD 88 elsewhere (effective 2004). adv. bk.rev. back issues avail. **Document type:** *Newspaper, Trade.* **Description:** Features aviation news and history of interest to pilots, historians, and lovers of aviation.
Address: 3355 Mission Ave, Ste 213, Oceanside, CA 92054-1334. TEL 760-439-4466, FAX 760-439-9666. Ed., Pub., R&P Wayman C Dunlap. Adv. contact Chris Dunlap. Circ: 100,000.

PACIFIC WINGS. *see* AERONAUTICS AND SPACE FLIGHT

387.7 CAN
PASSENGER FORECAST (ONLINE). Text in English. a. USD 2,499 (effective 2008). **Document type:** *Report, Trade.* **Description:** Forecast giving a collective view of the world's major airlines on scheduled international passenger traffic prospects in the coming five years. Includes global as well as regional forecasts and highlights major historical and projected trends.
Former titles (until 200?): Passenger Forecast (Print); (until 1998): International Scheduled Passenger Forecast; (until 1994): Passenger Traffic Forecast
Media: Online - full content. **Related titles:** CD-ROM ed.: USD 1,099 (effective 2008).
Published by: International Air Transport Association, 800 Place Victoria, PO Box 113, Montreal, PQ H4Z 1M1, Canada. TEL 514-390-6726, 800-716-6326, FAX 514-874-9659, sales@iata.org.

387.742 CAN ISSN 0256-3282
PASSENGER SERVICES CONFERENCE RESOLUTIONS MANUAL. Text in English. 1981. a., latest 21st ed. USD 305 includes CD-ROM (effective 2008). **Document type:** *Handbook/Manual/Guide, Trade.* **Description:** Contains all rules and regulations which have been universally accepted by airlines to process passengers and baggage in the international interline environment.
—**CCC.**
Published by: International Air Transport Association, 800 Place Victoria, PO Box 113, Montreal, PQ H4Z 1M1, Canada. TEL 514-390-6726, 800-716-6326, FAX 514-874-9659, sales@iata.org. Adv. contact Sandra Davies.

387.71 CAN
PASSENGER TARIFF COORDINATING CONFERENCES RESOLUTIONS MANUAL. Text in English. a. price varies. **Document type:** *Handbook/Manual/Guide, Trade.* **Description:** Contains the text of all resolutions adopted by the Passenger Tariff Coordinating Conferences together with details of corresponding Government Reservations.
Published by: International Air Transport Association, 800 Place Victoria, PO Box 113, Montreal, PQ H4Z 1M1, Canada. TEL 514-390-6726, 800-716-6326, FAX 514-874-9659, sales@iata.org. Ed. Karin Bengtsson.

387.736 GBR ISSN 1362-0770
PASSENGER TERMINAL WORLD. Text in English. 1994. q. free (effective 2009). adv. back issues avail. **Document type:** *Magazine, Trade.* **Description:** Provides an international communication platform for the views and opinions of experts in the field of passenger terminal facilities, design and technology.
Related titles: Online - full text ed.; Supplement(s):.
Indexed: HRIS.
—**CCC.**
Published by: U K & International Press (Subsidiary of: AutoIntermediates Ltd.), Abinger House, Church St, Dorking, Surrey RH4 1DF, United Kingdom. TEL 44-1306-743744, FAX 44-1306-887546, info@ukintpress.com, http://www.ukipme.com. Adv. contact Jasmy Kesavan. page GBP 3,905; trim 230 x 300.

387.744 HKG
PAYLOAD ASIA; the air cargo - courier - express magazine for the Asia - Pacific region. Text in Chinese. 1985. m. **Document type:** *Trade.*
Published by: (Federation of Asia - Pacific Aircargo Associations), Asian Media Services Ltd., PO Box 3580, Hong Kong, Hong Kong. TEL 852-893-3676, FAX 852-893-3676. Ed. Van Fenema. adv.: B&W page USD 2,595, color page USD 3,315; trim 295 x 210. Circ: 12,500 (controlled).

387.7 CAN
PERISHABLE CARGO HANDLING MANUAL. Text in English. biennial. USD 132 per issue (effective 2008). **Document type:** *Handbook/Manual/Guide, Trade.* **Description:** Addresses such subjects as: industry co-operation and interface between participants; cargo acceptance; general and special cargo handling.
Formerly: Principles of Cargo Handling and Perishable Cargo Handling Guide
Related titles: CD-ROM ed.: USD 127 per issue (effective 2008).
Published by: International Air Transport Association, 800 Place Victoria, PO Box 113, Montreal, PQ H4Z 1M1, Canada. TEL 514-390-6726, 800-716-6326, FAX 514-874-9659, sales@iata.org. Adv. contact Sandra Davies.

387.7 DEU ISSN 0175-0143
PILOT UND FLUGZEUG. Text in German. 1974. m. EUR 77 domestic; USD 85 in North America; EUR 84.32 elsewhere; EUR 6.60 newsstand/cover (effective 2007). adv. charts; illus. **Document type:** *Magazine, Consumer.*
Formerly: Luftfahrt International
Related titles: Online - full text ed.
Published by: Teegen Verlags GmbH, Regensburger Str 61, Straubing, 94315, Germany. TEL 49-9421-968454, 49-721-151415985. Ed. Jan Brill. Pub. Heiko Teegen. adv.: B&W page EUR 1,687, color page EUR 2,530; trim 145 x 200. Circ: 19,000 (paid and controlled).
Subscr. to: Bayerwaldstr 28, Falkenfels 94350, Germany.

387.7 FRA
PILOTES. Text in French. 2006. bi-m. EUR 39 (effective 2008). **Document type:** *Magazine, Consumer.*
Published by: Altipresse, 150 Rue Aristide Briand, Levallois-Perret, 92300, France. TEL 33-1-47305310, http://www.altipresse.com.

387 USA
PORT AUTHORITY OF NEW YORK AND NEW JERSEY. AVIATION DEPARTMENT. AIRPORT TRAFFIC REPORT (YEAR). Text in English. a. free. stat. **Document type:** *Government.*
Formerly: Port Authority of New York and New Jersey. Aviation Department. Airport Statistics
Published by: Port Authority of New York and New Jersey, Aviation Department, Customer & Marketing Services, One World Trade Center, 65 North, New York, NY 10048. TEL 212-466-7000.

387.736 USA
PORT AUTHORITY OF NEW YORK AND NEW JERSEY. AVIATION DEPARTMENT. AVIATION ANNUAL REPORT. Text in English. a.
Published by: Port Authority of New York and New Jersey, Aviation Department, Customer & Marketing Services, One World Trade Center, 65 North, New York, NY 10048.

PORT PROGRESS NEWS AND EVENTS. *see* TRANSPORTATION—Ships And Shipping

PRIVIUM UPDATE. *see* TRAVEL AND TOURISM—Airline Inflight And Hotel Inroom

387.7 USA ISSN 0191-6238
TL501
PROFESSIONAL PILOT MAGAZINE. Text in English. 1967. m. USD 50 domestic; USD 60 in Canada & Mexico; USD 80 elsewhere (effective 2005). adv. back issues avail.; reprints avail. **Document type:** *Magazine, Trade.* **Description:** Presents information of interest to corporate, charter, and commuter airlines pilots and associated personnel.
Indexed: CLT&T, HRIS.
—Ingenta.
Published by: Queensmith Communications Corporation, 30 S Quaker Ln, Ste 300, Alexandria, VA 22314-4599. TEL 703-370-0606, FAX 703-370-7082. Ed., Pub., R&P Murray Smith. Adv. contact Earlene Chandler. B&W page USD 8,050. Circ: 39,850 (paid and controlled).

PROPLINER; the international review of piston-engined and turboprop transport aircraft. *see* AERONAUTICS AND SPACE FLIGHT

387.74 387 PRI
PUERTO RICO. PORTS AUTHORITY. STATISTICAL SUMMARY. Text in English; Summaries in English. 1955. a. free. stat. back issues avail. **Document type:** *Government.*
Former titles: Puerto Rico. Ports Authority. Office of Economic Research. Statistical Summary; Puerto Rico. Ports Authority. Office of Economic Research. Statistical Report
Published by: Puerto Rico Ports Authority, G P O Box 362829, San Juan, 00936-2829, Puerto Rico. TEL 787-729-8649. Ed. Elsa I Berrios Suarez. Circ: 500.

387.744 388.324 USA
QUICK CALLER: ATLANTA AIR CARGO DIRECTORY. Text in English. a. USD 21.95 per issue (effective 2008). adv. charts; maps. 184 p./no.; back issues avail. **Document type:** *Directory, Trade.* **Description:** Features advertisers from 2,000+ business listings and over 150 itemized categories of air freight service in Atlanta.
Published by: Fourth Seacoast Publishing Co., Inc., 25300 Little Mack Ave, St. Clair Shores, MI 48081. TEL 586-779-5570, FAX 586-779-5547, info@fourthseacoastonline.com, http://www.fourthseacoast.com. Adv. contact Tom Buysse. B&W page USD 1,175; trim 5.25 x 8.5. Circ: 10,000.

387.744 388.324 USA
QUICK CALLER: BOSTON AREA AIR CARGO DIRECTORY. Variant title: Quick Caller: Boston - New England Area Air Cargo Directory. Text in English. 1976. a. USD 21.95 per issue (effective 2009). charts; maps. 160 p./no.; back issues avail. **Document type:** *Directory, Trade.* **Description:** Provides detailed reference information on air cargo service companies operating out of the Boston area.
Published by: Fourth Seacoast Publishing Co., Inc., 25300 Little Mack Ave, St. Clair Shores, MI 48081. TEL 586-779-5570, FAX 586-779-5547, info@fourthseacoastonline.com, http://www.fourthseacoast.com. Circ: 10,000.

387.7 388.324 USA
QUICK CALLER: CHICAGO AREA AIR CARGO DIRECTORY. Text in English. a. USD 21.95 per issue (effective 2009). adv. charts; maps. 348 p./no.; back issues avail. **Document type:** *Directory, Trade.* **Description:** Features advertisers from 2,000+ business listings and over 150 itemized categories of air freight service in Chicago.
Published by: Fourth Seacoast Publishing Co., Inc., 25300 Little Mack Ave, St. Clair Shores, MI 48081. TEL 586-779-5570, FAX 586-779-5547, info@fourthseacoastonline.com, http://www.fourthseacoast.com. Adv. contact Tom Buysse. B&W page USD 1,175; trim 5.25 x 8.5. Circ: 10,000.

387.744 388.324 USA
QUICK CALLER: DETROIT AREA AIR CARGO DIRECTORY. Text in English. 1973. a. USD 21.95 per issue (effective 2009). adv. 164 p./no.; back issues avail. **Document type:** *Directory, Trade.* **Description:** Features advertisers from 2,000+ business listings and over 150 itemized categories of air freight service in Detroit.
Published by: Fourth Seacoast Publishing Co., Inc., 25300 Little Mack Ave, St. Clair Shores, MI 48081. TEL 586-779-5570, FAX 586-779-5547, info@fourthseacoastonline.com, http://www.fourthseacoast.com. Adv. contact Tom Buysse. B&W page USD 1,175; trim 5.25 x 8.5. Circ: 10,000.

387.7 388.324 USA
QUICK CALLER: LOS ANGELES AREA AIR CARGO DIRECTORY. Text in English. a. USD 21.95 per issue (effective 2009). adv. charts; maps. 200 p./no.; back issues avail. **Document type:** *Directory, Trade.* **Description:** Features advertisers from 2,000+ business listings and over 150 itemized categories of air freight service in Los Angeles.
Published by: Fourth Seacoast Publishing Co., Inc., 25300 Little Mack Ave, St. Clair Shores, MI 48081. TEL 586-779-5570, FAX 586-779-5547, info@fourthseacoastonline.com, http://www.fourthseacoast.com. Adv. contact Tom Buysse. B&W page USD 1,175; trim 5.25 x 8.5. Circ: 10,000.

387.744 388.324 USA
QUICK CALLER: MIAMI - ORLANDO - FLORIDA AIR CARGO DIRECTORY. Text in English. 1975. a. USD 21.95 per issue (effective 2009). adv. charts; maps. 252 p./no.; back issues avail. **Document type:** *Directory, Trade.* **Description:** Features advertisers from 2,000+ business listings and over 150 itemized categories of air freight service in Miami - Orlando - Florida.
Formerly: Quick Caller: Miami Area Air Cargo Directory
Published by: Fourth Seacoast Publishing Co., Inc., 25300 Little Mack Ave, St. Clair Shores, MI 48081. TEL 586-779-5570, FAX 586-779-5547, info@fourthseacoastonline.com, http://www.fourthseacoast.com. Adv. contact Tom Buysse. B&W page USD 1,175; trim 5.25 x 8.5. Circ: 10,000.

387.744 388.324 USA
QUICK CALLER: NEW YORK- NEW JERSEY METRO AREA AIR CARGO DIRECTORY. Text in English. 1989. a. USD 21.95 per issue (effective 2009). adv. charts; maps. 376 p./no.; back issues avail. **Document type:** *Directory, Trade.* **Description:** Features advertisers from 2,000+ business listings and over 150 itemized categories of air freight service in New York- New Jersey Metro Area.
Formerly: Quick Caller: New York Metro Area Air Cargo Directory
Published by: Fourth Seacoast Publishing Co., Inc., 25300 Little Mack Ave, St. Clair Shores, MI 48081. TEL 586-779-5570, FAX 586-779-5547, info@fourthseacoastonline.com, http://www.fourthseacoast.com. Adv. contact Tom Buysse. B&W page USD 1,175; trim 5.25 x 8.5. Circ: 10,000.

338.324 USA
QUICK CALLER: PACIFIC NORTHWEST AREA AIR CARGO DIRECTORY. Text in English. 1996. a. USD 21.95 per issue (effective 2008). adv. charts; maps. 184 p./no.; back issues avail. **Document type:** *Directory, Trade.* **Description:** Features advertisers from 2,000+ business listings and over 150 itemized categories of air freight service in Pacific Northwest.
Published by: Fourth Seacoast Publishing Co., Inc., 25300 Little Mack Ave, St. Clair Shores, MI 48081. TEL 586-779-5570, FAX 586-779-5547, info@fourthseacoastonline.com, http://www.fourthseacoast.com. Adv. contact Tom Buysse. B&W page USD 1,175; trim 5.25 x 8.5. Circ: 10,000.

387.744 388.324 USA
QUICK CALLER: SAN FRANCISCO - OAKLAND BAY AREA AIR CARGO DIRECTORY. Text in English. 1982. a. USD 21.95 per issue (effective 2008). adv. charts; maps. 168 p./no.; back issues avail. **Document type:** *Directory, Trade.* **Description:** Features advertisers from 2,000+ business listings and over 150 itemized categories of air freight service in San Francisco - Oakland Bay.
Formerly (until 19??): Quick Caller: San Francisco Bay Area Air Cargo Directory
Published by: Fourth Seacoast Publishing Co., Inc., 25300 Little Mack Ave, St. Clair Shores, MI 48081. TEL 586-779-5570, FAX 586-779-5547, info@fourthseacoastonline.com, http://www.fourthseacoast.com. Adv. contact Tom Buysse. B&W page USD 1,175; trim 5.25 x 8.5. Circ: 10,000.

387.7 AUS ISSN 1839-146X
R A A A NEWS. Text in English. 2008. q. free (effective 2011). back issues avail. **Document type:** *Newsletter, Trade.* **Description:** Provides fast and regular passenger, aero-medical and freight services linking regional communities with each other and the major cities.
Media: Online - full text.
Published by: Regional Aviation Association of Australia Ltd., Unit 11, 26-28 Winchcombe Ct, Mitchell, ACT 2911, Australia. TEL 61-2-61620305, FAX 61-2-61620308, office@raaa.com.au.

387.7 BRA ISSN 2175-1927
▼ **R E T A@/JOURNAL OF EDUCATION AND TECHNOLOGY APPLIED TO AERONAUTICS.** (Revista de Educacao e de Tecnologia Aplicadas a Aeronautica) Text in Portuguese. 2009. s-a. **Document type:** *Journal, Academic/Scholarly.*
Related titles: Online - full text ed.: ISSN 1984-5944. free (effective 2011).
Published by: Escola de Especialistas de Aeronautica, Av Brigadeiro Ademar Lyrio s/n, Guaratingueta, SP 125000-000, Brazil. Ed. Elson de Campos.

387.74 GBR
RANDOM FLIGHT PLAN A F T N ADDRESS BOOK. (Aeronautical Fixed Telecommunications Network) Text in English. 19??. base vol. plus irreg. updates. looseleaf. **Document type:** *Government.* **Description:** Provides a guide to the selection of appropriate collective address codes to simplify addressing of flight safety messages via the AFTN.
Related titles: Online - full text ed.: free (effective 2010).
Published by: Civil Aviation Authority, Printing and Publication Services, C A A House, 45-59 Kingsway, London, WCB2 6TE, United Kingdom. TEL 44-20-73797311, FAX 44-20-74536097, infoservices@caa.co.uk. **Dist. by:** Westward Documedia Limited.

387.7 FRA ISSN 1769-4566
RAPPORT D'ACTIVITE ET DE DEVELOPPEMENT DURABLE. Text in French. 2003. a. **Document type:** *Magazine.*
Former titles (until 2003): Rapport Environnement et Partenariat (1638-6264); (until 2000): Bilan Environnement (1621-6334)
Related titles: Online - full text ed.: free.
Published by: Aeroports de Paris, Direction de l'Environnement et des Relations Territoriales, Orly Aerogare, Orly sud 103, Paris, Cedex 94396, France.

387.7 GBR
REDCOAT. Text in English. 1989. q. **Description:** Concerned with air communication specifically for the West African community in the diaspora.
Published by: Redcoat Express Ltd., Balcombe Rd, 12 Gatwick Metro Centre, Horley, Surrey RH6 9GA, United Kingdom. TEL 01293-774141, FAX 01293-774080, TELEX 87337 REDAIR.

REFERATIVNYI ZHURNAL. AVIASTROENIE; vypusk svodnogo toma. *see* TRANSPORTATION—Abstracting, Bibliographies, Statistics

REFERATIVNYI ZHURNAL. VOZDUSHNYI TRANSPORT; svodnyi tom. *see* TRANSPORTATION—Abstracting, Bibliographies, Statistics

REFERATIVNYI ZHURNAL. VOZDUSHNYI TRANSPORT. AEROPORTY; vypusk svodnogo toma. *see* TRANSPORTATION—Abstracting, Bibliographies, Statistics

387.7 USA
REGIONAL AIRLINE ASSOCIATION. ANNUAL REPORT. Text in English. 1974. a. USD 75 to non-members (effective 2000). adv. illus.; stat. **Document type:** *Directory, Corporate.* **Description:** Provides comprehensive analysis of issues and trends affecting the US domestic regional airline industry, with company information for airlines and suppliers.
Indexed: SRI.
Published by: Regional Airline Association, 1200 19th S, N W, Ste 300, Washington, DC 20036. TEL 202-857-1170, FAX 202-429-5113. Ed., R&P Deborah McElroy. Adv. contact Pat McGrane. Circ: 2,200 (controlled).

387.7 USA
REGIONAL AVIATION NEWS (ONLINE). Text in English. w. USD 997 (effective 2009). **Document type:** *Newsletter, Trade.*
Media: Online - full text.
Published by: Access Intelligence, LLC (Subsidiary of: Veronis, Suhler & Associates Inc.), 4 Choke Cherry Rd, 2nd Fl, Rockville, MD 20850. TEL 301-354-2000, 800-777-5006, FAX 301-340-3819, clientservices@accessintel.com, http://www.accessintel.com. Ed. Ramon Lopez.

387.742 CAN
REGIONAL CARGO AGENT'S HANDBOOKS (CD-ROM). Text in Multiple languages. 1981. a. USD 84 per issue (effective 2008). **Description:** Contains the Cargo Agent's Handbooks for different regions of the world and in several languages of interest.
Formerly: Cargo Agent's Handbook (Print)
Media: CD-ROM.
Published by: International Air Transport Association, 800 Place Victoria, PO Box 113, Montreal, PQ H4Z 1M1, Canada. TEL 514-390-6726, 800-716-6326, FAX 514-874-9659, sales@iata.org.

387.71 CAN ISSN 1012-6538
REGIONAL DIFFERENCES IN FARES, RATES AND COSTS FOR INTERNATIONAL AIR TRANSPORT (YEAR). Text in English. 1979. a. USD 9. back issues avail.
Related titles: French ed.; Russian ed.; Spanish ed.; ◆ Series of: I C A O Circulars. ISSN 1014-4412.
Published by: International Civil Aviation Organization (I C A O), External Relations and Public Information Office, 999 University St, Montreal, PQ H3C 5H7, Canada. TEL 514-954-8022, FAX 514-954-6769, icaohq@icao.int.

387.7 FRA ISSN 0080-066X
REGISTRE AERONAUTIQUE INTERNATIONAL. Text in French. 1966. a. bk.rev. Supplement avail. **Document type:** *Directory.* **Description:** Lists 73000 aircraft from 44 countries.
Related titles: Microfiche ed.
Published by: Bureau Veritas, 67-71 Bd. du Chateau, Neuilly-sur-Sene, Cedex 44 92077, France. TEL 33-1-55247000, FAX 33-1-55247001, http://www.bureauveritas.com. Ed. Gerard Hammer. Pub. Eric Renier. Circ: 1,000. **Co-sponsors:** Registro Aeronautico Italiano, IT; Civil Aviation Authority, UN.

387.71 CAN
REMITTANCES OF FOREIGN BALANCES SURVEY. Abbreviated title: R F B Survey. Text in English. a. (plus 1 update). USD 150 combined subscription (print & online eds.) (effective 2008). 35 p./no.; **Document type:** *Report, Trade.* **Description:** Details the worldwide industry position with respect to remittances of foreign balances. Contains individual country data, regional analyses, and executive summary and individual comments on the worst ten countries.
Related titles: Online - full content ed.
Published by: International Air Transport Association, 800 Place Victoria, PO Box 113, Montreal, PQ H4Z 1M1, Canada. TEL 514-390-6726, 800-716-6326, FAX 514-874-9659, sales@iata.org. Ed. Simon Ralph.

387.74 GBR
REPORTABLE ACCIDENTS TO U K REGISTERED AIRCRAFT AND TO FOREIGN REGISTERED AIRCRAFT IN U K AIRSPACE (YEAR). Text in English. 1949. a. charts; stat. reprints avail. **Document type:** *Government.* **Description:** Features compiles and analyzes accidents to U.K.-registered civilian aircraft during the year.
Formerly: Accidents to Aircraft on the British Register (0306-3550)
Related titles: Online - full text ed.: free (effective 2010).
Published by: Civil Aviation Authority, Printing and Publication Services, C A A House, 45-59 Kingsway, London, WCB2 6TE, United Kingdom. TEL 44-20-73797311, FAX 44-20-74536097, infoservices@caa.co.uk. **Dist. by:** Westward Documedia Limited.

387.742 CAN
RESERVATIONS SERVICES MANUAL. Text in English. 1983. a. USD 150 per issue includes CD-ROM (effective 2008). **Document type:** *Handbook/Manual/Guide, Trade.* **Description:** Contains all internationally agreed upon reservations rules and interline reservations message procedures.
Formerly: Passenger Reservations Manual (1013-4042)
Published by: International Air Transport Association, 800 Place Victoria, PO Box 113, Montreal, PQ H4Z 1M1, Canada. TEL 514-390-6726, 800-716-6326, FAX 514-874-9659, sales@iata.org. Adv. contact Sandra Davies.

387.71 657 CAN
REVENUE ACCOUNTING MANUAL. Text in English. a. USD 135 (effective 2001). **Description:** Explains the standard billing procedures for the interline accounting of passenger, cargo, Universal Air Travel and miscellaneous revenues.
Published by: International Air Transport Association, 800 Place Victoria, PO Box 113, Montreal, PQ H4Z 1M1, Canada. TEL 514-390-6726, 800-716-6326, FAX 514-874-9659.

387.7 629.1 USA ISSN 1073-8274
HE9769.A3
ROTOR ROSTER. Text in English. 1987. a. USD 29 (effective 1998). adv. charts; illus. back issues avail. **Document type:** *Directory.* **Description:** Provides worldwide listing of civil helicopter owners.
Related titles: CD-ROM ed.
Published by: Air Track, PO Box 610, Hilliard, FL 32046. TEL 912-496-3504, FAX 912-496-7513. Ed. Faye Wonnacott. Pub. Glenn Wonnacott. Adv. contact Sue B Hill. Circ: 10,000.

387.74 GBR ISSN 2042-0714
▼ **ROTORHUB HANDBOOK.** Text in English. 2009. a. GBP 60 per month (effective 2010). adv. back issues avail. **Document type:** *Directory, Trade.* **Description:** Contains information on operators, aircraft manufacturers, product and service suppliers around the world.
Formed by the merger of (1996-2009): Shephard's Civil Helicopter Handbook (1365-649X); Which was formerly (1994-1996): Helicopter Operators' and Buyers' Handbook (1355-4646); (2003-2009): Public Service Aviation Handbook (1740-9284); Which was formed by the merger of (1996-2003): Shephard's Police Aviation Handbook (1364-9698); Which was formerly until (198?-1996): Police Helicopter Handbook (0968-655X); (1995-2003): Shephard's Air Ambulance Handbook (1365-6597); Which was formerly (until 1995): Air Ambulance Handbook (1355-6061); (198?-1994): E M S Helicopter Handbook (0968-6541)
Related titles: ◆ Supplement to: Defence Helicopter. ISSN 1741-6043.
—Linda Hall.
Published by: Shephard Press Ltd., 268 Bath Rd, Slough, Berkshire SL1 4DX, United Kingdom. TEL 44-1753-727001, FAX 44-1753-727002, info@shephard.co.uk. Ed. Ian Kemp TEL 44-7532-426978. Adv. contact Jane Smith TEL 44-1753-727004.

387.736 IRL
RUNWAY AIRPORTS. Text in English. m. adv. **Document type:** *Magazine, Trade.*
Published by: Aer Rianta, Collinstown House, First Fl., Dublin Airport, Co. Dublin, Ireland. TEL 353-1-8144170, FAX 353-1-8144663. adv.: color page EUR 1,000; trim 210 x 297. Circ: 9,000 (controlled).

387.7 SGP
S A A REVIEW. Text in English. s-a. free to qualified personnel. back issues avail. **Document type:** *Newsletter, Trade.* **Description:** Covers current topical civil aviation issues and happenings in the academy.
Published by: Singapore Aviation Academy, 1 Aviation Dr., Singapore, 499867, Singapore. TEL 65-65-430433, FAX 65-65-429890, saa@caas.gov.sg, http://www.saa.com.sg/.

S P A WATER LANDING DIRECTORY. *see* AERONAUTICS AND SPACE FLIGHT

387.7 CHE
DIE SCHWEIZERISCHE ZIVILLUFTFAHRT; l'aviation civile Suisse. Text in French, German. 1925. a. CHF 17. **Document type:** *Government.*
Supersedes (in 1975): Schweizerische Luftverkehrsstatistik - Statistique du Trafic Aerien Suisse
Published by: Bundesamt fuer Zivilluftfahrt/Federal Office for Civil Aviation (Office Federal de l'Aviation Civile), Inselgasse, Bern, 3003, Switzerland. Ed. Daniel Ruhier. Circ: 1,400.

341.46 GBR
SHAWCROSS & BEAUMONT AIR LAW. Text in English. 1984. 3 base vols. plus updates 5/yr. looseleaf. GBP 1,117 base vol(s). (effective 2010). **Document type:** *Handbook/Manual/Guide, Trade.* **Description:** Contains an informed exposition of the principal legal rules governing the flight and operation of aircraft.
Published by: LexisNexis Butterworths, Halsbury House, 35 Chancery Ln, London, Mddx WC2A 1EL, United Kingdom. TEL 44-20-74002500, FAX 44-20-74002842, customer.services@lexisnexis.co.uk.

358.4 GBR ISSN 1365-6600
SHEPHARD'S MILITARY HELICOPTER HANDBOOK. Variant title: Military Helicopter Handbook. Text in English. 1996. a. GBP 60 per issue (effective 2010). adv. back issues avail. **Document type:** *Directory, Trade.* **Description:** Provides details of military operators and their fleets, aircraft and weapon specifications.
Related titles: ◆ Supplement to: Defence Helicopter. ISSN 1741-6043.
—BLDSC (5768.075500). **CCC.**
Published by: Shephard Press Ltd., 268 Bath Rd, Slough, Berkshire SL1 4DX, United Kingdom. TEL 44-1753-727001, FAX 44-1753-727002, info@shephard.co.uk. Ed. Ian Kemp TEL 44-7532-426978. Adv. contact Jane Smith TEL 44-1753-727004. color page GBP 650; 150 x 210.

387.742 688 HKG
SHOP. Text in English, Chinese. 2002. q. adv. **Document type:** *Magazine, Consumer.* **Description:** Offers wide range of exclusive duty-free items, fashion accessories, cosmetics, perfumes, jewelery and watches from some of the biggest international brand names. Also featured are a selection of the finest tobacco, liquor and wines, unique gifts and toys for the kids presented with English and Chinese descriptions.
Published by: Cathay Pacific Airways Ltd, 10/F Chung Nam Bldg 1, Lockhart Rd, Wanchai, Hong Kong. TEL 852-2527-3822, FAX 852-2861-3621. adv.: color page HKD 21,900; trim 205 x 273. Circ: 290,000 (free).

387.7 USA
SIGHT LECTURE. Text in English. a.
Published by: Wings Club, 52 Vanderbilt Ave, 18th Fl, New York, NY 10017. TEL 212-867-1770.

363.12 USA ISSN 2153-5612
SIGNAL CHARLIE. Text in English. 2007. m. free (effective 2010). back issues avail. **Document type:** *Journal, Trade.* **Description:** Promotes safety in high reliability organizations and helps people find aviation safety information.
Media: Online - full text.
Published by: Kent Blair, Pub. lewis.kent@gmail.com.

387.7 SGP ISSN 0217-5371
SINGAPORE AIRFREIGHT DIRECTORY. Text in English. 1984. a. USD 30 per issue (effective 2008). **Document type:** *Directory, Trade.*
Published by: (Civil Aviation Authority of Singapore), Marshall Cavendish Business Information Pty. Ltd. (Subsidiary of: Times Publishing Group), Times Centre, 1 New Industrial Rd, Singapore, 536196, Singapore. TEL 65-6213-9288, FAX 65-6285-0161, bizinfo@sg.marshallcavendish.com, http://www.marshallcavendish.com/.

387.7 SGP
SINGAPORE CHANGI AIRPORT TIMETABLE. Text in English. 1989. q. USD 10 (effective 2000). adv.
Published by: (Civil Aviation Authority of Singapore), Marshall Cavendish Business Information Pty. Ltd. (Subsidiary of: Times Publishing Group), Times Centre, 1 New Industrial Rd, Singapore, 536196, Singapore. TEL 65-6213-9288, FAX 65-6285-0161, bizinfo@sg.marshallcavendish.com, http://www.marshallcavendish.com/.

387.7 USA
SKYLIGHTS; the inflight magazine of Spirit Airlines. Text in English. 2005. bi-m. free to qualified personnel (effective 2011). back issues avail. **Document type:** *Magazine, Consumer.* **Description:** Features top celebrities, trendy destination hotspots and cool events in the city.
Related titles: Online - full text ed.: free (effective 2011).
Published by: Worth International Media Group, 5979 NW 151 St, Ste 120, Miami Lakes, FL 33014. TEL 305-828-0123, FAX 305-826-6950, info@worthit.com, http//www.worthit.com. Pub. Laurel A Herman.

387.7 USA ISSN 0271-2598
HD9711.2
SPEEDNEWS; a weekly publication for the aviation industry. Text in English. 1979. w. USD 727 (effective 2011). adv. bk.rev. **Document type:** *Newsletter, Trade.* **Description:** Keeps executives up-to-date on the week's aviation news, including new aircraft orders, leases, new product orders and innovations.

T U

Related titles: CD-ROM ed.: USD 595; Online - full text ed.
—CCC.
Published by: Penton Media, Inc., 1801 Ave of the Stars, Ste 210, Los Angeles, CA 90067. TEL 310-203-9603, FAX 310-203-9352, information@penton.com, http://www.penton.com. Ed. Steve Costley. Pub. Gilbert Speed. Circ: 4,000 (paid).

SPIC; revista de turismo. *see* TRAVEL AND TOURISM

387.74 CAN
STANDARD SCHEDULES INFORMATION MANUAL. Abbreviated title: S S I M. Text in English. 2/yr. USD 470 per issue includes CD-ROM (effective 2008). **Document type:** *Handbook/Manual/Guide, Trade.* **Description:** Designed to help originators and recipients of schedule information, both in terms of electronic data processing and for conventional manual processes.
Related titles: Online - full content ed.
Published by: International Air Transport Association, 800 Place Victoria, PO Box 113, Montreal, PQ H4Z 1M1, Canada. TEL 514-390-6726, 800-716-6326, FAX 514-874-9659, sales@iata.org.

STATISTIQUES DE TRAFIC. *see* TRANSPORTATION—Abstracting, Bibliographies, Statistics

387.71 CAN
SURVEYS OF INTERNATIONAL AIR TRANSPORT FARES AND RATES. Text in English. a. (issued in Sep.). USD 23. back issues avail.
Related titles: French ed.; Russian ed.; Spanish ed.; ◆ Series of: I C A O Circulars. ISSN 1014-4412.
Published by: International Civil Aviation Organization (I C A O), External Relations and Public Information Office, 999 University St, Montreal, PQ H3C 5H7, Canada. TEL 514-954-8022, FAX 514-954-6769, icaohq@icao.int.

380.5 HRV ISSN 0351-1898
SUVREMENI PROMET. Text in Croatian; Summaries in English. 1979. bi-m. USD 42. adv. bk.rev.
Indexed: A26.
Published by: Sveuciliste u Zagrebu, Faculty of Transportation/University of Zagreb, Vukeliceva 4, Zagreb, 41000, Croatia. TEL 041 215 767. Ed. Franko Rotim. Circ: 1,400.

363.7 CAN
TECHNICAL INSTRUCTIONS FOR THE SAFE TRANSPORT OF DANGEROUS GOODS BY AIR. Text in English. biennial. USD 88 (effective 2001).
Related titles: French ed.; Russian ed.; Spanish ed.
Published by: International Civil Aviation Organization (I C A O), External Relations and Public Information Office, 999 University St, Montreal, PQ H3C 5H7, Canada. TEL 514-954-8022, FAX 514-954-6769, icaohq@icao.int.

387.74 THA ISSN 0125-1090
THAILAND AIRLINE TIMETABLE. Text in English. 1976. m. adv.
Published by: Advertising and Media Consultants Ltd., Silom Condominium 12th Fl, 52-38 Soi Saladaeng 2, Bangkok, 10500, Thailand. TEL 266-9040, FAX 236-6764. Ed. Asha Narula Sehgal. R&P, Adv. contact Raui Sehgal. Circ: 40,000.

TRANSMIT. *see* AERONAUTICS AND SPACE FLIGHT

387.70971 629.13 CAN ISSN 1715-7382
TRANSPORT CANADA AERONAUTICAL INFORMATION MANUAL. Text in English. 1981. s-a. CAD 24 (effective 2006).
Supersedes in part (in 2005): A I P Canada (English Edition) (0825-5229)
Related titles: Online - full text ed.: ISSN 1715-7390. 2005.
Published by: Transport Canada/Transports Canada, 300 Sparks St, Ottawa, ON K1A 0N5, Canada. TEL 613-990-2309, FAX 613-954-4731.

TRAVEL AGENT'S HANDBOOK (CD-ROM). *see* TRAVEL AND TOURISM

387.742 DNK ISSN 0900-3606
TRAVEL MANAGER C P H. Text in Danish. 1980. q. adv. **Document type:** *Consumer.*
Formerly (until 1983): Copenhagen Airline Guide
Published by: European Traffic Guides, Valby Overdrev 6, Helsinge, 3200, Denmark. TEL 45-48-394545, FAX 45-48-394010.

387.74 CAN ISSN 0849-6811
U L D TECHNICAL MANUAL. (Unit Load Devices) Text in English. a. USD 192.50 per issue (effective 2008). illus. **Document type:** *Handbook/Manual/Guide, Trade.* **Description:** Contains all specifications agreed to within the airline industry and illustrates them with clear drawings.
Published by: International Air Transport Association, 800 Place Victoria, PO Box 113, Montreal, PQ H4Z 1M1, Canada. TEL 514-390-6726, 800-716-6326, FAX 514-874-9659, sales@iata.org. Adv. contact Sandra Davies.

387.7 USA ISSN 1541-5996
U P. Text in English. 2002 (Nov.). bi-m. USD 39 (effective 2003).
Published by: ShowMedia, LLC, 1600 SE 17th St. Ste. 200, Fort Lauderdale, FL 33316. TEL 954-525-8626, FAX 954-525-7954. Eds. Mark T. Masciarotte, James R. Gilbert. Pub. Lester S. Abberley II.

U.S. INTERNATIONAL AIR TRAVEL STATISTICS. *see* TRANSPORTATION—Abstracting, Bibliographies, Statistics

U S INTERNATIONAL AIR TRAVEL STATISTICS REPORT. *see* TRANSPORTATION—Abstracting, Bibliographies, Statistics

387.74 USA
U.S. NATIONAL TRANSPORTATION SAFETY BOARD. AIRCRAFT ACCIDENT REPORTS. Text in English. 19??. irreg. back issues avail.; reprints avail. **Document type:** *Report, Government.*
Related titles: Microfiche ed.: (from CIS); Online - full text ed.: free (effective 2011).
Indexed: AmStI.
Published by: (U.S. National Transportation Safety Board), U.S. Department of Commerce, National Technical Information Service, 5301 Shawnee Rd, Alexandria, VA 22312. TEL 703-605-6000, info@ntis.gov, http://www.ntis.gov.

387.74 341.46 GBR
UNITED KINGDOM AERONAUTICAL INFORMATION PUBLICATION. Abbreviated title: U K - A I P. Text in English. 19??. base vol. plus irreg. updates. looseleaf. **Document type:** *Government.* **Description:** Contains information on facilities, services, rules, regulations, and restrictions in U.K. airspace.
Formerly: U K Air Pilot
Related titles: Online - full text ed.: free (effective 2009); ◆ Includes: Aeronautical Information Circulars; ◆ Series: Great Britain. Civil Aviation Authority. Airport Surveys; ◆ Manual of Air Traffic Services - Part 1; ◆ Overseas Non-scheduled Flight Clearances Guide; ◆ Great Britain. Civil Aviation Authority. Mandatory Requirements for Airworthiness; ◆ Mandatory Aircraft Modifications and Inspections Summary; ◆ Civil Aircraft Airworthiness Information and Procedures; ◆ A A I B Recommendations - C A A Progress Report (Year); ◆ Air Traffic Services Engineering Requirements; ◆ Great Britain. Civil Aviation Authority. Annual Punctuality Statistics - Full Analysis (Year); ◆ Great Britain. Civil Aviation Authority. Annual Punctuality Statistics - Full and Summary Analysis (Year); ◆ Air Navigation - The Order and the Regulations; ◆ Air Traffic Control Licensing; ◆ Great Britain. Civil Aviation Authority. Approved Aerial Positions.
Published by: Civil Aviation Authority, C A A House, 45-59 Kingsway, London, WC2B 6TE, United Kingdom. TEL 44-20-73797311, infoservices@caa.co.uk, http://www.caa.co.uk. **Dist. by:** Westward Documedia Limited.

387.7 USA ISSN 0149-3965
HD9680.U54
UNITED TECHNOLOGIES. ANNUAL REPORT. Text in English. 1975. a.
Published by: United Technologies Corp., United Technologies Bldg., Hartford, CT 06101. TEL 860-728-7000, invrelations@corphq.utc.com, http://www.utc.com.

387.7 USA
UNIVERSITY AVIATION ASSOCIATION. NEWSLETTER. Text in English. bi-m. looseleaf. USD 35. adv. bk.rev. back issues avail. **Document type:** *Newsletter.*
Published by: University Aviation Association, 3410 Skyway Dr., Auburn, AL 36830. TEL 334-844-2434, FAX 334-844-2432. Adv. contact Carolyn Williamson. Circ: 650.

387.7 DEU
V C INFO. Text in German. 1972. m. free to members. **Document type:** *Magazine, Trade.*
Formerly: Cockpit Report
Published by: Vereinigung Cockpit/German Air Line Pilots' Association, Main Airport Center (MAC), Unterschweinstiege 10, Frankfurt, 60549, Germany. TEL 49-69-6959760, FAX 49-69-695976150, Office@VCockpit.de. Circ: 800.

387.7 USA ISSN 2151-6588
V L J NEWS. (Very Light Jet) Text in English. 2006. d. free to members (effective 2009). adv. back issues avail. **Document type:** *Newsletter, Trade.* **Description:** Provides news and information from the very light jet industry.
Media: Online - full content.
Published by: K R D Corporation

VERANTWOORD ONDERNEMEN OP AMSTERDAM AIRPORT SCHIPHOL. *see* BUSINESS AND ECONOMICS—Management

387.7 RUS
VOZDUSHNYI TRANSPORT. Text in Russian. 1936. w. USD 217 foreign (effective 2006). **Document type:** *Newspaper, Consumer.* **Description:** Contains information on Russia's aviation and cosmonautics, flight safety, analysis of social problems of civil aviation personnel, reports from international air and space fairs.
Published by: Izdatel'skii Dom Ekonomicheskaya Gazeta, Bumazhnyi proezd 14, Moscow, 101462, Russian Federation. TEL 7-495-2505858, akdi@akdi.ru. Ed. Sergey A Gusiakov TEL 7-095-2574085. Circ: 10,000. **Dist. by:** East View Information Services, 10601 Wayzata Blvd, Minneapolis, MN 55305. TEL 952-252-1201, 800-477-1005, FAX 952-252-1202, info@eastview.com, http://www.eastview.com.

WATER FLYING. *see* AERONAUTICS AND SPACE FLIGHT

WATER FLYING ANNUAL. *see* AERONAUTICS AND SPACE FLIGHT

387.7 USA ISSN 0509-9528
THE WEEKLY OF BUSINESS AVIATION. Text in English. 1965. w. (Mon.). looseleaf. USD 795 domestic; USD 895 foreign (effective 2008). adv. bk.rev. charts; illus.; stat.; tr.lit. q. cum.index. **Document type:** *Newsletter, Trade.* **Description:** Contains the latest information on regulatory changes, new and used business aircraft delivery data, operational costs and more.
Formerly: Business Aviation (0045-3617)
Related titles: E-mail ed.: USD 649 (effective 2008); Online - full text ed.
Indexed: A26, G08, I05, P48, PQC, SRI.
—CIS. **CCC.**
Published by: Aviation Week Group (Subsidiary of: McGraw-Hill Companies, Inc.), 2 Penn Plz, 25th Fl, New York, NY 10121. TEL 800-525-5003, FAX 888-385-1428, buccustserv@cdsfulfillment.com. Ed. David Collogan.

WEEKLY REVIEW OF COLLECTIVE BARGAINING. *see* LABOR UNIONS

WHO'S WHO LEGAL. AVIATION. *see* LAW

629.13 CAN ISSN 0701-1369
HE9761.1
WINGS. Text in English. 1959. bi-m. CAD 34 domestic; USD 50 in United States; USD 65 elsewhere (effective 2007). adv. bk.rev. back issues avail. **Document type:** *Magazine, Trade.* **Description:** Provides domestic and international coverage of corporate, commercial and military fixed-wing aviation.
Former titles (until 1976): Canadian Wings (0008-5367); (until 1964): Western Wings (0315-4645)
Related titles: Online - full text ed.
Published by: Annex Publishing & Printing, Inc., 105 Donly Dr S, PO Box 530, Simcoe, ON N3Y 4N5, Canada. TEL 519-429-3966, 800-265-2827, FAX 519-429-3112, 888-404-1129, mfredericks@annexweb.com, http://www.annexweb.com. Ed. Drew McCarthy TEL 888-599-2228 ext 265. Pub. Diane Kleer TEL 888-599-2228 ext 231. Circ: 11,468.

387.7 GBR ISSN 1471-2768
WINGSPAN INTERNATIONAL. Text in English. m. GBP 35.15 for 2 yrs. domestic; GBP 42.85 for 2 yrs. in Europe; GBP 61.70 for 2 yrs. in North America; GBP 84.60 for 2 yrs. elsewhere (effective 2004). adv. bk.rev. illus. back issues avail. **Document type:** *Magazine, Consumer.*
Former titles (until 2000): Wingspan (0955-9000); (until 1985): Planes
Address: Aldbury House, Dower Mews, Berkhamsted, Herts BP 2BL, United Kingdom. TEL 44-1442-866233, FAX 44-1442-862225. Ed. Alan Forberg.

387.7 USA
WORLD AEROSPACE DATABASE. BUYER'S GUIDE. Text in English. 1940. s-a. USD 265 domestic (effective 2007). **Document type:** *Directory, Trade.*
Former titles (until 2005): World Aviation Directory & Aerospace Database. Buyer's Guide (1550-0098); (until 2003): Aviation Week's World Aviation Directory. Buyer's Guide (1541-1486); (until 2001): World Aviation Directory & Buyer's Guide (1064-0509); (until 1992): World Aviation Buyer's Guide (1064-0495)
—CCC.
Published by: Aviation Week Group (Subsidiary of: McGraw-Hill Companies, Inc.), 2 Penn Plz, 25th Fl, New York, NY 10121. TEL 800-525-5003, FAX 888-385-1428, buccustserv@cdsfulfillment.com, http://www.aviationweek.com. Circ: 13,135 (controlled and free).

WORLD AIR TRANSPORT STATISTICS. *see* TRANSPORTATION—Abstracting, Bibliographies, Statistics

363.12465 GBR
WORLD AIRCRAFT ACCIDENT SUMMARY (CD-ROM). Text in English. 1950. a. GBP 500 per issue for PDF; GBP 1,250 per issue for WAAS Microsoft Access database (effective 2009). **Document type:** *Journal, Trade.* **Description:** Contains information and statistics on over 3,000 of the world's aircraft and helicopter accidents since 1990.
Former titles (until 2005): World Aircraft Accident Summary (Print) (1366-6800); (until 1995): World Airline Accident Summary (1461-5126)
Media: CD-ROM.
—BLDSC (9352.720000).
Published by: Ascend Worldwide Ltd., Cardinal Point, Newall Rd, Heathrow Airport, London, TW6 2AS, United Kingdom. TEL 44-20-85646700, FAX 44-20-88970300, ian.sheppard@airclaims.co.uk, uk@ascendworldwide.com.

387.7 629.13 GBR ISSN 0951-8673
WORLD AIRLINE FLEETS NEWS. Text in English. 1977. m. GBP 42 domestic; GBP 42 in Europe; GBP 53 elsewhere (effective 2010). adv. bk.rev. charts; illus.; stat. back issues avail. **Document type:** *Magazine, Trade.* **Description:** Covers the ever changing world of airlines and airliners - reporting new airlines, new and used airliner transactions, accidents, livery changes, orders and much more.
Former titles (until 1987): Airline Data News (0263-3272); (until 1982): World Airline Fleets Monthly (0140-6450)
Published by: W A F News Ltd., Caxton House, Trout Rd, West Drayton, Mddx UB7 7TQ, United Kingdom. TEL 44-1895-444159, FAX 44-1895-441228, info@wafnews.com. Ed. Ricky-Dene Halliday. Circ: 5,000.

387.736 GBR
WORLD AIRPORT GUIDE. Text in English. 19??. a. adv. **Document type:** *Directory, Trade.* **Description:** Contains information on the top 150 gateway airports in the world. Information for the business and leisure traveller include: Business and conference facilities, Information lines and help desks, airport facilities and amenities, car rental, airport parking, hotel accommodation, transfer times and on-going transport links.
Published by: Columbus Travel Media Ltd (Subsidiary of: Highbury House Communications Plc), Media House, Azalea Dr, Swanley, Kent BR8 8HU, United Kingdom. TEL 44-1322-611430, FAX 44-1322-616323, travelads@columbustravelmedia.com. Adv. contact David Simms TEL 44-1322-611335.

387.7 SGP
WORLD CIVIL AVIATION CHIEF EXECUTIVES FORUM (YEAR). PROCEEDINGS. Text in English. 2003. triennial. SGD 80 per issue (effective 2009). **Document type:** *Proceedings, Trade.* **Description:** Includes transcripts of all the presentations, panel discussions and speakers' biographies.
Published by: Singapore Aviation Academy, 1 Aviation Dr., Singapore, 499867, Singapore. TEL 65-65-430433, FAX 65-65-429890, saa@caas.gov.sg, http://www.saa.com.sg/.

WORLD METEOROLOGICAL ORGANIZATION. COMMISSION FOR AERONAUTICAL METEOROLOGY. ABRIDGED FINAL REPORT OF THE (NO.) SESSION. *see* METEOROLOGY

358.4 USA
WORLD MILITARY AND CIVIL AIRCRAFT BRIEFING. Abbreviated title: W M C A B. Text in English. 1990. m. looseleaf. USD 2,295; USD 3,920 combined subscription (print & online eds.); USD 3,345 combined subscription (print & CD-ROM eds.) (effective 2011). **Document type:** *Trade.* **Description:** Reports on over 300 programs covering the world market for military and civil aircraft. Provides comprehensive data and market analysis.
Related titles: CD-ROM ed.; Diskette ed.; Online - full text ed.: USD 2,245 (online or CD-ROM ed.); USD 3,870 combined subscription (online & CD-ROM eds.) (effective 2011).
Published by: Teal Group Corp., 3900 University Dr, Ste 220, Fairfax, VA 22030. TEL 703-385-1992, FAX 703-691-9591, custserv@tealgroup.com.

387.71 CAN
THE WORLD OF CIVIL AVIATION. (Subseries of: I C A O Circulars) Text in English. irreg. USD 50 (effective Nov. 2000). back issues avail. **Description:** Previews 4-year periods of civil aviation.
Indexed: IIS.
Published by: International Civil Aviation Organization (I C A O), Legal Affairs and External Relations Bureau, 999 University St, Montreal, PQ H3C 5H7, Canada. TEL 514-954-8022, FAX 514-954-6769, TELEX 05-24513, icaohq@icao.int.

387.7 USA
X L A EXPRESS. (Express Delivery & Logistics Association) Text in English. q. **Document type:** *Newsletter, Trade.*
Formerly (until 197?): A C C A Express
Published by: Express Delivery and Logistics Association (X L A), 14 W. Third Street, Suite 200, Kansas City, MO 64105. TEL 816-221-0254, 888-838-0761, FAX 816-472-7765. Circ: 1,500.

ZAKENREIS MAGAZINE; Business travel magazine for the Benelux. *see* TRAVEL AND TOURISM

387.7 ZMB
ZAMBIA. DEPARTMENT OF CIVIL AVIATION. ANNUAL REPORT. Text in English. a. **Document type:** *Government.*
Published by: (Zambia. Department of Civil Aviation), Government Printing Department, PO Box 30136, Lusaka, Zambia.

ZHONGGUO MINHANG BAO/CIVIL AVIATION ADMINISTRATION OF CHINA. JOURNAL. *see* TRAVEL AND TOURISM

TRANSPORTATION—Automobiles

388.3 ITA
A 4. AUTORUOTE 4 X 4. Text in Italian. 1986. m. (11/yr.). EUR 40 domestic (effective 2008). adv. back issues avail. **Document type:** *Magazine, Consumer.*
Formerly (until 2007): Autoruote 4 x 4 (1122-8342)
Published by: Cantelli Editore Srl, Via Saliceto 22c, Castelmaggiore, BO 40013, Italy. TEL 39-051-6328811, FAX 39-051-6328815, cantelli.editore@cantelli.net, http://www.cantelli.net.

343 USA ISSN 0093-4062
KF2210.Z95
A A A DIGEST OF MOTOR LAWS. (American Automobile Association) Key Title: Digest of Motor Laws. Text in English. a. USD 13.95 (effective 2003). **Document type:** *Monographic series.*
Published by: (Traffic Safety Department), A A A Government Relations, 1440 New York Ave., Ste 200, NW, Washington, DC 2005. TEL 202-942-2050, http://www.aaa.com. Circ: 80,000.

388.3 USA ISSN 1098-3767
A A A GOING PLACES (POTTSTOWN). Text in English. 1986. bi-m. USD 2 domestic to members (effective 2006). **Document type:** *Magazine, Consumer.*
Formerly (until 1998): A A A Today (Pottstown) (1049-8133); Which was formed by the merger of (1928-1986): Motor Travel (0027-2086); (19??-1986): Motorist
Published by: Greenfield Printing & Publishing Co., 1025 N. Washington St., Greenfield, OH 45123. TEL 614-228-4664. Ed. John T. Rice. Circ: 37,000 (paid).

A A A HORIZONS. *see* TRAVEL AND TOURISM

A A A JOURNEYS. *see* TRAVEL AND TOURISM

A A A LIVING (ILLINOIS/N. INDIANA EDITION). *see* TRAVEL AND TOURISM

A A A LIVING (MICHIGAN EDITION). *see* TRAVEL AND TOURISM

A A A LIVING (WISCONSIN EDITION). (American Automobile Association) *see* TRAVEL AND TOURISM

388.3 USA ISSN 1079-8943
A A A MOTORIST - WEST VIRGINIA. Text in English. bi-m. membership. adv. charts; illus. **Document type:** *Newspaper.*
Published by: A A A West Penn - West Virginia, 5900 Baum Blvd, Pittsburgh, PA 15206. TEL 412-365-7203, FAX 412-362-0926. Ed. Doug O'Neil. adv.: B&W page USD 2,600, color page USD 3,000. Circ: 72,000.

388.3 USA ISSN 1077-6060
A A A MOTORIST - WESTERN PENNSYLVANIA. Variant title: A A A Motorist - Uniontown Region. Text in English. 1980. bi-m. film rev.; rec.rev.; software rev.; video rev.; bk.rev. charts; illus.; stat.; tr.lit. **Document type:** *Magazine, Consumer.* **Description:** News and features about travel, automotive, and lifestyle opportunities available to members.
Incorporates: Western Pennsylvania Motorist (1066-6869); Former titles (until 1994): A A A Today (0890-5614); (until 1986): Motorist (0273-9283)
Published by: American Automobile Association, A A A East Central, 5900 Baum Blvd, Pittsburgh, PA 15206. TEL 412-365-7203, FAX 412-362-0926.

A A A READING - BERKS. *see* TRAVEL AND TOURISM

388.3 USA ISSN 0891-3153
A A A ROAD ATLAS. (American Automobile Association Road Atlas) Text in English. 1985. a.
Published by: American Automobile Association, 8111 Gatehouse Rd, Falls Church, VA 22042.

388.3 USA
A A A SOUTHERN TRAVELER. Text in English. 1998. bi-m. USD 3; USD 0.50 newsstand/cover (effective 2001). adv. illus. 40 p./no.; back issues avail. **Document type:** *Magazine, Consumer.*
Formerly (until Jan. 1999): Southern Traveler (1097-1912)
Published by: Automobile Club of Missouri, 12901 N. Forty Dr., St. Louis, MO 63141. TEL 314-523-7350, FAX 314-523-6982, http://www.aaamissouri.com. Ed., Pub., R&P Michael Right. Adv. contact Deborah Reinhardt TEL 314-523-7350 ext 6301. color page USD 5,585; 7 x 10. Circ: 170,000 (controlled).

A A A TODAY (CINCINNATI). *see* TRAVEL AND TOURISM

796.72 USA ISSN 1075-668X
A A A TRAVELER (ALLENTOWN). (American Automobile Association) Text in English. 1910. 6/yr. free membership (effective 2007). adv. charts; illus.; stat. 32 p./no.; **Document type:** *Newspaper, Consumer.*
Former titles (until 1994): A A A Motorist (Allentown) (1056-2532); (until 1991): A A A Today (Allentown) (0896-4874); Supersedes (in 1987): Lehigh Valley Motor Club News
Published by: American Automobile Association, East Penn, 1020 W. Hamilton St, Allentown, PA 18105-1910. TEL 610-434-5141, FAX 610-778-3381, http://www.aaaeastpenn.com/. Ed. Theresa E Deutsch. Circ: 169,000 (paid and controlled).

A A A TRAVELER (FLORHAM PARK). *see* TRAVEL AND TOURISM

796.72 917 USA
THE A A A VALLEY MOTORIST. Text in English. 1936. bi-m. USD 1. **Document type:** *Newspaper.*
Former titles (until Apr. 1997): Valley Motorist; Wyoming Valley Motorist (0049-822X)
Published by: A A A Mid-Atlantic, PO Box 820884, Philadelphia, PA 19182-0884. TEL 215-864-5000, FAX 215-568-1153. Ed. John C Moyer. Circ: 59,500.

388 USA
G149
A A A WORLD (HAMILTON). (American Automobile Association) Text in English. bi-m. USD 4 to non-members (effective 1999); USD 1 newsstand/cover. adv. **Description:** Focuses on automobile safety, automobile maintenance tips, travel tips, vacation destinations and a wide variety of miscellaneous topics.
Former titles (until 1999): Car & Travel. Central West Jersey Edition (1080-2231); (until 1995): Spotlight on Travel (1074-4436); Spotlight (Robbinsville) (0887-3453)
Published by: American Automobile Association, Central - West Jersey Division, 3 AAA Dr., Hamilton, NJ 08691-1898. TEL 609-890-2220, FAX 609-587-7345. Ed., R&P Sylvia Veitia. Pub. Doug Damerst. Adv. contact Bob Smarto. Circ: 420,000.

910.90 388.342 USA ISSN 1523-9403
A A A WORLD (YORK). Text in English. 1970. bi-m. free domestic to members (effective 2005). adv. 72 p./no. 3 cols./p.; **Document type:** *Magazine, Consumer.*
Incorporates (1911-1999): Keystone A A A Motorist (1055-1093); Former titles (until 199?): A A A Mid-Atlantic Motorist (1097-8755); (until 199?): A A A Delaware Motorist (1056-5086); Delaware Keystone Motorist (1042-5926)
Published by: American Automobile Association, 2840 Eastern Blvd., York, PA 17402. TEL 717-600-8900, FAX 717-755-3552. Ed. Kristen Brant. adv.: B&W page USD 7,654, color page USD 9,568. Circ: 151,000 (controlled).

388.3 USA ISSN 0001-0154
HE5623.A1
A A M V A BULLETIN. Text in English. 1935. m. USD 25; USD 30 in Canada; USD 40 elsewhere (effective 1999). charts; illus. **Document type:** *Newsletter.*
Indexed: HRIS, P06.
Published by: American Association of Motor Vehicle Administrators, 4301 Wilson Blvd, Ste 400, Arlington, VA 22203. TEL 703-522-4200, FAX 703-522-1553. Ed., R&P Melissa D Clague. Pub. Kenneth Beam. Circ: 2,500.

629.2 ZWE
A A MAGAZINE. Text in English. 1979. q. membership. charts; illus. **Description:** Motoring magazine of general interest to the motorist and up-to-date information for AAZ members.
Former titles: Wheels; Supersedes: Motoring Review; Which was formerly: Automobile Association of Rhodesia. Bulletin
Published by: Automobile Association of Zimbabwe, Fanum House, Samora Machel Ave 57, PO Box 585, Harare, Zimbabwe. Ed. Vivian Mitchell. Circ: 50,000.

914.1 GBR ISSN 0305-0742
A A MEMBERS HANDBOOK. IRELAND. Text in English. a. **Document type:** *Magazine, Consumer.*
—CCC.
Published by: Automobile Association, Lambert House, Stockport Rd, Cheadle, SK8 2DY, United Kingdom. TEL 44-161-4958945, FAX 44-161-4887544, customersupport@theAA.com, http://www.theaa.com.

796.7 IRL ISSN 0791-380X
A A MOTORING. (Automobile Association) Text in English. 1990. 10/yr. adv. **Document type:** *Magazine, Consumer.*
Published by: Automobile Association Ireland, 7 Cranford Centre, Montrose, Dublin, 4, Ireland. TEL 353-1-2600899, FAX 353-1-2600911. adv.: color page EUR 4,444; trim 210 x 297. Circ: 96,000 (paid and controlled).

388.3 910.09 DEU ISSN 0943-3945
A C E LENKRAD. Text in German. 1954. m. EUR 24; EUR 2 newsstand/cover (effective 2011). adv. bk.rev. **Document type:** *Magazine, Consumer.* **Description:** Automobile club magazine featuring the latest news on cars, parts and accessories. Articles also cover testing, road safety and travel. Includes readers' comments.
Formerly (until 1975): Lenkrad (0343-172X)
Published by: (Auto Club Europa e.V.), A C E Verlag GmbH, Schmidener Str 233, Stuttgart, 70374, Germany. TEL 49-711-53030, FAX 49-711-5303259, ace@ace-online.de, http://www.ace-online.de. Ed. Klaus-Michael Schaal. Adv. contact Ursula Hoerning. Circ: 546,274 (controlled).

388.3 ITA
A C I NEWS. (Automobile Club d'Italia) Text in Italian. 1949. bi-m. free to members. adv. **Document type:** *Newsletter, Consumer.*
Published by: Automobile Club Torino, Via Giovanni Giolitti 15, Turin, TO 10123, Italy. TEL 39-011-57791, http://www.acitorino.it. Ed. Tancredi Savaro. Circ: 129,000.

629.286 CHE
A C S ZURICH. (Automobil-Club de Schweiz) Text in Multiple languages. m.
Published by: Swiss Motor Club, International Werbung, PO Box, Zuerich 1, 8032, Switzerland. Circ: 15,000.

614.86 DEU
A C V PROFIL. Text in German. 1985. 10/yr. adv. **Document type:** *Magazine, Consumer.*
Published by: Automobil-Club Verkehr, Goldgasse 2, Cologne, 50668, Germany. TEL 49-221-9126910, FAX 49-221-91269126, acv@acv.de, http://www.acv.de. adv.: B&W page EUR 3,740, color page EUR 5,610; trim 182 x 262. Circ: 167,500 (controlled).

796.77 GBR ISSN 2043-0299
▼ **A D.** (Automotive Design) Text in English. 2010. bi-m. GBP 45 domestic; GBP 66 foreign; free to qualified personnel (effective 2010). adv. **Document type:** *Magazine, Trade.* **Description:** For automotive design engineers: the latest industry news; a comprehensive supplier directory; full technical and management feature archives; videos; white papers; interviews.
Related titles: Online - full text ed.: free (effective 2010).
Published by: (S A E International), AD Media Europe, Hawley Mill, Hawley Rd, Dartford, DA2 7TJ, United Kingdom. TEL 44-1322-221144, enquiries@automotivedesign.eu.com. Eds. Ian Adcock, Kevin Jost. Pub. Ed Tranter. Circ: 19,708.

796.77 DEU ISSN 1864-1059
A D A C AUTO TEST NEUWAGEN. Text in German. 19??. a. EUR 7.90 newsstand/cover (effective 2008). adv. **Document type:** *Magazine, Consumer.*
Former titles (until 2006): A D A C Special Auto Test (1610-3483); (until 2002): A D A C Special Auto (0934-7569)
Published by: (Allgemeiner Deutscher Automobil-Club e.V.), A D A C Verlag GmbH, Leonhard-Moll-Bogen 1, Munich, 81365, Germany. TEL 49-89-76760, FAX 49-89-76762500, verlag@adac.de, http://www.adac.de. adv.: page EUR 14,640. Circ: 180,000 (controlled).

388.3 DEU ISSN 0007-2842
A D A C MOTORWELT. Text in German. 1925. m. EUR 44.50 membership (effective 2008). adv. bibl.; charts; illus.; stat. **Document type:** *Magazine, Consumer.*
Indexed: DokStr.
Published by: (Allgemeiner Deutscher Automobil-Club e.V.), A D A C Verlag GmbH, Leonhard-Moll-Bogen 1, Munich, 81365, Germany. TEL 49-89-76760, FAX 49-89-76762500, verlag@adac.de, http://www.adac.de. Ed. Michael Ramstetter. Adv. contact Michael Behrend. B&W page EUR 76,000, color page EUR 105,280; trim 184 x 244. Circ: 13,879,722 (paid).

A D A C REISEMAGAZIN. *see* TRAVEL AND TOURISM

629.283 DEU
A D A C SIGNALE. Text in German. 1988. s-a. free (effective 2008). **Document type:** *Bulletin, Consumer.*
Published by: (Allgemeiner Deutscher Automobil-Club e.V.), A D A C Verlag GmbH, Leonhard-Moll-Bogen 1, Munich, 81365, Germany. TEL 49-89-76760, FAX 49-89-76762500, verlag@adac.de, http://www.adac.de. Circ: 3,000.

388 DEU ISSN 1613-2483
A D A C SPECIAL GEBRAUCHTWAGEN TEST. Text in German. 1990. a. adv. **Document type:** *Magazine, Consumer.*
Former titles (until 2004): A D A C Special Gebrauchtwagen-Ratgeber (1613-0545); (until 2002): A D A C Special Gebrauchtwagen (0937-2938)
Published by: (Allgemeiner Deutscher Automobil-Club e.V.), A D A C Verlag GmbH, Leonhard-Moll-Bogen 1, Munich, 81365, Germany. TEL 49-89-76760, FAX 49-89-76762500, verlag@adac.de, http://www.adac.de. adv.: B&W page EUR 10,200, color page EUR 10,200. Circ: 160,000 (controlled).

629.286 FRA ISSN 1631-1035
A D D X. Text in French. 2001. m. EUR 49 (effective 2008). **Document type:** *Magazine, Consumer.*
Published by: Mondadori France, 1 Rue du Colonel Pierre-Avia, Paris, Cedex 15 75754, France. TEL 33-1-41335001, contact@mondadori.fr, http://www.mondadori.fr.

388.3 DEU ISSN 1435-6074
A E P. (Automotive Engineering Partners) Text in German. 1999. 6/yr. **Document type:** *Magazine, Trade.* **Description:** Contains strategies for successful production and process optimization.
Published by: Vieweg und Sohn Verlagsgesellschaft mbH (Subsidiary of: Springer Science+Business Media), Abraham-Lincoln-Str 46, Wiesbaden, 65189, Germany. TEL 49-611-78780, FAX 49-611-7878400, vieweg.service@bertelsmann.de, http://www.vieweg.de.

338.476 USA ISSN 2154-977X
A F P D BOTTOM LINE. Text in English. 1990. m. **Document type:** *Magazine, Trade.* **Description:** Features the latest business and marketing trends, legislative issues impacting the industry, plus updates on AFPD business, activities and member benefits.
Former titles (until 2010): Food & Petroleum Report; (until 2006): Food and Beverage Report (1049-1899)
Published by: Associated Food & Petroleum Dealers, 30415 W 13 Mile, Farmington Hills, MI 48334. TEL 248-671-9600, FAX 866-601-9610, info@AFPDonline.org.

629.286 ARG
A G E S. (Asociacion de Garajes y Estaciones de Servicio) Text in Spanish. 1925. 6/yr. adv.
Published by: Asociacion de Garajes y Estaciones de Servico, Hipolito Yrigoyen 2738, Buenos Aires, 1090, Argentina. Circ: 1,000.

A G R R: AUTO GLASS REPLACEMENT & REPAIR; the magazine driving the auto glass industry. *see* CERAMICS, GLASS AND POTTERY

629.2 AUS
A I M NEWSLETTER. (Automotive Industry Matters) Variant title: Automotive Industry Matters. Newsletter. Text in English. 1967. s-m. (23/yr.). AUD 434.50 domestic; AUD 395 foreign (effective 2008). adv. **Document type:** *Newsletter, Trade.* **Description:** Brings news and views report of automotive industry developments in Australia and overseas.
Formerly (until 2004): A I M Newsletter (Print) (0044-5681)
Media: Online - full text. **Related titles:** Supplement(s): A I M Ads.
Published by: Automotive Industry Matters Pty. Ltd., PO Box 186, Albert Park, VIC 3206, Australia. TEL 61-3-59898440, FAX 61-3-59898666, aim@automotive-industry.com.au. adv.: page AUD 1,250; 175 x 225.

629.222 CAN ISSN 1924-1275
THE A L R E VILLAGE CRYER. Text in English. 2006. irreg., latest vol.1, 2006. **Document type:** *Newsletter, Consumer.*
Related titles: Online - full text ed.: free (effective 2010).
Published by: Alberta Land-Rover Enthusiasts, 4908-24 St, Edmonton, AB T6H 3T9, Canada. admin@alre.ca, http://www.alre.ca.

658 GBR
A M; the newspaper for the automotive industry. (Automotive Management) Text in English. 2002. fortn. GBP 149; free to qualified personnel (effective 2010). adv. **Document type:** *Newspaper, Trade.* **Description:** Features articles that analyse the critical issues facing the automobile industry, from Government legislation to consumer trends.
Formed by the merger of (19??-2002): Automotive Management; (1973-2002): Autotrade (0308-7476); Which incorporated (1993-1996): Autobusiness (1352-2868); Which was formerly (until 1993): Garage and Automotive Retailer (0267-8411); (until 1984): G & T. Garage and Transport. Garage Edition (0264-0163); (until 1982): Garage and Transport. Garage Edition (0264-0813); Which superseded in part (in 1974): G A T E. Garage and Transport Equipment (0046-5429); Which was formerly (until 1969): Garage and Transport Equipment (0264-0848)
Published by: H. Bauer Publishing Ltd. (Subsidiary of: Bauer Media Group), Media House, Lynchwood, Peterborough, Cambridgeshire PE2 6EA, United Kingdom. TEL 44-1733-468000, http://www.bauer.co.uk. Ed. Jeremy Bennett TEL 44-1733-468261. Adv. contact Sarah Wilson TEL 44-1733-468320. color page GBP 5,120; trim 248 x 342. Circ: 17,746.

629.222 388.3 USA
A M G B A OCTAGON. Text in English. 1976. bi-m. USD 30 domestic; USD 40 foreign (effective 2000 - 2001). adv. bk.rev. back issues avail. **Document type:** *Newsletter.* **Description:** Provides news for enthusiasts of MG automobiles, in particular the MGB, MGB-GT, and MG Midget.
Incorporates: A M G B A Quarterly (0199-6797)
Related titles: Online - full content ed.
Published by: American M G B Association, PO Box 11401, Chicago, IL 60611. TEL 773-878-5055, 800-723-MGMG, FAX 773-769-3240. Ed., R&P, Adv. contact Frank J Ochal. Circ: 2,500.

796.77 GBR
A M QUATERLY. (Aston Martin) Text in English. 1948. q. free to members (effective 2009). adv. bk.rev. back issues avail. **Document type:** *Magazine, Trade.* **Description:** Contains reports of club activity from all round the world, technical articles, historical items, factory news and so on.
Published by: Aston Martin Owners' Club Ltd., Drayton St Leonard, Wallingford, Oxon OX10 7BG, United Kingdom. TEL 44-1865-400400, FAX 44-1865-400200, secretary@amoc.org. Adv. contact Marcella Brown TEL 44-1865-893935. page GBP 965. Circ: 5,500.

629.2 GRC
A M S TEST BOOK. (Auto Motor eae Sport) Text in Greek. 2006. a. EUR 8.80 newsstand/cover (effective 2006). adv. **Document type:** *Magazine, Consumer.*
Published by: Motorpress Hellas (Subsidiary of: Gruner + Jahr AG & Co), 132 Lefkis Str, Krioneri, 14568, Greece. TEL 30-210-6262000, FAX 30-210-6262401, info@motorpress.gr, http://www.motorpress.gr. Circ: 35,000 (controlled).

388.3 DEU ISSN 0001-1983
A M Z; Das Fachmagazin fuer den Kfz-Service und den Teilehandel. (Auto Motor Zubehoer) Text in German. 1912. 10/yr. EUR 62, EUR 83; EUR 7 newsstand/cover (effective 2010). adv. bk.rev. illus.; stat.; tr.lit. index. **Document type:** *Magazine, Trade.*
Related titles: Online - full text ed.
Indexed: RefZh.
—CCC.
Published by: Schluetersche Verlagsgesellschaft mbH und Co. KG, Hans-Boeckler-Allee 7, Hannover, 30173, Germany. TEL 49-511-85500, FAX 49-511-85501100, info@schluetersche.de, http://www.schluetersche.de. Ed. Juergen Rinn. Adv. contact Christian Welc. B&W page EUR 4,865, color page EUR 5,975; trim 188 x 272. Circ: 24,533 (paid).

629.286 658 AUS
A P A JOURNAL. (Auto Parts and Accessories) Text in English. 1978. bi-m. AUD 49.50 domestic; AUD 70 in New Zealand; AUD 80 elsewhere (effective 2008). adv. back issues avail. **Document type:** *Magazine, Trade.* **Description:** Provides news, views, product releases and industry trends on the Australian automotive industry.
Formerly: Automotive Parts and Accessories Trade Journal
Published by: Glenvale Publications, 4 Palmer Ct, PO Box 50, Mt Waverley, VIC 3149, Australia. TEL 61-3-95442233, FAX 61-3-95431150, glenvale@glenv.com.au, http://www.glenv.com.au. Ed. Pierre Meneaud TEL 61-3-95506825. Pub. Graeme Cox. Adv. contact Nirma Ledford TEL 61-3-95506826. color page USD 2,360; trim 210 x 280. Circ: 7,106.

A P R A (YEAR) MEMBERSHIP DIRECTORY. *see* BUSINESS AND ECONOMICS—Trade And Industrial Directories

388.3 USA
A R A NEWSLETTER. Text in English. 1970. m. free to members. **Document type:** *Newsletter.*
Formerly: A D R A Newsletter
Published by: Automotive Recyclers Association, 3975 Fair Ridge Dr, Ste 20 N, Fairfax, VA 22033-2924. TEL 703-385-1001. Ed. Tammy Haire. Circ: 2,000.

388 USA
A S P A REPORT. Text in English. 1986. q. free to members (effective 2008). adv. **Document type:** *Magazine, Trade.*
Published by: American Salvage Pool Association, 2100 Roswell Rd, Ste 200 C, PMB 709, Marietta, GA 30062. TEL 678-560-6678, FAX 678-560-9112, natalie@aspa.com, http://www.aspa.com. adv.: page USD 695; bleed 8.5 x 11. Circ: 3,500 (paid).

796.7 SVK ISSN 1337-0987
A T MAGAZIN. Text in Slovak. 2000. m. EUR 25.90 (effective 2009). adv. **Document type:** *Magazine, Consumer.*
Former titles (until 2007): Autotuning Autohifi (1336-7803); (until 2004): Autotuning Mototuning (1335-9436); (until 2001): Autotuning Slovakia (1335-7352)
Published by: Almega s.r.o., Stara Vajnorska 4, Bratislava, 83104, Slovakia. Ed. Petr Vadkerti.

388.3 USA ISSN 1098-0423
A T V 4-WHEEL ACTION. (All Terrain Vehicle) Text in English. 1984. m. USD 19.99 domestic; USD 32.99 in Canada; USD 34.99 foreign; USD 4.99 newsstand/cover (effective 2011). adv. back issues avail. **Document type:** *Magazine, Consumer.*
Formerly (until 199?): 3 and 4 Wheel Action (0884-7126)
Related titles: Online - full text ed.
Published by: Hi-Torque Publications, Inc., 25233 Anza Dr, Valencia, CA 91355. TEL 661-295-1910, FAX 661-295-1278, michelle@hi-torque.com, http://www.hi-torque.com. Adv. contact Robert Rex TEL 661-367-2109.

388.3 USA ISSN 1086-5632
A T V MAGAZINE. (All Terrain Vehicle) Text in English. 1995. bi-m. USD 19.97 (effective 2008). adv. back issues avail. **Document type:** *Magazine, Trade.*
Related titles: Online - full text ed.
Indexed: G05, G06, G07, G08, I05.
Published by: Affinity Group Inc., 2575 Vista Del Mar, Ventura, CA 93001. TEL 805-667-4100, FAX 805-667-4419, info@affinitygroup.com, http://www.affinitygroup.com. Ed. Tim Erickson TEL 763-383-4400. Adv. contact Allison Gruhn. Circ: 241,518.

388.3 USA ISSN 1099-2103
A T V SPORT. (All Terrain Vehicle) Text in English. 1998. 10/yr. USD 13.97 (effective 2008). adv. back issues avail. **Document type:** *Magazine, Trade.* **Description:** Contains pro and amateur racing schedules and results, personality profiles, objective product reviews, and new ideas on where to ride.
Related titles: Online - full text ed.
Indexed: G05, G06, G07, G08, I05.
Published by: Affinity Group Inc., 2575 Vista Del Mar, Ventura, CA 93001. TEL 805-667-4100, FAX 805-667-4419, info@affinitygroup.com, http://www.affinitygroup.com. Ed. Jerrod Kelley TEL 763-383-4400. Adv. contact Lane Uherka. Circ: 70,000 (paid and controlled).

388.3 AUT
A T V UND QUAD. (All Terrain Vehicles) Text in German. bi-m. EUR 43 domestic; EUR 38 in Germany; EUR 50 in Europe; EUR 55 elsewhere; EUR 3.90 newsstand/cover (effective 2006). adv. **Document type:** *Magazine, Consumer.*
Published by: Rede & Antwort Verlag und Handels GmbH, Hauptplatz 3, Neulengbach, 3040, Austria. TEL 43-2772-568230, FAX 43-2772-568235. adv.: color page EUR 3,000, B&W page EUR 2,700; trim 195 x 265. Circ: 8,470 (paid).

629.2 DEU ISSN 0001-2785
CODEN: AUTZA6
A T Z; fuer Forschung, Entwicklung, Konstruktion, Versuch und Fertigung. (Automobiltechnische Zeitschrift) Text in German. 1929. 11/yr. EUR 224; EUR 85 to students; EUR 26 newsstand/cover (effective 2010). adv. bk.rev. bibl.; charts; illus.; stat. index, cum.index every 20 yrs. **Document type:** *Magazine, Trade.* **Description:** Trade publication for the automobile industry. Features construction, development, research, production engineering, and testing. Includes industry news, reports of meetings and events.
Formed by the merger of (1898-1929): Motorwagen (0369-1330); (1912-1929): Auto-Technik (0365-8090)
Related titles: Online - full text ed.
Indexed: A22, A28, APA, AcoustA, ApMecR, BrCerAb, C&ISA, CA/WCA, CIA, CISA, CerAb, CivEngAb, CorrAb, DIP, E&CAJ, E11, EEA, EMA, ESPM, EngInd, EnvEAb, FR, H15, IBR, IBZ, M&TEA, M09, MBF, METADEX, RefZh, S&VD, SCOPUS, SolStAb, T04, TM, WAA.
—BLDSC (1833.000000), IE, Infotrieve, Ingenta, INIST, Linda Hall. **CCC.**
Published by: Vieweg und Teubner Verlag (Subsidiary of: Springer Fachmedien Wiesbaden GmbH), Abraham-Lincoln-Str 46, Wiesbaden, 65189, Germany. TEL 49-611-78780, FAX 49-611-7878400, info@viewegteubner.de, http://www.viewegteubner.de. Ed. Johannes Winterhagen. Circ: 6,781 (paid and controlled).

338.476 DEU ISSN 1865-6536
HD9710.A1
A T Z AUTOTECHNOLOGY; international magazine for engineering, production and management. (Automobiltechnische Zeitschrift) Text in English. 2001. bi-m. EUR 86 (effective 2009). adv. **Document type:** *Magazine, Trade.* **Description:** Contains articles and news on current topics in the international automotive industry.
Formerly (until 2008): AutoTechnology (1616-8216)
Related titles: Online - full text ed.
Indexed: A28, APA, BrCerAb, C&ISA, CA/WCA, CIA, CPEI, CerAb, CivEngAb, CorrAb, E&CAJ, E11, EEA, EMA, EngInd, H15, M&TEA, M09, MBF, METADEX, SCOPUS, SolStAb, T04, WAA.
—Linda Hall. **CCC.**
Published by: Vieweg und Teubner Verlag (Subsidiary of: Springer Fachmedien Wiesbaden GmbH), Abraham-Lincoln-Str 46, Wiesbaden, 65189, Germany. TEL 49-611-78780, FAX 49-611-7878400, info@viewegteubner.de, http://www.viewegteubner.de. Ed. Roland Schedel. Adv. contact Heinrich Prinz Reuss. B&W page EUR 5,228, color page EUR 7,110; trim 175 x 240. Circ: 19,971 (controlled).

621.9816 DEU ISSN 1862-1791
A T Z ELEKTRONIK. (Automobiltechnische Zeitschrift) Text in German. 2006. bi-m. EUR 111; EUR 51 to students; EUR 26 newsstand/cover (effective 2010). adv. **Document type:** *Magazine, Trade.*
—CCC.
Published by: Vieweg und Teubner Verlag (Subsidiary of: Springer Fachmedien Wiesbaden GmbH), Abraham-Lincoln-Str 46, Wiesbaden, 65189, Germany. TEL 49-611-78780, FAX 49-611-7878400, info@viewegteubner.de, http://www.viewegteubner.de. Ed. Johannes Winterhagen. Adv. contact Heinrich Prinz Reuss. Circ: 8,939 (paid and controlled).

621.9816 DEU ISSN 1865-4908
A T Z PRODUKTION. (Automobiltechnische Zeitschrift) Text in German. 2007. bi-m. EUR 98; EUR 41 to students; EUR 26 newsstand/cover (effective 2009). adv. **Document type:** *Magazine, Trade.*
—CCC.
Published by: Vieweg und Teubner Verlag (Subsidiary of: Springer Fachmedien Wiesbaden GmbH), Abraham-Lincoln-Str 46, Wiesbaden, 65189, Germany. TEL 49-611-78780, FAX 49-611-7878400, info@viewegteubner.de, http://www.viewegteubner.de. Ed. Johannes Winterhagen. Adv. contact Sabine Roeck. B&W page EUR 3,400, color page EUR 5,950; trim 175 x 240. Circ: 11,250 (paid).

629.2 DEU ISSN 1436-2821
TL151
A U DATEN P K W UND TRANSPORTER. (Abgasuntersuchung) Text in German. 1955. a. EUR 36 (effective 2004). **Document type:** *Journal, Trade.*
Supersedes in part (in 1997): P K W Tabellen fuer die Werkstattpraxis (1433-4429); Which was formerly (until 1994): Krafthand-Taschenfachbuch fuer Inspektion und Reparatur (1433-4410); (until 1984): Taschenfachbuch fuer Inspektion und Reparatur (0171-4686); (until 197?): Taschenfachbuch der Kraftfahrzeugbetriebe (0171-4678)
Published by: Krafthand Verlag Walter Schulz, Walter-Schulz-Str 1, Bad Woerishofen, 86825, Germany. TEL 49-8247-30070, FAX 49-8247-300770, info@krafthand.de, http://www.krafthand.de. Ed. Walter Schulz.

388.3 910.09 DEU
A V D AUTO BORD UND SPORT BUCH. Text in German. a. EUR 4 newsstand/cover (effective 2008). **Document type:** *Magazine, Consumer.*
Formerly: A v D Auto Bordbuch
Published by: A v D Verlag GmbH, Lyoner Str 16, Frankfurt Am Main, 60528, Germany. TEL 49-69-66060, FAX 49-69-6606789, avd@avd.de.

ACCELERATOR. *see* ANTIQUES

796.7 FRA ISSN 1762-9314
ACTION AUTO MOTO. Text in French. 1994. 11/yr. EUR 34; EUR 2.90 newsstand/cover (effective 2008). adv. bk.rev. charts; illus. **Document type:** *Magazine, Consumer.*
Former titles (until 2003): Auto Moto (1626-8210); (until 2001): Action Auto Moto (1252-1353); Which was formed by the merger of (1934-1994): Action Automobile et Touristique (0001-7418); Which was formerly (until 1945): Action Automobile (0758-3168); (1957-1994): Auto - Moto (0769-8933); Which was formerly (until 1982): Prevention Routiere (0032-8022)
Related titles: Online - full content ed.
Published by: Hachette Filipacchi Medias S.A. (Subsidiary of: Lagardere Media), 149/151 Rue Anatole France, Levallois-Perret, 925340, France. TEL 33-1-413462, FAX 33-1-413469, lgardere@interdeco.fr, http://www.lagardere.com. Circ: 334,984.

ACTION CONTRE LA MARCHE AU RALENTI. *see* ENVIRONMENTAL STUDIES

ACTION ERA VEHICLE. *see* ANTIQUES

ACTION MAGAZINE. *see* HEATING, PLUMBING AND REFRIGERATION

388.3 CAN
ACURA STYLE. Text in English. 1986. s-a. free (effective 2008). adv. **Document type:** *Magazine, Consumer.* **Description:** Contains articles and features on Acura cars, their owners, travel, and lifestyles.
Formerly: Acura Driver
Published by: (American Honda Motor Co. USA, Acura Division USA), Javelin Custom Publishing, 31 Adelaide St, E, PO Box 980, Toronto, ON M5C 2K4, Canada. TEL 416-847-8050, FAX 416-644-0255, info@javelincp.com, http://www.javelincp.com. Ed. Susan Backus Wright. Adv. contacts Bridgitte Baron TEL 212-896-3844, Michael Grier TEL 416-847-8567. color page USD 27,500; trim 9 x 10.875. Circ: 865,000 (free). **Co-publisher:** Sunset Custom Publishing.

ADAJUR; Die juristische Datenbank des ADAC. *see* LAW—Abstracting, Bibliographies, Statistics

629.2 USA
➤ **ADVANCES IN ENGINEERING SERIES.** Text in English. 1962. irreg. **Document type:** *Monographic series, Academic/Scholarly.*
Formerly (until 1979): Advances in Engineering (0065-2555)
Published by: S A E Inc., 400 Commonwealth Dr, Warrendale, PA 15096. TEL 724-776-4841, 877-606-7323, FAX 724-776-0790, CustomerService@sae.org, http://www.sae.org.

388 USA
THE ADVANTAGE (ARLINGTON). Text in English. 1996. q. **Document type:** *Newsletter, Trade.* **Description:** Provides advice for limousine companies.
Published by: Charles Tenney & Associates, 2102 Roosevelt Dr., Ste. G, Pantego, TX 76013-5932. TEL 817-274-0054, FAX 817-274-1888.

AFRICAN AMERICANS ON WHEELS. *see* ETHNIC INTERESTS

388.3 USA ISSN 0892-1121
AFTERMARKET BUSINESS WORLD; the global resource for the automotive automarkets. Text in English. 1936. m. free to qualified personnel (effective 2011). adv. charts; illus.; stat. **Document type:** *Magazine, Trade.* **Description:** Previews of new products, industry news, merchandising trends and company and business activities of automotive aftermarket retailers and wholesalers.
Former titles (until 1986): Home and Auto (0162-8801); (until 19??): Home and Auto Retailer (0018-3911)
Related titles: Microform ed.: (from PQC); Online - full text ed.: ISSN 1938-0593. free (effective 2011).
Indexed: A09, A10, A15, ABIn, B01, B02, B03, B06, B07, B08, B09, B11, B15, B17, B18, BusI, C12, G04, G06, G07, G08, I05, M01, M02, P48, P51, P52, PQC, SRI, T&II, T02, T03, V02, V03, V04.
—CCC.
Published by: Advanstar Communications, Inc., 6200 Canoga Ave, 2nd Fl, Woodland Hills, CA 91367. TEL 818-593-5000, FAX 818-593-5020, info@advanstar.com, http://www.advanstar.com. Pub. Terri McMenamin TEL 610-397-1667.

338.476 CAN ISSN 0828-6116
AFTERMARKET CANADA. Text in English. 1985. m. CAD 40 domestic; USD 50 in United States; USD 75 elsewhere. adv. bk.rev. **Document type:** *Magazine, Trade.* **Description:** Industry news on the automotive aftermarket. Includes information on wholesaling and replacement parts.
Published by: S G B Communications, 2050 Speers Rd, Unit 1, Oakville, ON L6L 2X8, Canada. TEL 416-847-0277, FAX 416-847-7752. Ed. Steve Manning. Adv. contact Shirley Brown. Circ: 11,600.

338.476 USA
AFTERMARKET DISTRIBUTION. Text in English. 10/yr. **Document type:** *Newsletter, Trade.*
Formerly (until 1994): A W D A News
Published by: Automotive Warehouse Distributors Association, 9140 Ward Pkwy, Kansas City, MO 64114. TEL 816-444-3500, FAX 816-444-0330.

388 USA ISSN 1526-4475
HD9710.3.A1
AFTERMARKET INSIDER. Text in English. bi-m. free for members. **Document type:** *Magazine, Trade.* **Description:** Features articles and association news. Designed to help industry professionals to improve their aftermarket business and take advantage of AAIA products and services. Includes industry trends and outlooks.
Published by: Automotive Aftermarket Industry Association, 4600 East - West Hwy Ste 300, Bethesda, MD 20814-3415. TEL 301-654-6664, FAX 301-654-3299. Ed. Elizabeth Preston. Pub. Richard White.

629.2 658.8 NLD ISSN 2210-5034
▼ **AFTERSALES MAGAZINE.** Text in Dutch. 2010. 10/yr. EUR 47.50 (effective 2010). adv. **Document type:** *Magazine, Trade.*
Related titles: Online - full text ed.: ISSN 2210-5042.
Published by: Minervum Multi Media BV, Postbus 5691, Breda, 4801 EB, Netherlands. TEL 31-76-5780630, FAX 31-76-5780635. Eds. Barend Luiting, Jos Veldhuisen. Pub. Rob Kuechler. Adv. contact Wim van Baal. B&W page EUR 2,200; 210 x 280. Circ: 20,000.

629.286 USA
AIR CONDITIONING & HEATING SERVICE & REPAIR - DOMESTIC CARS, LIGHT TRUCKS & VANS. Text in English. 1977. a. USD 77 (effective 1997). illus. **Document type:** *Handbook/Manual/Guide, Trade.* **Description:** Auto service and repair manual for professional auto technicians.
Related titles: CD-ROM ed.; Microform ed.
Published by: Mitchell Repair Information Company, 9889 Willow Creek Rd, Box 26260, San Diego, CA 92196-0260. TEL 619-549-7809, FAX 619-578-4752.

629.2 FIN ISSN 0355-9610
AJA. Text in Finnish. 4/yr. adv.
Address: PL 16, Helsinki, 00381, Finland. Ed. Jukka Miettinen. Circ: 100,000.

338 USA ISSN 1061-8295
ALABAMA AUTOMOTIVE REPORT. Text in English. 1992. m. adv. **Document type:** *Newspaper, Trade.* **Description:** Business newspaper for regional automotive industries, including body shops, independent repair shops, car dealers and others. News coverage is local and national. Monthly features include a local business profile, racing notes, a humor column, industry feedback and much more.
Published by: Autographic Publishing Company, Inc., 1121 Airport Center Dr, Ste 101, Nashville, TN 37214. TEL 800-467-3666, FAX 615-391-3622, garnett@automotivereport.net, http://www.automotivereport.net. adv.: B&W page USD 1,200; trim 11.5 x 15. Circ: 6,200 (free).

388 USA ISSN 0364-930X
TL215.A35
ALFA OWNER. Text in English. 1958. m. USD 60 membership; USD 5.95 newsstand/cover (effective 2004). adv. bk.rev. illus. **Document type:** *Magazine, Consumer.*
Published by: (Alfa Romeo Owners Club), Parabolica Publishing, LLC, 5300 Orange Ave, Ste 211A, Cypress, CA 90630. TEL 714-236-8676, FAX 714-827-2304. Circ: 5,800.

796.77 ITA ISSN 1824-7717
ALFA ROMEO COLLECTION. Text in Italian. 2004. w. **Document type:** *Magazine, Consumer.*
Published by: R C S Libri (Subsidiary of: R C S Mediagroup), Via Mecenate 91, Milan, 20138, Italy. TEL 39-02-5095-2248, FAX 39-02-5095-2975, http://rcslibri.corriere.it/libri/index.htm.

629.24 USA ISSN 1058-9082
ALIGNMENT TECH-TALK. Text in English. 1990. m. USD 89 domestic (effective 2011). adv. **Document type:** *Newsletter, Trade.* **Description:** Contains technical updates and tips for automotive chassis alignment service.
Published by: M D Publications, Inc. (Springfield), 3057 E Cairo St, Springfield, MO 65802. TEL 417-866-3917, 800-274-7890, FAX 417-866-2781, http://www.mdpublications.com.

ALL-TERRAIN VEHICLE. *see* SPORTS AND GAMES—Outdoor Life

388.34 SWE ISSN 1101-7546
ALLA BILAR; uppslagsboken med data och priser paa alla modeller. Variant title: Teknikens Vaerld Alla Bilar. Text in Swedish. 1973. a. SEK 149 (effective 2010). adv. **Document type:** *Magazine, Consumer.*
Published by: Bonnier Tidskrifter AB, Sveavaegen 53, Stockholm, 10544, Sweden. TEL 46-8-7365200, FAX 46-8-7363842, info@bt.bonnier.se, http://www.bonniertidskrifter.se.

796.77 CAN ISSN 0821-7505
ALMANACH DE L'AUTO. Text in English. 1984. a. CAD 11.95. adv.
Published by: Publicor Inc., 7 Chemin Bates, Outremont, PQ H2V 1A6, Canada. TEL 514-270-1100, FAX 514-270-6900. Ed. Claude Bedard. Circ: 24,018.

629.331 NLD ISSN 1872-0803
ALPINE MAGAZINE. Text in Dutch. 1985. 4/yr.
Published by: Club Renault Sportives, c/o Geke Mulder, Sec., Dwergstern 45, Emmen, 7827 TG, Netherlands. TEL 31-61-5343868, FAX 31-591-677238, http://www.clubrenaultsportives.nl. Ed. Elmar Werkman.

796.72 ESP
ALTAGAMA MOTOR. Text in Spanish. m. EUR 3 newsstand/cover (effective 2009). adv. **Document type:** *Magazine, Consumer.*
Published by: Grupo V, C Valportillo Primera, 11, Alcobendas, Madrid, 28108, Spain. TEL 34-91-6622137, FAX 34-91-6622654, secretaria@grupov.es. Ed. Manuel Onieva. Adv. contact Rocio Marin. page EUR 11,350; trim 20 x 27. Circ: 49,093.

388.3 USA ISSN 1528-6746
ALTFUELS ADVISOR. Text in English. 1992. s-m. USD 367 domestic (effective 2007). Index. **Document type:** *Newsletter, Trade.*
Formerly (until 1999): N G V News (1065-3422)
Related titles: Online - full text ed.: USD 395 (effective 2008).
Published by: B C C Research, 40 Washington St, Wellesley, MA 02481. TEL 866-285-7215, FAX 781-489-7308, sales@bccresearch.com, http://www.bccresearch.com. Ed. Richard Hilton. Pub. David Nydam.

796.7 NOR ISSN 0802-7730
AMCAR. Text in Norwegian. 1976. 10/yr. NOK 650 in Europe; NOK 950 elsewhere (effective 2003). adv. 84 p./no. 3 cols./p.; back issues avail. **Document type:** *Magazine, Consumer.* **Description:** Contains articles and features on American cars of today and yesterday.
Related titles: Fax ed.; Online - full text ed.
Published by: Amcar Magazine A-S, PO Box 6006, Trondheim, 7434, Norway. TEL 47-72-89-60-00, 47-72-896000, FAX 47-72-89-60-30, 47-72-896020. Ed., Pub. Terje G Aasen. R&P Terje G Aasen TEL 47-72-89-60-08. Adv. contact Aud Oeyas Aasen TEL 47-92-884560. B&W page NOK 10,000, color page NOK 15,000; trim 190 x 277. Circ: 24,000.

796.77 USA
AMERICAN DRIVER. Text in English. 2006. bi-m. USD 40 (effective 2008). adv. illus. **Document type:** *Magazine, Consumer.* **Description:** Features the finest in luxury and exotic automobiles, motorcycles, boats, luxury living and accessories, dining, destinations and entertainment.
Published by: American Driver Media, Inc., 4546 Sunbelt Dr, Addison, TX 75001. TEL 972-733-9991, FAX 972-733-0153. Pub. Timothy Miller TEL 972-733-9991 ext 101. Adv. contact Frank Kopec TEL 682-553-3912. color page USD 13,750; trim 9.125 x 11.125. Circ: 90,000 (paid and controlled).

388 USA ISSN 0274-8215
AMERICAN TOWMAN. Text in English. 1977. m. USD 40 domestic; USD 55 foreign (effective 2006). adv. **Document type:** *Magazine, Trade.*
Incorporates: Road Service News
Published by: American Towman Network, 7 West St., Warwick, NY 10990-1447. Ed. Steven Calitri. Pub., R&P Charles Duke III. Adv. contact Chuck Messina. B&W page USD 2,810, color page USD 3,840; trim 7 x 10. Circ: 10,600 (paid); 15,900 (controlled).

338.47629 GBR ISSN 1750-7723
HD9710.A42
AMERICAS AUTOMOTIVES INSIGHT. Text in English. 2006. m. USD 1,010 combined subscription (print & online eds.) (effective 2010). adv. **Document type:** *Report, Trade.* **Description:** Provides analysis, forecasts and company profiles on a country-by-country basis, covering the key trends impacting automotive markets across the Americas.
Related titles: Online - full text ed.
Indexed: A15, ABIn, P48, P51, P52, PQC.
Published by: Business Monitor International Ltd., Senator House, 85 Queen Victoria St, London, EC4V 4AB, United Kingdom. TEL 44-20-72480468, FAX 44-20-72480467, subs@businessmonitor.com, http://www.businessmonitor.com. Adv. contact Leila Scott TEL 44-207-2465131.

629 388 USA ISSN 1534-9241
HD9999.C273
AMERICA'S CAR CARE BUSINESS. Text in English. m. **Document type:** *Magazine, Trade.*
Published by: Workhorse Publications, P O Box 25310, Scottsdale, AZ 85255. TEL 480-585-0455.

AMICALE X J. LE BULLETIN. *see* ANTIQUES

629.288 USA ISSN 2159-3914
TL7.A1
AMOS AUTO ENTHUSIAST. Text in English. 1957. m. USD 19.99 (effective 2011). adv. bk.rev. illus. index. back issues avail.; reprints avail. **Document type:** *Magazine, Consumer.* **Description:** For car collectors and hobbyists. Each issue contains how-to articles, in-depth marque history, pre- and post-war antique car features, hands-on restoration projects, collector car shows, auction results, salvage yard coverage, new parts reviews and evaluations, events listings, and more.
Formerly (until 2010): Cars & Parts (0008-6975)
Related titles: Online - full text ed.
Indexed: G06, G07, G08, I05, I07.
—Ingenta.
Published by: Amos Publishing, Automotive (Subsidiary of: Amos Publishing), 911 Vandemark Rd, PO Box 926, Sidney, OH 45365. TEL 800-448-3611, cuserv@amospress.com, http://www.amospress.com. Pub., Adv. contact John Nichols TEL 863-937-8097.

ANDREWS LITIGATION REPORTER: AUTOMOTIVE. *see* LAW

ANNALS OF ADVANCES IN AUTOMOTIVE MEDICINE. *see* MEDICAL SCIENCES

796.77 AUS
ANTIQUE & CLASSIC. Text in English. 1960. m. (11/yr.). free to members (effective 2009). back issues avail. **Document type:** *Magazine, Consumer.* **Description:** Covers the restoration, preservation and use of classic cars built before 1942.
Published by: Antique & Classic Motor Club Inc., PO Box 143, Burwood, NSW 2134, Australia. TEL 62-418-643505, FAX 62-2-96861913. Ed. Steve Bryant. Circ: 100 (controlled).

ANTIQUE AUTOMOBILE. *see* ANTIQUES

338.342 BRA
ANUARIO AUTOMOTOR. Text in Portuguese. 1992. a. BRL 18, USD 13. **Document type:** *Consumer.*
Published by: Casa Editorial Ltda., Rua Sampaio Vidal, 652, Jd Paulistano, Sao Paulo, SP 01443-000, Brazil. TEL 55-11-30613688, FAX 55-11-852-9430. adv.: page USD 16,000. Circ: 30,000.

388.3 ESP ISSN 1130-5983
ANUARIO ESPANOL DE LA AUTOMOCION. Text in Spanish. 1991. a. **Document type:** *Yearbook, Trade.*
Related titles: ◆ Print ed.: Automovilismo en Espana. ISSN 0005-1632.
Published by: Editorial Borrmart S.A., C. Don Ramon de la Cruz, 68 6o, Madrid, 28001, Spain. TEL 34-91-4029607, http://www.borrmart.es/.

388.3 BRA ISSN 1517-1663
ANUARIO ESTADISTICO DA INDUSTRIA AUTOMOBILISTICA BRASILEIRA. Text in Portuguese. 1999. a. **Document type:** *Yearbook, Academic/Scholarly.*
Published by: Associacao Nacional dos Fabricantes de Veiculos Automotores, Ave Indianapolis, 496, Sao Paulo, 04062-900, Brazil. TEL 55-11-50514044, FAX 55-11-50514044 ext. 225.

388.342 982 GBR ISSN 1748-975X
ARGENTINA AUTOS REPORT. Text in English. 2005. q. EUR 820, USD 1,030 combined subscription (print & email eds.) (effective 2010). **Document type:** *Report, Trade.* **Description:** Provides industry professionals and strategists, corporate analysts, auto associations, government departments and regulatory bodies with independent forecasts and competitive intelligence on the Argentinian automotives market.
Related titles: E-mail ed.
Indexed: A15, ABIn, B02, B15, B17, B18, G04, I05, P48, P51, P52, PQC.
Published by: Business Monitor International Ltd., Senator House, 85 Queen Victoria St, London, EC4V 4AB, United Kingdom. TEL 44-20-72480468, FAX 44-20-72480467, subs@businessmonitor.com.

388.3 FRA ISSN 0751-5545
TL2
L'ARGUS DE L'AUTOMOBILE ET DES LOCOMOTIONS. Text in French. 1927. w. adv. **Document type:** *Directory, Consumer.* **Description:** Reports on the results of car, van, and motorcycle tests, as well as new and used car prices and automotive data of the European and French markets.
Related titles: Supplement(s): Les Statistique de l'Automobile.
Published by: Societe Nouvelle d'Etudes d'Editions et de Publicite, 52, Rue de la Victoire, Paris, 75009, France. TEL 33-1-53291100, FAX 33-1-49270949. Ed., Pub. Jacques Loste. Adv. contact Jean Pierre Dagory. Circ: 110,000 (paid).

ARIZONA A A A HIGHROADS. *see* TRAVEL AND TOURISM

796.77 USA
ARNOLT-BRISTOL REGISTRY. Text in English. 1985. s-a. USD 10. adv. back issues avail. **Document type:** *Directory.*
Address: PO Box 60, Brooklandville, MD 21022. Ed. Lee Raskin. Circ: 275.

388 USA
ARROW (ROCHESTER). Text in English. 1957. q. USD 25 to members (effective 2000). illus.
Media: Duplicated (not offset).
Published by: Pierce-Arrow Society, Inc., 135 Edgerton St, Rochester, NY 14607. Ed., Pub., R&P Bernard J Weis. Circ: 1,100.

388.3 NLD ISSN 0004-3966
ARTS EN AUTO. Text in Dutch. 1934. m. bk.rev. illus. index. **Document type:** *Trade.*
Related titles: Online - full text ed.: ISSN 1876-4614.
Published by: Vereniging van Artsen, Postbus 8153, Utrecht, 3503 RD, Netherlands. TEL 31-30-2474341, FAX 31-30-2474561. Ed. Flip Vuijsje. Circ: 96,144 (controlled).

ARZT UND AUTO; der kraftfahrende Arzt. *see* MEDICAL SCIENCES

ASIAN AUTO ABSTRACTS. *see* TRANSPORTATION—Abstracting, Bibliographies, Statistics

ASIANS ON WHEELS. *see* ETHNIC INTERESTS

629.286 SAU
ASSAYARAT. Text in Arabic. m. adv.
Published by: Saudi Research & Publishing Co., P O Box 478, Riyadh, 11411, Saudi Arabia. TEL 966-1-4419933, FAX 966-1-4429555, editorial@majalla.com, http://www.srpc.com/main. Ed. Adel Issam Al-Deen.

629.2 GBR ISSN 2042-7743
THE ASSESSOR; your voice. Text in English. 2001. bi-m. free to members (effective 2010). adv.
Incorporates (1967-2001): Institute of Automotive Engineer Assessors. Journal (0309-1430); Which was formerly (until 1967): Institute of Automobile Assessors. Journal
Published by: Institute of Automotive Engineer Assessors, Brooke House, 24 Dam St, Lichfield, Staffs WS13 6AA, United Kingdom. TEL 44-1543-266906, FAX 44-1543-257848, secretary@iaea-online.co.uk. Ed. Rachel Deeson TEL 44-1795-535468. Adv. contact Paul Holness TEL 44-1795-542411.

ASSOCIATIONS SECTORIELLES PARITAIRES, LESIONS PROFESSIONNELLES, STATISTIQUES. TOME 8. ASSOCIATION PARITAIRE POUR LA SANTE ET LA SECURITE DU TRAVAIL DU SECTEUR DES SERVICES AUTOMOBILES. *see* OCCUPATIONAL HEALTH AND SAFETY—Abstracting, Bibliographies, Statistics

796.77 GBR ISSN 2045-3787
ASTON MARTIN. Text in English. 19??. q. **Document type:** *Magazine, Trade.*
Formerly (until 2007): Works Torque
Published by: Affinity Publishing, 21 Grosvenor St, London, W1K 4QJ, United Kingdom. TEL 44-20-73999580, FAX 44-20-73999589, info@affinitypublishing.co.uk, http://www.affinitypublishing.co.uk.

AUDI DISSERTATIONSREIHE. *see* ENGINEERING—Industrial Engineering

796.7 GBR ISSN 1369-4340
AUDI DRIVER. Text in English. 1997. m. GBP 38 domestic; GBP 44.99 in Europe; GBP 54.99 elsewhere; GBP 3 per issue (effective 2009). back issues avail. **Document type:** *Magazine, Consumer.* **Description:** Information on products and services for Audi enthusiasts.
Published by: (Autometrix Publications), T - A Autometrix Publications, Campion House, 1 Greenfield Rd, Westoning, Beds MK45 5JD, United Kingdom. TEL 44-1525-750500, FAX 44-1525-750700, mail@autometrix.co.uk. Ed. Paul Harris. **Dist. by:** Seymour Distribution Ltd, 86 Newman St, London W1T 3EX, United Kingdom.

796.77 DEU
AUDI MAGAZIN. Text in German. 1995. q. adv. **Document type:** *Magazine, Consumer.* **Description:** Contains lifestyle and product articles and features of interest to Audi owners.
Published by: (Audi AG), corps - Corporate Publishing Services GmbH, Kasernenstr 69, Duesseldorf, 40213, Germany. TEL 49-211-54227700, FAX 49-211-54227722, info@corps-verlag.de. Ed. Mirko Hackmann. adv.: B&W page EUR 10,500, color page EUR 13,200. Circ: 430,000 (controlled).

796.77 CZE ISSN 1211-9857
AUDI MAGAZIN. Text in Czech. 1996. q. CZK 290; CZK 72.50 newsstand/cover (effective 2008). adv. **Document type:** *Magazine, Consumer.*
Published by: Import Volkswagen Group, Radlicka 740/113d, Prague 5, 15800, Czech Republic. TEL 420-8-00110101.

656.1 NLD ISSN 1871-7918
AUDI MAGAZINE. Text in Dutch. 1986. q. free to customers (effective 2010).
Formerly (until 2005): Profile (1382-9025)
Published by: Pon's Automobielhandel BV, Postbus 72, Amersfoort, 3800 HD, Netherlands. TEL 31-33-4949944, FAX 31-33-4950304, autoinbedrijf@pah.nl, http://www.pon.nl. Circ: 140,000 (free).

796.77 DEU ISSN 1610-9899
AUDI SCENE LIVE. Text in German. 2000. bi-m. EUR 21 domestic; EUR 24 foreign; EUR 3.80 newsstand/cover (effective 2011). adv. **Document type:** *Magazine, Consumer.* **Description:** Provides specialist articles and information for Audi enthusiasts.
Published by: Vestische Mediengruppe Welke GmbH & Co. KG, Hertener Mark 7, Herten, 45699, Germany. TEL 49-2366-808400, FAX 49-2366-808499, info@vmw-verlag.de, http://vmw-verlag.de. Ed. Rudolf Welke. Pub. Arno Welke. Adv. contact Julia Wissing.

629.222 AUS
AUSSIE BRUTES. Text in English. bi-m. AUD 40.28 domestic (effective 2008). **Document type:** *Magazine, Consumer.* **Description:** Provides information on feature Utes.
Published by: Express Publications Pty. Ltd., 2-4 Stanley St, Locked Bag 111, Silverwater, NSW 2168, Australia. TEL 61-2-97480599, 61-2-97413800, subs@magstore.com.au, http://www.expresspublications.com.au. Ed. Andrew Broadley TEL 61-2-97413919. Adv. contact Michael Coiro TEL 61-2-97413911.

786.77 629.222 USA ISSN 1547-8807
AUSTIN - HEALEY MAGAZINE. Text in English. 1970. 10/yr. USD 35 (effective 1996). adv. bk.rev. charts; illus.; tr.lit. cum.index: 1970-1996. back issues avail. **Document type:** *Magazine, Consumer.* **Description:** Contains travel, technical information, and club news relating to Austin-Healey or Jenson-Healey sports cars.
Published by: Austin - Healey Club, Pacific Centre, PO Box 6197, San Jose, CA 95150. TEL 408-541-9608, FAX 408-541-9320. Ed., Adv. contact John Trifari. page USD 100; trim 10 x 7.25. Circ: 2,000 (paid). **Subscr. to:** 3807 Corina Way, Palo Alto, CA 94303.

388.342 994 GBR ISSN 1748-9768
AUSTRALIA AUTOS REPORTS. Variant title: Auto Reports for Australia. Text in English. 2005. q. EUR 820, USD 1,030 combined subscription (print & email eds.) (effective 2010). **Document type:** *Report, Trade.* **Description:** Provides industry professionals and strategists, corporate analysts, auto associations, government departments and regulatory bodies with independent forecasts and competitive intelligence on the Australian automotives market.

Related titles: E-mail ed.
Indexed: A15, ABIn, B01, B02, B15, B17, B18, G04, I05, P48, P51, P52, PQC.
Published by: Business Monitor International Ltd., Senator House, 85 Queen Victoria St, London, EC4V 4AB, United Kingdom. TEL 44-20-72480468, FAX 44-20-72480467, subs@businessmonitor.com.

AUSTRALIA. BUREAU OF STATISTICS. MOTOR VEHICLE CENSUS, AUSTRALIA (ONLINE). *see* TRANSPORTATION—Abstracting, Bibliographies, Statistics

AUSTRALIA. BUREAU OF STATISTICS. SURVEY OF MOTOR VEHICLE USE, AUSTRALIA TWELVE MONTHS ENDED (ONLINE). *see* TRANSPORTATION—Abstracting, Bibliographies, Statistics

AUSTRALIAN 4 W D ACTION. (Wheel Drive) *see* SPORTS AND GAMES

388.3 AUS ISSN 1836-1137
AUSTRALIAN 4 W D & S U V BUYERS GUIDE. Text in English. 2003. s-a. adv. **Document type:** *Magazine, Consumer.* **Description:** Provides tips, news and advice on the latest models of 4WD to towing and touring.
Former titles (until 2008): Australian 4 W D Buyers Guide (1832-7575); (until 2006): New & Used 4 W D Buyers Guide (1320-9914); Which was formed by the merger of (1994-2003): Used 4 W D Buyers Guide (1326-7434); (2002-2003): New Car & 4 W D Buyer (1446-733X); Which was formed by the merger of (2001-2002): New 4 W D Buyer (1446-5191); (1997-2002): New Car Buyer Australia (1326-0715); Which was formerly (1990-1997): New Car Buyers Guide (1035-1825)
Published by: Universal Magazines Pty. Ltd., Unit 5, 6-8 Byfield St, Private Bag 154, North Ryde, NSW 2113, Australia. TEL 61-2-98870300, FAX 61-2-98050714, info@universalmagazines.com.au. Ed. Bill McKinnon. Adv. contact Brian Sullivan TEL 61-3-95838377.

796.77 AUS ISSN 1329-4660
AUSTRALIAN CLASSIC CAR. Text in English. 1993. m. AUD 82 to non-members; AUD 74 to members; AUD 215 in US & Canada; AUD 165 in Asia & the Pacific (effective 2008). back issues avail. **Document type:** *Magazine, Consumer.* **Description:** Provides information on latest classic cars for sale. Also offers classified ads, auction results and classic car events for classic car enthusiasts.
Formerly (until 1996): Australian Classic Car Monthly (1321-7127)
Related titles: Online - full text ed.; Supplement(s): Australian Classic Car Yearbook & Desk Diary.
Published by: Australian Classic Motoring Press, Level 1, 9 George St, North Strathfield, NSW 2137, Australia. TEL 61-2-87416678, FAX 61-2-87416697.

388.3 AUS
AUSTRALIAN CONVENIENCE STORE NEWS. Text in English. 1993. bi-m. AUD 59 domestic; AUD 120 foreign (effective 2008). adv. 64 p./no.; back issues avail. **Document type:** *Magazine, Trade.* **Description:** Aims to help convenience retailers to improve their commercial performance in all areas of business.
Formerly (until 2001): Australian Service Station & Convenience Store News
Related titles: Online - full text ed.: free (effective 2008); Supplement(s): ACNielson Convenience Report.
Published by: Berg Bennett Pty. Ltd., Ste 6, The Atrium, 340 Darling St, Balmain, NSW 2041, Australia. TEL 61-2-95551355, FAX 61-2-95551434, exhibition@c-store.com.au. Ed. Keith Berg. Adv. contact Andrew Murphy TEL 61-2-91551325. color page AUD 5,682; 240 x 340. Circ: 20,431.

AUSTRALIAN INCAR ENTERTAINMENT. *see* SOUND RECORDING AND REPRODUCTION

796.77 AUS
THE AUSTRALIAN JAGUAR DRIVER. Text in English. 1963. m. free to members (effective 2009). adv. **Document type:** *Magazine, Trade.*
Related titles: Online - full text ed.
Published by: Jaguar Drivers Club of Australia, PO Box 1485, Macquarie Park, NSW 2113, Australia. magazine@jaguar.org.au, http://www.jaguar.org.au/.

678.32 AUS ISSN 1447-3127
AUSTRALIAN TYRE DEALER. Text in English. 1992. bi-m. AUD 36 domestic to non-members; AUD 65 foreign to non-members; AUD 6 per issue domestic; AUD 11 per issue foreign; free to members (effective 2009). adv. **Document type:** *Magazine, Trade.* **Description:** Provides the latest news, views and opinions of the industry, technical reports on products, the latest information on new products, and advice on industry activities.
Published by: (Australian Tyre Dealers and Retreaders Association), M T A - Q Publications, PO Box 3359, South Brisbane, QLD 4101, Australia. TEL 61-3-32378777, 800-177-951, FAX 61-3-38444488, info@mtaq.com.au. Adv. contact Jeff Dunlop TEL 61-7-32378740. page AUD 1,473; 185 x 276. Circ: 1,500.

388 AUT
AUSTRO CLASSIC; oesterreichische Magazin fuer Technik-Geschichte. Text in German. 1991. bi-m. EUR 32 domestic; EUR 40 foreign (effective 2005). adv. bk.rev. **Document type:** *Magazine, Consumer.*
Published by: Verein fuer Motorgeschichte, Lenaugasse 10, Kierling, N 3412, Austria. TEL 43-2243-87476, FAX 43-2243-87837. Ed., Pub. Wolfgang Buchta. R&P Ulrike Buchta. Adv. contact Peter Kronberger. Circ: 9,000.

629.222 796.7 SRB ISSN 0353-6866
AUTO; prvi srpski magazin za automobilizam i auto moto sport. Text in Serbo-Croatian. 1990. m.
Published by: Auto Press, Vojvode Misica 17, Belgrade. Ed. Dejan Danilovic.

629.286 CHE
AUTO. Variant title: A C S Auto. Text in German. 1901. 10/yr. CHF 40; CHF 60 foreign. adv. **Document type:** *Consumer.*
Published by: (Swiss Automobile Club), Vogt-Schild AG, Zuchwilerstr 21, Solothurn, 4501, Switzerland. TEL 41-32-6247474, FAX 065-247235. Ed. Erwin Thomann. Adv. contact Veronika Wegmueller. B&W page CHF 4,700, color page CHF 6,800; trim 260 x 185. Circ: 71,146.

629.286 ITA ISSN 1122-1674
AUTO; mensile di automobilismo e tecnica automobilistica. Text in Italian. 1985. m. adv. bk.rev. **Document type:** *Magazine, Consumer.*
Published by: Conti Editore SpA, Via del Lavoro 7, San Lazzaro di Savena, BO 40068, Italy. http://www.contieditore.it. Circ: 162,580.

796.7 HRV ISSN 1331-6672
AUTO. Text in Croatian. 1998. bi-m. **Document type:** *Magazine, Consumer.*
Published by: S I G, Ilica 205a, Zagreb, 10000, Croatia. TEL 385-1-3775356, FAX 385-1-3775356. Ed. Domagoj Kodzic.

796.77 USA
AUTO A FONDO; la guia para el fanatico del automovil. Text in Spanish; Text occasionally in English. 2005. q. USD 12.95; USD 1.95 newsstand/cover (effective 2007). adv. **Document type:** *Magazine, Consumer.*
Address: PO Box 5486, Fullerton, CA 92838. TEL 714-680-3828, FAX 714-441-1747. Ed. Ricardo Rodriguez-Long TEL 562-761-1999. adv.: color page USD 6,880; trim 8 x 10.5. Circ: 45,588 (paid).

629.2 GRC ISSN 1108-7838
AUTO ACCESSORIES. Text in Greek. 1991. a. EUR 8.80 newsstand/cover (effective 2006). adv. **Document type:** *Magazine, Consumer.*
Published by: Motorpress Hellas (Subsidiary of: Gruner + Jahr AG & Co), 132 Lefkis Str, Krioneri, 14568, Greece. TEL 30-210-6262000, FAX 30-210-6262401, info@motorpress.gr, http://www.motorpress.gr. Circ: 35,000 (paid and controlled).

388.3 USA ISSN 1553-8397
TL7.A1
AUTO AFICIONADO. Text in English. 2005. bi-m. USD 39.95; USD 9 newsstand/cover (effective 2007). adv. **Document type:** *Magazine, Consumer.* **Description:** Covers rare, exotic and fine cars.
Address: 848 Kari Dr., Ste. #4, Eau Claire, WI 54701. TEL 888-800-0505. Ed. Larry Crane TEL 805-241-5752. Pub. James Lopez TEL 352-359-2823. Adv. contact Fred Marik TEL 702-792-9309. B&W page USD 2,370, color page USD 3,385; trim 9 x 11.

388 SVK ISSN 1336-0876
AUTO AKTUAL. Text in Slovak. 1997. fortn. adv. **Document type:** *Magazine, Consumer.*
Published by: Motor-Presse Slovakia, s.r.o., Prievozska 18, Bratislava, 82451, Slovakia. TEL 421-2-53418351, FAX 421-2-53418351. Ed. Peter Nevicky. Pub. Jan Korecky. Adv. contact Slavka Plstekova. Circ: 25,000 (paid).

338 629.2 DEU ISSN 0179-4078
AUTO AKTUELL. Text in German. m. **Document type:** *Trade.*
Published by: Verband der Automobilindustrie e.V., Westendstr 61, Frankfurt Am Main, 60325, Germany. TEL 49-69-97507-0, FAX 49-69-97507261.

796.77 AUT
AUTO AKTUELL; Das Magazin fuer Auto-Tuning - 4x4. Text in German. bi-m. EUR 18.50 for 2 yrs. (effective 2005). adv. **Document type:** *Magazine, Consumer.*
Related titles: Online - full text ed.
Published by: C B Verlags GmbH, Kleingoepfink 44, Pfaffenschlag, N 3834, Austria. TEL 43-1-5974985, FAX 43-1-597498515, office@cbverlag.at, http://www.cbverlag.at. adv.: B&W page EUR 3,450, color page EUR 5,040; trim 210 x 297. Circ: 37,600 (paid and controlled).

AUTO AND FLAT GLASS JOURNAL; serving the interests of the auto glass replacement business. *see* CERAMICS, GLASS AND POTTERY

388 USA
AUTO & R V. Text in English. w. (Mon.). USD 40 (effective 2006). **Document type:** *Newspaper, Consumer.*
Published by: The Papers, Inc., 206 S. Main St, Milford, IN 46542. TEL 574-658-4111, FAX 574-658-4701. Pub. Della Baumgartner. Circ: 467,300 (free).

796.77 ITA ISSN 1827-9244
AUTO ANNUARIO. Text in Italian. 2006. a. **Document type:** *Catalog, Consumer.*
Published by: Conti Editore SpA, Via del Lavoro 7, San Lazzaro di Savena, BO 40068, Italy. http://www.contieditore.it.

796.7 HRV ISSN 1331-4173
AUTO AUTO. Text in Croatian. 1997. m. **Document type:** *Magazine, Consumer.*
Supersedes in part (1997-1997): Auto Moto Puls (1331-243X); Which was formed by the merger of (1993-1997): Auto Auto (1330-433X); (1996-1997): Moto Puls (1330-9943)
Published by: Auto Auto d.o.o., Preradoviceva 21, Zagreb, 10000, Croatia. TEL 385-1-4822073, FAX 385-1-4821386, auto-auto@zg.tel.hr. Ed. Goran Dijakovic.

388 ESP
AUTO BILD. Text in Spanish. 2005. m. EUR 54.60 (effective 2009). adv. back issues avail. **Document type:** *Magazine, Consumer.*
Published by: Grupo Axel Springer, C Santiago de Compostela, 84-2a Planta, Madrid, 28035, Spain. TEL 34-91-5140600, FAX 34-902-118633, http://www.axelspringer.es. Ed. Tito Klein. Adv. contact Teresa Angulo. page EUR 9,760; 23 x 29.7. Circ: 132,000.

388 DEU ISSN 0930-7095
AUTO BILD. Text in German. 1986. w. (Fri.). EUR 1.50 newsstand/cover (effective 2010). adv. **Document type:** *Magazine, Consumer.*
—CIS. **CCC.**
Published by: A S Autoverlag GmbH (Subsidiary of: Axel Springer Verlag AG), Axel-Springer-Platz 1, Hamburg, 20350, Germany. TEL 49-40-34725934, FAX 49-40-34727073, dk@autoverlag.de, http://www.autojournal.de. Ed. Bernd Wieland. Adv. contact Peter Hoffmann. color page EUR 38,050; trim 212 x 304. Circ: 592,245 (paid and controlled).

796.77 SRB ISSN 1452-3361
AUTO BILD. Text in Serbian. 2006. fortn. CSD 79 per issue (effective 2007). **Document type:** *Magazine, Consumer.*
Published by: Politika, Novine i Magazini/Politika Newspapers and Magazines, Makedonska 29, Belgrade, 11000. TEL 381-11-3301442, FAX 381-11-3373346, ilustrovana@politika.co.yu, http://www.politika.co.yu. **Dist. by:** Global Press, Francuska 56, Belgrade 11060. TEL 381-11-2769301, FAX 381-11-2764538, http://www.globalpress.co.yu.

388 ESP
AUTO BILD 4X4. Text in Spanish. 2007. m. EUR 25 (effective 2009). adv. back issues avail. **Document type:** *Magazine, Consumer.*
Published by: Grupo Axel Springer, C Santiago de Compostela, 84-2a Planta, Madrid, 28035, Spain. TEL 34-91-5140600, FAX 34-902-118633, http://www.axelspringer.es. Ed. Hector Del Prado. Adv. contact Teresa Angulo. page EUR 6,000; 21 x 28. Circ: 6,000.

388 DEU ISSN 1864-3264
AUTO BILD - ALLRAD. Text in German. 199?. m. EUR 3.50 newsstand/cover (effective 2011). adv. **Document type:** *Magazine, Consumer.*
Former titles (until 2007): Auto Bild Alles Allrad (1619-2125); (until 2002): Gelaendewagen Magazin (1437-9635)
Published by: A S Autoverlag GmbH (Subsidiary of: Axel Springer Verlag AG), Axel-Springer-Platz 1, Hamburg, 20350, Germany. TEL 49-40-34725934, FAX 49-40-34727073, dk@autoverlag.de, http://www.autojournal.de. Ed. Bernhard Weinbacher. Circ: 66,234 (paid).

388.3 DEU ISSN 2190-1619
AUTO-BILD CABRIO EXTRA. Text in German. 1999. a. EUR 3.90 newsstand/cover (effective 2011). adv. **Document type:** *Magazine, Consumer.*
Formerly (until 2010): Auto-Test Cabrio (1615-5173)
Published by: A S Autoverlag GmbH (Subsidiary of: Axel Springer Verlag AG), Axel-Springer-Platz 1, Hamburg, 20350, Germany. TEL 49-40-34725934, FAX 49-40-34727073, dk@autoverlag.de, http://www.autojournal.de. Circ: 109,000 (controlled).

388 ESP
AUTO BILD CLASSIC. Text in Spanish. 2008. m. adv. **Document type:** *Magazine, Consumer.*
Published by: Grupo Axel Springer, C Santiago de Compostela, 84-2a Planta, Madrid, 28035, Spain. TEL 34-91-5140600, FAX 34-902-118633, http://www.axelspringer.es. Ed. Tito Klein. Adv. contact Teresa Angulo. page EUR 4,900; 21 x 28.

629 GRC ISSN 1791-2822
AUTO BILD HELLAS. Text in Greek. 2007. w. EUR 1.50 newsstand/cover (effective 2011). adv. **Document type:** *Magazine, Consumer.*
Published by: Technical Press SA, 80 Ioannou Metaxa, Karelas, Koropi, 19400, Greece. TEL 30-210-9792500, FAX 30-210-9792528, info@technicalpress.gr, http://www.technicalpress.gr.

629.22205 DEU ISSN 2190-0744
AUTO BILD KLASSIK. Text in German. 2007. bi-m. EUR 3.90 newsstand/cover (effective 2011). adv. **Document type:** *Magazine, Consumer.*
Published by: A S Autoverlag GmbH (Subsidiary of: Axel Springer Verlag AG), Axel-Springer-Platz 1, Hamburg, 20350, Germany. TEL 49-40-34725934, FAX 49-40-34727073, dk@autoverlag.de, http://www.autojournal.de. Ed. Bernd Wieland. Circ: 108,892 (paid).

796.77 LVA
AUTO BILD LATVIJA. Text in Latvian. 2004 (May). m. LVL 1.29 newsstand/cover (effective 2004). adv. **Document type:** *Magazine, Consumer.*
Published by: Zurnals Santa, Balasta Dambis 3, PO Box 32, Riga, LV-1081, Latvia. TEL 371-762-8275, FAX 371-746-5450, santa@santa.lv. Ed. Martins Dzenitis.

796.77 HUN ISSN 1786-1071
AUTO BILD MAGYARORSZAG. Text in Hungarian. 2004. m. HUF 4,140 (effective 2010). adv. **Document type:** *Magazine, Consumer.*
Published by: Axel Springer - Budapest Kft., Varosmajor u 11, Budapest, 1122, Hungary. TEL 36-1-4885766, FAX 36-1-4885607, info@axelspringer.hu, http://www.axelspringer.hu. Ed. Robert Szabo.

629 DEU ISSN 1435-5213
AUTO BILD SPEZIAL. Text in German. 1990. irreg. adv. **Document type:** *Magazine, Consumer.*
Published by: A S Autoverlag GmbH (Subsidiary of: Axel Springer Verlag AG), Axel-Springer-Platz 1, Hamburg, 20350, Germany. TEL 49-40-34725934, FAX 49-40-34727073, dk@autoverlag.de, http://www.autojournal.de.

388 DEU ISSN 1861-5295
AUTO BILD SPORTSCARS. Text in German. 2001. m. EUR 3.30 newsstand/cover (effective 2011). adv. **Document type:** *Magazine, Consumer.*
Formerly (until 2005): Auto Bild Test & Tuning (1619-2133)
Published by: A S Autoverlag GmbH (Subsidiary of: Axel Springer Verlag AG), Axel-Springer-Platz 1, Hamburg, 20350, Germany. TEL 49-40-34725934, FAX 49-40-34727073, dk@autoverlag.de, http://www.autojournal.de. Ed. Olaf Schilling. Circ: 58,581 (paid).

388 ESP
AUTO BILD SPORTSCARS. Text in Spanish. 2008. m. adv. **Document type:** *Magazine, Consumer.*
Published by: Grupo Axel Springer, C Santiago de Compostela, 84-2a Planta, Madrid, 28035, Spain. TEL 34-91-5140600, FAX 34-902-118633, http://www.axelspringer.es. Ed. Tito Klein. Adv. contact Teresa Angulo. page EUR 5,000; 21 x 28.

796.77 FIN ISSN 1459-949X
AUTO BILD SUOMI. Text in Finnish. 2004 (Mar.). bi-w. EUR 73 (effective 2009). adv. **Document type:** *Magazine, Consumer.* **Description:** Presents the latest car models and test drive results.
Published by: Sanoma Magazines Finland Corporation, Lapinmaentie 1, Helsinki, 00350, Finland. TEL 358-9-1201, FAX 358-9-1205171, info@sanomamagazines.fi, http://www.sanomamagazines.fi. Ed. Jarmo Markkanen.

629.11 UKR
AUTO BILD UKRAINE. Text in Ukrainian. 2003 (Sep.). fortn. UAK 4 newsstand/cover (effective 2003). adv. **Document type:** *Magazine, Consumer.*
Published by: Autocentre Ltd., PO Box 2, Kiev, 03047, Ukraine. TEL 380-44-4596001, FAX 380-44-4584404, info@autocentr.kiev.ua, http://www.autocentre.ua. Ed. Oleg Vasylevskyy.

796.77 HRV ISSN 1330-8238
AUTO BLIC. Text in Croatian. 1995. m. adv. **Document type:** *Magazine, Consumer.*
Published by: Revije d.d., Slavonska avenija 4, Zagreb, 10000, Croatia. TEL 385-1-6161035, FAX 385-1-6161028, revije@revije.hr, http://www.revije.hr. Ed. Uros Soskic. Circ: 43,000 (paid).

338.476 GBR ISSN 0965-9374
AUTO BRIEFING. Text in English. 1990. s-a. back issues avail. **Document type:** *Magazine, Trade.*
Related titles: Online - full text ed.: ISSN 2046-4126.
Published by: Knibb, Gormezano and Partners, The Old Vicarage, Marketplace, Castle Donington, Derby DE74 2JB, United Kingdom. TEL 44-1332-856301, FAX 44-1332-856301, consult@kgpauto.com, http://www.kgpauto.com.

388.342 TUR
AUTO CAR. Text in Turkish. w. adv. **Document type:** *Magazine, Consumer.*

Published by: Merkez Dergi/Merkez Magazine Group, Medya Plaza, Basin Ekspres Yolu, Gunesli - Istanbul, 34540, Turkey. TEL 90-212-502-8840, FAX 90-212-502-8068.

388 659.13 POL ISSN 1233-8346
AUTO - CENTRUM. Text in Polish. 1994. m. free. **Document type:** *Newspaper.*
Published by: Auto - Centrum Przedsiebiorstwo Motoryzacyjne S.A., Ul Wojciechowskiego 7-17, Poznan, 60685, Poland. TEL 48-61-226851, FAX 48-61-226081. Ed. Raul Czywczynski. Pub. Bogdan Kozak.

629 ESP ISSN 1135-6774
AUTO-CLUB. Text in Spanish. 1964. bi-m. membership. adv. bk.rev. **Document type:** *Consumer.*
Published by: Real Automovil Club de Espana, Jose Abascal, 10, Madrid, 28003, Spain. TEL 34-902-404545, racetel@race.es, http://www.race.es/. Ed. Fernando Falco. Circ: 215,000.

629.2 ZAF ISSN 0378-522X
AUTO DATA DIGEST. Text in English. 1974. a. ZAR 165.30. **Document type:** *Journal, Trade.* **Description:** Provides concise, practical specification and tune up data for all cars marketed in South Africa.
Published by: Mead & McGrouther (Pty) Ltd., PO Box 1240, Randburg, Gauteng 2125, South Africa. TEL 27-11-789-3213, FAX 27-11-789-5218. Ed. W Calcutt. adv.: B&W page ZAR 3,400, color page ZAR 5,125. Circ: 7,500.

658.8 629.2 USA ISSN 1941-384X
AUTO DEALER MONTHLY. Text in English. 200?. m. USD 60 (effective 2008). **Document type:** *Magazine, Trade.* **Description:** Presents expert industry advice and and profiles of leading automobile dealerships with the aim of improving business and sales at automobile dealerships and repair facilities.
Related titles: Online - full text ed.: ISSN 1938-2529.
Published by: Auto Dealer Monthly LLC, PO Box 39, Osprey, FL 34229. TEL 888-300-8844, http://autodealermonthly.com. Ed. Harlene Doane.

388.3 USA
AUTO DEALER PAY PLANS FOR SERVICE DEPARTMENTS. Text in English. biennial. **Document type:** *Guide, Trade.*
Published by: W D & S Publishing, 10 W 7th St, 1st Fl, PO Box 606, Barnegat Light, NJ 08006. TEL 800-321-5312, http://www.dealersedge.com.

388.3 ZAF
AUTO DEALERS' GUIDE. Text in English. 1960. m. ZAR 492.48. **Document type:** *Handbook/Manual/Guide, Trade.* **Description:** Provides trade and retail values of used passenger cars traded throughout South Africa.
Formerly (until 1984): Auto Dealers' Digest (0005-0733)
Published by: Mead & McGrouther (Pty) Ltd., PO Box 1240, Randburg, Gauteng 2125, South Africa. TEL 27-11-789-3213, FAX 27-11-789-5218. adv.: B&W page ZAR 1,675, color page ZAR 2,575. Circ: 11,300.

388.3 ZAF
AUTO DEALERS' GUIDE - CARS AND LDV'S OVER 10 YEARS OLD. Text in English. 1994. bi-m. ZAR 409.72. illus. **Document type:** *Handbook/Manual/Guide, Trade.* **Description:** Provides trade and retail values for older used passenger cars traded throughout South Africa.
Former titles: Auto Dealers' Guide - Cars over 10 Years Old; Best Deal (1022-8330)
Published by: Mead & McGrouther (Pty) Ltd., PO Box 1240, Randburg, Gauteng 2125, South Africa. TEL 27-11-789-3213, FAX 27-11-789-5218. adv.: B&W page ZAR 715, color page ZAR 1,375. Circ: 1,200.

388.3 USA
AUTO DEALERSHIP SERVICE; million dollar ideas for boosting fixed operations profits. Text in English. a. adv. **Document type:** *Newsletter, Trade.*
Published by: W D & S Publishing, 10 W 7th St, 1st Fl, PO Box 606, Barnegat Light, NJ 08006. TEL 800-321-5312, http://www.dealersedge.com.

388.3 ITA ISSN 1827-6954
AUTO D'EPOCA. Text in Italian. w. adv. illus. **Document type:** *Magazine, Consumer.*
Published by: R C S Libri (Subsidiary of: R C S Mediagroup), Via Mecenate 91, Milan, 20138, Italy. TEL 39-02-5095-2248, FAX 39-02-5095-2975, http://rcslibri.corriere.it/libri/index.htm.

796.77 ITA ISSN 1827-9279
AUTO DOSSIER. Text in Italian. 2006. m. **Document type:** *Magazine, Consumer.*
Published by: Conti Editore SpA, Via del Lavoro 7, San Lazzaro di Savena, BO 40068, Italy. http://www.contieditore.it.

627.286 ITA ISSN 0393-8387
TL240
AUTO & DESIGN; concetto architettura immagine. Text in English, Italian. 1979. bi-m. EUR 51 domestic (effective 2008). adv. bk.rev. 96 p./no.; back issues avail. **Document type:** *Magazine, Consumer.* **Description:** Designed for auto industry's design centers, design studios, major designers and specialized schools.
Indexed: SCOPUS.
—BLDSC (1827.160000), IE, Infotrieve, Ingenta.
Published by: Auto & Design s.r.l., Corso Francia, 54, Turin, TO 10143, Italy. TEL 39-011-488225, FAX 39-011-488120. Ed., R&P Fulvio Cinti TEL 39-011-488225. Adv. contact Silvia Galli. Circ: 13,000.

388.3 ITA
AUTO & FUORISTRADA. Text in Italian. 1982. 10/yr. EUR 20 domestic (effective 2009). adv. back issues avail. **Document type:** *Magazine, Consumer.*
Formerly: Auto in Fouristrada (0393-7887)
Published by: Hachette Rusconi SpA (Subsidiary of: Hachette Filipacchi Medias S.A.), Viale Sarca 235, Milan, 20126, Italy. TEL 39-02-66192629, FAX 39-02-66192469, dirgen@rusconi.it, http://portale.hachettepubblicita.it. Ed. Daniele Buzzonetti. Adv. contact Eduardo Giliberti. Circ: 76,500.

629.2 NLD ISSN 0376-6918
AUTO + MOTOR TECHNIEK. Text in Dutch. 1940. m. (11/yr.). EUR 125 (effective 2009). adv. bk.rev. charts; illus. **Document type:** *Trade.* **Description:** Technical magazine dealing with the maintenance and repair of cars.
Formerly: A M T - V A M Orgaan; Incorporates (1962-1970): Auto Service (0005-0849)
—IE, Infotrieve.

Published by: Reed Business bv (Subsidiary of: Reed Business), Postbus 4, Doetinchem, 7000 BA, Netherlands. TEL 31-314-349911, FAX 31-314-343991, info@reedbusiness.nl, http://www.reedbusiness.nl. Ed. Auke N Cupedo. Pub. Geert van de Bosch. adv.: B&W page EUR 2,785, color page EUR 4,683; trim 215 x 285. Circ: 19,901.

796.71 NLD ISSN 1572-7238
AUTO & TUNING. Text in Dutch. 1996. 10/yr. EUR 36; EUR 4.95 newsstand/cover (effective 2009). adv. **Document type:** *Magazine, Consumer.*
Formerly (until 2003): GTi Tuning en Design (1389-3505)
Published by: Uitgeverij De Koppelenburg, Postbus 46, Brummen, 6970 AA, Netherlands. TEL 31-575-565455, FAX 31-575-566133, info@dekoppelenburg.nl, http://www.dekoppelenburg.nl. Ed. Gert te Lintelo.

629.22075 USA ISSN 1943-1910
AUTO EVENTS MAGAZINE. Text in English. 2003. bi-m. USD 18 (effective 2009). adv. **Document type:** *Magazine, Consumer.* **Description:** Keeps car collectors informed of upcoming car shows, concours d'elegance, rallyes, collector auctions and other significant events surrounding the world of the automobile.
Published by: Automobile Heritage & Communications, Inc., 800 E 8th St, New Albany, IN 47150. TEL 812-948-2886, FAX 812-948-2816. Ed., Pub. Gerry A Durnell TEL 812-948-2886. adv.: color page USD 2,400; trim 8.5 x 10.875. Circ: 7,500 (paid).

388 FRA ISSN 0150-7230
AUTO EXPERTISE. Text in French. 1966. bi-m. EUR 179.87 (effective 2009). **Document type:** *Magazine.* **Description:** Provides repair estimates for cars in accidents.
Formerly (until 1973): Assurances and Techniques de l'Expertise Automobile (0150-7370)
Related titles: ◆ Supplement(s): Tarif Pieces Detachees. ISSN 0153-9205.
—CCC.
Published by: Editions Techniques pour l'Automobile et l'Industrie (E T A I), 20 rue de la Saussiere, Boulogne-Billancourt, 92641, France. TEL 33-1-46992424, FAX 33-1-48255692, http://www.etai.fr. Ed. Jacques Dubroca. Circ: 10,554.

796.77 GBR ISSN 0954-8866
AUTO EXPRESS; car news weekly. Text in English. 1988. w. GBP 58.49 domestic; GBP 90 in Europe; GBP 150 elsewhere (effective 2009). adv. **Document type:** *Magazine, Consumer.*
Related titles: ◆ Supplement(s): Auto Express Special. ISSN 0967-4500.
—CCC.
Published by: Dennis Publishing Ltd., 30 Cleveland St, London, W1T 4JD, United Kingdom. TEL 44-20-79076000, FAX 44-20-79076835, reception@dennis.co.uk, http://www.dennis.co.uk/. Ed. David Johns TEL 44-20-79076202. Pub. Phil Parker. Adv. contact Sarah Perks TEL 44-20-79076744. page GBP 7,150; trim 216 x 300. Circ: 73,644. **Subscr. to:** Bradley Pavillions. **Dist. by:** USM Distribution Ltd.

796.77 GBR ISSN 0967-4500
AUTO EXPRESS SPECIAL. Text in English. 1992. m. adv. **Document type:** *Magazine, Consumer.* **Description:** Contains special features on new car models and other developments in the auto industry.
Related titles: ◆ Supplement to: Auto Express. ISSN 0954-8866.
—CCC.
Published by: Dennis Publishing Ltd., 30 Cleveland St, London, W1T 4JD, United Kingdom. TEL 44-20-79076000, FAX 44-20-79076020, reception@dennis.co.uk, http://www.dennis.co.uk/. **Subscr. to:** Bradley Pavillions. **Dist. by:** Seymour Distribution Ltd.

796.7 SVK ISSN 1336-8257
AUTO FILTER. Text in Slovak. 2006. q. **Document type:** *Magazine, Consumer.*
Published by: Auto Filter s.r.o., Tomasikova 10/B, Bratislava, 821 03, Slovakia.

AUTO FINANCE NEWS. *see* BUSINESS AND ECONOMICS—Banking And Finance

388 CHE
AUTO FLASH. Text in French. m.
Address: Case Postale 66, Cologny, 1223, Switzerland. TEL 022-482112. Ed. Gerald Henriod. Circ: 30,000.

388.342 PRT
AUTO FOCO. Text in Portuguese. 2000. w. adv. **Document type:** *Magazine, Consumer.*
Published by: Sociedade Vicra Desportiva Lda., Travessa da Queimada, 23, Lisbon, 1294-113, Portugal. TEL 351-213-232-100, FAX 351-213-432-215. Circ: 40,000 (paid).

629 ROM ISSN 1454-1149
AUTO FOCUS. Text in Romanian. 1997. m. adv. **Document type:** *Magazine, Consumer.*
Published by: Lahnmedia Press, Bd. Ficusului nr. 3-5, bl. XX/7, sector 1, Bucharest, Romania. TEL 40-21-2329874, FAX 40-21-2329873.

339.13 PRT ISSN 0874-0542
AUTO GUIA. Text in Portuguese. 196?. 3/yr. EUR 16.20 (effective 2004). adv. **Document type:** *Magazine, Consumer.*
Published by: Edimpresa Editora Lda., Rua Calvet de Magalhaes 242, Laveiras, Paco de Arcos, 2770-022, Portugal. TEL 351-21-4698000, FAX 351-21-4698501, edimpresa@edimpresa.pt, http://www.edimpresa.pt. adv.: page EUR 1,390; trim 145 x 220. Circ: 18,489 (paid).

629.286 CAN
AUTO HEBDO. Text in English, French. 1976. w. adv.
Address: 130 DeLiege St, Montreal, PQ H2P 1J2, Canada. Ed. Elio Vettes. Circ: 28,000.

796.72 FRA ISSN 0395-4366
AUTO HEBDO. Text in French. 1968. w. EUR 99 domestic; EUR 131 in Europe (effective 2011). adv. bk.rev. illus.
Formerly (until 1976): Scratch (0395-4358)
Address: 48-50 Bd Senard, Saint-Cloud, 92210, France. TEL 33-1-47112000, 33-5-56039090, courrier@autoh.hommell.com, http://www.autohebdo.fr. Ed. Etienne Moity. Circ: 95,000.

384 DEU ISSN 1860-1618
AUTO HIFI. Text in German. 1990. 6/yr. EUR 27.90; EUR 5 newsstand/cover (effective 2011). adv. **Document type:** *Magazine, Consumer.*
Related titles: Online - full text ed.

Published by: W E K A Media Publishing GmbH, Gruberstr 46a, Poing, 85586, Germany. TEL 49-8121-950, FAX 49-8121-951199, online@wekanet.de, http://www.weka-media-publishing.de. Eds. Vedran Budimir, Dirk Waasen. Circ: 30,000 (paid and controlled).

388 PRT
AUTO HOJE. Text in Portuguese. 1989. w. EUR 1.50 per issue (effective 2005). **Document type:** *Magazine, Consumer.* **Description:** Emphasis on topical reporting and auto testing.
Related titles: Online - full text ed.
Published by: Motorpress Lisboa, SA (Subsidiary of: Gruner + Jahr AG & Co), Rua Policarpio Anjos No. 4, Cruz Quebrada, Dafundo 1495-742, Portugal. TEL 351-21-4154500, FAX 351-21-4154501, buzine@motorpress.pt, http://www.mpl.pt. Ed. Luis Pimenta. Circ: 30,000 (paid).

388.342 629.2 POL ISSN 0867-7352
AUTO I ZYCIE. Text in Polish. 1991. w. **Document type:** *Newspaper, Consumer.*
Related titles: ◆ Supplement to: Zycie Warszawy. ISSN 0137-9437.
Published by: Dom Prasowy Sp. z o.o., al Jana Pawla II 80, Warsaw, 00175, Poland. TEL 48-22-6256990, FAX 48-22-252829, redakcja@zw.com.pl, http://www.zw.com.pl.

388 CHE ISSN 1424-0130
AUTO ILLUSTRIERTE; das Schweizer Auto-Magazin. Text in German. 1977. m. CHF 6 newsstand/cover (effective 2001). adv. back issues avail. **Document type:** *Magazine, Consumer.*
Published by: Motor-Presse (Schweiz) AG, Bahnstr 24, Schwerzenbach, 8603, Switzerland. TEL 41-1-8065555, FAX 41-1-8065500, verlag@motorpresse.ch. Ed. Stefan Luescher. Pubs. August Hug, Richard Stolz. Adv. contact August Hug. Circ: 24,000 (paid).

388.3 AUS ISSN 1833-7317
AUTO INDUSTRY NEWS. Text in English. 1919. m. bk.rev. charts; stat. index. back issues avail. **Document type:** *Magazine, Trade.*
Former titles (until 2005): Auto Industry Australia (1322-3690); (until 1994): Motor Industry Journal (0729-0799); (until 1982): V A C C Journal (0004-8712); (until 1970): Australian Automobile Trade Journal (0810-2082)
Indexed: ARI.
Published by: Victorian Automobile Chamber of Commerce, 464 St, Kilda Rd, Melbourne, VIC 3004, Australia. TEL 61-3-98291111, FAX 61-3-98203401, vacc@vacc.com.au, http://www.vacc.com.au.

796.7 IRL ISSN 0791-7635
AUTO IRELAND. Text in English. 1969. 10/yr. adv. **Document type:** *Magazine, Consumer.*
Published by: Harmonia Ltd., Rosemount House, Dundrum Rd, Dublin, 14, Ireland. TEL 353-1-2405300, FAX 353-1-6619757, fneeson@harmonia.ie, http://www.harmonia.ie.

796.77 GBR ISSN 1357-4515
AUTO ITALIA. Text in English. 1995. 13/yr. GBP 44 domestic; GBP 62 in Europe; GBP 75 elsewhere (effective 2009). adv. back issues avail. **Document type:** *Magazine, Consumer.* **Description:** Covers all aspects of Italian automobiles- new, historic, classic, motorsport, motorbikes, clubs, etc.
Published by: C H Publications Ltd., Nimax House, 20 Ullswater Cresent, Ullswater Business Park, Coulsdon, Surrey CR5 2HR, United Kingdom. TEL 44-20-86556400, FAX 44-20-87631001, chp@chpltd.com, http://www.chpltd.com. Adv. contact Frank Archer TEL 44-208-6556400.

629.222 ZAF ISSN 1021-8505
AUTO ITALIANA. Text in English. 1993. bi-m. ZAR 42. adv. illus.; maps. **Document type:** *Journal, Consumer.*
Published by: Spartan Communication, PO Box 9344, Pretoria, 0001, South Africa.

388.3 BEL
AUTO JOURNAL; journal du XXe siecle. Text in English, French. 26/yr. adv.
Published by: Diffusion et Publicite S.A., Rue Vanderkindere 318, Brussels, 1180, Belgium. Ed. P de Vanssay. Circ: 20,000.

388.3 FRA ISSN 0005-0768
TL2
L'AUTO-JOURNAL. Text in French. 1950. bi-w. EUR 65 (effective 2008). adv. bibl.; charts; illus. **Document type:** *Magazine, Consumer.*
Related titles: ◆ Supplement(s): L' Auto-Journal. Hors-Serie. ISSN 1275-8493.
—CCC.
Published by: Mondadori France, 1 Rue du Colonel Pierre-Avia, Paris, Cedex 15 75754, France. TEL 33-1-41335001, contact@mondadori.fr, http://www.mondadori.fr. Circ: 161,505 (paid).

388.3 FRA ISSN 2106-9964
L'AUTO-JOURNAL EVASION & 4 X 4. Text in French. 2002. q. EUR 17 (effective 2011). **Document type:** *Magazine, Consumer.*
Formerly (until 2010): L' Auto Journal 4 x 4 (1634-2844)
Published by: Mondadori France, 1 Rue du Colonel Pierre-Avia, Paris, Cedex 15 75754, France. TEL 33-1-41335001, contact@mondadori.fr, http://www.mondadori.fr. Ed. Mathieu Chevalier.

338.3 POL
AUTO KATALOG. Text in Polish. 1991. a. PLZ 24.40 newsstand/cover (effective 2001). adv. **Document type:** *Magazine, Consumer.*
Published by: Motor-Presse Polska, ul Przyjazni 2-4, Wroclaw, 53 030, Poland. TEL 48-71-3397011, FAX 48-71-3397012. Ed. Roman Skapski. Pub. Krzysztof Komar. Adv. contact Maciej Ignaczak. Circ: 100,000 (paid).

388 SVK
AUTO KATALOG. Text in Slovak. 1993. a. adv. **Document type:** *Magazine, Consumer.*
Published by: Motor-Presse Slovakia, s.r.o., Prievozska 18, Bratislava, 82451, Slovakia. TEL 421-753-418351, FAX 421-753-417189. Ed. Kamil Pecho. Pub., Adv. contact Jan Korecky. Circ: 18,000 (paid).

629.2 GRC ISSN 1108-782X
AUTO KATALOG. Text in Greek. 1991. a. EUR 8.80 newsstand/cover (effective 2006). adv. **Document type:** *Magazine, Consumer.*
Published by: Motorpress Hellas (Subsidiary of: Gruner + Jahr AG & Co), 132 Lefkis Str, Krioneri, 14568, Greece. TEL 30-210-6262000, FAX 30-210-6262401, info@motorpress.gr, http://www.motorpress.gr. Circ: 45,000 (paid and controlled).

TU

629.2 DEU ISSN 0949-0884
AUTO KATALOG. Variant title: Auto Motor Sport Spezial Auto Katalog. Text in German. 1956. a. EUR 7.90 newsstand/cover (effective 2010). adv. abstr. index. **Document type:** *Magazine, Consumer.*
Description: Provides a reliable directory on cars from around the world; detailed presentation of 1,900 cars in text and photos; available in 16 international editions.
Formerly (until 1974): Auto-Modelle (0463-6589)
Published by: Motor Presse Stuttgart GmbH & Co. KG (Subsidiary of: Gruner + Jahr AG & Co), Leuschnerstr 1, Stuttgart, 70174, Germany. TEL 49-711-18201, FAX 49-711-1821779, internet-redaktion@motor-presse-stuttgart.de, http://www.motorpresse.de. Ed. Bernd Ostmann. Adv. contact Andrea Bantle. Circ: 150,000 (paid).

388 HUN ISSN 0865-3518
AUTO KATALOGUS. Text in Hungarian. 1989. a. HUF 2,180 newsstand/cover (effective 2006). adv. **Document type:** *Catalog, Consumer.*
Published by: Motor-Presse Budapest Lapkiado kft, Hajogyari-sziget 307, Budapest, 1033, Hungary. TEL 36-1-4369244, FAX 36-1-4369248, mpb@motorpresse.hu, http://www.motorpresse.hu. Ed. Viktor Balazs. Pub. Dietmar Metzger. Adv. contacts Andrea Poz, Dietmar Metzger. Circ: 55,000 (paid).

796.7 HRV ISSN 0353-5355
AUTO KLUB. Text in Croatian. 1989. w. adv. **Document type:** *Magazine, Consumer.*
Published by: Arena d.d., Slavonska Avenija 4, Zagreb, 10000, Croatia. TEL 385-1-341573, FAX 385-1-342053. Ed. Igor Stazic.

388.3 USA ISSN 0005-0776
HD9999.C27
AUTO LAUNDRY NEWS; the voice of the car care industry. Text in English. 1953. m. USD 72 domestic; USD 83 in Canada; USD 125 elsewhere; USD 7 per issue domestic; USD 10 per issue in Canada; USD 18 per issue elsewhere (effective 2008). adv. charts; illus.; stat.; tr.mk. back issues avail. **Document type:** *Magazine, Trade.*
Related titles: Supplement(s): Auto Laundry News Directory.
Published by: E.W. Williams Publications Co., 2125 Center Ave, Ste 305, Fort Lee, NJ 07024. TEL 201-592-7007, FAX 201-592-7171, philpl@ewwpi.com, http://www.williamspublications.com. Ed. Stefan Budricks. Pub. Andrew H Williams. Adv. contact Joanne Gambert. B&W page USD 2,825, color page USD 3,575; 7 x 10. Circ: 16,049 (paid).

388.342 TUR
AUTO LIFE. Text in Turkish. m. **Document type:** *Magazine, Trade.*
Published by: Star Intermedya, PK 25, Yenikoy - Istanbul, Turkey. TEL 90-212-2754115, FAX 90-212-2674494.

388.3 BEL
AUTO LOISIRS MOTOR REVUE. Text in French. 1921. bi-m. free to members (effective 2005). adv. **Document type:** *Magazine, Consumer.*
Former titles: Motor Revue Belgium (1374-531X); (until 1998): Motor Revue (1374-5301); (until 1951): Motor
Published by: Royal Motor Union, Boulevard d'Avroy, 254/1, Bte 1, Liege, 4000, Belgium. TEL 32-4-252-7030, FAX 32-4-252-8301, http://www.rmu.be/index.asp. Circ: 30,000.

388 HUN ISSN 0864-8492
AUTO MAGAZIN. Text in Hungarian. 1989. m. HUF 8,340; HUF 695 newsstand/cover (effective 2006). adv. 100 p./no.; **Document type:** *Magazine, Consumer.*
Related titles: Online - full text ed.: ISSN 1786-1462; ◆ Supplement(s): Transzport. ISSN 1217-9582.
Published by: Motor-Presse Budapest Lapkiado kft, Hajogyari-sziget 307, Budapest, 1033, Hungary. TEL 36-1-4369244, FAX 36-1-4369248, mpb@motorpresse.hu, http://www.motorpresse.hu. Ed. Viktor Balazs. Pub. Dietmar Metzger. Adv. contacts Andrea Poz, Dietmar Metzger. page USD 2,250; bleed 215 x 280. Circ: 40,000 (paid). **Dist. by:** Lapker Rt, 1097 Tablas utca, Budapest, Hungary.

388 PRT
AUTO MAGAZINE. Text in Portuguese. 1992. m. EUR 3 newsstand/cover (effective 2005). adv. **Document type:** *Magazine, Consumer.*
Related titles: Online - full text ed.
Published by: Motorpress Lisboa, SA (Subsidiary of: Gruner + Jahr AG & Co), Rua Policarpio Anjos No. 4, Cruz Quebrada, Dafundo 1495-742, Portugal. TEL 351-21-4154500, FAX 351-21-4154501, buzine@motorpress.pt, http://www.mpl.pt. Ed. Luis Pimenta. Adv. contact Rita Vidreiro. Circ: 30,000 (paid).

796.7 HRV ISSN 1330-4984
AUTO MANIA. Text in Croatian. 1994. m. **Document type:** *Magazine, Consumer.*
Address: Drenovacka 2, Zagreb, 10000, Croatia. TEL 385-1-395648, FAX 385-1-395164.

388.3 796.77 BEL ISSN 1782-4397
AUTO MAX (DUTCH EDITION). Text in Dutch. 2006. bi-m. EUR 30 (effective 2007). back issues avail. **Document type:** *Magazine, Consumer.*
Related titles: ◆ French ed.: Auto Max (French Edition). ISSN 1782-4389.
Published by: Maxteam, 14 Rue Petite-Coyarde, Mont-Saint-Andre, 1367, Belgium. info@automaxxx.be.

388.3 796.77 BEL ISSN 1782-4389
AUTO MAX (FRENCH EDITION). Text in French. 2006. bi-m. EUR 30 (effective 2007). back issues avail. **Document type:** *Magazine, Consumer.*
Related titles: ◆ Dutch ed.: Auto Max (Dutch Edition). ISSN 1782-4397.
Published by: Maxteam, 14 Rue Petite-Coyarde, Mont-Saint-Andre, 1367, Belgium. info@automaxxx.be.

388 DEU ISSN 1434-4084
AUTO-MOBILES. Text in German. 1989. fortn. **Document type:** *Magazine, Trade.*
Published by: D A Z Verlag GmbH und Co. KG, An der Strusbek 23, Ahrensburg, 22926, Germany. TEL 49-4102-47870, FAX 49-4102-478795, info@daz-verlag.de. Circ: 72,001 (controlled).

388 MEX
AUTO MODELOS. Text in Spanish. 1994. a. MXN 25 newsstand/cover (effective 2001). adv. **Document type:** *Magazine, Consumer.*
Published by: Editorial Motorpress Televisa (Subsidiary of: Gruner + Jahr AG & Co), Av Vasco de Quiroga 2000, Edif E, Mexico, Col Santa Fe, Mexico City, DF 01210, Mexico. TEL 525-2612672, FAX 525-2612731. Ed. Juan Manuel Garcia Rubio. Pubs. Carlos Mendez, Jesus Carrera. Adv. contact Otilia Perez. Circ: 37,500 (paid).

388 IND
AUTO MONITOR. Text in English. 19??. bi-m. INR 770 domestic; INR 4,000 foreign (effective 2011). **Document type:** *Magazine, Trade.*
Description: Monitors, analyzes and reports on news from auto industries in India and around the world.
Published by: Infomedia 18 Ltd., A Wing, Ruby House, J K Sawant Marg, Dadar (West), Mumbai, 400 028, India. TEL 91-22-30245000, FAX 91-22-30034499, ho@infomedia18.in. Adv. contact Ruby Roy TEL 91-22-30034582.

388.3 POL ISSN 1643-4862
AUTO MOTO. Text in Polish. 1997. m. PLZ 4.99 newsstand/cover (effective 2011). adv. **Document type:** *Magazine, Consumer.*
Formerly (until 2002): Auto Dzis i Jutro (1429-3919)
Published by: Wydawnictwo Bauer Sp. z o.o. (Subsidiary of: Bauer Media Group), ul Motorowa 1, Warsaw, 04-035, Poland. TEL 48-22-5170500, FAX 48-22-5170125, kontakt@bauer.pl, http://www.bauer.pl. Ed. Krzysztof Burmajster. Adv. contact Marcin Gudowicz.

614.86 SRB ISSN 0352-4523
AUTO MOTO REVIJA. Text in Serbo-Croatian. 1984. m.?. free membership. **Document type:** *Magazine, Trade.*
Published by: Auto Moto Savez Srbije i Crne Gore/Automobile and Motorcycle Association of Serbia and Montenegro, Ruzveltova 18, Belgrade, 11000. TEL 381-11-9800, ic@amss.org.yu, http://www.amsj.co.yu. Ed. Ranko Jovicevic.

629.2 BEL ISSN 1784-9128
AUTO-MOTO-REVUE. Text in Dutch, French. 11/yr. **Document type:** *Trade.* **Description:** Contains new car prices.
Published by: Federauto a.s.b.l., Bd de la Woluwe 46, Bte 9, Bruxelles, 1200, Belgium. TEL 32-2-7786200, FAX 32-2-7786222, mail@federauto.be, http://www.federauto.be. Ed., Pub. Bob Pauwels. R&P, Adv. contact Yves Sprumont. Circ: 8,000.

629.286 POL ISSN 1231-0131
AUTO MOTO SERWIS. Text in Polish. 1993. m. EUR 102 foreign (effective 2006). **Document type:** *Magazine, Trade.*
Published by: Instalator Polski Sp. z o.o., ul Koniczynowa 11, Warsaw, 03612, Poland. TEL 48-22-6783760, FAX 48-22-6795203, http://www.instalator.com.pl. Ed. Krzysztof Trzeciak. **Dist. by:** Ars Polona, Obroncow 25, Warsaw 03933, Poland. TEL 48-22-5098609, FAX 48-22-5098610, arspolona@arspolona.com.pl, http://www.arspolona.com.pl.

388.3 HUN ISSN 0005-0792
AUTO-MOTOR. Text in Hungarian. 1946. fortn. HUF 4,140; HUF 225 newsstand/cover (effective 2010). adv. bk.rev. charts; illus. **Document type:** *Magazine, Consumer.*
Formerly (until 1951): Auto (0200-2620)
Published by: Axel Springer - Budapest Kft., Varosmajor u 11, Budapest, 1122, Hungary. TEL 36-1-4885766, FAX 36-1-4885607, info@axelspringer.hu, http://www.axelspringer.hu. Ed. Robert Szabo. Circ: 34,394 (paid).

388 SVK ISSN 1336-2038
AUTO MOTOR A SPORT. Text in Slovak. 1992. m. EUR 21.91 (effective 2011). adv. **Document type:** *Magazine, Consumer.*
Published by: Motor-Presse Slovakia, s.r.o., Prievozska 18, Bratislava, 82451, Slovakia. TEL 421-2-53418351, FAX 421-2-53418351. Circ: 30,000 (paid).

388 CZE ISSN 1212-1355
AUTO MOTOR A SPORT. Text in Czech. 1993. m. CZK 621 (effective 2009). adv. **Document type:** *Magazine, Consumer.*
Formerly (until 1998): Automagazin (1212-0553)
Published by: Motor-Presse Bohemia, U Krcskeho Nadrazi 36, Prague 4, 14000, Czech Republic. TEL 420-2-24109340, FAX 420-2-41721905, motopresse@motorpresse.cz, http://www.motorpresse.cz. Ed. Michael Kudela. Adv. contact Renata Ben. page CZK 32,000. Circ: 30,000 (paid).

796.7 SWE ISSN 1400-951X
AUTO MOTOR & SPORT. Text in Swedish. 1994. 26/yr. SEK 1,195 (effective 2009). adv. **Document type:** *Magazine, Consumer.*
Published by: Auto Motor & Sport Sverige AB, Gardsvaegen 4, Solna, 16970, Sweden. TEL 46-8-470-92-60, FAX 46-8-470-92-61. Ed. Alrik Soederlind. Pub. Gunnar Dackevall. Adv. contact Svante Svensson TEL 46-8-7596075.

796.7 TUR
AUTO MOTOR & SPORT. Text in Turkish. 2006 (Aug.). m. TRY 32 domestic (effective 2009). adv. **Document type:** *Magazine, Consumer.* **Description:** Covers a broad variety of topics, all shaped by unchallenged writing and testing competence. The emphasis is on car news, driving reviews, individual and comparative vehicle tests and motorsport features. It follows in the footsteps of the famous German "auto motor und sport" pattern - tailored to the specific requirements of the Turkish market.
Published by: Merkez Motor Presse Dergi Yayincilik, Tevfikbey Mahallesi, 20 Temmuz Cad. No.24, Sefakoy, Istanbul, 34295, Turkey. TEL 90-212-4112227, http://www.turkuvazdergi.com.tr. Ed. Halit Bolkan. Adv. contact Ebru Alisan. color page TRY 22,500. Circ: 11,123 (paid).

796.7 GRC ISSN 1106-6776
AUTO MOTOR & SPORT. Text in Greek. 1991. fortn. EUR 4.98 newsstand/cover (effective 2006). adv. **Document type:** *Magazine, Consumer.* **Description:** Contains articles and reviews of the latest car models on the market.
Published by: Motorpress Hellas (Subsidiary of: Gruner + Jahr AG & Co), 132 Lefkis Str, Krioneri, 14568, Greece. TEL 30-210-6262000, FAX 30-210-6262401, info@motorpress.gr, http://www.motorpress.gr. Ed. Mihalis Stauropoulos. Pub. Aristotelis Kokkas. Adv. contact Kleopatra Sofianoroulou. Circ: 45,000 (paid).

388.3 796.92 POL ISSN 1426-6385
AUTO MOTOR I SPORT. Text in Polish. 1991. m. PLZ 6.50 newsstand/cover (effective 2001). adv. **Document type:** *Magazine, Consumer.*
Description: Covers motorization, tourism, road safety.
Formerly (until 1996): Auto International (1230-8145)
Published by: Motor-Presse Polska, ul Przyjazni 2-4, Wroclaw, 53 030, Poland. TEL 48-71-3397011, FAX 48-71-3397012. Ed. Roman Skapski. Pub. Krzysztof Komar. Adv. contact Maciej Ignaczak. Circ: 120,000 (paid).

796.77 NLD ISSN 1380-9040
AUTO MOTOR KLASSIEK. Text in Dutch. 1985. m. EUR 32.50 (effective 2010). adv. bk.rev. **Document type:** *Consumer.*
Published by: Wilbers Publishing BV, Postbus 10, Ulft, 7070 AA, Netherlands. TEL 31-315-681326, FAX 31-315-630813, info@wilberspublishing.nl, http://www.wilberspublishing.nl. Ed. Maarten Wilbers. Adv. contact Christina Djermor. color page EUR 2,695; 213 x 290. Circ: 40,000.

629.222 NOR ISSN 1503-819X
AUTO MOTOR OG SPORT. Text in Norwegian. 2004. m. NOK 350 (effective 2009). adv. **Document type:** *Magazine, Consumer.*
Published by: Hjemmet Mortensen AS, Gullhaugveien 1, Nydalen, Oslo, 0441, Norway. TEL 47-22-585000, FAX 47-22-585959, firmapost@hm-media.no, http://www.hm-media.no. adv.: page NOK 36,000.

796.72 ROM ISSN 1453-5769
AUTO MOTOR SI SPORT. Text in Romanian. 1997. m. ROL 402,696 (effective 2006). adv. **Document type:** *Magazine, Consumer.*
Published by: Motor-Presse Romania, Bul Ficusului nr 44, Romaero, corp A, et 1, sector 1, Bucharest, 013975, Romania. TEL 40-21-2329920, FAX 40-21-2329873, web.redactia@motorpresse.ro.

388.3 DEU
AUTO MOTOR SPORT SPEZIAL CROSS-ROAD. Variant title: Cross-Road. Text in German. 2003. a. EUR 4.20 newsstand/cover (effective 2010). adv. **Document type:** *Magazine, Consumer.*
Formerly (until 2004): Auto Motor Sport Spezial Off-Road
Published by: Motor Presse Stuttgart GmbH & Co. KG (Subsidiary of: Gruner + Jahr AG & Co), Leuschnerstr 1, Stuttgart, 70174, Germany. TEL 49-711-18201, FAX 49-711-1821779, cgolla@motorpresse.de, http://www.motorpresse.de. Ed. Bernd Ostmann. Adv. contact Andrea Bantle. Circ: 40,000 (paid).

388.3 796.72 DEU ISSN 0005-0806
AUTO MOTOR UND SPORT. Text in German. 1946. fortn. EUR 83.20; EUR 3.50 newsstand/cover (effective 2010). adv. charts; illus. **Document type:** *Magazine, Consumer.* **Description:** Provides comprehensive test reports and technical articles, accompanied by broad coverage of the work of cars, motoring and sport.
Related titles: CD-ROM ed.
Indexed: A22, RefZh.
—IE, Infotrieve.
Published by: Motor Presse Stuttgart GmbH & Co. KG (Subsidiary of: Gruner + Jahr AG & Co), Leuschnerstr 1, Stuttgart, 70174, Germany. TEL 49-711-18201, FAX 49-711-1821779, cgolla@motorpresse.de, http://www.motorpresse.de. Ed. Bernd Ostmann. Adv. contact Jochen Bechtle. Circ: 408,523 (paid).

388.3 796.72 DEU ISSN 1430-0729
AUTO MOTOR UND SPORT SPEZIAL GEBRAUCHTWAGEN. Text in German. 1976. a. EUR 4.30 newsstand/cover (effective 2010). adv. charts; illus.; stat.; tr.lit. **Document type:** *Magazine, Consumer.*
Description: Provides concise information on the used car market; consumer advice, checklists, data and prices for over 8000 used cars.
Supersedes in part (in 1993): Auto Motor und Sport Spezial (0940-3833)
Published by: Motor Presse Stuttgart GmbH & Co. KG (Subsidiary of: Gruner + Jahr AG & Co), Leuschnerstr 1, Stuttgart, 70174, Germany. TEL 49-711-18201, FAX 49-711-1821779, internet-redaktion@motor-presse-stuttgart.de, http://www.motorpresse.de. Ed. Bernd Ostmann. Adv. contact Andrea Bantle. Circ: 100,000 (controlled).

388.3 796.72 DEU ISSN 0178-9643
AUTO MOTOR UND SPORT TESTJAHRBUCH. Text in German. 1984. a. EUR 5.50 newsstand/cover (effective 2010). adv. charts; illus.; stat.; tr.lit. **Document type:** *Magazine, Consumer.* **Description:** Contains reliable tests, reports, technical data and advice on the most important car models of the year.
Published by: Motor Presse Stuttgart GmbH & Co. KG (Subsidiary of: Gruner + Jahr AG & Co), Leuschnerstr 1, Stuttgart, 70174, Germany. TEL 49-711-18201, FAX 49-711-1821779, internet-redaktion@motor-presse-stuttgart.de, http://www.motorpresse.de. Ed. Bernd Ostmann. Adv. contact Andrea Bantle. Circ: 70,000 (paid).

388 629.286 DEU
AUTO MOTORRAD FREIZEIT. Text in German. 1986. bi-m. EUR 17.40; EUR 2.90 newsstand/cover (effective 2008). adv. **Document type:** *Magazine, Consumer.*
Published by: A M O Verlag GmbH, Sattlerstr 7, Luebeck, 23556, Germany. TEL 49-1805-151165, FAX 49-190-151050, info@amo-verlag.de, http://www.amo-verlag.de. Ed. Juergen Koslowski. adv.: B&W page EUR 400, color page EUR 500; trim 204 x 280.

796.77 DEU
AUTO NEWS. Text in German. bi-m. EUR 16; EUR 2.99 newsstand/cover (effective 2008). adv. **Document type:** *Magazine, Consumer.*
Published by: New Look Electronic Publishing GmbH, Hans-Pinsel-Str 10a, Haar, 85540, Germany. TEL 49-89-4623700, FAX 49-89-466096, mail@newlook.de, http://www.newlook.de. adv.: color page EUR 6,000. Circ: 20,824 (paid and controlled).

388.34 USA
AUTO NEWS FAST NEWSLETTER. Text in English. 1998. w. **Document type:** *Newsletter.* **Description:** Designed to give an overview of the automotive industry activities in Central Europe.
Media: Online - full text.
Published by: Central Europe Automotive Report, 4800 Baseline Rd, Ste E 104-34D, Boulder, CO 80303. Ed. Jeffrey Jones.

629.2 GRC
AUTO NEWSPAPER. Text in Greek. 2005. w. free newsstand/cover (effective 2006). adv. **Document type:** *Newspaper, Consumer.*
Published by: Motorpress Hellas (Subsidiary of: Gruner + Jahr AG & Co), 132 Lefkis Str, Krioneri, 14568, Greece. TEL 30-210-6262000, FAX 30-210-6262401, info@motorpress.gr, http://www.motorpress.gr. Circ: 50,000 (controlled).

629.286 ITA ISSN 1120-494X
AUTO OGGI; settimanale di auto e consigli pratici sul mondo dei motori. Text in Italian. 1986. w. EUR 39 (effective 2009). adv. **Document type:** *Magazine, Consumer.*
Published by: (Automobile Club d'Italia), A C I Mondadori SpA, Via Cassanese 224, Segrate, MI 20090, Italy. TEL 39-02-26937550, FAX 39-02-26937560. Ed. Giancarlo Pini. Circ: 45,690 (paid).

388.342 TWN ISSN 1682-2609
AUTO ONLINE. Text in Chinese, English. 2002. m. **Document type:** *Magazine, Consumer.*
Published by: Wangsuo Keji Guofenyouxian Gongsi, 4F, 131 Zhiyuan 3rd, Taipei, 112, Taiwan. TEL 886-2-28234643, FAX 886-2-81461006. Ed. Liao Sutl.

AUTO PARTS & ACCESSORIES BUYERS' GUIDE. *see* BUSINESS AND ECONOMICS—Trade And Industrial Directories

629.28 368 USA ISSN 1939-0424
TL145
AUTO PHYSICAL DAMAGE BASICS. Text in English. irreg. USD 42 per issue (effective 2008). **Document type:** *Handbook/Manual/Guide, Trade.* **Description:** Teaches the terms and functions relating to each part and system of an automobile.
Published by: Kaplan Financial, 1905 Palace St, La Crosse, WI 54603. TEL 608-779-8301, 800-824-8742, contactus@kaplan.com, http://www.kaplanfinancial.com.

388 ARG ISSN 1668-8333
AUTO PLUS. Text in Spanish. 2004. m. ARS 7.90 newsstand/cover (effective 2010). **Document type:** *Magazine, Trade.*
Published by: Motorpress Argentina, S.A. (Subsidiary of: Gruner + Jahr AG & Co), Ituzaingo, 642-648, Buenos Aires, 1141, Argentina. TEL 54-114-3077672, FAX 54-114-3077858, http://www.motorpress.com.ar/.

388.3 FRA ISSN 0992-8154
AUTO PLUS. Text in French. 1988. w. EUR 75 (effective 2008). **Document type:** *Magazine, Consumer.*
Published by: Mondadori France, 1 Rue du Colonel Pierre-Avia, Paris, Cedex 15 75754, France. TEL 33-1-41335001, contact@mondadori.fr, http://www.mondadori.fr. Circ: 550,000 (paid).

388 ROM ISSN 1223-6772
AUTO PRO. Text in Romanian. 1994. m. adv. **Document type:** *Magazine, Consumer.*
Published by: Motor-Presse Romania, Bul Ficusului nr 44, Romaero, corp A, et 1, sector 1, Bucharest, 013975, Romania. TEL 40-1-2121843, FAX 40-1-2121407. Ed. Dan Vardie. Adv. contact Bogdan Paun. Circ: 19,500 (paid).

388 CZE ISSN 1214-8342
AUTO PRUVODCE. Text in Czech. 1992. a. CZK 325 per issue (effective 2009). adv. **Document type:** *Catalog, Consumer.*
Formerly (until 2004): Autokatalog (1212-0545)
Published by: Motor-Presse Bohemia, U Krcskeho Nadrazi 36, Prague 4, 14000, Czech Republic. TEL 420-2-24109340, FAX 420-2-41721905, motopresse@motorpresse.cz. Ed. Jan Blasek. Adv. contact Renata Ben. Circ: 40,000 (paid).

388.3 USA
AUTO REMARKETING NEWS MAGAZINE. Text in English. 1990. m. USD 24.95 (effective 2007). adv. **Document type:** *Magazine, Trade.* **Description:** Reports on changes in the automotive industry and their effects on the buying and selling of used cars. Covers the used car operations of franchised and independent dealers and the preparation of cars for resale.
Former titles: Auto Remarketing; Used Car Merchandising
Related titles: ♦ Alternate Frequency ed(s).: Auto Remarketing Weekly. w.
Published by: Cherokee Publishing Co., Westview at Weston, 301 Cascade Pointe Ln. #101, Cary, NC 27513-5778. TEL 919-674-6020, 800-608-7500, FAX 919-674-6027. Ed. Kerry Watson Garner. Pub. Ronald H Smith. Circ: 22,000 (paid and controlled).

AUTO RENTAL NEWS; the magazine of the car and truck rental industry. *see* BUSINESS AND ECONOMICS—Marketing And Purchasing

629.288 USA ISSN 1523-178X
AUTO RESTORER; the how-to guide for vintage car enthusiasts. Text in English. 1989. m. USD 20 domestic; USD 38 foreign (effective 2008). adv. bk.rev. illus. back issues avail. **Document type:** *Newsletter, Consumer.* **Description:** Features old cars, restoration information, parts sources, auto club listings and auctions and events.
Formerly (until 199?): Classic Auto Restorer (1042-5683)
Published by: BowTie, Inc., 2401 Beverly Blvd, PO Box 57900, Los Angeles, CA 90057. TEL 213-385-2222, FAX 213-385-8565, adtraffic@bowtieinc.com, http://www.bowtieinc.com. Ed. Ted Kade.

629.22075 FRA ISSN 0247-1469
AUTO RETRO. Variant title: Auto Moto Retro. Text in French. 1980. 11/yr. EUR 41 domestic; EUR 55 foreign (effective 2009). adv. bk.rev. back issues avail. **Document type:** *Magazine, Consumer.*
Published by: Editions L V A, BP 40419, Fontainebleau Cedex, France. Circ: 60,000.

629.114 NLD ISSN 1574-9134
AUTO REVIEW. Text in Dutch. 2005. m. EUR 22.50; EUR 2.99 newsstand/cover (effective 2009). adv. **Document type:** *Magazine, Consumer.*
Published by: F & L Automotive Publications B.V., Meijhorst 60-10, Postbus 31331, Nijmegen, 6503 CH, Netherlands. TEL 31-24-3723636, FAX 31-24-3723630, info@fnl.nl, http://www.fnl.nl. Ed. Arjan Kropman. Adv. contact Dick Verbeeten. color page EUR 4,200; trim 210 x 280.

388.3 USA ISSN 1068-980X
AUTO REVISTA. Text in English, Spanish. 1988. w. free. adv. **Document type:** *Magazine, Consumer.* **Description:** Focuses on the retail auto market in the Dallas - Fort Worth Metroplex.
Published by: Revista Communications, Inc., 14330 Midway Rd, Ste 202, Dallas, TX 75244-3514. TEL 972-386-0040, FAX 972-386-4255. Ed., R&P Aaron Esslinger. Pub. Ray Lozano. Adv. contact Barbra Einsohn. Circ: 41,000 (controlled).

388.3 ESP ISSN 0005-1691
AUTO REVISTA. Text in Spanish, English. 1959. m. (11/yr.). EUR 224.14 combined subscription domestic (print, online & email eds.); EUR 295 combined subscription foreign (print, online & email eds.) (effective 2009). bk.rev. bibl.; charts; illus.; mkt.; pat.; stat.; tr.lit. **Document type:** *Magazine, Consumer.* **Description:** Covers the automobile business and industry. Contains prices and test results.
Related titles: E-mail ed.: ISSN 1988-5504. 2000. EUR 168.28 (effective 2002); Online - full text ed.: Auto Revista Digital. ISSN 1988-8694. 2000; English ed.
Published by: Tecnipublicaciones Espana, S.L., Avda de Manoteras 44, 3a Planta, Madrid, 28050, Spain. TEL 34-91-2972000, FAX 34-91-2972154, tp@tecnipublicaciones.com. Circ: 12,000.

796.77 FRA ISSN 1951-977X
AUTO RIDE. Text in French. 2006. m. EUR 36 (effective 2007); free newsstand/cover. **Document type:** *Magazine, Consumer.*
Address: 1900 Rte des Cretes, Sophia Antipolis, 06560, France. TEL 33-4-97216130, FAX 33-4-92270235, http://www.autoride.fr. **Subscr. to:** S R S Concept, Service Abonnement, 10 Av. de Lyon, Cannes 06400, France.

794.7 DEU
AUTO SAISON. Text in German. 2001. q. EUR 6 newsstand/cover (effective 2006). adv. **Document type:** *Magazine, Consumer.*
Published by: Pro Publica International Verlag GmbH, Hansaallee 289, Duesseldorf, 40549, Germany. TEL 49-211-5581866, FAX 49-211-5578657, http://www.peil-pp.de. adv.: B&W page EUR 6,720, color page EUR 8,000. Circ: 60,000 (controlled).

629.286 DEU ISSN 1437-1162
AUTO-SERVICE-PRAXIS; das Fachmagazin fuer den Werkstattprofi. Text in German. 1997. m. EUR 72.90 domestic; EUR 83.90 foreign; EUR 7.50 newsstand/cover (effective 2008). adv. **Document type:** *Magazine, Trade.*
Published by: Springer Automotive Media (Subsidiary of: Springer Fachmedien Muenchen GmbH), Neumarkter Str 18, Munich, 81673, Germany. TEL 49-89-43721121, FAX 49-89-43721266, vertriebsservice@springer.com, http://www.springerautomotivemedia.de. adv.: B&W page EUR 5,495, color page EUR 7,447. Circ: 26,669 (paid and controlled).

629.11 ROM ISSN 1582-5043
AUTO-SHOP IN IMAGINI. Text in Romanian. 2000. s-m. adv. **Document type:** *Magazine, Consumer.*
Published by: Hiparion, Str. Mihai Veliciu 15-17, Cluj-Napoca, 3400, Romania. TEL 40-64-411100, FAX 40-64-411700, office@hiparion.ro.

388.342 TUR ISSN 1300-5863
AUTO SHOW. Text in Turkish. 1992. w. adv. **Document type:** *Magazine, Consumer.*
Related titles: Online - full text ed.
Published by: D B R - Dogan Burda Rizzoli Dergi Yayyncylyk ve Pazarlama A.S., Hurriyet Medya Towers, Gunesli - Istanbul, 34212, Turkey. TEL 90-212-4780300, FAX 90-212-4103200, abone@dbr.com.tr, http://www.dbr.com.tr.

796.77 USA
AUTO SHOW WEEKLY. Text in English. 1991. bi-w. USD 19.95. adv. bk.rev. **Document type:** *Magazine, Consumer.*
Formerly: Auto Exotica
Published by: Fantasy Publications, 6034 S. Lindbergh Blvd., St. Louis, MO 63123-7041. TEL 314-487-0054, FAX 314-487-7284. Ed. Robert Schneider Jr. Pub. James Smoot. Adv. contact Barry Sterneck. Circ: 50,000.

388 336.2 DEU ISSN 1613-0774
AUTO, STEUERN, RECHT. Text in German. 1974. m. EUR 94.50 for 6 mos. (effective 2010). **Document type:** *Journal, Trade.*
Formerly (until 2004): Steuer-Erfahrungsaustausch Kraftfahrzeuggewerbe (0344-1016)
Related titles: Online - full text ed.
Published by: (I W W - Institut fuer Wirtschaftspublizistik), Vogel Business Media GmbH & Co.KG, Max-Planck-Str 7-9, Wuerzburg, 97064, Germany. TEL 49-931-4180, FAX 49-931-4182750, info@vogel.de, http://www.vogel-media.de. Ed. Ruth Hilgendorf. **Subscr. to:** DataM-Services GmbH, Fichtestr 9, Wuerzburg 97074, Germany. TEL 49-931-417001, FAX 49-931-4170499, http://www.datam-services.de.

388.3 ITA ISSN 1124-9978
AUTO SUPER MARKET. Text in Italian. 1991. 11/yr. **Document type:** *Magazine, Consumer.* **Description:** Contains classified announcements of automobiles for sale in Italy. Each announcement includes a photo, description, price and telephone number.
Formerly (until 1991): Auto Market (1124-9986)
Published by: Edizeta Srl, Via Lussinpiccolo 19, Mestre, VE 30174, Italy. TEL 39-041-5459500, FAX 39-041-5459555, redazione@edizeta.com, http://www.edizeta.it. **Dist. by:** A. Pieroni S.r.l., Viale Vittorio Veneto, 28, Milan, MI 20124, Italy.

796.77 POL ISSN 1234-0294
AUTO SWIAT. Text in Polish. 1995. w. PLZ 2.30 newsstand/cover (effective 2011). adv. **Document type:** *Magazine, Consumer.*
Published by: Ringier Axel Springer Polska, ul Domaniewska 52, Warsaw, 02672, Poland. TEL 48-22-2321400, FAX 48-22-2325540, asp@axelspringer.com.pl, http://www.ringieraxelspringer.pl. Ed. Stanislaw Sewastianowicz. Adv. contact Wojciech Mistewicz.

796.77 POL ISSN 1427-3535
AUTO SWIAT KATALOG. Text in Polish. 1998. q. **Document type:** *Magazine, Consumer.*
Published by: Ringier Axel Springer Polska, ul Domaniewska 52, Warsaw, 02672, Poland. TEL 48-22-2321400, FAX 48-22-2325540, asp@axelspringer.com.pl, http://www.ringieraxelspringer.pl. Circ: 100,000 (paid).

388.33 AUT
AUTO TANKSTELLE GARAGE; Tankstellen- und Werkstaettenjournal. Text in German. 1930. 11/yr. EUR 59.10 domestic; EUR 78.50 foreign (effective 2005). adv. **Document type:** *Magazine, Trade.*
Former titles: Tankstelle und Garage; Garage, Tankstelle und Servicestation (0016-4550)
Published by: Bohmann Druck und Verlag GmbH & Co. KG, Leberstr 122, Vienna, W 1110, Austria. TEL 43-1-740950, FAX 43-1-74095183, 43-1-74095-183, http://www.bohmann.at. Ed. Peter Tajmar. Adv. contact Eveline Kern-Nagler TEL 43-1-7409543. page EUR 3,633; trim 185 x 270. Circ: 7,000 (controlled).

388 ARG ISSN 1514-0016
AUTO TEST. Text in Spanish. 1991. m. ARS 7 newsstand/cover (effective 2001). adv. **Document type:** *Magazine, Consumer.*
Formerly (until 1998): Road Test (0329-3300)
Published by: Motorpress Argentina, S.A. (Subsidiary of: Gruner + Jahr AG & Co), Ituzaingo, 642-648, Buenos Aires, 1141, Argentina. TEL 54-114-3077672, FAX 54-114-3077858, http://www.motorpress.com.ar/. Ed. Carlos Figueras. Pub. Jesus Carrera. Adv. contact Adrian Lualdi. Circ: 16,000 (paid).

388.3 DEU ISSN 1869-9855
AUTO TEST. Text in German. 1990. m. EUR 2.20 newsstand/cover (effective 2011). adv. **Document type:** *Magazine, Consumer.*
Former titles (until 2007): Automobil Test (1613-9445); (until 2003): Automobil (1434-2863); (until 1996): Auto-Magazin (1432-4245)
Published by: A S Autoverlag GmbH (Subsidiary of: Axel Springer Verlag AG), Axel-Springer-Platz 1, Hamburg, 20350, Germany. TEL 49-40-34725934, FAX 49-40-34727073, dk@autoverlag.de, http://www.autojournal.de. Ed. Olaf Schilling. Circ: 213,924 (paid).

388 ARG ISSN 0329-3327
AUTO TEST LIBRO DE PRUEBAS. Text in Spanish. 1996. a. adv. **Document type:** *Magazine, Consumer.*
Published by: Motorpress Argentina, S.A. (Subsidiary of: Gruner + Jahr AG & Co), Ituzaingo, 642-648, Buenos Aires, 1141, Argentina. TEL 54-114-3077672, FAX 54-114-3077858, http://www.motorpress.com.ar/. Ed. Carlos Figueras. Pub. Jesus Carrera. Adv. contact Adrian Lualdi.

388 PRT
AUTO TESTES. Text in Portuguese. 1994. a. EUR 5 newsstand/cover (effective 2005). adv. **Document type:** *Magazine, Consumer.*
Formerly: Auto Hoje Testes
Published by: Motorpress Lisboa, SA (Subsidiary of: Gruner + Jahr AG & Co), Rua Policarpio Anjos No. 4, Cruz Quebrada, Dafundo 1495-742, Portugal. TEL 351-21-4154500, FAX 351-21-4154501, buzine@motorpress.pt, http://www.mpl.pt. Circ: 20,000 (paid).

388.3 CZE ISSN 1803-8476
AUTO TIP SPORTSCARS. Text in Czech. 1998. s-a. CZK 69 newsstand/cover (effective 2011). 122 p./no. 4 cols./p.; **Document type:** *Magazine, Consumer.*
Former titles (until 2008): Auto Tip Extra (1214-6323); (until 2003): Auto Exclusive (1212-1681)
Published by: Axel Springer Praha a.s., Rosmarin Business Center, Dilnicka 12, Prague 7, 17000, Czech Republic. TEL 420-2-34692111, FAX 420-2-34692102. Ed. Vitezslav Kodym. Adv. contact Petra Kardova. Circ: 20,000 (paid). **Subscr. to:** SEND Predplatne s.r.o., PO Box 141, Prague 4 140 21, Czech Republic. TEL 420-225-985225, FAX 420-225-341425, send@send.cz.

388.3 AUT ISSN 0001-2688
AUTO TOURING. Text in German. 1947. m. membership. adv. illus. 100 p./no.; **Document type:** *Magazine, Consumer.*
Published by: (Oesterreichischer Automobil-, Motorrad- und Touring-Club DEU), Oe A M T C Verlag GmbH, Tauchnergasse 5, Klosterneuburg, N 3400, Austria. TEL 43-2243-4042700, FAX 43-2243-4042721, autotouring.verlag@oeamtc.at, http://www.oeamtc.at. Ed. Peter Pisecker. Adv. contact Gerhard Schinhan. B&W page EUR 13,800, color page EUR 20,700; trim 185 x 250. Circ: 1,291,845 (paid and controlled).

388 NZL
AUTO TRADER. Text in English. 1981. w. NZD 199 (effective 2008). adv. **Document type:** *Magazine, Consumer.* **Description:** Features thousand's of New Zealand's best cars for sale and the latest in road tests and motorsport news.
Published by: A C P Media New Zealand (Subsidiary of: A C P Magazines Ltd.), Private Bag 92512, Auckland, 1036, New Zealand. TEL 64-9-3082700, FAX 64-9-3082878. Adv. contact Glen Spry.

388.3 USA
AUTO TRADER. Text in English. 1991. w. free (effective 2011). **Document type:** *Magazine, Trade.*
Published by: Trader Publishing Co., 150 Granby St, Norfolk, VA 23510. TEL 757-640-4020, http://www.traderonline.com/.

629.11 IRL
AUTO TRADER. Text in English. w. adv. **Document type:** *Magazine, Consumer.*
Published by: Auto Trader Ireland, Unit 1, Bracken Business Park, Bracken Rd., Sandyford, Dublin, 18, Ireland. TEL 353-1-2950787, FAX 353-1-2950812. adv.: color page EUR 1,158. Circ: 38,668 (paid and controlled).

388 USA ISSN 1548-3223
TL152.5
AUTO TRAVEL IN THE U.S. Text in English. 2004. irreg. USD 225 per issue to non-members; USD 135 per issue to members (effective 2009). **Document type:** *Monographic series, Trade.* **Description:** Provides a detailed profile of U.S. trips that are taken by owned cars and trucks, camper/recreation vehicles and rental cars as primary modes of transportation.
Related titles: Online - full text ed.: ISSN 1549-7984.
Published by: Travel Industry Association of America, 1100 New York Ave, NW, Ste 450, Washington, DC 20005. TEL 202-408-8422, FAX 202-408-1255, feedback@tia.org.

388.3 USA ISSN 1049-9601
TL1
AUTO TRIM & RESTYLING NEWS; maintenance and repair of auto upholstery, etc. Abbreviated title: A T R N. Text in English. 1953. 11/school-academic yr. USD 19.95 domestic; USD 60 in Canada; USD 90 elsewhere (effective 2008). adv. bk.rev. charts; illus. back issues avail.; reprints avail. **Document type:** *Magazine, Trade.* **Description:** Provides innovative ideas and programs that enhance and strengthen the auto trim and restyling industry.
Formerly (until 1990): Auto Trim News (0005-0865)
Related titles: Online - full text ed.
—CCC.
Published by: (National Association of Auto Trim Shops), Bobit Business Media, 3520 Challenger St, Torrance, CA 90503. TEL 310-533-2400, FAX 310-533-2500, order@bobit.com, http://www.bobit.com. Ed. Mark Becker. Adv. contact Brett Potter TEL 310-533-2578. Circ: 9,000.

629.2 GRC ISSN 1108-779X
AUTO TRITI. Text in Greek. 1993. w. EUR 1.98 newsstand/cover (effective 2006). adv. **Document type:** *Magazine, Consumer.*
Published by: Motorpress Hellas (Subsidiary of: Gruner + Jahr AG & Co), 132 Lefkis Str, Krioneri, 14568, Greece. TEL 30-210-6262000, FAX 30-210-6262401, info@motorpress.gr, http://www.motorpress.gr. Circ: 43,000 (paid).

629.2 GRC
AUTO TRITI 4 X 4 & S U V TEST BOOK. Text in Greek. 2005. a. EUR 5.95 newsstand/cover (effective 2006). adv. **Document type:** *Magazine, Consumer.*
Published by: Motorpress Hellas (Subsidiary of: Gruner + Jahr AG & Co), 132 Lefkis Str, Krioneri, 14568, Greece. TEL 30-210-6262000, FAX 30-210-6262401, info@motorpress.gr, http://www.motorpress.gr. Circ: 35,000 (paid and controlled).

629.2 GRC ISSN 1108-7684
AUTO TRITI AGGELIES. Text in Greek. 1993. fortn. EUR 2.95 newsstand/cover (effective 2006). adv.
Published by: Motorpress Hellas (Subsidiary of: Gruner + Jahr AG & Co), 132 Lefkis Str, Krioneri, 14568, Greece. TEL 30-210-6262000, FAX 30-210-6262401, info@motorpress.gr, http://www.motorpress.gr. Circ: 25,000 (paid).

TU

629.2 GRC
AUTO TRITI BEST VALUE FOR MONEY. Text in Greek. 2004. a. EUR 4.95 newsstand/cover (effective 2006). adv. **Document type:** *Magazine, Consumer.*
Published by: Motorpress Hellas (Subsidiary of: Gruner + Jahr AG & Co), 132 Lefkis Str, Krioneri, 14568, Greece. TEL 30-210-6262000, FAX 30-210-6262401, info@motorpress.gr, http://www.motorpress.gr. Circ: 35,000 (paid and controlled).

629.2 GRC
AUTO TRITI EPAGGELMATIKA. Text in Greek. 2002. m. EUR 2.95 newsstand/cover (effective 2006). adv. **Document type:** *Magazine, Consumer.*
Published by: Motorpress Hellas (Subsidiary of: Gruner + Jahr AG & Co), 132 Lefkis Str, Krioneri, 14568, Greece. TEL 30-210-6262000, FAX 30-210-6262401, info@motorpress.gr, http://www.motorpress.gr. Circ: 17,000 (paid and controlled).

629.2 GRC
AUTO TRITI EPAGGELMATIKA TEST BOOK. Text in Greek. 2005. a. EUR 5.95 newsstand/cover (effective 2006). adv. **Document type:** *Magazine, Trade.*
Published by: Motorpress Hellas (Subsidiary of: Gruner + Jahr AG & Co), 132 Lefkis Str, Krioneri, 14568, Greece. TEL 30-210-6262000, FAX 30-210-6262401, info@motorpress.gr, http://www.motorpress.gr. Circ: 35,000 (paid and controlled).

629.2 GRC
AUTO TRITI IKANOPIISI KATOCHOU. Text in Greek. 2004. a. EUR 4.95 newsstand/cover (effective 2006). adv. **Document type:** *Magazine, Consumer.*
Published by: Motorpress Hellas (Subsidiary of: Gruner + Jahr AG & Co), 132 Lefkis Str, Krioneri, 14568, Greece. TEL 30-210-6262000, FAX 30-210-6262401, info@motorpress.gr, http://www.motorpress.gr. Circ: 35,000 (paid and controlled).

629.2 GRC ISSN 1108-7803
AUTO TRITI TEST BOOK. Text in Greek. 1995. 2/yr. EUR 5.95 newsstand/cover (effective 2006). adv. **Document type:** *Magazine, Consumer.*
Published by: Motorpress Hellas (Subsidiary of: Gruner + Jahr AG & Co), 132 Lefkis Str, Krioneri, 14568, Greece. TEL 30-210-6262000, FAX 30-210-6262401, info@motorpress.gr, http://www.motorpress.gr. Circ: 35,000 (paid).

629.2 GRC ISSN 1108-7811
AUTO TRITI TOURING. Text in Greek. 1994. 2/yr. EUR 5.95 newsstand/cover (effective 2006). adv. **Document type:** *Magazine, Consumer.*
Published by: Motorpress Hellas (Subsidiary of: Gruner + Jahr AG & Co), 132 Lefkis Str, Krioneri, 14568, Greece. TEL 30-210-6262000, FAX 30-210-6262401, info@motorpress.gr, http://www.motorpress.gr. Circ: 35,000 (paid).

629.2 GRC
AUTO TRITI VOREIA ELLADA. Text in Greek. 1995. m. **Document type:** *Magazine, Consumer.*
Published by: Motorpress Hellas (Subsidiary of: Gruner + Jahr AG & Co), 132 Lefkis Str, Krioneri, 14568, Greece. TEL 30-210-6262000, FAX 30-210-6262401, info@motorpress.gr, http://www.motorpress.gr. Circ: 16,000 (controlled).

629.286 ITA ISSN 1971-0232
AUTO TUNING. Text in Italian. 2006. s-a. **Document type:** *Magazine, Consumer.*
Published by: Eurosport Editoriale, Via della Bufalotta 378, Rome, 00139, Italy. TEL 39-06-45231508, FAX 39-06-45231599, info@eurosporteditoriale.com, http://www.eurosporteditoriale.com.

388 AUT
AUTO UND WIRTSCHAFT. Text in German. 1988. 11/yr. EUR 68; EUR 8 newsstand/cover (effective 2005). adv. **Document type:** *Magazine, Trade.*
Published by: Auto und Wirtschaft Verlag GmbH, Inkustr 16, Klosterneuburg, 3403, Austria. TEL 43-2243-368400, FAX 43-2243-36840593. Ed. Lutz Holzinger. Pub. Helmut Lederer. Adv. contact Andreas Dusovsky. B&W page EUR 2,850, color page EUR 4,240; trim 180 x 255. Circ: 13,500 (paid and controlled).

AUTO WEEKLY. *see* BUSINESS AND ECONOMICS

620 DEU ISSN 0944-5005
AUTO WELT. Text in German. 1970. 2/yr. EUR 6 newsstand/cover (effective 2006). adv. **Document type:** *Magazine, Consumer.*
Published by: Pro Publica International Verlag GmbH, Hansaallee 289, Duesseldorf, 40549, Germany. TEL 49-211-5581866, FAX 49-211-5578657, http://www.peil-pp.de. adv.: B&W page EUR 9,350, color page EUR 11,000. Circ: 100,000 (paid and controlled).

796.7 IRL ISSN 1393-7634
AUTO WOMAN. Text in English. 1998. q. adv. **Document type:** *Magazine, Consumer.*
Published by: Auto Ireland, Rattoo House, 1a Palmerston Villas, Rathmines, Dublin, 6, Ireland. TEL 353-1-4965439, FAX 353-1-4965995. adv.: B&W page EUR 1,400, color page EUR 1,700. Circ: 17,500 (paid and controlled).

796.77 USA
AUTO WORLD MAGAZINE. Variant title: A M I Auto World Magazine. Text in English. 2000 (Jun.). m. adv. **Document type:** *Magazine, Consumer.* **Description:** Presents information and articles on various new car models.
Formerly (until 2001): A M I's Auto World Weekly (1529-9082)
Published by: American Media, Inc., 4950 Communication Ave, Ste 100, Boca Raton, FL 33431. TEL 212-743-6527, 800-998-0731, kslivken@amilink.com, http://www.americanmediainc.com. Ed. William Jeanes. Pub., Adv. contact Steve Harrison.

388.3 DEU ISSN 0171-8452
TL3
AUTO ZEITUNG. Text in German. 1969. fortn. EUR 52; EUR 2 newsstand/cover (effective 2010). adv. bk.rev. charts; illus. **Document type:** *Magazine, Consumer.*
Incorporates (1951-1999): Kraftfahrzuegtechnik (0023-4419); Formerly (until 1971): Deutsche Auto Zeitung (0171-8444)
Published by: Heinrich Bauer Smaragd KG (Subsidiary of: Bauer Media Group), Charles-de-Gaulle-Str 8, Munich, 81737, Germany. TEL 49-89-67860, FAX 49-89-6702033, kommunikation@hbv.de, http://www.hbv.de. Ed. Volker Koerdt. Adv. contact Martin Rabe. color page EUR 20,885. Circ: 214,184 (paid and controlled).

388 DEU
AUTO ZUBEHOER MARKT: AUTOFAHRERHANDBUCH. Text in German. 1995. a. adv. **Document type:** *Magazine, Consumer.* **Description:** Contains information on activities and services associated with long car trips.
Published by: Verlag Kaufhold GmbH, Philipp-Nicolai-Weg 3, Herdecke, 58313, Germany. TEL 49-2330-918311, FAX 49-2330-13570, info@verlag-kaufhold.de, http://www.verlag-kaufhold.de. Ed. Claudia Pfleging. Pub. Manfred Kaufhold. Adv. contact Selina Wannke. B&W page EUR 2,310, color page EUR 3,600; trim 105 x 148. Circ: 100,000 (paid).

629.286 338.476 DEU ISSN 0939-7329
AUTO ZUBEHOER MARKT: DIE SONDERSEITEN; unabhaengige Monatszeitschrift fuer den Fachhandel Auto - Teile - Zubehoer. Text in German. 1988. 9/yr. EUR 30 (effective 2004). adv. **Document type:** *Magazine, Trade.*
Published by: Verlag Kaufhold GmbH, Philipp-Nicolai-Weg 3, Herdecke, 58313, Germany. TEL 49-2330-91830, FAX 49-2330-13570, info@verlag-kaufhold.de, http://www.verlag-kaufhold.de. Ed., R&P Claudia Pfleging. Pub. Manfred Kaufhold. Adv. contact Selina Wannke. B&W page EUR 1,693, color page EUR 2,237; trim 184 x 265. Circ: 3,000.

629.33 SVK ISSN 1336-7900
AUTO ZURNAL. Text in Slovak. 1992. m. EUR 0.66 newsstand/cover (effective 2011). adv. **Document type:** *Magazine, Consumer.*
Published by: Car Press, Bellova 4, Bratislava, 831 01, Slovakia. TEL 421-02-54772971, FAX 421-02-62316136.

796.75 CZE ISSN 1214-6781
AUTO7. Text in Czech. 2004. w. CZK 741 (effective 2009). adv. **Document type:** *Magazine, Consumer.*
Published by: Motor-Presse Bohemia, U Krcskeho Nadrazi 36, Prague 4, 14000, Czech Republic. TEL 420-2-24109340, FAX 420-2-41721905, motorpresse@motorpresse.cz, http://www.motorpresse.cz. Ed. Jan Blasek. Adv. contact Renata Ben. page CZK 110,000; trim 210 x 297. Circ: 43,000 (paid).

388 GBR ISSN 1360-9416
AUTOASIA. Text in English. 1992. bi-m. GBP 450, USD 725; includes AutoAsia Data. adv. back issues avail. **Document type:** *Magazine, Trade.* **Description:** Covers Asia's automotive industry.
Former titles: Asian Auto Digest (1355-6118); (until 1994): Japan Auto Digest
Related titles: Online - full text ed.
Published by: Newspeed, South Pavilion, 31 Oval Rd, London, NW1 7EA, United Kingdom. TEL 44-171-4289220, FAX 44-171-4289171. Ed. Paul Fisher. Adv. contact Stephen Fisher. **Subscr. to:** AutoAsia, Alban House, Brownfields, Welwyn Garden City, Herts AL7 1AY, United Kingdom. TEL 44-1707-320598, FAX 44-1707-320626.

388 GBR ISSN 1462-4095
AUTOASIA DATA. Text in English. m. GBP 450, USD 725; includes AutoAsia. adv. **Document type:** *Report, Trade.* **Description:** Includes details of sales by maker and vehicle type right across the Asia-Pacific region.
Related titles: Online - full text ed.
Published by: Newspeed, South Pavilion, 31 Oval Rd, London, NW1 7EA, United Kingdom. TEL 44-171-4289220, FAX 44-171-4289171. Ed. Paul Fisher. Adv. contact Stephen Fisher. **Subscr. to:** AutoAsia, Alban House, Brownfields, Welwyn Garden City, Herts AL7 1AY, United Kingdom. TEL 44-1707-320598, FAX 44-1707-320626.

388.3 629.2 DNK ISSN 1903-4695
AUTOBRANCHEN.INFO. Text in Danish. 2004. 10/yr. DKK 619 (effective 2008). adv. index. reprints avail. **Document type:** *Journal, Trade.*
Formerly (until 2008): Autobranchen (1603-970X); Which was formed by the merger of (1946-2004): Bil og Motor (0006-2332); (1991-2004): Auto (0906-4419); Which was formed by the merger of (1939-1991): Motor-Service (0906-5032); Which was formerly (until 1988): Motor-Service & Autoteknisk Tidsskrift (0027-1993); (1967-1991): Lak & Karrosseri (0905-9326); Which was formerly (until 1989): F A I Bladet (0903-0514)
Related titles: Online - full text ed.: ISSN 1903-4709. 2004.
Published by: Autobranchen I/S, Islands Brygge 26, Copenhagen S, 2300, Denmark. TEL 45-32-630460, FAX 45-32-630464, fai@fai.dk. Ed. Erik Holme Bertelsen. Adv. contact Anita Rasmussen. Circ: 5,450.

AUTOBUS. *see* TRANSPORTATION

388.3 ITA ISSN 1973-7807
AUTOCAPITAL S U V. (Sport Utility Vehicle) Text in Italian. 1996. m. **Document type:** *Magazine, Consumer.*
Former titles (until 2008): Off Road Capital (1827-6261); (until 2006): Auto in 4 X 4 (1124-707X)
Published by: Piscopo Editore Srl, Via di Villa Sacchetti 11, Rome, 00197, Italy. TEL 39-06-3200105, FAX 39-06-3200143, http://www.piscopoeditore.it. Ed. Alberto Franzoni.

388.3 GBR ISSN 1355-8293
TL1
AUTOCAR. Text in English. 1988. w. GBP 95.63 (effective 2009). adv. bk.rev. charts; illus.; stat. index. back issues avail.; reprints avail. **Document type:** *Magazine, Consumer.* **Description:** Specializes in revealing details of secret new cars. Its famous road tests, invented by the magazine 75 years ago, are used by industry and consumers alike as the authoritative benchmark.
Formerly (until 1994): Autocar and Motor (0955-5889); Which was formed by the merger of (1903-1988): Motor (0143-6945); Which was formerly (until 1903): Motor Cycling; (1895-1988): Autocar (0005-092X)
Related titles: Microfilm ed.: (from BHP); Microform ed.: (from PMC, PQC); Online - full text ed.
Indexed: E11, G08, HRIS, I05, T04.
—BLDSC (1828.000000), IE, Infotrieve, Linda Hall. **CCC.**
Published by: Haymarket Publishing Ltd. (Subsidiary of: Haymarket Media Group), Teddington Studios, Broom Rd, Teddington, Middlesex, TW11 9BE, United Kingdom. TEL 44-20-82675630, FAX 44-20-82675759, info@haymarket.com, http://www.haymarket.com. Eds. Chas Hallett TEL 44-20-82675735, Steve Cropley. Adv. contact Julia Dear TEL 44-20-82675739. Circ: 52,366. **Subscr. to:** PO Box 568, Haywards Heath RH16 3XQ, United Kingdom. TEL 44-8456-777800, Haymarket.subs@qss-uk.com, http://www.themagazineshop.com.

629.3 CZE ISSN 1803-2273
AUTOCAR. Text in Czech. 2002. w. CZK 1,435 (effective 2011). adv. **Document type:** *Magazine, Consumer.*
Former titles (until 2008): Carauto (1214-987X); (until 2005): Autocar (1213-9688)
Published by: Stratosfera s.r.o., Drtinova 8, Prague 5, 150 00, Czech Republic. TEL 420-234-109540, FAX 420-234-109264, online@stratosfera.cz, http://www.stratosfera.cz. Adv. contact Martina Palkoskova. Circ: 11,219 (paid and controlled). **Subscr. to:** SEND Predplatne s.r.o., PO Box 141, Prague 4 140 21, Czech Republic. TEL 420-225-985225, FAX 420-225-341425, send@send.cz, http://www.send.cz.

796.7 ITA ISSN 1828-339X
AUTOCAR - ITALIA. Text in Italian. 2006. m. adv. **Document type:** *Magazine, Consumer.*
Published by: De Agostini Editore, Via G da Verrazzano 15, Novara, 28100, Italy. TEL 39-0321-4241, FAX 39-0321-424305, info@deagostini.it, http://www.deagostini.it.

629.26 ESP ISSN 1699-1990
AUTOCASION CATALUNA. Text in Spanish. 2005. m. adv. **Document type:** *Magazine, Trade.*
Published by: MaxiPress Comunicacion, C Pasaje de Biscal, 6 1o A, Madrid, 28028, Spain. TEL 34-91-7262748, FAX 34-91-3615030, info@autocasion.com, http://www.autocasion.com/.

388 ARG ISSN 0329-3335
AUTOCATALOGO. Text in Spanish. 1996. a. ARS 10 newsstand/cover (effective 2001). adv. **Document type:** *Magazine, Consumer.* **Description:** Contains descriptions and reviews of car models from all over the world.
Published by: Motorpress Argentina, S.A. (Subsidiary of: Gruner + Jahr AG & Co), Ituzaingo, 642-648, Buenos Aires, 1141, Argentina. TEL 54-114-3077672, FAX 54-114-3077858. Ed. Carlos Figueras. Pub. Jesus Carrera. Adv. contact Adrian Lualdi. Circ: 13,000 (paid).

629.22 BEL ISSN 0778-3574
AUTOCCASION. Text in French. 1987. bi-w. adv. **Document type:** *Newspaper.*
Published by: Maxipress S.A., Rue Broodcoorens 52, La Hulpe, 1310, Belgium. TEL 32-2-6520020, FAX 32-2-6521129. Circ: 35,000 (controlled).

629.11 UKR ISSN 1605-5330
AUTOCENTRE. Text in Ukrainian. 1997. w. adv. **Document type:** *Magazine, Consumer.*
Related titles: Online - full text ed.: ISSN 1563-647X. 1998.
Published by: Autocentre Ltd., PO Box 2, Kiev, 03047, Ukraine. TEL 380-44-4596001, FAX 380-44-4584404, info@autocentr.kiev.ua.

796.77 DEU ISSN 1867-9838
AUTOCLASSIC. Text in German. 2006. bi-m. EUR 21; EUR 4.20 newsstand/cover (effective 2010). adv. **Document type:** *Magazine, Consumer.*
Published by: GeraMond Verlag GmbH, Infanteriestr 11a, Munich, 80797, Germany. TEL 49-89-1306990, FAX 49-89-130699100, info@geramond.de, http://www.geramond.de. Adv. contact Judith Fischl. color page EUR 3,350. Circ: 64,800 (paid and controlled).

388.3 ARG ISSN 0005-0946
AUTOCLUB; revista del automovilismo, turismo e informaciones. Text in Spanish. 1961. q. membership. adv. bk.rev. abstr.; charts; illus.; mkt.; stat.; tr.lit. **Document type:** *Magazine, Consumer.*
Published by: Automovil Club Argentino, Ave del Libertador 1850, 3er Piso, Buenos Aires, 1425, Argentina. TEL 54-114-8026061, FAX 54-114-8027282, http://www.aca.org.ar. Ed. Carlos A Vaquer. Circ: 450,000.

AUTOCOURSE; the world's leading Grand Prix annual. *see* SPORTS AND GAMES

629.3 CZE ISSN 1801-6766
AUTODESIGN & STYLING. Text in Czech. 2006. bi-m. CZK 640 (effective 2011). adv. **Document type:** *Magazine, Consumer.*
Published by: Signum, PO Box 21, Roztoky u Prahy, 25263, Czech Republic. Ed. Radek Laube. Pub., Adv. contact Jindrich Dusek.

796 FRA ISSN 2106-329X
▼ **AUTODIVA.** Text in French. 2009. q. **Document type:** *Magazine, Consumer.*
Address: 54 Rue Chevreul, Lyon, 69007, France.

629.2 AUS ISSN 1444-8599
AUTOENGINEER AUSTRALASIA. Text in English. 1940. q. AUD 90 domestic; AUD 110 foreign (effective 2008). adv. bk.rev. illus. index. back issues avail. **Document type:** *Magazine, Trade.* **Description:** Automotive industry news, reports and analysis, technical briefings for automotive engineers, workshop personnel, enthusiasts, tradesmen.
Former titles (until 2000): S A E - Australasia (0036-0651); (until 1967): I A A E Journal
Indexed: ARI, HRIS.
—BLDSC (1828.148000), IE, Ingenta.
Published by: Society of Automotive Engineers, Suite 3, 21 Vale St, North Melbourne, VIC 3051, Australia. TEL 61-3-93267166, FAX 61-3-93267244, enquiries@sae-a.com.au. Circ: 3,500.

796.77 629.2 BRA ISSN 1413-9308
AUTOESPORTE. Text in Portuguese. 1964. m. BRL 87 (effective 2005). adv. illus. **Document type:** *Magazine, Consumer.* **Description:** Reviews sports cars and other vehicles of interest to car aficianados.
Related titles: Online - full text ed.
Published by: Editora Globo S.A., Av. Jaguare 1487, Sao Paulo, SP 05346 902, Brazil. TEL 55-11-37677400, FAX 55-11-37677870, atendimento@edglobo.com.br, http://editoraglobo.globo.com. adv.: page BRL 38,600. Circ: 65,000.

629.331 CZE ISSN 1211-2380
AUTOEXPERT. Text in Czech. 1995. 10/yr. CZK 750 (effective 2011). adv. **Document type:** *Magazine, Trade.* **Description:** Contains technical information on car repair, service and motor vehicle sales.
Published by: Autopress, s. r. o., U Seradiste 7, Prague, 10100, Czech Republic. TEL 420-2-67216122, FAX 420-2-67216103, autopress@autopress.cz, http://www.autopress.cz. Ed. Jaromir Martinec TEL 420-2-67216122. Adv. contact Eliska Loufkova.

388.3 USA
AUTOEXTREMIST.COM; the bare-knuckled, unvarnished, high-octane truth. Text in English. 1999. w. adv. back issues avail. **Document type:** *Magazine, Trade.* **Description:** Reports on news and issues about the automotive industry.
Media: Online - full content.
Published by: Autoextremist.com, Inc., P O Box 13, Birmingham, MI 48012. editor@autoextremist.com, http://www.autoextremist.com/.

388.3 DEU
AUTOFACHMANN. Text in German. 1952. 11/yr. EUR 82.20 domestic; EUR 90 foreign (effective 2010). adv. bk.rev. abstr.; charts; illus.; stat. cum.index. **Document type:** *Magazine, Trade.*
Formerly: Junghandwerker im Kraftfahrzeug Betrieb (0022-6432)
Published by: (Zentralverband des Kraftfahrzeughandwerks), Vogel Business Media GmbH & Co.KG, Max-Planck-Str 7-9, Wuerzburg, 97064, Germany. TEL 49-931-4180, FAX 49-931-4182750, info@vogel.de, http://www.vogel-media.de. Ed. Werner Degen. adv.: B&W page EUR 3,510, color page EUR 5,130; trim 190 x 270. Circ: 64,904 (paid and controlled).

629.222 NOR ISSN 1503-318X
AUTOFIL. Text in Norwegian. 2002. 11/yr. NOK 499 (effective 2009). adv. **Document type:** *Magazine, Consumer.*
Published by: Aller Forlag AS, Stenersgaten 2, Sentrum, Oslo, 0189, Norway. TEL 47-21-301000, FAX 47-21-301205, allerforlag@aller.no, http://www.aller.no. adv.: page NOK 44,000; bleed 234 x 305. Circ: 30,569 (paid).

629.2 NZL ISSN 0112-3475
AUTOFILE. Text in English. 1979. w. NZD 255 (effective 2008). **Document type:** *Newsletter, Consumer.*
Formerly (until 1984): Auto Industry Data (0112-0069)
Published by: Armada Publishing Ltd., Parnell, PO Box 37745, Auckland, New Zealand. TEL 64-9-3772114, FAX 64-9-3772115, info@armadapublishing.co.nz?, http://www.armadapublishing.co.nz/.

388.3 DEU ISSN 0948-6682
AUTOFLOTTE; das Fachmagazin fuer Unternehmensmobilitaet. Text in German. 1995. m. EUR 54.90 domestic; EUR 60.90 foreign; EUR 5.50 newsstand/cover (effective 2008). adv. **Document type:** *Magazine, Trade.*
Published by: Springer Automotive Media (Subsidiary of: Springer Fachmedien Muenchen GmbH), Neumarkter Str 18, Munich, 81673, Germany. TEL 49-89-43721121, FAX 49-89-43721266, vertriebsservice@springer.com, http://www.springerautomotivemedia.de. adv.: B&W page EUR 4,689, color page EUR 5,985. Circ: 31,555 (paid and controlled).

796.77 CZE ISSN 1212-351X
AUTOFORUM. Text in Czech. 1998. bi-m. CZK 333 (effective 2011). adv. **Document type:** *Magazine, Consumer.*
Published by: MotorCom s.r.o., Nam 14 rijna 1307/2, Prague 5, 15000, Czech Republic. FAX 420-2-57210770.

629.286 DEU ISSN 1865-8644
DAS AUTOGAS JOURNAL. Text in German. 2008. bi-m. EUR 21; EUR 3.90 newsstand/cover (effective 2009). adv. **Document type:** *Magazine, Trade.*
Published by: Dr. Martin Steffan Media, Markgrafenstr 3-5, Bielefeld, 33602, Germany. TEL 49-521-5251310, FAX 49-521-5251311. Circ: 19,168 (paid and controlled).

388.3 BEL ISSN 0773-3380
DE AUTOGIDS. Text and summaries in Dutch. 1979. bi-w. EUR 78 domestic; EUR 160 in the European Union; EUR 186 elsewhere (effective 2005). adv. bk.rev. mkt.; stat. back issues avail. **Document type:** *Consumer.* **Description:** Gives a detailed and objective view of the motoring world for the reader and consumer.
Related titles: Online - full text ed.
Published by: Uitgeverij Auto - Magazine N.V., Gen Dumonceaulaan 56-1, Brussels, 1190, Belgium. TEL 32-2-333-3229, FAX 32-2-333-3210, contact@automagazine.be. Ed. Anthony Verhelle. Pub. Eric Decroix. Adv. contact Myriam Merckx. Circ: 45,000.

AUTOGLASS. *see* CERAMICS, GLASS AND POTTERY

629.222 IND
AUTOGUIDE. Text in English. 1966. m. INR 250 domestic; USD 50 foreign (effective 2001); INR 40 per issue (effective 2011). adv. 100 p./no. 3 cols./p.; **Document type:** *Journal, Trade.*
Address: 1010 Faiz Rd, Karol Bagh, New Delhi, t 110 005, India. TEL 91-11-41051000, FAX 91-11-41051005, autoguide@autoguideindia.com.

659.132 CZE ISSN 1212-6284
AUTOHANDL. Text in Czech. 1999. m. CZK 348 (effective 2010). adv. **Document type:** *Magazine, Trade.*
Published by: Annonce Prague, Na Porici 30, Prague 1, 11406, Czech Republic. TEL 420-2-21626216, FAX 420-2-21626678, redakce@annonce.cz, http://www.annonce.cz.

388.3 DEU ISSN 0005-0989
AUTOHAUS. Text in German. 1957. fortn. EUR 174.90, EUR 196.90; EUR 9.30 newsstand/cover (effective 2008). adv. bk.rev. charts; illus.; tr.lit. **Document type:** *Magazine, Trade.*
—CCC.
Published by: (Zentralverband Deutsches Kfz-Gewerbe e.V.), Springer Automotive Media (Subsidiary of: Springer Fachmedien Muenchen GmbH), Neumarkter Str 18, Munich, 81673, Germany. TEL 49-89-43721121, FAX 49-89-43721266, vertriebsservice@springer.com, http://www.springerautomotivemedia.de. Ed. Hannes Brachat. adv.: B&W page EUR 5,495, color page EUR 7,447. Circ: 18,232 (paid and controlled).

796.77 CZE ISSN 1212-8791
AUTOHIT. Text in Czech. 2000. fortn. CZK 455 domestic; CZK 24.90 newsstand/cover (effective 2010). adv. **Document type:** *Magazine, Consumer.* **Description:** Contains extensive new and used car comparisons, repair shop and tire tests, service and personal tips, as well as travel information and insurance advice.
Related titles: ◆ Supplement(s): Autohit Special.
Published by: Burda Praha spol. s.r.o., Premyslovska 2845/43, Prague 2, 13000, Czech Republic. TEL 420-2-21589111, FAX 420-2-21589368, burda@burda.cz, http://www.burda.cz.

796.77 CZE
AUTOHIT SPECIAL. Text in Czech. s-a. included with subscr. to Autohit. adv. **Document type:** *Magazine, Consumer.*
Related titles: ◆ Supplement to: Autohit. ISSN 1212-8791.
Published by: Burda Praha spol. s.r.o., Premyslovska 2845/43, Prague 2, 13000, Czech Republic. TEL 420-2-21589111, FAX 420-2-21589368, burda@burda.cz, http://www.burda.cz.

AUTOHOF GUIDE. *see* TRAVEL AND TOURISM

388 PRT
AUTOHOJE CATALOGO. Text in Portuguese. 1992. a. EUR 5 newsstand/cover (effective 2005). adv. **Document type:** *Magazine, Consumer.*
Published by: Motorpress Lisboa, SA (Subsidiary of: Gruner + Jahr AG & Co), Rua Policarpio Anjos No. 4, Cruz Quebrada, Dafundo 1495-742, Portugal. TEL 351-21-4154500, FAX 351-21-4154501, buzine@motorpress.pt, http://www.mpl.pt. Circ: 30,000 (paid).

629.2 USA ISSN 1047-5559
AUTOINC. Text in English. 1952. m. USD 25 domestic; USD 30 in Canada & Mexico; USD 85 elsewhere (effective 2005). adv. stat.; tr.lit. 52 p./no. 3 cols./p.; back issues avail. **Document type:** *Magazine, Trade.* **Description:** Covers industry issues that relate to the automotive repair business. Includes legislative, technical and management articles.
Former titles (until 1989): Automotive Independent (0199-6908); Independent Garageman
Related titles: Online - full text ed.
Published by: Automotive Service Association, PO Box 929, Bedford, TX 76095-0929. TEL 817-283-6205, 800-272-7467, FAX 817-685-0225, asainfo@asashop.org, http://www.asashop.org. Ed. Leona Dalavai Scott. Pub. Angie Wilson. Adv. contact Kevin Ploetz. B&W page USD 2,154, color page USD 3,832; trim 10.88 x 8.38. Circ: 14,000 (paid).

629.286 MEX
AUTOINDUSTRIA. Text in Spanish. 1971. m. adv. bk.rev.
Published by: Grupo Editorial Aviare, Queretaro 229, Desp. 402, Apdo. 71339, Mexico City, DF 06700, Mexico. TEL 5-584-31-94, FAX 2-584-48-21. Ed. Alfredo Villagran Arevalo. Circ: 30,384.

AUTOJOURNALIST. *see* JOURNALISM

388.3 NLD ISSN 0005-0997
AUTOKAMPIOEN. Text in Dutch. 1908. 24/yr. EUR 84 to non-members; EUR 71.45 to members (effective 2008). adv. Website rev. bibl.; charts; illus.; mkt.; stat. **Document type:** *Consumer.*
Formerly (until 1930): Motorkampioen
—IE, Infotrieve.
Published by: (ANWB BV/Royal Dutch Touring Club), Algemene Nederlandse Wielrijders Bond (A N W B) Media/Dutch Automobile Association Media, Postbus 93200, The Hague, 2509 BA, Netherlands. TEL 31-70-3141470, FAX 31-70-3146538, http://www.anwbmedia.nl. adv.: B&W page EUR 3,530, color page EUR 5,200; bleed 215 x 300. Circ: 37,648.

388.3 DEU ISSN 0174-6863
AUTOKAUFMANN. Text in German. 1983. 11/yr. EUR 119.40 domestic; EUR 127.20 foreign (effective 2010). adv. abstr.; charts; illus.; stat. index. **Document type:** *Journal, Trade.*
Published by: (Zentralverband des Kraftfahrzeuggewerbes), Vogel Business Media GmbH & Co.KG, Max-Planck-Str 7-9, Wuerzburg, 97064, Germany. TEL 49-931-4180, FAX 49-931-4182750, info@vogel.de, http://www.vogel-media.de. Ed. Werner Degen. adv.: B&W page EUR 3,510, color page EUR 5,130; trim 190 x 270. Circ: 11,230 (paid and controlled).

388 NLD ISSN 1385-6669
AUTOKOMPAS. Text in Dutch. 1989. 16/yr. EUR 70 domestic (effective 2009); EUR 90 foreign (effective 2005). adv. 52 p./no. 5 cols./p.; back issues avail. **Document type:** *Trade.*
Published by: RAI Langfords bv, Postbus 10099, Amsterdam, 1001 EB, Netherlands. TEL 31-20-5042800, FAX 31-20-5042888, http://www.railangfords.nl. Ed. Jos Veldhuisen. Pub. Rob Kuechler. Adv. contact Wim van Baal. B&W page EUR 2,230, color page EUR 2,660; trim 210 x 280. Circ: 20,102.

388.3 DEU ISSN 0937-3381
AUTOKOSTEN UND STEUERN AKTUELL; Kosten und Steuern. Text in German. 1977 (vol.11). a. **Document type:** *Directory, Consumer.*
Former titles (until 1990): A D A C Handbuch - Geschaeftswagen (0931-0053); (until 1987): Was Kostet der Geschaeftswagen? (0179-6097); (until 1980): Was Kostet Mein Auto?
Published by: (Allgemeiner Deutscher Automobil-Club e.V.), A D A C Verlag GmbH, Leonhard-Moll-Bogen 1, Munich, 81365, Germany. TEL 49-89-76760, FAX 49-89-76762500, verlag@adac.de, http://www.adac.de. Circ: 5,000.

388 USA
THE AUTOMARKET. Text in English. w. (Thu.). free. **Document type:** *Newspaper, Trade.*
Published by: Newspaper Publishers, Llc., 1035 Conklin Rd, Conklin, NY 13748. TEL 607-775-0472, FAX 607-775-5863. Ed. Elizabeth Einstein. Pub. Donald Einstein. Circ: 7,000 (paid and controlled).

HET AUTOMOBIEL; klassieker magazine. *see* ANTIQUES

388.3 NLD ISSN 0929-1083
AUTOMOBIEL MANAGEMENT; vakblad voor de automobielmanager. Text in Dutch. 1980. 22/yr. EUR 109.20 (effective 2009). adv. illus. **Document type:** *Trade.* **Description:** For managers and decision makers in the automotive and transport sector.
Published by: Uitgeverij Nassau (Subsidiary of: MYbusinessmedia b.v.), Postbus 58, Deventer, 7400 AB, Netherlands. TEL 31-570-504300, FAX 31-570-504399. Ed. Peter Brouwer TEL 31-570-504370. Pub. Pascal van Sluijs. adv.: B&W page EUR 2,745; trim 257 x 385. Circ: 11,000.

388.3 ZAF ISSN 0304-8721
HD9710.S7
AUTOMOBIL. Text and summaries in Afrikaans, English. 1909. m. ZAR 48. adv. bk.rev.
Formerly: Automobile in Southern Africa (0005-139X)
Published by: (Motor Industries' Federation), M & M Publications, PO Box 8859, Johannesburg, 2000, South Africa. TEL 27-11-880-5790, FAX 27-11-880-5789. Ed. R W Emslie. Circ: 9,833.

388.3 SWE ISSN 0280-1981
AUTOMOBIL. Text in Swedish. 1982. m. SEK 475 (effective 2004). adv. 84 p./no. 4 cols./p.; **Document type:** *Magazine, Consumer.*
Related titles: Online - full text ed.: ISSN 1402-893X.
Published by: O K Forlaget AB, Sveavaegen 155, PO Box 23800, Stockholm, 10435, Sweden. TEL 46-8-7361240, FAX 46-8-7652554. Ed. Eric Lund TEL 46-8-7361242. Adv. contact Cecilia Erman TEL 46-8-7361235. B&W page SEK 12,000, color page SEK 15,000; trim 173 x 244.

629.11 ROM ISSN 1582-5248
AUTOMOBIL. Text in Romanian. 2001. s-a. **Document type:** *Magazine, Consumer.*
Published by: Sapte Seri, Calea Mosilor nr. 296, bloc 46, scara 1, apartament 2, Bucharest, Romania. TEL 40-21-2116706, FAX 40-21-2102316.

629.286 DEU ISSN 0939-5326
AUTOMOBIL-ELEKTRONIK; Das Magazin fuer Manager in der Automobil-, Automobilzuliefer- und Elektronikindustrie. Text in German. 1989. bi-m. EUR 98 domestic; EUR 113 in Europe; EUR 19 newsstand/cover (effective 2010). adv. **Document type:** *Magazine, Trade.*
Published by: Verlag Moderne Industrie AG & Co. KG, Justus-von-Liebig-Str 1, Landsberg, 86899, Germany. TEL 49-8191-1250, FAX 49-8191-125211, info@mi-verlag.de, http://www.mi-verlag.de. Circ: 11,018 (paid and controlled).

629.2 DEU ISSN 0005-1306
TL3
AUTOMOBIL-INDUSTRIE; research, design, manufacturing. Text in German. 1955. 10/yr. EUR 117 domestic; EUR 123 foreign (effective 2010). adv. bk.rev. illus.; tr.lit. **Document type:** *Magazine, Trade.*
Related titles: Online - full text ed.
Indexed: A22, A28, APA, BrCerAb, C&ISA, CA/WCA, CIA, CerAb, CivEngAb, CorrAb, E&CAJ, E11, EEA, EMA, ESPM, EnvEAb, H15, IBR, IBZ, Inspec, M&TEA, M09, MBF, METADEX, SolStAb, T04, TM, WAA.
—IE, Infotrieve, INIST, Linda Hall. **CCC.**
Published by: Vogel Business Media GmbH & Co.KG, Max-Planck-Str 7-9, Wuerzburg, 97064, Germany. TEL 49-931-4180, FAX 49-931-4182750, info@vogel.de, http://www.vogel-media.de. Ed. Wilhelm Missler. adv.: B&W page EUR 4,140, color page EUR 5,760; trim 190 x 270. Circ: 14,878 (controlled). **Subscr. to:** DataM-Services GmbH, Fichtestr 9, Wuerzburg 97074, Germany. TEL 49-931-4170-01, FAX 49-931-4170499, swestenberger@datam-services.de, http://www.datam-services.de.

388.3 DEU ISSN 1614-3418
AUTOMOBIL JAHRBUCH. Text in German. 2000. a. adv. **Document type:** *Magazine, Consumer.*
Formerly (until 2004): Das Neue Automobil. Testjahrbuch (1616-0525)
Published by: A S Autoverlag GmbH (Subsidiary of: Axel Springer Verlag AG), Axel-Springer-Platz 1, Hamburg, 20350, Germany. TEL 49-40-34725934, FAX 49-40-34727073, dk@autoverlag.de, http://www.autojournal.de.

629.2305 DEU ISSN 1866-9131
AUTOMOBIL-KONSTRUKTION. Text in German. 2007. 4/yr. EUR 18.40 (effective 2011). adv. **Document type:** *Magazine, Trade.*
Published by: Konradin Verlag Robert Kohlhammer GmbH, Ernst Mey Str 8, Leinfelden-Echterdingen, 70771, Germany. TEL 49-711-75940, FAX 49-711-7594390, info@konradin.de, http://www.konradin.de. Ed. Herbert Neumann. Adv. contact Walter Schwager. Circ: 13,538 (paid).

338.476 DEU ISSN 0934-0394
AUTOMOBIL PRODUKTION; Management - Maerkte - Technologien. Text in German. 1987. bi-m. EUR 182 domestic; EUR 193 foreign; EUR 19 newsstand/cover (effective 2011). adv. **Document type:** *Magazine, Trade.* **Description:** Provides a forum for the German automotive and supplier industry as well as for all service providers and factory outfitters involved in automotive manufacturing.
Indexed: A22, B03.
—IE, Infotrieve. **CCC.**
Published by: Verlag Moderne Industrie AG & Co. KG, Justus-von-Liebig-Str 1, Landsberg, 86899, Germany. TEL 49-8191-1250, FAX 49-8191-125211, info@mi-verlag.de, http://www.mi-verlag.de. Ed. Bettin Mayer. Adv. contact Michael Klotz. color page EUR 5,740; trim 178 x 257. Circ: 15,628 (paid and controlled).

629.2 796.7 388.34 CZE ISSN 1211-9555
AUTOMOBIL REVUE; technicky mesicnik. Text in Czech, Slovak; Summaries in English, German, Russian. 1955. m. CZK 374 (effective 2008). adv. charts; illus. **Document type:** *Magazine, Consumer.*
Formerly (until 1992): Automobil (0404-3529)
Related titles: Supplement(s): Stavba Automobilu.
Published by: Springer Media CZ, s. r. o., Nadrazni 32, Prague, 15000, Czech Republic. TEL 420-2-25351212, FAX 420-2-25351404, predplatne@bmczech.cz, http://www.businessmedia.cz. Ed. Tomas Hyan. Circ: 60,000.

388 CAN ISSN 1711-7526
L'AUTOMOBILE; carrosserie et mecanique. Text in French. 2004. m. CAD 27.95 domestic; USD 41.95 foreign (effective 2008). **Document type:** *Magazine, Trade.*
Formed by the merger of (1939-2003): Automobile (0005-1330); (1999-2003): Bodyshop (1494-0124); Which was formerly (1994-1999): Carrossier (1199-8199)
Published by: Business Information Group, 12 Concorde Pl, Ste 800, Toronto, ON M3C 4J2, Canada. TEL 416-442-2122, 800-668-2374, FAX 416-442-2191, orders@businessinformationgroup.ca, http://www.businessinformationgroup.ca.

388.3 ITA ISSN 0005-1349
AUTOMOBILE. Text in Italian. 1945. m. adv. bk.rev.; film rev. charts; illus.; stat.; tr.lit. **Document type:** *Magazine, Consumer.*
Published by: (Automobile Club d'Italia), A C I Mondadori SpA, Via Cassanese 224, Segrate, MI 20090, Italy. TEL 39-02-26937550, FAX 39-02-26937560. Ed. Giancarlo Pini. Circ: 727,945 (controlled).

388.3 USA
AUTOMOBILE. Text in English. 1986. m. USD 10 domestic; USD 23 in Canada; USD 25 elsewhere (effective 2008). adv. illus. back issues avail.; reprints avail. **Document type:** *Magazine, Consumer.* **Description:** Focuses on taking interesting cars to interesting places and meeting interesting people along the way.
Former titles (until 1988): Automobile (0897-8360); (until 1987): Automobile Magazine (0894-3583)
Related titles: Online - full text ed.: USD 5 (effective 2008); Special ed(s).: Automobile Magazine's Guide to Buying & Leasing. USD 4.95 newsstand/cover (effective 2001); Automobile Magazine's Field Guide to Sport-Utility Vehicles, Pickups, & Vans.
Indexed: A10, A22, ASIP, G08, I05, S23, V03.
—CCC.
Published by: Source Interlink Companies, 6420 Wilshire Blvd, 10th Fl, Los Angeles, CA 90048. TEL 323-782-2000, FAX 323-782-2585, dheine@sourceinterlink.com, http://www.sourceinterlinkmedia.com. Eds. Gavin Conway, Jean Jennings. Pub. Brad Gerber TEL 323-782-2727. adv.: B&W page USD 66,480, color page USD 94,960; trim 8 x 10.8. Circ: 561,338 (paid).

TU

AUTOMOBILE ASSOCIATION MEMBERS HANDBOOK. *see* TRAVEL AND TOURISM

388 ZWE
AUTOMOBILE ASSOCIATION OF ZIMBABWE. MEMBERS' HANDBOOK. Text in English. 1923. biennial. membership. adv. **Description:** Information on services for members.
Published by: Automobile Association of Zimbabwe, Fanum House, Samora Machel Ave 57, PO Box 585, Harare, Zimbabwe. FAX 752552, TELEX 22167 ZW. Ed. J M Rowett. Adv. contact Mrs. F M Steblicki. Circ: 50,000.

388.3 USA
AUTOMOBILE DEALERS & THE LAW. Text in English. a. **Document type:** *Journal, Trade.*
Published by: W D & S Publishing, 10 W 7th St, 1st Fl, PO Box 606, Barnegat Light, NJ 08006. TEL 800-321-5312, http://www.dealersedge.com.

AUTOMOBILE DESIGN LIABILITY. *see* LAW

338 USA
THE AUTOMOBILE INDUSTRY: DOMESTIC & FOREIGN AUTO MANUFACTURERS. Text in English. 1992. a. **Description:** Examins the major foreign and domestic automobile manufacturers with an analysis of industry issues.
Published by: Dun & Bradstreet Information Services (Subsidiary of: Dun & Bradstreet, Inc.), 103 JFK Pkwy, Short Hills, NJ 07078. TEL 973-921-5500, 800-234-3867, SMSinfo@dnb.com, http://www.dnb.com.

338.476 JPN
THE AUTOMOBILE INDUSTRY - TOYOTA AND JAPAN. Text in English. 1972. a. free. charts; illus.; stat. **Document type:** *Corporate.*
Formerly: Motor Industry of Japan; Incorporates: Toyota in Brief
Indexed: JCT.
Published by: Toyota Motor Corporation, International Public Affairs Division, 1-4-18 Koraku, Bunkyo-ku, Tokyo, 112-0004, Japan. TEL 03-3817-9930, FAX 03-3817-9017. Circ: 15,000.

AUTOMOBILE INSURANCE LOSSES, COLLISION COVERAGES, VARIATIONS BY MAKE AND SERIES. *see* INSURANCE

388.342 796.7 FRA ISSN 0982-9156
L'AUTOMOBILE MAGAZINE. Text in French. 1945. m. EUR 51 (effective 2010). illus. Supplement avail. **Document type:** *Magazine, Consumer.* **Description:** Contains information on exclusive and in-depth tests for cars, guidance for choosing a better car, as well as details on major sporting events.
Formerly (until 1981): L' Automobile (0758-6957)
Indexed: A22.
—IE. **CCC.**
Published by: Motor Presse France, 12 rue Rouget de Lisle, Issy-les-Moulineaux, 92442, France. http://www.motorpresse.fr. Circ: 280,000 (paid).

388 FRA
L'AUTOMOBILE MAGAZINE HORS-SERIE - TOUTES LES VOITURES DU MONDE (YEAR). Text in French. 1978. irreg. **Document type:** *Magazine, Consumer.*
Published by: Motor Presse France, 12 rue Rouget de Lisle, Issy-les-Moulineaux, 92442, France. http://www.motorpresse.fr. Circ: 250,000 (paid).

796.77 USA
AUTOMOBILE MAGAZINE'S ULTIMATE NEW CAR GUIDE. Variant title: Ultimate New Car Guide. Text in English. 2008. a. USD 5.99 newsstand/cover (effective 2008). adv. **Document type:** *Guide, Consumer.* **Description:** Features reviews of every vehicle sold in America for enthusiasts and in-market buyers.
Published by: Source Interlink Companies, 261 Madison Ave, 6th Fl, New York, NY 10016. TEL 212-915-4000, FAX 212-915-4422, edisupport@sourceinterlink.com. Ed. Jean Jennings. adv.: B&W page USD 25,560, color page USD 29,210; trim 8.375 x 10.875.

629.2 FRA ISSN 1961-4047
L'AUTOMOBILE PASSION; le mensuel gratuit des passionnes de l'automobile. Text in French. 2008. m. free. **Document type:** *Magazine, Consumer.*
Related titles: Online - full text ed.
Published by: Automobile Passion, 08 Av. de la Marne, Tourcoing, 59200, France. contact@lautomobilepassion.com.

388.3 USA ISSN 0005-1438
TL1
AUTOMOBILE QUARTERLY; the connoisseur's magazine of motoring today, yesterday and tomorrow. Text in English. 1962. q. USD 79.95 domestic; USD 99.95 in Canada; USD 109.95 elsewhere; USD 24.95 per issue (effective 2007). adv. bk.rev. charts; illus. cum.index: 1962-1987, 1988-1993. back issues avail.; reprints avail. **Document type:** *Magazine, Consumer.* **Description:** Contains articles on contemporary, modern, classic, collectible, historic, special interest, sports, racing, postwar and pre-war cars.
Indexed: A05, A20, A22, A23, A24, AS&TA, AS&TI, B04, B13, IBR, IBZ, ISR.
—Ingenta, Linda Hall.
Published by: Automobile Heritage & Communications, Inc., 800 E 8th St, New Albany, IN 47150. TEL 812-948-2886, FAX 812-948-2816. Ed., Pub., R&P Gerry A Durnell TEL 812-948-2886. adv.: color page USD 5,950; trim 8.375 x 10.4375. Circ: 8,150.

388.3 FRA ISSN 1637-6129
AUTOMOBILE REVUE. Text in French. 2002. q. EUR 44 for 2 yrs. (effective 2010). **Document type:** *Magazine, Consumer.*
Published by: Lafont Presse, 53 Rue du Chemin Vert, Boulogne-Billancourt, 92100, France. TEL 33-1-46102121, FAX 33-1-45792211.

AUTOMOBILE REVUE. SPECIAL 4 X 4. *see* SPORTS AND GAMES

388.3 363.7 FRA ISSN 2101-6267
▼ **AUTOMOBILE REVUE VERTE.** Text in French. 2009. q. **Document type:** *Magazine, Consumer.*
Published by: Lafont Presse, 53 Rue du Chemin Vert, Boulogne-Billancourt, 92100, France. TEL 33-1-46102121, FAX 33-1-45792211.

388.3 FRA ISSN 1960-2286
AUTOMOBILE STORY. Text in French. 2006. q. **Document type:** *Magazine, Consumer.*
Published by: Lafont Presse, 53 Rue du Chemin Vert, Boulogne-Billancourt, 92100, France. FAX 33-1-45792211, http://www.lafontpresse.fr.

629.2 CHE ISSN 0084-7674
AUTOMOBILE YEAR. Text in English. 1953. a. CHF 85 (effective 2001). adv. illus. 272 p./no.; back issues avail. **Document type:** *Yearbook, Consumer.*
Related titles: German ed.; French ed.
Published by: Editions J R, PO Box 756, Lausanne 9, 1000, Switzerland. TEL 41-21-3116733, FAX 41-21-3116734, edijr@urbanet.ch. Ed. Ian Norris. Pub. J.-R. Piccard. Circ: 39,000. **Dist. in UK by:** Vine House Distribution Ltd., Waldenbury, North Common, Chailey, E Sussex BN8 4DR, United Kingdom. TEL 44-1825-723398, FAX 44-1825-724188, sales@vinehouseuk.co.uk, http://www.vinehouseuk.co.uk; **Dist. in US by:** Motorbooks International, PO Box 2, Osceola, WI 54020. TEL 800-826-6600, http://www.motorbooks.com.

388 USA
AUTOMOBILER. Text in English. 1923. bi-m. USD 2. adv.
Published by: (Automobile Club of Hartford), Hartford Automobiler, 815 Farmington Ave, West, Hartford, CT 06119. TEL 203-236-3261. Circ: 177,000.

388.3 FRA ISSN 0759-6065
AUTOMOBILES CLASSIQUES. Text in French. 1977. m. adv. bk.rev. **Document type:** *Magazine, Consumer.* **Description:** Features dream cars, collector's items and cars of the future.
Formerly: Enthousiaste
Published by: Editions T T M, 101 Bd Murat, Paris, 75016, France. TEL 33-1-53843150, FAX 33-1-53843199. Circ: 31,892 (controlled).

629.22075 FRA ISSN 1270-217X
AUTOMOBILIA; la revue de l'histoire automobile. Text in French. 1996. q. EUR 38.50 domestic; EUR 46 foreign (effective 2009). back issues avail. **Document type:** *Magazine, Consumer.* **Description:** Explores various automobiles of the past and also highlights their latest miniatures.
Published by: Histoire et Collection, 5 Av. de la Republique, Paris, 75011, France. TEL 33-1-40211820, FAX 33-1-47005111, fredbey@club-internet.fr, http://www.histoireetcollections.com.

796.77 ITA ISSN 0394-0128
AUTOMOBILISMO. Text in Italian. 1985. m. EUR 47 domestic; EUR 90 in the European Union; EUR 157 elsewhere (effective 2009). adv. bk.rev. charts; illus. index. **Document type:** *Magazine, Consumer.* **Description:** Provides information on cars, industrial news and results of tests. Includes technical and sport reports.
Related titles: Online - full text ed.
Published by: Edisport Editoriale SpA, Via Gradisca 11, Milan, MI 20151, Italy. TEL 39-02-38085, FAX 39-02-38010393, edisport@edisport.it, http://www.edisport.it. Circ: 170,000.

796.77 ITA ISSN 1723-4549
AUTOMOBILISMO D'EPOCA. Text in Italian. 2003. 10/yr. EUR 47 domestic; EUR 60 in the European Union; EUR 75 elsewhere (effective 2009). **Document type:** *Magazine, Consumer.*
Related titles: Online - full text ed.
Published by: Edisport Editoriale SpA, Via Gradisca 11, Milan, MI 20151, Italy. TEL 39-02-38085, FAX 39-02-38010393, edisport@edisport.it, http://www.edisport.it.

338.476 DEU ISSN 1616-654X
AUTOMOBILWIRTSCHAFT. Text in German. 1999. q. EUR 30; EUR 10 newsstand/cover (effective 2007). adv. **Document type:** *Magazine, Trade.*
Published by: Krafthand Verlag Walter Schulz, Walter-Schulz-Str 1, Bad Woerishofen, 86825, Germany. TEL 49-8247-30070, FAX 49-8247-300770, info@krafthand.de. adv.: B&W page EUR 4,944, color page EUR 6,591. Circ: 22,993 (paid and controlled).

338.476 DEU ISSN 1619-0327
AUTOMOBILWOCHE. Text in German. 2001. fortn. EUR 128 (effective 2009). adv. **Document type:** *Magazine, Trade.* **Description:** Contains articles and information on all aspects of the automobile industry.
Related titles: Online - full text ed.
Published by: Crain Communications GmbH, Technopark Oberpfaffenhofen, Argelsrieder Feld 13, Oberpfaffenhofen, 82234, Germany. TEL 49-8153-907400, FAX 49-8153-907426. Ed. Guido Reinking. Pub. Helmut Kluger TEL 49-8153-907402. Adv. contact Thomas Heringer. B&W page EUR 7,790, color page EUR 9,320; trim 285 x 403. Circ: 39,329 (paid and controlled).

388 DEU ISSN 1862-3883
AUTOMONAT; Alle Infos fuer den Autokauf. Text in German. 2006. q. EUR 20; EUR 5 newsstand/cover (effective 2010). adv. **Document type:** *Magazine, Consumer.*
Published by: Motor Presse Stuttgart GmbH & Co. KG (Subsidiary of: Gruner + Jahr AG & Co), Leuschnerstr 1, Stuttgart, 70174, Germany. TEL 49-711-18201, FAX 49-711-1821779, internet-redaktion@motor-presse-stuttgart.de, http://www.motorpresse.de.

AUTOMOTIVE AFTERMARKET IN CHINA. *see* BUSINESS AND ECONOMICS—Marketing And Purchasing

621.9816 DEU ISSN 1867-495X
AUTOMOTIVE AGENDA. Text in German. 2008. 4/yr. EUR 200; EUR 55 newsstand/cover (effective 2009). adv. **Document type:** *Magazine, Trade.*
—**CCC.**
Published by: Vieweg und Teubner Verlag (Subsidiary of: Springer Fachmedien Wiesbaden GmbH), Abraham-Lincoln-Str 46, Wiesbaden, 65189, Germany. TEL 49-611-78780, FAX 49-611-7878400, info@viewegteubner.de, http://www.viewegteubner.de. Ed. Elisabeth Massfeller. adv.: page EUR 7,000; trim 216 x 285. Circ: 10,000 (paid).

AUTOMOTIVE & AEROSPACE TEST REPORT. *see* ENGINEERING—Electrical Engineering

629 USA ISSN 0192-0995
TL255
AUTOMOTIVE BODY REPAIR NEWS; the voice of the collision repair industry. Short title: A B R N. Text in English. 1962. m. USD 69 domestic; USD 78 in Canada & Mexico; USD 109 elsewhere; USD 14 newsstand/cover domestic; USD 15 newsstand/cover in Canada & Mexico; USD 19 newsstand/cover elsewhere (effective 2011). adv. bk.rev. back issues avail. **Document type:** *Magazine, Trade.* **Description:** For professional businesses engaged in automotive collision repair and paint-refinish.
Formerly (until 19??): Automotive Service and Body News
Related titles: Online - full text ed.: ISSN 1558-5743. USD 55 (effective 2011).
Indexed: A09, A10, A15, ABIn, B01, B02, B06, B07, B09, B15, B17, B18, G04, G08, I05, P16, P48, P51, P52, P53, P54, PQC, S22, T02, V02, V03, V04.
—**CCC.**
Published by: Advanstar Communications, Inc., 6200 Canoga Ave, 2nd Fl, Woodland Hills, CA 91367. TEL 818-593-5000, FAX 818-593-5020, info@advanstar.com, http://www.advanstar.com. Pub. Terri McMenamin TEL 610-397-1667. Circ: 60,030 (controlled).

388 USA ISSN 0191-6459
THE AUTOMOTIVE BOOSTER OF CALIFORNIA. Text in English. 1928. 7/yr. USD 6 (effective 2007). adv. back issues avail. **Document type:** *Magazine, Trade.* **Description:** Covers the automotive parts aftermarket and industry in California and the West.
Published by: KAL Publications Inc., 559 S Harbor Blvd, #A, Anaheim, CA 92805-4525. TEL 714-563-9300, FAX 714-563-9310. Ed., Pub., R&P Kathy Laderman. adv.: B&W page USD 650, color page USD 1,100. Circ: 4,800 (controlled).

338.3 USA
AUTOMOTIVE CONTACT. Text in English. 194?. m. adv. bk.rev.
Address: PO Box 517, Terre Haute, IN 47808. TEL 812-232-2441. Ed. T L Spelman. Circ: 5,000.

338.3 USA
AUTOMOTIVE CONTACT DIRECTORY. INDIANA. Text in English. a. USD 27.95. adv. **Document type:** *Directory.*
Formerly: Indiana Automotive Directory
Published by: Automotive Contact, PO Box 517, Terre Haute, IN 47808. TEL 812-232-2441. Ed. T L Spelman. Circ: 3,250.

388.3 629.2 USA ISSN 0005-1497
AUTOMOTIVE COOLING JOURNAL. Abbreviated title: A C J. Text in English. 1956. m. USD 30 domestic; USD 48.50 in Canada; USD 75 elsewhere (effective 2007). adv. bk.rev. bibl. Index. 65 p./no.; back issues avail. **Document type:** *Magazine, Trade.* **Description:** Provides management and technical articles for the owners and operators of automotive cooling system service and air conditioning shops.
Published by: National Automotive Radiator Service Association, 15000 Commerce Pkwy, Ste C, Mt. Laurel, NJ 08054. TEL 856-439-1575, 800-551-3232, FAX 856-439-9596, info@narsa.org. Ed., R&P Michael Dwyer TEL 215-541-4500 ext 128. adv.: B&W page USD 1,595, color page USD 2,630; bleed 8.375 x 10.875. Circ: 10,000 (paid and controlled). **Co-sponsor:** Mobile Air Conditioning Society.

629 330 USA
AUTOMOTIVE DEALERS DIGEST. Text in English. fortn.
Published by: Davco, Inc., 800 SE 20th Ave., Apt. 405, Deerfield Bch, FL 33441-5143. TEL 908-583-2100. Ed. Raphael Cohen.

629.286 GBR
▼ **AUTOMOTIVE DESIGN.** Text in English. 2010 (Mar.). bi-m. **Document type:** *Magazine, Trade.* **Description:** Focuses on design and engineering elements of the automotive industry.
Published by: (Society of Automotive Engineers International USA), Findlay Publications Ltd., Hawley Mill, Hawley Rd, Horton Kirby, Kent DA2 7TJ, United Kingdom. TEL 44-1322-221144, FAX 44-1322-221188, enquiries@findlay.co.uk, http://www.findlay.co.uk/.

388 USA ISSN 1536-8823
TJ1180.A1 CODEN: PDTNAG
AUTOMOTIVE DESIGN & PRODUCTION. Abbreviated title: A D P. Text in English. 1934. m. USD 89 domestic; USD 99 in Canada; USD 200 elsewhere; free in North America to qualified personnel (effective 2008). adv. charts; illus.; tr.lit.; stat. Index. back issues avail.; reprints avail. **Document type:** *Magazine, Trade.* **Description:** Covers the interrelationships between automotive product development and manufacturing processes.
Former titles (until 2001): Automotive Manufacturing and Production (1094-1746); (until 1996): Automotive Production (1086-9298); (until 1995): Production (0032-9819); (until 1953): Production Engineering & Management; (until 19??): The Tool Engineer; (until 1935): A S T E Journal
Related titles: Online - full text ed.
Indexed: A09, A10, A12, A13, A15, A17, A22, ABIn, AIA, B01, B02, B06, B07, B08, B09, B11, B15, B17, B18, BPIA, BusI, C12, CA, CADCAM, G04, G06, G07, G08, I05, Inspec, M01, M02, ManagCont, ORMS, P48, P51, P53, P54, PQC, PROMT, QC&AS, RoboAb, S22, SRI, T02, V02, V03, V04.
—AskIEEE, IE, Linda Hall. **CCC.**
Published by: Gardner Publications, Inc., 6915 Valley Ave, Cincinnati, OH 45244. TEL 513-527-8800, 800-950-8020, FAX 513-527-8801, skline2@gardnerweb.com. Eds. Kevin Kelly, Gary Vasilash TEL 734-416-9705. adv.: B&W page USD 6,840, color page USD 9,040; trim 8.75 x 10.875. Circ: 60,015 (paid).

388.34 GBR ISSN 1749-1819
AUTOMOTIVE ELECTONICS. Abbreviated title: A E. Text in English. 2005. bi-m. free to qualified personnel (effective 2009). adv. **Document type:** *Magazine, Trade.*
Related titles: Online - full text ed.
Published by: M T Publications Ltd., Prudence Pl, Proctor Way, Luton, Bedfordshire, LU2 9PE, United Kingdom. TEL 44-1582-722460, FAX 44-1582-722470. Ed. Steve Rogerson. Pub. David Williams. Adv. contact Jonathan Kirk.

388.3 AUS
AUTOMOTIVE, ELECTRICAL & AIR CONDITIONING NEWS. Abbreviated title: A E A C News. Text in English. 1992. bi-m. AUD 59 domestic; AUD 79 foreign (effective 2008). adv. back issues avail. **Document type:** *Magazine, Trade.*
Formerly: A A E N Auto Electrical News
Related titles: Online - full text ed.
Published by: A A E N Pty Ltd., PO Box 271, Lutwyche, QLD 4030, Australia. TEL 61-7-33566155, FAX 61-7-33566130, office@aaen.com.au. Ed. Anthony McMahon. Circ: 3,200 (paid).

629.2 AUS
AUTOMOTIVE ENGINEER. Text in English. 1933. 6/yr. free to members (effective 2008). adv. bk.rev. charts; illus.; tr.lit. **Document type:** *Journal, Trade.*
Formerly (until 1977): Australian Automotive Engineering and Equipment (0004-8720)
Indexed: HRIS.

Published by: Institute of Automotive Mechanical Engineers Inc., 11-13 Byrne St, Auburn, NSW 2144, Australia. TEL 61-2-96481412, FAX 61-2-96484241, inbox@iame.com.au. Ed., R&P Ralph Goss. Adv. contacts Kim O'Mara TEL 61-2-96481412, Ralph Gross. B&W page AUD 1,675, color page AUD 2,005; trim 205 x 270. Circ: 26,823.

629.2 GBR ISSN 0307-6490
TL1
AUTOMOTIVE ENGINEER. Text in English. 1975. 11/yr. EUR 475 in Europe to institutions; USD 842 in North America to institutions; GBP 432 to institutions in the UK & elsewhere (effective 2012). adv. bk.rev. charts; illus.; pat.; tr.lit. back issues avail.; reprints avail. **Document type:** *Magazine, Trade.* **Description:** News and informational briefs and research papers on technological, design, and product development pertaining to the mechanical, electronic, and operational aspects of on- and off-highway vehicles.
Formed by the merger of (1962-1975): Automotive Design Engineering (0005-1500); Which incorporated: Farm Machine Design Engineering; (1971-1975): J A E. Journal of Automotive Engineering (0307-1820); Which was formerly: Journal of Automotive Engineering (0047-2247); Institution of Mechanical Engineers. Automobile Division. Proceedings (0367-8822); Institution of Automobile Engineers, London. Proceedings (0369-9838); Which incorporated: Incorporated Institution of Automobile Engineers. Proceedings
Related titles: Online - full text ed.
Indexed: A01, A03, A05, A08, A09, A10, A15, A22, A23, A24, A26, A28, ABIn, APA, APICat, APIH&E, APIOC, APIPR, APIPS, APITS, ARI, AS&TA, AS&TI, AcoustA, B01, B03, B04, B06, B07, B09, B13, BMT, BrCerAb, BrTechI, C&ISA, C10, CA, CA/WCA, CBNB, CIA, CerAb, CivEngAb, CorrAb, E&CAJ, E11, EEA, EMA, ESPM, EngInd, EnvAb, H15, HRIS, I05, Inspec, M&TEA, M09, MBF, METADEX, P26, P34, P48, P51, P52, P54, PQC, R18, S01, SCOPUS, SolStAb, T01, T02, T04, TM, TTI, V03, V04, WAA.
—BLDSC (1833.818000), IE, Infotrieve, Ingenta, INIST, Linda Hall. **CCC.**
Published by: (European Automotive Engineers Cooperation AUT), Caspian Media, 198 Kings Rd., London, SW3 5XP, United Kingdom. http://caspianmedia.com/. Circ: 20,000. **Subscr. to:** Portland Customer Services, Commerce Way, Colchester CO2 8HP, United Kingdom. TEL 44-1206-796351, FAX 44-1206-799331, sales@portland-services.com, http://www.portland-services.com.

629.2 USA ISSN 1543-849X
TL1 CODEN: AUEGBB
AUTOMOTIVE ENGINEERING INTERNATIONAL. Abbreviated title: A E I. Text in English. 1917. m. USD 140 in North America to non-members; USD 245 elsewhere to non-members; free to members (effective 2009). adv. illus. back issues avail.; reprints avail. **Document type:** *Magazine, Trade.* **Description:** Covers the latest information in automotive technology that can be applied to the design of new or improved vehicle systems for the automotive engineer.
Incorporates (1989-1998): Truck Engineering (1048-9584); Former titles (until 1998): Automotive Engineering (0098-2571); (until 1972): S A E Journal of Automotive Engineering (0097-711X); Which superseded in part (in 1970): S A E Journal (0036-066X); Which was formerly (until 1928): Society of Automotive Engineers. Journal (0097-2010); (until Jun.1917): S A E Bulletin
Related titles: Microfiche ed.: (from PMC); Microfilm ed.: (from PMC); Online - full text ed.: ISSN 1939-7453; Spanish ed.: Automotive Engineering International - en Espanol. ISSN 1579-3524. 2001. EUR 70.99 domestic; EUR 80.17 foreign (effective 2004); ◆ Supplement(s): S A E Off-Highway Engineering. ISSN 1528-9702.
Indexed: A05, A22, A23, A24, A25, A26, A28, APA, APICat, APIH&E, APIOC, APIPR, APIPS, APITS, AS&TA, AS&TI, AcaI, B02, B04, B13, B15, B16, B17, B18, BCIRA, BMT, BrCerAb, C&ISA, C10, CA, CA/WCA, CIA, CLT&T, Cadscan, CerAb, CivEngAb, CorrAb, E&CAJ, E08, E11, EEA, EMA, ESPM, EnvEAb, ErgAb, G04, G06, G07, G08, GeotechAb, H15, HRIS, I05, ISR, Inspec, L09, LeadAb, M&TEA, M09, MBF, METADEX, P02, P10, P13, P26, P48, P53, P54, PQC, PROMT, R18, S08, S09, S10, SCOPUS, SolStAb, T&II, T02, T04, WAA, Zincscan.
—CASDDS, IE, Ingenta, INIST, Linda Hall. **CCC.**
Published by: S A E Inc., 400 Commonwealth Dr, Warrendale, PA 15096. TEL 724-772-8509, FAX 724-776-9765, CustomerService@sae.org, http://www.sae.org/automag. Pub. Scott R Sward TEL 610-399-5279. Adv. contact Linda Risch TEL 724-772-4039. B&W page USD 9,910, color page USD 12,110; trim 206 x 276. Circ: 85,813.

AUTOMOTIVE EXPORTS. *see* BUSINESS AND ECONOMICS—International Commerce

AUTOMOTIVE FINE ART; a journal by the Automotive Fine Arts Society. *see* ART

388.3 USA ISSN 0005-1519
TL165
AUTOMOTIVE FLEET; the car and truck fleet and leasing management magazine. Text in English. 1961. m. (plus Factbook in April). free to qualified personnel (effective 2009). adv. charts; illus.; mkt.; stat. back issues avail. **Document type:** *Magazine, Trade.* **Description:** Covers the car and light truck fleet market.
Related titles: Online - full text ed.
Indexed: CLT&T, HRIS, SRI.
Published by: Bobit Business Media, 3520 Challenger St, Torrance, CA 90503. TEL 310-533-2400, FAX 310-533-2500, order@bobit.com, http://www.bobit.com. Pub. Sherb Brown. Adv. contact Eric Bearly TEL 310-533-2579. color page USD 10,850; 7 x 10. Circ: 20,000. **Subscr. to:** PO Box 1068, Skokie, IL 60076.

629 USA ISSN 1056-2729
TL15
AUTOMOTIVE HISTORY REVIEW. Text in English. s-a. USD 40 membership (effective 2005).
Indexed: AmH&L, HistAb.
Published by: Society of Automotive Historians, 1102 Long Cove Rd, Gales Ferry, CT 06335. http://www.autohistory.org.

629.2 USA ISSN 1099-4130
AUTOMOTIVE INDUSTRIES. Abbreviated title: A I. Text in English. 1895. m. adv. bk.rev. charts; illus.; tr.lit. s-a. index. Supplement avail.; back issues avail.; reprints avail. **Document type:** *Magazine, Trade.* **Description:** Contains comprehensive information on all aspects of the automobile industry.
Former titles (until 1994): Chilton's Automotive Industries (0273-656X); (until 1976): Automotive Industries (0886-4675); (until 1972): Chilton's Automotive Industries; (until 1970): Automotive Industries; (until 1947): Automotive and Aviation Industries (0097-7071); (until 1942): Automotive Industries (0005-1527); (until 1917): Automobile and Automotive Industries; Incorporated (1923-1934): Automotive Abstracts (0097-708X); and incorporated in part (in 1917): The Horseless Age
Related titles: Microfiche ed.: (from CIS, PQC); Microfilm ed.: (from PMC, PQC); Online - full text ed.: free (effective 2009).
Indexed: A05, A09, A10, A15, A22, A23, A24, A26, A28, ABIn, APA, AS&TA, AS&TI, B01, B02, B03, B04, B06, B07, B08, B09, B10, B11, B13, B15, B17, B18, BPI, BRD, BrCerAb, BusI, C&ISA, C10, C12, CA/WCA, CADCAM, CIA, CLT&T, CWI, CerAb, CivEngAb, CorrAb, E&CAJ, E08, E11, EEA, EMA, ESPM, EngInd, EnvAb, EnvEAb, G04, G06, G07, G08, H15, HRIS, I05, ISR, M&TEA, M09, MBF, METADEX, P06, P26, P48, P51, P52, P54, PQC, RoboAb, S04, S09, SCOPUS, SRI, SolStAb, T&II, T02, T04, V02, V03, V04, W01, W02, W03, W05, WAA.
—BLDSC (1834.000000), IE, Ingenta, Linda Hall. **CCC.**
Published by: Diesel & Gas Turbine Publications, 20855 Watertown Rd, Ste 220, Waukesha, WI 53186. TEL 262-832-5000, FAX 262-832-5075, http://www.dieselpub.com. Ed. Edward Richardson TEL 27-41-5823750. Pub. John Larkin TEL 313-262-5702. Adv. contact Kara Kane. color page USD 11,990; bleed 209 x 273. Circ: 25,722.

388 USA
THE AUTOMOTIVE INDUSTRY: A LOOK AT DEALERSHIP, REPAIR SERVICES AND AUTO PARTS RETAILERS. Text in English. 1992. a. **Description:** Examines dealerships, repair services and auto parts retailers to determine the effect of economic conditions.
Published by: Dun & Bradstreet Information Services (Subsidiary of: Dun & Bradstreet, Inc.), 103 JFK Pkwy, Short Hills, NJ 07078. TEL 973-921-5500, 800-234-3867, http://www.dnb.com.

388 338.478 GBR ISSN 0951-158X
AUTOMOTIVE INDUSTRY DATA NEWSLETTER. Short title: A I D Newsletter. Text in English. 1983. s-m. GBP 479 in Europe (effective 2009); USD 770 elsewhere (effective 2000). stat. s-a. index. back issues avail. **Document type:** *Newsletter, Trade.* **Description:** Provides statistical analysis of motor industry.
Related titles: Online - full text ed.
Published by: Automotive Industry Data Ltd., 30 Cape Rd, Warwick, Warcs CV34 4JP, United Kingdom. TEL 44-1926-410040, FAX 44-1926-776252, info@eagleaid.com. Ed. Peter Schmidt.

338.476 GBR ISSN 2046-3073
AUTOMOTIVE INSIGHT. Text in English. 1987. m. free to members (effective 2011). **Document type:** *Magazine, Trade.*
Incorporates: Forecourt (1741-4539)
Published by: Retail Motor Industry Federation Ltd., 201 Great Portland St, London, W1W 5AB, United Kingdom. TEL 44-20-75809122, FAX 44-20-75806376, feedback@rmif.co.uk, http://www.rmif.co.uk.

388.3
AUTOMOTIVE INTELLIGENCE NEWS. Text in English. w. adv. back issues avail. **Document type:** *Journal, Trade.* **Description:** Reports on news and issues about the automotive industry.
Media: Online - full content.
Published by: Automotive Intelligence editor@autointell.com, http://www.autointell.com.

388.3 GBR ISSN 1471-6038
TL278
AUTOMOTIVE MANUFACTURING SOLUTIONS. Abbreviated title: A M S. Text in English. 2000. bi-m. free to qualified personnel (effective 2009). adv. back issues avail. **Document type:** *Magazine, Trade.* **Description:** Provides coverage of global automotive manufacturing.
Related titles: Online - full text ed.
Indexed: A10, A28, APA, B01, B07, BrCerAb, C&ISA, CA/WCA, CIA, CerAb, CivEngAb, CorrAb, E&CAJ, E11, EEA, EMA, ESPM, EnvEAb, H15, M&TEA, M09, MBF, METADEX, SolStAb, T02, T04, V03, WAA.
—Linda Hall. **CCC.**
Published by: Ultima Media Ltd., Lamb House, Church St, London, W4 2PD, United Kingdom. TEL 44-20-89870900, FAX 44-20-89870948, info@ultimamedia.com, http://www.ultimamedia.org/. Ed. Julian Buckley TEL 44-20-89870979. Pub. Andrew Fallon TEL 44-20-89870931.

388.3 USA ISSN 0733-2084
AUTOMOTIVE MARKET REPORT. Text in English. 1951. bi-w. USD 130; USD 10 newsstand/cover (effective 2005). adv. mkt. **Document type:** *Magazine, Trade.*
Formerly: Automotive Market Report and Auto Week (0005-1543)
Published by: Automotive Auction Publishing, Inc., 607 Laurel Dr, Monroeville, VA 15146. TEL 412-373-6383, FAX 412-373-6388. Ed., Pub. Clyde K Hillwig. Circ: 6,000.

629.286 DEU ISSN 1613-9321
AUTOMOTIVE MATERIALS. Text in German. 2004. bi-m. adv. **Document type:** *Magazine, Trade.*
—IE.
Published by: Giesel Verlag GmbH (Subsidiary of: Schluetersche Verlagsgesellschaft mbH und Co. KG), Rehkamp 3, Isernhagen, 30916, Germany. TEL 49-511-73040, FAX 49-511-7304157, giesel@giesel.de, http://www.giesel.de. Circ: 8,968 (paid and controlled).

388.3 629.2 USA ISSN 0005-1551
AUTOMOTIVE NEWS; engineering, financial, manufacturing, sales, marketing, servicing. Text in English. 1925. w. (Mon.). USD 159 domestic (print or online ed.); USD 239 in Canada (print or online ed.); USD 395 elsewhere (print or online ed.) (effective 2009). adv. bk.rev. charts; illus.; mkt.; stat.; tr.lit. back issues avail.; reprints avail. **Document type:** *Newspaper, Trade.* **Description:** Covers news and developments in the automobile manufacturing, servicing and sales industries for car and truck manufacturers, their franchised dealers, and original-equipment suppliers.
Incorporates (1939-1942): Automotive Service; Formerly (until 1938): Automotive Daily News
Related titles: Microfiche ed.: (from CIS); Microform ed.: (from PMC, PQC); Online - full text ed.: ISSN 1557-7686. USD 155 (effective 2009); Supplement(s): Automotive News. Market Data Book. ISSN 1931-6542.
Indexed: A09, A10, A11, A15, A22, A23, A25, A26, A28, ABIn, APA, AcaI, B01, B02, B03, B04, B06, B07, B08, B09, B11, B13, B15, B16, B17, B18, BPI, BRD, BrCerAb, BusI, C&ISA, C05, C12, CA/WCA, CIA, CLT&T, CPerI, CWI, CerAb, CivEngAb, CorrAb, E&CAJ, E08, E11, EEA, EMA, ESPM, EnvEAb, G04, G06, G07, G08, H15, HRIS, I05, M&TEA, M01, M02, M06, M09, MBF, METADEX, P02, P06, P10, P13, P34, P48, P51, P52, P53, P54, PQC, S08, S09, S22, SRI, SolStAb, T&II, T02, T04, V02, V03, V04, W01, W02, W03, W05, WAA.
—CIS, Linda Hall. **CCC.**
Published by: Crain Communications, Inc., 1155 Gratiot Ave, Detroit, MI 48207. TEL 313-446-6000, 888-909-9111, FAX 313-446-1616, info@crain.com, http://www.crain.com. Ed. David Sedgwick TEL 313-446-0376. Pub. Keith E Crain TEL 313-446-6001. adv.: B&W page USD 13,310, color page USD 17,105. Circ: 80,000 (paid).

388.3 629.2 GBR
AUTOMOTIVE NEWS EUROPE (ONLINE). Text in English. 1999. d. free (effective 2010). adv. **Document type:** *Newspaper, Trade.* **Description:** Covers automotive engineering as well as financial, manufacturing, sales and marketing news affecting the automobile industry.
Media: Online - full text.
Indexed: A09, B06, B08, B09.
Published by: Crain Communications, Ltd., 3rd Fl, 21 St Thomas St, London, SE1 9RY, United Kingdom. TEL 44-20-74571400, FAX 44-20-74571440, http://www.crain.co.uk. Eds. Jason Stein TEL 313-446-0376, Keith Crain TEL 313-446-6001.

388.3 USA ISSN 0005-156X
AUTOMOTIVE NEWS OF THE PACIFIC NORTHWEST. Text in English. 1919. 6/yr. USD 10 (effective 2007). adv. bk.rev. illus.; tr.lit. **Document type:** *Magazine, Trade.* **Description:** Covers news of the automotive trade, especially directed to the Pacific Northwest. Includes new car and truck sales in Oregon, Washington, and Idaho, gasoline sales, new products, literature, and personal items.
Address: 6090 S W Willow Ln, Milwaukie, OR 97267-1821. TEL 503-656-1456, FAX 503-656-1547. Ed., Adv. contact William H Boyer. Circ: 4,000.

629 USA ISSN 1058-9376
TL154
AUTOMOTIVE RECYCLING. Text in English. 1975. bi-m. USD 30 domestic; USD 45 foreign (effective 2005). **Document type:** *Magazine, Trade.*
Former titles (until 1990): Dismantlers Digest (0192-0316); Automotive Recycler and Merchandiser; Auto Wrecker
Indexed: A28, APA, BrCerAb, C&ISA, CA/WCA, CIA, CerAb, CivEngAb, CorrAb, E&CAJ, E11, EEA, EMA, ESPM, EnvEAb, H15, M&TEA, M09, MBF, METADEX, SolStAb, T04, WAA.
—Linda Hall.
Published by: Automotive Recyclers Association, 3975 Fair Ridge Dr, Ste 20 N, Fairfax, VA 22033-2924. TEL 703-385-1001, FAX 703-385-1494. Eds. Caryn Suko-Smith, Tammy Haire. Pub. George K Eliades. Circ: 2,000.

629.286 CAN ISSN 0068-9629
AUTOMOTIVE SERVICE DATA BOOK. Text in English. 1935. a. (Dec.). CAD 34.95 per issue domestic; USD 34.95 per issue foreign (effective 2007). adv. **Document type:** *Handbook/Manual/Guide, Trade.* **Description:** Book of detailed service specifications for all cars and light trucks sold in Canada for the last 10 years.
Related titles: CD-ROM ed.: CAD 25 per issue domestic; USD 25 per issue foreign (effective 2006).
Published by: Business Information Group, 12 Concorde Pl, Ste 800, Toronto, ON M3C 4J2, Canada. TEL 416-442-2122, 800-668-2374, FAX 416-442-2191, orders@businessinformationgroup.ca. Ed. David Booth.

629.286 338 FRA ISSN 1622-860X
AUTOMOTIVE SUPPLY. Text in French, English. 1987. bi-m. EUR 68 domestic; EUR 85 in Europe; EUR 96 elsewhere (effective 2009). adv. maps; stat. 100 p./no.; **Document type:** *Magazine, Corporate.*
Formerly (until 2000): Equipement pour Vehicules Automobiles (0984-3922)
Indexed: A28, APA, BrCerAb, C&ISA, CA/WCA, CIA, CerAb, CivEngAb, CorrAb, E&CAJ, E11, EEA, EMA, H15, M&TEA, M09, MBF, METADEX, SolStAb, T04, WAA.
Published by: (Federation des Industries des Equipement pour Vehicules), Editions V B, 7 Rue Jean Mermoz, Versailles, 78000, France. TEL 33-1-39208805, FAX 33-1-39208806, vblcda@lcda.fr. Ed. Eric Bigourdan. Adv. contact Sebastien Gourdon. Circ: 10,000.

388.3 658 USA ISSN 0889-3918
AUTOMOTIVE WEEK; the Greensheet. Variant title: Automotive Week / The Greensheet. Text in English. 1975. 46/yr. USD 260 (effective 2007). adv. s-a. index. 8 p./no. 3 cols./p.; back issues avail.; reprints avail. **Document type:** *Newsletter, Trade.* **Description:** Covers mergers, acquisitions, marketing, personnel moves,trends, commentary and news of auto replacement market retailers, wholesalers, distributors and manufacturers.
Formerly: Automotive Buyer
Related titles: E-mail ed.: USD 195 (effective 2007).
Published by: Molinaro Communications, 100 Merle Blvd, Munroe Falls, OH 44262-1642. TEL 330-688-4960, FAX 330-688-4909, greensheet@auto-week.com, http://www.auto-week.com. Ed., Pub. Gary Molinaro. adv.: col. inch USD 180. Circ: 3,100 (paid).

629.2 338.476 GBR ISSN 1755-5558
AUTOMOTIVEWORLD.COM. MANUFACTURING MONTHLY DIGEST; essential monthly analysis of key trends in vehicle manufacturing. Text in English. 1998. m. free (effective 2009). stat.
Former titles (2007): Light Vehicle Manufacturing (1751-6773); (until 2006): World Automotive Manufacturing (Online) (1749-527X); (until 200?): World Automotive Manufacturing (Print) (1463-1857)
Media: Online - full text.
—**CCC.**
Published by: Automotive World, 19 Neptune Ct, Vanguard Way, Cardiff, CF24 5PJ, United Kingdom. TEL 44-29-20468902, FAX 44-29-20468903, subscriptions@automotiveworld.com, https://www.automotiveworld.com/.

388.342 TUR
AUTOMOTO. Text in Turkish. w. **Document type:** *Magazine, Trade.*
Published by: D M G Magazines, Evren Oto Sanayi Sitesi Yani, Esenyurt - Istanbul, 34850, Turkey. TEL 90-212-6221535, FAX 90-212-6221533.

629.2 PRT ISSN 0871-6153
AUTOMOTOR. Text in Portuguese. 1989. m. adv. illus. **Document type:** *Magazine, Consumer.*
Related titles: Online - full text ed.
Published by: Edirevistas (Subsidiary of: Cofina Media), Av Joao Crisostomo 72, Lisbon, 1069-043, Portugal. TEL 351-213-307700, FAX 351-213-307799.

338.3 ESP
AUTOMOVIL. Text in Spanish. 1978. m. adv. **Document type:** *Magazine, Consumer.*
Related titles: ◆ Supplement(s): Los Mejores Automoviles del Mundo.
Published by: Motorpress Iberica (Subsidiary of: Gruner + Jahr AG & Co), Ancora 40, Madrid, 28045, Spain. TEL 34-91-3470100, FAX 34-91-3470152, http://www.motorpress-iberica.es. Ed. Fernando Gomez Blanco. Circ: 94,750 (paid and controlled).

388.3 VEN ISSN 0005-1616
AUTOMOVIL DE VENEZUELA. Text in Spanish. 1961. m. USD 25 (effective 2001). adv. back issues avail. **Document type:** *Magazine, Consumer.*
Published by: Ortiz y Asociados, s.r.l., Av. Caurimare, Qta. Expo., Colinas de Bello Monte, Caracas, Venezuela. TEL 58-212-7511355, FAX 58-212-7511122, ortizauto@cantv.net. Ed. Armando Ortiz P. Adv. contact Maria Ortiz TEL 58-212-7511755. Circ: 7,500 (controlled).

629.28 MEX
AUTOMOVIL PANAMERICANO. Text in Spanish. 1995. m. adv. index. back issues avail. **Document type:** *Magazine, Consumer.*
Description: Provides results of new car tests, comparative tests, prices and news of the car industry.
Published by: Editorial Motorpress Televisa (Subsidiary of: Gruner + Jahr AG & Co), Av Vasco de Quiroga 2000, Edif E, Mexico, Col Santa Fe, Mexico City, DF 01210, Mexico. TEL 525-2612672, FAX 525-2612731. adv.: page USD 5,300; trim 207 x 257. Circ: 52,700 (paid).

388.3 ESP ISSN 0005-1632
AUTOMOVILISMO EN ESPANA. Text in Spanish. 1942. m. EUR 35 domestic; EUR 84 elsewhere (effective 2009). adv. bk.rev. bibl.; illus.; stat. index. Supplement avail.; back issues avail. **Document type:** *Magazine, Trade.*
Related titles: ◆ Print ed.: Anuario Espanol de la Automocion. ISSN 1130-5983.
Published by: Editorial Borrmart S.A., C. Don Ramon de la Cruz, 68 6o, Madrid, 28001, Spain. TEL 34-91-4029607, http://www.borrmart.es/. Ed. Ramon Borreda Garcia. Circ: 16,500.

388 ZAF
AUTONEWS INTERNATIONAL. Text in English. 1998. m. ZAR 7,800, ZAR 15; ZAR 6 newsstand/cover (effective 2000). adv. software rev. charts; illus.; maps; mkt.; stat. 24 p./no. 4 cols./p.; back issues avail. **Document type:** *Magazine, Trade.* **Description:** Aims specifically at fleet and corporate buyers of cars and light trucks.
Published by: Autonews cc, Ste 136, Private Bag X3, North Riding, Johannesburg 2162, South Africa. TEL 27-11-462-5824, FAX 27-11-462-5826. Ed., Pub., Adv. contact Colin Windell. R&P Michelle Windell. B&W page ZAR 9,718, color page ZAR 16,809; trim 280 x 410. Circ: 8,900 (paid).

388.34029 ZAF
AUTOPART; a directory of companies supplying the motor trade. Text in English. a. adv. illus. **Document type:** *Directory.*
Published by: M & M Publications, PO Box 8859, Johannesburg, 2000, South Africa. TEL 27-11-880-5790, FAX 27-11-880-5789. Circ: (controlled).

388.3 USA ISSN 1045-1978
THE AUTOPARTS REPORT; news and analysis of the changing autoparts industry. Text in English. 1986. s-m. USD 445 in North America; USD 510 elsewhere (effective 2006). charts; stat. 10 p./no.; back issues avail.; reprints avail. **Document type:** *Newsletter, Trade.* **Description:** Provides analysis of new marketing techniques, tracks the forces of consolidation, and explains the effects of industry changes.
Formerly (until 1992): Automotive Parts International (0896-3614)
Related titles: Online - full text ed.
Indexed: PROMT.
Published by: International Trade Services, PO Box 5950, Bethesda, MD 20824-5950. TEL 301-229-4070, FAX 301-229-3995, itsron@bellatlantic.net, http://www.theautoreport.com. Ed., Pub., R&P Ronald J DeMarines.

388 HUN ISSN 0239-0426
AUTOPIAC. Text in Hungarian. 1989. fortn. adv. 48 p./no.; **Document type:** *Magazine, Consumer.*
Media: Large Type.
Published by: Motor-Presse Budapest Lapkiado kft, Hajogyari-sziget 307, Budapest, 1033, Hungary. TEL 36-1-4369244, FAX 36-1-4369248, mpb@motorpresse.hu, http://www.motorpresse.hu. Eds. Zoltan Toth, Viktor Balazs. Pub. Dietmar Metzger. Adv. contacts Andrea Poz, Dietmar Metzger. page USD 2,000; bleed 230 x 300. Circ: 50,000 (paid). **Dist. by:** Lapker Rt, 1097 Tablas utca, Budapest, Hungary.

614.86 CAN ISSN 0836-1630
AUTOPINION. Text in English. 1981. a. CAD 7.20. **Document type:** *Journal, Consumer.* **Description:** Published for the car buyer and automobile enthusiast. Contains specifications, editorial copy and feature articles on new and used automobiles.
Published by: Canadian Automobile Association, 1145 Hunt Club Rd, Ste 200, Ottawa, ON K1V 0Y3, Canada. TEL 613-247-0117, FAX 613-247-0118. Ed. David Steventon.

629.2 ESP ISSN 0567-2392
AUTOPISTA. Text in Spanish. 1961. w. adv. back issues avail. **Document type:** *Magazine, Consumer.*
Related titles: Online - full text ed.
Published by: Motorpress Iberica (Subsidiary of: Gruner + Jahr AG & Co), Ancora 40, Madrid, 28045, Spain. TEL 34-91-3470100, FAX 34-91-3470152. Ed. Juan Carlos Payo. Circ: 67,000 (paid and controlled).

629.286 ITA ISSN 1129-3330
AUTOPRO. Text in Italian. 1998. m. **Document type:** *Magazine, Consumer.*
Related titles: ◆ Supplement to: Quattroruote. ISSN 0033-5916.
Published by: Editoriale Domus, Via Gianni Mazzocchi 1/3, Rozzano, MI 20089, Italy. TEL 39-02-824721, editorialedomus@edidomus.it, http://www.edidomus.it.

629.33 CZE ISSN 1210-7441
AUTOPROFI. Text in Czech. 1993. m. (11/yr.). CZK 59 newsstand/cover (effective 2011). adv. **Document type:** *Magazine, Consumer.*
Published by: Axel Springer Praha a.s., Rosmarin Business Center, Dilnicka 12, Prague 7, 17000, Czech Republic. TEL 420-2-34692111, FAX 420-2-34692102. Ed. Ladislav Cerny. Adv. contact Petra Kardova. Circ: 15,000 (paid). **Subscr. to:** SEND Predplatne s.r.o., PO Box 141, Prague 4 140 21, Czech Republic. TEL 420-225-985225, FAX 420-225-341425, send@send.cz.

388.3 ITA ISSN 0005-1683
AUTORAMA; mensile d'informazione e cultura del mondo dei motori. Text in Italian. 1958. m. **Document type:** *Magazine, Consumer.*
Published by: Vega Editrice S.r.l., Via Ramazzotti 20, Monza Parco, MI 20052, Italy. TEL 39-039-493101, FAX 39-039-493102. Circ: 30,000 (paid).

388.3 AUS
AUTOREV. Text in English. d. **Document type:** *Report, Consumer.*
Description: Reports on news and trends about the motor industry in Australasia and worldwide.
Media: Online - full content.
Address: P O Box 574, Victoria Park, W.A. 6979, Australia. info@autorev.com.au, http://www.autorev.com.au.

629.2 LUX
AUTOREVUE. Text in French. 1948. m. illus.
Address: B.P. 231, Luxembourg, L-2012, Luxembourg. TEL 22-99-3. Ed. Paul Neyens. Circ: 10,000.

629.331 CZE ISSN 1214-1895
AUTOREVUE.CZ. Text in Czech. 2001. d. free. adv. **Document type:** *Consumer.*
Media: Online - full content.
Published by: Computer Press a.s., Spielberk Office Centre, Holandska 8, Brno, 639 00, Czech Republic. TEL 420-545-113777, FAX 420-545-113701, webmaster@cpress.cz, http://www.cpress.cz. Ed. Petr Broza.

796.77 796.75 EST ISSN 0868-4405
AUTOREVUU. Text in Estonian. 1990. m. USD 42 (effective 1993). stat.
Published by: Kirjastus Perioodika, Voorimehe 9, Tallinn, 10146, Estonia. TEL 372-627-6421, FAX 372-627-6420. Ed. Vello Kala. Circ: 4,700.
Subscr. to: Akateeminen Kirjakauppa, PO Box 128, Helsinki 10 00101, Finland.

629 DEU
AUTOS BIS 5,000 EUROS. Text in German. m. EUR 2.50 newsstand/cover (effective 2011). adv. **Document type:** *Magazine, Consumer.*
Published by: Der Heisse Draht Verlag GmbH und Co., Drostestr 14, Hannover, 30161, Germany. TEL 49-511-390910, FAX 49-511-39091196, zentrale@dhd.de, http://www.dhd.de. Adv. contact Lars Schnatmann.

629.113 ARG ISSN 0329-3319
AUTOS DE EPOCA. Text in Spanish. 1996. q. ARS 6 newsstand/cover (effective 2001). adv. **Document type:** *Magazine, Consumer.*
Published by: Motorpress Argentina, S.A. (Subsidiary of: Gruner + Jahr AG & Co), Ituzaingo, 642-648, Buenos Aires, 1141, Argentina. TEL 54-114-3077672, FAX 54-114-3077858. Ed. Jorge Auge. Pub. Jesus Carrera. Adv. contact Adrian Lualdi. Circ: 4,500 (paid).

388.342 USA
AUTOS Y MAS. Text in Spanish. 2004. w. adv. **Description:** Used automobile guide.
Related titles: Online - full content ed.
Published by: ImpreMedia, LLC., 6001 N Clark St, Chicago, IL 60660. TEL 773-273-2900, FAX 773-273-2926. Ed. Jorge Mederos. Pub. Robert Armband TEL 773-273-2901. Adv. contact Joe Matessa TEL 773-273-2937. B&W page USD 395; trim 8.25 x 10. Circ: 17,984 (free).

629.331 CZE ISSN 1212-7264
AUTOSALON. Text in Czech. 1997. a. adv. **Document type:** *Magazine, Consumer.*
Supersedes in part (in 1998): Cesky Autosalon (1211-7641)
Published by: Axel Springer Praha a.s., Rosmarin Business Center, Dilnicka 12, Prague 7, 17000, Czech Republic. TEL 420-2-34692111, FAX 420-2-34692102, v.kodym@axelspringer.cz, http://www.axelspringer.cz.

388.3 CAN ISSN 1480-347X
AUTOSERVICE QUARTERLY. Text in English. 1947. q. CAD 18 domestic; USD 18 foreign (effective 1999). adv. bk.rev. **Document type:** *Magazine, Trade.* **Description:** For the automotive repair and aftermarket industries in western Canada.
Formerly (until 1997): Automotive Retailer (0005-1578)
Related titles: Microform ed.: (from PQC).
Indexed: C03, CBCABus, CBPI, PQC.
Published by: Automotive Retailers' Publishing Co. Ltd., 8980 Fraserwood Ct, Unit 1, Burnaby, BC V5J 5H7, Canada. TEL 604-432-7987, FAX 604-432-1756. Ed., R&P Reg Romero. Adv. contact Lea Allen. Circ: 8,000.

388.342 TUR
AUTOSHOW. Text in Turkish. w. **Document type:** *Magazine, Trade.*
Published by: D M G Magazines, Evren Oto Sanayi Sitesi Yani, Esenyurt - Istanbul, 34850, Turkey. TEL 90-212-6221441, FAX 90-212-6221442.

796.72 GBR ISSN 0269-946X
AUTOSPORT. Text in English. 1950. w. GBP 125 combined subscription (print & online eds.) (effective 2009). adv. charts; illus.; stat. back issues avail. **Document type:** *Magazine, Consumer.* **Description:** Covers all aspects of the sport, from the major international series such as Formula 1, IndyCar and World Rally to grass roots UK club motorsport.
Related titles: Microform ed.: (from PQC); Online - full text ed.: GBP 32.50, EUR 42, USD 65 (effective 2009).
—CCC.
Published by: Haymarket Publishing Ltd. (Subsidiary of: Haymarket Media Group), 174 Hammersmith Rd, London, W6 7JP, United Kingdom. TEL 44-20-82674210, info@haymarket.com, http://www.haymarket.com. Ed. Andy Van De Burgt TEL 44-20-82675974. Pub. Rob Aherne TEL 44-20-82675428. Adv. contact Matthew Witham TEL 44-20-82675146. Circ: 34,442. **Subscr. to:** PO Box 568, Haywards Heath RH16 3XQ, United Kingdom. TEL 44-8456-777800, Haymarket.subs@qss-uk.com, http://www.themagazineshop.com.

796.77 PRT ISSN 0870-1857
AUTOSPORT. Text in Portuguese. 1977. w. **Document type:** *Newsletter, Consumer.*
Related titles: Online - full text ed.
Published by: Medipress Sociedade Editora de Publicacoes, Lda., Av. Infante D. Henrique 334, Lisbon, 1900, Portugal. TEL 351-21-8542000, FAX 351-21-8530732. Ed., Pub. Rui Freire. Adv. contact Luis Caramelo. Circ: 75,000 (controlled).

AUTOSPRINT. *see* SPORTS AND GAMES

796.77 ROM
AUTOSTRADA. Text in Romanian. w. **Document type:** *Magazine, Consumer.*
Published by: R H Press srl, Calea Plevnei nr. 114, sector 6, Bucharest, Romania. TEL 40-21-3102052, FAX 40-21-3123764.

629.331 ESP ISSN 1134-2080
AUTOTEC. Text in Spanish. 1994. m. EUR 50 domestic (effective 2010). adv. **Document type:** *Magazine, Consumer.*
Published by: R D M Editorial, Poligono Industrial Norte, c/ Gomera, 10-2 B, San Sebastian de los Reyes, 28700, Spain. TEL 34-91-6518227, FAX 34-91-6518227, rdm@rdmeditorial.com.

629.286 ITA ISSN 1121-3450
AUTOTECNICA; research projects development production testing. Key Title: Auto Tecnica. Text in Italian. 1981. m. EUR 50 domestic (effective 2009). Website rev. 110 p./no.; back issues avail. **Document type:** *Magazine, Trade.*
Published by: Nuovi Periodici Milanesi, Via Molise 3, Locate Triulzi, MI 20085, Italy. http://www.nuoviperiodicimilanesi.com. Circ: 65,000 (paid).

796.77 CZE ISSN 1210-1087
AUTOTIP. Text in Czech. 1991. fortn. CZK 690; CZK 29.90 newsstand/cover (effective 2011). adv. 50 p./no. 4 cols./p.; **Document type:** *Magazine, Consumer.*
Published by: Axel Springer Praha a.s., Rosmarin Business Center, Dilnicka 12, Prague 7, 17000, Czech Republic. TEL 420-2-34692111, FAX 420-2-34692102, http://www.axelspringer.cz. Ed. Vitezslav Kodym. Adv. contact Petra Kardova. Circ: 53,000 (paid). **Subscr. to:** SEND Predplatne s.r.o., PO Box 141, Prague 4 140 21, Czech Republic. TEL 420-225-985225, FAX 420-225-341425, send@send.cz.

388.3 363.7 USA
AUTOTRADER GREEN. Text in English. w. **Document type:** *Magazine, Consumer.* **Description:** Covers fuel-efficient vehicles that get 30 miles per gallon or more.
Published by: AutoTrader Publishing, 5775 Peachtree Dunwoody Rd, Bldg A, Ste 200, Atlanta, GA 30342. http://www.autotraderpub.com/.

AUTOUNI - SCHRIFTENREIHE. *see* ENGINEERING—Industrial Engineering

▼ **AUTOUNI - SKRIPTENREIHE.** *see* ENGINEERING—Industrial Engineering

388.321 ESP
AUTOVERDE 4 X 4. Text in Spanish. 1988. m. adv. **Document type:** *Magazine, Consumer.*
Related titles: ◆ Supplement(s): Catalogo Autoverde 4 x 4.
Published by: Motorpress Iberica (Subsidiary of: Gruner + Jahr AG & Co), Ancora 40, Madrid, 28045, Spain. TEL 34-91-3470100, FAX 34-91-3470152, http://www.motorpress-iberica.es. Circ: 14,500 (paid).

388.3 DEU ISSN 0931-2366
DER AUTOVERMIETER. Text in German. 1955. q. EUR 32 domestic; EUR 44 foreign; EUR 7.65 newsstand/cover (effective 2007). adv. bk.rev. illus. index. **Document type:** *Magazine, Trade.* **Description:** Discusses automobile rentals.
Formerly (until 1986): Kraftfahrzeugvermieter (0023-4400)
—CCC.
Published by: (Bundesverband der Automieter Deutschlands e.V.), U P E - Unternehmens Presse Verlag Eckl GmbH, Karlstr 69, Bedburg, 50181, Germany. TEL 49-2272-91200, FAX 49-2272-912020, info@upe-verlag.de, http://www.upe-verlag.de. Ed., Pub. Christian Eckl. adv.: B&W page EUR 1,950, color page EUR 2,600. Circ: 1,500 (paid and controlled).

388 ESP
AUTOVIA. Text in Spanish. 1990. m. adv. **Document type:** *Magazine, Consumer.*
Published by: Motorpress Iberica (Subsidiary of: Gruner + Jahr AG & Co), Ancora 40, Madrid, 28045, Spain. TEL 34-91-3470100, FAX 34-91-3470152, http://www.motorpress-iberica.es. Ed. Adolfo Randulfe. Circ: 39,500 (paid).

388.3 NLD ISSN 0005-0873
AUTOVISIE. Text in Dutch. 1956. fortn. EUR 83; EUR 3.95 newsstand/cover (effective 2009). adv. bk.rev. **Document type:** *Consumer.*
—IE, Infotrieve.
Published by: De Telegraaf Tijdschriftengroep, Postbus 127, Amsterdam, 1000 AC, Netherlands. TEL 31-20-5852871, FAX 31-20-5853176, ttg@telegraaf.nl, http://www.ttg.nl. Eds. Ben Kuenen, Ton Roks. adv.: page EUR 4,874; trim 225 x 285. Circ: 47,565 (paid and controlled).

338.476 DEU
DIE AUTOWAESCHE. Text in German. 1972. bi-m. EUR 43.87 (effective 2010). adv. **Document type:** *Magazine, Trade.*
Published by: (Bundesverband Tankstellen und Gewerbliche Autowaesche Deutschland e.V.), Witas GmbH, Postfach 2227, Minden, 32379, Germany. TEL 49-571-886080, info@witas-minden.de, http://www.witas-minden.de. adv.: B&W page EUR 1,290, color page EUR 1,290. Circ: 3,400 (controlled).

388.3 USA ISSN 0192-9674
AUTOWEEK. Text in English. 1958. bi-w. (w. until 2009). USD 29.95 (effective 2008). adv. bk.rev. illus. reprints avail. **Document type:** *Magazine, Consumer.* **Description:** Provides information for those especially interested in the most up-to-date news on new vehicles, product eveluations, motorsports and automotive trends.

Former titles: Autoweek and Competition Press; (until 196?): Competition Press
Related titles: Online - full text ed.: AutoWeek Online. USD 32 (effective 2002); ◆ Includes: AutoWeek Racing Fan Guide; ◆ AutoWeek Strategic Buyer's Guide.
Indexed: A09, A10, A11, A15, A22, ABIn, B01, B06, B07, B08, B09, C05, C12, CPerl, G08, I05, I07, M01, M02, M06, MASUSE, P48, P51, P52, PQC, PROMT, S22, T02, V02, V03, V04.
—CIS, Linda Hall. **CCC.**
Published by: Crain Communications, Inc., 1155 Gratiot Ave, Detroit, MI 48207. TEL 313-446-6000, FAX 313-446-1616, http://www.crain.com. Eds. Dutch Mandel, Keith Craine. Pub. K. C. Crain Jr. adv.: B&W page USD 21,093, color page USD 32,855. Circ: 350,000 (paid).

629.222 NLD ISSN 1381-7973
AUTOWEEK. Text in Dutch. 1990. w. EUR 65; EUR 2.30 newsstand/cover (effective 2011). adv. charts; illus. **Document type:** *Magazine, Consumer.* **Description:** Profiles new cars, offering first impressions and technical analyses.
Related titles: Online - full text ed.
Published by: Sanoma Men's Magazines, Capellalaan 65, Hoofddorp, 2132 JL, Netherlands. TEL 31-88-7518380, sales@smm.nl, http://www.smm.nl. Ed. Tonie Broekhuijsen. Pub. Eric Ariens. Circ: 105,000 (paid).

388.3 USA
AUTOWEEK RACING FAN GUIDE. Text in English. 1994. 3/yr. adv. back issues avail.; reprints avail. **Document type:** *Guide, Consumer.* **Description:** Contains a complete run-down of all major racing series, top teams, drivers and tracks.
Formerly (until 199?): AutoWeek's Official Racing Fan Guide
Related titles: ◆ Issued with: AutoWeek. ISSN 0192-9674.
Published by: Crain Communications, Inc., 1155 Gratiot Ave, Detroit, MI 48207. TEL 313-446-6000, FAX 313-446-1616, info@crain.com, http://www.crain.com.

388.3 USA
AUTOWEEK STRATEGIC BUYER'S GUIDE. Variant title: AutoFile. Text in English. 1991. q. back issues avail.; reprints avail. **Document type:** *Guide, Consumer.*
Formerly: AutoWeek Complete Buyer's Guide
Related titles: ◆ Issued with: AutoWeek. ISSN 0192-9674.
Published by: Crain Communications, Inc., 1155 Gratiot Ave, Detroit, MI 48207. TEL 313-446-6000, FAX 313-446-1616, info@crain.com, http://www.crain.com.

629.33 658 NLD ISSN 1871-9821
AUTOZAKEN. Text in Dutch. 3/yr. adv.
Published by: Brand Communications, Westerkade 18 a, Postbus 835, Groningen, 9700 AV, Netherlands. TEL 31-50-3171717, FAX 31-50-3119366, info@brandcommunications.nl, http://www.brandcommunications.nl. adv.: color page EUR 1,590; trim 210 x 297. Circ: 10,000.

629.22 USA ISSN 0889-6267
TL215.A94
AVANTI MAGAZINE. Text in English. q. free to members (effective 2008). **Document type:** *Newsletter.*
Former titles (until 198?): Avanti Newsletter (0741-9252); (until 19??): Avanti Owners Association Newsletter (0149-1911)
Published by: Avanti Owners Association International, c/o Cornerstone Registration Ltd., P O Box 1743, Maple Grove, MN 55311-6743. backissues@aoai.org, http://www.aoai.org.

796.77 DEU
AVENUE. Text in German. 1992. q. EUR 4.50 newsstand/cover (effective 2006). adv. **Document type:** *Magazine, Consumer.*
Published by: Journal International Verlags- und Werbegesellschaft mbH, Hanns-Seidel-Platz 5, Munich, 81737, Germany. TEL 49-89-6427970, FAX 49-89-64279777, info@journal-international.de, http://www.journal-international.de. Ed. Jens Leichsenring. Adv. contact Josef Rindert. color page EUR 8,500; trim 210 x 295. Circ: 280,000 (controlled).

629.286 UKR
AVISO-AVTO. Text in Russian. free (effective 2002). **Document type:** *Newspaper, Consumer.*
Published by: Aviso, PO Box 182, Kiev, 252042, Ukraine. TEL 380-44-2681716, 380-44-2689016, http://www.aviso.com.ua. Circ: 60,000.

388.3 RUS
AVTO. Text in Russian. w. USD 239.95 in United States.
Published by: Izdatel'stvo Avto, Butyrskii val 24, Moscow, 125047, Russian Federation. TEL 7-095-9789414, FAX 7-095-9784655. Ed. V A Simonyan. **Dist. by:** East View Information Services, 10601 Wayzata Blvd, Minneapolis, MN 55305. TEL 952-252-1201, 800-477-1005, FAX 952-252-1202, info@eastview.com, http://www.eastview.com.

388.3 MDA
AVTO-EKSPRESS/AUTO-EXPRESS. Text in Russian. w. **Document type:** *Newspaper, Consumer.* **Description:** Devoted to matters of efficient use of vehicles, conditions of roads, traffic safety, information on how to operate and look after your car.
Published by: Nezavisimaya Moldova, Ul Pushkin 22, Chisinau, 2012, Moldova. TEL 373-2-233605, FAX 373-2-233141, tis@nemo.moldova.su, http://www.mldnet.com/nezmold/index.html. Ed. Nikolai Varikash TEL 373-2-233104.

629.114 SVN ISSN 1580-1195
AVTO FOKUS. Text in Slovenian. 1999. m. USD 83 foreign (effective 2007). adv. **Document type:** *Magazine, Consumer.*
Related titles: Online - full content ed.: ISSN 1581-002X. 2001.
Published by: Avto Medija d. o. o, Dimiceva ul 16, Ljubljana, 1000, Slovenia. TEL 386-1-2361000, FAX 386-1-2361010, http://www.polet-press.si. Ed. Semo Sadikovic.

388.3 UKR
AVTO FOTO PRODAZHA. Text in Ukrainian. 1995. w. USD 601 in United States (effective 2008). **Document type:** *Magazine, Consumer.*
Address: vul Marshala Grechka, 13, Kyiv, Ukraine. **Dist. by:** East View Information Services, 10601 Wayzata Blvd, Minneapolis, MN 55305. TEL 952-252-1201, 800-477-1005, FAX 952-252-1202, info@eastview.com, http://www.eastview.com.

629.2 796.7 388.3 SVN ISSN 0352-5368
AVTO MAGAZIN. Text in Slovenian. 1967. fortn. EUR 72.80 (effective 2008). adv. **Document type:** *Magazine, Consumer.* **Description:** Reports on the latest trends and models in the automobile industry.
Published by: Adria Media Ljubljana, Zaloznistvo in Trzenje, d.o.o., Vosnjakova ulica 3, Ljubljana, 1000, Slovenia. TEL 386-1-3000700, FAX 386-1-3000713, info@adriamedia.si, http://www.adriamedia.si. adv.: page EUR 1,800; trim 210 x 280. Circ: 16,000 (paid).

629.113 RUS ISSN 1682-2390
AVTO STIL'. Text in Russian. 2001. bi-m. **Document type:** *Magazine, Consumer.*
Published by: S K Press, Marksistkaya 34, str 10, Moscow, 109147, Russian Federation. deliver@skpress.ru, http://www.skpress.ru.

388.3 028.5 RUS
AVTO-YUNIOR. Text in Russian. s-a. USD 65 in United States.
Published by: Novaya Igrushechka, B Nikitskaya 50-5, kab 24, Moscow, 121069, Russian Federation. TEL 7-095-2916022, FAX 7-095-2916325. Ed. N D Eremchenko. **Dist. by:** East View Information Services, 10601 Wayzata Blvd, Minneapolis, MN 55305. TEL 952-252-1201, 800-477-1005, FAX 952-252-1202, info@eastview.com, http://www.eastview.com.

388.3 RUS
AVTOGID. Text in Russian. m. USD 85 in United States.
Published by: Izdatel'stvo Dorogi, Ul Shchepkina 11, Moscow, 129090, Russian Federation. TEL 7-095-2843189, FAX 7-095-2843838. Ed. V F Polyakov. **Dist. by:** East View Information Services, 10601 Wayzata Blvd, Minneapolis, MN 55305. TEL 952-252-1201, 800-477-1005, FAX 952-252-1202, info@eastview.com, http://www.eastview.com.

629.11 UKR ISSN 1681-3154
AVTOMIR. Text in Ukrainian. 1998. w. adv. **Document type:** *Magazine, Consumer.* **Description:** Contains extensive new and used car comparisons, repair shop and tire tests, service and personal tips, and travel information.
Published by: Burda Ukraina, Zhyljanskaja ul. 29, Kiev, 01033, Ukraine. TEL 38-044-4908363, FAX 38-044-4908364, zhestkov@burda.ua, http://www.burda.ua. Ed. Vitalii Novak TEL 380-44-4908361. adv.: page USD 2,500. Circ: 30,000 (paid and controlled).

629.113 RUS ISSN 1560-5396
AVTOMIR. Text in German. 1997. w. adv. **Document type:** *Magazine, Consumer.* **Description:** Contains extensive new and used car comparisons, repair shop and tire tests, service and personal tips, as well as travel information and insurance advice.
Published by: Izdatel'skii Dom Burda, ul Pravdy 8, Moscow, 125040, Russian Federation. TEL 7-095-7979849, FAX 7-095-2571196, vertrieb@burda.ru, http://www.burda.ru. adv.: page USD 4,800. Circ: 200,000 (paid and controlled).

629.113 RUS ISSN 1607-9663
AVTOMIR. AVTOKATALOG. Text in Russian. 2000. s-a. adv. **Document type:** *Magazine, Consumer.*
Published by: Izdatel'skii Dom Burda, ul Pravdy 8, Moscow, 125040, Russian Federation. TEL 7-095-7979849, FAX 7-095-2571196, vertrieb@burda.ru, http://www.burda.ru. adv.: page USD 3,000. Circ: 100,000 (paid and controlled).

629.113 UKR
AVTOMIR. AVTOKATALOG. Text in Russian. s-a. **Document type:** *Catalog, Consumer.*
Published by: Burda Ukraina, Zhyljanskaja ul. 29, Kiev, 01033, Ukraine. TEL 38-044-4908363, FAX 38-044-4908364, zhestkov@burda.ua, http://www.burda.ua.

388.3 UKR
AVTOMOBIL'. Text in Russian. 24/yr. USD 125 in United States.
Published by: Tovarystvo Intertekh, Aerovokzal'naya ul 3, Kiev, Ukraine. TEL 224-40-57. **Dist. by:** East View Information Services, 10601 Wayzata Blvd, Minneapolis, MN 55305. TEL 952-252-1201, 800-477-1005, FAX 952-252-1202, info@eastview.com, http://www.eastview.com.

388.3 RUS ISSN 1811-0037
AVTOMOBILI. Text in Russian. m. USD 142 in United States (effective 2004). **Document type:** *Magazine, Consumer.*
Address: Lubyanskii pr-d 5, ofis 3, Moscow, 101958, Russian Federation. TEL 7-095-9217211. **Dist. by:** East View Information Services, 10601 Wayzata Blvd, Minneapolis, MN 55305. TEL 952-252-1201, 800-477-1005, FAX 952-252-1202, info@eastview.com, http://www.eastview.com.

338.3 RUS ISSN 0005-2337
TL4 CODEN: AVPRA3
AVTOMOBIL'NAYA PROMYSHLENNOST'. Text in Russian. 1930. m. USD 634 foreign (effective 2004). adv. bk.rev. bibl.; charts; illus. index. **Document type:** *Academic/Scholarly.* **Description:** Introduces the reader to new developments in the theory and practice of the automobile industry as well as to the state-of-the-art and trends in the automovile industry in foreign countries.
Indexed: C&ISA, CIN, ChemAb, ChemTitl, CorrAb, E&CAJ, RASB, RefZh, SCOPUS, SolStAb, TM, WAA.
—CASDDS, East View, INIST, Linda Hall. **CCC.**
Published by: (Komitet Rossiiskoi Federatsii po Mashinostroeniyu), Izdatel'stvo Mashinostroenie, Stromynskii per 4, Moscow, 107076, Russian Federation. TEL 7-095-2683858, mashpubl@mashin.ru, http://www.mashin.ru. Ed. V P Morozov. adv.: page MRK 4,000. Circ: 8,000. **Dist. by:** M K - Periodica, ul Gilyarovskogo 39, Moscow 129110, Russian Federation. TEL 7-095-2845008, FAX 7-095-2813798, info@periodicals.ru, http://www.mkniga.ru. **Co-sponsor:** AO Avtosel'khozmash-Kholding.

AVTOMOBIL'NYE DOROGI. *see* ENGINEERING—Civil Engineering

388.3 RUS ISSN 0005-2345
TL4 CODEN: AVTRAN
AVTOMOBIL'NYI TRANSPORT. Short title: A T. Text in Russian. 1923. m. USD 156 (effective 1998). charts; illus. **Description:** Covers all aspects of transportation.
Indexed: ChemAb, RASB, RefZh.
—BLDSC (0005.000000), East View.
Published by: (Russia. Ministerstvo Transporta), Concern Rosavtotrans, Likhov per 3, str 1, Moscow, 103051, Russian Federation. TEL 7-095-2092778, FAX 7-095-2829558. Ed. E P Kuprin. **US dist. addr.:** East View Information Services, 10601 Wayzata Blvd, Minneapolis, MN 55305. TEL 952-252-1201, 800-477-1005, FAX 952-252-1202, info@eastview.com, http://www.eastview.com.

388.3 UKR ISSN 2219-8342
➤ **AVTOMOBIL'NYI TRANSPORT.** Text in Russian, Ukrainian, English. 1998. s-a. **Document type:** *Journal, Academic/Scholarly.*
Related titles: Online - full text ed.: free (effective 2011).
Published by: Kharkivs'kyi Natsional'nyi Avtomobil'no-Dorozhnii Universytet, vul Petrovs'kogo 25, Kharkivukr, 61002, Ukraine. TEL 380-57-7073799, rio@khadi.kharkov.ua. Ed. A M Turenko. Circ: 110.

388.3 RUS
AVTOPANORAMA. Text in Russian. m. USD 179 in United States.
Address: Volgogradskii pr-t 26, ofis 1405, Moscow, 109316, Russian Federation. TEL 7-095-2708852. **Dist. by:** East View Information Services, 10601 Wayzata Blvd, Minneapolis, MN 55305. TEL 952-252-1201, 800-477-1005, FAX 952-252-1202, info@eastview.com, http://www.eastview.com.

388.3 RUS
AVTOPILOT. Text in Russian. 1994. m. USD 235 in United States (effective 2008). **Document type:** *Magazine, Consumer.* **Description:** An automotive trend-setting magazine.
Published by: Izdatel'skii Dom Kommersant, ul Vrubelya 4, str 1, Moscow, 125080, Russian Federation. TEL 7-095-9439771, FAX 7-095-9439728, kommersant@kommersant.ru, http://www.kommersant.ru. Ed. Nikolai Fomenko. **Dist. by:** East View Information Services, 10601 Wayzata Blvd, Minneapolis, MN 55305. TEL 952-252-1201, FAX 952-252-1202, info@eastview.com, http://www.eastview.com.

388.3 UKR
AVTOPROFI. Text in Ukrainian. 24/yr. USD 145 in United States.
Published by: Izdatel'skii Dom Avtoprofi, A-ya 112, Kiev, 252055, Ukraine. TEL 417-21-15. **Dist. by:** East View Information Services, 10601 Wayzata Blvd, Minneapolis, MN 55305. TEL 952-252-1201, 800-477-1005, FAX 952-252-1202, info@eastview.com, http://www.eastview.com.

388.1 RUS
AVTOREVYU/AUTOREVIEW. Text in Russian. 1990. s-m. USD 197 foreign (effective 2005). adv. **Document type:** *Newspaper, Consumer.* **Description:** Provides news on both foreign and domestic automotive industries, as well as extensive performance testing on new cars, trucks, tires, tools, and equipment. Reports from auto shows and exhibitions throughout the world and takes a look at motor sports.
Published by: Autoreview Ltd., A-ya 21, Moscow, 121170, Russian Federation. TEL 7-095-1290710, FAX 7-095-1248383. Ed., Pub. Mikhail Podorozhansky. R&P, Adv. contact Oleg Selikhov. B&W page USD 6,400, color page USD 8,000. Circ: 200,000. **Dist. by:** East View Information Services, 10601 Wayzata Blvd, Minneapolis, MN 55305. TEL 952-252-1201, 800-477-1005, FAX 952-252-1202, info@eastview.com, http://www.eastview.com.

388.3 RUS
AVTOSHOP. Text in Russian. m. USD 185 in United States.
Published by: Izdatel'skii Dom Pasport Interneishnl, Leningradskii pr-t 80-2, 5-a, Moscow, 125178, Russian Federation. TEL 7-095-1589754, FAX 7-095-1587376. Ed. S Yu Esenin. **Dist. by:** East View Information Services, 10601 Wayzata Blvd, Minneapolis, MN 55305. TEL 952-252-1201, 800-477-1005, FAX 952-252-1202, info@eastview.com, http://www.eastview.com.

388.3 RUS ISSN 1684-7725
AVTOSTROENIE ZA RUBEZHOM. Text in Russian. 1961. m. USD 626 foreign (effective 2004). **Document type:** *Journal, Trade.*
Formerly (until 1998): Avtomobil'naya Promyshlennost' (0320-6890)
Indexed: RefZh.
—East View.
Published by: Izdatel'stvo Mashinostroenie, Stromynskii per 4, Moscow, 107076, Russian Federation. TEL 7-095-2683858, mashpubl@mashin.ru. Ed. B I Trifontsev. **Dist. by:** M K - Periodica, ul Gilyarovskogo 39, Moscow 129110, Russian Federation. TEL 7-095-2845008, FAX 7-095-2813798, info@periodicals.ru, http://www.mkniga.ru.

388 RUS ISSN 1683-2841
AVTOTRIO. Text in Russian. 2002. m. **Document type:** *Magazine, Consumer.*
Address: ul Stromynka, 11, str 1, Moscow, 107014, Russian Federation.

388.3 UKR
AVTOVISNYK-LYUDYNA, DOROGA, AVTOMOBIL'. Text in Ukrainian. 24/yr. USD 145 in United States.
Address: Ul B Khmel'nitskogo 54, Kiev, Ukraine. TEL 291-39-44. **Dist. by:** East View Information Services, 10601 Wayzata Blvd, Minneapolis, MN 55305. TEL 952-252-1201, 800-477-1005, FAX 952-252-1202, info@eastview.com, http://www.eastview.com.

388.342 TUR
AYLIK ISTATISTIKI BILGILER BULTENI/MONTHLY STATISTICAL BULLETIN. Text in Turkish. m. **Document type:** *Magazine, Trade.*
Related titles: Online - full text ed.: free (effective 2009).
Published by: Otomotiv Sanayii Dernegi/Automotive Manufacturers Association, Atilla Sokak No 8, Altunizade - Istanbul, 81190, Turkey. TEL 90-216-3182994, FAX 90-216-3219497.

796.77 PHL
B B C TOP GEAR. Variant title: Top Gear. Text in English. 2004. m. PHP 1,275 (effective 2005). **Document type:** *Magazine, Consumer.* **Description:** Contains features on all auto makes and models, from everyday passenger sedans to the most exotic supercars money can buy.
Published by: Summit Media, Level 1, Robinsons Galleria, Ortigas Ave, Quezon City, 1100, Philippines. TEL 63-2-6317738, FAX 63-2-6372206, luz.bolos@summitmedia.com.ph, http://www.summitmedia.com.ph. Ed. Mike Black. Pub. Denis del Callar. Circ: 23,637 (paid).

796.77 GBR ISSN 1350-9624
B B C TOP GEAR. (British Broadcasting Corporation) Text in English. 1993. s-a. GBP 51.35 (effective 2009). adv. **Document type:** *Magazine, Consumer.* **Description:** Contains reviews of all the very latest cars, as well as head-to-head road tests with similar cars.
Related titles: Online - full text ed.
Published by: (British Broadcasting Corporation (B B C)), B B C Worldwide Ltd., 2nd Fl A, Energy Centre, Media Centre, 201 Wood Ln, London, W12 7TQ, United Kingdom. TEL 44-20-84333598, bbcworldwide@bbc.co.uk, http://www.bbcmagazines.com. Adv. contact Bernie Scranney TEL 44-20-84331677. **Subscr. to:** Dovetail Services UK Ltd, 800 Guillat Ave, Kent Science Park, Sittingbourne, Kent ME9 8GU, United Kingdom. TEL 44-844-8489767, http://www.dovetailservices.com/. **Dist. by:** Frontline, Midgate House, Midgate, Peterborough PE1 1TN, United Kingdom. TEL 44-1733-555161, FAX 44-1733-562788, http://www.frontline.ltd.uk/frontline.

B F P - FUHRPARK UND MANAGEMENT. *see* BUSINESS AND ECONOMICS—Management

388.342 HKG
B M W. Text in Chinese. q. free. adv. back issues avail.
Published by: Hachette Filipacchi Hong Kong Ltd., 15-F, East Wing, Warwick House, Taikoo Place, 979 King s Rd, Quarry Bay, Hong Kong, Hong Kong. TEL 852-2567-8707, FAX 852-2568-4650. Ed. Ma Waiying. Pub. Sandy Kwong. Adv. contact Tony Lo. page HKD 38,600; trim 215 x 280. Circ: 25,450.

629.222 GBR ISSN 1353-7954
B M W CAR; the independent BMW magazine. (Bayerische Motoren Werke) Text in English. 1994. m. GBP 43.20 domestic; GBP 62 in Europe; GBP 78 elsewhere; GBP 5 per issue (effective 2009). adv. illus. back issues avail. **Document type:** *Magazine, Consumer.* **Description:** Reviews new BMW cars and performance enhancements to existing models.
Published by: Unity Media PLC, Becket House, Vestry Rd, Sevenoaks, Kent TN14 5EJ, United Kingdom. TEL 44-1732-748000, FAX 44-1732-748001, http://www.unity-media.com/. Ed. Bob Harper TEL 44-1732-748033. Pub. Colin Wilkinson. Adv. contact Claire Greenland TEL 44-1732-748052. page GBP 1,650; trim 220 x 285.

629.2 DEU ISSN 0946-8390
B M W MAGAZIN. Text in English. 1991. q. EUR 14 (effective 2009). adv. **Document type:** *Magazine, Consumer.* **Description:** Lifestyle magazine targeting BMW owners and enthusiasts.
Published by: (Bayerische Motoren Werke AG), Hoffmann und Campe Verlag (Subsidiary of: Ganske Verlagsgruppe), Harvestehuder Weg 42, Hamburg, 20149, Germany. TEL 49-40-441880, FAX 49-40-44188202, email@hoca.de, http://www.hoffmann-und-campe.de. Ed. Bernd Zerelles. adv.: B&W page EUR 10,600, color page EUR 13,900. Circ: 559,618 (paid and controlled).

629.2 AUS ISSN 1444-402X
B M W MAGAZINE. (Bayerische Motoren Werke) Text in English. 2002. q. AUD 27.90 (effective 2008). back issues avail. **Document type:** *Magazine, Consumer.* **Description:** Provides information on BMW products, personalities, exotic travels and gourmet foods.
Related titles: Online - full text ed.
Published by: B M W Australia, PO Box 661, Mulgrave North, VIC 3170, Australia. TEL 800-813-299, FAX 800-350-528.

796.77 DEU ISSN 1610-9902
B M W SCENE LIVE. (Bayerische Motoren Werke) Text in German. 2001. bi-m. EUR 21 domestic; EUR 24 foreign; EUR 3.80 newsstand/cover (effective 2011). adv. **Document type:** *Magazine, Consumer.*
Published by: Vestische Mediengruppe Welke GmbH & Co. KG, Hertener Mark 7, Herten, 45699, Germany. TEL 49-2366-808400, FAX 49-2366-808499, info@vmw-verlag.de, http://vmw-verlag.de. Ed. Karlheinz Schnelzer. Pub. Arno Welke. Adv. contact Julia Wissing. Circ: 21,000 (paid and controlled).

796.77 GBR ISSN 0267-9841
BACK STREET HEROES. Text in English. 1983. m. GBP 43.89 domestic; GBP 55.89 in Europe; GBP 67.89 elsewhere (effective 2009). adv. bk.rev. back issues avail. **Document type:** *Magazine, Consumer.* **Description:** Covers motorcycles with particular emphasis on customizing and performance.
Published by: Ocean Media Group Ltd. (Subsidiary of: Trinity Mirror Plc.), 1 Canada Sq, 19th Fl, Canary Wharf, London, E14 5AP, United Kingdom. TEL 44-20-77728300, FAX 44-20-77728599, Pamela.McSweeney@oceanmedia.co.uk, http://www.oceanmedia.co.uk. Adv. contact Justin Driver TEL 44-207-7728327.

388.342 953.65 GBR ISSN 1748-9776
BAHRAIN AUTOS REPORT. Text in English. 2005. q. EUR 820, USD 1,030 combined subscription (print & email eds.) (effective 2010). **Document type:** *Report, Trade.* **Description:** Provides industry professionals and strategists, corporate analysts, auto associations, government departments and regulatory bodies with independent forecasts and competitive intelligence on the Bahraini automotives market.
Related titles: E-mail ed.
Indexed: A15, ABIn, B02, B15, B17, B18, G04, I05, P48, P51, P52, PQC.
Published by: Business Monitor International Ltd., Senator House, 85 Queen Victoria St, London, EC4V 4AB, United Kingdom. TEL 44-20-72480468, FAX 44-20-72480467, subs@businessmonitor.com.

796.77 GBR ISSN 1468-456X
BANZAI; Japanese performance magazine. Text in English. 1999. m. GBP 43.20 domestic; GBP 60 in Europe; GBP 71 elsewhere (effective 2009). adv. back issues avail. **Document type:** *Magazine, Consumer.* **Description:** Provides information about cars currently available in markets.
Related titles: Online - full text ed.
Published by: Unity Media PLC, Becket House, Vestry Rd, Sevenoaks, Kent TN14 5EJ, United Kingdom. TEL 44-1732-748000, FAX 44-1732-748001, http://www.unity-media.com/. Ed. Joe Clifford TEL 44-1732-748030. Pub. Colin Wilkinson. Adv. contact Cinnamon Lacey TEL 44-1732-748055. page GBP 950; trim 210 x 297.

388.3 USA ISSN 1939-4217
THE BARRETT - JACKSON EXPERIENCE. Text in English. 2005 (Dec.). q. USD 6.99 newsstand/cover (effective 2007). **Document type:** *Magazine, Consumer.* **Description:** Covers car collecting, trends, and information about the annual auction.
Published by: (Barrett - Jackson Auction Co.), Source Interlink Companies, 6420 Wilshire Blvd, 10th Fl, Los Angeles, CA 90048. TEL 323-782-2000, FAX 323-782-2585, dheine@sourceinterlink.com, http://www.sourceinterlinkmedia.com.

BATTERIES INTERNATIONAL. *see* ENGINEERING—Electrical Engineering

629.2 621.38 USA ISSN 0005-6359
THE BATTERY MAN; international journal for starting, lighting, ignition & generating systems. Text in English. 1921; N.S. 1959. 10/yr. USD 36 domestic; USD 47 foreign (effective 2005). adv. bk.rev. charts; illus.; tr.lit. index. reprints avail. **Document type:** *Magazine, Trade.* **Description:** Covers the battery industry, including the manufacture and sale of batteries, new developments and applications for batteries and general industry news.
Indexed: A22, Cadscan, LeadAb, Zincscan.
—IE, Ingenta, Linda Hall.
Published by: Battery Council International, 401 N Michigan Ave, Chicago, IL 60611. TEL 312-245-1074, FAX 312-527-6640, http://www.batterycouncil.org. Ed. Amy Carlton. Circ: 4,800 (controlled and free).

BELGIUM. INSTITUT NATIONAL DE STATISTIQUE. STATISTIQUES DU TRANSPORT. PARC DES VEHICULES A MOTEUR AU (YEAR). *see* TRANSPORTATION—Abstracting, Bibliographies, Statistics

BELGIUM. NATIONAAL INSTITUUT VOOR DE STATISTIEK. VERVOERSTATISTIEKEN. MOTORVOERTUIGENPARK OP (YEAR). *see* TRANSPORTATION—Abstracting, Bibliographies, Statistics

BENCHMARK REPAIR; the ultimate buyers guide for Taiwan auto repair tools. *see* BUSINESS AND ECONOMICS—Trade And Industrial Directories

BENCHMARK TOOL. *see* BUSINESS AND ECONOMICS—Trade And Industrial Directories

388 DEU ISSN 0945-0742
BERICHTE AUS DER FAHRZEUGTECHNIK. Text in German. 1994. irreg., latest 2009. price varies. **Document type:** *Monographic series, Academic/Scholarly.*
Published by: Shaker Verlag GmbH, Kaiserstr 100, Herzogenrath, 52134, Germany. TEL 49-2407-95960, FAX 49-2407-95969, info@shaker.de.

629.231 GBR ISSN 1751-2670
BERNOULLI AERODYNAMICS INTERNATIONAL. Text in English. 2006. q. GBP 40 domestic; GBP 49 in Europe; GBP 53 in United States; GBP 60 elsewhere (effective 2009). adv. **Document type:** *Magazine, Consumer.* **Description:** Contents include road and race car aero design and development studies and insights into wind tunnel design and operation, the use of CFD and on-track aero testing techniques.
Published by: Racecar Graphic Ltd., 841 High Rd, Finchley, London, N12 8PT, United Kingdom. TEL 44-20-84462100, FAX 44-20-84462191, info@racetechmag.com. Ed. William Kimberley. adv.: color page GBP 1,600, color page USD 3,200, B&W page GBP 1,400, B&W page USD 2,800; trim 210 x 297.

388 JPN
BEST CAR. Text in Japanese. 1978. s-m. **Document type:** *Magazine, Consumer.* **Description:** For car enthusiasts.
Formerly: Best Car Guide
Published by: Kodansha Ltd., 2-12-21 Otowa, Bunkyo-ku, Tokyo, 112-8001, Japan. TEL 81-3-3946-6201, FAX 81-3-3944-9915, http://www.kodansha.co.jp. Ed. Yu Katsumata. Circ: 470,000.

388.3 FRA ISSN 1291-3960
BEST CARS MAGAZINE. Text in French. 1998. m. **Document type:** *Magazine, Consumer.*
Published by: Editions Lariviere, 6 Rue Olof Palme, Clichy, 92587, France. TEL 33-1-47565400, http://www.editions-lariviere.fr.

796.77 ITA ISSN 1971-0224
BEST MOTORING. Text in Italian. 2006. bi-m. **Document type:** *Magazine, Consumer.*
Published by: Eurosport Editoriale, Via della Bufalotta 378, Rome, 00139, Italy. TEL 39-06-45231508, FAX 39-06-45231599, info@eurosporteditoriale.com, http://www.eurosporteditoriale.com.

796.77 USA ISSN 1527-9197
BEST OF LOWRIDER. Text in English. 1995. a. USD 7.95 newsstand/cover (effective 2007). adv. **Document type:** *Magazine, Consumer.*
Published by: Source Interlink Companies, 2400 E Katella Ave, 11th Fl, Anaheim, CA 92806. TEL 714-939-2400, FAX 714-978-6390, dheine@sourceinterlink.com, http://www.sourceinterlink.com.

BEST OF TATTOO REVUE PRESENTS: HOT ROD TATTOO. *see* HOBBIES

629.1 DEU ISSN 0933-2553
BEWERTUNG VON NUTZFAHRZEUGEN. Text in German. 1987. irreg. **Document type:** *Monographic series, Trade.*
Published by: D E K R A - AG, Handwerkstr 15, Stuttgart, 70565, Germany. TEL 49-711-78610, FAX 49-711-78612204, info@dekra.de, http://www.dekra.de.

388 629.2 NOR ISSN 0800-5850
BIL. Text in Norwegian. 1975. 10/yr. NOK 395 (effective 2005). adv. **Document type:** *Magazine, Trade.* **Description:** Includes results of testing of new cars and car related products. Covers technical features, in-car entertainment equipment. Company cars and used cars.
Incorporates (1984-2002): Firmabil (0800-5869)
Related titles: Online - full text ed.
—CCC.
Published by: Bilforlaget, Urtegaten 9, PO Box 9247, Oslo, 0134, Norway. TEL 47-23-036600, FAX 47-23-036640. Ed. Jon Winding-Soerensen. Adv. contact Magne Stenberg TEL 47-23-036625. B&W page NOK 26,300, color page NOK 36,800; 192 x 260. Circ: 56,383.

629.22 796.77 DNK ISSN 0906-5474
BIL MAGASINET. Variant title: Bilmagasinet. Bilmarkedet Plus. Text in Danish. 1989. m. DKK 479 (effective 2009). adv. back issues avail. **Document type:** *Magazine, Consumer.* **Description:** Publishes articles and information on automobiles, new engineering and design.
Formerly (until 1991): Bil Markedet (0906-5172); Incorporates (1974-2001): Bilen (0106-9470); Which was formerly (until 1975): Bilen, Baaden og Motor-Journalen (0106-9462); Which was formed by the merger of (1967-1974): Bilen og Baaden (0006-2464); (1973-1974): Motor-Journalen (0106-9454)
Published by: Benjamin Media A/S, Finsensvej 6 D, Frederiksberg, 2000, Denmark. TEL 45-70-220255, FAX 45-70-220056, http://www.benjamin.dk. Ed. Mikkel Thomsager. adv.: page DKK 38,200; 202 x 267. Circ: 41,596 (paid).

629.22 DNK ISSN 0107-0924
BIL-REVYEN. Text in Danish. 1965. a. DKK 148 per issue (effective 2009). adv. mkt. **Document type:** *Yearbook, Consumer.* **Description:** Full color catalogue of more than 1200 cars from all over the world.
Published by: Benjamin Media A/S, Finsensvej 6 D, Frederiksberg, 2000, Denmark. TEL 45-70-220255, FAX 45-70-220056, http://www.benjamin.dk.

629.113 ISL ISSN 1025-255X
BILABLADID BILLINN. Text in Icelandic. 1984. bi-m. ISK 2,874. adv.
Former titles (until 1995): Billinn (1017-351X); Bilabladid Billinn; Bilabladid Oekuthor
Published by: (Icelandic AAA), Humall Ltd., Myrargata 26, Reykjavik, 101, Iceland. TEL 354-552-6090, FAX 354-515-5599. Ed. Leo M Jonsson. Adv. contact Sjoefn Sigurgeirsdottir. B&W page ISK 46,900, color page ISK 81,800; trim 190 x 270. Circ: 8,000.

629.222 DNK ISSN 1603-8347
BILARBOGEN. Text in Danish. 2004. a. DKK 128 (effective 2009). adv. **Document type:** *Magazine, Consumer.*
Published by: Egmont Magasiner A/S, Hellerupvej 51, Hellerup, 2900, Denmark. TEL 45-39-457500, FAX 45-39-457404, abo@egmontmagasiner.dk, http://www.egmont-magasiner.dk. Ed. Michael Rasmussen.

659 SWE ISSN 1650-5913
BILBOERSEN. Text in Swedish. 2001. 12/yr. SEK 25 newsstand/cover (effective 2010). adv. mkt. **Document type:** *Magazine, Consumer.*
Published by: Foerlags AB Albinsson & Sjoeberg, PO Box 529, Karlskrona, 37123, Sweden. TEL 46-455-335325, FAX 46-455-311715, fabas@fabas.se, http://www.fabas.se. Ed. Fredrik Lund. Adv. contact Stefan Janeld. page SEK 6,000; trim 190 x 275.

388.3 NOR ISSN 0006-2367
BILBRANSJEN - BILTEKNISK FAGBLAD. Text in Norwegian. 1929. m. NOK 420 domestic; NOK 450 elsewhere (effective 2002). adv. charts; illus.; stat.; tr.lit.
Incorporates (1981-1985): Dekk Aktuelt (0333-3523); Incorporates (1931-1978): Oljebladet (0030-2120); Incorporates (1942-1964): Bilteknisk Fagblad (0332-6829); Formerly (until 1949): Automobilforhandleren (0806-2420)
—CCC.
Published by: Norges Bilbransjeforbund, Drammensveien 97, PO Box 2804, Solli, Oslo, 0204, Norway. TEL 47-22-54-21-00, FAX 47-22-54-21-40. Ed. Oyvind Holmvik. Circ: 5,000.

388.3 SWE ISSN 0282-0536
BILISMEN I SVERIGE. Text in Swedish. 1948. a.
Related titles: ◆ Swedish ed.: Motor Traffic in Sweden. ISSN 0077-1619.
Published by: AB Bilstatistik, Fack 26173, Stockholm, 10041, Sweden.

796.77 SWE ISSN 0347-2035
BILSPORT. Text in Swedish. 1962. 24/yr. SEK 995 (effective 2010). adv. back issues avail. **Document type:** *Magazine, Consumer.* **Description:** Contains articles about car racing and its personalities.
Published by: Foerlags AB Albinsson & Sjoeberg, PO Box 529, Karlskrona, 37123, Sweden. TEL 46-455-335325, FAX 46-455-311715, fabas@fabas.se, http://www.fabas.se. Ed. Mikael Johansson. Adv. contact Per Oestman. color page SEK 32,400; trim 190 x 275. Circ: 36,900 (controlled).

629.1 SWE ISSN 1404-0506
BILSPORT CLASSIC. Text in Swedish. 1999. m. SEK 249 for 6 mos. (effective 2010). adv. **Document type:** *Magazine, Consumer.*
Published by: Foerlags AB Albinsson & Sjoeberg, PO Box 529, Karlskrona, 37123, Sweden. TEL 46-455-335325, FAX 46-455-311715, fabas@fabas.se, http://www.fabas.se. Ed. Magnus Karlsson. Adv. contact Therese Lindell Antonsson. page SEK 14,000; trim 190 x 275. Circ: 27,800 (paid).

629.2 SWE ISSN 1653-9060
BILSPORT GATBILAR.SE. Text in Swedish. 2006. bi-m. SEK 149 for 4 nos. (effective 2010). adv. **Document type:** *Magazine, Consumer.*
Published by: Foerlags AB Albinsson & Sjoeberg, PO Box 529, Karlskrona, 37123, Sweden. TEL 46-455-335325, FAX 46-455-311715, fabas@fabas.se, http://www.fabas.se. Ed. Daniel Lindstedt. Adv. contact Per Oestman. page SEK 11,700; trim 202 x 265. Circ: 9,100 (paid).

BILSPORT JUNIOR. *see* CHILDREN AND YOUTH—For

388.3 USA ISSN 1097-7465
TL215.B25
BIMMER; the magazine about B M W. Text in English. 1998. 8/yr. USD 19.99 domestic; USD 28 in Canada; USD 36 elsewhere; USD 4.99 per issue (effective 2011). adv. back issues avail. **Document type:** *Magazine, Consumer.*
Published by: Ross Periodicals, 42 Digital Dr, Ste 5, Novato, CA 94949. TEL 415-382-0580, FAX 415-382-0587. Adv. contact Holly Lundgren TEL 415-382-2860.

388.3 AUS ISSN 1036-3165
BLACK & WHITE DATA BOOK. Text in English. 1990. a. AUD 99 per issue (effective 2008). adv. **Document type:** *Directory, Trade.* **Description:** Provides key automotive industry contacts, previous and future import trends and industry web listings.
Related titles: Online - full text ed.
Published by: Glass' Guide Pty. Ltd., 48 La Trobe St, Melbourne, VIC 3000, Australia. TEL 61-3-96633009, FAX 61-3-96633049, customers@glassguide.com.au, http://www.glassguide.com.au. adv.: color page USD 800; trim 156 x 225.

BLACK BOOK. C P I VALUE GUIDE. (Cars of Particular Interest) *see* BUSINESS AND ECONOMICS—Trade And Industrial Directories

BLACK BOOK. HISTORICAL USED CAR XPRESS. *see* BUSINESS AND ECONOMICS—Trade And Industrial Directories

BLACK BOOK. HISTORY XPRESS. *see* BUSINESS AND ECONOMICS—Trade And Industrial Directories

BLACK BOOK. MONTHLY USED CAR XPRESS. *see* BUSINESS AND ECONOMICS—Trade And Industrial Directories

BLACK BOOK. NEW CAR XPRESS. *see* BUSINESS AND ECONOMICS—Trade And Industrial Directories

BLACK BOOK. OFFICIAL OLD CAR MARKET GUIDE. *see* BUSINESS AND ECONOMICS—Trade And Industrial Directories

BLACK BOOK. OFFICIAL RESIDUAL VALUE GUIDE. *see* BUSINESS AND ECONOMICS—Trade And Industrial Directories

BLACK BOOK. OFFICIAL USED CAR MARKET GUIDE MONTHLY. *see* BUSINESS AND ECONOMICS—Trade And Industrial Directories

388.329 640.73 USA ISSN 1544-9637
BLACK BOOK. ORIGINAL NEW CAR COST GUIDE. Variant title: New Car Cost Guide. Original New Car Cost Guide. Text in English. 19??. 7/yr. USD 90 (effective 2008). **Document type:** *Directory, Trade.*
Formerly (until 19??): Black Book. New Car Cost Guide (0731-4787)
Related titles: Online - full text ed.
Published by: Black Book National Auto Research (Subsidiary of: Hearst Corporation), PO Box 758, Gainesville, GA 30503. TEL 770-532-4111, 800-554-1026, info@BlackBookUSA.com, http://www.blackbookusa.com.

BLACK BOOK. TRUCK AND VAN GUIDE. see BUSINESS AND ECONOMICS—Trade And Industrial Directories

BLACK BOOK. WEEKLY USED CAR GUIDE. see BUSINESS AND ECONOMICS—Trade And Industrial Directories

BLACK BOOK XPRESS. see BUSINESS AND ECONOMICS—Trade And Industrial Directories

BLACK BOOK. XPRESS FOR EXOTIC AND OLDER CARS. see BUSINESS AND ECONOMICS—Trade And Industrial Directories

BLACK BOOK XPRESS FOR NEW CARS. see BUSINESS AND ECONOMICS—Trade And Industrial Directories

BLACK BOOK XPRESS FOR USED VEHICLES. see BUSINESS AND ECONOMICS—Trade And Industrial Directories

388.3 USA
THE BLUE SEAL TECH NEWS. Text in English. 1984. q. free (effective 2009). illus.; stat. back issues avail. **Document type:** *Newsletter, Trade.* **Description:** Provides information for automotive technicians and parts specialists who have passed ASE certification exams and their employers.
Formerly (until 1995): Blue Seal (0897-9421)
Related titles: Online - full text ed.
Published by: National Institute for Automotive Service Excellence, 101 Blue Seal Dr, SE Ste 101, Leesburg, VA 20175. TEL 703-669-6600, 888-273-8378, FAX 703-669-6123, asehelp@act.org. Ed. Martin Lawson.

388.3 330 USA
BLUE SKY. Text in English. 2005. q. **Document type:** *Magazine, Trade.* **Description:** Provides information for Honda and Acura dealers, including customer experience, business efficiency, and market development.
Published by: (America Honda), Tendo Communications, 340 Brannan St., Ste. 500, San Francisco, CA 94107. TEL 415-369-8200, FAX 415-369-8222, inquiries@tendocom.com, http://www.tendocom.com/.

338 USA
BLUEGRASS AUTOMOTIVE REPORT. Text in English. 1995. m. free to qualified personnel (effective 2008). adv. **Document type:** *Newspaper, Trade.* **Description:** Business newspaper for regional automotive industries, including body shops, independent repair shops, car dealers and others. News coverage is local and national. Monthly features include a local business profile, racing notes, a humor column, industry feedback and much more.
Indexed: V03.
Published by: Autographic Publishing Company, Inc., 1121 Airport Center Dr, Ste 101, Nashville, TN 37214. TEL 615-391-3666, 800-467-3666, FAX 615-391-3622, garnett@automotivereport.net, http://www.automotivereport.net. Ed. Garnett Forkum. Pub. Allen Forkum. adv.: B&W page USD 1,200; trim 11.5 x 15. Circ: 7,000 (free).

388.33 629.2 GBR ISSN 0006-5501
BODY. Text in English. 1914. m. GBP 40 domestic; GBP 55 in Europe; GBP 65 includes Middle East, Africa, Canada and USA; GBP 70 includes Pacific and Far East (effective 2009). adv. illus.; stat.; tr.lit. back issues avail. **Document type:** *Magazine, Trade.* **Description:** Features company profiles, news analysis, new product information, health and safety/environmental/employment legislation updates, as well as information on new vehicle manufacturing and repair techniques.
—BLDSC (2117.200000).
Published by: Vehicle Builders and Repairers Association Ltd., Belmont House, 102 Finkle Ln, Gildersome, Leeds, W Yorks LS27 7TW, United Kingdom. TEL 44-113-2538333, FAX 44-113-2380496, vbra@vbra.co.uk, http://www.vbra.co.uk/. Ed. Judi Barton TEL 44-1423-733120. Adv. contact Sophie Dickson TEL 44-1536-747333.

629.286 USA
BODY ENGINEERING. Text in English. s-a. free to members; USD 20 to non-members (effective 2005). adv. tr.lit. reprints avail. **Document type:** *Magazine, Trade.*
Published by: American Society of Body Engineers, 2122 15 Mile Rd, Sterling Heights, Macomb, MI 48310. TEL 586-268-8360, FAX 586-268-2187. Eds. Elfriede Schlenker, Robert Szefi. Pub. Mike Hopper. Circ: 5,800 (paid).

629.286 USA
BODY LANGUAGE. Text in English. 1982. m. USD 90 domestic; USD 110 foreign (effective 2001); includes Collision Parts Journal & Buyers Directory. **Document type:** *Newsletter.* **Description:** Covers automobile repair industry including updates on legislation, regulation and legal activities as they affect the state of collision repair and the use of aftermarket (non-OEM) replacement body parts.
Published by: (Automotive Body Parts Association), Sarco Management and Publications, P O Box 820689, Houston, TX 77282-0689. TEL 800-323-5832. Ed., Pub. Stanley A Rodman. Circ: 400.

388.3 CAN ISSN 0045-2319
BODYSHOP (ENGLISH EDITION). Text in English. 1970. 8/yr. CAD 36.95 domestic; USD 40.95 foreign (effective 2008). **Document type:** *Magazine, Trade.* **Description:** Contains industry news, technical and business management, shop profiles, new products as well as features of interest to the trade.
Related titles: Online - full text ed.; ◆ French ed.: Bodyshop (French Edition). ISSN 1494-0124.
Indexed: C03, CBCABus, P48, P52, PQC.
Published by: Business Information Group, 12 Concorde Pl, Ste 800, Toronto, ON M3C 4J2, Canada. TEL 416-442-2122, 800-668-2374, FAX 416-442-2191, orders@businessinformationgroup.ca, http://www.businessinformationgroup.ca. Ed. Cindy Macdonald TEL 416-510-6839. Pub. Joe Plati TEL 416-510-6850. Circ: 12,105.

629.286 USA ISSN 0730-7241
BODYSHOP BUSINESS; the Babcox magazine for the body repair industry. Text in English. 1982. m. free domestic to qualified personnel (effective 2009). adv. tr.lit. reprints avail. **Document type:** *Magazine, Trade.* **Description:** Designed for the owners, managers and salespeople of collision repair shops and the authorized jobbers and distributors who serve them.
Related titles: Online - full text ed.
Indexed: A15, A26, ABIn, B02, B15, B17, B18, G04, G08, I05, P16, P48, P51, P52, P53, P54, PQC.
Published by: Babcox Publications, Inc., 3550 Embassy Pky, Akron, OH 44333. TEL 330-670-1234, FAX 330-670-0874, bbabcox@babcox.com, http://www.babcox.com. Ed. Jason Stahl TEL 330-670-1234 ext 226. Adv. contact Kelly McAleese TEL 330-670-1234 ext 284. B&W page USD 6,240. Circ: 55,123 (paid).

BODYSHOP BUYER'S GUIDE. see BUSINESS AND ECONOMICS—Trade And Industrial Directories

629.286 USA
BODYSHOP EXPO. Text in English. 1992. bi-m. USD 32; USD 64 foreign (effective 1999). adv. **Document type:** *Magazine, Trade.*
Formerly: Bodyshop Tool and Equipment News
Published by: Cygnus Business Media, Inc., 1233 Janesville Ave, PO Box 803, Fort Atkinson, WI 53538. TEL 920-563-6388, FAX 920-563-1702, http://www.cygnusb2b.com. Ed. Anthony J Ross. Pub., R&P, Adv. contact Rudy Wolf. B&W page USD 4,350, color page USD 6,175; trim 10.75 x 7.75. Circ: 62,406.

380 GBR ISSN 1465-9514
BODYSHOP MAGAZINE. Text in English. 1988. m. GBP 55 domestic; GBP 90 in Europe; GBP 130 elsewhere (effective 2010). adv. charts; mkt.; stat.; tr.lit. back issues avail. **Document type:** *Magazine, Trade.* **Description:** Directed to proprietors, directors, and managers of bodyshops, factors, and distributors.
Related titles: Fax ed.
—CCC.
Published by: Plenham Ltd., The Firs, High St, Whitchurch, Buckinghamshire HP22 4JU, United Kingdom. TEL 44-1296-642800, FAX 44-1296-640044, http://www.autorefinish.com. Ed. Kelly Dalwood TEL 44-1296-642828. Adv. contact Gavin Higginson TEL 44-1296-642802.

388.3 NLD ISSN 1380-5320
DE BOVAGKRANT. Text in Dutch. 1938. 24/yr. EUR 126 (effective 2009). adv. bk.rev. **Document type:** *Newspaper, Trade.* **Description:** For managers in automobile service and leasing companies, repair shops and tire shops, motoring schools, and related firms.
Formerly (until 1994): Bovagblad (0006-839X); Incorporates (1994-1994): Bovag Magazine (1380-5339)
Published by: (Bond van Garagehouders (BOVAG)), RAI Langfords bv, Postbus 10099, Amsterdam, 1001 EB, Netherlands. TEL 31-20-5042800, FAX 31-20-5042888, http://www.railangfords.nl. Ed. Freek Van Leeuwen. Pub. Ron Brokking.

629.286 AUS
BOYCE'S SERVICE STATION MANUAL. Text in English. 1984. a. **Document type:** *Handbook/Manual/Guide, Trade.* **Description:** For mechanics servicing the auto industry.
Published by: David Boyce Publishing and Associates, 44 Regent St, Redfern, NSW 2016, Australia.

388.33 USA ISSN 0193-726X
TL275.A1
BRAKE & FRONT END; the complete undercar service magazine. Text in English. 1931. 12/yr. USD 64 domestic; USD 84 in Canada & Mexico; USD 124 elsewhere (effective 2008). adv. bk.rev. illus.; charts. index. Supplement avail. **Document type:** *Magazine, Trade.* **Description:** Features the latest information on brake, chassis, exhaust, front-end, front-wheel alignment, Each issue also profiles the newest product and service offerings from aftermarket suppliers.
Formerly: Brake and Front End Service (0006-9019)
Related titles: Online - full text ed.; ◆ Special ed(s).: Aftermarket Training Guide. ISSN 1069-9996.
Indexed: A15, A26, ABIn, B02, B15, B17, B18, G04, G08, I05, P16, P48, P51, P52, P53, P54, PQC.
—Linda Hall.
Published by: Babcox Publications, Inc., 3550 Embassy Pky, Akron, OH 44333. TEL 330-670-1234, FAX 330-670-0874, bbabcox@babcox.com. Ed. Andrew Markel TEL 330-670-1234 ext 296. R&P Greg Cira. adv.: B&W page USD 6,365. Circ: 40,863 (controlled); 509 (paid).

629.246 USA ISSN 1058-3610
BRAKE TECH-TALK. Text in English. 1990. m. USD 89 domestic (effective 2011). adv. **Document type:** *Newsletter, Trade.* **Description:** Aftermarket technical updates and tips for repairs and service of automotive brake systems.
Published by: M D Publications, Inc. (Springfield), 3057 E Cairo St, Springfield, MO 65802. TEL 417-866-3917, 800-274-7890, FAX 417-866-2781, http://www.mdpublications.com.

▼ **BRANDENBURGISCHE TECHNISCHE UNIVERSITAET COTTBUS. LEHRSTUHL FAHRZEUGTECHNIK UND ANTRIEBE. SCHRIFTENREIHE.** see ENGINEERING—Mechanical Engineering

388.3 NLD ISSN 1871-2312
BRANDSTOFVERBRUIKBOEKJE. Text in Dutch. a.
Published by: (ANWB BV/Royal Dutch Touring Club), Rijksdienst voor het Wegverkeer, Postbus 777, Zoetermeer, 2700 AT, Netherlands. http://www.rdw.nl. Circ: 40,000.

388.342981 GBR ISSN 1748-9784
BRAZIL AUTOS REPORT. Text in English. 2005. q. EUR 820, USD 1,030 combined subscription (print & email eds.) (effective 2010). **Document type:** *Report, Trade.* **Description:** Provides industry professionals and strategists, corporate analysts, auto associations, government departments and regulatory bodies with independent forecasts and competitive intelligence on the Brazilian automotives market.
Related titles: E-mail ed.
Indexed: A15, ABIn, B01, B02, B15, B17, B18, G04, I05, P48, P51, P52, PQC.
Published by: Business Monitor International Ltd., Senator House, 85 Queen Victoria St, London, EC4V 4AB, United Kingdom. TEL 44-20-72480468, FAX 44-20-72480467, subs@businessmonitor.com.

388.3 USA ISSN 1052-0929
BRITISH CAR. Text in English. 1985. bi-m. USD 22.95 domestic; USD 26 in Canada & Mexico; USD 35 elsewhere; USD 2.99 newsstand/cover (effective 2001). adv. bk.rev. **Document type:** *Magazine, Consumer.* **Description:** Addresses the needs, tastes, and interests of the British automobile buyer, collector, and enthusiast.
Formerly: British Car and Bike
Published by: Enthusiast Publications Ltd., 361 N. San Antonio Rd., # H, Los Altos, CA 94022-2248. TEL 650-949-9680, 800-520-8292, FAX 650-949-9685, editor@britishcar.com, ads@britishcar.com. Ed., Pub., R&P Gary G Anderson. Adv. contact Nina Wichman. Circ: 35,000. **Subscr. to:** PO Box 1683, Los Altos, CA 94023-1683. **Dist. in UK by:** Comag, Tavistock Rd, W Drayton, Middlesex UB7 7QE, United Kingdom. TEL 44-1895-444055, FAX 44-1895-433602.

796.77 DEU
BRITISH CLASSICS; cars - bikes - technik - lifestyle. Text in German. bi-m. EUR 24.30 domestic; EUR 32.60 foreign; EUR 4.50 newsstand/cover (effective 2011). adv. **Document type:** *Magazine, Consumer.*
Published by: V F Verlagsgesellschaft mbH, Lise-Meitner-Str 2, Mainz, 55129, Germany. TEL 49-6131-9920, FAX 49-6131-992103, info@vfmz.de, http://www.vfmz.de. Ed. Martin Brueggemann. Adv. contact Michael Kaiser TEL 49-6131-992130. Circ: 25,000 (controlled).

796.72 CAN ISSN 0045-3226
BROKEN SPOKE. Text in English. 1958. bi-m. CAD 10. adv. **Document type:** *Newsletter.* **Description:** Covers club, regional and national motorsport news, coming events in the western Canada area and technical articles pertaining to racing automobiles.
Published by: Calgary Sports Car Club, Kensington Postal Sta, P O Box 61143, Calgary, AB T2N 4S6, Canada. TEL 403-285-1177, FAX 403-289-7256. Eds. Akio Nagatomi, Steve Barry. Circ: 200 (controlled).

BULB HORN. see ANTIQUES

338.3429499 GBR ISSN 1748-9792
BULGARIA AUTOS REPORT. Text in English. 2005. q. EUR 820, USD 1,030 combined subscription (print & email eds.) (effective 2010). **Document type:** *Report, Trade.* **Description:** Provides industry professionals and strategists, corporate analysts, auto associations, government departments and regulatory bodies with independent forecasts and competitive intelligence on the Bulgarian automotives market.
Related titles: E-mail ed.
Indexed: A15, ABIn, B02, B15, B17, B18, G04, I05, P48, P51, P52, PQC.
Published by: Business Monitor International Ltd., Senator House, 85 Queen Victoria St, London, EC4V 4AB, United Kingdom. TEL 44-20-72480468, FAX 44-20-72480467, subs@businessmonitor.com.

BUSINESS DRIVER. see BUSINESS AND ECONOMICS—Marketing And Purchasing

BUSINESS FLEET; managing 10-50 company vehicles. see BUSINESS AND ECONOMICS—Marketing And Purchasing

388 GBR ISSN 1472-992X
BUSINESS RATIO REPORT. THE NEW CAR INDUSTRY (YEAR). Text in English. 1975. a., latest no.36, 2008, Oct. GBP 365 per issue (effective 2010). charts; stat. back issues avail. **Document type:** *Report, Trade.* **Description:** Covers companies active in the new car industry.
Former titles (until 2000): Business Ratio. The New Car Industry (1468-893X); (until 1999): Business Ratio Plus. The New Car Industry (1358-2127); (until 1994): Business Ratio Report: New Car Industry (1352-4208); (until 1992): Business Ratio Report: Foreign Vehicle Distributors (0261-815X)
Published by: Key Note Ltd. (Subsidiary of: Bonnier Business Information), Harlequin House, 5th Fl, 7 High St, Teddington, Richmond upon Thames, TW11 8EE, United Kingdom. TEL 44-845-5040452, FAX 44-845-5040453, sales@keynote.co.uk.

388 658.8 GBR ISSN 1474-6050
BUSINESS RATIO REPORT. VEHICLE DEALERS. Text in English. 1994. a. GBP 365 per issue (effective 2010). charts; stat. back issues avail. **Document type:** *Report, Trade.* **Description:** Covers companies active as vehicle dealers.
Former titles (until 2001): Business Ratio. Vehicle Dealers (1468-4284); (until 1999): Business Ratio Plus: Vehicle Dealers (1463-953X); (until 1998): Business Ratio Plus: Car Dealers (1355-8978); Which was formed by the 1994 merger of: Business Ratio Report. Car Dealers. Intermediate (0954-2159); Business Ratio Report. Car Dealers. Major (0954-2140); Both of which superseded in part (in 1988): Business Ratio Report. Car Dealers (0261-7544)
Published by: Key Note Ltd. (Subsidiary of: Bonnier Business Information), Harlequin House, 5th Fl, 7 High St, Teddington, Richmond upon Thames, TW11 8EE, United Kingdom. TEL 44-845-5040452, FAX 44-845-5040453, sales@keynote.co.uk.

388.3 629.2 USA ISSN 1539-624X
BUYER'S GUIDE. Spine title: Road & Track Car Buyer's Guide. Text in English. 1978. a. charts; illus.; stat. reprints avail. **Document type:** *Directory, Consumer.* **Description:** Offers persons seeking to purchase an automobile advice and reviews.
Former titles (until 2001): Car Buyer's Guide (1539-6231); (until 1999): Complete Road & Track Car Buyer's Guide (1539-6223); (until 1995): The Complete Car Buyer's Guide (1060-8400); (until 1991): Road and Track Car Buyer's Guide (1058-5125); (until 1990): Road & Track Buyer's Guide (1539-6215); Which superseded in part (in 1978): Road & Track's Road Test Annual & Buyer's Guide (0278-2669)
Related titles: ◆ Supplement to: Road & Track. ISSN 0035-7189.
Published by: Hachette Filipacchi Media U.S., Inc. (Subsidiary of: Hachette Filipacchi Medias S.A.), 1633 Broadway, New York, NY 10019. TEL 212-767-6000, FAX 212-767-5600, flyedit@hfmus.com, http://www.hfmus.com.

796.77 USA ISSN 1932-779X
C 16 AUTOSTYLE. Variant title: C16 Autostyle. Text in English. 2000. bi-m. USD 14.95; USD 4.95 newsstand/cover (effective 2006). adv. **Document type:** *Magazine, Consumer.* **Description:** Features a unique perspective on modified car culture with a focus on the lifestyle created by the influencers of this rapidly growing market. The latest trends in electronic entertainment, events and fashion are showcased alongside the modified automobiles that fuel the scene.
Published by: Overamerica Media Group, 6725 Sunset Blvd, Ste 320, Los Angeles, CA 90028. TEL 323-655-9600, FAX 323-978-7925, staff@overamerica.com, http://www.overamerica.com/overamerica.html. Pub. Steve Levy. Adv. contact Justin Lim. color page USD 4,000; trim 8.625 x 10.75. Circ: 60,000 (paid and controlled).

C A M S MAGAZINE. see SPORTS AND GAMES

TU

388.3 GBR
C A T. (Car & Accessory Trader) Text in English. 1979. m. free to qualified personnel (effective 2009). adv. back issues avail. **Document type:** *Magazine, Trade.* **Description:** Contains news, features on trends, and information about the distribution of car components and accessories in the UK within the automotive aftermarket.
Published by: Haymarket Publishing Ltd. (Subsidiary of: Haymarket Media Group), Teddington Studios, Broom Rd, Teddington, Middlesex, TW11 9BE, United Kingdom. TEL 44-20-82675630, FAX 44-20-82675759, info@haymarket.com, http://www.haymarket.com. Ed. Emma Butcher TEL 44-20-82675906. Pub. Jim Foster TEL 44-20-82675049. Adv. contact Martin Lee TEL 44-20-82675839. color page GBP 3,950; trim 210 x 297. Circ: 17,083.

910.202 796.77 GBR
C S M A CLUB MAGAZINE. (Civil Service Motoring Association) Text in English. 1924. m. free (effective 2009). bk.rev. back issues avail. **Document type:** *Magazine, Consumer.* **Description:** Contains news, articles and special offers to help you get more out of life.
Former titles (until 2008): Motoring & Leisure; (until 1986): Civil Service Motoring
Published by: Civil Service Motoring Association Club, Britannia House, 21 Station St, Brighton, BN1 4DE, United Kingdom. TEL 44-1273-744773, club.activities@csmaclub.co.uk, http://www.csmaclub.co.uk.

629.2 FRA ISSN 1950-6643
CAHIER TECHNIQUE AUTOMOBILE. Text in French. 1997. irreg. back issues avail. **Document type:** *Monographic series, Consumer.*
Published by: Editions Techniques pour l'Automobile et l'Industrie (E T A I), 20 rue de la Saussiere, Boulogne-Billancourt, 92641, France. TEL 33-1-46992424, FAX 33-1-48255692, http://www.etai.fr.

388.3 USA
CALIFORNIA DEPARTMENT OF TRANSPORTATION. JOURNAL. Text in English. m. **Document type:** *Magazine, Consumer.*
Published by: California Department of Transportation, 1120 North St, Sacramento, CA 94273. TEL 916-654-5266.

796.77 USA ISSN 0747-0223
CALIFORNIA SPORTS CAR. Text in English. 1980. m. adv.
Formerly (until 1984): Finish Line (0199-5936)
Published by: Pfanner Communications, Inc., 1371 E Warner Ave, Ste E, Tustin, CA 92680-6442. TEL 714-259-8240, FAX 714-259-9377. Ed. Jane Shaw. Circ: 3,787.

388.342 USA ISSN 1944-8589
TL215.C33
CAMARO PERFORMERS; super Chevy. Text in English. 9/yr. USD 19.97 domestic; USD 31.97 in Canada; USD 43.97 elsewhere (effective 2008). adv. 100 p./no.; back issues avail.; reprints avail. **Document type:** *Magazine, Consumer.* **Description:** Covers custom Camaros, classics, and other related topics.
—CCC.
Published by: Source Interlink Companies, 6420 Wilshire Blvd, 10th Fl, Los Angeles, CA 90048. TEL 323-782-2000, FAX 323-782-2585, dheine@sourceinterlink.com, http://www.sourceinterlink.com. Ed. Nick Licata. Pub. Ed Zinke TEL 714-939-2626. adv.: B&W page USD 5,555, color page USD 8,225.

388.3 CAN ISSN 1912-3132
CAMAUTO. Text in French. 1995. bi-m. CAD 24 domestic; CAD 35 foreign (effective 2006). **Document type:** *Magazine, Consumer.*
Formerly (until 2006): Camauto Plus (1203-1372)
Related titles: Supplement(s): Camauto Plus (Annual Edition). ISSN 1719-7856.
Published by: Publications J R S, Inc., 1329 rue Belanger, Montreal, PQ H2G 1A2, Canada. TEL 514-278-6659.

388.3 ITA
CAMBIO PANORAMAUTO. Text in Italian. 2001. m. adv. **Document type:** *Magazine, Consumer.*
Formerly (until 2008): Cambio l'Automobile (1591-9994)
Published by: A C I Mondadori SpA, Via Cassanese 224, Segrate, MI 20090, Italy. TEL 39-02-26937550, FAX 39-02-26937560. Ed. Giancarlo Pini. Circ: 133,511 (controlled).

▼ **CAMPER MAGAZINE.** *see* SPORTS AND GAMES—Outdoor Life

388.3 AUS
CAMPERTRAILER AUSTRALIA. Text in English. bi-m. AUD 35.90 in Australia & New Zealand; AUD 43.90 elsewhere; AUD 6.95 newsstand/cover (effective 2008). adv. **Document type:** *Magazine, Trade.* **Description:** Provides information and reviews on the best camper trailers, top spots to travel around with RV and technical talk sections for a camper trailer owner.
Formerly: Camper Trailer Guide
Published by: A C P Trader International Group (Subsidiary of: P B L Media Pty Ltd.), 73 Atherton Rd, Oakleigh, VIC 3166, Australia. TEL 61-3-95674200, FAX 61-3-95634554. Eds. Carlisle Rogers TEL 61-3-95674256, Greg Leech TEL 61-3-95674194. Adv. contact Justine Schuller. color page AUD 1,595; trim 225 x 297. Circ: 13,000. **Subscr. to:** Magshop, Reply Paid 4967, Sydney, NSW 2001, Australia. TEL 61-2-136116, subs@magstore.com.au, http://shop.magstore.com.au.

796.7099405 AUS ISSN 1441-6417
CAMPERVAN & MOTORHOME TRADER. Text in English. 1991. m. AUD 59.95 domestic; AUD 79.95 in New Zealand; AUD 83.95 elsewhere; AUD 5.50 newsstand/cover (effective 2008). adv. **Document type:** *Magazine, Consumer.* **Description:** Provides information on new and used motorhomes, campervans and accessories posted for sale by private advertisers and dealers.
Published by: A C P Trader International Group (Subsidiary of: P B L Media Pty Ltd.), 73 Atherton Rd, Oakleigh, VIC 3166, Australia. TEL 61-3-95674200, FAX 61-3-95634554. Ed. Greg Leech TEL 61-3-95674194. Adv. contact Justine Schuller. color page AUD 1,500, B&W page AUD 850; trim 195 x 275. Circ: 9,500. **Subscr. to:** Magshop, Reply Paid 4967, Sydney, NSW 2001, Australia. TEL 61-2-136116, subs@magstore.com.au, http://shop.magstore.com.au.

388.346 FRA
CAMPING-CAR MAGAZINE SPECIAL FOURGONS. Text in French. 1995. a. EUR 8.50 newsstand/cover (effective 2009). adv. **Document type:** *Magazine, Consumer.*
Published by: Motor Presse France, 12 rue Rouget de Lisle, Issy-les-Moulineaux, 92442, France. http://www.motorpresse.fr. Circ: 28,190 (paid).

388.3 971 GBR ISSN 1748-9806
CANADA AUTOS REPORT. Text in English. 2005. q. EUR 820, USD 1,030 combined subscription (print & email eds.) (effective 2010). **Document type:** *Report, Trade.* **Description:** Provides industry professionals and strategists, corporate analysts, auto associations, government departments and regulatory bodies with independent forecasts and competitive intelligence on the Canadian automotives market.
Related titles: E-mail ed.
Indexed: B01, C05, P34.
Published by: Business Monitor International Ltd., Senator House, 85 Queen Victoria St, London, EC4V 4AB, United Kingdom. TEL 44-20-72480468, FAX 44-20-72480467, subs@businessmonitor.com.

388 658 CAN ISSN 1715-8737
CANADIAN AUTO DEALER. Text in English. 2005. 8/yr. CAD 16.95 in Canada; USD 29.95 in United States (effective 2008). adv. **Document type:** *Magazine, Trade.*
Related titles: E-mail ed.: free (effective 2006).
Published by: C L B Media, Inc. (Subsidiary of: Canada Law Book Inc.), 240 Edward St, Aurora, ON L4G 3S9, Canada. TEL 905-727-0077, FAX 905-727-0017, http://www.clbmedia.ca. Ed. Gerry Malloy TEL 905-372-4957. Pub., Adv. contact Niel Hiscox. page CAD 3,904.

CANADIAN AUTOMOBILE AGREEMENT. *see* LAW—International Law

388.3 CAN ISSN 0707-624X
CANADIAN AUTOMOBILE ASSOCIATION. ANNUAL REPORT. Text in English, French. 1959. a. free. **Document type:** *Corporate.*
Published by: Canadian Automobile Association, 1145 Hunt Club Rd, Ste 200, Ottawa, ON K1V 0Y3, Canada. TEL 613-247-0117, FAX 613-247-0118.

388 CAN ISSN 0702-2441
CANADIAN AUTOMOBILE ASSOCIATION. STATEMENT OF POLICY. Text in English. 1975. a. **Document type:** *Bulletin.*
Formerly: Canadian Automobile Association. Policies and Resolutions
Published by: Canadian Automobile Association, 1145 Hunt Club Rd, Ste 200, Ottawa, ON K1V 0Y3, Canada. TEL 613-247-0117, FAX 613-247-0118. Ed. David Leonhardt. Circ: 4,000.

629.286 CAN ISSN 0828-2161
CANADIAN AUTOMOTIVE FLEET. Text in English. 1984. 7/yr. CAD 35 domestic; USD 40 in United States; USD 50 elsewhere (effective 2006). adv. **Document type:** *Magazine, Trade.*
Related titles: Supplement(s): Canadian Automotive Fleet. Fact Book. ISSN 1187-5356. 1985.
Published by: Bobit Publishing Canada Limited, 295 The West Mall, Ste 110, Toronto, ON M9C 4Z4, Canada. TEL 416-383-0302, FAX 416-383-0313, http://www.fleetbusiness.com. Ed., Pub. Jake McLaughlin. Circ: 12,200.

388.3 CAN ISSN 1192-2745
CANADIAN AUTOWORLD. Text in English. 1992. m. adv. **Document type:** *Magazine, Trade.*
Published by: Formula Publications (Subsidiary of: Torstar Corp.), 447 Speers Rd, Ste 4, Oakville, ON L6K 3S7, Canada. TEL 905-842-6592, FAX 905-842-6843, circ@formulapublications.com. Circ: 5,600.

CANADIAN BLACK BOOK. VEHICLE INFORMATION GUIDE. *see* BUSINESS AND ECONOMICS—Trade And Industrial Directories

388.3 CAN ISSN 0045-527X
CANADIAN RED BOOK; official used car valuations. Text in English, French. 1959. m. CAD 85 (effective 2000). adv. back issues avail.
Related titles: Supplement(s): Canadian Older Car & Light Duty Truck Red Book. CAD 22.95 newsstand/cover (effective 2000).
Published by: Healthcare and Financial Publishing (Subsidiary of: Rogers Publishing Ltd./Les Editions Rogers Limitee), 777 Bay Street, 5th Fl, Toronto, ON M5W 1A7, Canada. TEL 416-596-5082. Pub. Imants Grotans. Circ: 16,000.

629.2 CAN ISSN 1710-7644
CANADIAN TECHNICIAN; for automotive repair shop owners, managers & technicians. Text in English. 1996. 10/yr. CAD 35.70 domestic; USD 40 in United States; USD 65 elsewhere (effective 2008). adv. **Document type:** *Magazine, Trade.* **Description:** Written for the men and women who keep Canada's fleet of cars and light trucks on the road.
Formerly (until 2004): Automotive Parts & Technology (1204-9921)
Published by: Newcom Business Media, Inc., 451 Attwell Dr, Toronto, ON M9W 5C4, Canada. TEL 416-614-2200, FAX 416-614-8861, http://www.newcom.ca/. Ed. Allan Janssen TEL 416-614-5814. Pub. Mark Vreugdenhil TEL 416-614-5826.

388.3 CAN ISSN 1913-0295
CANAUTO FLEET MANAGEMENT. Text in English. 2007. bi-m. **Document type:** *Magazine, Trade.*
Published by: Publications Rousseau, 2938 Terrasse Abenaquis, bureau 110, Longueuil, PQ J4M 2B3, Canada. TEL 450-448-2220, 888-748-2220, FAX 450-448-1041, admin@p-rousseau.com.

388.3 GBR ISSN 0008-5987
CAR. Text in English. 1962. m. GBP 41.99 domestic; GBP 79.99 foreign (effective 2009). adv. illus.; mkt. back issues avail.; reprints avail. **Document type:** *Magazine, Consumer.* **Description:** Features information on world's best cars.
Incorporates (1968-199?): Performance Car (0265-6183); Which was formerly (until 1983): Hot Car (0018-6007); Formerly (until 1965): Small Car
Indexed: R18.
—IE, Infotrieve. **CCC.**
Published by: H. Bauer Publishing Ltd. (Subsidiary of: Bauer Media Group), Media House, Lynchwood, Peterborough, Cambridgeshire PE2 6EA, United Kingdom. TEL 44-1733-468485, FAX 44-1733-468660, http://www.bauer.co.uk. Adv. contact Mathew Vernon TEL 44-1733-468063. page GBP 6,741. **Subscr. to:** Tower House, Sovereign Park, Market Harborough, Leicestershire LE16 9EF, United Kingdom. TEL 44-1858-438866, subs@greatmagazines.co.uk.

388.3 ZAF ISSN 0008-5995
CAR; the motoring journal of Southern Africa. Text in English. 1957. m. ZAR 162 domestic; ZAR 542 foreign (effective 2004). adv. charts; illus.; mkt.; stat. **Document type:** *Journal, Consumer.* **Description:** Publishes articles on new cars, motor sport, exotic cars, do-it-yourself repairs, technical articles and car prices.
Incorporates: Technicar (0040-1013)
Indexed: ISAP.
Published by: Ramsay, Son & Parker (Pty) Ltd., PO Box 180, Howard Place, Cape Town 7450, South Africa. TEL 27-21-530-3100, FAX 27-21-5313333. Ed. Harold Eedes. Pub., R&P, Adv. contact Rob Cowan. Circ: 114,404 (paid).

796.77 THA
CAR. Text in Thai. m. THB 90 newsstand/cover (effective 2010). adv. **Document type:** *Magazine, Consumer.*
Published by: Inspire Entertainment Co., 115-66 Moo 12, Soi Ramintra 40, Ramintra Rd, Klong-kum, Bung-kum, Bangkok, 10230, Thailand. TEL 662-508-8100, FAX 662-693-3287, contact@inspire.co.th, http://www.inspire.co.th. Adv. contact Amara Thitithamraksa. Circ: 100,000 (paid).

629.331 UAE ISSN 1817-1427
CAR (MIDDLE EAST EDITION). Text in English. 2007. m. AED 90 domestic; AED 109 GCC countries; AED 149 elsewhere (effective 2007). adv. **Document type:** *Magazine, Consumer.*
Published by: I T P Consumer Publishing (Subsidiary of: I T P Publishing Group), PO Box 500024, Dubai, United Arab Emirates. TEL 971-4-2108000, FAX 971-4-2108080, info@itp.com, http://www.itp.com. Ed. Shahzad Sheikh. Adv. contact Andrew Wingrove. page USD 6,000; trim 210 x 297.

388.3 GBR ISSN 2041-2088
▼ **CAR (TRAVEL EDITION).** Text in English. 2009. m. **Document type:** *Magazine, Consumer.* **Description:** Features information on world's best cars.
Published by: H. Bauer Publishing Ltd. (Subsidiary of: Bauer Media Group), Media House, Lynchwood, Peterborough, Cambridgeshire PE2 6EA, United Kingdom. TEL 44-1733-468485, FAX 44-1733-468660, http://www.bauermedia.co.uk.

796.77 CHE ISSN 1662-6923
CAR 4WOMAN. Text in German. 2008. 2/yr. adv. **Document type:** *Magazine, Consumer.*
Published by: Flash Media GmbH, Sonnenstr 8, Au SG, 9434, Switzerland. TEL 41-71-7449490, FAX 41-71-7449491. Ed. Nicole Caloz Schnyder. Adv. contact Harald Fessler. Circ: 18,000 (controlled).

388 ITA ISSN 1827-076X
CAR & CAR. Text in Italian. 2006. bi-w. **Document type:** *Magazine, Consumer.*
Published by: De Agostini Editore, Via G da Verrazzano 15, Novara, 28100, Italy. TEL 39-0321-4241, FAX 39-0321-424305, info@deagostini.it, http://www.deagostini.it.

388.3 ESP
CAR AND DRIVER. Text in Spanish. 1995. m. EUR 2.80 newsstand/cover (effective 2009). adv. back issues avail. **Document type:** *Magazine, Consumer.*
Related titles: Online - full text ed.
Published by: Hachette Filipacchi SA, Avda Cardenal Herrera Oria 3, Madrid, 28034, Spain. TEL 34-91-7287000, FAX 34-91-3585473, comunicacion@hachette.es, http://www.hachette.es. Ed. Agustin De Tena. adv.: color page EUR 5,250; 228 x 297. Circ: 44,344.

388.3 USA ISSN 0008-6002
TL236
CAR AND DRIVER. Text in English. 1956. m. USD 10 (effective 2008). adv. bk.rev. illus. back issues avail.; reprints avail. **Document type:** *Magazine, Consumer.* **Description:** Examines the new technology, new directions and new ideas put forth by the automobile industry.
Formerly: Sports Cars Illustrated
Related titles: Online - full text ed.: USD 8 (effective 2008).
Indexed: A01, A02, A03, A08, A09, A10, A11, A22, A25, A26, AcaI, B04, B07, BRD, C05, C12, CPerI, ConsI, E08, G05, G06, G07, G08, G09, HRIS, I05, I07, M01, M02, M06, MASUSE, MagInd, P02, P10, P16, P48, P53, P54, PMR, PQC, R03, R04, R06, RGAb, RGPR, S08, S09, SPI, T02, TOM, V03, V04, W03.
—IE, Infotrieve, Ingenta.
Published by: Hachette Filipacchi Media U.S., Inc. (Subsidiary of: Hachette Filipacchi Medias S.A.), 1633 Broadway, New York, NY 10019. TEL 212-767-6000, FAX 212-767-5600, flyedit@hfmus.com, http://www.hfmus.com. Ed. Csaba Csere. adv.: B&W page USD 95,650, color page USD 147,265; trim 7.88 x 10.5. Circ: 1,300,000.

629.28 388.3 HKG ISSN 1017-3323
CAR AND DRIVER/REN CHE ZHI; Hong Kong. Text in Chinese. 1986. m. HKD 432; HKD 1,300 foreign. adv. **Document type:** *Consumer.*
Published by: Hachette Filipacchi Hong Kong Ltd., 15-F, East Wing, Warwick House, Taikoo Place, 979 King s Rd, Quarry Bay, Hong Kong, Hong Kong. TEL 852-2567-8707, FAX 852-2568-4650. Ed. Edmond Lau. Pub. Sandy Kwong. Adv. contact Tony Lo. color page HKD 38,350; trim 275 x 214. Circ: 36,000.

629.2 USA
TL162
CAR AND DRIVER BUYING GUIDE. Text in English. 1957. a. USD 5.95 newsstand/cover (effective 2007). adv. charts; illus.; stat. **Document type:** *Magazine, Consumer.* **Description:** Offers persons contemplating the purchase of a new car or light truck advice on every vehicle in the US, with comparisons on price, dimensions, and performance.
Former titles (until 1997): Car and Driver the Thinking Buyer's New Car Guide (1087-6073); Car and Driver Buyers Guide (1060-8141); Car and Driver Yearbook (0069-0260)
Published by: Hachette Filipacchi Media U.S., Inc. (Subsidiary of: Hachette Filipacchi Medias S.A.), 1633 Broadway, New York, NY 10019. TEL 212-767-6000, http://www.hfmus.com. Ed. Tony Swan. Pub. Edward Abramson. Circ: 125,254.

CAR AND DRIVER TRUCK BUYERS GUIDE. *see* TRANSPORTATION—Trucks And Trucking

629.222 USA ISSN 1546-4687
TL1
CAR AND DRIVER ULTIMATE ROAD TEST COMPARISONS. Text in English. 1985. a. USD 5.95 newsstand/cover (effective 2007). charts; illus.; stat. **Document type:** *Magazine, Consumer.* **Description:** Compiles road test evaluations of the preceding year, with comparisons of the most popular models.
Formerly (until 1997): Car and Driver Road Test Annual (8755-626X)
Published by: Hachette Filipacchi Media U.S., Inc. (Subsidiary of: Hachette Filipacchi Medias S.A.), 1633 Broadway, New York, NY 10019. TEL 212-767-6000, FAX 212-767-5600, saleshfmbooks@hfmus.com, http://www.hfmus.com. Ed. Csaba Csere. Pub. Edward Abramson. Circ: 75,000 (paid).

629.286 DEU ISSN 0940-9157
CAR & HIFI; das internationale Car-Hifi-Magazin. Text in German. 1990. bi-m. EUR 20.40; EUR 3.80 newsstand/cover (effective 2011). adv.
Document type: *Magazine, Consumer.*
Published by: Michael E. Brieden Verlag GmbH, Gartroper Str 42, Duisburg, 47138, Germany. TEL 49-203-42920, FAX 49-203-4292149, info@brieden.de, http://www.brieden.de. Circ: 15,381 (paid).

CAR & MONEY NEWS. *see* BUSINESS AND ECONOMICS—Investments

796.75 CHN ISSN 1009-0231
CAR & MOTOR. Text in Chinese. 1998. m. USD 62.40 (effective 2009).
Document type: *Magazine, Consumer.*
—East View.
Published by: G + J - C L I P Publishing Consulting Co. Ltd. (Subsidiary of: Gruner + Jahr AG & Co), Commercial Office Bldg, 4th Fl, No 8 Gongyuan West St, Jianguomennei, Dongcheng District, Beijing, 100005, China. TEL 86-10-65235020, FAX 86-10-65235021, kohl.wolfgang@gjclip.com.cn. Circ: 50,000 (paid and controlled).

388.3 USA ISSN 1080-2290
G149
CAR & TRAVEL MONTHLY. Text in English. 1926. m. adv. bk.rev. illus. back issues avail. **Document type:** *Magazine, Consumer.*
Description: Features legislative, governmental and traffic safety developments of significance to motorists, and information on travel and vacation opportunities.
Formerly (until 1995): New York Motorist (0028-7385)
Related titles: Microform ed.
Published by: Automobile Club of New York, Inc., 1415 Kellum Pl, Garden City, NY 11530. TEL 516-746-7730, 888-780-8552. Adv. contact Erich W Berger.

629.222 GBR ISSN 0955-3703
CAR AUCTION. Text in English. 1986. q. GBP 1.95 newsstand/cover. adv.
Document type: *Handbook/Manual/Guide, Consumer.* **Description:** Serves as a complete reference guide to anyone in need of buying or selling a car in the UK.
Published by: Centre House Publications, 1 Bradenham Pl, Penarth, Vale Of Glam CF64 2AG, United Kingdom. TEL 44-1222-700078. Ed. Andy Johnson. **Dist. by:** Diamond Magazine Distribution, Rye Wharf, Harbour Rd, Rye, E Sussex TN31 7TE, United Kingdom. TEL 44-1797-225229, FAX 44-1797-225657.

CAR AUDIO & ELECTRONICS. *see* SOUND RECORDING AND REPRODUCTION

388.3 CZE
CAR BUSTERS. Text in English. 1998. q. CZK 190, EUR 12, USD 18, GBP 9 (effective 2008). adv. bk.rev. illus. **Document type:** *Magazine, Consumer.*
Address: Kratka 26, Praha 10, 100 00, Czech Republic. Circ: 3,000.

388.34 IRL ISSN 2009-3020
▼ **CAR BUYERS GUIDE (DUBLIN, 2010).** Text in English. 2010. w. adv.
Document type: *Magazine, Trade.* **Description:** Provides variety of classifieds of Irish cars for sale.
Formed by the merger of (2004-2010): Car Buyers Guide (Dublin Edition) (1649-3214); (2004-2010): Car Buyers Guide (Connaught Edition) (1649-489X); (2004-2010): Car Buyers Guide (Munster Edition) (1649-4873); (2004-2010): Car Buyers Guide (Ulster Edition) (1649-5403); (2007-2010): Car Buyers Guide (Dublin. Leinster Edition) (2009-0404); Which was formed by the merger of (2004-2007): Car Buyers Guide (South Leinster Edition) (1649-539X); (2004-2007): Car Buyers Guide (North Leinster Edition) (1649-4881)
Related titles: Online - full text ed.: free (effective 2010).
Published by: Car Buyers Guide, Penthouse Fl, Arena House, Arena Rd, Sandyford Industrial Estate, Dublin, 18, Ireland. TEL 353-1-2405555, FAX 353-1-2943303.

388.34 IRL ISSN 1649-038X
CAR BUYERS GUIDE. IRISH NEW CAR GUIDE. Text in English. 2001. q. adv. **Document type:** *Magazine, Consumer.*
Published by: Car Buyers Guide, Penthouse Fl, Arena House, Arena Rd, Sandyford Industrial Estate, Dublin, 18, Ireland. TEL 353-1-2405555, FAX 353-1-2943303, info@cbg.ie, http://www.cbg.ie. adv.: color page EUR 2,438. Circ: 31,265 (paid and controlled).

388 CAN ISSN 1920-731X
▼ **CAR CARE BUSINESS.** Text in English. 2009. 7/yr. USD 27.95; USD 5.95 newsstand/cover; free to qualified personnel (effective 2010). adv. back issues avail. **Document type:** *Magazine, Trade.*
Description: Brings out industry's image via articles and testimonies with an emphasis on human resources, professional management, ongoing training and the environment.
Published by: Rousseau Automotive Communication, 455, Notre-Dame Est, Ste 311, Montreal, PQ H2Y 1C9, Canada. TEL 514-289-0888, 877-989-0888, FAX 514-289-5151, info@autosphere.ca. Ed., Pub. Remy L Rousseau.

629.222 USA ISSN 1094-3579
TL1
CAR COLLECTOR. Text in English. 1979. m. USD 21.95 domestic; USD 32.95 foreign (effective 2003). adv. bk.rev. illus. reprints avail.
Document type: *Magazine, Consumer.* **Description:** Features factual articles on car history and opinion articles on trends.
Former titles (until 1997): Car Collector & Car Classics (1072-3668); (until 1993): Car Collector & Car Classics Magazine (1057-4441); (until 1991): Car Collector and Car Classics (0164-5552); Which incorporates (in 1988): Nostalgic Cars; Which was formerly (1979-1987): Car Exchange (0164-0836); Formed by the merger of (1966-1979): Car Classics (0095-0556); (1977-1979): Car Collector (0734-5046)
Related titles: Online - full text ed.
Published by: Car Collector Magazine, Inc., 5095 S. Washington Ave., Ste. 207, Titusville, FL 32780-7333. TEL 321-268-5010, FAX 321-269-2025, editorial@carcollector.com. Ed. Dennis Adler. Pub., Adv. contact Jeff Broadus TEL 321-268-5010 ext 102. Circ: 40,000 (paid).

388.3 USA
THE CAR CONNECTION; the web's automotive authority. Text in English. w. adv. **Document type:** *Magazine, Consumer.* **Description:** Provides news, reviews and opinions about the automotive industry.
Media: Online - full content.
Published by: The Car Connection, 22 Cambridge, Pleasant Ridge, MI 48069. letters@thecarconnection.com. Ed. Martin Padgett. Pub. Paul A. Eisenstein. Adv. contact Miranda E. Leaver TEL 248-544-8762.

796.72 USA ISSN 0008-6010
CAR CRAFT; do-it-yourself street performance. Text in English. 1953. m. USD 12 domestic; USD 24 in Canada; USD 36 elsewhere (effective 2008). adv. illus. back issues avail.; reprints avail. **Document type:** *Magazine, Consumer.* **Description:** Focuses on practical performance, technical how-tos, engine buildups and product evaluations.
Formerly: Honk
Related titles: Online - full text ed.: USD 6 (effective 2008).
Indexed: A10, A22, G06, G07, G08, I05, I07, S23, V03.
—**CCC.**
Published by: Source Interlink Companies, 6420 Wilshire Blvd, 10th Fl, Los Angeles, CA 90048. TEL 323-782-2000, FAX 323-782-2585, dheine@sourceinterlink.com, http://www.sourceinterlink.com. Ed. Douglas Glad. Pub. John Gallagher TEL 323-782-2733. adv.: B&W page USD 13,690, color page USD 19,560; trim 10.5 x 7.75. Circ: 288,524 (paid).

388.3 USA ISSN 1052-407X
CAR DEALER INSIDER. Text in English. 1965. w. (48/yr.). bk.rev. charts; tr.lit. back issues avail.; reprints avail. **Document type:** *Newsletter.*
Description: For automobile dealers in the new car retailing business.
Former titles (until 1990): Car Dealer Insider Newsletter (1043-6456); (until 198?): Car Dealer Insider (0148-6721); Incorporated (1965-1989): Truck Insider Newsletter (0041-3399)
—**CCC.**
Published by: Argosy Group (Subsidiary of: United Communications Group), Two Washingtonian Ctr, 9737 Washingtonian Blvd, Ste 100, Gaithersburg, MD 20878. TEL 301-287-2700, FAX 301-287-2039, http://www.ucg.com/argosy.html. Pub. Dennis Sullivan TEL 301-287-2211.

796.77 ITA ISSN 1722-6546
CAR DESIGN. Text in Italian. 2000. s-a. EUR 8 domestic (effective 2009).
Document type: *Magazine, Trade.*
Published by: Design Diffusion Edizioni, Via Lucano 3, Milan, 20135, Italy. TEL 39-02-5516109, FAX 39-02-59902431, info@designdiffusion.com, http://www.designdiffusion.com. Circ: 40,000.

388.3 USA ISSN 1546-3117
CAR DESIGN NEWS. Text in English. 2000 (Jan.). d. adv. **Document type:** *Newsletter, Trade.* **Description:** Reports on news, trends and events in the automotive styling design industry.
Media: Online - full content.
Published by: Car Design News, Inc., 43311 Joy Rd. Ste. 411, Canton, MI 48187. info@cardesignnews.com. Ed., Pub. Brett Patterson. Adv. contact Patrick Wong.

796.77 ITA ISSN 1825-5183
CAR EMOTION. Text in Italian. 2004. m. **Document type:** *Magazine, Consumer.*
Published by: Editoriale Domus, Via Gianni Mazzocchi 1/3, Rozzano, MI 20089, Italy. TEL 39-02-824721, editorialedomus@edidomus.it, http://www.edidomus.it.

629.22 JPN ISSN 0915-1702
CAR GRAPHIC. Key Title: C G. Car Graphic. Text in Japanese. 1962. m. JPY 18,300. adv. bk.rev. **Description:** Provides graphic and professional information to new and classic car enthusiasts.
Indexed: JTA.
Published by: Nigensha Publishing Co. Ltd., 6-2-1 Honkomagome, Bunkyo-ku, Tokyo, 113-0021, Japan. TEL 81-3-5395-0953, FAX 81-3-5395-0954. Ed. K Saka. Adv. contact T Miyasaka. B&W page JPY 440,000, color page JPY 800,000; trim 295 x 222. Circ: 200,000.

629.2 GBR ISSN 0008-6037
CAR MECHANICS. Text in English. 1958. m. GBP 43.92 domestic; GBP 49.44 in Europe; GBP 54.96 elsewhere (effective 2010). adv. bk.rev. illus. back issues avail. **Document type:** *Magazine, Consumer.*
Description: Targeted at the do-it-yourself enthusiast and the secondhand car buyer.
Related titles: Online - full text ed.
—**CCC.**
Published by: Kelsey Publishing Ltd., PO Box 978, Peterborough, PE1 1JA, United Kingdom. TEL 44-1959-541444, FAX 44-1959-541400, info@kelsey.co.uk, http://www.kelsey.co.uk. Ed. Martyn Knowles. Adv. contact Ian Hamilton.

388 JPN
CAR ROAD. Text in Japanese. 1978. m. JPY 2,640.
Published by: Kotsu Times Co. Ltd., 4-3 Uchikanda 2-chome, Chiyoda-ku, Tokyo, 101-0047, Japan. Ed. Takayoshi Yamada.

796.77 USA ISSN 1949-3274
THE CAR ROOM MAGAZINE. Text in English. 2008. bi-m. USD 24.95 domestic; USD 36.95 in Canada; USD 87.95 elsewhere; USD 5.99 per issue domestic; USD 8.99 per issue in Canada; USD 14.95 per issue elsewhere (effective 2009). adv. back issues avail. **Document type:** *Magazine, Trade.*
Published by: O.K. Daddy Productions, Ltd, 1069 Main St, Ste 118, Holbrook, NY 11741. TEL 631-648-3481. Ed., Pub. Joe Kelly. Adv. contact Jeff Stalling.

629.296 JPN
CAR STYLING. Text in English, Japanese. 1973. bi-m. USD 216. adv. bk.rev. back issues avail. **Description:** Primarily features automobile design, but also includes other design fields.
Indexed: D05, JTA, RASB.
Published by: San'ei Shobo Publishing Co., 4-8-16 Kita-Shinjuku, Shinjuku-ku, Tokyo, 169-0074, Japan. TEL 03-364-4819, FAX 03-364-4819. Ed. Akira Fujimoto. Circ: 30,000. **Dist. by:** International Marketing Corp., I.P.O. Box 5056, Tokyo 100-30, Japan. TEL 81-3-3661-7458, FAX 81-3-3667-9646.

388 JPN
CAR TOP. Text in Japanese. 1968. m. JPY 2,640.
Published by: Kotsu Times Co. Ltd., 4-3 Uchikanda 2-chome, Chiyoda-ku, Tokyo, 101-0047, Japan. Ed. Shuichi Miyasaka.

796.77 TUR
CAR TURKIYE. Text in Turkish. 2000. m. adv. **Document type:** *Magazine, Consumer.* **Description:** Offers entertaining perspectives on all aspects of motoring from dreamcars to mainstream family cars.
Published by: Dogus Yayin Group Corporation, Old Buyukdere St, USO Center No.61, Maslak, Istanbul, 80660, Turkey. TEL 90-212-3354820, FAX 90-212-3300323, info@dogusiletisim.com, http://www.dogusiletisim.com.

796.77 BRA ISSN 1679-3560
CARANGOS ESPECIAIS. Text in Portuguese. 2003. m. BRL 5.90 newsstand/cover (effective 2006). adv. **Document type:** *Magazine, Consumer.*
Published by: Editora Escala Ltda., Av Prof Ida Kolb, 551, Casa Verde, Sao Paulo, 02518-000, Brazil. TEL 55-11-38552100, FAX 55-11-38579643, escala@escala.com.br, http://www.escala.com.br.

CARAVAN & MOTORHOME. *see* TRAVEL AND TOURISM

CARAVAN BUYER; your ultimate caravan buying guide. *see* TRAVEL AND TOURISM

388.3 AUS ISSN 1449-633X
CARAVAN TRADER; Australia's magazine for buying and selling your caravan. Text in English. 1991. m. AUD 59.95 in Australia & New Zealand; AUD 71.95 elsewhere; AUD 5.50 newsstand/cover (effective 2008). adv. **Document type:** *Magazine, Consumer.* **Description:** Provides information on new and used caravans, camping trailers and caravanning accessories posted for sale by private advertisers and dealers.
Published by: A C P Trader International Group (Subsidiary of: P B L Media Pty Ltd.), 73 Atherton Rd, Oakleigh, VIC 3166, Australia. TEL 61-3-95674200, FAX 61-3-95634554. Eds. Ros Bromwich TEL 61-3-95674251, Greg Leech TEL 61-3-95674194. Adv. contact Justine Schuller. color page AUD 1,500, B&W page AUD 850; trim 195 x 275. Circ: 7,000. **Subscr. to:** Magshop, Reply Paid 4967, Sydney, NSW 2001, Australia. TEL 61-2-136116, subs@magstore.com.au, http://shop.magstore.com.au.

629.286 665.5 ESP ISSN 1130-8907
CARBUROL. Text in Spanish. 1991. 11/yr. EUR 75 domestic; EUR 135 in Europe; EUR 159 elsewhere (effective 2010). adv. **Document type:** *Magazine, Trade.* **Description:** Covers service stations.
Published by: Sede Tecnica S.A., Avda Brasil, 17 planta 12, Madrid, 28020, Spain. TEL 34-91-5565004, FAX 34-91-5560962, editorial@sedetecnica.com, http://www.sedetecnica.com/. Ed. Carlos Alvarez. Pub. Carlos Martin. Adv. contact Alfonso Villanueva. Circ: 72,000.

CAREER DRIVEN. *see* OCCUPATIONS AND CAREERS

796.77 CAN ISSN 0384-9309
CARGUIDE. Text in English. 1971. bi-m. CAD 17.99 domestic; CAD 25.99 foreign (effective 2005). adv. charts; illus.; stat. **Document type:** *Magazine, Consumer.* **Description:** Official program for Toronto International Auto Show and Ottawa-Hull Auto Show. Lists complete mechanical specifications, photos, suggested retail price and fuel consumption of every new car available in Canada.
Incorporates: Light Truck Guide
Related titles: French ed.: Magazine Carguide. ISSN 1187-9475; ♦ Supplement(s): Toronto International Auto Show Program. ISSN 0704-7339.
Published by: Formula Publications (Subsidiary of: Torstar Corp.), 447 Speers Rd, Ste 4, Oakville, ON L6K 3S7, Canada. TEL 905-842-6591, FAX 905-842-6843, circ@formulapublications.com. Ed. Josef Knycha. Pub. J Scott Robinson. R&P J Robinson. adv.: B&W page CAD 4,250, color page CAD 5,000; trim 8.13 x 10.88. Circ: 89,000.

388.3 USA
CARLAW. Text in English. m. USD 6,500 (effective 2001); Discount available for qualified subscribers. **Document type:** *Magazine, Trade.* **Description:** Covers legal developments in the automobile lease and finance industry.
Related titles: Online - full text ed.: USD 5,500 (effective 2001); Discount available to qualified subscribers.
Published by: Consumer Credit Compliance Company, LLC, 971 Corporate Blvd, Ste 301, Linthicum, MD 21090. TEL 410-684-6800, 877-464-8326, FAX 410-684-6923, trohwedder@hudco.com, http://www.creditcompliance.com. Ed. Thomas B. Hudson.

CARLINK NEWS. *see* BUSINESS AND ECONOMICS—Marketing And Purchasing

388.3 796.72 SGP
CARMA. Text in English. m. USD 48 (effective 2008). **Document type:** *Magazine, Consumer.* **Description:** Covers automotive information and entertainment for enthusiasts between the ages of 25 and 45.
Related titles: Online - full content ed.
Published by: Hardware Zone Pte Ltd. (Subsidiary of: S P H Magazines Pte Ltd.), Blk 20, Ayer Rajah Crescent, Technopreneur Centre, #09-14, Singapore, 139964, Singapore. TEL 65-6872-2725, FAX 65-6872-2724, info.sg@hwzcorp.com, http://www.hwzcorp.com.

388.34 IRL ISSN 1649-878X
CARMART. Text in English. 2006. fortn. adv.
Address: Unit 3, Charvey Court, Rathnew Business Park, Rathnew, Co. Wicklow, Ireland. TEL 353-1850-444999, FAX 353-1850-678888, info@carmart.ie, http://www.carmart.ie.

796.77 GBR ISSN 0957-0632
CARNOISSEUR. Text in English. 1982. 3/yr. GBP 3.50 newsstand/cover. adv. **Document type:** *Handbook/Manual/Guide, Consumer.*
Description: Provides information on parts and accessories for all types of cars.
Published by: Carnoisseur Retail Ltd., Brittany Ct., High Street South, Dunstable, Beds. LU6 3HR, United Kingdom. TEL 44-1582-471589, FAX 44-1582-475427. **Dist. by:** Comag, Tavistock Rd, W Drayton, Middlesex UB7 7QE, United Kingdom. TEL 44-1895-444055, FAX 44-1895-433602.

388 BRA ISSN 0104-5733
CARRO. Text in Portuguese. 1993. m. BRL 4.90 newsstand/cover (effective 2001). adv. **Document type:** *Magazine, Consumer.*
Published by: MotorPress Brasil (Subsidiary of: Gruner + Jahr AG & Co), Rua Benjamin Mota 86, Sao Paulo, SP 04727-070, Brazil. TEL 55-11-56413454, FAX 55-11-56413858. Ed. Priscilla Cortezze. Pubs. Isabel Reis, Sergio Quintanilha. Adv. contact Dario Castilho. Circ: 22,000 (paid).

629.114 NLD ISSN 1380-5037
CARROS. Text in Dutch. 1994. 8/yr. EUR 29 (effective 2011). **Document type:** *Magazine, Consumer.*

TU

Published by: Pelican Magazines Hearst, Delflandlaan 4, Amsterdam, 1062 EB, Netherlands. TEL 31-20-7581000, FAX 31-20-7581003, info@pelicanmags.nl, http://www.pelicanmags.nl. Ed. Carlo Brantsen. Pub. Frank Kloppert.

629.331 NLD ISSN 1872-3640
CARROS. AUTOJAARBOEK. Text in Dutch. 1978. a. EUR 14 (effective 2009).
Formerly (until 2002): Auto (1872-3632)
Published by: Pelican Magazines Hearst, Postbus 69530, Amsterdam, 1060 CN, Netherlands. TEL 31-20-7581000, info@pelicanmags.nl, http://www.pelicanmags.nl.

388.3 NLD ISSN 1385-559X
CARROSSERIE. Text in Dutch. 1934. 9/yr. EUR 58 (effective 2010). adv. bk.rev. 48 p./no.; **Document type:** *Magazine, Trade.* **Description:** For car body shops, car body builders, car sprayers, motorcycle damage repairers, and car cleaners.
Former titles (until 1993): F O C W A Magazine (0926-1826); (until 1989): Carrosserie (0008-6940); (until 1961): Eenheid (0926-1818)
Indexed: KES.
Published by: Nederlandse Vereniging van Ondernemers in het Carrosseriebedrijf, Postbus 299, Sassenheim, 2170 AG, Netherlands. TEL 31-252-265222, FAX 31-252-265255, info@focwa.nl, http://www.focwa.nl. adv.: B&W page EUR 871, color page EUR 1,681; trim 210 x 297. Circ: 3,250.

629.286 FRA ISSN 0750-8131
CARROSSERIE. Text in French. 1945. 8/yr. EUR 74; EUR 186 combined subscription print & online eds. (effective 2009). adv. bk.rev. **Document type:** *Magazine, Trade.* **Description:** Contains information on bodywork and body repair of trucks and lorries, light commercial vehicles and cars.
Related titles: Online - full text ed.
Published by: Wolters Kluwer France (Subsidiary of: Wolters Kluwer N.V.), 1 Rue Eugene et Armand Peugeot, Rueil-Malmaison, Cedex 92856, France. FAX 33-1-76733040, www.wk-transport-logistique.fr. Circ: 4,500 (paid).

629.286 CAN ISSN 1718-5653
JOURNAL LE CARROSSIER. Text in French. 199?. bi-m. **Document type:** *Magazine, Trade.* **Description:** About auto body repair.
Published by: Publications Rousseau, 2938 Terrasse Abenaquis, bureau 110, Longueuil, PQ J4M 2B3, Canada. TEL 450-448-2220, 888-748-2220, FAX 450-448-1041, admin@p-rousseau.com, http://www.publicationsrousseau.com. Ed. Remy L Rousseau.

796 790.13 USA ISSN 1937-2698
CARS & PLACES MAGAZINE. Text in English. 2006. 9/yr. USD 14.95 (effective 2007). adv. **Document type:** *Magazine, Consumer.* **Description:** Features news about car shows, car clubs, antique and classic cars, and news and reviews of new cars on the market, as well as feature articles about driving.
Published by: C N P Publishing LLC, 11917 Mid County Dr, Monrovia, MD 21770. TEL 301-865-2118, FAX 301-865-2119. Ed. Cindy Trawick. Pub. Rick Trawick.

796.71 ZAF ISSN 1027-8346
CARS IN ACTION. Text in English. 1997. m. ZAR 220 domestic; ZAR 1,100 foreign (effective 2006).
Published by: Action Publications cc, PO Box 70174, Bryanston, South Africa. FAX 27-11-4632466. Pub. Michele Lupini.

796.77 GBR ISSN 1363-2493
CARSPORT MAGAZINE. Text in English. 1982. m. GBP 33 domestic; GBP 43 in Ireland; GBP 53 elsewhere (effective 2009). adv. bk.rev. **Document type:** *Magazine, Consumer.* **Description:** Contains news and in-depth coverage of motoring and motorsport in Northern Ireland.
—CCC.
Published by: Greer Publications, 5B Edgewater Business Park, Belfast Harbour Estate, Belfast, BT3 9JQ, United Kingdom. TEL 44-28-90783200, FAX 44-28-90783210, info@greerpublications.com, http://www.greerpublications.com. Ed. Pat Burns TEL 44-28-90783200 ext 220. Pub. Gladys Greer. Adv. contact Jason Curran TEL 44-28-90783237.

629.2 ROM ISSN 1454-9433
CATALOG AUTO SPECIAL. Text in Romanian. 2000. a. ROL 16.90 newsstand/cover. adv. **Document type:** *Magazine, Consumer.*
Published by: Burda Romania, Bd Carol I, nr 31-33, complexul Asirom, corpul 4, Sector 2, Bucharest, 020912, Romania. TEL 40-372-106000, FAX 40-372-106055, publicitate@burda.ro, http://www.burda.ro. Adv. contact Adina Gheorghe. Circ: 18,000 (controlled).

388.321 ESP
CATALOGO AUTOVERDE 4 X 4. Text in Spanish. 1993. irreg. price varies. adv. **Document type:** *Catalog, Consumer.*
Related titles: ◆ Supplement to: Autoverde 4 x 4.
Published by: Motorpress Iberica (Subsidiary of: Gruner + Jahr AG & Co), Ancora 40, Madrid, 28045, Spain. TEL 34-91-3470100, FAX 34-91-3470152, http://www.motorpress-iberica.es. Ed. Ignacio Salvador. Pub. Javier Recio. Adv. contact Choni Garcia. Circ: 18,000 (paid).

688.1029 ITA
CATALOGO MOTORISTICO. Text in English, French, German, Italian, Russian, Spanish, Portuguese. 1962. a. free (effective 2009). abstr.; tr.mk. 600 p./no.; **Document type:** *Catalog, Trade.* **Description:** Contains information on Italian production of parts, accessories, equipment and machinery for cars, motorcycles, trucks, agricultural machines, carts, boats, and more.
Related titles: CD-ROM ed.; Online - full text ed.
Published by: Edizioni Collins Sas, Via Giovanni Pezzotti, 4, Milan, MI 20141, Italy. TEL 39-02-8372897, FAX 39-02-58103891, collins@collins.com, http://www.netcollins.com. Pub. David Giardino. Adv. contact Natascia Giardino TEL 39-02-8372897. Circ: 10,000 (free).

388.3 BEL ISSN 1374-6227
CATALOGUE GENERAL DU COMMERCE ET DE LA REPARATION AUTOMOBILES ET DES SECTEURS CONNEXES. Text in Dutch, French. 1950. a. **Document type:** *Catalog.*
Formerly (until 1998): Catalogue General de l'Industrie et du Commerce Automobile de Belgique (1374-6219)
Published by: Federauto a.s.b.l., Bd de la Woluwe 46, Bte 9, Bruxelles, 1200, Belgium. TEL 32-2-7786200, FAX 32-2-7786222, mail@federauto.be, http://www.federauto.be. Pub. Bob Pauwels. R&P Luc Missnate. Adv. contact Luc Missante. Circ: 8,000.

388.3 USA ISSN 0889-2504
CAVALLINO MAGAZINE; the magazine of Ferrari. Text in English. 1978. s-m. USD 30. adv. bk.rev. **Document type:** *Magazine, Trade.*
Published by: Cavallino Inc., PO Box 810819, Boca Raton, FL 33481-0819. TEL 561-994-1345, FAX 561-994-9473. Ed., Pub. John W Barnes Jr. Adv. contact Anne Bluntschli. Circ: 16,500 (paid).

388.3 918.904 URY
CENTUR. Text in Spanish. 1977. a. free. adv.
Published by: Centro Automovilista del Uruguay, Cn. Artigas, 1773, Montevideo, 12413, Uruguay. Ed. Ever Cabrera Tornielli. Circ: 10,000.

388.3 NLD ISSN 1877-1408
C'EST RENAULT. Text in Dutch. 1962. s-a. **Document type:** *Magazine, Consumer.*
Former titles (until 2008): Createur (1877-1394); (until 2006): Createur d'Automobiles (1872-0285); (until 2004): Renault Magazine (1380-2364); Which superseded in part (in 1992): Renault Revue (1380-2356)
Published by: Renault Nederland, Postbus 75784, Schiphol, 1118 ZX, Netherlands.

CHAIYOUJI SHEJI YU ZHIZAO/DESIGN & MANUFACTURE OF DIESEL ENGINE. *see* ENGINEERING—Mechanical Engineering

CHAUFFOEREN. *see* LABOR UNIONS

388.3 CHN ISSN 1005-1473
CHE WANG/AUTOTRENDS. Variant title: Champion Racers. Text in Chinese. 1993. m. USD 106.80 (effective 2009). **Document type:** *Magazine, Consumer.*
Related titles: Online - full content ed.
—East View.
Published by: Zhongguo Tiyubao Yezongshe, 8, Tiyuguan Lu, Chongwen-qu, Beijing, 100061, China. TEL 86-10-64284462, FAX 86-10-64284475. **Dist. by:** China International Book Trading Corp, 35 Chegongzhuang Xilu, Haidian District, PO Box 399, Beijing 100044, China. TEL 86-10-68412045, FAX 86-10-68412023, cibtc@mail.cibtc.com.cn, http://www.cibtc.com.cn.

388.3 HKG ISSN 1727-6152
CHE WANG ZAZHI/CAR PLUS. Text in Chinese. 1993. m. HKD 198 domestic; HKD 1,296 in Southeast Asia; HKD 1,536 elsewhere (effective 2010); includes subscr. to HIM. adv. **Document type:** *Magazine, Consumer.*
Related titles: Online - full text ed.
Published by: South China Media Limited/Nan-Hua Chuanmei, 3/F., Wah Shing Centre, 5 Fung Yip St., Chai Wan, Hong Kong. TEL 852-2202-5000, FAX 852-2963-0515, http://www.scmedia.com.hk/.

388 355.8 CHN ISSN 1009-4687
CHELIANG YU DONGLI JISHU/VEHICLE & POWER TECHNOLOGY. Text in Chinese. 1979. q. CNY 6 newsstand/cover (effective 2006). **Document type:** *Journal, Academic/Scholarly.*
Formerly (until 2000): Binggong Xuebao. Tanke Zhuangjiache yu Fadongji Fence/Acta Armamentarii. Volume of Tank, Armored Vehicle and Engine (1009-5411)
Related titles: Online - full text ed.
Published by: Zhongguo Binggong Xuehui/China Ordnance Society, c/o Beijing Ligong Daxue, 5, Zhongguan Nan Dajie, Beijing, 100081, China. TEL 86-10-68910491.

388.3 CHN ISSN 1008-3561
CHENGCAI ZHI LU/ROAD TO SUCCESS. Text in Chinese. 1999. every 10 days. **Document type:** *Magazine, Consumer.*
Related titles: Online - full text ed.
Published by: Chengcai zhi Lu Zazhishe, Daowai-qu Dafanglixiao-qu, 228-dong, 5-men, Ha'erbin, 150020, China. TEL 86-451-82513098, FAX 86-451-82513098.

388.3 ZAF ISSN 1016-5312
CHEQUERED FLAG. Text in English. fortn. ZAR 50. adv.
Formerly: S A Motorscene (0256-0550)
Published by: Titan Publications (Pty) Ltd., Rodland House, 382 Jan Smuts Ave, Craighall, Gauteng 2196, South Africa. Ed. Justin Haler. Circ: 25,000.

388.3 CHN ISSN 1009-7929
CHESHIDAI/AUTO TIME. Text in Chinese. 2001. m. **Document type:** *Magazine, Trade.*
Published by: Beifang Baokan Fazhan Zhongxin/North Press Development Center, 15, Ningshan Zhong Lu, Shenyang, 110031, China. TEL 86-24-86203120, http://www.npdc.cn/index1.htm.

388.3 USA ISSN 1056-2974
CHEVY ACTION. Text in English. 2/yr. USD 3.95 per issue.
Published by: Dobbs Publishing Group, 3816 Industry Blvd, Lakeland, FL 33811. TEL 813-646-5743, FAX 813-644-8373.

388.3 USA ISSN 1062-192X
CHEVY HIGH PERFORMANCE. Text in English. 1985. m. USD 17 domestic; USD 29 in Canada; USD 41 elsewhere (effective 2008). adv. illus. back issues avail. **Document type:** *Magazine, Consumer.* **Description:** Provides an authoritative source for all Chevy enthusiasts who are interested in buying, selling, restoring and modifying high-performance Chevy vehicles.
Formerly (until 199?): Chevrolet High Performance (1052-5491)
Related titles: Online - full text ed.: USD 8.50 (effective 2008).
Indexed: A10, G06, G07, G08, I05, S23, V03.
—CCC.
Published by: Source Interlink Companies, 774 S Placentia Ave, Placentia, CA 92870. TEL 714-939-2559, FAX 714-572-3502, dheine@sourceinterlink.com, http://www.sourceinterlinkmedia.com. Ed. Henry De Santos. Pub. Ed Zinke TEL 714-939-2626. adv.: B&W page USD 12,695, color page USD 18,135. Circ: 140,103 (paid).

388 USA ISSN 1081-2059
CHEVY TRUCKIN'. Text in English. q. USD 3.50 newsstand/cover (effective 2007). adv. **Document type:** *Magazine, Consumer.* **Description:** Original GM truck specialty publication with editorial features that include current industry news, manufacturer support, product installations and reviews, and road tests.
Published by: Source Interlink Companies, 6420 Wilshire Blvd, 10th Fl, Los Angeles, CA 90048. TEL 323-782-2000, FAX 323-782-2585, dheine@sourceinterlink.com, http://www.sourceinterlinkmedia.com.

621.4 CHN ISSN 1001-2222
CHEYONG FADONGJI/VEHICLE ENGINE. Text in English. 1978. bi-m. CNY 4.50 per issue domestic (effective 2003). back issues avail. **Document type:** *Journal, Academic/Scholarly.*
Related titles: Online - full content ed.; Online - full text ed.
Published by: Shanxi Cheyong Fadongji Yanjiusuo/Chian North Engine Research Institute, PO Box 22, Datong, Shanxi 037036, China. TEL 86-352-4088609, FAX 86-352-4088602. Ed., Adv. contact Jiwen Ren.

388.3 CHN ISSN 1009-4911
CHEZHU ZHI YOU/CAR OWNERS. Text in Chinese. 1982. m. **Document type:** *Magazine, Consumer.*
Former titles (until 2000): Tuolaji Qiche Jiashiyuan/Tractor and Automobile Drivers (1002-6118); (until 1985): Tuola Jishou
Published by: Chezhu zhi You Zazhishe (Subsidiary of: Beijing Zhuozhong Chuban Youxian Gongsi/Prominion Publishing), 1-16, Bei Shatan, Deshengmen wai, Beijing, 100083, China. TEL 86-10-64882403, FAX 86-10-64882329.

CHI E CHI DEL GIORNALISMO DELL'AUTO. *see* JOURNALISM

388.413 USA
CHICAGO DISPATCHER. Text in English. 2002. m. USD 36 (effective 2006). adv. **Document type:** *Newsletter, Trade.* **Description:** Forum open to everyone with an interest in the industry including taxi owners, cab companies, government officials, special interest groups, and especially drivers and passengers.
Address: 3935 N Elston, Ste B, Chicago, IL 60618. Ed. Jonathan Bullington. Pub. George Lutfallah. adv.: B&W page USD 999; trim 11.5 x 16.875. Circ: 8,000 (free).

629.2 NLD ISSN 1879-7687
▼ **CHICANE MAGAZINE.** Text in Dutch. 2010. q. EUR 17.50; EUR 4.99 newsstand/cover (effective 2010). adv. **Document type:** *Magazine, Consumer.*
Published by: Chicane Mediaprodukties B.V., Postbus 53095, The Hague, 2505 AB, Netherlands. TEL 31-6-5180869. Ed. Peter Dielissen. Circ: 10,000.

388.342 983 GBR ISSN 1748-9822
CHILE AUTOS REPORT. Text in English. 2005. a. EUR 820, USD 1,030 combined subscription per issue (print & email eds.) (effective 2010). **Document type:** *Report, Trade.* **Description:** Provides industry professionals and strategists, corporate analysts, auto associations, government departments and regulatory bodies with independent forecasts and competitive intelligence on the Chilean automotives market.
Related titles: E-mail ed.
Indexed: A15, ABIn, B02, B15, B17, B18, G04, I05, P48, P51, P52, PQC.
Published by: Business Monitor International Ltd., Senator House, 85 Queen Victoria St, London, EC4V 4AB, United Kingdom. TEL 44-20-72480468, FAX 44-20-72480467, subs@businessmonitor.com.

629.286 USA ISSN 1930-2037
TL152
CHILTON ASIAN DIAGNOSTIC SERVICE. Text in English. 200?. a., latest 2006. **Document type:** *Handbook/Manual/Guide, Trade.* **Description:** Provides technicians with the diagnostic information they need to identify and solve engine performance problems for all Asian vehicles.
Published by: Delmar Cengage Learning (Subsidiary of: Cengage Learning), PO Box 6904, Florence, KY 41022. TEL 800-354-9706, FAX 800-487-8488, schoolcustomerservice@cengage.com, http://www.delmarhealthcare.com.

388.3 USA ISSN 1557-2781
CHILTON EUROPEAN MECHANICAL SERVICE. Text in English. 2004. a., latest 2006.
Formerly (until 2005): Chilton European Service Manual (1558-1047)
Published by: Delmar Cengage Learning (Subsidiary of: Cengage Learning), PO Box 6904, Florence, KY 41022. TEL 800-354-9706, FAX 800-487-8488, schoolcustomerservice@cengage.com, http://www.delmarhealthcare.com.

CHINA AUTO/ZHONGGUO QICHE. *see* TRANSPORTATION—Abstracting, Bibliographies, Statistics

388.3 HKG ISSN 1021-1322
➤ **CHINA AUTOMOTIVE JOURNAL/XIANDAI QICHE;** an automotive journal for P.R. China. Text mainly in Chinese; Contents page in Chinese, English. 1985. bi-m. HKD 455 domestic; USD 90 in Asia; USD 100 elsewhere (effective 2003). adv. abstr.; charts; illus.; bibl.; stat. back issues avail. **Document type:** *Journal, Academic/Scholarly.* **Description:** Provides an international perspective for the automotive industry in China.
Incorporates (1994-1997): Auto Trend - Xiandai Qiche Qingbao
Published by: (China Automotive Technology and Research Center CHN), Yashi Chuban Gongsi/Adsale Publishing Ltd., 4-F, Stanhope House, 734 King's Rd, North Point, Hong Kong. TEL 852-2811-8897, FAX 852-2516-5119, circulation@adsalepub.com.hk, http://www.adsalepub.com.hk. Ed. Pandora Hui. Pub. Annie Chu. Adv. contact Mandy Luk. B&W page USD 3,365, color page USD 4,785; trim 280 x 215. Circ: 33,786 (controlled). **Co-sponsors:** China Automobile Circulation Association; China Automotive Trade Corporation; Ministry of the Machine, Building Industry.

388 USA ISSN 1548-1166
HD9710.C528
CHINA AUTOMOTIVE REVIEW; automotive journal. Abbreviated title: C A R. C B U. Text in English. 1995. m. USD 687.60 (effective 2009). **Document type:** *Newspaper, Trade.*
Formerly (until 2006): China Business Update. Automotive (1080-4080)
Related titles: Supplement(s): China Business Update Heavy-Duty. ISSN 2154-1310. 2010.
Published by: China Business Update, PO Box 1368, Amherst, MA 01004. TEL 413-253-5477, FAX 413-253-2775, http://www.chinaautoreview.com/default_paid.asp.

388.342 951 GBR ISSN 1748-9830
CHINA AUTOS REPOPRT. Text in English. 2005. q. EUR 820, USD 1,030 combined subscription (print & email eds.) (effective 2010). **Document type:** *Report, Trade.* **Description:** Provides industry professionals and strategists, corporate analysts, auto associations, government departments and regulatory bodies with independent forecasts and competitive intelligence on the Chinese automotives market.
Related titles: E-mail ed.
Indexed: A15, ABIn, B02, B15, B17, B18, G04, I05, P48, P51, P52, PQC.

Published by: Business Monitor International Ltd., Senator House, 85 Queen Victoria St, London, EC4V 4AB, United Kingdom. TEL 44-20-72480468, FAX 44-20-72480467, subs@businessmonitor.com.

CHINESE MARKETS FOR AUTOMOTIVE COATINGS. *see* BUSINESS AND ECONOMICS—Marketing And Purchasing

CHINESE MARKETS FOR AUTOMOTIVE COMPONENTS. *see* BUSINESS AND ECONOMICS—Marketing And Purchasing

CHINESE MARKETS FOR AUTOMOTIVE ELECTRONICS. *see* BUSINESS AND ECONOMICS—Marketing And Purchasing

796.77 USA ISSN 1099-9396
CHRISTIAN MOTORSPORTS ILLUSTRATED. Text in English. 1996. q. USD 19.96; USD 4.99 newsstand/cover (effective 2007). adv. bk.rev. illus.; mkt.; stat. 40 p./no. 3 cols./p.; back issues avail. **Document type:** *Magazine, Consumer.* **Description:** Reports on "God's invasion of the world of motorsports." Features Christian racers in all motorsports, as well as technical information and a buyer's guide.
Incorporates (in 1999): Chrysler Power (0885-663X)
Published by: C P O, PO Box 929, Bristow, OK 74010-0929. TEL 607-742-3407. Ed. Tom Winfield. Pub., Adv. contact Roland Osborne. page USD 1,000; trim 10.88 x 8. Circ: 15,000 (paid and controlled).

796.77 DEU ISSN 0412-3417
CHRISTOPHORUS (STUTTGART); Porsche Magazine. Text in English, French, German. 1952. bi-m. EUR 24; EUR 6 newsstand/cover (effective 2010). adv. back issues avail. **Document type:** *Magazine, Consumer.*
Published by: Dr. Ing. h.c. F. Porsche AG, Porscheplatz 1, Stuttgart, 70435, Germany. TEL 49-6232-310214, FAX 49-6232-310215. adv.: color page EUR 11,100; trim 187 x 247. Circ: 265,000 (paid and controlled).

388 DEU ISSN 0777-8473
CHROM UND FLAMMEN. Text in German. 1982. m. EUR 44 domestic; EUR 49 foreign; EUR 3.90 newsstand/cover (effective 2011). adv. **Document type:** *Magazine, Consumer.*
Published by: Vestische Mediengruppe Welke GmbH & Co. KG, Hertener Mark 7, Herten, 45699, Germany. TEL 49-2366-808400, FAX 49-2366-808499, info@vmw-verlag.de, http://vmw-verlag.de. Ed. Michael Stein. Pub. Arno Welke. Circ: 50,688 (paid and controlled).

388.3 USA
CHRYSLER CAR ENTHUSIAST ENGINES ETC. MAGAZINE. Text in English. 1984. bi-m. USD 15. adv. back issues avail. **Document type:** *Magazine, Consumer.* **Description:** Covers Chrysler cars from the '50s through current models, with particular emphasis on the muscle car period.
Former titles: Performance for the Chrysler Car Enthusiast (1068-4131); (until 1991): Morperformance
Published by: R H O Publications, 1580 Hampton Rd, Bensalem, PA 19020-4610. TEL 215-639-4456, FAX 215-639-6642. Ed., Pub. Robert Oskiera. Adv. contact Robert Henry. Circ: 60,000 (controlled).

796.77 USA
CITROEN. Text in English. 1987. q. USD 20; USD 25 foreign (effective 1999). adv. back issues avail. **Document type:** *Newsletter.* **Description:** For owners and aficionados of Citroen automobiles from 1919 to the present.
Published by: Citroen Concours of America, 8585 Commerce Ave, San Diego, CA 92121. TEL 619-566-2860, FAX 619-566-2432. Ed., Adv. contact Rudy A Heilig.

388.3 ESP
CLASICOS DE OCASION. Text in Spanish. bi-m. EUR 3.95 newsstand/cover (effective 2009). adv. **Document type:** *Magazine, Consumer.*
Published by: Grupo V, C Valportillo Primera, 11, Alcobendas, Madrid, 28108, Spain. TEL 34-91-6622137, FAX 34-91-6622654, secretaria@grupov.es, http://www.grupov.es/. Adv. contact Isidro Iglesias. page EUR 1,350; trim 19.5 x 25.5. Circ: 30,000.

629.222 GBR ISSN 0263-3183
TL1
CLASSIC & SPORTS CAR. Abbreviated title: C & S C. Text in English. 1963. m. GBP 43.86 (effective 2009). adv. back issues avail. **Document type:** *Magazine, Consumer.* **Description:** Provides authoritative and entertaining coverage of all types of classic cars, from mainstream favourites such as MGBs and Jaguar E-types to one-offs, prototypes and great racers.
Former titles (until 1982): Old Motor (0030-2023); (until 1966): Old Motor and Vintage Commercial
Related titles: Supplement(s): Classic & Sports Car Owner's Bible.
—CCC.
Published by: Haymarket Publishing Ltd. (Subsidiary of: Haymarket Media Group), Teddington Studios, Broom Rd, Teddington, Middlesex, TW11 9BE, United Kingdom. TEL 44-20-82675630, FAX 44-20-82675759, info@haymarket.com, http://www.haymarket.com. Ed. James Elliot TEL 44-20-82675399. Adv. contacts Kane Dalton TEL 44-20-82675277, Ben Guynan TEL 44-20-82675408. Circ: 74,008. **Subscr. to:** PO Box 568, Haywards Heath RH16 3XQ, United Kingdom. TEL 44-8456-777800, Haymarket.subs@qss-uk.com, http://www.themagazineshop.com.

388 GBR ISSN 1362-9484
CLASSIC AND VINTAGE COMMERCIALS. Abbreviated title: C V C. Text in English. 1994. m. GBP 43.92 domestic; GBP 49.44 in Europe; GBP 54.96 elsewhere; GBP 4 per issue in domestic; GBP 5 per issue in Europe; GBP 5.50 per issue elsewhere (effective 2010). adv. back issues avail. **Document type:** *Magazine, Trade.* **Description:** Covers the whole world of historic commercials - veteran, vintage and classic.
Related titles: Online - full text ed.
Published by: Kelsey Publishing Ltd., Cudham Tithe Barn, Berry's Hill, Cudham, Kent TN16 3AG, United Kingdom. TEL 44-1959-541444, FAX 44-1959-541400, info@kelsey.co.uk, http://www.kelsey.co.uk. Eds. Ted Connolly, Phil Weeden TEL 44-1733-353372. Adv. contact Julia Johnston TEL 44-1733-353353.

796.77 SWE
CLASSIC BOERSEN. Text in Swedish. 2008. m. adv. **Document type:** *Magazine, Consumer.*
Published by: Foerlags AB Albinsson & Sjoeberg, PO Box 529, Karlskrona, 37123, Sweden. TEL 46-455-335325, FAX 46-455-311715, fabas@fabas.se, http://www.fabas.se. Ed. Lars-Ake Krantz. Adv. contact Therese Lindell Antonsson. page SEK 7,700; trim 190 x 275.

▼ **CLASSIC CAR BUYER.** *see* ANTIQUES

629.222 796.77 GBR ISSN 1351-1203
CLASSIC CAR MART. Text in English. 1993. m. GBP 40.68 domestic; GBP 46.20 in Europe; GBP 51.72 elsewhere; GBP 4.20 per issue domestic; GBP 4.70 per issue in Europe; GBP 5.20 per issue elsewhere (effective 2009). illus. back issues avail. **Document type:** *Magazine, Consumer.* **Description:** Aims to serve as a market place for classic cars. Contains news and features on several brands including American, MG, Triumph, Rolls Royce-Bentley, and Jaguar. Also includes sections on insurance, transport, spares and parts, and restoration services.
Published by: Kelsey Publishing Ltd., Cudham Tithe Barn, Berry's Hill, Cudham, Kent TN16 3AG, United Kingdom. TEL 44-1959-541444, FAX 44-1959-541400, info@kelsey.co.uk, http://www.kelsey.co.uk. Ed. Phil Weeden TEL 44-1733-353372. Adv. contact Wendy Loftus Martin. **Subscr. to:** PO Box 978, Peterborough PE1 1JA, United Kingdom. TEL 44-1959 543530.

CLASSIC CAR WEEKLY. *see* ANTIQUES

629.222 GBR ISSN 1365-9537
CLASSIC CARS. Text in English. 1973. m. GBP 42.50 domestic; GBP 69.99 foreign (effective 2009). adv. bibl.; charts; illus.; tr.lit. back issues avail. **Document type:** *Magazine, Consumer.* **Description:** Covers classic cars past and present with an emphasis on those built 1950-1975.
Former titles (until 1996): Thoroughbred & Classic Cars (0143-7267); (until 1974): Classic Car; Thoroughbred & Classic Cars incorporated (1979-1981): Collector's Car (0143-7259); Which was formerly (until 1979): Veteran and Vintage Magazine (0042-4773)
Related titles: Microform ed.: (from PQC).
Published by: H. Bauer Publishing Ltd. (Subsidiary of: Bauer Media Group), Media House, Lynchwood, Peterborough, Cambridgeshire PE2 6EA, United Kingdom. TEL 44-1733-468582, FAX 44-1733-468582, http://www.bauer.co.uk. Ed. Phil Bell. Adv. contact Louise Rizzo TEL 44-1733-468435. page GBP 4,582. **Subscr. to:** Tower House, Sovereign Park, Market Harborough, Leicestershire LE16 9EF, United Kingdom. TEL 44-1858-438866, subs@greatmagazines.co.uk.

629.222 388.324 USA ISSN 2151-0563
CLASSIC CARS & PARTS. Text in English. 19??. m. USD 39.95 domestic; USD 79.95 in Canada; USD 139.95 elsewhere (effective 2009). adv. **Document type:** *Magazine, Trade.* **Description:** Lists thousands of cars for sale, a wide selection of hard-to-find parts, services and accessories, as well as event listings throughout the country.
Formerly (until 2008): Old Car Trader
Published by: AutoTrader Classics, 5775 Peachtree-Dunwoody Rd, Ste A-100, Atlanta, GA 30342. TEL 800-548-8889. Adv. contact Debbie Reetz TEL 404-568-8383.

629.222 GBR ISSN 1468-9235
CLASSIC CARS FOR SALE. Text in English. 2000. m. GBP 59.95 (effective 2010). adv. back issues avail. **Document type:** *Magazine, Trade.* **Description:** Provides latest information on vintage cars.
—CCC.
Published by: M S Publications, 9 Cashmere Way, Vange, Essex SS16 4RE, United Kingdom. TEL 44-750-7173101. Adv. contact Jo Kelshaw TEL 44-1206-506250.

629.286 NZL ISSN 1176-2993
CLASSIC DRIVER. Text in English. 2003. bi-m. adv. **Document type:** *Magazine, Consumer.*
Published by: Straight 8 Publishing, Symonds St, PO Box 8673, Auckland, New Zealand. TEL 64-9-3695412, FAX 64-9-3695422, admin@straight8.co.nz, http://www.drivermagazine.co.nz.

796.77 DEU ISSN 1611-5082
CLASSIC DRIVER (ONLINE). Text in German. 2002. w. adv. **Document type:** *Magazine, Consumer.*
Formerly (until 2003): Classic Driver (Print)
Media: Online - full content. **Related titles:** Online - full text ed.
Published by: Classic Driver, Mittelweg 159, Hamburg, 20148, Germany. TEL 49-40-2800830, FAX 49-40-28008350. Ed. Jan-Christian Richter.

629.222 GBR ISSN 1367-8809
CLASSIC FORD. Text in English. 1993. m. GBP 47.51 domestic; GBP 67.99 in Europe; GBP 89.99 elsewhere; GBP 4.25 newsstand/cover (effective 2010). adv. illus. back issues avail. **Document type:** *Magazine, Consumer.* **Description:** Dedicated to the modified classic Ford scene in the UK and around the world. Features buying and service guides, readers' projects, practical hands-on features and a free readers' classified section.
Formerly (until 1997): Ford Heritage (0968-6436)
Related titles: Online - full text ed.: GBP 55.25; GBP 4.25 per issue (effective 2010).
—CCC.
Published by: Future Publishing Ltd., Beauford Ct, 30 Monmouth St, Bath, Avon BA1 2BW, United Kingdom. TEL 44-1225-442244, FAX 44-1225-446019, customerservice@subscription.co.uk, http://www.futureplc.com. Ed. Simon Woolley TEL 44-1225-732365. Adv. contact Lara Jaggon TEL 44-1225-224422 ext 2136. **Subscr. to:** Tower House, Sovereign Park, Market Harborough, Leicestershire LE16 9EF, United Kingdom. TEL 44-844-8481602, FAX 44-1858-438795, future@subscription.co.uk.

388.3 SWE ISSN 1400-5506
CLASSIC MOTOR MAGASIN. Text in Swedish. 1969. 10/yr. SEK 487 (effective 2005). adv. **Document type:** *Magazine, Consumer.*
Former titles (until 1994): Classic Motor, Signalhornet (0282-7670); (until 1985): Veteranmagasinet Signalhornet (0280-5138); (until 1979): Signalhornet
Published by: Hjemmet Mortensen AB (Subsidiary of: Hjemmet-Mortensen AS), Gaevlegatan 22, Stockholm, 11378, Sweden. TEL 46-8-6920100, FAX 46-8-6509705, info@hjemmetmortensen.se, http://www.hjemmetmortensen.se. Eds. Rickard Johansson Wolrath TEL 46-8-6920164, Thomas Sjoelund TEL 46-8-6920167. Adv. contact Dan Larsson TEL 46-8-6920135. B&W page SEK 12,295, color page SEK 15,950. Circ: 53,400.

796.77 DEU
CLASSIC SAISON. Text in German. 2001. 3/yr. EUR 7 newsstand/cover (effective 2006). adv. **Document type:** *Magazine, Consumer.*
Published by: Pro Publica International Verlag GmbH, Hansaallee 289, Duesseldorf, 40549, Germany. TEL 49-211-5581866, FAX 49-211-5578657, http://www.peil-pp.de. adv.: B&W page EUR 6,380, color page EUR 7,500. Circ: 60,000 (controlled).

388 USA ISSN 1097-7988
CLASSIC TRUCKS. Text in English. 1991. m. USD 22.95 domestic; USD 34.95 in Canada; USD 46.95 elsewhere (effective 2008). adv. back issues avail. **Document type:** *Magazine, Consumer.* **Description:** Provides technical upgrading, how-to features for the do-it-yourselfer presented with detailed photos and text.
Formerly (until 199?): Truckin' Classic Trucks (1081-2067)
Indexed: G06, G07, G08, I05, S23.
—CCC.
Published by: Source Interlink Companies, 774 S Placentia Ave, Placentia, CA 92870. dheine@sourceinterlink.com, http://www.sourceinterlinkmedia.com. Ed. Rob Fortier. Pub. Tim Foss TEL 714-939-2409. adv.: B&W page USD 5,335, color page USD 7,625. Circ: 69,759 (paid).

629.222 GBR ISSN 1748-071X
CLASSICS MONTHLY. Text in English. 1995. m. GBP 46.68 domestic; GBP 75 in Europe; GBP 89 in United States; GBP 100 elsewhere; GBP 4.10 newsstand/cover (effective 2010). adv. **Document type:** *Magazine, Consumer.* **Description:** Features articles on classic cars, including prices and advice.
Former titles (until 2005): Classics (1369-1007); (until 1997): Retro Classics (1366-4441); (until Jan.1997): Retro (1360-5771)
Related titles: Online - full text ed.: GBP 51.87 domestic; GBP 3.99 per issue (effective 2010).
—CCC.
Published by: Future Publishing Ltd., Beauford Ct, 30 Monmouth St, Bath, Avon BA1 2BW, United Kingdom. TEL 44-1225-442244, FAX 44-1225-446019, customerservice@subscription.co.uk, http://www.futureplc.com. Ed. Jim Douglas. Pub. Charley Davies TEL 44-1225-442244 ext 2194. Adv. contact Lara Jaggon TEL 44-1225-224422 ext 2136. **Subscr. to:** Tower House, Sovereign Park, Market Harborough, Leicestershire LE16 9EF, United Kingdom. TEL 44-844-8481602, FAX 44-1858-438795.

388.3 USA
CLEAN CITIES NEWS. Text in English. 1997. 4/yr. free. 16 p./no.; back issues avail. **Document type:** *Newsletter, Government.* **Description:** Provides information about Clean Cities projects, designations, and conferences, and is dedicated to publishing the most unbiased and up-to-date information about developments in the alternative fuels industry.
Formerly (until 2004): Alternative Fuel News; Which was formed by the merger of (1995-1997): A F D C Update; (1995-1997): Clean Cities Drive
Related titles: Online - full text ed.
Published by: U.S. Department of Energy, Office of Energy Efficiency and Renewable Energy, Vehicle Technologies Program, Clean Cities, EE-2G, Rm 5G-030, 1000 Independence Ave, SW, Washington, DC 20585. http://www1.eere.energy.gov/vehiclesandfuels/. Circ: 8,200 (controlled).

796.77 GBR ISSN 1751-1313
CLOUD NINE CLASSICS YEARBOOK. Text in English. 2006. a. GBP 12.99 per issue domestic; GBP 17.99 per issue in Europe; GBP 22.99 per issue elsewhere (effective 2007). **Document type:** *Yearbook, Consumer.*
Published by: Cloud Nine Vehicles, 18 St George Sq, Stamford, Lincs PE9 2BN, United Kingdom. TEL 44-1780-766787, FAX 44-1780-752225.

388.3 ESP ISSN 1988-091X
COCHE ACTUAL. Text in Spanish. 1987. w. adv. **Document type:** *Magazine, Consumer.*
Related titles: ◆ Supplement(s): Gran Guia de Coche Actual.
Published by: Motorpress Iberica (Subsidiary of: Gruner + Jahr AG & Co), Ancora 40, Madrid, 28045, Spain. TEL 34-91-3470100, FAX 34-91-3470152, http://www.motorpress-iberica.es. Ed. Rafel Guitart. Circ: 29,000 (paid).

388.3 ESP
COCHES CLASICOS. Text in Spanish. m. EUR 5 newsstand/cover (effective 2009). adv. **Document type:** *Magazine, Consumer.*
Published by: Grupo V, C Valportillo Primera, 11, Alcobendas, Madrid, 28108, Spain. TEL 34-91-6622137, FAX 34-91-6622654, secretaria@grupov.es. Ed. Ivan Vicario-Martin. Adv. contact Isidro Iglesias. page EUR 3,350; trim 19.5 x 25.5. Circ: 30,000.

388.3 ESP
COCHES DE OCASION. Text in Spanish. m. **Document type:** *Magazine, Consumer.* **Description:** Contains descriptions and reviews of secondhand automobiles available on the market.
Published by: Editorial Moredi S.L., Hiedra no 2-C, Madrid, 28036, Spain. TEL 34-91-7339713, FAX 34-91-7339673, administrador@moredi.com, http://www.moredi.com. Circ: 32,261 (paid and controlled).

629.222 USA ISSN 0742-812X
TL7.U6
COLLECTIBLE AUTOMOBILE. Variant title: Automobile. Text in English. 1984. bi-m. adv. bk.rev. charts; illus. back issues avail.; reprints avail. **Description:** Publishes articles of interest to automobile collectors, concerning historic and special cars.
Formerly: Consumer Guide Elite Cars
Published by: Publications International Ltd., 7373 N Cicero Ave, Lincolnwood, IL 60712. TEL 847-329-5339, 847-676-3470, FAX 847-676-3671, customer_service@pubint.com, http://www.pubint.com. Ed. John Biel. Pub. Frank E Peiler. Circ: 100,000.

629.222075 USA ISSN 1556-2840
COLLECTOR CAR MARKET REVIEW. Text in English. 1994. bi-m. USD 18.95 (effective 2006). adv. back issues avail. **Document type:** *Magazine, Consumer.* **Description:** Lists prices for collectible automobiles built between 1946 and 1979. Each issue features articles relating to the market for old cars and covers some of the latest big auctions.
Former titles (until 2005?): Collector Car & Truck Market Guide (1098-3678); (until 1998): Collector Car & Truck Prices (1073-869X)
—CCC.
Published by: V M R International, Inc., 607, North Grafton, MA 01536-0607. TEL 508-839-6707, FAX 508-839-6266. Ed., Pub., R&P John Iafolla. Adv. contact Linda Mekulsia. Circ: 16,000 (paid). **Dist. by:** I C D - Hearst, 250 W 55th St, New York, NY 10019. TEL 212-649-4443.

388.3 USA ISSN 1931-9819
TL7.A1
COLLECTOR CAR PRICE GUIDE. Text in English. 1989. a. USD 19.99 (effective 2008). charts; illus. 744 p./no.; **Document type:** *Magazine, Consumer.* **Description:** Contains more than 250,000 values determined from auction data, collector input and market research to help accurately rate the condition of a car and identify the difference between classic, antique, special interest, collector and milestone models.
Former titles (until 2006): Standard Guide to Cars & Prices (1048-1001); Collector Car Price Guide
Published by: Krause Publications, Inc. (Subsidiary of: F + W Media Inc.), 700 E State St, Iola, WI 54990. TEL 715-445-2214, 888-457-2873, FAX 715-445-2164, info@krause.com, http://www.krause.com. Ed. Ron Kowalke TEL 715-445-2214 ext 246.

624.286 USA ISSN 0739-7437
COLLISION; dedicated to the improvement of the auto body trade. Text in English. 1960. bi-m. USD 18 domestic (effective 2001). adv. bk.rev. charts; illus.; stat.; tr.lit. **Document type:** *Magazine, Trade.* **Description:** News and instructions for owners, buyers, managers of dealerships, and auto body repair shops serving northeastern U.S.
Formerly (until 1974): Shop Talk
Indexed: HRIS.
Published by: Collision Magazine, Inc., PO Box M, Franklin, MA 02038-0822. TEL 508-528-6211, FAX 508-528-6211. Ed. Jay Kruza. R&P B. Call. Circ: 15,000 (paid and controlled).

COLLISION (KIRKLAND); the international compendium for crash research. *see* PUBLIC HEALTH AND SAFETY

388 USA ISSN 1526-8934
COLLISION PARTS JOURNAL. Text in English. 1983. q. USD 45 (effective 2001). **Document type:** *Newspaper.* **Description:** Covers happenings in the collision parts industry as they pertain to members of the Automotive Body Parts Association, and the manufacturer and distributor of replacement collision parts.
Formerly: A B P D A Journal
Published by: (Automotive Body Parts Association), Sarco Management and Publications, P O Box 820689, Houston, TX 77282-0689. TEL 800-323-5832, 800-323-5832, FAX 281-531-9411. Ed., Pub., R&P, Adv. contact Stanley A Rodman. Circ: 2,300.

629.286 CAN ISSN 1483-0256
COLLISION QUARTERLY. Text in English. 1997. q. CAD 16; CAD 5 newsstand/cover. adv. back issues avail. **Document type:** *Newsletter, Trade.*
Published by: Automotive Retailers' Publishing Co. Ltd., 8980 Fraserwood Ct, Unit 1, Burnaby, BC V5J 5H7, Canada. TEL 604-432-7987, FAX 604-432-1756. Ed. Reg Romero. Adv. contact Lea Allen. page USD 1,595; trim 10.88 x 8.13. Circ: 5,347 (controlled).

388.342 629.222 USA ISSN 1554-6543
COLLISION REPAIR PRODUCT NEWS. Text in English. 2004. bi-m. USD 48; USD 7 newsstand/cover (effective 2005). adv. **Document type:** *Magazine, Trade.* **Description:** Focuses on PBE tools, equipment and supplies.
Published by: Cygnus Business Media, Inc., 1233 Janesville Ave, PO Box 803, Fort Atkinson, WI 53538. TEL 920-563-6388, FAX 920-563-1702, http://www.cygnusb2b.com. Ed. Jeff Reinke TEL 920.568-8363. Pub. Tom Lynch TEL 920-563-1640. adv.: color page USD 3,810. Circ: 60,000.

388.342 GBR ISSN 1748-9849
COLOMBIA AUTOS REPORT. Text in English. 2005. a. EUR 820, USD 1,030 combined subscription per issue (print & email eds.) (effective 2010). **Document type:** *Report, Trade.* **Description:** Provides industry professionals and strategists, corporate analysts, auto associations, government departments and regulatory bodies with independent forecasts and competitive intelligence on the Colombian automotives market.
Related titles: E-mail ed.
Indexed: A15, ABIn, B02, B15, B17, B18, G04, I05, P48, P51, P52, PQC.
Published by: Business Monitor International Ltd., Senator House, 85 Queen Victoria St, London, EC4V 4AB, United Kingdom. TEL 44-20-72480468, FAX 44-20-72480467, subs@businessmonitor.com.

388.3 345 USA
COLORADO CRIMINAL CORRECTION VEHICLES AND RELATED STATUTES. Text in English. 1996. a. USD 49.95 (effective 2000). **Document type:** *Handbook/Manual/Guide, Trade.* **Description:** Contains up-to-date presentation of Colorado Corrections (Title 17), Criminal Code (Title 18), Vehicles and traffic (Title 42) besides related Statutes, Rules of Criminal Prosecution and selected sections of the Colorado and U.S. Constitutions with legislative changes in text.
Related titles: CD-ROM ed.
Published by: Gould Publications, Inc. (Subsidiary of: LexisNexis North America), 1333 North US Hwy 17-92, Longwood, FL 32750. TEL 800-533-1637, 877-374-2919, criminaljustice@lexisnexis.com, http://www.gouldlaw.com.

COMMERCIAL AUTO INSURANCE. *see* INSURANCE

629.287405 GBR ISSN 1757-577X
COMMERCIAL VEHICLE WORKSHOP. Text in English. 2004. 11/school-academic yr. adv. **Document type:** *Magazine, Trade.* **Description:** Provides technical, product and business information to commercial automotive technicians.
—CCC.
Published by: Hamerville Magazines Ltd., Regal House, Regal Way, Watford, Herts WD24 4YF, United Kingdom. TEL 44-1923-237799, FAX 44-1923-246901, office@hamerville.co.uk. Ed. Tim Franklin. Adv. contact Rob Gilham. page GBP 2,090; 180 x 255. Circ: 9,479.

338.476 GBR ISSN 1755-1374
COMMERCIAL VEHICLES MONTHLY DIGEST. Text in English. 1999. m. free (effective 2009). **Document type:** *Magazine, Trade.*
Former titles (until 2007): World Commercial Vehicles (Online) (1755-442X); (until 200?): World Commercial Vehicles (Print) (1467-386X)
Media: Online - full content.
—CCC.
Published by: Automotive World, 19 Neptune Ct, Vanguard Way, Cardiff, CF24 5PJ, United Kingdom. TEL 44-29-20468902, FAX 44-29-20468903, https://www.automotiveworld.com/.

629.23 GBR ISSN 1754-1271
COMPLETE KIT CAR. Text in English. 1988. m. GBP 45 domestic; GBP 65 in Europe; GBP 85 elsewhere (effective 2010). **Document type:** *Magazine, Consumer.* **Description:** Features road tests, articles and up-to-date news on the kit car industry.
Former titles (until 2007): Which Kit Car (1743-6923); (until 2004): Which Kit? (0955-7954)
—CCC.
Published by: Performance Publishing Ltd., 12 Thesiger Close, Worthing, W Sussex BN11 2RN, United Kingdom. Ed. Ian Stent TEL 44-1823-335443. Adv. contact Karen O'Riordan.

338.476 GBR ISSN 1755-1366
COMPONENTS MONTHLY DIGEST. Variant title: Automotiveworld.com. Components Monthly Digest. Text in English. 200?. m. free (effective 2009). **Document type:** *Magazine, Trade.*
Former titles (until 2007): Automotive Components Manufacturers (1755-4411); (until 2005): Automotive Components Analyst (Online) (1755-4403)
Media: Online - full text.
Published by: Automotive World, 19 Neptune Ct, Vanguard Way, Cardiff, CF24 5PJ, United Kingdom. TEL 44-29-20468902, FAX 44-29-20468903, https://www.automotiveworld.com/.

388.3 USA
CONNECTICUT MOTOR VEHICLE LAWS. Text in English. 1994. a. USD 9.95 (effective 2000). **Document type:** *Handbook/Manual/Guide, Trade.* **Description:** Contains complete Connecticut Motor Laws (Title 14), including selected sections from Transportation (Title 13b) and Navigation and Aeronautics (Title 15). Includes a comprehensive index.
Related titles: CD-ROM ed.
Published by: Gould Publications, Inc. (Subsidiary of: LexisNexis North America), 1333 North US Hwy 17-92, Longwood, FL 32750. TEL 800-533-1637, 877-374-2919, criminaljustice@lexisnexis.com, http://www.gouldlaw.com.

629.22 USA ISSN 0097-8337
TL5
CONSUMER GUIDE MAGAZINE. Text in English. 1966. m. illus.
Related titles: Online - full text ed.
Indexed: G05, G06, G07, G08, G09, HlthInd, I05, MagInd, P02, P10, P48, P53, P54, PQC.
Published by: Publications International Ltd., 7373 N Cicero Ave, Lincolnwood, IL 60712. TEL 847-676-3470, FAX 847-676-3671, SA_CS@pubint.com, http://www.pilbooks.com. Ed. Charles Giametta. Circ: 220,000.

CONSUMER REPORTS BEST & WORST NEW CARS. *see* CONSUMER EDUCATION AND PROTECTION

388 USA ISSN 1935-4002
TL162
CONSUMER REPORTS CARS. NEW CAR RATINGS & REVIEWS. Text in English. 200?. a., latest 2007. USD 6.99 per issue (effective 2008). **Document type:** *Magazine, Consumer.*
Published by: Consumers Union of the United States, Inc., 101 Truman Ave, Yonkers, NY 10703. TEL 914-378-2000, 800-234-1645, FAX 914-378-2900, http://www.consumersunion.org.

CONSUMER REPORTS CARS: RATINGS & PRICING GUIDE. *see* CONSUMER EDUCATION AND PROTECTION

629.222 USA ISSN 1044-3045
TL162
CONSUMER REPORTS NEW CAR BUYING GUIDE. Variant title: New Car Buying Guide. Text in English. 1989. a. USD 9.99 per issue (effective 2008). back issues avail. **Document type:** *Magazine, Consumer.* **Description:** Contains extensive reports from the Consmers Union product testing center on 200 new cars, sport-utility vehicles, minivans, and pickups, each with reliability details and prices, along with the year's top 10 picks.
Formerly (until 1989): Guide to New Cars
Published by: Consumers Union of the United States, Inc., 101 Truman Ave, Yonkers, NY 10703. TEL 914-378-2000, 800-234-1645, FAX 914-378-2900, http://www.consumerreports.org. Eds. Gordon Hard, Rik Paul.

629.222 USA ISSN 1551-3009
TL162
CONSUMER REPORTS NEW CAR PREVIEW. Text in English. 1994. a. USD 6.99 per issue (effective 2009). back issues avail. **Document type:** *Magazine, Consumer.* **Description:** Contains objective information on more than 150 new cars.
Former titles (until 2000): Consumer Reports Preview (1528-3267); (until 1999): Consumer Reports New Car Yearbook
Published by: Consumers Union of the United States, Inc., 101 Truman Ave, Yonkers, NY 10703. TEL 914-378-2000, 800-234-1645, FAX 914-378-2900, http://www.consumerreports.org. Eds. Gordon Hard, Rik Paul.

614.86 640.73 USA ISSN 1555-7464
TL162
CONSUMER REPORTS S U V'S, WAGONS, MINIVANS, TRUCKS. Text in English. 1999. a. **Document type:** *Magazine, Consumer.* **Description:** Provides the results of test and reviews conducted on all makes and models of sport utility vehicles available on the market.
Formerly (until 200?): Consumer Reports Sport Utility Special (1530-3853)
Published by: Consumers Union of the United States, Inc., 101 Truman Ave, Yonkers, NY 10703. TEL 914-378-2000, 800-234-1645, FAX 914-378-2900, http://www.consumersunion.org. **Dist. by:** Murdoch Magazines Distribution.

629.222 USA ISSN 1042-9476
TL154
CONSUMER REPORTS USED CAR BUYING GUIDE. Variant title: Used Car Buying Guide. Text in English. 1979. a. USD 9.99 per issue (effective 2008). back issues avail. **Document type:** *Magazine, Consumer.* **Description:** Provides a comprehensive guide to finding the most reliable used cars available.
Former titles (until 1989): Guide to Used Cars (1045-6090); (until 1986): Consumer Reports Guide to Used Cars (0162-4091)
Published by: Consumers Union of the United States, Inc., 101 Truman Ave, Yonkers, NY 10703. TEL 914-378-2000, 800-234-1645, FAX 914-378-2900, http://www.consumerreports.org. Eds. Gordon Hard, Rik Paul.

629.2 621.38 USA
CONVERGENCE: INTERNATIONAL CONGRESS ON TRANSPORTATION ELECTRONICS. PROCEEDINGS. Text in English. 1984. irreg. **Document type:** *Proceedings.*
Formerly: Convergence: International Colloquium on Automotive Electronic Technology. Proceedings
Related titles: Online - full text ed.
Published by: (I E E E), S A E Inc., 400 Commonwealth Dr, Warrendale, PA 15096. TEL 724-776-4841, 877-606-7323, FAX 724-776-0790, CustomerService@sae.org, http://www.sae.org.

338.3 IRL ISSN 1649-6809
CORK'S MOTOR TRADER. Text in English. 2002. bi-w. EUR 2.50 newsstand/cover (effective 2006). adv. **Document type:** *Magazine, Trade.*
Supersedes in part (in 2005): Ireland's Motor Trader (1649-6353); Which was formerly (until 2004): The Motor-Trader (1649-2072)
Published by: Motor Trader, Box 338, Naas, Co. Kildare, Ireland. TEL 353-45-893343, FAX 353-45-893342, info@motortrader.ie, http://www.motortrader.ie/.

CORMORANT NEWS BULLETIN. *see* ANTIQUES

388.3 ARG
CORSA. Text in Spanish. 1966. w. adv. illus.; tr.lit.
Published by: Editorial Abril S.A., Leandro N Alem 896, Buenos Aires, 1001, Argentina. Circ: 75,000.

629.222 388.324 USA ISSN 2151-0571
CORVETTE & CHEVY. Text in English. 19??. m. USD 32.95 domestic; USD 69.95 in Canada; USD 124.95 elsewhere (effective 2009). adv. **Document type:** *Magazine, Trade.* **Description:** Contains articles on technology, events, and special feature cars written by authorities in the field, including the National Corvette Museum and Bloomington Gold.
Formerly (until 2009): Corvette & Chevy Trader
Published by: AutoTrader Classics, 5775 Peachtree-Dunwoody Rd, Ste A-100, Atlanta, GA 30342. TEL 800-548-8889. Adv. contact Debbie Reetz TEL 404-568-8383.

CORVETTE ENTHUSIAST. *see* SPORTS AND GAMES

796.77 USA ISSN 0195-1661
CORVETTE FEVER. Text in English. 1978. m. USD 27.97 domestic; USD 39.97 in Canada; USD 51.97 elsewhere (effective 2008). adv. bk.rev. illus.; tr.lit. back issues avail. **Document type:** *Magazine, Consumer.* **Description:** Provides Corvette enthusiasts with a forum to pursue their restoration and high-performance modification goals.
Incorporates (1976-1991): Keepin' Track of Vettes (0191-474X)
Related titles: Online - full text ed.
Indexed: G05, G06, G07, G08, I05, I07, S23.
—CCC.
Published by: Source Interlink Companies, 9036 Brittany Way, Tampa, FL 33619. TEL 813-675-3500, dheine@sourceinterlink.com, http://www.sourceinterlinkmedia.com. Ed. Alan Colvin. Pubs. Jim Foos, John Gallagher TEL 323-782-2733. adv.: B&W page USD 5,590, color page USD 7,445. Circ: 34,277 (paid).

796.77 USA
CORVETTE INFORMANT. Text in English. 1997. q. USD 12.95. adv. **Document type:** *Newsletter.*
Published by: Corvette Mike Southern California, 1133 N Tustin Ave, Anaheim, CA 92807. TEL 800-327-8388. Ed. Mike Vietro.

796.77 USA
CORVETTE LIFESTYLES. Text in English. 2002. m. USD 27.95 (effective 2002). adv. **Document type:** *Magazine, Consumer.* **Description:** Focuses on the lifestyles of Corvette owners and enthusiasts.
Published by: CorvetteMagazine.com, 5151 S. Lakeland Dr., Ste. 3, Lakeland, FL 33813. Ed. Donald Farr.

796.77 USA
CORVETTE MAGAZINE. Text in English. m. adv. **Document type:** *Magazine, Consumer.*
Media: Online - full content.
Published by: CorvetteMagazine.com, 5151 S. Lakeland Dr., Ste. 3, Lakeland, FL 33813. Ed. Donald Farr.

629.222 796.77 USA
CORVETTE TRADER & CHEVYS. Text in English. m.
Published by: Trader Publishing Company, 24771 US 19 N, Clearwater, FL 34623. TEL 800-548-8889, FAX 727-712-0034.

388.3 USA
COSTCO AUTO BUYER'S GUIDE. Text in English. 2002. bi-m. adv. **Description:** Provides up-to-date automotive information for Costco members to assist them in making a new car buying decision.
Published by: Custom Publishing Group, 3920 Conde St, San Diego, CA 92110. TEL 858-777-5119, FAX 619-297-2610. Pub. Peter J Gottfredson. adv.: color page USD 76,518; trim 8 x 10.5. Circ: 12,000,000 (free).

629.222 NLD ISSN 1569-4283
COTE & PROVENCE. Text in Dutch. 2001. 4/yr. EUR 19.50 domestic; EUR 20.50 in Belgium; EUR 25 in Europe (effective 2010). adv. bk.rev.; Website rev. 80 p./no.; back issues avail.; reprints avail. **Document type:** *Magazine, Consumer.* **Description:** Life in the south of France.
Related titles: Online - full content ed.
Published by: De Bladenfabriek, Postbus 19217, Utrecht, 3501 DE, Netherlands. TEL 31-30-2302530, FAX 31-30-2302501, http://www.debladenfabriek.nl.

COTE AUTO. *see* TRAVEL AND TOURISM

658.8 USA ISSN 0739-3695
COUNTERMAN; the magazine for the jobber sales team. Abbreviated title: C M. (Technical Sales Seminars published in April; Tech-Forum published in Aug.; Top 25 Influences in Aftermarket Distribution in Dec.) Text in English. 1983. m. free domestic to qualified personnel (effective 2008). adv. tr.lit. back issues avail.; reprints avail. **Document type:** *Magazine, Trade.* **Description:** Designed for professionals at every level of the automotive parts distribution channel, from retail chain, program group and corporate headquarters to independent WDs and company-owned distribution centers, to retail chain, company-owned and independent parts stores.
Related titles: Online - full text ed.
Indexed: P16, P48, P52, P53, P54, PQC.

Published by: Babcox Publications, Inc., 3550 Embassy Pky, Akron, OH 44333. TEL 330-670-1234, FAX 330-670-0874, bbabcox@babcox.com, http://www.babcox.com. Ed. Mark Phillips. Adv. contact Ellen Mays TEL 330-670-1234 ext 275. B&W page USD 7,725. Circ: 46,288 (paid).

614.86 GBR
CRASH TEST TECHNOLOGY INTERNATIONAL. Text in English. 2004 (Sep.). s-a. free (effective 2009). adv. back issues avail. **Document type:** *Magazine, Trade.* **Description:** Covers the area of crash test technology and implementation.
Published by: U K I P Media & Events Ltd. (Subsidiary of: AutoIntermediates Ltd.), Abinger House, Church St, Dorking, Surrey RH4 1DF, United Kingdom. TEL 44-1306-743744, FAX 44-1306-887546, info@ukintpress.com.

388.342 497 GBR ISSN 1748-9857
CROATIA AUTOS REPORT. Text in English. 2005. a. EUR 820, USD 1,030 combined subscription per issue (print & email eds.) (effective 2010). **Document type:** *Report, Trade.* **Description:** Provides industry professionals and strategists, corporate analysts, auto associations, government departments and regulatory bodies with independent forecasts and competitive intelligence on the Croatian automotives market.
Related titles: E-mail ed.
Indexed: A15, ABIn, B02, B15, B17, B18, G04, I05, P48, P51, P52, PQC.
Published by: Business Monitor International Ltd., Senator House, 85 Queen Victoria St, London, EC4V 4AB, United Kingdom. TEL 44-20-72480468, FAX 44-20-72480467, subs@businessmonitor.com.

388 USA ISSN 1946-7605
CROSLEY QUARTERLY. Text in English. 196?. q. free to members (effective 2009). adv. **Document type:** *Newsletter, Trade.*
Formerly (until 1982): Crosley Automobile Club Quarterly
Published by: Crosley Automobile Club Inc., 307 Schaeffer Rd, Blandon, PA 19510. CAC@CrosleyAutoClub.com, http://crosleyautoclub.com. Ed. Fred Syrdal. adv.: B&W page USD 150, color page USD 265.

388.342 COL ISSN 2011-2297
CROSSCAR. Text in Spanish. 2007. m. **Document type:** *Magazine, Consumer.*
Published by: Casa Editorial el Tiempo, Cra 69 No 43-B-44 Piso 3, Bogota, Colombia. TEL 57-1-5714444, FAX 57-1-4166227, http://eltiempo.com/.

388.3 FRA ISSN 1951-4506
CROSSLINE. Text in French. 2006. q. EUR 14 (effective 2010). **Document type:** *Magazine, Consumer.*
Published by: Motor Presse France, 12 rue Rouget de Lisle, Issy-les-Moulineaux, 92442, France. http://www.motorpresse.fr.

388.3 AUS ISSN 1444-5352
CRUZIN. Text in English. m. AUD 7.95 per issue (effective 2009). back issues avail. **Document type:** *Magazine, Consumer.* **Description:** Features from pre-49 hot rods to American muscle cars and Aussie classics.
Published by: Drive Publishing Pty. Ltd., PO Box 2487, Logan City DC, QLD 4114, Australia. TEL 61-7-32902222, FAX 61-7-32902422, info@drivepublishing.com.au, http://www.drivepublishing.com.au.

388.3 796.7 USA
CRUZIN' SOUTH MAGAZINE. Text in English. 2007 (Jan.). bi-m. adv. **Document type:** *Magazine, Consumer.* **Description:** Covers the south custom car and bike scene, including events, races, and shows.
Published by: D & G Productions, 8200 Highway178, Olive Branch, MS 38654. TEL 901-212-3262. Ed. Donna Wadford. adv.: page USD 900. Circ: 10,000 (controlled).

629 ESP ISSN 2174-0569
▼ **CURUXARALLYE.** Text in Multiple languages. 2010. m. back issues avail. **Document type:** *Magazine, Consumer.*
Media: Online - full text.
Address: Ave da Peregrina, 1, Bertamnans Ames, Coruna, 15220, Spain. TEL 34-981-891120. Ed. Martino De Lopo.

388 GBR ISSN 0591-2334
CUSTOM CAR. Abbreviated title: C C. Text in English. 1970. m. GBP 43.92 domestic; GBP 49.44 in Europe; GBP 54.96 elsewhere; GBP 4 per issue domestic; GBP 5 per issue in Europe; GBP 5.50 per issue elsewhere (effective 2010). adv. bk.rev. back issues avail. **Document type:** *Magazine, Trade.* **Description:** Contains feature articles and photography on automobile customizing, with profiles of models, owners, customizers, technical advice, and announcements of events and competitions.
Incorporates: Hot Rod and Custom U.K.
Related titles: Online - full text ed.
Published by: Kelsey Publishing Ltd., Cudham Tithe Barn, Berry's Hill, Cudham, Kent TN16 3AG, United Kingdom. TEL 44-1959-541444, FAX 44-1959-541400, info@kelsey.co.uk, http://www.kelsey.co.uk. Eds. Dave Biggadyke, Phil Weeden TEL 44-1733-353372. Adv. contact Gavin Williams.

388.3 USA
CYLINDER HEAD & BLOCK IDENTIFICATION GUIDE. Text in English. biennial. USD 74 to non-members; USD 69 to members.
Published by: Automotive Engine Rebuilders Association, 330 Lexington Dr, Buffalo, IL 60089-6998. TEL 847-541-6550, FAX 847-541-5808. Circ: 4,300.

388.34294371 GBR ISSN 1748-9865
CZECH REPUBLIC AUTOS REPORT. Text in English. 2005. q. EUR 820, USD 1,030 combined subscription (print & email eds.) (effective 2010). **Document type:** *Report, Trade.* **Description:** Provides industry professionals and strategists, corporate analysts, auto associations, government departments and regulatory bodies with independent forecasts and competitive intelligence on the Czech automotives market.
Related titles: E-mail ed.
Indexed: A15, ABIn, B02, B15, B17, B18, G04, I05, P48, P51, P52, PQC.
Published by: Business Monitor International Ltd., Senator House, 85 Queen Victoria St, London, EC4V 4AB, United Kingdom. TEL 44-20-72480468, FAX 44-20-72480467, subs@businessmonitor.com.

D A R. (Deutsches Autorecht) *see* LAW

388 DEU ISSN 1434-4076
D A Z. (Der Auto-Anzeiger) Text in German. 19??. fortn. EUR 29 (effective 2009). **Document type:** *Magazine, Trade.*
Published by: D A Z Verlag GmbH und Co. KG, An der Strusbek 23, Ahrensburg, 22926, Germany. TEL 49-4102-47870, FAX 49-4102-478795, info@daz-verlag.de, http://www.daz24.de. Circ: 93,986 (controlled).

388 DEU ISSN 1861-6216
D A Z CARAVAN. (Der Auto-Anzeiger) Text in German. 2005. m. EUR 20 (effective 2009). **Document type:** *Magazine, Trade.*
Published by: D A Z Verlag GmbH und Co. KG, An der Strusbek 23, Ahrensburg, 22926, Germany. TEL 49-4102-47870, FAX 49-4102-478795, info@daz-verlag.de, http://www.daz24.de. Circ: 50,000 (paid).

796.5 DEU ISSN 1430-0966
D C C - CARAVAN UND MOTORCARAVAN MODELLFUEHRER. Text in German. 1971. a. adv. **Document type:** *Magazine, Consumer.*
Former titles (until 1985): D C C - Caravan Modellfuehrer; (until 1979): D C C - Caravanfuehrer
Published by: (Deutscher Camping Club e.V.), D C C - Wirtschaftsdienst und Verlag GmbH, Mandlstr 28, Munich, 80802, Germany. TEL 49-89-3801420, FAX 49-89-334737, info@campingpresse.de, http://www.campingpresse.de. Ed., R&P Hermann Groenert. Adv. contact Rosemarie Swoboda. Circ: 15,000.

351.81 DEU ISSN 0721-7315
D E K R A - FACHSCHRIFTENREIHE. Text in German. 1975. irreg. **Document type:** *Monographic series, Trade.*
Published by: D E K R A - AG, Handwerkstr 15, Stuttgart, 70565, Germany. TEL 49-711-78610, FAX 49-711-78612204, info@dekra.de, http://www.dekra.de.

629.286 DEU
D E K R A SOLUTIONS. Text in German. 2002. q. adv. **Document type:** *Magazine, Trade.*
Published by: D E K R A - AG, Handwerkstr 15, Stuttgart, 70565, Germany. TEL 49-711-78610, FAX 49-711-78612204, info@dekra.de. Circ: 46,000 (controlled).

796.77 DEU ISSN 1617-7290
DACABRIO; Touren - Lifestyle - Genuss. Text in German. 2001. 4/yr. EUR 16; EUR 4.50 newsstand/cover (effective 2006). adv. **Document type:** *Magazine, Consumer.*
Published by: Muc Automotive Medien- und Verlags GmbH, Richard-Strauss-Str 7, Munich - Bogenhausen, 81677, Germany. TEL 49-89-45554870, FAX 49-89-45708979. adv.: B&W page EUR 3,800, color page EUR 6,200; trim 180 x 255. Circ: 50,000 (paid and controlled).

629.286 USA
DAMAGE REPORT. Text in English. m. adv. **Document type:** *Report, Trade.* **Description:** Offers news and information about the collision repair industry to all licensed auto body repair shops in Massachusetts and Rhode Island.
Incorporates (1980-199?): Automotive Times
Published by: Thomas Greco Publishing Co., 244 Chestnut St, Nutley, NJ 07110. TEL 973-667-6922, FAX 973-235-1963.

388.3 CHN ISSN 1673-7172
DANGDAI QICHE/MODERN CAR. Text in Chinese. 1986. m. USD 36 (effective 2009). **Document type:** *Magazine, Consumer.*
Related titles: Online - full text ed.
Published by: Chongqing Qiche Yanjiusuo, 3, Shuanggang Lu, Kexie Dasha 10/F, Chongqing, 400013, China. TEL 86-23-63658888 ext 39093, FAX 86-23-63658965. **Dist. by:** China International Book Trading Corp, 35 Chegongzhuang Xilu, Haidian District, PO Box 399, Beijing 100044, China. TEL 86-10-68412045, FAX 86-10-68412023, cibtc@mail.cibtc.com.cn, http://www.cibtc.com.cn.

388.3222 DNK ISSN 1399-5219
DANSKE BUSVOGNMAEND. Text in Danish. 1999. 11/yr. DKK 375 (effective 2009). adv. 48 p./no.; **Document type:** *Magazine, Trade.*
Formed by the merger of (1951-1999): Vognmanden (0108-2167); (1974-1999): Bilruten (0901-3229); Which was formerly (1922-1974): Danmarks Bilruter (1398-4047)
Address: Sundkrogsgade 13, Copenhagen OE, 2100, Denmark. TEL 45-70-227099, FAX 45-70-221099, db@db-dk.dk, http://www.db-dk.dk.

DARMSTAEDTER LICHTTECHNIK. *see* ENGINEERING—Engineering Mechanics And Materials

388.3 CHN ISSN 1006-9836
DAZHONG QICHE. Text in Chinese. 1994. m. **Document type:** *Magazine, Consumer.*
Published by: Dazhong Qiche Zazhishe (Subsidiary of: Jilin Chuban Jituan/Jilin Publishing Group), Jike Zhongda Chuanmei Guanggao, 16-17, A225, Chunshuyuan Xiao-qu, Beijing, 100052, China. TEL 86-10-63109491.

388.3 910.2 CHN
DAZHONG QICHE (QICHE LUXING)/AUTO TRAVEL. Text in Chinese. 2007. m.
Published by: Dazhong Qiche Zazhishe (Subsidiary of: Jilin Chuban Jituan/Jilin Publishing Group), Jike Zhongda Chuanmei Guanggao, 16-17, A225, Chunshuyuan Xiao-qu, Beijing, 100052, China. TEL 86-10-63109491.

796.77 USA
DEALER FIXED OPERATIONS. Text in English. 2005. m. USD 48; USD 4 per issue; free to qualified personnel (effective 2006). adv. **Document type:** *Magazine, Trade.*
Published by: Dealer Communications, 330 Franklin Rd, Ste 135-A, Box 386, Brentwood, TN 37027. TEL 615-370-1515. Ed. Lance Helgeson TEL 615-370-1515 ext 203. adv.: B&W page USD 8,228, color page USD 10,128; trim 8.25 x 10.75.

DEALER MARKETING MAGAZINE. *see* BUSINESS AND ECONOMICS—Trade And Industrial Directories

388.3 USA
DEALERS' CHOICE. Text in English. 1961. q. avail. only to franchised Texas dealers of new cars and trucks. adv. bk.rev. index. back issues avail. **Document type:** *Magazine, Trade.* **Description:** Provides automotive and business information for franchised new car and truck dealers in Texas.
Published by: Texas Automobile Dealers Association, 1108 Lavaca St, Box 1028, Austin, TX 78767-1028. TEL 512-476-2686, FAX 512-476-2179. Ed., R&P Patricia M Bardole. Adv. contact Sylvia Coker. Circ: 1,800 (controlled).

388.3 USA ISSN 1088-1727
DEALER'S EDGE. Text in English. 1995. w. **Document type:** *Newsletter, Trade.* **Description:** Provides information and news on the automotive industry.
Related titles: Online - full text ed.
Published by: W D & S Publishing, 10 W 7th St, 1st Fl, PO Box 606, Barnegat Light, NJ 08006. TEL 800-321-5312, mbowers@dealersedge.com. Pub. Jim Muntz.

388.3 330 USA
DEALERSEDGE C F O REPORT. Text in English. m. **Document type:** *Report, Trade.*
Published by: W D & S Publishing, 10 W 7th St, 1st Fl, PO Box 606, Barnegat Light, NJ 08006. TEL 800-321-5312, http://www.dealersedge.com. Pub. Jim Muntz.

388.3 USA
DEALERSEDGE PARTS MANAGER. Text in English. 1997. m. USD 299 (effective 2008). adv. back issues avail. **Document type:** *Newsletter, Trade.* **Description:** Provides management tips for improved parts department operation and profits.
Formerly: The Parts Manager (1522-7871)
Related titles: Online - full text ed.
Published by: W D & S Publishing, 10 W 7th St, 1st Fl, PO Box 606, Barnegat Light, NJ 08006. TEL 800-321-5312, http://www.dealersedge.com. Ed. Mike Bowers. Pub., Adv. contact Jim Muntz.

388.3 USA
DEALERSEDGE SERVICE MANAGER; parts & service profit report. Text in English. 1981. m. USD 299 (effective 2008). adv. back issues avail. **Document type:** *Newsletter, Trade.* **Description:** Aimed at the automobile parts and service sector of the automobile industry.
Formerly: Fixed Coverage (Parts & Service Profit Report) (1084-3272)
Published by: W D & S Publishing, 10 W 7th St, 1st Fl, PO Box 606, Barnegat Light, NJ 08006. TEL 800-321-5312, http://www.dealersedge.com. Ed. Michael Causey. Pub., Adv. contact Jim Muntz.

629.222 USA ISSN 2151-0601
DEALS ON WHEELS (ATLANTA). Text in English. 1998. m. USD 26.95 domestic; USD 51.95 in Canada; USD 99.95 elsewhere (effective 2009). adv. **Document type:** *Magazine, Consumer.* **Description:** Contains listing of vehicles for sale nationwide, ranging from classic and muscle cars to vintage trucks, street rods, trailers, and even high end automobiles.
Published by: AutoTrader Classics, 5775 Peachtree-Dunwoody Rd, Ste A-100, Atlanta, GA 30342. TEL 800-548-8889, http://www.autotraderclassics.com. Adv. contact Debbie Reetz TEL 404-568-8383. color page USD 6,900; trim 7.375 x 10.625. Circ: 6,305 (paid).

629.286 FRA ISSN 1777-6287
DECISION ATELIER; toute l'information pour l'univers du garage. Text in French. 2005. m. EUR 85 (effective 2009). **Document type:** *Magazine, Trade.*
Published by: Editions Techniques pour l'Automobile et l'Industrie (E T A I), 20 rue de la Saussiere, Boulogne-Billancourt, 92641, France. TEL 33-1-46992424, FAX 33-1-48255692, http://www.groupe-etai.com.

629.222 USA
DELOREAN WORLD. Text in English. 1983. q. USD 60 (effective 2001). adv. back issues avail. **Description:** Provides DeLorean maintenance, how-to, parts, suppliers, services and more.
Published by: DeLorean Owners Association, 2651 Altamira Dr, W Covina, CA 91792. TEL 626-965-5190, 818-352-7232, FAX 818-352-7232, 626-965-5190. Adv. contact Jim Hales. Circ: 2,000. **Subscr. to:** Membership Data Center, 879 Randolph Rd, Santa Barbara, CA 93111.

338 USA ISSN 1078-5663
DELTA AUTOMOTIVE REPORT. Text in English. 1994. m. free to qualified personnel (effective 2009). adv. **Document type:** *Newspaper, Trade.* **Description:** Provides monthly news for the local automotive industry in Louisiana and Southern Mississippi.
Related titles: Online - full text ed.: free (effective 2009).
Published by: Autographic Publishing Company, Inc., 1121 Airport Center Dr, Ste 101, Nashville, TN 37214. TEL 615-391-3666, 800-467-3666, FAX 615-391-3622, garnett@automotivereport.net. Ed. Garnett Forkum. Pub. Allen Forkum. adv.: B&W page USD 1,200; trim 11.5 x 15. Circ: 5,900 (free).

629.22075 USA
DESOTO DAYS; Desoto days bi-monthly newsletter. Text in English. 1975. USD 20 domestic membership; USD 25 foreign membership. **Description:** Provides information on the preservation and the restoration of the Desoto automobile.
Published by: The Desoto Club of America, 403 S Thornton, Richmond, MO 64085. TEL 816-470-3048. Ed. Walter O'Kelly.

343.489 DNK ISSN 0108-1306
DETAILFORSKRIFTER FOR KOERETOEJER/DETAILED REGULATIONS FOR VEHICLES. Text in Danish. 1977. irreg. price varies. **Document type:** *Government.*
Related titles: Online - full text ed.
Published by: Transportministeriet, Faerdselsstyrelsen/Ministry of Transportation, Road Safety and Transport Agency, Adelgade 13, PO Box 9039, Copenhagen K, 1304, Denmark. TEL 45-33-929100, FAX 45-33-932292, fstyr@fstyr.dk. **Dist. by:** Schultz Information A-S, Herstedvang 12, Albertslund 2620, Denmark. schultz@schultz-information.dk, http://www.schultz-information.dk.

DIASPORA - M I V A; Verkehrshilfe des Bonifatiuswerkes. (Motorisierende Innerdeutsche Verkehrs-Arbeitsgemeinschaft) *see* RELIGIONS AND THEOLOGY—Roman Catholic

DICK BERGGREN'S SPEEDWAY ILLUSTRATED. *see* SPORTS AND GAMES

629.222 GBR ISSN 2045-6069
DIESEL CAR. Text in English. 1988. m. GBP 38 domestic; GBP 66 foreign (effective 2011). adv. bk.rev. charts; illus.; stat. index. back issues avail. **Document type:** *Magazine, Consumer.* **Description:** Provides the UK's car buyers with the definitive guide to buying a diesel car, whether it's brand new or used.
Former titles (until 2010): What Diesel (1759-9709); (until 2007): What Diesel Car (1753-0334); (until 2006): Diesel Car (1472-4359); (until 1998): Diesel Car & 4 X 4 (1361-9446); (until 1996): Diesel Car (0956-3806)
—CCC.

Published by: Blaze Publishing, Lawrence House, Morrell St, Leamington Spa, Warwickshire CV32 5SZ, United Kingdom. TEL 44-1926-339808, FAX 44-1926-470400, info@blazepublishing.co.uk, http://www.blazepublishing.co.uk/.

DIESEL FORECAST; the leading source for diesel technology news. *see* ENERGY

DIESEL - LEHTI. *see* ENGINEERING—Mechanical Engineering

665.5 388.3 USA ISSN 1934-4988
DIESEL POWER. Text in English. 2005. m. USD 19.95 domestic; USD 31.95 in Canada; USD 43.95 elsewhere (effective 2008). adv. back issues avail. **Document type:** *Magazine, Consumer.* **Description:** Designed for diesel enthusiasts, showing Ford Powerstroke, Dodge Cummins and GM Duramax owners what is on the market to improve their trucks' engine, transmission and driveline.
Related titles: Online - full text ed.: USD 10 (effective 2008).
Indexed: A10, G06, G07, G08, I05, S23, V03.
—CCC.
Published by: Source Interlink Companies, 2570 E Cerritos Ave, Anaheim, CA 92806. TEL 714-941-1400, FAX 714-978-6390, dheine@sourceinterlink.com, http://www.sourceinterlinkmedia.com. Ed. David Kennedy. Pub. Steve VonSeggern TEL 714-939-2581. adv.: color page USD 10,835. Circ: 143,738 (paid).

796.71 ZAF ISSN 1810-2700
DIESELCAR. Text in English. 2003. bi-m. ZAR 200 (effective 2007). adv. **Document type:** *Magazine, Consumer.*
Published by: DieselCar Publications, Hangar 2, Pharazyn Way, Oribi Airport, Pietermaritzburg, 3201, South Africa. TEL 27-33-3867750, FAX 27-33-3868531. Adv. contact Hilton Botha.

658 USA
DIGITAL DEALER. Text in English. 2005. m. USD 48; USD 4 per issue (effective 2006). adv. **Document type:** *Magazine, Trade.* **Description:** Edited for Internet professionals working at new franchised vehicle dealerships. It focuses on technology, the Internet, marketing services related to new vehicle dealership sales and the software that supports those processes.
Related titles: Online - full text ed.
Published by: Dealer Comminications, 330 Franklin Rd, Ste 135-A, Box 386, Brentwood, TN 37027. TEL 615-370-1515, FAX 615-370-8181. Ed. Mark Dubis. Pub. Greg Noonan. adv.: B&W page USD 8,228, color page USD 10,128; trim 8.25 x 10.25.

629.286 VEN
DIRECTORIO AUTOMOR DE VENEZUELA/VENEZUELAN AUTOMOTIVE GUIDE. Text in Spanish. 1970. a. USD 25 (effective 2001). adv. **Document type:** *Directory, Trade.*
Formerly (until 2001): Guia Automotriz de Venezuela
Published by: Ortiz y Asociados, s.r.l., Av. Caurimare, Qta. Expo., Colinas de Bello Monte, Caracas, Venezuela. TEL 58-212-7511355, FAX 58-212-7511122, ortizauto@cantv.net. Ed. Armando Ortiz P. Adv. contact Maria Ortiz TEL 58-212-7511755. Circ: 8,000 (controlled).

796.7 USA ISSN 1553-7633
DIRTSPORTS. Text in English. 2004. m. adv. back issues avail. **Document type:** *Magazine, Consumer.* **Description:** Covers the exciting world of off-road motor sports.
Indexed: A09, A10, B04, G06, G07, G08, G09, I05, M01, M02, P10, P48, P52, P53, P54, PQC, R03, RGAb, RGPR, T02, V03, V04, W03, W05.
—CCC.
Published by: Advanstar Communications, Inc., 6200 Canoga Ave, 2nd Fl, Woodland Hills, CA 91367. TEL 818-593-5000, FAX 818-593-5020, info@advanstar.com, http://www.advanstar.com.

629.28 USA ISSN 1041-4290
TL152
DOMESTIC CARS SERVICE & REPAIR; engine performance, electrical, mechanical. Text in English. 1967. a. (in 2 vols.). USD 434 (effective 1997). illus. **Description:** Auto service and repair manual for professional auto technicians.
Formerly (until 1971): National Service Data: Domestic (0272-8745)
Related titles: CD-ROM ed.
Published by: Mitchell Repair Information Company, 9889 Willow Creek Rd, Box 26260, San Diego, CA 92196-0260. TEL 619-549-7809, 888-724-6742, FAX 619-578-4752. Circ: 27,000.

629.28 USA
DOMESTIC LIGHT TRUCKS & VANS SERVICE & REPAIR. Text in English. 1917. a. USD 434 (effective 1997). illus. **Document type:** *Handbook/Manual/Guide, Trade.* **Description:** Auto service and repair manual for professional auto technicians.
Formerly (until 1967): Domestic Cars. Tune-up, Mechanical Transmission Service & Repair
Related titles: CD-ROM ed.; Microform ed.
Published by: Mitchell Repair Information Company, 9889 Willow Creek Rd, Box 26260, San Diego, CA 92196-0260. TEL 619-549-7809, FAX 619-578-4752. Circ: 27,000.

345.730247 USA ISSN 0730-2568
KF2231.A15
DRINKING / DRIVING LAW LETTER. Text in English. 1982. bi-w. looseleaf. USD 1,114.56 (effective 2010). bk.rev. index. 30 p./no.; back issues avail. **Document type:** *Newsletter, Trade.* **Description:** Contains the latest legal, technical and procedural information on the latest issues in drunk driving cases.
—CCC.
Published by: Thomson West (Subsidiary of: Thomson Reuters Corp.), 610 Opperman Dr, Eagan, MN 55123. TEL 651-687-7000, 800-344-5008, west.customer.service@thomson.com. Circ: 2,000.

DRIVE. *see* LIFESTYLE

388.342 USA
DRIVE!, your #1 event guide & part source across the USA. Text in English. 1987. m. free (effective 2008). adv. **Document type:** *Magazine, Consumer.* **Description:** Features the nation's hottest rods, customs, classics and trucks with the latest trackside action with technical articles, full coverage of events, and interviews with important personalities.
Former titles: Swap Talk
Published by: Drive! Media, 1300 Galaxy Way, Ste 15, Concord, CA 94520. TEL 925-682-9900, 800-764-6278, FAX 925-682-9907. Ed. Scott Ross. Pub., R&P, Adv. contact Mike Calamusa. Circ: 185,000 (paid and free).

796.7 IRL ISSN 1393-8576
DRIVE!. Text in English. 198?. 10/yr. adv. **Document type:** *Magazine, Consumer.*
Formerly (until 1999): Car Driver (0791-1793)
Address: 7 Cranford Centre, Montrose, Dublin, 4, Ireland. TEL 353-1-2600899, FAX 353-1-2600911. adv.: color page EUR 2,220. Circ: 10,028 (paid and controlled).

796.77 DEU
DRIVE FORD SCENE INTERNATIONAL. Text in German. 1993. q. EUR 21 domestic; EUR 24 foreign; EUR 3.80 newsstand/cover (effective 2011). adv. **Document type:** *Magazine, Consumer.*
Published by: Vestische Mediengruppe Welke GmbH & Co. KG, Hertener Mark 7, Herten, 45699, Germany. TEL 49-2366-808400, FAX 49-2366-808499, info@vmw-verlag.de, http://vmw-verlag.de. Ed. Rudolf Welke. Pub. Arno Welke. Adv. contact Michaela de Verdin. Circ: 21,000 (paid and controlled).

796.77 USA
DRIVE PERFORMANCE. Text in English. s-a. free. **Document type:** *Magazine, Consumer.*
Published by: Subaru of America, Inc., PO Box 514025, Milwaukee, WI 53203-3425. TEL 800-926-8293.

388.34 FRA ISSN 1957-4223
DRIVEN. Text in French. 2007. bi-m. EUR 17.50; EUR 3.90 newsstand/cover (effective 2008). adv. **Document type:** *Magazine, Consumer.*
Published by: Hachette Filipacchi Medias S.A. (Subsidiary of: Lagardere Media), 149/151 Rue Anatole France, Levallois-Perret, 925340, France. TEL 33-1-413462, FAX 33-1-413469, lgardere@interdeco.fr, http://www.lagardere.com.

388.3 NZL ISSN 1175-7388
DRIVER. Text in English. 1994. m. adv. **Document type:** *Magazine, Consumer.*
Formerly (until 2001): Driver Magazine (1173-5902)
Published by: Straight 8 Publishing, Symonds St, PO Box 8673, Auckland, New Zealand. TEL 64-9-3695412, FAX 64-9-3695422, admin@straight8.co.nz. Ed. Allan Dick.

629.286 CAN ISSN 1920-6135
THE DRIVER MAGAZINE. Text in English. 2003. bi-m. USD 23.99 domestic; USD 41.99 foreign (effective 2010). adv. back issues avail. **Document type:** *Magazine, Trade.*
Published by: Driver Inc., 1315 Finch Ave W, Ste 408, Toronto, ON M3J 2G6, Canada. TEL 416-398-2700, 800-728-5771, FAX 416-398-3272, info@thedrivermagazine.com.

629.283 GBR ISSN 0265-7716
DRIVING. Key Title: Driving Magazine. Text in English. 1980. bi-m. GBP 22.50 domestic to non-members; GBP 47.50 foreign to non-members; free to members (effective 2010). adv. bk.rev. illus. **Document type:** *Magazine, Trade.* **Description:** Covers discerning and advanced drivers and driving instructors on motoring and safety matters.
Published by: D I A International Ltd., Safety House, Beddington Farm Rd, Croydon, Surrey CR0 4XZ, United Kingdom. TEL 44-20-8665-5151, FAX 44-20-8665-5565. Ed. Stephen Picton.

614.86 CAN
DRIVING COSTS. Text in English. 1972. a. **Document type:** *Bulletin.* **Description:** Describes how to calculate costs of owning and operating an automobile in Canada.
Formerly: Car Costs (0705-1298)
Published by: Canadian Automobile Association, 1145 Hunt Club Rd, Ste 200, Ottawa, ON K1V 0Y3, Canada. TEL 613-247-0117, FAX 613-247-0118. Ed. Rosalinda Weisbrod.

629.2830715 GBR ISSN 0265-8747
DRIVING INSTRUCTOR. Text in English. 1984. bi-m. free to members (effective 2010). adv. bk.rev. 24 p./no.; **Document type:** *Newspaper, Trade.* **Description:** Provides driving instructors with news and views on matters affecting them and their profession.
Published by: (Driving Instructor's Association), D I A International Ltd., Safety House, Beddington Farm Rd, Croydon, Surrey CR0 4XZ, United Kingdom. TEL 44-20-8665-5151, FAX 44-20-8665-5565. Ed. Stephen Picton.

629.2830715 GBR
DRIVING INSTRUCTOR'S MANUAL. Variant title: D I A Instructor's Manual. Text in English. 1984. base vol. plus a. updates. looseleaf. GBP 45 per issue to non-members; free to members (effective 2010). stat. 825 p./no.; **Document type:** *Handbook/Manual/Guide, Trade.* **Description:** Covers activities of the organization which enables people to work in partnership with public authorities, government, and business and voluntary organizations in order to regenerate their communities.
Published by: (Driving Instructor's Association), D I A International Ltd., Safety House, Beddington Farm Rd, Croydon, Surrey CR0 4XZ, United Kingdom. TEL 44-20-8665-5151, FAX 44-20-8665-5565, dia@driving.org, http://www.driving.org. Ed. Graham R J Fryer.

796.77 USA ISSN 1536-3562
DUB MAGAZINE. Text in English. 2000. 9/yr. USD 24.99 domestic (effective 2006). adv. **Document type:** *Magazine, Consumer.* **Description:** Profiles the automobiles of celebrities from the worlds of music, sports and movies.
Related titles: Online - full text ed.
Published by: Dub Publishing, Inc., 16815 E Johnson Dr, City of Industry, CA 91745. TEL 626-336-3821, FAX 626-336-2282, herman@dubmagazine.com. Ed. Myles Kovacs. Adv. contact Rich Calbay. color page USD 12,025; trim 8.125 x 10.875. Circ: 104,522.

388.34 IRL ISSN 1649-6361
DUBLIN'S MOTOR TRADER. Text in English. 2002. bi-w. adv.
Supersedes in part (in 2004): Ireland's Motor Trader (1649-6353); Which was formerly: The Motor-Trader (1649-2072)
Published by: Motor Trader, Box 338, Naas, Co. Kildare, Ireland. TEL 353-45-893343, FAX 353-45-893342, info@motortrader.ie, http://www.motortrader.ie/. adv.: color page EUR 2,195; 260 x 340. Circ: 9,000.

796.77 NLD ISSN 1385-1489
DUEMILA. Text in Dutch. 1986. q. free membership (effective 2010). adv. back issues avail. **Document type:** *Magazine, Consumer.* **Description:** Includes information on the history of Alfa Romeo cars, experiences of members, technical information, and upcoming events.
Published by: Vereniging Alfa Romeo Liefhebbers Nederland, Dorpstraat 4a, Veldhoven, 5504 HH, Netherlands. TEL 31-40-2548682, FAX 31-40-2531005, secretariaat@varln.nl, http://www.varln.nl.

388.3 USA ISSN 0012-7132
TL236.7
DUNE BUGGIES & HOT V WS; the fun car journal. Text in English. 1967. m. USD 19.97 domestic; USD 31.97 in Canada; USD 37.97 elsewhere (effective 2004). adv. bk.rev.; video rev. charts; illus.; stat. index. 144 p./no. 3 cols./p.; back issues avail. **Document type:** *Magazine, Consumer.*
Published by: Wright Publishing Co., 2950 Airway A7, Box 2260, Costa Mesa, CA 92628. TEL 714-979-2560, FAX 714-979-3998. Ed., R&P Bruce Simurda. Pub. Judy Wright. Adv. contacts Steve Gotoski, Linda Dill. B&W page USD 1,980, color page USD 2,870; 7 x 10. Circ: 86,645 (paid).

629 USA ISSN 0890-362X
DUPONT REGISTRY: A BUYER'S GALLERY OF FINE AUTOMOBILES. Key Title: DuPont Registry. Text in English. 1985. m. USD 49.95 domestic; USD 69.95 in Canada; USD 109.95 elsewhere; USD 10.80 per issue domestic; USD 13.95 per issue in Canada; USD 15.95 per issue elsewhere (effective 2009). adv. back issues avail. **Document type:** *Magazine, Consumer.* **Description:** Showcase of exotic, luxury and collectible automobiles for sale.
Related titles: Online - full text ed.
Published by: DuPont Publishing, Inc., 3051 Tech Dr, Saint Petersburg, FL 33716. TEL 727-573-9339, 800-233-1731, http://www2.dupontregistry.com. Pub. Thomas L Dupont.

DUSTY TIMES. *see* SPORTS AND GAMES—Bicycles And Motorcycles

E-DRIVE E-REPORT. *see* ENGINEERING—Mechanical Engineering

629.222 USA
E I U AUTOMOTIVE. Text in English. base vol. plus bi-m. updates. USD 750 (effective 2004). **Description:** Provides EIU's latest research into global automotive trends, passenger car distribution and global car components.
Media: Online - full content. **Related titles:** ◆ Series of: Motor Business Japan. ISSN 1359-4524.
Published by: Economist Intelligence Unit Ltd. (Subsidiary of: Economist Intelligence Unit Ltd.), 111 W 57th St, New York, NY 10019. TEL 212-554-0600, FAX 212-586-1181, http://www.eiu.com.

388.3 NLD ISSN 1383-2247
E V O MAGAZINE. Text in Dutch. m. EUR 200 to non-members; EUR 140 to members (effective 2009). adv. **Document type:** *Trade.*
Former titles (until 1995): Bedrijfsvervoer (0921-2000); Which Incorporated (1987-1991): Goederenstroom Management (0927-7072); (until 1987): E V O Bedrijfsvervoer (0165-425X); (until 1977): E V O Bedrijfstransport
—IE, Infotrieve.
Published by: (Eigen Vervoer Organisatie), E V O, Signaalrood 60, Zoetermeer, 2718 SG, Netherlands. TEL 31-79-3467346, FAX 31-79-3467800, evo@evo.nl, http://www.evo.nl.

629.2502 USA
E V WORLD. (Electric Vehicles) Text in English. w. free. bk.rev. **Description:** Includes news and previews of latest developments in advanced electric and hybrid vehicles.
Media: Online - full text.
Published by: Digital Revolution, PO Box 461132, Papillion, NE 68046. TEL 402-339-9877.

388.3 USA
EAST COAST RYDERS. Text in English. bi-m. **Document type:** *Magazine, Consumer.*
Published by: M I A Entertainment, Inc., PO Box 693097, Miami, FL 33269-3097. TEL 305-493-3278, FAX 305-402-3900.

796.77 GBR
▼ **EAST OF ENGLAND AUTO TRADER.** Text in English. 2009. w. adv. **Document type:** *Magazine, Consumer.*
Formed by the merger of (1988-2008): Anglia Auto Trader (0958-2495); (2005-2008): Herts, Beds & Essex Auto Trader (1747-6844); Which was formerly (1989-2005): E. London & Essex Auto Trader (0958-2878)
Published by: Auto Trader Publications Ltd. (Subsidiary of: Trader Media Group Ltd.), 3rd and 4th Fl, 41-47 Hartfield Rd., Wimbeldon, London, SW19 3RQ, United Kingdom. TEL 44-20-85447000, FAX 44-20-88791879, editorial@autotrader.co.uk, enquiries@autotrader.co.uk, http://www.autotrader.co.uk.

796.77 FRA ISSN 0765-1457
L'ECHAPPEMENT; le magazine du sport automobile. Key Title: Echappement. Text in French. 1968. m. EUR 45 domestic; EUR 59 in Europe (effective 2009). adv. back issues avail. **Document type:** *Magazine, Consumer.*
Published by: Groupe de Presse Michel Hommell, 48-50 bd. Senard, St Cloud, 92210, France. TEL 33-1-47112000. Ed. William Pac. Pub. Michel Hommell. R&P Olivier Quesnel. Adv. contact Bertrand Piot. Circ: 59,000.

388 USA ISSN 1086-5470
EDMUND'S NEW CARS; prices and reviews. Text in English. 1969. 4/yr. USD 39.96 to individuals; USD 26.80 to libraries; USD 14.99 newsstand/cover (effective Nov. 2000). illus.; stat. back issues avail. **Document type:** *Magazine, Consumer.* **Description:** Consumer guide to help consumers purchase new cars, detailing options, specifications, gas mileage and standard equipments.
Formerly: Edmund's New Car Prices (1047-0751)
Published by: Edmund Publications Corp., 2401 Colorado Blvd, Ste 250, Santa Monica, CA 90404. TEL 310-309-6300, FAX 310-309-6400. Ed. Peter Steinlauf. Circ: 47,000. **Subscr. to:** NexTech, PO Box 338, Shrub Oak, NY 10588. **Dist. by:** Curtis, 433 Hackensack Ave, Hackensack, NJ 07601.

796.7 USA ISSN 0046-1326
EDSELETTER. Text in English. 1969. m. USD 25 domestic membership; USD 30 foreign membership (effective 2005). adv. bk.rev. **Document type:** *Newsletter, Consumer.* **Description:** Contains information on the repair and preservation of the Edsel, folklore, club events, and cars and parts for sale.
Published by: International Edsel Club, c/o Lois Barrow, 238 Fairview St, Paris, TN 38242. ebarrow@wk.net. Circ: 1,000.

388.3 USA
EFFECTIVE USE OF G M'S LABOR TIME GUIDE. (General Motors) Text in English. a. **Document type:** *Guide, Trade.*
Published by: W D & S Publishing, 10 W 7th St, 1st Fl, PO Box 606, Barnegat Light, NJ 08006. TEL 800-321-5312, http://www.dealersedge.com.

388.342962 GBR ISSN 1748-9873
EGYPT AUTOS REPORT. Text in English. 2005. q. EUR 820, USD 1,030 combined subscription (print & email eds.) (effective 2010). **Document type:** *Report, Trade.* **Description:** Provides industry professionals and strategists, corporate analysts, auto associations, government departments and regulatory bodies with independent forecasts and competitive intelligence on the Egyptian automotives market.
Related titles: E-mail ed.
Indexed: A15, ABIn, B02, B15, B17, B18, G04, I05, P48, P51, P52, PQC.
Published by: Business Monitor International Ltd., Senator House, 85 Queen Victoria St, London, EC4V 4AB, United Kingdom. TEL 44-20-72480468, FAX 44-20-72480467, subs@businessmonitor.com.

388 910.2 NLD ISSN 1872-1389
EILEEN MAGAZINE. Text in Dutch. 2005. s-a. free (effective 2010). adv. **Document type:** *Magazine, Consumer.*
Published by: YPCA, Your Personal Call Assistant B.V., Postbus 132, Hilversum, 1200 AC, Netherlands. TEL 31-35-6777280, FAX 31-35-6777281, info@ypca.nl, http://www.ypca.nl.

388.4 GBR ISSN 1467-5560
ELECTRIC AND HYBRID VEHICLE TECHNOLOGY INTERNATIONAL. Text in English. 1995. s-a. free (effective 2009). adv. **Document type:** *Magazine, Trade.* **Description:** International showcase for innovation in electric and hybrid vehicle development. Contains interviews, feature reports and contributed papers by expert authors, focusing on electric and hybrid vehicles as well as infrastructural issues, user perspectives and trial projects.
Formerly (until 1998): Electric and Hybrid Vehicle Technology (1362-5217)
Related titles: Online - full text ed.
Indexed: HRIS.
—BLDSC (3671.290020), IE, Ingenta. **CCC.**
Published by: U K & International Press (Subsidiary of: AutoIntermediates Ltd.), Abinger House, Church St, Dorking, Surrey RH4 1DF, United Kingdom. TEL 44-1306-743744, FAX 44-1306-887546, info@ukintpress.com. Adv. contact Simon Edmands. color page GBP 3,450.

629.286 ESP
ELECTROCAR; la revista del especialista en electronica del automovil. Text in Spanish. 1999. m. EUR 91 (effective 2008). adv. back issues avail. **Document type:** *Magazine, Trade.* **Description:** Contains technical data for car repairing workshops, automotive electronics specialists and persons in the auxiliary automotive industry.
Related titles: E-mail ed.; Fax ed.
Published by: C E I Arsis S.L., C Paris, 150, 4o 3a, Barcelona, 08036, Spain. TEL 34-93-4395564, FAX 34-93-4306853. Ed. Ernest Vinals. Pub. Pilar Grau. Adv. contact Gloria Vinals. page EUR 1,380; 210 x 297. Circ: 3,500.

621.3 629.2 FRA ISSN 1630-7062
ELECTRONIC AUTO VOLT. Text in French. 2001. m. EUR 232.36 (effective 2009). **Document type:** *Magazine, Trade.* **Description:** Covers the electric and electronic aspects of car repair.
Formed by the merger of (1999-2001): Electronique Auto (1292-8860); (1929-2001): Auto-Volt (0005-0881)
—AskIEEE.
Published by: Editions Techniques pour l'Automobile et l'Industrie (E T A I), 20 rue de la Saussiere, Boulogne-Billancourt, 92641, France. TEL 33-1-46992424, FAX 33-1-48255692, http://www.etai.fr.

629.222 DEU ISSN 0934-6805
ELEKTRO- UND SOLARMOBILBRIEF; electric and solar vehicle letter. Abbreviated title: E S B. Text in German; Summaries in English. 1988. m. bk.rev. 12 p./no.; back issues avail. **Document type:** *Magazine, Consumer.*
Published by: Goldener Turm Verlag, Wahlenstr 21, Regensburg, 93047, Germany. TEL 49-941-53866, FAX 49-941-53866. Ed., R&P Erwin Litschel.

621.3 DEU ISSN 1614-0125
ELEKTRONIK AUTOMOTIVE; Fachmedium fuer Entwicklungen in der Kfz-Elektronik und Telematik. Text in German. 2000. 10/yr. EUR 72 domestic; EUR 84.40 foreign; EUR 9 newsstand/cover (effective 2011). adv. **Document type:** *Magazine, Trade.*
Indexed: TM.
Published by: W E K A Fachzeitschriften-Verlag GmbH, Gruberstr 46a, Poing, 85586, Germany. TEL 49-8121-950, FAX 49-8121-951396, info@elektroniknet.de, http://www.wekanet.de. Ed. Stephan Janouch. Adv. contact Peter Eberhard. Circ: 20,105 (paid).

EMERGENCY RESPONSE GUIDEBOOK. *see* PUBLIC HEALTH AND SAFETY

629.222 ZAF
EMERGENCY ROAD SERVICES GUIDE. Text in English. a. membership only. illus. **Document type:** *Directory.*
Formerly (until 1992): Emergency Road Services Directory
Related titles: Afrikaans ed.: Noodpaddiensgids.
Published by: Automobile Association of South Africa/Automobiel-Assosiasie van Suid-Afrika, PO Box 596, Johannesburg, 2000, South Africa.

338 GBR ISSN 1755-1358
EMERGING MARKETS MONTHLY DIGEST. Text in English. 1997. m. free (effective 2009). mkt.; stat. **Document type:** *Newsletter.* **Description:** Provides analysis of the latest industry news, views, facts and figures. Includes features and detailed information on developing automotive markets.
Former titles (until 2007): Automotive Emerging Markets (Online) (1755-4438); (until 200?): Automotive Emerging Markets (Print) (1460-552X)
Media: Online - full text.
—CCC.
Published by: Automotive World, 19 Neptune Ct, Vanguard Way, Cardiff, CF24 5PJ, United Kingdom. TEL 44-29-20468902, FAX 44-29-20468903, https://www.automotiveworld.com/.

629.288 USA ISSN 1535-041X
TL1
ENGINE BUILDER; serving engine builders and rebuilders since 1964. Text in English. 1964. m. free domestic to qualified personnel (effective 2009). adv. Supplement avail.; back issues avail. **Document type:** *Magazine, Trade.* **Description:** Provides in-depth technical and market overview articles along with numerous columns direct from the shop floor.
Formerly (until 2001): Automotive Rebuilder (0567-2317)
Related titles: Online - full text ed.
Indexed: B02, B15, B17, B18, G04, G08, I05, P16, P48, P52, P53, P54, PQC.
Published by: Babcox Publications, Inc., 3550 Embassy Pky, Akron, OH 44333. TEL 330-670-1234, FAX 330-670-0874, bbabcox@babcox.com, http://www.babcox.com. Ed. Douglas Kaufman TEL 330-670-1234 ext 262. Pub. Dave Wooldridge TEL 330-670-1234 ext 214. adv.: B&W page USD 5,150. Circ: 18,000 (paid).

629.286 USA ISSN 1559-9787
TL214.C64
ENGINE CONTROL MODULE WIRING DIAGRAMS & P I N IDENTIFICATION. Variant title: Motor Engine Control Module, Wiring Diagrams & P I N Identification, includes Light Trucks, Vans & SUV's. Text in English. 2004. a. **Document type:** *Journal, Trade.*
Published by: Motor Information Systems (Subsidiary of: Hearst Corporation), 5600 Crooks Rd, Ste 200, Troy, MI 48098. TEL 248-312-2700, 800-288-6828, FAX 248-879-8603, motorbookscallcenter@motor.com, http://www.motor.com.

ENGINE PROFESSIONAL. *see* MACHINERY

621 AUS
ENGINE RECONDITIONER AUSTRALIA. Short title: E R A. Text in English. 2002. 6/yr. adv. **Document type:** *Magazine, Trade.* **Description:** Provides news, views and opinions to the industry, technical reporting of products, information on new products, and advice on industry activities.
Published by: (Engine Reconditioners Association of Australia), M T A - Q Publications, PO Box 3359, South Brisbane, QLD 4101, Australia. TEL 61-3-32378777, 800-177-951, FAX 61-3-38444488, info@mtaq.com.au, http://www.mtaq.com.au. Ed. Tony Tranchida. R&P Gunther Jurkschat. Adv. contact Laura Ray. B&W page AUD 650, color page AUD 1,500; trim 275 x 212. Circ: 2,000.

629.286 GBR ISSN 1460-9509
ENGINE TECHNOLOGY INTERNATIONAL. Text in English. 1997. q. free (effective 2009). adv. back issues avail. **Document type:** *Magazine, Trade.* **Description:** Aims to bring its global audience the latest world news, interviews with leading industry figures, powertrain case studies, product reviews, technology features, and engine appraisals.
Related titles: Online - full text ed.
—CCC.
Published by: U K & International Press (Subsidiary of: AutoIntermediates Ltd.), Abinger House, Church St, Dorking, Surrey RH4 1DF, United Kingdom. TEL 44-1306-743744, FAX 44-1306-887546, info@ukintpress.com, http://www.ukipme.com. Ed. Dean Slavnich. Adv. contact Simon Willard.

629.1 DEU ISSN 0930-7389
ENTWICKLUNG DER REPARATURKOSTEN UNFALLBESCHAEDIGTER PKW UND MOTORRAEDER. Text in German. 1979. irreg. **Document type:** *Monographic series, Trade.*
Formerly (until 1985): Entwicklung der Reparaturkosten Unfallbeschaedigter Pkw (0723-273X)
Published by: D E K R A - AG, Handwerkstr 15, Stuttgart, 70565, Germany. TEL 49-711-78610, FAX 49-711-78612204, info@dekra.de, http://www.dekra.de.

338.476 GBR ISSN 1755-554X
ENVIRONMENT MONTHLY DIGEST. Variant title: Automotiveworld.Com. Environment Monthly Digest. Text in English. 200?. m. free (effective 2009). **Document type:** *Magazine, Trade.*
Formerly (until 2007): Automotive Environment Analyst (Online) (1747-3314)
Media: Online - full text.
Published by: Automotive World, 19 Neptune Ct, Vanguard Way, Cardiff, CF24 5PJ, United Kingdom. TEL 44-29-20468902, FAX 44-29-20468903, https://www.automotiveworld.com/.

796.5 910.09 USA ISSN 1556-7486
ESCAPEES. Text in English. 1978. q. USD 50 (effective 2000). adv. bk.rev. back issues avail. **Document type:** *Magazine, Consumer.* **Description:** Information on travel as it applies to extended travel in recreational vehicles.
Related titles: Online - full text ed.: ISSN 1556-7966.
Published by: (Escapees Club), RoVing Press, 100 Rainbow Dr, Livingston, TX 77351. TEL 936-327-8873, 888-757-2582, FAX 936-327-4388. Ed. Kay Peterson. Pub. Cathie Carr. R&P Jan Lasko. Adv. contact Marolyn Will. Circ: 30,000.

388.3 USA
ESCAPEES CLUB. ANNUAL DIRECTORY. Text in English. a. membership only. adv. **Document type:** *Directory.*
Published by: RoVing Press, 100 Rainbow Dr, Livingston, TX 77351. TEL 936-327-8873, 888-757-2582, FAX 936-327-4388. Ed. Kay Peterson. Pub. Cathie Carr. R&P Jan Lasko. Adv. contact Marolyn Will.

629.226 FRA ISSN 1961-6740
ESPRIT CAMPING-CAR. Text in French. 2007. bi-m. **Document type:** *Magazine, Consumer.*
Published by: Editions Riva, 16 Rue de la Fontaine-au-Roi, Paris, 75011, France.

388 796.77 FRA ISSN 1620-5154
L'ESSENTIEL DE L'AUTO. Text in French. 1994. bi-m. EUR 43 for 2 yrs. (effective 2010). **Document type:** *Magazine, Consumer.*
Published by: Lafont Presse, 53 Rue du Chemin Vert, Boulogne-Billancourt, 92100, France. FAX 33-1-45792211.

629.286 ESP ISSN 1888-7864
ESTACIONES DE SERVICIO. Text in Spanish. 1988. m. EUR 135.34 combined subscription domestic (print, online & email eds.); EUR 195 combined subscription foreign (print, online & email eds.) (effective 2009). **Document type:** *Magazine, Trade.*
Related titles: E-mail ed.: ISSN 1988-9119; Online - full text ed.: Estaciones de Servicio Digital. ISSN 1988-902X; Supplement(s): Guia de Estaciones de Servicio, Proveedores y Operadores. ISSN 1888-7872.
Published by: Tecnipublicaciones Espana, S.L., Avda de Manoteras 44, 3a Planta, Madrid, 28050, Spain. TEL 34-91-2972000, FAX 34-91-2972154, tp@tecnipublicaciones.com.

388 GBR ISSN 0963-6498
ESTATE CAR AND M P V. (Multi-Purpose Vehicle) Text in English. ceased 1994; resumed 1991. bi-m. GBP 9.95. adv. back issues avail. **Document type:** *Magazine, Consumer.*
Published by: U.K. and International Press, Talisman House, 120 South St, Dorking, Surrey RH4 2EU, United Kingdom. TEL 0306-743744, FAX 0306-742525. Ed. Tony Robinson. Adv. contact Joy Robinson. Circ: 11,000 (paid).

388.642 GBR ISSN 1748-9881
ESTONIA AUTOS REPORT. Text in English. 2005. a. EUR 820, USD 1,030 combined subscription per issue (print & email eds.) (effective 2010). **Document type:** *Report, Trade.* **Description:** Provides industry professionals and strategists, corporate analysts, auto associations, government departments and regulatory bodies with independent forecasts and competitive intelligence on the automotives industry.
Related titles: E-mail ed.
Indexed: A15, ABIn, B02, B15, B17, B18, G04, I05, P48, P51, P52, PQC.
Published by: Business Monitor International Ltd., Senator House, 85 Queen Victoria St, London, EC4V 4AB, United Kingdom. TEL 44-20-72480468, FAX 44-20-72480467, subs@businessmonitor.com.

ETOILES PASSION. *see* HOBBIES

338.3 FRA ISSN 0153-906X
ETUDES ET DOCUMENTATION DE LA REVUE TECHNIQUE AUTOMOBILE. Text in French. 1946. irreg. adv. charts; illus.
Published by: Editions pour l'Automobile et l'Industrie, 20-22 rue de la Saussiere, Boulogne-Billancourt, 92100, France. TEL 46-04-81-13, FAX 48-25-56-92, TELEX 204850F. Ed. Pascal Cromback. Circ: 2,500.

388.3 DEU ISSN 1862-1724
EUROPARKING. Text in German. 2006. q. EUR 25; EUR 7.20 per issue (effective 2011). adv. **Document type:** *Magazine, Trade.*
Published by: Verlag F.H. Kleffmann GmbH, Herner Str 299, Bochum, 44809, Germany. TEL 49-234-953910, FAX 49-234-9539130, service@kleffmann-verlag.de. Ed. Jana Kolb. Adv. contact Karoline Bruse TEL 49-234-9539115. Circ: 9,000 (paid).

338.476292 GBR ISSN 2040-6045
EUROPEAN AUTOMOTIVE COMPONENTS NEWS (ONLINE). Text in English. 2005. bi-m. free (effective 2009). adv. **Document type:** *Magazine, Trade.* **Description:** Highlights the latest contract, appointment and product news from within the European automotive industry, as well as featuring interviews with leading figures from major vehicle manufacturers and component suppliers.
Formerly (until 2007): European Automotive Components News (Print) (1747-5279)
Media: Online - full text.
—CCC.
Published by: U K I P Media & Events Ltd. (Subsidiary of: AutoIntermediates Ltd.), Abinger House, Church St, Dorking, Surrey RH4 1DF, United Kingdom. TEL 44-1306-743744, FAX 44-1306-887546, info@ukintpress.com, http://www.ukipme.com.

796.77 620.1 GBR ISSN 1368-552X
EUROPEAN AUTOMOTIVE DESIGN. Text in English. 1997. m. free to qualified personnel (effective 2009). charts; illus.; tr.lit. **Document type:** *Magazine, Trade.* **Description:** Aimed at professionally qualified engineers in automotive industry - OEMs and supplier network. Covers advances in components, systems and materials used in the development of cars, trucks and buses.
Related titles: Online - full text ed.
Indexed: P16, P48, P52, P53, P54, PQC.
—CCC.
Published by: Findlay Publications Ltd., Hawley Mill, Hawley Rd, Horton Kirby, Kent DA2 7TJ, United Kingdom. TEL 44-1322-221144, FAX 44-1322-221188, enquiries@findlay.co.uk, http://www.findlay.co.uk/. Eds. Graham Pitcher, Ken Hurst TEL khurst@findlay.co.uk. Circ: 24,000.

388.3 USA ISSN 1056-8476
TL55
EUROPEAN CAR. Text in English. 1971. m. USD 11.97 domestic; USD 24.97 in Canada; USD 26.97 elsewhere (effective 2008). adv. back issues avail. **Document type:** *Magazine, Consumer.* **Description:** Presents information on the new, late-model and classic European cars on sale in the U.S. and around the world.
Former titles (until 1991): V W and Porsche Etc (0273-6748); V W and Porsche; Volkswagen Greats (0049-6723)
Related titles: Online - full text ed.
Indexed: G05, G06, G07, G08, I05, I07, S23.
—CCC.
Published by: Source Interlink Companies, 2400 E Katella Ave, Ste 700, Anaheim, CA 92806. dheine@sourceinterlink.com, http://www.sourceinterlinkmedia.com. Ed. Les Bidrawn. Pub. Howard Lim. adv.: B&W page USD 5,955, color page USD 7,325. Circ: 41,019 (paid).

658 USA ISSN 0960-5436
HD9710.3.E9
EUROPE'S AUTOMOTIVE COMPONENTS BUSINESS. Text in English. 1990. q. GBP 635, USD 1,095 (effective 2000). **Description:** Provides regular analysis of the issues and prospects facing the sector.
Related titles: ◆ Series of: Motor Business Japan. ISSN 1359-4524.
—CCC.
Published by: Economist Intelligence Unit Ltd. (Subsidiary of: Economist Intelligence Unit Ltd.), 111 W 57th St, New York, NY 10019. TEL 212-554-0600, FAX 212-586-1181, newyork@eiu.com, http://www.eiu.com.

388 CHE
EUROTAX - AUTO - INFORMATION. Text in German. w. CHF 492 (effective 2008). **Document type:** *Magazine, Trade.*
Published by: EurotaxGlass's International AG, Wolleraustr 11a, Freienbach, 8807, Switzerland. TEL 41-55-4158100, FAX 41-55-4158200, ccc@eurotaxglass.ch, http://www.eurotaxglass.ch.

796.77 USA ISSN 1538-2079
EUROTUNER. Text in English. 1998. m. USD 15 domestic; USD 28 in Canada; USD 30 elsewhere (effective 2008). adv. back issues avail. **Document type:** *Magazine, Consumer.* **Description:** Features the latest European automotive performance, styling and technological trends to readers.
Formerly (until 2002): Max Speed (1099-5153)
Related titles: Online - full text ed.: USD 7.50 (effective 2008).
Indexed: A10, G06, G07, G08, I05, S23, V03.
—CCC.

TU

Published by: Source Interlink Companies, 2400 E Katella Ave, Ste 700, Anaheim, CA 92806. TEL 714-939-2400, dheine@sourceinterlink.com, http://www.sourceinterlinkmedia.com. Ed. Greg Emmerson. Pub. Maria Brown. adv.: B&W page USD 4,695, color page USD 7,540. Circ: 31,265 (paid).

388.3 ITA ISSN 1590-8461
EVO. Text in Italian. 2000. 10/yr. EUR 34 (effective 2009). adv. **Document type:** *Magazine, Consumer.*
Published by: A C I Mondadori SpA, Via Cassanese 224, Segrate, MI 20090, Italy. TEL 39-02-26937550, FAX 39-02-26937560. Ed. Giancarlo Pini. Circ: 46,000 (paid).

629.222105 GBR ISSN 1464-2786
EVO; the thrill of driving. Text in English. 1998. m. GBP 48.20 in Europe; USD 99 in United States; USD 78.40 elsewhere (effective 2009). adv. back issues avail. **Document type:** *Magazine, Consumer.*
Description: Contains news and features for hardcore car enthusiasts.
—CCC.
Published by: Evo Publications Ltd. (Subsidiary of: Dennis Publishing Ltd.), Tower Ct, Irchester Rd, Wollaston, Northants NN29 7PJ, United Kingdom. TEL 44-20-79076310, FAX 44-1933-663367, reception@dennis.co.uk, http://www.dennis.co.uk. Eds. Harry Metcalfe TEL 44-20-79076312, Paul Sanders. Adv. contact Sarah Perks TEL 44-20-79076744. page GBP 4,563; trim 222 x 285.

629.222 USA
AN EXAMINATION OF THE AUTOMOTIVE PARTS INDUSTRY. Text in English. 1992. a. **Description:** Examines the original equipment manufacturers and the aftermarket to determine performance.
Published by: Dun & Bradstreet Information Services (Subsidiary of: Dun & Bradstreet, Inc.), 103 JFK Pkwy, Short Hills, NJ 07078. TEL 973-921-5500, 800-234-3867, SMSinfo@dnb.com, http://www.dnb.com.

388.3 USA ISSN 0896-0798
EXCELLENCE (NOVATO); the magazine about Porsche. Text in English. 1986. 9/yr. USD 25 domestic; USD 35 in Canada; USD 45 elsewhere; USD 5.99 per issue (effective 2011). adv. back issues avail. **Document type:** *Magazine, Consumer.* **Description:** Provides current news and information about the Porsche and the people who drive it.
Formerly (until 1987): Porsche Magazine (0894-2587)
Published by: Ross Periodicals, PO Box 1529, Ross, CA 94957. TEL 415-382-0580, FAX 415-382-0587. Adv. contact Stan Michelman TEL 415-382-2864.

796.77 CZE ISSN 1803-0971
EXCLUSIVE TOP CARS. Text in Czech. 2008. q. CZK 316 (effective 2009). **Document type:** *Magazine, Consumer.*
Published by: R F Hobby s.r.o., Bohdalecka 6, Prague 10, 110 00, Czech Republic. TEL 420-281-090610, FAX 420-281-090623, sekretariat@rf-hobby.cz, http://www.rf-hobby.cz. Ed. Petr Prokopec. Adv. contact Petr Doul. Circ: 30,000.

388.3 USA
EXITSOURCE R V DIRECTORY (YEAR). (Recreational Vehicle) Text in English. 1997. a. adv. **Document type:** *Directory.* **Description:** Lists truck stops in the US and Canada for recreational vehicle users and tour bus operators.
Formerly: Travel Centers & Truck Stops (1534-0791)
Published by: Exitsource, 5715-B Oakbrook Parkway, Norcross, GA 30093. TEL 770-248-1300, 800-494-5566, FAX 770-248-1302.

796.77 USA ISSN 1054-8084
TL236
EXOTIC CARS QUARTERLY. Text in English. q.
Published by: Diamandis Communications, 1499 Monrovia Ave, Newport Beach, CA 92663-2752. TEL 714-720-5300, FAX 714-631-2374. Ed. Ron Sessions. Circ: 100,000.

388.3 FRA ISSN 0755-110X
L'EXPERT AUTOMOBILE; la revue des reparateurs. Text in French. 1965. m. adv. illus.; stat. Supplement avail.
Related titles: CD-ROM ed.
Published by: Editions Techniques pour l'Automobile et l'Industrie (E T A I), 20 rue de la Saussiere, Boulogne-Billancourt, 92641, France. TEL 33-1-46992424, FAX 33-1-48255692. Circ: 25,000.

629.2 GBR
THE EXPRESS GUIDE TO WORLD CARS. Text in English. 1954. a. GBP 5.99 newsstand/cover (effective 2000). illus. **Document type:** *Magazine, Consumer.* **Description:** Provides pictures and details of the latest automobiles from manufacturing companies around the world.
Former titles: Daily Express Guide to World Cars (0142-3282); (until 1978): Daily Express Review of the Motor Show
Published by: Express Newspapers PLC, Ludgate House, 245 Blackfriars Rd, London, SE1 9UX, United Kingdom. TEL 44-20-79227373, FAX 44-20-7-9227960. Circ: 70,000.

629.222 AUS ISSN 1834-5107
EXTREME STREET. Text in English. 2006. 13/yr. AUD 87.26; AUD 8.95 newsstand/cover (effective 2008). back issues avail. **Document type:** *Magazine, Consumer.* **Description:** Provides information on powerful and well-built automotive machinery to the thousands of loyal readers.
Formerly: Extreme (1447-9249)
Published by: Express Publications Pty. Ltd., 2-4 Stanley St, Locked Bag 111, Silverwater, NSW 2168, Australia. TEL 61-2-97413800, 800-801-647, FAX 61-2-97378017, subs@magstore.com.au, http://www.expresspublications.com.au. Ed. Paul Beck TEL 61-2-42560722. Adv. contact Nathan Wellington TEL 61-2-87193614. **Subscr. to:** ISubscribe Pty Ltd., 25 Lime St, Ste 303, Level 3, Sydney, NSW 2000, Australia. TEL 61-2-92621722, FAX 61-2-92625044, info@isubscribe.com.au, http://www.isubscribe.com.au.

658 USA ISSN 2154-1728
F & I AND SHOWROOM. (Finance & Insurance) Text in English. 1998. m. free (effective 2008). adv. back issues avail. **Document type:** *Magazine, Trade.* **Description:** Provide knowledge, news, techniques, procedures and skill sets at a high level, presented by some of the leading names in the field of automotive finance and insurance.
Formerly (until 2010): F & I Management and Technology (1529-5656)
Related titles: Online - full text ed.
Published by: Bobit Business Media, 3520 Challenger St, Torrance, CA 90503. TEL 310-533-2400, FAX 310-533-2500, order@bobit.com, http://www.bobit.com. Ed. Steve Elliott. Pub. Sherb Brown. Circ: 21,139.

338.3 DEU
FAHRLEHRERBRIEF. Text in German. 1997. 10/yr. EUR 82.90 domestic; EUR 94.90 foreign (effective 2010). **Document type:** *Newsletter, Trade.*
Published by: Verlag Heinrich Vogel (Subsidiary of: Springer Science+Business Media), Neumarkterstr 18, Munich, 81664, Germany. TEL 49-89-2030431100, FAX 49-89-2030432100, kontakt@verlag-heinrich-vogel.de, http://www.springerfachmedien-muenchen.de.

388.3 DEU ISSN 0014-6838
FAHRSCHULE; Zeitschrift fuer die Kraftfahrlehrer. Text in German. 1949. m. EUR 87.90 domestic; EUR 99.90 foreign (effective 2010). adv. bk.rev. **Document type:** *Magazine, Trade.* **Description:** Contains information for driving school owners and instructors throughout Germany.
—CCC.
Published by: Verlag Heinrich Vogel (Subsidiary of: Springer Science+Business Media), Neumarkterstr 18, Munich, 81664, Germany. TEL 49-89-43722878, FAX 49-89-2030432100, kontakt@verlag-heinrich-vogel.de, http://www.springerfachmedien-muenchen.de. Ed. Anne K Peters. Adv. contact Elisabeth Huber. B&W page EUR 3,875, color page EUR 5,560; trim 185 x 250. Circ: 17,774 (paid).

388.3 DEU
FAHRSCHULPRAXIS. Text in German. 1970. m. EUR 15 newsstand/cover (effective 2007). adv. **Document type:** *Magazine, Trade.*
Published by: Fahrlehrerverband Baden-Wuerttemberg e.V., Zuffenhauser Str 3, Korntal-Muenchingen, 70825, Germany. TEL 49-711-8398750, FAX 49-711-8380211, hotline@flvbw.de, http://www.flvbw.de. adv.: B&W page EUR 599, color page EUR 1,382. Circ: 2,950 (paid and controlled).

629.2 DEU ISSN 0014-6862
FAHRZEUG UND KAROSSERIE. Text in German. 1947. m. EUR 132.60 domestic; EUR 140.40 foreign (effective 2010). adv. **Document type:** *Magazine, Trade.*
Indexed: IBR, IBZ, RefZh.
Published by: (Zentralverband Karosserie und Fahrzeugtechnik), Gentner Verlag Stuttgart, Forststr 131, Stuttgart, 70193, Germany. TEL 49-711-636720, FAX 49-711-63672747, gentner@gentnerverlag.de, http://www.gentnerverlag.de. Adv. contact Mareike Zander. Circ: 6,251 (paid and controlled).

388.3 NOR ISSN 0809-280X
FALKEN MAGASINET. Text in Norwegian. 1975. q. NOK 12.
Former titles (until 1996): Falken (0809-2796); (until 1991): Falken Nytt (0809-2788)
Published by: Falken Redningskorps A-S, Blasbortveien 1, Oslo, 0873, Norway. Ed. Arve Andreson. Circ: 105,000.

FAMILY SITES. *see* SPORTS AND GAMES—Outdoor Life

796.77 GBR ISSN 0951-7499
FAST CAR. Text in English. 1987. 13/yr. adv. back issues avail. **Document type:** *Magazine, Consumer.* **Description:** Covers engine modifications, body styling, and engine building.
Related titles: Supplement(s): Fast Car. The Guide. GBP 4.99 per issue (effective 2003).
—CCC.
Published by: Future Publishing Ltd., Beauford Ct, 30 Monmouth St, Bath, Avon BA1 2BW, United Kingdom. TEL 44-1225-442244, FAX 44-1225-446019, customerservice@subscription.co.uk, http://www.futureplc.com. **Subscr. to:** Tower House, Sovereign Park, Market Harborough, Leicestershire LE16 9EF, United Kingdom. TEL 44-844-8481602, FAX 44-1858-438795, future@subscription.co.uk.

629.22 GBR ISSN 0958-0522
FAST FORD. Text in English. 1985. m. GBP 49.72 domestic; GBP 85 in Europe; GBP 110 elsewhere; GBP 4.25 newsstand/cover (effective 2010). adv. back issues avail. **Document type:** *Magazine, Consumer.* **Description:** Features the best performance Ford road cars, product news and reviews, buyers guides, technical advice, information on engine tuning, body styling and ICE.
Related titles: Online - full text ed.
Published by: Future Publishing Ltd., Beauford Ct, 30 Monmouth St, Bath, Avon BA1 2BW, United Kingdom. TEL 44-1225-442244, FAX 44-1225-446019, customerservice@subscription.co.uk, http://www.futureplc.com. Ed. Dan White. **Subscr. to:** Tower House, Sovereign Park, Market Harborough, Leicestershire LE16 9EF, United Kingdom. TEL 44-844-8481602, FAX 44-1858-438795, future@subscription.co.uk.

796.77 AUS
FAST FOURS & ROTARIES. Text in English. m. AUD 59.20 (effective 2009). adv. **Document type:** *Magazine, Consumer.* **Description:** Covers modified-four cylinder and rotary-engine cars.
Formerly (until 2008): Fast Fours
Published by: Express Publications Pty. Ltd., 2-4 Stanley St, Locked Bag 111, Silverwater, NSW 2168, Australia. TEL 61-2-97413800, 800-801-647, FAX 61-2-97378017, subs@magstore.com.au, http://www.expresspublications.com.au. Ed. Andrew Mara. Adv. contact Michael Coiro TEL 61-2-97413911. page AUD 1,859. Circ: 38,535.

388.3 USA ISSN 2152-8004
▼ **FEDERAL FLEET FILES.** Text in English. 2009. m. free (effective 2010). back issues avail. **Document type:** *Government.*
Media: Online - full text.
Published by: U.S. Department of Energy, Federal Energy Management Program, 1000 Independence Ave, SW, Washington, DC 20585. TEL 202-586-5772, http://www1.eere.energy.gov/femp/index.html.

388 USA ISSN 1555-0524
KF2265.A15
FEDERAL MOTOR CARRIER SAFETY ADMINISTRATION REGISTER; a daily summary of motor carrier applications and of decisions and notices. Text in English. d. USD 995 (effective 2001). **Document type:** *Government.*
Published by: U.S. Department of Transportation, Federal Motor Carrier Safety Administration, 400 Seventh St SW, Washington, DC 20590. TEL 202-366-2519, http://www.fmcsa.dot.gov. **Subscr. to:** U.S. Government Printing Office, Superintendent of Documents, PO Box 371954, Pittsburgh, PA 15250. TEL 202-512-1800, FAX 202-512-2250, orders@gpo.gov, http://www.access.gpo.gov.

354.8 USA ISSN 0093-0180
JK1677.M7
FEDERAL MOTOR VEHICLE FLEET REPORT. Text in English. 1948. a., latest 1996. free. charts; stat. **Document type:** *Government.*
Description: Report summarizes statistical data for vehicles operated by Federal employees and authorized Federal contractors. Includes data for vehicles both federally owned and commercially leased.
Formerly (until 1972): Annual Motor Vehicle Report (0566-8166)
Related titles: CD-ROM ed.; Online - full text ed.
Published by: (Federal Vehicle Management Policy Division (MTV)), U.S. General Services Administration, Office of Policy, Planning and Evaluation, G S A Bldg, 1800 F St, N W, Rm 1221, Washington, DC 20405. TEL 202-501-2507, FAX 202-501-6742. Ed. William T Rivers.

629.283 USA ISSN 0364-6858
KF2212
FEDERAL MOTOR VEHICLE SAFETY STANDARDS AND REGULATIONS. (Comprises 3 parts: Procedural Rules and Regulations; Standards; Rulings and Additional Regulations) Text in English. 1972. base vol. plus irreg. updates. looseleaf. back issues avail. **Document type:** *Government.*
Supersedes (in 19??): Motor Vehicle Safety Standards, With Amendments and Onterpretations.
Related titles: Online - full text ed.: free (effective 2011).
Published by: U.S. Department of Transportation, National Highway Traffic Safety Administration, 1200 New Jersey Ave, SE, West Bldg, Washington, DC 20590. TEL 202-366-4000, 888-327-4236.

629.222 CHE
FEDERATION DES CARROSSIERS ROMANDS. JOURNAL. Text in French. q.
Address: Route de Glane 16, Fribourg, 1700, Switzerland. TEL 037-243048. Ed. O Maradan. Circ: 500.

629.2 BEL
FEDERAUTO MAGAZINE; la revue des professionnels de l'automobile - het vakblad van de autosektor. Text in Dutch. 1981. 10/yr. **Document type:** *Trade.* **Description:** Deals with the following columns: life and action of the trade associations; market evolution; current events in the automobile world; new equipment and tools; mobility and environmental problems; social, fiscal, and legal items; technical items; EC regulations; and automobile economy in belgium and Europe.
Former titles (until 1995): Autotechnica (0771-4912); Chambre Syndicale du Commerce Automobile de Belgique. Bulletin Mensuel
Related titles: French ed.
Published by: Federauto a.s.b.l., Bd de la Woluwe 46, Bte 9, Bruxelles, 1200, Belgium. TEL 32-2-7786200, FAX 32-2-7786222, mail@federauto.be, http://www.federauto.be. Ed. Eugene Charbonnier. Pub. Bob Pauwels. Adv. contact Jacques Ambinet. Circ: 12,000.

FENDER BENDER (MIDWEST EDITION). *see* BUSINESS AND ECONOMICS—Management

796.77 ITA
FERRARI. Text in English. 2008. q. EUR 250 (effective 2008); free to qualified personnel. **Document type:** *Magazine, Consumer.*
Published by: (Ferrari S.p.A.), Edizioni Conde Nast SpA (Subsidiary of: Arnoldo Mondadori Editore SpA), Piazza Castello 27, Milan, MI 20122, Italy. info@condenet.it, http://www.condenast.it. **Subscr. to:** Ferrari S.p.A. subscriptionmagazine@ferrari.it.

LA FERRARI GRANTURISMO. *see* SPORTS AND GAMES

796.77 DEU
FERRARI SPEZIAL. Text in German. 1997. a. EUR 7 newsstand/cover (effective 2006). adv. **Document type:** *Magazine, Consumer.*
Published by: Pro Publica International Verlag GmbH, Hansaallee 289, Duesseldorf, 40549, Germany. TEL 49-211-5581866, FAX 49-211-5578657, http://www.peil-pp.de. adv.: B&W page EUR 6,380, color page EUR 7,500. Circ: 80,000 (controlled).

796.77 DEU ISSN 0939-723X
FERRARI WORLD. Text in German. 1991. q. EUR 6.50 newsstand/cover (effective 2010). adv. video rev.; bk.rev. bibl.; illus. 112 p./no.; back issues avail. **Document type:** *Magazine, Consumer.*
Published by: Heel-Verlag GmbH, Gut Pottscheidt, Koenigswinter, 53639, Germany. TEL 49-2223-92300, FAX 49-2223-92301326, info@heel-verlag.de, http://www.heel-verlag.de. R&P Karin Michelberger.

338.3 FRA ISSN 0153-9108
FICHES TECHNIQUES R T C. (Revue Technique Carrosserie) Text in French. irreg. looseleaf. charts; illus.
Related titles: ◆ Supplement to: Revue Technique Carrosserie. ISSN 0150-7206.
Published by: Editions Techniques pour l'Automobile et l'Industrie (E T A I), 20-22 rue de la Saussiere, Boulogne Billancourt, 92100, France. TEL 33-1-46992424, FAX 33-1-48255692, http://www.etai.fr.

338.3 FRA ISSN 0153-9094
FICHES TECHNIQUES R T D. (Revue Technique Diesel) Text in French. irreg.
Published by: Editions Techniques pour l'Automobile et l'Industrie (E T A I), 20-22 rue de la Saussiere, Boulogne Billancourt, 92100, France. TEL 33-1-46992424, FAX 33-1-48255692, http://www.groupe-etai.com.

388.3 DEU ISSN 1618-4998
FIRMEN AUTO; Geschaeftewagen - Flotten-Management - Finanzen. Text in German. 1995. 12/yr. EUR 36; EUR 4 newsstand/cover (effective 2011). adv. back issues avail. **Document type:** *Magazine, Consumer.*
Published by: EuroTransportMedia Verlags- und Veranstaltungs-GmbH, Handwerkstr 15, Stuttgart, 70565, Germany. TEL 49-711-784980, FAX 49-711-7849888, info@eurotransport.de, http://www.etm-verlag.de. Circ: 51,505 (paid).

388 AUT
DER FIRMENWAGEN; Das Magazin fuer Flottenbetreiber und kostenbewusste Vielfahrer. Text in German. 1996. bi-m. EUR 30 domestic; EUR 48 foreign; EUR 5.50 newsstand/cover (effective 2005). adv. mkt.; tr.lit.; illus. **Document type:** *Magazine, Consumer.* **Description:** Contains articles, reviews and tests on new automobile models.
Related titles: E-mail ed.; Fax ed.; Online - full text ed.
Published by: Springer Business Media Austria GmbH (Subsidiary of: Springer Science+Business Media), Inkustr 16, Klosterneuburg, 3403, Austria. TEL 43-2243-301110, FAX 43-2243-30111222, office@springer-sbm.at, http://www.springer-sbm.at. Ed. Andreas Uebelbacher. adv.: B&W page EUR 4,259, color page EUR 6,236; trim 185 x 255. Circ: 29,500 (controlled).

796.77 USA
FIXED OPS MAGAZINE; the auto dealer's original fixed operations resource. Text in English. 2004. m. free domestic to qualified personnel; USD 60 domestic to individuals; USD 85 in Canada to individuals; USD 180 elsewhere to individuals (effective 2008). adv. back issues avail. **Document type:** *Magazine, Trade.* **Description:** Keep abreast of important news, industry events, tips, trends and expert advice essential for managing the profitability of this vital department.
Related titles: Online - full text ed.: free.
Published by: Prism Automotivre Llc., 17853 Santiago Blvd, Ste 107-467, Villa Park, CA 92861. TEL 877-349-3367. Pub. Nick West. adv.: B&W page USD 5,986; trim 8.375 x 10.875. Circ: 24,000 (paid).

796.77 DEU ISSN 1438-2075
FLASH OPEL SCENE. Text in German. 1995. m. EUR 42 domestic; EUR 48 foreign; EUR 3.80 newsstand/cover (effective 2011). adv. **Document type:** *Magazine, Consumer.*
Published by: Vestische Mediengruppe Welke GmbH & Co. KG, Hertener Mark 7, Herten, 45699, Germany. TEL 49-2366-808400, FAX 49-2366-808499, info@vmw-verlag.de, http://vmw-verlag.de. Pub. Arno Welke. Adv. contact Julia Wissing. Circ: 21,806 (paid).

388.3 SVK ISSN 1337-6306
FLEET; firemne automobily. Text in Slovak. 2007. q. SKK 350 (effective 2011). adv. **Document type:** *Magazine, Trade.*
Published by: Auto Business Media s.r.o., Racianska 62, Bratislava, 83102, Slovakia. TEL 421-2-44632936, FAX 421-2-44632936. Ed. Peter Krc. Adv. contact Jan Keder.

629.040289 363.12 USA ISSN 1558-3759
FLEET ADMINISTRATOR SAFETY REPORT; the nation's only report on fleet driver and vehicle safety. Abbreviated title: F A S R. Text in English. 2005 (Nov.). s-m. USD 395 (effective 2011). **Document type:** *Newsletter, Trade.*
Related titles: Online - full text ed.: USD 345 (effective 2011).
Published by: Stamler Publishing Co., PO Box 3367, Branford, CT 06405. TEL 203-488-9808, 800-422-4121, FAX 203-488-3129, newsgroup@trafficsafetynews.com.

388.3 BEL ISSN 0778-9165
FLEET & BUSINESS (EDITION FRANCAISE); le magazine automobile des gestionnaires. Text in French. 1987. 7/yr. EUR 47 (effective 2005). illus. **Document type:** *Trade.*
Formerly (until 1992): Mini Maxi Fleet (0778-0346)
Related titles: Dutch ed.: ISSN 0778-9157; Regional ed(s).: Fleet & Business (Luxembourg Edition).
Published by: Multi Media Management, Parc Artisanal 11-13, Blegny-Barchon, 4670, Belgium. TEL 32-4-3878787, FAX 32-4-3879087. Ed. Caroline Thonnon. Circ: 9,000.

FLEET ASSOCIATION DIRECTORY. *see* BUSINESS AND ECONOMICS—Marketing And Purchasing

FLEET FINANCIALS; executive vehicle management. *see* BUSINESS AND ECONOMICS—Marketing And Purchasing

629.286 658 USA ISSN 1084-2519
FLEET MANAGEMENT. Text in English. 1981. m. looseleaf. USD 195 (effective 2004). charts; illus.; stat. back issues avail.; reprints avail. **Document type:** *Newsletter, Trade.*
Formerly (until 199?): Runzheimer Reports on Transportation (0730-8655)
—CCC.
Published by: Skyline Publishing Co., PO Box 599, Brookfield, IL 60513-0599. TEL 708-485-6015, FAX 708-485-4237. Ed., Pub. Ralph McDarmont.

388.3 GBR
FLEET NEWS DIRECTORY (YEAR). Text in English. 1980. a. GBP 65 per issue (effective 2009). stat. index. back issues avail. **Document type:** *Directory, Trade.* **Description:** Provides contact information for every supplier offering services to the fleet marketplace.
Formerly: Fleet Operators Handbook (0953-9085)
Published by: H. Bauer Publishing Ltd. (Subsidiary of: Bauer Media Group), Media House, Lynchwood, Peterborough, Cambridgeshire PE2 6EA, United Kingdom. TEL 44-1733-468000, http://www.bauer.co.uk.

388 GBR
FLEET NORTH. Text in English. 1986. 8/yr. GBP 19; GBP 35 elsewhere. back issues avail. **Document type:** *Magazine, Trade.*
Published by: Tweedprint Ltd., 97 Heaton St, Standish, Wigan, Lancs WN6 0DA, United Kingdom. TEL 0257-427332, FAX 0257-422054. Ed. Alan Fawcett. Circ: 17,100 (controlled).

388.342 FRA ISSN 1252-6134
FLOTTES AUTOMOBILES. Text in French. 1994. 10/yr. EUR 70 (effective 2010). back issues avail. **Document type:** *Magazine, Consumer.*
Published by: Varenne Entreprises, 6 cite Paradis, Paris, 75010, France. TEL 33-1-53242400, redaction@flotauto.com. Ed. M P Dyens. Adv. contact Christian de Romanet.

388.3 DEU
FLOW. Text in German. 2004. 4/yr. free to qualified personnel (effective 2006). adv. **Document type:** *Magazine, Consumer.*
Published by: Thomssen Communications, Kollaustr 122, Hamburg, 22453, Germany. TEL 49-40-58916950, FAX 49-40-58916951, info@thomssen.com, http://thomssen.com. adv.: page EUR 7,500. Circ: 75,500 (controlled).

388.3 USA ISSN 0015-4830
FLYING LADY. Text in English. 1951. bi-m. membership. adv. bk.rev. charts; illus. index. **Description:** Includes historical and technical articles.
Published by: Rolls-Royce Owners' Club, Inc., 191 Hempt Rd, Mechanicsburg, PA 17055. Circ: 7,500 (paid).

FOCUS (RESEARCH TRIANGLE PARK). *see* BUSINESS AND ECONOMICS—Marketing And Purchasing

796.77 USA
FOR VETTES ONLY. Text in English. 1975. m. looseleaf. USD 25 to non-members; USD 20 to members (effective 2000). adv. **Document type:** *Newsletter.*
Published by: National Corvette Owners Association, 900 S Washington St, Ste G 13, Falls Church, VA 22046. TEL 703-533-7222, FAX 703-533-1153. Adv. contact Donna Sandoval. Circ: 19,000.

796.77 790.13 USA
FORD ENTHUSIAST MAGAZINE. Text in English. 1980. bi-m. USD 22 domestic; USD 30 in Canada; USD 47 elsewhere. adv. bk.rev. back issues avail. **Description:** For those interested in Ford powered vehicles, especially models of the 1950's and later. Includes a sale-wanted section.
Published by: Performance Ford Club of America Inc., 13155 U S R 23, Ashville, OH 43103. TEL 740-983-2273, FAX 740-983-9691. Ed., R&P, Adv. contact Wanda Nelson. Circ: 6,000.

629.222 388.324 USA
FORD TRADER. Text in English. m.
Published by: Trader Publishing Company, 24771 US 19 N, Clearwater, FL 34623. TEL 800-548-8889, FAX 727-712-0034.

FORD WORLD. *see* BUSINESS AND ECONOMICS—Labor And Industrial Relations

796.77 ITA ISSN 1825-1838
FORMULA 1. Text in Italian. 2005. a. **Document type:** *Magazine, Consumer.*
Published by: De Agostini Editore, Via G da Verrazzano 15, Novara, 28100, Italy. TEL 39-0321-4241, FAX 39-0321-424305, info@deagostini.it, http://www.deagostini.it.

▼ **FORMULE1.NL.** *see* SPORTS AND GAMES

629 DEU ISSN 0178-9449
FORTSCHRITT-BERICHTE V D I. REIHE 12: VERKEHRSTECHNIK - FAHRZEUGTECHNIK. Text in German. 1965. irreg., latest vol.729, 2010. price varies. **Document type:** *Monographic series, Academic/Scholarly.*
Former titles (until 1986): Fortschritt-Berichte V D I. Reihe 12: Verkehrstechnik (0933-0992); (until 1985): Fortschrittberichte der V D I Zeitschriften. Reihe 12: Verkehrstechnik (0506-3167)
Indexed: A22, TM.
—BLDSC (4018.590500), IE, Ingenta. **CCC.**
Published by: V D I Verlag GmbH, VDI-Platz 1, Duesseldorf, 40468, Germany. TEL 49-211-61880, FAX 49-211-6188112, info@vdi-nachrichten.com, http://www.vdi-verlag.de.

388.3 USA ISSN 1093-0949
FORZA; the magazine about Ferrari. Text in English. 1996. 8/yr. USD 28 domestic; USD 35 in Canada; USD 45 elsewhere; USD 4.99 per issue (effective 2011). adv. back issues avail. **Document type:** *Magazine, Consumer.* **Description:** Contains information about Ferrari automobiles.
Published by: Ross Periodicals, PO Box 1529, Ross, CA 94957. Adv. contact Holly Lundgren TEL 415-382-2860.

388.3 USA ISSN 0015-9123
TL235.6
FOUR WHEELER MAGAZINE; world's leading four wheel drive magazine. Text in English. 1962. m. USD 10 domestic; USD 22 in Canada; USD 34 elsewhere (effective 2008). adv. bk.rev. charts; illus.; mkt.; tr.lit. back issues avail.; reprints avail. **Document type:** *Magazine, Consumer.* **Description:** Explores the high-adventure and global nature of off-roading.
Related titles: Online - full text ed.: USD 5 (effective 2008).
Indexed: G06, G07, G08, I05, S23.
—CCC.
Published by: Source Interlink Companies, 6420 Wilshire Blvd, 10th Fl, Los Angeles, CA 90048. TEL 323-782-2000, FAX 323-782-2585, dheine@sourceinterlink.com, http://www.sourceinterlink.com. Eds. Douglas McColloch, Ken Brubaker. Pub. Steve VonSeggern TEL 714-939-2581. adv.: B&W page USD 16,950, color page USD 26,715. Circ: 235,957.

796.77 FRA ISSN 0765-0698
FRANCE AUTO; la revue du licencie. Text in French. 1956. bi-m. back issues avail. **Document type:** *Magazine, Consumer.*
Published by: Federation Francaise du Sport Automobile (F F S A), 32 Av. de New-York, Paris, Cedex 16 75781, France. TEL 33-1-44302400, FAX 33-1-42241680.

388.342 944 GBR ISSN 1748-989X
FRANCE AUTOS REPORT. Text in English. 2005. q. EUR 820, USD 1,030 combined subscription (print & email eds.) (effective 2010). **Document type:** *Report, Trade.* **Description:** Provides industry professionals and strategists, corporate analysts, auto associations, government departments and regulatory bodies with independent forecasts and competitive intelligence on the automotives industry.
Related titles: E-mail ed.
Indexed: A15, ABIn, B01, B02, B15, B17, B18, G04, I05, P48, P51, P52, PQC.
Published by: Business Monitor International Ltd., Senator House, 85 Queen Victoria St, London, EC4V 4AB, United Kingdom. TEL 44-20-72480468, FAX 44-20-72480467, subs@businessmonitor.com.

338.3 GBR ISSN 1351-4822
FRANCHISE NETWORKS. Text in English. 1989. a. GBP 1,050 per issue (effective 2010). software rev. tr.lit.; stat. back issues avail. **Document type:** *Directory, Trade.* **Description:** Covers specially commissioned research with data provided by all manufacturers and importers operating within the UK.
Related titles: Online - full text ed.
Published by: Sewells Information and Research (Subsidiary of: H. Bauer Publishing Ltd.), Bauer Automotive Media House, Peterborough Business Park, Lynchwood, Peterborough, Northants PE2 6EA, United Kingdom. TEL 44-1733-468254, FAX 44-1733-468349, sewells@emap.com, http://www.sewells.co.uk.

388 796.6 AUT
FREIE FAHRT. Text in German. m. membership. **Document type:** *Newsletter.*
Published by: A R B Oe - Auto- Motor- und Radfahrerbund Oesterreichs, Mariahilfer Str 180, Vienna, W 1150, Austria. TEL 43-1-891210, FAX 43-1-89121236, id@arboe.at, http://www3.arboe.at. Ed. Leo Musil. Pubs. Karl Damisch, Rudolf Hellar. Adv. contact Peter Burger. Circ: 400,000 (controlled).

629.286 DEU
FREIE WERKSTATT. Text in German. 1994. 10/yr. EUR 33.36 (effective 2011). adv. **Document type:** *Magazine, Trade.*
Former titles (until 2007): Auto, Reparatur, Markt: Freie Werkstatt; (until 2003): Freie Werkstatt : Auto, Reparatur, Markt; (until 2000): Auto Zubehoer Markt: Freie Werkstatt (1436-0543)
Published by: Verlag Kaufhold GmbH, Philipp-Nicolai-Weg 3, Herdecke, 58313, Germany. TEL 49-2330-918311, FAX 49-2330-13570, info@verlag-kaufhold.de, http://www.verlag-kaufhold.de. Ed. Claudia Pfleging. Pub. Manfred Kaufhold. adv.: B&W page EUR 2,322, color page EUR 4,273; trim 184 x 265. Circ: 18,947 (paid).

629.22075 USA ISSN 1934-6255
FRESH COAST. Text in English. 2002. q. USD 13 (effective 2007). adv. **Document type:** *Magazine, Consumer.* **Description:** Designed for custom car aficionados. Includes information about car shows, new products and interviews with notable custom car owners.
Published by: Fresh Coast Media, LLC, 264 S La Cienega Blvd #310, Beverly Hills, CA 90211. info@freshcoastmagazine.com. Ed. Mykose Hufana.

796.77 USA ISSN 2157-6823
▼ **FUEL MAGAZINE (METAIRIE).** Text in English. 2010. bi-m. free (effective 2010). adv. **Document type:** *Magazine, Trade.* **Description:** Showcase automobiles and highlight regional events for readers.
Related titles: Online - full text ed.
Published by: Fat City Publishing, Llc., 4401 Division St, Ste A, Metairie, LA 70002. TEL 504-218-7526.

796.77 BRA ISSN 1676-8256
FULLPOWER. Text in Portuguese. 2002. m. BRL 7.90 newsstand/cover (effective 2010). adv. **Document type:** *Magazine, Consumer.*
Published by: B7 Editorial Ltda., Rua LaPlace, 74 4o Andar Brooklin, Sao Paulo, 04622-000, Brazil. TEL 55-11-50900000, FAX 55-11-50900029, http://www.editorab7.com.br.

629.2 GRC
FURIOUS TUNING. Text in Greek. 2005. m. EUR 4.95 newsstand/cover (effective 2006). adv. **Document type:** *Magazine, Consumer.*
Published by: Motorpress Hellas (Subsidiary of: Gruner + Jahr AG & Co), 132 Lefkis Str, Krioneri, 14568, Greece. TEL 30-210-6262000, FAX 30-210-6262401, info@motorpress.gr, http://www.motorpress.gr. Circ: 60,000 (paid and controlled).

629.2 SWE ISSN 1654-224X
FYNDBOERSEN. Text in Swedish. 2006. m. SEK 60 newsstand/cover (effective 2010). adv. **Document type:** *Magazine, Consumer.*
Formerly (until 2007): Fyndboersxtra (1654-1146)
Published by: Foerlags AB Albinsson & Sjoeberg, PO Box 529, Karlskrona, 37123, Sweden. TEL 46-455-335325, FAX 46-455-311715, fabas@fabas.se, http://www.fabas.se. Ed. Fredrik Lund. adv.: page SEK 7,700; trim 190 x 275.

388.3 JPN
G I A DIAAROGU KOEN SHIRYOSHU/G I A DIALOGUE. Text in Japanese. irreg. JPY 1,050 per issue (effective 2009).
—BLDSC (4169.170000).
Published by: Jidosha Gijutsukai/Society of Automotive Engineers of Japan, Inc., 10-2 Goban-cho, Chiyoda-ku, Tokyo, 102-0076, Japan. TEL 81-3-3262-8211, FAX 81-3-3261-2204, http://www.jsae.or.jp/.

388.3 USA
G M C DIRECTIONS. (General Motors Corporation) Text in English. 1997. 3/yr. adv.
Published by: Sandy Corporation, 1500 W Big Beaver Rd, Troy, MI 48084. TEL 800-733-4739, FAX 248-816-2305. Ed. Duane Roose.

388 USA ISSN 1523-9454
G M HIGH TECH PERFORMANCE. (General Motors) Text in English. 198?. 9/yr. USD 19.95 domestic; USD 28.95 in Canada; USD 37.95 elsewhere (effective 2008). adv. back issues avail. **Document type:** *Magazine, Consumer.* **Description:** Covers fuel injection, supercharging, nitrous oxide systems, turbo technology, suspension technology, electronic engine management, cutting-edge engine hardware and various other things in the modern arsenal of GM power.
Former titles (until 1996): High Tech Performance (1088-8446); (until 199?): Hot Rod Mechanix (1084-3728); (until 19??): Tex Smith's Hot Rod Mechanix (0897-6899)
Indexed: A10, G06, G07, G08, I05, S23, V03.
—CCC.
Published by: Source Interlink Companies, 365 West Passaic St, Rochelle Park, NJ 07662. dheine@sourceinterlink.com, http://www.sourceinterlinkmedia.com. Ed. Rick Jensen. Pub. Ed Zinke TEL 714-939-2626. adv.: B&W page USD 3,640, color page USD 4,420; bleed 8.125 x 10.75. Circ: 24,227 (paid).

796.7 ZAF ISSN 1812-1373
G Q CARS. (Gentlemen's Quarterly) Text in English. 2004. s-a. **Document type:** *Magazine, Consumer.*
Published by: Conde Nast Independent Magazines, PO Box 16414, Vlaeberg, 8018, South Africa. TEL 27-21-4802300, FAX 27-21-4246222. Adv. contact Madeleine Stoltz.

629.11 NLD ISSN 1571-5256
G T O. (Gran Turismo Omologato) Text in Dutch. 2003. bi-m. EUR 29.40; EUR 5.25 newsstand/cover (effective 2009). adv. **Document type:** *Magazine, Consumer.*
Published by: Sanoma Men's Magazines, Haaksbergweg 75, Amsterdam (ZO), 1101 BR, Netherlands. TEL 31-20-7518000, FAX 31-20-7518301, sales@smm.nl, http://www.smm.nl. Ed. Tonie Broekhuijsen. Pub. Eric Ariens. Circ: 28,036.

629.2222 GBR ISSN 1474-6549
G T PURELY PORSCHE. Text in English. 2001. m. GBP 40.50 domestic; GBP 58 in Europe; GBP 73.35 elsewhere; GBP 5 per issue (effective 2009). adv. back issues avail. **Document type:** *Magazine, Consumer.* **Description:** Provides information about cars.
Published by: Unity Media PLC, Becket House, Vestry Rd, Sevenoaks, Kent TN14 5EJ, United Kingdom. TEL 44-1732-748000, FAX 44-1732-748001, http://www.unity-media.com/. Ed. Stuart Gallagher. Pub. Colin Wilkinson. Adv. contact Helen Rush TEL 44-1732-748054. page GBP 750; trim 220 x 285.

629 DEU
G W TRENDS. (Gebrauchtwagen) Text in German. bi-m. EUR 119 domestic; EUR 125 foreign (effective 2008). adv. **Document type:** *Magazine, Trade.*
Published by: Springer Automotive Media (Subsidiary of: Springer Fachmedien Muenchen GmbH), Neumarkter Str 18, Munich, 81673, Germany. TEL 49-89-43721121, FAX 49-89-43721266, vertriebsservice@springer.com, http://www.springerautomotivemedia.de. Ed. Martin Endlein. Adv. contact Michael Harms. color page EUR 5,980. Circ: 13,410 (paid and controlled).

620 JPN ISSN 0919-1364
GAKUJUTSU KOENKAI MAEZURISHU. Text in Japanese. s-a. **Document type:** *Journal.*
Formerly (until 1959): Koenkaiyo Maezurishu
—BLDSC (5073.724800). **CCC.**
Published by: Jidosha Gijutsukai/Society of Automotive Engineers of Japan, Inc., 10-2 Goban-cho, Chiyoda-ku, Tokyo, 102-0076, Japan. TEL 81-3-3262-8211, FAX 81-3-3261-2204, http://www.jsae.or.jp/.

796.77 796.72 ITA
GALLERIA FERRARI. YEARBOOK. Text in English, Italian. a. back issues avail. **Document type:** *Yearbook, Consumer.* **Description:** Provides coverage of special events, previously unpublished images of the Formula 1 racing season, and other related information on Ferrari automobiles.
Published by: Galleria Ferrari, Via Dino Ferrari, 43, Maranello, 41053, Italy. FAX 39-0536-949714, shop@ferrari.it, http://www.ferrari.com/.

796.7 ITA ISSN 1826-9079
GALLERIA RUOTECLASSICHE. Text in Italian. 2002. m. **Document type:** *Magazine, Consumer.*
Published by: Editoriale Domus, Via Gianni Mazzocchi 1/3, Rozzano, MI 20089, Italy. TEL 39-02-824721, editorialedomus@edidomus.it, http://www.edidomus.it.

629.286 CAN
GARAGE & SERVICE STATION NEWS. Text in English. 1934. m. USD 7. adv. illus.; tr.lit.
Published by: Garage & Service Station News Publishing Co., 204, 260 Raymur Ave, Vancouver, BC, Canada. Ed. Theodore L Coates. Circ: (controlled).

629.2 GBR
GARAGE TRADER; the magazine for Ireland's automotive repair market. Abbreviated title: G T. Text in English. 19??. q. free to qualified personnel (effective 2010). adv. **Document type:** *Magazine, Trade.* **Description:** Contains material of interest to new and used car dealers, managers of service stations, fleet operators, body repair shop owners, electrical system specialists, and engine and component reconditioners.
Published by: Greer Publications, 5B Edgewater Business Park, Belfast Harbour Estate, Belfast, BT3 9JQ, United Kingdom. TEL 44-28-90783200, FAX 44-28-90783210, info@greerpublications.com, http://www.greerpublications.com. Ed. Pat Burns TEL 44-28-90783200 ext 220. Adv. contact Jackie Stott TEL 44-28-90783200 ext 232.

629.222 SWE ISSN 1653-3771
GASOLINE MAGAZINE. Text in Swedish. 2006. bi-m. SEK 269 (effective 2006). adv. **Document type:** *Magazine, Consumer.*
Published by: Rivstart AB, PO Box 65, Kungsoer, 73622, Sweden. TEL 46-227-12140. Ed., Pub. Mattias Hammarstedt.

629.222 NOR
GATEBIL. Text in Norwegian. 10/yr. NOK 449 (effective 2009). adv. **Document type:** *Magazine, Consumer.*
Published by: Aller Forlag AS, Stenersgaten 2, Sentrum, Oslo, 0189, Norway. TEL 47-21-301000, FAX 47-21-301205, allerforlag@aller.no, http://www.aller.no. Adv. contact Lars Bruto. page NOK 25,000; bleed 234 x 295. Circ: 20,068 (paid).

388.342 629.2 POL ISSN 1232-1923
GAZETA MOTORYZACYJNA. Text in Polish. 1991. irreg.
Related titles: ◆ Supplement to: Gazeta Wyborcza. ISSN 0860-908X.
Published by: Agora S.A., ul Czerska 8/10, Warsaw, 00732, Poland. TEL 48-22-6994301, FAX 48-22-6994603, http://www.agora.pl.

629.286 AUS ISSN 1449-8650
GEARED. Text in English. 2004. s-a. free (effective 2008). 65 p./no.; **Document type:** *Magazine, Consumer.* **Description:** Covers article on driving, latest in safety, road rules and information about how to get and keep your licence.
Related titles: Online - full text ed.: free (effective 2008).
Published by: Roads and Traffic Authority of N S W, PO Box K198, Haymarket, NSW 1240, Australia. TEL 61-2-92186888, FAX 61-2-92186286, Communication_Enquiries@rta.nsw.gov.au, http://www.rta.nsw.gov.au.

GEARHEAD MAGAZINE. *see* LIFESTYLE

388 DEU ISSN 0721-278X
GEBRAUCHTWAGEN-PRAXIS. Text in German. 1981. m. EUR 180 (effective 2010). **Document type:** *Journal, Trade.*
Related titles: Online - full text ed.
Published by: (I W W - Institut fuer Wirtschaftspublizistik), Vogel Business Media GmbH & Co.KG, Max-Planck-Str 7-9, Wuerzburg, 97064, Germany. TEL 49-931-4180, FAX 49-931-4182750, info@vogel.de, http://www.vogel-media.de. **Subscr. to:** DataM-Services GmbH, Fichtestr 9, Wuerzburg 97074, Germany. TEL 49-931-417001, FAX 49-931-4170499, http://www.datam-services.de.

388 DEU ISSN 0941-6080
GEFAHRGUT-PROFI; Transport, Umschlag und Lagerung. Text in German. 1991. bi-m. EUR 54; EUR 9.80 newsstand/cover (effective 2010). adv. **Document type:** *Magazine, Consumer.*
—IE, Infotrieve.
Published by: T Ue V Media GmbH, Am Grauen Stein 1, Cologne, 51105, Germany. TEL 49-221-8063535, FAX 49-221-8063510, tuev-media@de.tuv.com, http://www.tuev-media.de.

388 629.2 USA
GENERAL MOTORS RESEARCH LABORATORIES SYMPOSIA SERIES. Text in English. 1988. irreg., latest 1988. price varies. **Document type:** *Proceedings, Trade.*
Published by: Springer New York LLC (Subsidiary of: Springer Science+Business Media), 233 Spring St, New York, NY 10013. TEL 212-460-1500, FAX 212-460-1575, service-ny@springer.com, http://www.springer.com/.

629.226 796.54 FRA ISSN 1953-650X
GENERATION CAMPING CAR; Le Magazine de l'art de vivre en camping-car. Text in French. 2006. q. EUR 15 (effective 2007). back issues avail. **Document type:** *Magazine, Consumer.*
Published by: Agence Impact Auto Moto, 215 Rue Jean Jacques Rousseau, Issy les Moulineaux, 92136 Cedex, France. TEL 33-1-46447096, FAX 33-1-47362148, http://www.agenceimpact.com/.

796.77 USA ISSN 2157-4073
▼ **GENERATION FIVE CAMARO.** Variant title: Generation V Camaro. Text in English. 2010. a. USD 8 per issue domestic; USD 12 per issue in Canada; USD 20 per issue elsewhere (effective 2010). **Document type:** *Catalog, Trade.*
Related titles: CD-ROM ed.: ISSN 2157-4081; Online - full text ed.: ISSN 2157-4162. free (effective 2010).
Published by: Classic Industries, Inc., 18460 Gothard St, Huntington Beach, CA 92648. TEL 714-847-6887, 800-300-3081, FAX 714-848-9501, info@classicindustries.com.

388.3 ITA ISSN 0393-7860
GENTE MOTORI. Text in Italian. 1972. m. EUR 15.60 (effective 2009). adv. bk.rev. **Document type:** *Magazine, Consumer.*
Published by: Hachette Rusconi SpA (Subsidiary of: Hachette Filipacchi Medias S.A.), Viale Sarca 235, Milan, 20126, Italy. TEL 39-02-66192629, FAX 39-02-66192469, dirgen@rusconi.it, http://portale.hachettepubblicita.it. Ed. Daniele Buzzonetti. Adv. contact Eduardo Giliberti. Circ: 210,000.

388.342 943 GBR ISSN 1748-9903
GERMANY AUTO REPORT. Text in English. 2005. q. EUR 820, USD 1,030 combined subscription (print & email eds.) (effective 2010). **Document type:** *Report, Trade.* **Description:** Provides industry professionals and strategists, corporate analysts, auto associations, government departments and regulatory bodies with independent forecasts and competitive intelligence on the German automotives market.
Related titles: E-mail ed.
Indexed: A15, ABIn, B01, B02, B15, B17, B18, G04, I05, P48, P51, P52, PQC.
Published by: Business Monitor International Ltd., Senator House, 85 Queen Victoria St, London, EC4V 4AB, United Kingdom. TEL 44-20-72480468, FAX 44-20-72480467, subs@businessmonitor.com.

629.2 796.77 DEU ISSN 0939-5849
GESAMTVERBAND AUTOTEILE-HANDEL. MITGLIEDERVERZEICHNIS. Text in German. 1969. a. adv. stat. back issues avail. **Document type:** *Directory, Trade.* **Description:** Contains contact information for car parts dealers and automotive suppliers as well as information on the German automobile aftermarket.
Formerly (until 1990): V K G Jahrbuch (0171-5046)
Published by: Gesamtverband Autoteile-Handel e.V., Gothaer Str 17, Ratingen, 40880, Germany. TEL 49-2102-770770, FAX 49-2102-7707717, info@gva.de, http://www.gva.de. Ed. Thomas Kobudzinski. Circ: 1,500.

GHANA. STATISTICAL SERVICE. MOTOR VEHICLE REGISTRATION. *see* TRANSPORTATION—Abstracting, Bibliographies, Statistics

629.286 ITA ISSN 1120-8287
IL GIORNALE DEL MECCANICO. Text in Italian. 1991. 9/yr. EUR 45 domestic; EUR 68 foreign (effective 2009). adv. **Document type:** *Trade.*
Published by: Reed Business Information Spa (Subsidiary of: Reed Business Information International), Viale Giulio Richard 1, Milan, 20143, Italy. TEL 39-02-818301, FAX 39-02-81830406, info@reedbusiness.it, http://www.reedbusiness.it. Circ: 17,000.

388 GBR
GLASS'S CAR CHECKBOOK. Text in English. a. adv. back issues avail. **Document type:** *Handbook/Manual/Guide, Trade.*
Published by: Glass's Information Services Ltd., 1 Princes Rd, Weybridge, Surrey KT13 9TU, United Kingdom. TEL 44-1932-823823, FAX 44-1932-849299, customer@glass.co.uk, http://www.glass.co.uk.

338.476 GBR
GLASS'S GUIDE TO CAR VALUES. Text in English. 1933. m. adv. **Document type:** *Handbook/Manual/Guide, Trade.* **Description:** Offers dealers valuation information on new and used cars.
Formerly: Glass's Guide to Used Car Values
Related titles: Diskette ed.: USD 360 (effective 1999).
Published by: Glass's Information Services Ltd., 1 Princes Rd, Weybridge, Surrey KT13 9TU, United Kingdom. TEL 44-1932-823823, FAX 44-1932-849299, customer@glass.co.uk, http://www.glass.co.uk. Circ: 17,649 (paid).

338.476 GBR
GLASS'S GUIDE TO COMMERCIAL VEHICLE VALUES. Text in English. 1951. m. adv. **Document type:** *Handbook/Manual/Guide, Trade.* **Description:** Includes lightweights, pick ups and motor caravans through to trucks, tippers, boxes, tractors, trailers and specialist vehicles up to 38 tons, for over 44 chassis manufacturers. Special features include top van and 4x4 values and a new premium section for top condition models.
Formerly (until 1985): Glass's Guide to Used Commercial Vehicle Values
Related titles: Diskette ed.: GBP 360 (effective 2000).
Published by: Glass's Information Services Ltd., 1 Princes Rd, Weybridge, Surrey KT13 9TU, United Kingdom. TEL 44-1932-823823, FAX 44-1932-846564, customer@glass.co.uk, http://www.glass.co.uk. Ed. George Alexander.

338.476 336 GBR
GLASS'S GUIDE TO COMPANY CAR TAX. Text in English. 1993. q. adv. **Document type:** *Handbook/Manual/Guide, Trade.* **Description:** Provides price information for new company cars and their options.
Formerly (until 1999): Company Car Tax
Related titles: Diskette ed.: GBP 182 (effective 2001).
Published by: Glass's Information Services Ltd., 1 Princes Rd, Weybridge, Surrey KT13 9TU, United Kingdom. TEL 44-1932-823823, FAX 44-1932-846564, customer@glass.co.uk, http://www.glass.co.uk.

338.476 SGP
GLOBAL SOURCES AUTO PARTS & ACCESSORIES. Short title: Auto Parts & Accessories. Text in English. 2005. m. USD 75 (effective 2007). **Document type:** *Magazine, Consumer.* **Description:** Provides information on new auto part and accessory products and suppliers.
Published by: Global Sources, c/o Media Data Systems Pte Ltd, PO Box 0203, Raffles City, 911707, Singapore. TEL 65-6547-2800, FAX 65-6547-2888, service@globalsources.com.

388 AUT
GO!; das Fahrschuelermagazin. Text in German. 1989. s-a. adv. **Document type:** *Magazine, Consumer.*
Published by: Elektro und Wirtschaft Verlagsgesellschaft mbH, Wilhelminenstrasse 91-IIC, Vienna, W 1160, Austria. TEL 43-1-4853149-0, FAX 43-1-4869032-30, redaktion@elektro.at, http://www.elektro.at. Ed., Adv. contact Ronald Rockenbauer. page EUR 4,500; trim 185 x 270. Circ: 60,000 (controlled).

GO MAGAZINE (CHARLOTTE). *see* TRAVEL AND TOURISM

614 CAN ISSN 0832-5448
GOING PLACES (MANITOBA). Text in English. 1958. q. adv.
Former titles (until 1987): Westworld (Manitoba) (0831-1560); (until 1985): Drive (Winnipeg) (0712-5755); (until 1981): Manitoba Motorist (0380-0172)
Related titles: ◆ Supplement to: C A A Magazine. ISSN 1910-0140.
Published by: C A A Manitoba, 870 Empress St, Winnipeg, MB R3G 3H3, Canada. TEL 204-262-6161, http://www.caaneo.on.ca. Circ: 42,000.

629.222 USA
GOLD BOOK CLASSICS & ANTIQUES. Text in English. s-a. looseleaf. USD 35. **Document type:** *Guide, Consumer.* **Description:** Provides values in four condition categories for more than 6,000 antique vehicles manufactured between 1897 and 1942.
Published by: Gold Book, Inc., 1400 Lake Hearn Dr, 2nd Fl, Atlanta, GA 30319. TEL 800-842-6848, FAX 404-847-6507. Ed. John Apen. R&P Brandi Keesey.

629.2 USA ISSN 1057-0535
GOLD BOOK CONTEMPORARY VEHICLES. Text in English. 6/yr. looseleaf. USD 66. **Document type:** *Guide, Consumer.* **Description:** Provides values in three condition categories plus wholesale and loan values for more than 10,000 domestic and imported cars and trucks manufactured since 1976.
Supersedes in part: Gold Book Used Car Value Guide
Published by: Gold Book, Inc., 1400 Lake Hearn Dr, 2nd Fl, Atlanta, GA 30319. TEL 800-842-6848, FAX 404-847-6507. Ed. Patrick Keating. R&P Brandi Keesey.

629.2 USA ISSN 1057-0136
GOLD BOOK OLDER VEHICLES. Text in English. q. looseleaf. USD 46. **Document type:** *Consumer.* **Description:** Provides values in three condition categories plus loan value for more than 10,000 domestic and imported cars and truck manufactured between 1945 and 1975.
Supersedes in part: Gold Book Used Car Value Guide
Published by: Gold Book, Inc., 1400 Lake Hearn Dr, 2nd Fl, Atlanta, GA 30319. TEL 800-842-6848, FAX 404-847-6507. Ed. John Apen. R&P Brandi Keesey.

388.3 GBR ISSN 0017-2111
GOOD MOTORING. Text in English. 1935. q. free to members (effective 2009). adv. bk.rev. illus. **Document type:** *Magazine, Consumer.* **Description:** General motoring journal published for the members of the Guild of Experienced Motorists.
Published by: (G E M Motoring Assist), Good Motoring (Publishers) Ltd., c/o Guild of Experienced Motorists, Station Rd, Forest Row, East Sussex RH18 5EN, United Kingdom. TEL 44-845-3700940, FAX 44-1342-824847.

GOODGUYS GOODTIMES GAZETTE. *see* SPORTS AND GAMES

388.3 USA
GOVERNMENT FLEET. Text in English. 2003. bi-m. free to qualified personnel (effective 2008). adv. **Document type:** *Magazine, Consumer.* **Description:** Provides information to government fleet decision makers at the federal, state and local levels throughout the U.S. market.
Published by: Bobit Business Media, 3520 Challenger St, Torrance, CA 90503. TEL 310-533-2400, FAX 310-533-2500, order@bobit.com, http://www.bobit.com. Pub. Sherb Brown. adv.: color page USD 9,850; trim 7.875 x 10.75. Circ: 18,000 (controlled).

796.77 ITA
GRACE; classic & sport cars. Text in Italian. m. EUR 60 (effective 2008). 130 p./no.; **Document type:** *Magazine, Consumer.*
Published by: Barbero Editori Srl, Via Galileo Galilei 3, Chieri, TO 10023, Italy. TEL 39-011-9470400, FAX 39-011-9470577.

338.3 ESP
GRAN GUIA DE COCHE ACTUAL. Text in Spanish. 1991. a. **Document type:** *Directory, Consumer.*
Related titles: ◆ Supplement to: Coche Actual. ISSN 1988-091X.
Published by: Motorpress Iberica (Subsidiary of: Gruner + Jahr AG & Co), Ancora 40, Madrid, 28045, Spain. TEL 34-91-3470100, FAX 34-91-3470152, http://www.motorpress-iberica.es. Circ: 19,000 (paid).

629 CZE ISSN 1802-3304
GRAND AUTO-MOTO. Text in Czech. 2002. m. CZK 216 (effective 2009). adv. **Document type:** *Magazine, Consumer.*
Related titles: Online - full text ed.: ISSN 1802-3312.
Published by: Grand Princ s.r.o., Vinohradska 138, Prague 3, 130 00, Czech Republic. TEL 420-272-107111, FAX 420-272-107000, grandprinc@grandprinc.cz, http://www.grandprinc.cz. adv.: page CZK 42,000; trim 215 x 270. Circ: 60,000 (paid and controlled).

388.3 USA ISSN 1047-0298
GRASSROOTS MOTORSPORTS. Key Title: Auto-X and Grassroots Motorsports. Text in English. 1984. 8/yr. USD 19.95 domestic; USD 27.95 in Canada; USD 31.95 elsewhere (effective 2005). adv. bk.rev. **Document type:** *Magazine, Consumer.*
Formerly (until 1989): Auto-X (1043-1748)
Published by: Motorsport Marketing, Inc., 310 Division Ave, Ormond Beach, FL 32174. TEL 386-673-4148, FAX 386-673-6040, grmhq@aol.com. Ed., R&P David Wallens. Pub., Adv. contact Tim Suddard. page USD 1,315. Circ: 35,000.

GREATER WASHINGTON - MARYLAND SERVICE STATION AND AUTOMOTIVE REPAIR ASSOCIATION. MEMBERSHIP DIRECTORY & BUYER'S GUIDE. *see* BUSINESS AND ECONOMICS—Trade And Industrial Directories

388.342 GBR ISSN 1748-9911
GREECE AUTOS REPORT. Text in English. 2005. q. EUR 820, USD 1,030 combined subscription (print & email eds.) (effective 2010). **Document type:** *Report, Trade.* **Description:** Provides industry professionals and strategists, corporate analysts, auto associations, government departments and regulatory bodies with independent forecasts and competitive intelligence on the automotives industry in Greece.
Related titles: E-mail ed.
Indexed: A15, ABIn, B02, B15, B17, B18, G04, I05, P48, P51, P52, PQC.
Published by: Business Monitor International Ltd., Senator House, 85 Queen Victoria St, London, EC4V 4AB, United Kingdom. TEL 44-20-72480468, FAX 44-20-72480467, subs@businessmonitor.com.

GREEN CAR JOURNAL. *see* ENERGY

629.3 FIN ISSN 1457-6058
GTI-MAGAZINE. Text in Finnish. 2000. 12/yr. EUR 69 (effective 2009). adv. **Document type:** *Magazine, Consumer.* **Description:** Contains information and advice on improving the driving properties and enhancing the appearance of cars.
Published by: Sanoma Magazines Finland Corporation, Lapinmaentie 1, Helsinki, 00350, Finland. TEL 358-9-1201, FAX 358-9-1205171, info@sanomamagazines.fi, http://www.sanomamagazines.fi.

388.3 ESP ISSN 0211-657X
GUIA DEL COMPRADOR DE COCHES. Text in Spanish. 1982. m. **Document type:** *Magazine, Consumer.*
Published by: Editorial Moredi S.L., Hiedra no 2-C, Madrid, 28036, Spain. TEL 34-91-7339713, FAX 34-91-7339673, administrador@moredi.com, http://www.moredi.com. Ed. Luis Miguel Dominguez. Pub. Ignacio de Lucas. Circ: 38,281 (paid and controlled).

796.2 ESP
GUIA DEL COMPRADOR DE FURGONETAS Y TODO TERRENO. Text in Spanish. 1988. m. **Document type:** *Magazine, Consumer.* **Description:** Contains articles and information on vans, pickup trucks, commercial vans and other 4x4s.
Published by: Editorial Moredi S.L., Hiedra no 2-C, Madrid, 28036, Spain. TEL 34-91-7339713, FAX 34-91-7339673, administrador@moredi.com, http://www.moredi.com. Eds. Carlos Espinosa, Luis Miguel Dominguez, Marta Lopez. Pub. Ignacio de Lucas. Circ: 10,500 (paid and controlled).

388 PRT
GUIA DO ACESSORIO AUTO E SERVICOS. Text in Portuguese. 2000. a. EUR 2.49 newsstand/cover (effective 2005). **Document type:** *Magazine, Trade.*
Published by: Motorpress Lisboa, SA (Subsidiary of: Gruner + Jahr AG & Co), Rua Policarpio Anjos No. 4, Cruz Quebrada, Dafundo 1495-742, Portugal. TEL 351-21-4154500, FAX 351-21-4154501, buzine@motorpress.pt, http://www.mpl.pt.

388 PRT
GUIA DO AUTOMOVEL; precos do novo e usado. Text in Portuguese. 1985. m. EUR 18; EUR 2 per issue (effective 2005). adv. **Document type:** *Magazine, Consumer.* **Description:** Lists the prices of new and used cars.
Related titles: Online - full text ed.
Published by: Motorpress Lisboa, SA (Subsidiary of: Gruner + Jahr AG & Co), Rua Policarpio Anjos No. 4, Cruz Quebrada, Dafundo 1495-742, Portugal. TEL 351-21-4154500, FAX 351-21-4154501, buzine@motorpress.pt, http://www.mpl.pt. Ed. Luis Pimenta. Adv. contact Rita Vidreiro. page EUR 1,795.67; 13.5 x 19.5. Circ: 55,000 (paid).

388.3 ESP
GUIA UTIL DEL AUTOMOVIL DE COCHE ACTUAL. Text in Spanish. 1992. m. adv. **Document type:** *Magazine, Consumer.* **Description:** Price guide for new and used cars.
Published by: Motorpress Iberica (Subsidiary of: Gruner + Jahr AG & Co), Ancora 40, Madrid, 28045, Spain. TEL 34-91-3470100, FAX 34-91-3470152, http://www.motorpress-iberica.es. Circ: 37,300 (paid).

388.3 CAN ISSN 1719-7104
GUIDE COMPLET DES PRIX, AUTOMOBILES USAGEES. Text in French. 1996. a. **Document type:** *Directory, Consumer.*
Supersedes in part (in 2004): Guide Complet de Prix Autos, Fourgonnettes et Camions Usages (1209-8558); Which was formerly (until 1997): Autos et Camions Usages, Guide Complet de Prix (1207-5515); Which was formed by the merger of (1995-1996): Guide de Prix, Autos Usagees (1202-7049); Which was formerly (1994-1995): Guide des Prix Automobile (1202-7030); (1995-1996): Guide de Prix, Camions Usages (1202-7065); Which was formerly (1994-1995): Guide des Prix, Camions, Fourgonnettes, Vehicules Recreatifs (1202-7057)
Published by: Edutile Inc., 44, chemin du Vieux-Moulin, Notre-Dame-de-l'Ile Perrot, PQ J7V 8P6, Canada. TEL 514-236-3365, FAX 514-453-8871.

388.3 CAN ISSN 1719-7112
GUIDE COMPLET DES PRIX, FOURGONNETTES, V U S ET CAMIONS USAGES. Text in French. 1996. a. **Document type:** *Directory, Consumer.*
Supersedes in part (in 2005): Guide Complet de Prix Autos, Fourgonnettes et Camions Usages (1209-8558); Which was formerly (until 1997): Autos et Camions Usages, Guide Complet de Prix (1207-5515); Which was formed by the merger of (1995-1996): Guide de Prix, Autos Usagees (1202-7049); Which was formerly (1994-1995): Guide des Prix Automobile (1202-7030); (1995-1996): Guide de Prix, Camions Usages (1202-7065); Which was formerly (1994-1995): Guide des Prix, Camions, Fourgonnettes, Vehicules Recreatifs (1202-7057)
Published by: Edutile Inc., 44, chemin du Vieux-Moulin, Notre-Dame-de-l'Ile Perrot, PQ J7V 8P6, Canada. TEL 514-236-3365, FAX 514-453-8871.

388.3 USA
GUIDE TO FORD'S 126 REPORT, THE W C P, AUDIT PREP. & NEGOTIATIONS. Text in English. a. **Document type:** *Guide, Trade.*
Published by: W D & S Publishing, 10 W 7th St, 1st Fl, PO Box 606, Barnegat Light, NJ 08006. TEL 800-321-5312, http://www.dealersedge.com.

629.222 HKG
GUOJI QICHE GONGCHENG/AUTOMOTIVE ENGINEERING INTERNATIONAL. Text in Chinese. bi-m. **Document type:** *Magazine, Trade.*
Published by: B I T F (Publishing) Ltd (Subsidiary of: Business & Industrial Trade Fairs Ltd.), Unit 1101, Kowloon Plaza, 485 Castle Peak Rd, Kowloon, Hong Kong. TEL 852-2865-2633, FAX 852-2866-1770, enquiry@bitf.com.hk, http://www.bitf.com.hk/.

388.3 DEU ISSN 0017-5765
GUTE FAHRT; Alles ueber Volkswagen und Audi. Text in German. 1950. m. EUR 36.30 domestic; EUR 48 foreign; EUR 3.30 newsstand/cover (effective 2011). adv. illus. **Document type:** *Magazine, Consumer.*
Related titles: ◆ Supplement(s): V W Classic.
—CCC.
Published by: Delius Klasing Verlag GmbH, Siekerwall 21, Bielefeld, 33602, Germany. TEL 49-521-5590, FAX 49-521-559113, info@delius-klasing.de, http://www.delius-klasing.de. Ed. Joachim Fischer. Pub. Markus Gries. Adv. contact Marion Bertelmann. Circ: 74,273 (paid).

796.7 HRV ISSN 1331-2596
H A K. Text in Croatian. 1991. m. adv. **Document type:** *Magazine, Consumer.*
Published by: Hrvatski Auto-Klub, Draskoviceva 25, Zagreb, 10000, Croatia. TEL 385-1-4557949, FAX 385-1-4613040. Circ: 115,000 (controlled).

790.13 USA
HAGERTY'S; the voice of the car collector community. Text in English. 2006. q. adv. **Document type:** *Magazine, Consumer.* **Description:** Covers topics that surround the hobby: showing, buying, selling, running a business, appraising and repairing classic vehicles, offering insight from highly respected figures in the hobby.
Published by: Campbell - Ewald Publishing, 30400 Van Dyke, Warren, MI 48093-2316. TEL 586-558-5202, http://www.campbell-ewald.com/. Adv. contact Tom Krempel TEL 586-558-4502. color page USD 12,921; trim 8 x 10.5. Circ: 250,000 (paid).

388.3 DEU ISSN 0949-9288
HALLO TAXI; Das Magazin fuer Taxiunternehmer. Text in German. 1982. m. EUR 19; EUR 1.80 newsstand/cover (effective 2007). adv. **Document type:** *Magazine, Trade.*
Published by: Taxi-Fachverlag, Jakobistr 20, Bremen, 28195, Germany. TEL 49-421-170470, FAX 49-421-170473. Ed. Raimund Cassalette. adv.: B&W page EUR 4,994, color page EUR 7,904. Circ: 24,000 (paid and controlled).

HANDBOEK AUTO EN VERKEER. *see* TRAVEL AND TOURISM

THE HANSEN REPORT ON AUTOMOTIVE ELECTRONICS; a business and technology newsletter. *see* ENGINEERING

519 DEU ISSN 1860-5699
HANSER AUTOMOTIVE; electronics - systems. Text in German. 2002. 7/yr. EUR 86.70 domestic; EUR 93 foreign; EUR 15.20 newsstand/cover (effective 2011). adv. **Document type:** *Magazine, Trade.*
Formerly (until 2005): Automotive Electronics and Systems (1619-8190)
Published by: Carl Hanser Verlag GmbH & Co. KG, Kolbergerstr 22, Munich, 81679, Germany. TEL 49-89-998300, FAX 49-89-984809, info@hanser.de, http://www.hanser.de. Ed. Klaus Oertel. Adv. contact Lutz Benecke. Circ: 16,738 (paid and controlled).

HAWAII WESTWAYS. *see* TRAVEL AND TOURISM

629.286 USA
HEADLINER. Text in English. m. adv. **Document type:** *Magazine, Trade.* **Description:** Offers news and information about the collision repair industry to all licensed auto body repair shops in Connecticut.
Published by: Thomas Greco Publishing Co., 244 Chestnut St, Nutley, NJ 07110. TEL 973-667-6922, FAX 973-235-1963.

796.77 796.72 USA ISSN 1947-3761
TL255.2
HEAVY HITTERS; live large, floss daily. Abbreviated title: H H. Text in English. 2008. m. USD 5.99 per issue domestic; USD 7.99 per issue in Canada (effective 2009). adv. **Document type:** *Magazine, Consumer.* **Description:** Provides an insight into behind the scenes of the urban automotive lifestyle and the culture of "bling". Contains interviews, features, and photos chronicle this genre of younger, affluent consumers and the dynamic force behind the desire to stand out and showcase all the "toys" that money can buy.
—CCC.
Published by: Source Interlink Media, LLC, 261 Madison Ave, 6th Fl, New York, NY 10016. TEL 212-915-4000, FAX 212-915-4422. Ed. John Jarasa. Adv. contact Christina Ponce. color page USD 8,975.

388.3 USA ISSN 1550-8730
TL1
HEMMINGS CLASSIC CAR. Text in English. 2004. m. **Document type:** *Magazine, Consumer.* **Description:** Focuses on American-built collector cars and features all eras of autos, primarily post-war vehicles.
—CCC.
Published by: Hemmings Motor News, 222 Main Sr, Bennington, VT 05201. http://www.hemmings.com.

629.222 USA
HEMMINGS MOTOR NEWS. Text in English. 1954. m. USD 31.95 domestic; USD 56.14 in Canada; USD 98.95 in Mexico; USD 118.95 in Central America; USD 163.95 elsewhere (effective 2009). adv. back issues avail. **Document type:** *Magazine, Consumer.* **Description:** Provides automotive enthusiasts and historians with significant information on cars.
Related titles: Online - full text ed.: USD 12; USD 1 per issue (effective 2009).
Published by: Hemmings Publishing (Subsidiary of: American City Business Journals, Inc.), 222 Main St, PO Box 256, Bennington, VT 05201. TEL 802-442-3101, FAX 802-447-1561, hmnmail@hemmings.com, http://www.hemmings.com. Ed. Richard Lentinello. Pub. Jim Menneto. adv.: B&W page USD 4,305, color page USD 6,930; trim 8 x 10.75. **Subscr. to:** PO Box 100, Bennington, VT 05201. TEL 800-227-4373 ext 79550, FAX 802-447-9631.

HEMMINGS MUSCLE MACHINES. *see* SPORTS AND GAMES

HEMMINGS SPORTS & EXOTIC CAR. *see* SPORTS AND GAMES

629.22 AUS
HIGH PERFORMANCE IMPORTS. Abbreviated title: H P I. Text in English. 1997. 13/yr. AUD 77.51 domestic; AUD 159.50 in New Zealand; AUD 189.50 elsewhere; AUD 7.95 newsstand/cover (effective 2008). adv. back issues avail. **Document type:** *Magazine, Consumer.* **Description:** Offers technical features on modifications and feature articles on modified cars.
Related titles: Optical Disk - DVD ed.
Published by: Express Publications Pty. Ltd., 2-4 Stanley St, Locked Bag 111, Silverwater, NSW 2168, Australia. TEL 61-2-97413800, 800-801-647, FAX 61-2-97378017, subs@magstore.com.au, http://www.expresspublications.com.au. Ed. Jason Round. Adv. contact Chantal Capablanca TEL 61-2-97413835. **Subscr. to:** ISubscribe Pty Ltd., 25 Lime St, Ste 303, Level 3, Sydney, NSW 2000, Australia. TEL 61-2-92621722, FAX 61-2-92625044, info@isubscribe.com.au, http://www.isubscribe.com.au.

796.77 USA ISSN 0745-5941
HIGH-PERFORMANCE PONTIAC. Text in English. 1979. m. USD 24.97 domestic; USD 36.97 in Canada; USD 48.97 elsewhere (effective 2008). adv. back issues avail. **Document type:** *Magazine, Consumer.* **Description:** Covers today's high-tech, fuel-injected screamers to the massive muscle cars of the past, as well as restored and competition Pontiacs replete with histories, performance capabilities and technical highlights.
Formerly (until 198?): Thunder Am Magazine (0199-1957)
Indexed: A10, G06, G07, G08, I05, S23, V03.
—CCC.
Published by: Source Interlink Companies, 2570 E Cerritos Ave, Anaheim, CA 92806. TEL 714-941-1400, dheine@sourceinterlink.com, http://www.sourceinterlinkmedia.com. Ed. Tom DeMauro TEL 814-849-5254. Pubs. Jim Foos, Michael Essex TEL 813-675-3492. adv.: B&W page USD 4,900, color page USD 3,675; bleed 8.125 x 10.75. Circ: 28,713 (paid).

629.222 USA
HIGH - TECH PERFORMANCE. Text in English. 1995. bi-m. USD 16.95 domestic; USD 23.50 in Canada; USD 26 elsewhere (effective 2007). **Document type:** *Magazine, Consumer.* **Description:** Covers late-model American power cars. Features new technology, after-market modifications, performance tips, track coverage and how-to's.
Published by: Source Interlink Companies, 27500 Riverview Ctr Blvd, Bonita Springs, FL 34134. TEL 239-949-4450, edisupport@sourceinterlink.com, http://www.sourceinterlink.com. Ed. Richard Lentinello.

HIGHWAY LOSS DATA INSTITUTE. VEHICLE DESCRIPTIONS. *see* INSURANCE

HISTOCAR REVUE. *see* ANTIQUES

388.3 USA
HISTORIC MOTOR RACING. Text in English. 2000. bi-m. USD 48 domestic; CAD 68 in Canada; GBP 30 in United Kingdom; USD 8 newsstand/cover (effective 2001). adv. **Document type:** *Magazine, Consumer.* **Description:** Covers today's major historic car racing events as well as the histories of cars and drivers, both successful and failed.
Published by: H M R Publishing LLC, PO Box 63038, Grand Rapids, MI 49516. TEL 616-262-7834. Ed. Graham Gauld. Pub. Jos W Moch. **Dist. by:** International Publishers Direct, 27500 Riverview Center Blvd, Bonita Springs, FL 34134. TEL 858-320-4563, FAX 858-677-3220.

388.3 GBR ISSN 1472-2135
HISTORIC MOTOR RACING NEWS. Text in English. 1994. 11/yr. GBP 50 in Europe; GBP 55 elsewhere (effective 2009). bk.rev.; software rev.; Website rev. 20 p./no.; **Document type:** *Magazine, Consumer.* **Description:** Features informative articles on historic racing and rallying.
Published by: Historic Motor Racing News Ltd., 26-30 Old Church St, London, SW3 5BY, United Kingdom. TEL 44-20-73493193, FAX 44-20-73493160, contact@historicmotorracingnews.com.

HOLIDAY PARKS GUIDE. *see* TRAVEL AND TOURISM

HOME & AWAY (INDIANAPOLIS EDITION). *see* TRAVEL AND TOURISM

910.2 USA ISSN 2152-7377
HOME & AWAY (MIAMI COUNTY EDITION). Text in English. 1988. bi-m. free to members (effective 2010). adv. back issues avail. **Document type:** *Magazine, Trade.*
Former titles (until 2010): Journeys (1554-2114); (until 2005): A A A Today (1041-8229)
Related titles: Online - full text ed.
Published by: (American Automobile Association), H&A Media Group, PO Box 3535, Omaha, NE 68103. TEL 402-592-5000, FAX 402-331-5194. Ed. Gary Peterson. Pub., Adv. contact Terry Ausenbaugh.

HOME & AWAY (MINNEAPOLIS EDITION). *see* TRAVEL AND TOURISM

HOME & AWAY (NORTH DAKOTA EDITION). *see* TRAVEL AND TOURISM

629.222 USA
HONDA TUNING; sport compact car. Text in English. 1988. 9/yr. USD 14.95 domestic; USD 27.95 in Canada; USD 29.95 elsewhere (effective 2008). adv. 100 p./no.; back issues avail.; reprints avail. **Document type:** *Magazine, Consumer.* **Description:** Contains tech tips, dyno testing, new product evaluations and comprehensive how-to articles.
Indexed: V03.
Published by: Source Interlink Companies, 2400 E Katella Ave, Ste 700, Anaheim, CA 92806. TEL 714-939-2400, dheine@sourceinterlink.com, http://www.sourceinterlinkmedia.com. Ed. Aaron Bonk. adv.: B&W page USD 5,635, color page USD 6,885. Circ: 36,146 (paid).

388.342 GBR ISSN 1748-992X
HONG KONG AUTOS REPORT. Text in English. 2005. q. EUR 820, USD 1,030 combined subscription (print & email eds.) (effective 2010). **Document type:** *Report, Trade.* **Description:** Provides industry professionals and strategists, corporate analysts, auto associations, government departments and regulatory bodies with independent forecasts and competitive intelligence on the automotives industry in Hong Kong.
Related titles: E-mail ed.
Indexed: A15, ABIn, B02, B15, B17, B18, G04, I05, P48, P51, P52, PQC.

TU

Published by: Business Monitor International Ltd., Senator House, 85 Queen Victoria St, London, EC4V 4AB, United Kingdom. TEL 44-20-72480468, FAX 44-20-72480467, subs@businessmonitor.com.

629.2 AUS
HORIZONS (PERTH). Text in English. 1930. bi-m. free to members (effective 2009). adv. bk.rev. charts; illus. **Document type:** *Magazine, Consumer.* **Description:** Contains interesting articles on travel, motoring, home and finance.
Formerly (until 2007): Road Patrol (0810-8285)
Indexed: ARI.
Published by: Royal Automobile Club of Western Australia, PO Box C 140, Perth, W.A. 6839, Australia. TEL 61-8-94364471, FAX 61-8-94365030, fame@rac.com.au, http://www.rac.com.au. Eds. Margaret Rafferty, Susan Bell. Adv. contact Lindsay Every. **Co-sponsor:** R.A.C. Insurance Pty. Ltd.

HORSELESS CARRIAGE GAZETTE. *see* ANTIQUES

796.77 AUS
HOT 4S & PERFORMANCE CARS. Text in English. 1991. 14/yr. AUD 83.48 domestic; AUD 93.98 in New Zealand; AUD 7.95 newsstand/cover (effective 2008). adv. back issues avail. **Document type:** *Magazine, Consumer.* **Description:** Provides latest industry trends, news and products, high-performance contemporary road and racecars and technical informations about cars.
Formerly (until 1994): Hot 4s & Wild Rotaries (1037-2415)
Related titles: Optical Disk - DVD ed.
Published by: Express Publications Pty. Ltd., 2-4 Stanley St, Locked Bag 111, Silverwater, NSW 2168, Australia. TEL 61-2-97413800, 800-801-647, FAX 61-2-97378017, subs@magstore.com.au, http://www.expresspublications.com.au. Circ: 40,000 (paid and controlled). **Subscr. to:** ISubscribe Pty Ltd., 25 Lime St, Ste 303, Level 3, Sydney, NSW 2000, Australia. TEL 61-2-92621722, FAX 61-2-92625044, info@isubscribe.com.au, http://www.isubscribe.com.au.

796.72 USA ISSN 0018-6031
TL236
HOT ROD. Text in English. 1948. m. USD 14 domestic; USD 26 in Canada; USD 38 elsewhere (effective 2009). adv. bk.rev.; music rev.; tel.rev.; Website rev. charts; illus. 150 p./no.; back issues avail.; reprints avail. **Document type:** *Magazine, Consumer.* **Description:** Covers the gamut of hot rodding with an unrivaled mix of technical information, industry commentary, and new trends.
Formerly (until 1953): Hot Rod Magazine
Related titles: Microform ed.: (from PQC); Online - full text ed.: USD 7 (effective 2009).
Indexed: A11, A22, A25, ARG, B04, BRD, C03, C05, CBCARef, CPerI, ConsI, G05, G06, G07, G08, G09, I05, I06, I07, JHMA, M01, M02, M04, MASUSE, MagInd, P02, P10, P16, P48, P52, P53, P54, PMR, PQC, R03, R04, R06, RGAb, RGPR, S08, S09, S23, SPI, T02, TOM, W03.
—Ingenta. **CCC.**
Published by: Source Interlink Companies, 6420 Wilshire Blvd, 10th Fl, Los Angeles, CA 90048. TEL 323-782-2000, FAX 323-782-2223, edisupport@sourceinterlink.com, http://www.sourceinterlink.com. Ed. Rob Kinnan. Pub. Jerry Pitt TEL 323-782-2612. Adv. contact Bruce Miller TEL 313-967-5125. B&W page USD 56,830, color page USD 92,020; trim 7.625 x 10.5. Circ: 675,535. **Subscr. to:** PO Box 420235, Palm Coast, FL 32142. TEL 800-800-4681.

HOT WHEELS DERGI. *see* CHILDREN AND YOUTH—For

796.72 USA ISSN 1936-4962
HOTROD & RESTORATION. Text in English. 1998. m. free in US & Canada to qualified personnel; USD 80 elsewhere (effective 2008). adv. **Document type:** *Magazine, Consumer.* **Description:** Features business strategies, tradeshow and product information for hot rod and restoration industry professionals.
Published by: Bobit Business Media, 3520 Challenger St, Torrance, CA 90503. TEL 310-533-2400, FAX 310-533-2500, order@bobit.com, http://www.bobit.com. Pub. Debbie Lewis. adv.: page USD 2,020. Circ: 12,000 (controlled).

388.3 USA
HOW TO CODE AND MANAGE GM BODY SHOP CLAIMS. Text in English. 19??. a. **Document type:** *Handbook/Manual/Guide, Trade.*
Published by: W D & S Publishing, 10 W 7th St, 1st Fl, PO Box 606, Barnegat Light, NJ 08006. TEL 800-321-5312, http://www.dealersedge.com. Pub. Jim Muntz.

388.342 GBR ISSN 1748-9938
HUNGARY AUTOS REPORT. Text in English. 2005. q. EUR 820, USD 1,030 combined subscription (print & email eds.) (effective 2010). **Document type:** *Report, Trade.* **Description:** Provides industry professionals and strategists, corporate analysts, auto associations, government departments and regulatory bodies with independent forecasts and competitive intelligence on the automotives industry in Hungary.
Related titles: E-mail ed.
Indexed: A15, ABIn, B02, B15, B17, B18, G04, I05, P48, P51, P52, PQC.
Published by: Business Monitor International Ltd., Senator House, 85 Queen Victoria St, London, EC4V 4AB, United Kingdom. TEL 44-20-72480468, FAX 44-20-72480467, subs@businessmonitor.com.

629.222 USA ISSN 1548-7997
CODEN: EVEPEO
HYBRID & ELECTRIC VEHICLE PROGRESS; industry news and technical developments in elctric, hybrid and fuel cell vehicles. Text in English. 1979. s-m. USD 590 combined subscription domestic (print & online eds.); USD 640 combined subscription foreign (print & online eds.) (effective 2008). bk.rev. charts; illus. 8 p./no.; back issues avail.; reprints avail. **Document type:** *Newsletter, Trade.* **Description:** Provides in-depth news, data and information on worldwide electric vehicle commercialization with articles on new vehicles, research and development, demonstration projects, business and government and project developments.
Formerly: Electric Vehicle Progress (0190-4175)
Related titles: Online - full text ed.: USD 495 (effective 2008).
Indexed: Cadscan, LeadAb, Zincscan.
Published by: Alexander Communications Group, Inc., 712 Main St, Ste 187B, Boonton, NJ 07005. TEL 973-265-2300, FAX 973-402-6056, info@alexcommgrp.com, http://www.alexcommgrp.com. Eds. Don Saxman, Layne Holley. Pub. David Nydam.

HYDROGEN FORECAST. *see* ENERGY

I A D A SERVICE DIRECTORY. *see* INSURANCE

614.86 388 JPN ISSN 0386-1112
HE5601
➤ **I A T S S RESEARCH.** Text in English. 1977. s-a. USD 66 (effective 2003). stat.; tr.lit.; abstr. back issues avail. **Document type:** *Journal, Academic/Scholarly.* **Description:** For administrators, policy-makers, and scientists on traffic and its safety.
Related titles: Online - full content ed.; Online - full text ed.: ISSN 2210-4240 (from ScienceDirect).
Indexed: EIP, HRIS, JTA, SCOPUS, T02.
—BLDSC (4359.577000), IE, Ingenta. **CCC.**
Published by: International Association of Traffic and Safety Sciences, 6-20 Yaesu 2-chome, Chuo-ku, Tokyo, 104-0028, Japan. TEL 81-3-3273-7884, FAX 81-3-3272-7054, iatss@db3.so-net.ne.jp, http://wwwsoc.nii.ac.jp/iatss/. Pub. Hiroshi Ishizuki. Circ: 1,100.

629.286 330 USA
I C A UPDATE (CHICAGO). Text in English. m.
Formerly: I C A Letter
Published by: International Carwash Association, 401 N Michigan Ave, Chicago, IL 60611-4212. TEL 708-495-0144. Ed. Tina Gonsalves. Pub. Bob Paisner.

388.3 GBR
I C M E MANUAL FOR CARS; repair times, service times, intervals and operations. (Institute of Consulting Motor Engineers) Text in English. 1932. a. adv. **Document type:** *Handbook/Manual/Guide, Trade.* **Description:** Data covers 49 manufacturers and over 19,000 models for vehicles produced from 1978 onwards.
Published by: Glass's Information Services Ltd., 1 Princes Rd, Weybridge, Surrey KT13 9TU, United Kingdom. TEL 44-1932-823823, FAX 44-1932-846564, customer@glass.co.uk, http://www.glass.co.uk.

388 GBR
I C M E MANUAL FOR HEAVY GOODS VEHICLES. (Institute of Consulting Motor Engineers) Text in English. 1989. a. adv. **Document type:** *Handbook/Manual/Guide, Trade.* **Description:** Covers vehicles from 3.5 to 38 tonnes GVW - chassis, engines and derivatives included. Both rigid and tractor versions included.
Published by: Glass's Information Services Ltd., 1 Princes Rd, Weybridge, Surrey KT13 9TU, United Kingdom. TEL 44-1932-823823, FAX 44-1932-846564, customer@glass.co.uk, http://www.glass.co.uk.

388 GBR
I C M E MANUAL FOR LIGHT COMMERCIAL VEHICLES. (Institute of Consulting Motor Engineers) Text in English. 1989. a. adv. **Document type:** *Handbook/Manual/Guide, Trade.* **Description:** Covers car-derived vans and other light commercial vehicles up to 3.5 tonnes GVW.
Formerly (until 2004): I C M E Manual: Manufacturers' Service Schedules and Repair Times
Published by: Glass's Information Services Ltd., 1 Princes Rd, Weybridge, Surrey KT13 9TU, United Kingdom. TEL 44-1932-823823, FAX 44-1932-846564, customer@glass.co.uk, http://www.glass.co.uk.

629.2 USA ISSN 1550-2252
TK6570.M6
I E E E V T S VEHICULAR TECHNOLOGY CONFERENCE. PROCEEDINGS. (Institute of Electrical and Electronics Engineers Vehicular Technology Society) Text in English. 19??. s-a. adv. illus. reprints avail. **Document type:** *Proceedings, Trade.*
Former titles (until 1999): I E E E Vehicular Technology Conference. Papers (1090-3038); (until 1993): I E E E Vehicular Technology Conference. Proceedings (1069-6377); (until 1992): I E E E Vehicular Technology Conference. Papers (1042-4369); (until 1984): I E E E Vehicular Technology Conference. Conference Record of Papers Presented (1550-2279); (until 1981): I E E E Vehicular Technology Society. Annual Conference. Proceedings (1042-458X); (until 1980): I E E E Vehicular Technology Conference. Conference Record of Papers Presented at the Annual Conference (0739-5140); (until 1978): I E E E Vehicular Technology Conference. Annual Conference. Conference Record (0740-0551); (until 1975): I E E E Vehicular Technology Conference. Record (0098-3551)
Related titles: CD-ROM ed.; Microfiche ed.; Online - full text ed.
Indexed: EngInd, SCOPUS.
—IE, Ingenta. **CCC.**
Published by: I E E E, 445 Hoes Ln, Piscataway, NJ 08854. TEL 732-981-0060, 800-678-4333, FAX 732-562-6380, customer.service@ieee.org, http://www.ieee.org.

796.77 AUS ISSN 1834-0717
IGNITION MAGAZINE. Text in English. 2006. bi-m. **Document type:** *Magazine, Consumer.*
Published by: Ozworld Marketing, PO Box 21, Gisborne, VIC 3437, Australia. FAX 61-3-5428-1123, 321ignition@austarnet.com.au, http://www.ignitionmagazine.com.

388.3 ITA
ILLUSTRATOFIAT. Text in Italian. 1952. m. adv. bk.rev. illus. **Document type:** *Magazine, Consumer.*
Published by: Fiat, Corso Guglielmo Marconi, 10, Turin, TO 10125, Italy. http://www.fiat.com. Circ: 245,000.

346 614.86 USA ISSN 0162-4989
KF1297.A8
IMPACT (WASHINGTON, 1975). Text in English. 1975. bi-m. USD 100; USD 125 foreign (effective 2000). bk.rev. illus. index. back issues avail.; reprints avail. **Document type:** *Newsletter, Consumer.* **Description:** Reports on the auto safety work of CAS. Covers safety legislation, auto defects, lemon laws, recalls and federal and state investigations.
Published by: Center for Auto Safety, 1825 Connecticut Ave N W Ste 330, Washington, DC 20009. TEL 202-328-7700, http://www.autosafety.org, http://www.essential.org/cas. Ed. Debra Barclay. Circ: 1,000 (paid).

614.86 340 USA ISSN 1091-4684
HE5620.D72
IMPAIRED DRIVING UPDATE. Abbreviated title: I D U. Variant title: Impaired Driving. Text in English. 1996. q. USD 179.95 domestic; USD 194.95 in Canada; USD 209.95 elsewhere (effective 2008). back issues avail. **Document type:** *Newsletter, Trade.* **Description:** Designed to help professionals engaged in the fight against drunk driving stay current with the programs, policies, technologies and practices for treatment, prevention, enforcement and education.
—**CCC.**
Published by: Civic Research Insitute, 4478 US Rte 27, PO Box 585, Kingston, NJ 08528. TEL 609-683-4450, FAX 609-683-7291, order@civicresearchinstitute.com. Ed. Denis Foley.

629.286 USA ISSN 0199-4468
IMPORT AUTOMOTIVE PARTS & ACCESORIES. Text in English. 1979. m. USD 45 (effective 2000). adv. **Document type:** *Journal, Trade.*
Published by: Meyers Publishing Corp., 799 Camarillo Springs Rd., Camarillo, CA 93012-8111. TEL 818-785-3900, FAX 818-785-4397. Ed. Steve Releya. Pub. Len Meyers. R&P Elyse Wilson. Adv. contact Lana Meyers. Circ: 35,000 (controlled).

796.77 USA ISSN 1528-0845
IMPORT TUNER. Text in English. 1998. m. USD 14.97 domestic; USD 27.97 in Canada; USD 29.97 elsewhere (effective 2008). adv. back issues avail. **Document type:** *Magazine, Consumer.* **Description:** Provides information on cars and various shows, as well as features articles that detail how to select, purchase and install aftermarket parts and accessories.
Related titles: Online - full text ed.: USD 7.50 (effective 2008).
Indexed: A10, G06, G07, G08, I05, S23, V03.
—**CCC.**
Published by: Source Interlink Companies, 2400 E Katella Ave, Ste 700, Anaheim, CA 92806. TEL 714-939-2400, dheine@sourceinterlink.com, http://www.sourceinterlinkmedia.com. Ed. Carter Jung. adv.: B&W page USD 5,785, color page USD 7,070. Circ: 70,160 (paid).

629.28 USA ISSN 1069-4714
TL159
IMPORTCAR; the complete import service magazine. Text in English. 1979. m. free domestic to qualified personnel (effective 2009). adv. charts; illus.; stat.; tr.lit. back issues avail. **Document type:** *Magazine, Trade.* **Description:** Provides direct reach into import specialist repair shops with targeted underhood and undercar technical features that help readers make profitable and professional import vehicle repairs.
Former titles (until 1993): ImportCar and Truck (1040-5267); (until 1988): ImportCar (0735-7877); (until 1982): Babcox's ImportCar (0278-6532); (until 1980): ImportCar (0271-6712); (until 1979): Babcox's ImportCar (0194-2492)
Related titles: Online - full text ed.; Supplement(s): Automotive Aftermarket Training Guide.
Indexed: A26, B02, B15, B17, B18, G04, G08, I05.
Published by: Babcox Publications, Inc., 3550 Embassy Pky, Akron, OH 44333. TEL 330-670-1234, FAX 330-670-0874, bbabcox@babcox.com, http://www.babcox.com. Ed. Mary DellaValle. Pub. Jeff Stankard TEL 330-670-1234 ext 282. adv.: B&W page USD 4,895. Circ: 29,310 (paid).

629.283 USA
IN MOTION (NORTHBROOK); the guide to safe driving. Text in English. 1977. a. adv. illus. **Document type:** *Magazine, Consumer.* **Description:** Publishes articles on safety, driving skills, maintenance.
Former titles (until 1986): New Driver (0279-6384); (until 19??): Scholastic Wheels (0161-2727)
Published by: (General Motors), General Learning Communications, 900 Skokie Blvd, Ste 200, Northbrook, IL 60062. TEL 847-205-3000, 800-641-3912, FAX 847-564-8197, jcimba@glcomm.com, http://www.glcomm.com.

629.2 CAN ISSN 0702-5785
IN THE DRIVER'S SEAT. Text in English. m. free. **Document type:** *Newsletter, Government.*
Published by: Access Toronto, Toronto City Hall, 100 Queen St. West, Main Floor, Toronto, ON M5H 2N2, Canada. TEL 416-392-7410, FAX 416-338-0685, http://www.toronto.ca/publications. Circ: (controlled).

388.342 GBR ISSN 1748-9946
INDIA AUTOS REPORT. Text in English. 2005. q. EUR 820, USD 1,030 combined subscription (print & email eds.) (effective 2010). **Document type:** *Report, Trade.* **Description:** Provides industry professionals and strategists, corporate analysts, auto associations, government departments and regulatory bodies with independent forecasts and competitive intelligence on the automotives industry in India.
Related titles: E-mail ed.
Indexed: A15, ABIn, B02, B15, B17, B18, G04, I05, P48, P51, P52, PQC.
Published by: Business Monitor International Ltd., Senator House, 85 Queen Victoria St, London, EC4V 4AB, United Kingdom. TEL 44-20-72480468, FAX 44-20-72480467, subs@businessmonitor.com.

388.342 GBR ISSN 1748-9954
INDONESIA AUTOS REPORT. Text in English. 2005. q. EUR 820, USD 1,030 combined subscription (print & email eds.) (effective 2010). **Document type:** *Report, Trade.* **Description:** Provides industry professionals and strategists, corporate analysts, auto associations, government departments and regulatory bodies with independent forecasts and competitive intelligence on the automotives industry in Indonesia.
Related titles: E-mail ed.
Indexed: A15, ABIn, B02, B15, B17, B18, G04, I05, P48, P51, P52, PQC.
Published by: Business Monitor International Ltd., Senator House, 85 Queen Victoria St, London, EC4V 4AB, United Kingdom. TEL 44-20-72480468, FAX 44-20-72480467, subs@businessmonitor.com.

388 MEX ISSN 0187-4861
HD9710.M42
INDUSTRIA AUTOMOTRIZ EN MEXICO. Text in Spanish. 1981. a. MXN 53 (effective 1999).
Published by: Instituto Nacional de Estadistica, Geografia e Informatica, Secretaria de Programacion y Presupuesto, Prol. Heroe de Nacozari 2301 Sur, Puerta 11, Acceso, Aguascalientes, 20270, Mexico. TEL 52-4-918-1948, FAX 52-4-918-0739. Circ: 2,000.

796.77 USA
INDYCAR SERIES; the ultimate open wheel magazine. Text in English. bi-m. USD 15.95; USD 4.99 newsstand/cover (effective 2007). adv. **Document type:** *Magazine, Consumer.* **Description:** Provides an insider's perspective on the FedEx Championship Series.
Formerly (until 2003): Champ Car
Published by: Haymarket Worldwide Inc. (Subsidiary of: Haymarket Media Inc.), 16842 Von Karman Ave, Ste 125, Irvine, CA 92606. TEL 949-417-6700, FAX 949-417-6116. Pub. Ian Howard. Adv. contact Raelyn Powell.

629.2 ITA
TL4 CODEN: AIAUEK
INGEGNERIA DELL'AUTOVEICOLO. Text in English, Italian. 1948. bi-m. EUR 60 domestic; EUR 90 foreign (effective 2008). adv. bk.rev. abstr.; bibl.; charts; illus.; pat. index. **Document type:** *Magazine, Trade.*
Formerly (until 2003): A T A Ingegneria Automotoristica (0001-2661)
Indexed: A22, ApMecR.
—IE, Ingenta, INIST.
Published by: Associazione Tecnica dell'Automobile (A T A), Strada Torino 32 A, Orbassano, TO 10043, Italy. TEL 39-011-9032364, FAX 39-011-9080400, http://www.ata.it. Circ: 3,000.

629.2 FRA ISSN 0020-1200
TL2I5
INGENIEURS DE L'AUTOMOBILE. Text in French, English. 1927. 6/yr. EUR 130 domestic; EUR 149 in Europe; EUR 167 elsewhere (effective 2009). adv. bk.rev. abstr.; illus. 100 p./no.; **Document type:** *Magazine, Corporate.* **Description:** Overviews of scientific advances in the automobile industry.
Indexed: A22, A28, APA, BrCerAb, C&ISA, CA/WCA, CIA, CISA, CerAb, CivEngAb, CorrAb, E&CAJ, E11, EEA, EMA, H15, M&TEA, M09, MBF, METADEX, RefZh, SCOPUS, SolStAb, T04, WAA.
—IE, Infotrieve, INIST, Linda Hall. **CCC.**
Published by: (Societe des Ingenieurs de l'Automobile), Editions V B, 7 Rue Jean Mermoz, Versailles, 78000, France. TEL 33-1-39208805, FAX 33-1-39208806, vblcda@lcda.fr. Ed. Eric Bigourdan. Adv. contact Patricia Hernandez. Circ: 8,500.

INJURY, COLLISION AND THEFT LOSSES. *see* PUBLIC HEALTH AND SAFETY

796.77 USA ISSN 2154-5596
▼ **INLAND EMPIRE AUTOMOTIVE MAGAZINE**; the automotive voice of the inland empire. Variant title: IEAM. Text in English. 2009. m. free (effective 2010). adv. back issues avail. **Document type:** *Magazine, Trade.* **Description:** Provides articles, news, reviews, product and technical information on a variety of automotive-related topics.
Related titles: Online - full text ed.
Published by: Chris Sawyer, Ed. & Pub., 5198 Arlington Ave, Ste 617, Riverside, CA 92504. TEL 951-565-3435, FAX 951-354-5638, info@ieautomag.com. Ed., Pub. Chris Sawyer. Adv. contact Curt Rigney.

621 GBR ISSN 0954-4070
TJ1 CODEN: PMDEEA
➤ **INSTITUTION OF MECHANICAL ENGINEERS. PROCEEDINGS. PART D: JOURNAL OF AUTOMOBILE ENGINEERING.** Text in English. 1984. m. USD 3,726 combined subscription in North America to institutions (print & online eds.); GBP 2,017 combined subscription elsewhere to institutions (print & online eds.) (effective 2011). stat.; bibl.; illus. index, cum.index. back issues avail.; reprint service avail. from PSC. **Document type:** *Journal, Academic/Scholarly.* **Description:** Provides a forum for those involved in research, design, development, manufacture, operation, servicing and repair of cars, commercial vehicles, public service vehicles, off-highway vehicles and industrial and agricultural tractors throughout the world.
Supersedes in part (in 1989): Institution of Mechanical Engineers. Proceedings. Part D: Transport Engineering (0265-1904); Which superseded in part (1847-1982): Institution of Mechanical Engineers. Proceedings (0020-3483)
Related titles: Online - full text ed.: ISSN 2041-2991. USD 3,357 in North America to institutions; GBP 1,817 elsewhere to institutions (effective 2011); ♦ Series: Institution of Mechanical Engineers. Proceedings.
Indexed: A01, A03, A05, A08, A22, A28, APA, AS&TA, AS&TI, ASCA, AcoustA, ApMecR, B01, B06, B07, B09, B21, BCIRA, BMT, BrCerAb, BrRB, BrTechI, C&ISA, C10, CA, CA/WCA, CIA, CPEI, CerAb, ChemAb, CivEngAb, CorrAb, CurCont, E&CAJ, E01, E11, EEA, EMA, ESPM, EngInd, EnvEAb, FLUIDEX, H&SSA, H15, HRIS, ISMEC, ISR, Inspec, M&TEA, M09, MBF, METADEX, MathR, P26, P48, P52, P54, PQC, PollutAb, S01, SCI, SCOPUS, SolStAb, T02, T04, TM, W07, WAA.
—BLDSC (6724.900770), AskIEEE, IE, Infotrieve, Ingenta, INIST, Linda Hall. **CCC.**
Published by: (Institution of Mechanical Engineers), Sage Publications Ltd. (Subsidiary of: Sage Publications, Inc.), 1 Oliver's Yard, 55 City Rd, London, EC1Y 1SP, United Kingdom. TEL 44-20-73248500, FAX 44-20-73248600, info@sagepub.co.uk, http://www.uk.sagepub.com/home.nav.

➤ **INSURANCE INJURY REPORT PASSENGER CARS, CARGO VANS, PICKUPS, AND UTILITY VEHICLES.** *see* INSURANCE

➤ **INSURANCE SPECIAL REPORT: VARIOUS TOPICS.** *see* INSURANCE

➤ **INSURANCE THEFT REPORT PASSENGER CARS, CARGO VANS, PICKUPS AND UTILITY VEHICLES.** *see* INSURANCE

388.3 ITA ISSN 1970-6243
INTERAUTONEWS. Text in Italian. 1988. m. (11/yr.). EUR 75 (effective 2008). **Document type:** *Magazine, Consumer.*
Related titles: ♦ Supplement(s): InterTruckNews. ISSN 1970-6251; InterAuto Fleet & Mobility. ISSN 1970-6235. 2005; InterAutoNews Data Book. ISSN 1970-626X. 1991. EUR 50 (effective 2007).
Published by: Press Multi Service (P M S), Via Ermete Novelli 11, Rome, 00197, Italy.

INTERIORMOTIVES. *see* INTERIOR DESIGN AND DECORATION

INTERNATIONAL AUTO STATISTICS. *see* TRANSPORTATION—Abstracting, Bibliographies, Statistics

629.286 USA ISSN 1557-7104
INTERNATIONAL AUTOMOTIVE BODY CONGRESS. PROCEEDINGS. Text in English. a. **Document type:** *Proceedings, Trade.*
Published by: International Automotive Body Congress, 166 South Industrial, Saline, MI 48176. TEL 734-944-5850, FAX 734-944-5840, info@bodycongress.org, http://www.bodycongress.org.

629.286 USA
INTERNATIONAL CONFERENCE ON VEHICLE STRUCTURAL MECHANICS. PROCEEDINGS. Text in English. 1974. irreg. **Document type:** *Proceedings.*
Published by: S A E Inc., 400 Commonwealth Dr, Warrendale, PA 15096. TEL 724-776-4841, 877-606-7323, FAX 724-776-0790, CustomerService@sae.org, http://www.sae.org.

THE INTERNATIONAL DIRECTORY OF AUTOMOTIVE EQUIPMENT, PARTS AND ACCESSORIES IMPORTERS. *see* BUSINESS AND ECONOMICS—Trade And Industrial Directories

THE INTERNATIONAL DIRECTORY OF TIRES AND TUBES IMPORTERS. *see* BUSINESS AND ECONOMICS—Trade And Industrial Directories

388.3 DEU ISSN 1229-9138
TL158
➤ **INTERNATIONAL JOURNAL OF AUTOMOTIVE TECHNOLOGY.** Text in English. 2000. bi-m. EUR 979, USD 1,312 combined subscription to institutions (print & online eds.) (effective 2012). reprint service avail. from PSC. **Document type:** *Journal, Academic/Scholarly.* **Description:** Covers original research in all fields of automotive technology, science and engineering.
Related titles: Online - full text ed.: ISSN 1976-3832.
Indexed: A12, A17, A22, A26, ABIn, CPEI, CurCont, E01, E08, P26, P48, P51, P53, P54, PQC, S09, SCI, SCOPUS, W07.
—BLDSC (4542.125100), IE. **CCC.**
Published by: (Korea Society of Automotive Engineers KOR), Springer (Subsidiary of: Springer Science+Business Media), Tiergartenstr 17, Heidelberg, 69121, Germany. TEL 49-6221-4870, FAX 49-6221-345229, subscriptions@springer.com. Eds. H C Wolf, J Wolters, Paul T Welfens.

629.286 GBR ISSN 1470-9511
HD9710.A1 CODEN: IJATB7
➤ **INTERNATIONAL JOURNAL OF AUTOMOTIVE TECHNOLOGY AND MANAGEMENT.** Abbreviated title: I J A T M. Text in English. 2001. 4/yr. EUR 494 to institutions (print or online ed.); EUR 672 combined subscription to institutions (print & online eds.) (effective 2012). abstr.; bibl.; charts; illus.; stat. back issues avail.; reprints avail. **Document type:** *Journal, Academic/Scholarly.* **Description:** Provides a source of information in the field of automotive technology, automotive management, and related disciplines.
Related titles: Online - full text ed.: ISSN 1741-5012 (from IngentaConnect).
Indexed: A12, A17, A26, A28, ABIn, APA, B01, B02, B06, B07, B09, B15, B17, B18, BrCerAb, C&ISA, CA, CA/WCA, CIA, CPEI, CerAb, CivEngAb, CorrAb, E&CAJ, E08, E11, EEA, EMA, ESPM, EngInd, EnvEAb, ErgAb, G04, G08, H15, I05, Inspec, M&TEA, M09, MBF, METADEX, P48, P51, P53, P54, PQC, RiskAb, S09, SCOPUS, SolStAb, T02, T04, WAA.
—BLDSC (4542.125250), IE, Ingenta, INIST, Linda Hall. **CCC.**
Published by: Inderscience Publishers, PO Box 735, Olney, Bucks MK46 5WB, United Kingdom. TEL 44-1234-240519, FAX 44-1234-240515, editorial@inderscience.com. Eds. Dr. Giuseppe Giulio Calabrese, Jean-Jacques Chanaron. **Subscr. to:** World Trade Centre Bldg, 29 Rte de Pre-Bois, Case Postale 856, Geneva 15 1215, Switzerland. FAX 41-22-7910885, subs@inderscience.com.

➤ **INTERNATIONAL JOURNAL OF ELECTRIC AND HYBRID VEHICLES.** *see* ENERGY—Electrical Energy

▼ ➤ **INTERNATIONAL JOURNAL OF RENEWABLE ENERGY VEHICLES.** *see* ANTIQUES

388.3 GBR ISSN 1745-3194
▼ ➤ **INTERNATIONAL JOURNAL OF VEHICLE PERFORMANCE.** Text in English. forthcoming 2011. 4/yr. EUR 494 to institutions (print or online ed.); EUR 672 combined subscription to institutions (print & online eds.) (effective 2012). **Document type:** *Journal, Academic/Scholarly.*
Related titles: Online - full text ed.: ISSN 1745-3208. forthcoming.
—CCC.
Published by: Inderscience Publishers, PO Box 735, Olney, Bucks MK46 5WB, United Kingdom. TEL 44-1234-240519, FAX 44-1234-240515, editorial@inderscience.com. **Subscr. to:** World Trade Centre Bldg, 29 Rte de Pre-Bois, Case Postale 856, Geneva 15 1215, Switzerland. FAX 41-22-7910885, subs@inderscience.com.

388.3 GBR ISSN 1745-6436
➤ **INTERNATIONAL JOURNAL OF VEHICLE SYSTEMS MODELLING AND TESTING.** Text in English. 2005. 4/yr. EUR 494 to institutions (print or online ed.); EUR 672 combined subscription to institutions (print & online eds.) (effective 2012). bk.rev. illus.; charts; abstr.; bibl. **Document type:** *Journal, Academic/Scholarly.* **Description:** Provides a resource of information for the scientific and engineering community working with ground vehicles. Emphases are placed on novel computational and testing techniques that are used by automotive engineers and scientists.
Related titles: Online - full text ed.: ISSN 1745-6444 (from IngentaConnect).
Indexed: A26, A28, APA, B21, BrCerAb, C&ISA, CA/WCA, CIA, CPEI, CerAb, CivEngAb, CorrAb, E&CAJ, E08, E11, EEA, EMA, ESPM, EnvEAb, G08, H&SSA, H15, I05, Inspec, M&TEA, M09, MBF, METADEX, S09, SCOPUS, SSciA, SolStAb, T04, WAA.
—BLDSC (4542.697707), IE, Ingenta, INIST, Linda Hall. **CCC.**
Published by: (International Association for Vehicle Design CHE), Inderscience Publishers, PO Box 735, Olney, Bucks MK46 5WB, United Kingdom. TEL 44-1234-240519, FAX 44-1234-240515, editorial@inderscience.com. Ed. Dr. Johan P Wideberg. **Subscr. to:** World Trade Centre Bldg, 29 Rte de Pre-Bois, Case Postale 856, Geneva 15 1215, Switzerland. FAX 41-22-7910885, subs@inderscience.com.

➤ **INTERNATIONAL JOURNAL OF VEHICULAR TECHNOLOGY.** *see* ENGINEERING—Mechanical Engineering

796.77 GBR ISSN 1473-7620
INTERSECTION; on the road, at sea and in the air. Text in English. 2002. s-a. GBP 9.99 domestic; GBP 25 in Europe; GBP 45 elsewhere (effective 2009). back issues avail. **Document type:** *Magazine, Consumer.*
Published by: Intersection Magazine, 116 Old St, London, EC1V 9BG, United Kingdom. TEL 44-207-6081166, FAX 44-207-6081090. **Subscr. to:** Studio 9, 49-59 Old St, London EC1V 9HX, United Kingdom.

INTERSTANDOX; information for the world of the car repair painter. *see* PAINTS AND PROTECTIVE COATINGS

INTERSTANDOX EXTRA. *see* PAINTS AND PROTECTIVE COATINGS

629.2 IND
➤ **INVENTI RAPID AUTO.** Text in English. q. INR 1,000 domestic; USD 20 foreign (effective 2011). adv. abstr. a. index. back issues avail.; reprints avail. **Document type:** *Journal, Academic/Scholarly.* **Description:** Publishes research reports, review articles and scientific commentaries on automobile engineering.
Media: Online - full text.
Published by: Inventi Journals Pvt. Ltd., SDX 33, Minal Residency, JK Rd, Bhopal, Madhya Pradesh 462 023, India. TEL 91-9425536487, FAX 91-11-66173705, info@inventi.in, editor@inventi.in, http://www.inventi.in. Ed. Dr. Tarun Kant. Pub. V B Gupta. R&P Emmanuel Toppo. Circ: 50.

388.473 GBR ISSN 1748-9962
IRAN AUTOS REPORT. Text in English. 2005. q. EUR 820, USD 1,030 combined subscription (print & email eds.) (effective 2010). **Document type:** *Report, Trade.* **Description:** Provides industry professionals and strategists, corporate analysts, auto associations, government departments and regulatory bodies with independent forecasts and competitive intelligence on the Iranian automotives market.
Related titles: E-mail ed.
Indexed: A15, ABIn, B02, B15, B17, B18, G04, I05, P48, P51, P52, PQC.
Published by: Business Monitor International Ltd., Senator House, 85 Queen Victoria St, London, EC4V 4AB, United Kingdom. TEL 44-20-72480468, FAX 44-20-72480467, subs@businessmonitor.com.

388.3 IRL ISSN 1649-6353
IRELAND'S MOTOR TRADER. Text in English. 2002. bi-w. EUR 2.50 newsstand/cover (effective 2006). adv.
Formerly (until 2004): The Motor-Trader (1649-2072)
Published by: Motor Trader, Box 338, Naas, Co. Kildare, Ireland. TEL 353-45-893343, FAX 353-45-893342, info@motortrader.ie, http://www.motortrader.ie/. adv.: color page EUR 2,195; trim 260 x 340. Circ: 25,000.

388.34 IRL ISSN 1649-668X
IRELAND'S USED CAR PRICE GUIDE. Text in English. 2005. m. EUR 35 (effective 2006).
Published by: Car Buyers Guide, Penthouse Fl, Arena House, Arena Rd, Sandyford Industrial Estate, Dublin, 18, Ireland. TEL 353-1-2405555, info@cbg.ie, http://www.cbg.ie.

629.2 IRL ISSN 1393-5011
IRISH 4 X 4 & OFF ROAD. Text in English. 1997. q. adv. **Document type:** *Magazine, Consumer.*
Published by: I M P Ltd., Riverview House, Barrett St., Ballina, Co. Mayo, Ireland. TEL 353-96-70941, FAX 353-96-73167. adv.: page EUR 2,158; 206 x 297. Circ: 12,000 (paid and controlled).

796.7 IRL ISSN 0791-4792
IRISH CAR. Text in English. 1990. m. adv. **Document type:** *Magazine, Consumer.*
Published by: I M P Ltd., Riverview House, Barrett St., Ballina, Co. Mayo, Ireland. TEL 353-96-70941, FAX 353-96-73167. adv.: page EUR 2,158; trim 206 x 297. Circ: 15,000 (paid and controlled).

388.3 IRL ISSN 1649-976X
IRISH MOTOR MANAGEMENT. Text in English. 1968. bi-m. adv. bk.rev. **Document type:** *Magazine, Trade.* **Description:** Provides in-depth news and features relevant to managerial level readers within the Irish motor industry.
Formerly (until 2003): Irish Motor Industry (0790-0317)
Indexed: B01, B07, T02.
Published by: (Society of the Irish Motor Industry), I F P Media, 31 Deansgrange Rd., Blackrock, Co. Dublin, Ireland. TEL 353-1-2893305, FAX 353-1-2896406. Ed. Daniel Attwood. Adv. contact Rebecca Markey. color page EUR 1,500; trim 210 x 297. Circ: 4,200.

IRISH MOTORSPORT ANNUAL. *see* SPORTS AND GAMES

629.2482 IRL ISSN 1393-4996
IRISH TYRE TRADE JOURNAL. Text in English. 1997. bi-m. adv. **Document type:** *Magazine, Trade.*
Published by: Automotive Publications Ltd., Glencree House, Lanesborough Rd., Roscommon, Ireland. TEL 353-903-25676, FAX 353-903-25636, info@autopub.ie. Ed. Padraic Deane. adv.: B&W page EUR 2,032, color page EUR 2,349. Circ: 6,250 (controlled).

629.2 IRL ISSN 1393-533X
IRISH VAN & TRUCK. Text in English. 1997. q. adv. **Document type:** *Magazine, Consumer.*
Formed by the merger of (1994-1997): Irish Van Plus 4 X 4 (1393-0494); (1997-1997): Irish Van (1393-5003)
Published by: I M P Ltd., Riverview House, Barrett St., Ballina, Co. Mayo, Ireland. TEL 353-96-70941, FAX 353-96-73167. adv.: page EUR 2,158; 206 x 297. Circ: 12,000 (paid and controlled).

388.342 GBR ISSN 1748-9970
ISRAEL AUTOS REPORT. Text in English. 2005. a. EUR 820, USD 1,030 combined subscription per issue (print & email eds.) (effective 2010). **Document type:** *Report, Trade.* **Description:** Provides industry professionals and strategists, corporate analysts, auto associations, government departments and regulatory bodies with independent forecasts and competitive intelligence on the Israeli automotives market.
Related titles: E-mail ed.
Indexed: A15, ABIn, B02, B15, B17, B18, G04, I05, P48, P51, P52, PQC.
Published by: Business Monitor International Ltd., Senator House, 85 Queen Victoria St, London, EC4V 4AB, United Kingdom. TEL 44-20-72480468, FAX 44-20-72480467, subs@businessmonitor.com.

388.342 GBR ISSN 1748-9989
ITALY AUTOS REPORT. Text in English. 2005. q. EUR 820, USD 1,030 combined subscription (print & email eds.) (effective 2010). **Document type:** *Report, Trade.* **Description:** Provides industry professionals and strategists, corporate analysts, auto associations, government departments and regulatory bodies with independent forecasts and competitive intelligence on the Italian automotives market.
Related titles: E-mail ed.
Indexed: A15, ABIn, B01, B02, B15, B17, B18, G04, I05, P48, P51, P52, PQC.
Published by: Business Monitor International Ltd., Senator House, 85 Queen Victoria St, London, EC4V 4AB, United Kingdom. TEL 44-20-72480468, FAX 44-20-72480467, subs@businessmonitor.com.

ITALY. ISTITUTO NAZIONALE DI STATISTICA. STATISTICA DEGLI INCIDENTI STRADALI. *see* TRANSPORTATION—Abstracting, Bibliographies, Statistics

T
U

338.476 JPN
J A N CORPORATION. FACTS & INFO; annual guide to Japan's auto industry. Text in English. 1981. a. JPY 8,400 domestic; JPY 9,740 in Asia; JPY 9,960 elsewhere (effective 2001). adv. **Document type:** *Handbook/Manual/Guide, Trade.* **Description:** Provides pictures and major specifications for all production vehicles built by Japanese makers at home and abroad. Also includes sections on technology, and market trends as well as a "Facts and Figures" section.
Formerly (until 1991): Automotive Herald. Facts and Info
Published by: J A N Corporation, DIK Shinbashi Bldg, 415, 5-4 Shinbashi 6-chome, Minato-ku, Tokyo, 105-0004, Japan. TEL 81-3-3438-0361, FAX 81-3-3438-0362, janinfo@japan-autonews.com. Ed. Makio Sakurazawa. R&P, Adv. contact Hijiri Ito. B&W page JPY 150,000, color page JPY 350,000; trim 257 x 182. Circ: 6,200.

796.77 GBR ISSN 1744-4721
J-TUNER. Cover title: jtuner. Text in English. 2005. 13/yr. GBP 44.09 domestic; GBP 65 in Europe; GBP 85 elsewhere (effective 2006). adv. **Document type:** *Magazine, Consumer.*
Published by: Future Publishing Ltd., Beauford Ct, 30 Monmouth St, Bath, Avon BA1 2BW, United Kingdom. TEL 44-1225-442244, FAX 44-1225-446019, customerservice@subscription.co.uk, http://www.futureplc.com.

388.3 GBR ISSN 1473-2408
JAGUAR. Text in Multiple languages. 2000. s-a. free to qualified personnel (effective 2009). adv. **Document type:** *Magazine, Consumer.*
Formerly (until 2001): Jaguar Racing (1470-0050)
—CCC.
Published by: Haymarket Network (Subsidiary of: Haymarket Media Group), Teddington Studios, Broom Rd, Teddington, TW11 9BE, United Kingdom. TEL 44-20-82675013, enquiries@haymarket.com, http://www.haymarketnetwork.com. Ed. Simon Kanter TEL 44-20-82675434.

388.3 AUS ISSN 1833-1378
JAGUAR. Text in English. 2005. s-a. **Document type:** *Magazine, Consumer.*
Published by: Haymarket Media Pty. Ltd., 52 Victoria St, McMahons Point, Sydney, NSW 2060, Australia. TEL 61-2-83993611, FAX 61-2-83993622, http://www.haymarketmedia.com.au.

796.77 GBR
JAGUAR ENTHUSIAST. Text in English. 1985. m. free to members (effective 2009). back issues avail. **Document type:** *Magazine, Consumer.*
Published by: Jaguar Enthusiasts' Club, Abbeywood Office Park, Emma Chris Way, Bristol, BS34 7JU, United Kingdom. TEL 44-1179-698186, FAX 44-1179-791863. Ed. Nigel Thorley.

629.222 GBR ISSN 1476-4350
JAGUAR WORLD MONTHLY. Abbreviated title: J W M. Text in English. 2002. m. GBP 49.20 domestic; GBP 54.60 in Europe; GBP 60 elsewhere (effective 2010). adv. illus.; mkt. back issues avail. **Document type:** *Magazine, Trade.* **Description:** Lively, entertaining magazine for those interested in buying and using Jaguars, and the Jaguar "lifestyle".
Formed by the merger of (1998-2002): Jaguar Monthly (1462-3633); (2000-2002): Classic Jaguar World (1474-2500); Which was formerly (until 2000): Jaguar World (1357-4264); (until 1992): Jaguar Quarterly (0957-0608)
Related titles: Online - full text ed.
Published by: Kelsey Publishing Ltd., PO Box 13, Westerham, Kent TN16 3WT, United Kingdom. TEL 44-1959-541444, FAX 44-1959-541400, info@kelsey.co.uk, http://www.kelsey.co.uk. Ed. Matt Skelton. Adv. contact Alex Oliver TEL 44-1959-543571.

796.72 AUS
JAGUARS WEST. Text in English. m. free membership (effective 2008). adv. **Document type:** *Magazine, Consumer.*
Formerly (until 1990): Jaguar Torque
Published by: Jaguar Car Club of Western Australia, PO Box 1438, Osborne Park, W.A., Australia. FAX 61-8-92422563, hbradstreet@bigpond.com. Eds. Inger Ward, Mark Ward. Circ: 400.

JAPAN AUTO ABSTRACTS; real time database. *see* TRANSPORTATION—Abstracting, Bibliographies, Statistics

388.3 CAN ISSN 1487-9409
JAPAN AUTOMOBILE MANUFACTURERS ASSOCIATION OF CANADA. ANNUAL REVIEW. Text in English. a. **Document type:** *Journal, Trade.*
Formerly (until 1998): J A M A Canada Annual Report (1482-4280)
Related titles: CD-ROM ed.: ISSN 1719-5926.
Published by: Japan Automobile Manufacturers Association of Canada, Ste 460, 151 Bloor St West, Toronto, ON M5S 1S4, Canada. TEL 416-968-0150, FAX 416-968-7095, JAMA@jama.ca, http://www.jama.ca.

388.3 JPN ISSN 0021-4329
JAPAN AUTOMOTIVE NEWS. Text in English. 1959. m. JPY 9,990 domestic; JPY 11,500 in Asia; JPY 12,000 elsewhere (effective 2001). adv. bk.rev. charts; illus.; stat. **Document type:** *Newspaper, Trade.* **Description:** Serves as a trade paper for the industry. Aims to help decision makers worldwide learn about Japan's automotive industry.
Indexed: JCT, JTA.
Published by: J A N Corporation, DIK Shinbashi Bldg, 415, 5-4 Shinbashi 6-chome, Minato-ku, Tokyo, 105-0004, Japan. TEL 81-3-3438-0361, FAX 81-3-3438-0362, janinfo@japan-autonews.com. Ed. Makio Sakurazawa. R&P, Adv. contact Hijiri Ito. B&W page JPY 355,000; trim 410 x 273. Circ: 5,180.

388.342 GBR ISSN 1748-9997
JAPAN AUTOS REPORT. Text in English. 2005. q. EUR 820, USD 1,030 combined subscription (print & email eds.) (effective 2010). **Document type:** *Report, Trade.* **Description:** Provides industry professionals and strategists, corporate analysts, auto associations, government departments and regulatory bodies with independent forecasts and competitive intelligence on the Japanese automotives market.
Related titles: E-mail ed.
Indexed: A15, ABIn, B02, B15, B17, B18, G04, I05, P48, P51, P52, PQC.
Published by: Business Monitor International Ltd., Senator House, 85 Queen Victoria St, London, EC4V 4AB, United Kingdom. TEL 44-20-72480468, FAX 44-20-72480467, subs@businessmonitor.com.

388.3 ITA ISSN 1722-8107
JAPAN CAR MAGAZINE. Text in Italian. 1990. m. adv. **Document type:** *Magazine, Consumer.*
Related titles: Online - full text ed.: ISSN 1722-8115.
Published by: Edizioni Oriente s.r.l., Via Adeodato Ressi, 12, Milan, MI 20125, Italy. TEL 39-2-66711711, FAX 39-2-66710170. Circ: 40,000.

629.286 JPN ISSN 0289-6087
JAPAN MOTOR INDUSTRY. Text in Japanese. 6/yr. USD 110.
Published by: Intercontinental Marketing Corp., I.P.O. Box 5056, Tokyo, 100-3191, Japan.

796.77 GBR ISSN 1467-7792
JAPANESE PERFORMANCE. Abbreviated title: J P. Text in English. 1999. m. GBP 40 domestic; GBP 58 in Europe; GBP 70 elsewhere; GBP 4.25 per issue domestic; GBP 5.25 per issue in Europe; GBP 6.75 per issue elsewhere (effective 2009). adv. back issues avail. **Document type:** *Magazine, Consumer.* **Description:** Contains reports on news and trends about Japanese high-performance cars.
Published by: C H Publications Ltd., Nimax House, 20 Ullswater Cresent, Ullswater Business Park, Coulsdon, Surrey CR5 2HR, United Kingdom. TEL 44-20-86556400, FAX 44-20-87631001, chp@chpltd.com, http://www.chpltd.com. Ed. Chris Rees.

JESSICAR. *see* WOMEN'S INTERESTS

629.286 CHN ISSN 1561-2406
JIASHI YUAN/DRIVER'S WORLD. Text in Chinese. 1989. m. CNY 42 (effective 2004). **Document type:** *Magazine, Consumer.*
Related titles: Online - full content ed.
Address: PO Box 1848, Beijing, 100006, China. TEL 86-10-64811308. **Dist. outside of China by:** China International Book Trading Corp, 35 Chegongzhuang Xilu, Haidian District, PO Box 399, Beijing 100044, China. TEL 86-10-68412045, FAX 86-10-68412023, cibtc@mail.cibtc.com.cn, http://www.cibtc.com.cn/.

629.286 JPN ISSN 0385-7298
TL105 CODEN: JDGJA9
JIDOSHA GIJUTSU/SOCIETY OF AUTOMOTIVE ENGINEERS OF JAPAN. JOURNAL. Text in Japanese. 1947. m. JPY 31,500 to non-members; JPY 25,200 to members (effective 2004). **Document type:** *Journal, Trade.*
Former titles (until 1949): Jidosha Gijutsukai Kaiho; (until 1948): J S A E. News Edition
Indexed: A22, CIN, ChemAb, ChemTitl, JCT.
—BLDSC (4880.910000), CASDDS, IE, Ingenta, INIST, Linda Hall. **CCC.**
Published by: Jidosha Gijutsukai/Society of Automotive Engineers of Japan, Inc., 10-2 Goban-cho, Chiyoda-ku, Tokyo, 102-0076, Japan.

629.286 JPN ISSN 0287-8321
TL240 CODEN: JGRODZ
JIDOSHA GIJUTSUKAI RONBUNSHU/SOCIETY OF AUTOMOTIVE ENGINEERS OF JAPAN. TRANSACTIONS. Text in Japanese; Summaries in English. 1970. q. USD 18,000 (effective 1999). **Document type:** *Trade.*
Indexed: A22, JCT.
—BLDSC (9005.600000), CASDDS, IE, Ingenta, Linda Hall. **CCC.**
Published by: Jidosha Gijutsukai/Society of Automotive Engineers of Japan, Inc., 10-2 Goban-cho, Chiyoda-ku, Tokyo, 102-0076, Japan.

629.286 JPN ISSN 0387-3803
TL105
JIDOSHA KENKYU/JAPAN AUTOMOBILE RESEARCH INSTITUTE. JOURNAL. Text in Japanese. 1979. m. **Document type:** *Academic/Scholarly.* **Description:** Covers automotive research, automotive safety, pollution control, conservation, management of test courses and laboratory facilities.
Indexed: A22.
—BLDSC (4662.869000), IE, Ingenta.
Published by: Nihon Jidosha Kenkyujo/Japan Automobile Research Institute, 2530 Karima, Tsukuba, Ibaraki 305-0822, Japan. TEL 81-29-8561112, FAX 81-29-8561122, http://www.jari.or.jp/.

629.286 621 JPN ISSN 0388-3841
JIDOSHA KOGAKU/AUTOMOBILE ENGINEERING. Text in Japanese. 1952. m. JPY 650.
Indexed: JCT, JTA.
Published by: Tetsudo Nihon-sha, 1-4 Nishi-Kanda 2-chome, Chiyoda-ku, Tokyo, 101-0065, Japan. Ed. M Okasawa. adv.: B&W page JPY 120,000, color page JPY 320,000; trim 257 x 182. Circ: 98,000.

629.286 JPN ISSN 0919-1356
JIDOSHA SHOGENHYO/MOTOR VEHICLE ENGINEERING SPECIFICATIONS - JAPAN. Text in Japanese. 1968. a. JPY 14,000 (effective 1999). **Document type:** *Trade.*
Published by: Jidosha Gijutsukai/Society of Automotive Engineers of Japan, Inc., 10-2 Goban-cho, Chiyoda-ku, Tokyo, 102-0076, Japan.

388.3 USA
JOB DESCRIPTIONS FOR DEALERSHIP STAFF. Text in English. biennial. USD 297 per issue (effective 2008). adv. **Document type:** *Handbook/Manual/Guide, Trade.*
Related titles: CD-ROM ed.
Published by: W D & S Publishing, 10 W 7th St, 1st Fl, PO Box 606, Barnegat Light, NJ 08006. TEL 800-321-5312, http://www.dealersedge.com. Pub., Adv. contact Jim Muntz.

388.3 CAN ISSN 0021-7050
JOBBER NEWS; for Canadian automotive wholesalers and salesmen warehouse distributors and automotive rebuilders. Text in English. 1931. m. CAD 49.95 domestic; USD 62.95 foreign (effective 2008). adv. charts; illus.; tr.lit. **Document type:** *Magazine, Trade.* **Description:** Provides business management and product technology information to enhance the professionalism and overall profitability of warehouse distributors and jobbers nationally. Also provides shop management and technical rebuilding information for the engine rebuilder and machine shop trade across Canada.
Related titles: Online - full text ed.
Indexed: C03, CBCABus, P48, P52, PQC.
Published by: Business Information Group, 12 Concorde Pl, Ste 800, Toronto, ON M3C 4J2, Canada. TEL 416-442-2122, 800-668-2374, FAX 416-442-2191, orders@businessinformationgroup.ca, http://www.businessinformationgroup.ca. Ed., Pub. Andrew Ross TEL 416-510-6763. Circ: 11,029.

388.3 CAN
JOBBER NEWS ANNUAL MARKETING GUIDE. Text in English. a. (in Nov.). CAD 75.95 per issue domestic; USD 75.95 per issue foreign (effective 2008). **Document type:** *Handbook/Manual/Guide, Trade.* **Description:** Lists the automotive aftermarket manufacturers, products, warehouse distributors, re-manufacturers agents, automotive jobbers, and industry facts & statistics.
Supersedes in part: Automotive Marketer Annual Buyer's Guide
Published by: Business Information Group, 12 Concorde Pl, Ste 800, Toronto, ON M3C 4J2, Canada. TEL 416-442-2122, 800-668-2374, 800-268-7742, FAX 416-442-2191, orders@businessinformationgroup.ca.

388 DEU
DAS JOURNAL; fuer Menschen im Raum der Kirchen. Text in German. 1976. q. EUR 1.15 newsstand/cover (effective 2003). adv. **Document type:** *Bulletin, Consumer.*
Former titles (until 1999): Bruderhilfe Journal (0724-5955); (until 1982): Bruderhilfe - Nachrichten (0172-7508)
Published by: Publikom Z Verlagsgesellschaft mbH, Frankfurter Str 168, Kassel, 34121, Germany. TEL 49-561-2031742, FAX 49-561-2032745, publikom_z@dierichs.de, http://www.publikom-z.de. Ed. Armin Noll. Adv. contact Erika Metz. B&W page EUR 6,400, color page EUR 9,500. Circ: 448,610 (paid and controlled).

388.3 FRA ISSN 0242-0805
JOURNAL DE L'AUTOMOBILE. Text in French. 1979. 44/yr. EUR 90 (effective 2010).
Related titles: Online - full text ed.
Address: 89 Rue du Gouverneur General Felix Eboue, Issy les Moulineaux, 92130, France. TEL 33-1-46902000. Ed. Alexandre Guillet TEL 33-1-46900943. Adv. contact David chatelon TEL 33-1-46900925. Circ: 8,074.

388.3 355 GBR ISSN 2042-7778
▼ **JOURNAL OF THE MILITARY JEEP IN ACTION.** Text in English. 2010. bi-m. GBP 39.99 domestic; GBP 49.99 in Europe; GBP 59.99 elsewhere; GBP 9.99 per issue domestic; GBP 14.99 per issue foreign (effective 2010). **Document type:** *Magazine, Trade.* **Description:** Designed for those who are into military jeeps or those restoring a Willys MB or Ford GPW jeep.
Published by: Jeep Promotions Ltd., 5 Chestnut Ave, Wheatley Hills, Doncaster, S Yorkshire DN2 5SW, United Kingdom. TEL 44-1302-739000, FAX 44-1302-739001, info@jeepworld.co.uk.

629.283 614.8 USA ISSN 0164-1344
HE5614.3.C3
JOURNAL OF TRAFFIC SAFETY EDUCATION. Text in English. 1970. q. USD 8. adv. bk.rev.
Related titles: Online - full text ed.
Indexed: B04, BRD, E02, EdA, EdI, HRIS, W03.
Published by: California Association for Safety Education, 5151 State University Dr, Los Angeles, CA 90032. TEL 213-343-4622, rmikulik@casewebsite.org, http://www.casewebsite.org/. Ed. William Cole. Circ: 2,800.

629.222 USA ISSN 1097-2730
JP MAGAZINE. (Jeep) Text in English. 1996. every 10 yrs. USD 20 domestic (effective 2007); USD 30 in Canada; USD 40 elsewhere (effective 2008). adv. back issues avail. **Document type:** *Magazine, Consumer.* **Description:** Covers the entire world of Jeep for Jeep owners and enthusiasts.
Formerly (until 199?): J P (1088-3428)
Related titles: Online - full text ed.: USD 10 (effective 2008).
Indexed: G06, G07, G08, I05, S23.
—CCC.
Published by: Source Interlink Companies, 6420 Wilshire Blvd, 10th Fl, Los Angeles, CA 90048. TEL 323-782-2000, FAX 323-782-2585, dheine@sourceinterlink.com, http://www.sourceinterlinkmedia.com. Ed. John Cappa. Pub. Jeff Nasi TEL 323-782-2649. adv.: B&W page USD 5,420, color page USD 8,130. Circ: 92,982 (paid).

629.28 DEU
JURID - TIP. Text in German. 1956. 3/yr. free. **Document type:** *Magazine, Trade.*
Published by: Jurid Werke GmbH, Glinder Weg, Glinde, 21509, Germany. TEL 49-40-72710. Circ: 60,000.

388.3 790.13 AUS ISSN 1833-2439
JUST HOLDENS MAGAZINE. Text in English. 2005. bi-m. AUD 58.40; AUD 7.95 newsstand/cover (effective 2009). back issues avail. **Document type:** *Magazine, Consumer.* **Description:** Provides all information about Holdens.
Published by: Investment Vehicles, PO Box 85, St. Andrews, VIC 3761, Australia. TEL 61-3-97101722, FAX 61-3-97101530, pitcrew@motormania.com.au.

388.3 BEL ISSN 0022-7242
K A C B AUTO REVUE/ROYAL AUTO. Text in French. 1905. 4/yr. membership. bk.rev. charts; illus. index. **Document type:** *Magazine, Consumer.*
Related titles: Dutch ed.
Published by: Koninklijke Automobiel Club van Belgie/Royal Automobile Club of Belgium, Rue d'Arlon 53, Boite 3, Brussels, 1040, Belgium. TEL 32-2-287-0911, FAX 32-2-230-7584, autoclub@racb.com, http://www.racb.com. Ed., R&P Philippe Brasseur. Adv. contact L Janssens. Circ: 40,000 (controlled).

388.3 DEU ISSN 0942-3613
K F Z BETRIEB. (Kraftfahrzeug) Text in German. 1990. w. EUR 166.40 (effective 2010). adv. **Document type:** *Newspaper, Trade.*
Related titles: Online - full text ed.
Published by: (Zentralverband des Kraftfahrzeughandwerks), Vogel Business Media GmbH & Co.KG, Max-Planck-Str 7-9, Wuerzburg, 97064, Germany. TEL 49-931-4180, FAX 49-931-4182750, info@vogel.de, http://www.vogel-media.de. Ed. Rainer Simon. adv.: B&W page EUR 5,390, color page EUR 7,220; trim 288 x 437. Circ: 30,190 (controlled).

388.3 DEU
K F Z BOERSE. (Kraftfahrzeug) Text in German. 1996. m. EUR 2.50 newsstand/cover (effective 2011). adv. **Document type:** *Magazine, Consumer.*
Published by: Der Heisse Draht Verlag GmbH und Co., Drostestr 14, Hannover, 30161, Germany. TEL 49-511-390910, FAX 49-511-39091196, zentrale@dhd.de, http://www.dhd.de. Adv. contact Lars Schnatmann. Circ: 82,000 (paid and controlled).

388.3 AUT
K F Z PERFEKT. Text in German. m. **Document type:** *Magazine, Trade.*
Related titles: ◆ Supplement to: K F Z Wirtschaft.
Published by: Oesterreichischer Wirtschaftsverlag GmbH (Subsidiary of: Sueddeutscher Verlag GmbH), Wiedner Hauptstr 120-124, Vienna, W 1051, Austria. TEL 43-1-546640, FAX 43-1-54664406, office@wirtschaftsverlag.at, http://www.wirtschaftsverlag.at. Ed. Erhard Zagler. Adv. contact Markus Prikowitsch. Circ: 5,000.

388.3 AUT
K F Z WIRTSCHAFT; Fachmagazin fuer Fahrzeughandel, -reparatur und -industrie. Text in German. 1948. m. EUR 60 domestic; EUR 75 foreign (effective 2005). adv. bk.rev. charts; illus. **Document type:** *Magazine, Trade.*
Former titles: K F Z Werkstaette (0022-7323); Kraftfahrzeug
Related titles: ◆ Supplement(s): K F Z Perfekt.
Indexed: RASB.
Published by: (Bundesinnung der Kraftfahrzeugmechaniker), Oesterreichischer Wirtschaftsverlag GmbH (Subsidiary of: Sueddeutscher Verlag GmbH), Wiedner Hauptstr 120-124, Vienna, W 1051, Austria. TEL 43-1-546640, FAX 43-1-54664406, office@wirtschaftsverlag.at, http://www.wirtschaftsverlag.at. Eds. Erhard Zagler, Thomas Ableidinger. Adv. contact Markus Prikowitsch. color page EUR 4,060; trim 168 x 245. Circ: 8,233 (paid and controlled).

796.7 USA
KART RACER. Text in English. bi-m. adv. illus. **Document type:** *Magazine, Consumer.* **Description:** Contains technical articles and illustrated stories on improving your driving technique on the kart track.
Published by: Challenge Publications, Inc., 9509 Vassar Ave, Unit A, Chatsworth, CA 91311. TEL 818-700-6868, FAX 818-700-6282, challpubs@aol.com, http://www.challengeweb.com/. Ed. Dan Kahn. Pub., R&P Edwin Schnepf. Adv. contact Flint Burckart.

796.77 USA ISSN 0744-5962
KART SPORT. Text in English. 1982. m. adv. illus.
Address: 5510 Ashborn Rd, Baltimore, MD 21227. Ed. Joe Xavier.

796.7 USA ISSN 0096-3216
GV1029.5
KARTER NEWS. Text in English. 1957. m. adv. **Document type:** *Newsletter, Trade.*
Published by: International Kart Federation, 1609 South Grove Ave, Ste 105, Ontario, CA 91761. TEL 909-923-4999, FAX 909-923-6940, support@ikfkarting.com. Ed. Deborah Davidson-Harpur. Circ: 6,000 (controlled).

388.3 GBR ISSN 0022-913X
KARTING MAGAZINE. Text in English. 1960. m. GBP 36 domestic; GBP 44 in Europe; GBP 52 elsewhere; GBP 3.80 newsstand/cover (effective 2009). adv. bk.rev.; software rev. charts; illus.; mkt.; tr.lit. index. 100 p./no. 3 cols./p.; back issues avail. **Document type:** *Magazine, Consumer.* **Description:** Features technical developments, race reports, track and club news about the game of kart racing.
Related titles: Online - full text ed.: GBP 14.99; GBP 1.50 per issue (effective 2009).
Indexed: SportS.
Published by: Lodgemark Press, 15 Moorfield Rd, Orpington, Kent BR6 OXD, United Kingdom. TEL 44-1689-897123, FAX 44-1689-890998. adv.: B&W page GBP 600, color page GBP 800; trim 210 x 280. Circ: 12,800.

338.342958 GBR ISSN 2044-317X
KAZAKHSTAN AND CENTRAL ASIA AUTOS REPORT. Text in English. 2005. a. USD 1,150 combined subscription per issue (print & e-mail eds.) (effective 2010). **Document type:** *Report, Trade.* **Description:** Provides industry professionals and strategists, corporate analysts, auto associations, government departments and regulatory bodies with independent forecasts and competitive intelligence on the Kyrgyzstani, Kazakhstani, Tajikistani, Turkmen, Uzbekistani automotives market.
Formerly (until 2009): Central Asia Autos Report (1748-9814)
Related titles: E-mail ed.
Indexed: A15, ABIn, B02, B15, B17, B18, G04, I05, P48, P51, P52, PQC.
Published by: Business Monitor International Ltd., Senator House, 85 Queen Victoria St, London, EC4V 4AB, United Kingdom. TEL 44-20-72480468, FAX 44-20-72480467, subs@businessmonitor.com, http://www.businessmonitor.com.

388.3 CHN ISSN 1006-6861
KECHE JISHU/COACH TECHNOLOGY. Text in English. 1986. bi-m. **Document type:** *Magazine, Trade.*
Published by: Liaoning Huanghai Automobile (Group) Co., Ltd., 544 Huanghai Ave, Dandong, 118008, China. TEL 86-415-6272437, FAX 86-415-6224270, http://www.huanghaibus.com.cn/index.htm.

796.77 790.13 USA ISSN 1939-6481
TL215.C6
KEITH MARTIN'S CORVETTE MARKET. Text in English. 2007. q. USD 29.95 (effective 2011). **Document type:** *Magazine, Trade.*
Related titles: Online - full text ed.: ISSN 2162-1713.
Published by: Automotive Investor Media Group, 401 NE 19th St, Ste 100, Portland, OR 97232. TEL 877-219-2605, FAX 503-253-2234. Pub. Keith Martin.

388.3 USA ISSN 1932-6351
KELLEY BLUE BOOK AUTO RESIDENTIAL GUIDE. Text in English. 198?. bi-m.
Published by: Kelley Blue Book Company, 195 Technology Dr., Irvine, CA 92618-2402. kelley@kbb.com, http://www.kbb.com.

388 USA ISSN 0897-6171
TL162
KELLEY BLUE BOOK NEW CAR PRICE MANUAL. Cover title: Kelley Blue Book Auto Price Manual. Text in English. q. USD 89 (effective 2004).
Published by: Kelley Blue Book Company, 195 Technology Dr., Irvine, CA 92618-2402. kelley@kbb.com, http://www.kbb.com. Pub. Paul Johnson.

658 GBR ISSN 1473-6675
KEY NOTE MARKET ASSESSMENT. MOTOR FINANCE. Variant title: Motor Finance Market Assessment. Text in English. 2000. irreg., latest 2005, Sep. GBP 799 per issue (effective 2010). **Document type:** *Report, Trade.* **Description:** Provides an in-depth strategic analysis across a broad range of industries and contains an examination on the scope, dynamics and shape of key UK markets in the consumer, financial, lifestyle and business to business sectors.
—CCC.
Published by: Key Note Ltd. (Subsidiary of: Bonnier Business Information), Harlequin House, 5th Fl, 7 High St, Teddington, Richmond upon Thames, TW11 8EE, United Kingdom. TEL 44-845-5040452, FAX 44-845-5040453, info@keynote.co.uk.

KEY NOTE MARKET ASSESSMENT. VEHICLE BREAKDOWN SERVICES. *see* BUSINESS AND ECONOMICS—Production Of Goods And Services

388 GBR ISSN 1363-7959
KEY NOTE MARKET REPORT: AUTOMOTIVE SERVICES. Variant title: Automotive Services Market Report. Text in English. 1996. irreg., latest 2008, May. GBP 460 per issue (effective 2010). **Document type:** *Report, Trade.* **Description:** Provides an overview of a specific UK market segment and includes executive summary, market definition, market size, industry background, competitor analysis, current issues, forecasts, company profiles, and more.
Published by: Key Note Ltd. (Subsidiary of: Bonnier Business Information), Harlequin House, 5th Fl, 7 High St, Teddington, Richmond upon Thames, TW11 8EE, United Kingdom. TEL 44-845-5040452, FAX 44-845-5040453, info@keynote.co.uk.

629.222 GBR ISSN 1366-7890
KEY NOTE MARKET REPORT: AUTOPARTS. Variant title: Autoparts Market Report. Text in English. 199?. irreg., latest 2009, Jan. GBP 460 per issue (effective 2010). **Document type:** *Report, Trade.* **Description:** Provides an overview of a specific UK market segment and includes executive summary, market definition, market size, industry background, competitor analysis, current issues, forecasts, company profiles, and more.
Formerly (until 1995): Key Note Report: Autoparts (0269-1086)
Related titles: CD-ROM ed.; Online - full text ed.
Published by: Key Note Ltd. (Subsidiary of: Bonnier Business Information), Harlequin House, 5th Fl, 7 High St, Teddington, Richmond upon Thames, TW11 8EE, United Kingdom. TEL 44-845-5040452, FAX 44-845-5040453, info@keynote.co.uk.

388 338 GBR ISSN 1460-7638
KEY NOTE MARKET REPORT: COMMERCIAL VEHICLES. Variant title: Commercial Vehicles Market Report. Text in English. 1981. irreg., latest 2009, Jan. GBP 460 per issue (effective 2010). **Document type:** *Report, Trade.* **Description:** Provides an overview of the UK commercial vehicles market, including industry structure, market size and trends, developments, prospects, and major company profiles.
Formerly (until 1997): Key Note Report: Commercial Vehicles (0951-6727)
Related titles: CD-ROM ed.; Online - full text ed.
Published by: Key Note Ltd. (Subsidiary of: Bonnier Business Information), Harlequin House, 5th Fl, 7 High St, Teddington, Richmond upon Thames, TW11 8EE, United Kingdom. TEL 44-845-5040452, FAX 44-845-5040453, info@keynote.co.uk.

388 GBR
KEY NOTE MARKET REPORT: VEHICLE SECURITY. Variant title: Vehicle Security Market Report. Text in English. 1995. irreg., latest 2007, Feb. GBP 440 per issue (effective 2010). **Document type:** *Report, Trade.* **Description:** Provides an overview of a specific UK market segment and includes executive summary, market definition, market size, industry background, competitor analysis, current issues, forecasts, company profiles, and more.
Formerly (until 1995): Key Note Report: Vehicle Security
Related titles: CD-ROM ed.; Online - full text ed.
Published by: Key Note Ltd. (Subsidiary of: Bonnier Business Information), Harlequin House, 5th Fl, 7 High St, Teddington, Richmond upon Thames, TW11 8EE, United Kingdom. TEL 44-845-5040452, FAX 44-845-5040453, info@keynote.co.uk.

KEY NOTE MARKET REVIEW: MOTOR INDUSTRY. *see* BUSINESS AND ECONOMICS—Production Of Goods And Services

KILLER ROADS: FROM CRASH TO VERDICT. *see* LAW

388.3 USA
KING OF THE STREET. Text in English. 2007 (Sep.). bi-m. USD 35 (effective 2007). **Document type:** *Magazine, Consumer.* **Description:** Covers urban style automotive customization.
Published by: M I A Entertainment, Inc., PO Box 693097, Miami, FL 33269-3097. TEL 305-493-3278, FAX 305-402-3900. Ed. Phil Gordon. Pub. Daniel Perez.

388 USA
KIPLINGER'S NEW CAR BUYER'S GUIDE (YEAR). Text in English. 1991. a. **Document type:** *Directory.*
Formerly: Kiplinger's Cars
Published by: Kiplinger Washington Editors, Inc., 1729 H St, NW, Washington, DC 20006. TEL 202-887-6400, 800-544-0155, http://www.kiplinger.com.

388 USA ISSN 1529-8493
TL162
KIPLINGER'S PERSONAL FINANCE NEW CARS & TRUCKS BUYER'S GUIDE. Text in English. a.
Former titles (until 1999): Kiplinger's New Cars & Trucks Buyer's Guide; (until 1998): Kiplinger's Buyers Guide to New Cars & Trucks; (until 1997): Kiplinger's Buyer's Guide the New Cars
Published by: Kiplinger Washington Editors, Inc., 1729 H St, NW, Washington, DC 20006. TEL 202-887-6400, 800-544-0155, FAX 202-331-1206, http://www.kiplinger.com.

629.222 GBR ISSN 0955-4076
KIT CAR; biggest & best value kit car magazine. Text in English. 1981. m. GBP 45 domestic; GBP 55 foreign; GBP 4.30 per issue (effective 2009). adv. back issues avail. **Document type:** *Magazine, Consumer.* **Description:** Features information relevant to the kit car industry.
Formerly (until 1984): Alternative Cars
—BLDSC (5098.064800).
Published by: Kit Cars International Ltd., 11 Meadow Close, Hove, Sussex BN3 6QQ, United Kingdom. FAX 44-20-83952653, kitcarman@ntlworld.com. Ed. Ian Hyne. Pub. Den Tanner.

796.77 SWE ISSN 1653-4956
KLASSISKA BILAR. Variant title: Teknikens Vaerld Klassiska Bilar. Text in Swedish. 2005. a. SEK 129 newsstand/cover (effective 2010). adv. **Document type:** *Magazine, Consumer.*
Published by: Bonnier Tidskrifter AB, Sveavaegen 53, Stockholm, 10544, Sweden. TEL 46-8-7365200, FAX 46-8-7363842, info@bt.bonnier.se, http://www.bonniertidskrifter.se. Ed. Daniel Frodin TEL 46-8-7365890. adv.: page SEK 14,000; trim 217 x 280. Circ: 20,500 (controlled).

388.3 790.13 FRA ISSN 2106-895X
▼ **KM/H.** Text in French. 2009. m. **Document type:** *Magazine, Consumer.*
Published by: Riva Corporate, 16 Rue de la Fontaine du Roi, Paris, 75011, France.

338 USA ISSN 1054-254X
KNOXVILLE AUTOMOTIVE REPORT. Text in English. 1990. m. free to qualified personnel (effective 2008). adv. **Document type:** *Newspaper, Trade.* **Description:** Provides monthly news for the local automotive industry in East Tenn., West N.C., Southeast Ky., North Ga., and parts of Va. and Ala.
Published by: Autographic Publishing Company, Inc., 1121 Airport Center Dr, Ste 101, Nashville, TN 37214. TEL 615-391-3666, 800-467-3666, FAX 615-391-3622, garnett@automotivereport.net, http://www.automotivereport.net. Ed. Garnett Forkum. Pub. Allen Forkum. adv.: B&W page USD 1,200; trim 11.5 x 15. Circ: 6,900 (free).

796.77 SWE ISSN 2000-4117
▼ **KOEPA BIL.** Variant title: Teknikens Vaerld Koepa Bil. Text in Swedish. 2009. a. SEK 69 newsstand/cover (effective 2010). adv. **Document type:** *Magazine, Consumer.*
Published by: Bonnier Tidskrifter AB, Sveavaegen 53, Stockholm, 10544, Sweden. TEL 46-8-7365200, FAX 46-8-7363842, http://www.bonniertidskrifter.se. Ed. Daniel Frodin TEL 46-8-7365890. Adv. contact Christer Johansson. page SEK 14,000; trim 217 x 280. Circ: 30,000 (paid).

KOERELAERAREN. *see* LABOR UNIONS

KOMMUNALE FAHRZEUGE. *see* PUBLIC ADMINISTRATION—Municipal Government

388.3 KOR
KOREA BUYERS GUIDE AUTOMOTIVE. Text in English. bi-m. USD 50 in East Asia; USD 60 elsewhere (effective 2008). **Document type:** *Magazine, Trade.* **Description:** Covers auto parts, accessories, and repair equipment.
Related titles: Online - full text ed.
Published by: Maekyung Buyers Guide Corp., Fl. 2-3, 161-7, Samseong-dong, Gangnam-gu, Seoul, 135-090, Korea, S. TEL 82-2-5585607, FAX 82-2-5584915, info@bg21.co.kr, http://www.buyersguide.co.kr/.

388 678.2 USA
KOVACH TIRE REPORT. Text in English. 1984. m. free to qualified personnel (effective 2003). **Document type:** *Report, Trade.* **Description:** For executives of tire manufacturers and tire dealers in North America.
Published by: Quality Design Systems, 390 E Corporate Dr, Meridian, ID 83642. TEL 800-657-6409, info@qds-solutions.net, http://www.qds-solutions.com/.

629.222 388.324 USA ISSN 2151-0555
KUSTOMS & HOT RODS. Text in English. 1984. m. USD 26.95 domestic; USD 51.95 in Canada; USD 99.95 elsewhere (effective 2009). adv. **Document type:** *Magazine, Trade.* **Description:** Features tech articles with information on making your ride the best it can be.
Formerly (until 2008): Specialty Car Marketplace
Published by: AutoTrader Classics, 5775 Peachtree-Dunwoody Rd, Ste A-100, Atlanta, GA 30342. TEL 800-548-8889. Adv. contact Debbie Reetz TEL 404-568-8383. color page USD 1,900; trim 7.375 x 10.625.

388.342 953.67 GBR ISSN 1749-0006
KUWAIT AUTOS REPORT. Text in English. 2005. q. EUR 820, USD 1,030 combined subscription (print & email eds.) (effective 2010). **Document type:** *Report, Trade.* **Description:** Provides industry professionals and strategists, corporate analysts, auto associations, government departments and regulatory bodies with independent forecasts and competitive intelligence on the Kuwaiti automotives market.
Related titles: E-mail ed.
Indexed: A15, ABIn, B02, B15, B17, B18, G04, I05, P48, P51, P52, PQC.
Published by: Business Monitor International Ltd., Senator House, 85 Queen Victoria St, London, EC4V 4AB, United Kingdom. TEL 44-20-72480468, FAX 44-20-72480467, subs@businessmonitor.com.

796.77 USA
LANCIA ENTHUSIAST. Text in English. 1983. m. membership. adv.
Published by: American Lancia Club, c/o Armand Giglio, Turk Hill Rd, Brewster, NY 10509. Ed. Neil Pering. Circ: 1,000. **Subscr. to:** Keith Goring, Rt 1, Box 136, Norfolk, CT 06058.

388.3 USA ISSN 0023-7515
LANCIANA. Text in English. 1954. q. membership. adv. bk.rev.
Published by: American Lancia Club, c/o Armand Giglio, Turk Hill Rd, Brewster, NY 10509. Ed. Paul Feine. Circ: 1,000. **Subscr. to:** Keith Goring, Rt 1, Box 136, Norfolk, CT 06058.

388.342 GBR ISSN 1471-7077
LAND ROVER ENTHUSIAST. Text in English. 2001. m. GBP 36 domestic; GBP 45 foreign (effective 2009). adv. **Document type:** *Magazine, Consumer.* **Description:** Features information on custom Rovers, travel, editorial, owner information, activities and events.
Published by: Green House Publishing, PO Box 178, Wallingford, Oxon OX10 8PD, United Kingdom. TEL 44-131-6697465, sales@landroverenthusiast.com. Ed. James Taylor. Pub. Richard Green. Adv. contact Debe Stocks. page GBP 595; trim 210 x 297.

629.222 GBR ISSN 1463-1202
LAND ROVER MONTHLY. Abbreviated title: L R M. Text in English. m. GBP 30 domestic; GBP 40 in Europe; GBP 2.75 newsstand/cover (effective 2001). adv. **Document type:** *Magazine, Consumer.* **Description:** Provides Land Rover enthusiasts with information on maintenance, performance, driving tips and the latest news on accessories and equipment.

TU

Published by: Four by Four Productions, Prior Cottage, Gedding, Suffolk IP30 0QE, United Kingdom. TEL 44-1449-736966, FAX 44-1449-736977. Ed. Richard Howell Thomas. Pub., R&P Cathie Howell Thomas. Adv. contact Terri Longhorne TEL 44-1449-737756. **Dist. by:** M M C Distribution Ltd, Octagon House, White Hart Meadows, Ripley, Woking, Surrey GU23 6HR, United Kingdom. TEL 44-1483-211222, FAX 44-1483-211731.

629.222 GBR ISSN 1351-1742
LAND ROVER OWNER INTERNATIONAL. Text in English. 1987. 13/yr. GBP 51 domestic; GBP 66.50 foreign (effective 2009). adv. bk.rev. back issues avail. **Document type:** *Magazine, Consumer.* **Description:** Covers off-road and four-wheel vehicles for sale, technical tips, travel features, club news, and competitions.
Formerly (until 199?): Land Rover Owner (0954-1403)
Related titles: Online - full text ed.
Published by: H. Bauer Publishing Ltd. (Subsidiary of: Bauer Media Group), Media House, Lynchwood, Peterborough, Cambridgeshire PE2 6EA, United Kingdom. TEL 44-1733-468582, http://www.bauer.co.uk. Ed. John Pearson. Adv. contact Kelly Millis TEL 44-1733-468422.

629.2222 GBR ISSN 1351-8313
LAND ROVER WORLD. Text in English. 1993. m. GBP 43.92 domestic; GBP 49.44 in Europe; GBP 54.96 elsewhere; GBP 4 per issue domestic; GBP 5 per issue in Europe; GBP 5.50 per issue elsewhere (effective 2009). illus. back issues avail. **Document type:** *Magazine, Consumer.* **Description:** Provides technical and practical advice on purchasing, driving, and maintaining a Land Rover.
Published by: Kelsey Publishing Ltd., Cudham Tithe Barn, Berry's Hill, Cudham, Kent TN16 3AG, United Kingdom. TEL 44-1959-541444, FAX 44-1959-541400, info@kelsey.co.uk, http://www.kelsey.co.uk. Eds. Mike Gould, Phil Weeden TEL 44-1733-353372. Adv. contact Julia Johnston TEL 44-1733-353353. **Subscr. to:** PO Box 13, Westerham, Kent TN16 3WT, United Kingdom. TEL 44-1959-543530.

388 DEU ISSN 0023-866X
LASTAUTO OMNIBUS. Text in German. 1924. m. EUR 46.20 (effective 2011). adv. charts; illus.; mkt.; pat.; tr.lit. index. **Document type:** *Magazine, Trade.* **Description:** Technically oriented magazine covering the whole spectrum of trucks, goods vehicles, and omnibuses.
Incorporates: Kraftverkehr
—IE, Infotrieve. **CCC.**
Published by: EuroTransportMedia Verlags- und Veranstaltungs-GmbH, Handwerkstr 15, Stuttgart, 70565, Germany. TEL 49-711-784980, FAX 49-711-7849888, info@eurotransport.de, http://www.etm-verlag.de. Ed. Andreas Wolf. Adv. contact Roland Schaefer. Circ: 15,153 (paid).

796.75 CZE ISSN 1214-679X
LASTAUTO OMNIBUS. Text in Czech. 2004. m. CZK 621 (effective 2009). adv. **Document type:** *Magazine, Trade.*
Published by: Motor-Presse Bohemia, U Krcskeho Nadrazi 36, Prague 4, 14000, Czech Republic. TEL 420-2-24109340, FAX 420-2-41721905, motopresse@motorpresse.cz, http://www.motorpresse.cz. Ed. Jan Kvartek. Adv. contact Renata Ben. page CZK 45,000; trim 210 x 297. Circ: 8,000 (paid).

796.75 CZE ISSN 1801-142X
LASTAUTO OMNIBUS PRUVODCE. Text in Czech. 2005. a. CZK 250 per issue (effective 2006). adv. **Document type:** *Magazine, Consumer.*
Published by: Motor-Presse Bohemia, U Krcskeho Nadrazi 36, Prague 4, 14000, Czech Republic. TEL 420-2-24109340, FAX 420-2-41721905, motopresse@motorpresse.cz, http://www.motorpresse.cz. Ed. Jan Kvartek. Adv. contact Renata Ben. page CZK 69,000; trim 210 x 297.

790.13 USA
THE LATEST SCOOP. Text in English. 1990. 9/yr. USD 12 domestic; USD 20 foreign (effective 2002). adv. illus. back issues avail. **Document type:** *Magazine, Consumer.* **Description:** The source for auto events in the Rocky Mountains region.
Published by: Latest Scoop Publishing, PO Box 7477, Loveland, CO 80537-0477. Scoopautoevents@aol.com. Ed., Pub. Tracey L Ellis. Circ: 3,000.

LATINOS ON WHEELS. *see* ETHNIC INTERESTS

388.3 AUS ISSN 1833-1122
LEADED. Text in English. 2006. bi-m. AUD 33 (effective 2007). 60 p./no.; **Document type:** *Magazine, Consumer.* **Description:** About classic, club and sports cars.
Published by: Leaded Magazine, 15 Arunga St, Petrie, QLD 4502, Australia. TEL 61-4-1772-6870, FAX 61-7-3285-1064, http://www.leadedmagazine.com.au.

796.77 CAN ISSN 0709-7093
LEISURE WHEELS. Text in English. 1969. m. illus.
Formerly (until 1979): Taylor's Leisure Wheels (0318-3467)
Published by: Murray Publications, P O Box 40, Irricana, AB T0M 1B0, Canada. TEL 403-935-4688.

629.22 CAN ISSN 0834-2423
LEMON AID MAGAZINE. Text in English. 1972. 4/yr. CAD 12.84 (effective 2001). **Document type:** *Magazine, Consumer.*
Former titles: Lemon Aid Bulletin - Auto Conseils (0821-3747); Consumer Bulletin - Bulletin aux Consommateurs (0708-3963)
Related titles: Online - full text ed.; French ed.: Roulez sans Vous Faire Rouler. ISSN 0840-8475. 1972.
Indexed: C03, CBCARef, CBPI, PQC.
Published by: Automobile Protection Association Consumer Publications Co. Inc./Association pour la Protection Automobile, 292 Blvd Saint Joseph, Ouest, Montreal, PQ H2V 2N7, Canada. TEL 514-273-5555, FAX 514-273-0797. Ed. Antoinette Greco. Circ: 25,000.

629.222 CAN ISSN 1700-7593
TL162
LEMON-AID NEW CARS AND MINIVANS. Text in English. 1976. a. CAD 30 (effective 2006).
Former titles (until 2002): Lemon-Aid New Cars (1481-4188); (until 1998): Lemon-Aid New Car Guide (0714-5861); Which superseded in part (in 1982): Lemon-Aid (0383-7084)
Published by: Penguin Group Canada, 90 Eglinton Ave E, Suite 700, Toronto, ON M4P 2Y3, Canada. TEL 416-925-2249, FAX 416-925-0068, info@penguin.ca, http://www.penguin.ca.

629.223 CAN ISSN 1701-1884
LEMON-AID S U VS, VANS AND TRUCKS. Text in English. 2002. a. CAD 30 (effective 2006). **Document type:** *Directory, Consumer.*
Formed by the merger of (1988-2002): Lemon-Aid New 4 x 4s, Vans and Trucks (1485-5682); Which was formerly (until 1998): Lemon-Aid 4 x 4, Van and Truck Guide (1205-4569); (1999-2002): Lemon-Aid Used 4 x 4s, Vans and Trucks (1487-041X)
Published by: Penguin Group Canada, 90 Eglinton Ave E, Suite 700, Toronto, ON M4P 2Y3, Canada. TEL 416-925-2249, FAX 416-925-0068, info@penguin.ca, http://www.penguin.ca.

629.222 CAN ISSN 1701-6908
LEMON-AID USED CARS AND MINIVANS. Text in English. 1976. a. CAD 30 (effective 2006).
Former titles (until 2003): Lemon-Aid Used Cars (1485-1121); (until 1998): Lemon-Aid Used Car Guide (0714-587X); Which superseded in part (in 1982): Lemon-Aid (0383-7084)
Published by: Penguin Group Canada, 90 Eglinton Ave E, Suite 700, Toronto, ON M4P 2Y3, Canada. TEL 416-925-2249, FAX 416-925-0068, info@penguin.ca, http://www.penguin.ca.

614.86 640.73 USA
LEMON TIMES. Text in English. 1979. q. USD 20 (effective 2000). **Description:** Highlights important actions and findings, including such topics as airbags, tips for using small claims court and car defect.
Indexed: CLT&T.
Published by: Center for Auto Safety, 1825 Connecticut Ave N W Ste 330, Washington, DC 20009. TEL 202-328-7700, http://www.essential.org/cas, http://www.autosafety.org. Ed. Sanja Pesek. Circ: 13,000.

388.3 IRL ISSN 1649-6922
LIMERICK'S MOTOR TRADER. Text in English. 2002. bi-w. EUR 2.50 newsstand/cover (effective 2006). adv.
Supersedes in part (in 2005): Ireland's Motor Trader (1649-6353); Which was formerly (until 2004): The Motor-Trader (1649-2072)
Published by: Motor Trader, Box 338, Naas, Co. Kildare, Ireland. TEL 353-45-893343, FAX 353-45-893342, info@motortrader.ie, http://www.motortrader.ie/.

388.3 USA ISSN 1097-4814
LIMOUSINE & CHAUFFEURED TRANSPORTATION. Text in English. 1983. m. (plus Factbook in July). USD 30 (effective 2008). adv. illus. back issues avail. **Document type:** *Magazine, Trade.* **Description:** Serves the information needs of the limousine service industry.
Formerly (1998): Limousine and Chauffeur (8750-7374)
Related titles: Online - full text ed.
Published by: Bobit Business Media, 3520 Challenger St, Torrance, CA 90503. TEL 310-533-2400, FAX 310-533-2500, order@bobit.com, http://www.bobit.com. Pub. Sara Eastwood-McLean. adv.: color page USD 6,300, B&W page USD 5,500; trim 7.875 x 10.75. Circ: 10,000 (paid).

388.3 USA
LIMOUSINE DIGEST. Text in English. 1990. m. **Document type:** *Magazine, Trade.*
Published by: Digest Publications, 29 Fostertown Rd, Medford, NJ 08055. TEL 609-953-4900, FAX 609-953-4905, http://www.limodigest.com. Ed. Kathryn Stadel. Pub. Jennifer Lutes TEL 888-LIMO-DIG. Circ: 16,000 (controlled).

388.3 USA
LION OF BELFORT. Text in English. 1970. bi-m. USD 12. adv. bk.rev. back issues avail. **Document type:** *Newsletter.*
Published by: Peugeot Owners' Club, 6649 E 65th St, Indianapolis, IN 46220-4301. TEL 317-845-5050. Ed. Marvin A Needler. Circ: 650.

LIV; it's Swedish for life. *see* GENERAL INTEREST PERIODICALS—Great Britain

388 PRT
LIVRO D'OURO DO CARRO USADO. Text in Portuguese. 1997. a. EUR 4.50 newsstand/cover (effective 2005). **Document type:** *Directory, Consumer.*
Published by: Motorpress Lisboa, SA (Subsidiary of: Gruner + Jahr AG & Co), Rua Policarpio Anjos No. 4, Cruz Quebrada, Dafundo 1495-742, Portugal. TEL 351-21-4154500, FAX 351-21-4154501, buzine@motorpress.pt, http://www.mpl.pt. Circ: 20,000.

THE LOCATOR. *see* BUSINESS AND ECONOMICS—Trade And Industrial Directories

388.33 USA
LOCATOR UPFRONT MAGAZINE. Text in English. 1996. bi-m. USD 36; USD 7.75 per issue (effective 2007). adv. 56 p./no. 3 cols./p.; **Document type:** *Magazine, Trade.* **Description:** Magazine of used auto and truck parts.
Related titles: Online - full content ed.
Published by: John Holmes Publishing, 521 Main St, Whiting, IA 51063-0286. TEL 712-458-2213, 800-831-0820, FAX 712-458-2687. Ed. Wendy Lloyd. Pub. John F Holmes. adv.: page USD 2,740; trim 7.75 x 10.5. Circ: 6,000 (paid and controlled).

796.77 USA ISSN 0199-9362
LOWRIDER. Text in English. 1977. m. USD 20 domestic; USD 33 in Canada; USD 35 elsewhere (effective 2008). adv. illus. back issues avail.; reprints avail. **Document type:** *Magazine, Consumer.* **Description:** Provides information on lowriding and comprises of four main categories - departments, shows, vehicle showcases and technical how-tows.
Related titles: Online - full text ed.: USD 10 (effective 2008).
Indexed: ChPerI, Chicano, I05, S23.
—**CCC.**
Published by: Source Interlink Companies, 2400 E Katella Ave, 11th Fl, Anaheim, CA 92806. TEL 714-939-2400, FAX 714-978-6390, dheine@sourceinterlink.com, http://www.sourceinterlinkmedia.com. Eds. Joe Ray, Ralph Fuentes. adv.: B&W page USD 10,085, color page USD 18,975. Circ: 84,835 (paid).

LOWRIDER ARTE. *see* ART

▼ **LOWSIDE MAGAZINE**; garage built suicide machines. *see* SPORTS AND GAMES—Bicycles And Motorcycles

LUXEMBOURG. SERVICE CENTRAL DE LA STATISTIQUE ET DES ETUDES ECONOMIQUES. INDICATEURS RAPIDES. SERIE D. IMMATRICULATIONS DE VEHICULES AUTOMOTEURS. *see* TRANSPORTATION—Abstracting, Bibliographies, Statistics

M A C S SERVICE REPORTS. *see* HEATING, PLUMBING AND REFRIGERATION

M C 2 (BREMERTON); the independent American magazine for all Mini owners. (Mini Classic Mini Cooper) *see* SPORTS AND GAMES

796.77 GBR ISSN 0950-3307
M G ENTHUSIAST MAGAZINE. Text in English. 1986. m. GBP 38.25 domestic; GBP 42 in Europe; GBP 49 elsewhere (effective 2009). adv. illus. back issues avail. **Document type:** *Magazine, Consumer.* **Description:** Covers all aspects of MG ownership of interest to MG drivers throughout the world. Features news, events, historical features, DIY advice, hints and tips, what's-on guide, shows and the sporting scene.
Incorporates (2004-2005): Total M G (1743-6087)
Published by: Hothouse Publishing, 1st Fl, 2 King St, Peterborough, PE1 1LT, United Kingdom. TEL 44-1733-246500, FAX 44-1733-246555. Ed. Simon Goldsworthy. Adv. contact Madeline Lillywhite.

M S A COMPETITORS AND OFFICIALS YEARBOOK. *see* SPORTS AND GAMES

388.3 629.2 DEU ISSN 0024-8525
TJ751 CODEN: MOTZAS
M T Z; Verbrennungsmotor und Gasturbine. (Motortechnische Zeitschrift) Text in German. 1939. 11/yr. EUR 224; EUR 85 to students; EUR 26 newsstand/cover (effective 2010). adv. bk.rev. abstr.; bibl.; charts; illus.; stat. index, cum.index every 20 yrs. **Document type:** *Magazine, Trade.* **Description:** For the engine and turbine industry. Features research and development, product engineering, tests and measurement. Also includes events, news, and new products.
Related titles: Online - full text ed.
Indexed: A22, A28, APA, ApMecR, BMT, BrCerAb, C&ISA, CA/WCA, CIA, CerAb, CivEngAb, CorrAb, DIP, E&CAJ, E11, EEA, EMA, Englnd, H15, IBR, IBZ, M&TEA, M09, MBF, METADEX, RefZh, S&VD, SCOPUS, SolStAb, T04, TM, WAA.
—IE, Infotrieve, Ingenta, INIST, Linda Hall. **CCC.**
Published by: Vieweg und Teubner Verlag (Subsidiary of: Springer Fachmedien Wiesbaden GmbH), Abraham-Lincoln-Str 46, Wiesbaden, 65189, Germany. TEL 49-611-78780, FAX 49-611-7878400, info@viewegteubner.de, http://www.viewegteubner.de. Ed. Johannes Winterhagen. Adv. contact Sabine Roeck. Circ: 6,729 (paid and controlled).

629.2872 NZL ISSN 1177-6757
M V P. (Most Valuable Players) Variant title: MVPMagazine. Text in English. 2007. bi-m. **Document type:** *Magazine, Consumer.*
Published by: Kings Productions Ltd, PO Box 33-698, Takapuna North Shore, Auckland, New Zealand. FAX 64-9-8288502. Ed. Brendon White.

388.8 USA ISSN 1052-4568
HE5614.2
M V R BOOK. (Motor Vehicle Report) Text in English. 19??. a. USD 14.95 per issue (effective 2011). **Document type:** *Handbook/Manual/Guide, Trade.*
Related titles: Online - full text ed.
Published by: B R B Publications, Inc., PO Box 27869, Tempe, AZ 85285. TEL 800-929-3811, FAX 800-929-4981, brb@brbpub.com, http://www.brbpub.com.

388.3 ITA ISSN 1825-7275
MACCHINE MOTORI. Text in Italian. 2005. bi-m. **Document type:** *Magazine, Trade.*
Published by: Orsa Maggiore Edizioni, Corso Sempione 104, Milan, 20154, Italy. TEL 39-02-34934189.

629.286 CAN ISSN 1910-6157
LE MAG DE L'AUTORELEVE. Text in French. 2004. a. **Document type:** *Magazine, Trade.*
Published by: Comite Sectoriel de Main-d'Oeuvre des Services Automobiles, 5110, boul. Cousineau, bureau 200-C, Saint-Hubert, PQ J3Y 7G5, Canada. TEL 450-656-3445, 866-677-5999, FAX 450-677-8888.

MALAYSIA AUTOMOTIVE DIRECTORY. *see* BUSINESS AND ECONOMICS—Trade And Industrial Directories

388 336.2 DEU
MANDANTEN-INFORMATION FUER DAS KFZ-GEWERBE. Text in German. 1991. m. EUR 1.91 per issue (effective 2011). **Document type:** *Journal, Trade.*
Formerly (until 2007): Steuer-Brief fuer das Kfz-Gewerbe (0940-3078)
Published by: Deubner Verlag GmbH & Co. KG, Oststr 11, Cologne, 50996, Germany. TEL 49-221-9370180, FAX 49-221-93701890, kundenservice@deubner-verlag.de, http://www.vrp.de.

388.3 USA
MARKETPLACE (GLEN ELLYN). Text in English. bi-m. membership. **Document type:** *Newsletter, Consumer.* **Description:** For car enthusiasts dedicated to promoting the history, preservation and restoration of the Nash and related automobiles.
Published by: Nash Car Club of America, 1N274 Prairie, Glen Ellyn, IL 60137. bracewell@nashcarclub.org, http://www.nashcarclub.org. Ed. Jeff Griffith.

MARYLAND MOTOR VEHICLE INSURANCE. *see* INSURANCE

MARYLAND MOTORIST. *see* TRAVEL AND TOURISM

MASSACHUSETTS PRACTICE SERIES. MOTOR VEHICLE LAW AND PRACTICE WITH FORMS. *see* LAW

629.286 DEU
MATZE. Text in German. 1998. 3/yr. adv. **Document type:** *Magazine, Trade.*
Published by: Verlag Kaufhold GmbH, Philipp-Nicolai-Weg 3, Herdecke, 58313, Germany. TEL 49-2330-918311, FAX 49-2330-13570, info@verlag-kaufhold.de, http://www.verlag-kaufhold.de. Ed. Claudia Pfleging. Pub. Manfred Kaufhold. Adv. contact Selina Wannke. page EUR 5,000. Circ: 300,000 (controlled).

629.222 GBR ISSN 0968-8714
MAX POWER. Text in English. 1993. m. GBP 35 domestic; GBP 62 foreign (effective 2009). adv. back issues avail. **Document type:** *Magazine, Consumer.* **Description:** Features articles on the latest in tuning, styling and in car entertainment.
Related titles: Online - full text ed.
—**CCC.**
Published by: H. Bauer Publishing Ltd. (Subsidiary of: Bauer Media Group), Media House, Lynchwood, Peterborough, Cambridgeshire PE2 6EA, United Kingdom. TEL 44-1733-468000, http://www.bauer.co.uk. Ed. Mark Guest. Adv. contact Sarah Dodd. page GBP 8,400.

796.71 ZAF ISSN 1990-4568
MAX POWER. Text in English. 2006. m. ZAR 260 domestic; ZAR 441.46 in Namibia; ZAR 473.56 in Zimbabwe; ZAR 752.56 elsewhere (effective 2006). **Document type:** *Magazine, Consumer.*
Published by: Media24 Ltd., Naspers Centre, 40 Heerengracht St, PO Box 1802, Cape Town, 8000, South Africa. http://www.media24.com.

796.75 ESP
MAXI MOTO TUNING. Text in Spanish. 1994. m. **Document type:** *Magazine, Consumer.*
Published by: Motorpress Iberica (Subsidiary of: Gruner + Jahr AG & Co), Ancora 40, Madrid, 28045, Spain. TEL 34-91-3470100, FAX 34-91-3470152, http://www.motorpress-iberica.es. Ed. Ramon A Castella. Circ: 166,000 (paid and controlled).

796.5 CZE ISSN 1801-1594
MAXI TUNING. Text in Czech. 2005. m. CZK 455 (effective 2009). adv. **Document type:** *Magazine, Consumer.*
Published by: Motor-Presse Bohemia, U Krcskeho Nadrazi 36, Prague 4, 14000, Czech Republic. TEL 420-2-24109340, FAX 420-2-41721905, motopresse@motorpresse.cz, http://www.motorpresse.cz. Ed. Daniel Palat. Pub. Jan Blasek. Adv. contact Renata Ben. page CZK 30,000; trim 185 x 247.

388 PRT
MAXI TUNNING. Text in Portuguese. 2004. m. EUR 3.50 newsstand/cover (effective 2005). **Document type:** *Magazine, Consumer.*
Published by: Motorpress Lisboa, SA (Subsidiary of: Gruner + Jahr AG & Co), Rua Policarpio Anjos No. 4, Cruz Quebrada, Dafundo 1495-742, Portugal. TEL 351-21-4154500, FAX 351-21-4154501, buzine@motorpress.pt, http://www.mpl.pt. Ed. Luis Pimenta. Adv. contact Cristina Dias. Circ: 19,154 (paid).

656.1 CHE ISSN 1661-657X
MAXXTUNER. Text in German. 2006. q. CHF 19.80 (effective 2007). adv. **Document type:** *Magazine, Consumer.*
Published by: MaxxTuner GmbH, Muehlenweg 10, Diessenhofen, 8253, Switzerland. TEL 41-52-2129060, FAX 41-52-6573724, abo@maxxtuner.ch. Adv. contact Adrian Koch. page CHF 4,480; trim 210 x 297.

388.3 USA
MAZDASPORT. Text in English. 2001. bi-m. USD 19.95 domestic; USD 29.95 in Canada; USD 39.95 elsewhere; USD 6.99 newsstand/cover (effective 2005). adv. **Document type:** *Magazine, Consumer.*
Formerly (until 2003): Miata (1079-1337)
Published by: MediaSource Publishing Group, 770 Sycamore Ave, Ste J-445, Vista, CA 92083. TEL 760-631-1202. Ed. Alan Paradise. Pub. Barbara Beach.

388.3 ESP
LOS MEJORES AUTOMOVILES DEL MUNDO. Text in Spanish. 1992. a. **Document type:** *Catalog, Consumer.*
Related titles: ◆ Supplement to: Automovil.
Published by: Motorpress Iberica (Subsidiary of: Gruner + Jahr AG & Co), Ancora 40, Madrid, 28045, Spain. TEL 34-91-3470100, FAX 34-91-3470152. Circ: 25,000 (paid).

629.113 MEX
LOS MEJORES AUTOMOVILES DEL MUNDO. Text in Spanish. 1994. a. MXN 40 newsstand/cover (effective 2001). adv. **Document type:** *Magazine, Consumer.*
Published by: Editorial Motorpress Televisa (Subsidiary of: Gruner + Jahr AG & Co), Av Vasco de Quiroga 2000, Edif E, Mexico, Col Santa Fe, Mexico City, DF 01210, Mexico. TEL 525-2612672, FAX 525-2612731. Ed. Juan Manuel Garcia Rubio. Pubs. Carlos Mendez, Jesus Carrera. Adv. contact Otilia Perez. Circ: 18,750 (paid).

629.113 ARG ISSN 0329-3343
LOS MEJORES AUTOMOVILES DEL MUNDO. Text in Spanish. 1996. a. ARS 20 newsstand/cover (effective 2010). adv. **Document type:** *Magazine, Consumer.*
Published by: Motorpress Argentina, S.A. (Subsidiary of: Gruner + Jahr AG & Co), Ituzaingo, 642-648, Buenos Aires, 1141, Argentina. TEL 54-114-3077672, FAX 54-114-3077858, http://www.motorpress.com.ar/. Ed. Carlos Figueras. Pub. Jesus Carrera. Adv. contact Adrian Lualdi. Circ: 12,000 (paid).

388 PRT
OS MELHORES AUTOMOVEIS DO MUNDO. Text in Portuguese. 1994. a. EUR 3.75 newsstand/cover (effective 2005). adv. **Document type:** *Magazine, Consumer.*
Published by: Motorpress Lisboa, SA (Subsidiary of: Gruner + Jahr AG & Co), Rua Policarpio Anjos No. 4, Cruz Quebrada, Dafundo 1495-742, Portugal. TEL 351-21-4154500, FAX 351-21-4154501, buzine@motorpress.pt, http://www.mpl.pt. Circ: 9,529 (paid).

338 USA ISSN 1054-2558
MEMPHIS AUTOMOTIVE REPORT. Text in English. 1998. m. free to qualified personnel (effective 2008). adv. **Document type:** *Newspaper, Trade.* **Description:** Provides monthly news for the local automotive industry in West Tennessee, Arkansas, North Mississippi and Southeast Missouri.
Indexed: V03.
Published by: Autographic Publishing Company, Inc., 1121 Airport Center Dr, Ste 101, Nashville, TN 37214. TEL 615-391-3666, 800-467-3666, FAX 615-391-3622, garnett@automotivereport.net, http://www.automotivereport.net. Ed. Garnett Forkum. Pub. Allen Forkum. adv.: B&W page USD 1,200; trim 11.5 x 15. Circ: 5,800 (free).

MEN'S CAR. *see* LIFESTYLE

796.7 ZAF ISSN 1811-9069
MERCEDES. Text in English. 2004. s-a. **Document type:** *Magazine, Consumer.*
Published by: (DaimlerChrysler in South Africa (Pty) Ltd.), New Media Publishing, PO Box 440, Green Point, 8051, South Africa. TEL 27-21-4171111, FAX 27-21-4171112, newmedia@newmediapub.co.za, http://www.newmediapub.co.za. Ed. Adelle Horier.

796.77 DEU ISSN 1610-8043
MERCEDES-BENZ CLASSIC. Text in German. 2002. q. EUR 5 newsstand/cover (effective 2010). adv. **Document type:** *Magazine, Consumer.*
Related titles: English ed.: ISSN 1610-8051. EUR 6 newsstand/cover (effective 2003).
Published by: (Daimler AG, Kommunikation), W D V Gesellschaft fuer Medien & Kommunikation mbH & Co. OHG, Siemensstr 6, Bad Homburg, 61352, Germany. TEL 49-6172-6700, FAX 49-6172-670144, info@wdv.de, http://www.wdv.de. adv.: page EUR 7,500; trim 187 x 244. Circ: 126,000 (controlled).

629.2222 GBR ISSN 1474-7030
MERCEDES ENTHUSIAST. Text in English. 2001 (Oct.). m. GBP 43 domestic; GBP 55.20 in Europe; GBP 61 elsewhere; GBP 5.10 per issue domestic; GBP 5.80 per issue in Europe; GBP 6.70 per issue elsewhere; GBP 3.99 newsstand/cover (effective 2010). adv. back issues avail. **Document type:** *Magazine, Consumer.* **Description:** Offers practical guidance to buyers of pre-owned Mercedes and down-to-earth tips on keeping cars in top condition.
Published by: Sundial Magazines Ltd., 17 Wickham Rd, Beckenham, Kent BR3 5JS, United Kingdom. TEL 44-20-86394411, 44-20-86394400, info@sundialmagazines.co.uk, http://www.sundialmagazines.co.uk/. adv.: B&W page GBP 875, color page GBP 1,095; trim 297 x 210. **Subscr. addr.:** Mercedes Enthusiast Subscriptions, 800 Guillat Ave, Kent Science Park, Sittingbourne ME8 8GU, United Kingdom. TEL 44-8448-488430, FAX 44-8448-560650, mercedes@servicehelpline.co.uk.

629.22 NLD ISSN 1877-6663
▼ **MERCEDES MAGAZINE.** Text in French, Dutch. 2009. 4/yr. adv. **Document type:** *Magazine, Consumer.*
Published by: (Mercedes-Benz Belgium/Luxembourg BEL), Hemels BV, PO Box 369, Hilversum, 1200 AJ, Netherlands. TEL 31-35-6899900, FAX 31-35-6899999, mail@hemels.com, http://www.hemels.com. Circ: 60,000 (controlled).

388.3 ITA ISSN 1721-3932
LA MIA 4 X 4; extreme & trendy car magazine. Variant title: La Mia Quattro per Quattro. Text in Italian. 2002. m. EUR 50 (effective 2008). **Document type:** *Magazine, Consumer.*
Published by: Barbero Editori Srl, Via Galileo Galilei 3, Chieri, TO 10023, Italy. TEL 39-011-9470400, FAX 39-011-9470577.

388.3 ITA ISSN 1128-3653
LA MIA AUTO. Text in Italian. 1999. m. EUR 44 (effective 2008). **Document type:** *Magazine, Consumer.*
Published by: Barbero Editori Srl, Via Galileo Galilei 3, Chieri, TO 10023, Italy. TEL 39-011-9470400, FAX 39-011-9470577.

388 USA
MID-WESTERN 4-WHEELER. Text in English. 1979. 6/yr. USD 8. adv. **Description:** Covers events and issues of special interest to owners of four-wheel drive vehicles.
Published by: Midwest 4-Wheel Drive Association, 25624 Eaton Ave., Fairbault, MN 55021-8283. TEL 414-898-4598. Eds. Jim Schrot, Mel Schrot. Circ: 1,600.

338.476 GBR ISSN 0958-5893
MIDLAND AUTO TRADER. Text in English. 1988. w. **Document type:** *Magazine, Consumer.* **Description:** Provides detailed information on cars and other vehicles for sale. Area of covereage includes: Birmingham, Black Country, Leicestershire, Coventry, Nottingham, Derby & Northampton.
Incorporates in part (in 2009): Lincolnshire Auto Trader
Published by: Auto Trader Publications Ltd. (Subsidiary of: Trader Media Group Ltd.), Auto Trader House, Danehill, Cutbush Park, Lower Earley Reading, Berkshire RG6 4UT, United Kingdom. TEL 44-845-0501766, FAX 44-118-9239159, enquiries@autotrader.co.uk. Circ: 34,264 (paid).

MIDWEST RACING NEWS. *see* SPORTS AND GAMES

388.3 USA ISSN 1524-5268
MIDWEST TRAVELER. Variant title: A A A Midwest Traveler. Text in English. 1915. bi-m. USD 3 to non-members; USD 0.50 per issue to non-members; free to members (effective 2005). adv. bk.rev. illus. 52 p./no.; **Document type:** *Magazine, Consumer.* **Description:** Fetures local and world travel, safety and transportation news.
Former titles (until 199?): Midwest Motorist (0026-3435); Auto Club News
Published by: Automobile Club of Missouri, 12901 N. Forty Dr., St. Louis, MO 63141. TEL 314-523-7350, 800-222-7623, FAX 314-523-6982, http://www.aaamissouri.com. Ed., Pub., R&P Michael J Right. Adv. contact Debbie Reinhardt. Circ: 470,000 (controlled).

629.286 790.1 USA
MIGHTY MOPARS. Text in English. 1981. 6/yr. USD 25 (effective 1999). adv. bk.rev.; software rev. maps; mkt.; stat.; charts; illus. back issues avail. **Document type:** *Newsletter.* **Description:** Dedicated to the preservation of Chrysler Corporation muscle cars. Includes articles on restoration tips, services, parts and technical information.
Published by: Mopar Scat Pack Club, PO Box 2303, Dearborn, MI 48123-2303. TEL 313-278-2240. Ed. J Bielenda. adv.: B&W page USD 150; trim 10 x 7.

MILE POST. *see* HOBBIES

388.3 GBR ISSN 0026-380X
MILESTONES. Text in English. 1946. 3/yr. GBP 0.30 per issue. adv. bk.rev. charts; illus.
Published by: (Institute of Advanced Motorists), Advanced Mile-Posts Publications Ltd., I A M House, Advanced Mile-Posts Publications Ltd, Flat 359, 365 Chiswick High Rd, London, W4 4HS, United Kingdom. TEL 081-994-4403, FAX 081-994-9249. Ed. Ian Webb. Circ: 102,000.

MILITARY VEHICLES MAGAZINE. *see* MILITARY

388.3 CHN ISSN 1009-6892
MINGCHEZHI/CAR AND DRIVER. Text in Chinese. 2000. m. CNY 145 (effective 2009). **Document type:** *Magazine, Consumer.*
Related titles: Online - full text ed.
Published by: Beijing Bierde Guanggao Youxian Gongsi/Beijing Hachette Advertising Co., Ltd. (Subsidiary of: Hachette Filipacchi Medias S.A.), 19, Deguomen wai Dajie, Guoji Dasha 2202, Beijing, 100004, China. Adv. contact Alex Lei TEL 86-21-6133 5199.

796.77 AUS ISSN 1449-8960
THE MINI EXPERIENCE. Text in English. 2004. q. AUD 32 domestic; AUD 39 in New Zealand; AUD 55 elsewhere; AUD 9.95 newsstand/cover domestic; NZD 10.90 newsstand/cover in New Zealand (effective 2008). adv. back issues avail. **Document type:** *Magazine, Consumer.*
Published by: Autofan Media, PO Box 186, Newcomb, VIC 3219, Australia. TEL 61-3-52504842, FAX 61-3-52504846, advertising@miniexperience.com.au, http://www.autofan.com.au.

629.222 GBR ISSN 1362-7252
MINI MAGAZINE. Text in English. 1996. m. GBP 45 domestic; GBP 80 in Europe; GBP 110 elsewhere; GBP 3.99 newsstand/cover (effective 2010). adv. illus. back issues avail. **Document type:** *Magazine, Consumer.* **Description:** Features Minis from the UK and abroad - classic to custom, retro to racer. Practical advise on maintenance, tuning and restoration, buying guides, the latest news and products, plus a massive free readers' classified section.
Related titles: Online - full text ed.: GBP 45; GBP 3.99 per issue (effective 2010); Supplement(s): Mini Expert. ISSN 1752-0630. 2006.
Published by: Future Publishing Ltd., Beauford Ct, 30 Monmouth St, Bath, Avon BA1 2BW, United Kingdom. TEL 44-1225-442244, FAX 44-1225-446019, customerservice@subscription.co.uk, http://www.futureplc.com. Ed. Mark Robinson TEL 44-1225-442244 ext 5127. **Subscr. to:** Tower House, Sovereign Park, Market Harborough, Leicestershire LE16 9EF, United Kingdom. TEL 44-844-8481602, FAX 44-1858-438795, future@subscription.co.uk.

629.222 796.77 GBR ISSN 0963-1186
MINIWORLD; the magazine for the mighty mini. Text in English. 1991. m. GBP 34.99 domestic; USD 90.90 in United States; USD 93.30 in Canada; EUR 72 in Europe; GBP 56.80 elsewhere; GBP 4.10 newsstand/cover (effective 2010). adv. illus. back issues avail. **Document type:** *Magazine, Consumer.* **Description:** Covers all aspects of buying, selling, and owning a Morris Mini.
Published by: I P C Country & Leisure Media Ltd. (Subsidiary of: I P C Media Ltd.), Leon House, 233 High St, Croydon, CR9 1HZ, United Kingdom. TEL 44-20-87268364, http://www.ipcmedia.com. Ed. Monty Watkins TEL 44-20-87268357. Pub. Richard Marcroft TEL 44-20-87268343. Adv. contact Ian James TEL 44-20-87268333. B&W page GBP 790, color page GBP 1,139; trim 210 x 297. **Subscr. to:** Rockwood House, Perrymount Rd, Haywards Heath RH16 3DH, United Kingdom. TEL 44-845-1231231, IPCsubs@quadrantsubs.com, http://www.magazinesdirect.co.uk. **Dist. by:** MarketForce UK Ltd. salesinnovation@marketforce.co.uk, http://www.marketforce.co.uk/.

388 USA
MINNESOTA. METROPOLITAN COUNCIL. ANNUAL REPORT. Text in English. 1969. a. free. **Description:** Examines the activities of the organizations' previous year.
Former titles: St. Paul, Minnesota. Twin Cities Area Metropolitan Transit Commission. Annual Report; St. Paul, Minnesota. Metropolitan Transit Commission. Annual Report (0082-710X)
Published by: Metropolitan Council, Mears Park Centre, 230 E. Fifth St., St. Paul, MN 55101. TEL 651-602-1000, FAX 651-602-1464. Ed. Judy Hohmann. Circ: 3,000.

629.2222 GBR ISSN 1358-829X
MINOR MONTHLY. Text in English. 1995. m. GBP 27; GBP 2.75 newsstand/cover (effective 2010). adv. illus. back issues avail. **Document type:** *Magazine, Consumer.* **Description:** Dedicated to the Morris Minor car and enthusiast.
Related titles: Online - full text ed.: GBP 20 (effective 2010).
Published by: Poundbury Publishing Ltd., Middle Farm, Middle Farm Way, Acland Rd, Poundbury, Dorset DT1 3RS, United Kingdom. TEL 44-1305-266360, FAX 44-1305-262760, admin@poundbury.co.uk, http://www.poundbury.co.uk. Ed. Russ Harvey.

MINORAGE. *see* ANTIQUES

629.288 USA
MINUTIA. Text in English. 1986. q. USD 20 (effective 1998). adv. illus. back issues avail. **Document type:** *Newsletter.*
Formerly (until 1991): M und M Rapper (0888-4641)
Published by: Microcar and Minicar Club, PO Box 43137, Upper Montclair, NJ 07043. Ed. John Luttrop. Circ: 250.

MISS INFORMATION'S AUTOMOTIVE CALENDAR OF EVENTS. *see* ANTIQUES

MOBILE ELECTRONICS. *see* COMMUNICATIONS

629.286 621.8 SRB ISSN 1450-5304
MOBILITY AND VEHICLES MECHANICS. Abbreviated title: M V M. Text in Serbian, English. 1975. q.
Formerly (until 1992): Motorna Vozila. Motori (0350-1027)
Published by: Univerzitet u Kragujevcu, Masinski Fakultet/University of Kragujevac, Faculty of Mechanical Engineering, Sestre Janjic 6, Kragujevac, 34000. TEL 381-34-335990, FAX 381-34-333192, mfkg@kg.ac.yu, http://www.mfkg.kg.ac.yu.

796.7 USA
MODEL A NEWS. Text in English. 1953. bi-m. USD 20; USD 24 foreign. adv. index. back issues avail.
Published by: Model A Restorer's Club, 6721 Merriman Rd., Garden City, MI 48135-1956. TEL 313-278-1455. Ed. Kenneth Keeley. Circ: 9,000.

388.3 USA
MODERN CAR CARE. Text in English. m. USD 47 domestic; USD 60 in Canada; USD 97 elsewhere (effective 2008). adv. **Document type:** *Magazine, Trade.* **Description:** Contains trade information and news for owners and operators of full-serve, self-serve carwashes and detail shops.
Related titles: Online - full text ed.
Published by: Virgo Publishing, Llc, PO Box 40079, Phoenix, AZ 85067. TEL 480-990-1101, FAX 480-990-0819, jsiefert@vpico.com, http://www.vpico.com. Ed. Tony Jones TEL 480-990-1101 ext 1261. Pub. George Spelius TEL 480-990-1101 ext 1023. adv.: B&W page USD 2,235, color page USD 4,435; bleed 8.375 x 11.125. Circ: 20,170 (paid and controlled).

MODERN TIRE DEALER; covering tire sales and car service. *see* RUBBER

796.77 CAN
MODIFIED LUXURY & EXOTICS. Text in English. 2004 (Oct.). bi-m. USD 24.95; USD 5.99 newsstand/cover (effective 2004). adv. **Document type:** *Magazine, Consumer.*
Published by: Modified Automotive Media Group (Subsidiary of: Source Interlink Companies), 111 Peter St, Ste 700, Toronto, ON M5V 2H1, Canada. TEL 416-341-8950, FAX 416-341-8959, info@verticalscope.com, http://www.verticalscope.com/. Adv. contact Paul Murphy TEL 416-341-8950 ext 263. color page USD 7,800; trim 8 x 10.875.

796.77 796.72 CAN
MODIFIED MAGAZINE. Text in English. 2002. m. USD 37.50 domestic; USD 23.88 in United States; USD 59.88 elsewhere (effective 2003). adv. **Document type:** *Magazine, Consumer.*
Related titles: Online - full content ed.

TU

Published by: Modified Automotive Media Group (Subsidiary of: Source Interlink Companies), 111 Peter St, Ste 700, Toronto, ON M5V 2H1, Canada. TEL 416-341-8950, FAX 416-341-8959, info@verticalscope.com, http://www.verticalscope.com/. Ed. David Pankew. Pub. Rob Laidlaw. adv.: color page USD 4,000; trim 8 x 10.875.

769.77 CAN ISSN 1715-4448
MODIFIED MUSTANGS; the performance magazine for Mustang enthusiasts. Text in English. m. USD 19.95; USD 4.99 newsstand/cover (effective 2006). adv. **Document type:** *Magazine, Consumer.*
—CCC.
Published by: Modified Automotive Media Group (Subsidiary of: Source Interlink Companies), 111 Peter St, Ste 700, Toronto, ON M5V 2H1, Canada. TEL 416-341-8950, FAX 416-341-8959, info@verticalscope.com, http://www.verticalscope.com/. Ed. Huw Evans. Pub. Rob Laidlaw. Adv. contact Mark Borbo TEL 416-324-9768. color page USD 4,000; trim 8 x 10.875. Circ: 80,000 (paid).

MODIFIED MUSTANGS & FORDS. *see* ANTIQUES

629 USA ISSN 2152-4106
▼ **MOMENTUM (WARRENDALE)**; a student magazine of S A E International. Text in English. 2010 (Feb.). bi-m. USD 30 in North America; USD 50 elsewhere (effective 2011). **Document type:** *Magazine, Consumer.* **Description:** For student members of the Society of Automobile Engineers. Includes student, chapter and team news, guides for undergraduate and graduate schools, and career and continuing education tips.
Published by: S A E International, 400 Commonwealth Dr, Warrendale, PA 15096. TEL 724-776-4970, FAX 724-776-0790, CustomerService@sae.org, http://www.sae.org.

388.3 CAN ISSN 0831-2958
LE MONDE DE L'AUTO. Text in English. 1985. 6/yr. CAD 12. adv. bk.rev. **Document type:** *Magazine, Consumer.* **Description:** Includes articles of general interest to car owners and operators such as information and prices on new cars, maintenance information and tips.
Published by: World of Wheels Publishing, Inc. (St. Laurent), 7575 Rte Transcanadienne, Bur 401, St Laurent, PQ H4T 1V6, Canada. TEL 514-956-1361, FAX 514-956-1461. Ed., R&P Luc Gagne. Pub. Lynn R Helpard. Adv. contact John McGouran. Circ: 42,000.

629.2 BEL
LE MONITEUR DE L'AUTOMOBILE. Text in French. 1979. fortn. EUR 65 domestic; EUR 160 in the European Union; EUR 186 elsewhere (effective 2005). **Document type:** *Directory, Consumer.*
Related titles: Dutch ed.: Auto Gids.
Published by: Editions Automagazine S.A., Ch de la Hulpe 181, Brussels, 1170, Belgium. TEL 32-2-3333212. Ed. Etienne Visart. Circ: 390,000.

796.7 FIN ISSN 0359-7636
MOOTTORI. Text in Finnish; Summaries in Swedish. 1925. m. EUR 52 (effective 2007). adv. bk.rev. charts; illus. **Document type:** *Magazine, Consumer.*
Former titles (until 1983): Auto ja Liikenne (0356-4827); (until 1978): Moottori (0027-0970)
Published by: (Autoliitto r.y./Automobile and Touring Club of Finland), Kynamies Oy, Koydenpunojankatu 2 A, Helsinki, 00180, Finland. TEL 358-9-15668510, FAX 358-9-15668600, http://www.kynamies.fi. Ed. Eila Parviainen. Circ: 83,000.

629.286 USA
MOPAR ENGINES & TECH; high performance mopar. Text in English. 2000. a. USD 4 newsstand/cover domestic; USD 5.99 newsstand/cover in Canada (effective 2007). adv. 100 p./no.; back issues avail.; reprints avail. **Document type:** *Magazine, Consumer.* **Description:** Focuses on mopars and engines, including engine buildup features, carb and intakemanifold testing, restoration, detailing and more.
Published by: Source Interlink Companies, 6420 Wilshire Blvd, 10th Fl, Los Angeles, CA 90048. TEL 323-782-2000, FAX 323-782-2585, dheine@sourceinterlink.com, http://www.sourceinterlinkmedia.com.

796.77 790.13 USA ISSN 1056-2966
MOPAR MUSCLE. Text in English. 1998. m. USD 29.97 domestic; USD 41.97 in Canada; USD 53.97 elsewhere (effective 2008). adv. back issues avail.; reprints avail. **Document type:** *Magazine, Consumer.* **Description:** Provides "how-to" and technical information. Includes parts and service sources, restoration and repair data, buying tips, news on Mopar events nationwide.
Formerly: High Performance Mopar Combined With Mopar Muscle
Related titles: Online - full content ed.
Indexed: G06, G07, G08, I05, S23.
—CCC.
Published by: Source Interlink Companies, 9036 Brittany Way, Tampa, FL 33619. TEL 813-675-3500, FAX 813-675-3556, dheine@sourceinterlink.com, http://www.sourceinterlinkmedia.com. Ed. Randy Bolig. Pub. Michael Essex TEL 813-675-3492. adv.: B&W page USD 4,980, color page USD 7,340. Circ: 67,924 (paid).

796.77 USA
MOPAR NOW!. Text in English. 2000. q. USD 5.95 per issue domestic; USD 6.95 per issue in Canada (effective 2009). **Document type:** *Magazine, Consumer.*
Published by: Harris Publications, Inc., 1115 Broadway, New York, NY 10010. TEL 212-807-7100, FAX 212-924-2352, subscriptions@harris-pub.com, http://www.harris-pub.com. Ed. Cliff Gromer. Pub. Stanley R Harris. Adv. contact Brett Underwood TEL 704-896-1959.

388.3 CAN ISSN 1719-6442
MOST FUEL-EFFICIENT VEHICLES. Text in English. 1999. a. **Document type:** *Journal, Consumer.*
Media: Online - full text. **Related titles:** French ed.: Vehicules les Plus Econergetiques. ISSN 1719-6450. 1999.
Published by: Natural Resources Canada, Office of Energy Efficiency (Subsidiary of: Natural Resources Canada/Ressources Naturelles Canada), 580 Booth St, 18th Flr, Ottawa, ON K1A 0E4, Canada. TEL 613-995-2943, 800-387-2000, FAX 613-943-1590, euc.cec@nrcan.gc.ca.

796.77 ITA ISSN 1828-1141
MOTO DESIGN. Text in Multiple languages. 2006. s-a. EUR 6 (effective 2009). **Document type:** *Magazine, Trade.*
Published by: Design Diffusion Edizioni, Via Lucano 3, Milan, 20135, Italy. TEL 39-02-5516109, FAX 39-02-59902431, info@designdiffusion.com. Circ: 40,000.

796.7 HRV ISSN 1331-3266
MOTO PULS. Text in Croatian. 1997. bi-m. adv. **Document type:** *Magazine, Consumer.*
Supersedes in part (1997-1997): Auto Moto Puls (1331-243X); Which was formed by the merger of (1993-1997): Auto Auto (1330-433X); (1996-1997): Moto Puls (1330-9943)
Published by: Moto Puls d.o.o., Savica Sanci 115, Zagreb, 10000, Croatia. TEL 385-1-249149, FAX 385-1-249154, moto-puls@zg.tel.hr. Ed. Boris Puscenik.

629.326 CZE ISSN 1213-3086
MOTOHOUSE. Text in Czech. 2001. 10/yr. CZK 750; CZK 99 per issue (effective 2011). adv. **Document type:** *Magazine, Consumer.*
Published by: MediaForce, s.r.o., Veselska 699, Prague 9, 19900, Czech Republic. TEL 420-2-606667650. Ed. Karel Taborsky. Adv. contact Hilda Liptakova. Circ: 25,000 (paid and controlled).

629.326 CZE ISSN 1212-3412
MOTOHOUSE KATALOG. Text in Czech. 1998. a. CZK 100 per issue (effective 2008). **Document type:** *Catalog, Consumer.*
Incorporates (1999-2005): Autohouse Katalog (1212-7485)
Published by: MediaForce, s.r.o., Veselska 699, Prague 9, 19900, Czech Republic. TEL 420-2-606667650, FAX 420-2-96361636, motohouse@motohouse.cz, http://www.motohouse.cz. Ed. Karel Taborsky.

629.2 NLD ISSN 1872-6410
MOTOPLUS. Text in Dutch. 2006. 24/yr. EUR 59; EUR 3.95 newsstand/cover (effective 2010). adv.
Published by: Volgas TTG Producties bv, Postbus 90, Varsseveld, 7050 AB, Netherlands. FAX 31-88-6686737, http://www.ttg.nl. Eds. Jeroen Hidding, Eric Bulsink. adv.: B&W page EUR 1,050, color page EUR 1,500; trim 215 x 280. Circ: 25,000.

388.3 SWE ISSN 0027-1764
MOTOR. Variant title: Nya Motor. Text in Swedish. 1943. 10/yr. SEK 395 (effective 2004). adv. bk.rev. illus. **Document type:** *Magazine, Consumer.*
Related titles: Online - full text ed.
Indexed: A09, A10, A11, T02, V03, V04.
Published by: Motormaennens Riksfoerbund, Sveavaegen 159 3tr, Box 23142, Stockholm, 10435, Sweden. TEL 46-8-6903800, FAX 46-8-6903824, service@motormannen.se. Ed. Lars Arnborg. Pub. Martin Andreae. adv.: B&W page SEK 18,800, color page SEK 25,000; trim 194 x 258. Circ: 121,300 (paid).

388.3 RUS ISSN 1028-8910
MOTOR. Text in Russian. 1996. m. USD 179 in North America (effective 2004). adv. bk.rev. **Document type:** *Magazine, Consumer.*
Related titles: Online - full text ed.
Published by: Motor Press, a/ya 626, Moscow, 119049, Russian Federation. TEL 7-095-7271895, FAX 7-095-3177100. Ed., Adv. contact Michael Galkin. Circ: 75,000. **Dist. by:** East View Information Services, 10601 Wayzata Blvd, Minneapolis, MN 55305. TEL 952-252-1201, 800-477-1005, FAX 952-252-1202, info@eastview.com, http://www.eastview.com.

388.3 USA ISSN 0027-1748
TL1
MOTOR; covering the world of automotive service. Text in English. 1903. m. USD 48 domestic; USD 60 foreign; USD 6 newsstand/cover; free to qualified personnel (effective 2011). adv. bk.rev. illus.; mkt.; stat.; tr.lit.; charts. Index. back issues avail.; reprints avail. **Document type:** *Magazine, Trade.* **Description:** Provides the readers with the information needed to fix their vehicles, along with the guidance on running their businesses and reports on the newest tools, equipment and repair techniques.
Related titles: Microform ed.: (from PQC); Online - full text ed.: free to qualified personnel; USD 90 (effective 2008); Supplement(s): MOTOR Source Guide. 1992. USD 19.95 newsstand/cover (effective 2011).
Indexed: A15, A22, ABIn, G09, P10, P16, P48, P51, P52, P53, P54, PQC, WMB.
—Ingenta, Linda Hall.
Published by: Hearst Business Media, 1301 W. Long Lake Rd, Ste 300, Troy, MI 48098. TEL 248-312-2700, http://www.hearst.com. Ed., Pub. John Lypen. Circ: 3,225 (paid); 141,202 (free).

388.321 796.7 DNK ISSN 0047-8199
MOTOR. Text in Danish. 1906. m. DKK 605 membership (effective 2009). adv. bk.rev. charts; illus.; pat.; stat.; tr.lit. index. back issues avail. **Document type:** *Magazine, Consumer.*
Related titles: Online - full text ed.
—CCC.
Published by: Forenede Danske Motorejere/Federation of Danish Motorists, Firskovvej 32, Kgs. Lyngby, 2800, Denmark. TEL 45-45-270707, FAX 45-45-270993, fdm@fdm.dk. Adv. contact Henning Olesen. Circ: 232,000 (controlled).

629.2 NOR ISSN 0027-173X
MOTOR. Text in Norwegian. 1933. m. NOK 405 membership (effective 2005). adv. bk.rev. illus. **Document type:** *Magazine, Consumer.*
Formerly (until 1966): Motortidende (0332-897X)
Related titles: Online - full text ed.
—CCC.
Published by: Hjemmet Mortensen AS, Gullhaugveien 1, Nydalen, Oslo, 0441, Norway. TEL 47-22-585000, FAX 47-22-585959, firmapost@hm-media.no, http://www.hm-media.no. Ed. Svein Ola Hope. Adv. contact Anne Schwarz. page NOK 68,000; trim 210 x 280. Circ: 400,000 (paid).

629.33 SVK ISSN 1336-4200
MOT'OR. Text in Slovak. 1991. m. EUR 0.90 newsstand/cover (effective 2011). adv. **Document type:** *Magazine, Consumer.*
Formerly (until 2003): MOT (1210-2083)
Published by: Elektro-Energo s.r.o., Drotarska Cesta 21/A, Bratislava, 81102, Slovakia. TEL 421-2-62527077, FAX 421-2-62527077. Ed. Samuel Bibza.

796.71 KEN ISSN 1991-0991
MOTOR; East Africa's only independent cars and motorsport magazine. Text in English. 1995. m. KES 1,750 (effective 2006). adv. **Document type:** *Magazine, Consumer.*
Published by: Media 7 Group Kenya Ltd., PO Box 50087, City Square, Nairobi, 00200, Kenya. TEL 254-20-550957, FAX 254-20-551997, info@media7group.com. adv.: B&W page KES 79,750, color page KES 99,750; trim 210 x 276.

796.77 POL ISSN 0580-0447
MOTOR. Text in Polish. 1952. w. PLZ 1.99 newsstand/cover (effective 2011). adv. **Document type:** *Magazine, Consumer.*
Published by: Wydawnictwo Bauer Sp. z o.o. (Subsidiary of: Bauer Media Group), ul Motorowa 1, Warsaw, 04-035, Poland. TEL 48-22-5170500, FAX 48-22-5170125, kontakt@bauer.pl, http://www.bauer.pl. Ed. Krzysztof Burmajster. Adv. contact Marcin Gudowicz.

388.3 796.72 AUS
MOTOR (SYDNEY); the power, the prestige, the passion. Text in English. 1954. m. AUD 79.95; AUD 8.50 newsstand/cover (effective 2008). adv. bk.rev. illus.; pat. index. **Document type:** *Magazine, Consumer.* **Description:** Provides information on latest trends among performance and prestige cars. Offers comprehensive coverage of international racing events.
Formerly (until 1992): Modern Motor (0026-8143)
Related titles: Online - full text ed.
Indexed: GdIns.
Published by: A C P Magazines Ltd. (Subsidiary of: P B L Media Pty Ltd.), 54-58 Park St, Sydney, NSW 2000, Australia. TEL 61-2-92828000, FAX 61-2-91263769, research@acpaction.com.au. Ed. Michael Taylor. Adv. contact Michael Merckel. color page AUD 6,490; trim 225 x 297. Circ: 43,171. **Subscr. to:** Magshop, Reply Paid 4967, Sydney, NSW 2001, Australia. TEL 61-2-136116, subs@magstore.com.au, http://shop.magstore.com.au.

MOTOR A DIESEL. *see* ENGINEERING—Mechanical Engineering

388.3 USA ISSN 1520-9385
TL1
MOTOR AGE; for the professional automotive import & domestic service industry. Text in English. 1899. m. USD 70 domestic; USD 106 foreign; USD 14 newsstand/cover domestic; USD 15 newsstand/cover in Canada & Mexico; USD 21 newsstand/cover elsewhere (effective 2011). adv. illus.; mkt.; stat.; tr.lit. index. back issues avail.; reprints avail. **Document type:** *Magazine, Trade.* **Description:** Provides a technical publication that covers the domestic and import automotive service industry for owners, managers and professional service technicians and mechanics.
Incorporates (1921-2002): Motor Service (0027-1977); Former titles (until 1997): Chilton's Motor Age (0193-7022); (until 1970): Motor Age (0027-1772); (until 1961): Chilton's Motor Age; (until 1950): Motor Age; (until 1943): Motor Age for Automotive Servicemen; (until 1940): Motor Age
Related titles: Microfiche ed.: (from PQC); Microfilm ed.: (from PQC); Online - full text ed.: ISSN 1558-2892. USD 60 (effective 2011).
Indexed: A09, A10, A15, A22, A26, ABIn, B01, B02, B04, B06, B07, B09, B15, B17, B18, BPI, BusI, E08, G04, G06, G07, G08, I05, I07, M01, M02, MASUSE, P48, P51, P52, PQC, S09, T&II, T02, V02, V03, V04, W01, W02, W03, W05.
—CCC.
Published by: Advanstar Communications, Inc., 6200 Canoga Ave, 2nd Fl, Woodland Hills, CA 91367. TEL 818-593-5000, FAX 818-593-5020, info@advanstar.com, http://www.advanstar.com. Ed. Larry Silvey TEL 440-891-2612. Pub. Terri McMenamin TEL 610-397-1667.

629.2 USA ISSN 0098-1745
TL152
MOTOR AUTO REPAIR MANUAL. Text in English. 1938. a. (in 2 vols.). adv. index. **Document type:** *Handbook/Manual/Guide, Trade.* **Description:** Deals with mechanical repair for American made cars.
Former titles (until 1973): Motor's Auto Repair Manual; (until 19??): Motor's Factory Shop Manual
Published by: Motor Information Systems (Subsidiary of: Hearst Corporation), 5600 Crooks Rd, Ste 200, Troy, MI 48098. TEL 248-312-2700, 800-288-6828, FAX 248-879-8603, motorbookscallcenter@motor.com, http://www.motor.com.

388 USA ISSN 1359-4524
HD9710.3.E9
MOTOR BUSINESS JAPAN. Text in English. 4/yr. GBP 635, USD 1,095 (effective 2000). **Description:** Examines the impact of the Japanese market on the international automotive markets.
Formerly (until Oct. 1995): Japanese Motor Business (0266-898X)
Related titles: Microform ed.: (from PQC); Online - full text ed.; ◆ Series: E I U Automotive; ◆ Europe's Automotive Components Business. ISSN 0960-5436.
Indexed: A12, A17, ABIn, P48, P51, P53, P54, PQC.
Published by: Economist Intelligence Unit Ltd. (Subsidiary of: Economist Intelligence Unit Ltd.), 111 W 57th St, New York, NY 10019. TEL 212-554-0600, FAX 212-586-1181, newyork@eiu.com, http://www.eiu.com.

MOTOR CARAVAN. *see* SPORTS AND GAMES—Outdoor Life

338.3 ESP
MOTOR CLASICO. Text in Spanish. 1986. m. adv. **Document type:** *Magazine, Consumer.* **Description:** For classic car enthusiasts.
Published by: Motorpress Iberica (Subsidiary of: Gruner + Jahr AG & Co), Ancora 40, Madrid, 28045, Spain. TEL 34-91-3470100, FAX 34-91-3470152, http://www.motorpress-iberica.es. Ed. Luis Alberto Izquierdo. Circ: 16,000 (paid).

796.77 PRT
MOTOR CLASSICO (PORTUGAL). Text in Portuguese. 199?. m. EUR 37.80 (effective 2011). adv.
Published by: Motorpress Lisboa, SA (Subsidiary of: Gruner + Jahr AG & Co), Rua Policarpio Anjos No. 4, Cruz Quebrada, Dafundo 1495-742, Portugal. TEL 351-21-4154500, FAX 351-21-4154501, http://www.mpl.pt.

629.28 USA
MOTOR DOMESTIC CAR CRASH ESTIMATING GUIDE. Text in English. 1955. 12/yr. USD 376 (effective 2007). adv. **Document type:** *Handbook/Manual/Guide, Trade.* **Description:** Provides information necessary for assessing vehicle collision damage.
Formerly (until 19??): Motor Crash Estimating Data (1532-9445); Which superseded in part: Motor Crash Estimating Guide (0194-9411)
Published by: Motor Information Systems (Subsidiary of: Hearst Corporation), 5600 Crooks Rd, Ste 200, Troy, MI 48098. TEL 248-312-2700, 800-288-6828, FAX 248-879-8603, motorbookscallcenter@motor.com, http://www.motor.com. Circ: 15,000.

614.86 USA ISSN 0160-1644
TL152
MOTOR EARLY MODEL CRASH ESTIMATING GUIDE. Variant title: Crash Estimating Guide. Early Model Crash Estimating Guide. Text in English. 1977. q. USD 400 (effective 2007). adv. **Description:** Covers information about domestic and imported cars, light trucks, vans and SUVs early models.
Published by: Motor Information Systems (Subsidiary of: Hearst Corporation), 5600 Crooks Rd, Ste 200, Troy, MI 48098. TEL 248-312-2700, 800-288-6828, FAX 248-879-8603, motorbookscallcenter@motor.com, http://www.motor.com.

388.3 AUS ISSN 0129-1483
MOTOR EQUIPMENT NEWS. Abbreviated title: M E N. Text in English. 1982. m. AUD 60.50 (effective 2009). adv. bk.rev. **Document type:** *Magazine, Trade.* **Description:** Covers all aspects of the automotive industry trade including service and repair and parts and accessories.
Published by: Trade Press Australia, PO Box 229, Potts Point, NSW 1335, Australia. TEL 61-2-96648900, FAX 61-2-96648911, neilthomas@ausauto.com.au. Ed. Tony Tannous. Pub. Neil Thomas. Adv. contact David Newton Ross. page AUD 5,820; trim 270 x 370. Circ: 22,000.

788.3 NZL ISSN 1175-1908
MOTOR EQUIPMENT NEWS. Text in English. 1985. m. NZD 59 domestic; NZD 110 in Australia; NZD 120 elsewhere (effective 2008). adv. **Document type:** *Magazine, Trade.* **Description:** Contains a range of news and features of interest to those involved in the automotive repair industry.
Incorporates (2006-2006): Diesel Industry News (1177-3286); (in 1999): Automotive Industry Magazine
Indexed: A09, A10, A11, B01, B07, T02, V03, V04.
Published by: Adrenalin Publishing Ltd, 14C Vega Pl, North Shore City, 0754, New Zealand. TEL 64-9-4784771, FAX 64-9-4784779, http://www.adrenalin.co.nz/. Ed. Robert Barry. Pub. Cathy Parker. Adv. contact Ben McDonald.

338.4 USA ISSN 0164-6346
TL152
MOTOR IMPORTED CAR CRASH ESTIMATING GUIDE. Text in English. m. USD 414 (effective 2007). illus. **Document type:** *Handbook/ Manual/Guide, Trade.* **Description:** Provides information necessary for assessing vehicle collision damage.
Published by: Motor Publications, Crash Books Department, 5600 Crooks Rd, Ste 102, Troy, MI 48098. Ed. Philip C Cunningham.

621.4 GBR ISSN 1742-5204
MOTOR INDUSTRY MAGAZINE. Abbreviated title: M I M. Text in English. 1946. 10/yr. GBP 45 in Europe to non-members; GBP 50 elsewhere to non-members; free to members (effective 2009). adv. bk.rev. abstr.; bibl.; charts; illus. index, cum.index. back issues avail. **Document type:** *Magazine, Trade.* **Description:** Contains authoritative editorial coverage on subjects of concern to the motor industry, plus news and specialist features.
Former titles (until 2003): Motor Industry Management (0265-0843); (until 1983): Motor Management (0020-2746); (until 1970): Institute of the Motor Industry. Journal (0020-3173)
Indexed: M&MA.
—CCC.
Published by: Institute of the Motor Industry, Fanshaws, Brickendon, Hertford, Herts SG13 8PQ, United Kingdom. TEL 44-1992-511521, FAX 44-1992-511548, imi@motor.org.uk. Ed. Chris Phillips. Adv. contact Michael Linegar TEL 44-870-3000690. B&W page GBP 1,443, color page GBP 1,984; trim 216 x 291.

629.222 GBR
MOTOR INDUSTRY OF GREAT BRITAIN (YEAR) WORLD AUTOMOTIVE STATISTICS. Text in English. 1926. a., latest 2008. free to members (effective 2010). stat. back issues avail. **Document type:** *Yearbook, Trade.* **Description:** Provides information on vehicle production, new registrations, vehicles in use, used vehicle transactions and overseas trade from all over the world.
Formerly: Motor Industry of Great Britain (0077-1597)
—BLDSC (5975.010000).
Published by: Society of Motor Manufacturers and Traders Ltd., Forbes House, Halkin St, London, SW1X 7DS, United Kingdom. TEL 44-20-72357000, FAX 44-20-2357112, memberservices@smmt.co.uk.

388 CHE
MOTOR JOURNAL. Text in German. 18/yr.
Address: Villa Mueslischreck, Dietwil, 6042, Switzerland. TEL 041-912950. Ed. Alfred Wepf. Circ: 8,000.

796.72 CZE ISSN 1213-2527
MOTOR JOURNAL; nestranny a nezavisly mesicnik vsech automobilistu a motocyklistu. Text in Czech. 2000. m. CZK 1,000; CZK 100 newsstand/cover (effective 2008). adv. **Document type:** *Magazine, Consumer.*
Published by: Atelier Kupka s.r.o., Hvezdova 13, Brno, 60200, Czech Republic. Ed., Pub. Karel Kupka.

388 DEU ISSN 0177-8862
MOTOR KLASSIK; Das Oldtimermagazin. Text in German. 1984. m. EUR 4.50 newsstand/cover (effective 2010). adv. **Document type:** *Magazine, Consumer.* **Description:** Contains auto motor and sport news and features; with fascinating driving reports, servicing tips, club news and a large section of classified ads.
Incorporates (1983-1985): Automobil und Motorrad (0176-2176); Which was formerly (1974-1983): Automobil- und Motorrad-Chronik (0171-8428); Which superseded in part (1953-1974): Das Schnauferl (0487-6512)
Published by: Motor Presse Stuttgart GmbH & Co. KG (Subsidiary of: Gruner + Jahr AG & Co), Leuschnerstr 1, Stuttgart, 70174, Germany. TEL 49-711-18201, FAX 49-711-1821779, internet-redaktion@motor-presse-stuttgart.de, http://www.motorpresse.de. Ed. Malte Juergens. Adv. contact Stephen Brand. Circ: 80,410 (paid).

629.28 USA
MOTOR LIGHT TRUCK TUNE UP & REPAIR MANUAL. Text in English. 1984. a. adv. **Document type:** *Handbook/Manual/Guide, Trade.*
Formerly (uintil 1986): Motor Light Truck & Van Repair Manual; Which was formed by the 1984 merger of: Motor Truck Repair Manual (0098-3624); Motor Truck & Diesel Repair Manual (0362-6938); Which was formerly (until 19??): Motor's Truck & Diesel Repair Manual; Motor Truck and Diesel Repair Manual (0077-1724)
Published by: Motor Information Systems (Subsidiary of: Hearst Corporation), 5600 Crooks Rd, Ste 200, Troy, MI 48098. TEL 248-312-2700, 800-288-6828, FAX 248-879-8603, motorbookscallcenter@motor.com, http://www.motor.com.

381.456292 DNK ISSN 0109-7490
MOTOR-MAGASINET. Text in Danish. 1969. 44/yr. DKK 595 (effective 2010). adv. bk.rev. Supplement avail. **Document type:** *Magazine, Trade.* **Description:** Intends to provide the entire Danish automotive industry with objective and informative information.
Related titles: Online - full text ed.
Published by: Danske Fagmedier, Marielundvej 46 E, Herlev, 2730, Denmark. TEL 45-44-858899, FAX 45-44-858887, info@danskefagmedier.dk, http://www.danskefagmedier.dk. Ed. Michael Noerfelt TEL 45-44-857316. Adv. contact Suzanne Zabava. color page DKK 22,600; trim 266 x 360. Circ: 10,117 (controlled).

796.77 DEU
MOTOR MANIACS. Text in German. bi-m. EUR 27; EUR 5 newsstand/ cover (effective 2010). adv. **Document type:** *Magazine, Consumer.*
Published by: Huber Verlag GmbH & Co. KG, Markircher Str 9 a, Mannheim, 68229, Germany. TEL 49-621-483610, FAX 49-621-4836111, szeneshop@huber-verlag.de, http://www.huber-verlag.de. Ed. Boris Glatthaar. Adv. contact Oliver Langguth.

388 UKR
MOTOR NEWS. Text in Ukrainian. 1994. m. UAK 6 newsstand/cover (effective 2001). adv. **Document type:** *Magazine, Consumer.*
Published by: Artware Company Publishing Ltd., PO Box 47, Kiev, 03037, Ukraine. TEL 380-44-2514636, FAX 380-44-2514630. Ed. Oleg Vassilewski. Pub. Frank Schruhl. Adv. contact Alla Dolguschewa. Circ: 55,000 (paid).

388.3 AUS ISSN 0818-5549
MOTOR NEWS. Text in English. 1953. bi-m. bk.rev. **Document type:** *Newsletter, Consumer.*
Formerly (until 1985): Tasmanian Motor News (0039-9841)
Published by: Royal Automobile Club of Tasmania, GPO Box 1292, Hobart, TAS 7001, Australia. FAX 61-3-62348784, motornews@ract.com.au, http://www.ract.com.au.

629.20688 USA
MOTOR PARTS AND LABOR GUIDE. Text in English. 1930. a. adv. **Document type:** *Handbook/Manual/Guide, Trade.*
Former titles (until 199?): Motor Parts and Time Guide (0077-1716); Motor's Flat Rate and Parts Manual
Published by: Motor Information Systems (Subsidiary of: Hearst Corporation), 5600 Crooks Rd, Ste 200, Troy, MI 48098. TEL 248-312-2700, 800-288-6828, FAX 248-879-8603, motorbookscallcenter@motor.com, http://www.motor.com.

MOTOR RACING AUSTRALIA. *see* SPORTS AND GAMES

388.3 GBR ISSN 0027-2019
MOTOR SPORT. Text in English. 1924. m. GBP 46 (effective 2009). adv. bk.rev. charts; illus. index. back issues avail. **Document type:** *Magazine, Consumer.* **Description:** Covers the history of motor racing, from the dawn of the sport to the present day. Includes modern super cars as well.
Indexed: A10, SD, U01, V03.
—CCC.
Published by: Stratfield Publishing, 38 Chelsea Wharf, 15 Lots Rd, London, SW10 0QJ, United Kingdom. TEL 44-20-73498471, FAX 44-20-73498494, sales@motorsportmagazine.co.uk. Eds. Damien Smith, Nigel Roebuck. Adv. contact Matthew Blay TEL 44-20-73498496. page GBP 2,475; trim 230 x 285. Circ: 33,210.

388.3 AUS ISSN 0027-2035
MOTOR TRADE JOURNAL. Text in English. 1930. bi-m. adv. bk.rev. **Document type:** *Journal, Trade.*
Published by: (Motor Trade Association of S.A. Inc.), Boylen Media, 1 Richmond Rd, Keswick, SA 5035, Australia. TEL 61-8-82339433, FAX 61-8-83515633, vschmerl@boylen.com.au, http:// www.boylen.com.au. adv.: B&W page AUD 1,575, color page AUD 2,730; trim 210 x 297. Circ: 3,000 (controlled).

388.3 GBR ISSN 0027-2043
MOTOR TRADER. Text in English. 1905. m. GBP 95 domestic; GBP 130 foreign (effective 2009). adv. charts; illus. Index. back issues avail. **Document type:** *Magazine, Trade.* **Description:** Carries up-to-date news for car and auto component manufacturers, car importers and distributors, new and used car retailers, and independent service and repair garages.
Incorporates: Garage (0016-4526); Which was formerly (until 1975): Garage and Motor Agent
Related titles: Online - full text ed.; Supplement(s): Motor Trader Buyers Guide. ISSN 1465-1580.
—CCC.
Published by: Metropolis International Ltd, 6th Fl, Davis House, 2 Robert St, Croydon, Surrey CR0 1QQ, United Kingdom. TEL 44-20-82538600, FAX 44-20-82538727, metropolis@metropolis.co.uk, http://www.metropolis.co.uk/. Ed. Curtis Hutchinson TEL 44-20-82538711. Pub. Helen Lyons. Adv. contact Alan Toogood TEL 44-20-82538715. page GBP 2,995; trim 225 x 297.

388.3 AUS
MOTOR TRADER. Abbreviated title: A T D. Text in English. 1946. m. AUD 55 domestic to non-members; AUD 99 foreign to non-members; AUD 5 per issue domestic; AUD 9 per issue foreign; free to members (effective 2009). adv. illus. **Document type:** *Journal, Trade.* **Description:** Provides the latest news, views and opinions to the trade, technical reporting of products, latest information on new products, and advice on industry activities.
Formerly (until 1976): Q A C C Motor Trader (0310-5830); Which was formed by the merger of (1946-1972): Queensland Motor Industry (0033-6203); (1962-1972): Garage and Motor Trader (0016-4534)
Published by: (Motor Trades Association of Queensland), M T A - Q Publications, PO Box 3359, South Brisbane, QLD 4101, Australia. TEL 61-3-32378777, 800-177-951, FAX 61-3-38444488, info@mtaq.com.au. Adv. contact Jeff Dunlop TEL 61-7-32378740. page USD 1,530; 186 x 264. Circ: 2,700.

388.3 ZWE ISSN 0027-2051
MOTOR TRADER AND FLEET OPERATOR. Text in English. 1956. m. ZWD 181.20; ZWD 250.80 foreign (effective 1999). **Document type:** *Magazine, Trade.*
Published by: (Motor Trade Association), Thomson Publications Zimbabwe (Pvt) Ltd., Thomson House, PO Box 1683, Harare, Zimbabwe. TEL 263-4-736835, FAX 263-4-752390. **Co-sponsor:** Motor Industry Employers' Association.

388.3 AUS
MOTOR TRADERS ASSOCIATION JOURNAL. Text in English. 1919. m. AUD 82.50 domestic to non-members; AUD 90 foreign to non-members; free to members (effective 2009). adv. bk.rev. **Document type:** *Journal, Trade.* **Description:** Provides information relevant to the motor industry including technical updates, legal information, services and processes.
Former titles (until 2004): M T A The Magazine; (until 2000): M T A Journal (0047-5297); (until 1982): M T A; (until 1967): The M T A Official Journal
Indexed: ARI, ChemAb.
Published by: Motor Traders' Association of New South Wales, Locked Bag 5012, Darlinghurst, NSW 2010, Australia. TEL 61-2-92134222, FAX 61-2-92126889, mail@mtansw.com.au. Circ: 5,000.

388.3 SWE ISSN 0077-1619
HE5680.A1
MOTOR TRAFFIC IN SWEDEN. Text in Swedish. 1948. a. SEK 72. **Document type:** *Consumer.* **Description:** Contains statistics on vehicles in use, production, export, import and other useful information.
Related titles: ◆ Swedish ed.: Bilismen i Sverige. ISSN 0282-0536.
Published by: AB Bilstatistik, Fack 26173, Stockholm, 10041, Sweden. TEL 46-8-701-63-60, FAX 46-8-791-23-11, TELEX 119 23 BIL S. Circ: 1,500.

388.3 USA ISSN 0027-2094
TL1
MOTOR TREND. Text in English. 1949. m. USD 10 domestic; USD 23 in Canada; USD 25 elsewhere (effective 2008). adv. bk.rev. charts; illus. index. back issues avail.; reprints avail. **Document type:** *Magazine, Consumer.* **Description:** Features automotive information for new vehicle shoppers and dedicated enthusiasts.
Incorporates (in 19??): Car Life; (in 1971): Sports Car Graphic (0038-8165); (in 1971): Wheels Afield (0043-4787)
Related titles: CD-ROM ed.; Online - full text ed.: USD 5 (effective 2008).
Indexed: A01, A03, A08, A11, A22, A25, A26, ARG, B04, B07, BRD, C03, C05, C12, CBCARef, CPerI, ConsI, G05, G06, G07, G08, G09, I05, I06, I07, JHMA, M01, M02, M04, M06, MASUSE, MagInd, P02, P10, P13, P48, P52, P53, P54, PMR, PQC, R03, R04, R06, RGAb, RGPR, S08, S09, S23, SPI, T02, TOM, W03, W05.
—IE, Infotrieve, Ingenta, Linda Hall. **CCC.**
Published by: Source Interlink Companies, 6420 Wilshire Blvd, 10th Fl, Los Angeles, CA 90048. TEL 323-782-2000, FAX 323-782-2585, dheine@sourceinterlink.com, http://www.sourceinterlinkmedia.com. Ed. Angus MacKenzie. Pub. Ira Gabriel TEL 323-782-2724. adv.: B&W page USD 95,300, color page USD 160,100. Circ: 1,112,574 (paid).

629.22 USA
TL230.A1
MOTOR TREND SPORT UTILITY, TRUCK & VAN BUYER'S GUIDE. Text in English. s-a. **Document type:** *Magazine, Consumer.* **Description:** Contains descriptions and fact sheets for the buyer of a new truck or van.
Formerly: Motor Trend's Truck & Van Buyer's Guide (0190-3101)
Published by: Source Interlink Companies, 6420 Wilshire Blvd, 10th Fl, Los Angeles, CA 90048. TEL 323-782-2000, FAX 323-782-2585, dheine@sourceinterlink.com, http://www.sourceinterlinkmedia.com. Circ: 200,000.

629.28 USA ISSN 0160-8886
TL5
MOTOR TREND'S NEW CAR BUYERS' GUIDE. Text in English. 1976. a. **Document type:** *Magazine, Consumer.* **Description:** Highlights cars from the US, Japan and Europe.
Published by: Source Interlink Companies, 6420 Wilshire Blvd, 10th Fl, Los Angeles, CA 90048. TEL 323-782-2000, FAX 323-782-2585, dheine@sourceinterlink.com, http://www.sourceinterlinkmedia.com.

629.22 USA ISSN 1094-4370
MOTOR TREND'S TRUCK TREND. Text in English. 1998. bi-m. USD 10 domestic; USD 23 in Canada; USD 25 elsewhere (effective 2008). adv. back issues avail. **Document type:** *Magazine, Consumer.* **Description:** Provides a first-hand look at every aspect of the burgeoning SUV-light truck field for first-time buyers to dedicated enthusiasts.
Formerly: Truck Trends (0049-478X)
Related titles: Online - full text ed.: USD 5 (effective 2008).
Indexed: G05, G06, G07, G08, I05, I07, S23.
—CCC.
Published by: Source Interlink Companies, 6420 Wilshire Blvd, 10th Fl, Los Angeles, CA 90048. TEL 323-782-2000, FAX 323-782-2585, dheine@sourceinterlink.com, http://www.sourceinterlink.com. Ed. Mark Williams. Pub. Ira Gabriel TEL 323-782-2724. adv.: B&W page USD 95,300, color page USD 160,100. Circ: 1,112,574 (paid).

796.77 BRA ISSN 1806-3705
MOTOR TUNING CAR. Text in Portuguese. 2004. m. BRL 6.90 newsstand/cover (effective 2006). adv. **Document type:** *Magazine, Consumer.*
Published by: Editora Escala Ltda., Av Prof Ida Kolb, 551, Casa Verde, Sao Paulo, 02518-000, Brazil. TEL 55-11-38552100, FAX 55-11-38579643, escala@escala.com.br, http://www.escala.com.br.

388 910.202 DEU ISSN 0176-3792
MOTOR UND REISEN. Text in German. 1960. 6/yr. EUR 1.10 newsstand/ cover (effective 2006). adv. **Document type:** *Magazine, Consumer.*
Formerly (until 1984): Motor Reise Revue. Ausgabe E (0723-371X); Which superseded in part (in 1976): Motor Reise Revue (0027-1950)
Published by: (Automobilclub von Deutschland e.V.), A v D Verlag GmbH, Lyoner Str 16, Frankfurt Am Main, 60528, Germany. TEL 49-69-66060, FAX 49-69-6606789, avd@avd.de, http://www.avd.de. Ed. Karen-Nina Rhode. Adv. contact Norbert Mayer. color page EUR 9,620, B&W page EUR 5,310. Circ: 345,009 (controlled).

629.2 CAN ISSN 0316-6198
HD9710
MOTOR VEHICLE DATA BOOK. Text in English. 1947. a. CAD 42. **Description:** Identification and registration guide, listing 9 years of statistics including: curb weight, wheelbase, vehicle identification number, engine statistics and M.S. retail price.

TU

Published by: Sanford Evans Research Group A Subsidiary of Sun Media Corporation, 1700 Church Ave, Winnipeg, MB R2X 3A2, Canada. TEL 204-694-2022, FAX 204-632-4250. Ed. G B Henry. Pub., R&P Gary Henry.

354.7 USA
MOTOR VEHICLE REGULATION - STATE CAPITALS. Cover title: State Capitals Newsletters. Text in English. 1946. w. back issues avail. **Document type:** *Newsletter, Trade.* **Description:** Focuses on laws relating to motor vehicles. Monitors state efforts regarding inspection, tags, fees and taxes, emissions standards, drunken-driving laws, motorist licensing, insurance, and driver education.
Formerly (until 1996): From the State Capitals. Motor Vehicle Regulation (0016-1810)
Related titles: Online - full text ed.: USD 225 (effective 2001).
—CCC.
Published by: State Capitals Newsletters, PO Box 7376, Alexandria, VA 22307. TEL 703-768-9600, FAX 703-768-9690, newsletters@statecapitals.com.

629.287 USA ISSN 0565-7717
TL242
MOTOR VEHICLE SAFETY DEFECT AND RECALL CAMPAIGNS. Text in English. 1970. q. reprints avail. **Document type:** *Government.*
Related titles: Microfiche ed.: (from CIS).
Indexed: AmStI.
Published by: U.S. Department of Transportation, National Highway Traffic Safety Administration, 1200 New Jersey Ave, SE, West Bldg, Washington, DC 20590. TEL 202-366-4000, 888-327-4236.

388.34 310 JPN ISSN 0463-6635
MOTOR VEHICLE STATISTICS OF JAPAN. Text in Japanese. 1958. a. free. stat. **Document type:** *Trade.*
Published by: Japan Automobile Manufacturers Association, Otemachi Bldg, 1-6-1 Ote-Machi, Chiyoda-ku, Tokyo, 100-0004, Japan. FAX 03-287-2072. Circ: 7,500.

388 IND
MOTOR VIKATAN. Text in Tamil. 2007. m. INR 480 in state; INR 500 out of state; INR 2,100 elsewhere (effective 2011). **Document type:** *Magazine, Consumer.*
Published by: Vasan Publications Pvt. Ltd., 757 Anna Salai, Chennai, Tamil Nadu 600 002, India. TEL 91-44-28524074, pubonline@vikatan.com, http://www.vikatan.com.

338 AUS ISSN 1442-8148
MOTOR W A. (Western Australia) Text in English. 1935. 11/yr. AUD 99 (effective 2009). adv. illus.; mkt. **Document type:** *Magazine, Trade.* **Description:** Provides informative articles essential to the motor industry.
Former titles (until 1999): Motor Industry; (until 1980): W A A C C S Motor Industry (Western Australian Automobile Chamber of Commerce) (0042-9430); (until 1966): Service Station and Motor Trader
Published by: Motor Trade Association of Western Australia, Locked Bag 13, Belmont, W.A. 6984, Australia. TEL 61-8-94537900, 800-652-300, FAX 61-8-94537999, 800-623-759, mtawa@mtawa.com.au. Ed., Adv. contact David Lloyd TEL 61-8-93453466.

796.77 USA ISSN 1080-9929
MOTORACING. Text in English. 1994. m. USD 18 (effective 2001). adv. bk.rev. 32 p./no.; back issues avail. **Document type:** *Newspaper, Consumer.* **Description:** Reports on Sports Car Club of America activities in western states; oval track racing in Arizona, California, Oregon, Washington, Nevada.
Published by: Kelly Communications (Pleasanton), 3609 Virgin Islands Ct, Pleasanton, CA 94588. TEL 925-846-7728, FAX 925-846-0118. Ed., Pub., Adv. contact John F Kelly Jr. Circ: 2,500 (paid and controlled). **Subscr. to:** MotoRacing, PO Box 1203, Pleasanton, CA 94566-0120.

796.77 ESP
MOTORACING. Text in Spanish. m. EUR 2.95 (effective 2009). adv. **Document type:** *Magazine, Consumer.*
Published by: Grupo V, C Valportillo Primera, 11, Alcobendas, Madrid, 28108, Spain. TEL 34-91-6622137, FAX 34-91-6622654, secretaria@grupov.es, http://www.grupov.es/. Adv. contact Amador Moreno. page EUR 4,650; 20 x 27.5.

796.77 DEU
MOTORAVER MAGAZINE. Text in German. 4/yr. EUR 20; EUR 5 newsstand/cover (effective 2007). adv. **Document type:** *Magazine, Consumer.*
Published by: Motoraver Verlags GbR, St Pauli Hafenstr 98, Hamburg, 20359, Germany. TEL 49-40-39909686, FAX 49-40-39909687. adv.: color page EUR 2,950. Circ: 19,000 (paid and controlled).

388.3 SWE ISSN 0027-2140
MOTORBRANSCHEN. Text in Swedish. 1940. 9/yr. SEK 380; SEK 44 newsstand/cover (effective 2001). adv. charts; illus. **Document type:** *Magazine, Trade.*
Former titles (until vol.18, 1970): Motorbranschen med Laeckeraren; Formed by the 1961 merger of: Laeckeraren; Motorbranschen; Formed by the 1948 merger of: Tidskrift foer Motor- och Automobilbranschen; Bilverkstaederna
Published by: (Motorbranschens Riksfoerbund/Swedish National Association for Motor Trades; National Association of Tire Dealers and Repairers), Motorbranschens Foerlag, Karlavaegen 14 A, Box 5611, Stockholm, 11486, Sweden. TEL 46-8-701-63-19, FAX 46-8-20-67-47, forlaget@mrf.se. Ed., Pub. Hans Bister. Adv. contact Inger Zetterwall. B&W page SEK 10,000, color page SEK 14,000; trim 190 x 264. Circ: 5,400 (paid).

629.2 NOR ISSN 0332-8864
MOTORBRANSJEN. Text in Norwegian. 1976. 11/yr. NOK 400 (effective 2005). adv. bk.rev. stat. **Document type:** *Trade.*
Formerly (until 1978): Bilreparatoeren (0333-4287)
Related titles: Online - full text ed.
Published by: Bilforlaget, Urtegaten 9, PO Box 9247, Oslo, 0134, Norway. TEL 47-23-036600, FAX 47-23-036640, http://www.bilnorge.no. Ed. Tor Ivar Volla. Adv. contact Jorgen Dale TEL 47-23-036621. B&W page NOK 30,300, color page NOK 37,900; 250 x 370. Circ: 16,048.

629.22075 DNK ISSN 1902-4908
MOTORCLASSIC. Text in Danish. 2007. q. DKK 198; DKK 50 per issue (effective 2009). adv. **Document type:** *Magazine, Consumer.*
Published by: Forenede Danske Motorejere/Federation of Danish Motorists, Firskovvej 32, Kgs. Lyngby, 2800, Denmark. TEL 45-45-270707, FAX 45-45-270993, fdm@fdm.dk.

388 THA ISSN 0125-1732
MOTORCYCLE MAGAZINE. Text in Thai. 1974. m. THB 300. **Document type:** *Consumer.*
Published by: Grand Prix International Co. Ltd., Prachachuen Rd Bangsue, 129-133 Rim Klong Prapar, Bangkok, 10800, Thailand. TEL 662-02-587-0101, FAX 662-02-587-6567. Ed. Prachin Eamlumnow. Circ: 40,000.

388.3 SWE ISSN 0463-6678
MOTORFOERAREN. Text in Swedish. 1927. 7/yr. SEK 150 (effective 2001). adv. 48 p./no. 4 cols./p.; **Document type:** *Magazine, Consumer.*
Published by: Motorfoerarnas Helynykterhetsfoerbund, Vaestertorpsvaegen 131, Haegersten, 12944, Sweden. TEL 46-8-555-765-55, FAX 46-8-555-765-96, info@mhf.se. Ed. Soeren Sehlberg. Pub. Goeran Ohlson. Adv. contact Boerje Nilsson. B&W page SEK 15,000, color page SEK 19,000; trim 192 x 248. Circ: 40,800 (paid).

388.3 NOR ISSN 0027-2213
MOTORFOEREREN. Text in Norwegian. 1939. 6/yr. NOK 140; NOK 20 per issue (effective 2006). adv. bk.rev. illus. **Document type:** *Magazine, Consumer.*
—CCC.
Published by: Motorfoerernes Avholdsforbund, Stroemsveien 223, PO Box 80, Alnabru, Oslo, 0614, Norway. TEL 47-22-956969, FAX 47-22-956968, ma@ma-norge.no. Ed. Eivind Groenvold TEL 47-22-956966. adv.: B&W page NOK 10,600, color page NOK 13,200; 185 x 260. Circ: 11,597.

388.3 AUS
MOTORHOME WORLD. Text in English. 2006. bi-m. AUD 35.95 in Australia & New Zealand; AUD 44.45 elsewhere; AUD 6.95 newsstand/cover (effective 2008). adv. **Document type:** *Magazine, Trade.* **Description:** Provides reviews on the latest Australian and international motorhome models, inspirational travel stories and practical tips.
Published by: A C P Trader International Group (Subsidiary of: P B L Media Pty Ltd.), 73 Atherton Rd, Oakleigh, VIC 3166, Australia. TEL 61-3-95674200, FAX 61-3-95634554. Ed. Greg Leech TEL 61-3-95674194. Adv. contact Justine Schuller. color page AUD 1,486; trim 225 x 297. Circ: 25,000. **Subscr. to:** Magshop, Reply Paid 4967, Sydney, NSW 2001, Australia. TEL 61-2-136116, subs@magstore.com.au, http://shop.magstore.com.au.

388.3 IND ISSN 0027-223X
MOTORINDIA. Text in English. 1956. m. INR 300 domestic; USD 100 foreign (effective 2011). adv. bk.rev. 92 p./no.; **Document type:** *Magazine, Trade.*
Related titles: Online - full text ed.: free (effective 2011).
Published by: (Auto Dealers' & Fleet Operators' Associations), Gopali & Co., Quanta Zen Bldg, No.38, (Old No.2), Thomas Rd, 2nd St, Off. S Boag Rd, T.Nagar, Chennai, 600 017, India. TEL 91-44-42024951, FAX 91-44-24332413. Pub. R Natarajan. Adv. contact B Vijaya.

388.3 IND ISSN 0027-2248
MOTORING. Text in English. 1927. m. free to members (effective 2011).
Published by: Western India Automobile Association, Lalji Naranji Memorial Bldg, 76 Veer Nariman Rd, Mumbai, Maharashtra 400 020, India. TEL 91-22-2041085, FAX 91-22-2041382, wiaa@cybersteering.com, http://www.cybersteering.com/wiaa/index.html.

796.77 SGP ISSN 0217-393X
MOTORING. Text in English. 1982. bi-m. SGD 58 (effective 2008). **Document type:** *Magazine, Consumer.*
Published by: Eastern Publishing Pte Ltd (Subsidiary of: Eastern Holdings Ltd), 1100 Lower Delta Rd, #04-01, EPL Bldg, Singapore, 169206, Singapore. TEL 65-6-3792888, FAX 65-6-3792803. Circ: 20,000.

796.77 SGP
MOTORING ANNUAL. Text in English. a. **Document type:** *Magazine, Consumer.*
Published by: Eastern Publishing Pte Ltd (Subsidiary of: Eastern Holdings Ltd), 1100 Lower Delta Rd, #04-01, EPL Bldg, Singapore, 169206, Singapore. TEL 65-6-3792888, FAX 65-6-3792803.

388.3 IRL ISSN 0027-2256
MOTORING LIFE. Text in English. 1949-1991; N.S. m. adv. bk.rev. charts; illus.; tr.lit. **Document type:** *Magazine, Consumer.*
Published by: Private Motorist Protection Association, 48 N. Great Georges St., Dublin, 1, Ireland. adv.: B&W page EUR 1,771, color page EUR 1,898; trim 210 x 297. Circ: 8,000.

388.3 CAN
MOTORIST'S ADVOCATE. Text in English. 1991. bi-m. **Document type:** *Bulletin.*
Formerly: C A A News and Views
Related titles: French ed.
Published by: Canadian Automobile Association, 1145 Hunt Club Rd, Ste 200, Ottawa, ON K1V 0Y3, Canada. TEL 613-247-0117, FAX 613-247-0118, TELEX 053-4440. Ed. David Leonhardt. Circ: 1,200.

796.77 CZE ISSN 1801-5298
MOTORSPORT MAGAZIN. Text in Czech. 2005. m. CZK 599 (effective 2011). adv. **Document type:** *Magazine, Consumer.*
Published by: Fullerton s.r.o., Kutnohorska 181/64, Prague, 10900, Czech Republic. TEL 420-272-703410, FAX 420-272-703412, info@fullerton.cz. Ed. Karel Malina.

629.222 ZAF
MOTORSPORT - S.A. NEWS BULLETIN. Text in English. 1983; N.S. 1992; N.S. 1995. q. free. illus. **Document type:** *Bulletin.* **Description:** Publishes national and international motorsport information, club and calendar information, and changes in the official rules and regulations governing motorsporting for cars and motorcycles in South Africa.
Supersedes (in Dec. 1995): A A Motorsport News Bulletin; Which was formerly titled (until 1993): A A Motorsport. Official Bulletin; (until 1989): A A S A Motorsport. Official Bulletin; S A Motor Sport Control Bulletin (1010-8025)
Published by: Motorsport - South Africa, PO Box 11499, Vorna Valley, 1686, South Africa. TEL 27-11-4662440, FAX 27-11-4662450. Ed. Beulah Verolini.

MOTORSPORTS NOW!. *see* SPORTS AND GAMES

629.222 USA
MOTORWATCH. Text in English. 1988. bi-m. USD 22 to members (effective 2006). bk.rev. illus. reprints avail. **Document type:** *Newsletter, Trade.* **Description:** Covers all things automotive. Provides information and advice for the do-it-yourselfer and consumers interested in avoiding rip-offs.
Formerly: Nutz & Boltz Newsletter (1056-1714)
Related titles: Online - full text ed.: USD 9.95 (effective 2001).
Published by: Nutz & Boltz, Inc, PO Box 123, Butler, MD 21023. TEL 410-374-0900, FAX 410-374-1735. Ed. Carolyn Solomon. Pub. David R Solomon. Circ: 2,000 (paid and free).

629.286 CHN ISSN 1001-7666
MOTUOCHE JISHU/JOURNAL OF MOTORCYCLE TECHNOLOGY. Text in Chinese. 1988. m. USD 56.40 (effective 2009). adv. **Document type:** *Trade.* **Description:** Covers the motorcycle industry in China.
Published by: Zhongguo Qiche Jishu Yanjiu Zhongxin/China Automotive Technology & Research Center, PO Box 59, Tianjin 300162, China. TEL 86-22-473100, FAX 86-22-470846. Ed., R&P Yugui Lang. Adv. contact Houhua Liang. color page USD 1,200.

388.3 ESP ISSN 1139-8647
MUNDO RECAMBIO Y TALLER; revista tecnica de la automocion. Text in Spanish. 1980. 11/yr. EUR 82 (effective 2008). adv. back issues avail. **Document type:** *Magazine, Trade.* **Description:** For professionals in the automotive repair and spare parts industry, and its distribution, after-market.
Published by: C E I Arsis S.L., C Paris, 150, 4o 3a, Barcelona, 08036, Spain. TEL 34-93-4395564, FAX 34-93-4306853. Ed. Yvonne Rubio. Pub., R&P Pilar Grau. Adv. contact Gloria Vinals. page EUR 1,375; 210 x 295. Circ: 10,000.

388.3 USA ISSN 0891-4796
MUSCLE CAR REVIEW. Text in English. 1984. m. USD 19.97 domestic; USD 31.97 in Canada; USD 43.97 elsewhere (effective 2008). adv. illus. reprints avail. **Document type:** *Magazine, Consumer.* **Description:** Covers all aspects of muscle car restoration and performance in the past and present.
Formerly (until 1986): Popular and Performance Car Review (0747-1483)
Indexed: I05, S23.
—CCC.
Published by: Source Interlink Companies, 6420 Wilshire Blvd, 10th Fl, Los Angeles, CA 90048. TEL 323-782-2000, FAX 323-782-2585, dheine@sourceinterlink.com, http://www.sourceinterlink.com. Ed. Drew Hardin. Pub. Ed Zinke TEL 714-939-2626. adv.: B&W page USD 3,025, color page USD 8,830. Circ: 53,469 (paid).

388.3 USA ISSN 1054-8912
MUSCLE MUSTANGS & FAST FORDS. Variant title: Mustangs and Fast Fords. Text in English. 1987. m. USD 29.97 domestic; USD 41.97 in Canada; USD 53.97 elsewhere (effective 2008). adv. bk.rev. 284 p./no.; back issues avail.; reprints avail. **Document type:** *Magazine, Consumer.* **Description:** Provides enthusiasts with a practical guide to make their vehicles perform at peak level.
Related titles: Online - full text ed.: USD 15 (effective 2008).
Indexed: G06, G07, G08, I05, S23.
—CCC.
Published by: Source Interlink Companies, 365 West Passaic St, Rochelle Park, NJ 07662. dheine@sourceinterlink.com, http://www.sourceinterlink.com. Ed. Evan Smith. Pub. Don Parrish TEL 813-675-3482. adv.: B&W page USD 7,250, color page USD 9,065. Circ: 94,067 (paid).

388.3 USA ISSN 2151-061X
MUSTANG & FORD. Text in English. 19??. m. USD 32.95 domestic; USD 69.95 in Canada; USD 124.95 elsewhere (effective 2009). adv. **Document type:** *Magazine, Trade.* **Description:** Features classified ads for Ford enthusiasts.
Formerly (until 2008): Mustang & Ford Trader
Published by: AutoTrader Classics, 5775 Peachtree-Dunwoody Rd, Ste A-100, Atlanta, GA 30342. TEL 800-548-8889. Adv. contact Debbie Reetz TEL 404-568-8383.

796.77 USA ISSN 0274-8460
MUSTANG MONTHLY. Text in English. 1977. m. USD 24.97 domestic; USD 36.97 in Canada; USD 48.97 elsewhere (effective 2008). adv. back issues avail.; reprints avail. **Document type:** *Magazine, Consumer.* **Description:** Covers everything from do-it-yourself recommendations to the history of the Mustang.
Related titles: Online - full text ed.
Indexed: G05, G06, G07, G08, I05, I07, S23.
—CCC.
Published by: Source Interlink Companies, 9036 Brittany Way, Tampa, FL 33619. TEL 813-675-3500, FAX 813-675-3556, dheine@sourceinterlink.com, http://www.sourceinterlinkmedia.com. Ed. Donald Farr. Pub. Sandy Patterson TEL 813-675-3477. adv.: B&W page USD 6,890, color page USD 8,610. Circ: 51,452 (paid).

629.22 USA ISSN 0744-2572
MUSTANG TIMES. Text in English. 1976. m. USD 30 (effective 1998). adv. **Document type:** *Magazine, Consumer.*
Published by: Mustang Club of America, 3588 Highway 138, Ste 365, Stockbridge, GA 30281. TEL 770-477-1965, FAX 770-477-1965. Ed. Teresa Vickery. Adv. contact Marilyn Newcombe. B&W page USD 350. Circ: 8,500.

388.3 USA
N A D A AUCTIONNET AUCTION GUIDE. Text in English. 19??. bi-w. **Document type:** *Directory.*
Published by: National Automobile Dealers Association, Used Car Guide Co., 8400 Westpark Dr, 10th Fl, McLean, VA 22102. FAX 866-438-6232, 800-252-6232, guideinfo@nada.org, http://www.nada.org/.

388.3 USA
N A D A CLASSIC, COLLECTIBLE, EXOTIC AND MUSCLE CAR APPRAISAL GUIDE AND DIRECTORY. Text in English. 199?. 3/yr. USD 78 to non-members; USD 39 per issue to non-members; free to members (effective 2011). **Document type:** *Handbook/Manual/Guide, Trade.*
Former titles (until 2009): N A D A Classic, Collectible and Special Interest Car Appraisal Guide; (until 1996): N A D A Exotic, Collectible and Special Interest Car Appraisal Guide
Published by: (National Automobile Dealers Association), N.A.D.A. Appraisal Guides, PO Box 7800, Costa Mesa, CA 92628. http://www.nadaguides.com.

388.3 USA ISSN 0027-5794
N A D A OFFICIAL USED CAR GUIDE. (National Automobile Dealers Association) (Avail. in 9 Regional Editions) Text in English. 1933. m. USD 90 (effective 2009); monthly updates included. **Document type:** *Directory, Trade.* **Description:** Covers passenger cars, light-duty trucks and SUV pricing, including trade-in, M.S.R.P., loan and retail prices, photos, and weight specifications.
Related titles: Regional ed(s).: N A D A Official Used Car Guide (Eastern Edition). ISSN 0193-2780.
Published by: National Automobile Dealers Association, Used Car Guide Co., PO Box 7800, Costa Mesa, CA 92628. TEL 714-556-8511, FAX 714-556-8715, guideinfo@nada.org.

388.3 USA
N A D A OLDER USED CAR GUIDE. Variant title: N A D A Official Older Used Car Guide. Text in English. 19??. 3/yr. USD 75 to non-members; USD 38 per issue to non-members; free to members (effective 2011). **Document type:** *Handbook/Manual/Guide, Trade.*
Published by: (National Automobile Dealers Association), N.A.D.A. Appraisal Guides, PO Box 7800, Costa Mesa, CA 92628. http://www.nadaguides.com.

381 USA ISSN 0092-4601
HD9715.7.U6
N A D A RECREATION VEHICLE APPRAISAL GUIDE. Text in English. 19??. 3/yr. USD 137 to non-members; USD 69 per issue to non-members; free to members (effective 2011). back issues avail. **Document type:** *Handbook/Manual/Guide, Trade.*
Published by: (National Automobile Dealers Association), N.A.D.A. Appraisal Guides, PO Box 7800, Costa Mesa, CA 92628. http://www.nadaguides.com.

388.3 USA ISSN 0195-1564
HD9710.U52
N A D A'S AUTOMOTIVE EXECUTIVE. Variant title: Automotive Executive. Text in English. 1917. m. USD 24 domestic; USD 30 foreign (effective 2005). adv. illus. Index. back issues avail. **Document type:** *Magazine, Trade.*
Incorporates: N A D A Newsletter; Former titles (until 1979): Cars and Trucks (0164-3592); (until 1974): N A D A Magazine
—Ingenta.
Published by: National Automobile Dealers Association, 8400 Westpark Dr., 19th Fl., Mclean, VA 22102. TEL 703-821-7000, FAX 703-821-7234. Ed. Marc H Stertz. Adv. contact Diane Vance. Circ: 24,000.

388.3 USA
N A F A ANNUAL REFERENCE BOOK. Text in English. 1960. a. USD 45. adv. stat. **Document type:** *Handbook/Manual/Guide, Trade.*
Formerly: N A F A Conference Brochure and Reference Book (0550-8843)
Published by: National Association of Fleet Administrators, Inc., 100 Wood Ave S, Ste 310, Iselin, NJ 08830-2716. TEL 732-494-8100, FAX 732-494-6789, jsyp@nafa.org. Ed. Jessica Sypniewski. R&P Michael E Berel. Circ: 4,000.

388 USA
N A F R D INSIDE TRACKS. Text in English. q. USD 750 to members. adv. **Document type:** *Newsletter.*
Published by: National Association of Fleet Resale Dealers, 4700 W Lake Ave, Glenview, IL 60025. TEL 847-375-4729, 800-392-2536, FAX 847-375-4777. Ed. Arlene Burd. Adv. contact Kate Schooley.

796.77 USA ISSN 1931-2105
GV1029.9.S74
N A S C A R NEXTEL CUP SERIES. (National Association for Stock Car Auto Racing) Text in English. 2004. a., latest 2007. **Document type:** *Yearbook, Trade.*
Published by: U M I Publications, Inc., PO Box 30036, Charlotte, NC 28230. TEL 800-747-9287, status@umipub.com, http://www.umipub.com/.

629 USA
N A S C A R PERFORMANCE. (National Association for Stock Car Auto Racing) Text in English, Spanish. m. adv. **Document type:** *Magazine, Trade.*
Formerly (until 2003): N A S C A R Tech
Related titles: Online - full text ed.
Published by: Babcox Publications, Inc., 3550 Embassy Pky, Akron, OH 44333. TEL 330-670-1234, FAX 330-670-0874, bbabcox@babcox.com, http://www.babcox.com. Ed. Douglas Kaufman TEL 330-670-1234 ext 262. adv.: B&W page USD 20,370, color page USD 27,195; bleed 8.125 x 11.125.

796.77 NZL ISSN 1176-9920
N Z V8. (New Zealand) Text in English. 2005. m. NZD 79 domestic; NZD 120 elsewhere; NZD 8.95 newsstand/cover (effective 2008). adv. **Document type:** *Magazine, Consumer.* **Description:** Covers high-performance v8-engined vehicles.
Published by: Parkside Media, Herne Bay, PO Box 46020, Auckland, 1147, New Zealand. TEL 64-9-3601480, FAX 64-9-3601470, http://www.parksidemedia.co.nz. Ed. Todd Wylie. Pub. Greg Vincent.

▼ **NANREN FENGSHANG/LEON.** *see* MEN'S INTERESTS

629.286 USA
NASH TIMES. Text in English. 1970. bi-m. USD 30 domestic membership; USD 33 in Canada membership; USD 48 elsewhere membership (effective 2005). back issues avail. **Document type:** *Newsletter, Consumer.* **Description:** For car enthusiasts dedicated to promoting the history, preservation, and restoration of the Nash and related automobiles.
Published by: Nash Car Club of America, 1N274 Prairie, Glen Ellyn, IL 60137. bracewell@nashcarclub.org, http://www.nashcarclub.org. Circ: 2,000.

338 USA ISSN 1042-0282
NASHVILLE AUTOMOTIVE REPORT. Text in English. 1998. m. free to qualified personnel (effective 2008). adv. **Document type:** *Newspaper, Trade.* **Description:** Provides monthly news for the local automotive industry in Middle Tennessee, South Central Kentucky and Northern Alabama.
Indexed: V03.
Published by: Autographic Publishing Company, Inc., 1121 Airport Center Dr, Ste 101, Nashville, TN 37214. TEL 615-391-3666, 800-467-3666, FAX 615-391-3622, garnett@automotivereport.net, http://www.automotivereport.net. Ed. Garnett Forkum. Pub. Allen Forkum. adv.: B&W page USD 1,200; trim 11.5 x 15. Circ: 5,350 (free).

388.3 USA
NATIONAL AUTOMOTIVE PARTS ASSOCIATION. OUTLOOK. Text in English. 1967. 10/yr. adv. **Description:** For owners and managers of NAPA auto parts stores only.
Published by: National Automotive Parts Association, 2999 Circle 75 Parkway, Atlanta, GA 30339. TEL 404-956-2200, FAX 404-956-2211. Ed. Kathy Randall. Circ: 16,500.

796.72 USA ISSN 0466-2199
NATIONAL DRAGSTER. Text in English. 1960. 48/yr. USD 69; USD 3.95 newsstand/cover (effective 2007). adv. stat. **Document type:** *Magazine, Consumer.* **Description:** Covers drag racing and NHRA events. Features technical articles, new product data, performance standards, race previews, interviews and official rule changes.
Incorporates: N H R A Souvenir Program; Which was formerly: N H R A Souvenir Yearbook
Related titles: Online - full text ed.; Supplement(s): Annual N H R A Rulebook; Annual Fun Guide.
Indexed: G09, P02, P10, P48, P52, P53, P54, PQC.
Published by: National Hot Rod Association, 2035 Financial Way, Glendora, CA 91741. TEL 626-963-7695, FAX 626-335-4307, nhra@goracing.com. Ed. Phil Burgess. Adv. contact Jeff Morton. B&W page USD 3,483. Circ: 80,000 (paid).

629.222 GBR
NATIONAL MOTOR MUSEUM PICTORIAL GUIDE. Text in English. 1959. a. illus.; stat. **Document type:** *Bulletin.*
Published by: (National Motor Museum Trust), Montagu Ventures Ltd., Beaulieu, Brockenhurst, Hants SO42 7ZN, United Kingdom. TEL 44-1590-612345, FAX 44-1590-612624, 44-1590-612624, http://www.nationalmotormuseum.org.uk/. Ed. M E Ware. Circ: 120,000.

629.222 USA
NATIONAL TOWING NEWS. Text in English. 1982. m. USD 36. adv. bk.rev. charts; tr.lit. back issues avail. **Document type:** *Magazine, Trade.* **Description:** Covers legal, legislative and business issues affecting the towing and recovery industry.
Former titles: Towing News; National Towing News
Published by: Towing and Recovery Association of America, Inc., 2200 Mill Rd, Alexandria, VA 22314-4686. TEL 703-838-1897, FAX 703-684-6720. Ed. Patricia Harman. Pub. Fletcher R Hall. R&P, Adv. contact Patricia L Harman TEL 410-560-1749. Circ: 1,500.

629.286 UKR ISSN 2078-6840
➤ **NATSIONAL'NYI TEKHNICHESKII UNIVERSITET "KHAR'KOVSKII POLITEKHNICHESKII INSTITUT". VESTNIK. AVTOMOBILE- I TRAKTOROSTROENIE/NATSIONAL'NYI TEKHNICHNYI UNIVERSYTET "KHARKIVS'KYI POLITEKHNICHNYI INSTYTUT". VISNYK. AVTOMOBILE- TA TRAKTOROBUDUVANNYA.** Text in Russian, Ukrainian. 1968. a. **Document type:** *Journal, Academic/Scholarly.*
Formerly (until 2002): Khar'kovskii Politekhnicheskii Institut. Vestnik. Traktorostroenie (0207-1029)
Related titles: Online - full text ed.
Published by: Natsional'nyi Tekhnicheskii Universitet "Kharkovskii Politekhnicheskii Institut"/National Technical University "Kharkiv Polytechnical Institute", vul Frunze 21, Kharkiv, 310002, Ukraine. TEL 380-572-7076212, FAX 380-572-7076601, omsroot@kpi.kharkov.ua, http://www.kpi.kharkov.ua. Ed. V B Samorodov.

629.22 JPN ISSN 0289-6079
NAVI. Text in Japanese. 1984. m. JPY 13,800. adv. **Description:** Covers social and economic aspects of cars and motoring for car enthusiasts and car buyers.
Published by: Nigensha Publishing Co. Ltd., 6-2-1 Honkomagome, Bunkyo-ku, Tokyo, 113-0021, Japan. TEL 81-3-5395-0953, FAX 81-3-5395-0954. Ed. M Suzuki. Adv. contact T Miyasaka. color page JPY 780,000; trim 295 x 222. Circ: 230,000.

629.2 USA
NECKARSULM NEWS. Text in English. 1971. q. USD 15; USD 17 foreign (effective 1999). adv. illus. back issues avail. **Document type:** *Newsletter.* **Description:** Provides readers with news of vehicles produced by the N.S.U. company in Germany.
Published by: N S U Enthusiasts U S A, 2909 Utah Pl, Alton, IL 62002. TEL 618-462-9195. Ed., Pub., R&P Terry Stuchlik. Circ: 125 (paid).

621.43 CHN ISSN 1000-6494
NEIRANJI/INTERNAL COMBUSTION ENGINES. Text in Chinese. 1985. bi-m. USD 21.60 (effective 2009). **Document type:** *Journal, Academic/Scholarly.*
Related titles: Online - full text ed.
—East View.
Published by: Jixie Gongye Di-3 Shejie Yanjiuyuan/Third Design and Research Institute, Machine Industry China, No.17 Yuzhou Road, Shiqiaopu, Chongqing, 400039, China. http://www.cmtdi.com/.

629.11 DEU ISSN 0933-3312
NEUE REIFENZEITUNG. Text in German. 1981. m. EUR 119.60 domestic; EUR 156.60 in Europe; EUR 180.60 elsewhere; EUR 12 newsstand/cover (effective 2010). adv. **Document type:** *Magazine, Trade.*
Published by: Profil Verlag GmbH, Harsefelder Str 5, Stade, 21680, Germany. TEL 49-4141-53360, FAX 49-4141-609900, info@reifenpresse.de. Ed., Pub. Klaus Haddenbrock. Adv. contact Ute Monsees. B&W page EUR 2,300, color page EUR 3,600; trim 216 x 303. Circ: 6,500 (paid and controlled).

629.286 ESP ISSN 1579-2390
NEUMATICOS & MECANICA RAPIDA. Abbreviated title: N M R. Text in Spanish. 1999. m. adv. **Document type:** *Magazine, Trade.* **Description:** This magazine is for the auto repair shop operator.
Related titles: Online - full text ed.: ISSN 1989-0346.
Published by: Tecnipublicaciones Espana, S.L., Avda de Manoteras 44, 3a Planta, Madrid, 28050, Spain. TEL 34-91-2972000, FAX 34-91-2972154, tp@tecnipublicaciones.com, http://www.tecnipublicaciones.com.

344.047 USA ISSN 1534-6528
KFN1497.A29
NEW HAMPSHIRE SELECTED MOTOR VEHICLE, BOATING AND RELATED LAWS ANNOTATED. Text in English. a., latest 2007. USD 48 combined subscription (print & CD-ROM eds.) (effective 2008). 564 p./no.; **Document type:** *Handbook/Manual/Guide, Trade.* **Description:** Contains the latest motor vehicle statutes, fully annotated with history notes and case law.
Former titles (until 1997): New Hampshire Selected Motor Vehicle and Boating Laws; (until 1990): New Hampshire Motor Vehicle Laws and Related Laws (1050-5776)
Related titles: CD-ROM ed.: ISSN 1555-2721.
Published by: Michie Company (Subsidiary of: LexisNexis North America), 701 E Water St, Charlottesville, VA 22902. TEL 434-972-7600, 800-446-3410, FAX 434-972-7677, customer.support@lexisnexis.com, http://www.michie.com.

388.3 USA
NEW JERSEY AUTOMOTIVE; the official publication of the automotive service association of new jersey. Text in English. 1969. m. USD 48 (effective 1999). adv. back issues avail. **Document type:** *Magazine, Consumer.* **Description:** Informs readers about the current issues affecting the automotive industry.
Published by: (Automotive Service Association of New Jersey), Thomas Greco Publishing Co., 244 Chestnut St, Nutley, NJ 07110. TEL 973-667-6922, FAX 973-235-1963. Ed. Thomas Greco. R&P, Adv. contact Billy Joe Burns. Circ: 3,000 (controlled).

910.91 USA ISSN 1092-6186
F791
NEW MEXICO JOURNEY. Key Title: A A A New Mexico Journey. Text in English. 1997. bi-m. free to members (effective 2009). adv. stat.; illus.; tr.lit. 81 p./no. 3 cols./p.; **Document type:** *Magazine, Consumer.* **Description:** Describes tourist destinations of historical or cultural importance in New Mexico.
Supersedes in part (in 1997): Car and Travel (Houston Edition)
Published by: American Automobile Association, Texas and New Mexico Branches, 3333 Fairview Rd, A327, Costa Mesa, CA 92626. TEL 714-885-2376, FAX 714-885-2335, http://www.aaa-texas.com/index.asp. Adv. contact Betty Chew TEL 714-885-2356. B&W page USD 3,520, color page USD 4,390; trim 7.875 x 10.5. Circ: 107,715.

388.40941 GBR ISSN 2041-4536
NEW TRANSIT. Text in English. 1995. fortn. GBP 95 (effective 2009). adv. charts; illus.; stat. 5 cols./p.; back issues avail. **Document type:** *Magazine, Trade.* **Description:** Provides news, analysis, and background information in UK public transport for system managers and persons responsible for setting policy and regulation for operators, financial advisors, and analysts.
Formerly (until 2009): Transit (1358-4766)
Related titles: Online - full text ed.: ISSN 2041-4544.
—CCC.
Published by: (Local Transport Today Ltd.), Landor Publishing Ltd, Apollo House, 359 Kennington Ln, London, SE11 5QY, United Kingdom. TEL 44-845-2707950, business@landor.co.uk, http://www.landor.co.uk. Adv. contact Florence Branchu TEL 44-845-2707968.

388.33 USA ISSN 0028-713X
NEW YORK AUTO REPAIR NEWS. Text in English. 1948. m. USD 12; free to qualified personnel. adv. bk.rev.
Published by: Van Allen Publishing Co., PO Box 354, Hicksville, NY 11802. TEL 516-422-5521. Ed. Richard Van Allen. Circ: 11,300 (controlled).

388.3 NZL ISSN 1174-1600
NEW ZEALAND AUTOCAR. Text in English. 1996. m. NZD 79 domestic; NZD 185 in Australia; NZD 195 elsewhere; NZD 9.20 newsstand/cover (effective 2008). **Document type:** *Magazine, Consumer.*
Formerly (until 1997): Auto News and Car New Zealand (1174-1597); Which was formed by the merger of (1986-1996): New Zealand Car (0113-0196); (1989-1996): Auto News New Zealand (1172-6423); Which was formerly (until 1993): New Zealand Auto News (1171-9249); (until 1992): Auto News (1171-4123); (until 1991): Race & Rally (1170-9081); (until 1991): Road Race & Rally (0114-6866)
Related titles: Online - full content ed.
Published by: Fairfax Magazines (Subsidiary of: Fairfax Media), PO Box 6341, Auckland, 1036, New Zealand. TEL 64-9-9096800, FAX 64-9-9096802, info@fairfaxmedia.co.nz, http://www.fairfaxnz.co.nz.

629.222 NZL ISSN 1170-9332
NEW ZEALAND CLASSIC CAR. Text in English. 1991. m. NZD 75 domestic; NZD 135 Australia & Pacific; NZD 199 elsewhere; NZD 8.95 newsstand/cover (effective 2008). adv. bk.rev. mkt. back issues avail. **Document type:** *Magazine, Consumer.* **Description:** Presents articles, club listings, cars for sale advertisements.
Published by: Parkside Media, Herne Bay, PO Box 46020, Auckland, 1147, New Zealand. TEL 64-9-3601480, FAX 64-9-3601470, http://www.parksidemedia.co.nz. Ed. Allan Walton. Pub. Greg Vincent. Circ: 11,441. **Dist. by:** Gordon & Gotch, 2 Carr Rd, Mt Roskill, PO Box 3207, Auckland, New Zealand.

788.3 NZL
NEW ZEALAND COMPANY VEHICLE AND EXECUTIVE CARS. Text in English. 1992. bi-m. NZD 48 domestic; NZD 70 in Australia; NZD 80 elsewhere (effective 2008). adv. **Document type:** *Magazine, Trade.* **Description:** Covers a range of topics of interest to the company vehicle buyer and manager.
Published by: Adrenalin Publishing Ltd, 14C Vega Pl, North Shore City, 0754, New Zealand. TEL 64-9-4784771, FAX 64-9-4784779, http://www.adrenalin.co.nz/. Ed. Robert Barry. Pub. Cathy Parker. adv.: color page NZD 2,550; 18.5 x 26.5.

388.342 NZL ISSN 1170-2540
NEW ZEALAND IDENTICAR. Text in English. 1981. a. adv. bk.rev. illus. back issues avail. **Document type:** *Directory, Trade.* **Description:** Contains information on almost 30,000 model variants seen on NZ roads in the past 10 years, including vital chassis and manufacturers' codes. Plus full coverage of Japanese imports.
Formerly (until 1990): Identicar (0111-7629)
Published by: G C L Publishing, Ltd., 15 Bath St, 1st Fl., Parnell, PO Box 37-745, Auckland, New Zealand. TEL 64-9-3092444, FAX 64-9-3092449, info@gcl.co.nz, http://www.gcl.co.nz. adv.: B&W page NZD 1,750, color page NZD 2,250; trim 210 x 297. Circ: 5,000.

388.346 NZL ISSN 1177-1453
NEW ZEALAND MOTORHOMES, CARAVANS & DESTINATIONS. Text in English. m. NZD 55 (effective 2008). adv. **Document type:** *Magazine, Consumer.* **Description:** Features reviews of motorhomes, campervans and caravans along with information-packed profiles of great holiday destinations.
Published by: A C P Media New Zealand (Subsidiary of: A C P Magazines Ltd.), Private Bag 92512, Auckland, 1036, New Zealand. TEL 64-9-3082700, FAX 64-9-3082878. Adv. contact Clark Mitchell. page NZD 1,575; trim 225 x 297. Circ: 6,550.

629.222 NZL ISSN 1173-972X
NEW ZEALAND PERFORMANCE CAR. Text in English. 1996. m. NZD 85 domestic; NZD 155 in Australia; NZD 210 elsewhere (effective 2008). adv. back issues avail. **Document type:** *Magazine, Consumer.* **Description:** Includes technical articles on high-performance automobiles, along with reviews of audio equipment.
Published by: Parkside Media, Herne Bay, PO Box 46020, Auckland, 1147, New Zealand. TEL 64-9-3601480, FAX 64-9-3601470, http://www.parksidemedia.co.nz. Ed. Brad Lord. Pub. Greg Vincent.

388 AUT
NISSAN AKTUELL; das aktuelle Magazin fuer Auto, Reise und Freizeit. Text in German. 3/yr. **Document type:** *Magazine, Consumer.* **Description:** General interest publication for the owners of Nissan automobiles in Austria.
Published by: Nissan Oesterreich GmbH, Laaer Berg-Str 64, Vienna, N 1101, Austria. office@nissan.at. Ed. Manfred Waldenmair. Pub., Adv. contact Markus Auferbauer.

388.3 JPN ISSN 0029-0734
NISSAN DIESEL TECHNICAL REVIEW. Text in Japanese; Summaries in English, Japanese. 1950. a. free. bk.rev. abstr.; bibl.; charts; illus.
Published by: Nissan Diesel Motor Co. Ltd./Nihon Nissan Jizeru Kogyo K.K., 1-1 Ageoshi, Saitama-ken, 362, Japan. Circ: 4,000.

388 USA ISSN 1934-3949
NISSAN SPORT. Text in English. q. USD 16.95 domestic; USD 25.95 in Canada; USD 39.95 elsewhere (effective 2008). adv. back issues avail. **Document type:** *Magazine, Trade.*
Formerly (until 2006): Sport Z (1542-2895)
Published by: RAZ Publishing, 10219 Arroyo Crest Dr NW, Albuquerque, NM 87114-5805. TEL 505-890-1764, FAX 505-890-4640, publisher@sportzmagazine.com. Ed. David Muramoto TEL 303-752-9777. Pub. Dave Ochenreider TEL 505-890-1764.

629.222 JPN
NISSHA GIHO/NIPPON SHARYO TECHNICAL REVIEW. Text in Japanese. s-a.
Published by: Nippon Sharyo Seizo K.K., Kaihatsu Honbu, 1-1 Sanbonmatsu-cho, Atsuta-ku, Nagoya-shi, Aichi-ken 456-0032, Japan.

NO-FAULT / SUM ARBITRATION. *see* LAW

629.2 NOR ISSN 0803-5172
NORSK MOTORVETERAN. Text in Norwegian. 1991. 10/yr. NOK 420; NOK 60 newsstand/cover (effective 2009). adv. **Document type:** *Magazine, Consumer.*
Published by: Hjemmet Mortensen AS, Gullhaugveien 1, Nydalen, Oslo, 0441, Norway. TEL 47-22-585000, FAX 47-22-585959, firmapost@hm-media.no, http://www.hm-media.no. adv.: page NOK 6,800.

796.7 USA ISSN 1533-421X
NORTH AMERICAN CLASSIC M G MAGAZINE. Text in English. 2001. q. USD 20 domestic; USD 24 in Canada; USD 30 elsewhere (effective 2002).
Published by: Grand Prix Graphics, Inc., 8702 Taybrook Dr., Huntersville, NC 28078. TEL 704-948-1745, FAX 704-948-1746. Eds. Dick Lunney, Ken Smith.

796.72 USA ISSN 1053-4881
NORTH AMERICAN PYLON; dedicated to sports car autocrossing. Text in English. 1990. m. USD 24 (effective 2001). adv. bk.rev. 24 p./no.; back issues avail. **Document type:** *Newspaper, Consumer.* **Description:** Reports on autocross time trial events throughout the U.S. and Canada, with road tests of new cars and interviews of prominent drivers and personalities in the sport.
Published by: Kelly Communications (Pleasanton), PO Box 1203, Pleasanton, CA 94566-0120. TEL 925-846-7728, FAX 925-846-0118. Ed., Pub., Adv. contact John F Kelly Jr. Circ: 2,800.

388.476 GBR ISSN 2044-5164
NORTH EAST & YORKSHIRE AUTO TRADER. Text in English. 1988. w. GBP 2.20 newsstand/cover (effective 2010). adv. illus. **Document type:** *Magazine, Consumer.* **Description:** Provides information on buying and selling cars, bicycles, boats, caravans (trailers), and accessories.
Formerly (until 2009): North East Auto Trader (0958-3335)
Published by: Trader Publishing Ltd., Auto Trader House, Catherine St, Bewsey Industrial Estate, Warrington, Cheshire WA5 0LH, United Kingdom. TEL 845-345-6789, enquiries@autotrader.co.uk, http://www.tradermediagroup.com.

338 USA
NORTH TEXAS AUTOMOTIVE REPORT. Text in English. m. free to qualified personnel (effective 2008). adv. **Document type:** *Newspaper, Trade.* **Description:** Provides monthly news for the local automotive industry in North Eastern Texas, which includes body shops, mechanical shops and dealers.
Supersedes in part: Texas Automotive Report
Published by: Autographic Publishing Company, Inc., 1121 Airport Center Dr, Ste 101, Nashville, TN 37214. TEL 615-391-3666, 800-467-3666, FAX 615-391-3622, garnett@automotivereport.net, http://www.automotivereport.net. Ed. Garnett Forkum. Pub. Allen Forkum. adv.: B&W page USD 825; trim 11.5 x 15.

338.476 GBR ISSN 0958-4277
NORTH WEST AUTO TRADER. Text in English. 1989. w. adv. back issues avail. **Document type:** *Magazine, Consumer.* **Description:** Advertising medium for buying and selling vehicles and motor related products. Area of coverage includes: Cheshire, Lancashire, Merseyside, Manchester, Cumbria, N.Wales & Staffordshire.
Formerly: North West Automart
Published by: Auto Trader Publications Ltd. (Subsidiary of: Trader Media Group Ltd.), Auto Trader House, Danehill, Cutbush Park, Lower Earley Reading, Berkshire RG6 4UT, United Kingdom. TEL 44-845-0501766, FAX 44-118-9239159, enquiries@autotrader.co.uk. Circ: 33,094.

388.3 USA ISSN 0029-3148
NORTHERN LIGHTS (MINNEAPOLIS). Text in English. 1954. 8/yr. membership. adv. **Document type:** *Newsletter.*
Published by: Antique Automobile Club of America, Minnesota Region, 621 E 61st St, Minneapolis, MN 55417. TEL 612-869-1710. Ed. Priscilla Johansen. Circ: 550.

NORTHERN NEW ENGLAND JOURNEY. *see* TRAVEL AND TOURISM

388.3 USA
NORTHERN RODDER. Text in English. 2000. m. USD 24.95; USD 3.95 newsstand/cover (effective 2001). adv. **Document type:** *Magazine, Consumer.*
Published by: Pro-Motion Publication, 1400 Commerce Blvd, Ste 18, Anniston, AL 36207. TEL 256-831-7877, FAX 256-831-6705. Ed., Pub. Ron Zuetlau.

NOSTALGIA. *see* ANTIQUES

629.286 388.3 ITA
NOTIZIARIO ATTREZZATURE. Text in Italian, English. s-a. free. **Document type:** *Magazine, Trade.* **Description:** Covers the industry and trade of equipment and tools for auto garages, car electrician shops, body shops, tire specialists and vehicle inspection centers.
Related titles: Online - full text ed.
Published by: Edizioni Collins Sas, Via Giovanni Pezzotti, 4, Milan, MI 20141, Italy. TEL 39-02-8372897, FAX 39-02-58103891, collins@collins.com, http://www.netcollins.com.

388 388.324 ITA
NOTIZIARIO MOTORISTICO/MOTOR - NACHRICHTEN/MOTOR NEWS/NOUVELLES DE L'AUTOMOBILE; autoattrezzature-impiantistica-ricambi-accessori. Text in English, Italian. 1965. m. free. bk.rev.; Website rev. abstr.; illus.; pat.; tr.mk. 160 p./no.; **Document type:** *Magazine, Trade.* **Description:** Covers technical, financial, and commercial news for the automotive industry, with special issues during international exhibitions.
Related titles: CD-ROM ed.; Online - full text ed.
Published by: Edizioni Collins Sas, Via Giovanni Pezzotti, 4, Milan, MI 20141, Italy. TEL 39-02-8372897, FAX 39-02-58103891, collins@collins.com, http://www.netcollins.com. Pub. David Giardino. Adv. contact Natascia Giardino TEL 39-02-8372897. Circ: 23,000 (free).

388.3 USA
NOVA CHEVY'S LITTLE CLASSIC; Super Chevy. Text in English. 2000. a. USD 3.75 domestic; USD 4.50 in Canada (effective 2007). adv. **Document type:** *Magazine, Consumer.* **Description:** Covers Chevy Novas from restoring classics to building custom chassis.
Published by: Source Interlink Companies, 27500 Riverview Ctr Blvd, Bonita Springs, FL 34134. TEL 239-949-4450, edisupport@sourceinterlink.com, http://www.sourceinterlink.com.

388.3 USA ISSN 0029-5434
NOZZLE. Text in English. 1970. m. adv. charts; illus.
Published by: Greater Washington - Maryland Service Station & Automotive Repair Association, 9420 Annapolis Rd, Ste 307, Lanham, MD 20706-3021. TEL 301-577-2875. Ed. Roy Littlefield III. Circ: 3,500.

629.286 USA
THE NOZZLE & WRENCH. Text in English. 1950. a. free domestic to members (effective 2005). adv. **Document type:** *Magazine, Trade.*
Formerly: Nozzle, The
Published by: WMDA Service Station & Automotive Repair Assn., 1532 Pointer Ridge Pl., Ste. E, Bowie, MD 20716. TEL 301-390-0900, FAX 301-390-3161. Ed., Pub. Roy Littlefield. adv.: B&W page USD 450. Circ: 2,500 (controlled).

629.286 ESP
NUESTROS TALLERES/CHAPA Y PINTURA. Text in Spanish. 2001. m. adv. **Document type:** *Magazine, Trade.* **Description:** Covers the auto repair industry. Includes new equipment, legal articles and interviews.
Formed by the merger of (1980-2001): Nuestros Talleres (0212-8330); (1997-2001): Chapa y Pintura (1138-0667); Which was formerly (1986-1997): Cuadernos de Chapa y Pintura (1131-8856)
Published by: Tecnipublicaciones Espana, S.L., Avda de Manoteras 44, 3a Planta, Madrid, 28050, Spain. TEL 34-91-2972000, FAX 34-91-2972154, tp@tecnipublicaciones.com, http://www.tecnipublicaciones.com.

O B D I I DRIVE CYCLE GUIDE: DOMESTIC & IMPORT CARS, LIGHT TRUCKS, VANS & SUVS. (On Board Diagnostics) *see* ENGINEERING

388.3 FRA ISSN 1763-7155
OCCASIONS MAG. Text in French. 2004. q. EUR 18 (effective 2010). **Document type:** *Magazine, Consumer.*
Published by: Motor Presse France, 12 rue Rouget de Lisle, Issy-les-Moulineaux, 92442, France. http://www.motorpresse.fr.

388 AUT
OESTERREICHISCHE MOTORISTEN MAGAZIN. Text in German. 1992. 5/yr. EUR 31.50 domestic; EUR 39.50 foreign (effective 2005). adv. **Document type:** *Magazine, Consumer.*
Published by: Verlag Lorenz, Ebendorferstr 10, Vienna, W 1010, Austria. TEL 43-1-40566950, FAX 43-1-4068693, office@verlag-lorenz.at, http://www.verlag-lorenz.at. Ed., Adv. contact Hannelore Wachter-Sieg. B&W page EUR 1,750, color page EUR 3,035; trim 167 x 254. Circ: 12,000 (paid and controlled).

629.37 CZE ISSN 1211-6033
OFF ROAD. Text in Czech. 1995. bi-m. CZK 650 (effective 2011). adv. **Document type:** *Magazine, Consumer.*
Related titles: Online - full text ed.
Published by: Off Road Club s.r.o., Olomoucka 2332, Prague 9, 19800, Czech Republic. TEL 420-2-81933121, FAX 420-2-81933053. Ed. Mila Janacek. Adv. contact Dagmar Kubinova.

796.7 USA ISSN 0363-1745
TL235.6
OFF-ROAD. Text in English. 1969. m. USD 11.97 domestic; USD 23.97 in Canada; USD 35.97 elsewhere (effective 2008). adv. Supplement avail.; back issues avail.; reprints avail. **Document type:** *Magazine, Consumer.* **Description:** Emphasizes modifications of light-truck and four-wheel-drive vehicles for off-highway action.
Former titles (until 19??): Off Road Vehicles and Adventure; (until 19??): Off Road Vehicles
Related titles: Online - full text ed.
Indexed: A22, ConsI, G05, G06, G07, G08, G09, I05, MagInd, P02, P10, P53, P54, PQC, S23, T02.
—Ingenta. **CCC.**
Published by: Source Interlink Companies, 2400 E Katella Ave, 11th Fl, Anaheim, CA 92806. TEL 714-939-2400, FAX 714-978-6390, dheine@sourceinterlink.com, http://www.sourceinterlinkmedia.com. Eds. Jerrod Jones, Philip Howell. Pubs. Amber Pierce, Jeff Dahlin TEL 714-939-2512. adv.: B&W page USD 5,855, color page USD 8,275. Circ: 52,991 (paid).

796.77 DEU ISSN 0172-4185
OFF ROAD; das 4x4-Magazin fuer die Freiheit auf Raedern. Text in German. 1978. m. EUR 40.80 domestic; EUR 46 foreign; EUR 3.80 newsstand/cover (effective 2011). adv. **Document type:** *Magazine, Consumer.*
Related titles: Online - full text ed.
Published by: Off Road Verlag AG, Alte Landstr 21, Ottobrunn, 85521, Germany. TEL 49-89-608210, FAX 49-89-60821200, zentrale@off-road.de. Ed. Hanspeter Heckel. Pub. Juergen Flach. Adv. contact Christian Czerny. Circ: 57,077 (paid and controlled).

629.37 SVK ISSN 1337-7884
OFF ROAD 4X4 MAGAZIN. Text in Slovak. 2008. m. adv. **Document type:** *Magazine, Consumer.*
Published by: IPOM s.r.o., Velkoblahovska 75/39, Dunajska Streda, 92901, Slovakia. TEL 421-911-586844. Ed. Stefan Malak. Adv. contact Tomas Ladanyi.

629 USA ISSN 1082-0957
GV1029.9.S74
THE OFFICIAL N A S C A R PREVIEW AND PRESS GUIDE. (National Association for Stock Car Auto Racing) Text in English. 1986. a. 450 p./no.; back issues avail. **Document type:** *Handbook/Manual/Guide, Trade.*
Formerly (until 1994): The Official N A S C A R Yearbook and Press Guide (0891-4648)
Published by: U M I Publications, Inc., PO Box 30036, Charlotte, NC 28230. TEL 800-747-9287, status@umipub.com.

629.286 330 USA
OHIO & NORTHERN KENTUCKY GASOLINE DEALERS & GARAGE NEWS. Text in English. bi-m. adv. **Document type:** *Magazine, Trade.*
Published by: Greater Cincinnati Gasoline Dealers Association, 3410 Glenway Ave, Cincinnati, OH 45205-2902. TEL 513-921-3182. Ed., Pub. John Mike Kunnen. Adv. contact Mary Chitwood. Circ: 1,800.

THE OHIO MOTORIST. *see* TRAVEL AND TOURISM

629.2 CAN ISSN 0841-775X
OLD AUTOS. Text in English. 1987. s-m. CAD 30; CAD 80 foreign. adv.
Address: 348 Main St, P O Box 419, Bothwell, ON N0P 1C0, Canada. TEL 519-695-2303, FAX 519-695-3716. Ed. Murray McEwan. Circ: 16,000.

629.222 USA ISSN 0048-1637
OLD CARS; weekly news and marketplace. Variant title: Old Cars Weekly. Text in English. 1971. 56/yr. USD 79.98; USD 2.99 newsstand/cover (effective 2012). adv. bk.rev. charts; illus.; tr.lit. back issues avail.; reprints avail. **Document type:** *Magazine, Trade.* **Description:** Covers the entire field of collectible automobiles from classic touring cars and roadster of the early 1900s to the popular muscle cars of the 1960s and 1970s. Includes historical perspectives and facts on cars and their manufacturers, and reports on attractions at upcoming shows. Regular columns include: New Products, Questions & Answers, Restoration Basics, and an extensive classified word ad section. Hundreds of car show listings are included in each issue to help readers schedule their car show attendance over the upcoming two months.
Related titles: Online - full text ed.
Indexed: G08, I05.
—**CCC.**
Published by: F + W Media Inc., 4700 E Galbraith Rd, Cincinnati, OH 45236. TEL 513-531-2690, contact_us@fwmedia.com, http://www.fwmedia.com/. Ed. Angelo Van Bogart TEL 715-445-2214 ext 13228. Pub. Jamie Wilkinson TEL 715-445-2214 ext 13447. Circ: 62,846 (paid and free).

796.77 BRA ISSN 1806-7484
OLD CARS ESPECIAL. Text in Portuguese. 2004. irreg. BRL 5.90 newsstand/cover (effective 2006). adv. **Document type:** *Magazine, Consumer.*
Published by: Editora Escala Ltda., Av Prof Ida Kolb, 551, Casa Verde, Sao Paulo, 02518-000, Brazil. TEL 55-11-38552100, FAX 55-11-38579643, escala@escala.com.br, http://www.escala.com.br.

388.3 AUS
OLDER CARS & COMMERCIAL GUIDE. Text in English. 1987. q. USD 237 (effective 2000). adv. **Document type:** *Directory, Trade.* **Description:** Provides prices and identification on used passenger cars and commercial vehicles for the period in excess of 10 years back to 1968.
Published by: Glass' Guide Pty. Ltd., 48 La Trobe St, Melbourne, VIC 3000, Australia. TEL 61-3-96633009, FAX 61-3-96633049, customers@glassguide.com.au, http://www.glassguide.com.au. adv.: color page USD 100; trim 80 x 125.

629.2 ZAF
OLDER VEHICLE DATA DIGEST (CARS, LDV'S PRE - 1977). Text in English. biennial. **Description:** Provides concise, practical specifications and tune-up data for older model cars and Ldv's marketed in South Africa before 1977, which are no longer listed in the current Auto Data Digest and Commercial Vehicle Data Digest.
Published by: Mead & McGrouther (Pty) Ltd., PO Box 1240, Randburg, Gauteng 2125, South Africa. adv.: B&W page ZAR 2,700, color page ZAR 4,125; trim 200 x 130. Circ: 6,000.

OLDTIMER ANZEIGER; Klassische Automobile & Motorraeder - Zubehoer. *see* ADVERTISING AND PUBLIC RELATIONS

796.7 DEU
OLDTIMER BOERSE. Text in German. bi-m. EUR 17.40; EUR 2.90 newsstand/cover (effective 2008). adv. **Document type:** *Magazine, Consumer.*
Published by: A M O Verlag GmbH, Sattlerstr 7, Luebeck, 23556, Germany. TEL 49-1805-151165, FAX 49-190-151050, info@amo-verlag.de, http://www.amo-verlag.de. Ed. Juergen Koslowski. adv.: B&W page EUR 400, color page EUR 500; trim 204 x 270.

388 796.7 DEU
OLDTIMER HANDEL. Text in German. 1992. bi-m. EUR 17.40; EUR 2.90 newsstand/cover (effective 2008). adv. **Document type:** *Magazine, Consumer.*
Former titles: Auto und Motorrad Oldtimer; (until 1995): Auto Motorrad Oldtimer; Cabrio und Oldtimer Markt
Published by: A M O Verlag GmbH, Sattlerstr 7, Luebeck, 23556, Germany. TEL 49-1805-151165, FAX 49-190-151050, info@amo-verlag.de, http://www.amo-verlag.de. Ed. Juergen Koslowski. adv.: B&W page EUR 400, color page EUR 500; trim 204 x 270. Circ: 50,000 (paid).

OLDTIMER INSERAT. *see* ADVERTISING AND PUBLIC RELATIONS

796.77 DEU
OLDTIMER KATALOG. Text in German. 1983. a. EUR 17.90 (effective 2010). adv. back issues avail. **Document type:** *Catalog, Consumer.*
Published by: Heel-Verlag GmbH, Gut Pottscheidt, Koenigswinter, 53639, Germany. TEL 49-2223-92300, FAX 49-2223-92301326, info@heel-verlag.de, http://www.heel-verlag.de. Pub. Franz Christoph Heel.

796.77 DEU ISSN 0943-7320
OLDTIMER-MARKT; Europas groesste Zeitschrift fuer Klassische Autos und Motorraeder. Text in German. 1980. m. EUR 35.40 domestic; EUR 46.20 foreign; EUR 3.20 newsstand/cover (effective 2011). adv. bk.rev. mkt.; illus. back issues avail. **Document type:** *Magazine, Consumer.* **Description:** For classic automobile and motorcycle enthusiasts. Includes new products, readers' comments, and large classified listings for automobiles and parts for sale.
Former titles (until 1993): Markt (0939-9704); (until 1990): Markt fuer Klassische Automobile und Motorraeder (0175-9698)
Published by: V F Verlagsgesellschaft mbH, Lise-Meitner-Str 2, Mainz, 55129, Germany. TEL 49-6131-9920, FAX 49-6131-992103, info@vfmz.de, http://www.vfmz.de. Ed. Peter Steinfurth. Adv. contact Michael Kaiser TEL 49-6131-992130. Circ: 137,882 (paid).

388 DEU ISSN 0937-6291
OLDTIMER PRAXIS; Technik - Tipps - Termine. Text in German. 1990. m. EUR 23.20 domestic; EUR 32.80 foreign; EUR 2.10 newsstand/cover (effective 2011). adv. charts; illus.; maps. back issues avail. **Document type:** *Magazine, Consumer.*
Indexed: TM.
Published by: V F Verlagsgesellschaft mbH, Lise-Meitner-Str 2, Mainz, 55129, Germany. TEL 49-6131-9920, FAX 49-6131-992103, info@vfmz.de, http://www.vfmz.de. Ed. Lars Rosenbrock. Adv. contact Michael Kaiser TEL 49-6131-992130. Circ: 100,672 (paid).

388.3 DEU ISSN 1436-9974
OMNIBUS-REVUE. Text in German. 1950. m. EUR 96.90; EUR 8 newsstand/cover (effective 2010). adv. charts; illus.; tr.lit. index. **Document type:** *Magazine, Trade.* **Description:** Contains detailed articles on topical problems of the coach business, transportation products, bus tourism, and group travel operators.
Formerly (until 1995): Omnibusrevue (0030-2279)
—CCC.
Published by: Verlag Heinrich Vogel (Subsidiary of: Springer Science+Business Media), Neumarkterstr 18, Munich, 81664, Germany. TEL 49-89-43722878, FAX 49-89-2030432100, kontakt@verlag-heinrich-vogel.de, http://www.springerfachmedien-muenchen.de. Ed. Anne K Peters. Adv. contact Elisabeth Huber. B&W page EUR 3,200, color page EUR 4,500; trim 185 x 250. Circ: 4,335 (paid); 2,175 (controlled).

ON THE LINE (PENSACOLA). *see* LEISURE AND RECREATION

338.476 DEU
ON TOUR. Text in German. q. adv. **Document type:** *Magazine, Consumer.*
Published by: (Union Tank Eckstein GmbH & Co. KG), EuroTransportMedia Verlags- und Veranstaltungs-GmbH, Handwerkstr 15, Stuttgart, 70565, Germany. TEL 49-711-784980, FAX 49-711-7849888, info@etm-verlag.de, http://www.etm-verlag.de. Adv. contact Bettina Pfeffer. Circ: 143,000 (controlled).

796.77 USA ISSN 0279-2737
ON TRACK (CHARLOTTE); the auto racing magazine of record. Text in English. 1981. fortn. (25/yr.). bk.rev. illus. back issues avail. **Document type:** *Magazine, Consumer.* **Description:** Covers the most important open-wheel auto racing events worldwide, including Formula 1, Formula 3000, Indy Lights, NASCAR, Atlantics, Formula Ford, Barber Dodge, FIA GT, Trans-Am, and World Sports Car.
Related titles: Online - full text ed.: On Track Online.
—CCC.
Published by: (American City Business Journals, Inc.), Street & Smith's Sports Group (Subsidiary of: American City Business Journals, Inc.), 120 W Morehead St, Ste 230, Charlotte, NC 28202. TEL 704-973-1300, FAX 704-973-1576, annuals@streetandsmiths.com, http://www.streetandsmiths.com. Circ: 19,658 (paid).

338.3 CAN ISSN 0832-8269
ONTARIO. MINISTRY OF TRANSPORTATION. ONTARIO ROAD SAFETY ANNUAL REPORT. Text in English. 1957. a. free. illus.; stat. **Document type:** *Government.*
Former titles: Ontario. Ministry of Transportation and Communications. Ontario Road Safety Annual Report; (until 1985): Ontario. Ministry of Transportation and Communications. Motor Vehicle Accident Facts; Ontario. Ministry of Transportation and Communications. Highway Traffic Collisions
Published by: Ministry of Transportation, 1201 Wilson Ave, Downsview, ON M3M 1J8, Canada. TEL 416-235-3585, FAX 416-235-3633. Eds. Antoine Haroun, Landsay Tom. R&P Mark Robinson. **Subscr. to:** Publications Services Section, 880 Bay St, 5th Fl, Toronto, ON M7A 1N8, Canada. TEL 800-668-9938.

796.77 DEU
OPEL - DAS MAGAZIN. Text in German. 1983. q. adv. **Document type:** *Magazine, Consumer.*
Published by: Adam Opel GmbH, Friedrich-Lutzmann-Ring, Ruesselsheim, 65423, Germany. TEL 49-6142-770, FAX 49-6142-778800, kunden.info.center@de.opel.com, http://www.opel.de. adv.: B&W page EUR 7,500, color page EUR 7,500. Circ: 149,051 (controlled).

629.22 NLD ISSN 1872-5384
OPEL KLASSIEK. Text in Dutch. 1995. 5/yr. EUR 32 (effective 2009). adv.
Published by: Historische Opel Club Nederland, Middelburgseweg 89-A, Boskoop, 2771 NJ, Netherlands. secretaris@opelclub.nl, http://www.opelclub.nl. Ed. Paul Hermans.

388 AUS ISSN 1444-8807
OPEN ROAD. Text in English. 1921. bi-m. free to members (effective 2009). adv. bk.rev. back issues avail. **Document type:** *Magazine, Consumer.* **Description:** Features articles and news on travel, motoring, home and money.
Formerly (until 1927): Good Roads
Related titles: CD-ROM ed.: AUD 15 to non-members; AUD 10 to members (effective 2009); Online - full text ed.
Indexed: ARI.
Published by: (National Roads and Motorists Association), N R M A Publishing, Level 1, 9 George St., North Strathfield, NSW 2137, Australia. TEL 61-2-9292-9275, FAX 61-2-9292-9069. Ed. David Naylor. Pub. Charles Blackburn. Adv. contact Katherine Komorowski TEL 61-2-87416692. color page AUD 24,275; trim 200 x 275. Circ: 1,536,426.

388.3 USA ISSN 0279-0254
GV1029.9.S74
OPEN WHEEL. Text in English. 1980. m. USD 11.97 domestic; USD 3.99 newsstand/cover domestic; GBP 2.25 newsstand/cover in United Kingdom (effective 2007). adv. illus. back issues avail. **Document type:** *Magazine, Consumer.* **Description:** Covers sprint car, midget, supermodified and Indy car racing. Includes technical features, personality profiles, columns and race reports.
Published by: Source Interlink Companies, 6420 Wilshire Blvd, 10th Fl, Los Angeles, CA 90048. TEL 323-782-2000, FAX 323-782-2585, dheine@sourceinterlink.com, http://www.sourceinterlink.com. Circ: 61,000 (paid).

388.3 629.2 CAN
OPPORTUNITIES UNLIMITED. Text in English. biennial. free.
Published by: Automotive Industries Association of Canada/Association des Industries de l'Automobile du Canada, 1272 Wellington St, Ottawa, ON K1Y 3A7, Canada. TEL 613-728-5821, FAX 613-728-6021, info.aia@aiacanada.com. Ed. Mireille Schippers. Circ: 40,000.

796.72 388.3 FRA ISSN 1779-1006
OPTION 4 X 4; l'essentiel de l'equipement 4 X 4 et de la pratique tout terrain. Text in French. 2006. bi-m. **Document type:** *Magazine, Consumer.*
Published by: Editions Lariviere, 6 Rue Olof Palme, Clichy, 92587, France. TEL 33-1-47565400, http://www.editions-lariviere.fr.

796.77 USA ISSN 1084-8436
ORLIE'S LOWRIDING. Text in English. m. USD 32 domestic; USD 95 foreign; USD 4.50 newsstand/cover; USD 5.95 newsstand/cover in Canada (effective 2001). adv. **Document type:** *Magazine, Consumer.* **Description:** Contains articles and features on lowrider cars and the people who drive and build them.
Published by: Ristra Publishing, 1224 Bellamah NW, Albuquerque, NM 87104. TEL 505-842-8820, FAX 505-842-0202. Ed., Pub. Dana Buchanan. Adv. contact Karla Anderson. **Dist. by:** Rider Circulation Services, 3700 Eagle Rock Blvd, Los Angeles, CA 90065. TEL 213-344-1200, FAX 213-256-9999.

388.342 TUR ISSN 1300-8021
OTO HABER. Text in Turkish. 1991. w. **Document type:** *Magazine, Consumer.*
Published by: Turkuvaz Magazine Broadcasting Enterprises, Inc., Tevfik Bey Mah. 20 Temmuz Cad. No.24, Sefakoy - Istanbul, 34295, Turkey. TEL 90-212-4112323, FAX 90-212-3543792, http://www.calik.com/.

388.34 TUR ISSN 1301-4366
OTO MOTOR MARKETING. Text in Turkish. 1997. m. **Document type:** *Magazine, Trade.*
Published by: Merkez Dergi/Merkez Magazine Group, Medya Plaza, Basin Ekspres Yolu, Gunesli - Istanbul, 34540, Turkey. TEL 90-212-502-8840, FAX 90-212-502-8068.

388.342 TUR
OTO YEDEKPARCA. Text in Turkish. bi-m. **Document type:** *Magazine, Trade.*
Published by: Erem Uluslararasi Tanitim Hizmetleri Ltd., Emniyet Evleri, Yeniceri Sokak 2-4-14, Levent - Istanbul, 80650, Turkey. TEL 90-212-2807506, FAX 90-212-2787112.

388 TUR
OTOMOTIV ENDUSTRISI/AUTOMOTIVE INDUSTRY. Text in Turkish. bi-m. **Document type:** *Magazine, Trade.*
Published by: Sektor Reklamcilik ve Yayincilik Ltd., Rumeli Caddesi, No 55-14, Nisantasi - Istanbul, 80220, Turkey. TEL 90-212-2257181, FAX 90-212-2415042.

388 TUR
OTOMOTIVDE SERVIS, EKIPMAN VE YEDEKPARCA. Text in Turkish. bi-m. **Document type:** *Magazine, Trade.*
Published by: Sektor Reklamcilik ve Yayincilik Ltd., Rumeli Caddesi, No 55-14, Nisantasi - Istanbul, 80220, Turkey. TEL 90-212-2257181, FAX 90-212-2415042.

796.77 IND
OVERDRIVE. Text in English. 19??. m. INR 1,150 domestic; INR 4,250 foreign (effective 2011). **Document type:** *Magazine, Trade.* **Description:** Contains news, views, reviews and sneak previews of the very latest in the world of cars and motorcycles as well as motor sports updates.
Published by: Infomedia 18 Ltd., A Wing, Ruby House, J K Sawant Marg, Dadar (West), Mumbai, 400 028, India. TEL 91-22-30245000, FAX 91-22-30034499, ho@infomedia18.in. Adv. contact Ruby Roy TEL 91-22-30034582.

796.71 ZAF ISSN 1991-4962
OVERDRIVE MOTORING.COM. Variant title: O D. Text in English. 2006. d.
Media: Online - full text.
Address: mailbox@odmotoring.com, http://www.odmotoring.com. Ed. Ciro De Siena.

388.3 AUS ISSN 1030-9896 ♦
OVERLANDER 4WD TOURING GUIDE. Text in English. 1987. m. AUD 55 domestic; AUD 101 in New Zealand; AUD 166 elsewhere; AUD 8.50 newsstand/cover (effective 2008). adv. bk.rev. index. back issues avail. **Document type:** *Magazine, Consumer.* **Description:** Covers new vehicle road tests, comparison driving, and news on four wheel drives.
Published by: News Magazines Pty Ltd., Level 3, 2 Holt St, Surry Hills, NSW 2010, Australia. TEL 61-2-92883000, http://www.newsspace.com.au/magazines. Adv. contacts Andrew Byrne TEL 61-2-80622656, Paul Gilliland TEL 61-3-95396107. page AUD 2,590; trim 206 x 276. Circ: 24,679 (paid).

P L 8 S MAGAZINE. *see* HOBBIES

P M L; the market letter for Porsche automobiles. (Porsche Market Letter) *see* BUSINESS AND ECONOMICS—Marketing And Purchasing

388 DEU ISSN 0938-6645
P S; das Sport-Motorrad Magazin. (Pferdestaerke) Text in German. 1974. m. EUR 3.50 newsstand/cover (effective 2010). adv. **Document type:** *Magazine, Consumer.*
Published by: Motor Presse Stuttgart GmbH und Co. KG, Leuschnerstr 1, Stuttgart, 70174, Germany. TEL 49-711-18201, FAX 49-711-1821779, cgolla@motorpresse.de, http://www.motorpresse.de. Ed. Michael Pfeiffer. Pub. Peter Paul Pietsch. Adv. contact Marcus Schardt.

PACKARD CORMORANT. *see* ANTIQUES

796.77 USA ISSN 0887-9613
PANTERA INTERNATIONAL NEWS. Short title: P I News. Text in English. 1975. q. USD 75 domestic membership; USD 85 foreign membership (effective 2008). adv. charts; illus. index. back issues avail. **Document type:** *Magazine, Consumer.* **Description:** Features technical "how to" information on the repair, service and modification of the Pantera automobile. Includes reprints of out-of-print articles and want ads.
Published by: Pantera International, 330 Central Ave, #25, Fillmore, CA 93015. TEL 805-524-5248, FAX 805-378-7100, george@panteracars.com. Ed. David Adler. Circ: 500.

380.8 ARG ISSN 0328-4387
PARABRISAS. Text in Spanish. 1960. m. USD 78.68 (effective 2002). adv. **Document type:** *Magazine, Consumer.* **Description:** Covers all aspects of buying, owning and driving automobiles.
Related titles: Online - full text ed.; Supplement(s): Parabrisas Libro Guia Todos Los 4 x 4. ISSN 0328-8285. 1996; Parabrisas Libro de Los Tests. ISSN 0328-8269. 1996; Parabrisas Guia Total de Rutas. ISSN 1514-1934. 1999.
Published by: Editorial Perfil S.A., Chacabuco 271, Buenos Aires, Buenos Aires 1069, Argentina. TEL 54-11-43419000, FAX 54-11-43418988, perfilcom@perfil.com.ar, http://www.perfil.com.ar. Ed. Hector Chavalier. Circ: 23,000 (paid).

388 GBR ISSN 0958-0662
PARKER'S CAR PRICE GUIDE; used, new & trade. Variant title: Parker's Price Guide. Text in English. 1972. m. GBP 65 domestic; GBP 100 foreign (effective 2009). adv. back issues avail. **Document type:** *Magazine, Consumer.* **Description:** Lists used car prices between 1980 and 1989 including values for classic cars.
Published by: H. Bauer Publishing Ltd. (Subsidiary of: Bauer Media Group), Media House, Lynchwood, Peterborough, Cambridgeshire PE2 6EA, United Kingdom. TEL 44-1733-468000, http://www.bauer.co.uk. Adv. contact Stuart Adam TEL 44-1733-468589. **Subscr. to:** Tower House, Sovereign Park, Market Harborough, Leicestershire LE16 9EF, United Kingdom. TEL 44-1858-438866, subs@greatmagazines.co.uk.

388.3 USA ISSN 0031-2193
HE371.A2
PARKING; the premier magazine of the parking industry. Text in English. 1952. 10/yr. USD 99 domestic to non-members; USD 150 foreign to non-members (effective 2005); include Products & Services Directory. adv. bk.rev. charts; illus.; tr.lit. 64 p./no.; **Document type:** *Magazine, Trade.*
Incorporates (1973-1990): N P A Government Affairs Report; (1972-1990): Parking World; Which was formerly (1963-1971): National Parking Association Newsletter (0277-0970); Newsletter - National Parking Association (0027-9862)
Indexed: HRIS, P06, P30.
Published by: National Parking Association, 1112 16th St N W, Ste 300, Washington, DC 20036. TEL 202-296-4336, FAX 202-331-8523. Ed. Logan Hunter-Thompson. Adv. contact Patricia Langfeld. B&W page USD 1,292, color page USD 1,892. Circ: 4,500 (controlled).

388.3 USA ISSN 0896-2324
PARKING PROFESSIONAL. Text in English. 1984. m. USD 60; USD 72 foreign. adv. bibl.; charts; illus.; stat.; tr.lit. index. back issues avail. **Document type:** *Magazine, Trade.* **Description:** Focuses on the parking industry: construction, operation, enforcement, maintenance.
Indexed: HRIS.
Published by: Institutional and Municipal Parking Congress, 701 Kenmore Ave, Ste 200, Fredericksburg, VA 22404. TEL 703-371-7535, FAX 703-371-8022. Ed. Marie E Witmer. Pub. David L Ivey. Adv. contact Lynne Chiara. B&W page USD 965, color page USD 1,715; trim 11 x 8.5. Circ: 1,800.

388 GBR ISSN 0962-3566
PARKING REVIEW. Text in English. 1989. m. GBP 75 domestic; GBP 95 in Europe; GBP 110 elsewhere; GBP 10 per issue; free to members (effective 2009). adv. illus. back issues avail. **Document type:** *Magazine, Trade.* **Description:** Covers on and off street parking policy and equipment and services used by public and private car park operators.
Incorporates: International Car Park Design and Construction Trends (0966-4955)
Related titles: Online - full text ed.: GBP 60 (effective 2009).
—CCC.
Published by: Landor Publishing Ltd, Apollo House, 359 Kennington Ln, London, SE11 5QY, United Kingdom. TEL 44-845-2707950, business@landor.co.uk, http://www.landor.co.uk. Adv. contact Frank Kingaby TEL 44-20-79245885. color page GBP 1,900; trim 240 x 332.

388 AUS ISSN 1838-5613
PARKING WORLD. Text in English. 2008. s-a. free (effective 2011). adv. **Document type:** *Magazine, Trade.* **Description:** Covers and supply information on all aspects of the parking industry. Helps to keep the latest and greatest releases, be it policing, hardware, software, construction, revenue control or operations.
Related titles: Online - full text ed.: ISSN 1838-5621.
Published by: Bricepac Pty Ltd., Locked Bag 1235, North Melbourne, VIC 3051, Australia. TEL 310-390-5277. Ed. Jolyon Porter. Pub. John Van Horn. Adv. contact Neil Hartley TEL 44-77-69338285.

629.24 ITA ISSN 1120-1789
PARTS. Text in Italian. 1978. 11/yr. EUR 74 domestic; EUR 107 foreign (effective 2009). adv. **Document type:** *Magazine, Trade.*
Formerly (until 1985): Tutto Ricambi (0392-6826)
Published by: Reed Business Information Spa (Subsidiary of: Reed Business Information International), Viale Giulio Richard 1, Milan, 20143, Italy. TEL 39-02-818301, FAX 39-02-81830406, info@reedbusiness.it, http://www.reedbusiness.it. Circ: 8,000.

629.283 USA ISSN 1083-771X
PARTS & PEOPLE; the monthly publication for Rocky Mountain, Midwest and Northwest automotive specialists. Variant title: Northwest Motor. (In 3 eds.: Midwest, Mountain, Northwest) Text in English. 1986. m. free for automotive professionals; USD 36 (effective 2003). adv. 36 p./no. 4 cols./p.; **Document type:** *Newspaper, Newspaper-distributed.* **Description:** Focuses on business practices, industry issues, and education and training for automotive parts and service specialists.
Published by: Automotive Counseling & Publishing Co., Inc., 450 Lincoln St, Ste 110, Denver, CO 80203-3459. TEL 303-860-0545, 800-530-8557, FAX 303-860-0532. Ed. Kevin Loewen. Pub., R&P, Adv. contact Lance R Buchner TEL 303-765-4664. B&W page USD 1,495; 13.5 x 10.5. Circ: 41,500 all eds. combined.

388.3 USA
PARTS & PEOPLE (NORTHWEST MOTOR EDITION). Text in English. 1909. m. USD 36 (effective 2005). adv. bk.rev. illus.; stat.; tr.lit. 32 p./no. 4 cols./p.; back issues avail. **Document type:** *Magazine, Trade.* **Description:** Contains the news of the Northwest automotive industry. Includes products and new vehicle reviews, as well as business and legislative news, calendar of events, training and classes, and monthly special features.
Formerly: Northwest Motor (0029-3393)
Related titles: Microform ed.: (from PQC); Online - full text ed.
Published by: Automotive Counseling and Publishing Company, Inc.,, 7353-36th Ave SW, Seattle, WA 98126. TEL 206-935-3336, 800-530-8557, FAX 206-937-9732. Ed. Lance Buchner. adv.: B&W page USD 1,245. Circ: 12,500 (paid and controlled).

388.3 GBR
PASS. Text in English. q. GBP 2.95 newsstand/cover. **Document type:** *Handbook/Manual/Guide, Consumer.* **Description:** Offers hints and tips on how to cope with both the theoretical and practical aspects of the UK's driving test and how to avoid failing the test.
Published by: Future Publishing Ltd., Beauford Ct, 30 Monmouth St, Bath, Avon BA1 2BW, United Kingdom. TEL 44-1225-442244, FAX 44-1225-446019, customerservice@subscription.co.uk, http://www.futureplc.com. Ed. Alison Stewart.

388.3 AUS
PASSENGER VEHICLE GUIDE. Text in English. 1971. m. AUD 403.70 (effective 2008). adv. **Document type:** *Directory, Trade.* **Description:** Provides prices and identification on new and used passenger cars dating back 10 years.
Former titles (until 1991): Glass's Passenger Vehicles Guide; (until 1989): Glass's Dealers Guide. Passenger Vehicle Values; Glass's Dealers Guide. Used Vehicle Values
Published by: Glass' Guide Pty. Ltd., 48 La Trobe St, Melbourne, VIC 3000, Australia. TEL 61-3-96633009, FAX 61-3-96633049, customers@glassguide.com.au, http://www.glassguide.com.au. adv.: color page USD 200; trim 80 x 125.

629.286 ITA ISSN 1120-4176
LA PATENTE DI GUIDA. Text in Italian. 1990. s-w. **Document type:** *Magazine, Consumer.*
Related titles: CD-ROM ed.: ISSN 1824-5501. 2002; Online - full text ed.: 2006.
Published by: Edizioni Giuridico Amministrative e Formazione (E G A F), Via Filippo Guarini 2, Forli, 47100, Italy. TEL 39-0543-473347, FAX 39-0543-474133, gruppo@egaf.it, http://www.egaf.it.

388.3 USA
PAY PLANS FOR SALES & ADMINISTRATIVE STAFF. Text in English. biennial. USD 198 per issue (effective 2008). adv. **Document type:** *Handbook/Manual/Guide, Trade.*
Published by: W D & S Publishing, 10 W 7th St, 1st Fl, PO Box 606, Barnegat Light, NJ 08006. TEL 800-321-5312, http://www.dealersedge.com. Pub., Adv. contact Jim Muntz.

388.3 USA
PENNSYLVANIA VEHICLES LAW. Text in English. 1976. a. USD 27 base vol(s). (effective 2008). **Document type:** *Handbook/Manual/Guide, Trade.* **Description:** Concise summaries of the Pennsylvania Consolidated Statutes, including Title 67, Chapter 75, Driver's Licensing Examination, selected sections of Title 36, Highways and Bridges, and a comprehensive index.
Related titles: CD-ROM ed.; Online - full text ed.
Published by: Gould Publications, Inc. (Subsidiary of: LexisNexis North America), 1333 North US Hwy 17-92, Longwood, FL 32750. TEL 800-533-1637, 877-374-2919, FAX 407-695-2906, criminaljustice@lexisnexis.com, http://www.gouldlaw.com.

PEOPLE 'N PRIDE. *see* ENGINEERING—Mechanical Engineering

PERFORMANCE AUTO & SOUND. *see* SPORTS AND GAMES

629.22 GBR ISSN 1462-3110
PERFORMANCE B M W. Text in English. 1998. m. GBP 43.20 domestic; GBP 60 in Europe; GBP 71 elsewhere; GBP 5 per issue (effective 2009). adv. back issues avail. **Document type:** *Magazine, Consumer.* **Description:** Features all the latest developments in BMW motoring and offers regular reviews of new cars and the latest accessories. It contains the latest on engine tuning, body kits, suspension drops and lots more.
Published by: Unity Media PLC, Becket House, Vestry Rd, Sevenoaks, Kent TN14 5EJ, United Kingdom. TEL 44-1732-748000, FAX 44-1732-748001, http://www.unity-media.com/. Ed. Louise Woodhams TEL 44-1732-748028. Pub. Colin Wilkinson. Adv. contact Helen Rush TEL 44-1732-748054. page GBP 1,350; trim 210 x 297.

796.77 796.72 USA ISSN 1555-4325
PERFORMANCE BUSINESS. Text in English. 2003. m. free domestic to qualified personnel; USD 85 combined subscription in Canada & Mexico (print & online eds.); USD 110 combined subscription elsewhere (print & online eds.) (effective 2008). adv. back issues avail.; reprints avail. **Document type:** *Magazine, Trade.* **Description:** Presents readers with new profit centers and ways to diversify their product line.
Related titles: Online - full text ed.: free to qualified personnel (effective 2008).
Published by: National Business Media, Inc., PO Box 1416, Broomfield, CO 80038. TEL 303-469-0424, 800-669-0424, FAX 303-469-5730. Ed. Jef White TEL 303-469-0424 ext 254. Pub. Kent Bradley TEL 303-469-0424 ext 256. Adv. contact Adina Foster TEL 303-469-0424 ext 257. color page USD 3,745, B&W page USD 3,045; trim 8.125 x 10.875. Circ: 14,040.

629.222 GBR ISSN 0955-0526
PERFORMANCE FORD. Text in English. 1987. m. GBP 40.32 domestic; GBP 58 in Europe; GBP 72 elsewhere; GBP 5 per issue (effective 2009). adv. back issues avail. **Document type:** *Magazine, Consumer.* **Description:** Covers the Ford line of vehicles in terms of performance, technology, and maintanence. Includes a classified section.
Related titles: Online - full text ed.
Published by: Unity Media PLC, Becket House, Vestry Rd, Sevenoaks, Kent TN14 5EJ, United Kingdom. TEL 44-1732-748000, FAX 44-1732-748001, http://www.unity-media.com/. Ed. Luke Wood. Pub. Colin Wilkinson. Adv. contact Jamie Lawrence TEL 44-1732-748047. color page GBP 950; trim 210 x 297.

629.22 GBR ISSN 1759-0345
PERFORMANCE FRENCH CARS. Abbreviated title: P F C. Text in English. 2000. m. GBP 43.44 domestic; GBP 48.84 in Europe; GBP 54.36 elsewhere; GBP 3.95 per issue domestic; GBP 4.95 per issue in Europe; GBP 5.45 per issue elsewhere (effective 2010). adv. back issues avail. **Document type:** *Magazine, Trade.* **Description:** Contains articles about the features of new cars.
Former titles (until 2007): Performance G T I French Cars (1751-9489); (until 2006): Performance G T I (1471-7387)
Related titles: Online - full text ed.
Published by: Kelsey Publishing Ltd., Cudham Tithe Barn, Berry's Hill, Cudham, Kent TN16 3AG, United Kingdom. TEL 44-1959-541444, FAX 44-1959-541400, info@kelsey.co.uk, http://www.kelsey.co.uk. Eds. Ian Cushway, Phil Weeden TEL 44-1733-353372. Adv. contact Natasha Lewis.

PERFORMANCE RACING INDUSTRY. *see* SPORTS AND GAMES

629.222 GBR ISSN 1364-2502
PERFORMANCE V W. (Volkswagen) Text in English. 1996. m. GBP 43.20 domestic; GBP 60 in Europe; GBP 71 elsewhere; GBP 5 per issue (effective 2009). adv. illus. back issues avail. **Document type:** *Magazine, Consumer.* **Description:** Reviews new Volkswagen cars and accessories to enhance their performance.
Related titles: Online - full text ed.
Published by: Unity Media PLC, Becket House, Vestry Rd, Sevenoaks, Kent TN14 5EJ, United Kingdom. TEL 44-1732-748000, FAX 44-1732-748001, http://www.unity-media.com/. Ed. Elliott Roberts TEL 44-1732-748026. Pub. Colin Wilkinson. Adv. contact Sarah Church TEL 44-1732-748057. color page GBP 950; trim 210 x 297.

338.342 985 GBR ISSN 1749-0073
PERU AUTOS REPORT. Text in English. 2005. a. EUR 820, USD 1,030 combined subscription per issue (print & email eds.) (effective 2010). **Document type:** *Report, Trade.* **Description:** Provides industry professionals and strategists, corporate analysts, auto associations, government departments and regulatory bodies with independent forecasts and competitive intelligence on the automotives industry in Peru.
Related titles: E-mail ed.
Indexed: A15, ABIn, B02, B15, B17, B18, G04, I05, P48, P51, P52, PQC.
Published by: Business Monitor International Ltd., Senator House, 85 Queen Victoria St, London, EC4V 4AB, United Kingdom. TEL 44-20-72480468, FAX 44-20-72480467, subs@businessmonitor.com.

PETERSEN'S 4 WHEEL & OFF-ROAD. *see* SPORTS AND GAMES—Bicycles And Motorcycles

629.2 NLD ISSN 1573-3173
PEUGEOT EXPO MAGAZINE. Text in Dutch. 2004. q. adv. **Document type:** *Magazine, Consumer.*
Published by: Holland Media Consult, Burgemeester Fabiuspark 22, Bilthoven, 3721 CN, Netherlands. TEL 31-6-21210892, http://www.hollandmediaconsult.nl.

338.342 959.9 GBR ISSN 1749-0081
PHILIPPINES AUTOS REPORT. Text in English. 2005. q. EUR 820, USD 1,030 combined subscription (print & email eds.) (effective 2010). **Document type:** *Report, Trade.* **Description:** Provides industry professionals and strategists, corporate analysts, auto associations, government departments and regulatory bodies with independent forecasts and competitive intelligence on the automotives industry in the Philippines.
Related titles: E-mail ed.
Indexed: A15, ABIn, B02, B15, B17, B18, G04, I05, P48, P51, P52, PQC.
Published by: Business Monitor International Ltd., Senator House, 85 Queen Victoria St, London, EC4V 4AB, United Kingdom. TEL 44-20-72480468, FAX 44-20-72480467, subs@businessmonitor.com.

388.3 USA
PIERCE-ARROW SERVICE BULLETIN. Text in English. 1968. bi-m. USD 25 to members. **Document type:** *Bulletin.*
Media: Duplicated (not offset).
Published by: Pierce-Arrow Society, Inc., 135 Edgerton St, Rochester, NY 14607. Pub. Bernard J Weis. Circ: 1,100.

629.262 GBR ISSN 1753-805X
PINSTRIPING & KUSTOM GRAPHICS MAGAZINE. Text in English. 19??. bi-m. GBP 35 in the UK & Northern Ireland; GBP 42.50 rest of Europe; GBP 50 elsewhere; GBP 5.95 per issue in the UK & Northern Ireland; GBP 7.25 per issue rest of Europe; GBP 8.95 per issue elsewhere (effective 2009). back issues avail. **Document type:** *Magazine, Consumer.* **Description:** Designed for both artists and their prospective customers. Contains features, interviews, Hints and Tips and How To's from the artists.
Formerly (until 2007): Trickstriperist
Published by: P & K G, 35 Westley Business Park, West Ave, Wigston, Leics LE18 2FB, United Kingdom. TEL 44-116-2810009, FAX 44-116-2813370, sales@pandkg.com.

796.77 GBR
PISTONHEADS.COM. Text in English. 1988. irreg. free (effective 2009). adv. **Document type:** *Magazine, Consumer.* **Description:** Covers news and trends about the British sportscar and performance motoring industry.
Media: Online - full content.
Published by: Haymarket Publishing Ltd. (Subsidiary of: Haymarket Media Group), West Coast Labs, Unit 9 Oak Tree Ct, Mulberry Dr, Cardiff Gate Business Park, Cardiff, CF23 8RS, United Kingdom. TEL 44-29-20548400, sales@westcoast.com, http://www.haymarket.com.

PLATES. *see* HOBBIES

628.2 FRA
PLEINS PHARES; revue de la filiere automobile francaise. Text in French. 199?. 5/yr. EUR 90 (effective 2008). **Document type:** *Magazine, Trade.*
Address: 37 Rue d'Amsterdam, Paris, 75008, France. TEL 33-1-42821892, FAX 33-1-45268135, pp@pleinsphares.fr.

388 USA ISSN 1552-3004
HD9710.U5
PLUNKETT'S AUTOMOBILE INDUSTRY ALMANAC. Variant title: Automobile Industry Almanac. Text in English. 2003. a. USD 299 combined subscription (print, online & CD-ROM eds.); USD 399 combined subscription (print & CD-ROM eds.) (effective 2009). **Document type:** *Directory, Trade.* **Description:** Provides industry analysis, statistical tables and in-depth profiles of the 300 leading automotive industry firms.
Related titles: CD-ROM ed.: ISSN 1555-2713; Online - full text ed.: USD 299 (effective 2009).
Published by: Plunkett Research, Ltd, PO Drawer 541737, Houston, TX 77254. TEL 713-932-0000, FAX 713-932-7080, customersupport@plunkettresearch.com. Pub. Jack W Plunkett.

PLYMOUTH BULLETIN. *see* ANTIQUES

629.286 678.32 CAN ISSN 1710-422X
PNEU MAG. Text in French. 2004. q. **Document type:** *Magazine, Trade.*
Published by: Publications Rousseau, 2938 Terrasse Abenaquis, bureau 110, Longueuil, PQ J4M 2B3, Canada. TEL 450-448-2220, 888-748-2220, FAX 450-448-1041, admin@p-rousseau.com, http://www.publicationsrousseau.com.

678.32 CZE ISSN 1214-3936
PNEU REVUE. Text in Czech. 1995. q. adv. **Document type:** *Magazine, Trade.* **Description:** Provides information for professionals in the tire industry. Monitors the industry, its status and trends within the Czech Republic, but also across Europe and worldwide.
Published by: Club 91, 5 Kvetna 1323/9, Prague 4, 140 00, Czech Republic. TEL 420-2-61221953, FAX 420-2-41403333. adv.: page EUR 1,200; trim 191 x 232. Circ: 2,000 (paid and controlled).

LE PNEUMATIQUE; industrie - distribution - rechapage. *see* RUBBER

388.342 943.8 GBR ISSN 1749-009X
POLAND AUTOS REPORT. Text in English. 2005. q. EUR 820, USD 1,030 combined subscription (print & email eds.) (effective 2010). **Document type:** *Report, Trade.* **Description:** Provides industry professionals and strategists, corporate analysts, auto associations, government departments and regulatory bodies with independent forecasts and competitive intelligence on the automotives industry in Poland.
Related titles: E-mail ed.
Indexed: A15, ABIn, B02, B15, B17, B18, G04, I05, P48, P51, P52, PQC.
Published by: Business Monitor International Ltd., Senator House, 85 Queen Victoria St, London, EC4V 4AB, United Kingdom. TEL 44-20-72480468, FAX 44-20-72480467, subs@businessmonitor.com.

388.3 USA
PONTIAC DRIVING EXCITEMENT. Text in English. 3/yr. adv. **Description:** Lifestyle magazine targets Pontiac owners.
Published by: Sandy Corporation, 1500 W Big Beaver Rd, Troy, MI 48084. TEL 800-733-4739, FAX 248-816-2305. Ed. Barry Kluczyk.

388.3 USA
PONTIAC ENGINE GUIDE; high performance Pontiac. Text in English. 2001. a. USD 4 newsstand/cover domestic; USD 4.99 newsstand/cover in Canada (effective 2007). adv. 100 p./no.; reprints avail. **Document type:** *Magazine, Consumer.*
Published by: Source Interlink Companies, 6420 Wilshire Blvd, 10th Fl, Los Angeles, CA 90048. TEL 323-782-2000, FAX 323-782-2585, dheine@sourceinterlink.com, http://www.sourceinterlinkmedia.com.

629.286 USA
PONTIAC TECH SPECIAL. Text in English. 2000. a. USD 4 newsstand/cover (effective 2007). adv. **Document type:** *Magazine, Consumer.*
Published by: Source Interlink Companies, 6420 Wilshire Blvd, 10th Fl, Los Angeles, CA 90048. TEL 323-782-2000, FAX 323-782-2585, dheine@sourceinterlink.com, http://www.sourceinterlinkmedia.com.

388.3 USA ISSN 0032-4523
TL236
POPULAR HOT RODDING. Text in English. 1962. m. USD 13.97 domestic; USD 25.97 in Canada; USD 37.97 elsewhere (effective 2008). adv. illus. back issues avail.; reprints avail. **Document type:** *Magazine, Consumer.* **Description:** Provides readers with technical articles on high-performance engine building, high lateral g handling, paint and body restoration, sportsman-level drag racing, historical special features, and the latest performers out of Detroit.
Related titles: Online - full text ed.
Indexed: G06, G07, G08, I05, S23.
—CCC.
Published by: Source Interlink Companies, 774 S Placentia Ave, Placentia, CA 92870. dheine@sourceinterlink.com, http://www.sourceinterlinkmedia.com. Ed. Johnny Hunkins. Pubs. Ed Zinke TEL 714-939-2626, John Gallagher TEL 323-782-2733. adv.: B&W page USD 10,060, color page USD 16,085. Circ: 112,809 (paid).

629.286 USA
POPULAR MECHANICS CARCARE. Key Title: CarCare. Text in English. 2001. 4/yr. adv. **Document type:** *Magazine, Consumer.* **Description:** Designed to inform and entertain automotive do-it-yourself enthusiasts.
Published by: (AutoZone, Inc.), Hearst Magazines (Subsidiary of: Hearst Corporation), 300 W 57th St, 12th Fl, New York, NY 10019. TEL 212-649-2000, HearstMagazines@hearst.com, http://www.hearstcorp.com/magazines/.

796.77 DEU ISSN 1618-9256
PORSCHE CLUB. Text in German. 1981. q. adv. **Document type:** *Magazine, Consumer.*
Formerly (until 2001): Porsche Club Life (1438-5686)
Published by: (Porsche Club Deutschland e.V.), P C L Medien und Verlags GmbH, Adams-Lehmann-Str 61, Munich, 80797, Germany. TEL 49-89-32729990, FAX 49-89-327299928. Ed. Frank Gindler. Adv. contact Anna Maria Artinger. B&W page EUR 4,500, color page EUR 6,300. Circ: 25,814 (paid and controlled).

796.7 DEU ISSN 1864-4090
PORSCHE FAHRER; das unabhaengige Porsche Magazin. Text in German. 2007. q. EUR 5.90 newsstand/cover (effective 2010). adv. **Document type:** *Magazine, Consumer.*

Published by: Heel-Verlag GmbH, Gut Pottscheidt, Koenigswinter, 53639, Germany. TEL 49-2223-92300, FAX 49-2223-92301326, info@heel-verlag.de, http://www.heel-verlag.de.

796.77 USA ISSN 0147-3565
TL215.P75
PORSCHE PANORAMA. Text in English. 1955. m. USD 42 membership (effective 2000). adv. bk.rev. charts; illus.; stat. back issues avail.; reprints avail.
Related titles: Microfilm ed.
Indexed: A22.
Published by: Porsche Club of America, Inc., PO Box 30100, Alexandria, VA 22310. TEL 703-922-9300, FAX 404-377-7041. Ed. Betty Jo Turner. Circ: 31,000. **Subscr. to:** 912 Lullwater Rd, Atlanta, GA 30307.

796.77 DEU ISSN 1611-3381
PORSCHE SCENE LIVE. Text in German. 2003. m. EUR 47 domestic; EUR 54 foreign; EUR 4.30 newsstand/cover (effective 2011). adv. **Document type:** *Magazine, Consumer.*
Published by: Vestische Mediengruppe Welke GmbH & Co. KG, Hertener Mark 7, Herten, 45699, Germany. TEL 49-2366-808400, FAX 49-2366-808499, info@vmw-verlag.de, http://vmw-verlag.de. Ed. Rudolf Welke. Pub. Arno Welke. Adv. contact Julia Wissing. Circ: 30,000 (paid and controlled).

796.77 USA ISSN 0192-8481
PORSCHE UEBER ALLES. Text in English. 10/yr. USD 18 (effective 2008). **Document type:** *Newsletter, Consumer.*
Published by: Porsche Club of America, Western Michigan Region, 10085 Edgerton Ave. N.E., Rockford, MI 49341. http://wmi.pca.org. Ed. Craig Ackerman. Adv. contact John Kilgren TEL 616-393-6754.

POWER BUILDERS. *see* ENGINEERING—Mechanical Engineering

388.3 USA
POWER WAGON & SPORT UTES; for Dodge truck and Jeep enthusiasts. Text in English. 1994. q. USD 12; USD 18 foreign (effective 1999). adv. bk.rev. back issues avail. **Document type:** *Magazine, Consumer.* **Description:** Covers technical and historical how-to's and features on Dodge trucks and Jeeps.
Published by: R H O Publications, 1580 Hampton Rd, Bensalem, PA 19020-4610. TEL 215-639-4456, FAX 215-639-6642. Ed., Pub., R&P Robert Oskiera. Circ: 50,000 (paid). **Dist. by:** Curtis Circulation Co., 730 River Rd, New Milford, NJ 07646. TEL 856-488-5700.

629.222 GBR ISSN 0957-6975
PRACTICAL CLASSICS. Text in English. 1980. 13/yr. GBP 51.50 domestic; GBP 63.50 foreign (effective 2009). adv. bk.rev. illus. back issues avail. **Document type:** *Magazine, Consumer.* **Description:** Designed to take the readers through restoration projects and provides advice and answers to maintenance problems.
Incorporates (1989-1996): Popular Classics (0957-6541); Former titles (until 1996): Practical Classics & Car Restorer (0955-5862); (until 1985): Practical Classics (0260-2911)
Related titles: Online - full text ed.
Published by: H. Bauer Publishing Ltd. (Subsidiary of: Bauer Media Group), Media House, Lynchwood, Peterborough, Cambridgeshire PE2 6EA, United Kingdom. TEL 44-1733-468582, FAX 44-1733-468888, http://www.bauer.co.uk. Ed. Matt Wright. Adv. contact Louise Rizzo TEL 44-1733-468435.

796.7 USA ISSN 1547-1306
PRESTIGE MAGAZINE; the Mercedes-Benz enthusiasts magazine. Text in English. 2003. q. USD 16 (effective 2003). adv. **Document type:** *Magazine, Consumer.* **Description:** Features road tests of the newest Mercedes Benz, market reports/buyers guides to pre-owned models, step-by-step DIY projects, calendar of events, hot product reviews and more.
Address: P. O. Box 408, Gamerco, NM 87317. TEL 888-225-6920. Ed. Brian Minson. Pubs. Brian Minson, Darren Baade. adv.: B&W page USD 1,495, color page USD 2,190; bleed 8.625 x 11.25.

PREVIEW (TROY). *see* BUSINESS AND ECONOMICS—Personnel Management

629.286 614.86 FRA ISSN 1957-6021
PRIORITE; le magazine des nouveaux conducteurs. Text in French. 2006. q. free. **Document type:** *Magazine, Consumer.*
Related titles: Online - full text ed.
Published by: M M C Group, 17 Rue de la Felicite, Paris, 75017, France. TEL 33-1-40543000, FAX 33-1-40543001.

629.286 USA
PROFESSIONAL CAR CARE E-NEWS. Text in English. 19??. s-w. free (effective 2011). **Document type:** *Newsletter, Trade.* **Description:** Covers news in the automotive service and after market industry.
Media: E-mail. **Related titles:** Online - full text ed.: free (effective 2011).
Published by: N T P Media (Subsidiary of: Grand View Media Group, Inc.), 19 British American Blvd W, Latham, NY 12110. TEL 518-783-1281, FAX 518-783-1386, http://www.cleanfax.com.

629.286 USA ISSN 1087-3260
PROFESSIONAL CAR WASHING & DETAILING. Text in English. 1976. m. USD 74 domestic; USD 150 foreign (effective 2011). adv. back issues avail. **Document type:** *Magazine, Trade.* **Description:** Provides technical, sales and marketing information to investors, owners, operators and managers of professional car washing facilities.
Formerly: Professional Carwashing (0191-6823)
Related titles: Online - full text ed.: free (effective 2011).
Indexed: A09, A10, S22, V03, V04.
—CCC.
Published by: N T P Media (Subsidiary of: Grand View Media Group, Inc.), 19 British American Blvd W, Latham, NY 12110. TEL 518-783-1281, FAX 518-783-1386. Ed. Deb Gorgos TEL 518-640-9166. Circ: 16,588.

PROFESSIONAL DISTRIBUTOR. *see* ENGINEERING—Mechanical Engineering

338.476292 GBR ISSN 1757-5745
PROFESSIONAL MOTOR FACTOR. Text in English. 2002. m. **Document type:** *Magazine, Trade.* **Description:** Features essential information on all aspects of the business and includes substantive editorial coverage of product developments, new markets and industry news.
—CCC.
Published by: Hamerville Magazines Ltd., Regal House, Regal Way, Watford, Herts WD24 4YF, United Kingdom. TEL 44-1923-237799, FAX 44-1923-246901, office@hamerville.co.uk. Ed. Richard Bowler. Adv. contact Oliver Shannon. Circ: 3,167.

629.287205 GBR ISSN 1757-5753
PROFESSIONAL MOTOR MECHANIC. Text in English. 2000. m. (except Jul./Aug. combined). adv. **Document type:** *Magazine, Trade.* **Description:** Features technical advice, the latest products and equipment, plus business and training features for auto mechanics.
—CCC.
Published by: Hamerville Magazines Ltd., Regal House, Regal Way, Watford, Herts WD24 4YF, United Kingdom. TEL 44-1923-237799, FAX 44-1923-246901, office@hamerville.co.uk. Ed. Richard Bowler. Adv. contact Oliver Shannon. page GBP 2,750; trim 210 x 285. Circ: 58,911.

PROFESSIONAL MOTORSPORT WORLD. *see* SPORTS AND GAMES

629.286 USA ISSN 1081-4485
PROFESSIONAL TOOL AND EQUIPMENT NEWS; the independent tool authority. Abbreviated title: P T E N. Text in English. 1990. 10/yr. USD 59 domestic; USD 85 in Canada & Mexico; USD 120 elsewhere; free to qualified personnel (effective 2009). adv. Supplement avail.; back issues avail.; reprints avail. **Document type:** *Magazine, Trade.* **Description:** Reports on new tools and equipment available for diagnosing and repairing vehicles properly and profitably.
Related titles: Online - full text ed.: ISSN 2150-2072. free (effective 2009).
Indexed: A09, A10, A15, ABIn, B02, B15, B17, B18, G04, G08, I05, P16, P48, P51, P52, P53, P54, PQC, T02, V03, V04.
—CCC.
Published by: Cygnus Business Media, Inc., 1233 Janesville Ave, PO Box 803, Fort Atkinson, WI 53538. TEL 920-563-6388, 800-547-7377, FAX 920-563-1702, http://www.cygnusb2b.com. Ed. Brendan Dooley TEL 920-568-8363. Pub. Larry M Greenberger TEL 847-454-2722. Adv. contact Kylie Hahn TEL 920-563-1666. B&W page USD 13,245, color page USD 15,707; trim 7.875 x 10.75. Circ: 104,604.

388.3 910.202 DEU ISSN 0935-834X
PROMOBIL; Europas groesstes Reisemobil-Magazin. Text in German. 1982. m. EUR 41; EUR 3.70 newsstand/cover (effective 2010). adv. back issues avail. **Document type:** *Magazine, Consumer.* **Description:** Travel, touring and outfitting information for drivers of recreational vehicles.
Related titles: Supplement(s): Promobil Spezial. ISSN 0941-7176. 1989.
—CCC.
Published by: Motor Presse Stuttgart GmbH & Co. KG (Subsidiary of: Gruner + Jahr AG & Co), Leuschnerstr 1, Stuttgart, 70174, Germany. TEL 49-711-18201, FAX 49-711-1821779, internet-redaktion@motor-presse-stuttgart.de, http://www.motorpresse.de. Adv. contacts Michael Roy, Peter Steinbach. B&W page EUR 5,115, color page EUR 8,200; trim 185 x 248. Circ: 74,482 (paid and controlled).

796.76 ARG ISSN 1852-2289
PUESTA PUNTO. Text in Spanish. 2008. m. **Document type:** *Magazine, Consumer.*
Published by: Club Argentino de Karting, Ave Roca y Ave Gral. Puz, Buenos Aires, 1439, Argentina. TEL 54-11-46057323, info@clubargentinodekart.com.ar, http://www.clubargentinodekart.com.ar/.

PUGET SOUND JOURNEY. *see* TRAVEL AND TOURISM

388.3 338.4791 RUS
PUT' I VODITEL'. Text in Russian. q. illus. **Document type:** *Magazine, Consumer.*
Related titles: Online - full content ed.
Published by: Izdatel'stvo Ostrov, Ul Shchepkina, dom 58, str.3, Moskow, 129110, Russian Federation. TEL 7-095-9612760, FAX 7-095-9612761, ad@naostrove.ru, market@naostrove.ru, http://naostrove.ru. Ed. Sergey Burtiak. Adv. contact Alla Putko TEL 7-095-9612770.

338.476 330 GBR ISSN 2044-5768
QATAR AUTOS REPORT. Text in English. 200?. q. EUR 820, USD 1,150 combined subscription (print & email eds.) (effective 2010). **Document type:** *Report, Trade.* **Description:** Provides industry professionals and strategists, corporate analysts, auto associations, government departments and regulatory bodies with independent forecasts and competitive intelligence on the Qatari automotives market.
Related titles: E-mail ed.
Published by: Business Monitor International Ltd., Senator House, 85 Queen Victoria St, London, EC4V 4AB, United Kingdom. TEL 44-20-72480468, FAX 44-20-72480467, subs@businessmonitor.com.

388.3 CHN ISSN 1673-081X
QICHE BOLAN. Text in Chinese. 2005. m. CNY 150 (effective 2009). **Document type:** *Magazine, Consumer.*
Published by: Qiche Bolan Zazhishe, PO Box 4720, Beijing, 100027, China. TEL 86-10-64603932.

388.3 381.33 CHN ISSN 1671-900X
QICHE DAOGOU/CAR MARKET GUIDE. Text in Chinese. 197?. m. CNY 96; CNY 8 newsstand/cover (effective 2009). **Document type:** *Magazine, Consumer.*
Former titles (until 2002): Nongji Anquan Jianli (1009-492X); (until 2001): Nongcun Jixiehua/Rural Mechanization (1002-5294); (until 1986): Nongye Jixiehua; (until 1983): Nongye Jixiehua Yanjiu Tongxun
Published by: Zhonggo Jixie Gongye Lianhehui, Deshengmen Wai, 1, Bei Shatan, Xinxiang 16, Beijing, 100083, China. TEL 86-10-64882175, FAX 86-10-64870803.

QICHE DIANQI/AUTO ELECTRIC PARTS. *see* ENGINEERING—Electrical Engineering

629.286 CHN ISSN 1000-680X
TL4 CODEN: QIGOE4
QICHE GONGCHENG/AUTOMOTIVE ENGINEERING. Text in Chinese; Abstracts in English. 1979. m. USD 133.20 (effective 2009). adv. **Document type:** *Magazine, Trade.*
Related titles: Online - full text ed.
Indexed: CPEI, SCOPUS.
—BLDSC (1833.819800), East View, Linda Hall.
Published by: Zhongguo Qiche Gongcheng Xuehui/Society of Automotive Engineers of China, 1, Baiyun Rd., Rm. 1202, Beijing, 100045, China. TEL 86-10-63287786, FAX 86-10-63280627. Circ: 4,000. **Dist. by:** China International Book Trading Corp, 35 Chegongzhuang Xilu, Haidian District, PO Box 399, Beijing 100044, China.

388.3 620 CHN ISSN 1674-6546
QICHE GONGCHENGSHI/AUTO ENGINEER. Text in Chinese. 1974. m. **Document type:** *Magazine, Trade.*
Formerly (until 2009): Tianjin Qiche/Tianjin Auto (1007-3620)
Related titles: Online - full text ed.
Published by: Tianjin Shi Qiche Yanjiusuo/Tianjin Automobile Research Institute, 15, Tiantuo Bei Dao, Nankai-qu, Tianjin, 300190, China. TEL 86-22-27030751, FAX 86-22-27030750, http://www.tjzyw.com/. **Co-sponsor:** Tianjin Shi Qiche Gongcheng Xuehui/Society of Automotive Engineers of China, Tianjin Branch.

629.286 CHN ISSN 1003-8817
QICHE GONGYI YU CAILIAO/AUTOMOBLIE TECHNOLOGY & MATERIAL. Text in Chinese. 1992. m. CNY 6 newsstand/cover (effective 2006). **Document type:** *Journal, Academic/Scholarly.*
Related titles: Online - full text ed.
Published by: Changchun Qiche Cailiao Yanjiusuo/Changchun Automobile Material Research Institute, 1063, Chuangye Dajie, Changchun, Jilin 130011, China. TEL 86-431-5789860, FAX 86-431-5789810.

629.286 CHN ISSN 1000-3703
TL4 CODEN: QJISEX
QICHE JISHU/AUTOMOBILE TECHNOLOGY. Text in Chinese. 1970. m. USD 49.20 (effective 2009). 64 p./no.;
Related titles: Online - full text ed.
—East View.
Published by: Changchun Qiche Cailiao Yanjiusuo/Changchun Automobile Material Research Institute, 1063, Chuangye Dajie, Changchun, Jilin 130011, China. TEL 0431-5902445, FAX 0431-867780. Ed. Han Xuechun. **Dist. overseas by:** China International Book Trading Corp, 35 Chegongzhuang Xilu, Haidian District, PO Box 399, Beijing 100044, China. **Co-sponsor:** Zhongguo Qiche Gongcheng Xuehui/Society of Automotive Engineers of China.

388.3 620 CHN ISSN 1005-2550
QICHE KEJI/AUTOMOBILE SCIENCE & TECHNOLOGY. Text in Chinese. 1973. bi-m. **Document type:** *Journal, Academic/Scholarly.*
Former titles (until 1993): Erqi Keji; (until 1982): Shiyan Erqi Keji; (until 1978): Erqi Keji Tongxun
Related titles: Online - full text ed.
—BLDSC (7163.614000).
Published by: Dongfeng Qiche Youxian Gongsi, Keji Qingbaosuo/Dongfeng Motor Company, Technical Information Institute, 10, Dongfeng Rd., Wuhan Economic & Technological Development Zone, Wuhan, 430056, China. TEL 86-27-84283755, FAX 86-27-84283757. Ed. Qing-lu Zeng.

388.3 362.1 CHN ISSN 1006-6713
QICHE YU ANQUAN/AUTO & SAFETY. Text in Chinese. 1995. m. **Document type:** *Journal, Academic/Scholarly.*
Published by: Qiche yu Anquan Zazhishe, 1, Rongchang Dong Jie Jia, Beijing, 100176, China. TEL 86-10-67866688 ext 6436, FAX 86-10-67806846. **Co-sponsor:** Zhongguo Jidong Cheliang Anquan Jianding Jiance Zhongxin.

629.283 CHN ISSN 1000-6796
QICHE ZHI YOU/AUTO FAN. Text in Chinese. 1986. s-m. USD 124.80 (effective 2009). adv. **Document type:** *Magazine, Consumer.*
Related titles: Online - full text ed.
—East View.
Published by: Zhongguo Qiche Gongcheng Xuehui/Society of Automotive Engineers of China, 1, Baiyun Rd., Rm. 1202, Beijing, 100045, China. TEL 86-10-63286179, FAX 86-10-63280627. Circ: 250,000. **Dist. by:** China International Book Trading Corp, 35 Chegongzhuang Xilu, Haidian District, PO Box 399, Beijing 100044, China. TEL 86-10-68412045, FAX 86-10-68412023, cibtc@mail.cibtc.com.cn, http://www.cibtc.com.cn.

388 CHN
QICHE ZIZHAOYE/AUTOMOBIL INDUSTRIE. Text in Chinese. 17/yr. free to qualified personnel. **Document type:** *Magazine, Trade.*
Published by: Deguo Fuge Gongye Meiti Jituan/Vogel Media Group (Subsidiary of: Vogel Business Media GmbH & Co.KG), 11/F, 1, Baiyue Lu, Xicheng-qu, Beijing, 100045, China. TEL 86-10-63326090, FAX 86-10-63326099, http://www.vogel.com.cn/.

388.3 CHN ISSN 1009-2153
QICHE ZU/MOTOR TREND. Text in Chinese. 2000. m. CNY 240 (effective 2009). **Document type:** *Magazine, Consumer.*
Published by: Qiche Zu Zazhishe, 36, Bei San Huan Dong Lu, Huanqiu Maoyi Zhongxin A-8, Beijing, 100013, China. TEL 86-10-58256931, FAX 86-10-58256868.

388.3 FRA ISSN 1298-518X
QUAD PASSION MAGAZINE. Text in French. 2000. bi-m. EUR 22 (effective 2010). **Document type:** *Magazine, Consumer.*
Published by: Editions D G T, 204 Chemin de la Pertuade, Six-Fours-les-Plages, 83148, France.

QUATRO RODAS. *see* TRAVEL AND TOURISM

388.3 ITA ISSN 0033-5916
TL4
QUATTRORUOTE. Text in Italian. 1956. m. bk.rev. illus. index. **Document type:** *Magazine, Consumer.*
Related titles: ♦ Supplement(s): Autopro. ISSN 1129-3330.
Indexed: A22.
—IE, Infotrieve.
Published by: Editoriale Domus, Via Gianni Mazzocchi 1/3, Rozzano, MI 20089, Italy. TEL 39-02-824721, editorialedomus@edidomus.it, http://www.edidomus.it.

QUEENSLAND STREET CAR. *see* HOBBIES

796.77 AUS ISSN 1838-4439
▼ **QUEENSLAND STREET CAR (MARSDEN).** Text and summaries in English. 2010. 8/yr. AUD 55; AUD 7.95 per issue (effective 2011). **Document type:** *Magazine, Trade.* **Description:** Provides information about cars around Queensland.
Published by: Queensland Street Car, 41 Fourth Ave, Marsden, QLD 4132, Australia. Ed. Craig Muller TEL 61-4-06278737.

629.286 USA
TL214.L8
QUICK LUBRICATION GUIDE. Text in English. 1991. a. adv. **Document type:** *Handbook/Manual/Guide, Trade.* **Description:** Provides manufacturer's specifications for complete, accurate lube service of cars and light trucks.

Former titles (until 2002): Chek-Chart's Quick Lubrication Guide; (until 19??): Chilton's Quick Lubrication Guide (1055-6842); Chek-Chart Quick Lubrication Charts
Published by: Motor Information Systems (Subsidiary of: Hearst Corporation), 5600 Crooks Rd, Ste 200, Troy, MI 48098. TEL 248-312-2700, 800-288-6828, FAX 248-879-8603, motorbookscallcenter@motor.com.

388.3 NLD ISSN 1389-8205
R A I VOORRANG. (Rijwiel- en Automobiel Industrie) Text in Dutch. 1997. 19/yr. bk.rev. stat.; tr.mk. 8 p./no. 5 cols./p.;
Formed by the merger of (1973-1997): R A I Actueel (0166-1922); (1970-1997): R A I Trends (0928-4079); Which was formerly (until 1992): R A I Documentatie (0922-3568)
Indexed: KES.
Published by: (R A I Vereniging), RAI Langfords bv, Postbus 10099, Amsterdam, 1001 EB, Netherlands. TEL 31-20-5042800, FAX 31-20-5042888, http://www.railangfords.nl. Ed. M F Timmer.

629.22 SWE ISSN 2000-3544
▼ **R P M MAGAZINE.** (Reparation Produktion Motorfordon) Text in Swedish. 2009. bi-m. adv. **Document type:** *Magazine, Consumer.*
Published by: Foerlags AB Albinsson & Sjoeberg, PO Box 529, Karlskrona, 37123, Sweden. TEL 46-455-335325, FAX 46-455-311715, fabas@fabas.se, http://www.fabas.se. Ed. Gunnar Svensson. Adv. contact Svante Svensson. page SEK 20,280; trim 210 x 297.

388.3 USA
R V TRADER. (Recreational Vehicle) Text in English. 19??. w. free (effective 2011). adv. **Document type:** *Magazine, Trade.*
Related titles: Online - full text ed.
Published by: Trader Publishing Co., 150 Granby St, Norfolk, VA 23510. TEL 757-640-4020, http://www.traderonline.com/.

629.228 GBR ISSN 0961-1096
RACECAR ENGINEERING. Text in English. 1990. m. GBP 44.99 domestic; USD 110.90 in US & Canada; EUR 70.10 in Europe; GBP 58.30 elsewhere; GBP 5.25 newsstand/cover domestic (effective 2009). illus. back issues avail. **Document type:** *Magazine, Consumer.* **Description:** Features articles relevant to the worldwide motorsport industry.
—BLDSC (7225.963900), IE, Ingenta.
Published by: I P C Country & Leisure Media Ltd. (Subsidiary of: I P C Media Ltd.), Leon House, 233 High St, Croydon, CR9 1HZ, United Kingdom. TEL 44-20-87268000, http://www.ipcmedia.com. Ed. Graham Jones TEL 44-20-87268362. Adv. contact Tony Tobias TEL 44-20-87268328. **Subscr. to:** Rockwood House, Perrymount Rd, Haywards Heath RH16 3DH, United Kingdom. TEL 44-845-1231231, IPCsubs@quadrantsubs.com, http://www.magazinesdirect.co.uk. **Dist. by:** MarketForce UK Ltd, The Blue Fin Bldg, 3rd Fl, 110 Southwark St, London SE1 0SU, United Kingdom. TEL 44-20-31483300, FAX 44-20-31488105, salesinnovation@marketforce.co.uk, http://www.marketforce.co.uk/.

RACING. *see* SPORTS AND GAMES

786.72 PRT
RACING: FORMULA 1. Text in Portuguese. 1997. a. EUR 4 newsstand/cover (effective 2005). **Document type:** *Magazine, Consumer.*
Published by: Motorpress Lisboa, SA (Subsidiary of: Gruner + Jahr AG & Co), Rua Policarpio Anjos No. 4, Cruz Quebrada, Dafundo 1495-742, Portugal. TEL 351-21-4154500, FAX 351-21-4154501, buzine@motorpress.pt, http://www.mpl.pt. Circ: 16,059 (paid).

796.72 USA ISSN 1931-5082
RACING MILESTONES; America's race fan magazine. Text in English. 1996. m. USD 19.95 domestic; USD 29.95 in Canada; USD 42.95 elsewhere (effective 2001). **Document type:** *Magazine, Consumer.* **Description:** Covers the auto race actions, driver profiles, and behind the scenes look at America's fastest growing spectator sport.
Address: 100 West Plume St, Norfolk, VA 23510. TEL 757-664-3552, 888-372-3326, FAX 757-640-6363, bwalton@traderonline.com, http://www.racingmilestones.com/. Ed. Mary Scully.

RACING WHEELS. *see* SPORTS AND GAMES

338 NZL ISSN 1179-7800
RADIATOR. Text in English. 1920. m. NZD 99 to non-members; free to members (effective 2010). adv. tr.lit. back issues avail. **Document type:** *Magazine, Trade.* **Description:** Targets the motor trade and includes 95% of all service stations in New Zealand and approximately 80% of automotive repairers.
Former titles (until 2010): N Z Radiator Magazine (1174-5428); (until 1997): Radiator (1171-3968)
Related titles: ◆ Supplement(s): Shift. ISSN 1177-0775.
Published by: Motor Trade Association, Marion Sq, PO Box 9244, Wellington, 6141, New Zealand. TEL 64-4-3858859, FAX 64-4-3859517. Adv. contact Cathy La Ville TEL 64-9-4138577. page NZD 1,720; 210 x 297.

629.286 USA ISSN 1063-7958
RADIATOR REPORTER AND RADHOTLINE DATA BASE. Variant title: Radiator Reporter. Text in English. 1973. 10/yr. looseleaf. USD 140 domestic; CAD 195 in Canada; USD 175 foreign (effective 2001). charts; illus.; stat. back issues avail.; reprints avail. **Document type:** *Newsletter, Trade.*
Former titles: Radiator Reporter and Radinfo Data Base (0896-3347); Radiator Reporter (0739-2060)
—CCC.
Published by: Skyline Publishing Co., PO Box 599, Brookfield, IL 60513-0599. TEL 708-485-6015, 800-914-2599, FAX 708-485-4237. Ed., Pub. Ralph McDarmont.

796.77 USA ISSN 1533-4600
TL236
RAGTOPS AND ROADSTERS MAGAZINE. Text in English. 2000. bi-m. USD 19.95 in United States; USD 29.95 in Canada; USD 39.95 elsewhere; USD 4.99 newsstand/cover (effective 2001). **Document type:** *Magazine, Consumer.*
Published by: MediaSource California LLC, 770 Sycamore Ave, Ste J-445, Vista, CA 92083.

RALLY SPRINT. *see* SPORTS AND GAMES

796.72 ITA ISSN 1827-0778
RALLYE MONTE-CARLO. Text in Italian. 2006. bi-w. **Document type:** *Magazine, Consumer.*
Published by: De Agostini Editore, Via G da Verrazzano 15, Novara, 28100, Italy. TEL 39-0321-4241, FAX 39-0321-424305, info@deagostini.it, http://www.deagostini.it.

RALLYES MAGAZINE. *see* SPORTS AND GAMES

RANCHERO COURIER. *see* HOBBIES

629.286 USA ISSN 2159-6646
▼ **RATROD MAGAZINE.** Abbreviated title: R R M. Text in English. 2010. bi-m. USD 6.99 per issue (effective 2011). adv. **Document type:** *Magazine, Trade.*
Published by: Rat Rod Magazine, PO Box 435, Princeton, MN 55371. TEL 952-378-1447. Ed. Steve Thaemert TEL 952-378-1447.

388.3 USA
READING & USING YOUR GM WINS DA REPORT. Text in English. a. **Document type:** *Report, Trade.*
Published by: W D & S Publishing, 10 W 7th St, 1st Fl, PO Box 606, Barnegat Light, NJ 08006. TEL 800-321-5312, http://www.dealersedge.com.

388.3 USA ISSN 1936-1777
REBEL RODZ. Text in English. 2007 (May). bi-m. USD 19.97; USD 5.99 newsstand/cover (effective 2009). adv. back issues avail. **Document type:** *Magazine, Consumer.* **Description:** Contains product reviews, tech articles, band reviews and killer coverage from hot rod, bike and tattoo shows across the country.
Related titles: Online - full text ed.
Published by: Paisano Publications, Inc., 28210 Dorothy Dr, Box 3075, Agoura Hills, CA 91301. TEL 818-889-8740, 800-247-6246, FAX 818-735-6518, bulkmagazines@paisanopub.com. Adv. contact Tammy Porter TEL 818-889-8740 ext 1265. B&W page USD 1,450, color page USD 1,900; trim 7.75 x 10.5.

629.286 ESP ISSN 1132-1490
RECAMBIO LIBRE. Text in Spanish. 1991. m. EUR 80 domestic; EUR 100 in Europe; EUR 150 elsewhere (effective 2009). adv. back issues avail. **Document type:** *Magazine, Trade.* **Description:** For automobile spare parts and accessories dealers.
Published by: Reed Business Information SA (Subsidiary of: Reed Business Information International), C Albarracin 34, Madrid, 28037, Spain. TEL 34-91-3755800, FAX 34-91-4562499, rbi@rbi.es. Ed. Nuria Alvarez TEL 34-91-3755800. Circ: 3,000 (controlled).

629.286 ESP ISSN 1579-2404
RECAMBIOS & ACCESORIOS. Abbreviated title: R & A. Text in Spanish. 1982. m. EUR 143.10 combined subscription domestic (print & email eds.); EUR 215 combined subscription foreign (print & email eds.) (effective 2009). **Document type:** *Magazine, Trade.*
Formerly (until 1993): Tienda de Recambios y Accesorios (0212-0526)
Related titles: E-mail ed.: ISSN 1989-0362. 2001. EUR 225.38 (effective 2002); Supplement(s): Guia Grupo de Distribucion de Recambios. 1982. EUR 69.72 (effective 2002); Guia Distribucion No Agrupada. 1992. EUR 69.72 (effective 2002).
Published by: Tecnipublicaciones Espana, S.L., Avda de Manoteras 44, 3a Planta, Madrid, 28050, Spain. TEL 34-91-2972000, FAX 34-91-2972154, tp@tecnipublicaciones.com. Circ: 10,000.

790.13 USA
TL298
RECREATIONAL VEHICLE BLUE BOOK (ONLINE). Text in English. a. USD 99.95 (effective 2011). back issues avail. **Document type:** *Directory.* **Description:** Covers more than 20 years of travel trailer, motor home, tent trailer identification and values. Includes model description, factory SRP, weight, length and manufacturer-model cross reference guide.
Former titles (until 2009): Recreational Vehicle Blue Book (Print); (until 2001): Recreational Vehicle and Van Conversion Blue Book; Which was formed by the merger of (199?-1999): Recreational Vehicle Blue Book (0733-4745); (1984-1999): Van Conversion Blue Book Official Market Report (0884-7231)
Published by: Penton Media, Inc., 1300 E 9th St, Cleveland, OH 44114. TEL 216-696-7000, FAX 216-696-3432, information@penton.com, http://www.penton.com.

796.77 GBR ISSN 1462-463X
REDLINE; driving - buying - tuning - styling. Text in English. 1998. 13/yr. GBP 47.96 domestic; GBP 69 in Europe; GBP 99 elsewhere; GBP 4.35 newsstand/cover (effective 2010). adv. back issues avail. **Document type:** *Magazine, Consumer.* **Description:** Dedicated to showing the best way to maximise the performance of your road car.
—CCC.
Published by: Future Publishing Ltd., Beauford Ct, 30 Monmouth St, Bath, Avon BA1 2BW, United Kingdom. TEL 44-1225-442244, FAX 44-1225-446019, customerservice@subscription.co.uk, http://www.futureplc.com. Ed. Davy Lewis. Adv. contact Steve Grigg TEL 44-1225-732392. **Subscr. to:** Tower House, Sovereign Park, Market Harborough, Leicestershire LE16 9EF, United Kingdom. TEL 44-844-8481602, FAX 44-1858-438795, future@subscription.co.uk.

REFERATIVNYI ZHURNAL. AVTOMOBILESTROENIE; vypusk svodnogo toma. *see* TRANSPORTATION—Abstracting, Bibliographies, Statistics

REFERATIVNYI ZHURNAL. AVTOMOBIL'NYI I GORODSKOI TRANSPORT; svodnyi tom. *see* TRANSPORTATION—Abstracting, Bibliographies, Statistics

REFERATIVNYI ZHURNAL. AVTOMOBIL'NYI TRANSPORT; vypusk svodnogo toma. *see* TRANSPORTATION—Abstracting, Bibliographies, Statistics

629.288 AUS
REFINISHER. Text in English. 1958. 4/yr. adv. **Document type:** *Journal, Trade.*
Published by: P P G Industries Australia, Locked Bag 888, Clayton South, VIC 3169, Australia. TEL 61-3-92636000, FAX 61-3-92636970, http://corporateportal.ppg.com/ppg/. Circ: 17,000 (controlled).

388 DEU ISSN 2191-270X
REISEMOBIL INTERNATIONAL. Text in German. 1989. m. EUR 39.60 domestic; EUR 45 foreign; EUR 3.70 newsstand/cover (effective 2011). adv. **Document type:** *Magazine, Consumer.*
Published by: DoldeMedien Verlag GmbH, Postwiesenstr 5A, Stuttgart, 70327, Germany. TEL 49-711-134660, FAX 49-711-1346638, info@doldemedien.de, http://www.doldemedien.de. Ed. Michael Kirchberger. Adv. contact Sylke Wohlschiess. Circ: 84,053 (paid and controlled).

388.3 ISR
REKHEV. Text in Hebrew. 2002. m. ILS 232 (effective 2008). **Document type:** *Magazine, Consumer.*
Related titles: Online - full text ed.: ILS 102 (effective 2008).
Published by: S B C Group, 8 Shefa Tal St., Tel Aviv, 67013, Israel. TEL 972-3-565-2100, FAX 972-3-562-6476, sherut@sbc.co.il, http://www.sbc.co.il/Index.asp.

388.3 USA ISSN 1524-0428
REPAIR SHOP PRODUCT NEWS. Text in English. 6/yr. abstr. **Description:** Directed to qualified individuals in the automotive repair and maintenance industry.
Related titles: Online - full text ed.
Indexed: B02, B15, B17, B18, G04, G06, G07, G08, I05.
—CCC.
Published by: Adams Business Media, 2101 S Arlington Heights Rd, Ste 150, Arlington Heights, IL 60005-4142. http://www.abm.net.

629.2 DEU ISSN 1436-2848
REPARATUR-DATEN MOTORISIERTE ZWEIRAEDER. Text in German. 1955. a. EUR 36 (effective 2004). **Document type:** *Journal, Trade.*
Supersedes in part (in 1997): P K W Tabellen fuer die Werkstattpraxis (1433-4429); Which was formerly (until 1994): Krafthand-Taschenbuch fuer Inspektion und Reparatur (1433-4410); (until 1984): Taschenbuch fuer Inspektion und Reparatur (0171-4686); (until 197?): Taschenfachbuch der Kraftfahrzeugbetriebe (0171-4678)
Published by: Krafthand Verlag Walter Schulz, Walter-Schulz-Str 1, Bad Woerishofen, 86825, Germany. TEL 49-8247-30070, FAX 49-8247-300770, info@krafthand.de, http://www.krafthand.de.

629.2 DEU ISSN 1436-2856
REPARATUR-DATEN P K W. Text in German. 1955. a. EUR 36 (effective 2004). **Document type:** *Journal, Trade.*
Supersedes in part (in 1997): P K W Tabellen fuer die Werkstattpraxis (1433-4429); Which was formerly (until 1994): Krafthand-Taschenbuch fuer Inspektion und Reparatur (1433-4410); (until 1984): Taschenbuch fuer Inspektion und Reparatur (0171-4686); (until 197?): Taschenfachbuch der Kraftfahrzeugbetriebe (0171-4678)
Published by: Krafthand Verlag Walter Schulz, Walter-Schulz-Str 1, Bad Woerishofen, 86825, Germany. TEL 49-8247-30070, FAX 49-8247-300770, info@krafthand.de, http://www.krafthand.de.

629.2 DEU ISSN 1436-283X
REPARATUR- UND A U - DATEN NUTZFAHRZEUGE. Text in German. 1955. a. EUR 36 (effective 2004). **Document type:** *Journal, Trade.*
Supersedes in part (in 1997): P K W Tabellen fuer die Werkstattpraxis (1433-4429); Which was formerly (until 1994): Krafthand-Taschenbuch fuer Inspektion und Reparatur (1433-4410); (until 1984): Taschenbuch fuer Inspektion und Reparatur (0171-4686); (until 197?): Taschenfachbuch der Kraftfahrzeugbetriebe (0171-4678)
Published by: Krafthand Verlag Walter Schulz, Walter-Schulz-Str 1, Bad Woerishofen, 86825, Germany. TEL 49-8247-30070, FAX 49-8247-300770, info@krafthand.de, http://www.krafthand.de.

388.3 ZAF
RESIDUAL VALUES. Text in English. m. **Document type:** *Handbook/Manual/Guide, Trade.* **Description:** Provides residual values for leased vehicles in South Africa.
Published by: Mead & McGrouther (Pty) Ltd., PO Box 1240, Randburg, Gauteng 2125, South Africa. TEL 27-11-789-3213, FAX 27-11-789-5218. adv.: B&W page ZAR 1,000, color page ZAR 2,050. Circ: 350.

RESTORATION MAGAZINE (ONLINE). *see* ANTIQUES

629.286 AUS ISSN 0311-4163
RESTORED CARS. Text in English. 1973. bi-m. AUD 47.50 domestic; AUD 75.50 in Asia & the Pacific; AUD 88.50 elsewhere (effective 2011). adv. bk.rev. illus. back issues avail. **Document type:** *Magazine, Consumer.* **Description:** Devoted to the restored or original car. Includes veteran, vintage, classic and post-war period cars to cars of the '50s, '60s, and '70s, and muscle cars.
Published by: Eddie Ford Publications Pty. Ltd., 29 Lyons St, Newstead, VIC 3462, Australia. TEL 61-3-54762212, FAX 61-3-54762592.

629.2 USA
RESTYLING; the auto, truck and SUV accessory magazine. Text in English. 1998. m. free domestic to qualified personnel (effective 2005); USD 85 combined subscription in Canada & Mexico (print & online eds.); USD 110 combined subscription elsewhere (print & online eds.) (effective 2008). adv. illus. 88 p./no. 3 cols./p.; reprints avail. **Document type:** *Magazine, Trade.* **Description:** Provides the aftermarket accessory dealer with informative articles on everything - from working with dealerships to designing a top-notch showroom.
Related titles: Online - full text ed.: free to qualified personnel (effective 2008).
Published by: National Business Media, Inc., PO Box 1416, Broomfield, CO 80038. TEL 303-469-0424, 800-669-0424, FAX 303-469-5730, rpmpublisher@nbm.com. Eds. Alan Farb TEL 303-469-0424 ext 292, Jef White. Pub. Kent Bradley TEL 303-469-0424 ext 256. Adv. contact Adina Foster TEL 303-469-0424 ext 257. B&W page USD 3,045, color page USD 3,745; trim 8.125 x 10.875. Circ: 14,210.

629.222 GBR ISSN 1479-7992
RETRO CARS. Text in English. 2003. m. GBP 40.32 domestic; GBP 59 in Europe; GBP 72 elsewhere (effective 2010). adv. back issues avail. **Document type:** *Magazine, Consumer.* **Description:** Covers information about modified classic cars, back and ready to take the retro scene by storm.
—CCC.
Published by: Unity Media PLC, Becket House, Vestry Rd, Sevenoaks, Kent TN14 5EJ, United Kingdom. TEL 44-1732-748000, FAX 44-1732-748001, http://www.unity-media.com/. Ed. Simon Jackson. Adv. contact Cinnamon Lacey. page GBP 950; trim 210 x 297.

796.77 IRL ISSN 2009-3918
▼ **RETRO CLASSICS.** Text in English. 2011. 3/yr. EUR 5.95 per issue domestic; EUR 7.47 per issue in United Kingdom; EUR 11.05 per issue elsewhere (effective 2011). adv. back issues avail. **Document type:** *Magazine, Consumer.* **Description:** Covers a wide range of styles from historic rally cars and Italian sportsters to American muscle cars and Japanese legends.
Published by: Irish Vintage Scene Ltd., Unit 3D, Deerpark Business Ctr, Oranmore, Co.Galway, Ireland. TEL 353-91-388805, FAX 353-91-388806, irishvintage@gmail.com.

629.22 GBR ISSN 1750-2942
RETRO FORD. Text in English. 2006. m. GBP 40.32 domestic; GBP 58 in Europe; GBP 72 elsewhere; GBP 5 per issue (effective 2009). adv. back issues avail. **Document type:** *Magazine, Consumer.* **Description:** Aims to reflect the vibrancy of the cars and the scene with amazing pictures and entertaining, educational words.

Published by: Unity Media PLC, Becket House, Vestry Rd, Sevenoaks, Kent TN14 5EJ, United Kingdom. TEL 44-1732-748000, FAX 44-1732-748001, http://www.unity-media.com/. Ed. Ben Morley. Pub. Colin Wilkinson. Adv. contact Sarah Norwood TEL 44-1732-748075. page GBP 950; trim 210 x 297.

629.222 FRA ISSN 0992-5007
RETROVISEUR. Text in French. 1988. 11/yr. EUR 52 domestic; EUR 60 foreign (effective 2009). adv. illus. 160 p./no. 3 cols./p.; back issues avail. **Document type:** *Magazine, Consumer.* **Description:** Covers classic automobiles.
Published by: Editions L V A, Chateau de la Magdeleine, Samois-sur-Seine, 77920, France.

796.77 USA ISSN 1949-2820
TL215.A77
▼ **REUNION (AUBURN).** Text in English. 2009. a. USD 30 per issue (effective 2009). **Document type:** *Consumer.* **Description:** Event book of the Auburn Cord Duesenberg Club, Inc.
Published by: Auburn Cord Duesenberg Museum, 1600 S Wayne St, PO Box 271, Auburn, IN 46706. TEL 219-925-1444, FAX 219-925-6266, info@automobilemuseum.org, http://www.acdmuseum.org.

REV MAGAZINE. *see* SPORTS AND GAMES—Bicycles And Motorcycles

629.2 JPN ISSN 1349-4724
TL240 CODEN: JREVDY
REVIEW OF AUTOMOTIVE ENGINEERING. Text in English. 1978. q. JPY 18,900 to non-members; JMD 15,120 to members (effective 2008). back issues avail. **Document type:** *Journal, Trade.* **Description:** Disseminates advanced technical information on subjects such as fuel economy, automotive safety, emission and noise controls, electronics and production technology.
Formerly (until 2004): J S A E Review (0389-4304)
Related titles: Microform ed.: (from PQC); Online - full text ed.: (from IngentaConnect).
Indexed: A01, A03, A08, A22, APA, APIAb, C&ISA, CA, CPEI, ChemAb, ChemTitl, CorrAb, E&CAJ, EEA, HRIS, IBR, IBZ, JTA, S01, SCOPUS, SolStAb, T02, WAA.
—BLDSC (7788.180000), CASDDS, IE, Infotrieve, Ingenta, Linda Hall. **CCC.**
Published by: Society of Automotive Engineers of Japan, 10-2 Gobancho, Chiyoda-ku, Tokyo, 102-0076, Japan. TEL 81-3-32628211, FAX 81-3-32612204, webmaster@jsae.or.jp.

629.28 796.77 PRT ISSN 0870-273X
REVISTA A C P. Text in Portuguese. 1930. m. adv. illus. back issues avail. **Document type:** *Magazine, Trade.*
Published by: Automovel Club de Portugal, Rua Rosa Araujo, 24, Lisbon, 1250-195, Portugal. TEL 351-21-3180202, FAX 351-21-3180227, apoio.socio@acp.pt, https://www.acp.pt/. Ed. Dr. Antonio Raposo de Magalhaes. Adv. contact Leopoldo Ludovice. Circ: 188,000.

REVUE AUTOMOBILE; journal suisse de l'automobile. *see* TRANSPORTATION

REVUE AUTOMOBILE MEDICALE. *see* MEDICAL SCIENCES

629.22075 FRA ISSN 1953-0005
LA REVUE DE MEHARISTES. Text in French. 1992. q. **Document type:** *Newsletter, Consumer.*
Published by: Mehari Club de France, 12 Rue de Paris, Piscop, 95350, France. TEL 33-6-26032308, bulletin@mehariclubdefrance.com.

629.286 CAN ISSN 1711-2842
REVUE LE GARAGISTE. Variant title: Le Garagiste. Text in French. 1994. irreg. **Document type:** *Magazine, Trade.*
Supersedes in part (in 2003): Garagiste Mecanicien (1485-810X); Which was formerly (1994-1997): Garagiste (1202-614X)
Published by: Publications Rousseau, 2938 Terrasse Abenaquis, bureau 110, Longueuil, PQ J4M 2B3, Canada. TEL 450-448-2220, 888-748-2220, FAX 450-448-1041, admin@p-rousseau.com, http://www.publicationsrousseau.com.

388.3 629.2 FRA ISSN 0017-307X
REVUE TECHNIQUE AUTOMOBILE. Variant title: R T A Magazine. Text in French. 1946. m. EUR 348.10 (effective 2009). **Document type:** *Magazine, Trade.* **Description:** Technical review for professionals in the car repair field.
Formerly (until 1948): Vie et Technique Automobile (1639-9889)
—IE, INIST. **CCC.**
Published by: Editions Techniques pour l'Automobile et l'Industrie (E T A I), 96 rue de Paris, Boulogne Billancourt, 92100, France. TEL 33-1-46992424, FAX 33-1-48255692, http://www.groupe-etai.com. Ed. Bernard Rambaud. Pub. Pascal Cromback. Circ: 18,241.

338.476 FRA ISSN 0150-7206
REVUE TECHNIQUE CARROSSERIE. Text in French. 1963. bi-m. EUR 164.84 (effective 2009). charts; illus. **Document type:** *Magazine, Trade.* **Description:** Aimed at car body-builders, steel-workers and painters, details how to repair the car body and describes the tools to be used.
Related titles: ◆ Supplement(s): Fiches Techniques R T C. ISSN 0153-9108.
—**CCC.**
Published by: Editions Techniques pour l'Automobile et l'Industrie (E T A I), 20-22 rue de la Saussiere, Boulogne Billancourt, 92100, France. TEL 33-1-46992424, FAX 33-1-48255692, http://www.etai.fr. Ed. Jean Pierre Nicolas. Circ: 6,035.

629.2 FRA ISSN 0037-2579
REVUE TECHNIQUE DIESEL. Text in French. 1963. bi-m. EUR 178 (effective 2009). **Document type:** *Magazine, Trade.* **Description:** Deals with trucks, public works material and industrial engines. Describes a particular diesel oil truck and explains how to repair it.
Formerly: Service Diesel
—IE, Infotrieve, INIST. **CCC.**
Published by: Editions Techniques pour l'Automobile et l'Industrie (E T A I), 20-22 rue de la Saussiere, Boulogne Billancourt, 92100, France. TEL 33-1-46992424, FAX 33-1-48255692, http://www.groupe-etai.com. Ed. Bernard Adam. Circ: 6,659.

388.3 629.22 USA
RIDE & DRIVE.COM; the car magazine created for cyberspace. Text in English. w. adv. **Document type:** *Magazine, Consumer.* **Description:** Reports on news, issues and events about the automotive industry.
Media: Online - full content.
Address: P O Box 16355, Baltimore, MD 21210. TEL 410-235-6927, FAX 410-235-7681, ridedrive@aol.com, http://www.rideanddrive.com. Ed., Pub. Thomas E. Bonsall. Adv. contact Kevin S. Lowery.

796.77 USA
RIDES. Text in English. 2004. m. USD 12 in US & Canada; USD 24 elsewhere (effective 2009). adv. back issues avail. **Document type:** *Magazine, Consumer.*
Related titles: Online - full text ed.
Published by: Harris Publications, Inc., 1115 Broadway, New York, NY 10010. TEL 212-807-7100, FAX 212-924-2352, subscriptions@harris-pub.com, http://www.harris-pub.com. Ed. Willie G. Adv. contact Ben Harris. Circ: 150,000.

656.1 CHE ISSN 1661-6561
RIEGER. Text in German. 2006. a. CHF 6.90 newsstand/cover (effective 2007). **Document type:** *Magazine, Consumer.*
Published by: Forcar GmbH, Churerstr 154, Pfaeffikon, 8808, Switzerland. TEL 41-55-4155100, FAX 41-55-4155109, info@forcar.ch, http://www.forcar.ch.

388.3 AUS ISSN 0035-7170
ROAD AHEAD. Text in English. 1914. bi-m. free to members (effective 2009). adv. bk.rev. charts; illus. back issues avail. **Document type:** *Magazine, Consumer.* **Description:** Covers consumer-related issues, travel and motoring articles.
Related titles: Online - full text ed.
Published by: (Royal Automobile Club of Queensland, Brisbane), Road Ahead Publishing Co. Pty Ltd., PO Box 4, Springwood, QLD 4127, Australia. TEL 61-7-38728653, FAX 61-7-32571863, roadahead@racq.com.au. Adv. contact Jeff Bygraves TEL 61-7-38728640. color page AUD 17,369; trim 210 x 276. Circ: 956,623 (controlled).

388.3 USA ISSN 0035-7189
TL1
ROAD & TRACK. Text in English. 1947. m. USD 10 domestic; USD 20 in Canada; USD 38 elsewhere (effective 2010). adv. bk.rev.; rec.rev. charts; illus. index. back issues avail.; reprints avail. **Document type:** *Magazine, Consumer.* **Description:** Reports on all types of new cars. Includes features on such wide-ranging topics as racing, automotive art and photography, and travel stories.
Related titles: Online - full text ed.: USD 8 (effective 2008); ◆ Supplement(s): Buyer's Guide. ISSN 1539-624X.
Indexed: A01, A02, A03, A08, A09, A10, A11, A22, A25, A26, AcaI, B04, B07, BRD, C05, C12, CPerI, ConsI, E08, G05, G06, G07, G08, G09, I05, I07, M01, M02, M06, MASUSE, MagInd, P02, P10, P16, P48, P53, P54, PMR, PQC, R03, R04, R06, RGAb, RGPR, S08, S09, SPI, TOM, V03, V04, W03.
—IE, Infotrieve, Ingenta, Linda Hall.
Published by: Hachette Filipacchi Media U.S., Inc. (Subsidiary of: Hachette Filipacchi Medias S.A.), 1633 Broadway, New York, NY 10019. TEL 212-767-6000, FAX 212-767-5600, flyedit@hfmus.com, http://www.hfmus.com. Ed. Matt DeLorenzo. R&P Nadine Goody. Circ: 700,000 (paid).

388.3 USA ISSN 1067-9146
TL230.5.S66
ROAD & TRACK COMPLETE SPORT-UTILITY, PICKUP & VAN BUYER'S GUIDE. Text in English. 1993. a. USD 4.95 newsstand/cover (effective 2007). **Document type:** *Magazine, Consumer.*
Published by: Hachette Filipacchi Media U.S., Inc. (Subsidiary of: Hachette Filipacchi Medias S.A.), 1633 Broadway, New York, NY 10019. TEL 212-767-6000, FAX 212-767-5600, saleshfmbooks@hfmus.com, http://www.hfmus.com.

621.38
ROAD & TRACK ROAD GEAR (ONLINE). Text in English. 19??. bi-m. **Document type:** *Magazine, Consumer.* **Description:** Articles and test reports on car stereo and mobile electronics, video and DVD, navigation, and telematics equipment.
Media: Online - full text.
Published by: Hachette Filipacchi Media U.S., Inc. (Subsidiary of: Hachette Filipacchi Medias S.A.), 1633 Broadway, New York, NY 10019. TEL 212-767-6000.

796.77 USA ISSN 1551-398X
TL236
ROAD & TRACK SPEED (ONLINE). Text in English. 2005. bi-m. USD 11.95 (effective 2007). **Document type:** *Magazine, Consumer.*
Formerly (until 2006): Road & Track Speed (Print)
Published by: Hachette Filipacchi Media U.S., Inc. (Subsidiary of: Hachette Filipacchi Medias S.A.), 1633 Broadway, New York, NY 10019. TEL 212-767-6000, FAX 212-767-5600, saleshfmbooks@hfmus.com, http://www.hfmus.com.

796.77 388.3 USA ISSN 1060-8656
ROAD & TRACK SPORTS & G T CARS. Key Title: Sports & G T Cars. Text in English. 1965. a. adv. charts; illus.; stat. back issues avail.; reprints avail. **Document type:** *Magazine, Consumer.* **Description:** Presents scores of action packed tests and comprehensive evaluations of sports, sporty and exotic driving machines.
Related titles: Microform ed.: (from PQC).
Published by: Hachette Filipacchi Media U.S., Inc. (Subsidiary of: Hachette Filipacchi Medias S.A.), 1633 Broadway, New York, NY 10019. TEL 212-767-6000, FAX 212-767-5600, privacy@hfmus.com, http://www.hfmus.com. adv.: B&W page USD 9,380, color page USD 15,745; trim 7.88 x 10.5.

ROAD & TRACK TRUCK S U V VAN BUYER'S GUIDE. *see* TRANSPORTATION—Trucks And Trucking

388.3 USA
ROAD GEAR. Text in English. 2005. bi-m. adv. **Document type:** *Magazine, Trade.*
Published by: Hachette Filipacchi Media U.S., Inc. (Subsidiary of: Hachette Filipacchi Medias S.A.), 1633 Broadway, New York, NY 10019. TEL 212-767-6000, http://www.hfmus.com.

629.2 388.3 USA ISSN 1060-8664
ROAD TEST ANNUAL. Text in English. 1990. a. USD 5.99 newsstand/cover (effective 2007). adv. charts; illus.; stat. reprints avail. **Document type:** *Magazine, Consumer.* **Description:** Provides depth analysis of the hottest new cars on the market.
Former titles (until 1990): Road & Track Road Test Annual; (until 1987): Road & Track's Road Test Annual & Buyer's Guide (0278-2669)
Published by: Hachette Filipacchi Media U.S., Inc. (Subsidiary of: Hachette Filipacchi Medias S.A.), 1633 Broadway, New York, NY 10019. TEL 212-767-6000, FAX 212-767-5600, privacy@hfmus.com, http://www.hfmus.com. Ed. Don Canet. adv.: B&W page USD 11,720, color page USD 16,980; trim 10.5 x 7.88.

629.2 USA ISSN 1932-2925
TL1
ROBB REPORT SPORTS & LUXURY AUTOMOBILE. Variant title: Robb Report Sports & Luxury Automobile Buyer's Guide. Text in English. 2006. a. USD 7.99 per issue (effective 2009). adv. back issues avail.; reprints avail. **Document type:** *Magazine, Consumer.* **Description:** Provides an overview of automobiles on the markets and their specifications for prospective buyers of luxury automobiles.
Published by: CurtCo Robb Media LLC., 29160 Heathercliff Rd, Ste 200, Malibu, CA 90265. TEL 310-589-7700, FAX 310-589-7723, support@robbreport.com.

614.8 ZAF ISSN 0035-7391
ROBOT. Text in Afrikaans, English. 1962. q. free. adv. bk.rev.; film rev. illus.; stat. **Document type:** *Magazine, Trade.* **Description:** General interest road and traffic safety information.
Indexed: HRIS, RoboAb.
Published by: National Road Safety Council/Nasionale Verkeersveiligheidsraad, NRSC Bldg, Beatrix St, Private Bag X147, Pretoria, 0001, South Africa. TEL 27-12-328-5929, FAX 27-12-3232215, TELEX 320828. Ed. Ivor van Rensburg. Circ: 50,000.

388.3 USA
ROCKCRAWLER. Text in English. m.
Media: Online - full text.
Address: 1919 Oxmoor Rd Ate 104, Homewood, AL 35209. TEL 205-870-8181, FAX 603-658-9594, http://www.rockcrawler.com/. Ed. Mike Cohn.

629.28 USA ISSN 1053-2064
TL236
ROD & CUSTOM. Text in English. 1966. m. USD 17.97 domestic; USD 29.97 in Canada; USD 41.97 elsewhere (effective 2008). adv. illus. back issues avail.; reprints avail. **Document type:** *Magazine, Consumer.* **Description:** Features comprehensive event coverage, as well as innovative technical how-tos and styling ideas.
Former titles (until 1990): Petersen's Rod and Custom (1045-120X); (until 1988): Rod and Custom (0161-150X); Which incorporated in part: Hot Rod (0018-6031)
Indexed: G06, G07, G08, H20, I05, S23.
—**CCC.**
Published by: Source Interlink Companies, 774 S Placentia Ave, Placentia, CA 92870. TEL 714-939-2559, FAX 714-572-3502, dheine@sourceinterlink.com, http://www.sourceinterlink.com. Ed. Kevin Lee. Pub. Tim Foss TEL 714-939-2409. adv.: B&W page USD 7,505, color page USD 10,505. Circ: 116,381 (paid).

796.77 USA ISSN 0745-5739
RODDER'S DIGEST. Text in English. 1981. bi-m. USD 16.95 (effective 1999). adv. **Document type:** *Magazine, Consumer.*
Published by: Target Publications Inc., 668 2nd Ln., Vero Beach, FL 32962-2959. TEL 772-569-2122, FAX 772-569-2142. Ed., Pub., R&P Gerry Burger. Adv. contact Garry McWhirter.

796.77 USA
THE RODDER'S JOURNAL. Text in English. q. USD 40 domestic; USD 60 foreign; USD 12.95 newsstand/cover domestic; USD 19.95 newsstand/cover in Canada (effective 2004).
Published by: The Rodder's Journal, 263 Wattis Way, South San Francisco, CA 94080. Ed., Pub. Steve Coonan.

388.3 HKG
ROLLS-ROYCE PINNACLE. Text in English. 2004. q. **Document type:** *Magazine, Consumer.*
Published by: Blu Inc Media (HK) Ltd. (Subsidiary of: S P H Magazines Pte Ltd.), Ste 2901, 29/F Universal Trade Centre, No. 3 Arbuthnot Rd, Central, Hong Kong. TEL 852-2165-2800, FAX 852-2868-1799, queries@bluincmedia.com, http://www.bluincmedia.com.hk/.

388.342 GBR ISSN 1749-0103
ROMANIA AUTOS REPORT. Text in English. 2005. q. EUR 820, USD 1,030 combined subscription (print & email eds.) (effective 2010). **Document type:** *Report, Trade.* **Description:** Provides industry professionals and strategists, corporate analysts, auto associations, government departments and regulatory bodies with independent forecasts and competitive intelligence on the Romanian automotives market.
Related titles: E-mail ed.
Indexed: A15, ABIn, B02, B15, B17, B18, G04, I05, P48, P51, P52, PQC.
Published by: Business Monitor International Ltd., Senator House, 85 Queen Victoria St, London, EC4V 4AB, United Kingdom. TEL 44-20-72480468, FAX 44-20-72480467, subs@businessmonitor.com.

ROTAS & DESTINOS. *see* TRAVEL AND TOURISM

629.222 USA ISSN 0273-9453
ROUGH RIDER. Text in English. 1965. 10/yr. membership. adv. bk.rev. **Document type:** *Newsletter.* **Description:** News, features, technical information and other items of interest to Morgan car owners.
Published by: Morgan Car Club, Washington D.C., Inc., 616 Gist Ave, Silver Spring, MD 20910. TEL 301-858-0121. Ed. Edmund J Zielinski.

796.77 USA ISSN 0889-3225
ROUNDEL. Text in English. 1968. m. USD 35 membership. adv. **Document type:** *Magazine, Consumer.* **Description:** Covers BMW automobiles, maintenance, repair, driving, racing and club activities.
Published by: B M W Car Club of America, 640 S. Main St., Ste. 201, Greenville, SC 29601-2564. TEL 617-492-2500, 800-878-9292, FAX 617-876-3424. Ed. Satch Carlson. Pub., R&P Mark Luckman. Adv. contact Michael Slaff. Circ: 47,000 (paid).

388.3 FRA ISSN 0035-8568
ROUTE. Text in French. 1961. q. adv. charts; illus.; stat. **Document type:** *Magazine, Consumer.*
Published by: Comite National du Secours Routiers Francais, 50 quai Bleriot, Paris, 75016, France.

ROUTE 49. *see* LIFESTYLE

388.3 AUS ISSN 0035-9300
ROYALAUTO. Text in English. 1925. m. (except Jan.). free to members (effective 2009). adv. bk.rev. **Document type:** *Magazine, Consumer.*
Former titles (until 1960): Royalauto Journal; (until 1956): Royalauto Magazine; (until 1953): The Radiator; (until 1936): Royal Auto Journal; (until 1927): R A C V
Indexed: ARI.

Published by: (Royal Automobile Club of Victoria), R A C U Sales and Marketing Pty Ltd, 550 Princes Hwy, Noble Park, VIC 3174, Australia. TEL 61-3-97902759, FAX 61-3-97902636, claire_dickinson@racv.com.au. Ed. Jeremy Bourke. Adv. contact Robert McWaters TEL 61-3-97902759. page AUD 18,800; trim 203 x 275. Circ: 1,431,714.

▼ **RUKUS.** *see* LIFESTYLE

629.221 CAN ISSN 0048-8771
THE RUNNING BOARD. Text in English. 1961. 11/yr. adv. **Document type:** *Newsletter.* **Description:** Review of club events, tours and events coming up. Includes swap shop listings, executive reports and articles by members.
Formerly: Edmonton Antique Car Club. Bulletin
Published by: Edmonton Antique Car Club, P O Box 102, Edmonton, AB T5J 2G9, Canada. TEL 403-438-0404. Ed., Adv. contact Dave Jeffares. Circ: 90 (controlled).

RUOTECLASSICHE. *see* ANTIQUES

388.342947 GBR ISSN 1749-0111
RUSSIA AUTOS REPORT. Text in English. 2005. q. EUR 820, USD 1,030 combined subscription (print & email eds.) (effective 2010). **Document type:** *Report, Trade.* **Description:** Provides industry professionals and strategists, corporate analysts, auto associations, government departments and regulatory bodies with independent forecasts and competitive intelligence on the Russian automotives market.
Related titles: E-mail ed.
Indexed: A15, ABIn, B01, B02, B15, B17, B18, G04, I05, P48, P51, P52, PQC.
Published by: Business Monitor International Ltd., Senator House, 85 Queen Victoria St, London, EC4V 4AB, United Kingdom. TEL 44-20-72480468, FAX 44-20-72480467, subs@businessmonitor.com.

629.283 628.5 USA
TL273
S A E GROUND VEHICLE LIGHTING STANDARDS MANUAL. (Society of Automotive Engineers) Text in English. 19??. a. USD 340 per issue to non-members; USD 272 per issue to members (effective 2009). **Document type:** *Handbook/Manual/Guide, Trade.* **Description:** Contains informative articles on topics such as general, signaling and marking lighting devices, switches and flashers, test procedures and materials, warning lamps and devices, agricultural machinery, construction and industrial machinery, motorcycles, snowmobiles and electrical systems.
Formerly (until 1993): S A E Ground Vehicle Lighting Manual (1043-1896)
Published by: S A E Inc., 400 Commonwealth Dr, Warrendale, PA 15096. TEL 724-776-4841, 877-606-7323, FAX 724-776-0790, CustomerService@sae.org.

629.222 USA ISSN 1946-3936
TL210
➤ **S A E INTERNATIONAL JOURNAL OF ENGINES.** (Society of Automotive Engineers) Text in English. 1906. a. USD 375 per issue to non-members; USD 300 per issue to members (effective 2009). back issues avail. **Document type:** *Journal, Academic/Scholarly.* **Description:** Contains technical papers on engine research.
Supersedes in part (in 2009): S A E Transactions (0096-736X); Which was formerly (until 1927): Society of Automotive Engineers. Transactions
Related titles: Online - full text ed.: ISSN 1946-3944. USD 449.90 per issue to non-members; USD 359.92 per issue to members (effective 2009).
Indexed: SCOPUS.
—BLDSC (8062.950000), IE, Linda Hall.
Published by: S A E Inc., 400 Commonwealth Dr, Warrendale, PA 15096. TEL 724-776-4970, 877-606-7323, FAX 724-776-0790, CustomerService@sae.org, http://www.sae.org.

➤ **S A E INTERNATIONAL JOURNAL OF MATERIALS & MANUFACTURING.** (Society of Automotive Engineers) *see* ENGINEERING—Engineering Mechanics And Materials

➤ **S A E INTERNATIONAL JOURNAL OF PASSENGER CARS - ELECTRONIC AND ELECTRICAL SYSTEMS.** (Society of Automotive Engineers) *see* ENGINEERING—Electrical Engineering

➤ **S A E INTERNATIONAL JOURNAL OF PASSENGER CARS - MECHANICAL SYSTEMS.** (Society of Automotive Engineers) *see* ENGINEERING—Mechanical Engineering

621.9 USA ISSN 1528-9702
TA725 CODEN: OFENFH
S A E OFF-HIGHWAY ENGINEERING. (Society of Automotive Engineers) Text in English. 1993. 8/yr. USD 86 in North America to non-members; USD 127 elsewhere to non-members; free to members (effective 2009). adv. abstr. back issues avail.; reprints avail. **Document type:** *Magazine, Trade.* **Description:** Provides information for US and overseas automotive engineers and manufacturers of off-highway vehicle systems and components.
Formerly (until 199?): Off-Highway Engineering (1074-6919)
Related titles: Microfiche ed.; Microfilm ed.; Online - full text ed.: ISSN 1939-6686; ◆ Supplement to: Automotive Engineering International. ISSN 1543-849X.
Indexed: A28, APA, BrCerAb, C&ISA, CA/WCA, CIA, CerAb, CivEngAb, CorrAb, E&CAJ, E11, EEA, EMA, ESPM, EnvEAb, H15, Inspec, M&TEA, M09, MBF, METADEX, SolStAb, T04, WAA.
—BLDSC (8062.920600), IE, Ingenta, Linda Hall. **CCC.**
Published by: S A E Inc., 400 Commonwealth Dr, Warrendale, PA 15096. TEL 724-776-4841, 877-606-7323, FAX 724-776-0790, CustomerService@sae.org. Pub. Scott R Sward TEL 610-399-5279. Adv. contact Debby Catalano TEL 724-772-4014. Circ: 16,237.

S A E SPECIAL PUBLICATIONS. (Society of Automotive Engineers) *see* ENGINEERING

388 USA ISSN 0148-7191
TL1 CODEN: STPSDN
S A E TECHNICAL PAPERS. (Society of Automotive Engineers) Text in English. 197?. irreg. price varies. back issues avail. **Document type:** *Monographic series, Academic/Scholarly.*
Former titles (until 1979): Society of Automotive Engineers. Technical Paper Series (0740-6975); (until 1978): Society of Automotive Engineers. Technical Paper Series
Related titles: Online - full text ed.
Indexed: GeoRef.
—BLDSC (6392.350000), CASDDS, Infotrieve, Linda Hall. **CCC.**

Published by: S A E Inc., 400 Commonwealth Dr, Warrendale, PA 15096. TEL 724-776-4841, 877-606-7323, FAX 724-776-0790, CustomerService@sae.org, http://www.sae.org.

388.3 AUS ISSN 1030-8253
S A MOTOR. (South Australia) Text in English. 1913. bi-m. free to members (effective 2009). adv. back issues avail. **Document type:** *Magazine, Consumer.* **Description:** Provides travel and touring information, motoring tips, car reviews and a tackling a range of other topics.
Formerly (until 1986): South Australian Motor (1030-8245)
Related titles: Online - full text ed.: free (effective 2009).
Indexed: ARI, Pinpoint.
Published by: Royal Automobile Association of South Australia Inc., 101 Richmond Rd, Mile End, SA 5031, Australia. TEL 61-8-82024600, FAX 61-8-82024257. Adv. contacts John Ogden TEL 61-3-96969960, Richard Davis TEL 61-8-83799522. Circ: 351,425.

629.286 USA ISSN 0279-5051
S E M A NEWS. Text in English. 1968. m. free to qualified personnel. adv. **Document type:** *Magazine, Trade.* **Description:** Covers specialty automotive product news.
Incorporates (1988-1992): Performance and Specialty Aftermarket News (1060-4839); Which was formerly: Performance Aftermarket Magazine (1043-7991)
Published by: Specialty Equipment Market Association, PO Box 4910, Diamond Bar, CA 91765-0910. TEL 909-860-2961, FAX 909-860-1709, Julie@sema.org. Ed., Pub. William Groak. R&P Linda Czarkowski. Adv. contact Joann Tatar. Circ: 30,000.

388.33 CAN ISSN 0381-548X
S S G M. SERVICE STATION & GARAGE MANAGEMENT. Text in English. 1970. m. CAD 47.95 domestic; USD 66.95 foreign (effective 2008). adv. **Document type:** *Magazine, Trade.* **Description:** For the mechanical repair trade.
Formerly (until 1975): Service Station & Garage Management (0037-2668); Which was formed by the merger of (1934-1970): Automotive Service in Canada (0381-5498); (1955-1970): Service Station (0037-2676)
Related titles: Microfiche ed.: (from MML); Online - full text ed.
Indexed: C03, CBCABus, CBPI, P48, P51, P52, PQC.
Published by: Business Information Group, 12 Concorde Pl, Ste 800, Toronto, ON M3C 4J2, Canada. TEL 416-442-2122, 800-668-2374, FAX 416-442-2191, orders@businessinformationgroup.ca. Ed., Pub. Andrew Ross TEL 416-510-6763. Circ: 30,621.

796.77 ITA ISSN 1971-9310
S U V MAGAZINE. (Sport Utility Vehicle) Text in Italian. 2007. a. price varies. **Document type:** *Magazine, Consumer.*
Published by: Sprea Editori Srl, Via Torino 51, Cernusco sul Naviglio, MI 20063, Italy. TEL 39-02-92432222, FAX 39-02-92432236, editori@sprea.it, http://www.sprea.it.

SACRED OCTAGON. *see* ANTIQUES

796.77 GBR ISSN 0558-1222
SAFETY FAST; the marque of friendship. Text in English. 1959. m. GBP 3.50 per issue; free to members (effective 2009). bk.rev. charts; illus.; stat. back issues avail. **Document type:** *Magazine, Trade.* **Description:** Contains news and activities of MG car users and enthusiasts.
Related titles: Online - full text ed.
Published by: M G Car Club Ltd., Kimber House, Cemetery Rd, Abingdon, Oxfordshire OX14 1AS, United Kingdom. TEL 44-1235-555552, FAX 44-1235-533755. Ed. Andy Knott.

SAN DIEGO WESTWAYS; southern California's lifestyle magazine. *see* TRAVEL AND TOURISM

388.3 USA ISSN 1096-1941
SAND SPORTS MAGAZINE. Text in English. 1995. bi-m. USD 12.95; USD 4.99 newsstand/cover (effective 2007). **Document type:** *Magazine, Consumer.*
Published by: Wright Publishing Co., 2949 Century Place, Box 2260, Costa Mesa, CA 92628. TEL 714-979-2560, FAX 714-979-3998, http://www.sandsports.com. Pub. Judy Wright. Adv. contact Steve Gotoski. Circ: 25,000 (paid).

388 CAN ISSN 1197-6950
SANFORD EVANS GOLD BOOK OF OLDER CAR PRICES. Text in English. 1992. q. CAD 78. **Description:** Lists the previous eight models of cars and light duty trucks.
Published by: Sanford Evans Research Group A Subsidiary of Sun Media Corporation, 1700 Church Ave, Winnipeg, MB R2X 3A2, Canada. TEL 204-694-2022, FAX 204-632-4250. Ed., Pub. Gary Henry.

388 CAN ISSN 0381-8179
SANFORD EVANS GOLD BOOK OF USED CAR PRICES. Text in English. 1952. m. CAD 78. **Description:** Lists previous eight models of cars and light duty trucks. Valuations for three major Canadian markets, factory suggested price, and current wholesale and retail values.
Published by: Sanford Evans Research Group A Subsidiary of Sun Media Corporation, 1700 Church Ave, Winnipeg, MB R2X 3A2, Canada. TEL 204-694-2022, FAX 204-632-4250. Ed., Pub. Gary Henry.

629.222 CAN ISSN 1717-1865
SANFORD EVANS GOLD BOOK. SUPPLEMENT TO BOTH THE CAR AND TRUCK DATA GUIDES. Text in English. a. CAD 18 (effective 2006).
Former titles (until 2003): Supplement to Both the Motor Vehicle and Truck Data Books (0834-0714); (until 1985): Motor Vehicle Data Book Supplement (0316-6201)
Published by: Sanford Evans Research Group A Subsidiary of Sun Media Corporation, 1700 Church Ave, Winnipeg, MB R2X 3A2, Canada. TEL 204-632-2768, 800-840-7776, FAX 204-632-4250, goldbook@wpgsun.com, http://www.segoldbook.com.

629.224 JPN ISSN 0036-4398
SANGYO SHARYO/INDUSTRIAL VEHICLES. Text in Japanese. 1964. m. JPY 3,600, USD 12. adv.
Indexed: JTA.
Published by: Japan Industrial Vehicles Association/Nihon Sangyo Sharyo Kyokai, Tobu Bldg, 5-26, 1-chome, Moto-Akasaka, Minato-ku, Tokyo, 107, Japan. TEL 03-403-5556, FAX 03-403-5057. Ed. Masaru Terada. Circ: 1,000.

388.342 953.8 GBR ISSN 1749-012X
SAUDI ARABIA AUTOS REPORT. Text in English. 2005. q. EUR 820, USD 1,030 combined subscription (print & email eds.) (effective 2010). **Document type:** *Report, Trade.* **Description:** Provides industry professionals and strategists, corporate analysts, auto associations, government departments and regulatory bodies with independent forecasts and competitive intelligence on the Saudi automotives market.
Related titles: E-mail ed.
Indexed: A15, ABIn, B02, B15, B17, B18, G04, I05, P48, P51, P52, PQC.
Published by: Business Monitor International Ltd., Senator House, 85 Queen Victoria St, London, EC4V 4AB, United Kingdom. TEL 44-20-72480468, FAX 44-20-72480467, subs@businessmonitor.com.

629.222 UAE
AL-SAYYARAH AL-ARABIYYAH. Text in Arabic. 1989. m. **Description:** Provides news and information on cars for enthusiasts in the Gulf region, including road tests and safety topics.
Published by: Muhammad Rashid Amiri Prop., PO Box 8790, Dubai, United Arab Emirates. TEL 211123, FAX 213080, TELEX 48906. Ed. Abu Bakr Amiri. Circ: 2,000.

SCALE MILITARY MODELLER INTERNATIONAL. *see* HOBBIES

629.286 DEU
SCHWACKELISTE KALKULATION. Text in German. 1970. 2/yr. EUR 411; EUR 296 per issue (effective 2009). adv. **Document type:** *Magazine, Trade.*
Published by: EurotaxSchwacke GmbH, Wilhelm-Roentgen-Str 7, Maintal, 63477, Germany. TEL 49-6181-4050, FAX 49-6181-405111, info@schwacke.de, http://www.schwacke.de. adv.: B&W page EUR 1,000, color page EUR 1,900; trim 210 x 297. Circ: 985 (controlled).

629.113 DEU ISSN 0935-1493
SCHWACKELISTE LACKIERUNG. Text in German. 1970. 2/yr. EUR 486; EUR 333 per issue (effective 2009). adv. **Document type:** *Magazine, Trade.*
Published by: EurotaxSchwacke GmbH, Wilhelm-Roentgen-Str 7, Maintal, 63477, Germany. TEL 49-6181-4050, FAX 49-6181-405111, info@schwacke.de, http://www.schwacke.de. adv.: B&W page EUR 1,300, color page EUR 2,200; trim 105 x 297. Circ: 889 (paid and controlled).

629.286 DEU
SCHWACKELISTE P K W. Text in German. 1957. m. EUR 296; EUR 53 per issue (effective 2009). adv. **Document type:** *Magazine, Trade.*
Published by: EurotaxSchwacke GmbH, Wilhelm-Roentgen-Str 7, Maintal, 63477, Germany. TEL 49-6181-4050, FAX 49-6181-405111, info@schwacke.de, http://www.schwacke.de. adv.: B&W page EUR 900, color page EUR 1,800; trim 105 x 148. Circ: 4,520 (paid and controlled).

388.3 DEU
SCHWACKELISTE SUPERSCHWACKE. Text in German. 1957. m. EUR 672; EUR 87 per issue (effective 2009). adv. **Document type:** *Magazine, Trade.*
Published by: EurotaxSchwacke GmbH, Wilhelm-Roentgen-Str 7, Maintal, 63477, Germany. TEL 49-6181-4050, FAX 49-6181-405111, info@schwacke.de, http://www.schwacke.de. adv.: B&W page EUR 1,000, color page EUR 1,900. Circ: 3,940 (paid and controlled).

388 CHE
SCHWEIZER AUTO GEWERBE. Text in French, German, Italian. 21/yr.
Address: Mittelstr 32, Bern, 3001, Switzerland. TEL 031-238494, FAX 031-455463, TELEX 912641-BURI-CH. Ed. Rudolf Baldinger. Circ: 7,300.

388 GBR ISSN 0958-7969
SCOTTISH AUTO TRADER. Text in English. 1986. w. GBP 2.60 newsstand/cover (effective 2009). adv. back issues avail. **Document type:** *Magazine, Trade.*
Related titles: Online - full text ed.
Published by: Auto Mart Publications Ltd., Catherine St, Bewsey Industrial Estate, Warrington, Cheshire WA5 0LH, United Kingdom. TEL 44-845-3456789.

692.2 USA
SECRETARY OF ENERGY ANNUAL REPORT TO CONGRESS. Text in English. a. **Document type:** *Government.*
Published by: U.S. Department of Energy, Secretary of Energy, 1000 Independence Ave, SW, Washington, DC 20585.

388.3 USA
SECRETS OF A SUCCESSFUL CHRYSLER WARRANTY AUDIT. Text in English. a. **Document type:** *Journal, Trade.*
Published by: W D & S Publishing, 10 W 7th St, 1st Fl, PO Box 606, Barnegat Light, NJ 08006. TEL 800-321-5312, http://www.dealersedge.com.

388.3 USA
SECRETS OF A SUCCESSFUL G M WARRANTY AUDIT. (General Motors) Text in English. a. **Document type:** *Journal, Trade.*
Published by: W D & S Publishing, 10 W 7th St, 1st Fl, PO Box 606, Barnegat Light, NJ 08006. TEL 800-321-5312, http://www.dealersedge.com.

388.342 949.71 GBR ISSN 1754-3738
SERBIA AUTOS REPORT. Text in English. 2005. q. EUR 820, USD 1,030 combined subscription (print & email eds.) (effective 2010). **Document type:** *Report, Trade.* **Description:** Provides industry professionals and strategists, corporate analysts, auto associations, government departments and regulatory bodies with independent forecasts and competitive intelligence on the Serbian automotives market.
Formerly (until 2007): Serbia & Montenegro Autos Report (1749-0138)
Related titles: E-mail ed.
Indexed: A15, ABIn, B02, B15, B17, B18, G04, I05, P48, P51, P52, PQC.
Published by: Business Monitor International Ltd., Senator House, 85 Queen Victoria St, London, EC4V 4AB, United Kingdom. TEL 44-20-72480468, FAX 44-20-72480467, subs@businessmonitor.com.

388.3 USA
SERVICE EXECUTIVE (EMAIL EDITION). Text in English. 1997. 16/yr. USD 95 (effective 2005). 6 p./no. 3 cols./p.; **Document type:** *Newsletter, Trade.*
Formerly: Service Executive (Print Edition)
Media: E-mail.

Contact Owner: Molinaro Communications, 100 Merle Blvd, Munroe Falls, OH 44262-1642. TEL 330-688-4960, FAX 330-688-4909. Circ: 1,000 (paid).

629 DEU ISSN 1860-8175
SERVICEPROFI. Text in German. 2005. q. EUR 25.90 (effective 2008). adv. **Document type:** *Magazine, Trade.*
Published by: Springer Automotive Media (Subsidiary of: Springer Fachmedien Muenchen GmbH), Neumarkter Str 18, Munich, 81673, Germany. TEL 49-89-43721121, FAX 49-89-43721266, vertriebsservice@springer.com, http://www.springerautomotivemedia.de. Adv. contact Michael Harms. color page EUR 6,400; trim 300 x 400. Circ: 16,000 (controlled).

388.3 GBR
SEWELLS PAY GUIDE (YEAR). Text in English. 1988. a., latest 2007. GBP 249 per issue (effective 2010). software rev. **Document type:** *Directory, Trade.* **Description:** Covers the pay and benefits structures in the retail motor industry based on an extensive survey of salaries and benefits of almost 3,000 job holders in 21 key dealership job titles throughout seven regions of the UK mainland.
Related titles: Online - full text ed.
Published by: Sewells Information and Research (Subsidiary of: H. Bauer Publishing Ltd.), Bauer Automotive Media House, Peterborough Business Park, Lynchwood, Peterborough, Northants PE2 6EA, United Kingdom. TEL 44-1733-468254, FAX 44-1733-468349, sewells@emap.com, http://www.sewells.co.uk.

338 NZL ISSN 1177-0775
SHIFT. Variant title: Dealer News and Views. Text in English. 200?. m. **Document type:** *Magazine, Consumer.*
Related titles: ◆ Supplement to: Radiator. ISSN 1179-7800.
Published by: Motor Trade Association, Level 2, 79 Taranaki St, Marion Sq, PO Box 9244, Wellington, 6141, New Zealand. TEL 64-4-3858859, FAX 64-4-3859517, radiator@mta.org.nz.

338.342 959.57 GBR ISSN 1749-0146
SINGAPORE AUTOS REPORT. Text in English. 2005. q. EUR 820, USD 1,030 combined subscription (print & email eds.) (effective 2010). **Document type:** *Report, Trade.* **Description:** Covers independent forecasts and competitive intelligence on the automotives industry in Singapore.
Related titles: E-mail ed.
Indexed: A15, ABIn, B02, B15, B17, B18, G04, I05, P48, P51, P52, PQC.
Published by: Business Monitor International Ltd., Senator House, 85 Queen Victoria St, London, EC4V 4AB, United Kingdom. TEL 44-20-72480468, FAX 44-20-72480467, subs@businessmonitor.com.

628.286 388.324 FIN ISSN 0785-3793
SISUVIESTI. Text in Finnish. 1969. 3/yr. adv. **Document type:** *Magazine, Trade.*
Related titles: Online - full text ed.
Published by: Oy Sisu Auto AB/Sisu Truck Manufacturing Co., Tammisaarentie 45, PO Box 68, Karjaa, 10301, Finland. TEL 358-102751, FAX 358-19-236044. Ed. Hannu Kuosmanen TEL 358-10-2753441.

629.331 CZE ISSN 1801-934X
SKODA REVUE. Text in Czech. 2006. bi-m. CZK 140 (effective 2009). adv. **Document type:** *Magazine, Consumer.*
Published by: Max Power s.r.o., Prazska 18-810, Prague 10, 102 21, Czech Republic. TEL 420-281-017640. Ed. Jan Cerny. adv.: page CZK 55,000; trim 210 x 297.

388.3 USA
THE SKYLINER. Text in English. 1971. 10/yr. USD 32 domestic membership; USD 36 in Canada membership; USD 48 elsewhere membership (effective 2008). adv. charts; illus.; tr.lit. back issues avail. **Document type:** *Magazine, Consumer.* **Description:** Provides social and educational information on 1957-59 Ford retractable cars.
Related titles: E-mail ed.; Fax ed.
Published by: International Ford Retractable Club Inc., PO Box 157, Spring Park, MN 55384. TEL 952-472-3739, FAX 952-472-9116, albracht@accunet.net. Ed. Ed Albracht. R&P Ed. Albracitt. Circ: 1,200 (paid).

388.342 943.73 GBR ISSN 1749-0154
SLOVAKIA AUTOS REPORT. Text in English. 2005. q. EUR 820, USD 1,030 combined subscription (print & email eds.) (effective 2010). **Document type:** *Report, Trade.* **Description:** Covers independent forecasts and competitive intelligence on the automotives industry in Slovakia.
Related titles: E-mail ed.
Indexed: A15, ABIn, B02, B15, B17, B18, G04, I05, P48, P51, P52, PQC.
Published by: Business Monitor International Ltd., Senator House, 85 Queen Victoria St, London, EC4V 4AB, United Kingdom. TEL 44-20-72480468, FAX 44-20-72480467, subs@businessmonitor.com.

338.342 949.73 GBR ISSN 1749-0162
SLOVENIA AUTOS REPORT. Text in English. 2005. a. EUR 820, USD 1,030 combined subscription per issue (print & email eds.) (effective 2010). **Document type:** *Report, Trade.* **Description:** Covers independent forecasts and competitive intelligence on the automotives industry in Slovenia.
Related titles: E-mail ed.
Indexed: A15, ABIn, B02, B15, B17, B18, G04, I05, P48, P51, P52, PQC.
Published by: Business Monitor International Ltd., Senator House, 85 Queen Victoria St, London, EC4V 4AB, United Kingdom. TEL 44-20-72480468, FAX 44-20-72480467, subs@businessmonitor.com.

388.342 ESP
SOLO AUTO MONOVOLUMEN Y FAMILIARES. Text in Spanish. q. EUR 32.40 domestic; EUR 55.89 in Europe; EUR 85.94 elsewhere. adv. back issues avail. **Document type:** *Magazine, Consumer.* **Description:** Provides news of the family car market. Discusses equipment and improvements. Includes articles on travel.
Formerly: Solo Monovolumen
Related titles: Online - full text ed.
Published by: Alesport S.A., Gran Via 8-10, Hospitalet de Llobragat, Barcelona, 08902, Spain. TEL 34-93-4315533, FAX 34-93-2973905, http://www.alesport.com. Ed. Chema Huete. Pub. Jaime Alguersuari. Adv. contact Antonio Defebrer.

388.342 968 GBR ISSN 1749-0170
SOUTH AFRICA AUTOS REPORT. Text in English. 2005. q. EUR 820, USD 1,030 combined subscription (print & email eds.) (effective 2010). **Document type:** *Report, Trade.* **Description:** Covers independent forecasts and competitive intelligence on the automotives industry in South Africa.
Related titles: E-mail ed.
Indexed: A15, ABIn, B02, B15, B17, B18, G04, I05, P48, P51, P52, PQC.
Published by: Business Monitor International Ltd., Senator House, 85 Queen Victoria St, London, EC4V 4AB, United Kingdom. TEL 44-20-72480468, FAX 44-20-72480467, subs@businessmonitor.com.

796.72 ZAF
SOUTH AFRICAN 4 X 4. Text in English. 1992. bi-m. adv. illus. **Document type:** *Handbook/Manual/Guide, Consumer.* **Description:** Covers the South African 4 wheel drive vehicle market. Includes road tests, information on off-road driving, maintenance and tips.
Published by: Caravan Publications (Pty) Ltd., PO Box 15939, Vlaeberg, Cape Town 8018, South Africa. Ed. Godfrey Castle. Adv. contact Mandy Ahrens. B&W page USD 657, color page USD 1,114; trim 276 x 210. Circ: 15,000 (paid).

629.11 ZAF ISSN 1019-2093
SOUTH AFRICAN AUTO TRADER. Text in English. w. ZAR 5.50 newsstand/cover (effective 2002). adv. **Document type:** *Magazine, Consumer.*
Formerly (until 1992): Auto Trader (1010-6715)
Related titles: Online - full text ed.: Auto Trader Interactive. ISSN 1605-699X.
Address: PO Box 4825, Randburg, Gauteng 2125, South Africa. TEL 27-11-7895254, FAX 27-11-7896449, info@autotrader.co.za, http://www.autotrader.co.za.

388.34295195 GBR ISSN 1749-0189
SOUTH KOREA AUTOS REPORT. Text in English. 2005. q. EUR 820, USD 1,030 combined subscription (print & email eds.) (effective 2010). **Document type:** *Report, Trade.* **Description:** Provides industry professionals and strategists, corporate analysts, auto associations, government departments and regulatory bodies with independent forecasts and competitive intelligence on the automotives industry in South Korea.
Related titles: E-mail ed.
Indexed: A15, ABIn, B02, B15, B17, B18, G04, I05, P48, P51, P52, PQC.
Published by: Business Monitor International Ltd., Senator House, 85 Queen Victoria St, London, EC4V 4AB, United Kingdom. TEL 44-20-72480468, FAX 44-20-72480467, subs@businessmonitor.com.

338.476 GBR ISSN 1355-6789
SOUTH LONDON AUTO TRADER; cars - boats - bikes - caravans - commercials - accessories. Key Title: S. London Auto Trader. Text in English. 1994. w. GBP 1.20 newsstand/cover. **Document type:** *Handbook/Manual/Guide, Trade.* **Description:** Provides a buying and selling guide for various modes of transportation.
Published by: South London Auto Trader Ltd., Auto Trader House, 2 Jubilee Way, London, SW19 3XD, United Kingdom. TEL 44-181-543-8000, FAX 44-181-540-1041. Circ: 32,464 (paid).

388 USA
SOUTH TEXAS AUTOMOTIVE REPORT. Text in English. m. free to qualified personnel (effective 2009). adv. **Document type:** *Newspaper, Trade.* **Description:** Provides monthly news for the local automotive industry in Southeastern Texas, which includes body shops, mechanical shops and dealers.
Supersedes in part: Texas Automotive Report
Related titles: Online - full text ed.
Indexed: V03.
Published by: Autographic Publishing Company, Inc., 1121 Airport Center Dr, Ste 101, Nashville, TN 37214. TEL 615-391-3666, 800-467-3666, FAX 615-391-3622, garnett@automotivereport.net. Ed. Garnett Forkum. Pub. Allen Forkum. adv.: B&W page USD 825; trim 11.5 x 15. Circ: 5,050 (free).

338.376 GBR ISSN 0958-238X
SOUTH WEST AUTO TRADER. Text in English. 1982. w. GBP 1.10 newsstand/cover. **Document type:** *Handbook/Manual/Guide, Trade.* **Description:** Provides various types of information associated with the selling and buying of automobiles.
Published by: South West Auto Trader Ltd., Auto Trader House, Industrial Estate, Babbage Rd, Totnes Industrial Estate, Totnes, Devon TQ9 5JA, United Kingdom. TEL 44-1803-867777, FAX 44-1803-863248.

338.476 GBR ISSN 0958-2398
SOUTHERN AUTO TRADER. Text in English. 1981. w. **Document type:** *Magazine, Trade.* **Description:** Contains information on all types of automobiles available for purchase.
Published by: Auto Trader Publications Ltd. (Subsidiary of: Trader Media Group Ltd.), Auto Trader House, Danehill, Cutbush Park, Lower Earley Reading, Berkshire RG6 4UT, United Kingdom. TEL 44-845-0501766, FAX 44-118-9239159, enquiries@autotrader.co.uk. Circ: 7,775 (paid).

SOUTHERN MOTORACING. *see* SPORTS AND GAMES

796.72 USA
SOUTHERN RODDER. Text in English. 2000. m. USD 24.95; USD 3.95 newsstand/cover (effective 2001). **Document type:** *Magazine, Consumer.* **Description:** Features drivers & their muscle cars, rods, customs, street machines, trucks, including a how-to section and coming events.
Published by: Pro Motion Publication, 1400 Commerce Blvd Ste 18, Anniston, AL 36207. TEL 256-831-7877, FAX 256-831-6705, editor1@southernrodder.com, http://www.southernrodder.com/.

796.77 GBR
SOVEREIGN. Text in English, German, Spanish. 1991. 3/yr. free. adv. **Document type:** *Magazine, Consumer.* **Description:** Jaguar Cars magazine which contains a wide range of lifestyle features from fashion to sport, finance to culture, and food to travel.
Published by: Warwicks U K Ltds., Warwicks Uk Ltd, 45 Blondvil St, Coventry, Warks CV3 5QX, United Kingdom. TEL 44-2476-505339, FAX 44-2476-503185. Ed. Richard Madden. Pub., R&P John Lowe. Adv. contact Avril Tracy. Circ: 165,000 (controlled).

388.342 946 GBR ISSN 1749-0197
SPAIN AUTOS REPORT. Text in English. 2005. q. EUR 820, USD 1,030 combined subscription (print & email eds.) (effective 2010). **Document type:** *Report, Trade.* **Description:** Provides industry professionals and strategists, corporate analysts, auto associations, government departments and regulatory bodies with independent forecasts and competitive intelligence on the automotives industry in Spain.
Related titles: E-mail ed.
Indexed: A15, ABIn, B02, B15, B17, B18, G04, I05, P48, P51, P52, PQC.
Published by: Business Monitor International Ltd., Senator House, 85 Queen Victoria St, London, EC4V 4AB, United Kingdom. TEL 44-20-72480468, FAX 44-20-72480467, subs@businessmonitor.com.

796.77 USA
SPECIAL FINANCE INSIDER. Text in English. 2007. bi-m. USD 60 per issue (effective 2008). adv. **Document type:** *Magazine, Trade.* **Description:** Provides educational content and news related to the subprime segment of the retail automotive industry.
Published by: Auto Dealer Monthly LLC, PO Box 358, Evansville, IN 47703. TEL 812-424-6666, FAX 812-424-9999, http://autodealermonthly.com. Adv. contact Brian Ball. color page USD 4,840; trim 8.5 x 10.875. Circ: 11,364.

388.3 USA ISSN 0049-1845
SPECIAL INTEREST AUTOS. Text in English. 1970. bi-m. USD 29.95 (effective 2005). adv. charts. cum.index: 1970-1994. back issues avail. **Document type:** *Magazine, Consumer.* **Description:** Covers cars built from 1925-1980.
Published by: Watering, Inc., Special Interest Publications, PO Box 904, Bennington, VT 05201. TEL 802-442-3101, FAX 802-447-1561, hmnmail@hemmings.com, http://www.hemmings.com. Ed. Richard A Lentinello. Pub. James C Menneto. Adv. contact Bob Putnam. Circ: 35,000 (paid and free). **Subscr. to:** PO Box 196, Bennington, VT 05201.

796.77 USA ISSN 1075-9271
SPECIALTY AUTOMOTIVE MAGAZINE. Text in English. 1983. q. USD 30 (effective 2000). adv. tr.lit. reprints avail. **Document type:** *Magazine, Trade.*
Formerly: Specialty Automotive (0894-7414)
Published by: Meyers Publishing Corp., 799 Camarillo Springs Rd., Camarillo, CA 93012-8111. TEL 818-785-3900, FAX 818-785-4397. Ed. Steve Relyea. Pub. Len Meyers. R&P Elyse Wilson. Adv. contact Lana Meyers. Circ: 25,000.

SPECIALTY CAR (YEAR); your source for kit and component cars. *see* HOBBIES

338 CZE ISSN 1212-4583
SPEED. Text in Czech. 1998. m. CZK 825 (effective 2011). adv. **Document type:** *Magazine, Consumer.* **Description:** Contains articles, photos and features on a wide variety of automobiles.
Published by: Stratosfera s.r.o., Drtinova 8, Prague 5, 150 00, Czech Republic. TEL 420-234-109540, FAX 420-234-109264, online@stratosfera.cz, http://www.stratosfera.cz. Adv. contact Martina Palkoskova. Circ: 17,240 (paid). **Subscr. to:** SEND Predplatne s.r.o., PO Box 141, Prague 4 140 21, Czech Republic. TEL 420-225-985225, FAX 420-225-341425, send@send.cz, http://www.send.cz.

796.77 388.344 388.347 USA ISSN 1543-1428
SPEED STYLE & SOUND. Text in English. 2003 (Apr.). m. USD 19.99 domestic; USD 39.99 foreign (effective 2007). **Document type:** *Magazine, Consumer.*
Address: 15 E Jones Alley, Burford, GA 30518. TEL 770-932-7660, FAX 770-485-1870. Ed. Jonathan Wooley. Adv. contact Mike Sanders.

SPEEDWAY USA MAGAZINE. *see* SPORTS AND GAMES

388.3 NLD ISSN 1876-7915
THE SPITFIRE. Text in Dutch. 1981. bi-m. EUR 40 membership (effective 2010). adv. **Document type:** *Magazine, Consumer.*
Formerly (until 1988): Triumph Spitfire Clubkrant (2210-2825)
Published by: Triumph Spitfire Club, c/o Ron van der Schalie, Sec., Prins Vernhardstraat 46, Oud-Beijerland, 3262 SR, Netherlands. TEL 31-186-624272, http://www.spitfire.nl.

796 DEU ISSN 0940-4287
SPORT AUTO. Text in German. 1969. m. EUR 44.40; EUR 3.90 newsstand/cover (effective 2010). adv. bk.rev. index. back issues avail. **Document type:** *Magazine, Consumer.* **Description:** Covers the latest trends and styles, technology, tests, racing, and events; includes letters from readers.
Indexed: RASB.
Published by: Motor Presse Stuttgart GmbH & Co. KG (Subsidiary of: Gruner + Jahr AG & Co), Leuschnerstr 1, Stuttgart, 70174, Germany. TEL 49-711-18201, FAX 49-711-1821779, cgolla@motorpresse.de, http://www.motorpresse.de. Ed. Horst von Saurma-Jeltsch. Adv. contact Stefan Granzer. Circ: 50,411 (paid).

796.7 GRC ISSN 1109-7035
SPORT AUTO. Text in Greek. 2003. bi-m. EUR 4.95 newsstand/cover (effective 2006). adv. **Document type:** *Magazine, Consumer.*
Published by: Motorpress Hellas (Subsidiary of: Gruner + Jahr AG & Co), 132 Lefkis Str, Krioneri, 14568, Greece. TEL 30-210-6262000, FAX 30-210-6262401, info@motorpress.gr, http://www.motorpress.gr. Circ: 20,000 (paid and controlled).

796.77 LBN
SPORT AUTO MAGAZINE. Text in Arabic; Summaries in Arabic, English. 1973. m. USD 40 domestic; USD 60 foreign; LBP 7,000 newsstand/cover domestic; USD 5 newsstand/cover in United States (effective 2000). adv. charts; illus.; stat. back issues avail. **Document type:** *Consumer.* **Description:** Includes new model reviews, regional and international motor show information, road tests and evaluations, and international and regional motor sports coverage.
Published by: Barson Publications Ltd., P O Box 113 5358, Beirut, Lebanon. TEL 961-1-742726, FAX 961-1-746457. Ed., Pub. Gerard P Saunal. Adv. contact Nadim N Barrage. page USD 4,600. Circ: 103,075.

388.3 USA ISSN 1062-9629
SPORT COMPACT CAR. Text in English. 1988. m. USD 14.95 domestic; USD 27.95 in Canada; USD 29.95 elsewhere (effective 2008). adv. back issues avail. **Document type:** *Magazine, Consumer.* **Description:** Designed for the 18-34 year old male who has purchased and/or is interested in enhancing an existing personal sized, sport model performance car.
Indexed: A10, V03.

TU

—CCC.
Published by: Source Interlink Companies, 2400 E Katella Ave, 11th Fl, Anaheim, CA 92806. TEL 714-939-2400, FAX 714-978-6390, dheine@sourceinterlink.com, http://www.sourceinterlinkmedia.com. Eds. Scott Oldham, Joey Leh. Pub. Mark Han. adv.: B&W page USD 15,695, color page USD 19,880. Circ: 43,493 (paid).

388.3 USA
SPORT TUNING MAGAZINE; the authority for German auto performance and styling. Text in English. q. **Document type:** *Magazine, Consumer.*
Published by: Felge Publishing, 3208 Bluebird Cir., Simi Valley, CA 93063-5704. TEL 805-526-6844, FAX 805-526-8336, staff@sporttuningmag.com.

388.3 USA ISSN 0300-6387
TL1
SPORTS CAR; the official publication of The Sports Car Club of America. Text in English. 1944. m. USD 13.99 membership (effective 2007). adv. bk.rev. illus. **Document type:** *Magazine, Consumer.*
Indexed: G06, G07, G08, I05, I07, P48, PQC, SD.
—CCC.
Published by: (Sports Car Club of America), Haymarket Worldwide Inc. (Subsidiary of: Haymarket Media Inc.), 16842 Von Karman Ave, Ste 125, Irvine, CA 92606. TEL 949-417-6700, FAX 949-417-6116. Pub. Ian Howard. Adv. contact Raelyn Powell. B&W page USD 2,600, color page USD 3,320. Circ: 24,638.

388.3 USA ISSN 1042-9662
TL236
SPORTS CAR INTERNATIONAL. Text in English. 1985. bi-m. USD 14.99 domestic; USD 21 foreign; USD 3.99 newsstand/cover domestic; CAD 4.99 newsstand/cover in Canada; GBP 2 newsstand/cover in United Kingdom (effective 2005). adv. bk.rev. charts; illus. back issues avail.; reprints avail. **Document type:** *Magazine, Consumer.* **Description:** For performance car enthusiasts and those traditionalists who define cars as entertainment.
Formerly (until Jul. 1989): Sports Car Illustrated
Published by: S C I Publishing, Inc., 42 Digital Dr, 5, Novato, CA 94949. TEL 415-382-0580, FAX 415-382-0587. Ed. Eric Gustason. Pub. Tom Toldrian. Adv. contact Stan Michelman. Circ: 50,000 (paid).

796.77 USA ISSN 1527-859X
SPORTS CAR MARKET. Text in English. 199?. m. USD 58 (effective 2007). **Document type:** *Magazine, Consumer.* **Description:** Insider's information on collecting, investing, values, and trends in the collector car market.
Published by: Keith Martin Publications, PO Box 4797, Portland, OR 97208-4797. TEL 503-261-0555, 800-289-2819, FAX 503-253-2234.

SPORTSCAR. *see* SPORTS AND GAMES

388.3 USA
SPOT DELIVERY. Text in English. m. USD 199 (effective 2001). adv. back issues avail. **Document type:** *Newsletter, Trade.* **Description:** Covers legal developments in the auto dealership industry.
Related titles: Online - full text ed.
Published by: Consumer Credit Compliance Company, LLC, 971 Corporate Blvd, Ste 301, Linthicum, MD 21090. TEL 410-684-6800, 877-464-8326, FAX 410-684-6923, trohwedder@hudco.com, http://www.creditcompliance.com.

629.28 USA ISSN 1532-8546
TL6 CODEN: SCCCBR
STAPP CAR CRASH JOURNAL. Text in English. 19??. a. USD 129.95 per issue to non-members; USD 103.96 per issue to members (effective 2009). back issues avail. **Document type:** *Journal, Academic/Scholarly.* **Description:** Provides a forum for the presentation of research in impact biomechanics, human injury tolerance, and related fields that advance the knowledge of land-vehicle crash injury and occupant protection.
Former titles (until 2000): Stapp Car Crash Conference. Proceedings (0585-086X); (until 1990): Stapp Car Crash and Field Demonstration Conference (0883-2161); (until 1964): Stapp Car Crash Conference. Proceedings (0883-2153); (until 1963): Stapp Car Crash and Field Demonstration Conference. Proceedings
Related titles: Online - full text ed.
Indexed: EMBASE, ExcerpMed, HRIS, MEDLINE, P10, P20, P26, P30, P48, P51, P52, P53, P54, PQC, S10, SCOPUS.
—BLDSC (8434.510000), IE, Ingenta. **CCC.**
Published by: S A E Inc., 400 Commonwealth Dr, Warrendale, PA 15096. TEL 724-776-4841, 877-606-7323, FAX 724-776-0790, CustomerService@sae.org, http://www.sae.org.

629.222 USA ISSN 0744-155X
THE STAR (LAKEWOOD). Variant title: Mercedes-Benz Star. Text in English. 1956. bi-m. USD 45 domestic; USD 55 foreign (effective 2005). adv. bk.rev. back issues avail. **Document type:** *Magazine, Consumer.* **Description:** Contains features and articles on new and classic Mercedes-Benz cars from 1886 to present.
Published by: (Mercedes-Benz Club of America), Toad Hall Motorbooks, Inc., 1235 Pierce St, Lakewood, CO 80214-1936. TEL 303-235-0116, FAX 303-237-6080, vwtoad1@aol.com. Ed., Pub., R&P Frank Barrett. Adv. contact Norm Martin. Circ: 24,000 (paid). **Subscr. to:** M B C A, 1907 Lelaray St, Colorado Springs, CO 80909. TEL 800-637-2360, FAX 719-633-9283.

STARTLINE. *see* SPORTS AND GAMES

629.222 665.5 CAN
STATION REPORTER; serving Atlantic Canada's automotive service industry. Text in English. 1966. bi-m. CAD 19.95; CAD 3.95 newsstand/cover (effective 1997). adv. back issues avail. **Document type:** *Newsletter, Trade.* **Description:** Reports on news and events relating to the automotive aftermarket, petroleum retailing and bodyshop industries in Atlantic Canada.
Related titles: Online - full text ed.
Published by: Alfers Advertising & Publishing Inc., 3845 Dutch Village Rd, Ste 301, Halifax, NS B3L 4H9, Canada. TEL 902-423-6788, FAX 902-423-3354. Ed. Dale Mader. Pub., Adv. contact Robert D Alfers. page CAD 845; trim 10.75 x 8.25. Circ: 7,500 (controlled).

338.475 USA ISSN 0561-9726
TL200
STEAM AUTOMOBILE. Text in English. 1958. bi-m. USD 30 in North America membership; USD 40 elsewhere membership (effective 2008). adv. bk.rev. illus.; pat. back issues avail. **Document type:** *Bulletin.*
Published by: Steam Automobile Club of America, Inc., Tom Kimmel, Ed., PO Box 247, Berrien springs, MI 49103. http://www.steamautomobile.com/. Ed. Tom Kimmel TEL 269-471-7408. Circ: 915. **Subscr. to:** c/o Dave Lewis, Membership Sec., PO Box 31, Carson City, MI 48811.

388.3 USA
STOCK AND CUSTOM. Text in English. 2006. 4/yr. (bi-m. in 2007). USD 25 (effective 2006). **Document type:** *Magazine, Consumer.* **Description:** Covers various types of classics, modern, stock and customized vehicles for enthusiasts.
Published by: Big Runners Publishing, Inc., PO Box 1355, Bronx, NY 10475. TEL 718-652-4650. Pub. Michael Horton TEL 917-692-8255.

STOCK CAR RACING. *see* SPORTS AND GAMES

388.3 SVK ISSN 0139-6501
TL4
STOP; motoristicky magazin. Text in Slovak. 1971. fortn. USD 21. adv. illus. **Document type:** *Trade.* **Description:** Technical and sports motoring information.
Address: Exnarova 57, Bratislava, 82013, Slovakia. Ed., R&P Lubomir Kriz. Circ: 115,000. **Subscr. to:** Slovart G.T.G. s.r.o., Krupinska 4, PO Box 152, Bratislava 85299, Slovakia. TEL 421-2-63839472, FAX 421-2-63839485, http://www.slovart-gtg.sk.

796.77 SWE
STORA BEGBILBOKEN. Text in Swedish. 1998. a. SEK 149 newsstand/cover (effective 2010). adv. **Document type:** *Magazine, Consumer.*
Published by: Bonnier Tidskrifter AB, Sveavaegen 53, Stockholm, 10544, Sweden. TEL 46-8-7365200, FAX 46-8-7363842, info@bt.bonnier.se, http://www.bonniertidskrifter.se. Ed. Daniel Frodin TEL 46-8-7365890. Adv. contact Christer Johansson. page SEK 17,900; trim 220 x 300. Circ: 28,200 (controlled).

STRASSENATLAS DEUTSCHLAND UND EUROPA. *see* TRAVEL AND TOURISM

388 CHE ISSN 0259-5192
STRASSENVERKEHRSUNFAELLE IN DER SCHWEIZ/ACCIDENTS DE LA CIRCULATION ROUTIERE EN SUISSE. Text in French, German. 1963. a. CHF 22 (effective 2001). stat. **Document type:** *Government.*
Published by: Bundesamt fuer Statistik, Espace de l'Europe 10, Neuchatel, 2010, Switzerland. TEL 41-32-7136011, FAX 41-32-7136012, information@bfs.admin.ch, http://www.admin.ch/bfs.

629.22 AUS ISSN 1329-1475
STREET COMMODORES. Text in English. 1995. 14/yr. AUD 83.48 domestic; AUD 155 in New Zealand; AUD 185 elsewhere; AUD 7.95 newsstand/cover (effective 2008). adv. back issues avail. **Document type:** *Magazine, Consumer.* **Description:** Provides latest news, reviews, tips and products available for the Aussie automotive legend.
Related titles: Optical Disk - DVD ed.; Supplement(s): Street Commodores Car of the Year (Year).
Published by: Express Publications Pty. Ltd., 2-4 Stanley St, Locked Bag 111, Silverwater, NSW 2168, Australia. TEL 61-2-97413800, 800-801-647, FAX 61-2-97378017, subs@magstore.com.au, http://www.expresspublications.com.au. Eds. Ben Nightingale TEL 61-2-97413941, Ben Hosking TEL 61-2-97413921. Adv. contact Michael Coiro TEL 61-2-97413911. page AUD 2,306; trim 230 x 297. **Subscr. to:** ISubscribe Pty Ltd., 25 Lime St, Ste 303, Level 3, Sydney, NSW 2000, Australia. TEL 61-2-92621722, FAX 61-2-92625044, info@isubscribe.com.au, http://www.isubscribe.com.au.

STREET CUSTOMS. *see* SPORTS AND GAMES

629.222 AUS
STREET FORDS. Text in English. 1995. 14/yr. AUD 83.48 domestic; AUD 155 in New Zealand; AUD 185 elsewhere; AUD 7.95 newsstand/cover (effective 2008). back issues avail. **Document type:** *Magazine, Consumer.* **Description:** Provides the latest news and gossip from around the Ford world, interviews, road tests of the latest Ford vehicles, technical reviews and budget DIY tips.
Published by: Express Publications Pty. Ltd., 2-4 Stanley St, Locked Bag 111, Silverwater, NSW 2168, Australia. TEL 61-2-97413800, 800-801-647, FAX 61-2-97378017, subs@magstore.com.au, http://www.expresspublications.com.au. Ed. Roy Velardi TEL 61-2-97413993. Adv. contact Michael Coiro TEL 61-2-97413911. **Subscr. to:** ISubscribe Pty Ltd., 25 Lime St, Ste 303, Level 3, Sydney, NSW 2000, Australia. TEL 61-2-92621722, FAX 61-2-92625044, info@isubscribe.com.au, http://www.isubscribe.com.au.

796.77 BRA ISSN 1807-5746
STREET MOTORS. Text in Portuguese. 2004. bi-m. BRL 9.90 newsstand/cover (effective 2007). adv. **Document type:** *Magazine, Consumer.*
Published by: Digerati Comunicacao e Tecnologia Ltda., Rua Haddock Lobo 347, 12o andar, Sao Paulo, 01414-001, Brazil. TEL 55-11-32172600, FAX 55-11-32172617, http://www.digerati.com.br.

796.77 USA ISSN 1931-7670
STREET N' STRIP PERFORMANCE. Text in English. 2006. bi-m. **Document type:** *Magazine, Consumer.* **Description:** Enthusiast magazine devoted to street and sports drag race performance.
Published by: Performance Media Group, PO Box 488, Hebron, IN 46341. TEL 219-996-7832, FAX 219-996-7749, http://www.streetnstripmagazine.com.

STREET RODDER; America's street rodding authority. *see* SPORTS AND GAMES

629.286 USA
STREET RODDER PRESENTS: A GUIDE TO BUILDING STREET RODS. Text in English. 2000. a. adv. **Document type:** *Magazine, Consumer.*
Published by: Source Interlink Companies, 6420 Wilshire Blvd, 10th Fl, Los Angeles, CA 90048. TEL 323-782-2000, FAX 323-782-2585, dheine@sourceinterlink.com, http://www.sourceinterlink.com.

796.77 388.342 USA ISSN 1557-5640
STREET THUNDER. Text in English. 2005 (Feb./Mar.). bi-m. free to members (effective 2008). adv. 80 p./no.; back issues avail. **Document type:** *Magazine, Consumer.* **Description:** Designed for guys who love to build fearsome street machines of all eras and styles including rods, customs and muscle cars from the '20's to present.
Published by: North American Media Group, Inc. (Subsidiary of: North American Membership Group, Inc.), 12301 Whitewater Dr, Minnetonka, MN 55343. TEL 952-936-9333, 800-922-4888, FAX 952-936-9755, namghq@namginc.com, http://www.northamericanmediagroup.com/. Ed. Scott Parkhurst. Pub. Del Austin TEL 951-264-1898. adv.: B&W page USD 10,040, color page USD 14,660; trim 7.75 x 10.5. Circ: 191,305.

629.286 USA ISSN 1525-1918
STREET TRUCKS. Text in English. 1999. m. USD 24.95; USD 5.99 per issue (effective 2011). adv. **Document type:** *Magazine, Consumer.* **Description:** Provides information for all aspects of the custom truck market.
Published by: Beckett Media Llc, 2400 E Katella Ave, Ste 300, Anaheim, CA 92806. TEL 714-939-9991, 800-764-6287, FAX 714-456-0146, customerservice@beckett.com, http://www.beckett.com. Ed. Travis Noack TEL 714-939-9991 ext 350. Adv. contact Gabe Frimmel TEL 800-332-3330 ext 238.

388.3 USA ISSN 1550-462X
STREETTRENZ MAGAZINE. Text in English. 2004. m. USD 36 (effective 2007). **Document type:** *Magazine, Consumer.*
Related titles: Online - full text ed.: ISSN 1550-4638.
Address: 1148 Pulaski Hwy, Ste. 461, Bear, DE 19701. TEL 302-221-5477, FAX 302-221-5478, info@streettrenz.com.

STRUCTURE OF THE JAPANESE AUTO PARTS INDUSTRY. *see* BUSINESS AND ECONOMICS—Economic Situation And Conditions

658.8 USA ISSN 1941-3491
HD9710.A1
STYLING & PERFORMANCE. Text in English. 2007 (July). m. back issues avail. **Document type:** *Magazine, Trade.* **Description:** Designed to connect manufacturers with the entire aftermarket distribution system, including traditional and specialty warehouses, jobbers, retailers, service providers and new car and truck dealers.
Incorporates (2005-200?): Off-Road Business (1559-4203); Which was formerly (2004-2005): Off-Road Retailer (1554-0596)
Related titles: Online - full text ed.: ISSN 1941-3505.
Published by: Advanstar Communications, Inc., 6200 Canoga Ave, 2nd Fl, Woodland Hills, CA 91367. TEL 818-593-5000, FAX 818-593-5020, info@advanstar.com, http://www.advanstar.com. Circ: 50,000 (controlled).

388.3 USA
SUBIESPORT. Text in English. 2004 (Oct.). bi-m. USD 19.99 (effective 2005). adv. back issues avail. **Document type:** *Magazine, Consumer.* **Description:** Provides information for Subaru owners and enthusiasts.
Published by: Jelsoft Enterprises Ltd., PO BOX 2866, Kirkland, WA 98083. TEL 800-927-4344.

332 USA
SUBPRIME; auto finance news. Text in English. 2005. bi-m. USD 24.95; free to qualified personnel (effective 2010). adv. **Document type:** *Magazine, Trade.* **Description:** Focuses on the subprime finance segment of the auto industry.
Published by: Cherokee Publishing Co., Westview at Weston, 301 Cascade Pointe Ln. #101, Cary, NC 27513-5778. TEL 919-674-6020, 800-608-7500, FAX 919-674-6027. Pub. Bill Zadeits. adv.: color page USD 6,610. Circ: 40,000.

388 DEU ISSN 0937-8030
SUCH & FIND KRAFTFAHRZEUG. Text in German. 1983. w. EUR 1.95 newsstand/cover (effective 2006).
Published by: Kempen Verlag GmbH, Hinter der Jugenstr 22, Muelheim-Kaerlich, 56218, Germany. TEL 49-261-27020, FAX 49-261-2702244, info@sufi.de, http://www.sufi.de. Ed. A Kempen.

388.3 FIN ISSN 0355-2691
SUOMEN AUTOLEHTI; the automotive magazine of Finland. Text in Finnish. 1933. m. EUR 42 domestic; EUR 77 foreign (effective 2002). adv. bk.rev. **Document type:** *Trade.*
Published by: Kustannusliike Autotieto Oy, Koeydenpunojankatu 8, Helsinki, 00180, Finland. FAX 358-9-6944027. Ed. Heikki Haapaniemi. Adv. contact Eija Haapaniemi TEL 358-9-6944807. B&W page EUR 1,270; 195 x 255. Circ: 7,800 (paid); 150 (controlled).

388.3 ESP
SUPER AUTO. Text in Spanish. m. back issues avail. **Document type:** *Magazine, Consumer.*
Published by: Grupo Zeta, O'Donnell 12, 5a planta, Madrid, 28009, Spain. TEL 34-91-5869721, FAX 34-91-5869780, http://www.grupozeta.es.

388.3 USA ISSN 0146-2628
TL215.C5
SUPER CHEVY. Text in English. 1973. m. USD 18 domestic; USD 30 in Canada; USD 42 elsewhere (effective 2008). adv. illus. back issues avail. **Document type:** *Magazine, Consumer.* **Description:** Contains technical, performance how-to editorials and features modification theories, classic restorations and engine upgrades.
Formerly: Chevy Hi-Performance
Related titles: Online - full text ed.
Indexed: G05, G06, G07, G08, I05, S23.
—CCC.
Published by: Source Interlink Companies, 365 West Passaic St, Rochelle Park, NJ 07662. dheine@sourceinterlink.com, http://www.sourceinterlinkmedia.com. Ed. Jim Campisano. Pub. Ed Zinke TEL 714-939-2626. adv.: B&W page USD 12,820, color page USD 18,315. Circ: 164,784 (paid).

388.342 PRT
SUPER MOTORES MAGAZINE. Text in Portuguese. m. adv. **Document type:** *Magazine, Consumer.* **Description:** Contains detailed information and specifications for various types of automobiles.
Published by: Super Motores, Rua Ruben A.Leitao, 4-1 Dto, Lisbon, 1200, Portugal. TEL 351-1-343-3111, FAX 351-1-343-3114, super.motores@ip.pt, http://www.supermotores-magazine.pt. Ed. Tulio Goncalves. Adv. contact Christina Nunes. **Dist. by:** VASP Soc. de Transportes e Distribuicoes, Complexo Crel Bela-Vista, Rua da Tascoa, piso 4, Massama, Massama, Queluz 2745, Portugal. TEL 351-1-439-8500, FAX 351-1-430-2499; **Dist. in Brazil by:** Fernando Chinaglia Distribuidora, Rua Teodoro da Silva 907, CEP, Grajau, RJ 20563-900, Brazil. TEL 55-21-577-1117, 55-21-575-7828.

796.77 USA
SUPER STREET. Text in English. 1996. m. USD 14.97 domestic; USD 27.97 in Canada; USD 29.97 elsewhere (effective 2008). adv. back issues avail. **Document type:** *Magazine, Consumer.* **Description:** Focuses on the technical and how-to aspects of personalization and performance enhancement of compact cars.
Published by: Source Interlink Companies, 2400 E Katella Ave, 11th Fl, Anaheim, CA 92806. TEL 714-939-2400, FAX 714-978-6390, dheine@sourceinterlink.com, http://www.sourceinterlinkmedia.com. Ed. Jonathan Wong. adv.: B&W page USD 12,825, color page USD 20,495. Circ: 86,886 (paid).

796.77 FRA
SUPER V W. Text in French. q.
Published by: (Super VW Magazine), Auto Hebdo (Subsidiary of: Groupe de Presse Michel Hommell), 48-50 Bd Senard, Saint-Cloud, 92210, France. TEL 33-5-56039090.

796.77 NOR
SUPERCARS. Text in Norwegian. 2002. a. adv.
Published by: Amcar Magazine A-S, PO Box 6006, Trondheim, 7434, Norway. TEL 47-72-896000, FAX 47-72-896020, amcar@amcar.no, http://www.amcar.no. Circ: 17,000 (paid).

629.286 USA
SUPERCHARGER. Text in English. 1928. 8/yr. (Oct.-May). membership only. adv. **Document type:** *Magazine, Trade.*
Published by: Society of Automotive Engineers, Detroit Section, 21000 W Ten Mile Rd, Southfield, MI 48075. TEL 313-357-3340. Ed. Sandra Bouckley. Circ: 9,819.

629.326 CZE ISSN 1212-2408
SUPERMOTO. Text in Czech. 1998. m. CZK 662 (effective 2008). **Document type:** *Magazine, Consumer.*
Published by: Springer Media CZ, s. r. o., Nadrazni 32, Prague, 15000, Czech Republic. TEL 420-2-25351212, FAX 420-2-25351404, predplatne@bmczech.cz, http://www.businessmedia.cz. Ed. Frantisek Gorczyca.

SUPPLY LINE. *see* HOBBIES

629.286 USA
SURGEONS OF STEEL. Text in English. 1982. m. free to members. **Document type:** *Newsletter.* **Description:** Covers automotive collision-repair.
Related titles: Online - full content ed.
Published by: Nebraska Autobody Association, Inc., PO Box 145, Clay Center, NE 68933. Pub. Norbert Zaenglein. Circ: 1,300.

338.476 GBR ISSN 1364-5994
SUSSEX, EAST SURREY AND SOUTH EAST AUTO TRADER. Text in English. 1996. w. GBP 1.20 newsstand/cover. **Document type:** *Handbook/Manual/Guide, Trade.* **Description:** Serves as a guide to buying and selling various types of vehicles.
Published by: South London Auto Trader Ltd., Auto Trader House, 2 Jubilee Way, London, SW19 3XD, United Kingdom. TEL 44-181-543-8000, FAX 44-181-540-1041.

629.286 SWE ISSN 1100-5416
DET SVENSKA MOTOR-MAGASINET. Variant title: Motor-Magasinet. Text in Swedish. 1978. 40/yr. SEK 880 (effective 2007). adv. illus. **Document type:** *Magazine, Trade.*
Former titles (until 1989): Motor-Magasinet (0282-4981); (until 1984): Svenska Motor-Magasinet (0348-3304)
Published by: Aller Business AB (Subsidiary of: Aller Business AS), Berga Alle 1, PO Box 52, Helsingborg, 25053, Sweden. TEL 46-42-168300, FAX 46-42-163915, info@allerbusiness.se, http://www.allerbusiness.se. Eds. Staffan Johnsson TEL 46-42-168309, Olle Holm TEL 46-42-168303. Adv. contact Dagmar Wendelblom TEL 46-42-168311. B&W page SEK 31,800, color page SEK 38,700; 253 x 365. Circ: 15,700.

388.3 CZE ISSN 0039-7016
TL4
SVET MOTORU. Text in Czech. 1947. w. CZK 970 (effective 2011). adv. charts; illus. index. **Document type:** *Magazine, Consumer.*
Published by: Axel Springer Praha a.s., Rosmarin Business Center, Dilnicka 12, Prague 7, 17000, Czech Republic. TEL 420-2-34692111, FAX 420-2-34692102, http://www.axelspringer.cz. Ed. Zbysek Pechr. Adv. contact Petra Kardova. Circ: 100,000. **Subscr. to:** SEND Predplatne s.r.o., PO Box 141, Prague 4 140 21, Czech Republic. TEL 420-225-985225, FAX 420-225-341425, send@send.cz, http://www.send.cz.

796.77 POL ISSN 1230-9397
SWIAT MOTOCYKLI. Text in Polish. 1993. m. PLZ 65 domestic; PLZ 156.20 in United States; PLZ 6.90 newsstand/cover (effective 2011). **Document type:** *Magazine, Consumer.*
Published by: Agora S.A., ul Czerska 8/10, Warsaw, 00732, Poland. TEL 48-22-5556000, FAX 48-22-5554850, pomoc@agora.pl, http://www.agora.pl. Ed. Lech Potynski. Adv. contact Beata Remjasz. Circ: 49,413.

T 3. *see* TECHNOLOGY: COMPREHENSIVE WORKS

388.3 FIN ISSN 0786-2016
T M. TEKNIIKAN MAAILMA. AUTOMAAILMA. Variant title: T M. Automaailma. Text in Finnish. 1988. a. price varies. adv. **Document type:** *Consumer.*
Related titles: ◆ Supplement to: T M. Tekniikan Maailma. ISSN 0355-4287.
Published by: Yhtyneet Kuvalehdet Oy/United Magazines Ltd., Maistraatinportti 1, Helsinki, 00015, Finland. TEL 358-9-15661, FAX 358-9-145650, http://www.kuvalehdet.fi.

388 DEU
T UE V REPORT. Variant title: Auto Bild TueV Report. Text in German. 1972. a. EUR 3.90 newsstand/cover (effective 2010). adv. **Document type:** *Magazine, Consumer.*
Formerly (until 2007): T Ue V Autoreport (0341-6844); Which incorporated (19??-1998): Gebrauchtwagen (0949-491X)
Published by: (Vereinigung der Technischen Ueberwachungs-Vereine e.V.), T Ue V Media GmbH, Am Grauen Stein 1, Cologne, 51105, Germany. TEL 49-221-8063535, FAX 49-221-8063510, tuev-media@de.tuv.com, http://www.tuev-media.de.

388.4 DEU
TACHOMETER. Text in German. 1980. bi-m. EUR 35 (effective 2011). adv. **Document type:** *Magazine, Trade.*
Published by: (Verband des Kraftfahrzeuggewerbes NRW), Verlagsanstalt Handwerk GmbH, Postfach 105162, Duesseldorf, 40042, Germany. TEL 49-211-390980, FAX 49-211-3909829, info@verlagsanstalt-handwerk.de, http://www.verlagsanstalt-handwerk.de. Ed. Dieter Paust. Adv. contact Erwin Klein. B&W page EUR 1,229, color page EUR 1,741. Circ: 7,794 (paid and controlled).

338.342 951.249 GBR ISSN 1749-0200
TAIWAN AUTOS REPORT. Text in English. 2005. q. EUR 820, USD 1,030 combined subscription (print & email eds.) (effective 2010). **Document type:** *Report, Trade.* **Description:** Provides industry professionals and strategists, corporate analysts, auto associations, government departments and regulatory bodies with independent forecasts and competitive intelligence on the Taiwanese automotives market.
Related titles: E-mail ed.
Indexed: A15, ABIn, B02, B15, B17, B18, G04, I05, P48, P51, P52, PQC.
Published by: Business Monitor International Ltd., Senator House, 85 Queen Victoria St, London, EC4V 4AB, United Kingdom. TEL 44-20-72480468, FAX 44-20-72480467, subs@businessmonitor.com.

629.286 DEU ISSN 0342-622X
TANKSTELLE; aktuell - kritisch - praxisnah. Text in German. 1954. m. EUR 49.20; EUR 4.70 newsstand/cover (effective 2010). adv. **Document type:** *Magazine, Trade.*
Formed by the merger of (1958-1975): Tankstellen- und Garagengewerbe (0494-6871); (1969-1975): Tankstelle und Servicestation (0342-6211); Which was formerly (1961-1969): Die Tankstelle (0342-6238)
Related titles: Online - full text ed.
—CCC.
Published by: (Bundesverband Tankstellen und Gewerbliche Autowaesche Deutschland e.V.), Verlag Kirchheim und Co. GmbH, Kaiserstr 41, Mainz, 55116, Germany. TEL 49-6131-960700, FAX 49-6131-9607070, info@kirchheim-verlag.de, http://www.kirchheim-verlag.de. Ed. Matthias Heinz. Circ: 15,544 (paid). **Co-sponsors:** Arbeitsgemeinschaft der Bundesautobahntankstellen e.V.; Zentralverband des Tankstellen- und Garagengewerbes e.V.

338.476 DEU ISSN 0940-7871
TANKSTELLEN-MARKT. Text in German. 1991. m. adv. **Document type:** *Magazine, Trade.*
Published by: Springer Automotive Media (Subsidiary of: Springer Fachmedien Muenchen GmbH), Neumarkter Str 18, Munich, 81673, Germany. TEL 49-89-43721121, FAX 49-89-43721266, vertriebsservice@springer.com, http://www.springerautomotivemedia.de. Ed. Manfred Ruopp. adv.: B&W page EUR 3,800, color page EUR 5,660. Circ: 17,675 (paid and controlled).

656.016 DEU ISSN 0178-983X
DER TANKSTELLENBERATER. Text in German. 1975. bi-m. EUR 43.87 (effective 2010). adv. **Document type:** *Magazine, Trade.*
Published by: (Bundesverband Tankstellen und Gewerbliche Autowaesche Deutschland e.V.), Witas GmbH, Postfach 2227, Minden, 32379, Germany. TEL 49-571-886080, info@witas-minden.de, http://www.witas-minden.de. adv.: B&W page EUR 870, color page EUR 1,410. Circ: 4,850 (paid and controlled).

338 629.2 DEU ISSN 1619-2877
TATSACHEN UND ZAHLEN; verband der automobilindustrie. Text in German. 1927. a. EUR 113 to non-members; EUR 67 to members (effective 2006). back issues avail. **Document type:** *Trade.*
Formerly (until 2001): Tatsachen und Zahlen aus der Kraftverkehrswirtschaft (0083-548X)
Published by: Verband der Automobilindustrie e.V., Westendstr 61, Frankfurt Am Main, 60325, Germany. TEL 49-69-975070, FAX 49-69-97507261, info@vda.de, http://www.vda.de.

388 DEU ISSN 1437-0336
TAXI. Text in German. 1994. 8/yr. EUR 35.90; EUR 5.10 newsstand/cover (effective 2010). adv. **Document type:** *Magazine, Trade.* **Description:** Reports on all important issues involving taxi and rental operators in Germany, including road safety, law, traffic planning, education, technology and insurance.
Published by: Verlag Heinrich Vogel (Subsidiary of: Springer Science+Business Media), Neumarkterstr 18, Munich, 81664, Germany. TEL 49-89-43722878, FAX 49-89-2030432100, kontakt@verlag-heinrich-vogel.de, http://www.springerfachmedien-muenchen.de. Ed. Anne K Peters. Adv. contact Elisabeth Huber. B&W page EUR 5,215, color page EUR 8,095; trim 185 x 253. Circ: 36,095 (paid).

388.3 DEU ISSN 0174-3775
TAXI HEUTE; das bundesweite Fachblatt fuer den erfolgreichen Taxi- und Mietwagenunternehmer. Text in German. 1978. 8/yr. EUR 46; EUR 6.50 newsstand/cover (effective 2010). adv. **Document type:** *Magazine, Trade.*
Published by: Huss-Verlag GmbH, Joseph-Dollinger-Bogen 5, Munich, 80807, Germany. TEL 49-89-323910, FAX 49-89-32391416, management@huss-verlag.de, http://www.huss-verlag.de. Ed. Juergen Hartmann. Adv. contact Angelika Koenig. Circ: 20,175 (paid).

388.3 DEU
TAXI KURIER. Text in German. m. adv. **Document type:** *Magazine, Trade.*
Published by: Taxi Muenchen e.G., Engelhardstr 6, Munich, 81369, Germany. TEL 49-89-773077, FAX 49-89-772462, laermann@taxi-muenchen.de, http://www.taxizentrale-muenchen.de. Ed. Hans Meissner. adv.: page EUR 2,040; trim 210 x 297. Circ: 8,000 (controlled).

629.222 388.324 DEU ISSN 0943-9919
TECHNISCHE VORSCHRIFTEN FUER KRAFTFAHRZEUGE. Text in German. 1962. 3 base vols. plus updates 2/yr. EUR 128 base vol(s).; EUR 29.80 updates per issue (effective 2009). **Document type:** *Monographic series, Trade.*
Published by: Erich Schmidt Verlag GmbH & Co. (Berlin), Genthiner Str 30 G, Berlin, 10785, Germany. TEL 49-30-2500850, FAX 49-30-250085305, vertrieb@esvmedien.de, http://www.erich-schmidt-verlag.de.

629 USA
TECHSHOP; equipment and tool showcase. Text in English. 2000. m. free domestic to qualified personnel (effective 2008). adv. back issues avail. **Document type:** *Magazine, Trade.* **Description:** Designed for automotive technicians and repair shop owners who want the latest information on shop equipment, tools and supplies.
Related titles: Online - full text ed.
Published by: Babcox Publications, Inc., 3550 Embassy Pky, Akron, OH 44333. TEL 330-670-1234, FAX 330-670-0874, bbabcox@babcox.com, http://www.babcox.com. Pub. Beth Skove. Circ: 95,357 (paid).

388 DEU
TEILEHANDEL. Text in German. 1998. 10/yr. EUR 33.36 (effective 2011). adv. **Document type:** *Magazine, Trade.* **Description:** General information for car drivers and enthusiasts.
Formerly (until 2007): Auto Zubehoer Markt: Teilehandel
Published by: Verlag Kaufhold GmbH, Philipp-Nicolai-Weg 3, Herdecke, 58313, Germany. TEL 49-2330-918311, FAX 49-2330-13570, info@verlag-kaufhold.de, http://www.verlag-kaufhold.de. Ed. Claudia Pfleging. Pub. Manfred Kaufhold. adv.: B&W page EUR 1,693, color page EUR 2,237; trim 223 x 320. Circ: 2,000 (paid and controlled).

629.13 SWE ISSN 0346-5373
TEKNIKENS VAERLD; allt om bilen. Text in Swedish. 1947. fortn. SEK 1,195 (effective 2010). adv. Supplement avail.; back issues avail. **Document type:** *Magazine, Consumer.*
Formed by the merger of (1944-1947): Populaer-Teknik; Which was formerly (until 1946): Teknik och Hobby; (1920-1947): Flyg (1100-2182); Which was formerly (until 1942): Flygning (1100-8970); Flyg incorporated (1943-1945): Svensk Flygtidning; Which was formerly (1939-1942): Flygtidningen
Published by: Bonnier Tidskrifter AB, Sveavaegen 53, Stockholm, 10544, Sweden. TEL 46-8-7365200, FAX 46-8-7363842, info@bt.bonnier.se, http://www.bonniertidskrifter.se. Ed. Daniel Frodin TEL 46-8-7365890. Adv. contact Anders Blomqvist TEL 46-8-7365465. color page SEK 39,900; 217 x 280. Circ: 48,100 (paid). **Subscr. to:** Pressdata AB, Fack 3217, Stockholm 10364, Sweden.

796.71 ZAF ISSN 1812-6685
TESTDRIVEN. Text in English. 2004. bi-w.
Published by: Giant Man Multi Media, 18 Dairy Rd, Pelham, Pietermaritzburg, 3201, South Africa. TEL 27-33-3867750.

910.91 USA
TEXAS JOURNEY. Text in English. 1997. bi-m. free to members (effective 2009). adv. illus.; tr.lit. 80 p./no. 3 cols./p.; **Document type:** *Magazine, Consumer.* **Description:** Describes tourist destinations of historical or cultural importance in the Lone Star State.
Formerly (until 1997): A A A Texas Journey (1092-6178); Which superseded in part (in 1997): Car and Travel (Houston Edition)
Related titles: Online - full text ed.
Published by: American Automobile Association, Texas and New Mexico Branches, 3333 Fairview Rd, A327, Costa Mesa, CA 92626. TEL 714-885-2376, FAX 714-885-2335, http://www.aaa-texas.com/index.asp. Adv. contact Betty Chew TEL 714-885-2356. B&W page USD 14,780, color page USD 18,480; trim 7.875 x 10.5. Circ: 779,106.

388.342 959.3 GBR ISSN 1749-0219
THAILAND AUTOS REPORT. Text in English. 2005. q. EUR 820, USD 1,030 combined subscription (print & email eds.) (effective 2010). **Document type:** *Report, Trade.* **Description:** Provides industry professionals and strategists, corporate analysts, auto associations, government departments and regulatory bodies with independent forecasts and competitive intelligence on the Thai automotives market.
Related titles: E-mail ed.
Indexed: A15, ABIn, B02, B15, B17, B18, G04, I05, P48, P51, P52, PQC.
Published by: Business Monitor International Ltd., Senator House, 85 Queen Victoria St, London, EC4V 4AB, United Kingdom. TEL 44-20-72480468, FAX 44-20-72480467, subs@businessmonitor.com.

338.476 GBR
THAMES VALLEY & SOUTHERN AUTO TRADER. Text in English. 19??. w. GBP 2.70 newsstand/cover (effective 2010). illus. **Document type:** *Magazine, Consumer.* **Description:** Provides pictures and other information on various types of automobiles available for purchase. Area of covereage includes: Berkshire, Buckinghamshire, Surrey, Wiltshire, Oxford, Middlesex & London.
Former titles (until 200?): London & Thames Valley Auto Trader (1747-6852); (until 2008): Thames Valley Auto Trader (0958-4269); (until 1987): Thames Valley Trader
Published by: Auto Trader Publications Ltd. (Subsidiary of: Trader Media Group Ltd.), Auto Trader House, Danehill, Cutbush Park, Lower Earley Reading, Berkshire RG6 4UT, United Kingdom. TEL 44-845-0501766, FAX 44-118-9239159, enquiries@autotrader.co.uk.

388.3 CAN
THUNDER BAY CAR & TRUCK NEWS. Text in English. m. CAD 50. **Document type:** *Magazine, Trade.*
Published by: North Superior Publishing Inc., 1145 Barton St, Thunder Bay, ON P7B 5N3, Canada. TEL 807-623-2348, FAX 807-623-7515. Ed., Pub. Scott A Sumnr. Circ: 30,000.

388 629.222 USA ISSN 1062-5755
THUNDERBIRD SCOOP. Text in English. 1972. bi-m. USD 26; USD 45 foreign. adv. bk.rev. charts; illus. **Document type:** *Newsletter.* **Description:** Informs, educates, and entertains owners of the 1958 to today's Ford Motor Company's Thunderbird series with articles about restoration, maintenance, and collecting. Also contains the current agenda, activities, events, and conventions of the club.
Published by: Vintage Thunderbird Club International, PO Box 2250, Dearborn, MI 48123-2250. TEL 316-794-8061. Ed. Terry Gibbs. Pub., R&P Alan H Tast. Adv. contact Rick Solors. B&W page USD 75; 7.75 x 4.56. Circ: 3,200 (paid).

388.3 CHN
TIANJIN QICHE BAO/TIANJIN AUTOMOBILE GAZETTE. Text in Chinese. 1987. 3/m. CNY 48 (effective 2004). **Document type:** *Consumer.*
Published by: Tianjin Ribao Baoye Jituan, 873, Dagu Nanlu, Tianjin, 300211, China.

388.3 USA
TIGER TALES. Text in English. 1969. m. free to members (effective 2008). adv. **Document type:** *Newsletter.* **Description:** Provides a medium through which Sunbeam Tiger and Alpine owners may pool ideas and resources on the care and maintenance of their vehicles.
Published by: California Association of Sunbeam Tiger Owners, c/o Michels, 6684 Pageant Dr, Huntington Beach, CA 92648. TEL 714-854-2561, rootes@ix.netcom.com. Ed., Pub., Adv. contact Steve Sage. Circ: 850 (paid).

▼ **TIGER TANK**; build the model and discover the history of tanks. *see* MILITARY

388.3 IRL ISSN 1649-6930
TIPPERARY'S MOTOR TRADER. Text in English. 2002. bi-w. EUR 2.50 newsstand/cover (effective 2006). adv.
Supersedes in part (in 2005): Ireland's Motor Trader (1649-6353); Which was formerly (until 2004): The Motor-Trader (1649-2072)
Published by: Motor Trader, Box 338, Naas, Co. Kildare, Ireland. TEL 353-45-893343, FAX 353-45-893342, info@motortrader.ie, http://www.motortrader.ie/.

388 388.3 USA
TIRE BUSINESS. Text in English. 1983. bi-w. USD 79 domestic; USD 107 in Canada; USD 119 elsewhere; USD 4 per issue (effective 2009). adv. back issues avail. **Document type:** *Newspaper, Trade.* **Description:** Provides timely news and features on the North American tire and automotive service business for independent tire dealers, retreaders, wholesalers and others involved in tire marketing.
Formerly (until 19??): Crain's Tire Business (0746-9071)
Related titles: Online - full text ed.: TireBusiness.com.
Indexed: A09, A10, B01, B06, B07, B09, I05, P34, PROMT, T02, V03, V04.
—BLDSC (8858.350000), CIS. **CCC.**
Published by: Crain Communications, Inc., 1725 Merrimen Rd, Ste 300, Akron, OH 44313. TEL 330-836-9180, FAX 330-836-2831, info@crain.com, http://www.crain.com. Eds. David E. Zielasko, Keith E Crain TEL 313-446-6001. adv.: B&W page USD 7,140, color page USD 9,440. Circ: 20,868 (paid and controlled).

678.32 USA ISSN 0040-8085
TS1870
TIRE REVIEW; the authority on tire dealer profitability. Text in English. 1901. m. free in US & Canada to qualified personnel (effective 2009). adv. **Document type:** *Magazine, Trade.* **Description:** Provides information pertaining to all aspects of operating a successful dealership - including market overviews, product applications, technical service-related issues, insightful industry research, business operation issues, and annual directories and guides.
Former titles (until 1966): Tire and T B A Review; (until 1955): Tire Review; (until 1934): India Rubber & Tire Review (0096-5782); (until 1925): India Rubber Review
Related titles: Online - full text ed.; Supplement(s): Annual Sourcebook and Purchasing Directory.
Indexed: ChemAb, G08, I05, PROMT.
—Linda Hall.
Published by: Babcox Publications, Inc., 3550 Embassy Pky, Akron, OH 44333. TEL 330-670-1234, FAX 330-670-0874, bbabcox@babcox.com, http://www.babcox.com. Ed. Jim Smith TEL 330-670-1234 ext 298. Pub. David Moniz TEL 330-670-1234 ext 215. adv.: B&W page USD 7,395. Circ: 32,023 (paid).

340 USA ISSN 1088-2340
KF2215.Z95
TITLE AND REGISTRATION TEXT BOOK; summary of procedures, fees, and regulations. Text in English. 1977. a. USD 160 per issue to non-members; free to members (effective 2011). **Document type:** *Handbook/Manual/Guide, Trade.*
Formerly (until 1996): N A D A Title and Registration Book
Published by: (National Automobile Dealers Association), N.A.D.A. Appraisal Guides, PO Box 7800, Costa Mesa, CA 92628. http://www.nadaguides.com.

629.113 ARG ISSN 1666-0617
TM. TRANSPORTE MUNDIAL. CATALOGO ESPECIAL. Text in Spanish. 2000. a. ARS 12 newsstand/cover (effective 2010). back issues avail. **Document type:** *Directory, Trade.*
Related titles: ◆ Supplement to: Transporte Mundial. ISSN 1514-5255.
Published by: Motorpress Argentina, S.A. (Subsidiary of: Gruner + Jahr AG & Co), Ituzaingo, 642-648, Buenos Aires, 1141, Argentina. TEL 54-114-3077672, FAX 54-114-3077858, http://www.motorpress.com.ar/.

388 USA ISSN 1947-5128
▼ **TODAY'S AUTO GUIDE.** Text in English. 2009. w. free (effective 2009). **Document type:** *Magazine, Consumer.* **Description:** For the consumer shopping for new and pre-owned, cars, SUVs, trucks and vans in Charlotte, North Carolina.
Published by: High Rev Publishing, LLC, 13016 Eastfield Rd, Ste 200-258, Huntersville, NC 28078. TEL 704-400-9826, chris@todaysautoguide.com.

629.222 USA
TODAY'S TRUCK & SPORT UTILITY PERFORMANCE. Text in English. bi-m. USD 3.95 newsstand/cover. **Document type:** *Magazine, Consumer.*
Published by: Mag-Tec Productions, 9582 Hamilton Ave, Huntington Beach, CA 92646. TEL 962-932-7795, FAX 714-965-2268. Ed. Eva Griffey.

629 USA ISSN 1539-9532
TOMORROW'S TECHNICIAN; dedicated to today's automotive student. Text in English. 2002. m. free domestic to qualified personnel (effective 2009). adv. **Document type:** *Magazine, Consumer.* **Description:** Designed exclusively for a core target audience of 17-to-25-year-old automotive students.
Related titles: Online - full text ed.
Indexed: A26, B02, B15, B17, B18, G04, G08, I05.
Published by: Babcox Publications, Inc., 3550 Embassy Pky, Akron, OH 44333. TEL 330-670-1234, FAX 330-670-0874, bbabcox@babcox.com, http://www.babcox.com. Ed. Edward Sunkin. Adv. contact Ellen Mays TEL 330-670-1234 ext 275. Circ: 50,098 (paid).

629.11 ESP
TOP AUTO. Text in Spanish. m. adv. **Document type:** *Magazine, Consumer.*
Published by: R B A Edipresse, Perez Galdos 36, Barcelona, 08012, Spain. TEL 34-93-4157374, FAX 34-93-2177378, http://www.rbaedipresse.es. Circ: 28,500 (paid).

629.2 GRC
TOP CARS. Variant title: Auto Triti Top Cars. Text in Greek. 2006. a. EUR 5.95 newsstand/cover (effective 2006). adv. **Document type:** *Magazine, Consumer.*
Published by: Motorpress Hellas (Subsidiary of: Gruner + Jahr AG & Co), 132 Lefkis Str, Krioneri, 14568, Greece. TEL 30-210-6262000, FAX 30-210-6262401, info@motorpress.gr, http://www.motorpress.gr. Circ: 35,000 (paid and controlled).

796.77 SVK ISSN 1337-2432
TOP CARS. Text in Slovak. 2007. q. adv. **Document type:** *Magazine, Consumer.*
Published by: Star Production, s.r.o., Dr Vladimira Clementisa 10, Bratislava 2, 821 02, Slovakia. TEL 421-2-48282140, FAX 421-2-48282148, office@starproduction.sk.

388.3 NZL ISSN 1177-0198
TOP GEAR. Text in English. 2005. bi-m. NZD 69.85 domestic; NZD 170 in Australia; NZD 360 elsewhere (effective 2008). adv. **Document type:** *Magazine, Consumer.* **Description:** Offers a unique mix of hardcore buying advice and high entertainment values, and brings Kiwi car fans a unique blend of fantastic local features, reviews, gadgetry and opinion.
Published by: Jones Publishing, Victoria St W, PO Box 91344, Auckland, 1142, New Zealand. TEL 64-9-3606424, FAX 64-9-3587291, info@jonespublishing.co.nz, http://www.jonespublishing.co.nz/. Ed. Cameron Officer TEL 64-9-3587298. Adv. contact Martin Shanahan TEL 64-9-3580786. color page NZD 4,185; trim 230 x 300. Circ: 12,094.

796.77 CZE ISSN 1801-8866
TOP GEAR. Variant title: B B C Top Gear. Text in Czech. 2006. m. CZK 935 (effective 2011). adv. **Document type:** *Magazine, Consumer.*
Published by: Stratosfera s.r.o., Drtinova 8, Prague 5, 150 00, Czech Republic. TEL 420-234-109540, FAX 420-234-109264, online@stratosfera.cz, http://www.stratosfera.cz. Adv. contact Martina Palkoskova. **Subscr. to:** SEND Predplatne s.r.o., PO Box 141, Prague 4 140 21, Czech Republic. TEL 420-225-985225, FAX 420-225-341425, send@send.cz, http://www.send.cz.

796.77 POL ISSN 1898-3731
TOP GEAR. Text in Polish. 2008. m. PLZ 58.80; PLZ 4.90 newsstand/cover (effective 2010). adv. **Document type:** *Magazine, Consumer.*
Published by: Hubert Burda Media, ul Warecka 11a, Warsaw, 00034, Poland. TEL 48-22-4488000, FAX 48-22-4488001, kontakt@burdamedia.pl, http://www.burdamedia.pl. Ed. Piotr Frankowski. Adv. contact Janusz Jedrzejczak TEL 48-22-4488467.

796.77 ROM ISSN 1841-3781
TOP GEAR. Text in Romanian. 2005. m. **Document type:** *Magazine, Consumer.*
Published by: Media Sport Promotion, Str. Feleacu nr. 23, bl. 13A, sc. 3, ap. 34, sector 1, Bucharest, Romania. TEL 40-21-2330551, FAX 40-21-2330551, office@motorxtrem.ro.

338.476 GBR
TOP GEAR (LONDON). Text in English. 13/yr. GBP 51.35 domestic; GBP 92 in United States; USD 10.25 newsstand/cover in United States (effective 2007). **Document type:** *Magazine, Consumer.*
Published by: Top Gear, Woodlands, 80 Wood Ln, London, W12 0TT, United Kingdom. tgweb@bbc.co.uk. Ed. Michael Harvey.

629.286 GBR ISSN 2042-0277
TOP GEAR PORTFOLIO. Text in English. 200?. a. adv. **Document type:** *Magazine, Trade.* **Description:** Covers beautiful car shots by leading photographers.
Published by: B B C Magazines Ltd. (Subsidiary of: B B C Worldwide Ltd.), Second Fl A, Energy Ctr, Media Ctr, 201 Wood Ln, London, W12 7TQ, United Kingdom. TEL 44-20-84333598, bbcworldwide@bbc.co.uk, http://www.bbcmagazines.com.

629.73 ROM ISSN 1454-0436
TOP GUN SPECIAL. Text in Romanian. 1998. m. adv. **Document type:** *Magazine, Consumer.*
Published by: Hiparion, Str. Mihai Veliciu 15-17, Cluj-Napoca, 3400, Romania. TEL 40-64-411100, FAX 40-64-411700, office@hiparion.ro.

388 GBR
TOP MARQUES. Text in English. 1994. fortn. GBP 92.50 (effective 2009). adv. **Document type:** *Magazine, Trade.* **Description:** Information and listings on buying and selling prestige automobiles.
Related titles: Online - full text ed.
Published by: Auto Trader Publications Ltd. (Subsidiary of: Trader Media Group Ltd.), Optimum House, Clippers Quay, Salfords Quay, Salfords, Manchester, M50 3XP, United Kingdom. TEL 44-845-0710427, enquiries@autotrader.co.uk, http://www.autotrader.co.uk. Circ: 17,869.

796.77 DEU
TOP SPEED. Text in German. 1995. m. EUR 35; EUR 1.50 newsstand/cover (effective 2010). adv. **Document type:** *Magazine, Consumer.*
Published by: Vestische Mediengruppe Welke GmbH & Co. KG, Hertener Mark 7, Herten, 45699, Germany. TEL 49-2366-808400, FAX 49-2366-808499, info@vmw-verlag.de, http://vmw-verlag.de.

388.3 ESP
TOP TUNING. Text in Spanish. m. EUR 4.95 newsstand/cover (effective 2009). adv. **Document type:** *Magazine, Consumer.*
Published by: Grupo V, C Valportillo Primera, 11, Alcobendas, Madrid, 28108, Spain. TEL 34-91-6622137, FAX 34-91-6622654, secretaria@grupov.es. Ed. Eduardo Caro. Adv. contact Isidro Iglesias. page EUR 2,355; trim 18 x 26.5. Circ: 85,000.

388.3 FRA ISSN 0984-9068
TOP'S CARS. Text in French. 1987. fortn. adv. mkt. **Document type:** *Magazine, Consumer.*
Published by: Motor Presse France, 12 rue Rouget de Lisle, Issy-les-Moulineaux, 92442, France. http://www.motorpresse.fr.

796.77 CAN ISSN 0704-7339
TORONTO INTERNATIONAL AUTO SHOW PROGRAM. Text in English. 1974. a. CAD 4 (effective 2001). adv. **Document type:** *Journal, Consumer.*
Related titles: ◆ Supplement to: Carguide. ISSN 0384-9309.
Published by: Formula Publications (Subsidiary of: Torstar Corp.), 447 Speers Rd, Ste 4, Oakville, ON L6K 3S7, Canada. TEL 905-842-6591, FAX 905-842-6843. Ed. Josef Knycha. Pub. J Scott Robinson. R&P J Robinson. Circ: 50,000.

388.3 JOR ISSN 1999-6683
TL114
TORQUE. Text in English. 2007. m. **Document type:** *Magazine, Consumer.*
Published by: Near East Media, PO Box 940166, Amman, 11194, Jordan. TEL 962-6-516-3357, FAX 962 6 516 3267.

388.3 SGP
TORQUE. Text in English. m. SGD 60 (effective 2008). **Document type:** *Magazine, Consumer.*
Published by: S P H Magazines Pte Ltd. (Subsidiary of: Singapore Press Holdings Ltd.), 82 Genting Ln Level 7, Media Centre, Singapore, 349567, Singapore. TEL 65-6319-6319, FAX 65-6319-6345, sphmag@sph.com.sg, http://www.sphmagazines.com.sg/. Ed. Lee Nian Tjoe.

796.77 MYS ISSN 1511-5658
TORQUE. Text in English. 1999. m. MYR 96 in Penisular Malaysia; MYR 114 in East Malaysia (effective 2008). **Document type:** *Magazine, Consumer.*
Published by: Blu Inc Media Sdn Bhd (Subsidiary of: S P H Magazines Pte Ltd.), Lot 7, Jalan Bersatu 13/4, Section 13, Petaling Jaya, Selangor 46200, Malaysia. TEL 60-3-79527000, FAX 60-3-79555191.

629.22 NLD ISSN 2211-2359
▼ **TOTAL 911.** Text in Dutch. 2010. 10/yr. EUR 40 (effective 2011). **Document type:** *Magazine, Consumer.*
Published by: F & L Life Publications B.V. (Subsidiary of: F & L Publishing Group B.V.), Postbus 31331, Nijmegen, 6503 CG, Netherlands. TEL 31-24-3723643, FAX 31-24-3723632.

721.84 GBR ISSN 1746-613X
TOTAL 911; the Porsche magazine. Text in English. 2005. m. GBP 52.65 domestic; GBP 60 in Europe; GBP 70 elsewhere; GBP 4.50 newsstand/cover (effective 2009). adv. back issues avail. **Document type:** *Magazine, Consumer.* **Description:** Features informative articles on the Porsche.
Related titles: Online - full text ed.
Published by: Imagine Publishing Ltd., Richmond House, 33 Richmond Hill, Bournemouth, Dorset BH2 6EZ, United Kingdom. TEL 44-1202-586200, md@imagine-publishing.co.uk, http://www.imagine-publishing.co.uk. Ed. Phil Raby. Adv. contact Darren Moseley TEL 44-1452-554911.

771.38 GBR ISSN 1471-4299
TOTAL B M W. Text in English. 2000. m. GBP 49.20 domestic; GBP 54.60 in Europe; GBP 60 elsewhere; GBP 4.50 per issue domestic; GBP 5.50 per issue in Europe; GBP 6 per issue elsewhere (effective 2010). adv. illus. back issues avail. **Document type:** *Magazine, Consumer.* **Description:** Covers everything from modified newer cars to 70's and 80's modern classics, includes product news and reviews, practical help, technical advice, buying guides and cars & parts for sale.
Published by: Kelsey Publishing Ltd., Cudham Tithe Barn, Berry's Hill, Cudham, Kent TN16 3AG, United Kingdom. TEL 44-1959-541444, FAX 44-1959-541400, info@kelsey.co.uk. Ed. Paul Wager. Adv. contact Ian Hamilton TEL 44-1733-353353.

629.222 GBR ISSN 1474-1393
TOTAL VAUXHALL. Text in English. 2001. 13/yr. GBP 44.95 domestic; GBP 60 in Europe; GBP 85 elsewhere; GBP 4.25 newsstand/cover (effective 2010). adv. back issues avail. **Document type:** *Magazine, Consumer.* **Description:** Dedicated performance car magazine is the enthusiast's bible, featuring the best modified vauxhalls around, expert technical advice, step-by-step DIY guides and the last word in tuning and stylin.
Published by: Future Publishing Ltd., Beauford Ct, 30 Monmouth St, Bath, Avon BA1 2BW, United Kingdom. TEL 44-1225-442244, FAX 44-1225-446019, customerservice@subscription.co.uk, http://www.futureplc.com. Ed. Barton Brisland. Adv. contact Jame Hammond. **Subscr. to:** Tower House, Sovereign Park, Market Harborough, Leicestershire LE16 9EF, United Kingdom. TEL 44-844-8481602, FAX 44-1858-438795, future@subscription.co.uk.

▼ **TOTALLY MODIFIED**; ultimate magazine for car modifiers by modifiers. *see* HOBBIES

TOURING; auto et lois. *see* TRAVEL AND TOURISM

TOURING. *see* TRAVEL AND TOURISM

TOURING. *see* TRAVEL AND TOURISM

388.3 FRA ISSN 0995-2268
TOUT TERRAIN MAGAZINE. Text in French. 1989. m. (includes two special issues). adv. **Document type:** *Magazine, Consumer.*
Published by: Edireqie, 12 rue Rouget de Lisle, Issy-les-Moulineaux, Cedex 92442, France. TEL 33-1-41333761, FAX 33-1-41334767. Ed. Bruno Fischer. Pub. Frederic Noizat. Adv. contact Eric Lebon. Circ: 70,577 (paid).

388.3 FRA
TOUT TERRAIN MAGAZINE ACCESSOIRES 4 X 4. Key Title: Accessoires 4 x 4. Text in French. 1998. a. adv. **Document type:** *Magazine, Consumer.*
Published by: Edireqie, 12 rue Rouget de Lisle, Issy-les-Moulineaux, Cedex 92442, France. TEL 33-1-41333761, FAX 33-1-41334767. Ed. Bruno Fischer. Pub. Frederic Noizat. Adv. contact Eric Lebon. Circ: 37,650 (paid).

388.3 FRA
TOUT TERRAIN MAGAZINE LES 4 X 4 D'OCCASION. Key Title: Les 4 x 4 d'Occasion. Text in French. 2000. a. adv. **Document type:** *Magazine, Consumer.*
Published by: Edireqie, 12 rue Rouget de Lisle, Issy-les-Moulineaux, Cedex 92442, France. TEL 33-1-41333761, FAX 33-1-41334767. Ed. Bruno Fischer. Pub. Frederic Noizat. Adv. contact Eric Lebon. Circ: 32,200 (paid).

388.3 FRA
TOUT TERRAIN MAGAZINE TOUS LES 4 X 4 DU MARCHE. Key Title: Tous Les 4 x 4 du Marche. Text in French. 1995. a. adv. **Document type:** *Magazine, Consumer.*
Published by: Edireqie, 12 rue Rouget de Lisle, Issy-les-Moulineaux, Cedex 92442, France. TEL 33-1-41333761, FAX 33-1-41334767. Ed. Bruno Fischer. Pub. Frederic Noizat. Adv. contact Eric Lebon. Circ: 57,390 (paid).

388.3 CAN
TOW CANADA. Text in English. 1998. q. CAD 16; CAD 16 foreign (effective 1999). **Document type:** *Magazine, Trade.*
Published by: Automotive Retailers' Publishing Co. Ltd., 8980 Fraserwood Ct, Unit 1, Burnaby, BC V5J 5H7, Canada. TEL 604-432-7987, FAX 604-432-1756. Ed. Reg Romero. Circ: 4,800.

629.222 JPN ISSN 0287-3427
TOYODA GOSEI GIHO/TOYODA GOSEI TECHNICAL REPORTS. Text in Japanese; Contents page in English. 1959. s-a. **Document type:** *Corporate.*
Formerly (until 1973): Nagoya Gomu Giho/Rubber, Plastics & Corks (0287-3419)
Related titles: Online - full content ed.

Indexed: A28, APA, BrCerAb, C&ISA, CA/WCA, CIA, CerAb, CivEngAb, CorrAb, E&CAJ, E11, EEA, EMA, H15, M&TEA, M09, MBF, METADEX, SolStAb, T04, WAA.
—Linda Hall.
Published by: Toyoda Gosei Co., Ltd., 1 Nagahata, Ochiai, Haruhi, Nishikasugai, Aichi 452-8564, Japan. TEL 81-52-4001055.

363.7 JPN
TOYOTA; environmental programs and activities. Text in English. 1991. irreg. free. **Description:** Introduces Toyota's stance on environment protection and its current and future technology development.
Formerly: Toyota and the Environment
Published by: Toyota Motor Corporation, International Public Affairs Division, 1-4-18 Koraku, Bunkyo-ku, Tokyo, 112-0004, Japan. TEL 03-3817-9930, FAX 03-3817-9017. Circ: 30,000 (controlled).

629.286 JPN
TOYOTA AND AUTOMOTIVE ELECTRONICS. Text in English. 1987. irreg. free.
Formerly (until 1991): Toyota and Automotive Electronic
Published by: Toyota Motor Corporation, International Public Affairs Division, 1-4-18 Koraku, Bunkyo-ku, Tokyo, 112-0004, Japan. TEL 03-3817-9930, FAX 03-3817-9017. Circ: 10,000.

629.286 JPN
TOYOTA AND AUTOMOTIVE SAFETY. Text in English. 1991. irreg. free.
Published by: Toyota Motor Corporation, International Public Affairs Division, 1-4-18 Koraku, Bunkyo-ku, Tokyo, 112-0004, Japan. TEL 03-3817-9930, FAX 03-3817-9017. Circ: 12,000.

629.222 NLD ISSN 2210-3996
TOYOTA CELICA CLUB NEDERLAND. CLUBMAGAZINE. Text in Dutch. 1987. q.
Published by: Toyota Celica Club Nederland, Bandeliersberg 204, Roosendaal, 4707 SE, Netherlands. TEL 31-168-395929, secretaris@tccn.nl, http://www.tccn.nl. Ed. Arie Hitzert TEL 31-6-25031966.

629.286 JPN
TOYOTA ENGINE TECHNOLOGY. Text in English. 1989. irreg. free. **Description:** Introduces Toyota's current engine technology and the future direction of its development.
Published by: Toyota Motor Corporation, International Public Affairs Division, 1-4-18 Koraku, Bunkyo-ku, Tokyo, 112-0004, Japan. TEL 03-3817-9930, FAX 03-3817-9017. Circ: 20,000 (controlled).

629.222 JPN ISSN 0916-7501
CODEN: TYGJBT
TOYOTA GIJUTSU. Text in Japanese. 1953. s-a. **Description:** Introduces Toyota's technical properties to engineers in automotive industries.
Formerly (until 1991): Toyota Engineering (0385-8898)
Related titles: ◆ English ed.: Toyota Technical Review. ISSN 0917-3706.
—BLDSC (8873.265000), CASDDS, Ingenta.
Published by: Toyota Motor Corporation, International Public Affairs Division, 1-4-18 Koraku, Bunkyo-ku, Tokyo, 112-0004, Japan. FAX 03-3817-9017.

796.77 DEU
TOYOTA MAGAZIN. Text in German. 1999. 4/yr. adv. **Document type:** *Magazine, Consumer.*
Published by: T P D Medien GmbH, Nymphenburger Str 81, Munich, 80636, Germany. TEL 49-89-35759310, FAX 49-89-35759359, info@tpd.de, http://www.tpd.de. adv.: page EUR 7,950. Circ: 370,435 (controlled).

629.286 JPN
TOYOTA MOTOR CORPORATION. ANNUAL REPORT. Text in English. 1969. a. free. **Document type:** *Corporate.*
Published by: Toyota Motor Corporation, International Public Affairs Division, 1-4-18 Koraku, Bunkyo-ku, Tokyo, 112-0004, Japan. TEL 03-3817-9930, FAX 03-3817-9017. Circ: 40,000.

629.222 JPN ISSN 0917-3706
TL1 CODEN: TTEREB
TOYOTA TECHNICAL REVIEW. Text in English. 1991. s-a. **Description:** Introduces Toyota's technical properties to engineers in automotive industries.
Related titles: ◆ Japanese ed.: Toyota Gijutsu. ISSN 0916-7501.
—IE.
Published by: Toyota Motor Corporation, International Public Affairs Division, 1-4-18 Koraku, Bunkyo-ku, Tokyo, 112-0004, Japan. FAX 03-3817-9017. Ed. Hideo Hattori.

TRACK & RACE CARS. *see* SPORTS AND GAMES

388 659.1 GBR ISSN 0960-8885
TRADE-IT. Text in English. 1990. w. **Document type:** *Magazine, Trade.* **Description:** Carries ads for buying and selling cars.
Related titles: Online - full text ed.
Published by: Friday-Ad Ltd., London Rd, Sayers Common, W Sussex BN6 9HS, United Kingdom. TEL 44-1646-680720, support@friday-ad.co.uk, http://www.friday-ad.co.uk.

TRADITIONAL ROD & KULTURE ILLUSTRATED. *see* HOBBIES

388.3 SWE
TRAFIK & MOTOR. Text in Swedish. 1960. 6/yr. SEK 80 to members. adv. 44 p./no. 3 cols./p.; **Document type:** *Consumer.*
Published by: Foersvarets Motorklubb (F M K), Fack 323, Akersberga, 18424, Sweden. TEL 46-8-540-640-20, FAX 46-8-540-635-36. Ed. Johnny Hansson. Pub. Bo Stenson. Adv. contact Patrik Irmer. B&W page SEK 14,500, color page SEK 19,500; trim 265 x 185. Circ: 65,800.

388.3 SWE ISSN 0349-9790
TRAILER. Text in Swedish. 1980. 11/yr. SEK 379 for 8 nos. (effective 2010). adv. 84 p./no. 4 cols./p.; **Document type:** *Magazine, Consumer.*
Published by: Foerlags AB Albinsson & Sjoeberg, PO Box 529, Karlskrona, 37123, Sweden. TEL 46-455-335325, FAX 46-455-311715, fabas@fabas.se, http://www.fabas.se. Ed. Rutger Anderson. Adv. contact Martin Lindstroem. color page SEK 38,900; trim 190 x 275. Circ: 34,200 (controlled).

629.286 USA ISSN 0277-8300
TRANSMISSION DIGEST; the automotive powertrain industry journal. Text in English. 1981. m. USD 39 domestic; USD 48 in Canada; USD 81 elsewhere; USD 4.75 per issue (effective 2011). adv. back issues avail. **Document type:** *Journal, Trade.* **Description:** Covers the automatic and standard transmission rebuilding, repair and service aftermarket.
Related titles: Online - full text ed.: free (effective 2011).
Published by: M D Publications, Inc. (Springfield), 3057 E Cairo St, Springfield, MO 65802. TEL 417-866-3917, 800-274-7890, FAX 417-866-2781, http://www.mdpublications.com. Ed. Gary Sifford. Pub. Bobby Mace.

388 USA ISSN 1058-479X
TRANSMISSION TECH - TALK. Text in English. 198?. m. looseleaf. USD 89 domestic (effective 2011). adv. illus. **Document type:** *Newsletter, Trade.* **Description:** Covers technical troubleshooting, diagnosis and updates on automotive automatic transmissions in a complaint, cause and correction format.
Published by: M D Publications, Inc. (Springfield), 3057 E Cairo St, Springfield, MO 65802. TEL 417-866-3917, 800-274-7890, FAX 417-866-2781, http://www.mdpublications.com.

338.476 CAN ISSN 1923-1040
TRANSPORT ACTION ONTARIO. ONTARIO REPORT. Text in English. 1981. bi-m. free to members (effective 2011). back issues avail. **Document type:** *Newsletter, Trade.* **Description:** Promotes an integrated network of public transportation for Ontario for the movement of both passengers and freight.
Former titles (until 2010): Transport 2000 Ontario (1924-5297); (until 2008): Transport 2000 Ontario Report (1713-6539); (until 2004): Transport 2000 Ontario Newsletter (1195-7476); (until 1993): Transport 2000 Ontario. Newsletter (1199-1143)
Related titles: Online - full text ed.: ISSN 1923-1059. free (effective 2011).
Published by: Transport Action Ontario, Sta A, PO Box 6418, Toronto, ON M5W 1X3, Canada. TEL 416-504-3934, 866-542-1067, ontario@transport-action.ca. Ed. Tony Turrittin.

388.3 340 FRA ISSN 1951-8323
TRANSPORT ET TOURISME PAR AUTOCAR. Text in French. 1996. base vol. plus updates 3/yr. looseleaf. EUR 317 combined subscription Print & CD-ROM eds. (effective 2010). **Document type:** *Trade.*
Related titles: CD-ROM ed.: ISSN 1292-8194. EUR 317 (effective 2010); Online - full text ed.
Published by: Lamy S.A. (Subsidiary of: Wolters Kluwer France), 1 Rue Eugene et Armand Peugeot, Rueil-Malmaison, 92856 Cedex, France. TEL 33-1-76733000, FAX 33-1-76734809, lamy@lamy.fr.

388.3 URY
TRANSPORTE AUTOMOTOR. Text in Spanish. 1977. m.
Published by: Confederacion Uruguay del Transporte Automotor, Lima, 1423, Montevideo, 11813, Uruguay. Ed. Jose M Camano Abal.

629.113 ARG ISSN 1514-5255
TRANSPORTE MUNDIAL. Key Title: TM. Transporte Mundial Catalogo. Text in Spanish. 1999. s-a. ARS 10.50 newsstand/cover (effective 2010). **Document type:** *Magazine, Trade.*
Related titles: ◆ Supplement(s): TM. Transporte Mundial. Catalogo Especial. ISSN 1666-0617.
Published by: Motorpress Argentina, S.A. (Subsidiary of: Gruner + Jahr AG & Co), Ituzaingo, 642-648, Buenos Aires, 1141, Argentina. TEL 54-114-3077672, FAX 54-114-3077858, http://www.motorpress.com.ar/.

TRANSPORTNYTT. *see* TRANSPORTATION—Ships And Shipping

388 HUN ISSN 1217-9582
TRANSZPORT. Text in Hungarian. 1994. q. 16 p./no.; **Document type:** *Magazine, Consumer.*
Related titles: ◆ Supplement to: auto Magazin. ISSN 0864-8492.
Published by: Motor-Presse Budapest Lapkiado kft, Hajogyari-sziget 307, Budapest, 1033, Hungary. TEL 36-1-4369244, FAX 36-1-4369248, mpb@motorpresse.hu, http://www.motorpresse.hu. Pub. Dietmar Metzger. Adv. contact Andrea Poz. **Dist. by:** Lapker Rt, 1097 Tablas utca, Budapest, Hungary.

629.286 ESP ISSN 1888-4512
TRAVESIA. Text in Spanish. 2004. m. **Document type:** *Magazine, Trade.*
Published by: Etrasa Editorial Trafico Vial, S.A. (Subsidiary of: Springer Science+Business Media), Puerto de Navacerrada, 128, Poligono Industrial Las Nieves, Mostoles, 28935, Spain. TEL 34-91-6658000, FAX 34-91-6658009, http://www.etrasa.com.

338 USA ISSN 1069-2274
TREND SETTER. Text in English. 1980. bi-m. USD 28; USD 36 in Canada; USD 48 elsewhere. adv. **Document type:** *Magazine, Trade.*
Published by: Kustom Kemps of America, 26 Main St, Cassville, MO 65625-9400. Ed. L Cecetka. R&P Jerry E Titus. Adv. contact Devona Titus. Circ: 4,400 (paid).

388 GBR ISSN 1357-4248
TRIUMPH WORLD. Text in English. 1995. m. GBP 42 domestic; GBP 47.40 in Europe; GBP 53.40 elsewhere; GBP 3.85 per issue domestic; GBP 4.85 per issue in Europe; GBP 5.35 per issue elsewhere (effective 2010). adv. back issues avail. **Document type:** *Magazine, Consumer.* **Description:** Focuses on the news stand dedicated to all standard-triumph cars.
Related titles: Online - full text ed.
Published by: Kelsey Publishers Group, Cudham Tithe Barn, Berry's Hill, Cudham, Kent TN16 3AG, United Kingdom. TEL 44-1959-541444, FAX 44-1959-541400, info@kelsey.co.uk, http://www.kelsey.co.uk. Ed. Simon Goldsworthy. Adv. contact Madeleine Lillywhite.

629.222 388.324 USA ISSN 2151-0547
TRUCK, RACE, CYCLE AND REC. MARKETPLACE. Variant title: AutoTrader Classics Truck, Race Cycle and Rec. Marketplace. Text in English. 1983. m. USD 22.95 domestic; USD 45.95 in Canada; USD 87.95 elsewhere (effective 2009). adv. **Document type:** *Magazine, Trade.* **Description:** Contains information on range of vehicles for sale, including trucks, SUVs, race cars, motorcycles, recreational vehicles, monster trucks, trailers, repairable vehicles, and parts and services.
Published by: AutoTrader Classics, 5775 Peachtree-Dunwoody Rd, Ste A-100, Atlanta, GA 30342. TEL 800-548-8889. Adv. contact Debbie Reetz TEL 404-568-8383. color page USD 3,175; trim 7.375 x 10.625. Circ: 1,361 (paid).

629.35 CZE ISSN 1212-334X
TRUCKSALON. Text in Czech. 1998. a. adv. **Document type:** *Magazine, Consumer.*
Published by: Axel Springer Praha a.s., Rosmarin Business Center, Dilnicka 12, Prague 7, 17000, Czech Republic. TEL 420-2-34692111, FAX 420-2-34692102, http://www.axelspringer.cz.

629.222 367 USA
TUCKER TOPICS. Text in English. 1948. m. USD 25 domestic; USD 40 foreign (effective 2001). adv. back issues avail. **Document type:** *Newsletter.* **Description:** Presents original and reprinted articles relating to Preston Tucker, the Tucker Corporation, Tucker automobiles, and automobiles in general.
Published by: Tucker Automobile Club of America, Inc., 9509 Hinton Dr., Santee, CA 92071. TEL 619-596-3028, FAX 866-728-8895, tuckerclub@home.com, http://www.tuckerclub.org. Adv. contact William E. Pommering. Circ: 450 (paid).

629.2 NOR ISSN 1504-0534
TUNGVEKTER'N. Text in Norwegian. 199?. bi-m. **Document type:** *Magazine, Consumer.*
Published by: Transporthistorisk Forening, PO Box 915, Drammen, 3002, Norway. TEL 47-63-903273, thf@lmk.no, http://www.thf.lmk.no. Ed. Jan-Willy Solberg.

796.77 DEU ISSN 0936-1383
TUNING; Autotechnik und Design. Text in German. 1987. bi-m. EUR 19.20 domestic; EUR 28.60 foreign; EUR 3.50 newsstand/cover (effective 2011). adv. **Document type:** *Magazine, Consumer.* **Description:** Contains articles and features on a wide variety of automobiles.
Published by: Delius Klasing Verlag GmbH, Siekerwall 21, Bielefeld, 33602, Germany. TEL 49-521-5590, FAX 49-521-559113, info@delius-klasing.de, http://www.delius-klasing.de. Ed. Sven Alisch. Adv. contact Sigrid Pinke.

TUNING & CAR AUDIO. *see* ELECTRONICS

629.286 ITA ISSN 1824-3428
TUNING GENERATION. Text in Italian. 2004. bi-m. EUR 19.90 (effective 2009). **Document type:** *Magazine, Consumer.*
Published by: Sprea Editori Srl, Via Torino 51, Cernusco sul Naviglio, MI 20063, Italy. TEL 39-02-92432222, FAX 39-02-92432236, editori@sprea.it, http://www.sprea.it.

796.77 DEU
TUNING SCENE LIVE. Text in German. 2004. m. adv. **Document type:** *Magazine, Consumer.*
Published by: Vestische Mediengruppe Welke GmbH & Co. KG, Hertener Mark 7, Herten, 45699, Germany. TEL 49-2366-808400, FAX 49-2366-808499, info@vmw-verlag.de, http://vmw-verlag.de.

656.1 CHE ISSN 1661-6553
TUNINGGUIDE.CH. Text in German. 2006. a. CHF 6.90 newsstand/cover (effective 2007). **Document type:** *Magazine, Consumer.*
Published by: Forcar GmbH, Churerstr 154, Pfaeffikon, 8808, Switzerland. TEL 41-55-4155100, FAX 41-55-4155109, info@forcar.ch, http://www.forcar.ch.

388 FIN ISSN 1795-0546
TURBO. Text in Finnish. 2004. q. adv. **Document type:** *Magazine, Consumer.* **Description:** All about used cars.
Published by: A-Lehdet Oy, Risto Rytin tie 33, Helsinki, 00081, Finland. TEL 358-9-75961, FAX 358-9-7598600, a-tilaus@a-lehdet.fi. Ed. Lauri Larmela. Adv. contact Matti Sahravuo TEL 358-9-7596385. color page EUR 6,235; 192 x 254.

796.7 PRT ISSN 0874-0534
TURBO. Text in Portuguese. 1981. m. EUR 24; EUR 3.20 newsstand/cover (effective 2007). adv. **Document type:** *Magazine, Consumer.*
Published by: Edimpresa Editora Lda., Rua Calvet de Magalhaes 242, Laveiras, Paco de Arcos, 2770-022, Portugal. TEL 351-21-4698000, FAX 351-21-4698501, edimpresa@edimpresa.pt, http://www.edimpresa.pt. Ed. Henrique Sequerra. adv.: page EUR 4,750; trim 230 x 297. Circ: 21,059 (paid).

388.3 USA ISSN 0894-5039
TL1
TURBO & HIGH TECH PERFORMANCE. (Formerly published by (until 2007): Primedia Enthusiast Media) Text in English. 1985. m. USD 27.97 domestic; USD 40.97 in Canada; USD 42.97 elsewhere (effective 2008). adv. 132 p./no.; back issues avail.; reprints avail. **Document type:** *Magazine, Consumer.* **Description:** Designed for knowledgeable enthusiasts who want to wring every last horsepower, squeeze every last G out of their high-performance imports.
Formerly: Turbo
Indexed: A10, V03.
—CCC.
Published by: Source Interlink Companies, 2400 E Katella Ave, 11th Fl, Anaheim, CA 92806. TEL 714-939-2400, FAX 714-978-6390, dheine@sourceinterlink.com, http://www.sourceinterlink.com. Eds. Evan Griffey, Scott Tsuneishi. Pub. Howard Lim. adv.: B&W page USD 5,475, color page USD 6,690. Circ: 16,521 (paid).

388.3 USA
TURBOZINE. Text in English. w.
Media: Online - full content.
Indexed: SpeleolAb.
Published by: Intrigue HTML Design joeg@magicnet.net, http://www.magicnet.net/~joeg/turbo_mag. Ed. Joe Gallagher.

388.342 956.1 GBR ISSN 1749-0227
TURKEY AUTOS REPORT. Text in English. 2005. q. EUR 820, USD 1,030 combined subscription (print & email eds.) (effective 2010). **Document type:** *Report, Trade.* **Description:** Provides industry professionals and strategists, corporate analysts, auto associations, government departments and regulatory bodies with independent forecasts and competitive intelligence on the Turkish automotives market.
Related titles: E-mail ed.
Indexed: A15, ABIn, B02, B15, B17, B18, G04, I05, P48, P51, P52, PQC.
Published by: Business Monitor International Ltd., Senator House, 85 Queen Victoria St, London, EC4V 4AB, United Kingdom. TEL 44-20-72480468, FAX 44-20-72480467, subs@businessmonitor.com.

388 388.324 USA ISSN 1052-3251
TURNING WHEELS. Text in English. 1968. m. USD 27.50 (effective 2000). adv. bk.rev.; film rev. cum.index. back issues avail. **Description:** Provides articles on the history, restoration, maintenance, and current happenings concerning Studebaker cars, trucks and buggies manufactured from 1852 to 1966.
Published by: Studebaker Drivers Club, Inc., PO Box 1040, Oswego, IL 60543. TEL 800-527-3452, FAX 209-634-2163. Ed., Adv. contact Linda Fox. Pub. Laurence Swanson. Circ: 12,800 (paid).

629.286 ITA ISSN 1971-0240
TUTTO TUNING. Text in Italian. 2006. 3/yr. **Document type:** *Magazine, Consumer.*
Published by: Eurosport Editoriale, Via della Bufalotta 378, Rome, 00139, Italy. TEL 39-06-45231508, FAX 39-06-45231599, info@eurosporteditoriale.com, http://www.eurosporteditoriale.com.

388.3 ITA
TUTTOFUORISTRADA OSSERVATORE MOTORISTICO. Text in Italian. 1975. 10/yr. EUR 28 (effective 2009). adv. 100 p./no.; **Document type:** *Magazine, Consumer.*
Formerly: Osservatore Motoristico
Published by: Free Wheels Srl, Via XXV Aprile, 99, Peschiera Borromeo, MI 20068, Italy. redazione@tuttofuoristrada.it.

TWO-LANE ROADS; a nostalgic backroad adventure. *see* TRAVEL AND TOURISM

388.3 AUS
TWOWHEELS SCOOTER. Text in English. s-a. AUD 33 domestic; AUD 52.50 in New Zealand; AUD 75 elsewhere (effective 2008). adv. **Document type:** *Magazine, Consumer.* **Description:** Covers the wide variety of machines and the freedom-loving people who ride scooters. Brings out the fun, the freedom and pure joy of riding a scooter.
Published by: News Magazines Pty Ltd., Level 3, 2 Holt St, Surry Hills, NSW 2010, Australia. TEL 61-2-92883000, subscriptions@newsmagazines.com.au, http://www.newsspace.com.au/magazines. Ed. Jeremy Bowdler. Adv. contact Luke Finn TEL 61-2-80622738. color page AUD 2,000; trim 276 x 412.

THE TYRE AND RIM ASSOCIATION OF AUSTRALIA STANDARDS MANUAL. *see* RUBBER

678.32 640.73 GBR
TYRES-ONLINE. Text in English. 1996. irreg. free (effective 2009). adv. **Document type:** *Magazine, Consumer.* **Description:** Provides information and reviews on tire products, manufacturers and dealers.
Media: Online - full content.
Published by: Retreading Business Ltd, PO Box 320, Crewe, Cheshire CW2 6WY, United Kingdom. TEL 44-1270-668718, FAX 44-1270-668801, retreadingbusiness@btconnect.com. Ed., Pub. David Wilson.

388.3 NLD ISSN 1873-037X
TYREZONE. Text in Dutch. 2003. s-a. EUR 8; EUR 4.95 newsstand/cover (effective 2008). adv. **Document type:** *Magazine, Consumer.*
Published by: (Profile International N.V.), FK Media b.v., Gouverneurlaan 4, Postbus 155, Weert, 6000 AD, Netherlands. TEL 31-495-450105, FAX 31-495-539485, info@efka-uitgevers.nl. adv.: color page EUR 2,500; trim 230 x 297. Circ: 75,000.

UIT; het V T B - V A B magazine. *see* TRAVEL AND TOURISM

629.222 GBR ISSN 1470-4528
THE UK MOTOR INDUSTRY DIRECTORY (YEAR). Abbreviated title: M I D. Text in English. 1980. a. free to members (effective 2010). **Document type:** *Directory.* **Description:** Provides information about the companies and organisations that make up the UK automotive industry covering all aspects of the industry from design and development of vehicles and components through to their production, after-sales, servicing as well as disposal and recycling.
Former titles (until 1999): Motor Industry Directory (1363-6782); (until 1996): U K Suppliers Directory (1364-6877); (until 1995): Buyers' Guide to the Motor Industry of Great Britain
Published by: Society of Motor Manufacturers and Traders Ltd., Forbes House, Halkin St, London, SW1X 7DS, United Kingdom. TEL 44-20-72357000, FAX 44-20-2357112, http://www.smmt.co.uk.

388.342 947.7 GBR ISSN 1749-0235
UKRAINE AUTOS REPORT. Text in English. 2005. q. EUR 820, USD 1,030 combined subscription (print & email eds.) (effective 2010). **Document type:** *Report, Trade.* **Description:** Provides industry professionals and strategists, corporate analysts, auto associations, government departments and regulatory bodies with independent forecasts and competitive intelligence on the automotives industry in Ukraine.
Related titles: E-mail ed.; Online - full text ed.
Indexed: A15, ABIn, B02, B15, B17, B18, G04, I05, P48, P51, P52, PQC.
Published by: Business Monitor International Ltd., Senator House, 85 Queen Victoria St, London, EC4V 4AB, United Kingdom. TEL 44-20-72480468, FAX 44-20-72480467, subs@businessmonitor.com.

THE ULTIMATE CAR BOOK (YEAR); an indispensable guide to the safest, most economical new cars. *see* CONSUMER EDUCATION AND PROTECTION

629.22 GBR ISSN 1740-7028
ULTRA V W. (Volks World) Text in English. 2003. m. GBP 37 domestic; GBP 48 in Europe; GBP 70 elsewhere; GBP 3.99 per issue domestic; GBP 5 per issue in Europe; GBP 6.50 per issue elsewhere (effective 2009). adv. back issues avail. **Document type:** *Magazine, Consumer.* **Description:** Contains reports on news and trends about ultra high-performance cars.
Published by: C H Publications Ltd., Nimax House, 20 Ullswater Cresent, Ullswater Business Park, Coulsdon, Surrey CR5 2HR, United Kingdom. TEL 44-20-86556400, FAX 44-20-87631001, chp@chpltd.com, http://www.chpltd.com. Ed. Paul Knight.

629.286 USA ISSN 0893-6943
UNDERCAR DIGEST. Text in English. 1976. m. USD 39 domestic; USD 48 in Canada; USD 81 elsewhere; USD 4.75 per issue (effective 2011). adv. bk.rev. charts; illus.; tr.lit. back issues avail. **Document type:** *Magazine, Trade.* **Description:** Covers the undercar repair and service aftermarket including exhaust, ride control, chassis alignment and brakes.
Formerly (until 1987): Muffler Digest (0164-6044)
Related titles: Online - full text ed.: free (effective 2011).
Published by: M D Publications, Inc. (Springfield) http://www.mdpublications.com. Eds. Gary Sifford, Jim Wilder.

388.3 AUS ISSN 1446-5353
UNDERCAR REVIEW. Text in English. 2001. bi-m. AUD 66 domestic; AUD 80 in New Zealand; AUD 100 elsewhere; AUD 22 per issue domestic (effective 2008). adv. **Document type:** *Magazine, Trade.* **Description:** Provides the latest information on automotive industry.
Formed by the merger of (1989-2001): Brake & Suspension (1034-3083); (1984-2001): Exhaust & Undercar (1030-2077); Which was formerly (until 1987): Exhaust (1030-2069)
Published by: (Exhaust Systems Professional Association), Auto Media Pty. Ltd., PO Box 303, Fairy Meadow, NSW 2519, Australia. TEL 61-2-42832500, FAX 61-2-42832737, noelwynn@ozemail.com.au, http://www.automedia.com.au/. adv.: B&W page AUD 1,323, color page AUD 1,985; trim 210 x 270. Circ: 3,000 (controlled).

629.286 USA ISSN 1079-6177
TL153
UNDERHOOD SERVICE. Text in English. 1995. m. free domestic to qualified personnel (effective 2008). adv. back issues avail. **Document type:** *Magazine, Trade.* **Description:** Addresses various things under the hoods of cars and light trucks such as electronics, cooling systems, air conditioning, emissions controls, fuel systems, ignition, internal engine repair and electrical/charging systems.
Related titles: Online - full text ed.
Indexed: A26, B02, B15, B17, B18, G04, G08, I05, P16, P48, P52, P53, P54, PQC.
Published by: Babcox Publications, Inc., 3550 Embassy Pky, Akron, OH 44333. TEL 330-670-1234, FAX 330-670-0874, bbabcox@babcox.com, http://www.babcox.com. Ed. Edward Sunkin. Pub. Jeff Stankard TEL 330-670-1234 ext 282. adv.: B&W page USD 5,335. Circ: 39,380 (paid).

388.3 AUS ISSN 1449-6682
UNIQUE CARS. Text in English. 1985. 13/yr. AUD 75 in Australia & New Zealand; AUD 93.50 elsewhere; AUD 7.95 newsstand/cover (effective 2008). adv. **Document type:** *Magazine, Consumer.* **Description:** Provides information on Australia's finest vintage, classic, sports, modified and luxury cars.
Formerly (until 1987): Unique Cars Magazine
Published by: A C P Trader International Group (Subsidiary of: P B L Media Pty Ltd.), 73 Atherton Rd, Oakleigh, VIC 3166, Australia. TEL 61-3-95674200, FAX 61-3-95634554. Eds. Chris Fincham TEL 61-3-95674171, Greg Leech TEL 61-3-95674194. Adv. contact Justine Schuller. color page AUD 3,450; trim 195 x 275. Circ: 61,007. **Subscr. to:** Magshop, Reply Paid 4967, Sydney, NSW 2001, Australia. TEL 61-2-136116, subs@magstore.com.au, http://shop.magstore.com.au.

338.342 953.57 GBR ISSN 1749-0243
UNITED ARAB EMIRATES AUTOS REPORT. Text in English. 2005. q. EUR 820, USD 1,030 combined subscription (print & email eds.) (effective 2010). **Document type:** *Report, Trade.* **Description:** Covers independent forecasts and competitive intelligence on the automotives industry in the UAE.
Related titles: E-mail ed.; Online - full text ed.
Indexed: A15, ABIn, B02, B15, B17, B18, G04, I05, P48, P51, P52, PQC.
Published by: Business Monitor International Ltd., Senator House, 85 Queen Victoria St, London, EC4V 4AB, United Kingdom. TEL 44-20-72480468, FAX 44-20-72480467, subs@businessmonitor.com.

388.342 941 GBR ISSN 1749-0251
UNITED KINGDOM AUTOS REPORT. Variant title: U K Autos Report. Text in English. 2005. q. EUR 820, USD 1,030 combined subscription (print & email eds.) (effective 2010). **Document type:** *Report, Trade.* **Description:** Covers independent forecasts and competitive intelligence on the automotives industry in UK.
Related titles: E-mail ed.; Online - full text ed.
Indexed: A15, ABIn, B01, B02, B15, B17, B18, G04, I05, P48, P51, P52, PQC.
Published by: Business Monitor International Ltd., Senator House, 85 Queen Victoria St, London, EC4V 4AB, United Kingdom. TEL 44-20-72480468, FAX 44-20-72480467, subs@businessmonitor.com.

338.342 973 GBR ISSN 1749-026X
UNITED STATES AUTOS REPORTS. Text in English. 2005. q. EUR 820, USD 1,030 combined subscription (print & email eds.) (effective 2010). **Document type:** *Report, Trade.* **Description:** Covers independent forecasts and competitive intelligence on the automotives industry in the US.
Related titles: E-mail ed.; Online - full text ed.
Indexed: B01, P34.
Published by: Business Monitor International Ltd., Senator House, 85 Queen Victoria St, London, EC4V 4AB, United Kingdom. TEL 44-20-72480468, FAX 44-20-72480467, subs@businessmonitor.com.

388.3 IND ISSN 0500-6813
THE UPPER INDIA MOTORIST. Text in English. 1954. m. INR 20 newsstand/cover to non-members; free to members (effective 2011). back issues avail. **Document type:** *Magazine, Consumer.* **Description:** Contains information relating to road safety, developments in automobiles and environment air pollution.
Published by: Automobile Association of Upper India, C-8 Institutional Area, Behind Qutab Hotel, New Delhi, 110 016, India. TEL 91-11-26965397, FAX 91-11-26857304, aauindia@airtelmail.in. Ed., Pub. T K Malhotra.

388.3 GBR ISSN 1461-1686
USED CAR BUYER. Text in English. 1998. m. GBP 20 (effective 2000). **Document type:** *Magazine, Consumer.*
Published by: The/Realty Motoring Group Ltd., Winchester Court, 1 Forum Place, Hatfield, Herts, AL10 0RN, United Kingdom. TEL 01707-273999, FAX 01707-276555, mike@trmg.co.uk. Ed. Mike Penny. Pub. Ian Wearing.

388.3 USA ISSN 0279-425X
USED CAR DEALER. Text in English. 1981. m. free to members; USD 60 to non-members (effective 2005). adv. charts; illus.; stat. **Document type:** *Magazine, Trade.* **Description:** Covers items of interest to the used car dealer industry, including profit centers and legislative issues.
Published by: National Independent Automobile Dealers Association, 2521 Brown Blvd, Ste 100, Arlington, TX 76006-5203. TEL 817-640-3838, FAX 817-649-2377. Ed. Darrin Scheid. Pub. Michael R Lynn. adv.: page USD 1,642, color page USD 2,392. Circ: 19,000 (paid).

629.23105 NZL ISSN 1178-4229
USED CAR SAFETY RATINGS (ONLINE). Text in English. irreg. **Document type:** *Monographic series, Trade.*
Media: Online - full text.
Published by: New Zealand Transport Agency, Lambton Quay, PO Box 5084, Wellington, 6145, New Zealand. TEL 64-4-8945200, FAX 64-4-8943305, info@nzta.govt.nz, http://www.nzta.govt.nz/.

388.3 USA
USED CARS. Text in English. 1993. q. USD 18 in United States; USD 22 in Canada & Mexico; USD 28 elsewhere (effective 2000). back issues avail. **Document type:** *Magazine, Consumer.* **Description:** Lists US prices of cars, vans, light trucks for ten years. Contains editorial and consumer information and articles.
Published by: V M R International, Inc., 607, North Grafton, MA 01536-0607. TEL 508-839-6707, FAX 508-839-6266, http://www.vmrintl.com. Ed., Pub., R&P John Iafolla. Circ: 28,000 (paid). **Dist. by:** I C D - Hearst, 250 W 55th St, New York, NY 10019. TEL 212-649-4465.

V 8 BATHURST MAGAZINE. *see* SPORTS AND GAMES

388.3 FIN ISSN 0355-4295
V M. (Vauhdin Maailma) Key Title: VM. Vauhdin Maailma. Text in Finnish. 1965. 14/yr. EUR 61.20 (effective 2005). adv. **Document type:** *Magazine, Consumer.* **Description:** Devoted to motor sports in Finland.
Related titles: Online - full text ed.
Published by: Yhtyneet Kuvalehdet Oy/United Magazines Ltd., Maistraatinportti 1, Helsinki, 00015, Finland. TEL 358-9-15661, FAX 358-9-145650, http://www.kuvalehdet.fi. Ed. Peter Geitel. adv.: color page EUR 2,300; trim 280 x 217. Circ: 32,903.

629.222 USA ISSN 1069-8779
V M R STANDARD USED CAR PRICES. Text in English. 1993. 6/yr. USD 22 (effective 2002). back issues avail. **Document type:** *Magazine, Consumer.* **Description:** Lists U.S. prices of cars, vans, and light trucks for the past 14 years.
—CCC.
Published by: V M R International, Inc., 607, North Grafton, MA 01536-0607. TEL 508-839-6707, FAX 508-839-6266, http://www.vmrintl.com. Ed., Pub., R&P John Iafolla. Circ: 28,000 (paid). **Dist. by:** I C D - Hearst, 250 W 55th St, New York, NY 10019. TEL 212-649-4465.

796.7 USA
THE V W AUTOIST. (Volkswagen) Text in English. 1955. bi-m. USD 15; USD 21 foreign (effective 1999). adv. illus.; stat. back issues avail. **Document type:** *Newsletter.* **Description:** For owners and enthusiasts of Volkswagen and Audi automobiles.
Published by: Volkswagen Club of America, PO Box 154, N Aurora, IL 60542-0154. TEL 603-896-2803. Ed., R&P Fred Ortlip TEL 314-821-9091. Adv. contact Shell Tomlin. B&W page USD 88; trim 6.44 x 6.31. Circ: 2,500.

796.77 DEU
▼ **V W CLASSIC**; Magazin fuer historische Volkswagen. (Volkswagen) Text in German. 2010 (Nov.). 2/yr. EUR 5.50 newsstand/cover (effective 2011). adv. **Document type:** *Magazine, Consumer.*
Related titles: ◆ Supplement to: Gute Fahrt. ISSN 0017-5765.
Published by: Delius Klasing Verlag GmbH, Siekerwall 21, Bielefeld, 33602, Germany. TEL 49-521-5590, FAX 49-521-559113, info@delius-klasing.de, http://www.delius-klasing.de. Ed. Thomas Fuths. Adv. contact Sigrid Pinke. Circ: 120,000 (controlled).

629.222 GBR ISSN 1751-4770
V W GOLF PLUS. (Volkswagen) Text in English. 1995. m. GBP 47.28 domestic; GBP 52.80 in Europe; GBP 58.32 elsewhere; GBP 4.30 per issue domestic; GBP 5.30 per issue in Europe; GBP 5.80 per issue elsewhere (effective 2010). back issues avail. **Document type:** *Magazine, Consumer.* **Description:** Features information about VW Golfs, featuring the coolest cars, technical advice and content about the VW scene and its people.
Former titles (until 2006): The Golf Plus (1751-4762); (until 2004): Golf (1359-4982)
Published by: Kelsey Publishing Ltd., PO Box 978, Peterborough, PE1 1JA, United Kingdom. TEL 44-1959-541444, FAX 44-1959-541400, info@kelsey.co.uk, http://www.kelsey.co.uk. Eds. Ian Cushway, Phil Weeden. Adv. contact Gavin Williams. **Subscr. to:** PO Box 13, Westerham, Kent TN16 3WT, United Kingdom. TEL 44-1959-543530.

796.77 DEU ISSN 0942-3257
V W SCENE INTERNATIONAL. Variant title: Volkswagen Scene International. Text in German. 1989. m. EUR 42 domestic; EUR 48 foreign; EUR 3.80 newsstand/cover (effective 2011). adv. **Document type:** *Magazine, Consumer.* **Description:** Covers all aspects of owning and driving Volkswagen automobiles.
Published by: Vestische Mediengruppe Welke GmbH & Co. KG, Hertener Mark 7, Herten, 45699, Germany. TEL 49-2366-808400, FAX 49-2366-808499, info@vmw-verlag.de, http://vmw-verlag.de. Ed. Rudolf Welke. Pub. Arno Welke. Adv. contact Julia Wissing. Circ: 33,272 (paid and controlled).

388.3 DEU ISSN 1433-4542
V W SPEED; Magazin fuer Volkswagen-Fans. (Volkswagen) Text in German. 1995. m. EUR 39.50 domestic; EUR 53.40 Austria & Switzerland; EUR 57 elsewhere; EUR 3.80 newsstand/cover (effective 2011). adv. **Document type:** *Magazine, Consumer.*
Related titles: Online - full text ed.; Supplement(s): Kaefer Revue. 2004. EUR 4.90 newsstand/cover (effective 2011).
—CCC.
Published by: Delius Klasing Verlag GmbH, Siekerwall 21, Bielefeld, 33602, Germany. TEL 49-521-5590, FAX 49-521-559113, info@delius-klasing.de, http://www.delius-klasing.de. Ed. Joachim Fischer. Adv. contact Sigrid Pinke.

796.72 FIN ISSN 0780-2102
V8 - MAGAZINE. Text in Finnish. 1978. 10/yr. EUR 69 (effective 2009). adv. **Document type:** *Magazine, Consumer.* **Description:** Contains technological secrets and distributes useful information on American cars.
Formerly: Street and Race (0782-4033)
Published by: Sanoma Magazines Finland Corporation, Lapinmaentie 1, Helsinki, 00350, Finland. TEL 358-9-1201, FAX 358-9-1205171, info@sanomamagazines.fi, http://www.sanomamagazines.fi. Circ: 31,388 (paid and controlled).

388 GBR ISSN 0269-1825
VAN USER. Text in English. 1985. m. GBP 22.50 domestic; free to qualified personnel (effective 2009). adv. tr.lit. 4 cols./p.; back issues avail. **Document type:** *Magazine, Trade.* **Description:** Provides constantly updated sources of information.
Published by: Countrywide Publications, 27 Norwich Rd, Halesworth, Suffolk IP19 8BX, United Kingdom. TEL 44-1986-834250, info@micropress.co.uk. Ed. Dan Gilkes TEL 44-1284-788388. Adv. contact Jo Leverett TEL 44-1986-834253.

388.3 620 GBR ISSN 1479-7747
VEHICLE DYNAMICS INTERNATIONAL. Text in English. 2003. q. free (effective 2009). adv. back issues avail. **Document type:** *Magazine, Trade.* **Description:** Covers the latest news, technologies and developments relating to suspension, chassis engineering, stability and traction controls, steering, braking, ride, handling and corner module engineering.
Related titles: Online - full text ed.
—CCC.
Published by: U K & International Press (Subsidiary of: AutoIntermediates Ltd.), Abinger House, Church St, Dorking, Surrey RH4 1DF, United Kingdom. TEL 44-1306-743744, FAX 44-1306-887546, info@ukintpress.com, http://www.ukipme.com. Ed. Graham Heeps. Adv. contact Rob Hughes.

388.3 330 USA
VEHICLE LEASING TODAY. Text in English. 1981. bi-m. USD 39; USD 50 foreign. adv. **Document type:** *Magazine, Trade.* **Description:** Covers issues affecting the leasing of consumer and commercial vehicles.
Published by: National Vehicle Leasing Association, PO Box 281230, San Francisco, CA 94128-1230. TEL 650-548-9135, FAX 650-548-9155. Ed. Rod Couts. Adv. contact Judy Flanagan. Circ: 3,000.

629 USA ISSN 1948-4674
▼ **VEHICLE M D**; a driver's guide to maintaining a healthy car. (Medical Doctor) Text in English. 2009. q. free (effective 2009). **Document type:** *Magazine, Consumer.* **Description:** Features information about common services offered at most automotive maintenance and repair facilities.
Related titles: Online - full text ed.
Published by: National Oil & Lube News, Inc., 4418 74th St, Ste 66, Lubbock, TX 79424. TEL 806-762-4464, garrett.mckinnon@noln.net, http://www.noln.net/.

VEHICLE RECOVERY LINK. *see* TRANSPORTATION—Trucks And Trucking

388.3 USA
VEHICLE REMARKETING. Text in English. 1984. bi-m. free to qualified personnel (effective 2006). adv. back issues avail. **Document type:** *Magazine, Trade.* **Description:** Covers and reports the automotive needs of the remarketing industry, that includes fleet management companies, retail lessors, auto manufacturers and captive finance companies, banks and daily retail companies.
Media: Online - full content.
Published by: Bobit Business Media, 3520 Challenger St, Torrance, CA 90503. TEL 310-533-2400, FAX 310-533-2500, order@bobit.com, http://www.bobit.com. Ed. Mike Antich. Circ: 2,000 (paid and controlled).

338 629.2 GBR ISSN 1362-7171
➤ **VEHICLE TECHNOLOGY.** Text in English. 1974. q. free to members (effective 2009). adv. bk.rev. illus.; pat.; abstr. 36 p./no.; back issues avail. **Document type:** *Journal, Academic/Scholarly.* **Description:** Provides articles on the OEM sector of the automotive industry. Covers new developments, trends, and safety issues within the industry. Includes IVEHE members' news.
Former titles (until Mar.1996): I B C A M Journal (1360-3663); (until 1990): News from I B C A M; I B C A M Journal (0306-2910); Supersedes: Institute of British Carriage and Automobile Manufacturers. Institute Bulletin
Related titles: CD-ROM ed.; Online - full text ed.: free (effective 2009).
Published by: S A E International, PO Box 13312, Birmingham, B28 1BG, United Kingdom. TEL 44-121-2706592, FAX 44-121-2706596, info@sae-uk.org, http://www.sae-uk.org. Ed. Anthony Mc Donagh-Smith. Adv. contact Jonathan Masding. page GBP 1,000; 210 x 297.

➤ **VEHICLE THERMAL MANAGEMENT SYSTEMS CONFERENCE PROCEEDINGS.** *see* ENGINEERING—Engineering Mechanics And Materials

388.3 ITA ISSN 1824-548X
I VEICOLI: PROFILI AMMINSTRATIVI. Text in Italian. 2003. m. **Document type:** *Magazine, Trade.*
Related titles: CD-ROM ed.: ISSN 1824-5498. 2004; Online - full text ed.: ISSN 1826-879X.
Published by: Edizioni Giuridico Amministrative e Formazione (E G A F), Via Filippo Guarini 2, Forli, 47100, Italy. TEL 39-0543-473347, FAX 39-0543-474133, gruppo@egaf.it, http://www.egaf.it.

388 PRT
VEICULOS COMERCIAIS. Text in Portuguese. 1992. q. EUR 4 newsstand/cover (effective 2005). adv. **Document type:** *Magazine, Consumer.*
Formerly (until 2000): Guia dos Comerciais
Published by: Motorpress Lisboa, SA (Subsidiary of: Gruner + Jahr AG & Co), Rua Policarpio Anjos No. 4, Cruz Quebrada, Dafundo 1495-742, Portugal. TEL 351-21-4154500, FAX 351-21-4154501, buzine@motorpress.pt, http://www.mpl.pt. Circ: 14,310 (paid).

796.72 ARG ISSN 0049-5913
VELOCIDAD. Text in Spanish. 1950. bi-m.
Address: Avda. Belgrano, 1735, Buenos Aires, 1093, Argentina. Ed. Gilberto Julian Riega.

388.3 USA
VELOCITY (MARINA DEL REY); journal of the honda-acura club. Text in English. 2000. q. USD 35; USD 3.95 newsstand/cover (effective 2001). adv. **Document type:** *Journal, Consumer.*
Published by: Honda-Acura Club, Inc., 4324 Promenade Way, Ste 109, Marina del Rey, CA 90292. TEL 310-822-6163, FAX 310-822-5030, staff@hondaclub.com, http://www.hondaclub.com. Ed. Peter Frey. Pub. Burton Merrill.

388.342 987 GBR ISSN 1749-0278
VENEZUELA AUTOS REPORT. Text in English. 2005. q. EUR 820, USD 1,030 combined subscription (print & email eds.) (effective 2010). **Document type:** *Report, Trade.* **Description:** Covers independent forecasts and competitive intelligence on the automotives industry in Venezuela.
Related titles: E-mail ed.
Indexed: A15, ABIn, B02, B15, B17, B18, G04, I05, P48, P51, P52, PQC.
Published by: Business Monitor International Ltd., Senator House, 85 Queen Victoria St, London, EC4V 4AB, United Kingdom. TEL 44-20-72480468, FAX 44-20-72480467, subs@businessmonitor.com.

629.2 338 DEU ISSN 0171-4317
VERBAND DER AUTOMOBILINDUSTRIE. AUTO. Text in German. 1956. a. free. **Document type:** *Corporate.*
Former titles (until 1974): Verband der Automobilindustrie. Jahresbericht (0506-6573); (until 1965): Verband der Automobilindustrie. Taetigkeitsbericht (0083-5471)
Related titles: English ed.: ISSN 0939-8937.
Indexed: DokStr.
Published by: Verband der Automobilindustrie e.V., Westendstr 61, Frankfurt Am Main, 60325, Germany. TEL 49-69-97507-0, FAX 49-69-97507261.

796.77 DEU ISSN 1860-8167
VERKAUFSPROFI. Text in German. 2005. q. adv. **Document type:** *Magazine, Trade.*
Published by: Springer Automotive Media (Subsidiary of: Springer Fachmedien Muenchen GmbH), Neumarkter Str 18, Munich, 81673, Germany. TEL 49-89-43721121, FAX 49-89-43721266, vertriebsservice@springer.com, http://www.springerautomotivemedia.de. adv.: color page EUR 4,400. Circ: 5,700 (controlled).

629.286 DEU
VERKEHRSSICHERHEITSREPORT. Text in German. 1977. a. **Document type:** *Journal, Trade.*
Former titles (until 2005): Technische Sicherheit im Strassenverkehr; (until 2001): Technische Sicherheit und Mobilitaet (1616-1661); (until 1997): Technische Mangel an Kraftfahrzeugen (0721-7307)
Published by: D E K R A - AG, Handwerkstr 15, Stuttgart, 70565, Germany. TEL 49-711-78610, FAX 49-711-78612204, info@dekra.de, http://www.dekra.de.

629.286 DEU ISSN 0724-2050
VERKEHRSUNFALL UND FAHRZEUGTECHNIK; Verkehrsunfall Fachblatt fuer Kraftfahrzeugsachverstaendige. Text in German. 1961. 11/yr. EUR 299; EUR 157 to students; EUR 35 newsstand/cover (effective 2010). adv. illus.; charts. **Document type:** *Magazine, Trade.*
Former titles (until 1983): Verkehrsunfall (0341-2210); (until 1972): Information (0341-2202)
Indexed: RefZh, TM.
—CCC.
Published by: Vieweg und Teubner Verlag (Subsidiary of: Springer Fachmedien Wiesbaden GmbH), Abraham-Lincoln-Str 46, Wiesbaden, 65189, Germany. TEL 49-611-78780, FAX 49-611-7878400, info@viewegteubner.de, http://www.viewegteubner.de. Ed. Johannes Winterhagen. Adv. contact Sabine Roeck. Circ: 1,400 (paid and controlled).

629.286 SVN
VESTNIK A C; galsilo delavnihljudi W.O. A C. Text and summaries in Serbo-Croatian, Slovenian. 1962. bi-m. free. back issues avail.
Published by: W.O. Autocomerce, Trinova 4, Ljubljana, Slovenia. TEL 61 323-046, FAX 061-317-196, TELEX 31299 YUAC. Ed. Miran Juvancic.

VETERAN. *see* ANTIQUES

796.7 HUN ISSN 1417-1406
VETERAN AUTO ES MOTOR. Text in Hungarian. 1991. bi-m. HUF 7,800 (effective 2005). adv. **Document type:** *Magazine, Consumer.*
Formerly (until 1997): Auto Motor Veteran (1215-1580)
Published by: Oldtimer Media, Postafiok 66, Budapest, 1755, Hungary. TEL 36-1-4253668, FAX 36-1-2780475.

388.3 GBR ISSN 0042-4781
VETERAN CAR. Text in English. 1938. bi-m. membership. adv. bk.rev. charts; illus. index. back issues avail. **Document type:** *Magazine, Consumer.*
Published by: Veteran Car Club of Great Britain, Jessamine Court, 15 High St, Ashwell, Baldock, Herts SG7 5NL, United Kingdom. Ed. Elizabeth Bennett. R&P Margaret Goding TEL 44-1462-742818. Adv. contact Margaret Goding. Circ: 1,600.

796.77 USA ISSN 0199-7890
VETTE. Text in English. 1976. m. USD 32.95 domestic; USD 44.95 in Canada; USD 56.95 elsewhere (effective 2008). adv. bk.rev. back issues avail. **Document type:** *Magazine, Consumer.* **Description:** Provides Corvette enthusiasts with coverage of the cars, the people and the events that make up the hobby.
Indexed: G06, G07, G08, I05, S23.
—CCC.
Published by: Source Interlink Companies, 9036 Brittany Way, Tampa, FL 33619. TEL 813-675-3500, dheine@sourceinterlink.com, http://www.sourceinterlinkmedia.com. Ed. Jay Heath. Pubs. Jim Foos, John Gallagher TEL 323-782-2733. adv.: B&W page USD 5,275, color page USD 7,035; bleed 8.125 x 10.75. Circ: 27,684 (paid).

388.3 790.1 SWE ISSN 0346-4210
VI BILAEGARE; sveriges stoerste bil- och fritidstidning. Variant title: Nya Vi Bilaegare. Text in Swedish. 1929. 18/yr. SEK 411 domestic (effective 2005). adv. bk.rev. charts; illus. **Document type:** *Magazine, Consumer.* **Description:** Directed to car owners. Extends to homes, gardening, traveling and leisure, hunting, boats and fishing.
Former titles (until 1975): Vi Bilaegare med Hem och Hobby; (until vol.19, 1970): Vi Bilaegare (0042-4943); (until vol.2, 1949): Meddelanden fraan Bilaegarnas Inkoepsfoerening, Stockholm
Published by: O K Foerlaget AB, Yngligagatan 12, Box 23800, Stockholm, 10435, Sweden. TEL 46-8-7361220, FAX 46-8-7361227. Ed. Haakon Baecklund TEL 46-8-7361207. Pub. Nils-Erik Frendin TEL 46-8-7361201. Adv. contact Madeleine Ehrensparre TEL 46-8-7361226. B&W page SEK 46,900, color page SEK 61,000; trim 186 x 275. Circ: 205,200.

629.222 NOR ISSN 1501-0325
VI MENN BIL. Text in Norwegian. 1998. 8/yr. adv. **Document type:** *Magazine, Consumer.*
Published by: Hjemmet Mortensen AS, Gullhaugveien 1, Nydalen, Oslo, 0441, Norway. TEL 47-22-585000, FAX 47-22-585959, firmapost@hm-media.no, http://www.hm-media.no. adv.: page NOK 49,000.

388.3 ITA
VIA!. Text in Italian. 1948. m. free to members. adv. bk.rev. abstr.; illus.; stat. **Document type:** *Magazine, Consumer.*
Formerly: Autoclub and Via (0005-0962)
Published by: Automobile Club di Milano, Corso Venezia 43, Milan, 20121, Italy. TEL 39-02-77451, FAX 39-02-781844, http://www.acimi.it. Ed. Paolo Montagna. Circ: 180,000.

388.3 USA
VIA (PORTLAND); A A A traveler's companion. Text in English. 1920. bi-m. free to members (effective 2009). adv. illus. 60 p./no.; **Document type:** *Magazine, Consumer.* **Description:** Designed for the AAA members in Northern California, Nevada, Utah, Montana, Wyoming, Alaska, Oregon, and southern Idaho.
Formerly (until 1996): Oregon Motorist (0274-5844)
Related titles: Online - full text ed.
Published by: A A A Oregon - Idaho, 100 Van Ness Ave, San Francisco, CA 94102. TEL 415-565-2451, FAX 415-863-4726, aaasales@aaaoregon.com, http://www.aaaorid.com. Ed. Bruce Anderson. Pub. Mary D'Agostino.

VIA (SAN FRANCISCO). *see* TRAVEL AND TOURISM

796.77 USA
VIALE CIRO MENOTTI; a magazine for Maserati enthusiasts. Text in English. 1976. q. USD 60. adv. bk.rev. index. back issues avail.
Published by: M I E Corporation, PO Box 772, Mercer Island, WA 98040. TEL 206-455-4449, FAX 206-646-5458. Ed. Francis G Mandarano. Circ: 3,500.

LA VIE DE L'AUTO. *see* ANTIQUES

388.342 959.7 GBR ISSN 1749-0286
VIETNAM AUTOS REPORT. Text in English. 2005. q. EUR 820, USD 1,030 combined subscription (print & email eds.) (effective 2010). **Document type:** *Report, Trade.* **Description:** Covers independent forecasts and competitive intelligence on the automotives industry in Vietnam.
Related titles: E-mail ed.
Indexed: A15, ABIn, B02, B15, B17, B18, G04, I05, P48, P51, P52, PQC.
Published by: Business Monitor International Ltd., Senator House, 85 Queen Victoria St, London, EC4V 4AB, United Kingdom. TEL 44-20-72480468, FAX 44-20-72480467, subs@businessmonitor.com.

388 USA ISSN 1535-556X
TL236
VINTAGE RACECAR JOURNAL AND MARKET REPORT. Text in English. 1999 (Sept.). m. USD 45 domestic; USD 65 in Canada & Mexico; USD 90 elsewhere; USD 5 newsstand/cover (effective 2001). adv. **Document type:** *Magazine, Consumer.* **Description:** Contains articles and reviews of products and services of interest to the vintage car racer.
Published by: Parabolica Publishing, LLC, 5300 Orange Ave, Ste 211A, Cypress, CA 90630. TEL 714-236-8676, FAX 714-827-2304. Ed., Pub. Casey Annis. **Dist. by:** International Publishers Direct, 27500 Riverview Center Blvd, Bonita Springs, FL 34134. TEL 858-320-4563, FAX 858-677-3220.

629.222 USA ISSN 0147-9695
TL215.T7
VINTAGE TRIUMPH. Text in English. 1975. q. USD 25; USD 38 foreign (effective 1998). adv. bk.rev. back issues avail. **Document type:** *Newsletter.* **Description:** Contains articles and information which fosters the ownership, operation and preservation of Triumph automobiles.
Published by: Vintage Triumph Register, 15218 W Larren Ave, Dearborn, MI 48126. TEL 609-758-8749. Ed. Chris Hansel. Circ: 3,000.

388.3 USA
VIPER MAGAZINE; the magazine for dodge viper enthusiasts. Text in English. 1995. q.
Published by: J.R. Thompson Co., 26970 Haggerty Rd, Farmington, MI 48331. TEL 248-553-4566, FAX 248-553-2138, jrt@jrthompson.com. Eds. Mark Giannatta, John Thompson. Circ: 15,000.

796.77 DNK ISSN 1399-2864
VMAX. (Velocity Maximum) Text in Danish. 1999. m. DKK 479 (effective 2009). adv. **Document type:** *Magazine, Consumer.*
Published by: Benjamin Media A/S, Finsensvej 6 D, Frederiksberg, 2000, Denmark. TEL 45-70-220255, FAX 45-70-220056, info@benjamin.dk, http://www.benjamin.dk. Ed. Michael Holt. adv.: page DKK 24,600; 223 x 297. Circ: 27,328 (controlled).

629.22 USA
THE VOICE (BEAVERTON). Text in English. q. free to members. bk.rev. **Document type:** *Newsletter.* **Description:** Features reports from Association's officers, plus articles and news from member associations and clubs, both from the United States and from around the world.
Formerly: National Four Wheel Drive Association News
Published by: United Four Wheel Drive Associations, 14525 SW Millikan Way, #22622, Beaverton, OR 97005-2343. TEL 619-390-8747, http://www.ufwda.org.

796.77 DEU
VOILA. Text in German. 1986. 3/yr. adv. **Document type:** *Magazine, Consumer.*
Published by: Journal International Verlags- und Werbegesellschaft mbH, Hanns-Seidel-Platz 5, Munich, 81737, Germany. TEL 49-89-6427970, FAX 49-89-64279777, info@journal-international.de, http://www.journal-international.de. Ed. Robert Hauke. Adv. contact Josef Rindert. color page EUR 4,850; trim 185 x 250. Circ: 100,000 (controlled).

388 AUT
VOLKSBLATT MOTOR JOURNAL. Text in German. s-a.
Address: Hafenstrasse 1-3, Postfach 63, Linz, O 4020, Austria. TEL 0732-281901, FAX 0732-279242. Ed. Hans Gilbert Mueller. Circ: 150,000.

629.226 GBR ISSN 1756-2007
VOLKSWAGEN CAMPER & COMMERCIAL. Text in English. 2000. bi-m. GBP 19.98 domestic; GBP 28.74 in Europe; GBP 35.46 elsewhere; GBP 3.95 per issue domestic; GBP 5.41 per issue in Europe; GBP 6.53 per issue elsewhere (effective 2009). adv. back issues avail. **Document type:** *Magazine, Consumer.* **Description:** Celebrates the VW bus, in all its forms, and caters for all things bus related.
Related titles: Online - full text ed.: GBP 25.50; GBP 4.25 per issue (effective 2009).
Published by: Jazz Fashion Publishing Ltd., The Old School, Main Rd, Higher Kinnerton, Chester, Ches. CH4 9AJ, United Kingdom. TEL 44-1244-663400, FAX 44-1244-660611, info@jazzpublishing.co.uk, http://www.jazzpublishing.co.uk. Ed. David Eccles. Pub. Stuart Mears TEL 44-1244-663400 ext 234. Adv. contact Wendy Lennon TEL 44-1244-663400 ext 314. page GBP 730; 210 x 297. Circ: 13,892.

796.7 GBR
VOLKSWAGEN DRIVER. Text in English. 1953. m. GBP 47.40 domestic; GBP 44.99 in Europe; GBP 54.99 elsewhere; GBP 3 per issue (effective 2009). bk.rev. illus. cum.index. back issues avail.; reprints avail. **Document type:** *Magazine, Consumer.* **Description:** Reviews new Volkswagen and Audi automobiles and accessories.
Former titles (until June 2000): Volkswagen Audi Car (0956-9294); (until 1982): Beetling
Related titles: Online - full text ed.
Published by: AutoMetrix Publications, Campion House, 1 Greenfield Rd, Westoning, Bedford, Beds MK45 5JD, United Kingdom. TEL 44-1525-750500, FAX 44-1525-750700, mail@autometrix.co.uk, http://www.autometrix.co.uk. **Dist. by:** M M C Ltd.

796.77 DEU ISSN 1867-6286
VOLKSWAGEN MAGAZIN. Text in German. 1983. q. adv. **Document type:** *Magazine, Consumer.*
Formerly (until 1995): Auto, Mobil (0179-3926)
Published by: (Volkswagen AG), G + J Corporate Editors GmbH (Subsidiary of: Gruner + Jahr AG & Co), Stubbenhuk 10, Hamburg, 20459, Germany. TEL 49-40-37030, FAX 49-40-37035010, info@corporate-editors.com, http://www.corporate-editors.com. Adv. contact Gerdt Groos. page EUR 19,900. Circ: 623,400 (controlled).

629.222 796.77 GBR ISSN 0954-0164
VOLKSWORLD. Text in English. 1987. 13/yr. GBP 40.51 domestic; GBP 4.20 newsstand/cover (effective 2010). adv. illus. back issues avail. **Document type:** *Magazine, Consumer.* **Description:** Addresses all aspects of owning, restoring, maintaining, and customizing a Volkswagen Beetle.
Related titles: Online - full text ed.: GBP 15.23; GBP 3.26 per issue (effective 2010); Supplement(s): V W Camper & Bus. ISSN 1749-9127.
Published by: I P C Country & Leisure Media Ltd. (Subsidiary of: I P C Media Ltd.), Leon House, 233 High St, Croydon, CR9 1HZ, United Kingdom. TEL 44-20-87268000, FAX 44-20-87268296, http://www.ipcmedia.com. Ed. Ivan McCutcheon TEL 44-20-87268347. Pub. Richard Marcroft TEL 44-20-87268343. Adv. contact Ian James TEL 44-20-87268333. page GBP 1,200. **Subscr. to:** Rockwood House, Perrymount Rd, Haywards Heath RH16 3DH, United Kingdom. TEL 44-845-1231231, IPCsubs@quadrantsubs.com, http://www.magazinesdirect.co.uk. **Dist. by:** MarketForce UK Ltd, The Blue Fin Bldg, 3rd Fl, 110 Southwark St, London SE1 0SU, United Kingdom. TEL 44-20-31483300, FAX 44-20-31488105, salesinnovation@marketforce.co.uk, http://www.marketforce.co.uk/.

388.3 HRV ISSN 0351-6296
VOZAC. Text in Croatian. 1948. m. **Document type:** *Journal, Trade.*
Formerly (until 1980): Vozac i Saobracaj (0350-9958)
Published by: Hrvatska Unija Vozaca i Automehanicara, Draskoviceva 27, Zagreb, 10000, Croatia. TEL 385-1-4613001, FAX 385-1-4613001. Ed. Zeljko Stergar.

629.2293 BEL
W E V A JOURNAL. Text in English. 2007. a. **Document type:** *Journal, Academic/Scholarly.* **Description:** Covers studies related to battery, hybrid, and fuel cell electric vehicles. Contains papers selected at EVS (Worldwide International Battery, Hybrid and Fuel Cell Electric Vehicle Symposium).
Media: CD-ROM.
Published by: (World Electric Vehicle Association JPN), European Association for Battery, Hybrid and Fuel Cell Electric Vehicles (AVERE), c/o VUB-TW-ETEC, Bd. de la Plaine, 2, Brussels, BE 1050, Belgium. avere@vub.ac.be, http://www.avere.org/.

388.286 USA ISSN 0886-5175
HD9710.U5
WARD'S AUTOMOTIVE REPORTS. Text in English. 19??. w. USD 1,540 (effective 2011). **Document type:** *Newsletter, Trade.* **Description:** Provides statistics and news on the automotive industry, including production numbers, sales figures, and marketing trends.
Incorporates (198?-2001): Ward's Automotive International (0895-2191)
Related titles: Online - full text ed.
Indexed: G08, I05.
—CCC.
Published by: Ward's Automotive Group (Subsidiary of: Penton Media, Inc.), 3000 Town Ctr, Ste 2750, Southfield, MI 48075. TEL 248-357-0800, FAX 248-357-0810, wards@wardsauto.com, http://www.wardsauto.com.

WARD'S AUTOMOTIVE YEARBOOK. *see* TRANSPORTATION—Abstracting, Bibliographies, Statistics

388.3 USA ISSN 0043-0315
HD9710.U5
WARD'S AUTOWORLD. Text in English. 1964. m. USD 69 domestic; USD 85 in Canada; USD 99 elsewhere; free domestic to qualified personnel (effective 2011). adv. bk.rev. charts; illus.; stat. index. reprints avail. **Document type:** *Magazine, Trade.* **Description:** Covers the automotive manufacturing industry. Provides news and analysis of all aspects of the vehicle manufacturing industry.
Formerly: Ward's Quarterly
Related titles: Online - full text ed.
Indexed: A09, A10, A12, A13, A15, A17, A22, A28, ABIn, APA, B01, B02, B04, B06, B07, B08, B09, B15, B17, B18, BPI, BRD, BrCerAb, BusI, C&ISA, C12, CA/WCA, CIA, CLT&T, CerAb, CivEngAb, CorrAb, E&CAJ, E11, EEA, EMA, ESPM, EnvEAb, G04, G06, G07, G08, G09, H15, HRIS, I05, M&TEA, M01, M02, M06, M09, MBF, METADEX, MMI, P10, P52, P53, P54, PQC, S22, SolStAb, T&II, T02, T04, V02, V03, V04, W01, W02, W03, W05, WAA.
—CIS, Ingenta, Linda Hall. **CCC.**
Published by: Ward's Automotive Group (Subsidiary of: Penton Media, Inc.), 3000 Town Ctr, Ste 2750, Southfield, MI 48075. TEL 248-357-0800, FAX 248-357-0810, wards@wardsauto.com, http://www.wardsauto.com. Ed. Barbara L McClellan. Circ: 68,200 (controlled).

388.1 USA ISSN 1086-1629
WARD'S DEALER BUSINESS; the management magazine for auto dealership professionals. Text in English. 1966. m. USD 52 domestic; USD 72 in Canada; USD 104 elsewhere; free domestic to qualified personnel (effective 2011). illus. back issues avail. **Document type:** *Magazine, Trade.* **Description:** For new car and light truck dealers.
Former titles (until 1995): Auto Age Dealer Business (1070-8294); (until 1992): Auto Age (0894-1270); (until 1986): Automotive Age (0005-1470)
Related titles: Online - full text ed.
Indexed: A09, A10, A15, ABIn, B01, B03, B06, B07, B09, B11, BPI, BRD, CA, G06, G07, G08, I05, P52, PQC, S22, T02, V03, V04, W01, W02, W03, W05.
—CIS, Ingenta. **CCC.**
Published by: Ward's Automotive Group (Subsidiary of: Penton Media, Inc.), 3000 Town Ctr, Ste 2750, Southfield, MI 48075. TEL 248-357-0800, FAX 248-357-0810, wards@wardsauto.com, http://www.wardsauto.com. Circ: 27,512 (controlled).

629.286 USA ISSN 1088-6869
TL210
WARD'S ENGINE AND VEHICLE TECHNOLOGY UPDATE. Text in English. 1975. s-a. USD 1,110 (effective 2011). **Document type:** *Newsletter, Trade.* **Description:** Provides technical information on the world of automotive technology. Covers the latest developments in engine design, drive trains, materials and components.
Former titles (until 1990): Ward's Engine Update; (until 19??): Ward's Wankel Report
—CCC.
Published by: Ward's Automotive Group (Subsidiary of: Penton Media, Inc.), 3000 Town Ctr, Ste 2750, Southfield, MI 48075. TEL 248-357-0800, FAX 248-357-0810, wards@wardsauto.com, http://www.wardsauto.com.

388.3 USA ISSN 1088-1743
WARRANTY DOLLARS & SENSE FOR FORD DEALERS. Text in English. 1981. 24/yr. adv. **Document type:** *Newsletter, Trade.*
Published by: W D & S Publishing, 10 W 7th St, 1st Fl, PO Box 606, Barnegat Light, NJ 08006. TEL 800-321-5312, http://www.dealersedge.com. Pub. James M Muntz.

388.3 USA ISSN 1088-1735
WARRANTY DOLLARS & SENSE FOR G M DEALERS. (General Motors) Text in English. 1981. 24/yr. adv. **Document type:** *Newsletter, Trade.*
Published by: W D & S Publishing, 10 W 7th St, 1st Fl, PO Box 606, Barnegat Light, NJ 08006. TEL 800-321-5312, http://www.dealersedge.com. Ed. Rob Campbell. Pub., Adv. contact Jim Muntz.

WASHINGTON JOURNEY. *see* TRAVEL AND TOURISM

WEGRY. *see* TRAVEL AND TOURISM

388.3 USA ISSN 0043-3977
TL1
WESTERN NEW YORK MOTORIST. Text in English. 1909. m. USD 1.50. abstr.; charts; illus.; stat.
Formerly: Buffalo Motorist
Published by: Automobile Club of Western New York, 100 International Dr, Buffalo, NY 14221. Ed. Earle V Charles III. Circ: 250,000.

WESTWAYS. *see* TRAVEL AND TOURISM

614.86 790.01 CAN ISSN 0831-1579
WESTWORLD ALBERTA MAGAZINE. Text in English. 1974. 5/yr. CAD 9.95 domestic to non-members; CAD 16.95 foreign to non-members; free to members (effective 2005). adv. bk.rev. charts; illus.; stat. **Document type:** *Magazine, Consumer.* **Description:** Features automotive-related tips; club news; and general interest, national and international travel articles.
Former titles (until 1985): Alberta Motorist (0826-4937); (until 1980): Alberta Magazine (0228-1082); Alberta Motorist (0002-4856)
Published by: (Alberta Motor Association), Canada Wide Media Ltd., 4180 Lougheed Hwy, 4th Fl, Burnaby, BC V5C 6A7, Canada. TEL 604-299-7311, FAX 604-299-9188, cwm@canadawide.com. adv.: B&W page CAD 8,240, color page CAD 10,300; trim 10.88 x 8.13. Circ: 443,000.

614.86 CAN ISSN 0843-3356
WESTWORLD MAGAZINE (BRITISH COLUMBIA EDITION). Text in English. 1975. 5/yr. CAD 9.95. adv. bk.rev. illus. index. **Document type:** *Magazine, Consumer.* **Description:** Features automotive-related tips, club news and national and international travel.
Former titles (until 1982): Westworld Magazine (Vancouver) (0316-1315); (until 1975): B C Motorist (0005-2884)
Related titles: Online - full text ed.
Indexed: C03, CBCARef, P48, PQC.
Published by: Canada Wide Media Ltd., 4180 Lougheed Hwy, 4th Fl, Burnaby, BC V5C 6A7, Canada. TEL 604-299-7311, FAX 604-299-9188, cwm@canadawide.com. Ed. Anne Rose. Pub. Peter Legge. Adv. contact Rick McMorran. Circ: 102,000.

388.3 CAN ISSN 0831-1552
WESTWORLD SASKATCHEWAN. Text in English. 1984. 4/yr. membership. adv. bk.rev. illus. **Document type:** *Journal, Consumer.*
Formerly: Saskatchewan Motorist (0036-4940)
Published by: (C A A Saskatchewan), Canada Wide Media Ltd., 4180 Lougheed Hwy, 4th Fl, Burnaby, BC V5C 6A7, Canada. TEL 604-299-7311, FAX 604-299-9188, cwm@canadawide.com, http://www.canadawide.com. Ed. Pat Price. Pub. Peter Legge. Adv. contact Rick McMorran. Circ: 108,000.

388.34 IRL ISSN 1649-7376
WEXFORD'S MOTOR TRADER. Text in English. 2002. bi-w. EUR 2.50 newsstand/cover (effective 2006). adv.
Supersedes in part (in 2005): Ireland's Motor Trader (1649-6353); Which was formerly (until 2004): The Motor-Trader (1649-2072)
Published by: Motor Trader, Box 338, Naas, Co. Kildare, Ireland. TEL 353-45-893343, FAX 353-45-893342, info@motortrader.ie, http://www.motortrader.ie/.

388.3 USA
WHALES ON WHEELS. Text in English. 1981. q. USD 6 (effective 2001). 12 p./no. 2 cols./p.; **Document type:** *Newsletter.* **Description:** Gives technical information on the ongoing care and maintenance of the ultra van.
Published by: Group Ultra Van, c/o Louis C. Griggs, Treasurer, 626 Brookfield Ave, Cumberland, MD 21502. TEL 505-585-8035, finchbird@juno.com. Ed. Mazziotti Gillan. R&P W Christy Barden. Circ: 250.

388.3 RUS ISSN 1816-4765
WHAT CAR?. Text in Russian. 2001. m. RUR 880 (effective 2006). **Document type:** *Magazine, Consumer.*
Formerly (until 2005): Avtomobili (1609-3569)
Published by: Izdatel'stvo Otkrytye Sistemy/Open Systems Publications, ul Rustaveli, dom 12A, komn 117, Moscow, 127254, Russian Federation. TEL 7-095-2539206, FAX 7-095-2539204, info@osp.ru, http://www.osp.ru. Pub. Roman Filipov. Circ: 80,000.

629.22 GBR ISSN 0307-2991
TL1
WHAT CAR?. Text in English. 1973. 13/yr. GBP 39.60 (effective 2009). adv. mkt.; illus. back issues avail. **Document type:** *Magazine, Consumer.* **Description:** Contains reviews of new cars and comparison tests between similar cars. Also includes used car prices and budget search, Q & A, and information on all aspects of cars, such as security and parts.
Incorporates (2004-2006): Test Drive (1744-9308)
Related titles: Online - full text ed.
—BLDSC (9309.660000). **CCC.**
Published by: Haymarket Publishing Ltd. (Subsidiary of: Haymarket Media Group), Teddington Studios, Broom Rd, Teddington, Middlesex, TW11 9BE, United Kingdom. TEL 44-20-82675630, FAX 44-20-82675759, info@haymarket.com, http://www.haymarket.com. Ed. Steve Fowler TEL 44-20-82675550. Adv. contacts David Poole TEL 44-20-82675547, Sean Costa TEL 44-20-82675715. Circ: 92,102. **Subscr. to:** PO Box 568, Haywards Heath RH16 3XQ, United Kingdom. TEL 44-8456-777800, Haymarket.subs@qss-uk.com, http://www.themagazineshop.com.

629.22 GBR ISSN 1746-8906
WHAT CAR? NEW CAR GUIDE. Text in English. 2001. m. GBP 5.99 newsstand/cover (effective 2009). back issues avail. **Document type:** *Directory, Consumer.* **Description:** Contains information on every new car on sale in the UK, complete with pictures, test verdicts and specification data.
Formerly (until 2005): What Car? Road Test Directory (1475-0546)
Related titles: Optical Disk - DVD ed.: ISSN 1749-0928.
Published by: Haymarket Publishing Ltd. (Subsidiary of: Haymarket Media Group), 174 Hammersmith Rd, London, W6 7JP, United Kingdom. TEL 44-20-82674210, info@haymarket.com. Ed. Steve Fowler TEL 44-20-82675550.

388.342 GBR ISSN 1752-7317
WHAT CAR? PRICE GUIDE; trade, private, new & part-ex prices. Text in English. 1996. m. charts; illus. back issues avail. **Document type:** *Magazine, Consumer.* **Description:** Provides car buyers with accurate prices for used cars, valuations, plus reliable and well-informed views on buying cars.
Formerly (until 2006): What Car? Used Car Price Guide (1365-8271); Which incorporated (1996-1998): Book - Used Car Price Guide (1362-1483)
—CCC.
Published by: Haymarket Publishing Ltd. (Subsidiary of: Haymarket Media Group), 174 Hammersmith Rd, London, W6 7JP, United Kingdom. TEL 44-20-82674210, info@haymarket.com. Ed. Steve Fowler TEL 44-20-82675550. **Dist. by:** Frontline.

388.3 JPN ISSN 0049-755X
HE277.A1
THE WHEEL EXTENDED; a Toyota quarterly review. Text in English. 1971. q. free. charts; illus. **Document type:** *Monographic series.* **Description:** Covers issues relating to the automobile and transportation fields.
Indexed: AIAP, BAS, EIP, F&EA, HRIS, IBR, IBZ, P06.
—Ingenta.
Published by: Toyota Motor Corporation, International Public Affairs Division, 1-4-18 Koraku, Bunkyo-ku, Tokyo, 112-0004, Japan. TEL 03-3817-9930, FAX 03-3817-9017. Circ: 11,000 (controlled).

388.3 AUS ISSN 0043-4779
WHEELS. Text in English. 1953. m. AUD 89.95 domestic; AUD 116.65 in New Zealand; AUD 132.55 elsewhere; AUD 8.50 newsstand/cover (effective 2008). adv. bk.rev. charts; illus. index. back issues avail. **Document type:** *Magazine, Consumer.* **Description:** Contains news and reviews on cars and motor sports.
Related titles: Microfiche ed.; Online - full text ed.
Indexed: A11, ARI, Pinpoint, T02.
Published by: A C P Magazines Ltd. (Subsidiary of: P B L Media Pty Ltd.), 54-58 Park St, Sydney, NSW 2000, Australia. TEL 61-2-92828000, FAX 61-2-91263769, research@acpaction.com.au, http://www.acp.com.au. Ed. Ged Bulmer. Adv. contact Kylie Taylor TEL 61-2-92639731. color page AUD 7,385; trim 225 x 297. Circ: 64,488. **Subscr. to:** Magshop, Reply Paid 4967, Sydney, NSW 2001, Australia. TEL 61-2-136116, subs@magstore.com.au, http://shop.magstore.com.au.

388.3 SWE ISSN 0348-0313
WHEELS MAGAZINE; wheels rod & classic - foer aekta bilentusiaster. Text in Swedish. 1977. m. SEK 427 domestic; SEK 450 in Scandinavia; SEK 500 in Europe; SEK 550 elsewhere (effective 2003). adv. 100 p./no. 3 cols./p.; back issues avail. **Document type:** *Magazine, Consumer.* **Description:** Covers automobile hobbies, restoring older cars, building hot rods, and more.
Incorporates (1982-1984): Hojmagasinet (0280-9370)
Published by: Wheels Magazine AB, Fack 6040, Taeby, 18706, Sweden. TEL 46-8-7567375, FAX 46-8-7567096. Eds. Olof Svenningsson, Sture Torngren. Pub. Sture Torngren. Adv. contact Mikael Henrikssson. page SEK 12,200; trim 190 x 260. Circ: 29,700.

629.226 796.5 GBR ISSN 2043-6416
WHICH MOTORCHOME. Text in English. 1986. m. GBP 31.99 per issue domestic; GBP 52.99 per issue in Europe; GBP 74.99 per issue elsewhere; GBP 3.50 per issue (effective 2010). adv. bk.rev. charts; illus.; maps; stat. 140 p./no.; **Document type:** *Magazine, Trade.* **Description:** Reviews motorhomes in terms of safety, value, and convenience. Gives advice on buying a new or used motorhome and includes information on accessories.
Formerly (until 2010): Which Motorcaravan (0950-9291)
Published by: Warners Group Publications Plc., The Maltings, Manor Ln, Bourne, Lincs PE10 9PH, United Kingdom. TEL 44-1778-391000, FAX 44-1778-425437, wgpsubs@warnersgroup.co.uk, http://www.warnersgroup.co.uk. Ed. Peter Vaughan TEL 44-1778-391118. Pub. John Greenwood TEL 44-1778-391116.

WHO IS WHO IM P K W - FLOTTENMARKT. *see* BUSINESS AND ECONOMICS—Trade And Industrial Directories

388.3 GBR
WHO OWNS WHO. Text in English. 19??. s-a. GBP 425; GBP 250 per issue (effective 2010). software rev. **Document type:** *Directory, Trade.* **Description:** Lists UK-based companies which own three or more franchised retail motor trade sites.
Related titles: Online - full content ed.: GBP 848.94; GBP 499.38 per issue (effective 2010).

Published by: Sewells Information and Research (Subsidiary of: H. Bauer Publishing Ltd.), Bauer Automotive Media House, Peterborough Business Park, Lynchwood, Peterborough, Northants PE2 6EA, United Kingdom. TEL 44-1733-468254, FAX 44-1733-468349, sewells@bauermedia.co.uk, http://www.sewells.co.uk.

388.3 NLD ISSN 1876-620X
WIJZER. Variant title: Vier en Zes Wijzer. Text in Dutch. 2006. bi-m. EUR 30 membership (effective 2008).
Formerly (until 2008): 4 en 6 Wijzer (1875-1873)
Published by: 2CV Club Nederland, Rembrandtstr 40, Amersfoort, 3817 RV, Netherlands. TEL 31-33-4481232, ledenadministratie@2cvclub.nl, http://www.2cvclub.nl.

629.266 USA
WINDSHIELD AND GLASS REPAIR MAGAZINE. Text in English. 1994. bi-m. software rev. back issues avail. **Document type:** *Magazine, Trade.* **Description:** Covers topics of interest to professionals who repair windshields.
Published by: Key Communications, Inc., PO Box 569, Garrisonville, VA 22463. TEL 540-720-5584, FAX 540-720-5687, http://www.key-com.com/.

388 051 USA ISSN 1523-5742
WOMAN MOTORIST; Internet magazine. Text in English. 1996. d. adv. **Document type:** *Magazine, Consumer.* **Description:** Automotive, car and motorsports magazine for women.
Media: Online - full text.
Published by: CyberAd, 2674 E Main St, Ste D 240, Ventura, CA 93003-2899. TEL 805-641-2400, FAX 805-641-2400. Ed., Pub. Sandra Kinsler. Adv. contact Maria Perez.

388.3 305.4 USA
WOMEN WITH WHEELS (ONLINE); the online publication on automobiles for women. Text in English. 2000. irreg. (update as needed). free. **Document type:** *Magazine, Consumer.* **Description:** Provides information on automotive industry; educates and informs women on automotive industry; educates and informs women on auto-related topics, such as, buying, leasing, maintenance.
Media: Online - full content.
Published by: Women with Wheels, 1885 Willowview Terrace, Northfield, IL 60093-2934. Ed., Pub., Adv. contact Susan Frissell.

WOODALL'S SOUTHERN R V. *see* SPORTS AND GAMES—Outdoor Life

WORLD OF SPECIAL FINANCE. *see* BUSINESS AND ECONOMICS—Banking And Finance

629 CAN ISSN 0824-5487
WORLD OF WHEELS. Text in English. 1983. bi-m. CAD 17.99 domestic; CAD 27.99 foreign (effective 2005). adv. illus. reprints avail. **Document type:** *Magazine, Consumer.* **Description:** Publishes industry news pertaining to the Canadian market, product reviews and tests, features on automobiles and automotive issues, direct vehicle comparisons, motorsports, columns and comment.
Indexed: CPerI, G08.
Published by: Formula Publications (Subsidiary of: Torstar Corp.), 447 Speers Rd, Ste 4, Oakville, ON L6K 3S7, Canada. TEL 905-842-6592, FAX 905-842-6843, circ@formulapublications.com. Circ: 59,000.

388.3 629.22 USA
WORLD WIDE WHEELS. Text in English. w. adv. **Document type:** *Magazine, Consumer.* **Description:** Provides information on new cars, car dealers, and classifieds of used cars.
Media: Online - full content.
Address: 340 W Butterfield Rd, Suite 3C, Elmhurst, IL 60126. TEL 630-953-1989, FAX 630-953-8403, http://wwwheels.com/.

388.3 CHN
XING BAO/AUTO WEEK. Text in English. w. CNY 51.96; CNY 1 newsstand/cover (effective 2004). **Document type:** *Newspaper, Consumer.*
Related titles: Online - full content ed.
Published by: Wenhui Xinmin Lianhebao Yejietuan/Wenhui Xinmin United Press Group, 840, Luochuan Zhonglu, 4th Fl, no.1, Shanghai, 200072, China.

621.38 ESP
XTR TUNING. Text in Spanish. 2003. m. EUR 3.50 newsstand/cover (effective 2005). back issues avail. **Document type:** *Magazine, Consumer.*
Published by: Hachette Filipacchi SA, Avda Cardenal Herrera Oria 3, Madrid, 28034, Spain. TEL 34-91-7287000, FAX 34-91-3585473, comunicacion@hachette.es, http://www.hachette.es. Circ: 35,751.

629.222 AUS
XTREME FORDS. Text in English. bi-m. AUD 40.28; AUD 8.95 newsstand/cover (effective 2008). back issues avail. **Document type:** *Magazine, Consumer.* **Description:** Provides information on brutal street and strip cars, DIY tech articles and coverage of the latest events from all over Australia, stunning feature photography and articles.
Published by: Express Publications Pty. Ltd., 2-4 Stanley St, Locked Bag 111, Silverwater, NSW 2168, Australia. TEL 61-2-97413800, 800-801-647, FAX 61-2-97378017, subs@magstore.com.au, http://www.expresspublications.com.au. **Subscr. to:** ISubscribe Pty Ltd., 25 Lime St, Ste 303, Level 3, Sydney, NSW 2000, Australia. TEL 61-2-92621722, FAX 61-2-92625044, info@isubscribe.com.au, http://www.isubscribe.com.au.

629.222 AUS
XTREME HOLDENS. Text in English. 9/yr. AUD 60.41; AUD 8.95 newsstand/cover (effective 2008). back issues avail. **Document type:** *Magazine, Consumer.* **Description:** Provides information about the feature cars, the best show coverage and the most in depth and relevant technical content.
Published by: Express Publications Pty. Ltd., 2-4 Stanley St, Locked Bag 111, Silverwater, NSW 2168, Australia. TEL 61-2-97413800, 800-801-647, FAX 61-2-97378017, subs@magstore.com.au, http://www.expresspublications.com.au. Ed. Andrew Broadley TEL 61-2-97413919. Adv. contact Michael Coiro TEL 61-2-97413911. **Subscr. to:** ISubscribe Pty Ltd., 25 Lime St, Ste 303, Level 3, Sydney, NSW 2000, Australia. TEL 61-2-92621722, FAX 61-2-92625044, info@isubscribe.com.au, http://www.isubscribe.com.au.

388.3 ZAF ISSN 1728-3086
XTREME MACHINES. Variant title: Extreme Machines. Text in English. 2003. q. ZAR 120 (effective 2006). adv. **Document type:** *Magazine, Consumer.*
Published by: Xtreme Publications, PO Box 83775, Doornpoort, 0017, South Africa. TEL 27-12-5480147.

YINXIANG GAIZHUANG JISHU/AUTO AUDIOMOD. *see* ELECTRONICS

338.476 GBR ISSN 1367-7438
YORKSHIRE AUTO TRADER. Text in English. 1982. w. GBP 2.20 per issue (effective 2010). adv. 340 p./no. 5 cols./p.; **Document type:** *Journal, Consumer.* **Description:** Contains trade and private advertisements of cars, motor bikes, caravans, buying and selling.
Incorporates in part (in 2009): Lincolnshire Auto Trader; Formerly (until 1997): Yorkshire & Humberside Auto Trader (0958-4013)
Related titles: Online - full content ed.
Published by: Auto Trader Publications Ltd. (Subsidiary of: Trader Media Group Ltd.), 3rd and 4th Fl, 41-47 Hartfield Rd., Wimbeldon, London, SW19 3RQ, United Kingdom. TEL 44-20-85447000, FAX 44-20-88791879, editorial@autotrader.co.uk, enquiries@autotrader.co.uk. Circ: 32,075 (paid).

629.22075 NLD ISSN 2210-3643
▼ **YOUNGTIMER MAGAZINE.** Text in Dutch. 2010. bi-m. EUR 21; EUR 4.25 newsstand/cover (effective 2010). adv. **Document type:** *Magazine, Consumer.*
Published by: Uitgeverij De Koppelenburg, Postbus 53, Tolkamer, 6916 ZH, Netherlands. TEL 31-316-544474, FAX 31-316-541344, info@dekoppelenburg.nl, http://www.dekoppelenburg.nl. adv.: color page EUR 750; trim 230 x 297.

796.77 DEU
▼ **YOUNGTIMER SCENE**; Das Magazin fuer Youngtimer-Enthusiasten. Text in German. 2009. bi-m. EUR 22 domestic; EUR 25 foreign; EUR 3.90 newsstand/cover (effective 2011). adv. **Document type:** *Magazine, Consumer.*
Published by: Vestische Mediengruppe Welke GmbH & Co. KG, Hertener Mark 7, Herten, 45699, Germany. TEL 49-2366-808400, FAX 49-2366-808499, info@vmw-verlag.de, http://vmw-verlag.de. Adv. contact Julia Wissing.

388 629.22 RUS ISSN 0321-4249
ZA RULEM. Text in Russian. 1928. m. USD 209 foreign (effective 2005). adv. 232 p./no. 3 cols./p.; **Document type:** *Magazine, Trade.*
Related titles: CD-ROM ed.; Diskette ed.
—East View.
Published by: Izdatel'stvo Za Rulem, Seliverstov per 10, Moscow, 103045, Russian Federation. TEL 7-095-2072733, FAX 7-095-7374307, info@zr.ru, http://www.zr.ru. Ed. Petr Menshikh. Adv. contact Semion Shadrin TEL 7-095-9780389. page USD 10,000; trim 270 x 200. Circ: 480,000. **Dist. by:** East View Information Services, 10601 Wayzata Blvd, Minneapolis, MN 55305. TEL 952-252-1201, 800-477-1005, FAX 952-252-1202, info@eastview.com, http://www.eastview.com.

338.476 CHN
ZHONGGUO QICHE BAO/CHINA AUTOMOTIVE NEWS. Text in Chinese. 5/w. CNY 198 (effective 2004). **Document type:** *Newspaper, Trade.*
Address: Xicheng-qu, 22, Baiwanzhuang Dajie, Beijing, 100037, China. TEL 86-10-68329915. **Dist. by:** China International Book Trading Corp, 35 Chegongzhuang Xilu, Haidian District, PO Box 399, Beijing 100044, China. TEL 86-10-68412045, FAX 86-10-68412023, cibtc@mail.cibtc.com.cn, http://www.cibtc.com.cn.

629.22 AUS
ZOOM. Text in English. 13/yr. AUD 77.51 domestic; AUD 129.90 in New Zealand; AUD 154.90 elsewhere; AUD 7.95 newsstand/cover (effective 2008). adv. back issues avail. **Document type:** *Magazine, Consumer.* **Description:** Covers technical articles, mechanical theory, engine conversions, DIY performance tips, supercharger and turbocharger installations, bolt on upgrades and product review etc.
Published by: Express Publications Pty. Ltd., 2-4 Stanley St, Locked Bag 111, Silverwater, NSW 2168, Australia. TEL 61-2-97413800, 800-801-647, FAX 61-2-97378017, subs@magstore.com.au, http://www.expresspublications.com.au. Ed. Greg Conway TEL 61-2-97413812. Adv. contact Chantal Capablanca TEL 61-2-97413835. **Subscr. to:** ISubscribe Pty Ltd., 25 Lime St, Ste 303, Level 3, Sydney, NSW 2000, Australia. TEL 61-2-92621722, FAX 61-2-92625044, info@isubscribe.com.au, http://www.isubscribe.com.au.

629.222 CHN ISSN 1672-9196
ZUOJIA/AUTOSTYLE. Text in Chinese. m. CNY 200 (effective 2008). adv. **Document type:** *Magazine, Consumer.*
Formelry (until 2000): Dazhong Jixieshi (1009-3982)
—East View.
Published by: Trends Communication Co. Ltd., 20/F, Trends Bldg., 9, Guanghua Rd., Beijing, 100020, China. TEL 86-10-65871611, FAX 86-10-65871638, http://www.trends.com.cn/.

388.3 DEU
ZWEITE HAND AUTOBILDER. Text in German. 2001. m. EUR 2.50 newsstand/cover (effective 2010). adv. **Document type:** *Magazine, Consumer.*
Published by: Zweite Hand Verlag, Askanischer Platz 3, Berlin, 10963, Germany. TEL 49-30-290210, FAX 49-30-2902199935, service@zweitehand.de, http://www.zweitehand.de. adv.: color page EUR 900. Circ: 17,400 (paid and controlled).

388.3 DEU
ZWEITE HAND AUTOHANDEL. Text in German. 1993. w. EUR 2.50 newsstand/cover (effective 2010). adv. **Document type:** *Magazine, Consumer.*
Published by: Zweite Hand Verlag, Askanischer Platz 3, Berlin, 10963, Germany. TEL 49-30-290210, FAX 49-30-2902199935, service@zweitehand.de, http://www.zweitehand.de. adv.: page EUR 2,322. Circ: 16,800 (paid and controlled).

388.3 DEU
ZWEITE HAND AUTONET. Text in German. 1998. m. EUR 2.60 newsstand/cover (effective 2010). adv. **Document type:** *Magazine, Consumer.*
Published by: Zweite Hand Verlag, Askanischer Platz 3, Berlin, 10963, Germany. TEL 49-30-290210, FAX 49-30-2902199935, service@zweitehand.de, http://www.zweitehand.de. adv.: color page EUR 770. Circ: 14,600 (paid and controlled).

629.286 GRC ISSN 1105-1280
4 TROCHOI/4 WHEELS. Text in Greek. 1970. m. EUR 5.50 newsstand/cover (effective 2011). adv. Website rev. illus.; mkt. back issues avail. **Document type:** *Magazine, Consumer.* **Description:** Presents new car models, new technologies, environmental issues, and driving tests.
Related titles: Online - full content ed.; ◆ Supplement(s): 4 Trochoi Test. ISSN 1105-1329.
Published by: Technical Press SA, 80 Ioannou Metaxa, Karelas, Koropi, 19400, Greece. TEL 30-210-9792500, FAX 30-210-9792528, info@technicalpress.gr, http://www.technicalpress.gr. Ed. Michael Stavropoulos. Adv. contact Chrisanthi Bitsori.

380.5 GRC ISSN 1105-1329
4 TROCHOI TEST/4 WHEELS TEST. Text in Greek. 1979. a. adv. Website rev. illus. back issues avail. **Document type:** *Magazine, Consumer.* **Description:** Discusses new car models and driving tests.
Related titles: ◆ Supplement to: 4 Trochoi. ISSN 1105-1280.
Published by: Technical Press SA, 80 Ioannou Metaxa, Karelas, Koropi, 19400, Greece. TEL 30-210-9792500, FAX 30-210-9792528, info@technicalpress.gr, http://www.technicalpress.gr. Ed. Michael Stavropoulos. Adv. contact Chrisanthi Bitsori.

629.22 388.3 AUT
4 W D; internationales Allradmagazin und Allrad-Trucker. Text in German. bi-m. EUR 22.80; EUR 3.50 newsstand/cover (effective 2005). **Document type:** *Magazine, Consumer.*
Published by: Exclusiv Verlagsgesellschaft mbH und Co. KG, Schloss Lichtenegg 1, Wels, O 4800, Austria. TEL 43-7242-67823, FAX 43-7242-29707. Ed. Helmut Moser. Adv. contact Ernst Tavernini. Circ: 25,000 (controlled).

388.3 629.22 NLD ISSN 1872-5708
4 W D & S U V AUTO-MAGAZINE. Variant title: Four Wheel Drive and Sports Utility Vehicle Auto-Magazine. Text in Dutch. m. (11/yr.). EUR 39; EUR 4.20 newsstand/cover (effective 2009). adv. **Document type:** *Magazine, Consumer.*
Formerly (until 2004): 4 W D Auto-Magazine (1381-8198)
Published by: K V Z Publications, Koningin Wilhelminaweg 441, Groenekan, 3737 BE, Netherlands. TEL 31-346-213154, FAX 31-346-213234. Ed. D van Zijl. Circ: 25,500.

796.72 ZAF
4 WHEEL ACTION; the 4wd adventure magazine. Text in English. 1990. m. ZAR 3.30 newsstand/cover. adv. illus. **Document type:** *Magazine, Consumer.*
Former titles (until no.19, 1995): Off Road (1021-0636); (until 1992): 4 x 4 Action (1017-2343)
Published by: Four Wheel Drive Club of Southern Africa, PO Box 8860, Edenglen, 1613, South Africa. fwdcsa@icon.co.za, http://www.fourwheeldrive.co.za.

629.22 388.3 SWE ISSN 0281-3580
4 WHEEL DRIVE; terraeng & transpport. Text in Swedish. 1983. 10/yr. SEK 249 for 6 nos.; SEK 60 newsstand/cover (effective 2010). adv. 70 p./no. 4 cols./p.; **Document type:** *Magazine, Consumer.*
Published by: Foerlags AB Albinsson & Sjoeberg, PO Box 529, Karlskrona, 37123, Sweden. TEL 46-455-335325, FAX 46-455-311715, fabas@fabas.se, http://www.fabas.se. Ed. Gunnar Svensson. Adv. contact Malini Karlsson. color page SEK 19,600; trim 190 x 275. Circ: 13,700 (controlled).

388.3 USA ISSN 1097-7066
4 WHEEL DRIVE & SPORT UTILITY. Text in English. 1984. m. USD 15.95 domestic; USD 27.95 in Canada; USD 39.95 elsewhere (effective 2008). adv. back issues avail. **Document type:** *Magazine, Consumer.* **Description:** Features in-depth articles about Jeeps, Broncos, Explorers, Blazers, and domestic and imported four-wheel drive trucks and sport utility vehicles.
Formerly (until 1992): 4 W D sport utility magazine
Indexed: G06, G07, G08, I05, S23.
—CCC.
Published by: Source Interlink Companies, 2400 E Katella Ave, Anaheim, CA 92806. TEL 714-939-2400, dheine@sourceinterlink.com, http://www.sourceinterlinkmedia.com. Ed. Philip Howell. Pub. Jeff Dahlin TEL 714-939-2512. adv.: B&W page USD 4,095, color page USD 5,315; bleed 8.125 x 10.75. Circ: 38,786 (paid).

388.3 621.9 GBR ISSN 1475-6188
4 X 4. Text in English. m. GBP 46.20 domestic; EUR 51.60 in Europe; GBP 27.12 elsewhere (effective 2009). adv. bk.rev. charts; illus. back issues avail. **Document type:** *Magazine, Consumer.* **Description:** Covers the entire four-by-four arena, both working and sport vehicles, on and off the road.
Former titles (until 2001): Off Road and 4 Wheel Drive (0953-203X); (until 1986): Off Road and 4 Wheel Driver (0268-4586); (until 1984): Overlander 4 x 4
Related titles: Supplement(s): What 4 x 4 ?. ISSN 1478-808X. 2003.
Published by: I P C Country & Leisure Media Ltd. (Subsidiary of: I P C Media Ltd.), The Blue Fin Bldg, 110 Southwark St, London, SE1 0SU, United Kingdom. TEL 44-20-31485000, FAX 44-20-31486439, magazinesales@ipcmedia.com, http://www.ipcmedia.com. Ed. Hils Everitt. Adv. contact Adam Fergar. Circ: 40,000. **Dist. by:** MarketForce UK Ltd, The Blue Fin Bldg, 3rd Fl, 110 Southwark St, London SE1 0SU, United Kingdom. TEL 44-20-31483300, FAX 44-20-31488105, salesinnovation@marketforce.co.uk, http://www.marketforce.co.uk/.

629.4 GRC
4 X 4. Text in Greek. 2003. m. EUR 4.95 newsstand/cover (effective 2006). adv. **Document type:** *Magazine, Consumer.*
Published by: Motorpress Hellas (Subsidiary of: Gruner + Jahr AG & Co), 132 Lefkis Str, Krioneri, 14568, Greece. TEL 30-210-6262000, FAX 30-210-6262401, info@motorpress.gr, http://www.motorpress.gr. Circ: 18,000 (paid and controlled).

388.3 NZL ISSN 1177-1100
4 X 4 ACTION MAGAZINE. Text in English. 2003. m. NZD 71 per issue (effective 2008). adv. **Document type:** *Magazine, Consumer.*
Published by: 4x4 Action Magazine, PO Box 14248, Tauranga, New Zealand. Ed. Bobbie Kincaid. Adv. contact John Reid.

629.222 GBR ISSN 1745-4700
4 X 4 & M P V DRIVER. Variant title: Four by Four and Multi-Purpose Vehicle Driver. Text in English. 2002. bi-m. GBP 16.55 (effective 2010). adv. **Document type:** *Magazine, Consumer.*
Former titles (until 2005): What M P V and 4 x 4? (1741-1491); (until 2003): What M P V? and Four Wheel Drive (1476-5357)

TU

—CCC.
Published by: M S Publications, 2nd Fl, Ewer House, 44-46 Crouch St, Colchester, CO3 3HH, United Kingdom. TEL 44-1206-506249, FAX 44-1206-500180.

388.3 AUS ISSN 0726-2418
4 X 4 AUSTRALIA. Text in English. 1980. m. AUD 8.50 newsstand/cover (effective 2008). adv. **Document type:** *Magazine, Consumer.* **Description:** Covers the latest trends and the best tracks for four wheel drive enthusiasts.
Formerly (until 199?): Australian Off-Road Action (0159-723X)
Indexed: A11.
Published by: A C P Magazines Ltd. (Subsidiary of: P B L Media Pty Ltd.), 54-58 Park St, Sydney, NSW 2000, Australia. TEL 61-2-92828000, FAX 61-2-91263769. Ed. Dean Mellor. Adv. contact Cameron Davis. color page AUD 2,947; bleed 235 x 307. Circ: 20,521. **Subscr. to:** Magshop, Reply Paid 4967, Sydney, NSW 2001, Australia. TEL 61-2-136116, subs@magstore.com.au, http://shop.magstore.com.au.

388.3 USA
4 X 4 PERFORMANCE. Text in English. bi-m. USD 16.95 domestic; USD 23.50 in Canada; USD 26 elsewhere (effective 2007). **Document type:** *Magazine, Consumer.* **Description:** Emphasis is on affordable hands-on how-to articles, practical technical information, and tricks and tips to help everyone from hardcore to casual four-wheelers enjoy their vehicles to the max.
Published by: Source Interlink Companies, 6420 Wilshire Blvd, 10th Fl, Los Angeles, CA 90048. TEL 323-782-2000, FAX 323-782-2585, dheine@sourceinterlink.com, http://www.sourceinterlinkmedia.com.

388.3 BEL ISSN 0779-9500
4 X 4 PLUS (FRENCH EDITION). Text in French. 1972. 8/yr. EUR 4.45 per issue domestic; EUR 5.30 per issue foreign (effective 2005). adv. back issues avail. **Description:** Includes news on SUVs, test reports, and travel.
Related titles: Dutch ed.: 4 x 4 Plus (Nederlandse Edition). ISSN 0779-9497.
Published by: Plus Media, Kalkstraat 23, St-Niklaas, 9100, Belgium. TEL 32-3-766-0695, FAX 32-3-777-7204, info@plusmedia.be. Ed., Pub. Lubo de Ravet. Circ: 35,000.

388.346 AUS ISSN 1449-6224
4 X 4 TRADER. Text in English. 1991. m. AUD 50 in Australia & New Zealand; AUD 70 elsewhere; AUD 3.95 newsstand/cover (effective 2008). adv. **Document type:** *Magazine, Consumer.* **Description:** Provides deals on recreational market of 4WD's, motorhomes and caravans; offers a list of new and used AWD's and specialist 4WD's available for sale.
Published by: A C P Trader International Group (Subsidiary of: P B L Media Pty Ltd.), 73 Atherton Rd, Oakleigh, VIC 3166, Australia. TEL 61-3-95674200, FAX 61-3-95634554. Eds. Mike Sinclair, Greg Leech TEL 61-3-95674194. Adv. contact Justine Schuller. color page AUD 1,600; trim 195 x 275. Circ: 13,535. **Subscr. to:** Magshop, Reply Paid 4967, Sydney, NSW 2001, Australia. TEL 61-2-136116, subs@magstore.com.au, http://shop.magstore.com.au.

629.22 DEU ISSN 0946-2937
4WHEEL FUN; das Gelaendewagen-Magazin. Text in German. 1994. m. EUR 29.90; EUR 2.90 newsstand/cover (effective 2007). adv. **Document type:** *Magazine, Consumer.*
Published by: Motor Presse Stuttgart GmbH und Co. KG, Leuschnerstr 1, Stuttgart, 70174, Germany. TEL 49-711-18201, FAX 49-711-1821779, cgolla@motorpresse.de, http://www.motorpresse.de. Ed. Roland Korioth. Adv. contact Stefan Granzer. color page EUR 7,000; trim 185 x 260. Circ: 33,177 (paid).

629.331 CZE ISSN 1212-7043
4X4 AUTOMAGAZIN. Text in Czech. 1999. m. CZK 790; CZK 79 newsstand/cover (effective 2010). adv. **Document type:** *Magazine, Consumer.*
Published by: Polygraf Net, s.r.o., Jana Masaryka 26, Prague 2, 120 00, Czech Republic. TEL 420-222-522321, FAX 420-222-514677. Ed. Petr Zikmund. Adv. contact Dagmar Janouskova.

388.3 FRA ISSN 2105-7753
▼ **4X4 MAGAZINE & AUTO VERTE.** Text in French. 2009. m. **Document type:** *Magazine, Consumer.*
Formed by the merger of (1981-2009): 4x4 Magazine (0247-6886); (1981-2009): Auto Verte (0242-9292)
Published by: Editions Lariviere, 6 Rue Olof Palme, Clichy, 92587, France. TEL 33-1-47565400, http://www.editions-lariviere.fr.

629.222 NOR ISSN 1504-3665
4X4GUIDEN; autofilaarbok. Spine title: Den Store 4x4-guiden. Variant title: Autofil Aarbok 4x4guiden. Text in Norwegian. 2004. a. **Document type:** *Magazine, Consumer.*
Published by: Aller Forlag AS, Stenersgaten 2, Sentrum, Oslo, 0189, Norway. TEL 47-21-301000, FAX 47-21-301205, allerforlag@aller.no, http://www.aller.no.

796.77 USA ISSN 1547-4364
5.0 MUSTANG & SUPER FORDS. Text in English. 1994. m. USD 15 domestic; USD 27 in Canada; USD 39 elsewhere (effective 2008). adv. back issues avail. **Document type:** *Magazine, Consumer.* **Description:** Provides readers with a mix of performance how-tos, technical advice, competition tips, new product evaluations and latest innovations in street performance.
Formed by the merger of (1994-200?): 5.0 Mustang (1073-4740); (19??-2000): Super Ford (1054-318X); Which was formerly (until 19??): Super Ford Magazine (0279-2184)
Related titles: Online - full text ed.: USD 7.50 (effective 2008).
—CCC.
Published by: Source Interlink Companies, 9036 Brittany Way, Tampa, FL 33619. TEL 813-675-3500, FAX 813-675-3556, dheine@sourceinterlink.com, http://www.sourceinterlinkmedia.com. Ed. Steve Turner. Pub. Don Parrish TEL 813-675-3482. adv.: B&W page USD 6,880, color page USD 8,605. Circ: 85,667 (paid).

629.2 GRC
5 ASTERIA TIS ASFALIAS. Text in Greek. 2005. a. EUR 5.95 newsstand/cover (effective 2006). adv. **Document type:** *Magazine, Consumer.*
Published by: Motorpress Hellas (Subsidiary of: Gruner + Jahr AG & Co), 132 Lefkis Str, Krioneri, 14568, Greece. TEL 30-210-6262000, FAX 30-210-6262401, info@motorpress.gr, http://www.motorpress.gr. Circ: 25,000 (controlled).

385.34 RUS
5 KOLESO. Text in Russian. m. **Document type:** *Magazine, Consumer.* **Description:** Designed for car owners, professional drivers and car dealers. Contains information on the latest models from Russian and foreign car manufacturers as well as design proposals, test drives, advice for drivers, etc.
Published by: Izdatel'skii Dom S P N, ul Kedrova, 15, Moscow, 117036, Russian Federation. valle@spn.ru, http://www.spn.ru/publishing. Circ: 93,000.

796.77 USA ISSN 1540-1448
9 MAGAZINE; the porsche enthusiasts magazine. Text in English. 2002 (Feb.). 4/yr. USD 19.97; USD 3.99 newsstand/cover (effective 2002). adv. **Document type:** *Magazine, Consumer.* **Description:** Contains articles and features on and for Porsche owners and their cars.
Address: 107 W. Wilson, Ste. C, Gallup, NM 87301. adv.: B&W page USD 1,400, color page USD 1,850; trim 8.25 x 10.75.

629.222 ITA ISSN 1724-9392
100 ANNI DI ITALIA IN AUTOMOBILE. Text in Italian. 2004. s-m. **Document type:** *Magazine, Consumer.*
Published by: De Agostini Editore, Via G da Verrazzano 15, Novara, 28100, Italy. TEL 39-0321-4241, FAX 39-0321-424305, info@deagostini.it, http://www.deagostini.it.

796.7 GBR ISSN 0306-6312
750 BULLETIN. Text in English. 1939. m. GBP 45 domestic membership; GBP 50 foreign membership (effective 2010). adv. bk.rev. **Document type:** *Magazine, Consumer.*
Published by: Seven Fifty Motor Club Ltd., Rose Farm, Upper St, Oakley, Diss, Norfolk IP21 4AX, United Kingdom. TEL 44-1379-741641, FAX 44-1379-741941, 750mc@btconnect.com, http://www.750mc.co.uk/. adv.: B&W page GBP 120, color page GBP 180. Circ: 2,300.

388 GBR ISSN 0959-8782
911 AND PORSCHE WORLD. Text in English. 1990. m. GBP 45 domestic; GBP 80 foreign; GBP 4.50 per issue domestic; GBP 7.25 per issue foreign (effective 2009). adv. back issues avail. **Document type:** *Magazine, Consumer.* **Description:** Contains information about classical cars.
Related titles: Online - full text ed.
Published by: C H Publications Ltd., Nimax House, 20 Ullswater Cresent, Ullswater Business Park, Coulsdon, Surrey CR5 2HR, United Kingdom. TEL 44-20-86556400, FAX 44-20-87631001, chp@chpltd.com, http://www.chpltd.com. Ed. Steve Bennett. **Dist. by:** M M C Ltd.

TRANSPORTATION—Computer Applications

388.0285 DEU
NAVI TEST. Text in German. 2007. irreg. EUR 2.30 newsstand/cover (effective 2011). adv. **Document type:** *Magazine, Consumer.*
Formerly (until 2009): Navigation
Published by: Michael E. Brieden Verlag GmbH, Gartroper Str 42, Duisburg, 47138, Germany. TEL 49-203-42920, FAX 49-203-4292149, info@brieden.de, http://www.brieden.de.

352.7 624 GBR
P T R C SUMMER ANNUAL MEETING. PROCEEDINGS. (Planning and Transport Research and Computation) Text in English. 1968. irreg., latest 1998. price varies. back issues avail. **Document type:** *Proceedings.*
Indexed: HRIS.
Published by: P T R C Education and Research Services Ltd., Glenthorne House, 5-17 Hammersmith Grove, London, W6 0LG, United Kingdom. info@ptrc-training.co.uk. Circ: 350.

SIGNAL UND DRAHT; Railsignalling & Telecommunication. *see* TRANSPORTATION—Railroads

625 001.642 ZAF
SOUTH AFRICA. DIVISION OF ROADS AND TRANSPORT TECHNOLOGY. USER MANUALS AND COMPUTER PROGRAMS/ DIVISIE VIR PAD- EN VERVOERTEGNOLOGIE. GEBRUIKERSHANDBOEKE EN REKENAARPROGRAMME. Text in English. 1976. irreg., latest 1990. price varies. **Document type:** *Government.*
Formerly: National Institute for Transport and Road Research. User Manuals for Computer Programs
Published by: (South Africa. Computer Information Centre for Transportation), Division of Roads and Transport Technology, PO Box 395, Pretoria, 0001, South Africa. **Co-sponsor:** Great Britain. Department for Transport.

TETSUDO SAIBANE. SHINPOJUMU RONBUNSHU (CD-ROM)/ RAILWAY CYBERNETICS. SYMPOSIUM. PAPERS. *see* COMPUTERS—Cybernetics

TRANSPORTATION MANAGEMENT & ENGINEERING. *see* TRANSPORTATION

TRANSPORTATION—Railroads

385 USA ISSN 1934-4449
TF501
A A R S JOURNAL. Text in English. 1996. q. USD 75 membership (effective 2007). **Document type:** *Journal, Trade.*
Published by: American Association of Railroad Superintendents, PO Box 456, Tinley Park, IL 60477. TEL 708-342-0210, FAX 708-342-0257, aars@supt.org, http://www.supt.org.

385 USA ISSN 1076-6693
A C & Y H S NEWS. Text in English. 1994. q. USD 5 newsstand/cover to non-members; USD 4 newsstand/cover to members (effective 2005). **Document type:** *Magazine, Consumer.*
Published by: Akron, Canton and Youngstown Railroad Historical Society, PO Box 196, Sharon Center, OH 44274. http://www.acyhs.org. Ed. Robert E Lucas.

A M R A JOURNAL. *see* HOBBIES

385 GBR
A S L E F JOURNAL. Text in English. 1884. m. free to members (effective 2009). adv. bk.rev. illus. back issues avail. **Document type:** *Journal, Trade.* **Description:** Features up to date on key issues within the rail industry as well as the trade union movement.
Former titles (until 2006): Locomotive Journal; (until 1904): Locomotive Engineers' and Firemen's Monthly Journal
Related titles: Online - full text ed.: free (effective 2009).
Published by: Associated Society of Locomotive Engineers and Firemen, 9 Arkwright Rd, Hampstead, London, NW3 6AB, United Kingdom. TEL 44-20-73178600, FAX 44-20-77946406, info@aslef.org.uk. Ed. Keith Norman. Adv. contact David Lancaster TEL 44-20-78782316.

385 625 DNK ISSN 1902-6242
AARET PAA BANEN. Text in Danish. 2007. a. **Document type:** *Yearbook, Government.*
Related titles: Online - full text ed.: ISSN 1902-6250.
Published by: Banedanmark/Rail Net Denmark, Amerika Plads 15, Copenhagen OE, 2100, Denmark. TEL 45-82-340000, FAX 45-82-344572, banedanmark@bane.dk.

385 CAN ISSN 1912-7286
ALBERTA RAILWAY PROPERTY ASSESSMENT MINISTER'S GUIDELINES. Text in English. 1999. a. **Document type:** *Government.*
Former titles (until 2004): Alberta Railway Assessment Minister's Guidelines (1910-2607); (until 2003): Alberta Railway Assessment Manual (1707-9268)
Published by: Alberta Municipal Affairs and Housing, 18th Flr, Commerce Pl, 10155-102 St, Edmonton, AB T5J 4L4, Canada. TEL 780-427-2732, FAX 780-422-1419, comments@gov.ab.ca, http://www.municipalaffairs.gov.ab.ca/index.htm.

625.1 690 USA ISSN 1542-9253
AMERICAN RAILWAY ENGINEERING AND MAINTENANCE-OF-WAY ASSOCIATION. ANNUAL CONFERENCE. PROCEEDINGS. Text in English. 2000. a. USD 125 to non-members; USD 65 to members (effective 2008).
Formed by the 2000 merger of: American Railway Bridge and Building Association. Proceedings; American Railway Engineering Association. Proceedings; Which was formerly (until 1983): American Railway Engineering Association. Proceedings, Technical Conference (0271-4450); (until 1974): American Railway Engineering Association. Annual Convention. Proceedings (0096-0268); (until 1912): American Railway Engineering and Maintenance-of-Way Association. Annual Convention. Proceedings
Related titles: CD-ROM ed.: ISSN 1543-8279.
—Linda Hall.
Published by: American Railway Engineering and Maintenance-of-Way Association, 10003 Derekwood Lane, Ste 210, Lanham, MD 20706. TEL 301-459-3200, FAX 301-459-8077, http://www.arema.org.

621 385 USA
AMERICAN SOCIETY OF MECHANICAL ENGINEERS. RAIL TRANSPORTATION DIVISION. NEWSLETTER. Text in English. irreg. (2-3/yr). free to members (effective 2009). back issues avail.
Related titles: Online - full text ed.
Indexed: C&ISA, E&CAJ.
Published by: A S M E International, Three Park Ave, New York, NY 10016. TEL 212-591-7158, 800-843-2763, FAX 212-591-7739, infocentral@asme.org, http://www.asme.org.

385 USA ISSN 0097-7039
HE2791
AMTRAK ANNUAL REPORT. Text in English. 1971. a. charts; illus.; stat. **Document type:** *Corporate.* **Description:** Reviews Amtrak's activities for the previous year, along with the company's plans for the future.
Published by: National Railroad Passenger Corporation, 60 Massachusetts Ave, N E, Washington, DC 20002. TEL 202-906-3000. Circ: 15,000.

ARBEIT UND VERKEHR. *see* LABOR UNIONS

ARRIVE (ARLINGTON). *see* TRAVEL AND TOURISM—Airline Inflight And Hotel Inroom

385 ARG
ASOCIACION DEL CONGRESO PANAMERICANO DE FERROCARRILES. BOLETIN. Text in Spanish. 1916. bi-m. membership. adv. bk.rev. charts; stat.
Published by: Asociacion del Congreso Panamericano de Ferrocarriles/ Pan-American Railway Congress Association, Avda. 9 de Julio 1925, Piso 13, Buenos Aires, 1332, Argentina. TEL 54-114-8141823, FAX 54-114-8141823. Ed. Juan Carlos de Marchi. Circ: 800.

385 FRA ISSN 0760-548X
ASSOCIATION FRANCAISE DES AMIS DES CHEMINS DE FER. REVUE. Text in French. 1937. bi-m. adv. bk.rev. charts; illus. **Document type:** *Magazine, Consumer.* **Description:** Discusses worldwide railways of yesterday, today and the future.
Formerly (until 1979): Chemins de Fer (0009-2924)
Published by: Association Francaise des Amis des Chemins de Fer, Gare de l'Est, Paris, Cedex 10 75475, France. TEL 33-1-40382092. Ed. Bernard Porcher. Circ: 5,000.

625.1 USA
ASSOCIATION OF RAILROAD EDITORS. PROOF. Text in English. 1922. m. **Document type:** *Newsletter.*
Published by: Association of Railroad Editors, c/o Paula Newbaker, Association of American Railroads, 50 F St, N W, Washington, DC 20001. TEL 202-639-2562, FAX 202-639-2559.

AUSTRALIA. BUREAU OF STATISTICS. FREIGHT MOVEMENTS, AUSTRALIA, SUMMARY (ONLINE). *see* TRANSPORTATION—Abstracting, Bibliographies, Statistics

AUSTRALIAN MODEL RAILWAY MAGAZINE. *see* HOBBIES

AUSTRALIAN RAIL TRAM & BUS WORKER. *see* LABOR UNIONS

625.1 790.133 AUS ISSN 1030-021X
AUSTRALIAN RAILWAY ENTHUSIAST. Text in English. 1961. q. free to members (effective 2008). adv. bk.rev. illus.; maps. back issues avail. **Document type:** *Magazine, Consumer.* **Description:** Provides information on interesting developments taking place in the operation of railways and tram-ways around Australia.
Published by: Association of Railway Enthusiasts Ltd., GPO Box 4810, Melbourne, VIC 3001, Australia. http://www.steamengine.com.au/railways/are/. Ed. Warren Banfield. Circ: 1,400.

385 AUS ISSN 1449-6291
TF121
AUSTRALIAN RAILWAY HISTORY. Abbreviated title: A R H. Text in English. 1950. m. AUD 73 domestic to non-members; free to members (effective 2008). bk.rev.; film rev. charts; illus.; stat. index. back issues avail. **Document type:** *Bulletin, Consumer.* **Description:** Contain historical articles about the Australian Railway Historical Society.

Former titles (until 2004): Australian Railway Historical Society. Bulletin (0005-0105); (until 1952): Australasian Railway and Locomotive Historical Society. Bulletin; Which superseded in part (in 1948): Railways in Australia and A R L H S Bulletin
Published by: Australian Railway Historical Society, New South Wales Division, 67 Renwick St, Redfern, NSW 2016, Australia. TEL 61-2-96994595, FAX 61-2-96991714, mail@arhsnsw.com.au. Ed. Andrew Hayne. Circ: 2,600.

385 AUS ISSN 1837-915X
▼ **AUSTRALIAN RAILWAYS ILLUSTRATED.** Text in English. 2010. bi-m. AUD 49.75 domestic; AUD 95 in New Zealand; AUD 120 elsewhere; AUD 9.75 per issue (effective 2011). adv. back issues avail. **Document type:** *Magazine, Trade.*
Published by: Australian Railways Illustrated Pty Ltd, PO Box 886, Kings Langley, NSW 2147, Australia. TEL 61-2-413183080, mike@arimagazine.com.au. Ed. Stewart Anderson.

AUSTRALIAN RAILWAYS UNION. NATIONAL OFFICE NEWS. *see* LABOR UNIONS

385 USA ISSN 0362-2711
TF25.B8
B & M BULLETIN. (Boston & Maine) Text in English. 1971. irreg. USD 10 newsstand/cover to non-members; free to members (effective 2008). bk.rev. charts; illus. **Document type:** *Newsletter, Consumer.* **Description:** Historical record of the B&M and its predecessor railroads.
Published by: Boston & Maine Railroad Historical Society, Inc., c/o Editor, PO Box 469, Derry, NH 03038-0469. TEL 978-454-3600. Ed. Andrew Andrew Wilson. Circ: 2,000.

385 DEU
B D E F - JAHRBUCH. Text in German. 1982. a. EUR 5 per issue (effective 2011). back issues avail. **Document type:** *Yearbook, Trade.*
Published by: Bundesverband Deutscher Eisenbahn-Freunde, Postfach 1140, Hannover, 30011, Germany. TEL 49-5101-13340, FAX 49-5101-13370, bdef@bdef.de. Circ: 3,000.

B M W E JOURNAL. *see* LABOR UNIONS

385 GBR ISSN 0955-5382
BACKTRACK; britain's leading historical railway monthly. Text in English. 1986. m. GBP 42 domestic; GBP 60 in Europe; GBP 70 elsewhere; GBP 3.70 newsstand/cover (effective 2009). illus. back issues avail. **Document type:** *Magazine, Consumer.* **Description:** Presents articles and features on the history of railways and locomotives.
Incorporates (1991-199?): Modellers' Backtrack (0961-5466)
Related titles: Online - full text ed.
Published by: Pendragon Publishing, PO Box No 3, Easingwold, York Y061 3YS, United Kingdom. TEL 44-1347-824397, pendragonpublishing@btinternet.com. Ed. Michael Blakemore. **Subscr. to:** c/o Warners, W S, Bourne, Lincolnshire PE10 9PH, United Kingdom. TEL 44-1778-392024, FAX 44-1778-421706, subscriptions@warnersgroup.co.uk.

556 DEU ISSN 1860-143X
DAS BAHN-ADRESSBUCH. Variant title: D B A. Text in German. 195?. a. EUR 52 (effective 2009). **Document type:** *Directory, Trade.*
Former titles (until 2004): Deutsches Bahn-Adressbuch (0947-8426); (until 1994): Deutsche Bundesbahn. Adressbuch. Teil 1: Dienststellen (0943-0636); (until 1991): Deutsche Bundesbahn-Adressbuch. Teil 1: Dienststellen und Aemter (0932-4348); (until 1986): Deutsches Bundesbahn-Adressbuch. Teil 1: Dienststellen und Aemter der Deutschen Bundesbahn (0415-715X)
Published by: Eurailpress Tetzlaff-Hestra GmbH & Co. KG (Subsidiary of: Deutscher Verkehrs Verlag GmbH), Nordkanalstr 36, Hamburg, 20097, Germany. TEL 49-40-2371403, FAX 49-40-23714259, info@eurailpress.com, http://www.eurailpress.com. Circ: 6,000 (paid and controlled).

629.4 DEU ISSN 0937-7174
BAHN-EXTRA. Text in German. 1990. bi-m. EUR 63.72; EUR 12.50 newsstand/cover (effective 2010). adv. **Document type:** *Magazine, Consumer.*
Published by: GeraMond Verlag GmbH, Infanteriestr 11a, Munich, 80797, Germany. TEL 49-89-1306990, FAX 49-89-130699100, info@geramond.de, http://www.geramond.de. Adv. contact Judith Fischl. B&W page EUR 1,440, color page EUR 1,980. Circ: 14,936 (paid and controlled).

625.1 DEU ISSN 0178-4528
BAHN-REPORT. Text in German. 1983. bi-m. EUR 31.20; EUR 5.50 newsstand/cover (effective 2007). adv. **Document type:** *Magazine, Trade.*
Published by: Interessengemeinschaft Schienenverkehr e.V., Moritzstr 15, Chemnitz, 09111, Germany. TEL 49-371-6662980, FAX 49-371-6662992. Ed., Adv. contact Matthias Hansen. B&W page EUR 439, color page EUR 799. Circ: 6,300 (controlled).

385 CHE
BAHNHOFBLATT. Text in German. q.
Published by: Schweizerischer Bundesbahnen SBB, Kreisdirektion 111, Zuerich, 8021, Switzerland. TEL 01-8093111, FAX 01-8106002. Circ: 220,000.

385 DNK ISSN 1904-3228
▼ **BANEBRANCHEN.** Variant title: Magasinet BaneBranchen. Text in Danish. 2010. a. adv. **Document type:** *Trade.*
Related titles: Online - full text ed.: ISSN 1904-4046.
Published by: Banebranchen, c/o Peter Sonne, Bombardier, Kay FiskersPlads 9, Copenhagen S, 2300, Denmark. TEL 45-36-394600, info@banebranchen.dk. Ed. Peter Sonne. Circ: 5,000.

385 625 DNK ISSN 1604-309X
BANEDANMARK. AARSRAPPORT. Text in Danish. 1999. a. stat. back issues avail. **Document type:** *Government.*
Former titles (until 2004): Banestyrelsen. Aarsrapport (1604-3081); (until 2002): Banestyrelsen. Virksomhedsregnskab (Online) (1601-3948); (until 2002): Banestyrelsen. Virksomhedsregnskab (Print) (1600-4442)
Media: Online - full content.
Published by: Banedanmark/Rail Net Denmark, Amerika Plads 15, Copenhagen OE, 2100, Denmark. TEL 45-82-340000, FAX 45-82-344572, banedanmark@bane.dk.

385 NLD ISSN 0282-888X
BENELUX RAIL. Text in Dutch, French. 1981. irreg., latest vol.8, 1994. EUR 22 (effective 2009). illus. back issues avail. **Document type:** *Academic/Scholarly.* **Description:** Provides information on events and developments affecting all railroads (including urban transport, industrial and museum railways) in the Benelux countries during the preceding two years. Includes network maps and list of all railways stations and depots.
Published by: Het Nijvere Lezerke, Hoebigerweg 10, Eys, 6287 AT, Netherlands. TEL 31-43-4512152, FAX 31-43-4511949, marhann@planet.nl, http://www.nijverepublishers.nl. Ed., Pub., R&P Marcel Vleugels.

385 GBR ISSN 0263-0125
BLASTPIPE. Text in English. 1981. q. free membership (effective 2009). illus. **Document type:** *Magazine, Consumer.*
—BLDSC (2109.033000).
Published by: Scottish Railway Preservation Society, Bo'ness Station, Union St, Bo'ness, W Lothian, Scotland EH51 9AQ, United Kingdom. TEL 44-1506-825855, society@srps.org.uk, http://www.srps.org.uk/.

385 USA
BOSTON & MAINE RAILROAD HISTORICAL SOCIETY. NEWSLETTER. Text in English. 6/yr. free to members (effective 2008). **Document type:** *Newsletter, Consumer.* **Description:** Serves to notify members of upcoming events and Society business. It also contains news articles that have been submitted by members.
Published by: Boston & Maine Railroad Historical Society, Inc., c/o Editor, PO Box 469, Derry, NH 03038-0469. TEL 978-454-3600.

385 GBR ISSN 1354-0947
BRANCH LINE NEWS. Abbreviated title: B L N. Text in English. 1955. s-m. looseleaf. free to members (effective 2009). adv. bk.rev. index. back issues avail. **Document type:** *Newsletter, Trade.* **Description:** Covers both the history of and the current evolution of railways, especially in Britain, but also around the world.
Related titles: Diskette ed.: Passenger Train Services Over Unusual Lines.
Published by: Branch Line Society, c/o Hon General Secretary S R Chandler, 37 Osberton Pl, Hunters Bar, Sheffield, S Yorks S11 8XL, United Kingdom. TEL 44-114-2680429, FAX 44-114-263-1094, info@branchline.org.uk. Circ: 1,020 (paid). **Dist. by:** D.J. Monger, Distribution Officer, 6 Underhill Close, Godalming, Surrey GU7 1NU, United Kingdom.

385.2 CAN ISSN 0824-233X
BRANCHLINE; Canada's rail newsmagazine. Text in English. 1965. m. CAD 32, USD 26. adv. bk.rev. back issues avail. **Description:** Promotes an interest in railways and railway history. Provides current news.
Published by: Bytown Railway Society, P O Box 141, Sta A, Ottawa, ON K1N 8V1, Canada. TEL 613-745-1201. Eds. David Stremes, Earl Roberts. Adv. contact Leslie Goodwin. Circ: 1,800 (paid); 70 (controlled).

BRITAIN BY BRITRAIL; touring Britain by train. *see* TRAVEL AND TOURISM

385 CAN ISSN 1713-2738
BRITISH COLUMBIA RAILWAY COMPANY ANNUAL REPORT. Text in English. 1959. a.
Former titles (until 2002): B C R Group of Companies. Annual Report (1208-0845); (until 1994): British Columbia Railway Group Annual Report (0846-4847); (until 1988): British Columbia Railway. Annual Report (0702-9438); (until 1972): Pacific Great Eastern Railway. Annual Report (0702-942X)
Published by: British Columbia Railway Company, 400-221 W Esplanade, North Vancouver, BC V7M 3J3, Canada. TEL 604-678-4735, FAX 604-678-4736.

385.264 GBR
BRITISH INTERNATIONAL FREIGHT ASSOCIATION. YEARBOOK. Text in English. 1944. a. GBP 95 (effective 2000). adv. **Document type:** *Yearbook, Trade.*
Formerly: Institute of Freight Forwarders. Yearbook
Published by: British International Freight Association, Redfern House, Browells Ln, Feltham, Mddx TW13 7EP, United Kingdom. TEL 44-020-88442266, FAX 44-020-88905546, bifa@bifa.org, http://www.bifa.org. Ed. Emma Murray. R&P Colin Beaumont. Adv. contact Ray Girvan. Circ: 6,000.

385.094 GBR ISSN 0961-8244
BRITISH RAILWAYS ILLUSTRATED. Text in English. 1991. m. GBP 45.60 domestic; GBP 61.70 in Europe; GBP 73.80 elsewhere; GBP 3.80 per issue (effective 2009). illus. back issues avail. **Document type:** *Magazine, Consumer.* **Description:** Provides extensive articles and photographs on the history of British railways and trains.
Published by: Irwell Press, 59a High St, Clophill, Beds MK45 4BE, United Kingdom. TEL 44-1525-861888, FAX 44-1525-862044, george@irwellpress.demon.co.uk.

BULLETIN DES TRANSPORTS ET DE LA LOGISTIQUE. *see* LAW

385 340 CHE ISSN 1011-3797
HE1001
BULLETIN DES TRANSPORTS INTERNATIONAUX FERROVIAIRES. Text in French, German, English. 1983. q. CHF 48 (effective 2001). **Document type:** *Bulletin, Trade.*
Formerly (until 1985): Bulletin des Transports Internationaux par Chemin de Fer (1015-2156)
Indexed: A22.
—IE, Infotrieve.
Published by: Organisation Intergouvernementale pour les Transports Internationaux Ferroviaires/Zwischenstaatliche Organisation fuer den Internationalen Eisenbahnverkehr, Gryphenhuebeliweg 30, Bern, 3006, Switzerland. TEL 41-31-3591010, FAX 41-31-3591011, otif@otif.ch, http://www.otif.ch. Circ: 350.

385 CMR
CAMEROON. REGIE NATIONALE DES CHEMINS DE FER. CHEMINOT CAMEROUNAIS. Text in French. q. **Document type:** *Newspaper.*
Published by: Regie Nationale des Chemins de Fer, BP 304, Douala, Cameroon. TEL 00-237-406045, FAX 00-237-407159. Ed. Jean Moto Moto.

385.1 CMR
CAMEROON. REGIE NATIONALE DES CHEMINS DE FER. RAPPORT D'ACTIVITES. Text in French. s-a. **Document type:** *Trade.*
Formerly: Cameroon. Regie Nationale des Chemins de Fer. Compte Rendu de Gestion
Published by: Regie Nationale des Chemins de Fer, BP 304, Douala, Cameroon. TEL 00-237-406045, FAX 00-237-407159. Ed. Jean Moto Moto.

385 CMR
CAMEROON. REGIE NATIONALE DES CHEMINS DE FER. STATISTIQUES DE GESTION. Text in French. q. illus. **Document type:** *Trade.*
Formerly: Cameroon. Regie Nationale des Chemins de Fer. Statistiques
Published by: Regie Nationale des Chemins de Fer, BP 304, Douala, Cameroon. TEL 00-237-406045, FAX 00-237-407159. Ed. Jean Moto Moto.

385 CAN ISSN 0008-4875
HE2801
CANADIAN RAIL/RAIL CANADIEN. Text in English, French. 1949. bi-m. CAD 36, USD 31 (effective 2000). bk.rev. illus. index. **Document type:** *Bulletin.*
Indexed: AmH&L.
Published by: Canadian Railroad Historical Association, 120 rue St. Pierre, St. Constant, PQ J5A 2G9, Canada. Eds. Douglas N W Smith, Frederick F Angus. Circ: 1,100 (controlled).

385 CAN ISSN 0226-157X
CANADIAN RAILWAY CLUB. NEWSLETTER. Text in English. 1908. 3/yr. CAD 120 to members. adv. **Document type:** *Newsletter.* **Description:** Concerned with the construction, operation and maintenance of railroads and railroad equipment.
Formerly (until 1978): Canadian Railway Club. Official Proceedings (0008-4883)
—Linda Hall.
Published by: Canadian Railway Club, Inc., P O Box 162, Sta A, Montreal, PQ H3C 1C5, Canada. TEL 514-634-4515, FAX 514-631-2280. Ed. J H Glatzmayer. Adv. contact J.H. Glatzmayer. Circ: 1,500.

385.2 CAN ISSN 0829-3023
CANADIAN TRACKSIDE GUIDE. Text in English. 1982. a. CAD 23.95, USD 24 (effective 2001). adv. 700 p./no.; **Document type:** *Directory.* **Description:** Lists mainline, shortline and industrial locomotives, passenger cars, preserved equipment, urban rail transit equipment, cabooses, cranes, spreaders, plows, work service equipment, former passenger equipment now in non-revenue service, railway reporting marks, detailed listings for every mainline railway subdivision in Canada, and AAR reporting marks.
Published by: Bytown Railway Society, P O Box 141, Sta A, Ottawa, ON K1N 8V1, Canada. TEL 613-745-1201. Eds. David Stremes, Earl Roberts. Circ: 1,850 (paid).

625.2 USA
CAR AND LOCOMOTIVE CYCLOPEDIA. Text in English. 1879. irreg., latest 1997. looseleaf. USD 150 per issue binder; USD 225 per issue hardcover (effective 2001). adv. charts; illus. reprints avail. **Document type:** *Monographic series, Trade.* **Description:** Features state-of-the-art technical resource information, with extensive descriptions and technical drawings of freight cars, passenger cars, and locomotives in use today, along with those still in the planning stages.
Formed by the 1966 merger of: Car Builders Cyclopedia; Locomotive Cyclopedia
Published by: Simmons - Boardman Books Inc., 1809 Capitol Ave, Omaha, NE 10014. TEL 402-346-4300, 800-228-9670, FAX 402-346-1783, customer_service@transalert.com, http://www.transalert.com. Ed. William Kratville. R&P Jan Benson TEL 402-449-1661. Adv. contact Pat Kentner TEL 402-449-1677. Circ: 6,000.

385 ESP
CARRIL; revista de divulgacion ferroviaria. Text in Spanish. 1978. 4/yr. EUR 23.50 domestic; EUR 37 in Europe; EUR 43.50 elsewhere (effective 2008). adv. bk.rev. back issues avail. **Document type:** *Magazine, Consumer.*
Published by: Asociacion de Amigos del Ferrocarril de Barcelona, Estacion de Francia, Ocata, s-n, Apdo. 1923, Barcelona, 08080, Spain. TEL 34-93-3105297, aafcb@iespana.es, http://www.ieaspana.es/aafcb. Adv. contact Marta Balletbo Coll.

385 PRT ISSN 1647-6379
▼ **CARRIS. NEWSLETTER.** Key Title: Newsletter Carris. Text in Portuguese. 2010. bi-m. **Document type:** *Newsletter, Consumer.*
Published by: Companhia Carris de Ferro de Lisboa, Alameda Antonio Sergio 62, Oeiras, 2795, Portugal. TEL 351-213-613000, http://www.carris.pt.

625 USA ISSN 0069-1623
TF701 CODEN: GPTLFY
CENTRAL ELECTRIC RAILFANS' ASSOCIATION. BULLETIN. Text in English. 1938. irreg., latest vol.133, 2000. USD 32 membership; USD 25 Associate Membership (effective 2000). **Document type:** *Bulletin.* **Description:** Books pertaining to the history of electric-powered trolleys, streetcars, and railroad systems.
Published by: Central Electric Railfans' Association, PO Box 503, Chicago, IL 60690. TEL 312-346-3723. Ed., R&P Walter Keevil. Circ: 1,800 (paid).

385 USA ISSN 0008-9532
CENTRAL RAILWAY CHRONICLE. Text in English. 1890. 4/yr. USD 3. adv.
—Linda Hall.
Published by: Central Railway Club of Buffalo, 960 French St, Buffalo, NY 14227-3632. TEL 716-825-0248. Ed. Clarence Michael Voll. Circ: 295 (controlled).

625.1 CHN ISSN 1000-2499
CHANGSHA TIEDAO XUEYUAN XUEBAO/CHANGSHA RAILWAY INSTITUTE. JOURNAL. Text in Chinese. 1979. q. CNY 6 newsstand/cover (effective 2004). **Document type:** *Journal, Academic/Scholarly.*
Related titles: Online - full text ed.; Ed.
Published by: Changsha Tiedao Xueyuan/Changsha Railway Institute, 22, Shaoshan Nanlu, Changsha, 410075, China. TEL 86-731-2655133, FAX 86-731-5583754. **Dist. by:** China International Book Trading Corp, 35 Chegongzhuang Xilu, Haidian District, PO Box 399, Beijing 100044, China. TEL 86-10-68412045, FAX 86-10-68412023, cibtc@mail.cibtc.com.cn, http://www.cibtc.com.cn.

CHEMINOT DE FRANCE. *see* LABOR UNIONS

CHEMINOT RETRAITE. *see* LABOR UNIONS

TU

385 USA ISSN 0886-6287
TF25.C45
CHESAPEAKE AND OHIO HISTORICAL MAGAZINE. Text in English. 1969. m. USD 30 (effective 1999). bk.rev. charts; illus. **Document type:** *Monographic series.*
Formerly (until 1986): Chesapeake and Ohio Historical Newsletter (0883-587X)
Related titles: Microfilm ed.: (from PQC); Online - full text ed.
Indexed: A22, P10, P48, P53, P54, PQC.
—Ingenta.
Published by: Chesapeake and Ohio Historical Society, Inc., PO Box 79, Clifton, VA 24422. TEL 540-862-2210, FAX 540-863-9159, cohs@cfs.com, http://www.cohs.org. Circ: 2,500.

625.1 CHN ISSN 1005-0485
CHINESE RAILWAYS (ENGLISH EDITION). Text in English. 1993. s-a. USD 142 (effective 2009). **Document type:** *Journal, Academic/Scholarly.* **Description:** Provides information on the scientific and technological development of Chinese railways.
Related titles: ◆ Chinese ed.: Zhongguo Tielu. ISSN 1001-683X.
—BLDSC (3181.048855), East View.
Published by: Zhongguo Tiedao Kexue Yanjiuyuan/China Academy of Railway Sciences, 2, Daliushu Rd., Xizhimenwai, Haidian District, Beijing, 100081, China. TEL 86-10-51849182, http://www.rails.com.cn/.

385 USA ISSN 1527-0718
TF1
CLASSIC TRAINS. Text in English. 2000. q. USD 23.50 domestic; USD 29.50 in Canada; USD 30.50 elsewhere; USD 6.95 per issue (effective 2009). adv. back issues avail. **Document type:** *Magazine, Trade.* **Description:** Contains articles and features on steam engines, early diesels, famous passenger trains, and colorful old-time stories from the golden years of railroading.
Related titles: Online - full text ed.
Indexed: H20, T02.
—Linda Hall.
Published by: Kalmbach Publishing Co., 21027 Crossroads Circle, PO Box 1612, Waukesha, WI 53187. TEL 262-796-8776, 800-533-6644, FAX 262-796-1615, customerservice@kalmbach.com, http://www.kalmbach.com. Eds. Alice Korach, Dave Ingles, Rob McGonigal. Pub. Kevin P Keefe. Adv. contact Scott Bong. B&W page USD 2,477, color page USD 3,468; bleed 8.5 x 11. Circ: 58,603 (paid).

385 531.64 USA ISSN 1538-9340
COAL TRANSPORTATION REPORT (ONLINE). Variant title: Coal Transportation. Text in English. 1982. w. bk.rev. **Document type:** *Newsletter, Trade.* **Description:** Studies all aspects of coal transportation and railroad legislation and regulation.
Formerly (until 199?): Coal Transportation Report (Print) (0732-8397)
Media: Online - full text.
—CCC.
Published by: Energy Argus, Inc. (Subsidiary of: Argus Media Inc.), 1012 Fourteenth St NW, Ste 1500, Washington, DC 20005. TEL 202-775-0240, FAX 202-872-8045, washington@argusmediagroup.com, http://www.argusmediagroup.com. Circ: 250 (paid).

385.264 USA
COMMON, CARRIER CONFERENCE-IRREGULAR ROUTE. NEWSLETTER. Text in English. 1941. bi-m.
Published by: Common, Carrier Conference-Irregular Route, 2200 Mill Rd, Ste 600, Alexandria, VA 22314. TEL 703-838-1950.

385 FRA ISSN 1638-3281
CONNAISSANCE DU RAIL. Text in French. 1979. m. adv. bk.rev. bibl. cum.index. back issues avail. **Document type:** *Magazine, Consumer.*
Former titles (until 2002): Rail (1636-4384); (until 2001): Connaissance du Rail (0222-4844)
Published by: Editions de l'Ormet, Valignat, 03330, France. TEL 33-4-70585319, FAX 33-4-70585436. Ed. Pierre Laederich. Adv. contact Patricia Laederich. Circ: 10,000.

385 CAN ISSN 0319-8332
COUPLER. Text in English. 1957. bi-m. free.
Published by: B C Rail Ltd., P O Box 8770, Vancouver, BC V6B 4X6, Canada. TEL 604-984-5248, FAX 604-984-5090. Ed. K Korbin. Circ: 4,000.

625.143 USA ISSN 0097-4536
TF252
CROSSTIES. Text in English. 1919. bi-m. USD 35 (effective 1999). adv. charts; illus.; stat. index. **Description:** Covers all aspects of the railroad crosstie industry, including forest management, timber processing, worker safety, legislative and engineering issues.
Formerly: Cross Tie Bulletin (0011-197X)
Indexed: CLT&T, ChemAb, HRIS.
Published by: (Railway Tie Association), Convention South, PO Box 2267, Gulf Shores, AL 36547. TEL 251-968-5300, FAX 251-968-4532. Ed., Adv. contact J. Talty O'Connor. Pub. J Talty O'Connor. R&P Kristen McIntosh. Circ: 3,000.

385 DEU ISSN 1615-0295
D B MOBIL. (Deutsche Bahn) Text in German. 1957. m. adv. **Document type:** *Magazine, Consumer.*
Former titles (until 1999): Zug; (until 1994): Intercity; (until 1990): Schoene Welt; (until 1968): Durch die Schoene Welt
Published by: (Deutsche Bahn AG), G + J Corporate Editors GmbH (Subsidiary of: Gruner + Jahr AG & Co), Stubbenhuk 10, Hamburg, 20459, Germany. TEL 49-40-37030, FAX 49-40-37035010, info@corporate-editors.com, http://www.corporate-editors.com. Adv. contact Lena Voges. page EUR 17,300. Circ: 508,730 (controlled).

D B - SELECT. (Deutsche Bahn) *see* TRANSPORTATION—Abstracting, Bibliographies, Statistics

385 DEU ISSN 0948-7263
DEINE BAHN; Fachzeitschrift von DB Training, Learning & Consulting und des Verbandes Deutscher Eisenbahnfachschulen. Text in German. 1973. m. EUR 64.80; EUR 52.80 to students; EUR 5.40 newsstand/cover (effective 2009). adv. bk.rev. charts; illus. **Document type:** *Magazine, Trade.*
Former titles (until 1992): D B - D R Deine Bahn (0948-7638); (until 1990): D B - Deine Bahn (0172-4479); Which was formed by the merger of (1948-1973): Eisenbahner. Ausgabe A (0172-2808); (1948-1973): Eisenbahner. Ausgabe B (0172-2816); Both of which superseded in part (in 1949): Eisenbahner (0172-2824)
Published by: (Deutsche Bahn AG), Bahn Fachverlag GmbH, Am Linsenberg 16, Mainz, 55131, Germany. TEL 49-6131-28370, FAX 49-6131-283737, mail@bahn-fachverlag.de. adv.: B&W page EUR 1,800, color page EUR 2,300; trim 210 x 297. Circ: 5,886 (paid).
Co-sponsor: Verband Deutscher Eisenbahn-Fachschulen.

385.748 USA ISSN 1073-6859
DELAWARE VALLEY RAIL PASSENGER. Text in English. 1983 (Jan.). m. USD 16 (effective 2005). Website rev. stat. index. 16 p./no. 2 cols./p.; back issues avail. **Document type:** *Newsletter, Consumer.* **Description:** Contains news and analysis of passenger trains and mass transit in the Philadelphia area.
Related titles: Diskette ed.; Online - full content ed.
Published by: Delaware Valley Association of Railroad Passengers, 1601 Walnut St, Ste 1129, Philadelphia, PA 19102. TEL 215-724-5929, FAX 215-564-9415. Eds. Matthew D Mitchell, Tony DeSantis. R&P, Adv. contact Matthew D Mitchell. Circ: 2,000.

625.1 333.7932 CHN ISSN 1672-1187
DIANLI JICHE YU CHENGGUI CHELIANG/ELECTRIC LOCOMOTIVES & MASS TRANSIT VEHICLES. Text in Chinese. 1978. bi-m. USD 18 (effective 2009). **Document type:** *Journal, Academic/Scholarly.*
Formerly (until 2002): Dianli Jiche Jishu/Technology for Electric Locomotives (1007-0656)
Related titles: Online - full text ed.
—East View.
Published by: Zhuzhou Dianli Jiche Youxian Gongsi/Zhuzhou Electric Locomotive Co., Ltd., Tianxin, Zhuzhou, Hunan 412001, China. http://www.zeloco.com/.

385.264 USA
HF5686.F67
DIRECTORY OF FREIGHT ACCOUNTING OFFICES AND OVERCHARGE CLAIMS. Text in English. a. looseleaf. USD 12. **Document type:** *Directory, Trade.*
Published by: Association of American Railroads, Operations and Maintenance Department, 50 F St, N W, Washington, DC 20001. TEL 202-639-2325.

385 DEU ISSN 0934-2230
DREHSCHEIBE (COLOGNE). Text in German. 1983. 8/yr. EUR 3.80 newsstand/cover (effective 2008). adv. bk.rev. back issues avail. **Document type:** *Magazine, Trade.*
Published by: ArGe Drehscheibe e.V., Haselnusshof 1, Cologne, 50767, Germany. TEL 49-9191-704378, versandleitung@drehscheibe-online.de.

385 DEU ISSN 0936-3475
Z7233
DUMJAHN'S JAHRBUCH FUER EISENBAHNLITERATUR; ein kritischer Wegweiser zu lieferbaren, angezeigten und empfehlenswerten Buechern "rund um die Eisenbahn". Text in German. 1983. a. adv. bk.rev. back issues avail. **Document type:** *Journal, Bibliography.*
Formerly (until 1988): Jahrbuch fuer Eisenbahnliteratur (0175-2537)
Published by: Horst-Werner Dumjahn Verlag, Immenhof 12, Mainz, 55128, Germany. TEL 49-6131-330810, eisenbahn@dumjahn.de, http://www.dumjahn.de. Ed. Horst Werner Dumjahn.

385 CHN ISSN 1672-6073
DUSHI KUAIGUI JIAOTONG. Text in Chinese. 2004. bi-m. USD 31.20 (effective 2009). **Document type:** *Journal, Academic/Scholarly.*
Related titles: Online - full text ed.
Indexed: B21, ESPM, H&SSA, SSciA.
—East View.
Published by: Beijing Jiaotong Daxue, Xizhimen Wai, 3, Shangyuancun, Siyuanlou 809-2 shi, Beijing, 100044, China. TEL 86-10-68318887 ext 6198, FAX 86-10-51683783.

DYNAMIC. *see* LABOR UNIONS

385 JPN
EAST JAPAN RAILWAY COMPANY. SEMI-ANNUAL REPORT. Text in English. s-a. free for 6 mos. to corporations. charts; illus.; maps; stat. **Document type:** *Corporate.* **Description:** Contains information on the financial status of JR-East, operational summaries, and future planes during a period of 6 months.
Published by: East Japan Railway Co., 2-2 Yoyogi 2-chome, Shibuya-ku, Tokyo, 151-8578, Japan. TEL 81-3-5334-1310, FAX 81-3-5334-1297, ir@jreast.co.jp, bond@jreast.co.jp, http://www.jreast.co.jp.

385 USA
EASTERN RAILROAD NEWS. Text in English. 1998. m. USD 20 domestic; CAD 28 in Canada (effective 2001). back issues avail. **Document type:** *Magazine, Trade.* **Description:** Covers industry news pertaining to railroads running in the eastern U.S.
Media: Online - full text.
Address: 2 Pin Oak St., Palmyra, PA 17078-2945. TEL 717-975-0281, 717-838-2301, kburkholder@eastrailnews.com, http://www.eastrailnews.com. Ed. Kevin Burkholder.

EISENBAHN-AMATEUR; Schweizerische Zeitschrift fuer Eisenbahn- und Modellbaufreunde. *see* HOBBIES

385 DEU ISSN 1611-6283
EISENBAHN GESCHICHTE. Text in German. 1969. bi-m. EUR 32.50; EUR 6.50 newsstand/cover (effective 2009). adv. bk.rev. charts; illus. 32 p./no.; back issues avail. **Document type:** *Magazine, Trade.*
Former titles (until 2003): Deutsche Gesellschaft fuer Eisenbahngeschichte. Nachrichten (0722-0170); (until 1976): D G E G Nachrichten (0722-0162); (until 1974): Deutsche Gesellschaft fuer Eisenbahngeschichte. Rundschreiben (0722-0154)
Published by: Deutsche Gesellschaft fuer Eisenbahngeschichte e.V., Kleinsorgenring 14, Werl, 59457, Germany. TEL 49-2922-84970, FAX 49-2922-84927, gs@dgeg.de. Circ: 2,500.

625.1 DEU ISSN 0934-5930
EISENBAHN INGENIEUR KALENDER (YEAR). Text in German. a. adv. back issues avail. **Document type:** *Trade.* **Description:** Part A covers material required by railway engineers in their daily work; Part B covers building, machine engineering, electrical engineering, signalling and telecommunications.
Formerly: Elsners Taschenbuch der Eisenbahntechnik (0071-0075)
Published by: Tetzlaff Verlag GmbH & Co. KG, Nordkanalstr 36, Hamburg, 20097, Germany. kapke@eurailpress.com. Ed. Klaus Wehrum. Adv. contact Riccardo Di Stefano. Circ: 7,500.

385 DEU ISSN 0720-051X
EISENBAHN-JOURNAL. Text in German. 1975. m. EUR 78; EUR 7.40 newsstand/cover (effective 2011). adv. bk.rev. bibl.; charts; illus.; stat. index. back issues avail. **Document type:** *Magazine, Consumer.*
Formerly (until 1980): M und F Journal (0171-3671)
Published by: Verlagsgruppe Bahn GmbH, Am Fohlenhof 9a, Fuerstenfeldbruck, 82256, Germany. TEL 49-8141-534810, FAX 49-8141-53481100, info@vgbahn.de, http://www.vg-bahn.de. Ed. Gerhard Zimmermann. Adv. contact Elke Albrecht. Circ: 14,500 (paid and controlled).

385 625.19 DEU ISSN 0342-1902
EISENBAHN MODELLBAHN MAGAZIN. Text in German. 1963. m. EUR 72 domestic; EUR 78 foreign; EUR 6.50 newsstand/cover (effective 2010). adv. bk.rev. illus. Index. back issues avail.; reprints avail. **Document type:** *Magazine, Consumer.* **Description:** Covers all aspects of rail transport and model railroading.
Formerly (until 1973): Moderne Eisenbahn (0342-1880)
—CCC.
Published by: Alba Publikation Alf Teloeken GmbH & Co. KG, Willstaetterstr 9, Duesseldorf, 40549, Germany. TEL 49-211-520130, FAX 49-211-5201358, braun@alba-verlag.de. adv.: B&W page EUR 2,700, color page EUR 3,610. Circ: 24,254 (controlled).

385 625.1 CHE ISSN 1421-2900
EISENBAHN OESTERREICH; Geschichte, Technik, Aktualitaeten. Text in German. 1948. m. adv. abstr.; illus. index. **Document type:** *Magazine, Trade.*
Formerly (until 1995): Eisenbahn (0254-5322)
Published by: Minirex AG, Maihofstr 63, Luzern, 6002, Switzerland. TEL 41-41-4297090, FAX 41-41-4297099, redaktion@minirex.ch, http://www.minirex.ch. Circ: 8,500.

385 CHE ISSN 1421-2811
EISENBAHN REVUE INTERNATIONAL. Text in German. 1994. 10/yr. CHF 99.80; CHF 109.80 foreign (effective 1999). adv. **Document type:** *Bulletin.*
Published by: Minirex AG, Maihofstr 63, Luzern, 6002, Switzerland. redaktion@minirex.ch, http://www.minirex.ch. Ed. Walter von Andrian. Adv. contact C Roelli. B&W page CHF 1,975, color page CHF 2,955; 257 x 188. Circ: 12,000.

385 AUT ISSN 0013-2799
EISENBAHNER. Text in German. 1892. m. bk.rev.; play rev. abstr.; charts; illus. **Document type:** *Magazine, Trade.*
Published by: Oesterreichischer Gewerkschaftsbund, Gewerkschaft der Eisenbahner, Margaretenstr 166, Vienna, W 1050, Austria. TEL 43-1-54641411, FAX 43-1-54641504, gde@eisenbahner.at, http://www.eisenbahner.at. Ed. Sylvia Reiss. Circ: 108,000.

625.1 DEU ISSN 0013-2810
TF3 CODEN: ESBGAP
DER EISENBAHNINGENIEUR; Fachzeitschrift fuer Eisenbahntechnik. Text in German. 1949. m. EUR 128; EUR 15 newsstand/cover (effective 2009). adv. bk.rev. bibl.; charts; illus.; pat. index. back issues avail. **Document type:** *Magazine, Trade.* **Description:** Complete coverage of railway engineering including specialized branches such as building, building construction, surveying, signalling, telecommunications, machines, and electrical engineering.
Formerly (until 1951): Verein Deutscher Eisenbahningenieure. Zeitschrift (0174-7649); Incorporates (1965-1990): Schienenfahrzeuge (0036-6021); Which was formerly (1957-1965): Die Werkstatt (0323-8733); (1966-1990): Eisenbahnpraxis (0013-2780); Which was formerly (1957-1966): Der Operative Dienst (0323-8539); (1957-1990): Signal und Schiene (0037-5004)
Indexed: A22, EngInd, IBR, IBZ, Inspec, RefZh, SCOPUS, TM.
—AskIEEE, IE, Infotrieve, INIST, Linda Hall. **CCC.**
Published by: (Verband Deutscher Eisenbahningenieur), Eurailpress Tetzlaff-Hestra GmbH & Co. KG (Subsidiary of: Deutscher Verkehrs Verlag GmbH), Nordkanalstr 36, Hamburg, 20097, Germany. TEL 49-40-2371403, FAX 49-40-23714259, info@eurailpress.com, http://www.eurailpress.com. Ed. Rolf Stenner. Adv. contact Silke Haertel. B&W page EUR 2,880, color page EUR 3,870; trim 182 x 266. Circ: 8,506 (paid).

385 625.1 DEU ISSN 0013-2845
TF3
EISENBAHNTECHNISCHE RUNDSCHAU. Text in German; Summaries in English, French, Spanish. 1952. 10/yr. EUR 176; EUR 16.80 newsstand/cover (effective 2009). adv. bk.rev. abstr.; bibl.; charts; illus. index. **Document type:** *Magazine, Trade.*
Indexed: A22, GeotechAb, HRIS, IBR, IBZ, RefZh, TM.
—IE, Infotrieve, INIST, Linda Hall. **CCC.**
Published by: Eurailpress Tetzlaff-Hestra GmbH & Co. KG (Subsidiary of: Deutscher Verkehrs Verlag GmbH), Nordkanalstr 36, Hamburg, 20097, Germany. TEL 49-40-2371403, FAX 49-40-23714259, info@eurailpress.com, http://www.eurailpress.com. Ed. Ursula Hahn. Adv. contact Silke Haertel. B&W page EUR 2,970, color page EUR 3,960; trim 182 x 265. Circ: 4,581 (paid and controlled).

385 GBR ISSN 1750-8266
THE ELECTRIC RAILWAY. Text in English. 1946. bi-m. free to members (effective 2009). adv. bk.rev. index. back issues avail. **Document type:** *Newsletter, Trade.* **Description:** Presents both topical and historical articles on electric railways worldwide.
Former titles (until 2001): Electric Railway Society. Journal (0013-4147); (until 1956): The Electric Railway
Indexed: CLT&T, HRIS.
Published by: Electric Railway Society, 17 Catherine Dr, Sutton Coldfield, West Midlands B73 6AX, United Kingdom. iwfrew@tiscali.co.uk.

385 621.38 DEU ISSN 0013-5437
TF701 CODEN: ELBAAQ
ELEKTRISCHE BAHNEN; Elektrotechnik im Verkehrswesen. Short title: E B. Text in German. 1903. 11/yr. EUR 289; EUR 144.50 to students; EUR 33 newsstand/cover (effective 2011). adv. abstr.; bibl.; charts; illus. index. reprints avail. **Document type:** *Journal, Trade.* **Description:** Reports on the latest developments of the use of electronics in railroads and tramways. Focuses on high speed engineering, efficiency and automatic controls.
Formerly (until 1957): Elektrische Bahnen (0341-7271)
Related titles: Microform ed.: (from PQC).
Indexed: A22, BrRB, CPEI, EngInd, Inspec, RefZh, SCOPUS, TM.
—BLDSC (3711.000000), AskIEEE, IE, Infotrieve, Ingenta, INIST, Linda Hall. **CCC.**
Published by: Oldenbourg Industrieverlag GmbH (Subsidiary of: Oldenbourg Wissenschaftsverlag GmbH), Rosenheimer Str 145, Munich, 81671, Germany. TEL 49-89-450510, FAX 49-89-45051207, oiv-info@oldenbourg.de, http://www.oldenbourg-industrieverlag.de. Ed. Eberhard Buhl. Adv. contact Inge Matos Feliz. Circ: 1,149 (paid and controlled).

385 BEL ISSN 0777-933X
EN LIGNES - P F T. (Patrimoine Ferroviaire Touristique) Text in French. 1990. q. EUR 36 domestic; EUR 42 foreign (effective 2005). **Document type:** *Newsletter, Consumer.*
Related titles: Dutch ed.: Op de Baan - T S P. ISSN 0777-9321.
Published by: Patrimoine Ferroviaire Touristique (PFT)/Toeristisch Spoor Patrimonium (TSP), BP 5, Brussels, 1140, Belgium. TEL 32-75-956893, FAX 32-65-664541. Ed. Jean-Luc van der Haegen.

625.1 USA ISSN 0013-8142
S671
ENGINEERS AND ENGINES MAGAZINE. Text in English. 1955. bi-m. USD 18 domestic; USD 22 foreign (effective 2000). adv. charts; illus. **Document type:** *Magazine, Consumer.*
Published by: Donald D. Knowles, Ed. & Pub., 2240 Oak Leaf St, Box 2757, Joliet, IL 60434-2757. TEL 815-741-2240, FAX 815-741-2243. Circ: 9,500.

ESTATISTICAS DOS TRANSPORTES RODOVIARIOS DE PASSAGEIROS E DE MERCADORIAS. *see* TRANSPORTATION—Abstracting, Bibliographies, Statistics

EURAIL AND TRAIN TRAVEL GUIDE TO EUROPE. *see* TRAVEL AND TOURISM

385 HRV ISSN 1330-0555
EUROCITY. Text in Croatian. 1992. q. **Document type:** *Magazine, Trade.*
Published by: Hrvatske Zeljeznice, Mihanoviceva 12, Zagreb, 10000, Croatia. TEL 385-1-3872999, FAX 385-1-3783396, hrvatske.zeljeznice@hz.tel.hr, http://www.hznet.hr. Ed. Biljana Limpic-Donadic.

EUROPE BY EURAIL; touring Europe by train. *see* TRAVEL AND TOURISM

385.1 CHE ISSN 0071-2264
EUROPEAN COMPANY FOR THE FINANCING OF RAILWAY ROLLING STOCK. ANNUAL REPORT. Short title: E U R O F I M A Annual Report. Text in English, French, German. 1957. a. free. **Document type:** *Corporate.* **Description:** For the business year of Eurofima.
Published by: European Company for the Financing of Railway Rolling Stock (EUROFIMA), Rittergasse 20, PO Box 1764, Basel, 4001, Switzerland. TEL 41-61-2873340, FAX 41-61-2873240, info@eurofima.org, http://www.eurofima.org. Circ: 4,000.

385 GBR ISSN 1351-1599
EUROPEAN RAILWAY REVIEW. Text in English. 1995. bi-m. GBP 70 combined subscription (print & online eds.) (effective 2009). adv. 96 p./no.; back issues avail. **Document type:** *Magazine, Trade.* **Description:** Provides information on the latest technology, major projects and the current purchasing and operational strategies in the rail industry.
Related titles: Online - full text ed.: free to qualified personnel (effective 2009); Supplement(s): European Railway Review and Eurotransport Industry Focus. ISSN 1759-0531. 2009.
—CCC.
Published by: Russell Publishing Ltd., Court Lodge, Hogtrough Hill, Brasted, Kent TN16 1NU, United Kingdom. TEL 44-1959-563311, FAX 44-1959-563123, info@russellpublishing.com, http://www.russellpublishing.com/. Adv. contact Ben Holliday TEL 44-1959-563311. page GBP 4,081; trim 210 x 297.

EXPORAIL NEWS. *see* MUSEUMS AND ART GALLERIES

385 790.13 CAN ISSN 0014-1380
TF1
EXTRA 2200 SOUTH; locomotive news magazine. Text in English. 1961. q. USD 4.95 newsstand/cover (effective 2003). bk.rev. charts; illus.; stat.; tr.lit. cum.index. back issues avail. **Document type:** *Magazine, Consumer.*
Published by: Iron Horse Publishers, 27-2801 Ellerslie Ave, Burnaby, BC V5B 4R9, Canada. TEL 604-444-3506, FAX 604-444-3507, ihp@paralynx.com. Ed., Pub., R&P Doug Cummings. Circ: 10,000.

F E L A REPORTER & RAILROAD LIABILITY MONITOR. (Federal Employees Liability Act) *see* LAW

385 DEU ISSN 1430-6891
TF3
FERN EXPRESS. Text in German. 1986. q. EUR 39.80; EUR 10.80 newsstand/cover (effective 2005). bk.rev. **Document type:** *Magazine, Consumer.*
Formerly: Dampf und Reise - Ueberseeische Bahnen (0933-7598); Which was formed by the merger of (1986-1988): Dampf und Reise (0930-6684); (1986-1988): Ueberseeische Bahnen (1010-5093)
Published by: Roehr-Verlag GmbH, Brandenburger Str 10, Krefeld, 47809, Germany. TEL 49-6593-989260, FAX 49-6593-989261. Ed., Adv. contact K.W. Koch. R&P K W Koch.

385 MEX ISSN 0186-8543
FERROCARRILES MEXICANOS; revista tecnica. Text in Spanish; Summaries in English. N.S. 1966 (vol.4). q. free. charts; illus.; stat.
Formerly (until 1972): Ferrocarriles (0186-8535)
Published by: Asociacion del Congreso Panamericano de Ferrocarriles, Comision Nacional Mexicana, Calle Navarra No. 210, 2o. Piso, Col. Alamos, Mexico, D.F., 03400, Mexico. Ed. Aurelio Diaz Arzoz.

385 ITA ISSN 0021-3128
FERROVIE DELLO STATO. INFORMAZIONI DOC. Text in Italian. 1961. bi-m. abstr.; bibl. index. **Document type:** *Magazine, Consumer.*
Published by: Ferrovie dello Stato, Piazza della Croce Rossa 1, Rome, RM 00161, Italy. TEL 39-06-44101, http://www.ferroviedellostato.it.

385.37 FRA ISSN 1961-5035
FERROVISSIME. Text in French. 2008. m. EUR 70 domestic; EUR 83 foreign (effective 2010). **Document type:** *Magazine, Consumer.*
Formed by the merger of (2004-2007): Ferrovissimo (1772-1202); (2006-2007): Correspondances Ferroviaires (1779-4145); Which was formerly (until 2006): Correspondances (1634-8206)
Published by: L R Presse, 12 Rue de Sablen, Auray, 56401 Cedex, France. TEL 33-2-97240165, FAX 33-2-97242830, http://www.lrpresse.fr.

385 GBR ISSN 0015-0355
FFESTINIOG RAILWAY MAGAZINE. Abbreviated title: F R Magazine. Text in English. 1958. q. free to members (effective 2009). adv. bk.rev. charts; illus. back issues avail. **Document type:** *Magazine, Consumer.* **Description:** Contains news on the railway, updates on the associated Welsh Highland Railway, official announcements, articles on new developments and historic matters, correspondence from members and advertisements for accommodation in the area.
Published by: Ffestiniog Railway Society, c/o John Dobson, Editor, Harbour Station, Porthmadog, Gwynedd LL49 9NF, United Kingdom. Ed. John Dobson.

385 GBR
FIVE FOOT THREE. Text in English. 1966. a. free to members (effective 2009). bk.rev. illus. back issues avail. **Document type:** *Journal, Trade.* **Description:** Designed for the members of the Railway Preservation Society of Irelands.
Related titles: Online - full text ed.
Published by: Railway Preservation Society of Ireland, Whitehead Excursion Station, PO Box 461, Newtownabbey, Co Antrim, N Ireland BT36 9BT, United Kingdom. TEL 44-28-93373968, rpsitrains@hotmail.com.

385 PRT ISSN 1647-7073
O FOGUETE. Text in Portuguese. 2002. q. **Document type:** *Newspaper, Consumer.*
Published by: Associacao de Amigos do Museu Nacional Ferroviario, Rua Eng Ferreira de Mesquita, Entroncamento, 2334-909, Portugal.

FOOTPLATE/VOETPLAAT. *see* LABOR UNIONS

FRACHT-DIENST; Fachzeitschrift fuer Lager, Logistik, Transport und Verkehr. *see* TRANSPORTATION—Ships And Shipping

385.264 USA ISSN 1548-4629
FREIGHT CAR NEWS & NOTES. Text in English. 2003. irreg. free (effective 2004). **Document type:** *Newsletter, Trade.*
Media: Online - full text.
Published by: Society of Freight Car Historians, PO Box 2480, Monrovia, CA 91017.

385.264 USA ISSN 1548-4610
FREIGHT CARS TODAY. Text in English. 2003. irreg. free (effective 2004). **Document type:** *Monographic series, Trade.*
Media: Online - full text.
Published by: Society of Freight Car Historians, PO Box 2480, Monrovia, CA 91017.

385 ESP ISSN 2174-0194
▼ **FUNDACION DE LOS FERROCARRILES ESPANOLES. COLECCION TECNICA.** Text in Spanish. 2011. a. **Document type:** *Monographic series, Academic/Scholarly.*
Media: Online - full text.
Published by: Fundacion de los Ferrocarriles Espanoles, Santa Isabel 44, Madrid, 28012, Spain. TEL 34-91-1511071, FAX 34-915-281003, vlibre@ffe.es, http://www.ffe.es.

385 DEU ISSN 1438-0099
G D L MAGAZIN VORAUS. Text in German. 1919. 10/yr. adv. bk.rev. **Document type:** *Magazine, Trade.*
Formerly (until 1999): Voraus (0171-8290)
Published by: Gewerkschaft Deutscher Lokomotivfuehrer, Baumweg 45, Frankfurt Am Main, 60316, Germany. TEL 49-69-4057090, FAX 49-69-40570940, info@gdl.de, http://www.gdl.de. Ed. Gerda Seibert. Adv. contact Ulrike Niggemann. B&W page EUR 1,250, color page EUR 2,050. Circ: 39,500 (controlled).

385 DEU
G D L TASCHENBUCH. Text in German. 1968. base vol. plus updates 2/yr. looseleaf. EUR 99 base vol(s).; EUR 45 updates (effective 2010). adv. **Document type:** *Trade.*
Published by: (Gewerkschaft Deutscher Lokomotivfuehrer), Walhalla Fachverlag, Haus an der Eisernen Bruecke, Regensburg, 93042, Germany. TEL 49-941-56840, FAX 49-941-5684111, walhalla@walhalla.de. adv.: B&W page EUR 310. Circ: 600 (controlled).

385 CHN ISSN 1674-8247
▼ **GAOSU TIELU JISHU/HIGH SPEED RAILWAY TECHNOLOGY.** Text in Chinese. 2010. bi-m. **Document type:** *Journal, Academic/Scholarly.*
Related titles: Online - full text ed.
Published by: Zhongguo Zhong-tie Eryuan Gongcheng Jituan Youxian Zeren Gongsi/China Railway Eryuan Engineering Group Co. Ltd., 3, Tongjin Lu, Chengdu, 610031, China. TEL 86-28-86445484, FAX 86-28-87664889, http://www.creegc.com.

385 GBR ISSN 0969-952X
GARDENRAIL. Text in English. 1993. m. GBP 46.20 domestic; GBP 62 in Europe; USD 120 in United States; GBP 72 elsewhere; GBP 3.65 newsstand/cover; USD 10 per issue in United States (effective 2009). adv. illus. back issues avail. **Document type:** *Magazine, Consumer.* **Description:** Contains layout articles, short pieces, practical tips, and photographs for garden railway hobbyists.
Incorporates (1988-1993): Garden Railway World (0957-6355); Which was formerly (until 1988): Steamlines (0268-6260); (until 1985): Live Steam Model Railway Review
Related titles: Online - full text ed.: GBP 29.50 (effective 2009).
Published by: Atlantic Transport Publishers, 83 Parkanaur Ave, Southend on Sea, Essex SS1 3JA, United Kingdom. Ed. Tag Gorton TEL 44-1752-845938. **Subscr. to:** The Maltings, W St, Bourne, Lincolnshire PE10 9PH, United Kingdom. **Dist. by:** Comag.

385 USA ISSN 1098-5239
THE GRAND SCALES QUATERLY. Text in English. 1997. q. USD 20 domestic; USD 25 foreign; USD 6 newsstand/cover (effective 2003). bk.rev.; film rev.; video rev. illus. back issues avail. **Document type:** *Magazine, Consumer.* **Description:** Presents information, news, and layout tours of scale railroads 12" gauge and larger.
Published by: Robinson & Associates, PO Box 8953, Red Bluff, CA 96080. TEL 530-527-0141, FAX 530-527-0420, info@grandscales.com, http://www.grandscales.com. Ed. Gregory Robinson.

385 GBR ISSN 0307-3319
GREAT NORTH REVIEW. Text in English. 1964. q. GBP 15 membership (effective 2009). adv. bk.rev. illus. cum.index. **Document type:** *Journal, Consumer.* **Description:** Contains a wide range of articles, long and short, members exchange information and keep up to date with what is happening.
—BLDSC (4214.546000).
Published by: Great North of Scotland Railway Association, 31 Brackley Ln, Abthorpe, Towcester, Northants NN12 8QJ, United Kingdom. TEL 44-1327-857083. Ed. Keith Fenwick. Circ: 195.

385 GBR ISSN 1362-2153
GREAT WESTERN ECHO. Text in English. 1963. q. GBP 18. adv. bk.rev. bibl.; charts; illus.; tr.lit. 16 p./no.; **Document type:** *Magazine, Consumer.*
Published by: Great Western Society Ltd., Didcot, Oxon, United Kingdom. TEL 44-1235-817200, FAX 44-1235-510621, didrlyc@globalnet.co.uk, http://www.didcotrailwaycentre.org.uk. Ed., Adv. contact Michael Baker. Circ: 4,500 (paid).

GREAT WESTERN RAILWAY JOURNAL. *see* HOBBIES

315 USA
GREEN BLOCK. Text in English. 1965. m. USD 6 to non-members (effective 2000). bk.rev. 12 p./no.; **Document type:** *Newsletter, Newspaper-distributed.*
Published by: National Railway Historical Society, Inc., Central New York Chapter, PO Box 229, Marcellus, NY 13108. cnynrns@aol.com, http://www.rrhistorical-2.com/cnynrns. Ed. George Read.

385 RUS
GUDOK; ezhednevnaya transportnaya gazeta. Text in Russian. 1917. d. (5 d./w.; 260/yr.). USD 480 in United States (effective 2004). **Document type:** *Newspaper, Consumer.*
Related titles: Microfiche ed.: (from IDC); Microfilm ed.: (from PQC); Online - full content ed.
Indexed: CDSP, RASB.
Published by: (Redaktsiya Gazety Gudok), Ministerstvo Putei Soobshcheniya Rossiiskoi Federatsii, B Nikitskaya, Khlynovskii tup 8, Moscow, 103858, Russian Federation. Ed. Igor T Yanin. Circ: 167,000. **Dist. by:** East View Information Services, 10601 Wayzata Blvd, Minneapolis, MN 55305. TEL 952-252-1201, 800-477-1005, FAX 952-252-1202, info@eastview.com, http://www.eastview.com.

385 DEU
GUETERBAHNEN; Gueterverkehr auf der Schiene: Markt - Technik - Verkehrspolitik. Text in German. 2002. 4/yr. EUR 40; EUR 10 newsstand/cover (effective 2008). adv. **Document type:** *Magazine, Trade.*
Published by: Alba Fachverlag GmbH und Co., Willstaetterstr 9, Duesseldorf, 40549, Germany. TEL 49-211-520130, FAX 49-211-5201328, braun@alba-verlag.de, http://www.alba-verlag.de. Ed. Lothar Kuttig. Adv. contact Beatrice van Dijk. B&W page EUR 1,670, color page EUR 2,310. Circ: 1,000 (paid and controlled).

625.1 USA
GUNDERSON NEWS. Text in English. 1987. q. free. back issues avail. **Document type:** *Newsletter.* **Description:** Covers general happenings in the railroad car manufacturing shop, informs of upcoming company events.
Published by: Gunderson Inc., 4350 N W Front Ave, Portland, OR 97210. TEL 503-228-9281, FAX 503-242-0683. Ed., R&P Julie Ward. Circ: 7,000.

385 SWE ISSN 0281-7411
GURKLISTEN. Text in Swedish. 1975. q. SEK 150 to members (effective 1999). adv. **Document type:** *Newsletter.* **Description:** Contains news about the museum railway and publishes articles on railway history, particularly Swedish narrow-gauge railways.
Published by: Wadstena-Faagelsta Jaernvaeg, Jaernvaegsstationen, Vadstena, 59230, Sweden. TEL 46-13-17-67-54. Ed., R&P, Adv. contact Christer Brimalm. Circ: 400.

385 NLD ISSN 1574-6011
HAAGSE TRAMHISTORIE. Text in Dutch. 1987. q. EUR 12.50 (effective 2010).
Published by: Stichting Haags Tram Museum, Ter Borchstraat 7, The Hague, 2525 XG, Netherlands. TEL 31-70-4451559, FAX 31-70-4450472, info@hovm.nl, http://www.hovm.nl.

385 CHN ISSN 1674-2451
HAERBIN TIEDAO KEJI/HAREBIN RAILWAY SCIENCE & TECHNOLOGY. Text in Chinese. 1958. q. **Document type:** *Journal, Academic/Scholarly.*
Former titles (until 1998): Ha-tie Keji Tongxun; (until 1978): Ha-tie Keji Jianbao
Published by: Haerbin Tieluju Kexue Jishu Yanjiusuo/Harbin Railway Bureau. Science And Technology Research Institute, 364, Youzheng Jie, Ha'erbin, 150006, China. TEL 86-451-86426813. **Co-sponsor:** Haerbin Tieluju Kexue Jishu Weiyuanhui.

385 NLD ISSN 1872-3861
HANDBOEK REGELING VERVOER OVER DE SPOORWEG GEVAARLIJKE STOFFEN / REGLEMENT CONCERNANT LE TRANSPORT INTERNATIONAL FERROVIAIRE DES MARCHANDISES DANGEREUSES. Key Title: Handboek V S G/R I D. Cover title: Vervoer Gevaarlijke Stoffen over de Spoorwegen. Text in Dutch. 2001. biennial. EUR 100 (effective 2009).
Published by: GDS Europe BV, Postbus 3111, Hoofddorp, 2130 KC, Netherlands. TEL 31-23-5542970, FAX 31-23-5542971, info@gdscrossmediagroup.nl, http://www.gds-europe.com.

385 DEU
HANDBUCH FUER MITARBEITER DER DEUTSCHE BAHN AG. Text in German. 1968. base vol. plus updates 4/yr. looseleaf. EUR 99 base vol(s).; EUR 45 updates (effective 2010). adv. **Document type:** *Trade.*
Related titles: CD-ROM ed.
Published by: Walhalla Fachverlag, Haus an der Eisernen Bruecke, Regensburg, 93042, Germany. TEL 49-941-56840, FAX 49-941-5684111, walhalla@walhalla.de. adv.: B&W page EUR 310. Circ: 800 (paid and controlled).

385.20942925 GBR ISSN 1369-4138
HERITAGE GROUP JOURNAL. Text in English. 1984. q. free to members (effective 2009). back issues avail. **Document type:** *Journal, Consumer.* **Description:** Contains news of the Group's as well as articles of historic interest not just on the Festiniog Railway, but also on the local area, especially if they have a connection to the Railway.
Formerly (until 1989): Heritage Group Newsletter
Published by: Festiniog Railway Heritage Group, c/o Peter Harrison, Membership Sec., 1 Peel St, Runcorn, Cheshire WA7 1JP, United Kingdom. TEL 44-1928-576185, membership@frheritage.org.uk. Ed. Paul Harris.

385.094105 GBR ISSN 1466-3562
HERITAGE RAILWAY. Text in English. 1999. 13/yr. GBP 39 domestic; GBP 50 in Europe; GBP 60 elsewhere (effective 2009). adv. **Document type:** *Magazine, Consumer.* **Description:** Contains topical features combined with stunning photography from Britain's top lineside cameramen.
Related titles: Online - full text ed.
—BLDSC (4300.056500).

TU

Published by: Mortons Heritage Media (Subsidiary of: Mortons Media Group Ltd.), PO Box 43, Horncastle, LN9 6JR, United Kingdom. TEL 44-1507-529300, FAX 44-1507-529490, http://www.mortonsmediagroup.com. Ed. Robin Jones. Adv. contact Carol Woods TEL 44-1507-529411.

385 GBR
HERITAGE RAILWAY ASSOCIATION. INFORMATION PAPERS. Text in English. irreg. **Document type:** *Monographic series, Trade.*
Former titles: Heritage Railways Information Papers; A R P S Information Papers
Published by: Heritage Railway Association, c/o John M. Crane, 7 Robert Close, Potters Bar, Herts EN6 2DH, United Kingdom. http://www.ukhrail.uel.ac.uk/.

385 GBR
HERITAGE RAILWAY. JOURNAL. Text in English. 1979. q. adv. **Document type:** *Newsletter.* **Description:** Provides news, commentary and articles on subjects of special interest to the railway preservation movement. Includes details of society meetings and seminars.
Published by: Heritage Railway Association, c/o John M. Crane, 7 Robert Close, Potters Bar, Herts EN6 2DH, United Kingdom. http://www.ukhrail.uel.ac.uk/. Ed. S Gamble. Adv. contact J Crane. Circ: 1,000.

385.264 DEU ISSN 1435-411X
HESSISCHER VERKEHRSSPIEGEL. Text in German. 1970. m. **Document type:** *Journal, Consumer.*
Published by: Fachverband Gueterkraftverkehr und Logistik Hessen e.V., Waldschulstr 128, Frankfurt Am Main, 65933, Germany. TEL 49-69-395232, FAX 49-69-387579, info@gueterkraft.de, http://www.gueterkraft.de.

385 USA
HIGH SPEED RAIL - MAGLEV ASSOCIATION. YEARBOOK. Text in English. 1984. a. USD 25 (effective 1997). **Document type:** *Proceedings.* **Description:** Covers proceedings of the convention, High Speed Rail directory and information about new transportation mode and industry of high speed rail.
Formerly: High Speed Rail Yearbook (0898-4611)
Published by: High Speed Ground Transportation Association, 1666 K St., NW, Ste. 1100, Washington, DC 20006-1215. TEL 202-261-6020, FAX 202-496-4349, info@hsgta.com, http://www.hsgt.org. Ed. Robert J Casey. Circ: 5,000.

385 625.1 FRA ISSN 1957-5971
HISTORAIL. Text in French. 2007. q. EUR 30 domestic; EUR 37 in Europe; EUR 39 in North America (effective 2010). **Document type:** *Magazine, Consumer.* **Description:** Explores the history of railroads.
Related titles: Online - full text ed.: free.
Published by: La Vie du Rail, 11 rue de Milan, Paris, Cedex 9 75440, France. TEL 33-1-49701200, FAX 33-1-49701269, info@laviedurail.com, http://www.laviedurail.com. Ed. Olivier Bertrand.

385 SWE ISSN 1100-5165
HJULET. Text in Swedish. 1968. 10/yr. SEK 120 (effective 1991).
Formerly (until 1987): Tidningen Hjulet; Supersedes: Spaarvaegnsmaennens Tidning
Address: Fack 19039, Stockholm, 10432, Sweden.

625 790.133 USA ISSN 1937-6790
TJ630
THE HOME RAILWAY JOURNAL. Text in English. 2006. q. USD 25 domestic; USD 41 foreign (effective 2007). **Document type:** *Magazine, Consumer.* **Description:** Covers rideable steam railroads built at home, including technical aspects of building live steam locomotives, new products and product reviews.
Published by: MDR Media, 9647 Folsom Blvd, #106, Sacramento, CA 95827. Ed. Matthew Mason.

HORNBY MAGAZINE. *see* HOBBIES

HORSE BRASS. *see* HOBBIES

HOTBOX; the magazine of model railroaders. *see* HOBBIES

625.1 USA
TF858.A2
I E E E - A S M E JOINT RAIL CONFERENCE. PROCEEDINGS. (Institute of Electrical and Electronics Engineers - American Society of Mechanical Engineers) Text in English. 19??. a. adv. back issues avail. **Document type:** *Proceedings, Trade.* **Description:** Contains design and technical characteristics of current hardware used to improve the operation of systems in the railroad or transit industries.
Former titles (until 2006): I E E E - A S M E Joint Rail Conference. Proceedings (1559-9531); (until 2003): Joint A S M E - I E E E Railroad Conference. Proceedings (1066-5528); (until 1991): Technical Papers Presented at the A S M E - I E E E Joint Railroad Conference (1054-0253); (until 1987): I E E E Technical Papers Presented at the Joint A S M E - I E E E Railroad Conference (0885-3800); (until 1981): I E E E Technical Papers Presented at the Joint A S M E - I E E E - A A R Railroad Conference (0885-3819); (until 1977): Joint A S M E - I E E E Railroad Technical Conference. I E E E Papers; (until 1975): Joint Railroad Conference. I E E E Papers; (until 19??): Joint Railroad Conference Record; Which superseded: Joint Railroad Technical Conference. Preprint (0075-3998)
Related titles: CD-ROM ed.; Microfiche ed.; Online - full text ed.
Indexed: A22.
—BLDSC (6844.166645). **CCC.**
Published by: I E E E, 445 Hoes Ln, Piscataway, NJ 08855. contactcenter@ieee.org, http://www.ieee.org.

385 AUT ISSN 0005-0504
I F E F AUSTRIA SEKCIO. BULTENO. (Federacio Esperantista Fervojista) Text in Esperanto, German. 1956. 4/yr. free. illus.
Published by: Oesterreichischer Eisenbahner Esperant Verband, Postfach 117, Vienna, W 1103, Austria. Ed. Leopold Patek.

385.262 DEU
IHR REISEPLAN. Text in German. m. adv. **Document type:** *Bulletin, Consumer.*
Published by: Stroeer D E R G Media GmbH (Subsidiary of: Stroeer Out-of-Home Media AG), Buergermeister-Brunner-Str 2, Kassel, 34117, Germany. TEL 49-561-70020, FAX 49-561-7002230, info@derg.de. adv.: B&W page EUR 320, color page EUR 410; trim 120 x 230. Circ: 5,200,000 (controlled).

385 ITA ISSN 1128-5192
IN TRENO; l'orario ufficiale. Text in Italian. 1899. s-a. **Document type:** *Directory, Consumer.*
Former titles (until 1992): Il Treno (1972-8468); (until 1977): Ferrovie Italiane dello Stato. Orario Ufficiale (1972-8476)
Published by: Ferrovie dello Stato, Piazza della Croce Rossa 1, Rome, RM 00161, Italy. TEL 39-06-44101, http://www.ferroviedellostato.it.

625.1 IND ISSN 0019-6266
INDIAN RAILWAY TECHNICAL BULLETIN. Abbreviated title: I R T B. Text in English. 1954. q. free (effective 2011). abstr.; charts; illus.; stat. back issues avail. **Document type:** *Bulletin, Government.*
Related titles: Online - full text ed.
Indexed: BrRB.
Published by: Indian Railways Institute of Civil Engineering, Government of India, Ministry of Railways, Pune, Maharastra 411 001, India. TEL 91-20-26123680, mail@iricen.gov.in, http://www.iricen.gov.in.

385 625.1 GBR
INDUSTRIAL LOCOMOTIVE. Text in English. 1947. q. free to members (effective 2009). bk.rev. bibl.; illus. back issues avail. **Document type:** *Magazine, Academic/Scholarly.* **Description:** Contains articles based on original research into the history of industrial railway systems and locomotives.
Formerly (until 1976): Industrial Locomotive Society. Journal
Published by: Industrial Locomotive Society, c/o W.Wright "Fermain", 31 Lower Brimley Rd, Teignmouth, Devon, TQ14 2LH, United Kingdom. secretary@industrial-loco.org.uk, http://www.industrial-loco.org.uk.

385 USA
INFO MAGAZINE. Text in English. 1968. m.
Incorporates (in Sept. 1996): Southern Pacific Bulletin; Formerly: Infonews
Indexed: CLT&T.
Published by: Union Pacific Railroad, Employee Communications Department, 1400 Douglas St., Omaha, NE 68179-1610. Ed. J H Beck. Circ: 78,000 (controlled).

385 625.1 ITA ISSN 0020-0956
TF4 CODEN: INFEAE
INGEGNERIA FERROVIARIA; rivista di tecnica ed economia dei trasporti. Text in Italian; Summaries in English, French, German. 1904. m. EUR 75 domestic; EUR 130 in the European Union; EUR 150 elsewhere (effective 2008). adv. bk.rev. abstr.; bibl.; charts; illus. index. **Document type:** *Magazine, Trade.*
Indexed: C&ISA, CISA, CPEI, ChemAb, E&CAJ, EngInd, GeoRef, GeotechAb, ISMEC, Inspec, RefZh, SCOPUS, SolStAb, SpeleolAb.
Published by: Collegio Ingegneri Ferroviari Italiani, Via Giovanni Giolitti 48, Rome, RM 00185, Italy. TEL 39-06-4882129, FAX 39-06-4742987, cifi@mclink.it. Circ: 3,500 (paid).

385 GBR ISSN 0954-4097
TF1 CODEN: PMFTEV
➤ **INSTITUTION OF MECHANICAL ENGINEERS. PROCEEDINGS. PART F: JOURNAL OF RAIL AND RAPID TRANSIT.** Text in English. 1847. bi-m. USD 1,621 combined subscription in North America to institutions (print & online eds.); GBP 905 combined subscription elsewhere to institutions (print & online eds.) (effective 2011). charts; illus. back issues avail.; reprint service avail. from PSC. **Document type:** *Journal, Academic/Scholarly.* **Description:** Devoted to engineering in its widest interpretation applicable to rail and rapid transit.
Supersedes in part (in 1989): Institution of Mechanical Engineers. Proceedings. Part D: Transport Engineering (0265-1904); Which superseded in part (in 1984): Institution of Mechanical Engineers. Proceedings (0020-3483)
Related titles: Online - full text ed.: ISSN 2041-3017. USD 1,460 in North America to institutions; GBP 815 elsewhere to institutions (effective 2011); ◆ Series: Institution of Mechanical Engineers. Proceedings.
Indexed: A01, A03, A05, A08, A22, A28, APA, AS&TA, AS&TI, ASCA, AcoustA, ApMecR, B21, BrCerAb, BrTechI, C&ISA, C10, CA, CA/WCA, CIA, CPEI, CerAb, CivEngAb, CorrAb, CurCont, E&CAJ, E01, E11, EEA, EMA, ESPM, EngInd, EnvEAb, FLUIDEX, H&SSA, H15, HRIS, Inspec, M&TEA, M09, MBF, METADEX, P02, P26, P48, P52, P54, PQC, S01, SCI, SCOPUS, SolStAb, T02, T04, TM, W07, WAA.
—BLDSC (6724.900850), AskIEEE, IE, Infotrieve, Ingenta, INIST, Linda Hall. **CCC.**
Published by: (Institution of Mechanical Engineers), Sage Publications Ltd. (Subsidiary of: Sage Publications, Inc.), 1 Oliver's Yard, 55 City Rd, London, EC1Y 1SP, United Kingdom. TEL 44-20-73248500, FAX 44-20-73248600, info@sagepub.co.uk, http://www.uk.sagepub.com/home.nav.

625.1 385 GBR ISSN 0073-9839
CODEN: PRWEAY
INSTITUTION OF RAILWAY SIGNAL ENGINEERS. PROCEEDINGS. Text in English. 1912. a. free to members (effective 2009). back issues avail. **Document type:** *Proceedings.* **Description:** Contains papers on modern railway signaling and telecommunications developments.
Indexed: Inspec.
—AskIEEE.
Published by: Institution of Railway Signal Engineers, 4th Fl, 1 Birdcage Walk, Westminster, London, SW1H 9JJ, United Kingdom. TEL 44-20-78081180, FAX 44-20-78081196, hq@irse.org, http://www.irse.org.

385.264 CHE ISSN 1012-4020
INTERCONTAINER. Text in English. 3/yr.
Published by: International Company for the Transport by Transcontainers, Margarethenstr 38, Basel, 4008, Switzerland. TEL 061-452525, TELEX 62298.

385 USA
INTERLINE SETTLEMENT SYSTEM RULES. Text in English. base vol. plus s-a. updates. USD 22 per vol. **Document type:** *Handbook/Manual/Guide, Trade.*
Published by: Association of American Railroads, Operations and Maintenance Department, 50 F St, N W, Washington, DC 20001. TEL 202-639-2325. Ed. K Eric Wolfe.

INTERNATIONAL BULK JOURNAL. *see* TRANSPORTATION—Ships And Shipping

385 GBR ISSN 1742-4267
▼ ➤ **INTERNATIONAL JOURNAL OF POWERTRAINS.** Text in English. forthcoming 2011. 4/yr. **Document type:** *Journal, Academic/Scholarly.*
Related titles: Online - full text ed.: ISSN 1742-4275. forthcoming.
Indexed: B02, G04, I05.
—**CCC.**
Published by: Inderscience Publishers, PO Box 735, Olney, Bucks MK46 5WB, United Kingdom. TEL 44-1234-240519, FAX 44-1234-240515, editorial@inderscience.com. Ed. Dr. Xubin Song TEL xubinsong@eaton.com. **Subscr. to:** World Trade Centre Bldg, 29 Rte de Pre-Bois, Case Postale 856, Geneva 15 1215, Switzerland. FAX 41-22-7910885, subs@inderscience.com.

385 USA ISSN 2161-7376
TE1
INTERNATIONAL RAILWAY JOURNAL. Abbreviated title: I R J. Text in English; Summaries in French, German, Spanish. 1960. m. free (effective 2011). charts; illus.; stat.; tr.lit. index. back issues avail.; reprints avail. **Document type:** *Magazine, Trade.*
Former titles (until 2001): International Railway Journal and Rapid Transit Review (0744-5326); (until 1979): International Railway Journal (0020-8450)
Related titles: E-mail ed.; Microform ed.: (from PQC); Online - full text ed.: ISSN 2161-7368. free (effective 2011).
Indexed: A15, A26, ABIn, B02, B15, B17, B18, BrRB, E08, G04, G06, G07, G08, HRIS, I05, Inspec, P48, P51, P52, PQC, RefZh, S09.
—IE, Ingenta, INIST, Linda Hall. **CCC.**
Published by: Simmons-Boardman Publishing Corp., 345 Hudson St, New York, NY 10014. TEL 212-620-7200, FAX 212-633-1165, http://www.simmonsboardman.com/. Pub. Robert P DeMarco TEL 212-620-7244.

INTERNATIONAL RAILWAY STATISTICS (YEAR). *see* TRANSPORTATION—Abstracting, Bibliographies, Statistics

INTERNATIONAL RAILWAY TRAVELER. *see* TRAVEL AND TOURISM

INTERNATIONALES VERKEHRSWESEN; Fachzeitschrift fuer Wissenschaft und Praxis. *see* TRANSPORTATION—Roads And Traffic

385 JPN ISSN 0447-2322
TF4
J R E A. Text in Japanese. 1958. m. **Document type:** *Journal, Academic/Scholarly.*
Published by: Japan Railway Engineers Association/Nihon Tetsudo Gijutsu Kyokai, 1-28-6, Kameido, Koto-ku, Tokyo, 136-0071, Japan. TEL 81-3-56262322, FAX 81-3-56262325, http://www.jrea.or.jp/.

385 625.19 SWE
JAERNVAEGAR (ONLINE); specialtidning foer fullskala och modell. Text in Swedish. 1981-1989; resumed 1990. bi-m. back issues avail. **Document type:** *Magazine, Consumer.*
Formerly (until 1998): Jaernvaegar (Print) (0349-5434)
Media: Online - full content.
Published by: Rax Media, c/o Palm, Hjaertervaegen 13, Traangsund, 14266, Sweden. TEL 46-9-7490520, FAX 46-9-7490600, torgny@jarnvagar.se. Ed., Pub. Torgny Palm.

385 SWE ISSN 0281-0522
JAERNVAEGSBLADET FOERSTLINGEN. Text in Swedish. 1976. q. SEK 80 to members.
Former titles (until 1989): S W B Nytt; (until 1978): Informationsblad - Utgivet af mfSWB
Published by: Nora Bergslags Veteran-Jernvaeg (NBVJ), Fack 52, Nora, 71322, Sweden.

625.1 DEU ISSN 1434-4343
HE3071
JAHRBUCH DES BAHNWESENS. Text in German. 1950. a. EUR 39 (effective 2009). adv. **Document type:** *Directory, Trade.*
Formerly: Jahrbuch des Eisenbahnwesens (0075-2479)
—INIST.
Published by: (Verband Deutscher Verkehrsunternehmen), Eurailpress Tetzlaff-Hestra GmbH & Co. KG (Subsidiary of: Deutscher Verkehrs Verlag GmbH), Nordkanalstr 36, Hamburg, 20097, Germany. TEL 49-40-2371403, FAX 49-40-23714259, info@eurailpress.com, http://www.eurailpress.com. Circ: 4,000 (paid and controlled).

385.264 DEU
JAHRBUCH FUER DAS BAYERISCHE TRANSPORTGEWERBE. Text in German. a.
Published by: Landesverband Bayerischer Transport- und Logistikunternehmen e.V., Leonrodstr 48, Munich, 80636, Germany. info@lbt.de, http://www.lbt.de.

385.1 625.1 GBR ISSN 0075-3084
TF1
JANE'S WORLD RAILWAYS. Cover title: Jane's World Railways and Rapid Transit Systems. Text in English. 1950. a. GBP 595 per issue (2010-2011 ed.) (effective 2010). adv. illus. index. **Document type:** *Yearbook, Trade.* **Description:** Covers trends and developments of the rail industry worldwide; includes a country-by-country survey of railway systems and equipment manufacturers.
Related titles: CD-ROM ed.: GBP 1,340 (effective 2010); Microfiche ed.: USD 1,045 in the Americas for complete set 1950-1993; GBP 675 elsewhere for complete set 1950-1993; USD 525 in the Americas per individual set; GBP 345 elsewhere per individual set (effective 2002); individual microfiche sets are cumulative and available for each of the following years 1950-1959, 1960-1969, 1970-1979, and 1980-1993; Online - full text ed.: GBP 1,845 (effective 2010).
—BLDSC (4647.150000). **CCC.**
Published by: I H S Jane's (Subsidiary of: I H S), Sentinel House, 163 Brighton Rd, Coulsdon, Surrey CR5 2YH, United Kingdom. TEL 44-20-87003700, FAX 44-20-87003751, info@janes.co.uk, http://www.janes.com. Ed. Ken Harris. Adv. contact Janine Boxall TEL 44-20-87003852. **Dist. in Asia by:** Jane's Information Group Asia, 60 Albert St, #15-01 Albert Complex, Singapore 189969, Singapore. TEL 65-331-6280, FAX 65-336-9921, info@janes.com.sg; **Dist. in Australia by:** Jane's Information Group Australia, PO Box 3502, Rozelle, NSW 2039, Australia. TEL 61-2-8587-7900, FAX 61-2-8587-7901, info@janes.thomson.com.au; **Dist. in the Americas by:** 1340 Braddock Pl, Ste 300, Alexandria, VA 22314-1651. TEL 703-683-3700, 800-824-0768, FAX 703-836-0297, 800-836-0297, info@janes.com.

625.1 JPN ISSN 0448-8938
TF4 CODEN: JAREBT
JAPANESE RAILWAY ENGINEERING. Text in English; Summaries in French, Spanish. 1959. q. free to members. **Document type:** *Journal, Academic/Scholarly.*

Indexed: A28, APA, BrCerAb, BrRB, C&ISA, CA/WCA, CIA, CLT&T, CPEI, CerAb, CivEngAb, CorrAb, E&CAJ, E11, EEA, EMA, ESPM, Englnd, EnvEAb, H15, HRIS, Inspec, JTA, M&TEA, M09, MBF, METADEX, SCOPUS, SolStAb, T04, WAA.
—BLDSC (4661.200000), AskIEEE, IE, Ingenta, INIST, Linda Hall.
Published by: Japan Railway Engineers Association/Nihon Tetsudo Gijutsu Kyokai, 1-28-6, Kameido, Koto-ku, Tokyo, 136-0071, Japan. TEL 81-3-56262321, FAX 81-3-56262325, http://www.jrea.or.jp/. Circ: 3,000.

385.09489 DNK ISSN 0107-3702
JERNBANEN. Text in Danish. 1961. bi-m. DKK 400 domestic to individual members; EUR 64 foreign to individual members; DKK 1,000 to institutional members (effective 2008). adv. bk.rev. **Document type:** *Magazine, Consumer.*
Published by: Dansk Jernbane-Klub/Danish Railway Club, Kalvebod Brygge 40, Copenhagen V, 1560, Denmark. TEL 45-33-338697, FAX 45-33-338696, djk@jernbaneklub.dk. Ed. Tommy O Jensen TEL 45-49-194235. Adv. contact Gunnar W Christensen.

385 SWE ISSN 0347-1845
JERNVAEGSNYTT. Text in Swedish. 1966. q. SEK 60 (effective 1990).
Published by: Museifoereningen Anten-Graefsnaes Jaernvaeg, Fack 300, Alingsas, 44126, Sweden.

385 CAN ISSN 0453-4441
HE1001
KEEPING TRACK. Text in English. 1966. 10/yr. **Description:** For active and retired employees of CN. Covers news and events about the company.
Former titles (until 1958): Canadian National Magazine (0703-5306); (until 1938): Canadian National Railways Magazine (0703-5128)
Published by: Canadian National, 935 de La Gauchetiere St W, Montreal, PQ H3B 2M9, Canada. TEL 514-399-8041, FAX 514-399-5344. Ed. Louise Cardella. Circ: 73,400.

385 KEN
KENRAIL. Text in English, Swahili. 1955. q. free. adv. bk.rev. illus. 2 cols./p.; **Document type:** *Newspaper.* **Description:** Contains railway information geared primarily toward employees of Kenya Railways.
Supersedes in part: Sikio (0037-5136)
Published by: Kenya Railways Corporation, PO Box 30121, Nairobi, Kenya. TEL 254-2-221211, FAX 254-2-340049, TELEX 22254 RAIL KE. Ed. J N Luseno. Circ: 10,000.

385 MYS ISSN 0047-3375
KERETAPI. Text in English, Malay. 1957. q. MYR 0.60 per issue. charts; illus.; stat.
Published by: Malaya Railway Administration/Pertadbiran Keretapi Tawah Malaya, PO Box 1, Kuala Lumpur, Malaysia. Circ: 2,400.

KEY, LOCK AND LANTERN. *see* ANTIQUES

385 GBR
KEY NOTE MARKET ASSESSMENT. RAIL TRANSPORT LOGISTICS. Variant title: Rail Transport Logistics Market Assessment. Text in English. 2003. irreg., latest 2003, Mar. GBP 775 per issue (effective 2010). **Document type:** *Report, Trade.* **Description:** Provides an in-depth strategic analysis across a broad range of industries and contains an examination on the scope, dynamics and shape of key UK markets in the consumer, financial, lifestyle and business to business sectors.
Published by: Key Note Ltd. (Subsidiary of: Bonnier Business Information), Harlequin House, 5th Fl, 7 High St, Teddington, Richmond upon Thames, TW11 8EE, United Kingdom. TEL 44-845-5040452, FAX 44-845-5040453, info@keynote.co.uk.

385 GBR ISSN 1460-5961
KEY NOTE MARKET REPORT: RAIL TRAVEL. Text in English. 1997. irreg., latest 2008, May. GBP 460 per issue (effective 2009). **Document type:** *Report, Trade.* **Description:** Provides an overview of a specific UK market segment and includes executive summary, market definition, market size, industry background, competitor analysis, current issues, forecasts, company profiles, and more.
Published by: Key Note Ltd. (Subsidiary of: Bonnier Business Information), Field House, 72 Oldfield Rd, Hampton, Mddx TW12 2HQ, United Kingdom. TEL 44-20-84818750, FAX 44-20-87830049, info@keynote.co.uk, http://www.keynote.co.uk. Ed. Jacob Howard.

KEY NOTE MARKET REVIEW: RAILWAY INDUSTRY. *see* BUSINESS AND ECONOMICS—Production Of Goods And Services

385 DEU
KURSBUCH DER DEUTSCHEN MUSEUMS - EISENBAHNEN. Text in German. 1978. a. EUR 5.50 per issue (effective 2011). back issues avail.
Published by: Verlag Uhle und Kleimann, Postfach 1543, Luebbecke, 32295, Germany. Ed. Bernhard Uhle. Circ: 15,000.

385 DEU ISSN 0344-7146
L O K REPORT; Europaeisches Nachrichtenmagazin fuer Eisenbahnfreunde. Text in German. 1972. m. EUR 65 domestic; EUR 75 foreign (effective 2008). adv. bk.rev. illus.; stat. back issues avail. **Document type:** *Magazine, Trade.*
Published by: Arbeitsgruppe L O K Report e.V., Regensburgerstr 25, Berlin, 10777, Germany. TEL 49-30-86409263, FAX 49-30-86409264. Ed., R&P, Adv. contact Martin Stertz. Circ: 10,000.

385 DEU ISSN 0170-4621
L O K REPORT REISEFUEHRER; Europa-Reisefuehrer fuer Eisenbahnfreunde. Text in German. 1978. biennial. EUR 19.80 per issue (effective 2009). illus.; stat. index. back issues avail. **Document type:** *Magazine, Consumer.*
Published by: Arbeitsgruppe L O K Report e.V., Regensburgerstr 25, Berlin, 10777, Germany. TEL 49-30-86409263, FAX 49-30-86409264, info@lok-report.de, http://www.lok-report.de. Ed., Pub. Konrad Koschinski. Circ: 5,000.

385 GBR ISSN 1749-8082
L Y R FOCUS. Abbreviated title: Focus on the L & Y R. Text in English. 2005. biennial. GBP 5 per issue to non-members; free to members (effective 2010). back issues avail. **Document type:** *Journal, Trade.* **Description:** Contains articles, drawings and historical photographs pertaining to Lancashire and Yorkshire Railway society.
Formed by the merger of (200?-2005): Focus on the Lancashire & Yorkshire Railway (1462-5520); (1978-2005): Platform (0143-8875); Both of which superseded in part (1998-2001): Lancashire & Yorkshire Railway Society. Branchline; Which was formerly (until 1998): Branchline Series
Published by: Lancashire & Yorkshire Railway Society, c/o Ken Carter, 11 Waveney Close, Arnold, Nottingham, NG5 6QH, United Kingdom. membership.officer@lyrs.org.uk.

385 GBR ISSN 1478-8837
LANCASHIRE & YORKSHIRE RAILWAY SOCIETY. MAGAZINE. Text in English. 1950. q. GBP 3.50 per issue to non-members; free to members (effective 2009). back issues avail. **Document type:** *Magazine, Trade.* **Description:** Features articles that deal with the more transient aspects of a Society including letters, book offers, membership news, days out, modelling and preservation news.
Formerly (until 2002): Lancashire & Yorkshire Railway Society. Newsletter (0263-2896)
Published by: Lancashire & Yorkshire Railway Society, c/o Ken Carter, 11 Waveney Close, Arnold, Nottingham, NG5 6QH, United Kingdom. membership.officer@lyrs.org.uk.

LAVORO E TRANSPORTI. *see* LABOR UNIONS

385.9 USA ISSN 0888-7837
LEXINGTON QUARTERLY. Text in English. 1942. q. looseleaf. USD 15 (effective 2001). bk.rev. back issues avail. **Document type:** *Newsletter, Trade.*
Published by: Lexington Group in Transportation History, St. Cloud State University, Department of History, St. Cloud, MN 56301. TEL 320-255-4906, FAX 320-654-5198. Ed. Don L Hofsommer. Circ: 525.

385.264 USA
THE LIGHT (ARLINGTON). Text in English. 1918. w. **Document type:** *Magazine, Trade.*
Formerly: Southern Traffic Light
Published by: Southern Transportation Logistics Association, Inc., 3426 N Washington Blvd, Arlington, VA 22201. TEL 703-525-4050.

385 622 AUS ISSN 0727-8101
LIGHT RAILWAYS; Australia's magazine of industrial and narrow gauge railways. Text in English. 1960. bi-m. AUD 5.96 per issue to members (effective 2008). adv. back issues avail. **Document type:** *Magazine, Consumer.* **Description:** Covers current news, research, and history of industrial, narrow-gauge and light railways in Australia and its territories, past and present.
Incorporates (1977-1997): Light Railway News (0155-2260)
Related titles: CD-ROM ed.; Supplement(s): L R R S A Sales List.
Published by: Light Railway Research Society of Australia Inc., PO Box 21, Surrey Hills, VIC 3127, Australia. FAX 61-3-59682484, lrrsa@lrrsa.org.au, http://www.lrrsa.org.au/.

385 FRA ISSN 2105-7273
LIGNES D'AVENIR. Text in French. 2002. 3/yr. **Document type:** *Magazine.*
Formerly (until 2008): Reseau Ferre de France. Le Journal (1635-4362)
Published by: Languedoc-Roussillon, 1030 Av Jean Mermoz, Montpellier, 34000, France. TEL 33-4-67179469, FAX 33-4-67179470, contact@lr2l.fr, http://www.lr2l.fr.

385 GBR ISSN 0142-7326
LIVE RAIL. Text in English. 1970. bi-m. GBP 2.10 per issue to non-members; free to members (effective 2009). adv. bk.rev. index. back issues avail. **Document type:** *Magazine, Consumer.* **Description:** Contains both topical and historical information about the development and operation of the third rail system.
Published by: Southern Electric Group, Flat 2, The Old Manor House, The Goffs, Eastbourne, BN21 9HF, United Kingdom. TEL 44-1903-501029, FAX 44-1903-501029. Ed. Simon Jeffs.

LOCO REVUE; la passion du train miniature. *see* HOBBIES

331.88 USA ISSN 1549-6422
LOCOMOTIVE ENGINEERS AND TRAINMEN NEWS. Text in English. 1987. m. membership only. 8 p./no. 4 cols./p.; **Document type:** *Newsletter, Trade.* **Description:** Covers union activities, safety issues in the rail industry, collective bargaining issues, and labor/management relations.
Formerly (until 2004): Locomotive Engineer Newsletter (0898-8625); Which superseded in part (in 1987): Locomotive Engineer (0024-5747); Which incorporated (1907-1959): Locomotive Engineers Journal (0738-6036)
Related titles: Online - full text ed.
—Linda Hall.
Published by: International Brotherhood of Locomotive Engineers, 1370 Ontario St, Mezzanine, Cleveland, OH 44113-1702. TEL 216-241-2630, FAX 216-861-0932. Ed. John Bentley Jr. Circ: 55,000 (paid and controlled).

385 GBR ISSN 1353-7091
LOCOMOTIVES INTERNATIONAL. Text in English. 1989. q. GBP 18 domestic; GBP 19 in Europe; GBP 24 elsewhere; GBP 4.25 per issue (effective 2009). adv. bk.rev.; video rev. illus.; maps; stat. back issues avail. **Document type:** *Magazine, Consumer.* **Description:** Covers all aspects of railways throughout the world, including steam locomotives, and railway history and photography. For rail enthusiasts, travelers, and mail order purchasers of books and videos.
Published by: Paul Catchpole Ltd., World of Model Railways, Meadow St, Mevagissey, Cornwall PL26 6UL, United Kingdom. TEL 44-1726-842457, FAX 44-1726-844998.

385 DEU ISSN 0458-1822
TJ605
LOK MAGAZIN; Aktuelles, Fahrzeuge, Geschichte. Text in German. 1962. m. EUR 81; EUR 7.50 newsstand/cover (effective 2010). adv. **Document type:** *Magazine, Consumer.* **Description:** Magazine for railroad enthusiasts. Features the history, the present state and future development of steam engines. Includes national and international news, list of exhibitions, and special trips.
Indexed: IBR, IBZ.
—CCC.
Published by: GeraMond Verlag GmbH, Infanteriestr 11a, Munich, 80797, Germany. TEL 49-89-1306990, FAX 49-89-130699100, info@geramond.de, http://www.geramond.de. Adv. contact Judith Fischl. B&W page EUR 950, color page EUR 1,150; trim 140 x 217. Circ: 11,885 (paid and controlled).

621 385.1 RUS ISSN 0869-8147
LOKOMOTIV; massovyi proizvodstvennyi zhurnal. Text and summaries in Russian. 1957. 12/yr. USD 86 foreign (effective 2003). adv. back issues avail. **Document type:** *Journal, Corporate.* **Description:** Provides technical and economic information mostly for the locomotive and maintenance crews, as well as for the railway engineers, constructors, power supply services.
Formerly (until 1994): Elektricheskaya i Teplovoznaya Tyaga (0422-9274)
Related titles: Diskette ed.
Indexed: Inspec, RefZh.
—East View, Linda Hall.
Address: Panteleyevskaya ul 26, Moscow, 129110, Russian Federation. TEL 7-095-2621232, FAX 7-095-2621232. Ed., Pub., R&P Vladimir N Bzhitsky. adv.: B&W page USD 1,000, color page USD 3,000. Circ: 4,300 (paid and controlled). **Dist. by:** M K - Periodica, ul Gilyarovskogo 39, Moscow 129110, Russian Federation. TEL 7-095-2845008, FAX 7-095-2813798, info@periodicals.ru, http://www.mkniga.ru; **Dist. in US by:** Victor Kamkin Inc., 220 Girard St, Ste 1, Gaithersburg, MD 20877. http://www.kamkin.com.

LOKOMOTIVET; tidsskrift om jernbaner i virkelighed og model. *see* HOBBIES

LOKOMOTIVET. SAERSKRIFT. *see* HOBBIES

385 DEU ISSN 0170-379X
DIE LOKRUNDSCHAU. Text in German. 1969. bi-m. EUR 26 domestic; EUR 30 foreign; EUR 4.90 newsstand/cover (effective 2008). adv. bk.rev. back issues avail. **Document type:** *Magazine, Trade.*
Published by: Arbeitsgemeinschaft Lokrundschau e.V., Postfach 800107, Hamburg, 21001, Germany. TEL 49-4151-896913, FAX 49-4151-82889, verlag@lokrundschau.de. Ed. Dietmar Braemert. Adv. contact Heike Heitmann TEL 49-4151-896913. Circ: 5,000.

385 GBR ISSN 0140-8356
LONDON UNDERGROUND ROLLING STOCK. Text in English. 1976. a. GBP 9.95 per issue (effective 2009). **Document type:** *Directory, Trade.* **Description:** Contains details of all current rolling stock on the underground, plus disposed stock still in existence.
—CCC.
Published by: Capital Transport Publishing, 38 Long Elmes, Harrow Weald, Middlesex HA3 5JL, United Kingdom. FAX 44-20-84274707, info@transport-of-delight.com.

M I B A - DIE EISENBAHN IM MODELL. (Miniaturbahnen) *see* HOBBIES

M I B A MESSE. (Miniaturbahnen) *see* HOBBIES

M I B A SPEZIAL. (Miniaturbahnen) *see* HOBBIES

MAERKLIN-MAGAZIN; Die ganze Welt der Modellbahnen. *see* HOBBIES

385 GBR ISSN 0264-7028
MAIN LINE. Text in English. 1969. q. GBP 15 to students includes senior citizens; free to members (effective 2009). adv. bk.rev. back issues avail. **Document type:** *Magazine, Trade.* **Description:** Explores historical concerns of this preserved steam railway, covering news and developments.
Published by: Great Central Railway, Main Line Steam Trust, Great Central Rd, Loughborough, Leics LE11 1RW, United Kingdom. TEL 44-1509-230726, FAX 44-1509-239791, mail_line@compuserve.com, http://www.gcrailway.co.uk.

385 MWI ISSN 0076-3330
MALAWI RAILWAYS. ANNUAL REPORTS AND ACCOUNTS. Variant title: Malawi Railways. Directors' Reports and Accounts. Text in English. 1932. a. free. **Document type:** *Report, Trade.*
Published by: Central East African Railway Co., PO Box 5144, Limbe, Malawi. TEL 265-459024. Circ: 500.

385 IND
MAZDOOR NEWS. Text in Telugu. 19??. m. **Document type:** *Newsletter, Trade.*
Formerly: Rail Mazdoor
Published by: South Central Railway Mazdoor Union, 7-C Railway Bldg, FA & CAO's Compound, Secunderabad, Andhra Pradesh 500 025, India. TEL 91-40-27834279, FAX 91-40-27821351, scrmu@rediffmail.com.

385 DNK ISSN 1603-7383
METRO NYT; information om metroen. Variant title: Metronyt. Text in Danish. 2004. m. free. back issues avail. **Document type:** *Newsletter, Consumer.*
Related titles: Online - full text ed.
Published by: Metroselskabet I/S, Metrovej 5, Copenhagen S, 2300, Denmark. TEL 45-33-111700, FAX 45-33-112301, info@m.dk. Circ: 30,000.

385 USA ISSN 1082-5584
THE MIDLANDER. Text in English. 1994. q. USD 20 (effective 2001). adv. illus.; stat. 20 p./no.; back issues avail. **Document type:** *Newsletter.* **Description:** Publishes historical articles on railroads in northern New Jersey, southern New York, and eastern Pennsylvania.
Published by: New Jersey Midland Railroad Historical Society, PO Box 6125, Parsippany, NJ 07054. TEL 973-331-2739. Ed., Pub., R&P, Adv. contact Timothy O Stuy. Circ: 500 (paid).

625.1 NLD ISSN 1875-5674
MILJOENENLIJN EXPRESSE. Text in Dutch. 1989. q.
Published by: Stichting Zuid-Limburgse Stroomtrein Maatschappij, Postbus 21071, Simpelveld, 6369 ZH, Netherlands. TEL 31-45-5440018, FAX 31-45-5688128, info@miljoenenlijn.nl, http://www.zlsm.nl.

625.190 GBR ISSN 0267-3207
TF197
MODEL RAILWAY JOURNAL. Text in English. 1985. 8/yr. GBP 3.75 newsstand/cover (effective 2009). back issues avail. **Document type:** *Magazine, Consumer.*
Published by: Wild Swan Publications Ltd., 1-3 Hagbourne Rd, Didcot, Oxfordshire OX11 8DP, United Kingdom. TEL 44-1235-816478. **Dist. by:** Seymour Distribution Ltd.

621.2 USA
MODERN LOCOMOTIVE HANDBOOK. Text in English. 1950. irreg. USD 10 per vol. (effective 2008). **Document type:** *Journal, Trade.*
Published by: International Association of Railway Operating Officers, c/o Ted Hagemo, 6645 MacArthur Dr, Missoula, MT 59808. TEL 406-370-6977, 2070cooper@msn.com, http://www.iaroo.org.

385 625.2 GBR ISSN 0026-8356
TF1 CODEN: MORABC
MODERN RAILWAYS. Text in English. 1962. m. GBP 45.60 domestic; GBP 55 in Europe; GBP 60.40 elsewhere; GBP 3.80 per issue (effective 2009). adv. bk.rev. charts; illus. 80 p./no.; back issues avail.; reprints avail. **Document type:** *Magazine, Consumer.* **Description:** Provides the up to the minute information of the latest industry events.
Incorporates: Locomotive, Railway Carriage; Wagon Review
Related titles: Microform ed.: (from PQC).
Indexed: A22, BrRB, H20, HRIS, IBR, IBZ, Inspec, T02.

—BLDSC (5894.900000), IE, Infotrieve, Ingenta, INIST. **CCC.**
Published by: (Railway Study Association), Ian Allan Publishing Ltd., Riverdene Business Park, Riverdene Industrial Estate, Molesey Rd, Walton-on-Thames, Surrey KT12 4RG, United Kingdom. TEL 44-1932-266622, FAX 44-1932-266633, magazines@ianallanpublishing.co.uk, http://www.ianallanpublishing.com. Ed. James Abbott TEL 44-1892-525339. Adv. contact Paul Edwards TEL 44-1303-267456. **Dist. by:** MarketForce UK Ltd, The Blue Fin Bldg, 3rd Fl, 110 Southwark St, London SE1 0SU, United Kingdom. TEL 44-20-31483333, FAX 44-20-31488105, salesinnovation@marketforce.co.uk, http://www.marketforce.co.uk/.

385.2 CAN ISSN 1709-870X
MOMENTUM (CALGARY). Text in English. 1971. q. free (effective 2008).
Former titles (until 2003): Canadian Pacific Railway News (1208-865X); (until 1996): C P Rail System News (1189-363X); (until 1992): C P Rail News (0229-8694)
Published by: Canadian Pacific, Communications & Public Affairs, 401 9th Ave SW, Suite 500, Calgary, AB T2P 4Z4, Canada. TEL 403-319-6200.

385 RUS
MOSKOVSKII ZHELEZNODOROZHNIK. Text in Russian. w. (50/yr.). USD 199.95 in United States.
Address: Krasnoprudnaya ul 20, Moscow, 107140, Russian Federation. TEL 7-095-2663769. Ed. Z M Shingareva. **Dist. by:** East View Information Services, 10601 Wayzata Blvd, Minneapolis, MN 55305. TEL 952-252-1201, 800-477-1005, FAX 952-252-1202, info@eastview.com, http://www.eastview.com.

385 CAN ISSN 0704-1500
MOVIN'. Text in English. 1968. 6/yr. **Description:** Keeps customers informed about Canadian National's new services and equipment and the results of the latest developments in technology.
Related titles: French ed.: En Voie. ISSN 0704-1519.
Indexed: CLT&T, HRIS.
Published by: Canadian National, 935 de La Gauchetiere St W, Montreal, PQ H3B 2M9, Canada. TEL 514-399-5822, FAX 514-399-5344. Ed. Patricia Tokai. Circ: 28,500.

385 DEU ISSN 0936-4609
MUSEUMS - EISENBAHN; Zeitschrift fuer Kleinbahn Geschichte. Text in German. 1966. q. EUR 17 domestic; EUR 21 foreign; EUR 5.50 newsstand/cover (effective 2009). adv. bk.rev. **Document type:** *Magazine, Consumer.*
Published by: Deutscher Eisenbahn-Verein e.V., Postfach 1106, Bruchhausen-Vilsen, 27300, Germany. TEL 49-4252-93000, FAX 49-4252-930012, info@museumseisenbahn.de, http://www.museumse.senbabn.de. Ed. Wolfram Baeumer.

385 USA ISSN 0740-672X
HE2791
MUTUAL MAGAZINE. Text in English. 1914. bi-m. USD 1.20 (effective 2005). adv. 54 p./no.; **Document type:** *Magazine, Trade.* **Description:** Serves as a railroad fraternal monitor. Also covers insurance-related news.
Published by: Mutual Beneficial Association of Rail Transportation Employees, Inc., 1301 Lancaster Ave, Ste 102, Berwyn, PA 19312-1290. TEL 610-722-0253, 800-456-0402, FAX 610-722-0256. Ed. Stephen M Santarlasci. adv.: page USD 240. Circ: 8,000.

N C E ROAD RAIL AND TRANSPORT DIRECTORY. *see* ENGINEERING—Civil Engineering

385 USA ISSN 1947-5659
▼ **N C F R P REPORT.** (National Cooperative Freight Research Program) Text in English. 2009. 5/yr. Varies by page count. **Document type:** *Report, Trade.* **Description:** Reports of the NCFRP intended for freight shippers and carriers, service providers, suppliers, and public officials.
—Linda Hall.
Published by: Transportation Research Board, 500 Fifth St, NW, Washington, DC 20001. TEL 202-334-3213, FAX 202-334-2519, TRBSales@nas.edu, http://www.trb.org.

N M R A MAGAZINE. (National Model Railroad Association) *see* HOBBIES

385 970 USA ISSN 1940-3615
HE2715
N R H S BULLETIN. (National Railway Historical Society) Text in English. 1935. 5/yr. free to members (effective 2010). bk.rev. illus. back issues avail.; reprints avail. **Document type:** *Bulletin, Trade.* **Description:** Covers US railroads in the nineteenth and twentieth centuries.
Former titles (until 2005): National Railway Bulletin (0885-5099); (until 1976): National Railway Historical Society. Bulletin
Indexed: CLT&T, HRIS.
—Ingenta.
Published by: National Railway Historical Society, 100 N 20th St, Ste 400, Philadelphia, PA 19103. TEL 215-557-6606, FAX 215-963-9785, info@nrhs.com. Ed. Jeffrey S Smith.

385 GBR ISSN 0142-5587
THE NARROW GAUGE. Text in English. 1953. q. GBP 18 domestic to individual members; GBP 24 foreign to individual members (effective 2009). adv. bk.rev. charts; illus.; tr.lit. back issues avail. **Document type:** *Magazine, Consumer.* **Description:** Records the history and development of narrow gauge rail transport, and also publishes feature length articles on the current scene that are beyond the scope of the Society's Newsletter.
Formerly: Narrow Gauge Illustrated
Published by: Narrow Gauge Railway Society, c/o Alan Burgess, Ed., 6 The Crescent, Orton, Longueville, Peterborough, PE2 7DT, United Kingdom. TEL 44-1733-234498, http://www.ngrs.org/. Ed. Alan Burgess. Circ: 1,250. **Subscr. to:** c/o Lawson Little, NGRS Membership Secretary, Dept.WWW, 1 Archers Dr, Old Bilsthorpe, Newark, Notts NG22 8SD, United Kingdom. littlerail@talktalk.net.

NARROW GAUGE AND SHORT LINE GAZETTE. *see* HOBBIES

385 GBR ISSN 0142-5595
NARROW GAUGE NEWS. Text in English. 1953. bi-m. GBP 18 domestic to individual members; GBP 24 foreign to individual members (effective 2009). adv. bk.rev.; video rev. illus.; tr.lit. back issues avail. **Document type:** *Newsletter, Consumer.* **Description:** Features up-to-date company, pleasure, preservation and industrial news of both the current Narrow Gauge and the Miniature scene in the UK and overseas.
Published by: Narrow Gauge Railway Society, c/o Paul Bennett, Ed., 90 Stortford Hall Park, Bishop's Stortford, CM23 5AN, United Kingdom. http://www.ngrs.org/. Ed. Paul Bennett. **Subscr. to:** c/o Lawson Little, NGRS Membership Secretary, Dept.WWW, 1 Archers Dr, Old Bilsthorpe, Newark, Notts NG22 8SD, United Kingdom. littlerail@talktalk.net.

385.1 GBR ISSN 2046-0457
NARROW GAUGE WORLD. Text in English. 1991. bi-m. GBP 23.70 domestic; USD 49.95 in United States; GBP 31 in Europe; GBP 35.50 elsewhere (effective 2011). **Document type:** *Magazine, Trade.*
Former titles (until 2010): Narrow Gauge World & N G Modelling (1747-4523); (until 2004): Narrow Gauge World (1466-0180)
Related titles: Online - full text ed.: GBP 19.50 (effective 2011).
Published by: Atlantic Publishers, The Maltings, W St, Bourne, Lincolnshire PE10 9PH, United Kingdom. TEL 44-1778-392469. Pub. Trevor Ridley. Adv. contact Bev Francis TEL 44-1778-392055.

385 USA ISSN 0739-3490
NATIONAL ASSOCIATION OF RAILROAD PASSENGERS NEWS. Text in English. 1969. m. (11/yr.). USD 24 to members. back issues avail. **Document type:** *Newsletter.* **Description:** News and advocacy articles on rail passenger and transit service.
Indexed: CLT&T, HRIS.
Published by: National Association of Railroad Passengers, 900 Second St, N E, Ste 308, Washington, DC 20002-3557. TEL 202-408-8362, FAX 202-408-8287. Ed. Ross Capon. Circ: 11,500 (paid); 2,300 (controlled).

385.3 GBR ISSN 2043-8400
NATIONAL RAILWAY MUSEUM REVIEW. Variant title: N R M Review. Text in English. 19??. q. free to members (effective 2010). **Document type:** *Magazine, Trade.* **Description:** Features articles of general railway interest and includes authoritative reviews of books and videos.
Formerly (until 1998): Friends of the National Railway Museum. Newsletter
Published by: Friends of the National Railway Museum, Leeman Rd, York, YO26 4XJ, United Kingdom. TEL 44-1904-636874, nrm.friends@nrm.org.uk.

385 ZWE
NATIONAL RAILWAYS OF ZIMBABWE. ANNUAL REPORT. Text in English. 1991 (no.42). a. adv. **Document type:** *Newsletter, Corporate.*
Published by: National Railways of Zimbabwe, Publications Dept, PO Box 596, Bulawayo, Zimbabwe. TEL 263-9-363528, FAX 263-9-363543. Ed. M Gumede. Adv. contact Fanuel Masikati TEL 263-9-363526.

NATIONALE MAATSCHAPPIJ VAN BELGISCHE SPOORWEGEN. INFORMATIE EN AANWINSTEN. *see* TRANSPORTATION—Abstracting, Bibliographies, Statistics

385 625.1 AUT
NEUE BAHN; oesterreichische Fachzeitschrift fuer modernen Eisenbahntechnik und umweltbewusste Verkehrspolitik. Text in German. 1966. q. EUR 18.90 domestic; EUR 29.80 foreign (effective 2005). adv. abstr.; illus. index. **Document type:** *Magazine, Trade.*
Formerly: Eisenbahntechnik (0013-2829)
Indexed: BrRB.
Published by: Bohmann Druck und Verlag GmbH & Co. KG, Leberstr 122, Vienna, W 1110, Austria. TEL 43-1-740950, FAX 43-1-74095183. Ed. Josef Mueller. Adv. contact Rudolf Ortner. B&W page EUR 3,888, color page EUR 4,902; trim 260 x 365. Circ: 4,900 (controlled).

NEW ZEALAND MODEL RAILWAY JOURNAL. *see* HOBBIES

385 NZL ISSN 0028-8624
NEW ZEALAND RAILWAY OBSERVER. Text in English. 1944. bi-m. NZD 63 membership (effective 2009). adv. bk.rev. charts; illus.; maps. index. **Document type:** *Magazine, Consumer.* **Description:** Provides information on the design, construction, operation, development and history of railways in New Zealand.
Indexed: INZP.
—CCC.
Published by: New Zealand Railway & Locomotive Society, Inc., Lambton Quay, PO Box 5134, Wellington, 6145, New Zealand. TEL 64-4-5684938, FAX 64-4-5865554, nzrls@actrix.co.nz. Ed. G T Carter. R&P, Adv. contact G.T. Carter. Circ: 1,200 (paid).

385 IND
NEWS (SECUNDERABAD). Text in English. m.
Published by: South Central Railway Mazdoor Union, 7-C Railway Bldg, FA & CAO's Compound, Secunderabad, Andhra Pradesh 500 025, India. TEL 91-40-27834279, FAX 91-40-27821351, scrmu@rediffmail.com, http://scrmu.co.

385.2 NLD ISSN 1879-5145
NIEUWSBRIEF SPOORTECHNIEK.NL. Abbreviated title: Spoortechniek.nl. Text in Dutch. 2007. m. free (effective 2011). **Document type:** *Magazine, Consumer.*
Media: Online - full text.
Published by: Spoortechniek.nl beheer@spoortechniek.nl. Eds. Kars Cleveringa, Marc Schouwenaars.

385 COD
NJANJA. Text in French. m.
Published by: Societe Nationale des Chemins de Fer Zairois, Lubumbashi, P.O.B. 297, BP 10597, Kinshasa, Congo, Dem. Republic.

385 SWE ISSN 0029-1382
NORDISK JAERNBANETIDSKRIFT. Short title: N J T. Text in Danish, Finnish, Norwegian, Swedish; Text occasionally in English, German. 1874. 5/yr. adv. bk.rev. charts; illus. index. **Document type:** *Magazine, Trade.*
Formerly (until 1925): Jernbanebladet
Published by: Forum foer Nordiskt Jaernvaegssamarbete/Forum for Nordic Railway Association, c/o Per Olof Lingwall, Trafikverket, Borlaenge, 78189, Sweden. http://www.njsforum.com. Ed. Mikael Prenler. Adv. contact Ronald Carlsson TEL 46-35-106018. Circ: 4,000.

385.264 DEU ISSN 0171-2012
NORDRHEIN VERKEHR. Text in German. 195?. m. **Document type:** *Journal, Trade.*
Published by: Verband Gueterkraftverkehr und Logistik Nordrhein e.V., Erkrather Str 141, Duesseldorf, 40233, Germany. TEL 49-211-734780, FAX 49-211-7347831, duesseldorf@vvwl.de, http://www.vgln.de.

385 USA ISSN 0894-0800
NORTHWESTERNER. Text in English. 1987. s-a. membership. adv. bk.rev. back issues avail. **Document type:** *Bulletin.* **Description:** Information on the history of the Redwood Empire Route.
Published by: Northwestern Pacific Railroad Historical Society, PO Box 667, Santa Rosa, CA 95402-0667. TEL 415-459-7082. Ed., R&P, Adv. contact Frederick P Codoni. Circ: 1,000.

385 USA ISSN 0030-0373
TF340
OFFICIAL RAILWAY EQUIPMENT REGISTER. Abbreviated title: O R E R. Text in English. 1886. q. adv. **Document type:** *Directory, Trade.* **Description:** Contains complete descriptions of freight cars operated by railroads and private companies in N.A. including series numbers, dimensions and capacities.
Related titles: CD-ROM ed.; Magnetic Tape ed.
—CCC.
Published by: Commonwealth Business Media, Inc. (Subsidiary of: United Business Media Limited), 400 Windsor Corporate Park, 50 Millstone Rd, Ste 200, East Windsor, NJ 08520. TEL 800-221-5488, FAX 609-371-7883, cbizservices@sunbeltfs.com, http://www.cbizmedia.com. Pub. Susan C Murray. Adv. contact Kathy Keeney TEL 410-788-0376. Circ: 7,000.

380.5 USA ISSN 1069-1715
THE OFFICIAL RAILWAY GUIDE. Text in English. 1868. bi-m. USD 279 domestic; USD 309 foreign (effective 2008). adv. **Document type:** *Directory, Trade.* **Description:** Contains maps, contact personnel, intermodal terminal locations, freight schedules and route profiles for all railroads.
Incorporates: Railway Line Clearances (0190-6763); Former titles (until 1993): Official Railway Guide. North American Freight Service Edition (0190-6704); Official Guide of the Railways and Steam Navigation Lines of the United States, Puerto Rico, Canada, Mexico and Cuba, Airline Schedules (0030-0322)
—CCC.
Published by: Commonwealth Business Media, Inc. (Subsidiary of: United Business Media Limited), 400 Windsor Corporate Park, 50 Millstone Rd, Ste 200, East Windsor, NJ 08520. TEL 609-371-7700, 800-221-5488, 888-215-6084, FAX 609-371-7883, cbizservices@sunbeltfs.com, http://www.cbizmedia.com. Pub. Kathy Keeney TEL 410-788-0376.

385.262 IRL
ON TRACK. Text in English. q. adv. **Document type:** *Magazine, Consumer.*
Published by: Mainstream Publications, Coolbracken House, Church Terrace, Bray, Co. Wicklow, Ireland. TEL 353-1-2868246, FAX 353-1-2868241. Adv. contact Leslie Magill. color page EUR 2,800; trim 210 x 297. Circ: 50,000 (controlled).

385 USA
ON TRACK (WASHINGTON); railroad construction membership newsletter. Text in English. 1977. m. free to members. adv. bk.rev. stat.; tr.lit. index. back issues avail. **Document type:** *Newsletter.*
Formerly: Clear Track (0193-3477)
Published by: National Railroad Construction and Maintenance Association, Inc., 122 C St, NW, Ste 850, Washington, DC 20001-2109. FAX 202-638-1045, info@nrcma.org, http://www.nrcma.org. Ed. Richard Sherman. Circ: 1,500 (controlled).

385 NLD ISSN 0030-3321
OP DE RAILS. Text in Dutch. 1931. m. EUR 7.90 newsstand/cover (effective 2009). adv. bk.rev. illus. index. **Document type:** *Magazine, Trade.*
Published by: Nederlandse Vereniging van Belangstellenden in het Spoor- en Tramwegwezen, Postbus 777, Leiden, 2300 AT, Netherlands. TEL 31-71-5724014, nvbswinkel@nvbs.com, http://www.nvbs.com.

ORANGE EMPIRE RAILWAY MUSEUM GAZETTE. *see* MUSEUMS AND ART GALLERIES

051 USA
P A T H WAYS. Text in English. 1968. bi-m. free. **Document type:** *Newspaper.* **Description:** News of the PATH rail transit system and its services.
Published by: (Port Authority of New York and New Jersey), Port Authority Trans-Hudson Corporation, 1 PATH Plaza, Jersey City, NJ 07306. TEL 800-234-PATH, FAX 201-216-6266. Ed. Joann M Breslin.

385 NZL ISSN 1170-4810
PANTOGRAPH. Text in English. 1956. bi-m. NZD 55 membership (effective 2009). bk.rev. **Document type:** *Journal, Trade.*
Former titles (until 1990): Smokebox (0114-1104); (until 1988): Pantograph (1170-5140); (until 1977): Pantograph News (1170-5132); (until 1972): Pantograph (0031-1014)
Published by: Silver Stream Railway Inc., Reynolds Bach Dr, Silverstream, PO Box 48177, Upper Hutt, New Zealand. TEL 63-4-5637348, rickkimj@ihug.co.nz, http://www.silverstreamrailway.org.nz/. Ed. A Collins. Circ: 120.

385 GBR ISSN 0031-5524
PERMANENT WAY INSTITUTION. JOURNAL AND REPORT OF PROCEEDINGS. Text in English. 1884. q. free to members (effective 2009). adv. bk.rev. abstr.; charts; illus.; stat. index. back issues avail. **Document type:** *Proceedings, Academic/Scholarly.* **Description:** Reports of all activities, meetings, seminars, formal business meetings (council agm etc.) technical papers as read at meetings etc. Domestic information, sales, officials addresses etc.
Indexed: A28, APA, BrCerAb, BrRB, BrTechI, C&ISA, CA/WCA, CIA, CerAb, CivEngAb, CorrAb, E&CAJ, E11, EEA, EMA, ESPM, EnvEAb, H15, M&TEA, M09, MBF, METADEX, SolStAb, T04, WAA.
—BLDSC (4934.000000), INIST. **CCC.**
Published by: Permanent Way Institution, Lucks Cottage, Lucks Lane, Patdduck Wood, Kent TN12 GQL, United Kingdom. pwi.bjn@virgin.net. Ed. Martin Fairbrother. Adv. contact Charles Croft.

385 GBR
PINES EXPRESS. Text in English. 1966. bi-m. free to members (effective 2009). bk.rev. back issues avail. **Document type:** *Bulletin.*
Formerly (until 1993): Somerset and Dorset Railway Trust. Bulletin

Published by: Somerset and Dorset Railway Trust, The Railway Station, Washford, Somers TA23 OPP, United Kingdom. TEL 44-1984-640869, info@sdrt.org, http://www.sdrt.org.uk/. Ed. Jonathan Edwards.

385 USA ISSN 0032-1826
HE2723
POCKET LIST OF RAILROAD OFFICIALS. Text in English. 1895. q. USD 249 (effective 2008). adv. Supplement avail. **Document type:** *Directory, Trade.* **Description:** Presents detailed information on over 20,000 officials in freight railroad, rail transit and rail supply companies.
Related titles: Online - full text ed.: free (effective 2008).
—CCC.
Published by: Commonwealth Business Media, Inc. (Subsidiary of: United Business Media Limited), 400 Windsor Corporate Park, 50 Millstone Rd, Ste 200, East Windsor, NJ 08520. TEL 800-221-5488, 888-215-6084, FAX 609-371-7883, cbizservices@sunbeltfs.com, http://www.cbizmedia.com. Pub. Kathy Keeney TEL 410-788-0376. Circ: 5,600.

385 USA ISSN 1044-4688
HE1009
POCKET LIST OF RAILROAD OFFICIALS INTERNATIONAL EDITION. Text in English. 1989. a. adv. **Description:** Provides detailed corporate listings for freight and passenger railroads, rail transit, rail supply companies and related organizations outside N. America.
Related titles: Online - full text ed.; Special ed(s).: Pocket List of Railroad Officials International Edition. Buyer's Guide.
Published by: Commonwealth Business Media, Inc. (Subsidiary of: United Business Media Limited), 400 Windsor Corporate Park, 50 Millstone Rd, Ste 200, East Windsor, NJ 08520. TEL 800-221-5488, FAX 609-371-7883, cbizservices@sunbeltfs.com, http://www.cbizmedia.com. Pub. Kathy Keeney TEL 410-788-0376.

385 DEU ISSN 1865-0163
PRIVATBAHN-MAGAZIN. Text in German. 2007. bi-m. EUR 30; EUR 5 newsstand/cover (effective 2009). adv. **Document type:** *Magazine, Trade.*
Published by: Bahn Media, Marktplatz 15, Suhlendorf, 29562, Germany. TEL 49-5820-9701770, FAX 49-5820-97017720. Ed., Pub. Christian Wiechel-Kramueller. Adv. contact Irina Schober. page EUR 2,900. Circ: 5,000 (paid and controlled).

385 USA ISSN 1047-9473
TF455
PRIVATE VARNISH. Text in English. 1985. bi-m. USD 22; USD 25 foreign. adv. **Document type:** *Journal, Trade.*
Published by: American Association of Private Railcar Owners, PO Box 50221, Pasadena, CA 91115. TEL 708-891-2030. Ed. John Kuehl. adv.: B&W page USD 460, color page USD 667. Circ: 3,200 (paid and controlled).

385 USA ISSN 0033-0817
HE2714
PROGRESSIVE RAILROADING. Text in English. 1958. m. free to qualified personnel (effective 2008). adv. illus.; tr.lit. Supplement avail.; back issues avail.; reprints avail. **Document type:** *Magazine, Trade.* **Description:** Covers critical industry areas such as freight, transit, mechanical, engineering, communications and signaling, finance, labor and technology.
Related titles: Online - full text ed.
Indexed: A22, A28, APA, BrCerAb, BrRB, C&ISA, CA/WCA, CIA, CerAb, CivEngAb, CorrAb, E&CAJ, E11, EEA, EMA, ESPM, EnvEAb, H15, HRIS, LogistBibl, M&TEA, M09, MBF, METADEX, SolStAb, T04, WAA.
—IE, Infotrieve, Linda Hall.
Published by: Trade Press Publishing Corp., 2100 W Florist Ave, Milwaukee, WI 53209. TEL 414-228-7701, 800-727-7995, FAX 414-228-1134, info@tradepress.com, http://www.tradepress.com. Ed. Patrick Foran. Pub. Steve Bolte TEL 561-743-7373. Adv. contact Ray Kosakowski TEL 412-788-6988. B&W page USD 5,765, color page USD 8,215; trim 7 x 10. Circ: 25,059.

385 USA ISSN 1534-3901
TF1
PROGRESSIVE RAILROADING'S CAR & LOCOMOTIVE YEARBOOK & BUYERS' GUIDE. Variant title: Car & Locomotive Yearbook. Text in English. 1988. a. USD 55 domestic; USD 65 foreign (effective 2009). adv. **Document type:** *Directory, Trade.*
Formerly (until 1990): Freight Car Yearbook & Buyers Guide
Published by: Trade Press Publishing Corp., 2100 W Florist Ave, Milwaukee, WI 53209. TEL 414-228-7701, 800-727-7995, FAX 414-228-1134, info@tradepress.com, http://www.tradepress.com. Ed. Patrick Foran. Pub. Steve Bolte TEL 561-743-7373. adv.: B&W page USD 5,645, color page USD 7,865; 7 x 10. Circ: 6,000.

385 NLD ISSN 1872-5880
PRORAIL MAGAZINE. Text in Dutch. 2005. q.
Published by: ProRail, Postbus 2038, Utrecht, 3500 GA, Netherlands. TEL 31-30-2357104, FAX 31-30-2359056, http://www.prorail.nl.

385 GBR
PUSH & PULL. Text in English. 1965. q. free to members (effective 2009). tel.rev.; video rev.; bk.rev. illus. back issues avail. **Document type:** *Magazine, Consumer.* **Description:** Magazine for Railway Society members.
Published by: Keighley & Worth Valley Railway, Haworth Sta, Keighley, W Yorks BD22 8NJ, United Kingdom. TEL 44-1535-645214, admin@kwvr.co.uk.

385 RUS ISSN 0033-4715
PUT' I PUTEVOE KHOZYAISTVO. Text in Russian. 1957. m. USD 80 foreign (effective 2004). bk.rev.
Indexed: RefZh.
—East View.
Published by: Ministerstvo Putei Soobshcheniya Rossiiskoi Federatsii, Novoryazanskaya ul 12, Moscow, 107226, Russian Federation. TEL 7-095-2621232. Ed. A I Ratnikov. Circ: 25,000. **Dist. by:** M K - Periodica, ul Gilyarovskogo 39, Moscow 129110, Russian Federation. TEL 7-095-2845008, FAX 7-095-2813798, info@periodicals.ru, http://www.mkniga.ru.

385 GBR
R M T NEWS. Text in English. 1880. m. free to members (effective 2009). adv. bk.rev. illus.; stat. back issues avail. **Document type:** *Newsletter, Trade.*
Former titles (until 1994): Transport Review; (until 1976): Railway Review (0033-8974)
Published by: Rail Maritime & Transport Union, 205 Euston Rd, London, NW1 2BN, United Kingdom. info@rmt.org.uk. Ed. Bob Crow.

385 629.8 USA ISSN 0096-2309
R S C, RAILWAY SYSTEM CONTROLS; the newsletter for railway C&S and IT professionals. Text in English. 1907. m. USD 148 to institutions (effective 2009). back issues avail.; reprints avail. **Document type:** *Newsletter, Trade.* **Description:** Provides most up-to-date domestic and international news, features, and commentary to keep you on top of this dynamic segment of the railway industry.
Supersedes (in 1970): R S C, Railway Signaling and Communications (0096-2295); Which was formerly (19??): Railway Signaling and Communications; (until 1949): Railway Signaling; (until 1923): Railway Signal Engineer; (until 1916): Signal Engineer
Related titles: Online - full text ed.
Indexed: Inspec.
—CCC.
Published by: Simmons-Boardman Publishing Corp., 345 Hudson St, New York, NY 10014. TEL 212-620-7200, FAX 212-633-1863, jsnyder@sbpub.com, http://www.simmonsboardman.com/. Ed. William C Vantuono. Pub. Robert P DeMarco TEL 212-620-7244. **Subscr. to:** PO Box 10, Omaha, NE 68101. TEL 402-346-4740, FAX 402-346-3670.

385 GBR ISSN 0953-4563
RAIL. Text in English. 1981. fortn. GBP 80 domestic; GBP 90 foreign (effective 2009). adv. bk.rev. back issues avail. **Document type:** *Magazine, Consumer.* **Description:** Provides the most comprehensive and up-to-date news, comment and analysis on the modern rail.
Formerly (until 1988): Rail Enthusiast (0262-561X)
Related titles: Online - full text ed.; Supplement(s): Comprehensive Guide to Britain's Railways. ISSN 1471-0404.
Indexed: CLT&T.
Published by: H. Bauer Publishing Ltd. (Subsidiary of: Bauer Media Group), Bushfield House, Orton Centre, Peterborough, PE2 5UW, United Kingdom. TEL 44-1733-237111, http://www.bauer.co.uk. Ed. Robyn Bewsey-Holden TEL 44-1733-465810. Adv. contact Mary McCormack TEL 44-1733-288120.

385 FRA ISSN 0989-8220
LE RAIL. Text in French; Summaries in English. 1954. bi-m. (plus 2 special issues). EUR 60 domestic; EUR 80 in the European Union; EUR 90 elsewhere (effective 2009). adv. bk.rev. **Document type:** *Magazine, Trade.*
Former titles (until 1988): Rail et Le Monde (0181-1878); (until no.286, 1979): Vie du Rail Outremer (0049-6278)
Indexed: RASB.
—CCC.
Published by: Groupe Actis, 82 Rue Anatole France, Levallois-Perret, 92300, France. FAX 33-1-80825047. Ed. Christian Scasso TEL 33-1-46225371. Circ: 18,000.

385 GBR ISSN 1757-9910
RAIL ALLIANCE MATRIX. Text in English. 2008. q. free to members (effective 2010). **Document type:** *Magazine, Trade.*
Related titles: Online - full text ed.: free (effective 2010).
Published by: The Rail Alliance, The Control Tower, Long Marston Storage, Campden Rd, Stratford on Avon, CV37 8QR, United Kingdom. TEL 44-1789-720026, Info@railalliance.co.uk.

385 USA
RAIL AND WIRE. Text in English. 1957. bi-m. looseleaf. USD 30 to members (effective 2000). bk.rev. **Document type:** *Newsletter.* **Description:** Contains news and articles about the restoration and history of railroad equipment at IRM.
Published by: Illinois Railway Museum, Inc., PO Box 427, Union, IL 60180. TEL 815-923-4391, FAX 815-923-2006. Ed. Peter J Schmidt. Pub., R&P Nick Kallas. Circ: 2,500 (paid).

385 GBR ISSN 1472-5428
RAIL BUSINESS INTELLIGENCE. Text in English. 1995 (Mar.). fortn. GBP 642 (print or online ed.); GBP 742 combined subscription (print & online eds.) (effective 2010). **Document type:** *Newsletter, Trade.* **Description:** Provides reporting on the transformation of Britain's railways since privatisation.
Formerly (until 1998): Rail Privatisation News (1358-5479)
Related titles: Online - full text ed.
Indexed: A09, A10, A15, ABIn, B01, B06, B07, B09, CA, P34, P48, P51, P52, PQC, T02, V03, V04.
—CCC.
Published by: Reed Business Information Ltd. (Subsidiary of: Reed Business), Quadrant House, The Quadrant, Sutton, Surrey SM2 5AS, United Kingdom. TEL 44-20-86523500, FAX 44-20-86528932, rbi.subscriptions@qss-uk.com, http://www.reedbusiness.co.uk/. Adv. contact Sheena Rennie TEL 44-20-86525200.

385 USA CODEN: LHAEAE
RAIL BUSINESS WEEK (ONLINE). Text in English. 1995. w. price varies. **Document type:** *Newsletter, Trade.* **Description:** Provides news in the US railroad industry and analyses of the issues, from railroad and shipper perspectives.
Former titles (until 200?): Rail Business Week (Print) (1092-289X); (until 1997): Rail Business (1080-2851)
Media: E-mail.
—CCC.
Published by: Energy Argus, Inc. (Subsidiary of: Argus Media Inc.), 1012 Fourteenth St NW, Ste 1500, Washington, DC 20005. TEL 202-775-0240, FAX 202-872-8045, washington@argusmediagroup.com, http://www.argusmediagroup.com. Circ: 325 (paid).

625.1 NLD ISSN 0141-4615
TF1 CODEN: REGIAX
RAIL ENGINEERING INTERNATIONAL. Text in English. 1971. q. adv. bk.rev. charts; illus. back issues avail. **Document type:** *Journal, Trade.* **Description:** Aims to keep readers informed about developments and innovations in railway technology.
Indexed: BrRB, HRIS.
—BLDSC (7242.827000), IE, Infotrieve, Ingenta, Linda Hall.
Published by: De Rooi Publications, PO Box 543, Veenendaal, 3900 AM, Netherlands. TEL 31-318-515012, FAX 31-318-511243. Ed. Wilhelmina M. de Rooi. Pub., R&P, Adv. contact Wilhelmina M de Rooi.

385 GBR ISSN 1362-234X
RAIL EXPRESS; keeping in touch with the railway today. Text in English. 1966. m. GBP 43 domestic; GBP 57 in Europe; GBP 71 elsewhere (effective 2009). adv. bk.rev. illus. back issues avail. **Document type:** *Magazine, Consumer.* **Description:** Packed with news, features, nostalgia, and updates on all aspects of trains and railways.
Published by: Foursight Publications Ltd., 20 Park St, Kings Cliffe, Peterborough, Cambs PE8 6XN, United Kingdom. TEL 44-1780-470086, FAX 44-1780-470060. Ed. Philip Sutton. Adv. contact Paul Lawrinson. **Subscr. to:** Customer Interface Ltd. **Dist. by:** Seymour Distribution Ltd.

385.1 GBR ISSN 1352-3937
RAIL INDUSTRY MONITOR. Text in English. 1993. a. (in 5 vols.). looseleaf. GBP 299 per issue (effective 2009). **Document type:** *Report, Trade.* **Description:** Contains information about the railway industry, including the latest franchise remapping.
Related titles: CD-ROM ed.: ISSN 1752-5004. 2002. GBP 280 per issue (effective 2009); Online - full text ed.: ISSN 1752-6523. 2006. GBP 275 per issue (effective 2009).
—CCC.
Published by: T A S Publications & Events Ltd., Ross Holme, West End, Long Preston, Skipton, N Yorks BD23 4QL, United Kingdom. TEL 44-1729-840756, FAX 44-1729-840705, info@taspublications.co.uk.

385 CHE ISSN 0020-8442
TF1 CODEN: RAIIAF
RAIL INTERNATIONAL/SCHIENEN DER WELT. Text in English. 1924-2004; N.S. 2007. q. adv. bk.rev. bibl.; charts; illus.; stat. index. back issues avail.; reprints avail. **Document type:** *Journal, Trade.* **Description:** Promotes exchanges of experience among railway networks throughout the world.
Formerly (until 1969): International Railway Congress Association. Monthly Bulletin (0368-8828)
Related titles: German ed.: ISSN 0771-1344; French ed.: ISSN 1022-4076.
Indexed: A22, A28, APA, BAS, BrCerAb, BrRB, C&ISA, CA/WCA, CIA, CISA, CerAb, CivEngAb, CorrAb, DIP, E&CAJ, E11, EEA, EMA, ESPM, EnvEAb, H15, HRIS, IBR, IBZ, Inspec, M&TEA, M09, MBF, METADEX, SCOPUS, SolStAb, T04, WAA.
—AskIEEE, IE, Infotrieve, Ingenta, Linda Hall. **CCC.**
Published by: Minirex AG, Maihofstr 63, Luzern, 6002, Switzerland. TEL 41-41-4297090, FAX 41-41-4297099, redaktion@minirex.ch, http://www.minirex.ch. Ed. Walter von Andrian. adv.: B&W page EUR 1,900, color page EUR 2,950; trim 188 x 257. Circ: 4,000.
Co-sponsor: International Union of Railways.

385.094253 GBR ISSN 1350-0031
RAIL LINCS. Text in English. 1991. 3/yr. **Document type:** *Magazine, Trade.* **Description:** Keeps readers up-to-date on local rail news and issues in the Lincolnshire region.
—CCC.
Published by: Railfuture, Lincolnshire Branch, c/o David Harby, 6 Carral Close, Lincoln, LN5 9BD, United Kingdom. TEL 44-1724-710528, david.harby@ntlworld.com, http://www.railfuture.org.uk/tiki-index.php?page=Lincolnshire%20Branch.

385 FRA ISSN 1960-9515
LE RAIL MAGHREB. Text in French. 2007. bi-m. EUR 48 domestic; EUR 60 in the European Union; EUR 70 elsewhere (effective 2008). back issues avail. **Document type:** *Magazine, Trade.*
Published by: Groupe Actis, 82 Rue Anatole France, Levallois-Perret, 92300, France. FAX 33-1-80825047. Ed. Christian Scasso TEL 33-1-46225371.

385 625.1 FRA ISSN 1261-3665
RAIL PASSION. Text in French. 1995. m. EUR 70 domestic; EUR 90 in Europe; EUR 97 in North America (effective 2010). **Document type:** *Magazine, Consumer.* **Description:** Reports on everything to do with the railway systems of today including where there is work taking place on them and also includes reports on foreign railroads.
Related titles: Online - full text ed.: free.
Published by: La Vie du Rail, 11 rue de Milan, Paris, Cedex 9 75440, France. TEL 33-1-49701200, FAX 33-1-49701269, info@laviedurail.com, http://www.laviedurail.com.

LE RAIL SYNDICALISTE. *see* LABOR UNIONS

RAIL TEAMSTER; a magazine for teamster rail members. *see* LABOR UNIONS

625.100 GBR ISSN 1471-0668
RAIL TECHNOLOGY MAGAZINE. Abbreviated title: R T M. Text in English. 2000. bi-m. free to qualified personnel (effective 2009). adv. **Document type:** *Magazine, Trade.* **Description:** Contains technology news and developments in the UK's rail network.
—CCC.
Published by: Cognitive Publishing Ltd., Ste 102, International House, 82-86 Deansgate, Manchester, Lancashire M3 2ER, United Kingdom. TEL 44-161-8336320, FAX 44-161-8320571, info@cognitivepublishing.com, http://www.cognitivepublishing.com. Ed. Stephen Lewis. Adv. contact Chris Greenhalgh. Circ: 8,000.

385 IND ISSN 0970-3187
HE3291
RAIL TRANSPORT JOURNAL. Text in English. 1965. q. INR 50; INR 15 per issue; free to members (effective 2011). adv. bk.rev. charts. 52 p./no. 3 cols./p.; **Document type:** *Journal, Academic/Scholarly.* **Description:** Covers the production and track of railway and ancillary equipments like locomotives, coaches, wagons, signaling and telecommunication equipments, electrical appliances and allied products.
Formerly (until 1987): Institute of Rail Transport. Journal (0020-3114)
Published by: Institute of Rail Transport, Rm. 17 Rail Bhavan, Raisina Rd., New Delhi, 110 001, India. TEL 91-11-3384171, FAX 91-11-3384005, irt@nde.vsnl.net.in. Circ: 2,500.

385 USA ISSN 0896-4440
HE2561
RAIL TRAVEL NEWS. Abbreviated title: R T N. Text in English. 1970. s-m. USD 30 domestic; USD 39 foreign (effective 2010). bk.rev. illus. reprints avail. **Document type:** *Magazine, Trade.*
Formerly (until 1974): Rail Travel Newsletter
Indexed: CLT&T, HRIS.
Published by: Message Media, PO Box 9007, Berkeley, CA 94709.

385 USA ISSN 0163-7266
TF1
RAILFAN & RAILROAD. Text in English. 1979. m. USD 37.95 domestic; USD 50 foreign (effective 2010). adv. bk.rev. illus. 72 p./no.; back issues avail.; reprints avail. **Document type:** *Magazine, Consumer.*
Formed by the merger of (1974-1979): Railfan (0098-0714); (1937-1979): Railroad Magazine (0033-8761); Which was formerly (until 1937): Railroad Stories; (until 1932): Railroad Man's magazine
Indexed: CLT&T, HRIS, P06.
Published by: Carstens Publications, Inc., 108 Phil Hardin Rd, Newton, NJ 07860. TEL 973-383-3355, FAX 973-383-4064, carstens@carstens-publications.com, http://www.carstens-publications.com. Pub. Henry Carstens. Adv. contact John Earley.

385 GBR ISSN 0033-8745
RAILNEWS. Text in English. 1963. m. looseleaf. GBP 28.40 foreign (effective 2009). adv. bk.rev. charts; illus. 6 cols./p.; **Document type:** *Newspaper, Trade.* **Description:** Contains news of the British Railways industry.
—CCC.
Published by: Rail News, King's Cross Business Ctr, 180-186 King's Cross Rd, London, WC1X 9DE, United Kingdom. TEL 44-20-72786100, FAX 44-20-72786145, advertising@railnews.co.uk. Ed. Paul Whiting. Adv. contact Laurence Butters TEL 44-7947-948585. Circ: 60,000. **Subscr. to:** Cats Solutions, Two Caen View, Rushy Platt, Swindon, Wiltshire SN5 8WQ, United Kingdom. TEL 44-1793-868868, FAX 44-1793-490270, railnews@cats-solutions.co.uk, http://www.cats-solutions.co.uk/.

385 USA ISSN 0745-5267
TF1
RAILPACE NEWSMAGAZINE. Text in English. m. adv.
Address: 927, Piscataway, NJ 08855-0927. TEL 908-463-1091. Ed. Thomas Nemeth. Circ: 8,500.

385 USA ISSN 0090-7847
TF1
➤ **RAILROAD HISTORY.** Text in English. 1921. s-a. USD 12.50 per issue to non-members; USD 7.50 per issue to members (effective 2010). bk.rev. bibl.; charts; illus. cum.index 1921-1984; then every 2 yrs. 160 p./no. 1 cols./p.; back issues avail.; reprints avail. **Document type:** *Journal, Academic/Scholarly.* **Description:** Features scholarly articles, based on original research of all facets of US railroads 1828 to present, and including articles on railroad preservation and historical libraries as well as book review section of railroad topics.
Formerly (until 1972): Railway and Locomotive Historical Society. Bulletin (0033-8842)
Indexed: AmH&L, CA, CLT&T, HRIS, P06, T02.
—Ingenta, Linda Hall.
Published by: Railway & Locomotive Historical Society, c/o Peter A. Hansen, 15621 W 87th St, PO Box 152, Lenexa, KS 66219. Ed. Peter A Hansen.

➤ **RAILROAD MODEL CRAFTSMAN.** *see* HOBBIES

385.26 USA ISSN 0887-347X
TF302.U54
RAILROAD STATION HISTORICAL SOCIETY. RAILROAD STATION MONOGRAPH. Text in English. 1970. a. free. bibl.; illus. **Document type:** *Monographic series.*
Published by: Railroad Station Historical Society, Inc, c/o Jim Dent, Business Manager, 33 Third Ave, Hawthorne, NJ 07506-2411. jdent@erols.com, http://www.rrshs.org. Circ: 500.

385 USA ISSN 0147-0027
TF302.U54
RAILROAD STATION HISTORICAL SOCIETY. THE BULLETIN. Text in English. 1968. bi-m. USD 10 domestic membership; USD 15 foreign (effective 2000). adv. bk.rev. abstr.; charts; illus.; stat. index. **Document type:** *Bulletin.*
Indexed: AIAP.
Published by: Railroad Station Historical Society, Inc, c/o Jim Dent, Business Manager, 33 Third Ave, Hawthorne, NJ 07506-2411. jdent@erols.com, http://www.rrshs.org. Circ: 500.

385 GBR
RAILTRACK SAFETY AND STANDARDS BOARD. INFORMATION BULLETIN; railway safety is everyone's business. Text in English. 1998. bi-m. free to members (effective 2009). **Document type:** *Newsletter, Trade.* **Description:** Aims to keep Railway Group members informed of RSSB's activities. News relating to new safety initiatives, risk management, updates on research projects, Railway Group Standards and other progress is reported.
Formerly (until 2003): Railtrack Safety and Standards Directorate. Information Bulletin
Related titles: Online - full text ed.
Published by: R S S B, Block 2, Angel Sq, 1 Torrens St, London, EC1V 1NY, United Kingdom. TEL 44-20-31425300, FAX 44-20-31425663, enquirydesk@rssb.co.uk.

385 GBR ISSN 0267-5943
RAILWATCH. Text in English. 19??. q. GBP 6 to non-members; free to members (effective 2009). adv. bk.rev. 20 p./no.; back issues avail. **Document type:** *Magazine, Trade.* **Description:** Contains reports on railways and rail user groups.
Former titles (until 1985): Railway Development News (0266-724X); (until 1978): Railway Invigoration Society. Progress Reports
Related titles: Online - full text ed.
—CCC.
Published by: Railfuture, 4 Christchurch Sq, London, E9 7HU, United Kingdom. TEL 44-20-89858548, FAX 44-20-89858212, media@railfuture.org.uk, http://www.railfuture.org.uk/. Eds. Ray King, Robert Stevens. adv.: page GBP 190.

657 385 USA
RAILWAY ACCOUNTING RULES. Text in English. base vol. plus s-a. updates. USD 22. **Document type:** *Handbook/Manual/Guide, Trade.*
Published by: Association of American Railroads, Operations and Maintenance Department, 50 F St, N W, Washington, DC 20001. TEL 202-639-2325. Ed. K Eric Wolfe.

385 625.1 USA ISSN 0033-8826
TF1 CODEN: RAAGA3
RAILWAY AGE; serving the railway industry since 1856. Text in English. 1876. m. free to qualified personnel (effective 2011). adv. illus.; charts; maps; mkt.; stat. Supplement avail.; back issues avail.; reprints avail. **Document type:** *Magazine, Trade.* **Description:** Emphasizes on technology, operations, strategic planning, marketing and other issues such as legislative and labor/management developments.
Incorporates (1982-1991): Modern Railroads (0736-2064); Which was formerly (until 1982): Modern Railroads - Rail Transit (0193-3272); (until 1977): Modern Railroads (0026-8348); Railway Locomotives and Cars (0033-8915); Former titles (until 1918): Railway Age Gazette (0096-2317); (until 1910): Railroad Age Gazette (0149-4406); Which was formed by the merger of (1870-1908): Railroad Gazette (0097-6679); Which was formerly (until 1870): Western Railroad Gazette; (1900-1908): Railway Age (0149-4430); Which was formerly (until 1900): Railway Age and Northwestern Railroads (0149-4422); Which was formed by the merger of (1876-1891): Railway Age (0149-4414); (1887-1891): Northwestern Railroads
Related titles: Microfiche ed.: (from CIS); Microform ed.: (from PQC); Online - full text ed.: ISSN 2161-511X.
Indexed: A09, A10, A12, A13, A14, A15, A17, A22, A23, A24, A28, ABIn, APA, B01, B02, B04, B06, B07, B08, B09, B13, B15, B16, B17, B18, B21, BPI, BRD, BrCerAb, BrRB, BusI, C&ISA, C12, CA/WCA, CIA, CerAb, CivEngAb, CorrAb, E&CAJ, E11, EEA, EIA, EMA, ESPM, EngInd, EnvAb, EnvEAb, G04, G05, G06, G07, G08, H&SSA, H15, HRIS, I05, I07, ISMEC, Inspec, KES, M&TEA, M01, M02, M09, MBF, METADEX, MagInd, P02, P06, P10, P13, P34, P48, P51, P52, P53, P54, PAIS, PQC, RefZh, S10, S23, SCOPUS, SRI, SolStAb, T&II, T02, T04, V02, V03, V04, W01, W02, W03, W05, WAA.
—IE, Infotrieve, Ingenta, Linda Hall. **CCC.**
Published by: Simmons-Boardman Publishing Corp., 345 Hudson St, New York, NY 10014. TEL 212-620-7200, http://www.simmonsboardman.com/. Ed. William C Vantuono. Pub. Robert P DeMarco TEL 212-620-7244. **Subscr. to:** PO Box 10, Omaha, NE 68101. TEL 800-895-4389.

385 GBR ISSN 0033-8834
➤ **THE RAILWAY AND CANAL HISTORICAL SOCIETY.JOURNAL.** Abbreviated title: R & C H S Journals. Text in English. 1955. 3/yr. free to members (effective 2009). bk.rev. bibl.; charts; illus.; maps. index. back issues avail. **Document type:** *Journal, Academic/Scholarly.* **Description:** Presents a history of railways, canals and other forms of transport.
Related titles: Microform ed.: (from PQC).
—BLDSC (4845.400000), IE, Ingenta.
Published by: Railway and Canal Historical Society, c/o M Searle, 3 W Ct, W St, Oxford, OX2 0NP, United Kingdom. Ed. P S M Cross-Rudkin.

385 USA
RAILWAY & LOCOMOTIVE HISTORICAL SOCIETY NEWSLETTER. Text in English. 1981. s-a. membership. **Document type:** *Newsletter.*
Indexed: CLT&T, HRIS.
Published by: Railway & Locomotive Historical Society (East Irvine), PO Box 215, East Irvine, CA 92650. Ed. C Zlatkovich. Circ: 3,000.

385 GBR ISSN 1360-2098
RAILWAY BYLINES. Text in English. 1985. m. GBP 49.20 domestic; GBP 65.30 in Europe; GBP 77.40 elsewhere; GBP 4.10 per issue (effective 2009). illus. back issues avail. **Document type:** *Magazine, Consumer.*
Published by: Irwell Press, 59a High St, Clophill, Beds MK45 4BE, United Kingdom. TEL 44-1525-861888, FAX 44-1525-862044, george@irwellpress.demon.co.uk. Ed. Martin Smith.

385 AUS ISSN 0157-2431
RAILWAY DIGEST. Text in English. 1963. m. AUD 90 domestic; AUD 115 in Asia & the Pacific; AUD 110 in New Zealand; AUD 140 elsewhere (effective 2008). back issues avail. **Document type:** *Magazine, Consumer.* **Description:** Provides latest news on Australian railways.
Formerly (until 1982): New South Wales Digest
Published by: Australian Railway Historical Society, New South Wales Division, 67 Renwick St, Redfern, NSW 2016, Australia. TEL 61-2-96994595, FAX 61-2-96991714, mail@arhsnsw.com.au. Ed. Chris Walters TEL 61-2-83949016. Circ: 6,000.

385 GBR ISSN 1747-2989
HE1009
RAILWAY DIRECTORY. Text in English. 1895. a. EUR 430 per issue; EUR 560 combined subscription per issue (print & online eds.) (effective 2010). adv. **Document type:** *Directory.* **Description:** Contains contact and statistical information about railway operators, suppliers, regulatory authorities, consultants and support services.
Former titles (until 1989): Railway Directory and Yearbook (0079-9513); (until 1968): Directory of Railway Officials & Year Book; (until 1950): Universal Directory of Railway Officials and Railway Year Book
Related titles: CD-ROM ed.: GBP 320 in Europe; USD 545 in United States; GBP 340 elsewhere (effective 1999); Online - full text ed.: EUR 445 per issue (effective 2010).
Indexed: H&TI.
—CCC.
Published by: D V V Media UK Ltd., NINE, Sutton Court Rd, Sutton, Surrey SM1 4SZ, United Kingdom. TEL 44-20-86528608, FAX 44-20-86523738. Ed. Andrew Hellawell TEL 44-20-86525200. Pub. Sheena Rennie TEL 44-20-86525211. Adv. contact Paul Davis TEL 44-20-86525212.

385 USA ISSN 0079-9521
TF501
RAILWAY FUEL AND OPERATING OFFICERS ASSOCIATION. PROCEEDINGS. Text in English. a. USD 30 membership (effective 2008). **Document type:** *Proceedings, Trade.*
—Linda Hall.
Published by: International Association of Railway Operating Officers, c/o Ted Hagemo, 6645 MacArthur Dr, Missoula, MT 59808. TEL 406-370-6977, 2070cooper@msn.com, http://www.iaroo.org.

625.1 GBR ISSN 0373-5346
TF1 CODEN: RWGIAN
RAILWAY GAZETTE INTERNATIONAL; a journal of management, engineering and operation. Text in English. 1835. m. GBP 68.40 domestic; EUR 133 in Europe Eurozone; USD 188.55 in United States; GBP 115.50 elsewhere (effective 2004). adv. bk.rev. charts; illus.; stat.; tr.lit. index. reprints avail. **Document type:** *Magazine, Trade.* **Description:** Provides coverage of engineering, commercial and management issues affecting the railway business worldwide.
Former titles (until 1971): International Railway Gazette (0374-3349); (until 19??): Railway Gazette (0033-8907); Which incorporated (1880-1935): Railway Engineer (0370-8004); Railway News; Railway Times; Transport and Railroad Center
Related titles: Online - full text ed.
Indexed: A09, A10, A15, A22, A28, ABIn, APA, B01, B02, B06, B07, B09, B15, B17, B18, BrCerAb, BrRB, C&ISA, CA, CA/WCA, CIA, CISA, CerAb, CivEngAb, CorrAb, E&CAJ, E11, EEA, EMA, ESPM, EngInd, EnvEAb, G04, G08, H15, HRIS, I05, ICEA, ISMEC, Inspec, M&TEA, M09, MBF, METADEX, P34, P48, P51, P52, P53, P54, PQC, SCOPUS, SoftAbEng, SolStAb, T02, T04, V03, V04, WAA.
—BLDSC (7247.500000), IE, Infotrieve, Ingenta, INIST, Linda Hall. **CCC.**
Published by: Reed Business Information Ltd. (Subsidiary of: Reed Business), Quadrant House, The Quadrant, Sutton, Surrey SM2 5AS, United Kingdom. TEL 44-20-86523500, FAX 44-20-86528932, rbi.subscriptions@qss-uk.com, http://www.reedbusiness.co.uk/. Ed. Murray Hughes TEL 44-20-8652-3056. Pub. Giles Grant. Adv. contact Sheena Rennie TEL 44-20-86525200. B&W page USD 2,650, color page USD 4,375. Circ: 9,616. **Subscr. to:** Quadrant Subscription Services, PO Box 302, Haywards Heath, W Sussex RH16 3YY, United Kingdom. TEL 44-1444-475603, FAX 44-1444-445447.

385 GBR ISSN 1367-4293
RAILWAY GROUP STANDARD. Text in English. 1995. irreg. **Document type:** *Monographic series.* **Description:** Aims to facilitate the management and operation of the shared system that is the mainline railway.
Related titles: Online - full text ed.
Published by: R S S B, Block 2, Angel Sq, 1 Torrens St, London, EC1V 1NY, United Kingdom. TEL 44-20-31425300, FAX 44-20-31425663, enquirydesk@rssb.co.uk, http://www.rssb.co.uk.

385 USA ISSN 0093-8505
TF15
RAILWAY HISTORY MONOGRAPH. Text in English. 1972. irreg. illus. index. **Document type:** *Monographic series.*
—Ingenta.
Published by: Raildroad Station Historical Society, 26 Thackeray Road, Oakland, NJ 07436-3312. jdent1@optonline.net, http://www.rrshs.org/. Ed. James Dent. Circ: 100.

625.23 GBR ISSN 1744-2281
RAILWAY INTERIORS INTERNATIONAL. Text in English. 2004 (Jun.). a. free (effective 2009). **Document type:** *Newspaper, Trade.* **Description:** Covers the growing field of passenger railway interior design, branding, furnishing and completion.
Related titles: Online - full text ed.
—CCC.
Published by: U K & International Press (Subsidiary of: AutoIntermediates Ltd.), Abinger House, Church St, Dorking, Surrey RH4 1DF, United Kingdom. TEL 44-1306-743744, FAX 44-1306-887546, info@ukintpress.com.

385 GBR ISSN 0033-8923
TF1
THE RAILWAY MAGAZINE. Text in English. 1897. m. GBP 34.49 domestic; USD 81 in United States; USD 97.30 in Canada; EUR 74.40 in Europe; GBP 55.80 elsewhere; GBP 3.65 newsstand/cover (effective 2010). adv. bk.rev. charts; illus. index. back issues avail.; reprints avail. **Document type:** *Magazine, Consumer.* **Description:** Clear and trusted voice for the railway community, covering all aspects of the scene from steam through to modern rail developments.
Incorporates: Railway & Travel Monthly
Related titles: Microform ed.: (from PQC).
Indexed: P06.
—BLDSC (7248.150000), Linda Hall. **CCC.**
Published by: I P C Country & Leisure Media Ltd. (Subsidiary of: I P C Media Ltd.), The Blue Fin Bldg, 110 Southwark St, London, SE1 0SU, United Kingdom. TEL 44-20-31485000, http://www.ipcmedia.com. Ed. Nick Pigott TEL 44-20-31484680. Pub. Lindsay Greatbatch TEL 44-203-1484324. Adv. contact Lee Morris TEL 44-20-31482517. color page GBP 1,045; trim 210 x 297. Circ: 35,100. **Subscr. to:** Rockwood House, Perrymount Rd, Haywards Heath RH16 3DH, United Kingdom. TEL 44-845-1231231, IPCsubs@quadrantsubs.com, http://www.magazinesdirect.co.uk. **Dist. by:** MarketForce UK Ltd, The Blue Fin Bldg, 3rd Fl, 110 Southwark St, London SE1 0SU, United Kingdom. TEL 44-20-31483300, FAX 44-20-31488105, salesinnovation@marketforce.co.uk, http://www.marketforce.co.uk/.

385 USA ISSN 1934-4414
TF6.U5
RAILWAY MUSEUM QUARTERLY. Text in English. 199?. q. USD 20 to individual members (effective 2007). **Document type:** *Bulletin, Trade.*
Indexed: HRIS.
Published by: Association of Railway Museums, 1016 Rosser St, Conyers, GA 30012. TEL 770-278-0088, FAX 770-388-7772, http://www.railwaymuseums.org.

385 USA ISSN 0094-2278
TF455
RAILWAY PASSENGER CAR ANNUAL. Text in English. 1974. a. price varies. **Description:** Compilation of photographs of passenger cars taken when they were built. Shows exteriors, interiors, and mechanical details.
Published by: R P C Publications, PO Box 503, Alton, IL 62002-0503. Ed. W David Randall. Circ: 1,500.

385 658 GBR ISSN 1467-0399
RAILWAY STRATEGIES; for senior rail management. Text in English. 1999. bi-m. back issues avail. **Document type:** *Magazine, Trade.* **Description:** Designed to help senior executives within the rail industry.
Published by: Hartford Publications Limited (Subsidiary of: Schofield Publishing), Essex Technology & Innovation Ctr, The Gables, Fyfield Rd, Ongar, CM5 0GA, United Kingdom. TEL 44-1277-368318, FAX 44-1277-368291, http://www.schofieldmediagroup.com/.

625.1 JPN ISSN 0033-9008
TF1 CODEN: QRTIA8
RAILWAY TECHNICAL RESEARCH INSTITUTE. QUARTERLY REPORT. Key Title: Quarterly Report of R T R I. Text in English. 1960. q. USD 134 (effective 2005). charts; illus. index. back issues avail. **Document type:** *Journal, Academic/Scholarly.*
Related titles: Online - full text ed.: ISSN 1880-1765. 2004.
Indexed: A22, A28, APA, ApMecR, B21, BrCerAb, BrRB, C&ISA, CA/WCA, CIA, CPEI, CerAb, CivEngAb, CorrAb, E&CAJ, E11, EEA, EMA, ESPM, EngInd, EnvEAb, H&SSA, H15, HRIS, ISMEC, Inspec, JTA, M&TEA, M09, MBF, METADEX, RefZh, SCOPUS, SolStAb, T04, WAA.
—BLDSC (7201.855000), AskIEEE, IE, Infotrieve, Ingenta, Linda Hall.

Published by: (Railway Technical Research Institute/Tetsudo Gijutsu Kenkyujo), Ken-yusha, Inc., 2-8-38, Hikari-cho, Kokubunji-shi, 185-0034, Japan. TEL 81-42-572-7157, FAX 81-425-73-7255. Ed., R&P Kanji Wakoh. Circ: 700.

625.1 DEU ISSN 0079-9548
RAILWAY TECHNICAL REVIEW. Text in English. 1952. q. EUR 50 domestic; EUR 54.50 in Europe; EUR 58.50 elsewhere; EUR 12.50 newsstand/cover (effective 2008). adv. **Document type:** *Magazine, Trade.*
Indexed: BrRB, C&ISA, CorrAb, E&CAJ, HRIS, SolStAb, WAA. —Linda Hall.
Published by: Eurailpress Tetzlaff-Hestra GmbH & Co. KG (Subsidiary of: Deutscher Verkehrs Verlag GmbH), Nordkanalstr 36, Hamburg, 20097, Germany. TEL 49-40-2371403, FAX 49-40-23714259, info@eurailpress.com, http://www.eurailpress.com. Ed. Eberhard Jaensch. Adv. contact Silke Haertel. B&W page EUR 2,520, color page EUR 3,510. Circ: 5,258 (paid and controlled).

625.1 USA ISSN 0033-9016
TF1 CODEN: RTSTAR
RAILWAY TRACK & STRUCTURES. Text in English. 1885. m. USD 16 in North America to qualified personnel (print or online ed.); USD 42 in North America (print or online ed.); USD 72 elsewhere (print or online ed.); USD 24 combined subscription in North America to qualified personnel (print & online eds.); USD 63 combined subscription in North America (print & online eds.); USD 108 combined subscription elsewhere (print & online eds.) (effective 2011). illus. Index. back issues avail.; reprints avail. **Document type:** *Magazine, Trade.* **Description:** Reaches railway engineering professionals, including maintenance-of-way and c&s engineering decision-makers.
Former titles (until 1953): Railway Engineering and Maintenance (0097-6687); (until 1923): Railway Maintenance Engineer
Related titles: E-mail ed.; Microform ed.: (from PQC); Online - full text ed.: ISSN 2160-2514.
Indexed: A15, A22, A28, ABIn, APA, B02, B15, B17, B18, BrCerAb, BrRB, C&ISA, CA/WCA, CIA, CerAb, ChemAb, CivEngAb, ConcrAb, CorrAb, E&CAJ, E11, EEA, EMA, ESPM, EngInd, EnvEAb, G04, G06, G07, G08, H15, HRIS, I05, Inspec, M&TEA, M09, MBF, METADEX, P48, P51, P52, PQC, SCOPUS, SolStAb, T04, WAA. —IE, Infotrieve, Ingenta, Linda Hall. **CCC.**
Published by: Simmons-Boardman Publishing Corp., 345 Hudson St, New York, NY 10014. TEL 212-620-7200, http://www.simmonsboardman.com/. Ed. Mischa Wanek-Libman. Pub. Robert P DeMarco TEL 212-620-7244.

RAILWAYS. *see* TRAVEL AND TOURISM

625.1 ZAF ISSN 1029-2756
TF1
RAILWAYS AFRICA. Key Title: Railways. Text in English. 1957. bi-m. ZAR 160 domestic; ZAR 310 in Africa; ZAR 435 elsewhere (effective 2006). adv. bk.rev. charts; illus.; tr.lit. back issues avail. **Document type:** *Magazine, Consumer.* **Description:** Covers developments, opinions, and news on the railroad industry in Africa.
Former titles (1957-1991): Railways in Southern Africa (1029-2845); S.A. Railway Engineering (0033-8885)
Indexed: ISAP, Inspec.
Published by: Rail Link Communications, PO Box 4794, Randburg, Gauteng 2125, South Africa. TEL 27-11-463-4330, FAX 27-11-463-4224. Ed. Helmuth Hagen. Pub., R&P Barbara Sheat. Adv. contact J Thompson. B&W page ZAR 8,827.50, color page ZAR 9,704.75; trim 180 x 260. Circ: 2,500 (controlled).

385 GBR ISSN 1479-2230
RAILWAYS ILLUSTRATED. Text in English. 1939. m. GBP 44.40 domestic; GBP 54 in Europe; GBP 59.20 elsewhere; GBP 3.70 newsstand/cover (effective 2009). adv. back issues avail. **Document type:** *Magazine, Consumer.* **Description:** Provides a comprehensive round-up of the latest news and topical events from the UK across the present day railway, including heritage traction in operation on the main lines.
Former titles (until 2003): Railway World (0033-9032); (until 1952): Railways
Indexed: H20, T02.
—CCC.
Published by: Ian Allan Publishing Ltd., Foundry Rd, Stamford, Lincolnshire PE9 2PP, United Kingdom. TEL 44-1780-484630, FAX 44-1780-763388, magazines@ianallanpublishing.co.uk, http://www.ianallanpublishing.com. Ed. Pip Dunn TEL 44-1775-723849. Adv. contact David Smith TEL 44-1775-767184. **Subscr. to:** Riverdene Business Park, Riverdene Industrial Estate, Molesey Rd, Walton-on-Thames, Surrey KT12 4RG, United Kingdom. TEL 44-1932-266622, FAX 44-1932-266633, subs@ianallanpublishing.co.uk.

385 AUS ISSN 0033-9040
RAILWAYS INSTITUTE MAGAZINE. Text in English. 1897. m. bk.rev. illus. **Document type:** *Newsletter.*
Published by: Railways Institute Council, Perth Business Ctr, PO Box 8436, Perth, W.A. 6849, Australia. TEL 61-9-3262461, FAX 61-9-3262754.

385 GBR
RAILWAYS OF SOUTHERN AFRICA: LOCOMOTIVE GUIDE. Text in English. a. **Document type:** *Monographic series.*
Formerly (until 1990): South African Railways Locomotive Allocations
Indexed: Inspec.
Address: 39 Nightingale Rd, Hitchin, Herts HP3 2DF, United Kingdom. Ed., Pub., R&P John N Middleton TEL 44-1235-814876.

385 GBR ISSN 0269-0608
RAILWAYS RESTORED (YEAR). Text in English. 19??. a. GBP 15.99 per issue (effective 2010). back issues avail. **Document type:** *Directory, Consumer.* **Description:** Gives details of more than 100 railways, museums and steam centers, including locomotives, rolling stock and associated organizations.
Formerly (until 1980): Steam
Published by: (Association of Railway Preservation Socieities), Ian Allan Publishing Ltd., Riverdene Business Park, Riverdene Industrial Estate, Molesey Rd, Walton-on-Thames, Surrey KT12 4RG, United Kingdom. TEL 44-1932-266622, FAX 44-1932-266633, magazines@ianallanpublishing.co.uk. Ed. Allan C Butcher.

385 ARG
REALIDAD FERROVIARIA. Variant title: R F. Text in Spanish. 1997. bi-m. USD 48 domestic; USD 100 foreign (effective 2002). **Description:** Provides information regarding freight, passenger and metropolitan services of all operating systems in Latin America. A complete world agenda of rail events is included.
Related titles: Online - full text ed.
Published by: Fundacion Instituto Argentino de Ferrocarriles, Cap.Gral.Ramon Freire, Buenos Aires, C1428CYC, Argentina. admin@fiaf.org.ar, http://www.fiaf.org.ar. Ed., Pub. Marcos F Pipan.

REFERATIVNYI ZHURNAL. AVTOMATIKA, TELEMEKHANIKA I SVIAZ' NA ZHELEZNYKH DOROGAKH; vypusk svodnogo toma. *see* TRANSPORTATION—Abstracting, Bibliographies, Statistics

REFERATIVNYI ZHURNAL. LOKOMOTIVOSTROENIE I VAGONOSTROENIE; vypusk svodnogo toma. *see* TRANSPORTATION—Abstracting, Bibliographies, Statistics

REFERATIVNYI ZHURNAL. STROITELSTVO ZHELEZNYKH DOROG. PUT' I PUTEVOE KHOZYAISTVO; vypusk svodnogo toma. *see* TRANSPORTATION—Abstracting, Bibliographies, Statistics

REFERATIVNYI ZHURNAL. TEKHNICHESKAYA EKSPLUATATSIYA PODVIZHNOGO SOSTAVA I TYAGA POEZDOV; vypusk svodnogo toma. *see* TRANSPORTATION—Abstracting, Bibliographies, Statistics

REFERATIVNYI ZHURNAL. UPRAVLENIE PEREVOZOCHNYM PROTSESSOM NA ZHELEZNYKH DOROGAKH; vypusk svodnogo toma. *see* TRANSPORTATION—Abstracting, Bibliographies, Statistics

REFERATIVNYI ZHURNAL. ZHELEZNODOROZHNYI TRANSPORT; svodnyi tom. *see* TRANSPORTATION—Abstracting, Bibliographies, Statistics

556 DEU ISSN 1615-7281
REGIONALVERKEHR. Text in German. 1997. 8/yr. EUR 42; EUR 6 newsstand/cover (effective 2008). adv. **Document type:** *Magazine, Trade.*
Published by: Regionalverkehr - Verlag Jochen Neu, Rohrdommelweg 10, Munich, 81249, Germany. TEL 49-89-86487344, FAX 49-89-86487333. Ed., Pub. Tim Schulz. adv.: B&W page EUR 1,258, color page EUR 1,882. Circ: 5,600 (paid and controlled).

385 COL
REIL. Text in Spanish. 1961. m. adv.
Address: Calle 13 No. 18-24, Bogota, CUND, Colombia. Circ: 13,500.

385 USA ISSN 1949-033X
▼ **REMNANTS OF THE RAILS**; a journey of Illinois railroad depots. Text in English. 2010 (Oct.). q. **Document type:** *Magazine, Consumer.* **Description:** Contains photography of Illinois railroad depots.
Related titles: Online - full text ed.: ISSN 1949-0348.
Published by: In a Bind Publishing, PO Box 17673, Urbana, IL 61802. TEL 217-384-7036, mtwigg@gmail.com, http://98.212.61.143/4_Bind.htm.

385 CHN
RENMIN TIEDAO/PEOPLE'S RAILWAYS. Text in Chinese. d. CNY 276, USD 99.60 (effective 2005). **Document type:** *Newspaper.*
Published by: Renmin Tiedao Baoshe, Fuxingmen Wai, 3, Beifengwo, Beijing, 100038, China. TEL 86-10-51842209, FAX 86-10-51844433. **Dist. by:** China International Book Trading Corp, 35 Chegongzhuang Xilu, Haidian District, PO Box 399, Beijing 100044, China. TEL 86-10-68412045, FAX 86-10-68412023, cibtc@mail.cibtc.com.cn, http://www.cibtc.com.cn.

385 BRA ISSN 0034-950X
REVISTA FERROVIARIA. Text in Portuguese. 1939. m. BRL 340,000, USD 50. adv. bk.rev. charts; illus.; stat. Supplement avail. **Description:** Covers the economics, politics and technology of the railway world in Brazil and abroad.
Published by: Empresa Jornalistica dos Transportes, Rua Mexico, 41-S-904, Centro, Rio De Janeiro, RJ 20031-144, Brazil. TEL 021-532-0260, FAX 021-240-0139. Ed. Gerson Toller Gomes. Circ: 10,000.

385.262 DEU
RHEINBAHN EXTRA. Text in German. 1980. irreg. **Document type:** *Consumer.*
Formerly (until 1993): Steig Ein
Published by: Rheinische Bahngesellschaft AG, Postfach 104263, Duesseldorf, 40033, Germany. TEL 49-211-58201, FAX 49-211-5821966. Ed. Hermann Josef Vetten. Circ: 50,000.

385 USA
RIDER INSIDER. Text in English. 1995. q. free. **Document type:** *Magazine, Consumer.*
Published by: Dallas Area Rapid Transit, 1401 Pacific Ave., Dallas, TX 75266. TEL 214-749-2577, FAX 214-749-3668. Ed. Jeff Hampton. Circ: 50,000 (free).

385 USA
ROSTER OF NORTH AMERICAN RAPID TRANSIT CARS (YEAR). Text in English. irreg., latest 1993. USD 100 to non-members; USD 45 to members. **Document type:** *Report, Trade.* **Description:** Lists costs, performance, dimensions, weights, H.V.A.C. systems, propulsion equipment, trucks and suspensions for transit cars in North America.
Published by: (Rolling Stock Equipment Committee), American Public Transportation Association, 1666 K St, NW Ste 1100, Washington, DC 20006. TEL 202-898-4089, FAX 202-989-4049.

385.1 658.3 CHE ISSN 1422-6553
S B B ZEITUNG; Informationen fuer die Mitarbeiterinnen und Mitarbeiter der Schweizerischen Bundesbahnen. Text in German. 1985. fortn. back issues avail. **Document type:** *Bulletin, Trade.* **Description:** Contains news for and about employees of the Swiss Federal Railways.
Related titles: Italian ed.: Corriere F F S. ISSN 1422-6588; French ed.: Courrier C F F. ISSN 1422-6561.
Published by: Schweizerischen Bundesbahnen, Hochschulstr 6, Bern 65, 3000, Switzerland. TEL 41-512-204260, FAX 41-512-204358, via@sbb.ch. Pub. Ruedi Eichenberger. Circ: 43,805 (controlled).

385 SWE ISSN 0037-5985
S J - NYTT. Text in Swedish. 1943. 16/yr. SEK 120; SEK 20 to senior citizens (effective 2000). bk.rev. illus. **Description:** Provides an internal information publication for the Swedish State Railways.
Published by: Statens Jaernvaegar/Swedish State Railways, Stockholm, 10550, Sweden. TEL 46-031-10-42-60, FAX 46-8-762-35-81. Ed. Gunnel Sundbom. Circ: 40,000.

385 363.12 GBR
SAFETYEXCHANGE; railway safety is everyone's business. Text in English. **Document type:** *Newsletter.*
Published by: Railway Safety, Evergreen House, 160 Euston Rd, London, NW1 2DX, United Kingdom. enquiries@railwaysafety.org.uk, http://www.railwaysafety.org.uk/. Ed. Helen Goodman TEL 44-20-7904-7704.

385 JPN
SAIBANETIKUSU/CYBERNETICS. Text in Japanese. 2006 (vol.11, no.1). m. **Document type:** *Journal, Academic/Scholarly.*
Published by: Japan Railway Engineers Association/Nihon Tetsudo Gijutsu Kyokai, 1-28-6, Kameido, Koto-ku, Tokyo, 136-0071, Japan. FAX 81-3-56262325, http://www.jrea.or.jp/.

385 RUS ISSN 0202-1250
SBORNIK OPISANII IZOBRETENII, REKOMENDOVANNYKH DLYA VNEDRENIYA NA ZHELEZNODOROZHNOM TRANSPORTE. Text in Russian. bi-m. USD 85 in United States.
Published by: Sbornik Opisanii Izobretenii Rekomendovannykh dlya Vnedreniya na Zheleznodorozhnom Transporte, Rizhskaya pl 3, Moscow, 129855, Russian Federation. TEL 7-095-2621331. **Dist. by:** East View Information Services, 10601 Wayzata Blvd, Minneapolis, MN 55305. TEL 952-252-1201, 800-477-1005, FAX 952-252-1202, info@eastview.com, http://www.eastview.com.

385 CHE ISSN 1022-7113
SCHWEIZER EISENBAHN REVUE. Text in German. 1978. 10/yr. CHF 106.80 (effective 1999). **Document type:** *Bulletin.*
Published by: Minirex AG, Maihofstr 63, Luzern, 6002, Switzerland. redaktion@minirex.ch, http://www.minirex.ch. Ed. W von Andrian. adv.: B&W page CHF 2,365, color page CHF 3,345; trim 257 x 188. Circ: 12,300.

SEASHORE TROLLEY MUSEUM DISPATCH. *see* MUSEUMS AND ART GALLERIES

614.8 AUT ISSN 0037-4539
SICHERHEIT ZUERST. Text in German. 1958. q. free. **Document type:** *Magazine, Trade.*
Indexed: CISA.
Published by: Versicherungsanstalt fuer Eisenbahnen und Bergbau, Linke Wienzeile 48-52, Vienna, W 1061, Austria. TEL 43-1-588480, FAX 43-1-58848332, direktion@vaeb.at, http://www.vaeb.at. Circ: 20,000.

385 DEU ISSN 0037-4997
CODEN: SIGDAN
SIGNAL UND DRAHT; Railsignalling & Telecommunication. Text in German. 1906. 10/yr. EUR 124; EUR 15 newsstand/cover (effective 2008). adv. bk.rev. abstr.; bibl.; charts; illus.; pat.; tr.lit.; tr.mk. index. **Document type:** *Magazine, Trade.* **Description:** Computer technology used in railway engineering, including signalling and telecommunications, data processing, and data processing equipment for office use and selling.
Incorporates: Signal und Schiene (0037-5004)
Indexed: A22, HRIS, Inspec, RefZh, TM. —BLDSC (8276.000000), AskIEEE, IE, Ingenta, INIST, Linda Hall. **CCC.**
Published by: Eurailpress Tetzlaff-Hestra GmbH & Co. KG (Subsidiary of: Deutscher Verkehrs Verlag GmbH), Nordkanalstr 36, Hamburg, 20097, Germany. TEL 49-40-2371403, FAX 49-40-23714259, info@eurailpress.com, http://www.eurailpress.com. Ed. Karl-Heinz Suwe. Adv. contact Silke Haertel. B&W page EUR 2,210, color page EUR 3,200. Circ: 3,013 (paid and controlled).

385 DNK ISSN 1902-7206
SIKKERHEDSRAPPORT FOR JERNBANEN. Text in Danish. 2005. a. **Document type:** *Government.*
Formerly (until 2006): Trafikstyrelsens Sikkerhedsrapport (1901-6247)
Related titles: Online - full text ed.: ISSN 1902-7214. 2005.
Published by: Trafikstyrelsen/Public Transport Authority, Gammel Moent 4, Copenhagen K, 1117, Denmark. TEL 45-72-267000, FAX 45-33-690548, info@trafikstyrelsen.dk.

385 SWE ISSN 1650-3627
SKAANSKA JAERNVAEGAR. Text in Swedish. 1978. q. free membership (effective 2002). adv.
Formerly (until 2000): S K J -Nytt
Published by: Museifoereningen Skaanska Jaernvaegar, Jaernvaegsstationen, Broesarp, 27755, Sweden. TEL 46-414-730-15, FAX 46-40-22-47-09. adv.: page SEK 1,500.

385 SWE ISSN 0281-109X
SKENBLADET. Text in Swedish. 1978. q. SEK 175 membership (effective 2011). illus. **Document type:** *Bulletin, Consumer.* **Description:** Includes news of OKBv activities, historical articles on Swedish railroads, and articles on modern Swedish railroads.
Published by: Ostkustbanans Vaenner, Svartviksvaegen 22, Kvissleby, 86233, Sweden. okbv@telia.com, http://www.okbv.se.

625.1 385 SWE ISSN 1101-9727
SMALSPAARSINFORM/NARROW GAUGE INFORM. Text in Swedish. 1989. q. SEK 125 to members (effective 1995). adv. bk.rev. **Document type:** *Newsletter.*
Published by: Foereningen Smalspaaret Vaexjoe-Vaestervik, c/o Claes Swendsen, Hoehhult, Landsbro, 57022, Sweden. TEL 46-495-100-61, FAX 46-495-141-42. Ed. Claes Swendsen.

385 USA ISSN 1083-1606
SMOKE AND CINDERS. Text in English. 1961. q. USD 25 (effective 2000). bk.rev. **Document type:** *Newsletter.*
Published by: Tennessee Valley Railroad Museum, Inc., 4119 Cromwell Rd, Chattanooga, TN 37421. TEL 423-894-8028, FAX 423-894-8029. Ed. Steven R Freer. Circ: 850.

385 BEL ISSN 0081-119X
SOCIETE NATIONALE DES CHEMINS DE FER BELGES. RAPPORT ANNUEL. Text in French. 1926. a. **Document type:** *Corporate.*
Related titles: English ed.; Dutch ed.
Published by: Societe Nationale des Chemins de Fer Belges/Nationale Maatschappij de Belgische Spoorwegen, Strategy & Development SD 2, De Merdestraat 38-40, Brussels, 1060, Belgium. TEL 32-2-5254423, FAX 32-2-5253901. R&P G Thomas. Circ: 1,700.

385 IND ISSN 0038-450X
SOUTHERN RAILWAYS. Text in English. 1949. m. **Document type:** *Newsletter, Trade.*
Related titles: Online - full text ed.: free (effective 2011).
Address: GM Secretariet, Head Quarters Office, Parktown, Chennai, Tamil Nadu 600 003, India. srailway@gmail.com.

385 BEL ISSN 0773-5901
HET SPOOR. Text in Dutch. 1956. m. bk.rev. charts; illus.; tr.lit.
Related titles: French ed.: De Rail. ISSN 0033-8729.
Published by: Nationale Maatschappij der Belgische Spoorwegen/ Societe Nationale des Chemins de Fer Belges, Rue de France 85, Bureau 05-322, Brussels, 1060, Belgium. FAX 32-2-5253516. Ed. M Bouquiaux. Circ: 107,000.

385 NLD ISSN 2211-2634
SPOOR. Text in Dutch. 1990. a. price varies.
Former titles (until 2010): Spoor en Tram (1871-7004); (until 2005): Spoor en Trein (0926-2695)
Published by: Uitgeverij de Alk bv, Postbus 9006, Alkmaar, 1800 GA, Netherlands. TEL 31-72-5113965, FAX 31-72-5129989, info@alk.nl, http://www.alk.nl.

385 DNK ISSN 0106-6927
SPORVEJSMUSEET SKJOLDENAESHOLM. AARSBERETNING. Text in Danish. 1979. a. illus. **Document type:** *Consumer.*
Published by: Sporvejshistorisk Selskab/Danish Tram Historical Society, c/o Mikael Lund, Ellinorsvej 9, Charlottenlund, 2920, Denmark. http://www.sporvejsmuseet.dk. Ed. Per Soegaard.

385 USA ISSN 1049-9024
STAYING ON TRACK. Text in English. 1989. m. free to members. **Document type:** *Newsletter.*
Published by: BayRail Alliance, 3921 E Bayshore Rd, Palo Alto, CA 94303. TEL 866-267-8024, http://www.bayrailalliance.org/.

385 GBR ISSN 0269-0020
TF1
STEAM DAYS; steam nostalgia and railway history at its best. Text in English. 1968. m. GBP 41 domestic; GBP 52.50 in Europe; GBP 72 elsewhere (effective 2009). adv. bk.rev. charts; illus. 64 p./no. 3 cols./p.; back issues avail.; reprints avail. **Document type:** *Magazine, Consumer.* **Description:** Illustrated feature articles on steam railways.
Formerly (until 1986): Trains Illustrated (0141-9935)
Published by: Redgauntlet Publications, PO Box 2471, Bournemouth, BH7 7WF, United Kingdom. TEL 44-1202-304849, FAX 44-1202-304849, red.gauntlett@btconnect.com. **Subscr. to:** PO Box 464, Berkhamsted, Herts HP4 2UR, United Kingdom. TEL 44-1442-879097, FAX 44-1442-872279.

385.1 USA ISSN 0081-542X
STEAM PASSENGER SERVICE DIRECTORY. Text in English. 1966. a. USD 14.95 (effective 1997). adv. back issues avail. **Document type:** *Directory.* **Description:** Includes locations, operating hours, admission prices, and discount coupons for many attractions.
Published by: (Empire State Railway Museum), Great Eastern Publishing, PO Box 246, Richmond, VT 05477-0246. TEL 802-434-2351, FAX 802-434-2364. Ed. Michelle Giroux. Pub. Mark Smith. Adv. contact Kathleen Truax. Circ: 14,000.

385 GBR ISSN 0143-7232
STEAM RAILWAY. Text in English. 1979. m. GBP 45 domestic; GBP 55 foreign (effective 2009). bk.rev. illus.; tr.lit. back issues avail. **Document type:** *Magazine, Consumer.* **Description:** Provides latest news and views from the steam railway industry and the preservation movement.
Incorporates (1981-19??): Steam World (0263-0877)
Published by: H. Bauer Publishing Ltd. (Subsidiary of: Bauer Media Group), Bushfield House, Orton Centre, Peterborough, PE2 5UW, United Kingdom. TEL 44-1733-237111, http://www.bauer.co.uk. Ed. Jane Cutteridge TEL 44-1733-465792. Adv. contact Trevor Newman TEL 44-1733-288097.

385 GBR ISSN 0039-1190
STEPHENSON LOCOMOTIVE SOCIETY. JOURNAL. Text in English. 1924. bi-m. free to members (effective 2009). adv. bk.rev. charts; illus.; stat. back issues avail. **Document type:** *Journal, Trade.* **Description:** Features articles on locomotives and the railway scene, past and present, home and overseas, together with the latest stock changes.
Published by: Stephenson Locomotive Society, c/o M A Green, 3 Cresswell Ct, Hartlepool, TS26 0ES, United Kingdom. MAGreenBq@aol.com. Ed. Bruce I Nathan.

385 NLD ISSN 1382-8649
STOOMTRACTIE. Text in Dutch. q. adv. bk.rev.
Published by: Stoom Stichting Nederland, Postbus 2968, Rotterdam, 3000 CZ, Netherlands. TEL 31-10-2829282, FAX 31-10-2829286, info@stoomstichting.nl.

385 NLD ISSN 1382-8770
DE STOOMTRAM. Text in Dutch. 1977-1989 (no.39); resumed. q. EUR 7.50 (effective 2010). adv. bk.rev. **Document type:** *Newsletter.* **Description:** Includes news and historical background on steam trams.
Published by: Stichting Museum Stoomtram, Postbus 137, Hoorn, 1620 AC, Netherlands. TEL 31-229-214862, FAX 31-229-216653, info@museumstoomtram.nl, http://www.museumstoomtram.nl.

385 DEU ISSN 0340-7071
STRASSENBAHN MAGAZIN; Nahverkehr. Text in German. 1970. m. EUR 85.32; EUR 7.90 newsstand/cover (effective 2010). adv. bk.rev. illus.; maps. **Document type:** *Magazine, Consumer.* **Description:** Publication devoted to the history and the present state of the tramway in Germany and other European countries.
Indexed: IBR, IBZ.
—CCC.
Published by: GeraMond Verlag GmbH, Infanteriestr 11a, Munich, 80797, Germany. TEL 49-89-1306990, FAX 49-89-130699100, info@geramond.de, http://www.geramond.de. Adv. contact Judith Fischl. B&W page EUR 820, color page EUR 1,080; trim 140 x 221. Circ: 8,963 (paid and controlled).

385.264 CHE
STRASSENTRANSPORT. Text in German. fortn. CHF 82 domestic; CHF 100 foreign (effective 2000). **Document type:** *Journal, Trade.*
Published by: (Schweizerischer Nutzfahrzeugverband), Huber und Co. AG, Promenadenstr 16, Frauenfeld, 8501, Switzerland. TEL 41-54-271111.

385.264 DEU
SUEDDEUTSCHER VERKEHRSKURIER. Text in German. m. adv. **Document type:** *Magazine, Trade.*
Published by: Landesverband Bayerischer Transport- und Logistikunternehmen e.V., Leonrodstr 48, Munich, 80636, Germany. TEL 49-89-1266290, FAX 49-89-12662925, info@lbt.de, http://www.lbt.de. adv.: B&W page EUR 1,278, color page EUR 2,337; trim 175 x 240. Circ: 4,455 (paid and controlled).

385 900 AUS ISSN 0726-5093
SUNSHINE EXPRESS. Text in English. 1963. m. free (effective 2008). Website rev. illus.; maps. 32 p./no.; back issues avail. **Document type:** *Magazine, Consumer.* **Description:** Provides history of railways in Queensland for all those who are interested in railways.
Formerly: Australian Railway Historical Society. Queensland Division. Bulletin. Supplement
Published by: Australian Railway Historical Society, Queensland Division, GPO Box 682, Brisbane, QLD 4001, Australia. TEL 61-7-32521759, FAX 61-7-32521767, jacob@arhs-qld.org.au, http://www.arhs-qld.org.au. Ed. Paul de Sauty. Circ: 700 (paid).

SUVREMENI PROMET. *see* TRANSPORTATION—Air Transport

352.63 SWE ISSN 0346-2323
SVENSKA JAERNVAEGSTIDNINGEN. Text in Swedish. m. adv.
Published by: Jaernvaeg Statstjaenstemannafoerbundet, Fack 5308, Stockholm, 10247, Sweden. Circ: 2,923.

625.1 CZE ISSN 1213-7219
SVET ZELEZNICE. Text in Czech. 2002. q. CZK 636; CZK 159 newsstand/cover (effective 2010). adv. **Document type:** *Magazine, Consumer.*
Published by: Nakladatelstvi Corona s.r.o., Vybiralova 971/11, Prague 9, 190 00, Czech Republic. TEL 420-281-910544, corona.publ@volny.cz, http://corona-books.sweb.cz.

385.264 CHE ISSN 1423-4319
SWISS CAMION. Text in French, German. 1959. m. (11/yr.). CHF 60 domestic; CHF 80 foreign; CHF 6 newsstand/cover (effective 2001). adv. **Document type:** *Bulletin, Trade.*
Published by: Routiers Suisses, Rue de la Chocolatiere 26, Echandens, 1026, Switzerland. TEL 41-21-7062000, FAX 41-21-7062009, dpiras@routiers.ch, http://www.routiers.ch. Ed. Hans-Peter Steiner. Adv. contact R Dieboldswyler. B&W page CHF 2,880, color page CHF 3,850; trim 210 x 297. Circ: 20,000.

385 GBR ISSN 2047-024X
▼ **T L C**; in the top left hand corner of Wales.. Text in English. 2011. s-a. GBP 3.50 per issue (effective 2011). **Document type:** *Magazine, Trade.* **Description:** Explains the story behind the original railway and describes how it was brought back to life by a team of dedicated volunteers in addition to a look behind the scenes at Boston lodge and shots of the FR's heritage locomotives in action.
Related titles: Online - full text ed.: ISSN 2047-0258. free (effective 2011).
Published by: Ffestiniog & Welsh Highland Railways, Harbour Sta, Porthmadog, Gwynedd LL49 9NF, United Kingdom. TEL 44-1766-516000, FAX 44-1766-516005, enquiries@festrail.co.uk.

385 SWE ISSN 0039-8683
TAAG/TRAINS. Text in Swedish. 1966. 10/yr. SEK 400 domestic membership; SEK 450 in Scandinavia membership; SEK 500 elsewhere membership (effective 2004). adv. bk.rev. charts; illus. Cum Index: 1978-1996. **Document type:** *Consumer.*
Formed by the merger of (1961-1965): Svenska Jaernvaegsklubbens Medlemsblad; Meddelanden fraan Svenska Jaernvaegsklubben
Published by: Svenska Jaernvaegsklubben/Swedish Railway Club, PO Box 4175, Stockholm, 10264, Sweden. TEL 46-8-840401, FAX 46-8-840406. Ed. Jan Lindahl. Adv. contact Lars-Olof Broberg.

TABI TO TETSUDO. *see* TRAVEL AND TOURISM

385.3 USA
TACOMA TRAINSHEET. Text in English. 1965. m. (except Jul. & Aug.). USD 5 to libraries. bk.rev. illus. Supplement avail. **Document type:** *Newsletter.*
Formerly (until 1994): Trainsheet (0041-0845)
Media: Duplicated (not offset). **Related titles:** Microform ed.: (from PQC).
Published by: National Railway Historical Society, Tacoma Chapter, PO Box 340, Tacoma, WA 98401. TEL 206-752-0047. Ed. Rudy Jaskar. R&P Rick Bacon. Circ: 275.

385 TWN ISSN 1011-6850
TAITEI ZILIAO/TAIWAN RAILWAY. Text in Chinese, English. 1963. q. (m. until no.228; bi-m. until no.246). illus. **Document type:** *Journal, Academic/Scholarly.*
Published by: Taiwan Tielu Guanliju/Taiwan Railway Administration, 3, Beiping Xi Lu, Taipei, 10026, Taiwan. TEL 886-2-23815226, http://www.railway.gov.tw/. Circ: 2,000.

385 GBR ISSN 0300-3272
TALYLLYN NEWS. Text in English. 1953. q. free to members (effective 2009). adv. bk.rev. illus. **Document type:** *Newsletter.*
Published by: Talyllyn Railway Preservation Society, Wharf Sta, Tywyn, Gwynedd, Wales LL36 9EY, United Kingdom. Enquiries@talyllyn.co.uk.

385 TZA
TANZANIA RAILWAYS CORPORATION. HABARI ZA RELI. Text in Swahili. 1977. m. TZS 12 per issue. adv. bk.rev.
Supersedes in part: Sikio (0037-5136)
Published by: Tanzania Railways Corporation, PO Box 468, Dar Es Salaam, Tanzania. TELEX 41308 TRC DSM. Ed. Winston Makamba. Circ: 10,000.

385 AUS ISSN 1321-0238
TASMANIAN RAIL NEWS. Text in English. 1965. q. AUD 23 domestic; AUD 29 in New Zealand; AUD 34 elsewhere; AUD 5.75 per issue domestic (effective 2008). back issues avail. **Document type:** *Magazine, Consumer.* **Description:** Covers all aspects of Tasmanian railways.
Formerly (until 1968): News Sheet of the Tasmanian Subdivision of the Australian Railway Historical Society
Published by: Australian Railway Historical Society, PO Box 162, Sandy Bay, TAS 7006, Australia. TEL 300-220-220, arhs@railtasmania.com. Ed. Michael Dix. Circ: 350.

625.1 AUT
TECHNISCHE UNIVERSITAET WIEN. INSTITUT FUER EISENBAHNWESEN. ARBEITEN. Text in German. 1971. irreg. **Document type:** *Monographic series.*
Formerly (until 1991): Technische Universitaet Wien. Institut fuer Eisenbahnwesen, Spezialbahnen und Verkehrswirtschaft. Arbeiten
Published by: Technische Universitaet Wien, Institut fuer Eisenbahnwesen, Karlsplatz 13, Vienna, W 1040, Austria. FAX 43-1-5055415. Ed. Edwin Engel.

625.1 ITA
TECNICA PROFESSIONALE. Text in Italian. 1933. m. USD 31 domestic; USD 65 foreign (effective 2008). adv. bk.rev. bibl.; charts; illus. **Document type:** *Magazine, Trade.*
Published by: Collegio Ingegneri Ferroviari Italiani, Via Giovanni Giolitti 48, Rome, RM 00185, Italy. TEL 39-06-4882129, FAX 39-06-4742987, cifi@mclink.it. Circ: 17,000.

385 331.8 USA
TELLING IT LIKE IT IS. Text in English. bi-m. looseleaf. **Document type:** *Journal, Trade.* **Description:** Examines economic trends and collective bargaining agreements affecting members employed in the transportation industry, especially railroads.
Formerly (until 1991): Leadership Action Lines
Published by: Transportation Communications International Union, 3 Research Pl, Rockville, MD 20850. TEL 301-948-4910, FAX 301-948-1369. Ed. R A Scardelletti. Circ: 2,000 (controlled).

385 JPN ISSN 0040-4047
TETSUDO PIKUTORIARU/RAILWAY PICTORIAL. Text in Japanese. 1951. m. JPY 3,480, USD 9.70. adv. charts; illus.; stat.
Published by: Tetsudo Toshokankai, New Kokusai Bldg, 3-4-1 Marunochi, Chiyoda-ku, Tokyo, 100-0005, Japan. Ed. Ryuzo Tanaka.

385 GBR ISSN 0144-2708
TIDDLY DYKE. Text in English. 1978. q.
Published by: Swindon & Cricklade Railway Society, 36 Parklands Rd, Swindon, Wilts SN3 1EG, United Kingdom.

385 CHN ISSN 1006-2106
➤ **TIEDAO GONGCHENG XUEBAO/RAILWAY ENGINEERING SOCIETY. JOURNAL.** Text in Chinese; Abstracts in Chinese, English. 1984. m. CNY 240, USD 240; CNY 20 per issue (effective 2009). **Document type:** *Journal, Academic/Scholarly.*
Related titles: Online - full text ed.
Indexed: B21, ESPM, H&SSA, RiskAb.
Published by: (Zhongguo Tiedao Xuehui/China Railway Society), Zhongguo Tielu Gongcheng Zonggongsi/China Railway Group Ltd., A912, Zhong-tie Engineering Bldg., S. Sq. of Beijing West Railway Station, Beijing, 100055, China. TEL 86-10-51847497, http://www.crecg.com/. Ed. Ning He. Circ: 2,000.

625.1 CHN ISSN 1003-1995
TIEDAO JIANZHU/RAILWAY ENGINEERING. Text in Chinese. 1961. m. USD 62.40 (effective 2009). **Document type:** *Journal, Academic/ Scholarly.*
Related titles: Online - full text ed.
—East View.
Published by: Zhongguo Tiedao Kexue Yanjiuyuan/China Academy of Railway Sciences, 2, Daliushu Rd., Xizhimenwai, Haidian District, Beijing, 100081, China. TEL 86-10-51849235, FAX 86-10-62256572, http://www.rails.com.cn/.

385 CHN ISSN 1009-4539
TIEDAO JIANZHU JISHU/RAILWAY CONSTRUCTION TECHNOLOGY. Text in Chinese. 1984. bi-m. CNY 7.50 newsstand/cover (effective 2006). **Document type:** *Journal, Academic/Scholarly.*
Related titles: Online - full text ed.
Published by: Zhongguo Tiedao Jianzhu Zonggongsi, Daxingxian Kang Zhuang Lu #9, Beijing, 102600, China. TEL 86-10-51011591, FAX 86-10-51011595.

385 CHN ISSN 1008-7842
TIEDAO JICHE CHELIANG/RAILWAY LOCOMOTIVE & CAR. Text in Chinese. 1981. bi-m. USD 31.20 (effective 2009). **Document type:** *Journal, Academic/Scholarly.*
Related titles: Online - full text ed.
—East View.
Published by: Zhongguo Tiedao Kexue Yanjiuyuan/China Academy of Railway Sciences, 2, Daliushu Rd., Xizhimenwai, Haidian District, Beijing, 100081, China. http://www.rails.com.cn/.

385 364 CHN
TIEDAO JINGGUAN GAODENG ZHUANKE XUEXIAO XUEBAO/ RAILWAY POLICE COLLEGE. JOURNAL. Text in Chinese. 1987. q. CNY 10 newsstand/cover (effective 2006). **Document type:** *Journal, Academic/Scholarly.*
Former titles (until 2001): Tiedaobu Zhengzhou Gongan Guanli Ganbu Xueyuan Xuebao/Railway Ministry Zhengzhou Police College. Journal (1009-3192); Tiedao Gongan Xuekan
Related titles: Online - full text ed.
Published by: Tiedao Jingguan Gaodeng Zhuanke Xuexiao, 31, Nongye Lu, Zhengzhou, 450053, China. TEL 86-371-63830924.

385 CHN ISSN 1006-9178
TIEDAO JISHU JIANDU/RAILWAY QUALITY CONTROL. Text in Chinese. 1973. m. CNY 96; CNY 8 newsstand/cover (effective 2006). **Document type:** *Journal, Academic/Scholarly.*
Formerly (utnil 1996): Tiedao Biaozhunhua/Railway Standardization (1003-2037)
Related titles: Online - full text ed.
Published by: Zhongguo Tiedao Kexue Yanjiuyuan/China Academy of Railway Sciences, 2, Daliushu Rd., Xizhimenwai, Haidian District, Beijing, 100081, China. http://www.rails.com.cn/.

385 CHN
TIEDAO KEYANBAO. Text in Chinese. 1959. s-m. **Document type:** *Newspaper, Trade.*
Formerly (until 1985): Zhongguo Tiedao Kexue Yanjiuyuan Yuankan
Published by: Zhongguo Tiedao Kexue Yanjiuyuan/China Academy of Railway Sciences, 2, Daliushu Rd., Xizhimenwai, Haidian District, Beijing, 100081, China. http://www.rails.com.cn/.

385 613.62 363.7 CHN ISSN 1003-1197
TIEDAO LAODONG ANQUAN WEISHENG YU HUAN-BAO/RAILWAY OCCUPATIONAL SAFETY HEALTH & ENVIRONMENTAL PROTECTION. Text in Chinese. 1974. q. CNY 40; CNY 10 newsstand/cover (effective 2006). **Document type:** *Journal, Academic/Scholarly.*
Former titles (until 1986): Tiedao Laodong Weisheng Tongxun; (until 1975): Jiaotong Laodong Weisheng Tongxun
Related titles: Online - full text ed.
Published by: Zhongguo Tiedao Kexue Yanjiuyuan/China Academy of Railway Sciences, 2, Daliushu Rd., Xizhimenwai, Haidian District, Beijing, 100081, China. TEL 86-10-51893783, FAX 86-10-51893412, http://www.rails.com.cn/.

385 384 CHN ISSN 1000-7458
TF615 CODEN: TTXIEB
TIEDAO TONGXIN XINHAO/RAILWAY SIGNALLING & COMMUNICATION. Text in Chinese. 1957. m. USD 49.20 (effective 2009). **Document type:** *Journal, Academic/Scholarly.*
Related titles: Online - full text ed.
—East View.
Published by: Zhongguo Tiedao Kexue Yanjiuyuan/China Academy of Railway Sciences, 2, Daliushu Rd., Xizhimenwai, Haidian District, Beijing, 100081, China. TEL 86-10-51849476, http://www.rails.com.cn/.

385 CHN ISSN 1001-8360
➤ **TIEDAO XUEBAO/CHINA RAILWAY SOCIETY. JOURNAL.** Text in Chinese; Abstracts in English. 1979. bi-m. USD 48 (effective 2009). bk.rev. abstr.; bibl.; charts; illus.; maps; pat.; stat. Index. 120 p./no.; back issues avail. **Document type:** *Journal, Academic/Scholarly.* **Description:** Contains academic research papers on the latest development and theories of management of Chinese railways.
Related titles: Online - full text ed.
Indexed: A28, APA, B21, BrCerAb, C&ISA, CA/WCA, CIA, CPEI, CerAb, CivEngAb, ConcrAb, CorrAb, E&CAJ, E11, EEA, EMA, ESPM, EngInd, EnvEAb, H&SSA, H15, M&TEA, M09, MBF, METADEX, RefZh, SCOPUS, SolStAb, T04, WAA.
—East View, Linda Hall.
Published by: Zhongguo Tiedao Xuehui/China Railway Society, 10 Fuxing Rd., Beijing, 100844, China. TEL 86-10-51892393, FAX 86-10-51892424, http://www.crs.org.cn. Circ: 1,200 (paid). **Dist. overseas by:** China International Book Trading Corp, 35 Chegongzhuang Xilu, Haidian District, PO Box 399, Beijing 100044, China. TEL 86-10-68412045, FAX 86-10-68412023, cibtc@mail.cibtc.com.cn, http://www.cibtc.com.cn.

385 CHN ISSN 1003-1421
TIEDAO YUNSHU YU JINGJI/RAILWAY TRANSPORTATION AND ECONOMICS. Text in Chinese; Abstracts in English. 1979. m. USD 49.20 (effective 2009). adv. **Document type:** *Journal, Academic/Scholarly.*
Related titles: Online - full text ed.
—East View.
Published by: Zhongguo Tiedao Kexue Yanjiuyuan/China Academy of Railway Sciences, 2, Daliushu Rd., Xizhimenwai, Haidian District, Beijing, 100081, China. TEL 86-10-51849452, http://www.rails.com.cn/. adv.: page USD 4,000. Circ: 6,000 (paid).

385 CHN ISSN 1000-0372
TIEDAO ZHISHI/RAILWAY KNOWLEDGE. Text in Chinese. 1980. bi-m. USD 21.60 (effective 2009). adv. **Description:** News about China railway construction and international railroad developments.
—East View.
Published by: China Railway Society/Zhongguo Tiedao Xuehui, 10 Fuxing Lu, Beijing, 100844, China. TEL 8645811. Ed. Ni Hannong. Adv. contact Wei Zhongyan. Circ: 80,000. **Dist. overseas by:** China International Book Trading Corp, 35 Chegongzhuang Xilu, Haidian District, PO Box 399, Beijing 100044, China.

385 CHN ISSN 1004-2024
TIEDAO ZHUANGXIE YU JIZHUANGXIANG YUNSHU/RAILWAY FREIGHT TRANSPORT. Text in Chinese. 1983. bi-m. USD 43.20 (effective 2009). **Document type:** *Journal, Academic/Scholarly.*
Related titles: Online - full text ed.
—East View.
Published by: Zhongguo Tiedao Kexue Yanjiuyuan/China Academy of Railway Sciences, 2, Daliushu Rd., Xizhimenwai, Haidian District, Beijing, 100081, China. http://www.rails.com.cn/.

385 CHN ISSN 1673-7121
TIELU CAIGOU YU WULIU/RAILWAY PURCHASE AND LOGISTICS. Text in Chinese. 1982. m. CNY 144; CNY 12 per issue (effective 2010). **Document type:** *Journal, Academic/Scholarly.*
Formerly (until 2006): Tiedao Wuzi Kexue Guanli (1007-9637)
Published by: Tielu Caigou yu Wuliu Zazhishe, 11, Huayuan Jie, Xicheng-qu, Tianjin, 300011, China. TEL 86-22-24416845, FAX 86-22-24416849.

385 CHN ISSN 1005-8451
➤ **TIELU JISUANJI YINGYONG/RAILWAY COMPUTER APPLICATION.** Text in Chinese; Abstracts in Chinese, English. 1992. m. CNY 36, USD 36; CNY 6 per issue (effective 2011). **Document type:** *Journal, Academic/Scholarly.* **Description:** Covers the latest developments of applied researches in the fields of railway computer.
Related titles: Online - full text ed.: (from WanFang Data Corp.).
Indexed: B21, ESPM, H&SSA, Inspec, RefZh.
—East View.
Published by: Zhongguo Tiedao Kexue Yanjiuyuan/China Academy of Railway Sciences, 2, Daliushu Rd., Xizhimenwai, Haidian District, Beijing, 100081, China. TEL 86-10-51849246, FAX 86-10-51849330. Circ: 5,000.

385 GBR ISSN 1354-2753
TODAY'S RAILWAYS. Text in English. 1994. m. GBP 35.40 domestic; USD 79 in United States; GBP 42 rest of world; GBP 2.95 newsstand/cover. adv. bk.rev.; video rev. charts; illus. index. back issues avail. **Document type:** *Magazine, Consumer.* **Description:** Presents all the latest news and events from the railways of Europe as well as efforts in the preservation of the past.
Published by: Platform 5 Publishing Ltd., 3 Wyvern House, Sark Rd, Sheffield, S Yorks S2 4HG, United Kingdom. TEL 44-114-255-2625, FAX 44-114-255-2471. Ed. David Haydock. Pub., Adv. contact Peter Fox. B&W page GBP 400, color page GBP 600; trim 210 x 297. Circ: 8,000 (paid). **Subscr. in US to:** Wise Owl Worldwide Publications, 5674 El Camino Real., Ste. D, Carlsbad, CA 92008-7130. TEL 310-375-6258. **Dist. by:** Seymour Distribution Ltd, 86 Newman St, London W1T 3EX, United Kingdom. TEL 44-20-73968000, FAX 44-20-73968002.

385 NZL
TOLL N Z. ANNUAL REPORT. (New Zealand) Text in English. 188?. a. free. illus.; stat. **Document type:** *Corporate.*
Former titles: Tranz Rail.Holdings Limited. Annual Report; (until 1996): Tranz Rail. Annual Report; (until 1994): New Zealand Rail. Annual Report (1171-266X); Which superseded in part (in 1991): New Zealand Railways Corporation. Annual Report (0114-0434); (until 1988): New Zealand Railways Corporation. Report (0112-2215); (until 1983): New Zealand. Railways Department. Annual Report (0110-2974); (until 1958): Railways Statement
Published by: Toll N Z Ltd., Toll Bldg., Smales Farm, Corner, Northcote and Taharoto Rds, Takapuna, Auckland, New Zealand. TEL 64-4-2705000, FAX 64-4-2705039, http://www.toll.co.nz/. Circ: 750.

385.264 388.324 JPN
TORAKKU YUSO JOHO. Text in Japanese. 1948. 3/m.
Published by: Japan Trucking Association, 19th FL Shinjuku L Tower, 6-1 Nishi-shinjuku 1-chome, Shinjuku-ku, Tokyo, 163-1519, Japan. TEL 81-3-5323-7109, FAX 81-3-5323-7230, http://www.jta.or.jp/.

385 CAN ISSN 0040-9553
TORONTO RAILWAY CLUB. OFFICIAL PROCEEDINGS. Text in English. 1931. 3/yr. membership only. adv. charts; illus. **Document type:** *Newsletter.*
Published by: Toronto Railway Club, P O Box 114, Union Station, Toronto, ON M5J 1E6, Canada. Ed., Pub. John Glatzmayer. Circ: 1,200.

385 AUS ISSN 1327-418X
TF1
TRACK & SIGNAL. Text in English. 1964. q. AUD 44 domestic; AUD 83 foreign (effective 2009). adv. bk.rev. **Document type:** *Magazine, Trade.*
Supersedes in part (in 1996): Network Rail (1328-2468); Which was formerly (until 1997): Network (0159-7302)
Indexed: CLT&T, HRIS.
Published by: Star Media Services, PO BOX 1063-G, Balwyn North, VIC 3104, Australia. admin@trackandsignal.com. Adv. contact John Reeves TEL 61-3-98578818. color page AUD 2,300. Circ: 10,000 (controlled).

625.1 USA
TRACK YEARBOOK & BUYERS' GUIDE. Text in English. 1982. a. USD 55 domestic; USD 65 foreign (effective 2008). adv. **Document type:** *Yearbook, Trade.*
Formerly (until 1986): Track Yearbook
Indexed: CLT&T.
Published by: Trade Press Publishing Corp., 2100 W Florist Ave, Milwaukee, WI 53209. TEL 414-228-7701, 800-727-7995, FAX 414-228-1134, info@tradepress.com, http://www.tradepress.com. Ed. Pat Foran. Pub. Steve Bolte TEL 561-743-7373. adv.: B&W page USD 5,645, color page USD 7,865; bleed 7 x 10. Circ: 7,000.

625.1 GBR ISSN 1354-2680
TRACTION. Text in English. 1994. m. GBP 52.95 domestic; GBP 60 in Europe; GBP 80 elsewhere; GBP 3.75 per issue (effective 2009); includes Traction Annual. adv. bk.rev. illus. back issues avail. **Document type:** *Magazine, Trade.* **Description:** Dedicated to classic diesels and electrics past and present, including information on the national network and developments on the preserved lines and nostalgia-filled features on the heyday of diesel and electric power.
Related titles: Online - full text ed.: GBP 37.50 domestic; GBP 52 in Europe; GBP 64 elsewhere (effective 2009); includes Traction Annual; Supplement(s): Traction Annual.
—CCC.
Published by: Warners Group Publications Plc., The Maltings, Manor Ln, Bourne, Lincs PE10 9PH, United Kingdom. TEL 44-1778-391000, wgpsubs@warnersgroup.co.uk, http://www.warnersgroup.co.uk. Pub. John Greenwood TEL 44-1778-391116. Adv. contact Patrick Raphael Sisko.

TRAIN COLLECTORS QUARTERLY. *see* HOBBIES

TRAIN DISPATCHER. *see* LABOR UNIONS

385.22 USA ISSN 0896-4424
TRAIN RIDER MAGAZINE. Text in English. 1986. bi-m. USD 6.50. illus.
Formerly: Train Rider Monthly
Published by: Message Media, PO Box 9007, Berkeley, CA 94709. TEL 510-525-3030. Ed. James Russell. Circ: 750.

385 USA ISSN 0041-0926
THE TRAINMASTER. Text in English. 1956. m. USD 32 domestic membership (effective 2002). bk.rev. **Document type:** *Newsletter, Consumer.* **Description:** Contains information on chapter business and activities, and original material, contributed by members, pertaining to railroad history and preservation.
Media: Duplicated (not offset).
Published by: National Railway Historical Society, Pacific Northwest Chapter, c/o TM Editor, PNWC NRHS, Union Sta, Rm 1, 800 N W Sixth Ave, Portland, OR 97209-3715. TEL 503-226-6747, FAX 503-230-0572, pnwc@pnwc-nrhs.org, http://www.pnwc-nrhs.org. Ed. Glenn Laubaugh. R&P Jim Loomis. Circ: 600.

385 USA ISSN 0041-0934
TF1
TRAINS. Text in English. 1940. m. USD 42.95 domestic (effective 2008); USD 52.95 in Canada; USD 57.95 elsewhere (effective 2006). adv. bk.rev. charts; illus.; stat. index. back issues avail.; reprints avail. **Document type:** *Magazine, Consumer.* **Description:** Covers the broad spectrum of railroading with authoritative content, dazzling photography and a mix of content designed to appeal to everyone from the casual enthusiast to the seasoned professional railroader.
Formerly: Trains & Travel
Related titles: Online - full text ed.
Indexed: A15, A22, ABIn, B16, G05, G06, G07, G08, HRIS, I05, I07, M01, M02, MASUSE, MagInd, P02, P06, P10, P48, P51, P52, P53, P54, PQC, S23, T02.
—Ingenta, Linda Hall.
Published by: Kalmbach Publishing Co., 21027 Crossroads Circle, PO Box 1612, Waukesha, WI 53187. TEL 262-796-8776, FAX 262-796-1142, customerservice@kalmbach.com, http://www.kalmbach.com. Eds. Jim Wrinn, Matt Van Hattem. adv.: B&W page USD 3,230, color page USD 4,716. Circ: 106,000 (paid).

385 GBR ISSN 0041-1019
TF701
TRAMWAY REVIEW. Text in English. 1950. q. GBP 16 domestic; GBP 18 foreign (effective 2009). adv. bk.rev.; video rev. index. 40 p./no. 1 cols./p.; back issues avail. **Document type:** *Magazine, Consumer.* **Description:** Provides information about the history of British and Irish tramway systems, occasionally others overseas.
Indexed: HRIS.
—BLDSC (8884.590000). **CCC.**
Published by: Light Rail Transit Association, 8 Berwick Pl, Welwyn Garden City, Herts AL7 4TU, United Kingdom. TEL 44-1179-517785, FAX 44-1179-517785, office@lrta.org, http://www.lrta.org. Ed. Rev. Richard Buckley.

388.4 625 GBR ISSN 1460-8324
TF701
TRAMWAYS & URBAN TRANSIT; international light rail magazine. Text in English. 1938. m. free to members (effective 2009). adv. bk.rev. charts; illus. index. back issues avail.; reprints avail. **Document type:** *Magazine, Consumer.* **Description:** Provides news, features and articles about light rail and urban transit systems around the world.
Former titles (until 1997): Light Rail and Modern Tramway (0964-9255); (until 1992): Modern Tramway and Light Rail Transit (0144-1655); (until 1980): Modern Tramway and Rapid Transit (0309-8222); (until 1977): Modern Tramway and Light Railway Review (0026-850X)
Indexed: BrTechI, E11, HRIS, RefZh, T04.
—BLDSC (8884.560000), IE, Ingenta, Linda Hall. **CCC.**
Published by: Light Rail Transit Association, 8 Berwick Pl, Welwyn Garden City, Herts AL7 4TU, United Kingdom. TEL 44-1179-517785, FAX 44-1179-517785, office@lrta.org, http://www.lrta.org. Ed. Howard Johnston. Adv. contact Vicky Binley. Circ: 8,793.

385 USA
TRANSALERT. Text in English. 1998. bi-m. free. **Document type:** *Magazine, Trade.* **Description:** Provides information resources for transportation professionals.
Published by: (Railway Educational Bureau), Simmons - Boardman Books Inc., 1809 Capitol Ave, Omaha, NE 10014. TEL 402-346-4300, 800-228-9670, FAX 402-346-1783. Ed., Adv. contact Pat Kentner TEL 402-449-1677. R&P Jan Benson TEL 402-449-1661.

TRANSFER. *see* TRANSPORTATION—Ships And Shipping

385 625.1 AUS ISSN 0818-5204
TRANSIT AUSTRALIA; the Australian urban transit magazine. Text in English. 1946. m. AUD 105 domestic to individuals; AUD 110 in Asia & the Pacific to individuals; AUD 130 elsewhere to individuals; AUD 140 in Asia & the Pacific to institutions; AUD 155 elsewhere to institutions (effective 2009). adv. bk.rev. charts; illus.; stat. index. back issues avail. **Document type:** *Journal, Trade.* **Description:** Features articles that focus on the developments in the urban passenger transport industry across Australia and New Zealand.
Former titles (until 1987): E T (0013-4163); (until 1985): Electric Traction; (until 1951): Railways in Australia and A R L H S. Bulletin; (until 1948): Tram Tracks
Indexed: ARI, HRIS.
Published by: Transit Australia Publishing, GPO Box 1017, Sydney, NSW 2001, Australia. Ed., Adv. contact Tony Bailey TEL 61-2-93418700. Pub. Hugh Ballment TEL 61-3-98363338.

385 USA
TRANSIT TIMES. Text in English, Spanish. 1949. m. free (effective 2011). adv. bk.rev. illus. back issues avail. **Document type:** *Newsletter, Trade.*
Related titles: Online - full text ed.
Indexed: CLT&T, HRIS.
Published by: Metropolitan Atlanta Rapid Transit Authority, Department of Marketing and Communications, 2424 Peidmont Rd, NE, Atlanta, GA 30324. TEL 404-848-5112, custserv@itsmarta.com.

385 SWE ISSN 0348-3118
TRANSPORT-JOURNALEN. Text in Swedish. 1955. 4/yr. free. bk.rev. charts; illus.
Published by: (Sweden. Freight Division), Statens Jaernvaegar/Swedish State Railways, Stockholm, 10550, Sweden. TEL 46-8-762-44-70. Ed. Christer Beijbom. Circ: 29,800.

385 RUS ISSN 0131-4300
TA4
TRANSPORTNOE STROITEL'STVO. Text in English, Russian. 1951. m. USD 150 foreign (effective 2004). bk.rev. bibl.; charts; illus. index.
Indexed: GeoRef, GeotechAb, RASB, RefZh, SpeleolAb.
—East View, INIST.
Published by: Tsentr Transstroiizdat, Sadovaya-Spasskaya 21, kom 832, Moscow, 107807, Russian Federation. TEL 7-095-2621919, FAX 7-095-9245566. Ed. O Makarov. **Dist. by:** M K - Periodica, ul Gilyarovskogo 39, Moscow 129110, Russian Federation. TEL 7-095-2845008, FAX 7-095-2813798, info@periodicals.ru, http://www.mkniga.ru.

388 NOR
TRANSPORTOEKONOMISK INSTITUTT. AARSBERETNING. Text in Norwegian. 1965. a. free.
Formerly: Norges Teknisk-Naturvitenskapelige Forskningsraad. Transportoekonomisk Institutt. Aarsberetning (0078-124X)
Published by: Transportoekonomisk Institutt/Institute of Transport Economics, Postboks 6110, Etterstad, Oslo, 0602, Norway. Ed. Kirsten Vaas.

TRAVAIL ET TRANSPORT. *see* LABOR UNIONS

385 790.13 900 ITA
I TRENI. Text in Italian. 1980. m. (11/yr.). adv. bk.rev. illus. back issues avail. **Document type:** *Magazine, Consumer.* **Description:** Covers railroads, railroad history and railway modelling.
Formerly (until 1993): I Treni Oggi (0392-4602)
Published by: Editrice Trasporti su Rotaie, Piazza Vittorio Emanuele II, 42, Salo', BS 25087, Italy. http://itreni.com. Circ: 14,000.

TROLLEY FARE. *see* MUSEUMS AND ART GALLERIES

TUTTO TRENO. *see* HOBBIES

TUTTO TRENO & STORIA. *see* HOBBIES

TUTTO TRENO MODELLISMO. *see* HOBBIES

TUTTO TRENO TEMA. *see* HOBBIES

385 FRA
U I C E-NEWS. (International Union of Railways) Text in English. 1995. q. **Document type:** *Newsletter.*
Formerly (until 2004): International Union of Railways. Panorama (1025-7896)
Media: Online - full text. **Related titles:** French ed.: ISSN 1815-4611; German ed.: ISSN 1815-462X.
Published by: International Union of Railways, 16 Rue Jean Rey, Paris, 75015, France. TEL 33-1-44492020, FAX 33-1-44492029, http://www.uic.asso.fr.

U.S. DEPARTMENT OF TRANSPORTATION. FEDERAL RAILROAD ADMINISTRATION. OFFICE OF SAFETY ANALYSIS. RAILROAD SAFETY STATISTICS. ANNUAL REPORT (YEAR). *see* TRANSPORTATION—Abstracting, Bibliographies, Statistics

385 USA ISSN 0275-3758
U S RAIL NEWS. Text in English. 1978. 25/yr. looseleaf. USD 437 in North America (print or E-mail ed.); USD 453 out of North America (print or E-mail ed.) (effective 2008). adv. back issues avail.; reprints avail. **Document type:** *Newsletter, Trade.* **Description:** Provides information to readers that can help to monitor and manage rail system issues developing in industry, government and communities across America.
Incorporates (in 2008): Urban Transport News (0195-4695); Which incorporated (in 1986): Public Transit Report (0148-4087)
Related titles: E-mail ed.; Online - full text ed.: ISSN 1545-7443. USD 387 (effective 2005).
Indexed: A26, B01, B02, B07, B15, B17, B18, G04, G06, G07, G08, I05, M06.
—CCC.
Published by: Capitol Press LLC, 3600 Leesburg Pike, West Bldg, Ste 300, Falls Church, VA 22043. TEL 800-248-6426, FAX 703-905-8040, customer@capitolpub.com, http://www.capitolpub.com. Ed. Tom Ramstack. Pub. Steve Sturm.

U T U NEWS. *see* LABOR UNIONS

385.09489 DNK ISSN 0106-7850
UD OG SE. Text in Danish. 1973. m. DKK 215 in Scandinavia; DKK 339 in Europe (effective 2009). adv. back issues avail. **Document type:** *Magazine, Consumer.*
Former titles (until 1980): Kupe (0105-502X); (until 1975): D S B Nyt (0105-5011)
Related titles: Online - full text ed.
Published by: D S B/The Danish State Railroads, Soelvgade 40, Copenhagen K, 1349, Denmark. TEL 45-70-131415. Eds. Oliver Stilling, Anna Vinding. Adv. contact Lars Schau Nielsen TEL 45-33-853026. Circ: 191,210 (paid and controlled).

385 DEU
UESTRALINIE. Text in German. 1930. q. adv. back issues avail. **Document type:** *Magazine, Consumer.*
Former titles (until 1997): Linie (0720-8456); (until 1980): Linien (0344-5232); (until 1977): Linie (0344-5240)
Published by: Uestra Hannoversche Verkehrsbetriebe AG, Postfach 2540, Hannover, 30025, Germany. TEL 49-511-1668-0, FAX 49-511-16682666, presse@uestra.de, http://www.uestra.de. R&P Dirk Sarnes. Circ: 5,000.

385.264 NLD ISSN 1381-6578
UITVAARTWEZEN. Text in Dutch. 10/yr. EUR 79.50 (effective 2009). adv.
Published by: (Nederlandse Unie van Erkende Uitvaartondernemingen (NUVU)), Uitvaart Media, Postbus 80532, Den Haag, 2508 GM, Netherlands. TEL 31-70-3518818, FAX 31-70-3518809, info@uitvaartmedia.com, http://www.uitvaartmedia.com. Ed. Marjon Weijzen.

385 HUN ISSN 0133-0314
VAROSI KOZLEKEDES/URBAN TRANSPORT. Text in Hungarian; Summaries in English. 1968. bi-m. HUF 1,500; HUF 250 newsstand/cover (effective 2004). adv. bk.rev. charts; illus.; maps; stat. index. **Document type:** *Magazine, Trade.* **Description:** Covers urban public and private transport; includes national and international information.
Formerly (until 1968): Fovrosi Villamosvasut Muszaki Szemle (0324-458X)
Address: Akacfa u 15, V em 506, Budapest 7, 1980, Hungary. TEL 36-1-3227074, FAX 36-1-4616575, nagyj@bkv.hu, http://www.bkv.hu. Ed. Kovacs Zoltan. Circ: 1,200.

385.264 DEU
VERBAND DES WURTTEMBURGISCHEN VERKEHRSGEWERBES. SUEDDEUTSCHER VERKEHRSURIER. Text in German. m.
Published by: Verband des Wurttemburgischen Verkehrsgewerbes, Hedelfinger Str 25, Stuttgart, 70327, Germany. TEL 0711-423066, TELEX 22846.

385 DEU ISSN 0232-9042
VERKEHRSGESCHICHTLICHE BLAETTER. Text in German. 1974. bi-m. EUR 2.50 newsstand/cover (effective 2006). adv. bk.rev. index. **Document type:** *Newsletter, Trade.*
Related titles: CD-ROM ed.: EUR 24.80 domestic; EUR 27.50 foreign (effective 2010).
Published by: Verkehrsgeschichtliche Blaetter e.V., c/o Wolf-Dietger Machel, Zingster Str. 30 (neu), Berlin, 13051, Germany. TEL 49-30-68814184, FAX 49-30-68814184. Ed. Michael Guenther. adv.: B&W page EUR 200. Circ: 1,650 (paid and controlled).

385 ESP ISSN 1134-1416
VIA LIBRE. Text in Spanish. 1964. m. EUR 40 domestic; EUR 65 in Europe; EUR 85 elsewhere (effective 2009). adv. bk.rev. illus. back issues avail. **Document type:** *Magazine, Trade.*
Related titles: Online - full text ed.
Indexed: GeoRef, SpeleolAb.
Published by: Fundacion de los Ferrocarriles Espanoles, Santa Isabel 44, Madrid, 28012, Spain. TEL 34-91-1511071, FAX 34-915-281003, vlibre@ffe.es, http://www.ffe.es. Ed. Pilar Lozano. Adv. contact Paz Ayuso. Circ: 13,000.

385.22 CAN ISSN 0706-5698
HE2591.C3
VIA RAIL CANADA. ANNUAL REPORT. Text in English, French. 1977. a.
Related titles: Online - full text ed.: ISSN 1700-0289.
Published by: VIA Rail Canada, 3 Place Ville-Marie, Suite 500, Montreal, PQ H3B 2C9, Canada. TEL 514-871-6000.

385 FRA ISSN 0042-5478
LA VIE DU RAIL. Variant title: La Vie du Rail et des Transports. Text in French. 1938. w. EUR 90 domestic; EUR 133 in Europe; EUR 141 in North America (effective 2010). bk.rev.; film rev. **Document type:** *Magazine, Consumer.* **Description:** Technical and general railroad and transport information including tourism and travel by rail.
Related titles: Online - full text ed.: free.
Indexed: A22, HRIS.
—IE.
Published by: La Vie du Rail, 11 rue de Milan, Paris, Cedex 9 75440, France. TEL 33-1-49701200, FAX 33-1-49701269, info@laviedurail.com, http://www.laviedurail.com. Ed. Francis Dumont. Adv. contact Vincent Lalu. Circ: 173,804 (paid).

385 USA
VIEWS AND NEWS. Text in English. 1933. w. membership only. **Document type:** *Newsletter.*
Published by: American Short Line and Regional Railroad Association, 50 F St NW, Ste. 7020, Washington, DC 20001-1507. TEL 202-628-4500, FAX 202-628-4500. Ed. A C Saylor. Circ: 1,400.

388.22 FRA ISSN 2104-0028
▼ **VILLE, RAIL & TRANSPORTS.** Text in French. 2009. s-m. EUR 149 combined subscription domestic print & online eds. (effective 2010). **Document type:** *Magazine, Trade.* **Description:** Covers all aspects of the rairoad industry including political and technical developments.
Formed by the merger of (2007-2009): La Vie du Rail International (1771-2769); (2005-2009): Ville et Transports (1774-3869); Which was formerly (until 2005): Rail et Transports (1634-5851); (1997-2002): La Vie du Rail et des Transports - Edition Professionnelle (1249-2892)
Related titles: Online - full text ed.
Published by: La Vie du Rail, 11 rue de Milan, Paris, Cedex 9 75440, France. TEL 33-1-49701200, FAX 33-1-49701269, info@laviedurail.com, http://www.laviedurail.com.

VOIE LIBRE. *see* HOBBIES

385 FRA ISSN 0249-4914
VOIES FERREES. Text in French. 1980. bi-m. EUR 57 domestic; EUR 73 in Europe; EUR 119 elsewhere (effective 2009).
Published by: Presses et Editions Ferroviaires, 4 av. Albert 1er de Belgique, Grenoble, 38000, France. TEL 33-4-76426922, FAX 33-4-76427955. Ed. Philippe Morel. Pub. Patrice Bouillin. Circ: 19,000.

385 615.1 RUS ISSN 0869-8163
CODEN: VVNZAA
VSEROSSIISKII NAUCHNO-ISSLEDOVATEL'SKII INSTITUT ZHELEZNODOROZHNOVO TRANSPORTA. VESTNIK. Text in Russian; Summaries in English, French, German, Russian. 1942. 7/yr. USD 106 foreign (effective 2001). adv. illus. index. back issues avail. **Document type:** *Proceedings.* **Description:** Covers research and development of Russian railroads.
Formerly: Vsesoyuznyi Nauchno-issledovatel'skii Institut Zheleznodorozhnovo Transporta. Vestnik (0042-4749)
Indexed: RASB, RefZh.
—CASDDS, Linda Hall.
Published by: Vserossiiskii Nauchno-issledovatel'skii Institut Zheleznodorozhnovo Transporta, 3-ya Mytishchinskaya ul 10, Moscow, 129851, Russian Federation. TEL 7-095-2871331, FAX 7-095-2877236. Ed. V S Kalinikov. Adv. contact V S Kalinnikov. page USD 300. Circ: 1,100.

385 CAN ISSN 1204-072X
W C R A NEWS. Text in English. 1961. m. CAD 40 (effective 1999). bk.rev. **Document type:** *Newsletter.* **Description:** Provides updates on Association activities, rail stories of interest, rail travel and tours.
Published by: West Coast Railway Association, P O Box 2790, Vancouver, BC V6B 3X2, Canada. TEL 604-524-1011, FAX 604-986-7660. Ed., R&P Don Evans TEL 604-988-3435. Circ: 600 (paid).

385 USA ISSN 0897-7577
WAYBILL. Text in English. 1970. q. USD 6 domestic; USD 12 foreign (effective 2007). adv. bk.rev. 8 p./no. 4 cols./p.; **Document type:** *Newsletter, Consumer.* **Description:** Provides education in the field of railroad transportation.
Published by: Mystic Valley Railway Society, Inc., PO Box 365486, Hyde Park, MA 02136-0009. TEL 617-361-4445, FAX 617-361-4445 ext 51. Ed. Dorothy Dear. R&P W R Rylko. Adv. contact Mary P Rylko. col. inch USD 10. Circ: 12,000 (paid and free).

385 USA
TF23.6
WESTERN RAILROADER. Text in English. 1937. bi-m. USD 37 (effective 2000). bk.rev. charts; illus.; maps.
Former titles: Western Railroader and Western Railfan (0149-4996); Western Railroader (0043-4108)
Published by: Railway & Locomotive Historical Society (Folsom), Pacific Coast Chapter, Milepost 1 Railroad Bookstore, 198 Wool St, Folsom, CA 95630. http://mp1.com. Circ: 1,000.

385 USA ISSN 0043-4744
HE5351
WHEEL CLICKS. Text in English. 1938. m. USD 25 domestic; USD 34 in Canada; USD 43 elsewhere (effective 2000). bk.rev. charts; illus. Index. reprints avail. **Document type:** *Newsletter.* **Description:** Details railway operation. Covers Amtrak, UP & BNSF, Peninsula CalTrain and western U.S. rail transit, commuter and tourist lines.
Published by: Pacific Railroad Society, Inc., PO Box 80726, San Marino, CA 91118-8726. TEL 562-692-4858. Ed. Dick Finley. Circ: 700.

385 JPN
WHITE PAPER ON TRAFFIC SAFETY IN JAPAN. Text in English. 1978. a. USD 25 (effective 2003). back issues avail. **Document type:** *Government.*
Formerly: White Paper on Transportation Safety in Japan (0386-1716)
Published by: International Association of Traffic and Safety Sciences, 6-20 Yaesu 2-chome, Chuo-ku, Tokyo, 104-0028, Japan. TEL 81-3-3273-7884, FAX 81-3-3272-7054, iatss@db3.so-net.ne.jp, http://wwwsoc.nii.ac.jp/iatss/.

385 CHN ISSN 1672-7533
XIANDAI CHENGSHI GUIDAO JIAOTONG/MODERN URBAN TRANSIT. Text in Chinese. 2004. bi-m. USD 48 (effective 2009). **Document type:** *Journal, Academic/Scholarly.*
—East View.
Published by: Zhongguo Tiedao Kexue Yanjiuyuan/China Academy of Railway Sciences, 2, Daliushu Rd., Xizhimenwai, Haidian District, Beijing, 100081, China. TEL 86-10-51893693, FAX 86-10-51849570.

385 NZL ISSN 0044-023X
Y A R N. (Your Auckland Railway News) Text in English. 1952. m. free to members. adv. bk.rev. **Document type:** *Magazine, Consumer.*
—CCC.
Published by: Auckland Railway Enthusiasts Society, Inc., Onehunga, PO Box 13-684, Auckland, New Zealand. office@railfan.org.nz, http://www.railfan.org.nz/. Circ: 680.

385 625.1 DEU ISSN 1618-8330
T3 CODEN: GLANAE
Z E VRAIL - GLASERS ANNALEN; Zeitschrift fuer das gesamte System Bahn. (Zeitschrift fuer Eisenbahnwesen und Verkehrstechnik) Text in German; Summaries in English, French. 1877. m. EUR 18 newsstand/cover (effective 2010). adv. bk.rev. charts; illus. index. back issues avail. **Document type:** *Journal, Trade.*
Former titles (until 2002): Z E V und D E T Glasers Annalen - Die Eisenbahntechnik (0941-0589); (until 1990): Zeitschrift fuer Eisenbahnwesen und Verkehrstechnik (0373-322X); (until 1972): Glasers Annalen (0017-0844)
Indexed: A22, CPEI, ChemAb, EngInd, Inspec, SCOPUS, TM.
—IE, Ingenta, INIST, Linda Hall. **CCC.**
Published by: Georg Siemens Verlag GmbH & Co. KG, Boothstr 11, Berlin, 12207, Germany. TEL 49-30-7699040, FAX 49-30-76990418. Ed. Heinz Kurz. Adv. contact Sascha Plambeck.

385.264 BEL
ZEE. Text in Dutch. s-a. **Document type:** *Bulletin, Trade.*
Published by: Belgische Transportarbeidersbond, Paardenmarkt 66, Antwerp, 2000, Belgium. TEL 32-3-224-3411, FAX 32-3-234-0149. Ed. Frank van Thillo.

385 CHE
ZEITSCHRIFT FUER DEN INTERNATIONALEN EISENBAHNVERKEHR. Text in German, English. 1893. q. bk.rev. **Document type:** *Magazine, Government.*
Published by: Organisation Intergouvernementale pour les Transports Internationaux Ferroviaires/Zwischenstaatliche Organisation fuer den Internationalen Eisenbahnverkehr, Gryphenhuebeliweg 30, Bern, 3006, Switzerland. TEL 41-31-3591010, FAX 41-31-3591011, otif@otif.ch, http://www.otif.ch.

385 HRV ISSN 1333-7971
ZELJEZNICE 21. Text in Croatian. 2002. q. **Document type:** *Magazine, Trade.*
Formed by the merger of (1976 -2000): Zeljeznica u Teoriji i Praksi (0353-5282); (1994-2000): I T H Z (1330-4429)
Related titles: Online - full text ed.
Published by: Hrvatske Zeljeznice, d.o.o., Petrinjska 89, Zagreb, 10000, Croatia. TEL 385-1-3782858, FAX 385-1-4577709. Ed. Marko Odak.

385 RUS ISSN 0044-4448
HE7
ZHELEZNODOROZHNYI TRANSPORT. Text in Russian. 1919. m. USD 231 in United States (effective 2007). adv. bk.rev. abstr.; bibl.; charts; illus.; stat. index.
Related titles: Microfiche ed.: (from EVP).
Indexed: CISA, ChemAb, RASB, RefZh.
—East View, INIST.
Published by: Izdatel'stvo Transport, Aviamotornaya ul, dom 34/2, Moscow, 107174, Russian Federation. Ed. A V Gogolev TEL 7-095-2626767. Circ: 14,325. **Dist. by:** East View Information Services, 10601 Wayzata Blvd, Minneapolis, MN 55305. TEL 952-252-1201, 800-477-1005, FAX 952-252-1202, info@eastview.com, http://www.eastview.com.

385 RUS ISSN 0203-1884
ZHELEZNODOROZHNYI TRANSPORT. SERIYA. BEZOPASNOST' TRUDA. Text in Russian. 7/yr.
—East View.
Address: Rizhskaya pl 3, Moscow, 129855, Russian Federation. TEL 7-095-2621331. **Dist. by:** East View Information Services, 10601 Wayzata Blvd, Minneapolis, MN 55305. TEL 952-252-1201, 800-477-1005, FAX 952-252-1202, info@eastview.com, http://www.eastview.com.

385 RUS ISSN 0135-9673
ZHELEZNODOROZHNYI TRANSPORT. SERIYA. EKOLOGIYA I ZHELEZNODOROZHNYI TRANSPORT. Text in Russian. s-a.
—East View.
Address: Rizhskaya pl 3, Moscow, 129855, Russian Federation. TEL 7-095-2621331. **Dist. by:** East View Information Services, 10601 Wayzata Blvd, Minneapolis, MN 55305. TEL 952-252-1201, 800-477-1005, FAX 952-252-1202, info@eastview.com, http://www.eastview.com.

385 RUS
ZHELEZNODOROZHNYI TRANSPORT. SERIYA. EKONOMIKA. OBSHCHETRANSPORTNYE RASKHODY. ORGANIZATSIYA DVIZHENIYA. GRUZOVAYA I KOMMERCHESKAYA RABOTA. KONTEINERNYE PEREVOZKI. Text in Russian. bi-m.
Address: Rizhskaya pl 3, Moscow, 129855, Russian Federation. TEL 7-095-2621331. **Dist. by:** East View Information Services, 10601 Wayzata Blvd, Minneapolis, MN 55305. TEL 952-252-1201, 800-477-1005, FAX 952-252-1202, info@eastview.com, http://www.eastview.com.

385 RUS ISSN 0321-3218
ZHELEZNODOROZHNYI TRANSPORT. SERIYA. ELEKTRIOFIKATSIYA. AVTOMATIKA I SVYAZ'. Text in Russian. bi-m.
—East View.
Address: Rizhskaya pl 3, Moscow, 129855, Russian Federation. TEL 7-095-2621331. **Dist. by:** East View Information Services, 10601 Wayzata Blvd, Minneapolis, MN 55305. TEL 952-252-1201, 800-477-1005, FAX 952-252-1202, info@eastview.com, http://www.eastview.com.

385 RUS ISSN 0236-3593
ZHELEZNODOROZHNYI TRANSPORT. SERIYA. ELEKTROSNABZHENIE ZHELEZNYKH DOROG. Text in Russian. q.
—East View.
Address: Rizhskaya pl 3, Moscow, 129855, Russian Federation. TEL 7-095-2621331. **Dist. by:** East View Information Services, 10601 Wayzata Blvd, Minneapolis, MN 55305. TEL 952-252-1201, 800-477-1005, FAX 952-252-1202, info@eastview.com, http://www.eastview.com.

385 RUS ISSN 0203-1841
ZHELEZNODOROZHNYI TRANSPORT. SERIYA. GRUZOVAYA I KOMMERCHESKAYA RABOTA. KONTEINERNYE PEREVOZKI. Text in Russian. q.
—East View.
Address: Rizhskaya pl 3, Moscow, 129855, Russian Federation. TEL 7-095-2621331. **Dist. by:** East View Information Services, 10601 Wayzata Blvd, Minneapolis, MN 55305. TEL 952-252-1201, 800-477-1005, FAX 952-252-1202, info@eastview.com, http://www.eastview.com.

385 RUS ISSN 0203-1876
ZHELEZNODOROZHNYI TRANSPORT. SERIYA. ORGANIZATSIYA DVIZHENIYA I PASSAZHIRSKIE PEREVOZKI. Text in Russian. q.
—East View.

Address: Rizhskaya pl 3, Moscow, 129855, Russian Federation. TEL 7-095-2621331. **Dist. by:** East View Information Services, 10601 Wayzata Blvd, Minneapolis, MN 55305. TEL 952-252-1201, 800-477-1005, FAX 952-252-1202, info@eastview.com, http://www.eastview.com.

385 RUS ISSN 0203-1914
ZHELEZNODOROZHNYI TRANSPORT. SERIYA. PODVIZHNOI SOSTAV. LOKOMOTIVNOE I VAGONNOE KHOZYAISTVO. Text in Russian. bi-m.
—East View.
Address: Rizhskaya pl 3, Moscow, 129855, Russian Federation. TEL 7-095-2621331. **Dist. by:** East View Information Services, 10601 Wayzata Blvd, Minneapolis, MN 55305. TEL 952-252-1201, 800-477-1005, FAX 952-252-1202, info@eastview.com, http://www.eastview.com.

385 RUS ISSN 0134-7365
ZHELEZNODOROZHNYI TRANSPORT. SERIYA. PUT'I PUTEVOE KHOZYAISTVO. PROEKTIROVANIE I STROITEL'STVO. Text in Russian. bi-m.
—East View.
Address: Rizhskaya pl 3, Moscow, 129855, Russian Federation. TEL 7-095-2621331. **Dist. by:** East View Information Services, 10601 Wayzata Blvd, Minneapolis, MN 55305. TEL 952-252-1201, 800-477-1005, FAX 952-252-1202, info@eastview.com, http://www.eastview.com.

385 RUS
ZHELEZNODOROZHNYI TRANSPORT. SERIYA. PUT'I PUTEVOE KHOZYAISTVO. PROEKTIROVANIE I STROITEL'STVO. NAUCHNO-TEKHNICHESKII REFERATIVNYI SBORNIK. Text in Russian. bi-m.
Published by: Zheleznodorozhnyi Transport. Seriya. Put'i Putevoe Khozyaistvo. Proektirovanie i Stroitel'stvo, Rizhskaya pl 3, Moscow, 129855, Russian Federation. TEL 7-095-2621331. **Dist. by:** East View Information Services, 10601 Wayzata Blvd, Minneapolis, MN 55305. TEL 952-252-1201, 800-477-1005, FAX 952-252-1202, info@eastview.com, http://www.eastview.com.

385 RUS ISSN 0236-3607
ZHELEZNODOROZHNYI TRANSPORT. SERIYA. SIGNALIZATSIYA I SVYAZ'. Text in Russian. q.
—East View.
Address: Rizhskaya pl 3, Moscow, 129855, Russian Federation. TEL 7-095-2621331. **Dist. by:** East View Information Services, 10601 Wayzata Blvd, Minneapolis, MN 55305. TEL 952-252-1201, 800-477-1005, FAX 952-252-1202, info@eastview.com, http://www.eastview.com.

385 RUS ISSN 0233-612X
ZHELEZNODOROZHNYI TRANSPORT. SERIYA. STROITEL'STVO. PROEKTIROVANIE. Text in Russian. q.
Address: Rizhskaya pl 3, Moscow, 129855, Russian Federation. TEL 7-095-2621331. **Dist. by:** East View Information Services, 10601 Wayzata Blvd, Minneapolis, MN 55305. TEL 952-252-1201, 800-477-1005, FAX 952-252-1202, info@eastview.com, http://www.eastview.com.

385 RUS ISSN 0236-3615
ZHELEZNODOROZHNYI TRANSPORT. SERIYA. VYCHISLITEL'NAYA TEKHNIKA I AVTOMATIZIROVANNYE SISTEMY UPRAVLENIYA. Text in Russian. q.
—East View.
Address: Rizhskaya pl 3, Moscow, 129855, Russian Federation. TEL 7-095-2621331. **Dist. by:** East View Information Services, 10601 Wayzata Blvd, Minneapolis, MN 55305. TEL 952-252-1201, 800-477-1005, FAX 952-252-1202, info@eastview.com, http://www.eastview.com.

385 RUS ISSN 0321-1487
ZHELEZNODOROZHNYI TRANSPORT V ROSSIISKOI FEDERATSII, S.N.G. I ZA RUBEZHOM. Text in Russian. s-a.
Indexed: RASB.
Published by: Zheleznodorozhnyi Transport v Rossiiskoi Federatsii S.N.G. i Za Rubezhom, Rizhskaya pl 3, Moscow, 129855, Russian Federation. TEL 7-095-2621331. **Dist. by:** East View Information Services, 10601 Wayzata Blvd, Minneapolis, MN 55305. TEL 952-252-1201, 800-477-1005, FAX 952-252-1202, info@eastview.com, http://www.eastview.com.

385 RUS ISSN 0321-1495
ZHELEZNYE DOROGI MIRA. Text in Russian; Summaries in English, Russian. 1961. m. USD 125 in United States. adv. bibl.; illus. index. back issues avail. **Document type:** *Newsletter.* **Description:** Covers transportation of passengers and goods; railroad tracks and structures; signalization and communication.
Related titles: Diskette ed.
Indexed: RefZh.
—East View.
Published by: Transport, Spiridonovka ul 22/2, Moscow, 103001, Russian Federation. TEL 7-095-2900927, FAX 7-095-2900927. Ed. A T Golovaty. Adv. contact A Yu Efremov. page USD 400. Circ: 1,050. **Dist. by:** East View Information Services, 10601 Wayzata Blvd, Minneapolis, MN 55305. TEL 952-252-1201, 800-477-1005, FAX 952-252-1202, info@eastview.com, http://www.eastview.com.

385 BGR ISSN 1310-683X
ZHELEZOPUTEN TRANSPORT. Text in Bulgarian; Summaries in German. 1990. m. USD 52 foreign (effective 2002).
Published by: Bulgarski Durzhavni Zhelezhnitsi/Bulgarian State Railroad, 3 Ivan Vazov Street, Sofia, 1000, Bulgaria. TEL 359-2-873045. **Dist. by:** Sofia Books, ul Silivria 16, Sofia 1404, Bulgaria. TEL 359-2-9586257, info@sofiabooks-bg.com, http://www.sofiabooks-bg.com.

625.1 CHN ISSN 1001-4632
TF4
ZHONGGUO TIEDAO KEXUE/CHINA RAILWAY SCIENCE. Text in Chinese. 1979. bi-m. USD 48 (effective 2009). **Document type:** *Journal, Academic/Scholarly.*
Related titles: Online - full text ed.
Indexed: A28, APA, B21, BrCerAb, C&ISA, CA/WCA, CIA, CPEI, CerAb, CivEngAb, CorrAb, E&CAJ, E11, EEA, EMA, ESPM, EngInd, EnvEAb, H&SSA, H15, M&TEA, M09, MBF, METADEX, RefZh, SCOPUS, SolStAb, T04, WAA.
—BLDSC (3180.231500), East View.
Published by: Zhongguo Tiedao Kexue Yanjiuyuan/China Academy of Railway Sciences, 2, Daliushu Rd., Xizhimenwai, Haidian District, Beijing, 100081, China. **Dist. by:** China International Book Trading Corp, 35 Chegongzhuang Xilu, Haidian District, PO Box 399, Beijing 100044, China. TEL 86-10-68412045, FAX 86-10-68412023, cibtc@mail.cibtc.com.cn, http://www.cibtc.com.cn.

625.1 CHN ISSN 1001-683X
ZHONGGUO TIELU. Text in Chinese. 1962. m. USD 74.40 (effective 2009). stat. **Document type:** *Journal, Academic/Scholarly.*
Formerly (until 1990): Recent Developments in Railway Science and Technology
Related titles: Online - full text ed.; ◆ English ed.: Chinese Railways (English Edition). ISSN 1005-0485.
—BLDSC (9512.823000), East View.
Published by: Zhongguo Tiedao Kexue Yanjiuyuan/China Academy of Railway Sciences, 2, Daliushu Rd., Xizhimenwai, Haidian District, Beijing, 100081, China. TEL 86-10-51849182, FAX 86-10-51874317, http://www.rails.com.cn/.

385 DEU
ZUEGE. Text in German. 6/yr. EUR 27; EUR 4.50 newsstand/cover (effective 2011). adv. **Document type:** *Magazine, Consumer.*
Published by: Verlagsgruppe Bahn GmbH, Am Fohlenhof 9a, Fuerstenfeldbruck, 82256, Germany. TEL 49-8141-534810, FAX 49-8141-53481100, info@vgbahn.de, http://www.vg-bahn.de. adv.: B&W page EUR 1,240, color page EUR 1,840. Circ: 18,512 (controlled).

TRANSPORTATION—Roads And Traffic

see also ENGINEERING—Civil Engineering

338.31 624 USA
A A S H T O JOURNAL; weekly transportation report. Text in English. 19??. w. free to members (effective 2011). cum.index: 1988-1997. back issues avail. **Document type:** *Journal, Trade.* **Description:** Covers current transportation events.
Related titles: Online - full text ed.
Published by: American Association of State Highway and Transportation Officials, 444 N Capitol St, NW, Ste 249, Washington, DC 20001. TEL 202-624-5800, 800-231-3475, FAX 202-624-5806, info@aashto.org, http://www.transportation.org.

A D A C AUTOATLAS DEUTSCHLAND - EUROPA. *see* TRAVEL AND TOURISM

388.1 ITA ISSN 1971-5730
A I S C A T INFORMAZIONI. Text in Italian. 1985. m. free (effective 2009). bk.rev. charts; stat. **Document type:** *Bulletin, Trade.*
Related titles: Online - full text ed.: ISSN 1972-6503; ◆ Alternate Frequency ed(s).: A I S C A T Informazioni. ISSN 0044-975X. q.
Indexed: DokStr.
—BLDSC (0785.450000).
Published by: Associazione Italiana Societa Concessionarie Autostrade e Trafori, Via Sardegna, 40, Rome, RM 00187, Italy. TEL 39-6-4827163, FAX 39-6-4746968, aiscat@mclink.it. Ed. Giancarlo Valori.

388.1 ITA ISSN 0044-975X
A I S C A T INFORMAZIONI. (Associazione Italiana Societa Concessionarie Autostrade e Trafori) Text in Italian. 1966. q.
Related titles: Online - full text ed.: ISSN 1972-6511; ◆ Alternate Frequency ed(s).: A I S C A T Informazioni. ISSN 1971-5730. m.
—BLDSC (0785.450000).
Published by: Associazione Italiana Societa Concessionarie Autostrade e Trafori, Via Sardegna, 40, Rome, RM 00187, Italy. TEL 39-6-4827163, FAX 39-6-4746968, aiscat@mclink.it.

388.31 AUS ISSN 1328-7206
A R R B TRANSPORT RESEARCH. BRIEFING. Text in English. 1989. q. free (effective 2008). illus. back issues avail. **Document type:** *Newsletter, Corporate.* **Description:** Provides information on forthcoming conferences and new ARRB and Austroads publications.
Formerly (until 1993): Australian Road Research Board. Briefing
Related titles: Online - full content ed.
Published by: A R R B Group Ltd., 500 Burwood Hwy, Vermont South, VIC 3133, Australia. TEL 61-3-98811555, FAX 61-3-98878104, info@arrb.com.au. Eds. John Best TEL 61-3-98811531, Peter Milne. Circ: 1,700.

388 625.7 AUS ISSN 0572-1431
➤ **A R R B TRANSPORT RESEARCH. PROCEEDINGS (CD-ROM EDITION).** Text in English. 1998. a., latest 2003. AUD 55 (effective 2005). **Document type:** *Proceedings, Academic/Scholarly.*
Media: CD-ROM.
Indexed: A22, EngInd, SCOPUS.
—Linda Hall. **CCC.**
Published by: A R R B Group Ltd., 500 Burwood Hwy, Vermont South, VIC 3133, Australia. TEL 61-3-98811555, FAX 61-3-98878104, info@arrb.com.au, http://www.arrb.com.au.

388.411 388.3 AUS
A R R B TRANSPORT RESEARCH. RESEARCH REPORT. Text in English. 1975. irreg. AUD 45 (effective 2003). illus. back issues avail. **Document type:** *Report, Academic/Scholarly.*
Formerly: Australian Road Research Board. Reseach Report (0158-0728)
Indexed: CPEI, DokStr, EngInd, GeoRef, SCOPUS.
—BLDSC (7760.260000), IE, Ingenta.
Published by: A R R B Group Ltd., 500 Burwood Hwy, Vermont South, VIC 3133, Australia. TEL 61-3-98811555, FAX 61-3-98878104, info@arrb.com.au, http://www.arrb.com.au. R&P John Best TEL 61-3-98811531. Circ: 200.

380.5 388.3 AUS
A R R B TRANSPORT RESEARCH. SPECIAL REPORT. Text in English. 1966. irreg. price varies. back issues avail. **Document type:** *Report, Academic/Scholarly.*
Formerly: Australian Road Research Board. Special Report (0572-144X)
Indexed: AESIS, EngInd, GeoRef, SCOPUS.
—Linda Hall.
Published by: A R R B Group Ltd., 500 Burwood Hwy, Vermont South, VIC 3133, Australia. TEL 61-3-98811555, FAX 61-3-98878104, info@arrb.com.au, http://www.arrb.com.au. R&P John Best TEL 61-3-98811531. Circ: 200.

624 690 USA
A R T B A TRANSPORTATION OFFICIALS AND ENGINEERS DIRECTORY, STATE AND FEDERAL TRANSPORTATION AGENCY PERSONNEL. Text in English. a. USD 47. adv. **Document type:** *Directory.*
Formerly: A R B A Officials and Engineers Directory, Transportation Agency Personnel (0360-6996)
Published by: American Road & Transportation Builders Association, 1010 Massachusetts Ave, N W, Washington, DC 20001. TEL 202-289-4434, FAX 202-289-4435. Ed., R&P, Adv. contact Noelle Sotack.

388.3 USA ISSN 1082-6521
HV8079.55
ACCIDENT INVESTIGATION QUARTERLY. Text in English. 1994. q. USD 27 domestic (effective 2005). back issues avail. **Document type:** *Magazine, Trade.*
Indexed: HRIS.
Address: PO Box 234, Waldorf, MD 20604-0234. TEL 301-843-1371, FAX 301-884-5066. Ed., R&P Victor T Craig. Circ: 3,600.

ADVANCED PUBLIC TRANSPORTATION SYSTEMS: STATE OF THE ART UPDATE (YEAR). *see* TRANSPORTATION—Abstracting, Bibliographies, Statistics

388.314 DNK ISSN 0908-4037
AKSELTRYKMAALINGER. Text in Danish. 1993. irreg. charts; stat. **Document type:** *Government.*
Related titles: ◆ Series of: Denmark. Vejdirektoratet. Rapport. ISSN 0909-4288.
Published by: Vejdirektoratet, Vejteknisk Institut/Road Directorate, Danish Road Institute, Guldalderen 12, Hedehusene, 2640, Denmark. TEL 45-46-307000, FAX 45-46-307105, vd@vd.dk, http://www.vejdirektoratet.dk.

976.1 388.1 690 USA
THE ALABAMA ROADBUILDER. Text in English. 2003. q. free to members (effective 2009). adv. back issues avail. **Document type:** *Magazine, Trade.*
Related titles: Online - full text ed.
Published by: (Alabama Road Builders Association, Inc.), Naylor LLC, 5950 NW 1st Pl, Gainesville, FL 32607. TEL 800-369-6220, FAX 352-331-3525, http://www.naylor.com. Ed. Julie Bancroft. Pub. Kathleen Gardner. Adv. contact Mark Tumarkin. B&W page USD 1,639.50, color page USD 2,509.50; trim 8.375 x 10.875.

388.041 USA
AMERICAN DRIVER AND TRAFFIC SAFETY EDUCATION ASSOCIATION. CHRONICLE. Text in English. 1994. irreg.
Indexed: BRD, CA, ERI, EdA, MASUSE.
Published by: American Driver and Traffic Safety Education Association, Highway Safety Center, R & P Bldg, Indiana, PA 15705. TEL 724-357-4051, FAX 724-357-7595, 800-896-7703.

388.1 USA ISSN 1942-3691
AMERICA'S BYWAYS BULLETIN. Text in English. 2003. bi-m. free (effective 2008). **Document type:** *Newsletter, Government.* **Description:** Serves as a forum for promotion and exchange of ideas and programs about America's Scenic Byway Progam.
Media: Online - full content.
Published by: U.S. Department of Transportation, Federal Highway Administration, c/o Karen Timpone, Office of Safety HSSI, E71 318, 1200 New Jersey Ave, SE, Washington, DC 20590. TEL 202-366-2327.

388.1 CAN
ANNOTATED BRITISH COLUMBIA MOTOR VEHICLE ACT. Text in English. 1999. base vol. plus a. updates. looseleaf. CAD 110 per vol. (effective 2005). charts. **Document type:** *Handbook/Manual/Guide, Trade.* **Description:** Provides the full text to the British Columbia Municipal Act, with annotations and expert citations and summaries. Includes a table of relevant cases.
Published by: Canada Law Book Inc., 240 Edward St, Aurora, ON L4G 3S9, Canada. TEL 905-841-6472, 800-263-3269, FAX 905-841-5085, b.loney@canadalawbook.ca, http://www.canadalawbook.ca. Eds. Douglas B Muir, Michael J Libby. R&P Nancy Nesbitt.

388.1 EGY ISSN 1110-046X
ARAB ROADS. Text in English. 1965. q. EGP 1,000 domestic (effective 2004); USD 7 foreign (effective 2008). **Document type:** *Magazine, Consumer.*
Published by: Arab Roads Association, 33 Qasr El-Nil Str, Cairo, Egypt. TEL 20-2-3932186. Ed. Ahmad El-Haddad.

ARCHIVIO DELLA CIRCOLAZIONE E DEI SINISTRI STRADALI. *see* LAW

ARIZONA CRIMINAL CODE, TRANSPORTATION AND RELATED STATUTES. *see* LAW—Criminal Law

388.1 USA ISSN 0403-1792
ARKANSAS HIGHWAYS. Text in English. 1953. q. free. charts; illus. **Document type:** *Government.*
Published by: State Highway and Transportation Department, PO Box 2261, Little Rock, AR 72203. TEL 501-569-2000, FAX 501-569-2698. Ed. Randy Ort. Circ: 5,000.

388.1 USA ISSN 1043-0962
TE270
ASPHALT. Text in English. 1949. 3/yr. free. adv. illus. **Document type:** *Catalog, Trade.*
Formerly (until 1986): Asphaltnews (0276-1912); Supersedes (in 1976): Asphalt Institute. Newsletter
—BLDSC (1745.980000), IE, Ingenta, Linda Hall.
Published by: Asphalt Institute, PO Box 14052, Lexington, KY 40512-4052. FAX 606-288-4999. Ed., R&P John Davis. Adv. contact Kelly Pinson TEL 606-288-4983. Circ: 16,000 (controlled).

665.5 USA
ASPHALT EMULSION MANUFACTURERS ASSOCIATION. NEWSLETTER. Text in English. 1973. q. membership. adv. **Document type:** *Newsletter.*
Published by: Asphalt Emulsion Manufacturers Association, 3 Church Circle, PMB 250, Annapolis, MD 21401. TEL 410-267-0023. Ed., R&P Michael R Krissoff. Circ: 1,200.

363.7282 USA
ASPHALT RECYCLING AND RECLAIMING ASSOCIATION NEWSLETTER. Text in English. q. free for members. **Document type:** *Newsletter.*

Published by: Asphalt Recycling and Reclaiming Association, 3 Church Circle, PMB 250, Annapolis, MD 21401. TEL 410-267-0023. Ed., R&P Michael R Krissoff. Circ: 2,000.

388.1 USA ISSN 1083-687X
ASPHALT TECHNOLOGY NEWS. Text in English. 1989. s-a. back issues avail. **Document type:** *Newsletter, Consumer.*
Related titles: Online - full text ed.: free (effective 2011).
Published by: National Center for Asphalt Technology, 277 Technology Pky, Auburn, AL 36830. TEL 334-844-6228, FAX 334-844-6248, karen.hunley@auburn.edu, http://www.ncat.us. Ed. Courtney Jones.

388.31 GBR ISSN 1369-9776
THE ASPHALT YEARBOOK. Text in English. 1992. a. free to members. **Document type:** *Yearbook, Trade.* **Description:** Publishes papers concerned with the manufacture and use of bituminous materials in highway engineering, civil engineering and building construction.
—BLDSC (1746.230000).
Published by: The Institute of Asphalt Technology, Paper Mews Place, 290 High St, Dorking, Surrey TW19 7QU, United Kingdom. TEL 44-1306-742792, FAX 44-1306-888902, secretary@instofasphalt.org, http://www.instofasphalt.org/.

388.1 ITA
ASSOCIAZIONE ITALIANA INGEGNERIA DEL TRAFFICO E DEI TRASPORTI. NEWSLETTER. Text in Italian. m. free to members. **Document type:** *Newsletter, Trade.*
Published by: Associazione Italiana per l'Ingegneria del Traffico e dei Trasporti (A I I T), Via Magenta 5, Rome, 00185, Italy.

AUSTRALASIAN COLLEGE OF ROAD SAFETY. JOURNAL. *see* TRANSPORTATION

388.4131 AUS ISSN 1324-8626
AUSTRALIAN INSTITUTE OF TRAFFIC PLANNING AND MANAGEMENT. NEWSLETTER. Text in English. 19??. biennial. back issues avail. **Document type:** *Newsletter, Trade.*
Formerly (until 199?): A I T P M Newsletter (1324-745X)
Related titles: Online - full text ed.: ISSN 1838-305X.
Published by: Australian Institute of Traffic Planning and Management, Blackwood, PO Box 357, Adelaide, SA 5051, Australia. TEL 61-8-82783424, FAX 61-8-82789535, aitpm@aitpm.com.

AUSTRALIAN RAIL TRAM & BUS WORKER. *see* LABOR UNIONS

AUSTROPACK; Zeitschrift fuer alle Gebiete des Verpackungswesens fuer Transport und Verkehr. *see* PACKAGING

388.31 DEU ISSN 1860-0514
AUTO STRASSENVERKEHR. Text in German. 1952. fortn. EUR 35; EUR 1.40 newsstand/cover (effective 2011). adv. bk.rev. charts; illus.; mkt.; maps; stat. back issues avail. **Document type:** *Magazine, Consumer.* **Description:** Consists of a practical everyday guide for men and women who have interests in cars.
Former titles (until 1993): Auto - Der Deutsche Strassenverkehr (0863-3940); (until 1990): Deutsche Strassenverkehr (0012-0804)
Related titles: ◆ Supplement(s): Auto Kaufen Leicht Gemacht.
Published by: Motor Presse Stuttgart GmbH & Co. KG (Subsidiary of: Gruner + Jahr AG & Co), Leuschnerstr 1, Stuttgart, 70174, Germany. TEL 49-711-18201, FAX 49-711-1821779, internet-redaktion@motor-presse-stuttgart.de, http://www.motorpresse.de. Ed. Jens Katemann. Adv. contact Stephen Brand. Circ: 178,511 (controlled).

AUTOKAMPIOEN. *see* TRANSPORTATION—Automobiles

AUTOREVUU. *see* TRANSPORTATION—Automobiles

388.1 UKR ISSN 0365-8392
AVTOSHLYAKHOVYK UKRAINY; naukovo-vyrobnychyi zhurnal. Text in Ukrainian. 1960. bi-m. USD 160 in United States (effective 2008). **Document type:** *Journal, Trade.*
—East View.
Address: prospekt Peremogy 57, ofis 1308, Kyiv, 03113, Ukraine. **Dist. by:** East View Information Services, 10601 Wayzata Blvd, Minneapolis, MN 55305. TEL 952-252-1201, 800-477-1005, FAX 952-252-1202, info@eastview.com, http://www.eastview.com. **Co-sponsor:** Ministerstvo Transportu Ukrainy/Ministry of Transport of Ukraine.

388.31 DEU
B G L JAHRESBERICHT. (Bundesverband Gueterkraftverkehr Logistik und Entsorgung) Text in German. 1984. a. free (effective 2009). **Document type:** *Bulletin, Trade.*
Formerly (until 1997): B D F Jahresbericht
Published by: Bundesverband Gueterkraftverkehr Logistik und Entsorgung e.V., Breitenbachstr 1, Frankfurt Am Main, 60487, Germany. TEL 49-69-79190, FAX 49-69-7919227, bgl@bgl-ev.de.

THE BALTIC JOURNAL OF ROAD AND BRIDGE ENGINEERING. *see* ENGINEERING—Civil Engineering

388.4131 362.1 CHN ISSN 1009-4261
BAN NI TONGXING/COMPANION. Text in Chinese. 1996. m. **Document type:** *Magazine, Government.*
Published by: Ban Ni Tongxing Zazhishe, 147, Jianmin Lu, Zhuhai, 519015, China. TEL 86-756-2634906, FAX 86-756-2634050.

BELGIUM. INSTITUT NATIONAL DE STATISTIQUE. TRANSPORT. VEHICULES A MOTEUR NEUFS ET D'OCCASION MIS EN CIRCULATION EN (ANNEE). *see* TRANSPORTATION—Abstracting, Bibliographies, Statistics

BELGIUM. NATIONAAL INSTITUUT VOOR DE STATISTIEK. VERVOER. IN HET VERKEER GEBRACHTE NIEUWE EN TWEEDEHANDS MOTORVOERTUIGEN IN (YEAR). *see* TRANSPORTATION—Abstracting, Bibliographies, Statistics

BETTER ROADS. *see* ENGINEERING—Civil Engineering

BIL. *see* TRANSPORTATION—Automobiles

388.31 USA
BOHMAN TRAFFIC NEWS SUMMARY. Text in English. m. USD 29.95 (effective 1999).
Published by: Bohman Industrial Traffic Consultants, Inc., 32 Pleasant St, Box 889, Gardner, MA 01440. TEL 617-632-1913. Ed. Raynard R Bohman Jr.

386 COL ISSN 0120-2251
BOLETIN DE VIAS. Text in Spanish. 1974. s-a. back issues avail. **Document type:** *Bulletin, Consumer.*
Indexed: HRIS.
—Linda Hall.
Published by: Universidad Nacional de Colombia. Sede Manizales, Facultad de Ingenieria y Arquitectura, Carrera 27 No 64-60, Manizales, Caldas, Colombia. TEL 57-6-8810000. Ed. Julio Robledo Isaza.

388 BRA
BRASILIA. DEPARTAMENTO DE ESTRADAS DE RODAGEM DO DISTRITO FEDERAL. DIRETORIA GERAL. RELATORIO DE ATIVIDADES. Text in Portuguese. 1978. a. free.
Formerly: Brasilia. Departamento de Estradas de Rodagem do Distrito Federal. Diretoria Geral. Relatorio Anual.
Published by: Departamento de Estrados de Rodagem do Distrito Federal, Divisao de Programacao, Brasilia, DF 70000, Brazil. Circ: 300.

BUTTERWORTHS ROAD TRAFFIC SERVICE. *see* LAW

C R O W ET CETERA. (Centrum voor Regelgeving en Onderzoek in de Grond-, Water- en Wegenbouw en de Verkeerstechniek) *see* ENGINEERING—Civil Engineering

388.411 CAN ISSN 1183-2282
C U T A FORUM A C T U. Text in English, French. 1977. bi-m. membership. adv. illus. **Document type:** *Journal, Trade.* **Description:** Serves providers of urban transit services, associated manufacturers and suppliers and related organizations.
Formerly (until 1991): Transit Topics (1185-2208)
Published by: Canadian Urban Transit Association, 55 York St, Ste 1401, Toronto, ON M5J 1R7, Canada. TEL 416-365-9800, FAX 416-365-1295, transit@cutaactu.ca. Adv. contact David Onodera. Circ: 1,000.

388 FRA ISSN 1162-6925
CAHIERS DE L'OBSERVATOIRE; les informations du C N R. Text in French. 1987. m. (11/yr.). EUR 67 domestic; EUR 75 foreign (effective 2005).
Published by: Comite National Routier, 88 Bd de la Villette, Paris, 75019, France. TEL 33-1-53591272, FAX 33-1-53591273.

388.1 FRA ISSN 0244-6316
HE363.F7
CAISSE NATIONALE DES AUTOROUTES. RAPPORT ANNUEL. Text in French. 1963. a. free. **Document type:** *Corporate.* **Description:** Report by the board of directors on the activities for the year of the Caisse Nationale des Autoroutes.
Published by: Caisse Nationale des Autoroutes, 15 Quai Anatole France, Paris, 75356, France. TEL 33-1-58508387, FAX 33-1-58500566, 33-1-40493330. Ed. Albert Hayem. Circ: 2,000.

388.4131 GBR
CAMBRIDGESHIRE COUNTY COUNCIL. ROAD NETWORK MANAGEMENT PLAN. Text in English. a., latest 2001. charts; illus.; stat. **Document type:** *Government.* **Description:** Covers forth policies, strategies, and annual targets for work on the highway infrastructure in Cambridgeshire.
Published by: Cambridgeshire County Council, Shire Hall, Castle Hill, Cambridge, CB3 0AP, United Kingdom. TEL 44-345-0455200, FAX 44-1223-717201, info@cambridgeshire.gov.uk, http://www.cambridgeshire.gov.uk.

388.4131 GBR
CAMBRIDGESHIRE COUNTY COUNCIL. ROAD SAFETY PLAN (YEAR). Text in English. a., latest 2001. charts; stat. **Document type:** *Government.* **Description:** Covers reviews the previous year's road safety activity in Cambridgeshire and sets out action plans for the following year.
Published by: Cambridgeshire County Council, Shire Hall, Castle Hill, Cambridge, CB3 0AP, United Kingdom. TEL 44-345-0455200, FAX 44-1223-717201, info@cambridgeshire.gov.uk, http://www.cambridgeshire.gov.uk.

388.314 GBR
CAMBRIDGESHIRE COUNTY COUNCIL. TRAFFIC MONITORING REPORT (YEAR). Text in English. 19??. a. free (effective 2009). charts; stat. **Document type:** *Government.* **Description:** Examines traffic patterns on rural and urban roads in Cambridgeshire over the past year and provides projections for the following year.
Related titles: Online - full text ed.
Published by: Cambridgeshire County Council, Shire Hall, Castle Hill, Cambridge, CB3 0AP, United Kingdom. TEL 44-345-0455200, FAX 44-1223-717201, info@cambridgeshire.gov.uk.

CAR FREE CITIES MAGAZINE; network for a new mobility culture. *see* HOUSING AND URBAN PLANNING

CARE ON THE ROAD. *see* PUBLIC HEALTH AND SAFETY

388 CHE ISSN 0255-5263
CENSUS OF MOTOR TRAFFIC ON MAIN INTERNATIONAL TRAFFIC ARTERIES. Text in English, French. quinquennial. USD 80 (effective 2000). **Document type:** *Bulletin, Government.*
Formerly: Census of Traffic on Main International Traffic Arteries (0566-7631)
Related titles: CD-ROM ed.: USD 100 (effective 2000); Microfiche ed.
Indexed: IIS.
Published by: United Nations, Economic Commission for Europe (ECE), Palais des Nations, Geneva 10, 1211, Switzerland. TEL 41-22-9174444, FAX 41-22-9170505, info.ece@unece.org, http://www.unece.org.

CESTE I MOSTOVI/ROADS AND BRIDGES. *see* ENGINEERING—Civil Engineering

388.31 CHN ISSN 1671-8879
CHANG'AN DAXUE XUEBAO. ZIRAN KEXUE BAN/XI'AN HIGHWAY UNIVERSITY. JOURNAL. Text in Chinese. 1983. q. USD 31.20 (effective 2009). **Document type:** *Journal, Academic/Scholarly.*
Former titles (until 2002): Xi'an Gonglu Jiaotong Daxue Xuebao (1007-4112); (until 1995): Xi'an Gonglu Xueyuan Xuebao (1000-2774)
Related titles: Online - full content ed.; Online - full text ed.
Indexed: ESPM, EngInd, EnvEAb, SCOPUS.
—BLDSC (3129.639900), East View, Linda Hall.
Published by: Xi'an Gonglu Jiaotong Daxue/Xi'an Highway University, 3, Cuihua Lu, Xi'an, 710064, China. TEL 86-29-5268346 ext 4383, FAX 86-29-5261532.

CHENGSHI DAO-QIAO YU FANGHONG/URBAN ROADS BRIDGES & FLOOD CONTROL. *see* ENGINEERING—Civil Engineering

388.1 USA
THE CONSTANT RIDER; stories from the transportation front. Text in English. 2003. irreg. price varies for each issue. **Document type:** *Magazine, Consumer.* **Description:** Offers Kate Lopresti travel stories. Travels on the Tri-Met (Portland, Oregon's public transit authority) and other interesting and amusing travel stories on trains and planes.
Published by: The Constant Rider, P O Box 6753, Portland, OR 97228. kate@constantrider.com. Ed., Pub. Kate Lopresti.

CONSTRUCTION INDUSTRIES OF MASSACHUSETTS DIRECTORY; a directory and catalog of highway and heavy construction in New England. *see* BUSINESS AND ECONOMICS—Trade And Industrial Directories

THE CONTROLLER; journal of air traffic control. *see* AERONAUTICS AND SPACE FLIGHT

388.1 CRI
COSTA RICA. MINISTERIO DE OBRAS PUBLICAS Y TRANSPORTES. MEMORIAS. Text in Spanish. irreg., latest 1997-98. per issue exchange basis. **Document type:** *Corporate.*
Formerly: Costa Rica. Ministerio de Transportes. Memoria (0589-8617)
Published by: Ministerio de Obras Publicas y Transportes, Apdo 10176, San Jose, 1000, Costa Rica. TEL 506-527-7798, FAX 506-265-4560.

388.31 USA
COUNTRY ROADS AND CITY STREETS. Text in English. 1985. q. free. 12 p./no. 3 cols./p.; back issues avail. **Document type:** *Newsletter.* **Description:** Contains articles about road and bridge problem solving, regulations, maintenance techniques, safety issues, and design features.
Related titles: Online - full content ed.
Published by: West Virginia Transportation Technology Transfer Center, PO Box 6103, Department of Civil Engineering, Engineering Sc, Morgantown, WV 26506. TEL 304-293-3031, FAX 304-293-7109, blanken@cemr.wvu.edu. Ed., R&P Michael Blankenship. Circ: 1,450.

388 624 GBR ISSN 1464-1380
TA1057.A1
CURRENT TOPICS IN TRANSPORT. Text in English. 1992. irreg. price varies. back issues avail. **Document type:** *Monographic series, Trade.* **Description:** Provides abstracts of recent research on topics of current interest to transport researchers.
—IE, Ingenta. **CCC.**
Published by: Transport Research Laboratory, Crowthorne House, Nine Mile Ride, Wokingham, Berks RG40 3GA, United Kingdom. TEL 44-1344-773131, FAX 44-1344-770356, enquiries@trl.co.uk, http://www.trl.co.uk.

388.31 DEU ISSN 0940-9025
D V R REPORT; Fachmagazin fuer Verkehrssicherheit. Text in German. 1969. 4/yr. **Document type:** *Magazine, Trade.*
Formerly (until 1991): Partner Report
Published by: Deutscher Verkehrssicherheitsrat e.V., Beueler Bahnhofsplatz 16, Bonn, 53225, Germany. TEL 49-228-400010, FAX 49-228-4000167, info@dvr.de. Ed. Sven Rademacher. Pub. Ute Hammer. Circ: 20,000.

338.31 DEU ISSN 0342-166X
D V Z. (Deutsche Verkehrs - Zeitung) Text in German. 1947. 3/w. EUR 312 (effective 2009). adv. bk.rev. charts; illus. **Document type:** *Newspaper, Trade.* **Description:** International trade journal for transport and logistics, transport policy, forwarding, warehousing and transhipment.
Related titles: Online - full text ed.
Published by: Deutscher Verkehrs Verlag GmbH, Nordkanalstr 36, Hamburg, 20097, Germany. TEL 49-40-2371401, FAX 49-40-23714205, info@dvv-gruppe.de, http://www.dvv-gruppe.de. Ed. Bjoern Helmke. Adv. contact Oliver Detje. B&W page EUR 9,100, color page EUR 15,925; trim 281 x 430. Circ: 14,893 (paid and controlled).

388.4131 CHN ISSN 1004-504X
DAOLU JIAOTONG GUANLI/ROAD TRAFFIC MANAGEMENT. Text in Chinese. 1986. m.
Published by: Zhongguo Daolu Jiaotong Anquan Xiehui, Peixin Jie, 4F, Peixinbin Guan, Beijing, 100061, China. TEL 86-10-67152945, FAX 86-10-67152943, zlh0605@sina.com.

388.4131 CHN ISSN 1008-2522
DAOLU JIAOTONG YU ANQUAN/ROAD TRAFFIC & SAFETY. Text in Chinese. 1981. bi-m. **Document type:** *Journal, Academic/Scholarly.*
Formerly (until 2000): Jiaotong Gongcheng
Published by: Beijing Jiaotong Gongcheng Xuehui/Beijing Traffic Engineering Association, 5 Peixin St, Chongwen District, Beijing, 100061, China. TEL 86-10-68398458, FAX 86-10-68398458, jtgcxu@bjkp.gov.cn, http://www.bast.net.cn/bjkx/xstt/gkl/bjjtgcxh/index.shtml.

388 USA ISSN 0070-329X
DELAWARE. DEPARTMENT OF HIGHWAYS AND TRANSPORTATION. TRAFFIC SUMMARY. Text in English. 1957. a. USD 20. **Document type:** *Government.*
Published by: Department of Transportation, Bureau of Traffic, PO Box 778, Dover, DE 19901. TEL 302-739-4366, FAX 302-739-6792. Ed. James Ho. Circ: 400.

388.1 DNK
DENMARK. VEJDIREKTORATET. AARSRAPPORT. Text in Danish. 2001. a. free. illus. back issues avail. **Document type:** *Government.*
Formerly (until 2003): Denmark. Transport- og Energiministeriet. Vejdirektoratet. Aarsrapport (1603-3574); Which was formed by the merger of (1999-2001): Denmark. Vejdirektoratet. Virksomhedsregnskab (1602-1711); (1983-2001): Denmark. Trafikministeriet. Vejdirektoratet. Aarsberetning (0109-2405); Which was formerly (1980-1982): Denmark. Vejdirektoratet. Aarsrapport (0107-0355)
Related titles: Online - full text ed.: ISSN 1604-780X.
Published by: Vejdirektoratet/The Danish Road Directorate, Niels Juels Gade 13, PO Box 9018, Copenhagen K, 1022, Denmark. TEL 45-72-443333, vd@vd.dk.

388.31 DNK ISSN 0909-8410
DENMARK. VEJDIREKTORATET. NOTAT/DENMARK. MINISTRY OF TRANSPORT AND ENERGY. DANISH ROAD DIRECTORATE. NOTE. Text in Danish, English. 1981. irreg., latest vol.121, 2009. free. back issues avail. **Document type:** *Monographic series, Government.*
Formerly (until 1994): Vejdatalaboratoriet. Notat (0907-9343)

Related titles: Online - full text ed.
Published by: Vejdirektoratet/The Danish Road Directorate, Niels Juels Gade 13, PO Box 9018, Copenhagen K, 1022, Denmark. TEL 45-72-443333, vd@vd.dk.

DENMARK. VEJDIREKTORATET. RAPPORT. *see* ENGINEERING—Civil Engineering

624 388.1 ARG ISSN 0011-5177
DIRECCION DE VIALIDAD. PUBLICACIONES TECNICAS. Text in Spanish. 1933. 10/yr. free. charts; illus.; stat.
Published by: Direccion de Vialidad, Calle 7, 1175, La Plata, Buenos Aires 1900, Argentina. Circ: 1,500.

DOBOKU GAKKAI ROMBUNSHUU. D (DVD-ROM). *see* ENGINEERING—Civil Engineering

DOROKYO NENPO/ANNUAL REPORT OF ROAD BRIDGES. *see* ENGINEERING—Civil Engineering

388.1 DEU
EINKAUFSFUEHRER FUER DEN STRASSENBAU DEUTSCHLAND. Text in German. a. EUR 10 (effective 2009). adv. **Document type:** *Journal, Trade.*
Published by: Aweto Verlag, Am Hambuch 7, Meckenheim, 53340, Germany. TEL 49-2225-921631, FAX 49-2225-921655, verlag@aweto.de, http://www.aweto.de. Ed., Adv. contact Friedhelm Todtenhoefer. B&W page EUR 1,400, color page EUR 1,600. Circ: 10,000 (controlled).

388 340 GBR ISSN 0142-2952
ENCYCLOPEDIA OF HIGHWAY LAW AND PRACTICE. Text in English. 1965. 4 base vols. plus updates 3/yr. looseleaf. GBP 823 base vol(s). domestic; EUR 1,087 base vol(s). in Europe; USD 1,415 base vol(s). elsewhere (effective 2011). **Document type:** *Handbook/Manual/Guide, Trade.* **Description:** Provide the full text of all relevant legislation, complete with annotations and includes an authoritative general introduction to the law covering the interests of the highway authority, the rights of the public, statutory undertakers, and the rights and duties of adjoining landowners.
Related titles: CD-ROM ed.; Online - full text ed.
Published by: Sweet & Maxwell Ltd. (Subsidiary of: Thomson Reuters Corp.), 100 Avenue Rd, London, NW3 3PF, United Kingdom. TEL 44-20-73937000, FAX 44-20-74491144, sweetandmaxwell.customer.services@thomson.com. Ed. Stephen Sauvain. **Subscr. to:** PO Box 1000, Andover SP10 9AF, United Kingdom. TEL 44-20-73938051, sweetandmaxwell.international.queries@thomson.com.

388 340 GBR ISSN 0142-2847
ENCYCLOPEDIA OF ROAD TRAFFIC LAW AND PRACTICE. Text in English. 1960. 6 base vols. plus updates 3/yr. looseleaf. GBP 1,106 base vol(s). domestic; EUR 1,461 base vol(s). in Europe; USD 1,901 base vol(s). elsewhere (effective 2011). **Document type:** *Handbook/Manual/Guide, Trade.* **Description:** Provides comprehensive, authoritative and up-to-date information on all aspects of road traffic law and practice.
Related titles: CD-ROM ed.: GBP 2,820 base vol(s). domestic to institutions; EUR 3,723.60 base vol(s). in Europe to institutions; USD 4,039 base vol(s). elsewhere to institutions (effective 2011); Online - full text ed.
Published by: Sweet & Maxwell Ltd. (Subsidiary of: Thomson Reuters Corp.), 100 Avenue Rd, London, NW3 3PF, United Kingdom. TEL 44-20-73937000, FAX 44-20-74491144, sweetandmaxwell.customer.services@thomson.com. Eds. Alexandra Ward, Hannah Willcocks, Mark Lucraft. **Subscr. to:** PO Box 1000, Andover SP10 9AF, United Kingdom. TEL 44-20-73938051, sweetandmaxwell.international.queries@thomson.com.

ESTADISTICA PANAMENA. SITUACION SOCIAL. SECCION 451. ACCIDENTES DE TRANSITO. *see* TRANSPORTATION—Abstracting, Bibliographies, Statistics

FLORIDA CRIMINAL LAW AND MOTOR VEHICLE HANDBOOK. *see* LAW—Criminal Law

FLORIDA TRAFFIC & D U I PRACTICE MANUAL. *see* LAW

DER FLUGLEITER. *see* TRANSPORTATION—Air Transport

388 DEU
FORSCHUNGSGESELLSCHAFT FUER STRASSEN- UND VERKEHRSWESEN. ARBEITSGRUPPE GESTEINSKOERNUNGEN, UNGEBUNDENE BAUWEISEN. SCHRIFTENREIHE. Text in German. 1977. irreg. price varies. **Document type:** *Monographic series, Trade.*
Former titles (until 2008): Forschungsgesellschaft fuer Strassen- und Verkehrswesen. Arbeitsgruppe Mineralstoffe im Strassenbau. Schriftenreihe; (until 1983): Forschungsgesellschaft fuer das Strassenwesen. Arbeitsgruppe Mineralstoffe im Strassenbau. Schriftenreihe
Published by: Forschungsgesellschaft fuer Strassen- und Verkehrswesen, An Lyskirchen 14, Cologne, 50676, Germany. TEL 49-221-935830, FAX 49-221-9358373, koeln@fgsv.de, http://www.fgsv.de.

388.3 USA
GARDEN STATE PARKWAY TRAFFIC REPORT. Text in English. 1972. m. free. charts; illus.
Formerly: Garden State Parkway Quarterly Report
Related titles: Microfilm ed.
Published by: Highway Authority, Garden State Parkway, Traffic Division, Woodbridge, NJ 07095. TEL 201-442-8600. Ed. Jude T Depko. Circ: 750.

388 CHN ISSN 0451-0712
GONG LU/ROADS. Text in Chinese. m. USD 48 (effective 2009).
Related titles: Online - full text ed.
—East View.
Published by: Jiaotong-bu, Gonglu Guihua Shejiyuan/Ministry of Communications and Transportation, Road Planning and Designing Institute, 33 Qianchaomian Hutong, Dongsi, Beijing, 100010, China. TEL 5125565. Ed. He Xiumei.

625.7 CHN ISSN 1002-0268
TA1101 CODEN: GJKEER
➤ **GONGLU JIAOTONG KEJI/JOURNAL OF HIGHWAY AND TRANSPORTATION RESEARCH AND DEVELOPMENT.** Text in Chinese; Abstracts in Chinese, English. 1984. m. CNY 144; CNY 12 newsstand/cover (effective 2008). **Document type:** *Journal, Academic/Scholarly.*
Related titles: Online - full text ed.
Indexed: A28, APA, BrCerAb, C&ISA, CA/WCA, CIA, CerAb, CivEngAb, CorrAb, E&CAJ, E11, EEA, EMA, ESPM, EnvEAb, H15, HRIS, M&TEA, M09, MBF, METADEX, SCOPUS, SolStAb, T04, WAA.
—BLDSC (4998.675000).
Address: 8 Xi Tu Cheng Lu, Beijing, 100088, China. TEL 86-10-62079557 ext 813, FAX 86-10-62058207, zhiyan.li@rioh.cn. Ed. Hua-yong Zhang. R&P Zhi-yan Li. Circ: 3,500 (paid and controlled).

388.1 CHN ISSN 1671-2668
GONGLU YU QIYUN/HIGHWAYS & AUTOMOTIVE APPLICATIONS. Text in Chinese. 1985. bi-m. **Document type:** *Journal, Academic/Scholarly.*
Related titles: Online - full text ed.
Published by: Changsha Ligong Daxue/Changsha University of Science and Technology, 45, Chiling Lu, Xinxiang #8, Changsha, 410076, China. TEL 86-731-85258189.

388.411 388.4131 GBR
GREAT BRITAIN. DEPARTMENT FOR TRANSPORT. ROAD SAFETY STRATEGY DIVISION RESEARCH PROGRAMME. SUMMARY OF PLANNED RESEARCH (ONLINE). Text in English. biennial.
Former titles (until 200?): Great Britain. Department for Transport. Transport Strategy and Local Transport Research Programme. Summary of Planned Research (Print); Great Britain. Department for Transport, Local Government and the Regions. Roads and Local Transport Research Programme. Summary of Planned Research
Media: Online - full text.
Published by: Great Britain. Department for Transport, Great Minster House, 76 Marsham St, London, SW1P 4DR, United Kingdom. TEL 44-20-79443078, FAX 44-20-79449643, publications@communities.gsi.gov.uk, http://www.dft.gov.uk.

388.411 388.4131 GBR
GREAT BRITAIN. DEPARTMENT OF COMMUNITIES AND LOCAL GOVERNMENT. REGENERATION RESEARCH SUMMARY (ONLINE). Text in English. irreg., latest no.37, 2006. **Document type:** *Government.*
Formerly: Great Britain. Department for Transport, Local Government and the Regions. Regeneration Research Summary (Print)
Media: Online - full text.
Published by: Great Britain. Department of Communities and Local Government, Eland House, Bressenden Pl, London, SW1E 5DU, United Kingdom. TEL 44-20-79444400, contactus@communities.gov.uk, http://www.communities.gov.uk.

388.1 355 CHN ISSN 1672-3953
GUOFANG JIAOTONG GONGCHENG YU JISHU/TRAFFIC ENGINEERING AND TECHNOLOGY FOR NATIONAL DEFENCE. Text in Chinese. 2003. q. USD 23.40 (effective 2009). **Document type:** *Journal, Academic/Scholarly.*
Related titles: Online - full text ed.
Published by: Shijiazhuang Tiedao Xueyuan, 17, Beierhua Dong Lu, Shijiazhuang, 050043, China.

388.312 USA
H M A T. (Hot Mix Asphalt Technology) Text in English. 1964. bi-m. USD 50; free to qualified personnel (effective 2011). adv. bk.rev. 64 p./no.; back issues avail.; reprints avail. **Document type:** *Magazine, Trade.* **Description:** Contains information and news for public works officials, pavement consulting engineers, architects, and others involved with paving materials and pavement design, construction and maintenance.
Former titles: Focus on H M A T; H M A T; Supersedes (in 1986): National Asphalt Pavement Association. Paving Forum (0048-3079)
Related titles: Online - full content ed.
Indexed: HRIS.
Published by: National Asphalt Pavement Association, 5100 Forbes Blvd, Lanham, MD 20706-4407. TEL 301-731-4748, 888-468-6499, FAX 301-731-4621, napa@hotmix.org, http://www.hotmix.org. Ed. Patricia D Long. Pub. Mike Acott. Circ: 28,000 (controlled).

388.31 ITA ISSN 2035-4215
H P TRASPORTI CLUB. Text in Italian. 1974. m. free to qualified personnel (effective 2009). adv. bk.rev. bibl.; charts; illus.; stat. **Document type:** *Magazine, Trade.*
Former titles (until 1979): H P Energia Trasporti (0391-2019); (until 1974): Segnalazioni Stradali (0037-0959)
Published by: (Automobile Club d'Italia), A C I Mondadori SpA, Via Cassanese 224, Segrate, MI 20090, Italy. TEL 39-02-26937550, FAX 39-02-26937560. Ed. Giancarlo Pini. Circ: 35,000 (paid).

HIGHWAY FINANCING & CONSTRUCTION - STATE CAPITALS. *see* LAW

HIGHWAY RESEARCH RECORD. *see* ENGINEERING—Civil Engineering

388 USA
HIGHWAY SAFETY DIRECTIONS. Text in English. 1970. s-a. free. **Document type:** *Newsletter.* **Description:** Reports on research being conducted by the Highway Safety Research Center on alcohol and highway safety, roadway alignment and engineering, accident investigation and analysis, driver behavior, education and licensing, bicycle and pedestrian safety, facility design, adult and child passenger safety, seat belts and child car seats. Looks at passenger protection laws, injury prevention, and North Carolina passenger and highway safety efforts.
Formed by the 1987 merger of: Totline; Highway Safety Highlights (0162-6205)
Indexed: HRIS.
Published by: University of North Carolina at Chapel Hill, Highway Safety Research Center, Chapel Hill, NC 27514. Circ: 4,000.

THE HUB. *see* SPORTS AND GAMES—Bicycles And Motorcycles

HUGHES GUIDE TO TRAFFIC LAW. *see* LAW

HUNGARY. KOZPONTI STATISZTIKAI HIVATAL. KOZLEKEDESI EVKONYV. *see* TRANSPORTATION—Abstracting, Bibliographies, Statistics

I A T S S RESEARCH. *see* TRANSPORTATION—Automobiles

388.411 JPN ISSN 0386-1104
HE5613.5
➤ **I A T S S REVIEW.** Text in English, Japanese. 1975. q. JPY 4,320 (effective 2003). back issues avail. **Document type:** *Journal, Academic/Scholarly.*
Related titles: Online - full content ed.
Published by: International Association of Traffic and Safety Sciences, 6-20 Yaesu 2-chome, Chuo-ku, Tokyo, 104-0028, Japan. TEL 81-3-3273-7884, FAX 81-3-3272-7054, iatss@db3.so-net.ne.jp, http://wwwsoc.nii.ac.jp/iatss/. Pub. Hiroshi Ishizuki.

388.31 USA ISSN 1064-2560
TA1250
I M S A JOURNAL. Text in English. 1965. bi-m. USD 60 (effective 2006). adv. charts; illus. 80 p./no. 3 cols./p.; **Document type:** *Magazine, Trade.* **Description:** Contains articles on traffic signals, signs and markings, fire alarms, dispatch and roadway lighting.
Former titles (until 1979): Municipal Signals (1064-4652); (until 1979): I M S A Signal Magazine (0019-0055)
Indexed: HRIS.
Published by: International Municipal Signal Association, 165 E Union St, Box 539, Newark, NY 14513. TEL 315-331-2182, 800-723-4672, FAX 315-331-8205, sne@imsasafety.org. Ed. Marilyn Lawrence. Pubs. Marilyn Lawrence, Sharon Earl. R&P, Adv. contact Sharon Earl. B&W page USD 874; trim 8.5 x 11. Circ: 11,000 (paid and free).

388.1 IND
I R C SPECIAL PUBLICATION. Text in English. 1966. irreg. bibl.; charts. **Document type:** *Monographic series, Trade.*
Published by: Indian Roads Congress, The Secretary General, Sector 6, (Near RBI Quarters), R K Puram, New Delhi, 110 022, India. TEL 91-11-26185303, FAX 91-11-26183669, secretarygen@irc.org.in, http://www.irc.org.in.

388.31 USA ISSN 0162-8178
HE331 CODEN: ITEJDZ
➤ **I T E JOURNAL.** Text in English. 1930. m. USD 65 in North America to non-members; USD 85 elsewhere to non-members; free to members (effective 2010). adv. bk.rev. illus. 68 p./no.; back issues avail.; reprints avail. **Document type:** *Journal, Academic/Scholarly.* **Description:** Covers articles and technical papers dealing with all phases and modes of surface traffic transportation engineering with emphasis on safe, convenient, efficient and economic private and public transportation via highway, roads, streets, rail, planning and geometric design of related facilities, vehicles and abutting lands in rural, suburban and urban areas.
Former titles (until 1978): Transportation Engineering (0148-0170); (until 1977): Traffic Engineering (0041-0675); (until 1937): Traffic Digest
Related titles: CD-ROM ed.; Microfilm ed.: (from PQC); Online - full text ed.
Indexed: A05, A12, A13, A17, A20, A22, A23, A24, A28, ABIn, APA, AS&TA, AS&TI, ASCA, B04, B13, B21, BRD, BrCerAb, C&ISA, C10, CA, CA/WCA, CADCAM, CIA, CPEI, Cadscan, CerAb, CivEngAb, CorrAb, CurCont, DokStr, E&CAJ, E11, EEA, EIA, EMA, ESPM, EngInd, EnvAb, EnvEAb, EnvInd, GeotechAb, H&SSA, H15, HRIS, ICEA, LeadAb, M&TEA, M09, MBF, METADEX, P06, P26, P45, P48, P51, P52, P53, P54, P56, PQC, PetrolAb, S04, SCI, SCOPUS, SUSA, SoftAbEng, SolStAb, T02, T04, W03, W05, W07, WAA, Zincscan.
—BLDSC (4588.550000), IE, Infotrieve, Ingenta, Linda Hall.
Published by: Institute of Transportation Engineers, 1099 14th St, NW Ste 300 W, Washington, DC 20005. TEL 202-289-0222, FAX 202-289-7722, ite_staff@ite.org. Adv. contact Christina Garneski TEL 202-289-0222 ext 128. B&W page USD 1,850, color page USD 2,850; trim 8.25 x 10.875. Circ: 17,367.

625.7 USA ISSN 0019-1175
IDAHO TRANSPORTATION DEPARTMENT. HIGHWAY INFORMATION. Text in English. 1920. bi-m. free. charts; illus.; stat.
Formerly: Idaho Department of Highways. Highway Information
Published by: Transportation Department, PO Box 7129, Boise, ID 83707-1129. TEL 208-334-8000, TELEX 334-3858. Ed. Barbara Babic. Circ: 1,500.

388 IND
CODEN: HREBDK
INDIAN ROADS CONGRESS. HIGHWAY RESEARCH JOURNAL. Text in English. 1947. s-a. **Document type:** *Journal, Trade.* **Description:** Devoted to research papers under four topics, namely pavements, soil engineering, traffic engineering and bridge engineering.
Former titles (until 2007): Indian Roads Congress. Highway Research Bulletin (0376-4788); (until 1975): Indian Roads Congress. Road Research Bulletin
Indexed: A22, CRIA, GeoRef, HRIS, SpeleolAb.
—Linda Hall.
Published by: Indian Roads Congress, The Secretary General, Sector 6, (Near RBI Quarters), R K Puram, New Delhi, 110 022, India. TEL 91-11-26185303, FAX 91-11-26183669, secretarygen@irc.org.in.

624 IND ISSN 0258-0500
CODEN: JIRCAA
INDIAN ROADS CONGRESS. JOURNAL. Text in English. 1944. q. INR 300 per issue (effective 2011). adv. **Document type:** *Journal, Academic/Scholarly.* **Description:** Publishes papers on standards, specification, construction of important road and bridge works in addition to sections on plant, machinery & apparatus, information services, research, statistics etc.
Formerly (until 1975): Indian Roads Congress. Journal (0046-905X)
Indexed: CRIA, CRICC, GeotechAb, HRIS.
—Linda Hall.
Published by: Indian Roads Congress, The Secretary General, Sector 6, (Near RBI Quarters), R K Puram, New Delhi, 110 022, India. TEL 91-11-26185303, FAX 91-11-26183669, secretarygen@irc.org.in. **Subscr. to:** I N S I O Scientific Books & Periodicals, PO Box 7234, Indraprastha HPO, New Delhi 110 002, India.

388.31 USA
INDIANA L T A P NEWSLETTER. (Local Technical Assistance Program) Text in English. 1982. q. free (effective 2010). back issues avail. **Document type:** *Newsletter, Trade.* **Description:** Covers maintenance techniques, management, engineering and design for local roads and streets.
Former titles (until 2008): Pothole Gazette; (until 19??): H E R P I C C Pothole Gazette; (until 1984): Newsletter of Roads and Streets
Related titles: Online - full text ed.
Published by: (Indiana Local Technical Assistance Program), Purdue University, 1435 Win Hentschel Blvd, B100, West Lafayette, IN 47906. TEL 765-494-2164, 800-428-7639, FAX 765-496-1176, http://www.purdue.edu/. Circ: 3,500.

388.31 USA ISSN 2158-2343
INNOVATOR; accelerating innovation for the American driving experience. Text in English. 2007. bi-m. back issues avail.; reprints avail. **Document type:** *Journal, Trade.* **Description:** Designed for transportation professionals in highway agencies, trade and research groups, academia and the private sector, and the driving public. Advances implementation of innovative technologies and processes in the highway industry.
Related titles: Online - full text ed.: free (effective 2011).
Published by: U.S. Department of Transportation, Federal Highway Administration, c/o Kathleen Bergeron, HIHL, Rm E76-331, 1200 New Jersey Ave, SE, Washington, DC 20590. TEL 202-366-5508, kathleen.bergeron@fhwa.dot.gov.

388.413 DEU
INSTITUT FUER VERKEHR UND STADTBAUWESEN. VEROEFFENTLICHUNGEN. Text in German. 1967. irreg. (approx. 2/yr.). cum.index. **Document type:** *Journal, Academic/Scholarly.*
Formerly: Institut fuer Stadtbauwesen. Veroeffentlichungen (0341-5805)
Indexed: GeoRef, SpeleolAb.
—INIST.
Published by: Institut fuer Verkehr und Stadtbauwesen, T U Braunschweig, Pockelsstr 3, Braunschweig, 38106, Germany. TEL 49-531-391-7929, FAX 49-531-3918100, f.schroeter@tu-bs.de, http://www.tu-bs.de/institute/ivs. Circ: 250.

INSTYTUT BADAWCZY DROG I MOSTOW. PRACE. *see* ENGINEERING

INSURANCE INSTITUTE FOR HIGHWAY SAFETY. STATUS REPORT. *see* PUBLIC HEALTH AND SAFETY

388.1 USA ISSN 0959-6631
INTELLIGENT HIGHWAY; global road transport technology update. Text in English. 1990. s-m. looseleaf. USD 790 combined subscription domestic (print & online eds.); USD 840 combined subscription foreign (print & online eds.) (effective 2008). adv. reprints avail. **Document type:** *Newsletter, Trade.* **Description:** Covers intelligent transport systems and transport telematics.
Related titles: Online - full text ed.: USD 695 (effective 2008).
—IE, Infotrieve. **CCC.**
Published by: B C C Research, 40 Washington St, Wellesley, MA 02481. TEL 866-285-7215, FAX 781-489-7308, sales@bccresearch.com, http://www.bccresearch.com. Ed. Kieran Lindsey. Pub. David Nydam.

388.3 USA
INTERMODAL SURFACE TRANSPORTATION ACT: FLEXIBLE FUNDING OPPORTUNITIES FOR TRANSIT (YEAR). Short title: I S T E A: Flexible Funding Opportunities for Transit (Year). Text in English. a. **Document type:** *Government.* **Description:** Informs state, county, and local officials on the flexible funding opportunities the Surface Transportation Efficiency Act of 1991 offers each year.
Published by: U.S. Federal Transit Administration, Office of Planning, U S Department of Transportation, TGM 20, 400 Seventh St, S W, Rm 9301, Washington, DC 20590. TEL 202-366-2360, FAX 202-366-7951.

625.7 USA
INTERNATIONAL CONFERENCE ON ASPHALT PAVEMENTS. PROCEEDINGS. Text in English. 1963. quinquennial. USD 100. **Document type:** *Proceedings.*
Formerly: International Conference on the Structural Design of Asphalt Pavements. Proceedings (0074-3348)
Published by: International Society for Asphalt Pavements, 2602 Dellana La, Austin, TX 78746. TEL 512-327-4211, FAX 512-328-7246. Ed. Morris C Reinhardt.

388.1 625.7 FRA ISSN 0074-7815
INTERNATIONAL ROAD CONGRESSES. PROCEEDINGS. Text in English. quadrennial (since 1964; 20th 1995, Montreal). **Document type:** *Proceedings.*
Related titles: French ed.
Published by: Association Mondiale de la Route - AIPCR/World Road Association - PIARC, La Grande Arche, Paroi Nord, Niveau 8, Paris La Defense, Cedex 92055, France. TEL 33-1-47968121, FAX 33-1-49000202, piarc@wanadoo.fr, http://www.piarc.org. Ed., Adv. contact Jean-Francois Coste.

388.3 DEU ISSN 0020-9511
HE5
INTERNATIONALES VERKEHRSWESEN; Fachzeitschrift fuer Wissenschaft und Praxis. Text in German. 1949. 10/yr. EUR 146; EUR 15 newsstand/cover (effective 2010). adv. bk.rev. abstr.; bibl.; charts; illus. index. **Document type:** *Magazine, Trade.* **Description:** Technical and scientific publication covering all fields of traffic and transport, including traffic policy, traffic legislation, and traffic and transport related technology.
Incorporates (1968-1990): DDR Verkehr (0011-4820); Formerly: Internationales Archiv fuer Verkehrswesen
Indexed: A22, DokStr, HRIS, IBR, IBZ, KES, RASB, SCIMP, TM.
—IE, Infotrieve, INIST. **CCC.**
Published by: (Deutsche Verkehrswissenschaftliche Gesellschaft e.V.), Deutscher Verkehrs Verlag GmbH, Nordkanalstr 36, Hamburg, 20097, Germany. TEL 49-40-2371401, FAX 49-40-23714205, info@dvv-gruppe.de, http://www.dvv-gruppe.de. Ed. Gerd Aberle. Adv. contact Silke Haertel. B&W page EUR 2,940, color page EUR 3,930; trim 180 x 252. Circ: 4,983 (paid and controlled).

388.4131 GBR ISSN 2042-7204
▼ **INTERTRAFFIC WORLD.** Text in English. 2010. a. free to qualified personnel (effective 2010). adv. **Document type:** *Magazine, Trade.* **Description:** Focuses on the major service and technology disciplines that can be found within the halls of intertraffic, i.e. traffic management, vehicle safety, road infrastructure and parking.
Related titles: Online - full text ed.: free (effective 2010).
Published by: UKIP Media & Events Ltd, Abinger House, Church St, Dorking, Surrey RH4 1DF, United Kingdom. TEL 44-1306-743744, FAX 44-1306-887546, info@ukintpress.com. Ed. Jon Lawson. Adv. contact Mike Robinson TEL 44-1306-742525. Circ: 20,000.

388.4131 CHN
JIAOTONG GUANLI GANBU XUEYUAN XUEBAO. Text in Chinese. 1991. s-a. **Document type:** *Journal, Academic/Scholarly.*
Formerly (until 2008): Beijing Jiaotong Guanli Ganbu Xueyuan Xuebao/ Beijing Communications Management Institute for Executives. Journal (1008-1976)
Published by: Jiaotong Yunshu Bu Jiaotong Guanli Ganbu Xueyuan/ Ministry of Transport of the People's Republic of China. Transportation Management Institute of China, 24, Dongyanjiao Xinggong Xi Dajie, Beijing, 101601, China.

388.4131 CHN ISSN 1673-8098
JIAOTONG JIANSHE YU GUANLI/TRAFFIC CONSTRUCTION AND ADMINISTRATION. Text in Chinese. 1964. m. USD 85.20 (effective 2009). **Document type:** *Journal, Academic/Scholarly.*
Formerly: Shuilu Yunshu Wenzhai/Waterway Transportation Digest (1002-5138)
—East View.
Published by: Jiaotong Bu Kexue Yanjiuyuan, 240, Huixinli, Beijing, 100029, China. TEL 86-10-64912277 ext 2305, FAX 86-10-64972152.

JIAOTONG YUNSHU GONGCHENG XUEBAO/JOURNAL OF TRAFFIC AND TRANSPORTATION ENGINEERING. *see* ENGINEERING—Civil Engineering

388.1 CHN ISSN 1009-6744
JIAOTONG YUNSHU XITONG GONGCHENG YU XINXI. Text in Chinese. 2001. bi-m. USD 53.40 (effective 2009). **Document type:** *Journal, Academic/Scholarly.*
Related titles: Online - full text ed.; English ed.: Journal of Transportation Systems Engineering and Information Technology. ISSN 1570-6672.
Indexed: B21, ESPM, H&SSA, SCOPUS.
—BLDSC (4668.705150), East View. **CCC.**
Address: Zhimen Wai Shangyuancun #3, Beijing, 100044, China. TEL 86-10-51684836, FAX 86-10-51684109. **Dist. by:** China International Book Trading Corp, 35 Chegongzhuang Xilu, Haidian District, PO Box 399, Beijing 100044, China. TEL 86-10-68412045, FAX 86-10-68412023, cibtc@mail.cibtc.com.cn, http://www.cibtc.com.cn.

JURISPRUDENTIEWIJZER VERKEERSRECHT. *see* LAW

▼ **KENGETALLEN ONDERHOUD WEGVERHARDINGEN.** *see* BUSINESS AND ECONOMICS—Accounting

388.4131 JPN ISSN 0910-9749
➤ **KOTSU SHINRIGAKU KENKYU/JAPANESE JOURNAL OF TRAFFIC PSYCHOLOGY.** Text in Japanese. 1985. a. membership. **Document type:** *Journal, Academic/Scholarly.*
—BLDSC (5115.075500).
Published by: Nihon Kotsu Shinri Gakkai/Japanese Association of Traffic Psychology, Yokoyama Bldg, 1-29-4 Shinjuku, Shinjuku-ku, Tokyo, 160-0022, Japan. FAX 81-3-33515120, staff@jatp-web.jp, bch13032@nifty.com.

➤ **KOZUTI ES MELYEPITESI SZEMLE/SCIENTIFIC REVIEW OF CIVIL ENGINEERING.** *see* ENGINEERING—Civil Engineering

656 AUT ISSN 1992-173X
KURATORIUM FUER VERKEHRSSICHERHEIT. RESEARCH LETTER. Text in German. 2006. irreg. **Document type:** *Newsletter, Academic/Scholarly.*
Published by: Kuratorium fuer Verkehrssicherheit, Schleiergasse 18, Vienna, 1100, Austria. TEL 43-1-5770770, FAX 43-1-5770771186, kfv@kfv.at, http://www.kfv.at.

LANDWERK. *see* AGRICULTURE—Crop Production And Soil

388.31 DEU ISSN 0942-4849
LEHRSTUHL FUER VERKEHRS- UND STADTPLANUNG. SCHRIFTENREIHE. Text in German; Summaries in English, German. 1991. irreg. back issues avail. **Document type:** *Academic/Scholarly.*
Published by: (Lehrstuhl fuer Verkehrs- und Stadtplanung), Technische Universitaet Muenchen, Arcisstr 21, Munich, 80290, Germany. TEL 49-89-28922438, FAX 49-89-285577. Ed. Dr. Peter Kirchhoff.

388.4131 GBR
LEICESTERSHIRE CITY COUNCIL. LOCAL TRANSPORT PLAN. ANNUAL PROGRESS REPORT. Text in English. 2001. a.
Published by: Leicester City Council, New Walk Centre, Welford Pl, Leicester, LE1 6ZG, United Kingdom. TEL 44-116-2657095, tps@leics.gov.uk.

388.31 DEU ISSN 0939-3188
LEXIKON STRASSENVERKEHRSRECHTLICHER ENTSCHEIDUNGEN. Text in German. 1955. base vol. plus updates 2/yr. looseleaf. EUR 58 base vol(s).; EUR 19.80 updates per issue (effective 2009). **Document type:** *Monographic series, Trade.*
Published by: Erich Schmidt Verlag GmbH & Co. (Berlin), Genthiner Str 30 G, Berlin, 10785, Germany. TEL 49-30-2500850, FAX 49-30-250085305, vertrieb@esvmedien.de, http://www.erich-schmidt-verlag.de.

LIIKENNETURVA. REPORTS. *see* PUBLIC HEALTH AND SAFETY

LIIKENNETURVA. TUTKIMUKSIA. *see* PUBLIC HEALTH AND SAFETY

363.7 GBR ISSN 1366-2694
LINACRE LECTURES. Text in English. 199?. irreg., latest 2004. price varies. **Document type:** *Monographic series, Academic/Scholarly.*
—BLDSC (5220.160000). **CCC.**
Published by: Oxford University Press, Great Clarendon St, Oxford, OX2 6DP, United Kingdom. TEL 44-1865-556767, FAX 44-1865-556646, enquiry@oup.co.uk, http://www.oup-usa.org/catalogs/general/series/, http://www.oup.co.uk/.

LINKS UND RECHTS DER AUTOBAHN. *see* HOTELS AND RESTAURANTS

388.31 GBR ISSN 1465-5780
LONDON CYCLIST. Text in English. 19??. bi-m. free to members (effective 2009). adv. bk.rev. back issues avail. **Document type:** *Magazine, Consumer.* **Description:** Includes practical information, news and views on all issues of interest to cyclists in London; provides updates on campaigning for better conditions for cyclists and gives a voice to the typical urban cyclists.
Formerly (until 1990): Daily Cyclist
—BLDSC (5293.200500).
Published by: London Cycling Campaign, 2 Newhams Row, London, SE1 3UZ, United Kingdom. TEL 44-20-72349310, 44-20-72349319, office@lcc.org.uk. Adv. contact Matt Styrka TEL 44-20-73060300 ext 112.

388.312 692.8 USA ISSN 0024-7030
LOW BIDDER. Text in English. 1928. bi-m. USD 25. adv. illus.; mkt. **Document type:** *Magazine, Trade.* **Description:** Provides highway contracting technical and news information.
Published by: Associated General Contractors of America, N.Y. State Chapter, 1900 Western Ave, Albany, NY 12203. TEL 518-456-1134, FAX 518-456-1198. Ed., R&P, Adv. contact Liz Elvin. Circ: 1,700 (controlled).

388.1 DEU
▼ **MARKTPLATZ STRASSENWESEN.** Text in German. 2009. biennial. EUR 22.50 newsstand/cover (effective 2011). adv. **Document type:** *Directory, Trade.*
Published by: Kirschbaum Verlag GmbH, Siegfriedstr 28, Bonn, 53179, Germany. TEL 49-228-954530, FAX 49-228-9545327, info@kirschbaum.de, http://www.kirschbaum.de. Circ: 14,000 (paid and controlled).

388.3 USA ISSN 0094-6265
MARYLAND. STATE HIGHWAY ADMINISTRATION. TRAFFIC TRENDS. Key Title: Traffic Trends. Text in English. 1963. a. free. stat. **Document type:** *Government.*
Published by: State Highway Administration, Department of Transportation, 707 Calvert St, Baltimore, MD 21203. TEL 410-545-5511, FAX 410-545-1023. Ed. Mike Baxter. Circ: 200 (controlled).

MASKINKONTAKT. *see* MACHINERY

388.4131 AUS
MONASH UNIVERSITY ACCIDENT RESEARCH CENTRE. CONSULTANTS' REPORTS SERIES. Text in English. 1979. irreg., latest 2006. back issues avail.
Former titles: Australian Transport Safety Bureau. Road Safety Research Report (1445-4467); (until 199?): C R Canberra (0810-770X)
Related titles: Online - full text ed.: free (effective 2009).
—BLDSC (7996.479100).
Published by: Monash University, Accident Research Centre, Bldg 70, Melbourne, VIC 3800, Australia. TEL 61-3-99054371, FAX 61-3-99054363, enquire@muarc.monash.edu.au, http://www.monash.edu.au/muarc/.

388.4131 AUS
MONASH UNIVERSITY ACCIDENT RESEARCH CENTRE. MINOR REPORTS SERIES. Text in English. 1989. irreg., latest 1996. back issues avail. **Document type:** *Report, Trade.*
Related titles: Online - full text ed.: free (effective 2009).
Published by: Monash University, Accident Research Centre, Bldg 70, Melbourne, VIC 3800, Australia. TEL 61-3-99054371, FAX 61-3-99054363, enquire@muarc.monash.edu.au, http://www.monash.edu.au/muarc/.

388.4131 AUS
MONASH UNIVERSITY ACCIDENT RESEARCH CENTRE. OTHER REPORTS SERIES. Text in English. 1979. irreg., latest 2008. back issues avail. **Document type:** *Report, Trade.*
Related titles: Online - full text ed.: free (effective 2009).
Published by: Monash University, Accident Research Centre, Bldg 70, Melbourne, VIC 3800, Australia. TEL 61-3-99054371, FAX 61-3-99054363, enquire@muarc.monash.edu.au, http://www.monash.edu.au/muarc/.

MOT - BAU; Baumaschinen Baufahrzeuge Baustoffe Baulogistik. *see* ENGINEERING—Civil Engineering

MOTOR AND TRAFFIC LAW NEW SOUTH WALES. *see* LAW—Civil Law

MOTOR & TRAFFIC LAW - VICTORIA. *see* LAW—Civil Law

MOTOR VEHICLE LAW. QUEENSLAND. *see* LAW

MOTOR VEHICLE LAW SOUTH AUSTRALIA. *see* LAW—Civil Law

388.4131 310 CAN ISSN 1719-3842
N W T TRAFFIC COLLISION FACTS. (Northwest Territories) Text in English. 1989. a. **Document type:** *Government.*
Formerly (until 2004): N W T Traffic Accident Facts (1714-2695)
Published by: Northwest Territories, Department of Transportation, Road Licensing and Safety Division (Subsidiary of: Northwest Territories, Department of Transportation), PO Box 1320, Yellowknife, NT X1A 2L9, Canada. TEL 867-873-7406, FAX 867-873-0120, http://www.gov.nt.ca/Transportation.

625.7 388.31 USA ISSN 0077-5614
TE7 CODEN: NCHRDA
NATIONAL COOPERATIVE HIGHWAY RESEARCH PROGRAM REPORTS. Text in English. 1964. irreg., latest no.670, 2010. price varies. illus. back issues avail.; reprints avail. **Document type:** *Monographic series, Trade.* **Description:** Contains research project materials such as appendixes, which describes technical details, information-gathering activities, or survey instruments, glossaries and bibliographies.
Related titles: Microfiche ed.; Online - full text ed.: free (effective 2010).
Indexed: A22, DokStr, GeoRef, HRIS, SpeleolAb.
—BLDSC (6021.863000), IE, Ingenta, Linda Hall.
Published by: U.S. National Research Council, Transportation Research Board, The National Academies, 500 Fifth St, NW, Washington, DC 20001. TEL 202-334-3213, FAX 202-334-2519, TRBsales@nas.edu.

625.7 USA ISSN 0547-5570
CODEN: NCHSBB
NATIONAL COOPERATIVE HIGHWAY RESEARCH PROGRAM SYNTHESIS OF HIGHWAY PRACTICE. Text in English. 1969. irreg., latest no.408, 2010. price varies. back issues avail. **Document type:** *Monographic series, Trade.* **Description:** Provides reports on the state of the practice based on literature reviews and surveys of recent activities in critical areas.
Related titles: Microfiche ed.; Online - full text ed.: free (effective 2010).
Indexed: A22, DokStr, GeoRef, HRIS, SpeleolAb.
—BLDSC (6021.866000), IE, Ingenta, Linda Hall.
Published by: U.S. National Research Council, Transportation Research Board, The National Academies, 500 Fifth St, NW, Washington, DC 20001. TEL 202-334-3213, FAX 202-334-2519, TRBsales@nas.edu. **Co-sponsor:** American Association of State Highway and Transportation Officials.

388.3 GBR ISSN 0260-7735
NATIONAL COUNCIL ON INLAND TRANSPORT. NEWSLETTER. Text in English. 196?. irreg. (2-3/yr.). free to members (effective 2009). back issues avail. **Document type:** *Newsletter, Trade.*
Formerly (until 1978): Civilised Transport
Published by: National Council on Inland Transport, c/o Derek Leggetter, 6 Merrivale Ave, Redbridge, Ilford, Essex IG4 5PO, United Kingdom. http://www.ncit.org.uk.

388.4 NZL ISSN 1176-1024
NATIONAL LAND TRANSPORT PROGRAMME. Text in English. 1990. a. **Document type:** *Handbook/Manual/Guide, Trade.*
Former titles (until 2003): National Roading Program (1174-2151); (until 1997): Transit New Zealand. National Land Transport Programme (1170-2761)
Related titles: Online - full text ed.: ISSN 1177-8504.
Published by: New Zealand Transport Agency, Lambton Quay, PO Box 5084, Wellington, 6145, New Zealand. TEL 64-4-8945200, FAX 64-4-8943305, info@nzta.govt.nz, http://www.nzta.govt.nz/.

625.7 388 USA ISSN 0360-859X
HE131 CODEN: SRTBDC
NATIONAL RESEARCH COUNCIL. TRANSPORTATION RESEARCH BOARD. SPECIAL REPORT. Text in English. 1952. irreg., latest no.301, 2010. price varies. illus. back issues avail.; reprints avail. **Document type:** *Monographic series, Government.* **Description:** Addresses transportation policy issues of national significance.
Formerly (until no.144, 1974): National Research Council. Highway Research Board. Special Report (0077-5622)
Related titles: Microfiche ed.; Microfilm ed.: (from BHP); Online - full text ed.: free (effective 2010).
Indexed: ConcrAb, DokStr, GeoRef, GeotechAb, HRIS, SCOPUS, SpeleolAb.
—BLDSC (8401.007800), CASDDS, Ingenta, Linda Hall.
Published by: U.S. National Research Council, Transportation Research Board, The National Academies, 500 Fifth St, NW, Washington, DC 20001. TEL 202-334-3213, FAX 202-334-2519, TRBsales@nas.edu.

NEBRASKA. DEPARTMENT OF ROADS. NEBRASKA SELECTED TRANSPORTATION STATISTICS. *see* TRANSPORTATION—Abstracting, Bibliographies, Statistics

388 USA ISSN 0091-844X
HE371.N25
NEBRASKA. DEPARTMENT OF ROADS. TRAFFIC ANALYSIS UNIT. CONTINUOUS TRAFFIC COUNT DATA AND TRAFFIC CHARACTERISTICS ON NEBRASKA STREETS AND HIGHWAYS. Text in English. 1968. a. free. **Description:** Contains traffic data from permanent counter, organized by day, hour, and vehicle type.
Published by: Department of Roads, Transportation Planning Division, 1500 Nebraska Hwy 2, Box 94759, Lincoln, NE 68509-4759. TEL 402-471-4567, FAX 402-479-4325. Circ: (controlled).

388.31 USA
NEBRASKA HIGHWAY PROGRAM. Text in English. 1970. a. free. charts; illus.; stat. **Document type:** *Government.*
Former titles: Challenge of the 80's; Focus on Nebraska Highways
Media: Duplicated (not offset).
Published by: Nebraska Department of Roads, 1500 NE Hwy 2, Box 94759, Lincoln, NE 68509-4759. TEL 402-479-4512, FAX 402-479-4325. Circ: 3,850 (controlled).

625.7 388.31 USA ISSN 0028-5242
NEW HAMPSHIRE HIGHWAYS. Text in English. 1970 (vol.25). bi-m. USD 25 (effective 2004). adv. bk.rev. bibl.; charts; illus.; stat.; tr.lit. **Document type:** *Magazine, Trade.*
Published by: New Hampshire Good Roads Association, Inc., 261 Sheep Davis Rd, Ste 5, Concord, NH 03301-5750. TEL 603-224-1823, FAX 603-224-9399. Ed. Brenda Clemons. Circ: 1,000 (paid and controlled).

NEW JERSEY CRIMINAL LAW AND MOTOR VEHICLE HANDBOOK. *see* LAW—Criminal Law

NEW YORK CITY TRAFFIC RULES AND REGULATIONS. *see* LAW

338.413 BEL
NIEUWSBRIEF VERKEERSPECIALIST. Text in Flemish. s-m. Supplement avail. **Description:** Provides information on traffic legislation and technical aspects of traffic control.
Published by: C E D Samsom (Subsidiary of: Wolters Samsom Belgie n.v.), Kouterveld 14, Diegem, 1831, Belgium. TEL 32-2-7231111.

354.485 SWE ISSN 1101-5179
NORDIC ROAD & TRANSPORT RESEARCH; news from Denmark, Finland, Iceland, Norway, and Sweden. Text in English. 1989. 3/yr. SEK 150 in Scandinavia; free elsewhere (effective 2003). 32 p./no. 3 cols./p.; **Document type:** *Journal, Academic/Scholarly.* **Description:** Latest research findings from 6 public research organizations in Denmark, Finland, Iceland, Norway, and Sweden.
Incorporates (1982-1988): V T I Topics (Vaeg och Trafik Institutet) (0280-896X)
Related titles: Online - full text ed.: free (effective 2011).
Indexed: A39, C27, C29, D03, D04, E13, GeoRef, HRIS, R14, S14, S15, S18.
Published by: (Vejdirektoratet/The Danish Road Directorate DNK, Transportoekonomisk Institutt/Institute of Transport Economics NOR, Vegdirektoratet, Statens Vegvesen (SVV)/Norwegian Directorate of Public Roads (NRPA) NOR, Vegagerdin/Public Roads Administration (PRA), Iceland ISL, V T T Rakennus-Ja Yhdyskunta-Tekniikka/V T T Building and Transport FIN), Statens Vaeg- och Transportforskningsinstitut/Swedish National Road and Transport Research Institute, Linkoeping, 58195, Sweden. TEL 46-13-204000, FAX 46-13-141436. Eds. Thomas Lange, Tarja Magnusson.

388.1 DEU
NORDVERKEHR. Text in German. 10/yr. adv. **Document type:** *Magazine, Trade.*
Published by: S V G - Strassenverkehrsgenossenschaft Hamburg e G, Bullerdeich 36, Hamburg, 20537, Germany. TEL 49-40-254500, FAX 49-40-25450301, info@svg-hamburg.de, http://www.svg-hamburg.de. adv.: B&W page EUR 695, color page EUR 1,442; trim 183 x 262. Circ: 1,200 (controlled).

388 614 USA
NORTH DAKOTA'S HIGHWAY SAFETY PLAN. Text in English. 1967. a. looseleaf. free to qualified personnel. **Document type:** *Government.*
Formerly: North Dakota's Highway Safety Work Programs
Published by: Department of Transportation, Driver's License and Traffic Safety, Traffic Safety Programs Section, 608 E Blvd Ave, Bismarck, ND 58505-0700. TEL 701-224-2600, FAX 701-224-4545. Circ: 150 (controlled).

388.4131 310 AUS ISSN 1838-5710
NORTHERN TERRITORY. DEPARTMENT OF LANDS AND PLANNING. ANNUAL TRAFFIC REPORT. Variant title: Northern Territory. Department of Lands and Planning. Transport Group. Annual Traffic Report. Text in English. 2003. a. back issues avail. **Document type:** *Report, Government.* **Description:** Provides the provision of traffic statistics pertaining to roads managed by the Northern Territory Government.
Media: Online - full text.
Published by: Northern Territory, Department of Lands and Planning, GPO Box 2520, Darwin, N.T. 0801, Australia. TEL 61-8-89995511, FAX 61-8-89247044, feedback.dpi@nt.gov.au, http://www.nt.gov.au/dpi/.

388.3 AUT
OESTERREICHISCHE VERKEHRSWISSENSCHAFTLICHE GESELLSCHAFT. MITTEILUNGEN. Text in German; Summaries in French, English. 1951. irreg. adv. bk.rev. bibl.; charts. **Document type:** *Journal, Trade.*
Published by: Oesterreichische Verkehrswissenschaftliche Gesellschaft, Kolingasse 13/2/7, Vienna, W 1090, Austria. TEL 43-1-5879727, FAX 43-1-5853615, office@oevg.at, http://www.oevg.at. Ed. Otto Seidelmann.

388.31 624 USA ISSN 0030-0861
OHIO CONTRACTOR. Text in English. 1961. bi-m. USD 25 to members; USD 30 to non-members (effective 2005). adv. bk.rev. charts; illus. **Document type:** *Magazine, Trade.* **Description:** Focuses on job stories, new equipment, industry trends and articles on individuals in the field,.
Published by: Ohio Contractors Association, PO Box 909, Columbus, OH 43216-0000. TEL 614-488-0724, FAX 614-846-8763, info@ohiocontractors.org, http://www.ohiocontractors.org/. Ed. C Clark Street. Adv. contact Carrie Silverstein. page USD 897. Circ: 5,000 (paid and controlled).

388.1 USA
OKLAHOMA. DEPARTMENT OF TRANSPORTATION. SUFFICIENCY RATING REPORT AND NEEDS STUDY: OKLAHOMA STATE TRANSPORTATION. Text in English. 1966. biennial. free. illus. **Document type:** *Government.*
Formerly: Oklahoma. Department of Highways. Sufficiency Rating Report and Needs Study: Oklahoma State Highways (0094-6230)
Published by: Department of Transportation, Planning Division, 200 N E 21st, Oklahoma City, OK 73105. TEL 405-521-2705, FAX 405-521-6917. Circ: 200.

388.31 USA
OKLAHOMA TURNPIKE AUTHORITY. ANNUAL REPORT TO THE GOVERNOR. Text in English. 1954. a. free. charts; stat.
Published by: Turnpike Authority, 3500 Martin Luther King Blvd, Box 11357, Oklahoma City, OK 73136-0357. TEL 405-425-3600, FAX 405-427-8246. Circ: 1,000.

388.31 USA
OKLAHOMA TURNPIKE AUTHORITY. REPORT TO BONDHOLDERS. Text in English. a.
Published by: Turnpike Authority, 3500 Martin Luther King Blvd, Box 11357, Oklahoma City, OK 73136-0357. TEL 405-425-3600, FAX 405-427-8246.

388.1 ITA ISSN 1120-6276
ONDAVERDE. Text in Italian. 1989. 6/yr. **Document type:** *Magazine, Trade.*
Published by: Associazione Italiana per l'Ingegneria del Traffico e dei Transporti (A I I T), Via Magenta 5, Rome, 00185, Italy. TEL 39-06-46959209, FAX 39-06-46959540, http://www.aiit.it.

ONTARIO HIGHWAY TRANSPORT BOARD. ANNUAL REPORT. *see* PUBLIC ADMINISTRATION

388.1 IND
ORISSA STATE ROAD TRANSPORTATION CORPORATION. ANNUAL ADMINISTRATION REPORT. Text in English. 1974. a. stat. **Document type:** *Report, Trade.*
Published by: State Road Transportation Corporation, Paribahan Bhavan, Sachivalaya Marg, Bhubaneswar, Orissa 753 001, India. TEL 91-674-530208, FAX 91-674-530719, osrtc@orissa.nic.in, http://www.rtiorissa.gov.in/.

388.1 GBR ISSN 0951-8797
OVERSEAS ROAD NOTE. Text in English. 1981. irreg. price varies. back issues avail. **Document type:** *Monographic series, Academic/Scholarly.*
—CCC.
Published by: Transport Research Laboratory, Crowthorne House, Nine Mile Ride, Wokingham, Berks RG40 3GA, United Kingdom. TEL 44-1344-773131, FAX 44-1344-770356, enquiries@trl.co.uk, http://www.trl.co.uk.

P C M - LE PONT. *see* ENGINEERING—Civil Engineering

351 GBR ISSN 0960-9938
P T R C PERSPECTIVES. (Planning and Transport Research and Computation) Text in English. 1991. irreg., latest vol.4, 2000. price varies. **Document type:** *Monographic series, Trade.*
—BLDSC (6946.603500). **CCC.**
Published by: P T R C Education and Research Services Ltd., 1 Vernon Mews, Vernon St, London, W14 0RL, United Kingdom. TEL 44-20-73481970, FAX 44-20-73481989, info@ptrc-training.co.uk.

388.411 DEU
PARKEN AKTUELL; Das Magazin fuer Parkraum - Management, Konzeption, Technik. Text in German. 1992. q. EUR 22; EUR 6 newsstand/cover (effective 2011). adv. **Document type:** *Magazine, Trade.*
Formerly: Parkhaus Aktuell
Published by: (Bundesverband Parken e.V.), Maenken Kommunikation GmbH, Von-der-Wettern-Str 25, Cologne, 51149, Germany. TEL 49-2203-35840, FAX 49-2203-3584185, info@maenken.com, http://www.maenken.com. Ed. Marko Ruh. Adv. contact Wolfgang Locker. Circ: 3,700 (controlled).

388 352 690 624 GBR ISSN 1470-8361
PARKING NEWS. Text in English. 1969. 11/yr. free to members (effective 2009). bk.rev. tr.lit. 60 p./no.; **Document type:** *Journal, Trade.* **Description:** Aimed at local authority, central government, world parking associations, private and commercial sectors, security industry, hospitals, airports, universities, consultancies, architects, and other persons/organizations interested in the parking of vehicles.
Formerly (until 1988): Parking Newsletter
Published by: British Parking Association, Stuart House, 41-43 Perrymount Rd, Haywards Heath, W Sussex RH16 3BN, United Kingdom. TEL 44-1444-447300, FAX 44-1444-454105, info@britishparking.co.uk, http://www.britishparking.co.uk. Ed. Simon O Brien. Adv. contact Richard Langrish.

PAVEMENT (FORT ATKINSON); maintenance & reconstruction. *see* ENGINEERING—Civil Engineering

PAVING AND TRANSPORTATION CONFERENCE. PROCEEDINGS. *see* ENGINEERING—Civil Engineering

388 USA ISSN 1944-8848
PEDESTRIAN FORUM. Variant title: Pedestrian Forum Newsletter. Text in English. 1997. q. free (effective 2011). back issues avail. **Document type:** *Newsletter, Government.* **Description:** Aims to improve highway safety by reducing highway fatalities and injuries by 20 percent in ten years.
Media: Online - full text.
Published by: U.S. Federal Highway Administration (Subsidiary of: U.S. Department of Transportation), 1200 New Jersey Ave, SE, Washington, DC 20590. TEL 202-366-4000, execsecretariat.fhwa@fhwa.dot.gov, http://www.fhwa.dot.gov.

625.7 USA ISSN 0079-8142
PURDUE UNIVERSITY. ROAD SCHOOL. PROCEEDINGS OF ANNUAL ROAD SCHOOL. Text in English. 1924. a. **Document type:** *Proceedings.*
Related titles: Series: Engineering Bulletin. Engineering Extension Series.
Published by: Purdue University, School of Civil Engineering, 1284 Civil Engineering Building, W. Lafayette, IN 47907-1284. TEL 317-494-2211, FAX 317-496-1105. Ed. K C Sinha. Circ: 2,500.

625.7 388.1 BGR ISSN 1310-6848
PUTISHTA/ROADS. Text in Bulgarian; Summaries in English. 1961. bi-m. USD 10 (effective 1997). adv. bk.rev. **Document type:** *Bulletin, Government.* **Description:** Scientific and technical magazine highlighting problems in the field of research, design, construction, repair, maintenance and operation of roads, bridges and tunnels, as well as of road construction equipment.
Indexed: BSLGeo.
Published by: Ministerstvo na Transporta, Glavno Upravlenie na Putishchata, 3 Macedonia blvd, Sofia, 1606, Bulgaria. TEL 359-2-521354, FAX 359-2-9806151, TELEX 22679 GUP BG. Ed., R&P Tanya Kremencka. Adv. contact Kristina Daskalova. Circ: 1,500 (paid). **Dist. by:** Roads Agency, 3 Macedonia pl, Sofia 1000, Bulgaria.

388.1 CHN ISSN 1672-6189
QINGHAI JIAOTONG KEJI. Text in Chinese. 1988. bi-m. CNY 10 newsstand/cover (effective 2006). **Document type:** *Journal, Academic/Scholarly.*
Related titles: Online - full text ed.
Published by: Qinghai Sheng Gonglu Xuehui, 72, Wu-Xi Dajie, Xining, 810008, China. TEL 86-971-6116598 ext 66312.

R C: REVISTA DE RESPONSABILIDAD CIVIL, CIRCULACION Y SEGURO. *see* LAW

388.1 USA ISSN 2157-796X
R S A NEWSLETTER. (Road Safety Audits) Text in English. 2008. q. free (effective 2010). back issues avail. **Document type:** *Newsletter, Government.* **Description:** Includes an overview of State RSA programs, current resources to assist you in performing RSAs, and a compilation of RSA-related news stories.
Media: Online - full text.
Published by: U.S. Department of Transportation, Federal Highway Administration, c/o Karen Timpone, Office of Safety HSSI, E71 318, 1200 New Jersey Ave, SE, Washington, DC 20590. TEL 202-366-2327, Karen.Timpone@dot.gov.

388.31 AUT
DAS RECHT DES KRAFTFAHRERS. Text in German. 1980. m. **Document type:** *Bulletin, Consumer.*
Published by: Verlag Dr. Herta Ranner, Zeismannsbrunngasse 1, Vienna, W 1070, Austria. TEL 43-1-5235387, FAX 43-1-52353874.

REFERATIVNYI ZHURNAL. AVTOMOBIL'NYE DOROGI. OTDEL'NYI VYPUSK. *see* TRANSPORTATION—Abstracting, Bibliographies, Statistics

REFERATIVNYI ZHURNAL. GORODSKOI TRANSPORT; vypusk svodnogo toma. *see* TRANSPORTATION—Abstracting, Bibliographies, Statistics

388 SWE ISSN 0284-0707
REFLEXEN. Text in Swedish. 1983. 7/yr. SEK 150 to members (effective 1999). adv. bk.rev. **Document type:** *Newsletter.*
Published by: T F - Trafiktekniska Foereningen, c/o Aasa vaegland, Ed, Inregia, Fack 12519, Stockholm, 10229, Sweden. TEL 46-8-737-4400. R&P, Adv. contact Aasa Vaegland. Circ: 1,000.

388.4131 CHN
RENMIN GONGAN BAO. JIAOTONG ANQUAN ZHOUKAN. Text in Chinese. w. CNY 61.20 (effective 2004). **Document type:** *Newspaper, Government.*
Related titles: Online - full content ed.
Published by: Renmin Gongan Baoshe, Fengtai-qu, 15, Fangzhuang Fangxingyuan, Beijing, 100078, China. **Dist. by:** China International Book Trading Corp, 35 Chegongzhuang Xilu, Haidian District, PO Box 399, Beijing 100044, China. TEL 86-10-68412045, FAX 86-10-68412023, cibtc@mail.cibtc.com.cn, http://www.cibtc.com.cn.

385.1 GBR
REPORTED ROAD CASUALTIES GREAT BRITAIN. Text in English. 1969. a., latest 2009. GBP 40 (effective 2010). stat. back issues avail. **Document type:** *Government.* **Description:** Presents detailed statistics about the circumstances of personal injury road accidents.
Former titles (until 2009): Road Casualties Great Britain; (until 2002): Road Accidents in Great Britain (0307-6822)
—CCC.
Published by: (Great Britain. Office for National Statistics, Great Britain. Department for Transport), The Stationery Office, St Crispins, Duke St, Norwich, NR3 1PD, United Kingdom. TEL 44-1603-622211, customer.services@tso.co.uk, http://www.tso.co.uk. **Subscr. to:** PO Box 29, Norwich NR3 1GN, United Kingdom. TEL 44-870-6005522, FAX 44-870-6005533, subscriptions@tso.co.uk.

388.1 BRA
REVISTA RODOVIARIA. Text in Portuguese. 1972. m. illus.

Published by: Departamento Autonomo del Estradas de Rodagem, Divisao de Servicos Especiais, Av Borges de Medeiros, 1555, Pr Belas, Porto Alegre, RGS 90110-150, Brazil.

387.73 FRA ISSN 1290-256X
TE2
REVUE GENERALE DES ROUTES. Text in French; Summaries in English, French, Spanish. 1926. 11/yr. EUR 250 in Europe; EUR 260 elsewhere; EUR 75 to students (effective 2009). adv. bk.rev. abstr.; bibl.; charts; illus. index. **Document type:** *Newspaper.*
Former titles (until 1996): Revue Generale des Routes et des Aerodromes (0035-3191); (until 1948): Revue Generale des Routes et de la Circulation Routiere (1155-7621)
Indexed: DokStr, GeoRef, GeotechAb, HRIS, ICEA, RefZh, SoftAbEng, SpeleolAb.
—IE, Infotrieve, INIST, Linda Hall.
Published by: Revue Generale des Routes et des Aerodromes, 9 rue Magellan, Paris, 75008, France. TEL 33-1-40738003, FAX 33-1-49520180. Ed. Marie Francoise Ossola. Pub. Francois Bonis Charancle. R&P Marie-Francoise Ossola. Circ: 3,250.

RIJ - INSTRUCTIE; onafhankelijk vakblad voor de verkeersopleiding. *see* EDUCATION—Adult Education

388.1 GBR
ROAD CASUALTIES IN GREAT BRITAIN. QUARTERLY PROVISIONAL ESTIMATES. Text in English. q. free (effective 2009). Index. back issues avail. **Document type:** *Bulletin, Government.* **Description:** Provides statistics on road casualties in personal injury road accidents reported to the police in Great Britain for each quarter.
Former titles (until 1996): Quarterly Road Casualties Great Britain (0951-2071); (until 1985): Road Accidents and Casualties in Great Britain
Related titles: Online - full text ed.
—CCC.
Published by: Great Britain. Department for Transport, Great Minster House, 76 Marsham St, London, SW1P 4DR, United Kingdom. TEL 44-20-79443078, FAX 44-20-79449643, publications@communities.gsi.gov.uk.

385.21 AUS ISSN 1449-1168
ROAD DEATHS AUSTRALIA. Text in English. 1994. m. free (effective 2008). back issues avail. **Document type:** *Bulletin, Government.*
Former titles (until 2004): Road Fatalities Australia (Online); (until 2003): Road Fatalities Australia (Print) (1323-3688)
Media: Online - full text.
Published by: Australian Government. Department Of Infrastructure, Transport, Regional Development And Local Government, Infrastructure and Surface Transport Policy Division, GPO Box 594, Canberra, ACT 2601, Australia. roadsafety@infrastructure.gov.au, http://www.atsb.gov.au/.

388.1 GBR ISSN 2045-2942
ROAD FILE. Text in English. 2002. a. GBP 10 per issue (effective 2010). **Document type:** *Trade.* **Description:** Provides useful information to improve the UK's network of roads, footways and cycle paths, for the people and goods to travel freely without getting caught in unnecessary jams.
Related titles: Online - full text ed.: free (effective 2010).
Published by: Road Users Allian, Delegate House, 30A Hart St, Henley-on-Thames, Oxon RG9 2AL, United Kingdom. TEL 44-1491-578761, FAX 44-1491-579835.

388.1 340 ZAF ISSN 1682-0746
ROAD TRAFFIC AND TRANSPORT LIBRARY. Variant title: Juta's Road Traffic and Transport Library. Text in English, Afrikaans. 2000. m. ZAR 1,118 single user; ZAR 560 per additional user (effective 2006).
Media: Online - full text. **Related titles:** CD-ROM ed.: ISSN 1024-2503.
Published by: Juta & Company Ltd., Juta Law, PO Box 14373, Lansdowne, 7779, South Africa. TEL 27-21-7970121, FAX 27-11-7970121, cserv@juta.co.za, http://www.jutalaw.co.za.

388.1 GBR ISSN 0306-5286
KD2595.A2
ROAD TRAFFIC REPORTS. Text in English. 1970. bi-m. GBP 367, EUR 484, USD 631 (effective 2012). cum.index. **Document type:** *Report, Trade.* **Description:** Contains reports of decisions in higher courts on road traffic law.
Related titles: Online - full text ed.: 1970.
—BLDSC (7997.130000). **CCC.**
Published by: Sweet & Maxwell Ltd. (Subsidiary of: Thomson Reuters Corp.), 100 Avenue Rd, London, NW3 3PF, United Kingdom. TEL 44-20-73937000, FAX 44-20-74491144, sweetandmaxwell.customer.services@thomson.com. Eds. Carol Ellis, Clare Noon. **Subscr. to:** PO Box 1000, Andover SP10 9AF, United Kingdom. TEL 44-20-73938051, sweetandmaxwell.international.queries@thomson.com.

388.1 NZL ISSN 1176-9297
ROAD USER CHARGES. Text in English. 2005. a. **Document type:** *Newsletter, Trade.*
Published by: New Zealand Transport Agency, Lambton Quay, PO Box 5084, Wellington, 6145, New Zealand. TEL 64-4-8945200, FAX 64-4-8943305, info@nzta.govt.nz, http://www.nzta.govt.nz/.

388.1 GBR ISSN 2044-7442
ROADS AND ROAD TRANSPORT HISTORY ASSOCIATION. JOURNAL. Text in English. 1991. q. free to members (effective 2010). back issues avail. **Document type:** *Journal, Trade.*
Formerly (until 2009): Roads and Road Transport History Association. Newsletter (1750-9408)
Published by: Roads and Road Transport History Association, c/o P Jaques, Secretary, 21, The Oaklands, Droitwich, WR9 0QE, United Kingdom. enquiries@rrtha.org.uk. Ed. Roy Larkin.

388.4131 AUS ISSN 1833-1769
ROADS AND TRAFFIC AUTHORITY OF N S W. RESEARCH REPORT. Variant title: R T A of N S W. Research Report. Text in English. 1986. irreg. free (effective 2008). **Document type:** *Monographic series, Government.* **Description:** Provides roads and traffic authority of New South Wales.
Former titles (until 1996): Roads and Traffic Authority of NSW, Road Safety and Traffic Management Directorate. Research Note (1324-079X); (until 1994): Roads and Traffic Authority (NSW). Road Safety Bureau. Research Note (1035-5855); (until 1988): Traffic Authority, New South Wales. Research Note (1032-6669); Traffic Authority of New South Wales. Traffic Accident Research Unit. Research Note

Published by: Roads and Traffic Authority of N S W, PO Box K198, Haymarket, NSW 1240, Australia. TEL 61-2-92186888, FAX 61-2-92186286, Communication_Enquiries@rta.nsw.gov.au, http://www.rta.nsw.gov.au.

388 FRA ISSN 1156-4865
ROUTE ACTUALITE/ROAD NEWS; chantiers, procedes, produits, materiels, techniques nouvelles. Text in English, French. 8/yr. EUR 67 domestic; EUR 85 foreign (effective 2009). adv. tr.lit. **Document type:** *Magazine, Trade.* **Description:** Covers topical methods and equipment for road construction, activities or regional road constructors and reference sites.
Indexed: RefZh.
Published by: (Societe Technique d'Editions pour l'Entreprise), Groupe Chantiers de France, Bord de Seine, 202 quai de Clichy, Clichy, 92110, France. TEL 33-1-47561723, FAX 33-1-47561432, contact@chantiersdefrance.com, http://www.chantiersdefrance.com. Ed., Pub. Arlette Surchamp. Adv. contact Karine Colin. Circ: 8,000.

388.1 CAN ISSN 0319-3780
TE2R6
ROUTES ET TRANSPORTS. Text in French. 1971. 4/yr. CAD 50, USD 10. adv. bk.rev. back issues avail. **Document type:** *Journal, Academic/Scholarly.*
Formerly: Routes du Quebec
Indexed: HRIS, PdeR.
Published by: Association Quebecoise du Transport et des Routes Inc., 1595 rue Saint Hubert, Montreal, PQ H2L 3Z2, Canada. TEL 514-523-6444, FAX 514-523-2666. Ed. Jean Audet. Adv. contact Marie Josee Huot. B&W page CAD 850, color page CAD 1,125; trim 10 x 7.5. Circ: 2,000.

388.1 FRA ISSN 1011-1891
ROUTES - ROADS. Text in English, French. 1911. 4/yr. USD 51 (effective 2000). adv. illus. back issues avail.
Formerly: Association Internationale Permanente des Congres de la Route. Bulletin (0004-556X)
Indexed: DokStr, GeotechAb, HRIS, SpeleolAb.
—BLDSC (7997.451000), IE, Ingenta.
Published by: Association Mondiale de la Route - AIPCR/World Road Association - PIARC, La Grande Arche, Paroi Nord, Niveau 8, Paris La Defense, Cedex 92055, France. TEL 33-1-47968121, FAX 33-1-49000202, piarc@wanadoo.fr, http://www.piarc.org. Ed., Adv. contact Jean-Francois Coste. Circ: 7,000.

LES ROUTIERS. *see* TRANSPORTATION—Trucks And Trucking

388 624 ESP ISSN 1130-7102
RUTAS. Text in Spanish. 198?. 6/yr. EUR 60.10 to members; EUR 66.11 to non-members (effective 2008). adv. bk.rev. **Document type:** *Magazine, Consumer.*
Indexed: IECT.
Published by: Asociacion Tecnica de Carreteras, Monte Esquinza, 24 4o dcha, Madrid, 28010, Spain. TEL 34-91-3082318, FAX 34-91-3082319, http://www.atc-piarc.com/index.php. Ed. V Barbera. Circ: 5,000.

388.3 CAN
S G I - AUTO FUND. ANNUAL REPORT. Text in English. 1946. a. free. adv.
Former titles: SaskAuto Annual Report; Saskatchewan. Government Insurance Office. Province of Saskatchewan Motor Vehicle Traffic Accidents. Annual Report
Published by: Saskatchewan Government Insurance, 2260 11th Ave, Regina, SK S4P 0J9, Canada. TEL 306-751-1347, FAX 306-757-7477, TELEX 306-071-2417. Ed., R&P, Adv. contact Maureen MacCuish. Circ: 2,500.

388.1 NLD ISSN 1380-703X
S W O V RESEARCH ACTIVITIES. Text in English. 1994. s-a. free (effective 2011). illus. 8 p./no. 3 cols./p.; back issues avail. **Document type:** *Newsletter, Trade.*
Related titles: Online - full text ed.
Published by: Stichting Wetenschappelijk Onderzoek Verkeersveiligheid/ S W O V Institute for Road Safety Research, Postbus 1090, Leidschendam, 2260 BB, Netherlands. TEL 31-70-3173333, FAX 31-70-3201261, info@swov.nl, http://www.swov.nl. Ed. Hansje Weijer.

388.1 NLD ISSN 1380-7021
S W O V-SCHRIFT. (Stichting Wetenschappelijk Onderzoek Verkeersveiligheid) Text in Dutch. 1979. q. free (effective 2010). back issues avail. **Document type:** *Newsletter, Trade.* **Description:** Includes summaries of research carried out by the institute.
Related titles: Online - full text ed.
Published by: Stichting Wetenschappelijk Onderzoek Verkeersveiligheid/ S W O V Institute for Road Safety Research, Postbus 1090, Leidschendam, 2260 BB, Netherlands. TEL 31-70-3173333, FAX 31-70-3201261, info@swov.nl, http://www.swov.nl. Ed. Hansje Weijer. Circ: 3,000 (controlled).

388 553.6 USA
SALT AND HIGHWAY DEICING NEWSLETTER. Text in English. s-a. free (effective 2000). **Document type:** *Newsletter.*
Formerly: Salt and Highway Digest
Published by: Salt Institute, 700 N Fairfax St, Ste 600, Alexandria, VA 22314-2040. TEL 703-549-4648, FAX 703-548-2194. Ed. Andrew Briscoe. Circ: 9,500.

388.31 NOR ISSN 0332-8988
SAMFERDSEL. Text in Norwegian. 1925. 10/yr. NOK 475 (effective 1999). adv. bk.rev. charts; illus.; tr.lit. index. **Document type:** *Academic/Scholarly.*
Formerly: Norsk Veitidsskrift
Indexed: DokStr, HRIS.
Published by: Transportoekonomisk Institutt/Institute of Transport Economics, Postboks 6110, Etterstad, Oslo, 0602, Norway. TEL 47-2-57-38-00, FAX 47-2-57-02-90. Ed. Harald Aas. Adv. contact Anne Vera Lystad. Circ: 3,400.

388.31 SRB ISSN 0558-6208
➤ **SAOBRACAJ.** Text in Serbian; Summaries in English. 1954. bi-m. adv. bk.rev. abstr.; bibl.; illus.; stat. 24 p./no. 2 cols./p.; **Document type:** *Journal, Academic/Scholarly.*
Related titles: ◆ Supplement to: Masinstvo. ISSN 0461-2531.
Published by: Savez Inzenjera i Tehnicara Srbije, Kneza Milosa 7, Belgrade, 11000. TEL 381-11-3237363, sits@beotel.yu, http://www.sits.org.yu. Ed. Smiljan Vukanovic. Adv. contact Ivanka Vuletic. Circ: 1,000.

388.4131 ESP ISSN 1888-9697
SECURITAS VIALIS. Text in Spanish. 2008. 3/yr. EUR 193 combined subscription to institutions (print & online eds.) (effective 2011). **Document type:** *Journal, Academic/Scholarly.*
Related titles: Online - full text ed.: ISSN 1989-1679. 2008.
Indexed: A22, E01, SCOPUS.
—IE. **CCC.**
Published by: Etrasa Editorial Trafico Vial, S.A. (Subsidiary of: Springer Science+Business Media), Puerto de Navacerrada, 128, Poligono Industrial Las Nieves, Mostoles, 28935, Spain. TEL 34-91-6658000, FAX 34-91-6658009, http://www.etrasa.com.

SECURITE ROUTIERE. *see* TRANSPORTATION—Abstracting, Bibliographies, Statistics

388.4131 JPN
SHISUTEMU NIIKOUTSUU; koutsuu purojekuto nyuusu. Text in Japanese. w. JPY 73,500 (effective 2008). **Document type:** *Journal, Academic/Scholarly.*
Published by: Kogyo Jiji Tsushinsha/Industrial News Agency, 5th Fl, Tosho Bldg, 332, Yamabuki-cho, Shinjuku-ku, Tokyo, 162-0801, Japan. TEL 81-3-52250227, FAX 81-3-32696517, mail@ina-info.com, http://www.ina-info.com/.

SIGNAL. *see* OCCUPATIONAL HEALTH AND SAFETY

388.41 624 CZE ISSN 0322-7154
SILNICNI OBZOR; mesicnik pro otazky vystavby a udrzby silnic, dalnic, mistnich kominikaci, letist, mostu, tunelu a silnicniho a mestskeho dopravniho inzynyrstvi. Text in Czech, Slovak; Summaries in English, French, German, Russian. 1922. m. CZK 69 per issue (effective 2009). adv. **Document type:** *Journal, Trade.* **Description:** Covers traffic engineering, construction and maintenance of highways, local roads, airports, bridges, tunnels.
Formerly: Silnicni Doprava (0037-5292)
Indexed: GeotechAb.
Published by: Ceska Silnicni Spolecnost, Novotneho lavka 5, Prague 1, 11668, Czech Republic. Circ: 1,100.

SITE & ROAD. *see* ENGINEERING—Civil Engineering

388.1 GBR ISSN 2044-1363
▼ **SMARTER TRAVEL.** Text in English. 2010. q. GBP 6.95 per issue (effective 2011). **Document type:** *Report, Trade.*
Published by: Local Transport Today Ltd., Apollo House, 359 Kennington Ln, London, SE11 5QY, United Kingdom. info@transportxtra.com.

388.413 DNK ISSN 1395-3354
SORTE PLETTER; vurdering af trafiksikkerhedsprojekter paa hovedlandsveje. Text in Danish. 1975. irreg. free. illus. **Document type:** *Government.*
Former titles (until 1995): Sikkerhedsmaessig Vurdering og Prioritering af Mindre Anlaegsarbejder paa Hovedlandeveje (0107-5179); (until 1974): Denmark. Vejdirektoratet. Black-Spotundersoegelse paa Hovedlandeveje
Related titles: ◆ Series of: Denmark. Vejdirektoratet. Rapport. ISSN 0909-4288.
Published by: Vejdirektoratet/The Danish Road Directorate, Niels Juels Gade 13, PO Box 9018, Copenhagen K, 1022, Denmark. TEL 45-72-443333, vd@vd.dk, http://www.vejdirektoratet.dk.

625 ZAF
SOUTH AFRICA. DEPARTMENT OF TRANSPORT. TECHNICAL METHODS FOR HIGHWAYS. Text in Afrikaans, English. 1978. irreg., latest vol.5, 1991. price varies.
Former titles: South Africa. Division of Roads and Transport Technology. Technical Methods for Highways; South Africa. National Institute for Transport and Road Research. Technical Methods for Highways
Published by: Department of Transport, Private Bag X193, Pretoria, 0001, South Africa.

388.312 ZAF
SOUTH AFRICA. DEPARTMENT OF TRANSPORT. TECHNICAL RECOMMENDATIONS FOR HIGHWAYS. Text in Afrikaans, English. 1970. irreg., latest vol.25, 1994. price varies.
Former titles: South Africa. Division of Roads and Transport Technology. Technical Recommendations for Highways; South Africa. National Institute for Transport and Road Research. Technical Recommendations for Highways
Indexed: DokStr.
Published by: Department of Transport, Private Bag X193, Pretoria, 0001, South Africa.

388.1 ZAF
SOUTH AFRICA. DIVISION OF ROADS AND TRANSPORT TECHNOLOGY. P A D SERIES. Variant title: C S I R Special Reports. Text in Afrikaans, English. irreg., latest vol.70, 1989.
Formerly: National Institute for Transport and Road Research. P A D Series
Indexed: SpeleolAb.
Published by: Division of Roads and Transport Technology, PO Box 395, Pretoria, 0001, South Africa. FAX 841-32-32, TELEX 3-213125A.

388.31 ZAF
SOUTH AFRICAN ROAD FEDERATION OFFICIAL NEWSLETTER. Variant title: S A R F Newsletter. Text in Afrikaans, English. 1955. q. membership. adv. **Document type:** *Newsletter.* **Description:** Discusses transport economic issues in South Africa.
Formerly (until 1996): Southern Africa Road Federation Newsletter
Published by: South African Road Federation, Lippert House, 104 Pritchard St., Johannesburg, 2001, South Africa. TEL 27-11-299181, FAX 27-11-3375713. Ed. R H Kingdon. R&P K P Gregg. Adv. contact R.H. Kingdon. Circ: 1,200.

388.31 ESP
HE5681
SPAIN. MINISTERIO DE JUSTICIA E INTERIOR. DIRECCION GENERAL DE TRAFICO. REVISTA TRAFICO. Text in Spanish. 1960. bi-m. free. illus.; stat. **Document type:** *Newsletter, Consumer.* **Description:** Presents articles on traffic, driver education and safety, and new cars.
Former titles: Spain. Direccion General de Trafico. Boletin Informativo (0210-9220); (until 1974): Spain. Direccion General de la Jefatura Central de Trafico. Boletin Informativo (0210-9212); (until 1969): Spain. Jefatura Central de Trafico. Boletin Informativo (0210-9670)
Related titles: Online - full text ed.
—CCC.
Published by: Ministerio del Interior, Direccion General de Trafico, General Aranaz, 86, Madrid, 28027, Spain. TEL 34-91-3018100, FAX 34-1-3204138. Circ: 350,000.

STRADE & AUTOSTRADE. *see* ENGINEERING—Civil Engineering

388.31 DEU ISSN 0943-4577
STRASSENBAU A-Z. Text in German. 1949. 10 base vols. plus updates 8/yr. looseleaf. EUR 198 base vol(s).; EUR 38 updates per issue (effective 2009). **Document type:** *Monographic series, Trade.*
Published by: Erich Schmidt Verlag GmbH & Co. (Berlin), Genthiner Str 30 G, Berlin, 10785, Germany. TEL 49-30-2500850, FAX 49-30-250085305, vertrieb@esvmedien.de, http://www.erich-schmidt-verlag.de.

STRASSENVERKEHRSRECHT TEXTE CD. *see* LAW

388.31 DEU ISSN 0039-2219
HE363.G29 CODEN: SVKTAC
STRASSENVERKEHRSTECHNIK. Text in German; Summaries in English, French, German. 1965. m. EUR 114.40; EUR 9.50 newsstand/cover (effective 2011). adv. bk.rev. charts; illus.; tr.lit. index. **Document type:** *Magazine, Trade.*
Indexed: A22, DokStr, HRIS, ICEA, Inspec, SoftAbEng.
—IE, Infotrieve, Linda Hall. **CCC.**
Published by: (Forschungsgesellschaft fuer Strassen- und Verkehrswesen), Kirschbaum Verlag GmbH, Siegfriedstr 28, Bonn, 53179, Germany. TEL 49-228-954530, FAX 49-228-9545327, info@kirschbaum.de, http://www.kirschbaum.de. Ed. Hans Walter Horz. Adv. contact Volker Rutkowski. Circ: 3,509 (paid and controlled).

388.411 DEU
STRASSENWAERTER; Fachorgan fuer den Verband Deutscher Strassenwaerter. Text in German. 1906. m. adv. **Document type:** *Magazine, Trade.*
Published by: Verband Deutscher Strassenwaerter, Roesrather Str 565, Cologne, 51107, Germany. TEL 49-221-986700, FAX 49-221-986706. adv.: B&W page EUR 980, color page EUR 2,054. Circ: 22,000 (controlled).

388.31 USA
T A B BRIEFS NEWSLETTER. Text in English. irreg. **Document type:** *Newsletter.* **Description:** For outdoor advertising industry.
Formerly: Traffic Audit Bureau. Newsletter
Published by: Traffic Audit Bureau for Media Measurement, Inc., 271 Madison Avenue, Ste 1504, New York, NY 10016. TEL 212-972-8075, inquiry@tabonline.com.

690 FRA ISSN 0397-6513
TA1001
T E C. (Transport Environnement Circulation) Text in French. 1973. q. EUR 180 domestic; EUR 196 foreign (effective 2008). adv. bk.rev. index. **Document type:** *Magazine, Trade.*
Indexed: A22, DokStr, HRIS, Inspec.
—BLDSC (9025.602000), IE, Ingenta, INIST.
Published by: Association pour le Developpement des Techniques de Transport d'Environnement et de Circulation (ATEC), 51 bis av. de Versailles, Paris, 75016, France. TEL 33-1-45240909, FAX 33-1-45240994. Ed. Andre Imbert. Adv. contact Laurent Fraysse. Circ: 3,000.

388.31 GBR
T R L NEWS. (Transport Research Laboratory) Text in English. 1992. q. free (effective 2009). back issues avail. **Document type:** *Newsletter, Academic/Scholarly.* **Description:** Provides solutions to the ever-changing needs of the transport sector.
Related titles: Online - full text ed.
Indexed: CLT&T, HRIS.
Published by: Transport Research Laboratory, Crowthorne House, Nine Mile Ride, Wokingham, Berks RG40 3GA, United Kingdom. TEL 44-1344-773131, FAX 44-1344-770356, enquiries@trl.co.uk.

388 625.7 GBR ISSN 0968-4107
T R L REPORTS. Text in English. 1985. irreg. price varies. back issues avail. **Document type:** *Monographic series, Academic/Scholarly.* **Description:** Covers a wide range of road transportation topics, including urban planning, traffic and vehicle safety, environmental issues, and highway, bridge and tunnel engineering.
Formerly (until 1994): Transport Research Laboratory. Project Report (0968-4093); Which superseded in part (in 1985): Road Notes (0080-3294); Transport and Road Research; Which was formerly: Road Research (0080-3308)
Related titles: E-mail ed.
Indexed: DokStr.
—BLDSC (9050.782390), INIST. **CCC.**
Published by: Transport Research Laboratory, Crowthorne House, Nine Mile Ride, Wokingham, Berks RG40 3GA, United Kingdom. TEL 44-1344-773131, FAX 44-1344-770356, enquiries@trl.co.uk.

353.9 USA ISSN 0095-1994
HE5614.3.T2
TENNESSEE. DEPARTMENT OF SAFETY. ANNUAL REPORT. Text in English. 1971. a. free to qualified personnel. **Document type:** *Government.* **Description:** Covers department's statewide activity related to highway traffic.
Published by: Department of Safety, 1148 Foster Ave., Nashville, TN 37210-4406. TEL 615-251-5313, FAX 615-251-5242. Ed. Lt Jerry Strain. Circ: 500 (controlled).

388.4131 SWE ISSN 0283-7986
TIDNINGEN TRAFIKMAGASINET. Text in Swedish. 1986. 5/yr. SEK 180 (effective 2001). adv. **Document type:** *Magazine, Trade.*
Published by: Transvision Media AB, Box 3089, Stockholm, 10361, Sweden. TEL 46-8-645-07-10, FAX 46-8-20-00-70. Ed., Pub. Johan Rietz. Adv. contact Ove Lindholm. page SEK 33,300; trim 210 x 297. Circ: 22,400 (paid and controlled).

TIE JA LIIKENNE. *see* ENGINEERING—Civil Engineering

388 382.7 USA
TOLLWAYS. Text in English. s-a. free (effective 2011). back issues avail. **Document type:** *Journal, Academic/Scholarly.* **Description:** Provides toll industry news, listings of events and other items of interest to members.
Published by: International Bridge, Tunnel & Turnpike Association, 1146 19th St NW, Ste 800, Washington, DC 20036. TEL 202-659-4620, FAX 202-659-0500, info@ibtta.org.

TOW TIMES; the international communications medium for the automotive towing and recovery industry. *see* TRANSPORTATION—Trucks And Trucking

388.409 GBR ISSN 0959-5996
TRAFFIC ADVISORY LEAFLET. Text in English. 198?. irreg., latest 2009. free (effective 2009). back issues avail. **Document type:** *Monographic series, Academic/Scholarly.*
Formerly (until 1989): Traffic Advisory Unit Leaflet
Related titles: Online - full text ed.
—**CCC.**
Published by: Great Britain. Department for Transport, PO Box 236, Wetherby, West Yorkshire LS23 7NB, United Kingdom. TEL 44-300-1231102, FAX 44-300-1231103, publications@communities.gsi.gov.uk.

388.31 USA
TRAFFIC AUDIT BUREAU. ANNUAL REPORT. Text in English. a. **Document type:** *Report, Trade.* **Description:** For outdoor advertisers.
Published by: Traffic Audit Bureau for Media Measurement, Inc., 271 Madison Avenue, Ste 1504, New York, NY 10016. TEL 212-972-8075, inquiry@tabonline.com.

388.31 GBR ISSN 0041-0683
HE331 CODEN: TENCA4
TRAFFIC ENGINEERING & CONTROL; the international journal of traffic management and transportation planning. Abbreviated title: T E C. Text in English. 1960. m. (11/yr.). GBP 110, USD 220, EUR 160 combined subscription (print & online eds.) (effective 2009). adv. bk.rev. charts; illus. index. back issues avail.; reprints avail. **Document type:** *Magazine, Trade.* **Description:** Designed for international traffic managers and planning professionals.
Incorporates (1953-1967): International Road Safety and Traffic Review
Related titles: Microform ed.: (from PQC); Online - full text ed.; Supplement(s): I T S Solutions (Sherborne). ISSN 1751-9462.
Indexed: A22, A26, A28, APA, BrCerAb, BrRB, BrTechI, C&ISA, CA/WCA, CIA, CIS, CPEI, CerAb, CivEngAb, CorrAb, DokStr, E&CAJ, E08, E11, EEA, EMA, EngInd, ErgAb, GEOBASE, H15, HRIS, I05, ICEA, Inspec, M&TEA, M09, MBF, MEA&I, METADEX, RefZh, S09, SCOPUS, SoftAbEng, SolStAb, T04, WAA.
—BLDSC (8882.100000), IE, Infotrieve, Ingenta, INIST, Linda Hall. **CCC.**
Published by: Hemming Information Services Ltd. (Subsidiary of: Hemming Group Ltd.), 32 Vauxhall Bridge Rd, London, SW1V 2SS, United Kingdom. TEL 44-20-79736694, FAX 44-20-79734797, customer@hgluk.com, http://www.hemminginfo.co.uk. Ed. Carol Debell TEL 44-1935-816030. Adv. contact Kasia Brzeska-Reffell TEL 44-20-79734769. B&W page GBP 1,100, color page GBP 1,600. Circ: 22,500.

388 USA ISSN 0082-5859
K24
TRAFFIC LAWS COMMENTARY. Text in English. 1963. irreg., latest 1982. price varies.
Published by: National Committee on Uniform Traffic Laws and Ordinances, 405 Church St, Box 1409, Evanston, IL 60204.

614.86 USA ISSN 0041-0721
CODEN: TRHUAH
TRAFFIC SAFETY (ITASCA). Text in English. 1927. m. USD 34.30 to non-members; USD 26.40 to members (effective 2009). bibl.; illus.; stat.; tr.lit. index. 4 p./no.; **Document type:** *Newsletter, Trade.* **Description:** Provides statistics on motor vehicle deaths by state as compared with the previous month and previous years.
Formerly (until 1957): Public Safety
Related titles: Microfiche ed.: (from CIS, PQC).
Indexed: A05, A22, AS&TA, AS&TI, ASCA, B01, B06, B07, B09, BPI, BRD, C10, CA, CISA, CJPI, HRIS, P06, P48, PQC, T02, W01, W02, W03.
—BLDSC (8882.190000), IE, Ingenta.
Published by: National Safety Council, 1121 Spring Lake Dr, Itasca, IL 60143. TEL 630-775-2056, 800-621-7619, FAX 630-285-0797, customerservice@nsc.org, http://www.nsc.org.

388.1 USA
HE5614.2
TRAFFIC SAFETY FACTS. (Supplementary reports include: Alcohol, Children, Large Trucks, Occupant Protection, Motorcycles, Pedestrians, Pedal-Cyclists, School Buses, Young Drivers, State Traffic Data, State Alcohol Estimates, and Speed) Text in English. 1992. a. free. **Document type:** *Government.* **Description:** Presents descriptions of all fatal accidents reported within the 50 states, the District of Columbia, and Puerto Rico, with coded data elements that characterize the accident, the vehicles, and the persons involved. Includes analyses based on data from sample jurisdictions.
Formed by the merger of (1988-1992): General Estimate System; (1975-1992): Fatal Accident Reporting System (0732-9792); Which was formerly (until 1979): Fatal Accident Reporting System. Annual Report (0147-6939)
Related titles: Microfiche ed.
Published by: U.S. Department of Transportation, National Highway and Traffic Safety Administration, National Center for Statistics and Analysis, 400 Seventh St, SW, Washington, DC 20590. TEL 202-366-4198, FAX 202-366-7078. Circ: 8,000.

TRAFFIC TECH. *see* TECHNOLOGY: COMPREHENSIVE WORKS

388.4131 GBR ISSN 1356-9252
TE228
TRAFFIC TECHNOLOGY INTERNATIONAL. Text in English. 1994. bi-m. free (effective 2009). **Document type:** *Magazine, Trade.* **Description:** Covers advanced traffic management and intelligent transportation systems industry.
Related titles: Online - full text ed.; Supplement(s): Traffic Technology International. Annual Review. ISSN 1352-8548. 1994.
Indexed: HRIS, RefZh.
—BLDSC (8882.360000), IE, Ingenta. **CCC.**
Published by: U K & International Press (Subsidiary of: AutoIntermediates Ltd.), Abinger House, Church St, Dorking, Surrey RH4 1DF, United Kingdom. TEL 44-1306-743744, FAX 44-1306-887546, info@ukintpress.com, http://www.ukipme.com. Adv. contact Mike Robinson TEL 44-1306-742525.

388.4131 AUS
TRAFFIC VOLUME DATA. Text in English. 19??. irreg., latest 2006. free (effective 2009). **Document type:** *Government.* **Description:** Provides Australian traffic information.
Formerly (until 2003): Traffic Volume Data for South Western Region (1449-941X)
Published by: Roads and Traffic Authority of N S W, PO Box K198, Haymarket, NSW 1240, Australia. TEL 61-2-92186888, FAX 61-2-92186286, Communication_Enquiries@rta.nsw.gov.au.

338.41 ESP
TRAFIKO-ISTRIPUAK E.A.E.KO ERREPIDEETAN/ACCIDENTES DE TRAFICO EN CARRETERAS DE LA C.A.V. Text in Basque, Spanish. 1991. a., latest 1989. **Document type:** *Government.* **Description:** Statistical tables of road traffic accidents in the Basque region for the year.
Published by: (Basque Region. Herrizaingo Saila/Departamento de Interior, Basque Region. Bidezaingo Zuzendaritza/Direccion de Trafico), Eusko Jaurlaritzaren Argitalpen-Zerbitzu Nagusia/Servicio Central de Publicaciones del Gobierno Vasco, Donostia-San Sebastian, 1, Vitoria-gasteiz, Alava 01010, Spain. TEL 34-945-018561, FAX 34-945-189709, hac-sabd@ej-gv.es, http://www.ej-gv.net/publicaciones. Circ: 1,500.

388.1 338 DNK
TRAFIKOEKONOMISKE ENHEDSPRISER (ONLINE). Variant title: Noegletalskatalog. Text in Danish. 1977. irreg. free. **Document type:** *Government.*
Formerly (until 2003): Trafikoekonomiske Enhedspriser (Print) (0106-1852)
Media: Online - full content.
Published by: Vejdirektoratet/The Danish Road Directorate, Niels Juels Gade 13, PO Box 9018, Copenhagen K, 1022, Denmark. TEL 45-72-443333, vd@vd.dk.

388.31 NZL ISSN 1176-3140
TRANSIT NEW ZEALAND'S 10-YEAR STATE HIGHWAY PLAN. Variant title: State Highway Forecast. State Highway Plan. Text in English. 200?. a.
Published by: Transit New Zealand, PO Box 5084, Wellington, New Zealand. TEL 64-4-4996600, FAX 64-4-4966666.

TRANSPORT EN LOGISTIEK; weekblad voor het goedenvervoer. *see* TRANSPORTATION

388.4131 POL ISSN 1732-5153
TRANSPORT MIEJSKI I REGIONALNY. Text in Polish. 1982. m. PLZ 180 domestic; PLZ 15 per issue domestic; USD 6 per issue foreign (effective 2004).
Formerly (until 2004): Transport Miejski (0209-0333)
Indexed: B22.
Published by: Stowarzyszenie Inzynierow i Technikow Komunikacji (SITK)/Polish Association of Engineers & Technicians of Transportation, Ul Czackiego 3-5, Warsaw, 00043, Poland.

388.4 GBR ISSN 1475-2298
TRANSPORT RESEARCH FOUNDATION. FELLOWSHIP LECTURE. Text in English. 2001. irreg., latest 2007. **Document type:** *Monographic series, Academic/Scholarly.*
—**CCC.**
Published by: Transport Research Foundation, Crowthorne House, Nine Mile Ride, Wokingham, Berkshire RG40 3GA, United Kingdom. TEL 44-1344-773131, FAX 44-1344-770356, enquiries@trl.co.uk, http://www.transportresearchfoundation.co.uk.

TRANSPORT STATISTICS GREAT BRITAIN. *see* TRANSPORTATION—Abstracting, Bibliographies, Statistics

388.31 USA ISSN 1524-1912
TRANSPORTATION ALTERNATIVES. Text in English. 1989. bi-m. USD 30 domestic; USD 40 foreign (effective 2000). adv. bk.rev. back issues avail. **Document type:** *Newsletter.* **Description:** Promotes the use of alternative means of transportation, such as bicycling, walking, or using public transportation instead of driving.
Formerly: Auto Free Press (1063-0899)
Related titles: Online - full text ed.
Indexed: A10, B07, CA, E04, E05, T02, V03.
Address: 115 W 30th St, Ste 1207, New York, NY 10001-4010. TEL 212-629-8080, FAX 212-629-8334. Ed., Pub. John Kachny. R&P Sharon Soons. Adv. contact Catherine Fennell. B&W page USD 470. Circ: 5,000.

625.7 690 USA ISSN 1043-4054
TE1
TRANSPORTATION BUILDER. Text in English. 1923. m. USD 95 (effective 2005). adv. bk.rev. charts; illus. index. **Document type:** *Magazine, Trade.* **Description:** For transportation construction professionals.
Former titles: American Transportation Builder (0149-4511); American Road Builder (0003-0856)
Indexed: A26, G08, HRIS.
—Linda Hall.
Published by: American Road & Transportation Builders Association, 1010 Massachusetts Ave, N W, Washington, DC 20001. TEL 202-289-4434, FAX 202-289-4435. Ed. Carrie Halpern. Adv. contact Tom Kirby. Circ: 10,000 (paid and controlled).

388.413 USA
TRANSPORTATION IMPROVEMENT PROGRAM. Abbreviated title: T I P. Text in English. 19??. a. free (effective 2011). **Document type:** *Government.* **Description:** Identifies all transportation capital and service improvement projects scheduled for the following 5 years in Douglas, Sarpy, and Washington counties in Nebraska, and Mills and Pottawattamie counties in Iowa.
Related titles: Online - full text ed.
Published by: Omaha - Council Bluffs Metropolitan Area Planning Agency, 2222 Cuming St, Omaha, NE 68102. TEL 402-444-6866, FAX 402-342-0949, mapa@mapacog.org.

TRANSPORTATION JOURNAL. *see* TRANSPORTATION

TRANSPORTATION PROFESSIONAL. *see* ENGINEERING—Civil Engineering

625.7 388 USA ISSN 0361-1981
TE7 CODEN: TRREDM
➤ **TRANSPORTATION RESEARCH RECORD.** Abbreviated title: T R R. Text in English. 1963. irreg. (50 issues/yr), latest 2010. USD 2,300 in North America; USD 2,475 out of North America; USD 2,980 combined subscription in North America (print & online eds.); USD 3,155 combined subscription out of North America (print & online eds.) (effective 2010). illus. back issues avail.; reprints avail. **Document type:** *Monographic series, Academic/Scholarly.* **Description:** Consists of collection of papers on specific transportation modes and subject areas.

T U

Former titles (until 1974): Highway Research Record (0073-2206); Which incorporates (1927-1963): Highway Research Board. Annual Meeting. Proceedings (0096-1027); Which was formerly (until 1927): Annual Meeting. Proceedings; (until 1963): Highway Research Board. Bulletin (0099-944X)
Related titles: Microfiche ed.; Online - full text ed.: USD 1,700 (effective 2010).
Indexed: A22, A28, A34, A36, A37, APA, B21, BrCerAb, C&ISA, CA/WCA, CABA, CIA, CerAb, ChemAb, CivEngAb, CorrAb, DokStr, E&CAJ, E11, E12, EEA, EMA, ESPM, EngInd, EnvEAb, F08, F11, F12, GH, GeoRef, GeotechAb, H&SSA, H15, HRIS, I11, ICEA, ISMEC, ISR, LT, M&TEA, M09, MBF, METADEX, N02, NPPA, P30, PollutAb, R12, RRTA, RiskAb, S02, S03, S13, S16, SCI, SCOPUS, SSciA, SoftAbEng, SolStAb, SpeleolAb, T04, T05, W07, W11, WAA, WildRev.
—BLDSC (9026.275000), CASDDS, IE, Infotrieve, Ingenta, INIST, Linda Hall.
Published by: U.S. National Research Council, Transportation Research Board, The National Academies, 500 Fifth St, NW, Washington, DC 20001. TEL 202-334-3213, FAX 202-334-2519, trbsales@nas.edu.

388.31 665.5 CAN ISSN 1499-2450
TRANSPORTATION SAFETY REFLEXIONS. PIPELINE. Text in English. 1994. irreg.
Formerly: Pipeline Safety Reflexions (1201-1541)
Published by: Transportation Safety Board of Canada, 200 Promenade de Portage, Place du Centre 4th Fl, Gatineau, PQ KIA 1K8, Canada. TEL 819-994-3741, FAX 819-997-2239, http://www.tsb.gc.ca.

388.31 USA
TRANSPORTATION TOPICS. Text in English. 1960. m. (Apr.-Oct.). free. maps. back issues avail. **Document type:** *Newsletter, Government.* **Description:** Provides information on a variety of subjects related to transportation in Wyoming, ranging from road construction and systems planning to law enforcement.
Formerly: Road Construction News
Related titles: E-mail ed.; Fax ed.; Online - full text ed.
Published by: Department of Transportation, Public Affairs Office, PO Box 1708, Cheyenne, WY 82003-1708. TEL 307-777-4439, FAX 307-777-4289. Ed., Pub. Bruce Burrows. Circ: 2,000.

388 CAN ISSN 0581-8079
TRAVEL ON SASKATCHEWAN HIGHWAYS. Text in English. 1958. biennial. free. **Document type:** *Government.*
Published by: Department of Highways and Transportation, 1855 Victoria Ave, Regina, SK S4P 3V5, Canada. TEL 306-787-8334, FAX 306-787-1007. R&P Tom Anderson. Circ: 300 (controlled).

388.3 USA
U.S. DEPARTMENT OF TRANSPORTATION. INTELLIGENT VEHICLE HIGHWAY SYSTEMS PROJECTS. Text in English. irreg. **Document type:** *Monographic series, Government.* **Description:** Profiles research into the application of emerging computer and information-management technologies to improve the efficiency and reduce the negative effects of ground transportation.
Published by: U.S. Federal Highway Administration, Office of Traffic Management and I V H S, U S Department of Transportation, 400 Seventh St, S W, Rm 3401, Washington, DC 20590. TEL 202-366-2196. **Co-sponsor:** Federal Transit Administration, National Highway Traffic Safety Administration.

380.5 USA ISSN 0547-5554
TE1
U.S. NATIONAL COOPERATIVE HIGHWAY RESEARCH PROGRAM. RESEARCH RESULTS DIGEST. Text in English. 1968. irreg., latest no.349, 2010. price varies. back issues avail. **Document type:** *Monographic series, Government.* **Description:** Publishes informal reports providing early awareness of results of N.C.H.R.P. research projects.
Related titles: Online - full text ed.: free (effective 2010).
Indexed: DokStr, HRIS.
—BLDSC (7769.587500), Linda Hall.
Published by: U.S. National Research Council, Transportation Research Board, The National Academies, 500 Fifth St, NW, Washington, DC 20001. TEL 202-334-3213, FAX 202-334-2519, TRBsales@nas.edu.

388.413 DEU
➤ **UNIVERSITAET MUENSTER. INSTITUT FUER VERKEHRSWISSENSCHAFT. BEITRAEGE.** Text in German. 1954. irreg., latest vol.160, 2009. price varies. back issues avail. **Document type:** *Proceedings, Academic/Scholarly.*
Published by: (Westfaelische Wilhelms-Universitaet Muenster, Universitaet zu Koeln, Wirtschafts- und Sozialwissenschaftliche Fakultaet, Institut und Seminar fuer Verkehrswissenschaft/University of Cologne, Faculty of Management, Economics and Social Sciences, Institute and Seminar for Transport Economics), Vandenhoeck und Ruprecht, Theaterstr 13, Goettingen, 37073, Germany. TEL 49-551-508440, FAX 49-551-5084422, info@v-r.de.

388.411 NLD ISSN 2210-917X
▼ **UPDATE (UTRECHT).** Text in Dutch. 2009. s-a.
Published by: Kennisplatform Verkeer en Vervoer, Postbus 24051, Utrecht, 3521 AM, Netherlands. TEL 31-30-2918200, FAX 31-30-2918299, info@kpvv.nl, http://www.kpvv.nl.

388 SWE ISSN 0347-9382
V T I AKTUELLT. (Vaeg-och Transportforskningsinstitut) Text in Swedish. 1977. bi-m. **Document type:** *Newsletter.* **Description:** News and commentaries abour VTI's research.
Published by: Statens Vaeg- och Transportforskningsinstitut/Swedish National Road and Transport Research Institute, Linkoeping, 58195, Sweden. TEL 46-13-204000, FAX 46-13-141436.

388 SWE ISSN 1403-4905
V T I EC RESEARCH. (Statens Vaeg- och Transportforskningsinstitut) Text in English. 1998. irreg. (5-10/year). price varies. **Document type:** *Monographic series, Academic/Scholarly.*
Published by: Statens Vaeg- och Transportforskningsinstitut/Swedish National Road and Transport Research Institute, Linkoeping, 58195, Sweden. TEL 46-13-204000, FAX 46-13-141436.

388.31 SWE
V T I FACTS AND FIGURES. ANNUAL REPORT. Text in English. 1971. a. free. charts. **Document type:** *Monographic series.*
Former titles: V T I Annual Report (0283-7021); (until 1984): Vaeg- och Trafikinstitut. Annual Report (0283-5940); (until 1983): National Swedish Road and Traffic Research Institute. Annual Report (0346-752X)
Related titles: ◆ Swedish ed.: V T I i Siffror.

Indexed: DokStr.
Published by: Statens Vaeg- och Transportforskningsinstitut/Swedish National Road and Transport Research Institute, Linkoeping, 58195, Sweden. TEL 46-13204000, FAX 46-13141436. Ed., R&P Ulla Kaisa Knutsson. Circ: 2,000.

354.485 SWE
V T I I SIFFROR. (Statens Vaeg- och Transportforskningsinstitut) Text in Swedish. a. free. **Document type:** *Monographic series.*
Former titles: Sweden. Statens Vaeg- och Transportforskningsinstitut. Verksamhetsberaettelse; Sweden. Statens Vaeg- och Trafikinstitut. Verksamhetsberaettelse (0282-5996)
Related titles: ◆ English ed.: V T I Facts and Figures. Annual Report.
Published by: Statens Vaeg- och Transportforskningsinstitut/Swedish National Road and Transport Research Institute, Linkoeping, 58195, Sweden. TEL 46-13-204000, FAX 46-13-141436. Ed., R&P Ulla Kaisa Knutsson.

388 SWE ISSN 1104-7267
V T I KONFERENS. (Statens Vaeg- och Transportforskningsinstitut) Text in Danish. 1994. irreg. price varies. **Document type:** *Proceedings, Academic/Scholarly.*
Related titles: CD-ROM ed.; Online - full content ed.: 2000.
—INIST.
Published by: Statens Vaeg- och Transportforskningsinstitut/Swedish National Road and Transport Research Institute, Linkoeping, 58195, Sweden. TEL 46-13-204000, FAX 46-13-141436.

338.1 351.81 SWE ISSN 0347-6049
TE89
V T I MEDDELANDE. Text in Swedish; Summaries in English. 1976. irreg. (50-60/yr.). price varies. **Document type:** *Monographic series, Academic/Scholarly.*
Related titles: Print ed.: 2000.
Indexed: DokStr, GeoRef, HRIS.
—INIST.
Published by: Statens Vaeg- och Transportforskningsinstitut/Swedish National Road and Transport Research Institute, Linkoeping, 58195, Sweden. TEL 46-13204000, FAX 46-13141436. Ed., Pub., Adv. contact Thomas Lange.

338.1 351.81 SWE ISSN 0347-6030
V T I RAPPORT. Text in English, Swedish; Summaries in English. 1971. irreg. (15-20/yr.). price varies. **Document type:** *Monographic series, Academic/Scholarly.*
Formerly (until 1977): Statens Vaef- och Trafikinstitut. Rapport (0373-4706); Which was formed by the 1971 merger of: Statens Vaeginstitut. Meddelande (0081-5713); Statens Vaeginstitut. Rapport
Related titles: Online - full text ed.: 2000.
Indexed: GeoRef, SpeleolAb.
—BLDSC (9258.905000), INIST.
Published by: Statens Vaeg- och Transportforskningsinstitut/Swedish National Road and Transport Research Institute, Linkoeping, 58195, Sweden. Ed., Pub., Adv. contact Thomas Lange.

351.81 SWE ISSN 1102-626X
➤ **V T I SAERTRYCK.** (Statens Vaeg- och Transportforskningsinstitut) Text in English. 1972. irreg. (20-30 times a year). price varies. **Document type:** *Monographic series, Academic/Scholarly.*
Indexed: GeoRef.
Published by: Statens Vaeg- och Transportforskningsinstitut/Swedish National Road and Transport Research Institute, Linkoeping, 58195, Sweden. TEL 46-13-204000, FAX 46-13-141436, http://www.vti.se.

388.4131 DEU ISSN 0340-9554
V UND T SCHRIFTENREIHE FUER VERKEHR UND TECHNIK. Text in German. 1957. irreg., latest vol.96, 2009. price varies. **Document type:** *Monographic series, Academic/Scholarly.*
Formerly (until 196?): Schriftenreihe fuer Verkehr und Technik (0487-7381)
Published by: Erich Schmidt Verlag GmbH & Co. (Berlin), Genthiner Str 30 G, Berlin, 10785, Germany. TEL 49-30-2500850, FAX 49-30-250085305, vertrieb@esvmedien.de.

388 310 DEU ISSN 0083-5021
V W Z. (Verkehrswirtschaftliche Zahlen) Text in German. 1954. a. **Document type:** *Journal, Trade.*
Formerly (until 1967): Verkehrswirtschaftliche Zahlen (0171-5003)
Indexed: DokStr.
Published by: Bundesverband Gueterkraftverkehr Logistik und Entsorgung e.V., Breitenbachstr 1, Frankfurt Am Main, 60487, Germany. TEL 49-69-79190, FAX 49-69-7919227, bgl@bgl-ev.de, http://www.bgl-ev.de. Ed. Karlheinz Schmidt. Circ: 6,500.

VAARE VEGER. *see* ENGINEERING—Civil Engineering

VAROSI KOZLEKEDES/URBAN TRANSPORT. *see* TRANSPORTATION—Railroads

VEHICLE RECOVERY LINK. *see* TRANSPORTATION—Trucks And Trucking

388.4 NLD ISSN 1567-8725
➤ **VEILIGHEID VOOROP.** Text in Dutch. 2000. q. EUR 25 to individuals; EUR 70 to institutions (effective 2010). bk.rev. illus. **Document type:** *Academic/Scholarly.* **Description:** Discusses all aspects of pedestrian safety, including government road safety policies, society initiatives to improve road safety, with particular emphasis on urban areas.
Formed by the merger of (1977-2000): Mensen op Straat (0166-4654); Which was formerly (19??-1977): Voetganger; Feiten, Cijfers, Meningen (0014-9721); (1993-2000): Kinderen Voorrang! (1380-0337); Which was formerly (1979-1993): Veerkeert (0165-9987); (1997-2000): Wegwijs Verkeerskrant (1386-8152); Which was formerly (1957-1997): Wegwijs (0166-4735)
Published by: Veilig Verkeer Nederland, Postbus 66, Amersfoort, 3800 AB, Netherlands. TEL 31-88-5248800, FAX 31-88-5248899, info@vvn.nl, http://www.veiligverkeernederland.nl.

388.312 CHE
VEREINIGUNG SCHWEIZERISCHER STRASSENFACHLEUTE. FORSCHUNGSBERICHTE. Text in German. 1974 (vol.5). irreg. price varies. charts; stat. **Document type:** *Academic/Scholarly.*
Former titles: Vereinigung Schweizerischer Strassenfachleute. Versuchsberichte; Vereinigung Schweizerischer Strassenfachmaenner. Versuchsbericht
Published by: Vereinigung Schweizerischer Strassenfachleute/Union des Professionnels Suisses de la Route, Seefeldstr 9, Zuerich, 8008, Switzerland. TEL 41-1-2516914, FAX 41-1-2523130. Circ: 140.

388.4131 NLD ISSN 1878-9277
VERKEER IN BEELD. Text in Dutch. 2007. bi-m. EUR 52.50 (effective 2011). adv. **Document type:** *Magazine, Trade.*
Published by: Acquire Publishing bv, Faradaystraat 4a, Zwolle, 8013 PH, Netherlands. TEL 31-38-4606384, FAX 31-38-4606318, info@acquirepublishing.nl, http://www.acquirepublishing.nl. Circ: 6,500.

388.31 NLD ISSN 0377-8495
VERKEERSKUNDE; vaktijdschrift over verkeer en vervoer. Text in Dutch. 1949. 10/yr. EUR 94.90 to non-members (effective 2008). adv. bk.rev. illus. 60 p./no.; **Document type:** *Magazine, Trade.* **Description:** Covers technical, social and political developments affecting all phases of the transport and traffic sector, from pedestrians to high-speed trains.
Formerly (until 1975): Verkeerstechniek (0042-3998)
Indexed: A22, DokStr, HRIS, KES.
—IE, Infotrieve.
Published by: ANWB BV/Royal Dutch Touring Club, Wassenaarseweg 220, Postbus 93200, The Hague, 2509 BA, Netherlands. TEL 31-70-3146533, FAX 31-70-3147404, http://www.anwb.nl. Eds. Rene Welmers, Nettie Bakker. adv.: B&W page EUR 1,145, color page EUR 2,110; trim 180 x 267. Circ: 1,840.

338.4131 343.093 NLD ISSN 1389-4005
VERKEERSRECHT (ALPHEN AAN DEN RIJN). Variant title: Tekstuitgave Verkeersrecht. Text in Dutch. 1997. a. EUR 35.50 (effective 2011).
Related titles: Online - full text ed.: ISSN 1568-492X.
Published by: Kluwer B.V. (Subsidiary of: Wolters Kluwer N.V.), Postbus 4, Alphen aan den Rijn, 2400 MA, Netherlands. TEL 31-172-466633, info@kluwer.nl, http://www.kluwer.nl.

VERKEERSVEILIGHEID. *see* TRANSPORTATION—Abstracting, Bibliographies, Statistics

388 AUT ISSN 0254-5314
VERKEHR; internationale Fachzeitung fuer Verkehrswirtschaft. Text in German. 1945. w. adv. **Document type:** *Magazine, Trade.*
Indexed: DokStr.
Published by: Bohmann Druck und Verlag GmbH & Co. KG, Leberstr 122, Vienna, W 1110, Austria. TEL 43-1-740950, FAX 43-1-74095183. Ed. Peter Tajmar. Adv. contact Rudolf Ortner. B&W page EUR 3,888, color page EUR 4,902; trim 260 x 365. Circ: 4,900.

388 DEU ISSN 0340-4536
TF3
VERKEHR UND TECHNIK. Text in German. 1948. m. EUR 119.40; EUR 11.90 newsstand/cover (effective 2012). adv. bk.rev. charts; illus.; pat.; stat. index. **Document type:** *Newspaper, Trade.*
Related titles: Online - full text ed.: ISSN 1868-7911. EUR 119.40 (effective 2012).
Indexed: A22, DIP, DokStr, HRIS, IBR, IBZ, RefZh.
—IE, INIST, Linda Hall.
Published by: Erich Schmidt Verlag GmbH & Co. (Berlin), Genthiner Str 30 G, Berlin, 10785, Germany. TEL 49-30-2500850, FAX 49-30-250085305, esv@esvmedien.de, http://www.esv.info. Ed. Juergen Hille. Adv. contact Peter Taprogge. Circ: 1,920 (paid and controlled).

VERKEHRS RUNDSCHAU. *see* TRANSPORTATION

388.31 DEU ISSN 0042-4013
VERKEHRSBLATT. Text in German. 1947. fortn. EUR 78.60 (effective 2010). adv. bk.rev. bibl.; illus. index, cum.index. **Document type:** *Journal, Trade.*
Related titles: Microfilm ed.: (from BHP); Online - full text ed.: EUR 68 (effective 2010).
Indexed: A22, DokStr.
—IE, Infotrieve.
Published by: (Germany. Bundesministerium fuer Verkehr, Bau und Stadtentwicklung/Federal Ministry of Transport, Building and Urban Affairs), Verkehrsblatt Verlag Borgmann GmbH, Hohe Str 39, Dortmund, 44139, Germany. TEL 49-231-128047, FAX 49-231-128009, info@verkehrsblatt.de, http://www.verkehrsblatt.de. adv.: page EUR 1,280; trim 167 x 245. Circ: 10,320 (controlled).

388.413 DEU ISSN 0341-4388
VERKEHRSDIENST. Text in German. 1955. m. EUR 109.80 domestic; EUR 112.80 foreign (effective 2010). **Document type:** *Magazine, Trade.*
—CCC.
Published by: Verlag Heinrich Vogel (Subsidiary of: Springer Science+Business Media), Neumarkterstr 18, Munich, 81664, Germany. TEL 49-89-2030431100, FAX 49-89-2030432100, vertriebsservice@springer.com, http://www.springerfachmedien-muenchen.de. Ed. Matthias Schmidt.

VERKEHRSGESCHICHTLICHE BLAETTER. *see* TRANSPORTATION—Railroads

388.31 AUT ISSN 0042-4048
VERKEHRSPSYCHOLOGISCHER INFORMATIONSDIENST. Text in German. 1962. a. free. **Document type:** *Corporate.*
Indexed: DokStr.
Published by: Kuratorium fuer Verkehrssicherheit, Verkehrspsychologisches Institut, Oelzeltgasse 3, Vienna, W 1031, Austria. TEL 43-1-71770145, FAX 43-1-717709, wernerklemenjak@kfv.or.at, http://www.kfv.or.at. Ed. Werner Klemenjak. Circ: 2,000.

388.31 CHE
VERKEHRSVERBAND OBERAARGAU. OFFIZIELLES BULLETIN. Text in German. 10/yr.
Published by: Orell Fuessli Werbe AG, Aarwangenstr 4, Postfach 338, Langenthal, 4900, Switzerland. TEL 063-231812. Circ: 5,500.

388 BEL ISSN 0775-9002
VIA SECURA. Text in French. 1953; N.S. 1987. q. EUR 7.44 (effective 2005). bk.rev. illus. **Document type:** *Trade.* **Description:** Publishes news and information on road safety, including pedestrian- and cycling-related issues, and European initiatives.
Related titles: Dutch ed.: ISSN 0775-9010. 1956.
Published by: Institut Belge pour la Securite Routiere/Belgisch Instituut voor de Verkeersveiligheid, Ch de Haecht 1405, Brussels, 1130, Belgium. TEL 32-2-2441511, FAX 32-2-2164342, info@bivv.be. Ed., R&P, Adv. contact Werner De Dobbeleer TEL 32-2-2441582. Pub. Christian van den Meersschaut. Circ: 3,200.

388.1 BRA
VIA URBANA; politica, negocios e sistemas de transporte urbano. Text in Portuguese. 1991. m. BRL 430,000, USD 50 (effective 1993). illus.
Description: Covers problems and issues in city transportation.
Published by: Empresa Jornalistica dos Transportes, Rua Mexico, 41-S-904, Centro, Rio De Janeiro, RJ 20031-144, Brazil. TEL 021-532-0260, FAX 021-240-0139.

388.1 351 AUS ISSN 1832-0732
VICROADS. ANNUAL REPORT. Text in English. 1990. a. back issues avail. **Document type:** *Government.*
Formed by the merger of (1984-1989): Road Traffic Authority. Annual Report (0817-0754); Which was formerly (until 1984): Road Safety and Traffic Authority. Annual Report (0813-1910); (1984-1989): Road Construction Authority. Annual Report (0816-3499); Which was formerly (until 1983): Country Roads Board. Activity Report (0814-9852); Which superseded in part (in 1983): Country Road Board. Annual Report
Related titles: Online - full text ed.
Indexed: HRIS.
Published by: VicRoads, 60 Denmark St, Kew, VIC 3101, Australia. TEL 61-3-98542782, FAX 61-3-98542468, bookshop@roads.vic.gov.au, http://www.vicroads.vic.gov.au/.

388.411 GBR ISSN 0266-8947
VINTAGE ROADSCENE. Text in English. 1984. q. GBP 9.60 in United Kingdom; GBP 12.60 overseas (effective 2001). bk.rev. charts; illus. 48 p./no. 3 cols./p.; reprints avail. **Document type:** *Magazine, Consumer.* **Description:** Publishes news and features from the field of historic road transport.
Published by: Vintage Roadscene Publications, 40 Fairfield Way, Ewell, Epsom, Surrey KT19 0EF, United Kingdom. Ed. S W Stevens Stratten. Adv. contact S W Stevens Stratter. Circ: 10,500.

388.1 USA
VIRGINIA DEPARTMENT OF TRANSPORTATION BULLETIN. Text in English. 1934. m. free to qualified personnel and libraries. illus. **Document type:** *Newsletter.*
Former titles: Virginia Department of Highways and Transportation Bulletin; (until 1974): Virginia Highway Bulletin (0042-6547)
Published by: Department of Transportation, 1401 E Broad St, Richmond, VA 23219. TEL 804-786-4243, FAX 804-786-6250. Ed. Charles M Armstrong. Circ: 16,000.

388.1 USA ISSN 1526-5188
HE202.5
VOLPE JOURNAL. Text in English. 1997. s-a. back issues avail. **Document type:** *Journal, Trade.*
Formerly (until 1999): Volpe Transportation Journal (1095-3752)
Related titles: Online - full text ed.: ISSN 1946-343X.
Published by: John A Volpe National Transportation Systems Center, 55 Broadway, Cambridge, MA 02142. TEL 617-494-2000.

385.264 BEL
WEGWIJS - U B O T EN ROUTE. Text in Dutch. q. **Document type:** *Bulletin.*
Published by: Belgische Transportarbeidersbond, Paardenmarkt 66, Antwerp, 2000, Belgium. TEL 32-3-224-3411, FAX 32-3-234-0149. Ed. Bob Baete.

▼ **WEGWIJZER VERKEERSRECHT.** *see* LAW

388.1 USA ISSN 2152-8012
WHEELS & WINGS. Text in English. 2007. m. free (effective 2010). back issues avail. **Document type:** *Newsletter, Government.*
Media: Online - full text.
Published by: U.S. General Services Administration, Office of Governmentwide Policy, 1800 F St, NW, Washington, DC 20405. TEL 202-501-8880, http://www.gsa.gov/Portal/gsa/ep/home.do?tabId=7. Eds. Elizabeth Allison, Jacquie Perry.

WISCONSIN. DEPARTMENT OF TRANSPORTATION. DIVISION OF PLANNING AND BUDGET. HIGHWAY MILEAGE DATA. *see* TRANSPORTATION—Abstracting, Bibliographies, Statistics

388.1 USA
WOODALL'S FLORIDA R V TRAVELER. Text in English. 11/yr. USD 20 (effective 2007). **Document type:** *Magazine, Consumer.*
Published by: Woodall Publications Corp. (Subsidiary of: Affinity Group Inc.), 2575 Vista Del Mar Dr, Ventura, CA 93001. TEL 805-667-4100, 877-680-6155, FAX 805-667-4122, info@woodallpub.com, http://www.woodalls.com. Eds. Barbara Leonard, Judy Steele, Kristopher Bunker, Malina Baccanari, Timothy Conway. Pub. Ron Epstein. Adv. contacts Julie Bruce, Terry Thompson, Chuck Lasley.

388.1 USA
WOODALL'S MIDWEST R V TRAVELER. Text in English. 19??. 11/yr. USD 20 (effective 2007). adv. **Document type:** *Magazine, Consumer.*
Published by: Woodall Publications Corp. (Subsidiary of: Affinity Group Inc.), 2575 Vista Del Mar Dr, Ventura, CA 93001. TEL 805-667-4100, 877-680-6155, FAX 805-667-4122, info@woodallpub.com, http://www.woodalls.com. Adv. contact Chuck Lasley. B&W page USD 1,630.

388.1 GBR ISSN 0964-4598
TE1
WORLD HIGHWAYS/ROUTES DU MONDE. Text in English. 1950. 10/yr. GBP 86, EUR 136, USD 152 combined subscription (print & online eds.) (effective 2009). adv. bk.rev. charts; illus.; stat. back issues avail.; reprints avail. **Document type:** *Magazine, Trade.* **Description:** Features highways infrastructure industry worldwide. Each issue updates readers on leading construction projects, from the latest highway, bridge and tunnel contracts, to innovations in construction equipment, products and ITS technology.
Former titles (until 1991): World Highways; (until 1954): World Highway Report
Related titles: Online - full text ed.
Indexed: DokStr, HRIS.
—CCC.
Published by: (International Road Federation USA), Route One Publishing Ltd., Horizon House, Azalea Dr, Swanley, Kent BR8 8JR, United Kingdom. TEL 44-1322-612055, FAX 44-161-6030891, media@ropl.com, http://www.routeonepub.com. Eds. Mike Woof, Alan Peterson. Adv. contact Yvonne Tindall. Circ: 15,542.

388.413 USA ISSN 0511-0440
WYOMING TRUCKER. Text in English. 1952. q. free. adv. 32 p./no. 3 cols./p.; back issues avail. **Document type:** *Magazine, Trade.* **Description:** Geared to trucking industry in Wyoming. Reflects viewpoint of organized industry and publicity favorable thereto. Covers news, legislation and regulations of interest to truckers.
Published by: Wyoming Trucking Association, Inc., PO Box 1909, Casper, WY 82602. TEL 307-234-1579, FAX 307-234-7082. R&P Kathy Cundall. Adv. contacts Kathy Cundall, Kathy Cundall. Circ: 3,300 (free).

Z F K - ZEITUNG FUER KOMMUNALE WIRTSCHAFT; das Fachblatt fuer Energie, Wasser, Entsorgung, Stadtverkehr und Umweltschutz. *see* HOUSING AND URBAN PLANNING

388.3124 DEU ISSN 0948-2210
ZEITSCHRIFT FUER VERKEHRSERZIEHUNG. Text in German. 1955. 4/yr. EUR 26 (effective 2010). adv. bk.rev. **Document type:** *Magazine, Trade.* **Description:** Features traffic safety and education for children. Deals with risks, bicycles, traffic rules, and accidents. Includes statistics and charts.
Former titles (until 1995): Verkehr und Erziehung (0942-2803); (until 1992): Zeitschrift fuer Verkehrserziehung (0341-2334); (until 1972): Schulverkehrswacht (0341-2342)
Published by: Verlag Heinrich Vogel (Subsidiary of: Springer Science+Business Media), Neumarkterstr 18, Munich, 81664, Germany. TEL 49-89-43722878, FAX 49-89-2030432100, kontakt@verlag-heinrich-vogel.de, http://www.springerfachmedien-muenchen.de. Ed. Dieter Hohenadel.

388.31 DEU ISSN 0044-3654
HE331
ZEITSCHRIFT FUER VERKEHRSSICHERHEIT. Text mainly in German; Text occasionally in English. 1955. q. EUR 85 (effective 2010). adv. bk.rev. abstr.; bibl.; charts; illus. index. **Document type:** *Magazine, Consumer.*
Indexed: A22, CLT&T, DIP, DokStr, ErgAb, GJP, IBR, IBZ, P06, PAIS. —IE, Infotrieve. **CCC.**
Published by: T Ue V Media GmbH, Am Grauen Stein 1, Cologne, 51105, Germany. TEL 49-221-8063535, FAX 49-221-8063510, tuev-media@de.tuv.com, http://www.tuev-media.de. Ed. Walter Schneider. Adv. contact Gudrun Karafiol.

380.5 DEU ISSN 0044-3670
HE5
ZEITSCHRIFT FUER VERKEHRSWISSENSCHAFT. Text in German. 1921. q. EUR 60 (effective 2010). adv. bk.rev. **Document type:** *Journal, Trade.*
Indexed: A22, CLT&T, DIP, DokStr, IBR, IBSS, IBZ, KES, PAIS, RefZh. —IE, Infotrieve.
Published by: (Universitaet zu Koeln, Wirtschafts- und Sozialwissenschaftliche Fakultaet, Institut und Seminar fuer Verkehrswissenschaft/University of Cologne, Faculty of Management, Economics and Social Sciences, Institute and Seminar for Transport Economics), Verkehrs-Verlag J. Fischer GmbH & Co. KG, Postfach 140265, Duesseldorf, 40072, Germany. TEL 49-211-991930, FAX 49-211-6801544, vvf@verkehrsverlag-fischer.de, http://www.verkehrsverlag-fischer.de. Ed. Rainer Willeke. adv.: page EUR 200; 129 x 184. Circ: 685 (controlled).

338.31 CHN ISSN 1001-7372
TE4
➤ **ZHONGGUO GONGLU XUEBAO/CHINA JOURNAL OF HIGHWAY AND TRANSPORT.** Text in Chinese; Abstracts in Chinese, English. 1988. q. USD 37.20 (effective 2009). reprints avail. **Document type:** *Journal, Academic/Scholarly.* **Description:** Covers traffic engineering, road construction machinery, automobile, trailer, and transportation.
Related titles: Online - full text ed.
Indexed: A28, APA, B21, BrCerAb, C&ISA, CA/WCA, CIA, CPEI, CerAb, CivEngAb, CorrAb, E&CAJ, E11, EEA, EMA, ESPM, EngInd, EnvEAb, H&SSA, H15, M&TEA, M09, MBF, METADEX, RefZh, SCOPUS, SolStAb, T04, WAA.
—BLDSC (3180.182000), East View, Linda Hall.
Published by: Chang'an Daxue Zazhishi/Chang'an University Magazines Company, Nan Erhuan Lu, Zhongduan, Xi'an, 710064, China. TEL 86-29-82334387. Circ: 1,500.

388.1 CHN ISSN 1671-2579
ZHONGWAI GONGLU/JOURNAL OF CHINA & FOREIGN HIGHWAY. Text in Chinese. 1989. bi-m. USD 40.20 (effective 2009). **Document type:** *Journal, Academic/Scholarly.*
Formerly (until 2001): Guowai Gonglu (1003-6512)
Related titles: Online - full text ed.
—East View.
Published by: Changsha Ligong Daxue/Changsha University of Science and Technology, 45, Chiling Lu, Changsha, 410076, China.

ZHULU JIXIE YU SHIGONG JIXIEHUA/ROAD MACHINERY & CONSTRUCTION MECHANIZATION. *see* MACHINERY

TRANSPORTATION—Ships And Shipping

387.1 USA
A A P A SEAPORTS. Text in English. 2004. 3/yr. USD 350 to non-members; free to members (effective 2011). adv. back issues avail. **Document type:** *Magazine, Trade.* **Description:** Covers industry issues, news and events, feature articles of immediate interest to the port industry at large, and the latest updates of port data, statistics and personnel changes throughout the industry.
Related titles: Online - full text ed.: free (effective 2011).
Published by: (American Association of Port Authorities), Seaports Publications Group (Subsidiary of: Commonwealth Business Media, Inc.), 3400 Lakeside Dr, Ste 515, Miramar, FL 33027. TEL 954-628-0058, FAX 954-628-0085, publisher@seaportsinfo.com, http://www.seaportsinfo.com/. Ed. Paul Scott Abbott. Adv. contact Ray Venturino.

387.1 USA
A A P A SEAPORTS OF THE AMERICAS. Variant title: A A P A Port & Industry Services Directory. Text in English. 1986. a. USD 350 to non-members; free to members (effective 2011). adv. **Document type:** *Directory, Trade.* **Description:** Provides a comprehensive guide to the seaports, port authorities and port services industry of the Western Hemisphere and a premier reference resource for the ports industry.
Formerly (until 1996): Seaports of the Western Hemisphere
Related titles: Online - full text ed.
Published by: (American Association of Port Authorities), Seaports Publications Group (Subsidiary of: Commonwealth Business Media, Inc.), 3400 Lakeside Dr, Ste 515, Miramar, FL 33027. TEL 954-628-0058, FAX 954-628-0085, publisher@seaportsinfo.com, http://www.seaportsinfo.com/. Adv. contact David Cantwell.

387.029 GBR ISSN 1358-1783
HE557.G7
A B P PORTS HANDBOOK. (Associated British Port) Text in English. 1982. a. adv. **Document type:** *Handbook/Manual/Guide, Trade.*
Former titles (until 1994): A B P Ports (1369-5932); (until 1987): Ports (0262-1630)
Indexed: HRIS.
—BLDSC (0549.739730).
Published by: Associated British Port Holdings, Aldwych House, 71 - 91 Aldwych, London, WC2B 4HN, United Kingdom. TEL 44-20-74301177, FAX 44-20-74067896, pr@abports.co.uk, http://www.abports.co.uk/. Circ: 12,000.

627.2 NLD ISSN 1877-699X
▼ **A D WERELDHAVEN.** (Algemeen Dagblad) Text in Dutch. 2009. m. **Document type:** *Magazine, Trade.*
Published by: AD NieuwsMedia BV, Marten Meesweg 35, Rotterdam, 3068 AV, Netherlands. TEL 31-10-4066077, FAX 31-10-4066950, ad@ad.nl, http://www.ad.nl.

387 USA ISSN 0517-5828
A W O LETTER. Text in English. 1944. bi-w. USD 75 (effective 2001). back issues avail. **Document type:** *Newsletter, Trade.*
Formerly: A W O Weekly Letter
Related titles: Duplicated (not offset) ed.; Online - full content ed.
Published by: American Waterways Operators, 801 N Quincy St, Arlington, VA 22203. TEL 703-841-9300, FAX 703-841-0389. Ed., R&P Traci L King. Circ: 1,500.

A W T A O ANNUAL REPORT. *see* BUSINESS AND ECONOMICS—Accounting

A W T A O BULLETIN. *see* BUSINESS AND ECONOMICS—Accounting

387.109 BEL ISSN 0776-3468
➤ **ACADEMIE ROYALE DE MARINE DE BELGIQUE. COMMUNICATIONS/KONINKLIJKE BELGISCHE MARINE ACADEMIE. MEDEDELINGEN.** Text in Dutch, French; Summaries in English, French, Dutch. 1935. irreg., latest vol.31, 1997-2000. adv. bibl.; illus. back issues avail. **Document type:** *Proceedings, Academic/Scholarly.* **Description:** Dedicated to the study of shipping and maritime history, including shipbuilding, navigation, and maritime economics, mainly in Belgium and Congo.
Formerly (until 1982): Academie de Marine. Communications - Marine Academie. Mededelingen (0776-345X)
Published by: Academie Royale de Marine de Belgique/Koninklijke Belgische Marine Academie, Steenplein 1, Antwerp, 2000, Belgium. TEL 32-3-232-08-50. Ed., R&P C Koninckx TEL 32-2-6292605.

387 PRT
ADMINISTRACAO DO PORTO DE LISBOA. RELATORIO E CONTAS. Text in Portuguese. 1935. a. free. **Document type:** *Government.*
Former titles: Administracao do Porto de Lisboa. Relatorio; Administracao Geral do Porto de Lisboa. Relatorio
Published by: Administracao do Porto de Lisboa, Divisao de Relacoes Publicas e Marketing, Rua Junqueira, 94, Lisbon, 1300, Portugal. TEL 351-1-3637151, FAX 351-1-3643114, TELEX 18529-PORLI. Circ: 1,000.

623.89 GBR ISSN 1464-1607
VK798
ADMIRALTY NOTICES TO MARINERS. Text in English. 19??. w. GBP 2.30 per issue (effective 2009). **Document type:** *Newsletter, Trade.* **Description:** Contains important changes to charts and lights (including temporary ones), radio signals and sailing directions.
Related titles: CD-ROM ed.: A Update. ISSN 1464-1682; Diskette ed.: ISSN 1464-1674; Online - full text ed.: free.
Published by: United Kingdom Hydrographic Office, Admiralty Way, Taunton, Somerset TA1 2DN, United Kingdom. TEL 44-1823-337900, FAX 44-1823-284077, helpdesk@ukho.gov.uk.

623.89 GBR
ADMIRALTY NOTICES TO MARINERS. ANNUAL SUMMARY. Text in English. 1961. a. GBP 5.10 per issue (effective 2009). **Document type:** *Journal, Trade.* **Description:** Contains the annual statutory notices to mariners numbers 1-25, a summary of temporary and preliminary notices to mariners still in force at the start of the year, and a cumulative summary of amendments to admiralty sailing directions.
Related titles: Online - full text ed.: free.
Published by: United Kingdom Hydrographic Office, Admiralty Way, Taunton, Somerset TA1 2DN, United Kingdom. TEL 44-1823-337900, FAX 44-1823-284077, helpdesk@ukho.gov.uk.

387 ITA
L'AGENDA NAUTICA. Text in Italian. 1955. a. EUR 20 (effective 2009). **Document type:** *Directory, Consumer.* **Description:** Provides seaman and navigation information.
Published by: Istituto Idrografico della Marina, Passo dell' Osservatorio 4, Genoa, GE 16100, Italy. TEL 39-010-24431, FAX 39-010-261400, http://www.marina.difesa.it/idro/index.asp. Circ: 21,000.

387 ITA ISSN 1590-9131
ALMANACCO NAVALE. Text in Italian. 1937. biennial. price varies. **Document type:** *Catalog, Trade.* **Description:** Provides a detailed description of military ships and analyzes the characteristics of the world's navies.
Formerly (until 1938): Almanacco Navale Italiano (1590-9123)
Published by: Istituto Idrografico della Marina, Passo dell' Osservatorio 4, Genoa, GE 16100, Italy. TEL 39-010-24431, FAX 39-010-261400, http://www.marina.difesa.it/idro/index.asp.

387 USA ISSN 0740-588X
AMERICAN CANALS. Text in English. 1972. q. USD 20 (effective 2000). bk.rev. **Document type:** *Newspaper.* **Description:** For canal buffs, professional planners, historians and archeologists. Covers canal news, history, activities and practical information from the US and around the world.
Indexed: HRIS.
Published by: American Canal Society, 840 Rinks Lane, Savannah, TN 38372-6774. TEL 901-925-0099. Ed., R&P David F Ross. Circ: 900; 900 (paid).

387 USA
AMERICAN INSTITUTE FOR SHIPPERS ASSOCIATIONS. NEWS. Text in English. m. **Document type:** *Newsletter.*

TU

Published by: American Institute for Shippers Associations, PO Box 33457, Washington, DC 20033. TEL 202-628-0933, FAX 202-296-7374, gcella@shippers.org. Ed. Glenn R Cella.

AMERICAN MARITIME OFFICER. *see* LABOR UNIONS

387.5 USA ISSN 0364-7374
HE745
AMERICAN MERCHANT MARINE CONFERENCE. PROCEEDINGS. Text in English. 1935. a. free. **Document type:** *Proceedings.*
Media: Online - full content.
Published by: Propeller Club of the United States, 3927 Old Lee Hwy, Ste 101A, Fairfax, VA 22030. propellerclubhq@aol.com, http://www.propellerclubhq.com.

387.00973 USA ISSN 1074-8350
HF1
AMERICAN SHIPPER; ports, transportation and industry. Text in English. 1959. m. USD 36 (print or online ed.) (effective 2010). adv. charts; illus.; mkt.; stat. 100 p./no. 3 cols./p.; reprints avail. **Document type:** *Magazine, Trade.* **Description:** Designed to serve the information needs of shippers, carriers and third parties involved in international transportation and for executives managing international logistics and supply chains.
Former titles (until 1991): American shipper international; (until 1990): American Shipper Magazine (0160-225X); (until 1976): Florida Journal of Commerce - American Shipper (0097-6237); (until 1974): Florida Journal of Commerce (0015-413X)
Related titles: Microform ed.: (from PQC); Online - full text ed.; ◆ Supplement(s): Southern Shipper. ISSN 1054-7150.
Indexed: A22, B02, B03, B04, B11, B15, B17, B18, BPI, BRD, BusI, CLT&T, G04, G06, G07, G08, HRIS, I05, LogistBibl, OceAb, P06, T&II, W01, W02, W03.
—BLDSC (0857.100000), IE, Infotrieve, Ingenta. **CCC.**
Published by: Howard Publications (Subsidiary of: Lee Enterprises, Inc.), 10322 Globe Dr, Ellicott City, MD 21042. FAX 410-461-5668, billbeachy@hotmail.com, http://www.howardpub.com. Ed. Christopher Gillis.

AN BORD; das Magazin fuer Schiffsreisen und Seewesen. *see* TRAVEL AND TOURISM

387.2 GBR
ANCHOR HANDLING TUGS AND SUPPLY VESSELS OF THE WORLD. Text in English. 199?. a. GBP 460, USD 828, EUR 575 per issue (print or online ed.) (effective 2009). adv. **Document type:** *Directory, Trade.* **Description:** Features general data includes flag, ownership, builder and classification, the tonnage and dimension section also includes important free deck measurements and deck cargo capacity as well as machinery details, in addition to engine/thrusters data, includes bollard pull and information on maneuvering /control systems (i.e. joystick, dynpos etc).
Incorporates: Noble Denton Towing Vessel Register
Related titles: CD-ROM ed.; Online - full text ed.
Published by: Oilfield Publications Ltd., PO Box 11, Ledbury, Herefordshire HR8 1BN, United Kingdom. TEL 44-1531-634561, FAX 44-1531-634239, sales@crsl.com. Adv. contact Shaun Sturge.

387 USA
ANCHOR NEWS. Text in English. 1969. q. USD 40 (effective 2003). adv. **Document type:** *Newsletter, Consumer.* **Description:** Includes articles on the maritime history of the Great Lakes region.
Published by: Wisconsin Maritime Museum, 75 Maritime Dr, Manitowoc, WI 54220. TEL 920-684-0218, FAX 920-684-0219. Ed. Jay C Martin. R&P Joy C Martin. Adv. contact Veronica Franz. Circ: 1,000.

623.89 387.5 FRA ISSN 0373-3629
VK798 CODEN: AHDGAG
ANNALES HYDROGRAPHIQUES. Text in French. 1848. irreg., latest 2009. price varies. charts; illus. index, cum.index. **Document type:** *Government.*
Indexed: ASFA, B21, ChemAb, ESPM, GEOBASE, GeoRef, SCOPUS, SpeleolAb.
—CASDDS, INIST.
Published by: Service Hydrographique et Oceanographique de la Marine (S H O M), 13 Rue du Chatellier, Brest, 29200, France. TEL 33-2-98220573, FAX 33-2-98220591, http://www.shom.fr. Circ: 400. **Subscr. to:** EPSHOM, B.P. 426, Brest Cedex 29275, France.

387 FRA ISSN 1257-6360
ANNUAIRE DE LA MARINE MARCHANDE. Text in French. 1904. a. EUR 100. adv.
Formerly (until 1910): Comite Central des Armateurs de France. Annuaire (1257-6352)
Published by: Comite Central des Armateurs de France, 47 rue de Monceau, Paris, 75008, France. FAX 33-4-42657189, 33-1-53895253, ccaf@ccaf.asso.fr. Circ: 650.

623.89 AUS ISSN 1035-6878
VK927
ANNUAL AUSTRALIAN NOTICES TO MARINERS. Text in English. 1933. a. free (effective 2009). illus. index. Supplement avail.; back issues avail.; reprints avail. **Document type:** *Government.* **Description:** Covers mariners information of Australia.
Formerly (until 1989): Annual Summary of Australian Notices to Mariners (0727-2405)
Related titles: Online - full text ed.
Published by: Royal Australian Navy Hydrographic Service, Locked Bag 8801, Wollongong, NSW 2500, Australia. TEL 61-2-42218500, FAX 61-2-42218599, hydro.ntm@defence.gov.au. Ed. Mark Bolger TEL 61-2-42218590. Circ: 3,000 (controlled).

623.82 JPN ISSN 0448-3294
ANNUAL STATISTICS OF MARITIME SAFETY. Text in Japanese. 1950. a. stat.
Published by: Kaijo Hoancho, 1-3, Kasumigaseki 2-chome, Chiyoda-ku, Tokyo, 100, Japan.

387.164 381 FRA ISSN 0395-8582
L'ANTENNE; seul quotidien francais des transports. Text in French. 1828. d. (5/wk.). EUR 298 (effective 2008). adv. 12 p./no.; back issues avail. **Document type:** *Newspaper.*
Former titles (until 1947): Antenne de Marseille (1153-8473); (until 1946): Marseille Maritime (1153-8465); (until 1939): Semaphore
Related titles: Online - full text ed.: ISSN 1958-5470. EUR 197 (effective 2008).
Published by: l' Antenne, B P 36, Marseille, Cedex 16 13321, France. TEL 33-4-91332581, FAX 33-4-91555897, redaction@lantenne.com. Ed., R&P Edmond Oliva. Adv. contact Laurence Acedo. Circ: 8,000.

387 623.8 DEU ISSN 0003-6080
ANTRIEB; Fachzeitschrift fuer Schiffstechnik und Seeverkehrswirtschaft. Text in German. 1955. q. EUR 4.50 newsstand/cover (effective 2007). adv. bk.rev. stat.; tr.lit. **Document type:** *Magazine, Trade.*
Published by: Verein der Schiffsingenieure in Bremen e.V., Senator-Boemers-Str 4, Bremen, 28197, Germany. TEL 49-421-5288314, FAX 49-421-544949. Ed. Herwig Pollem. Adv. contact Wilhelm Groeneveld. B&W page EUR 750, color page EUR 1,209; trim 170 x 246. Circ: 1,360 (paid and controlled).

621.8 658 HUN ISSN 0003-6242
A+CS. Text in Hungarian; Summaries in English, German, Russian. 1956. m. adv. bk.rev. bibl.; charts; illus. **Document type:** *Magazine, Trade.* **Description:** Technical and economic review for materials handling, packaging and logistics.
Formerly (until 1965): Csomagolastechnika (0324-6825)
Indexed: FS&TA, HBB, PST.
Published by: Kovacs Erzsebet, Ujszolo u. 9/B. III.1, Dunakeszi, 2120, Hungary. TEL 36-27-630731. Ed. Kovacs Erzsebet. Circ: 1,600.

387 USA ISSN 1946-1208
THE ARBITRATOR (ONLINE). Text in English. 1969. q. free (effective 2009). back issues avail. **Document type:** *Newsletter, Trade.* **Description:** Contains announcements about recent developments in the field as well as summaries of interesting awards.
Formerly (until 19??): The Arbitrator (Print)
Media: Online - full text.
Published by: Society of Maritime Arbitrators, Inc., 30 Broad St, 7th Fl, New York, NY 10004. TEL 212-344-2400, FAX 212-344-2402, info@smany.org. Ed. Manfred W Arnold.

387 971 CAN ISSN 0842-0866
V1
ARGONAUTA. Text in English, French. 1984. q. CAD 30 to individuals; CAD 55 to institutions. adv. bk.rev. **Document type:** *Magazine, Academic/Scholarly.* **Description:** Publishes articles, news and information on publications and conferences of interest to Canadian maritime historians.
Formerly (until 1986): Canadian Nautical Research Society. Newsletter (0842-0858)
Published by: Memorial University of Newfoundland, Maritime Studies Research Unit, PO Box 4920, St. John's, NF A1C 5R3, Canada. TEL 709-737-8424, FAX 709-737-4569, TELEX 016-4677. Eds. Lewis R Fischer, Olf U Janzen. Circ: 325. **Subscr. to:** Canadian Nautical Research Society, P O Box 21076, Sta J, Ottawa, ON K2A 3Z6, Canada.

388.044 GBR ISSN 1751-309X
ARGUS FREIGHT; daily international freight rates and market commentary. Text in English. 2006. d. **Document type:** *Newsletter, Trade.* **Description:** Features prices and market commentary in the international shipping spot market for crude, petroleum products, LPG and coal together with prices for bunker in the main bunkering centers.
Media: Online - full text.
Published by: Argus Media Ltd., Argus House, 175 St. John St, London, EC1V 4LW, United Kingdom. TEL 44-20-77804200, FAX 44-20-77804201, enquiries@argusmedia.com, http://www.argusmedia.com. Ed. Ian Bourne. Pub. Adrian Binks.

387.54 GBR ISSN 1352-8033
ARROWSMITH'S BRISTOL CHANNEL TIDE TABLE. Text in English. 1835. a. GBP 3.90 per issue (effective 2009). back issues avail. **Document type:** *Directory.*
Published by: J.W. Arrowsmith Ltd., Winterstoke Rd, Bristol, BS3 2NT, United Kingdom. TEL 44-117-9406902. Pub. Victoria Arrowsmith-Brown.

387 GBR
ASSOCIATED BRITISH PORTS HOLDINGS. ANNUAL REPORT AND ACCOUNTS (YEAR). Text in English. 1983. a. free. **Document type:** *Corporate.*
Formerly: British Transport Docks Board. Annual Report and Accounts (0068-2659)
—BLDSC (1500.753500).
Published by: Associated British Ports Holdings PLC, Aldwych House, 71-91 Aldwych, London, EC1N 2LR, United Kingdom. TEL 44-20-7430-1177, FAX 44-20-7430-1384. Ed. Bo Lerenius. R&P M Collins.

359.97 FRA ISSN 0373-9090
VK1000
ASSOCIATION INTERNATIONALE DE SIGNALISATION MARITIME. BULLETIN/I A L A BULLETIN. Key Title: Bulletin de l'A.I.S.M. Text in English, French. 1958. q. adv. bk.rev. **Document type:** *Bulletin.* **Description:** Technical papers and general information articles on aids to navigation technique and history.
—INIST.
Published by: Association Internationale de Signalisation Maritime/ International Association of Marine Aids to Navigation and Lighthouse Authorities, 20 ter rue Schnapper, Saint-germain-en-laye, 78100, France. TEL 33-1-34517001, FAX 33-1-34518205, iala-aism@wanadoo.fr, http://www.iala-aism.org. Ed. Paul Ridgway. Adv. contact G Josse. Circ: 700.

387 FRA ISSN 0066-9814
VM2 CODEN: BATMA8
ASSOCIATION TECHNIQUE MARITIME ET AERONAUTIQUE BULLETIN. Text in French; Summaries in English, French. 1890. a. index. back issues avail.
Indexed: ApMecR.
—INIST, Linda Hall. **CCC.**
Published by: Association Technique Maritime et Aeronautique, 19-21 Rue du Colonel Pierre Avia, Paris, 75015, France. FAX 33-1-40935772, contact@atma.asso.fr, http://www.atma.asso.fr/. Circ: 1,000.

AUSMARINE. *see* FISH AND FISHERIES

387 AUS ISSN 0314-0377
AUSTRALASIAN SHIPPING RECORD. Text in English. 1970. q. AUD 22 in Australia & New Zealand membership; AUD 30 elsewhere membership (effective 2009). bk.rev. index. back issues avail. **Document type:** *Journal, Consumer.* **Description:** Contains news of current nautical events in Australia and New Zealand plus historial material touching on nautical matters concerning Australia and New Zealand.
Published by: Australasian Maritime Historical Society, PO Box 2307, Murray Bridge, SA 5253, Australia. TEL 61-8-85354105, amhs@lm.net.au, http://oceans.customer.netspace.net.au/amhs.html. Ed. Ronald H Parsons.

AUSTRALIA. BUREAU OF STATISTICS. INFORMATION PAPER: FREIGHT MOVEMENTS, AUSTRALIA. *see* TRANSPORTATION—Abstracting, Bibliographies, Statistics

387.5 639.2 343.096 AUS
AUSTRALIAN MARITIME DIGEST. Text in English. 1991. m. (except Jan.). AUD 110 combined subscription domestic to members (print & online eds.); AUD 115 combined subscription in Asia & the Pacific to members (print & online eds.); AUD 122 combined subscription elsewhere to members (print & online eds.); AUD 121 combined subscription domestic to non-members (print & online eds.); AUD 125 combined subscription in Asia & the Pacific to non-members (print & online eds.); AUD 132 combined subscription elsewhere to non-members (print & online eds.) (effective 2008). 8 p./no.; back issues avail. **Document type:** *Journal, Academic/Scholarly.* **Description:** Publishes articles on various aspects of maritime affairs, Includes inquiries undertaken by government in the maritime field.
Related titles: Online - full text ed.: AUD 66 domestic to members; AUD 60 foreign to members; AUD 77 domestic to non-members; AUD 70 foreign to non-members (effective 2008).
Indexed: P26.
Published by: Australian Centre for Maritime Studies, PO Box 55, Red Hill, ACT 2603, Australia. TEL 61-2-62950056, FAX 61-2-62953367, acmarst@bigpond.com. Ed. Ernie Davitt.

387.1 AUS ISSN 1039-0626
AUSTRALIAN MARITIME SAFETY AUTHORITY. ANNUAL REPORT. Text in English. 1992. a. **Document type:** *Journal, Trade.*
—**CCC.**
Published by: Australian Maritime Safety Authority, GPO Box 2181, Canberra, ACT 2601, Australia. TEL 61-2-62795000, FAX 61-2-62795950, http://www.amsa.gov.au.

623.8949 AUS ISSN 0812-2245
VK727
AUSTRALIAN NATIONAL TIDE TABLES. Text in English. 196?. a. free (effective 2009). Supplement avail.; reprints avail. **Document type:** *Government.* **Description:** Covers tidal prediction of Australia.
Published by: Royal Australian Navy Hydrographic Service, Locked Bag 8801, Wollongong, NSW 2500, Australia. TEL 61-2-42218500, FAX 61-2-42218599, hydro.ntm@defence.gov.au.

AUSTRALIAN SEA HERITAGE. *see* MUSEUMS AND ART GALLERIES

623.89 CAN ISSN 1719-7694
AVIS AUX NAVIGATEURS. PUBLICATION (EAST EDITION). Text in French. 1997. m. **Document type:** *Journal, Trade.*
Former titles (until 2004): Avis aux Navigateurs. Edition de l'Est (1493-5759); (until 2000): Edition de l'Est des Avis aux Navigateurs (1493-5732)
Media: Online - full text. **Related titles:** English ed.: ISSN 1719-7678. 1997; Regional ed(s).: Avis aux Navigateurs (East Edition). ISSN 1719-7716. 1997.
Published by: Department of Fisheries and Oceans, Canadian Coast Guard Marine Navigation Services Directorate, 200 Kent St, Sta 5150, Ottawa, ON K1A 0E6, Canada. TEL 613-990-3016, FAX 613-998-8428.

387 ITA
AVVISATORE MARITTIMO. Text in Italian. d. **Document type:** *Newspaper, Trade.*
Related titles: Online - full text ed.
Address: Via San Vincenzo, 42, Genoa, GE 16121, Italy. Circ: 15,000.

387 797.1 ITA ISSN 1971-5250
AVVISO AI NAVIGANTI. Text in Italian. 1984. 3/yr. **Document type:** *Magazine, Trade.*
Published by: Istituto Idrografico della Marina, Passo dell' Osservatorio 4, Genoa, GE 16100, Italy. TEL 39-010-24431, FAX 39-010-261400, http://www.marina.difesa.it/idro/index.asp.

387 CAN ISSN 1925-4865
▼ **B C SHIPPING NEWS.** (British Columbia) Text in English. 2011. 10/yr. CAD 37.50 (effective 2011). adv. back issues avail. **Document type:** *Magazine, Trade.* **Description:** Provides new multi-media information source for the commercial marine industry on the west coast.
Published by: McIvor Communications Inc., 300-1275 W 6th Ave, Vancouver, BC V6H 1A6, Canada. TEL 604-893-8800, http://www.mcivor-communications.com. Adv. contact Jane McIvor.

387 DNK ISSN 0901-814X
HE381.A2
B I M C O BULLETIN. Text in English. 1969. bi-m. EUR 135 membership; EUR 250 to non-members (effective 2008). adv. bk.rev. index. back issues avail. **Document type:** *Bulletin, Trade.* **Description:** Articles on developments affecting the shipping industry at large containing details on new charter parties and other documents, reports from regulatory bodies, commentaries on new legislation and other articles on current aspects of shipping.
Formerly (until 1970): Baltic and International Maritime Conference. Bulletin (0903-4242)
Indexed: CLT&T.
Published by: Baltic and International Maritime Council, Bagsvaerdvej 161, Bagsvaerd, 2880, Denmark. TEL 45-44-366800, FAX 45-44-366868, mailbox@bimco.org, http://www.bimco.org. Circ: 3,000. **Dist. by:** BIMCO Informatique AS. sales@bimco.org.

387 DNK ISSN 1819-5709
B I M C O ICE HANDBOOK. (Baltic and International Maritime Council) Text in English. 2005. irreg. EUR 65 per issue membership; EUR 119 per issue to non-members (effective 2008). **Document type:** *Handbook/Manual/Guide, Trade.*
Published by: Baltic and International Maritime Council, Bagsvaerdvej 161, Bagsvaerd, 2880, Denmark. TEL 45-44-366800, FAX 45-44-366868, mailbox@bimco.org, http://www.bimco.org. **Dist. by:** BIMCO Informatique AS. sales@bimco.org.

B M T ABSTRACTS; international maritime technology. *see* TRANSPORTATION—Abstracting, Bibliographies, Statistics

387 GBR
B M T FOCUS. (British Maritime Technology) Text in English. 1980. s-a. free (effective 2009). charts; illus. **Document type:** *Corporate.*
Former titles (until 1996): B M T News; (until 1991): N M I News (0260-4817)
Related titles: Online - full text ed.: free (effective 2009).

Published by: British Maritime Technology Ltd., Goodrich House, 1 Waldegrave Rd, Teddington, Middx TW11 8LZ, United Kingdom. TEL 44-20-89435544, FAX 44-20-89435347, enquiries@bmtmail.com. Ed. Jenni Williamson. Circ: 7,000 (controlled).

387 THA
B S A A (YEAR) THAILAND SHIPPING HANDBOOK; official BSAA (year) handbook of shipping, transportation and services for industry, trade and commerce in Thailand and worldwide. Text in English. 1989. biennial. USD 24. adv. **Document type:** *Directory.*
Published by: (Bangkok Shipowners and Agents Association), Cosmic Group of Companies, 4th Fl Phyathai Bldg, Rajthevi, 31 Phyathai Rd, Bangkok, 10400, Thailand. TEL 245-3850, FAX 246-4737. adv.: color page USD 1,200. Circ: 5,000 (controlled).

387 910.09 GBR
B W MONTHLY; the British Waterways staff newspaper. (British Waterways) Text in English. 1971. 10/yr. **Document type:** *Newspaper, Trade.*
Former titles (until 1997): British Waterways Board. New Ways; (until 1989): Waterways News; Which superseded: Waterways
—BLDSC (2937.244000).
Published by: British Waterways Board, 64 Clarendon Rd, Watford, Herts WD17 1DA, United Kingdom. TEL 44-1923-201120, FAX 44-1923-201400, enquiries.hq@britishwaterways.co.uk, http://www.british-waterways.org/. Ed. Sheila Doeg. Circ: 10,000.

387 BHS
BAHAMAS. MINISTRY OF TRANSPORT. PORT AND MARINE DEPARTMENT. ANNUAL REPORT. Text in English. a.
Published by: Ministry of Transport, Port and Marine Department, P.O. Box N-8175, Nassau N.p., Bahamas. TEL 242-322-8832, FAX 242-322-5545. Ed. Harvey A Sweeting.

334.644 GBR ISSN 0967-0394
THE BALTIC. Text in English. 1992. q. free to members. adv. **Document type:** *Journal, Trade.* **Description:** Source of maritime market information for the trading and settlement of physical and derivative contracts.
Related titles: Online - full text ed.: free.
Published by: (The Baltic Exchange), Maritime Media (Subsidiary of: Roxby Media Ltd.), The Diary House, Rickett St, London, SW6 RU1, United Kingdom. TEL 44-20-73866100, FAX 44-20-73818890, inbox@mar-media.com. Ed. Lucy Budd TEL 44-20-73866120. Pub. W H Robinson.

387 ESP
BARCELONA PORT; guia de servicios del puerto de Barcelona. Text in Spanish. 1978. a. adv. back issues avail. **Document type:** *Magazine, Trade.*
Formerly: Port (Year)
Published by: Grupo Editorial Men-Car, Passeig de Colom, 24, Barcelona, 08002, Spain. TEL 34-93-301-5749, FAX 34-93-302-1779, men-car@men-car.com, http://www.men-car.com. Eds. Juan Cardona, Manuel Cardona. Circ: 15,000.

387 NLD ISSN 1383-0252
BATAVIA JOURNAAL. Text in Dutch; Abstracts occasionally in English, German. 1989. q. EUR 20 to individuals; EUR 250 to institutions (effective 2010). illus. **Document type:** *Newsletter.* **Description:** News for donors regarding the background and progress of building historic wooden ships at the Batavia shipyard.
Published by: (Stichting Batavia), Stichting Nederland Bouwt V O C Retourschip, Postbus 119, Lelystad, 8200 AC, Netherlands. TEL 31-320-261409, FAX 31-320-261360, info@bataviawerf.nl, http://www.bataviawerf.nl. Circ: 25,000.

386.0916346 386.09749 USA ISSN 1540-9465
THE BAY PILOT. Text in English. 1998. q.
Published by: Delaware River and Bay Lighthouse Foundation, P. O. Box 708, Lewes, DE 19958. TEL 302-644-7046, FAX 302-644-7062. Ed. Bob Trapani Jr.

387 BEL
BELGIUM. ADMINISTRATION DES AFFAIRES MARITIMES ET DE LA NAVIGATION. RAPPORT ANNUEL SUR L'EVOLUTION DE LA FLOTTE DE PECHE. Text in French. a. **Document type:** *Government.*
Former titles: Belgium. Administration de la Marine et de la Navigation Interieure. Rapport Annuel sur l'Evolution de la Flotte de Peche; Belgium. Administration de la Marine. Rapport Annuel sur l'Evolution de la Flotte de Peche
Published by: Administration des Affaires Maritimes et de la Navigation, Rue d'Arlon 104, Brussels, 1040, Belgium. TEL 32-2-233-1211, FAX 32-2-230-3002. Ed. M Joseph TEL 32-2-233-1321.

BELGIUM. INSTITUT NATIONAL DE STATISTIQUE. STATISTIQUE DU TRAFIC INTERNATIONAL DES PORTS (U E B L). *see* TRANSPORTATION—Abstracting, Bibliographies, Statistics

BELGIUM. INSTITUT NATIONAL DE STATISTIQUE. TRANSPORT. NAVIGATION INTERIEURE. *see* TRANSPORTATION—Abstracting, Bibliographies, Statistics

BELGIUM. NATIONAAL INSTITUUT VOOR DE STATISTIEK. STATISTIEK OVER DE INTERNATIONALE TRAFIEK (B.L.E.U.) IN DE HAVENS. *see* TRANSPORTATION—Abstracting, Bibliographies, Statistics

BELGIUM. NATIONAAL INSTITUUT VOOR DE STATISTIEK. VERVOER. BINNENSCHEEPVAART (JAAR). *see* TRANSPORTATION—Abstracting, Bibliographies, Statistics

BENEDICT ON ADMIRALTY. *see* LAW—Maritime Law

BERMUDA JOURNAL OF ARCHAEOLOGY AND MARITIME HISTORY. *see* ARCHAEOLOGY

387.54409489 DNK ISSN 0901-781X
DEN BLAA BESEJLINGSLISTE (YEAR)/DANISH EXPORT AND IMPORT SHIPPING GUIDE. Text in Danish. 1958. a. adv. **Document type:** *Directory, Trade.*
Former titles (until 1975): Besejlingslisten for Koebenhavn og Vigtigste Danske Provinshavne (0901-7828); (until 1967): Besejlingslisten for Koebenhavn (0525-5899); (until 1962): Besejlingsliste
Related titles: ♦ Includes: Den Roede Transportliste (Year). ISSN 0901-7801.
Published by: TechMedia A/S, Naverland 35, Glostrup, 2600, Denmark. TEL 45-43-242628, FAX 45-43-242626, info@techmedia.dk, http://www.techmedia.dk. Ed. Helle Hansen. Adv. contact Bent Henriksen. B&W page DKK 12,800; 195 x 270. Circ: 2,000.

387 623.8 NLD ISSN 0006-4661
DE BLAUWE WIMPEL; maandblad voor scheepvaart en scheepsbouw in de lage landen. Text in Dutch. 1946. m. EUR 50 domestic; EUR 57.50 in Belgium; EUR 67.65 elsewhere; EUR 6.15 newsstand/cover (effective 2009). adv. bk.rev. charts; illus. index. **Document type:** *Trade.* **Description:** Discusses ship building and shipping in the Netherlands.
Published by: Van der Veer Media, Korbeel 34, Blaricum, 1261 LC, Netherlands. TEL 31-35-5254558, FAX 31-35-5254652, vanderveer.media@hetnet.nl. Pub. Wim J van der Veer.

BOAT INTERNATIONAL. *see* SPORTS AND GAMES—Boats And Boating

BOATBUILDER'S INTERNATIONAL DIRECTORY; the boatbuilder's source book of designers, kit makers and suppliers. *see* SPORTS AND GAMES—Boats And Boating

387 CAN
BOATING INDUSTRY CANADA. Text in English. bi-m. free to qualified personnel (effective 2005). **Document type:** *Magazine, Trade.*
Published by: Kerrwil Publications Ltd., 49 Bathurst St, Ste 201B, Toronto, ON M5V 2P2, Canada. TEL 416-703-7167, FAX 416-703-1330, info@kerrwil.com, http://www.kerrwil.com. Pub. Rob Macleod TEL 905-577-2391.

BOATING INDUSTRY MARINE BUYERS' GUIDE. *see* BUSINESS AND ECONOMICS—Trade And Industrial Directories

623.8 797.1 USA
VM321
BOATWORKS; how to rewire your boat. Text in English. 2004 (Spr.). q. USD 4.99 per issue elsewhere (effective 2008). adv. 100 p./no. 3 cols./p.; back issues avail. **Document type:** *Magazine, Consumer.*
Formerly: Boatworks for the Hands-On Sailor (1551-6113)
Published by: Source Interlink Companies, 6420 Wilshire Blvd, 10th Fl, Los Angeles, CA 90048. TEL 323-782-2000, FAX 323-782-2585, dheine@sourceinterlink.com, http://www.sourceinterlinkmedia.com. Ed. Peter Nielsen TEL 617-720-8629. Pubs. Glen Bernard, Josh Adams TEL 617-720-8605. adv.: page USD 3,530; trim 7.875 x 10.75. Circ: 75,000.

387 USA
BOHMAN OCEAN SHIPPING NEWS SUMMARY. Text in English. 1982. m. USD 29.95 (effective 1999). **Document type:** *Newsletter.*
Published by: Bohman Industrial Traffic Consultants, Inc., 32 Pleasant St, Box 889, Gardner, MA 01440. TEL 617-632-1913. Ed. Raynard F Bohman Jr.

387.1 USA ISSN 1948-9951
BREAK BULK. Text in English. 2006. q. Included with subscr. to The Journal of Commerce. adv. **Document type:** *Magazine, Trade.* **Description:** Contains insightful analysis of current events that affect the global breakbulk and project-cargo industry, targeted directories offering a glimpse of the carriers and ports plying the trade, and breaking news that helps readers get to the heart of the issue.
Published by: Commonwealth Business Media, Inc. (Subsidiary of: United Business Media Limited), 400 Windsor Corporate Park, 50 Millstone Rd, Ste 200, East Windsor, NJ 08520. TEL 888-215-6084, FAX 609-371-7883, cbizservices@sunbeltfs.com, http://www.cbizmedia.com. Ed. Janet Nodar TEL 251-476-0197. Pub. Liam Power TEL 973-848-7191.

387 GBR
THE BRISTOL PORT COMPANY. Text in English. 1886. a. free to qualified personnel. adv.
Former titles: Port of Bristol Authority; Port of Bristol. Handbook
Published by: The Bristol Port Company, St Andrews Rd, Avonmouth, Bristol, Glos BS11 9DQ, United Kingdom. TEL 44-117-982-0000, FAX 44-117-982-0698, TELEX 44240. Ed. Julie Gough. Circ: 3,000.

623.82 GBR
BRITISH MARINE INDUSTRIES FEDERATION YEARBOOK. Text in English. 1947. a. GBP 15 (effective 1998). adv. **Document type:** *Yearbook, Trade.*
Formerly: Ship and Boat Builders National. Federation Handbook
Published by: (British Marine Industries Federation), Charles Smith Publications, Meadlake Pl, Thorpe Lea Rd, Egham, Surrey TW20 8HE, United Kingdom. TEL 44-1784-473377, FAX 44-1784-439678. Ed., Pub. Susan Grant. Adv. contact Charles Smith. Circ: 1,500.

386 GBR
HE663
BRITISH WATERWAYS BOARD. ANNUAL REPORT AND ACCOUNTS. Text in English. 1963. a. free (effective 2009). back issues avail. **Document type:** *Report, Trade.* **Description:** Contains a operational and financial review for the past year.
Former titles (until 1997): British Waterways. Report and Accounts; (until 1985): British Waterways Board. Annual Report and Accounts (0068-2683)
Related titles: Online - full text ed.
Published by: British Waterways Board, 64 Clarendon Rd, Watford, Herts WD17 1DA, United Kingdom. TEL 44-8456-715530, FAX 44-1923-201400, enquiries.hq@britishwaterways.co.uk, http://www.british-waterways.org/.

623.8 HRV ISSN 0007-215X
BRODOGRADNJA/SHIPBUILDING; journal of naval architecture and shipbuilding industry. Text in Croatian, English; Summaries in English. 1950. q. HRK 60; USD 50 foreign (effective 2001 - 2002). adv. bk.rev. abstr.; bibl.; illus. index. 110 p./no. 2 cols./p.; **Document type:** *Journal, Consumer.* **Description:** Publishes scientific and professional papers, current topics, reviews and news in the areas of naval architecture, shipbuilding, marine engineering aND supporting industry.
Indexed: A22, ASFA, BMT, CA, EngInd, OceAb, RefZh, SCI, SCOPUS, T02, W07.
—BLDSC (2349.200000), IE, Ingenta, Linda Hall.
Published by: (Croatia. Ministry of Science of the Republic of Croatia), Brodarski Institut, Av V Holjevca 20, Zagreb, 10020, Croatia. TEL 385-1-6504444, FAX 385-1-6504222. Ed. Rajko Grubisic. Adv. contact Zdenko Barisic. B&W page USD 800, color page USD 1,200. Circ: 1,100.

623.8 POL ISSN 1732-078X
BUDOWNICTWO OKRETOWE. Text in Multiple languages. 1990. m. EUR 98 foreign (effective 2006). adv. bk.rev. illus. index. **Document type:** *Magazine, Trade.* **Description:** Covers safety of ships, building of ships, boarding platforms, protection of sea environment.
Formerly (until 2003): Budownictwo Okretowe i Gospodarka Morska (1230-7718); Which was formed by the merger of (1956-1990): Budownictwo Okretowe (0007-3008); (1951-1990): Technika i Gospodarka Morska (0040-1137)
Indexed: B22.
Published by: (Stowarzyszenie Inzynierow i Technikow Mechanikow Polskich), Oficyna Wydawnicza S I M P Press Ltd., ul Swietokrzyska 14a, Warsaw, 00050, Poland. TEL 48-22-3361476. Ed. Zbigniew Grzywaczewski. adv.: page USD 1,000. Circ: 1,000. **Dist. by:** Ars Polona, Obroncow 25, Warsaw 03933, Poland. TEL 48-22-5098609, FAX 48-22-5098610, arspolona@arspolona.com.pl, http://www.arspolona.com.pl.

387.2 GBR ISSN 2042-9355
▼ **BUILD THE ENDEAVOUR.** Text in English. 2010. w. GBP 5.99 per issue (effective 2010). back issues avail. **Document type:** *Magazine, Consumer.* **Description:** Describes to build the beautiful historical ships and learns about the greatest ships from every era of maritime exploration.
Published by: Eaglemoss Publications Ltd., 1st Fl, Beaumont House, Kensington Village, Avonmore Rd, London, W14 8TS, United Kingdom. TEL 44-20-76051200, FAX 44-20-76051201, emmathackara@eaglemoss.co.uk, http://www.eaglemoss.co.uk. Pub. Maggie Calmels.

627 GBR ISSN 0305-0122
THE BULK CARRIER REGISTER. Text in English. 1969. a. (plus m. & q. updates). GBP 250, USD 450 (effective 2011). adv. charts; stat. back issues avail. **Document type:** *Directory, Trade.* **Description:** Contains details of the world fleet of over 6,978 dry bulk and combined carriers of 10,000 dwt and above.
Related titles: CD-ROM ed.: Bulk Carrier Fleet CD. GBP 575, USD 1,035 (effective 2011).
Published by: Clarkson Research Services Ltd., St Magnus House, 3 Lower Thames St, London, EC3R 6HE, United Kingdom. TEL 44-20-73343134, FAX 44-20-75220330, sales@crsl.com, http://www.crsl.com.

387 NOR ISSN 1504-1301
BULK CARRIER UPDATE; newsletter from DNV to the bulk carrier industry. Text in English. 2003. 3/yr. free. back issues avail. **Document type:** *Newsletter, Trade.*
Related titles: Online - full text ed.
Published by: Det Norske Veritas, Veritasveien 1, Hoevik, 1363, Norway. TEL 47-67-579900, FAX 47-67-579911, dnv.corporate@dnv.com, http://www.dnv.com. Ed. Ulf Freudendahl.

BULLETIN FROM JOHNNY CAKE HILL. *see* HISTORY—History Of North And South America

387 343.09 USA ISSN 1062-6506
C I B DAILY MARITIME NEWSLETTER. Text in English. 1897. d. (230/yr.). looseleaf. USD 1,500 (effective 2008). cum.index. back issues avail. **Document type:** *Newsletter.* **Description:** Maritime news, including regulation, promotion, congressional activities, courts, steamship lines, legal matters, conventions and seminars.
Related titles: Online - full text ed.
—CCC.
Published by: Congressional Information Bureau, Inc., P O Box 146, Wachapreague, VA 23480-0146. TEL 757-787-2451, FAX 757-787-2230, cibaech@erols.com, info@cibpubs.com, http://www.cibpubs.com. Ed., Pub. Robert Cazalas. Circ: 1,000.

387 343.09 USA
C I B DAILY MARITIME NEWSLETTER INDEX. Text in English. 4/yr. included in subscription to newsletter. index. back issues avail. **Document type:** *Abstract/Index.*
Published by: Congressional Information Bureau, Inc., P O Box 146, Wachapreague, VA 23480-0146. TEL 757-787-2451, FAX 757-787-2230, info@cibpubs.com, http://www.cibpubs.com. Ed., Pub. Robert Cazalas.

387 BEL
C M I YEARBOOKS & NEWS LETTERS. Text in English, French. 1975. 3/yr. GBP 89, USD 147 to institutions (effective 2004). **Document type:** *Newsletter, Academic/Scholarly.* **Description:** Maritime law.
Formed by the merger of: C M I News Letter (0778-9882); C M I Yearbook; Which both superseded in part (in 1978): International Maritime Committee. Documentation (0538-8643)
Indexed: A01, A03, A08, B01, B06, B07, B09, CA, T02.
Published by: Comite Maritime International/International Maritime Committee, Mechelsesteenweg 196, Antwerp, 2018, Belgium. TEL 32-3-2273526, FAX 32-3-2273528, admini@cmi-imc.org, http://www.comitemaritime.org. Ed. Francesco Berlingieri.

C N A CORPORATION ANNUAL REPORT. *see* MILITARY

CAHIER STATISTIQUE MARITIME. *see* TRANSPORTATION—Abstracting, Bibliographies, Statistics

CAILIAO KAIFA YU YINGYONG/DEVELOPMENT AND APPLICATION OF MATERIALS. *see* ENGINEERING—Engineering Mechanics And Materials

387 CAN ISSN 1193-9893
VK1026
CANADIAN AIDS TO NAVIGATION SYSTEM. Text in English. 196?. irreg.
Supersedes in part: Systeme Canadien d'Aides a la Navigation (1193-9915)
Published by: Department of Fisheries and Oceans, Canadian Coast Guard Marine Navigation Services Directorate, 200 Kent St, Sta 5150, Ottawa, ON K1A 0E6, Canada. TEL 613-990-3016, FAX 613-998-8428, http://www.notmar.gc.ca.

623.894 CAN ISSN 0590-9384
VK1026
CANADIAN COAST GUARD. LIST OF LIGHTS, BUOYS AND FOG SIGNALS: ATLANTIC COAST. Text in English. 1944. a.
Formerly (until 1967): Canada. Department of Transport. List of Lights and Fog Signals: Atlantic Coast (0382-1064)
Published by: Department of Fisheries and Oceans, Canadian Coast Guard Marine Navigation Services Directorate, 200 Kent St, Sta 5150, Ottawa, ON K1A 0E6, Canada. TEL 613-990-3016, FAX 613-998-8428. **Dist. by:** Department of Fisheries and Oceans, Hydrographic Chart Distribution Office, PO Box 8080, Ottawa, ON K1G 3H6, Canada. TEL 613-998-4931, FAX 613-998-1217, chs_sales@dfo-mpo.gc.ca, http://www.charts.gc.ca.

623.894 CAN ISSN 0382-1072
VK1027.N4
CANADIAN COAST GUARD. LIST OF LIGHTS, BUOYS AND FOG SIGNALS: NEWFOUNDLAND. Text in English. 1950. a.
Formerly (until 1967): Canada. Department of Transport. List of Lights and Fog Signals: Newfoundland (0576-1476)
Published by: Department of Fisheries and Oceans, Canadian Coast Guard Marine Navigation Services Directorate, 200 Kent St, Sta 5150, Ottawa, ON K1A 0E6, Canada. TEL 613-990-3016, FAX 613-998-8428. **Dist. by:** Department of Fisheries and Oceans, Hydrographic Chart Distribution Office, PO Box 8080, Ottawa, ON K1G 3H6, Canada. TEL 613-998-4931, FAX 613-998-1217, chs_sales@dfo-mpo.gc.ca, http://www.charts.gc.ca.

387 CAN ISSN 0821-5944
HE561
CANADIAN SAILINGS. Text in English. 1937. w. CAD 100 domestic; CAD 120 in United States; CAD 140 elsewhere (effective 2000). adv. illus.; stat.; tr.lit. **Document type:** *Report, Trade.* **Description:** Covers ocean sailing schedules, ports and shipping as well as shipbuilding and world trade surveys.
Incorporates: Seaports and the Shipping World. Annual Issue (0080-8423); Incorporates: Seaports and the Shipping World (0037-0150)
Related titles: Online - full text ed.
Indexed: A10, B01, B02, B07, B15, B17, B18, BPI, BRD, C03, CBCABus, CBPI, G04, G08, I05, P34, PQC, T02, V03, W01, W02, W03, W05.
—CCC.
Published by: Premedia Information Inc., 4634 St Catherine St W, Montreal, PQ H3Z 1S3, Canada. TEL 514-934-0373, FAX 514-934-4708. Ed. Leo Ryan. Pub., Adv. contact Joyce Hammock. B&W page CAD 1,990. Circ: 10,000.

CANAL SOCIETY OF OHIO. NEWSLETTER. *see* HISTORY—History Of North And South America

387 GBR ISSN 0957-8668
CAPITAL FOR SHIPPING. Text in English. 1989. a. includes subscr. with Lloyd's Shipping Economist. **Document type:** *Directory, Trade.*
—CCC.
Published by: Informa Maritime & Transport (Subsidiary of: T & F Informa plc), Telephone House, 69-77 Paul St, London, EC2A 4LQ, United Kingdom. TEL 44-20-70174482, FAX 44-20-70175007, http://www.informaprofessional.com.

387.2 GBR ISSN 2045-9386
▼ **CAPTAIN COOK'S ENDEAVOUR.** Text in English. 2011. w. GBP 5.99 per issue (effective 2011). back issues avail. **Document type:** *Magazine, Trade.* **Description:** About beautiful historical ships and greatest ships from every era of maritime exploration.
Published by: Eaglemoss Publications Ltd., Unit 4, Pullman Business Park, Pullman Way, Ringwood, Hampshire BH24 1HD, United Kingdom. TEL 44-20-76051200, FAX 44-20-76051201, emmathackara@eaglemoss.co.uk, http://www.eaglemoss.co.uk. Ed. Maggie Calmels.

387 USA ISSN 1944-3323
HE561
CARGO BUSINESS NEWS. Text in English. 1922. m. USD 28 domestic; USD 70 foreign (effective 2006). adv. bk.rev. **Document type:** *Magazine, Trade.* **Description:** Serves the maritime and shipping community of the US and Pacific Rim.
Former titles (until 2008): Marine Digest and Cargo Business News (1547-478X); (until Nov.2002): Marine Digest (1542-5568); (until 1999): Marine Digest and Transportation News (1059-2970); (until 1987): Marine Digest (0025-3197)
Indexed: CLT&T, HRIS.
Published by: Northwest Publishing Center, 1710 S Norman St, Seattle, WA 98144. TEL 206-709-1840, FAX 206-324-8939. Ed. Eric Watkins. Pub. Peter Hurme. Circ: 10,000.

387.164 HKG
CARGO CLAN (QUARRY BAY). Text in English. 1976. q. free. adv. back issues avail. **Document type:** *Magazine, Trade.* **Description:** Features cargo news of Cathay Pacific Airways and topics of general interest to the airfreight industry.
Related titles: Chinese ed.
Published by: Emphasis HK Ltd., 505-508 Westlands Centre, 20 Westlands Rd, Quarry Bay, Hong Kong, Hong Kong. TEL 852-25161000, FAX 852-25613306. Eds. Mark Caldwell, Stuart Lawrence. R&P, Adv. contact Geraldine Moor TEL 852-2516-1009. Circ: 8,000 (controlled).

388.044 GBR
CARGO WORLD. Text in English. 1993. a. free to members (effective 2010). adv. **Document type:** *Magazine, Trade.* **Description:** Provides analysis of trends and developments in cargo handling and transportation in the following geographic regions: North America, South America, Europe, Africa, the Middle East, the Far East, FSU, Indian Sub-Continent, and Australasia.
Formerly: The World of Cargo Handling (1028-5288)
—Infotrieve.
Published by: (International Cargo Handling Co-ordination Association), I C H C A Publications, Ste 2, 85 Western Rd, Romford, Essex RM1 3LS, United Kingdom. TEL 44-1708-735295, FAX 44-1708-735225, publications@ichcainternational.co.uk, http://www.ichca.org.uk.

387.150986114 GBR ISSN 1461-9113
CARTAGENA PORT HANDBOOK. Text in English. 1999. biennial. **Document type:** *Handbook/Manual/Guide, Trade.*
Related titles: Online - full text ed.: free (effective 2010).
Published by: Land & Marine Publications Ltd., 1 Kings Ct, Newcomen Way, Severalls Business Park, Colchester, Essex CO4 9RA, United Kingdom. TEL 44-1206-752902, FAX 44-1206-842958, publishing@landmarine.com, http://www.landmarine.com. Ed. John Tavner. Adv. contact Judith Gimson.

623.89 387.1 FRA ISSN 0989-5973
LE CATALOGUE DES CARTES MARINES ET DES OUVRAGES NAUTIQUES. Text in French. 1983. a., latest 2009. free (effective 2009). **Document type:** *Catalog, Government.* **Description:** Lists and describes marine charts and nautical publications.
Published by: Service Hydrographique et Oceanographique de la Marine (S H O M), 13 Rue du Chatellier, Brest, 29200, France. TEL 33-2-98220573, FAX 33-2-98220591, http://www.shom.fr. **Subscr. to:** EPSHOM, B.P. 426, Brest Cedex 29275, France.

387 ARG
CENTRO DE NAVEGACION. HANDBOOK. RIVER PLATE HANDBOOK FOR SHIPOWNERS AND AGENTS. Cover title: River Plate Shipping Guide; Ship Owners', Masters' and Agents' Handbook, River Plate Ports. Text in English. 1972. triennial. USD 100. **Document type:** *Directory, Trade.*
Formerly: Centro de Navegacion Transatlantica. C.N.T. Handbook. River Plate Handbook for Shipowners and Agents; Which superseded (1933-1966): M A R Year Book
Published by: Centro de Navegacion, Maipu 521, Buenos Aires, 1006, Argentina. TEL 54-114-3221423, FAX 54-114-3250042, TELEX 25572 CNT AR. adv.: B&W page USD 1,050; 200 x 130. Circ: 2,500.

387 LKA
CEYLON SHIPPING CORPORATION. ANNUAL REPORT & STATEMENT OF ACCOUNTS. Text in English. a.
Published by: Ceylon Shipping Corporation, P O Box 1718, Colombo, Sri Lanka.

387 USA
CHARTERING ANNUAL. Text in English. 1954. a. USD 120 (effective 1999). adv. abstr.; charts. index. **Document type:** *Directory.* **Description:** Offers the shipping industry a yearly listing of charter fixture information.
Published by: Maritime Research, Inc., 499 Ernston Rd, Box 805, Parlin, NJ 08859. mri499@aol.com, http://www.maritime-research.com.

387 GBR ISSN 0969-9139
THE CHEMICAL TANKER REGISTER. Text in English. 1993. a. GBP 250, USD 450 per issue (effective 2011). adv. charts; stat. **Document type:** *Directory, Trade.* **Description:** Contains lists of chemical tankers by name and type including ship size and weight, age, capacity, and other technical characteristics.
Supersedes in part (in 1993): Tanker Register (0305-179X); Which was formerly (until 1960): Register of Tank Vessels of the World
Related titles: CD-ROM ed.: Chemical Tanker Fleet CD. GBP 575, USD 1,035 updates (effective 2011).
Published by: Clarkson Research Services Ltd., St Magnus House, 3 Lower Thames St, London, EC3R 6HE, United Kingdom. TEL 44-20-73343134, FAX 44-20-75220330, sales@crsl.com, http://www.crsl.com.

387 GBR ISSN 2040-9710
▼ **CHINA SHIPPING REPORT.** Text in English. 2009. q. EUR 820, USD 1,030 combined subscription (print & email eds.) (effective 2010). **Document type:** *Report, Trade.* **Description:** Provides industry professionals and strategists, sector analysts, business investors, trade associations and regulatory bodies with independent forecasts and competitive intelligence on the shipping industry in China.
Related titles: E-mail ed.
Published by: Business Monitor International Ltd., Senator House, 85 Queen Victoria St, London, EC4V 4AB, United Kingdom. TEL 44-20-72480468, FAX 44-20-72480467, subs@businessmonitor.com.

387 TWN
CHINESE SEAMEN'S NEWS. Text in Chinese. m.
Published by: National Chinese Seamen's Union, 2nd Fl, No 115 Changchow S. Rd, Sec 1, Taipei, Taiwan.

387.54 BGD
CHITTAGONG PORT AUTHORITY. PORT FOLIO, PORT OF CHITTAGONG. Text in English. m.
Supersedes: Chittagong Port Authority. Monthly Bulletin
Published by: Chittagong Port Authority, PO Box 2013, Chittagong, Bangladesh.

387 BGD
CHITTAGONG PORT AUTHORITY. YEARBOOK. Text in English. a.
Formerly: Chittagong Port Trust. Yearbook of Information (0069-3723)
Published by: Chittagong Port Authority, PO Box 2013, Chittagong, Bangladesh.

387 621.3 CHN ISSN 1003-4862
CHUAN-DIAN JISHU/MARINE ELECTRIC & ELECTRONIC ENGINEERING. Text in Chinese. 1971. m. CNY 8.50 per issue. **Document type:** *Journal, Academic/Scholarly.*
Formerly (until 1980): Dianqi Jishu
Related titles: Online - full text ed.: (from WanFang Data Corp.).
Published by: (Zhongguo Zaochuan Gongcheng Xuehui Lunji Xueshu Weiyuanhui), Wuhan Chuanyong Dianli Tuijin Zhuangzhi Yanjiusuo/Wuhan Institute of Marine Electric Propulsion (Subsidiary of: Zhongguo Chuanbo Zhonggong Jituan Gongsi/China Shipbuilding Industry Corporation), PO Box 64311-25, Wuhan, 430064, China. TEL 86-27-68896677, FAX 86-27-88035934.

387 CHN ISSN 1671-7953
CHUAN-HAI GONGCHENG/SHIP & OCEAN ENGINEERING. Text in Chinese. 1972. bi-m. **Document type:** *Journal, Academic/Scholarly.*
Formerly (until 2001): Wuhan Zaochuan/Wuhan Shipbuilding (1001-1684)
Related titles: Online - full text ed.
Published by: Wuhan Ligong Daxue/Wuhan University of Technology, 1040, Heping Dadao, PO Box 50, Wuhan, 430063, China. TEL 86-27-86551694 ext 3296, 3806, 86-27-86551247, http://www.whut.edu.cn/index.html. **Co-sponsor:** Wuhan Zaochuan Gongcheng Xuehui.

623.8 CHN ISSN 1001-9855
CHUANBO/SHIP R & D. Text in Chinese. 1990. bi-m. **Document type:** *Journal, Academic/Scholarly.*
Formed by the merger of (1986-1989): Chuanbo yu Haiyang Gongcheng; (1974-1989): Jianchuan Keyan yu Sheji
Related titles: Online - full text ed.: (from WanFang Data Corp.).
Published by: Zhongguo Chuanbo ji Haiyang Gongcheng Sheji Yanjiuyuan/Marine Design & Research Institute of China, 1688, Xizang Nan Lu, Shanghai, 200011, China. TEL 86-21-63161688 ext 8242.

623.82 CHN ISSN 1000-6982
VM4
CHUANBO GONGCHENG/SHIP ENGINEERING. Text in Chinese; Abstracts in English. 1979. bi-m. USD 40.20 (effective 2009). adv. bk.rev.
Related titles: Online - full text ed.
Indexed: BMT.
—BLDSC (8258.600000), East View, IE, Ingenta.
Published by: Zhongguo Zaochuan Gongcheng Xuehui/Chinese Society of Naval Architecture and Marine Engineering, 71 Sipailou Lu, PO Box 040 002, Shanghai, 200010, China. TEL 3203055, FAX 86-21-3290929. Ed. Yu Fengchang. Circ: 5,000. **Dist. overseas by:** China International Book Trading Corp, 35 Chegongzhuang Xilu, Haidian District, PO Box 399, Beijing 100044, China.

387.51 CHN ISSN 1008-1054
CHUANBO JINGJI MAOYI/SHIP ECONOMY AND TRADE. Text in Chinese. m. **Document type:** *Journal, Academic/Scholarly.*
Formerly: Chuanbo Baojia Cankao
Related titles: Online - full text ed.: (from WanFang Data Corp.).
Published by: Zhongguo Chuanbo Baoshe, 5 Yuetan Beijie, Beijing, 100861, China. TEL 86-10-59517980, FAX 86-10-59517978.

623.8 CHN ISSN 1007-7294
VM595
CHUANBO LIXUE/JOURNAL OF SHIP MECHANICS. Text in Chinese. 1997. bi-m. USD 53.40 (effective 2009). **Document type:** *Journal, Academic/Scholarly.*
Related titles: Online - full text ed.
Indexed: A22, A28, APA, BrCerAb, C&ISA, CA/WCA, CIA, CPEI, CerAb, CivEngAb, CorrAb, E&CAJ, E11, EEA, EMA, ESPM, EngInd, EnvEAb, H15, M&TEA, M09, MBF, METADEX, RefZh, SCOPUS, SolStAb, T04, WAA.
—BLDSC (5064.270000), East View, IE, Ingenta.
Address: 1, Yuanjiawan, Wuxi, 214082, China. TEL 86-510-5555510, FAX 86-510-5555193.

387 CHN ISSN 1001-4624
CHUANBO SHEJI TONGXUN/JOURNAL OF SHIP DESIGN. Text in Chinese. 1972. q. USD 5. adv. bk.rev. **Document type:** *Academic/Scholarly.*
Related titles: Online - full text ed.
Published by: Shanghai Chuanbo Yanjiu Shejiyuan/Shanghai Merchant Ship Design & Research Institute, 221 Zhaojiabang Lu, PO Box 020 017, Shanghai, 200032, China. TEL 86-21-6431-3600, FAX 86-21-6433-8213. Ed. Jiajun Ni. R&P Jingyu Yan. Adv. contact Jingjiu Yan. Circ: 3,000.

387 380.1029 GBR
CLARKSON REGISTER CD. (Avail. in 2 editions: Standard Edition & Professional Edition) Text in English. a. GBP 895, USD 1,611 standard ed.; GBP 1,695, USD 3,051 professional ed. (effective 2011). **Document type:** *Directory, Trade.* **Description:** Contains details of cargo ships over 5,000 dwt (and specialised tankers over 1,000 dwt), divided into 9 main registers and 74 sub-registers. Professional edition includes additional data: Demolition data, ship sales, and enhanced capabilities.
Media: CD-ROM.
Published by: Clarkson Research Services Ltd., 12 Camomile St, London, EC3A 7BH, United Kingdom. TEL 44-20-73343134, FAX 44-20-75220330, sales@crsl.com.

387 665.5 USA ISSN 1931-1893
CLEAN TANKERWIRE. Text in English. 19??. d. USD 4,585 combined subscription (online & E-mail eds.) (effective 2008). back issues avail. **Document type:** *Newsletter, Trade.* **Description:** Contains an extensive listings and analysis of the latest tanker freight and fixture rates as a percentage of the worldscale figure and an additional $/mt conversion.
Media: Online - full content. **Related titles:** E-mail ed.
Published by: Platts (Subsidiary of: McGraw-Hill Companies, Inc.), 1200 G St NW, Ste 1000, Washington, DC 20005. TEL 212-904-3070, 800-752-8878, FAX 202-383-2024, support@platts.com.

387.164 622.33 GBR ISSN 1478-159X
COALTRANS INTERNATIONAL. Cover title: Coal Trans International. Text in English. 1979. bi-m. GBP 130, USD 260, EUR 170 (effective 2009). adv. bk.rev. back issues avail. **Document type:** *Magazine, Trade.* **Description:** Information on the international coal market: mined product trading, transportation, end-user technology.
Former titles (until 2002): CoalTrans Magazine (1472-197X); (until 2000): CoalTrans (0269-381X); (until 1986): Bulk Systems International (0143-7852)
Related titles: Online - full content ed.
Indexed: CLT&T, HRIS, RefZh.
—BLDSC (3292.216000), IE, Infotrieve, Ingenta.
Published by: W C N Publications, Northbank House, 5 Bridge St, Leatherhead, Surrey KT22 8BL, United Kingdom. TEL 44-1372-375511, FAX 44-1372-370111, info@wcnpublishing.com, http://www.wcnpublishing.com. Ed. Anne Wilkinson. Adv. contact Simon Peskett. B&W page GBP 1,895, color page GBP 2,745; trim 210 x 297.

359.97 GBR
COASTGUARD. Text in English. 1946. q. free. adv. bk.rev.; film rev. illus.; stat. **Document type:** *Government.* **Description:** Features training, equipment and good practice for mariners and carries news of activities of organizations.
Published by: Department of Transport, H.M. Coastguard, Rm S13-03 2, Marsham St, London, SW1P 4LA, United Kingdom. TEL 0171-276-5082, FAX 0171-276-6080. Ed. Ian Fraser. Adv. contact Peter Barnes. Circ: 16,000 (controlled).

623.88 USA ISSN 1946-1313
GV771
COMPASS (RALEIGH). Text in English. 2007. bi-m. free to members (effective 2009). back issues avail. **Document type:** *Newsletter, Trade.* **Description:** Provides the members and friends of United States Power Squadrons with the latest USPS news and information.
Media: Online - full content.
Published by: United States Power Squadrons, PO Box 30423, Raleigh, NC 27622. TEL 888-367-8777, FAX 888-304-0813, ns@usps.org.

387 USA
CONNECTIONS (TOLEDO, 1956). Text in English. 1956. q. free. charts; illus. **Document type:** *Newsletter.* **Description:** Contains news and information on the Port of Toledo area airports and economic development.
Formerly (until 1989): Port of Toledo News (0032-4868)
Published by: Toledo-Lucas County Port Authority, One Maritime Plaza, 7th Fl, Toledo, OH 43604-1866. TEL 419-243-8251, FAX 419-243-1835. Ed. T Mark Sweeney. Circ: 7,000.

378 GBR ISSN 1467-0488
CONTAINER INTELLIGENCE MONTHLY. Abbreviated title: C I M. Text in English. 1999. m. GBP 575, USD 1,035 (effective 2011). adv. **Document type:** *Journal, Trade.* **Description:** Aims to track developments in the container shipping market.
Related titles: Online - full text ed.: ISSN 1741-4652.
Published by: Clarkson Research Services Ltd., St Magnus House, 3 Lower Thames St, London, EC3R 6HE, United Kingdom. TEL 44-20-73343134, FAX 44-20-75220330, sales@crsl.com.

387 GBR ISSN 1478-9779
CONTAINER INTELLIGENCE QUARTERLY. Abbreviated title: C I Q. Text in English. 2002. q. GBP 1,195, USD 2,151 (effective 2011). adv. illus. 130 p./no.; **Document type:** *Catalog, Trade.* **Description:** Provides comprehensive source of information on the container shipping market.
Related titles: Online - full text ed.: ISSN 2044-0448.
Published by: Clarkson Research Services Ltd., St Magnus House, 3 Lower Thames St, London, EC3R 6HE, United Kingdom. TEL 44-20-73343134, FAX 44-20-75220330, sales@crsl.com.

387.164 GBR ISSN 0269-7726
CONTAINER MANAGEMENT. Abbreviated title: C M. Text in English. 1984 (Oct.). m. GBP 180, EUR 280, USD 380 (effective 2009). adv. back issues avail. **Document type:** *Magazine, Trade.* **Description:** Addresses cargo-handling issues.
Related titles: Regional ed(s).: Container Management Americas. 1986.
Indexed: CLT&T, HRIS.
Published by: Container Management Ltd, Drewry House, 213 Marsh Wall, London, EC14 9FJ, United Kingdom. TEL 44-20-75100015, FAX 44-20-75102344. Pub. Stuart Fryer. Adv. contact Marie-Anne Hoffer TEL 44-20-86487113.

387 NOR ISSN 1504-2529
CONTAINER SHIP UPDATE; the container ship newsletter from DNV. Text in English. 2002. 3/yr. free. back issues avail. **Document type:** *Newsletter, Trade.*
Related titles: Online - full text ed.
Published by: Det Norske Veritas, Veritasveien 1, Hoevik, 1363, Norway. TEL 47-67-579900, FAX 47-67-579911, dnv.corporate@dnv.com, http://www.dnv.com. Ed. Knut A Doehlie.

387 GBR ISSN 0010-7379
CONTAINERISATION INTERNATIONAL. Text in English. 1967. m. GBP 795 combined subscription domestic (print & online eds.); EUR 1,105, GBP 885 combined subscription in Europe (print & online eds.); USD 1,640, GBP 995 combined subscription elsewhere (print & online eds.) (effective 2010). adv. illus.; tr.lit. back issues avail.; reprints avail. **Document type:** *Magazine, Trade.* **Description:** Provides industry executives with instant access to high quality, real-time business information.
Related titles: Online - full text ed.: GBP 250 domestic; EUR 350 in Europe; USD 498 elsewhere (effective 2009).
Indexed: A22, BMT, CLT&T, HRIS, IPackAb, SCOPUS.
—BLDSC (3425.080000), IE, Infotrieve, Ingenta. **CCC.**
Published by: Informa Trade & Energy (Subsidiary of: Informa U K Ltd.), Telephone House, 69-77 Paul St, London, EC2A 4LQ, United Kingdom. TEL 44-20-33773204, FAX 44-20-70177860, http://www.informa.com/divisions/commercial/informa_Informa_Trade_and_Energy. Ed. John Fossey TEL 44-20-70174891. Pub. Tim Budgen TEL 44-20-70176771. Adv. contact Ed Andrews TEL 44-20-70174294. B&W page GBP 4,107, color page GBP 4,884; trim 208 x 273. Circ: 10,000.

387 GBR ISSN 0305-7402
TA1215
CONTAINERISATION INTERNATIONAL YEARBOOK. Text in English. 1968. a. GBP 395 per issue domestic; EUR 585 per issue in Europe; USD 780 per issue elsewhere (effective 2010). adv. illus. **Document type:** *Directory, Trade.* **Description:** Contains a series of industry overviews by liner shipping experts including an easy to use reference section that covers container leasing, repair, second hand container sales, tank container operators, freight forwarding, road haulage and much more.
Formerly (until 1969): Container Guide
—BLDSC (3425.090000).
Published by: Informa Trade & Energy (Subsidiary of: Informa U K Ltd.), Informa House, 30-32 Mortimer St, London, W1W 7RE, United Kingdom. TEL 44-20-70175000, http://www.informa.com/divisions/commercial/informa_Informa_Trade_and_Energy. adv.: B&W page GBP 3,774, color page GBP 4,551; trim 208 x 273.

387.5442 GBR ISSN 1750-3752
THE CONTAINERSHIP REGISTER (LONDON, 2002). Text in English. 1999. a. GBP 250, USD 450 per issue (effective 2011). adv. 1381 p./no.; **Document type:** *Directory, Trade.* **Description:** Provides the liner industry with a definitive guide to the global liner fleet.
Formerly (until 2001): Liner Register (1467-7806); Which was formed by the merger of (19??-1999): Container Ship Register; (1997-1999): The Multi-Purpose Vessel Register; (19??-1999): The Ro-ro Vessel Register
Related titles: CD-ROM ed.: Container Fleet CD. GBP 575, USD 1,035 (effective 2011).
Published by: Clarkson Research Services Ltd., St Magnus House, 3 Lower Thames St, London, EC3R 6HE, United Kingdom. TEL 44-20-73343134, FAX 44-20-75220330, sales@crsl.com, http://www.crsl.com.

387 USA
COOL CARGOES. Text in English. 1995. q. Inculdes with subscr. to: The Journal of Commerce and Pacific Shipper magazines. adv. **Document type:** *Magazine, Trade.* **Description:** A guide to transporting perishable goods.
Related titles: Online - full text ed.; ◆ Supplement to: Pacific Shipper. ISSN 0030-8900.
Published by: The Journal of Commerce Shipper Group (Subsidiary of: Commonwealth Business Media, Inc.), 33 Washington St, 13th Fl, Newark, NJ 07102. TEL 800-223-0243, FAX 973-848-7167, production@joc.com, http://www.jocshippergroup.com/. Ed. Nall Stephanie TEL 909-389-9222. Pub. Noreen Murray TEL 973-848-7082.

387 ITA ISSN 0010-9193
CORRIERE DEI TRASPORTI; settimanale indipendente di informazioni. Text in Italian. 1958. w. adv. illus.; stat. 28 p./no.; **Document type:** *Newspaper, Trade.*
Related titles: Online - full text ed.
Address: Via Livenza 3, Rome, 00198, Italy. TEL 39-06-8413718, FAX 39-06-90286841.

COSTRUZIONI; tecnica ed organizzazione dei cantieri. *see* ENGINEERING—Civil Engineering

387 BEL
COURTIER NAUTIQUE. Text in Flemish, French. 1970. m. adv.
Address: Rue du Sceptre 8, Brussels, 1040, Belgium. Circ: 13,400.

623.89 GBR ISSN 2046-5009
THE CREW REPORT.COM. Text in English. 2006. 9/yr. adv. back issues avail. **Document type:** *Magazine, Consumer.*
Formerly (until 2009): Crew Report
Published by: T R P Magazines, Lansdowne House, 3-7 Northcote Rd, London, SW11 1NG, United Kingdom. TEL 44-20-79244004, FAX 44-20-79241004, http://www.trpmagazine.com/. Eds. Esther Barney, Martin H Redmayne, Don Hoyt Gorman.

CRUISE INDUSTRY NEWS (NEWSLETTER). *see* TRAVEL AND TOURISM

CRUISE INDUSTRY NEWS ANNUAL. *see* TRAVEL AND TOURISM

CRUISE INDUSTRY NEWS QUARTERLY. *see* TRAVEL AND TOURISM

387.2 AUS ISSN 1834-5913
CRUISE WEEKLY. Text in English. 2006. w. **Document type:** *Newsletter, Consumer.*
Media: Online - full text.
Address: info@cruiseweekly.com.au, http://www.cruiseweekly.com.au/default.htm. Ed. Mike Heard.

CURRENTS (NEW YORK, NY). *see* TRAVEL AND TOURISM

387 623 DNK ISSN 0905-3549
D M I NEWS. (Dansk Maritimt Institut) Text in English. 1979. 2/yr. free. bk.rev. illus. **Document type:** *Newsletter, Trade.* **Description:** Covers naval architecture, maritime safety, wind engineering, and industrial fluid mechanics.
Former titles (until 1989): D M I Update (0903-112X); (until 1987): D M I News (0902-851X); (until 1983): S L News (0903-9619)
Related titles: Online - full text ed.: ISSN 1602-8554; French ed.: ISSN 0909-8348. 1993.
Published by: Force Technology, Park Alle 345, Broendby, 2605, Denmark. TEL 45-43-267000, FAX 45-43-267011, info@forcetechnology.com, http://www.forcetechnology.com. Ed. Nadia Maria Lind. Circ: 4,000.

387.2 NOR ISSN 0803-7108
D N V FORUM. (Det Norske Veritas) Text in English. 1955. 3/yr. free. adv. bk.rev. cum.index: 1983-1988. back issues avail. **Document type:** *Newsletter, Trade.* **Description:** Covers marine, offshore and other industries worldwide with particular reference to advanced technologies. classification, certification, verification and advisory services.
Former titles (until 1992): Veritas Forum (0801-714X); (until 1986): Veritas (0042-3963)
Related titles: Online - full text ed.
Indexed: BMT, CLT&T, HRIS, PetrolAb.
—BLDSC (3605.739000), PADDS. **CCC.**
Published by: Det Norske Veritas, Veritasveien 1, Hoevik, 1363, Norway. TEL 47-67-579900, FAX 47-67-579911, dnv.corporate@dnv.com. Ed. Eva Halvorsen. Circ: 20,000 (controlled and free).

387 BRA
DADOS ESTATISTICOS DA MOVIMENTACAO DE CARGA E PASSAGEIROS. Cover title: Dados Estatisticos da Navegacao. Text in Portuguese. a. stat.
Published by: Empresa de Navegacao de Amazonia, S.A., Setor de Processamento de Dados Estatisticos, Av. Presidente Vargas 41, Belem, PARA, Brazil.

387.164 USA
DAILY SHIPPING NEWS. Text in English. 1920. w. USD 78; USD 1 newsstand/cover (effective 2004). adv. **Document type:** *Newspaper, Trade.*
Address: PO Box 1029, Camas, WA 98607-0029. TEL 360-254-5504, FAX 360-254-7145. Ed., Pub. James Egger. adv.: col. inch USD 5. Circ: 1,000 morning (paid).

387 DNK ISSN 0107-8011
DANSK ILLUSTRERET SKIBSLISTE. Text in Danish. 1980. a. DKK 350 per issue (effective 2009). adv. illus. **Document type:** *Directory.*
Published by: Seapress ApS, c/o Soefart, Stenvej 21 A, Hoejbjerg, 8270, Denmark. TEL 45-86-205898, FAX 45-86-258900.

387 USA
DEEPWATER. Text in English. 1956. q. free. adv. **Document type:** *Newsletter.*
Published by: Greater Baton Rouge Port Commission, 2425 Ernest Wilson Dr, PO Box 380, Port Allen, LA 70767. TEL 225-342-1660, FAX 225-342-1666. Ed. Karen St Cyr. Adv. contact Karen St. Cyr. Circ: 1,000 (controlled).

621.384 JPN ISSN 0287-6450
DENPA KOHO/ELECTRONIC NAVIGATION REVIEW. Text in Japanese. 1960. m. JPY 2,000 per issue. adv. charts; illus.; stat. **Document type:** *Proceedings, Academic/Scholarly.*
Indexed: JTA.
Published by: Japanese Committee for Radio Aids to Navigation/Denpa Koho Kenkyukai, c/o Kaijo Hoan-cho Todai-bu, 2-1-3 Kasumigaseki, Chiyoda-ku, Tokyo, 100-0013, Japan. TEL 81-3-3591-6361 ext. 652, FAX 81-3-3591-5468. Ed., Adv. contact Yukishige Nishida.

DETROIT NEWSPAPER AGENCY. TRAVEL DIRECTORY. *see* TRANSPORTATION—Air Transport

387 DEU ISSN 0948-9002
DEUTSCHE SEESCHIFFAHRT. Text in German. 1995. m. EUR 51.40 (effective 2007). adv. bk.rev. **Document type:** *Magazine, Trade.*
Formed by the merger of (1952-1995): Deutsche Kuestenschiffahrt (0415-5963); (1957-1995): Kehrwieder (0176-473X)
Published by: (Verband Deutscher Reeder e.V.), K.O. Storck Verlag, Striepenweg 31, Hamburg, 21147, Germany. TEL 49-40-7971301, FAX 49-40-79713101, webmaster@storck-verlag.de. adv.: B&W page EUR 1,690, color page EUR 2,425; trim 184 x 264. Circ: 7,500 (paid and controlled).

387 DEU ISSN 0070-4377
DEUTSCHER KUESTEN-ALMANACH; ein Nachschlagewerk fuer die Berufs- und Sportschiffahrt in Nord- und Ostsee und auf den deutschen Seeschiffahrts-strassen. Text in German. 197?. 4 base vols. plus a. updates. EUR 198 base vol(s).; EUR 138 updates (effective 2009). **Document type:** *Monographic series, Trade.*
Formerly: Deutscher Fischerei-Almanach
Published by: Carl Heymanns Verlag KG (Subsidiary of: Wolters Kluwer Deutschland GmbH), Luxemburger Str 449, Cologne, 50939, Germany. TEL 49-221-943730, FAX 49-221-94373901, marketing@heymanns.com, http://www.heymanns.com.

387 DEU ISSN 0343-3668
DEUTSCHES SCHIFFAHRTSARCHIV. Text in German. 1975. a. EUR 19.50 (effective 2009). adv. **Document type:** *Journal, Academic/Scholarly.*
Indexed: DIP, IBR, IBZ.
Published by: Deutsches Schiffahrtsmuseum Bremerhaven, Hans-Scharoun-Platz 1, Bremerhaven, 27568, Germany. TEL 49-471-482070, FAX 49-471-4820755, info@dsm.de, http://www.dsm.de. Circ: 250 (controlled).

623.87 GBR ISSN 1369-7587
DIRECTORY OF MARINE DIESEL ENGINES. Text in English. 1988. a. 3 cols./p.; back issues avail. **Document type:** *Directory, Trade.*
Formerly (until 199?): Marine Engineers Review. Directory of Marine Diesel Engines (0954-2604)
Related titles: ◆ Supplement to: M E R. Marine Engineers Review. ISSN 0047-5955.
—**CCC.**
Published by: Institute of Marine Engineering, Science and Technology, 80 Coleman St, London, EC2R 5BJ, United Kingdom. TEL 44-20-73822600, FAX 44-20-73822670, info@imarest.org, http://www.imarest.org/.

DIRITTO MARITTIMO; rivista trimestrale di dottrina giurisprudenza legislazione italiana e straniera. *see* LAW

387 NLD ISSN 1571-7615
DIRKZWAGER'S DUTCH PORT GUIDE. Text in English. 1873. a. EUR 38.50 (effective 2009). **Document type:** *Directory.* **Description:** Covers port regulations and navigation information, ports and port facilities, pilotage, helicopter and airport services, weather information, nautical, medical, social and legal information.
Former titles (until 2002): Dirkzwager's Guide for the Rotterdam Port Area (1387-828X); (until 1995): Dirkzwager's Guide (Year) (0927-3581); (until 1940): G. Dirkzwager M. Zoon's Guide to the New Waterway (0928-0081); (until 1884): M. Dirkzwager G. Zoon's Guide to the New Waterway (0928-0073)
Published by: Koninklijke Scheepsagentuur Dirkzwager BV, Postbus 14, Maassluis, 3140 AA, Netherlands. TEL 31-10-5931600, FAX 31-10-5925767, info@dirkzwager.com, http://www.dirkzwager.com.

387 665.5 USA ISSN 1931-1931
DIRTY TANKERWIRE. Text in English. 1984. d. USD 4,085; USD 4,585 combined subscription (online & E-mail eds.) (effective 2008). back issues avail. **Document type:** *Newsletter, Trade.* **Description:** OfferProvides extensive listings and analysis of the latest tanker freight and fixture rates as a percentage of the worldscale figure and an additional $/mt conversion.
Media: Online - full content. **Related titles:** E-mail ed.
Published by: Platts (Subsidiary of: McGraw-Hill Companies, Inc.), 1200 G St NW, Ste 1000, Washington, DC 20005. TEL 212-904-3070, 800-752-8878, FAX 202-383-2024, support@platts.com.

387.1 AUS
THE DOG WATCH. Text in English. 1943. a. bk.rev. illus.; maps. 120 p./no. 1 cols./p.; back issues avail. **Document type:** *Journal, Academic/Scholarly.*
Formerly (until 1971): Annual Dog Watch (0066-3921)
Published by: (Shiplovers' Society of Victoria), Research Publications Pty Ltd., 27 A Boronia Rd, Vermont, VIC 3133, Australia. TEL 61-3-98731450, FAX 61-3-98730100, respub@access.net.au.

387 JPN ISSN 0910-6197
DOKKUMASUTA. Text in Japanese. 1960. 3/yr. membership. **Document type:** *Academic/Scholarly.*
Published by: Nihon Senkyocho Kyokai/Japan Dockmasters Association, 1 Yamashita-cho, Naka-ku, Yokohama-shi, Kanagawa-ken 231-0023, Japan. Ed. Kunizo Kasahara. R&P Akemi Ino.

387 910.202 GBR ISSN 1351-640X
DREAM WORLD CRUISE DESTINATIONS. Text in English. 1993. a. GBP 35 per issue (effective 2010). adv. illus. back issues avail. **Document type:** *Magazine, Trade.*
Related titles: Online - full text ed.: free (effective 2010); ◆ Supplement to: International Cruise and Ferry Review. ISSN 0957-7696.
Indexed: G08, I05.
—CCC.
Published by: Ashcroft & Associates, PO Box 57940, London, W4 5RD, United Kingdom. TEL 44-20-89944123, info@ashcroftandassociates.com. Ed., Pub. Chris Ashcroft.

387 623.8 GBR ISSN 0264-4835
DREDGING & PORT CONSTRUCTION. Abbreviated title: D & P C. Text in English. 19??. m. GBP 430 combined subscription (print & online eds.) (effective 2009). adv. Supplement avail.; back issues avail. **Document type:** *Magazine, Trade.* **Description:** Provides articles focusing on port construction, development and dredging campaigns of all types.
Formerly (until 1977): International Dredging and Port Construction (0579-546X)
Related titles: Online - full text ed.
Indexed: A09, A10, A28, APA, B01, B06, B07, B08, B09, BMT, BrCerAb, C&ISA, C12, CA/WCA, CIA, CerAb, CivEngAb, CorrAb, E&CAJ, E11, EEA, EMA, ESPM, EngInd, EnvEAb, FLUIDEX, GEOBASE, H15, KES, M&TEA, M09, MBF, METADEX, P34, SCOPUS, SolStAb, T02, T04, V03, V04, WAA.
—IE, Infotrieve, Linda Hall. **CCC.**
Published by: (Central Dredging Association NLD, Eastern Dredging Association MYS), Lloyd's Register - Fairplay Ltd., Lombard House, 3 Princess Way, Redhill, Surrey RH1 1UP, United Kingdom. TEL 44-1737-379000, FAX 44-1737-379001, info@lrfairplay.com, http://www.lrfairplay.com/. Ed. Tony Slinn TEL 44-1737-379159. Adv. contact Daniel Goncalves TEL 44-1737-379706. color page GBP 2,813; trim 210 x 297.

TU

387.5 GBR
DRY BULK MARKET. QUARTERLY REPORT. Text in English. 1982. q. GBP 1,045 (effective 2000). charts; stat. back issues avail.
Document type: *Report, Trade.* **Description:** Gives a thorough overview of the fast-moving world of bulk shipping. Comments on the developments and trades in the market, monitors the economics, and records fleet changes.
Published by: Drewry Shipping Consultants Ltd., Drewry House, Meridian Gate - S Quay, 213 Marsh Wall, London, E14 9FJ, United Kingdom. TEL 44-2075-380191, FAX 44-2079-879396, http://www.drewry.co.uk.

387 GBR ISSN 1361-3189
DRY BULK TRADE OUTLOOK. Abbreviated title: D B T O. Text in English. 1995. m. GBP 575, USD 1,035 (effective 2011). adv.
Document type: *Report, Trade.* **Description:** Aims to trackc and analyze the dry bulk trades.
Related titles: Online - full text ed.: ISSN 1741-461X.
Published by: Clarkson Research Services Ltd., St Magnus House, 3 Lower Thames St, London, EC3R 6HE, United Kingdom. TEL 44-20-73343134, FAX 44-20-75220330, sales@crsl.com.

387.5448 GBR ISSN 1466-3643
DRY CARGO INTERNATIONAL. Abbreviated title: D C I. Text in English. 1999. m. GBP 140 domestic; GBP 180 in Europe; GBP 230 elsewhere (effective 2009). adv. back issues avail. **Document type:** *Magazine, Trade.*
—CCC.
Address: Clover House, 24 Drury Rd, Colchester, Essex CO2 7UX, United Kingdom. TEL 44-1206-562560, FAX 44-1206-562566. Adv. contact Jason Chinnock. B&W page GBP 1,408, color page GBP 2,200; trim 185 x 275.

623.82 GBR
DRYDOCK MAGAZINE; international journal of ship repair & maintenance. Text in English. 1979. q. GBP 69 domestic; GBP 72 foreign (effective 2009). adv. illus. **Document type:** *Magazine, Trade.*
Description: Provides shipowners, managers and operators with the latest developments in the technical and commercial aspects of ship repair, maintenance and conversion.
Former titles (until 1999): Drydock (0143-5000); (until 1979): Shipping World & Shipbuilder. Ship Repair Number
Indexed: BMT, BioDAb, WSCA.
—IE, Infotrieve, Linda Hall.
Published by: Marine Publications International Ltd., Peel House, Upper S View, Farnham, Surrey GU9 7JN, United Kingdom. TEL 44-1252-732220, FAX 44-1252-732221, info@drydock.co.uk. Ed. Mark Langdon. Pub. Andrew Deere. Adv. contact Patricia Nichols.

387 IRL
DUBLIN PORT AND DOCKS YEARBOOK. Text in English. a. adv.
Document type: *Yearbook, Trade.*
Published by: Tara Publishing Co. Ltd., Poolbeg House, 1-2 Poolbeg St, Dublin, 2, Ireland. TEL 353-1-6719244, FAX 353-1-2413020, info@tarapublishingco.com. Ed. Fergus Farrell. Adv. contact Tony Murphy. B&W page EUR 1,710, color page EUR 2,375; trim 210 x 297. Circ: 3,000.

ED RACHAL FOUNDATION NAUTICAL ARCHAEOLOGY SERIES. *see* ARCHAEOLOGY

387 GBR ISSN 2040-994X
▼ **EGYPT SHIPPING REPORT.** Text in English. 2009. q. USD 975, EUR 695 combined subscription (print & email eds.) (effective 2011).
Document type: *Report, Trade.* **Description:** Provides industry professionals and strategists, sector analysts, business investors, trade associations and regulatory bodies with independent forecasts and competitive intelligence on the shipping industry in Egypt.
Related titles: E-mail ed.
Published by: Business Monitor International Ltd., Senator House, 85 Queen Victoria St, London, EC4V 4AB, United Kingdom. TEL 44-20-72480468, FAX 44-20-72480467, subs@businessmonitor.com.

387 BRA
EMPRESA DE NAVEGACAO DA AMAZONIA. ESTATISTICA DA NAVEGACAO. Text in Portuguese. a. charts.
Published by: Empresa de Navegacao da Amazonia, Av. Presidente Vargas 41, Belem, Para Para, Brazil. Ed. Eugenio Marques Frazao.

387.2 USA ISSN 0744-3129
THE ENSIGN; boating, education, fun and safety. Text in English. 1914. bi-m. USD 15 (effective 2009). adv. 48 p./no.; back issues avail.
Document type: *Magazine, Trade.*
Related titles: Online - full text ed.: ISSN 1949-2294. free (effective 2009).
Published by: (United States Power Squadrons), The Ensign, PO Box 31664, Raleigh, NC 27622. TEL 888-367-8777, FAX 888-304-0813. Ed. Yvonne Hill. Adv. contacts Jim Ocello TEL 704-425-5509, Ted Taylor TEL 704-489-0323. page USD 3,600; 7.5 x 9.75.

387 BEL
EUROPEAN COMMUNITY SHIPOWNERS' ASSOCIATIONS. ANNUAL REPORT. Text in English. a. free. charts; illus. **Document type:** *Corporate.* **Description:** Reports on ECSA actvities and achievements over the past year.
Supersedes: Comite des Associations d'Armateurs des Communautes Europeens. Annual Report
Published by: European Community Shipowners' Associations, Rue Ducale 45, Brussels, 1000, Belgium. TEL 32-2-511-3949, FAX 32-2-511-8092. Ed. Alfons Guinier.

387 BEL
EUROPEAN COMMUNITY SHIPOWNERS' ASSOCIATIONS. NEWSLETTER. Text in English. 1997. m. membership only. illus.
Document type: *Newsletter, Trade.*
Published by: European Community Shipowners' Associations, Rue Ducale 45, Brussels, 1000, Belgium. TEL 32-2-511-3949, FAX 32-2-511-8092.

387 NLD ISSN 1568-881X
EUROPOORT KRINGEN. Text in Dutch. 1962. m. EUR 75; EUR 8.75 newsstand/cover (effective 2009). adv. bk.rev. charts; illus.; stat.
Document type: *Magazine, Trade.*
Formerly (until 2000): Uit Europoortkringen (0041-588X); Which incorporated (1955-1988): Isolatie (0165-2141)
—IE.
Published by: Europoort Producties, Postbus 33050, Rotterdam, 3005 EB, Netherlands. TEL 31-10-4613000, FAX 31-10-4612401, info@europoortproducties.nl. adv.: B&W page EUR 1,845, color page EUR 2,695; trim 210 x 297. Circ: 5,575.

387 USA ISSN 1556-3782
EXPLORATIONS IN WORLD MARITIME HISTORY. Text in English. 2005. irreg., latest 2005. USD 51.95, GBP 35.95 per issue (effective 2010). **Document type:** *Monographic series, Academic/Scholarly.*
Published by: Praeger Publishers (Subsidiary of: Greenwood Publishing Group Inc.), 88 Post Rd W, Westport, CT 06881. TEL 800-368-6868, tech.support@greenwood.com, http://www.greenwood.com. Ed. Lincoln Paine.

F A M E N A. TRANSACTIONS. (Faculty of Mechanical Engineering and Naval Architecture) *see* ENGINEERING—Mechanical Engineering

387 GBR
F I D I FOCUS. Text in English, French, German. 1982. 9/yr. EUR 100 to non-members; EUR 60 to members (effective 2009). adv. back issues avail. **Document type:** *Magazine, Trade.* **Description:** Contains news items, feature articles, photography, and personalized advertisements pertaining to the activities of this organization for overseas furniture moving and storage facilities.
Published by: (Federation Internationale des Demenageurs Internationaux BEL), Quarrington-Curtis Ltd., No 3, Trinity Barns, Weston, Petersfield, Hampshire GU32 3NN, United Kingdom. TEL 44-1730-269262, FAX 44-7836-590479, qcl@qcpr.co.uk. Ed. Colin Quarrington. Adv. contact Pam Quarrington. color page EUR 871.

387.5 DNK ISSN 1902-1712
FACTS ABOUT SHIPPING. Text in English. 2004. a. back issues avail.
Document type: *Government.*
Formerly (until 2006): The Danish Maritime Authority and Shipping (1901-2454)
Related titles: Online - full text ed.: ISSN 1902-1720; ◆ Danish ed.: Fakta om Soefart. ISSN 1901-2438.
Published by: Soefartsstyrelsen/Danish Maritime Authority, Vermundsgade 38 C, Copenhagen OE, 2100, Denmark. TEL 45-39-174400, FAX 45-39-174401, sfs@dma.dk.

387 GBR ISSN 1745-5456
HE561
FAIRPLAY; the international shipping weekly. Text in English. 1883. w. GBP 495, EUR 695 in Europe; USD 850 in United States; USD 1,150 elsewhere (effective 2010). adv. bk.rev. charts; illus.; mkt.; pat.; tr.lit.; stat. back issues avail.; reprints avail. **Document type:** *Magazine, Trade.* **Description:** Provides news, insight, analysis, markets summary, topical features and commentary.
Former titles (until 1992): Fairplay International (0960-6165); (until 1989): Fairplay International Shipping Weekly (0307-0220); (until 1974): Fairplay International Shipping Journal; (until 1966): Fairplay Shipping Journal; (until 1962): Fairplay Weekly Shipping Journal
Related titles: Online - full text ed.
Indexed: CLT&T, ELJI, HRIS, KES, LJI, RASB.
—BLDSC (3865.505500), IE, Ingenta. **CCC.**
Published by: Lloyd's Register - Fairplay Ltd., Lombard House, 3 Princess Way, Redhill, Surrey RH1 1UP, United Kingdom. TEL 44-1737-379000, FAX 44-1737-379001, info@lrfairplay.com, http://www.lrfairplay.com/. Ed. Richard Clayton. Adv. contact Ian Parker TEL 44-1737-379725.

387 GBR
FAIRPLAY NEWBUILDINGS (ONLINE). Text in English. 1964. m. included with subscr. to Fairplay Magazine. stat. **Document type:** *Directory, Consumer.* **Description:** Contains a complete summary of all vessels currently under construction, on order or under negotiation, along with the operator and builder's address details. For professionals in both the shipbuilding and shipowning sectors of the shipping industry.
Former titles (until 200?): Fairplay Newbuildings (Print); (until 1995): World Ships on Order (0043-9010)
Media: Online - full text. **Related titles:** ◆ Supplement to: Fairplay Solutions. ISSN 1367-1227.
Published by: Fairplay Publications Ltd., Lombard House, 3 Princess Way, Redhill, Surrey RH1 1UP, United Kingdom. TEL 44-1737-379000, FAX 44-1737-379001, info@lrfairplay.com.

387 GBR ISSN 1367-1227
HE561
FAIRPLAY SOLUTIONS. Text in English. 1996. m. Included with subscr. to Fairplay. adv. back issues avail. **Document type:** *Magazine, Trade.*
Description: Aims to make life easier and more profitable for shipowners by highlighting technical solutions to the commercial problems faced by the shipping industry.
Incorporates: Fairplay Newbuildings
Related titles: ◆ Supplement(s): Fairplay Newbuildings (Online).
—BLDSC (3865.508070). **CCC.**
Published by: Lloyd's Register - Fairplay Ltd., Lombard House, 3 Princess Way, Redhill, Surrey RH1 1UP, United Kingdom. TEL 44-1737-379000, FAX 44-1737-379001, info@lrfairplay.com, http://www.lrfarplay.com/. Ed. Malcolm Latarche.

387.5 DNK ISSN 1901-2438
FAKTA OM SOEFART. Text in Danish. 2004. a. stat. back issues avail.
Document type: *Government.*
Related titles: Online - full text ed.: ISSN 1901-2446; ◆ English ed.: Facts about Shipping. ISSN 1902-1712.
Published by: Soefartsstyrelsen/Danish Maritime Authority, Vermundsgade 38 C, Copenhagen OE, 2100, Denmark. TEL 45-39-174400, FAX 45-39-174401, sfs@dma.dk, http://www.dma.dk.

623.8 NOR ISSN 0807-3201
FARTOEYVERN. Text in Multiple languages. 1996. a. NOK 85 (effective 2006). back issues avail.
Published by: Hardanger Fartoeyvernsenter/Centre for Ship Preservation, Norheimsund, 5600, Norway. TEL 47-56-553350, FAX 47-56-553351, info@fartoyvern.no.

629.3 GBR ISSN 0954-3988
VM362 CODEN: FFINE5
FAST FERRY INTERNATIONAL. Text in English. 1961. 10/yr. GBP 85 in Europe; GBP 95 elsewhere (effective 2009). bk.rev. charts; illus.; pat. index. 40 p./no. 3 cols./p.; back issues avail.; reprints avail.
Document type: *Magazine, Trade.* **Description:** Provides a primary source of information for the fast ferry industry worldwide including new vessels, designs and components, ferry operations, company profiles, conference reports and annual statistics.
Former titles (until 1989): High-Speed Surface Craft (0144-7823); (until 1979): Hovering Craft and Hydrofoil (0018-6775)
Indexed: A22, AcoustA, ApMecR, BMT, BrRB, CLT&T, GeoRef, HRIS, SCOPUS, SpeleolAb.
—BLDSC (3897.170000), IE, Infotrieve, Ingenta, INIST, Linda Hall. **CCC.**
Published by: Fast Ferry Information Ltd., 14 Marston Gate, Winshester, SO23 7DS, United Kingdom. TEL 44-1962-869842, FAX 44-1962-843863.

387.1 GBR ISSN 1746-7403
FAXAFLOHAFNIR. HANDBOOK. Text in English. 1995. biennial.
Document type: *Handbook/Manual/Guide, Trade.*
Formerly (until 2005): Reykjavik Port Handbook (1356-8175)
Published by: Lamd and Marine Publications Ltd., 1 Kings Court, Newcomen Way, Severalls Business Park, Colchester, Essex CO4 9RA, United Kingdom. TEL 44-1206-752902, FAX 44-1206-842958, info@landmarine.com, http://www.landmarine.com/.

FISKERBLADET; magasinet for nordisk fiskeri og fiskeindustri. *see* FISH AND FISHERIES

387 USA ISSN 1067-1455
THE FLORIDA SHIPPER MAGAZINE. Text in English. 1975. w.
Document type: *Magazine, Trade.*
Former titles (until 19??): Florida Shipper (0884-8548); South Florida Shipper
Related titles: Online - full text ed.
Indexed: A10, B01, B02, B07, B15, B17, B18, BPI, BRD, G04, G08, I05, P34, T02, V03, W01, W02, W03, W05.
—CCC.
Published by: Journal of Commerce, Inc. (Subsidiary of: Commonwealth Business Media, Inc.), 2 Penn Plz E, Newark, NJ 07105. TEL 973-776-8660, customersvs@joc.com, http://www.joc.com.

387 USA
FOGHORN (ARLINGTON). Text in English. 19??. m. free (effective 2011). adv. back issues avail. **Document type:** *Magazine, Trade.*
Description: Designed to address the issues which directly affect owners and operators of commercial passenger vessels. Contains reports by expert PVA staff members on regulatory, legislative and safety matters as they affect the passenger vessel community.
Published by: (Passenger Vessel Association), Philips Publishing Group, 2201 W Commodore Way, Seattle, WA 98199. TEL 206-284-8285, FAX 206-284-0391, http://www.philipspublishing.com. Ed. Chris Philips. Pub. Peter Philips. Adv. contact Mike Morris.

FORD'S FREIGHTER TRAVEL GUIDE AND WATERWAYS OF THE WORLD. *see* TRAVEL AND TOURISM

387 DEU ISSN 0939-7965
FRACHT-DIENST; Fachzeitschrift fuer Lager, Logistik, Transport und Verkehr. Text in German. 1945. bi-m. EUR 12 (effective 2007). adv. bk.rev. back issues avail. **Document type:** *Magazine, Trade.*
Indexed: RefZh.
Address: Jasperallee 82, Braunschweig, 38102, Germany. TEL 49-531-2346197, FAX 49-531-2347101. Ed. Olaf Kortegast. Adv. contact J R Lodiga. B&W page EUR 2,000, color page EUR 3,200; trim 185 x 270. Circ: 7,893 (paid and controlled).

387 NOR ISSN 0015-9352
FRAKTEMANN. Text in Norwegian. 1935. 5/yr. NOK 60, USD 3.50. adv.
—CCC.
Published by: Fraktefartoyenes Rederiforening, Postboks 2020, Nordnes, Bergen, 5024, Norway. Ed. Einar Haakon Kirkefjord. Circ: 1,000.

387 FRA ISSN 2024-9950
FRANCE. COMMISSION CENTRALE POUR LA NAVIGATION DU RHIN. RAPPORT ANNUEL. Text in French, German, Dutch. 1835. a. charts; stat. **Document type:** *Government.* **Description:** Contains reviews and statistical information about the Rhine river for each year as well as statistics about the preceding decades.
Published by: Commission Centrale pour la Navigation du Rhin, Palais du Rhin, 2 Place de la Republique, Strasbourg, Cedex 67082, France. TEL 33-3-88522010, FAX 33-3-88321072, http://www.ccr-zkr.org. Ed. Hans van der Werf. Circ: 500 (controlled).

387.1 AUS
FREMANTLE PORT NEWS. Variant title: Port News. Text in English. 1961. q. bk.rev. illus. **Document type:** *Newsletter, Trade.*
Description: Explores port development, export trade and shipping lines. Includes staff appointments and port activities.
Former titles (until 1998): Western Australia. Fremantle Port Authority. News; (until 1991): Port of Fremantle; (until 1976): Port of Fremantle Quarterly
Related titles: Online - full text ed.: free (effective 2009).
Published by: Fremantle Port Authority, PO Box 95, Fremantle, W.A. 6959, Australia. TEL 61-8-94303555, FAX 61-8-93361391, mail@fremantleport.com.au, http://www.fremantleport.com.au.

FRIES SCHEEPVAART MUSEUM EN OUDHEIDKAMER. JAARBOEK. *see* MUSEUMS AND ART GALLERIES

FUNE TO KAIJO KISHO/SHIP AND MARITIME METEOROLOGY. *see* METEOROLOGY

387.1 USA
G P A PORTS GUIDE & DIRECTORY. Text in English. 200?. a. adv. back issues avail. **Document type:** *Directory, Trade.*
Related titles: Online - full text ed.: free (effective 2011).
Published by: (Georgia Ports Authority), Seaports Publications Group (Subsidiary of: Commonwealth Business Media, Inc.), 3400 Lakeside Dr, Ste 515, Miramar, FL 33027. TEL 954-628-0058, FAX 954-628-0085, publisher@seaportsinfo.com, http://www.seaportsinfo.com/. Adv. contact David Cantwell TEL 954-628-0058 ext 173.

387.54 661.46 GBR
GARSTON DOCKS TIDE TABLE. Text in English. a. **Document type:** *Report, Trade.*
Published by: Associated British Ports (Liverpool) (Subsidiary of: Associated British Ports Holdings PLC), Port Office, Garston, Liverpool, Merseyside L19 2JW, United Kingdom. TEL 44-151-4275971, FAX 44-151-4943232, bgreen@abports.co.uk, http://www.abports.co.uk/custinfo/ports/garston.htm.

387 662 GBR ISSN 1478-4610
HE566.T3
THE GAS CARRIER REGISTER. Text in English. 1966. a. GBP 250, USD 450. adv. charts; stat. **Document type:** *Directory, Trade.*
Description: Contains lists of liquid gas carrier ships by name; also includes ship size and weight, age, capacity, and other technical characteristics.
Former titles (until 2002): The Liquid Gas Carrier Register (0305-1803); (until 1967): Liquid Gas Tanker Register
Related titles: CD-ROM ed.: Gas Carrier Fleet CD. GBP 575, USD 1,035 updates (effective 2011).
Published by: Clarkson Research Services Ltd., St Magnus House, 3 Lower Thames St, London, EC3R 6HE, United Kingdom. TEL 44-20-73343134, FAX 44-20-75220330, sales@crsl.com, http://www.crsl.com.

387 USA ISSN 0016-8149
HE554.A3
GEORGIA ANCHORAGE. Text in English. 1959. q. free (effective 2005). adv. charts; illus. **Document type:** *Magazine, Trade.* **Description:** News articles on the export and import trade and shipping industry in the state, as well as news on the activities of the State's Ports Authority.
Indexed: CLT&T.
Published by: Georgia Ports Authority, State Hwys. 307 & 25N, Garden City, GA 31408. TEL 912-964-3811, FAX 912-964-3921. Ed., R&P Robert Morris. adv.: color page USD 975, B&W page USD 550. Circ: 13,000 (free).

387 DEU ISSN 0723-2667
HE565.G3
GERMAN MERCHANT FLEET; die Deutsche Handelsflotte. Text in German, English. 1954. a. EUR 390 per issue (effective 2009). adv. **Document type:** *Journal, Trade.*
Formerly (until 1982): Die Deutsche Handelsflotte (0070-4148)
Published by: Seehafen Verlag GmbH, Nordkanalstr 36, Hamburg, 20097, Germany. TEL 49-40-23714228, FAX 49-40-23714259, http://www.schiffundhafen.de.

387 JPN
GLOBAL PORT/YOKOHAMA. Text in English, Japanese. a. free. 10 p./no.
Published by: Port of Yokohama Promotion Association, Industry and Trade Center Bldg, 2 Yamashita-cho, Naka-ku, Yokohama-shi, Kanagawa-ken 231-0023, Japan. TEL 81-45-671-7241, FAX 81-45-671-7350.

THE GREAT CIRCLE. *see* HISTORY

387 USA
GREAT LAKER; lighthouses, lake boats, travel & leisure. Text in English. 1970. q. USD 30 (effective 2011). **Document type:** *Magazine, Consumer.* **Description:** Exposure to cultural tourism in the Great Lakes maritime community and maritime.
Published by: Harbor House Publishers, Inc., 221 Water St, Boyne City, MI 49712. TEL 800-491-1760, FAX 866-906-3392, harbor@harborhouse.com, http://www.harborhouse.com. Ed. Janenne Irene Pung. Pub. Michelle Cortright. Adv. contact James Fish.

387 CAN ISSN 0824-8583
HE554.A5
GREAT LAKES NAVIGATION. Text in English. 1917. a. adv. **Document type:** *Handbook/Manual/Guide, Trade.*
Published by: Canadian Marine Publications Ltd., Ste 512, 1434 St Catherine St W, Montreal, PQ H3G 1R4, Canada. TEL 514-861-6715, FAX 514-861-0966. Ed. Megan Perkins. R&P John McManus. Adv. contact Marilyn Belanger.

386 CAN ISSN 1910-3468
GREAT LAKES PILOTAGE AUTHORITY. ANNUAL REPORT (ONLINE). Text in English. 2001. a., latest 2005. **Document type:** *Report, Trade.*
Media: Online - full text. **Related titles:** ◆ Print ed.: Great Lakes Pilotage Authority. Annual Report (Print). ISSN 0711-0707; French ed.: Administration de Pilotage des Grands Lacs. Rapport Annuel. ISSN 1910-3476.
Published by: Canada, Great Lakes Pilotage Authority, PO Box 95, Cornwall, ON K6H 5R9, Canada. TEL 613-933-2991, FAX 613-932-3793, http://www.glpa-apgl.com/homePage_e.asp.

386 CAN ISSN 0711-0707
GREAT LAKES PILOTAGE AUTHORITY. ANNUAL REPORT (PRINT). Text in English, French. 1972. a., latest 2005. **Document type:** *Government.*
Related titles: ◆ Online - full text ed.: Great Lakes Pilotage Authority. Annual Report (Online). ISSN 1910-3468.
Published by: Canada, Great Lakes Pilotage Authority, PO Box 95, Cornwall, ON K6H 5R9, Canada. TEL 613-933-2991, FAX 613-932-3793, http://www.glpa-apgl.com/homePage_e.asp.

387 USA
HE381.A2
GREAT LAKES/SEAWAY REVIEW; the international transportation magazine of midcontinent North America. Text in English. 1970. q. USD 32 (effective 2011). adv. bk.rev. charts; illus.; stat. back issues avail.; reprints avail. **Document type:** *Magazine, Trade.* **Description:** Edited for the bi-national transportation industry and infrastructure of the Great Lakes - St. Lawrence transportation system. Articles concern international trade, port development, shipbuilding, shipping, economics, maritime technology and hardware, ship maintenance, foreign and U.S. liner services and cargo handling.
Former titles: Great Lakes Seaway Log; (until 1998): Seaway Review (0037-0487); Which incorporated (1968-1977): Limnos (0024-3604)
Related titles: Microfilm ed.: (from PQC).
Indexed: A22, BMT, CLT&T, GeoRef, HRIS, MMI, SpeleolAb.
—Linda Hall. **CCC.**
Published by: Harbor House Publishers, Inc., 221 Water St, Boyne City, MI 49712. TEL 800-491-1760, FAX 866-906-3392, harbor@harborhouse.com, http://www.harborhouse.com. Ed. Janenne Irene Pung. Pub. Michelle Cortright. Adv. contact James Fish.

386 USA
GREATER CHICAGO OCEAN FREIGHT DIRECTORY. Text in English. 1991. a. USD 21.95 per issue (effective 2008). adv. charts; maps; stat. back issues avail. **Document type:** *Directory, Trade.*
Description: Features many advertisers from ocean cargo and intermodal companies that serve the port of Chicago, the port of Indiana and the Chicago intermodal container industry.
Published by: Fourth Seacoast Publishing Co., Inc., 25300 Little Mack Ave, St. Clair Shores, MI 48081. TEL 586-779-5570, FAX 586-779-5547, info@fourthseacoastonline.com, http://www.fourthseacoast.com. Adv. contact Tom Buysse. B&W page USD 1,115; trim 8.5 x 11. Circ: 15,000.

387.5 CAN ISSN 1924-2026
▼ **GREEN MARINE MAGAZINE**; a wave worth riding. Text in English. 2009. s-a. adv. **Document type:** *Magazine, Trade.* **Description:** Designed to highlight and reward environmental excellence in initiatives taken by the marine industry around the world.
Related titles: Online - full text ed.: free (effective 2010).
Published by: Canadian Sailings, 5165 Sherbrooke St W, Ste 200, Montreal, PQ H4A 1T6, Canada. TEL 514-934-0373, FAX 514-934-4708, http://www.canadiansailings.ca. Ed., Pub. Joyce Hammock TEL 514-934-0373 ext 1. Adv. contact Wendy Hennick TEL 514-934-0373 ext 27.

387.1 GBR ISSN 2045-6085
▼ **GREENPORT.** Text in English. 2010. q. GBP 104 (effective 2011). adv. **Document type:** *Magazine, Trade.* **Description:** Provides business information on environmental best practice and corporate responsibility centered around marine ports and terminals.
Published by: E W P Communications, The Old Mill, Lower Quay, Fareham, Hampshire PO16 0RA, United Kingdom. TEL 44-1329-825335, FAX 44-1329-825330, corporate@mercatormedia.com, http://www.mercatormedia.com. Circ: 5,500.

386 USA ISSN 0072-7490
HE630.G7
GREENWOOD'S GUIDE TO GREAT LAKES SHIPPING. Text in English. 1959. a. USD 69 (effective 2000). adv.
Published by: Freshwater Press, Inc., 1700 E 13th St, Ste 3R E, Cleveland, OH 44114. TEL 216-241-0373. Ed. John O Greenwood. Circ: 3,000.

387 GRD
GRENADA PORTS AUTHORITY. (YEAR) HANDBOOK. Text in English. irreg. (every 3-5 yrs.). free.
Published by: Grenada Ports Authority, P.O. Box 494, Carenage, St. George's, Grenada. TEL 809-440-3013, FAX 809-440-3418.

387 GRD
GRENADA PORTS AUTHORITY ANNUAL REPORT & ACCOUNTS. Text in English. a. free. **Document type:** *Corporate.*
Published by: Grenada Ports Authority, P.O. Box 494, Carenage, St. George's, Grenada. TEL 809-440-3013, FAX 809-440-3418.

387 DEU ISSN 1861-0986
GUETERTRANSPORT; handbuch fuer transport und logistik. Text in German. 1954. a. EUR 36.30 (effective 2006). **Document type:** *Directory, Trade.*
Former titles (until 2004): Guetertransport im Land-, See- und Luftverkehr (1430-6336); (until 1991): Guetertransport in Seeverkehr (1430-7596); (until 1984): Fracht-Schiffahrts-Konferenzen (0344-144X)
Published by: K.O. Storck Verlag, Striepenweg 31, Hamburg, 21147, Germany. TEL 49-40-7971301, FAX 49-40-79713101, webmaster@storck-verlag.de, http://www.storck-verlag.de. Ed. H Meder.

387 PRT
GUIA DO PORTO DE LISBOA. Text in Portuguese. 1965. a. free.
Published by: Administracao do Porto de Lisboa, Divisao de Relacoes Publicas e Marketing, Rua Junqueira, 94, Lisbon, 1300, Portugal. Circ: 3,000.

387 PER ISSN 1726-0841
GUIA MARITIMA. Text in Spanish. 1999. m.
Related titles: Online - full text ed.: ISSN 1726-085X. 2002.
Published by: Asociacion Peruana de Derecho Maritimo, Ave. Conquistadores 333 Ofi. 203, San Isidro, Lima, Peru. TEL 51-1-4225064. Ed. Unices Martes Espinoza.

GUIA MARITIMA, PORTUARIA Y DE LA INDUSTRIA NAVAL DE VENEZUELA/MARITIME, PORT AND NAVAL INDUSTRY GUIDE OF VENEZUELA. *see* BUSINESS AND ECONOMICS—Trade And Industrial Directories

387.2 ESP ISSN 1137-2516
GUIA PRACTICA DEL MAR NAVEGAR. Variant title: Navegar Guia Practica del Mar. Text in Spanish. 1994. a. adv. **Document type:** *Magazine, Consumer.*
Published by: Motorpress Iberica (Subsidiary of: Gruner + Jahr AG & Co), Ancora 40, Madrid, 28045, Spain. TEL 34-91-3470100, FAX 34-91-3470152, http://www.motorpress-iberica.es. Ed. Erik Tarres. Circ: 20,000 (paid and controlled).

387 GBR ISSN 1467-0968
THE GUIDE ON CD; ther port information resource. Text in English. 1997. q. GBP 320 per vol. (effective 2010). charts; illus.; maps. **Document type:** *Directory, Trade.* **Description:** Contains general port description, pre-arrival information, maximum size of vessel, health, safety and security, communications, berthing location and operations, cargo ports facilities, shore facilities, pollution and local information.
Media: CD-ROM.
Published by: Shipping Guides Ltd., 28 Reigate Hill, Reigate, Surrey RH2 9NG, United Kingdom. TEL 44-1737-242255, FAX 44-1737-222449, info@portinfo.co.uk.

387 GBR
GUIDE TO PORT ENTRY (YEAR). Text in English. 1971. biennial, latest 20th eds. GBP 360 combined subscription per issue (print & CD-ROM eds.) (effective 2010). **Document type:** *Directory, Trade.*
Description: Provides detailed port information including port plans, mooring diagrams, regulations, maximum size, port restrictions, port access, required documentation, customs allowances, berthing times and availability for masters and owners.
Related titles: CD-ROM ed.
Published by: Shipping Guides Ltd., 28 Reigate Hill, Reigate, Surrey RH2 9NG, United Kingdom. TEL 44-1737-242255, FAX 44-1737-222449, info@portinfo.co.uk.

387.1 GBR ISSN 1467-0976
GUIDE TO TANKER PORTS. Text in English. 1976. base vol. plus q. updates. looseleaf. GBP 530 per vol. domestic; GBP 610 per vol. in Europe; GBP 590 per vol. in Europe Union & USA; GBP 690 per vol. elsewhere (effective 2010). maps. **Document type:** *Directory, Trade.*
Description: Provides essential information for major oil companies, tanker operators and marine specialists.
Published by: Shipping Guides Ltd., 28 Reigate Hill, Reigate, Surrey RH2 9NG, United Kingdom. TEL 44-1737-242255, FAX 44-1737-222449, info@portinfo.co.uk.

387 USA ISSN 1086-1807
HE561
GULF SHIPPER. Text in English. 1990. w. **Document type:** *Magazine, Trade.*
Related titles: Online - full text ed.
Indexed: A10, B01, B02, B07, B15, B17, B18, BPI, BRD, G04, G08, I05, T02, V03, W01, W02, W03, W05.
—CCC.
Published by: Journal of Commerce, Inc. (Subsidiary of: Commonwealth Business Media, Inc.), 2 Penn Plz E, Newark, NJ 07105. TEL 973-776-8660, customersvs@joc.com, http://www.joc.com.

387.5 388.324 GBR ISSN 1362-7716
H C B TANK GUIDE. (Hazardous Cargo Bulletin) Text in English. 1991. a. GBP 365, EUR 540, USD 720 per issue (effective 2009). **Document type:** *Directory, Trade.* **Description:** 'Who's Who' directory for the tank container and road tanker industry. Allowing purchasers of tank services and equipment instant access to a wealth of information on the top companies worldwide. Provides comprehensive contact details and company descriptions. Covering tank containers and road tanker, rail tank cars, cleaning and repair depots and other support services, also contains web site and e-mail addresses.
Published by: Informa Trade & Energy (Subsidiary of: Informa U K Ltd.), Informa House, 30-32 Mortimer St, London, W1W 7RE, United Kingdom. TEL 44-20-70175000, http://www.informa.com/divisions/commercial/informa_Informa_Trade_and_Energy.

387 DEU
H H L A REPORT. Text in German. 1974. irreg. free. **Document type:** *Magazine, Trade.*
Published by: Hamburger Hafen- und Lagerhaus-Aktiengesellschaft, Bei St Annen 1, Hamburg, 20457, Germany. TEL 49-40-30881, FAX 49-40-30883355, info@hhla.de, http://www.hhla.de. Circ: 4,500.

387 ISR ISSN 0334-715X
HADSHOT SAPPANUT UTEUFAH - YIDION; shipping and aviation news. Text in Hebrew. 1971. m. **Document type:** *Bulletin, Trade.*
Description: News and statistics on shipping and aviation.
Formerly (until 1983): Israel Shipping and Aviation Research Institute. Yidion (0334-2808)
Published by: Haifa University, Wydra Institute of Shipping and Aviation Research, University of Haifa, Eshkol Tower, Haifa, 31905, Israel. TEL 972-4-8240186, FAX 972-4-8348908, estiw@univ.haifa.ac.il, http://wydra.haifa.ac.il/html/html_eng/index.htm. Ed. M Ofek.

387 NLD
HAMBURG - LE HAVRE RANGE; ontwikkelingsplannen en infrastructurele projecten in de belangrijkste Duitse, Belgische en Franse Havens. Text in Dutch. 1989. a. free (effective 2009). **Document type:** *Trade.* **Description:** Describes infrastructure development projects at the main German, Dutch, Belgian and French seaports.
Formerly (until 1996): Ontwikkelingsplannen van de Havens in de Hamburg - Le Havre Range
Published by: Nationale Havenraad, Koningskade 4, Postbus 20906, The Hague, 2500 EX, Netherlands. TEL 31-70-3517615, FAX 31-70-3517600, info@havenraad.nl, http://www.havenraad.nl.

387.5 NLD ISSN 1872-3977
HANDBOEK INTERNATIONAL MARITIME DANGEROUS GOODS. Key Title: Handboek I M D G. Cover title: Vervoer Gevaarlijke Stoffen over Zee. Text in Dutch. 2002. biennial. EUR 100 (effective 2009).
Published by: GDS Europe BV, Postbus 3111, Hoofddorp, 2130 KC, Netherlands. TEL 31-23-5542970, FAX 31-23-5542971, info@gdscrossmediagroup.nl, http://www.gds-europe.com.

387.009489 DNK ISSN 0085-1418
HF61
HANDELS- OG SOEFARTSMUSEET PAA KRONBORG. AARBOG. Text in Danish, German, Swedish; Summaries in English. 1942. a. DKK 250 domestic membership; DKK 1,700 membership (effective 2009). adv. illus. cum.index. back issues avail. **Document type:** *Yearbook, Academic/Scholarly.*
Indexed: MLA-IB.
Published by: (Selskabet Handels- og Soefartsmuseets Venner/Friends of the Danish Maritime Museum), Handels- og Soefartsmuseet paa Kronborg, Helsingoer, 3000, Denmark. TEL 45-49-210685, FAX 45-49-213440, info@maritime-museum.dk, http://www.maritime-museum.dk.

387 CHN ISSN 1000-0356
VK4
HANG HAI. Text in Chinese. bi-m. USD 18 (effective 2009).
Related titles: Online - full text ed.
—East View.
Published by: Shanghai Hanghai Xuehui, No2, Rm.1001, Yuanping Nanlu Alley 590, Shanghai, 200030, China. TEL 4385774. Ed. Zhou Yiheng.

HANGHAI JIAOYU YANJIU/MARITIME EDUCATION RESEARCH. *see* EDUCATION

387 CHN ISSN 1006-1738
HANGHAI JISHU/MARINE TECHNOLOGY. Text in Chinese. 1979. bi-m. USD 24.
Related titles: Online - full text ed.
Published by: Zhongguo Hanghai Xuehui, No2, Rm. 1005, Aijian Dasha, Yuanping Nanlu, Alley 590, Shanghai, 200030, China. TEL 021-4385457. Ed. Jin Zhongming. Circ: 15,000 (paid).

623.8 DEU ISSN 0017-7504
VK3 CODEN: NNGZB2
HANSA; international maritime journal. Text in German; Summaries in English. 1864. m. adv. bk.rev. abstr.; bibl.; charts; illus.; stat. index. **Document type:** *Magazine, Trade.*
Indexed: A22, ASFA, B21, BMT, CISA, CLT&T, DIP, ESPM, IBR, IBZ, KES, RefZh, TM.
—BLDSC (4262.250000), IE, Infotrieve, Ingenta, Linda Hall.
Published by: Schiffahrts Verlag Hansa, Striepenweg 31, Hamburg, 21147, Germany. TEL 49-40-79713225, FAX 49-40-79713208. Ed. Ralf Hinrichs. Adv. contact Ruediger Spieckermann. B&W page EUR 2,460, color page EUR 3,270; 180 x 266. Circ: 6,378 (controlled).

HARBIN GONGCHENG DAXUE XUEBAO/HARBIN ENGINEERING UNIVERSITY. JOURNAL. *see* ENGINEERING

TU

387 CAN ISSN 0017-7636
HARBOUR AND SHIPPING. Text in English. 1918. m. CAD 48.15, USD 85.60. adv. illus.; tr.lit. **Document type:** *Journal, Trade.*
Indexed: BMT.
Published by: Progress Publishing Co. Ltd., 1865 Marine Dr, Ste 200, West Vancouver, BC V7V 1J7, Canada. TEL 604-922-6717, FAX 604-922-1739. Circ: 2,000.

387 CAN ISSN 1203-5564
HARBOUR AUTHORITIES FORUM/FORUM DES ADMINISTRATIONS PORTUAIRES. Text in English. s-a. **Document type:** *Newsletter, Government.*
Related titles: Online - full text ed.: ISSN 1719-7015. 1998.
Published by: Fisheries and Oceans Canada, 200 Kent St, 13th Fl, Sta 13E228, Ottawa, ON K1A 0E6, Canada. TEL 613-993-0999, FAX 613-990-1866, info@dfo-mpo.gc.ca.

623.8 NOR ISSN 1503-9927
HARDANGER FARTOEYVERNSENTER. RAPPORT. Text in Norwegian. 2001. irreg. back issues avail. **Document type:** *Monographic series.*
Published by: Hardanger Fartoeyvernsenter/Centre for Ship Preservation, Norheimsund, 5600, Norway. TEL 47-56-553350, FAX 47-56-553351, info@fartoyvern.no, http://www.fartoyvern.no.

385.264 BEL
HAVEN. Text in Dutch. 1913. s-a. **Document type:** *Bulletin, Trade.*
Published by: Belgische Transportarbeidersbond, Paardenmarkt 66, Antwerp, 2000, Belgium. TEL 32-3-224-3411, FAX 32-3-234-0149. Ed. Bob Baete.

338.0029 BEL ISSN 0775-7034
HAVEN GENT. JAARBOEK/GHENT PORT ANNUAL/HAFEN VON GENT. JAHRBUCH/PORT DE GAND. ANNUAIRE. Text in Dutch, English, French, German. 1987. a. charts; illus.; stat. **Document type:** *Directory.* **Description:** Provides a comprehensive reference for the activities of the Port of Ghent. Discusses the management and operation of the port and provides directory listings for ancillary services, chambers of commerce, consulates, and trade and professional associations.
Published by: De Lloyd N.V./Le Lloyd S.A., Vleminckstraat 18, Antwerpen, 2000, Belgium. TEL 32-3-234-0550, FAX 32-3-234-0850, info@lloyd.be, http://www.anlloyd.be. Ed. Bernard Van den Bossche. Pub. Guy Dubois.

387.5 BEL
HAVEN VAN ANTWERPEN. INDEX/PORT D'ANVERS. INDEX. Text in Dutch, French. a. adv. charts; stat. **Document type:** *Directory, Trade.* **Description:** Reviews warehouses and depots, administrative issues, port services, and technical data of cranes and docks. Lists all docks and berths, along with shipping lines.
Published by: De Lloyd N.V./Le Lloyd S.A., Vleminckstraat 18, Antwerpen, 2000, Belgium. TEL 32-3-234-0550, FAX 32-3-234-0850, info@lloyd.be, http://www.anlloyd.be. Ed. Bernard Van den Bossche. Pub. Guy Dubois.

338.0229 BEL ISSN 0774-7365
HAVENS ZEEBRUGGE EN OOSTENDE. JAARBOEK/HAVEN VON ZEEBRUGGE UND OSTENDE. JAHRBUCH/PORTS DE ZEEBRUGGE ET D'OSTENDE. ANNUAIRE/ZEEBRUGGE AND OSTEND PORTS. ANNUAL. Text in Dutch, English, French, German. 1986. a. charts; illus.; stat. **Document type:** *Directory.* **Description:** Offers a comprehensive reference for the activities of the ports of Zeebrugge and Ostend, along with detailed directory listings of consulates, chambers of commerce, trade and professional associations, and transportation companies.
Published by: De Lloyd N.V./Le Lloyd S.A., Vleminckstraat 18, Antwerpen, 2000, Belgium. TEL 32-3-234-0550, FAX 32-3-234-0850, info@lloyd.be, http://www.anlloyd.be. Ed. Bernard Van den Bossche. Pub. Guy Dubois.

387 DNK ISSN 1395-4466
HAVNE & SKIBSFART. Text in Danish. 1995. bi-m. adv. tr.lit. **Document type:** *Magazine, Trade.*
Related titles: Online - full text ed.: 2007.
Published by: ErhvervsMagasinerne, Jaegergaardsgade 152, Bygning 03 I, Aarhus C, 8000, Denmark. TEL 45-70-204155, FAX 45-70-204156, rw@erhvervsmagasinerne.dk, http://www.erhvervsmagasinerne.dk. Ed., Pub. Rene Wittendorff. Adv. contact Kasper Kristensen.

HAZARDS OF CONFINED SPACES FOR SHIPPING AND TRANSPORTATION INDUSTRIES. *see* PUBLIC HEALTH AND SAFETY

623.82 JPN
HINKAN JIHO. Text in Japanese. m.
Published by: Nihon Senpaku Hinshitsu Kanri Kyokai/Japan Ship Machinery Quality Control Association, 1-9 Kanda-Sakuma-cho, Chiyoda-ku, Tokyo, 101-0025, Japan.

387 GBR ISSN 1476-3575
HONOURABLE COMPANY OF MASTER MARINERS. JOURNAL. Text in English. 1933. q. free to members (effective 2009). bk.rev. illus. cum.index every 3 yrs. back issues avail. **Document type:** *Journal, Trade.*
Related titles: Online - full text ed.
Published by: Honourable Company of Master Mariners, HQS Wellington, Temple Stairs, Victoria Embankment, London, WC2R 2PN, United Kingdom. TEL 44-20-78368179, FAX 44-20-72403082, info@hcmm.org.uk, http://www.hcmm.org.uk. Ed. David Squire TEL 44-1282-814998.

388.044 GBR ISSN 1028-8821
I C H C A NEWS AND CARGO MANAGEMENT. Text in English. 1995. irreg. **Document type:** *Monographic series, Trade.*
Related titles: ◆ Supplement to: I C H C A News and Cargo Today. ISSN 1029-1768.
Published by: International Cargo Handling Co-ordination Association, Ste 2, 85 Western Rd, Romford, Essex RM1 3LS, United Kingdom. TEL 44-1708-735295, FAX 44-1708-735225, info@ichcainternational.co.uk, http://www.ichcainternational.co.uk.

623.8 JPN ISSN 0018-9820
TA1 CODEN: IHERA6
I H I ENGINEERING REVIEW. Text in English. 1968. q. membership. bk.rev. reprints avail.
Related titles: Microfilm ed.: (from PQC); Japanese ed.: Ishikawajima-Harima Giho. ISSN 0578-7904.
Indexed: A22, BMT, CIN, ChemAb, ChemTitl, INIS AtomInd, Inspec, JCT, JTA, SCOPUS, SpeleolAb.
—BLDSC (4363.570000), CASDDS, IE, Ingenta, INIST, Linda Hall.
Published by: Ishikawajima-Harima Heavy Industries Co. Ltd./Ishikawajima Harima Jukogyo K.K., 2-16 Toyosu 3-chome, Koto-ku, Tokyo, 135-0061, Japan. Ed. Akira Tsutsui.

387.2 GBR ISSN 0253-8199
HE561.5
I M O NEWS. Text in English. 1962. q. free to qualified personnel (effective 2009). adv. bk.rev. illus. back issues avail. **Document type:** *Magazine, Trade.* **Description:** Provides news on maritime safety and pollution prevention.
Former titles (until 1982): I M C O News (0140-6434); (until 1977): I M C O Bulletin (0047-0422)
Related titles: Online - full text ed.: ISSN 1564-5134. free (effective 2009); French ed.: Organisation Maritime Internationale. Nouvelles. ISSN 1010-6197. 1982.
Indexed: BMT, CLT&T, HRIS, RASB.
—BLDSC (4369.790000). **CCC.**
Published by: International Maritime Organization/Organisation Maritime Internationale, 4 Albert Embankment, London, SE1 7SR, United Kingdom. TEL 44-20-77357611, FAX 44-20-75873210, info@imo.org. Adv. contact Hanna Moreton TEL 44-20-77357611.

THE I N A QUARTERLY. *see* ARCHAEOLOGY

387 IND ISSN 0970-4299
HE561
INDIAN SHIPPING. Text in English. 1949. m. INR 625 (effective 2011). bk.rev. **Document type:** *Journal, Trade.*
Indexed: BMT, CLT&T, HRIS.
—IE, Ingenta.
Published by: Indian National Shipowners' Association, 22 Maker Tower F, 2nd Fl, Cuffe Parade, Mumbai, Maharashtra 400 005, India. TEL 91-22-22182103, FAX 91-22-22182104. Ed. B V Nilkund.

INFOMARINE; technology and business in the marine industries. *see* LAW—Maritime Law

387 URY ISSN 0797-3101
INFORMATIVO A L A M A R. Text in Spanish. 1976. m.
Published by: Asociacion Latinoamericana de Armadores/Latinamerican Shipowners Association, Rio Negro 1394 Of. 502, Montevideo, Uruguay. TEL 05982-987449, FAX 05982-920732. Circ: 500.

797.1 551.5 ITA ISSN 1971-5242
INFORMAZIONI NAUTICHE. Text in Italian. 1984. 3/yr. **Document type:** *Magazine, Consumer.*
Published by: Istituto Idrografico della Marina, Passo dell' Osservatorio 4, Genoa, GE 16100, Italy. TEL 39-010-24431, FAX 39-010-261400, http://www.marina.difesa.it/idro/index.asp.

387.58 GBR ISSN 1752-573X
THE INFOSPECTRUM DIRECTORY. Text in English. 2000. a. GBP 45, USD 72 per issue (effective 2006). **Document type:** *Directory, Trade.*
Formerly (until 200?): The Book (1473-0227)
Published by: (International Bunkering Industry Association), Infospectrum Ltd., 59 St. Aldates, Oxford, OX1 1ST, United Kingdom. TEL 44-1865-420400, FAX 44-1865-420401, info@infospectrum.net, http://www.infospectrum.net. **Subscr. in Australia to:** Infospectrum Australia, 50 Easter Parade, North Avoca, NSW 2260, Australia; **Subscr. in the Americas to:** Infospectrum Americas, 8410 N W 53rd Terrace, Miami, FL 33166. TEL 305-479-2904, FAX 305-359-3801.

623.8 ESP ISSN 0020-1073
➤ **INGENIERIA NAVAL.** Text in Spanish. 1929. m. EUR 70 domestic; EUR 100 in Portugal; EUR 115 in Europe; EUR 138 elsewhere; EUR 7 newsstand/cover (effective 2008). adv. bk.rev. abstr.; illus. index. back issues avail. **Document type:** *Journal, Academic/Scholarly.* **Description:** Reports on technical developments in ship design, naval architecture, and maritime construction.
Indexed: A22, BMT, ChemAb, IECT.
—Linda Hall.
Published by: Asociacion de Ingenieros Navales y Oceanicos de Espana/Spanish Association of Naval Architects and Marine Engineers, Castello, 66 6a Planta, Madrid, 28001, Spain. TEL 34-91-5784383, FAX 34-91-5892510, rin@iies.es. Ed., R&P Belen Garcia de Pablos. Pub. Pedro Penas Vargas. Adv. contact Rafael Crespo Fortun. B&W page EUR 740, color page EUR 1,300; trim 210 x 297. Circ: 3,500 (controlled).

387.1 USA ISSN 2156-7611
▼ **INLAND PORT MAGAZINE.** Text in English. 2009. bi-m. USD 50; free to qualified personnel (effective 2010). adv. **Document type:** *Magazine, Trade.* **Description:** Aims to bring the varied organizations in this industry together to form one outlet to cover the spectrum of interests in the U.S. Inland Waterways.
Related titles: Online - full text ed.: free (effective 2010).
Published by: Hudson Jones Publications, Llc., PO Box 10398, Midland, TX 79702. TEL 281-602-5400, jhudson@inlandportmagazine.com. Ed. Daron Jones.

386 USA ISSN 0198-859X
HE627
INLAND RIVER GUIDE. Text in English. 1972. a. USD 75 per issue (print or CD-ROM ed.); USD 90 combined subscription per issue (print & CD-ROM eds.) (effective 2011). adv. **Document type:** *Handbook/Manual/Guide, Trade.* **Description:** Contains more than 600 pages of vital information about companies servicing all industry segments.
Related titles: CD-ROM ed.
Published by: Waterways Journal, Inc., 319 N 4th St, Ste 650, St. Louis, MO 63102. TEL 314-241-7354, FAX 314-241-4207. Ed. Dan Owen.

386 USA
INLAND RIVER RECORD. Text in English. 1945. a. USD 40 per issue (print or CD-ROM ed.); USD 50 combined subscription per issue (print & CD-ROM eds.) (effective 2011). adv. **Document type:** *Handbook/Manual/Guide, Trade.* **Description:** Contains lists in detail more than 3,500 commercial towboats and tugs, U.S. engineer vessels and coast guard vessels navigating the Mississippi and Ohio, their tributaries and the Gulf intracoastal waterway.
Related titles: CD-ROM ed.
Published by: Waterways Journal, Inc., 319 N 4th St, Ste 650, St. Louis, MO 63102. TEL 314-241-7354, FAX 314-241-4207. Ed. Dan Owen.

INLAND SEAS. *see* HISTORY—History Of North And South America

387 JPN ISSN 0386-1198
INSTITUTE FOR SEA TRAINING. JOURNAL. Text in Japanese; Summaries in English. 1951. irreg. free. **Document type:** *Academic/Scholarly.* **Description:** Covers navigation, equipment and outfit of ships, marine engineering, and education for seafarers.
Published by: Ministry of Transport, Institute for Sea Training, 57 Kita-Nakadori 5-chome, Naka-ku, Yokohama-shi, Kanagawa-ken 231-0003, Japan. TEL 81-45-211-7312, FAX 81-45-211-7317, kenkikan@ho-ist.mariner.com, http://www.motnet.go.jp/int/index.htm. Ed. Capt. Kunzou Yamamoto. Circ: 300.

623.87 GBR
➤ **INSTITUTE OF MARINE ENGINEERING, SCIENCE & TECHNOLOGY. CONFERENCE PROCEEDINGS.** Text in English. 19??. irreg., latest 2008. GBP 150 per vol. (effective 2009). back issues avail. **Document type:** *Proceedings, Academic/Scholarly.* **Description:** Publishes papers presented at conferences on a diverse range of maritime engineering topics such as fire safety, maritime defense, and offshore oil platform design and development.
Former titles (until 2008): Institute of Marine Engineering, Science & Technology. Conference Proceedings. Part D; (until 2003): Institute of Marine Engineers. Conference Proceedings
Indexed: BMT.
Published by: Institute of Marine Engineering, Science and Technology, 80 Coleman St, London, EC2R 5BJ, United Kingdom. TEL 44-20-73822600, FAX 44-20-73822670, info@imarest.org, http://www.imarest.org/.

623.89 USA
INSTITUTE OF NAVIGATION. PROCEEDINGS OF THE ANNUAL MEETING. Text in English. 19??. a. free to members (effective 2010). back issues avail. **Document type:** *Proceedings.*
Published by: Institute of Navigation, 3975 University Dr, Ste 390, Fairfax, VA 22030-2520. membership@ion.org.

623.8 GBR ISSN 0020-3289
INSTITUTION OF ENGINEERS AND SHIPBUILDERS IN SCOTLAND. TRANSACTIONS. Text in English. 1872. a. free to members. charts; illus. index, cum.index: vols.1-100. **Document type:** *Proceedings, Academic/Scholarly.*
Indexed: BMT, ChemAb, Inspec.
—BLDSC (8964.200000).
Published by: Institution of Engineers and Shipbuilders in Scotland, Clydeport, 16 Robertson St, Glasgow, G2 8DS, United Kingdom. TEL 44-141-2483721, FAX 44-141-2212698, Secretary@iesis.org, http://www.iesis.org/.

387 620 GBR ISSN 1475-0902
VM595
➤ **INSTITUTION OF MECHANICAL ENGINEERS. PROCEEDINGS. PART M: JOURNAL OF ENGINEERING FOR THE MARITIME ENVIRONMENT.** Variant title: Journal of Engineering for the Maritime Environment. Text in English. 2002 (Sept.). q. USD 1,101 combined subscription in North America to institutions (print & online eds.); GBP 603 combined subscription elsewhere to institutions (print & online eds.) (effective 2011). back issues avail.; reprint service avail. from PSC. **Document type:** *Journal, Academic/Scholarly.* **Description:** Provides a forum for engineers from a variety of disciplines with a common interest in the design, production and operation of engineering artefacts for the maritime environment.
Related titles: Online - full text ed.: ISSN 2041-3084. USD 992 in North America to institutions; GBP 543 elsewhere to institutions (effective 2011); ◆ Series: Institution of Mechanical Engineers. Proceedings.
Indexed: A01, A03, A08, A22, A28, APA, B21, BrCerAb, C&ISA, CA, CA/WCA, CIA, CPEI, CerAb, CivEngAb, CorrAb, CurCont, E&CAJ, E01, E04, E05, E11, EEA, EMA, ESPM, EngInd, EnvEAb, FLUIDEX, H&SSA, H15, Inspec, M&TEA, M09, MBF, METADEX, OceAb, P26, P48, P52, P54, P56, PQC, S01, SCI, SCOPUS, SSciA, SolStAb, T02, T04, W07, WAA.
—BLDSC (6724.904000), IE, Infotrieve, Ingenta, Linda Hall. **CCC.**
Published by: (Institution of Mechanical Engineers), Sage Publications Ltd. (Subsidiary of: Sage Publications, Inc.), 1 Oliver's Yard, 55 City Rd, London, EC1Y 1SP, United Kingdom. TEL 44-20-73248500, FAX 44-20-73248600, info@sagepub.co.uk, http://www.uk.sagepub.com/home.nav.

363.12 FRA ISSN 0223-534X
INSTRUCTIONS NAUTIQUES. Text in French. 1902. irreg. price varies. **Document type:** *Government.* **Description:** Provides mariners with all the information not provided on charts to ensure a safe journey.
Published by: Service Hydrographique et Oceanographique de la Marine (S H O M), 13 Rue du Chatellier, Brest, 29200, France. TEL 33-2-98220573, FAX 33-2-98220591, http://www.shom.fr. **Subscr. to:** EPSHOM, B.P. 426, Brest Cedex 29275, France.

387 GBR ISSN 0260-1087
HE593
INTERNATIONAL BULK JOURNAL. Text in English. 1981. bi-m. adv. bk.rev. charts; illus.; mkt.; stat. 60 p./no. 4 cols./p.; **Document type:** *Magazine, Trade.*
Indexed: A22, CLT&T, FLUIDEX, FR, GEOBASE, GeoRef, HRIS, SCOPUS.
—BLDSC (4537.678000), IE, Infotrieve, Ingenta.
Published by: Glenbuck Publishing Ltd., Bryn Siriol, Llangollen, LL20 7BE, United Kingdom. TEL 44-1691-718045. Ed. Giles Large TEL 44-20-88860653. Pub. Ray Girvan TEL 44-20-82755561. Adv. contact Dave Maddox TEL 44-20-76899009. page GBP 4,275; trim 210 x 297.

623.89 FRA ISSN 0538-6128
INTERNATIONAL CONFERENCE ON LIGHTHOUSES AND OTHER AIDS TO NAVIGATION. REPORTS. Text in French. 1929. every 4 yrs. **Document type:** *Proceedings.* **Description:** Technical reports, some with photographs and-or drawings covering the conferences.
Published by: Association Internationale de Signalisation Maritime/International Association of Marine Aids to Navigation and Lighthouse Authorities, 20 ter rue Schnapper, Saint-germain-en-laye, 78100, France. TEL 33-1-34517001, FAX 33-1-34518205, iala-aism@wanadoo.fr. Ed. Paul Ridgway. Adv. contact G Josse.

387 910.09 GBR ISSN 0957-7696
INTERNATIONAL CRUISE AND FERRY REVIEW. Text in English. 1989. s-a. free to qualified personnel (effective 2010). back issues avail. **Document type:** *Magazine, Trade.* **Description:** Contains reports on current trends and future developments in the passenger shipping industry.
Related titles: Online - full text ed.; ◆ Supplement(s): Dream World Cruise Destinations. ISSN 1351-640X.
Indexed: B01, B02, B07, B15, B17, B18, G04, G06, G07, G08, I05.
—**CCC.**

Published by: Euromoney Institutional Investor Plc., Nestor House, Playhouse Yard, London, EC4V 5EX, United Kingdom. TEL 44-20-77798752, FAX 44-20-77798960, information@euromoneyplc.com, http://www.euromoneyplc.com/. Ed., Pub. Nolan Andrews.

387 GBR
INTERNATIONAL FEDERATION OF SHIPMASTERS ASSOCIATIONS. ANNUAL REPORT. Text in English. a. free. adv. 30 p./no.; **Document type:** *Corporate.*
Published by: International Federation of Shipmasters Associations, 202 Lambeth Rd, London, SE1 7JY, United Kingdom. TEL 44-20-7261-0450, FAX 44-20-7928-9030, http://www.ifsma.org. Ed. Capt. Roger Clipsham.

387 GBR
INTERNATIONAL FEDERATION OF SHIPMASTERS ASSOCIATIONS. NEWSLETTER. Text in English. 19??. 3/yr. free to members (effective 2009). 30 p./no. 2 cols./p.; back issues avail. **Document type:** *Newsletter, Trade.*
Related titles: Online - full text ed.: free (effective 2009).
Published by: International Federation of Shipmasters Associations, 202 Lambeth Rd, London, SE1 7JY, United Kingdom. TEL 44-20-7261-0450, FAX 44-20-7928-9030, hq@ifsma.org, http://www.ifsma.org. Ed. Capt. Paul Owen. Circ: 600.

387 GBR ISSN 0032-5007
INTERNATIONAL FREIGHTING WEEKLY; the voice of freight. Abbreviated title: I F W. Text in English. 1962. w. looseleaf. GBP 285 domestic; EUR 500 in Europe; USD 740, GBP 390 elsewhere (effective 2010). bk.rev. charts; illus.; stat.; tr.lit. back issues avail. **Document type:** *Newspaper, Trade.* **Description:** Covers all aspects of the commercial transport chain.
Former titles (until 1970): Ports and Terminals International Freighting; (until 1966): Ports and Terminals
Related titles: Online - full text ed.; ◆ Supplement(s): Routes.
Indexed: BMT, CPerI, G08.
—CCC.
Published by: Informa Trade & Energy (Subsidiary of: Informa U K Ltd.), Informa House, 30-32 Mortimer St, London, W1W 7RE, United Kingdom. TEL 44-20-70175000, http://www.informa.com/divisions/commercial/informa_Informa_Trade_and_Energy. Adv. contact Fergus Gregory TEL 44-20-70176773.

387.5 GBR
INTERNATIONAL GRAINS COUNCIL. OCEAN FREIGHT RATES (ONLINE). Text in English. 19??. w. GBP 450, USD 740, EUR 540 combined subscription (online & e-mail eds.) (effective 2009). charts; stat. **Document type:** *Directory.*
Former titles: International Grains Council. Ocean Freight Rates (Print); International Wheat Council. Ocean Freight Rates
Media: Online - full text. **Related titles:** E-mail ed.
Published by: International Grains Council, One Canada Sq, Canary Wharf, London, E14 5AE, United Kingdom. TEL 44-20-75131122, FAX 44-20-75130630, igc@igc.org.uk, http://www.igc.org.uk.

387 971 CAN ISSN 0843-8714
VK15
➤ **INTERNATIONAL JOURNAL OF MARITIME HISTORY.** Text in English. 1989. s-a. adv. bk.rev. **Document type:** *Journal, Academic/Scholarly.* **Description:** Publishes scholarly articles, notes, and reviews on maritime economic and social history.
Related titles: Microform ed.
Indexed: A22, AmH&L, BAS, C03, CA, CBCARef, GeoRef, H05, HRIS, HistAb, IBR, IBZ, P30, P48, P52, P56, PCI, PQC, T02.
—BLDSC (4542.329500), IE, Infotrieve, Ingenta. **CCC.**
Published by: International Maritime Economic History Association (I M E H A), Memorial University of Newfoundland, Saint John's, NF A1C 5S7, Canada. TEL 709-737-2602, http://www.mun.ca/mhp/imeha.htm.

387.5 GBR ISSN 1752-6582
TC1501
➤ **INTERNATIONAL JOURNAL OF OCEAN SYSTEMS MANAGEMENT.** Text in English. 2007 (Apr.). q. EUR 494 to institutions (print or online ed.); EUR 672 combined subscription to institutions (print & online eds.) (effective 2012). charts; illus. **Document type:** *Journal, Academic/Scholarly.* **Description:** Covers the business and government management aspects of ocean systems and activities, including ocean transportation, marine resource development, public policy and ocean use.
Related titles: Online - full text ed.: ISSN 1752-6590 (from IngentaConnect).
Indexed: A28, APA, BrCerAb, C&ISA, CA/WCA, CIA, CerAb, CivEngAb, CorrAb, E&CAJ, E11, EEA, EMA, ESPM, EnvEAb, GEOBASE, H15, M&TEA, M09, MBF, METADEX, SolStAb, T04, WAA.
—IE. **CCC.**
Published by: Inderscience Publishers, PO Box 735, Olney, Bucks MK46 5WB, United Kingdom. TEL 44-1234-240519, FAX 44-1234-240515, editorial@inderscience.com. Eds. Dr. Efstratios Georgoudis, Dr. Miltiadis Lytras. **Subscr. to:** World Trade Centre Bldg, 29 Rte de Pre-Bois, Case Postale 856, Geneva 15 1215, Switzerland. FAX 41-22-7910885, subs@inderscience.com.

387 GBR ISSN 1756-6517
▼ ➤ **INTERNATIONAL JOURNAL OF SHIPPING AND TRANSPORT LOGISTICS.** Text in English. 2009. 4/yr. EUR 494 to institutions (print or online ed.); EUR 672 combined subscription to institutions (print & online eds.) (effective 2012). abstr.; bibl.; charts; illus. **Document type:** *Journal, Academic/Scholarly.* **Description:** Provides a vehicle to help professionals, academics, researchers and policy makers, working in the field of shipping and transport logistics, to disseminate information and to learn from one another's work.
Related titles: Online - full text ed.: ISSN 1756-6525 (from IngentaConnect).
Indexed: A26, CurCont, E08, SSCI, W07.
—CCC.
Published by: Inderscience Publishers, PO Box 735, Olney, Bucks MK46 5WB, United Kingdom. TEL 44-1234-240519, FAX 44-1234-240515, editorial@inderscience.com. Eds. Dr. C T Daniel Ng, Dr. Kee-Hung Lai, Dr. Y H Venus Lun. **Subscr. to:** World Trade Centre Bldg, 29 Rte de Pre-Bois, Case Postale 856, Geneva 15 1215, Switzerland. FAX 41-22-7910885, subs@inderscience.com.

387.5 341 346.07 GBR
INTERNATIONAL MARITIME AND COMMERCIAL LAW YEARBOOK (YEAR). Text in English. 2002. a. includes subscr. with (Lloyd's Maritime and Commercial Law Quarterly). **Document type:** *Yearbook, Trade.* **Description:** It Comprises surveys of international maritime and commercial law developments which previously appeared as articles in Lloyd's Maritime and Commercial Law Quarterly.
Published by: Informa Professional (Subsidiary of: T & F Informa plc), Telephone House, 69-77 Paul St, London, EC2A 4LQ, United Kingdom. TEL 44-20-70175532, FAX 44-20-70175274, professional.enquiries@informa.com, http://www.informaprofessional.com/.

623.8 387.2 GBR
INTERNATIONAL MARITIME ORGANIZATION. INTERNATIONAL CODE FOR THE CONSTRUCTION AND EQUIPMENT OF SHIPS CARRYING LIQUEFIED GASES IN BULK. Abbreviated title: I B C Code. Text in French. 1983. a. GBP 14. Supplement avail.
Incorporates (in 1994): Index of Dangerous Chemicals Carried in Bulk
Published by: International Maritime Organization/Organisation Maritime Internationale, 4 Albert Embankment, London, SE1 7SR, United Kingdom. TEL 44-20-77357611, FAX 44-20-75873210, publications-sales@imo.org, http://www.imo.org/.

623.8 387.2 GBR
INTERNATIONAL MARITIME ORGANIZATION. TESTING AND EVALUATION OF LIFE-SAVING APPLIANCES. Text in French. a. GBP 8.
Published by: International Maritime Organization/Organisation Maritime Internationale, 4 Albert Embankment, London, SE1 7SR, United Kingdom. TEL 44-20-77357611, FAX 44-20-75873210, publications-sales@imo.org, http://www.imo.org/.

623.89 BEL
INTERNATIONAL NAVIGATION ASSOCIATION. TECHNICAL BRIEFS. Text in English. irreg. EUR 1 per issue (effective 2003). **Document type:** *Monographic series, Academic/Scholarly.*
Media: Online - full content.
Published by: International Navigation Association/Association Internationale de Navigation, Graaf de Ferraris, 11th Fl, 20 Boulevard du Roi Albert II, Brussels, 1000, Belgium. TEL 32-2-5537157, FAX 32-2-5537155, info@pianc-aipcn.org, http://www.pianc-aipcn.org.

623.89 BEL ISSN 1015-9568
INTERNATIONAL NAVIGATION CONGRESS. PAPERS. Text in English, French; Summaries in English, French. 1901. quadrennial. price varies. **Document type:** *Proceedings, Academic/Scholarly.* **Description:** Publishes papers presented at the international congress.
Published by: International Navigation Association/Association Internationale de Navigation, Graaf de Ferraris, 11th Fl, 20 Boulevard du Roi Albert II, Brussels, 1000, Belgium. TEL 32-2-5537157, FAX 32-2-5537155, info@pianc-aipcn.org, http://www.pianc-aipcn.org.

INTERNATIONAL SAFETYNET MANUAL. *see* COMMUNICATIONS

387 USA ISSN 1040-6530
INTERNATIONAL SHIP REGISTRY REVIEW. Text in English. 1988. m. USD 300 (effective 2004). **Document type:** *Newsletter, Trade.* **Description:** Contains information on every open, national and second ship registry and corporate domicile worldwide.
Media: Online - full content.
Published by: International Marketing Strategies, Inc., 62 Southfield Ave., Ste. 214, Stamford, CT 06902-7229. inquiries@marinemoney.com.

623.82 NLD ISSN 0020-868X
VM1 CODEN: ISBPAS
➤ **INTERNATIONAL SHIPBUILDING PROGRESS.** Text in English. 1954. q. USD 491 combined subscription in North America (print & online eds.); EUR 350 combined subscription elsewhere (print & online eds.) (effective 2012). reprints avail. **Document type:** *Journal, Academic/Scholarly.* **Description:** Reports on advances in ship design and construction.
Related titles: Online - full text ed.: ISSN 1566-2829.
Indexed: A22, A28, APA, ApMecR, B21, BMT, BrCerAb, C&ISA, C10, CA, CA/WCA, CIA, CPEI, CerAb, CivEngAb, CorrAb, E&CAJ, E01, E11, EEA, EMA, ESPM, EngInd, EnvEAb, H&SSA, H15, M&TEA, M09, MBF, METADEX, OceAb, SCOPUS, SolStAb, T02, T04, WAA.
—BLDSC (4549.300000), IE, Infotrieve, Ingenta, INIST, Linda Hall.
Published by: Delft University Press (Subsidiary of: I O S Press), Nieuwe Hemweg 6B, Amsterdam, 1013 BG, Netherlands. TEL 31-20-6883355, FAX 31-20-6870039, info.dupress@iospress.nl, http://www.dupress.nl. Ed. Rene Huijsmans. **Dist. by:** I O S Press, Nieuwe Hemweg 6B, Amsterdam 1013 BG, Netherlands. TEL 31-20-6883355, FAX 31-20-6203419.

387 GBR ISSN 1463-1555
INTERNATIONAL TUG AND SALVAGE. Abbreviated title: I T & S. Text in English. 1995. bi-m. GBP 65 to non-members; free to members (effective 2009); subscr. includes TugWorld Annual Review. adv. back issues avail. **Document type:** *Magazine, Trade.* **Description:** Covers the activities of the salvage and towage operators, the vessels used, the yards that build them, the specialist skills involved and the equipment employed.
Formerly (until 1998): I T S Report (1361-7451)
Related titles: Online - full text ed.
—CCC.
Published by: A B R Company Ltd., The Barn, Ford Farm, Bradford Leigh, Bradford-on-Avon, Wiltshire BA15 2RP, United Kingdom. TEL 44-1225-868821, FAX 44-1225-868831, tugsrus@tugandsalvage.com. Ed. Dawn Gorman. Pub. Allan Brunton-Reed. adv.: color page GBP 1,500; 184 x 262.

387 GBR
INTERNATIONAL TUG & SALVAGE CONVENTION. PROCEEDINGS. Text in English. 1969. biennial. GBP 100 per issue (effective 2009). adv. back issues avail. **Document type:** *Proceedings.* **Description:** Designed for all those involved in the international tug, towage and salvage industries.
Former titles (until 1994): The International Tug & Salvage Convention. Proceedings; (until 1992): International Tug Convention and Marine Salvage Symposium. Proceedings; (until 1990): The International Tug Convention. Proceedings; (until 1975): International Tug Conference. Proceedings
Indexed: BMT.
Published by: A B R Company Ltd., The Barn, Ford Farm, Bradford Leigh, Bradford-on-Avon, Wiltshire BA15 2RP, United Kingdom. TEL 44-1225-868821, FAX 44-1225-868831, tugsrus@tugandsalvage.com. Pub. Allan Brunton-Reed.

INTERNATIONALE TRANSPORT ZEITSCHRIFT. *see* TRANSPORTATION

387.1097296 GBR ISSN 2042-7344
INVEST GRAND BAHAMA. Text in English. 2007. biennial. **Document type:** *Journal, Trade.*
Formerly (until 2009): Grand Bahamas Port Authority Handbook (1754-3258)
Related titles: Online - full text ed.: free (effective 2010).
Published by: Land & Marine Publications Ltd., 1 Kings Ct, Newcomen Way, Severalls Business Park, Colchester, Essex CO4 9RA, United Kingdom. TEL 44-1206-752902, FAX 44-1206-842958, publishing@landmarine.com.

387 POL ISSN 0867-4299
➤ **INZYNIERIA MORSKA I GEOTECHNIKA.** Text in Polish. 1951. bi-m. EUR 264 foreign (effective 2006). adv. bk.rev. stat. index. **Document type:** *Journal, Academic/Scholarly.*
Former titles: Inzynieria Morska (0138-0540); (until 1980): Technika i Gospodarka Morska (0040-1137); Which was formed by the merger of (1948-1951): Gospodarka Morska (0860-6129); (1946-1951): Technika Morza i Wybrzeza (0860-6110)
Indexed: B22, PST.
Published by: Politechnika Gdanska, Wydzial Inzynierii Ladowej i Srodowiska, ul Narutowicza 11/12, Gdansk, 80952, Poland. TEL 48-58-3472205, FAX 48-58-3472044, http://cenwil.bl.pg.gda.pl/wilis. Circ: 400. **Dist. by:** Ars Polona, Obroncow 25, Warsaw 03933, Poland. TEL 48-22-5098609, FAX 48-22-5098610, arspolona@arspolona.com.pl, http://www.arspolona.com.pl.

387 GBR ISSN 2040-9958
▼ **IRAN SHIPPING REPORT.** Text in English. 2009. q. USD 975, EUR 695 combined subscription (print & email eds.) (effective 2011). **Document type:** *Report, Trade.* **Description:** Provides industry professionals and strategists, sector analysts, business investors, trade associations and regulatory bodies with independent forecasts and competitive intelligence on the shipping industry in Iran.
Related titles: E-mail ed.
Published by: Business Monitor International Ltd., Senator House, 85 Queen Victoria St, London, EC4V 4AB, United Kingdom. TEL 44-20-72480468, FAX 44-20-72480467, subs@businessmonitor.com.

IRELAND. CENTRAL STATISTICS OFFICE. STATISTICS OF PORT TRAFFIC. *see* TRANSPORTATION—Abstracting, Bibliographies, Statistics

387 IRL ISSN 1649-5225
IRISH MARITIME TRANSPORT ECONOMIST. Text in English. 2004. q.
Published by: (Ireland. Marine Institute), Irish Maritime Development Office, 80 Harcourt St, Dublin, 2, Ireland. TEL 353-1-4766500, FAX 353-1-4784988, imdo@marine.ie, http://www.imdo.ie.

IRISH SKIPPER. *see* FISH AND FISHERIES

623.89 DNK ISSN 1903-0037
GB2511
IS- OG BESEJLINGSFORHOLDENE I DE DANSKE FARVANDE I VINTEREN (ONLINE)/ICE AND NAVIGATIONAL CONDITIONS IN DANISH WATERS DURING THE WINTER. Text in Danish, English. 1932. a. illus. **Document type:** *Yearbook, Government.*
Formerly (until 2005): Is- og Besejlingsforholdene i de Danske Farvande i Vinteren (Print) (0106-5076)
Media: Online - full text.
—BLDSC (4582.300000).
Published by: Soevaernets Operative Kommando, Istjenesten/Admiral Danish Fleet, Ice Service, Soedalsparken 20, PO Box 1483, Brabrand, 8220, Denmark. TEL 45-89-433099, FAX 45-89-433171, http://forsvaret.dk/sok/nationalt/istjenesten.

ITALY. ISTITUTO NAZIONALE DI STATISTICA. STATISTICHE DEI TRASPORTI MARITTIMI. *see* TRANSPORTATION—Abstracting, Bibliographies, Statistics

JAARBOEK WETGEVING VOOR DE SCHEEPVAART. *see* LAW—Maritime Law

387 POL ISSN 0867-4337
JACHTING. Text in Polish. 1991. m. PLZ 99; PLZ 11.50 newsstand/cover (effective 2011). **Document type:** *Magazine, Consumer.*
Published by: Twoje Media, ul Saska 9a, Warsaw, 03968, Poland. TEL 48-22-6161604, FAX 48-22-6161524, poczta@twojemedia.pl, http://www.twojemedia.pl.

387 POL ISSN 1897-5062
JACHTING MOTOROWY. Text in Polish. 2007. m. PLZ 276; PLZ 14.90 newsstand/cover (effective 2011). **Document type:** *Magazine, Consumer.*
Published by: Twoje Media, ul Saska 9a, Warsaw, 03968, Poland. TEL 48-22-6161604, FAX 48-22-6161524, poczta@twojemedia.pl, http://www.twojemedia.pl. Ed. Wlodzimierz Kluczynski.

387 JAM
JAMAICA PORT NEWS. Text in English. 1968. q. **Document type:** *Newsletter.* **Description:** Highlights shipping and cruise line innovations. Lists promotions and appointments.
Published by: Port Authority, 15-17 Duke St., Kingston, Jamaica. TEL 809-922-0290, FAX 809-924-9437, TELEX 2386-PORTOPS. Ed. Jennifer McDonald. Circ: 700.

JANE'S AMPHIBIOUS AND SPECIAL FORCES. *see* MILITARY

JANE'S FIGHTING SHIPS. *see* MILITARY

387 GBR ISSN 1364-9647
JANE'S HIGH-SPEED MARINE TRANSPORTATION; hydrofoils, builders of air-cushion vehicles and other civil and military vessels, civil operators, engineering components, associations. Variant title: High-Speed Marine Transportation. Text in English. 1967. a. GBP 515 per issue (2010-2011 ed.) (effective 2010). adv. illus. index. **Document type:** *Yearbook, Trade.* **Description:** Provides comprehensive and detailed specifications complete with images, on all types of high-speed marine craft including component and propulsion systems. Accurate coverage of the design, build and operation of high-speed marine craft along with manufacturer details.
Former titles: Jane's High-Speed Marine Craft (0960-7994); (until 1989): Jane's High-Speed Marine Craft and Air Cushion Vehicles (0951-3124); (until 1986): Jane's Surface Skimmers (0075-305X)

Related titles: CD-ROM ed.: GBP 1,235 (effective 2010); Online - full text ed.: GBP 1,700 (effective 2010).
—BLDSC (4647.061000). **CCC.**
Published by: I H S Jane's (Subsidiary of: I H S), Sentinel House, 163 Brighton Rd, Coulsdon, Surrey CR5 2YH, United Kingdom. TEL 44-20-87003700, FAX 44-20-87003751, info@janes.co.uk, http://www.janes.com. Ed. Stephen Phillips. **Dist. in Asia by:** Jane's Information Group Asia, 60 Albert St, #15-01 Albert Complex, Singapore 189969, Singapore. TEL 65-331-6280, FAX 65-336-9921, info@janes.com.sg; **Dist. in Australia by:** Jane's Information Group Australia, PO Box 3502, Rozelle, NSW 2039, Australia. TEL 61-2-8587-7900, FAX 61-2-8587-7901, info@janes.thomson.com.au; **Dist. in the Americas by:** 1340 Braddock Pl, Ste 300, Alexandria, VA 22314-1651. TEL 703-683-3700, 800-824-0768, FAX 703-836-0297, 800-836-0297, info@janes.com.

623.8 GBR ISSN 1748-2550
JANE'S MARINE PROPULSION. Text in English. 1997. s-a. GBP 920 (effective 2010). illus. **Document type:** *Magazine, Trade.*
Description: Provides up-to-date information on marine engine technology and markets throughout the world.
Related titles: CD-ROM ed.: GBP 1,505 (effective 2010); Online - full text ed.: GBP 2,065 (effective 2010).
—CCC.
Published by: I H S Jane's (Subsidiary of: I H S), Sentinel House, 163 Brighton Rd, Coulsdon, Surrey CR5 2YH, United Kingdom. TEL 44-20-87003700, FAX 44-20-87003751, info@janes.co.uk, http://www.janes.com. Ed. Keith Henderson. **Dist. in Asia by:** Jane's Information Group Asia, 60 Albert St, #15-01 Albert Complex, Singapore 189969, Singapore. TEL 65-331-6280, FAX 65-336-9921, info@janes.com.sg; **Dist. in Australia by:** Jane's Information Group Australia, PO Box 3502, Rozelle, NSW 2039, Australia. TEL 61-2-8587-7900, FAX 61-2-8587-7901, info@janes.thomson.com.au; **Dist. in the Americas by:** 1340 Braddock Pl, Ste 300, Alexandria, VA 22314-1651. TEL 703-683-3700, 800-824-0768, FAX 703-836-0297, 800-836-0297, info@janes.com.

387 GBR ISSN 0263-7030
JANE'S MERCHANT SHIPS. Text in English. 1982. a. GBP 460 per issue (2010-2011 ed.) (effective 2010). adv. illus. **Document type:** *Yearbook, Trade.* **Description:** Comprehensive guide allows you to identify merchant ships quickly and easily. Each section consists of illustrations of ships in an order that is based on the recognition system, making it easy for you to recognise merchant ships worldwide.
Related titles: CD-ROM ed.: GBP 1,155 (effective 2010); Online - full text ed.: GBP 1,575 (effective 2010).
—BLDSC (4647.082000). **CCC.**
Published by: I H S Jane's (Subsidiary of: I H S), Sentinel House, 163 Brighton Rd, Coulsdon, Surrey CR5 2YH, United Kingdom. TEL 44-20-87003700, FAX 44-20-87003751, info@janes.co.uk, http://www.janes.com. Ed. David Greenman. Adv. contact Janine Boxall TEL 44-20-87003852. **Dist. in Asia by:** Jane's Information Group Asia, 60 Albert St, #15-01 Albert Complex, Singapore 189969, Singapore. TEL 65-331-6280, FAX 65-336-9921, info@janes.com.sg; **Dist. in Australia by:** Jane's Information Group Australia, PO Box 3502, Rozelle, NSW 2039, Australia. TEL 61-2-8587-7900, FAX 61-2-8587-7901, info@janes.thomson.com.au; **Dist. in the Americas by:** 1340 Braddock Pl, Ste 300, Alexandria, VA 22314-1651. TEL 703-683-3700, 800-824-0768, FAX 703-836-0297, 800-836-0297, info@janes.com.

387 JPN ISSN 0447-3728
JAPAN. MARITIME SAFETY AGENCY. HYDROGRAPHIC DEPARTMENT. NOTICES TO MARINERS/SUIRO TSUHO. Text in English, Japanese. 1889. w. per issue exchange basis. stat. **Document type:** *Government.*
Published by: Kaijo Hoancho, Suirobu/Maritime Safety Agency, Hydrographic Department, 3-1 Tsuki-Ji 5-chome, Chuo-ku, Tokyo, 104-0045, Japan. TEL 81-3-3541-4296, FAX 81-3-3545-2885, TELEX 2522222 JAHYD J.

387 JPN
JAPAN PORT INFORMATION. Text in English. 1969. biennial. JPY 20,000 (effective 2000). adv.
Published by: (Japan Association of Foreign - Trade Ship Agencies), Japan Press, Ltd., C.P.O. Box 6, Tokyo, 100-8691, Japan. TEL 81-3-3404-5161, FAX 81-3-3404-5152. Ed. Yoshio Wada. Adv. contact M Oish.

387.2 620 389.6 CHN ISSN 1005-7560
JIANCHUAN BIAOZHUNHUA YU HUANJING TIAOJIAN/SHIP STANDARDIZATION ENGINEER. Text in Chinese. 1998. bi-m. **Document type:** *Journal, Academic/Scholarly.*
Published by: Zhongguo Chuanbo Zhonggong Jituan Gongsi. Di-7 Yanjiuyuan. Di-704 Yanjiusuo, 851, Zhongshan Nan Er Lu, Shanghai, 200031, China. TEL 86-21-54591998 ext 802, FAX 86-21-54595766, smeri@stn.sh.cn, http://www.chinasmeri.com/.

387 CHN ISSN 1672-7649
JIANCHUAN KEXUE JISHU/SHIP SCIENCE AND TECHNOLOGY. Text in Chinese. 1962. m. **Document type:** *Journal, Academic/Scholarly.*
Related titles: Online - full text ed.
—BLDSC (4668.449000).
Published by: Zhongguo Jianchuan Yanjiuyuan, 2, Shuangquanbao Jia, PO Box 2854, Beijing, 100192, China. TEL 86-10-64831773 ext 810, FAX 86-10-64837398, postdoct@shipol.com.cn, http://csrda.shipol.com.cn/7yuan/index.htm. **Co-sponsor:** Zhongguo Chuanbo Xinxi Zhongxin/China Ship Information Center.

359 CHN ISSN 1000-7148
VM4
JIANCHUAN ZHISHI. Text in Chinese. 1979. m. USD 49.20 (effective 2009).
—East View.
Published by: (Zhongguo Zaochuan Gongcheng Xuehui/Chinese Society of Naval Architecture and Marine Engineering), Jianchuan Zhishi Bianjibu, 70 Xueyuan Nanlu, Beijing, 100081, China. TEL 8315522. Ed. Yang Pu.

387 CHN ISSN 1001-5388
➤ **JIANGSU CHUANBO/JIANGSU SHIP.** Text in Chinese. 1980. bi-m. CNY 24; HKD 60 in Hong Kong; USD 50 elsewhere. adv. **Document type:** *Academic/Scholarly.*
Related titles: Online - full text ed.
Published by: Jiangsu Sheng Chuanbo Sheji Yanjiusuo/Ship Design & Research Institute of Jiangsu Province, 37 Zhengdong Rd, Zhenjiang, Jiangsu 212003, China. TEL 86-511-4422493, FAX 86-511-4424389. Ed. Zhu Minhu. adv.: B&W page USD 300, color page USD 600. Circ: 3,000. **Co-sponsor:** Jiangsu Provincial Society of Naval Architecture and Marine Engineering.

➤ **JIB.** *see* SPORTS AND GAMES—Boats And Boating

➤ **JIDIAN SHEBEI/MECHANICAL AND ELECTRICAL EQUIPMENT.** *see* MACHINERY

623.89 NLD ISSN 1566-2659
JOURNAAL ZEEVAART. Text in Dutch. 1999. q. EUR 90 (effective 2009). **Document type:** *Journal, Trade.*
—IE.
Published by: Sdu Uitgevers bv, Postbus 20025, The Hague, 2500 EA, Netherlands. TEL 31-70-3789911, FAX 31-70-3854321, sdu@sdu.nl. Eds. J Huisman, M Tiemens, R Akerboom.

387.5 FRA ISSN 1633-7921
VK2 CODEN: JMMMED
JOURNAL DE LA MARINE MARCHANDE. Text in French. 1919. w. adv. bk.rev. abstr.; charts; illus.; stat. **Document type:** *Magazine, Trade.*
Former titles (until 2001): Journal de la Marine Marchande et du Transport Multimodal (0983-0537); (until 1986): Journal de la Marine Marchande (0762-3151); (until 1982): Journal de la Marine Marchande et de la Navigation Aerienne (0397-6467); (until 1938): Journal de la Marine Marchande (0021-7786)
Indexed: A22, BMT, KES.
—IE, Infotrieve, INIST.
Published by: Wolters Kluwer France (Subsidiary of: Wolters Kluwer N.V.), 1 Rue Eugene et Armand Peugeot, Rueil-Malmaison, Cedex 92856, France. TEL 33-1-76734809, FAX 33-1-76733040, www.wk-transport-logistique.fr, www.wkf.fr.

387 GBR ISSN 2153-3369
▼ ➤ **JOURNAL FOR MARITIME RESEARCH.** Abbreviated title: J M R. Text in English. 2010 (Feb.). q. GBP 158 combined subscription in United Kingdom to institutions (print & online eds.); EUR 209, USD 261 combined subscription to institutions (print & online eds.) (effective 2012). bk.rev. back issues avail. **Document type:** *Journal, Academic/Scholarly.* **Description:** Features articles covering contemporary issues to the political, economic, cultural and social aspects of maritime history.
Related titles: Online - full text ed.: ISSN 1469-1957. 199?. GBP 144 in United Kingdom to institutions; EUR 189, USD 237 to institutions (effective 2012).
Indexed: AmH&L, CA, HistAb, P30, T02.
—CCC.
Published by: (National Maritime Museum), Routledge (Subsidiary of: Taylor & Francis Group), 4 Park Square, Milton Park, Abingdon, Oxon OX14 4RN, United Kingdom. TEL 44-1235-828600, FAX 44-1235-829000, info@routledge.co.uk, http://www.tandf.co.uk/journals.

623.87 623.888 GBR ISSN 1476-1556
VM1
➤ **JOURNAL OF MARINE DESIGN AND OPERATIONS.** Abbreviated title: J M D O. Variant title: Proceedings of the Institute of Marine Engineering, Science and Technology. Text in English. 1889. s-a. free to members (effective 2009). back issues avail. **Document type:** *Proceedings, Academic/Scholarly.* **Description:** Contains practical based papers featuring real life examples of design, manufacture, operation, safety and environmental aspects of marine and offshore concepts, equipment and systems.
Supersedes in part (in 2002): International Maritime Technology (1475-0414); Which was formerly (until 1999): Institute of Marine Engineers. Transactions (1358-3956); (until 1988): Institute of Marine Engineers. Transactions T M (0268-4152); (until 1979): Institute of Marine Engineers. Transactions. Series A. Technical Reports (0309-3948); (until 1977): Institute of Marine Engineers. Transactions. Series A (0950-530X); Which superseded in part (in 1973): Institute of Marine Engineers. Transactions (0020-2924)
Related titles: Online - full text ed.
Indexed: A28, APA, ASFA, BrCerAb, C&ISA, CA/WCA, CIA, CerAb, CivEngAb, CorrAb, E&CAJ, E11, EEA, EMA, ESPM, EngInd, EnvEAb, H15, M&TEA, M09, MBF, METADEX, SCOPUS, SolStAb, T04, WAA.
—BLDSC (6715.612000), IE, Ingenta, INIST, Linda Hall. **CCC.**
Published by: Institute of Marine Engineering, Science and Technology, 80 Coleman St, London, EC2R 5BJ, United Kingdom. TEL 44-20-73822600, FAX 44-20-73822670, info@imarest.org.

623.87 GBR ISSN 2046-4177
VM595 CODEN: TIMTDD
➤ **JOURNAL OF MARINE ENGINEERING AND TECHNOLOGY.** Abbreviated title: J M E T. Text in English. 1889. 3/yr. GBP 120 to institutions (effective 2011). abstr.; charts; illus. index. **Document type:** *Proceedings, Academic/Scholarly.* **Description:** Contains peer reviewed papers of a specialist academic nature covering research, theory and scientific studies concerned with all aspects of marine engineering and technology.
Formerly (until 2011): Institute of Marine Engineering, Science and Technology. Proceedings. Part A. Journal of Marine Engineering and Technology (1476-1548); Supersedes in part (in 2002): International Maritime Technology (1475-0414); Which was formerly (until 1999): Institute of Marine Engineers. Transactions (1358-3956); (until 1988): Institute of Marine Engineers. Transactions T M (0268-4152); (until 1979): Institute of Marine Engineers. Transactions. Series A. Technical Reports (0309-3948); (until 1977): Institute of Marine Engineers. Transactions. Series A (0950-530X); Which superseded in part (in 1973): Institute of Marine Engineers. Transactions (0020-2924)
Related titles: Microfilm ed.: (from WMP); Online - full text ed.: (from IngentaConnect).
Indexed: A28, APA, APIAb, APICat, APIH&E, APIPR, APITS, ASFA, B21, BMT, BrCerAb, C&ISA, CA/WCA, CIA, CPEI, CerAb, ChemAb, CivEngAb, CorrAb, E&CAJ, E11, EEA, EMA, ESPM, EngInd, EnvEAb, H&SSA, H15, Inspec, M&TEA, M09, MBF, METADEX, SCI, SCOPUS, SolStAb, T04, W07, WAA.
—BLDSC (5011.775500), IE, Ingenta, INIST, Linda Hall. **CCC.**
Published by: Institute of Marine Engineering, Science and Technology, 80 Coleman St, London, EC2R 5BJ, United Kingdom. TEL 44-20-73822600, FAX 44-20-73822670, info@imarest.org. Eds. Dr. Alistair Greig, Dr. Richard Bucknall.

387 620 ROM ISSN 1844-6116
➤ **JOURNAL OF MARINE TECHNOLOGY AND ENVIRONMENT.** Text in English. 2008. s-a. (Apr. & Nov.). abstr. **Document type:** *Journal, Academic/Scholarly.*
Indexed: E04, E05, M&GPA, OceAb, T02.
Published by: (Universitatea Maritima Constanta/Constanta Maritime University), "Nautica" Publishing House/Editura Nautica, Mircea cel Batran St.,104, Constanta, 900663, Romania. TEL 40241664740, FAX 40241617260, info@imc.ro, http://www.cmu-edu.eu/editura.html. Ed. Feiza Memet.

➤ **JOURNAL OF MARITIME LAW AND COMMERCE.** *see* LAW—Maritime Law

623.8 GBR ISSN 0373-4633
VK1 CODEN: JONVAL
➤ **JOURNAL OF NAVIGATION.** Text in English. 1947. q. GBP 322, USD 579 to institutions; GBP 332, USD 612 combined subscription to institutions (print & online eds.) (effective 2012). bk.rev. charts; illus.; maps. index, cum.index every 15 yrs. back issues avail.; reprint service avail. from PSC. **Document type:** *Journal, Academic/Scholarly.* **Description:** Presents papers on every aspect of navigation - air, land, sea, and space - and papers on every type - scientific, historical, and narrative.
Formerly (until 1972): Institute of Navigation. Journal (0020-3009)
Related titles: Online - full text ed.: ISSN 1469-7785. GBP 292, USD 532 to institutions (effective 2012).
Indexed: A01, A03, A08, A20, A22, A28, A33, APA, ASCA, ASFA, B21, BMT, BrCerAb, BrTechI, C&ISA, CA, CA/WCA, CIA, CLT&T, CerAb, CivEngAb, CorrAb, CurCont, E&CAJ, E01, E11, EEA, EMA, ESPM, EnvEAb, ErgAb, FLUIDEX, GEOBASE, GeoRef, H&SSA, H15, HRIS, Inspec, LID&ISL, M&TEA, M09, MBF, METADEX, OceAb, P26, P48, P52, P54, P56, PQC, RefZh, SCI, SCOPUS, SolStAb, T02, T04, TM, W07, WAA.
—BLDSC (5021.320000), AskIEEE, IE, Infotrieve, Ingenta, INIST, Linda Hall. **CCC.**
Published by: (Royal Institute of Navigation), Cambridge University Press, The Edinburgh Bldg, Shaftesbury Rd, Cambridge, CB2 8RU, United Kingdom. TEL 44-1223-312393, FAX 44-1223-315052, journals@cambridge.org, http://www.cambridge.org/uk. Ed. Norman Hughes. R&P Linda Nicol TEL 44-1223-325702. Adv. contact Rebecca Roberts TEL 44-1223-325083. Circ: 3,500. **Subscr. to:** Cambridge University Press, 32 Ave of the Americas, New York, NY 10013. TEL 212-337-5000, FAX 212-691-3239, journals_subscriptions@cup.org.

➤ **JOURNAL OF OPERATIONAL OCEANOGRAPHY.** *see* EARTH SCIENCES—Oceanography

623.8 USA ISSN 2158-2866
VM1
➤ **JOURNAL OF SHIP PRODUCTION AND DESIGN.** Abbreviated title: J S P D. Text in English. 1985. q. USD 335 in North America to non-members; USD 365 elsewhere to non-members; USD 75 in North America to members; USD 90 elsewhere to members (effective 2011). adv. illus. index. 70 p./no. 2 cols./p.; back issues avail.; reprints avail. **Document type:** *Journal, Academic/Scholarly.* **Description:** Contains technical papers that address the problems of shipyard techniques and production of merchant and naval ships.
Formerly (until May 2010): Journal of Ship Production (8756-1417)
Related titles: Online - full text ed.: ISSN 2158-2874 (from IngentaConnect).
Indexed: A22, A28, APA, BMT, BrCerAb, C&ISA, CA/WCA, CIA, CLT&T, CPEI, CerAb, CivEngAb, CorrAb, E&CAJ, E11, EEA, EMA, EngInd, H15, HRIS, M&TEA, M09, MBF, SCOPUS, SolStAb, T04, WAA.
—BLDSC (5064.355000), IE, Ingenta, INIST, Linda Hall.
Published by: The Society of Naval Architects and Marine Engineers, 601 Pavonia Ave, Jersey City, NJ 07306. TEL 201-798-4800, 800-798-2188, FAX 201-798-4975, tfaix@sname.org. Ed. David J Singer.

623.8 USA ISSN 0022-4502
VM1 CODEN: JSRHAR
➤ **JOURNAL OF SHIP RESEARCH.** Abbreviated title: J S R. Text in English. 1957. q. USD 320 in North America to non-members; USD 350 elsewhere to non-members; USD 80 in North America to members; USD 95 elsewhere to members (effective 2009). adv. charts; illus.; stat. index. 70 p./no. 2 cols./p.; back issues avail.; reprints avail. **Document type:** *Journal, Academic/Scholarly.* **Description:** Presents technical papers on applied research in hydrodynamics, propulsion, ship motions, structures and vibrations.
Related titles: CD-ROM ed.; Online - full text ed.: ISSN 1542-0604 (from IngentaConnect).
Indexed: A22, A28, APA, ASCA, ApMecR, BMT, BrCerAb, C&ISA, CA, CA/WCA, CIA, CPEI, CerAb, CivEngAb, CorrAb, CurCont, E&CAJ, E11, EEA, EMA, ESPM, EngInd, EnvEAb, H15, M&TEA, M09, MBF, METADEX, OceAb, S&VD, SCI, SCOPUS, SolStAb, T02, T04, W07, WAA.
—BLDSC (5064.400000), IE, Infotrieve, Ingenta, INIST, Linda Hall. **CCC.**
Published by: The Society of Naval Architects and Marine Engineers, 601 Pavonia Ave, Jersey City, NJ 07306. TEL 201-798-4800, 800-798-2188, FAX 201-798-4975, tfaix@sname.org. Adv. contact Bob Rogaski.

623.8 IND ISSN 0973-1423
JOURNAL OF SHIP TECHNOLOGY. Text in English. 2005. s-a. INR 800 domestic; USD 70 foreign (effective 2011). adv. back issues avail. **Document type:** *Journal, Trade.* **Description:** Explores emerging opportunities and problems regarding ship technology.
Published by: Institution of Naval Architects, Delhi Chapter, Block IV, Department of Applied Mechanics, Indian Institute of Technology, Hauzkhas, New Delhi, 110 016, India. TEL 91-11-26596259, editor@jstindia.org, www.jstindia.org. Ed. R K Whig.

387 USA ISSN 2159-5879
▼ ➤ **JOURNAL OF SHIPPING AND OCEAN ENGINEERING.** Text in English. 2011. m. **Document type:** *Journal, Academic/Scholarly.*
Related titles: Online - full text ed.: ISSN 2159-5887.
Published by: David Publishing Co., Inc., 1840 Industrial Dr, Ste 160, Libertyville, IL 60048. TEL 847-281-9822, FAX 847-281-9855, order@davidpublishing.com, http://www.davidpublishing.com.

387 624 USA ISSN 0733-950X
TC1 CODEN: JWPED5
➤ **JOURNAL OF WATERWAY, PORT, COASTAL, AND OCEAN ENGINEERING.** Text in English. 1873. bi-m. USD 491 domestic to institutions; USD 521 foreign to institutions; USD 560 combined subscription domestic to institutions (print & online eds.); USD 590 combined subscription foreign to institutions (print & online eds.) (effective 2012). adv. bk.rev. illus. index. back issues avail.; reprints avail. **Document type:** *Journal, Academic/Scholarly.* **Description:** Presents information regarding the engineering aspects of dredging, floods, ice, pollution, sediment transport, and tidal wave action that affect shorelines, waterways, and harbors.
Former titles (until 1983): American Society of Civil Engineers. Waterway, Port, Coastal and Ocean Division. Journal (0148-9895); (until 1977): American Society of Civil Engineers. Waterways, Harbors, and Coastal Engineering Division. Journal (0044-8028); (until 1970): American Society of Civil Engineers. Waterways and Harbors Division. Journal (0569-8103); (until 1956): American Society of Civil Engineers. Waterways Division. Journal; (until 1955): American Society of Civil Engineers. Proceedings (0097-417X)
Related titles: CD-ROM ed.: USD 49 to members for CD-ROM and online eds.; USD 74 to individuals for CD-ROM and online eds.; USD 220 to institutions for CD-ROM and online eds. (effective 2000); Microform ed.: (from PQC); Online - full text ed.: ISSN 1943-5460. USD 431 to institutions (effective 2012).
Indexed: A01, A02, A03, A05, A08, A22, A23, A24, A25, A26, A28, A32, APA, AS&TA, AS&TI, ASCA, ASFA, B04, B13, B21, BMT, BrCerAb, C&ISA, C10, CA, CA/WCA, CIA, CPEI, CerAb, CivEngAb, CorrAb, CurCont, E&CAJ, E&PHSE, E04, E05, E08, E11, EEA, EIA, EMA, ESPM, EngInd, EnvAb, EnvEAb, EnvInd, FLUIDEX, G01, G08, GEOBASE, GP&P, GeoRef, H&SSA, H15, HRIS, I05, ICEA, ISR, M&GPA, M&TEA, M05, M06, M09, MBF, METADEX, OceAb, OffTech, PetrolAb, PollutAb, RefZh, S01, S08, S09, SCI, SCOPUS, SWRA, SolStAb, SpeleolAb, T02, T04, W07, WAA.
—BLDSC (5072.545000), IE, Infotrieve, Ingenta, INIST, Linda Hall, PADDS. **CCC.**
Published by: (Waterway, Port, Coastal, and Ocean Division), American Society of Civil Engineers, 1801 Alexander Bell Dr, Reston, VA 20191. TEL 703-295-6300, FAX 703-295-6333. Ed. Vijay Panchang. Adv. contact Dianne Vance TEL 703-295-6234.

➤ **JURISPRUDENCE DU PORT D'ANVERS/ANTWERP MARITIME LAW REPORTS/RECHTSPRAAK DER HAVEN VAN ANTWERPEN.** *see* LAW—Maritime Law

387 PAK
K P T NEWS BULLETIN. Text in English. 1966. fortn. PKR 2.40 per issue. charts; illus.; stat.
Published by: Karachi Port Trust, P O Box 4725, Karachi, Pakistan. TEL 201305, FAX 2415567, TELEX 2739 KPT PK. Ed. Kafil Ahmed Khan. Circ: 2,000.

387 JPN
KAIJI KANREN GYOSHA YORAN/MARITIME DIRECTORY IN JAPAN. Text in Japanese. 1940. a. JPY 16,500 (effective 2000). **Document type:** *Directory, Trade.*
Related titles: Diskette ed.
Published by: Nihon Kaiun Shukaijo/Japan Shipping Exchange Inc., Wajun Bldg, 2-22-2 Koishi-Kawa, Bunkyo-ku, Tokyo, 112-0002, Japan. TEL 81-3-5802-8368, FAX 81-3-5802-8371, jmis@jseinc.org, http://www.jseinc.org.

387 JPN ISSN 0286-9152
KAIJI SANGYO KENKYUJOHO/JAPAN MARITIME RESEARCH INSTITUTE. BULLETIN. Text in Japanese. 1966. m. JPY 12,600 (effective 2001). bk.rev. index. **Document type:** *Academic/Scholarly.* **Description:** Journal of shipping, shipbuilding and port research.
Published by: Japan Maritime Research Institute/Kaiji Sangyo Kenkyusho, Kaiun Bldg, 2-6-4 Hirakawa-cho, Chiyoda-ku, Tokyo, 102-0093, Japan. TEL 81-3-3265-5231, FAX 81-3-3265-5035, henshu@jamri.or.jp. Ed. Masaru Iwata. Circ: 1,300.

KAIJO HOANCHO. SUIROBU KANSOKU HOKOKU. EISEI SOKUCHI HEN/DATA REPORT OF HYDROGRAPHIC OBSERVATIONS. SERIES OF SATELLITE GEODESY. *see* EARTH SCIENCES—Geophysics

387 JPN ISSN 0022-7803
KAIUN/SHIPPING. Text in Japanese. 1922. m. JPY 15,120 (effective 2006). adv. bk.rev. stat. Index. **Document type:** *Magazine, Trade.*
Published by: Nihon Kaiun Shukaijo/Japan Shipping Exchange Inc., Wajun Building, 3/F, 2-22-2 Koishikawa, Bunkyo-ku, Tokyo, 112-0002, Japan. TEL 86-3-58028365, FAX 86-3-58028371. Circ: 8,000.

KAIYO KOGAKU SHINPOJUMU/OCEAN ENGINEERING SYMPOSIUM. *see* EARTH SCIENCES—Oceanography

623.82 JPN
KAKI KOZA ATARASHII ZOZENGAKU/SUMMER SEMINAR ON NEW TOPICS IN NAVAL ARCHITECTURE. Text in Japanese. a.
Published by: Nihon Zosen Gakkai/Society of Naval Architects of Japan, 1Hamamatsucho Yazaki White Bldg., 2-12-9 Shibadaimon, Minato-ku, Tokyo, 105-0012, Japan.

359.97 FIN ISSN 1795-4614
KALKHOLM NEWS. Text in Finnish. 1993. q. **Document type:** *Magazine, Trade.*
Published by: S M P S Paraisten Meripelastajat ry/Finnish Lifeboat Society, Parainen Division, PO Box 29, Parainen, 21601, Finland. http://www.kuulalaakeri.fi. Ed. Jarmo Saarinen.

387 620 359 JPN ISSN 1880-3725
VM4
KANRIN/JAPAN SOCIETY OF NAVAL ARCHITECTS AND OCEAN ENGINEERS. BULLETIN. Text in Japanese. 2005. bi-m. **Document type:** *Bulletin, Academic/Scholarly.*
Formed by the merger of (1988-2004): Ran/Kansai Society of Naval Architects, Japan. Bulletin (0916-0981); (1992-2005): Techno Marine/Nihon Zosen Gakkaishi (0916-8699); Which was formerly (until 1991): Nihon Zosen Gakkaishi/Society of Naval Architects of Japan. Bulletin (0386-1597); (1952-1967): Zosen Kyokaishi (0386-1503)
Published by: Nihon Sempaku Kaiyou Kougakkai/Japan Society of Naval Architects and Ocean Engineers, 2-12-9 Shiba Daimon. Minato-Ku, Hamamatsu-cho Yazaki White Bldg. 3F, Tokyo, 105-0012, Japan. TEL 81-3-34382014, FAX 81-3-34382016, info@jasnaoe.or.jp.

623.82 JPN ISSN 0919-7591
KANSAI ZOSEN KYOKAI KOEN RONBUNSHU/KANSAI SOCIETY OF NAVAL ARCHITECTS. PREPRINTS OF MEETING. Text in English, Japanese; Summaries in English. 2/yr.
Formerly (until 1993): Kansai Zosen Kyokai Koenkai Ronbun Maezuri
Published by: Kansai Zosen Kyokai/Kansai Society of Naval Architects, c/o Osaka Daigaku Kogakubu Senpaku-Kaiyou Kyoshitsu, 2-1 Yamada-Oka, Suita-shi, Osaka-fu 565-0871, Japan. TEL 81-6-879-7593, FAX 81-6-879-7594.

KEY NOTE MARKET ASSESSMENT. THE CRUISE MARKET. *see* BUSINESS AND ECONOMICS—Production Of Goods And Services

387.5 GBR
KEY NOTE MARKET FOCUS. WATER TRANSPORT LOGISTICS. Variant title: Water Transport Logistics Market Focus. Text in English. 2003. irreg., latest 2003, Mar. GBP 315 per issue (effective 2010). **Document type:** *Report, Trade.* **Description:** Provides an overview of a specific UK market segment and includes executive summary, market definition, market size, industry background, competitor analysis, current issues, forecasts, company profiles, and more.
Published by: Key Note Ltd. (Subsidiary of: Bonnier Business Information), Harlequin House, 5th Fl, 7 High St, Teddington, Richmond upon Thames, TW11 8EE, United Kingdom. TEL 44-845-5040452, FAX 44-845-5040453, info@keynote.co.uk.

387.1 NOR ISSN 1504-7601
KNUTEPUNKT. Text in Norwegian. 1999. m. NOK 690 domestic; NOK 890 in Scandinavia; NOK 1,190 elsewhere (effective 2007). adv. **Document type:** *Magazine, Trade.*
Former titles (until 2007): Havne@visen (1502-573X); (until 2000): Norsk Havneavis (1501-9624)
Published by: Innovation Publishing AS, PO Box 1, Kyrksaeteroera, 7201, Norway. TEL 47-72-450095, FAX 47-72-450091, innovationpublishing.no. Ed. Lasse Krog. Adv. contact Richard Oelmheim.

355 DEU ISSN 0075-6474
KOEHLERS FLOTTENKALENDER; internationales Jahrbuch der Seefahrt. Text in German. 1901. a. EUR 13.90 (effective 2005). bk.rev. abstr.; charts; illus.; stat. **Document type:** *Directory, Trade.*
Published by: Koehlers Verlagsgesellschaft mbH, Striepenweg 31, Hamburg, 21147, Germany. TEL 49-40-7971303, FAX 49-40-79713324, vertrieb@koehler-mittler.de, http://www.koehler-mittler.de. Ed. Hans J Witthoft. R&P Juergen Rohweder. Adv. contact Rainer Metzner. Circ: 22,500.

623.8 386 BGR
KORABOSTROENE I KORABOPLAVANE/SHIPBUILDING AND SHIPPING. Text in Bulgarian; Summaries in English. 1956. m. USD 11.
Indexed: BMT.
Published by: Ministerstvo na Transporta, 9 Levski ul, Sofia, 1080, Bulgaria. Ed. S Popov. Circ: 2,017. **Dist. by:** Hemus, 6 Rouski Blvd., Sofia 1000, Bulgaria. **Co-sponsor:** Bulgaria Ministerstvo na Mashinostroeneto i Metalurgiiata.

387 KOR
KOREA SHIPPING GAZETTE. Text in English, Korean. 1971. w. KRW 35,000 (effective 2009). adv. bk.rev. illus. **Document type:** *Newspaper, Trade.*
Related titles: Online - full text ed.
Published by: (Korea Maritime Research Institute), Korea Shipping Gazette Co., Ltd./kori-a Swiping Gajeteu, 43-1,Tongeui-Dong Jongno-gu, Seoul, 110-040, Korea, S. TEL 82-2-7330040, FAX 82-2-7323771. Ed. Jong Ok Lee. Circ: 5,000.

627.2 JPN
KOWAN GIJUTSU KENKYUJO. GAIDO/PORT AND HARBOUR RESEARCH INSTITUTE. GUIDE. Text in Japanese. irreg. per issue exchange basis. illus.
Formerly: Port and Harbour Technical Research Institute. Guide
Indexed: GeotechAb.
Published by: Un'yu-sho, Kowan Gijutsu Kenkyujo/Ministry of Transportation, Port and Harbour Research Institute, 1-1 Nagase 3-chome, Yokosuka-shi, Kanagawa-ken 239-0826, Japan.

387.5 665.5 GBR ISSN 1746-0603
L N G WORLD SHIPPING. (Liquefied Natural Gas) Text in English. 2004. bi-m. GBP 299 combined subscription (print & online eds.) (effective 2009). adv. back issues avail. **Document type:** *Journal, Trade.* **Description:** Covers every aspect of the dynamic LNG carrier sector - from new participants, new projects and breakthroughs in ship propulsion systems and ship size to streamlined shipyard production capabilities, advances in offshore technology, new higher-capacity shipboard equipment and the expanding catalogue of sophisticated, back-up services available to ship operators.
Related titles: Online - full text ed.
—CCC.
Published by: Riviera Maritime Media, Mitre House, 66 Abbey Rd, Enfield, EN1 2QN, United Kingdom. TEL 44-20-83641551, FAX 44-20-83641331, info@rivieramm.com. Eds. Mike Corkhill TEL 44-1252-721693, Tony Wilson TEL 44-1803-213161. adv.: color page GBP 3,040; trim 210 x 297. Circ: 3,637.

387.5448 GBR ISSN 1754-2790
L P G WORLD SHIPPING. (Liquid Petroleum Gas) Text in English. 2007. a. GBP 199 combined subscription (print & online eds.) (effective 2010). adv. back issues avail. **Document type:** *Journal, Trade.* **Description:** Covers all technical, commercial and operational aspects of the LPG shipping industry and the full range of cargoes, from LPG and ammonia to ethylene and the other petrochemical gases.
Related titles: Online - full text ed.
Published by: Riviera Maritime Media, Mitre House, 66 Abbey Rd, Enfield, EN1 2QN, United Kingdom. TEL 44-20-83641551, FAX 44-20-83641331, info@rivieramm.com. Ed. Tony Wilson TEL 44-1803-213161. adv.: color page EUR 3,540, color page GBP 2,950; trim 210 x 297. Circ: 4,475.

387 USA
LAKE BOATS. Text in English. 1965. a. USD 12 (effective 2000).
Published by: Freshwater Press, Inc., 1700 E 13th St, Ste 3R E, Cleveland, OH 44114. TEL 216-241-0373.

386.5 USA ISSN 0075-7748
HE564.A4
LAKE CARRIERS' ASSOCIATION. ANNUAL REPORT. Text in English. 1885. a. USD 10 (effective 2000). index. **Document type:** *Corporate.*
Indexed: GeoRef.
Published by: Lake Carriers' Association, 614 W Superior Ave, Ste 915, Cleveland, OH 44113. TEL 216-861-0592, FAX 216-241-8262, ggn@lcaships.com. Ed. Glen G Nekvasil. Circ: 1,500.

551.482 USA
LAKE LEVELS FOR THE GREAT LAKES. MONTHLY BULLETIN. Text in English. m. **Description:** Covers water levels of Lake Superior, Lake Michigan-Huron, Lake Erie, Lake Ontario. Tables of possible storm induced rises at key locations on the Great Lakes are also available on request.
Published by: Department of the Army, Detroit District Corps of Engineers, Attn: CELRE-EP-HW, P O Box 1027, Detroit, MI 48231. TEL 313-226-6443.

387 IDN ISSN 1411-7959
DS625
LATITUDES. Text in Indonesian. 2001. m.
Related titles: Online - full text ed.
Indexed: A01, A03, A08, E03, ERI, P04.
Published by: P T Teduh Mitra Utama, Jl.Sulatri I/6, Denpasar, Bali, Indonesia.

LEADING LIGHT. *see* MUSEUMS AND ART GALLERIES

387.5 ITA ISSN 0024-032X
LEGA NAVALE. Text in Italian. 1897. 9/yr. free to members. bk.rev. illus.; stat. **Document type:** *Magazine, Consumer.* **Description:** Covers the merchant marine.
Published by: Lega Navale Italiana, Via Guidobaldo del Monte 54, Rome, 00197, Italy. TEL 39-06-80913701, FAX 39-06-809137205, presidenza@leganavale.it.

623.8 GBR ISSN 0308-7441
VK1473
LIFEBOAT INTERNATIONAL. Text in English. 1975. a. **Document type:** *Bulletin.*
Published by: Royal National Lifeboat Institution, West Quay Rd, Poole, Dorset BH15 1HZ, United Kingdom, TEL 44-1202-663000, FAX 44-1202-663238. Ed. Edward Wake Walker. **Co-sponsor:** International Lifeboat Federation.

359.97 USA ISSN 0565-1557
VK1214
LIGHT LIST. Text in English. 19??. a. back issues avail. **Document type:** *Trade.* **Description:** Contains a list of lights, sound signals, buoys, daybeacons, and other aids to navigation for each Coast Guard District.
Related titles: Online - full text ed.: free (effective 2010).
—Linda Hall.
Published by: U.S. Coast Guard, 2100 Second St, SW, Washington, DC 20593. TEL 202-372-4620, gchappell@comdt.uscg.mil, http://www.uscg.mil/default.asp.

LIGHTHOUSE DIGEST. *see* ARCHITECTURE

387.029 GBR
HE565.A3
LIST OF SHIPOWNERS & MANAGERS. Text in English. 1876. a. USD 650 per issue (effective 2010). 760 p./no.; back issues avail. **Document type:** *Directory, Trade.* **Description:** Lists approximately 40,000 shipowners, managers and managing agents: addresses, telephone, telex and fax numbers, and fleet lists.
Former titles (until 2004): List of Shipowners, Managers and Managing Agents; (until 1996): List of Shipowners (0260-7387)
Related titles: CD-ROM ed.
Published by: Lloyd's Register - Fairplay Ltd., Lombard House, 3 Princess Way, Redhill, Surrey RH1 1UP, United Kingdom. TEL 44-1737-379000, FAX 44-1737-379001, info@lrfairplay.com.

387 CAN ISSN 0833-5672
HE565.C2
LIST OF SHIPS. Text in English, French. 1953. irreg.
Formerly (until 1984): List of Shipping (0701-7588)
Published by: Transport Canada/Transports Canada, 300 Sparks St, Ottawa, ON K1A 0N5, Canada. TEL 613-990-2309, FAX 613-954-4731.

387.2 BEL
LISTE OFFICIELLE DES NAVIRES DE MER BELGES ET DE LA FLOTTE DE LA FORCE NAVALE. Text in French. a. charts; illus. **Document type:** *Government.*
Published by: Administration des Affaires Maritimes et de la Navigation, Rue d'Arlon 104, Brussels, 1040, Belgium. TEL 32-2-233-1211, FAX 32-2-230-3002. Ed. M Joseph TEL 32-2-233-1321.

387.5 343.09 BEL
DE LLOYD (DUTCH EDITION); dagblad voor transporteconomie. Text in Dutch, English. 1979. d. (Mon.-Fri.). adv. illus. back issues avail. **Document type:** *Newspaper, Trade.* **Description:** Covers developments in shipping in and around the Port of Antwerp, along with marine casualties, legal issues and notices, ship sales, and bankruptcies and labor actions.
Published by: De Lloyd N.V./Le Lloyd S.A., Vleminckstraat 18, Antwerpen, 2000, Belgium. TEL 32-3-234-0550, FAX 32-3-234-0850, info@lloyd.be, http://www.anlloyd.be. Ed. Bernard Van den Bossche. Pub. Guy Dubois. Circ: 13,000.

387.5 343.09 BEL
LE LLOYD (FRENCH EDITION); l'economie des transports au quotodien. Text in French, English. 1853. d. (Mon.-Fri.). adv. illus. back issues avail. **Document type:** *Newspaper.* **Description:** Covers developments in shipping in and around the Port of Antwerp, along with marine casualties, legal issues and notices, ship sales, and bankruptcies and labor actions.
Formerly: Quotidien International des Transports
Published by: De Lloyd N.V./Le Lloyd S.A., Vleminckstraat 18, Antwerpen, 2000, Belgium. TEL 32-3-234-0550, FAX 32-3-234-0850, info@lloyd.be, http://www.anlloyd.be. Ed. Bernard Van den Bossche. Pub. Guy Dubois. Circ: 13,000.

LLOYD'S CASUALTY WEEK. *see* INSURANCE

387.505 GBR ISSN 0144-820X
LLOYD'S LIST. Text in English. 1734. d. (Mon.-Fri.). GBP 970, EUR 1,640, USD 3,370 combined subscription (print & online eds.) (effective 2009). adv. bk.rev. **Document type:** *Newspaper, Trade.* **Description:** Covers shipping, insurance, energy, transportation and finance, with special reports on selected business topics.
Incorporates: Shipping and Mercantile Gazette; Formerly: Shipping Gazette and Lloyd's List

TU

Related titles: Microfilm ed.: (from PQC, RPI, WMP); Online - full text ed.: GBP 900, EUR 1,125, USD 800 (effective 2009); ◆ Supplement(s): Lloyd's List Maritime Americas.
Indexed: BMT, RASB.
—BLDSC (5287.260000), CIS. **CCC.**
Published by: Informa U K Ltd. (Subsidiary of: T & F Informa plc), Sheepen Pl, Colchester, Essex CO3 3LP, United Kingdom. TEL 44-1206-772223, FAX 44-1206-772771, enquiries@informa.com, http://www.llplimited.com. Ed. Tom Leander TEL 44-20-70175248. Adv. contact Ryan Hanley TEL 44-20-33773356. Circ: 14,650. **Subscr. in the US to:** L L P Inc, Customer Service, PO Box 1017, Westborough, MA 01581-6017. TEL 1-800-493-4080, FAX 508-231-0856, enquiries.usa@informa.com.

387 AUS
LLOYD'S LIST DAILY COMMERCIAL NEWS. Abbreviated title: L L D C N. Variant title: Lloyd's List D C N. Text in English. 1999. w. AUD 407 domestic; AUD 680 in New Zealand; AUD 855 in Asia & the Pacific; AUD 1,035 elsewhere; AUD 583 combined subscription domestic (print & online eds.); AUD 850 combined subscription in New Zealand (print & online eds.); AUD 1,090 combined subscription in Asia & the Pacific (print & online eds.); AUD 1,325 combined subscription elsewhere (print & online eds.) (effective 2008). adv. Supplement avail. **Document type:** *Newspaper, Trade.* **Description:** Features articles in maritime, transport and trade industries; comprehensive shipping guide and sailing schedules.
Formed by the merger of (1900-1999): Lloyd's List Australia Weekly; (1891-1999): Daily Commercial News; Which was formerly (until 1976): D C N; (until 1975): Daily Commercial News and Shipping List
Related titles: Online - full text ed.: AUD 506 domestic; AUD 460 foreign (effective 2008); Supplement(s): Rail Express. AUD 126.50 domestic; AUD 175 in New Zealand; AUD 190 in Asia & the Pacific; AUD 220 elsewhere; free to members (effective 2008).
Indexed: ABIX.
Published by: Informa Australia Pty Ltd., Level 2, 120 Sussex St, GPO Box 2728, Sydney, NSW 2001, Australia. TEL 61-2-90804300, FAX 61-2-92902577, enquiries@informa.com.au, http://www.informa.com.au/. Ed. Sam Collyer TEL 61-2-90804414. Pub. Peter Attwater TEL 61-2-90804480. Adv. contact Lynn Cavanagh TEL 61-2-90804419. page AUD 6,310; 262 x 380.

387.5098 GBR
LLOYD'S LIST MARITIME AMERICAS. Variant title: Maritime Americas. Text in English. 2007. irreg. included with subscr. to "Lloyd's List Newspaper". **Document type:** *Magazine, Trade.* **Description:** Provides shipowners throughout the world with the information required to capitalise on the latest regional trends and places the spotlight on leading operators in the region.
Related titles: ◆ Supplement to: Lloyd's List. ISSN 0144-820X.
—BLDSC (5287.269500).
Published by: Informa U K Ltd. (Subsidiary of: T & F Informa plc), Albert House, 1-4 Singer St, London, EC2A 4BQ, United Kingdom. TEL 44-20-70175000, http://www.informa.com.

387 HKG
HE873
LLOYD'S LIST MARITIME ASIA. Text in English. 1979. 10/yr. GBP 112 in UK; GBP 112 in Europe; USD 190 in North America; GBP 112 elsewhere (effective 2002). adv. bk.rev. charts; illus.; stat.; tr.lit. back issues avail. **Document type:** *Magazine, Trade.*
Incorporates: Intermodal Asia (1015-2253); Formerly: Lloyd's Maritime Asia (1015-227X)
—IE, Ingenta.
Published by: L L P Asia Ltd., 6th Fl Hollywood Centre, 233 Hollywood Rd, Hong Kong, Hong Kong. TEL 852-2854-3222, FAX 852-2854-1538, informa.asia@informa.com, http://www.maritmeasiaawards.com. Ed. Corey Bousen. Adv. contact Bianca Fernandes. Circ: 8,260. **Subscr. to:** 69-77 Paul St, London EC2A 4LQ, United Kingdom.

387.029 GBR ISSN 2041-2711
HE951
LLOYD'S LIST MARITIME DIRECTORY. Text in English. 19??. a. (in 3 vols.). GBP 499, EUR 624, USD 898, SGD 1,287 per issue (effective 2010). adv. **Document type:** *Directory, Trade.* **Description:** Provides names and addresses of more than 5,500 shipowners, managers and agents arranged in alphabetical order under countries, details of the 34,000 vessels under their control, with listings of maritime service industry firms, from shipbuilding to salvage.
Formed by the merger of (2008-2009): The Lloyd's List Maritime Directory of Shipping Services (1758-2849); (2008-2009): The Lloyd's List Maritime Directory of Shipowners, Managers and Operators (1758-2857); Both of which superseded in part (until 2008): Lloyd's Maritime Directory (Year) (0268-327X); (until 1982): International Shipping and Shipbuilding Directory
Related titles: Online - full text ed.: Lloyd's Electronic Maritime Directory. ISSN 1368-6437. 1997.
—BLDSC (5287.261500). **CCC.**
Published by: Lloyd's M I U (Subsidiary of: Informa Maritime & Transport), 69 - 77 Paul St, London, EC2A 4LQ, United Kingdom. TEL 44-20-70174482, FAX 44-20-70175007, enquiries@lloydsmiu.com, http://www.lloydsmiu.com.

387 GBR ISSN 1478-4696
LLOYD'S LIST PORTS OF THE WORLD (YEAR). Text in English. 1896. a. GBP 399 per vol. (effective 2010). adv. maps. back issues avail. **Document type:** *Directory, Trade.* **Description:** Provides the list of 2,800 ports worldwide, with name and address of the relevant port authority, approach hazards, and facilities for anyone involved in international trade.
Former titles (until 2001): Lloyd's Ports of the World (Year) (0266-6197); (until 1982): Ports of the World (0079-4066); (until 1947): Port Directory of the World
Related titles: CD-ROM ed.: ISSN 1478-4645.
—BLDSC (5287.261800). **CCC.**
Published by: Lloyd's M I U (Subsidiary of: Informa Maritime & Transport), 69 - 77 Paul St, London, EC2A 4LQ, United Kingdom. TEL 44-20-70174482, FAX 44-20-70175007, enquiries@lloydsmiu.com, http://www.lloydsmiu.com. **Subscr. addr. in the US:** L L P Inc.

387 GBR ISSN 0144-6681
LLOYD'S LOADING LIST. Text in English. 1853. w. GBP 495 domestic; EUR 956 in Europe; USD 1,396, GBP 846 elsewhere (effective 2010). adv. **Document type:** *Directory, Trade.* **Description:** Provides coverage of freighting services by sea, road, rail and air from the UK to more than 1,000 destinations in all parts of the world.
Related titles: Supplement(s): Consular Requirements. ISSN 0958-7691.
—BLDSC (5287.263000). **CCC.**
Published by: Informa Trade & Energy (Subsidiary of: Informa U K Ltd.), Informa House, 30-32 Mortimer St, London, W1W 7RE, United Kingdom. TEL 44-20-70175000, http://www.informa.com/divisions/commercial/informa_Informa_Trade_and_Energy. Adv. contact Martin Carter TEL 44-20-70174869.

LLOYD'S MARITIME & COMMERCIAL LAW QUARTERLY. *see* LAW—Maritime Law

387 GBR ISSN 1479-1005
G1060
LLOYD'S MARITIME ATLAS OF WORLD PORTS AND SHIPPING PLACES. Text in English. 1951. biennial, latest 25th ed. GBP 120 per issue (effective 2010). maps. index. back issues avail. **Document type:** *Directory, Trade.* **Description:** Gives reference to more than 10,000 ports and shipping places around the world. Includes maps, economic information, distance tables, text and other shipping information.
Formerly (until 1987): Lloyd's Maritime Atlas (0076-020X)
—CCC.
Published by: Lloyd's M I U (Subsidiary of: Informa Maritime & Transport), 69 - 77 Paul St, London, EC2A 4LQ, United Kingdom. TEL 44-20-70174482, FAX 44-20-70175007, enquiries@lloydsmiu.com, http://www.lloydsmiu.com. **Subscr. addr. in the US:** L L P Inc.

LLOYD'S MARITIME LAW NEWSLETTER. *see* LAW—Maritime Law

387 GBR ISSN 1477-3236
HE561
LLOYD'S REGISTER FAIRPLAY WORLD SHIPPING DIRECTORY. Abbreviated title: W S D. Text in English. 1975. a. USD 700 per issue (effective 2010). adv. back issues avail. **Document type:** *Directory, Trade.* **Description:** Lists more than 40,000 companies in the maritime industry and more than 6,000 shipowners with fleets totaling some 34,000 vessels.
Former titles (until 2002): Fairplay World Shipping Directory (Year) (0959-3101); (until 1990): Fairway World Shipping Year Book (0142-6974); (until 1978): Fairplay International World Shipping Year Book (0140-5047); (until 1977): Financial Times World Shipping Year Book (0141-8629)
Related titles: Online - full text ed.
—CCC.
Published by: Fairplay Publications Ltd., Lombard House, 3 Princess Way, Redhill, Surrey RH1 1UP, United Kingdom. TEL 44-1737-379000, FAX 44-1737-379001, info@lrfairplay.com, http://www.fairplay.co.uk.

387 GBR ISSN 0141-4909
HE565.A3
LLOYD'S REGISTER OF SHIPS. Text in English. 1764. a. USD 2,200 per issue (effective 2010). 5700 p./no.; back issues avail. **Document type:** *Directory, Trade.* **Description:** Provides information on more than 80,000 merchant ships, listed in alphabetical order by ship name.
Former titles (until 1967): Lloyd's Register of Shipping. Register Book. Volume 1, Register of Ships; (until 195?): Lloyd's Register of Shipping; (until 1914): Lloyd's Register of British and Foreign Shipping
Related titles: CD-ROM ed.
—CCC.
Published by: Lloyd's Register - Fairplay Ltd., Lombard House, 3 Princess Way, Redhill, Surrey RH1 1UP, United Kingdom. TEL 44-1737-379000, FAX 44-1737-379001, info@lrfairplay.com.

387 GBR ISSN 0265-2455
VK200
LLOYD'S SHIP MANAGER. Text in English. 1977. m. GBP 305 (effective 2010). adv. bk.rev. illus. **Document type:** *Magazine, Trade.* **Description:** Provides monthly information service on all management, technical and operational aspects relating to the safe and profitable operation of ocean-going tonnage.
Formerly (until 1980): Nautical Review (0309-6254); Incorporates (1985-1987): Shipping News International (0800-9163); Which was formerly (until 1985): Norwegian Shipping News (0029-3709); (1972-1984): Shipbuilding and Marine Engineering International (0262-463X); Which was formed by the merger of (19??-1972): Shipbuilding International (0583-0745); (1949-1972): Marine Engineer and Naval Architect (0025-3200); Which was formerly (until 1949): The Marine Engineer (1759-6157); (until 1933): Marine Engineer and Motorship Builder (1759-6149); (until 1924): Marine Engineer and Naval Architect
Indexed: BMT, P06, PAIS.
—BLDSC (5287.735000), IE, Infotrieve, Ingenta, INIST. **CCC.**
Published by: Informa U K Ltd. (Subsidiary of: T & F Informa plc), 69-77 Paul St, London, EC2A 4LQ, United Kingdom. TEL 44-20-70175000, FAX 44-20-70174975, http://www.informa.com. Ed. Tom Leander TEL 44-20-70175248. Adv. contact Russell Borg TEL 44-20-70174495. **Subscr. to:** Sheepen Pl, Colchester, Essex CO3 3LP, United Kingdom.

387 GBR ISSN 0144-6673
HE561
LLOYD'S SHIPPING ECONOMIST. Text in English. 1979. m. GBP 950 domestic; EUR 1,450, GBP 1,035 in Europe; USD 2,230, GBP 1,115 elsewhere (effective 2010). adv. charts; maps; mkt. 50 p./no.; back issues avail. **Document type:** *Magazine, Trade.* **Description:** Provides information, analysis and commentary on supply-and-demand factors in the international shipping markets.
Indexed: CLT&T, HRIS, PAIS.
—BLDSC (5287.743000), IE, Infotrieve. **CCC.**
Published by: Informa U K Ltd. (Subsidiary of: T & F Informa plc), 69-77 Paul St, London, EC2A 4LQ, United Kingdom. TEL 44-20-70174187, FAX 44-20-70174973, http://www.informa.com. Ed. Steve Matthews TEL 44-20-70174709. Adv. contact Nigel Gray TEL 44-20-70174367. B&W page GBP 2,140, color page GBP 2,950; trim 297 x 420. **Subscr. to:** Sheepen Pl, Colchester, Essex CO3 3LP, United Kingdom.

387 GBR ISSN 0144-4549
VM1
LLOYD'S SHIPPING INDEX. Text in English. 1880. w. **Document type:** *Directory, Trade.* **Description:** Presents the current voyages, latest reported movements and vital particulars of 23,000 merchant ships, together with any casualty or other information reported.
Former titles (until 1936): Lloyd's Daily Shipping Index; (until 1932): Lloyd's Daily Index; (until 1918): Lloyd's Weekly Index; (until 1914): Lloyd's Weekly Shipping Index; (until 1880): Weekly Shipping Record
Related titles: Online - full text ed.
—CCC.
Published by: Informa U K Ltd. (Subsidiary of: T & F Informa plc), 69-77 Paul St, London, EC2A 4LQ, United Kingdom. TEL 44-20-70174482, FAX 44-20-70175007, http://www.lloydslist.com/.

387 GBR ISSN 2041-5796
HE730
LLOYD'S VOYAGE RECORD (ONLINE). Text in English. 1946. m. **Document type:** *Directory, Trade.* **Description:** Records vessels' movements chronologically, providing details of the last four ports of call for tankers, six for bulk carriers and eight for dry cargo vessels.
Former titles (until 2009): Lloyd's Voyage Record (Print) (0144-4557); (until 1972): Lloyd's Shipping Index. Voyage Supplement
Media: Online - full text. **Related titles:** Microfiche ed.
—CCC.
Published by: Informa U K Ltd. (Subsidiary of: T & F Informa plc), 69-77 Paul St, London, EC2A 4LQ, United Kingdom. TEL 44-20-70174482, FAX 44-20-70175007, http://www.lloydslist.com/.

387 AUS ISSN 0815-0052
LOG. Text in English. 1954. q. AUD 27.50 domestic to individuals; NZD 27.50 in New Zealand to individuals; AUD 30 elsewhere to individuals; AUD 35.20 to institutions (effective 2008). adv. bk.rev. illus. index. back issues avail.
Published by: Nautical Association of Australia, c/o John b Labrum, Treas, PO Box 142, Caulfield South, VIC 3162, Australia. TEL 61-3-95281223, info@nautical.asn.au. Ed. Russell A Priest.

387.029 GBR ISSN 0260-8839
LONDON PORT HANDBOOK (YEAR). Text in English. 1981. a. adv. **Document type:** *Directory, Trade.*
Published by: Compass Publications Ltd., Marcon House, Bailey St, Castle Acre, Kings Lynn, Norfolk, United Kingdom. TEL 44-1760-755783, FAX 44-1760-755942, http://www.compass-publications.co.uk.

387 SWE ISSN 0024-6328
LONGITUDE; tidskrift fraan de sju haven/magazine of the seven seas. Text in Swedish. 1966. a. SEK 225. charts; illus.
Published by: Carlstedt Foerlag AB, Artillerigatan 2, Stockholm, 11451, Sweden. Ed. J E Carlstedt.

353.987 NZL ISSN 1177-2654
LOOKOUT!. Text in English. 1994. q. free (effective 2009). **Document type:** *Newsletter, Trade.* **Description:** Features the lessons to be learnt from maritime accidents or incidents. Stories cover both recreational and commercial accidents.
Formerly (until 2006): Maritime Accidents (1173-700X)
Published by: Maritime New Zealand, Level 8, gen-i Tower, 109 Featherston St, PO Box 27006, Wellington, New Zealand. TEL 64-4-4730111, FAX 64-4-4941263, http://www.maritimenz.govt.nz.

387 USA ISSN 0882-9004
HE745
M A R A D (YEAR). Text in English. 1950. a. free (effective 2011). **Document type:** *Report, Government.* **Description:** Incorporates reports by the Congress on the following topics: acquisition of obsolete vessels in exchange for vessel trade-in credit; war-risk insurance activities; scrapping or removal of obsolete vessels owned by the U.S.; and U.S.-flag carriage of government-sponsored cargoes. Includes information on the state of the maritime industry, as well as other MARAD activities.
Formerly (until 1969): U.S. Maritime Administration. Annual Report (0083-1670); Which superseded in part (in 1962): Federal Maritime Board and Maritime Administration. Annual Report (0499-3950)
Related titles: Online - full text ed.: ISSN 1942-3853.
Published by: U.S. Maritime Administration, U.S. Department of Transportation, W Bldg, 1200 New Jersey Ave, SE, Washington, DC 20590. TEL 800-996-2723.

623.8 NOR ISSN 0802-622X
M A R I N T E K. ANNUAL REPORT. (Norwegian Marine Technology Research Institute) Text in English. 1987. a. **Document type:** *Report, Consumer.*
Related titles: Online - full text ed.
Published by: M A R I N T E K/Norwegian Marine Technology Research Institute (Subsidiary of: S I N T E F Group/Foundation for Scientific and Industrial Research), Valentinlystvegen, PO Box 4125, Trondheim, 7450, Norway. TEL 47-73-595500, FAX 47-73-595776, marintek@marintek.sintef.no, http://www.marintek.sintef.no.

623.81 NOR ISSN 0801-1818
M A R I N T E K REVIEW. (Norwegian Marine Technology Research Institute) Text in English. 1959. irreg. (1-2/yr). back issues avail. **Document type:** *Magazine, Trade.*
Former titles (until 1985): N S F I-Nytt (0333-0230); (until 1972): S F I-Nytt (0333-032X)
Related titles: Online - full text ed.: ISSN 0805-8253.
Published by: (S I N T E F Group/Foundation for Scientific and Industrial Research), M A R I N T E K/Norwegian Marine Technology Research Institute (Subsidiary of: S I N T E F Group/Foundation for Scientific and Industrial Research), Valentinlystvegen, PO Box 4125, Trondheim, 7450, Norway. TEL 47-73-595500, FAX 47-73-595776, marintek@marintek.sintef.no, http://www.marintek.sintef.no.

387 SWE ISSN 1403-7785
MACGREGOR NEWS. Text in English. 1956. s-a. **Document type:** *Magazine, Consumer.* **Description:** Provides information and news to the cargo handling industry.
Indexed: FLUIDEX, SCOPUS.
Published by: MacGregor Group AB, PO Box 4114, Gothenburg, 400 40, Sweden. TEL 46-31-850900, FAX 46-31-850901, info@macgregor-group.com. Circ: 12,000.

MADE IN HOLLAND. MARITIME INDUSTRY. *see* BUSINESS AND ECONOMICS—International Commerce

387 ESP
MADRID PORT. Text in Spanish. 1983. a. adv. back issues avail. **Document type:** *Magazine, Trade.*
Published by: Grupo Editorial Men-Car, Passeig de Colom, 24, Barcelona, 08002, Spain. TEL 34-93-301-5749, FAX 34-93-302-1779, men-car@men-car.com, http://www.men-car.com. Eds. Juan Cardona, Manuel Cardona. Circ: 15,000.

MAILING SYSTEMS TECHNOLOGY; managing strategies for business communications. *see* COMMUNICATIONS—Postal Affairs

387 NLD ISSN 1389-7101
MAINPORT NEWS. Text in Dutch. 1962. 10/yr. EUR 122 (effective 2009). adv. software rev. stat.; tr.lit. back issues avail. **Document type:** *Newspaper, Trade.* **Description:** Contains logistical, distribution and industrial issues and developments in the port and city of Rotterdam.
Formerly (until 1998): Havennieuws (1381-0162); Incorporates (1962-1999): Port of Rotterdam Magazine (Netherlands Edition) (0922-7148); Which was formerly (until 1988): Rotterdam Europoort Delta (0035-8487)
—IE, Infotrieve.
Published by: NT Publishers B.V., Postbus 200, Rotterdam, 3000 AE, Netherlands. TEL 31-10-2801000, FAX 31-10-2801005, informatie@ntpublishers.nl, http://www.ntpublishers.nl. Ed. Donald Suidman. Pub. Miranda Keuters. adv.: B&W page EUR 2,425, color page EUR 3,136; trim 210 x 297. Circ: 4,293.

387.2 GBR ISSN 2041-7659
MAINSHEET. Text in English. 2008. irreg. free to members (effective 2010).
Former titles (until 2008): Society for Sailing Barge Research (1749-5776); (until 2005): S S B R Newsletter (0951-4589); (until 1986): Society for Spritsail Barge Research Newsletter (0951-3000); (until 1985): Society for Spritsail Barge Research. News-Sheet (0141-1217)
Published by: Society for Sailing Barge Research, c/o Fleur de Lis Heritage Ctr, 13,Preston St, Faversham, Kent ME13 8NS, United Kingdom. john.white6@talk21.com, http://www.sailingbargeresearch.org.uk.

387.2 979 USA ISSN 1540-3386
VM1
MAINS'L HAUL; a journal of pacific maritime history. Text in English. 1964 (Sept.). q. USD 40 (effective 2002). illus. **Document type:** *Journal, Academic/Scholarly.* **Description:** Covers Pacific heritage.
Indexed: AmH&L, CA, HistAb, P30, T02.
Published by: Maritime Museum Association of San Diego, 1492 N. Harbor Dr., San Diego, CA 92101. TEL 619-234-9153, FAX 619-234-8345, editor@sdmaritime.com. Ed. Mark Allen TEL 619-234-9153 ext 118.

387 GBR ISSN 2040-9761
MALAYSIA SHIPPING REPORT. Text in English. 200?. q. EUR 820, USD 1,030 combined subscription (print & email eds.) (effective 2010). **Document type:** *Report, Trade.* **Description:** Provides industry professionals and strategists, sector analysts, business investors, trade associations and regulatory bodies with independent forecasts and competitive intelligence on the shipping industry in Malaysia.
Related titles: E-mail ed.
Published by: Business Monitor International Ltd., Senator House, 85 Queen Victoria St, London, EC4V 4AB, United Kingdom. TEL 44-20-72480468, FAX 44-20-72480467, subs@businessmonitor.com.

MALTA. CENTRAL OFFICE OF STATISTICS. SHIPPING AND AVIATION STATISTICS. *see* TRANSPORTATION—Abstracting, Bibliographies, Statistics

387 CHL ISSN 0047-5866
MAR. Text in Spanish. 1914. a. adv. charts; illus. **Document type:** *Magazine.*
Published by: Liga Maritima de Chile, Errazurriz 471, Piso 2o, Valparaiso, Chile. ligamar@armada.cl, http://www.ligamar.cl. Ed. Alejandro Navarette Torres. Circ: 2,000 (controlled).

387.5 PRT ISSN 0874-5846
HE861
MAR (LISBOA). Variant title: Instituto Maritimo Portuario. Boletim. Text in Portuguese. 1975. q.
Former titles (until 1999): Direccao Geral da Navegacao e dos Transportes Maritimos. Boletim (0022-6742); (until 1989): Marinha de Comercio. Direccao Geral. Boletim (0871-9810)
Published by: Instituto Maritimo Portuario, Edificio Vasco da Gama, Cais de Alcantara, Lisboa, 1399-005, Portugal. TEL 351-21-3957866, FAX 351-21-3957863.

LE MARIN. *see* FISH AND FISHERIES

387 AUS ISSN 1445-9043
MARINE BUSINESS. Text in English. 1989. 11/yr. AUD 88 domestic; AUD 105 in New Zealand; AUD 120 in Asia; AUD 160 elsewhere (effective 2008). adv. **Document type:** *Magazine, Trade.* **Description:** Provides industry-specific news comments, in-depth analysis and detailed business-to-business features servicing the marine sector.
Formerly (until 2001): Marine Industry News (1320-5889)
Published by: Yaffa Publishing Group Pty Ltd., 17-21 Bellevue St, Surry Hills, NSW 2010, Australia. TEL 61-2-92812333, FAX 61-2-92812750, info@yaffa.com.au, http://www.yaffa.com.au. Ed. Scott Thomas TEL 61-2-92138278. Adv. contact Guy Yaffa TEL 61-2-92138264. B&W page AUD 1,670, color page AUD 1,930; trim 220 x 297. Circ: 4,004. **Subscr. to:** GPO Box 606, Sydney, NSW 2001, Australia.

387.5 NGA ISSN 1596-7891
MARINE BUSINESS INTERNATIONAL. Text in English. 2002. m. **Document type:** *Magazine, Trade.* **Description:** Covers news and events in the maritime industry.
Address: PO Box 11130, Ikeja, Lagos, Nigeria. TEL 234-1-7939210, FAX 234-1-3209527.

623.82 JPN ISSN 0287-203X
MARINE ENGINEER. Text in Japanese. 1962. m. JPY 600 per issue.
Published by: Japan Marine Engineers' Association/Nihon Senpaku Kikanshi Kyokai, 4-5 Koji-Machi, Chiyoda-ku, Tokyo, 102-0083, Japan.

623.87 387 USA ISSN 0076-4469
MARINE ENGINEERING LOG ANNUAL MARITIME REVIEW AND YEARBOOK ISSUE. Text in English. 1942. a. (June). **Document type:** *Yearbook, Trade.*
Related titles: Microform ed.: 1942 (from PQC).
Indexed: BMT.
Published by: Simmons-Boardman Publishing Corp., 345 Hudson St, New York, NY 10014. TEL 212-620-7200, FAX 212-633-1165, jsnyder@sbpub.com, http://www.simmonsboardman.com/. Pub. John R Snyder TEL 212-620-7254.

623.8 387 AUS
MARINE ENGINES & PROPULSION SYSTEMS. Text in English. 1995. a. free (effective 2010). illus. **Document type:** *Directory, Trade.*
Former titles (until 200?): World Marine Engines & Propulsion Systems (CD-ROM); World Marine Engines & Propulsion Systems (Print) (1324-7875)
Media: Online - full text.
Published by: Baird Publications Pty. Ltd., 135 Sturt St, South Bank, Melbourne, VIC 3006, Australia. TEL 61-3-96450411, FAX 61-3-96450475, marinfo@baird.com.au, http://www.baird.com.au. Eds. Steven Kelleher, Neil Baird.

623.81 USA ISSN 0882-1984
VM781
MARINE EQUIPMENT CATALOG. Text in English. 1984. a. USD 65. adv. **Document type:** *Catalog.*
Published by: Maritime Activity Reports Inc., 118 E 25th St, 2nd Fl, New York, NY 10010. http://www.marinelink.com. Ed. Laura Ann Sciame. Circ: 12,000.

387 USA ISSN 0824-8729
VM470
MARINE EQUIPMENT DIRECTORY. Text in English. 1917. a. adv. **Document type:** *Directory, Trade.* **Description:** Provides a purchasing guide for users of a wide range of marine equipment and services. Contains more than 4600 product classifications, and more than 2000 companies serving the marine industry worldwide.
Published by: Anchor Publications, Inc., PO Box 953548, Lake Mary, FL 32795. TEL 407-324-9970, FAX 407-324-0616, http://www.marinetrac.com/, info@marinetrac.com. Ed. Sonia C Silva. Pub. Olaf J Silva.

623.87 USA ISSN 0897-0491
VM1
MARINE LOG. Text in English. 1876. m. USD 75 in North America (print or online ed.); USD 175 elsewhere (print or online ed.); USD 113 combined subscription in North America (print & online eds.); USD 263 combined subscription elsewhere (print & online eds.); USD 20 per issue; free to qualified personnel (effective 2008). adv. bk.rev. charts; illus.; stat.; tr.lit. index. 3 cols./p.; back issues avail.; reprints avail. **Document type:** *Magazine, Trade.* **Description:** Reports on emerging trends in marine business and technology.
Former titles (until 1987): Marine Engineering - Log (0732-5460); (until 1979): Marine Engineering - Log International (0885-4912); (until 1977): Marine Engineering - Log (0025-3219); (until 1956): Marine Engineering (0272-2887); (until 1953): Marine Engineering Shipping and Review (0096-9435); (until 1935): Marine Engineering & Shipping Age (0272-2895); (until 1921): Marine Engineering (0272-2909); (until 1920): International Marine Engineering (0272-2879); (until 1906): Marine Engineering (0272-2860)
Related titles: Microform ed.: (from PQC); Online - full text ed.
Indexed: A05, A15, A22, A23, A24, ABIn, AS&TA, AS&TI, B04, B13, BMT, CLT&T, DM&T, EIA, EnvAb, EnvInd, HRIS, I05, L09, P48, P51, P52, PQC, PROMT, SCOPUS.
—BLDSC (5376.030000), IE, Infotrieve, Ingenta, Linda Hall. **CCC.**
Published by: Simmons-Boardman Publishing Corp., 345 Hudson St, New York, NY 10014. TEL 212-620-7200, FAX 212-633-1165, http://www.simmonsboardman.com/. Ed., Pub. John R Snyder TEL 212-620-7254. Adv. contact Roland Espinosa TEL 212-620-7225. Circ: 27,458.

387 USA
MARINE LOG BUYER'S GUIDE. Text in English. 1943. a. USD 89.95 per issue (effective 2009). adv. **Document type:** *Directory, Trade.*
Former titles (until 2008): Marine Catalog and Buyers Guide; Marine Catalog (0076-4450)
Published by: Simmons-Boardman Publishing Corp., 345 Hudson St, New York, NY 10014. TEL 212-620-7200, FAX 212-633-1165, jsnyder@sbpub.com, http://www.simmonsboardman.com/. Ed., Pub. John R Snyder TEL 212-620-7254. adv.: B&W page USD 1,975, color page USD 2,650; trim 8 x 10.875.

387 USA ISSN 1087-3864
HE745
MARINE NEWS. Text in English. 19??. m. USD 29 (effective 2007). **Document type:** *Magazine, Trade.*
Related titles: Online - full text ed.: ISSN 1559-7539.
—Linda Hall.
Published by: Maritime Activity Reports Inc., 118 E 25th St, 2nd Fl, New York, NY 10010. TEL 212-477-6700, FAX 212-254-6271, mren@marinelink.com, http://www.marinelink.com. Pub. John C O'Malley.

623.87 USA ISSN 1075-9069
VM595
MARINE OFFICER. Text in English. 1906. bi-m. free to members (effective 2008). charts; illus. **Document type:** *Magazine, Trade.*
Formed by the merger of (1906- 1991): American Marine Engineer (0002-9866); (1985-1991): The Marine Journal (0887-6738)
Related titles: Online - full content ed.
—Linda Hall.
Published by: National Marine Engineers Beneficial Association, 444 N Capitol, Ste 800, Washington, DC 20001. TEL 202-638-5355, FAX 202-638-5369. Ed. Victor Rollo.

623.8 GBR ISSN 1742-2825
CODEN: MPRIEC
MARINE PROPULSION & AUXILIARY MACHINERY. Text in English. 1981. bi-m. GBP 299 combined subscription (print & online eds.) (effective 2010). adv. illus. back issues avail. **Document type:** *Magazine, Trade.* **Description:** Dedicated to reporting and analysing developments in prime movers, drives and propulsors, as well as in auxiliary power and other below-deck engineering plant, for all types of commercial tonnage and naval and paramilitary vessels.
Formerly (until 2003): Marine Propulsion International (0143-3709)
Related titles: Online - full text ed.
Indexed: ASFA, B21, BMT, ESPM, OceAb.
—IE, Infotrieve. **CCC.**
Published by: Riviera Maritime Media, Mitre House, 66 Abbey Rd, Enfield, EN1 2QN, United Kingdom. TEL 44-20-83641551, FAX 44-20-83641331, info@rivieramm.com. Ed. Duncan Payne TEL 44-20-83701745. Adv. contact Rob Gore TEL 44-20-83707007. color page EUR 2,985, color page GBP 2,485; trim 210 x 297. Circ: 13,519.

387 USA ISSN 1075-9549
MARINE REGULATORY BULLETIN. Text in English. 1994. fortn. USD 260 (effective 2000). **Document type:** *Newsletter.*
Published by: Newman-Burrows Publishing, 1710 S Norman St, Seattle, WA 98144-2819. TEL 206-709-1840, FAX 206-324-8939.

MARINE SAFETY AND SECURITY COUNCIL. PROCEEDINGS. *see* MILITARY

387 343.096 CAN ISSN 1484-8473
CA1T12-7
MARINE SAFETY REVIEW. Variant title: Examen de la Securite Maritime. Securite Maritime en Rubrique. Text in English, French. 1997. a. **Document type:** *Newsletter.* **Description:** Informs the maritime community about marine legislation, relevant research, projects, and events.
Related titles: Online - full text ed.: ISSN 1494-5711.
Published by: Transport Canada, Marine Safety Directorate (Subsidiary of: Transport Canada/Transports Canada), Mailstop AMS, 330 Sparks St, Ottawa, ON K1A 0N5, Canada. TEL 613-991-3135, FAX 613-990-6191, marinesafety@tc.gc.ca.

577 GBR
MARINE SERVICES DIRECTORY. Text in English. a. **Description:** Aims to produce a directory which embraces all the disciplines involved in port development projects, land reclamation, coastal engineering, as well as manufacturers of dredging, civil engineering and port equipment.
Published by: Foxlow Publications Ltd., 20 Harcourt St, London, W1H 2AX, United Kingdom. TEL 44-171-724-6547, FAX 44-171-724-3442.

387 GBR ISSN 1462-6101
MARINE TECHNOLOGY. Text in English. 1999. irreg., latest vol.3, 2003. price varies. back issues avail. **Document type:** *Monographic series, Academic/Scholarly.* **Description:** Covers many of the changes which have recently taken place in the areas of ship design, building and operation.
Published by: W I T Press, Ashurst Lodge, Ashurst, Southampton, Hants SO40 7AA, United Kingdom. TEL 44-238-0293223, FAX 44-238-0292853, marketing@witpress.com.

623.8 USA
MARINE TECHNOLOGY SOCIETY. ANNUAL CONFERENCE PROCEEDINGS. Short title: Oceans (Year). Text in English. 1974 (no.9). a. bibl.; charts. **Document type:** *Proceedings, Academic/Scholarly.*
Indexed: AcoustA, SpeleolAb.
Published by: (I E E E), Marine Technology Society, 5565 Sterrett Pl, Ste 108, Columbia, MD 21044. TEL 410-884-5330, FAX 410-884-9060, mtspubs@erols.com, http://www.mtsociety.org/shop/. **Co-sponsor:** I E E E Oceanic Engineering Society, Marine Technology Society.

387 DEU ISSN 0172-8539
MARINEFORUM. Text in German. 1925. 10/yr. EUR 59.90; EUR 6.75 newsstand/cover (effective 2011). adv. bk.rev. abstr.; charts; illus.; stat. **Document type:** *Magazine, Trade.*
Published by: Verlag E.S. Mittler und Sohn GmbH, Ulrich-von-Hassell-Str.2, Bonn, 53123, Germany. TEL 49-228-9191521, FAX 49-228-9191522, vertrieb@koehler-mittler.de, http://www.koehler-mittler.de. Ed. Juergen Kratzmann. adv.: B&W page EUR 2,500, color page EUR 3,460; trim 185 x 270. Circ: 9,060 (paid).

387 NLD ISSN 2211-2286
MARITIEM AKTUEEL. Text in Dutch. 3/yr. EUR 15; EUR 3.50 newsstand/cover (effective 2011). adv. **Document type:** *Magazine, Consumer.*
Published by: Stichting Promotie Maritieme Tradities, Postbus 37670, Amsterdam, 1030 BH, Netherlands. TEL 31-20-6343482, promotiemaritiem@xs4all.nl, http://www.mahu880.nl.

387.5 069 NLD ISSN 1877-3486
MARITIEM MUSEUM MAGAZINE. Text in Dutch. 1980. 3/yr. **Document type:** *Magazine, Consumer.*
Former titles (until 2008): M M Journaal (1569-3384); (until 2002): Plaatsbepaling (1382-0001)
Published by: (Vereniging Vrienden van het Maritiem Museum Rotterdam), Maritiem Museum Rotterdam, Postbus 988, Rotterdam, 3000 AZ, Netherlands. TEL 31-10-4132680, FAX 31-10-4137342, http://www.maritiemmuseum.nl. Ed. Froukje Aben.

387 623.8 NLD ISSN 1380-6742
MARITIEM NEDERLAND; scheepvaart - techniek - marine - havens - offshore. Text in Dutch. 1911. 10/yr. EUR 65 (effective 2009). adv. bk.rev. illus. **Document type:** *Magazine, Trade.* **Description:** Examines the Navy, the Merchant Navy, shipbuilding, national and international harbor services and offshore activities.
Formed by the 1994 merger of: Maritiem (0927-6637); Which was formerly (1984-1991): Maritiem Gezien (0927-6645); Zeewezen (0165-8182); Which was formerly: Ons Zeewezen (0030-2791)
Published by: (Koninklijke Nederlandse Vereniging Onze Vloot), Beta Publishers, Postbus 249, Leidschendam, 2260 AE, Netherlands. TEL 31-70-4440600, FAX 31-70-3378799, info@betapublishers.nl, http://www.betapublishers.nl. Pub. Dr. Roeland Dobbelaer. adv.: B&W page EUR 1,550, color page EUR 2,150; trim 210 x 297. Circ: 5,600.

387 DNK ISSN 0106-7818
VK69
MARITIM KONTAKT. Text in Danish. 1980. a. DKK 150 membership (effective 2009). back issues avail. **Document type:** *Monographic series, Academic/Scholarly.* **Description:** For all with interest in Danish maritime history.
Published by: Kontaktudvalget for Dansk Maritim Historie- og Samfundsforskning/Committee for Danish Maritime History and Anthropology, c/o Erik Housted, Dyvekes Alle 6, Copenhagen S, 2300, Denmark. TEL 45-32-596910, forlaget@maritimkontakt.dk, http://www.maritimkontakt.dk. Eds. Morten Ravn TEL 45-22-445221, Erik Goebel TEL 45-33-922386.

387 NOR ISSN 1890-6095
MARITIM LOGG; paa sjoemannens side. Text in Norwegian. 2008. 10/yr. adv. back issues avail. **Document type:** *Magazine, Trade.*

TU

Formed by the merger of (1999-2008): Loggen (1501-4622); Which superseded in part (in 1999): Norsk Sjoemannsforbund. Medlemsblad (0029-2079); Which was formerly (1911-1934): Fagblad for Norsk Matros- og Fyrboeterunion (0806-7139); (1995-2008): Norsk Maskin Tidende (0805-598X); (1995-2008): Sjoeoffiseren (0805-7656); Both of which superseded in part (in 1995): Norsk Skibsfoerertidende, Norsk Maskin-Tidende, Norsk Styrmandsblad (0801-8715); Which was formed by the merger of (1917-1987): Norsk Skibsfoerertidende (0048-0606); (1986-1987): Norsk Maskin-Tidende, Norsk Styrmandsblad (0801-1400); Which incorporated (1911-1985): Norsk Styrmandsblad (0029-215X); (1896-1985): Norsk Maskin-Tidende (0333-0192)
Related titles: Online - full text ed.: ISSN 1891-8271.
Published by: (Norsk Sjoemannsforbund, Norsk Sjoeoffisersforbund/ Norwegian Maritime Officers' Association), Norske Maskinistforbund/ Norwegian Union of Marine Engineers, PO Box 2000, Vika, Oslo, 0125, Norway. TEL 47-22-825800, FAX 47-22-336618, firmapost@sjomannsunion.no, http://www.sjomannsforbundet.no. Eds. Omar Joergensen, Roy Ervin Solstad, Tore Bjoerkan, Arnljot Muren. Adv. contact Tore Bjoerkan. page NOK 18,000. Circ: 30,000. **Co-publishers:** Norsk Sjoemannsforbund; Norsk Sjoeoffisersforbund/Norwegian Maritime Officers' Association.

387 ESP ISSN 0213-3067
MARITIMAS. Text in Spanish. 1951. d. adv. illus. back issues avail. **Document type:** *Newsletter, Consumer.*
Formerly (until 1956): Informacion Maritima Comercial (0213-3075)
Published by: Grupo Editorial Men-Car, Passeig de Colom, 24, Barcelona, 08002, Spain. TEL 34-93-301-5749, FAX 34-93-302-1779, men-car@men-car.com, http://www.men-car.com. Circ: 11,600.

387.5 IND ISSN 0973-3159
HF3785
➤ **MARITIME AFFAIRS.** Text in English. 2005. s-a. GBP 191 combined subscription in United Kingdom to institutions (print & online eds.); EUR 278, USD 346 combined subscription to institutions (print & online eds.) (effective 2012). adv. back issues avail. **Document type:** *Journal, Academic/Scholarly.* **Description:** Contains international studies and research material on issues related to oceanic activity such as shipbuilding, maritime security, port modernization, disaster management, and laws of the sea.
Related titles: Online - full text ed.: ISSN 1946-6609. GBP 173 in United Kingdom to institutions; EUR 250, USD 312 to institutions (effective 2012).
Indexed: A01, I02, T02.
—CCC.
Published by: (National Maritime Foundation), Anamaya Publishers, F-154/2, Lado Sarai, New Delhi, 110 030, India. TEL 91-11-29523205, FAX 91-11-29523205, anamayapub@vsnl.net. Ed. C Uday Bhaskar. **Co-publisher:** Taylor & Francis Ltd.

387.5 GBR
MARITIME AND COASTGUARD AGENCY. M NOTICES. Text in English. irreg. **Document type:** *Bulletin.*
Formerly: Maritime Safety Agency. Marine Guidance Note
Published by: Maritime and Coastguard Agency, Spring Pl, 105 Commercial Rd, Southampton, Hants SO15 1EG, United Kingdom. TEL 44-1703-329106, FAX 44-1703-329388. **Subscr. to:** Lisa Gates, MCA, 3-23 Spring Pl, Southampton, Hamshire SO15 1EG, United Kingdom. TEL 44-1703-329106, FAX 44-1703-329388.

387.5 GBR ISSN 1462-6160
MARITIME AND COASTGUARD AGENCY. MARINE INFORMATION NOTE. Text in English. irreg., latest 2007. **Document type:** *Government.*
Formerly: Marine Safety Agency. Marine Information Note
Related titles: Online - full text ed.: free.
—BLDSC (5375.571450).
Published by: Maritime and Coastguard Agency, Spring Pl, 105 Commercial Rd, Southampton, Hants SO15 1EG, United Kingdom. TEL 44-1703-329297, FAX 44-1442-229050. **Paper subscr. to:** Mail Marketing (Scotland) Ltd., 42 Methil St, Glasgow G14 0SZ, United Kingdom. TEL 44-141-9502222, FAX 44-141-9502726, mca@promo-solutions.com.

387 SGP
MARITIME AND PORT AUTHORITY OF SINGAPORE. ANNUAL REPORT. Text in English. 1974. a. free. **Document type:** *Government.*
Published by: Maritime and Port Authority of Singapore, 460 Alexandra Rd, #19-00 PSA Bldg, Singapore, 119963, Singapore. TEL 65-63751600, media_enquiries@mpa.gov.sg. Circ: 800.

387.5 USA
MARITIME ASSOCIATION OF THE PORT OF NEW YORK - NEW JERSEY. MARITIME NEWSLETTER. Text in English. 1973. fortn. membership. adv. bk.rev. charts; illus.; stat. **Document type:** *Newsletter.*
Formerly: Maritime Association of the Port of New York. Newsletter; Which supersedes: Maritime Exchange Bulletin (0025-3421)
Published by: Maritime Association of the Port of New York - New Jersey, 17 Battery Place, Ste 1115, New York, NY 10004. Circ: 1,500.

623.82 NLD ISSN 2211-3444
VM77
MARITIME BY HOLLAND. Text in English. 1952. bi-m. EUR 79 in Europe; EUR 129 elsewhere; EUR 40 to students (effective 2011). adv. bk.rev. charts; illus.; mkt.; pat.; tr.lit. back issues avail. **Document type:** *Magazine, Trade.* **Description:** Covers shipbuilding, dredging, engineering, oil and gas industry, ports and shipping, industry, maintenance and corrosion prevention.
Former titles (until 2011): Holland Shipbuilding (1877-1661); (until 2008): H S B International (0923-666X); (until 1988): Holland Shipbuilding (0018-3571); Holland Shipbuilding, Marine Engineering and Shipping Herald
Indexed: A22, A28, APA, ASFA, BMT, BrCerAb, C&ISA, CA/WCA, CIA, CerAb, CivEngAb, CorrAb, E&CAJ, E11, EEA, EMA, ESPM, EngInd, EnvEAb, FLUIDEX, GEOBASE, H15, KES, M&TEA, M09, MBF, METADEX, OceAb, SCOPUS, SolStAb, T04, WAA.
—IE, Infotrieve, Linda Hall.
Published by: Navingo BV, Westerlaan 1, Rotterdam, 3016 CK, Netherlands. TEL 31-10-2092600, FAX 31-10-4368134, info@navingo.com, http://www.navingo.com. Ed. Gail van den Hanenberg.

623 USA
MARITIME DIRECTORY AND MARINE INDUSTRY CENSUS. Text in English. a. USD 145. **Document type:** *Directory.*
Published by: Maritime Directory Reports Inc., 118 E 25th St, New York, NY 10010. TEL 212-477-6700, FAX 212-254-6271.

387 GBR ISSN 1479-2931
HE561
➤ **MARITIME ECONOMICS & LOGISTICS.** Abbreviated title: M E L. Text in English. 1999. q. USD 1,031 in North America to institutions; GBP 554 elsewhere to institutions (effective 2011). adv. back issues avail.; reprint service avail. from PSC. **Document type:** *Journal, Academic/Scholarly.* **Description:** Committed to the advancement of maritime economics as a distinct and well-defined branch of applied economics.
Formerly (until 2003): International Journal of Maritime Economics (1388-1973)
Related titles: Online - full text ed.: ISSN 1479-294X (from IngentaConnect).
Indexed: A12, A22, ABIn, B16, E01, EconLit, HRIS, IBR, IBZ, ICEA, JEL, P10, P48, P51, P52, P53, P54, P56, PQC, SCOPUS.
—BLDSC (5381.352750), IE, Ingenta. **CCC.**
Published by: (International Association of Maritime Economists AUS, Erasmus Universiteit Rotterdam, Rotterdam School of Economics NLD), Palgrave Macmillan Ltd. (Subsidiary of: Macmillan Publishers Ltd.), Houndmills, Basingstoke, Hants RG21 6XS, United Kingdom. TEL 44-1256-329242, FAX 44-1256-479476, orders@palgrave.com, http://www.palgrave.com. Ed. H E Haralambides. Pub. David Bull TEL 44-1256-329242. Circ: 600. **Subscr. to:** Subscription Department, Brunel Rd, Houndmills, Basingstoke, Hants RG21 2XS, United Kingdom. TEL 44-1256-357893, FAX 44-1256-328339, subscriptions@palgrave.com.

➤ **THE MARITIME EXECUTIVE**; intellectual capital for executives. *see* BUSINESS AND ECONOMICS—Management

➤ **MARITIME HANDBOOK OF SOUTHERN AFRICA.** *see* ENGINEERING—Industrial Engineering

387 GBR ISSN 0957-7009
MARITIME JOURNAL; insight for european commercial marine industries. Text in English. 1987. m. GBP 70 domestic; GBP 80 in Europe; GBP 106.50 elsewhere; free to qualified personnel (effective 2010). bk.rev. **Document type:** *Magazine, Trade.* **Description:** Professional marine trade guide to equipment, sales and services relating to European ports and harbours, workboats, maritime safety matters and short sea operations.
Related titles: Online - full text ed.: free (effective 2010).
—CCC.
Published by: Mercator Media Ltd., The Old Mill, Lower Quay, Fareham, Hampshire PO16 0RA, United Kingdom. TEL 44-1329-825335, FAX 44-1329-825330, corporate@mercatormedia.com, http://www.mercatormedia.com. Ed. Larz Bourne.

387 DEU ISSN 1868-369X
▼ **MARITIME LOGISTICS/MARITIME LOGISTIK.** Text in English. 2009. irreg. price varies. **Document type:** *Monographic series, Academic/Scholarly.*
Published by: Peter Lang GmbH (Subsidiary of: Peter Lang Publishing Group), Eschborner Landstr 42-50, Frankfurt Am Main, 60489, Germany. TEL 49-69-7807050, FAX 49-69-78070550, zentrale.frankfurt@peterlang.com, http://www.peterlang.com.

387.2 USA ISSN 1545-7648
MARITIME MUSEUM NEWS. Text in English. 1993 (Apr.). m. USD 12 (effective 2003).
Published by: Cubberley & Shaw, PO Box 607, Groton, MA 01450-0607. cubberley@aol.com.

387.2 NOR ISSN 1891-747X
MARITIME NEWS (HOEVIK). Text in English. 1990. bi-m. free. back issues avail. **Document type:** *Journal, Trade.*
Former titles (until 2009): D N V Maritime News (1504-8772); (until 2007): Classification News (1503-6650); (until 1998): Safety Update (1500-7197); (until 1996): Classification Newsletter (0806-8909); (until 1995): Classification News (0806-8895)
Related titles: Online - full text ed.
Published by: Det Norske Veritas, Veritasveien 1, Hoevik, 1363, Norway. TEL 47-67-579900, FAX 47-67-579911, dnv.corporate@dnv.com, http://www.dnv.com.

MARITIME NEWSLETTER. *see* LABOR UNIONS

387 GBR ISSN 0308-8839
HC92
➤ **MARITIME POLICY AND MANAGEMENT**; an international journal of shipping and port research. Text in English. 1973. bi-m. GBP 1,400 combined subscription in United Kingdom to institutions (print & online eds.); EUR 1,853, USD 2,330 combined subscription to institutions (print & online eds.) (effective 2012). adv. bk.rev. illus. Index. back issues avail.; reprint service avail. from PSC. **Document type:** *Journal, Academic/Scholarly.* **Description:** Emphasizes organizational, economic, sociolegal, and management topics at port, community, shipping company, and shipboard levels.
Formerly (until 1976): Maritime Studies and Management (0306-1957)
Related titles: Online - full text ed.: ISSN 1464-5254. GBP 1,259 in United Kingdom to institutions; EUR 1,668, USD 2,097 to institutions (effective 2012) (from IngentaConnect).
Indexed: A01, A03, A08, A22, A28, APA, APEL, ASFA, B01, B06, B07, B09, B21, BMT, BrCerAb, C&ISA, CA, CA/WCA, CIA, CISA, CREJ, CerAb, CivEngAb, CorrAb, E&CAJ, E01, E04, E05, E11, EEA, EMA, ESPM, EconLit, EnvEAb, FLUIDEX, FR, GEOBASE, H15, HPNRM, HRIS, JEL, M&TEA, M09, MAB, MBF, METADEX, OceAb, P26, P34, P52, P54, P56, PAIS, PQC, PollutAb, SCOPUS, SSciA, SolStAb, T02, T04, WAA.
—IE, Infotrieve, Ingenta, Linda Hall. **CCC.**
Published by: Routledge (Subsidiary of: Taylor & Francis Group), 4 Park Sq, Milton Park, Abingdon, Oxon OX14 4RN, United Kingdom. FAX 44-20-70176336, subscriptions@tandf.co.uk, http://www.routledge.com. Eds. Heather Leggate McLaughlin, Kevin Li. Adv. contact Linda Hann TEL 44-1344-779945. **Subscr. in N. America to:** Taylor & Francis Inc., Customer Services Dept, 325 Chestnut St, 8th Fl, Philadelphia, PA 19106. TEL 215-625-8900, 800-354-1420, FAX 215-625-2940, customerservice@taylorandfrancis.com; **Subscr. to:** Taylor & Francis Ltd., Journals Customer Service, Sheepen Pl, Colchester, Essex CO3 3LP, United Kingdom. TEL 44-20-70175544, FAX 44-20-70175198, tf.enquiries@tfinforma.com.

623.8 387 USA ISSN 0025-3448
VM1
MARITIME REPORTER AND ENGINEERING NEWS. Text in English. 1939. m. free to qualified personnel (effective 2005). adv. bk.rev. illus. **Document type:** *Magazine, Trade.*
Indexed: BMT, T&II.
Published by: Maritime Activity Reports Inc., 118 E 25th St, 2nd Fl, New York, NY 10010. TEL 212-477-6700, FAX 212-254-6271, mren@marinelink.com, http://www.marinelink.com. Pub. John C O'Malley. Circ: 30,000 (controlled).

387 USA ISSN 1084-2713
MARITIME RESEARCH CHARTER NEWSLETTER. Text in English. 1953. w. USD 280 domestic; USD 300 foreign (effective 2005). adv. index. back issues avail. **Document type:** *Newsletter, Trade.* **Description:** Contains a listing of all charter fixtures reported worldwide in the tramp charter market.
Published by: Maritime Research, Inc., 499 Ernston Rd, Box 805, Parlin, NJ 08859. TEL 732-727-8040, FAX 732-727-0243, mri499@aol.com, http://www.maritime-research.com. Ed. Jay Lillianthal. Circ: 5,000 (paid and controlled).

387 EGY ISSN 1110-0664
VK4
MARITIME RESEARCH JOURNAL/MAGALLAT BUHUTH AL-NAQL AL-BAHARI. Text in English. 1976. s-a. USD 25, EGP 15. **Document type:** *Journal, Academic/Scholarly.*
Formerly (until 198?): Maritime Research Bulletin (1110-1490)
Published by: Maritime Research and Consultancy Center, Gamal Abd-El Nasser Str, Maimi, PO Box 1029, Alexandria, Egypt. TEL 20-3-5576826, FAX 20-3-5408374, info@mrcc.aast.edu, http://www.aast.edu:8282/en/portal/media-type/html/role/user/page/maritime_research?p=38001. Ed. Dr. Abdel-Halim Basyouni.

623.8 FIN ISSN 0784-6010
MARITIME RESEARCH NEWS. Text in English. 1987. s-a. free.
Indexed: GeoRef.
Published by: Maritime Institute of Finland, c/o VTT Industrial Systems, PO Box 1705, Espoo, 02044, Finland. TEL 358-9-4561, FAX 358-9-4550619. Ed. Saara Hanninen TEL 358-9-4566866. **Co-publisher:** Helsinki University of Technology, Ship Laboratory.

387 GBR ISSN 1365-7542
MARITIME REVIEW. Text in English. 1997. s-a. GBP 95 domestic; GBP 95 in Europe; GBP 114 rest of world (effective 2001). back issues avail. **Document type:** *Magazine, Trade.* **Description:** Covers trends and developments within various sectors of the global shipping industry.
Related titles: Online - full content ed.; Supplement(s): Cruise & Ferry Supplement.
Published by: Pacific Press Ltd., 197-199 City Rd, London, EC1V 1JN, United Kingdom. TEL 44-20-72532080, FAX 44-20-72532090, pacific.press@btinternet.com.

MARITIME RISK INTERNATIONAL. *see* INSURANCE

387.5 639.2 AUS ISSN 0726-6472
➤ **MARITIME STUDIES.** Text in English. 1981. bi-m. (11/yr.). AUD 99 combined subscription domestic to members (print & online eds.); AUD 107 combined subscription in Asia & the Pacific to members (print & online eds.); AUD 115 combined subscription elsewhere to members (print & online eds.); AUD 110 combined subscription domestic to non-members (print & online eds.); AUD 117 combined subscription in Asia & the Pacific to non-members (print & online eds.); AUD 125 combined subscription elsewhere to non-members (print & online eds.) (effective 2008). bk.rev. 36 p./no. 2 cols./p.; back issues avail. **Document type:** *Journal, Academic/Scholarly.* **Description:** Covers all aspects of marine affairs relevant to Australia and its region.
Related titles: Online - full text ed.: AUD 66 domestic to members; AUD 60 foreign to members; AUD 77 domestic to non-members; AUD 70 foreign to non-members (effective 2008).
Indexed: ASFA, B21, ESPM, P48, P52, P54, P56, PQC.
Published by: Australian Centre for Maritime Studies, PO Box 55, Red Hill, ACT 2603, Australia. TEL 61-2-62950056, FAX 61-2-62953367, acmarst@bigpond.com. Circ: 350.

387 EGY ISSN 1110-6328
MARITIME TECHNOLOGY/TIKNULUGYA AL-NAQL AL-BAHARI. Text in English. 1983. s-a. **Document type:** *Bulletin, Academic/Scholarly.*
Published by: Maritime Research and Consultancy Center, Gamal Abd-El Nasser Str, Maimi, PO Box 1029, Alexandria, Egypt. TEL 20-3-5576826, FAX 20-3-5408374, info@mrcc.aast.edu, http://www.aast.edu:8282/en/portal/media-type/html/role/user/page/maritime_research?p=38001. Ed. Dr. Abdel-Halim Basyouni.

387 ROM ISSN 2065-2909
MARITIME TRANSPORT & NAVIGATION JOURNAL. Text in English. 2004. q. **Document type:** *Journal, Academic/Scholarly.*
Formerly (until 2009): Transporturi Navale (1582-0319)
Published by: (Universitatea Maritima Constanta, Catedra de Navigatie si Transport Maritim), "Nautica" Publishing House/Editura Nautica, Mircea cel Batran St.,104, Constanta, 900663, Romania. TEL 40241664740, FAX 40241617260, info@imc.ro, http://www.cmu-edu.eu/editura.html.

387 AUS ISSN 1324-3268
MARITIME WORKERS' JOURNAL. Abbreviated title: M W J. Text in English. 1938. m. (11/yr.). bk.rev.; play rev. illus.; stat. **Document type:** *Journal, Trade.* **Description:** Union magazine covering stevedoring and industrial issues.
Supersedes (in Jul. 1993): Maritime Worker (0025-3464)
Related titles: Online - full text ed.: free (effective 2009).
Published by: Maritime Union of Australia, 365 Sussex St, Sydney, NSW 2000, Australia. TEL 61-2-92679134, FAX 61-2-92613481, info@mua.org.au. Ed. Paddy Crumlin.

MARPOL 1973 - 1978 AMENDMENTS. *see* CONSERVATION

MASTER, MATE & PILOT. *see* LABOR UNIONS

THE MASTHEAD (PHILADELPHIA). *see* MUSEUMS AND ART GALLERIES

MEER & YACHTEN. *see* SPORTS AND GAMES—Boats And Boating

MELBOURNE PORT & SHIPPING HANDBOOK (YEAR). *see* BUSINESS AND ECONOMICS—Trade And Industrial Directories

387 DNK ISSN 1902-164X
MERCATOR; maritime innovation, research and education. Text in Danish, English, Norwegian. 2007. q. DKK 350 (effective 2009). adv. back issues avail. **Document type:** *Magazine, Academic/Scholarly.*
Related titles: Online - full text ed.
Published by: Iver C. Weilbach & Co. A/S, Toldbodgade 35, Copenhagen K, 1253, Denmark. TEL 45-33-343560, FAX 45-33-343561, nautical@weilbach.dk, http://www.weilbach.dk. Ed. Kristen D Nedergaard. Adv. contact Ditte Kragh. color page DKK 5,000. **Subscr. to:** Europas Maritime Udviklingscenter, Amaliegade 33 B, Copenhagen K 1256, Denmark. TEL 45-33-337488, FAX 45-33-327938, info@maritimecenter.dk, http://www.maritimecenter.dk. **Co-publisher:** Europas Maritime Udviklingscenter/Maritime Development Center of Europe.

387 FIN ISSN 1456-7814
MERENKULKULAITOS. JULKAISUJA/FINNISH MARITIME ADMINISTRATION. PUBLICATIONS. Text in Multiple languages. 1999. irreg., latest 2007. back issues avail. **Document type:** *Monographic series, Trade.*
Related titles: Online - full text ed.
Published by: Merenkulkulaitos/Finnish Maritime Administration, Porkkalankatu 5, Helsiki, 00180, Finland. TEL 358-204-481, FAX 358-204-484355, kirjaamo@fma.fi.

387 FIN ISSN 1455-7525
MERIVAYLA. Text mainly in Finnish; Text occasionally in Swedish. 1998. 3/yr. EUR 10 (effective 2008). back issues avail. **Document type:** *Magazine, Trade.*
Related titles: Online - full text ed.
Published by: Merenkulkulaitos/Finnish Maritime Administration, Porkkalankatu 5, Helsiki, 00180, Finland. TEL 358-204-481, FAX 358-204-484355, kirjaamo@fma.fi. Ed. Maire Salonen.

623.82 JPN ISSN 0911-5234
MESSAGE. Text in Japanese. 1985. 3/yr. free. **Document type:** *Trade.*
Description: Introduces the company's activities.
Indexed: Perlslam.
Published by: Mitsui Zosen K.K./Mitsui Engineering and Shipbuilding Co., Ltd., 6-4 Tsuki-Ji 5-chome, Chuo-ku, Tokyo, 104-0045, Japan. TEL 81-3-3544-3147, FAX 81-3-3544-3050. Ed. M. Gomi. R&P M Gomi. Circ: 10,000.

623.8 JPN ISSN 0026-6825
CODEN: MIZGAR
MITSUI ZOSEN TECHNICAL REVIEW/MITSUI ZOSEN GIHO. Text in Japanese; Summaries in English, Japanese. 1952. q. free to qualified organizations or personnel. bk.rev. abstr.; bibl.; charts; illus. cum.index. **Description:** Examines the computer applications as well as latest developments and research in engineering and shipbuilding.
Related titles: Microfilm ed.
Indexed: BMT, ChemAb, INIS AtomInd, Inspec, RefZh.
—BLDSC (5829.833000), AskIEEE, CASDDS, Linda Hall.
Published by: Mitsui Engineering & Shipbuilding Co. Ltd., Corporate Technical Research & Development Headquarters/Mitsui Zosen K.K. Gijutsu Soukatsu Honbu, 6-4 Tsuki-Ji 5-chome, Chuo-ku, Tokyo, 104-0045, Japan. Ed. K Nagata. Circ: 1,900.

LE MODELE REDUIT DE BATEAU. *see* HOBBIES

387 RUS
MORSKAYA KOLLEKTSIYA. Text in Russian. bi-m. USD 51 foreign (effective 2003).
Published by: Redaktsiya Zhurnala Modelist - Konstruktor, Novodmitrovskaya ul 5-a, Moscow, 127015, Russian Federation. TEL 7-095-2851704. Ed. A S Raguzin. **Dist. by:** East View Information Services, 10601 Wayzata Blvd, Minneapolis, MN 55305. TEL 952-252-1201, 800-477-1005, FAX 952-252-1202, info@eastview.com, http://www.eastview.com; M K - Periodica, ul Gilyarovskogo 39, Moscow 129110, Russian Federation. TEL 7-095-2845008, FAX 7-095-2813798, info@periodicals.ru, http://www.mkniga.ru.

MORSKOI ASTRONOMICHESKII EZHEGODNIK/NAVAL ASTRONOMICAL YEARBOOK. *see* ASTRONOMY

387 RUS ISSN 0369-1276
VM4 CODEN: MORFAQ
MORSKOI FLOT. Text in Russian; Summaries in English. 1886. m. USD 90 foreign (effective 2003). adv. bk.rev. abstr.; bibl.; charts; illus.; stat. index. **Description:** Covers Russian and foreign sea transport, international maritime law, domestic and foreign shipbuilding and ship repair, maritime academies and research institutions, and Russian fleet's history.
Related titles: Microform ed.
Indexed: A33, BMT, ChemAb, RASB, RefZh.
—East View, Linda Hall.
Published by: Ministerstvo Transporta R F, Otdel Morskogo Transporta, Ul Rozhdestvenka 1-4, Moscow, 103759, Russian Federation. TEL 7-095-9261585, FAX 7-095-9261381. Ed. Leonid Grankov. Circ: 10,000. **Dist. by:** M K - Periodica, ul Gilyarovskogo 39, Moscow 129110, Russian Federation. TEL 7-095-2845008, FAX 7-095-2813798, info@periodicals.ru, http://www.mkniga.ru; East View Information Services, 10601 Wayzata Blvd, Minneapolis, MN 55305. TEL 952-252-1201, 800-477-1005, FAX 952-252-1202, info@eastview.com, http://www.eastview.com.

387.51 RUS ISSN 0236-1205
MORSKOI TRANSPORT. SERIYA: EKONOMIKA I KOMMERCHESKAYA RABOTA NA MORSKOM TRANSPORTE. Text in Russian. m. USD 99.95 in United States.
Indexed: RASB.
Published by: Mortekhinformreklama, Volokolamskoe shosse 14, Moscow, 125080, Russian Federation. TEL 7-095-1581617. **Dist. by:** East View Information Services, 10601 Wayzata Blvd, Minneapolis, MN 55305. TEL 952-252-1201, 800-477-1005, FAX 952-252-1202, info@eastview.com, http://www.eastview.com.

387 RUS
MORSKOI TRANSPORT. SERIYA: ORGANIZATSIYA I UPRAVLENIE MORSKIM TRANSPORTOM. Text in Russian. m. USD 179.95 in United States.
Published by: Mortekhinformreklama, Volokolamskoe shosse 14, Moscow, 125080, Russian Federation. TEL 7-095-1581617. **Dist. by:** East View Information Services, 10601 Wayzata Blvd, Minneapolis, MN 55305. TEL 952-252-1201, 800-477-1005, FAX 952-252-1202, info@eastview.com, http://www.eastview.com.

387 RUS ISSN 0205-4108
MORSKOI TRANSPORT. SERIYA: SUDOREMONT. Text in Russian. m. USD 179.95 in United States.
Published by: Mortekhinformreklama, Volokolamskoe shosse 14, Moscow, 125080, Russian Federation. TEL 7-095-1581617. **Dist. by:** East View Information Services, 10601 Wayzata Blvd, Minneapolis, MN 55305. TEL 952-252-1201, 800-477-1005, FAX 952-252-1202, info@eastview.com, http://www.eastview.com.

387 RUS
MORSKOI TRANSPORT. SERIYA: SUDOVOZHDENIE, SVIAZ' I BEZOPASNOST' MOREPLAVANIYA. Text in Russian. m. USD 179.95 in United States.
Published by: Mortekhinformreklama, Volokolamskoe shosse 14, Moscow, 125080, Russian Federation. TEL 7-095-1581617. **Dist. by:** East View Information Services, 10601 Wayzata Blvd, Minneapolis, MN 55305. TEL 952-252-1201, 800-477-1005, FAX 952-252-1202, info@eastview.com, http://www.eastview.com.

623.8 RUS ISSN 0205-4027
MORSKOI TRANSPORT. SERIYA: TEKHNICHESKAYA EKSPLUATATSIYA FLOTA. Text in Russian. 18/yr. USD 139.95 in United States.
Published by: Mortekhinformreklama, Volokolamskoe shosse 14, Moscow, 125080, Russian Federation. TEL 7-095-1581617. **Dist. by:** East View Information Services, 10601 Wayzata Blvd, Minneapolis, MN 55305. TEL 952-252-1201, 800-477-1005, FAX 952-252-1202, info@eastview.com, http://www.eastview.com.

623.8 RUS ISSN 0205-406X
MORSKOI TRANSPORT. SERIYA: TEKHNOLOGIYA MORSKIKH PEREVOZOK I MORSKIE PORTY. Text in Russian. m. USD 179.95 in United States.
Published by: Mortekhinformreklama, Volokolamskoe shosse 14, Moscow, 125080, Russian Federation. TEL 7-095-1581617. **Dist. by:** East View Information Services, 10601 Wayzata Blvd, Minneapolis, MN 55305. TEL 952-252-1201, 800-477-1005, FAX 952-252-1202, info@eastview.com, http://www.eastview.com.

387.5 POL ISSN 1426-529X
MORZA, STATKI I OKRETY. Text in Polish. 1996. bi-m. EUR 41 foreign (effective 2006). **Document type:** *Magazine, Trade.*
Published by: Wydawnictwo Magnum-X, ul Skrajna 1/25, Warsaw, 03209, Poland. TEL 48-22-8103330, magnum@hbz.com.pl. **Dist. by:** Ars Polona, Obroncow 25, Warsaw 03933, Poland. TEL 48-22-5098609, FAX 48-22-5098610, arspolona@arspolona.com.pl, http://www.arspolona.com.pl.

623.82 GBR ISSN 0027-2000
VM1 CODEN: MOSHA3
THE MOTOR SHIP. Text in English. 1920. m. (11/yr.). GBP 133.50; free to qualified personnel (effective 2010). adv. bk.rev. charts; illus.; tr.lit. index. reprints avail. **Document type:** *Magazine, Trade.* **Description:** Encompasses all technical developments affecting modern tonnage. Directed at technical managers in ship-owning companies and allied industries.
Former titles (until 1957): The British Motor Ship; (until 19??): Motor Ship
Related titles: Online - full text ed.: free (effective 2010).
Indexed: A22, A28, APA, APIAb, ASFA, B02, B03, B15, B17, B18, BMT, BrCerAb, BusI, C&ISA, CA/WCA, CIA, CerAb, CivEngAb, CorrAb, E&CAJ, E11, EEA, EMA, ESPM, EngInd, EnvEAb, G04, G06, G07, G08, GeoRef, H15, HRIS, I05, ISMEC, Inspec, M&TEA, M09, MBF, METADEX, OceAb, SCOPUS, SolStAb, T&II, T04, WAA.
—BLDSC (5975.540000), IE, Infotrieve, Ingenta, Linda Hall. **CCC.**
Published by: Mercator Media Ltd., The Old Mill, Lower Quay, Fareham, Hampshire PO16 0RA, United Kingdom. TEL 44-1329-825335, FAX 44-1329-825330, corporate@mercatormedia.com, http://www.mercatormedia.com. Ed. Bill Thomson. Circ: 7,124.

623.8 USA ISSN 2153-4721
VM1
➤ **(MT) MARINE TECHNOLOGY.** Variant title: Marine Technology. Text in English. 19??. q. USD 320 domestic; USD 350 foreign (effective 2009). adv. charts; illus. index. back issues avail.; reprints avail. **Document type:** *Journal, Academic/Scholarly.* **Description:** Features selected meeting papers and news about the society.
Former titles (until 2010): Marine Technology and S N A M E News (1945-3582); (until 1987): Marine Technology (0025-3316); (until 1964): S N A M E News; (until 19??): Society of Naval Architects and Marine Engineers. Bulletin
Related titles: CD-ROM ed.; Online - full text ed.: ISSN 2153-473X (from IngentaConnect).
Indexed: A05, A15, A22, A23, A24, ABIn, APICat, APIH&E, APIOC, APIPR, APIPS, APITS, AS&TA, AS&TI, ASCA, ASFA, B04, B13, BMT, BRD, C10, CA, CLT&T, CPEI, ChemAb, CurCont, EngInd, FR, HRIS, OceAb, P26, P48, P51, P52, P54, P56, PQC, S04, SCOPUS, T02, TM, W03, W05.
—IE, Ingenta, INIST, Linda Hall. **CCC.**
Published by: The Society of Naval Architects and Marine Engineers, 601 Pavonia Ave, Jersey City, NJ 07306. TEL 201-798-4800, 800-798-2188, FAX 201-798-4975, tfaix@sname.org. Adv. contact Bob Rogaski.

➤ **N K K NEWS**; steelmaking, engineering, construction & shipbuilding, advanced materials, electronics, urban development, biotechnology. (Nippon Kokan K.K.) *see* ENGINEERING—Mechanical Engineering

387 NGA
N P A ANNUAL REPORT. (Nigerian Ports Authority) Text in English. a.
Published by: Nigerian Ports Authority, Public Relations Department, 26-28 Marina, PMB 12588, Lagos, Nigeria.

387 NGA ISSN 0794-3008
N P A BULLETIN. (Nigerian Ports Authority) Text in English. q. free.
Published by: Nigerian Ports Authority, Public Relations Department, 26-28 Marina, PMB 12588, Lagos, Nigeria. TELEX 21500 ONPNPA NG.

387 NGA ISSN 0547-0730
N P A NEWS. Text in English. 1973. q. free. illus. **Document type:** *Government.*
Published by: Institute of Transport, Nigerian Ports Authority, Headquarters, 26-28 Marina, Lagos, Nigeria. Ed. Agidi Ovurevu.

387 DEU ISSN 0027-7444
VK798
NACHRICHTEN FUER SEEFAHRER. Text in German. 1849. w. EUR 10 per month; EUR 3 newsstand/cover (effective 2009). index. **Document type:** *Magazine, Trade.*
Published by: Bundesamt fuer Seeschifffahrt und Hydrographie, Bernhard-Nocht-Str 78, Hamburg, 20359, Germany. TEL 49-40-31900, FAX 49-40-31905000, posteingang@bsh.de. Circ: 2,400 (paid).

387 GRC ISSN 0047-861X
NAFTIKA CHRONIKA. Text in English, Greek. 1931. m. USD 100. adv. bk.rev. charts; illus.; stat. **Document type:** *Journal, Trade.* **Description:** Presents information about shipping.
Published by: Rigas Ekdotiki, 7 Ipsilantou St, Athens, 106 75, Greece. TEL 30-1-7229-614, FAX 30-1-7229-607, TELEX 212845. Ed. D Rigas Cottakis. Circ: 4,000.

387 GRC
NAFTILIAKI; Greek shipping review. Text in English, Greek. 1957. q. USD 50; subscr. includes supplements plus a. index. adv. bk.rev. index. back issues avail. **Document type:** *Journal, Trade.* **Description:** Provides news and analysis of Greek merchant shipping and shipping-related business worldwide.
Related titles: ◆ Supplement(s): Newsfront.
Published by: Diorama Publishers Ltd., 4-6 Efplias St, PO Box 80 162, Piraeus, 185 37, Greece. TEL 30-1-428 2788, FAX 30-1-428-3193, TELEX 212310 NAFT GR. Ed. David Glass. Pub. Themistocles Vokos. Adv. contact Natassa Vassilaki. Circ: 3,400.

387 JPN
NAIKO SENPAKU MEISAISHO/REGISTER OF SHIPS (IN JAPANESE COASTAL SHIPPING SERVICE). Text in Japanese. 1998. a. JPY 20,000 (effective 2000). **Document type:** *Directory, Trade.*
Supersedes in part (in 1998): Nihon Senpaku Meisaisyo
Related titles: Diskette ed.
Published by: Nihon Kaiun Shukaijo/Japan Shipping Exchange Inc., Wajun Bldg, 2-22-2 Koishi-Kawa, Bunkyo-ku, Tokyo, 112-0002, Japan. TEL 81-3-5802-8368, FAX 81-3-5802-8371, jmis@jseinc.org, http://www.jseinc.org. Circ: 8,000.

387.5 PAK
NATIONAL SHIPPING CORPORATION. REPORT AND ACCOUNTS. Text in English. a. free. **Document type:** *Corporate.*
Published by: National Shipping Corporation, N S C Bldg., Moulvi Tamizuddin Khan Rd., Karachi, Pakistan.

387 NLD
NATIONALE HAVENRAAD. JAARVERSLAG (YEAR). Text in Dutch. 1970. a. free (effective 2009). back issues avail. **Document type:** *Journal, Trade.* **Description:** Reports on the activities of the Dutch National Seaports Council, developments in Dutch seaports, including infrastructure, industry, labor and environmental issues. Provides statistical data concerning seaborne traffic, employment and land use.
Former titles: Netherlands. Provisional National Ports Council. Jaarverslag; (until 1978): Netherlands. Commissie Zeehavenoverleg. Jaarverslag (0077-7552)
Published by: Nationale Havenraad, Koningskade 4, Postbus 20906, The Hague, 2500 EX, Netherlands. TEL 31-70-3517615, FAX 31-70-3517600, info@havenraad.nl.

387.5 797.1 ITA
NAUTIC SERVICE. Text in Italian, English. 5/yr. free. **Document type:** *Magazine, Trade.*
Related titles: Online - full text ed.
Published by: Edizioni Collins Sas, Via Giovanni Pezzotti, 4, Milan, MI 20141, Italy. TEL 39-02-8372897, FAX 39-02-58103891, collins@collins.com, http://www.netcollins.com. Circ: 5,000 (free).

623.89 528 USA ISSN 0077-619X
QB8
THE NAUTICAL ALMANAC. Text in English. 1960. a. USD 43 per issue (effective 2011). back issues avail. **Document type:** *Government.* **Description:** Contains the astronomical data required for marine navigation.
Formerly (until 1960): American Nautical Almanac
—**CCC.**
Published by: U.S. Naval Observatory, c/o Dr D D McCarthy, Department of the Navy, Washington, DC 20392-5100. **Subscr. to:** The Stationery Office, PO Box 29, Norwich NR3 1GN, United Kingdom. TEL 44-870-6005522, FAX 44-870-6005533; U.S. Government Printing Office, Superintendent of Documents. **Co-sponsors:** Royal Greenwich Observatory; H.M. Nautical Almanac Office.

387.2 GBR ISSN 0028-1336
V1
NAUTICAL MAGAZINE; for those interested in ships and the sea. Text in English. 1832. m. GBP 34.20 domestic; GBP 39.60 foreign (effective 2010). adv. bk.rev. s-a. index. **Document type:** *Magazine, Consumer.* **Description:** Discusses nautical arts and science.
Related titles: Microfiche ed.: (from BHP).
—**CCC.**
Published by: Brown, Son and Ferguson Ltd., 4-10 Darnley St, Glasgow, Scotland G41 2SD, United Kingdom. TEL 44-141-4291234, FAX 44-141-4201694, info@skipper.co.uk. Ed. L Ingram Brown. R&P L. Ingram-Brown. Adv. contact David H Provan. Circ: 1,100.

387 623.82 USA ISSN 0738-7245
V1
NAUTICAL RESEARCH JOURNAL. Text in English. 1949. q. USD 35 domestic; USD 40 in Canada; USD 43 elsewhere (effective 2005). adv. bk.rev. illus. index, cum.index: vols.1-40. reprints avail. **Description:** For marine artists, model builders, and those interested in marine history. Provides information on maritime lore and model building.
Related titles: Microfilm ed.; Microform ed.: (from PQC).
Indexed: AmH&L, CA, HistAb, MLA-IB, T02.
—BLDSC (6063.000000), IE, Ingenta, Linda Hall.
Published by: Nautical Research Guild, Inc., 31 Water St, Cuba, NY 14727-1030. TEL 301-622-2635, nrg@a-znet.com, http://www.nautres-guild.org. Ed. Rob Napier. R&P Eugene Larson TEL 703-360-2111. Adv. contact Ken Dorr. Circ: 1,600.

387 NLD ISSN 1873-9067
NAUTILUS MARITIEM MAGAZINE. Text in Dutch. 1966. 5/yr. EUR 13; EUR 4 newsstand/cover (effective 2009). adv. bk.rev. charts; illus.; stat. index. **Document type:** *Magazine, Trade.*
Formerly (until 2006): F W Z Maritiem Magazine (0929-4678); Which was formed by the merger of (1967-1993): Federatie van Werknemersorganisaties in de Zeevaart. Journaal (0014-9292); (1968-1993): Peiling (0031-4099)
—IE, Infotrieve.

Published by: (Nautilus NL), Media Business Press BV, Postbus 8632, Rotterdam, 3009 AP, Netherlands. TEL 31-10-2894078, FAX 31-10-2894076, info@mbp.nl, http://www.mbp.nl/. Ed. E Sarton. adv.: B&W page EUR 1,124, color page EUR 2,059; trim 210 x 297.

387 SWE ISSN 0028-1379
VK4
NAUTISK TIDSKRIFT; organ foer svensk sjoefart. Text in Swedish. 1908. 8/yr. SEK 350 (effective 2011). adv. bk.rev. charts; illus.; tr.lit. index. **Document type:** *Magazine, Trade.*
Related titles: Online - full text ed.: 2010.
Published by: Sveriges Fartygsbefaelsfoerening/Swedish Ship Officers' Association, Gamla Brogatan 19, Stockholm, 11120, Sweden. TEL 46-8-106015, FAX 46-8-106772, info@sfbf.a.se, http://www.sfbf.a.se. Ed. Marie Halvdanson. Adv. contact Ankie Nilsson. Circ: 5,100.

623.81 GBR ISSN 0306-0209
VM1 CODEN: NVARA3
➤ **THE NAVAL ARCHITECT.** Text in English. 1960. 10/yr. GBP 120 domestic to non-members; GBP 125 in Europe to non-members; GBP 135 elsewhere to non-members; free to members (effective 2009); subscr. includes Warship Technology, Offshore Marine Technology. adv. bk.rev. bibl.; charts; illus. **Document type:** *Journal, Academic/Scholarly.* **Description:** News items and research articles on legislation, architectural and technological developments, and products and services pertaining to the construction and operation of ocean-going vessels.
Supersedes in part (in 1971): Royal Institution of Naval Architects. Transactions (0035-8967); Which incorporated (1971-1987): Royal Institution of Naval Architects. Supplementary Papers (0373-529X); Transactions was formerly (until 1959): Institution of Naval Architects. Transactions
Related titles: CD-ROM ed.: GBP 32 to members; GBP 37 to non-members (effective 2005); Online - full text ed.; ◆ Supplement(s): Warship Technology. ISSN 0957-5537; Offshore Marine Technology. ISSN 1757-7977.
Indexed: A22, A28, APA, APIAb, ASCA, ApMecR, BMT, BrCerAb, C&ISA, CA/WCA, CIA, CerAb, CivEngAb, CorrAb, CurCont, E&CAJ, E11, EEA, EMA, ESPM, Englnd, EnvEAb, FLUIDEX, H15, Inspec, M&TEA, M09, MBF, METADEX, RefZh, SCI, SCOPUS, SolStAb, T04, W07, WAA.
—BLDSC (6063.850000), IE, Ingenta, INIST, Linda Hall. **CCC.**
Published by: Royal Institution of Naval Architects, 10 Upper Belgrave St, London, SW1X 8BQ, United Kingdom. TEL 44-20-72354622, FAX 44-20-72595912, publications@rina.org.uk. Ed. Hugh O'Mahony. Adv. contact John Payten.

➤ **NAVAL INSTITUTE GUIDE TO COMBAT FLEETS OF THE WORLD.** *see* MILITARY

387 JPN ISSN 0919-9985
VK4
NAVIGATION/KOKAI GAKKAISHI. Text in English, Japanese. 1954. q. JPY 2,000, USD 14 per issue. back issues avail. **Document type:** *Bulletin.*
Formerly (until 1993): Kokai (0450-660X)
Indexed: A22, BMT, Inspec, JTA, RefZh.
—BLDSC (6067.100000), AskIEEE, IE, Ingenta, Linda Hall. **CCC.**
Published by: Nihon Kokai Gakkai/Japan Institute of Navigation, c/o Tokyo University of Mercantile Marine, 2-1-6 Etchujima, Koto-ku, Tokyo, 135-0044, Japan. Ed. Houhei Ohtu. Circ: 1,900.

623.89 FRA ISSN 0028-1530
VK2 CODEN: NVGNAL
NAVIGATION; revue technique de navigation aerienne, maritime, spatiale et terrestre. Text in French; Summaries in English. 1953. q. EUR 76 domestic to individuals; EUR 86 foreign to individuals; EUR 56 domestic to members; EUR 66 foreign to members (effective 2009). adv. bk.rev. abstr.; illus. index, cum.index every 5 yrs. **Document type:** *Journal, Trade.* **Description:** Dedicated to scientific and technical problems arising from positioning and routing of ships, aircraft and land vehicles.
Indexed: A22, A28, APA, ASFA, BibCart, BrCerAb, C&ISA, CA/WCA, CIA, CerAb, CivEngAb, CorrAb, E&CAJ, E11, EEA, EMA, ESPM, EnvEAb, GeoRef, H15, Inspec, M&TEA, M09, MBF, METADEX, RefZh, SolStAb, SpeleolAb, T04, WAA.
—BLDSC (6067.000000), AskIEEE, IE, Ingenta, INIST, Linda Hall. **CCC.**
Published by: Institut Francais de Navigation, 3 av. Octave Greard, Paris, 75007, France. TEL 33-1-44384043, FAX 33-1-40619319. Ed. C Ville. Circ: 1,500.

387 GBR ISSN 0268-6317
NAVIGATION NEWS. Text in English. 1986. bi-m. free to members. adv. bk.rev. back issues avail. **Document type:** *Magazine, Trade.*
—CCC.
Published by: Royal Institute of Navigation, 1 Kensington Gore, London, SW7 2AT, United Kingdom. TEL 44-20-75913130, FAX 44-20-75913131, info@rin.org.uk, http://www.rin.org.uk. Circ: 4,000 (paid).

623.8 FRA ISSN 1769-8588
HE387.R5
NAVIGATION PORTS ET INDUSTRIES. Short title: Navigation, Ports and Industries. Text in French. 1922. m. EUR 185 domestic; EUR 210 foreign (effective 2009). adv. bk.rev. charts; illus.; bibl. index. **Document type:** *Journal.* **Description:** Covers current events in navigation such as productivity, port traffic as well as inter model issues in Europe and various projects and developments taking place in ports world-wide.
Formerly (until 2004): Revue de la Navigation Fluviale Europeenne, Ports et Industries (0767-094X)
Indexed: A22, CLT&T.
—IE, Infotrieve, INIST.
Published by: Navigation Ports et Industries (N P I), 5 Rue du Port du Rhin, Strasbourg, 67000, France. TEL 33-3-88362844, FAX 33-3-88370482, npi@n-pi.fr. Ed. Maurice Ruscher. Adv. contact Jean Marie Lochert. Circ: 2,500.

NAVIGATIONAL RADIO AIDS. *see* COMMUNICATIONS—Radio

387 FIN ISSN 0355-7871
NAVIGATOR; merenkulun aikakauslehti. Text in Finnish. 1926. 6/yr. EUR 45 (effective 2004). adv. bk.rev. stat. **Document type:** *Journal, Trade.* **Description:** News about Finnish shipping and its maritime industries.
Incorporates (1985-1991): Kauppamerenkulka (0785-7578); Which was formerly (until 1988): Varustamoyhdistyksen (0782-7598)
Published by: Edita Press Oy, Siltasaarenkatu 14, PO Box 739, Edita, 00043, Finland. FAX 358-0-566-0374, http://www.edita.fi. Ed. M Pervilae. Adv. contact M Poijaerui. Circ: 4,000.

359.97 USA ISSN 2152-4653
VG53
NAVIGATOR (ST. LOUIS). Text in English. 19??. q. free to members (effective 2010). **Document type:** *Magazine, Trade.*
Formerly (until 19??): Under the Blue Ensign
Related titles: Online - full text ed.: ISSN 1938-985X.
Published by: Coast Guard Auxiliary Association, Inc., Coast Guard Auxiliary Ctr, 9449 Watson Industrial Park, St. Louis, MO 63126. TEL 314-962-8828, executivedirector@cgauxa.org.

623.89 NLD ISSN 1872-6550
NAVIGATOR NL. Text in English. s-a. **Document type:** *Magazine, Trade.*
Former titles (until 2004): Loodswezen Visie (1380-8508); (until 1994): Nederlandse Loods (0166-6142)
Published by: Nederlandse Loodsencorporatie, Postbus 830, Rotterdam, 3000 AV, Netherlands. TEL 31-10-4000500, FAX 31-10-4115588, http://www.loodswezen.nl. Ed. Clarinda van den Bor.

NAVIRES & HISTOIRE. *see* MILITARY

NAVTEX MANUAL. *see* COMMUNICATIONS

387.5 NLD
NEDERLAND MARITIEM LAND/DUTCH MARITIME NETWORK. Text in Dutch. 1997. irreg., latest vol.32, 2007. price varies. **Document type:** *Monographic series.* **Description:** Discusses technical details in shipping facilities in the Netherlands.
Published by: Delft University Press (Subsidiary of: I O S Press), Nieuwe Hemweg 6B, Amsterdam, 1013 BG, Netherlands. TEL 31-20-6883355, FAX 31-20-6870039, info.dupress@iospress.nl.

387 PRT
NEPTUNO. Text in Portuguese. 1914. q. free. back issues avail. **Document type:** *Bulletin.* **Description:** Includes technical matters related with merchant navy, maritime environment, fisheries, safety and law, work health and safety, welfare.
Published by: Sindicato dos Capitaes Oficiais Pilotos Comissarios e Radiotecnicos da Marinha Mercante, Pc. D. Luis I, 9-1o D., Lisbon, Lisboa 1200-148, Portugal. TEL 351-1-3960433, FAX 351-1-3961099. Ed. Luis Armando Fernandes Garcia de Almeida. Circ: 1,200.

387 BEL ISSN 0028-2790
NEPTUNUS; info marine. Text in Dutch, French. 1952. q. EUR 15 domestic; EUR 33 foreign; EUR 4.50 per issue (effective 2005). bk.rev. bibl.; charts; illus. 72 p./no. 3 cols./p.; back issues avail. **Document type:** *Bulletin.* **Description:** Contains historical and present articles on the navy.
Published by: Belgian Navy, Postbus 17, Oostende, 8400, Belgium. Ed. J C VanBostal. Adv. contact Chris Cappon. Circ: 1,200.

387 665.5 USA ISSN 0953-9336
NEW WORLDWIDE TANKER NOMINAL FREIGHT SCALE; code name Worldscale. Text in English. 1969. a., latest 2001. USD 1,875 (effective 2001). back issues avail. **Document type:** *Handbook/Manual/Guide, Trade.*
Formerly (until Jul. 1988): Worldwide Tanker Nominal Freight Scale (0267-1913)
Related titles: Online - full content ed.
Published by: Worldscale Association (NYC), Inc., 63 Wall St, New York, NY 10005-3001. TEL 212-422-2786, FAX 212-344-4169, TELEX 62351 WSCALE UW. Eds. Robert Porter, Sara Bierman. Circ: 1,200.

623.89 NZL ISSN 0113-5597
Z6027.N54
NEW ZEALAND CHART CATALOGUE. Text in English. 1978. biennial. **Document type:** *Handbook/Manual/Guide, Trade.* **Description:** Includes an index to charts by region, a numerical chart list, ocean sounding charts, general bathymetric chart of the oceans (GEBCO), and a record of chart corrections published in Notices to Mariners.
Supersedes: Chart Catalogue and Index (0110-5523)
Related titles: Online - full text ed.: ISSN 1176-1822.
Published by: Land Information New Zealand, Lambton House, 160 Lambton Quay, Private Box 5501, Wellington, 6145, New Zealand. TEL 64-4-4600110, FAX 64-4-4722244, info@linz.govt.nz.

387 NZL ISSN 0549-0502
NEW ZEALAND MARINE NEWS. Text in English. 1949. q. bk.rev. back issues avail. **Document type:** *Magazine, Trade.* **Description:** For laypersons interested in historical and general aspects of shipping and nautical matters, particularly in reference to New Zealand.
Indexed: INZP.
—CCC.
Published by: New Zealand Ship and Marine Society Inc., P.O. Box 5104, Wellington, New Zealand. pryce@xtra.co.nz. Circ: 600.

387 NZL ISSN 1172-2134
HE932.5
NEW ZEALAND SHIPPING AND TRANSPORT DIRECTORY. Text in English. 1962. a. adv. illus. **Document type:** *Directory, Trade.*
Formerly (until 1993): New Zealand Shipping Directory (0545-7866)
Published by: Mercantile Gazette Marketing Ltd., Freepost 5003, Bishopdale, PO Box 20-034, Christchurch, New Zealand. TEL 64-3-3583219, FAX 64-3-3584490, johannes@mgpublications.co.nz, http://www.mgpublications.co.nz/. Ed. G Everts. Circ: 2,500.

387 NZL ISSN 0027-724X
NEW ZEALAND SHIPPING GAZETTE. Text in English. w. NZD 167 (effective 2008). **Document type:** *Newspaper, Trade.* **Description:** Contains vital news and advertising for importers, exporters, manufacturers and those companies allied to the shipping industry.
—CCC.
Published by: Mercantile Gazette Marketing Ltd., Freepost 5003, Bishopdale, PO Box 20-034, Christchurch, New Zealand. TEL 64-3-3583219, FAX 64-3-3584490, johannes@mgpublications.co.nz.

387.2 NZL ISSN 1176-3086
NEW ZEALAND WORK BOAT REVIEW. Text in English. 2005. a. NZD 10.50 (effective 2009). adv. **Document type:** *Magazine, Trade.*
Published by: VIP Publications, 4 Prince Regent Dr, Half Moon Bay, Auckland, New Zealand. TEL 64-9-5334336, FAX 64-9-5334337. Ed. Keith Ingram. adv.: page NZD 1,850; trim 210 x 297.

387 JPN
NIHON KAIJI SHIMBUN/JAPAN MARITIME DAILY. Text in Japanese. 1942. d. (Mon.-Fri.). JPY 6,180; JPY 310 newsstand/cover. adv. **Document type:** *Newspaper.*
Published by: Nihon Kaiji Shimbunsha, 19-2, Shimbashi 5-chome, Minato-ku, Tokyo, Japan. TEL 81-3-3436-3221, FAX 8-3-3436-6553. Ed. Minoru Takashimizu. Pub. Takaaki Ohyma. Adv. contact Kikuo Matsumoto. page JPY 1,600,000.

387 551.46 629.13 JPN ISSN 0388-7405
VK1 CODEN: NKGRDR
NIHON KOKAI GAKKAI RONBUNSHU/JAPAN INSTITUTE OF NAVIGATION. JOURNAL. Text in English, Japanese; Summaries in English. 1949. s-a. JPY 3,000 newsstand/cover (effective 2005). back issues avail. **Document type:** *Journal, Academic/Scholarly.*
Formerly (until 1941): Nihon Kokai Gakkaishi/Nautical Society of Japan. Journal (0466-6607)
Indexed: BMT, Inspec, JTA, RefZh.
—BLDSC (4805.300000), AskIEEE, Linda Hall. **CCC.**
Published by: Nihon Kokai Gakkai/Japan Institute of Navigation, c/o Tokyo University of Mercantile Marine, 2-1-6 Etchujima, Koto-ku, Tokyo, 135-0044, Japan. FAX 81-3-36303093, navigation@nifty.com. Ed. H Imazu. Circ: 1,700.

387 620 359 JPN ISSN 1880-3717
VM4
NIHON SEMPAKU KAIYOU KOUGAKKAI ROMBUNSHUU/JAPAN SOCIETY OF NAVAL ARCHITECTS AND OCEAN ENGINEERS. JOURNAL. Text in Japanese. 2005. s-a. **Document type:** *Journal, Academic/Scholarly.*
Formed by the merger of (1949-2005): Seibu Zosenkai Kaiho/West-Japan Society of Naval Architects. Transactions (0389-911X); (1952-2004): Nihon Zosen Gakkai Ronbunshu/Society of Naval Architects of Japan. Journal (0514-8499); (2001-2005): Kansai Zousen Kyoukai Rombunshuu/Kansai Society of Naval Architects, Japan. Journal (1346-7727); Which was formerly (1912-2000): Kansai Zosen Kyokaishi/Kansai Society of Naval Architects, Japan. Journal (0389-9101)
Indexed: A28, APA, BrCerAb, C&ISA, CA/WCA, CIA, CerAb, CivEngAb, CorrAb, E&CAJ, E11, EEA, EMA, ESPM, EnvEAb, H15, M&TEA, M09, MBF, METADEX, SolStAb, T04, WAA.
—BLDSC (6113.511000), IE, Ingenta.
Published by: Nihon Sempaku Kaiyou Kougakkai/Japan Society of Naval Architects and Ocean Engineers, 2-12-9 Shiba Daimon. Minato-Ku, Hamamatsu-cho Yazaki White Bldg. 3F, Tokyo, 105-0012, Japan. TEL 81-3-34382014, FAX 81-3-34382016, info@jasnaoe.or.jp, http://www.jasnaoe.or.jp/.

387 JPN
NIHON SENPAKU MEISAISHO I/JAPAN REGISTER OF SHIPS I. Text in Japanese. 1930. a. JPY 19,500 (effective 2000). adv. **Document type:** *Directory, Trade.*
Supersedes in part (in 1998): Nihon Senpaku Meisaisyo
Related titles: Diskette ed.
Published by: Nihon Kaiun Shukaijo/Japan Shipping Exchange Inc., Wajun Bldg, 2-22-2 Koishi-Kawa, Bunkyo-ku, Tokyo, 112-0002, Japan. TEL 81-3-5802-8368, FAX 81-3-5802-8371. Ed. Toshio Matsumoto. Adv. contact Miss Hiroe Goto. Circ: 6,000.

387 JPN
NIHON SENPAKU MEISAISHO II/JAPAN REGISTER OF SHIPS II (OF JAPANESE FLAG, UNDER 100 GT). Text in Japanese. 1998. a. JPY 10,000 (effective 2000). **Document type:** *Directory, Trade.*
Supersedes in part (in 1998): Nihon Senpaku Meisaisyo
Related titles: Diskette ed.
Published by: Nihon Kaiun Shukaijo/Japan Shipping Exchange Inc., Wajun Bldg, 2-22-2 Koishi-Kawa, Bunkyo-ku, Tokyo, 112-0002, Japan. TEL 81-3-5802-8368, FAX 81-3-5802-8371, jmis@jseinc.org, http://www.jseinc.org. Circ: 2,000.

NIHON SHOSEN SENPUKU TOKEI. *see* TRANSPORTATION—Abstracting, Bibliographies, Statistics

387 JPN
NIPPON YUSEN. ANNUAL REPORT. Text in Japanese. a. **Document type:** *Corporate.*
Published by: (Corporate Communication Chamber), Nippon Yusen Kaisha, 2-3-2 Marunochi, Chiyoda-ku, Tokyo, 100-0005, Japan. TEL 81-3-3284-5193, FAX 81-3-3284-6382.

NOR'EASTER (DULUTH). *see* HISTORY—History Of North And South America

387 NOR ISSN 0801-6593
NORSK SJOEFARTSMUSEUM. SKRIFT. Text in Norwegian. 1929. irreg., latest vol.50, 2006. **Document type:** *Monographic series, Academic/Scholarly.*
—BLDSC (1591.976000).
Published by: Norsk Maritimt Museum/Norwegian Maritime Museum, Bygdoeynesveien 37, Oslo, 0286, Norway. TEL 47-24-114150, FAX 47-24-114151, http://www.marmuseum.no.

387 NOR ISSN 0804-2462
DET NORSKE VERITAS. ANNUAL REPORT. Text in English. 18??. a. **Document type:** *Report, Trade.*
Related titles: Online - full text ed.
Published by: Det Norske Veritas, Veritasveien 1, Hoevik, 1363, Norway. TEL 47-67-579900, FAX 47-67-579911, dnv.corporate@dnv.com.

NORTH AMERICAN SOCIETY FOR OCEANIC HISTORY. NEWSLETTER. *see* HISTORY—History Of North And South America

NORTH SEA SUPPLY VESSEL FORECAST. *see* PETROLEUM AND GAS

NORTHERN MARINER. *see* HISTORY

623.89 NLD ISSN 1871-9244
NOTICE TO MASTER MARINERS. Text in Dutch. 1943. 5/yr.
Former titles (until 2005): Mededelingen voor de Kapitein (1571-9111); (until 2000): Mededelingen voor de Gezagvoerder (1382-2365)
Published by: Nederlandse Vereniging van Kapiteins ter Koopvaardij, Parklaan 5, Driebergen, 3972 JX, Netherlands. TEL 31-343-520572, info@nvkk.nl, http://www.nvkk.nl.

623.89 CAN ISSN 1714-0218
NOTICES TO MARINERS PUBLICATION (EASTERN EDITION, PRINT). Text in English. 1997. m. **Document type:** *Government.*
Former titles (until 2004): Notices to Mariners (Eastern Edition) (1493-7859); (until 2000): Eastern Edition of Notices to Mariners (1482-8812); Which superseded in part (in 1997): National Edition of Notices to Mariners (1200-7900); Which was formerly (until 1995): Notices to Mariners (0700-1800); (until 1976): Canadian Notices to Mariners (0700-1819)

Related titles: Online - full text ed.: ISSN 1719-7678. 1997; ◆ Regional ed(s).: Notices to Mariners Publication (Western Edition, Print). ISSN 1714-0196.
Published by: Department of Fisheries and Oceans, Canadian Coast Guard Marine Navigation Services Directorate, 200 Kent St, Sta 5150, Ottawa, ON K1A 0E6, Canada. TEL 613-990-3016, FAX 613-998-8428. **Dist. by:** Canadian Hydrographic Chart Dealers, Fisheries and Oceans, Ottawa, ON K1G 3H6, Canada. TEL 613-998-4931, FAX 613-998-1217, chs_sales@dfo-mpo.gc.ca, http://www.charts.gc.ca.

623.89 CAN ISSN 1714-0196
NOTICES TO MARINERS PUBLICATION (WESTERN EDITION, PRINT). Text in English. 1995. m. **Document type:** *Government.*
Former titles (until 2004): Notices to Mariners (Western Edition) (1493-7352); (until 2000): Western Edition of Notices to Mariners (1482-8839); (until 1997): National Edition of Notices to Mariners (1200-7900)
Related titles: Online - full text ed.: ISSN 1719-7708. 1997; ◆ Regional ed(s).: Notices to Mariners Publication (Eastern Edition, Print). ISSN 1714-0218.
Published by: Department of Fisheries and Oceans, Canadian Coast Guard Marine Navigation Services Directorate, 200 Kent St, Sta 5150, Ottawa, ON K1A 0E6, Canada. TEL 613-990-3016, FAX 613-998-8428, http://www.notmar.gc.ca.

359.97 ITA
NOTIZIARIO DELLA GUARDIA COSTIERA. Text in Italian. 1987. bi-m. EUR 25 domestic; EUR 50 foreign (effective 2009). adv. **Document type:** *Newsletter, Trade.*
Published by: Ministero delle Infrastrutture e dei Trasporti, Comando Generale del Corpo delle Capitanerie di Porto, Viale dell'Arte 16, Rome, 00144, Italy. TEL 39-06-5908, guardiacostiera@guardiacostiera.it.

387 910.09 USA
OCEAN & CRUISE NEWS. Text in English. 1980. m. USD 30 (effective 2000). adv. back issues avail. **Document type:** *Magazine, Consumer.* **Description:** Covers the latest news about cruises and cruise ships.
Published by: World Ocean & Cruise Liner Society, PO Box 92, Stamford, CT 06904. TEL 203-329-2787, FAX 203-329-2787. Ed., Pub., Adv. contact George C Devol III. R&P George Devol. Circ: 9,000.

387 IND ISSN 0029-8123
OCEANITE. Text in English. 1945. q. illus.; stat.; tr.lit. 58 p./no.; **Document type:** *Magazine, Trade.* **Description:** Includes information on the International Transportworkers' Federation. Covers fuels, repairs, provisions, and job opportunities in the Indian shipping industry.
Related titles: Fax ed.
Published by: Maritime Union of India, Udyog Bhavan, 4th Fll, 29 Walchand Hirachand Marg, Ballard Estate, Mumbai, Maharashtra 400 001, India. TEL 91-22-22613052, FAX 91-22-22620606, http://www.mui.in/.

OFFSHORE INDUSTRY. *see* ENGINEERING—Industrial Engineering

387.544 USA ISSN 1742-7959
OFFSHORE MARINE MONTHLY. Text in English. 1984. m. **Document type:** *Newsletter, Trade.* **Description:** Examines from a global perspective the latest newbuilds, market trends and fixtures of supply vessels as well as the major stories involving standby vessels, FPSOs and other support vessels.
Formerly (until 2003): Offshore Fleet Economics (0266-3112)
Related titles: Online - full text ed.
—CCC.
Published by: O D S - Petrodata, 3200 Wilcrest Dr, Ste 170, Houston, TX 77042. TEL 832-463-3000, FAX 832-463-3100, general@ods-petrodata.com, http://www.ods-petrodata.com. Ed. Shaun Heywood. Pub. Tom Marsh.

387.5 665.5 GBR ISSN 1463-581X
OFFSHORE SUPPORT JOURNAL. Abbreviated title: O S J. Text in English. 1998. bi-m. GBP 249 combined subscription (print & online eds.) (effective 2010). adv. **Document type:** *Journal, Trade.* **Description:** Contains a wealth of information regarding the marketplace for offshore support vessels and the organizations involved in it.
Related titles: Online - full text ed.
—CCC.
Published by: Riviera Maritime Media, Mitre House, 66 Abbey Rd, Enfield, EN1 2QN, United Kingdom. TEL 44-20-83641551, FAX 44-20-83641331, info@rivieramm.com, http://www.rivieramm.com. Ed. David Foxwell TEL 44-1252-717898. Adv. contact Ian Glen TEL 44-7919-263737. color page GBP 2,205, color page EUR 2,646; trim 210 x 297.

387 GBR ISSN 1477-5395
THE OFFSHORE VESSEL REGISTER. Text in English. 1977. a. adv. **Document type:** *Directory, Trade.* **Description:** Contains full details of the more than 3,000 offshore service ships and the 1,200 companies that own or manage them; statistics of each ship are compiled in regard to size, age, capacity, and registry.
Formerly (until 2002): The Offshore Service Vessel Register (0309-040X)
Published by: Clarkson Research Services Ltd., St Magnus House, 3 Lower Thames St, London, EC3R 6HE, United Kingdom. TEL 44-20-73343134, FAX 44-20-75220330, sales@crsl.com.

387 HRV ISSN 0030-0713
OGLAS ZA POMORCE/NOTICES TO MARINERS. Text in Serbo-Croatian. 1924. m. USD 15. bk.rev.
Published by: Hidrografski Institut Jugoslavenske Ratne Mornarice, Split, 58000, Croatia. FAX 058-47045, TELEX 26270.

387 GBR ISSN 1363-9617
OIL & TANKER TRADES OUTLOOK. Text in English. 199?. m. GBP 575, USD 1,035 (effective 2011). adv. **Document type:** *Journal, Trade.* **Description:** Contains "at a glance" reviews of the VLCC, Suezmax, Aframax, Panamax and products tanker markets.
Formerly (until 1996): Oil and Tanker Report (1364-0291)
Related titles: CD-ROM ed.: Tanker Fleet CD. GBP 575, USD 1,035 (effective 2011); Online - full text ed.: ISSN 1742-4399.
Published by: Clarkson Research Services Ltd., St Magnus House, 3 Lower Thames St, London, EC3R 6HE, United Kingdom. TEL 44-20-73343134, FAX 44-20-75220330, sales@crsl.com.

387.2 POL ISSN 1231-014X
OKRETY WOJENNE; magazyn milosnikow spraw wojennomorskich. Text in Polish. 1993. q. EUR 66 foreign (effective 2005).
Published by: Wydawnictwo Okrety Wojenne, ul Krzywoustego 16, Tarnowskie Gory, 42605, Poland. TEL 48-32-3844861, okrety@ka.home.pl. **Dist. by:** Ars Polona, Obroncow 25, Warsaw 03933, Poland. TEL 48-22-5098609, FAX 48-22-5098610, arspolona@arspolona.com.pl, http://www.arspolona.com.pl.

623.89 BEL
ON COURSE/ASSOCIATION INTERNATIONALE DE NAVIGATION. BULLETIN. Text in French, English. 1926; N.S. 1961; N.S. 1968. 3/yr. EUR 80 (effective 2005). adv. back issues avail. **Document type:** *Bulletin, Trade.*
Former titles (until 2004): International Navigation Association. Bulletin (1680-1059); (until 1997): Permament International Association of Navigation Congresses. Bulletin (0374-1001)
Indexed: A22, BMT, GeoRef, HRIS, RefZh.
—IE, Ingenta, INIST, Linda Hall.
Published by: International Navigation Association/Association Internationale de Navigation, Graaf de Ferraris, 11th Fl, 20 Boulevard du Roi Albert II, Brussels, 1000, Belgium. TEL 32-2-5537157, FAX 32-2-5537155, info@pianc-aipcn.org, http://www.pianc-aipcn.org. Ed. Louis Van Schel. adv.: B&W page EUR 420. Circ: 4,000.

387 USA ISSN 0093-2124
VK1323
ON SCENE (WASHINGTON); the journal of U. S. Coast Guard search and rescue. Text in English. 1969. s-a. bibl.; charts; illus. back issues avail.; reprints avail. **Document type:** *Journal, Trade.* **Description:** Provides a forum for information on maritime search and rescue.
Formerly (until 1972): National Maritime S A R Review (0047-8946)
Related titles: Microform ed.: (from PQC); Online - full text ed.: ISSN 1931-3772.
Indexed: A22, CLT&T, HRIS.
—Ingenta, Linda Hall.
Published by: (Office of Navigation Safety and Waterway Services), U.S. Coast Guard, 2100 Second St, SW, Washington, DC 20593. TEL 202-267-1061, FAX 202-267-4402, gchappell@comdt.uscg.mil, http://www.uscg.mil/default.asp.

387 USA ISSN 1062-6484
P M A UPDATE. Text in English. 1989. m. looseleaf. membership. charts; stat. **Document type:** *Newsletter.* **Description:** Provides updates and statistics for shoreside workers in wage rate, annual earnings, consumer price index, registration statistics for 52 payroll weeks, port hours, and tonnage by port area.
Related titles: Online - full text ed.
Published by: (Pacific Maritime Association), P M A Research, PO Box 7861, San Francisco, CA 94120-7861.

387 USA ISSN 0741-7586
PACIFIC MARITIME MAGAZINE; marine business for the operations sector. Text in English. 1983. m. USD 39 domestic; USD 78 foreign (effective 2011). adv. bk.rev. back issues avail. **Document type:** *Magazine, Trade.* **Description:** Geared toward owner-operators of steamship lines, their agents and representatives, tug and barge lines, terminal operators, stevedores and port and harbor operations executives in the Pacific.
Formerly (until 1984): Port Reporter (0738-4165)
Indexed: HRIS.
Published by: Philips Publishing Group, 2201 W Commodore Way, Seattle, WA 98199. TEL 206-284-8285, FAX 206-284-0391, http://www.philipspublishing.com. Pub. Peter Philips. Adv. contact Mike Morris.

387 USA ISSN 0030-8900
HE8.9
PACIFIC SHIPPER. Text in English. 1926. w. **Document type:** *Magazine, Trade.*
Related titles: Online - full text ed.: ISSN 1542-8443; ◆ Supplement(s): Cool Cargoes; Pacific Shipper's Transportation Services Shipper.
Indexed: A10, B01, B02, B07, B15, B17, B18, BPI, BRD, G04, G08, I05, P34, T02, V03, W01, W02, W03, W05.
—CCC.
Published by: Journal of Commerce, Inc. (Subsidiary of: Commonwealth Business Media, Inc.), 2 Penn Plz E, Newark, NJ 07105. TEL 973-776-8660, customersvs@joc.com, http://www.joc.com.

387 GBR
PADDLE WHEELS. Text in English. 1959. q. membership. adv. bk.rev. illus. **Document type:** *Newsletter.*
Published by: Paddle Steamer Preservation Society, 26 Wood St, Mitcham Junction, Surrey CR4 4JS, United Kingdom. TEL 0181-640-0838. Ed. M Allen. Circ: 3,500.

386 GBR ISSN 1758-7255
PASSENGER SHIP TECHNOLOGY. Text in English. 2008. q. GBP 129 (print or online ed.); GBP 179 combined subscription (print & online eds.) (effective 2010). adv. back issues avail. **Document type:** *Magazine, Trade.* **Description:** Provides technical information about all types of passenger and passenger/vehicle ferries worldwide.
Formed by the merger of (Mar.2008-Jul.2008): The Cruise Ship (1757-062X); (2005-2008): Ferry Technology (1746-1111); Which was formerly (until 2005): Speed at Sea (1359-4222)
Related titles: Online - full text ed.
Indexed: BAS, BMT.
—CCC.
Published by: Riviera Maritime Media, Mitre House, 66 Abbey Rd, Enfield, EN1 2QN, United Kingdom. TEL 44-20-83641551, FAX 44-20-83641331, info@rivieramm.com. Eds. Clive Woodbridge TEL 44-20-83932853, Susan Parker TEL 44-20-73730793. Adv. contact Rob Gore TEL 44-20-83707007. color page GBP 2,365, color page EUR 2,838; trim 164 x 232. Circ: 4,056 (paid).

387.029 GBR
PETERHEAD PORT HANDBOOK. Text in English. 1985. irreg. adv. illus. **Document type:** *Directory, Trade.*
Published by: Compass Publications Ltd., Marcon House, Bailey St, Castle Acre, Kings Lynn, Norfolk, United Kingdom. TEL 44-1760-755783, FAX 44-1760-755942, http://www.compass-publications.co.uk.

387 GBR ISSN 2040-9788
PHILIPPINES SHIPPING REPORT. Text in English. 200?. q. EUR 820, USD 1,030 combined subscription (print & email eds.) (effective 2010). **Document type:** *Report, Trade.* **Description:** Provides industry professionals and strategists, sector analysts, business investors, trade associations and regulatory bodies with independent forecasts and competitive intelligence on the shipping industry in the Philippines.
Related titles: E-mail ed.
Published by: Business Monitor International Ltd., Senator House, 85 Queen Victoria St, London, EC4V 4AB, United Kingdom. TEL 44-20-72480468, FAX 44-20-72480467, subs@businessmonitor.com.

387.5 NOR ISSN 0802-0213
PLATOU REPORT. Text in English. 1947. a., latest 2005. free. illus. **Document type:** *Report, Trade.* **Description:** This publication covers the previous year's development in the tanker, dry bulk and offshore markets. In addition, the report covers the next year's outlook for the same markets.
Related titles: Online - full text ed.
Published by: R. S. Platou Shipbrokers A-S, Haakon VII Gate 10, PO Box 1604, Vika, Oslo, 0119, Norway. TEL 47-23-112000, FAX 47-23-112300, office@platou.com.

387 GBR ISSN 2040-9877
POLAND SHIPPING REPORT. Text in English. 200?. q. EUR 820, USD 1,030 combined subscription (print & email eds.) (effective 2010). **Document type:** *Report, Trade.* **Description:** Provides industry professionals and strategists, sector analysts, business investors, trade associations and regulatory bodies with independent forecasts and competitive intelligence on the shipping industry in Poland.
Related titles: E-mail ed.
Published by: Business Monitor International Ltd., Senator House, 85 Queen Victoria St, London, EC4V 4AB, United Kingdom. TEL 44-20-72480468, FAX 44-20-72480467, subs@businessmonitor.com.

387.2 620.1 POL ISSN 1233-2585
VK4
➤ **POLISH MARITIME RESEARCH.** Text in English. 1994. q. USD 80 foreign (effective 2011). abstr.; bibl.; illus. 32 p./no. 2 cols./p.; back issues avail. **Document type:** *Journal, Academic/Scholarly.* **Description:** Publishes technical scientific papers on naval architecture, marine engineering, corrosion protection, operation and economy, other maritime subjects.
Media: Large Type. **Related titles:** Online - full text ed.: free (effective 2011).
Indexed: A28, APA, AgrAg, B22, BMT, BrCerAb, C&ISA, CA/WCA, CIA, CerAb, CivEngAb, CorrAb, E&CAJ, E11, EEA, EMA, H15, Inspec, M&TEA, M09, MBF, METADEX, RefZh, SCI, SCOPUS, SolStAb, T04, W07, WAA.
—BLDSC (6543.684000).
Published by: Politechnika Gdanska, Wydzial Oceanotechniki i Okretownictwa, ul Narutowicza 11/12, Gdansk-Wrzeszcz, 80952, Poland. TEL 48-58-3471662, FAX 48-58-3414712, sekoce@pg.gda.pl, http://www.pg.gda.pl/~wwwoce/WOiOSite/HTMLdocs/Home.htm. Circ: 300 (paid); 200 (controlled).

623.8 POL ISSN 0373-868X
POLITECHNIKA GDANSKA. ZESZYTY NAUKOWE. BUDOWNICTWO OKRETOWE. Text in English, Polish; Summaries in Russian. 1957. irreg. price varies. bibl.; charts; illus. **Document type:** *Monographic series, Academic/Scholarly.* **Description:** Research on ship design and equipment, steam and gas turbines, mechanics and hydromechanics of structures and power installations.
—INIST, Linda Hall.
Published by: Politechnika Gdanska/Gdansk University of Technology, ul Narutowicza 11-12, Gdansk, 80233, Poland. **Dist. by:** Osrodek Rozpowszechniania Wydawnictw Naukowych PAN, Palac Kultury i Nauki, Warsaw 00901, Poland.

387 639.2 HRV ISSN 1332-0718
Q69.3.S56
POMORSTVO (RIJEKA); journal of maritime studies. Variant title: Maritime Affairs. Text in Croatian, English. 1964. a. **Document type:** *Journal, Academic/Scholarly.*
Former titles (until 1999): Pomorski Fakultet. Zbornik Radova (1330-0938); (until 1992): Fakultet za Pomorstvo i Saobracaj u Rijeci. Zbornik Radova (0352-4159); (until 1984): Fakultet za Pomorstvo i Saobracaj u Rijeci. Zbornik (1332-4365); (until 1969): Visa Pomorska Skola u Rijeci. Zbornik (1332-4373); (until 1964): Visa Pomorska Skola u Rijeci. Zbornik (1332-4357)
Related titles: Online - full text ed.: free (effective 2011).
Indexed: A01, ASFA, CA, GEOBASE, HRIS, OceAb, SCOPUS, T02.
Published by: (Sveuciliste u Rijeci, Pomorski Fakultet/University of Rijeka, Faculty of Maritime Studies), Sveuciliste u Rijeci, Odjel za Pomorstvo, Studentska 2, Rijeka, 51000, Croatia. TEL 385-51-338411, FAX 385-51-336755, odjel@pfri.hr, http://www.pfri.hr/odjel/index1.htm.

387 382 USA
HE564.A4
PORT CHARLESTON. Text in English. 1947. m. free to qualified personnel. adv. charts; illus.; stat. **Document type:** *Magazine, Trade.* **Description:** Covers news relevant to the Port of Charleston. Features customers and stories of general interest to the community.
Former titles (until 2001): Port News (0896-2278); (until 1984): South Carolina Port News
Published by: South Carolina State Ports Authority, PO Box 22287, Charleston, SC 29413-2286. TEL 843-577-8622, 800-382-1721, FAX 843-577-8710, SCSPAMktg_Sales@scspa.com. Ed., Pub. Marion L Bull. Circ: 11,200.

387 GBR ISSN 0965-8203
PORT ENGINEERING MANAGEMENT; the international journal of dredging, port development and ocean technology. Abbreviated title: P E M. Text in English. 1991. bi-m. GBP 55 domestic; GBP 63 foreign (effective 2009). adv. back issues avail. **Document type:** *Magazine, Trade.* **Description:** Contains information on dredging, port development as well as on Ocean technology.
Incorporates (1989-1991): World Port Construction and Ocean Technology (0959-9320); Which was formerly (until 1989): Port Construction and Ocean Technology; (until 1986): Port Construction International
Related titles: Online - full text ed.: free (effective 2009).
Indexed: BMT, SCOPUS.

—IE, Infotrieve.
Published by: A & A Thorpe, 131a Furtherwick Rd, Canvey Island, Essex SS8 7AT, United Kingdom. TEL 44-1268-511300, FAX 44-1268-510467. Ed. Alan Thorpe. Circ: 4,000.

387.1 USA
PORT EVERGLADES FACILITIES GUIDE & DIRECTORY. Text in English. 200?. a. adv. back issues avail. **Document type:** *Directory, Trade.*
Published by: (Broward County Port Everglades Department), Seaports Publications Group (Subsidiary of: Commonwealth Business Media, Inc.), 3400 Lakeside Dr, Ste 515, Miramar, FL 33027. TEL 954-628-0058, FAX 954-628-0085, publisher@seaportsinfo.com, http://www.seaportsinfo.com/. Adv. contact David Cantwell TEL 954-628-0058 ext 173.

338.0029 BEL
PORT OF ANTWERP YEARBOOK. Text in Dutch, English, French. 1905. a. charts; illus.; stat. **Document type:** *Directory.* **Description:** Provides a comprehensive reference for the activities of the Port of Antwerp. Discusses the management and operation of the port, provides directory listings of government services, railways, consulates, chambers of commerce, trade and professional associations, and transportation companies, with the important persons at each of these organizations. Covers infrastructure and port equipment and reviews data on seaborne traffic through the port.
Former titles: Antwerp Port Annual; Annuaire Maritime
Published by: De Lloyd N.V./Le Lloyd S.A., Vleminckstraat 18, Antwerpen, 2000, Belgium. TEL 32-3-234-0550, FAX 32-3-234-0850, info@lloyd.be, http://www.anlloyd.be. Ed. Bernard Van den Bossche. Pub. Guy Dubois. Circ: 7,000.

387 USA
PORT OF BALTIMORE MAGAZINE. Text in English. 1946. m. free. adv. **Document type:** *Magazine, Trade.* **Description:** Carries news, featues and business profiles focused on the diverse activities of the Port of Baltimore.
Formerly: Port of Baltimore Handbook (0079-3981)
Indexed: HRIS.
Published by: Maryland Port Administration, Media Two, 1031 Cromwell Bridge Rd, Baltimore, MD 21286. TEL 410-828-0120, FAX 410-825-1002. Ed. Merrill Witty. Pub. Jonathan Witty. Adv. contact Dana Scott. Circ: 12,000 (controlled).

386.8 USA ISSN 0160-5526
HE554.D4
PORT OF DETROIT WORLD HANDBOOK. Text in English. 1973. a. USD 21.95 per issue (effective 2008). adv. illus.; maps. 104 p./no.; back issues avail. **Document type:** *Directory, Trade.* **Description:** Features advertisers from 1,600+ Detroit Ocean maritime and intermodal business listings and over 150 itemized categories of port and intermodal services.
Formerly (until 1975): Official Port of Detroit World Handbook (0093-1799)
Published by: Fourth Seacoast Publishing Co., Inc., 25300 Little Mack Ave, St. Clair Shores, MI 48081. TEL 586-779-5570, FAX 586-779-5547, info@fourthseacoastonline.com, http://www.fourthseacoast.com. Pub. Roger J Buysse. adv.: B&W page USD 1,115; trim 8.5 x 11. Circ: 10,000.

387 DEU ISSN 0968-6886
PORT OF HAMBURG HANDBOOK. Text in German. 1969. a. adv. **Document type:** *Journal, Trade.*
Former titles (until 1987): Hamburger Hafen Handbuch (0072-954X); Hamburger Hafen-Jahrbuch
Published by: Hafen Hamburg Marketing e.V., Mattentwiete 2, Hamburg, 20457, Germany. TEL 49-40-37709-0, FAX 49-40-37709199, info@hafen-hamburg.de, http://www.mainport-hamburg.de. Circ: 5,000.

380 USA ISSN 1064-7686
HE554.H65
PORT OF HOUSTON. Text in English. 1959. bi-m. free (effective 2004). adv. charts; illus. 40 p./no.; **Document type:** *Magazine, Trade.*
Formerly (until 1987): Port of Houston Magazine (0032-4825)
Indexed: CLT&T, HRIS.
Published by: Port of Houston Authority, PO Box 2562, Houston, TX 77252. TEL 713-670-2644, FAX 713-670-2425. adv.: page USD 2,950; trim 8 x 10.5. Circ: 14,000.

387 FRA ISSN 0338-1927
PORT OF LE HAVRE FLASHES. Text in English. 1972. bi-m. **Document type:** *Newsletter, Consumer.* **Description:** Covers news concerning the Port of Le Havre Authority.
Published by: Port Autonome du Havre, Terre-Plein de la Barre, BP 1413, Le Havre, Cedex 76067, France. TEL 33-2-32747400, FAX 33-2-32747429, TELEX PAHAVRE 190 663 F. Ed. Bernard Coloby. Circ: 7,200. **U.S. orders to:** Port of Le Havre Authority, 425 Madison Av, Ste 500, New York, NY 10017. TEL 212-486-1158, 212-486-1157.

387 JPN
PORT OF OSAKA/OOSAKA-KO. Text in English, Japanese. 1955. a. free. stat.
Published by: Port and Harbor Bureau City of Osaka/Osaka-shi Kowan-Kyoku, 2-8-24 Chikko, Minato-ku, Osaka-shi, 552-0000, Japan. TEL 81-6-572-0554, FAX 81-6-572-0554, TELEX 525-6320.

387.109 GBR ISSN 1755-8751
PORT OF OULU HANDBOOK. Text in English. 1996. biennial. **Document type:** *Handbook/Manual/Guide, Trade.* **Description:** Contains information on Oulu Port in Finland.
Formerly (until 2005): Oulu Port Handbook (1362-7562)
Related titles: Online - full text ed.: free (effective 2010).
Published by: Land & Marine Publications Ltd., 1 Kings Ct, Newcomen Way, Severalls Business Park, Colchester, Essex CO4 9RA, United Kingdom. TEL 44-1206-752902, FAX 44-1206-842958, publishing@landmarine.com, http://www.landmarine.com.

387 SGP ISSN 0219-2195
HE560.S5
PORT OF SINGAPORE. Text in English. 1993. 3/yr. **Document type:** *Magazine, Government.*
Published by: Maritime and Port Authority of Singapore, 460 Alexandra Rd, #19-00 PSA Bldg, Singapore, 119963, Singapore. TEL 65-63751643, media_enquiries@mpa.gov.sg.

315.2 JPN
PORT OF YOKOHAMA. ANNUAL REPORT. Text in Chinese, English, Japanese. a. free. stat. **Document type:** *Corporate.*
Published by: Port and Harbor Bureau, Industry and Trade Center Bldg, 2 Yamashita-cho, Naka-ku, Yokohama-shi, Kanagawa-ken 231-0023, Japan. TEL 81-45-671-7241, FAX 81-45-671-7350.

387 USA
PORT PROGRESS NEWS AND EVENTS. Text in English. 1964. q. free. **Document type:** *Newsletter.* **Description:** Covers personnel, facilities and transport service developments at the Oakland seaport and airport.
Published by: Port of Oakland, 530 Water St, Oakland, CA 94607. TEL 510-272-1100, FAX 510-272-1172. Ed. Robert Middleton. Circ: 15,000 (controlled).

387 USA
HF3163.N5
PORT RECORD. (Overseas edition avail.) Text in English. 1942-1991 (Jul.); N.S. bi-m. free to qualified personnel. adv. charts; illus.; stat.; tr.lit. **Document type:** *Magazine, Trade.* **Description:** News on the port and its international customers.
Former titles: Port of New Orleans Record (1046-9265); (until 1989): Port Record (0194-1836); (until 1979): New Orleans Port Record (0028-6397)
Indexed: P06, PAIS.
—Linda Hall.
Published by: Board of Commissioners Port of New Orleans, PO Box 60046, New Orleans, LA 70160. TEL 504-528-3234, FAX 504-528-3376, craigu@portno.com. Eds. Chris Bonura, Scott McCrossen. Adv. contact Chris Bonura. Circ: 5,000 (controlled).

387 CAN ISSN 1912-872X
PORT STATE CONTROL ANNUAL REPORT. Text in English. 1998. a. **Document type:** *Report, Trade.*
Formerly (until 1999): Port State Control. Annual Report (1912-8614)
Media: Online - full text. **Related titles:** Print ed.: ISSN 1912-2217. 2000; French ed.: Controle des Navires par l'Etat du Port. Rapport Annuel. ISSN 1912-8738.
Published by: Transport Canada, Marine Safety Directorate (Subsidiary of: Transport Canada/Transports Canada), Mailstop AMS, 330 Sparks St, Ottawa, ON K1A 0N5, Canada. TEL 613-991-3135, FAX 613-990-6191, marinesafety@tc.gc.ca.

387.106 GBR ISSN 1740-2638
PORT STRATEGY; insight for port executives. Text in English. 2003. m. (10/yr.). GBP 142; free to qualified personnel (effective 2010). adv. **Document type:** *Journal, Trade.* **Description:** Provides news on world information for senior port executives.
Related titles: Online - full text ed.: free (effective 2010).
Indexed: RefZh.
—CCC.
Published by: Mercator Media Ltd., The Old Mill, Lower Quay, Fareham, Hampshire PO16 0RA, United Kingdom. TEL 44-1329-825335, FAX 44-1329-825330, corporate@mercatormedia.com, http://www.mercatormedia.com. Ed. Carly Fields.

PORTHOLE; cruise magazine. *see* TRAVEL AND TOURISM

387 ITA ISSN 0032-4957
IL PORTO DI SAVONA. Text in Italian. 1956. m. adv. charts; illus.; stat. index. Supplement avail. **Document type:** *Newsletter, Consumer.* **Description:** Covers shipping activities and statistics in the port of Savona.
Published by: Autorita Portuale di Savona, Via Gramsci 14, Savona, 17100, Italy. TEL 39-019-85541, FAX 39-019-827399, http://www.porto.sv.it.

387 GBR ISSN 1478-4947
HE951
PORTS AND TERMINALS GUIDE. Text in English. 1990. a. USD 640 (print or CD-ROM ed.) (effective 2010). adv. maps. **Document type:** *Directory, Trade.* **Description:** Lists the latest port information on ports and terminals worldwide. Includes vessel and harbor dues, berthing and mooring dues, wharfage and commodity dues, and pilotage, towage and water charges. Also contains update details on port facilities and accommodations for nearly 4,300 ports and waterways, along with more than 17,700 addresses of port services and authorities.
Former titles (until 2002): Fairplay Ports Guide (Year) (1360-5577); (until 1995): Fairplay World Ports Directory (Year) (0961-2181); Which was formed by the 1990 merger of: Fairplay World Ports Directory. Vol. 1: North European Ports (0952-9659); Which superseded in part (in 1988): Fairplay World Ports Directory. Vol. 2: Port Dues and Charges (0264-2840); Fairplay World Ports Directory. Vol. 2: The Americas (0952-9667); Fairplay World Ports Directory. Vol. 3. The Mediterranean, Africa and the Middle East (0952-9675); Fairplay World Ports Directory. Vol. 4: Indian and Pacific Ocean Ports (0952-9683); All of which superseded in part (in 1988): Fairplay World Ports Directory. Vol. 1: Port Information (0261-2356); Which was formerly (1869-1981): Port Dues, Charges and Accomodation (0305-4357)
Related titles: CD-ROM ed.: GBP 345, USD 595 (effective 2000).
—CCC.
Published by: Fairplay Publications Ltd., Lombard House, 3 Princess Way, Redhill, Surrey RH1 1UP, United Kingdom. TEL 44-1737-379000, FAX 44-1737-379001, info@lrfairplay.com, http://www.fairplay.co.uk.

387.1 CAN ISSN 0225-5456
PORTS ANNUAL. Text in English. 1972. a. adv. illus.
Published by: Canadian Marine Publications Ltd., Ste 512, 1434 St Catherine St W, Montreal, PQ H3G 1R4, Canada. TEL 514-861-6715, FAX 514-861-0966. Ed. Megan Perkins. R&P John McManus. Adv. contact Marilyn Belanger.

380.5 CAN ISSN 0846-555X
PORTS CANADA. ANNUAL REPORT. Text in English. 1936. a. free.
Former titles (until 1988): Ports Canada. Report to the Minister (0844-7128); (until 1983): Canada. National Harbours Board. Annual Report (0068-7928)
Published by: Ports Canada, Ottawa, ON K1A 0N6, Canada. Circ: 8,000.

387 USA
HE554.A6
PORTS SERVICES DIRECTORY. PACIFIC NORTHWEST. Text in English. 1996. a. USD 17 (effective 1998). **Document type:** *Directory.*
Formerly: Pacific Northwest Ports Handbook (1075-9522)
Published by: Newman-Burrows Publishing, 1710 S Norman St, Seattle, WA 98144-2819. TEL 206-709-1840, FAX 206-324-8939.

387 USA ISSN 0048-489X
PORTSIDE. Text in English. 1971. q. free. **Document type:** *Magazine, Trade.* **Description:** News of the Port of Portland: marine cargo, aviation, land development, activities, trends in international trade in the region.
Indexed: CLT&T, HRIS.
Published by: Port of Portland, PO Box 3529, Portland, OR 97208. TEL 503-231-5000. Ed., R&P Darrel Buttice. Circ: 10,000 (controlled).

387 USA ISSN 2154-5928
➤ **POWERSHIPS.** Text in English. 1940. q. free to members (effective 2010). adv. bk.rev. charts; illus. cum.index: 1940-1974, 1975-1989. back issues avail.; reprints avail. **Document type:** *Magazine, Consumer.* **Description:** Provides information about ships.
Former titles (until 2010): Steamboat Bill (0039-0844); (until 1958): Steamboat Bill of Facts
Related titles: Microform ed.: (from PQC).
Indexed: AmH&L, HRIS, HistAb.
Published by: The Steamship Historical Society of America, Inc., 1029 Waterman Ave, E Providence, RI 02914. TEL 401-274-0805, FAX 401-274-0836, info@sshsa.org. Ed. John H Shaum. Adv. contact Susan V Ewen TEL 401-274-0805. Circ: 3,400 (paid).

387 NLD ISSN 1876-4274
PRAKTIJKBOEK BINNENVAART. Text in Dutch. 2004. a. EUR 38.90 (effective 2008).
Published by: (Scheepvaart en Transport College), Sdu Uitgevers bv, Postbus 20025, The Hague, 2500 EA, Netherlands. TEL 31-70-3789911, FAX 31-70-3854321, sdu@sdu.nl. Ed. R van Reem.

387 ESP
PROA A LA MAR. Text in Spanish. 4/yr. **Document type:** *Magazine, Consumer.*
Related titles: Online - full text ed.
Published by: Real Liga Naval Espanola, C Mayor 16, Madrid, 28013, Spain. TEL 34-91-3664494, FAX 34-91-3661284, http://www.hispamar.com/PAG_HISPAMAR/ProaAlamar1.htm.

387 USA ISSN 1066-2774
HE730
PROFESSIONAL MARINER; journal of the maritime industry. Variant title: Journal of Professional Seamanship. Text in English. 1993. 8/yr. USD 29.95 domestic; USD 39.95 in Canada; USD 44.95 elsewhere (effective 2009). adv. bk.rev. illus. back issues avail. **Document type:** *Magazine, Trade.* **Description:** Contains news of the commercial maritime industry written for professionals working at all levels. Also includes coverage of maritime casualties and accidents.
Related titles: Online - full text ed.; Supplement(s): American Ship Review. ISSN 1546-4792.
Indexed: ASFA, HRIS, OceAb.
—CCC.
Published by: Navigator Publishing LLC., 58 Fore St, Portland, ME 04101-4842. TEL 207-772-2466, FAX 207-772-2879, http://www.navigatorpublishing.com. Ed. Evan True. Pub., Adv. contact Alex Agnew TEL 207-822-4350 ext 219. B&W page USD 2,995, color page USD 4,494; 7 x 10. Circ: 29,000.

387 USA ISSN 0048-5551
THE PROPELLER CLUB QUARTERLY. Text in English. 1972. q. free (effective 2011). adv. illus. back issues avail. **Document type:** *Magazine, Trade.* **Description:** Features expanded editorial coverage of Propeller Club activities, including legislative and regulatory reports, feature-length member profiles, regional news and expanded coverage of national maritime issues.
Published by: (Propeller Club of the United States), Philips Publishing Group, 2201 W Commodore Way, Seattle, WA 98199. TEL 206-284-8285, FAX 206-284-0391, http://www.philipspublishing.com. Ed. Chris Philips. Pub. Peter Philips. Adv. contact Mike Morris.

387.5 PRT
PROPULSOR. Text in Portuguese. 1971. bi-m. free. adv. bk.rev. charts; illus. **Description:** Contains scientific and technical news on shipping, marine engineering and marine pollution.
Published by: Centro Cultural dos Oficiais e Engenheiros Maquinistas da Marinha Mercante, Avda. D. Carlos I No. 101 1o. Esq., Lisbon, 1200, Portugal. TEL 351-1-3961775, FAX 351-1-3977212. Ed., Adv. contact Joao Correia Neves. Circ: 1,750.

PUERTO RICO. PORTS AUTHORITY. STATISTICAL SUMMARY. *see* TRANSPORTATION—Air Transport

387 ESP ISSN 1695-8985
PUERTOS Y NAVIERAS Y TRANSPORTE MARITIMO. Text in Spanish. 2002. m. **Document type:** *Magazine, Trade.*
Formerly (until 2002): Puertos y Navieras (1695-5315)
Published by: Medios de Distribucion 2000 S.L., El Algabeno 53, Madrid, 28043, Spain. TEL 34-91-721895, FAX 34-91-721902, correo@logisticaytransporte.es, http://www.logisticaytransporte.es.

387 CHN ISSN 1671-7996
QINGDAO YUANYANG CHUANYUAN XUEYUAN XUEBAO/QINGDAO OCEAN SHIPPING MARINERS COLLEGE. JOURNAL. Text in Chinese. 1980. q. **Document type:** *Journal, Academic/Scholarly.*
Related titles: Online - full text ed.
Published by: Qingdao Yuanyang Chuanyuan Xueyuan, 84, Jiangxi Lu, Qingdao, 266071, China. TEL 86-532-85752124, FAX 86-532-85752555.

QUARTERDECK. *see* MUSEUMS AND ART GALLERIES

387 DEU
QUER DURCH ANTWERPEN. PORT AND SHIPPING. Text in German. 1978. a. EUR 22 (effective 2006). adv. **Document type:** *Trade.*
Formerly: Quer Durch Port and Shipping of Antwerp (0170-2068)
Published by: Seehafen Verlag GmbH, Nordkanalstr 36, Hamburg, 20097, Germany. TEL 49-40-23714228, FAX 49-40-23714259, info@seehafen-verlag.de, http://www.schiffundhafen.de. adv.: page EUR 985; trim 82 x 122.

387 DEU ISSN 1617-9536
QUER DURCH BREMEN. NIEDERSACHSISCHE HAEFEN. Text in German. 1977. a. EUR 26.50 (effective 2006). adv. **Document type:** *Trade.*
Former titles (until 1999): Quer Durch Bremen. Unterweser (1436-4425); (until 1985): Quer Durch Bremen. Schiffahrt - Spedition - Transport (0170-1576)
Published by: Seehafen Verlag GmbH, Nordkanalstr 36, Hamburg, 20097, Germany. TEL 49-40-23714228, FAX 49-40-23714259, info@seehafen-verlag.de, http://www.schiffundhafen.de. Ed. Sabine Radzuweit. adv.: page EUR 1,040; trim 82 x 122. Circ: 3,500.

387 DEU ISSN 0936-0603
QUER DURCH HAMBURG. SCHIFFAHRT UND HAFEN. Text in German. 1954. a. EUR 26.50 (effective 2006). adv. **Document type:** *Trade.*
Former titles (until 1985): Quer Durch Schiffahrt und Hafen Hamburg (0170-5997); (until 1978): Quer Durch Hamburgs Schiffahrt und Hafen (0170-1142)
Published by: Seehafen Verlag GmbH, Nordkanalstr 36, Hamburg, 20097, Germany. TEL 49-40-23714228, FAX 49-40-23714259, info@seehafen-verlag.de, http://www.schiffundhafen.de. Ed. Sabine Radzuweit. adv.: page EUR 1,135; trim 82 x 155. Circ: 8,500.

387 DEU
QUER DURCH ROTTERDAM. PORT AND SHIPPING. Text in German. 197?. a. EUR 22 (effective 2006). adv. **Document type:** *Trade.*
Formerly: Quer Durch Port and Shipping of Rotterdam (0173-6051)
Published by: Seehafen Verlag GmbH, Nordkanalstr 36, Hamburg, 20097, Germany. TEL 49-40-23714228, FAX 49-40-23714259, info@seehafen-verlag.de, http://www.schiffundhafen.de. adv.: page EUR 985; trim 82 x 122.

RADIO AIDS TO MARINE NAVIGATION. ATLANTIC, ST. LAWRENCE, GREAT LAKES, LAKE WINNIPEG AND EASTERN ARCTIC. *see* COMMUNICATIONS—Radio

RADIO AIDS TO MARINE NAVIGATION. PACIFIC AND WESTERN ARCTIC. *see* COMMUNICATIONS—Radio

623.89 FRA
RADIOCOMMUNICATIONS MARITIMES. Text in French. 1991. irreg., latest 2008. price varies. **Document type:** *Monographic series, Government.* **Description:** Covers communications between ships and land-based radio stations.
Related titles: ◆ Series of: Les Ouvrages de Radiosignaux.
Published by: Service Hydrographique et Oceanographique de la Marine (S H O M), 13 Rue du Chatellier, Brest, 29200, France. TEL 33-2-98220573, FAX 33-2-98220591, http://www.shom.fr. **Subscr. to:** EPSHOM, B.P. 426, Brest Cedex 29275, France.

THE RAILWAY AND CANAL HISTORICAL SOCIETY.JOURNAL. *see* TRANSPORTATION—Railroads

387 ESP
REAL CLUB NAUTICO DE VALENCIA. REVISTA. Text in Spanish. 4/yr.
Published by: Real Club Nautico de Valencia, Canal 91, Valencia, 46024, Spain. TEL 34-96-3679011, FAX 34-96-3677737, http://www.rcnauticovalencia.com/. Ed. J M Lajara.

387 RUS ISSN 0034-1290
TC601 CODEN: RETRAN
RECHNOI TRANSPORT. Text in Russian. 1918. q. USD 99.95. bk.rev. bibl.; charts; illus.; stat. index.
Indexed: ChemAb, RASB.
Published by: Departament Rechnogo Transporta Mintransa, Nagatinskaya Poima, Proektiruemyi pr 4062, d 6, Moscow, 109432, Russian Federation. TEL 7-095-2776696. Ed. L A Sabolev. Circ: 15,490. **Dist. by:** East View Information Services, 10601 Wayzata Blvd, Minneapolis, MN 55305. TEL 952-252-1201, 800-477-1005, FAX 952-252-1202, info@eastview.com, http://www.eastview.com.

623.89 GBR
REEDS CHANNEL ALMANAC (YEAR). Text in English. 2000. a. GBP 26.99 per issue (effective 2010); subscr. includes Reeds Marina Guide. 272 p./no.; back issues avail. **Document type:** *Handbook/Manual/Guide, Trade.* **Description:** Covers the south coast of England from the Scillies to Dover, the Channel Islands and northern France from Calais to L'Aberildut. Topics include pilotage, tides, safety, navigation, radio, lights, waypoints, weather and forecasts around UK and European waters, communications, MAYDAY and distress procedures.
Former titles (until 2009): Reeds Oki Channel Almanac; (until 2005): Macmillan Reeds Channel Almanac
Related titles: ◆ Regional ed(s).: Reeds Eastern Almanac (Year); Reeds Western Almanac (Year). GBP 24.99 per issue (effective 2007); Includes Reeds Marina Guide.
Published by: Adlard Coles Nautical (Subsidiary of: A & C Black Publishers Ltd), 38 Soho Sq, London, W1D 3HB, United Kingdom. TEL 44-20-77580200, FAX 44-20-77580222, adlardcoles@acblack.com, http://www.acblack.com/nautical/.

623.89 GBR
REEDS EASTERN ALMANAC (YEAR). Text in English. 2002. a. GBP 26.99 per issue (effective 2010); subscr. includes Reeds Marina Guide. 240 p./no.; back issues avail. **Document type:** *Handbook/Manual/Guide, Trade.* **Description:** Covers the east coast of the UK from Ramsgate to Cape Wrath, the Orkney and Shetland Isles plus the Continental coast from Dunkerque to Hookseil and Helgoland.
Former titles (until 2007): Reeds Oki Eastern Almanac; (until 2005): Macmillan Reeds Eastern Almanac
Related titles: ◆ Regional ed(s).: Reeds Channel Almanac (Year); Reeds Western Almanac (Year). GBP 24.99 per issue (effective 2007); Includes Reeds Marina Guide.
Published by: Adlard Coles Nautical (Subsidiary of: A & C Black Publishers Ltd), 38 Soho Sq, London, W1D 3HB, United Kingdom. TEL 44-20-77580200, FAX 44-20-77580222, adlardcoles@acblack.com, http://www.acblack.com/nautical/.

REEDS LOOSELEAF ALMANAC. *see* ENCYCLOPEDIAS AND GENERAL ALMANACS

387 GBR
REEDS MARINA GUIDE (YEAR). Text in English. 2003. a., latest 2003. GBP 4.99 per issue (effective 2010); Included with subscr. to Reeds Nautical Almanac. adv. back issues avail. **Document type:** *Handbook/Manual/Guide, Trade.* **Description:** Provides all the data required to navigate Atlantic coastal waters from the UK, Ireland, Channel Islands and the entire European coastline from the tip of Denmark right down to Gibraltar.
Formerly (until 2007): Reeds Waypoint & Marina Guide (Year)
Published by: Adlard Coles Nautical (Subsidiary of: A & C Black Publishers Ltd), 38 Soho Sq, London, W1D 3HB, United Kingdom. TEL 44-20-77580200, FAX 44-20-77580222, adlardcoles@acblack.com, http://www.acblack.com/nautical/.

387 623.8 GBR ISSN 1753-139X
REEDS NAUTICAL ALMANAC (YEAR). Text in English. 1980. a. GBP 34.99 per issue (effective 2010); subscr. includes Reeds Marina Guide. index. back issues avail. **Document type:** *Handbook/Manual/Guide, Trade.* **Description:** Provides all the data required to navigate Atlantic coastal waters from the UK, Ireland, Channel Islands and the entire European coastline from the tip of Denmark right down to Gibraltar.
Former titles (until 2007): Reeds Oki Nautical Almanac (1748-5835); (until 2005): Macmillan-Reeds Nautical Almanac (1470-9813); (until 2000): Macmillan Nautical Almanac (1366-3968); (until 1996): Macmillan & Silk Cut Nautical Almanac (0260-2709)
—BLDSC (7331.421600).
Published by: Adlard Coles Nautical (Subsidiary of: A & C Black Publishers Ltd), 38 Soho Sq, London, W1D 3HB, United Kingdom. TEL 44-20-77580200, FAX 44-20-77580222, adlardcoles@acblack.com, http://www.acblack.com/nautical/.

623.89 GBR
REEDS P B O SMALL CRAFT ALMANAC (YEAR). (Practical Boat Owner) Text in English. 19??. a. USD 15.99 per issue (effective 2010). **Document type:** *Handbook/Manual/Guide, Trade.* **Description:** Covers tidal information, area planning charts, distress, comprehensive list of waypoints, radio data, light recognition, principal lights and their characteristics, weather information, IALA buoyage, international code and flags, sun/moon rise and set, Navtex and Marinecall data.
Formerly (until 2001): Macmillan Reeds Small Craft Alamnac
Published by: Adlard Coles Nautical (Subsidiary of: A & C Black Publishers Ltd), 38 Soho Sq, London, W1D 3HB, United Kingdom. TEL 44-20-77580200, FAX 44-20-77580222, adlardcoles@acblack.com, http://www.acblack.com/nautical/.

REEFER INTERNATIONAL. *see* HEATING, PLUMBING AND REFRIGERATION

387 GBR
THE REEFER REGISTER (ONLINE). Text in English. 1995. a. GBP 125, USD 225 per issue (effective 2011). adv. **Document type:** *Directory, Trade.* **Description:** Provides information on the reefer and reefer containership fleet.
Formerly: The Reefer Register (Print)
Media: Online - full text. **Related titles:** CD-ROM ed.: Reefer Fleet CD. GBP 575, USD 1,035 (effective 2011).
Published by: Clarkson Research Services Ltd., St Magnus House, 3 Lower Thames St, London, EC3R 6HE, United Kingdom. TEL 44-20-73343134, FAX 44-20-75220330, sales@crsl.com, http://www.crsl.com.

REFERATIVNYI ZHURNAL. SUDOSTROENIE; vypusk svodnogo toma. *see* TRANSPORTATION—Abstracting, Bibliographies, Statistics

REFERATIVNYI ZHURNAL. VODNYE PEREVOZKI. TEKHNICHESKAYA EKSPLUATATSIYA I REMONT FLOTA; vypusk svodnogo toma. *see* TRANSPORTATION—Abstracting, Bibliographies, Statistics

REFERATIVNYI ZHURNAL. VODNYI TRANSPORT; svodnyi tom. *see* TRANSPORTATION—Abstracting, Bibliographies, Statistics

387.54 GBR ISSN 1460-0625
REGISTER OF INTERNATIONAL SHIPOWNING GROUPS. Text in English. 19??. 3/yr. 830 p./no.; **Document type:** *Directory, Trade.*
Formerly (until 1997): Lloyd's World Shipowning Groups (0963-6722)
Related titles: CD-ROM ed.
—CCC.
Published by: Lloyd's Register - Fairplay Ltd., Lombard House, 3 Princess Way, Redhill, Surrey RH1 1UP, United Kingdom. TEL 44-1737-379000, FAX 44-1737-379001, info@lrfairplay.com, http://www.lrfairplay.com/.

387 FRA ISSN 0152-9994
REGISTRE MARITIME. Text in French. 1829. a.
Supersedes in part: Registre International de Classification de Navires et d'Aeronefs (0080-0678)
Related titles: Microfilm ed.; ◆ Supplement(s): Supplement Trimestriel au Registre Maritime. ISSN 0153-6052; ◆ Supplement au Registre Maritime. ISSN 0153-6001.
Published by: Bureau Veritas, 67-71 Bd. du Chateau, Neuilly-sur-Sene, Cedex 44 92077, France. TEL 33-1-55247000, FAX 33-1-55247001, http://www.bureauveritas.com. Circ: 800.

REIHE MARITIM. *see* HISTORY—History Of Europe

RENENG DONGLI GONGCHENG/JOURNAL OF ENGINEERING FOR THERMAL ENERGY AND POWER. *see* ENGINEERING—Mechanical Engineering

REPERTOIRE DES RADIOSIGNAUX. *see* COMMUNICATIONS—Radio

387.1 ESP ISSN 2172-6558
▼ **RESPONSIBILIDAD SOCIAL CORPORATIVA.** Text in Spanish. 2010. a. **Document type:** *Monographic series, Academic/Scholarly.*
Published by: Autoridad Portuaria de las Palmas, Tomas Quevedo Ramirez, s-n, Las Palmas, Spain. TEL 34-92-8214507, FAX 34-92-8214460, mvida@palmasport.es, http://www.palmasport.es/.

387.2 USA ISSN 0566-7682
HE730
REVIEW OF MARITIME TRANSPORT. Text in English. 1968. a. USD 90 (effective 2008). back issues avail. **Document type:** *Journal, Trade.* **Description:** Focuses on developments concerning maritime activities in developing countries as compared with other groups of countries.
Related titles: Online - full text ed.: USD 72 (effective 2008); Spanish ed.: El Transporte Maritimo en.. ISSN 0252-5410; French ed.: Etude sur les Transports Maritimes. ISSN 0252-5429; Russian ed.: Obzor Morskogo Transporta. ISSN 0252-5453; Arabic ed.: Isti'rau al-Naql al-Bauri 'am. ISSN 0252-5437; Chinese ed.: Nian Haiyun Gailan. ISSN 0252-5445.
Indexed: A26, ASFA, B21, E08, ESPM, G06, G07, G08, I05, IIS, RASB.
Published by: (United Nations, Conference on Trade and Development (U N C T A D)), United Nations Publications, 2 United Nations Plaza, Rm DC2-853, New York, NY 10017. TEL 212-963-8302, 800-253-9646, FAX 212-963-3489, publications@un.org, https://unp.un.org. **Subscr. to:** United Nations Publications, Sales Office and Bookshop, Bureau E4, Geneva 10 1211, Switzerland.

387 PRT ISSN 0034-8546
REVISTA DE MARINHA. Text in Portuguese. 1937. m. adv. bk.rev.
Indexed: RASB.
Published by: Editora Nautica Nacional, Apdo. 3115, Lisbon, 1303, Portugal. TEL 351-21-4391485. Ed. Gabriel Lobo Fialho. Circ: 5,000.

380 DNK ISSN 0901-7801
DEN ROEDE TRANSPORTLISTE (YEAR)/DANISH EXPORT AND IMPORT TRANSPORT GUIDE. Text in Danish. 1975. a. adv. **Document type:** *Directory, Trade.*
Related titles: ◆ Issued with: Den Blaa Besejlingsliste (Year). ISSN 0901-781X.
Published by: TechMedia A/S, Naverland 35, Glostrup, 2600, Denmark. TEL 45-43-242628, FAX 45-43-242626, info@techmedia.dk, http://www.techmedia.dk. Ed. Helle Hansen. Adv. contact Bent Henriksen. B&W page DKK 12,800; 195 x 270. Circ: 2,000.

623.82 ESP ISSN 0211-2892
ROTACION; revista mensual de la industria naval, maritima y pesquera. Text in Spanish. 1968. m. (10/yr.). EUR 117 domestic; EUR 196 in Europe; EUR 270 elsewhere (effective 2009). adv. bk.rev. illus.; tr.lit. **Document type:** *Magazine, Trade.*
Indexed: IECT.
Published by: TPI Edita, Ave Manoteras, 26 3a Planta, Madrid, 28050, Spain. TEL 34-91-3396807, FAX 34-91-3396096, info@grupotpi.es, http://www.tpiedita.es. Circ: 7,500.

623.81 GBR ISSN 1479-8751
ROYAL INSTITUTION OF NAVAL ARCHITECTS. TRANSACTIONS. PART A. INTERNATIONAL JOURNAL OF MARITIME ENGINEERING. Abbreviated title: I J M E. Text in English. 1960. q. GBP 60 combined subscription to non-members (print & online eds.); GBP 30 combined subscription to members (print & online eds.); GBP 18 per issue to non-members; GBP 9 per issue to members (effective 2009). back issues avail. **Document type:** *Proceedings, Academic/Scholarly.* **Description:** Provides a forum for the reporting and discussion on technical and scientific issues associated with the design and construction of marine vessels and offshore structures.
Supersedes in part (in 2003): Royal Institution of Naval Architects. Transactions (0035-8967); Which incorporated (1971-1987): Royal Institution of Naval Architects. Supplementary Papers (0373-529X); Transactions was formerly (until 1959): Institution of Naval Architects. Transactions
Related titles: CD-ROM ed.: ISSN 1740-2700; Microform ed.: 1860 (from PMC); Online - full text ed.: ISSN 1740-0716.
Indexed: ASFA, BMT, CPEI, CurCont, OceAb, SCI, SCOPUS, W07.
—BLDSC (8998.230000), INIST, Linda Hall. **CCC.**
Published by: Royal Institution of Naval Architects, 10 Upper Belgrave St, London, SW1X 8BQ, United Kingdom. TEL 44-20-72354622, FAX 44-20-72595912, publications@rina.org.uk. Ed. P A Wilson.

387 GBR ISSN 1740-0694
ROYAL INSTITUTION OF NAVAL ARCHITECTS. TRANSACTIONS. PART B. INTERNATIONAL JOURNAL OF SMALL CRAFT TECHNOLOGY. Abbreviated title: I J S C T. Text in English. 1960. s-a. GBP 32 combined subscription to non-members (print & online eds.); GBP 18 combined subscription to members (print & online eds.); GBP 9 per issue to members (effective 2009). back issues avail. **Document type:** *Proceedings, Academic/Scholarly.* **Description:** Provides a forum for the reporting and discussion on technical and scientific issues associated with research and development of recreational and commercial small craft.
Supersedes in part (in 2003): Royal Institute of Naval Architects. Transactions (0035-8967); Which incorporated (1971-1987): Royal Institution of Naval Architects. Supplementary Papers (0373-529X); Transactions was formerly (until 1959): Institution of Naval Architects. Transactions
Related titles: CD-ROM ed.: ISSN 1740-2719; Online - full text ed.: ISSN 1740-0708.
Indexed: ASFA, CPEI, OceAb, SCOPUS.
—BLDSC (8998.230000), INIST, Linda Hall. **CCC.**
Published by: Royal Institution of Naval Architects, 10 Upper Belgrave St, London, SW1X 8BQ, United Kingdom. TEL 44-20-72354622, FAX 44-20-72595912, publications@rina.org.uk. Ed. R Birmingham.

387 JPN ISSN 0286-8474
RYOKAKUSEN/PASSENGERBOAT. Text in Japanese. 1955. q. JPY 400 per issue.
Published by: Nihon Ryokakusen Kyokai/Japan Passengerboat Association, 1-1 Uchisaiwai-cho 2-chome, Chiyoda-ku, Tokyo, 100-0011, Japan.

S A R STATISTICS. (Search and Rescue) *see* TRANSPORTATION—Abstracting, Bibliographies, Statistics

623.82 JPN
S R C NEWS. Text in Japanese. 1987. q.
Published by: Shipbuilding Research Center of Japan/Nihon Zosen Gijutsu Senta, 3-8 Mejiro 1-chome, Toshima-ku, Tokyo, 171-0031, Japan.

387 CHE ISSN 1423-5471
S V S JOURNAL; Zeitschrift fuer Schiffahrt und Hafenwirtschaft. Text in German. 1906. 6/yr. membership. adv. bk.rev. charts; illus.; tr.lit. index. **Document type:** *Magazine, Trade.*
Former titles (until 1998): Strom und See (0039-2510); (until 1943): Rheinquellen (1421-8992)
Published by: Schweizerische Vereinigung fuer Schiffahrt und Hafenwirtschaft/Swiss Association for Navigation and Harbour Economy, Suedquaistr 14, Basel, 4019, Switzerland. TEL 41-61-6312727, FAX 41-61-6311483, svs@swissonline.ch. adv.: B&W page CHF 1,665; trim 185 x 261. Circ: 3,000.

623.8 NLD ISSN 1876-0236
VM4
S W Z MARITIME. (Schip en Werf de Zee) Text in Dutch. 1991. m. (11/yr.). EUR 95 domestic; EUR 130.95 foreign; EUR 36.95 to students (effective 2009). adv. index. **Document type:** *Magazine, Trade.*
Formerly (until 2007): Schip en Werf de Zee (0926-4213); Which was formed by the merger of (1934-1991): Schip en Werf (0036-6099); (1985-1991): N T T De Zee (0921-2450); Which was formerly (until 1985): Nautisch Technisch Tijdschrift de Zee (0165-6236)
Indexed: A22, BMT, CISA, KES, SCOPUS.
—IE, Infotrieve, Linda Hall.

Published by: (Nederlandsche Vereniging van Technici op Scheepvaartgebied/Dutch Welding Institute), Media Business Press BV, Postbus 8632, Rotterdam, 3009 AP, Netherlands. TEL 31-10-2894078, FAX 31-10-2894076, info@mbp.nl, http://www.mbp.nl/. Ed. C Dirkse. Pub. Judith Verbeek. adv.: B&W page EUR 1,935, color page EUR 2,990; trim 225 x 297. Circ: 4,553. **Co-sponsors:** Nederlandse Vereniging van Kapiteins ter Koopvaardij; Nautilus NL; Koninklijk Nederlands Meteorologisch Instituut.

387 623.888 GBR ISSN 1751-1984
VK200
SAFETY AT SEA INTERNATIONAL. Abbreviated title: S A S I. Text in English. 1967. m. USD 490 combined subscription (print & online eds.) (effective 2010). adv. bk.rev. abstr.; illus. back issues avail. **Document type:** *Magazine, Trade.* **Description:** Aims to keep the readers up-to-date with legislation, safety standards, maritime safety and security, technical and market developments, ongoing research projects, conference and exhibition reports, the latest equipment and services.
Former titles (until 1991): Safety at Sea (0142-0666); (until 1978): Safety at Sea International (0036-2441)
Related titles: Online - full text ed.
Indexed: ASFA, B02, B15, B17, B18, BMT, CLT&T, ESPM, G04, G06, G07, G08, I05, OceAb.
—BLDSC (8069.130000), IE, Infotrieve, Ingenta. **CCC.**
Published by: Lloyd's Register - Fairplay Ltd., Lombard House, 3 Princess Way, Redhill, Surrey RH1 1UP, United Kingdom. TEL 44-1737-379700, 44-1737-379000, info@lrfairplay.com, http://www.lrfairplay.com/. Ed. Nick Blackmore TEL 44-1737-379176. Adv. contact Daniel Goncalves TEL 44-1737-379706.

387 JPN ISSN 0287-590X
SAGYOSEN/WORKVESSEL. Text in Japanese. 1959. bi-m. JPY 2,240 (effective 1999). adv. **Description:** Covers port construction including planning, construction, managing and instruments. Also covers work vessels including dredgers, floating cranes, tug-boats and more.
Published by: Nihon Sagyosen Kyokai/Japan Work Vessel Association, 9-7 Yaesu 2-chome, Chuo-ku, Tokyo, 104-0028, Japan. TEL 81-3-3271-5618, FAX 81-3-3281-2975. Ed. Yasuji Saotome. Pub., R&P Akimitsu Aramaki. Circ: 1,200.

623.89 BEL
SAILING AHEAD. Text in English. quadrennial. **Document type:** *Newsletter, Academic/Scholarly.*
Media: Online - full content.
Published by: International Navigation Association/Association Internationale de Navigation, Graaf de Ferraris, 11th Fl, 20 Boulevard du Roi Albert II, Brussels, 1000, Belgium. TEL 32-2-5537157, FAX 32-2-5537155, info@pianc-aipcn.org, http://www.pianc-aipcn.org.

623.8922 CAN ISSN 1701-8773
VK986
SAILING DIRECTIONS: CAPE CANSO TO CAPE SABLE, INCLUDING SABLE ISLAND. Text in English. 2001. irreg. CAD 18.95 per issue (effective 2004). **Description:** Contains natural characteristics, geography, climatic variations, and wharves for the region.
Published by: Department of Fisheries and Oceans, Canadian Hydrographic Service, 615 Booth St, Ottawa, ON K1A 0E6, Canada. TEL 613-995-5249, FAX 613-996-9053, chsinfo@dfo-mpo.gc.ca. **Dist. by:** Department of Fisheries and Oceans, Hydrographic Chart Distribution Office, PO Box 8080, Ottawa, ON K1G 3H6, Canada. TEL 613-998-4931, FAX 613-998-1217, chs_sales@dfo-mpo.gc.ca, http://www.charts.gc.ca.

623.8922 CAN ISSN 1701-879X
VK986
SAILING DIRECTIONS: CAPE NORTH TO CAPE CANSO, INCLUDING BRAS D'OR LAKE. Text in English. 2001. irreg. CAD 14.95 per issue (effective 2004). **Description:** Contains natural characteristics, geography, climatic variations, and wharves for the region.
Published by: Department of Fisheries and Oceans, Canadian Hydrographic Service, 615 Booth St, Ottawa, ON K1A 0E6, Canada. TEL 613-995-5249, FAX 613-996-9053, chsinfo@dfo-mpo.gc.ca. **Dist. by:** Department of Fisheries and Oceans, Hydrographic Chart Distribution Office, PO Box 8080, Ottawa, ON K1G 3H6, Canada. TEL 613-998-4931, FAX 613-998-1217, chs_sales@dfo-mpo.gc.ca, http://www.charts.gc.ca.

623.89 CAN ISSN 1482-0978
VK984.D48
SAILING DIRECTIONS: DETROIT RIVER, LAKE ST. CLAIR, ST. CLAIR RIVER. Text in English. 1996. irreg. CAD 9.95 per issue (effective 2006).
Published by: Department of Fisheries and Oceans, Canadian Hydrographic Service, 615 Booth St, Ottawa, ON K1A 0E6, Canada. TEL 613-995-5249, FAX 613-996-9053, chsinfo@dfo-mpo.gc.ca. **Dist. by:** Department of Fisheries and Oceans, Hydrographic Chart Distribution Office, PO Box 8080, Ottawa, ON K1G 3H6, Canada. TEL 613-998-4931, FAX 613-998-1217, chs_sales@dfo-mpo.gc.ca, http://www.charts.gc.ca.

623.89 CAN ISSN 1482-6968
VK983
SAILING DIRECTIONS: GENERAL INFORMATION. GREAT LAKES. Text in English. 1996. irreg. CAD 14.95 per issue (effective 2006).
Published by: Department of Fisheries and Oceans, Canadian Hydrographic Service, 615 Booth St, Ottawa, ON K1A 0E6, Canada. TEL 613-995-5249, FAX 613-996-9053, chsinfo@dfo-mpo.gc.ca. **Dist. by:** Department of Fisheries and Oceans, Hydrographic Chart Distribution Office, PO Box 8080, Ottawa, ON K1G 3H6, Canada. TEL 613-998-4931, FAX 613-998-1217, chs_sales@dfo-mpo.gc.ca, http://www.charts.gc.ca.

623.8922 CAN ISSN 1701-8811
VK987
SAILING DIRECTIONS: GULF OF MAINE AND BAY OF FUNDY. Text in English. 2001. irreg. CAD 18.95 (effective 2004). **Description:** Provides the natural characteristics, geography, climatic variations, and wharves for the region.
Published by: Department of Fisheries and Oceans, Canadian Hydrographic Service, 615 Booth St, Ottawa, ON K1A 0E6, Canada. TEL 613-995-3065, 613-995-5249, FAX 613-996-9053, chsinfo@dfo-mpo.gc.ca.

623.8922 CAN ISSN 1495-9836
VK984.H8
SAILING DIRECTIONS: LAKE HURON, ST. MARYS RIVER, LAKE SUPERIOR. Text in English. 2000. irreg. CAD 19.95 per issue (effective 2004). **Description:** Contains natural characteristics, geography, climatic variations, and wharves for the region.
Published by: Department of Fisheries and Oceans, Canadian Hydrographic Service, 615 Booth St, Ottawa, ON K1A 0E6, Canada. TEL 613-995-5249, FAX 613-996-9053, chsinfo@dfo-mpo.gc.ca. **Dist. by:** Department of Fisheries and Oceans, Hydrographic Chart Distribution Office, PO Box 8080, Ottawa, ON K1G 3H6, Canada. TEL 613-998-4931, FAX 613-998-1217, chs_sales@dfo-mpo.gc.ca, http://www.charts.gc.ca.

623.8922 CAN ISSN 1494-6653
VK984.H8
SAILING DIRECTIONS: NORTH CHANNEL OF LAKE HURON. Text in English. 2000. irreg. CAD 14.95 per issue (effective 2004). **Description:** Contains natural characteristics, geography, climatic variations, and wharves for the area.
Published by: Department of Fisheries and Oceans, Canadian Hydrographic Service, 615 Booth St, Ottawa, ON K1A 0E6, Canada. TEL 613-995-5249, FAX 613-996-9053, chsinfo@dfo-mpo.gc.ca. **Dist. by:** Department of Fisheries and Oceans, Hydrographic Chart Distribution Office, PO Box 8080, Ottawa, ON K1G 3H6, Canada. TEL 613-998-4931, FAX 613-998-1217, chs_sales@dfo-mpo.gc.ca, http://www.charts.gc.ca.

623.8922 CAN ISSN 1498-8909
VK988
SAILING DIRECTIONS: ST. LAWRENCE RIVER, CAP-ROUGE TO MONTREAL AND RIVIERE RICHELIEU. Text in English. 1992. irreg. **Document type:** *Consumer.* **Description:** Provides information on the natural characteristics, geography, climatic variations, and wharves for the region.
Formerly (until 2001): Sailing Directions: St. Lawrence River, Cap-Rouge to Montreal (1498-8623)
Published by: Department of Fisheries and Oceans, Canadian Hydrographic Service, 615 Booth St, Ottawa, ON K1A 0E6, Canada. TEL 613-995-5249, FAX 613-996-9053, chsinfo@dfo-mpo.gc.ca. **Dist. by:** Department of Fisheries and Oceans, Hydrographic Chart Distribution Office, PO Box 8080, Ottawa, ON K1G 3H6, Canada. TEL 613-998-4931, FAX 613-998-1217, chs_sales@dfo-mpo.gc.ca, http://www.charts.gc.ca.

623.89 CAN ISSN 1482-1214
VK984.E6
SAILING DIRECTIONS: WELLAND CANAL AND LAKE ERIE. Text in English. 1996. irreg. CAD 14.95 per issue (effective 2006).
Published by: Department of Fisheries and Oceans, Canadian Hydrographic Service, 615 Booth St, Ottawa, ON K1A 0E6, Canada. TEL 613-995-5249, FAX 613-996-9053, chsinfo@dfo-mpo.gc.ca. **Dist. by:** Department of Fisheries and Oceans, Hydrographic Chart Distribution Office, PO Box 8080, Ottawa, ON K1G 3H6, Canada. TEL 613-998-4931, FAX 613-998-1217, chs_sales@dfo-mpo.gc.ca, http://www.charts.gc.ca.

SAILING LETTERS JOURNAAL. *see* LITERATURE

387 CAN ISSN 0581-3298
ST. LAWRENCE SEAWAY AUTHORITY. ANNUAL REPORT. Text in English, French. 1955. a. free. **Document type:** *Corporate.*
Published by: St. Lawrence Seaway Management Corporation, 202 Pitt St, Cornwall, ON K6J 3P7, Canada. TEL 613-932-5170, FAX 613-932-7286. Circ: 3,000.

387.2 NLD ISSN 1877-0061
SCHEEPSBOUW NEDERLAND MAGAZINE. Text in Dutch. 2008. q. adv. **Document type:** *Magazine, Trade.*
Published by: Scheepsbouw Nederland, Postbus 138, Zoetermeer, 2700 AC, Netherlands. TEL 31-79-3531165, FAX 31-79-3531155, info@scheepsbouw.nl, http://www.scheepsbouw.nl. Circ: 2,000.

623.8 627.2 DEU ISSN 1436-8498
VM3 CODEN: SHASEZ
SCHIFF UND HAFEN; Zeitschrift fuer Maritime Technik und Seewirtschaft. Text in English, German. 1990. m. EUR 186.18 domestic; EUR 193 in Europe; EUR 216 elsewhere; EUR 111.71 domestic to students; EUR 123.40 in Europe to students; EUR 146.40 elsewhere to students (effective 2008). adv. bk.rev. charts; illus. index. **Document type:** *Magazine, Trade.*
Formerly (until 1993): Schiff und Hafen Seewirtschaft (0938-1643); Which was formed by the merger of (1949-1990): Schiff und Hafen (0036-603X); (1969-1990): Seewirtschaft (0037-0886); Which was formed by the merger of (1961-1968): Seeverkehr (0037-086X); (1963-1968): Schiffbau-, Schiffsbetriebs-, Fischerei-, Hafentechnik (0323-6048); Which was formerly (1951-1963): Schiffbautechnik (0581-9695)
Indexed: A22, ASFA, B21, BMT, CISA, ChemAb, ESPM, IBR, IBZ, RefZh, SCOPUS, TM.
—BLDSC (8088.702000), IE, Infotrieve, Ingenta, Linda Hall. **CCC.**
Published by: (Schiffbautechnische Gesellschaft e.V.), Seehafen Verlag GmbH, Nordkanalstr 36, Hamburg, 20097, Germany. TEL 49-40-23714228, FAX 49-40-23714259, info@seehafen-verlag.de, http://www.schiffundhafen.de. Ed. Silke Sadowski. adv.: B&W page EUR 2,870; trim 185 x 260. Circ: 6,683 (paid).

387.2 DEU ISSN 1432-7880
SCHIFF UND ZEIT. Text in German. 1973. s-a. EUR 25.40 (effective 2006). adv. illus. **Document type:** *Magazine, Trade.*
Incorporates (1976-1992): Panorama Maritim (0232-5233); Which was formerly (until 1981): D D R-Arbeitskreis Schiffahrts- und Marinegeschichte. Mitteilungsblatt (0232-5284)
Indexed: DIP, IBR, IBZ.
Published by: (Deutsche Gesellschaft fuer Schiffahrts-und Marinegeschichte e. V.), Koehlers Verlagsgesellschaft mbH, Striepenweg 31, Hamburg, 21147, Germany. TEL 49-40-7971303, FAX 49-40-79713324, vertrieb@koehler-mittler.de, http://www.koehler-mittler.de. Ed. Jan Heitmann. **Subscr. to:** AWU, Kleine Bahnstr 6, Hamburg 22525, Germany.

623.8 DEU ISSN 0036-6056
VM156
SCHIFFBAUFORSCHUNG; Schriftenreihe fuer Ingenieurwissenschaften. Text in German; Abstracts and contents page in English, German, Russian, Spanish. 1962. q. bk.rev. charts; illus. **Document type:** *Academic/Scholarly.* **Description:** Reports on research and developments in naval engineering.
Indexed: BMT, IBR, IBZ, TM.
—INIST, Linda Hall.
Published by: Universitaet Rostock, Fachbereich Maschinenbau und Schiffstechnik, Albert-Einstein-Str 2, Rostock, 18059, Germany. TEL 49-381-4405322, FAX 49-381-4405253. Eds. I Grabow, Mathias Paschen. Circ: 450.

387.2 DEU
SCHIFFE - MENSCHEN - SCHICKSALE. Abbreviated title: S M S. Text in German. m. EUR 44 in Europe; EUR 69 in North America (effective 2011). **Document type:** *Magazine, Consumer.*
Published by: Verlag Rudolf Stade, Holtenauer Str 67, Kiel, 24105, Germany. TEL 49-431-566496, FAX 49-431-566461.

387 DEU ISSN 1432-9891
SCHIFFS-INGENIEUR JOURNAL. Text in German. 1953. bi-m. EUR 30 membership (effective 2005). adv. **Document type:** *Journal, Academic/Scholarly.*
Published by: Verein der Schiffs-Ingenieure zu Hamburg e.V., Gurlittstr 32, Hamburg, 20099, Germany. TEL 49-40-2803883, FAX 49-40-2803565, VSIH-VDSI@t-online.de, http://www.schiffsingenieure.de. Ed., R&P Joachim Ortlepp. adv.: page EUR 452.50; trim 170 x 250. Circ: 1,500 (controlled).

387 621.9 DEU ISSN 0177-1116
SCHIFFSBETRIEBSTECHNIK FLENSBURG. Text in German. 1954. q. EUR 3 per issue (effective 2005). adv. bk.rev. back issues avail. **Document type:** *Journal, Trade.* **Description:** Trade publication for the shipbuilding industry. Features the latest technology, marketing, industry and trade school information. Includes list of events and exhibitions.
Formerly (until 1982): Schiffsbetriebstechnische Gesellschaft Flensburg. Mitteilungsblatt (0177-1124)
Published by: Schiffsbetriebstechnische Gesellschaft Flensburg e.V., Kanzleistr 91-93, Flensburg, 24943, Germany. TEL 49-461-979430, stgf-kux@foni.net. Ed. Dagmar Schmitz TEL 49-461-1607187. Circ: 1,100.

387 340 NLD ISSN 0165-103X
SCHIP EN SCHADE; beslissingen op het gebied van zee- en binnenvaartrecht, transport en brandverzekeringsrecht. Text in Dutch. 1957. m. EUR 300; EUR 151 to students; EUR 28.90 newsstand/cover (effective 2009). adv. **Document type:** *Magazine, Trade.*
Related titles: CD-ROM ed.; Online - full text ed.; ◆ Supplement(s): Schip en Schade, Kaarten. ISSN 0165-1080.
Published by: Kluwer B.V. (Subsidiary of: Wolters Kluwer N.V.), Postbus 23, Deventer, 7400 GA, Netherlands. TEL 31-570-673555, FAX 31-570-691555, juridisch@kluwer.nl, http://www.kluwer.nl.

387 GBR ISSN 0308-2253
THE SEA. Text mainly in English; Section in Russian, Spanish, Chinese. 1953. bi-m. GBP 3.50, USD 5 (effective 2009). back issues avail. **Document type:** *Newspaper, Trade.* **Description:** Contains practical information for seafarers, as well as news about the shipping industry.
Related titles: Online - full text ed.: free (effective 2009).
Published by: Mission to Seafarers, Saint Michael Paternoster Royal, College Hill, London, EC4R 2RL, United Kingdom. TEL 44-20-72485202, FAX 44-20-72484761, pr@missiontoseafarers.org. Ed. Gillian Ennis.

387 GBR ISSN 0036-9977
HE753.P32
SEA BREEZES; the worldwide magazine of ships and the sea. Text in English. 1919. m. GBP 39 domestic; GBP 58 foreign (effective 2010). bk.rev. tr.lit. index. back issues avail. **Document type:** *Magazine, Trade.* **Description:** Features articles devoted to the worldwide shipping industry with a focus on the latest maritime news, including specialist coverage of naval, ferry, coastal, Asia-pacific, sail and cruise sectors.
Related titles: Online - full text ed.
—BLDSC (8213.560000), IE, Ingenta.
Published by: Sea Breezes Publications Ltd., Media House, Cronkbourne, Douglas, Isle of Man, IM4 4SB, United Kingdom. TEL 44-1624-696573, FAX 44-1624-661655. Ed. Capt. Andrew C Douglas. Pub. Hamish C Ross. Adv. contact Sara Kilduff. **Dist. by:** Comag.

387 970 USA ISSN 0582-3471
F897.P9
➤ **SEA CHEST.** Text in English. 1967. q. free to members (effective 2010). bk.rev. illus. index. back issues avail. **Document type:** *Journal, Academic/Scholarly.* **Description:** Aims to record historical maritime events of greater Puget Sound, British Columbia and Alaska.
Related titles: Microfiche ed.
Published by: Puget Sound Maritime Historical Society, PO Box 9731, Seattle, WA 98109. TEL 206-324-1685 ext 41, president@pugetmaritime.org. Ed. Ronald R Burke.

387 USA ISSN 0048-9867
VM1
SEA CLASSICS. Text in English. m. adv. illus. back issues avail. **Document type:** *Magazine, Consumer.* **Description:** Contains articles on scale ship modeling.
Incorporates: Sea Combat (0199-087X)
Related titles: Online - full text ed.
Indexed: H20, P10, P48, P53, P54, PQC.
Published by: Challenge Publications, Inc., 9509 Vassar Ave, Unit A, Chatsworth, CA 91311. TEL 818-700-6868, FAX 818-700-6282, challpubs@aol.com, http://www.challengeweb.com/. Ed., Pub., R&P Edwin Schnepf. Adv. contact Flint Burckart.

387 USA ISSN 0896-1646
VK23
SEA HISTORY GAZETTE. Text in English. 1987. bi-m. USD 18.75 domestic to members; USD 28.75 foreign to members; USD 28.75 domestic to non-members; USD 38.75 foreign to non-members (effective 2000). **Description:** Digest of maritime heritage news.
Published by: National Maritime Historical Society, 5 John Walsh Blvd, Box 68, Peekskill, NY 10566-0068. TEL 914-271-2177. Ed. Justine Ahlstrom. Circ: 1,000.

SEA POWER. *see* MILITARY

370 GBR ISSN 0037-007X
VK1
➤ **THE SEAFARER.** Text in English. 1933. 3/yr. GBP 8 domestic; GBP 13 foreign; GBP 3 newsstand/cover (effective 2009). adv. bk.rev. illus. back issues avail. **Document type:** *Magazine, Academic/Scholarly.* **Description:** Designed for the marine society and sea cadets.
Indexed: ASFA.
Published by: The Marine Society & Sea Cadets, 202 Lambeth Rd, London, SE1 7JW, United Kingdom. TEL 44-20-76547000, FAX 44-20-79288914, info@ms-sc.org. Ed. Nick Blackmore. Adv. contact Charlotte Vogel.

➤ **SEAFARERS LOG.** *see* LABOR UNIONS

387 GBR ISSN 1476-3680
HE561
SEATRADE. Text in English. 1971. m. GBP 92 domestic; EUR 142 in Europe; USD 180 elsewhere (effective 2009). adv. bk.rev. Supplement avail.; back issues avail. **Document type:** *Magazine, Trade.* **Description:** Provides in-depth reporting and analysis of the world's most dynamic shipping regions and sectors.
Former titles (until 2001): Seatrade Review (0964-8895); (until 1992): Seatrade Business Review (0951-6832); (until 1986): Seatrade (0037-0428)
Related titles: Online - full text ed.
Indexed: BMT, F&EA, HRIS, KES, P06, PAIS.
—BLDSC (8216.055000), IE, Ingenta.
Published by: Seatrade Communications Ltd., Seatrade House, 42 North Station Rd, Colchester, Essex CO1 1RB, United Kingdom. TEL 44-1206-545121, FAX 44-1206-545190, mail@seatrade-global.com. Ed. Bob Jaques. Adv. contact Andrew Callaghan. color page GBP 4,080, color page EUR 6,650; bleed 216 x 305. Circ: 6,466.

387 GBR
SEATRADE WEEK NEWSFRONT. Text in Chinese. 1982. w. USD 695; includes Seatrade Review. bk.rev. **Document type:** *Newsletter, Trade.* **Description:** Shipping news and market data.
Formerly: Seatrade Week Information Service
Published by: Seatrade Communications Ltd., Seatrade House, 42 North Station Rd, Colchester, Essex CO1 1RB, United Kingdom. TEL 44-1206-545121, FAX 44-1206-545190, mail@seatrade-global.com, http://www.seatrade-global.com. Circ: 1,200.

387 GBR ISSN 0144-1019
SEAWAYS. Text in English. 1980. m. free membership. adv. bk.rev. charts; illus. index. back issues avail. **Document type:** *Journal, Trade.* **Description:** Vehicle which links professionals worldwide and enables members to be kept up-to-date with changes in legislation, new books, charts and announcements. It is the source of new ideas and a steadying influence on impractical proposals.
Supersedes in part (in 1980): Nautical Review (0309-6254)
Indexed: ASFA, B21, BMT, E11, ESPM, H&SSA, PollutAb, T04.
—BLDSC (8216.055600), IE, Ingenta.
Published by: Nautical Institute, 202 Lambeth Rd, London, SE1 7LQ, United Kingdom. TEL 44-20-79281351, FAX 44-20-74012817, sec@nautinst.org. Ed. Claire Walsh. Pub. Julian Parker. Adv. contact Tina Scott. Circ: 6,389.

SEAWAYS' SHIPS IN SCALE. *see* HOBBIES

SEIBU ZOSENKAI RONBUN KOGAI/WEST JAPAN SOCIETY OF NAVAL ARCHITECTS. ABSTRACTS FROM RESEARCH REPORT. *see* TRANSPORTATION—Abstracting, Bibliographies, Statistics

387 JPN ISSN 1340-4229
SEKAI KOWAN JIJO SOKUHO/WORLD PORT JOURNAL. Text in Chinese, English, Japanese. 1955. m. JPY 15,600; USD 130 foreign. bibl.; charts; illus.; maps. index. back issues avail.
Formerly: Kowan Jijo Sokuho - Port and Harbour News (0910-0423)
Related titles: Fax ed.
Published by: Kaijo Hoan Kyokai/Maritime Safety Association, 3-1 Tsuki-Ji 5-chome, Chuo-ku, Tokyo, 104-0045, Japan. TEL 81-3-3542-3678, FAX 81-3-3541-9085.

SEKAI NO KANSEN/SHIPS OF THE WORLD. *see* MILITARY

SELLING CRUSING. *see* TRAVEL AND TOURISM

623.81 JPN
SENPAKU GIJUTSU KENKYUJO HAPPYO RONBUN HYODAISHU/ SHIP RESEARCH INSTITUTE. LIST OF PAPERS. Text in Japanese. 1966. every 5 yrs. **Document type:** *Government.*
Published by: Un'yusho, Senpaku Gijutsu Kenkyujo/Ministry of Transport, Ship Research Institute, 38-1 Shinkawa 6-chome, Mitaka-shi, Tokyo-to 181-0004, Japan.

623.81 JPN ISSN 0285-7332
SENPAKU GIJUTSU KENKYUJO KENKYU HAPPYOKAI KOENSHU/ SHIP RESEARCH INSTITUTE. REPORTS OF MEETING. Text in English, Japanese. 1974. s-a. **Document type:** *Government.*
Published by: Un'yusho, Senpaku Gijutsu Kenkyujo/Ministry of Transport, Ship Research Institute, 38-1 Shinkawa 6-chome, Mitaka-shi, Tokyo-to 181-0004, Japan.

623.8 JPN
SENPAKU GIJUTSU KENKYUJO KIKAN DORYOKUBU KIYO/SHIP RESEARCH INSTITUTE. POWER AND ENERGY ENGINEERING DIVISION. MEMOIRS. Text in English, Japanese; Summaries in English. 1991. irreg.
Published by: Un'yusho, Senpaku Gijutsu Kenkyujo/Ministry of Transport, Ship Research Institute, 38-1 Shinkawa 6-chome, Mitaka-shi, Tokyo-to 181-0004, Japan.

623.81 JPN
SENPAKU GIJUTSU KENKYUJO NENPO/SHIP RESEARCH INSTITUTE. ANNUAL REPORT. Text in Japanese. 1950. a. **Document type:** *Government.*
Published by: Un'yusho, Senpaku Gijutsu Kenkyujo/Ministry of Transport, Ship Research Institute, 38-1 Shinkawa 6-chome, Mitaka-shi, Tokyo-to 181-0004, Japan.

623.8 JPN ISSN 0916-8672
SENPAKU KAIHATSU GIHO/SHIP RESEARCH REPORT. Text in Japanese. 1975. a.
Formerly (until 1986): Kaihatsu Giho (0911-6702)
Published by: Kaijo Hoancho, Sobi Gijutsubu/Maritime Safety Agency, Equipment and Technology Department, 1-3 Kasumigaseki 2-chome, Chiyoda-ku, Tokyo, 100, Japan.

387 ESP ISSN 0211-304X
SERNAVAL; informe mensual sobre la actividad naval y maritima. Text in English, Spanish. 1972. m. EUR 496 domestic; EUR 605 foreign (effective 2009). stat. back issues avail. **Document type:** *Bulletin, Trade.*
Published by: TPI Edita, Ave Manoteras, 26 3a Planta, Madrid, 28050, Spain. TEL 34-91-3396807, FAX 34-91-3396096, info@grupotpi.es. Circ: 1,000.

387 CHN ISSN 1674-5949
SHANGHAI CHUANBO YUNSHU KEXUE YANJIUSUO XUEBAO/ SHANGHAI SHIP & SHIPPING RESEARCH INSTITUTE. JOURNAL. Text in Chinese. s-a. **Document type:** *Journal, Academic/Scholarly.*
Formerly (until 2005): Jiaotongbu Shanghai Chuanbo Yunshu Kexue Yanjiusuo Xuebao/Shanghai Scientific Research Institute of Shipping. Journal (1000-4696)
Related titles: Online - full text ed.
Published by: Shanghai Chuanbo Yunshu Kexue Yanjiusuo/Shanghai Ship and Shipping Research Institute, 600, Minsheng Lu, Pudongxin-qu, Shanghai, 200135, China. TEL 86-21-58856638 ext 2219, FAX 86-21-58522151.

387 CHN ISSN 1672-9498
SHANGHAI HAISHI DAXUE XUEBAO/SHANGHAI MARITIME UNIVERSITY. JOURNAL. Text in Chinese. 1979. q. CNY 10 newsstand/cover (effective 2006). **Document type:** *Journal, Academic/Scholarly.*
Formerly (until 2003): Shanghai Haiyun Xueyuan Xuebao (Wenli Zonghe Ban) (1000-5188)
Related titles: Online - full text ed.
Indexed: A28, APA, BrCerAb, C&ISA, CA/WCA, CIA, CerAb, CivEngAb, CorrAb, E&CAJ, E11, EEA, EMA, ESPM, EnvEAb, H15, M&TEA, M09, MBF, METADEX, SCOPUS, SolStAb, T04, WAA.
Published by: Shanghai Haishi Daxue/Shanghai Maritime University, 1550 Pudong Dadao, Shanghai, 200135, China. TEL 86-21-38820091. Ed. Wan-You Huang.

387 CHN ISSN 1006-7728
HE561
➤ **SHIJIE HAIYUN/WORLD SHIPPING.** Text in Chinese. 1978. m. (bi-m. until 2009). CNY 192, USD 120; CNY 16 per issue (effective 2010 & 2011). **Document type:** *Journal, Academic/Scholarly.*
Related titles: Online - full text ed.
—East View.
Published by: Dalian Haishi Daxue Qikanshe, 7, Gangwan St., Rm.401, Times Bldg., Dalian, 116001, China. TEL 86-411-82550880, FAX 86-411-82550889. Ed. Yue-hui Wang. Circ: 3,000.

387 GBR ISSN 0037-3834
VM320
SHIP & BOAT INTERNATIONAL. Text in English. 1937. bi-m. GBP 92 domestic to non-members; GBP 97 in Europe to non-members; GBP 110 elsewhere to non-members; GBP 23 to members (effective 2009). adv. bk.rev. charts; illus.; mkt.; pat.; stat.; tr.lit.; tr.mk. back issues avail. **Document type:** *Journal, Trade.* **Description:** Covers all aspects of the workboat, small craft and small ship industry worldwide.
Incorporates (1981-1989): Small Craft; Former titles (until 1969): Ship and Boat; (until 1968): Ship and Boat Builder International; (until 1964): Ship and Boat Builder and Marine Trader; (until 1960): Ship and Boat Builder and Naval Architect
Related titles: Online - full text ed.
Indexed: A22, BMT, E11, SCOPUS, SPPI, T04.
—BLDSC (8258.550000), IE, Infotrieve, Ingenta, Linda Hall. **CCC.**
Published by: Royal Institution of Naval Architects, 10 Upper Belgrave St, London, SW1X 8BQ, United Kingdom. TEL 44-20-72354622, FAX 44-20-72595912, publications@rina.org.uk. Ed. Angela Velasco. Adv. contact Donna McGrath.

623.81 GBR ISSN 0969-0174
SHIP REPAIR AND CONVERSION TECHNOLOGY. Text in English. 1989. q. GBP 41 domestic to non-members; GBP 46 in Europe to non-members; GBP 51 elsewhere to non-members; GBP 15 to members (effective 2009). adv. **Document type:** *Magazine, Trade.* **Description:** Covers all aspects of repair and conversion work ranging from fishing vessels and workboats to cruise liners, ferries, container ships and supertankers.
Related titles: Online - full text ed.
Indexed: BMT, FLUIDEX, GEOBASE, RefZh, SCOPUS.
—IE. **CCC.**
Published by: Royal Institution of Naval Architects, 10 Upper Belgrave St, London, SW1X 8BQ, United Kingdom. TEL 44-20-72354622, FAX 44-20-72595912, publications@rina.org.uk. Ed. Clive Woodbridge. Adv. contact Rosemary Little.

387.2 ZAF ISSN 1996-7446
SHIP SHAPE. Text in English. 2006. a. adv.
Published by: (South African Oil and Gas Alliance), Red Ink Media, 156 Main Rd, Muizenberg, 7945, South Africa. TEL 27-21-7885698, FAX 27-21-7884506, http://www.redinkmedia.co.za. adv.: color page ZAR 19,500.

338.476238 GBR ISSN 1362-7198
THE SHIP SUPPLIER. Text in English. 1997. q. free to members (effective 2009). adv. back issues avail. **Document type:** *Magazine, Trade.* **Description:** Provides latest ship supply news and information from around the world.
—**CCC.**
Published by: (International Shipsuppliers & Services Association), Elaborate Communications Ltd., Acorn Farm Business Ctr, Cublington Rd, Wing, Leighton Buzzard, LU7 0LB, United Kingdom. TEL 44-1296-682051, FAX 44-1296-682156, sales@elaborate.co.uk, http://www.elabor8.co.uk. Ed. Spencer Eade. Pub. Sean Moloney. adv.: color page GBP 2,000; trim 210 x 297. Circ: 5,605.

623.8 ZAF ISSN 1029-1865
SHIP YEAR. Text in English. 1998. a. adv.
Published by: (South African Institute of Marine Engineers and Naval Architects), Cape Media Corporation, Sanclare Bldg, 4th Flr, 21 Dreyer St, Claremont, Cape Town 7735, South Africa. TEL 27-21-6573800, FAX 27-21-6573866, info@capemedia.co.za. Ed. Kenny MacNeill. adv.: page ZAR 19,800; trim 210 x 275. Circ: 10,000.

387 SWE ISSN 2000-169X
▼ **SHIPGAZ.** Text in English. 2009. bi-m. adv. back issues avail. **Document type:** *Magazine, Trade.*
Related titles: Online - full text ed.; ◆ English ed.: Sjoefartstidningen. ISSN 2000-933X.
Published by: Svensk Sjoefarts Tidnings Foerlag AB, Soedra Hamngatan 53, PO Box 370, Goeteborg, 40125, Sweden. TEL 46-31-7121750, FAX 46-31-802750, info@shipgaz.com. Ed. Rolf Nilsson TEL 46-31-7121765. Adv. contact Lars Adrians TEL 46-31-629571. page EUR 2,150; 213 x 297.

THE SHIPPER ADVOCATE. *see* TRANSPORTATION—Trucks And Trucking

387 HKG ISSN 1561-1175
SHIPPERS TODAY. Text in Chinese, English. 1977. bi-m. HKD 120 domestic; USD 35 foreign (effective 2000). adv. bk.rev. back issues avail. **Document type:** *Journal, Trade.* **Description:** Covers international trade and transportation topics of interest to shippers in Hong Kong.
Indexed: HongKongiana.
Published by: Hong Kong Shippers Council, Rm 2407, Hopewell Centre, 183 Queen's Rd E, Wanchai, Hong Kong. TEL 852-2834-0010, FAX 852-2891-9787, http://www.hkshippers.org.hk. Ed. Gina Giron Urquiola. Pub., R&P Sunny Ho. Adv. contact Czarina Shum. Circ: 6,000.

▼ **SHIPPING.** *see* LAW—Corporate Law

387 910.09 GRC
SHIPPING AND TOURISM. Text in Greek. 1991. a. adv. **Document type:** *Trade.*
Related titles: ◆ Supplement to: Epilogi. ISSN 1105-2503.
Published by: Electra Press, 4 Stadiou St, Athens, 105 64, Greece. TEL 30-1-3233-303, FAX 30-1-3255-160. Ed. Christos Papaioannou. Circ: 9,000.

387 382 JPN
SHIPPING AND TRADE NEWS. Text in English. 1949. d. (plus m. special issues). JPY 42,900. **Document type:** *Newspaper.*
Published by: Tokyo Nyusu Tsushinsha/Tokyo News Service Ltd., Tsukiji Hamarikyu Bldg 10th Fl, 3-3 Tsuki-Ji 5-chome, Chuo-ku, Tokyo, 104-8004, Japan. TEL 03-3542-8521. Ed. Chiaki Sakurai. Circ: 15,000.

387 GBR
HE603
SHIPPING FINANCE REVIEW (YEAR). Text in English. 1993. a. GBP 245, EUR 325, USD 425 per issue (print or online ed.) (effective 2010). back issues avail. **Document type:** *Directory, Trade.* **Description:** Covers all financial aspects of ships and shipping, profiling more than 900 companies active in the marketplace.
Formerly (until 2006): Shipping Finance Annual (0969-9635)
Related titles: Online - full text ed.
—**CCC.**
Published by: Euromoney Institutional Investor Plc., Nestor House, Playhouse Yard, London, EC4V 5EX, United Kingdom. TEL 44-20-77798673, information@euromoneyplc.com. Ed. Adrian Hornbrook.

387 JPN ISSN 0037-3915
SHIPPING GAZETTE; weekly of shipping schedules and news digest. Text in English, Japanese. 1951. w. JPY 24,000 (effective 2000). adv.
Published by: Japan Press, Ltd., C.P.O. Box 6, Tokyo, 100-8691, Japan. TEL 81-3-3404-5151, FAX 81-3-3404-5152. Ed. Yoshio Wada. Adv. contact M Oish. Circ: 15,000. **Subscr. to:** 2-12-8 Kita-Aoyama, Minato-ku, Tokyo 107-0061, Japan.

387 NLD ISSN 1872-2482
SHIPPING INDUSTRY ALMANAC. Text in English. 199?. a.
Published by: (Ernst & Young, International Shipping Group), Ernst & Young Nederland, Postbus 488, Rotterdam, 3000 AL, Netherlands. TEL 31-10-4068888, FAX 31-10-4065351, http://www.ey.nl.

387 GBR ISSN 1358-8028
SHIPPING INTELLIGENCE WEEKLY. Abbreviated title: S I W. Text in English. 1992. w. GBP 700, USD 1,260 (effective 2011). adv. charts; stat. **Document type:** *Report, Trade.* **Description:** Covers reports on developments across the range of shipping markets.
Related titles: Online - full text ed.: ISSN 1741-3303.
Published by: Clarkson Research Services Ltd., St Magnus House, 3 Lower Thames St, London, EC3R 6HE, United Kingdom. TEL 44-20-73343134, FAX 44-20-75220330, sales@crsl.com.

387 USA
SHIPPING INTERNATIONAL; the maritime net magazine. Text in English. 1995. w. **Document type:** *Magazine, Trade.* **Description:** Publishes news and press releases about the international maritime shipping industry.
Media: Online - full content.
Published by: Ship Publishing Group, 10515 Pearl Drive, Houston, TX 77064. TEL 281-897-0660, FAX 281-897-0662, publisher@shipint.com, http://www.shipint.com.

387 GBR ISSN 1360-8061
SHIPPING REVIEW & OUTLOOK. Abbreviated title: S R O. Text in English. 1994. s-a. GBP 450 (effective 2011); USD 810 (effective 2009). adv. stat. **Document type:** *Catalog, Trade.* **Description:** Aims to analyzes developments in 16 shipping industry market segments, includes a comprehensive time-series statistical section.
Related titles: Online - full text ed.: ISSN 1743-7296.
Published by: Clarkson Research Services Ltd., St Magnus House, 3 Lower Thames St, London, EC3R 6HE, United Kingdom. TEL 44-20-73343134, FAX 44-20-75220330, sales@crsl.com.

SHIPPING STATISTICS AND MARKET REVIEW. *see* TRANSPORTATION—Abstracting, Bibliographies, Statistics

SHIPPING STATISTICS YEARBOOK. *see* TRANSPORTATION—Abstracting, Bibliographies, Statistics

387 GBR ISSN 0958-7683
SHIPPING - TODAY AND YESTERDAY. Variant title: Shipping T&Y. Text in English. 1990. m. GBP 37 domestic; GBP 52 in Europe; GBP 68 elsewhere (effective 2009). adv. back issues avail. **Document type:** *Magazine, Consumer.* **Description:** Covers many aspects of sea transport including ocean liners, ferries, merchant ships and docks and ports around the world.
Published by: H P C Publishing, Drury Ln, St Leonards-on-Sea, E Sussex TN38 9BJ, United Kingdom. TEL 44-1424-205530, FAX 44-1424-443693, http://www.hpcpublishing.com. Ed. Nigel Lawrence. Pub. Derek Knoll. Adv. contact Rosemary Beckwith TEL 44-1825-766597. **Dist. by:** Seymour Distribution Ltd.

623.82 GBR ISSN 0037-3931
CODEN: SWSBA5
SHIPPING WORLD & SHIPBUILDER. Abbreviated title: S W & S. Text in English. 1883. 10/yr. GBP 78 (effective 2009). adv. bk.rev. illus. reprints avail. **Document type:** *Journal, Trade.* **Description:** Provides invaluable insight into the complete maritime environment, and is read by key players such as shipowners, operators and managers, shipbuilders, naval architects, insurers and fleet managers.
Formerly (until 1964): Shipping World; Incorporates (1931-1964): Shipbuilder and Marine Engine-Builder; Which was formerly (1906-1930): Shipbuilder; Which incorporated (1904-1906): Mid-Tyne Link
Related titles: Microform ed.: (from PQC).
Indexed: A22, A28, APA, ASFA, ApMecR, BMT, BrCerAb, BrTechI, C&ISA, CA/WCA, CIA, CISA, CerAb, CivEngAb, CorrAb, E&CAJ, E11, EEA, EMA, ESPM, EngInd, EnvEAb, H15, HRIS, KES, M&TEA, M09, MBF, METADEX, OceAb, RefZh, SCOPUS, SolStAb, T04, WAA, WSCA.
—BLDSC (8263.300000), IE, Infotrieve, Ingenta, Linda Hall.
Published by: Institute of Marine Engineering, Science and Technology, 80 Coleman St, London, EC2R 5BJ, United Kingdom. TEL 44-20-73822600, FAX 44-20-73822670, info@imarest.org, http://www.imarest.org/. Ed. Patrick Wheater. Pub. John Butchers. adv.: page GBP 2,840; trim 210 x 297. Circ: 5,982.

387 623.8 AUS
SHIPS AND BOATS ON ORDER. Text in English. m. free (effective 2010); includes Australia and the Sea. charts; illus. **Document type:** *Directory, Trade.* **Description:** Provides details of recently delivered vessels, newbuilding orders announced by shipyards around the world, and contact details of ship and boat builders.
Media: Online - full text.
Published by: Baird Publications Pty. Ltd., 135 Sturt St, South Bank, Melbourne, VIC 3006, Australia. TEL 61-3-96450411, FAX 61-3-96450475, marinfo@baird.com.au, http://www.baird.com.au. Eds. Steven Kelleher, Neil Baird.

623.8 GBR ISSN 1744-5302
➤ **SHIPS AND OFFSHORE STRUCTURES.** Text in English. 2006. q. GBP 463 combined subscription in United Kingdom to institutions (print & online eds.); EUR 702, USD 880 combined subscription to institutions (print & online eds.) (effective 2012). reprint service avail. from PSC. **Document type:** *Journal, Trade.* **Description:** Covers the entire range of issues and technologies related to both ships and offshore structures, with a strong emphasis on practical design, construction and operation.
Related titles: Online - full text ed.: ISSN 1754-212X. GBP 416 in United Kingdom to institutions; EUR 632, USD 792 to institutions (effective 2012) (from IngentaConnect).
Indexed: A22, ASFA, C10, CA, CPEI, CurCont, E01, E14, Inspec, OceAb, P26, P48, P52, P54, P56, PQC, PetrolAb, SCI, T02, W07.
—BLDSC (8266.077550), IE, PADDS. **CCC.**
Published by: Taylor & Francis Ltd. (Subsidiary of: Taylor & Francis Group), 4 Park Sq, Milton Park, Abingdon, Oxfordshire OX14 4RN, United Kingdom. TEL 44-20-70176000, FAX 44-20-70176336, subscriptions@tandf.co.uk. Ed. Jeon Kee Paik.

387 AUS
SHIPS AND SHIPPING. Text in English. m. AUD 175, USD 175, GBP 115, EUR 130 (effective Jul. 2010).
Formed by the 2006 merger of: World Shipbuilding; (2000-2006): Asia Pacific Shipping (1444-4976); Which was formed by the merger of (1978-2001): Asian Shipping; (1988-2001): Australasian Ships & Ports (1032-3449)
Published by: Baird Publications Pty. Ltd., 135 Sturt St, South Bank, Melbourne, VIC 3006, Australia. TEL 61-3-96450411, FAX 61-3-96450475, http://www.baird.com.au.

387 USA ISSN 1052-6862
G521
SHIPS & SHIPWRECKS. Text in English. 1990. bi-m. USD 24. bk.rev. **Document type:** *Newsletter.*
Published by: Riderwood Publishing Co., 5049 Smith Rd, Rohrersville, MD 21779-1039. TEL 301-432-4815. Ed. Lynn K Sibley.

387 GBR
THE SHIPS ATLAS. Text in English. 1984. biennial, latest 13th ed. GBP 140 per vol. (effective 2010). maps. **Document type:** *Directory, Trade.* **Description:** Contains port information listed in over 70 headings, including a general port description, pre-arrival information, maximum size of vessel, health, safety and security, communications, berthing location and operations, cargo ports facilities, shore facilities, pollution and local information.
Published by: Shipping Guides Ltd., 28 Reigate Hill, Reigate, Surrey RH2 9NG, United Kingdom. TEL 44-1737-242255, FAX 44-1737-222449, info@portinfo.co.uk.

387 GBR ISSN 0037-394X
VM1
SHIPS MONTHLY; the international magazine for shiplovers ashore and afloat. Text in English. 1966. m. GBP 47.40 domestic; GBP 70.10 in Europe; GBP 81.64 elsewhere; GBP 3.80 newsstand/cover (effective 2009). adv. bk.rev. charts; illus.; stat. index. back issues avail. **Document type:** *Magazine, Consumer.* **Description:** Features articles regarding the history of ships and their use today as well as readers' letters.
Indexed: A22.
—BLDSC (8266.150000), IE, Ingenta.
Published by: I P C Country & Leisure Media Ltd. (Subsidiary of: I P C Media Ltd.), 222 Branston Rd, Burton-on-Trent, DE14 3BT, United Kingdom. TEL 44-1283-542721, FAX 44-1283-546436, http://www.ipcmedia.com. Ed. Iain Wakefield TEL 44-1283-542741. Pub. Jake Cassels TEL 44-20-31484286. Adv. contact Susan Philo TEL 44-1367-820181. B&W page GBP 430, color page GBP 650; 188 x 267. Circ: 18,000. **Dist. by:** MarketForce UK Ltd, The Blue Fin Bldg, 3rd Fl, 110 Southwark St, London SE1 0SU, United Kingdom. TEL 44-20-31483300, FAX 44-20-31488105, salesinnovation@marketforce.co.uk, http://www.marketforce.co.uk/.

387.54 GBR
SHIPS' ROUTEING. Text in English. 19??. irreg., latest 2008. GBP 110 per issue (print or online ed.) (effective 2009). **Document type:** *Directory, Trade.*
Related titles: CD-ROM ed.; Online - full text ed.
Published by: International Maritime Organization/Organisation Maritime Internationale, 4 Albert Embankment, London, SE1 7SR, United Kingdom. TEL 44-20-77357611, FAX 44-20-75873210, info@imo.org, http://www.imo.org/.

SHIPYARD & I M F LOG. (Intermediate Maintenance Facility) *see* MILITARY

623.82 USA
SHIPYARD BULLETIN. Text in English. 1927. m. free. **Description:** Includes news on company business as well as employee features.
Published by: Newport News Shipbuilding, Newport, VA 23607. TEL 804-380-2342, FAX 804-380-3867. Ed. Pam Curley. Circ: 30,000 (controlled).

387 USA ISSN 1061-9224
SHIPYARD CHRONICLE. Text in English. 1975. bi-m. bk.rev. stat. **Document type:** *Newsletter.* **Description:** Contains news and opinions related to shipbuilding and repair.
Formerly: Shipyard Weekly
Published by: Shipbuilders Council of America, 1455 F Street NW, Suite 225, Washington, DC 20005. TEL 202-347-5462, FAX 202-347-5464, http://www.shipbuilders.org/. Ed. Franklin W Losey. Circ: 1,200.

359.97 CAN ISSN 1206-5676
SHORELINES. Text in English. 1997. s-a.
Published by: Canadian Coast Guard, Pacific Region, 401 Burrard St, Suite 200, Vancouver, BC V6C 3S4, Canada. TEL 604-775-8809, FAX 604-666-1847. Ed. Dan Bate TEL 604-666-0384.

387 CHN ISSN 1672-0156
SHUISHANG XIAOFANG/MARINE FIRE. Text in Chinese. 1981. m.
Formerly (until 2002): Hanghai Keji Dongtai/Marine Technical News and Trends (1000-4688)
Published by: Zhongguo Shuishang Xiaofang Xiehui, 4053, Jungong Lu, Shanghai, 200438, China. TEL 86-21-51185291, FAX 86-21-65321951. **Co-sponsor:** Shanghai Chuanbo Yunshu Kexue Yanjiusuo/Shanghai Ship and Shipping Research Institute.

387 658 CHN ISSN 1000-8799
SHUIYUN GUANLI/WATER TRANSPORTATION MANAGEMENT. Text in Chinese. 1979. m. CNY 108 (effective 2006). **Document type:** *Journal, Academic/Scholarly.*
Related titles: Online - full text ed.
Published by: Shanghai Haishi Daxue/Shanghai Maritime University, 1550 Pudong Dadao, Shanghai, 200135, China. TEL 86-21-58855200 ext 4041, FAX 86-21-58218976.

SIGNALS. *see* MUSEUMS AND ART GALLERIES

387 SGP
SINGAPORE MARITIME DIRECTORY (YEAR). Text in English. a. USD 40 per issue (effective 2008). adv. **Document type:** *Directory.* **Description:** Shipping directory contains in-depth editorial coverage of the dynamic port of Singapore and a comprehensive listing of companies concerned with shipping and maritime as well as those in the supporting industries.
Related titles: Online - full text ed.
Published by: Marshall Cavendish Business Information Pty. Ltd. (Subsidiary of: Times Publishing Group), Times Centre, 1 New Industrial Rd, Singapore, 536196, Singapore. TEL 65-6213-9288, FAX 65-6285-0161, bizinfo@sg.marshallcavendish.com, http://www.marshallcavendish.com/.

387 GBR ISSN 2040-9796
▼ **SINGAPORE SHIPPING REPORT.** Text in English. 2009. q. USD 975, EUR 695 combined subscription (print & email eds.) (effective 2011). **Document type:** *Report, Trade.* **Description:** Provides industry professionals and strategists, sector analysts, business investors, trade associations and regulatory bodies with independent forecasts and competitive intelligence on the shipping industry in Singapore.
Related titles: Online - full text ed.
Published by: Business Monitor International Ltd., Senator House, 85 Queen Victoria St, London, EC4V 4AB, United Kingdom. TEL 44-20-72480468, FAX 44-20-72480467, subs@businessmonitor.com.

SINGAPORE SHIPREPAIRING, SHIPBUILDING & OFFSHORE INDUSTRIES DIRECTORY. *see* BUSINESS AND ECONOMICS—Trade And Industrial Directories

623.8 SWE ISSN 1650-2353
SJOEBEFAEL. Text in Swedish; Section in English. 1891. 8/yr. SEK 200 (effective 2004). adv. bk.rev. charts; illus. index. 32 p./no. 2 cols./p.; **Document type:** *Journal, Trade.* **Description:** Technical and trade magazine for Swedish marine engineers and other ship officers.
Former titles (until 2000): Maskinbefaelet (0025-4622); (until 1944): Maskinbefaelsfoerbundets Tidskrift; (until 1928): Tidskrift foer Maskinister
Published by: (Svenska Maskinbefaelsfoerbundet/Swedish Engineer Officers' Association), Sjoebefaelsfoerbundet, PO Box 12100, Stockholm, 10223, Sweden. TEL 46-8-59899106, FAX 46-8-6510848. Ed. Benkt Lundgren TEL 46-859899121. Adv. contact Ankie Nilsson TEL 46-739861649. B&W page SEK 6,070, color page SEK 12,760; trim 185 x 262. Circ: 4,300 (controlled).

387.9 070.5 NOR ISSN 0080-9888
➤ **SJOEFARTSHISTORISK AARBOK/NORWEGIAN YEARBOOK OF MARITIME HISTORY.** Text in Norwegian; Summaries in English. 1928. a. NOK 290 domestic membership; NOK 340 foreign membership (effective 2011). adv. charts; illus. back issues avail. **Document type:** *Report, Academic/Scholarly.*
Formerly (until 1965): Foreningen "Bergens Sjoefartsmuseum". Aarshefte (0802-5843)
Indexed: HistAb, RASB.
Published by: Stiftelsen Bergens Sjoefartsmuseum/Bergen Maritime Museum, PO Box 7800, Bergen, 5020, Norway. TEL 47-55-549600, FAX 47-55-549610, venneforeningen@bsj.uib.no, bergenssjofartsmuseum@bsj.uib.no, http://www.bsj.uib.no.

387 SWE ISSN 2000-933X
VK4 CODEN: SSTIF8
SJOEFARTSTIDNINGEN/SCANDINAVIAN SHIPPING GAZETTE. Text in English, Swedish. 1905. 11/yr. SEK 750; SEK 795 combined subscription domestic to individuals (inc. Shipgaz); SEK 1,270 combined subscription in Europe (inc. Shipgaz); SEK 1,550 combined subscription domestic to institutions (inc. Shipgaz); SEK 2,025 combined subscription in Europe (inc. Shipgaz) (effective 2010). adv. bk.rev. illus. index. back issues avail. **Document type:** *Magazine, Trade.* **Description:** Scandinavian and international shipping, shipbuilding and associated industries.
Formerly (until 2011): Svensk Sjoefartstidning (0039-6702)
Related titles: Online - full text ed.; ◆ English ed.: Shipgaz. ISSN 2000-169X.
Indexed: BMT.
Published by: Svensk Sjoefartstidnings Foerlag AB, Soedra Hamngatan 53, PO Box 370, Goeteborg, 40125, Sweden. TEL 46-31-7121750, FAX 46-31-802750, info@shipgaz.com, http://www.shipgaz.com. Ed. Rolf Nilsson TEL 46-31-7121765. Adv. contact Lars Adrians TEL 46-31-629571.

362.6 ISL
SJOMANNADAGSBLADID. Text in Icelandic. 1938. a. ISK 450 (effective 1992). back issues avail. **Description:** Devoted to the interests of seamen, their life and work.
Published by: (Sjomannadagsrad), Seamen's Welfare Organization, Hrafnista D A S, Reykjavik, 104, Iceland. TEL 354-553-8465. Circ: 4,500.

387 DNK ISSN 0900-9132
SKIPPEREN. Text in Danish. 1910. m. adv. **Document type:** *Magazine, Trade.*
Formerly (until 1943): Medlemsblad for Dansk Sejlskibsredeeriforening
Published by: Rederiforeningen for Mindre Skibe/Shipowners Association for Smaller Vessels, c/o Danmarks Rederiforening, Amaliegade 33, Copenhagen K, 1256, Denmark. TEL 45-33-114088, FAX 45-33-116210, info@shipowners.dk, http://www.danmarksrederiforening.dk, http://www.shipowners.dk.

387 NOR
SKIPSFARTENS INNKJOEPSBOK. (Published in 2 volumes) Text mainly in Norwegian. 1960. a. adv. **Document type:** *Catalog, Consumer.* **Description:** Listing of suppliers and their products to the shipping and off shore industry.
Published by: Instituttet for Merkantil Informasjon AS, Ranviksvingen 7C, Sandefjord, 3212, Norway. TEL 47-33-612414, imi@imi.no, http://www.imi.no.

387.2 623.8 NOR ISSN 0800-2282
SKIPSREVYEN. Text mainly in Norwegian. 1978. bi-m. NOK 890 domestic; NOK 990 elsewhere (effective 2007). adv. index. back issues avail. **Document type:** *Newspaper, Trade.*
Incorporates (1926-1986): Skipsnytt (0332-558X); Which was formerly: Skipsteknikk (0037-6361); (until 1977): Skandinavisk Smaaskipsfart (0332-5342); (until 1970): Smaaskipsfart (0037-7171); (until 1963): Skibsfart (0333-2179)
Related titles: Online - full text ed.
Indexed: BMT.
Published by: Skipsrevyen AS, PO Box 34, Nyborg, Bergen, 5871, Norway. TEL 47-55-197770, FAX 47-55-197780. Eds. Jan Einar Zachariassen, Asle B. Stroenen. Adv. contact Per Haukedal. page NOK 23,700. Circ: 10,000.

387 623.89 NOR ISSN 0809-6287
SKVAERRIGGERNE. Text in Norwegian. 2005. **Document type:** *Magazine, Consumer.* **Description:** Magazine featuring the 3 former Norwegian training ships, the Christian Radich, the Staatsraad Lehmkuhl and the Soerlandet.
Published by: Stiftelsen Skoleskipet Christian Radich, Akershusstrande, Skur 32, PO Box 666, Sentrum, Oslo, 0106, Norway. TEL 47-22-478270, FAX 47-22-478271, postmaster@radich.no, http://www.radich.no.

387.2 NLD ISSN 1386-3797
SLEEP & DUWVAART. Text in Dutch. 1986. bi-m. EUR 44 domestic; EUR 70 in Europe; EUR 105 elsewhere (effective 2010). adv. bk.rev. **Document type:** *Consumer.*
Formerly (until 1997): Sleepboot (0921-8033)
Published by: Stichting tot Behoud van Authentieke Stoomvaartuigen en Motorsleepboten, PO Box 190, Wormerveer, 1520 AD, Netherlands. TEL 31-6-22516238, FAX 31-75-6420536, basmbehoud@xs4all.nl, htpp://www.sleepduwvaart.nl.

387 USA
SOCIETY OF MARITIME ARBITRATORS. AWARD SERVICE. Text in English. 1965. a. USD 495. **Document type:** *Journal, Trade.*
Published by: Society of Maritime Arbitrators, Inc., 30 Broad St, 7th Fl, New York, NY 10004. TEL 212-587-0033, FAX 212-587-6179. Circ: 300.

623.8 USA ISSN 0081-1661
VM1 CODEN: SNAMAL
SOCIETY OF NAVAL ARCHITECTS AND MARINE ENGINEERS. TRANSACTIONS. Text in English. 1893. a. index. **Document type:** *Proceedings, Academic/Scholarly.* **Description:** Contains papers and annual reports presented at the Society of Naval Architects and Marine Engineers's annual meeting, including certain award-winning technical papers.
Indexed: BMT, CLT&T, CPEI, EngInd, PetrolAb, SCOPUS.
—Ingenta, INIST, Linda Hall.
Published by: The Society of Naval Architects and Marine Engineers, 601 Pavonia Ave, Jersey City, NJ 07306. TEL 201-798-4800, 800-798-2188, FAX 201-798-4975, tfaix@sname.org, http://www.sname.org.

387 DNK ISSN 0038-0520
SOEFART; Danmarks maritime fagblad. Text in Danish. 1950. 40/yr. DKK 950 print ed.; DKK 713 to students print ed.; DKK 1,125 combined subscription print & online eds. (effective 2009). adv. bk.rev. charts; illus. **Document type:** *Trade.*
Incorporates (1972-1985): Position (0900-5609)
Related titles: Online - full text ed.
Published by: Foreningen til Soefartens Fremme/Association for the Promotion of the Danish Merchant Marine, Amaliegade 33 B, Copenhagen K, 1256, Denmark. TEL 45-33-327933, FAX 45-33-327938, info@soefart-frem.dk, http://www.soefart-frem.dk. Ed. Erik Brandt-Jensen TEL 45-86-205893. Adv. contact Kim E Thoegersen TEL 45-86-205899. B&W page DKK 27,850, color page DKK 29,450; 253 x 350.

387 623.89 DNK ISSN 1901-4899
SOEFARTENS LEDERE. Text in Danish; Summaries in English. 1907. 10/yr. DKK 500 (effective 2009). adv. bk.rev. index. back issues avail. **Document type:** *Magazine, Trade.*
Former titles (until 2006): Navigatoer (0902-7076); Which incorporated (1967-1991): Dansk Skibsfart (0901-361X); Which incorporated (1980-1989): Coasterfarten (0107-4814); Navigatoer was formerly (until 1986): Navigatoer Nyt (0107-4806); (until 1980): Nyt Navigatoer, Navigatoer Nyt (0900-3495)
Related titles: Online - full text ed.: ISSN 1901-5674.

Address: Havnegade 55, Copenhagen K, 1058, Denmark. TEL 45-33-455565, FAX 45-33-455566, mail@soefartens.org. Ed. Per O Frederiksen. Adv. contact Peter Friis Jespersen. page DKK 12,225; 210 x 297. Circ: 5,936 (controlled).

387 DNK ISSN 1901-8657
SOEFARTSSTYRELSEN. AARSRAPPORT. Text in Danish. 1997. a. back issues avail. **Document type:** *Government.*
Former titles (until 2004): Soefartsstyrelsen. Virksomhedsregnskab (1399-2708); (until 1999): Soefartsstyrelsens Virksomhedsregnskab (1398-5035); (until 1998): Soefartsstyrelsen. Virksomhedsregnskab og -Beretning (1397-5145)
Related titles: Online - full text ed.: ISSN 1901-8665. 2004.
Published by: Soefartsstyrelsen/Danish Maritime Authority, Vermundsgade 38 C, Copenhagen OE, 2100, Denmark. TEL 45-39-174400, FAX 45-39-174401, sfs@dma.dk, http://www.dma.dk.

SOEHESTEN. *see* WOMEN'S INTERESTS

387.009489 DNK ISSN 0107-6647
SOEHISTORISKE SKRIFTER. Text in Danish, English. 1947. irreg., latest vol.25, 2009. price varies. back issues avail. **Document type:** *Monographic series, Academic/Scholarly.*
Published by: Handels- og Soefartsmuseet paa Kronborg, Helsingoer, 3000, Denmark. TEL 45-49-210685, FAX 45-49-213440, info@maritime-museum.dk, http://www.maritime-museum.dk.

SOLAS - INTERNATIONAL CONVENTION FOR THE SAFETY OF LIFE AT SEA. AMENDMENTS. *see* ENVIRONMENTAL STUDIES—Toxicology And Environmental Safety

SOUNDINGS (MILWAUKEE). *see* HISTORY—History Of North And South America

387 ARG
SOUTH AMERICAN PORTS HANDBOOK. Text in English. 1974. biennial. USD 80. illus.
Formerly (until 1976): Owners, Masters, Brokers and Agents Handbook on South American Caribbean and Pacific Ports in Venezuela, Colombia, Panama, Ecuador, Peru, Bolivia and Chile
Published by: Agencia Maritima Internacional S.A., 25 de Mayo 555, Piso 20, Buenos Aires, 1002, Argentina. FAX 54-114-3131996, TELEX 21115. Circ: 1,500.

387.1 GBR
SOUTH WALES PORTS TIDES TABLES. Text in English. 19??. a. GBP 4.30 per issue (effective 2009). **Document type:** *Bulletin, Trade.*
Published by: Associated British Ports (Cardiff) (Subsidiary of: Associated British Ports Holdings PLC), Queen Alexandra House, Cargo Rd, Cardiff, CF10 4LY, United Kingdom. TEL 44-870-6096699, severnvts@abports.co.uk. Circ: 5,000.

387 ZAF
HE561
SOUTHERN AFRICAN SHIPPING NEWS. Variant title: S.A. Shipping News. Text in English. 1946-1983; resumed. bi-m. ZAR 106 domestic; ZAR 166 in Namibia (effective 2003). adv. bk.rev. charts; illus.; tr.lit. **Document type:** *Magazine, Trade.* **Description:** Provides a forum within the industry by publishing stories on a wide range of marine related topics such as news and features on ships, cargoes, ports, marine engineering, ship building, repairs and maintenance, ship service facilities, marine exploration and exploitation, as well as maritime law and insurance.
Incorporated: South African Shipping News and Fishing Industry Review (0038-2671)
Indexed: BMT, CLT&T, HRIS, ISAP.
—Linda Hall.
Published by: George Warman Publications (Pty.) Ltd., Rondebosch, PO Box 705, Cape Town, 7701, South Africa. TEL 27-21-6892640, FAX 27-21-6893408, info@gwarmanpublications.co.za, http://www.gwarmanpublications.co.za. Ed. Colleen Jacka. Circ: 1,150.

387 USA ISSN 1054-7150
HE554.J3
SOUTHERN SHIPPER. Text in English. 1952. m. included in subscr. to American Shipper. adv. reprints avail. **Document type:** *Magazine, Trade.*
Former titles (until 1991): Seafarer (0882-7788); (until 1984): Jacksonville Seafarer (0447-2462); Which was Incorporated: Jacksonville Port Handbook (0160-2241); Miami Port Handbook; South Florida Ports Handbook; Georgia Port Handbook; Savannah Port Handbook
Related titles: Microform ed.: 1952 (from PQC); ◆ Supplement to: American Shipper. ISSN 1074-8350.
Indexed: P06.
Published by: Howard Publications (Subsidiary of: Lee Enterprises, Inc.), 300 W Adams St, Ste 600, Jacksonville, FL 32201. TEL 904-355-2601, FAX 904-791-8836, publisher@shippers.com, http://www.americanshipper.com. Ed. Joseph A Bonney. Circ: 7,321.

623.82 GBR ISSN 1464-1046
SOVIET MARITIME NEWSLETTER. Text in English. m. GBP 195 (effective 2000). adv. **Document type:** *Newsletter, Trade.*
Published by: Marine Publications International Ltd., The Orchard, Elvetham Ln, Hartley Wintney, Hants RG27 8AJ, United Kingdom. TEL 44-1256-840444, FAX 44-1256-817877, info@drydock.co.uk. Ed. Derek Deere. Pub. Andrew Deere. Adv. contact Helen Read.

STAYING AT A LIGHTHOUSE; America's romantic and historic lighthouse inns. *see* TRAVEL AND TOURISM

STEAMBOATING; steamboater's handbook. *see* SPORTS AND GAMES—Boats And Boating

387.2 NLD ISSN 1875-0265
STOOMSCHIP VEREENIGING. Text in Dutch. 2007. s-a.
Published by: Vriendenkring Stoomschip Vereeniging, Oldewierde 114, Almere, 1353 HN, Netherlands. TEL 31-36-5310673, info@stoomschipvereeniging.nl, http://www.stoomschipvereeniging.nl. Eds. Bert van der Weijde, Dirk Vlaar.

387.164029 DEU ISSN 0934-6260
STOWAGE AND SEGREGATION GUIDE TO I M D G CODE. Text in German. 1973. a. EUR 249 (effective 2006). **Document type:** *Directory, Trade.*
Formerly (until 1981): Stowage and Segregation to I M D G Code (0172-8660)
Published by: K.O. Storck Verlag, Striepenweg 31, Hamburg, 21147, Germany. TEL 49-40-7971301, FAX 49-40-79713101, webmaster@storck-verlag.de, http://www.storck-verlag.de. Ed. H Meder.

387 UKR
SUDOKHODSTVO. Text in Ukrainian. 8/yr. USD 180 in United States.
Address: Per Sabanskii 1-10, Odessa, Ukraine. TEL 380-482-226319, FAX 380-42-25-0966. **Dist. by:** East View Information Services, 10601 Wayzata Blvd, Minneapolis, MN 55305. TEL 952-252-1201, 800-477-1005, FAX 952-252-1202, info@eastview.com, http://www.eastview.com.

623.8 RUS ISSN 0039-4580
CODEN: SUDOAN
SUDOSTROENIE/SHIPBUILDING. Text in Russian; Contents page in English. 1898. bi-m. USD 120 foreign (effective 2005). bibl.; charts; illus.; tr.lit. 80 p./no.; **Document type:** *Journal, Trade.*
Related titles: Microfiche ed.: (from EVP).
Indexed: ApMecR, CISA, ChemAb, RASB, RefZh.
—CASDDS, East View, INIST, Linda Hall. **CCC.**
Published by: (Nauchno-tekhnicheskoe Obshchestvo Sudostroietel'noi Promyshlennosti im. A.N. Krylova/A. N. Krylov Scientific and Technical Society of Shipbuilders), Tsentral'nyi Nauchno-Issledovatel'skii Institut Tekhnologii Sudostroeniya/Central Reseal Institute of Shipbuilding Technology, Redaktsiya Zhurnala Sudostroenie, Promyshlennaya ul 7, St Petersburg D-65, 198095, Russian Federation. TEL 7-812-1860530, FAX 7-812-1860459, info@crist.ru. Ed. G G Pulyaevskii. Circ: 4,000 (controlled). **Dist. by:** M K - Periodica, ul Gilyarovskogo 39, Moscow 129110, Russian Federation. TEL 7-095-2845008, FAX 7-095-2813798, info@periodicals.ru, http://www.mkniga.ru. **Co-sponsor:** Ministerstvo Sudostroeniya.

SUISAN KOGAKU KENKYUJO GIHO/NATIONAL RESEARCH INSTITUTE OF FISHERIES ENGINEERING. TECHNICAL REPORT. *see* FISH AND FISHERIES

SUPERPORTS. *see* SPORTS AND GAMES—Boats And Boating

387.2 NLD ISSN 1875-015X
SUPERYACHT INDUSTRY. Variant title: S Y I. Text in English. 2006. bi-m. EUR 110 (effective 2011). **Document type:** *Magazine, Trade.* **Description:** For yacht builders, designers, naval architects, suppliers, yacht owners, and brokers, as well as charter companies and manning and crewing agencies around the world.
Published by: Yellow & Finch Publishers, Voorborch 2, Middelburg, 4335 AV, Netherlands. TEL 31-118-473398, FAX 31-118-461150, info@ynfpublishers.com, http://www.ynfpublishers.com. Ed., Pub. Dennis Vinkoert.

623.89 GBR ISSN 2046-4983
THE SUPERYACHT REPORT. Text in English. 1993. 10/yr. adv. back issues avail. **Document type:** *Magazine, Consumer.*
Formerly (until 2011): Yacht Report (1464-8253); Which incorporated (1993-1998): Wood Report (0969-6091)
Published by: T R P Magazines, Lansdowne House, 3-7 Northcote Rd, London, SW11 1NG, United Kingdom. TEL 44-20-79244004, FAX 44-20-79241004, http://www.trpmagazine.com/. Eds. Martin H Redmayne, Don Hoyt Gorman.

387 FRA ISSN 0153-6001
SUPPLEMENT AU REGISTRE MARITIME. Text in French. 1976.
Related titles: ◆ Supplement to: Registre Maritime. ISSN 0152-9994.
Published by: Bureau Veritas, 67-71 Bd. du Chateau, Neuilly-sur-Sene, Cedex 44 92077, France. TEL 33-1-55247000, FAX 33-1-55247001, http://www.bureauveritas.com.

387 FRA ISSN 0153-6052
SUPPLEMENT TRIMESTRIEL AU REGISTRE MARITIME. Text in French. 1976. q.
Related titles: ◆ Supplement to: Registre Maritime. ISSN 0152-9994.
Published by: Bureau Veritas, 67-71 Bd. du Chateau, Neuilly-sur-Sene, Cedex 44 92077, France. TEL 33-1-55247000, FAX 33-1-55247001, http://www.bureauveritas.com.

SUVREMENI PROMET. *see* TRANSPORTATION—Air Transport

387 DEU ISSN 1618-5234
T H B DEUTSCHE SCHIFFAHRTSZEITUNG. (Taeglicher Hafen Bericht) Text in German. 1947. d. (Mon.-Fri.). EUR 1,262.60 domestic; EUR 1,229 foreign (effective 2006). adv. bk.rev. charts; illus.; stat. **Document type:** *Newspaper, Trade.*
Former titles (until 1998): T H B - Taeglicher Hafenbericht (0933-0984); Which incorporated (1989-1994): Via Hafen Hamburg (0936-9783); Which was formerly (1971-1989): Hamburger Hafen-Nachrichten (0341-0862); (1961-1971): Hamburger Hafen-Nachrichten und Schiffsabfahrten (0017-694X); (until 1979): T H B - Taeglicher Hafenbericht. Ausgabe A (0933-0976); (until 1976): Taeglicher Hafenbericht. Ausgabe A (0341-0870)
Published by: Seehafen Verlag GmbH, Nordkanalstr 36, Hamburg, 20097, Germany. TEL 49-40-23714228, FAX 49-40-23714259, info@seehafen-verlag.de, http://www.schiffundhafen.de. Ed. Jens Meyer. Adv. contact Florian Visser. page EUR 2,530; trim 184 x 270. Circ: 2,017 (paid and controlled).

387 THA
T I F F A FREIGHT FORWARDING HANDBOOK. Text in Thai. 1991. biennial. USD 24 per issue. adv. **Document type:** *Directory.* **Description:** Covers multimodal transport, scope of freight forwarding services, container types, and seaports of Thailand.
Published by: (Thai International Freight Forwarders Association), Cosmic Group of Companies, 4th Fl Phyathai Bldg, Rajthevi, 31 Phyathai Rd, Bangkok, 10400, Thailand. TEL 245-3850, FAX 246-4737. adv.: color page USD 1,200. Circ: 5,000 (controlled).

387 GBR ISSN 0305-179X
HE566.F7
THE TANKER REGISTER. Text in English. 19??. a. GBP 250, USD 450 per issue (effective 2011). adv. charts; stat. Supplement avail. **Document type:** *Directory, Trade.* **Description:** Contain lists of oil tankers by name with technical characteristics, including ship size, capacity, weight, age, and registry.
Formerly (until 1960): Register of Tank Vessels of the World
Related titles: CD-ROM ed.: Tanker Fleet CD. GBP 575, USD 1,035 (effective 2011).
Published by: Clarkson Research Services Ltd., St Magnus House, 3 Lower Thames St, London, EC3R 6HE, United Kingdom. TEL 44-20-73343134, FAX 44-20-75220330, sales@crsl.com, http://www.crsl.com.

387 ITA ISSN 1721-758X
TECNOLOGIE E TRASPORTI MARE; international magazine of advanced marine technology, transportation and logistics. Text in English, Italian. 1969. bi-m. free to members. adv. bk.rev. charts; illus.; mkt.; maps; stat. back issues avail. **Document type:** *Magazine, Trade.* **Description:** Deals with ships, ports, shipyards, maritime communication, transportation, environment activities and marine operators. Includes informative articles on development and progress in boating technology in Italy; Eastern Europe; the Mediterranean; North, Central and South America; and the Far East.
Former titles (until 1994): Tecnologie e Trasporti per il Mare. L'Automazione Navale (1721-7571); (until 1986): L' Automazione Navale (0392-2294)
Related titles: Online - full text ed.: ISSN 1721-7598.
Indexed: BMT, RefZh.
Published by: Associazione Italiana di Tecnica Navale (ATENA), c/o Prof Antonio Fiorentino, Via Stazio 118, Naples, 80122, Italy. http://www.atenanazionale.it.

387 GBR ISSN 0040-2575
TELEGRAPH. Text in English. 1969. m. GBP 38 domestic to non-members; GBP 76 foreign to non-members; GBP 2.85, EUR 3 per issue to non-members; free to members (effective 2009). adv. bk.rev. charts; illus.; stat. back issues avail. **Document type:** *Newspaper, Trade.* **Description:** Contains news, features and special reports on a wide range of issues related to maritime professionals.
Formed by the merger of: Merchant Navy Journal; Ships' Telegraph
Related titles: Online - full text ed.: free (effective 2009).
Indexed: BMT.
—CCC.
Published by: Nautilus International, Oceanair House, 750-760 High Rd, Leytonstone, London, E11 3BB, United Kingdom. TEL 44-20-89896677, FAX 44-20-85301015, enquiries@nautilusint.org. Ed. Andrew Linington. Adv. contact Oliver Kirkman TEL 44-1727-739184. Circ: 34,000.

387.2 USA ISSN 1933-5008
VM1
THE TELEGRAPH. Text in English. q. **Document type:** *Newsletter, Consumer.*
Formerly (until 2006): Billlet
Published by: The Steamship Historical Society of America, Inc., 1029 Waterman Ave, E Providence, RI 02914. TEL 401-274-0805, FAX 401-274-0836, info@sshsa.org, http://www.sshsa.org.

387.1 NLD ISSN 0376-6411
TC187 CODEN: TEAQEJ
➤ **TERRA ET AQUA.** Text in English. 1972. q. free to qualified personnel (effective 2009). bk.rev. charts; illus.; stat. back issues avail. **Document type:** *Journal, Academic/Scholarly.* **Description:** Aimed at individuals and organizations with a professional interest in development of ports and waterways, particularly dredging work and environmental dredging of channels, harbours, and rivers.
Formerly (until 1972): Terra
Related titles: Online - full text ed.
Indexed: BMT, CLT&T, CTO, EngInd, EnvAb, EnvInd, FLUIDEX, GEOBASE, GeoRef, HRIS, SCOPUS, SpeleolAb, WildRev.
—BLDSC (8794.760000), IE, Ingenta, INIST, Linda Hall.
Published by: International Association of Dredging Companies, PO Box 80521, The Hague, 2508 GM, Netherlands. TEL 31-70-3523334, FAX 31-70-3512654, info@iadc-dredging.com, http://www.iadc-dredging.com. Ed. Marsha R Cohen. Circ: 3,000 (controlled).

387.54 551.46 GBR ISSN 1748-0043
TIDE TABLES. Text in English. 1927. a. GBP 1.50 per issue (effective 2009). **Document type:** *Report, Trade.*
Published by: Associated British Ports (Southampton) (Subsidiary of: Associated British Ports Holdings PLC), Ocean Gate, Atlantic Way, Southampton, SO14 3QN, United Kingdom. TEL 44-23-80488800, FAX 44-23-80336402, southampton@abports.co.uk, http://www.southamptonvts.co.uk.

387 NLD ISSN 0167-9988
D27
TIJDSCHRIFT VOOR ZEEGESCHIEDENIS. Text in Dutch, English, German. 1961. s-a. EUR 27 (effective 2009). adv. bk.rev. abstr.; bibl. cum.index. **Document type:** *Journal, Academic/Scholarly.*
Formerly (until 1982): Nederlandse Vereniging voor Zeegeschiedenis. Mededelingen (0028-2340)
Indexed: A22, EI, RASB.
—IE, Infotrieve.
Published by: (Nederlandse Vereniging voor Zeegeschiedenis), Uitgeverij Verloren, Torenlaan 25, Hilversum, 1211 JA, Netherlands. TEL 31-35-6859856, FAX 31-35-6836557, info@verloren.nl.

387 USA ISSN 1068-896X
THE TILLER. Text in English. 1980. q.
Published by: Virginia Canals & Navigations Society, Inc, 6826 Rosemont Dr, McLean, VA 22101. TEL 703-356-4027, http://organizations.rockbridge.net/canal. Ed. Ruth Harris.

387 GBR
TIME CHARTERS. Text in English. 1987. irreg., latest vol.6, 2008. GBP 470 per issue (effective 2010). **Document type:** *Handbook/Manual/Guide, Trade.* **Description:** Provides current reference to law and arbitration on the chartering and operation of ships on both sides of the Atlantic.
Published by: Informa U K Ltd. (Subsidiary of: T & F Informa plc), Albert House, 1-4 Singer St, London, EC2A 4BQ, United Kingdom. TEL 44-20-70175000, http://www.informa.com. **Subscr. to:** Sheepen Pl, Colchester, Essex CO3 3LP, United Kingdom.

387 USA ISSN 0040-8182
TITANIC COMMUTATOR. Text in English. 1963. q. membership only. adv. bk.rev. charts; illus. back issues avail. **Description:** Contains articles on the Titanic and other White Star and North Star Atlantic liners. Includes biographies from survivors and others, maritime art, photographs and deck plans. Many accounts contain the results of original research about the liners of the past, the people who built and sailed in them as well as contemporary issues on the subject.
Published by: Titanic Historical Society, Inc., PO Box 51053 0053, Indian Orchard, MA 01151-0053. TEL 413-543-4770. Eds. Edward Kamuda, Karen Kamuda. Circ: 5,000.

387 621.39 JPN ISSN 0387-9283
TOBA SHOSEN KOTO SENMON GAKKO KIYO/TOBA NATIONAL COLLEGE OF MARITIME TECHNOLOGY. ANNUAL REPORTS. Text in English, Japanese; Summaries in English. 1979. a. **Document type:** *Bulletin, Academic/Scholarly.* **Description:** Covers ships and shipping, computers and engineering.
Published by: Toba Shosen Koto Senmon Gakko, 1-1 Ikegami-cho, Toba-shi, Mie-ken 517-0012, Japan. TEL 81-599-25-8015, FAX 81-599-25-8016. R&P Yukito Iijima. Circ: 250.

TOKYO SHOSEN DAIGAKU KENKYU HOKOKU. SHIZEN KAGAKU/ TOKYO UNIVERSITY OF MERCANTILE MARINE. JOURNAL. NATURAL SCIENCES. *see* SCIENCES: COMPREHENSIVE WORKS

TOWPATHS. *see* HISTORY—History Of North And South America

387.5 JPN
TOYAMA SHOSEN KOTO SENMON GAKKO KENKYU SHUROKU/ TOYAMA NATIONAL COLLEGE OF MARITIME TECHNOLOGY. RESEARCH STUDIES. Text in Japanese; Summaries in English. 1968. a. illus.
Published by: Toyama Shosen Koto Senmon Gakko, 1-2 Ebieneriya, shinminato-shi, Toyama-ken 933-0235, Japan. Ed. Henshu Iinkai. Circ: 140.

387 NZL
TRADE-A-BOAT. Text in English. 1994. m. NZD 65 (effective 2008). adv. bk.rev. **Document type:** *Magazine, Consumer.* **Description:** Features the latest in boat and product reviews as well as thousand's of NZ's best boats for sale.
Published by: A C P Media New Zealand (Subsidiary of: A C P Magazines Ltd.), Private Bag 92512, Auckland, 1036, New Zealand. TEL 64-9-3082700, FAX 64-9-3082878, http://www.acpmedia.co.nz/. Adv. contact Cliff Bowman.

387 NOR ISSN 0803-9364
TRADEWINDS; international shipping gazette. Text in English. 1990. w. NOK 5,800 domestic; GBP 460 in United Kingdom; EUR 630 in rest of Europe and Africa; USD 775 elsewhere (effective 2006). adv. **Document type:** *Newspaper, Trade.* **Description:** Covers international shipping news.
Related titles: Online - full text ed.: Tradewinds Archive. 1999. USD 495 subscribers; USD 1,175 non-subscribers (effective 2001); TradeWinds Today. ISSN 1503-9528. 1995. USD 675 combined subscription paper and online editions (effective 2001).
—CCC.
Published by: Norges Handels og Sjoefartstidende/N H S T Media Group, Grev Wedells Plass 9, PO Box 1182, Sentrum, Oslo, 0107, Norway. TEL 47-22-001200, FAX 47-22-001210, help@tradewinds.no, http://www.nhst.no. Ed. Trond Lillestolen. adv.: B&W page NOK 61,875, color page NOK 100,125; trim 246 x 374. Circ: 7,650.

387 385 USA ISSN 1543-1886
TRANSFER. Text in English. 1994. s-a. (2-4/yr.). **Description:** Presents information about the transportation of railroad equipment over water.
Published by: Rail-Marine Information Group, c/o John Teichmoeller, 12107 Mt. Albert Rd., Elliott City, MD 21042. http://www.trainweb.org/ rmig/index.html. Pub. John G. Teichmoeller.

387 CHE
TRANSHELVETIQUE. Text in French. q.
Address: Rue des Amis 5, Lausanne, 1018, Switzerland. TEL 021-363661. Ed. Daniel Jaquinet. Circ: 3,000.

389 CAN ISSN 1497-8075
TRANSPORT CANADA. PORT PROGRAMS AND DIVESTITURE. ANNUAL REPORT ON PORT DIVESTITURE AND OPERATIONS. Text in English. a.
Formerly (until 1999): Annual Report on the Financial Operations of Canada's Public Harbours and Ports (1485-5445)
Published by: Transport Canada, Port Programs and Divestiture (Subsidiary of: Transport Canada/Transports Canada), 330 Sparks St, Ottawa, ON K1A 0N5, Canada. TEL 613-990-2309, FAX 613-954-4731.

387 SWE ISSN 0041-1523
TRANSPORTNYTT. Text in Swedish. 1958. 10/yr. SEK 720 (effective 2011). adv. bk.rev. charts; illus. **Document type:** *Magazine, Trade.* **Description:** Directed to users of trucks, lifters, warehouse equipment, as well as persons involved in shipping, overland and air cargo.
Related titles: Online - full text ed.
Published by: Foerlags AB Verkstadstidningen, PO Box 2082, Solna, 16902, Sweden. TEL 46-8-51493400, FAX 46-8-51493409, vt@vts.se, http://www.verkstadtidningen.se. Ed. Mats Udika TEL 46-8-51493471. Adv. contact Katarina Ungman TEL 46-8-51493472.

TRAVLTIPS. *see* TRAVEL AND TOURISM

623.8 GBR ISSN 0049-4690
TRIDENT; Portsmouth Naval Base newspaper. Text in English. 1969. m. GBP 60. adv. bk.rev. charts; illus. **Document type:** *Newspaper.*
—CCC.
Published by: Great Britain. Ministry of Defence, Business Information Centre, Rm 110, Somerset Hall, Somerset St, Bath, BA1 1TS, United Kingdom. Ed. D Moore. Circ: 2,500.

387.1 GBR ISSN 2044-3633
THE TRINIDAD & TOBAGO PORTS AND OUTPORTS HANDBOOK. Text in English. 19??. biennial. **Document type:** *Handbook/Manual/ Guide, Trade.* **Description:** Dedicated to the development of the local maritime industry and by extension national development through the provision of services such as advocacy, technical advice services etc.
Formerly (until 2010): Marine Ports and Outports Handbook of Trinidad and Tobago
Related titles: Online - full text ed.: ISSN 2044-3641. free (effective 2011).
Published by: Land & Marine Publications Ltd., 1 Kings Ct, Newcomen Way, Severalls Business Park, Colchester, Essex CO4 9RA, United Kingdom. TEL 44-1206-752902, FAX 44-1206-842958, publishing@landmarine.com, http://www.landmarine.com. Ed. John Tavner. Adv. contact Judith Gimson.

387 351.46 JPN
TSUKUBA INSTITUTE. TECHNICAL REPORT/TSUKUBA KENKYUJO GIHO. Text in English, Japanese; Summaries in English. 1981. a.
Published by: Ship and Ocean Foundation, Tsukuba Institute, 2, Minamihara, Tsukuba-shi, Ibaraki-ken 305, Japan.

TUNISIA. OFFICE DES PORTS NATIONAUX. BULLETIN ANNUEL DES STATISTIQUES. *see* TRANSPORTATION—Abstracting, Bibliographies, Statistics

387.1 TUN
TUNISIA. OFFICE DES PORTS NATIONAUX. BULLETIN TRIMESTRIEL. Text in French. q. charts; stat. **Document type:** *Bulletin, Government.*
Published by: Office des Ports Nationaux, Tunis, Tunisia.

359.97 USA ISSN 2152-6990
VG53
▼ **U S COAST GUARD FORUM**; dedicated to those who are always ready. Text in English. 2009. bi-m. free to qualified personnel (effective 2010). adv. back issues avail. **Document type:** *Magazine, Trade.* **Description:** Focuses on the people and technologies that allows the Guard to perform the spectrum of tasks it is assigned from port security and homeland defense, humanitarian and rescue relief, military support and protection missions, immigration and drug enforcement, to safe navigation of our waterways.
Related titles: Online - full text ed.: ISSN 2152-7008.
Published by: Kerrigan Media International, Inc., 15800 Crabbs Branch Way, Ste 300, Rockville, MD 20855. TEL 301-670-5700, 888-299-8292, FAX 301-670-5701, kmi@kmimediagroup.com, http:// www.kerriganmedia.com. Eds. Mark Fitzgerald, Jeff McKaughan. Adv. contact Stephen Karp. B&W page USD 6,219, color page USD 7,259; trim 8.375 x 10.875.

U.S. COAST GUARD. MARINE SAFETY MANUAL. VOLUME 1: ADMINISTRATION AND MANAGEMENT. *see* MILITARY

U.S. COAST GUARD. MARINE SAFETY MANUAL. VOLUME 10: INTERAGENCY AGREEMENTS AND ACRONYMS. *see* MILITARY

U.S. COAST GUARD. MARINE SAFETY MANUAL. VOLUME 2: MATERIEL INSPECTION. *see* MILITARY

U.S. COAST GUARD. MARINE SAFETY MANUAL. VOLUME 3: MARINE INDUSTRY PERSONNEL. *see* MILITARY

U.S. COAST GUARD. MARINE SAFETY MANUAL. VOLUME 4: TECHNICAL. *see* MILITARY

U.S. COAST GUARD. MARINE SAFETY MANUAL. VOLUME 5: INVESTIGATIONS. *see* MILITARY

U.S. COAST GUARD. MARINE SAFETY MANUAL. VOLUME 6: PORTS AND WATERWAYS ACTIVITIES. *see* MILITARY

U.S. COAST GUARD. MARINE SAFETY MANUAL. VOLUME 9: ENVIRONMENTAL PROTECTION. *see* MILITARY

387 USA
U.S. COAST GUARD. NAVIGATION AND VESSEL INSPECTION CIRCULARS. Abbreviated title: N V I C. Text in English. 19??. irreg. looseleaf. back issues avail. **Document type:** *Government.* **Description:** Provides guidance about the enforcement or compliance with a certain Federal marine safety regulations and Coast Guard marine safety programs.
Related titles: Online - full text ed.: free (effective 2010).
Published by: U.S. Coast Guard, 2100 Second St, SW, Washington, DC 20593. TEL 202-267-1061, FAX 202-267-4402, gchappell@comdt.uscg.mil, http://www.uscg.mil/default.asp. **Subscr. to:** U.S. Government Printing Office, Superintendent of Documents.

287 USA ISSN 0083-0755
U.S. FEDERAL MARITIME COMMISSION. ANNUAL REPORT. Text in English. 1962. a. free. **Document type:** *Government.*
Published by: U.S. Federal Maritime Commission, 800 N Capital St, N W, Washington, DC 20573. TEL 202-523-5725.

387.5 USA
U S S REPORTS. Text in English. 1942. s-a. free. **Document type:** *Newsletter, Corporate.* **Description:** Reports on USS and AMMLA's activities.
Published by: United Seamen's Service, One World Trade Center, Ste 2161, New York, NY 10048. FAX 212-432-5492, TELEX 222146 UNS UR. Ed., R&P Kevon Storie TEL 212-775-1033. Circ: 5,000.

387 USA ISSN 0558-149X
HD1694
U.S. SAINT LAWRENCE SEAWAY DEVELOPMENT CORPORATION. ANNUAL REPORT. Text in English. 1955. a., latest 2003. **Document type:** *Corporate.*
—Linda Hall.
Published by: U.S. Saint Lawrence Seaway Development Corporation, 400 Seventh St, S W., Rm 5424, Washington, DC 20026-4090. TEL 202-366-0091, 800-785-2779, FAX 202-366-7147.

UNDERWATER MAGAZINE. *see* BUSINESS AND ECONOMICS—Marketing And Purchasing

623.81 JPN
UNDO SEINO KENKYU IINKAI SHINPOJUMU/MARINE DYNAMICS SYMPOSIUM. Text in Japanese. a.
Published by: Nihon Zosen Gakkai/Society of Naval Architects of Japan, 1Hamamatsucho Yazaki White Bldg., 2-12-9 Shibadaimon, Minato-ku, Tokyo, 105-0012, Japan.

UNIVERSITATEA "DUNAREA DE JOS" DIN GALATI. ANALELE. FASCICULA XI. CONSTSRUCTII NAVALE. *see* ENGINEERING

387 620 500 ROM ISSN 1582-3601
➤ **UNIVERSITATII MARITIME CONSTANTA. ANALELE/NAVIGATION AND MARITIME TRANSPORT.** Text in English. 2000. s-a. EUR 10 per issue (effective 2011). abstr.; bibl.; charts; illus.; maps; pat.; stat. back issues avail. **Document type:** *Journal, Academic/Scholarly.* **Description:** Contains articles and reserach results by academics from the university, other Romanian and European polytechnics universities. Covers navigation,maritime transport, mechanical engineering, electrical engineering, mathematics, physics, maritime English, environment engineering, and economics. Includes 4 series: A series, navigation and maritime transport; B series, mathematical science and physics; C series, electrical engineering and computer science; D series - mechanical engineering.
Formerly (until 2001): Institutului de Marina Civila. Analele (1454-8887)
Indexed: A01, P52, P56.
Published by: (Universitatea Maritima Constanta/Constanta Maritime University), "Nautica" Publishing House/Editura Nautica, Mircea cel Batran St.,104, Constanta, 900663, Romania. TEL 40241664740, FAX 40241617260, info@imc.ro, http://www.cmu-edu.eu/editura.html. Ed. Violeta Ciucur. Circ: 123.

387.1 UAE
UPDATE. Text in English. **Document type:** *Magazine, Consumer.* **Description:** Covers news about the Dubai ports and Jebel Ali Free Zone.
Related titles: Online - full content ed.
Published by: Dubai Ports and Jebel Ali Free Zone Authorities, P O Box 17000, Dubai, United Arab Emirates. TEL 971-4-815000, FAX 971-4-817777, sids@sids.com, http://sids.com/update/.

386 333.72 USA
UPPER MISSISSIPPI RIVER-ILLINOIS WATERWAY NAVIGATION SYSTEM STUDY. Text in English. 1993. irreg. **Document type:** *Newsletter, Government.*
Related titles: Online - full content ed.: ISSN 1939-2745.
Published by: U.S. Army Corps of Engineers, Rock Island, PM-A (Simmons) Clock Tower Building, PO Box 2004, Rock Island, IL 61204, IL 61204.

387.2 NLD ISSN 1877-797X
▼ **V H Z C SCHEEPS JOURNAAL.** Text in Dutch, Frisian. 2009. 4/yr. free (effective 2011). adv.
Published by: Verenigde Hollandse Zeil Compagnie, Postbus 2254, Leiden, 2301 CG, Netherlands. info@vhzc.nl. Circ: 2,500 (free).

386 333.91 ESP
VALENCIA PORT; guia del servicios del puerto de Valencia. Text in Spanish. 1978. a. adv. back issues avail. **Document type:** *Magazine, Trade.*
Published by: Grupo Editorial Men-Car, Passeig de Colom, 24, Barcelona, 08002, Spain. TEL 34-93-301-5749, FAX 34-93-302-1779, men-car@men-car.com, http://www.men-car.com. Eds. Juan Cardona, Manuel Cardona. Circ: 15,000.

387 FIN ISSN 1797-3988
VENEILY.FI (ONLINE). Text in Finnish. 2005. a.
Formerly (until 2008): Veneily.fi (Print) (1795-5564)
Media: Online - full content. **Related titles:** Ed.
Published by: Merenkulkulaitos/Finnish Maritime Administration, Porkkalankatu 5, Helsiki, 00180, Finland. TEL 358-204-481, FAX 358-204-484355, kirjaamo@fma.fi, http://www.fma.fi.

623.82 DEU
VERBAND FUER SCHIFFBAU UND MEERESTECHNIK. JAHRESBERICHT. Text in German. 1962. a. free. bk.rev. stat. **Document type:** *Trade.* **Description:** Comprehensive report covering current situation, development, industry, political and technical questions.
Formerly (until 1987): Deutscher Shiffbau
Published by: Verband fuer Schiffbau und Meerestechnik e.V., An der Alster 1, Hamburg, 20099, Germany. TEL 49-40-280152-0, FAX 49-40-280152-30, info@vsm.de, http://www.vsm.de. Circ: 1,750.

387.09 NLD ISSN 1387-1536
VEREENIGING NEDERLANDSCH HISTORISCH SCHEEPVAART MUSEUM TE AMSTERDAM. JAARBOEK. Text in Dutch. 1991. a. EUR 40 (effective 2010). **Description:** Describes important objects groups of objects collections in the museum.
Published by: Vereeniging Nederlandsch Historisch Scheepvaart Museum, Kattenburgerplein 7, Amsterdam, 1018 KK, Netherlands. TEL 31-20-5232222, FAX 31-20-5232213, vereeniging@scheepvaartmuseum.nl, http:// www.scheepvaartmuseum.nl.

▼ **VERVOER VAN GEVAARLIJKE STOFFEN OVER DE BINNENWATEREN.** *see* ENVIRONMENTAL STUDIES—Waste Management

387 USA ISSN 1065-7096
HE554.N7
VIA INTERNATIONAL PORT OF NEW YORK - NEW JERSEY. Text in English. 1949. bi-m. USD 36; free to export-import shippers. adv. bk.rev. illus. **Document type:** *Magazine, Trade.*
Former titles: Via Port of New York - New Jersey (0193-6565); Via Port of New York (0042-5001)
Indexed: HRIS, P06, PAIS.
Published by: Port Authority of New York and New Jersey, One World Trade Ctr, Rm 34E, New York, NY 10048. TEL 212-435-6614, FAX 212-435-6032. Ed., R&P Margot O Pagan. Adv. contact James Wilson. Circ: 30,000 (controlled).

387 GBR ISSN 2040-9834
▼ **VIETNAM SHIPPING REPORT.** Text in English. 2009. q. EUR 820, USD 1,030 combined subscription (print & email eds.) (effective 2010). **Document type:** *Report, Trade.* **Description:** Provides industry professionals and strategists, sector analysts, business investors, trade associations and regulatory bodies with independent forecasts and competitive intelligence on the shipping industry in Vietnam.
Related titles: E-mail ed.
Published by: Business Monitor International Ltd., Senator House, 85 Queen Victoria St, London, EC4V 4AB, United Kingdom. TEL 44-20-72480468, FAX 44-20-72480467, subs@businessmonitor.com.

387 VIR
VIRGIN ISLANDS PORT AUTHORITY. ANNUAL REPORT. Text in English. 1968. a. reprints avail.
Published by: Virgin Islands Port Authority, PO Box 1707, St Thomas, 00803-1707, Virgin Isl., US. TEL 809-774-3140, FAX 809-774-0025. Ed. Jean M Bozzuto. Circ: 500.

387 VIR
VIRGIN ISLANDS PORT AUTHORITY DIRECTORY. Text in English. 1988. irreg. (every 2-3 yrs.), latest 1991. free. **Document type:** *Directory.* **Description:** Provides complete description of cruise shipping, marine cargo and airport facilities and the companies that provide various services to their operations throughout the territory.
Published by: Virgin Islands Port Authority, PO Box 1707, St Thomas, 00803-1707, Virgin Isl., US. TEL 809-774-3140, FAX 809-774-0025.

387 USA
VIRGINIA MARITIMER. Text in English. bi-m. free to qualified personnel. **Document type:** *Magazine, Trade.* **Description:** Reports international trade development news and information about Virginia's ports, in both the public and private sectors.
Former titles: Ports of Virginia; Port of Hampton Roads Monthly Log; (until Oct. 1981): Virginia Ports
Indexed: CLT&T.

Published by: Virginia Port Authority, 600 World Trade Center, Norfolk, VA 23510. TEL 757-683-2140, FAX 757-683-2897, lford@vaports.com, http://www.vaports.com. Pub. Linda Ford. Circ: 9,500 (controlled).

VOKABULAIRE. *see* COLLEGE AND ALUMNI

WARSHIP INTERNATIONAL. *see* MILITARY

623.81 GBR ISSN 0957-5537
V750
WARSHIP TECHNOLOGY. Text in English. 1987. 5/yr. includes subscr. with The Naval Architect. adv. **Document type:** *Journal, Trade.* **Description:** Adopts a technical rather than political approach to naval defense, giving in-depth coverage to the design, construction and outfitting of naval vessels worldwide.
Related titles: Online - full text ed.; ◆ Supplement to: The Naval Architect. ISSN 0306-0209.
Indexed: A28, APA, BMT, BrCerAb, C&ISA, CA/WCA, CIA, CerAb, CivEngAb, CorrAb, E&CAJ, E11, EEA, EMA, ESPM, EngInd, EnvEAb, FLUIDEX, H15, M&TEA, M09, MBF, METADEX, RefZh, SCOPUS, SolStAb, T04, WAA.
—BLDSC (9261.869250), IE, Ingenta, Linda Hall. **CCC.**
Published by: Royal Institution of Naval Architects, 10 Upper Belgrave St, London, SW1X 8BQ, United Kingdom. TEL 44-20-72354622, FAX 44-20-72595912, publications@rina.org.uk. Ed. David Foxwell. Pub. Mark J Staunton-Lambert. Adv. contact Donna McGrath.

387 USA ISSN 0083-7725
HE563.U5
WATERBORNE COMMERCE OF THE UNITED STATES. (In 5 parts: Atlantic Coast; Gulf Coast, Mississippi River System & Antilles (Puerto Rico & Virgin Islands); The Great Lakes; Pacific Coast, Alaska & Hawaii; National Summary of Data from vols. 1-4) Text in English. 1952. a. price varies. stat. **Document type:** *Government.*
Published by: U.S. Army Corps of Engineers, Water Resources Support Center, PO Box 61280, New Orleans, LA 70161-1280. TEL 504-862-1424, FAX 504-862-1423. Ed. Thomas Mire. Circ: 1,100.
Subscr. to: U.S. Army Engineer District, CEKMN-ED-SX, P O Box 60267, New Orleans, LA. TEL 504-862-2715, FAX 504-862-1091.

387 AUS ISSN 1324-4043
WATERLINE. Text in English. 1994. s-a. free (effective 2008). adv. charts; stat.; tr.lit. back issues avail. **Document type:** *Magazine, Government.* **Description:** Provides information on freight movements in both the wharf side and the landside of five Australian major city port terminals.
Related titles: E-mail ed.; Online - full text ed.: free (effective 2008).
Published by: Bureau of Infrastructure, Transport and Regional Economics, GPO Box 501, Canberra City, ACT 2600, Australia. TEL 61-2-62747111, FAX 61-2-62747614, avstats@dotrs.gov.au, http://www.dotrs.gov.au/aviation/avstats.htm. Eds. Godfrey Lubulwa, Tony Carmdoy. Circ: 1,000.

387 USA ISSN 0043-1524
HE623
WATERWAYS JOURNAL. Text in English. 1887. w. USD 39 domestic; USD 104 in Canada & Mexico (effective 2010). bk.rev. charts; illus.; tr.lit. Supplement avail.; back issues avail.; reprints avail. **Document type:** *Journal, Trade.* **Description:** Delivers news to members of the industry and promote the industry to those not as familiar with the benefits of marine transportation.
Related titles: Online - full text ed.
Indexed: HRIS.
Published by: Waterways Journal, Inc., 319 N 4th St, Ste 650, St. Louis, MO 63102. TEL 314-241-7354, FAX 314-241-4207. Ed. John Shoulberg. Pub. Nelson H Spencer.

387 NLD ISSN 0165-490X
WEEKBLAD SCHUTTEVAER; vakblad voor de Rijn- en binnenvaart, kustvaart, visserij, offshore, scheepsbouw. Text in Dutch. 1888. w. (Sat.). EUR 145.90; EUR 95.50 to senior citizens; EUR 72.50 to students (effective 2009). adv. **Document type:** *Newspaper, Trade.* **Description:** Covers the Rhine, inland and coastal shipping industries in the Netherlands, including fishing, shipbuilding, offshore, recreational and professional sailing.
Incorporates (1992-1993): Watersport Aktueel (0928-9399)
—IE, Infotrieve.
Published by: (Koninklijke Schippersvereniging Schuttevaer), Uitgeverij Nassau (Subsidiary of: MYbusinessmedia b.v.), Postbus 58, Deventer, 7400 AB, Netherlands. TEL 31-570-504300, FAX 31-570-504399. Eds. Patrick Naaraat TEL 31-570-504365, Dirk van der Meulen TEL 31-570-504360. Pub. Hein Bronk. adv.: B&W page EUR 4,320, color page EUR 4,835; trim 398 x 530.

387 USA ISSN 1057-5863
HF1
WEEKLY COMMERCIAL NEWS AND SHIPPING GUIDE. Text in English. w. adv. **Document type:** *Newspaper, Trade.*
Formerly (until 1991): Daily Commercial News and Shipping Guide (1053-9042)
Indexed: RASB.
Published by: C.A. Page Publishing Co., PO Box 530, Redondo Beach, CA 90277-0530. TEL 213-568-4560, FAX 213-568-4567. Ed. Shay Ramos. Adv. contact Mark Wagner. Circ: 2,000.

387 USA ISSN 0273-4699
WEST COAST SAILORS. Text in English. m.
Published by: Sailors' Union of the Pacific, 450 Harrison St, San Francisco, CA 94105. TEL 415-777-3400. Ed. Teresa Anibale.

387 796.95 CAN ISSN 0844-5567
WESTCOAST MARINER. Text in English. 1989. m. CAD 32.10 domestic; USD 40 foreign. adv. **Description:** For skippers and crews who work the Pacific Coast.
Published by: Bellwether Publishing Ltd., 101-4438 Juneau St, Burnaby, BC V5C 4C8, Canada. TEL 604-299-7433, FAX 604-299-2924, michael@bellwetherpublishingltd.com. Ed. Michael Siddall. Circ: 10,500.

WHAT CRUISE. *see* TRAVEL AND TOURISM

381.029 NOR ISSN 0807-9439
WHERE TO BUILD & WHERE TO REPAIR. Text in English. 1953. a. NOK 600, EUR 200, USD 250; NOK 600, EUR 80, USD 100 combined subscription (online, print & CD-ROM eds.) (effective 2007). adv. **Document type:** *Directory, Trade.* **Description:** Technical and commercial information about more than 600 ship builders across the world.
Formerly (until 1996): Year Book Where to Build - Where to Repair (0800-1200)
Related titles: CD-ROM ed.: ISSN 1890-1271. 1998; Online - full text ed.
Published by: Selvig Publishing A-S, Anthon Walles Vei 36, PO Box 384, Sandvika, 1301, Norway. TEL 47-67-808026, FAX 47-67-564762, adm@seadirectory.com, sales@seadirectory.com.

387.2 IRL ISSN 1649-8585
WHITE STAR JOURNAL. Text in English. 1993. q. EUR 15 domestic; GBP 13 in United Kingdom; EUR 20 in Europe; USD 30 in United States; EUR 30 elsewhere (effective 2006). **Description:** Covers maritime issues of historical interest and up-to-date news and reviews.
Published by: Irish Titanic Historical Society, 4 Fancourt Rd, Bilbriggan, Co. Dublin, Ireland. Ed. Kilian Harford.

343.096 GBR ISSN 1756-0128
WHO'S WHO LEGAL. SHIPPING & MARITIME. Text in English. 2007. biennial. USD 200 per issue (effective 2011). **Document type:** *Handbook/Manual/Guide, Trade.*
Published by: Law Business Research Ltd., 87 Lancaster Rd, London, W11 1QQ, United Kingdom. TEL 44-20-79081188, FAX 44-20-72296910, http://www.lbresearch.com/.

380.1029 DEU ISSN 0172-990X
WIE ERREICHE ICH WEN?. Text in German. 1958. a. EUR 15.60 (effective 2006). adv. **Document type:** *Directory, Trade.*
Published by: K.O. Storck Verlag, Striepenweg 31, Hamburg, 21147, Germany. TEL 49-40-7971301, FAX 49-40-79713101, webmaster@storck-verlag.de, http://www.storck-verlag.de. Ed. H Meder. adv.: B&W page EUR 1,050, color page EUR 1,830; 105 x 210. Circ: 11,500.

387 AUS ISSN 1037-3748
WORK BOAT WORLD. Text in English. 1982. m. AUD 175, USD 175, GBP 115, EUR 130 (effective Jul. 2010). adv. illus. back issues avail. **Document type:** *Magazine, Trade.* **Description:** Provides latest news on all types of commercial, military and government vessels that are around 130 meters in length and their operation, including ferries, patrol boats, tugs, offshore support vessels, harbor craft, oil spill vessels, tourist vessels, fishing/aquaculture vessels, rescue boats, dredgers, small naval vessels, and general workboats.
Incorporates (in 2006): Fishing Boat World; Workboats; Former titles (until 1989): Work and Patrol Boat World (0812-1648); (until 1983): Asia - Pacific Work and Patrol Boat (0726-3724)
Indexed: A10, B07, C12, M01, M02, P26, P48, P52, P54, P56, PQC, RefZh, S22, SCOPUS, V03.
Published by: Baird Publications Pty. Ltd., 135 Sturt St, South Bank, Melbourne, VIC 3006, Australia. TEL 61-3-96450411, FAX 61-3-96450475, marinfo@baird.com.au, http://www.baird.com.au. Eds. Steven Kelleher, Neil Baird. adv.: B&W page AUD 2,300, color page AUD 3,000; trim 210 x 297. Circ: 4,000.

387 USA ISSN 0043-8014
VK1 CODEN: WOBOAF
WORKBOAT. Text in English. 1943. m. free to qualified personnel (effective 2010). adv. bk.rev. charts; illus.; stat. back issues avail.; reprints avail. **Document type:** *Magazine, Trade.* **Description:** Designed for owners, operators, builders and designers of US commercial shallow-draft vessels under 400 feet. Contains trade-related news, waterway development, economic trends and new legislation.
Incorporates (1954-1959): Offshore Drilling; Southern Marine Review
Related titles: Online - full text ed.
Indexed: B02, B15, B17, B18, G04, G06, G07, G08, HRIS, I05.
Published by: Diversified Business Communications, 121 Free St, Portland, ME 04101. TEL 207-842-5600, FAX 207-842-5611, custserv@divcom.com, http://www.divbusiness.com. Ed. David Krapf TEL 504-891-4100. Pub. Michael Lodato. Adv. contact John D Allen TEL 207-359-2516. B&W page USD 2,575, color page USD 3,570; 7 x 10. Circ: 25,563.

387.2 GBR ISSN 1363-5018
WORLD BUNKERING. Text in English. 1996 (May). q. free to qualified personnel. adv. **Document type:** *Magazine, Trade.* **Description:** Provides an international forum to address the concerns of all sectors of the Bunker Industry.
Related titles: Online - full text ed.: free.
Published by: (International Bunkering Industry Association), Maritime Media (Subsidiary of: Roxby Media Ltd.), The Diary House, Rickett St, London, SW6 RU1, United Kingdom. TEL 44-20-73866100, FAX 44-20-73818890, inbox@mar-media.com. Ed. David Hughes. Pub. W H Robinson.

WORLD CASUALTY STATISTICS. *see* TRANSPORTATION—Abstracting, Bibliographies, Statistics

387.51 790.1 GBR ISSN 0954-1500
WORLD CRUISE INDUSTRY REVIEW. Text in English. 1989. s-a. GBP 5.95 per issue domestic; EUR 8 per issue in Europe; USD 8.95 per issue in United States; free to qualified personnel (effective 2010). back issues avail. **Document type:** *Magazine, Trade.* **Description:** Features up-to-date information on ports and destinations, shipbuilding and repair, marine equipment and technology, environment and safety, interiors and design.
Related titles: Online - full text ed.
Indexed: BMT.
Published by: (International Council of Cruise Lines USA), S P G Media Ltd. (Subsidiary of: Sterling Publishing Group Plc.), Brunel House, 55-57 N Wharf Rd, London, W2 1LA, United Kingdom. TEL 44-20-79159660, FAX 44-20-77242089, info@spgmedia.com, http://www.spgmedia.com/. Eds. Christopher Kanal, John Lawrence. Pub. William Crocker.

WORLD DIRECTORY OF LINER SHIPPING AGENTS (YEAR). *see* BUSINESS AND ECONOMICS—Trade And Industrial Directories

387 623.8 AUS ISSN 1327-9408
WORLD FAST FERRY MARKET. Text in English. 1996. irreg., latest no.2, 1998. AUD 400, USD 400, GBP 240, EUR 240 (effective 2010). illus. **Document type:** *Directory, Trade.*
Published by: Baird Publications Pty. Ltd., 135 Sturt St, South Bank, Melbourne, VIC 3006, Australia. TEL 61-3-96450411, FAX 61-3-96450475, marinfo@baird.com.au, http://www.baird.com.au. Ed. Neil Baird.

387.5 GBR ISSN 2042-0633
▼ **WORLD FLEET MONITOR.** Text in English. 2010. m. GBP 625, USD 1,125 (effective 2011). 32 p./no.; **Document type:** *Catalog, Trade.* **Description:** Provides a completely new perspective on fleet data.
Related titles: Online - full text ed.: GBP 1,800, USD 3,240 single user license (effective 2011).
Published by: Clarkson Research Services Ltd., St Magnus House, 3 Lower Thames St, London, EC3R 6HE, United Kingdom. TEL 44-20-73343134, FAX 44-20-75220330, sales@crsl.com.

WORLD FLEET STATISTICS. *see* TRANSPORTATION—Abstracting, Bibliographies, Statistics

387.5 DEU ISSN 1651-436X
VK1
➤ **WORLD MARITIME UNIVERSITY. JOURNAL OF MARITIME AFFAIRS.** Text in English. 2002. biennial. EUR 156, USD 192 combined subscription to institutions (print & online eds.) (effective 2012). **Document type:** *Journal, Academic/Scholarly.* **Description:** Aims to present fresh ideas and information to a broad audience of professionals in the international maritime transportation sector.
Related titles: Online - full text ed.: ISSN 1654-1642 (from IngentaConnect).
Indexed: A22, E01, SCOPUS.
—BLDSC (9341.605700), IE, Ingenta. **CCC.**
Published by: (International Maritime Organization, World Maritime University SWE), Springer (Subsidiary of: Springer Science+Business Media), Tiergartenstr 17, Heidelberg, 69121, Germany. TEL 49-6221-4870, FAX 49-6221-345229, subscriptions@springer.com. Ed. Jens Schroeder-Hinrichs.

➤ **WORLD METEOROLOGICAL ORGANIZATION. COMMISSION FOR MARINE METEOROLOGY. ABRIDGED FINAL REPORT OF THE (NO.) SESSION.** *see* METEOROLOGY

➤ **WORLD METEOROLOGICAL ORGANIZATION. WEATHER REPORTING. VOLUME D: INFORMATION FOR SHIPPING.** *see* METEOROLOGY

387 GBR ISSN 1369-3565
WORLD OIL TANKER TRENDS. Text in English. 1921. s-a. GBP 395, USD 745 (effective 2009). charts; stat. **Document type:** *Journal, Trade.* **Description:** Detailed half-yearly review of oil tanker supply and charter markets, including extensive time-series data.
Formerly (until 1996): World Tanker Fleet Review (0049-8157)
Published by: S S Y Consultancy & Research Ltd., Lloyds Chambers, 1 Portsoken St, London, E1 8PH, United Kingdom.

WORLD SHIPBUILDING STATISTICS. *see* TRANSPORTATION—Abstracting, Bibliographies, Statistics

387 GBR ISSN 1358-8788
WORLD SHIPYARD MONITOR. Abbreviated title: W S M. Text in English. 1994. m. GBP 670, USD 1,206 (effective 2011). adv. **Document type:** *Catalog, Trade.* **Description:** Provides coverage of supply-demand trends in the ship-building market.
Related titles: Online - full text ed.: ISSN 1741-329X.
Published by: Clarkson Research Services Ltd., St Magnus House, 3 Lower Thames St, London, EC3R 6HE, United Kingdom. TEL 44-20-73343134, FAX 44-20-75220330, sales@crsl.com.

623.8 387 AUS
WORLD SHIPYARDS. Text in English. irreg., latest 2000. AUD 337, USD 337, GBP 205, EUR 205 (effective 2010). **Document type:** *Directory, Trade.*
Published by: Baird Publications Pty. Ltd., 135 Sturt St, South Bank, Melbourne, VIC 3006, Australia. TEL 61-3-96450411, FAX 61-3-96450475, marinfo@baird.com.au, http://www.baird.com.au. Ed. Neil Baird.

387.5 POL ISSN 0860-8806
WYZSZA SZKOLA MORSKA W SZCZECINIE. STUDIA. Text in Polish. 1980. irreg.
Indexed: ASFA, B21, B22, ESPM.
Published by: Wyzsza Szkola Morska w Szczecinie, Ul. Waly Chrobrego 1/2, Szczecin, 70500, Poland. TEL 48-91-4809400, http://www.wsm.szczecin.pl.

387.5 POL
WYZSZA SZKOLA MORSKA. ZESZYTY NAUKOWE. Text in Polish. irreg. PLZ 103.
Indexed: AgrLib.
Published by: Wyzsza Szkola Morska w Gdyni/Merchant Marine Academy, Czerwonych Kosynierow 83, Gdynia, 81225, Poland. Ed. Bozena Sobolewska. **Dist. by:** Ars Polona, Obroncow 25, Warsaw 03933, Poland.

387 CHN ISSN 1003-2339
XIANDAI JIANCHUAN/MODERN SHIPS. Text in Chinese. 1986. s-m. **Document type:** *Magazine, Trade.*
Published by: (Zhongguo Chuanbo Xinxi Zhongxin/China Shipbuilding Information Center), Xiandai Jianchuan Zazhshe, 2, Shuangchuanbao Jia, Beijing, 100085, China. TEL 86-10-64831783, FAX 86-10-64837389, http://www.shipnet.com.cn/mseo/index.htm.

387.20423 HKG ISSN 1996-1014
YACHT STYLE. Text in English. q. HKD 165 in Hong Kong & Macau; USD 43 in Asia, excluding Japan; USD 45 elsewhere (effective 2010). adv. **Document type:** *Magazine, Consumer.* **Description:** Contains 4 sections: Logbook, which covers news, Asian regattas, boat shows, parties and people. Features, which includes articles on sailing yachts, power boats, superyachts, extreme machines and classic craft. On Board and Style includes sea trials of the last yachts or cruisers on offer, as well as the cool toys and must-haves for every sailor.
Related titles: Online - full text ed.
Published by: Edipresse Asia Ltd., 6th Fl., Guardian House, 32 Oi Kwan Rd., Wanchai, Hong Kong. TEL 852-2547-7117, FAX 852-2858-2671, enquiry@edipresse.com.hk, http://www.edipresseasia.com/home.html. Circ: 23,500.

387.20423 CHN
YACHT STYLE (CHINA). Text in Chinese. s-a. **Document type:** *Magazine, Consumer.*
Published by: Edipresse Asia Ltd. (China) (Subsidiary of: Edipresse Asia Ltd.), 8F, No.2, Lane 139, Anshun Rd., Shanghai, 200052, China. TEL 86-21-52587666, FAX 86-21-62802377, http://www.edipresseasia.com/home.html.

TU

387.544 NOR ISSN 1501-7133
HE563.N8
YEARBOOK OF SCANDINAVIAN SHIPOWNERS AND SHIP MANAGEMENT COMPANIES. Text in Multiple languages. 1936. a. NOK 600, EUR 80, USD 110 print edition; NOK 995, EUR 133, USD 166 combined subscription online, print & CD-ROM eds. (effective 2007). adv. **Document type:** *Directory, Trade.*
Former titles (unitl 1997): Skandinaviske Skipsrederier (0806-9387); (until 1994): Aarbok over Skandinaviske Skipsrederier og Management Selskaper (0806-9379); (until 1986): Aarbok over Skandinaviske Skipsrederier (0800-1235); (until 1949): Aarbok over Norske Skipsrederier (0800-1243); (until 1938): Norske Skipsrederier (0806-9360)
Related titles: CD-ROM ed.: Scandinavian Shipowners and Ship Management Companies. ISSN 1890-128X; Online - full text ed.: Scandinavian Ship Owners Online.
Published by: Selvig Publishing A-S, Anthon Walles Vei 36, PO Box 384, Sandvika, 1301, Norway. TEL 47-67-808026, FAX 47-67-564762, sales@seadirectory.com, adm@seadirectory.com. adv.: color page NOK 6,900.

387 JPN ISSN 0388-449X
YOKOHAMA PORT NEWS. Text in English. s-a. **Description:** Covers current activities as well as future plans of the port of Yokohama.
Published by: Port and Harbor Bureau, Industry and Trade Center Bldg, 2 Yamashita-cho, Naka-ku, Yokohama-shi, Kanagawa-ken 231-0023, Japan. TEL ta-45-671-7190, FAX 81-45-671-7310.

387 CHN ISSN 1674-5388
YOUTING/YACHT. Text in Chinese. 1990. bi-m. **Document type:** *Magazine, Trade.*
Former titles (until 2009): Chuan Ting/Ships & Yachts (1673-5056); (until 2006): Chuanbo Gongye Jishu Jingji Xinxi/Technology Economy Information (1001-9065)
Published by: Zhongguo Chuanbo Gongye Jituan Gongsi/China State Shipbuilding Corporation, 5, Yuetan Bei Jie, Beijing, 100861, China. TEL 86-10-68038833, FAX 86-10-68034592, cssc@cssc.net.cn, http://www.cssc.net.cn/.

387 CHN
YOUTINGYE/CHINA YACHTING. Text in Chinese. 2002. bi-m. **Document type:** *Magazine, Trade.*
Formerly (until 2005): Youting Gongye/Yacht Industry (1008-5386)
Published by: Zhongguo Jianchuan Yanjiuyuan, 2, Shuangquanbao Jia, PO Box 2854, Beijing, 100192, China. TEL 86-10-64831783 ext 800, postdoct@shipol.com.cn, http://csrda.shipol.com.cn/7yuan/index.htm.

387 CHN ISSN 1000-3878
CODEN: ZAJIEA
ZAOCHUAN JISHU/MARINE TECHNOLOGY. Text in Chinese. 1973. m. USD 31.20 (effective 2009). adv. **Document type:** *Trade.*
Description: Deals with shipbuilding and offshore engineering. Also covers new designs, materials, equipment and technology related to shipbuilding and shiprepairing industry.
Related titles: Online - full text ed.
Published by: Zhongguo Chuanbo Gongye Zonggongsi, Chuanbo Gongyi Yanjiusuo, PO Box 032 201, Shanghai, 200032, China. TEL 86-21-6439-9626, FAX 86-21-6439-0908. Ed. Nihua Sun. Pub. Yongliang Dai. R&P Rongbo Lan. Adv. contact Huajun Liang. Circ: 2,500 (paid).

387 NLD ISSN 1569-7304
ZEEHAVENS AMSTERDAM/AMSTERDAM SEAPORTS. Text in German, English. 1966. bi-m. free outside the Netherlands. adv.
Description: Publishes news on shipping and transport via the port of Amersterdam.
Former titles (until 2006): Haven Amsterdam (0920-3753); (until 1986): Haven Bulletin (0920-4466)
Indexed: CLT&T, HRIS.
Published by: Amsterdam Ports Association, Het Havengebouw, 13e stock, De Ruyterkade 7, Amsterdam, 1013 AA, Netherlands. TEL 31-20-6273706, FAX 31-20-6264969, amports@amports.nl, http://www.amports.nl. adv.: B&W page EUR 997, color page EUR 1,797; bleed 210 x 297. Circ: 6,100.

387.1 GBR ISSN 1751-2298
ZEELAND SEAPORTS PORT HANDBOOK. Text in English. 2003. biennial. **Document type:** *Handbook/Manual/Guide, Trade.*
Formerly (until 2006): Terneuzen-Vlissingen Port Handbook (1740-7990); Which was formed by the merger of (1997-2000): Terneusen Ports Handbook (1460-7379); Which was formerly (until 1997): Havenschap Terneuzen Handbook (0968-7440); Terneusen Ports Handbook incorporated (1994-1997): Vlissingen Ports Handbook (1357-3497); Which was formerly (1992-1994): Flushing Ports Handbook (0966-839X)
Related titles: Online - full text ed.: free (effective 2010).
Published by: Land & Marine Publications Ltd., 1 Kings Ct, Newcomen Way, Severalls Business Park, Colchester, Essex CO4 9RA, United Kingdom. TEL 44-1206-752902, FAX 44-1206-842958, publishing@landmarine.com, http://www.landmarine.com.

387.330 CHN ISSN 1671-9360
ZHONG-CHUAN ZHONGGONG. Text in Chinese. 2001. w. CNY 240 (effective 2009). **Document type:** *Newspaper, Trade.*
Published by: Zhongguo Chuanbo Zhonggong Jituan Gongsi/China Shipbuilding Industry Corporation, 5, Yuetan Bei Jie, Beijing, 100861, China. TEL 86-10-59518792, FAX 86-10-59518799, csic@csic.com.cn.

387 CHN
ZHONGGUO CHUANBO BAO/CHINA SHIP NEWS. Text in Chinese. 1990. w. (Mon.). adv. **Document type:** *Newspaper, Trade.*
Description: Reports up-to-date developments in marine policy, economic and trade information, new product and technology.
Formed by the merger of (1979-1990): Chuanbo Shijie; (1983-1990): Chuanbo Gongye
Related titles: Online - full text ed.
Published by: (Zhongguo Chuanbo Gongye Zonggongsi), Zhongguo Chuanbo Baoshe, 5 Yuetan Beijie, Beijing, 100861, China. TEL 86-10-68058257, 86-10-59517980, FAX 86-10-59517855. Ed. Huo Rusu. Adv. contact Zhenqing Wang. B&W page CNY 50,000, color page CNY 90,000; 35 x 48. Circ: 59,000. **Dist. overseas by:** China International Book Trading Corp, 35 Chegongzhuang Xilu, Haidian District, PO Box 399, Beijing 100044, China.

387 CHN ISSN 1006-124X
HE559.C5
ZHONGGUO GANGKOU/PORTS OF CHINA. Text in Chinese. 1986. m. USD 74.40 (effective 2009). adv. **Document type:** *Trade.*
Description: Covers the exchanges between domestic and foreign harbors, management and administration, and the construction of Chinese ports and harbors.
Related titles: Online - full text ed.
Published by: Zhongguo Gangkou Zashishe, Room 415, 12 Zhongshan E 2 Lu, Shanghai, 200002, China. TEL 86-21-64314037, FAX 86-21-64314037, TELEX 33023 SHACO CN. Ed., R&P Tang Shaowu. Pub. Liu Lizhu. Adv. contact Xizhang Xu. Circ: 20,000.

ZHONGGUO GUANXING JISHU XUEBAO/JOURNAL OF CHINESE SOCIETY OF INERTIAL TECHNOLOGY. *see* ENGINEERING

387 363.11 CHN ISSN 1673-2278
ZHONGGUO HAISHI/CHINA MARITIME SAFETY. Text in Chinese. 1980. m. CNY 15, USD 10 per issue (effective 2011). adv. back issues avail. **Document type:** *Journal, Academic/Scholarly.*
Former titles (until 2005): Jiaotong Huanbao/Environmental Protection in Transportation (1673-405X); (until 1980): Jiaotong Huanbao (Shuiyun Ban)/Environmental Protection in Transportation (Water Transportation Edition) (1006-4281)
Related titles: Online - full text ed.
Published by: (Zhonghua Renming Gonghe Haishiju/Maritime Safety Administration of the People's Republic of China, Zhonghua Renming Gonghe Tianjin Hashiju/Tianjin Maritime Safety Administration of P.R.C.), Zhongguo Haishi Zazhishe, 34, Heiniucheng Dao, Hexi-qu, Tianjin, 300211, China. TEL 86-22-28235119, FAX 86-22-28226358. Ed. Yaping Ma.

387 CHN
ZHONGGUO HAIYUAN/CHINESE SEAMEN. Text in Chinese. bi-m.
Published by: Zhongguo Haiyuan Gonghui/China Seamen's Union, 1441 Changyang Lu, Shanghai, 200090, China. TEL 5462878. Ed. Tong Menghou.

387 CHN ISSN 1000-4653
ZHONGGUO HANGHAI/CHINESE NAVIGATION. Text in Chinese. s-a. USD 32 (effective 2009).
Related titles: Online - full text ed.
Indexed: A28, APA, ASFA, BrCerAb, C&ISA, CA/WCA, CIA, CerAb, CivEngAb, CorrAb, E&CAJ, E11, EEA, EMA, ESPM, EnvEAb, H15, M&TEA, M09, MBF, METADEX, OceAb, RefZh, SolStAb, T04, WAA.
—East View, Linda Hall.
Published by: Jiaotong-bu, Shanghai Chuanbo Yunshu Kexue Yanjiusuo/Ministry of Transportation, Shanghai Institute of Shipping Transportation Science, 200 Minsheng Lu, Shanghai, 200135, China. TEL 8840348. Ed. Qiu Min. **Co-sponsor:** Zhongguo Hanghai Xuehui.

387 CHN ISSN 1006-2149
ZHONGGUO HANGWU ZHOUKAN/CHINA SHIPPING GAZETTE. Text in Chinese. 1993. w. USD 462.80 (effective 2009). **Document type:** *Magazine, Trade.*
—East View.
Published by: Zhongguo Jiaotong Yunshu Xiehui/China Communications and Transportation Association, 23 Shijin Huayuan Hutong, Dongsi, Beijing, 100007, China. TEL 86-10-84514532, FAX 86-10-64610196.

387 CHN ISSN 1673-3185
➤ **ZHONGGUO JIANCHUAN YANJIU/CHINESE JOURNAL OF SHIP RESEARCH.** Text in Chinese; Abstracts in Chinese, English. 2006. bi-m. CNY 120, USD 60; CNY 20 per issue (effective 2009). **Document type:** *Journal, Academic/Scholarly.* **Description:** Covers the latest developments of theoretical and applied researches in the fields of Naval Architecture, Shipbuilding and Marine engineering.
Related titles: Online - full text ed.
Address: 268 Ziyang Rd., Wuchang District, Wuhan, 430064, China. TEL 86-27-88730832, FAX 86-27-88730832. Ed. Ying-fu Zhu.

387 CHN ISSN 1001-8328
ZHONGGUO XIUCHUAN/CHINA SHIPREPAIR. Text in Chinese. 1987. bi-m. CNY 6.50 newsstand/cover (effective 2004). adv. index.
Description: Provides news and technical developments in the Chinese ship repairing industry.
Related titles: Online - full text ed.
Published by: Zhongguo Chuanbo Zonggongsi Tianjin Xiuchuan Jishu Yianjiusuo/The China State Ship-building Corporation, Ship-repairing Technology Research Institute of Tianjin, PO Box 562, Tianjin, 300456, China. TEL 86-22-5792835, FAX 86-22-5794559, TELEX 23166 TJSIC CN. Ed. Wang Ying. **Dist. by:** China International Book Trading Corp, 35 Chegongzhuang Xilu, Haidian District, PO Box 399, Beijing 100044, China. TEL 86-10-68412045, FAX 86-10-68412023, cibtc@mail.cibtc.com.cn, http://www.cibtc.com.cn.

387 CHN ISSN 1673-6664
ZHONGGUO YUANYANG HANGWU/CHINA MARITIME. Text in Chinese. 1995. m. **Document type:** *Magazine, Trade.* **Description:** Covers domestic and international shipping outlook, markets, and logistics, including information on schedules, movements, and trade and freight rates.
Formerly (until 2006): Zhongguo Yuanyang Hangwu Gonggao/China Shipping Bulletin (1006-4265)
Related titles: Online - full text ed.
Published by: Zhongguo Yuanyang Yunshu (Jituan) Zonggongsi/China Ocean Shipping (Group) Company, Rm.812, Lucky Tower A, 3 Dong San Huan Bei Rd., Chaoyang District, Beijing, 100027, China. TEL 86-10-64616218, FAX 86-10-64616131, http://www.cosco.com.cn.

387 TWN ISSN 1023-4535
ZHONGGUO ZAOCHUAN JI LUNJI GONGCHENG XUEKAN/NAVAL ARCHITECTS AND MARINE ENGINEERS, REPUBLIC OF CHINA. SOCIETY. Text in Chinese. 1989. s-a. TWD 300 to non-members; free to members (effective 2008). **Document type:** *Journal, Academic/Scholarly.*
Indexed: CPEI, SCOPUS.
—BLDSC (9512.835050).
Published by: Zhongguo Zaochuan ji Lunji Gongcheng Shixuehui/Society of Naval Architects and Marine Engineers, Republic of China, 10F, No.7, Sec.2, Anho Rd., Taipei, Taiwan. TEL 886-2-27050753, sname@seed.net.tw, http://www.ship.org.tw/. Pub. J.L. Hwang.

623.82 JPN ISSN 0387-2203
VM4
ZOSEN GIJUTSU/SHIPBUILDING AND ENGINEERING. Text in Japanese. 1968. m. JPY 1,400 per issue. **Document type:** *Trade.*
Published by: Japan Industrial Publishing Co., Ltd., Yubinkyo-ku, P.O. Box 9, shirai, Chiba-ken 270-14, Japan.

623.82 JPN
ZOSEN GIJUTSU KENKYU KAIHATSU KADAI CHOSHO/REPORTS OF DEVELOPMENT OF SHIPBUILDING TECHNIQUE. Text in Japanese. a. **Document type:** *Trade.*
Published by: Zosen Gijutsu Kaihatsu Kyogi Kiko/Organization for Development of Shipbuilding Techniques, Nihon Zosen Kenkyu Kyokai, 15-16 Toranomon 1-chome, Minato-ku, Tokyo, 105-0001, Japan.

623.82 JPN
ZOSEN GIJUTSU KENKYU KAIHATSU KADAISHU/RESEARCH SUBJECT FOR DEVELOPMENT SHIPBUILDING TECHNIQUES. Text in Japanese. 1969. a. **Document type:** *Trade.*
Published by: Zosen Gijutsu Kaihatsu Kyogi Kiko/Organization for Development of Shipbuilding Techniques, Nihon Zosen Kenkyu Kyokai, 15-16 Toranomon 1-chome, Minato-ku, Tokyo, 105-0001, Japan.

623.82 JPN
ZOSEN GIJUTSU, KIKAN. Text in Japanese. 1988. q. JPY 2,000 per issue.
Published by: Japan Industrial Publishing Co., Ltd., Yubinkyo-ku, P.O. Box 9, shirai, Chiba-ken 270-14, Japan.

623.82 JPN ISSN 0514-7999
ZOSEN KENKYU/SHIPBUILDING RESEARCH. Text in Japanese. 1960. q. **Document type:** *Trade.*
Published by: Nihon Zosen Kenkyu Kyokai/Shipbuilding Research Association of Japan, 15-16 Toranomon 1-chome, Minato-ku, Tokyo, 105-0001, Japan.

623.82 JPN
ZOSEN ZOKI TOKEI GEPPO/MONTHLY REPORT OF SHIPBUILDING AND MACHINE MAKING. Text in Japanese. 1950. m. **Document type:** *Government.*
Published by: (Japan. Joho Kanribu), Un'yusho, Un'yu Seisakukyoku/Ministry of Transport, Transport Policy Bureau, Research and Data Processing Department, 1-3 Kasumigaseki 2-chome, Chiyoda-ku, Tokyo, 100-0013, Japan.

623.82 JPN
ZOSENGYO DAYORI/SHIPBUILDING NEWS. Text in Japanese. 1963. m. JPY 200 per issue. **Document type:** *Trade.*
Published by: Nihon Kogata Senpaku Kogyoka/Cooperative Association of Japan Shipbuilders, c/o Chuzoko Secretariat, Senpaku Shinko Bldg, 15-16, Toranomon 1-chome, Minato-ku, Tokyo, 105, Japan. TEL 81-3-35022061, FAX 81-3-35031479, info@chuzoko.or.jp, http://www.cajs.or.jp/.

TRANSPORTATION—Trucks And Trucking

A M S A SCALE DIRECTORY. *see* BUSINESS AND ECONOMICS—Trade And Industrial Directories

629.222 USA ISSN 1091-045X
A T H S SHOW TIME. Text in English. 1994. a., latest 2000. USD 20 (effective 2000). illus. back issues avail. **Document type:** *Journal, Trade.*
Published by: American Truck Historical Society, PO Box 901611, Kansas City, MO 64190-1611. TEL 205-870-0566, FAX 205-870-3069. R&P Larry L Scheef. Circ: 4,000.

388.324 SWE ISSN 0348-0356
AAKERI & TRANSPORT. Abbreviated title: Aa T. Text in Swedish. 1941. m. (9/yr.). SEK 220 (effective 1990). adv. bk.rev. charts; illus.
Former titles (until 1987): Aakeri och Transport; (until 1977): Aakerifoeretagaren - Transportoeren; Which was formed by the 1942 merger of: Transportoeren; Aakerifoeretagaren (0001-298X)
Published by: Aakeriaegarnas Centralfoerbund, Vimmerby, 59810, Sweden. Ed. Alf Wesik. Circ: 26,000.

388.324 ITA ISSN 1825-2958
ACCESSO ALL'AUTOTRASPORTO DI MERCI. COMMISSIONE D'ESAME. Text in Italian. 2005. a. **Document type:** *Magazine, Trade.*
Published by: Edizioni Giuridico Amministrative e Formazione (E G A F), Via Filippo Guarini 2, Forli, 47100, Italy. TEL 39-0543-473347, FAX 39-0543-474133, gruppo@egaf.it, http://www.egaf.it.

388.324 ITA ISSN 1825-2966
ACCESSO ALL'AUTOTRASPORTO DI MERCI. GESTIONE CORSI E QUIZ. Text in Italian. 2005. a. **Document type:** *Magazine, Trade.*
Published by: Edizioni Giuridico Amministrative e Formazione (E G A F), Via Filippo Guarini 2, Forli, 47100, Italy. TEL 39-0543-473347, FAX 39-0543-474133, gruppo@egaf.it, http://www.egaf.it.

388.324 ITA ISSN 1825-294X
ACCESSO ALL'AUTOTRASPORTO DI VIAGGIATORI. Text in Italian. 2005. a. **Document type:** *Magazine, Trade.*
Published by: Edizioni Giuridico Amministrative e Formazione (E G A F), Via Filippo Guarini 2, Forli, 47100, Italy. TEL 39-0543-473347, FAX 39-0543-474133, gruppo@egaf.it, http://www.egaf.it.

388.329 ITA ISSN 1824-5668
ACCORDO A T P E NORME COMPLEMENTARI SUL TRASPORTO DI MERCI DETERIORABILI. Text in Italian. 1997. m. **Document type:** *Magazine, Trade.*
Related titles: Online - full text ed.: ISSN 1826-8722. 2006.
Published by: Edizioni Giuridico Amministrative e Formazione (E G A F), Via Filippo Guarini 2, Forli, 47100, Italy. TEL 39-0543-473347, FAX 39-0543-474133, gruppo@egaf.it, http://www.egaf.it.

388.324 USA
ADVANCED FLEET. Text in English. 2005 (Aug.). q. **Document type:** *Magazine, Trade.* **Description:** Targets automobile and truck fleet managers and organizational strategists at corporations and organizations who are using or monitoring the advanced vehicle technology industry.
Published by: R P Publishing, Inc., 2696 S Colorado Blvd, Ste 595, Denver, CO 80222-5944. TEL 303-863-0521, FAX 303-863-1722, info@rppublishing.com, http://www.rppublishing.com.

AIR CONDITIONING & HEATING SERVICE & REPAIR - DOMESTIC CARS, LIGHT TRUCKS & VANS. *see* TRANSPORTATION—Automobiles

388.324 USA ISSN 0897-0807
AMERICAN MOTOR CARRIER DIRECTORY: NORTH AMERICAN EDITION. Text in English. a. USD 499 per issue (effective 2008). adv. **Document type:** *Directory, Trade.*

Incorporates: American Motor Carrier Directory: Specialized Services Edition (0569-6364); Formerly: American Motor Carrier Directory: National Edition (0569-6356)
Published by: Commonwealth Business Media, Inc. (Subsidiary of: United Business Media Limited), 400 Windsor Corporate Park, 50 Millstone Rd, Ste 200, East Windsor, NJ 08520. TEL 609-371-7700, 800-221-5488, FAX 609-371-7883, cbizservices@sunbeltfs.com, http://www.cbizmedia.com.

388.324 USA ISSN 1090-9680
AMERICAN TRUCKER (CENTRAL EDITION). Text in English. 1980. m. USD 48 (effective 2011). adv. **Document type:** *Magazine, Trade.* **Description:** Advertises new and used trucks for sale, equipment, supplies, financing and other services geared to the trucking industry.
Formerly: Central States Trucker (1049-006X)
Related titles: ◆ Regional ed(s).: American Trucker (East Edition).
Published by: Penton Media, Inc., 8109 Greeley Blvd, Springfield, VA 22152. TEL 703-569-1829, information@penton.com, http://www.penton.com. Ed. Sean Kilcarr. adv.: page USD 1,282. Circ: 32,000 (paid and controlled).

388.324 USA
AMERICAN TRUCKER (EAST EDITION). Text in English. 1980. m. USD 48 (effective 2011). adv. **Document type:** *Magazine, Trade.* **Description:** Advertises new and used trucks for sale, equipment, supplies, financing and other services geared to the trucking industry.
Former titles: American Trucker (Metro East Edition) (1090-9737); (until 199?): Keystone / Jersey Truck Exchange (1049-0582)
Related titles: ◆ Regional ed(s).: American Trucker (Central Edition). ISSN 1090-9680.
Published by: Penton Media, Inc., 8109 Greeley Blvd, Springfield, VA 22152. TEL 703-569-1829, 800-827-7468, information@penton.com, http://www.pentonmedia.com. Ed. Sean Kilcarr. adv.: page USD 1,345. Circ: 29,700 (paid and controlled).

338.324 USA
AMERICAN TRUCKER (WEST EDITION). Text in English. m. USD 48 (effective 2011). **Document type:** *Magazine, Trade.*
Published by: Penton Media, Inc., 8109 Greeley Blvd, Springfield, VA 22152. TEL 703-569-1829, 800-827-7468, information@penton.com, http://www.pentonmedia.com. Ed. Sean Kilcarr.

388.324 USA ISSN 1091-9384
AMERICA'S DRIVING FORCE. Variant title: Driving Force. Text in English. 1996. m. adv. bk.rev.; software rev. maps; stat. back issues avail. **Document type:** *Magazine, Trade.* **Description:** Targeted to long-haul truck drivers and includes industry news, product information, and career opportunities.
Published by: American Graphics Group, LLC, 1001 Noble St, Ste 300, Anniston, AL 36207-4658. TEL 256-241-2060, 800-755-0288, FAX 256-241-2065. Pub. Brad Bentley. Adv. contact Bill Summerlin. page USD 1,895; trim 5.25 x 8.25. Circ: 175,000 (controlled).

388.324 USA
ANTIQUE TRUCK REGISTRY. Text in English. 1985. irreg. USD 10 (effective 2001). **Document type:** *Directory.* **Description:** Lists over 6,000 trucks, tractors and trailers, representing 249 manufacturers owned by 2,015 members of the society.
Published by: American Truck Historical Society, PO Box 901611, Kansas City, MO 64190-1611. TEL 205-870-0566, FAX 205-870-3069. R&P Larry L Scheef.

388.324 USA
ARKANSAS TRUCKING REPORT; regional journal of the Arkansas Trucking Association. Text in English. s-a. free to qualified personnel. adv. 48 p./no. 3 cols./p.; back issues avail.; reprints avail. **Document type:** *Newsletter, Trade.* **Description:** Items and articles of interest to those in the trucking industry.
Former titles: A M C A Trucking Report; Arkansas Motor Carrier
Related titles: Online - full text ed.
Published by: Arkansas Trucking Association, Inc., PO Box 3476, Little Rock, AR 72203-2798. Pub. Jennifer Matthews-Kidd. adv.: color page USD 1,425. Circ: 9,000 (controlled and free).

388.324 CAN ISSN 0830-1808
ATLANTIC TRUCKING. Text in English. 1956. q. CAD 20. adv. illus. **Document type:** *Magazine, Trade.* **Description:** Features people in the industry, new product news and industry updates.
Former titles: Atlantic Truck Transport Review (0004-6868); Maritime Truck Transport Review
Indexed: CLT&T.
Published by: Atlantic Provinces Trucking Association, 407 Dieppe Blvd, Dieppe, NB E1A 6P8, Canada. TEL 506-855-2782, FAX 506-853-7424. Ed. Ralph Boyd. Circ: 2,000.

AUSTRALASIAN TRANSPORT NEWS. *see* BUSINESS AND ECONOMICS—Management

388.324 NLD ISSN 1382-0559
AUTO- EN TRANSPORTWERELD. Text in Dutch. 1948. bi-w. EUR 81.50 domestic; EUR 115 in Belgium; EUR 230 in Europe; EUR 275 elsewhere (effective 2010). adv.
—IE, Infotrieve.
Published by: Peters Uitgevers Maatschappij B.V., Postbus 160, Deventer, 7400 AD, Netherlands. TEL 31-570-628092, FAX 31-570-636129. Ed. H Peters. Adv. contact R Eijkelenkamp. B&W page EUR 1,825; 280 x 380. Circ: 11,000.

AUTODOPRAVA V PRAXI. *see* LAW

388.324 DEU
B G L INFODIENST. (Bundesverband Gueterkraftverkehr Logistik und Entsorgung) Text in German. 1992. s-m. free (effective 2009). **Document type:** *Bulletin, Trade.*
Formerly (until 1997): B D F Infodienst
Published by: Bundesverband Gueterkraftverkehr Logistik und Entsorgung e.V., Breitenbachstr 1, Frankfurt Am Main, 60487, Germany. TEL 49-69-79190, FAX 49-69-7919227, bgl@bgl-ev.de, http://www.bgl-ev.de. Ed. Karlheinz Schmidt.

388.324 ZAF ISSN 1991-6450
BAKKIE AND TRUCK ACTION. Text in English. 1997. bi-m. adv. **Document type:** *Magazine, Consumer.* **Description:** Focuses on light commercial and utility vehicles.
Formerly (until 2006): Bakkie and Recreational Vehicle (1027-8354)
Published by: Action Publications cc, PO Box 70174, Bryanston, South Africa. TEL 27-11-4631191, FAX 27-11-4632466. Ed. Jesse Adams. Pub. Michele Lupini. adv.: page ZAR 15,000; trim 220 x 285. Circ: 10,534.

388.324 USA
BIG RIG OWNER. Text in English. 2005. m. free to qualified personnel (effective 2006). adv. **Document type:** *Magazine, Trade.*
Related titles: Online - full text ed.
Published by: American Graphics Group, LLC, 1001 Noble St, Ste 300, Anniston, AL 36207-4658. TEL 256-241-3317, 800-755-0288, FAX 256-241-2065. adv.: B&W page USD 1,895; trim 5.5 x 8.5. Circ: 130,000 (controlled).

BLACK BOOK. HEAVY DUTY TRUCK GUIDE. *see* BUSINESS AND ECONOMICS—Trade And Industrial Directories

BLACK BOOK. TRUCK XPRESS. *see* BUSINESS AND ECONOMICS—Trade And Industrial Directories

388.324 NOR ISSN 1504-4017
BLADET NORSK TRANSPORT. Text in Norwegian. 1991. 11/yr. (11/yr.). NOK 400 domestic; NOK 510 foreign (effective 2006). adv. charts. **Document type:** *Trade.*
Formerly (until 2005): Lastebilen (0023-8686)
Related titles: Online - full text ed.
—CCC.
Published by: Norges Lastebileier-Forbund/Norwegian Haulier's Association, PO Box 7134, St. Olavs Plass, Oslo, 0130, Norway. TEL 47-22-033200, FAX 47-22-205615, post@lastebil.no. Ed. Rolf Kristansen. Pub. Gunnar Apeland. Adv. contact Gunvor Samuelsen TEL 47-22-620403. page NOK 17,800; 196 x 263. Circ: 13,274 (controlled).

388.324 AUT
BLICKPUNKT L K W UND BUS. Text in German. 9/yr. **Document type:** *Trade.*
Address: Schuetzenstrasse 11, Kufstein, T 6330, Austria. TEL 43-5372-62332, FAX 43-5372-623324. Ed. Harald Gamper.

388.324 USA ISSN 1555-3795
TN860
BULK TRANSPORTER. Text in English. 1937. m. USD 47 in US & Canada; USD 93 foreign; free in US & Canada to qualified personnel (effective 2011). adv. charts; illus.; stat.; tr.lit. back issues avail.; reprints avail. **Document type:** *Magazine, Trade.* **Description:** Offers detailed coverage of important developments in regulations, equipment, services and operations affecting the safe and timely transport of pure bulk products.
Former titles (until 2005): Modern Bulk Transporter (0031-6431); (until 1970): Petroleum and Chemical Transporter
Related titles: Online - full text ed.
Indexed: A10, B01, B02, B03, B06, B07, B09, B11, B15, B17, B18, BPI, BRD, CA, CLT&T, G04, G06, G07, G08, HRIS, I05, LogistBibl, P34, T02, V03, W01, W02, W03, W05.
—CIS, Ingenta. **CCC.**
Published by: Penton Media, Inc., 4200 S Shepherd Dr, Ste 200, Houston, TX 77098. TEL 713-523-8124, FAX 713-523-8384, information@penton.com, http://www.penton.com. Ed. Charles E Wilson. Circ: 16,000 (paid and controlled).

388.324 USA
HE5613.6.U5
C T B S S P RESEARCH RESULTS DIGESTS. Text in English. 2002 (Oct.). irreg., latest 2005. **Document type:** *Government.*
Indexed: HRIS.
Published by: Commercial Truck and Bus Safety Synthesis Program, c/o Christopher W. Jenks, Transportation Research Board, 500 Fifth St., NW, Washington, DC 20001. TEL 202-334-3089, FAX 202-334-2006, cjenks@nas.edu, http://www4.trb.org/trb/crp.nsf/reference/appendices/ctbssp.

388.324 USA ISSN 1544-6808
TL230.A1
C T B S S P SYNTHESIS REPORTS/SYNTHESIS REPORTS. Text in English. 2003. irreg. **Document type:** *Government.*
Indexed: HRIS.
—BLDSC (8586.785500), IE, Linda Hall.
Published by: Commercial Truck and Bus Safety Synthesis Program, c/o Christopher W. Jenks, Transportation Research Board, 500 Fifth St., NW, Washington, DC 20001. TEL 202-334-3089, FAX 202-334-2006, cjenks@nas.edu, http://www4.trb.org/trb/crp.nsf/reference/appendices/ctbssp.

388.324 USA ISSN 1940-2880
CALIFORNIA TRANSPORTATION NEWS. Text in English. 19??. m. free to members (effective 2007). **Document type:** *Magazine, Trade.*
Published by: California Dump Truck Owners Association, 334 N. Euclid Ave, Upland, CA 91786. TEL 909-982-9898, FAX 909-985-2348, http://www.cdtoa.org/home.asp.

388.324 USA ISSN 1040-2705
CALTRUX. Variant title: California Trucking Association. Newsletter. Text in English. 1949. w. membership. adv. charts; illus. **Document type:** *Newsletter.*
Published by: California Trucking Association, 1251 Beacon Blvd, West Sacramento, CA 95691. TEL 916-329-3554. Ed. Deborah B Smith. Circ: 4,400.

388.324 ITA ISSN 1128-6229
CAMION SUPERMARKET. Text in Italian. 1999. m. **Document type:** *Magazine, Consumer.*
Published by: Edizeta Srl, Via Lussinpiccolo 19, Mestre, VE 30174, Italy. TEL 39-041-5459500, FAX 39-041-5459555, redazione@edizeta.com, http://www.edizeta.it.

388.324 USA
CAMIONES. Text in Spanish. 1994. q. USD 20. adv. **Document type:** *Magazine, Trade.* **Description:** For Mexican truck fleet managers. Includes information on state of the art equipment and operating procedures. Also covers new products, regulations, maintenance, and cross-border trucking news.
Published by: Newport Communications (Irvine) (Subsidiary of: H.I.C. Corporation), 38 Executive Pk, Ste 300, Irvine, CA 92614. TEL 949-261-1636, FAX 949-261-2904, aryder@truckinginfo.com. Ed. Andrew Ryder. Circ: 6,500 (controlled).

388.324 FRA ISSN 1961-0203
CAMIONS D'HIER ET D'AUJOURD'HUI. Text in French. 2007. bi-m. EUR 34.50 domestic; EUR 41.50 foreign (effective 2008). **Document type:** *Magazine, Consumer.*
Published by: Histoire et Collection, 5 Av. de la Republique, Paris, 75011, France. TEL 33-1-40211820, FAX 33-1-47005111, fredbey@club-internet.fr, http://www.histoireetcollections.com.

388.324 USA
CAR AND DRIVER TRUCK BUYERS GUIDE. Text in English. 1993. a. USD 4.99 newsstand/cover (effective 2009). adv. charts; illus.; stat. **Document type:** *Magazine, Consumer.* **Description:** Covers the market of pickups, trucks, vans, minivans, sport-utility vehicles and 4-wheel drive vehicles with complete coverage of all models sold in the US.
Published by: Hachette Filipacchi Media U.S., Inc. (Subsidiary of: Hachette Filipacchi Medias S.A.), 1633 Broadway, New York, NY 10019. TEL 212-767-6000, FAX 212-767-5600, privacy@hfmus.com, http://www.hfmus.com. Pub. Edward Abramson. adv.: B&W page USD 18,761, color page USD 28,758. Circ: 25,000.

363.17 USA
CARGO TANK HAZARDOUS MATERIAL REGULATIONS. Text in English. a. USD 75 to non-members; USD 53 to members (effective 2000).
Published by: National Tank Truck Carriers, Inc., 2200 Mill Rd, Alexandria, VA 22314-4677. TEL 703-838-1960, FAX 703-684-5753. Circ: 3,000.

388.324 CHE
CARROSSIER. Text in German. 1976 (vol.4). bi-m. CHF 49 domestic; CHF 56 foreign (effective 2000). adv. charts; illus. **Document type:** *Journal, Trade.*
Published by: (Verband der Schweizerischen Carrosserie-Industrie), Huber und Co. AG, Promenadenstr 16, Frauenfeld, 8501, Switzerland. TEL 41-54-271111.

CATALOGO MOTORISTICO. *see* TRANSPORTATION—Automobiles

388.324 USA ISSN 1932-250X
CHANGING LANES. Text in English. 2005. m. adv. back issues avail. **Document type:** *Magazine, Trade.*
Related titles: Online - full text ed.: free (effective 2011).
Published by: Randall-Reilly Publishing Company, 3200 Rice Mine Rd NE, Tuscaloosa, AL 35406. TEL 800-633-5953, http://www.randallpub.com. Ed. Brad Bentley. Pub. Scott Miller TEL 800-633-5953 ext 1393.

629.222 FRA ISSN 1240-2346
CHARGE UTILE MAGAZINE. Text in French. 1992. m. EUR 67 domestic; EUR 80 foreign (effective 2009). back issues avail. **Document type:** *Magazine, Consumer.* **Description:** Covers the history and collecting of trucks and utility vehicles of all kinds.
Published by: Histoire et Collection, 5 Av. de la Republique, Paris, 75011, France. TEL 33-1-40211820, FAX 33-1-47005111, fredbey@club-internet.fr, http://www.histoireetcollections.com.

629.224 USA
CHEVY TRUCK WORLD. Text in English. q. adv. **Document type:** *Magazine, Consumer.*
Published by: T E N Magazines, 1760 California Ave, Ste 101, Corona, CA 92881. TEL 951-371-8361, press@TenMagazines.com, http://www.tenmagazines.com.

CHEVY TRUCKIN'. *see* TRANSPORTATION—Automobiles

CHINA AUTOMOTIVE JOURNAL/XIANDAI QICHE; an automotive journal for P.R. China. *see* TRANSPORTATION—Automobiles

629.2230941 GBR ISSN 2042-3152
CLASSIC CAR WORLD. Text in English. 2000 (Nov.). m. adv. back issues avail. **Document type:** *Magazine, Trade.* **Description:** Covers an incisive range of topics including news, events and shows, readers' projects and analysis of vehicles available for sale, together with historical perspectives and an active classified section.
Supersedes in part (in 2010): Classic Car & Van World (2042-1516); Which was formerly (until 2009): Classic Van and Pick-Up (1472-1821)
Related titles: Online - full text ed.
Published by: Kelsey Publishing Ltd., Cudham Tithe Barn, Berry's Hill, Cudham, Kent TN16 3AG, United Kingdom. TEL 44-1959-541444, FAX 44-1959-541400, info@kelsey.co.uk. Ed. Paul Wager. Adv. contact Sarah Garrod TEL 44-1733-353353.

CLASSIC CARS & PARTS. *see* TRANSPORTATION—Automobiles

629.2230941 GBR ISSN 2042-4140
▼ **CLASSIC VAN AND PICK-UP.** Text in English. 2010. m. GBP 36 domestic; GBP 41.40 in Europe; GBP 47.28 elsewhere; GBP 3.30 per issue domestic; GBP 4.30 per issue in Europe; GBP 4.80 per issue elsewhere (effective 2010). adv. back issues avail. **Document type:** *Magazine, Consumer.* **Description:** Covers news, events and shows, readers' projects and analysis of vehicles available for sale, together with historical perspectives and an active classified section.
Published by: Kelsey Publishing Ltd., Cudham Tithe Barn, Berry's Hill, Cudham, Kent TN16 3AG, United Kingdom. TEL 44-1959-541444, FAX 44-1959-541400, info@kelsey.co.uk, http://www.kelsey.co.uk. Eds. Ted Connolly, Phil Weeden TEL 44-1733-353372. Adv. contact Adam Fergar.

388.324 DEU ISSN 1864-3000
CLICK; Truck - Bus - Bau. Text in German. 2000. a. EUR 4 newsstand/cover (effective 2010). adv. **Document type:** *Magazine, Trade.*
Published by: Stuenings Medien GmbH, Diessemer Bruch 167, Krefeld, 47805, Germany. TEL 49-2151-51000, FAX 49-2151-5100101, medien@stuenings.de, http://www.stuenings.de. Ed. Lutz Gerritzen. Adv. contact Cornelia Assem.

CODE DE LA SECURITE ROUTIERE ANALYTIQUE. *see* LAW

388.324 USA ISSN 1533-7502
TL1
COMMERCIAL CARRIER JOURNAL. Abbreviated title: C C J. Text in English. 1911. m. USD 48 domestic; USD 78 in Canada; USD 6 per issue domestic; USD 9 per issue in Canada & Mexico; USD 12 per issue elsewhere; free to qualified personnel (effective 2011). adv. bk.rev. charts; illus.; stat.; tr.lit. index. back issues avail.; reprints avail. **Document type:** *Magazine, Trade.* **Description:** For transportation managers with 10 or more heavy-duty vehicles. Articles encompass the spectrum of fleet management concerns - maintenance, operations, productivity, information technologies, safety, enviornment, drivers, new products and services, regulations, news on fleets, labor and more.

Incorporates (in 1999): Trucking Company (1532-1053); Former titles (until 1999): Commercial Carrier Journal for Professional Fleet Managers (1099-4173); (until 1997): Chilton's Commercial Carrier Journal for Professional Fleet Managers (1062-0060); (until 1990): Commercial Carrier Journal for Professional Fleet Managers (1062-0052); (until 1989): Chilton's C C J (8755-2531); (until 1984): Chilton's Commercial Carrier Journal (0734-1423); (until 1982): Chilton's C C J (0193-628X); (until 1977): Commercial Car Journal (0010-292X)
Related titles: Microfiche ed.: (from CIS); Microfilm ed.: (from PQC); Online - full text ed.: free (effective 2011).
Indexed: A09, A10, A22, B01, B03, B06, B07, B09, B11, CLT&T, HRIS, I05, P06, PROMT, S22, SRI, T02, V03, V04.
—CCC.
Published by: Randall-Reilly Publishing Company, 3200 Rice Mine Rd NE, Tuscaloosa, AL 35406. TEL 800-633-5953, http://www.randallpub.com. Eds. Jeff Crissey, Avery Vise TEL 205-248-1386. Pub. Stacy McCants. Circ: 96,500.

388.324 GBR ISSN 0010-3063
TL1
COMMERCIAL MOTOR. Text in English. 1905. w. GBP 116 domestic; EUR 252 in Europe; USD 375 elsewhere (effective 2010). adv. bk.rev. charts; illus.; mkt.; stat. s-a. index. **Document type:** *Magazine, Trade.* **Description:** Depicts as road transport industry's weekly giving its readers industry news, road tests, features, special supplements, and vehicle classified section in the business.
Incorporates (19??-1972): Commercial Vehicles (0010-3136)
Related titles: Microform ed.: (from PMC, PQC); Online - full text ed.
Indexed: A09, A10, A15, ABIn, B01, B02, B06, B07, B09, B15, B17, B18, BPI, BRD, BrTechI, CA, CISA, E11, G04, G08, HRIS, I05, P34, P48, P51, P52, PQC, SCOPUS, T02, T04, V03, V04, W01, W02, W03, W05.
—CIS, IE, Infotrieve, Linda Hall. **CCC.**
Published by: Reed Business Information Ltd. (Subsidiary of: Reed Business), Quadrant House, The Quadrant, Sutton, Surrey SM2 5AS, United Kingdom. TEL 44-20-86523500, FAX 44-20-86528932, rbi.subscriptions@qss-uk.com. Ed. Justin Stanton TEL 44-20-86523303. **Subscr. to:** Quadrant Subscription Services, Rockwood House, 9-17 Perrymount Rd, Haywards Heath, W. Sussex RH16 3DH, United Kingdom. TEL 44-845-0778844, FAX 44-845-6760030, qss.customer.services@quadrantsubs.com, http://www.quadrantsubs.com.

388.324 658 ZAF ISSN 1812-271X
COMMERCIAL TRADER. Text in English. 2004. bi-w.
Published by: Car Trader (Pty) Ltd., PO Box 4825, Randburg, 2125, South Africa. TEL 27-11-6860900, FAX 27-11-7896449, info@autotrader.co.za.

388 ZAF
COMMERCIAL TRANSPORT. Text in English. 1945. m. ZAR 88 domestic; ZAR 170 in Namibia; ZAR 196 elsewhere (effective 2000). adv. bk.rev. charts; illus.; mkt.; tr.lit. **Document type:** *Magazine, Trade.*
Supersedes in part: Commercial Transport and Freight (0376-5849); Which was formed by the merger of: Commercial Transport (0036-2107); Freight (0016-0857)
Indexed: ISAP.
Published by: T M L Business Publishing (Subsidiary of: Times Media Ltd.), PO Box 182, Pinegowrie, Gauteng 2123, South Africa. TEL 27-11-789-2144, FAX 27-11-789-3196. Ed. Elvira Whitmore. Adv. contact Reardon Sandderson. Circ: 7,309.

388.324 ZAF ISSN 1019-0899
COMMERCIAL VEHICLE DATA DIGEST. Text in English. 1982. a. ZAR 179.80. **Document type:** *Journal, Trade.* **Description:** Provides concise, practical specifications and tune up data for all trucks marketed in South Africa.
Published by: Mead & McGrouther (Pty) Ltd., PO Box 1240, Randburg, Gauteng 2125, South Africa. TEL 27-11-789-3213, FAX 27-11-789-5218. adv.: B&W page ZAR 2,700, color page ZAR 4,100. Circ: 4,667.

388.324 ZAF
COMMERCIAL VEHICLE DEALERS' GUIDE. Text in English. 1978. m. ZAR 456.91. **Document type:** *Handbook/Manual/Guide, Trade.* **Description:** Provides trade and retail values of used commercial vehicles traded throughout South Africa.
Formerly: Commercial Vehicle Dealers' Digest (0250-0132)
Published by: Mead & McGrouther (Pty) Ltd., PO Box 1240, Randburg, Gauteng 2125, South Africa. TEL 27-11-789-3213, FAX 27-11-789-5218. Ed. O Peruch. adv.: B&W page ZAR 1,300, color page ZAR 2,075. Circ: 7,963.

CONTRAILO: Container - Trailer - Logistik. *see* BUSINESS AND ECONOMICS—Production Of Goods And Services

CORVETTE & CHEVY. *see* TRANSPORTATION—Automobiles

388.3 GBR ISSN 0070-1610
CRONER'S ROAD TRANSPORT OPERATION. Key Title: Road Transport Operation. Text in English. 1977. base vol. plus m. updates. looseleaf. GBP 567; GBP 679.01 combined subscription (print, online & CD-ROM eds.) (effective 2010). **Document type:** *Handbook/Manual/Guide, Trade.* **Description:** Provides information on U.K. and European legislation affecting operators of commercial vehicles.
Related titles: CD-ROM ed.: GBP 568 (effective 2010); Online - full text ed.: GBP 422 (effective 2010); ◆ Supplement(s): Road Transport Briefing. ISSN 0963-536X.
Published by: Croner C C H Group Ltd. (Subsidiary of: Wolters Kluwer UK Ltd.), 145 London Rd, Kingston upon Thames, Surrey KT2 6SR, United Kingdom. TEL 44-20-85473333, FAX 44-20-85472638, info@croner.co.uk.

796.72 USA ISSN 1544-4813
CUSTOM CLASSIC TRUCKS. Text in English. 1994. m. USD 15 domestic; USD 27 in Canada; USD 39 elsewhere (effective 2008). adv. back issues avail. **Document type:** *Magazine, Consumer.* **Description:** Focuses on the full range of issues related to American-manufactured vintage pickups, panels, deliveries and other trucks manufactured prior to 1985.
Former titles (until 2002): Petersen's Custom Classic Trucks (1544-4805); (until 199?): Custom & Classic Trucks (1073-4732)
Related titles: Online - full text ed.
Indexed: G06, G07, G08, I05, S23.
—CCC.
Published by: Source Interlink Companies, 774 S Placentia Ave, Placentia, CA 92870. TEL 714-939-2559, FAX 714-572-3502, dheine@sourceinterlink.com, http://www.sourceinterlinkmedia.com. Ed. John Gilbert. Pub. Tim Foss TEL 714-939-2409. adv.: B&W page USD 5,335, color page USD 7,625. Circ: 45,712 (paid).

388.324 USA ISSN 1941-4595
CUSTOM RIGS; for truckers who take pride in their ride. Text in English. 2008 (Mar.). q. USD 19.95 domestic; USD 29.95 in Canada; USD 34.95 elsewhere; USD 6 per issue domestic; USD 9 per issue in Canada & Mexico; USD 12 per issue elsewhere (effective 2011). adv. back issues avail. **Document type:** *Magazine, Trade.* **Description:** Devoted to customizing trucks and big rigs, including specialized cutomizing shops, new products, customizing tricks and award-winning show trucks.
Related titles: Online - full text ed.: ISSN 1941-4609. free (effective 2011).
Published by: Randall-Reilly Publishing Company, 3200 Rice Mine Rd NE, Tuscaloosa, AL 35406. TEL 800-633-5953, http://www.randallpub.com. Eds. Bruce W Smith TEL 205-248-1709, Max Heine.

388 DEU ISSN 1861-6208
D A Z TRANSPORTER. (Der Auto-Anzeiger) Text in German. 2004. m. EUR 29; EUR 2.90 newsstand/cover (effective 2009). adv. **Document type:** *Magazine, Trade.*
Published by: D A Z Verlag GmbH und Co. KG, An der Strusbek 23, Ahrensburg, 22926, Germany. TEL 49-4102-47870, FAX 49-4102-478795, info@daz-verlag.de, http://www.daz24.de. adv.: page EUR 1,420. Circ: 35,000 (controlled).

388.324 DNK ISSN 1902-5173
D T L MAGASINET. (Dansk Transport og Logistik) Text in Danish. 1948. m. DKK 395 (effective 2009). adv. charts; illus.; mkt.; stat. index. back issues avail. **Document type:** *Magazine, Trade.*
Former titles (until 2007): Transport og Logistik (1399-7688); (until 1999): Danske Vognmaend (0011-6629)
Related titles: Online - full text ed.: ISSN 1902-5181. 200?.
Published by: Dansk Transport og Logistik, Groenningen 7, PO Box 2250, Copenhagen K, 1019, Denmark. TEL 45-70-159500, FAX 45-70-159502, dtl@dtl-dk.eu. Ed. John Larsen. adv.: page DKK 19,200; 297 x 210. Circ: 4,863.

388.324 DNK
D T L - NYT (ONLINE). (Dansk Transport og Logistik) Text in Danish. 1999. s-m. **Document type:** *Newsletter, Trade.*
Formerly (until 2002): D T L - Nyt (Print) (1600-5902)
Media: Online - full content.
Published by: Dansk Transport og Logistik, Groenningen 7, PO Box 2250, Copenhagen K, 1019, Denmark. TEL 45-70-159500, FAX 45-70-159502, dtl@dtl-dk.eu.

388.324 NZL
DEALS ON WHEELS. Text in English. m. NZD 55 domestic; NZD 169 in Australia; NZD 269 elsewhere (effective 2008). adv. **Document type:** *Magazine, Consumer.* **Description:** Includes news, reviews, profiles, new product guides and features across trucks, construction, forestry, and mining machinery.
Related titles: Online - full text ed.
Published by: A C P Media New Zealand (Subsidiary of: A C P Magazines Ltd.), Private Bag 92512, Auckland, 1036, New Zealand. TEL 64-9-3082700, FAX 64-9-3082878, http://www.acpmedia.co.nz/. Adv. contact Terry Williams King. page NZD 1,600; trim 192 x 260. Circ: 8,436.

388.324 AUS ISSN 1449-6348
DEALS ON WHEELS. Text in English. 1983. 13/yr. AUD 110 in Australia & New Zealand; AUD 130 elsewhere; AUD 6.50 newsstand/cover (effective 2008). adv. **Document type:** *Magazine, Consumer.* **Description:** Provides information on transport, trucks, trailers, buses, truck parts, engines and forklifts available for sale.
Published by: A C P Trader International Group (Subsidiary of: P B L Media Pty Ltd.), 73 Atherton Rd, Oakleigh, VIC 3166, Australia. TEL 61-3-95674200, FAX 61-3-95634554. Eds. Peter Lawson-Hanscombe TEL 61-3-98826191, Greg Leech TEL 61-3-95674194. Adv. contact Justine Schuller. B&W page AUD 1,408, color page AUD 3,289; trim 195 x 275. Circ: 26,351. **Subscr. to:** Magshop, Reply Paid 4967, Sydney, NSW 2001, Australia. TEL 61-2-136116, subs@magstore.com.au, http://shop.magstore.com.au.

388.324 USA ISSN 1098-0903
HF5487
DIRECTION (ALEXANDRIA); for the moving and storage industry. Text in English. 1986. m. USD 90 domestic to non-members (single subscription); USD 45 domestic to members (single subscription); USD 65 in Canada & Mexico; USD 70 elsewhere (effective 2009). adv. bk.rev. charts; illus.; tr.lit. index, cum.index. back issues avail. **Document type:** *Magazine, Consumer.* **Description:** Provides news and in-depth feature articles to members that help them to operate their companies more profitably.
Formerly (until 1998): American Mover (0886-9707); Incorporates: Direction (0092-7449); Which was formerly (until 1973): Furniture Warehouseman (0016-3082)
Indexed: CLT&T, HRIS.
Published by: American Moving and Storage Association, 1611 Duke St, Alexandria, VA 22314. TEL 703-683-7410, 888-849-2672, FAX 703-683-7527, info@moving.org, http://www.moving.org. Ed. John Bisney TEL 703-706-4986. Adv. contact Norma Gyovai TEL 703-706-4965. B&W page USD 780, color page USD 1,002; trim 8.25 x 10.875. Circ: 3,600.

DIVCO NEWS; the magazine of multi-stop delivery. *see* ANTIQUES

629.224 USA
DODGE TRUCK WORLD. Text in English. q. adv. **Document type:** *Magazine, Consumer.*
Published by: T E N Magazines, 1760 California Ave, Ste 101, Corona, CA 92881. TEL 951-371-8361, press@TenMagazines.com, http://www.tenmagazines.com.

388.324 CZE ISSN 1212-3277
DOPRAVA A SILNICE. Text in Czech. 1994. m. CZK 671; CZK 69.90 per issue (effective 2008). adv. **Document type:** *Magazine, Consumer.*
Published by: Springer Media CZ, s. r. o., Nadrazni 32, Prague, 15000, Czech Republic. TEL 420-2-25351212, FAX 420-2-25351404. Ed. Jiri Stepanek. Circ: 10,000 (paid and controlled).

388.324 CAN ISSN 0705-7040
L'ECHO DU TRANSPORT. Text in French. 1977. 10/yr. CAD 25 domestic; CAD 45 foreign (effective 1999). adv. bk.rev. tr.lit. **Document type:** *Journal, Trade.* **Description:** Covers all areas of local, national and international road transportation industry.
—CCC.
Published by: Editions Bomart Ltee., 7493 TransCanada Hwy, Ste 103, St Laurent, PQ H4T 1T3, Canada. TEL 514-337-9043, FAX 514-337-1862. Ed. Eric Berard. Pub. Pierre Gravel. Adv. contact Claude Boutin. color page CAD 4,905; trim 10 x 7. Circ: 21,000 (controlled).

388.324 USA
EXCISE TAX QUARTERLY. Text in English. 1979. q. looseleaf. USD 37 to non-members; USD 16 to members (effective 2011). back issues avail. **Document type:** *Newsletter, Trade.* **Description:** Review of I.R.S. releases and court cases concerning federal excise tax on motor vehicles.
Published by: National Truck Equipment Association, 37400 Hills Tech Dr, Farmington, MI 48331. TEL 248-489-7090, FAX 248-489-8590, info@ntea.com.

388.324 DEU
FAHRERPOST. Text in German. bi-m. **Document type:** *Trade.*
Published by: Iveco Magirus AG, Robert-Schuman-Str 1, Munich, 85716, Germany. TEL 089-31771120, FAX 089-31771452. Circ: 50,000.

388.324 USA
FASTLINE: BLUEGRASS EDITION. Text in English. 1978. a. USD 18 domestic; USD 45 in Canada & Mexico; USD 95 elsewhere; free to qualified personnel (effective 2008). adv. **Document type:** *Directory, Trade.* **Description:** Provides equipment buying guide for the trucking industry.
Former titles: Fastline for Kentucky Truckers; Bluegrass Trucker
Related titles: Online - full text ed.
Published by: Fastline Publications, Inc., 4900 Fox Run Rd, PO Box 248, Buckner, KY 40010. TEL 502-222-0146, 800-626-6409, FAX 502-222-0615, custcare@fastline.com, http://www.fastlinepublications.com.

388.324 659.1 USA
FASTLINE: DIXIE EDITION. Text in English. 1981. a. USD 18 domestic; USD 45 in Canada & Mexico; USD 95 elsewhere; free to qualified personnel (effective 2008). adv. **Document type:** *Directory, Trade.* **Description:** Provides equipment buying guide for the trucking edition.
Former titles: Fastline for Dixie Truckers; Dixie Trucker; Dixie Truck Trader
Related titles: Online - full text ed.
Published by: Fastline Publications, Inc., 4900 Fox Run Rd, PO Box 248, Buckner, KY 40010. TEL 502-222-0146, 800-626-6409, FAX 502-222-0615, custcare@fastline.com, http://www.fastlinepublications.com.

388.324 USA
FASTLINE: FLORIDA EDITION. Text in English. 1980. a. USD 18 domestic; USD 45 in Canada & Mexico; USD 95 elsewhere; free to qualified personnel (effective 2008). adv. **Document type:** *Directory, Trade.* **Description:** Provides equipment buying guide for the trucking industry.
Former titles: Fastline for Florida Truckers; Florida Trucker
Related titles: Online - full text ed.
Published by: Fastline Publications, Inc., 4900 Fox Run Rd, PO Box 248, Buckner, KY 40010. TEL 502-222-0146, 800-626-6409, FAX 502-222-0615, custcare@fastline.com, http://www.fastlinepublications.com.

388.324 USA
FASTLINE: GEORGIA EDITION. Text in English. 1979. a. USD 18 domestic; USD 45 in Canada & Mexico; USD 95 elsewhere; free to qualified personnel (effective 2008). adv. **Document type:** *Directory, Trade.* **Description:** Provides equipment buying guide for the trucking industry.
Former titles: Fastline for Georgia Truckers; Georgia Trucker
Related titles: Online - full text ed.
Published by: Fastline Publications, Inc., 4900 Fox Run Rd, PO Box 248, Buckner, KY 40010. TEL 502-222-0146, 800-626-6409, FAX 502-222-0615, custcare@fastline.com, http://www.fastlinepublications.com.

388.324 659.1
FASTLINE: TENNESSEE (TRUCK EDITION). Text in English. 1979. a. USD 18 domestic; USD 45 in Canada & Mexico; USD 95 elsewhere; free to qualified personnel (effective 2008). adv. **Document type:** *Directory, Trade.* **Description:** Provides equipment buying guide for the trucking industry.
Formerly: Fastline for Tennessee Truckers
Related titles: Online - full text ed.
Published by: Fastline Publications, Inc., 4900 Fox Run Rd, PO Box 248, Buckner, KY 40010. TEL 502-222-0146, 800-626-6409, FAX 502-222-0615, custcare@fastline.com, http://www.fastlinepublications.com.

388.324 USA ISSN 1931-9789
KF2248
FEDERAL MOTOR CARRIER SAFETY REGULATIONS: ADMINISTRATOR EDITION. Text in English. 200?. irreg. USD 89.83 combined subscription per issue (print & CD-ROM eds.); USD 29.95 per issue (effective 2011). **Document type:** *Handbook/Manual/Guide, Trade.*
Related titles: CD-ROM ed.: USD 59.88 per issue (effective 2011).
Published by: Mangan Communications, Inc., 315 W 4th St, Davenport, IA 52801. TEL 563-323-6245, 877-626-2666, FAX 888-398-6245, safetyinfo@mancomm.com.

388.324 USA ISSN 1931-4175
KF2248
FEDERAL MOTOR CARRIER SAFETY REGULATIONS: DRIVER EDITION. Text in English. 200?. a. USD 4.95 per issue (effective 2011). **Document type:** *Handbook/Manual/Guide, Trade.*
Published by: Mangan Communications, Inc., 315 W 4th St, Davenport, IA 52801. TEL 563-323-6245, 877-626-2666, FAX 888-398-6245, safetyinfo@mancomm.com.

388.324 DEU ISSN 0257-3180
FERNFAHRER; das internationale Truck-Magazin. Text in German. 1981. m. EUR 39; EUR 3.50 newsstand/cover (effective 2011). adv. bk.rev. **Document type:** *Magazine, Trade.* **Description:** Publication of interest to truckers. Features travel reports, technical information, new truck designs, road testing, traffic and transportation, new product information. Includes reports and calendar of events, readers' letters, classified ads.
Formerly (until 1983): Fernfahrer-Zeitung (0722-8236)
Published by: EuroTransportMedia Verlags- und Veranstaltungs-GmbH, Handwerkstr 15, Stuttgart, 70565, Germany. TEL 49-711-784980, FAX 49-711-7849888, info@etm-verlag.de, http://www.etm-verlag.de. Circ: 52,216 (paid).

388.324 USA ISSN 0747-2544
TL230.2
FLEET EQUIPMENT. Abbreviated title: F E. Variant title: Fleet Maintenance & Specifying. Text in English. 1974. m. free domestic to qualified personnel (effective 2008). adv. **Document type:** *Magazine, Trade.*
Formerly (until 1984): Fleet Maintenance and Specifying (0095-3245)
Related titles: Online - full text ed.
Indexed: A09, A10, A12, A13, A15, A17, A22, ABIn, B01, B02, B06, B07, B08, B09, B15, B17, B18, C12, G04, G06, G07, G08, I05, M01, M02, P48, P51, P52, P53, P54, PQC, S22, T02, V03, V04.
—BLDSC (3950.321800), IE, Ingenta.
Published by: Babcox Publications, Inc., 3550 Embassy Pky, Akron, OH 44333. TEL 330-670-1234, FAX 330-670-0874, bbabcox@babcox.com, http://www.babcox.com. Eds. Carol Birkland TEL 952-476-0230, Eric Brothers. Pub. David Moniz TEL 330-670-1234 ext 215. adv.: B&W page USD 10,675, color page USD 13,325. Circ: 60,000 (paid).

388.324 USA ISSN 1070-194X
FLEET OWNER. Text in English. 1928. m. USD 64 domestic; USD 75 in Canada; USD 95 elsewhere; free domestic to qualified personnel (effective 2011). adv. bk.rev. illus.; tr.lit. reprints avail. **Document type:** *Magazine, Trade.*
Formerly: Fleet Owner: Big Fleet Edition; Superseded in part: Fleet Owner (0731-9622)
Related titles: Microform ed.: (from PQC); Online - full text ed.
Indexed: A09, A10, A12, A13, A15, A17, A22, ABIn, B01, B02, B03, B04, B06, B07, B08, B09, B11, B15, B17, B18, BPI, BRD, BusI, C12, CLT&T, ChemAb, G04, G06, G07, G08, HRIS, I05, P52, P53, P54, PQC, S22, T&II, T02, V03, V04, W01, W02, W03, W05.
—BLDSC (3950.350000), IE, Ingenta, Linda Hall. **CCC.**
Published by: Penton Media, Inc., 11 River Bend Dr South, PO Box 4949, Stamford, CT 06907-0949. TEL 203-358-9900, FAX 203-358-5823, information@penton.com, http://www.pentonmedia.com. Ed. Jim Mele. Pub. Thomas Duncan. adv.: B&W page USD 12,715, color page USD 16,327; trim 10.75 x 7.88. Circ: 105,000 (controlled).

388.324 USA ISSN 0015-4334
FLORIDA TRUCK NEWS. Text in English. 1946. m. USD 25 to non-members; free to members (effective 2005). adv. bk.rev. illus. **Document type:** *Magazine, Trade.*
Published by: Florida Trucking Association, Inc., 350 E College Ave, Tallahassee, FL 32301. TEL 850-222-9900, FAX 850-222-9363, http://www.fltrucking.org. Ed. Charles Brantley. Adv. contacts Ed Pooser, Jim Long. Circ: 2,300 (controlled).

FORD TRADER. *see* TRANSPORTATION—Automobiles

629.224 USA
FORD TRUCK WORLD. Text in English. q. **Document type:** *Magazine, Consumer.*
Published by: T E N Magazines, 1760 California Ave, Ste 101, Corona, CA 92881. TEL 951-371-8361, press@TenMagazines.com, http://www.tenmagazines.com.

388.324 AUS
FREIGHT CARRIERS. Text in English. 1950. m. adv. charts; illus.
Former titles (until 1994): Freight Carriers (0727-9752); (until 1973): Master Carriers Journal (0025-5009)
Published by: (New South Wales Road Transport Association), Percival Publishing Company Pty Ltd., 862-870 Elizabeth St, Waterloo Dc, NSW 2017, Australia.

388.324 ITA ISSN 1825-862X
FURGONI MAGAZINE. Text in Italian. 2005. s-a. **Document type:** *Magazine, Consumer.*
Published by: Sprea Editori Srl, Via Torino 51, Cernusco sul Naviglio, MI 20063, Italy. TEL 39-02-92432222, FAX 39-02-92432236, editori@sprea.it, http://www.sprea.it.

388.324 USA
FURNITURE TRANSPORTER. Text in English. 1965. m. USD 49 (effective 1999).
Published by: Bohman Industrial Traffic Consultants, Inc., 32 Pleasant St, Box 889, Gardner, MA 01440. TEL 617-632-1913. Ed. Raynard F Bohman Jr.

388.324 USA ISSN 1942-4108
G3. Variant title: Gears.Guts.Glory. Text in English. 2007. m. adv. back issues avail. **Document type:** *Magazine, Trade.*
Related titles: Online - full text ed.: ISSN 1942-4116.
Published by: Randall-Reilly Publishing Company, 3200 Rice Mine Rd NE, Tuscaloosa, AL 35406. TEL 800-633-5953, http://www.randallpub.com.

388.324 DEU ISSN 0935-090X
GUETERKRAFTVERKEHRSRECHT. Text in German. 1953. 3 base vols. plus updates 4/yr. looseleaf. EUR 148 base vol(s).; EUR 34.95 updates per issue (effective 2009). **Document type:** *Monographic series, Trade.*
Published by: Erich Schmidt Verlag GmbH & Co. (Berlin), Genthiner Str 30 G, Berlin, 10785, Germany. TEL 49-30-2500850, FAX 49-30-250085305, vertrieb@esvmedien.de, http://www.erich-schmidt-verlag.de.

388.324 DEU ISSN 0017-5137
GUETERVERKEHR; Fachzeitschrift fuer Transport und Technik. Text in German. 1951. 9/yr. EUR 71.50; EUR 6 newsstand/cover (effective 2011). adv. bk.rev. charts; illus. index. back issues avail. **Document type:** *Magazine, Trade.*
—IE, Infotrieve. **CCC.**
Published by: Kirschbaum Verlag GmbH, Siegfriedstr 28, Bonn, 53179, Germany. TEL 49-228-954530, FAX 49-228-9545327, info@kirschbaum.de, http://www.kirschbaum.de. Ed. Dirk Sanne. Pub. Bernhard Kirschbaum. Adv. contact Volker Rutkowski. Circ: 26,199 (paid and controlled).

388.324 NLD ISSN 1872-3837
HANDBOEK REGELING VERVOER OVER LAND VAN GEVAARLIJKE STOFFEN / ACCORD EUROPEEN RELATIF AU TRANSPORT INTERNATIONAL DES MARCHANDISES DANGEREUSES PAR ROUTE. Key Title: Handboek V L G/A D R. Cover title: Vervoer Gevaarlijke Stoffen over de Weg. Text in Dutch. 2001. biennial. EUR 100 (effective 2009).
Published by: GDS Europe BV, Postbus 3111, Hoofddorp, 2130 KC, Netherlands. TEL 31-23-5542970, FAX 31-23-5542971, info@gdscrossmediagroup.nl, http://www.gds-europe.com.

388.324 GBR ISSN 1746-3653
HAULAGE MANUAL. Abbreviated title: The R H A Haulage Manual. Text in English. 1970. biennial. GBP 30 per issue to non-members; GBP 25 per issue to members (effective 2009). adv. stat. index. **Document type:** *Handbook/Manual/Guide, Trade.*
Published by: Road Haulage Association, Roadway House, 35 Monument Hill, Weybridge, Surrey KT13 8RN, United Kingdom. TEL 44-1932-841515, enquiries@rhaonline.co.uk, http://www.rha.uk.net/.

388.324 363.728 USA
THE HAULER MAGAZINE. Text in English. 1978. m. USD 15 domestic (effective 2001); Free to qualified subscribers. adv. **Document type:** *Magazine, Trade.* **Description:** Provides information on new and used equipment for hauling waste and recycling materials.
Published by: The Hauler Magazine, 1 Highland Drive, Chalfont, PA 18914. TEL 800-220-6029, mag@thehauler.com, http://www.thehauler.com. Pub. Thomas N. Smith.

HAZARDOUS MATERIALS REGULATION GUIDE. *see* ENVIRONMENTAL STUDIES—Toxicology And Environmental Safety

388.324 USA
HEAVY DUTY NEWSLETTER. Text in English. 1989. bi-m. free to members. **Document type:** *Newsletter.* **Description:** Keeps top executives of truck component manufacturers informed of industry trends and government regulations.
Published by: Heavy Duty Manufacturers Association, PO Box 13966, Research Triangle Park, NC 27709-3966. TEL 919-549-4800. Ed. J J Conner. Circ: 500.

388.3 CAN ISSN 1493-1338
HIGHWAYSTAR; for Canada's professional truckers. Text in English. 1999. m. CAD 28 domestic; CAD 81.60 in United States; CAD 100 elsewhere (effective 2008). adv. **Document type:** *Magazine, Trade.*
Formerly (until 1999): Canada Roadstar (1493-4353)
Published by: Newcom Business Media, Inc., 451 Attwell Dr, Toronto, ON M9W 5C4, Canada. TEL 416-614-2200, FAX 416-614-8861, http://www.newcom.ca/. Ed. Jim Park. Pub. Rolf Lockwood.

388.324 DEU
HISTORISCHER KRAFTVERKEHR. Text in German. bi-m. EUR 36 domestic; EUR 44 foreign; EUR 6 per issue (effective 2011). adv. **Document type:** *Magazine, Consumer.*
Published by: Verlag Klaus Rabe, Giesserallee 9, Postfach 250428, Willich, 57877, Germany. TEL 49-2154-48280, info@verlagrabe.de.

388.324 USA ISSN 2152-0550
▼ **HOT LINE TRANSPORTATION DIMENSION GUIDE.** Text in English. 2009. a. USD 50 per issue (effective 2009). **Document type:** *Magazine, Consumer.* **Description:** A reference guide on transportation dimensions for construction, lifting, hauling and agricultural equipment. Includes manufacturers and hauling estimates.
Related titles: Online - full text ed.: ISSN 2152-0569. 2009.
Published by: Heartland Communications Group, Inc., 1003 Central Ave, Fort Dodge, IA 50501. TEL 515-955-1600, http://www.hlipublishing.com.

629.2 CHE
I N U F A KATALOG. (Internationaler Nutzfahrzeugkatalog) Text in German. 1958. a. CHF 45. adv. bk.rev. **Document type:** *Catalog.*
Formerly: I N U F A: Internationaler Nutzfahrzeug-Katalog - International Catalogue for Commercial Vehicles (0073-4292)
Published by: Vogt-Schild AG, Zuchwilerstr 21, Solothurn, 4501, Switzerland. TEL 41-32-6247474, FAX 065-247235. Ed. Andre Vollmar. Adv. contact Andreas Benz. B&W page CHF 3,320, color page CHF 4,520; trim 260 x 185. Circ: 5,000.

388.324 USA ISSN 2158-2696
I T INTERNET TRUCKSTOP. Text in English. 2006. bi-m. free to members (effective 2010). **Document type:** *Magazine, Trade.* **Description:** Provides customer service and transportation related tools for reasonable cost.
Related titles: Online - full text ed.: ISSN 2158-270X. free (effective 2010).
Published by: Internet Truckstop, PO Box 99, New Plymouth, ID 83655. TEL 208-278-5097, 800-203-2540, FAX 208-248-5015, leigh@truckstop.com.

388.324 AUT ISSN 0019-0845
I T R; Die Oesterreichische Fachzeitschift fuer Fuhrparkmanagement, Transport-, Foerder- und Lagertechnik. (International Transport Revue) Text in German. 1962. 10/yr. EUR 30 domestic; EUR 45 foreign; EUR 4 newsstand/cover (effective 2005). adv. bk.rev. illus. **Document type:** *Magazine, Trade.*
Indexed: CISA.
Published by: Springer Business Media Austria GmbH (Subsidiary of: Springer Science+Business Media), Inkustr 16, Klosterneuburg, 3403, Austria. TEL 43-2243-301110, FAX 43-2243-30111222, office@springer-sbm.at. Ed. Ernst Mueller. Adv. contact Wolfgang Kreissl. B&W page EUR 3,420, color page EUR 4,830; trim 185 x 260. Circ: 12,530 (paid and controlled).

388.324 USA ISSN 0019-2309
ILLINOIS TRUCK NEWS. Text in English. 1935. q. USD 15; free to members (effective 2006). adv. bk.rev. **Document type:** *Magazine, Trade.* **Description:** Includes items on election issues, safety and maintenance, legislation and management.
Indexed: CLT&T.
Published by: Illinois Trucking Association, 7000 Adams, Ste 130, Willow Brook, IL 60527. TEL 630-654-0884, FAX 630-654-0899, gbillows@iltrucking.org. Ed. Laurel Thompson. Circ: 5,500 (free).

388.324 GBR ISSN 1471-115X
INDUSTRIAL VEHICLE TECHNOLOGY INTERNATIONAL. Variant title: I V T International. Text in English. 1997. q. free (effective 2009). adv. back issues avail. **Document type:** *Magazine, Trade.* **Description:** Provides news-driven coverage of the industrial vehicle market and examines the design and engineering of all classes of vehicles.
Formerly (until 2000): Industrial Vehicle Technology. Europe (1461-0450)
Related titles: Online - full text ed.; ◆ Supplement(s): Industrial Vehicle Technology. Off-Highway. ISSN 1355-2627; ◆ Industrial Vehicle Technology. Lift Truck & Materials Handling.
Indexed: HRIS.
—**CCC.**
Published by: U K & International Press (Subsidiary of: AutoIntermediates Ltd.), Abinger House, Church St, Dorking, Surrey RH4 1DF, United Kingdom. TEL 44-1306-743744, FAX 44-1306-887546, info@ukintpress.com, http://www.ukipme.com. Ed. Richard Carr. Adv. contact Kevin Barrett. page GBP 3,800; trim 215 x 275.

388.324 GBR
INDUSTRIAL VEHICLE TECHNOLOGY. LIFT TRUCK & MATERIALS HANDLING. Text in English. 1993. a. Included with subscr. to I V T International. adv. **Document type:** *Magazine, Trade.* **Description:** Provides news-driven coverage of the industrial vehicle market and examines the design and engineering of all classes of vehicles.
Formerly (until 1999): Industrial Vehicle Technology. Materials Handling (1462-7531)
Related titles: ◆ Supplement to: Industrial Vehicle Technology International. ISSN 1471-115X.
—**CCC.**
Published by: U K & International Press (Subsidiary of: AutoIntermediates Ltd.), Abinger House, Church St, Dorking, Surrey RH4 1DF, United Kingdom. TEL 44-1306-743744, FAX 44-1306-887546, info@ukintpress.com. Ed. Richard Carr. Adv. contact Kevin Barrett. page GBP 4,995; trim 210 x 297.

388.324 GBR ISSN 1355-2627
INDUSTRIAL VEHICLE TECHNOLOGY. OFF-HIGHWAY. Text in English. 1993. a. Included with subscr. to I V T International. adv. **Document type:** *Magazine, Trade.* **Description:** Provides news-driven coverage of the industrial vehicle market and examines the design and engineering of all classes of vehicles.
Related titles: ◆ Supplement to: Industrial Vehicle Technology International. ISSN 1471-115X.
—**CCC.**
Published by: U K & International Press (Subsidiary of: AutoIntermediates Ltd.), Abinger House, Church St, Dorking, Surrey RH4 1DF, United Kingdom. TEL 44-1306-743744, FAX 44-1306-887546, info@ukintpress.com. Ed. Richard Carr. Adv. contact Kevin Barrett. page GBP 4,995; trim 210 x 297.

388.324 CAN ISSN 1912-242X
LES INFRACTIONS ET LES SANCTIONS RELIEES A LA CONDUITE D'UN VEHICULE ROUTIER. Text in French. 1994. a. **Document type:** *Journal, Trade.*
Published by: Societe de l'Assurance Automobile du Quebec, PO Box 19600, Quebec, PQ G1K 8J6, Canada. TEL 418-643-7620, 800-361-7620, http://www.saaq.gouv.qc.ca/en/index.php.

388.324 GBR ISSN 0960-0035
HF5415.7 CODEN: IPDMEC
➤ **INTERNATIONAL JOURNAL OF PHYSICAL DISTRIBUTION & LOGISTICS MANAGEMENT.** Abbreviated title: I J P D L M. Text in English. 1970. 10/yr. EUR 14,519 combined subscription in Europe (print & online eds.); USD 15,599 combined subscription in the Americas (print & online eds.); GBP 9,769 combined subscription in the UK & elsewhere (print & online eds.); AUD 19,139 combined subscription in Australasia (print & online eds.) (effective 2012). bk.rev. illus. cum.index. back issues avail.; reprint service avail. from PSC. **Document type:** *Journal, Academic/Scholarly.* **Description:** Covers transport and inventory management, materials purchasing management, distribution planning and costs, customer service policy and order processing systems.
Former titles (until 1990): International Journal of Physical Distribution and Materials Management (0269-8218); (until 1977): International Journal of Physical Distribution (0020-7527); Which incorporated (in 1975): International Journal of Physical Distribution Monograph (0308-4264); Which was formerly (1970-1974): P D M. Physical Distribution Monograph (0305-2214)
Related titles: CD-ROM ed.; Online - full text ed.: ISSN 1758-664X (from IngentaConnect).
Indexed: A12, A13, A17, A22, A26, A28, ABIn, ADPA, APA, B01, B02, B06, B07, B08, B09, B11, B15, B16, B17, B18, BPIA, BrCerAb, BusI, C&ISA, C12, CA, CA/WCA, CIA, CPM, CerAb, CivEngAb, CorrAb, CurCont, E&CAJ, E01, E10, E11, EEA, EMA, ESPM, EmerIntel, Emerald, EnvEAb, G04, G06, G07, G08, H15, I05, IAOP, Inspec, KES, LogistBibl, M&TEA, M05, M06, M09, MBF, METADEX, ManagCont, P06, P10, P41, P47, P48, P51, P52, P53, P54, PAIS, PQC, SCIMP, SCOPUS, SSCI, SolStAb, T02, T04, W07, WAA.
—BLDSC (4542.461500), AskIEEE, IE, Infotrieve, Ingenta. **CCC.**
Published by: Emerald Group Publishing Ltd., Howard House, Wagon Ln, Bingley, W Yorks BD16 1WA, United Kingdom. TEL 44-1274-777700, FAX 44-1274-785201, information@emeraldinsight.com. Eds. Michael R Crum, Richard F Poist Jr. Pub. Lucy Sootheran. **Subscr. addr in N America:** Emerald Group Publishing Limited, One Mifflin Pl, Ste 400, Harvard Sq, Cambridge, MA 02138. TEL 617-576-5782, 888-309-7810, FAX 617-576-5883

388.324 ITA ISSN 1970-6251
INTERTRUCKNEWS. Text in Italian. 1999. m. (11/yr.). EUR 40 (effective 2008). **Document type:** *Magazine, Consumer.*
Related titles: ◆ Supplement to: InterAutoNews. ISSN 1970-6243.
Published by: Press Multi Service (P M S), Via Ermete Novelli 11, Rome, 00197, Italy.

388.324 USA
IOWA TRUCKING LIFELINER. Text in English. 1943. m. USD 4 (effective 2005). adv. illus. **Document type:** *Magazine, Trade.*
Former titles: Lifeliner (Des Moines); Motor Truck News (0027-2116)
Published by: Iowa Motor Truck Association, 717 E Court, Des Moines, IA 50309. TEL 515-244-5193, FAX 515-244-2204, http://www.ia-truck.com. Ed., Pub. Brenda Neville. Circ: 3,500 (controlled).

388.324 DEU ISSN 0341-9681
K F Z ANZEIGER; Truck und Transport in Europa. Text in German. 1947. fortn. EUR 81; EUR 4.50 newsstand/cover (effective 2010). adv. bk.rev. **Document type:** *Magazine, Trade.*
Formerly (until 1976): Kraftfahrzeug Anzeiger (0341-1559)

Published by: Stuenings Medien GmbH, Diessemer Bruch 167, Krefeld, 47805, Germany. TEL 49-2151-51000, FAX 49-2151-5100101, medien@stuenings.de, http://www.stuenings.de. Ed. Lutz Gerritzen. Adv. contact Manfred Schenk. B&W page EUR 5,100, color page EUR 7,650. Circ: 38,000 (paid and controlled).

388.324 USA ISSN 1539-6142
KEEP ON TRUCKIN' NEWS. Text in English. 1974. m. membership only. adv. software rev.; Website rev. maps. **Document type:** *Magazine, Trade.* **Description:** Information on activities in the trucking industry.
Related titles: Online - full content ed.
Published by: Mid-West Truckers Association, Inc., 2727 N Dirksen Parkway, Springfield, IL 62702. TEL 217-525-0310, FAX 217-525-0342, http://www.mid-westtruckers.com. Ed. Robert Jasmon. Pub., Adv. contact Don Schaefer. B&W page USD 265; trim 10 x 7.5. Circ: 4,000 (controlled).

388.324 USA ISSN 1041-8296
KELLER'S HAZARDOUS MATERIALS TRANSPORTATION REPORT. Variant title: Hazardous Materials Transportation Report. Text in English. 1989. m. looseleaf. USD 189 (effective 2008). **Document type:** *Newsletter, Trade.* **Description:** Explores important regulatory issues and alerts about the key developments affecting Hazmat shippers, handlers and transporters.
—CCC.
Published by: J.J. Keller & Associates, Inc., 3003 W Breezewood Ln, PO Box 368, Neenah, WI 54957. TEL 877-564-2333, FAX 800-727-7516, kellersoft@jjkeller.com. Ed. Randall Skoog.

388.324 USA ISSN 1092-1788
KELLER'S TRANSPORTATION RECRUITING AND RETENTION INSIGHTS. Variant title: Transportation Recruiting and Retention Insights. Text in English. 1997. m. looseleaf. USD 145 (effective 2008). **Document type:** *Newsletter, Trade.* **Description:** Discusses driver turnover, how to conduct a thorough interview, orientation sessions, re-hiring drivers, and more.
Published by: J.J. Keller & Associates, Inc., 3003 W Breezewood Ln, PO Box 368, Neenah, WI 54957. TEL 877-564-2333, FAX 800-727-7516, kellersoft@jjkeller.com, http://www.jjkeller.com. Pub. John J Keller.

388.324 GBR
KEY NOTE MARKET REPORT: ROAD HAULAGE. Variant title: Road Haulage Market Report. Text in English. 19??. irreg., latest 2009, Jan. GBP 460 per issue (effective 2010). **Document type:** *Report, Trade.* **Description:** Provides an overview of a specific UK market segment and includes executive summary, market definition, market size, industry background, competitor analysis, current issues, forecasts, company profiles, and more.
Formerly (until 1995): Key Note Report: Road Haulage (0954-5174)
Related titles: CD-ROM ed.; Online - full text ed.
Published by: Key Note Ltd. (Subsidiary of: Bonnier Business Information), Harlequin House, 5th Fl, 7 High St, Teddington, Richmond upon Thames, TW11 8EE, United Kingdom. TEL 44-845-5040452, FAX 44-845-5040453, info@keynote.co.uk.

388.324 DNK ISSN 1604-1720
KONJUNKTURUNDERSOEGELSE AF VOGNMANDSERHVERVET I DANMARK; analysereport. Text in Danish. 2002. a. back issues avail. **Document type:** *Monographic series, Trade.*
Related titles: Online - full text ed.: ISSN 1901-8258.
Published by: Dansk Transport og Logistik, Groenningen 7, PO Box 2250, Copenhagen K, 1019, Denmark. TEL 45-70-159500, FAX 45-70-159502.

388.324 FIN ISSN 1236-066X
KULJETUSYRITTAJA. Text in Finnish, Swedish. 1945. 10/yr. adv. **Document type:** *Magazine, Trade.* **Description:** Covers legislation, transport economy, taxation, and product news.
Formerly (until 1993): Ammattiautoilija (0355-7286)
Published by: Suomen Kuljetus ja Logistiikka SKAL ry/Finnish Transport and Logistics, Nuijamiestentie 7, Helsinki, 00400, Finland. TEL 358-9-478-999, 358-9-478999, FAX 358-9-587-8520, 358-9-5878520, TELEX 19100648 VDX SF, http://www.skal.fi. Ed. Pasi Moisio. adv.: color page EUR 2,650; 185 x 270. Circ: 11,000.

KUSTOMS & HOT RODS. *see* TRANSPORTATION—Automobiles

388.324 SWE ISSN 1101-0010
LAETTA LASTBILAR. Text in Swedish. 1990. 10/yr. SEK 200 (effective 2000). adv. 40 p./no. 4 cols./p.; **Document type:** *Journal, Trade.*
Published by: Cobra Foerlag AB, Fack 82, Hallekis, 53304, Sweden. TEL 46-510-86200, FAX 46-510-86220. Ed. Roland Goetblad. Adv. contact Ove Johansson. B&W page SEK 10,400, color page SEK 14,900; trim 275 x 192. Circ: 800.

388.324 USA ISSN 0279-6503
LAND LINE MAGAZINE; the business magazine of owner-operator truckers. Text in English. 1975. 9/yr. USD 18; free to members (effective 2005). adv. bk.rev. 140 p./no.; **Document type:** *Magazine, Trade.* **Description:** For the small business men and women of commercial trucking. Provides news for the serious decision-makers in this segment of the industry.
Incorporates: Owner Operator News
Related titles: Online - full text ed.
Indexed: HRIS.
Published by: Owner-Operator Independent Drivers Association, PO Box 1000, Grain Valley, MO 64029. TEL 816-229-5791, FAX 816-443-2227, http://www.ooida.com. Ed. Jami Jones. Pub. Todd Spencer. Adv. contact Alex Gates. Circ: 200,000 (controlled).

388.324 USA
LAND ROVER LIFESTYLE. Text in English. 2006 (Jan.). bi-m. USD 29.95 domestic; USD 51.95 foreign (effective 2006). **Document type:** *Magazine, Consumer.*
Published by: SlickRock Publishing LLC., PO Box 105, Rehoboth, NM 87322. TEL 888-575-6247. Pub. Douglas E. Evilsizor.

388.324 DEU ISSN 1613-1606
LAST UND KRAFT; Das Nutzfahrzeug-Oldtimer-Magazin. Text in German. 1992. bi-m. EUR 54; EUR 9.80 newsstand/cover (effective 2011). adv. **Document type:** *Magazine, Trade.*
Published by: V F Verlagsgesellschaft mbH, Lise-Meitner-Str 2, Mainz, 55129, Germany. TEL 49-6131-9920, FAX 49-6131-992103, info@vfmz.de, http://www.vfmz.de. Circ: 12,000 (paid).

388.324 DEU ISSN 0941-6285
LASTAUTO OMNIBUS KATALOG. Text in German. 1970. a. EUR 14.90 newsstand/cover (effective 2011). adv. charts; illus. **Document type:** *Catalog, Trade.*
Published by: EuroTransportMedia Verlags- und Veranstaltungs-GmbH, Handwerkstr 15, Stuttgart, 70565, Germany. TEL 49-711-784980, FAX 49-711-7849888, info@eurotransport.de, http://www.etm-verlag.de. Circ: 25,000 (paid and controlled).

388.324 DNK ISSN 1398-9014
LASTBIL AARBOGEN. Text in Danish. 1998. a. DKK 99 per issue (effective 2009). adv. back issues avail. **Document type:** *Trade.*
Published by: Lastbil Magasinet, Kongensgade 72, Odense C, 5000, Denmark. TEL 45-66-161647, FAX 45-66-160147, http://www.lastbilmagasinet.dk. Ed. Lorents B Rasmussen. Adv. contact Bjarne Routhe TEL 45-70-250350.

388.324 DNK ISSN 1397-6168
LASTBIL MAGASINET. Text in Danish. 1997. m. DKK 459 (effective 2009). adv. **Document type:** *Magazine, Trade.*
Related titles: Online - full text ed.
Address: Kongensgade 72, Odense C, 5000, Denmark. TEL 45-66-161647, FAX 45-66-160147. Ed. Lorents B Rasmussen. Adv. contact Bjarne Routhe TEL 45-70-250350. color page DKK 17,100; 219 x 297. Circ: 10,500.

388.324 NOR ISSN 0047-4126
LASTEBILEIEREN. Text in Norwegian. 1928. m. adv. **Document type:** *Magazine, Trade.*
Published by: (Andelsselskap av Lastbileiere), Begraf Forlag AS, c/o Bjoern-Erik Eriksen, Maridalsveien 10, Oslo, 0178, Norway. TEL 47-22-110082, FAX 47-22-208861, begraf@c2i.net.

343.094 USA
THE LAW OF COMMERCIAL TRUCKING; damages to persons and property. Text in English. 1994. irreg. (in 2 vols.), latest 2005, 3rd ed. USD 186 3rd ed. (effective 2008). Supplement avail. **Document type:** *Monographic series, Trade.* **Description:** Provides essential resource helps judges, lawyers, risk managers, and other interested parties understand the myriad legal issues that are specific to interstate.
Related titles: Online - full text ed.
Published by: Michie Company (Subsidiary of: LexisNexis North America), 701 E Water St, Charlottesville, VA 22902. TEL 434-972-7600, 800-446-3410, FAX 434-972-7677, customer.support@lexisnexis.com, http://www.michie.com. Ed. David N Nissenberg.

388.324 690 USA ISSN 1045-442X
HE5623.A1
LIFTING & TRANSPORTATION INTERNATIONAL. Text in English. 1953. 9/yr. free domestic to qualified personnel; USD 65 domestic; USD 98 in Canada & Mexico; USD 145 elsewhere (effective 2005). adv. bk.rev. illus.; tr.lit. 48 p./no. 3 cols./p.; reprints avail. **Document type:** *Magazine, Trade.* **Description:** Contains the latest news from the crane, rigging and specialized transportation industries worldwide.
Formerly (until 1988): Transportation Engineer (0041-1604)
Related titles: Supplement(s): Lifting & Transportation International. Buyer's Guide. USD 35 per issue domestic; USD 50 per issue foreign (effective 2004).
Indexed: HRIS.
—Linda Hall. **CCC.**
Published by: (Specialized Carriers & Rigging Association), M L S, Inc, 2895 Chad Dr, Eugene, OR 97408-7345. TEL 541-341-4650, 800-352-0642, FAX 541-342-3307. adv.: B&W page USD 3,205, color page USD 4,240; trim 7 x 10. Circ: 14,800 (controlled).

THE LIGHT (ARLINGTON). *see* TRANSPORTATION—Railroads

388.324 USA ISSN 1091-9651
LIGHT AND MEDIUM TRUCK; the business magzine for light and medium truck operators. Text in English. 1981. 10/yr. free domestic to qualified personnel (effective 2005). adv. back issues avail.; reprints avail. **Document type:** *Magazine, Trade.* **Description:** Concerned with the day-to-day management of light- and medium-duty trucks.
Formerly (until 1996): P and D Magazine (1042-2641)
Related titles: Online - full text ed.
Indexed: A15, ABIn, B16, HRIS, P10, P48, P51, P52, P53, P54, PQC.
—CCC.
Published by: T T Publishing, 2200 Mill Rd, Alexandria, VA 22314-4686. TEL 703-838-1785, FAX 703-549-5408. Ed., R&P Jim Galligan. Adv. contact Kirsten Welton TEL 703-838-1746. Circ: 53,000 (controlled).

LOGISTIIKKA/LOGISTICS. *see* TRANSPORTATION

388.33 USA ISSN 1942-5562
THE LONGHAUL MAGAZINE. Text in English. q. free (effective 2008). **Document type:** *Magazine, Trade.*
Published by: Flying J, 1104 Country Hills Dr, Ogden, UT 84403. TEL 801-624-1000, http://www.flyingj.com. Pub. Virginia Parker.

388.324 USA
M M C A NEWS. Text in English. 1990. m. free to members (effective 2005). **Document type:** *Magazine, Trade.*
Published by: Montana Motor Carriers Association, Inc., 501 N Sanders, Ste 201, Helena, MT 59624. TEL 406-442-6600, FAX 406-443-4281. Ed. Barry Stang. Circ: 850 (free).

388.306 GBR ISSN 1356-9104
M T LOGISTICA. (Motor Transport) Text in English. 1993. 10/yr. adv. **Document type:** *Report, Trade.* **Description:** Reports on developments in every sector of distribution, storage and cost management.
Related titles: ◆ Supplement to: Motor Transport. ISSN 0027-206X.
—BLDSC (5980.874545). **CCC.**
Published by: Reed Business Information Ltd. (Subsidiary of: Reed Business), Quadrant House, The Quadrant, Sutton, Surrey SM2 5AS, United Kingdom. TEL 44-20-86523500, FAX 44-20-86528932, rbi.subscriptions@qss-uk.com, http://www.reedbusiness.co.uk/. Ed., R&P John Towers TEL 44-18-1652-3711. Pub. Geoff Hadwick. Adv. contact Mike Spray.

MACCHINE MOTORI. *see* TRANSPORTATION—Automobiles

388.324 USA
MAINE MOTOR TRANSPORT NEWS. Text in English. 1946. 10/yr. USD 25 to members; USD 35 to non-members (effective 2005). adv. 24 p./no. 3 cols./p.; reprints avail. **Document type:** *Magazine, Trade.* **Description:** Covers the trucking industry.
Published by: Maine Motor Transport Association, Inc., 142 Whitten Rd, Augusta, ME 04330. TEL 207-623-4128, FAX 207-629-5184, http://www.mmta.com/. Ed. Dale E Hanington. Circ: 6,000 (controlled).

388.324 USA
MARYLAND MOTOR TRUCK. Text in English. 1984. q. **Document type:** *Magazine, Trade.*
Published by: (M M T A), Naylor LLC, 5950 NW 1st Pl, Gainesville, FL 32607. TEL 800-369-6220, FAX 352-331-3525, http://www.naylor.com.

388.324 USA
METROPOLITAN AREA WAGE ANALYSIS. Text in English. a. **Document type:** *Report, Trade.* **Description:** Provides wage information in the moving industry; contains regional analysis. For anyone who deals with the moving business.
Formerly: Standard Metropolitan Wage Analysis
Published by: American Moving and Storage Association, 1611 Duke St, Alexandria, VA 22314. TEL 703-683-7410, 888-849-2672, FAX 703-683-7527, info@moving.org, http://www.moving.org.

388.324 USA
MICHIGAN TRUCKING TODAY. Text in English. 1952. q. USD 4; free to members (effective 2005). adv. bk.rev. illus. **Document type:** *Magazine, Trade.*
Formerly: Michigan Motor Carrier-Folks (0026-2323)
Published by: Michigan Trucking Association, 1131 Centennial Way, Lansing, MI 48917. TEL 517-321-1951, FAX 517-321-0884. Ed. Jill Skutar. Circ: 900 (free).

388.324 USA
MID-SOUTH TRUCKING NEWS. Text in English. fortn. USD 28 (effective 2000). **Document type:** *Newspaper, Trade.*
Address: 9 Lucy Lane, Sherwood, AR 72120. TEL 501-834-8600, FAX 501-834-8120. Ed., Pub. Gene Williams.

388.324 SWE ISSN 0026-3710
MIL. Text in Swedish. 1955. q. free. adv. illus. **Document type:** *Trade.*
Incorporates (in 1981): Scania World Wide
Related titles: Dutch ed.: ISSN 0280-4832; German ed.: ISSN 0280-4816; French ed.: ISSN 0280-4824; English ed.: Scania World Wide (English edition). ISSN 0280-4808.
Published by: Tidningen Mil, c/o Scania AB, Soedertaelje, 151187, Sweden. TEL 46-8-55381000, FAX 46-8-55381037. Circ: 67,000 (controlled).

388.324 USA
MILEAGE GUIDE (NO.). Text in English. 1993. every 3 yrs. USD 299 combined subscription to non-members (print & CD-ROM eds.); USD 249 combined subscription to members (print & CD-ROM eds.) (effective 2008). **Document type:** *Guide, Consumer.* **Description:** Guides to calculate the distances between more than 140,000 locations across North America.
Related titles: CD-ROM ed.
Published by: American Moving and Storage Association, 1611 Duke St, Alexandria, VA 22314. TEL 703-683-7410, 888-849-2672, FAX 703-683-7527, info@moving.org, http://www.moving.org.

388.324 USA ISSN 0199-2317
MILK AND LIQUID FOOD TRANSPORTER. Text in English. 1960. m. USD 15 (effective 2005). adv. 16 p./no. 3 cols./p.; back issues avail. **Document type:** *Magazine, Trade.* **Description:** Covers articles and feature stories on timely issues affecting the business of transporting milk and other liquid food products such as vegetable oils, corn sweeteners, potable water and fruit juice. Includes new products, upcoming meetings and people.
Published by: Glen Street Publications, Inc., W 4652 Glen Street, Appleton, WI 54913-9563. TEL 920-749-4880, FAX 920-749-4877. Ed., Adv. contact Jane Plout. B&W page USD 800. Circ: 4,830 (paid and free).

388.324 USA ISSN 1052-0961
MINI TRUCKIN'. Text in English. 1986. m. USD 18 domestic; USD 30 in Canada; USD 42 elsewhere (effective 2008). adv. back issues avail. **Document type:** *Magazine, Consumer.* **Description:** Addresses the expanding market for customized mini-trucks, both domestic and import.
Indexed: G06, G07, G08, I05, S23.
—CCC.
Published by: Source Interlink Companies, 2400 E Katella Ave, Ste 700, Anaheim, CA 92806. TEL 714-939-2400, dheine@sourceinterlink.com, http://www.sourceinterlink.com. Ed. Mike Alexander. Pub. Brad Christopher TEL 714-939-2509. adv.: B&W page USD 4,805, color page USD 5,755. Circ: 33,382 (paid).

388.3 USA ISSN 1537-8349
MOTOR CARRIER PERMIT & TAX BULLETIN. Text in English. 1968. m. looseleaf. USD 189 (effective 2008). **Document type:** *Bulletin, Trade.* **Description:** Covers federal and state regulatory requirements governing operating authority, vehicle licensing and registration, proration and reciprocity, and taxes.
Formerly (until 1993): Trucking Permit and Tax Bulletin
—GNLM. **CCC.**
Published by: J.J. Keller & Associates, Inc., 3003 W Breezewood Ln, PO Box 368, Neenah, WI 54957. TEL 877-564-2333, FAX 800-727-7516, kellersoft@jjkeller.com. Ed. Vicky L Hart.

388.324 USA ISSN 0886-8778
MOTOR FREIGHT CONTROLLER. Text in English. 19??. bi-m. **Document type:** *Journal, Trade.*
Indexed: HRIS.
Published by: American Trucking Associations, Inc., 950 N Glebe Rd, Ste 210, Alexandria, VA 22203. TEL 703-838-1700, orders@trucking.org, http://www.truckline.com.

388.324 GBR ISSN 0027-206X
MOTOR TRANSPORT. Text in English. 1905. w. GBP 114 domestic; EUR 236 in Europe (eurozone); USD 300 elsewhere (effective 2009). adv. bk.rev. illus. **Document type:** *Newspaper, Trade.* **Description:** Concentrates on the business of running a commercial vehicle fleet for profit.
Related titles: Online - full text ed.; ◆ Supplement(s): M T Logistica. ISSN 1356-9104.
Indexed: A09, A10, A15, ABIn, B01, B02, B06, B07, B08, B09, B15, B17, B18, CA, CISA, G04, I05, P34, P48, P51, P52, PQC, PROMT, S22, T02, V03, V04.
—CCC.
Published by: Reed Business Information Ltd. (Subsidiary of: Reed Business), Quadrant House, The Quadrant, Sutton, Surrey SM2 5AS, United Kingdom. TEL 44-20-86523500, FAX 44-20-86528932, rbi.subscriptions@qss-uk.com. Ed. Justin Stanton TEL 44-20-86523303. Pub. Geoff Hadwick. Adv. contact Mike Spray. Circ: 20,314 (controlled).

MOTOR TREND SPORT UTILITY, TRUCK & VAN BUYER'S GUIDE. *see* TRANSPORTATION—Automobiles

388.324 CAN ISSN 0027-2108
MOTOR TRUCK. Text in English. 1934. m. CAD 33.95 domestic; USD 62.95 foreign (effective 2008). adv. illus.; stat.; tr.lit. **Document type:** *Magazine, Trade.* **Description:** Published specifically for heavy duty truck fleet managers and fleet operators.
Related titles: Online - full text ed.
Indexed: A15, A22, ABIn, C03, CBCABus, CBPI, P16, P48, P51, P52, P53, P54, PQC.
—CCC.
Published by: Business Information Group, 12 Concorde Pl, Ste 800, Toronto, ON M3C 4J2, Canada. TEL 416-442-2122, 800-668-2374, FAX 416-442-2191, orders@businessinformationgroup.ca, http://www.businessinformationgroup.ca. Pub. Rob Wilkins TEL 416-510-5123. Circ: 29,800.

388.324 USA ISSN 8750-1155
MOVERS NEWS. Text in English. 1937. bi-m. USD 40 (effective 2005). adv. **Document type:** *Magazine, Trade.*
Published by: N Y S Movers & Warehousemen's Association, 561 Hudson St, Ste 96, New York, NY 10014-2463. TEL 718-278-9090, FAX 718-937-4646, nymovers@msm.com, http://www.newyorkstatemovers.com/. Ed. David Blake. Circ: 1,200.

MOVICARGA. *see* BUSINESS AND ECONOMICS—Production Of Goods And Services

388.324 USA
MOVIN' OUT. Text in English. 1975. m. USD 12 (effective 2001). adv. bk.rev.; music rev.; software rev. **Document type:** *Newspaper, Trade.* **Description:** Features about truckers, trucking companies, truckstops and other trucking industry related subjects.
Related titles: Online - full text ed.
Address: 118 1/2 Franklin St, Box 97, Slippery Rock, PA 16057. TEL 724-794-6857, FAX 724-794-1314, movingout@pathway.net. Ed. Pamela S Pollock. Pub., R&P Steven M Pollock. Adv. contact Steve Pollock. B&W page USD 1,100, color page USD 2,200; trim 16 x 10.7. Circ: 60,000 (controlled).

388.324 USA
THE MOVING INDUSTRY PROFESSIONAL SOURCEBOOK. Text in English. a. adv. **Document type:** *Directory, Trade.* **Description:** Contains information on nearly 3,800 domestic and international moving companies, industry suppliers and state and local movers' associations.
Incorporates (in 1996): Directory of Movers; Former titles: A M C - H G C B Joint Membership Directory; A M C Membership Directory
Published by: American Moving and Storage Association, 1611 Duke St, Alexandria, VA 22314. TEL 703-683-7410, 888-849-2672, FAX 703-683-7527, info@moving.org, http://www.moving.org. Adv. contact Norma Gyovai TEL 703-706-4965. B&W page USD 1,020, color page USD 1,170; trim 7 x 10. Circ: 3,400.

MOVING INDUSTRY TRANSPORTATION STATISTICS (YEAR); demographic, economic and financial data of the moving industry. *see* TRANSPORTATION—Abstracting, Bibliographies, Statistics

380.14 USA
MY LITTLE SALESMAN TRUCK AND TRAILER CATALOG. Text in English. 1958. m. USD 24.95 domestic; USD 70 in Canada & Mexico; USD 110 elsewhere (effective 2006). adv. back issues avail.; reprints avail. **Document type:** *Catalog, Trade.* **Description:** Provides information to those buying or selling trucks and trucking equipment.
Formerly: My Little Salesman Truck Catalog (0192-7027)
Related titles: Online - full text ed.
Published by: M L S, Inc, 2895 Chad Dr, Eugene, OR 97408-7345. TEL 541-341-4650, 800-352-0642, FAX 541-342-3307. Pub. Richard Pierce. Adv. contacts Don Lindsey, Rod Womack. color page USD 1,595; trim 6.292 x 9.083. Circ: 75,000 (paid and controlled).

388.3 USA ISSN 1066-6494
N A D A OFFICIAL HEAVY DUTY TRUCK GUIDE. (National Automobile Dealers Association) Text in English. 1993. bi-m. back issues avail. **Document type:** *Directory, Trade.*
Published by: National Automobile Dealers Association, Used Car Guide Co., 8400 Westpark Dr, 10th Fl, McLean, VA 22102. FAX 800-252-6232, guideinfo@nada.org, http://www.nada.org/.

328.344 DEU ISSN 1435-2788
N F Z WERKSTATT; Das Magazin fuer den Werkstattprofi. (Nutzfahrzeug) Text in German. 1997. q. adv. **Document type:** *Magazine, Trade.*
Published by: Stuenings Medien GmbH, Diessemer Bruch 167, Krefeld, 47805, Germany. TEL 49-2151-51000, FAX 49-2151-5100101, medien@stuenings.de, http://www.stuenings.de. Ed. Lutz Gerritzen. Adv. contact Cornelia Assem. B&W page EUR 4,920, color page EUR 6,420. Circ: 40,000 (controlled).

388.324 DEU ISSN 1437-6229
N K W - PARTNER; fuer Ersatzteile und Reparaturen von Nutzfahrzeugen. (Nutzkraftwagen) Text in German. 1994. 4/yr. EUR 31 domestic; EUR 46 foreign; EUR 8 newsstand/cover (effective 2010). adv. **Document type:** *Magazine, Trade.*
Formerly (until 1997): Partner fuer Ersatzteile, Service und Reparatur von Nutzfahrzeugen (0946-8420)
Published by: Schluetersche Verlagsgesellschaft mbH und Co. KG, Hans-Boeckler-Allee 7, Hannover, 30173, Germany. TEL 49-511-85500, FAX 49-511-85501100, info@schluetersche.de, http://www.schluetersche.de. Ed. Olaf Tewes. Adv. contact Christian Welc. B&W page EUR 3,870, color page EUR 4,650; trim 188 x 272. Circ: 19,653 (paid and controlled).

388.324 USA
N T E A TECHNICAL REPORT. Text in English. 19??. irreg. (10-20/yr). looseleaf. USD 125 to non-members; free to members (effective 2011). illus. back issues avail. **Document type:** *Report, Trade.*
Published by: National Truck Equipment Association, 37400 Hills Tech Dr, Farmington, MI 48331. TEL 248-489-7090, 800-441-6832, FAX 248-489-8590, info@ntea.com.

388.324 USA
N T E A WASHINGTON UPDATE. Text in English. 1979. m. looseleaf. USD 99 to non-members; free to members (effective 2011). back issues avail. **Document type:** *Newsletter, Trade.* **Description:** Discussion of legislative and current federal and state regulatory activities, includes updates on congressional committee action and pending congressional bills.
Formerly: National Truck Equipment Association. Legislative Report; Incorporates: National Truck Equipment Association. Regulations Report
Related titles: Fax ed.; Online - full text ed.: membership.
Published by: National Truck Equipment Association, 37400 Hills Tech Dr, Farmington, MI 48331. TEL 248-489-7090, FAX 248-489-8590, info@ntea.com.

388.324 USA ISSN 0077-586X
HE5623.A45
NATIONAL TANK TRUCK CARRIER DIRECTORY. Text in English. 1954. a. USD 78 to non-members; USD 52 to members (effective 2000). adv. **Document type:** *Directory.*
Published by: National Tank Truck Carriers, Inc., 2200 Mill Rd, Alexandria, VA 22314-4677. TEL 703-838-1960, FAX 703-684-5753. Ed. George Mead. Circ: 2,000.

388.324 USA
NATIONAL TRUCK EQUIPMENT ASSOCIATION ANNUAL REPORT. Text in English. 200?. a. back issues avail. **Document type:** *Report, Trade.* **Description:** Illustrates how the Association helped position its members and the industry at large.
Related titles: Online - full text ed.: free (effective 2011).
Published by: National Truck Equipment Association, 37400 Hills Tech Dr, Farmington, MI 48331. TEL 248-489-7090, FAX 248-489-8590, info@ntea.com.

388.324 USA
NEBRASKA TRUCKER. Text in English. 1940. m. USD 24 (effective 2007). adv. **Document type:** *Magazine, Trade.*
Formerly: Midwestern Trucker and Shipper
Published by: Truck Services, Inc., 1701 K St, Box 81010, Lincoln, NE 68508-1010. TEL 402-476-8504, FAX 402-476-0579, nharris@navix.net. Ed., R&P Nance Harris TEL 402-476-8504. Adv. contact Sue Wilson. B&W page USD 600, color page USD 800. Circ: 2,100 (controlled).

388.324 USA ISSN 1554-2610
NEW JERSEY MOTOR TRUCK ASSOCIATION. BULLETIN. Text in English. 1964. m. free to members (effective 2005). adv. bk.rev. illus. **Document type:** *Bulletin, Trade.*
Former titles (until 2005): Moving Forward (East Brunswick) (1534-7613); (until 2001): New Jersey Motor Truck Association. Bulletin (0028-5838)
Published by: New Jersey Motor Truck Association, 160 Tices Ln, E Brunswick, NJ 08816-2083. TEL 732-254-5000, FAX 732-613-1745, http://www.njmta.org. Ed. Jennifer Duigon. Circ: 2,100 (controlled).

388.324 NZL ISSN 1174-7935
NEW ZEALAND TRUCK AND DRIVER MAGAZINE. Text in English. 1999. 11/yr. NZD 72 domestic; NZD 150 in Australia; NZD 195 in North America; NZD 215 in Europe; NZD 230 elsewhere (effective 2008). **Document type:** *Magazine, Trade.*
Published by: Allied Publications Ltd., PO Box 112-062, Penrose, Auckland, New Zealand. TEL 64-9-5713544, FAX 64-9-5713549.

388.324 NZL ISSN 1177-0007
NEW ZEALAND TRUCKBODY & TRAILER. Variant title: Truckbody & Trailer. Text in English. 2005. 6/yr. NZD 40 domestic; NZD 70 in Australia; NZD 85 in North America; NZD 90 in Europe; NZD 95 elsewhere (effective 2008). adv. **Document type:** *Magazine, Trade.*
Published by: Allied Publications Ltd., PO Box 112-062, Penrose, Auckland, New Zealand. TEL 64-9-5713544, FAX 64-9-5713549. Ed. Phil White TEL 64-9-5252029. Adv. contact Sandra DeJob. page NZD 3,920; trim 170 x 230.

388.344 NZL ISSN 0112-6393
NEW ZEALAND TRUCKING MAGAZINE. Text in English. 1984. 11/yr. NZD 61 domestic; NZD 110 in Australia; NZD 190 elsewhere; NZD 7.20 newsstand/cover (effective 2008). adv. back issues avail. **Document type:** *Magazine, Trade.* **Description:** Features articles on trucks, trucking roads and transportation in general.
Published by: Fairfax Magazines (Subsidiary of: Fairfax Media), Level 1, 274 Church St, Penrose, PO Box 12965, Auckland, New Zealand. TEL 64-9-6341800, FAX 64-9-6342948, info@fairfaxmedia.co.nz. Ed. John Murphy. Adv. contact Steven Ferrall. Circ: 9,901.

388.324 USA
HE5601
NEWPORT'S HEAVY DUTY TRUCKING; the fleet business authority. Abbreviated title: H D T. Text in English. 1925. m. USD 65 domestic; USD 130 foreign; free to qualified personnel (effective 2009). adv. illus. back issues avail.; reprints avail. **Document type:** *Magazine, Trade.* **Description:** Covers new equipment, design, safety, cost-cutting in heavy truck fleet operations.
Former titles (until 1999): Heavy Duty Trucking (0017-9434); (until 1968): Western Trucking and Motor Transportation; (until 1959): Western Trucking and Motor Transportation in the West; (until 195?): Motor Transportation; (until 1951): Motor Transportation of the West; (until 1949): Motor Transportation
Related titles: Online - full text ed.
Indexed: CLT&T, HRIS.
—Ingenta. **CCC.**
Published by: Newport Communications (Irvine) (Subsidiary of: H.I.C. Corporation), 38 Executive Pk, Ste 300, Irvine, CA 92614. TEL 949-261-1636, FAX 949-261-2904, http://www.newportcommunicationsgroup.com. Ed. Deborah Whistler. Adv. contact Keith Holsey TEL 949-225-7913. B&W page USD 14,299, color page USD 18,449; trim 7.875 x 10.75. Circ: 127,105.

338.3 658.8 USA ISSN 1538-6988
HD9710.35.U6
NEWPORT'S TRUCK SALES & LEASING. Text in English. 1983. bi-m. bk.rev. tr.lit. back issues avail.; reprints avail. **Document type:** *Magazine, Trade.* **Description:** Provides efficient, economical access to the vast but highly fragmented retail truck market.
Former titles (until 199?): Truck Sales & Leasing (1053-5942); (until 1990): Heavy Truck Salesman (0740-3941)
Related titles: Online - full text ed.
—CCC.
Published by: Newport Communications (Irvine) (Subsidiary of: H.I.C. Corporation), 38 Executive Pk, Ste 300, Irvine, CA 92614. TEL 949-261-1636, FAX 949-261-2904, http://www.newportcommunicationsgroup.com.

388.324 USA
NEWS BRIEFS (COLUMBUS). Text in English. 1961. bi-w. free to members (effective 2005). **Document type:** *Newsletter, Trade.*
Related titles: Supplement(s): Ohio Government Directory.
Published by: Ohio Trucking Association, 50 W Broad St, Ste 1111, Columbus, OH 43215. TEL 614-221-5375, FAX 614-221-3717, http://www.ohiotruckingassn.org/. Ed. David F Bartosic. Circ: 1,400 (controlled and free).

388.3 USA ISSN 1932-8311
NEXT TRUCK. Text in English. 2006. s-m. free (effective 2011). adv. back issues avail. **Document type:** *Magazine, Trade.* **Description:** Advertises trucks and trucking equipment available for purchase in the southeastern region of the U.S.
Related titles: Online - full text ed.
Published by: Randall-Reilly Publishing Company, 3200 Rice Mine Rd NE, Tuscaloosa, AL 35406. TEL 800-633-5953, http://www.randallpub.com. Pub. Chip Magner.

NISSAN DIESEL TECHNICAL REVIEW. *see* TRANSPORTATION—Automobiles

NOTIZIARIO MOTORISTICO/MOTOR - NACHRICHTEN/MOTOR NEWS/NOUVELLES DE L'AUTOMOBILE; autoattrezzature-impiantistica-ricambi-accessori. *see* TRANSPORTATION—Automobiles

388.324 ITA
NOTIZIARIO VEICOLI INDUSTRIALI. Text in English, Italian. 1965. 3/yr. free. **Document type:** *Magazine, Trade.*
Related titles: Online - full text ed.
Published by: Edizioni Collins Sas, Via Giovanni Pezzotti, 4, Milan, MI 20141, Italy. TEL 39-02-8372897, FAX 39-02-58103891, collins@collins.com, http://www.netcollins.com.

388.324 DEU ISSN 1436-994X
NUTZFAHRZEUG KATALOG. Text in German. 1992. a. EUR 6.90 per issue (effective 2010). adv. **Document type:** *Catalog, Trade.* **Description:** Provides comprehensive information on buying and using commercial vehicles.
Published by: Verlag Heinrich Vogel (Subsidiary of: Springer Science+Business Media), Neumarkterstr 18, Munich, 81664, Germany. TEL 49-89-2030431100, FAX 49-89-2030432100, vertriebsservice@springer.com, http://www.springerfachmedien-muenchen.de. Ed. Oliver Willms. adv.: B&W page EUR 4,420, color page EUR 8,650; trim 185 x 253. Circ: 30,000 (paid).

388.324 DEU ISSN 1614-1229
NUTZFAHRZEUGE-MANAGEMENT. Variant title: N F M. Text in German. 1989. m. EUR 3.30 newsstand/cover (effective 2008). adv. **Document type:** *Magazine, Trade.*
Formerly (until 2002): N F M - NutzFahrzeugeMarkt (1437-5516)
Published by: N F M Verlag, Am Hafen 10, Bremervoerde, 27432, Germany. TEL 49-4761-99470, FAX 49-4761-994722, nfm@transmoneymaker.de, http://www.transmoneymaker.com. adv.: page EUR 6,300. Circ: 24,086 (paid).

388.324 CAN ISSN 1491-2511
O T A NEWS. Text in English. 1980. bi-w. adv. bk.rev. stat.; tr.lit. **Document type:** *Newsletter, Trade.* **Description:** Provides Ontario Trucking Association members, government and industry with information on the Ontario truck transport industry.
Former titles (until 1998): OTA fax news (1485-3094); (until 1997): Update - Ontario Trucking Association (0841-2472); (until 1989): Ontario trucking update (0713-8482); (until 1982): O T A News Round-up (0822-5966)
Published by: Ontario Trucking Association, 555 Dixon Rd, Etobicoke, ON M9W 1H8, Canada. TEL 416-249-7401, FAX 416-245-6152, info@ontruck.org, http://www.ontruck.org/. Ed. Rebecka Torn. Circ: 1,100.

388.344 388.342 388.343 USA ISSN 1932-5835
OFF-ROAD ADVENTURES. Text in English. 1999. m. adv. 112 p./no.; **Document type:** *Magazine, Consumer.* **Description:** Aimed at the hands-on pickup truck, jeep and four wheel drive enthusiast. Focuses on vehicle modification and customizing, new truck and product reviews, and more.
Published by: Transamerican Auto Parts, 801 W Artesia Blvd, Compton, CA 90220. TEL 310-900-8626, FAX 310-762-9666, adventures@pacbell.net. Ed. Denis Snow. adv.: B&W page USD 18,600, color page USD 22,720; trim 7.75 x 10.5. Circ: 480,836.

388.324 CAN
OFFICIAL MANITOBA SHIP BY TRUCK DIRECTORY. Text in English. 1958. a. CAD 27. adv. **Document type:** *Directory.*
Former titles: Manitoba Ship by Truck Directory (0713-8776); M T A Ship by Truck Directory
Published by: Manitoba Trucking Association, 25 Bunting St, Winnipeg, MB R2X 2P5, Canada. Ed. Dianne Milton. R&P Al Harris. Circ: 1,000.

388.324 USA ISSN 0472-6243
HE5623.A45
OFFICIAL MOTOR CARRIER DIRECTORY. Text in English. 1958. s-a. USD 65.50. adv. charts. **Document type:** *Directory.*
Published by: Official Motor Freight Guide, Inc., 1700 W Cortland St, Chicago, IL 60622-1150. TEL 773-278-2454, FAX 773-489-0482. Ed. Edward K Koch. Pub., R&P Eric J Robison. Adv. contact Sam Donnelly. Circ: 5,200.

388.324 USA
OFFICIAL TRUCKING SAFETY GUIDE. Text in English. 197?. base vol. plus s-a. updates. looseleaf. USD 189; USD 232 combined subscription (print & online eds.) (effective 2011). **Document type:** *Handbook/Manual/Guide, Trade.* **Description:** Reference to federal and state safety requirements.
Formerly: Trucking Safety Guide
Related titles: Online - full text ed.
Published by: J.J. Keller & Associates, Inc., 3003 W Breezewood Ln, PO Box 368, Neenah, WI 54957. TEL 877-564-2333, 800-558-5011, FAX 800-727-7516.

629.2 380.5 FRA ISSN 1259-2439
L'OFFICIEL DES TRANSPORTEURS. Text in French. 1925. w. EUR 196; EUR 381 combined subscription print & online eds. (effective 2009). adv. **Document type:** *Magazine, Trade.*
Former titles (until 1994): L' Officiel des Transports (1156-3133); (until 1990): Officiel des Transporteurs (1163-0736); (until 194?): L' Officiel des Transporteurs et Garagistes (1243-4248); (until 1934): Garage Revue et Moto-Velo (1243-423X); (until 1932): Garage Revue (1242-1391)
Related titles: Online - full text ed.

Published by: Wolters Kluwer France (Subsidiary of: Wolters Kluwer N.V.), 1 Rue Eugene et Armand Peugeot, Rueil-Malmaison, Cedex 92856, France. TEL 33-1-76734809, FAX 33-1-76733040. Circ: 25,841.

320.025 USA
OHIO GOVERNMENT DIRECTORY - OHIO TRUCKING TIMES. Text in English. 1950. biennial. USD 5. adv. bk.rev. illus.
Former titles: Ohio Truck Times; (until 1974): Ohio Trucking News (0030-1191)
Published by: Ohio Trucking Association, 50 W Broad St, Ste 1111, Columbus, OH 43215. TEL 614-221-5375, FAX 614-221-3717. Ed. David F Bartosic. Circ: 8,000.

388.324 USA
OKLAHOMA MOTOR CARRIER. Text in English. 1937. q. USD 4; USD 1 newsstand/cover (effective 2005). adv. charts; illus.; stat. **Document type:** *Magazine, Trade.* **Description:** Presents general industry news including legislative and regulatory information, personnel news, economic and safety related news, photos of awards and new facilities.
Former titles: Truck and Commerce; Oklahoma Motor Carrier
Published by: Oklahoma Trucking Association, PO Box 14620, Oklahoma City, OK 73113. TEL 405-843-9488, FAX 405-843-7310. Ed. Rachel Meinke. Circ: 3,500 (controlled).

388.324 USA
OPEN ROAD NEWSLETTER. Text in English. 1946. a. USD 250 to non-members; free to members (effective 2005). **Document type:** *Newsletter, Consumer.*
Published by: Louisiana Motor Transport Association, Inc., 4838 Bennington Ave., Baton Rouge, LA 70808. TEL 225-928-5682, FAX 225-928-0500, http://www.truckinginfo.com. Pub. Cathy F. Gautreaux. Circ: 500 (controlled).

388.324 USA
OVER THE ROAD. Text in English. 1977. m. USD 59.95. adv. **Document type:** *Directory, Trade.*
Formerly: Owner and Operator Directory
Published by: Ramp Enterprises, Inc., 610 Colonial Park Dr, Roswell, GA 30075-3746. TEL 404-587-0338, FAX 770-642-8874. Ed. Penny Shefsky.

388.324 USA ISSN 0030-7394
HE5623
OVERDRIVE; the voice of the American trucker. Text in English. 1961. m. USD 34.97 domestic; USD 65 foreign; USD 6 per issue domestic; USD 9 per issue in Canada & Mexico; USD 12 per issue elsewhere; free to qualified personnel (effective 2011). adv. charts; illus.; tr.lit. back issues avail.; reprints avail. **Document type:** *Magazine, Trade.*
Incorporates (1970-2001): Owner Operator (1099-4246)
Related titles: Online - full text ed.: free (effective 2011).
Indexed: A09, A10, B01, B02, B06, B07, B08, B09, B15, B17, B18, BusI, C12, CLT&T, G04, G06, G07, G08, HRIS, I05, M01, M02, P34, T&II, T02, V03, V04.
Published by: Randall-Reilly Publishing Company, 3200 Rice Mine Rd NE, Tuscaloosa, AL 35406. TEL 800-633-5953, http://www.randallpub.com. Ed. Max Heine. Circ: 90,000.

388.324 AUS ISSN 1321-6279
OWNER - DRIVER; dedicated to the success of the person behind the wheel. Text in English. 1992. m. (except Jan.). AUD 69 domestic; AUD 79.35 in New Zealand; AUD 89.70 elsewhere (effective 2008). adv. **Document type:** *Newspaper, Consumer.* **Description:** Provides truck owner-drivers with up-to-date information on what affects them - from industry news, business aspects to equipments and services.
Published by: A C P Trader International Group (Subsidiary of: P B L Media Pty Ltd.), 73 Atherton Rd, Oakleigh, VIC 3166, Australia. TEL 61-3-95674200, FAX 61-3-95634554, http://www.tradergroup.com.au/. Eds. Gary Worral TEL 61-7-31662335, Graham Gardiner TEL 61-7-31662339. Adv. contact Jacky Acton TEL 61-7-31662307. B&W page AUD 2,500, color page AUD 4,950; trim 260 x 373. Circ: 33,579.

388.324 USA
HE5601
OWNER OPERATOR / COMPANY DRIVER. Text in English. 1970. m. adv. bk.rev. charts; illus.; tr.lit. back issues avail.; reprints avail. **Document type:** *Magazine, Trade.* **Description:** Business magazine for independent truckers and small fleet owner-operators that features technical information, vehicle selection information, equipment specifications, record-keeping information and methods of business management.
Incorporates (in 1999): Truck Owner; Former titles (until 2001): Owner Operator (1099-4246); (until 1997): Chilton's Owner Operator (1099-4254); (until 1990): Owner Operator (0475-2112)
Related titles: Microfiche ed.: (from PQC); Microfilm ed.: (from PQC); Online - full text ed.: free (effective 2011).
Indexed: CLT&T.
Published by: Randall-Reilly Publishing Company, 3200 Rice Mine Rd NE, Tuscaloosa, AL 35406. TEL 205-349-2990, 800-633-5953, FAX 205-248-1317. Pub. Scott Miller TEL 800-633-5953 ext 1393.

388.324 USA
PENNTRUX. Text in English. 1933. m. free membership only (effective 2005). index. **Document type:** *Magazine, Trade.* **Description:** Covers state and federal developments affecting the trucking industry, and chapter relations, member news.
Indexed: RASB.
Published by: Pennsylvania Motor Truck Association, 910 Linda Ln, Camp Hill, PA 17011-6409. TEL 717-761-7122, FAX 717-761-8434. Eds. Kristin Townsend, Kristin Townsend. R&P, Adv. contact Kristin Townsend. Circ: 2,300 (controlled).

388.324 ARG ISSN 1852-303X
PLANETA CAMION. Text in Spanish. 2004. bi-m. **Document type:** *Magazine, Consumer.*
Published by: Armadafilms, S.R.L., Calle Guatemala 1o., Buenos Aires, 1465, Argentina. TEL 54-11-47778034, FAX 54-11-47728909, info@armadafilms.ar, http://www.armadafilms.ar/. Ed. Ricardo Docimo.

388.324 USA
PRIDE & CLASS. Text in English. 2005. q. **Document type:** *Magazine, Consumer.* **Description:** Contains news, peer profiles and valuable specials on parts and services geared toward owner-operators.
Related titles: Online - full content ed.
Published by: Peterbilt Motors Co., 21420 W. Greenfield Ave., New Berlin, WI 53146. Circ: 100,000.

388.324 USA
PRO TRUCKER. Text in English. 1988. m. USD 29.95. adv. **Description:** For professional truck drivers, owner operators, fleet owners and drivers in the trucking industry. Covers industry news, and new products.
Formerly (until 1988): Pro Driver
Published by: Ramp Enterprises, Inc., 610 Colonial Park Dr, Roswell, GA 30075-3746. TEL 770-587-0338, FAX 770-642-8874. Ed. Pete Horner. Circ: 50,000.

388.324 ITA ISSN 1126-2648
PROFESSIONE CAMIONISTA. Text in Italian. 1998. m. EUR 27.90 (effective 2009). **Document type:** *Magazine, Consumer.*
Published by: Sprea Editori Srl, Via Torino 51, Cernusco sul Naviglio, MI 20063, Italy. TEL 39-02-92432222, FAX 39-02-92432236, editori@sprea.it, http://www.sprea.it.

338.47 GBR ISSN 1757-0255
PUBLIC SERVICE REVIEW: TRANSPORT. Text in English. 2001. q. GBP 50 (effective 2011). adv. back issues avail. **Document type:** *Magazine, Trade.* **Description:** Aims to focus on every aspect of the transport industry and its relationship with the public sector.
Formerly (until 2008): Freight Transport Review (1474-6506)
Related titles: Online - full text ed.: ISSN 2046-6153. free (effective 2011).
—CCC.
Published by: P S C A International Ltd., Ebenezer House, Rycroft, Newcastle-under-Lyme, Staffs ST5 2UB, United Kingdom. TEL 44-1782-630200, FAX 44-1782-625533, mailbox@publicservice.co.uk. Ed. Jonathan Miles. Adv. contact Gerrod Mellor TEL 44-1782-630200.

388.324 NLD ISSN 2211-5978
PULLING POWER. Text in Dutch. bi-m. EUR 34 domestic; EUR 46.50 foreign (effective 2011). adv. **Document type:** *Magazine, Consumer.*
Formerly (until 2011): Truck en Tractor Pulling Magazine (1877-4385)
Published by: Nederlandse Truck en Tractor Pulling Organisatie, Den Bramel 28, Ugchelen, 7339 JD, Netherlands. info@ntto.nl. Ed. Ton Herbrink.

QUARTERLY OPERATING STATISTICS; of major household goods carriers. *see* TRANSPORTATION—Abstracting, Bibliographies, Statistics

QUICK CALLER: ATLANTA AIR CARGO DIRECTORY. *see* TRANSPORTATION—Air Transport

QUICK CALLER: BOSTON AREA AIR CARGO DIRECTORY. *see* TRANSPORTATION—Air Transport

QUICK CALLER: CHICAGO AREA AIR CARGO DIRECTORY. *see* TRANSPORTATION—Air Transport

QUICK CALLER: DETROIT AREA AIR CARGO DIRECTORY. *see* TRANSPORTATION—Air Transport

QUICK CALLER: LOS ANGELES AREA AIR CARGO DIRECTORY. *see* TRANSPORTATION—Air Transport

QUICK CALLER: MIAMI - ORLANDO - FLORIDA AIR CARGO DIRECTORY. *see* TRANSPORTATION—Air Transport

QUICK CALLER: NEW YORK- NEW JERSEY METRO AREA AIR CARGO DIRECTORY. *see* TRANSPORTATION—Air Transport

QUICK CALLER: PACIFIC NORTHWEST AREA AIR CARGO DIRECTORY. *see* TRANSPORTATION—Air Transport

QUICK CALLER: SAN FRANCISCO - OAKLAND BAY AREA AIR CARGO DIRECTORY. *see* TRANSPORTATION—Air Transport

388.324 USA ISSN 0745-0389
R V TRADE DIGEST; your source for management, marketing & product information. (Recreational Vehicle) Text in English. 1981. 10/yr. USD 61 domestic; USD 77 in Canada & Mexico; USD 120 elsewhere; free to qualified personnel (effective 2008). adv. bk.rev. back issues avail.; reprints avail. **Document type:** *Magazine, Trade.* **Description:** Contains new product information and important industry news for RV dealers, manufacturers, wholesale distributors, suppliers and manufacturer reps.
Related titles: Online - full text ed.: free (effective 2008).
Indexed: A09, A10, A15, ABIn, G06, G07, G08, I05, P48, P51, P52, PQC, T02, V03, V04.
—CIS. **CCC.**
Published by: Cygnus Business Media, Inc., 1233 Janesville Ave, PO Box 803, Fort Atkinson, WI 53538. TEL 920-563-6388, 800-547-7377, FAX 920-563-1702, http://www.cygnusb2b.com. Eds. Dana Nelsen TEL 800-547-7377 ext 1349, Greg Gerber. Pubs. Bob Carnahan TEL 800-547-7377 ext 1682, Wolfgang Neuwirth. Adv. contacts Lani Bieberitz TEL 800-547-7377 ext 1633, Darci Bartley. B&W page USD 4,877, color page USD 6,437; trim 7.875 x 10.75. Circ: 16,000.

388.324 USA ISSN 1932-6769
TL153
THE R VER'S FRIEND. (Recreational Vehicle) Text in English. 1995. a. **Document type:** *Directory, Consumer.* **Description:** For use by RVers and other motorists to find diesel, gasoline, propane, large-vehicle parking, and other truck stop services.
Published by: T R Information Publishers, PO Box 476 DEPT 83, Clearwater, FL 33757. TEL 800-338-6317, FAX 727-443-4921, rdevos@truckstops.com, http://www.truckstops.com/default.asp.

388.324 USA
RAND MCNALLY MOTOR CARRIERS' ROAD ATLAS. Text in English. 1982. a. price varies. **Document type:** *Directory, Consumer.* **Description:** Privides coverage of state-designated truck routes and National Network routes will help truckers get where they're going on schedule with the best route possible in this easy to use motor carrier road atlas.
Published by: Rand McNally & Co., PO Box 7600, Chicago, IL 60680. TEL 800-777-6277, 800-678-7263, FAX 800-934-3479, http://www.randmcnally.com.

REEFER INTERNATIONAL. *see* HEATING, PLUMBING AND REFRIGERATION

REFERATIVNYI ZHURNAL. TRANSPORT PROMYSHLENNYKH PREDPRIYATII. LOGISTIKA. SKLADY. AVTOMATIZATSIYA POGRUZOCHNO-RAZGRUZOCHNYKH RABOT; vypusk svodnogo toma. *see* TRANSPORTATION—Abstracting, Bibliographies, Statistics

REFERATIVNYI ZHURNAL. VZAIMODEISTVIE RAZNYKH VIDOV TRANSPORTA I KONTEINERNYE PEREVOZKI; otdel'nyi vypusk. *see* TRANSPORTATION—Abstracting, Bibliographies, Statistics

388.324 USA
THE RESOURCE. Text in English. 1989. 3/yr. free. adv. **Document type:** *Corporate.* **Description:** Informs customers of Ryder transportation and logistics services.
Formerly (until 1998): Ryder Resource
Published by: Ryder System, Inc., 11690 NW 105th St., Medley, FL 33178-1103. TEL 305-500-3888, FAX 305-500-3203. Ed. Scott H Mall. Pub. David C Dawson. R&P Francine Williams TEL 305-500-3212. Circ: 30,000 (controlled).

388.344 BRA
REVISTA CAMINHONEIRO. Text in Portuguese, Spanish. 1985. m. free. adv. **Document type:** *Magazine, Trade.* **Description:** Designed for Brazilian and Mercosur truck drivers. Features news on roads, trucks, the truck driver's life, and related issues.
Formerly: Caminhoneiro
Published by: Takano Editora Grafica Ltda., Av Dr Silva Melo, 45 Jardim Marajoara, Jd Anhanguera, Sao Paulo, SP 04675-010, Brazil. TEL 55-11-5227934, FAX 55-11-56815763, http://www.caminhoneiro.net. Ed. Domingos Costa. Pub. Antonio Takano. Adv. contact Saulo P Muniz Furtado. color page USD 8,000. Circ: 80,000.

388.324 629.2 USA ISSN 1060-8397
ROAD & TRACK TRUCK S U V VAN BUYER'S GUIDE. Text in English. 1990. a. available at newsstands and not by subscription. charts; illus.; stat. reprints avail. **Document type:** *Guide, Consumer.* **Description:** Offers advice and guidance to persons seeking to purchase a light-duty truck: pickup, van, or sport utility vehicle.
Published by: Hachette Filipacchi Media U.S., Inc. (Subsidiary of: Hachette Filipacchi Medias S.A.), 1633 Broadway, New York, NY 10019. TEL 212-767-6000, FAX 212-767-5600, saleshfmbooks@hfmus.com, http://www.hfmus.com.

388.324 USA ISSN 1077-1581
ROAD KING; the magazine for the professional driver. Text in English. 1963. bi-m. USD 15 domestic (effective 2005). adv. bk.rev. **Document type:** *Magazine, Trade.* **Description:** Leisure reading about and for long haul truckers. Also includes equipment and product articles as well as new product announcements.
Published by: Travel Centers of America, 28 White Bridge Rd., Ste. 209, Nashville, TN 37205. TEL 615-627-2214, FAX 615-627-2197. Circ: 275,000 (controlled).

388.3 GBR ISSN 0963-536X
ROAD TRANSPORT BRIEFING. Text in English. 1991. bi-w. included with subscr. to Road Transport Operation. **Document type:** *Newsletter, Trade.*
Related titles: CD-ROM ed.; ◆ Supplement to: Croner's Road Transport Operation. ISSN 0070-1610.
Published by: Croner C C H Group Ltd. (Subsidiary of: Wolters Kluwer UK Ltd.), 145 London Rd, Kingston upon Thames, Surrey KT2 6SR, United Kingdom. TEL 44-20-85473333, FAX 44-20-85472638, info@croner.co.uk.

388.324 GBR ISSN 0035-7316
ROAD WAY. Text in English. 1935. m. GBP 36 domestic to non-members; GBP 48 in Europe to non-members; free to members (effective 2009). adv. bk.rev. illus.; stat. **Document type:** *Bulletin, Trade.*
Indexed: HRIS.
Published by: Road Haulage Association, Roadway House, 35 Monument Hill, Weybridge, Surrey KT13 8RN, United Kingdom. TEL 44-1932-841515, FAX 44-1932-838916, enquiries@rhaonline.co.uk. Adv. contact Nick Payne TEL 44-1453-882804.

388.324 GBR
ROADS GOODS VEHICLES TRAVELLING TO MAINLAND EUROPE (ANNUAL) (ONLINE). Text in English. 1979. a. **Document type:** *Government.*
Former titles (unil 200?): Roads Goods Vehicles Travelling to Mainland Europe (Print); International Road Haulage by United Kingdom Registered Vehicles (0262-6195); (until 1980): International Road Haulage by British Registered Vehicles (0262-4508)
Media: Online - full text. **Related titles:** Online - full text ed.
—CCC.
Published by: Great Britain. Department for Transport, Great Minster House, 76 Marsham St, London, SW1P 4DR, United Kingdom. TEL 44-20-79443078, FAX 44-20-79449643, publications@communities.gsi.gov.uk. Circ: 180.

388.324 USA
ROADWISE. Text in English. 1949. a. (Sep.). free to members (effective 2004). adv. **Document type:** *Bulletin, Trade.*
Published by: (Montana Motor Carriers Association, Inc.), Motor Carrier Service Inc., PO Box 1714, Helena, MT 59624. TEL 406-442-6600, FAX 406-443-4281. Ed. Barry Stang. Circ: 1,000 (controlled).

388.324 388.312 FRA ISSN 0243-6795
LES ROUTIERS. Text in French. 1934. 11/yr. EUR 38 domestic; EUR 48 foreign (effective 2009). adv. bk.rev. **Document type:** *Magazine.*
Published by: Societe d'Exploitation des Journaux Techniques, 21 rue Martissot, Clichy, 92110, France. TEL 33-1-41279737, FAX 33-1-41279730, sejt@sejt.com. Ed. Patrice de Saulieu. R&P Colette Fontanilles. Adv. contact Francois Deneuter. Circ: 45,000.

388.324 USA
S C & R A NEWSLETTER. Text in English. w. membership. **Description:** Industry news on legislation, industrial relations, management and safety.
Published by: Specialized Carriers & Rigging Association, 2750 Prosperity Ave, 620, Fairfax, VA 22031. TEL 703-698-0291, FAX 703-698-0297. Circ: 775.

388.324 USA
S C T A HI-LIGHTS. (South Carolina Trucking Association) Text in English. 1937. bi-m. free to members. **Document type:** *Magazine, Trade.*
Contact Owner: South Carolina Trucking Association, 2425 Devine St., Columbia, SC 29205. TEL 803-799-4306. Circ: 2,500 (controlled).

388.324 USA
SAFETY, INDUSTRIAL RELATIONS, AND GOVERNMENT AFFAIRS SPECIAL REPORT. Text in English. m. membership. **Description:** For transportation, crane, millwrighting and rigging professionals.
Published by: Specialized Carriers & Rigging Association, 2750 Prosperity Ave, 620, Fairfax, VA 22031. TEL 703-698-0291, FAX 703-698-0297. Circ: 775.

388.324 CAN ISSN 0229-9666
SASKATCHEWAN TRUCKING. Text in English. 1980. q. adv.

Published by: ProWest Publications, 208, 438 Victoria Ave E, Regina, SK S4N 0N7, Canada. TEL 306-352-3400, FAX 306-525-0960. Circ: 4,795.

388.324 CAN
SASKATCHEWAN TRUCKING - SHIP BY TRUCK DIRECTORY. Text in English. 1973. a. CAD 11. adv. **Document type:** *Directory.*
Formerly: Saskatchewan Motor Transport Guide (0707-0365)
Published by: Saskatchewan Trucking Association, 1335 Wallace St, Regina, SK S4N 3Z5, Canada. TEL 306-569-9696. Circ: 2,000.

388.324 DEU
SCHLEPPER POST. Text in German. 1992. bi-m. EUR 36 domestic; EUR 44 foreign; EUR 6 per issue (effective 2011). adv. **Document type:** *Magazine, Consumer.* **Description:** Contains articles on antique and historical trucks.
Published by: Verlag Klaus Rabe, Giesserallee 9, Postfach 250428, Willich, 57877, Germany. TEL 49-2154-48280, info@verlagrabe.de, http://www.verlagrabe.de.

388.324 DEU
SCHWACKELISTE NUTZFAHRZEUGE. Text in German. 1959. q. EUR 264; EUR 104 per issue (effective 2009). adv. **Document type:** *Magazine, Trade.*
Published by: EurotaxSchwacke GmbH, Wilhelm-Roentgen-Str 7, Maintal, 63477, Germany. TEL 49-6181-4050, FAX 49-6181-405111, info@schwacke.de, http://www.schwacke.de. adv.: B&W page EUR 1,000, color page EUR 1,900; trim 148 x 210. Circ: 2,655 (paid and controlled).

388.324 CAN ISSN 1717-872X
THE SHIPPER ADVOCATE. Text in English. s-a. adv. **Document type:** *Magazine, Trade.*
Formerly (until 2004): Canadian Shipper (0833-2932)
Indexed: CLT&T.
Published by: (Canadian Industrial Transportation Association/ Association Canadienne de Transport Industriel), Naylor (Canada), 100 Sutherland Ave., Winnipeg, MB R2W 3C7, Canada. TEL 800-665-2456, FAX 204-947-2047. Ed. Fiola Lilliane.

SISUVIESTI. *see* TRANSPORTATION—Automobiles

SOCIETY OF MOTOR MANUFACTURERS AND TRADERS. QUARTERLY STATISTICAL REVIEW. *see* TRANSPORTATION—Abstracting, Bibliographies, Statistics

388.324 ESP
SOLO CAMION; industrial ligero y derivados de turismo. Text in Spanish. 1989. m. (11/yr.). USD 36 domestic; USD 60 in Europe; USD 90 elsewhere (effective 2009). adv. back issues avail. **Document type:** *Magazine, Trade.* **Description:** Provides news from truck and components manufacturers, information on special transports and fleets, and truck tests.
Published by: Alesport S.A., Gran Via 8-10, Hospitalet de Llobragat, Barcelona, 08902, Spain. TEL 34-93-4315533, FAX 34-93-2973905, http://www.alesport.com. Ed. Juan Montenegro. Pub. Jaime Alguersuari. Adv. contact Maite Vinals. Circ: 39,000.

388.324 ESP
SOLO FURGO. Text in Spanish. m. EUR 31.20 domestic; EUR 60 in Europe; EUR 90 elsewhere (effective 2009). adv. **Document type:** *Magazine, Consumer.*
Published by: Alesport S.A., Gran Via 8-10, Hospitalet de Llobragat, Barcelona, 08902, Spain. TEL 34-93-4315533, FAX 34-93-2973905, http://www.alesport.com.

388.324 USA
SOUTH DAKOTA TRUCKING NEWS. Text in English. 1935. m. USD 35 (effective 2005). Supplement avail. **Document type:** *Magazine, Trade.*
Published by: South Dakota Trucking Association, PO Box 89008, Sioux Falls, SD 57105. TEL 605-334-8871, FAX 605-334-1938. Ed. Michelle Wells. Circ: 850 (controlled).

796.72 USA ISSN 1044-7903
SPORT TRUCK. Text in English. 1988. m. USD 12 domestic; USD 24 in Canada; USD 36 elsewhere (effective 2008). adv. back issues avail. **Document type:** *Magazine, Consumer.* **Description:** Designed for light-truck and SUV owners with an avid interest in the on-pavement performance and appearance of their vehicles.
Incorporates (in 1991): Hot Truck
Related titles: Online - full text ed.
Indexed: G05, G06, G07, G08, I05, I07.
—CCC.
Published by: Source Interlink Companies, 2400 E Katella Ave, Ste 700, Anaheim, CA 92806. TEL 714-939-2400, dheine@sourceinterlink.com, http://www.sourceinterlink.com. Ed. Mike Finnegan. Pub. Brad Christopher TEL 714-939-2509. adv.: B&W page USD 10,810, color page USD 17,435. Circ: 56,101 (paid).

STANDARD TRUCKING AND TRANSPORTATION STATISTICS. *see* TRANSPORTATION—Abstracting, Bibliographies, Statistics

388.33 USA ISSN 1942-2113
STOP WATCH. Text in English. 200?. bi-m. **Document type:** *Magazine, Trade.*
Published by: National Association of Truck Stop Operators, 1737 King St, Ste 200, Alexandria, VA 22314. TEL 703-549-2100, 888-275-6287, tpmembership@natso.com. Ed. Mindy Long.

STYLING & PERFORMANCE. *see* TRANSPORTATION—Automobiles

629.22 USA ISSN 0161-6080
SUCCESSFUL DEALER; delivering innovation in sales, service and support. Text in English. 1978. 7/yr. adv. charts; illus.; stat. back issues avail. **Document type:** *Magazine, Trade.* **Description:** Aims at dealer organizations selling medium and heavy-duty trucks, construction equipment, industrial trucks, trailers, diesel engines and for leasing-rental companies.
Related titles: Online - full text ed.
Published by: Randall-Reilly Publishing Company, 3200 Rice Mine Rd NE, Tuscaloosa, AL 35406. TEL 800-633-5953, http://www.randallpub.com. Ed. Denise L Rondini TEL 847-636-5069. Pub. Alan Welborn TEL 800-633-5953 ext 1422. Adv. contact Kim Ehrenhaft TEL 847-544-5348.

388.324 SWE ISSN 1404-1022
SVENSK AAKERITIDNING. Text in Swedish. 1918. 15/yr. SEK 583; SEK 42 newsstand/cover (effective 2004). bk.rev. illus.; stat. **Document type:** *Magazine, Trade.*
Former titles (until 1998): Lastbilen (0023-8678); Which incorporated (1971-1984): Transportveteranen; (1979-1982): Direkt till Medlemmerna; (until 1944): Lasttrafikbilaegaren
Published by: Aakerifoerlaget AB/Road Haulage Association of Sweden, Box 508, Danderyd, 18215, Sweden. TEL 46-8-7535440, FAX 46-8-7558895, http://www.akeri.se. Ed., Pub. Eric Bjoerklund TEL 46-8-7535441. Adv. contact Inger Kalin TEL 46-8-7535447.

388.324 USA
T A R A NEWS & TOPICS. Text in English. 1966. m. free. **Document type:** *Magazine, Trade.* **Description:** Contains information about truck repairs.
Published by: Truck-Frame & Axle Repair Association, PO Box 122, Adelphia, NJ 07710-0122. TEL 800-733-1851, FAX 732-577-9464. Circ: 1,000.

388.324 383.344 ESP ISSN 1139-9384
T M. TRANSPORTE MUNDIAL. Text in Spanish. 1984. m. **Document type:** *Magazine, Consumer.* **Description:** For the commercial trucking industry.
Formerly (until 1987): Transporte Mundial (1139-9147)
Published by: Motorpress Iberica (Subsidiary of: Gruner + Jahr AG & Co), Ancora 40, Madrid, 28045, Spain. TEL 34-91-3470100, FAX 34-91-3470152, http://www.motorpress-iberica.es. Ed. Pedro Guiterrez. Circ: 15,600 (paid).

388.324 NLD ISSN 1380-2852
T T M. (Truck en Transport Management) Text in Dutch. 1976. m. EUR 197.50 (effective 2009). adv. bk.rev. **Document type:** *Magazine, Trade.* **Description:** For executives and managers responsible for the management of road haulage companies and, in conjunction, for the purchase, operation and control of road transport vehicles in the road haulage industry as well as in industrial enterprises with their own vehicle fleets.
Formerly (until 1985): Eigen Vervoer (0165-2796)
—IE, Infotrieve.
Published by: Reed Business bv (Subsidiary of: Reed Business), Postbus 4, Doetinchem, 7000 BA, Netherlands. TEL 31-314-349911, info@reedbusiness.nl, http://www.reedbusiness.nl. Ed. Pieter Wieman. Pub. Geert van de Bosch. adv.: B&W page EUR 3,106, color page EUR 4,800; trim 215 x 285. Circ: 9,985.

TEAMSTER CONVOY DISPATCH; voice of the teamster rank and file since 1975. *see* LABOR UNIONS

TECHNISCHE VORSCHRIFTEN FUER KRAFTFAHRZEUGE. *see* TRANSPORTATION—Automobiles

388.324 USA
TENNESSEE TRUCKING NEWS. Text in English. bi-m. USD 25. adv. **Description:** Covers various topics in transportation.
Formerly: Transport News of Tennessee
Published by: Tennessee Trucking Association, 4531 Trousdale Rd, Nashville, TN 37204-4513. TEL 615-360-9200, FAX 615-777-2024. Ed. Lyn Hutchins. Circ: 1,000 (controlled).

388.324 CAN ISSN 0837-1512
TODAY'S TRUCKING. Text in English. 1987. m. free to qualified personnel (effective 2008). adv. bk.rev. charts; illus.; stat.; tr.lit. back issues avail. **Document type:** *Magazine, Trade.* **Description:** For owners and operators of heavy-duty trucks: news about trucking management, operation and maintenance.
Related titles: Online - full content ed.
—CCC.
Published by: Newcom Business Media, Inc., 451 Attwell Dr, Toronto, ON M9W 5C4, Canada. TEL 416-614-2200, FAX 416-614-8861, http://www.newcom.ca/. Ed. Peter Carter. Pub. Mark Vreugdenhil TEL 416-614-5826. adv.: B&W page CAD 5,570; trim 8 x 10.75. Circ: 30,000.

TORAKKU YUSO JOHO. *see* TRANSPORTATION—Railroads

388.344 FRA ISSN 1961-6341
TOUS LES VEHICULES UTILITAIRES MAG. Text in French. 200?. bi-m. EUR 30 (effective 2007). **Document type:** *Magazine, Consumer.*
Published by: Vehicule-Utilitaire.com, 14 Av. du Garric, Village d'Entreprises, Aurillac, 15000, France. TEL 33-4-71634182, FAX 33-4-71638928, contact@net-truck.com.

388.324 USA
TOW-AGE. Text in English. 1974. 6/yr. USD 18. adv. bk.rev. illus.; stat.; tr.lit. **Document type:** *Magazine, Trade.* **Description:** For towing and road service personnel who recover vehicles.
Formerly: Tow-Line
Published by: Collision Magazine, Inc., PO Box 389, Franklin, MA 02038. FAX 508-528-6211. Ed. J A Kruza. Circ: 8,000.

388 USA
TOW TIMES; the international communications medium for the automotive towing and recovery industry. Text in English. 1983. m. USD 34 domestic; USD 49 in Canada; USD 60 in Mexico; USD 70 elsewhere (effective 2000). adv. tr.lit. back issues avail. **Document type:** *Magazine, Trade.* **Description:** Covers all aspects of the automotive towing industry: economics and law, new products, technical data, recovery reviews, and company profiles.
Published by: T T Publications, Inc., 203 State Rd 434 W, Winter Springs, FL 32708-2598. TEL 407-327-4817, FAX 407-327-2603. Ed., R&P Tim Jackson. Pub. Clarissa Powell. Adv. contact Eleanor Joyce. Circ: 31,000 (controlled). **Subscr. to:** PO Box 522020, Longwood, FL 32752-2020.

388.324 USA
TOWING AND RECOVERY PHOOTNOTES. Text in English. 1991. m. USD 45 (effective 1999). adv. **Document type:** *Magazine, Trade.* **Description:** Provides towing and road service company owners and managers with business management ideas to improve profitability and quality of service.
Published by: Phootnotes, 100 W Plume St, Norfolk, VA 23510. TEL 877-219-7734, FAX 757-314-2411, phootnotes@traderonline.com, http://www.towtruckdrivers.com/advert/phhotnotes.htm. Ed. Clark Carriker. Pub. Shirley Thornton. R&P Jon A Lehman. adv.: B&W page USD 2,950; trim 15 x 10.13. Circ: 42,000 (controlled).

TRACK AND TIRE. *see* BUILDING AND CONSTRUCTION

388.324 USA ISSN 0041-0772
TRAILER / BODY BUILDERS. Text in English. 1959. m. USD 47 in US & Canada; USD 94 elsewhere; free in US & Canada to qualified personnel (effective 2011). adv. illus. **Document type:** *Magazine, Trade.* **Description:** Contains factual stories on production, sales, and management from the manufacturers or distributors of truck bodies, truck trailers, bus bodies, tank transports and van containers. Features stories on new products and new types of truck bodies and truck trailers.
Related titles: Online - full text ed.
Indexed: A09, A10, A15, ABIn, B01, B06, B07, B09, BPI, BRD, CA, I05, P52, PQC, PROMT, T02, V03, V04, W01, W02, W03, W05.
—CIS, Ingenta. **CCC.**
Published by: Penton Media, Inc., 4200 S Shepherd Dr, Ste 200, Houston, TX 77098. TEL 713-523-8124, FAX 713-523-8384, information@penton.com, http://www.penton.com. Ed. Bruce Sauer. Pub. Ray Anderson. Circ: 15,554 (controlled).

388.324 DEU ISSN 1869-4659
TRAILER-JOURNAL; der europaeische Einkaufsfuehrer. Text in German. 2005. biennial. EUR 8 newsstand/cover (effective 2010). adv. **Document type:** *Magazine, Trade.*
Published by: Stuenings Medien GmbH, Diessemer Bruch 167, Krefeld, 47805, Germany. TEL 49-2151-51000, FAX 49-2151-5100101, medien@stuenings.de, http://www.stuenings.de. Ed. Joerg Montag. Adv. contact Cornelia Assem. Circ: 50,000 (controlled).

388.324 AUT
TRAKTUELL; Partner in der Wirtschaft - Partner im Verkehr. Text in German. 1994. 10/yr. EUR 34 domestic; EUR 65 foreign; EUR 3.80 newsstand/cover (effective 2005). adv. **Document type:** *Magazine, Trade.*
Related titles: Online - full text ed.
Published by: Springer Business Media Austria GmbH (Subsidiary of: Springer Science+Business Media), Inkustr 16, Klosterneuburg, 3403, Austria. TEL 43-2243-301110, FAX 43-2243-30111222, office@springer-sbm.at, http://www.springer-sbm.at. Ed. Helmut Tober. Adv. contact Renate Greiter. B&W page EUR 3,224, color page EUR 4,730; trim 185 x 255. Circ: 8,000 (paid and controlled).

TRANSMISSION TECH - TALK. *see* TRANSPORTATION—Automobiles

388.324 NLD ISSN 1382-9033
TRANSMOBIEL; truck & bus magazine. Text in Dutch. 1985. 5/yr. EUR 26.25 (effective 2009). adv. bk.rev. 44 p./no.; back issues avail. **Document type:** *Magazine, Trade.* **Description:** Includes articles on trucks, buses, cranes, heavy transports, firefighting vehicles, and military vehicles.
Published by: Uitgeverij Transmobiel, Postbus 45, Zevenbergen, 4760 AA, Netherlands. TEL 31-168-335034, transmobiel@xs4all.nl, http://www.transmobiel.com.

388.3 ZAF ISSN 1015-5287
TRANSPORT MANAGER'S HANDBOOK AND TRUCKER'S GUIDE. Text in English. 1978. a. price varies. adv. **Document type:** *Handbook/Manual/Guide, Trade.*
Formerly (until 1989): Transport Manager's Handbook; Incorporates: Commercial Transport Equipment Index; Supersedes (1964-1978): Commercial Transport Handbook and Buyer's Guide for S A (0069-6676)
Published by: T M L Business Publishing (Subsidiary of: Times Media Ltd.), PO Box 182, Pinegowrie, Gauteng 2123, South Africa. TEL 27-11-789-2144, FAX 27-11-789-3196. Circ: 1,000.

388.324 GBR ISSN 0306-2252
TRANSPORT NEWS DIGEST. Text in English. 1968. m. GBP 24, USD 40 (effective 2000). bk.rev. **Document type:** *Newsletter.* **Description:** Contains trucks, law and industry news.
—BLDSC (9025.800000).
Published by: Transport Press Services, 38 Portobello Rd, London, W11 3DH, United Kingdom. TEL 44-171-727-0253, FAX 44-171-229-5909. Ed., Pub. John Dickson-Simpson. Circ: 500 (paid).

388.3240971405 CAN ISSN 1494-6564
TRANSPORT ROUTIER. Text in English, French. bi-m. adv. **Document type:** *Magazine, Trade.*
Published by: Newcom Business Media, Inc., 451 Attwell Dr, Toronto, ON M9W 5C4, Canada. TEL 416-614-2200, FAX 416-614-8861, http://www.newcom.ca/. Ed. Steve Bouchard. Pub. Rolf Lockwood.

629.2 CHE ISSN 1423-2707
TRANSPORT RUNDSCHAU; Unabhaengige Zeitschrift fuer Nutzfahrzeuge, Strassentransport, Logistik, und Werkstatt und Betrieb. Text in German. 1980. m. adv. illus. **Document type:** *Magazine, Trade.*
Formerly (until 1992): I N U F A Rundschau (0255-6871); Which incorporated (1986-1990): Garage und Transport (0257-8549); Which was formerly (1954-1986): Motor-Service (0027-1985)
Published by: Swiss Professional Meda AG - Rittmann (Subsidiary of: Sueddeutscher Verlag GmbH), Hochbergerstr 15, Postfach, Basel, 4002, Switzerland. TEL 41-58-9589500, FAX 41-61-6391095, info@s-p-m.ch, http://www.swissprofessionalmedia.ch. adv.: B&W page CHF 2,170, color page CHF 3,270; trim 260 x 185. Circ: 12,290.

388.324 USA ISSN 0041-1558
TRANSPORT TOPICS; national newspaper of the trucking industry. Text in English. 1935. w. (Mon.). USD 109 domestic; USD 149 in Canada & Mexico; USD 299 elsewhere; free to members (effective 2009). adv. charts; illus.; mkt.; stat.; tr.lit. 50 p./no. 5 cols./p.; back issues avail.; reprints avail. **Document type:** *Newspaper, Trade.* **Description:** Provides trucking news for anyone involved in the management, traffic and maintenance of regulated haulers for hire and private carriers engaged in interstate distribution.
Formerly (until 19??): A T A News Bulletin
Related titles: Microform ed.: (from PQC); Online - full text ed.
Indexed: A15, A22, ABIn, B16, CLT&T, HRIS, LogistBibl, P10, P48, P51, P52, P53, P54, PQC.
—CCC.
Published by: American Trucking Associations, Inc., 950 N Glebe Rd, Ste 210, Alexandria, VA 22203. TEL 703-838-1770, FAX 703-838-7916, orders@trucking.org, http://www.truckline.com. Ed., Pub. Howard S. Abramson TEL 703-838-1922. Circ: 28,666 (paid). Wire service: AP.

T U

388.324 USA ISSN 1532-0294
TRANSPORTATION EQUIPMENT NEWS. Abbreviated title: T E N. Variant title: Transportation. Text in English. 1998. m. adv. **Document type:** *Magazine, Trade.* **Description:** Aims to be the fleet owner's comprehensive source of information on trucking equipment, products and services.
Published by: Grand View Media Group, Inc. (Subsidiary of: EBSCO Industries, Inc.), 200 Croft St, Ste 1, Birmingham, AL 35242. TEL 888-431-2877, FAX 205-408-3797, webmaster@grandviewmedia.com, http://www.gvmg.com. adv.: color page USD 5,000; trim 8 x 10.875.

388.324 USA
TRANSPORTATION EQUIPMENT NEWS ANNUAL DIRECTORY. Abbreviated title: T E N Annual Directory. Text in English. a. **Document type:** *Directory, Trade.* **Description:** Contains product and services information for active fleet equipment buyers throughout the country.
Published by: Grand View Media Group, Inc. (Subsidiary of: EBSCO Industries, Inc.), 200 Croft St, Ste 1, Birmingham, AL 35242. TEL 888-431-2877, FAX 205-408-3797, webmaster@grandviewmedia.com, http://www.gvmg.com.

388.324 658 USA ISSN 0897-8077
TRANSPORTATION EXECUTIVE UPDATE. Text in English. 1987. bi-m. USD 48. **Description:** For upper level management of the general freight trucking industry.
Published by: Regular Common Carrier Conference, 2200 Mill Rd, Ste 350, Alexandria, VA 22314-4654. TEL 703-838-1970. Ed. Shawn Fields. Circ: 2,000.

388.324 USA ISSN 1097-6280
TRANSPORTATION MANAGEMENT TODAY. Text in English. 1999. m. looseleaf. **Document type:** *Newsletter.* **Description:** Provides information on communication, managing people, employee relations, problem solving, time management, training, customer service, and more.
Formerly: Transportation - Trucks and Trucking
—CCC.
Published by: J.J. Keller & Associates, Inc., 3003 W Breezewood Ln, PO Box 368, Neenah, WI 54957. TEL 877-564-2333, FAX 800-727-7516, http://www.jjkeller.com.

388.324 305.868 USA ISSN 1934-3264
TRANSPORTISTA; la revista de la industria del transporte. Text in Spanish. 2005 (Jan.). m. adv. back issues avail. **Document type:** *Magazine, Trade.* **Description:** Serves over-the-road Hispanic truckers by providing them with timely news, in-depth reporting of industry issues, and technical and operational information, as well as spotlighting their unique lifestyles and showing respect for their diverse cultural backgrounds.
Formerly (until 2006): Truckers News en Espanol (1555-8282)
Related titles: ◆ English ed.: Truckers News. ISSN 1040-2284.
Published by: (National Association of Truck Stop Operators), Randall-Reilly Publishing Company, 3200 Rice Mine Rd NE, Tuscaloosa, AL 35406. TEL 800-633-5953, http://www.randallpub.com.

388.3 NLD ISSN 1381-690X
TRANSPORTVISIE. Text in Dutch. 1993. bi-m. EUR 30.85 domestic; EUR 43.50 foreign; EUR 7.95 newsstand/cover (effective 2009). adv. bk.rev. back issues avail. **Document type:** *Magazine, Trade.*
Formerly (until 1995): Nederlands Goederenvervoer (0929-6875)
Related titles: ◆ Supplement to: Nederlands Vervoer. ISSN 0924-6584.
—IE.
Published by: Koninklijke Nederlands Vervoer, Postbus 19365, The Hague, 2500 CJ, Netherlands. TEL 31-70-3751751, FAX 31-70-3455853, postbus@knv.nl, knvmedia@knv.nl, http://www.knv.nl. Ed. Jos Haas. adv.: B&W page EUR 1,453, color page EUR 2,207; trim 210 x 297. Circ: 7,000 (paid).

TRUCK & BUS ENGINEERING. *see* ENGINEERING

388.324 ZAF ISSN 0258-9281
TRUCK & BUS, SOUTH AFRICA. Text in English. 1980. m. ZAR 40. adv. illus. **Document type:** *Magazine, Trade.*
Indexed: ISAP.
Published by: Titan Publications (Pty) Ltd., Rodland House, 382 Jan Smuts Ave, Craighall, Gauteng 2196, South Africa. Ed. John Marsh. Adv. contact R Considine. Circ: 4,000.

388.324 SVK ISSN 1337-897X
TRUCK & BUSINESS. Text in Slovak. 2008. q. SKK 350 (effective 2011). adv. **Document type:** *Magazine, Trade.*
Published by: Auto Business Media s.r.o., Racianska 62, Bratislava, 83102, Slovakia. TEL 421-2-44632936, FAX 421-2-44632936. Ed. Peter Krc. Adv. contact Jan Keder.

388.324 BEL ISSN 0772-5000
TRUCK & BUSINESS (DUTCH EDITION). Text in Dutch. 8/yr. EUR 50 (effective 2005). **Document type:** *Trade.*
Formerly (until 1992): Mini-Maxi-Truck (0770-5441)
Related titles: French ed.: Truck & Business (French Edition). ISSN 0778-838X.
Published by: Multi Media Management, Parc Artisanal 11-13, Blegny-Barchon, 4670, Belgium. TEL 32-4-3878787, FAX 32-4-3879087, http://www.mmm.be. Ed. Jean-Marie Becker. R&P Jean Marie Becker. Adv. contact Pola Dorthu. Circ: 10,500.

338.324 GBR ISSN 0966-3533
TRUCK & DRIVER MAGAZINE. Text in English. 1974. m. GBP 35 domestic; USD 88 elsewhere; GBP 2.85 newsstand/cover (effective 2010). adv. back issues avail. **Document type:** *Magazine, Trade.* **Description:** Includes news, reviews, letters, and questions and answers for the driver and owner-driver.
Supersedes in part (in 1992): Truck Magazine (0308-0641); Which incorporated (1984-1990): Truck & Driver (0266-7819)
Related titles: Online - full text ed.
Indexed: A09, A10, B01, B02, B06, B07, B09, B15, B17, B18, G04, G06, G07, G08, I05, P48, P51, P52, PQC, S22, T02, V03, V04.
—CCC.
Published by: Reed Business Information Ltd. (Subsidiary of: Reed Business), Quadrant House, The Quadrant, Sutton, Surrey SM2 5AS, United Kingdom. TEL 44-20-86523500, FAX 44-20-86528932, rbi.subscriptions@qss-uk.com. Eds. Will Shiers TEL 44-20-86523712, Brian Weatherley TEL 44-20-8652-3303. Adv. contact David Smith TEL 44-20-86523686. color page GBP 2,500; trim 210 x 297. Circ: 27,973. **Subscr. to:** Quadrant Subscription Services, Rockwood House, 9-17 Perrymount Rd, Haywards Heath, W. Sussex RH16 3DH, United Kingdom. TEL 44-845-0778844, FAX 44-845-6760030, qss.customer.services@quadrantsubs.com, http://www.quadrantsubs.com.

388.324 USA ISSN 1947-9751
▼ **TRUCK AND EQUIPMENT POST.** Text in English. 2009. bi-w. USD 1.50 per issue (effective 2009). **Document type:** *Magazine, Trade.* **Description:** For buyers and sellers in the trucking industry.
Published by: Optative Group, 116 Arbor Dr, Providence, RI 02908. TEL 401-644-9387, tmcvet@cox.net.

388.324 GBR ISSN 1745-624X
TRUCK & PLANT TRADER. Text in English. 1989. w. GBP 125 domestic; GBP 62 for 6 mos. domestic (effective 2010). adv. **Document type:** *Magazine, Consumer.* **Description:** Features the widest selection of trucks, LGVs, trailers and plant vehicles in the UK and Ireland.
Former titles (until 2004): Truck Trader (1745-5995); (until 1996): Truck Trader Weekly (0958-9597)
Published by: Trader Media Group Ltd., Auto Trader House, Cutbush Park Industrial Estate, Danehill, Lower Earley, Reading, Berks RG6 4UT, United Kingdom. TEL 44-208-5447000, FAX 44-208-8791879, enquiries@autotrader.co.uk, http://www.tradermediagroup.com/.

388.324 USA ISSN 1534-2107
TRUCK & S U V PERFORMANCE; products and trends for retailers. Text in English. 1994. 9/yr. USD 40 domestic; USD 60 in Canada; USD 99 elsewhere; free to qualified personnel (effective 2006). adv. illus. back issues avail. **Document type:** *Magazine, Trade.* **Description:** Features useful articles full of technical insight and business tips designed to help retailers run a successful specialty equipment business.
Formerly (until 2003): Truck Accessory News (1075-8178)
Related titles: Online - full text ed.
Indexed: B02, B15, B17, B18, G04, G06, G07, G08.
Published by: Bobit Business Media, 3520 Challenger St, Torrance, CA 90503. TEL 310-533-2400, FAX 310-533-2500, order@bobit.com, http://www.bobit.com. Ed. Steve Stillwell. Circ: 11,000.

388.324 CAN ISSN 0319-7492
TRUCK & TRAILER. Text in English. 1975. m. adv. **Document type:** *Magazine, Trade.* **Description:** Catalog of new and used trucks, trailers, parts for sale; services available; owner-operator recruitment section.
Related titles: Online - full text ed.
Published by: Newcom Business Media, Inc., 451 Attwell Dr, Toronto, ON M9W 5C4, Canada. TEL 416-614-2200, FAX 416-614-8861, http://www.newcom.ca/. Pub. Rolf Lockwood. Circ: 34,000.

388.324 AUS ISSN 1445-7806
TRUCK & TRAILER AUSTRALIA. Text in English. 1977. bi-m. AUD 6.95 per issue (effective 2008). adv. **Document type:** *Magazine, Trade.* **Description:** Aimed at truck fleet managers, covers local and international news, latest equipment tests, technology, management issues.
Former titles (until 1999): Truck Australia (0815-9211); (until 1985): C A R T (0727-5447)
Indexed: ARI.
Published by: News Magazines Pty Ltd., Level 3, 2 Holt St, Surry Hills, NSW 2010, Australia. TEL 61-2-92883000, http://www.newsspace.com.au/magazines. Adv. contact Andrew Byrne TEL 61-2-80622656. color page AUD 3,300; trim 206 x 276. Circ: 12,449.

388.324 USA ISSN 0273-9402
TRUCK BLUE BOOK. Text in English. 1911. q. USD 124.95 (effective 2011). adv. **Document type:** *Directory.*
Related titles: Online - full content ed.: USD 339.95 (effective 2011).
—CCC.
Published by: Penton Media, Inc., 9800 Metcalf Ave, Overland Park, KS 66212. TEL 913-341-1300, FAX 913-967-1898, information@penton.com, http://www.penton.com.

388.324 CAN ISSN 0564-3392
TL5
TRUCK DATA BOOK; identification data for all makes and models of trucks found in Canada. Text in English. 1949. a. CAD 42. **Document type:** *Directory.* **Description:** Nine model years listed. Identification and registration data includes, GVW and curb weight, wheelbase, engine stats and vehicle identification number for light, medium and heavy duty trucks. MSR price for light trucks featured.
Published by: Sanford Evans Research Group A Subsidiary of Sun Media Corporation, 1700 Church Ave, Winnipeg, MB R2X 3A2, Canada. TEL 204-694-2022, FAX 204-632-4250. Ed. Gary Henry.

388.324 USA
TRUCK EQUIPMENT NEWS. Text in English. 19??. m. free to qualified personnel (effective 2011). 12 p./no.; back issues avail. **Document type:** *Newsletter, Trade.* **Description:** Truck body and equipment industry newsletter.
Formerly (until Feb.2001): T E News
Published by: National Truck Equipment Association, 37400 Hills Tech Dr, Farmington, MI 48331. TEL 248-489-7090, FAX 248-489-8590, info@ntea.com, http://www.ntea.com.

388.324 USA
TRUCK EQUIPMENT OUTLOOK. Text in English. 19??. q. **Document type:** *Trade.*
Published by: National Truck Equipment Association, 37400 Hills Tech Dr, Farmington, MI 48331. TEL 248-489-7090, 800-441-6832, FAX 248-489-8590, info@ntea.com, http://www.ntea.com.

629.35 CZE ISSN 1214-4185
TRUCK MAGAZIN. Text in Czech. 2003. m. CZK 550 (effective 2011). adv. **Document type:** *Magazine, Trade.*
Published by: 66 Media s.r.o., Zirovnicka 3133/6, Prague 10, Czech Republic. TEL 420-2-34090320, FAX 420-2-34090301, info@66media.cz, http://www.66media.cz. Ed. Roman Repa. **Subscr. to:** SEND Predplatne s.r.o., PO Box 141, Prague 4 140 21, Czech Republic. TEL 420-225-985225, FAX 420-225-341425, send@send.cz, http://www.send.cz.

629.13 DEU
TRUCK-MAGAZIN MOTOR UND SPORT. Text in German. 1997. m. EUR 2.50 newsstand/cover (effective 2006). adv. **Document type:** *Magazine, Trade.*
Published by: Truck-Media Verlag Ltd., Bachstr 37, Iserlohn, 58642, Germany. TEL 49-2374-2688, FAX 49-2374-2689, info@truckmagazin.de. Ed. Bernd Schulte. Adv. contact Merima Mulic. color page EUR 1,950. Circ: 28,550 (paid and controlled).

388.324 DEU
TRUCK MARKET. Text in German. fortn. EUR 39.90; EUR 1 newsstand/cover (effective 2010). adv. **Document type:** *Magazine, Trade.*
Formerly: Truck und Trailer Markt
Published by: Verlag Heinrich Vogel (Subsidiary of: Springer Science+Business Media), Neumarkterstr 18, Munich, 81664, Germany. TEL 49-89-2030431100, FAX 49-89-2030432100, vertriebsservice@springer.com, http://www.springerfachmedien-muenchen.de. adv.: B&W page EUR 715, color page EUR 1,070. Circ: 40,000 (paid and controlled).

388.324 DEU ISSN 1434-4106
TRUCK-MOBILES. Text in German. 1994. fortn. adv. **Document type:** *Magazine, Trade.*
Published by: D A Z Verlag GmbH und Co. KG, An der Strusbek 23, Ahrensburg, 22926, Germany. TEL 49-4102-47870, FAX 49-4102-478795, info@daz-verlag.de, http://www.daz24.de. Pub. Joerg Walter. Circ: 74,845 (paid and controlled).

388.324 USA
TRUCK 'N TRAILER MAGAZINE. Variant title: Truck and Trailer Magazine. Text in English. 1966. bi-w. USD 65 domestic (effective 2001); Free to qualified subscribers. adv. **Document type:** *Magazine, Trade.* **Description:** Features the advertising of light and heavy-duty trucks, specialized equipment, auctions and related industries.
Related titles: Online - full content ed.
Published by: W.P. Lynagh Associates, Inc., 830 Barnesville Drive, P O Box 68, Barnesville, PA 18214. TEL 570-467-2528, FAX 570-467-3720, tntmail@ptd.net, http://www.truckntrailer.com/.

388.324 CAN ISSN 0712-2683
TRUCK NEWS. Text in English. 1981. m. CAD 38.95 domestic; USD 99.95 foreign (effective 2007). **Document type:** *Newspaper, Trade.* **Description:** Covers Canadian truck operators' concerns: regulations, products, events.
Incorporates: Eastern Trucker; Which was formerly: Eastern Western Trucker
Related titles: Online - full text ed.
Indexed: C03, CBCABus, P48, P52, PQC.
—CCC.
Published by: Business Information Group, 12 Concorde Pl, Ste 800, Toronto, ON M3C 4J2, Canada. TEL 416-442-2122, 800-668-2374, FAX 416-442-2191. Circ: 39,128.

388.324 USA
TRUCK PAPER. Text in English. 1981. w. USD 59; free to qualified personnel (effective 2008). adv. **Document type:** *Magazine, Trade.* **Description:** Contains informations on the buying and selling of heavy trucks and trailers.
Related titles: Online - full text ed.; Alternate Frequency ed(s).: bi-w. USD 38 (effective 2004); m. USD 24 (effective 2004).
Published by: Sandhills Publishing Co., PO Box 82545, Lincoln, NE 68501. TEL 402-479-2181, 800-331-1978, FAX 402-479-2195, feedback@sandhills.com, http://www.sandhills.com.

629.224 388.3 USA ISSN 0895-3856
TRUCK PARTS & SERVICE; the aftermarket authority. Text in English. 1966. m. USD 50; free to qualified personnel (effective 2011). adv. back issues avail. **Document type:** *Magazine, Trade.* **Description:** Aimed at owners, partners, managers and executives of truck specialists; truck trailer, bus dealers, truck stops and heavy duty parts distributors.
Former titles (until Aug.1987): Heavy-Duty Distribution (0191-6777); (until 19??): Fleet Distribution
Related titles: Online - full text ed.: free (effective 2011).
Published by: Randall-Reilly Publishing Company, 3200 Rice Mine Rd NE, Tuscaloosa, AL 35406. TEL 800-633-5953, http://www.randallpub.com. Ed. Avery Vise TEL 205-248-1386. Pub. Alan Welborn TEL 800-633-5953 ext 1422.

TRUCK, RACE, CYCLE AND REC. MARKETPLACE. *see* TRANSPORTATION—Automobiles

388.324 DEU
TRUCK SPORT BOOK. Text in German. 2002. a. EUR 15 newsstand/cover (effective 2011). adv. **Document type:** *Magazine, Consumer.*
Published by: Paul Pietsch Verlage GmbH & Co. KG, Olgastr 86, Stuttgart, 70180, Germany. TEL 49-711-210800, FAX 49-711-2360415, ppv@motorbuch.de, http://www.paul-pietsch-verlage.de. Circ: 10,000 (paid).

388.324 DEU
TRUCK SPORT GUIDE. Text in German. 1996. a. adv. **Document type:** *Magazine, Consumer.*
Formerly (until 2005): Truck Race Guide
Published by: EuroTransportMedia Verlags- und Veranstaltungs-GmbH, Handwerkstr 15, Stuttgart, 70565, Germany. TEL 49-711-784980, FAX 49-711-7849888, info@eurotransport.de, http://www.etm-verlag.de. Circ: 35,000 (controlled).

388.324 DEU ISSN 1865-0988
TRUCK SPORT MAGAZIN. Text in German. 2007. 3/yr. EUR 10; EUR 2.50 newsstand/cover (effective 2011). adv. **Document type:** *Magazine, Consumer.*
Published by: EuroTransportMedia Verlags- und Veranstaltungs-GmbH, Handwerkstr 15, Stuttgart, 70565, Germany. TEL 49-711-784980, FAX 49-711-7849888, info@etm-verlag.de, http://www.etm-verlag.de. Adv. contact Oliver Trost. Circ: 35,000 (paid and controlled).

388.3 USA
TRUCK TRADER. Text in English. 19??. w. free (effective 2011). adv. back issues avail. **Document type:** *Magazine, Trade.*
Related titles: Online - full text ed.
Published by: Trader Publishing Co., 150 Granby St, Norfolk, VA 23510. TEL 757-640-4020, http://www.traderonline.com/.

388.324 NZL
TRUCK TRADER. Text in English. 11/yr. (Jan./Feb. comb. issue). adv. **Document type:** *Magazine, Trade.*

Published by: Fairfax Magazines (Subsidiary of: Fairfax Media), Level 1, 274 Church St, Penrose, PO Box 12965, Auckland, New Zealand. TEL 64-9-6341800, FAX 64-9-6342948, info@fairfaxmedia.co.nz. Adv. contact Trish Bexley.

388.324 CAN ISSN 1185-3409
TRUCK WEST. Text in English. 1990. m. CAD 41.28 domestic; USD 99.95 foreign (effective 2008). adv. **Document type:** *Newspaper, Trade.*
Description: A newspaper for Western Canada trucking industry, with particular emphasis on small fleet and owner/operators.
Related titles: Online - full text ed.
Indexed: C03, CBCABus, P48, P52, PQC.
—CCC.
Published by: Business Information Group, 12 Concorde Pl, Ste 800, Toronto, ON M3C 4J2, Canada. TEL 416-442-2122, 800-668-2374, FAX 416-442-2191, orders@businessinformationgroup.ca, http://www.businessinformationgroup.ca. Pub. Rob Wilkins TEL 416-510-5123. Circ: 22,000.

388.324 USA ISSN 1526-0127
THE TRUCKER; America's Trucking Newspaper. Text in English. 1987. bi-w. USD 29.95 domestic (effective 2000). adv. bk.rev. charts; illus.; mkt.; stat.; tr.lit. 75 p./no. 4 cols./p.; back issues avail. **Document type:** *Newspaper, Trade.* **Description:** Provides information for the truckload freight industry, featuring news and information of critical interest to both drivers and managers.
Related titles: E-mail ed.; Fax ed.
Published by: Belmont Publishing, Inc., PO Box 3413, Little Rock, AR 72203-3413. TEL 501-666-0500, 800-666-2770, FAX 501-666-0700. Ed., R&P Emily Roberts. Pub. Ray Wittenberg. adv.: B&W page USD 2,725, color page USD 3,075; trim 11.5 x 10. Circ: 100,000 (paid and controlled).

388.324 DEU ISSN 0946-3216
TRUCKER; Fernfahrer Magazin. Text in German. 1979. m. EUR 38.90 domestic; EUR 44.40 foreign (effective 2011). adv. **Document type:** *Magazine, Trade.* **Description:** Contains articles and information on all aspects of trucks and trucking.
Published by: Verlag Heinrich Vogel (Subsidiary of: Springer Science+Business Media), Neumarkterstr 18, Munich, 81664, Germany. TEL 49-89-2030431100, FAX 49-89-2030432100, vertriebsservice@springer.com, http://www.springerfachmedien-muenchen.de. Ed. Johannes Reichel. Circ: 55,765 (paid and controlled).

388.324 CZE ISSN 1335-4531
TRUCKER (PRAGUE). Text in Czech, Slovak. 1991. m. CZK 460 (effective 2008). **Document type:** *Magazine, Trade.*
Published by: Springer Media CZ, s. r. o., Nadrazni 32, Prague, 15000, Czech Republic. TEL 420-2-25351212, FAX 420-2-25351404, predplatne@bmczech.cz, http://www.businessmedia.cz. Ed. Stano Cvengros.

388.324 USA
TRUCKER'S CONNECTION. Text in English. 1987. m. **Document type:** *Magazine, Trade.* **Description:** Contains industry and carrier news, information on new and used trucks, vehicle operation, and safety.
Address: 5960 Crooked Creek Rd, Ste 15, Norcross, GA 30092. TEL 770-416-0927, 800-948-0154, FAX 770-416-1734, megan@truckersconnection.com. Adv. contact David Guthrie.

388.324 NOR ISSN 1504-3487
TRUCKERS GUIDE; for kjoering i Norge. Text in Multiple languages. 2004. a. **Document type:** *Consumer.* **Description:** Truckers' Guide to driving in Norway.
Related titles: Online - full text ed.
Published by: Vegdirektoratet, Statens Vegvesen (SVV)/Norwegian Directorate of Public Roads (NRPA), P O Box 8142, Dep, Oslo, 0033, Norway. TEL 47-22-073500, FAX 47-22-073768, firmapost@vegvesen.no.

388.324 USA ISSN 1040-2284
TRUCKERS NEWS. Variant title: N A T S O Truckers News. Text in English. 1977. m. USD 26 domestic; USD 125 foreign (effective 2011). adv. back issues avail. **Document type:** *Magazine, Trade.*
Description: Features news and articles of interest to professional truck drivers.
Related titles: Online - full text ed.: free (effective 2011); ♦ Spanish ed.: Transportista. ISSN 1934-3264.
Indexed: DBA.
—CCC.
Published by: (National Association of Truck Stop Operators), Randall-Reilly Publishing Company, 3200 Rice Mine Rd NE, Tuscaloosa, AL 35406. TEL 800-633-5953, http://www.randallpub.com. Ed. Randy Grider. Circ: 130,025.

388.324 USA
THE TRUCKER'S PAGE. Text in English. 1995. m. free. **Description:** Covers the trucking life from drivers' point of view.
Formerly: Internet Trucking Magazine
Media: Online - full text.
Published by: Ramblin Publishing, PO Box 651, Kaysville, UT 84037. Ed., Pub. Keith A Hamblin.

388.324 USA ISSN 0277-5743
TRUCKIN'; world's leading sport truck publication. Text in English. 1975. 13/yr. USD 24.95 domestic; USD 37.95 in Canada; USD 50.95 elsewhere (effective 2008). adv. bk.rev. charts; illus. back issues avail.; reprints avail. **Document type:** *Magazine, Consumer.*
Description: Covers a wide gamut of the truck market - from street trucks to classic trucks, SUVs to minis and lifteds to lowereds.
Related titles: Online - full text ed.
Indexed: G06, G07, G08, I05, S23.
—CCC.
Published by: Source Interlink Companies, 2400 E Katella Ave, Ste 700, Anaheim, CA 92806. TEL 714-939-2400, dheine@sourceinterlink.com, http://www.sourceinterlinkmedia.com. Ed. Steve Warner. Pub. Brad Christopher TEL 714-939-2509. adv.: B&W page USD 15,370, color page USD 20,280. Circ: 133,353 (paid).

388.324 AUS ISSN 0155-9648
TRUCKIN' LIFE; the voice of the Australian truck driver. Text in English. 1976. 11/yr. AUD 65 domestic; AUD 91 in New Zealand; AUD 156 elsewhere; AUD 7.95 newsstand/cover (effective 2008). adv. bk.rev. back issues avail. **Document type:** *Magazine, Consumer.*
Description: Covers innovations in the trucking industry, freight rates and new motor truck models.
Related titles: Supplement(s): Rig of Truckin' Life.

Published by: News Magazines Pty Ltd., Level 3, 2 Holt St, Surry Hills, NSW 2010, Australia. TEL 61-2-92883000, subscriptions@newsmagazines.com.au, http://www.newsspace.com.au/magazines. Adv. contact Andrew Byrne TEL 61-2-80622656. color page AUD 3,600; trim 206 x 276. Circ: 20,088.

388.324 GBR ISSN 1740-066X
TRUCKING. Text in English. 1983. m. GBP 34.98 domestic; GBP 55 in Europe; GBP 80 elsewhere; GBP 2.99 newsstand/cover (effective 2010). adv. back issues avail. **Document type:** *Magazine, Trade.*
Description: Contains features and news of the UK trucking industry with an emphasis on material of interest to small fleet operators and owner drivers.
Formerly (until 2001): Trucking International (0950-1738)
Published by: Future Publishing Ltd., Beauford Ct, 30 Monmouth St, Bath, Avon BA1 2BW, United Kingdom. TEL 44-1225-442244, FAX 44-1225-446019, customerservice@subscription.co.uk, http://www.futureplc.com. Ed. Steev Hayes TEL 44-1225-442244 ext 2953. Pub. Charley Davies TEL 44-1225-442244 ext 2194. Adv. contact Catherine Turner TEL 44-1225-442244 ext 2109. **Subscr. to:** Tower House, Sovereign Park, Market Harborough, Leicestershire LE16 9EF, United Kingdom. TEL 44-844-8481602, FAX 44-1858-438795, future@subscription.co.uk.

TRUCKING ACTIVITY REPORT. *see* TRANSPORTATION—Abstracting, Bibliographies, Statistics

388.324 CAN ISSN 0829-8947
TRUCKING IN CANADA. Text in Multiple languages. 1975. a. CAD 42 (effective 2004). **Document type:** *Journal, Trade.*
Formerly (until 1984): Motor Carriers. Freight and Household Goods Movers (0705-5978); Which was formed by the merger of (1960-1975): Moving and Storage Household Goods (0575-9137); (1941-1975): Motor Carriers. Freight (0383-5758); Which was formerly (until 1974): Motor Carriers. Freight. Common and Contract (0575-9064); (until 1958): Motor Carriers. Freight (0822-3157); Which superseded in part (in 1956): Motor Carriers. Freight. Passenger (0410-5540)
Related titles: Online - full text ed.: ISSN 1481-0719. 1995; French ed.: Le Camionnage au Canada. ISSN 1718-4355. 2004.
Published by: (Statistics Canada, Surface and Marine Transport Division), Statistics Canada/Statistique Canada, Publications Sales and Services, Ottawa, ON K1A 0T6, Canada. TEL 613-951-8116, 800-267-6677, infostats@statcan.ca, http://www.statcan.gc.ca.

388.324 USA
TRUCKING MINNESOTA. Text in English. 1935. m. membership only. adv. stat.; tr.lit. **Document type:** *Newsletter.* **Description:** Provides members of the Minnesota Trucking Association with information regarding rules, regulations, laws and events that affect the trucking industry.
Formerly: Midwest Motor Transport News (0026-3427)
Published by: Minnesota Trucking Association, 2277 Highway 36 W., Ste. 302, Saint Paul, MN 55113-3894. TEL 612-646-7351, FAX 612-641-8995. Ed. Diane Haseltine. Adv. contact Shannon Litchfield. B&W page USD 325, color page USD 825; trim 11 x 8.5. Circ: 1,100.

388.324 USA
TRUCKING PERMIT GUIDE. Text in English. 1975. base vol. plus s-a. updates. looseleaf. USD 189; USD 232 combined subscription (print & online eds.) (effective 2011). 800 p./no.; **Document type:** *Handbook/Manual/Guide, Trade.* **Description:** Descriptions of the Federal Heavy Vehicle Use Tax.
Related titles: Online - full text ed.
Published by: J.J. Keller & Associates, Inc., 3003 W Breezewood Ln, PO Box 368, Neenah, WI 54957. TEL 877-564-2333, 800-558-5011, FAX 800-727-7516.

629.2 SWE ISSN 1652-2001
TRUCKING SCANDINAVIA. Text in Swedish. 2003. 11/yr. SEK 385 for 8 nos. (effective 2010). adv. **Document type:** *Magazine, Consumer.*
Published by: Foerlags AB Albinsson & Sjoeberg, PO Box 529, Karlskrona, 37123, Sweden. TEL 46-455-335325, FAX 46-455-311715, fabas@fabas.se, http://www.fabas.se. Ed. Henrik Kindwall. Adv. contact Frida Sanjiva. page SEK 13,400; trim 190 x 275. Circ: 15,600 (paid).

388.324 USA ISSN 1524-1009
TRUCKING TECHNOLOGY. Text in English. 1993. 6/yr. **Description:** For fleet executives, equipment dealers, and manufacturers.
Related titles: Online - full text ed.
Indexed: A26, CompD, E08, G06, G07, G08, I05, S09.
Published by: Adams Business Media, 2101 S Arlington Heights Rd, 150, Arlington, IL 60005. http://www.abm.net.

388.344029 USA ISSN 1935-6331
TRUCKING TIMES (YEAR); work,play and SUV. Text in English. 199?. bi-m. free to qualified personnel (effective 2009). adv. charts; illus.; tr.lit. back issues avail. **Document type:** *Directory, Trade.*
Description: Aims to serve the retailers, warehouse distributors, jobbers and other industry observers in the huge light-truck and SUV accessory aftermarket.
Former titles (until 2006): Trucking Times and Sport Utility News (1524-8232); (until 199?): Trucking Times (1069-8965)
Related titles: Online - full text ed.
Published by: Wiesner Media, LLC (Subsidiary of: Summit Business Media LLC), 307 Maryhill Dr, Cedar Falls, IA 50613. http://www.wiesnermedia.com. Ed. Dave Herrmeyer. Pub. Bart Taylor. adv.: page USD 3,595; trim 10.88 x 8.25. Circ: 13,800 (controlled).

388.324 NLD ISSN 2210-772X
TRUCKS. Text in Dutch. 1999. m. (11/yr.). EUR 39; EUR 4.50 newsstand/cover (effective 2010). adv. **Document type:** *Magazine, Trade.*
Published by: Powerline bv, Postbus 146, Hazerswoude, 2394 ZG, Netherlands. TEL 31-71-3416843, FAX 31-71-3416874. Ed. Dick van Zijl TEL 31-346-213029. Adv. contact Frans van den Hul. Circ: 30,000.

629.224 USA ISSN 1553-7811
TRUCKS. Text in English. 2000. m. USD 21.99 domestic; USD 31.99 in Canada; USD 36.99 elsewhere (effective 2006). adv. **Document type:** *Magazine, Consumer.*
Published by: T E N Magazines, 1760 California Ave, Ste 101, Corona, CA 92881. TEL 951-371-8361, press@TenMagazines.com, http://www.tenmagazines.com.

388.324 NLD ISSN 1382-9017
TRUCKSTAR. Text in Dutch. 1979. 13/yr. EUR 52; EUR 4.75 newsstand/cover (effective 2009). adv. **Document type:** *Magazine, Consumer.*
—Infotrieve.
Published by: Sanoma Men's Magazines, Haaksbergweg 75, Amsterdam (ZO), 1101 BR, Netherlands. TEL 31-20-7518000, FAX 31-20-7518301, sales@smm.nl, http://www.smm.nl. adv.: B&W page EUR 2,285, color page EUR 4,570; trim 230 x 300. Circ: 45,248.

TRUCKSTOP TRAVEL PLAZA. *see* BUSINESS AND ECONOMICS—Small Business

388.324 NLD ISSN 1874-9097
TRUCKWERK. Text in Dutch. 199?. q.
Published by: BOVAG, Truck Dealers Associatie (TDA), Postbus 1100, Bunnik, 3980 DC, Netherlands. TEL 31-30-6595211, FAX 31-30-6567835, bovag@bovag.nl, http://www.bovag.nl.

388.324 USA
TRUCKWORLD ONLINE!. Text in English. 1996. d. **Document type:** *Newsletter, Trade.* **Description:** Covers 4 x 4, street trucks, SUVs, new truck test, accessory and product reviews, and truck industry news.
Media: Online - full text.
Published by: AutoWeb Worldwide Publishing, Inc., PO Box 590, Cottage Grove, OR 97424. Eds. Duane Elliott, Tom Morr.

388.324 USA
TRUX. Text in English. 1949. q. adv. illus. **Document type:** *Magazine, Trade.* **Description:** Contains information for and about southeastern truckers and shippers. Includes how-to articles, general interest (sales, personnel, public relations), and features unusual personalities in the trucking or shipping world.
Published by: (Georgia Motor Trucking Association), Naylor LLC, 5950 NW 1st Pl, Gainesville, FL 32607. TEL 800-369-6220, FAX 352-331-3525, http://www.naylor.com. Ed. Carla S Gossett. Pub. Shane Holt. adv.: B&W page USD 1,150;. Circ: 3,405 (free).

TURNING WHEELS. *see* TRANSPORTATION—Automobiles

388.324 ITA ISSN 1121-5585
TUTTOTRASPORTI. Text in Italian. 11/yr. adv. **Document type:** *Magazine, Consumer.*
Published by: Editoriale Domus, Via Gianni Mazzocchi 1/3, Rozzano, MI 20089, Italy. TEL 39-02-824721, editorialedomus@edidomus.it, http://www.edidomus.it. Circ: 70,000.

388.324 USA
U - HAUL NEWS. Text in English. bi-m. free domestic to members qualified. **Document type:** *Magazine, Trade.*
Published by: U-Haul International, Inc., 2727 N. Central Ave., Phoenix, AZ 85004. TEL 602-263-6641, FAX 602-277-5207. Circ: 34,000 (controlled).

388.324 331.8 USA ISSN 1551-8973
U P S TEAMSTER. (United Parcel Service) Text in English. 2004 (Fall). q.
Published by: A F L - C I O, International Brotherhood of Teamsters, 25 Louisiana Ave, N W, Washington, DC 20001. TEL 202-624-6800, FAX 202-624-6918, communications@teamster.org, http://www.teamster.org.

388.324 USA ISSN 1053-4903
UTILITY FLEET MANAGEMENT; the transport topics publishing group magazine for utility and public works fleet professionals. Text in English. 1983. 10/yr. USD 49.95; free to qualified personnel (effective 2005). adv. Website rev. reprints avail. **Document type:** *Magazine, Trade.* **Description:** Serves personnel involved in work fleets engaged in gas, electric and water utility, public works, fire, rescue, police, telecommunications, cable TV, university and airport physical plants, overnight couriers military, manufacturers, distributors and others allied to the field.
Formerly: Electric Utility Fleet Management (0744-3501)
Related titles: Online - full text ed.
Indexed: A15, ABIn, B16, HRIS, P10, P48, P51, P52, P53, P54, PQC.
—CCC.
Published by: T T Publishing, 2200 Mill Rd, Alexandria, VA 22314-4686. TEL 703-838-1967, FAX 703-838-6259, http://www.TTnews.com. Pub. Howard Abramson. Adv. contact Kirsten Welton TEL 703-838-1746. B&W page USD 3,345. Circ: 21,000 (paid and free).

388.324 ITA ISSN 0042-2096
VADO E TORNO; magazine for truck drivers. Text in Italian. 1962. 11/yr. EUR 27 (effective 2009). bk.rev. illus. **Document type:** *Magazine, Trade.*
Published by: Vado e Torno Edizioni S.r.l., Via Cassano d'Adda 20, Milan, 20139, Italy. TEL 39-02-55230950, FAX 39-02-55230592, abbonamenti@vadoetorno.com. Ed. Paolo Scarpat. Pub. Gianni Sacerdoti. Adv. contact Ornella Cavalli. Circ: 55,000.

388 GBR
VEHICLE RECOVERY LINK. Text in English. 1992. bi-m. GBP 39 (effective 2009). stat.; tr.lit. back issues avail. **Document type:** *Magazine, Trade.* **Description:** Aimed at vehicle recovery and breakdown operators. Contains news, views, and features for the road rescue industry.
Published by: Lead Media Ltd, Dixies, High St, Ashwell, Herts S67 5NT, United Kingdom. Ed. Phil Renno. Adv. contact Michael Linegar. Circ: 3,000.

388.324 USA
VEHICLE SIZES AND WEIGHTS MANUAL. Text in English. 197?. base vol. plus s-a. updates. USD 189; USD 232 combined subscription (print & online eds.) (effective 2011). **Document type:** *Handbook/Manual/Guide, Trade.* **Description:** Describes federal, state and Canadian requirements for overdimensional movements.
Related titles: Online - full text ed.
Published by: J.J. Keller & Associates, Inc., 3003 W Breezewood Ln, PO Box 368, Neenah, WI 54957. TEL 877-564-2333, 800-558-5011, FAX 800-727-7516.

388.324 USA ISSN 1543-5059
VINTAGE TRUCK. Text in English. 1991. bi-m. USD 26.95 in North America; USD 5.95 newsstand/cover (effective 2005). adv. bk.rev. Index. back issues avail. **Document type:** *Magazine, Consumer.*
Description: Devoted to the interests of antique light truck enthusiasts. Contains recollections of their use, restoration tips, show information, color photographs, historical research.
Former titles: This Old Truck (1068-1744); (until 1993): Classic Trucks; Plugs 'n Points
Published by: Antique Power Inc., PO Box 838, Yellow Springs, OH 45387. TEL 937-767-1433, FAX 937-767-2726, http://www.thisoldtruck.com. Ed., Pub. Patrick W Ertel. R&P Patrick Ertel. Adv. contact Kathy Pence. Circ: 26,000 (paid).

388.324 AUS ISSN 1838-0492
▼ **VINTAGE TRUCKS AND COMMERCIALS MAGAZINE.** Abbreviated title: V T C M. Text in English. 2010. bi-m. AUD 45 domestic; AUD 65 in New Zealand & Pacific; AUD 76 elsewhere; AUD 9.50 per issue domestic; AUD 14 per issue in New Zealand & Pacific; AUD 15 per issue elsewhere (effective 2011). back issues avail. **Document type:** *Magazine, Consumer.* **Description:** Features truck and commercial vehicles of all makes and models that were produced at least 25 years ago.
Published by: V T C Magazine, PO Box 5660, Port Macquarie, NSW 2444, Australia. TEL 61-2-65844225, FAX 61-2-65844077.

388.324 CAN ISSN 0843-6207
VOIX DU VRAC. Text in English. 1972. 6/yr. free. **Document type:** *Journal, Trade.*
Published by: Association Nationale des Camionneurs Artisans Inc., 670 Bouvier St, Ste 235, Quebec, PQ G2J 1A7, Canada. TEL 418-623-7923, FAX 418-623-0448. Ed. Gabriel Berberi. adv.: B&W page CAD 1,195, color page CAD 1,875. Circ: 15,000.

VRAAGBAAK ARBEIDSTIJDEN WEGVERVOER. *see* BUSINESS AND ECONOMICS—Labor And Industrial Relations

388.3 USA ISSN 1075-0282
HF5415.6
WAREHOUSING - DISTRIBUTION DIRECTORY. Text in English. 1963. 2/yr. USD 73 (effective 2000). adv. **Document type:** *Directory.* **Description:** A comprehensive guide to warehousing facilities and distribution serviced throughout North America. Provides over 1000 detailed listings on dependable warehousing facilities.
Former titles (until 1992): M C D's Warehousing Distribution Directory (1075-0517); National Distribution Directory of Local Cartage - Short-Haul Carriers Warehousing (0364-9539); National Distribution Directory (0077-4219)
Published by: K-III Directory Corp., 155 Village Blvd., Princeton, NJ 08540-5765. TEL 609-371-7700, FAX 609-371-7885, http://www.primediainfo.com. Ed., R&P Karen Rae. Pub. John Capers. Adv. contact Christina Correia. B&W page USD 1,845; 7.25 x 9.5625. Circ: 20,000.

388.324 USA
WEST VIRGINIA TRANSPORTER. Text in English. 1972 (vol.29). m. membership. adv. **Document type:** *Magazine, Trade.*
Published by: West Virginia Motor Truck Association, PO Box 5187, Charleston, WV 25361. TEL 304-345-2800. Ed. Elizabeth Szerokman. Adv. contact Leslee Wilhelm. Circ: 1,000.

388.324 CAN
WESTERN CANADA HIGHWAY NEWS MAGAZINE. Text in English. 1971. 4/yr. CAD 12 (effective 2003). adv. back issues avail. **Document type:** *Magazine, Trade.*
Formerly (until 1995): Manitoba Highway News (0380-4852)
Published by: (Manitoba Trucking Association), Craig Kelman & Associates Ltd., 3C 2020 Portage Ave, Winnipeg, MB R3J 0K4, Canada. TEL 204-985-9780, FAX 204-985-9795. Ed. Terry Ross. Adv. contact Scott Browning. Circ: 4,000 (controlled). **Co-sponsors:** Saskatchewan Trucking Association; Alberta Motor Transport Association; B.C. Trucking Association.

388.324 GBR ISSN 1350-6404
WHAT VAN?. Text in English. 1986. m. GBP 42 domestic; EUR 88 in Europe; USD 135 in North America; USD 150 elsewhere (effective 2010). adv. back issues avail. **Document type:** *Magazine, Trade.* **Description:** Designed for fleet managers and controllers as well as owner-drivers. Includes new van test drives, long term tests reports and industry news.
Formerly (until 1993): Good Van Guide (0953-2951)
Related titles: Online - full text ed.: GBP 32 domestic; EUR 46.02 in Europe; USD 66.07 elsewhere (effective 2010).
—CCC.
Published by: Wilmington Media & Entertainment (Subsidiary of: Wilmington Group Plc), Progressive House, 2 Maidstone Rd, Foots Cray, Sidcup, DA14 5HZ, United Kingdom. TEL 44-20-82697766, FAX 44-20-82697804, investorinfo@wilmington.co.uk, http://www.wilmington.co.uk/. Ed. Neil Mcintee TEL 44-20-89418263.

388.324 629.222 USA ISSN 0738-565X
TL230.A1
WHEELS OF TIME. Text in English. 1980. bi-m. USD 25 domestic membership; USD 35 foreign membership (effective 2001). adv. back issues avail. **Document type:** *Magazine, Trade.* **Description:** Covers the history of trucks, the trucking industry, and its pioneers.
Indexed: HRIS.
Published by: American Truck Historical Society, PO Box 901611, Kansas City, MO 64190-1611. TEL 205-870-0566, FAX 205-870-3069. Ed. Shirley Sponholtz. R&P Larry Scheef. Adv. contact Pat Datka. Circ: 22,000.

388.324 USA
WORK TRUCK MAGAZINE. Text in English. 2007. bi-m. free to qualified personnel (effective 2008). adv. **Document type:** *Magazine, Trade.* **Description:** Features stories on managing fleet operations comprised of highly diversified vehicle and equipment assets.
Related titles: Online - full text ed.
Published by: Bobit Business Media, 3520 Challenger St, Torrance, CA 90503. TEL 310-533-2400, FAX 310-533-2500, order@bobit.com, http://www.bobit.com. adv.: color page USD 12,080; trim 7.875 x 10.75. Circ: 60,000 (controlled).

388.324 621 NOR ISSN 0333-1911
YRKESBIL. Text in Norwegian. 1980. 15/yr. NOK 375 (effective 2005). adv. **Document type:** *Newspaper, Trade.*
Related titles: Online - full text ed.
Published by: Bilforlaget, Urtegaten 9, PO Box 9247, Oslo, 0134, Norway. TEL 47-23-036600, FAX 47-23-036640, http://www.bilnorge.no. Ed. Torstein Magelssen. Adv. contact Erik Rusten TEL 47-23-036623. B&W page NOK 38,500, color page NOK 47,500; 250 x 370. Circ: 32,260.

388.324 CHN ISSN 1674-0378
YUEYE SHIJIE/OVERLANDER 4 W D. Text in Chinese. 2001. m. **Document type:** *Magazine, Consumer.*
Formerly: Wuhuan Mingxing/Olympic (1009-6930)
Related titles: Online - full content ed.
—East View.
Published by: Yueye Shijie Zazhishe, Renjishanzhuang C-5-1904, 1, Zizhuyuan, Haidian-qu, Beijing, 100048, China. TEL 86-10-51298136, FAX 86-10-88554234. **Dist. by:** China International Book Trading Corp, 35 Chegongzhuang Xilu, Haidian District, PO Box 399, Beijing 100044, China. TEL 86-10-68412045, FAX 86-10-68412023, cibtc@mail.cibtc.com.cn, http://www.cibtc.com.cn.

388.324 POL ISSN 0514-809X
Z M P D KWARTALNY BIULETYN INFORMACYJNY. Text in Polish. 1965. q. free. **Document type:** *Bulletin.*
Media: Duplicated (not offset).
Published by: Zrzeszenie Miedzynarodowych Przewoznikow Drogowych, Grojecka 17, Warsaw, 02021, Poland. Ed. Boleslaw Rajkowski. Circ: (controlled).

796.72 USA
4 X 4 MECHANIX. Text in English. 1995. bi-m. USD 16.95. **Document type:** *Magazine, Consumer.* **Description:** Covers the maintenance and enjoyment of four-wheel-drive sport trucks.
Published by: C S K Publishing Co., Inc., 299 Market St, Saddle Brook, NJ 07662. TEL 201-712-9300, FAX 201-712-7899. Ed. Brian Brennan.

388.324 USA
10-4 MAGAZINE. Text in English. m. USD 20 (effective 2002). **Document type:** *Magazine, Trade.*
Address: PO Box 7377, Huntington Beach, CA 92615-7377. TEL 714-378-9990.

TRAVEL AND TOURISM

see also GEOGRAPHY ; HOTELS AND RESTAURANTS ; TRAVEL AND TOURISM—Airline Inflight And Hotel Inroom

910.91 USA
A A A ARIZONA HIGHROADS. (American Automobile Association) Text in English. bi-m. free to members (effective 2005). 52 p./no.; back issues avail. **Document type:** *Magazine, Consumer.*
Published by: American Automobile Association Arizona, 3144 N 7th Ave, Phoenix, AZ 85013. TEL 602-274-1116, FAX 602-277-1194. Ed. Becky Antioco. Circ: 390,000 (controlled).

910.2 USA
A A A GOING PLACES (TAMPA). Text in English. 1982. bi-m. free to members (effective 2007). 64 p./no. 3 cols./p.; **Document type:** *Magazine, Consumer.*
Published by: A A A Auto Club South, PO Box 31087, Tampa, FL 33631. Ed. Sandy Klim. Pub. Bill Latta. Adv. contact Michael Eisman. Circ: 2,500,130 (paid and controlled).

388.3 USA
A A A HORIZONS. Text in English. m. USD 45 membership (effective 2004). adv.
Published by: A A A Southern New England, 110 Royal Little Dr, Providence, RI 02904. TEL 401-868-2000, FAX 401-868-2014. Ed. Jennifer Reed TEL 401-868-2000 ext 2123. Adv. contact Kathy Parker TEL 401-868-2000 ext 2122. color page USD 30,375; trim 9.75 x 13.5. Circ: 1,000,569.

388.3 USA ISSN 1527-2575
A A A JOURNEYS. Text in English. bi-m. USD 54.95 membership (effective 2004). adv. **Document type:** *Magazine, Consumer.* **Description:** Contains news and informative articles about activities of the local club and the AAA national organization.
Published by: H & A Publishing, 815 Farmington Ave, Hartford, CT 06119. TEL 860-236-3261, 800-842-4320, http://www.aaahartford.com, http://aaa.com. Adv. contact Ann Taylor TEL 402-592-5000 ext 294. color page USD 6,775; trim 7.875 x 10.875. Circ: 249,000.

910.2 388.3 USA ISSN 1932-1775
A A A LIVING (ILLINOIS/N. INDIANA EDITION). Text in English. bi-m. **Document type:** *Magazine, Consumer.*
Formerly (until 2005): A A A Living (Illinois Edition)
Published by: American Automobile Association, Chicago Motor Club, 6234 N Northwest Hwy 800, Chicago, IL 60631. TEL 773-222-4357.

910.202 USA ISSN 1932-1767
A A A LIVING (IOWA EDITION). (American Automobile Association) Text in English. 1980. bi-m. free to members (effective 2005). **Document type:** *Magazine, Consumer.*
Formerly (until Mar.-Apr. 2005): Home & Away (0744-1576)
Published by: Home & Away Publishing, Inc., 10703 J St., Omaha, NE 68127. TEL 402-592-5000, FAX 402-331-5194. Ed., Pub. Brian Nicol. Adv. contact Terry Ausenbaugh. Circ: 3,400,000 (paid).

796.7 USA ISSN 1554-2130
TL1
A A A LIVING (MICHIGAN EDITION). Text in English. 1918. bi-m. USD 1 to members (effective 2009). bk.rev. illus. reprints avail. **Document type:** *Magazine, Consumer.* **Description:** Provides entertaining information on AAA services, including travel, automotive, financial services, insurance and safety advocacy.
Former titles (until 2005): Michigan Living (0735-1798); (until 1981): Michigan Living Motor News (0161-2859); (until 1972): Motor News (0027-1934); (until 1936): Michigan Motor News; (until 1931): Detroit Motor News
Related titles: Online - full text ed.
Indexed: MMI.
Published by: Automobile Club of Michigan, One Auto Club Dr, Dearborn, MI 48126. TEL 313-336-1506, 800-659-7651, FAX 313-336-1344. Ed. Ron Garbinski. Pub. Betty M Schick.

910.09 USA ISSN 1932-1791
A A A LIVING (MINNESOTA EDITION). Text in English. 1980. bi-m. USD 6 to non-members; free to members (effective 2004). adv. **Document type:** *Magazine, Trade.*
Former titles (until Mar.-Apr. 2005): Home & Away (Minnesota/Iowa Edition) (1049-7692); (until 199?): Home and Away. Minnesota (0199-5383)
Indexed: CLT&T, HRIS.
Published by: American Automobile Association, Minnesota - Iowa Division, 2900 AAA Court, Bettendorf, IA 52722. Circ: 43,000 (controlled).

796.7 USA ISSN 1554-2602
G149
A A A LIVING (WISCONSIN EDITION). (American Automobile Association) Text in English. 1937. q. USD 1 to members (effective 2009). adv. bk.rev. charts; illus. **Document type:** *Magazine, Consumer.*
Former titles (until 2005): Home & Away (Wisconsin Edition) (1089-2672); (until Jul.1996): Car and Travel (Wisconsin Edition) (1080-2355); (until 1995): A A A World: Wisconsin Edition (0277-1411); (until 1981): A A A Traveler (0162-3591); Wisconsin A A A Motor News (0043-6348)
Related titles: Online - full text ed.
Published by: American Automobile Association, A A A Wisconsin, 1 Auto Club Dr, Dearborn, MI 48126. TEL 800-659-7651, http://www.autoclubgroup.com. Eds. Chad Kirtland, Ron Garbinski. Pub. Betty Schick.

910.09 USA
A A A MOTORIST OF NORTHEASTERN PENNSYLVANIA. Text in English. bi-m.
Published by: American Automobile Association of Northeastern Pennsylvania, 1035 N Washington Ave, Scranton, PA 18509-2917. TEL 717-348-2513. Ed. Craig H Smith. Circ: 92,000.

388.3 USA
A A A READING - BERKS. Text in English. 1930. bi-m. membership. adv. **Document type:** *Magazine, Consumer.*
Formerly: Reading - Berks Auto Club Magazine (0744-7043)
Published by: (American Automobile Association, Reading-Berks Auto Club), Roberts & Company, PO Box 716, Reading, PA 19603. TEL 610-375-4525, FAX 610-478-1269. Ed., R&P Bob Gerhart. Circ: 95,500.

A A A ROAD ATLAS. (American Automobile Association Road Atlas) *see* TRANSPORTATION—Automobiles

A A A SOUTHERN TRAVELER. *see* TRANSPORTATION—Automobiles

910.202 388.3 USA ISSN 1051-3701
A A A TODAY (CINCINNATI). Text in English. 1923. bi-m. USD 10. adv. **Document type:** *Magazine, Consumer.*
Formerly: Motour
Published by: (American Automobile Association, Cincinnati Division), Banta Publications, 1025 N Washington St, Greenfield, OH 45123. FAX 613-762-8741. R&P, Adv. contact Merrilee F Campbell. Circ: 195,000.

910.2 USA
A A A TOUCH. Text in English. 2004. bi-m. USD 15; USD 2 per issue (effective 2005). adv. **Document type:** *Magazine, Consumer.*
Published by: A A A Central Penn, 2023 Market St, Harrisburg, PA 17103. TEL 717-898-6900. Ed. Grace Palsgrove. Adv. contact Terry Ausenbaugh TEL 402-592-5000 ext 452. B&W page USD 4,405, color page USD 4,961; trim 7.875 x 10.375. Circ: 225,000 (paid).

910.09 USA
A A A TRAVEL TOPICS. (American Automobile Association) Text in English. 5/yr.
Published by: American Automobile Association, Central Pennsylvania Automobile Club, 2023 Market St, Harrisburg, PA 17103-2531. TEL 717-236-4021. Ed. Thomas G Miller. Circ: 80,000.

629.286 USA ISSN 1082-3700
A A A TRAVELER (FLORHAM PARK). Text in English. 1924. 6/yr. USD 4; USD 1 newsstand/cover (effective 2008). adv. 28 p./no. 4 cols./p.; back issues avail. **Document type:** *Newspaper, Consumer.* **Description:** Features travel advice, car care and buying information, safety, legislation, insurance information, and financial services for motorists and travelers.
Former titles (until 1994): Driving; (until 1969): New Jersey Autoist
Published by: (American Automobile Association), New Jersey Automobile Club, 1 Hanover Rd, Florham Park, NJ 07932. TEL 973-377-7200, FAX 973-377-2979, htrtp://www.aaa.com. Ed. Michele Mount. Pub. Frederick Gruel. adv.: B&W page USD 6,101, color page USD 8,274; trim 10.5 x 13. Circ: 225,000 (controlled).

910.91 USA ISSN 2158-2424
A A A WESTERN AND CENTRAL NEW YORK. MEMBER CONNECTION. (American Automobile Association) Variant title: A A A Member Connection. Text in English. 19??. q. free to members (effective 2011). adv. **Document type:** *Magazine, Consumer.* **Description:** Features articles will highlight destination spots, day trips, family getaways, lifestyles, history, and tourist activities in New York state.
Former titles (until 2011): A A A Going Places (1529-0506); (until 2000): Going Places (1528-784X); (until 1999): The Traveler (0279-7224)
Related titles: Online - full text ed.: free (effective 2011).
Published by: American Automobile Association, Western & Central New York, 100 International Dr, Buffalo, NY 14221. TEL 716-633-9860, 800-836-2582, FAX 716-631-5925. Adv. contact Jennifer Fidanza TEL 716-633-9860.

A A A WORLD (HAMILTON). (American Automobile Association) *see* TRANSPORTATION—Automobiles

914.2 GBR ISSN 1461-1694
A A BED AND BREAKFAST. Text in English. 1989. a. GBP 10.39 per issue (effective 2009). **Document type:** *Directory, Consumer.*
Formerly (until 1994): A A Inspected Bed and Breakfast in Britain (0964-9085)
—CCC.
Published by: Automobile Association, Lambert House, Stockport Rd, Cheadle, SK8 2DY, United Kingdom. TEL 44-161-4958945, FAX 44-161-4887544, customersupport@theAA.com, http://www.theaa.com.

914.2 GBR
A A BED & BREAKFAST GUIDE (YEAR). (Automobile Association) Text in English. 19??. a. GBP 10.39 per issue (effective 2009). **Document type:** *Handbook/Manual/Guide, Consumer.* **Description:** Provides clear and detailed descriptions of over 3, 500 AA inspected B&Bs, Guest Houses, Farmhouses and Inns in Britain, rated for quality from 1 to 5 stars.
Former titles: Bed & Breakfast Guide to Britain & Ireland (Year); (until 1996): Inspected Bed and Breakfasts in Britain; Guesthouses, Farmhouses and Inns in Britain; Automobile Association. Budget Guide

Published by: A A Publishing, Contact Ctr, Lambert House, Stockport Rd, Cheadle, Hants SK8 2DY, United Kingdom. TEL 44-161-4958945, FAX 44-161-4887544, customer.services@theAA.com, http://www.theaa.com.

916.8 ZAF
A A HOTELS, LODGES, GUEST HOUSES, BED & BREAKFASTS; south africa, namibia and other neighbouring states - south africa's best selling accomodation and touring guide. Variant title: Hotels, Lodges, Guest Houses, Bed & Breakfasts. Text in English. 1994. a. ZAR 99 per vol. (effective 2005). illus.; maps. **Document type:** *Directory, Consumer.* **Description:** Guide to hotels, game lodges, guest hoses, and bed and breakfasts in southern Africa including South Africa, Namibia, and Zimbabwe.
Published by: (Automobile Association GBR), R & V Business Services (Pty) Ltd., PO Box 787040, Sandton, 2146, South Africa. TEL 27-11-7132000, FAX 27-11-7283086, info@aatravel.co.za, http://www.aatravel.co.za. Ed. Helen de Coster. Pub., R&P, Adv. contact Vanessa Sand.

916.8 ZAF
A A SELF-CATERING GETAWAYS; suites, chalets, national parks/reserves, caravan - resorts, b&bs - south africa, namibia and other neighbouring states. Variant title: Self-Catering Getaways. Text in English. 1988. a. ZAR 69 newsstand/cover (effective 2005). adv. illus.; maps. **Document type:** *Directory, Consumer.* **Description:** Detailed guide to all types of self-catering accomodation in Southern Africa, including South Africa, Namibia and Zimbabwe.
Published by: (Automobile Association GBR), R & V Business Services (Pty) Ltd., PO Box 787040, Sandton, 2146, South Africa. TEL 27-11-7132000, FAX 27-11-7283086, info@aatravel.co.za, http://www.aatravel.co.za. Ed. Helen de Coster. Pub., R&P, Adv. contact Vanessa Sand.

796.5 910.202 ITA
A C AUTOCARAVAN. Text in Italian. 1975. m. EUR 40 domestic; EUR 90 foreign (effective 2008). adv. bk.rev. **Document type:** *Magazine, Consumer.* **Description:** Provides vacation ideas and information on campervans.
Former titles: Auto Caravan Notizie; Caravan Notizie
Published by: Cantelli Editore Srl, Via Saliceto 22c, Castelmaggiore, BO 40013, Italy. TEL 39-051-6328811, FAX 39-051-6328815, cantelli.editore@cantelli.net, http://www.cantelli.net. Circ: 60,000.

A C E LENKRAD. *see* TRANSPORTATION—Automobiles

910.202 DEU ISSN 1434-4335
A D A C AUTOATLAS DEUTSCHLAND - EUROPA. Text in German. 1984. a. EUR 29.90 (effective 2008). **Document type:** *Bulletin, Consumer.*
Former titles (until 1996): A D A C Atlas Deutschland - Europa (0936-6326); (until 1989): A D A C Strassen-Atlas (0179-5546)
Published by: (Allgemeiner Deutscher Automobil-Club e.V.), A D A C Verlag GmbH, Leonhard-Moll-Bogen 1, Munich, 81365, Germany. TEL 49-89-76760, FAX 49-89-76762500, verlag@adac.de, http://www.adac.de.

A D A C CAMPING-CARAVANING-FUEHRER. BAND 2: DEUTSCHLAND, NORDEUROPA. *see* SPORTS AND GAMES—Outdoor Life

A D A C CAMPING-CARAVANING-FUEHRER. SUEDEUROPA. *see* SPORTS AND GAMES—Outdoor Life

A D A C FREIZEIT MOBIL. *see* SPORTS AND GAMES—Outdoor Life

A D A C HANDBUCH: REISERECHT ENTSCHEIDUNGEN. *see* LAW

A D A C HANDBUCH: UNFALL IM AUSLAND - SCHADENSREGULIERUNG. *see* LAW

A D A C HANDBUCH: UNFALL RATGEBER. *see* LAW

A D A C MOTORWELT. *see* TRANSPORTATION—Automobiles

910.202 DEU ISSN 1610-2290
G153.4
A D A C REISEMAGAZIN. Text in German. 1990. bi-m. EUR 39.90; EUR 7.80 newsstand/cover (effective 2008). adv. **Document type:** *Magazine, Consumer.*
Formerly (until 1997): A D A C Special Reise (0939-4206)
Published by: (Allgemeiner Deutscher Automobil-Club e.V.), A D A C Verlag GmbH, Leonhard-Moll-Bogen 1, Munich, 81365, Germany. TEL 49-89-76760, FAX 49-89-76762500, verlag@adac.de, http://www.adac.de. adv.: B&W page EUR 13,080, color page EUR 18,120. Circ: 140,596 (controlled).

A D A C SKI-GUIDE. *see* SPORTS AND GAMES—Outdoor Life

910.202 DEU ISSN 1869-3644
A D A C SKIMAGAZIN. (Allgemeiner Deutscher Automobil-Club) Text in German. 1990. a. EUR 6.95 newsstand/cover (effective 2010). adv. **Document type:** *Magazine, Consumer.*
Former titles (until 2009): A D A C Reisemagazin Ski (1869-4055); (until 2002): A D A C Reisemagazin Extra Ski (1610-3475); (until 19??): A D A C Special Ski (0937-9096)
Published by: (Allgemeiner Deutscher Automobil-Club e.V.), A D A C Verlag GmbH, Leonhard-Moll-Bogen 1, Munich, 81365, Germany. TEL 49-89-76760, FAX 49-89-76762500, verlag@adac.de, http://www.adac.de. Circ: 90,000 (controlled).

910.2 USA ISSN 1553-9598
F317.E9
A FALCONGUIDE TO EVERGLADES NATIONAL PARK AND THE SURROUNDING AREA. Variant title: Everglades National Park and the Surrounding Area. Falcon Guide to Everglades National Park and the Surrounding Area. Text in English. 2005. biennial, latest 2005, 1st ed. USD 12.95 per issue (effective 2008). **Document type:** *Directory, Consumer.* **Description:** Guides through the 2.5 million acres of pristine and diverse landscapes and wildlife habitats- from dry, rocky pineland to open marshes.
Published by: Falcon Publishing (Subsidiary of: The Globe Pequot Press, Inc.), 246 Goose Ln, PO Box 480, Guilford, CT 06437. TEL 203-458-4500, http://www.falcon.com. Ed. Shelley Wolf.

910.91 USA ISSN 1555-4902
F817.S18
A FALCONGUIDE TO SAGUARO NATIONAL PARK & THE SANTA CATALINA MOUNTAINS GUIDE BOOK. Variant title: Falcon Guide to Saguaro National Park and the Santa Catalina Mountains. Saguaro National Park and the Santa Catalina Mountains. Text in English. 2006. biennial, latest 2005, 1st ed. USD 14.95 per issue (effective 2008). **Document type:** *Directory, Consumer.* **Description:** Guides through the best trails for walking, hiking and horseback riding, great campgrounds, unforgettable scenic drives and fascinating attractions in Tucson.
Published by: Falcon Publishing (Subsidiary of: The Globe Pequot Press, Inc.), 246 Goose Ln, PO Box 480, Guilford, CT 06437. TEL 203-458-4500, http://www.falcon.com. Ed. Shelley Wolf.

910.91 USA ISSN 1553-1112
F897.S2
A FALCONGUIDE TO THE SAN JUAN ISLANDS. Variant title: Falcon Guide to the San Juan Islands. San Juan Islands. Text in English. 2006. biennial, latest 2005, 1st ed. USD 14.95 per issue (effective 2008). **Document type:** *Directory, Consumer.* **Description:** Guides through the forty-two of the best scenic vistas, wildlife viewing areas, historical locations and fishing and camping sites on the San Juan islands.
Published by: Falcon Publishing (Subsidiary of: The Globe Pequot Press, Inc.), 246 Goose Ln, PO Box 480, Guilford, CT 06437. TEL 203-458-4500, http://www.falcon.com. Ed. Shelley Wolf.

910.4 MEX
A I M; a newsletter on retirement and travel in Mexico. (Adventures in Mexico Newsletter) Text in English. 1974. bi-m. USD 18 (effective 2000). **Document type:** *Newsletter.* **Description:** Attempts to portray intriguing Mexico as it really is today - its places, living costs, adventures, frustrations and fun. Includes practical tips on how to cope for a week, a month, or the rest of your life.
Published by: AIM, S.A., Apdo. Postal 31-70, Guadalajara, JALISCO, Mexico. Ed. David Alexander. Circ: 1,920 (paid).

910.2 CAN ISSN 1718-7362
A LA MONTREAL. Text in French. 2000. bi-m. free (effective 2006). **Document type:** *Bulletin, Consumer.* **Description:** Listing of cultural and sporting events, festivals, exhibitions, shows and other activities which are for a specific time period.
Formerly (until 2006): Quoi Faire a Montreal (1492-2509)
Related titles: English ed.: ISSN 1718-7370.
Published by: E F F Communication Marketing, 430 Sainte-Helene St, Ste 301, Montreal, PQ H2Y 2K7, Canada. TEL 514-842-5161, FAX 514-842-5413, production@effcommunication.com, http://www.effcommunication.com.

338.4791 AUT
A P A - JOURNAL. TOURISTIK. Text in German. w. EUR 380 combined subscription for print & online eds. (effective 2003). **Document type:** *Journal, Trade.*
Related titles: Online - full text ed.
Published by: Austria Presse Agentur, Gunoldstr 14, Vienna, W 1190, Austria. TEL 43-1-360600, FAX 43-1-360603099, kundenservice@apa.at, http://www.apa.at.

910.029 GBR
A P R O DIRECTORY. Text in English. 1990. a. adv. **Document type:** *Directory, Trade.* **Description:** Provides journalists with comprehensive media contact information about its members, including addresses, telephone, email, website and after-hour contacts.
Published by: (Airline Public Relations Organisation), B M I Publications Limited, Suffolk House, George St, Croydon, Surrey CR9 1SR, United Kingdom. TEL 44-20-86497233, FAX 44-20-86497234, sales@bmipublications.com, http://www.bmipublications.com. Pub. Sally Parker. Adv. contact Steve Thompson. Circ: 1,000 (controlled).

910.91 USA
A R T A AGENT. (Association of Retail Travel Agents) Text in English. bi-m. **Document type:** *Magazine, Consumer.*
Published by: Group Travel Leader, Inc., 401 W Main St, Ste 222, Lexington, KY 40507-1630. TEL 859-253-0455, http://www.grouptravelleader.com. Pub. Mac T Lacy.

338.4 IDN ISSN 1412-2073
➤ **A S E A N JOURNAL ON HOSPITALITY AND TOURISM.** (Association of South East Asian Nations) Text in English. s-a. USD 10 (effective 2007). **Document type:** *Journal, Academic/Scholarly.*
—BLDSC (1739.956555).
Published by: Institut Teknologi Bandung, Jalan Ganesha 10, Bandung, 40132, Indonesia. TEL 62-22-2534272, FAX 62-22-2506285. Ed. Wiwik Dwi Pratiwi.

338.4 GBR
A S T A NETWORK. Text in English. q. free to members (effective 2009). adv. **Document type:** *Magazine, Trade.* **Description:** Contains news and information from ASTA including diary events, seminars, membership updates and member services.
Related titles: E-mail ed.
Published by: (American Society of Travel Agents USA), Absolute Publishing Ltd., 197-199 City Rd, London, EC1V 1JN, United Kingdom. TEL 44-20-72539909, FAX 44-20-72539907, sales@absolutepublishing.com. Ed. Katie Reich-Storer. Pub. Peter Levinger. Adv. contact Matthew Midworth TEL 44-20-72539909. page USD 17,500, page GBP 8,750; trim 206 x 246.

910 USA
A S U TRAVEL GUIDE; the airline employee's discount directory. (Airline Services Unlimited) Text in English. 1970. q. USD 34.95; USD 17.50 newsstand/cover (effective 2005). adv. bk.rev. **Document type:** *Magazine, Trade.*
Formerly: Interline Tour Guide
Related titles: Online - full text ed.
Published by: A S U Travel Guide, Inc., 448 Ignacio Blvd., Ste. 333, Novato, CA 94901. TEL 415-898-9500, 866-459.0300, FAX 415-898-9501, http://www.asuguide.com. Ed. Christopher Gil. Pub. Ronald Folkenflik. adv.: B&W page USD 3,195, color page USD 4,190. Circ: 4,000.

A V D AUTO BORD UND SPORT BUCH. *see* TRANSPORTATION—Automobiles

910.09 DEU ISSN 0176-5388
ABENTEUER & REISEN; das Erlebnis-Magazin. Text in German. 1981. 10/yr. EUR 44 domestic; EUR 111.50 foreign; EUR 4.80 newsstand/cover (effective 2010). adv. **Document type:** *Magazine, Consumer.*
Published by: W D V Gesellschaft fuer Medien & Kommunikation mbH & Co. OHG, Siemensstr 6, Bad Homburg, 61352, Germany. TEL 49-6172-6700, FAX 49-6172-670144, info@wdv.de, http://www.wdv.de. Ed. Peter Pfaender. Pub. Wolfgang C Ehrnsperger. Adv. contact Sabine Nieth. B&W page EUR 7,175, color page EUR 10,250; trim 182 x 246. Circ: 107,510 (paid).

914.09 GRC
ABOUT TESSALONIKI KALOKERINES APODRASIS. Variant title: Kalokerines Apodrasis. Text in Greek. 2005. a. EUR 2.50 newsstand/cover (effective 2006). adv. **Document type:** *Magazine, Consumer.*
Published by: Motorpress Hellas (Subsidiary of: Gruner + Jahr AG & Co), 132 Lefkis Str, Krioneri, 14568, Greece. TEL 30-210-6262000, FAX 30-210-6262401, info@motorpress.gr, http://www.motorpress.gr. Circ: 50,000 (paid and controlled).

914.09 GRC
ABOUT THESSALONIKI CHIMERINES APODRASIS. Variant title: Chimerines Apodrasis. Text in Greek. 2005. a. EUR 2.50 newsstand/cover (effective 2006). adv. **Document type:** *Magazine, Consumer.*
Published by: Motorpress Hellas (Subsidiary of: Gruner + Jahr AG & Co), 132 Lefkis Str, Krioneri, 14568, Greece. TEL 30-210-6262000, FAX 30-210-6262401, info@motorpress.gr, http://www.motorpress.gr. Circ: 50,000 (paid and controlled).

910.91 001.3 ITA
ABRUZZO E SABINA DI IERI E DI OGGI. Text in Italian. 1995. irreg. **Document type:** *Magazine, Consumer.*
Media: Online - full text.
Published by: Editrice Nova Italica, Via Firenze 169, Pescara, 65122, Italy. info@novaitalica.com, http://www.novaitalica.com. Ed. Benedetto Grassi.

910.91 001.3 ITA
ABRUZZO OGGI. Text in Italian. 1986. irreg. **Document type:** *Magazine, Consumer.*
Related titles: Online - full text ed.
Published by: Editrice Nova Italica, Via Firenze 169, Pescara, 65122, Italy. info@novaitalica.com, http://www.novaitalica.com.

915.6 UAE
ABU DHABI NEWS. Text in English. w.
Published by: Department of Information and Tourism, Abu Dhabi, United Arab Emirates.

910.09 USA ISSN 0740-0365
ACCENT WEST AMARILLO; chronicle of the Southwestern lifestyle. Text in English. 1972. m. USD 14.98 (effective 1998). adv. bk.rev. **Document type:** *Magazine, Consumer.* **Description:** Covers city and regional issues for greater Amarillo, focusing on the life-styles of middle- to upper-income adults.
Published by: Accent West, Inc., PO Box 1504, Amarillo, TX 79105. TEL 806-371-8411, FAX 806-371-7347. Ed., Pub., R&P, Adv. contact Don Cantrell.

910.91 663.2 USA ISSN 1935-0937
F867.5
ACCESS CALIFORNIA WINE COUNTRY. Text in English. biennial (8th ed.). USD 21.95 per issue (effective 2008). **Document type:** *Guide, Consumer.*
Published by: Harper Collins Publishers, 10 East 53rd St, New York, NY 10022. TEL 212-207-7000, http://www.harpercollins.com. Ed. Richard Saul Wurman.

914.4 USA ISSN 1097-5837
ACCESS: PARIS. Text in English. 1987. biennial. USD 19.95 newsstand/cover (effective 2006).
Published by: Access Press (Subsidiary of: HarperCollins Publishers, Inc.), 10 E 53rd St, New York, NY 10022. TEL 212-207-7000.

917.104 CAN ISSN 1202-6395
ACCOMMODATION AND CAMPGROUND GUIDE. Cover title: Manitoba Accommodation and Campground Guide. Text in English. a. free. adv. illus. **Document type:** *Handbook/Manual/Guide, Consumer.* **Description:** Offers hotel and motel listings, campgrounds, resorts, farm vacations and bed and breakfast homes in Winnipeg and throughout the rest of Manitoba.
Formerly (until 1992): Accommodations and Travel Services (0846-7641)
Published by: Travel Manitoba, 155 Carlton St, 7th Fl, Department SS0, Winnipeg, MB R3C 3H8, Canada. TEL 800-665-0040, http://www.travelmanitoba.com. Pub. Colette Fontaine.

910.202 657 GBR
ACCOMMODATION LONDON (YEAR). Text in English. 1980. a. back issues avail. **Document type:** *Handbook/Manual/Guide, Trade.* **Description:** Provides guidance to all types of accommodation in London.
Former titles (until 2007): London: Where to Stay; (until 2005): Where to Stay and What to Do in London
Related titles: Online - full text ed.: free (effective 2009).
Published by: Visit London Ltd, 2 More London Riverside, London, SE1 2RR, United Kingdom. TEL 44-8701-566366. Adv. contact John Brown TEL 44-20-75653000. Circ: 40,000.

ACCOMMODATOR; the management magazine for O A A members. *see* HOTELS AND RESTAURANTS

338.4791 HRV ISSN 0353-4316
G155.C7
ACTA TURISTICA. Text in Multiple languages. 1989. s-a.
Indexed: A12, A17, A22, ABIn, CA, CABA, E12, EconLit, GH, H&TI, H06, LT, N02, N03, P48, P51, P53, P54, PQC, R12, RRTA, S13, S16, T02, W11.
—BLDSC (0668.034000), IE, Ingenta.
Published by: Ekonomski Fakultet Sveucilista, Katedra za Trgovinu i Turizam, Trg. J.F Kennedyja 6, Zagreb, 10000, Croatia. TEL 1-2331111, FAX 1-2335633, http://www.efzg.hr/html/acta-turistica.htm. Ed. Boris Vuconic.

915 HKG ISSN 1019-4630
GV649
ACTION ASIA. Text in English. 1992. bi-m. HKD 280 domestic; USD 60 in Indonesia, Philippines & China; USD 23 in Malaysia; USD 26 in Singapore; USD 32 in Thailand; USD 70 in United Arab Emirates; USD 80 elsewhere in Asia; USD 130 in United States; USD 155 elsewhere (effective 2008). adv. 136 p./no.; back issues avail. **Document type:** *Journal, Consumer.* **Description:** Covers adventure travel in the Asian region, focusing on action sports and ecotourism.
Related titles: Abridged ed.; Regional ed(s).: Action Asia (Singapore Edition).
Published by: Blu Inc Media (HK) Ltd. (Subsidiary of: S P H Magazines Pte Ltd.), Ste 2901, 29/F Universal Trade Centre, No. 3 Arbuthnot Rd, Central, Hong Kong. TEL 852-2165-2800, FAX 852-2868-1799, queries@bluincmedia.com, http://www.bluincmedia.com.hk/. adv.: page USD 8,500; trim 278 x 210. Circ: 36,000.

ACTIVE TRAVEL CYMRU NEWS. *see* SPORTS AND GAMES—Bicycles And Motorcycles

ACTIVE TRAVEL NEWS. *see* SPORTS AND GAMES—Bicycles And Motorcycles

910.91 FRA ISSN 2108-8829
ACTIVITES DE BORDEAUX-ACCUEILLE. BULLETIN. Text in French. 200?. a. **Document type:** *Bulletin, Consumer.*
Published by: Bordeaux-Accueille, 46, Rue Vital Carles, Bordeaux, 33000, France. http://www.bordeaux-accueille.com.

ACTUALIDAD HOSTELERA Y TURISTICA. *see* HOTELS AND RESTAURANTS

913.919 DEU ISSN 0947-2096
ADESSO. Text in Italian; Summaries in German. 1994. m. EUR 69.60; EUR 59.40 to students; EUR 6.50 newsstand/cover (effective 2011). adv. **Document type:** *Magazine, Consumer.*
Published by: Spotlight Verlag GmbH (Subsidiary of: Verlagsgruppe Georg von Holtzbrinck GmbH), Fraunhoferstr 22, Planegg, 82152, Germany. TEL 49-89-856810, FAX 49-89-85681105, info@spotlight-verlag.de, http://www.spotlight-online.de. Ed. Alessandra Albertoni. Adv. contact Axel Zettler. Circ: 24,091 (paid).

ADIRONDACK LIFE. *see* SPORTS AND GAMES—Outdoor Life

910.2 USA
ADJOURN MAGAZINE. Text in English. 1993. bi-m. USD 47.50 (effective 2000). **Document type:** *Newsletter.* **Description:** Informs upscale California lawyers of the best hotels, restaurants, cities, airlines, and other travel facilities.
Published by: National Association of Business Travel Agents, 3699 Wilshire Blvd, Ste 700, Los Angeles, CA 90010. TEL 213-382-3335, FAX 213-480-7712. Ed. Stuart J Faber. Circ: 80,000.

910.202 ITA ISSN 1970-0652
L'ADRIATICO. Text in Italian. 2006. m. **Document type:** *Magazine, Consumer.*
Published by: Editrice Millennium, Piazza Campo Marzio 12, Arzignano, VI 36071, Italy. TEL 39-0444-450693, FAX 39-0444-478247, info@editricemillennium.it.

338.4791 GBR ISSN 1871-3173
G155.7
ADVANCES IN CULTURE, TOURISM AND HOSPITALITY RESEARCH. Text in English. 2007. irreg., latest vol.2, 2008. price varies. **Document type:** *Monographic series, Academic/Scholarly.*
—CCC.
Published by: Emerald Group Publishing Ltd., Howard House, Wagon Ln, Bingley, W Yorks BD16 1WA, United Kingdom. TEL 44-1274-777700, FAX 44-1274-785201, information@emeraldinsight.com, http://www.emeraldinsight.com.

177.1 GBR ISSN 1745-3542
TX901
➤ **ADVANCES IN HOSPITALITY AND LEISURE.** Text in English. 2005. a. price varies. back issues avail. **Document type:** *Monographic series, Academic/Scholarly.* **Description:** Provides a platform to galvanize thoughts on contemporary issues and emerging trends essential to theory advancement as well as professional practices from a global perspective.
Related titles: Online - full text ed.
Indexed: SCOPUS.
—BLDSC (0709.062700). **CCC.**
Published by: J A I Press Ltd. (Subsidiary of: Elsevier Science & Technology), Howard House, Wagon Ln, Bingley, BD16 1WA, United Kingdom. TEL 44-1274-777700, FAX 44-1274-785201, emerald@emeraldinsight.com, http://www.emeraldinsight.com. Ed. Joseph S Chen.

338.4 NLD ISSN 1572-560X
ADVANCES IN TOURISM RESEARCH. Text in English. 2000. irreg., latest 2009. price varies. **Document type:** *Monographic series, Academic/Scholarly.* **Description:** Provides a forum for the study of tourism research, with particular emphasis on management issues faced by decision-makers, policy analysts and the public sector.
Published by: Elsevier BV (Subsidiary of: Elsevier Science & Technology), Radarweg 29, PO Box 211, Amsterdam, 1000 AE, Netherlands. TEL 31-20-4853911, FAX 31-20-4852457, JournalsCustomerServiceEMEA@elsevier.com, http://www.elsevier.com. Ed. Stephen Page.

910.202 USA
ADVENTURE ANNUAL. Text in English. 1970. a. adv. **Document type:** *Catalog.*
Published by: Mountain Travel - Sobek, 1266 66th St., Ste. 4, Emeryville, CA 94608-1159. TEL 510-527-8100, FAX 510-525-7710. Ed., R&P Dena Bartolome. Adv. contact David Ripley. Circ: 100,000 (controlled).

ADVENTURE CYCLIST. *see* SPORTS AND GAMES—Bicycles And Motorcycles

910.2 USA ISSN 1559-3827
DC708
ADVENTURE GUIDE. PARIS & ILE-DE-FRANCE. Text in English. 2004. irreg. USD 15.99 per issue (effective 2011). adv. 400 p./no.; **Document type:** *Handbook/Manual/Guide, Consumer.*
Published by: Hunter Publishing, PO Box 746, Walpole, MA 02081. TEL Comments@HunterPublishing.com, 800-255-0343.

910.2 USA ISSN 1099-4068
F2041
ADVENTURE GUIDE TO BARBADOS. Text in English. 19??. irreg., latest 4th Ed. USD 15.19 per issue (effective 2011). adv. **Document type:** *Handbook/Manual/Guide, Consumer.*
Published by: Hunter Publishing, PO Box 746, Walpole, MA 02081. TEL Comments@HunterPublishing.com, 800-255-0343.

910.2 USA ISSN 1544-3817
F2048.5
ADVENTURE GUIDE TO THE CAYMAN ISLANDS. Text in English. 1998. irreg., latest 3rd ed. USD 15.19 per issue (effective 2011). adv. **Document type:** *Handbook/Manual/Guide, Consumer.*
Published by: Hunter Publishing, PO Box 746, Walpole, MA 02081. TEL Comments@HunterPublishing.com, 800-255-0343.

910.2 AUS ISSN 1834-5204
THE ADVENTURE JOURNAL. Text in English. 2007. a. AUD 9.95 (effective 2008). adv. back issues avail. **Document type:** *Journal, Consumer.* **Description:** Contains Australia's biggest adventure tour directory and a long-term equipment field test.
Published by: Adventure Publishing, 2 Victoria St, Leura, NSW 2780, Australia. TEL 61-2-47841029, FAX 61-2-82128163, admin@adventurepublishing.com.au. Adv. contact Lucas Trihey. page AUD 2,195; trim 210 x 297.

910.202 796.1 GBR ISSN 1368-0773
ADVENTURE TRAVEL. Text in English. 1995. bi-m. GBP 15 domestic; GBP 26 in the European Union; GBP 28 elsewhere (effective 2009). back issues avail. **Document type:** *Magazine, Consumer.* **Description:** Features outdoor adventure travel stories from around the world, as well as advice on where to go and what type of gear to buy.
Formerly (until 1997): Independent & Specialist Travel (1360-3361)
Related titles: Online - full text ed.: free (effective 2009).
Published by: Independent & Specialist Travel, PO Box 6254, Alcester, Warks B49 6PF, United Kingdom. TEL 44-1789-450000, FAX 44-1789-459046. Ed., Pub. Alun Davies. Adv. contact Lara Dunn TEL 44-1684-576113.

910 USA
ADVENTURE TRAVEL NORTH AMERICA. Text in English. 1972. irreg., latest 1999. USD 16.95 (effective 2000). illus. **Document type:** *Directory.* **Description:** Provides specific information for vacationers wanting to arrange guided adventure trips on foot, by horse, on wheels, on water, in wilderness, in snow and in the air.
Formerly (until 1976): Adventure Trip Guide (0084-5965)
Published by: Adventure Guides, Inc., 5101 N. Casa Blanca Dr., Unit 306, Paradise Vly, AZ 85253-6989. TEL 602-596-0226, FAX 602-596-1722. Ed. Pat Dickerman.

910.21 USA
ADVENTURES N W MAGAZINE; race - play - experience. (North West) Text in English. 2006. q. USD 15 (effective 2006). adv. **Document type:** *Magazine, Consumer.* **Description:** Devoted to the Pacific Northwest's outdoor adventure activities and sports, focusing on all that Island, San Juan, Skagit and Whatcom counties have to offer, whether you are a serious athlete or just like to play outside.
Published by: Adventures N W Publishing, Inc., PO Box 2426, Bellingham, WA 98227. TEL 360-927-1843, FAX 360-733-5337, paul@adventuresnwmagazine.com. Ed. Alaine Borgias TEL 360-927-1842. Pub. Paul Haskins. Adv. contact Andrea Solberg TEL 360-739-6419. color page USD 2,100; trim 8.5 x 11. Circ: 25,973 (paid).

910.91 USA
ADVENTURESEEK.COM. Text in English. m. **Document type:** *Magazine, Consumer.*
Media: Online - full content.
Published by: Unexplored Network, 569 Mission St, San Francisco, CA 94105. freelance@adventureseek.com, http://www.adventureseek.com. Ed. Diana Grossman.

AERZTLICHES JOURNAL REISE UND MEDIZIN. *see* MEDICAL SCIENCES

910.202 USA ISSN 1947-4377
G1
▼ **AFAR**; where travel can take you. Text in English. 2009. bi-m. USD 19.95 domestic; USD 29.95 in Canada; USD 39.95 elsewhere (effective 2010). adv. **Document type:** *Magazine, Consumer.* **Description:** Features experiential travel, including stories of culture, geopolitics, active and eco-travel, and personal transformation.
Published by: AFAR Media, 40 Gold St, San Francisco, CA 94133. TEL 415-814-1414, FAX 415-391-1566, info@afar.com, http://www.afar.com/about. Ed. Susan West. Pub. John Sheehy. adv.: B&W page USD 4,900, color page USD 6,495.

338.4 910.2 SWE ISSN 1100-5149
AFFARSRESENAREN; the Swedish business traveller's magazine. Text in Swedish. 1988. bi-m. SEK 298 (effective 2005). adv. illus. **Document type:** *Magazine, Trade.* **Description:** Presents business travelers with ideas to make business travel more time- and cost effective.
Related titles: E-mail ed.; Online - full content ed.: ISSN 1402-4055. 1996.
Published by: Affarsresenaren Forlags AB, Sveavaegen 62, Stockholm, 11134, Sweden. TEL 46-8-7340070, FAX 46-8-242210, info@affarsresenaren.se. Ed. Bertil Hulten TEL 46-8-7340071. Adv. contact Robert Hertzman. B&W page SEK 35,100, color page SEK 42,900. Circ: 80,000.

338.4791 647.9 CYP
AFFINITY. Text in English. 1996. q. adv. bk.rev. illus. back issues avail. **Document type:** *Magazine, Consumer.*
Published by: Action Publications Ltd, PO Box 24676, Nicosia, 1302, Cyprus. TEL 357-2-590555, FAX 357-2-590048. Ed., Pub. Tony Christodoulou. R&P Dina Wilde TEL 357-2-590555. Adv. contact Oriana Patala. **Dist. by:** Action Publications.

338.4 916.8 ZAF
AFRICA CONFERENCE DIRECTORY. Text in English. 1993. a., latest vol.8. Website rev. illus. **Document type:** *Directory, Trade.* **Description:** Information resource for all hotels, convention centers, conference facilities and game lodges in southern Africa.
Formerly (until 2001): Comprehensive Directory to Hotels, Conference Venues, Country Guest Houses & Game Lodges in Southern Africa
Related titles: Online - full content ed.
Published by: Reservations Hotline, PO Box 782902, Sandton, 2146, South Africa. http://www.reservations-hotline.co.za. Ed. Wayne Stevens-Jennings. R&P Wayne Stevens Jennings. Adv. contacts Irene Hawes, Nadine Steven-Jennings. Circ: 20,000.

910 USA ISSN 0194-4584
AFRICA UPDATE (NEW YORK); annual newsletter with congress program. Text in English. 1978. s-a. USD 10. **Document type:** *Newsletter.*
Address: c/o Africa Travel Association, 347 Fifth Ave, Ste 610, New York, NY 10016. TEL 212-447-1926, FAX 212-725-8253. Ed. Mira Berman.

916 ZAF ISSN 1726-9164
AFRICA WILD. Text in English. 2003. m. **Document type:** *Magazine, Consumer.* **Description:** Promotes the continent of Africa and neighboring islands as preferred travel and holiday destinations.
Published by: Africa Wild Publishing (Pty) Ltd., PO Box 13333, Dowerglen, Gauteng 1612, South Africa. TEL 27-11-4540535, FAX 27-11-4540538, info@africawildgroup.co.za, http://www.africawildgroup.co.za.

910.91 305.896 USA
AFRICAN AMERICAN HERITAGE GUIDE. Text in English. 2008. irreg. free. **Document type:** *Magazine, Consumer.*
Published by: Georgia Department of Economic Development, 75 Fifth St, NW, Ste 1200, Atlanta, GA 30308. TEL 404-962-4000, http://www.georgia.org/Home.

910.4 ZAF ISSN 1813-1360
AFRICAN SAFARIS; the luxury bush experience. Text in English. 2004. q. adv.
Published by: Tau Sports & Media, CCMA House, 3rd Flr, 78 Darling St, Cape Town, 8000, South Africa. TEL 27-21-4612856, FAX 27-21-4617580, taumedia@telkomsa.net. adv.: color page ZAR 24,000. Circ: 30,000.

916 USA ISSN 1946-5211
▼ **AFRIKA TRAVEL & TOURISM MAGAZINE.** Variant title: Afrika Travel and Tourism Magazine. Text in English. 2009. q. USD 12; USD 4 per issue (effective 2009). **Document type:** *Magazine, Consumer.* **Description:** Articles on travel and tourism in Africa.
Published by: 255 America Global Publishers, LLC, PO Box 88572, Los Angeles, CA 90009. TEL 323-496-4920. Ed. Rosemary McClure.

658 USA
AGENCYINC. Text in English. m. adv. **Document type:** *Magazine, Trade.* **Description:** Provides business and marketing advice to travel agencies.
Published by: Source Publications, Inc., 5555 E. 71st St., Ste. 8300, Tulsa, OK 74136-6555. http://www.sourcepub.com. Pub. Rick Long.

910.2 ITA ISSN 1122-8539
AGENDA REGIONE CAMPANIA. Text in Italian. 1985. a. **Document type:** *Consumer.*
Published by: Guida Monaci SpA, Via Salaria 1319, Rome, 00138, Italy. TEL 39-06-8887777, FAX 39-06-8889996, guida.monaci@italybygm.it, http://www.italybygm.it.

910.2 ITA ISSN 1122-8571
AGENDA REGIONE PUGLIA. Text in Italian. 1985. a. **Document type:** *Consumer.*
Published by: Guida Monaci SpA, Via Salaria 1319, Rome, 00138, Italy. TEL 39-06-8887777, FAX 39-06-8889996, guida.monaci@italybygm.it, http://www.italybygm.it.

338.4 USA ISSN 1559-3428
AGENT@HOME. Text in English. 2004. m. free to qualified personnel. adv. **Document type:** *Magazine, Trade.* **Description:** Addresses the specific needs of the fastest growing segment of the travel agency business: agents who work from home.
Published by: Performance Media Group LLC, 593 Rancocas Rd, Westampton, NJ 08060. TEL 856-727-0035, FAX 856-727-0136, info@agentathome.com. Pub. Scott Whitley. Adv. contact Shaun Whitley. color page USD 7,286; trim 8.375 x 10.875. Circ: 17,244 (controlled).

910 ESP ISSN 1136-8632
AGENTTRAVEL. Text in Spanish. 1987. m. EUR 60.10 (effective 2005). index. **Document type:** *Magazine, Trade.* **Description:** For travel agents, tour operators, hotel and restaurant managers, airline workers, and government tourism agency personnel.
Related titles: ◆ Supplement(s): Empresas y Empresarios.
Published by: Ediciones Jaguar, C Laurel, 23 1o, Madrid, 28005, Spain. TEL 34-91-4741140, FAX 34-91-4744074, jaguar@edicionesjaguar.com, http://www.edicionesjaguar.com/. Ed. Marisa Lopez de Pariza. Circ: 10,000.

910.2 ITA ISSN 0002-0869
AGENZIA DI VIAGGI; quotidiano di notizie di interesse professionale. Text in Italian. 1965. d. (6/w.). adv. illus. **Document type:** *Newspaper, Consumer.*
Related titles: Online - full text ed.
Published by: Editrice Turistica s.r.l., Via Rasella 155, Rome, 00187, Italy. TEL 39-06-4821539, FAX 39-06-4826721.

338.4 ITA ISSN 1825-1862
AGRITURISMO. Text in Italian. 2005. a. **Document type:** *Magazine, Consumer.*
Published by: De Agostini Editore, Via G da Verrazzano 15, Novara, 28100, Italy. TEL 39-0321-4241, FAX 39-0321-424305, info@deagostini.it, http://www.deagostini.it.

910.202 ITA ISSN 1828-4701
AGRITURISTI. Text in Italian. 1975. bi-m. 64 p./no.; **Document type:** *Magazine, Consumer.*
Published by: Associazione Nazionale per l'Agricoltura, l'Ambiente e il Territorio, Corso Vittorio Emanuele 101, Rome, 00186, Italy. TEL 39-06-6852337, agrit@confagricoltura.it, http://www.agriturist.it. Circ: 15,000.

THE AIR CHARTER GUIDE. *see* TRANSPORTATION—Air Transport

910 FRA ISSN 1290-1563
AIR FRANCE MAGAZINE. Text in English, French. 1982. m. free (effective 2005). **Document type:** *Magazine, Consumer.*
Former titles (until 1997): Atlas - Air France (0767-5240); Atlas (Paris, 1960) (0004-6922); Atlas Histoire (0519-3273)
Published by: Editions Gallimard, 15 Rue Sebastien-Bottin, Paris, 75328 Cedex 07, France. TEL 33-1-49544200, FAX 33-1-45449403, catalogue@gallimard.fr, http://www.gallimard.fr. Circ: 400,000 (free).

910.09 USA
AIR TRAVEL JOURNAL. Text in English. 1971. s-m. USD 55 (effective 1998). adv. **Document type:** *Newspaper.* **Description:** Covers news of Logan International Airport in Boston. Includes news of the Massachusetts port authority, airlines and regional events.
Published by: Air Travel Publications, 256 Marginal St, East, Boston, MA 02128-2800. TEL 617-561-4000, FAX 617-561-2821. Ed., Pub., R&P, Adv. contact Bob Weiss. Circ: 15,000.

338.4791 ESP ISSN 1133-1208
AIRELIBRE; aventura, deporte, viajes, cultura, naturaleza. Text in Spanish. 1993. m. EUR 12 (effective 2009). adv. bibl.; illus.; mkt.; maps. back issues avail. **Document type:** *Magazine, Consumer.* **Description:** Covers hiking, bicycling, horseback riding, adventure sports, cultural trips, geographical material, nature tours and other touring activities.
Published by: Outside Comunicacion Integral, P. Marquez de Monistrol, 7, Madrid, 28011, Spain. TEL 34-91-5268080, FAX 34-91-5261012, outside@airelibre.com, http://www.airelibre.com/. Circ: 75,000.

910 AUT
AIRMAIL. Text in Croatian, Czech, Hungarian, Polish, Slovak. 6/yr. **Document type:** *Magazine, Trade.* **Description:** Covers all aspects of the travel trade in Eastern European countries.
Published by: Profi Reisen Verlagsgesellschaft mbH, Seidlgasse 22, Vienna, 1030, Austria. TEL 43-1-7142414, FAX 43-1-71424144, office@profireisen.at, http://www.profireisen.at. Ed. Rainer Pilcik. Circ: 12,000 (controlled).

AIRSTREAM LIFE; the official Airstream lifestyle magazine. *see* SPORTS AND GAMES—Outdoor Life

910.91 FRA ISSN 2108-2413
▼ **AIX PAUSES.** Text in French. 2010. bi-m. free (effective 2010). **Document type:** *Guide, Consumer.*
Published by: Sarl Aix Pauses Editions, 400, chemin de Granet, Aix-en-Provence, 13090, France.

AJUUS MAGAZINE. *see* BUSINESS AND ECONOMICS—Macroeconomics

AKRON LIFE & LEISURE. *see* GENERAL INTEREST PERIODICALS—United States

917.61 USA ISSN 1551-1316
F326.6
ALABAMA CURIOSITIES; quirky characters, roadside oddities, & other offbeat stuff. Text in English. 2004. biennial, latest 2005, 1st ed. USD 13.95 per issue (effective 2008). **Document type:** *Guide, Consumer.* **Description:** Provides tourist information about Dixie.
Published by: The Globe Pequot Press, Inc., 246 Goose Ln, PO Box 480, Guilford, CT 06437. TEL 203-458-4500, 888-249-7586, FAX 203-458-4603, 800-820-2329, info@globepequot.com, http://www.globepequot.com.

910.202 USA
ALABAMA VACATION GUIDE. Text in English. a. free. adv. **Document type:** *Magazine, Consumer.*
Formed by the merger of: Alabama Tourist Guide; Alabama Book of Surprises
Published by: Bureau of Tourism and Travel, 401 Adams Ave, Box 4927, Montgomery, AL 36103-4927. TEL 334-242-4169, FAX 334-242-4554. Ed. Marilyn Townsend. R&P, Adv. contact April Boone TEL 334-968-4600.

910.202 USA ISSN 1935-7583
F902.3
ALASKA (AMERICAN EDITION). Text in English. 2006. irreg. USD 25 per issue (effective 2008). **Document type:** *Guide, Consumer.*
Published by: D K Publishing (Subsidiary of: Penguin Books U S A, Inc.), 375 Hudson St, New York, NY 10014. TEL 212-213-4800, 800-631-8571, FAX 212-689-4828, publicity@dk.com, http://us.dk.com.

ALASKA ALMANAC: FACTS ABOUT ALASKA. *see* ENCYCLOPEDIAS AND GENERAL ALMANACS

910.91 CAN ISSN 1910-0124
ALASKA YUKON TRAVEL MAGAZINE. Text in English. 1994. a. (13th ed.), latest 2006. free (effective 2006). **Document type:** *Magazine, Consumer.*
Former titles (until 2006): Alaska Yukon Community Travel Guide (1713-4552); (until 2003): Alaska Yukon Travel Guide (1713-4544); Guide to the Goldfields (1498-4105)
Related titles: German ed.: Alaska Yukon Deutsches Reisemagazin.
Published by: Harper Street Publishing, Box 988, Dawson City, YT Y0B 1G0, Canada. TEL 888-848-6671, Greg@AlaskaYukon.com, http://www.alaskayukon.com. Ed. Krystal Karais. Pub. Greg Karais.

ALBERGHI D'ITALIA. *see* HOTELS AND RESTAURANTS

338.4 CAN ISSN 1718-1429
ALBERTA TOURISM QUICK FACTS. Text in English. 2006. q. **Document type:** *Government.*
Published by: Alberta, Tourism, Parks, Recreation & Culture, 4th Flr, Commerce Pl, 10155 - 102 St, Edmonton, AB T5J 4L6, Canada. TEL 780-422-1058, 310-0000, FAX 780-422-0061.

910.2 USA
ALL BREVARD MAGAZINE. Text in English. irreg. **Description:** Offers history and local culture from Brevard County, Florida.
Media: Online - full text.
Address: 1801 N Wickham Rd, Ste 5, Melbourne, FL 32935. TEL 407-242-1868. Pub. Warren Dodd.

ALL INN HOME MAGAZINE. *see* REAL ESTATE

910.91 USA
ALL ROADS LEAD TO BRANSON. Text in English. 1993. q. USD 19.95 (effective 2001). adv. **Description:** Includes show reviews and coverage of tourist attractions in Branson, Misouri.
Published by: Grant Publications Group, PO Box 10848, Springfield, MO 65808. TEL 417-889-9115, FAX 417-823-3837. Pub. Grant Cotton. Adv. contact Robert Alder.

910.2 USA
ALL TERRAIN ADVENTURES. Text in English. irreg. **Document type:** *Magazine, Consumer.* **Description:** Focuses on adventure trips and travel to interesting off-beat places.
Media: Online - full text. Ed. John Misage.

910.202 DEU
ALLMOUNTAIN; Bergsport - Reisen - Ausruestung. Text in German. 1998. bi-m. EUR 21.20 domestic; EUR 31.20 foreign; EUR 4 newsstand/cover ' (effective 2009). adv. **Document type:** *Magazine, Consumer.* **Description:** Contains articles and features on various trekking destinations around the world.
Formerly (until 2007): Trekkers World (1436-2295)
Related titles: Online - full text ed.
Published by: Brinkmann Henrich Medien GmbH, Heerstr 5, Meinerzhagen, 58540, Germany. TEL 49-2354-77990, FAX 49-2354-779977, info@bhmg.de, http://www.bhmg.de. Ed. Petra Thaller. adv.: color page EUR 4,631, B&W page EUR 2,779; trim 196 x 260. Circ: 34,327 (paid).

910 SWE ISSN 1653-6959
ALLT OM HOTELL & RESOR. Text in Swedish. 2005. q. SEK 149 (effective 2006). adv. **Document type:** *Magazine, Consumer.*
Published by: Next World Media AB, Midskogsgraend 13, Stockholm, 11543, Sweden. TEL 46-8-6631500, FAX 46-8-6615260, http://www.nextworld.se, info@nextworld.se. Ed. Kristina Andersson. Adv. contact Nicholas Phsaros TEL 46-8-6631586.

338.48 SWE ISSN 1403-6967
ALLT OM RESOR. Text in Swedish. 1998. 13/yr. SEK 520 (effective 2010). adv. **Document type:** *Magazine, Consumer.*
Published by: Bonnier Tidskrifter AB, Sveavaegen 53, Stockholm, 10544, Sweden. TEL 46-8-7365200, FAX 46-8-7363842, info@bt.bonnier.se, http://www.bonniertidskrifter.se. Ed. Niclas Blixt. Adv. contact Karolina Huelphers. page SEK 34,900; trim 217 x 280. Circ: 41,100 (paid).

914 DEU
ALPENADRIA. Text in German. 2002. q. EUR 18; EUR 5 newsstand/cover (effective 2009). adv. **Document type:** *Magazine, Consumer.*
Formerly: Alpen-Journal
Published by: D P Destination Publishing KG, Voelklinger Str 18, Wuppertal, 42285, Germany. TEL 49-202-94600226, FAX 49-202-94600229, verlag@alpen-journal.de. Ed. Snezana Simicic. adv.: color page EUR 4,900; trim 215 x 280. Circ: 31,500 (paid and controlled).

914.4 FRA ISSN 1250-0089
ALPES LOISIRS. Text in French. 1993. q. EUR 25 (effective 2008). **Document type:** *Magazine, Consumer.*
Formed by the merger of (1986-1991): AlpesNeige (0981-8383); (1988-1993): Alpes Vertes (0989-8719)
Related titles: Supplement(s): Balades.
Address: Les Iles Cordees, Veurey-Voroize, Cedex 38913, France. TEL 33-4-76887100, FAX 33-4-76887114. Ed. Patrick Peletier. Pub. Denis Huertas. Circ: 60,000.

ALPINE GARDENER. *see* BIOLOGY—Botany

THE ALPINE JOURNAL; a record of mountain adventure and scientific observation. *see* SPORTS AND GAMES—Outdoor Life

L'ALSACE. *see* GEOGRAPHY

338.4 SGP
ALWAYS THAILAND. Text in English. 2003. m. free to qualified personnel. **Document type:** *Newspaper, Trade.* **Description:** Reports on travel related news and events specific to Thailand for travel agents.
Published by: T T G Asia Media Pte Ltd, 6 Raffles Quay #16-02, Singapore, 048580, Singapore. TEL 65-6395-7575, FAX 65-6536-8639, contact@ttgasia.com, http://www.ttgasiamedia.com/.

AM-CAN REPORT; marketing & trade journal. *see* BUSINESS AND ECONOMICS—Marketing And Purchasing

910.91 DEU
AMADEUS MAGAZIN. Text in German. 1993. bi-m. EUR 22; EUR 2.20 newsstand/cover (effective 2005). adv. **Document type:** *Magazine, Trade.*
Published by: Konzept Verlagsgesellschaft mbH, Ludwigstr 33-37, Frankfurt Am Main, 60327, Germany. TEL 49-69-97460621, FAX 49-69-974608621, hann.wagner@konzept-verlagsgesellschaft.de, http://www.konzept-verlagsgesellschaft.de. Ed. Maren Cornils. Adv. contact Thomas Knopp. B&W page EUR 3,470, color page EUR 5,120. Circ: 39,610 (paid and controlled).

910.1 DEU ISSN 0939-3382
AMERICA. Text in German. 1990. bi-m. EUR 24; EUR 4.50 newsstand/cover (effective 2006). adv. bk.rev.; music rev. back issues avail. **Document type:** *Magazine, Consumer.* **Description:** Contains information and features about North America for frequent travelers and the travel trade.
Related titles: Online - full text ed.
—CCC.
Published by: J. Latka Verlag GmbH, Heilsbachstr 17-19, Bonn, 53123, Germany. TEL 49-228-919320, FAX 49-228-9193217, info@latka.de, http://www.latka.de. Ed. Sigrid Latka Joehring. Pub. Joachim Latka. Adv. contact Elisabet A Oleson. B&W page EUR 3,800, color page EUR 4,940; trim 210 x 297. Circ: 35,240 (paid). **Dist. in US by:** G L P International, PO Box 9868, Englewood, NJ 07631-6868. TEL 201-871-1010, FAX 201-871-0870.

917 NLD ISSN 1571-0351
AMERICA. Text in Dutch. 1993. q. EUR 18.50 domestic; EUR 21.50 in Belgium; EUR 4.95 newsstand/cover (effective 2009). adv. **Document type:** *Magazine, Consumer.*
Formerly (until 2003): Amerika (0929-5577)
Published by: dOrizon Media, Postbus 135, Castricum, 1900 AC, Netherlands. TEL 31-251-672136, FAX 31-251-654578, info@dorizon.nl, http://www.dorizon.nl. Adv. contact Harald Kolkman. color page EUR 1,550; trim 230 x 297. Circ: 10,000.

910.09 GBR
AMERICAN IN BRITAIN. Text in English. 1980. q. GBP 20 (effective 2009). adv. bk.rev. back issues avail. **Document type:** *Magazine, Consumer.* **Description:** Examines all areas of expatriate life for Americans living and working in the UK.
Formerly: American in London (0957-0667)
Published by: American in Britain Publications Ltd., PO Box 921, Sutton, SM1 2WB, United Kingdom. TEL 44-20-86610186. Pub., Adv. contact Helen Elliott. B&W page GBP 2,200, color page GBP 2,800; 180 x 264. Circ: 20,000.

AMERICAN ROAD. *see* HISTORY—History Of North And South America

910.202 USA
AMERICAN ROADS. Text in English. 2002. bi-m. back issues avail.
Media: Online - full text. Ed. Kathleen Walls.

910.202 USA ISSN 1070-3365
G151
AMERICANS TRAVELING ABROAD: WHAT YOU SHOULD KNOW BEFORE YOU GO; an international traveler's resource guide. Text in English. 1994. biennial. USD 39.99. **Document type:** *Directory.*
Published by: World Travel Institute, Inc., 8268 Streamwood Dr, Box 32674, Baltimore, MD 21208. TEL 410-922-4903, FAX 410-922-8115. Ed., Pub., R&P Gladson I Nwanna.

910.09 917.206 790.1 MEX
AMISTAD. Text in English. 1942. m. USD 42. adv. **Document type:** *Bulletin.*
Formerly: American Society of Mexico. Bulletin
Published by: American Society of Mexico, A.C., Apdo. 555, Mexico City, DF 06000, Mexico. TEL 525-202-4600, FAX 525-208-9675. Ed. Carlos Marban. Pub. James S Wright. Circ: 4,000 (paid).

910.09 USA ISSN 0275-5564
AMOCO TRAVELER. Text in English. 1981. q. membership.
Published by: (Amoco Travel Club), Amoco Enterprises, Inc., 200 E Randolph Dr, Chicago, IL 60601. TEL 212-303-6987, FAX 312-856-2379. Circ: 75,000 (controlled).

910.2 NLD ISSN 1872-132X
AMSTERDAM INDEX; a shortcut to creative Amsterdam. Text in English. 2005. a. EUR 24 (effective 2009).
Related titles: ◆ Supplement(s): Creative City Guide. ISSN 1872-1338.
Published by: BIS Publishers, Het Sieraad, Postjesweg 1, Amsterdam, 1057 DT, Netherlands. TEL 31-20-5150230, FAX 31-20-5150239, bis@bispublishers.nl, http://www.bispublishers.nl.

338.4791 LIE ISSN 1010-1241
AMT FUER VOLKSWIRTSCHAFT. FREMDENVERKEHRSSTATISTIK. Text in German. 19??. a. **Document type:** *Trade.*
Published by: Amt fuer Volkswirtschaft, Giessenstr 3, Vaduz, 9490, Liechtenstein. TEL 423-2366876, FAX 423-2366931, http://www.llv.li/amtsstellen/llv-avw-home.htm.

910.202 387.5 DEU
AN BORD; das Magazin fuer Schiffsreisen und Seewesen. Text in German. 1989. bi-m. EUR 29.50 domestic; EUR 39.40 foreign; EUR 5.10 newsstand/cover (effective 2006). adv. bk.rev. back issues avail. **Document type:** *Magazine, Consumer.*
Published by: J. Humburg Verlags GmbH, Am Hilgeskamp 51-57, Bremen, 28325, Germany. TEL 49-421-427980, FAX 49-421-4279899, verlag@humburg.de. Ed. Hans Dieter Hain. adv.: B&W page EUR 2,757, color page EUR 5,149; trim 198 x 265. Circ: 49,575 (paid).

910.91 794 USA
ANAHEIM / ORANGE COUNTY OFFICIAL VISITORS GUIDE. Text in English. a. free. adv. **Document type:** *Magazine, Consumer.*
Published by: Weaver Publications, Inc., 2420 Alcott St, Denver, CO 80211. TEL 303-458-1211, FAX 303-477-0724, info@weaver-group.com, http://www.weaver-group.com. adv.: color page USD 13,275; trim 7 x 9.5. Circ: 350,000.

338.479 GBR ISSN 1303-2917
G155.A53
➤ **ANATOLIA**; an international journal of tourism and hospitality research. Text in English. 1997. 3/yr. GBP 183 combined subscription in United Kingdom to institutions (print & online eds.); EUR 241, USD 302 combined subscription to institutions (print & online eds.) (effective 2012). bk.rev. bibl. index, cum.index. 136 p./no.; back issues avail.; reprint service avail. from PSC. **Document type:** *Journal, Academic/Scholarly.* **Description:** Provides an outlet for innovative studies that will contribute to the understanding of tourism and hospitality. Aims to heighten awareness of the Mediterranea region as a significant player in international tourism.
Related titles: Online - full text ed.: ISSN 2156-6909. GBP 164 in United Kingdom to institutions; EUR 217, USD 271 to institutions (effective 2012).
Indexed: A01, A34, CA, CABA, E12, F08, F12, GEOBASE, GH, H&TI, H06, LT, N02, P32, R12, RRTA, S13, S16, SD, T02, T05, W11.
—BLDSC (0897.919000). **CCC.**
Published by: Routledge (Subsidiary of: Taylor & Francis Group), 4 Park Sq, Milton Park, Abingdon, Oxon OX14 4RN, United Kingdom. TEL 44-20-70176000, FAX 44-20-70176336, subscriptions@tandf.co.uk.

338.4791 TUR ISSN 1300-4220
ANATOLIA TURIZM VE CEVRE KULTURU DERGISI. Text in Turkish. 1990. q. **Document type:** *Journal.*
Related titles: Online - full text ed.
Indexed: CA, ESPM, H&TI, H06, HPNRM, IBR, IBZ, M10, PEI, SCOPUS, SD, SSciA, T02.
—BLDSC (0897.919000), IE, Ingenta.
Published by: Anatolia, Yenisehir, P K 589, Ankara, 06444, Turkey. anatolia@tr.net. Ed. Nazmi Kozak.

ANDALUCIA COSTA DEL SOL. *see* LIFESTYLE

910.202 GBR ISSN 1363-7517
ANDALUCIA HANDBOOK. Text in English. 1997. irreg., latest 6th ed. GBP 14.99 per issue (effective 2010). adv. **Document type:** *Handbook/Manual/Guide, Consumer.* **Description:** Covers all the basics from where to stay and where to eat to cycling, walking and how to get around the Andalucia.
—CCC.
Published by: Footprint Handbooks Ltd., 6 Riverside Ct, Lower Bristol Rd, Bath, Avon BA2 3DZ, United Kingdom. TEL 44-1225-469141, FAX 44-1225-469461, wwwinfo@footprintbooks.com.

ANDARES. *see* GENERAL INTEREST PERIODICALS—Peru

910.91 USA
THE ANDREW HARPER COLLECTION. Text in English. 1983. m. looseleaf. USD 295 (effective 2003). maps. **Document type:** *Magazine, Consumer.*
Formerly: The Harper Collection
Media: Online - full content. **Related titles:** Print ed.
Published by: Harper Associates, Inc., PO Box 888, Liberty Lake, WA 99019. TEL 208-622-3183, 800-235-9622, subscriptions@andrewharpertravel.com, http://www.andrewharpertravel.com. Ed., Pub. Andrew Harper. R&P Ted Johnson TEL 406-862-3480. Circ: 9,500 (paid). **Subscr. to:** 888, Liberty Lake, WA 99019-0888.

TU

910 USA ISSN 0884-7622
ANDREW HARPER'S HIDEAWAY REPORT; a connoisseur's worldwide guide to peaceful and unspoiled places. Text in English. 1979. m. USD 99 domestic; USD 109 foreign (effective 2005). bk.rev. illus.; maps. index. 8 p./no. 2 cols./p.; back issues avail.; reprints avail. **Document type:** *Newsletter, Consumer.* **Description:** Provides independent reviews of the world's most exclusive and stylish resorts.
Related titles: Online - full text ed.
Published by: Harper Associates, Inc., PO Box 888, Liberty Lake, WA 99019. TEL 509-928-2077, 800-235-9622, FAX 509-928-4055, 888-701-6177, subscriptions@andrewharpertravel.com. Ed., Pub. Andrew Harper. R&P Ted Johnson TEL 406-862-3480. Circ: 26,500 (paid).

910.2 IRL
ANGLERS GUIDE TO IRELAND. Text in English. a. adv. **Document type:** *Directory, Consumer.*
Published by: In Europe Publishing, 4 Cumberland St., Dun Laoghaire, Co. Dublin, Ireland. TEL 353-1-6604805, FAX 353-1-6604165, info@ineurope.ie. adv.: page EUR 2,539; trim 210 x 297. Circ: 30,000 (paid and controlled).

910.91 GBR ISSN 1754-1824
ANGLESEY VISITOR. Text in English. 2006. s-a. free. **Document type:** *Magazine, Consumer.*
Published by: Coastal Property Management Ltd., 14 Bridge St, Menai Bridge, Anglesey, LL59 5DW, United Kingdom. TEL 44-1248-715390, info@coastalpropertymanagement.co.uk, http://www.coastalpropertymanagement.co.uk.

ANGLO-MALAGASY SOCIETY. NEWSLETTER. *see* POLITICAL SCIENCE

ANIMAN; Wunder der Welt. *see* GEOGRAPHY

ANN ARBOR MAGAZINE. *see* GENERAL INTEREST PERIODICALS—United States

910.91 ESP ISSN 1575-443X
ANNALS OF TOURISM RESARCH EN ESPANOL. Text in Multiple languages. 1999. s-a. **Document type:** *Journal, Academic/Scholarly.*
Related titles: ◆ English ed.: Annals of Tourism Research. ISSN 0160-7383.
Published by: (Universitat de les Illes Balears, Laboratori de Investigacio y Documentacio Turistica), Universitat de les Illes Balears, Servei de Publicacions i Intercanvi Cientific, Carr. de Valdemosa, Km. 7.5, Palma de Mallorca, 07071, Spain. informacio@uib.es, http://www.uib.es.

910.91 GBR ISSN 0160-7383
G155.A1
➤ **ANNALS OF TOURISM RESEARCH**; a social sciences journal. Text in English; Summaries in French. 1973. 4/yr. EUR 815 in Europe to institutions; JPY 108,400 in Japan to institutions; USD 910 elsewhere to institutions (effective 2012). adv. bk.rev.; film rev. illus. index. back issues avail.; reprints avail. **Document type:** *Journal, Academic/Scholarly.* **Description:** Provides a forum for academic perspectives on tourism.
Related titles: Microfilm ed.: (from PQC); Online - full text ed.: ISSN 1873-7722. 199? (from IngentaConnect, ScienceDirect); ◆ Multiple languages ed.: Annals of Tourism Resarch en Espanol. ISSN 1575-443X.
Indexed: A20, A22, A26, A34, A36, ABS&EES, APEL, ASCA, AbAn, B04, BPI, BRD, CA, CABA, CommAb, CurCont, E-psyche, E12, EI, ESPM, Emerald, F08, F12, FR, GEOBASE, GH, GeoRef, H&TI, H06, I05, IndVet, LT, N02, P03, P32, P34, PAIS, PGegResA, PsycInfo, PsycholAb, R12, RASB, RRTA, RiskAb, S02, S03, S13, S16, SCOPUS, SD, SOPODA, SSCI, SSciA, SociolAb, SportS, T02, VS, W01, W02, W03, W07, W11, WildRev.
—BLDSC (1044.800000), IE, Infotrieve, Ingenta, INIST. **CCC.**
Published by: Pergamon (Subsidiary of: Elsevier Science & Technology), The Blvd, Langford Ln, East Park, Kidlington, Oxford OX5 1GB, United Kingdom. TEL 44-1865-843000, FAX 44-1865-843010, JournalsCustomerServiceEMEA@elsevier.com. Ed. John Tribe. **Subscr. to:** Elsevier BV, Radarweg 29, PO Box 211, Amsterdam 1000 AE, Netherlands. TEL 31-20-4853757, FAX 31-20-4853432, http://www.elsevier.nl.

917 USA ISSN 1081-3454
TX907.2
ANNUAL DIRECTORY OF AMERICAN AND CANADIAN BED & BREAKFAST; in 5 regional volumes. Text in English. 1990. a. USD 19.95. adv. **Document type:** *Directory.* **Description:** Comprehensive listing of bed and breakfasts, and their accomodations throughout US and Canada.
Formerly: Annual Directory of American Bed and Breakfasts
Published by: Barbour Publishing Inc, 1810 Barbour Dr, Uhrichsville, OH 44683. Ed. Paul Muckley. R&P Heather Rodweller. Adv. contact Amy Veigel. Circ: 20,000.

ANTARCTIC. *see* GEOGRAPHY

917.52 USA ISSN 1949-0623
F187.W3
▼ **ANTIETAM**; a guided tour through history. Text in English. 2009. triennial. USD 15.95 per issue (effective 2009). **Document type:** *Guide, Consumer.* **Description:** Travel guide for the Antietam battlefield.
Published by: G P P Travel (Subsidiary of: The Globe Pequot Press, Inc.), 246 Goose Ln, PO Box 480, Guilford, CT 06437. TEL 203-458-4500, 888-249-7586, FAX 800-820-2329, info@globepequot.com.

338.4791 CAN ISSN 1910-1988
ANTIGONISH AND EASTERN SHORE. Text in English. a. **Document type:** *Magazine, Consumer.*
Published by: Antigonish Eastern Shore Tourism Association, 9042 #7 Hwy, Head Jeddore, NS B0J 1P0, Canada. http://www.novascotiaseacoast.com.

917 USA ISSN 1947-850X
▼ **ANTONIO THE EXPLORER.** Text in English. 2009. m. USD 100; USD 10 per issue (effective 2009). **Document type:** *Magazine, Consumer.* **Description:** A series of travel articles and digital photographs about a father and son on travel adventures mostly through Northern California and other parts of the United States.
Media: Online - full content.
Published by: A.M. Benjamin Services, 835 O'Farrell St, Ste 404, San Francisco, CA 94109. TEL 415-596-3164, ambenjamin79@yahoo.com.

910.2 ARG ISSN 1666-504X
ANUARIO DE ESTUDIOS DE TURISMO. Text in Spanish. 2001. a. ARS 20 (effective 2006). **Document type:** *Monographic series, Academic/Scholarly.*
Published by: Universidad Nacional del Comahue, Facultad de Turismo, Buenos Aires, 14000, Neuquen, 8300, Argentina. TEL 54-299-4490378, FAX 54-299-4490377, fatu@uncoma.edu.ar, http://fatu.uncoma.edu.ar/. Ed. Jose Luis Bosch. Circ: 300.

910.202 DEU
ANYWAY. Text in English. 2005. bi-m. EUR 5 newsstand/cover (effective 2008). adv. **Document type:** *Magazine, Consumer.* **Description:** Covers international travel and lifestyle.
Related titles: German ed.
Published by: ahead media GmbH, Schlesische Str 29-30, Berlin, 10997, Germany. TEL 49-30-6113080, FAX 49-30-6113088, ahead@aheadmedia.com, http://www.aheadmedia.com/. adv.: B&W page EUR 5,800, color page EUR 7,800. Circ: 68,000 (controlled).

910 ARG ISSN 0329-2045
G155.A7
APORTES Y TRANSFERENCIAS. TIEMPO LIBRE: TURISMO Y RECREACION. Text in Spanish. 1997. s-a. ARS 5 newsstand/cover (effective 2010). **Document type:** *Journal, Academic/Scholarly.*
Published by: Universidad Nacional de Mar del Plata, Facultad de Ciencias Economicas y Sociales, Funes 3250, Mar del Plata, Buenos Aires, 7600, Argentina. TEL 54-223-4749696, economic@mdp.edu.ar, http://www.mdp.edu.ar/. Ed. Juan Carlos Mantero.

APPALACHIAN HERITAGE; a magazine of southern Appalachian life and culture. *see* GENERAL INTEREST PERIODICALS—United States

910.2 USA ISSN 1075-1351
GV199.42.A68
APPALACHIAN TRAIL DATA BOOK. Text in English. 1982. a. USD 2 (effective 2005).
Published by: Appalachian Trail Conservancy, 799 Washington St, PO Box 807, Harpers Ferry, WV 25425. TEL 304-535-6331, FAX 304-535-2667, http://www.appalachiantrail.org.

AQUAMONDE; le magazine de l'image et des voyages subaquatiques. *see* BIOLOGY—Zoology

917.204 HND
AQUI Y AHORA. Text in Spanish. 1976. q. illus.
Published by: Secretaria de Cultura, Turismo e Informacion, Tegucigalpa DC, Honduras.

917.204 USA ISSN 1095-8886
F1219
ARCHAEOLOGICAL MEXICO. Text in English. 1998. triennial, latest 2001. USD 21.95 per issue (effective 2009).
Published by: Avalon Travel Publishing, 1700 4th St, Berkeley, CA 94710. TEL 510-595-3664, avalon.publicity@perseusbooks.com, http://www.avalontravelbooks.com.

910.202 GBR ISSN 1369-1406
ARGENTINA HANDBOOK. Text in English. 1998. biennial. GBP 15.99 per issue (effective 2010). adv. back issues avail. **Document type:** *Handbook/Manual/Guide, Consumer.* **Description:** Covers all the basics from where to stay and where to eat to cycling, walking and how to get around the Argentina.
—**CCC.**
Published by: Footprint Handbooks Ltd., 6 Riverside Ct, Lower Bristol Rd, Bath, Avon BA2 3DZ, United Kingdom. TEL 44-1225-469141, FAX 44-1225-469461, wwwinfo@footprintbooks.com.

388.3 USA
ARIZONA A A A HIGHROADS. Text in English. 1968. bi-m. USD 2 to non-members (effective 1998). adv. **Document type:** *Guide, Trade.* **Description:** Covers Arizona and foreign travel; automotive, civic and legislative activities; club seminars and benefits.
Published by: Arizona Automobile Association, PO Box 33119, 3144 N 7th Ave, Phoenix, AZ 85013. TEL 602-274-1116, FAX 602-277-1194. Ed. Pamela Heck. Circ: 295,000 (controlled).

910.2 USA ISSN 1559-6230
F809.3
ARIZONA & THE GRAND CANYON. Text in English. 2006. a., latest 2007. USD 19.95 per issue (effective 2008). **Document type:** *Guide, Consumer.* **Description:** Provides up-to-date information on Arizona and the Grand Canyon and includes full-color pullout map.
Published by: Fodor's Travel Publications, Inc. (Subsidiary of: Random House Inc.), 1745 Broadway, 15th Fl, New York, NY 10019. TEL 212-572-2313, editors@fodors.com, http://www.fodors.com.

917.904 979 USA
ARIZONA COAST. Text in English. 1988. bi-m. free. adv. bk.rev. back issues avail. **Document type:** *Magazine, Consumer.* **Description:** Covers tourism along the Colorado River in Western Arizona and Old West history.
Published by: Hale Communications, 1212 Fourth St, PO Box 5054, Parker, AZ 85344. TEL 602-669-6464, FAX 602-669-6464. Ed. Jerry Hale. Circ: 15,000.

917.91 USA ISSN 1545-6633
F809.3
ARIZONA CURIOSITIES; quirky characters, roadside oddities, & other offbeat stuff. Text in English. 2003. biennial, latest 2007, 2nd ed. USD 14.95 per issue (effective 2008). **Document type:** *Guide, Consumer.* **Description:** Provides tourist information about the Grand Canyon State.
Published by: The Globe Pequot Press, Inc., 246 Goose Ln, PO Box 480, Guilford, CT 06437. TEL 203-458-4500, 888-249-7586, FAX 203-458-4603, 800-820-2329, info@globepequot.com, http://www.globepequot.com.

917 USA ISSN 0004-1521
TE24.A6 CODEN: AZHIAW
ARIZONA HIGHWAYS. Text in English. 1921. m. USD 24 domestic; USD 44 foreign; USD 3.99 per issue (effective 2009). bk.rev. maps; illus. 56 p./no.; back issues avail. **Document type:** *Magazine, Consumer.* **Description:** Contains articles on Arizona's history, nature, travel, personalities, Native American art and archeology.
Related titles: Online - full text ed.: USD 24 (effective 2009).
Indexed: A06, A22, ASIP, B04, BRD, C12, ChPerI, G09, GeoRef, M01, M02, MLA-IB, MagInd, P02, P06, P10, P48, P53, P54, PMR, PQC, R03, R04, RGAb, RGPR, SpeleolAb, T02, W03.
Address: 2039 W Lewis Ave, Phoenix, AZ 85009. TEL 800-543-5432, FAX 602-254-4505, arizonahighways@emailcustomerservice.com. Ed. Robert Stieve. Pub. Win Holden.

917.67 USA ISSN 2154-2880
▼ **ARKANSAS CURIOSITIES.** Text in English. 2010 (Jun.). triennial. USD 15.95 per issue (effective 2011). **Document type:** *Consumer.* **Description:** Travel guide for quirky characters, roadside odditites and other offbeat stuff in Arkansas.
Published by: The Globe Pequot Press, Inc., 246 Goose Ln, PO Box 480, Guilford, CT 06437. TEL 203-458-4500, FAX 203-458-4603, info@globepequot.com.

338.4 USA
ARKANSAS TRAVEL AND TOURISM REPORT. Text in English. 1972. a., latest 2001. free. illus.; stat.; charts. **Document type:** *Yearbook, Government.*
Formerly: Tourism in Arkansas. Activity Report
Published by: Department of Parks and Tourism, 2312 Cantrell Road, Little Rock, AR 72202. TEL 501-324-1521, FAX 501-324-1525. Ed. Charles McLemore. Circ: 900.

910.2 USA ISSN 1949-064X
F234.A7
▼ **ARLINGTON NATIONAL CEMETERY**; a guided tour through history. Text in English. 2009. triennial. USD 15.95 per issue (effective 2010). **Document type:** *Consumer.* **Description:** Provides a guide for touring Arlington National Cemetery.
Published by: G P P Travel (Subsidiary of: The Globe Pequot Press, Inc.), 246 Goose Ln, PO Box 480, Guilford, CT 06437. TEL 888-249-7586, FAX 800-820-2329, info@globepequot.com, http://www.globepequot.com.

915.66 USA ISSN 1933-074X
DK682.9
ARMENIA AND KARABAGH. Text in English. 2004. irreg. USD 24.95 per issue (effective 2007). **Document type:** *Guide, Consumer.*
Published by: Stone Garden Productions, PO Box 7758, Northridge, CA 91327. TEL 888-266-7331, http://www.stonegardenproductions.com.

▼ **AROUND THE PANHANDLE**; things to do, places to go & people to know. *see* LIFESTYLE

910.202 USA
AROUND THE WORLD WITH BONNIE KOGOS. Text in English. 1981. q. USD 40 (effective 2000). **Document type:** *Newsletter, Consumer.*
Published by: Kogos Publications Co., 104 E 37th St, New York, NY 10016. TEL 212-679-9438, FAX 212-686-8103. Ed. Bonnie Kogos. Circ: 5,000.

917 USA ISSN 1549-6767
ARRINGTON'S INN TRAVELER. Text in English. q. USD 19.99 domestic; USD 23.99 in Canada; USD 40 elsewhere; USD 6.95 newsstand/cover domestic; USD 7.95 newsstand/cover in Canada (effective 2004). adv. **Document type:** *Magazine, Consumer.*
Published by: Arrington Publishing, 214 W Texas Ste 400, Midland, TX 79701. TEL 432-684-6800, FAX 432-684-5374, info@bnbjournal.com. Ed., Pub. David H Arrington.

914 747 664 FRA ISSN 2101-678X
▼ **ART DE VIVRE (BOULOGNE-BILLANCOURT).** Text in French. 2009. q. EUR 32 for 2 yrs. (effective 2010). **Document type:** *Magazine, Consumer.*
Published by: Lafont Presse, 53 Rue du Chemin Vert, Boulogne-Billancourt, 92100, France. TEL 33-1-46102121, FAX 33-1-45792211, http://www.lafontpresse.fr.

910.202 USA ISSN 1521-5210
G151
ARTHUR FROMMER'S BUDGET TRAVEL; vacations for real people. Variant title: Budget Travel. Text in English. 1998. 10/yr. USD 12 domestic; USD 22 in Canada; USD 32 elsewhere (effective 2009). adv. back issues avail. **Document type:** *Magazine, Consumer.* **Description:** Contains essential information on travel destinations.
Related titles: Online - full text ed.: free (effective 2009).
Indexed: A11, B04, BRD, C05, G09, M02, P10, P48, P53, P54, PQC, R03, RGAb, RGPR, T02, U01, W03, W05.
Published by: Arthur Frommer's Budget Travel, Inc., 530 Seventh Ave, 2nd Fl, New York, NY 10018. Custhelp@BudgetTravel.com. Pub. Bernadette H Haley TEL 646-695-6740. adv.: page USD 52,575. **Subscr. to:** PO Box 5609, Harlan, IA 51593. TEL 800-829-9121, NBTcustserv@cdsfulfillment.com, http://btsub.com.

ARTISTIC TRAVELER; architecture & travel with art & photography. *see* ARCHITECTURE

910.2 USA
ARUBA, BONAIRE & CURACAO ALIVE!. Text in English. 1997. irreg., latest 3rd ed. USD 15.99 per issue (effective 2011). **Document type:** *Handbook/Manual/Guide, Consumer.*
Formerly (until 2008): Aruba, Bonaire and Curacao Alive Guide
Published by: Hunter Publishing, PO Box 746, Walpole, MA 02081. TEL Comments@HunterPublishing.com, 800-255-0343.

917.2 CAN
ARUBA NIGHTS. Text in English. q. **Document type:** *Journal, Consumer.*
Published by: Nights Publications, 1831 Rene Levesque Blvd W, Montreal, PQ H3H 1R4, Canada. FAX 514-931-6273, editor@nightspublications.com. Ed. Stephen Trotter.

914.18 IRL
ASHFORD CASTLE AND DROMOLAND CASTLE. Text in English. a. adv. **Document type:** *Magazine, Consumer.*
Published by: Ashville Media Group, Apollo House, Tara St., Dublin, 2, Ireland. TEL 353-1-4322200, FAX 353-1-6727100, info@ashville.com, http://www.ashville.com. Ed. Anthea Savage. Adv. contact Brian O'Neill. B&W page EUR 2,533, color page EUR 3,168. Circ: 25,000 (controlled).

910.202 USA ISSN 1930-3718
ASIA-PACIFIC HARRIER. Text in English. 2002. q. USD 24 (effective 2007). **Document type:** *Magazine, Consumer.*
Published by: Asia-Pacific Harrier Magazine, PMB 3093, 3133 Waialae Ave, Ste 3, Honolulu, HI 96816-1533. Pub. Jim Edens.

338.4791 GBR ISSN 1094-1665
G155.A74 CODEN: APJRF4
➤ **ASIA PACIFIC JOURNAL OF TOURISM RESEARCH.** Abbreviated title: A P J T R. Text in English. 1995. q. GBP 419 combined subscription in United Kingdom to institutions (print & online eds.); EUR 556, USD 696 combined subscription to institutions (print & online eds.) (effective 2012). adv. bk.rev. illus. back issues avail.; reprint service avail. from PSC. **Document type:** *Journal, Academic/Scholarly.* **Description:** Publishes empirical and theoretical research on tourism, tourism education, and the tourism industry in the Asia Pacific region.
Related titles: Online - full text ed.: ISSN 1741-6507. GBP 377 in United Kingdom to institutions; EUR 501, USD 626 to institutions (effective 2012) (from IngentaConnect).
Indexed: A22, BAS, CA, CABA, CurCont, E01, E12, F08, F12, GEOBASE, GH, H&TI, H06, LT, N02, P32, PGegResA, PHN&I, R12, RRTA, S13, S16, SCOPUS, SOPODA, SSCI, T02, T05, W07, W11. —IE, Ingenta. **CCC.**
Published by: (Asia Pacific Tourism Association HKG), Routledge (Subsidiary of: Taylor & Francis Group), 4 Park Square, Milton Park, Abingdon, Oxon OX14 4RN, United Kingdom. subscriptions@tandf.co.uk, http://www.routledge.com. Ed. Kaye S Chon TEL 852-27666382. R&P Kaye Chon TEL 852-27666382. Adv. contact Linda Hann TEL 44-1344-779945. Circ: 500. **Subscr. to:** Taylor & Francis Ltd., Journals Customer Service, Sheepen Pl, Colchester, Essex CO3 3LP, United Kingdom. TEL 44-20-70175544, FAX 44-20-70175198.

338.4 PAK
ASIA TRAVEL NEWS. Text in English. 1988. fortn. PKR 200 domestic; USD 40 foreign (effective 2000). adv. illus. **Document type:** *Newspaper, Trade.* **Description:** Publishes international and Pakistani news affecting the travel industry, including financial issues, reports on changes in airline services, new hotels, and other items of interest.
Published by: Phoenix Publications Co., Chundrigar Rd., Muhammadi House 101, Karachi, 74000, Pakistan. TEL 92-21-2412591, FAX 92-21-2420797. Ed. Javed Mushtaq. Pub. M Anwar Mushtaq. Adv. contact Haseeb Ahmed.

910 GBR
ASPECTS OF TOURISM. Text in English. 2000. irreg., latest 2008. price varies. back issues avail. **Document type:** *Monographic series, Academic/Scholarly.* **Description:** Provides readers with the latest thinking on tourism world-wide and in so doing will push back the frontiers of tourism knowledge.
Published by: Channel View Publications (Subsidiary of: Multilingual Matters Ltd.), St Nicholas House, 31-34 High St, Bristol, BS1 2AW, United Kingdom. TEL 44-117-3158562, FAX 44-117-3158563, info@multilingual-matters.com, http://www.multilingual-matters.com/default.asp?TAG=&CID=. Eds. Dr. C Michael Hall, Chris Cooper, Dallen J Timothy.

910.91 USA
ASPEN MAGAZINE'S GUIDE. Text in English. 1985. s-a. adv.
Published by: Ridge Publications, PO Box G 3, Aspen, CO 81612. TEL 970-920-4040, FAX 970-920-4044. Pub. Randy Beier.

910.202 GBR ISSN 2046-7257
▼ **ASPIRE (LONDON)**; the luxury travel club from travel weekly. Text in English. 2010. q. free to members (effective 2011). **Document type:** *Magazine, Trade.* **Description:** Provides travel information.
Related titles: Online - full text ed.: free (effective 2011).
Published by: TWgroup Ltd., 52 Grosvenor Gardens, London, SW1W 0AU, United Kingdom. Ed. Lucy Huxley TEL 44-207-8814854.

910.2 FRA ISSN 2108-8209
ASSOCIATION POUR L'ESSOR PROVENCAL, EXCURSIONNISTES MARSEILLAIS. BULLETIN TRIMESTRIEL. Text in French. 1897. q. **Document type:** *Bulletin, Consumer.*
Former titles (until 2010): Societe des Excursionnistes Marseillais (1777-2230); (until 2005): La Societe des Excursionnistes Marseillais. Bulletin Periodique (1777-2222)
Published by: Association pour l'Essor Provencal, Excursionnistes Marseillais, 16, Rue de la Rotonde, Marseille, 13001, France. TEL 33-4-91847552, contact@excurs.com, http://www.excurs.com/index.php.

ATLANTIC CITY MAGAZINE. *see* GENERAL INTEREST PERIODICALS—United States

910.202 CAN
ATLANTIC EXPLORER TRAVELMAG. Text in English. 1996. irreg. **Document type:** *Newsletter.* **Description:** Travel, tourism, recreation and accomodations links and articles about the four Canadian provinces of Nova Scotia, New Brunswick, Newfoundland-Labrador and Prince Edward Island.
Media: Online - full text.
Published by: Atlantic Explorer Travel Group, 3889 Kencrest Ave, Halifax, NS B3K 3L4, Canada. Ed. Tony Thibault.

910.202 TUR ISSN 1300-5901
G80
ATLAS; aylik cografya ve kesir dergisi. Text in Turkish. 1993 (Apr.). m. TRY 115 domestic (effective 2009). adv. **Document type:** *Magazine, Consumer.*
Related titles: Online - full text ed.
Published by: D B R - Dogan Burda Rizzoli Dergi Yayyncylyk ve Pazarlama A.S., Hurriyet Medya Towers, Gunesli - Istanbul, 34212, Turkey. TEL 90-212-4103566, FAX 90-212-4103564, abone@dbr.com.tr, http://www.dbr.com.tr.

910.2 FRA ISSN 2107-4313
AU COEUR DE L'INFO. Text in French. 2003. 3/yr. **Document type:** *Magazine, Consumer.*
Formerly (until 2010): Communaute de Communes Epernay Pays de Champagne. Le Journal (1760-1401)
Published by: Communaute de Communes Epernay Pays de Champagne, BP 80526, Epernay, 51331, France. TEL 33-3-26564766, http://www.ccepc.fr.

919.304 NZL
AUCKLAND TOURIST TIMES. Text in English. w. free newsstand/cover. adv. **Document type:** *Newspaper, Consumer.* **Description:** Provides national and international visitors with in-depth information on Auckland and the rest of New Zealand.
Address: Newton, PO Box 68-126, Auckland, New Zealand. TEL 64-9-379-6982, FAX 64-9-377-4987, communities@communitynewsakl.co.nz. Ed. Margaret Taylor. Adv. contact Ross Preston. page NZD 750. Circ: 8,000 (controlled).

914 DEU ISSN 0004-7961
AUGSBURGER KULTURNACHRICHTEN. Text in German. 1948. m. adv. illus. **Document type:** *Bulletin, Government.*
Related titles: Microform ed.
Published by: Stadt Augsburg, Kulturbuero, Bahnhofstr 18 1-3a, Augsburg, 86150, Germany. TEL 49-821-324-3250, FAX 49-821-324-3252. Ed. Irmgard Baur. Circ: 15,000.

AURA. *see* ADVERTISING AND PUBLIC RELATIONS

379.85 DEU ISSN 0179-3543
AUSLANDSREISEN. Text in German. 1959. 2/yr. adv. **Document type:** *Magazine, Consumer.*
Published by: (Deutscher Sparkassenverlag GmbH), S V Corporate Media GmbH (Subsidiary of: Sueddeutscher Verlag GmbH), Emmy-Noether-Str 2, Munich, 80992, Germany. TEL 49-89-5485201, FAX 49-89-54852192, info@sv-medien-service.de, http://www.sv-medien-service.de/svcm/. Adv. contact Lutz Boden. B&W page EUR 5,130, color page EUR 7,380. Circ: 240,000 (controlled).

919.404 AUS
AUSSIE BACKPACKER; the budget travellers guide to Australia. Text in English. 1989. bi-m. free domestic; AUD 15 per issue foreign (effective 2009); subscr. includes Aussie Backpacker Accommodation Guide. 164 p./no.; back issues avail. **Document type:** *Magazine, Consumer.* **Description:** Provides backpackers and budget travellers in Australia with up-to-date and useful information about budget travel in Australia.
Related titles: Online - full text ed.; ◆ Special ed(s).: Aussie Backpacker Accommodation Guide.
Published by: North Australian Publishing Co. Pty. Ltd., PO Box 1264, Townsville, QLD 4810, Australia. TEL 61-7-47723244, FAX 61-7-47723250. Ed. Marie Erker. Pub., Adv. contact Warren Gardner.

AUSTIN MEETING PLANNER & DESTINATION GUIDE. *see* MEETINGS AND CONGRESSES

913.764 USA
AUSTIN OFFICIAL VISITORS GUIDE. Text in English. s-a. free. adv. **Document type:** *Guide, Consumer.* **Description:** Contains color photography, extensive maps and detailed listings of accommodations, dining, shopping and activities in the Austin area.
Published by: Weaver Publications, Inc., 2420 Alcott St, Denver, CO 80211. TEL 303-458-1211, FAX 303-477-0724, info@weaver-group.com, http://pub.weaver-group.com. adv.: color page USD 6,125; trim 5.25 x 8.375. Circ: 220,000 (free).

AUSTRALASIAN BUS AND COACH; the management magazine for bus and coach operators. *see* TRANSPORTATION

910.91 GBR ISSN 1748-6874
AUSTRALIA & NEW ZEALAND. Text in English. 2005. m. GBP 34 (effective 2010). **Document type:** *Magazine, Consumer.* **Description:** Covers the region's food, wine, culture, migration, property, travel, and real-life stories.
Related titles: Online - full text ed.
Published by: Evolve Digital Publishing, Unit 3, The Old Estate Yard, N Stoke Ln, Upton Cheyney, Bristol, BS30 6ND, United Kingdom. http://www.edpltd.co.uk/.

338.4791 GBR ISSN 2041-7233
▼ **AUSTRALIA TOURISM REPORT.** Text in English. 2009. q. EUR 850, USD 1,150 combined subscription (print & email eds.) (effective 2011). **Document type:** *Report, Trade.* **Description:** Provides industry professionals and strategists, corporate analysts, associations, government departments and regulatory bodies with independent forecasts and competitive intelligence on the Australian tourism industry.
Related titles: E-mail ed.
Published by: Business Monitor International Ltd., Senator House, 85 Queen Victoria St, London, EC4V 4AB, United Kingdom. TEL 44-20-72480468, FAX 44-20-72480467, enquiry@businessmonitor.com.

910.202 AUS ISSN 1442-6730
AUSTRALIAN COAST & COUNTRY. Text in English. 1999. q. AUD 31.80 domestic; AUD 60 foreign; AUD 7.95 newsstand/cover (effective 2009). adv. charts; illus.; maps. 120 p./no.; back issues avail. **Document type:** *Magazine, Consumer.* **Description:** Devoted to the enjoyment of travel and living.
Formerly (until 2004): Coast & Country Magazine
Related titles: E-mail ed.; Fax ed.; Online - full text ed.
Published by: Palm Acres Publications Pty. Ltd., 17 Madden Grove, Richmond, VIC 3121, Australia. TEL 61-3-94294493, 300-667-580, FAX 61-3-94281668, office@coastandcountry.com.au. Ed. Christopher Akehurst. Adv. contact Georgie Kirk. page AUD 3,875; trim 230 x 300.

AUSTRALIAN GEOGRAPHIC. *see* GEOGRAPHY

910.202 AUS ISSN 1034-9006
AUSTRALIAN GOURMET TRAVELLER. Text in English. 1988. m. AUD 74.95 domestic; AUD 125 in New Zealand; AUD 155 elsewhere; AUD 8.50 newsstand/cover (effective 2008). adv. bk.rev. **Document type:** *Magazine, Consumer.* **Description:** Contains recipes, reviews and food news, and explores exotic destinations, special properties and unique experiences around the globe.
Former titles (until 1989): Gourmet Traveler (1032-8009); (until 1989): Australian Gourmet with Traveler (1031-5799); Which was formed by the merger of (1970-1988): Australian Gourmet (0155-3380); (1986-1988): Traveler (1030-3758); Which was formerly (until 1987): Travel and Leisure (0818-9587)
Related titles: Online - full text ed.; ◆ Supplement(s): Australian Gourmet Traveller Wine. ISSN 1446-9510.
Indexed: A11, G06, G07, G08, H&TI, H06, I05, T02. —Ingenta.
Published by: A C P Magazines Ltd. (Subsidiary of: P B L Media Pty Ltd.), 54-58 Park St, Sydney, NSW 2000, Australia. TEL 61-2-92828000, FAX 61-2-91263769, research@acpaction.com.au, http://www.acp.com.au. Ed. Anthea Loucas. Adv. contact Justine Romanis TEL 61-2-92828981. color page AUD 10,190; trim 225 x 297. Circ: 75,207. **Subscr. to:** Magshop, Reply Paid 4967, Sydney, NSW 2001, Australia. TEL 61-2-136116, subs@magstore.com.au, http://shop.magstore.com.au.

AUSTRALIAN HOTELIER. *see* HOTELS AND RESTAURANTS

910.202 AUT
AUSTRIA NACHRICHTEN. Text in German. 6/yr. **Document type:** *Bulletin, Consumer.*
Address: Rotenturmstrasse 14, Vienna, W 1010, Austria. TEL 43-1-5131003, FAX 43-1-513100317. Ed. Hans Wallner. Circ: 15,000.

L'AUTO-JOURNAL. *see* TRANSPORTATION—Automobiles

AUTO TOURING. *see* TRANSPORTATION—Automobiles

910.2 DEU ISSN 0045-1010
AUTO UND REISE; Zeitschrift des Auto- und Reiseclubs Deutschland ARCD. Text in German. 1955. 10/yr. adv. bk.rev. illus.; stat.; tr.lit. **Document type:** *Magazine, Consumer.*
Formerly (until 1969): Kraftfahrervereinigung Deutscher Beamter E.V. K V D B Mitteilungen
Published by: Auto und Reise GmbH Verlag und Wirtschaftsdienst, Postfach 440, Bad Windsheim, 91427, Germany. TEL 49-9841-4090, FAX 49-9841-409264, redaktion@arcd.de, http://www.arcd.de. Ed. Joseph Harrer. Pub. Bernd Opolka. Adv. contact Ingrid Pohl. B&W page EUR 7,300, color page EUR 7,300; trim 185 x 250. Circ: 95,451 (paid and controlled).

910.202 ITA ISSN 1828-0811
AUTOCAPITAL TRAVEL. Text in Italian. 2003. q. **Document type:** *Magazine, Consumer.*
Formerly (until 2006): Best Travel (1724-1952)
Published by: Piscopo Editore Srl, Via di Villa Sacchetti 11, Rome, 00197, Italy. TEL 39-06-3200105, FAX 39-06-3200143, http://www.piscopoeditore.it. Ed. Monica Ciccolini.

010.91 DEU
AUTOHOF GUIDE. Text in German. 2000. a. EUR 2.50 newsstand/cover (effective 2010). adv. **Document type:** *Directory, Consumer.*
Published by: EuroTransportMedia Verlags- und Veranstaltungs-GmbH, Handwerkstr 15, Stuttgart, 70565, Germany. TEL 49-711-784980, FAX 49-711-7849888, info@etm-verlag.de, http://www.etm-verlag.de. adv.: page EUR 5,010. Circ: 120,000 (controlled).

910 FIN ISSN 1796-7031
AUTOILLEN EUROOPASSA. Text in Finnish. 1965. biennial. adv. **Document type:** *Consumer.*
Former titles (until 2007): Autolla Ulkomaille (0355-2896); (until 1976): Kansainvalinen Automatkailu (0075-4900)
Published by: Autoliitto r.y./Automobile and Touring Club of Finland, Hameentie 105 A, Helsinki, 00550, Finland. TEL 358-9-72584400, FAX 358-9-72584460, autoliitto@autoliitto.fi, http://www.autoliitto.fi.

910.09 GBR
AUTOMOBILE ASSOCIATION MEMBERS HANDBOOK. Text in English. 19??. biennial. free to members (effective 2009). maps. **Document type:** *Handbook/Manual/Guide, Consumer.* **Description:** Covers services offered by the association, lists hotels, and includes road maps for members.
Published by: (Automobile Association), A A Publishing, Contact Ctr, Lambert House, Stockport Rd, Cheadle, Hants SK8 2DY, United Kingdom. TEL 44-161-4958945, FAX 44-161-4887544, customer.services@theAA.com.

912 ARG ISSN 1852-3641
▼ **AUTOS Y VIAJES.** Text in Spanish. 2009. q. **Document type:** *Magazine, Consumer.*
Address: General E. Bonorino, 181-4B, Buenos Aires, 1406, Argentina. TEL 54-11-46191457, info@autosyviajes.com.ar, http://www.autosyviajes.com.ar/. Ed. Alicia Solari.

AUTOSPORT. *see* SPORTS AND GAMES

910.2 USA ISSN 1559-8861
F548.18
AVANT GUIDE. CHICAGO. Text in English. 2005. irreg. **Document type:** *Guide, Consumer.*
Published by: Empire Press Media, Inc., 444 Madison Ave. 35th Flr, New York, NY 10022. TEL 646-257-2457, http://avantguide.com.

AVIATION & SPACE JOURNAL. *see* TRANSPORTATION—Air Transport

910.2 051 USA
AVIATOR'S GUIDE. Text in English. 2003. bi-m. USD 14.95 domestic; USD 24.95 foreign; USD 4.95 per issue (effective 2004). adv. back issues avail. **Document type:** *Magazine, Consumer.* **Description:** Designed for the general aviation community. Provides aviators and their families with a definitive source of quality information on where to go and what to do when traveling by personal aircraft.
Published by: J & S Media, Inc., 14 Vandeventer Ave, Port Washington, NY 11050. TEL 888-426-0007, FAX 516-767-3485, subscriptions@aviatorsguide.com. Ed. Sean Fulton TEL 516-767-3325 ext 203. Pub. Joanne Persico TEL 516-767-3325 ext 204. Adv. contact Tom Ward. color page USD 4,785; trim 7.75 x 10.5. Circ: 40,000 (paid).

917.304 USA
AVIS TRAVELER. Text in English. 1989. s-a. USD 2 newsstand/cover (effective 2001). adv. **Description:** Offers maps, local business information, restaurant and entertainment guides, points of interest and things to do.
Published by: Wieland Publishing Company, Inc., 5457 Roswell Rd, 302, Atlanta, GA 30342. TEL 404-257-1682, FAX 404-256-3619. Ed. Erik Calonius. Pub. Louis A Wieland Jr. Circ: 2,500,000.

910.09 ITA
AVVENTURE NEL MONDO. Text in Italian. 1972. bi-m. adv. back issues avail. **Document type:** *Magazine, Consumer.* **Description:** Reports on adventure trips internationally.
Related titles: Online - full content ed.
Published by: Viaggi nel Mondo, Largo C. Grigioni, 7, Rome, RM 00152, Italy. TEL 39-6-532931, FAX 39-6-53293440, manager@viaggiavventurenelmondo.it. Circ: 100,000.

910.202 GBR
AWAY FROM IT ALL; guide to retreat houses and centres for spiritual renewal. Text in English. 1976. irreg., latest 1992, 5th ed. GBP 9.99, USD 19.99 (effective 2009). **Document type:** *Directory.* **Description:** Designed to guide nearly 200 guest houses, monasteries, convents, Buddhist and other retreat houses.
Published by: The Lutterworth Press, PO Box 60, Cambridge, Cambs CB1 2NT, United Kingdom. TEL 44-1223-350865, FAX 44-1223-366951, publishing@lutterworth.com.

B; a fashion and lifestyle magazine from Bloomingdale's. (Bloomingdale's) *see* CLOTHING TRADE—Fashions

910.09 GBR
B H & H P A JOURNAL. (British Holiday & Home Parks Association) Text in English. 1958. bi-m. free to members (effective 2009). adv. stat.; tr.lit. **Document type:** *Journal, Trade.* **Description:** Provides information on the holiday and home park industry, including reports on legislation and regulations affecting parks. Geared toward commercial operators of trailer parks in the U.K.
Formerly: N F S O Journal (National Federation of Site Operations)
Published by: British Holiday & Home Parks Association Ltd., Chichester House, 6 Pullman Ct, Great Western Rd, Gloucester, GL1 3ND, United Kingdom. TEL 44-1452-526911, FAX 44-1452-508508, enquiries@bhhpa.org.uk, http://www.bhhpa.org.uk.

B INTERNATIONAL. *see* GENERAL INTEREST PERIODICALS—Hong Kong, Special Administrative Region Of P R C

338.4 SGP ISSN 0218-9356
B T N ASIA-PACIFIC. (Business Travel News) Text in English. 1995. m. free to qualified personnel. **Document type:** *Newspaper, Trade.*
Published by: T T G Asia Media Pte Ltd, 6 Raffles Quay #16-02, Singapore, 048580, Singapore. TEL 65-6395-7575, FAX 65-6536-8639, contact@ttgasia.com, http://www.ttgasiamedia.com/. Ed. Raini Hamdi. Circ: 12,600.

B W MONTHLY; the British Waterways staff newspaper. (British Waterways) *see* TRANSPORTATION—Ships And Shipping

910.4 AUS ISSN 1328-6749
BACKPACKER ESSENTIALS; inspiration for independent travellers. Text in English. 1997. q. free to members (effective 2009). bk.rev. **Document type:** *Magazine, Consumer.* **Description:** Provides news and information on backpacker travel in Australia and around the world and YHA accommodation news.
Formerly (until 1997): On the Move
Related titles: Online - full text ed.
Published by: Y H A of N S W Inc., 422 Kent St, Near Town Hall Station and Queen Victoria Bldg, GPO Box 5276, Sydney, NSW 2001, Australia. TEL 61-2-92611111, FAX 61-2-92611969, yha@yhansw.org.au, http://www.yha.com.au. Circ: 110,000.

943 DEU ISSN 1434-6672
BAD TOELZ AKTUELL; Informationen und Veranstaltungen. Text in German. 1950. m. adv. play rev. **Document type:** *Magazine, Consumer.* **Description:** Information for visitors to Bad Toelz, including local events and health treatments.
Formerly: Kurjournal - Bad Toelz
Published by: Tourist-Information, Ludwigstr 11, Bad Toelz, 83646, Germany. TEL 49-8041-7867-0, FAX 49-8041-786756, info@bad-toelz.de, http://www.bad-toelz.de. Ed. Corinna Ewerdwalbesloh. Adv. contact Stephanie Lackermeier TEL 49-8041-7551936. B&W page EUR 290. Circ: 6,000 (controlled).

914 DEU
BAD WIESSEE AKTUELL. Text in German. m. adv. **Document type:** *Magazine, Consumer.*
Published by: Tourist Information Bad Wiessee, Adrian-Stoop-Str 20, Bad Wiessee, 83707, Germany. TEL 49-8022-86030, FAX 49-8022-860330, info@bad-wiessee.de, http://www.bad-wiessee.de. adv.: B&W page EUR 660. Circ: 5,400 (controlled).

908 DEU
BAEDERLAND BAYERISCHE RHOEN ERLEBEN. Text in German. 2003. s-a. EUR 2 newsstand/cover (effective 2010). adv. **Document type:** *Magazine, Consumer.*
Formerly (until 2006): Willkommen im Baederland Bayerische Rhoen
Published by: Mediengruppe Main-Post GmbH, Berner Str 2, Wuerzburg, 97084, Germany. TEL 49-931-60010, FAX 49-931-6001420, service.center@mainpost.de, http://www.mainpost.de.

BAHAMAS DATELINE. *see* BUSINESS AND ECONOMICS—Investments

910.2 CAN ISSN 1719-8895
BAIE - JAMES. Text in French. 2000. a. **Document type:** *Journal, Consumer.*
Former titles (until 2006): Baie - James, Nord-du-Quebec (1719-8879); (until 2004): Nord - du - Quebec, Baie - James (1495-8341); (until 2001): Guide Touristique, Nord - du - Quebec, Baie - James (1488-1845)
Related titles: English ed.: James Bay. ISSN 1719-8909.
Published by: Tourisme Baie-James, CP 134, Chibougamau, PQ G8P 2K6, Canada. TEL 418-748-8140, 888-748-8140, FAX 418-748-8150, info@tourismebaiejames.com, http://www.tourismebaiejames.com.

917.2 USA
BAJA LIFE; the magazine of Mexico's magnificent peninsula. Text in English. a. **Document type:** *Magazine, Consumer.*
Published by: Baja Life Magazine, Box 4917, Laguna Beach, CA 92652. TEL 949-376-2252, FAX 949-376-7575, erik@bajalife.com, http://www.bajalife.com. Ed. Erik Cutter.

910.2 USA ISSN 1941-3076
BAJA TRAVELER (CHULA VISTA). Text in English. 1999. a. USD 9.95 domestic; USD 14.95 in Canada; USD 19.90 elsewhere (effective 2008). adv. bk.rev. maps. 148 p./no. 3 cols./p.; back issues avail. **Document type:** *Magazine, Consumer.* **Description:** Covers vacation packages, hotels, food & entertainment in the Baja Peninsula.
Published by: I M C Publications, PO Box 210485, Chula Vista, CA 91921-0485. TEL 619-216-8035, FAX 619-216-8036.

944 796 FRA ISSN 1291-9896
BALADES NATURE. Text in French. 1999. irreg. EUR 12.16 newsstand/cover. back issues avail. **Document type:** *Monographic series, Consumer.*
Published by: Dakota Editions, 45 Rue Saint-Sebastien, Paris, 75011, France. TEL 33-1-55283700, FAX 33-1-55283707, contact@wdakota.com, http://www.wdakota.com/.

LE BALADEUR. *see* HANDICAPPED

379.8 ESP
BALEARES.COM. Text in English, German, Spanish. 1992. q. GBP 4.50 newsstand/cover. **Document type:** *Magazine, Consumer.* **Description:** Provides information on leisure activities and interests in the Mallorca region of Spain.
Formerly (until 200?): Baleares Magazine (Spanish Edition) (1578-8636); Which superseded in part (in 2001): Baleares Magazine (1134-1149); Which was formerly (until 1993): Baleares Golf (1134-6779)
Media: Online - full text.
Address: http://www.baleares.com.

910.91 330 USA
BANK TRAVEL MANAGEMENT; the magazine for bank loyalty directors. Text in English. 19??. bi-m. USD 49; free to qualified personnel (effective 2011). adv. **Document type:** *Magazine, Trade.*
Related titles: Online - full text ed.: free (effective 2011).
Published by: Group Travel Leader, Inc., 301 E High St, Lexington, KY 40507. TEL 859-253-0455. Pub. Mac T Lacy.

919.704 BRB
BARBADOS TOURISM AUTHORITY. ANNUAL REPORT. Text in English. 1972 (no.14). a. free. charts; illus. **Document type:** *Corporate.* **Description:** Records the Barbados Tourism Authority's function, structure, achievements, and undertakings.
Formerly: Barbados Tourist Board. Annual Report
Published by: Barbados Tourism Authority, PO Box 242, Bridgetown, Barbados. TEL 246-427-2623, FAX 246-426-4080, TELEX WB 2420. Ed. Kim Thorpe. Circ: 400.

338.4791 POL ISSN 0867-4264
BARBAKAN. Text in Polish. 1969. q.
Formerly (until 1990): Barbakan Warszawski (0209-1844)
Published by: Polskie Towarzystwo Turystyczno-Krajoznawcze, Zarzad Glowny, Ul Senatorska 11, Warsaw, 00075, Poland. TEL 48-22-8262251, FAX 48-22-8262505, cb@pttk.pl, http://www.pttk.pl. Ed. Jerzy Glownia TEL 48-42-6352752.

914 USA ISSN 1937-0393
DP402.B25
BARCELONA. Variant title: Eyewitness Travel Guide: Barcelona. Text in English. 2007. a. USD 20 (effective 2008). **Document type:** *Guide, Consumer.* **Description:** Provides information on local customs, currency, medical services and transportation facilities available in Barcelona.
Published by: D K Publishing (Subsidiary of: Penguin Books U S A, Inc.), 375 Hudson St, New York, NY 10014. TEL 800-631-8571, FAX 201-256-0000, specialsales@dk.com.

BARCOS. *see* SPORTS AND GAMES—Boats And Boating

910.91 914.204 GBR ISSN 1466-6634
BARNABY'S RELOCATION GUIDES. Text in English. 1999. irreg. GBP 14.95 per issue domestic; GBP 17, USD 24 per issue foreign (effective 2001).
Indexed: CA, M02, T02.
—CCC.
Published by: Cv Publications, 10 Barley Mow Passage, Cheswick, London, W4 4PH, United Kingdom. TEL 44-20-8400-6160, cvpub@tracksdirectory.ision.co.uk, http://www.tracksdirectory.ision.co.uk. Ed. Anna James. Pub., R&P Nick Wegner.

BASSMASTER'S TOP BASS DESTINATIONS; the travel guide for bass fishermen. *see* SPORTS AND GAMES—Outdoor Life

910.202 DEU
BAYERN ZEITUNG MAGAZIN; Nachrichten, Tips und Information aus dem Urlaubsland Bayern. Text in German. 1983. q. free. adv. back issues avail. **Document type:** *Newspaper, Consumer.* **Description:** Information about tourism in Bavaria.
Published by: (Bayerischer Tourismusverband), M T M Muenchen, Postfach 151505, Munich, 80049, Germany. TEL 49-89-747277-0, FAX 49-89-7250981. Ed. W E Matthaeus. Adv. contact Harald Zirnstein. Circ: 150,000.

338.4791 ZAF ISSN 1814-6619
BE MY GUEST. Text in English. 2005. a. free (effective 2006).
Published by: G S A Marketing Pty. Ltd., PO Box 2595, Claireinch, 7740, South Africa. TEL 27-21-6834433, FAX 27-21-6835100, http://www.the-gas.co.za. Pub. Jeff Hawthorne.

910.202 USA
BEACH HOUSES; for beach lovers everywhere!. Text in English. 2004. q. USD 9.99 (effective 2004). adv. **Document type:** *Magazine, Consumer.* **Description:** Showcases vacation beach houses around the world.
Published by: Rent101.com, 28 Clinton St, Saratoga Springs, NY 12866. TEL 518-581-1849, FAX 518-581-1492, info@rent101.com, http://www.rent101.com. adv.: color page USD 2,999; trim 8.375 x 10.875.

910.91 746.92 USA ISSN 1526-3908
BEACHSTYLE; your guide to sun fashion and travel. Text in English. 2000. bi-m. USD 3.99 newsstand/cover (effective 2001). adv.
Published by: Roxbury Media, LLC, 27 Glen Rd, PO Box 140, Sandy Hook, CT 06482.

910.91 746.92 USA
BEACHSTYLE PRESENTS SWIM IN STYLE. Text in English. 2000. q. adv. **Document type:** *Magazine, Consumer.*
Published by: Roxbury Media, LLC, 27 Glen Rd, PO Box 140, Sandy Hook, CT 06482. Ed. Bruce Shoengood. Pub. Kevin Montanaro.

338.4 USA
THE BEAT. Text in English. 200?. 49/yr. USD 425 (effective 2011). adv. back issues avail. **Document type:** *Newsletter, Trade.* **Description:** Contains information on travel distribution, business travel and business travel technology.
Media: Online - full text.
Published by: Business Travel Media Group, 116 W 32nd St, 14th Fl, New York, NY 10001. TEL 847-559-7533, 800-697-8859, FAX 847-291-4816, nbtn@omeda.com, http://www.promedia.travel/.

910.22 USA
BED & BREAKFAST NORTH AMERICA; a national directory for B & B travel. Text in English. irreg., latest vol.8. USD 15.95. illus. **Document type:** *Directory.* **Description:** Features historic Victorian Inns, intimate urban hotels, country inns, guesthouses and reservation services with details on prices, amenities, facilities, and attractions.
Published by: Betsy Ross Publications, 24406 S. Ribbonwood Dr., Sun Lakes, AZ 85248. TEL 602-895-2795. Pub. Norma Buzan.

914.2 GBR ISSN 0267-3363
BED & BREAKFAST STOPS. Text in English. 1975. a. GBP 8.99 per issue (effective 2009). adv. **Document type:** *Handbook/Manual/Guide, Consumer.* **Description:** Lists over 1400 overnight stops throughout the UK.
Published by: F H G Guides Ltd. (Subsidiary of: F H G Publications Ltd.), Abbey Mill Business Ctr, Seedhill, Paisley, PA1 1TJ, United Kingdom. TEL 44-141-8870428, FAX 44-141-8897204, sales@fhguides.co.uk, http://www.fhguides.co.uk.

910.202 USA
BED AND BREAKFAST U S A; guide to tourist homes and guest houses. Text in English. 1977. a.
Formerly: Guide to Tourist Homes and Guest Houses
Published by: Penguin Books U S A, Inc., 375 Hudson St, New York, NY 10014. TEL 800-526-0275, FAX 800-227-9604. Ed. Peggy Ackerman.

338.4791 CHE
BEITRAEGE ZUM OEFFENTLICHEN MANAGEMENT. Variant title: Institut fuer Oeffentliche Dienstleistungen und Tourismus. Schriftenreihe. Text in German. 1999. irreg., latest vol.6, 2002. price varies. **Document type:** *Monographic series, Academic/Scholarly.*
Published by: (Institut fuer Oeffentliche Dienstleistungen und Tourismus), Paul Haupt AG, Falkenplatz 14, Bern, 3001, Switzerland. TEL 41-31-3012425, FAX 41-31-3014669, verlag@haupt.ch, http://www.haupt.ch.

914.41670405 IRL ISSN 1747-0021
BELFAST IN YOUR POCKET. Text in English. 2005. bi-m. adv. **Document type:** *Handbook/Manual/Guide, Consumer.*
Related titles: Online - full text ed.: ISSN 1747-003X.
Address: 100 Sandown Rd, Belfast, BT5 6GW, Ireland. TEL 44-28-90913510, editorial_enquiry@inyourpocket.com.

913.0493 USA
BELGIUM TODAY. Text in English. 1997. bi-m.
Media: Online - full content.
Published by: Embassy of Belgium, Investments Office, 3330 Garfield St N W, Washington, DC 20008. BelgiumToday@diplobel.org, http://www.diplobel.org/usa/.

918 USA ISSN 1521-2815
BELIZE FIRST MAGAZINE. Text in English. 1993. q. USD 29 domestic; USD 49 foreign (effective 2000). bk.rev. **Document type:** *Magazine, Consumer.* **Description:** Covers travel, life and potential retirement in Belize.
Related titles: Online - full text ed.
Address: 280 Beaverdam Rd, Candler, NC 28715. Ed., Pub. Lan Sluder. Circ: 4,500 (paid); 40,000 (controlled).

910.202 ITA ISSN 1124-8408
BELL'EUROPA; alla scoperta del contiente piu bello del mondo. Text in Italian. 1993. m. EUR 34 domestic; EUR 72 foreign (effective 2008). adv. illus. **Document type:** *Magazine, Consumer.* **Description:** Presents the art, architecture, geography, history, culture and traditions of Europe.
Published by: Editoriale Giorgio Mondadori SpA (Subsidiary of: Cairo Communication SpA), Via Tucidide 56, Torre 3, Milan, 20134, Italy. TEL 39-02-748111, FAX 39-02-70100102, info@cairocommunication.it, http://www.cairocommunication.it. Ed. Luciano Di Pietro. Circ: 140,000.

910.09 ITA ISSN 0394-7203
DG401
BELL'ITALIA; alla scoperta del paese piu bello del mondo. Text in Italian. 1986. m. EUR 36 domestic; EUR 74 foreign (effective 2008). adv. illus. **Document type:** *Magazine, Consumer.*
Published by: Editoriale Giorgio Mondadori SpA (Subsidiary of: Cairo Communication SpA), Via Tucidide 56, Torre 3, Milan, 20134, Italy. TEL 39-02-748111, FAX 39-02-70100102, info@cairocommunication.it, http://www.cairocommunication.it. Ed. Luciano Di Pietro. Circ: 140,000.

910.09 USA ISSN 1543-0014
DG401
BELL'ITALIA; discover Italy's beauty and hidden treasures. Text in English. 2003. bi-m. USD 18.95 domestic; USD 30.95 in Canada; USD 36.95 elsewhere (effective 2003). adv. **Document type:** *Magazine, Consumer.* **Description:** Provides indepth information and an up-close look at the art, architecture, history, culture and traditions of Italy.
Published by: Beautiful Publishing Inc., PO Box 4137, Grand Central Sta, New York, NY 10169. Ed. Steven Wagner. Pub. Amedeo Angiolillo. Adv. contact Deneen M Vukelic.

910.91 AUS ISSN 1833-1289
BENDIGO MAGAZINE. Text in English. 2005. q. **Document type:** *Magazine, Consumer.*
Address: PO Box 2523, Bendigo Delivery Centre, VIC 3554, Australia. FAX 61-3-5444-1044, mail@bendigomagazine.com, http://www.bendigomagazine.com/index.html.

910.2 USA ISSN 1556-2468
THE BERKSHIRE SAVANT; a savvy guide to the Berkshires. Text in English. 2005. q. **Document type:** *Guide, Consumer.*
Published by: Berkshire Publishing Group, 314 Main St, Great Barrington, MA 01230. TEL 413-528-0206, FAX 413-528-5241, http://berkshirepublishing.com.

914 USA ISSN 1937-0407
DD859
BERLIN. Variant title: Eyewitness Travel Guide: Berlin. Text in English. 2007. a. USD 25 (effective 2008). **Document type:** *Guide, Consumer.* **Description:** Provides information on monuments, museums and art collections of Berlin.
Published by: D K Publishing (Subsidiary of: Penguin Books U S A, Inc.), 375 Hudson St, New York, NY 10014. TEL 800-631-8571, FAX 201-256-0000, specialsales@dk.com.

914 DEU ISSN 0005-9250
BERLIN PROGRAMM. Text in German. 1951. m. EUR 20; EUR 1.75 newsstand/cover (effective 2006). adv. illus. **Document type:** *Magazine, Consumer.* **Description:** Covers restaurants, museums, operas, theaters and galleries in the Berlin and Potsdam areas.
Published by: Rimbach Verlag GmbH, Postfach 370144, Berlin, 14131, Germany. TEL 49-30-8021071, FAX 49-30-8029988. Adv. contact Rainer Rimbach. B&W page EUR 1,500, color page EUR 2,625. Circ: 31,827 (paid and controlled).

BERLIN VON HINTEN; das Schwule Reisebuch. *see* HOMOSEXUALITY

919.404 USA
DU95
BERLITZ AUSTRALIA POCKET GUIDE. Variant title: Australia Berlitz Travel Guide. Text in English. 1989. a. USD 10.95 per issue (effective 2009). illus.; maps. **Document type:** *Magazine, Consumer.* **Description:** Contains must-see sights on and off the beaten track in Australia as well as current hotel and restaurant recommendations.
Former titles: Berlitz Travellers Guide to Australia (1057-4689); (until 1992): Penguin Guide to Australia (0897-6880)
Related titles: French ed.

Published by: Berlitz International, Inc., 400 Alexander Park Dr, Princeton, NJ 08540. TEL 609-514-3055, FAX 609-514-9681, publishing@berlitz.com, http://www.berlitz.com.

914.304 USA
DD859
BERLITZ BERLIN POCKET GUIDE. Variant title: Berlin Berlitz Travel Guide. Text in English. 1993. a. USD 8.95 per issue (effective 2009). illus.; maps. **Document type:** *Magazine, Consumer.* **Description:** Features information on various attractions and also contains photographs and detailed, easy-to-use maps.
Formerly: Berlitz Travellers Guide to Berlin (1065-6294)
Related titles: French ed.
Published by: Berlitz International, Inc., 400 Alexander Park Dr, Princeton, NJ 08540. TEL 609-514-3055, FAX 609-514-9681, publishing@berlitz.com, http://www.berlitz.com.

917.904 USA
BERLITZ CALIFORNIA POCKET GUIDE. Variant title: Berliz California. Text in English. 1991. a. illus.; maps. **Document type:** *Magazine, Consumer.* **Description:** Offers a handy reference and guide to what to see and do and where to stay throughout California.
Supersedes in part: Berlitz Travellers Guide to San Francisco and Northern California (1057-4727); Which was formerly (until 1992): Penguin Guide to San Francisco and Northern California (1049-1449)
Related titles: Spanish ed.; French ed.
Published by: Berlitz International, Inc., 3333 E Camelback Rd, Ste 160, Phoenix, AZ 85018. TEL 888-281-9704, http://www.berlitz.us/.

917.104 USA
F1009
BERLITZ CANADA POCKET GUIDE. Text in English. 1989. a. illus.; maps. **Document type:** *Magazine, Consumer.* **Description:** Offers a handy reference and guide to what to see and do and where to stay throughout Canada.
Former titles: Berlitz Travellers Guide to Canada (1057-4778); (until 1992): Penguin Guide to Canada (0897-6872)
Related titles: French ed.
Published by: Berlitz International, Inc., 3333 E Camelback Rd, Ste 160, Phoenix, AZ 85018. TEL 888-281-9704, http://www.berlitz.us/.

917.204 USA ISSN 1527-8824
F1543.5
BERLITZ COSTA RICA POCKET GUIDE. Variant title: Costa Rica Berlitz Travel Guide. Text in English. 1994. a. USD 8.95 per issue (effective 2009). illus.; maps. **Document type:** *Magazine, Consumer.* **Description:** Contains must-see sights on and off the beaten track in Costa Rica as well as current hotel and restaurant recommendations.
Formerly (until 199?): The Berlitz Travellers Guide to Costa Rica (1067-7135)
Related titles: German ed.
Published by: Berlitz International, Inc., 400 Alexander Park Dr, Princeton, NJ 08540. TEL 609-514-3055, FAX 609-514-9681, publishing@berlitz.com, http://www.berlitz.com.

914.404 USA ISSN 1528-2937
DC16
BERLITZ FRANCE POCKET GUIDE. Variant title: Berlitz France. Text in English. 1989. a. illus.; maps. **Document type:** *Magazine, Consumer.* **Description:** Offers a handy reference and guide to what to see and do and where to stay throughout France.
Former titles (until 1994): The Berlitz Travellers Guide to France (1057-476X); (until 1992): The Penguin Guide to France (0897-683X)
Published by: Berlitz International, Inc., 3333 E Camelback Rd, Ste 160, Phoenix, AZ 85018. TEL 888-281-9704, http://www.berlitz.us/.

914.9504 USA ISSN 1527-8751
DF895
BERLITZ GREEK ISLANDS OF THE AEGEAN POCKET GUIDE. Text in English. 1990. a. illus.; maps. **Document type:** *Magazine, Consumer.* **Description:** Offers a handy guide to what to see and do and where to stay throughout the Greek islands.
Supersedes in part: Berlitz Travellers Guide to Greece (1057-4670); Which was formerly (until 1992): Penguin Guide to Greece (1043-4607)
Related titles: French ed.
Published by: Berlitz International, Inc., 3333 E Camelback Rd, Ste 160, Phoenix, AZ 85018. TEL 888-281-9704, http://www.berlitz.us/.

917.904 USA ISSN 1528-2988
DU622
BERLITZ HAWAII POCKET GUIDE. Variant title: Hawaii Berlitz Travel Guide. Text in English. 1990. a. USD 8.95 per issue (effective 2009). illus.; maps. **Document type:** *Magazine, Consumer.* **Description:** Contains must-see sights on and off the beaten track in Hawaii as well as current hotel and restaurant recommendations.
Former titles (until 199?): Berlitz Travellers Guide to Hawaii (1057-4700); (until 1992): Penguin Guide to Hawaii (1043-4569)
Published by: Berlitz International, Inc., 400 Alexander Park Dr, Princeton, NJ 08540. TEL 609-514-3055, FAX 609-514-9681, publishing@berlitz.com, http://www.berlitz.com. **Subscr. to:** PO Box 3239, Princeton, NJ 08543.

914.104 USA
DA980
BERLITZ IRELAND POCKET GUIDE. Text in English. 1989. a. illus.; maps. **Document type:** *Magazine, Consumer.* **Description:** Offers a handy reference and guide to what to see and do and where to stay in Ireland.
Former titles: Berlitz Travellers Guide to Ireland (1057-4719); (until 1992): Penguin Guide to Ireland (0897-6856)
Related titles: French ed.
Published by: Berlitz International, Inc., 400 Alexander Park Dr, Princeton, NJ 08540. TEL 609-514-3055, FAX 609-514-9681, publishing@berlitz.com, http://www.berlitz.com.

914.504 USA
DG416
BERLITZ ITALY POCKET GUIDE. Variant title: Italy Berlitz Travel Guide. Text in English. 1989. a. USD 10.95 per issue (effective 2009). illus.; maps. **Document type:** *Magazine, Consumer.* **Description:** Contains must-see sights on and off the beaten track in Italy as well as current hotel and restaurant recommendations.
Supersedes in part: Berlitz Travellers Guide to Northern Italy and Rome (1057-4654); Berlitz Travellers Guide to Southern Italy and Rome (1057-4662); Both of which superseded in part (in 1992): Penguin Guide to Italy (0897-6848)
Related titles: French ed.
Published by: Berlitz International, Inc., 400 Alexander Park Dr, Princeton, NJ 08540. TEL 609-514-3055, FAX 609-514-9681, publishing@berlitz.com, http://www.berlitz.com.

914.204 USA ISSN 1528-493X
DA679
BERLITZ LONDON POCKET GUIDE. Variant title: Berlitz London. London Pocket Guide. Text in English. 1991. a. illus.; maps. **Document type:** *Magazine, Consumer.* **Description:** Offers a handy reference guide to what to see and do and where to stay in London and the surrounding area.
Former titles (until 1996): The Berlitz Travellers Guide to London (1057-4751); (until 1992): The Penguin Guide to London (1049-1457)
Related titles: Spanish ed.; French ed.
Published by: Berlitz International, Inc., 3333 E Camelback Rd, Ste 160, Phoenix, AZ 85018. TEL 888-281-9704, http://www.berlitz.us/.

917.204 USA
F1209
BERLITZ MEXICO POCKET GUIDE. Text in English. 1990. a. illus.; maps. **Document type:** *Magazine, Consumer.* **Description:** Provides a handy tourist reference of what to see and do in Mexico.
Former titles: Berlitz Travellers Guide to Mexico (1057-4786); (until 1992): Penguin Guide to Mexico (1043-4577)
Related titles: Spanish ed.
Published by: Berlitz International, Inc., 3333 E Camelback Rd, Ste 160, Phoenix, AZ 85018. TEL 888-281-9704, http://www.berlitz.us/.

914.304 USA ISSN 1527-8794
D901.M76
BERLITZ MUNICH POCKET GUIDE. Text in English. 1990. a. illus.; maps. **Document type:** *Magazine, Consumer.* **Description:** Offers a handy reference to what to see and do and where to stay in Munich.
Supersedes in part: Berlitz Travellers Guide to Germany (1057-462X); Which was formerly (until 1992): Penguin Guide to Germany (1043-4615)
Related titles: Spanish ed.; French ed.
Published by: Berlitz International, Inc., 400 Alexander Park Dr, Princeton, NJ 08540. TEL 609-514-3055, FAX 609-514-9681, publishing@berlitz.com, http://www.berlitz.com.

917.404 USA ISSN 1528-4956
F128.18
BERLITZ NEW YORK POCKET GUIDE. Variant title: New York City Berlitz Travel Guide. Text in English. 1989. a. USD 8.95 per issue (effective 2009). illus.; maps. **Document type:** *Magazine, Consumer.* **Description:** Contains must-see sights on and off the beaten track in New York as well as current hotel and restaurant recommendations.
Former titles (until 1994): Berlitz Travellers Guide to New York City (1057-4743); (until 1992): Penguin Guide to New York City (0898-8072)
Related titles: Spanish ed.; French ed.
Published by: Berlitz International, Inc., 400 Alexander Park Dr, Princeton, NJ 08540. TEL 609-514-3055, FAX 609-514-9681, publishing@berlitz.com, http://www.berlitz.com.

914.604 USA ISSN 1528-459X
DP516
BERLITZ PORTUGAL POCKET GUIDE. Text in English. 1990. a. illus.; maps. **Document type:** *Magazine, Consumer.* **Description:** Offers a handy reference of what to do and see in Portugal.
Former titles (until 1996): Berlitz Travellers Guide to Portugal (1057-4646); (until 1992): Penguin Guide to Portugal (1043-4585)
Related titles: French ed.
Published by: Berlitz International, Inc., 400 Alexander Park Dr, Princeton, NJ 08540. TEL 609-514-3055, FAX 609-514-9681, publishing@berlitz.com, http://www.berlitz.com.

917.904 USA
F869.S33
BERLITZ SAN FRANCISCO POCKET GUIDE. Variant title: San Francisco Berlitz Travel Guide. Text in English. 1991. a. USD 8.95 per issue (effective 2009). illus.; maps. **Document type:** *Magazine, Consumer.* **Description:** Contains must-see sights on and off the beaten track in San Francisco as well as current hotel and restaurant recommendations.
Supersedes in part: Berlitz Travellers Guide to San Francisco and Northern California (1057-4727); Which was formerly (until 1992): Penguin Guide to San Francisco and Northern California (1049-1449)
Related titles: French ed.
Published by: Berlitz International, Inc., 400 Alexander Park Dr, Princeton, NJ 08540. TEL 609-514-3055, FAX 609-514-9681, publishing@berlitz.com, http://www.berlitz.com.

917.204 USA ISSN 1528-7831
F1609
BERLITZ SOUTHERN CARIBBEAN POCKET GUIDE. Variant title: Berlitz Southern Caribbean. Text in English. 1989. a. illus.; maps. **Description:** Offers a practical guide and reference to what to see and do in the southern Caribbean islands.
Supersedes in part (199?): The Berlitz Travellers Guide to the Caribbean (1057-4697); Which was formerly (until 1992): The Penguin Guide to the Caribbean (0897-6821)
Related titles: French ed.
Published by: Berlitz International, Inc., 3333 E Camelback Rd, Ste 160, Phoenix, AZ 85018. TEL 888-281-9704, http://www.berlitz.us/.

914.604 USA ISSN 1528-4913
DP14
BERLITZ SPAIN POCKET GUIDE. Variant title: Spain Berlitz Travel Guide. Text in English. 1990. a. USD 10.95 per issue (effective 2009). illus.; maps. **Document type:** *Magazine, Consumer.* **Description:** Contains must-see sights on and off the beaten track in Spain as well as current hotel and restaurant recommendations.
Former titles (until 1996): Berlitz Travellers Guide to Spain (1057-4638); (until 1992): Penguin Guide to Spain (1043-4593)
Related titles: French ed.
Published by: Berlitz International, Inc., 400 Alexander Park Dr, Princeton, NJ 08540. TEL 609-514-3055, FAX 609-514-9681, publishing@berlitz.com, http://www.berlitz.com.

915.6104 USA ISSN 1528-4921
DR416
BERLITZ TURKEY POCKET GUIDE. Key Title: Turkey (Princeton, N.J.). Text in English. 19??. a. illus.; maps. **Document type:** *Magazine, Consumer.* **Description:** Offers a handy guide to what to see and do and where to stay in Turkey.
Former titles (until 199?): Berlitz Travellers Guide to Turkey (1049-1465); (until 1992): Penguin Guide to Turkey
Related titles: French ed.
Published by: Berlitz International, Inc., 400 Alexander Park Dr, Princeton, NJ 08540. TEL 609-514-3055, FAX 609-514-9681, publishing@berlitz.com, http://www.berlitz.com.

910.91 BMU
BERMUDA. Text in English. q. USD 19.85; USD 3.95 newsstand/cover (effective 2001). adv. **Description:** Contains travel information for those planning to visit Bermuda.
Published by: Bermuda Marketing Ltd, Continenatl Bldg, 25 Church St, Hamilton, HM 12, Bermuda. TEL 441-292-7279, FAX 441-295-3189. Pub. Ian Coles. Adv. contact Lissa Fisher.

914 CHE ISSN 1661-3856
BERN EVENTS/SEMAINE A BERNE/THIS WEEK IN BERNE. Text in English, French, German. 1943. m. illus. **Document type:** *Magazine, Consumer.*
Former titles (until 2005): What's On (1660-5322); (until 2002): Bern Aktuell (1660-5314); (until 1994): Berner Wochen Bulletin (0005-9412)
Published by: Bern Tourismus, Amthausgasse 4, PO Box 169, Bern 7, 3000, Switzerland. TEL 41-31-3281242, FAX 41-31-3281299, info@berninfo.com, http://www.berninfo.com. Circ: 7,200.

910 330 CHE ISSN 1420-6927
BERNER STUDIEN ZU FREIZEIT UND TOURISMUS. Text in German. 1966. irreg., latest vol.52, 2010. price varies. **Document type:** *Monographic series, Academic/Scholarly.*
Formerly (until 1989): Berner Studien zum Fremdenverkehr (0067-6152)
Published by: Universitaet Bern, Forschungsinstitut fuer Freizeit und Tourismus (Subsidiary of: Universitaet Bern), Schanzeneckstr 1, Bern, 3001, Switzerland. TEL 41-31-6313711, FAX 41-31-6313415, fif@fif.unibe.ch, http://www.fif.unibe.ch.

912 USA ISSN 1054-4089
TX907.5.G7
BEST BED & BREAKFAST IN ENGLAND, SCOTLAND & WALES. Text in English. 1992. a., latest 2008, 23rd ed. USD 19.95 per issue (effective 2008). back issues avail. **Document type:** *Guide, Consumer.* **Description:** Provides information on bed and breakfast accommodations in England, Scotland and Wales.
Formerly (until 1991): Best Bed and Breakfast in the World (1057-5472)
Published by: The Globe Pequot Press, Inc., 246 Goose Ln, PO Box 480, Guilford, CT 06437. TEL 203-458-4500, 888-249-7586, FAX 203-458-4603, 800-820-2329, info@globepequot.com, http://www.globepequot.com.

917.2 USA ISSN 1541-1397
GV199.42.C22
BEST EASY DAY HIKES: SEQUOIA AND KINGS CANYON NATIONAL PARKS. Text in English. 2002. irreg., latest 2002, 1st ed. USD 7.95 per issue (effective 2008). back issues avail. **Document type:** *Guide, Consumer.* **Description:** Includes concise descriptions and detailed maps for twenty mostly short, easy-to-follow trails that lead to some of the parks' most scenic destinations.
Published by: The Globe Pequot Press, Inc., 246 Goose Ln, PO Box 480, Guilford, CT 06437. TEL 203-458-4500, 888-249-7586, FAX 203-458-4603, 800-820-2329, info@globepequot.com.

BEST EVENTS BOSTON; special events resource directory. *see* MEETINGS AND CONGRESSES

▼ **BEST EVENTS CALIFORNIA**; special events resource directory. *see* MEETINGS AND CONGRESSES

BEST EVENTS CHICAGO; special events resource directory. *see* MEETINGS AND CONGRESSES

BEST EVENTS NEW YORK; special events resource directory. *see* MEETINGS AND CONGRESSES

BEST EVENTS WASHINGTON; special events resource directory. *see* MEETINGS AND CONGRESSES

910.09 USA
BEST OF MAUI; best of Maui sports, recreation, dining and shopping. Text in English. 1988. a. USD 15. adv. bk.rev. back issues avail. **Document type:** *Magazine, Consumer.*
Published by: Sandwich Islands Publishing Co., PO Box 10669, Lahaina, HI 96761. TEL 808-661-5844, FAX 808-661-9878. Ed., R&P Joe Harabin. Pub. Jamir Arnold. Adv. contact Jaime S Arnold. Circ: 20,000.

917 USA
BEST OF NEW ORLEANS; ultimate guide for visitors. Text in English. 1996. m. USD 32 (effective 2002). adv. **Document type:** *Magazine, Consumer.*
Former titles: Natives' Guide to New Orleans (1093-6955); (until 1997): Best of New Orleans (1090-6665)
Published by: Gambit Communications, Inc., 3923 Bienville St, New Orleans, LA 70119. TEL 504-486-5900, response@bestofneworleans.com, http://www.bestofneworleans.com. Ed. Michael Tisserand. Pub. Margo DuBos. Adv. contact Sandy Stein.

910 AUS
BEST OF THE GOLD COAST MAGAZINE. Text in English. 1986. q. free (effective 2009). adv. **Document type:** *Magazine, Trade.* **Description:** Includes news on tourism for the gold coast.
Formerly (until 1994): PointOut Magazine
Published by: PointOut Productions, PO Box 1, Molendinar, QLD 4215, Australia. TEL 61-7-55842744, FAX 61-7-55842784, info@pointout.com.au, http://www.pointout.com.au.

910.202 USA ISSN 1546-7686
F350.3
BEST OF THE MIDWEST. Variant title: Best Vacations. Midwest Living Best of the Midwest. Text in English. 2001. a. USD 29.95 per issue (effective 2009). **Document type:** *Magazine, Consumer.* **Description:** Provides travel advice and information for exploring the Midwest United States.
Formerly: Midwest Living Best Vacations
Related titles: ◆ Supplement to: Midwest Living. ISSN 0889-8138.
Published by: Meredith Corporation, 1716 Locust St, Des Moines, IA 50309. TEL 515-284-3000, 800-678-8091, FAX 515-284-3058, patrick.taylor@meredith.com, http://www.meredith.com.

917.954 USA
BEST PLACES PORTLAND. Text in English. 1990. irreg. USD 19.95 newsstand/cover (effective 2006).

TU

Formerly (until 2001): Portland Best Places (1095-9742)
Published by: Sasquatch Books, 119 S Main, Ste 400, Seattle, WA 98104. TEL 206-467-4300, 800-775-0817, FAX 206-467-4301, custserv@sasquatchbooks.com, http://www.sasquatchbooks.com. Ed. John Gottberg.

919.3 NZL ISSN 1179-8955
BEST WEEKENDS & SHORT BREAKS. Text in English. 2007. q. free to qualified personnel (effective 2010). **Document type:** *Magazine, Consumer.*
Formerly (until 2010): Weekend (1178-1254)
Published by: People Publishing Ltd., Ground Fl, 26 Albert St, PO Box 7070, Wellesley St, Auckland, 1141, New Zealand. TEL 64-9-3666879, FAX 64-9-3666838, info@peoplepublishing.co.nz, http://www.peoplepublishing.co.nz. Ed. Patrick Smith.

DIE BESTEN! GOLFCLUBS UND GOLFRESORTS. *see* SPORTS AND GAMES—Ball Games

910.2 USA
BEYOND FUN; the ultimate family activities guide. Text in English. 20??. m. **Document type:** *Magazine, Consumer.*
Published by: Churm Media, 1451 Quail St, Ste 201, Newport Beach, CA 92660. TEL 949-757-1404 ext 303, FAX 949-757-1996, info@churmpublishing.com, http://www.churmmedia.com.

910.91 USA
BIG ISLAND VISITOR. Text in English. m. 80 p./no.; **Document type:** *Magazine, Consumer.*
Related titles: Online - full content ed.
Published by: Visitor Magazines LLC, 1498 Lower Main St, Ste F, Wailuku, HI 96793. http://www.visitormagazines.com/.

BILDUNG+ REISEN. *see* CHILDREN AND YOUTH—About

BILL STRONG'S MISSISSIPPI PHOTOGRAPHY TRAVEL CULTURE. *see* PHOTOGRAPHY

910.2 USA ISSN 1931-0390
F2165
BIRNBAUM'S DISNEY CRUISE LINE. Text in English. 2004. a., latest 2007. USD 13.95 per issue (effective 2007). **Document type:** *Guide, Consumer.*
Published by: Disney Editions, 114 Fifth Ave, New York, NY 10011-5690. TEL 212-633-4400.

910.202 DEU
BIZTRAVEL; Geschaeftsreisen besser planen und einkaufen. Text in German. 2006. q. EUR 10 domestic; EUR 18 foreign (effective 2010). adv. **Document type:** *Magazine, Trade.*
Published by: Verlag Dieter Niedecken GmbH, Wandsbeker Allee 1, Hamburg, 22041, Germany. TEL 49-40-414480, FAX 49-40-41448999, info@niedeckenmedien.de, http://www.niedeckenmedien.de. Ed. Oliver Graue. adv.: page EUR 8,250. Circ: 31,463 (paid).

BLACK DIAMOND LIVING; celebrating the jewels of the East Bay. *see* GENERAL INTEREST PERIODICALS—United States

910.2 060 305.896 USA
BLACK MEETINGS & TOURISM. Text in English. 1993. bi-m. USD 45; USD 6 newsstand/cover (effective 2009). adv. **Document type:** *Magazine, Trade.* **Description:** Resource for all business and leisure travel needs. Provides vital information about professional accomplishments, achievements, career opportunities, and cultural events related to the travel, meetings and hospitality industries.
Published by: Black Meetings & Tourism / Sunglo Enterprises, 20840 Chase St, Winnetka, CA 91306-1207. TEL 818-709-0646, FAX 818-709-4753, info@blackmeetingsandtourism.com. Ed., Pub. Solomon J Herbert. Adv. contact Regina Buggs. B&W page USD 5,605, color page USD 7,198; trim 8.375 x 10.875. Circ: 20,150 (paid).

338.4791 305.896 USA
BLACK TRAVELER MAGAZINE. Text in English. 1991. m. USD 15; USD 20 foreign. adv. **Document type:** *Magazine, Consumer.* **Description:** News of the Black tourism, leisure, convention and business traveler.
Formerly: Black Convention Magazine
Published by: A & E Publishing, Inc., PO Box 15716, N. Hollywood, CA 91615-5716. TEL 818-753-9198, FAX 818-753-8405. Ed. Elizabeth Flournoy. Pub. Stanley Bethel. adv.: B&W page USD 6,300, color page USD 8,085; trim 10.88 x 8.13. Circ: 150,000.

796.95 914.2 GBR
BLAKES HOLIDAY BOATING. Text in English. 1974. a. free. illus. **Document type:** *Magazine, Consumer.*
Former titles: Blakes Holiday Boating in Britain and Abroad; Blakes Boating in Britain; Which superseded in part: Blakes Boating Holidays; Which superseded: Blakes Boating in Britain; Blakes Boating in Europe; Blakes Boating in Britain & Blakes Boating in Europe; Which superseded in part: Blakes Holidays Afloat; Which was formed by the merger of: Blakes International Holidays Afloat & Norfolk Broads Holidays Afloat (0078-1142)
Published by: Blakes Holidays Ltd., Spring Mill, Earby, Barnoldswick, Lancs BB94 0AA, United Kingdom. TEL 44-845-6043985, http://www.blakes.co.uk. Ed. T E Howes. Circ: 400,000.

910.202 AUT
BLICK. Text in German. m.
Address: Postfach 4, Groebming, St 8962, Austria. TEL 3685-22191, FAX 3685-22476. Ed. Winfried Halasz. Circ: 30,600.

910.2 USA
BLUE. Text in English. bi-m. USD 19.95 domestic; CAD 29.95 in Canada; USD 34.95 elsewhere (effective 2002). **Document type:** *Magazine, Consumer.*
Address: 611 Broadway, Ste 405, New York, NY 10012. Ed., Pub. Amy Schrier.

BLUE BOOK OF EUROPEAN SKI RESORTS. *see* SPORTS AND GAMES—Outdoor Life

BLUE BOOK: THE DIRECTORY OF GEOGRAPHIC, TRAVEL & DESTINATION STOCK PHOTOGRAPHY. *see* PHOTOGRAPHY

910.92 796 CAN ISSN 1710-3215
BLUE LAKE INFORMATION GUIDE. Text in English. 2004. a. **Document type:** *Handbook/Manual/Guide, Consumer.*
Published by: Ontario Ministry of Natural Resources, Ontario Parks, PO Box 7000, Peterborough, ON K9J 8M5, Canada. TEL 705-755-2000, http://www.ontarioparks.com, http://www.mnr.gov.on.ca.

910.91 051 USA
BLUE RIDGE HIGHLANDER; the most creative e-zine on the Blue Ridge and North Georgia mountains. Text in English. 1998. m. free. back issues avail.
Media: Online - full text.
Address: P O Box 2487, Blue Ridge, GA 30513. TEL 706-632-3471, FAX 706-374-4617. Pubs. Charles Wayne Dukes, Sherry Bell Dukes.

910.2 DEU
BLUE TRAVEL. Text in German. bi-m. EUR 29.60; EUR 4.80 newsstand/cover (effective 2006). adv. **Document type:** *Magazine, Consumer.*
Published by: J. Fink Verlag GmbH & Co. KG, Zeppelinstr 32, Ostfildern, 73760, Germany. TEL 49-711-4506463, FAX 49-711-4506459, verlag@jfink.de, http://www.jfink.de. Eds. Georgia van Uffelen, Gertrud Schmid-Heupel. Pub. Frieder Stein. Adv. contact Sandra Wilderer. page EUR 6,800. Circ: 70,000 (paid and controlled).

910.91 CAN
BOATING EAST CRUISING & VACATION GUIDE. Text in English. 1982. s-a. free. adv. bk.rev.; play rev. **Document type:** *Handbook/Manual/Guide, Consumer.* **Description:** Guide to supplies and services in Marinas in eastern Ontario and northern New York.
Published by: Marble Rock Publishing, R R 2, Gananoque, ON K7G 2V4, Canada. TEL 613-382-5735, FAX 613-382-1118. Ed. Morison Bock. Pub., R&P, Adv. contact Kathrine Christensen. B&W page CAD 1,000. Circ: 25,000.

BOBIL & CARAVAN; fritidsmagasinet. *see* SPORTS AND GAMES—Outdoor Life

BOCA RATON MAGAZINE. *see* GENERAL INTEREST PERIODICALS—United States

379.85 DEU ISSN 0178-4692
BODENSEE MAGAZIN. Text in German. 1985. a. EUR 5 newsstand/cover (effective 2006). adv. **Document type:** *Magazine, Consumer.*
Published by: Labhard Verlag GmbH, Zum Hussenstein 7, Konstanz, 78462, Germany. TEL 49-7531-9071-0, FAX 49-7531-907131. adv.: B&W page EUR 5,290, color page EUR 6,590. Circ: 115,000 (controlled).

BOLERO; Das Schweizer Magazin fuer Mode, Beauty, Lifestyle. *see* CLOTHING TRADE—Fashions

333.3 NOR ISSN 0809-6562
BOLIG I UTLANDET. Text in Norwegian. 2005. bi-m. NOK 375 (effective 2009). **Document type:** *Magazine, Consumer.*
Published by: Aller Forlag AS, Stenersgaten 2, Sentrum, Oslo, 0189, Norway. TEL 47-21-301000, FAX 47-21-301205, allerforlag@aller.no, http://www.aller.no.

910.202 GBR ISSN 1368-4264
F3308
BOLIVIA HANDBOOK. Text in English. 1997. biennial, latest 2008. GBP 14.99 per vol. (effective 2009). adv. **Document type:** *Directory, Consumer.*
—CCC.
Published by: Footprint Handbooks Ltd., 6 Riverside Ct, Lower Bristol Rd, Bath, Avon BA2 3DZ, United Kingdom. TEL 44-1225-469141, FAX 44-1225-469461, info@footprintbooks.com.

917.2 CAN
BONAIRE NIGHTS. Text in English. q. **Document type:** *Journal, Consumer.*
Published by: Nights Publications, 1831 Rene Levesque Blvd W, Montreal, PQ H3H 1R4, Canada. FAX 514-931-6273, editor@nightspublications.com. Ed. Stephen Trotter.

910.2 ITA ISSN 1972-6015
I BORGHI PIU BELLI D'ITALIA. Text in Italian. 2003. a. **Document type:** *Consumer.*
Published by: Societa Editrice Romana (S E R), Piazza Cola di Rienzo 85, Rome, 00192, Italy. TEL 39-06-36004654, FAX 39-06-36001296, http://www.editriceromana.com.

910.2 USA
BOSTON & CAMBRIDGE OFFICIAL VISITORS GUIDE. Variant title: Boston and Cambridge Official Visitors Guide. Text in English. 2007. s-a. adv. **Document type:** *Guide, Consumer.* **Description:** Offers information about accommodations, restaurants, shopping, attractions, transportation and more.
Published by: Weaver Publications, Inc., 2420 Alcott St, Denver, CO 80211. TEL 303-458-1211, 800-303-9328, FAX 303-477-0724, info@weaver-group.com, http://pub.weaver-group.com. adv.: color page USD 8,440; trim 5.25 x 8.375. Circ: 350,000 (free).

338.4791 CAN ISSN 1198-1903
BOTTIN TOURISTIQUE DU QUEBEC. Text in English. a. CAD 29.95 (effective 2000). **Document type:** *Directory.* **Description:** Contains listings of names, coordinates and areas of activity relating to tourism in Quebec.
Published by: Quebec dans le Monde, C P 8503, Sainte Foy, PQ G1V 4N5, Canada. TEL 418-659-5540, FAX 418-659-4143.

916.78 USA
THE BRADT TRAVEL GUIDE: TANZANIA. Text in English. 1993. biennial, latest 2007, 5th ed. USD 16.99 per issue (effective 2008). **Document type:** *Guide, Consumer.* **Description:** Contains information on planning a trip, whether visitors are seeking advice on independent travel or all-inclusive safaris in luxury game lodges.
Published by: The Globe Pequot Press, Inc., 246 Goose Ln, PO Box 480, Guilford, CT 06437. TEL 203-458-4500, 888-249-7586, FAX 203-458-4603, 800-820-2329, info@globepequot.com, http://www.globepequot.com.

980 DEU
DO BRASIL. Text in German, Portuguese. bi-m. EUR 26 domestic; EUR 30 foreign (effective 2004). adv. **Document type:** *Magazine, Consumer.* **Description:** Contains news and information on all aspects of Brazil, including travel and culture.
Published by: Mediengruppe Koenig, Aeussere Zeulenrodaer Str 11, Greiz, 07973, Germany. TEL 49-3661-674213, FAX 49-3661-674214, verlag-koenig@t-online.de, http://www.mediengruppe-koenig.de. Adv. contact Uwe Hilke. B&W page EUR 1,500, color page EUR 2,750; trim 185 x 265. Circ: 15,000 (paid and controlled).

910.09 BRA
BRASILTURIS JORNAL. Text in Portuguese. 1981. bi-w. USD 90 (effective 2002). **Description:** News on the development and promotion of tourism worldwide, covering all areas of transportation, hotels, excursions and related activities.
Published by: Markturis Editora Jornalistica Ltda, Rua General Jardim 633, 2o Andar, Sao Paulo, SP 01223-904, Brazil. TEL 55-11-2592400, FAX 55-11-2565818, jornal@brasilturis.com.br. Ed. Horacio Neves. Circ: 10,000.

659.1 ROM ISSN 1454-2757
BRASOV - WHAT, WHERE, WHEN. Text in Romanian, English. 1999. q. ROL 50,000 domestic; USD 12 foreign (effective 2002). adv. **Document type:** *Magazine, Consumer.*
Published by: Crystal Publishing Group, 253, Calea Calarasilor, bl. 67 A, Ste. 4, Bucharest, Romania. TEL 40-21-3233829, FAX 40-21-3234706, office@bucurestiwww.ro, http://www.bucurestiwww.ro. Circ: 25,000 (paid and controlled).

914.37 SVK ISSN 1335-8251
BRATISLAVA IN YOUR POCKET. Text in English. 2001. 5/yr. USD 25; USD 5 newsstand/cover (effective 2002). adv. **Document type:** *Magazine, Consumer.*
Address: Ul. Klariska c.12, Bratislava, Slovakia. TEL 421-7-54644431.

918.1 GBR
BRAZIL BUSINESS BRIEF (ONLINE). Text in English. 1942. bi-m. free to members (effective 2009). adv. bk.rev. **Document type:** *Bulletin, Trade.*
Former titles (until 2001): Brazil Business Brief (Print) (1351-4520); (until Apr.1993): Brazilian Chamber of Commerce in Great Britain. News Update (0968-1035); (until 1989): Brazil Journal; (until 1952): Brazilian Chamber of Commerce and Economic Affairs in Great Britain. Journal; (until 1943): Brazilian Press
Media: Online - full text.
Published by: Brazilian Chamber of Commerce, 32 Green St, London, W1K 7AT, United Kingdom. TEL 44-20-73999281, FAX 44-20-74990186, brazilianchamber@brazilianchamber.org.uk. Ed. Nadia Kerecuk. Circ: 400.

918.104 GBR ISSN 1363-7401
F2509.5
BRAZIL HANDBOOK. Text in English. 1998. biennial. GBP 15.99 per issue (effective 2010). adv. back issues avail. **Document type:** *Handbook/Manual/Guide, Consumer.* **Description:** Covers all the basics from where to stay and where to eat to cycling, walking and how to get around the Brazil.
—CCC.
Published by: Footprint Handbooks Ltd., 6 Riverside Ct, Lower Bristol Rd, Bath, Avon BA2 3DZ, United Kingdom. TEL 44-1225-469141, FAX 44-1225-469461, wwwinfo@footprintbooks.com.

910 USA
BREAK; the magazine for STA travel. Text in English. 2003. s-a. USD 19.97; USD 3.95 per issue (effective 2004). adv. **Document type:** *Magazine, Consumer.* **Description:** Edited for the student traveler and covers travel, lifestyle and study abroad with a fresh hip voice.
Published by: (S T A Travel, Inc.), Jungle Media Group, 632 Broadway, 7th Fl, New York, NY 10012. TEL 212-352-0840, FAX 212-352-9282, smcduffy@junglemediagroup.com, http://www.junglemediagroup.com/. Ed. Rogier Van Bakel. adv.: color page USD 16,835; trim 8 x 10.875.

914.410 FRA ISSN 1957-4800
BRETAGNE CULTURE & DECOUVERTE. Text in French. 2007. bi-m. **Document type:** *Magazine, Consumer.*
Published by: Euro Services Internet, 60 rue Vitruve, Paris, 75020, France.

▼ **BRIDES ABROAD**; weddings & honeymoons. *see* MATRIMONY

914.210 GBR ISSN 1757-9732
DA650
BRITAIN. Text in English. 1930. bi-m. GBP 19.50 domestic; USD 29.95 in United States; CAD 34.95 in Canada; AUD 54.95 in Australia; GBP 27.50 elsewhere; GBP 3.25 per issue (effective 2010). adv. back issues avail. **Document type:** *Magazine, Consumer.* **Description:** Provides insight into how to enjoy Britain's heritage and landscapes, style and design, arts and crafts, accommodations, food and fun.
Former titles (until 2009): In Britain (0019-3143); (until 1966): Coming Events in Britain; (until 1949): Coming Events in the British Isles; (until 1946): Coming Events in Great Britain and Ireland
Related titles: Online - full text ed.
Indexed: A01, A11, C05, C12, H&TI, H06, IBR, IBZ, M01, M02, RASB, T02, U01, WBA, WMB.
Published by: (VisitBritain), Chelsea Magazine Company Ltd., 26-30 Old Church St, London, SW3 5BY, United Kingdom. TEL 44-20-73493150, FAX 44-20-73493160, info@chelseamagazines.com, http://www.chelseamagazines.com. Ed. Andrea Spain. Pub. Steve Ross.

942 USA ISSN 1081-1117
DA650
BRITAIN BY BRITRAIL; touring Britain by train. Text in English. 1980. a., latest 2008, 29th ed. USD 17.95 per issue (effective 2009). back issues avail. **Document type:** *Guide, Consumer.* **Description:** Provides information on fares, schedules, pass options, hotel recommendations and sightseeing options for Britain train.
Published by: The Globe Pequot Press, Inc., 246 Goose Ln, PO Box 480, Guilford, CT 06437. TEL 203-458-4500, 888-249-7586, FAX 203-458-4603, 800-820-2329, info@globepequot.com, http://www.globepequot.com. Ed. LaVerne Ferguson-Kosinski.

914.2 GBR
BRITAIN'S BEST LEISURE & RELAXATION GUIDE. Text in English. 1968. a. **Document type:** *Handbook/Manual/Guide, Consumer.* **Description:** Guide to all types of holiday opportunities throughout England, Scotland and Wales.
Former titles (until 2007): Britain's Best Holidays - A Quick Reference Guide (0267-1468); (until 1983): Guide to Britain's Best Holidays
Published by: F H G Guides Ltd. (Subsidiary of: F H G Publications Ltd.), Abbey Mill Business Ctr, Seedhill, Paisley, PA1 1TJ, United Kingdom. TEL 44-141-8870428, FAX 44-141-8897204, sales@fhguides.co.uk, http://www.holidayguides.com.

917 CAN ISSN 1709-4623
F1086
BRITISH COLUMBIA MAGAZINE. Text in English. 1959. q. CAD 19.95 domestic; CAD 28.95 foreign (effective 2010). adv. bk.rev. illus. index. back issues avail.; reprints avail. **Document type:** *Magazine, Consumer.* **Description:** Explores British Columbia through photographs, educational articles and travel information.
Formerly (until 2002): Beautiful British Columbia (0005-7460)
Related titles: Magnetic Tape ed.; Microfiche ed.; Online - full text ed.

Indexed: C03, C04, C05, C12, CBCARef, CBPI, CPerI, G05, G06, G07, G08, I05, M02, P48, PQC, T02, WildRev.
—CIS, Ingenta.
Published by: Tourism British Columbia, 1803 Douglas St, Victoria, BC V8T 5C3, Canada. TEL 250-356-5860, FAX 250-356-5896, cs@bcmag.ca. Ed. Anita Willis. Pub. Don Foxgord. Adv. contact Michelle Hughes TEL 604-660-3702. color page CAD 9,750; trim 8.5 x 10.75. Circ: 114,156.

BRITISH CONFERENCE DESTINATIONS DIRECTORY (YEAR). *see* MEETINGS AND CONGRESSES

BRITISH HERITAGE. *see* HISTORY—History Of Europe

910.202 VGB
BRITISH VIRGIN ISLANDS WELCOME TOURIST GUIDE; the welcome. Text in English. 1971. bi-m. USD 25 in United States; USD 38 foreign (effective 2000). adv. **Document type:** *Handbook/Manual/Guide, Consumer.* **Description:** Supplying information about the British Virgin Islands to visitors. Articles on the history, people and locales of the BVI, as well as guide information on accomodations, charter boats, dinning and shopping.
Related titles: Online - full text ed.
Published by: Island Publishing Co., P.O. Box 133, Road Town, Tortola, Virgin Isl., UK. TEL 284-494-2413, FAX 284-494-6589, cpcips@surfbri.com. Ed., Adv. contact Claudia Colli. Pub., R&P Paul Bachshall. B&W page USD 1,560, color page USD 2,130; trim 11.25 x 8.75. Circ: 29,000 (free).

BRITISH WATERWAYS BOARD. ANNUAL REPORT AND ACCOUNTS. *see* TRANSPORTATION—Ships And Shipping

914.7 ROM ISSN 1454-5276
BUCHAREST IN YOUR POCKET. Text in English. 1999. 5/yr. USD 5 newsstand/cover (effective 2002). adv. **Document type:** *Magazine, Consumer.*
Address: Calea Victoriei 32-34, Sc C, 3rd Fl., Apt. 110, PO Box 1-544, Bucharest, 76000, Romania. TEL 40-1-3147923, FAX 40-1-3147924.

BUCHAREST NIGHTLIFE. *see* LEISURE AND RECREATION

BUCKS; the art + culture + lifestyle magazine. *see* GENERAL INTEREST PERIODICALS—United States

659 ROM ISSN 1454-119X
BUCURESTI PAGES FOR RESIDENTS & VISITORS. Text in Multiple languages. 1998. a. adv. **Document type:** *Magazine, Consumer.*
Published by: Crystal Publishing Group, 253, Calea Calarasilor, bl. 67 A, Ste. 4, Bucharest, Romania. TEL 40-21-3233829, FAX 40-21-3234706, office@bucurestiwww.ro, http://www.bucurestiwww.ro.

659.1 ROM ISSN 1222-5703
BUCURESTI - WHAT, WHERE, WHEN. Text in Multiple languages. 1994. bi-m. ROL 100,000 domestic; USD 18 foreign (effective 2002). adv. **Document type:** *Magazine, Consumer.*
Published by: Crystal Publishing Group, 253, Calea Calarasilor, bl. 67 A, Ste. 4, Bucharest, Romania. TEL 40-21-3233829, FAX 40-21-3234706, office@bucurestiwww.ro, http://www.bucurestiwww.ro. Circ: 35,000 (paid and controlled).

914.704 HUN ISSN 1585-1907
BUDAPEST IN YOUR POCKET. Text in English. 1999. 5/yr. USD 25; USD 5 newsstand/cover (effective 2002). adv. **Document type:** *Magazine, Consumer.*
Address: Dohany u. 37, fszt 3-4, Budapest, 1074, Hungary. TEL 36-1-4131869, FAX 36-1-4131868.

917.204 MEX
BUEN VIAJE!; convenciones - viajes de incentivo - sunshine - grupos. Text in English, Spanish. 1990. bi-m. MXN 10, USD 29.95. **Description:** Contains travel information for business travelers.
Published by: Grupo Editorial Aviare, Queretaro 229, Desp. 402, Apdo. 71339, Mexico City, DF 06700, Mexico. TEL 2-584-31-94, FAX 2-584-48-21. Ed. Alfredo Villagran Arevalo. adv.: B&W page MXN 3,000, color page MXN 4,000. Circ: 25,000.

BUITENLEVEN. *see* SPORTS AND GAMES—Outdoor Life

BUITENSPOOR. *see* SPORTS AND GAMES—Outdoor Life

791.43 ZWE
BULAWAYO THIS MONTH. Text in English. 1972. m. free. adv. illus.
Published by: Modern Publications, PO Box 1183, Bulawayo, Zimbabwe. Ed. Les Broughton. Circ: 2,500.

910 CAN ISSN 0706-215X
BULLETIN VOYAGES. Text in French. 1978. bi-m. free. adv. back issues avail. **Document type:** *Bulletin, Trade.*
Incorporates in 1987: Tour Hebdo (0835-1503)
Published by: Editions Acra Ltee., 5115, De Gaspe, Ste 330, Montreal, PQ H2T 3B7, Canada. TEL 514-287-9773, FAX 514-842-6180, info@bulletinvoyages.com. Ed. Gary Lawrence. Pub. Jean Pierre Kerten. Adv. contact Jose Lapierre. B&W page CAD 1,380, color page CAD 2,170. Circ: 9,000.

914.504 DEU
BUONGIORNO ITALIA. Text in German. 2003. 10/yr. EUR 4.50 newsstand/cover (effective 2009). adv. **Document type:** *Magazine, Trade.*
Published by: ChefMedia Verlag, Bechsteinstr 27, Weimar, 99423, Germany. TEL 49-3643-415800, FAX 49-3643-415819, info@chefmedia.de. Ed. Donatella Del Vecchio. Adv. contact Johann Scheid. color page EUR 3,790; trim 210 x 297. Circ: 10,634 (paid and controlled).

910.202 USA
BUREAU BRIEFS (MADISON, WI). Text in English. s-a. free (effective 2005). tr.lit. **Document type:** *Newsletter, Consumer.*
Published by: Greater Madison Convention & Visitors Bureau, 615 E Washington Ave, Madison, WI 53703. TEL 608-255-2537, FAX 608-258-4950.

BUS ET CAR MAGAZINE. *see* TRANSPORTATION

388.3 DEU ISSN 0341-5244
BUS-FAHRT; Das Magazin fuer Technik und Touristik. Text in German. 1952. m. EUR 68 domestic; EUR 81 foreign; EUR 7.50 newsstand/cover (effective 2010). adv. bk.rev. charts; illus.; stat. **Document type:** *Magazine, Trade.* **Description:** Focuses on bus travel and tourism.
Published by: Stuenings Medien GmbH, Diessemer Bruch 167, Krefeld, 47805, Germany. TEL 49-2151-51000, FAX 49-2151-5100101, medien@stuenings.de, http://www.stuenings.de. Ed. Lutz Gerritzen. Adv. contact Ulrich Miggel. B&W page EUR 2,480, color page EUR 3,890. Circ: 8,000 (paid and controlled).

910.09 DEU ISSN 1610-3882
BUS-TOURIST; Das Magazin fuer Reisen mit dem Bus. Text in German. 1981. q. EUR 20 domestic; EUR 30 foreign (effective 2010). adv. **Document type:** *Magazine, Trade.*
Former titles (until 2002): Bus-Tourist International (1430-726X); (until 1993): Bus-Tourist (0721-9652)
Published by: P A C S Gesellschaft fuer Promotion, Advertising & Communication Services mbH, Gewerbestr 9, Staufen, 79219, Germany. TEL 49-7633-982007, FAX 49-7633-982060, pacs@pacs-online.com, http://www.pacs-online.com. Circ: 12,000 (paid).

BUS TOURS MAGAZINE. *see* TRANSPORTATION

910.202 AUT
BUS- UND HOTELREPORT. Text in German. 1986. q. **Document type:** *Magazine, Trade.*
Published by: C B Verlags GmbH, Kleingoepfink 44, Pfaffenschlag, N 3834, Austria. TEL 43-1-5974985, FAX 43-1-597498515, office@cbverlag.at, http://www.cbverlag.at. Ed. Angelika Maier. Pub. Christian Boehm. Circ: 10,800.

910.09 DEU
BUS ZIELE. Text in German. 1989. a. EUR 5 newsstand/cover (effective 2010). adv. back issues avail. **Document type:** *Magazine, Trade.*
Formerly (until 1992): Tourist auf Reisen (0936-3637)
Published by: Stuenings Medien GmbH, Diessemer Bruch 167, Krefeld, 47805, Germany. TEL 49-2151-51000, FAX 49-2151-5100101, medien@stuenings.de, http://www.stuenings.de. Circ: 50,000 (controlled).

THE BUSINESS OF TOURISM. *see* HOTELS AND RESTAURANTS

910.2 GBR ISSN 1474-0923
BUSINESS RATIO REPORT. TRAVEL AGENTS & TOUR OPERATORS. Text in English. 1979. a., latest no.26, 2008, Nov. GBP 365 per issue (effective 2010). back issues avail. **Document type:** *Report, Trade.*
Former titles (until 2001): Business Ratio. Travel Agents & Tour Operators (1470-7047); (until 2000): Business Ratio Plus: Travel Agents & Tour Operators (1354-4470); (until 1994): Business Ratio Report: Travel Agents and Tour Operators (0261-9652)
Published by: Key Note Ltd. (Subsidiary of: Bonnier Business Information), Harlequin House, 5th Fl, 7 High St, Teddington, Richmond upon Thames, TW11 8EE, United Kingdom. TEL 44-845-5040452, FAX 44-845-5040453, sales@keynote.co.uk.

910.202 IRL ISSN 1393-967X
BUSINESS TRAVEL. Text in English. 1994. q. adv. **Document type:** *Magazine, Trade.*
Published by: Belgrave Group, A12 Calmount Pk., Ballymount, Dublin, 12, Ireland. TEL 353-1-4502422, FAX 353-1-4502954. adv.: B&W page EUR 1,695, color page EUR 2,489; trim 210 x 297. Circ: 6,500 (controlled).

THE BUSINESS TRAVEL MAGAZINE; for corporate travel and meetings arrangers. *see* BUSINESS AND ECONOMICS

338.4 USA ISSN 8750-3670
G156.5.B86
BUSINESS TRAVEL NEWS; news and ideas for business travel management. Abbreviated title: B T N. Text in English. 1984. 26/yr. USD 129 domestic; USD 142 in Canada; USD 210 elsewhere; free to qualified personnel (effective 2009). adv. back issues avail.; reprints avail. **Document type:** *Magazine, Trade.* **Description:** Focuses on the corporate business travel market news with "how-to" features and trend stories for corporate and travel agency personnel who are involved in business travel and meeting planning.
Formerly (until Apr. 1995): Corporate Travel (0882-8709)
Related titles: Online - full text ed.; Supplement(s): The Incentive Travel Buyer's Handbook. ISSN 1941-4277.
Indexed: A09, A10, A15, A22, ABIn, B01, B06, B07, B09, B11, G06, G07, G08, H&TI, H06, I05, M01, M02, P34, P48, P51, PQC, T02, V03, V04.
—CIS, Ingenta. **CCC.**
Published by: Nielsen Business Publications (Subsidiary of: Nielsen Business Media, Inc.), 770 Broadway, New York, NY 10003. TEL 646-654-4500, FAX 646-654-4948, bmcomm@nielsen.com, http://www.nielsenbusinessmedia.com. Eds. Jay Boehmer TEL 646-654-4434, David Meyer TEL 646-654-4431. Pub. John Dejesu TEL 646-654-4461. adv.: B&W page USD 20,800, color page USD 25,380; trim 9 x 10.5. Circ: 55,167 (controlled). **Subscr. to:** PO Box 1187, Skokie, IL 60076.

917 USA
BUSINESS TRAVEL PLANNER (ONLINE). Text in English. 2004. irreg. USD 169 (for one user) (effective 2011). **Document type:** *Guide, Trade.* **Description:** A resource for corporate travel agents and travel managers, it's an almanac-style index to hotels and airports around the world.
Formed by the merger of (2000-2004): Business Travel Planner. Europe, Africa, Middle East Edition (Print) (1532-0952); Which was formerly (until 2000): O A G Business Travel Planner. Europe, Africa, Middle East (1529-7632); (until 2000): OAG Travel Planner (European Edition) (1075-1548); (until 1992): O A G Travel Planner, Hotel & Motel Redbook (European Edition) (0894-1718); (200?-2004): Business Travel Planner. Asia Pacific Edition (Print) (1532-0960); Which was formerly (in 2000): O A G Business Travel Planner (Asia Pacific Edition) (1529-7624); (until 2000): O A G Travel Planner. Pacific Asia Edition (1069-2150); (until 1992): O A G Travel Planner Hotel and Motel Redbook. Pacific Asia Edition (0894-1734); (200?-2004): Business Travel Planner. North American Edition (Print) (1532-0944); Which was formerly (until 2000): O A G Business Travel Planner. North American Edition (1053-0002); (until 1990): O A G Travel Planner Hotel and Motel Redbook. North American Edition (0894-1726); Each of the three O A G Travel Planner, Hotel & Motel Redbook. Editions: European, North American, & Pacific Asia were formed by the merger of their corresponding edition (1978-1987): O A G Travel Planner and Hotel - Motel Guide. Pacific Area Edition (8750-8672); (197?-1987): O A G Travel Planner and Hotel - Motel Guide (European Edition) (0162-735X); (1978-1987): O A G Travel Planner and Hotel Motel Guide. North American Edition (0193-3299); Which was formerly (19??-1977): O A G Travel Planner and Hotel - Motel Guide (0090-0869); and part of (1987-1987): Red Book (0896-1565); Which was formerly (until 1986): Hotel and Motel Red Book (0073-3490); (until 1962): Hotel Red Book; (until 1954): Official Hotel Red Book and Directory; (until 1902): United States Official Hotel Directory; (1886-1892): United States Official Hotel Directory and Railroad Indicator
Media: Online - full text.

Indexed: H19, M01, M02, T02.
—**CCC.**
Published by: Northstar Travel Media LLC (Subsidiary of: Boston Ventures Management, Inc.), 100 Lighting Way, Secaucus, NJ 07094. TEL 201-902-2000, FAX 201-902-2045, http://www.northstartravelmedia.com/.

910.09 330 USA ISSN 1935-9896
BUSINESS TRAVELER (USA EDITION). Text in English. 1976. 10/yr. USD 39.99 domestic; USD 54.99 foreign (effective 2007). adv. bk.rev. illus. back issues avail.; reprints avail. **Document type:** *Magazine, Consumer.* **Description:** Provides travel tips, feature articles for the international business traveler.
Related titles: Online - full text ed.; ◆ Regional ed(s).: Business Traveller (UK Edition); ◆ Business Traveller (Asia - Pacific Edition). ISSN 0255-7312; ◆ Business Traveller (German Edition). ISSN 1430-810X; Business Traveller (Middle East Edition). USD 17 in the Middle East; USD 22 in Europe; USD 24 elsewhere (effective 2002).
Published by: Perry Publications Inc (Subsidiary of: Euromoney Institutional Investor Plc.), 72 Madison Ave, 5th Fl, New York, NY 10016. TEL 212-754-6983, 800-726-1243, FAX 212-754-6987, http://www.btonline.com. Ed. Eva Leonard. adv.: B&W page USD 13,400, color page USD 16,000; trim 10.875 x 8.125. Circ: 48,000 (paid).

910.202 HKG ISSN 0255-7312
BUSINESS TRAVELLER (ASIA - PACIFIC EDITION). Text in English. 1982. m. HKD 360 domestic; AUD 75 in Australia; NZD 100 in New Zealand; PHP 1,450 in Philippines; USD 75 elsewhere (effective 2002). adv. **Document type:** *Journal, Consumer.*
Related titles: Online - full text ed.; ◆ Regional ed(s).: Business Traveller (UK Edition); ◆ Business Traveler (USA Edition). ISSN 1935-9896; ◆ Business Traveller (German Edition). ISSN 1430-810X; Business Traveller (Middle East Edition). USD 17 in the Middle East; USD 22 in Europe; USD 24 elsewhere (effective 2002).
Indexed: A12, ABIn, B01, B03, B07, B11, G05, G06, G07, G08, I05.
—IE.
Published by: Perry Publications Asia Ltd., Unit 404 Printing House, 6 Duddell St, Central Hong Kong, Hong Kong. TEL 852-2511-9317, FAX 852-2519-6846. Ed. Jonathan Wall TEL 852-2594-9362. Pub., R&P Peggy Teo TEL 852-2594-9377. adv.: B&W page USD 7,200, color page USD 8,220. Circ: 24,465.

380.8 DEU ISSN 1430-810X
BUSINESS TRAVELLER (GERMAN EDITION); Das Geschaeftsreisemagazin. Text in German. 1992. bi-m. EUR 3.50 newsstand/cover (effective 2011). adv. **Document type:** *Magazine, Trade.*
Incorporates (1995-2000): B R T Travel (0949-7196); Which was formerly (until 1995): Besttravel (0947-9902)
Related titles: ◆ Regional ed(s).: Business Traveller (UK Edition); ◆ Business Traveller (Asia - Pacific Edition). ISSN 0255-7312; ◆ Business Traveler (USA Edition). ISSN 1935-9896; Business Traveller (Middle East Edition). USD 17 in the Middle East; USD 22 in Europe; USD 24 elsewhere (effective 2002).
Published by: Business Traveller, Schulstr 34, Munich, 80634, Germany. FAX 49-89-1679937, BT@businesstraveller.de. Ed. Marc Tuegel. Adv. contact Christian Buck TEL 49-89-16783914. Circ: 64,694 (paid).

330 GBR
BUSINESS TRAVELLER (UK EDITION). Text in English. 1976. m. GBP 42.95 domestic; GBP 65.65 in Europe; GBP 78.75 elsewhere (effective 2009). adv. bk.rev. illus. index. back issues avail. **Document type:** *Magazine, Consumer.* **Description:** Provides practical information for the regular individual traveler on every aspect of service provided by the travel industry.
Former titles: Business Traveler International (0955-7288); (until 1988): Business Traveller (British Edition) (0309-9334)
Related titles: Online - full text ed.; ◆ Regional ed(s).: Business Traveller (Asia - Pacific Edition). ISSN 0255-7312; ◆ Business Traveler (USA Edition). ISSN 1935-9896; ◆ Business Traveller (German Edition). ISSN 1430-810X; Business Traveller (Middle East Edition). USD 17 in the Middle East; USD 22 in Europe; USD 24 elsewhere (effective 2002).
Indexed: A26, B01, B03, B07, B11, BMT, G05, G06, G07, G08, I05.
—BLDSC (2934.901000), IE, Ingenta. **CCC.**
Published by: Panacea Publishing International, 2nd Fl, Cardinal House, 39-40 Albemarle St, London, W1S 4TE, United Kingdom. TEL 44-20-76476363, FAX 44-20-76476331, enquiries@panaceapublishing.co.uk, http://www.panaceapublishing.com/. Ed. Tom Otley. Pub. Rania Apthorpe TEL 44-20-76476360. Adv. contact Toni Mears TEL 44-20-76476361.

910 DNK ISSN 1901-3191
BUSINESS TRAVELLER DENMARK. Text in Danish. 2006. 8/yr. DKK 785 (effective 2008). adv. **Document type:** *Magazine, Consumer.*
Published by: Business Traveller Denmark Aps, Kildegaards Plads 1, Gentofte, 2920, Denmark. TEL 45-33-114413, FAX 45-33-114414, info@btdk.com, http://www.businesstravellerdenmark.com. Ed. Michael Boejes. adv.: page DKK 19,500. Circ: 10,000 (paid and controlled).

338.479 DEU
BUSPLANER INTERNATIONAL. Text in German. 1976. 10/yr. EUR 78; EUR 39 to students (effective 2010). adv. **Document type:** *Magazine, Trade.*
Former titles (until 1996): Buskontakt-Planer International; (until 1994): Buskontakt
Published by: Huss-Verlag GmbH, Joseph-Dollinger-Bogen 5, Munich, 80807, Germany. TEL 49-89-323910, FAX 49-89-32391416, management@huss-verlag.de, http://www.huss-verlag.de. Ed. Stephan Brummet. Adv. contact Ulrike Schnauf. Circ: 6,762 (controlled).

338.4 GBR ISSN 2041-4242
BUYING BUSINESS TRAVEL. Text in English. 2003. bi-m. GBP 35 in UK & Ireland; GBP 47 elsewhere; free to qualified personnel (effective 2010). adv. back issues avail. **Document type:** *Magazine, Trade.* **Description:** Provides company travel buyers, arrangers and agents with the latest news, product and destination information, technology updates, special offers and a wealth of vital information.
Indexed: A09, B06, B08, B09, H&TI, S22, V04.

Published by: Panacea Publishing International, 2nd Fl, Cardinal House, 39-40 Albemarle St, London, W1S 4TE, United Kingdom. TEL 44-20-76476363, FAX 44-20-76476331, enquiries@panaceapublishing.co.uk, http://www.panaceapublishing.com/. Ed. Mike Toynbee. Pub., Adv. contact Chris Mihalop. page GBP 4,500; bleed 216 x 303. Circ: 18,078.

910.09 USA
BYWAYS (FAIRFAX). Text in English. 1984. 6/yr. USD 17.95. adv. **Document type:** *Guide, Trade.* **Description:** Features travel destinations in U.S. and Canada.
Published by: Byways, Inc., PO Box 7430, Fairfax Sta, VA 22039-7430. TEL 703-503-3613, FAX 703-250-1477. Ed., R&P Steve Kirchner. Adv. contact Amy E Slagle. Circ: 15,000 (controlled).

C; California style. *see* GENERAL INTEREST PERIODICALS—United States

910.2 CAN ISSN 1910-0140
C A A MAGAZINE. Text in English. 2006. q. **Document type:** *Magazine, Consumer.*
Formed by the 2005 merger of: Going Places; (2000-2005): Journey (1704-0507); (1982-2005): Leisureways (0712-5747); Which was formerly (1946-1981): Canadian Motorist (0008-4530)
Related titles: Online - full text ed.; ◆ Supplement(s): Going Places (Manitoba). ISSN 0832-5448.
—CIS.
Published by: (Canadian Automobile Association), Totem Communications Group Inc., 37 Front St. E., Toronto, ON M5E 1B3, Canada. TEL 416-360-7339, info@totembrandstories.com, http://www.totembrandstories.com/. Circ: 1,500,000.

C A R A 'MAG'. (Communaute d'Agglomeration Royan Atlantique) *see* PUBLIC ADMINISTRATION

910 USA ISSN 1529-4617
C E O TRAVELER. Text in English. 1994. 3/yr. USD 15 (effective 2000). **Document type:** *Newsletter.* **Description:** Covers upscale travel, resorts, hotels, destinations, cruises, and spas.
Related titles: Online - full text ed.
Address: 40 Fifth Ave, Ste 16c, New York, NY 10011. TEL 212-674-0877, FAX 212-254-7936. Ed. Vivian Kramer Fancher. Pub. Edwin C Fancher. Circ: 2,000 (controlled).

914.504 ITA ISSN 0394-1434
C I R V I BOLLETTINO. (Centro Interuniversitario di Ricerche sul Viaggio in Italia) Text in English, French, Italian. 1980. s-a. bk.rev. **Document type:** *Journal, Academic/Scholarly.*
Indexed: MLA-IB.
Published by: Centro Interuniversitario di Ricerche sul Viaggio in Italia (C I R V I), Strada Revigliasco 6, Moncalieri, TO 10024, Italy. cirvi@cirvi.it, http://www.cirvi.it.

338.4 CAN ISSN 1715-5533
C I T Q. ANNUAL REPORT. (Corporation de l'Industrie Touristique du Quebec) Text in English. 2004. a. **Document type:** *Report, Trade.*
Published by: Corporation de l'Industrie Touristique du Quebec, 1010, rue De Serigny, bureau 810, Longueuil, PQ J4K 5G7, Canada. TEL 450-679-3737, 866-499-0550, FAX 450-679-1489, info@citq.qc.ca, http://www.citq.qc.ca.

910.2 FRA ISSN 2107-3201
C LE JOURNAL DU PARC NATUREL REGIONAL DE CHARTREUSE. Text in French. 1996. q. **Document type:** *Magazine, Consumer.*
Formerly (until 2008): Pt'Hibou de Chemin (1278-9682)
Published by: Parc Naturel Regional de Chartreuse, Maison du Parc, St-Pierre-de-Chartreuse, 38380, France. TEL 33-4-76887520, FAX 33-4-76887530, accueil@parc-chartreuse.net, http://www.parc-chartreuse.net/index.asp.

910.202 GBR ISSN 1740-441X
C N N TRAVELLER; for people going places. (Cable News Network) Text in English. 1995. bi-m. GBP 21 for 2 yrs. domestic; EUR 33 for 2 yrs. in Europe; USD 45 for 2 yrs. in the Americas, Asia & Africa (effective 2009). adv. back issues avail. **Document type:** *Magazine, Consumer.* **Description:** Provides information and entertainment for business and high-end leisure travelers, including articles on travel, news, and current affairs.
Formerly: Network (1358-8931)
Related titles: Online - full text ed.
Published by: (C N N USA), Cable News Network LP, LLLP., 4th Fl, Turner House, 16 Great Marlborough St, London, W1F 7HS, United Kingdom. Ed. Dan Hayes. Adv. contact Silvia Lehnert TEL 44-20-33558266.

C S M A CLUB MAGAZINE. (Civil Service Motoring Association) *see* TRANSPORTATION—Automobiles

910.202 USA
C T P A NEWS. Text in English. 1975. m. membership. adv. back issues avail. **Document type:** *Magazine, Trade.* **Description:** News of California, Nevada and Oregon RV park and campground industry.
Published by: California Travel Parks Association, Inc., PO Box 5648, Auburn, CA 95604. TEL 530-885-1624, FAX 530-823-6331. Ed. Judy Miller. Circ: 900.

910.91 USA
LOS CABOS. Text in English. 2001. q. USD 4.95 newsstand/cover (effective 2001). adv. **Document type:** *Magazine, Consumer.*
Published by: Promociones Tyson, S.A. de C.V., 2658 Del Mar Heights Rd. #455, Del Mar, CA 92014. TEL 858-569-0172, FAX 858-755-3966, loscabos@san.rr.com. Ed., Pub. Joseph A Tyson.

910.02 BRA ISSN 1677-6976
G155.B7
CADERNO VIRTUAL DE TURISMO. Text in Portuguese. 2001. 3/yr. free (effective 2011). **Document type:** *Journal, Academic/Scholarly.*
Media: Online - full text.
Indexed: CABA, E12, F08, F12, GH, LT, N02, P32, P33, PGegResA, R08, R12, RRTA, S13, S16, T02, TAR, W11.
Published by: Universidade Federal do Rio de Janeiro, Coordenacao dos Programas de Pos-Graduacao de Engenharia, Centro, Caixa Postal 1191 ZC 00, Rio de Janeiro, RJ 20001-970, Brazil. Ed. Roberto Bartholo.

CALENDAR OF COMMUNITY EVENTS; listings for Victoria. *see* LEISURE AND RECREATION

917.94 USA ISSN 1940-2414
CALIFORNIA CAMPING; the complete guide to more than 1,400 tent and RV campgrounds. Variant title: Moon California Camping. Text in English. 1987. biennial, latest 2009, 16th ed. USD 23.95 per issue (effective 2009). back issues avail. **Document type:** *Directory, Consumer.* **Description:** Features camping options from secluded Sierra hike-ins to convenient roadside stopovers, with advice on nearby recreation in California.
Former titles (until 2008): Foghorn Outdoors. California Camping (1531-8109); (until 2001): California Camping (1078-957X)
Published by: Avalon Travel Publishing, 1700 4th St, Berkeley, CA 94710. TEL 510-595-3664, info@travelmatters.com.

910.202 USA
CALIFORNIA R V & CAMPING GUIDE. Text in English. 1975. a. free. adv. charts; illus.; maps. **Document type:** *Directory, Consumer.*
Published by: (California Travel Parks Association, Inc.), Executive Services Group, PO Box 5578, Auburn, CA 95604. TEL 916-823-1076, 888-STA-YCTP, FAX 916-823-6331. Ed. Judy Miller. Circ: 250,000.

910.202 USA
CALIFORNIA TOUR & TRAVEL. Text in English. 2000. q. USD 19.95; USD 4.95 newsstand/cover (effective 2006). adv. **Document type:** *Magazine, Consumer.*
Published by: Market Interface, Inc., PO Box 3557, Grass Valley, CA 95945. TEL 530-273-5600, FAX 530-272-7261. Ed. Rudy Elbogen. Pub. Robert Bellezza. adv.: color page USD 3,195; trim 8.375 x 10.625. Circ: 34,098 (paid and controlled).

979.4 641.2 USA
CALIFORNIA VISITORS REVIEW. Text in English. 1981. w. USD 42. adv. **Document type:** *Magazine, Consumer.* **Description:** Visitors guide to Northern California wine country.
Address: PO Box 92, E. Verano, CA 95433. TEL 707-938-3494, FAX 707-938-3674. Ed. E Garneau. Adv. contact Greg Martin.

917.9 USA ISSN 1094-110X
TX907.3.C2
CALIFORNIA'S BEST BED & BREAKFASTS. Text in English. 1993. irreg.
Formerly (until 1995): Fodor's Bed & Breakfasts, Country Inns, and Other Weekend Pleasures. California (1079-1663)
Published by: Fodor's Travel Publications, Inc. (Subsidiary of: Random House Inc.), 1745 Broadway, 15th Fl, New York, NY 10019. TEL 212-572-2313, editors@fodors.com, http://www.fodors.com.

910.09 GBR ISSN 0575-6790
Q115
CAMBRIDGE EXPEDITIONS JOURNAL. Text in English. 1965. a. **Document type:** *Journal, Consumer.*
—Linda Hall.
Published by: University of Cambridge, Expeditions Society, The Old Schools, Trinity Lane, Cambridge, CB2 1TN, United Kingdom. TEL 44-1223-332300, FAX 44-1223-330262, http://www.srcf.ucam.org/cuex.

917 796.5 USA
CAMPBOOK: CALIFORNIA - NEVADA. Cover title: R V and Tent Sites in California, Nevada. Text in English. 1977. a. free to members (effective 2009). adv. **Document type:** *Magazine, Consumer.* **Description:** Features the list of privately operated campgrounds as well as publicly operated campgrounds in the California to Nevada.
Former titles (until 199?): California-Nevada Campbook; (until 1980): California-Nevada Camping
Published by: A A A Publishing, 1000 AAA Dr, Heathrow, FL 32746. TEL 407-444-8370, FAX 407-444-7766, AAATravelInfo-CustomerService@national.aaa.com, http://www.aaa.biz/. adv.: B&W page USD 7,960, color page USD 10,380. Circ: 445,530.

917 796.5 USA
GV191.46.M4
CAMPBOOK: EASTERN CANADA. Cover title: R V and Tent Sites in New Brunswick, Newfoundland, Nova Scotia, Ontario, Prince Edward Island, Quebec. Text in English. 19??. a. free to members (effective 2008). adv. illus. **Document type:** *Magazine, Consumer.* **Description:** Features the list of privately operated campgrounds as well as publicly operated campgrounds in the Eastern Canada.
Formerly (until 1980): Eastern Canada Camping (0363-2091)
Published by: A A A Publishing, 1000 AAA Dr, Heathrow, FL 32746. TEL 407-444-8370, FAX 407-444-7766, AAATravelInfo-CustomerService@national.aaa.com, http://www.aaa.biz/. adv.: color page USD 7,980, B&W page USD 6,250. Circ: 183,868. **Co-sponsor:** Canadian Automobile Association.

910.202 USA ISSN 0734-8517
GV198.65.G7
CAMPBOOK: GREAT LAKES. Cover title: R V and Tent Sites in Illinois, Indiana, Michigan, Ohio, Wisconsin. Text in English. 19??. a. free to members (effective 2008). adv. illus. **Document type:** *Magazine, Consumer.* **Description:** Features the list of privately operated campgrounds as well as publicly operated campgrounds in the Great Lakes.
Formerly (until 1981): Great Lakes Camping (0363-5171)
Published by: A A A Publishing, 1000 AAA Dr, Heathrow, FL 32746. TEL 407-444-8370, FAX 407-444-7766, AAATravelInfo-CustomerService@national.aaa.com, http://www.aaa.biz/. adv.: B&W page USD 7,020, color page USD 8,980. Circ: 267,660.

917 796.5 USA ISSN 0734-2705
GV191.42.A84
CAMPBOOK: MIDEASTERN. Cover title: R V and Tent Sites in Delaware, District of Columbia, Maryland, New Jersey, Pennsylvania, Virginia, West Virginia. Text in English. 19??. a. free to members (effective 2008). adv. illus. **Document type:** *Magazine, Consumer.* **Description:** Features the list of privately operated campgrounds as well as publicly operated campgrounds in the Mideastern.
Formerly (until 1980): Mideastern Camping (0147-7285)
Published by: A A A Publishing, 1000 AAA Dr, Heathrow, FL 32746. TEL 407-444-8370, FAX 407-444-7766, AAATravelInfo-CustomerService@national.aaa.com, http://www.aaa.biz/. adv.: B&W page USD 7,230, color page USD 9,260. Circ: 269,270.

917 796.5 USA ISSN 0732-2585
GV198.65.N67
CAMPBOOK: NORTH CENTRAL. Cover title: R V and Tent Sites in Iowa, Minnesota, Nebraska, North Dakota, South Dakota. Text in English. 19??. a. free to members (effective 2008). adv. illus. **Document type:** *Magazine, Consumer.* **Description:** Features the list of privately operated campgrounds as well as publicly operated campgrounds in the North Central.
Formerly (until 1980): North Central Camping (0147-8613)
Published by: A A A Publishing, 1000 AAA Dr, Heathrow, FL 32746. TEL 407-444-8370, FAX 407-444-7766, AAATravelInfo-CustomerService@national.aaa.com, http://www.aaa.biz/. adv.: B&W page USD 6,670, color page USD 8,540. Circ: 240,212.

647.94 USA ISSN 0732-7315
GV191.42.N74
CAMPBOOK: NORTHEASTERN. Cover title: R V and Tent Sites in Connecticut, Maine, Massachusetts, New Hampshire, New York, Rhode Island, Vermont. Text in English. 19??. a. free to members (effective 2008). adv. illus. **Document type:** *Magazine, Consumer.* **Description:** Features the list of privately operated campgrounds as well as publicly operated campgrounds in the Northeastern region.
Former titles (until 1980): Northeastern Camping (0196-6456); (until 19??): Northeastern Camping and Trailering
Published by: A A A Publishing, 1000 AAA Dr, Heathrow, FL 32746. TEL 407-444-8370, FAX 407-444-7766, AAATravelInfo-CustomerService@national.aaa.com, http://www.aaa.biz/. adv.: B&W page USD 6,970, color page USD 8,900. Circ: 245,140.

917.8 796 USA ISSN 0732-2577
GV191.35
CAMPBOOK: NORTHWESTERN. Cover title: R V and Tent Sites in Idaho, Montana, Oregon, Washington, Wyoming. Text in English. 19??. a. free to members (effective 2009). adv. illus. **Document type:** *Magazine, Consumer.* **Description:** Features the list of privately operated campgrounds as well as publicly operated campgrounds in the Northwestern region.
Former titles (until 1980): Northwestern Camping (0095-4411); (until 19??): Northwestern Camping and Trailering
Published by: A A A Publishing, 1000 AAA Dr, Heathrow, FL 32746. TEL 407-444-8370, FAX 407-444-7766, AAATravelInfo-CustomerService@national.aaa.com, http://www.aaa.biz/. adv.: B&W page USD 7,570, color page USD 9,680. Circ: 330,942.

917 796.5 USA ISSN 0731-535X
GV198.65.S68
CAMPBOOK: SOUTH CENTRAL. Cover title: R V and Tent Sites in Arkansas, Kansas, Missouri, Oklahoma, Texas. Text in English. 1977. a. free to members (effective 2009). adv. illus. **Document type:** *Magazine, Consumer.* **Description:** Features the list of privately operated campgrounds as well as publicly operated campgrounds in the South Central.
Formerly (until 1980): South Central Camping (0364-7161)
Published by: A A A Publishing, 1000 AAA Dr, Heathrow, FL 32746. TEL 407-444-8370, FAX 407-444-7766, AAATravelInfo-CustomerService@national.aaa.com, http://www.aaa.biz/. adv.: B&W page USD 6,620, color page USD 8,450. Circ: 203,362.

917 796.5 USA ISSN 0731-5112
GV191.42.S83
CAMPBOOK: SOUTHEASTERN. Cover title: R V and Tent Sites in Alabama, Florida, Georgia, Kentucky, Louisiana, Mississippi, North Carolina, South Carolina, Tennessee. Text in English. 19??. a. free to members (effective 2009). adv. illus. **Document type:** *Magazine, Consumer.* **Description:** Features the list of privately operated campgrounds as well as publicly operated campgrounds in the Southeastern.
Former titles (until 1980): Southeastern Camping (0162-9166); (until 19??): Southeastern Camping & Trailering (0093-1969)
Published by: A A A Publishing, 1000 AAA Dr, Heathrow, FL 32746. TEL 407-444-8370, FAX 407-444-7766, AAATravelInfo-CustomerService@national.aaa.com, http://www.aaa.biz/. adv.: color page USD 9,340, B&W page USD 7,310. Circ: 309,647.

917 796.5 USA ISSN 0731-8103
GV191.42.A165
CAMPBOOK: SOUTHWESTERN. Text in English. 19??. a. free to members (effective 2009). adv. illus. **Document type:** *Magazine, Consumer.* **Description:** Features the list of privately operated campgrounds as well as publicly operated campgrounds in the Southwestern.
Formerly (until 1980): Southwestern Camping (0094-2855); Which superseded in part (in 1972): Western Camping and Trailering
Published by: A A A Publishing, 1000 AAA Dr, Heathrow, FL 32746. TEL 407-444-8370, FAX 407-444-7766, AAATravelInfo-CustomerService@national.aaa.com, http://www.aaa.biz/. adv.: B&W page USD 7,570, color page USD 9,680. Circ: 309,647.

917.12 USA ISSN 0732-5347
GV198.67.C2
CAMPBOOK: WESTERN CANADA AND ALASKA. Cover title: R V and Tent Sites in Alberta, British Columbia, Manitoba, Northwest Territories, Saskatchewan, Yukon Territory and Alaska. Text in English. 19??. a. free to members (effective 2009). adv. illus. **Document type:** *Magazine, Consumer.* **Description:** Features the list of privately operated campgrounds as well as publicly operated campgrounds in the Western Canada and Alaska.
Formerly (until 1980): Western Canada. Alaska Camping (0146-6585)
Published by: A A A Publishing, 1000 AAA Dr, Heathrow, FL 32746. TEL 407-444-8370, FAX 407-444-7766, AAATravelInfo-CustomerService@national.aaa.com, http://www.aaa.biz/. adv.: B&W page USD 6,710, color page USD 8,590. Circ: 233,710. **Co-sponsor:** Canadian Automobile Association.

338.4791 796.54 NLD ISSN 2210-920X
▼ **CAMPERREISMAGAZINE.** Text in Dutch. 2010. q. EUR 19.95; EUR 5.95 newsstand/cover (effective 2010). adv. **Document type:** *Magazine, Consumer.*
Published by: V & L Media, Postbus 179, Raalte, 8100 AD, Netherlands. TEL 31-412-628489, FAX 31-412-656891, info@vlmedia.nl, http://www.vlmedia.nl. Eds. Christa Luijk, Rinus Vrijdag. adv.: color page EUR 2,250; trim 230 x 297. Circ: 15,000.

CAMPING DANMARK; godkendte campingpladser i Danmark. *see* SPORTS AND GAMES—Outdoor Life

910.202 ITA
CAMPING IN ITALY. Text in English, French, German, Italian. 1985. a. adv. bk.rev. charts; illus. **Document type:** *Catalog, Consumer.*
Published by: Editoriale Eurocamp Srl, Via Ludovico di Breme 79, Milan, MI 20156, Italy. TEL 39-02-38001954, FAX 39-02-38001940, info@guideuro.it, http://www.guideuro.it. Circ: 500,000.

CAMPING MAGAZINE. *see* SPORTS AND GAMES—Outdoor Life

CAMPING REVUE; Magazin des Oesterreichischen Camping Clubs. *see* SPORTS AND GAMES—Outdoor Life

338.4791 CAN ISSN 0837-4171
HC117.A6
CANADA. DEPARTMENT OF TOURISM. ANNUAL REPORT. Text in English. 1980. a.
Supersedes in part (in 1985): Canada. Department of Tourism and Small Business. Annual Report (0823-454X)
Published by: Alberta Tourism Education Council, #401-Centre 104, 5241 Calgary Trail, Edmonton, AB T6H 5G8, Canada. TEL 780-436-6112, FAX 780-436-5404, info@atec.ca, http://www.atec.ca.

917 NLD ISSN 1871-9317
CANADA MAGAZINE. Text in Dutch. 2006. s-a. EUR 15 membership; EUR 4.95 newsstand/cover (effective 2010). adv. **Document type:** *Magazine, Consumer.*
Published by: Walas Media, Postbus 590, Amersfoort, 3800 AN, Netherlands. TEL 31-33-4758326, FAX 31-33-4758359, info@walasmedia.com, http://www.walasmedia.com. Ed. Irma Verhoeven. adv.: color page EUR 1,350; trim 230 x 300. Circ: 15,000.

917.1021 CAN ISSN 1484-1177
CA1 CS 12-581
CANADA. STATISTICS CANADA. CANADA AT A GLANCE. Text in English. 1995. irreg.
Published by: Statistics Canada/Statistique Canada, Publications Sales and Services, Ottawa, ON K1A 0T6, Canada. TEL 613-951-7277, FAX 613-951-1584.

910.91 CAN ISSN 1910-0183
CANADA'S BEST DRIVES. Text in English. 2004. a. **Document type:** *Journal, Consumer.*
Published by: Canadian Tourism Commission/Commission Canadienne du Tourisme, Box 49230, Vancouver, BC V5P 1L2, Canada. TEL 604-638-8300, http://www.canadatourism.com.

338.4791 CAN ISSN 1481-3556
CANADIAN TOURISM COMMISSION. ANNUAL REPORT. Text in English. 1995. a.
Related titles: Online - full text ed.: ISSN 1493-5767.
Published by: Canadian Tourism Commission/Commission Canadienne du Tourisme, 55 Metcalfe St, Ste 600, Ottawa, ON K1P 6L5, Canada. TEL 613-946-1000, http://www.canadatourism.com.

338.4 330 CAN ISSN 1704-5630
CANADIAN TOURISM COMMISSION. CORPORATE PLAN SUMMARY. Text in English. 2001. a. **Document type:** *Journal, Trade.*
Related titles: Online - full text ed.: ISSN 1719-6515; French ed.: Commission Canadienne du Tourisme. Sommaire du Plan d'Entreprise. ISSN 1719-6523. 2001.
Published by: Canadian Tourism Commission/Commission Canadienne du Tourisme, Box 49230, Vancouver, BC V5P 1L2, Canada. TEL 604-638-8300.

917 CAN ISSN 1199-1615
CANADIAN TRAVEL PRESS. Text in English. 1968. w. CAD 80 domestic; USD 120 foreign (effective 2004). adv. bk.rev. **Document type:** *Magazine, Trade.* **Description:** Provides timely coverage of events of concern to the travel industry and carries in-depth destination reports from around the world.
Former titles (until 1994): Canadian Travel Press Weekly (0831-9138); (until 1986): Canadian Travel Press (0045-5490)
Indexed: A10, A33, H&TI, H06, RASB, T02, V03.
—CCC.
Published by: Baxter Publishing Co., 310 Dupont St, Toronto, ON M5R 1V9, Canada. TEL 416-968-7252, FAX 416-968-2377, ctp@baxter.net, http://www.baxter.net. Adv. contact Earl Lince. Circ: 3,000 (controlled).

910.09 USA
CANADIAN TRAVEL TO THE UNITED STATES. Text in English. 197?. a. stat. back issues avail. **Document type:** *Report, Government.* **Description:** Provides written analysis, graphics and data tables on Canadian travel of one or more nights to the U.S.
Formerly (until 1980): Vacation Travel by Canadians in the United States
Published by: International Trade Administration, Tourism Industries, 14th & Constitution Ave, NW Rm 1003, Washington, DC 20230. TEL 202-482-0140, FAX 202-482-2887, ron_erdmann@ita.doc.gov, http://www.tinet.ita.doc.gov.

917.1 CAN ISSN 1207-1463
CANADIAN TRAVELLER (VANCOUVER). Text in English. 1983. m. free for travel agents. adv. **Document type:** *Magazine, Trade.*
Former titles (until 1992): Canadian Traveller (1185-216X); (until 1991): TravelTrade Canada (0841-9191); (until 1988): TravelTrade, Travelexchange (0841-9183); (until 1988): Travelexchange (0841-9175)
Published by: Act Communications, 1260 Hornby St, Ste 104, Vancouver, BC V6Z 1W2, Canada. TEL 604-699-9990, FAX 604-699-9993. adv.: B&W page CAD 2,850, color page CAD 3,600; trim 10.88 x 8.13. Circ: 15,000 (controlled).

917.1 CAN ISSN 1911-5830
CANADIAN WINTER; Canada's coolest magazine. Text in English. 2007. a. **Document type:** *Magazine, Consumer.*
Published by: Griffintown Media Inc., 1336 Notre Dame West, Montreal, PQ H3C 1K7, Canada. TEL 888-934-2474.

917.2 CAN
CANCUN NIGHTS. Text in English. q. **Document type:** *Journal, Consumer.*
Published by: Nights Publications, 1831 Rene Levesque Blvd W, Montreal, PQ H3H 1R4, Canada. FAX 514-931-6273, editor@nightspublications.com. Ed. Stephen Trotter.

917.204 MEX
CANCUN TIPS - MAGAZINE. Text in English, Spanish. q. free (effective 2005). adv. illus.; maps. back issues avail. **Document type:** *Magazine, Consumer.* **Description:** Informs visitors to Cancun and surrounding areas of the many entertainment, shopping, and historical attractions of the region.
Published by: Cancun Tips S.A., Av. Tulum por Uxmal No.29, Locales 15 7 16, Cancun, QUINTANA ROO 77500, Mexico. TEL 52-998-8844044, FAX 52-998-8841868, http://www.cancuntips.com.mx/. Ed. Michelle Nieto Reynaud. Pub. Abel Minni Pugliese. Adv. contact Juan J Yanez. color page USD 10,710; 353 x 250. Circ: 120,000. **Subscr. outside of Mexico to:** ISCO, 3363 W. Commercial Blvd., Ste. 202, Ft. Lauderdale, FL 33309. TEL 800-930-5050.

917.204 MEX
CANCUN TIPS - TOURIST GUIDE. Text in English. 1987. s-a. free (effective 2005). adv. charts; illus.; maps. back issues avail. **Document type:** *Handbook/Manual/Guide, Consumer.* **Description:** Contains tourist information and tips on vacationing in Cancun and surrounding areas.
Formerly: Cancun Scene
Related titles: Spanish ed.: Cancun Tips - Guia Turistica.
Published by: Cancun Tips S.A., Av. Tulum por Uxmal No.29, Locales 15 7 16, Cancun, QUINTANA ROO 77500, Mexico. TEL 52-998-8844044, FAX 52-998-8841868, http://www.cancuntips.com.mx/. Ed. Michelle Nieto Reynaud. Pub. Abel Minni Pugliese. Adv. contact Juan J Yanez. color page USD 12,915; trim 184 x 134. Circ: 500,000.

914.613 ESP ISSN 1888-3915
A CANDEA; revista do caurel. Text in Gallegan. 2000. q. **Document type:** *Journal, Academic/Scholarly.*
Published by: Asociacion Fonte do Milagro, C. Froxan, 4, Lugo, 27325, Spain. TEL 34-982-210128, froxan.vila@terra.es, http://www.fontedomilagro.org/.

917.4 USA
CAPE COD GUIDE; the guide for the sophisticated traveller. Text in English. 1943. 9/yr. free to qualified personnel (effective 2009). illus. 96 p./no.; back issues avail. **Document type:** *Magazine, Consumer.* **Description:** Provides information on shopping, dining, entertainment and attractions in Cape Cod.
Published by: Rabideau Publishing, LLC, PO Box 208, Yarmouthport, MA 02675. TEL 508-771-6549, FAX 508-771-3769. Pub. Michael Rabideau. Adv. contact Julie Dalton.

917.4 USA ISSN 1074-4584
CAPE COD TRAVEL GUIDE. Text in English. 1993. a. USD 4.75 newsstand/cover; USD 5.75 newsstand/cover in Canada (effective 2001). adv. **Document type:** *Magazine, Consumer.* **Description:** Contains information and advice on getting the most out of vacationing on Cape Cod.
Published by: Northeast Publications, Inc., 143A Upper County Rd, Dennisport, MA 02639. TEL 508-398-6101, FAX 508-398-4711.

910.91 USA ISSN 1932-1813
F144.C23
CAPE MAY MAGAZINE. Text in English. 2006. bi-m. USD 24 (effective 2007). back issues avail. **Document type:** *Magazine, Consumer.*
Published by: Cape Publishing, Inc., PO Box 2383, Cape May, NJ 08204. TEL 609-898-4500, 888-898-2997, FAX 609-898-3585, info@capemay.com, http://www.capepublishing.com. Ed. Susan Tischler.

910.2 AUS ISSN 1832-2964
CAPE YORKER. Text in English. 2005. a. AUD 12.95 per issue (effective 2007). adv. 128 p./no.; **Document type:** *Magazine, Consumer.*
Published by: Cape Yorker Magazine, PO Box 710, Weipa, QLD 4874, Australia. TEL 61-7-4069-9204, FAX 61-7-4069-9274, mail@capeyorker.com, http://www.capeyorker.com/index.html. Ed. Anthony Gomes.

917.504 GBR ISSN 1366-6223
CAPITAL REGION U S A HOLIDAY GUIDE. Text in English. 19??. a. free (effective 2010). adv. **Document type:** *Handbook/Manual/Guide, Consumer.* **Description:** Holiday and travel planner aimed at consumers in Germany, the United Kingdom, and Europe.
Formerly (until 1995): Capital Region U S A (1360-7170)
Related titles: Online - full text ed.
Published by: (Capital Region USA, Inc.), Phoenix International Publishing, PO Box 615, Horsham, Sussex RH13 5WF, United Kingdom. marymooremason@phoenixip.com, http://www.phoenixip.com/. Ed. Neil Murrey. Pub. Simon Todd TEL 682-831-0133. Adv. contact Larry Cohen TEL 203-255-8800. **Dist. in US by:** Northeast Media Group.

914.504 ITA
CAPRI REVIEW. Text in Italian. 1994. s-a. **Document type:** *Magazine, Consumer.*
Related titles: Online - full text ed.
Published by: P R C Srl, Via Germanico 197, Rome, RM 00192, Italy. TEL 39-06-3215923, FAX 39-06-3242857.

388.3 BEL ISSN 1370-589X
CAR & BUS MAGAZINE (NEDERLANDSE EDITIE). Text in Dutch. 1928. m. (10/yr.). EUR 62 domestic; EUR 86.76 foreign (effective 2005). illus. **Document type:** *Trade.* **Description:** Covers news, information and travel destinations of interest to the tourist bus industry.
Former titles (until 1993): Transport en Toerisme (0773-6371); (until 1965): Transport langs de Baan (0773-638X)
Related titles: French ed.: Car & Bus Magazine (Edition Francaise). ISSN 1370-5903. 1945.
Published by: Federation Belge des Exploitants d'Autobus et d'Autocars/F.B.A.A. - Federatie van de Belgische Autobus- en Autocarondernemers, Moorseelsesteenweg 2, Roeselare, 8800, Belgium. TEL 32-51-226060, FAX 32-51-229273, info@fbaa.be, http://www.fbaa.be. Ed. Riet Espeel. Adv. contact Conny Desmet.

CAR & TRAVEL MONTHLY. *see* TRANSPORTATION—Automobiles

914.2 GBR ISSN 1475-9004
CARAVAN. Text in English. 1985. m. GBP 29.82 domestic; EUR 72.77 in Europe eurozone; GBP 47.25 in Europe non-eurozone; USD 101.99 in United States; GBP 70.83 in Canada; GBP 68.54 elsewhere (effective 2009). adv. bk.rev. charts; illus. **Document type:** *Magazine, Consumer.* **Description:** Informational and feature articles pertaining to touring trailer caravans, with reviews of products and equipment, technical advice, and ratings of sites.
Formerly (until 2001): Caravan Magazine (0268-0440); Which was formed by the merger of (1938-1984): Caravan (0008-6142); Which incorporated: Caravan Home (0528-0966); Caravan was formerly (1933-1937): Caravan and Trailer; (1978-1984): Caravanning Monthly (0262-8589); Which was formerly: Modern Caravanning; (until 1977): Modern Caravan (0026-7554)
Published by: I P C Country & Leisure Media Ltd. (Subsidiary of: I P C Media Ltd.), The Blue Fin Bldg, 110 Southwark St, London, SE1 0SU, United Kingdom. TEL 44-20-31485000, FAX 44-20-31486439. Ed. Victoria Bentley TEL 44-20-87268245. Pub. Clive Birch TEL 44-20-87268235. adv.: page GBP 2,208. Circ: 15,774 (paid). **Subscr. to:** I P C Media Ltd., PO Box 272, Haywards Heath, W Sussex RH16 3FS, United Kingdom. TEL 44-845-6767778, FAX 44-845-1238010, ipcsubs@qss-uk.com. **Dist. by:** MarketForce UK Ltd, The Blue Fin Bldg, 3rd Fl, 110 Southwark St, London SE1 0SU, United Kingdom. TEL 44-20-31483300, FAX 44-20-31488105, salesinnovation@marketforce.co.uk, http://www.marketforce.co.uk/.

CARAVAN AND CAMPING GUIDE - BRITAIN & IRELAND (YEAR). *see* SPORTS AND GAMES—Outdoor Life

728.76 AUS
CARAVAN & MOTORHOME. Text in English. 1998. 13/yr. AUD 90.55 domestic; AUD 160 in New Zealand; AUD 192.50 elsewhere; AUD 9.95 newsstand/cover (effective 2008). adv. back issues avail. **Document type:** *Magazine, Consumer.* **Description:** Provides motorhome and caravan reviews, photographed destinations, and travelling tips.
Formerly (until 1999): Australian Camper Caravan & Motorhome
Published by: Express Publications Pty. Ltd., 2-4 Stanley St, Locked Bag 111, Silverwater, NSW 2168, Australia. TEL 61-2-97413800, 800-801-647, FAX 61-2-97378017, subs@magstore.com.au, http://www.expresspublications.com.au. Ed. Greg Smith. Adv. contact Allan Goldby TEL 61-2-97413821. **Subscr. to:** ISubscribe Pty Ltd., 25 Lime St, Ste 303, Level 3, Sydney, NSW 2000, Australia. TEL 61-2-92621722, FAX 61-2-92625044, info@isubscribe.com.au, http://www.isubscribe.com.au.

796 ZAF ISSN 0379-4636
CARAVAN AND OUTDOOR LIFE. Text in English. 1960. m. ZAR 40; USD 25 foreign. adv. bk.rev. **Document type:** *Magazine, Consumer.* **Description:** Articles on travel and tourism for caravans(trailers), motorhomes, camping and backpacking. Includes vehicle tests, tips and hints for readers.
Formerly: Caravan
Published by: Caravan Publications (Pty) Ltd., PO Box 15939, Vlaeberg, Cape Town 8018, South Africa. TEL 27-21-241457, FAX 27-21-261809. Ed., Pub. Godfrey Castle. Adv. contact Mandy Ahrens. B&W page USD 800, color page USD 1,383; trim 276 x 210. Circ: 23,000.

910.2 388 GBR ISSN 2045-7901
CARAVAN BUYER; your ultimate caravan buying guide. Text in English. 2006. a. GBP 4.95 per issue (effective 2010). back issues avail. **Document type:** *Magazine, Consumer.* **Description:** Contains 227 new UK caravan models listed, bargain prices secondhand tourers and new and used buyers' guide.
Published by: I P C Focus Network, Leon House, 233 High St, Croydon, CR9 1HZ, United Kingdom. TEL 44-20-87268000, http://www.ipcmedia.com.

796.5 910.202 ITA ISSN 1121-7227
CARAVAN E CAMPER. Variant title: Caravan Camper Granturismo. Text in Italian. 1975. m. EUR 40 (effective 2008). **Document type:** *Magazine, Consumer.*
Formerly (until 1987): Caravanning. Vacanze Turismo (1121-7219)
Related titles: Online - full text ed.; Supplement(s): Almanacco. Caravan & Camper. ISSN 1121-7200. 1976.
Published by: M C M Editori srl, Via Eustachi 31, Milan, 20129, Italy. TEL 39-02-20241592, FAX 39-02-20249336.

914 GBR ISSN 1359-1223
CARAVAN INDUSTRY AND PARK OPERATOR. Text in English. 1969. m. GBP 3 per issue (effective 2009). adv. bk.rev. illus. 32 p./no.; **Document type:** *Magazine, Trade.* **Description:** Serves the camping trailer and caravan market, including developments, advice and special features for park operators, dealers and manufacturers.
Supersedes in part (in 1995): Caravan Business Plus Caravan Industry (0268-5558); Which was formed by the 1985 merger of: Caravan Business; Caravan Industry and Park Operator (0045-5725)
—CCC.
Published by: A.E. Morgan Publications Ltd., 8A High St, Epsom, Surrey KT19 8AD, United Kingdom. TEL 44-1372-741411, FAX 44-1372-744493, info@aemorgan.co.uk, http://www.aemorgan.co.uk/. Ed. David Ritchie. adv.: B&W page GBP 635, color page GBP 880; bleed 216 x 303.

388.346 AUS
CARAVAN WORLD. Text in English. 1972. m. AUD 71.50 in Australia & New Zealand; AUD 87.50 elsewhere; AUD 7.50 newsstand/cover (effective 2008). adv. charts; illus. **Document type:** *Magazine, Consumer.* **Description:** Provides information on new recreational vehicle reviews, tow tests of a range of suitable tow vehicles, travel stories and readers' own tales.
Former titles (until 2003): Caravan World and Outdoor Life (1320-2111); (until 1978): Australian Caravan World and Camper Trailering; Australian Caravan World
Published by: A C P Trader International Group (Subsidiary of: P B L Media Pty Ltd.), 73 Atherton Rd, Oakleigh, VIC 3166, Australia. TEL 61-3-95674200, FAX 61-3-95634554. Eds. Ros Bromwich TEL 61-3-95674251, Greg Leech TEL 61-3-95674194. Adv. contact Justine Schuller. color page AUD 2,415; trim 225 x 297. Circ: 13,322. **Subscr. to:** Magshop, Reply Paid 4967, Sydney, NSW 2001, Australia. TEL 61-2-136116, subs@magstore.com.au, http://shop.magstore.com.au.

796.5 ESP
CARAVANING & CAMPING. Text in Spanish. m. EUR 3.90 newsstand/cover (effective 2009). adv. **Document type:** *Magazine, Consumer.*
Published by: Grupo V, C Valportillo Primera, 11, Alcobendas, Madrid, 28108, Spain. TEL 34-91-6622137, FAX 34-91-6622654, secretaria@grupov.es. Ed. Oscar Munoz. Adv. contact Carmina Ferrer. page EUR 1,925; trim 19.5 x 25.5. Circ: 14,000.

CARAVANNEN!. *see* SPORTS AND GAMES—Outdoor Life

THE CARETAKER GAZETTE; number 1 source for caretaker jobs!. *see* OCCUPATIONS AND CAREERS

CARIBBEAN AVIATION AND TOURISM NEWS/NOTICIERO AERONAUTICO Y TURISMO CARIBENSE. *see* AERONAUTICS AND SPACE FLIGHT

CARIBBEAN DATELINE. *see* BUSINESS AND ECONOMICS—Investments

TU

910.202 USA ISSN 1935-3413
F2165
CARIBBEAN GUIDE. Text in English. 1998. irreg., latest 2nd ed. ILS 21.95 per issue (effective 2008). **Document type:** *Guide, Consumer.*
Published by: Open Road Publishing Co., PO Box 284, Cold Spring Harbor, NY 11724. TEL 631-692-7172, FAX 631-692-7193, jopenroad@aol.com, http://www.openroadguides.com/index.php. Ed. Janet Groene.

910.202 GBR ISSN 0967-4748
F1934.5
CARIBBEAN ISLANDS HANDBOOK (YEAR); with the Bahamas. Text in English. 1990. a. GBP 14.99 per issue (effective 2010). adv. maps. back issues avail. **Document type:** *Handbook/Manual/Guide, Consumer.* **Description:** Covers all the basics from where to stay and where to eat to cycling, walking and how to get around the Caribbean Islands.
—CCC.
Published by: Footprint Handbooks Ltd., 6 Riverside Ct, Lower Bristol Rd, Bath, Avon BA2 3DZ, United Kingdom. TEL 44-1225-469141, FAX 44-1225-469461, wwwinfo@footprintbooks.com.

917.29 USA ISSN 1941-1936
F2171.3
CARIBBEAN LIVING. Text in English. 2008 (Feb.). q. USD 20; USD 5.95 per issue (effective 2008). adv. **Document type:** *Magazine, Consumer.*
Published by: Caribbean Living Magazine, Inc, 10097 Cleary Blvd, Plantation, FL 33324. TEL 954-382-4533, FAX 954-382-4529. Pub. Peta Phipps. adv.: page USD 9,038.

910.09 USA ISSN 1052-1011
F2171.3
CARIBBEAN TRAVEL + LIFE. Abbreviated title: C T & L. Text in English. 1986. 9/yr. USD 16.97 domestic; USD 26.97 in Canada; USD 43.97 elsewhere; USD 4.99 per issue elsewhere (effective 2009). adv. bk.rev. illus. back issues avail.; reprints avail. **Document type:** *Magazine, Consumer.* **Description:** Provides a broad and deep package of inspiration and expert information to readers whose enthusiasm about traveling to the Caribbean goes beyond mere vacationing and amounts to an extension of their lifestyles.
Formerly (until 1987): Caribbean Travel and Life Magazine (0891-9496); Which incorporated (in 1987): Tropical Island Living
Related titles: Online - full text ed.
—CCC.
Published by: (Caribbean Tourism Organization), World Publications LLC (Subsidiary of: Bonnier Magazine Group), 460 N Orlando Ave, Ste 200, Winter Park, FL 32789. TEL 407-628-4802, FAX 407-628-7061, info@worldpub.net, http://www.bonniercorp.com. Eds. Sarah Greaves-Gabbadon, Dave Herndon. R&P Sue Gilman. Adv. contacts Jayne McAllister, Carol Johnson TEL 908-221-9122. color page USD 19,925. Circ: 154,811 (paid).

919 USA ISSN 1530-1176
F2171
CARIBBEAN TRAVELBOOK INCLUDING BERMUDA. Text in English. 1994. a. free to members (effective 2008). adv. illus. **Document type:** *Magazine, Consumer.* **Description:** Provides in-depth travel information and property listings on Caribbean includes Bermuda.
Former titles (until 1998): Bermuda, the Bahamas & Islands of the Caribbean TravelBook (1088-6532); (until 1995): Caribbean TravelBook (1082-7277); (until 1994): A A A Caribbean TravelGuide: Including the Bahamas & Bermuda; (until 1993): Travel Guide Caribbean, Bahamas, Bermuda, and other Ports of Call (0730-6873); (until 19??): Caribbean, Bahamas, Bermuda and other Ports of Call Travel Guide
Published by: A A A Publishing, 1000 AAA Dr, Heathrow, FL 32746. TEL 407-444-8370, FAX 407-444-8271, AAATravelInfo-CustomerService@national.aaa.com, http://www.aaa.biz/. adv.: B&W page USD 5,060, color page USD 6,600. Circ: 300,272 (controlled).

919 GBR ISSN 0963-2565
CARIBBEAN WORLD. Text in English. 1991. q. GBP 19.16 domestic; GBP 25.60 in Europe; GBP 35.60 elsewhere (effective 2009). back issues avail. **Document type:** *Magazine, Consumer.* **Description:** Comprehensive lifestyle magazine devoted to culture, living and travel in the Caribbean.
Published by: Caribbean World Magazine, W kensington, PO Box 4386, London, United Kingdom. TEL 44-20-77511689, publisher@caribbeanworld-magazine.com.

CARNET DE PROVENCE. *see* GENERAL INTEREST PERIODICALS—France

914 PRT
CARTAZ; revista mensal de cultura e informacao e turismo. Text in Portuguese. 1970 (vol.6). m. adv. charts; illus.
Address: Avenida de Roma, 72, 1 Esq. Frente, Lisbon, 1700, Portugal. Ed. A Borges Pires.

CATALOGUE OF CANADIAN RECREATION AND LEISURE RESEARCH. *see* LEISURE AND RECREATION

796.525 USA
CAVES AND CAVERNS; national caves association directory. Text in English. 1973. a. illus.; maps. **Document type:** *Directory.* **Description:** Includes names, addresses, phone numbers, and websites of current NCA members.
Published by: National Caves Association, 1904 Mammoth Cave Pkwy, PO Box 280, Park City, KY 42160. TEL 270-749-2228, FAX 270-749-2428, info@cavern.com, http://www.cavern.com.

910.202 URY
CENTAUR. Text in Spanish. 1977. a. adv.
Published by: Centro Automovilista del Uruguay, Cn. Artigas, 1773, Montevideo, 12413, Uruguay. Ed. Ever Cabrera Tornielli.

CENTRAL COAST (AVILA BEACH). *see* LIFESTYLE

914.704 USA
CENTRAL WISCONSIN RESORTER. Text in English. 1965. w. USD 30 out of county. adv.
Address: PO Box 838, Wautoma, WI 54982. TEL 414-787-3334, FAX 414-787-2883. Ed., Pub. Mary Kunasch. Circ: 11,000.

338.48 910.2 ARG ISSN 1852-4583
▼ **CENTRO DE ESTUDIOS DEL CONOCIMIENTO E INNOVACION EMPRESARIAL TURISTICO. NOTICIAS.** Text in Spanish. 2009. q. back issues avail. **Document type:** *Newsletter.*
Media: Online - full text.
Published by: Universidad Nacional del Comahue, Centro de Estudios del Conocimiento e Innovacion Empresarial Turistico, Buenos Aires, 1400, Neuquen, 8300, Argentina. TEL 54-299-4490378, FAX 54-299-4490380, centroestudios@ceciet.com.ar, http://www.ceciet.com.ar/cet/index.php.

CENTUR. *see* TRANSPORTATION—Automobiles

338.48 CZE ISSN 1801-7258
CESKOPIS. Text in Czech. 2006. m. CZK 380; CZK 38 newsstand/cover (effective 2008). adv. **Document type:** *Magazine, Consumer.*
Published by: Ceskopis, s.r.o., Pobrezni 21, Prague 4, 18000, Czech Republic. TEL 420-2-66312379. adv.: B&W page CZK 82,000, color page CZK 117,000; trim 165 x 235.

CHARLESTON MAGAZINE (CLEVELAND). *see* GENERAL INTEREST PERIODICALS—United States

CHARUTO ET CIA; pecadilhos e prazeres. *see* TOBACCO

917 910.91 USA ISSN 1934-2586
F73.18
THE CHEAP BASTARD'S GUIDE TO BOSTON; secrets of living the good life. Text in English. 2007. triennial, latest 2007, 1st ed. USD 14.95 per issue (effective 2008). **Document type:** *Guide, Consumer.* **Description:** Aims to act as a guide to unique places.
Published by: The Globe Pequot Press, Inc., 246 Goose Ln, PO Box 480, Guilford, CT 06437. TEL 203-458-4500, 888-249-7586, FAX 203-458-4603, 800-820-2329, info@globepequot.com, http://www.globepequot.com.

917 910.91 USA ISSN 1932-3514
F548.18
THE CHEAP BASTARD'S GUIDE TO CHICAGO; secrets of living the good life. Text in English. 2006. triennial, latest 2006, 1st ed. USD 14.95 per issue (effective 2008). **Document type:** *Guide, Consumer.*
Published by: The Globe Pequot Press, Inc., 246 Goose Ln, PO Box 480, Guilford, CT 06437. TEL 203-458-4500, 888-249-7586, FAX 203-458-4603, 800-820-2329, info@globepequot.com, http://www.globepequot.com.

917 USA ISSN 1549-5116
F128.18
THE CHEAP BASTARD'S GUIDE TO NEW YORK CITY; a native new yorker's secrets of living the good life. Text in English. 2002. triennial, latest 2008, 4th ed. USD 14.95 per issue (effective 2008). **Document type:** *Guide, Consumer.*
Published by: The Globe Pequot Press, Inc., 246 Goose Ln, PO Box 480, Guilford, CT 06437. TEL 203-458-4500, 888-249-7586, FAX 800-820-2329, info@globepequot.com, http://www.globepequot.com.

917 910.91 USA ISSN 1939-0777
F869.S33
THE CHEAP BASTARD'S GUIDE TO SAN FRANCISCO; secrets of living the good life. Text in English. 2007. triennial, latest 2007, 1st ed. USD 14.95 per issue (effective 2008). **Document type:** *Guide, Consumer.* **Description:** Aims to act as a guide to unique places.
Published by: The Globe Pequot Press, Inc., 246 Goose Ln, PO Box 480, Guilford, CT 06437. TEL 203-458-4500, 888-249-7586, FAX 203-458-4603, 800-820-2329, info@globepequot.com, http://www.globepequot.com.

975.3 USA ISSN 2151-5182
F192.3
▼ **CHEAP BASTARD'S GUIDE TO WASHINGTON, D.C.** Text in English. 2009. triennial. USD 14.95 per issue (effective 2009). **Document type:** *Guide, Consumer.* **Description:** Uncovers all the ins and outs and exclusive bargains in Washington, D.C.
Published by: The Globe Pequot Press, Inc., 246 Goose Ln, PO Box 480, Guilford, CT 06437. TEL 203-458-4500, FAX 203-458-4603, info@globepequot.com, http://www.globepequot.com.

917.52 917.5518 USA ISSN 1553-829X
THE CHESAPEAKE BAY BOOK; a complete guide. Text in English. 1992. irreg., latest 2005, 6th ed. USD 18.95 6th ed. (effective 2008). back issues avail. **Document type:** *Directory.* **Description:** Contains important contact information for lodging, dining, shopping and recreational activities, transportation details, a calendar of events, special 'if time is short' options, local history, over 60 photos and maps and essential information for residents.
Published by: The Countryman Press (Subsidiary of: W.W. Norton & Co., Inc.), PO Box 748, Woodstock, VT 05091. TEL 802-457-4826, 800-245-4151, FAX 802-457-1678, countrymanpress@wwnorton.com.

CHESAPEAKE BAY MAGAZINE. *see* SPORTS AND GAMES—Boats And Boating

917 USA ISSN 1937-0415
F548.18
CHICAGO. Variant title: Eyewitness Travel Guide: Chicago. Text in English. 2007. irreg., latest 2003. USD 20 per issue (effective 2008). **Document type:** *Guide, Consumer.* **Description:** Covers information on the north side, the downtown core, south loop, near south side and to parts further outside the Chicago.
Published by: D K Publishing (Subsidiary of: Penguin Books U S A, Inc.), 375 Hudson St, New York, NY 10014. TEL 800-631-8571, FAX 201-256-0000, specialsales@dk.com. Ed. Jane Ewart.

917.7311 USA ISSN 0362-4595
F548.1
CHICAGO MAGAZINE. Text in English. 1952. m. USD 1 per issue (effective 2009). adv. bk.rev. illus. **Document type:** *Magazine, Consumer.* **Description:** Presents extensive coverage of events, dining, culture, politics, personalities, design, fashion, entertainment and lifestyle issues.
Former titles (until 1975): Chicago Guide (0042-9651); Which incorporated (1973-1974): The Chicagoan (0092-2471); (until 1970): W F M T Guide; (until 1964): Chicago Perspective
Related titles: Microfiche ed.: (from PQC); Online - full text ed.; Supplement(s): Chicago Magazine Home. ISSN 1930-787X. 2002.
Indexed: A&ATA, A21, A22, ASIP, B04, BRD, G05, G06, G07, G08, G09, I05, M02, MagInd, P02, P10, P34, P48, P53, P54, PQC, R03, RGAb, RGPR, RI-1, RI-2, T02, W03.
—CCC.
Published by: Chicagoland Publishing Company (Subsidiary of: Chicago Tribune Company), 435 N Michigan Ave, Ste 1100, Chicago, IL 60611. TEL 312-222-8999, 800-874-2863, http://www.chicagotribune.com/. Ed. Richard Babcock. Adv. contact Tom Conradi.

913.773 USA
CHICAGO OFFICIAL VISITORS GUIDE. Text in English. 1984. 3/yr. free. adv. **Document type:** *Guide, Consumer.* **Description:** Includes features of Chicago goings-on: festivals, art exhibits, sports calendars and more.
Formerly (until 1988): Chicago, Dining, Shopping, Entertainment, Attractions
Published by: Weaver Publications, Inc., 2420 Alcott St, Denver, CO 80211. TEL 303-458-1211, FAX 303-477-0724, info@weaver-group.com, http://pub.weaver-group.com. Circ: 1,000,000.

913.773 USA
CHICAGO TRAVEL PROFESSIONALS GUIDE. Text in English. a. free. adv. **Document type:** *Guide, Consumer.* **Description:** Includes vital facts about visitor information centers, safety tips, phone facts, transportation information.
Published by: Weaver Publications, Inc., 2420 Alcott St, Denver, CO 80211. TEL 303-458-1211, FAX 303-477-0724, info@weaver-group.com, http://pub.weaver-group.com. Circ: 20,000.

910.202 GBR ISSN 1363-741X
F3059.5
CHILE HANDBOOK. Text in English. 1997. biennial. GBP 14.99 per issue (effective 2010). adv. back issues avail. **Document type:** *Handbook/Manual/Guide, Consumer.* **Description:** Contains up-to-date travel facts, lively listings and informative historical background and in-depth cultural context. Covers all the latest on the ever-growing adventure travel scene from climbing and trekking to skiing and rafting.
—CCC.
Published by: Footprint Handbooks Ltd., 6 Riverside Ct, Lower Bristol Rd, Bath, Avon BA2 3DZ, United Kingdom. TEL 44-1225-469141, FAX 44-1225-469461, wwwinfo@footprintbooks.com.

915.1 SGP ISSN 0218-6276
CHINA JOURNEY/ZHONGGUO XING. Text in Chinese. 1994. bi-m. SGD 25; SGD 60 in Asia; SGD 68 in Australia & New Zealand; SGD 82 elsewhere. adv. illus. **Document type:** *Trade.* **Description:** Focuses on places of interest, ancient relics, natural scenery, tradition of ethnic minorities, and tourist facilities, as well as business and economic development in China.
Published by: China Information Centre (Singapore) Pte. Ltd., Soon Seng Bldg, 25 Genting Rd 07-01, Singapore, 349482, Singapore. TEL 65-743-8606, FAX 65-743-6702. Ed., Pub. Tang Kin Eng. R&P Angela Tang. Adv. contact Janet Wong. Circ: 50,000.

951.04 HKG ISSN 1025-577X
DS712
CHINA TOURISM. Text in English. 1980. m. HKD 296 domestic; HKD 415 in PRC, Macao & Taiwan; USD 69 in Asia except Japan; USD 70 elsewhere (effective 2005). adv. illus.; maps. cum.index. back issues avail. **Document type:** *Magazine, Consumer.* **Description:** Contains feature articles on sights, scenery, customs, travel experiences, recent archeological discoveries, and places of historical interest in China.
Former titles: Culture, Arts and Crafts; China Tourism Pictorial
Related titles: Chinese ed.: Zhongguo Luyou. ISSN 1025-5761. USD 59 (effective 2001); French ed.: Voyage en Chine.
Indexed: RASB.
Published by: Hong Kong China Tourism Press, 24F Westlands Centre, 20 Westlands Rd, Quarry Bay, Hong Kong, Hong Kong. TEL 852-25618001, FAX 852-25618196. adv.: page HKD 20,600; trim 215 x 286. Circ: 96,000.

338.479151 GBR ISSN 1747-8855
CHINA TOURISM REPORT. Text in English. 2005. q. EUR 820, USD 1,030 combined subscription (print & email eds.) (effective 2010). **Document type:** *Report, Trade.* **Description:** Provides industry professionals and strategists, corporate analysts, associations, government departments and regulatory bodies with independent forecasts and competitive intelligence on the Chinese tourism industry.
Related titles: E-mail ed.
Indexed: B01, H&TI, H06, P34.
Published by: Business Monitor International Ltd., Senator House, 85 Queen Victoria St, London, EC4V 4AB, United Kingdom. TEL 44-20-72480468, FAX 44-20-72480467, subs@businessmonitor.com.

910.4 USA
CHINCOTEAGUE BEACHCOMBER. Text in English. 1959. 20/yr. free.
Address: PO Box 249, Onley, VA 23418-0249. TEL 804-787-1200, FAX 804-787-9567. Ed. Bill Sterling. Circ: 10,000.

639.950968 ZAF
CHRIS AND TILDE STUART'S GUIDE TO SOUTHERN AFRICAN GAME & NATURE RESERVES. Text in English. 1994 (3rd ed.). irreg. ZAR 79.99. illus. **Document type:** *Monographic series, Consumer.*
Published by: Struik Publishers, PO Box 1144, Cape Town, 8000, South Africa. TEL 27-21-4624360, FAX 27-21-4624379. Ed. Tilde Stuart.

910.2 CAN ISSN 1715-2186
CHUTES & MISSISSAGI, INFORMATION GUIDE. Text in English. 2005. a. **Document type:** *Handbook/Manual/Guide, Consumer.*
Published by: Ontario Ministry of Natural Resources, Ontario Parks, PO Box 7000, Peterborough, ON K9J 8M5, Canada. TEL 705-755-2000, http://www.mnr.gov.on.ca, http://www.ontarioparks.com.

CICLOTURISMO. *see* SPORTS AND GAMES—Bicycles And Motorcycles

910.91 ITA
LE CITTA DELLA CALABRIA. Text in Italian. 19??. bi-m. back issues avail. **Document type:** *Monographic series, Consumer.*
Published by: Rubbettino Editore, Viale Rosario Rubbettino 10, Soveria Mannelli, CZ 88049, Italy.

910.01 DEU ISSN 1610-0328
CITY FASZINATIONEN. Text in German. 1999. a. EUR 3.90 newsstand/cover (effective 2009). adv. **Document type:** *Magazine, Trade.*
Published by: Ella Verlag, Emil-Hoffmann-Str 55-59, Cologne, 50996, Germany. TEL 49-2236-84880, FAX 49-2236-848824, info@ella-verlag.de, http://www.ella-verlag.de. Adv. contact Elke Latuperisa. page EUR 2,660; trim 210 x 277. Circ: 8,994 (paid and controlled).

CITY LINE NEWS. *see* BUSINESS AND ECONOMICS—Economic Situation And Conditions

796.5 052 EST ISSN 1406-2208
DK502.3
CITY PAPER - THE BALTIC STATES. Variant title: City Paper. Text in English. 1995. bi-m. USD 54 in Europe; USD 62 elsewhere (effective 2002). adv. **Document type:** *Magazine, Consumer.* **Description:** Covers all three Baltic nations in a comprehensive, user-friendly way.
Related titles: Online - full text ed.
Address: Parnu mnt 142, Tallinn, 11317, Estonia. TEL 372-655-5095, FAX 372-655-5096. Ed. Eve Tarm. Adv. contact Riina Sepp. Circ: 25,000 (paid and controlled).

917.3 USA ISSN 1082-9938
E158
CITY PROFILES U S A; a traveler's guide to major U.S. and Canadian cities. Text in English. 1995. a., latest 9th ed. USD 175 (effective 2008). **Document type:** *Directory, Consumer.* **Description:** Provides key contact information for more than 200 major US cities and Canadian cities, including all state capitals. Includes information sources, lodging, food and travel, education, events and attractions.
Published by: Omnigraphics, Inc., PO Box 31-1640, Detroit, MI 48231. TEL 313-961-1340, 800-234-1340, FAX 313-961-1383, 800-875-1340, info@omnigraphics.com.

910.92 USA
CITYGUIDE U S A MAGAZINE. Text in Japanese. 1987. m. adv. **Description:** Tourist guide to Las Vegas caters to Japanese-speaking visitors.
Published by: Japan Convention & Translation Services, 535 E St. Louis Ave, Las Vegas, NV 89104. TEL 702-733-2880, FAX 702-734-8503.

910.2 973.7 USA ISSN 1541-8979
E641
CIVIL WAR SITES; the official guide to the civil war discovery trail. Text in English. 2003. biennial, latest 2007, 2nd ed. USD 17.95 per issue (effective 2008). **Document type:** *Guide, Consumer.* **Description:** Provides information and acts as the travel guide to more than 600 battlefields, antebellum mansions, state parks, cemeteries, memorials, museums, and other civil war related destinations.
Published by: The Globe Pequot Press, Inc., 246 Goose Ln, PO Box 480, Guilford, CT 06437. TEL 203-458-4500, 888-249-7586, FAX 203-458-4603, 800-820-2329, info@globepequot.com, http://www.globepequot.com.

910.09 DEU
CLEVER REISEN; das clevere Reise-Infomagazin. Text in German. 1986. q. EUR 20.40 domestic; EUR 25.50 in Europe; EUR 40.90 elsewhere; EUR 5.10 newsstand/cover (effective 2006). adv. bk.rev. **Document type:** *Magazine, Consumer.*
Formerly (until 2003): Fliegen & Sparen
Published by: Markt Control Multimedia Verlag GmbH & Co. KG, Postfach 180260, Duisburg, 47172, Germany. TEL 49-203-554248, FAX 49-203-547970. Eds. Juergen Zupancic, Wolfgang Grahl. adv.: B&W page EUR 1,880, color page EUR 3,110. Circ: 28,766 (paid and controlled).

914.3804 POL
CLUB. Text in English, Polish. 1996. m. free. adv. **Document type:** *Journal, Trade.* **Description:** Includes presentations of attractive Polish tourist regions, information about Polish carriers, Orbis news on events and undertakings important for the tourist sector, advice on recreation and restaurants in the Orbis Gold Club section, a review of cultural and artistic events in Poland.
Published by: (Orbis S.A.), Warsaw Voice S.A., Ksiecia Janusza 64, Warsaw, 01452, Poland. TEL 48-22-366377, FAX 48-22-371995, redakcja@terapia.com.pl. Ed. Przemyslaw Falnczynski. Adv. contact Kaja Dobrowolska. page PLZ 8,200.

CLUB DE GOURMETS; gastronomy & travel magazine - gastronomia y viajes. *see* HOTELS AND RESTAURANTS

917 USA
CLUBMEX; Baja California, Sea of Cortez, Mexico's west coast, interior Mexico. Text in English. 1976. m. USD 12.95 to members (effective Jul. 2001). adv. bk.rev. 16 p./no.; **Document type:** *Newsletter.* **Description:** Contains articles and news on vacations and travel to Mexico, focusing on auto or motorhome travel.
Formerly: Mexico West (0889-7107)
Address: 3450 Bonita Rd, 103, Chula Vista, CA 91902. TEL 619-585-3033, FAX 619-420-8133. Ed. Chuck Stein. Circ: 7,000.

659 ROM ISSN 1453-9527
CLUJ-NAPOCA - WHAT, WHERE, WHEN. Text in Multiple languages. 1998. q. ROL 50,000 domestic; USD 12 foreign (effective 2002). adv. **Document type:** *Magazine, Consumer.*
Published by: Crystal Publishing Group, 253, Calea Calarasilor, bl. 67 A, Ste. 4, Bucharest, Romania. TEL 40-21-3233829, FAX 40-21-3234706, office@bucurestiwww.ro, http://www.bucurestiwww.ro. Circ: 25,000 (paid and controlled).

COACH OPERATORS HANDBOOK. *see* TRANSPORTATION

910.2 GBR ISSN 2045-0257
COACH WORLD. Text in English. 19??. m. GBP 39; GBP 4 per issue (effective 2010). adv. back issues avail. **Document type:** *Magazine, Consumer.* **Description:** Offers travel and tour news, updates on destinations and events as well as route planners, theatre listings and event calendars.
Formerly (until 2010): Out & About (2044-7558)
Published by: Rouncy Media, Ltd., 3 The Office Village, Forder Way, Cygnet Park, Hampton, Peterborough, PE7 8GX, United Kingdom. TEL 44-1733-293240, FAX 44-845-2802927, cbwinbox@rouncymedia.co.uk. Ed. Andrew Sutcliffe TEL 44-1733-293242. Adv. contact Debbie Maclaren TEL 44-208-1819730.

910.2 USA
COAST MAGAZINE. Text in English. 1955. fortn. USD 29.95; free newsstand/cover (effective 2005). adv. bk.rev.; music rev.; video rev. illus. 48 p./no. 5 cols./p.; **Document type:** *Magazine, Consumer.*
Related titles: Online - full text ed.
Published by: Creative Communication Concepts Corp., PO Drawer 2485, Myrtle Beach, SC 29578. TEL 843-444-5556, 800-968-5819, FAX 843-444-5558. Pub. William E Darby. Adv. contact Lenore Flynn. Circ: 25,000 (paid and free).

910.91 USA ISSN 1097-8038
GV776.F62
COASTAL CHARTS FOR CRUISING GUIDE TO WESTERN FLORIDA. Text in English. 2001 (July). irreg. USD 65 per issue (effective 2008). **Document type:** *Guide, Consumer.*
Published by: Pelican Publishing Co., 1000 Burmaster St., Gretna, LA 70053. TEL 504-368-1175, 800-843-1724, FAX 504-368-1195, editorial@pelicanpub.com, http://www.pelicanpub.com. Ed. Claiborne S Young.

COASTAL CRUISING. *see* SPORTS AND GAMES—Boats And Boating

917.58 USA
COASTAL GEORGIA. Text in English. q. USD 10 (effective 2005). adv. **Document type:** *Magazine, Consumer.*
Published by: Anchor Media, Inc., PO Box 288, St. Marys, GA 31558. Ed. Susanne Talentino.

338.4 PRT ISSN 1647-0125
COGITUR; journal of tourism studies. Text in English. 2008. s-a. **Document type:** *Journal, Academic/Scholarly.*
Published by: Universidade Lusofona de Humanidades e Tecnologia, Edicoes Universitarias, Campo Grande 376, Lisbon, 1749-024, Portugal. TEL 351-217-515500, FAX 351-217-577006, http://ulusofona.pt.

338.4 910.9 ITA ISSN 2037-9382
COLLANA DI STUDI E RICERCHE SUL TURISMO. Text in Italian. 1988. irreg. **Document type:** *Monographic series, Academic/Scholarly.*
Published by: Franco Angeli Edizioni, Viale Monza 106, Milan, 20127, Italy. TEL 39-02-2837141, FAX 39-02-26144793, redazioni@francoangeli.it, http://www.francoangeli.it.

COLLECTION VILLES EN MOUVEMENT. *see* SOCIOLOGY

910 COL
COLOMBIA. CORPORACION NACIONAL DE TURISMO. BOLETIN INFORMATIVO C E N T U R. Text in Spanish. 1978. q. free. **Document type:** *Government.*
Published by: Corporacion Nacional de Turismo, Centro de Informacion Turistica, Calle 28 13A-15 Piso 17, Apartado Aereo 8400, Bogota, CUND, Colombia. TEL 57-1-284-3049. Circ: 700.

910 COL
COLOMBIA. CORPORACION NACIONAL DE TURISMO. CRONICA TURISTICA. Text in Spanish. 1988. q. free. **Document type:** *Government.*
Published by: Corporacion Nacional de Turismo, Centro de Informacion Turistica, Calle 28 13A-15 Piso 17, Apartado Aereo 8400, Bogota, CUND, Colombia. TEL 57-1-284-3049, TELEX 441350 COTUR. Circ: 700.

910.202 GBR ISSN 1369-1414
F2259.5
COLOMBIA HANDBOOK. Text in English. 1998. irreg., latest vol.3, 2009. GBP 14.99 per vol. (effective 2009). **Document type:** *Handbook/Manual/Guide, Consumer.*
—CCC.
Published by: Footprint Handbooks Ltd., 6 Riverside Ct, Lower Bristol Rd, Bath, Avon BA2 3DZ, United Kingdom. TEL 44-1225-469141, FAX 44-1225-469461, info@footprintbooks.com. Ed. Charlie Devereux.

COLORADO AVID GOLFER. *see* SPORTS AND GAMES—Ball Games

910.09 USA
COLORADO DIRECTORY OF CAMPING, CABINS, LODGES, COUNTRY B & B'S, FUN THINGS TO DO. Text in English. 1980. a. USD 8 per issue domestic includes territories; USD 14 per issue foreign (effective 2009). adv. **Document type:** *Directory, Consumer.* **Description:** Lists the best accommodations, cabins, lodges, hotels, motels, Country Bed and Breakfast inns and much more in Colorado.
Former titles: Colorado Directory of Camping, Cabins, Lodges, Fun Things to Do; Colorado Directory of Camping, R Vs, Cabins, Fun Things to Do; Colorado Directory of Camping, Cabins, Rafting, Fun Things to Do
Related titles: Online - full text ed.: free (effective 2009).
Published by: The Colorado Directory, Inc, 5101 Pennsylvania Ave, Boulder, CO 80303. TEL 303-499-9343, 888-222-4641, FAX 303-499-9333, caccl@caccl.com. Pub. Jenny Fitt Peaster. Adv. contact Violet Fitt.

917.88 USA ISSN 0146-9991
F771
COLORADO EXPRESS. Text in English. 1972. s-a. USD 20 for 2 yrs. adv. bk.rev. bibl.; charts; illus. cum.index for vols. 1-13 in vol. 13. back issues avail. **Description:** Explores alternative cultures.
Address: PO Box 18214, Capitol Hill Station, Denver, CO 80218. TEL 303-320-6976. Ed. Karl Kocivar. Circ: 18,000.

917.504 GBR ISSN 1365-5094
COLORADO HOLIDAY & TRAVEL GUIDE. Variant title: Colorado Holiday Planner. Text in English. 1996. a. free (effective 2010). adv. **Document type:** *Handbook/Manual/Guide, Consumer.* **Description:** Covers consumer and travel trade inquiries for vacation ideas.
Related titles: Online - full text ed.
Published by: Phoenix International Publishing, 18-20 Scrutton St, London, EC2A 4TG, United Kingdom. TEL 44-20-72470537, FAX 44-20-73772741, http://www.phoenixip.com/. Ed. Mary Moore Mason TEL 44-20-72436954. Pub. Simon Todd TEL 682-831-0133. Adv. contact Larry Cohen TEL 203-255-8800.

910.2 USA
COLORADO OFFICIAL STATE VACATION GUIDE. Text in English. 2005. a. free. adv. **Document type:** *Guide, Consumer.* **Description:** Offers information about accommodations, restaurants, shopping, attractions and transportation.
Published by: Weaver Publications, Inc., 2420 Alcott St, Denver, CO 80211. TEL 303-458-1211, 800-303-9328, FAX 303-477-0724, info@weaver-group.com, http://pub.weaver-group.com. adv.: B&W page USD 6,250, color page USD 7,600; trim 7.937 x 10.375. Circ: 800,000.

910.91 ITA ISSN 1828-6518
COLORI MARTINEGHESI. Text in Italian. 2006. q. **Document type:** *Magazine, Consumer.*
Published by: Pro Loco di Martinengo, Comune di Martinengo, Piazza Maggiore 1, Martinengo, BG 24057, Italy. TEL 39-0363-986011, FAX 39-0363-987765, http://www.comune.martinengo.bg.it.

COLUMBUS. *see* GEOGRAPHY

910 HND
COME TO HONDURAS. Text in English, Spanish. bi-m. **Document type:** *Magazine, Consumer.*
Published by: Editorial Hablemos Claro, Edificio Torre Libertad, Boulevard Suyapa, Residencial La Hacienda, Tegucigalpa, Honduras. http://www.hablemosclaro.com. Ed. Rodrigo Wong Arevalo.

910.2 GBR ISSN 2044-1932
▼ **COME TO NIGERIA.** Text in English. 2010. q. GBP 18 domestic; GBP 28 in Europe; GBP 35 includes United States and Canada, Middle East and Arab World; GBP 40 elsewhere (effective 2010). adv. back issues avail. **Document type:** *Magazine, Trade.* **Description:** Features information about getting people to come to Nigeria.
Published by: Jollof Ltd., 50-54 Mount Pleasant, Liverpool, L3 5SD, United Kingdom. info@cometonigeria.com.

COMMUNAUTE DE COMMUNES VARENNES FORTERRE. LA LETTRE D'INFORMATIONS. *see* PUBLIC ADMINISTRATION

917.97 USA ISSN 1539-3224
F889.3
COMPASS AMERICAN GUIDES: WASHINGTON. Text in English. 1995. irreg., latest vol.4, 2008. USD 21.95 per issue (effective 2011). **Document type:** *Handbook/Manual/Guide, Consumer.* **Description:** Provides coverage of the history, culture and character of one of America's most spectacular destinations.
Published by: Compass American Guides (Subsidiary of: Fodor's Travel Publications, Inc.), 1745 Broadway, 15th Fl, New York, NY 10019. tbuckley@fodors.com.

917.87 USA ISSN 1539-3283
F759.3
COMPASS AMERICAN GUIDES: WYOMING. Variant title: Wyoming: Compass American Guides. Text in English. 1991. irreg., latest vol.5, 2008. USD 21.95 per issue (effective 2011). back issues avail. **Document type:** *Handbook/Manual/Guide, Consumer.* **Description:** Provides coverage of the history, culture and character of one of America's most spectacular destinations.
Published by: Compass American Guides (Subsidiary of: Fodor's Travel Publications, Inc.), 1745 Broadway, 15th Fl, New York, NY 10019. tbuckley@fodors.com.

917.87 USA ISSN 1943-0094
▼ **COMPASS AMERICAN GUIDES: YELLOWSTONE & GRAND TETON NATIONAL PARKS.** Text in English. 2009. biennial (every 2 or 3 yrs.). USD 19.95 per issue (effective 2011). **Document type:** *Handbook/Manual/Guide, Consumer.* **Description:** Provides a true immersion experience for the culture, character and history of America's most spectacular destinations.
Published by: Compass American Guides (Subsidiary of: Fodor's Travel Publications, Inc.), 1745 Broadway, 15th Fl, New York, NY 10019. tbuckley@fodors.com.

910.91 USA
CONCIERGE PREFERRED - CHICAGO. Text in English. 2001. 5/yr. adv. **Document type:** *Magazine, Consumer.* **Description:** Covers dining, shopping, sightseeing and entertainment for both leisure and business/convention visitors to Chicago.
Published by: O'Malley-Magnusson Publishing Group, 1435 Plumb Grove Rd, Ste C, Schaumberg, IL 60173. TEL 847-585-0128, FAX 847-240-0969, http://www.conciergepreferred.com. Ed. Elizabeth Seymour. Pub., Adv. contact Tom O'Malley. color page USD 11,881; trim 3.625 x 8.5.

910.91 USA
CONCIERGE PREFERRED - ST. LOUIS. Text in English. 2004. q. free (effective 2004). adv. **Document type:** *Magazine, Consumer.* **Description:** Covers dining, shopping, sightseeing and entertainment for both leisure and business/convention visitors to St. Louis.
Published by: O'Malley-Magnusson Publishing Group, 1435 Plumb Grove Rd, Ste C, Schaumberg, IL 60173. TEL 847-585-0128, FAX 847-240-0969, http://www.conciergepreferred.com. Ed. Beth Custer. Pub. Tom O'Malley. Adv. contact Lynn Potts. color page USD 7,800; trim 3.625 x 8.5. Circ: 340,000 (free).

910.09 USA ISSN 0893-9683
AP2
CONDE NAST TRAVELER; truth in travel. Text in English. 1954. m. USD 10 domestic; USD 18.97 in Canada; USD 39.97 elsewhere; USD 4.50 newsstand/cover (effective 2009). adv. bk.rev. illus. Index. back issues avail.; reprints avail. **Document type:** *Magazine, Consumer.* **Description:** Guides to discover the best islands, cities, spas, castles and cruises.
Incorporates (1985-1992): European Travel & Life (0882-7737); Formerly (until 1987): Signature (0037-5039)
Related titles: Microform ed.: (from PQC); Online - full text ed.
Indexed: A22, A33, ASIP, B04, BRD, C05, CPerl, G05, G06, G07, G08, G09, GeoRef, I05, M01, M02, P02, P10, P48, P53, P54, PQC, R03, R06, RGAb, RGPR, SpeleolAb, T02, W03.
—CCC.
Published by: Conde Nast Publications, Inc. (Subsidiary of: Advance Publications, Inc.), 4 Times Sq, 6th Fl, New York, NY 10036. TEL 212-286-2860, FAX 212-286-6905, http://www.condenast.com. Ed. Klara Glowczewska. Pub. Lisa Henriques Hughes. Adv. contact Beth Lusko. B&W page USD 67,860, color page USD 100,660; trim 8 x 10.875. Circ: 820,217 (paid).

910 GBR ISSN 1368-597X
CONDE NAST TRAVELLER. Text in English. 1997. m. GBP 24 domestic; GBP 75 in Europe; GBP 60 in United States; GBP 89 elsewhere (effective 2010). adv. illus. **Document type:** *Magazine, Consumer.* **Description:** Provides an insider's guide to the outside world.
Published by: Conde Nast Publications Ltd. (Subsidiary of: Advance Publications, Inc.), Vogue House, Hanover Sq, London, W1S 1JU, United Kingdom. TEL 44-20-74999080, FAX 44-20-74951102, newbusiness@condenast.co.uk, http://www.condenast.co.uk. Ed. Sarah Miller.

910.202 ITA ISSN 1973-5669
CONDE NAST TRAVELLER. Text in Italian. 1998. m. **Document type:** *Magazine, Consumer.*
Formerly (until 2007): Conde Nast Traveller Gold (1127-8927)
Published by: Edizioni Conde Nast SpA (Subsidiary of: Arnoldo Mondadori Editore SpA), Piazza Castello 27, Milan, MI 20122, Italy. info@condenet.it, http://www.condenast.it.

910.202 GRC ISSN 1791-5562
CONDE NAST TRAVELLER. Text in Greek. 2008. q. adv. **Document type:** *Magazine, Consumer.*

TU

Published by: Liberis Publications S.A./Ekdoseon Lymperi A.E., Ioannou Metaxa 80, Karelas, Koropi 19400, Greece. TEL 30-210-6688000, FAX 30-210-6688300, info@liberis.gr, http://www.liberis.gr. Ed. Petros Bourovilis. Adv. contact Eirini Stathatou. Circ: 16,000 (paid).

910.202 DEU
CONDOR. Text in German. 2001. 3/yr. adv. **Document type:** *Magazine, Consumer.*
Former titles (until 2004): Thomas Cook; (until 2002): Condor Magazin
Published by: G + J Corporate Editors GmbH (Subsidiary of: Gruner + Jahr AG & Co), Stubbenhuk 10, Hamburg, 20459, Germany. TEL 49-40-37030, FAX 49-40-37035010, info@corporate-editors.com, http://www.corporate-editors.com. Adv. contact Sabrina Prumbs. page EUR 9,900. Circ: 161,182 (controlled).

910.09 GBR ISSN 0965-125X
CONFERENCE AND INCENTIVE TRAVEL. Abbreviated title: C & I T. Text in English. 1990. 10/yr. GBP 85 (effective 2009). adv. bk.rev. illus. reprints avail. **Document type:** *Magazine, Trade.* **Description:** Contains news, reviews and discussion, providing users with the tools they need to stay at the forefront of developments within the industry.
Formed by the merger of (1979-1990): Conference Britain (0142-7474); (1985-1990): Incentive Travel World (0950-0758); Incorporates (in 1993): C E I International (0967-6279); Which was formerly (until 1990): Conference and Exhibitions International (0260-8316); (until 1980): Conferences and Exhibitions (0306-9397); (until 1974): Conferences, Exhibitions and Executive Travel (0010-5597); Conference News
Related titles: Online - full text ed.
Indexed: A10, A15, ABIn, B01, B02, B07, B15, B17, B18, BldManAb, G04, G06, G07, G08, H&TI, H06, I05, P48, P51, PQC, R18, V03.
—BLDSC (3408.930000), IE, Ingenta. **CCC.**
Published by: Haymarket Publishing Ltd. (Subsidiary of: Haymarket Media Group), 174 Hammersmith Rd, London, W6 7JP, United Kingdom. TEL 44-20-82674210, info@haymarket.com, http://www.haymarket.com. Eds. Yasmin Arrigo TEL 44-20-82674362, Yasmin Razak TEL 44-20-82674362. Adv. contact Ian Porter TEL 44-20-82674565. page GBP 4,420; trim 210 x 297. Circ: 18,476. **Subscr. to:** 12-13 Cranleigh Gardens Industrial Estate, Southall UB1 2DB, United Kingdom. TEL 44-84-51557355, FAX 44-20-86067503, subscriptions@haymarket.com, http://www.haymarketbusinesssubs.com.

910.2 USA
CONNECTED TRAVELER. Text in English. 1996. irreg. adv. illus.
Media: Online - full text. Ed. Russell Johnson.

917.404 USA ISSN 0746-8636
CONNECTICUT TRAVELER. Text in English. 1983. m. free to members (effective 2005). adv. **Document type:** *Newspaper, Consumer.* **Description:** Focuses on travel, with features ranging from regional daytrips to international destinations. Also covers insurance and financial services, car care, traffic safety, local events and exclusive AAA member savings.
Published by: Connecticut Motor Club, Inc., 2276 Whitney Ave, Hamden, CT 06518. TEL 203-765-4222, FAX 203-799-0099. adv.: page USD 10,000. Circ: 250,000 (free).

974 USA
CONNECTICUT VACATION GUIDE. Text in English. 1950. a. free (effective 2009). adv. illus. back issues avail. **Document type:** *Magazine, Consumer.* **Description:** Provides a window to our state's beautiful scenery, arts, culture, events and destinations in a fun, easy to use resource for both residents and visitors.
Former titles (until 199?): ClassiConnecticut Vacation Guide; (until 1988): Connecticut Vacation Guide; (until 1982): Your .. Connecticut Vacation Guide; (until 1979): Your .. Connecticut Guide; (until 1978): Connecticut, So Much, So Near
Related titles: E-mail ed.; Online - full text ed.
Published by: Connecticut Commission on Culture & Tourism, One Financial Plz, 2nd Fl, 755 Main St, Hartford, CT 06103. TEL 860-256-2800, FAX 860-256-2811, ct.travelinfo@ct.gov, http://www.ctvisit.com/. Circ: 275,000 Spring; 175,000 Winter.

917 USA
CONNECTICUT WEST. Text in English. 1970. a. USD 2. adv. bibl.
Published by: Foothills Trader, Inc., 85 River Rd, Collinsville, CT 06022-1226. TEL 203-693-2990, FAX 203-693-2875. Ed. James Timpano. Circ: 30,000.

910.91 CAN ISSN 1194-8841
CONNECTING: SOLO TRAVEL NEWS. Text in English. bi-m. USD 28 domestic; CAD 40 in Canada; USD 40 elsewhere (effective 2002). **Document type:** *Newsletter, Consumer.*
Published by: Solo Travel Network, 689 Park Road, Unit 6, Gibsons, BC V0N 1V7, Canada. TEL 604-886-9099, FAX 604-608-2139, info@cstn.org, http://www.cstn.org. Pub. Diane Redfern. Circ: 1,800 (paid).

659.3 ROM ISSN 1454-573X
CONSTANTA - WHAT, WHERE, WHEN. Text in Multiple languages. 1999. q. ROL 50,000 domestic; USD 12 foreign (effective 2002). adv. **Document type:** *Magazine, Consumer.*
Published by: Crystal Publishing Group, 253, Calea Calarasilor, bl. 67 A, Ste. 4, Bucharest, Romania. TEL 40-21-3233829, FAX 40-21-3234706, office@bucurestiwww.ro, http://www.bucurestiwww.ro. Circ: 25,000 (paid and controlled).

910.202 USA ISSN 1548-9337
G149
CONSUMER REPORTS TRAVEL WELL FOR LESS. Variant title: Best Travel Ideas. Text in English. 1992. a. **Document type:** *Magazine, Consumer.*
Former titles (until 2001): Consumer Reports Best Travel Deals (1091-6288); (until 1995): Consumer Reports Travel Buying Guide (1060-1511)
Published by: Consumers Union of the United States, Inc., 101 Truman Ave, Yonkers, NY 10703. TEL 914-378-2000, 800-234-1645, FAX 914-378-2900, http://www.consumersunion.org.

910.91 USA ISSN 1558-710X
F92.3
CONSUMMATE CONNECTICUT; day trips with panache. Text in English. 2006. biennial. **Document type:** *Guide, Consumer.*
Published by: Cat Tales Press Inc., PO Box 382, Green Farms, CT 06838. TEL 203-268-3505, cattalespress@snet.net, http://www.cattalespress.com/index.htm. Ed., Pub. Stacy Lytwyn Maxwell.

910 PRY
CONTACTO TURISTICO. Text in Spanish. 1987. m. free. adv. **Description:** Features local and international tourist news, travel reports, events, interviews, airlines schedules, air fares from all destinations to and from Asuncion, Paraguay.
Address: Manduvira y Juan E. O'Leary, Edif. El Dorado Piso 3, Asuncion, 1255, Paraguay. TEL 595-21-497-264, FAX 595-21-497-264, contacto@conexion.com.py. Ed. Francisco Ramirez Vouga. Adv. contact Maria Evelina Rojas. color page USD 1,100, B&W page USD 1,000; trim 19 x 26. Circ: 2,000 (controlled).

362.7 THA ISSN 1684-6184
CONTOURS. Text in English. 1984. q. **Document type:** *Magazine, Consumer.*
Related titles: Online - full text ed.: ISSN 1684-6192.
Indexed: CA, H&TI, H06, T02.
—BLDSC (3425.742000), IE.
Published by: Ecumenical Coalition on Third World Tourism, c/o ECPAT Foundation in Thailand, 426/22 Mooban Kokgalae, Tambon Rimkok, Ampher Muang, Chiang Rai, Thailand. http://www.ecpat.net.

910.2 ITA
CONVEGNI B2B; yearly guide book to the best incentive destinations in the world. Text in Italian. 199?. a. price varies. adv. **Document type:** *Directory, Trade.*
Published by: Convegni Srl, Via Ezio Biondi 1, Milan, MI 20154, Italy. TEL 39-02-349921, FAX 39-02-34992290, convegni@convegni.it, http://www.convegni.it.

CONVEGNI INCENTIVE & COMUNICAZIONE. *see* MEETINGS AND CONGRESSES

919 NZL ISSN 2230-2611
▼ **COROMANDEL TOWN AND NORTH .. NAVIGATOR.** Text in English. 2011. 3/yr. adv. **Document type:** *Magazine, Consumer.*
Related titles: Online - full text ed.: free (effective 2011).
Published by: Jude Publishing Ltd., PO Box 148, Coromandel, 3543, New Zealand.

910.9 USA ISSN 0739-1587
CORPORATE & INCENTIVE TRAVEL. Text in English. 1983. m. USD 75 domestic; USD 150 foreign (effective 2008). adv. back issues avail.; reprints avail. **Document type:** *Magazine, Trade.* **Description:** Covers corporate meeting and incentive travel planners.
Published by: Coastal Communications Corp., 2700 N Military Trail, Ste 120, Boca Raton, FL 33431-6394. TEL 561-989-0600, FAX 561-989-9509, ccceditor1@att.net. Ed., Pub. Harvey Grotsky. Circ: 40,153 (controlled).

910.09 USA
CORPORATE CRUISE NEWS. Text in English. bi-m. free to qualified personnel.
Published by: Landry & Kling, Inc., 1390 S. Dixie Hwy., Ste. 1207, Coral Gables, FL 33146-2943. TEL 305-661-1880. Ed. Josephine King. Circ: (controlled).

CORPORATE EVENT. *see* BUSINESS AND ECONOMICS

CORPORATE EVENTS GUIDE; your essential guide to event planning. *see* BUSINESS AND ECONOMICS

CORPORATE MEETINGS & INCENTIVES. *see* MEETINGS AND CONGRESSES

914.504 ITA
CORTINA MAGAZINE. Text in Italian. 1987. 3/yr. **Document type:** *Magazine, Consumer.*
Published by: Renografica Srl, Via Seragnoli 13, Bologna, BO 40138, Italy. TEL 39-051-6026111, FAX 39-051-6026150, home@renografica.it, http://www.renografica.com.

910.91 USA ISSN 1930-6032
DP302.C8
COSTA BLANCA. D K EYEWITNESS TOP 10 TRAVEL GUIDES. Variant title: Eyewitness Top 10 Travel Guide: Costa Blanca. Text in English. 2005. irreg., latest 2007. USD 6.99 per issue (effective 2008). 144 p./no.; **Document type:** *Guide, Consumer.* **Description:** Provides information to save time and to find the 10 best of everything to see, buy, do, taste and avoid in Costa Blanca.
Published by: D K Publishing (Subsidiary of: Penguin Books U S A, Inc.), 375 Hudson St, New York, NY 10014. TEL 800-631-8571, FAX 212-689-4828, specialsales@dk.com, http://us.dk.com.

910.91 USA ISSN 1933-0774
F1543.5
COSTA RICA FOR DUMMIES. Text in English. 2005. irreg., latest 2009, 3rd ed. USD 21.99 per issue (effective 2010). adv. back issues avail.; reprints avail. **Document type:** *Guide, Consumer.*
Published by: John Wiley & Sons, Inc., 111 River St, Hoboken, NJ 07030. TEL 201-748-6000, FAX 201-748-6088, info@wiley.com, http://www.wiley.com/WileyCDA/.

914.502 ITA
COSTA SMERALDA MAGAZINE. Text and summaries in English, Italian. 1975. q. adv. bk.rev. back issues avail. **Document type:** *Magazine, Consumer.*
Published by: (Consorzio Costa Smeralda), P S E Editore, Largo Cairoli 2, Milan, 20121, Italy. TEL 39-02-72000758, FAX 39-02-8051429, info@pseeditore.it.

910.202 ITA ISSN 1970-0237
COSTA VIOLA MAGAZINE. Text in Italian. 2004. bi-m. EUR 28 (effective 2009). **Document type:** *Magazine, Consumer.*
Published by: Zerouno Italia Srl, Redazione Costa Viola Magazine, Via R Piria 36, Scilla, RC 89058, Italy. TEL 39-0965-754064. Ed. Andrea De Marco.

614.6 910.202 FRA ISSN 2107-3791
COTE AUTO. Text in French. 2002. m. **Document type:** *Magazine, Consumer.*
Formerly (until 2009): Mid'Ouest (1637-8768)
Published by: Union Nationale des Automobile Clubs, Automobile Club du Midi, 17 Bd de la Gare, BP 45866, Toulouse Cedex 5, 31506, France. TEL 33-5-62479330, FAX 33-5-62479339.

COUNTRY HOMES & INTERIORS. *see* INTERIOR DESIGN AND DECORATION

910.202 GBR ISSN 1479-2850
G155.A1
COUNTRY REPORTS. Variant title: Country Reports - Travel and Tourism. Text in English. 1971. q. GBP 175, USD 350, EUR 265 per issue (effective 2010). charts; stat. back issues avail. **Document type:** *Report, Trade.* **Description:** Presents detailed profiles of countries that constitute the world's tourist destinations.
Former titles (until 2002): T T I Country Reports (1466-612X); (until no.4, 1998): International Tourism Reports (0269-3747); (until 1985): International Tourism Quarterly (0306-4336)
Related titles: Online - full text ed.
Indexed: A22, B02, B15, B17, B18, CPM, Emerald, G04, G08, H&TI, H06, Hospl, I05, KES, RASB.
—BLDSC (3481.897016). **CCC.**
Published by: Mintel International Group Ltd., 18-19 Long Ln, London, EC1A 9PL, United Kingdom. TEL 44-20-76064533, FAX 44-20-77260849, info@mintel.com, http://www.mintel.com/.

917.94 USA ISSN 8756-906X
COUNTRY ROADS; adventures close to home. Text in English. 1983. m. adv. **Document type:** *Magazine, Consumer.* **Description:** Provides an in-depth guide to the historical, artistic, culinary and musical heritage of the Great River Road region between Natchez, Mississippi, and New Orleans, Louisiana.
Published by: Westmoreland Publishing, 340 St. Joseph St, Baton Rouge, LA 70802. TEL 800-582-1792, sales@countryroadsmag.com. Pub. Dorcas Brown. Adv. contact Rikki Broussard. B&W page USD 1,365, color page USD 1,665; trim 10.75 x 14.75. Circ: 4,000 (paid).

COUNTRY TRENDS (YEAR); the guide to performance and profitability of hotels in the UK, Europe, Middle East and South Africa. *see* HOTELS AND RESTAURANTS

338.4791 GBR ISSN 1465-7686
G155.A1
COUNTRY UPDATES. Text in English. 1999. q. **Document type:** *Handbook/Manual/Guide, Consumer.*
Indexed: H&TI, H06.
—BLDSC (3481.903510).
Published by: Travel and Tourism Intelligence, 48 Bedford Sq, London, WCIB 3DP, United Kingdom.

COUNTRYSIDE RECREATION. *see* LEISURE AND RECREATION

333.78 GBR ISSN 1350-7672
COUNTRYSIDE RECREATION RESEARCH. Text in English. 1993. a. **Document type:** *Journal, Trade.*
—**CCC.**
Published by: Countryside Recreation Network, c/o Magali Fleurot, Sheffield Hallam University, Unit 1, Sheffield Science Park. Howard St, Sheffield, S1 2LX, United Kingdom. TEL 44-114-2254494, FAX 44-144-2256319, CRN@shu.ac.uk, http://www.countrysiderecreation.org.uk.

910.09 USA ISSN 0279-4489
COURIER (LEXINGTON). Text in English. 1974. m. USD 36. adv.
—Ingenta.
Published by: National Tour Association, Inc., 546 E Main St, Lexington, KY 40508-2342. TEL 606-253-1036, FAX 606-231-9837. Ed. William A Bowden. Circ: 5,200 (controlled).

910.2 FRA ISSN 0154-733X
COURRIER DU QUEYRAS. Text in French. 1971. 2/yr. EUR 20 (effective 2009). adv. bk.rev. charts; illus.
Published by: Les Amis du Parc, Maison du Parc Naturel Regional du Queyras, Arvieux, 05350, France. FAX 33-1-92452720. Ed. Alain Bayrou. Circ: 2,000.

910.09 382 USA
CRAIGHEAD'S COUNTRY REPORTS. Text in English. 1988. m. USD 4,000 (effective 2000). **Document type:** *Report, Trade.* **Description:** Comprises 85 country reports discussing what it is like to live and do business overseas.
Formerly: Craighead's International Executive Travel and Relocation Service
Published by: Craighead.com, 50 Main St., Ste. 1675, White Plains, NY 10606-1971. Ed. Elizabeth W Weiss. Pub. Scott B Craighead.

910.09 USA ISSN 1058-3904
HF5549.5.E45
CRAIGHEAD'S INTERNATIONAL BUSINESS, TRAVEL AND RELOCATION GUIDE. Text in English. irreg., latest vol.4, 2004, 12th ed. USD 775 12th ed. (effective 2008). **Document type:** *Directory, Trade.* **Description:** Provides data necessary to understand and evaluate the political, economic and business environment and everyday living conditions of foreign destinations.
Former titles (until 1993): International Business Travel and Relocation Directory; (until 1980): Directory of International Business Travel and Relocation
Published by: Gale (Subsidiary of: Cengage Learning), 27500 Drake Rd, Farmington Hills, MI 48331. TEL 248-699-4253, 800-877-4253, FAX 877-363-4253, gale.galeord@thomson.com, http://gale.cengage.com.

910.2 NLD ISSN 1872-1338
CREATIVE CITY GUIDE. Text in English. 2005. a.
Related titles: ◆ Supplement to: Amsterdam Index. ISSN 1872-132X.
Published by: BIS Publishers, Het Sieraad, Postjesweg 1, Amsterdam, 1057 DT, Netherlands. TEL 31-20-5150230, FAX 31-20-5150239, bis@bispublishers.nl, http://www.bispublishers.nl.

910.2 USA
CRUISE AND RESORT. Text in English. 2002. 8/yr. USD 19.97 domestic; USD 40 in Canada; USD 80 for 3 yrs. elsewhere (effective 2003). **Document type:** *Magazine, Consumer.*
Published by: Cruise and Resort, Inc., 15303 Ventura Blvd. 9th Floor, Sherman Oaks, CA 91403. TEL 818-990-4290, FAX 888-652-6400. Ed. Ralph Grizzle. Pub. Anthony Dean Adler.

338.4 USA ISSN 0898-4867
CRUISE AND VACATION VIEWS; leisure travel sales and marketing. Text in English. 1987. bi-m. USD 48; USD 64 foreign (effective 1998). adv. bk.rev. **Document type:** *Magazine, Trade.* **Description:** Provides market-oriented information, trends analysis, and ideas to professional leisure travel retailers.
Formerly (until 1991): Cruise Views
Published by: Orban Communications, Inc., 25 Washington St, 4th Fl, Morristown, NJ 07960. TEL 973-605-2442, FAX 973-605-2722. Ed., Pub., R&P Michael Brown. Adv. contact George Skip Muns. Circ: 32,000 (controlled).

917.14 USA ISSN 0893-1240
CRUISE INDUSTRY NEWS (NEWSLETTER). Text in English. 1985. s-m. USD 495. **Document type:** *Newsletter, Trade.* **Description:** Inside news report of the cruise shipping industry worldwide.
Indexed: H&TI, H06, T02.
Published by: Nissen-Lie Communications, Inc., 441 Lexington Ave, Ste 1209 A, New York, NY 10017. TEL 212-986-1025, FAX 212-986-1033. Ed. Oivind Mathisen. Circ: 2,000.

917.04 USA ISSN 1047-3378
G550
CRUISE INDUSTRY NEWS ANNUAL. Text in English. 1988. a. USD 450. **Document type:** *Magazine, Trade.* **Description:** Covers the cruise shipping industry worldwide.
Former titles: Cruise Industry Annual (Year); North American Cruise Industry (Year)
Published by: Nissen-Lie Communications, Inc., 441 Lexington Ave, Ste 1209 A, New York, NY 10017. TEL 212-986-1025, FAX 212-986-1033. Ed. Oivind Mathisen. Circ: 1,100.

917.14 USA
CRUISE INDUSTRY NEWS QUARTERLY. Text in English. 1985. q. USD 40; USD 60 foreign (effective 1998). **Document type:** *Magazine, Trade.* **Description:** For cruise industry professionals.
Published by: Nissen-Lie Communications, Inc., 441 Lexington Ave, Ste 1209 A, New York, NY 10017. TEL 212-986-1025, FAX 212-986-1033. Circ: 10,000.

338.4791 GBR ISSN 1758-2326
CRUISE INTERNATIONAL. Text in English. 2008. bi-m. GBP 17.50 domestic; GBP 25 foreign (effective 2010). adv. back issues avail. **Document type:** *Magazine, Consumer.* **Description:** Features glorious photographs of exotic destinations, romantic ports and secret hideaways.
Published by: Chelsea Magazine Company Ltd., 26-30 Old Church St, London, SW3 5BY, United Kingdom. TEL 44-20-73493150, FAX 44-20-73493160, info@chelseamagazines.com, http://www.chelseamagazines.com. Ed. Sam Pears. Pub., Adv. contact Steve Ross. Circ: 50,000.

387.2 USA
CRUISE MAGAZINE. Text in English. 2005. bi-m. USD 15 domestic; USD 19 in Canada (effective 2005). adv. back issues avail. **Document type:** *Magazine, Consumer.* **Description:** Provides informative and engaging insights into the world of luxury travel.
Published by: Cruise Publishing, Inc., 4441 Six Forks Rd, Ste 106 - 311, Raleigh, NC 27609. TEL 919-532-7882, FAX 919-532-0685. adv.: color page USD 7,100; trim 8.3125 x 10.875. Circ: 51,000.

338.4791 USA
CRUISE REPORTS. Text in English. 1994. a. USD 49.95 (effective 2006). **Document type:** *Magazine, Trade.*
Formerly: Cruise & Vacation Views
Published by: Orban Communications, Inc., 25 Washington St, 4th Fl, Morristown, NJ 07960. TEL 973-605-2442, FAX 973-605-2722. Ed. Jessica Agate.

910.09 USA
CRUISE TRADE. Text in English. 19??. m. **Description:** Provides cruise sellers with news and marketing tools.
Published by: Travel Trade Publications, 122 E 42th St, New York, NY 10168. TEL 212-730-6600, FAX 212-730-7020, feedback@traveltrade.com, http://www.traveltrade.com. Ed. Nick Verrastro. Adv. contact Jeff Posner.

910.09 USA ISSN 0199-5111
G550
CRUISE TRAVEL; the worldwide cruise vacation magazine. Text in English. 1979. bi-m. USD 23.94 domestic; USD 40 in Canada; USD 50 foreign (effective 2009). adv. charts; illus.; stat. 68 p./no. 3 cols./p.; back issues avail.; reprints avail. **Document type:** *Magazine, Consumer.* **Description:** Includes features on cruise ships, ports-of-call, and itineraries, plus reviews of new and classsic vessels, tips on shore excursions and shopping.
Related titles: Online - full text ed.
Indexed: A10, A22, B07, C05, CPerI, G05, G06, G07, G08, H&TI, H06, I05, I07, M01, M02, S23, T02, V03.
Published by: World Publishing Co. (Subsidiary of: Century Publishing Inc.), 990 Grove St, Evanston, IL 60201. TEL 847-491-6440, FAX 847-491-0459. Adv. contact Irene Froehlich TEL 269-637-5790. B&W page USD 8,489, color page USD 12,128; trim 10.5 x 8. Circ: 175,000 (paid).

919.4 AUS
CRUISING THE CAPE. Text in English. bi-m. **Document type:** *Magazine, Consumer.* **Description:** Contains information on the Margaret River district in the soutwest of Western Australia including accomodations, what to do, events, wineries, and other attractions.
Related titles: Online - full text ed.
Published by: Augusta - Margaret River Mail, PO Box 820, Margaret River, W.A. 6285, Australia. TEL 61-8-97572266, FAX 61-8-97572830, amrmail@margaret-river.com.au. Adv. contact John Neeson.

914.6 ESP ISSN 1137-4837
LOS CUADERNOS DE EDITUR. TECNO AGENCIAS. Text in Spanish. 1995. irreg. **Document type:** *Magazine, Consumer.*
Related titles: ◆ Supplement to: Editur. ISSN 1134-6469.
Published by: Ediciones Turisticas, S.A., C. Consejo de Ciento 355 Piso 3o, Barcelona, 08007, Spain. TEL 34-93-4670229, FAX 34-93-4670218, direccion@editur.es, http://www.editur.com.

914.6 ESP ISSN 1137-4829
LOS CUADERNOS DE EDITUR. TECNO HOSTELERIA. Text in Spanish. 1990. irreg. **Document type:** *Magazine, Consumer.*
Related titles: ◆ Supplement to: Editur. ISSN 1134-6469.
Published by: Ediciones Turisticas, S.A., C. Consejo de Ciento 355 Piso 3o, Barcelona, 08007, Spain. TEL 34-93-4670229, FAX 34-93-4670218, direccion@editur.es, http://www.editur.com.

910 ESP ISSN 1139-7861
G155.A1
CUADERNOS DE TURISMO. Text in Spanish. 1998. s-a. **Document type:** *Journal, Academic/Scholarly.*
Published by: Universidad de Murcia, Escuela Universitaria de Turismo, Paseo del Malecon, 5, Murcia, 30004, Spain. TEL 34-968-293624, FAX 34-968-363924, elmurcia@nexo.es, http://www.um.es/eu-turismo/. Ed. Jose Luis Andres Sarasa.

914.6 ESP ISSN 1137-4683
CUADERNOS EDITUR. Text in Spanish. 1989. **Document type:** *Magazine, Consumer.*
Related titles: ◆ Supplement to: Editur. ISSN 1134-6469.
Published by: Ediciones Turisticas, S.A., C. Consejo de Ciento 355 Piso 3o, Barcelona, 08007, Spain. TEL 34-93-4670229, FAX 34-93-4670218, direccion@editur.es, http://www.editur.com.

910.91 CAN ISSN 1912-4694
CUBA. Text in French. 1993. irreg. CAD 29.95, EUR 22.99 per issue (effective 2007). 384 p./no.; **Document type:** *Monographic series, Consumer.*
Published by: Editions Ulysse, 4176, rue St-Denis, Montreal, PQ H2W 2M5, Canada. TEL 514-843-9447, FAX 514-843-9448, info@ulysse.com.

917 GBR ISSN 1369-1422
F1754.7
CUBA HANDBOOK. Text in English. 1998. irreg., latest vol.4, 2004. GBP 12.99 per vol. (effective 2009). **Document type:** *Handbook/Manual/Guide, Consumer.*
—**CCC.**
Published by: Footprint Handbooks Ltd., 6 Riverside Ct, Lower Bristol Rd, Bath, Avon BA2 3DZ, United Kingdom. TEL 44-1225-469141, FAX 44-1225-469461, info@footprintbooks.com. Ed. Sarah Cameron.

910.202 CUB
CUBA NOTICIAS TURISTICAS. Text in Spanish. m.
Published by: Instituto Nacional del Turismo, Malecon y G,, Vedado, La Habana, Cuba. TEL 7-32-9881, TELEX 511955.

917.29104 CAN ISSN 1911-4133
CUBA PLUS. Text in English. 2007. q. CAD 20 (effective 2007). **Document type:** *Magazine, Consumer.*
Related titles: French ed.: ISSN 1914-7945.
Published by: Taina Communications, 115-988 Beach Ave., Vancouver, BC V6Z 2N9, Canada. TEL 604-878-8900, 800-663-8013, FAX 604-685-2533, http://www.taina.com.

917.291 USA ISSN 1542-1538
F1765.3
CUBATRAVEL MAGAZINE. Text in Spanish. q.
Address: 12973 SW 122 St. Ste. 182, Miami, FL 33186. TEL 305-259-4747, FAX 305-259-3937. Ed. Josefina Hernandez.

CUISINE. *see* HOME ECONOMICS

CULTUURHISTORISCHE ROUTES IN NEDERLAND. *see* ARCHAEOLOGY

CUMBRIA LIFE. *see* GENERAL INTEREST PERIODICALS—Great Britain

917.2 CAN
CURACAO NIGHTS. Text in English. q. **Document type:** *Journal, Consumer.*
Published by: Nights Publications, 1831 Rene Levesque Blvd W, Montreal, PQ H3H 1R4, Canada. FAX 514-931-6273, editor@nightspublications.com. Ed. Stephen Trotter.

338.4 GBR ISSN 1368-3500
G155.E54
➤ **CURRENT ISSUES IN TOURISM.** Text in English. 1998. bi-m. GBP 544 combined subscription in United Kingdom to institutions (print & online eds.); EUR 818, USD 1,095 combined subscription to institutions (print & online eds.) (effective 2012). adv. bk.rev. back issues avail.; reprint service avail. from PSC. **Document type:** *Journal, Academic/Scholarly.* **Description:** Covers key questions within the subject of tourism.
Related titles: Online - full text ed.: ISSN 1747-7603. GBP 490 in United Kingdom to institutions; EUR 736, USD 986 to institutions (effective 2012).
Indexed: A10, A34, A36, C25, CA, CABA, CurCont, E12, ESPM, EnvAb, F08, F12, GEOBASE, GH, H&TI, H06, HPNRM, IndVet, LT, N02, P32, PAIS, PEI, PGegResA, R12, RRTA, S13, S16, SCOPUS, SSCI, SSciA, SociolAb, T02, T05, V03, VS, W07, W11.
—BLDSC (3499.078450), IE, Infotrieve, Ingenta. **CCC.**
Published by: Routledge (Subsidiary of: Taylor & Francis Group), 4 Park Sq, Milton Park, Abingdon, Oxon OX14 4RN, United Kingdom. TEL 44-20-70176000, FAX 44-20-70176336, subscriptions@tandf.co.uk, http://www.routledge.com. Eds. C Michael Hall, Chris Cooper. Adv. contact Linda Hann TEL 44-1344-779945. **Subscr. to:** Taylor & Francis Ltd., Journals Customer Service, Sheepen Pl, Colchester, Essex CO3 3LP, United Kingdom. TEL 44-20-70175544, FAX 44-20-70175198.

387.243 910.202 387.5 USA
CURRENTS (NEW YORK, NY). Text in English. 1989. 3/yr. **Document type:** *Magazine, Consumer.* **Description:** Provides past guests on Carnival Cruise Lines with travel insights on the Caribbean Islands, Mexico, Hawaii, Alaska and Northeast coast of Canada, as well as the latest cruise trends, new products to pack on vacation, new ship information, and special products.
Published by: Meredith Corporation, 1716 Locust St, Des Moines, IA 50309. TEL 515-284-3000, 800-678-8091, FAX 515-284-3058, patrick.taylor@meredith.com, http://www.meredith.com.

917.8 USA
CYBERWEST MAGAZINE. Text in English. 1995. 8/yr. adv. **Document type:** *Magazine, Consumer.* **Description:** A travel, recreation publication devoted to the American West. Contains travel features, news stories, science news, events listings and photos of the West.
Media: Online - full text.
Published by: David Iler, Ed. & Pub., PO Box 40239, Denver, CO 80204-0239. Adv. contact David Iler.

910.4 338 CYP ISSN 0256-1069
CYPRUS TIME OUT; tourist and business guide. Text in English. 1978. m. adv. bk.rev. back issues avail. **Document type:** *Directory.*
Published by: Comarts, Pygmalionos St, Christophides Bldg, 2nd Fl, AP 9, PO Box 3697, Nicosia, Cyprus. TEL 357-2-452079, FAX 357-2-360668. Ed. Lyn Haviland. Pub. Ellada Sophocleous. Adv. contact Myria Oleovoulou. Circ: 8,000.

910.4 382 CYP
CYPRUS. TOURISM ORGANISATION. ANNUAL REPORT. Text in English. 1972. a. charts; stat. **Document type:** *Bulletin, Government.*
Related titles: Greek ed.
Published by: Tourism Organisation, 19 Leoforos Lemesou, PO Box 4535, Nicosia, Cyprus. TEL 357-2-315715, FAX 357-2-313022, TELEX CYTOUR CY. Circ: 2,600.

910.2 DEU ISSN 1430-0192
D C C - CAMPING FUEHRER EUROPA. Text in German. 1950. a. EUR 10 (effective 2009). **Document type:** *Directory, Consumer.*
Former titles (until 1981): Offizieller Campingfuehrer Europa (0078-3943); (until 1968): Offizieller Campingfuehrer Deutschland und Europa (0302-6310); (until 1966): Campingfuehrer fuer das Westdeutsche Bundesgebiet (0340-2282)
Published by: (Deutscher Camping Club e.V.), D C C - Wirtschaftsdienst und Verlag GmbH, Mandlstr 28, Munich, 80802, Germany. TEL 49-89-3801420, FAX 49-89-334737, info@campingpresse.de, http://www.campingpresse.de. Circ: 100,000.

796.5 DEU
D C C - TOURISTIK SERVICE. Text in German. a. adv. **Document type:** *Directory, Consumer.*
Published by: (Deutscher Camping Club e.V.), D C C - Wirtschaftsdienst und Verlag GmbH, Mandlstr 28, Munich, 80802, Germany. TEL 49-89-3801420, FAX 49-89-334737, info@campingpresse.de, http://www.campingpresse.de.

647.94 NLD ISSN 2210-3678
▼ **DAARBUITEN.** Text in Dutch. 2010. 3/yr. **Document type:** *Magazine, Consumer.*
Published by: Stichting Stayokay, Postbus 92076, Amsterdam, 1090 AB, Netherlands. http://www.stayokay.com.

DALLAS MEETING PROFESSIONALS GUIDE. *see* MEETINGS AND CONGRESSES

913.764 USA
DALLAS OFFICIAL VISITORS GUIDE. Text in English. 19??. s-a. free. adv. **Document type:** *Magazine, Consumer.* **Description:** Covers dining, shopping, attractions, local transportation, day trips and a calendar of events.
Published by: Weaver Publications, Inc., 2420 Alcott St, Denver, CO 80211. TEL 303-458-1211, FAX 303-477-0724, info@weaver-group.com, http://www.weaver-group.com. adv.: color page USD 8,015; trim 5.25 x 8.375. Circ: 200,000.

910.09 USA ISSN 1525-1624
E158
DAMON WOMEN'S TRAVELLER. Text in English. 1989. a. USD 18.95 per issue (effective 2011). adv. 600 p./no.; **Document type:** *Handbook/Manual/Guide, Consumer.* **Description:** Complete travel guide for women. Provides information on women's accommodations, bookstores, festivals, and tours.
Formerly (until 1997): The Women's Traveller (1055-1905)
Related titles: Online - full text ed.: USD 15.16 per issue (effective 2011).
Published by: Damron Company, Inc., PO Box 422458, San Francisco, CA 94142. TEL 415-255-0404, 800-462-6654.

350 USA
DAMRON ACCOMODATIONS. Text in English. 1995. biennial. USD 23.95 per issue (effective 2011). adv. **Document type:** *Handbook/Manual/Guide, Consumer.* **Description:** Includes detailed listings and photographs of gay-friendly accomodations around the world.
Related titles: Online - full text ed.: USD 19.16 per issue (effective 2011).
Published by: Damron Company, Inc., PO Box 422458, San Francisco, CA 94142. TEL 415-255-0404, 800-462-6654.

910.09 USA ISSN 1534-3359
TX907.2
DAMRON MEN'S TRAVEL GUIDE. Text in English. 1964. a. USD 22.95 per issue (effective 2011). adv. 800 p./no.; **Document type:** *Handbook/Manual/Guide, Consumer.* **Description:** Gay pocket guide for U.S., Canada, Mexico, the Caribbean, and select cities in Europe.
Former titles (until 1999): Damron Address Book (1088-5250); (until 1993): Bob Damron's Address Book
Related titles: Online - full text ed.: USD 18.36 per issue (effective 2011).
Published by: Damron Company, Inc., PO Box 422458, San Francisco, CA 94142. TEL 415-255-0404, 800-462-6654.

910.202 USA ISSN 1551-8000
G1204
DAMRON ROAD ATLAS. Text in English. 1989. biennial. USD 19.95 (effective 2001). adv. illus.; maps. 330 p./no.; **Document type:** *Directory.* **Description:** Highlights gay locations and tourist attractions in major North American and European metropolitan areas.
Published by: Damron Company, Inc., PO Box 422458, San Francisco, CA 94142. TEL 415-255-0404, FAX 415-703-9049, https://damron.com. Ed., R&P Gina M Gatta. Circ: 50,000.

910.2 CHN ISSN 1671-7740
DANGDAI LUYOU/TOURISM TODAY. Text in Chinese. 1999. bi-m. **Document type:** *Magazine, Consumer.*
Published by: Heilongjiang Sheng Luyouju/Heilongjiang Province Tourism Agency, 247, Minjiang Lu, Nangang-qu, Ha'erbin, 150090, China. TEL 86-451-85978600, http://www.hljtour.gov.cn/.

DANSKE BUSVOGNMAEND. *see* TRANSPORTATION—Automobiles

919.4 AUS
DAWSONS ACCOMMODATION SOLUTIONS. Text in English. 1951. s-a. AUD 87.45 domestic; AUD 127.45 foreign (effective 2009). adv. **Document type:** *Directory.*
Formed by the merger of (2000-2005): Dawsons Accommodation Solutions. International; Which was formerly (until Jun.2000): Dawsons Hotel Guide. International Consultants Edition (0812-3667); (2000-2005): Dawsons Accommodation Solutions. Australia; Which was formerly (until 2000): Dawsons Hotel Guide. Australia; (1982-198?): Dawsons Hotel Guide. Domestic Consultants Edition (0814-575X); Both International Consultants Edition and Domestic Consultants Edition superseded in part(in 1982): Dawsons Guide (0812-3659); Which was formerly (until 1979): Dawsons Guide to Australian & Worldwide Hotels (0812-3640); (until 1976): Dawsons Australia and Worldwide Guide (0812-3632); (until 1968): Dawsons Guide to Hotels, Motels and Resorts
Related titles: CD-ROM ed.; Online - full text ed.
Published by: Dawson Magazines Pty. Ltd., PO Box 197, Cronulla, NSW 2230, Australia. TEL 61-2-85220000, FAX 61-2-85220088, admin@dawsons.com.au, http://www.dawsons.com.au. Ed. Larry Jamieson. adv.: page AUD 3,999; trim 297 x 210.

T U

910.202 AUS ISSN 1445-3592
DAWSONS VENUE SELECTIONS. Text in English. 1984. s-a. AUD 49.50 domestic; AUD 79.50 foreign (effective 2009). adv. index. **Document type:** *Directory.* **Description:** Directory of convention venues and incentive resorts throughout Australasia.
Former titles (until 2001): Dawsons Venue Directory (0815-6794); (until 1985): Dawsons Venues and Meeting Places (0815-5151)
Related titles: CD-ROM ed.; Online - full text ed.
Published by: Dawson Magazines Pty. Ltd., PO Box 197, Cronulla, NSW 2230, Australia. TEL 61-2-85220000, FAX 61-2-85220088, admin@dawsons.com.au, http://www.dawsons.com.au. Ed. Larry Jamieson. adv.: page AUD 3,628; trim 297 x 210. **Subscr. to:** PO Box 173, Frenchs Forest, NSW 2086, Australia.

917.71 USA ISSN 1540-675X
F499.C53
DAY TRIPS FROM CINCINNATI; getaway ideas for the local traveler. Variant title: Shifra Stein's Daytrips from Cincinnati. Text in English. 1984. biennial, latest 2007, 8th ed. USD 13.95 per issue (effective 2008). **Document type:** *Guide, Consumer.* **Description:** Describes hundreds of fascinating and exciting things to do, see and discover right in your own backyard.
Published by: The Globe Pequot Press, Inc., 246 Goose Ln, PO Box 480, Guilford, CT 06437. TEL 203-458-4500, 888-249-7586, FAX 203-458-4603, 800-820-2329, info@globepequot.com, http://www.globepequot.com.

917.71 910.2 USA ISSN 1536-3589
F499.C73
DAY TRIPS FROM COLUMBUS; getaways about two hours away. Text in English. 2002. biennial, latest 2004, 2nd ed. USD 12.95 per issue (effective 2008). back issues avail. **Document type:** *Guide, Consumer.* **Description:** Describes hundreds of fascinating and exciting things to do, many free of charge and most within a two-hour drive of Columbus.
Published by: The Globe Pequot Press, Inc., 246 Goose Ln, PO Box 480, Guilford, CT 06437. TEL 203-458-4500, 888-249-7586, FAX 203-458-4603, 800-820-2329, info@globepequot.com, http://www.globepequot.com.

917.64 USA ISSN 2155-5591
F394.D213
▼ **DAY TRIPS FROM DALLAS/FORT WORTH**; getaway ideas for the local traveler. Text in English. 2010 (Jun.). triennial. USD 14.95 per issue (effective 2011). **Document type:** *Guide, Consumer.* **Description:** Travel guide for day trips around the Dallas/Fort Worth, Texas area.
Published by: The Globe Pequot Press, Inc., 246 Goose Ln, PO Box 480, Guilford, CT 06437. TEL 203-458-4500, FAX 203-458-4603, info@globepequot.com.

917.72 USA ISSN 1547-7568
F534.I33
DAY TRIPS FROM INDIANAPOLIS; getaways about two hours away. Text in English. 2001. biennial (Evry 2-3/yrs). USD 12.95 per issue (effective 2008). **Document type:** *Guide, Consumer.* **Description:** Lists travel directions, destination highlights, other places to visit along the way, choice restaurants and lodging (including price ranges) and shopping.
Published by: The Globe Pequot Press, Inc., 246 Goose Ln, PO Box 480, Guilford, CT 06437. TEL 203-458-4500, 888-249-7586, FAX 203-458-4603, 800-820-2329, info@globepequot.com, http://www.globepequot.com.

917.633 338.4791 USA ISSN 1542-5169
F379.N53
DAY TRIPS FROM NEW ORLEANS. Text in English. 2002. irreg., latest 2005, 2nd ed. USD 12.95 per issue (effective 2008). 256 p./no.; **Document type:** *Guide, Consumer.* **Description:** Provides information about travel and tourism in New Orleans.
Published by: The Globe Pequot Press, Inc., 246 Goose Ln, PO Box 480, Guilford, CT 06437. TEL 203-458-4500, 888-249-7586, FAX 203-458-4603, 800-820-2329, info@globepequot.com, http://www.globepequot.com.

917.94 USA ISSN 2155-5540
F868.O6
▼ **DAY TRIPS FROM ORANGE COUNTY, CA**; getaway ideas for the local traveler. Text in English. 2010 (Jun.). triennial. USD 14.95 per issue (effective 2011). **Document type:** *Guide, Consumer.* **Description:** Tour guide for day trips around Orange County, California.
Published by: The Globe Pequot Press, Inc., 246 Goose Ln, PO Box 480, Guilford, CT 06437. TEL 203-458-4500, FAX 203-458-4603, info@globepequot.com.

917.592 910.91 USA ISSN 1541-0404
F319.O7
DAY TRIPS FROM ORLANDO. Text in English. 2002. biennial, latest 2005, 2nd ed. USD 14.95 per issue (effective 2008). **Document type:** *Guide, Consumer.*
Published by: The Globe Pequot Press, Inc., 246 Goose Ln, PO Box 480, Guilford, CT 06437. TEL 203-458-4500, 888-249-7586, FAX 203-458-4603, 800-820-2329, info@globepequot.com, http://www.globepequot.com.

917.565 USA ISSN 1543-1274
F264.R1
DAY TRIPS FROM RALEIGH-DURHAM; getaway ideas for the local traveler. Text in English. 2002. biennial, latest 2007, 3rd ed. USD 14.95 per issue (effective 2008). **Document type:** *Guide, Consumer.* **Description:** Describes hundreds of fascinating and exciting things to do, see and discover right in your own backyard.
Published by: The Globe Pequot Press, Inc., 246 Goose Ln, PO Box 480, Guilford, CT 06437. TEL 203-458-4500, 888-249-7586, FAX 203-458-4603, 800-820-2329, info@globepequot.com.

917.94 910.2 USA ISSN 1557-5470
F869.S12
DAY TRIPS FROM SACRAMENTO. Text in English. 2000. irreg., latest 2005, 2nd ed. USD 14.95 per issue (effective 2008). **Document type:** *Guide, Consumer.* **Description:** Contains information about day trips in Sacramento, California.
Published by: The Globe Pequot Press, Inc., 246 Goose Ln, PO Box 480, Guilford, CT 06437. TEL 203-458-4500, 888-249-7586, FAX 203-458-4603, 800-820-2329, info@globepequot.com, http://www.globepequot.com.

917.97 USA ISSN 2155-5567
F899.S43
▼ **DAY TRIPS FROM SEATTLE**; get away ideas for the local traveler. Text in English. 2010 (Jun.). triennial. USD 14.95 per issue (effective 2011). **Document type:** *Guide, Consumer.* **Description:** Travel guide for day trips around Seattle, Washington.
Published by: The Globe Pequot Press, Inc., 246 Goose Ln, PO Box 480, Guilford, CT 06437. TEL 203-458-4500, FAX 203-458-4603, info@globepequot.com.

917.53 USA ISSN 2155-5508
F192.3
▼ **DAY TRIPS FROM WASHINGTON, D.C.**; getaway ideas for the local traveler. Text in English. 2010 (Jun.). triennial. USD 14.95 per issue (effective 2011). **Document type:** *Guide, Consumer.* **Description:** Tour guide for day trips around Washington, DC.
Published by: The Globe Pequot Press, Inc., 246 Goose Ln, PO Box 480, Guilford, CT 06437. TEL 203-458-4500, FAX 203-458-4603, info@globepequot.com.

908 DEU ISSN 1439-3506
DAYDREAMS. Text in German. 1999. 4/yr. adv. **Document type:** *Magazine, Consumer.*
Published by: Vereinigte Verlagsanstalten GmbH, Hoeherweg 278, Duesseldorf, 40231, Germany. TEL 49-211-73570, FAX 49-211-7357123, info@vva.de, http://www.vva.de.

910.2 USA ISSN 1930-7594
F464.3
DAYTRIP MISSOURI; guide to the Show Me State. Text in English. 1996. biennial. **Document type:** *Guide, Consumer.*
Published by: Aphelion Publications, Inc., 5 Herring Dr., Fulton, MO 65251. Ed. Lee N Godley.

DAZHONG QICHE (QICHE LUXING)/AUTO TRAVEL. *see* TRANSPORTATION—Automobiles

THE DECCAN GEOGRAPHER. *see* GEOGRAPHY

910.202 CAN ISSN 1715-8281
DECKCHAIR; cruise lifestyle travel. Text in English. 2006. q. CAD 23.95 domestic; USD 24.95 in United States; CAD 6 per issue (effective 2006). **Document type:** *Magazine, Consumer.*
Published by: Dockside Media Group Inc., 17834-106 Ave, Ste 201, Edmonton, AB T5S 1V4, Canada. TEL 780-488-2224, info@docksidemedia.ca, http://www.docksidemedia.ca.

917.51 USA ISSN 1934-5852
F164.6
DELAWARE CURIOSITIES; quirky characters, roadside oddities & other offbeat stuff. Text in English. 2007. triennial, latest 2007, 1st ed. USD 14.95 per issue (effective 2008). **Document type:** *Guide, Consumer.* **Description:** Provides tourist information about Delaware.
Published by: The Globe Pequot Press, Inc., 246 Goose Ln, PO Box 480, Guilford, CT 06437. TEL 203-458-4500, 888-249-7586, FAX 203-458-4603, 800-820-2329, info@globepequot.com, http://www.globepequot.com.

DELTA MAGAZINE. *see* LIFESTYLE

338.4791 FRA ISSN 1264-4102
DEPARTEMENTS. Text in French. 1988. irreg. back issues avail. **Document type:** *Monographic series, Consumer.*
Published by: Editions Siloe, 18 rue des Carmelites, Nantes, 44000, France. TEL 33-2-43532601, FAX 33-2-43535601, contact@siloe.fr. Ed. Michel Thierry TEL 33-2-43538930.

052 USA ISSN 1542-1198
G1
DEPARTURES. Text in English. 1984. 7/yr. USD 10; free to qualified personnel Platinum & Centurion Card members (effective 2009). adv. back issues avail.; reprints avail. **Document type:** *Magazine, Consumer.* **Description:** Designed to be an essential resource that showcases the leading luxury brands.
Related titles: Online - full text ed.; Regional ed(s).: Departures (Europe Edition).
Published by: American Express Publishing Corp., 1120 Ave of the Americas, New York, NY 10036. TEL 212-382-5600, FAX 212-382-5879, ashields@amexpub.com, http://www.amexpub.com. Ed. Richard David Story. Pub. Kathi Doolan. Adv. contact Maria Kladopoulos TEL 212-382-5632. B&W page USD 54,195, color page USD 79,500; trim 7.875 x 9. Circ: 1,106,133.

910.13 DEU
DEPARTURES MAGAZIN. Variant title: American Express Departures Magazin. Text in German. 4/yr. adv. **Document type:** *Magazine, Consumer.*
Published by: Journal International Verlags- und Werbegesellschaft mbH, Hanns-Seidel-Platz 5, Munich, 81737, Germany. TEL 49-89-6427970, FAX 49-89-64279777, info@journal-international.de, http://www.journal-international.de. Ed. Thomas Midulla. Adv. contact Daniel Jaeger. color page EUR 9,970; trim 210 x 297. Circ: 32,500 (controlled).

910.2 PRT ISSN 1647-3396
▼ **DESCUBRA UMA REGIAO COM ALMA.** Text in Portuguese. 2009. a. **Document type:** *Guide, Consumer.*
Published by: Turismo Leiria Fatima, Jardim Luis de Camoes, Leiria, 2401-801, Portugal. info@rt-leiriafatima.pt, http://www.rt-leiriafatima.pt.

910.202 ESP ISSN 1954-8893
DESCUBRE. Text in Spanish. 2007. irreg. EUR 20 newsstand/cover (effective 2009). **Document type:** *Magazine, Consumer.* **Description:** Travel guides.
Related titles: ◆ French ed.: Michelin Voyager Pratique. ISSN 1772-5100.
Published by: Michelin Espana Portugal S.A., Avda. de los Encuartes 19, Tres Cantos, Madrid, 28760, Spain.

910.202 551.415 USA
DESERT GUIDE. Text in English. m.
Published by: Desert Publications, Inc., 303 N Indian Canyon Dr, Box 2724, Palm Springs, CA 92262-2724. TEL 760-325-2333, FAX 760-325-7008. Ed. Donna Curran.

DESERT U S A. *see* HISTORY—History Of North And South America

910.202 FRA ISSN 1957-5491
DESIRS DE VOYAGES. Text in French. 2007. bi-m. **Document type:** *Magazine, Consumer.*
Published by: Editions d'Ailleurs, 10 Rue Pergolese, Paris, 75016, France.

910.91 USA
DESTIN GEOGRAPHIC. Text in English. 2000. a. USD 19.95 (effective 2001). **Document type:** *Magazine, Consumer.*
Address: 6458, Miramar Beach, FL 32550-1004. http://www.destingeographic.com. Ed., Pub. Antonio Ceasar.

910.2 USA ISSN 2154-7734
▼ **DESTINATION AMERICA TRAVEL.** Text in English. 2009. m. free (effective 2010). adv. back issues avail. **Document type:** *Magazine, Consumer.* **Description:** Aims to provide readers information about North America's exciting and unique places to visit.
Media: Online - full text.
Published by: BlackFish Media, 136 Haggard Loop, Hot Springs, AR 71901.

917.104 CAN
DESTINATION CALGARY AND AREA. Text in English. 1987. bi-m. membership. back issues avail. **Document type:** *Newsletter.* **Description:** Includes news stories, features and reports about visitor industry events, activities and issues including marketing, industry trends and business in Calgary and the area.
Formerly: Destination Calgary
Published by: Calgary Convention & Visitors Bureau, 237 Eighth Ave, S E, Ste 200, Calgary, AB T2G 0K8, Canada. TEL 403-750-2391, FAX 403-262-3809. Ed. W A Bell. Circ: 1,100 (controlled).

DESTINATION FRANCE; the magazine with a passion for France. *see* SPORTS AND GAMES—Outdoor Life

DESTINATION I DO. *see* MATRIMONY

910.91 BHS
DESTINATION: ISLANDS OF THE BAHAMAS. Text in English. 1998. a. USD 24.50 (effective 1999). adv. **Document type:** *Directory, Consumer.* **Description:** Promotes tourism in the Bahamas.
Published by: (Bahamas Hotel Association), Symonette's Marketing Group, PO Box N 4846, Nassau, Bahamas. TEL 242-3562981, FAX 242-3565050. Ed. Michael A. J. Symonette. Pub. Michael A J Symonette. R&P Peter N Symonette. Adv. contact Brenda Grant. B&W page USD 7,990, color page USD 9,960. Circ: 150,000.

910.2 647.9 GBR ISSN 2045-6468
▼ **DESTINATION MOZAMBIQUE.** Text in English. 2011. a. adv. **Document type:** *Magazine, Consumer.*
Related titles: Online - full text ed.: free (effective 2011).
Published by: Land & Marine Publications Ltd., 1 Kings Ct, Newcomen Way, Severalls Business Park, Colchester, Essex CO4 9RA, United Kingdom. TEL 44-1206-752902, FAX 44-1206-842958, publishing@landmarine.com, http://www.landmarine.com. Eds. Robert Deaves, Denis Gathanju. Adv. contact Judith Gimson.

910.91 USA
DESTINATION SPA VACATIONS; retreats, resorts, & sanctuaries for the spa travelers. Text in English. 2000. a. USD 5.95 newsstand/cover (effective 2001). adv. 76 p./no.; **Document type:** *Magazine, Consumer.*
Published by: Destination Spa Group, 8600 E Rockcliff Rd, Tucson, AZ 85750. TEL 888-772-4363, http://www.destinationspa.com. Adv. contact Michelle Kleist.

338.4791 GBR ISSN 2046-0597
DESTINATION UK; promoting UK tourism to the world's travel trade. Text in English. 2006. m. GBP 40 domestic; GBP 50 foreign; free to qualified personnel (effective 2011). adv. back issues avail. **Document type:** *Magazine, Trade.* **Description:** Covers the latest news and information on tourist markets and attractions across England, Scotland and Wales and special areas of interest, market trends and growth opportunities.
Published by: Wharncliffe Publishing Ltd., 47 Church St, Barnsley, S Yorkshire S70 2AS, United Kingdom. TEL 44-1226-734639, FAX 44-1226-734478, editorial@wharncliffepublishing.co.uk, http://www.wharncliffepublishing.co.uk. Adv. contact Tony Barry TEL 44-1226-734333.

910.202 USA ISSN 1081-5546
DS556
DESTINATION: VIETNAM. Text in English. 1994. bi-m. USD 20; USD 60 foreign. adv. bk.rev. illus.; maps. **Document type:** *Magazine, Consumer.* **Description:** Covers the art, cuisine, culture, and history of Vietnam and its many tourist destinations. Includes travel essays and tips on shopping.
Published by: Global Directions, Inc., 3230 Scott St, San Francisco, CA 94123. TEL 415-921-1316, FAX 415-921-3432. Pub. Albert Wen. Adv. contact Lisa Spivey. Circ: 25,000 (paid).

DESTINATION WEDDINGS & HONEYMOONS. *see* MATRIMONY

917.9491 USA ISSN 1932-0159
DESTINATION WINE COUNTRY - SANTA BARBARA; a visitor's guide to wine tasting, shopping and dining in Santa Barbara County. Text in English. 2005 (Win.). 3/yr. USD 12; USD 4.95 newsstand/cover (effective 2006). adv. **Document type:** *Magazine, Consumer.*
Published by: Destination Media, LLC, P O Box 22008, Santa Barbara, CA 93121. TEL 805-565-9799, FAX 805-565-5916. Ed. Hillary D. Klein. Pub. Daniel Burgner. Adv. contact Jimmy Marshall.

919.5 NZL ISSN 1177-0740
DESTINATIONS; New Zealand's travel authority. Text in English. 1996. q. NZD 65 domestic; AUD 145 in Australia; EUR 145 in Europe; USD 145 elsewhere (effective 2008). adv. **Document type:** *Magazine, Consumer.*
Published by: Destinations Media, 74 Jervois Rd, Herne Bay, Auckland, New Zealand. TEL 64-9-3603978, FAX 64-9-3604097, mail@destinationsmagazine.com. Pub. Bruce Laybourn. adv.: page NZD 5,400; trim 215 x 297. Circ: 21,500.

910.4 USA ISSN 0279-8468
DESTINATIONS (WASHINGTON); motorcoach travel across North America. Text in English. 1979. m. membership; USD 25, USD 30 (effective 2001). adv. illus.; tr.lit. back issues avail. **Document type:** *Magazine, Trade.*
Published by: American Bus Association, 700 13th St NW, Ste. 575, Washington, DC 20005-5923. TEL 202-842-1645, FAX 202-842-0850, abainfo@buses.org, http://www.buses.org. Ed. Veronica Chao. Pub. Mary Jo Shapiro. Adv. contact Jane Herwig TEL 800-355-4051. B&W page USD 2,025; 7.5 x 10. Circ: 6,000.

917.204 ESP ISSN 1576-8511
DESTINO CUBA. Text in English, Spanish. 1997. q. included in subscription to Editur. **Document type:** *Magazine, Trade.*
Description: Provides information and facts for tourism professionals.
Related titles: ◆ Supplement to: Editur. ISSN 1134-6469.
Published by: Ediciones Turisticas, S.A., C. Consejo de Ciento 355 Piso 3o, Barcelona, 08007, Spain. TEL 34-93-4670229, FAX 34-93-4670218, direccion@editur.es, http://www.editur.com.

388.4 ESP
DETECTUR. Text in Spanish. fortn. adv. **Document type:** *Magazine, Trade.* **Description:** Provides classified ads for the tourism industry. Includes an article from an industry consultant.
Related titles: ◆ Supplement to: Editur. ISSN 1134-6469.
Published by: Ediciones Turisticas, S.A., C. Consejo de Ciento 355 Piso 3o, Barcelona, 08007, Spain. TEL 34-93-4670229, FAX 34-93-4670218, direccion@editur.es, http://www.editur.com. Ed. Pablo Morata. Pub. Miguel Vila Regard. Adv. contact Margarita Solernou.

914.406 FRA ISSN 1148-0858
DETOURS EN FRANCE (SAINTE-GENEVIEVE). Text in French. 6/yr. maps. **Document type:** *Magazine, Consumer.*
Published by: Detours en France, B.P. 270, Sainte-Genevieve, Cedex 60732, France. TEL 16-44-03-44-95, FAX 16-44-07-43-36.

DETROIT NEWSPAPER AGENCY. TRAVEL DIRECTORY. *see* TRANSPORTATION—Air Transport

382 DEU ISSN 0541-3370
DEUTSCHES WIRTSCHAFTSWISSENSCHAFTLICHES INSTITUT FUER FREMDENVERKEHR. SCHRIFTENREIHE. Text in German. 1953. irreg., latest vol.52, 2007. price varies. **Document type:** *Monographic series, Academic/Scholarly.*
Published by: Deutsches Wirtschaftswissenschaftliches Institut fuer Fremdenverkehr, Sonnenstr 27, Munich, 80331, Germany. TEL 49-89-267091, FAX 49-89-267613, info@dwif.de, http://www.dwif.de.

382 DEU ISSN 0580-6933
DEUTSCHES WIRTSCHAFTSWISSENSCHAFTLICHES INSTITUT FUER FREMDENVERKEHR. SONDERREIHE. Text in German. 1963. irreg., latest vol.74, 2007. price varies. **Document type:** *Monographic series, Academic/Scholarly.*
Published by: Deutsches Wirtschaftswissenschaftliches Institut fuer Fremdenverkehr, Sonnenstr 27, Munich, 80331, Germany. TEL 49-89-267091, FAX 49-89-267613, info@dwif.de, http://www.dwif.de. Ed. J Maschke.

338.4 ESP
DEVIAJES. Text in Spanish. 1999. m. EUR 2.70 newsstand/cover (effective 2009). adv. back issues avail. **Document type:** *Magazine, Consumer.*
Related titles: Online - full text ed.
Published by: Hachette Filipacchi SA, Avda Cardenal Herrera Oria 3, Madrid, 28034, Spain. TEL 34-91-7287000, FAX 34-91-3585473, comunicacion@hachette.es, http://www.hachette.es. Ed. Nuria Munoz. Adv. contact Luisa Ruiz de Velasco. B&W page EUR 5,300; 228 x 297. Circ: 32,885.

643.2 GRC ISSN 1106-8590
DIAKOPES. Text in Greek. 1967. a. **Document type:** *Magazine, Consumer.* **Description:** Provides information on destinations, hotels, restaurants, local customs and events, monuments, museums, as well as history and traditions in Greece of interest to tourists.
Published by: Lambrakis Press SA, Panepistimiou 18, Athens, 106 72, Greece. TEL 30-1-3686-452, FAX 30-1-3686-445, dolinfo@dol.gr, http://www.dol.gr. Circ: 33,646 (controlled).

DINE ONLINE; the independent UK dining and travel review. *see* HOTELS AND RESTAURANTS

910.202 DEU ISSN 0949-3131
DINERS CLUB MAGAZINE. Text in German. 1968. m. EUR 24.60; EUR 4.10 newsstand/cover (effective 2006). adv. bk.rev. 76 p./no.; **Document type:** *Magazine, Consumer.*
Published by: P M I Verlag AG, Oberfeldstr 29, Frankfurt Am Main, 60439, Germany. TEL 49-69-5480000, FAX 49-69-54800066, http://www.pmi-verlag.de. adv.: B&W page EUR 6,930, color page EUR 10,710. Circ: 65,769 (paid). **Subscr. to:** dsb Abo-Betreuung GmbH, Konrad-Zuse-Str 16, Neckarsulm 74172, Germany. TEL 49-1805-959500, FAX 49-1805-959511, gongverlag.abo@dsb.net, http://www.dsb.net.

DIRECTORY OF DESIGNATIONS OF NATIONAL HISTORIC SIGNIFICANCE; commemorating Canada's history. *see* HISTORY

338.4791 FRA ISSN 1957-0414
DIRIGER UN OFFICE DE TOURISME. Text in French. 200?. 3/yr. EUR 169 (effective 2011).
Related titles: CD-ROM ed.: ISSN 2103-6365. 200?.
Published by: Reseau Territorial, BP 215, Voiron, Cedex 38506, France. TEL 33-4-76657136, FAX 33-4-76050163, info@territorial.fr, http://www.territorial.fr.

DIRITTO DEL TURISMO. *see* LAW—International Law

973 USA ISSN 0898-6231
THE DISCERNING TRAVELER. Text in English. 1987. bi-m. USD 50 (effective 2005). bk.rev. **Document type:** *Newsletter, Consumer.* **Description:** Covers the east coast of the United States and Canada; includes what to do, where to stay and where to dine for each location covered.
Published by: Lida Limited, 504 W Mermaid Lane, Philadelphia, PA 19118. TEL 215-247-5578, FAX 215-247-6130. Ed. Linda Glickstein. Pub., R&P David Glickstein.

910.09 USA
DISCOVER COSTA RICA. Text in English, Spanish. 1989. a. adv. charts; illus. **Document type:** *Trade.* **Description:** Informs travelers about Costa Rica and supplies useful information.
Published by: Aboard Publishing, One Herald Plz, 4th Fl, Miami, FL 33132. TEL 305-376-5294, FAX 305-376-5274.

914.415 IRL
DISCOVER DUBLIN GUIDE. Text in English. a. adv. **Document type:** *Magazine, Consumer.*
Published by: Dublin Tourism Centre, Suffolk St., Dublin, 2, Ireland. TEL 353-1-6057700, FAX 353-1-6057757, http://www.visitdublin.com. adv.: color page EUR 1,651. Circ: 500,000 (controlled).

910.09 USA
DISCOVER GUATEMALA. Text in English, Spanish. 1989. a. free (effective 2011). adv. charts; illus. **Document type:** *Trade.* **Description:** Informs travelers about Guatemala and supplies useful information.
Published by: Aboard Publishing, One Herald Plz, 4th Fl, Miami, FL 33132. TEL 305-376-5294, FAX 305-376-5274.

918.04 USA
DISCOVER HONDURAS. Text in English, Spanish. 1990. a. free (effective 2011). adv. **Document type:** *Guide, Trade.* **Description:** Provides useful information for travelers to Honduras.
Published by: Aboard Publishing, One Herald Plz, 4th Fl, Miami, FL 33132. TEL 305-376-5294, FAX 305-376-5274. Pub. Garry Duell.

914.415 IRL
DISCOVER IRELAND. Text in English. 2/yr. adv. **Document type:** *Magazine, Consumer.*
Published by: Tudor Journals Ltd., 97 Botanic Ave, Belfast, BT7 1JN, Ireland. TEL 353-28-90320088, FAX 353-28-90323163, info@tudorjournals.com, http://www.tudorjournals.com. adv.: color page EUR 5,800; trim 210 x 297.

910.91 USA
DISCOVER OHIO; official state visitors guide & travel planner. Text in English. 1996. s-a. free. adv. **Document type:** *Magazine, Trade.* **Description:** Covers travel destinations in Ohio, including art, sports, parks, nature, and more.
Formerly: Ohiopass
Related titles: CD-ROM ed.; Online - full text ed.
Published by: Publishing Group, Ltd., 4500 Mobile Dr, Ste 100, Columbus, OH 43220. TEL 614-572-1240, FAX 614-572-1241, info@pubgroupltd.com, http://www.pubgroupltd.com/. Ed. Jeff Robinson.

913 NZL ISSN 1174-8001
DISCOVER RODNEY MAGAZINE; the tourism magazine for Rodney. Text in English. 2008. a. free (effective 2010). adv. **Document type:** *Magazine, Consumer.* **Description:** Presents articles on the unique and wide range of activities and destinations the Rodney district.
Published by: Discover Rodney Ltd., Albany, N Shore, PO Box 300-505, Auckland, 0752, New Zealand. TEL 64-9-4262050. Ed. Steve Hart TEL 64-9-4262050. Adv. contact Jackie Hart. page USD 1,790; 210 x 275. Circ: 2,000.

910.2 CAN ISSN 1910-0043
DISCOVER SOUTHWEST ALBERTA. Text in English. a. **Document type:** *Journal, Consumer.*
Former titles (until 2006): Official Alberta South Vacation Guide (1704-8079); (until 2002): Alberta South Vacation Guide (1704-8060)
Published by: Chinook Country Tourist Association, 2805 Scenic Dr, Lethbridge, AB T1K 5B7, Canada. TEL 403-320-1222, 800-661-1222, FAX 403-329-6177, info@chinookcountry.com, http://www.chinookcountry.com/index.html.

910.09 TTO
DISCOVER TRINIDAD AND TOBAGO. Text in English. 1991. a. **Document type:** *Magazine, Consumer.* **Description:** Contains a complete package of feature articles, pictures, listings and country information for visitors.
Published by: Media & Editorial Projects Ltd. (M E P), 6 Prospect Ave, Maraval, Port of Spain, Trinidad & Tobago. TEL 868-622-3821, FAX 868-628-0639, mep@wow.net, http://www.meppublishers.com. Ed. Brigitte Bento-Espinet. Pub. Jeremy Taylor. Circ: 150,000 (controlled).

917.9 USA
DISCOVER UTAH. Text in English. 19??. a. **Document type:** *Magazine, Consumer.* **Description:** Provides a guide to winter sports, dining, shopping, cultural activities and other items of interest to visitors to the state.
Published by: Morris Multimedia, Inc., 725 Broad St, Augusta, GA 30901. TEL 706-724-0851, http://www.morris.com.

916.8 338.4 ZAF ISSN 1810-4711
DISCOVERING S A; South African travel at your fingertips. Text in English. 2004. q.
Published by: Greg Vogt, Ed. & Pub., PO Box 2791, Knysna, 6570, South Africa.

910.91 AUS ISSN 1832-1046
DISCOVERING SYDNEY AND SURROUNDS. Variant title: Gregory's Discovering Sydney and Surrounds. Text in English. 1934. triennial, latest 2004, 38th ed. AUD 24.95 per issue (effective 2008). **Document type:** *Handbook/Manual/Guide, Consumer.* **Description:** Provides information on natural features, history, getting there, getting around, festivals and events, main localities and towns, national parks, parks and gardens, other attractions and recreation activities.
Former titles (until 2005): Gregory's 200 Kilometres Around Sydney (0156-4951); Gregory's 100 Miles 'Round Sydney
Published by: Universal Publishers Pty. Ltd., 1 Waterloo Rd, PO Box 1530, Macquarie Park, NSW 2113, Australia. TEL 61-2-98573700, 800-021-987, FAX 61-2-98889074, 800-636-197, dgardiner@universalpublishers.com.au, http://www.universalpublishers.com.au/index_html.

910.4 JPN
DISNEY FAN. Text in Japanese. 1990. bi-m. **Document type:** *Magazine, Consumer.* **Description:** Provides Disneyland information for the Disney fan.
Published by: Kodansha Ltd., 2-12-21 Otowa, Bunkyo-ku, Tokyo, 112-8001, Japan. TEL 81-3-3946-6201, FAX 81-3-3944-9915, http://www.kodansha.co.jp. Ed. Masataka Ono. Circ: 70,000.

DIVE; the magazine diving deserves. *see* SPORTS AND GAMES

DIVER MAGAZINE. *see* SPORTS AND GAMES

DIVERSION. *see* LIFESTYLE

910.2 DZA ISSN 0012-4311
DJEZAIR. Text in French. 1965. s-a. free. bk.rev. charts; illus.
Published by: (Algeria. Office National de l'Animation, de la Promotion et de l'Information Touristique), Ministere du Tourisme, 27 rue Khelifa Boukhalfa, Algiers, Algeria. Ed. Hafida Chaouch.

910.09 CAN ISSN 0821-5758
DOCTOR'S REVIEW; medicine on the move. Text in English. 1983. m. CAD 64 domestic; CAD 126 in United States; CAD 154 foreign (effective 2007). **Description:** A travel and lifestyle journal for doctors.
Published by: Parkhurst Publishing, 400 McGill St, 3rd Fl, Montreal, PQ H2Y 2G1, Canada. TEL 514-397-8833, FAX 514-397-0228, contact@parkpub.com, http://www.parkpub.com. Ed. Madeleine Partous. Pub. David Elkins. Circ: 36,220 (controlled).

917.44 636.7 USA ISSN 1546-2757
SF427.4574.M4
THE DOG LOVER'S COMPANION TO BOSTON; the inside scoop on where to take your dog. Text in English. 1996. triennial, latest 4th ed. USD 17.95 4th ed. (effective 2008). **Document type:** *Guide, Consumer.* **Description:** Provides information on the various canine-friendly parks, beaches, restaurants, accommodations and recreation spots in Boston.
Formerly (until 2003): The Boston Dog Lover's Companion (1089-2737)
Published by: Avalon Travel Publishing, 1700 4th St, Berkeley, CA 94710. TEL 510-595-3664, avalon.publicity@perseusbooks.com, http://www.avalontravelbooks.com.

917.94 636.7 USA ISSN 1539-5464
SF427.4574.C2
THE DOG LOVER'S COMPANION TO CALIFORNIA; the inside scoop on where to take your dog. Text in English. 1994. triennial, latest 6th ed. USD 24.95 6th ed. (effective 2008). **Document type:** *Guide, Consumer.* **Description:** Features information on dog runs, parks, beaches, hiking trails, camping areas, pet-friendly businesses, etc.
Formerly (until 199?): The California Dog Lover's Companion (1086-7856)
Published by: Avalon Travel Publishing, 1700 4th St, Berkeley, CA 94710. TEL 510-595-3664, avalon.publicity@perseusbooks.com, http://www.travelmatters.com.

917.73 636.7 USA ISSN 1545-2182
SF427.4574.I3
THE DOG LOVER'S COMPANION TO CHICAGO; the inside scoop on where to take your dog. Text in English. 2003. biennial, latest 2nd ed. USD 17.95 2nd ed. (effective 2008). **Document type:** *Guide, Consumer.* **Description:** Provides information on resources available to dogs in Chicago such as doggy spas, art openings, church and synagogue services and off-leash areas.
Published by: Avalon Travel Publishing, 1700 4th St, Berkeley, CA 94710. TEL 510-595-3664, avalon.publicity@perseusbooks.com, http://www.avalontravelbooks.com.

917.59 636.7 USA ISSN 1535-0312
SF427.4574.F6
THE DOG LOVER'S COMPANION TO FLORIDA; the inside scoop on where to take your dog. Text in English. 1996. triennial, latest 4th ed. USD 21.95 4th ed. (effective 2008). **Description:** Provides information on the various canine-friendly places in Florida.
Formerly (until 19??): The Florida Dog Lover's Companion (1089-2729)
Published by: Avalon Travel Publishing, 1700 4th St, Berkeley, CA 94710. TEL 510-595-3664, avalon.publicity@perseusbooks.com, http://www.travelmatters.com.

917.9494 636.7 USA ISSN 1555-9394
SF427.4574.C2
THE DOG LOVER'S COMPANION TO LOS ANGELES. Text in English. 2005. biennial, latest 1st ed. USD 17.95 1st ed. (effective 2008). **Document type:** *Guide, Consumer.* **Description:** Provides information on the various canine-friendly places in Los Angeles.
Published by: Avalon Travel Publishing, 1700 4th St, Berkeley, CA 94710. TEL 510-595-3664, avalon.publicity@perseusbooks.com, http://www.avalontravelbooks.com.

636.7 917.4 USA ISSN 1531-4243
SF427.4574.N427
THE DOG LOVER'S COMPANION TO NEW ENGLAND; the inside scoop on where to take your dog. Text in English. 2001. triennial, latest 3rd ed. USD 22.95 3rd ed. (effective 2008). **Document type:** *Guide, Consumer.* **Description:** Presents information on parks, dog runs, beaches, restaurants and pet-friendly businesses throughout the six states that make up New England.
Published by: Avalon Travel Publishing, 1700 4th St, Berkeley, CA 94710. TEL 510-595-3664, avalon.publicity@perseusbooks.com.

917.47 636.7 USA ISSN 1538-5027
SF415.45
THE DOG LOVER'S COMPANION TO NEW YORK CITY; the inside scoop on where to take your dog. Text in English. 2002. irreg., latest 2002. USD 23.50 per issue (effective 2008).
Published by: Avalon Travel Publishing, 1700 4th St, Berkeley, CA 94710. TEL 510-595-3664, avalon.publicity@perseusbooks.com, http://www.travelmatters.com.

917.9461 636.7 USA ISSN 1538-8824
SF427.4574
THE DOG LOVER'S COMPANION TO THE BAY AREA; the inside scoop on where to take your dog. Text in English. 1995. triennial, latest 2008. USD 17.95 newsstand/cover (effective 2003); USD 23.50 per issue (effective 2008).
Former titles (until 2002): The Bay Area Dog Lover's Companion (1078-8921); Dog Lover's Companion
Published by: Avalon Travel Publishing, 1700 4th St, Berkeley, CA 94710. TEL 510-595-3664, avalon.publicity@perseusbooks.com; http://www.travelmatters.com.

917.9 636.7 USA ISSN 1553-135X
SF427.4574.N85
THE DOG LOVER'S COMPANION TO THE PACIFIC NORTHWEST. Text in English. 2005. triennial, latest 1st ed. USD 19.95 1st ed. (effective 2008). **Document type:** *Guide, Consumer.* **Description:** Provides information on the various canine-friendly places in the Pacific Northwest including Oregon, Washington and British Columbia.
Published by: Avalon Travel Publishing, 1700 4th St, Berkeley, CA 94710. TEL 510-595-3664, avalon.publicity@perseusbooks.com, http://www.avalontravelbooks.com.

636.7 917.53 917.526 USA ISSN 1540-3300
F192.3
THE DOG LOVER'S COMPANION TO WASHINGTON D.C. & BALTIMORE. Text in English. 1998. biennial (Every two to three years), latest 2nd ed. USD 19.95 2nd ed. (effective 2008). **Document type:** *Guide, Consumer.* **Description:** Features information on several things - from parks and wildlife areas to restaurants, shops and hotels.
Formerly (until 2002): The Washington, D.C.-Baltimore Dog Lover's Companion (1521-2394)

TU

Published by: Avalon Travel Publishing, 1700 4th St, Berkeley, CA 94710. TEL 510-595-3664, avalon.publicity@perseusbooks.com, http://www.travelmatters.com.

917.95 636.7 USA ISSN 2151-7460
SF427.4574.O7

▼ **THE DOG LOVER'S GUIDE TO OREGON.** Text in English. 2010 (Mar.). triennial. USD 14.95 per issue (effective 2010). **Document type:** *Guide, Consumer.* **Description:** Features the best parks, restaurants, accommodations, recreation spots and pet-friendly businesses in Oregon.
Published by: Avalon Travel Publishing, 1700 4th St, Berkeley, CA 94710. TEL 510-595-3664, info@travelmatters.com, http://www.moon.com.

910.91 636 USA ISSN 1933-6268
GV198.56

DOGFRIENDLY.COM'S CAMPGROUND AND R V PARK GUIDE. (Recreational Vehicle) Text in English. 2006. a. **Document type:** *Guide, Consumer.*
Published by: Dogfriendly.com Inc., 6454 Pony Express Trail #33-233, Pollock Pines, CA 95726. TEL 877-475-2275, email@dogfriendly.com.

910.09 USA
G155.U6

DOMESTIC OUTLOOK FOR TRAVEL AND TOURISM. Text in English. 19??. a. charts. reprints avail. **Document type:** *Guide, Trade.* **Description:** Contains 28 separate presentations or white papers from TIA's 30th Marketing Outlook Forum, including topics such as the economy, consumer and demographic trends, technology, branding and consumer marketing, air travel, the hotel market, attraction industry, auto travel, business travel, cruise travel, rail travel; cultural and historic tourism, packaged travel; restaurant industry, the rv market, and family travel.
Former titles (until 2000): Outlook Forum. Outlook for Travel and Tourism; (until 1998): Outlook for Travel and Tourism (0737-8815); (until 1997): Travel Outlook Forum Proceedings (0160-4651)
Published by: Travel Industry Association of America, 1100 New York Ave, NW, Ste 450, Washington, DC 20005. TEL 202-408-8422, FAX 202-408-1255, feedback@tia.org, http://www.tia.org.

910.09 USA ISSN 1533-0435
G155.U6

DOMESTIC TRAVEL MARKET REPORT. Text in English. 1979. a. USD 300 per issue to non-members; USD 180 per issue to members (effective 2008). adv. back issues avail.; reprints avail. **Document type:** *Monographic series, Trade.* **Description:** Provides an overview of the size and composition of the 2 billion person-trips taken domestically by U.S. residents.
Former titles (until 2001): Travel Market Report (Year); (until 1993): National Travel Survey (0737-2620)
Related titles: Microfiche ed.: (from CIS); Online - full text ed.
Indexed: SRI.
Published by: Travel Industry Association of America, 1100 New York Ave, NW, Ste 450, Washington, DC 20005. TEL 202-408-8422, FAX 202-408-1255, feedback@tia.org. Pub. Dawn L Drew. Adv. contact Sarah Dickson TEL 202-408-2141.

910.2 USA ISSN 2157-054X

DOMINICAN REPUBLIC. D K EYEWITNESS TOP 10 TRAVEL GUIDES. Text in English. 2005. irreg. **Document type:** *Guide, Consumer.*
Published by: D K Publishing (Subsidiary of: Penguin Books U S A, Inc.), 375 Hudson St, New York, NY 10014. TEL 646-674-4000, specialsales@dk.com.

910.91 USA ISSN 1932-6459

DORDOGNE, BORDEAUX & THE SOUTHWEST COAST. Variant title: Eyewitness Travel Guide: Dordogne and Southwest France. Text in English. 2006. a. USD 25 per issue (effective 2008). 329 p./no.; **Document type:** *Magazine, Consumer.* **Description:** Contains beautiful new full color photos, maps and illustrations.
Published by: D K Publishing (Subsidiary of: Penguin Books U S A, Inc.), 375 Hudson St, New York, NY 10014. TEL 212-213-4800, FAX 201-256-0000, specialsales@dk.com.

DORSET; the magazine for people who like to explore. *see* SPORTS AND GAMES—Outdoor Life

DOS ALGARVES. *see* BUSINESS AND ECONOMICS—Management

914.504 ITA ISSN 1121-1792

DOVE. Text in Italian. 1991. m. (11/yr.). adv. illus. **Document type:** *Magazine, Consumer.* **Description:** Provides readers with detailed travel information on a particular city or region, including a forum for buying, selling, and renting properties in tourist areas.
Published by: R C S Periodici (Subsidiary of: R C S Mediagroup), Via San Marco 21, Milan, 20121, Italy. TEL 39-2-25844111, FAX 39-2-25845444, info@periodici.rcs.it, http://www.rcsmediagroup.it/siti/periodici.php. Ed. Carlo Montanaro. Circ: 114,440 (paid). **Dist. in UK by:** Seymour Distribution Ltd, 86 Newman St, London W1T 3EX, United Kingdom. FAX 44-207-396-8002, enquiries@seymour.co.uk.

990 NLD ISSN 1388-2325

DOWN UNDER. Cover title: Going Down Under. Text in Dutch. 1997. q. EUR 18.50 domestic; EUR 21.50 in Belgium; EUR 4.95 newsstand/cover (effective 2009). adv. **Document type:** *Magazine, Consumer.*
Incorporates (1990-1997): Newsletter Australia (0928-2351); Which was formerly (until 1991): Nieuwsbrief Australie (0928-2424)
Published by: dOrizon Media, Postbus 135, Castricum, 1900 AC, Netherlands. TEL 31-251-672136, FAX 31-251-654578, info@dorizon.nl, http://www.dorizon.nl. Adv. contact Harald Kolkman. color page EUR 1,550; trim 230 x 297. Circ: 10,000.

DREAM WORLD CRUISE DESTINATIONS. *see* TRANSPORTATION—Ships And Shipping

910.2 CAN ISSN 1710-6699

DRIFTWOOD, INFORMATION GUIDE. Text in English. 2004. a. **Document type:** *Handbook/Manual/Guide, Consumer.*
Published by: Ontario Ministry of Natural Resources, Ontario Parks, PO Box 7000, Peterborough, ON K9J 8M5, Canada. TEL 705-755-2000, http://www.mnr.gov.on.ca, http://www.ontarioparks.com.

917 790.13 051 USA ISSN 1534-5726

DRIVE AMERICA. Text in English. 1965. q. bk.rev. illus.; tr.lit. **Document type:** *Magazine, Consumer.* **Description:** Presents travel writing and photography for historical, tourist, and park destinations in North America.
Former titles (until 2001): Vista U S A (0507-1577); Vista
Published by: (Exxon Travel Club, Inc.), C - E Publishing (Subsidiary of: C - E Communications), 30400 Van Dyke Ave, Warren, MI 48093. TEL 586-574-3400, lturk@campbell-ewald.com, http://www.campbell-ewald.com.

910.4 USA ISSN 1546-2072
GV198.95

DUDE RANCH VACATIONS & HORSEBACK ADVENTURES. Text in English. 2004. a. USD 8.99 newsstand/cover domestic; USD 9.99 newsstand/cover in Canada (effective 2004). adv. **Description:** Travel Resource for Western and horseback riding vacations. Features dude & guest ranches, cattle prives, wagon train adventures and wilderness pack and trail ride outfitters.
Published by: TagMar, Inc., Gordon's Guide Travel Publications, 410 W. Fallbrook Ave., Ste 204, Fresno, CA 93711. TEL 559-490-2800 x121, FAX 559-490-2801, editor@gordonguide.com, http://www.cowboy-vacations-magazine.com, http://www.gordonsguide.com. Ed., R&P Rachel K Willis. Pub. Timothy E Gordon. Adv. contact Mark E Junette. page USD 4,860. **Dist. by:** Ingram Periodicals, 1240 Heil Quaker Blvd, La Vergne, TN 37086. TEL 800-627-6247, FAX 615-793-6043.

910.4 USA ISSN 1073-8533

DUDE RANCHER - DIRECTORY. Text in English. 1930. a. free. bk.rev. illus. back issues avail. **Document type:** *Directory, Consumer.* **Description:** Provides descriptions of the association's members and activities.
Formed by the merger of: Dude Rancher; Dude Rancher Directory
Published by: Dude Ranchers Association, PO Box 2307, Cody, WY 82414-2307. TEL 920-223-8440, FAX 970-223-0201. Eds. Bobbi Futterer, Jim Futterer. R&P Jim Futterer. Circ: 40,000.

910.2 CHN ISSN 1672-7517

DUJIA LUYOU. Text in Chinese. m. **Document type:** *Magazine, Consumer.*
Formerly (until 2004): Huangshan Luyou (1003-8175)
Published by: Huangshan Ribaoshe, 21, Xinan Nan Lu, Huangshan, 245041, China.

917.204 MEX

DURANGO. Text in Spanish. m.
Published by: (Durango Hotel Association), Editorial Bonanza S. de R.L., DR VELASCO 95, Ed. 5 Of. 203, Col Doctores Del. Cuauhtemoc, Mexico City, DF 06720, Mexico. TEL 525-5938720, FAX 525-7052492.

910.2 USA

DURANGO MAGAZINE. Text in English. s-a. USD 9.50; USD 3.95 newsstand/cover (effective 2001). **Document type:** *Magazine, Consumer.* **Description:** Covers area attractions, history, people, places and culture of Durango, Colorado.
Published by: Schultz and Associates, PO Box 8333, Durango, CO 81301. TEL 970-385-4030, FAX 970-385-4436, drgomag@frontier.net, http://www.durangomagazine.com/.

910.202 USA

E-HONG KONG. Text in Chinese. w. (English ed.; m. Japanese, Chinese eds.). **Description:** Covers Hong Kong sites of interest to tourists.
Former titles: Hong Kong Now! (Print); (until 1999): Hong Kong Digest (San Francisco)
Media: Online - full content. **Related titles:** Chinese ed.; Japanese ed.
Published by: Hong Kong Economic & Trade Office, 130 Montgomery St, San Francisco, CA 94104-4301. TEL 415-835-9300, FAX 415-421-0646. Circ: 26,000.

338.4 USA ISSN 1941-5842
G155.A1

E-REVIEW OF TOURISM RESEARCH. Text in English. 2003. 6/yr. free (effective 2010). **Document type:** *Journal, Academic/Scholarly.* **Description:** Promotes discourse and scholarship within the tourism research academic and professional communities.
Media: Online - full text.
Indexed: A39, C27, C29, CA, D03, D04, E13, F12, H&TI, H06, O01, R14, S13, S14, S15, S16, S18, SSciA, T02.
Published by: Texas A & M University, Department of Recreation, Park and Tourism Sciences, 106 Francis Hall, 2261 TAMU, College Station, TX 7784-2261. TEL 979-845-5411, FAX 979-845-0446, ugretzel@ag.tamu.edu, kangjae@tamu.edu. Ed. Sanjay Nepal.

338.4 658 GBR

E-TID.COM. Text in English. 1990. w. looseleaf. free to qualified personnel (effective 2009). back issues avail. **Document type:** *Newsletter, Trade.* **Description:** Covers business news, financial results, and trends and developments in the tourist trade.
Formerly (until 2000): Travel Industry Digest (Print)
Media: Online - full text. **Related titles:** Fax ed.
Published by: Travel Industry Digests Ltd., 4th Fl, Julia House, 40-42 Newman St, London, W1T 1QD, United Kingdom. TEL 44-20-74361088, FAX 44-20-73235752, ask@e-tid.com.

915.204 959 NLD ISSN 2211-8683

EAST!. Text in Dutch. 1998. q. EUR 21.50 domestic; EUR 27.50 foreign; EUR 5.95 newsstand/cover (effective 2011). adv. **Document type:** *Magazine, Consumer.*
Former titles (until 2011): Archipel (1566-7936); (until 1999): Archipelago (1389-6059)
Published by: Maasland Uitgeverij, Postbus 348, Oss, 5340 AH, Netherlands. TEL 31-412-628218, FAX 31-412-651367, info@maasland.com, http://www.maaslanduitgeverij.com. Pub. Peter van Riel.

914.2 GBR

EAST ANGLIA GUIDE. Text in English. 1973. a. GBP 3.95 (effective 1998). adv. **Document type:** *Directory, Consumer.* **Description:** Lists tourist attractions, restaurants, boat rentals, beaches, and historic towns in East Anglia.
Published by: East of England Tourist Board, Toppesfield Hall, Hadleigh, Suffolk, United Kingdom. FAX 44-1473-823063. Ed., Adv. contact Mark Dymond. Circ: 20,000 (paid).

910.91 USA

EASY ESCAPES. Text in English. 1995. 10/yr. USD 67.75 (effective 2001). **Document type:** *Newsletter, Consumer.*
Published by: Easy Escapes, Inc., Box 120365, Boston, MA 02112. TEL 800-221-0878, info@easyescapes.com, http://www.easyescapes.com. Ed. Catherine Clark.

641.05 DEU

EAT MAGAZINE. Text in German. 2008. 2/yr. EUR 20; EUR 12 newsstand/cover (effective 2011). adv. **Document type:** *Magazine, Consumer.*
Published by: abcverlag GmbH, Waldhofer Str 19, Heidelberg, 69123, Germany. TEL 49-6221-75704100, FAX 49-6221-75704109, info@abcverlag.de, http://www.abcverlag.de. Ed. Juergen Franke. Adv. contact Ingrid Gimbel. Circ: 25,000 (paid and controlled).

910.91 USA ISSN 1934-9904
TX907.3.C22

EATING NAPA & SONOMA; a food lover's guide to local produce & local dining. Abbreviated title: Eating Napa and Sonoma. Text in English. 2005. irreg. USD 15.95 per issue (effective 2008). **Document type:** *Guide, Consumer.* **Description:** Provides guidance on the places foodies love best: cheese makers, chocolatiers, wineries, olive oil presses, organic farms, cooking classes, herb farms, sausage makers, food and wine museums, orchards, specialty shops, ethnic grocery stores and neighborhoods, farmers markets, small specialty food producers of all sorts and outstanding restaurants.
Published by: The Countryman Press (Subsidiary of: W.W. Norton & Co., Inc.), PO Box 748, Woodstock, VT 05091. TEL 802-457-4826, 800-245-4151, FAX 802-457-1678, countrymanpress@wwnorton.com.

917.94 USA ISSN 2155-1308
F859.3

ECCENTRIC CALIFORNIA. Text in English. 2005. irreg. USD 19.95 per issue (effective 2010). **Document type:** *Guide, Consumer.* **Description:** Travel guide for California's oddest shops, wackiest festivals, and strangest tours.
Published by: The Globe Pequot Press, Inc., 246 Goose Ln, PO Box 480, Guilford, CT 06437. TEL 203-458-4500, FAX 203-458-4603, info@globepequot.com, http://www.globepequot.com.

910.09 FRA ISSN 1259-8682

L'ECHO TOURISTIQUE. Text in French. 1975. w. (42/yr). EUR 55 combined subscription to qualified personnel print & online eds.; EUR 79 combined subscription print & online eds. (effective 2009). adv. **Document type:** *Magazine, Trade.*
Former titles (until 1980): L' Echo Touristique. Tourisme Ces Derniers Jours (0150-6560); Which was formed by the merger of (1970-1975): Tourisme Ces Derniers Jours (0150-9365); Which was formerly (until 1972): Ces Derniers Jours (1259-8658); (1970-1975): L' Echo Touristique (0150-6552); Which was formerly (until 1972): L' Echo Touristique. Bonne Table et Tourisme (1259-8631); Which was formed by the merger (1950-1970): L' Echo Touristique (1259-8607); Which was formerly (until 1951): L' Echo Touristique et Municipal (1259-8593); (1950-1970): Bonne Table et Tourisme (1259-8623); Which was formerly (until 1953): Bonne Table (1259-8615)
Related titles: Online - full text ed.
Published by: Groupe Industrie Services Info, Antony Parc II, 10 Av. du General de Gaulle, Antony, 92160, France. TEL 33-1-77929775, http://www.librairie-gisi.fr. Ed. Thierry Beaurepere. Circ: 9,200.

917.5 USA ISSN 1526-7474
QH105.F6

ECOFLORIDA. Text in English. 4/yr. USD 12 domestic; CAD 28 in Canada; USD 3.95 newsstand/cover (effective 2003). adv. **Document type:** *Magazine, Consumer.* **Description:** Provides readers with detailed information about ecotourism and natural sites in Florida, with additional information related to enjoying Florida outdoors.
Published by: this little publishing co., 2141 N University Dr, Ste 253, Coral Springs, FL 33071. TEL 954-255-7010, 888-392-4832, FAX 954-255-7010. adv.: page USD 980.

917 910.2 USA ISSN 1540-6121

ECONOGUIDE DISNEYLAND RESORT, UNIVERSAL STUDIOS HOLLYWOOD; other major southern california attractionsincluding disney's california adventure. Text in English. 1996. a., latest 2007, 5th ed. USD 17.95 (effective 2008). **Document type:** *Guide, Consumer.* **Description:** Provides information on travel options, hotels, dining, and attractions for every budget.
Formerly (until 2000): Econoguide. Disneyland, Universal Studios Hollywood, and other Major Southern California Attractions (1090-6967)
Published by: The Globe Pequot Press, Inc., 246 Goose Ln, PO Box 480, Guilford, CT 06437. TEL 203-458-4500, 888-249-7586, FAX 203-458-4603, 800-820-2329, info@globepequot.com, http://www.globepequot.com.

917.13 910.2 USA ISSN 1544-8436
F839.3

ECONOGUIDE LAS VEGAS; also includes Reno, Lake Tahoe, and Laughlin. Text in English. 1994. biennial, latest 2007, 5th ed. USD 17.95 per issue (effective 2008). 464 p./no.; **Document type:** *Guide, Consumer.* **Description:** Provides travel and tourism information for Las Vegas and surrounding area.
Former titles (until 2003): Econoguide: Las Vegas, Reno, Laughlin, Lake Tahoe (1520-0256); (until 1996): Econoguide: Las Vegas, Reno, and Lake Tahoe; (until 1995): Econoguide to Las Vegas
Published by: The Globe Pequot Press, Inc., 246 Goose Ln, PO Box 480, Guilford, CT 06437. TEL 203-458-4500, 888-249-7586, FAX 203-458-4603, 800-820-2329, info@globepequot.com, http://www.globepequot.com.

917.5904 910.2 USA ISSN 1541-7158

ECONOGUIDE WALT DISNEY WORLD, UNIVERSAL ORLANDO; also includes SeaWorld and Central Florida. Text in English. 1993. a., latest 2007, 5th ed. USD 17.95 (effective 2008). **Document type:** *Guide, Consumer.* **Description:** Provides information on travel options, hotels, dining, and attractions for every budget.
Former titles (until 2000): Econoguide Walt Disney World, Universal Studios Florida, Epcot, and Other Major Central Florida attractions (1521-9267); (until 1995): Econoguide to Walt Disney World, Epcot Universal Studios (1521-933X)
Published by: The Globe Pequot Press, Inc., 246 Goose Ln, PO Box 480, Guilford, CT 06437. TEL 203-458-4500, 888-249-7586, FAX 203-458-4603, 800-820-2329, info@globepequot.com, http://www.globepequot.com.

910.09 USA ISSN 0733-642X
G155.U6

ECONOMIC REVIEW OF TRAVEL IN AMERICA (YEAR). Text in English. 19??. a. USD 195 per issue to non-members; USD 120 per issue to members (effective 2008). adv. back issues avail.; reprints avail. **Document type:** *Monographic series, Trade.* **Description:** Provides details about the economic impact of the U.S. travel industry on the economy and covers the United States' place in global tourism and the performance of major travel-related industries in the U.S.
Related titles: Online - full text ed.

Indexed: SRI.
Published by: Travel Industry Association of America, 1100 New York Ave, NW, Ste 450, Washington, DC 20005. TEL 202-408-8422, FAX 202-408-1255, feedback@tia.org. Pub. Dawn L Drew. Adv. contact Sarah Dickson TEL 202-408-2141.

338.4791 GBR ISSN 2042-3993
▼ **ECOTOURISM KENYA GUIDE.** Text in English. 2010. biennial. adv. **Document type:** *Handbook/Manual/Guide, Trade.* **Description:** Promotes ecotourism and sustainable tourism practices in Kenya.
Related titles: Online - full text ed.: free (effective 2010).
Published by: (Ecotourism Kenya KEN), Land & Marine Publications Ltd., 1 Kings Ct, Newcomen Way, Severalls Business Park, Colchester, Essex CO4 9RA, United Kingdom. TEL 44-1206-752902, FAX 44-1206-842958, publishing@landmarine.com. Adv. contact Lester Powell.

913.919 DEU ISSN 0176-9596
ECOUTE; Das Sprachmagazin fuer Frankreichliebhaber. Text in German. 1984. m. EUR 69.60; EUR 59.40 to students; EUR 6.50 newsstand/cover (effective 2011). adv. **Document type:** *Magazine, Consumer.*
Related titles: Online - full text ed.
Published by: Spotlight Verlag GmbH (Subsidiary of: Verlagsgruppe Georg von Holtzbrinck GmbH), Fraunhoferstr 22, Planegg, 82152, Germany. TEL 49-89-856810, FAX 49-89-85681105, info@spotlight-verlag.de, http://www.spotlight-online.de. Adv. contact Axel Zettler. Circ: 51,139 (paid and controlled).

910.202 GBR ISSN 1363-7398
F3709.5
ECUADOR AND GALAPAGOS HANDBOOK. Text in English. 1997. biennial, latest vol.6, 2007. GBP 14.99 (effective 2009). adv. **Document type:** *Handbook/Manual/Guide, Consumer.*
—CCC.
Published by: Footprint Handbooks Ltd., 6 Riverside Ct, Lower Bristol Rd, Bath, Avon BA2 3DZ, United Kingdom. TEL 44-1225-469141, FAX 44-1225-469461, info@footprintbooks.com. **Dist. in N. America by:** Passport Books, 130 E. Randolph St., Ste. 400, Chicago, IL 60601-6213. TEL 847-679-5500, FAX 847-679-6375.

910.91 USA ISSN 1930-6733
DA890.E3
EDINBURGH DIRECTIONS. Text in English. 2005. irreg., latest 2008, 2nd ed. USD 11.99 domestic 2nd ed.; USD 14.99 in Canada 2nd ed.; GBP 6.99 in United Kingdom 2nd ed. (effective 2008). back issues avail. **Document type:** *Guide, Consumer.*
Related titles: Online - full text ed.
Published by: Rough Guides, 375 Hudson St, 9th Fl, New York, NY 10014. TEL 212-414-3635, http://www.roughguides.com/default.aspx.

914.6 ESP ISSN 1134-6469
EDITUR; semanario del turismo. Text in Spanish. 1960. w. EUR 120 domestic; EUR 174 in Europe; EUR 235 elsewhere (effective 2009). adv. **Document type:** *Magazine, Trade.* **Description:** Includes subjects in the areas of tourism policy, product commercialization and tourism services.
Related titles: ◆ Online - full text ed.: Editur Online. ISSN 1575-3980; ◆ Supplement(s): Detectur; ◆ Destino Cuba. ISSN 1576-8511; ◆ Los Cuadernos de Editur. Tecno Hosteleria. ISSN 1137-4829; ◆ Las Guias de Editur. ISSN 1137-4764; ◆ Estudios de Gestion Turistica. ISSN 1137-4705; ◆ Cuadernos Editur. ISSN 1137-4683; ◆ Los Cuadernos de Editur. Tecno Agencias. ISSN 1137-4837; ◆ Editur Catalunya. ISSN 1135-9536; ◆ Mini Guias Editur. ISSN 1137-4713.
Published by: Ediciones Turisticas, S.A., C. Consejo de Ciento 355 Piso 3o, Barcelona, 08007, Spain. TEL 34-93-4670229, FAX 34-93-4670218, direccion@editur.es, http://www.editur.com. Ed. Pablo Morata Socias. Pub. Luisa Vila Regard. R&P, Adv. contact Anna Vera Llonch. B&W page USD 3,050, color page USD 3,300; 313 x 220. Circ: 6,950.

338.4 ESP ISSN 1135-9536
EDITUR CATALUNYA. Text in Catalan. 1995. m. included in subscription to Editur. adv. **Document type:** *Magazine, Trade.* **Description:** Contains the latest developments in the sector of specific interest to professionals in Catalonia.
Formerly (until 1995): Editur Catalunya i Andorra (1137-4845)
Related titles: ◆ Supplement to: Editur. ISSN 1134-6469.
Published by: Ediciones Turisticas, S.A., C. Consejo de Ciento 355 Piso 3o, Barcelona, 08007, Spain. TEL 34-93-4670229, FAX 34-93-4670218, direccion@editur.es, http://www.editur.com. Ed. Joan Miquel Gomis. Pub. Miguel Vila Regard. Adv. contact Maria Isabel Garcia.

338.4 ESP ISSN 1575-3964
EDITUR LATINOAMERICA. Text in Spanish. 1995. m. EUR 24 domestic; EUR 36 in Europe; EUR 53 elsewhere (effective 2009). adv. **Document type:** *Trade.* **Description:** Offers worldwide travel news of interest to Latinamerican travel professionals.
Related titles: Online - full text ed.: ISSN 1575-3999.
Published by: Ediciones Turisticas, S.A., C. Consejo de Ciento 355 Piso 3o, Barcelona, 08007, Spain. TEL 34-93-4670229, FAX 34-93-4670218, direccion@editur.es, http://www.editur.com. Ed. Pablo Morata. Pub. Cecilia Vila Regard. Adv. contact Monica Casares. page USD 1,200; 273 x 190.

914.6 ESP ISSN 1575-3980
EDITUR ONLINE. Text in Spanish. 1995. w. **Document type:** *Magazine, Consumer.*
Media: Online - full text. **Related titles:** ◆ Print ed.: Editur. ISSN 1134-6469.
Published by: Ediciones Turisticas, S.A., C. Consejo de Ciento 355 Piso 3o, Barcelona, 08007, Spain. http://www.editur.com.

910.202 GBR ISSN 1363-7983
EGYPT HANDBOOK. Text in English. 1996. biennial. GBP 14.99 per issue (effective 2010). adv. maps. back issues avail. **Document type:** *Handbook/Manual/Guide, Consumer.* **Description:** Covers all the basics from where to stay and where to eat to cycling, walking and how to get around the Egypt.
—CCC.
Published by: Footprint Handbooks Ltd., 6 Riverside Ct, Lower Bristol Rd, Bath, Avon BA2 3DZ, United Kingdom. TEL 44-1225-469141, FAX 44-1225-469461, wwwinfo@footprintbooks.com.

338.4 ZAF ISSN 1997-163X
➤ **EGYPTIAN JOURNAL OF TOURISM AND HOSPITALITY.** Text in English. s-a. **Document type:** *Journal, Academic/Scholarly.* **Description:** Covers best practices of tourism management, hospitality, tourism development and education, applied research studies, and critical review on major issues affecting the tourism sector.
Related titles: Online - full text ed.: ISSN 1998-3301.
Published by: (World Research Organization), Isis Press, PO Box 1919, Cape Town, 8000, South Africa. TEL 27-21-4471574, FAX 27-86-6219999, orders@unwro.org, http://www.unwro.org/isispress.html.

338.4791 DEU ISSN 1616-1718
EICHSTAETTER MATERIALIEN ZUR TOURISMUSFORSCHUNG. Text in German. 2000. irreg., latest vol.4, 2006. price varies. **Document type:** *Monographic series, Academic/Scholarly.*
Published by: (Katholische Universitaet Eichstaett-Ingolstadt), Profil Verlag GmbH, Veilchenstr 41, Munich, 80689, Germany. TEL 49-89-704924, FAX 49-89-704924, office@profilverlag.de, http://www.profilverlag.de.

EILEEN MAGAZINE. *see* TRANSPORTATION—Automobiles

910.202 929 USA ISSN 1092-6895
LC5451
ELDERHOSTEL. INTERNATIONAL CATALOG. Text in English. q. **Document type:** *Catalog, Consumer.*
Supersedes in part (in 19??): Elderhostel Catalog
Published by: Elderhostel, Inc., 11 Ave de Lafayette, Boston, MA 02111. TEL 800-454-5768, registration@elderhostel.org.

910.09 338 USA
ELECTRONIC TRAVEL ALERT. Text in English. 1987. 48/yr. USD 95 (effective 2001). **Document type:** *Bulletin, Consumer.* **Description:** Provides news of airfare wars and late-breaking events.
Formerly (until 2001): Fax Travel Bulletin
Media: Fax. **Related titles:** E-mail ed.
Published by: Nationwide Intelligence, PO Box 1922, Saginaw, MI 48605-1922. TEL 989-793-0123, 800-333-4130, FAX 989-793-8830, info@nationwideintelligence.com, http://www.nationwideintelligence.com. Ed., Pub. David W Oppermann.

910.202 USA ISSN 1536-5387
ELITE TRAVELER; the essence of luxury. Text in English. 2001. bi-m. USD 147 domestic; USD 182 foreign (effective 2002). adv. **Document type:** *Magazine, Consumer.* **Description:** Contains articles and features on luxurious travel destinations and services available to the affluent.
Address: Universal Media Bldg., 801 Second Ave., New York, NY 10017. TEL 212-986-5100, 800-571-0961, FAX 212-983-2548. Ed., Pub., Adv. contact Douglas D. Gollan. B&W page USD 19,940, color page USD 28,898. Circ: 125,000 (paid and controlled).

910.2 USA ISSN 1930-6660
TX907
ELITE TRAVELER'S HOTELS RESORTS SPAS. Text in English. 2003. a.
Published by: Elite Traveler, Universal Media Bldg., 801 Second Ave., New York, NY 10017. TEL 212-986-5100, 800-571-0961, FAX 212-983-2548.

915 USA ISSN 1933-4133
G155.C55
EMERGING TOURISM MARKETS; China & India. Text in English. 2006. irreg. USD 495 per issue to non-members; USD 300 per issue to members (effective 2009). **Document type:** *Magazine, Trade.* **Description:** Examines outbound travel and travel to the U.S. from China and India - two of the fastest growing economies and tourism markets in the world.
Related titles: Online - full text ed.: ISSN 1933-4141.
Published by: Travel Industry Association of America, 1100 New York Ave, NW, Ste 450, Washington, DC 20005. TEL 202-408-8422, FAX 202-408-1255, feedback@tia.org.

916 GBR ISSN 1362-3273
EMIGRATE (ANNUAL). Text in English. 1996. a. free to qualified personnel (effective 2009). **Document type:** *Magazine, Consumer.* **Description:** Gives practical information and advice to people who are considering emigrating to various parts of the world, particularly Australia, New Zealand, Canada, USA and South Africa.
Incorporates (2006-2008): Emigrate America (1749-9593); Which was formerly (1991-2005): Going U S A (0965-3732); (2006-2008): Emigrate New Zealand (1749-9542); Which was formerly (1994-2005): Destination New Zealand (1352-4771); (2006-2008): Emigrate Australia (1749-9550); Which was formerly (1992-2005): Australian News (0965-3740); (2006-2008): Emigrate Canada (1749-9577); Which was formerly (1987-2005): Canada News (0951-5267)
Related titles: Online - full text ed.
Published by: Outbound Media & Exhibitions, 1 Commercial Rd, Eastbourne, E Sussex BN21 3XQ, United Kingdom. TEL 44-1323-726040, FAX 44-1323-649249. Ed. Paul Beasley.

304.873041 GBR ISSN 1759-1139
▼ **EMIGRATE (MONTHLY).** Text in English. 2009. m. GBP 29; GBP 3.25 newsstand/cover (effective 2009). adv. bk.rev. back issues avail. **Document type:** *Magazine, Consumer.* **Description:** Provides potential migrants and travelers to the United States with information about immigration requirements, real estate, employment, education, investing and lifestyle.
Formed by the merger of (2006-2009): Emigrate America (1749-9593); Which was formerly (1991-2005): Going U S A (0965-3732); (2006-2009): Emigrate New Zealand (1749-9542); Which was formerly (1994-2005): Destination New Zealand (1352-4771); (2006-2009): Emigrate Australia (1749-9550); Which was formerly (1992-2005): Australian News (0965-3740); (2006-2009): Emigrate Canada (1749-9577); Which was formerly (until 2006): Canada News (0951-5267); (2006-2009): Emigrate South Africa (1749-9585); Which was formerly (1983-2005): South African News (0265-6787)
Published by: Outbound Media & Exhibitions, 1 Commercial Rd, Eastbourne, E Sussex BN21 3XQ, United Kingdom. TEL 44-1323-726040, FAX 44-1323-649249. Ed. Paul Beasley.

910.202 ITA ISSN 1826-2953
L'EMILIA ROMAGNA PAESE PER PAESE. Text in Italian. 2005. w. **Document type:** *Magazine, Consumer.*
Published by: Editrice Bonechi, Via dei Cairoli, 18BB, Florence, FI 50131, Italy. TEL 39-055-576841, FAX 39-055-5000766, bonechi@bonechi.it, http://www.bonechi.it.

EMPLOYEE SERVICES MANAGEMENT; the journal of employee services, recreation, health and education. *see* BUSINESS AND ECONOMICS—Management

914.4 NLD ISSN 1380-8249
EN FRANCE. Text in Dutch. 1993. 4/yr. EUR 17 (effective 2009). **Document type:** *Magazine, Consumer.*
Published by: Pelican Magazines Hearst, Delflandlaan 4, Amsterdam, 1062 EB, Netherlands. TEL 31-20-7581000, FAX 31-20-7581003, info@pelicanmags.nl, http://www.pelicanmags.nl. Ed. Nicky Bouwmeester. Pub. Frank Kloppert.

910.202 USA ISSN 1539-7696
ENCOMPASS. Text in English. 1922. bi-m. USD 1 (effective 2006). 60 p./no. 3 cols./p.; **Document type:** *Magazine, Consumer.*
Former titles (until 2002): The Motorist (1096-5858); (until 1997): Rocky Mountain Motorist (0273-6772)
Related titles: Online - full text ed.
—Ingenta.
Published by: A A A Colorado, 4100 E. Arkansas Ave., Denver, CO 80222. TEL 303-753-8800, FAX 303-300-7710, editor@colorado.aaa.com, http://www.aaacolorado.com. Ed. Jeff Miller. Circ: 310,000 (paid).

910.09 USA ISSN 0279-4853
TX907
ENDLESS VACATION. Text in English. 19??. bi-m. adv. bk.rev. illus. reprints avail. **Document type:** *Magazine, Consumer.* **Description:** Provides the readers with information needed to take a great trip, including where to play, eat, shop, relax and explore in plenty of destinations in the United States, Canada and Mexico, as well as Costa Rica, Cape Town and Beijing.
Incorporates (1980-198?): Resort Condominiums International. Annual Directory Edition (0276-9085); (19??-1984): Vacation Horizons International. Endless Vacation (0883-8852); Which incorporated (19??-198?): Vacation Horizons International. Annual Directory Edition (0749-4939)
Related titles: Online - full text ed.
Indexed: BRI, G08, I05.
Published by: (Resort Condominiums International), Endless Vacation Publications, 9998 N Michigan Rd, Carmel, IN 46032. TEL 317-805-9000, FAX 317-805-9335. Ed. Barbara Peck. Adv. contact Tammie Tullis TEL 212-481-3452. B&W page USD 65,600, color page USD 80,000; trim 8 x 10.5. Circ: 1,700,000.

918.3 CHL ISSN 0718-3836
ENFOQUE. Text in Spanish. 2001. m. CLP 19,000 (effective 2008).
Related titles: Online - full text ed.: ISSN 0718-3844. 2001.
Published by: Viento Sur Comunicacion Visual, Benavente 315 Ofic. 503, Puerto Montt, Chile. TEL 56-65-292474, doyarzun@revistaenfoque.cl. Circ: 7,000.

910.09 330 CAN ISSN 0703-0312
ENROUTE; your complimentary in-flight magazine. Text in English, French. 1973. m. free to Air Canada passengers. adv. bibl.; illus. back issues avail. **Document type:** *Magazine, Consumer.*
Indexed: CPerI, G08.
—CCC.
Published by: Spafax Canada Inc., 4200 Saint-Laurent Blvd, Ste 707, Montreal, PQ H2W 2R2, Canada. TEL 51-4-8442001, FAX 51-4-8446001, http://www.spafax.com/. adv.: color page CAD 18,500; trim 9 x 10.87. Circ: 145,000.

338.4 USA ISSN 1944-2246
ENTERTAINMENT & TRAVEL. Text in English. 2008. w. USD 2,295 in US & Canada; USD 2,495 elsewhere; USD 2,525 combined subscription in US & Canada (print & online eds.); USD 2,755 combined subscription elsewhere (print & online eds.) (effective 2011). adv. back issues avail. **Document type:** *Newsletter, Trade.* **Description:** Provides the latest in leisure and travel news, including airline security changes, casino, cruise and resort news, state tourism campaigns and rental car deals.
Related titles: E-mail ed.; Online - full text ed.: ISSN 1944-2254. USD 2,295 combined subscription (online & e-mail eds.) (effective 2011).
Indexed: A15, ABIn, P48, P51, PQC.
Published by: NewsRx, 2727 Paces Ferry Rd SE, Ste 2-440, Atlanta, GA 30339. TEL 770-435-8286, 800-726-4550, FAX 770-435-6800, pressrelease@newsrx.com, http://www.newsrx.com. Pub., Adv. contact Susan Hasty TEL 770-507-7777.

910.09 USA
ENTREE (SANTA BARBARA); an uncompromising and confidential luxury traveler's newsletter. Text in English. 1981. m. USD 75 domestic; USD 99 foreign (effective 2006). bk.rev.; film rev.; play rev. 8 p./no.; back issues avail. **Document type:** *Newsletter, Consumer.* **Description:** Upscale hotel and restaurant critiques; an insider's look at travel and dining; books, spas, cruises, shopping reviews.
Related titles: E-mail ed.
Published by: Entree Travel, PO Box 5148, Santa Barbara, CA 93150. TEL 805-969-5848, FAX 805-966-7095, wtomicki@aol.com. Ed., Pub., R&P William Tomicki. Circ: 8,000 (paid).

910.91 USA
ENTREE TRAVEL NEWSLETTER; an insider's uncompromising and confidential monthly look at hotels, restaurants and travel around the world. Text in English. 1982. m. USD 75 (effective 2007). 8 p./no.; **Document type:** *Newsletter, Consumer.*
Formerly: Entree
Published by: William Tomicki Ed. & Pub., 695 Olive Rd., Santa Barbara, CA 93108. TEL 805-969-5848, FAX 805-969-5849. Ed., Pub. William Tomicki. Circ: 15,000 (controlled and free).

910.202 ITA ISSN 1970-7541
ENTROTERRA. Text in Italian. 2006. m. EUR 25 to individuals; EUR 100 to institutions 5 copies of each issue (effective 2008). **Document type:** *Magazine, Consumer.*
Related titles: Online - full text ed.: ISSN 1970-755X.
Published by: Ecoprint Media, Via Airella 1, San Giorgio la Molara, BN, Italy.

908 DEU
ERLEBNISZEIT. Text in German. 2005. s-a. EUR 2 newsstand/cover (effective 2010). **Document type:** *Magazine, Consumer.*
Former titles (until 2008): Steigerwald und Fraenkisches Weinland; (until 2007): Fraenkisches Weinland Erleben; (until 2006): Willkommen in der Region Fraenkisches Weinland
Published by: Mediengruppe Main-Post GmbH, Berner Str 2, Wuerzburg, 97084, Germany. TEL 49-931-60010, FAX 49-931-6001420, service.center@mainpost.de, http://www.mainpost.de.

914.41 FRA ISSN 1969-3656
ESCALES. BAIE DE QUIBERON. Text in French, English. 2008. a. EUR 5 (effective 2008). **Document type:** *Magazine, Consumer.*
Published by: Editions Les Heliades, Parc Actilonne, Pepiniere d'Entreprise, B.P. 78, Olonne-sur-Mer, 85340, France. TEL 33-2-51213514, FAX 33-2-51968724, info@lesheliades.com, http://www.lesheliades.com.

914.41 FRA ISSN 1969-3664
ESCALES. GOLFE DU MORBIHAN. Text in French, English. 2008. a. EUR 5 (effective 2008). **Document type:** *Magazine, Consumer.*
Published by: Editions Les Heliades, Parc Actilonne, Pepiniere d'Entreprise, B.P. 78, Olonne-sur-Mer, 85340, France. TEL 33-2-51213514, FAX 33-2-51968724, info@lesheliades.com, http://www.lesheliades.com.

914.41 FRA ISSN 1969-3672
ESCALES. PAYS DE LORIENT. Text in French, English. 2008. a. EUR 5 (effective 2008). **Document type:** *Magazine, Consumer.*
Published by: Editions Les Heliades, Parc Actilonne, Pepiniere d'Entreprise, B.P. 78, Olonne-sur-Mer, 85340, France. TEL 33-2-51213514, FAX 33-2-51968724, info@lesheliades.com, http://www.lesheliades.com.

914.416 FRA ISSN 1776-1336
ESCALES VENDEENNES; sous l'egide du pole touristique international. Text in French, English. 2005. a. EUR 5 (effective 2008). **Document type:** *Magazine, Consumer.*
Published by: Editions Les Heliades, Parc Actilonne, Pepiniere d'Entreprise, B.P. 78, Olonne-sur-Mer, 85340, France. TEL 33-2-51213514, FAX 33-2-51968724, info@lesheliades.com, http://www.lesheliades.com.

910.2 SWE ISSN 1653-3682
ESCAPE 360. Text in Swedish. 2005. 3/yr. SEK 399 (effective 2006). adv. back issues avail. **Document type:** *Magazine, Consumer.*
Related titles: Online - full text ed.
Published by: Independent Publishing Group AB, PO Box 6320, Stockholm, 10235, Sweden. TEL 46-8-55591155, FAX 46-8-55591150, info@ipg-sweden.com, http://www.ipg-sweden.com. Adv. contact Anna-Mari Klaavuniemi. Circ: 30,000.

ESCAPEES. *see* TRANSPORTATION—Automobiles

ESPACES; tourisme et loisirs. *see* SPORTS AND GAMES—Outdoor Life

913 ESP ISSN 1577-6700
ESPANA DESCONOCIDA. Text in Spanish. 1995. m. EUR 22.50 domestic; EUR 34.50 foreign (effective 2010). **Document type:** *Magazine, Consumer.*
Published by: Revistas Profesionales, C/ Valentin Beato 42, 3a Planta, Madrid, 28037, Spain. revistasprofesionales@revistasprofesionales.com.

910 647.9 ESP ISSN 0211-0938
ESPANA HOSTELERA. Text in Spanish. 1957. m. USD 85. adv.
Published by: Espana Hostelera y Turistica, Padre Jesus Ordonez, 10 bajo, Madrid, 28002, Spain. TEL 262-95-49, FAX 262-00-35. Ed. Juan Romero Calvillo. Circ: 17,000.

910.202 FRA ISSN 2108-8292
▼ **ESPRIT PROVENCE.** Text in French. 2010. a. **Document type:** *Magazine, Consumer.*
Published by: l' Association Esprit Provence, 495 Route de Pernes, Saint-Didier, 84210, France. http://www.espritprovence.com. Pub. Gerard Bouscarat.

917 GBR ISSN 1352-2825
ESSENTIALLY AMERICA. Text in English. 1981. q. back issues avail. **Document type:** *Magazine, Consumer.* **Description:** Covers life styles and travel features in USA and Canadian regions.
Former titles (until 1994): Discover North America (0951-8126); (until 1985): Holiday U.S.A. and Canada Magazine; (until 19??): Holiday U.S.A.
Published by: Phoenix International Publishing, 18-20 Scrutton St, London, EC2A 4TG, United Kingdom. TEL 44-20-72470537, FAX 44-20-73772741, http://www.phoenixip.com/. Ed. Mary Moore Mason TEL 44-20-72436954. Pub. Simon Todd TEL 682-831-0133. Adv. contact Larry Cohen TEL 203-255-8800. **N. America dist. addr.:** Northeast Media Group.

914.6 ESP ISSN 1137-4705
ESTUDIOS DE GESTION TURISTICA. Text in Spanish. 1996. s-a. **Document type:** *Magazine, Consumer.*
Related titles: ◆ Supplement to: Editur. ISSN 1134-6469.
Published by: Ediciones Turisticas, S.A., C. Consejo de Ciento 355 Piso 3o, Barcelona, 08007, Spain. TEL 34-93-4670229, FAX 34-93-4670218, direccion@editur.es, http://www.editur.com.

914.604 ESP ISSN 0423-5037
ESTUDIOS TURISTICOS. Text in Spanish; Summaries in English, Spanish. 1963. q. bk.rev. stat. 128 p./no.; **Document type:** *Magazine, Government.* **Description:** Contains economic, geographic and sociological studies about tourism, travel, leisure and recreation. Includes a calendar of fairs, congresses and seminars and a review of tourism legislation.
Indexed: A22, CABA, E12, GH, LT, N02, P09, P32, PCI, PGegResA, R12, RRTA, S13, S16, W11.
—BLDSC (3812.816550), IE, Ingenta.
Published by: Ministerio de Economia, Instituto de Estudios Turisticos, Jose Lazaro Galdiano, 6 2a, Madrid, 28036, Spain. TEL 34-91-3433787, cdte@iet.tourspain.es. Circ: 1,000.

ESTUDIOS Y PERSPECTIVAS EN TURISMO. *see* SOCIAL SCIENCES: COMPREHENSIVE WORKS

ESTUDOS DE GEOGRAFIA HUMANA E REGIONAL. *see* GEOGRAPHY

379.8 ESP ISSN 1816-3521
ETHICS IN TOURISM. Text in Multiple languages. 2005. a. **Document type:** *Monographic series, Trade.*
Related titles: Online - full text ed.
—Ingenta.
Published by: World Tourism Organization, Capitan Haya 42, Madrid, 28020, Spain. TEL 34-91-5678100, FAX 34-91-5713733, omt@unwto.org, http://www.unwto.org.

914 385 USA
EURAIL AND TRAIN TRAVEL GUIDE TO EUROPE. Text in English. 1971. a. USD 14.95. **Document type:** *Magazine, Consumer.* **Description:** Covers train travel in 36 countries throughout Eastern and Western Europe, providing timetables and information on services available.
Formerly (until 1998): The Eurail Guide to Train Travel in the New Europe (0085-0330)
Published by: Houghton Mifflin Harcourt Publishing Company, 215 Park Ave S, New York, NY 10003. TEL 212-420-5800.

910.91 ITA
EURO TRAVEL NEWS; periodico di informazioni turistiche, spettacoli, beni culturali, ambiente. Text in Italian. 1991. bi-m. adv. bk.rev.; music rev.; play rev.; software rev.; tel.rev. bibl.; illus. **Document type:** *Magazine, Consumer.*
Related titles: E-mail ed.; Fax ed.
Address: Via Diomede Marvasi 15, Rome, 00165, Italy. TEL 39-06-66411358, FAX 39-06-66411359, eurotravelnews@it. Ed. Giulia Riccardo.

914 AUT
EUROCITY; das internationale Reisemagazin. Text in German. 1928. bi-m. EUR 13.80 domestic; EUR 30 foreign; EUR 2.70 newsstand/cover (effective 2005). adv. illus. **Document type:** *Magazine, Consumer.*
Former titles: Euro-City: Das Reisemagazin der Neuen Bahn; (until 1991): Reiseland Oesterreich (0254-5292); Fremdenverkehr-Reiseland - Oesterreich (0016-0954)
Published by: Bohmann Druck und Verlag GmbH & Co. KG, Leberstr 122, Vienna, W 1110, Austria. TEL 43-1-740950, FAX 43-1-74095183, http://www.bohmann.co.at. Ed. Georg Karp. Adv. contact Andrea Knopf TEL 43-1-7409548. page EUR 7,800; trim 185 x 250. Circ: 70,000 (paid and controlled).

EUROECONOMICA. *see* BUSINESS AND ECONOMICS

910 AUT
EUROGAST. Text in German. q.
Address: Rottweg 17, Salzburg, Sa 5020, Austria. TEL 0662-32395, FAX 0662-32396. Ed. H Kriechhammer. Circ: 46,500.

EUROPA CAMPING UND CARAVANING. INTERNATIONALER FUEHRER. *see* SPORTS AND GAMES—Outdoor Life

910.202 DEU ISSN 0721-5037
EUROPAEISCHE HOCHSCHULSCHRIFTEN. REIHE 10: FREMDENVERKEHR. Text in German. 1968. irreg., latest vol.12, 1991. price varies. **Document type:** *Monographic series, Academic/Scholarly.*
Formerly (until 1982): Europaeische Hochschulschriften. Reihe 10: Fremdenverkehr und Touristik (0531-738X)
Published by: Peter Lang GmbH (Subsidiary of: Peter Lang Publishing Group), Eschborner Landstr 42-50, Frankfurt Am Main, 60489, Germany. TEL 49-69-7807050, FAX 49-69-78070550, zentrale.frankfurt@peterlang.com, http://www.peterlang.com.

910 USA ISSN 1548-6788
D909
EUROPE BY EURAIL; touring Europe by train. Text in English. 1981. a. USD 18.95 per issue (effective 2009). back issues avail. **Document type:** *Guide, Consumer.* **Description:** Provides information on fares, schedules, pass options, hotel recommendations and sightseeing options for European trains.
Formerly (until 1999): Europe by Eurail (1081-1125)
Published by: The Globe Pequot Press, Inc., 246 Goose Ln, PO Box 480, Guilford, CT 06437. TEL 203-458-4500, 888-249-7586, FAX 203-458-4603, 800-820-2329, info@globepequot.com, http://www.globepequot.com. Ed. LaVerne Ferguson-Kosinski.

914.1 USA ISSN 1074-7516
D909
EUROPE TRAVELBOOK. Text in English. 19??. a. USD 17.95 domestic; USD 20.95 foreign; free to members (effective 2009). illus. **Document type:** *Magazine, Consumer.* **Description:** Provides a complete coverage of everything from specially selected lodgings and restaurants to driving distances and sightseeing suggestions essential for European travel.
Former titles (until 1994): Europe Travel Guide; (until 1988): Travel Guide to Europe; Which was formed by the 1997 merger of: British Isles and Ireland Travel Guide (0095-1579); Central Europe and Scandinavia Travel Guide (0094-3657); Eastern Europe Travel Guide (0094-8632); Southern Europe Travel Guide (0094-3614)
Published by: A A A Publishing, 1000 AAA Dr, Heathrow, FL 32746. TEL 407-444-8370, FAX 407-444-7766, AAATravelInfo-CustomerService@national.aaa.com, http://www.aaa.biz/. Circ: 347,323.

914.04 917.904 USA
EUROPEAN TRAVEL AND ENTERTAINMENT MAGAZINE. Text in English. 1969. m.
Address: PO Box 14545, Phoenix, AZ 85063. TEL 602-233-2342. Circ: 5,000.

910.202 TON
EVA, YOUR GUIDE TO TONGA. Text and summaries in English. 1989. q. USD 23 (effective 2001). adv. 24 p./no.; back issues avail. **Document type:** *Magazine, Consumer.* **Description:** Covers travel and tourism in Tonga.
Published by: Vava'u Press Ltd., PO Box 958, Nuku' alofa, Tonga. TEL 676-25779, FAX 676-24749. Ed., R&P Pesi Fonua. Adv. contact Mary Fonua. Circ: 5,000.

338 658 USA ISSN 1525-9951
GT3935 CODEN: FMETFJ
➤ **EVENT MANAGEMENT**; an international journal. Text in English. 1993. q. USD 525 combined subscription to institutions (print & online eds.) (effective 2011). adv. back issues avail. **Document type:** *Journal, Academic/Scholarly.* **Description:** Publishes articles intended to meet the needs of an evolving profession. Deal with the business of special events for non-profit and public organizations to carry out the missions and as a catalyst for community development.
Formerly (until 2000): Festival Management & Event Tourism (1065-2701)
Related titles: Online - full text ed.: ISSN 1943-4308. USD 445 (effective 2011) (from IngentaConnect).
Indexed: A34, CA, CABA, E12, GH, H&TI, H06, H16, HospAb, LT, N02, P03, PsycInfo, R12, RRTA, S13, S16, SCOPUS, SD, T02, VS, W11.
—BLDSC (3830.772560), IE, Ingenta. **CCC.**
Published by: Cognizant Communication Corp., 18 Peeksill Hollow Rd, P O Box 37, Putnam Valley, NY 10579. TEL 845-603-6440, FAX 845-603-6442, cogcomm@aol.com. Ed. Kenneth Backman. Pub. Robert N Miranda.

917.104 CAN ISSN 1491-4638
EVENTS GUIDE. Cover title: Manitoba (Year) Events Guide. Text in English. 1993. s-a. free. adv. illus. **Document type:** *Handbook/Manual/Guide, Consumer.* **Description:** Offers music, sports, exhibitions, events, festivals and theater listings.
Published by: Travel Manitoba, 155 Carlton St, 7th Fl, Department SS0, Winnipeg, MB R3C 3H8, Canada. TEL 800-665-0040, http://www.travelmanitoba.com. Pub. Colette Fontaine.

EVERY DAY WITH RACHAEL RAY. *see* LIFESTYLE

910.91 USA ISSN 1940-9613
EVERYWHERE; travel is all around you. Text in English. 2007 (Oct.). bi-m. USD 24.99 (effective 2008). adv. illus. **Document type:** *Magazine, Consumer.*
Published by: 8020 Publishing, 199 Fremont St 12th Fl, San Francisco, CA 94105. contact@8020publishing.com, http://www.8020publishing.com/. Ed. Todd Lappin.

910.09 USA ISSN 0890-9911
EXCHANGE BOOK; home exchange directory. Text in English. 1960. s-a. membership. adv. illus. **Document type:** *Directory, Consumer.*
Formerly: Home Exchange Directory
Published by: HomeLink International, 2937 NW 9th Terr, Fort Lauderdale, FL 33311. TEL 954-566-2687, 800-638-3841, us@homelink-usa.org, http://www.homelink.org/. Circ: 15,000.

914.2 GBR
EXCLUSIVE LONDON. Text in English. 1978. q. adv.
Published by: Exclusive Publications Ltd., 11 Dalmore Rd, London, SE21 8HD, United Kingdom. Ed. Robert Redman.

910.2 GBR ISSN 2041-4706
▼ **EXCURSIONS (LONDON).** Text in English. 2009. bi-m. GBP 220 domestic; EUR 268.97 in Europe; USD 367.41 in United States; GBP 3.50 newsstand/cover (effective 2011). adv. back issues avail. **Document type:** *Magazine, Consumer.* **Description:** Covers the best places to visit, best bargain breaks and best activity holidays in the UK.
Published by: Magnet Publishing Ltd., 28 Grafton Ter, London, NW5 4JJ, United Kingdom. TEL 44-20-74240027, http://www.magweb.co.

910.09 CAN ISSN 0847-933X
EXCURSIONS EN AUTOCAR. Text in English. 1988. m. CAD 40 (effective 2000). adv. **Document type:** *Newsletter, Trade.* **Description:** For group tour organizers.
Related titles: ◆ English ed.: Tours on Motorcoach. ISSN 0847-9348.
Published by: (Bus Owners Association), Publicom Inc., Place d Armes, C P 365, Montreal, PQ H2Y 3H1, Canada. TEL 514-274-0004, FAX 514-274-5884. Ed. Francois Marquis. Circ: 6,447 (controlled).

910.202 USA ISSN 2160-7257
EXECUTIVE TRAVEL. Text in English. 200?. bi-m. **Document type:** *Magazine, Trade.*
Published by: American Express Publishing Corp., 1120 Ave of the Americas, New York, NY 10036. TEL 212-382-5600, http://www.amexpub.com. Ed. Janet Libert.

917 330 USA ISSN 1547-9986
EXECUTIVE TRAVELER; the elite corporate retreat and client entertainment magazine. Text in English. 2003. bi-m. free (effective 2004). **Document type:** *Magazine, Trade.*
Published by: Hurley, Hargett & Sigler Media Group, 504 Brookwood Blvd. Ste. 110, Homewood, AL 35209. TEL 205-874-8600, FAX 205-874-8603. Ed., R&P Lee M. Hurley. Pub. Aaron Lisech.

EXHIBITION BULLETIN. *see* MEETINGS AND CONGRESSES

EXHIBITION BULLETIN YEARBOOK. *see* MEETINGS AND CONGRESSES

910.2 USA
EXITSOURCE (YEAR). Text in English. a. adv. **Document type:** *Directory.*
Published by: Exitsource, 5715-B Oakbrook Parkway, Norcross, GA 30093. TEL 770-248-1300, 800-683-3948.

910.19 306.38 USA
EXOTIC PLACES TO RETIRE. Text in English. 2001. q. USD 4.99 newsstand/cover (effective 2001). adv. **Document type:** *Magazine, Consumer.*
Published by: Places to Retire, Inc., 460 South Dixie Hwy., Ste. C, Coral Gables, FL 33146. TEL 305-866-5736, FAX 877-523-8495, karen@placestoretire.com, http://www.exoticplacestoretire.com. Ed. Greg Huneault. Pub. Karen Schellinck.

910.202 FRA ISSN 0247-8684
EXPANSION VOYAGES. Text in French. 1981. q. illus. **Document type:** *Magazine, Corporate.* **Description:** Appeals to senior executives, business men and professionals.
Published by: Groupe Express-Roularta, 29 Rue de Chateaudun, Paris Cede, 75308, France. TEL 33-1-75551000, http://www.groupe-exp.com. Circ: 140,000.

910.2 BRA ISSN 1519-0862
EXPEDICAO ECO TURISMO ESPECIAL. Text in Portuguese. 2001. irreg. BRL 6.90 newsstand/cover (effective 2006). **Document type:** *Magazine, Consumer.*
Published by: Editora Escala Ltda., Av Prof Ida Kolb, 551, Casa Verde, Sao Paulo, 02518-000, Brazil. TEL 55-11-38552100, FAX 55-11-38579643, escala@escala.com.br, http://www.escala.com.br.

910.202 USA ISSN 1526-8977
EXPEDITION NEWS. Text in English. 1994. m. USD 36 (effective 2004). 6 p./no.; back issues avail. **Document type:** *Newsletter, Consumer.*
Address: 137 Rowayton Ave, Ste 210, Rowayton, CT 06853. TEL 203-855-9400, FAX 203-855-9433, blumassoc@aol.com. Ed., Pub. Jeff Blumenfeld.

EXPEDITION PLANNERS' GUIDEBOOK AND DIRECTORY. *see* GEOGRAPHY

910.2 USA ISSN 1946-9160
EXPERIENCE A Z. (Arizona) Text in English. 2005. a. USD 9.95 newsstand/cover (effective 2009). adv. **Document type:** *Magazine, Consumer.* **Description:** Contains a travel guide for visitors and locals to some of the best places and secrets in the Grand Canyon State.
Related titles: Online - full text ed.

Published by: A Z Big Media, 3101 N Central Ave, Ste 1070, Phoenix, AZ 85012. TEL 602-277-6045, FAX 602-650-0827. Ed. Janet Perez. adv.: page USD 3,680; trim 8 x 10.875. Circ: 35,000.

919.404 AUS ISSN 1328-7850
EXPERIENCE VICTORIA. Text in English. 1996. a. AUD 16 (effective 2008). adv. **Document type:** *Directory, Consumer.* **Description:** Provides information on where to visit, what to see and how to get there in Victoria. Includes accommodation, attractions, events, tour operators, maps and other vital information.
Published by: A A A Tourism Pty Ltd., Level 3, 131 Queen St, Melbourne, VIC 3000, Australia. TEL 61-3-86012200, FAX 61-3-86012222, advertising@aaatourism.com.au. Ed. Garth Morrison. Adv. contact Jennifer Goldsmith. page AUD 5,395; trim 160 x 250. Circ: 24,000.

914 LUX
EXPLORATOR; city guide Luxembourg. Text in French, English. 1994. a. EUR 10 newsstand/cover (effective 2007).
Published by: Editions Mike Koedinger SA, P O Box 728, Luxembourg, L-2017, Luxembourg. TEL 35-2-2966181.

910.91 USA ISSN 1532-7094
EXPLORE! (ASHEVILLE). Text in English. 2000. 10/yr. USD 29.95; USD 3.95 newsstand/cover (effective 2001). adv. **Document type:** *Magazine, Consumer.*
Published by: Explore! Magazine, LLC, 39 Biltmore Ave, Asheville, NC 28801. TEL 877-817-4395, editor@exploremagazine.com, http://www.exploremagazine.com. Ed., Pub. Nat Belz. Adv. contact Elizabeth Belz TEL 828-254-9400 ext 12.

EXPLORE (CALGARY); Canada's outdoor magazine. see SPORTS AND GAMES—Outdoor Life

917.704 USA
EXPLORE MINNESOTA BED AND BREAKFAST - HISTORIC INNS. Text in English. 19??. a. free (effective 2009). adv. **Document type:** *Directory, Consumer.* **Description:** Lists and describes scenic and historic bed and breakfast establishments in the state of Minnesota.
Published by: Minnesota Office of Tourism, 121 Seventh Pl E, Metro Sq, Ste 100, St. Paul, MN 55101. TEL 651-296-5029, 800-868-7476, FAX 651-296-7095, explore@state.mn.us.

917 796.5 USA
EXPLORE MINNESOTA CAMPGROUNDS AND R V PARKS GUIDE. Text in English. 1984. a. free. adv. **Document type:** *Directory, Consumer.* **Description:** Lists or describes over 250 campgrounds and RV parks in Minnesota.
Former titles: Explore Minnesota Campground Guide; Explore Minnesota Campgrounds; Camping Guide
Published by: Minnesota Resort Association, Minnesota Alliance of Campground Operators, 305 E. Roselawn Ave., St Paul, MN 55117-2031. TEL 651-778-2400, FAX 651-778-2424. Ed. Julie Knowlton. Circ: 200,000.

916 ZAF ISSN 1728-2233
EXPLORE SOUTH AFRICA. Text in English. 2003. q. adv. **Document type:** *Magazine, Consumer.*
Published by: Cape Media Corporation, Sanclare Bldg, 4th Flr, 21 Dreyer St, Claremont, Cape Town 7735, South Africa. TEL 27-21-6573800, FAX 27-21-6573866, info@capemedia.co.za. Ed. Illana Strauss Dillon. adv.: page ZAR 21,750; trim 210 x 275. Circ: 10,000.

910.202 DEU
EXPLORER MAGAZIN. Text in German. m. **Document type:** *Consumer.* **Description:** Contains stories and features on travel and leisure activities in the great outdoors.
Media: Online - full text.
Published by: Kontext GmbH, Bergstr 5, Anzing, 85646, Germany. TEL 49-8121-5049, FAX 49-8121-3647.

914.15 USA ISSN 1066-5358
EXPLORING IRELAND. Text in English. 1990. 6/yr. USD 39. bk.rev. **Document type:** *Newsletter.* **Description:** Contains travel tips and articles that introduce towns, cities, hotels and restaurants in Ireland.
Address: 318 Pershing Ave, Roselle, NJ 07204. TEL 908-298-0315. Eds. Charlene Komar Storey, Gregory D Storey. Circ: 900 (paid).

338.4791 TUR ISSN 1302-0552
EXPO TOURISTIK. Text in Turkish. 1998. q. **Document type:** *Magazine, Trade.*
Published by: Dunya Yayincilik A.S., Balamir Sokak No 7, Kavacik-Beykoz, Istanbul, 34830, Turkey. TEL 90-216-6811814, FAX 90-216-6803971.

910.2 DEU
EXTRATOUR. Text in German. 1920; N.S. 1951. bi-m. free to members (effective 2009). adv. bk.rev. illus. **Document type:** *Magazine, Consumer.*
Formerly: Jugendherberge (0022-5932)
Published by: Deutsches Jugendherbergswerk, Hauptverband fuer Jugendwandern und Jugendherbergen, Leonardo-da-Vinci-Weg 1, Detmold, 32760, Germany. TEL 49-5231-99360, FAX 49-5231-993666, service@djh.de, http://www.jugendherberge.de. adv.: B&W page EUR 13,000, color page EUR 18,500. Circ: 768,792 (controlled).

910.09 DEU ISSN 1864-340X
F V W. (Fremdenverkehrswirtschaft) Text in German. 1967. bi-w. EUR 129.20 in Europe; EUR 200.50 elsewhere (effective 2010). adv. **Document type:** *Newspaper, Trade.*
Former titles (until 2007): F V W International (0939-6039); (until 1990): Fremdenverkehrswirtschaft International (0939-6020); (until 1972): Fremdenverkehrswirtschaft Wico Touristik (0939-6012); (until 1971): Fremdenverkehrwirtschaft (0939-6004)
Related titles: Online - full text ed.
Published by: Verlag Dieter Niedecken GmbH, Wandsbeker Allee 1, Hamburg, 22041, Germany. TEL 49-40-414480, FAX 49-40-41448999, info@niedeckenmedien.de, http://www.niedeckenmedien.de. Ed. Georg Jegminat. R&P Ines Niedecken. adv.: page EUR 9,150. Circ: 31,047 (paid and controlled).

910.202 USA
FABULOUS JOURNEYS. Text in English. 2005. **Document type:** *Newsletter, Consumer.* **Description:** Features Alice travel's recommendations for the very best travel offerings, crafted by experts to showcase these exceptional locales.
Published by: Alice Travel, Inc., 277 Fairfield Rd., Ste 218, Fairfield, NJ 07004. TEL 973-439-1700, 800-229-2542, sales@alicetravel.com, http://www.alicetravle.com.

FACTS AND ADVICE FOR AIRLINE PASSENGERS. see TRANSPORTATION—Air Transport

914 CHE
DAS FAEHREN-HANDBUCH. Text in German. a. **Document type:** *Consumer.*
Published by: Primus Verlag AG, Hammerstr 81, Postfach 1331, Zuerich, 8032, Switzerland. TEL 41-1-3875757, FAX 41-1-3875707, info@travelinside.ch, http://www.primusverlag.ch.

914.1504 IRL
FAILTE/WELCOME. Text in English. a. adv. **Document type:** *Magazine, Consumer.* **Description:** Contains articles and features for passengers of Irish ferries on both U.K. and continental routes.
Published by: Mac Communications, Taney Hall, Eglinton Terrace, Dundrum, Dublin, Dublin 14, Ireland. TEL 353-1-2960000, FAX 353-1-2960383, info@maccommunications.ie. Ed. Sarah McQuaid. Circ: 200,000 (controlled).

910.91 DEU
FAIRKEHR. Text in German. 1986. bi-m. EUR 23 (effective 2007). adv. **Document type:** *Magazine, Consumer.*
Published by: Fairkehr Verlagsgesellschaft mbH, Niebuhrstr 16b, Bonn, 53113, Germany. TEL 49-228-9858545, FAX 49-228-9858550. adv.: B&W page EUR 2,693, color page EUR 3,949. Circ: 67,000 (paid and controlled).

FAIRWAYS & GREENS (NEVADA EDITION). see SPORTS AND GAMES—Ball Games

FAMILY MOTOR COACHING. see TRANSPORTATION

910.202 USA
FAMILY TRAVEL LETTER. Text in English. 1998. m. USD 24 (effective 2000). **Document type:** *Newsletter, Consumer.* **Description:** Covers travel destinations, offerings and concepts for families.
Related titles: Online - full text ed.
Published by: Workstyles, Inc., 5 Rose Ave, Great Neck, NY 10021. TEL 516-829-8829. Ed., Pub. Karen Rubin. Adv. contact Neil Leiberman.

910.09 USA ISSN 1098-867X
FAMILY TRAVEL TIMES. Text in English. 1984. bi-m. USD 39 in US & Canada; USD 49 elsewhere (effective 2005). bk.rev. back issues avail. **Document type:** *Newsletter, Consumer.* **Description:** Contains news and in-depth reports about family travel in the U.S. and around the world.
Published by: F T T Marketing, 40 Fifth Ave, New York, NY 10011. TEL 212-477-5524, 888-822-4388, FAX 212-477-5173. R&P Dorothy Jordon TEL 212-477-5524. Circ: 2,500 (paid).

796 USA ISSN 0195-8437
TX907
FARM, RANCH & COUNTRY VACATIONS. Text in English. 1949. irreg. (every 2 or 3 yrs.), latest 1995. USD 12.95 (effective 2000). **Document type:** *Directory.*
Former titles: Country Vacations USA (0147-3867); Farm, Ranch and Country Vacations; Farm, Ranch and Countryside Guide; Farm and Ranch Vacation Guide (0085-0438)
Published by: Adventure Guides, Inc., 5101 N. Casa Blanca Dr., Unit 306, Paradise Vly, AZ 85253-6989. TEL 602-596-0226, FAX 602-596-1722. Ed. Pat Dickerman.

910.2 USA
FAVORITE HAUNTS. Text in English. 2001 (Oct.). q. USD 19.95 domestic; CAD 24.95 in Canada (effective 2001). adv. **Document type:** *Magazine, Consumer.* **Description:** Contains feature-length photo essays on haunted inns, haunted castles, and other places of interest, with emphasis on the accommodations, cuisine, and things to do in the area that may or may not have a sprectral slant.
Address: 100 Trade Center Dr Ste 204, Champaign, IL 61820. TEL 217-355-1458, subscribe@favoritehaunts.com, http://www.favoritehaunts.com/. Ed., Pub. Daniel Kennedy. adv.: page USD 1,000; trim 8.25 x 10.875. Circ: 50,000.

910.4 CHN ISSN 1003-5516
DS712
FENGJING MINGSHENG/SCENIC SPOTS AND HISTORICAL SITES. Text in Chinese. 1984. m. USD 74.40 (effective 2009). adv. **Document type:** *Consumer.* **Description:** Covers the construction, protection and management of senic spots and historical sites in China. Reports the latest development in gardening, archaeology, tourism, urban design, and environmental protection.
Published by: Hangzhou Yuanlin Wenwu Guanliju/Hangzhou Municipal Administration of Gardens and Cultural Relics, 12 Jiangyuan Nong, Xiaoying Xiang, Hangzhou, Zhejiang 310003, China. TEL 86-571-711944, FAX 86-571-7027890. Ed., Pub. Dawei Chen. R&P Jun Zhang. Adv. contact Jiaji Zhu. Circ: 40,000.

914.604 ISL ISSN 0256-8470
FERDAFELAG ISLANDS. ARBOK. Text in Icelandic. 1928. a. ISK 3,100.
Published by: Ferdafelag Islands/Iceland Touring Association, Moerkinni 6, Reykjavik, 108, Iceland. TEL 354-568-2533, FAX 354-568-2535. Ed. Hjalti Kristgeirsson. Circ: 9,500.

910.202 NOR ISSN 0801-5880
FERIEFORUM; magasin for reiseliv og turisme. Text in Norwegian. 1983. q. NOK 80, USD 16.
Address: Skogveien 85 A, Stabekk, 1320, Norway. TEL 02-534773. Ed. Reidar Nordheim. Circ: 20,000.

914.34 DEU
FERIENMAGAZIN EIDERSTEDT. Text in German. a. free. **Document type:** *Magazine, Consumer.*
Formerly (until 2007): Ferien Magazin Sankt Peter - Ording
Published by: Westholsteinische Verlagsanstalt Boyens und Co., Am Wulf Isebrand Platz, Heide, 25767, Germany. TEL 49-481-6886162, FAX 49-481-6886467, vertrieb@boyens-medien.de, http://www.buecher-von-boyens.de. Ed. Inken Boyens. Circ: 50,000.

FERN EXPRESS. see TRANSPORTATION—Railroads

917.904 USA
FERRY TRAVEL GUIDE. Text in English. 1984. 3/yr. USD 7 (effective 2001). adv. 48 p./no.; back issues avail. **Document type:** *Magazine, Consumer.* **Description:** Travel information for Washington State and British Columbia with maps, ferry schedules, resorts, cities and attractions.
Former titles: Olympic Travel Guide (0897-9618); Olympic Magazine
Published by: Dan Youra Studios, Inc., PO Box 1169, Port Hadlock, WA 98339-1169. TEL 360-379-8800, FAX 360-379-0819. Ed., Pub. Dan Youra. Circ: 180,000.

910.91 ITA ISSN 1592-9787
FESTE, SAGRE E MERCATINI. Text in Italian. 1997. bi-m. **Document type:** *Guide, Consumer.*
Published by: L' Ortensia Rossa, Circonvallazione Gianicolense 210, Rome, 00152, Italy. TEL 39-06-98387080, FAX 39-06-5349779, info@ortensiarossa.it, http://www.ortensiarossa.it.

910.91 USA
FESTIVALS DIRECTORY. Text in English. 1999. 3/yr. USD 48 domestic; USD 55 in Canada (effective 2003). adv. bk.rev.; music rev. illus. back issues avail. **Document type:** *Directory, Consumer.* **Description:** Covers detailed listings of 4000 festivals, fairs, music and art camps, and business conferences about arts and music in Washington, Oregon, Idaho, Montana, and British Columbia.
Formerly: Festival Northwest Quarterly
Address: PO Box 7515, Bonney Lake, WA 98390. TEL 253-863-6617, info@festivalsdirectory.com. Ed., Pub., R&P, Adv. contact Chris Lunn. B&W page USD 200; trim 7.75 x 10. Circ: 1,500.

FETES ET FESTIVALS. see BUSINESS AND ECONOMICS—Marketing And Purchasing

910.202 636.7 USA ISSN 1945-5828
FIDO FRIENDLY; the travel & lifestyle magazine for you & your dog. Text in English. 2001. m. USD 19.95 domestic; USD 31.95 in Canada; USD 39.95 elsewhere (effective 2008). adv. illus. **Document type:** *Magazine, Consumer.* **Description:** Contains articles and information on traveling in the United States and Canada with a pet dog.
Address: PO Box 160, Marsing, ID 83639. Eds. Arden Moore, Nicholas T Sveslovsky. Circ: 40,000.

910.4 FJI
FIJI MAGIC. Text in English. m.
Published by: Rubine Group Ltd., PO Box 12511, Suva, Fiji. TEL 679-313944. Ed. Mabel Howard. Circ: 10,000.

910 USA
FINE TRAVEL. Text in English. 1995. d. **Document type:** *Magazine, Consumer.* **Description:** Focuses on places of interest to residents of North America.
Formerly: Fine Food & Travel Magazine
Media: Online - full text.
Address: 1914 Conestoga St, Moscow, ID 83843. Ed. Louis Bignami. Pub. Frank Lucino. R&P Tony Smith.

FINE WINE FOLIO; an appreciation of vineyards and vintages. see BEVERAGES

910.2 USA
FIRST CLASS EXECUTIVE TRAVEL. Text in English. 1980. bi-m. USD 47.50 (effective 2000). **Document type:** *Newsletter, Trade.* **Description:** Informs business travelers on the best hotels, cities, airlines and auto rental centers.
Formerly: Business Traveler Magazine
Published by: National Association of Business Travel Agents, 3699 Wilshire Blvd, Ste 700, Los Angeles, CA 90010. TEL 213-382-3335, FAX 213-480-7712. Ed., R&P Stuart J Faber. Circ: 21,000 (paid).

910.91 USA
FIRST IMPRESSIONS NEWCOMER'S GUIDE. (Charlotte, NC, Triangle Area, NC, Upstate SC, Charleston, SC, Tampa, FL, Jacksonville, FL, South Florida, Central Florida, Wilmington, NC editions available.) Text in English. 1993. a. free domestic to members (effective 2007). adv. 96 p./no.; **Document type:** *Magazine, Trade.* **Description:** Covers the business climate, education, neighborhoods, sports and recreation, arts, religion, apartment living, places to go, things to do, and healthcare for the relocating newcomer.
Formerly: Builder Journal Of South Carolina
Published by: Knight Publishing Corporation, 8060 Melrose Ave, Los Angeles, CA 90046. TEL 323-653-8060, FAX 323-655-9452, psi@loop.com. Pub. James Molnar. adv.: B&W page USD 3,600, color page USD 1,650. Circ: 42,000 (controlled and free).

914.931 FRA ISSN 1957-3197
LA FLANDRE DES IRREGULIERS. Text in French. 2007. irreg., latest 2009. **Document type:** *Magazine, Consumer.*
Published by: Tourisme Belgique Flandre et Bruxelles, B P 143, Paris, Cedex 8 75363, France. TEL 33-1-56891442, contact@tourismebelgique.com, http://www.tourismebelgique.com.

FLATHEAD LIVING; Northwest Montana..the last best place. see GENERAL INTEREST PERIODICALS—United States

629.132 USA ISSN 0194-9039
FLIGHT REPORTS. Text in English. 1978. m. USD 36 (effective 2000). bk.rev.
Published by: Peter Katz Productions, Inc., PO Box 831, White Plains, NY 10602-0831. TEL 914-949-7443. Ed. Peter Katz.

910.91 USA ISSN 1933-0790
DG732
FLORENCE DIRECTIONS. Text in English. 2005. irreg., latest 2008, 2nd ed. USD 11.99 domestic 2nd ed.; USD 14.99 in Canada 2nd ed.; GBP 6.99 in United Kingdom 2nd ed. (effective 2008). 208 p./no.; back issues avail. **Document type:** *Guide, Consumer.*
Related titles: Online - full text ed.
Published by: Rough Guides, 375 Hudson St, 9th Fl, New York, NY 10014. TEL 212-414-3635, http://www.roughguides.com/default.aspx.

910.91 USA ISSN 0361-9796
F311
FLORIDA ALMANAC. Text in English. 2001 (Oct.). biennial. USD 17.95 per issue (effective 2007 - 2008). back issues avail. **Document type:** *Guide, Consumer.*
Published by: Pelican Publishing Co., 1000 Burmaster St., Gretna, LA 70053. TEL 504-368-1175, 800-843-1724, FAX 504-368-1195, editorial@pelicanpub.com, http://www.pelicanpub.com. Ed. Bernie McGovern.

917.59 USA ISSN 1541-7824
F311.6
FLORIDA CURIOSITIES; quirky characters, roadside oddities, & other offbeat stuff. Text in English. 2003. biennial, latest 2006, 2nd ed. USD 13.95 per issue (effective 2008). **Document type:** *Guide, Consumer.* **Description:** Provides tourist information about the Sunshine State.
Published by: The Globe Pequot Press, Inc., 246 Goose Ln, PO Box 480, Guilford, CT 06437. TEL 203-458-4500, 888-249-7586, FAX 203-458-4603, 800-820-2329, info@globepequot.com, http://www.globepequot.com.

TU

910.2 381.1 USA
FLORIDA OFFICIAL MEETING PLANNERS GUIDE. Text in English. 1983. a. free to qualified personnel (effective 2011). **Document type:** *Handbook/Manual/Guide, Trade.* **Description:** The guide to meeting properties and destinations in the Sunshine State, plus editorial covering key planner information, including new properties and facilities, event venues, and ideas for memorable events.
Related titles: E-mail ed.
Published by: Worth International Media Group, 5979 NW 151 St, Ste 120, Miami Lakes, FL 33014. TEL 305-828-0123, FAX 305-826-6950, info@worthit.com, http//www.worthit.com.

910.91 USA ISSN 1946-9918
▼ **FLORIDA PARKS & WILDLIFE.** Text in English. 2009. q. free to members (effective 2009). back issues avail. **Document type:** *Magazine, Trade.*
Incorporates: Real Florida (1098-2973)
Related titles: Online - full text ed.: ISSN 1946-9926.
Published by: (Friends of Florida State Parks Inc.), Florida Media Inc., 801 Douglas Ave, Ste 100, Altamonte Springs, FL 32714. Ed. Kristen M Cifers. Pub. E Douglas Cifers.

FLORIDA TRAVEL & LIFE. *see* LIFESTYLE

338.4 USA
FLORIDA VISITOR STUDY. Text in English. 1969. a. USD 75 to non-members. adv. charts; stat. **Document type:** *Government.* **Description:** Contains a summary of quarterly visitor surveys regarding the volume and composition of Florida's tourism industry.
Former titles: Florida's Visitors; Florida Tourist Study (0430-6953)
Published by: Visit Florida, 661 E Jefferson St, Ste 300, Tallahassee, FL 32304. TEL 850-488-4607, FAX 850-224-2938. Ed., R&P Chip Coggins TEL 850-488-5607. Adv. contact Jeanne Drewes. Circ: 20,000.

FLUGHAFEN-REVUE ZURICH AIRPORT MAGAZIN. *see* TRANSPORTATION—Air Transport

FLUGMEDIZIN - TROPENMEDIZIN - REISEMEDIZIN; Tauchmedizin - Bergmedizin - Expeditionsmedizin. *see* MEDICAL SCIENCES

FLYER INTERNATIONAL; aviation and tourism. *see* TRANSPORTATION—Air Transport

919 PAK ISSN 0046-4325
DS377
FOCUS ON PAKISTAN. Text in English. 1971-1973; resumed 1976. a. PKR 200, USD 5 per issue. adv. **Document type:** *Journal, Consumer.* **Description:** Articles on culture, customs, heritage, tourist attractions, and information on Pakistan.
Published by: Pakistan Tourist Development Corp., 36 St., House No. 17 F-10/1, P O Box 1465, Islamabad, 44000, Pakistan. TEL 92-51-294550, FAX 92-51-294540. Ed., R&P Salim Bokhari TEL 92-51-294189. Adv. contact Abdul Ghafoor Khan Qaisrani. Circ: 5,000; 5,000 (controlled).

918.6 PAN
FOCUS ON PANAMA. Text in English. 1971. s-a. USD 10 (effective 1999). adv. **Document type:** *Handbook/Manual/Guide, Consumer.* **Description:** Full color guide for visitors emphasizing both tourist attractions, business facilities and culture.
Related titles: Spanish ed.
Published by: Focus Publications (Int.) S.A., Apdo. 6-3287, El Dorado, Panama City, Panama. TEL 507-225-6638, FAX 507-225-0466, focusint@sinfo.net, http://focuspublicationsint.com. Ed. Kenneth J Jones. Circ: 70,000.

917 USA ISSN 2155-2339
▼ **FODOR'S 535 BEST BEACHES**; in the U.S., Caribbean, and Mexico. Variant title: 535 Best Beaches. Text in English. 2010 (Nov.). biennial. USD 18.99 per issue (effective 2011). **Document type:** *Guide, Consumer.* **Description:** Travel guide for beaches in the U.S., Caribbean and Mexico.
Published by: Fodor's Travel Publications, Inc. (Subsidiary of: Random House Inc.), 1745 Broadway, 15th Fl, New York, NY 10019. TEL 212-782-9000, 212-572-2313, editors@fodors.com, http://www.fodors.com.

917.204 USA ISSN 1070-8642
F1391.A15
FODOR'S ACAPULCO, IXTAPA, ZIHUATANEJO. Text in English. irreg. USD 9.
Former titles (until 199?): Fodor's Acapulco; (until 198?): Fodor's Fun in Acapulco; The Good Time Travel Guide to Acapulco
Published by: Fodor's Travel Publications, Inc. (Subsidiary of: Random House Inc.), 1745 Broadway, 15th Fl, New York, NY 10019. TEL 212-572-2313, editors@fodors.com, http://www.fodors.com. Ed. Craig Seligman. **Dist. by:** Random House Inc., 400 Hahn Rd, Westminster, MD 21157.

914.04 USA
D909
FODOR'S AFFORDABLE EUROPE. Text in English. 1972. biennial. USD 12.95.
Former titles: Fodor's Budget Europe (0197-4998); (until 1979): Fodor's Europe on a Budget (0276-0738)
Published by: Fodor's Travel Publications, Inc. (Subsidiary of: Random House Inc.), 1745 Broadway, 15th Fl, New York, NY 10019. TEL 212-572-2313, editors@fodors.com, http://www.fodors.com. **Dist. by:** Random House Inc., 400 Hahn Rd, Westminster, MD 21157.

914.404 USA ISSN 1068-3593
DC16
FODOR'S AFFORDABLE FRANCE. Text in English. 1980. biennial. USD 14. **Document type:** *Guide, Consumer.*
Former titles: Fodor's Great Travel Values: France; Fodor's Budget Travel France; Fodor's Budget France (0194-4150)
Published by: Fodor's Travel Publications, Inc. (Subsidiary of: Random House Inc.), 1745 Broadway, 15th Fl, New York, NY 10019. TEL 212-572-2313, editors@fodors.com, http://www.fodors.com. **Dist. by:** Random House Inc., 400 Hahn Rd, Westminster, MD 21157.

914.204 USA ISSN 1079-8439
DA650
FODOR'S AFFORDABLE GREAT BRITAIN. Text in English. 1979. biennial. USD 14. **Document type:** *Guide, Consumer.*
Former titles: Fodor's Great Travel Values: Britain; Fodor's Budget Travel Britain; Fodor's Budget Britain (0193-2381)
Published by: Fodor's Travel Publications, Inc. (Subsidiary of: Random House Inc.), 1745 Broadway, 15th Fl, New York, NY 10019. TEL 212-572-2313, editors@fodors.com, http://www.fodors.com. **Dist. by:** Random House Inc., 400 Hahn Rd, Westminster, MD 21157.

914.504 USA ISSN 1079-543X
DG416
FODOR'S AFFORDABLE ITALY. Text in English. 1980. biennial. USD 15. **Document type:** *Guide, Consumer.*
Former titles: Fodor's Great Travel Values: Italy; Fodor's Budget Travel Italy; Fodor's Budget Italy (0270-787X)
Published by: Fodor's Travel Publications, Inc. (Subsidiary of: Random House Inc.), 1745 Broadway, 15th Fl, New York, NY 10019. TEL 212-572-2313, editors@fodors.com, http://www.fodors.com. **Dist. by:** Random House Inc., 400 Hahn Rd, Westminster, MD 21157.

917.9804 USA ISSN 0271-2776
F902.3
FODOR'S ALASKA. Text in English. 1979. a., latest 2009. USD 19.95 per issue (effective 2008). **Document type:** *Guide, Consumer.* **Description:** Provides up-to-date information on Alaska and includes photo-features that impart the state's culture.
Published by: Fodor's Travel Publications, Inc. (Subsidiary of: Random House Inc.), 1745 Broadway, 15th Fl, New York, NY 10019. TEL 212-572-2313, editors@fodors.com, http://www.fodors.com. **Dist. by:** Random House Inc., 400 Hahn Rd, Westminster, MD 21157.

910.2 USA ISSN 1931-1826
DJ411.A5
FODOR'S AMSTERDAM'S 25 BEST. Text in English. a., latest 2007, 6th ed. USD 11.95 6th ed. (effective 2008). 128 p./no.; **Document type:** *Guide, Consumer.* **Description:** Focuses on the top 25 interesting sights in Amsterdam and includes a full-color pull-out map.
Formerly (until 2005): Fodor's Citypack Amsterdam's Best
Published by: Fodor's Travel Publications, Inc. (Subsidiary of: Random House Inc.), 1745 Broadway, 15th Fl, New York, NY 10019. TEL 212-572-2313, editors@fodors.com, http://www.fodors.com.

919.04 USA ISSN 1095-2675
DU95
FODOR'S AUSTRALIA (YEAR). Text in English. a. USD 24.94 (effective 2008). illus. **Description:** Provides up-to-date information on Australia and features a range of options for a variety of budgets, interests and tastes.
Former titles (until 1997): Fodor's Australia and New Zealand; (until 1993): Fodor's Australia; (until 1991): Fodor's Australia, New Zealand and the South Pacific (0191-2321)
Published by: Fodor's Travel Publications, Inc. (Subsidiary of: Random House Inc.), 1745 Broadway, 15th Fl, New York, NY 10019. TEL 212-572-2313, editors@fodors.com, http://www.fodors.com. **Dist. by:** Random House Inc.

914.3604 USA ISSN 0071-6340
DB16
FODOR'S AUSTRIA. Text in English. 1951. biennial, latest 2009, 13th ed. USD 21.95 per vol. (effective 2009). **Document type:** *Guide, Consumer.* **Description:** Provides up-to-date information on Austria and features a range of options for a variety of budgets, interests and tastes.
Formerly: Eugene Fodor. Austria (0572-1946)
Published by: Fodor's Travel Publications, Inc. (Subsidiary of: Random House Inc.), 1745 Broadway, 15th Fl, New York, NY 10019. TEL 212-782-9000, editors@fodors.com, http://www.fodors.com. **Dist. by:** Random House Inc.

919.704 USA
FODOR'S BAHAMAS. Text in English. 19??. a. USD 17.95 per issue (effective 2009). **Document type:** *Guide, Consumer.* **Description:** Contains choices for every traveler in Bahamas, from exploring deserted cays to bar hopping and boutique shopping, and much more.
Supersedes in part (1980-1985): Fodor's Caribbean and Bahamas (0271-4760)
Published by: Fodor's Travel Publications, Inc. (Subsidiary of: Random House Inc.), 1745 Broadway, 15th Fl, New York, NY 10019. TEL 212-782-9000, 212-572-2313, editors@fodors.com, http://www.fodors.com. Ed. Molly Moker. Pub. Tim Jarrell. **Dist. by:** Random House Inc., 400 Hahn Rd, Westminster, MD 21157.

917.204 USA
FODOR'S BAJA AND MEXICO'S PACIFIC COAST RESORTS. Text in English. irreg. USD 11.
Formerly: Fodor's Mexico's Baja
Published by: Fodor's Travel Publications, Inc. (Subsidiary of: Random House Inc.), 1745 Broadway, 15th Fl, New York, NY 10019. TEL 212-572-2313, editors@fodors.com, http://www.fodors.com. Ed. Carolyn Price. **Dist. by:** Random House Inc.

917.2904 USA ISSN 1050-9771
F2041
FODOR'S BARBADOS. Text in English. irreg. USD 8.
Formerly: Fodor's Fun in Barbados
Indexed: G08, I05.
Published by: Fodor's Travel Publications, Inc. (Subsidiary of: Random House Inc.), 1745 Broadway, 15th Fl, New York, NY 10019. TEL 212-572-2313, editors@fodors.com, http://www.fodors.com. Ed. Caroline Haberfeld. **Dist. by:** Random House Inc., 400 Hahn Rd, Westminster, MD 21157.

917.904 USA ISSN 1069-9007
TX907.3.P33
FODOR'S BED AND BREAKFASTS AND COUNTRY INNS AND OTHER WEEKEND PLEASURES: THE WEST COAST. Text in English. 1992. irreg. USD 15.
Published by: Fodor's Travel Publications, Inc. (Subsidiary of: Random House Inc.), 1745 Broadway, 15th Fl, New York, NY 10019. TEL 212-572-2313, editors@fodors.com, http://www.fodors.com. **Dist. by:** Random House Inc., 400 Hahn Rd, Westminster, MD 21157.

917.9 USA ISSN 1079-168X
TX907.3.G74
FODOR'S BED & BREAKFASTS, COUNTRY INNS, AND OTHER WEEKEND PLEASURES. THE UPPER GREAT LAKES REGION. Text in English. 1993. irreg.
Published by: Fodor's Travel Publications, Inc. (Subsidiary of: Random House Inc.), 1745 Broadway, 15th Fl, New York, NY 10019. editors@fodors.com, http://www.fodors.com.

914.9304 USA ISSN 1553-9164
FODOR'S BELGIUM. Text in English. 1992. biennial, latest 2009, 4th ed. USD 17.95 per issue (effective 2009). **Document type:** *Guide, Consumer.* **Description:** Provides up-to-date information on Belgium and features a range of options for a variety of budgets, interests and tastes.
Formerly (until 2001): Fodor's Belgium and Luxembourg (1533-2225); Which superseded in part (in 1999): Fodor's the Netherlands, Belgium, Luxembourg (1070-4590); Which was formed by the merger of (19??-1992): Fodor's Belgium and Luxembourg; (1969-1992): Fodor's Holland (0071-643X); Which was formerly (1951-1969): Holland
Published by: Fodor's Travel Publications, Inc. (Subsidiary of: Random House Inc.), 1745 Broadway, 15th Fl, New York, NY 10019. TEL 212-782-9000, editors@fodors.com, http://www.fodors.com. Ed. Nancy van Itallie. **Dist. by:** Random House Inc., 400 Hahn Rd, Westminster, MD 21157.

910.91 USA ISSN 1559-081X
F1443.5
FODOR'S BELIZE. Text in English. 1996. a., latest 2008, 3rd ed. USD 17.95 (effective 2008). adv. **Document type:** *Guide, Consumer.* **Description:** Features options for a variety of budgets, interests, and tastes, so you make the choices to plan your trip of a lifetime.
Formerly (until 2006): Fodor's Belize & Guatemala (1522-6123)
Indexed: G08, I05.
Published by: Fodor's Travel Publications, Inc. (Subsidiary of: Random House Inc.), 1745 Broadway, 15th Fl, New York, NY 10019. TEL 212-572-2313, editors@fodors.com, http://www.fodors.com.

914.304 USA ISSN 1065-4593
DD859
FODOR'S BERLIN. Text in English. 1992. a. USD 10.
Indexed: G08, I05.
Published by: Fodor's Travel Publications, Inc. (Subsidiary of: Random House Inc.), 1745 Broadway, 15th Fl, New York, NY 10019. TEL 212-572-2313, editors@fodors.com, http://www.fodors.com. **Dist. by:** Random House Inc., 400 Hahn Rd, Westminster, MD 21157.

919.704 USA ISSN 0192-3765
F1632
FODOR'S BERMUDA. Text in English. 1979. a. USD 17.95 (effective 2008). **Document type:** *Guide, Consumer.* **Description:** Provides up-to-date information on Bermuda and features a range of options for a variety of budgets, interests and tastes.
Supersedes in part (in 19??): Fodor's Caribbean, Bahamas and Bermuda (0098-2547); Which was formerly (until 19??): Fodor's Guide to the Caribbean, Bahamas, and Bermuda (0071-6561)
Indexed: G08, I05.
Published by: Fodor's Travel Publications, Inc. (Subsidiary of: Random House Inc.), 1745 Broadway, 15th Fl, New York, NY 10019. TEL 212-572-2313, editors@fodors.com, http://www.fodors.com. **Dist. by:** Random House Inc., 400 Hahn Rd, Westminster, MD 21157.

917.404 USA ISSN 0882-0074
F73.18
FODOR'S BOSTON. Text in English. 1984. a. USD 16.95 (effective 2008). adv. **Document type:** *Guide, Consumer.* **Description:** Presents information on the various hotels, restaurants, attractions and activities and also includes planning tools that are needed to tailor a trip.
Indexed: G08, I05.
Published by: Fodor's Travel Publications, Inc. (Subsidiary of: Random House Inc.), 1745 Broadway, 15th Fl, New York, NY 10019. TEL 212-572-2313, editors@fodors.com, http://www.fodors.com. **Dist. by:** Random House Inc., 400 Hahn Rd, Westminster, MD 21157.

918.104 USA ISSN 0163-0628
F2509.5
FODOR'S BRAZIL. Text in English. 1978. a., latest 5th ed. USD 22.95 (effective 2008). **Document type:** *Guide, Consumer.* **Description:** Provides up-to-date information on Brazil and features a range of options for a variety of budgets, interests and tastes.
Published by: Fodor's Travel Publications, Inc. (Subsidiary of: Random House Inc.), 1745 Broadway, 15th Fl, New York, NY 10019. TEL 212-572-2313, editors@fodors.com, http://www.fodors.com. **Dist. by:** Random House Inc., 400 Hahn Rd, Westminster, MD 21157.

910.09 USA ISSN 1554-3455
DB983.5
FODOR'S BUDAPEST. Text in English. 19??. irreg., latest 2007, 2nd ed. USD 17.95 per issue (effective 2011). **Document type:** *Handbook/Manual/Guide, Consumer.* **Description:** Provides information about best hotels, restaurants, attractions and activities in Budapest.
Supersedes in part (in 2005): Fodor's Prague and Budapest (1530-5384); Which was formerly (until 1998): Fodor's Budapest (1065-4607); Which superseded in part (in 1992): Fodor's Hungary (0361-9761)
Published by: Fodor's Travel Publications, Inc. (Subsidiary of: Random House Inc.), 1745 Broadway, 15th Fl, New York, NY 10019. TEL 212-782-9000, editors@fodors.com.

918.2 USA ISSN 1941-0182
F3001.A4
FODOR'S BUENOS AIRES; with side trips to Gaucho Country, Iguazu, and Uruguay. Text in English. 2008 (Mar.). biennial. USD 19.99 per issue (effective 2011). back issues avail. **Document type:** *Handbook/Manual/Guide, Consumer.*
Indexed: G08, I05.
Published by: Fodor's Travel Publications, Inc. (Subsidiary of: Random House Inc.), 1745 Broadway, 15th Fl, New York, NY 10019. TEL 212-782-9000, editors@fodors.com.

917.904 USA ISSN 0192-9925
F859.3
FODOR'S CALIFORNIA. Text in English. 19??. a. USD 21.95 (effective 2009). adv. **Document type:** *Guide, Consumer.* **Description:** Provides up-to-date information on California and features a range of options for a variety of budgets, interests and tastes.
Published by: Fodor's Travel Publications, Inc. (Subsidiary of: Random House Inc.), 1745 Broadway, 15th Fl, New York, NY 10019. TEL 212-572-2313, editors@fodors.com, http://www.fodors.com. **Dist. by:** Random House Inc., 400 Hahn Rd, Westminster, MD 21157.

917.104 USA ISSN 0160-3906
F1009
FODOR'S CANADA. Text in English. 1978. a., latest 29th ed. USD 22.95 (effective 2008). **Document type:** *Guide, Consumer.*

Published by: Fodor's Travel Publications, Inc. (Subsidiary of: Random House Inc.), 1745 Broadway, 15th Fl, New York, NY 10019. TEL 212-572-2313, editors@fodors.com, http://www.fodors.com. **Dist. by:** Random House Inc., 400 Hahn Rd, Westminster, MD 21157.

917.104 USA
FODOR'S CANADA'S GREAT COUNTRY INNS BY ANITA STEWART. Text in English. irreg. USD 13.
Published by: Fodor's Travel Publications, Inc. (Subsidiary of: Random House Inc.), 1745 Broadway, 15th Fl, New York, NY 10019. TEL 212-572-2313, editors@fodors.com, http://www.fodors.com. **Dist. by:** Random House Inc.

917.204 USA ISSN 1051-6336
F1376
FODOR'S CANCUN, COZUMEL & THE YUCATAN PENINSULA. Text in English. 1988. a. USD 17.95 (effective 2009). adv. **Description:** Provides up-to-date information on Cancun, Cozumel and the Yucatan Peninsula.
Formerly (until 1989): Fodor's Cancun, Cozumel, Merida and the Yucatan
Related titles: Online - full text ed.
Published by: Fodor's Travel Publications, Inc. (Subsidiary of: Random House Inc.), 1745 Broadway, 15th Fl, New York, NY 10019. TEL 212-572-2313, editors@fodors.com, http://www.fodors.com. Ed. Carolyn Price. **Dist. by:** Random House Inc.

917.404 USA ISSN 1934-5569
F72.C3
FODOR'S CAPE COD, NANTUCKET & MARTHA'S VINEYARD. Text in English. 1989. a. USD 17.95 (effective 2008). **Document type:** *Guide, Consumer.* **Description:** Provides up-to-date information on Cape Cod, Nantucket and Martha's Vineyard and features a range of options for a variety of budgets, interests and tastes.
Formed by the merger of (2001-2007): Fodor's Cape Cod (1542-3476); (2003-2007): Fodor's Martha's Vineyard and Nantucket (1541-2911); Both of which superseded in part (in 2001): Fodor's Cape Cod, Martha's Vineyard, Nantucket (1093-7986); Which was formerly (until 1992): Fodor's Cape Cod (1047-6768)
Indexed: G08, I05.
Published by: Fodor's Travel Publications, Inc. (Subsidiary of: Random House Inc.), 1745 Broadway, 15th Fl, New York, NY 10019. TEL 212-572-2313, editors@fodors.com, http://www.fodors.com. **Dist. by:** Random House Inc., 400 Hahn Rd, Westminster, MD 21157.

917.2904 USA ISSN 1524-9174
F1613
FODOR'S CARIBBEAN. Text in English. 1962. a. USD 23.95 (effective 2009). adv. **Document type:** *Guide, Consumer.* **Description:** Features options for a variety of budgets, interests, and tastes, so you make the choices to plan your trip of a lifetime.
Supersedes in part (in 1985): Fodor's Caribbean and the Bahamas (0271-4760); (in 19??): Fodor's Caribbean, Bahamas and Bermuda (0098-2547); Which was formerly (until 19??): Fodor's Guide to the Caribbean, Bahamas and Bermuda (0071-6561)
Published by: Fodor's Travel Publications, Inc. (Subsidiary of: Random House Inc.), 1745 Broadway, 15th Fl, New York, NY 10019. TEL 212-572-2313, editors@fodors.com, http://www.fodors.com. Ed. Caroline Haberfield. **Dist. by:** Random House Inc., 400 Hahn Rd, Westminster, MD 21157.

917.204 USA ISSN 0270-8183
F1429
FODOR'S CENTRAL AMERICA; Belize, Costa Rica, El Salvador, Guatemala, Honduras, Nicaragua, Panama. Text in English. 1980. irreg., latest 2008, 3rd ed. USD 22.95 3rd ed. (effective 2008). adv. **Document type:** *Guide, Consumer.* **Description:** Provides up-to-date information on Central America and includes various choices - from lounging on the beach in Honduras or scaling Mayan ruins in Guatemala to browsing open-air markets in Nicaragua, etc.
Published by: Fodor's Travel Publications, Inc. (Subsidiary of: Random House Inc.), 1745 Broadway, 15th Fl, New York, NY 10019. TEL 212-572-2313, editors@fodors.com, http://www.fodors.com. Ed. Carolyn Price. **Dist. by:** Random House Inc., 400 Hahn Rd, Westminster, MD 21157.

917.704 USA ISSN 0743-9326
F548.18
FODOR'S CHICAGO. Text in English. 1982. a. USD 17.95 (effective 2008). **Document type:** *Guide, Consumer.* **Description:** Provides up-to-date information on Chicago and features a range of options for a variety of budgets, interests and tastes.
Formerly (until 1984): Fodor's Chicago and the Great Lakes Recreation Areas
Indexed: G08, I05.
Published by: Fodor's Travel Publications, Inc. (Subsidiary of: Random House Inc.), 1745 Broadway, 15th Fl, New York, NY 10019. TEL 212-572-2313, editors@fodors.com, http://www.fodors.com. **Dist. by:** Random House Inc., 400 Hahn Rd, Westminster, MD 21157.

915.104 USA ISSN 1070-6895
DS705
FODOR'S CHINA. Text in English. 1979. a., latest 5th ed. USD 25.95 per issue (effective 2008). adv. **Document type:** *Guide, Consumer.* **Description:** Contains maps, a language guide and in-depth illustrated features on local food, culture and customs.
Formerly (until 19??): Fodor's People's Republic of China (0192-2378)
Published by: Fodor's Travel Publications, Inc. (Subsidiary of: Random House Inc.), 1745 Broadway, 15th Fl, New York, NY 10019. TEL 212-572-2313, editors@fodors.com, http://www.fodors.com. **Dist. by:** Random House Inc., 400 Hahn Rd, Westminster, MD 21157.

915.104 USA
FODOR'S CHINA'S GREAT CITIES. Text in English. irreg. USD 9.95.
Formerly: Fodor's Beijing, Guangzhou and Shanghai
Published by: Fodor's Travel Publications, Inc. (Subsidiary of: Random House Inc.), 1745 Broadway, 15th Fl, New York, NY 10019. TEL 212-572-2313, editors@fodors.com, http://www.fodors.com. **Dist. by:** Random House Inc., 400 Hahn Rd, Westminster, MD 21157.

917.804 USA ISSN 1941-5419
E160
FODOR'S COMPLETE GUIDE TO THE NATIONAL PARKS OF THE WEST. Text in English. 1992. irreg. USD 17.
Former titles: Fodor's National Parks of the West; Fodor's Road Guide USA. National Parks of the West (1538-7623); (until 1998): Fodor's National Parks of the West (1098-9633)
Published by: Fodor's Travel Publications, Inc. (Subsidiary of: Random House Inc.), 1745 Broadway, 15th Fl, New York, NY 10019. TEL 800-733-3000. Ed. Paula Consolo. **Dist. by:** Random House Inc., 400 Hahn Rd, Westminster, MD 21157.

914.204 USA
FODOR'S COTTAGES, BED AND BREAKFASTS AND COUNTRY INNS OF ENGLAND AND WALES BY ELIZABETH GUNDRY. Text in English. irreg. USD 15.
Published by: Fodor's Travel Publications, Inc. (Subsidiary of: Random House Inc.), 1745 Broadway, 15th Fl, New York, NY 10019. TEL 212-572-2313, editors@fodors.com, http://www.fodors.com. **Dist. by:** Random House Inc.

910.91 USA ISSN 1558-8181
DR1509
FODOR'S CROATIA AND SLOVENIA. Text in English. 2006. biennial, latest 2nd ed. USD 20.95 per issue 2nd ed. (effective 2008). adv. **Document type:** *Guide, Consumer.* **Description:** Features options for a variety of budgets, interests, and tastes, so you make the choices to plan your trip of a lifetime.
Published by: Fodor's Travel Publications, Inc. (Subsidiary of: Random House Inc.), 1745 Broadway, 15th Fl, New York, NY 10019. TEL 212-572-2313, editors@fodors.com, http://www.fodors.com.

917.13 USA ISSN 1543-6020
FODOR'S CUBA (NEW YORK, 2000). Text in English. 1996. irreg. USD 18 newsstand/cover (effective 2006).
Formerly (until 1997): Fodor's Cuba (New York, 1996) (1091-4749)
Published by: Fodor's Travel Publications, Inc. (Subsidiary of: Random House Inc.), 1745 Broadway, 15th Fl, New York, NY 10019. editors@fodors.com, http://www.fodors.com.

914.804 USA ISSN 1520-7765
DL107
FODOR'S DENMARK. Text in English. 1998. irreg., latest 5th ed. USD 18.95 5th ed. (effective 2008). **Document type:** *Guide, Consumer.*
Published by: Fodor's Travel Publications, Inc. (Subsidiary of: Random House Inc.), 1745 Broadway, 15th Fl, New York, NY 10019. TEL 212-782-9000, 212-572-2313, editors@fodors.com, http://www.fodors.com.

914.704 USA
DJK8
FODOR'S EASTERN AND CENTRAL EUROPE. Text in English. 1980. a., latest 21st ed. USD 24.95 (effective 2008). adv. **Document type:** *Guide, Consumer.* **Description:** Provides up-to-date information on Eastern and Central Europe and features options for a variety of budgets, interests and tastes.
Formerly (until 1994): Fodor's Eastern Europe (0734-8010)
Published by: Fodor's Travel Publications, Inc. (Subsidiary of: Random House Inc.), 1745 Broadway, 15th Fl, New York, NY 10019. TEL 212-572-2313, editors@fodors.com, http://www.fodors.com. **Dist. by:** Random House Inc., 400 Hahn Rd, Westminster, MD 21157.

916.204 USA ISSN 0147-8176
DT45
FODOR'S EGYPT. Text in English. 1977. biennial. USD 24.95 (effective 2009). adv. illus. **Document type:** *Guide, Consumer.*
Published by: Fodor's Travel Publications, Inc. (Subsidiary of: Random House Inc.), 1745 Broadway, 15th Fl, New York, NY 10019. TEL 212-572-2313, editors@fodors.com, http://www.fodors.com. Ed. Edie Jarolim. **Dist. by:** Random House Inc., 400 Hahn Rd, Westminster, MD 21157.

914 USA ISSN 1943-006X
D909
FODOR'S ESSENTIAL EUROPE. Short title: Essential Europe. Text in English. 1959. irreg., latest 2009, 1st ed. USD 24.95 per issue (effective 2011). **Document type:** *Handbook/Manual/Guide, Consumer.* **Description:** Travel guide for 16 countries in Europe.
Former titles (until 2009): Fodor's Europe (0362-0204); (until 19??): Fodor's Guide to Europe (0071-6375); (until 1963): Fodor's Jet Age Guide to Europe
Published by: Fodor's Travel Publications, Inc. (Subsidiary of: Random House Inc.), 1745 Broadway, 15th Fl, New York, NY 10019. TEL 212-782-9000, editors@fodors.com.

914.8 USA ISSN 1943-0078
DL4
FODOR'S ESSENTIAL SCANDINAVIA. Short title: Essential Scandinavia. Text in English. 1952. irreg., latest 2009, 1st ed. USD 23.95 per issue (effective 2011). adv. **Document type:** *Handbook/Manual/Guide, Consumer.* **Description:** Travel guide for Scandinavia.
Former titles (until 2009): Fodor's Scandinavia (0071-6529); (until 1969): Scandinavia in .
Published by: Fodor's Travel Publications, Inc. (Subsidiary of: Random House Inc.), 1745 Broadway, 15th Fl, New York, NY 10019. TEL 212-782-9000, editors@fodors.com.

917.3 USA ISSN 1946-3057
F207.3
▼ **FODOR'S ESSENTIAL SOUTH**; with the Carolinas, Georgia, Tennessee, the Gulf Coast & other top spots in 10 states. Short title: Essential South. Text in English. 2009. irreg., latest 2009, 1st ed. USD 21.99 per issue (effective 2011). **Document type:** *Handbook/Manual/Guide, Consumer.* **Description:** Travel guide for destinations in the U.S. South.
Published by: Fodor's Travel Publications, Inc. (Subsidiary of: Random House Inc.), 1745 Broadway, 15th Fl, New York, NY 10019. TEL 212-782-9000, editors@fodors.com.

914.404 USA ISSN 1074-4142
GV1853.4.F82
FODOR'S EURO DISNEY. Text in English. 1993. a. USD 10.
Published by: Fodor's Travel Publications, Inc. (Subsidiary of: Random House Inc.), 1745 Broadway, 15th Fl, New York, NY 10019. TEL 212-572-2313, editors@fodors.com, http://www.fodors.com. **Dist. by:** Random House Inc., 400 Hahn Rd, Westminster, MD 21157.

914 USA ISSN 1941-0204
D909
FODOR'S EUROPEAN PORTS OF CALL. Text in English. 2008 (May). irreg., latest 2011, 2nd ed. USD 16.99 per issue (effective 2011). back issues avail. **Document type:** *Handbook/Manual/Guide, Consumer.* **Description:** Filled with concise and practical overviews of over 70 major cruise ports throughout Europe, offering cruise passengers everything they need to know to make the most of their day ashore and enjoy unique shore excursions independently.
Published by: Fodor's Travel Publications, Inc. (Subsidiary of: Random House Inc.), 1745 Broadway, 15th Fl, New York, NY 10019. TEL 212-782-9000, editors@fodors.com.

914.04 USA ISSN 1074-1216
D909
FODOR'S EUROPE'S GREAT CITIES. Text in English. 19??. a., latest 5th ed. USD 15.95 per issue (effective 2005).
Published by: Fodor's Travel Publications, Inc. (Subsidiary of: Random House Inc.), 1745 Broadway, 15th Fl, New York, NY 10019. TEL 212-572-2313, editors@fodors.com, http://www.fodors.com. **Dist. by:** Random House Inc., 400 Hahn Rd, Westminster, MD 21157.

914.1504 USA ISSN 1524-6795
DA980
FODOR'S EXPLORING IRELAND. Text in English. 1994. biennial, latest 6th ed. USD 22 6th ed. (effective 2008).
Published by: Fodor's Travel Publications, Inc. (Subsidiary of: Random House Inc.), 1745 Broadway, 15th Fl, New York, NY 10019. TEL 212-782-9000, 212-572-2313, editors@fodors.com, http://www.fodors.com.

915.6904 USA ISSN 1520-7757
DS103
FODOR'S EXPLORING ISRAEL. Text in English. 1996. biennial, latest 4th ed. USD 22 4th ed. (effective 2006). **Document type:** *Guide, Consumer.* **Description:** Presents tips on dining and lodging for all budgets as well as tips on basics such as getting there and getting around and when to go and what to pack.
Published by: Fodor's Travel Publications, Inc. (Subsidiary of: Random House Inc.), 1745 Broadway, 15th Fl, New York, NY 10019. TEL 212-782-9000, 212-572-2313, editors@fodors.com, http://www.fodors.com.

915.204 USA ISSN 1095-4376
DS805.2
FODOR'S EXPLORING JAPAN. Text in English. 1996. biennial, latest 6th ed. USD 22 6th ed. (effective 2008). **Document type:** *Guide, Consumer.* **Description:** Provides a concise and comprehensive guide to Japan that contains practical information.
Published by: Fodor's Travel Publications, Inc. (Subsidiary of: Random House Inc.), 1745 Broadway, 15th Fl, New York, NY 10019. TEL 212-782-9000, 212-572-2313, editors@fodors.com, http://www.fodors.com.

917.404 USA ISSN 1098-7452
F128.18
FODOR'S EXPLORING NEW YORK CITY. Text in English. 1994. biennial, latest 7th ed. USD 22 7th ed. (effective 2008). **Document type:** *Guide, Consumer.* **Description:** Contains tips on dining and lodging for all budgets as well as tips on basics such as getting there and getting around and when to go and what to pack.
Published by: Fodor's Travel Publications, Inc. (Subsidiary of: Random House Inc.), 1745 Broadway, 15th Fl, New York, NY 10019. TEL 212-782-9000, 212-572-2313, editors@fodors.com, http://www.fodors.com.

917.44 USA ISSN 1943-0132
F73.18
▼ **FODOR'S FAMILY BOSTON WITH KIDS.** Variant title: Boston with Kids. Text in English. 2009. irreg., latest 2009, 1st ed. USD 10.95 per issue (effective 2011). **Document type:** *Handbook/Manual/Guide, Consumer.* **Description:** Guide for traveling to Boston with children.
Published by: Fodor's Travel Publications, Inc. (Subsidiary of: Random House Inc.), 1745 Broadway, 15th Fl, New York, NY 10019. TEL 212-782-9000, editors@fodors.com.

917.94 USA ISSN 1943-0159
F869.S33
▼ **FODOR'S FAMILY SAN FRANCISCO WITH KIDS.** Variant title: San Francisco with Kids. Text in English. 2009. irreg., latest 2009, 1st ed. USD 10.95 per issue (effective 2011). **Document type:** *Handbook/Manual/Guide, Consumer.* **Description:** Guide for traveling to San Francisco with kids.
Published by: Fodor's Travel Publications, Inc. (Subsidiary of: Random House Inc.), 1745 Broadway, 15th Fl, New York, NY 10019. TEL 212-782-9000, 212-572-2313, editors@fodors.com.

917.53 USA ISSN 1943-0140
▼ **FODOR'S FAMILY WASHINGTON, D.C. WITH KIDS.** Variant title: Washington, D.C. with Kids. Text in English. 2009. irreg., latest 2009, 1st ed. USD 10.95 per issue (effective 2011). **Document type:** *Handbook/Manual/Guide, Consumer.* **Description:** Guide for traveling to Washington, D.C. with kids.
Published by: Fodor's Travel Publications, Inc. (Subsidiary of: Random House Inc.), 1745 Broadway, 15th Fl, New York, NY 10019. TEL 212-782-9000, editors@fodors.com.

917.504 USA ISSN 0193-9556
F309.3
FODOR'S FLORIDA. Text in English. 19??. a. USD 19.95 (effective 2008). adv. **Document type:** *Guide, Consumer.* **Description:** Provides up-to-date information on Florida and includes various choices for travelers - from golfing, snorkeling, and swap-shopping to lounging on the beach, etc.
Published by: Fodor's Travel Publications, Inc. (Subsidiary of: Random House Inc.), 1745 Broadway, 15th Fl, New York, NY 10019. TEL 212-572-2313, editors@fodors.com, http://www.fodors.com. **Dist. by:** Random House Inc., 400 Hahn Rd, Westminster, MD 21157.

914.404 USA ISSN 0532-5692
DC16
FODOR'S FRANCE. Text in English. 1951. a. USD 23.95 (effective 2009). **Document type:** *Guide, Consumer.* **Description:** Provides up-to-date information on France and features a range of options for a variety of budgets, interests and tastes.

Published by: Fodor's Travel Publications, Inc. (Subsidiary of: Random House Inc.), 1745 Broadway, 15th Fl, New York, NY 10019. TEL 212-782-9000, editors@fodors.com, http://www.fodors.com. Ed. Jillian Magalaner. **Dist. by:** Random House Inc., 400 Hahn Rd, Westminster, MD 21157.

914.304 USA ISSN 1525-5034
DD16

FODOR'S GERMANY. Text in English. 1951. a., latest 24th ed. USD 24.95 (effective 2009). **Document type:** *Guide, Consumer.* **Description:** Provides up-to-date information on Germany and features a range of options for a variety of budgets, interests and tastes.
Former titles (until 1989): Fodor's Germany: West and East (0192-0952); Fodor's Germany (0071-6391)
Published by: Fodor's Travel Publications, Inc. (Subsidiary of: Random House Inc.), 1745 Broadway, 15th Fl, New York, NY 10019. TEL 212-572-2313, editors@fodors.com, http://www.fodors.com. Ed. Christopher Billy. **Dist. by:** Random House Inc., 400 Hahn Rd, Westminster, MD 21157.

914.304 USA ISSN 1543-1061
E158

FODOR'S GREAT AMERICAN VACATIONS. Text in English. irreg. USD 14.
Published by: Fodor's Travel Publications, Inc. (Subsidiary of: Random House Inc.), 1745 Broadway, 15th Fl, New York, NY 10019. TEL 212-572-2313, editors@fodors.com, http://www.fodors.com. **Dist. by:** Random House Inc., 400 Hahn Rd, Westminster, MD 21157.

914.104 USA ISSN 0071-6405
DA650

FODOR'S GREAT BRITAIN. Text in English. 1951. a., latest 36th ed. USD 22.95 (effective 2008). adv. **Document type:** *Guide, Consumer.* **Description:** Presents information on various hotels, restaurants, attractions and activities as well as planning tools that are needed to plan a trip.
Formerly (until 1969): Great Britain
Published by: Fodor's Travel Publications, Inc. (Subsidiary of: Random House Inc.), 1745 Broadway, 15th Fl, New York, NY 10019. TEL 212-572-2313, editors@fodors.com, http://www.fodors.com. **Dist. by:** Random House Inc., 400 Hahn Rd, Westminster, MD 21157.

910.91 USA ISSN 1559-078X
TX907.2

FODOR'S GREAT PLACES TO ESCAPE TO NATURE WITHOUT ROUGHING IT. Text in English. 2004. biennial. USD 19.95 per issue (effective 2007). **Document type:** *Guide, Consumer.*
Formerly (until 2006): Fodor's Escape to Nature without Roughing It (1549-4233)
Published by: Fodor's Travel Publications, Inc. (Subsidiary of: Random House Inc.), 1745 Broadway, 15th Fl, New York, NY 10019. TEL 212-572-2313, editors@fodors.com, http://www.fodors.com.

914.9504 USA ISSN 0071-6413
DF716

FODOR'S GREECE. Text in English. 1951. biennial, latest 8th ed. USD 21.95 per issue (effective 2008). **Document type:** *Guide, Consumer.* **Description:** Features photo-rich special sections on Greek culture, food and history and also provides practical itineraries and tips for planning a trip.
Formerly (until 1969): Greece
Published by: Fodor's Travel Publications, Inc. (Subsidiary of: Random House Inc.), 1745 Broadway, 15th Fl, New York, NY 10019. TEL 212-572-2313, editors@fodors.com, http://www.fodors.com. **Dist. by:** Random House Inc., 400 Hahn Rd, Westminster, MD 21157.

914.95 USA ISSN 1940-3291

FODOR'S GREEK ISLANDS. Text in English. 2008 (Apr.). irreg. USD 21.95 1st ed. (effective 2008). adv. **Document type:** *Guide, Consumer.* **Description:** Provides an overview of various islands that Greece has to offer as well as full coverage of Athens and the major mainland ports.
Related titles: Online - full text ed.
Published by: Fodor's Travel Publications, Inc. (Subsidiary of: Random House Inc.), 1745 Broadway, 15th Fl, New York, NY 10019. TEL 212-572-2313, editors@fodors.com, http://www.fodors.com.

919.6904 USA ISSN 0071-6421
DU622

FODOR'S HAWAII. Text in English. 1961. a. USD 19.95 (effective 2009). adv. **Document type:** *Guide, Consumer.* **Description:** Provides up-to-date information on Hawaii and features a range of options for a variety of budgets, interests and tastes.
Formerly (until 1969): Hawaii (0361-4271)
Published by: Fodor's Travel Publications, Inc. (Subsidiary of: Random House Inc.), 1745 Broadway, 15th Fl, New York, NY 10019. TEL 212-572-2313, editors@fodors.com, http://www.fodors.com. **Dist. by:** Random House Inc., 400 Hahn Rd, Westminster, MD 21157.

910.202 613.7 USA ISSN 1057-8048

FODOR'S HEALTHY ESCAPES. Text in English. 1989. irreg., latest 2003, 8th edition. USD 20 8th ed. (effective 2008). adv. **Document type:** *Guide, Consumer.* **Description:** Contains a selection of spas and fitness resorts in the U.S., Caribbean and Mexico.
Formerly (until 1990): Fodor's Health and Fitness Vacations (1047-5052)
Published by: Fodor's Travel Publications, Inc. (Subsidiary of: Random House Inc.), 1745 Broadway, 15th Fl, New York, NY 10019. TEL 212-572-2313, editors@fodors.com, http://www.fodors.com. **Dist. by:** Random House Inc., 400 Hahn Rd, Westminster, MD 21157.

914.9204 USA ISSN 1537-5617
DJ16

FODOR'S HOLLAND. Text in English. 1992. biennial, latest 3rd ed. USD 20 per issue (effective 2008). adv. **Document type:** *Guide, Consumer.* **Description:** Presents information on a wide variety of hotels, restaurants, attractions and activities as well as planning tools that are needed to plan a trip.
Supersedes in part (in 1999): Fodor's the Netherlands, Belgium, Luxembourg (1070-4590); Which was formed by the merger of (19??-1992): Fodor's Belgium and Luxembourg; (1969-1992): Fodor's Holland (0071-643X); Which was formerly (1951-1969): Holland
Published by: Fodor's Travel Publications, Inc. (Subsidiary of: Random House Inc.), 1745 Broadway, 15th Fl, New York, NY 10019. TEL 212-572-2313, editors@fodors.com, http://www.fodors.com. **Dist. by:** Random House Inc., 400 Hahn Rd, Westminster, MD 21157.

915.1204 USA ISSN 1070-6887
DS796.H74

FODOR'S HONG KONG; With Macau and the South China cities. Text in English. 1984. a., latest 21st ed. USD 19.95 (effective 2009). adv. **Document type:** *Guide, Consumer.* **Description:** Provides up-to-date information on Hong Kong and features options for a variety of budgets, interests and tastes.
Formerly (until 1988): Fodor's Hong Kong and Macau (0882-0066)
Indexed: G08, I05.
Published by: Fodor's Travel Publications, Inc. (Subsidiary of: Random House Inc.), 1745 Broadway, 15th Fl, New York, NY 10019. TEL 212-572-2313, editors@fodors.com, http://www.fodors.com. **Dist. by:** Random House Inc., 400 Hahn Rd, Westminster, MD 21157.

917.296 USA ISSN 1939-9855
F1652

FODOR'S IN FOCUS BAHAMAS. Text in English. 2008 (Jan.). irreg. USD 10.95 1st ed. (effective 2008). adv. **Document type:** *Guide, Consumer.* **Description:** Features options for a variety of budgets, interests and tastes for planning a trip to Bahamas.
Related titles: Online - full text ed.
Published by: Fodor's Travel Publications, Inc. (Subsidiary of: Random House Inc.), 1745 Broadway, 15th Fl, New York, NY 10019. TEL 212-572-2313, editors@fodors.com, http://www.fodors.com.

917.29 USA ISSN 1941-0212
F2041

FODOR'S IN FOCUS BARBADOS & ST. LUCIA. Text in English. 2008 (Jun.). biennial. USD 11.99 per issue (effective 2011). **Document type:** *Handbook/Manual/Guide, Consumer.*
Published by: Fodor's Travel Publications, Inc. (Subsidiary of: Random House Inc.), 1745 Broadway, 15th Fl, New York, NY 10019. TEL 212-782-9000, editors@fodors.com.

917.299 USA ISSN 1940-8366
F1632

FODOR'S IN FOCUS BERMUDA. Text in English. 2008 (Feb.). biennial, latest 1st ed. USD 10.95 per issue (effective 2008). adv. **Document type:** *Guide, Consumer.* **Description:** Features options for a variety of budgets, interests, and tastes, so you make the choices to plan your trip of a lifetime.
Published by: Fodor's Travel Publications, Inc. (Subsidiary of: Random House Inc.), 1745 Broadway, 15th Fl, New York, NY 10019. TEL 212-572-2313, editors@fodors.com, http://www.fodors.com.

917.94 USA ISSN 1940-3313
F867.5

FODOR'S IN FOCUS CALIFORNIA WINE COUNTRY. Text in English. 2008 (Apr.). biennial, latest 1st ed. USD 10.95 per issue (effective 2008). adv. **Document type:** *Guide, Consumer.* **Description:** Features options for a variety of budgets, interests, and tastes, so you make the choices to plan your trip of a lifetime.
Published by: Fodor's Travel Publications, Inc. (Subsidiary of: Random House Inc.), 1745 Broadway, 15th Fl, New York, NY 10019. TEL 212-572-2313, editors@fodors.com, http://www.fodors.com.

917.292 USA ISSN 1941-0220
F2048.5

FODOR'S IN FOCUS CAYMAN ISLANDS. Text in English. 2008 (Jul.). biennial. USD 11.99 per issue (effective 2011). **Document type:** *Handbook/Manual/Guide, Consumer.*
Published by: Fodor's Travel Publications, Inc. (Subsidiary of: Random House Inc.), 1745 Broadway, 15th Fl, New York, NY 10019. TEL 212-782-9000, editors@fodors.com.

917.58 USA ISSN 1943-0167
F279.C43

FODOR'S IN FOCUS CHARLESTON. Text in English. 2008. irreg., latest 2009, 1st ed. USD 10.95 per issue (effective 2011). **Document type:** *Handbook/Manual/Guide, Consumer.* **Description:** Prepares the reader for a trip to Charleston, South Carolina, by featuring options for a variety of budgets, interests, and tastes.
Supersedes in part (in 2009): Fodor's in Focus Savannah & Charleston (1939-9863)
Published by: Fodor's Travel Publications, Inc. (Subsidiary of: Random House Inc.), 1745 Broadway, 15th Fl, New York, NY 10019. TEL 212-782-9000, editors@fodors.com.

919.611 USA ISSN 1941-0263
DU600

FODOR'S IN FOCUS FIJI. Text in English. 2008 (Aug.). irreg., latest 2008, 1st ed. USD 10.95 per issue (effective 2011). **Document type:** *Handbook/Manual/Guide, Consumer.*
Published by: Fodor's Travel Publications, Inc. (Subsidiary of: Random House Inc.), 1745 Broadway, 15th Fl, New York, NY 10019. TEL 212-782-9000, editors@fodors.com.

917.9 USA ISSN 1941-0247
F788

FODOR'S IN FOCUS GRAND CANYON NATIONAL PARK. Text in English. 2008 (Jul.). irreg., latest 2008, 1st ed. USD 10.95 per issue (effective 2011). **Document type:** *Handbook/Manual/Guide, Consumer.*
Published by: Fodor's Travel Publications, Inc. (Subsidiary of: Random House Inc.), 1745 Broadway, 15th Fl, New York, NY 10019. TEL 212-782-9000, editors@fodors.com.

917.68 USA ISSN 1943-0108
F443.G7

▼ **FODOR'S IN FOCUS GREAT SMOKY MOUNTAINS NATIONAL PARK.** Variant title: Fodor's Great Smoky Mountains National Park. Great Smoky Mountains National Park. Text in English. 2009. biennial. USD 10.95 per issue (effective 2011). **Document type:** *Handbook/Manual/Guide, Consumer.* **Description:** Travel guide for the Great Smoky Mountains National Park.
Published by: Fodor's Travel Publications, Inc. (Subsidiary of: Random House Inc.), 1745 Broadway, 15th Fl, New York, NY 10019. TEL 212-782-9000, editors@fodors.com.

917.292 USA ISSN 1940-3283
F1869

FODOR'S IN FOCUS JAMAICA. Text in English. 2008 (Apr.). biennial. USD 10.95 1st ed. (effective 2008). adv. **Document type:** *Guide, Consumer.* **Description:** Features options for a variety of budgets, interests and tastes for planning a trip to Jamaica.
Related titles: Online - full text ed.
Published by: Fodor's Travel Publications, Inc. (Subsidiary of: Random House Inc.), 1745 Broadway, 15th Fl, New York, NY 10019. TEL 212-572-2313, editors@fodors.com, http://www.fodors.com.

917.44 USA ISSN 1940-3321
F72.M5

FODOR'S IN FOCUS MARTHA'S VINEYARD AND NANTUCKET. Text in English. 2008 (Apr.). biennial, latest 10.95. USD 10.95 per issue (effective 2008). adv. **Document type:** *Guide, Consumer.* **Description:** Features options for a variety of budgets, interests, and tastes, so you make the choices to plan your trip of a lifetime.
Published by: Fodor's Travel Publications, Inc. (Subsidiary of: Random House Inc.), 1745 Broadway, 15th Fl, New York, NY 10019. TEL 212-572-2313, editors@fodors.com, http://www.fodors.com.

917 USA ISSN 1941-0255
F884.P83

FODOR'S IN FOCUS PORTLAND. Text in English. 2008 (Jul.). biennial. USD 11.99 per issue (effective 2011). **Document type:** *Handbook/Manual/Guide, Consumer.*
Published by: Fodor's Travel Publications, Inc. (Subsidiary of: Random House Inc.), 1745 Broadway, 15th Fl, New York, NY 10019. TEL 212-782-9000, editors@fodors.com.

917.295 USA ISSN 1939-9871
F1959

FODOR'S IN FOCUS PUERTO RICO. Text in English. 2007 (Dec.). irreg. USD 10.95 1st ed. (effective 2008). adv. **Document type:** *Guide, Consumer.* **Description:** Features options for a variety of budgets, interests and tastes for planning a trip to Puerto Rico.
Related titles: Online - full text ed.
Published by: Fodor's Travel Publications, Inc. (Subsidiary of: Random House Inc.), 1745 Broadway, 15th Fl, New York, NY 10019. TEL 212-572-2313, editors@fodors.com, http://www.fodors.com.

917.58 USA ISSN 1943-0116
F294.S2

▼ **FODOR'S IN FOCUS SAVANNAH.** Text in English. 2009 (Dec.). irreg., latest 2009, 1st ed. USD 10.95 per issue (effective 2009). **Document type:** *Guide, Consumer.* **Description:** Features options for a variety of budgets, interests, and tastes, so you make the choices to plan your trip of a lifetime.
Supersedes in part (in 2008): Fodor's in Focus Savannah & Charleston (1939-9863)
Published by: Fodor's Travel Publications, Inc. (Subsidiary of: Random House Inc.), 1745 Broadway, 15th Fl, New York, NY 10019. TEL 212-782-9000, editors@fodors.com, http://www.fodors.com.

917.297 USA ISSN 1940-3305
F2136.A2

FODOR'S IN FOCUS VIRGIN ISLANDS. Text in English. 2008 (Apr.). biennial, latest 1st ed. USD 10.95 per issue (effective 2008). adv. **Document type:** *Guide, Consumer.* **Description:** Features options for a variety of budgets, interests, and tastes, so you make the choices to plan your trip of a lifetime.
Published by: Fodor's Travel Publications, Inc. (Subsidiary of: Random House Inc.), 1745 Broadway, 15th Fl, New York, NY 10019. TEL 212-572-2313, editors@fodors.com, http://www.fodors.com.

917.92 USA ISSN 1946-309X
F832.Z8

▼ **FODOR'S IN FOCUS ZION & BRYCE CANYON NATIONAL PARKS.** Short title: Zion & Bryce Canyon National Parks. Text in English. 2009. biennial. USD 10.99 per issue (effective 2011). **Document type:** *Handbook/Manual/Guide, Consumer.* **Description:** Travel guide for Zion and Bryce Canyon National Parks.
Published by: Fodor's Travel Publications, Inc. (Subsidiary of: Random House Inc.), 1745 Broadway, 15th Fl, New York, NY 10019. TEL 212-572-2313, editors@fodors.com.

915.404 USA ISSN 1079-6444
DS406

FODOR'S INDIA. Text in English. 1963. biennial, latest 2008, 6th ed. USD 24.95 per issue (effective 2008). adv. **Document type:** *Guide, Consumer.* **Description:** Provides up-to-date information on India and features a range of options for a variety of budgets, interests and tastes.
Former titles (until 1988): Fodor's India, Nepal and Sri Lanka (0737-1039); (until 1982): Fodor's India and Nepal (0276-5500); (until 1981): Fodor's India (0362-0212); (until 1969): Fodor's Guide to India (0071-6456)
Published by: Fodor's Travel Publications, Inc. (Subsidiary of: Random House Inc.), 1745 Broadway, 15th Fl, New York, NY 10019. TEL 212-572-2313, editors@fodors.com, http://www.fodors.com. Ed. Paula Consolo. **Dist. by:** Random House Inc., 400 Hahn Rd, Westminster, MD 21157.

914.1504 USA ISSN 0090-0648
DA978

FODOR'S IRELAND. Text in English. 1968. a. USD 22.95 (effective 2009). adv. **Document type:** *Guide, Consumer.* **Description:** Provides up-to-date information on Ireland and features a range of options for a variety of budgets, interests and tastes.
Formerly (until 1969): Ireland
Published by: Fodor's Travel Publications, Inc. (Subsidiary of: Random House Inc.), 1745 Broadway, 15th Fl, New York, NY 10019. TEL 212-572-2313, editors@fodors.com, http://www.fodors.com. Ed. Andrew Collins. **Dist. by:** Random House Inc., 400 Hahn Rd, Westminster, MD 21157.

915.6904 USA ISSN 0071-6588
DS103

FODOR'S ISRAEL. Text in English. 1967. a., latest 6th ed. USD 21.95 (effective 2008). adv. **Document type:** *Guide, Consumer.* **Description:** Contains information for today's travelers, is ideal for first time and return visitors who want to experience the country's awe-inspiring historical and religious sites and its vibrant modern culture.
Formerly: Israel
Published by: Fodor's Travel Publications, Inc. (Subsidiary of: Random House Inc.), 1745 Broadway, 15th Fl, New York, NY 10019. TEL 212-572-2313, editors@fodors.com, http://www.fodors.com. Ed. Paula Rackow. **Dist. by:** Random House Inc., 400 Hahn Rd, Westminster, MD 21157.

914.504 USA ISSN 0361-977X
DG416

FODOR'S ITALY. Text in English. 1951. a. USD 24.95 (effective 2009). adv. **Document type:** *Guide, Consumer.* **Description:** Provides up-to-date information on Italy and includes unique photo-features that impart the country's culture.
Formerly (until 1968): Italy in.. (0579-1332)

Published by: Fodor's Travel Publications, Inc. (Subsidiary of: Random House Inc.), 1745 Broadway, 15th Fl, New York, NY 10019. TEL 212-572-2313, editors@fodors.com, http://www.fodors.com. Ed. Holly Hughes. **Dist. by:** Random House Inc., 400 Hahn Rd, Westminster, MD 21157.

915.204 USA ISSN 0736-9956
DS811
FODOR'S JAPAN. Text in English. 1962. biennial, latest 2009, 19th ed. USD 25.95 per issue (effective 2009). adv. **Document type:** *Guide, Consumer.*
Supersedes in part (in 1983): Fodor's Japan and Korea (0098-1613); Which superseded in part (in 1975): Fodor's Japan and East Asia (0071-6480)
Published by: Fodor's Travel Publications, Inc. (Subsidiary of: Random House Inc.), 1745 Broadway, 15th Fl, New York, NY 10019. TEL 212-572-2313, editors@fodors.com, http://www.fodors.com. Ed. Paula Consolo. **Dist. by:** Random House Inc., 400 Hahn Rd, Westminster, MD 21157.

916.7604 USA ISSN 1537-5609
DT433.52 .F632
FODOR'S KENYA & TANZANIA. Text in English. irreg. USD 16.
Former titles (until 2002): Fodor's Kenya, Tanzania, Seychelles; (until 198?): Fodor's Kenya
Published by: Fodor's Travel Publications, Inc. (Subsidiary of: Random House Inc.), 1745 Broadway, 15th Fl, New York, NY 10019. TEL 212-572-2313, editors@fodors.com, http://www.fodors.com. Ed. Conrad Paulus. **Dist. by:** Random House Inc., 400 Hahn Rd, Westminster, MD 21157. TEL 410-848-1900, 800-733-3000, ecustomerservice@randomhouse.com, http://www.randomhouse.com.

917.904 USA ISSN 1542-345X
F849.L35
FODOR'S LAS VEGAS. Text in English. 1986. a. USD 18.95 per issue (effective 2009). **Document type:** *Guide, Consumer.* **Description:** Contains unique photo-features that impart the Las Vegas city's culture, covering the best spas, buffets, pool scenes and much more.
Former titles (until 2001): Fodor's Las Vegas, Reno, Tahoe (1070-6909); (until 1992): Fodor's .. Las Vegas; (until 1989): Fodor's Fun in Las Vegas, Including Reno & Lake Tahoe; (until 1988): Fodor's Fun in Las Vegas
Published by: Fodor's Travel Publications, Inc. (Subsidiary of: Random House Inc.), 1745 Broadway, 15th Fl, New York, NY 10019. TEL 212-782-9000, editors@fodors.com, http://www.fodors.com. Ed. Alexis C Kelly. Pub. Tim Jarrell. **Dist. by:** Random House Inc., 400 Hahn Rd, Westminster, MD 21157.

914.2104 USA ISSN 0149-631X
DA679
FODOR'S LONDON. Text in English. 1971. a. USD 18.95 (effective 2008). adv. **Document type:** *Guide, Consumer.* **Description:** Features options for a variety of budgets, interests, and tastes, so you make the choices to plan your trip of a lifetime.
Indexed: G08, I05.
Published by: Fodor's Travel Publications, Inc. (Subsidiary of: Random House Inc.), 1745 Broadway, 15th Fl, New York, NY 10019. TEL 212-572-2313, editors@fodors.com, http://www.fodors.com. Ed. Craig Seligman. **Dist. by:** Random House Inc., 400 Hahn Rd, Westminster, MD 21157.

917.904 USA ISSN 1095-3914
F869.L8
FODOR'S LOS ANGELES. Text in English. a. USD 16.95 (effective 2009). adv. **Document type:** *Guide, Consumer.* **Description:** Provides up-to-date information on Los Angeles and includes various choices - from prowling Hollywood to exploring the revitalized downtown to tapping the many music scenes, etc.
Formerly (until 1988): Fodor's Los Angeles and Nearby Attractions (0743-3336)
Indexed: G08, I05.
Published by: Fodor's Travel Publications, Inc. (Subsidiary of: Random House Inc.), 1745 Broadway, 15th Fl, New York, NY 10019. TEL 212-572-2313, editors@fodors.com, http://www.fodors.com. **Dist. by:** Random House Inc.

917.2 USA ISSN 1941-028X
F1246
FODOR'S LOS CABOS & THE BAJA PENINSULA. Text in English. 2008 (Jul.). biennial. USD 19.99 per issue (effective 2011). back issues avail. **Document type:** *Handbook/Manual/Guide, Consumer.* **Description:** Contains opinionated reviews, insider tips, and fantastic side-trip ideas. Also includes illustrated features about seeing Baja's gray whales, which resort spas offer the best services, the best colonial missions to explore, and where to find some of the most interesting up-and-coming wine south of Napa.
Indexed: G08, I05.
Published by: Fodor's Travel Publications, Inc. (Subsidiary of: Random House Inc.), 1745 Broadway, 15th Fl, New York, NY 10019. TEL 212-782-9000, editors@fodors.com.

914.604 USA
DP355
FODOR'S MADRID AND BARCELONA. Text in English. 1983. a. USD 11.
Formerly (until 1993): Fodor's Barcelona, Madrid & Seville; (until 1992): Fodor's Madrid and Barcelona (1095-3957); (until 1989): Fodor's Madrid (0884-0393)
Indexed: G08, I05.
Published by: Fodor's Travel Publications, Inc. (Subsidiary of: Random House Inc.), 1745 Broadway, 15th Fl, New York, NY 10019. TEL 212-572-2313, editors@fodors.com, http://www.fodors.com. **Dist. by:** Random House Inc., 400 Hahn Rd, Westminster, MD 21157.

917.404 USA ISSN 1073-6581
F17.3
FODOR'S MAINE, VERMONT, NEW HAMPSHIRE. Text in English. 1991. irreg., latest 11th ed. USD 19.95 per issue (effective 2008). adv. **Document type:** *Guide, Consumer.* **Description:** Provides the most accurate and up-to-date information available in a guidebook.
Published by: Fodor's Travel Publications, Inc. (Subsidiary of: Random House Inc.), 1745 Broadway, 15th Fl, New York, NY 10019. TEL 212-572-2313, editors@fodors.com, http://www.fodors.com. **Dist. by:** Random House Inc., 400 Hahn Rd, Westminster, MD 21157.

917.2904 USA ISSN 1559-0798
DU628.M3
FODOR'S MAUI WITH MOLOKAI AND LANAI. Text in English. 1986. a. USD 17.95 newsstand/cover (effective 2006). **Document type:** *Guide, Consumer.*
Former titles (until 2006): Fodor's Maui and Lanai (1525-5042); (until 1996): Fodor's Maui; (until 1988): Fodor's Fun in Maui
Indexed: G08, I05.
Published by: Fodor's Travel Publications, Inc. (Subsidiary of: Random House Inc.), 1745 Broadway, 15th Fl, New York, NY 10019. TEL 212-572-2313, editors@fodors.com, http://www.fodors.com. Ed. Larry Peterson. **Dist. by:** Random House Inc., 400 Hahn Rd, Westminster, MD 21157.

917.204 USA ISSN 0196-5999
F1216
FODOR'S MEXICO. Text in English. 1972. a. USD 21.95 (effective 2009). adv. **Document type:** *Guide, Consumer.* **Description:** Provides up-to-date information on Mexico and features a range of options for a variety of budgets, interests and tastes.
Published by: Fodor's Travel Publications, Inc. (Subsidiary of: Random House Inc.), 1745 Broadway, 15th Fl, New York, NY 10019. TEL 212-572-2313, editors@fodors.com, http://www.fodors.com. **Dist. by:** Random House Inc., 400 Hahn Rd, Westminster, MD 21157.

917.504 USA ISSN 1070-6399
F319.M6
FODOR'S MIAMI & THE KEYS. Text in English. a. USD 10.
Former titles: Fodor's Miami, Fort Lauderdale, Palm Beach; Fodor's Greater Miami, Fort Lauderdale, Palm Beach; Fodor's Greater Miami and the Gold Coast
Indexed: G08, I05.
Published by: Fodor's Travel Publications, Inc. (Subsidiary of: Random House Inc.), 1745 Broadway, 15th Fl, New York, NY 10019. TEL 212-572-2313, editors@fodors.com, http://www.fodors.com. Ed. Alison Hoffman. **Dist. by:** Random House Inc., 400 Hahn Rd, Westminster, MD 21157.

910.91 USA ISSN 1559-0801
F729.3
FODOR'S MONTANA & WYOMING. Text in English. 2004. biennial, latest 3rd ed. USD 19.95 per issue 3rd ed. (effective 2008). adv. 464 p./no.; **Document type:** *Guide, Consumer.* **Description:** Features options for a variety of budgets, interests, and tastes, so you make the choices to plan your trip of a lifetime.
Formerly (until 2006): Fodor's Montana, Wyoming and Idaho (1549-3784)
Published by: Fodor's Travel Publications, Inc. (Subsidiary of: Random House Inc.), 1745 Broadway, 15th Fl, New York, NY 10019. TEL 212-572-2313, editors@fodors.com, http://www.fodors.com.

917.104 USA ISSN 1525-5867
FODOR'S MONTREAL & QUEBEC CITY. Text in English. 1989. a. USD 16.95 (effective 2008). adv. **Description:** Provides up-to-date information on Montreal and Quebec and includes choices for every traveler, from shopping in Quebecois boutiques and exploring hip neighborhoods to hiking in the Laurentian Mountains.
Formerly (until 1989): Fodor's Montreal (1046-8102)
Related titles: Online - full text ed.
Indexed: G08, I05.
Published by: Fodor's Travel Publications, Inc. (Subsidiary of: Random House Inc.), 1745 Broadway, 15th Fl, New York, NY 10019. TEL 212-572-2313, editors@fodors.com, http://www.fodors.com. Ed. Conrad Paulus. **Dist. by:** Random House Inc.

910.2 USA ISSN 1939-5388
F1054.5.M83
FODOR'S MONTREAL'S 25 BEST. Text in English. irreg. **Document type:** *Guide, Consumer.*
Former titles (until 2005): Fodor's Citypack Montreal's 25 Best (1559-4254); (until 2003): Fodor's Citypack Montreal
Published by: Fodor's Travel Publications, Inc. (Subsidiary of: Random House Inc.), 1745 Broadway, 15th Fl, New York, NY 10019. editors@fodors.com, http://www.fodors.com.

916.104 USA ISSN 1527-4829
DT304
FODOR'S MOROCCO. Text in English. 1969. biennial, latest 4th ed. USD 22.95 per issue (effective 2009). adv. **Document type:** *Guide, Consumer.* **Description:** Provides up-to-date information and features options for a variety of budgets, interests and tastes.
Former titles (until 1990): Fodor's North Africa (0197-1271); (until 1979): Fodor's Morocco (0190-1508)
Published by: Fodor's Travel Publications, Inc. (Subsidiary of: Random House Inc.), 1745 Broadway, 15th Fl, New York, NY 10019. TEL 212-572-2313, editors@fodors.com, http://www.fodors.com. **Dist. by:** Random House Inc., 400 Hahn Rd, Westminster, MD 21157.

910.91 USA ISSN 1933-0936
DD901.M76
FODOR'S MUNICH'S 25 BEST. Text in English. 2001. irreg., latest 4th ed. **Document type:** *Guide, Consumer.*
Formerly (until 2005): Citypack Munich
Published by: Fodor's Travel Publications, Inc. (Subsidiary of: Random House Inc.), 1745 Broadway, 15th Fl, New York, NY 10019. TEL 800-733-3000, 212-572-2313, editors@fodors.com.

917.404 USA ISSN 0192-3412
F2.3
FODOR'S NEW ENGLAND. Text in English. 1975. a. USD 21.95 (effective 2009). adv. illus. **Document type:** *Guide, Consumer.* **Description:** Provides up-to-date information on New England and includes various choices for travelers - from hiking and skiing to beachcombing and antiquing, etc.
Published by: Fodor's Travel Publications, Inc. (Subsidiary of: Random House Inc.), 1745 Broadway, 15th Fl, New York, NY 10019. TEL 212-572-2313, editors@fodors.com, http://www.fodors.com. **Dist. by:** Random House Inc., 400 Hahn Rd, Westminster, MD 21157.

917.604 USA ISSN 0743-9385
F379.N53
FODOR'S NEW ORLEANS. Text in English. 1984. a. USD 17.95 (effective 2009). adv. **Description:** Provides up-to-date information on New Orleans and includes various choices for travelers - from shopping boutiques and walking historic neighborhoods to gallery hopping and late-night clubbing.
Related titles: Online - full text ed.
Indexed: G08, I05.

Published by: Fodor's Travel Publications, Inc. (Subsidiary of: Random House Inc.), 1745 Broadway, 15th Fl, New York, NY 10019. TEL 212-572-2313, editors@fodors.com, http://www.fodors.com. Ed. Nancy van Itallie. **Dist. by:** Random House Inc.

917.404 USA
F128.18
FODOR'S NEW YORK CITY. Text in English. 1975. a. USD 18.95 (effective 2008). illus. **Document type:** *Guide, Consumer.* **Description:** Provides up-to-date information on New York City and includes photo-features that impart the city's culture.
Supersedes in part (in 1987): Fodor's New York City with Atlantic City (0882-7338); Which was formerly (until 1985): Fodor's New York City and Nearby Attractions (0736-9395); (until 1982): Fodor's New York. City and State
Indexed: G08, I05.
Published by: Fodor's Travel Publications, Inc. (Subsidiary of: Random House Inc.), 1745 Broadway, 15th Fl, New York, NY 10019. TEL 212-572-2313, editors@fodors.com, http://www.fodors.com. Ed. Suzanne Degalan. **Dist. by:** Random House Inc.

917.404 USA ISSN 1554-5873
F117.3
FODOR'S NEW YORK STATE. Text in English. biennial, latest 2005, 1st ed. USD 19.95 per issue (effective 2008). adv. 704 p./no.; **Document type:** *Guide, Consumer.* **Description:** Presents information on various restaurants, attractions and activities and contains multi-day itineraries that can help readers build the right trip for them.
Former titles (until 2005): Fodor's Vacations in New York State; Fodor's New York State
Related titles: Online - full text ed.
Published by: Fodor's Travel Publications, Inc. (Subsidiary of: Random House Inc.), 1745 Broadway, 15th Fl, New York, NY 10019. TEL 212-572-2313, editors@fodors.com, http://www.fodors.com. **Dist. by:** Random House Inc.

919.304 USA ISSN 1531-0450
DU405.5
FODOR'S NEW ZEALAND. Text in English. a. USD 22.95 (effective 2009). adv. **Description:** Provides up-to-date information on New Zealand and includes various choices for travelers, from sunbathing and surfing to bushwalking and horseback riding.
Related titles: Online - full text ed.
Published by: Fodor's Travel Publications, Inc. (Subsidiary of: Random House Inc.), 1745 Broadway, 15th Fl, New York, NY 10019. TEL 212-572-2313, editors@fodors.com, http://www.fodors.com. Ed. Craig Seligman. **Dist. by:** Random House Inc.

917.404 USA ISSN 1073-6603
DL407
FODOR'S NORWAY. Text in English. 1992. irreg., latest 8th ed. USD 18.95 per issue (effective 2008). adv. **Document type:** *Guide, Consumer.* **Description:** Contains rely heavily on local experts who know the territory best - so you know you're seeing the real Norway.
Published by: Fodor's Travel Publications, Inc. (Subsidiary of: Random House Inc.), 1745 Broadway, 15th Fl, New York, NY 10019. TEL 212-572-2313, editors@fodors.com, http://www.fodors.com. **Dist. by:** Random House Inc., 400 Hahn Rd, Westminster, MD 21157.

917.104 USA ISSN 1558-8173
F1035.8
FODOR'S NOVA SCOTIA AND ATLANTIC CANADA. Text in English. 1985. irreg., latest 2008, 10th ed. USD 16.95 per issue (effective 2009). **Document type:** *Guide, Consumer.* **Description:** Contains choices for every traveler in Atlantic Canada, from traveling coastal cliffs on stunning scenic drives, to chowing down at a lobster boil, to spotting majestic whales, drifting icebergs, or nesting puffins.
Former titles (until 2006): Fodor's Nova Scotia, New Brunswick, Prince Edward Island (1079-0004); (until 1994): Fodor's Nova Scotia, Prince Edward Island and New Brunswick (1064-7643); (until 1992): Fodor's Canada's Atlantic Provinces (1060-0191); (until 1990): Fodor's Canada's Maritime Provinces (1043-6731); (until 1989): Fodor's Canada's Maritime Provinces Plus Newfoundland and Labrador (1042-525X); (until 1987): Fodor's Canada's Maritime Provinces (1042-5241)
Published by: Fodor's Travel Publications, Inc. (Subsidiary of: Random House Inc.), 1745 Broadway, 15th Fl, New York, NY 10019. TEL 212-782-9000, editors@fodors.com, http://www.fodors.com. Ed. Caroline Trefler. Pub. Tim Jarrell. **Dist. by:** Random House Inc., 400 Hahn Rd, Westminster, MD 21157.

917.904 USA ISSN 1523-8776
F874.3
FODOR'S OREGON. Text in English. 1998. irreg., latest 4th ed. USD 17.95 4th ed. (effective 2008). **Document type:** *Guide, Consumer.*
Published by: Fodor's Travel Publications, Inc. (Subsidiary of: Random House Inc.), 1745 Broadway, 15th Fl, New York, NY 10019. TEL 212-782-9000, 212-572-2313, editors@fodors.com, http://www.fodors.com.

917.904 USA ISSN 1098-6774
F852.3
FODOR'S PACIFIC NORTHWEST. Text in English. 1984. a., latest 17th ed. USD 19.95 17th ed. (effective 2008). **Document type:** *Guide, Consumer.* **Description:** Provides up-to-date information on Pacific Northwest and includes various choices for travelers - from rafting the Deschutes river to skiing Mt. Hood to relaxing in a Seattle coffeehouse, etc.
Formerly (until 1998): Fodor's Pacific North Coast (1072-0391)
Related titles: Online - full text ed.
Published by: Fodor's Travel Publications, Inc. (Subsidiary of: Random House Inc.), 1745 Broadway, 15th Fl, New York, NY 10019. TEL 212-572-2313, editors@fodors.com, http://www.fodors.com. **Dist. by:** Random House Inc., 400 Hahn Rd, Westminster, MD 21157.

914.404 USA ISSN 0149-1288
DC708
FODOR'S PARIS. Text in English. 1973. a. USD 18.95 (effective 2009). adv. **Document type:** *Guide, Consumer.* **Description:** Provides up-to-date information on Paris and features a range of options for a variety of budgets, interests and tastes as well as various customized trip planning tools.
Indexed: G08, I05.
Published by: Fodor's Travel Publications, Inc. (Subsidiary of: Random House Inc.), 1745 Broadway, 15th Fl, New York, NY 10019. TEL 212-572-2313, editors@fodors.com, http://www.fodors.com. **Dist. by:** Random House Inc., 400 Hahn Rd, Westminster, MD 21157.

TU

917.404 USA ISSN 1098-9358
F158.18
FODOR'S PHILADELPHIA & THE PENNSYLVANIA DUTCH COUNTRY. Text in English. 1985. biennial, latest 2007, 15th ed. USD 16.95 per issue (effective 2008). adv. **Description:** Presents information on the various hotels, restaurants, attractions and activities and also includes planning tools that are needed to tailor a trip.
Formerly (until 1990): Fodor's Philadelphia
Related titles: Online - full text ed.
Indexed: G08, I05.
Published by: Fodor's Travel Publications, Inc. (Subsidiary of: Random House Inc.), 1745 Broadway, 15th Fl, New York, NY 10019. TEL 212-572-2313, editors@fodors.com, http://www.fodors.com. Ed. Caroline Haberfeld. **Dist. by:** Random House Inc.

917.2904 USA ISSN 1074-1208
F1869
FODOR'S POCKET JAMAICA. Text in English. a. USD 7.
Formerly: Fodor's Fun in Jamaica
Published by: Fodor's Travel Publications, Inc. (Subsidiary of: Random House Inc.), 1745 Broadway, 15th Fl, New York, NY 10019. TEL 212-572-2313, editors@fodors.com, http://www.fodors.com. Ed. Caroline Haberfeld. **Dist. by:** Random House Inc., 400 Hahn Rd, Westminster, MD 21157.

914.2104 USA ISSN 1094-7124
DA679
FODOR'S POCKET LONDON. Text in English. a. USD 8.
Former titles (until 1990): Fodor's Pocket Guide to London; (until 198?): Fodor's Fun in London
Published by: Fodor's Travel Publications, Inc. (Subsidiary of: Random House Inc.), 1745 Broadway, 15th Fl, New York, NY 10019. TEL 212-572-2313, editors@fodors.com, http://www.fodors.com. Ed. Craig Seligman. **Dist. by:** Random House Inc., 400 Hahn Rd, Westminster, MD 21157.

917.404 USA
F128.18
FODOR'S POCKET NEW YORK CITY. Text in English. a. USD 8.
Former titles (until 1990): Fodor's Pocket Guide to New York City (1056-7712); (until 1989): Fodor's Fun in New York City
Published by: Fodor's Travel Publications, Inc. (Subsidiary of: Random House Inc.), 1745 Broadway, 15th Fl, New York, NY 10019. TEL 212-572-2313, editors@fodors.com, http://www.fodors.com. Ed. Suzanne Degalan. **Dist. by:** Random House Inc., 400 Hahn Rd, Westminster, MD 21157.

914.404 USA ISSN 1094-2998
DC708
FODOR'S POCKET PARIS. Text in English. a. USD 8.
Former titles (until 1990): Fodor's Pocket Guide to Paris; (until 198?): Fodor's Fun in Paris
Published by: Fodor's Travel Publications, Inc. (Subsidiary of: Random House Inc.), 1745 Broadway, 15th Fl, New York, NY 10019. TEL 212-572-2313, editors@fodors.com, http://www.fodors.com. Ed. Paula Consolo. **Dist. by:** Random House Inc., 400 Hahn Rd, Westminster, MD 21157.

917.204 USA ISSN 1523-0953
F1613
FODOR'S POCKET PUERTO RICO. Text in English. a. USD 7.
Published by: Fodor's Travel Publications, Inc. (Subsidiary of: Random House Inc.), 1745 Broadway, 15th Fl, New York, NY 10019. TEL 212-572-2313, editors@fodors.com, http://www.fodors.com. **Dist. by:** Random House Inc., 400 Hahn Rd, Westminster, MD 21157.

917.904 USA ISSN 1094-401X
F869.S33
FODOR'S POCKET SAN FRANCISCO. Text in English. a. USD 8.
Former titles (until 1990): Fodor's Pocket Guide to San Francisco (1046-8978); (until 1988): Fodor's Fun in San Francisco; The Good Time Travel Guide to San Francisco
Published by: Fodor's Travel Publications, Inc. (Subsidiary of: Random House Inc.), 1745 Broadway, 15th Fl, New York, NY 10019. TEL 212-572-2313, editors@fodors.com, http://www.fodors.com. Ed. Larry Peterson. **Dist. by:** Random House Inc.

917.504
FODOR'S POCKET WASHINGTON. Text in English. 1991. a. USD 8.
Published by: Fodor's Travel Publications, Inc. (Subsidiary of: Random House Inc.), 1745 Broadway, 15th Fl, New York, NY 10019. TEL 212-572-2313, editors@fodors.com, http://www.fodors.com. Ed. Suzanne Degalan. **Dist. by:** Random House Inc., 400 Hahn Rd, Westminster, MD 21157.

914.6904 USA ISSN 0071-6510
DP516
FODOR'S PORTUGAL. Text in English. 1951. a., latest 8th ed. USD 19.95 (effective 2008). adv. **Document type:** *Guide, Consumer.* **Description:** Presents information on a wide variety of hotels, restaurants, attractions and activities as well as planning tools that are needed to plan a successful trip.
Formerly (until 1969): Portugal (0196-1268); Which superseded in part (in 1967): Spain and Portugal
Published by: Fodor's Travel Publications, Inc. (Subsidiary of: Random House Inc.), 1745 Broadway, 15th Fl, New York, NY 10019. TEL 212-572-2313, editors@fodors.com, http://www.fodors.com. **Dist. by:** Random House Inc., 400 Hahn Rd, Westminster, MD 21157.

910.09 USA ISSN 1554-3447
DB2607
FODOR'S PRAGUE. Text in English. 2005. irreg., latest 2009, 3rd ed. USD 17.95 per issue (effective 2009). **Document type:** *Guide, Consumer.* **Description:** Contains choices for every traveler in Prague, from strolling past the cottages of Golden Lane and watching a black light theater performance to take the waters at a famous spa town, and much more.
Supersedes in part (in 2003): Fodor's Prague and Budapest (1530-5384); Which was formerly (until 1998): Fodor's Budapest (1065-4607); Which superseded in part: Fodor's Hungary (0361-9761)
Published by: Fodor's Travel Publications, Inc. (Subsidiary of: Random House Inc.), 1745 Broadway, 15th Fl, New York, NY 10019. TEL 212-782-9000, editors@fodors.com, http://www.fodors.com. **Dist. by:** Random House Inc., 400 Hahn Rd, Westminster, MD 21157.

910.91 USA ISSN 1933-0928
DB2607
FODOR'S PRAGUE'S 25 BEST. Text in English. irreg. **Document type:** *Guide, Consumer.*
Former titles (until 2006): Fodor's Citypack Prague's 25 Best; Citypack Prague
Published by: Fodor's Travel Publications, Inc. (Subsidiary of: Random House Inc.), 1745 Broadway, 15th Fl, New York, NY 10019. TEL 212-572-2313, editors@fodors.com, http://www.fodors.com.

914.4 USA ISSN 1944-2912
DC611.P958
FODOR'S PROVENCE & THE FRENCH RIVIERA. Variant title: Provence & the French Riviera. Text in English. 1993. biennial. USD 19.99 per issue (effective 2011). back issues avail. **Document type:** *Handbook/Manual/Guide, Consumer.* **Description:** Travel guide for Provence and the French Riviera.
Former titles (until 2009): Fodor's Provence and the Cote d'Azur (1532-6829); (until 1999): Fodor's Provence & the Riviera (1095-4007)
Published by: Fodor's Travel Publications, Inc. (Subsidiary of: Random House Inc.), 1745 Broadway, 15th Fl, New York, NY 10019. TEL 212-782-9000, editors@fodors.com.

918.1 USA ISSN 1941-0239
F2646.A4
FODOR'S RIO DE JANIERO & SAN PAULO. Text in English. 2008 (Aug.). irreg., latest 2008, 1st ed. USD 17.95 per issue (effective 2011). **Document type:** *Handbook/Manual/Guide, Consumer.*
Published by: Fodor's Travel Publications, Inc. (Subsidiary of: Random House Inc.), 1745 Broadway, 15th Fl, New York, NY 10019. TEL 212-782-9000, editors@fodors.com.

914.504 USA ISSN 0276-2560
DG804
FODOR'S ROME; with the best city walks and scenic day trips. Text in English. 1979. a., latest 7th ed. USD 18.95 (effective 2008). adv. **Document type:** *Guide, Consumer.* **Description:** Provides advice and tips on exploring Rome and covers the new hot locales and avant-garde sites.
Indexed: G08, I05.
Published by: Fodor's Travel Publications, Inc. (Subsidiary of: Random House Inc.), 1745 Broadway, 15th Fl, New York, NY 10019. TEL 212-572-2313, editors@fodors.com, http://www.fodors.com. **Dist. by:** Random House Inc., 400 Hahn Rd, Westminster, MD 21157.

910.91 USA ISSN 1932-6416
DG804
FODOR'S ROME'S 25 BEST. Text in English. irreg. **Document type:** *Guide, Consumer.*
Formerly (until 2006): Fodor's Citypack Rome's Best
Published by: Fodor's Travel Publications, Inc. (Subsidiary of: Random House Inc.), 1745 Broadway, 15th Fl, New York, NY 10019. TEL 212-572-2313, editors@fodors.com, http://www.fodors.com.

917.64 USA ISSN 1941-0298
F394.S2113
FODOR'S SAN ANTONIO, AUSTIN & HILL COUNTRY. Text in English. 2008 (Aug.). irreg., latest 2008, 1st ed. USD 16.95 per issue (effective 2011). **Document type:** *Handbook/Manual/Guide, Consumer.*
Published by: Fodor's Travel Publications, Inc. (Subsidiary of: Random House Inc.), 1745 Broadway, 15th Fl, New York, NY 10019. TEL 212-782-9000, editors@fodors.com.

917.904 USA ISSN 1053-5950
F869.S22
FODOR'S SAN DIEGO; with the north coast and tijuana. Text in English. a. USD 16.95 (effective 2008). adv. **Document type:** *Guide, Consumer.* **Description:** Presents information on the various hotels, restaurants, attractions and activities in San Diego and also includes planning tools that are needed to tailor a trip.
Formerly: Fodor's San Diego and Nearby Attractions
Indexed: G08, I05.
Published by: Fodor's Travel Publications, Inc. (Subsidiary of: Random House Inc.), 1745 Broadway, 15th Fl, New York, NY 10019. TEL 212-572-2313, editors@fodors.com, http://www.fodors.com. **Dist. by:** Random House Inc., 400 Hahn Rd, Westminster, MD 21157.

917.904 USA ISSN 1525-1829
F869.S33
FODOR'S SAN FRANCISCO. Text in English. 1982. a. USD 18.95 (effective 2008). adv. **Document type:** *Guide, Consumer.* **Description:** Provides up-to-date information and features options for a variety of budgets, interests and tastes.
Former titles (until 1989): Fodor's San Francisco Plus Marin County and the Wine Country; (until 1986): Fodor's San Francisco and Nearby Attractions (0743-9334)
Indexed: G08, I05.
Published by: Fodor's Travel Publications, Inc. (Subsidiary of: Random House Inc.), 1745 Broadway, 15th Fl, New York, NY 10019. TEL 212-572-2313, editors@fodors.com, http://www.fodors.com. **Dist. by:** Random House Inc., 400 Hahn Rd, Westminster, MD 21157.

917.804 USA ISSN 1095-3876
F804.S23
FODOR'S SANTA FE, TAOS, ALBUQUERQUE. Text in English. 1992. a., latest 2007, 1st ed. USD 16.95 (effective 2008). adv. **Description:** Presents information on the various hotels, restaurants, attractions and activities and also includes planning tools that are needed to tailor a trip.
Formerly: Fodor's New Mexico
Related titles: Online - full text ed.
Indexed: G08, I05.
Published by: Fodor's Travel Publications, Inc. (Subsidiary of: Random House Inc.), 1745 Broadway, 15th Fl, New York, NY 10019. TEL 800-733-3000. Ed. Julie Tomasz. **Dist. by:** Random House Inc., 400 Hahn Rd, Westminster, MD 21157.

914.804 USA
FODOR'S SCANDINAVIAN CITIES. Text in English. 1989. irreg. USD 9.
Formerly: Fodor's Stockholm, Copenhagen, Oslo, Helsinki and Reykjavik
Published by: Fodor's Travel Publications, Inc. (Subsidiary of: Random House Inc.), 1745 Broadway, 15th Fl, New York, NY 10019. TEL 212-572-2313, editors@fodors.com, http://www.fodors.com. **Dist. by:** Random House Inc., 400 Hahn Rd, Westminster, MD 21157.

914.104 USA ISSN 0743-0973
DA870
FODOR'S SCOTLAND. Text in English. 1983. a., latest 21st ed. USD 21.95 21st ed. (effective 2008). adv. **Document type:** *Guide, Consumer.* **Description:** Provides up-to-date information on Scotland and features options for a variety of budgets, interests and tastes.
Published by: Fodor's Travel Publications, Inc. (Subsidiary of: Random House Inc.), 1745 Broadway, 15th Fl, New York, NY 10019. TEL 212-572-2313, editors@fodors.com, http://www.fodors.com. **Dist. by:** Random House Inc., 400 Hahn Rd, Westminster, MD 21157.

917.904 USA ISSN 1531-3417
F899.S43
FODOR'S SEATTLE. Text in English. irreg., latest 2007, 4th ed. USD 16.95 per issue (effective 2009). **Document type:** *Guide, Consumer.* **Description:** Provides information on the best hotels, restaurants, attractions in Seattle.
Supersedes in part (in 2000): Fodor's Seattle and Vancouver (1525-5859)
Indexed: G08, I05.
Published by: Fodor's Travel Publications, Inc. (Subsidiary of: Random House Inc.), 1745 Broadway, 15th Fl, New York, NY 10019. http://www.fodors.com. Ed. Paul Eisenberg. Pub. Tim Jarrell. **Dist. by:** Random House Inc., 400 Hahn Rd, Westminster, MD 21157.

910.2 USA ISSN 1931-2598
F1543.5
FODOR'S SEE IT. COSTA RICA. Text in English. 2005. irreg., latest 2nd ed. USD 21.95 2nd ed. (effective 2008). 256 p./no.; **Document type:** *Guide, Consumer.* **Description:** Details various sights in Costa Rica and contains hundreds of hotel and restaurant reviews.
Published by: Fodor's Travel Publications, Inc. (Subsidiary of: Random House Inc.), 1745 Broadway, 15th Fl, New York, NY 10019. TEL 212-572-2313, editors@fodors.com, http://www.fodors.com.

910.91 USA ISSN 1930-7233
F1209
FODOR'S SEE IT. MEXICO. Text in English. 2005. irreg., latest 2nd ed. USD 23.95 2nd ed. (effective 2008). 336 p./no.; **Document type:** *Guide, Consumer.* **Description:** Details various sights in Mexico and contains hundreds of hotel and restaurant reviews.
Published by: Fodor's Travel Publications, Inc. (Subsidiary of: Random House Inc.), 1745 Broadway, 15th Fl, New York, NY 10019. TEL 212-572-2313, editors@fodors.com, http://www.fodors.com.

910.91 USA ISSN 1930-3491
DU405.5
FODOR'S SEE IT. NEW ZEALAND. Text in English. 2005. irreg., latest 2nd ed. USD 24.95 2nd ed. (effective 2008). 336 p./no.; **Document type:** *Guide, Consumer.* **Description:** Details various New Zealand's sights, hotels, restaurants and shops.
Published by: Fodor's Travel Publications, Inc. (Subsidiary of: Random House Inc.), 1745 Broadway, 15th Fl, New York, NY 10019. TEL 212-572-2313, editors@fodors.com, http://www.fodors.com.

910.91 USA ISSN 1932-6831
DB2607
FODOR'S SEE IT. PRAGUE. Text in English. 2006. irreg. USD 21.95 per issue (effective 2008). adv. **Document type:** *Guide, Consumer.* **Description:** Contains everthing from the latest dish on local hotels and restaurants to web sites, the nearest tram and metro stops, to prices.
Published by: Fodor's Travel Publications, Inc. (Subsidiary of: Random House Inc.), 1745 Broadway, 15th Fl, New York, NY 10019. TEL 212-572-2313, editors@fodors.com, http://www.fodors.com.

910.91 USA ISSN 1930-6717
DT1717
FODOR'S SEE IT. SOUTH AFRICA. Text in English. 2005. irreg., latest 2nd ed. USD 24.95 2nd ed. (effective 2008). 352 p./no.; **Document type:** *Guide, Consumer.* **Description:** Details various sights in South Africa and contains hundreds of hotel and restaurant reviews.
Published by: Fodor's Travel Publications, Inc. (Subsidiary of: Random House Inc.), 1745 Broadway, 15th Fl, New York, NY 10019. TEL 212-572-2313, editors@fodors.com, http://www.fodors.com.

915 USA ISSN 1939-540X
DS563
FODOR'S SEE IT. THAILAND. Text in English. 2006. irreg., latest 2nd ed. USD 22.95 2nd ed. (effective 2008). **Document type:** *Guide, Consumer.* **Description:** Details various sights in Thailand and contains hundreds of hotel and restaurant reviews.
Published by: Fodor's Travel Publications, Inc. (Subsidiary of: Random House Inc.), 1745 Broadway, 15th Fl, New York, NY 10019. TEL 212-572-2313, editors@fodors.com, http://www.fodors.com.

910.91 USA ISSN 1932-5363
DG672
FODOR'S SEE IT. VENICE. Text in English. 2006. irreg., latest 2nd ed. USD 21.95 per issue 2nd ed. (effective 2008). adv. 336 p./no.; **Document type:** *Guide, Consumer.* **Description:** Contains everything from the latest dish on local hotels and restaurants to web sites, the nearest tram and metro stops, to prices.
Published by: Fodor's Travel Publications, Inc. (Subsidiary of: Random House Inc.), 1745 Broadway, 15th Fl, New York, NY 10019. TEL 212-572-2313, editors@fodors.com, http://www.fodors.com.

910.91 USA ISSN 1930-6725
DS556.25
FODOR'S SEE IT. VIETNAM. Text in English. 2005. irreg., latest 2nd ed. USD 23.95 2nd ed. (effective 2008). 304 p./no.; **Document type:** *Guide, Consumer.* **Description:** Details various sights in Vietnam and contains hundreds of hotel and restaurant reviews.
Published by: Fodor's Travel Publications, Inc. (Subsidiary of: Random House Inc.), 1745 Broadway, 15th Fl, New York, NY 10019. TEL 212-572-2313, editors@fodors.com, http://www.fodors.com.

915.9504 USA ISSN 1533-5267
DS598.S72
FODOR'S SINGAPORE. Text in English. 1986. a., latest 2005, 12th ed. USD 18 (effective 2008). adv. **Document type:** *Guide, Consumer.* **Description:** Presents information on various restaurants, attractions and activities and contains multi-day itineraries that can help readers build the right trip for them.
Related titles: Online - full text ed.
Published by: Fodor's Travel Publications, Inc. (Subsidiary of: Random House Inc.), 1745 Broadway, 15th Fl, New York, NY 10019. TEL 212-572-2313, editors@fodors.com, http://www.fodors.com. **Dist. by:** Random House Inc.

917.04 796.93 USA
FODOR'S SKIING IN THE U S A & CANADA. Text in English. irreg. USD 15.
Formerly: Fodor's Ski Resorts of North America

Published by: Fodor's Travel Publications, Inc. (Subsidiary of: Random House Inc.), 1745 Broadway, 15th Fl, New York, NY 10019. TEL 212-572-2313, editors@fodors.com, http://www.fodors.com. **Dist. by:** Random House Inc., 400 Hahn Rd, Westminster, MD 21157.

918.04 USA ISSN 0362-0220
F2211
FODOR'S SOUTH AMERICA. Text in English. 1966. a., latest 8th ed. USD 27.95 (effective 2008). adv. **Document type:** *Guide, Consumer.* **Description:** Provides up-to-date information on South America and features a range of options for a variety of budgets, interests and tastes.
Formerly (until 1970): Fodor's Guide to South America (0071-6537)
Published by: Fodor's Travel Publications, Inc. (Subsidiary of: Random House Inc.), 1745 Broadway, 15th Fl, New York, NY 10019. TEL 212-572-2313, editors@fodors.com, http://www.fodors.com. Ed. Julie Tomasz. **Dist. by:** Random House Inc., 400 Hahn Rd, Westminster, MD 21157.

919.604 USA
FODOR'S SOUTH PACIFIC. Text in English. 1986. irreg. USD 12.
Published by: Fodor's Travel Publications, Inc. (Subsidiary of: Random House Inc.), 1745 Broadway, 15th Fl, New York, NY 10019. TEL 212-572-2313, editors@fodors.com, http://www.fodors.com. Ed. Craig Seligman. **Dist. by:** Random House Inc., 400 Hahn Rd, Westminster, MD 21157.

914.604 USA ISSN 0361-9648
DP14
FODOR'S SPAIN. Text in English. 1955. a. USD 22.95 (effective 2009). adv. **Document type:** *Guide, Consumer.* **Description:** Features options for a variety of budgets, interests, and tastes, so you make the choices to plan your trip of a lifetime.
Formerly (until 1969): Spain (0361-9680)
Published by: Fodor's Travel Publications, Inc. (Subsidiary of: Random House Inc.), 1745 Broadway, 15th Fl, New York, NY 10019. TEL 212-572-2313, editors@fodors.com, http://www.fodors.com. Ed. Suzanne Degalan. **Dist. by:** Random House Inc., 400 Hahn Rd, Westminster, MD 21157.

FODOR'S SPORTS: CYCLING. *see* SPORTS AND GAMES—Bicycles And Motorcycles

FODOR'S SPORTS: HIKING. *see* SPORTS AND GAMES—Outdoor Life

FODOR'S SPORTS: RUNNING. *see* SPORTS AND GAMES—Outdoor Life

FODOR'S SPORTS: SAILING. *see* SPORTS AND GAMES—Boats And Boating

917.404 USA
FODOR'S SUNDAY IN NEW YORK. Text in English. 1990. irreg. USD 11.
Published by: Fodor's Travel Publications, Inc. (Subsidiary of: Random House Inc.), 1745 Broadway, 15th Fl, New York, NY 10019. TEL 212-572-2313, editors@fodors.com, http://www.fodors.com. **Dist. by:** Random House Inc.

914.8504 USA ISSN 1528-3070
DL607
FODOR'S SWEDEN. Text in English. 1986. a., latest 2006, 14th ed. USD 18.95 (effective 2008). adv. **Description:** Presents information on the various hotels, restaurants, attractions and also includes planning tools that are needed to tailor a trip.
Related titles: Online - full text ed.
Published by: Fodor's Travel Publications, Inc. (Subsidiary of: Random House Inc.), 1745 Broadway, 15th Fl, New York, NY 10019. TEL 212-572-2313, editors@fodors.com, http://www.fodors.com. **Dist. by:** Random House Inc.

914.9404 USA ISSN 0071-6553
DQ16
FODOR'S SWITZERLAND. Text in English. 1951. a., latest 45th ed. USD 21.95 (effective 2009). adv. **Document type:** *Guide, Consumer.*
Formerly: Switzerland
Published by: Fodor's Travel Publications, Inc. (Subsidiary of: Random House Inc.), 1745 Broadway, 15th Fl, New York, NY 10019. TEL 212-572-2313, editors@fodors.com, http://www.fodors.com. Ed. Karen Cure. **Dist. by:** Random House Inc., 400 Hahn Rd, Westminster, MD 21157.

915.9304 USA ISSN 1064-0983
DS563
FODOR'S THAILAND; with side trips to Cambodia & Laos. Text in English. 1991. irreg., latest 10th ed. USD 23.95 per issue (effective 2008). adv. **Document type:** *Guide, Consumer.* **Description:** Presents information on the various hotels, restaurants, attractions and activities and also includes planning tools that are needed to tailor a trip.
Published by: Fodor's Travel Publications, Inc. (Subsidiary of: Random House Inc.), 1745 Broadway, 15th Fl, New York, NY 10019. TEL 212-572-2313, editors@fodors.com, http://www.fodors.com. **Dist. by:** Random House Inc., 400 Hahn Rd, Westminster, MD 21157.

910.202 USA ISSN 1522-5933
G550
FODOR'S THE BEST CRUISES. Text in English. 1977. a. USD 17.
Former titles (until 1998): Fodor's Worldwide Cruises and Ports of Call (1091-9163); (until 1996): Fodor's Cruises and Ports of Call (1070-4477); (until 19??): Fodor's Cruises Everywhere (0160-3914)
Published by: Fodor's Travel Publications, Inc. (Subsidiary of: Random House Inc.), 1745 Broadway, 15th Fl, New York, NY 10019. TEL 800-733-3000. Ed. Andrew Collins. **Dist. by:** Random House Inc., 400 Hahn Rd, Westminster, MD 21157.

917.504 USA ISSN 1525-5832
F252.3
FODOR'S THE CAROLINAS & GEORGIA. Text in English. a., latest 2007, 17th ed. USD 18.95 (effective 2008). adv. **Description:** Presents information on the various hotels, restaurants, attractions and activities and also includes planning tools that are needed to tailor a trip.
Formerly (until 1998): Fodor's Carolinas & the Georgia Coast
Related titles: Online - full text ed.
Published by: Fodor's Travel Publications, Inc. (Subsidiary of: Random House Inc.), 1745 Broadway, 15th Fl, New York, NY 10019. TEL 212-572-2313, editors@fodors.com, http://www.fodors.com. **Dist. by:** Random House Inc.

916 USA ISSN 1941-0336
QL337.E25
FODOR'S THE COMPLETE AFRICAN SAFARI PLANNER. Text and summaries in English. 2008 (Jul.). irreg., latest 2011, 2nd ed. USD 27.99 per issue (effective 2011). back issues avail. **Document type:** *Handbook/Manual/Guide, Consumer.*
Published by: Fodor's Travel Publications, Inc. (Subsidiary of: Random House Inc.), 1745 Broadway, 15th Fl, New York, NY 10019. TEL 212-782-9000, editors@fodors.com, http://www.fodors.com.

917.04 USA ISSN 0147-8680
F207.3
FODOR'S THE SOUTH. Text in English. 1975. irreg., latest 2003, 27th ed. USD 21. illus. **Document type:** *Guide, Consumer.*
Published by: Fodor's Travel Publications, Inc. (Subsidiary of: Random House Inc.), 1745 Broadway, 15th Fl, New York, NY 10019. TEL 212-572-2313, editors@fodors.com, http://www.fodors.com. **Dist. by:** Random House Inc., 400 Hahn Rd, Westminster, MD 21157.

915.204 USA ISSN 1554-5881
DS896.38
FODOR'S TOKYO. Text in English. 1985. biennial, latest 3rd ed. USD 16.95 per issue (effective 2009). adv. **Document type:** *Magazine, Consumer.*
Related titles: Online - full text ed.
Indexed: G08, I05.
Published by: Fodor's Travel Publications, Inc. (Subsidiary of: Random House Inc.), 1745 Broadway, 15th Fl, New York, NY 10019. TEL 212-572-2313, editors@fodors.com, http://www.fodors.com. **Dist. by:** Random House Inc.

910.91 USA ISSN 1933-0952
DS896.38
FODOR'S TOKYO'S 25 BEST. Text in English. biennial, latest 5th ed. **Document type:** *Guide, Consumer.*
Formerly (until 2006): Fodor's Citypack Tokyo's Best
Published by: Fodor's Travel Publications, Inc. (Subsidiary of: Random House Inc.), 1745 Broadway, 15th Fl, New York, NY 10019. TEL 212-572-2313, editors@fodors.com, http://www.fodors.com.

917.104 USA ISSN 1044-6133
F1059.5.T683
FODOR'S TORONTO. Text in English. 1984. a. USD 17.95 (effective 2009). adv. **Document type:** *Guide, Consumer.* **Description:** Provides up-to-date information on Toronto and includes various choices for travelers - from shopping tours and eclectic film festivals to hockey games and Lake Ontario getaways.
Formerly (until 1989): Fodor's Toronto and Nearby Attractions (1066-6141)
Related titles: Online - full text ed.
Indexed: G08, I05.
Published by: Fodor's Travel Publications, Inc. (Subsidiary of: Random House Inc.), 1745 Broadway, 15th Fl, New York, NY 10019. TEL 212-572-2313, editors@fodors.com, http://www.fodors.com. **Dist. by:** Random House Inc.

910.91 USA ISSN 1933-0944
F1059.5.T683
FODOR'S TORONTO'S 25 BEST. Text in English. biennial, latest 5th ed. USD 11.95 per issue (effective 2008). **Document type:** *Guide, Consumer.*
Formerly (until 2006): Fodor's Citypack Toronto's Best
Published by: Fodor's Travel Publications, Inc. (Subsidiary of: Random House Inc.), 1745 Broadway, 15th Fl, New York, NY 10019. TEL 212-572-2313, editors@fodors.com, http://www.fodors.com.

914.04 USA
FODOR'S TOURING EUROPE. Text in English. irreg. USD 14 (effective 2008). **Document type:** *Guide, Consumer.*
Formerly: Great European Itineraries
Published by: Fodor's Travel Publications, Inc. (Subsidiary of: Random House Inc.), 1745 Broadway, 15th Fl, New York, NY 10019. TEL 212-572-2313, editors@fodors.com, http://www.fodors.com. Ed. Nancy van Itallie. **Dist. by:** Random House Inc., 400 Hahn Rd, Westminster, MD 21157.

917.304 USA
FODOR'S TOURING U S A: EASTERN EDITION. Text in English. 1992. irreg. USD 16.
Published by: Fodor's Travel Publications, Inc. (Subsidiary of: Random House Inc.), 1745 Broadway, 15th Fl, New York, NY 10019. TEL 212-572-2313, editors@fodors.com, http://www.fodors.com. **Dist. by:** Random House Inc.

917.804 USA
FODOR'S TOURING U S A: WESTERN EDITION. Text in English. irreg. USD 16.
Published by: Fodor's Travel Publications, Inc. (Subsidiary of: Random House Inc.), 1745 Broadway, 15th Fl, New York, NY 10019. TEL 212-572-2313, editors@fodors.com, http://www.fodors.com. Ed. Craig Seligman. **Dist. by:** Random House Inc., 400 Hahn Rd, Westminster, MD 21157.

915.6104 USA ISSN 0071-6618
DR416
FODOR'S TURKEY. Text in English. 1969. a., latest 6th ed. USD 22.95 (effective 2008). adv. **Document type:** *Guide, Consumer.* **Description:** Includes extensive, updated, and accessible coverage of Istanbul; the Sea of Marmara; the Turquoise, Mediterranean, and Aegean coasts; and Cappadoccia.
Published by: Fodor's Travel Publications, Inc. (Subsidiary of: Random House Inc.), 1745 Broadway, 15th Fl, New York, NY 10019. TEL 212-572-2313, editors@fodors.com, http://www.fodors.com. **Dist. by:** Random House Inc., 400 Hahn Rd, Westminster, MD 21157.

919.704 USA ISSN 1070-6380
F2136.2
FODOR'S U S & BRITISH VIRGIN ISLANDS. Text in English. 1990. a. USD 16.95 (effective 2009). adv. **Description:** Provides up-to-date information on U.S. and British Virgin Islands and includes various choices for travelers - from scuba diving, kayaking, and horseback riding to beaches.
Formerly: Fodor's Virgin Islands (1048-1060)
Related titles: Online - full text ed.
Indexed: G08, I05.
Published by: Fodor's Travel Publications, Inc. (Subsidiary of: Random House Inc.), 1745 Broadway, 15th Fl, New York, NY 10019. TEL 212-572-2313, editors@fodors.com, http://www.fodors.com. **Dist. by:** Random House Inc.

917.11 USA ISSN 1941-0301
F1089.V3
FODOR'S VANCOUVER & VICTORIA. Text in English. 2008 (May). irreg., latest 2010, 2nd ed. USD 18.99 per issue (effective 2011). back issues avail. **Document type:** *Handbook/Manual/Guide, Consumer.*
Published by: Fodor's Travel Publications, Inc. (Subsidiary of: Random House Inc.), 1745 Broadway, 15th Fl, New York, NY 10019. TEL 212-782-9000, editors@fodors.com.

910.91 USA ISSN 1935-0333
DG672
FODOR'S VENICE'S 25 BEST. Text in English. irreg., latest 6th ed. USD 11.95 per issue (effective 2008). **Document type:** *Guide, Consumer.*
Formerly (until 2006): Fodor's Citypack Venice's Best
Published by: Fodor's Travel Publications, Inc. (Subsidiary of: Random House Inc.), 1745 Broadway, 15th Fl, New York, NY 10019. TEL 212-572-2313, editors@fodors.com, http://www.fodors.com.

914.304 USA ISSN 1554-5857
DB849
FODOR'S VIENNA TO SALZBURG. Text in English. 1984. irreg., latest 2009, 3rd Ed. USD 16.99 (effective 2009). **Document type:** *Guide, Consumer.*
Former titles (until 2005): Fodor's Vienna and the Danube Valley (1095-3922); (until 1990): Fodor's Vienna
Published by: Fodor's Travel Publications, Inc. (Subsidiary of: Random House Inc.), 1745 Broadway, 15th Fl, New York, NY 10019. TEL 212-572-2313, editors@fodors.com, http://www.fodors.com. **Dist. by:** Random House Inc., 400 Hahn Rd, Westminster, MD 21157.

917.504 USA ISSN 1075-0711
F224.3
FODOR'S VIRGINIA & MARYLAND. Text in English. 1991. a., latest 2007, 9th ed. USD 17.95 (effective 2008). adv. **Document type:** *Guide, Consumer.* **Description:** Presents information on the various hotels, restaurants, attractions and activities and also includes planning tools that are needed to tailor a trip.
Formerly: Fodor's Virginia
Related titles: Online - full text ed.
Published by: Fodor's Travel Publications, Inc. (Subsidiary of: Random House Inc.), 1745 Broadway, 15th Fl, New York, NY 10019. TEL 212-572-2313, editors@fodors.com, http://www.fodors.com. **Dist. by:** Random House Inc.

919.6904 USA ISSN 1044-923X
DU629.H7
FODOR'S WAIKIKI. Text in English. irreg. USD 9.
Formerly: Fodor's Fun in Waikiki
Published by: Fodor's Travel Publications, Inc. (Subsidiary of: Random House Inc.), 1745 Broadway, 15th Fl, New York, NY 10019. TEL 212-572-2313, editors@fodors.com, http://www.fodors.com. Ed. Jillian Magalaner. **Dist. by:** Random House Inc., 400 Hahn Rd, Westminster, MD 21157.

917.504 USA
GV1853.3.F62
FODOR'S WALT DISNEY WORLD. Cover title: Fodor's (Year) Walt Disney World and the Orlando Area. Text in English. 1989. a. USD 17.95 per issue (effective 2009). back issues avail. **Document type:** *Guide, Consumer.* **Description:** Features options for a variety of budgets, interests, and tastes, so you make the choices to plan your trip of a lifetime.
Former titles (until 2007): Fodor's Walt Disney World, Universal Orlando & Central Florida (1930-3505); (until 2004): Fodor's Walt Disney World Resort, Universal Orlando and Central Florida (1531-443X); (until 2000): Fodor's Disney World & the Orlando Area (1070-6402); (until 1989): Fodor's Fun in Disney World and the Orlando Area
Published by: Fodor's Travel Publications, Inc. (Subsidiary of: Random House Inc.), 1745 Broadway, 15th Fl, New York, NY 10019. TEL 212-782-9000, 212-572-2313, editors@fodors.com, http://www.fodors.com. **Dist. by:** Random House Inc.

917.504 USA ISSN 0743-9741
F192.3
FODOR'S WASHINGTON, D.C. Text in English. 19??. a. USD 17.95 (effective 2009). adv. **Document type:** *Guide, Consumer.* **Description:** Provides up-to-date information on Washington, D.C. and includes photo-features that impart the city's culture.
Formerly (until 19??): Fodor's Washington D.C. and Vicinity (0739-9383)
Related titles: Online - full text ed.
Indexed: G08, I05.
Published by: Fodor's Travel Publications, Inc. (Subsidiary of: Random House Inc.), 1745 Broadway, 15th Fl, New York, NY 10019. TEL 212-572-2313, editors@fodors.com, http://www.fodors.com. **Dist. by:** Random House Inc.

917.53 USA ISSN 1537-310X
FODOR'S WASHINGTON, D.C. WITH KIDS. Text in English. 2003 (Mar.). biennial. USD 16.95 4th ed. (effective 2008). adv. **Document type:** *Guide, Consumer.* **Description:** Provides a personal tour guide to Washington, D.C., and includes everything from historical sites, parks and monuments to inside information on activities for parents and teachers with kids of all ages.
Related titles: Online - full text ed.
Published by: Fodor's Travel Publications, Inc. (Subsidiary of: Random House Inc.), 1745 Broadway, 15th Fl, New York, NY 10019. TEL 212-572-2313, editors@fodors.com, http://www.fodors.com.

910.2 USA ISSN 1553-6092
GV199.42.V4
FOGHORN OUTDOORS. VERMONT HIKING. Text in English. 2005. biennial, latest 2005. USD 12.95 per issue (effective 2009). **Document type:** *Guide, Consumer.*
Published by: Avalon Travel Publishing, 1400 65th St, Ste 250, Emeryville, CA 94608. avalon.publicity@perseusbooks.com, http://www.avalontravelbooks.com.

FOGHORN OUTDOORS. WASHINGTON HIKING. *see* SPORTS AND GAMES—Outdoor Life

338.4 POL ISSN 0867-3888
FOLIA TURISTICA. Text in Polish, English. 1990. a. **Document type:** *Journal, Academic/Scholarly.*
Published by: Akademia Wychowanie Fizycznego im. Bronislawa Czecha, Instytut Turystyki i Rekreacji, Aleja Jana Pawla II 78, Krakow, 31571, Poland.

TU

641.514 910 GBR ISSN 1366-6967
FOOD AND TRAVEL. Text in English. 1997. m. GBP 45.60 domestic; GBP 56.50 in Europe; GBP 75 elsewhere (effective 2009). adv. illus. **Document type:** *Magazine, Consumer.* **Description:** Designed to help the world traveler find the perfect escape and the best restaurants.
—CCC.
Published by: Fox Publishing Ltd., Ste 51, The Business Centre, Ingate Pl, London, SW8 3NS, United Kingdom. TEL 44-20-75010511. Ed. Charlotte Swift. adv.: page GBP 3,900; trim 220 x 285. **Dist. by:** Comag.

917.5 USA
F252.3
FORBES TRAVEL GUIDE. COASTAL SOUTHEAST. Text in English. 19??. a. **Document type:** *Guide, Trade.*
Formerly (until 2010): Mobil Travel Guide: Coastal Southeast (1550-5456); Supersedes in part (in 200?): Mobil Travel Guide: Southeast (1040-1067); Which was formerly (until 1988): Mobil Travel Guide: Southeastern States (0076-9835); (until 1979): Mobil Travel Guide. Good Food, Lodging, and Sightseeing in Southeastern States
Published by: Mobil Travel Guide, 7373 N Cicero Ave, Lincolnwood, IL 60712. ratings@forbestravelguide.com, http://www.forbestravelguide.com/.

917.13 USA
FORBES TRAVEL GUIDE: FLORIDA. Text in English. 19??. a. **Document type:** *Guide, Trade.*
Formerly: Mobil Travel Guide: Florida (1096-7788)
Published by: Mobil Travel Guide, 7373 N Cicero Ave, Lincolnwood, IL 60712. ratings@forbestravelguide.com, http://www.forbestravelguide.com/.

917.12 USA
FORBES TRAVEL GUIDE. MID-ATLANTIC. Text in English. 1963. a. **Document type:** *Handbook/Manual/Guide, Consumer.*
Former titles (until 2010): Mobil Travel Guide. Mid-Atlantic (1090-6975); (until 1995): Mobil Travel Guide. Middle Atlantic States (0076-9797)
Published by: Mobil Travel Guide, 7373 N Cicero Ave, Lincolnwood, IL 60712. ratings@forbestravelguide.com, http://www.forbestravelguide.com/.

917.5 USA
F207.3
FORBES TRAVEL GUIDE. SOUTH. Text in English. 1966. a. **Document type:** *Handbook/Manual/Guide, Trade.*
Formely (until 2010): Mobil Travel Guide: South (1550-1930); Supersedes in part (in 2004): Mobil Travel Guide: Southeast (1040-1067); Which was formerly (until 1989): Mobil Travel Guide: Southeastern States (0076-9835); (until 1979): Mobil Travel Guide. Good Food, Lodging, and Sightseeing in Southeastern States
Published by: Mobil Travel Guide, 7373 N Cicero Ave, Lincolnwood, IL 60712. ratings@forbestravelguide.com, http://www.forbestravelguide.com/.

917.13 USA
F867
FORBES TRAVEL GUIDE: SOUTHERN CALIFORNIA. Text in English. 1998. a. **Document type:** *Guide, Trade.*
Formerly: Mobil Travel Guide: Southern California (1096-7796)
Published by: Mobil Travel Guide, 7373 N Cicero Ave, Lincolnwood, IL 60712. ratings@forbestravelguide.com, http://www.forbestravelguide.com/.

910.2 USA ISSN 1539-5227
HE556.F7
FORD'S FREIGHTER TRAVEL GUIDE AND WATERWAYS OF THE WORLD. Text in English. 1952. s-a. USD 24 domestic; USD 26.50 foreign (effective 2000). adv. illus. **Document type:** *Directory.* **Description:** Lists all freighter cruises, assorted waterway cruises, assorted sports and casual cruises, and major ferry travel.
Formerly: Ford's Freighter Travel Guide (0015-7058)
Published by: Ford's Travel Guides, 10520 Reseda Blvd., Northridge, CA 91326-3129. TEL 818-701-7414. Ed. Judith A Howard. Pub. Ron Howard. Circ: 12,408.

338.4791 AUS ISSN 1832-598X
FORECAST. Text in English. 1994. s-a. **Document type:** *Government.* **Description:** Provides the latest inbound, domestic, and outbound forecasts released by the Tourism Forecasting Committee.
Former titles (until 2004): Tourism Forecasting Council. Forecast (1449-1427)
Related titles: Online - full text ed.: ISSN 1833-0738.
Indexed: H&TI.
Published by: Tourism Research Australia, GPO Box 1110, Canberra, ACT 2616, Australia. TEL 61-62-286100, FAX 61-62-286180, tra@tourism.australia.com, http://www.tourism.australia.com.

FOREIGN TRAVEL & IMMUNIZATION GUIDE. *see* MEDICAL SCIENCES—Allergology And Immunology

913.919 GBR ISSN 0958-8213
FRANCE. Text in English. 1990. m. GBP 34; GBP 3.99 newsstand/cover (effective 2009). adv. illus. back issues avail.; reprints avail. **Document type:** *Magazine, Consumer.* **Description:** Covers the heritage, arts, culture, history, politics, cuisine, wine and regions of France.
Related titles: Online - full text ed.
Published by: Archant Life Ltd (Subsidiary of: Archant Group), Archant House, Oriel Rd, Cheltenham, Glos GL50 1BB, United Kingdom. TEL 44-1242-216050, http://www.archantlife.co.uk. Ed. Carolyn Boyd TEL 44-1242-216086. Adv. contact Stuart Ogden TEL 44-1242-216063. Circ: 53,896. **Subscr. to:** Market Harborough, Leicestershire LE16 9BR, United Kingdom.

944 GBR ISSN 1749-3153
FRANCE (BARNOLDSWICK). Spine title: Independent Traveller's Holiday Directory. Variant title: Chez Nous. Text in English. 1984. a. GBP 4 per issue (effective 2009). adv. **Document type:** *Directory, Consumer.* **Description:** Contains holiday property information of France.
Published by: Chez Nous, Spring Mill, Earby, Barnoldswick, Lancs BB94 0AA, United Kingdom. TEL 44-870-1971000, advertising@cheznous.co.uk.

910.91 647.9 FRA ISSN 1968-0163
FRANCE ART DE VIVRE. Text in French. 2008. q. EUR 64 for 2 yrs. (effective 2008). **Document type:** *Magazine, Consumer.* **Description:** Explores the world of dining and traveling in style in the most sophisticated places.
Formerly (until 2008): Entreprendre Art de Vivre (1961-0793)
Published by: Lafont Presse, 53 Rue du Chemin Vert, Boulogne-Billancourt, 92100, France. TEL 33-1-46102121, FAX 33-1-45792211, http://www.lafontpresse.fr.

914.404 USA
FRANCE INSIDER'S NEWS. Text in English. q. **Description:** Covers updates on museums, special events, hotel and restaurant openings throughout France. Also lets readers know about special offers and values.
Media: Online - full content.
Published by: French Government Tourist Office, 444 Madison ave., 16th Fl., New York, NY 10022. TEL 212-7450965, mfourestier@francetourism.com, http://www.franceguide.com.

914.404 USA
FRANCEGUIDE (YEAR). Text in English. 2001. a. free. **Document type:** *Magazine, Consumer.* **Description:** Magazine style travel planner which includes articles on Paris and other regions.
Related titles: French ed.; Spanish ed.
Published by: French Government Tourist Office, 444 Madison ave., 16th Fl., New York, NY 10022. TEL 212-7450965, mfourestier@francetourism.com, http://www.franceguide.com. Circ: 430,000.

914.4 DEU ISSN 1861-4256
FRANKREICH ERLEBEN. Text in German. 2006. bi-m. EUR 25.20 domestic; EUR 29.70 in Austria; CHF 51.80 in Switzerland; EUR 39.50 elsewhere; EUR 4.90 newsstand/cover (effective 2006). adv. **Document type:** *Magazine, Consumer.*
Published by: Globus Medien GmbH, Heckscherstr 29, Hamburg, 20253, Germany. TEL 49-40-43091648, FAX 49-40-38017863552. Ed. Jean-Charles Albert. Pub. Markus Harnau. Adv. contact Jeannette Kirchhoff. color page EUR 4,500. Circ: 40,000 (paid and controlled).

338.4791 BEL ISSN 0779-5696
FREESUN NEWS MAGAZINE. Text in English, French, Dutch. 1983. bi-m. back issues avail. **Document type:** *Magazine, Trade.* **Description:** Covers issues about the travel trade.
Address: Avenue Charles Plisnier 20, Brussels, 1070, Belgium. TEL 32-2-5213214, FAX 32-2-5217243, info@freesun.be, http://www.freesun.be/. Ed., Pub. Jacques Schoonjans.

910.2 USA ISSN 0016-089X
FREIGHTER TRAVEL NEWS. Text in English. 1958. m. USD 20 domestic; USD 24 foreign (effective 2001). adv. bk.rev. illus. index. **Document type:** *Newsletter.* **Description:** Contains first-hand reports of recent freighter or unusual water transportation. Features news bulletins about changes in freighter opportunities, answers specific questions and general information about freighter travel.
Published by: Freighter Travel Club of America, 3524 Harts Lake Rd, Roy, WA 98580. TEL 360-458-4178. Ed., Pub., Adv. contact Leland J Pledger. Circ: 3,000.

910 AUT
FREMDENVERKEHR. Text in German. m.
Indexed: RASB.
Address: Zieglergasse 1-3, Postfach 35, Vienna, W 1072, Austria. TEL 01-52131-0, FAX 01-939217, TELEX 112378-MUCHA-A. Ed. Christian Mucha. Circ: 18,200.

914.4 USA
FRENCH WALKER. Text in English. q. **Document type:** *Newsletter, Consumer.*
Address: 145 E 22nd Street, No 5E, New York, NY 10010. TEL 212-995-5869. Ed. Richard Bock.

910.91 SGP
FREQUENT TRAVELLER. Text in English. 8/yr. free in selected airlines and hotels. **Document type:** *Magazine, Consumer.*
Published by: Eastern Publishing Pte Ltd (Subsidiary of: Eastern Holdings Ltd), 1100 Lower Delta Rd, #04-01, EPL Bldg, Singapore, 169206, Singapore. TEL 65-6-3792888, FAX 65-6-3792804.

914.2 GBR
FRESHER'S GUIDE (YEAR). Text in English. 1950. a. free with subscr. to Cherwell. adv. **Document type:** *Handbook/Manual/Guide, Consumer.*
Former titles: In at the Deep End: The Cherwell Fresher's Guide; Cherwell Fresher's Guide; Cherwell Oxford Introduction; Cherwell Guide to Oxford (0955-4165)
Related titles: ◆ Supplement to: Cherwell. ISSN 0308-731X.
Published by: Oxford University Students' Union, Thomas Hull House, New Inn Hall St, Oxford, OX1 2DH, United Kingdom. TEL 44-1865-288450, enquiries@ousu.org. adv.: page GBP 1,300; 265 x 340. Circ: 4,000.

910.202 ITA ISSN 1974-6601
IL FRIULI VENZIA GIULIA PAESE PER PAESE. Text in Italian. 2008. w. **Document type:** *Magazine, Consumer.*
Published by: Editrice Bonechi, Via dei Cairoli, 18BB, Florence, FI 50131, Italy. TEL 39-055-576841, FAX 39-055-5000766, bonechi@bonechi.it, http://www.bonechi.it.

914.5 USA ISSN 2155-9201
DG416
FROMMER'S 25 GREAT DRIVES IN NORTHERN ITALY. Variant title: 25 Great Drives in Northern Italy. Text in English. 200?. biennial. USD 19.99 per issue (effective 2010). **Document type:** *Handbook/Manual/Guide, Consumer.* **Description:** Includes routes to see Northern Italy by car.
Published by: John Wiley & Sons, Inc., 111 River St, Hoboken, NJ 07030. TEL 201-748-6000, FAX 201-748-5915, info@wiley.com, http://www.wiley.com/WileyCDA/.

914 USA ISSN 1935-0317
DG975.A42
FROMMER'S AMALFI COAST WITH NAPLES, CAPRI & POMPEII. Text in English. 2006. irreg., latest 2010, 3rd ed. USD 19.99 per issue (effective 2010). adv. back issues avail.; reprints avail. **Document type:** *Guide, Consumer.*
Related titles: Online - full text ed.
Published by: John Wiley & Sons, Inc., 111 River St, Hoboken, NJ 07030. TEL 201-748-6000, FAX 201-748-6088, info@wiley.com, http://www.wiley.com/WileyCDA/.

915 USA ISSN 2153-7348
DS589.B2
▼ **FROMMER'S BANGKOK: DAY BY DAY.** Variant title: Bangkok: Day by Day. Text in English. 2009. irreg. USD 12.99 per issue (effective 2010). **Document type:** *Guide, Consumer.* **Description:** Travel guide for Bangkok, Thailand.
Published by: John Wiley & Sons, Inc., 111 River St, Hoboken, NJ 07030.

910.91 USA ISSN 1930-3513
DP402.B24
FROMMER'S BARCELONA. Text in English. 2005. irreg., latest 2009, 3rd ed. USD 16.99 per issue (effective 2010). adv. 352 p./no.; back issues avail.; reprints avail. **Document type:** *Guide, Consumer.* **Description:** Provides tips on where to see the magic of modernisme and where to find the best cava.
Published by: John Wiley & Sons, Inc., 111 River St, Hoboken, NJ 07030. TEL 201-748-6000, FAX 201-748-6088, info@wiley.com, http://www.wiley.com/WileyCDA/.

917.004 USA
F1632
FROMMER'S BERMUDA. Text in English. 19??. a. USD 18.99 per issue (effective 2011). adv. **Document type:** *Handbook/Manual/Guide, Consumer.*
Formerly (until 1996): Frommer's Comprehensive Travel Guide. Bermuda (1069-3572); Which superseded in part (in 199?): Frommer's Comprehensive Travel Guide. Bermuda & the Bahamas; Which was formerly (until 1993): Frommer's Bermuda and the Bahamas, plus Turks and Caicos (1044-2383); (until 1989): Frommer's Dollarwise Guide to Bermuda and the Bahamas (1042-8305); (until 1987): Frommer's Dollarwise Guide to the Caribbean, Including Bermuda & the Bahamas (0882-6919); (until 1983): Arthur Frommer's Dollarwise Guide to the Caribbean, Including Bermuda & the Bahamas (0198-7178)
Published by: Frommer Books (Subsidiary of: John Wiley & Sons, Inc.), 111 River St, 5th Fl, Hoboken, NJ 07030. TEL 201-748-6000, FAX 201-748-6088, info@frommers.biz.

917.94 USA ISSN 1534-8172
F859.3
FROMMER'S CALIFORNIA. Text in English. 19??. biennial. USD 23.99 per issue (effective 2011). adv. back issues avail. **Document type:** *Handbook/Manual/Guide, Consumer.*
Former titles (until 1996): Frommer's Comprehensive Travel Guide. California (1064-3044); (until 1992): Frommer's Comprehensive Travel Guide. California & Las Vegas; (until 1991): Frommer's California and Las Vegas (1044-2146); (until 1990): Frommer's Dollarwise California and Las Vegas (0899-3319); (until 1989): Frommer's Dollarwise Guide to California and Las Vegas (0277-187X)
Published by: Frommer Books (Subsidiary of: John Wiley & Sons, Inc.), 111 River St, 5th Fl, Hoboken, NJ 07030. TEL 201-748-6000, FAX 201-748-6088, info@frommers.biz.

915.96 USA ISSN 2155-7918
DS555.25
▼ **FROMMER'S CAMBODIA & LAOS.** Variant title: Cambodia & Laos. Text in English. 2010. irreg. USD 21.99 per issue (effective 2010). **Document type:** *Handbook/Manual/Guide, Consumer.* **Description:** Provides a tour guide for Cambodia and Laos.
Published by: John Wiley & Sons, Inc., 111 River St, Hoboken, NJ 07030. TEL 201-748-6000, FAX 201-748-6088, info@wiley.com, http://www.wiley.com/WileyCDA/.

917.104 USA ISSN 1530-4248
F1009
FROMMER'S CANADA. Text in English. 1981. biennial. USD 24.99 per issue (effective 2011). adv. back issues avail. **Document type:** *Handbook/Manual/Guide, Consumer.*
Former titles (until 1996): Frommer's Comprehensive Travel Guide. Canada (1064-3443); (until 1993): Frommer's Canada (1044-2251); (until 1990): Frommer's Dollarwise Guide to Canada (1042-8313); (until 1983): Arthur Frommer's Dollarwise Guide to Canada
Published by: Frommer Books (Subsidiary of: John Wiley & Sons, Inc.), 111 River St, 5th Fl, Hoboken, NJ 07030. TEL 201-748-6000, FAX 201-748-6088, info@frommers.biz.

914.6 USA ISSN 1064-3427
DP402.B24
FROMMER'S COMPREHENSIVE TRAVEL GUIDE. BARCELONA. Variant title: Frommer's Barcelona. Text in English. 1990. biennial. USD 17.99 per issue (effective 2011). adv. **Document type:** *Handbook/Manual/Guide, Consumer.* **Description:** Provides complete overview of insider knowledge on where and what to visit in this exciting Spanish city.
Formerly (until 1992): Frommer's Barcelona, plus Majorca, Ibiza, and Minorca (1045-9324)
Published by: Frommer Books (Subsidiary of: John Wiley & Sons, Inc.), 111 River St, 5th Fl, Hoboken, NJ 07030. TEL 201-748-6000, FAX 201-748-6088, info@frommers.biz.

916 USA ISSN 1053-2447
DT304
FROMMER'S COMPREHENSIVE TRAVEL GUIDE. MOROCCO. Variant title: Frommer's Morocco. Text in English. 1993. a. USD 24.99 per issue (effective 2011). adv. **Document type:** *Handbook/Manual/Guide, Consumer.*
Published by: Frommer Books (Subsidiary of: John Wiley & Sons, Inc.), 111 River St, 5th Fl, Hoboken, NJ 07030. TEL 201-748-6000, FAX 201-748-6088, info@frommers.biz.

910.91 USA ISSN 1935-2239
DR1509
FROMMER'S CROATIA. Text in English. 2006. irreg., latest 2010, 3rd ed. GBP 15.99, EUR 18.40, USD 21.99 per issue (effective 2010). adv. back issues avail.; reprints avail. **Document type:** *Guide, Consumer.* **Description:** Explores Croatia, gives an insider's look at everything from the country's famed beaches to it's less-traveled but equally stunning interior.
Published by: John Wiley & Sons, Inc., 111 River St, Hoboken, NJ 07030. TEL 201-748-6000, FAX 201-748-6088, info@wiley.com, http://www.wiley.com/WileyCDA/.

910.2 USA ISSN 1559-3797
G550
FROMMER'S CRUISES & PORTS OF CALL. Text in English. 2005. irreg., latest 2010. USD 24.99 per issue (effective 2010). adv. 735 p./no.; back issues avail.; reprints avail. **Document type:** *Guide, Consumer.* **Description:** Features photos of all the major ship classes that sail out of North American homeports.
Published by: John Wiley & Sons, Inc., 111 River St, Hoboken, NJ 07030. TEL 201-748-6000, FAX 201-748-6088, info@wiley.com, http://www.wiley.com/WileyCDA/.

917 USA ISSN 1534-9195
FROMMER'S DENVER, BOULDER & COLORADO SPRINGS. Text in English. 1990. a. USD 16.99 per issue (effective 2011). adv. back issues avail. **Document type:** *Handbook/Manual/Guide, Consumer.*
Former titles (until 1997): Frommer's Comprehensive Travel Guide. Denver, Boulder & Colorado Springs (1070-6410); (until 1993): Frommer's Denver, Boulder and Colorado Springs (1042-8763)
Published by: Frommer Books (Subsidiary of: John Wiley & Sons, Inc.), 111 River St, 5th Fl, Hoboken, NJ 07030. TEL 201-748-6000, FAX 201-748-6088, info@frommers.biz.

916.204 USA ISSN 1044-226X
DT45
FROMMER'S EGYPT. Text in English. 1982. biennial. USD 24.99 per issue (effective 2011). adv. back issues avail. **Document type:** *Handbook/Manual/Guide, Consumer.*
Formerly (until 1990): Frommer's Dollarwise Guide to Egypt (0731-4566)
Published by: Frommer Books (Subsidiary of: John Wiley & Sons, Inc.), 111 River St, 5th Fl, Hoboken, NJ 07030. TEL 201-748-6000, FAX 201-748-6088, info@frommers.biz.

917 USA ISSN 1534-8393
FROMMER'S FLORIDA. Text in English. 19??. a. USD 21.99 per issue (effective 2011). adv. back issues avail. **Document type:** *Handbook/Manual/Guide, Consumer.*
Former titles (until 1996): Frommer's Comprehensive Travel Guide. Florida (1057-2791); (until 1991): Frommer's Florida (1044-2391); (until 1990): Frommer's Dollarwise Guide to Florida (0732-0728)
Published by: Frommer Books (Subsidiary of: John Wiley & Sons, Inc.), 111 River St, 5th Fl, Hoboken, NJ 07030. TEL 201-748-6000, FAX 201-748-6088, info@frommers.biz.

914.3 USA ISSN 1094-0227
DD16
FROMMER'S GERMANY. Text in English. 19??. a. USD 24.99 per issue (effective 2011). adv. back issues avail. **Document type:** *Handbook/Manual/Guide, Consumer.*
Former titles (until 1996): Frommer's Comprehensive Travel Guide. Germany (1069-9031); (until 1991): Frommer's Germany (1044-2405); (until 1990): Frommer's Dollarwise Guide to Germany (0731-4442); (until 19??): Arthur Frommer's Dollarwise Guide to Germany (0272-0035)
Published by: Frommer Books (Subsidiary of: John Wiley & Sons, Inc.), 111 River St, 5th Fl, Hoboken, NJ 07030. TEL 201-748-6000, FAX 201-748-6088, info@frommers.biz.

914.509 USA ISSN 1529-6873
DG416
FROMMER'S ITALY. Text in English. 1982. a. USD 25.99 per issue (effective 2011). adv. back issues avail. **Document type:** *Handbook/Manual/Guide, Consumer.*
Former titles (until 1996): Frommer's Comprehensive Travel Guide. Italy (1529-6881); (until 1991): Frommer's Italy (1044-2170); (until 1990): Frommer's Dollarwise Italy (0899-336X); (until 1989): Frommer's Dollarwise Guide to Italy (0277-3244)
Published by: Frommer Books (Subsidiary of: John Wiley & Sons, Inc.), 111 River St, 5th Fl, Hoboken, NJ 07030. TEL 201-748-6000, FAX 201-748-6088, info@frommers.biz.

917.93 USA ISSN 2155-9198
F849.L35
FROMMER'S LAS VEGAS DAY BY DAY. Variant title: Las Vegas Day by Day. Text in English. 2008. a. USD 13.99 per issue (effective 2010). **Document type:** *Handbook/Manual/Guide, Consumer.* **Description:** Travel guide for the Las Vegas area.
Published by: John Wiley & Sons, Inc., 111 River St, Hoboken, NJ 07030. TEL 201-748-6000, FAX 201-748-5915, info@wiley.com, http://www.wiley.com/WileyCDA/.

910.2 USA ISSN 1544-0702
DA679
FROMMER'S LONDON WITH KIDS. Text in English. 2006. biennial. USD 17.99 per issue (effective 2010). adv. back issues avail.; reprints avail. **Document type:** *Guide, Consumer.*
Published by: John Wiley & Sons, Inc., 111 River St, Hoboken, NJ 07030. TEL 201-748-6000, FAX 201-748-6088, info@wiley.com, http://www.wiley.com/WileyCDA/.

917.2 USA ISSN 1933-0839
F1246
FROMMER'S LOS CABOS & BAJA. Text in English. 2006. irreg., latest 2009, 3rd ed. USD 17.99 per issue (effective 2010). adv. 214 p./no.; back issues avail.; reprints avail. **Document type:** *Guide, Consumer.* **Description:** Explores the craggy desert terrain of the Mid-Baja Peninsula.
Published by: John Wiley & Sons, Inc., 111 River St, Hoboken, NJ 07030. TEL 201-748-6000, FAX 201-748-6088, info@wiley.com, http://www.wiley.com/WileyCDA/.

914 USA ISSN 2153-8506
DG988.8
▼ **FROMMER'S MALTA & GOZO**; day by day. Text in English. 2009. irreg. USD 12.99 per issue (effective 2010). **Document type:** *Guide, Consumer.* **Description:** Tour guide for the islands of Malta and Gozo.
Published by: John Wiley & Sons, Inc., 111 River St, Hoboken, NJ 07030. TEL 201-748-6000, FAX 201-748-5915, info@wiley.com.

917.404 USA ISSN 1534-9055
F106
FROMMER'S MARYLAND & DELAWARE. Text in English. 1989. biennial. USD 18.99 per issue (effective 2011). adv. **Document type:** *Handbook/Manual/Guide, Consumer.*
Former titles (until 1996): Frommer's Comprehensive Travel Guide. Delaware & Maryland (1072-8015); (until 1995): Frommer's Comprehensive Travel Guide. Delaware, Maryland, Pennsylvania & the New Jersey Shore (1055-5382); (until 1993): Frommer's Mid-Atlantic States (1050-2939); (until 1991): Frommer's Dollarwise Guide to the Mid-Atlantic States, Including Pennsylvania, New Jersey, Delaware, Maryland, and Washington, D.C. (1042-8348)
Published by: Frommer Books (Subsidiary of: John Wiley & Sons, Inc.), 111 River St, 5th Fl, Hoboken, NJ 07030. TEL 201-748-6000, FAX 201-748-6088, info@frommers.biz.

910.91 USA ISSN 1935-2263
DK597
FROMMER'S MOSCOW & ST. PETERSBURG. Text in English. 2006. irreg., latest 2010, 3rd ed. USD 19.99 per issue (effective 2010). adv. back issues avail.; reprints avail. **Document type:** *Guide, Consumer.* **Description:** Offers authoritative, candid reviews that will help to find the choices that suit tastes and budget in Moscow & St. Petersburg.
Published by: John Wiley & Sons, Inc., 111 River St, Hoboken, NJ 07030. TEL 201-748-6000, FAX 201-748-6088, info@wiley.com, http://www.wiley.com/WileyCDA/.

917.3 USA ISSN 1935-2166
E160
FROMMER'S NATIONAL PARKS WITH KIDS. Text in English. 2006. irreg., latest 2008, 2nd ed. USD 21.99, GBP 14.99, EUR 14.70 per issue (effective 2010). adv. back issues avail.; reprints avail. **Document type:** *Guide, Consumer.* **Description:** Includes reviews of park lodges, camping, and nearby accommodations to help to plan all aspects of trip to all national parks.
Published by: John Wiley & Sons, Inc., 111 River St, Hoboken, NJ 07030. TEL 201-748-6000, FAX 201-748-6088, info@wiley.com.

917.404 USA
F2.3
FROMMER'S NEW ENGLAND. Text in English. 1978. biennial. USD 21.99 per issue (effective 2011). adv. back issues avail. **Document type:** *Handbook/Manual/Guide, Consumer.*
Former titles (until 1996): Frommer's Comprehensive Travel Guide. New England (1056-5787); (until 1991): Frommer's New England (1044-2286); (until 1990): Frommer's Dollarwise Guide to New England (0732-4871)
Published by: Frommer Books (Subsidiary of: John Wiley & Sons, Inc.), 111 River St, 5th Fl, Hoboken, NJ 07030. TEL 201-748-6000, FAX 201-748-6088, info@frommers.biz.

917.94 USA ISSN 1092-4477
F379.N53
FROMMER'S NEW ORLEANS. Text in English. 1982. a. USD 19.99 per issue (effective 2011). adv. back issues avail. **Document type:** *Handbook/Manual/Guide, Consumer.*
Former titles (until 1996): Frommer's Comprehensive Travel Guide. New Orleans (1057-7645); (until 1991): Frommer's New Orleans (0899-2908); (until 1990): Frommer's Guide to New Orleans (0277-4410)
Published by: Frommer Books (Subsidiary of: John Wiley & Sons, Inc.), 111 River St, 5th Fl, Hoboken, NJ 07030. TEL 201-748-6000, FAX 201-748-6088, info@frommers.biz.

917.404 USA ISSN 1544-0656
F117.3
FROMMER'S NEW YORK STATE. Text in English. 1989. biennial. USD 21.99 per issue (effective 2011). adv. back issues avail. **Document type:** *Handbook/Manual/Guide, Consumer.*
Former titles (until 2004): Frommer's Comprehensive Travel Guide. New York State (1064-5276); (until 1993): Frommer's New York State (1044-2308); (until 1991): Frommer's Dollarwise Guide to New York State (1042-8321)
Published by: Frommer Books (Subsidiary of: John Wiley & Sons, Inc.), 111 River St, 5th Fl, Hoboken, NJ 07030. TEL 201-748-6000, FAX 201-748-6088, info@frommers.biz.

944 USA ISSN 0899-3203
DC708
FROMMER'S PARIS. Text in English. 1982. a. USD 19.99 per issue (effective 2011). adv. back issues avail. **Document type:** *Handbook/Manual/Guide, Consumer.* **Description:** Informs readers of attractions, lodging and restaurants in the French capital.
Formerly (until 1990): Frommer's Guide to Paris (0277-3309)
Published by: Frommer Books (Subsidiary of: John Wiley & Sons, Inc.), 111 River St, 5th Fl, Hoboken, NJ 07030. TEL 201-748-6000, FAX 201-748-6088, info@frommers.biz.

917.296 USA ISSN 1940-4514
F1659.T9
FROMMER'S PORTABLE TURKS & CAICOS. Text in English. 2007. irreg., latest 2010, 3rd ed. USD 12.99 per issue (effective 2010). adv. back issues avail.; reprints avail. **Document type:** *Guide, Consumer.*
Published by: John Wiley & Sons, Inc., 111 River St, Hoboken, NJ 07030. TEL 201-748-6000, FAX 201-748-6088, info@wiley.com, http://www.wiley.com/WileyCDA/.

917.94 USA ISSN 1533-9777
F869.S33
FROMMER'S SAN FRANCISCO. Text in English. 19??. a. USD 19.99 per issue (effective 2011). adv. back issues avail. **Document type:** *Handbook/Manual/Guide, Consumer.*
Former titles (until 1996): Frommer's Comprehensive Travel Guide. San Francisco (1057-3399); (until 1991): Frommer's San Francisco (0899-3254); (until 1990): Frommer's Guide to San Francisco (0277-4429); (until 1982): Arthur Frommer's Guide to San Francisco
Published by: Frommer Books (Subsidiary of: John Wiley & Sons, Inc.), 111 River St, 5th Fl, Hoboken, NJ 07030. TEL 201-748-6000, FAX 201-748-6088, info@frommers.biz.

914 USA ISSN 1533-8045
DA650
FROMMER'S SCOTLAND. Text in English. 19??. a. USD 21.99 per issue (effective 2011). **Document type:** *Handbook/Manual/Guide, Consumer.* **Description:** Features gorgeous color photos of the quaint villages, misty moors, and offshore islands in Scotland.
Formerly (until 1996): Frommer's Comprehensive Travel Guide. Scotland (1055-5390); Which superseded in part (in 1993): Frommer's Comprehensive Travel Guide. England & Scotland (1057-4026); Which was formerly (until 1991): Frommer's England and Scotland (1044-2359); (until 1990): Frommer's Dollarwise Guide to England and Scotland (0276-8674)
Published by: Frommer Books (Subsidiary of: John Wiley & Sons, Inc.), 111 River St, 5th Fl, Hoboken, NJ 07030. TEL 201-748-6000, FAX 201-748-6088, info@frommers.biz.

917.104 USA ISSN 1534-3332
F1089.5.V22
FROMMER'S VANCOUVER AND VICTORIA. Text in English. 1990. a. USD 17.99 per issue (effective 2011). adv. back issues avail. **Document type:** *Handbook/Manual/Guide, Consumer.*
Former titles (until 1996): Frommer's Comprehensive Travel Guide. Vancouver & Victoria (1092-3500); (until 1994): Frommer's Vancouver and Victoria (1045-9316)
Published by: Frommer Books (Subsidiary of: John Wiley & Sons, Inc.), 111 River St, 5th Fl, Hoboken, NJ 07030. TEL 201-748-6000, FAX 201-748-6088, info@frommers.biz.

914.36 USA ISSN 2153-9820
DB849
▼ **FROMMER'S VIENNA: DAY BY DAY.** Text in English. 2009. irreg. USD 12.99 per issue (effective 2010). **Document type:** *Guide, Consumer.* **Description:** Tour guide for Vienna, Austria.
Published by: John Wiley & Sons, Inc., 111 River St, Hoboken, NJ 07030. info@wiley.com, http://www.wiley.com/WileyCDA/.

915.97 USA ISSN 1935-2247
DS556.25
FROMMER'S VIETNAM. Text in English. 2006. irreg., latest 2010, 3rd ed. USD 22.99 per issue (effective 2010). adv. back issues avail.; reprints avail. **Document type:** *Guide, Consumer.* **Description:** Gives all the details on the latest happenings in Vietnam.
Published by: John Wiley & Sons, Inc., 111 River St, Hoboken, NJ 07030. TEL 201-748-6000, FAX 201-748-6088, info@wiley.com, http://www.wiley.com/WileyCDA/.

919.704 USA
F2136.2
FROMMER'S VIRGIN ISLANDS. Text in English. 1993. biennial. USD 17.99 per issue (effective 2011). adv. back issues avail. **Document type:** *Handbook/Manual/Guide, Consumer.*
Formerly (until 1995): Frommer's Comprehensive Travel Guide. The Virgin Islands (1055-5447)
Published by: Frommer Books (Subsidiary of: John Wiley & Sons, Inc.), 111 River St, 5th Fl, Hoboken, NJ 07030. TEL 201-748-6000, FAX 201-748-6088, info@frommers.biz.

917.504 USA
F207.3
FROMMER'S VIRGINIA. Text in English. 19??. biennial. USD 18.99 per issue (effective 2011). adv. **Document type:** *Handbook/Manual/Guide, Consumer.*
Formerly (until 1996): Frommer's Comprehensive Travel Guide. Virginia (1058-4943); Which superseded in part (in 1993): Frommer's Southern Atlantic States (1044-2316); Which was formerly (until 1991): Frommer's Dollarwise Guide to the Southeast and New Orleans (0731-8588); (until 19??): Arthur Frommer's Dollarwise Guide to the Southeast and New Orleans (0731-857X)
Published by: Frommer Books (Subsidiary of: John Wiley & Sons, Inc.), 111 River St, 5th Fl, Hoboken, NJ 07030. TEL 201-748-6000, FAX 201-748-6088, info@frommers.biz.

910.2 USA ISSN 1559-3835
GV1853.3.F62
FROMMER'S WALT DISNEY WORLD & ORLANDO WITH KIDS. Text in English. 2004. irreg., latest 2010, 4th ed. USD 17.99 per issue (effective 2010). adv. back issues avail.; reprints avail. **Document type:** *Guide, Consumer.* **Description:** Offers the lowdown on all the major theme parks in Orlando and rates all attractions on their suitability for kids of all ages.
Published by: John Wiley & Sons, Inc., 111 River St, Hoboken, NJ 07030. TEL 201-748-6000, FAX 201-748-6088, info@wiley.com, http://www.wiley.com/WileyCDA/.

FRONTIER; the busniess magazine for travel retail. *see* BUSINESS AND ECONOMICS

917.91 910.2 USA ISSN 1545-6498
F809.3
FUN WITH THE FAMILY ARIZONA; hundreds of ideas for day trips with the kids. Text in English. 2002. biennial, latest 2006, 3rd ed. USD 12.95 per issue (effective 2008). back issues avail. **Document type:** *Guide, Consumer.* **Description:** Provides information about amusement parks, historical attractions, children's museums, wildlife habitats, festivals, parks and much more in Arizona.
Published by: The Globe Pequot Press, Inc., 246 Goose Ln, PO Box 480, Guilford, CT 06437. TEL 203-458-4500, 888-249-7586, FAX 203-458-4603, 800-820-2329, info@globepequot.com, http://www.globepequot.com.

917.46 910.2 USA ISSN 1540-2169
F92.3
FUN WITH THE FAMILY IN CONNECTICUT; hundreds of ideas for daytrips with the kids. Text in English. 199?. biennial, latest 2008, 7th ed. USD 13.95 per issue (effective 2008). **Document type:** *Guide, Consumer.*
Formerly: Connecticut
Published by: The Globe Pequot Press, Inc., 246 Goose Ln, PO Box 480, Guilford, CT 06437. TEL 203-458-4500, 888-249-7586, FAX 203-458-4603, 800-820-2329, info@globepequot.com, http://www.globepequot.com.

917.59 USA ISSN 1537-0518
F309.3
FUN WITH THE FAMILY IN FLORIDA; hundreds of ideas for day trips with the kids. Text in English. 1999. triennial, latest 2008, 6th ed. USD 13.95 per issue (effective 2008). back issues avail. **Document type:** *Guide, Consumer.* **Description:** Provides information about amusement parks, historical attractions, children's museums, wildlife habitats, festivals, parks and much more in Florida.
Published by: The Globe Pequot Press, Inc., 246 Goose Ln, PO Box 480, Guilford, CT 06437. TEL 203-458-4500, 888-249-7586, FAX 800-820-2329, info@globepequot.com, http://www.globepequot.com.

TU

919.69 910.91 USA ISSN 1541-8944
DU622
FUN WITH THE FAMILY IN HAWAII; hundreds of ideas for day trips with the kids. Text in English. 1997. triennial, latest 2008, 7th ed. USD 13.95 per issue (effective 2008). back issues avail. **Document type:** *Guide, Consumer.* **Description:** Provides information about amusement parks, historical attractions, children's museums, wildlife habitats, festivals, parks and much more in Hawaii.
Published by: The Globe Pequot Press, Inc., 246 Goose Ln, PO Box 480, Guilford, CT 06437. TEL 203-458-4500, 888-249-7586, FAX 203-458-4603, 800-820-2329, info@globepequot.com, http://www.globepequot.com.

917.73 USA ISSN 1546-3303
F539.3
FUN WITH THE FAMILY IN ILLINOIS; hundreds of ideas for day trips with the kids. Text in English. 1996. irreg., latest 2008, 6th ed. USD 13.95 per issue (effective 2008). **Document type:** *Guide, Consumer.* **Description:** Provides information on way to amusement parks, historical attractions, children's museums, wildlife habitats, festivals, parks.
Published by: The Globe Pequot Press, Inc., 246 Goose Ln, PO Box 480, Guilford, CT 06437. TEL 203-458-4500, 888-249-7586, FAX 203-458-4603, 800-820-2329, info@globepequot.com, http://www.globepequot.com.

917.72 USA ISSN 1540-1510
F524.3
FUN WITH THE FAMILY IN INDIANA; hundreds of ideas for day trips with the kids. Text in English. 1998. biennial, latest 2004, 5th ed. USD 12.95 per issue (effective 2008). **Document type:** *Guide, Consumer.* **Description:** Contains information on all family-friendly fun to be had in the Hoosier State.
Published by: The Globe Pequot Press, Inc., 246 Goose Ln, PO Box 480, Guilford, CT 06437. TEL 203-458-4500, 888-249-7586, FAX 203-458-4603, 800-820-2329, info@globepequot.com, http://www.globepequot.com.

917.77 910.2 USA ISSN 1542-6289
F619.3
FUN WITH THE FAMILY IN IOWA; hundreds of ideas for day trips with the kids. Text in English. 2003. irreg., latest 2003, 1st ed. USD 12.95 per issue (effective 2008). 232 p./no.; **Document type:** *Guide, Consumer.* **Description:** Provides information on day trips with kids in Iowa.
Published by: The Globe Pequot Press, Inc., 246 Goose Ln, PO Box 480, Guilford, CT 06437. TEL 203-458-4500, 888-249-7586, FAX 203-458-4603, 800-820-2329, info@globepequot.com, http://www.globepequot.com.

917.69 910.2 USA ISSN 1542-1783
F449.3
FUN WITH THE FAMILY IN KENTUCKY; hundreds of ideas for day trips with the kids. Text in English. 2003. biennial, latest 2007, 3rd ed. USD 13.95 per issue (effective 2008). **Document type:** *Guide, Consumer.* **Description:** Contains information on ways to amusement parks, water adventures, recreation trails, zoos, children's museums, festivals, performing arts, and much more.
Published by: The Globe Pequot Press, Inc., 246 Goose Ln, PO Box 480, Guilford, CT 06437. TEL 203-458-4500, 888-249-7586, FAX 203-458-4603, 800-820-2329, info@globepequot.com, http://www.globepequot.com.

917.93 790.1 USA ISSN 1536-9013
F839.3
FUN WITH THE FAMILY IN LAS VEGAS; hundreds of ideas for day trips with the kids. Text in English. 2002. biennial, latest 2007, 4th ed. USD 13.95 per issue (effective 2008). back issues avail. **Document type:** *Guide, Consumer.* **Description:** Contains hundreds of ideas to keep the kids entertained for an hour, a day, or a weekend.
Published by: The Globe Pequot Press, Inc., 246 Goose Ln, PO Box 480, Guilford, CT 06437. TEL 203-458-4500, 888-249-7586, FAX 203-458-4603, 800-820-2329, info@globepequot.com, http://www.globepequot.com.

917.41 790.1 USA ISSN 1536-6162
F17.3
FUN WITH THE FAMILY IN MAINE; hundreds of ideas for day trips with the kids. Text in English. 2000. biennial, latest 2007, 5th ed. USD 13.95 per issue (effective 2008). back issues avail. **Document type:** *Guide, Consumer.* **Description:** Contains hundreds of ideas to keep the kids entertained for an hour, a day, or a weekend.
Published by: The Globe Pequot Press, Inc., 246 Goose Ln, PO Box 480, Guilford, CT 06437. TEL 203-458-4500, 888-249-7586, FAX 203-458-4603, 800-820-2329, info@globepequot.com, http://www.globepequot.com.

917.52 910.2 USA ISSN 1548-4203
F179.3
FUN WITH THE FAMILY IN MARYLAND; hundreds of ideas for day trips with the kids. Text in English. 2004. irreg., latest 2001, 1st ed. USD 12.95 per issue (effective 2008). **Document type:** *Guide, Consumer.* **Description:** Covers information on Maryland's family attractions.
Published by: The Globe Pequot Press, Inc., 246 Goose Ln, PO Box 480, Guilford, CT 06437. TEL 203-458-4500, 888-249-7586, FAX 203-458-4603, 800-820-2329, info@globepequot.com, http://www.globepequot.com.

917.44 790.1 USA ISSN 1537-291X
F62.3
FUN WITH THE FAMILY IN MASSACHUSETTS; hundreds of ideas for day trips with the kids. Text in English. 1998. biennial, latest 2008, 6th ed. USD 13.95 per issue (effective 2008). back issues avail. **Document type:** *Guide, Consumer.* **Description:** Contains hundreds of ideas to keep the kids entertained for an hour, a day, or a weekend.
Published by: The Globe Pequot Press, Inc., 246 Goose Ln, PO Box 480, Guilford, CT 06437. TEL 203-458-4500, 888-249-7586, FAX 203-458-4603, 800-820-2329, http://www.globepequot.com.

917.78 USA ISSN 1535-8100
F464.3
FUN WITH THE FAMILY IN MISSOURI; hundreds of ideas for day trips with the kids. Text in English. 1999. irreg., latest 2004, 4th ed. USD 12.95 per issue (effective 2008). **Document type:** *Guide, Consumer.* **Description:** Contains hundreds of ideas to keep the kids entertained for an hour, a day, or a weekend.
Published by: The Globe Pequot Press, Inc., 246 Goose Ln, PO Box 480, Guilford, CT 06437. TEL 203-458-4500, 888-249-7586, FAX 203-458-4603, 800-820-2329, info@globepequot.com, http://www.globepequot.com.

917.49 USA ISSN 1543-9011
FUN WITH THE FAMILY IN NEW JERSEY; hundreds of ideas for day trips with the kids. Text in English. 2003. biennial. USD 13.95 per issue (effective 2008). **Document type:** *Guide, Consumer.*
Published by: The Globe Pequot Press, Inc., 246 Goose Ln, PO Box 480, Guilford, CT 06437. TEL 203-458-4500, 888-249-7586, FAX 203-458-4601, 800-820-2329, info@globepequot.com, http://www.globepequot.com. Ed. Amy Lyons TEL 203-458-4500.

917.89 USA ISSN 1545-7621
F794.3
FUN WITH THE FAMILY IN NEW MEXICO. Text in English. irreg., latest 2005, 4th ed. USD 12.95 per issue (effective 2008). **Document type:** *Magazine, Consumer.* **Description:** Provides information on way to pueblos, ski slopes, children's museums, zoos, festivals, parks and wildlife refuges.
Formerly: Family Adventure Guide. New Mexico
Published by: The Globe Pequot Press, Inc., 246 Goose Ln, PO Box 480, Guilford, CT 06437. TEL 203-458-4500, 888-249-7586, FAX 203-458-4603, 800-820-2329, info@globepequot.com, http://www.globepequot.com.

917.56 910.2 USA ISSN 1539-9044
F252.3
FUN WITH THE FAMILY IN NORTH CAROLINA; hundreds of ideas for day trips with the kids. Text in English. 1997. biennial, latest 2007, 6th ed. USD 13.95 per issue (effective 2008). **Document type:** *Guide, Consumer.* **Description:** Covers family fun in North Carolina.
Published by: The Globe Pequot Press, Inc., 246 Goose Ln, PO Box 480, Guilford, CT 06437. TEL 203-458-4500, 888-249-7586, FAX 203-458-4603, 800-820-2329, info@globepequot.com, http://www.globepequot.com.

917.94 910.2 USA ISSN 1540-305X
F867.5
FUN WITH THE FAMILY IN NORTHERN CALIFORNIA; hundreds of ideas for daytrips with the kids. Text in English. 1996. biennial, latest 2006, 6th ed. USD 13.95 per issue (effective 2008). **Document type:** *Guide, Consumer.*
Formerly: Northern California: Family Adventure Guide
Published by: The Globe Pequot Press, Inc., 246 Goose Ln, PO Box 480, Guilford, CT 06437. TEL 203-458-4500, 888-249-7586, FAX 203-458-4603, 800-820-2329, info@globepequot.com, http://www.globepequot.com.

917.68 910.2 USA ISSN 1537-3525
F434.3
FUN WITH THE FAMILY IN TENNESSEE; hundreds of ideas for day trips with the kids. Text in English. irreg., latest 2004, 4th ed. USD 12.95 per issue (effective 2008). **Document type:** *Guide, Consumer.* **Description:** Covers family fun in Tennessee.
Formerly: Tennessee Family Adventure Guide
Published by: The Globe Pequot Press, Inc., 246 Goose Ln, PO Box 480, Guilford, CT 06437. TEL 203-458-4500, 888-249-7586, FAX 203-458-4603, 800-820-2329, info@globepequot.com, http://www.globepequot.com.

917.47 USA ISSN 2155-5524
▼ **FUN WITH THE FAMILY METRO NEW YORK**; hundreds of ideas for day trips with the kids. Text in English. 2010 (Jun.). triennial. USD 14.95 per issue (effective 2011). **Document type:** *Guide, Consumer.* **Description:** Day trip ideas for families in the New York metropolitan area.
Published by: The Globe Pequot Press, Inc., 246 Goose Ln, PO Box 480, Guilford, CT 06437. TEL 203-458-4500, FAX 203-458-4603, info@globepequot.com.

917.47 910.91 USA
F128.18
FUN WITH THE FAMILY NEW YORK; hundreds of ideas for day trips with the kids. Text in English. 1997. biennial, latest 2007, 6th ed. USD 13.95 per issue (effective 2008). back issues avail. **Document type:** *Guide, Consumer.* **Description:** Provides information about amusement parks, historical attractions, children's museums, wildlife habitats, festivals, parks and much more in New York.
Formerly: Fun with the Family in New York (1542-4189)
Published by: The Globe Pequot Press, Inc., 246 Goose Ln, PO Box 480, Guilford, CT 06437. TEL 203-458-4500, 888-249-7586, FAX 203-458-4603, 800-820-2329, info@globepequot.com, http://www.globepequot.com.

917.95 USA
F874.3
FUN WITH THE FAMILY OREGON; hundreds of ideas for day trips with the kids. Text in English. 1995. biennial, latest 2007, 5th ed. USD 13.95 per issue (effective 2008). **Document type:** *Magazine, Consumer.* **Description:** Provides information on way to amusement parks, historical attractions, children's museums, wildlife habitats, festivals, parks.
Formerly: Fun with the Family in Oregon (1539-3569)
Published by: The Globe Pequot Press, Inc., 246 Goose Ln, PO Box 480, Guilford, CT 06437. TEL 203-458-4500, 888-249-7586, FAX 203-458-4603, 800-820-2329, info@globepequot.com, http://www.globepequot.com.

917.48 910.2 USA ISSN 1539-8730
F147.3
FUN WITH THE FAMILY PENNSYLVANIA; hundreds of ideas for day trips with the kids. Text in English. 1998. irreg., latest 2007, 6th ed. USD 13.95 per issue (effective 2008). back issues avail. **Document type:** *Magazine, Consumer.* **Description:** Provides information about day trips with the kids in Pennsylvania.
Formerly: Family Adventure Guide. Pennsylvania
Published by: The Globe Pequot Press, Inc., 246 Goose Ln, PO Box 480, Guilford, CT 06437. TEL 203-458-4500, 888-249-7586, FAX 203-458-4603, 800-820-2329, info@globepequot.com, http://www.globepequot.com.

917.949 790.1 USA
F867
FUN WITH THE FAMILY SOUTHERN CALIFORNIA; including channel islands vational park. Text in English. 1998. biennial, latest 2007, 6th ed. USD 13.95 per issue (effective 2008). **Document type:** *Guide, Consumer.* **Description:** Contains information on ways to amusement parks, water adventures, recreation trails, zoos, children's museums, festivals, performing arts, and much more.
Formerly: Fun with the Family in Southern California (1541-8952)
Published by: The Globe Pequot Press, Inc., 246 Goose Ln, PO Box 480, Guilford, CT 06437. TEL 203-458-4500, 888-249-7586, FAX 203-458-4603, 800-820-2329, info@globepequot.com, http://www.globepequot.com.

917.64 910.2 USA ISSN 1542-2313
F384.3
FUN WITH THE FAMILY TEXAS; hundreds of ideas for day trips with the kids. Text in English. 1997. biennial, latest 2006, 5th ed. USD 13.95 per issue (effective 2008). **Document type:** *Magazine, Consumer.* **Description:** Contains information on ways to amusement parks, water adventures, recreation trails, zoos, children's museums, festivals, performing arts, and much more.
Formerly (until 1997): Fun with the Family in Texas
Published by: The Globe Pequot Press, Inc., 246 Goose Ln, PO Box 480, Guilford, CT 06437. TEL 203-458-4500, 888-249-7586, FAX 203-458-4603, 800-820-2329, info@globepequot.com, http://www.globepequot.com.

917.47 USA ISSN 2155-5575
F128.18
▼ **FUN WITH THE FAMILY UPSTATE NEW YORK**; Hundreds of Ideas for Day Trips with the Kids. Text in English. 2010 (June). triennial. USD 14.95 per issue (effective 2011). **Document type:** *Guide, Consumer.* **Description:** Day trips for families in upstate New York.
Published by: The Globe Pequot Press, Inc., 246 Goose Ln, PO Box 480, Guilford, CT 06437. TEL 203-458-4500, 888-249-7586, FAX 203-458-4603, 800-820-2329, info@globepequot.com, http://www.globepequot.com.

917.92 910.2 USA
F824.3
FUN WITH THE FAMILY UTAH; hundreds of ideas for daytrips with the kids. Text in English. 1997. biennial, latest 2004, 4th ed. USD 12.95 per issue (effective 2008). **Document type:** *Guide, Consumer.* **Description:** Provides the information on all the family-friendly fun to be had in the land of the Great Salt Lake.
Former titles: Fun with the Family in Utah (1540-2150); Utah
Published by: The Globe Pequot Press, Inc., 246 Goose Ln, PO Box 480, Guilford, CT 06437. TEL 203-458-4500, 888-249-7586, FAX 203-458-4603, 800-820-2329, info@globepequot.com, http://www.globepequot.com.

917.4 USA
F47.3
FUN WITH THE FAMILY VERMONT AND NEW HAMPSHIRE; hundreds of ideas for day trips with the kids. Text in English. 2001. biennial (Every 2-3/yrs.). USD 12.95 per issue (effective 2008). **Document type:** *Magazine, Consumer.* **Description:** Provides information on way to amusement parks, historical attractions, children's museums, wildlife habitats, festivals, parks.
Formerly: Fun with the Family in Vermont and New Hampshire (1547-6804)
Published by: The Globe Pequot Press, Inc., 246 Goose Ln, PO Box 480, Guilford, CT 06437. TEL 203-458-4500, 888-249-7586, FAX 203-458-4603, 800-820-2329, info@globepequot.com, http://www.globepequot.com.

917.55 790.1 USA ISSN 1540-4366
F224.3
FUN WITH THE FAMILY VIRGINIA; hundreds of ideas for day trips with the kids. Text in English. 1990. biennial, latest 2008, 7th ed. USD 12.95 per issue (effective 2008). back issues avail. **Document type:** *Guide, Consumer.* **Description:** Contains information on amusement parks, water adventures, recreation trails, zoos, children's museums, festivals, performing arts, and much more.
Published by: The Globe Pequot Press, Inc., 246 Goose Ln, PO Box 480, Guilford, CT 06437. TEL 203-458-4500, 888-249-7586, FAX 203-458-4603, 800-820-2329, info@globepequot.com, http://www.globepequot.com.

FUN WITH THE FAMILY WISCONSIN. *see* LEISURE AND RECREATION

910.91 790.1 USA
G O R P TRAVEL NEWSLETTER. Text in English. m. **Document type:** *Newsletter, Consumer.*
Media: Online - full content.
Published by: G O R P, Inc., 22 W 19th St, 8th Fl, New York, NY 10011. TEL 212-675-8114, boettel@gorp.com, http://www.gorp.com. Ed. Bryan Oettel.

910.4 ZAF
THE G S A TRAVEL AGENTS' SALES GUIDE. Text in English. 1980. m. ZAR 35 per issue (effective 2000). adv. back issues avail. **Document type:** *Handbook/Manual/Guide, Trade.* **Description:** Provides comprehensive coverage of the South African travel industry.
Former titles (until vol.14, no.10, 1993): G S A Travel Marketing Magazine; (until 1983): G S A
Published by: G S A Marketing Pty. Ltd., PO Box 3239, Cape Town, 8000, South Africa. TEL 27-21-4191671, FAX 27-21-4194851, theqsa@icon.co.za, http://www.the-gas.co.za. Ed. Jeff Hawthorne. Circ: 5,200.

910.91 CAN
G S A TRAVEL MAGAZINE. Text in English. 1995. bi-w. **Document type:** *Magazine, Trade.*
Published by: G S A Publishing Group, 209-1015 Burrand St, Vancouver, BC V6Z 1Y5, Canada. TEL 604-689-2909, FAX 604-689-2989, editors@gsapublishing.com. Ed. Lynda Cumming.

910.4 MNG
GAL/FIRE. Text in Mongol. 1991. bi-m. **Description:** Covers non-political, cultural affairs.
Published by: Mongolian Cultural Foundation, PO Box 527, Ulan Bator, Mongolia. TEL 210611. Ed. Y Baatar.

914.83 NOR ISSN 0333-0869
DL596.V6
GAMALT FRAA VOSS. Text in Norwegian. 1969. a. NOK 200 per issue (effective 2006). **Document type:** *Yearbook.*
Indexed: RILM.
Published by: Voss Folkemuseum, Moelstervegen 143, Skulestadmo, 5710, Norway. TEL 47-56-511511, FAX 47-56-518815, voss.museum@c2i.net, http://home.c2i.net/voss-folkemuseum/index.html.

GAMBIA. CENTRAL STATISTICS DEPARTMENT. TOURIST STATISTICS. *see* TRAVEL AND TOURISM—Abstracting, Bibliographies, Statistics

910.202 664 641.5 CHE
GASTRONOMIE & TOURISME. Text and summaries in French, German, Italian. 1973. bi-m. CHF 52; CHF 80 foreign (effective 1998). **Document type:** *Trade.* **Description:** Covers international tourism and gastronomy.
Published by: Gastronomie & Tourisme SA, Case Postale 231, Lugano-Pregassona, 6963, Switzerland. TEL 41-91-9413828, FAX 41-91-9413825. Ed. Alberto Dell'Acqua. Circ: 20,000.

GASTROTOUR; gastronomie & tourisme. *see* HOME ECONOMICS

919.89 NZL ISSN 1177-0481
GATEWAY ANTARCTICA SPECIAL PUBLICATION SERIES. Text in English. 2005. irreg. price varies. **Document type:** *Monographic series, Academic/Scholarly.*
Published by: University of Canterbury, Centre for Antarctic Studies and Research, Gateway Antarctica, Private Bag 4800, Christchurch, New Zealand. TEL 64-3-3642136, FAX 64-3-3642197, gateway-antarctica@canterbury.ac.nz.

917 MEX ISSN 0016-5379
GAZER/MIRON. Text in Spanish. 1950. w. USD 30. adv. charts; illus.; stat. **Document type:** *Magazine, Consumer.* **Description:** Description and travel information on Mexico.
Published by: Editorial Monex S. de R.L. y C.V., Ave. Insurgentes Centro 132-204, Mexico City, DF 06030, Mexico. Ed. Raul Esquivel. Pub. Judith Esquivel. Circ: 25,000.

914 FRA ISSN 0016-5573
LA GAZETTE OFFICIELLE DU TOURISME; bulletin d'information et de documentation sur le tourisme. Text in French. w. EUR 260 domestic; EUR 285 foreign; EUR 155 to students (effective 2009). adv. **Document type:** *Newsletter, Trade.*
Indexed: RASB.
Published by: Office des Nouvelles Internationales, Zi Maysonnabe, 18, Allee Marie Politzer, Biarritz, 64200, France. TEL 33-5-5952-8400, FAX 33-5-5952-8401. Ed. Marie Pierre Bazin. Pub. Jacques Darrigrand. Adv. contact Nathalie Hutjens.

914.3804 POL
GDANSK IN YOUR POCKET. Text in English. 3/yr. USD 5 newsstand/cover (effective 2002). adv. **Document type:** *Magazine, Consumer.*
Address: ul. Heweliusza 11-818, Gdansk, 80890, Poland. TEL 48-58-3218161, FAX 48-58-3218161, http://www.inyourpocket.com.

910 ISR ISSN 1527-9812
GEMS IN ISRAEL. Text in English. 1999. bi-m. free (effective 2008). back issues avail. **Description:** Travel resource spotlighting Israel's lesser known gems.
Media: Online - full text.
Published by: Yael Zisling Marketing and Public Relations, PO Box 217, Gilboa, 18120, Israel. TEL 972-54-461-7677, 617-848-2011, gems@gemsinisrael.com. Pub. Yael Zisling Adar. Circ: 3,000.

910.91 USA
GENERAL STORE MAGAZINE. Text in English. 2000. q. USD 3.95 newsstand/cover (effective 2001). **Document type:** *Magazine, Consumer.*
Published by: Barley Sheaf & York, Inc., 246 Lyons Rd., Basking Ridge, NJ 07920. TEL 908-542-0873, FAX 908-542-0874, http://www.iGeneralStore.com. Ed., Pub. Lawrence E Bataille.

910.2 USA
GENEVA LAKES AREA VISITORS GUIDE. Text in English. a. free (effective 2009). **Document type:** *Magazine, Consumer.* **Description:** Features lodging, dining, shopping, and recreation options in the Geneva Lakes area.
Related titles: Online - full text ed.
Published by: Nei-Turner Media Group, 93 W Geneva St, PO Box 1080, Williams Bay, WI 53191. TEL 262-245-1000, 800-386-3228, FAX 262-245-2000, info@ntmediagroup.com. Ed. Sarah Hoke TEL 800-386-3228 ext 109. Pub. Gary Nei. Circ: 50,000 (free).

GENIETEN. *see* LIFESTYLE

910.09 ITA ISSN 0393-7895
GENTE VIAGGI. Text in Italian. 1979. m. adv. **Document type:** *Magazine, Consumer.*
Related titles: ◆ Supplement(s): Gente Viaggi Collection. ISSN 1720-1624.
Published by: Hachette Rusconi SpA (Subsidiary of: Hachette Filipacchi Medias S.A.), Viale Sarca 235, Milan, 20126, Italy. TEL 39-02-66192629, FAX 39-02-66192469, dirgen@rusconi.it, http://portale.hachettepubblicita.it. Ed. Giancarlo Pini. Adv. contact Eduardo Giliberti.

910.09 ITA ISSN 1720-1624
GENTE VIAGGI COLLECTION. Text in Italian. 2002. 2/yr. adv. **Document type:** *Magazine, Consumer.*
Related titles: ◆ Supplement to: Gente Viaggi. ISSN 0393-7895.
Published by: Hachette Rusconi SpA (Subsidiary of: Hachette Filipacchi Medias S.A.), Viale Sarca 235, Milan, 20126, Italy. TEL 39-02-66192629, FAX 39-02-66192469, dirgen@rusconi.it, http://portale.hachettepubblicita.it. adv.: page EUR 25,000; trim 167 x 224. Circ: 66,785 (controlled).

GEO. *see* ENVIRONMENTAL STUDIES

GEO; das neue Bild der Erde. *see* ENVIRONMENTAL STUDIES

GEO. *see* GEOGRAPHY

GEO. *see* GEOGRAPHY

GEO. *see* GEOGRAPHY

GEO. *see* GEOGRAPHY

GEO. *see* GEOGRAPHY

GEO. *see* GEOGRAPHY

GEO. *see* GEOGRAPHY

GEO; un nouveau monde: la terre. *see* GEOGRAPHY

910.91 SVN ISSN 1854-4479
GEO. Text in Slovenian. 2006. s-a. adv. **Document type:** *Magazine, Consumer.*
Published by: Adria Media Ljubljana, Zaloznistvo in Trzenje, d.o.o., Vosnjakova ulica 3, Ljubljana, 1000, Slovenia. TEL 386-1-3000700, FAX 386-1-3000713, info@adriamedia.si, http://www.adriamedia.si. Ed. Tadej Golob. adv.: page EUR 1,800; trim 213 x 270. Circ: 6,465 (paid).

GEO FOCUS. *see* GEOGRAPHY

910.202 DEU ISSN 0946-8773
GEO SAISON. Text in German. 1989. m. EUR 52.80; EUR 5 newsstand/cover (effective 2010). adv. **Document type:** *Magazine, Consumer.*
Formerly (until 1994): Saison (0936-7756)
Published by: Gruner + Jahr AG & Co, Am Baumwall 11, Hamburg, 20459, Germany. TEL 49-40-37030, FAX 49-40-37035601, info@gujmedia.de, http://www.guj.de. Adv. contact Korinna Koschek. color page EUR 16,200. Circ: 103,325 (paid).

910.2 DEU ISSN 1862-1449
GEO SAISON EXTRA. Text in German. 2006. 4/yr. EUR 8 newsstand/cover (effective 2010). adv. **Document type:** *Magazine, Consumer.*
Published by: Gruner + Jahr AG & Co, Am Baumwall 11, Hamburg, 20459, Germany. TEL 49-40-37030, FAX 49-40-37035601, info@gujmedia.de, http://www.guj.de. Adv. contact Korinna Koschek. page EUR 8,000. Circ: 50,000 (paid).

GEO TRAVELLER. *see* GEOGRAPHY

974 910.09 975.8 USA
F291.7
GEORGIA BACKROADS. Text in English. 1984 (Mar.). q. USD 27; USD 6 newsstand/cover (effective 2007). adv. bk.rev. 64 p./no.; back issues avail. **Document type:** *Magazine, Consumer.* **Description:** Provides a captivating source of information on travel opportunities, lifestyles, history, and historic real estate in Georgia.
Formerly (until 2002): North Georgia Journal (8756-9256)
Published by: Legacy Communications, Inc., PO Box 585, Armuchee, GA 30105-0585. TEL 706-295-7998, 800-547-1625, FAX 706-295-7725. Ed., Pub., Adv. contact Mr. D M Roper. B&W page USD 1,620, color page USD 2,045. Circ: 17,500 (paid).

917.58 USA ISSN 1542-1252
F284.3
GEORGIA CURIOSITIES; quirky characters, roadside oddities, & other offbeat stuff. Text in English. 2003. biennial, latest 2007, 2nd ed. USD 13.95 per issue (effective 2008). **Document type:** *Guide, Consumer.* **Description:** Provides tourist information about the Peach State.
Published by: The Globe Pequot Press, Inc., 246 Goose Ln, PO Box 480, Guilford, CT 06437. TEL 203-458-4500, 888-249-7586, FAX 203-458-4603, 800-820-2329, info@globepequot.com, http://www.globepequot.com.

910.202 USA ISSN 1067-4527
GEOTRAVELER. Text in English. 1993. bi-m. USD 39; USD 46 in Canada; USD 55 elsewhere. adv. bk.rev. **Document type:** *Newsletter.* **Description:** Provides its readers with unique information that will help them understand the places they visit, the things they see and the people they meet.
Published by: Geotravel Research Center, Inc., 160 Fiesta Dr, Ste 259, Kissimmee, FL 34743. TEL 407-348-9368. Ed. Bob Martin. Adv. contact Beverly Martin.

338.4 338.4791 COL ISSN 0121-9227
GERENCIA DE VIAJES; travel management for Latin American business & pleasure. Text in Spanish. 1993. bi-m. adv.
Published by: Latin Press Inc., Apartado Postal 67 252, Medellin, ANT, Colombia. TEL 57-4-4140169, FAX 57-4-2506990, http://www.latinpressinc.com.

GESTION DE HOTELES. *see* HOTELS AND RESTAURANTS

912 CHL ISSN 0717-1811
GESTION TURISTICA. Text in Spanish. 1995. s-a. CLP 3,000 domestic; USD 20 foreign (effective 2011). back issues avail. **Document type:** *Journal, Academic/Scholarly.*
Related titles: Print ed.: ISSN 0718-6428. 2008.
Published by: Universidad Austral de Chile, Instituto de Turismo, Casa 15, Campus Isla Teja, Valdivia, Chile. TEL 56-63-211158, FAX 56-63-221564, gestionturistica@uach.cl, http://www.economicas.uach.cl/institutos/turismo/. Ed. Pablo Szmulewicz. Circ: 300.

338.4791 USA
GET LOST MAGAZINE. Text in English. 1999. m. **Document type:** *Magazine, Consumer.* **Description:** Contains top-notch travel, adventure, natural history and lifestyle articles.
Address: 4509 Interlake Ave North, PO Box 136, Seattle, WA 98103.

916.8 ZAF ISSN 1013-8390
GETAWAY. Text in English. 1989. m. ZAR 115; ZAR 250 foreign; GBP 2.50 newsstand/cover (effective 1999). adv. **Document type:** *Magazine, Consumer.* **Description:** Publishes features on holidays, adventure travel and ecotourism in Southern Africa.
Indexed: ISAP.
Published by: Ramsay, Son & Parker (Pty) Ltd., PO Box 180, Howard Place, Cape Town 7450, South Africa. TEL 27-21-530-3100, FAX 27-21-5313846. Ed. D Steele. Pub. D. Steele. Circ: 90,580 (paid).

917.48 973 USA ISSN 1949-0631
F159.G5
▼ **GETTYSBURG**; a guided tour through history. Text in English. 2009. triennial. USD 15.95 per issue (effective 2009). **Document type:** *Guide, Consumer.* **Description:** Travel guide for the Gettysburg battlefield park with historical information.
Published by: G P P Travel (Subsidiary of: The Globe Pequot Press, Inc.), 246 Goose Ln, PO Box 480, Guilford, CT 06437. TEL 888-249-7586, FAX 800-820-2329, info@globepequot.com.

910.202 TUR
GEZI. Text in Turkish. m. adv. **Document type:** *Magazine, Consumer.*
Published by: Merkez Dergi/Merkez Magazine Group, Teyfik Mah., 20 Temmuz Cad., No. 24, Sefakoy, Istanbul, 34295, Turkey. TEL 90-212-4112000, FAX 90-212-3543884, http://www.parkgroup.com.tr/en/merdergi.htm.

973 USA
GIDEON'S TRUMPET. Text in English. 1979. bi-m. adv. **Document type:** *Newsletter.*
Published by: Granger Homestead Society, Inc., 295 N Main St, Canandaigua, NY 14424. TEL 716-394-1472, FAX 716-394-6958. Adv. contact Saralinda Hooker. Circ: 600.

GIRLFRIEND GETAWAYS. *see* WOMEN'S INTERESTS

917 910.91 USA ISSN 1933-9313
OH105.M9
GLACIER; a natural history guide. Text in English. 2000. irreg., latest 2007, 2nd ed. USD 17.95 per issue (effective 2008). **Document type:** *Guide, Consumer.* **Description:** Provides the information and acts as a guide to unique places.
Former titles (until 2002): Exploring Glacier National Park (1545-3324); Glacier National Park
Published by: The Globe Pequot Press, Inc., 246 Goose Ln, PO Box 480, Guilford, CT 06437. TEL 203-458-4500, 888-249-7586, FAX 203-458-4603, 800-820-2329, info@globepequot.com, http://www.globepequot.com.

▼ **GLOADVENTURER.** *see* CHILDREN AND YOUTH—For

GLOBE (LONDON). *see* CLUBS

916.8 ZAF ISSN 1819-6713
GO! (CAPE TOWN, 2006). Text in English. 2006. m. adv. **Document type:** *Magazine, Consumer.* **Description:** For outdoor enthusiasts looking for memorable travel experiences.
Related titles: ◆ Afrikaans ed.: Weg!. ISSN 1990-9896.
Published by: Media24 Ltd., Naspers Centre, 40 Heerengracht St, PO Box 1802, Cape Town, 8000, South Africa. Pub. John Relihan. adv.: color page ZAR 35,100; trim 230 x 275.

910.202 DEU
GO BRITAIN. Text in German. 2001. 4/yr. EUR 18.50; EUR 14.50 to students (effective 2003). adv. **Document type:** *Magazine, Consumer.*
Published by: Nordis Verlag GmbH, Maxstr 64, Essen, 45127, Germany. TEL 49-201-872290, FAX 49-201-8942511, verlag@nordis.com, http://www.nordis.de. Ed. Stephan Fennel. Adv. contact Gabriele Jaster TEL 49-211-7357885. B&W page EUR 6,240, color page EUR 10,400; trim 184 x 263.

796.7 USA ISSN 1077-1808
GO MAGAZINE (CHARLOTTE). Text in English. 1922. bi-m. free to members (effective 2009). adv. bk.rev. charts; illus.; stat. **Document type:** *Magazine, Consumer.* **Description:** Provides domestic and international travel and tourism information; includes automotive and insurance news and legislative issues.
Formerly (until 1991): Go (0017-1441)
Related titles: Online - full text ed.
Published by: American Automobile Association, Carolina Motor Club, 10703 J St Ste 100, Omaha, NE 68127. http://www.aaacarolinas.com. Ed. Tom Crosby TEL 704-569-7733. Adv. contact Lila Cloar TEL 800-307-4536. color page USD 27,000; trim 7.75 x 10.75. Circ: 1,100,000.

910.91 GBR ISSN 1759-7927
▼ **GO MOTORHOME.** Text in English. 2009. s-a. GBP 3.50 per issue to non-members; GBP 1.75 per issue to members (effective 2010). back issues avail. **Document type:** *Magazine, Consumer.*
Published by: Warners Group Publications Plc., The Maltings, Manor Ln, Bourne, Lincs PE10 9PH, United Kingdom. TEL 44-1778-391000, http://www.warnersgroup.co.uk.

778.051 910.91 USA
GOIN' TO KANSAS CITY; the official visitor's guide of the Convention & Visitors Bureau of Greater Kansas City. Text in English. 1999. q. adv. **Document type:** *Magazine, Consumer.* **Description:** Covers performing arts, dining, sports and entertainment for the Kansas City, Missouri area.
Published by: Grand Communications, 1729 Grand Blvd, Kansas City, MO 64108. TEL 816-234-4173, FAX 816-234-4123. Pub. Bill Gaier TEL 816-234-4194. Adv. contacts Michelle Jolles, Stacey Gresham TEL 816-234-4951. page USD 3,895; trim 8 x 10.875. Circ: 240,000 (free).

910.2 CAN ISSN 0835-1015
GOING NATURAL. Text in English. 1986. q. CAD 35 domestic; CAD 40 foreign; CAD 6, USD 4.95 newsstand/cover (effective 2002). adv. bk.rev.; film rev.; video rev.; Website rev. 48 p./no.; back issues avail. **Document type:** *Magazine, Consumer.* **Description:** Reports on naturist resorts, beaches, travel, events and all aspects of the naturist lifestyle.
Published by: Federation of Canadian Naturists, P O Box 186, Etobicoke, ON M9A 4X2, Canada. Ed., R&P Paul Rapoport TEL 905-304-4836. Adv. contact Ross Vickers TEL 416-233-2216. Circ: 2,400 (paid).

910.91 200 USA
GOING ON FAITH; the national newspaper for faith-based travel planners. Text in English. 19??. bi-m. USD 39; free to qualified personnel (effective 2011). adv. **Document type:** *Magazine, Consumer.*
Related titles: Online - full text ed.: free (effective 2011).
Published by: Group Travel Leader, Inc., 301 E High St, Lexington, KY 40507. TEL 859-253-0455. Ed. Brain Jewell. Pub. Mac T Lacy.

910.09 USA
GOING PLACES (MINOT). Text in English. 1990. m. USD 18.95; USD 28.95 foreign. adv. illus. **Document type:** *Magazine, Consumer.* **Description:** Promotes North Dakota's people, places and events.
Address: PO Box 1427, Minot, ND 58702-1427. TEL 701-858-1600, FAX 701-858-1644. Ed. Shirleyanne Keller. Pub. Debbie Schmidt Perdeu. Adv. contact Debbie Perdeu. Circ: 40,000 (controlled).

910.2 USA ISSN 1559-3819
F902.3
GOING PLACES: ALASKA AND THE YUKON FOR FAMILIES. Text in English. 2005. irreg. USD 21.95 per issue (effective 2007). **Document type:** *Guide, Consumer.*
Published by: Sasquatch Books, 119 S Main, Ste 400, Seattle, WA 98104. TEL 206-467-4300, 800-775-0817, FAX 206-467-4301, custserv@sasquatchbooks.com, http://www.sasquatchbooks.com.

910.09 GBR ISSN 0955-629X
GOING PLACES INTERNATIONAL; Britain's premier travel magazine. Text in English. 1984. q. GBP 2, USD 5.25. adv. bk.rev.
Formerly (until 1988): Going Places (0956-9626)
Published by: Pericles Press, 38 Buckingham Palace Rd, London, Mddx SW1W 0RE, United Kingdom. TEL 071-486-5353, FAX 071-486-2094, TELEX 27659. Ed. Daphne Aldis. Circ: 40,000.

914.415 IRL ISSN 1360-7766
GOLF DAYS. GOLF COURSES IN IRELAND. Variant title: Golfdays. Text in English. 1990. a. GBP 12.95, EUR 19.95 (effective 2005). adv. **Document type:** *Magazine, Consumer.*
Published by: Tudor Journals Ltd., 97 Botanic Ave, Belfast, BT7 1JN, Ireland. TEL 353-28-90320088, FAX 353-28-90323163, info@tudorjournals.com, http://www.tudorjournals.com. Adv. contact John Ferguson. color page EUR 2,380; 148.5 x 210.

910.91 796.352 NZL
GOLF DESTINATIONS. Text in English. 2006. a. **Document type:** *Magazine, Consumer.*
Related titles: Optical Disk - DVD ed.: ISSN 1177-2514.
Published by: Destinations Media, 74 Jervois Rd, Herne Bay, Auckland, New Zealand. TEL 64-9-3603978, FAX 64-9-3604097, mail@destinationsmagazine.com. Ed. Phillip Leishman.

GOLF & TURISMO. see SPORTS AND GAMES—Ball Games

GOLF ESTATE; wonen & reizen. see SPORTS AND GAMES—Ball Games

GOLF GUIDE - WHERE TO PLAY AND WHERE TO STAY. see SPORTS AND GAMES—Ball Games

GOLF JOURNAL. see SPORTS AND GAMES—Ball Games

GOLF MAGAZINE. see SPORTS AND GAMES—Ball Games

GOLF MEETINGS, RESORTS & DESTINATIONS. see SPORTS AND GAMES—Ball Games

GOLF ODYSSEY; the sophisticated guide to golf travel. see SPORTS AND GAMES—Ball Games

THE GOLFERS GUIDE TO IRELAND. see SPORTS AND GAMES—Ball Games

GOLF'S YELLOW PAGE DIRECTORY. see SPORTS AND GAMES—Ball Games

GOLFWELT REISE. see SPORTS AND GAMES—Ball Games

910.3 GBR
THE GOOD BED AND BREAKFAST GUIDE. Text in English. 1988. biennial. **Document type:** *Directory.* **Description:** Features information on over 1,200 good-value establishments.
Related titles: Online - full text ed.
Published by: (Consumers Association), Which? Ltd., 2 Marylebone Rd, London, NW1 4DF, United Kingdom. TEL 44-20-77707000, FAX 44-20-77707600, which@which.co.uk, http://www.which.co.uk. Ed. Elsie Dillard.

796.5 GBR ISSN 0963-1135
GOOD CAMPS GUIDE BRITAIN (YEAR). Variant title: Alan Rogers Campsite Guide Britain. Text in English. 1968. a. GBP 11.99 per issue (effective 2010). **Document type:** *Directory, Consumer.*
Formerly: Alan Rogers' Good Camps Guide Britain (0142-5978)
Related titles: ◆ Series of: Alan Rogers Directory of Camping and Caravanning, All Year Round. ISSN 0969-9708.
Published by: Mark Hammerton Group, Spelmonden Old Oast, Goudhurst, Kent TN17 1HE, United Kingdom. TEL 44-1580-214000, FAX 44-1580-214015, enquiries@markhammerton.com, http://www.markhammerton.com.

796.54 GBR ISSN 0955-9183
GOOD CAMPS GUIDE EUROPE (YEAR). Variant title: Alan Rogers Campsite Guide Europe. Text in English. 1968. a. GBP 13.99 per issue (effective 2010). illus. **Document type:** *Directory, Consumer.* **Description:** Provides information for campers, caravaners and motor caravaners regarding location, sanitary facilities, amenities, costs, cleanliness, and maintenance.
Former titles (until 1989): Selected Sites for Caravanning and Camping in Europe (0065-5686); Alan Rogers' Selected Sites for Caravanning and Camping in Europe (0000-6556)
Related titles: ◆ Series: Good Camps Guide France (Year). ISSN 0955-9205; Alan Rogers Good Camps Guide.
Published by: Mark Hammerton Group, Spelmonden Old Oast, Goudhurst, Kent TN17 1HE, United Kingdom. TEL 44-1580-214000, FAX 44-1580-214015, enquiries@markhammerton.com, http://www.markhammerton.com.

796.5 GBR ISSN 0955-9205
GOOD CAMPS GUIDE FRANCE (YEAR). Variant title: Alan Rogers Campsite Guide France. Text in English. 1985. a. GBP 13.99 per issue (effective 2010). illus. back issues avail. **Document type:** *Directory, Consumer.* **Description:** Covers special selected camping sites in France for the discerning camper.
Formerly: Alan Rogers' Good Camps Guide for France (0267-8934)
Related titles: ◆ Series of: Good Camps Guide Europe (Year). ISSN 0955-9183.
Published by: Mark Hammerton Group, Spelmonden Old Oast, Goudhurst, Kent TN17 1HE, United Kingdom. TEL 44-1580-214000, FAX 44-1580-214015, enquiries@markhammerton.com, http://www.markhammerton.com.

338.4791 POL ISSN 1642-0853
GOSCINIEC. Text in Polish. 1994. q. **Document type:** *Magazine.*
Formerly (until 2001): Polskie Towarzystwo Turystyczno-Krajoznawcze. Zarzad Glowny. Informacje (1234-1835)
Related titles: Online - full content ed.: 2001.
Published by: Polskie Towarzystwo Turystyczno-Krajoznawcze, Zarzad Glowny, Ul Senatorska 11, Warsaw, 00075, Poland. cb@pttk.pl, http://www.pttk.pl. Ed. Andrzej Gordon.

GOUR-MED; Das Magazin fuer Aerzte. see MEDICAL SCIENCES

GOURMETREISE; Das Magazin fuer Geniesser. see FOOD AND FOOD INDUSTRIES

910.2 USA ISSN 1931-5503
DP302.C45
GRAN CANARIA. D K EYEWITNESS TOP 10 TRAVEL GUIDES. AMERICAN EDITION. Variant title: Eyewitness Top 10 Travel Guide: Gran Canaria. Text in English. 2006. irreg. GBP 6.99 per issue (effective 2008). **Document type:** *Guide, Consumer.* **Description:** Features areas of natural beauty, exciting fiestas, liveliest night spots, fascinating museums, alluring beaches, most fun places for children and best restaurants in Gran Canaria.
Published by: D K Publishing (Subsidiary of: Penguin Books U S A, Inc.), 375 Hudson St, New York, NY 10014. TEL 800-631-8571, FAX 201-256-0000, specialsales@dk.com, http://us.dk.com.

656.2 CZE ISSN 1802-3398
GRAND PENDOLINO. Text in Czech. 2006. m. CZK 216 (effective 2009). adv. **Document type:** *Magazine, Consumer.*
Published by: Grand Princ s.r.o., Vinohradska 138, Prague 3, 130 00, Czech Republic. TEL 420-272-107111, FAX 420-272-107000, grandprinc@grandprinc.cz, http://www.grandprinc.cz. adv.: page CZK 47,000; trim 115 x 220. Circ: 30,000 (controlled).

910.202 ITA ISSN 1594-9532
GRAND TOUR CULT. Text in Multiple languages. 2002. bi-m. **Document type:** *Magazine, Consumer.*
Published by: Techne Editore, Viale Piave 11, Milan, 20129, Italy. TEL 39-02-76002856, FAX 39-02-76004252, info@techneditore.it, http://www.techneditore.it.

910 ITA ISSN 1825-4896
GRAND TOUR EMOZIONI IN VIAGGIO. COSTA SMERALDA. Text in Italian. 2005. s-m. **Document type:** *Magazine, Consumer.*
Published by: De Agostini Editore, Via G da Verrazzano 15, Novara, 28100, Italy. TEL 39-0321-4241, FAX 39-0321-424305, info@deagostini.it, http://www.deagostini.it.

910.91 ITA ISSN 1827-0085
GRAND TOUR EMOZIONI IN VIAGGIO. ITINERARI. Text in Italian. 2005. s-a. **Document type:** *Magazine, Consumer.*
Published by: De Agostini Editore, Via G da Verrazzano 15, Novara, 28100, Italy. TEL 39-0321-4241, FAX 39-0321-424305, info@deagostini.it, http://www.deagostini.it.

910 663.2 ITA ISSN 1825-4888
GRAND TOUR EMOZIONI IN VIAGGIO. L'ITALIA DEL VINO. Text in Italian. 2005. s-m. **Document type:** *Magazine, Consumer.*
Published by: De Agostini Editore, Via G da Verrazzano 15, Novara, 28100, Italy. TEL 39-0321-4241, FAX 39-0321-424305, info@deagostini.it, http://www.deagostini.it.

910.91 ITA ISSN 1827-0093
GRAND TOUR EMOZIONI IN VIAGGIO. LUOGHI. Text in Italian. 2005. s-a. **Document type:** *Magazine, Consumer.*
Published by: De Agostini Editore, Via G da Verrazzano 15, Novara, 28100, Italy. TEL 39-0321-4241, FAX 39-0321-424305, info@deagostini.it, http://www.deagostini.it.

910 ITA ISSN 1828-681X
GRAND TOUR EMOZIONI IN VIAGGIO. ORIZZONTI. Text in Italian. 2006. s-a. **Document type:** *Magazine, Consumer.*
Published by: De Agostini Editore, Via G da Verrazzano 15, Novara, 28100, Italy. TEL 39-0321-4241, FAX 39-0321-424305, info@deagostini.it, http://www.deagostini.it.

910 796.93 ITA ISSN 1825-487X
GRAND TOUR EMOZIONI IN VIAGGIO. SCI SULLE ALPI. Text in Italian. 2005. s-m. **Document type:** *Magazine, Consumer.*
Published by: De Agostini Editore, Via G da Verrazzano 15, Novara, 28100, Italy. TEL 39-0321-4241, FAX 39-0321-424305, info@deagostini.it, http://www.deagostini.it.

910 ITA ISSN 1825-4861
GRAND TOUR EMOZIONI IN VIAGGIO. TRENTINO. Text in Italian. 2005. s-m. **Document type:** *Magazine, Consumer.*
Published by: De Agostini Editore, Via G da Verrazzano 15, Novara, 28100, Italy. TEL 39-0321-4241, FAX 39-0321-424305, info@deagostini.it, http://www.deagostini.it.

910.91 ITA ISSN 1827-0107
GRAND TOUR EMOZIONI IN VIAGGIO. VIAGGI. Text in Italian. 2005. s-a.
Published by: De Agostini Editore, Via G da Verrazzano 15, Novara, 28100, Italy. TEL 39-0321-4241, FAX 39-0321-424305, info@deagostini.it, http://www.deagostini.it.

919 BEL ISSN 1379-4213
GRANDE; voyager c'est la vie. Text in French. 2003. m. EUR 52 (effective 2010). adv. **Document type:** *Magazine, Consumer.* **Description:** Contains information and articles on all aspects of travel in Europe and overseas.
Related titles: Dutch ed.: ISSN 1376-5515.
Published by: Roularta Media Group, Research Park, Zellik, 1731, Belgium. TEL 32-2-4675611, FAX 32-2-4675757, communication@roularta.be, http://www.roularta.be. Circ: 28,392 (paid).

910.2 ITA ISSN 2036-279X
▼ **I GRANDI ITINERARI DELLA FEDE.** Text in Italian. 2036. w. **Document type:** *Guide, Consumer.*
Published by: R C S Libri (Subsidiary of: R C S Mediagroup), Via Mecenate 91, Milan, 20138, Italy. TEL 39-02-5095-2248, FAX 39-02-5095-2975, http://rcslibri.corriere.it/libri/index.htm.

910.91 ITA ISSN 1824-100X
GRANDTOUR DOLOMITI. Text in Italian. 2004. s-a. **Document type:** *Magazine, Consumer.*
Published by: De Agostini Editore, Via G da Verrazzano 15, Novara, 28100, Italy. TEL 39-0321-4241, FAX 39-0321-424305, info@deagostini.it, http://www.deagostini.it.

910.91 ITA ISSN 1824-0992
GRANDTOUR SARDEGNA. Text in Italian. 2004. s-a. **Document type:** *Magazine, Academic/Scholarly.*
Published by: De Agostini Editore, Via G da Verrazzano 15, Novara, 28100, Italy. TEL 39-0321-4241, FAX 39-0321-424305, info@deagostini.it, http://www.deagostini.it.

910.91 ITA ISSN 1824-0984
GRANDTOUR TOSCANA. Text in Italian. 2004. s-a. **Document type:** *Magazine, Consumer.*
Published by: De Agostini Editore, Via G da Verrazzano 15, Novara, 28100, Italy. TEL 39-0321-4241, FAX 39-0321-424305, info@deagostini.it, http://www.deagostini.it.

910.202 DEU
DER GRAUE. Text in German. 1967. 60/yr. EUR 20 (effective 2006). adv. bk.rev. **Document type:** *Newsletter, Consumer.*
Published by: R B Marketing, Schraemelstr 126, Munich, 81247, Germany. TEL 49-89-88888888, FAX 49-89-882686, http://www.rb-marketing.de. Ed., Pub. Hans N Nechleba. Adv. contact Erika Nechleba. B&W page EUR 375, color page EUR 1,460; 185 x 275. Circ: 1,100 (paid).

914.2 GBR
THE GREAT BRITAIN GUIDE. Text in English. 19??. a. GBP 12 per issue (effective 2009). maps; illus. **Document type:** *Handbook/Manual/Guide, Consumer.* **Description:** Contains 1,000 main entries, 150 walks, 50 cycle rides, 24 car tours and hundreds of ideas for activities and places to visit.
Former titles (until 1998): Great Days Out and in Britain and Ireland; Days Out in Britain and Ireland; (until 1996): Days Out in Britain; 2000 Days Out in Britain; 2000 Places to Visit in Britain; Stately Homes, Museums, Castles and Gardens in Britain
Published by: (Automobile Association), A A Publishing, Contact Ctr, Lambert House, Stockport Rd, Cheadle, Hants SK8 2DY, United Kingdom. TEL 44-161-4958945, FAX 44-161-4887544, customer.services@theAA.com, http://www.theaa.com.

910.5 USA ISSN 0706-7682
GREAT EXPEDITIONS. Text in English. 1978. 4/yr. USD 11.95. adv. bk.rev. back issues avail. **Document type:** *Magazine, Consumer.* **Description:** Emphasizes independent, socially responsible travel outside the usual tourist areas.
Published by: Great Expeditions, Inc., PO Box 18036, Raleigh, NC 27619. TEL 919-846-3600, FAX 919-847-0780. Ed. George W Kane. Circ: 27,000.

GREAT GOLF RESORTS OF THE WORLD. see SPORTS AND GAMES—Ball Games

917.7 797.1 USA
GREAT LAKES CRUISER; the boater's travel guide. Text in English. 1994. m. CAD 24.95 domestic; CAD 29.95 in Canada; USD 2.95 newsstand/cover domestic; CAD 3.95 newsstand/cover in Canada (effective 2002). adv. bk.rev.; music rev.; software rev.; video rev. charts; illus. back issues avail. **Document type:** *Magazine, Consumer.* **Description:** Provides detailed travel information for boaters in the Great Lakes region. Each issue details three harbors including restaurants, history, museums and other attractions.
Published by: Great Lakes Cruiser, Ltd., 2510 Dallas Ave, Royal Oak, MI 48067. TEL 248-545-5999, FAX 248-545-6992. Pub., R&P, Adv. contact Bruce Jenvey. B&W page USD 1,000, color page USD 1,500; trim 11 x 8.5. Circ: 10,000 (paid); 2,000 (controlled). **Subscr. to:** PO Box 1722, Royal Oak, MI 48068-1722. **Dist. by:** Ingram Periodicals Inc., 1240 Heil Quaker Blvd, Box 7000, La Vergne, TN 37086. TEL 800-627-6247.

917.504 GBR
THE GREAT LAKES OF NORTH AMERICA. Text in English. 19??. a. adv. back issues avail. **Document type:** *Journal, Consumer.*
Related titles: Online - full text ed.: free (effective 2010).
Published by: Phoenix International Publishing, PO Box 615, Horsham, Sussex RH13 5WF, United Kingdom. marymooremason@phoenixip.com, http://www.phoenixip.com/. Ed. Simon Veness.

910.202 USA
GREAT LOCATIONS. Text in English, Spanish, German. 1992. s-a. **Description:** For international and domestic visitors, it contains information on local history, entertainment, shopping, dining and tourist attractions.
Published by: Great Locations, Inc., 1200 S Ocean Blvd, Pompano Beach, FL 33062. TEL 954-943-1188, 888-214-1188, FAX 954-943-1277, grlo@greatlocations.com, http://www.greatlocations.com.

GREATER LOUISVILLE RELOCATION GUIDE. see REAL ESTATE

338.4791 FRA ISSN 1960-825X
GREATER PARIS. Text in French, English. 2007. q. free. **Document type:** *Magazine, Consumer.*
Related titles: Online - full text ed.
Published by: France Brochure System, 33 Av. du Marechal Joffre, Chantilly, 60500, France. TEL 33-3-44672121.

914.95 GRC ISSN 0432-6105
DF727
GREECE. Text in English. 1950. a. illus.
Published by: National Tourist Organisation of Greece, General Direction of Promotion, 2 Amerikis St, Athens, Greece.

910.202 GRC ISSN 1107-3748
GREEK TRAVEL PAGES; Greede's monthly travel guide - magazine. Text in Greek. 1975. m. USD 250 in Europe; USD 280 elsewhere (effective 2000). adv. bk.rev. **Document type:** *Magazine, Consumer.* **Description:** Covers information and news concerning the Greek tourism sector.
Published by: International Publications Ltd., 6 Psylla kai Filellinon Sts, Athens, 105 57, Greece. TEL 30-210-324-7511, FAX 30-210-324-9996, info@gtpnet.com, http://www.gtpnet.com. Ed. Colin Chisholm. Pub. Eleftherios Theofanopoulos. Adv. contact Thanassis Caudas. B&W page GRD 260,000, color page GRD 350,000. Circ: 100,000.

919.404 AUS
GREEN TRIANGLE HOLIDAY NEWS. Text in English. 199?. q. maps. **Document type:** *Newspaper.* **Description:** Provides information on sightseeing and accommodation for tourists travelling within South-Western Victoria and South-Eastern South Australia.
Formerly: Green Triangle Visitors News
Published by: Hamilton Spectator Partnership, 59 Gray St, Hamilton, VIC 3300, Australia. TEL 61-3-55721011, FAX 61-3-55723800, specadmin@spec.com.au, http://www.spec.com.au.

910 DNK
GREENLAND GUIDE. Text in English. irreg. free. **Document type:** *Guide, Consumer.* **Description:** Presents news about traveling in Greenland, including hotel listing, airlines and cruise lines, travel agencies and local tourist services.
Media: Online - full text.
Published by: Pegasus Press, Blaagaards Plads 1, Copenhagen N, 2200, Denmark. TEL 45-40-454742, FAX 45-33-252835.

910.10 DEU
GREIFSWALDER BEITRAEGE ZUR REGIONAL-, FREIZEIT- UND TOURISMUSFORSCHUNG. Text in German. 1993. irreg., latest vol.17, 2007. price varies. **Document type:** *Monographic series, Academic/Scholarly.*
Formerly (until 1997): Greifswalder Beitraege zur Rekreationsgeographie, Freizeit- und Tourismusforschung (0943-7371)

Published by: Ernst-Moritz-Arndt-Universitaet Greifswald, Institut fuer Geographie und Geologie, Friedrich-Ludwig-Jahnstr 16, Greifswald, 17487, Germany. TEL 49-3834-864540, FAX 49-3834-864542, steingru@uni-greifswald.de, http://www.mnf.uni-greifswald.de/institute/geo.html.

338.4 GRD
GRENADA. BOARD OF TOURISM. QUARTERLY; overview of the tourism sector. Text in English. q.
Published by: Board of Tourism, Carenage, St. George's, Grenada.

▼ **GRENZELOOS.** *see* BUSINESS AND ECONOMICS—Marketing And Purchasing

914.9504 NLD ISSN 1571-0343
GRIEKENLAND MAGAZINE. Text in Dutch. 2003. q. EUR 21.95 domestic; EUR 26.50 foreign; EUR 5.95 newsstand/cover (effective 2010). adv. **Document type:** *Magazine, Consumer.*
Published by: Maasland Uitgeverij, Postbus 348, Oss, 5340 AH, Netherlands. TEL 31-412-628218, info@maasland.com, http://www.maaslanduitgeverij.com. Eds. Sanne Voets, Peter van Riel. Pub. Peter van Riel. adv.: page EUR 1,115; trim 230 x 297.

338.4791 USA
GROUP TOUR MAGAZINE. Text in English. 1987. q. free to qualified personnel (effective 2011). adv. back issues avail. **Document type:** *Magazine, Consumer.* **Description:** Provides the latest information on area suppliers and destinations across the United States and Canada for group travel planners.
Related titles: Online - full text ed.: free (effective 2011).
Published by: Shoreline Creations, Ltd., 2465 112th Ave, Holland, MI 49424. TEL 616-393-2077, 800-767-3489, FAX 616-393-0085, editor@grouptour.com, http://www.grouptour.com. Ed. Rick Martinez TEL 616-393-2077 ext 107. Pub. Elly DeVries TEL 616-393-2077 ext 130.

338.4791 USA
GROUP TOUR MAGAZINES INDUSTRY UPDATE. Text in English. 1998. a. **Document type:** *Magazine, Consumer.* **Description:** Includes insights into the group tour industry.
Published by: Shoreline Creations, Ltd., 2465 112th Ave, Holland, MI 49424. TEL 616-393-2077, 800-767-3489, FAX 616-393-0085, editor@grouptour.com, http://www.grouptour.com.

910 USA
THE GROUP TRAVEL LEADER. Text in English. 1991. m. USD 59; free to qualified personnel (effective 2011). adv. **Document type:** *Magazine, Trade.* **Description:** Contains industry news, destination features, and educational articles and information on group travel for seniors.
Related titles: Online - full text ed.: free (effective 2011).
Published by: Group Travel Leader, Inc., 301 E High St, Lexington, KY 40507. TEL 859-253-0455. Ed. Herbert L Sparrow. Pub. Mac T Lacy. Adv. contact Stacey Bowman.

338.4791 USA
GROUP TRAVEL LIFESTYLES. Text in English. 2000. q. **Document type:** *Magazine, Consumer.* **Description:** Provides assistance in planning tours.
Published by: Shoreline Creations, Ltd., 2465 112th Ave, Holland, MI 49424. TEL 616-393-2077, 800-767-3489, FAX 616-393-0085, editor@grouptour.com, http://www.grouptour.com.

910.202 GBR ISSN 0962-8266
GROUP TRAVEL ORGANISER. Abbreviated title: G T O. Text in English. 1988. 10/yr. GBP 24 domestic; GBP 36 in Europe; GBP 48 elsewhere; GBP 2.50 per issue; free to qualified personnel (effective 2009). adv. illus. back issues avail. **Document type:** *Magazine, Trade.* **Description:** Provides news and information for the group travel organizer.
Related titles: Online - full text ed.: free (effective 2009).
—CCC.
Published by: Landor Publishing Ltd, 47 Wellington Sq, Hastings, TN34 1PN, United Kingdom. TEL 44-845-1668120, FAX 44-1424-200478, business@landor.co.uk, http://www.landor.co.uk. Ed. Abbe Bates TEL 44-845-1668123. Pub. Peter Stonham. Adv. contact Tracy Hawley TEL 44-121-3235463. Circ: 9,872.

GROUP TRAVEL PLANET; the insider guide to group travel. *see* BUSINESS AND ECONOMICS

910.2 GBR
GROUPS WELCOME. Text in English. 19??. a. adv. **Document type:** *Directory, Trade.*
Former titles (until 2008): Coaches & Parties Welcome (0260-7573); (until 1977): Coaches Welcome
Published by: Lewis Productions Ltd., 167 Cranley Gardens, Muswell Hill, London, N10 3AG, United Kingdom.

338.4 TWN
GUANGUANG LIUYOU YANJIU XUEKAN/JOURNAL OF TOURISM AND TRAVEL RESEARCH. Text in Chinese. 2006. a. **Document type:** *Academic/Scholarly.*
Published by: Mingchuan University, School of Tourism/Mingchuan Daxue, Guanguang Xueyuan, 5 Teh-Ming Rd., Gwei Shan, Taoyuan, Taiwan. http://www.tourism.tj.mcu.edu.tw/.

910.2 USA
GUESTLIFE; Monterey Bay - New Mexico - El Paso - St. Petersburg - Clearwater. Text in English. 1979. a. **Document type:** *Magazine, Consumer.* **Description:** Highlights the attractions, hotels, restaurants, the arts, entertainment, nightlife, shopping, sports and detailed visitors guides of Monterey Bay, New Mexico, El Paso, Houston, Vancouver and other popular destinations.
Formerly: Monterey Bay GuestLife
Published by: Desert Publications, Inc., PO Box 2724, Palm Springs, CA 92263. TEL 760-325-2333, FAX 760-325-7008, sales@desertpublications.com. Pub. Milton W Jones. Adv. contact Franklin W Jones.

380.5 PER
GUIA AEREA. Text in Spanish. 1962. m. USD 140 in Peru to individuals; USD 260 in the Americas to individuals; USD 360 elsewhere to individuals (effective 2000). adv. back issues avail. **Document type:** *Directory, Trade.* **Description:** Airline guide and directory with news section covering the travel and airline industries.
Formerly: Guia Aerea y Maritima
Published by: Lima Editora S.A., Ave. Benavides, 1180, Miraflores, Lima 18, Peru. TEL 51-1-4440815, FAX 51-1-242-3669, info@limaedistora.com. Eds. Jose Luis Arrarte, Oscar Orgumanis. R&P Jose Luis Arrarte. Adv. contact Tana Servat. B&W page USD 600, color page USD 1,000. Circ: 3,450 (paid).

GUIA AEREA OFICIAL - CHILE. *see* TRANSPORTATION—Air Transport

GUIA AEREA Y MARITIMA DE VENEZUELA C.A.; Aruba, Curacao y Bonaire. *see* TRANSPORTATION

GUIA AERONAUTICO. *see* TRANSPORTATION—Air Transport

918 BRA
GUIA BRASIL. Text in Portuguese; Summaries in English, Spanish. 1966. a. price varies. charts; illus. **Document type:** *Magazine, Consumer.* **Description:** Details information on 744 cities, as well as various hotels, restaurants, and tourist attractions.
Published by: Editora Abril, S.A., Avenida das Nacoes Unidas 7221, Pinheiros, Sao Paulo, SP 05425-902, Brazil. TEL 55-11-50872112, FAX 55-11-50872100, abrilsac@abril.com.br, http://www.abril.com.br. Ed. Regner Camilo. Circ: 230,000.

338.4 MEX
GUIA DE TURISMO Y DE SERVICIOS. Text in Spanish. 1992. s-a.
Published by: Editorial del Norte Mexicano, Allende 980-1 pte., Torreon, COAHUILA, Mexico. TEL 169470.

917.204 MEX
GUIA DE VIAJES. Text in Spanish. m. free. illus.
Former titles: Visitors' Guide to Mexico; Now in Mexico
Published by: Editorial This Is Mexico, Calle Londres 166, Apdo. 6-728, Mexico City, DF 06600, Mexico. FAX 52-5-2082838. Circ: 20,000.

910.202 CUB
GUIA DEL SOL. Text in Spanish. s-a.
Published by: Instituto Nacional del Turismo, Malecon y G,, Vedado, La Habana, Cuba. TEL 7-32-9881.

338.479 BRA ISSN 1413-9049
GUIA DO TURISTA; descobrindo o Brasil. Text in Portuguese; Summaries in English, Spanish. 1988. a., latest vol.12, 1999. BRL 8 domestic; USD 4.50 foreign; USD 4.50 newsstand/cover (effective 2000). adv. illus.; maps. **Document type:** *Magazine, Consumer.* **Description:** Provides information on tourism in Brazil.
Related titles: CD-ROM ed.; Online - full text ed.
Published by: Editora Guia do Turista Ltda, Rua Pirai, Z67 - Alto da la Pa, Sao Paulo, SP 05059-100, Brazil. TEL 55-11-2601533, FAX 55-11-8328837, editora@guiadoturista.com.br. Ed., Pub., Adv. contact Romolo Ciuffo. page USD 4,000; 21 x 28. Circ: 40,000 (paid and controlled). **Dist. by:** R. Teodoro da Silva, 907, Rio de Janeiro, RJ 20563-900, Brazil. TEL 55-21-5783844.

918.104 BRA ISSN 0104-5024
G1776.P2
GUIA ESTRADAS - QUATRO RODAS. Text in Portuguese. 1988. a. BRL 140.40 (effective 2005). adv. back issues avail. **Document type:** *Magazine, Consumer.* **Description:** Includes detailed maps of Brazil with cities ande highways in small format.
Related titles: Online - full text ed.
Published by: Editora Abril, S.A., Avenida das Nacoes Unidas 7221, Pinheiros, Sao Paulo, SP 05425-902, Brazil. TEL 55-11-50872112, FAX 55-11-50872100, http://www.abril.com.br. Ed. Regner Camilo. adv.: page BRL 67,300. Circ: 143,030.

917.3 ESP ISSN 1888-4148
GUIA INTEGRADA DE HOSTELERIA. Text in Spanish. 2004. biennial. EUR 150 (effective 2009). back issues avail. **Document type:** *Directory, Trade.*
Published by: Informacion y Distribucion Anual, S.L., Ave Presidente Carmona, 2, Madrid, 28020, Spain. TEL 34-91-4177860, FAX 34-91-5567300, depto.comercial@indisa.es, http://www.indisa.es/.

910.202 ARG
GUIA INTERNACIONAL DE TRAFICO. Text in Spanish. 1963. m. USD 230 in the Americas; USD 300 elsewhere. adv. **Document type:** *Directory.* **Description:** Airline guide providing international travel information and news.
Formerly: Guia Internacional de Trafico - Division Viajes
Address: Suipacha, 207 Piso 3, Buenos Aires, 1008, Argentina. TEL 54-114-3949008, FAX 54-114-3949034. Ed. Alan Rodrigue. Circ: 10,000 (paid).

917.204 HND
GUIA OFICIAL DE CENTRO-AMERICA. Text in Spanish. 1922. irreg.
Address: Apartado 494, Tegucigalpa DC, Honduras.

910.09 BRA ISSN 0102-3225
GUIA PANROTAS. Text in Portuguese. 1972. m. USD 182. adv. **Document type:** *Trade.*
Published by: Panrotas Editora Ltda., Av. Jabaquara, 1761, CEP, Sao Paulo, SP 04045-901, Brazil. TEL 55-11-55840211, FAX 55-11-2761602, TELEX 11-56693. Ed. Luiz Sales. Pub. Jose G Condomi Alcorta. R&P Joao Batista Deresende Miranda. Adv. contact Fernando Begara. Circ: 11,000.

918.104 BRA ISSN 0104-5067
GUIA PRAIAS - QUATRO RODAS. Text in Portuguese. 1991. a. **Document type:** *Magazine, Consumer.*
Published by: Editora Abril, S.A., Avenida das Nacoes Unidas 7221, Pinheiros, Sao Paulo, SP 05425-902, Brazil. TEL 55-11-50872112, FAX 55-11-50872100, abrilsac@abril.com.br, http://www.abril.com.br. Ed. Regner Camilo. Circ: 75,000.

910.202 BRA ISSN 0104-4982
F2509.5
GUIA QUATRO RODAS BRASIL. Text in Portuguese. 1966. a. adv. charts. **Document type:** *Magazine, Consumer.* **Description:** Details information on 820 cities, including various hotels, restaurants and tourist attractions.
Published by: Editora Abril, S.A., Avenida das Nacoes Unidas 7221, Pinheiros, Sao Paulo, SP 05425-902, Brazil. TEL 55-11-50872112, FAX 55-11-50872100, abrilsac@abril.com.br, http://www.abril.com.br. Ed. Regner Camilo. Circ: 250,000.

910.202 BRA
GUIA QUATRO RODAS. SUL. Text in Portuguese. 1975. a. adv. charts; illus.; stat.
Published by: Editora Abril, S.A., Avenida das Nacoes Unidas 7221, Pinheiros, Sao Paulo, SP 05425-902, Brazil. TEL 55-11-50872112, FAX 55-11-50872100, abrilsac@abril.com.br, http://www.abril.com.br. Ed. Victor Civita. Circ: 38,000.

910.202 BRA
GUIA RODOVIARIO - QUATRO RODAS. Variant title: Guia Quatro Rodas. Rodoviario. Text in Portuguese. 1976. a. price varies. adv. charts. **Document type:** *Magazine, Consumer.* **Description:** Includes detailed maps of Brazil with cities and highways in large format.
Published by: Editora Abril, S.A., Avenida das Nacoes Unidas 7221, Pinheiros, Sao Paulo, SP 05425-902, Brazil. TEL 55-11-50872112, FAX 55-11-50872100, abrilsac@abril.com.br, http://www.abril.com.br. Ed. Regner Camilo. Circ: 113,000.

910.202 BRA ISSN 0104-4990
GUIA SAO PAULO - QUATRO RODAS. Variant title: Guia Quatro Rodas. Sao Paulo. Text in Portuguese. 1973. a. adv. charts; illus. **Document type:** *Consumer.* **Description:** Contains hotel, restaurant, service, tourist attraction, bus line and city information for the greater Sao Paulo region.
Published by: Editora Abril, S.A., Avenida das Nacoes Unidas 7221, Pinheiros, Sao Paulo, SP 05425-902, Brazil. TEL 55-11-50872112, FAX 55-11-50872100, abrilsac@abril.com.br, http://www.abril.com.br. Ed. Regner Camilo. Circ: 75,000.

918.104 ARG
GUIA TURISTICA DE ROSARIO Y SANTE FE. Text in Spanish. 1975 (vol.13). irreg. adv. illus.
Published by: Talleres Graficos Amalevi, Calle Mendoza, 1851, Rosario, Santa Fe 2000, Argentina. Ed. Rafael Vinas Paris.

914.6 ESP ISSN 1137-4764
LAS GUIAS DE EDITUR. Text in English. 1996. irreg. **Document type:** *Magazine, Consumer.*
Related titles: ◆ Supplement to: Editur. ISSN 1134-6469.
Published by: Ediciones Turisticas, S.A., C. Consejo de Ciento 355 Piso 3o, Barcelona, 08007, Spain. TEL 34-93-4670229, FAX 34-93-4670218, direccion@editur.es, http://www.editur.com.

910.2 ITA ISSN 1825-5434
GUIDA DEL VIAGGIATORE CURIOSO. Text in Italian. 1990. bi-m. **Document type:** *Magazine, Consumer.*
Former titles (until 1994): Ephemeris (1825-5418); (until 1992): Maecenas (1825-5426)
Related titles: Spanish ed.: Guia del Viajero Curioso. ISSN 1826-1809. 2004.
Published by: Franco Maria Ricci (F M R), Via Cavour 2, Villanova di Castenaso, BO 40055, Italy. TEL 39-051-6008911, http://www.artespa.it.

910.202 ITA
GUIDA EUROCAMPING EUROPA. Text in Italian. a. EUR 12 domestic; EUR 22 foreign (effective 2009). adv. charts; illus. **Document type:** *Catalog, Consumer.*
Published by: Editoriale Eurocamp Srl, Via Ludovico di Breme 79, Milan, MI 20156, Italy. TEL 39-02-38001954, FAX 39-02-38001940, info@guideuro.it, http://www.guideuro.it. Circ: 40,000.

910.202 ITA
GUIDA EUROCAMPING ITALIA E CORSICA. Text in Italian. a. EUR 12 domestic; EUR 22 foreign (effective 2009). adv. charts; illus. **Document type:** *Catalog, Consumer.*
Published by: Editoriale Eurocamp Srl, Via Ludovico di Breme 79, Milan, MI 20156, Italy. TEL 39-02-38001954, FAX 39-02-38001940, info@guideuro.it, http://www.guideuro.it. Circ: 60,000.

910.2 ITA ISSN 1828-4639
LA GUIDA MONACI DEL SISTEMA LAZIO. Text in Italian. 1985. a. **Document type:** *Consumer.*
Former titles (until 2005): Annuario Regione Lazio (1123-1300); (until 1993): Agenda Regione Lazio (1122-8547)
Published by: Guida Monaci SpA, Via Salaria 1319, Rome, 00138, Italy. TEL 39-06-8887777, FAX 39-06-8889996, guida.monaci@italybygm.it, http://www.italybygm.it.

910.202 ITA
GUIDA VIAGGI. Text in Italian. 1973. s-m. **Document type:** *Magazine, Trade.*
Related titles: Online - full text ed.
Published by: G I V I Srl, Via San Gregorio 6, Milan, MI 20124, Italy. TEL 39-02-2020431, FAX 39-02-20204343. Ed. Stefania Vicini. Pub. Giuliano Albani TEL 39-2-876936. R&P, Adv. contact Paolo Valenti. Circ: 7,000.

959.7 VNM
THE GUIDE; tourism - highlights - what's on - services - listings. Variant title: Vietnam Economic Times The Guide. Text in English. m. adv. **Document type:** *Magazine, Consumer.* **Description:** Contains articles and features on travel and tourism in Vietnam.
Related titles: ◆ Online - full text ed.: The Guide Online. ISSN 1563-8839.
Published by: Ringier Pacific (Vietnam) Ltd., 25 Thanh Mien St, Dong Da District, Hanoi, Viet Nam. ringier.sh@hn.vnn.vn, http://www.ringier.com.vn. Ed., Pub. Dao Nguyen Cat. Adv. contact Le Minh Anh. Circ: 10,000 (paid and controlled).

THE GUIDE (YEAR). *see* HOTELS AND RESTAURANTS

910.202 TUR ISSN 1303-054X
THE GUIDE ANKARA. Text in English. a. **Document type:** *Handbook/Manual/Guide, Consumer.*
Published by: Apa Tasarim Yayincilik ve Baski Hizmetleri, TEV-Dr. Orhan Birman Yp Merkezi, Barbaros Bulvary, No 149 Kat 10, Istanbul, 34349, Turkey. TEL 90-212-2746262.

338.476 FRA ISSN 1774-9484
LE GUIDE ANNUEL DES DEPLACEMENTS PROFESSIONNELS. Text in French. 1993. a., latest 2010. EUR 24.90 per issue; EUR 47 combined subscription incl. Voyages d'Affaires (effective 2010). **Document type:** *Directory, Consumer.*
Formerly (until 2000): Corporate Travel Management (1249-1098)
Published by: Varenne Entreprises, 6 cite Paradis, Paris, 75010, France. TEL 33-1-53242400, FAX 33-1-53242433.

910.202 TUR ISSN 1303-5762
THE GUIDE ANTALYA. Text in English. 1992. a. **Document type:** *Handbook/Manual/Guide, Consumer.*
Published by: Apa Tasarim Yayincilik ve Baski Hizmetleri, TEV-Dr. Orhan Birman Yp Merkezi, Barbaros Bulvary, No 149 Kat 10, Istanbul, 34349, Turkey. TEL 90-212-2746262.

GUIDE ARCHEOLOGICHE. *see* ARCHAEOLOGY

TU

910.202 FRA
GUIDE BEL AIR. Text in French. 1936. a. price varies. **Document type:** *Magazine, Consumer.*
Published by: Mondadori France, 1 Rue du Colonel Pierre-Avia, Paris, Cedex 15 75754, France. TEL 33-1-41335001, contact@mondadori.fr, http://www.mondadori.fr.

910.202 TUR ISSN 1303-0558
THE GUIDE BODRUM. Text in English. 1993. a. **Document type:** *Handbook/Manual/Guide, Consumer.*
Published by: Apa Tasarim Yayincilik ve Baski Hizmetleri, TEV-Dr. Orhan Birman Yp Merkezi, Barbaros Bulvary, No 149 Kat 10, Istanbul, 34349, Turkey. TEL 90-212-2746262.

659.1 ROM ISSN 1224-6689
THE GUIDE - BUCURESTI. Text in Multiple languages. 1996. a. adv. **Document type:** *Magazine, Consumer.*
Published by: Crystal Publishing Group, 253, Calea Calarasilor, bl. 67 A, Ste. 4, Bucharest, Romania. TEL 40-21-3233829, FAX 40-21-3234706, office@bucurestiwww.ro, http://www.bucurestiwww.ro.

910.202 CAN
GUIDE DE LA ROUTE: LA CAROLINE DU NORD, LA CAROLINE DU SUD ET LA GEORGIE. Text in English. 1993. a. CAD 10 newsstand/cover to members. adv. **Document type:** *Handbook/Manual/Guide, Consumer.*
Published by: Canadian Automobile Association, 1145 Hunt Club Rd, Ste 200, Ottawa, ON K1V 0Y3, Canada. TEL 613-247-0117, FAX 613-247-0118. Ed. Martine Trudeau. Adv. contact Nicole Villeneuve. Circ: 11,000.

910.202 CAN ISSN 0838-0015
GUIDE DE LA ROUTE: LA FLORIDE. Text in French. 1987. a. CAD 10 newsstand/cover to members. adv. **Document type:** *Handbook/Manual/Guide, Consumer.* **Description:** Listing accommodation, sites to see, things to do in the state of Florida.
Related titles: English Translation: American Automobile Association. Florida Tourbook.
Published by: Canadian Automobile Association, 1145 Hunt Club Rd, Ste 200, Ottawa, ON K1V 0Y3, Canada. TEL 613-247-0117, FAX 613-247-0118. Ed. Martine Trudeau. Adv. contact Nicole Villeneuve. Circ: 24,000.

917.504 CAN
GUIDE DE LA ROUTE: LE CENTRE DE LA COTE ATLANTIQUE. Text in French. 1992. a. CAD 10 newsstand/cover to members. adv. **Document type:** *Handbook/Manual/Guide, Consumer.* **Description:** Lists accomodations, sites to see in the states of Delaware, Maryland, Virginia, West Virginia and the District of Columbia.
Related titles: Translation of: American Automobile Association. Mid-Atlantic Tourbook.
Published by: Canadian Automobile Association, 1145 Hunt Club Rd, Ste 200, Ottawa, ON K1V 0Y3, Canada. TEL 613-247-0117, FAX 613-247-0118. Ed. Martine Trudeau. Adv. contact Nicole Villeneuve. Circ: 14,000.

910.202 CAN
GUIDE DE LA ROUTE: LE MAINE, LE NEW HAMPSHIRE, ET LE VERMONT. Text in French. 1991. a. CAD 10 newsstand/cover to members. adv. **Document type:** *Handbook/Manual/Guide, Consumer.* **Description:** Tourbook listing accommodations, sites to see, and things to do in Maine, New Hampshire and Vermont.
Related titles: English Translation: American Automobile Association. Maine, New Hampshire, Vermont TourBook.
Published by: Canadian Automobile Association, 1145 Hunt Club Rd, Ste 200, Ottawa, ON K1V 0Y3, Canada. TEL 613-247-0117, FAX 613-247-0118. Ed. Martine Trudeau. Adv. contact Nicole Villeneuve. Circ: 11,000.

910.202 CAN
GUIDE DE LA ROUTE: LE QUEBEC ET LES PROVINCES DE L'ATLANTIQUE. Text in French. 1978. a. CAD 10 newsstand/cover to members. adv. **Document type:** *Handbook/Manual/Guide, Consumer.* **Description:** Tourbook listing accommodations, sites to see, things to do in the province of Quebec and the maritime provinces.
Related titles: English Translation: American Automobile Association. Quebec and the Atlantic Provinces Tourbook.
Published by: Canadian Automobile Association, 1145 Hunt Club Rd, Ste 200, Ottawa, ON K1V 0Y3, Canada. TEL 613-247-0117, FAX 613-247-0118. Ed. Martine Trudeau. Adv. contact Nicole Villeneuve. Circ: 35,000.

910.202 CAN ISSN 1193-3569
GUIDE DE LA ROUTE, L'ONTARIO. Text in French. 1988. a. CAD 10 newsstand/cover to members. **Document type:** *Handbook/Manual/Guide, Consumer.* **Description:** Lists accomodations, sites to see in the province of Ontario.
Formerly (until 1988): Guide de la Route, Province de l'Ontario (0838-0023)
Related titles: ◆ English ed.: TourBook. Ontario.
Published by: Canadian Automobile Association, 1145 Hunt Club Rd, Ste 200, Ottawa, ON K1V 0Y3, Canada. TEL 613-247-0117, FAX 613-247-0118. Ed. Martine Trudeau. Circ: 17,500.

914.92 BEL
GUIDE DELTA DES HOTELS ET RESTAURANTS DE BRUXELLES. Text in French. 1978. a. EUR 22.25 (effective 2005). adv. 516 p./no.; **Document type:** *Directory.* **Description:** Provides a guide to more than 2000 restaurants and hotels in Brussels and suburbs, in all price ranges.
Formerly: Guide Delta des Hotels de Bruxelles (0771-7768)
Published by: Editions Delta, Rue Scailquin 55, Brussels, 1210, Belgium. TEL 32-2-217-5555, FAX 32-2-217-9393, editions.delta@skynet.be. Ed. Georges Francis Seingry.

910.91 796 FRA ISSN 1951-3143
GUIDE DES MERVEILLES DE LA NATURE. Text in French. 2000. irreg. **Document type:** *Monographic series, Consumer.*
Published by: Editions Arthaud (Subsidiary of: Editions Flammarion), Flammarion Groupe, 87 quai Panhard-et-levassor, Paris, 75647 Cedex 13, France. contact@artaud.fr, http://www.arthaud.fr.

910.202 CAN ISSN 1912-8096
GUIDE DES PLANIFICATEURS DE CONGRES ET DES VOYAGISTES. Text in French. 1998. a. **Document type:** *Handbook/Manual/Guide, Trade.*
Formerly (until 2004): Guide de Planification. l'Outaouais, Quebec (1489-6907)
Published by: Tourisme Outaouais, 103, rue Laurier, Gatineau, PQ J8X 3V8, Canada. TEL 819-778-2222, 800-265-7822, FAX 819-778-7758, info@tourisme-outaouais.ca, http://www.tourismeoutaouais.com/home/index_f.asp.

910 ITA ISSN 1824-0976
LE GUIDE DI CAMPAGNA AMICA VACANZE E NATURA. Text in Italian. 2004. a. **Document type:** *Magazine, Consumer.*
Published by: Edizioni Tellus, Via XXIV Maggio 43, Rome, 00187, Italy. TEL 39-06-4682324, FAX 39-06-4828865.

910.91 FRA ISSN 0768-2034
GUIDE DU ROUTARD. Text in French. 1975. irreg. **Document type:** *Monographic series, Consumer.*
—CCC.
Published by: Hachette Livre (Subsidiary of: Lagardere Media), 43, Quai de Grenelle, Paris Cedex 15, 75905, France.

910.2 ITA ISSN 1970-3953
GUIDE ILLUSTRATE. Text in Multiple languages. 1992. irreg. **Document type:** *Consumer.*
Published by: Salerno Editrice, Via Valadier 52, Rome, 00193, Italy. TEL 39-06-3608201, FAX 39-06-3223132, info@salernoeditrice.it, http://www.salernoeditrice.it.

910.2 ITA ISSN 1970-3783
GUIDE INSOLITE. Text in Italian. 1998. irreg. **Document type:** *Consumer.*
Published by: Newton Compton Editori, Via Portuense 1415, Rome, 00148, Italy. TEL 39-06-65002553, FAX 39-06-65002892, info@newtoncompton.com, http://www.newtoncompton.com.

910.202 TUR ISSN 1303-0574
THE GUIDE ISTANBUL. Text in English. 1991. a. **Document type:** *Handbook/Manual/Guide, Consumer.*
Published by: Apa Tasarim Yayincilik ve Baski Hizmetleri, TEV-Dr. Orhan Birman Yp Merkezi, Barbaros Bulvary, No 149 Kat 10, Istanbul, 34349, Turkey. TEL 90-212-2746262.

959.7 VNM ISSN 1563-8839
THE GUIDE ONLINE. Text in English. m. **Document type:** *Handbook/Manual/Guide, Consumer.*
Media: Online - full text. **Related titles:** ◆ Print ed.: The Guide.
Published by: Ringier Pacific (Vietnam) Ltd., 25 Thanh Mien St, Dong Da District, Hanoi, Viet Nam. TEL 84-4-8452411, FAX 84-4-8432755, http://www.ringier.com.vn.

910.202 MDG
GUIDE ROUTIER ET TOURISTIQUE: MADAGASCAR, REUNION, MAURICE, COMORES ET SEYCHELLES. Text in French. a. illus.
Formerly: Guide Routier (0572-2330)
Published by: Automobile Club de Madagascar, Service du Guide Routier, BP 571, Antananarivo, Madagascar.

GUIDE SKIRA. LE CITTA D'ARTE. *see* ART

796.5 GBR ISSN 0267-3355
GUIDE TO CARAVAN AND CAMPING HOLIDAYS. Text in English. 1975. a. GBP 7.99 per issue (effective 2009). adv. **Document type:** *Handbook/Manual/Guide, Consumer.* **Description:** Covers every type of caravan and camping facility.
Published by: F H G Guides Ltd. (Subsidiary of: F H G Publications Ltd.), Abbey Mill Business Ctr, Seedhill, Paisley, PA1 1TJ, United Kingdom. TEL 44-141-8870428, FAX 44-141-8897204, sales@fhguides.co.uk, http://www.fhguides.co.uk.

910.09 USA
GUIDE TO CHARLESTON'S ISLANDS MAGAZINE. Text in English. 1987. a. free. adv. tr.lit. back issues avail. **Document type:** *Magazine, Consumer.*
Formerly: Islands Magazine
Published by: Sea Islands Publishing, Inc., 2 Revenel Center, Kiawah Island, SC 29455. TEL 803-768-2304, FAX 803-768-8016. Ed. Robert H Moore. Pub., R&P Bob Moore. Adv. contact Kelly King. Circ: 100,000.

338.4791071 USA
TX911.5
GUIDE TO COLLEGE PROGRAMS IN HOSPITALITY, TOURISM & CULINARY ARTS (CD-ROM). Text in English. 1989. irreg. USD 29.95 to members; USD 59.95 to non-members (effective 2006). **Document type:** *Directory, Consumer.* **Description:** Lists programs by type of degree awarded ranging from certificates and diplomas to graduate degrees; by specialization; and by geographic location.
Former titles: A Guide to College Programs in Culinary Arts, Hospitality & Tourism (Print) (1525-6812); (until 1999): Guide to Hospitality and Tourism Education (1050-933X); Directory of C H R I E Member Schools
Media: CD-ROM.
Indexed: H&TI.
Published by: International Council on Hotel, Restaurant and Institutional Education (C H R I E), 2613 N Parham Rd, Ste 230, Richmond, VA 23294. TEL 804-346-4800, FAX 804-346-5009, info@chrie.org, http://www.chrie.org.

910.91 USA ISSN 1933-1622
GV1024
GUIDE TO COLORADO BACKROADS & 4-WHEEL DRIVE TRAILS. Text in English. 1998. irreg., latest 2nd ed. USD 24.95 per issue (effective 2008). **Document type:** *Guide, Consumer.*
Published by: FunTreks, Inc., PO Box 3127, Monument, CO 80132-3127. TEL 719-536-0722, 877-222-7623, FAX 719-277-7411, books@funtreks.com, http://www.funtreks.com/index.php.

GUIDE TO CRUISING THE CHESAPEAKE BAY. *see* SPORTS AND GAMES—Boats And Boating

914.18 IRL
GUIDE TO DUBLIN. Text in English. a. adv. **Document type:** *Magazine, Consumer.*
Published by: Dublin Tourism Centre, Suffolk St., Dublin, 2, Ireland. TEL 353-1-6057700, FAX 353-1-6057757, http://www.visitdublin.com. adv.: color page EUR 11,000. Circ: 250,000 (controlled).

916.8 647.94 ZAF
GUIDE TO GUEST FARMS AND COUNTRY LODGES IN SOUTHERN AFRICA. Text in English. 1994. biennial. ZAR 44.99 (effective 1996). maps. **Document type:** *Handbook/Manual/Guide, Consumer.* **Description:** Covers South Africa, Lesotho, Namibia and Swaziland.
Published by: Struik Publishers, PO Box 1144, Cape Town, 8000, South Africa. TEL 27-21-4624360, FAX 27-21-4624379.

910 GBR
GUIDE TO INTERNATIONAL TRAVEL. Text in English. q. GBP 67 (effective 2001). **Document type:** *Directory, Trade.* **Description:** Provides a guide to passport controls, visa regulations, vaccination requirements, currency regulation, and import allowances on more than 200 countries.
Former titles: O A G Guide to International Travel (1365-9758); (until 1996): A B C Guide to International Travel (0141-6278); (until 1972): International Travel Requirements
Indexed: RASB.
—CCC.
Published by: Reed Business Information Ltd. (Subsidiary of: Reed Business), DG&G Travel Information, Dukeminster House, Church St, Dunstable, Beds LU5 4HU, United Kingdom. TEL 44-1582-676845, FAX 44-1582-676893, http://www.reedbusiness.co.uk/. Ed. Ken Smith. Pub. Giles Harper. Adv. contact Shelley Cope TEL 44-1582-676851.

910.2 382 KOR
GUIDE TO LIVING IN KOREA. Text in English. a. free. maps; illus.; charts. **Document type:** *Magazine, Trade.* **Description:** Covers all aspects of relocating to Korea, including information on entry and departure, daily living, culture, and business.
Related titles: Online - full text ed.
Published by: Korea Trade-Investment Promotion Agency (K O T R A), KOTRA 13, Heolleungno, Seocho-gu, Seoul, 137-749, Korea, S. TEL 82-2-34607517, FAX 82-2-34607940, digitalkotra@kotra.or.kr, http://www.kotra.or.kr/.

917.04 910.2 USA ISSN 1537-3320
E160
GUIDE TO THE NATIONAL PARK AREAS: EASTERN STATES. Text in English. 1978. irreg., latest 2004, 8th edition. USD 18.95 per issue (effective 2008). back issues avail. **Document type:** *Magazine, Consumer.* **Description:** Acts as a comprehensive guide to nearly 250 sites east of the Mississippi.
Published by: The Globe Pequot Press, Inc., 246 Goose Ln, PO Box 480, Guilford, CT 06437. TEL 203-458-4500, 888-249-7586, FAX 203-458-4603, 800-820-2329, info@globepequot.com, http://www.globepequot.com. Ed. Jeff Serena TEL 203-458-4556.

910.09 CAN
GUIDE TO THE QUEEN CHARLOTTES. Text in English. biennial. USD 10.95.
Published by: Raincoast Books in Vancouver, 8680 Cambie St, Vancouver, BC V6P 6M9, Canada. TEL 604-323-7100.

641.2209687 ZAF
GUIDE TO THE WINELANDS OF THE CAPE. Text in English. irreg., latest 1994. ZAR 35.95. illus.; maps.
Published by: C G R Wine Enterprises, PO Box 435, Stellenbosch, 7599, South Africa. Ed. Christine Rudman.

910.91 USA ISSN 1066-7679
GUIDE TO UNIQUE MEETING AND EVENT FACILITIES. Text in English. 1988. a. USD 39.95 (effective 2000). adv. **Document type:** *Directory.* **Description:** Reference guide featuring colleges, universities, conference centers, camps and lodges, retreats, museums, mansions, national parks, zoos, aquariams, malls, movie theaters, executive suites, cultural, historical, and other unique meeting and event venues in North America. Over 5,000 meeting facilities are listed.
Published by: Amarc, Inc., PO Box 7920, Avon, CO 81620-7920. TEL 970-827-5500, FAX 970-827-9411. Ed., Pub. Michele Nicholes. Adv. contact Greg Clement.

910.2 ITA ISSN 2035-8598
▼ **LE GUIDE TRAVELER DI NATIONAL GEOGRAPHIC.** Text in Italian. 2009. w. **Document type:** *Guide, Consumer.*
Published by: Poligrafici Editoriale (Subsidiary of: Monrif Group), Via Enrico Mattei 106, Bologna, BO 40138, Italy. TEL 39-051-6006111, FAX 39-051-6006266, http://www.monrifgroup.net.

914.404 FRA
GUIDE VERT: ALPES DU NORD. Text in French. 1978. irreg. **Document type:** *Consumer.*
Supersedes in part: Michelin Green Guide Series: Alpes
Published by: Michelin, 46 Av de Breteuil, Paris, Cedex 7 75234, France. **Dist. in U.S. by:** Michelin Travel Publications, PO Box 19008, Greenville, SC 29602-9008. TEL 800-423-0485.

914.404 FRA
GUIDE VERT: ALPES DU SUD. Text in French. irreg., latest 1997. **Document type:** *Consumer.*
Supersedes in part: Michelin Green Guide Series: Alpes
Published by: Michelin, 46 Av de Breteuil, Paris, Cedex 7 75234, France. **Dist. in U.S by:** Michelin Travel Publications, PO Box 19008, Greenville, SC 29602-9008. TEL 800-423-0485.

914.404 FRA
GUIDE VERT: ALSACE ET LORRAINE. Text in French. irreg. **Document type:** *Consumer.*
Published by: Michelin, 46 Av de Breteuil, Paris, Cedex 7 75234, France. **Dist. in U.S. by:** Michelin Travel Publications, PO Box 19008, Greenville, SC 29602-9008. TEL 800-423-0485.

914.404 FRA
GUIDE VERT: AQUITAINE. Text in English. 1998. irreg. **Document type:** *Handbook/Manual/Guide, Consumer.*
Published by: Michelin, 46 Av de Breteuil, Paris, Cedex 7 75234, France. **Dist. in U.S. by:** Michelin Travel Publications, PO Box 19008, Greenville, SC 29602-9008. TEL 800-423-0485.

914.404 FRA
GUIDE VERT: AUVERGNE. Text in French. 1977. irreg. **Document type:** *Consumer.*
Published by: Michelin, 46 Av de Breteuil, Paris, Cedex 7 75234, France. **Dist. in U.S. by:** Michelin Travel Publications, PO Box 19008, Greenville, SC 29602-9008. TEL 800-423-0485.

914.404 FRA
GUIDE VERT: BORDEAUX. Text in English. 1998. irreg., latest 1999. **Document type:** *Handbook/Manual/Guide, Consumer.*
Formerly: Alsace Vosges Champagne
Published by: Michelin, 46 Av de Breteuil, Paris, Cedex 7 75234, France. **Dist. in U.S. by:** Michelin Travel Publications, PO Box 19008, Greenville, SC 29602-9008. TEL 800-423-0485.

914.404 FRA
GUIDE VERT: BOURGOGNE. Text in French. irreg. **Document type:** *Consumer.*

Published by: Michelin, 46 Av de Breteuil, Paris, Cedex 7 75234, France. **Dist. in U.S. by:** Michelin Travel Publications, PO Box 19008, Greenville, SC 29602-9008. TEL 800-423-0485.

914.4 FRA
GUIDE VERT: BRETAGNE. Text in French. irreg. **Document type:** *Consumer.*
Related titles: French ed.
Published by: Michelin, 46 Av de Breteuil, Paris, Cedex 7 75234, France. **Dist. in U.S. by:** Michelin Travel Publications, PO Box 19008, Greenville, SC 29602-9008. TEL 800-423-0485.

914.404 FRA
GUIDE VERT: CHAMPAGNE ARDENNE. Text in French. irreg. **Document type:** *Consumer.*
Published by: Michelin, 46 Av de Breteuil, Paris, Cedex 7 75234, France. **Dist. in U.S. by:** Michelin Travel Publications, PO Box 19008, Greenville, SC 29602-9008. TEL 800-423-0485.

914 FRA
GUIDE VERT: CHARENTE MARITIME. Text in French. irreg., latest 1997. **Document type:** *Consumer.*
Published by: Michelin, 46 Av de Breteuil, Paris, Cedex 7 75234, France. **Dist. in U.S. by:** Michelin Travel Publications, PO Box 19008, Greenville, SC 29602-9008. TEL 800-423-0485.

914.4 FRA
GUIDE VERT: CHATEAUX DE LA LOIRE. Text in French. irreg. **Document type:** *Consumer.*
Related titles: French ed.
Published by: Michelin, 46 Av de Breteuil, Paris, Cedex 7 75234, France. **Dist. in U.S. by:** Michelin Travel Publications, PO Box 19008, Greenville, SC 29602-9008. TEL 800-423-0485.

914.404 FRA
GUIDE VERT: CORSE. Text in French. irreg., latest 1997. **Document type:** *Consumer.*
Published by: Michelin, 46 Av de Breteuil, Paris, Cedex 7 75234, France. **Dist. in U.S. by:** Michelin Travel Publications, PO Box 19008, Greenville, SC 29602-9008. TEL 800-423-0485.

914.4 FRA
GUIDE VERT: COTE D'AZUR. Text in French. irreg., latest 1997. **Document type:** *Consumer.*
Published by: Michelin, 46 Av de Breteuil, Paris, Cedex 7 75234, France. **Dist. in U.S. by:** Michelin Travel Publications, PO Box 19008, Greenville, SC 29602-9008. TEL 800-423-0485.

914.404 FRA
GUIDE VERT: DEAUVILLE TROUVILLE HONFLEUR. Text in French. irreg. **Document type:** *Consumer.*
Published by: Michelin, 46 Av de Breteuil, Paris, Cedex 7 75234, France. **Dist. in U.S. by:** Michelin Travel Publications, PO Box 19008, Greenville, SC 29602-9008. TEL 800-423-0485.

914 FRA
GUIDE VERT: FLORENCE ET TOSCANE. Text in French. irreg., latest 1996. **Document type:** *Consumer.*
Related titles: English ed.
Published by: Michelin, 46 Av de Breteuil, Paris, Cedex 7 75234, France. **Dist. in U.S. by:** Michelin Travel Publications, PO Box 19008, Greenville, SC 29602-9008. TEL 800-423-0485.

914.4 FRA
GUIDE VERT: FRANCE. Text in French. irreg., latest 1997.
Related titles: Spanish ed.; French ed.
Published by: Michelin, 46 Av de Breteuil, Paris, Cedex 7 75234, France. **Dist. in U.S. by:** Michelin Travel Publications, PO Box 19008, Greenville, SC 29602-9008. TEL 800-423-0485.

914.404 FRA
GUIDE VERT: FRANCHE - COMTE JURA. Text in French. irreg., latest 1995.
Formerly: Michelin Green Guide Series: Burgundy
Published by: Michelin, 46 Av de Breteuil, Paris, Cedex 7 75234, France. **Dist. in U.S. by:** Michelin Travel Publications, PO Box 19008, Greenville, SC 29602-9008. TEL 800-423-0485.

914.9 FRA
GUIDE VERT: HOLLANDE. Text in French. 1990. irreg., latest 2004. USD 20. **Document type:** *Consumer.*
Published by: Michelin, 46 Av de Breteuil, Paris, Cedex 7 75234, France. **Dist. in U.S. by:** Michelin Travel Publications, PO Box 19008, Greenville, SC 29602-9008. TEL 800-423-0485.

914.4 FRA
GUIDE VERT: ILE DE FRANCE. Text in French. irreg., latest 1997. **Document type:** *Consumer.*
Published by: Michelin, 46 Av de Breteuil, Paris, Cedex 7 75234, France. **Dist. in U.S. by:** Michelin Travel Publications, PO Box 19008, Greenville, SC 29602-9008. TEL 800-423-0485.

914 FRA
GUIDE VERT: ITALIE. Text in French. irreg. **Document type:** *Consumer.*
Related titles: Spanish ed.
Published by: Michelin, 46 Av de Breteuil, Paris, Cedex 7 75234, France. **Dist. in U.S. by:** Michelin Travel Publications, PO Box 19008, Greenville, SC 29602-9008. TEL 800-423-0485.

914.4 FRA
GUIDE VERT: LA LOIRE. Text in French. irreg. **Document type:** *Consumer.*
Formerly (until 1998): Michelin Green Guide Series: Dordogne
Published by: Michelin, 46 Av de Breteuil, Paris, Cedex 7 75234, France. **Dist. in U.S. by:** Michelin Travel Publications, PO Box 19008, Greenville, SC 29602-9008. TEL 800-423-0485.

914.4 FRA
GUIDE VERT: LA MEUSE. Text in French. irreg.
Published by: Michelin, 46 Av de Breteuil, Paris, Cedex 7 75234, France. **Dist. in U.S. by:** Michelin Travel Publications, PO Box 19008, Greenville, SC 29602-9008. TEL 800-423-0485.

914.4 FRA
GUIDE VERT: LA MOSELLE. Text in French. irreg. **Document type:** *Consumer.*
Formerly: Michelin Green Guide Series: Pyrenees Roussillon - Gorges du Tarn
Published by: Michelin, 46 Av de Breteuil, Paris, Cedex 7 75234, France. **Dist. in U.S. by:** Michelin Travel Publications, PO Box 19008, Greenville, SC 29602-9008. TEL 800-423-0485.

914.2 FRA
GUIDE VERT: LONDRES. Text in French. irreg. **Document type:** *Consumer.*
Related titles: ◆ English ed.: Michelin Green Guides: London.
Published by: Michelin, 46 Av de Breteuil, Paris, Cedex 7 75234, France. **Dist. in U.S. by:** Michelin Travel Publications, PO Box 19001, Greenville, SC 29602-9001. TEL 800-423-0485.

916.4 FRA
GUIDE VERT: MAROC. Text in French. irreg., latest 1997. **Document type:** *Consumer.*
Published by: Michelin, 46 Av de Breteuil, Paris, Cedex 7 75234, France. **Dist. in U.S. by:** Michelin Travel Publications, PO Box 19008, Greenville, SC 29602-9008. TEL 800-423-0485.

914.404 FRA
GUIDE VERT: MIDI - PYRENEES. Text in French. irreg. **Document type:** *Consumer.*
Supersedes: Michelin Green Guide Series: Pyrenees
Published by: Michelin, 46 Av de Breteuil, Paris, Cedex 7 75234, France. **Dist. in U.S. by:** Michelin Travel Publications, PO Box 19008, Greenville, SC 29602-9008. TEL 800-423-0485.

914.404 FRA
GUIDE VERT: NORMANDIE CONTENTIN. Text in French. irreg. **Document type:** *Consumer.*
Published by: Michelin, 46 Av de Breteuil, Paris, Cedex 7 75234, France. **Dist in U.S. by:** Michelin Travel Publications, PO Box 19008, Greenville, SC 29602-9008. TEL 800-423-0485.

914.404 FRA
GUIDE VERT: NORMANDIE VALLEE DE LA SEINE. Text in French. irreg. **Document type:** *Consumer.*
Published by: Michelin, 46 Av de Breteuil, Paris, Cedex 7 75234, France. **Dist. in U.S. by:** Michelin Travel Publications, PO Box 19008, Greenville, SC 29602-9008. TEL 800-423-0485.

914.4 FRA
GUIDE VERT: PARIS. Text in French. irreg., latest 1996. **Document type:** *Consumer.*
Related titles: Spanish ed.; French ed.
Published by: Michelin, 46 Av de Breteuil, Paris, Cedex 7 75234, France. **Dist. in U.S. by:** Michelin Travel Publications, PO Box 19008, Greenville, SC 29602-9008. TEL 800-423-0485.

914.4 FRA
GUIDE VERT: PARIS ENFANTS. Text in French. irreg. **Document type:** *Consumer.*
Formerly: Michelin Green Guide Series: Euro-Disney
Published by: Michelin, 46 Av de Breteuil, Paris, Cedex 7 75234, France. **Dist. in U.S. by:** Michelin Travel Publications, PO Box 19008, Greenville, SC 29602-9008. TEL 800-423-0485.

914.404 FRA
GUIDE VERT: PERIGORD QUERCY DORDOGNE LOT. Text in French. irreg., latest 1997. **Document type:** *Consumer.*
Published by: Michelin, 46 Av de Breteuil, Paris, Cedex 7 75234, France. **Dist. in U.S. by:** Michelin Travel Publications, PO Box 19008, Greenville, SC 29602-9008. TEL 800-423-0485.

914.404 FRA
GUIDE VERT: POITOU CHARENTES VENDEE. Text in French. irreg., latest 1997. **Document type:** *Consumer.*
Published by: Michelin, 46 Av de Breteuil, Paris, Cedex 7 75234, France. **Dist. in U.S. by:** Michelin Travel Publications, PO Box 19008, Greenville, SC 29602-9008. TEL 800-423-0485.

914.404 FRA
GUIDE VERT: PROVENCE. Text in French. 1980. irreg. **Document type:** *Consumer.*
Related titles: French ed.
Published by: Michelin, 46 Av de Breteuil, Paris, Cedex 7 75234, France. **Dist. in U.S. by:** Michelin Travel Publications, PO Box 19008, Greenville, SC 29602-9008. TEL 800-423-0485.

914.3 FRA
GUIDE VERT: VIENNE. Text in French. 1997. irreg. **Document type:** *Consumer.*
Related titles: French ed.
Published by: Michelin, 46 Av de Breteuil, Paris, Cedex 7 75234, France. **Dist. in the U.S. by:** Michelin Travel Publications, PO Box 19008, Greenville, SC 29602-9008. TEL 800-423-0485.

914.3 FRA
GUIDE VERT: WEEK - END BERLIN. Text in French. 1997. irreg. **Document type:** *Consumer.*
Related titles: French ed.
Published by: Michelin, 46 Av de Breteuil, Paris, Cedex 7 75234, France. **Dist. in the U.S. by:** Michelin Travel Publications, PO Box 19008, Greenville, SC 29602-9008. TEL 800-423-0485.

914.9 FRA
GUIDE VERT: WEEK - END BRUXELLES. Text in French. irreg. **Document type:** *Consumer.*
Related titles: French ed.
Published by: Michelin, 46 Av de Breteuil, Paris, Cedex 7 75234, France. **Dist. in the U.S. by:** Michelin Travel Publications, PO Box 19008, Greenville, SC 29602-9008. TEL 800-423-0485.

910.4 FRA ISSN 0991-4781
GUIDES DE CHARME RIVAGES. Text in French. 1988. irreg.
Published by: Rivages, 106 bd. Saint Germain, Paris, 75006, France. Ed. Michelle Gastaut.

914.891 DNK ISSN 1901-8223
GUIDES.DK. Variant title: Turistfoererforeningen. Medlemsliste. Text in Danish. 1975. irreg. free. **Document type:** *Directory, Trade.*
Formerly (until 2002): Turistfoerer (0108-8734)
Related titles: Online - full text ed.
Published by: Turistfoererforeningen/Association of Authorized Guides in Copenhagen, Noerregade 41, 119C, Copenhagen K, 1165, Denmark. TEL 45-33-113310, FAX 45-33-113705, info@guides.dk.

338.4 CHN ISSN 1008-6080
GUILIN LUYOU GAODENG ZHUANKE XUEXIAO XUEBAO/GUILIN INSTITUTE OF TOURISM. JOURNAL. Text in Chinese. 1989. bi-m. CNY 6 newsstand/cover (effective 2006). **Document type:** *Journal, Academic/Scholarly.*
Formerly: Luyou Yanjiu yu Shijian
Related titles: Online - full text ed.
Published by: Guilin Luyou Gaodeng Zhuanke Xuexiao, 5, Canluan Lu, Guilin, 541004, China.

910.09 BHR
GULF TOURISM DIRECTORY. Text in English. 1990. a.?. **Document type:** *Directory.*
Address: PO Box 859, Manama, Bahrain. TEL 731224, FAX 731067. Ed. Rashid Bin Muhammad Al Khalifa.

910.09 ITA ISSN 1122-0627
GULLIVER. Text in Italian. 1993. m. (11/yr.). adv. illus. **Document type:** *Magazine, Consumer.* **Description:** Examines travel as not only a means to vacation but also explore trends in international lifestyles.
Published by: R C S Periodici (Subsidiary of: R C S Mediagroup), Via San Marco 21, Milan, 20121, Italy. TEL 39-2-25844111, FAX 39-2-25845444, info@periodici.rcs.it, http://www.rcsmediagroup.it/siti/periodici.php. Circ: 81,500 (paid). **Dist. in UK by:** Seymour Distribution Ltd, 86 Newman St, London W1T 3EX, United Kingdom. FAX 44-207-396-8002, enquiries@seymour.co.uk.

H O R E S C A - INFORMATIONS. (Hoteliers Restaurateurs et Cafetiers) *see* HOTELS AND RESTAURANTS

910.20 DEU ISSN 1868-2715
▼ **HAFF-MAGAZIN/MAGAZYN-ZALEWU SZCZECINSKIEGO;** die Zeitschrift der Regionalen Agenda fuer die Region Stettiner Haff. Text in German, Polish. 2009. 2/yr. **Document type:** *Journal, Trade.*
Published by: Callidus Verlag, Alter Holzhafen 19, Wismar, 23966, Germany. TEL 49-3841-7582760, FAX 49-3841-229985, callidus@callidusverlag.de, http://www.callidusverlag.de.

526 910 USA
HAGSTROM MAP AND TRAVEL NEWSLETTER. Text in English. 1986. q. free. bk.rev. **Document type:** *Newsletter.*
Formerly: Hagstrom Map and Travel Center Newsletter
Published by: Hagstrom Map and Travel, 51 W. 43rd St., New York, NY 10036-7407. TEL 212-398-1222. Ed. Douglas B Rose. Circ: 15,780.

HAKLUYT SOCIETY; works in the ordinary series. *see* HISTORY

914.04 DEU
HAMBURGER TOP INFO FOR VISITORS. Text in English. 1984. m. EUR 18.20 per issue (effective 2009). adv. illus. back issues avail. **Document type:** *Magazine, Consumer.*
Published by: Hamburg Fuehrer Verlag GmbH, Alter Wall 65, Hamburg, 20457, Germany. TEL 49-40-448185, FAX 49-40-452368, info@hamburg-fuehrer.de, http://www.hamburg-fuehrer.de. Adv. contact Sabine Mackprang. B&W page EUR 2,165, color page EUR 3,235; 90 x 185. Circ: 30,000.

910.91 388.3 NLD
HANDBOEK AUTO EN VERKEER. Text in Dutch. a. free to members (effective 2008). adv.
Published by: Algemene Nederlandse Wielrijders Bond (A N W B) Media/Dutch Automobile Association Media, Postbus 93200, The Hague, 2509 BA, Netherlands. TEL 31-70-3141470, FAX 31-70-3146538, http://www.anwbmedia.nl. adv.: color page EUR 2,820. Circ: 130,000.

914.04 NLD ISSN 1570-3649
HANDBOEK EUROPA. Text in Dutch. 2001. a. free to members (effective 2008). adv.
Formerly (until 2002): Reisinformatie Europa (1568-7988)
Published by: Algemene Nederlandse Wielrijders Bond (A N W B) Media/Dutch Automobile Association Media, Postbus 93200, The Hague, 2509 BA, Netherlands. TEL 31-70-3141470, FAX 31-70-3146538, http://www.anwbmedia.nl. adv.: color page EUR 8,652. Circ: 490,000.

910.91 796.6 NLD
HANDBOEK FIETSEN. Text in Dutch. a. free to members (effective 2008). adv.
Published by: Algemene Nederlandse Wielrijders Bond (A N W B) Media/Dutch Automobile Association Media, Postbus 93200, The Hague, 2509 BA, Netherlands. TEL 31-70-3141470, FAX 31-70-3146538, http://www.anwbmedia.nl. adv.: color page EUR 1,839. Circ: 85,000.

910.91 387.7 NLD
HANDBOEK VERRE REIZEN. Text in Dutch. a. free to members (effective 2008). adv.
Published by: Algemene Nederlandse Wielrijders Bond (A N W B) Media/Dutch Automobile Association Media, Postbus 93200, The Hague, 2509 BA, Netherlands. TEL 31-70-3141470, FAX 31-70-3146538, http://www.anwbmedia.nl. adv.: color page EUR 1,260. Circ: 60,000.

915.1 KOR
A HANDBOOK OF KOREA. Text in Korean. 1978. a.
Published by: The Korean Culture and Information Service (K O I S), 3-4 Fl., Fnc, Kolon Corp., 15, Hyojaro, Jongno-gu, Seoul, 110-040, Korea, S. TEL 82-2-3981-961, FAX 82-2-3981-882, http://www.korea.net/.

910.09 DEU
HANSESTADT LUEBECK TRAVEMUENDE AKTUELL; das offizielle Programm der Hansestadt Luebeck. Text in German. 1951. m. free (effective 2005). adv. **Document type:** *Magazine, Consumer.*
Published by: Max Schmidt-Roemhild KG, Mengstr 16, Luebeck, 23552, Germany. TEL 49-451-703101, FAX 49-451-7031253, info@schmidt-roemhild.de, http://www.beleke.de/unternehmen/verlage/schmidtroemhild/index.html. Circ: 10,500 (free).

HARTFORD MAGAZINE. *see* GENERAL INTEREST PERIODICALS—United States

910.91 FRA ISSN 1950-8271
HAUTES-ALPES LOISIR. Text in French. 200?. q. EUR 25 (effective 2009). **Document type:** *Magazine, Consumer.*
Published by: Dauphine Libere, Les Iles Cordees, Veurey-Voroize, Cedex 38913, France. TEL 33-4-76887100, src@ledl.com, http://www.ledauphine.com.

910.9178 790.1 USA
HAVE CHILDREN WILL TRAVEL. Text in English. q. price varies. back issues avail. **Document type:** *Newsletter, Consumer.* **Description:** Contains year-round family vacation ideas, practical travel information, information about family fun resorts, money saving ideas and travel tips, tricks and tactics.
Published by: Have Children Will Travel, Inc., PO Box 2766, Kamuela, HI 96743. TEL 808-885-0333. Pub. Deb Cornick.

TU

910.2 USA ISSN 1557-7961
DU622
HAWAII: AN EXPLORER'S GUIDE. Text in English. 2006. irreg., latest 2008, 2nd ed. USD 21.95 2nd ed. (effective 2008). **Document type:** *Directory, Consumer.* **Description:** Features updated listings of resorts, condos, vacation cottages and campgrounds as well as hundreds of dining recommendations, from plate lunches and local grinds to seared ahi and Kona lobster at haute eateries.
Published by: The Countryman Press (Subsidiary of: W.W. Norton & Co., Inc.), PO Box 748, Woodstock, VT 05091. TEL 802-457-4826, 800-245-4151, FAX 802-457-1678, countrymanpress@wwnorton.com.

910.202 USA
HAWAII DRIVE GUIDE. Text in English. 1974. 3/yr. USD 5 per issue (effective 2011). adv. **Document type:** *Magazine, Consumer.* **Description:** Touring guides for Oahu, Maui, Hawaii and Kauai, with detailed maps and descriptions of scenic and historical sites, visitor attractions, selected restaurants, shops and centers, things to do, sports and other information for the independent traveller.
Formerly (until 2004): Drive Guide. Hawaii
Related titles: Online - full text ed.: free (effective 2011); ◆ Regional ed(s).: Oahu Drive Guide. ISSN 0191-8478; Maui Drive Guide; Kauai Drive Guide.
Published by: Honolulu Publishing Company, Ltd., Ocean View Ctr, 707 Richards St, Ste 525, Honolulu, HI 96813. TEL 808-524-7400, 800-272-5245. Ed. Brett Uprichard. Pub. Maurina Borgatti TEL 808-935-9822.

HAWAII HOSPITALITY. *see* HOTELS AND RESTAURANTS

HAWAII HOTEL NETWORK. *see* TRAVEL AND TOURISM—Airline Inflight And Hotel Inroom

910.09 USA ISSN 1549-2109
HAWAII MAGAZINE. Text in English. 1982. bi-m. USD 20 domestic; USD 29 foreign (effective 2007). adv. bk.rev. illus. index. **Document type:** *Magazine, Consumer.* **Description:** Provides exploration of the natural and scenic richness of the Hawaiian islands, including tropical rainforests, local foods, lore and legend, and outdoor sports and activities.
Formerly: Hawaii (0892-0990)
Related titles: Microfilm ed.
Published by: PacificBasin Communications, LLC, 1000 Bishop St, Ste 405, Honolulu, HI 96813. TEL 808-537-9500, FAX 808-537-6455, info@pacificbasin.net, http://www.pacificbasin.net. Ed. John Heckathorn TEL 808-534-7545. Pub. John Alves TEL 808-534-7540. Adv. contact Helen McNeil TEL 808-534-7544. color page USD 7,910; trim 8.125 x 10.875. Circ: 64,846 (paid).

910.202 USA ISSN 1930-5974
DU628.H28
HAWAII, THE BIG ISLAND REVEALED. Text in English. 1997. irreg. (4th ed.). USD 15.95 per issue (effective 2007). **Document type:** *Guide, Consumer.*
Published by: Wizard Publications, Inc., PO Box 991, Lihue, HI 96766-0991. aloha@wizardpub.com, http://www.wizardpub.com/main/home.html.

910.91 388.3 USA ISSN 1524-8453
HAWAII WESTWAYS. Text in English. 199?. bi-m. **Document type:** *Magazine, Consumer.*
Published by: Automobile Club of Southern California, PO Box 25001, Santa Ana, CA 92799. TEL 877-428-2277, FAX 800-222-8794, http://www.aaa-calif.com.

910.09 DEU
HAYIT SPEZIAL. Text in German. 1998. bi-m. **Document type:** *Magazine, Consumer.*
Published by: Hayit Medien, Luxemburger Str 181, Cologne, 50939, Germany. TEL 49-221-9216590, FAX 49-221- 92163524, anzeigen@hayit.com, http://www.hayit.de. Ed., Pub. Ertay Hayit.

HEALTHCARE TRAVELER. *see* HEALTH FACILITIES AND ADMINISTRATION

910.91 614 USA
HEALTHY TRAVELER. Text in English. 2002. q. free with subscr. to National Geographic Traveler. **Document type:** *Magazine, Consumer.* **Description:** Contains information on regional health alerts, list of English speaking Hospitals and health facilities, medical information on travelling with the elderly or children, and other related travel health topics.
Related titles: ◆ Supplement to: National Geographic Traveler. ISSN 0747-0932.
Indexed: H&TI.
Published by: National Geographic Society, PO Box 98199, Washington, DC 20090. TEL 800-647-5463, askngs@nationalgeographic.com, http://www.nationalgeographic.com/.

917.42 051 USA ISSN 1559-3991
HEART OF NEW HAMPSHIRE MAGAZINE. Text in English. 2004 (Sept.). q. USD 25 (effective 2006). adv.
Related titles: Online - full content ed.: ISSN 1559-4009.
Published by: Heart of New Hampshire Adventure, P O Box 500, Rumney, NH 03266. TEL 603-786-9278. Pub. Wayne D King. Adv. contact Kathe Higgins.

338.4791 USA ISSN 1933-6853
HELIUM REPORT. Text in English. 2006. irreg. **Document type:** *Monographic series, Consumer.*
Media: Online - full text.
Published by: Helium Group, LLC, 625 Second St, 3rd flr, San Francisco, CA 94107. TEL 415-543-0520, helium@heliumreport.com, http://www.heliumreport.com.

914 FIN
HELSINKI IN YOUR POCKET. Text in English. 5/yr. USD 25 (effective 2002). adv. **Document type:** *Magazine, Consumer.*
Address: Pohjoinen Hesperiankatu 13B14, Helsinki, 00260, Finland. TEL 358-9-5662927, FAX 358-9-492295.

917.93135 USA
HERE IS LAS VEGAS; greater Las Vegas newcomers & relocation journal. Text in English. 1991. 2/yr. USD 5.95 newsstand/cover. **Document type:** *Magazine, Consumer.*
Related titles: Microfilm ed.: (from LIB).
Published by: DeCor Publishing, Inc., 3750 S Jones Blvd, Las Vegas, NV 89103. TEL 702-221-8836, FAX 702-253-9715. Ed. Ginger Tafoya. Pub. Bruce P Diebold. Circ: 115,000.

910.2 GBR ISSN 2044-3366
HEREFORDSHIRE & WORCESTERSHIRE SIGN POST. Text in English. 2003. a. GBP 2.95 per issue (effective 2010). adv. **Document type:** *Guide, Consumer.* **Description:** Contains interesting articles and information on local attractions, amenities and events.
Supersedes in part (in 2009): Shropshire, Herefordshire and Worcestershire Sign Post (1479-6414)
Related titles: Online - full text ed.: free (effective 2010).
Published by: County Signpost Ltd., Park Stile, Berriewood Ln, Condover, Shrewsbury, Shropshire SY5 7BY, United Kingdom. TEL 44-1743-874098, FAX 44-1743-874976, http://www.countysignpost.co.uk. Ed. Adam Davison.

917.13 USA ISSN 1524-5977
DU628.M3
HIDDEN MAUI; including Lahaina, Kaanapali, Haleakala and the Hana Highway. Text in English. 1996. irreg. USD 15.95 per issue (effective 2011). maps. **Document type:** *Guide, Trade.*
Published by: Ulysses Press, PO Box 3440, Berkeley, CA 94703. TEL 510-601-8301, FAX 510-601-8307, ulysses@ulyssespress.com.

917.94 USA ISSN 1097-1572
F867.5
HIDDEN SAN FRANCISCO & NORTHERN CALIFORNIA; including Napa, Sonoma, Mendocino, Santa Cruz, Monterey, Yosemite and Lake Tahoe. Text in English. 1984. biennial. USD 19.95 per issue (effective 2011). maps. **Document type:** *Handbook/Manual/Guide, Trade.*
Published by: Ulysses Press, PO Box 3440, Berkeley, CA 94703. TEL 510-601-8301, FAX 510-601-8307, ulysses@ulyssespress.com.

910.202 DEU ISSN 1430-4511
HIDEAWAYS; die schoensten Hotels und Destinationen der Welt. Text in German. 1996. q. EUR 30; EUR 8 newsstand/cover (effective 2007). adv. **Document type:** *Magazine, Consumer.*
Related titles: ◆ Supplement(s): Hideaways Beauty Special. ISSN 1439-7250; ◆ Hideaways Suite Dreams; ◆ Hideaways Golf Special.
Published by: Klocke Verlag GmbH, Hoefeweg 40, Bielefeld, 33619, Germany. TEL 49-521-911110, FAX 49-521-9111112, info@klocke-verlag.de, http://www.klocke-verlag.de. Ed. Thomas Klocke. Pubs. Martina Klocke, Thomas Klocke. Adv. contact Wolfgang Pohl. color page EUR 10,000. Circ: 57,434 (paid). **Subscr. to:** Leser-Club Merkur, Postfach 1118, Neckarsulm 74148, Germany. TEL 49-7132-959205. **Dist. by:** Special Interest, Waldstr 70, Dietzenbach 63128, Germany. TEL 49-6074-8235-0.

910.202 DEU ISSN 1439-7250
HIDEAWAYS BEAUTY SPECIAL. Text in German. 1999. a. EUR 7 newsstand/cover (effective 2007). adv. **Document type:** *Magazine, Consumer.*
Related titles: ◆ Supplement to: Hideaways. ISSN 1430-4511.
Published by: Klocke Verlag GmbH, Hoefeweg 40, Bielefeld, 33619, Germany. TEL 49-521-911110, FAX 49-521-9111112, info@klocke-verlag.de, http://www.klocke-verlag.de. adv.: color page EUR 8,500. Circ: 63,658 (paid and controlled).

796.352 DEU
HIDEAWAYS GOLF SPECIAL. Text in German. 2000. a. EUR 8 newsstand/cover (effective 2007). adv. **Document type:** *Magazine, Consumer.*
Related titles: ◆ Supplement to: Hideaways. ISSN 1430-4511.
Published by: Klocke Verlag GmbH, Hoefeweg 40, Bielefeld, 33619, Germany. TEL 49-521-911110, FAX 49-521-9111112, info@klocke-verlag.de, http://www.klocke-verlag.de. adv.: color page EUR 8,500. Circ: 46,812 (paid and controlled).

210.202 USA ISSN 1930-2622
HIDEAWAYS LIFE; know more get more travel better. Text in English. 1981. bi-m. USD 185 (effective 2006). adv. bk.rev. back issues avail. **Document type:** *Magazine, Consumer.* **Description:** Lists villa rentals worldwide, especially Caribbean, Mexico, Hawaii, and Europe. Includes articles about out-of-the-ordinary vacations.
Formerly (until Jan. 2006): Hideaways Guide (0741-1952)
Published by: Hideaways International, 767 Islington St, Portsmouth, NH 03801-4236. TEL 603-430-4433, FAX 603-430-4444, info@hideaways.com, http://www.hideaways.com/. Ed. Pat Chaudoin. Pub., R&P Michael F Thiel. Adv. contact Gail Richard. Circ: 20,000.

910.202 USA
HIDEAWAYS NEWSLETTER. Text in English. 1983. 4/yr. USD 99 membership (effective 2000). adv. back issues avail. **Document type:** *Newsletter.* **Description:** Lists villa rentals worldwide, especially Caribbean, Mexico, Hawaii, and Europe. Includes travel tips, features on less-traveled destinations, members' ratings on small resorts.
Published by: Hideaways International, 767 Islington St, Portsmouth, NH 03801-4236. TEL 603-430-4433, FAX 603-430-4444. Ed. Peg Aaronian. Pub., R&P Michael F Thiel. Adv. contact Gail Richard. Circ: 20,000.

910.202 DEU
HIDEAWAYS SUITE DREAMS. Text in English, German. a. EUR 8 newsstand/cover (effective 2009). adv. **Document type:** *Magazine, Consumer.*
Related titles: ◆ Supplement to: Hideaways. ISSN 1430-4511.
Published by: Klocke Verlag GmbH, Hoefeweg 40, Bielefeld, 33619, Germany. TEL 49-521-911110, FAX 49-521-9111112, info@klocke-verlag.de, http://www.klocke-verlag.de. adv.: color page EUR 9,000. Circ: 6,448 (controlled).

910.202 DEU
HIER; Urlaub - Fliegen - Reiselust. Text in German. 1996. q. EUR 6; EUR 1.80 newsstand/cover (effective 2003). adv. **Document type:** *Magazine, Consumer.*
Published by: Meyer's GmbH, Ellernstr 25, Hannover, 30175, Germany. TEL 49-511-2833970, FAX 49-511-28339779. Ed. Jutta Lemcke. Adv. contact Jan Hagemeister. color page EUR 7,798; trim 180 x 245. Circ: 250,000 (paid and controlled).

917.7271 USA
HIGHLIGHTS OF HUNTINGTON COUNTY. Text in English. a. **Document type:** *Magazine, Consumer.*
Published by: Michiana Business Publications, Inc., 7729 Westfield Dr, Fort Wayne, IN 46825. TEL 260-497-0433, FAX 260-497-0822, dcopeland@businesspeople.com, http://www.businesspeople.com.

910.91 USA ISSN 1558-6316
GV199.42.A4
HIKING ALASKA. Text in English. 1997. irreg., latest 2006, 2nd ed. USD 19.95 per issue (effective 2008). **Document type:** *Directory, Consumer.* **Description:** Provides firsthand descriptions and detailed maps for 100 of the states finest trails.
Published by: Falcon Publishing (Subsidiary of: The Globe Pequot Press, Inc.), 246 Goose Ln, PO Box 480, Guilford, CT 06437. TEL 203-458-4500, http://www.falcon.com. Ed. Shelley Wolf.

910.2 USA ISSN 1553-2259
GV199.42.N62
HIKING CARLSBAD CAVERNS AND GUADALUPE MOUNTAINS NATIONAL PARKS. Variant title: Carlsbad Caverns and Guadalupe Mountains National Parks. Text in English. 1996. biennial, latest 2005, 2nd ed. USD 12.95 per issue (effective 2008). 160 p./no.; **Document type:** *Directory, Consumer.* **Description:** Guides through all the thirty-six trails - both underground and aboveground - in Carlsbad Caverns and Guadalupe Mountains national parks.
Published by: Falcon Publishing (Subsidiary of: The Globe Pequot Press, Inc.), 246 Goose Ln, PO Box 480, Guilford, CT 06437. TEL 203-458-4500, sales@falconpublishing.com, http://www.falcon.com. Ed. Shelley Wolf.

910.91 USA ISSN 1933-4060
GV199.42.W22
HIKING MOUNT RAINIER NATIONAL PARK. Variant title: Mount Rainier National Park. National Park. Text in English. 1999. irreg., latest 2005, 2nd ed. USD 15.95 per issue (effective 2008). **Document type:** *Directory, Consumer.* **Description:** Features sixty-one of the finest trails in Washington - from short day hikes to backcountry treks.
Published by: Falcon Publishing (Subsidiary of: The Globe Pequot Press, Inc.), 246 Goose Ln, PO Box 480, Guilford, CT 06437. TEL 203-458-4500, http://www.falcon.com. Ed. Shelley Wolf.

910.202 USA ISSN 1930-7314
HIKING NEVADA; a guide to Nevada's greatest hiking adventures. Text in English. 1994. irreg., latest 2006, 2nd ed. USD 15.95 per issue (effective 2008). **Document type:** *Directory, Consumer.* **Description:** Features ninety-four hikes that include the shimmering desert salt flats, shady redrock canyons and dramatic alpine peaks.
Published by: Falcon Publishing (Subsidiary of: The Globe Pequot Press, Inc.), 246 Goose Ln, PO Box 480, Guilford, CT 06437. TEL 203-458-4500, http://www.falcon.com. Ed. Shelley Wolf.

917.8 910.2 USA ISSN 1540-0611
HIKING ROCKY MOUNTAIN NATIONAL PARK. Text in English. 1994. irreg., latest 2002, 9th ed. USD 14.95 per issue (effective 2008). 320 p./no.; **Document type:** *Guide, Consumer.* **Description:** Contains hike descriptions, which include detailed information on trail access, best times for hiking and points of interest along the way.
Formerly (until 1994): Rocky Mountain National Park Hiking Trails, Including Indian Peaks
Published by: The Globe Pequot Press, Inc., 246 Goose Ln, PO Box 480, Guilford, CT 06437. TEL 203-458-4500, 888-249-7586, FAX 203-458-4603, 800-820-2329, info@globepequot.com, http://www.globepequot.com.

917.604 USA ISSN 1524-2315
AN1.T4
HILL COUNTRY SUN. Text in English. 1990. m. USD 18 domestic; USD 25 foreign (effective 2001). adv. bk.rev.; music rev.; play rev. illus.; maps. **Document type:** *Magazine, Consumer.* **Description:** Focuses on interesting people, places and events in the scenic Central Texas Hill Country.
Related titles: Online - full text ed.
Published by: (Hill Country Sun), Sun Country Publications, PO Box 1482, Wimberley, TX 78676. TEL 512-847-5162, FAX 512-847-5162. Ed., R&P Allan C Kimball. Pub. Madonna M Kimball. Adv. contact Madonna Kimball. color page USD 975, B&W page USD 825; trim 10.75 x 13.75. Circ: 30,000 (paid and controlled).

338.4791 NPL
HIMALAYAN TRAVEL TRADE JOURNAL. Text in English. bi-m. free to tourism professionals worldwide. adv. **Document type:** *Journal, Consumer.* **Description:** Provides travel information on the Himalayas including hotel, resorts and news.
Related titles: Online - full content ed.
Published by: M D Publishing Co. Pvt. Ltd., Tripureswor, PO Box 3525, Kathmandu, Nepal. TEL 977-1-260418, 977-1-256003, 977-1-260327, FAX 977-1-260159, nttj@mos.com.np.

917 USA ISSN 1947-6205
▼ **HIPCOMPASS ESCAPES.** Variant title: Escapes. Text in English. 2009. q. free (effective 2009). **Document type:** *Magazine, Consumer.* **Description:** Presents information on a wide variety of travel options, from solo to family and budget to luxury.
Media: Online - full content.
Published by: HipCompass Inc., 3463 State St, No 404, Santa Barbara, CA 93105. TEL 800-609-4011, editor@hipcompassescapes.com, http://hipcompass.com/.

910.91 GBR ISSN 2044-1878
▼ **HISTORIC DAYS OUT.** Text in English. 2009. a. GBP 5.99 per issue (effective 2010). **Document type:** *Guide, Consumer.* **Description:** Contains information about the best places to visit in the summer in the UK.
Published by: B B C Magazines Bristol, 9th Fl, Tower House, Fairfax St, Bristol, BS1 3BN, United Kingdom. TEL 44-117-9279009, FAX 44-117-9349008, info@bbcmagazinesbristol.com, http://www.bbcmagazinesbristol.com. Ed. Dave Musgrove. Adv. contact Richard Gibson TEL 44-117-9338012.

338.4791 DEU ISSN 1863-9798
HOCHSCHULE BREMEN. SCHOOL OF INTERNATIONAL BUSINESS. INTERNATIONALER STUDIENGANG FUER TOURISMUSMANAGEMENT. SCHRIFTENREIHE. Text in German. 2006. irreg., latest vol.6, 2009. price varies. **Document type:** *Monographic series, Academic/Scholarly.*
Published by: (Hochschule Bremen, School of International Business), Ibidem Verlag, Melchiorstr 15, Stuttgart, 70439, Germany. TEL 49-711-9807954, FAX 49-711-9807952, ibidem@ibidem-verlag.de, http://www.ibidem-verlag.de.

HOERZU. *see* COMMUNICATIONS—Television And Cable

914.3 DEU
▼ **HOERZU HEIMAT**; so schoen ist Deutschland. Text in German. 2010. bi-m. EUR 3.50 newsstand/cover (effective 2011). adv. **Document type:** *Magazine, Consumer.*
Published by: Axel Springer Verlag AG, Axel-Springer-Platz 1, Hamburg, 20350, Germany. TEL 49-40-34700, FAX 49-40-34728460, information@axelspringer.de, http://www.asv.de.

910 AUT
HOLIDAY & BUSINESS IN AUSTRIA. Text in German. s-a.
Published by: Redaktionsbuero fuer Touristik, Am See 89, Deutsch Brodersdorf, N 2443, Austria. TEL 01-932745, FAX 01-5266116. Ed. Leo Froehlich. Circ: 50,000.

916.8 362.4 ZAF
HOLIDAY GUIDE O F S/VAKANSIEGIDS O V S. Text in English, Afrikaans. 1994. a. free. **Document type:** *Magazine, Consumer.* **Description:** Covers vacationing in the Orange Free State for disabled people.
Published by: Satour, Private Bag X164, Pretoria, 0001, South Africa.

910 GBR ISSN 1472-7110
HOLIDAY GUIDE. WINTER. Text in English. 1972. a. **Document type:** *Directory, Trade.* **Description:** Covers all commission-paying A.B.T.A. tour operators by country.
Former titles (until 2001): O A G Holiday Guide. Winter (1366-168X); (until 1997): A B C Holiday Guide. Winter (1462-9844); Which superseded in part (in 199?): A B C Holiday Guide (1357-1184)
—CCC.
Published by: Reed Travel Group, Church St, Dunstable, Beds LU5 4HB, United Kingdom. TEL 44-1582-600111, FAX 44-1582-695230. Ed. Bozena Briggs. Circ: 4,000.

919 AUS ISSN 1837-4662
▼ **HOLIDAY HOMES MAGAZINE.** Variant title: Holiday Homes Magazine Queensland Edition. Text in English. 2009. s-a. USD 7.95 newsstand/cover (effective 2010). adv. back issues avail. **Document type:** *Magazine, Trade.*
Published by: Holiday Media Pty Ltd., PO Box 140, Palm Cove, QLD 4879, Australia. FAX 44-7-40590125, info@holidaymedia.com.au. Adv. contact Paul McGilvery TEL 61-4-16874937.

910.2 GBR ISSN 1746-5125
HOLIDAY PARKS GUIDE. Text in English. 1971. a. free to members (effective 2009). **Document type:** *Directory, Consumer.* **Description:** Contains over 3,000 caravan and chalet sites.
Former titles (until 2004): Caravan & Chalet Parks Guide (0957-7335); (until 1990): Caravan and Chalet Sites Guide (0269-8730)
Published by: British Holiday & Home Parks Association Ltd., Chichester House, 6 Pullman Ct, Great Western Rd, Gloucester, GL1 3ND, United Kingdom. TEL 44-1452-526911, FAX 44-1452-508508, enquiries@bhhpa.org.uk, http://www.bhhpa.org.uk.

338.4791 796.54 ZAF ISSN 1995-9753
HOLIDAY RESORTS & DESTINATIONS. Text in English. 2004. a. ZAR 79.95 domestic; EUR 27 in United Kingdom; EUR 38 in Europe; USD 50 in United States (effective 2007). **Description:** Provides information on caravanning, camping and motorhome holidays in Southern Africa.
Published by: CaravanParks.com, PO Box 20232, Ashburton, 3213, South Africa. TEL 27-33-3261370, FAX 27-33-3261373, http://www.CaravanParks.com.

910.202 GBR ISSN 2041-1278
HOLIDAY VILLAS & COTTAGES. Abbreviated title: H V & C. Text in English. 1998. bi-m. GBP 2.95 per issue (effective 2009). illus.; maps. back issues avail. **Document type:** *Magazine, Consumer.* **Description:** Contains information for rented vacation properties worldwide with editorial and property advertising.
Formed by the merger of (1998-2009): Holiday Villas Magazine (1461-4170); (2003-2009): Holiday Cottages Magazine (1479-1102)
Related titles: Online - full text ed.
Published by: Merricks Publishing Ltd., Wessex Bldgs, Somerton Business Park, Somerton, Somers TA11 6SB, United Kingdom. TEL 44-1458-274447, FAX 44-1458-274059, info@merrickspublishing.com, http://www.merrickspublishing.com. Ed., Pub. John Kerswill. Adv. contact Carey-anne Perkins TEL 44-1458-271862.

338.4791 PAK
HOLIDAY WEEKLY. Text in English. 1978. w. PKR 250; USD 35 in United States. adv. 12 p./no. 6 cols./p.; **Document type:** *Newspaper.* **Description:** For the tourism and aviation industries in Pakistan. Seeks to promote tourism in Pakistan.
Published by: Asghar Ahmad Ed. & Pub., Bahadurabad 223, St.12, Karachi, 74800, Pakistan. TEL 92-21-4931124, FAX 92-21-4932820. Circ: 500.

910.202 GBR
HOLIDAY WEST HIGHLAND. Text in English. 1980. a. free newsstand/cover (effective 2009). adv. back issues avail. **Document type:** *Newspaper, Trade.* **Description:** Covers tourist attractions, hotels, restaurants, and events throughout the West Highlands and Islands.
Formerly (until 1992): Holiday West
Related titles: Online - full text ed.
Published by: Oban Times Ltd., PO Box 1, Oban, Argyll PA34 4HB, United Kingdom. TEL 44-1631-568000, FAX 44-1631-568001, letters@obantimes.co.uk, http://www.obantimes.co.uk/.

910.2 USA
HOLIDAYS. Text in English. bi-m. free domestic to qualified personnel (effective 2005). adv. **Document type:** *Magazine, Consumer.*
Published by: Monaco Coach Corp., 91320 Coburg Industrial Way, Coburg, OR 97408. TEL 800-634-0855, FAX 541-302-3800, http://www.monacocoach.com/. Eds. Randy Puckett, Mike Duncan. Pub. Christopher Phillips. Adv. contact Randy Puckett. B&W page USD 1,705, color page USD 2,015; trim 7.625 x 10.625. Circ: 34,145 (free).

916.8 ZAF
HOLIDAYS; your R C I travel quarterly. Text in English. 1993. q. ZAR 8.70 per issue. adv. illus.; maps. **Document type:** *Journal, Consumer.*
Published by: R C I Southern Africa, PO Box 783940, Sandton, Transvaal 2146, South Africa.

910.09 USA
HOME & AWAY. Text in English. 1980. bi-m. free to members (effective 2009). adv. **Document type:** *Magazine, Consumer.* **Description:** It is the official member publication for 9 different AAA clubs in the midwest.
Former titles (until 2005): A A A Chicago Motor Club Home & Away (0199-7521); (until 19??): Motor News (0194-8520)
Related titles: Regional ed(s).: Home & Away (Findlay, Ohio). ISSN 1933-4591. 1998; Journeys (Kansas). ISSN 1933-4605; Journeys (Cincinnati). ISSN 1933-4613.
Indexed: HRIS.
Published by: Home and Away Publishing, PO Box 3535, Omaha, NE 68103. TEL 402-592-5000, FAX 402-331-5194. Ed. Gary Peterson. Pub., Adv. contact Terry Ausenbaugh.

910.202 USA ISSN 8750-5649
HOME & AWAY (INDIANAPOLIS EDITION). Text in English. 1913. bi-m. USD 6 to non-members; free to members (effective 2005). adv. **Document type:** *Magazine, Consumer.* **Description:** Travel, finance and safety oriented magazine for AAA members in Central Indiana; promotes member services.
Formerly: Hoosier Motorist (0199-6975)
Published by: American Automobile Association, Hoosier Motor Club, PO Box 88505, Indianapolis, IN 46208-0505. TEL 317-923-1500, FAX 317-924-4669. Eds. Kathy Neff, Stephanie Hinds. Circ: 210,000 (controlled).

HOME & AWAY (MIAMI COUNTY EDITION). *see* TRANSPORTATION—Automobiles

910.202 USA ISSN 0274-8266
HOME & AWAY (MINNEAPOLIS EDITION). Text in English. bi-m. (plus special Dec. edition). USD 6 to non-members; USD 1 to members. adv. back issues avail. **Description:** Includes travel features, tours, member-only discounts, updates to club membership.
Published by: A A A Minneapolis, 10703 J St, PO Box 3535, Omaha, NE 68127. TEL 402-390-1000, FAX 402-331-5194. Ed. Brian Nicol. Circ: 2,850,000.

388.3 USA
HOME & AWAY (NORTH DAKOTA EDITION). Text in English. 1980. q. USD 4 to non-members; free to members (effective 2005). adv. **Document type:** *Magazine, Consumer.*
Published by: A A A North Dakota, PO Box 10338, Fargo, ND 58106. Ed. La Vonne Langord. Pub. Robert Stubblefield. Circ: 44,000 (paid).

910.09 USA ISSN 0889-4078
HOME & AWAY (OHIO EDITION). Text in English. 1986. bi-m. free to members (effective 2009). adv. back issues avail. **Document type:** *Magazine, Consumer.*
Formerly (until 1986): The A A A Traveler (0279-8883)
Related titles: Online - full text ed.
Published by: American Automobile Association, A A A Ohio Auto Club, PO Box 3535, Omaha, NE 68103. TEL 402-592-5000, FAX 402-331-5194, http://www.aaaohio.com/. Ed. Gary Peterson. Pub., Adv. contact Terry Ausenbaugh. B&W page USD 32,775, color page USD 38,558; trim 7.875 x 10.5. Circ: 1,259,423.

338.4 USA ISSN 1933-2262
G154
HOME-BASED TRAVEL AGENT. Text in English. 2006. 10/yr. USD 75 domestic; USD 90 in Canada & Mexico; USD 120 elsewhere; free domestic to qualified personnel (effective 2008). adv. back issues avail. **Document type:** *Magazine, Trade.* **Description:** Provides home-based agents with the knowledge they need to sell their client base on different destinations, cruises, tour packages, etc. as well as the information they need themselves to grow their businesses, choose effective technology and work as efficiently as possible.
Related titles: Online - full text ed.
Indexed: A09, CA, H&TI, V03.
Published by: Questex Media Group Inc., 275 Grove St, Bldg 2, Ste 130, Newton, MA 02466. TEL 617-219-8300, 888-552-4346, FAX 617-219-8310, questex@sunbeltfs.com, http://www.questex.com. Eds. Joe Pike TEL 212-895-8286, Mark Rogers TEL 818-227-4402. Pub. Kerry J Cannon. adv.: page USD 5,941; trim 8.875 x 10.75. Circ: 18,000 (controlled).

917.28304 USA ISSN 1523-9497
F1503.5
HONDURAS AND THE BAY ISLANDS. Text in English. 1998. irreg. USD 15.95 newsstand/cover (effective 2006).
Published by: Passport Press, PO Box 1346, Champlain, NY 12919.

910.09 HND
HONDURAS. CONSEJO SUPERIOR DE PLANIFICACION ECONOMICA. PLAN OPERATIVO ANUAL. SECTOR TURISMO. Text in Spanish. a.
Published by: Consejo Superior de Planificacion Economica, Secretaria Tecnica, Tegucigalpa DC, Honduras.

915 USA ISSN 2153-7402
DS796.H74
HONG KONG & MACAU. Variant title: Forbes Travel Guide: Hong Kong & Macau. Text in English. 2008. biennial. USD 13.95, CAD 15.95 per issue (effective 2010). **Description:** Travel guide for Hong Kong and Macau.
Published by: Mobil Travel Guide, 7373 N Cicero Ave, Lincolnwood, IL 60712. info@mobiltravelguide.com, http://www.mobiltravelguide.com/mtg.

915 HKG
HONG KONG GUIDE (YEAR). Text in Chinese, English. 1978. irreg. (every 1-2 yrs.). HKD 92 per issue (effective 2001). 352 p./no.; **Document type:** *Government.* **Description:** Comprehensive directory with maps for the Territory of Hong Kong.
Former titles: Hong Kong Guide - Streets and Places; (until 1988): Hong Kong Streets and Places
Published by: Survey and Mapping Office, Lands Department, Government Offices, 333 Java Rd, North Point, Hong Kong, Hong Kong. TEL 852-2231-3186. Ed. Cheung Chung Tong. R&P Wan Tak Chee TEL 852-2231-3188. Circ: 18,000.

338.47915125 GBR ISSN 1747-8901
HONG KONG TOURISM REPORT. Text in English. 2005. q. EUR 820, USD 1,030 combined subscription (print & email eds.) (effective 2010). **Document type:** *Report, Trade.* **Description:** Provides industry professionals and strategists, corporate analysts, associations, government departments and regulatory bodies with independent forecasts and competitive intelligence on the Hong Kong tourism industry.
Related titles: E-mail ed.
Indexed: B01, H&TI, H06, P34.
Published by: Business Monitor International Ltd., Senator House, 85 Queen Victoria St, London, EC4V 4AB, United Kingdom. TEL 44-20-72480468, FAX 44-20-72480467, subs@businessmonitor.com.

338.4791 BGR
HOREMAG. (Hotels & Restaurants Magazine) Text in Bulgarian. 2003. m. BGL 40 domestic; EUR 30 in Europe; USD 55 elsewhere (effective 2005). **Document type:** *Magazine.* **Description:** Reflects the current situation on Bulgaria's tourism market. Targets all who need information about the products, technologies and services in the tourism industry.
Published by: Economedia, ul Ivan Vazov 20, et. 2, Sofia, Bulgaria. TEL 359-2-9376444, FAX 359-2-9376236.

HOSEASONS BOATING HOLIDAYS IN UK AND EUROPE. *see* SPORTS AND GAMES—Boats And Boating

910.202 GBR
HOSEASONS HOLIDAY PARKS AND LODGES. Text in English. 1946. a. free (effective 2009). **Document type:** *Directory, Consumer.* **Description:** Featuring the very best in accommodation and locations for customers looking for holidays and short breaks.
Former titles: Hoseasons Holiday Homes in U K; (until 1970): Hoseasons Holiday-Homes
Published by: Hoseasons Holidays, Sunway House, Raglan Rd, Lowestoft, Suffolk NR32 2LW, United Kingdom. TEL 44-1502-500505, FAX 44-1502-514298, mail@hoseasons.co.uk, http://www.hoseasons.co.uk.

910.22 MEX ISSN 1665-1839
HOSPITALIDAD E S D A I. (Escuela Superior de Administracion de Instituciones) Text in Spanish. 2001. s-a. **Document type:** *Journal, Academic/Scholarly.*
Related titles: Online - full text ed.
Indexed: A01, AmHI, CA, F03, F04, H07, T02.
Published by: Universidad Panamericana, Escuela Superior de Administracion de Instituciones, Augusto Rodin, 498, Col. Insurgentes-Mixcoac, Mexico, D.F., 03920, Mexico. TEL 52-55-56615827, FAX 52-55-56610079, info@mx.up.mx, http://www.up.mx. Ed. Adriana Vazquez Gomez.

338.4 658 GBR ISSN 1464-9101
HOSPITALITY REVIEW. Text in English. 1999. q. back issues avail. **Document type:** *Journal, Trade.* **Description:** Covers news, hospitality and education, veterinary management, social science and history and classic crime fiction.
Indexed: A34, A37, CABA, D01, E12, GH, H&TI, H06, LT, N02, OR, PHN&I, R12, RRTA, W11.
Published by: Threshold Press Ltd., Norfolk House 75 Bartholomew St, Newbury, Berks RG14 5DU, United Kingdom. customer@threshold-press.co.uk, http://www.treshold-press.co.uk.

910.1 647.94 USA ISSN 1540-8116
HOSTELLING NORTH AMERICA: THE OFFICIAL GUIDE TO HOSTELS IN CANADA AND THE UNITED STATES OF AMERICA/AUBERGES DE JEUNESSE EN AMERIQUE DU NORD. Text in English. 1934. a. USD 3 (effective 2000). adv. **Document type:** *Directory, Consumer.* **Description:** Lists nearly 240 hostels in the U.S. and Canada, including location maps and travel information.
Former titles (until 1997): Hostelling U.S.A.: The Official Guide to Hostels in the United States of America; North American Hostels Handbook; American Youth Hostels Handbook; American Youth Hostels Guide and Handbook (0066-1201)
Published by: Hostelling International - American Youth Hostels, 8401 Colesville Rd., Ste. 600, Silver Spring, MD 20910-6339. TEL 202-783-6161, FAX 202-783-6171. Ed., R&P, Adv. contact Toby Pyle. Circ: 150,000.

914.3 910.2 USA ISSN 1540-4404
HOSTELS AUSTRIA & SWITZERLAND. Text in English. 2000. irreg., latest 2002, 2nd ed. USD 14.95 per issue (effective 2008). back issues avail. **Document type:** *Guide, Consumer.* **Description:** Provides information on 182 hostels throughout Austria and Switzerland.
Published by: The Globe Pequot Press, Inc., 246 Goose Ln, PO Box 480, Guilford, CT 06437. TEL 203-458-4500, 888-249-7586, FAX 203-458-4603, 800-820-2329, info@globepequot.com.

917.3 910.2 USA ISSN 1540-4390
TX907.2
HOSTELS U.S.A. Text in English. 1998. biennial, latest 2006, 6th ed. USD 15.95 per issue (effective 2008). back issues avail. **Document type:** *Guide, Consumer.* **Description:** Contains review on over 300 hostels throughout the United States and parts of Canada.
Published by: The Globe Pequot Press, Inc., 246 Goose Ln, PO Box 480, Guilford, CT 06437. TEL 203-458-4500, 888-249-7586, FAX 203-458-4603, 800-820-2329, info@globepequot.com, http://www.globepequot.com. Ed. Jeff Serena TEL 203-458-4556.

338.4 HRV ISSN 1330-7002
HOTEL. Text in Croatian. 1994. bi-m. **Document type:** *Magazine, Trade.*
Published by: U.T. Magazin, Jordanovac 1, Zagreb, 10000, Croatia. TEL 385-1-217817, FAX 385-1-217817. Ed. Drago Ferencic.

915.204 JPN
HOTEL. Text in Japanese. m. JPY 6,000, USD 100. adv. **Description:** Offers information on luxury hotels worldwide, and includes detailed coverage of special events, fairs, conventions, seminars, entertainment, arts, and fashion.
Published by: Ohta Publications Co. Ltd., Dame Ginza Bldg, 7-18 Ginza 6-chome, Chuo-ku, Tokyo, 104-0061, Japan. TEL 03-3571-1181, FAX 03-3574-1650. Ed. Minoru Murakami. Circ: 160,000.

910.2 USA ISSN 1935-1739
HOTEL AND TRAVEL INDEX WORLDWIDE. Abbreviated title: H T I. Text in English. 2007. a. **Document type:** *Handbook/Manual/Guide, Trade.*
Formed by the merger of (2001-2007): Official Hotel Guide International (1541-0285); (1994-2007): Hotel & Travel Index - International Edition (1082-782X); Which was formerly (until 1994): Hotel and Travel Index - A B C International Edition (1056-4713); Which superseded (in 1991): A B C Worldwide Hotel Guide; Which was formed by the merger of (19??-1986): A - Z Worldwide Hotel Guide; (1971-1986): A B C Hotel Guide (0141-6251)
Published by: Northstar Travel Media LLC (Subsidiary of: Boston Ventures Management, Inc.), 100 Lighting Way, Secaucus, NJ 07094. TEL 201-902-2000, FAX 201-902-2045, http://www.northstartravelmedia.com/.

910 AUT
HOTEL REVUE. Text in German. w.
Address: Kettenbrueckengasse 22, Postfach 57, Vienna, W 1040, Austria. TEL 01-5888150, FAX 01-5888166. Ed. Walter Norden. Circ: 12,400.

HOTEL UND TOURISMUS REVUE. *see* HOTELS AND RESTAURANTS

HOTEL & TOURISTIK. *see* HOTELS AND RESTAURANTS

914 NOR ISSN 0806-0029
HOTELL RESTAURANT OG REISELIV. Text in Norwegian. 1994. 9/yr. NOK 475; NOK 275 to students (effective 2007). adv. bk.rev. charts; illus. **Document type:** *Magazine, Consumer.*
Formerly (until 1994): Reiseliv (0804-9963); Which was formed by the merger of (1928-1994): Oss Verter imellom (0800-4560); Which was formerly (until 1981): Kafebladet (0800-4579); (1992-1994): Hotell - Restaurant og Reiseliv (0803-7019); Which was formed by the merger of (1973-1991): Reiseliv (0333-2373); (1989-1991): Hotell og Restaurant (0802-6203); Which was formerly (until 1989): Norsk Hotell og Restaurantblad (0332-7760); Which was formed by the merger of (1923-1943): Tidsskrift for Norsk Hotell og Restaurantforbund (0802-6262); Which was formerly (until 1923): Norsk Tidsskrift for Hotel og Turistvaesen (0802-6297); Norsk Hotell og Restaurantblad superseded in part (in 1942): Oslo Hotell og Restaurantblad (0802-6270); Which was formerly (until 1932): Norsk Hotell og Restaurantblad (0802-6289); Reiseliv was formerly (until 1973): Reiseliv i Norge (0034-3676); (until 1937): Turist og Reiseliv (0333-2381); (until 1934): Medlemsblad - Landslaget for Reiselivet i Norge (0333-239X); (until 1929): Reiseforeningens Medlemsblad (0333-2403)
Published by: (Landslaget for Reiselivet i Norge/Norway Travel Association, Hotell - Restaurant & Reiseliv), Nortra Produksjon A-S, Oevre Slottsgate 12, Oslo, 0157, Norway. TEL 47-22-417118, FAX 47-22-417199. Circ: 3,300. **Co-sponsor:** Norske Reisebyraaforening.

902 ESP ISSN 2013-049X
HOTELS CATALUNYA. Text in Catalan. 1989. a. **Document type:** *Handbook/Manual/Guide, Consumer.*
Published by: Generalitat de Catalunya, Departament d'Innovacio, Universitats i Empresa, Pg de Gracia, 105, Barcelona, 08008, Spain. TEL 34-93-4849500, FAX 34-93-4849599, http://www.gencat.cat/diue/departament/conseller/index.html.

919 BHS
HOTELS, MOTELS AND GUESTHOUSES AND RESTAURANTS: NEW PROVIDENCE, PARADISE ISLAND AND GRAND BAHAMA. Text in English. 1980. a. BSD 2.
Formerly: Hotels, Motels and Guest Houses in New Providence and Paradise Island
Published by: Department of Statistics, PO Box N 3904, Nassau, Bahamas.

910.91 CHN
HUADONG LUYOU BAO/EAST CHINA TOURISM NEWS. Text in Chinese. 1997. 3/w. CNY 78 (effective 2004). **Document type:** *Newspaper, Consumer.*
Published by: Wuxi Ribao Baoye Jituan, 1, Xueqian Donglu, Xinwen Dasha, Wuxi, Jiangsu 214002, China. TEL 86-510-2757557, wxrb@wxrb.com. **Dist. by:** China International Book Trading Corp, 35 Chegongzhuang Xilu, Haidian District, PO Box 399, Beijing 100044, China. TEL 86-10-68412045, FAX 86-10-68412023, cibtc@mail.cibtc.com.cn, http://www.cibtc.com.cn.

910.2 USA ISSN 1946-5246
HUDSON HEIGHTS. Variant title: Hot & Cool Guide. Text in English. 2008. s-a. USD 4.99 per issue (effective 2009). adv. back issues avail. **Document type:** *Directory, Consumer.* **Description:** Designed to show residents, new comers and tourists how to get around a neighborhood.
Published by: Hot and Cool Guide LLC, 1375 Broadway, 3rd Fl, New York, NY 10018. TEL 800-282-8144, FAX 646-417-8259, question@HotAndCoolGuide.com, http://hotandcoolguide.com. Pub. Enrique Gonzalez. adv.: page USD 1,350; 4.125 x 7.375.

910.2 USA ISSN 1559-3851
THE HUDSON VALLEY AND CATSKILL MOUNTAINS; an explorer's guide. Text in English. 1998. irreg., latest 2009, 7th ed. USD 21.95 per issue (effective 2009). 432 p./no.; back issues avail. **Document type:** *Guide, Consumer.* **Description:** Contains detailed maps and reviews of accommodations, eateries and activities to appeal to independent travelers and those seeking value for money.
Formerly (until 2002): The Best of the Hudson Valley and Catskill Mountains (1533-6867)
Published by: The Countryman Press (Subsidiary of: W.W. Norton & Co., Inc.), PO Box 748, Woodstock, VT 05091. TEL 802-457-4826, 800-245-4151, FAX 802-457-1678, countrymanpress@wwnorton.com.

HUDSON VALLEY CONNOISSEUR. *see* LIFESTYLE

914.04 DEU ISSN 1612-1589
HUSUM; graue stadt ganz bunt. Text in German. 1962. m. adv. **Document type:** *Bulletin, Consumer.*
Former titles (until 2000): Husumer Monatshefte (1430-9130); (until 1991): Husum (0343-5555); (until 1973): Husumer Monatshefte (0343-6454)
Published by: Husum Druck- und Verlagsgesellschaft, Postfach 1480, Husum, 25804, Germany. TEL 49-4841-83520, FAX 49-4841-835210, info@verlagsgruppe.de. Ed. Maike Barth. Adv. contact Ottilie van Kempen.

I A C V B NEWS. *see* MEETINGS AND CONGRESSES

374 910.202 USA
I C T A UPDATE. Text in English. bi-m. free to members. back issues avail. **Description:** Focuses on ICTA activities and programs, including members' accomplishments and management ideas.
Formerly: I C T A News
Published by: Institute of Certified Travel Agents, 148 Linden St, Box 812059, Wellesley, MA 02181-0012. TEL 617-237-0280, FAX 617-237-3860. Ed. Dawn Ringel. Circ: 28,000.

917.04 USA
I LOVE NEW YORK: THE FINGER LAKES TRAVEL GUIDE. Text in English. 1951. a. free. adv. **Document type:** *Directory.*
Formerly: Finger Lakes Travel Guide
Published by: Finger Lakes Association, Inc., 309 Lake Street, Penn Yan, NY 14527. TEL 315-536-7488, 800-548-4386, FAX 315-536-1237, http://FingerLakes.org. Ed. Ann Brink. Circ: 65,000 (controlled).

910.03 USA
I LOVE NEW YORK TRAVEL GUIDE. Text in English. a. free. illus.; maps. **Document type:** *Guide, Consumer.* **Description:** Lists tourist attractions and events in New York State.
Media: Online - full text.
Published by: Department of Economic Development, 30 South Pearl St., Albany, NY 12245. TEL 518-474-4116, FAX 518-474-6416. Ed. Mary Ellen Walsh.

910.91 USA
I LOVE ORLANDO. Text in English. q. adv.
Published by: C F I Resorts Management, 5601 Windhover Dr, 306, Orlando, FL 32819. TEL 407-351-3351, FAX 407-370-4394.

910.09 ITA
I T P EVENTS - INTERNATIONAL TOURIST PRESS. Text in Multiple languages. 12/yr. **Document type:** *Magazine, Consumer.*
Published by: C T A Bonelli, Viale Parioli 50, Rome, 00197, Italy. itpevents@studiobonelli.fastwebnet.it, http://www.bonelliconsulting.com. Ed. Antonio Bonelli.

659.1 ROM
IASI - WHAT, WHERE, WHEN. Text in Multiple languages. q. ROL 50,000 domestic; USD 12 foreign (effective 2002). adv. **Document type:** *Magazine, Consumer.*
Published by: Crystal Publishing Group, 253, Calea Calarasilor, bl. 67 A, Ste. 4, Bucharest, Romania. TEL 40-21-3233829, FAX 40-21-3234706, office@bucurestiwww.ro, http://www.bucurestiwww.ro. Circ: 25,000 (paid and controlled).

910.91 USA ISSN 1933-0731
DP302.B26
IBIZA & FORMENTERA DIRECTIONS. Text in English. 2005. irreg., latest 2008, 2nd ed. USD 11.99 domestic 2nd ed.; USD 15.99 in Canada 2nd ed.; GBP 6.99 in United Kingdom 2nd ed. (effective 2008). back issues avail. **Document type:** *Guide, Consumer.*
Related titles: Online - full text ed.
Published by: Rough Guides, 375 Hudson St, 9th Fl, New York, NY 10014. TEL 212-414-3635, http://www.roughguides.com/default.aspx.

338.4 USA
IMPACT OF INTERNATIONAL VISITOR SPENDING ON STATE ECONOMICS. Text in English. 1993. a. free (effective 2011). stat. **Document type:** *Government.* **Description:** Provides information on spending, payroll, employment and taxes supported by international travel to the U.S. and for all 50 states.
Published by: (US. Tourism Industries), U.S. Department of Commerce, International Trade Administration, 1401 Constitution Ave, NW, Washington, DC 20230. TEL 202-482-3251, FAX 202-482-5819, http://trade.gov/.

IN CORNWALL MAGAZINE. *see* GENERAL INTEREST PERIODICALS—Great Britain

910.09 USA
IN-FLIGHT SURVEY OF INTERNATIONAL AIR TRAVELERS: INBOUND NATIONAL REPORT. Text in English. 1983. a. stat. back issues avail. **Document type:** *Report, Government.* **Description:** Provides a comprehensive comparative analysis of overseas travelers to the US from nine world regions and 20 countries.
Published by: (US. Tourism Industries), U.S. Department of Commerce, International Trade Administration, 1401 Constitution Ave, NW, Washington, DC 20230. TEL 202-482-3251, FAX 202-482-5819, http://trade.gov/.

910.202 GBR ISSN 1358-7943
IN FOCUS (LONDON, 1990). Cover title: Tourism in Focus. Text in English. 1991. q. free to members (effective 2009). bk.rev. 16 p./no.; back issues avail. **Document type:** *Magazine, Consumer.* **Description:** Discusses the impact of tourism on host communities and the environment, promotes awareness of development issues relating to tourism, and encourages responsible and sustainable tourism.
Related titles: Online - full text ed.
Indexed: H&TI, H06.
—IE.
Published by: Tourism Concern, Stapleton House, 277-281 Holloway Rd, London, N7 8HN, United Kingdom. TEL 44-20-71333800, FAX 44-20-71333985, info@tourismconcern.org.uk. Ed. Kelly Haynes.

790.1 914 GBR ISSN 1742-0857
IN LONDON; Aussies and Kiwis at home abroad. Text in English. 1993. m. GBP 42 domestic; GBP 60 in Europe; GBP 80 elsewhere (effective 2009). adv. illus. back issues avail. **Document type:** *Magazine, Consumer.* **Description:** Provides up-to-date information on the best travel deals and entertainment news.
Formerly (until 2003): Londinium (1358-0329)
—CCC.
Published by: Blue Sky Publications, Unit 7 Commodore House, Battersea Reach, London, SW18 1TW, United Kingdom. TEL 44-845-4564910, FAX 44-845-4564912, info@blueskygroup.co.uk, http://www.blueskygroup.co.uk/. Ed. Paige Dorkin. Pub. Greg Eden. Adv. contact Bryce Lowry. Circ: 30,000.

910.91 GBR ISSN 1754-6257
IN LONDON (LONDON. 2003). Text in English. 2003. m. **Document type:** *Magazine, Consumer.*
Published by: Welcome Stranger Publishing, Fl 5, Threshold House, 65-69 Shepherd's Bush Green, London, W12 8TX, United Kingdom. TEL 44-20-31841000, FAX 44-20-31841020, info@welcomestranger.com, http://www.welcomestranger.com/.

917.47104 USA
IN NEW YORK. Text in English. 2001 (Mar.). m. **Document type:** *Magazine, Consumer.* **Description:** Contains feature articles on shopping, dining, entertainment, arts and antiques in New York City.
Published by: Morris Multimedia, Inc., 79 Madison Ave, 8th Fl, New York, NY 10016. TEL 212-636-2700, FAX 212-716-8578, http://www.morris.com/. Ed. Trisha S McMohan.

910.09 USA
IN - S I T E MAGAZINE. Text in English. 1987. bi-m. membership. adv. **Document type:** *Newsletter.* **Description:** Covers incentive travel as a tool to increase productivity in business.
Published by: Society of Incentive Travel Executives, 21 W 38th St, 10th Fl, New York, NY 10018. TEL 212-575-0910, FAX 212-575-1838. Ed. Maureen P Mangan. Circ: 2,500.

910.09 USA
IN THE QUIET TIME. Text in English. 1996. a. **Document type:** *Magazine, Consumer.*
Published by: Islands' Sounder, PO Box 758, Eastsound, WA 98245. TEL 360-376-4500, FAX 360-376-4501. Ed. Ted Grossman. Pub., R&P Jay Brodt TEL 360-378-5696. Adv. contact Elyse Van den Bosch.

910.2 AUS
IN TOWNSVILLE AND MAGNETIC ISLAND. Text in English. 19??. **Document type:** *Magazine, Consumer.* **Description:** Covers the accommodation, tours and site seeing in Toiwnsville, Magnetic Island and surrounding areas.
Published by: North Australian Publishing Co. Pty. Ltd., PO Box 1264, Townsville, QLD 4810, Australia. TEL 61-7-47723244, FAX 61-7-47723250, info@aussiebackpacker.com.au, http://www.aussiebackpacker.com.au/. Pub. Warren Gardner.

979.3 USA
IN-VEGAS NEWS AND REVIEWS. Text in English. 1999. w. **Document type:** *Newsletter.* **Description:** Includes reviews of hotels, casinos, attractions, dining, and shows.
Media: Online - full text.
Address: 2725 S Nellis Blvd, Ste 2136, Las Vegas, NV 89121. TEL 702-431-1465. Ed. Ted Newkirk.

910.91 ITA ISSN 1125-7334
IN VIAGGIO. Text in Italian. 1997. m. **Document type:** *Magazine, Consumer.*
Published by: Editoriale Giorgio Mondadori SpA (Subsidiary of: Cairo Communication SpA), Via Tucidide 56, Torre 3, Milan, 20134, Italy. TEL 39-02-748111, FAX 39-02-70100102, info@cairocommunication.it, http://www.cairocommunication.it. Ed. Luciano Di Pietro.

910.2 NLD ISSN 2210-5352
▼ **IN YOUR POCKET. 'S-HERTOGENBOSCH.** Text in English. 2010. 3/yr. adv. **Document type:** *Handbook/Manual/Guide, Consumer.*
Related titles: Online - full text ed.: ISSN 2210-5360.
Published by: In Your Pocket Netherlands, Weikesstraat 28, Alem, 5335 LE, Netherlands. TEL 31-653-799146, netherlands@inyourpocket.com. Eds. Isa McKechnie, Martins Zaprauskis, Theo Leerintveld. Adv. contact Bas van Haaren.

910.2 NLD ISSN 2210-545X
▼ **IN YOUR POCKET. UTRECHT.** Text in English. 2010. q. adv. **Document type:** *Handbook/Manual/Guide, Consumer.*
Related titles: Online - full text ed.: ISSN 2210-5484.
Published by: In Your Pocket Netherlands, Weikesstraat 28, Alem, 5335 LE, Netherlands. Eds. Isa McKechnie, Martins Zaprauskis, Theo Leerintveld. Adv. contact Ardi Lock. Circ: 60,000.

338.4791 GBR
INCENTIVE TRAVEL & CORPORATE MEETINGS. Text in English. 1988. bi-m. GBP 36 domestic; GBP 60 foreign; free to qualified personnel (effective 2009). adv. **Document type:** *Magazine, Trade.* **Description:** Contains reports on the developments in the MICE market from all around the world.
Formerly (until 1991): Incentive Travel (0957-820X)
Related titles: Online - full text ed.: free (effective 2009).
—CCC.
Address: Market House, 19-21 Market Pl, Wokingham, Berks RG40 1AP, United Kingdom. TEL 44-118-9793277, FAX 44-118-9793499, itcm@incentivetravel.co.uk. Ed. Sydney Paulden. Adv. contact Tim Manning.

910.202 GBR ISSN 1352-7851
DS334.5
INDIA HANDBOOK (YEAR). Text in English. 1991. a. GBP 18.99 per issue (effective 2010). adv. maps. back issues avail. **Document type:** *Handbook/Manual/Guide, Consumer.* **Description:** Covers all the basics from where to stay and where to eat to cycling, walking and how to get around the India.
Formerly (until 1994): South Asian Handbook (0968-0934)
—CCC.
Published by: Footprint Handbooks Ltd., 6 Riverside Ct, Lower Bristol Rd, Bath, Avon BA2 3DZ, United Kingdom. TEL 44-1225-469141, FAX 44-1225-469461, wwwinfo@footprintbooks.com.

338.479154 GBR ISSN 1747-8928
INDIA TOURISM REPORT. Text in English. 2005. q. EUR 820, USD 1,030 combined subscription (print & email eds.) (effective 2010). **Document type:** *Report, Trade.* **Description:** Provides industry professionals and strategists, corporate analysts, associations, government departments and regulatory bodies with independent forecasts and competitive intelligence on the Indian tourism industry.
Related titles: E-mail ed.
Indexed: B01, H&TI, H06.
—CCC.
Published by: Business Monitor International Ltd., Senator House, 85 Queen Victoria St, London, EC4V 4AB, United Kingdom. TEL 44-20-72480468, FAX 44-20-72480467, subs@businessmonitor.com.

338.4 IND ISSN 0974-2913
INDIAN JOURNAL OF INTERNATIONAL TOURISM AND HOSPITALITY RESEARCH. Text in English. 2007. a. **Document type:** *Journal, Academic/Scholarly.*
Published by: Kurukshetra University, Department of Tourism and Hotel Management, Kurukshetra, Haryana 136 119, India. http://kuk.ac.in.

917.72 USA ISSN 1932-7366
F526.6
INDIANA CURIOSITIES; quirky characters, roadside oddities & other offbeat stuff. Text in English. 2003. quadrennial, latest 2006, 2nd ed. USD 13.95 per issue (effective 2008). **Document type:** *Guide, Consumer.* **Description:** Provides tourist information about the Hoosier State.
Published by: The Globe Pequot Press, Inc., 246 Goose Ln, PO Box 480, Guilford, CT 06437. TEL 203-458-4500, 888-249-7586, FAX 203-458-4603, 800-820-2329, info@globepequot.com, http://www.globepequot.com. Ed. Mary Norris.

338.4791598 GBR ISSN 1747-8936
INDONESIA TOURISM REPORT. Text in English. 2005. q. EUR 820, USD 1,030 combined subscription (print & email eds.) (effective 2010). **Document type:** *Report, Trade.* **Description:** Provides industry professionals and strategists, corporate analysts, associations, government departments and regulatory bodies with independent forecasts and competitive intelligence on the Indonesian tourism industry.
Related titles: E-mail ed.

Indexed: A15, ABIn, B02, B15, B17, B18, G04, I05, P48, P51, PQC.
Published by: Business Monitor International Ltd., Senator House, 85 Queen Victoria St, London, EC4V 4AB, United Kingdom. TEL 44-20-72480468, FAX 44-20-72480467, subs@businessmonitor.com.

INDUSTRIEARCHAEOLOGIE; Zeitschrift fuer industrielle Kulturgueter, Kunst und Reisen. *see* HISTORY

INFORMATION TECHNOLOGY & TOURISM; application - methodology - techniques. *see* COMPUTERS—Information Science And Information Theory

914 ESP ISSN 1887-3499
INFORME ANUAL DEL TURISMO DE ANDALUCIA. Text in Spanish. 2006. a. back issues avail. **Document type:** *Monographic series, Academic/Scholarly.*
Published by: Analistas Economicos de Andalucia, C/ Ancla 2, 6a Planta, Malaga, 29015, Spain. TEL 34-952-225305, FAX 34-952-212073, aea@unicaja.es, http://www.analistaseconomicos.com. Ed. Francisco Villalba Cabello.

910.202 338.479 BEL
INFOTRAVEL (DUTCH EDITION); professioneel magazine voor de reiswereld. Text in Dutch. 1998. 9/yr. adv. charts; illus. **Document type:** *Trade.* **Description:** Offers travel agents in Belgium, the Netherlands, and Luxembourg news and information on inclusive tours; travel by air, train, ferry, or private car; rental car companies; tourist services; and hotels.
Related titles: ◆ French ed.: InfoTravel (French Edition).
Published by: Evolution Media Group s.p.r.l., Vlasstraat 17, Wielsbeke, 8710, Belgium. TEL 32-56-607333, FAX 32-56-610583, info@evolution.be, http://www.evolution.be. Ed. Danny Verheyden. Pub. Piet Desmyter. Adv. contact Michele Grasi. Circ: 4,200 (controlled).

910.202 338.479 BEL
INFOTRAVEL (FRENCH EDITION); magazine professionnel du secteur touristique. Text in French. 1998. 9/yr. adv. charts; illus. **Document type:** *Trade.* **Description:** Offers travel agents in Belgium, the Netherlands, and Luxembourg news and information on inclusive tours; travel by air, train, ferry, or private car; rental car companies; tourist services; and hotels.
Related titles: ◆ Dutch ed.: InfoTravel (Dutch Edition).
Published by: Evolution Media Group s.p.r.l., Vlasstraat 17, Wielsbeke, 8710, Belgium. TEL 32-56-607333, FAX 32-56-610583, info@evolution.be, http://www.evolution.be. Ed. Danny Verheyden. Pub. Piet Desmyter. Adv. contact Michele Grassi. Circ: 3,300 (controlled).

INN MARKETING DIGEST; country inns, small hotels and bed & breakfasts. *see* HOTELS AND RESTAURANTS

641.9 USA ISSN 1052-794X
TX907.2
THE INNKEEPERS' REGISTER. Text in English. 1990. a. USD 12.95 (effective 1998). adv. **Document type:** *Directory.*
Published by: Independent Innkeepers' Association, PO Box 150, Marshall, MI 49068. TEL 269-789-0393, 800-344-5244, FAX 269-789-0970. Ed. Slue C Moore. Adv. contact Judy Baker. Circ: 375,000.

910.2 DEU
DIE INSEL. Text in German. 1991. a. EUR 6 newsstand/cover (effective 2010). adv. **Document type:** *Magazine, Consumer.*
Published by: Guenter Kohl PR & Marketing, Gaertnerkoppel 3, Westensee, 24259, Germany. TEL 49-4305-992992, FAX 49-4305-992993, gkprkiel@t-online.de. Circ: 50,000 (controlled).

914 GBR ISSN 1362-5845
INSIDE CORNWALL; the what's on magazine. Text in English. 1990. m. GBP 27; GBP 4 per issue (effective 2009). adv. bk.rev. **Document type:** *Magazine, Consumer.* **Description:** Covers arts and crafts, dining, gardens and entertainment, with a calendar of cultural events and a listing of walks around Cornwall.
Formerly (until 1996): Whats on! in West Cornwall (0965-0024)
Related titles: Supplement(s): Taste Cornwall Magazine. ISSN 1748-5495. GBP 8 (effective 2009).
Published by: Creative Copy Limited, 2-4 The Fradgan, Newlyn, Penzance, Cornwall TR18 5BE, United Kingdom. TEL 44-1736-334800, FAX 44-1736-334808. Ed. Kathy Hill. Pub. Ian Waghorn. Circ: 8,000.

338.4 USA ISSN 1082-071X
INSIDE I T S. (Intelligent Transportation Systems) Text in English. 1991. s-m. USD 675 (effective 2007). **Document type:** *Newsletter, Trade.*
Formerly (until 1995): Inside I V H S (1054-2647)
Indexed: HRIS.
Published by: B C C Research, 40 Washington St, Wellesley, MA 02481. TEL 866-285-7215, FAX 781-489-7308, sales@bccresearch.com, http://www.bccresearch.com. Circ: 1,000 (paid).

914.1504 IRL ISSN 0332-2483
INSIDE IRELAND. Text in English. 1978. q. adv. **Document type:** *Magazine, Consumer.*
Address: PO Box 1886, Dublin, 16, Ireland. TEL 353-1-4931906, FAX 353-1-4934538. adv.: page EUR 1,016. Circ: 6,000 (controlled).

910.4 USA
INSIDE TRAVEL NEWS. Text in English. 1971. m. USD 9. adv.
Address: 6229 Bristol Pkwy, Culver City, CA 90230. TEL 213-296-8858. Ed. Lozetta Slaton. Circ: 6,000.

INSIDER VIEWPOINT OF LAS VEGAS. *see* SPORTS AND GAMES

917.95 USA ISSN 1545-1402
F882.P34
INSIDER'S GUIDE OREGON COAST. Key Title: Oregon Coast. Text in English. biennial, latest 2007, 3rd ed. USD 17.95 per issue (effective 2008). **Document type:** *Guide, Consumer.* **Description:** Describes how to live and thrive in the area, from the best family activities to the lowdown on real estate.
Formerly (until 2000): Oregon Coast
Published by: The Globe Pequot Press, Inc., 246 Goose Ln, PO Box 480, Guilford, CT 06437. TEL 203-458-4500, 888-249-7586, FAX 203-458-4603, 800-820-2329, info@globepequot.com, http://www.globepequot.com. Ed. Jeff Serena TEL 203-458-4556.

978.9 USA ISSN 2153-7801
F804.A3
▼ **INSIDERS' GUIDE TO ALBUQUERQUE.** Text in English. 2010 (Apr.). triennial. USD 18.95 per issue (effective 2011). **Document type:** *Consumer.* **Description:** Travel guide for Albuquerque, New Mexico.
Published by: The Globe Pequot Press, Insiders' Guide (Subsidiary of: The Globe Pequot Press, Inc.), PO Box 480, Guilford, CT 06437. TEL 203-458-4500, info@globepequot.com, http://www.globepequot.com/globepequot/index.cfm?fuseaction=customer.welcome.

917.63 USA ISSN 2153-8794
F379.B33
▼ **INSIDERS' GUIDE TO BATON ROUGE.** Text in English. 2010 (May). triennial. USD 16.95 per issue (effective 2011). **Document type:** *Consumer.* **Description:** Contains in-depth travel information for Baton Rouge, Louisiana.
Published by: The Globe Pequot Press, Insiders' Guide (Subsidiary of: The Globe Pequot Press, Inc.), PO Box 480, Guilford, CT 06437. TEL 203-458-4500, info@globepequot.com, http://www.globepequot.com/globepequot/index.cfm?fuseaction=customer.welcome.

910.91 USA ISSN 1931-3977
F899.B4
INSIDERS' GUIDE TO BELLINGHAM AND MOUNT BAKER. Text in English. 2006. irreg. USD 17.95 per issue (effective 2008). **Document type:** *Guide, Consumer.*
Published by: The Globe Pequot Press, Insiders' Guide (Subsidiary of: The Globe Pequot Press, Inc.), PO Box 480, Guilford, CT 06437. TEL 203-458-4500, 888-249-7586, FAX 800-820-2329, info@globepequot.com, http://www.globepequot.com/globepequot/index.cfm?fuseaction=customer.welcome.

917.2 USA ISSN 1541-4639
F869.B5
INSIDERS' GUIDE TO BERKELEY AND THE EAST BAY. Text in English. 2002. biennial. USD 18.95 per issue (effective 2008). back issues avail. **Document type:** *Guide, Consumer.* **Description:** offers information to travelers, newcomers and locals about Berkeley and the East Bay areas.
Published by: The Globe Pequot Press, Inc., 246 Goose Ln, PO Box 480, Guilford, CT 06437. TEL 203-458-4500, 888-249-7586, FAX 203-458-4603, 800-820-2329, info@globepequot.com.

917.886 910.2 USA ISSN 1532-592X
F784.B66
INSIDERS' GUIDE TO BOULDER AND ROCKY MOUNTAIN NATIONAL PARK. Text in English. 1994. a., latest 2007, 8th ed. USD 18.95 per issue (effective 2008). back issues avail. **Document type:** *Guide, Consumer.* **Description:** Describes how to live and thrive in the area, from the best places to shop and dine to neighborhoods and real estate.
Published by: The Globe Pequot Press, Inc., 246 Goose Ln, PO Box 480, Guilford, CT 06437. TEL 203-458-4500, 888-249-7586, FAX 203-458-4603, 800-820-2329, info@globepequot.com, http://www.globepequot.com. Ed. Amy Lyons TEL 203-458-4500.

917.787 910.2 USA ISSN 1539-3550
F474.B79
INSIDERS' GUIDE TO BRANSON AND THE OZARK MOUNTAINS. Text in English. 1995. irreg., latest 2006, 6th ed. USD 17.95 per issue (effective 2008). back issues avail. **Document type:** *Guide, Consumer.* **Description:** Provides information about top shopping, seasonal festivals, live entertainment offerings, restaurants, lodging and recreation opportunities in Branson and the Ozark Mountains.
Published by: The Globe Pequot Press, Inc., 246 Goose Ln, PO Box 480, Guilford, CT 06437. TEL 203-458-4500, 888-249-7586, FAX 203-458-4603, 800-820-2329, info@globepequot.com, http://www.globepequot.com. Ed. Amy Lyons TEL 203-458-4500.

917.941 910.2 USA ISSN 1539-9923
F868.N2
INSIDERS' GUIDE TO CALIFORNIA WINE COUNTRY; including napa, sonoma, mendocino, and lake counties. Text in English. 1997. irreg., latest 2009, 8th ed. USD 18.95 per issue (effective 2009). 336 p./no.; **Document type:** *Guide, Consumer.* **Description:** Provides travel and relocation information in California Wine Country.
Published by: The Globe Pequot Press, Inc., 246 Goose Ln, PO Box 480, Guilford, CT 06437. TEL 203-458-4500, 888-249-7586, FAX 203-458-4603, 800-820-2329, info@globepequot.com, http://www.globepequot.com. Ed. Amy Lyons TEL 203-458-4500.

917.449 USA ISSN 1532-6462
F72.C3
INSIDERS' GUIDE TO CAPE COD, NANTUCKET & MARTHA'S VINEYARD. Text in English. 1996. biennial. USD 18.95 per issue (effective 2008). **Document type:** *Guide, Consumer.*
Published by: The Globe Pequot Press, Inc., 246 Goose Ln, PO Box 480, Guilford, CT 06437. TEL 203-458-4500, 888-249-7586, FAX 203-458-4603, 800-820-2329, info@globepequot.com, http://www.globepequot.com. Ed. Jeff Ferina.

917.5791 USA ISSN 1546-329X
F279.C43
INSIDERS' GUIDE TO CHARLESTON. Text in English. a. USD 18.95 per issue (effective 2008). **Document type:** *Guide, Consumer.* **Description:** Provides information on in-depth travel and relocation.
Formerly (until 1997): Insiders' Guide to Greater Charleston
Published by: The Globe Pequot Press, Inc., 246 Goose Ln, PO Box 480, Guilford, CT 06437. TEL 203-458-4500, 888-249-7586, FAX 203-458-4603, 800-820-2329, info@globepequot.com, http://www.globepequot.com. Ed. Amy Lyons TEL 203-458-4500.

917.5676 910.2 USA ISSN 1523-8334
F264.C4
INSIDERS' GUIDE TO CHARLOTTE. Text in English. 1987. triennial, latest 2007, 10th ed. USD 17.95 per issue (effective 2008). back issues avail. **Document type:** *Guide, Consumer.* **Description:** Provides information about in-depth travel and relocation in Charlotte.
Published by: The Globe Pequot Press, Inc., 246 Goose Ln, PO Box 480, Guilford, CT 06437. TEL 203-458-4500, 888-249-7586, FAX 203-458-4603, 800-820-2329, info@globepequot.com, http://www.globepequot.com. Ed. Jeff Serena TEL 203-458-4556.

917.71 USA ISSN 1527-1188
F499.C53
INSIDERS' GUIDE TO CINCINNATI. Text in English. biennial. USD 18.95 per issue (effective 2008). **Document type:** *Guide, Consumer.* **Description:** Contains personal perspective of Cincinnati and its surroundings. Also includes three maps of the area.
Formerly: The Insiders' Guide to Greater Cincinnati : Including Northern Kentucky & Southeastern Indiana
Published by: The Globe Pequot Press, Inc., 246 Goose Ln, PO Box 480, Guilford, CT 06437. TEL 203-458-4500, 888-249-7586, FAX 203-458-4603, 800-820-2329, info@globepequot.com, http://www.globepequot.com. Ed. Amy Lyons TEL 203-458-4500.

917.5 973.7 USA ISSN 1528-5472
INSIDERS' GUIDE TO CIVIL WAR SITES IN THE EASTERN THEATER. Text in English. irreg., latest 2008, 3rd ed. USD 15.95 per issue (effective 2008). **Document type:** *Guide, Consumer.* **Description:** Contains a glossary of civil war terminology, listings of restaurants, accommodations and special events in each area.
Published by: The Globe Pequot Press, Inc., 246 Goose Ln, PO Box 480, Guilford, CT 06437. TEL 203-458-4500, 888-249-7586, FAX 203-458-4603, 800-820-2329, info@globepequot.com. Ed. Liz Taylor.

917.715 910.2 USA ISSN 1556-4479
F499.C73
INSIDERS' GUIDE TO COLUMBUS, OHIO. Text in English. 2006. biennial, latest 2008, 2nd ed. USD 18.95 per issue (effective 2008). 352 p./no.; **Document type:** *Guide, Consumer.* **Description:** Provides travel and relocation information for Columbus, Ohio.
Published by: The Globe Pequot Press, Inc., 246 Goose Ln, PO Box 480, Guilford, CT 06437. TEL 203-458-4500, 888-249-7586, FAX 203-458-4603, 800-820-2329, info@globepequot.com, http://www.globepequot.com. Ed. Jeff Serena TEL 203-458-4556.

976.4 USA ISSN 2153-7771
F394.D213
▼ **INSIDERS' GUIDE TO DALLAS & FORT WORTH.** Text in English. 2010 (Mar.). triennial. USD 18.95 per issue (effective 2011). **Document type:** *Consumer.* **Description:** Travel guide for Dallas and Fort Worth, Texas.
Published by: The Globe Pequot Press, Insiders' Guide (Subsidiary of: The Globe Pequot Press, Inc.), PO Box 480, Guilford, CT 06437. TEL 203-458-4500, info@globepequot.com, http://www.globepequot.com/globepequot/index.cfm?fuseaction=customer.welcome.

917.8883 910.2 USA ISSN 1534-2166
F784
INSIDERS' GUIDE TO DENVER. Text in English. 1994. biennial, latest 2007, 8th ed. USD 17.95 per issue (effective 2008). back issues avail. **Document type:** *Guide, Consumer.* **Description:** Describes how to live and thrive in the area, from the best family activities to the lowdown on real estate.
Formerly: Insiders' Guide to Greater Denver
Published by: The Globe Pequot Press, Inc., 246 Goose Ln, PO Box 480, Guilford, CT 06437. TEL 203-458-4500, 888-249-7586, FAX 203-458-4603, 800-820-2329, info@globepequot.com, http://www.globepequot.com. Ed. Amy Lyons TEL 203-458-4500.

917.469 910.2 USA ISSN 1552-7247
F102.F2
INSIDERS' GUIDE TO FAIRFIELD COUNTY. Text in English. 2004. irreg., latest 2004, 1st ed. USD 17.95 per issue (effective 2008). **Document type:** *Guide, Consumer.* **Description:** Provides travel and relocation information for Fairfield County.
Published by: The Globe Pequot Press, Inc., 246 Goose Ln, PO Box 480, Guilford, CT 06437. TEL 203-458-4500, 888-249-7586, FAX 203-458-4603, 800-820-2329, info@globepequot.com, http://www.globepequot.com. Ed. Stephen Hester.

917.4842 973.7349 910.2 USA ISSN 1930-3521
F159.G5
INSIDERS' GUIDE TO GETTYSBURG. Text in English. 2006. triennial, latest 2009, 2nd ed. USD 15.95 per issue (effective 2009). 240 p./no.; **Document type:** *Guide, Consumer.* **Description:** Serves as a travel and relocation guide to Gettysburg, Pennsylvania.
Published by: The Globe Pequot Press, Inc., 246 Goose Ln, PO Box 480, Guilford, CT 06437. TEL 203-458-4500, 888-249-7586, FAX 203-458-4603, 800-820-2329, info@globepequot.com, http://www.globepequot.com. Ed. Amy Lyons TEL 203-458-4500.

917.8652 USA ISSN 1544-4023
F737.G5
INSIDERS' GUIDE TO GLACIER NATIONAL PARK; including the Flathead Valley and Waterton Lakes National Park. Text in English. 1999. biennial, latest 2008, 5th ed. USD 16.95 per issue (effective 2008). **Document type:** *Guide, Consumer.* **Description:** Describes how to live and thrive in the area, from the best family activities to the lowdown on real estate.
Formerly (until 2001): The Insiders' Guide to Glacier (1536-8572)
Published by: The Globe Pequot Press, Inc., 246 Goose Ln, PO Box 480, Guilford, CT 06437. TEL 203-458-4500, 888-249-7586, FAX 203-458-4603, 800-820-2329, info@globepequot.com, http://www.globepequot.com. Ed. Jeff Serena TEL 203-458-4556.

917.913 USA
F788
INSIDERS' GUIDE TO GRAND CANYON AND NORTHERN ARIZONA. Text in English. 2001. biennial (Every 2-3 yrs.). USD 16.95 per issue (effective 2008). **Description:** Covers from ancient petroglyphs in Petrified Forest National Park to the western charms of Flagstaff, Williams, and Sedona, northern Arizona is rich in history and unsurpassed in geology. It also helps to navigate Grand Canyon's North and South Rims and Navajoland, home to the Navajo Nation.
Formerly: Insiders' Guide to Grand Canyon (1545-648X)
Published by: The Globe Pequot Press, Inc., 246 Goose Ln, PO Box 480, Guilford, CT 06437. TEL 203-458-4500, 888-249-7586, FAX 203-458-4601, 800-820-2329, info@globepequot.com.

917.47 USA ISSN 2154-7424
F127.H8
▼ **INSIDERS' GUIDE TO HUDSON RIVER VALLEY.** Text in English. 2009. irreg. USD 17.95 per issue (effective 2010). **Document type:** *Guide, Consumer.* **Description:** Travel guide for the Hudson River Valley, New York.
Published by: The Globe Pequot Press, Insiders' Guide (Subsidiary of: The Globe Pequot Press, Inc.), PO Box 480, Guilford, CT 06437. TEL 203-458-4500, FAX 800-820-2329, info@globepequot.com, http://www.globepequot.com/globepequot/index.cfm?fuseaction=customer.welcome.

977.2 USA ISSN 2153-7798
F534.I33
▼ **INSIDERS' GUIDE TO INDIANAPOLIS.** Text mainly in English. 2010 (Mar.). triennial. USD 18.95 per issue (effective 2011). **Document type:** *Consumer.* **Description:** Travel guide for Indianapolis, Indiana.

TU

Published by: The Globe Pequot Press, Insiders' Guide (Subsidiary of: The Globe Pequot Press, Inc.), PO Box 480, Guilford, CT 06437. TEL 203-458-4500, info@globepequot.com, http://www.globepequot.com/globepequot/index.cfm?fuseaction=customer.welcome.

917.5912 910.2 USA ISSN 1541-5597
F319.J1

INSIDERS' GUIDE TO JACKSONVILLE. Text in English. 2003. biennial, latest 2004, 2nd ed. USD 17.95 per issue (effective 2008). back issues avail. **Document type:** *Guide, Consumer.* **Description:** Describes how to navigate the area's historical landmarks, world-class resorts and golf courses, robust business scene, and massive urban park system.
Published by: The Globe Pequot Press, Inc., 246 Goose Ln, PO Box 480, Guilford, CT 06437. TEL 203-458-4500, 888-249-7586, FAX 203-458-4603, 800-820-2329, info@globepequot.com, http://www.globepequot.com. Ed. Amy Lyons TEL 203-458-4500.

917.78411 USA ISSN 1542-7404
F474.K23

INSIDERS' GUIDE TO KANSAS CITY. Text in English. 2003. biennial, latest 2008, 3rd ed. USD 18.95 per issue (effective 2008). **Document type:** *Guide, Consumer.* **Description:** Provides the information and acts as a guide for in-depth travel and relocation information about Kansas city.
Published by: The Globe Pequot Press, Inc., 246 Goose Ln, PO Box 480, Guilford, CT 06437. TEL 203-458-4500, 888-249-7586, FAX 203-458-4603, 800-820-2329, info@globepequot.com, http://www.globepequot.com. Ed. Liz Taylor.

917.47 USA ISSN 2154-4743
F127.L8

▼ **INSIDERS' GUIDE TO LONG ISLAND.** Text in English. 2010 (June). irreg. USD 18.95 per issue (effective 2011). **Document type:** *Consumer.* **Description:** Travel guide for the Long Island, New York region.
Published by: The Globe Pequot Press, Insiders' Guide (Subsidiary of: The Globe Pequot Press, Inc.), PO Box 480, Guilford, CT 06437. TEL 203-458-4500, FAX 800-820-2329, info@globepequot.com, http://www.globepequot.com/globepequot/index.cfm?fuseaction=customer.welcome.

917.41 910.2 USA ISSN 1549-1021
F17.3

THE INSIDERS' GUIDE TO MAINE'S MID-COAST. Text in English. 1997. irreg., latest 1998, 2nd ed. USD 15.95 per issue (effective 2008). **Document type:** *Guide, Consumer.* **Description:** Covers guides to maine's mid-coast.
Published by: The Globe Pequot Press, Inc., 246 Goose Ln, PO Box 480, Guilford, CT 06437. TEL 203-458-4500, 888-249-7586, FAX 203-458-4603, 800-820-2329, info@globepequot.com, http://www.globepequot.com. Ed. Jeff Serena TEL 203-458-4556.

917.6819 910.91 USA ISSN 1542-8451
F444.M53

INSIDERS' GUIDE TO MEMPHIS. Text in English. 2002. biennial, latest 2008, 4th ed. USD 17.95 per issue (effective 2008). **Document type:** *Guide, Consumer.* **Description:** Provides the information and acts as a guide for in-depth travel and relocation information about Memphis.
Published by: The Globe Pequot Press, Inc., 246 Goose Ln, PO Box 480, Guilford, CT 06437. TEL 203-458-4500, 888-249-7586, FAX 203-458-4603, 800-820-2329, info@globepequot.com, http://www.globepequot.com. Ed. Amy Lyons TEL 203-458-4500.

917.5787 USA ISSN 1544-4015
F279.M93

INSIDERS' GUIDE TO MYRTLE BEACH AND THE GRAND STRAND. Text in English. 1993. biennial, latest 2008, 9th ed. USD 17.95 per issue (effective 2008). **Document type:** *Guide, Consumer.* **Description:** Describes how to live and thrive in the area, from the best family activities to the lowdown on real estate.
Former titles (until 1996): Insiders' Guide to South Carolina's Myrtle Beach and the Grand Strand; (until 1995): Insiders' Guide to Myrtle Beach and the Grand Strand (1097-2617)
Published by: The Globe Pequot Press, Inc., 246 Goose Ln, PO Box 480, Guilford, CT 06437. TEL 203-458-4500, 888-249-7586, FAX 203-458-4603, 800-820-2329, info@globepequot.com. Ed. Liz Taylor.

917.2 USA ISSN 1525-8157
F444.N23

INSIDERS' GUIDE TO NASHVILLE. Text in English. 1996. biennial, latest 2007, 6th ed. USD 18.95 per issue (effective 2008). back issues avail. **Document type:** *Guide, Consumer.* **Description:** Provides travel and relocation information.
Published by: The Globe Pequot Press, Inc., 246 Goose Ln, PO Box 480, Guilford, CT 06437. TEL 203-458-4500, 888-249-7586, FAX 203-458-4603, 800-820-2329, info@globepequot.com. Ed. Amy Lyons TEL 203-458-4500.

917.6335 USA ISSN 1543-8686
F379.N53

INSIDERS' GUIDE TO NEW ORLEANS. Text in English. 1982. irreg., latest 2005, 3rd ed. USD 17.95 per issue (effective 2008). **Document type:** *Guide, Consumer.* **Description:** Describes how to live and thrive in the area, from the best family activities to the lowdown on real estate.
Published by: The Globe Pequot Press, Inc., 246 Goose Ln, PO Box 480, Guilford, CT 06437. TEL 203-458-4500, 888-249-7586, FAX 203-458-4603, 800-820-2329, info@globepequot.com. Ed. Amy Lyons TEL 203-458-4500.

917.56 910.2 USA ISSN 1525-8076
F262.A16

INSIDERS' GUIDE TO NORTH CAROLINA'S MOUNTAINS; including Asheville, Biltmore Estate, and the Blue Ridge Parkway. Text in English. 1995. a., latest 2008, 9th ed. USD 18.95 per issue (effective 2008). **Document type:** *Guide, Consumer.* **Description:** Aims to act as a travel and relocation guide to North Carolina's Mountains.
Published by: The Globe Pequot Press, Inc., 246 Goose Ln, PO Box 480, Guilford, CT 06437. TEL 203-458-4500, 888-249-7586, FAX 203-458-4601, 800-820-2329, info@globepequot.com, http://www.globepequot.com. Ed. Jeff Serena TEL 203-458-4556.

917.561 338.4791 USA ISSN 1082-9458
F262.O96

INSIDERS' GUIDE TO NORTH CAROLINA'S OUTER BANKS. Text in English. 1976. a., latest 2009, 30th ed. USD 18.95 per issue (effective 2009). **Document type:** *Guide, Consumer.* **Description:** Provides travel and tourism information for North Carolina's Outer Banks.
Formerly: Insiders' Guide to the Outer Banks of North Carolina
Published by: The Globe Pequot Press, Inc., 246 Goose Ln, PO Box 480, Guilford, CT 06437. TEL 203-458-4500, 888-249-7586, FAX 203-458-4603, 800-820-2329, info@globepequot.com, http://www.globepequot.com. Ed. Amy Lyons TEL 203-458-4500.

917.66 USA ISSN 2150-2536
F704.O41

▼ **INSIDERS' GUIDE TO OKLAHOMA CITY.** Text in English. 2009. triennial. USD 18.95 per issue (effective 2009). **Document type:** *Guide, Consumer.* **Description:** Travel guide for Oklahoma City.
Published by: The Globe Pequot Press, Insiders' Guide (Subsidiary of: The Globe Pequot Press, Inc.), PO Box 480, Guilford, CT 06437. TEL 203-458-4500, FAX 800-820-2329, info@globepequot.com, http://www.globepequot.com/globepequot/index.cfm?fuseaction=customer.welcome.

979.4 USA ISSN 2154-6797

▼ **INSIDERS' GUIDE TO ORANGE COUNTY.** Text in English. 2010 (June). triennial. USD 18.95 per issue (effective 2011). **Document type:** *Consumer.* **Description:** Provides an in-depth travel guide for Orange County, California.
Published by: The Globe Pequot Press, Insiders' Guide (Subsidiary of: The Globe Pequot Press, Inc.), PO Box 480, Guilford, CT 06437. TEL 203-458-4500, FAX 800-820-2329, info@globepequot.com, http://www.globepequot.com/globepequot/index.cfm?fuseaction=customer.welcome.

917.48 910.2 USA ISSN 1559-9582
F157.P44

INSIDERS' GUIDE TO PENNSYLVANIA DUTCH COUNTRY. Text in English. 2006. biennial, latest 2008, 2nd ed. USD 17.95 per issue (effective 2008). **Document type:** *Guide, Consumer.* **Description:** Acts as a travel and relocation guide to Dutch Country in Pennsylvania.
Published by: The Globe Pequot Press, Inc., 246 Goose Ln, PO Box 480, Guilford, CT 06437. TEL 203-458-4500, 888-249-7586, FAX 203-458-4603, 800-820-2329, info@globepequot.com, http://www.globepequot.com. Ed. Jeff Serena TEL 203-458-4556.

917.4886 USA ISSN 1546-3133
F159.P63

INSIDERS' GUIDE TO PITTSBURGH. Text in English. 2000. biennial, latest 2008, 4th ed. USD 18.95 per issue (effective 2008). **Document type:** *Guide, Consumer.* **Description:** Explores Pittsburgh and all its offerings.
Published by: The Globe Pequot Press, Inc., 246 Goose Ln, PO Box 480, Guilford, CT 06437. TEL 203-458-4500, 888-249-7586, FAX 203-458-4603, 800-820-2329, info@globepequot.com, http://www.globepequot.com. Ed. Jeff Serena TEL 203-458-4556.

917.9 USA ISSN 1541-7921
F884.P8

INSIDERS' GUIDE TO PORTLAND, OREGON; including the metro area and Vancouver, Washington. Text in English. 1999. irreg., latest 2009, 6th ed. USD 18.95 per issue (effective 2008). **Document type:** *Guide, Consumer.* **Description:** Explores personal and practical perspective of Portland and its surrounding environments.
Formerly (until 2002): The Insiders' Guide to Portland (1534-2689)
Published by: The Globe Pequot Press, Inc., 246 Goose Ln, PO Box 480, Guilford, CT 06437. TEL 203-458-4500, 888-249-7586, FAX 203-458-4603, 800-820-2329, info@globepequot.com, http://www.globepequot.com. Ed. Amy Lyons TEL 203-458-4500.

917.84 USA ISSN 2155-5583
F264.R1

▼ **INSIDERS' GUIDE TO RALEIGH, DURHAM & CHAPEL HILL**; North Carolina's triangle. Text in English. 2010 (Jul.). triennial. USD 18.95 per issue (effective 2011). **Document type:** *Guide, Consumer.* **Description:** Travel guide for Raleigh, Durham, and Chapel Hill, North Carolina.
Published by: The Globe Pequot Press, Inc., 246 Goose Ln, PO Box 480, Guilford, CT 06437. TEL 203-458-4500, FAX 203-458-4603, info@globepequot.com.

910.2 USA ISSN 1545-1399
TX307

INSIDERS' GUIDE TO RELOCATION; expert advice to move across the state, the country, or the world. Variant title: Guide to Relocation. Text in English. 2004. biennial, latest 2004, 2nd ed. USD 14.95 per issue (effective 2008). **Document type:** *Guide, Consumer.* **Description:** Provides relocation information for domestic moves as well as in-depth information about selecting the best relocation destination.
Published by: The Globe Pequot Press, Inc., 246 Goose Ln, PO Box 480, Guilford, CT 06437. TEL 203-458-4500, 888-249-7586, FAX 203-458-4603, 800-820-2329, info@globepequot.com, http://www.globepequot.com. Ed. Jeff Serena TEL 203-458-4556.

917.64351 910.91 USA ISSN 1542-846X
F394.S2113

INSIDERS' GUIDE TO SAN ANTONIO. Text in English. 2002. biennial, latest 2008, 4th ed. USD 17.95 per issue (effective 2008). **Document type:** *Guide, Consumer.* **Description:** Provides the information and acts as a guide for in-depth travel and relocation information about San Antonio.
Published by: The Globe Pequot Press, Inc., 246 Goose Ln, PO Box 480, Guilford, CT 06437. TEL 203-458-4500, 888-249-7586, FAX 203-458-4603, 800-820-2329, info@globepequot.com, http://www.globepequot.com. Ed. Amy Lyons TEL 203-458-4500.

917.94985 USA ISSN 1533-5224
F869.S22

INSIDERS' GUIDE TO SAN DIEGO. Text in English. 1999. biennial. USD 18.95 per issue (effective 2008). **Document type:** *Guide, Consumer.* **Description:** Covers travel and relocation information about Southern California city.
Published by: The Globe Pequot Press, Inc., 246 Goose Ln, PO Box 480, Guilford, CT 06437. TEL 203-458-4500, 888-249-7586, FAX 203-458-4603, 800-820-2329, info@globepequot.com, http://www.globepequot.com. Ed. Jeff Serena TEL 203-458-4556.

917.9491 910.2 USA ISSN 1536-8580
F869.S45

INSIDERS' GUIDE TO SANTA BARBARA; including Channel Islands National Park. Text in English. 1999. biennial, latest 2008, 4th ed. USD 18.95 per issue (effective 2008). back issues avail. **Document type:** *Guide, Consumer.* **Description:** Describes how to navigate Santa Barbara's abundance of natural and cultural sites and activities.
Published by: The Globe Pequot Press, Inc., 246 Goose Ln, PO Box 480, Guilford, CT 06437. TEL 203-458-4500, 888-249-7586, FAX 203-458-4603, 800-820-2329, info@globepequot.com, http://www.globepequot.com. Ed. Liz Taylor.

917.2 USA ISSN 1525-7959
F804.S2

INSIDERS' GUIDE TO SANTA FE. Text in English. 1998. biennial, latest 2005, 4th ed. USD 18.95 per issue (effective 2008). back issues avail. **Document type:** *Guide, Consumer.* **Description:** Offers information to travelers, newcomers and locals about Santa Fe.
Published by: The Globe Pequot Press, Inc., 246 Goose Ln, PO Box 480, Guilford, CT 06437. TEL 203-458-4500, 888-249-7586, FAX 203-458-4603, 800-820-2329, info@globepequot.com. Ed. Jeff Serena TEL 203-458-4556.

917.58 910.2 USA ISSN 1539-7378
F294.S23

INSIDERS' GUIDE TO SAVANNAH AND HILTON HEAD. Text in English. 1999. biennial, latest 2008, 7th ed. USD 21.95 per issue (effective 2008). 368 p./no.; **Document type:** *Guide, Consumer.* **Description:** Provides travel and relocation information.
Published by: The Globe Pequot Press, Inc., 246 Goose Ln, PO Box 480, Guilford, CT 06437. TEL 203-458-4500, 888-249-7586, FAX 203-458-4603, 800-820-2329, info@globepequot.com, http://www.globepequot.com. Ed. Jeff Serena TEL 203-458-4556.

917.5941 910.2 USA ISSN 1529-174X
F317.M7

INSIDERS' GUIDE TO THE FLORIDA KEYS AND KEY WEST. Text in English. 1996. a., latest 2008, 13th ed. USD 18.95 per issue (effective 2008). back issues avail. **Document type:** *Guide, Consumer.* **Description:** Provides information on visiting and relocating to the very sunny part of the state, from Key Largo to Key West.
Published by: The Globe Pequot Press, Inc., 246 Goose Ln, PO Box 480, Guilford, CT 06437. TEL 203-458-4500, 888-249-7586, FAX 203-458-4603, 800-820-2329, info@globepequot.com. Ed. Liz Taylor.

917.6889 USA ISSN 1542-5193
F443.G7

INSIDERS' GUIDE TO THE GREAT SMOKY MOUNTAINS. Text in English. biennial, latest 2009, 6th ed. USD 17.95 per issue (effective 2009). **Document type:** *Guide, Consumer.* **Description:** Provides travel and tourism information for the Great Smoky Mountains National Park.
Formerly: Great Smoky Mountains
Published by: The Globe Pequot Press, Inc., 246 Goose Ln, PO Box 480, Guilford, CT 06437. TEL 203-458-4500, 888-249-7586, FAX 203-458-4603, 800-820-2329, info@globepequot.com, http://www.globepequot.com. Ed. Jeff Serena TEL 203-458-4556.

917.49 910.91 USA ISSN 1542-7420
F142.A79

INSIDERS' GUIDE TO THE JERSEY SHORE. Text in English. 2002. irreg., latest 2004, 2nd ed. USD 17.95 per issue (effective 2008). **Description:** Provides the information and acts as a guide for in-depth travel and relocation information about Jersey Shore.
Published by: The Globe Pequot Press, Inc., 246 Goose Ln, PO Box 480, Guilford, CT 06437. TEL 203-458-4500, 888-249-7586, FAX 203-458-4601, 800-820-2329, http://www.globepequot.com. Ed. Jeff Serena TEL 203-458-4556.

917.74 910.2 USA ISSN 1549-1749
F612.S9

THE INSIDERS' GUIDE TO THE LAKE SUPERIOR REGION. Text in English. 1996. a., latest 2007, 1st ed. USD 14.95 per issue (effective 2008). **Document type:** *Guide, Consumer.* **Description:** Covers the history, attractions and accommodations along the shores of the Lake Superior.
Published by: The Globe Pequot Press, Inc., 246 Goose Ln, PO Box 480, Guilford, CT 06437. TEL 203-458-4500, 888-249-7586, FAX 203-458-4603, 800-820-2329, info@globepequot.com, http://www.globepequot.com.

917.41 USA ISSN 1547-8939
F27.A75

INSIDERS' GUIDE TO THE MAINE COAST. Text in English. 2004. biennial. USD 17.95 per issue (effective 2008). **Document type:** *Guide, Consumer.* **Description:** Covers cosmopolitan city and family vacation hot spots, as well as outlet shopping and national parks. It provides information on coastline, beaches and resort communities, rocky cliffs and tiny fishing villages.
Published by: The Globe Pequot Press, Inc., 246 Goose Ln, PO Box 480, Guilford, CT 06437. TEL 203-458-4500, 888-249-7586, FAX 203-458-4601, 800-820-2329. Ed. Jeff Serena TEL 203-458-4556.

917.947 910.91 USA ISSN 1540-1758
F868.M7

INSIDERS' GUIDE TO THE MONTEREY PENINSULA. Text in English. 1998. biennial, latest 2004, 4th ed. USD 17.95 per issue (effective 2008). **Document type:** *Guide, Consumer.*
Published by: The Globe Pequot Press, Inc., 246 Goose Ln, PO Box 480, Guilford, CT 06437. TEL 203-458-4500, 888-249-7586, FAX 203-458-4603, 800-820-2329, info@globepequot.com, http://www.globepequot.com. Ed. Jeff Serena TEL 203-458-4556.

917.482 USA ISSN 1541-048X
F157.P7

INSIDERS' GUIDE TO THE POCONO MOUNTAINS; including northeastern Pennsylvania. Text in English. 1996. irreg., latest 2005, 4th ed. USD 18.95 per issue (effective 2008). **Document type:** *Guide, Consumer.* **Description:** Describes how to live and thrive in the area, from the best family activities to the lowdown on real estate.
Published by: The Globe Pequot Press, Inc., 246 Goose Ln, PO Box 480, Guilford, CT 06437. TEL 203-458-4500, 888-249-7586, FAX 203-458-4603, 800-820-2329, info@globepequot.com. Ed. Jeff Serena TEL 203-458-4556.

917.76 USA ISSN 1525-7460
F614.M6

INSIDERS' GUIDE TO THE TWIN CITIES. Text in English. 1994. biennial, latest 2008, 6th ed. USD 18.95 per issue (effective 2008). **Document type:** *Guide, Consumer.* **Description:** Describes how to live and thrive in the area, from the best family activities to the lowdown on real estate.
Published by: The Globe Pequot Press, Inc., 246 Goose Ln, PO Box 480, Guilford, CT 06437. TEL 203-458-4500, 888-249-7586, FAX 203-458-4603, 800-820-2329, info@globepequot.com, http://www.globepequot.com. Ed. Jeff Serena TEL 203-458-4556.

917.91776 910.2 USA ISSN 1529-3459
F819.T93
THE INSIDERS' GUIDE TO TUCSON. Text in English. 1998. biennial, latest 2008, 6th ed. USD 16.95 per issue (effective 2008). 400 p./no.; **Document type:** *Guide, Consumer.* **Description:** Provides travel and relocation information.
Published by: The Globe Pequot Press, Inc., 246 Goose Ln, PO Box 480, Guilford, CT 06437. TEL 203-458-4500, 888-249-7586, FAX 203-458-4603, 800-820-2329, info@globepequot.com, http://www.globepequot.com. Ed. Jeff Serena TEL 203-458-4556.

917.66 USA ISSN 2150-2544
F704.T92
▼ **INSIDERS' GUIDE TO TULSA.** Text in English. 2009. triennial. USD 18.95 per issue (effective 2009). **Document type:** *Guide, Consumer.* **Description:** Travel guide for Tulsa, Oklahoma.
Published by: The Globe Pequot Press, Insiders' Guide (Subsidiary of: The Globe Pequot Press, Inc.), PO Box 480, Guilford, CT 06437. TEL 203-458-4500, FAX 800-820-2329, info@globepequot.com, http://www.globepequot.com/globepequot/index.cfm?fuseaction=customer.welcome.

917.55 USA ISSN 1092-4906
F232.B59
INSIDERS' GUIDE TO VIRGINIA'S BLUE RIDGE, INCLUDING THE SHENANDOAH VALLEY. Text in English. 1992. a. USD 16.95 per issue (effective 2008). **Document type:** *Guide, Consumer.* **Description:** Provides information on in-depth travel and relocation.
Published by: The Globe Pequot Press, Inc., 246 Goose Ln, PO Box 480, Guilford, CT 06437. TEL 203-458-4500, 888-249-7586, FAX 203-458-4603, 800-820-2329, info@globepequot.com, http://www.globepequot.com. Ed. Jeff Serena TEL 203-458-4556.

917.53 910.2 USA ISSN 1538-8174
F192.3
INSIDERS' GUIDE TO WASHINGTON, D.C. Text in English. 1993. a., latest 2007, 7th ed. USD 18.95 per issue (effective 2008). back issues avail. **Document type:** *Guide, Consumer.* **Description:** Describes how to live and thrive in the area, from the best shopping to the lowdown on real estate and education.
Formerly (until 1990): Insiders' Guide to Metropolitan Washington, D.C
Published by: The Globe Pequot Press, Inc., 246 Goose Ln, PO Box 480, Guilford, CT 06437. TEL 203-458-4500, 888-249-7586, FAX 203-458-4603, 800-820-2329, info@globepequot.com, http://www.globepequot.com. Ed. Jeff Serena TEL 203-458-4556.

917.554 910.2 USA ISSN 1541-454X
F234.W7
INSIDERS' GUIDE TO WILLIAMSBURG AND VIRGINIA'S HISTORIC TRIANGLE. Text in English. 1984. triennial, latest 2008, 15th ed. USD 18.95 per issue (effective 2008). back issues avail. **Document type:** *Guide, Consumer.* **Description:** Provides information about real estate, restaurants, accommodations, entertainment and recreational activities for Williamsburg and Virginia's Historic Triangle.
Formerly (until 19??): The Insiders' Guide to Williamsburg, Jamestown-Yorktown (1092-4922)
Published by: The Globe Pequot Press, Inc., 246 Goose Ln, PO Box 480, Guilford, CT 06437. TEL 203-458-4500, 888-249-7586, FAX 203-458-4603, 800-820-2329, info@globepequot.com, http://www.globepequot.com. Ed. Jeff Serena TEL 203-458-4556.

917.875 338.4791 USA ISSN 1539-6584
F722
INSIDERS' GUIDE TO YELLOWSTONE AND GRAND TETON. Text in English. 1998. biennial, latest 2009, 7th ed. USD 17.95 per issue (effective 2009). 344 p./no.; **Document type:** *Guide, Consumer.* **Description:** Provides travel and relocation information for Yellowstone and Grand Teton National Parks.
Formerly (until 1998): Insiders' Guide to Yellowstone (1536-9250)
Published by: The Globe Pequot Press, Inc., 246 Goose Ln, PO Box 480, Guilford, CT 06437. TEL 203-458-4500, 888-249-7586, FAX 203-458-4603, 800-820-2329, info@globepequot.com, http://www.globepequot.com. Ed. Jeff Serena TEL 203-458-4556.

917.5 USA ISSN 1531-4529
F232.S5
INSIGHTS (WINCHESTER); the magazine for the Shenandoah. Text in English. 1995. bi-m. adv.
Published by: Turning Point Publications, 2180 S. Loudoun St., Ste. 245, Winchester, VA 22601. TEL 540-247-7899. Ed. Heather B. Wilson. Pub. Wesley L. Wilson III.

INSITES (CHICAGO). *see* ARCHITECTURE

910.202 NZL ISSN 1177-7605
INSPIRE. Text in English. 2007. q. NZD 28.50 domestic; NZD 59.90 in Australia (effective 2008). adv. **Document type:** *Magazine, Consumer.*
Published by: (House of Travel), HB Media, Wellesley St, PO Box 7125, Auckland, New Zealand. TEL 64-9-9660999, FAX 64-9-3681034, info@hbmedia.co.nz, http://hbmedia.co.nz/. Ed. Sarah Heeringa. Adv. contact Ben Gibb TEL 64-9-9219217. color page NZD 4,990; trim 230 x 300.

910.202 GBR
INSTITUTE OF TRAVEL & TOURISM. JOURNAL. Text in English. 1955. bi-m. adv. bk.rev. charts; stat.; tr.lit. back issues avail. **Document type:** *Journal, Trade.* **Description:** Contains coverage on destinations, profiles, special travel offers and reader's letters.
Published by: Institute of Travel & Tourism, 113 Victoria St, St Albans, Herts AL1 3TJ, United Kingdom. TEL 44-1727-854395, FAX 44-1727-847415. Ed. Roger Edwards. Pub. Linda Gibson. adv.: color page GBP 1,200; trim 210 x 297. Circ: 8,000.

917.204 CRI
INSTITUTO COSTARRICENSE DE TURISMO. MEMORIA ANUAL. Text in Spanish. 1955. a. free. illus. **Document type:** *Government.*
Published by: Instituto Costarricense de Turismo, Apdo 777-1000, San Jose, Costa Rica. TEL 506-33-21-64, 506-2231733, FAX 223-54-52, http://www.tourism-costarica.com. Circ: 100.

INTERMEZZO (LEXINGTON). *see* LIFESTYLE

910 USA ISSN 1012-8042
INTERNATIONAL ACADEMY FOR THE STUDY OF TOURISM. NEWSLETTER. Text in English. 1986. q. USD 60. abstr. back issues avail. **Document type:** *Newsletter.* **Description:** Covers important events of the organization, as well as conferences and events.
Published by: Tourism Center, 1994 Buford Ave, 116 Classroom Office Bldg., University of Minnesota, St. Paul, MN 55108. TEL 612-624-4947, FAX 612-624-4264. Ed., Pub. Bill Gartner. Circ: 150 (controlled).

917.29 BHS
INTERNATIONAL BAHAMA LIFE. Text in English. m. USD 16.
Published by: Johnson Publications, PO Box N 1505, Nassau, Bahamas.

INTERNATIONAL CRUISE AND FERRY REVIEW. *see* TRANSPORTATION—Ships And Shipping

THE INTERNATIONAL DIRECTORY OF LEATHER GOODS, FOOTWEAR AND TRAVEL ACCESSORIES IMPORTERS. *see* BUSINESS AND ECONOMICS—Trade And Industrial Directories

910.2 BEL ISSN 0074-5979
INTERNATIONAL FEDERATION OF JOURNALISTS AND TRAVEL WRITERS. OFFICIAL LIST/REPERTOIRE OFFICIEL. Text in English, French. 1965. q. adv. bk.rev.
Published by: International Federation of Journalists and Travel Writers, Zavelstraat 62, Kortenberg, 3070, Belgium. Circ: 2,500.

INTERNATIONAL JOURNAL OF CONTEMPORARY HOSPITALITY MANAGEMENT. *see* HOTELS AND RESTAURANTS

338.4306 658.8 GBR ISSN 1750-6182
INTERNATIONAL JOURNAL OF CULTURE, TOURISM AND HOSPITALITY RESEARCH. Abbreviated title: I J C T H R. Text in English. 2007. q. EUR 339 combined subscription in Europe (print & online eds.); USD 479 combined subscription in the Americas (print & online eds.); GBP 239 combined subscription in the UK & elsewhere (print & online eds.); AUD 639 combined subscription in Australasia (print & online eds.) (effective 2012). reprint service avail. from PSC. **Document type:** *Journal, Academic/Scholarly.* **Description:** Focuses on building bridges in theory, research and practice across the fields of culture, tourism and hospitality.
Related titles: Online - full text ed.: ISSN 1750-6190 (from IngentaConnect).
Indexed: A12, A15, A17, A22, ABIn, CABA, E01, E12, ESPM, GEOBASE, LT, N02, P10, P48, P51, P53, P54, PQC, R12, RRTA, S13, S16, SD, SSciA, W11.
—BLDSC (4542.181300), IE. **CCC.**
Published by: Emerald Group Publishing Ltd., Howard House, Wagon Ln, Bingley, W Yorks BD16 1WA, United Kingdom. TEL 44-1274-777700, FAX 44-1274-785201, information@emeraldinsight.com. Ed. Arch Woodside. Pub. Valerie Robillard.

INTERNATIONAL JOURNAL OF DIGITAL CULTURE AND ELECTRONIC TOURISM. *see* COMPUTERS

▼ **INTERNATIONAL JOURNAL OF EVENT AND FESTIVAL MANAGEMENT.** *see* BUSINESS AND ECONOMICS—Management

INTERNATIONAL JOURNAL OF HOSPITALITY AND TOURISM ADMINISTRATION. *see* HOTELS AND RESTAURANTS

338.4791 IND ISSN 0974-6250
➤ **INTERNATIONAL JOURNAL OF HOSPITALITY AND TOURISM SYSTEMS.** Text in English. 2008. a. INR 750 combined subscription domestic to individuals (print & online eds.); USD 60 combined subscription foreign to individuals (print & online eds.); INR 1,200 combined subscription domestic to institutions (print & online eds.); USD 90 combined subscription foreign to institutions (print & online eds.) (effective 2011). **Document type:** *Journal, Academic/Scholarly.* **Description:** Dedicated to promoting excellence in teaching and stimulating research in hospitality and tourism internationally.
Related titles: Online - full text ed.: INR 500 domestic to individuals; USD 40 foreign to individuals; INR 800 domestic to institutions; USD 60 foreign to institutions (effective 2011).
Published by: Indian Journal of International Tourism & Hospitality Research, Department of Tourism & Hotel Management, Kurukshetra University, Kurushetra, Haryana 136 118, India. ijhts@in.com, http://hotelmgmt.tripod.com/. Ed. Suresh Kumar.

➤ **INTERNATIONAL JOURNAL OF HOSPITALITY MANAGEMENT.** *see* HOTELS AND RESTAURANTS

338.479105 GBR ISSN 1757-5567
➤ **INTERNATIONAL JOURNAL OF LEISURE AND TOURISM MARKETING.** Abbreviated title: I J L T M. Text in English. 2008. 4/yr. EUR 494 to institutions (print or online ed.); EUR 672 combined subscription to institutions (print & online eds.) (effective 2012). bk.rev. abstr.; bibl.; charts; illus. back issues avail. **Document type:** *Journal, Academic/Scholarly.* **Description:** Promotes discussion through original research that contributes innovative knowledge and understanding to the field of leisure, recreation and tourism studies.
Related titles: Online - full text ed.: ISSN 1757-5575 (from IngentaConnect).
Indexed: A26, E08.
—IE. **CCC.**
Published by: Inderscience Publishers, PO Box 735, Olney, Bucks MK46 5WB, United Kingdom. TEL 44-1234-240519, FAX 44-1234-240515, editorial@inderscience.com. Ed. Dr. . Rajagopal. **Subscr. to:** World Trade Centre Bldg, 29 Rte de Pre-Bois, Case Postale 856, Geneva 15 1215, Switzerland. subs@inderscience.com.

338.48 IND ISSN 0974-2603
INTERNATIONAL JOURNAL OF TOURISM AND TRAVEL. Abbreviated title: I J T & I. Text in English. 2008. s-a. INR 600 combined subscription domestic to individuals (print & online eds.); USD 100 combined subscription foreign to individuals (print & online eds.); INR 1,800 combined subscription domestic to institutions (print & online eds.); USD 200 combined subscription foreign to institutions (print & online eds.) (effective 2011). **Document type:** *Journal, Academic/Scholarly.* **Description:** Foresees to create value for enterprises and organisations in tourism, travel and related sectors.
Related titles: Online - full text ed.: INR 400 domestic to individuals; USD 80 foreign to individuals; INR 1,200 domestic to institutions; USD 150 foreign to institutions (effective 2011).
Published by: Indian Institute of Tourism and Travel Management, Research Unit, Gwalior, Madhya Pradesh 474 001, India. TEL 91-751-2345821, FAX 91-751-2344054, iittm@sancharnet.in, journal.iittm@gmail.com. Ed. Sithikanta Mishra.

338.4 GBR ISSN 1759-0442
▼ ➤ **INTERNATIONAL JOURNAL OF TOURISM ANTHROPOLOGY.** Text in English. 2010. 4/yr. EUR 494 to institutions (print or online ed.); EUR 672 combined subscription to institutions (print & online eds.) (effective 2012). abstr.; bibl. **Document type:** *Journal, Academic/Scholarly.* **Description:** Dedicated to advance theory, research and practice in the field of tourism anthropology.
Related titles: Online - full text ed.: ISSN 1759-0450 (from IngentaConnect).
Indexed: CABA, LT, W11.
—**CCC.**
Published by: Inderscience Publishers, PO Box 735, Olney, Bucks MK46 5WB, United Kingdom. TEL 44-1234-240519, FAX 44-1234-240515, editorial@inderscience.com. Ed. Dr. Cheng Li. **Subscr. to:** World Trade Centre Bldg, 29 Rte de Pre-Bois, Case Postale 856, Geneva 15 1215, Switzerland. FAX 41-22-7910885, subs@inderscience.com.

338.4 GBR ISSN 1750-4090
➤ **INTERNATIONAL JOURNAL OF TOURISM POLICY.** Abbreviated title: I J T P. Text in English. 2007. 4/yr. EUR 494 to institutions (print or online ed.); EUR 672 combined subscription to institutions (print & online eds.) (effective 2012). abstr.; bibl.; charts; illus.; stat. back issues avail. **Document type:** *Journal, Academic/Scholarly.* **Description:** Provides a forum for scholars and policy makers to exchange views and ideas at an international level on key issues that shape the growth of today's tourism industry.
Formerly announced as: International Journal of Tourism Policy and Research
Related titles: Online - full text ed.: ISSN 1750-4104 (from IngentaConnect).
Indexed: A26, A28, APA, BrCerAb, C&ISA, CA/WCA, CABA, CIA, CerAb, CivEngAb, CorrAb, E&CAJ, E11, E12, EEA, EMA, ESPM, EnvEAb, F08, F12, GEOBASE, H15, I05, LT, M&TEA, M09, MBF, METADEX, N02, R12, RRTA, S13, S16, SSciA, SolStAb, T04, TAR, W11, WAA.
—IE. **CCC.**
Published by: Inderscience Publishers, PO Box 735, Olney, Bucks MK46 5WB, United Kingdom. TEL 44-1234-240519, FAX 44-1234-240515, editorial@inderscience.com. Eds. Dr. George Agiomirgianakis, Konstantinos Andriotis. **Subscr. to:** World Trade Centre Bldg, 29 Rte de Pre-Bois, Case Postale 856, Geneva 15 1215, Switzerland. FAX 41-22-7910885, subs@inderscience.com.

338.4 GBR ISSN 1099-2340
G155.A1
➤ **INTERNATIONAL JOURNAL OF TOURISM RESEARCH.** Text in English. 1995. bi-m. GBP 501 in United Kingdom to institutions; EUR 631 in Europe to institutions; USD 980 elsewhere to institutions; GBP 576 combined subscription in United Kingdom to institutions (print & online eds.); EUR 727 combined subscription in Europe to institutions (print & online eds.); USD 1,127 combined subscription elsewhere to institutions (print & online eds.) (effective 2012). adv. back issues avail.; reprint service avail. from PSC. **Document type:** *Journal, Academic/Scholarly.* **Description:** Provides a platform for research practice in tourism and hospitality.
Formerly (until 1999): Progress in Tourism and Hospitality Research (1077-3509)
Related titles: Microform ed.: (from PQC); Online - full text ed.: ISSN 1522-1970. GBP 501 in United Kingdom to institutions; EUR 631 in Europe to institutions; USD 980 elsewhere to institutions (effective 2012).
Indexed: A10, A12, A13, A20, A22, A34, ABIn, B01, B07, CA, CABA, CurCont, E12, ESPM, EnvAb, EnvInd, F08, GEOBASE, GH, H&TI, H06, H16, HPNRM, IndVet, LT, N02, P03, P48, P51, P53, P54, PQC, PsycInfo, R12, RRTA, RiskAb, S02, S03, S13, S16, SCOPUS, SSCI, SSciA, T02, T05, V03, VS, W07, W11.
—IE, Ingenta. **CCC.**
Published by: (Consortium of Hospitality Research Information Services), John Wiley & Sons Ltd. (Subsidiary of: John Wiley & Sons, Inc.), 1-7 Oldlands Way, PO Box 808, Bognor Regis, West Sussex PO21 9FF, United Kingdom. TEL 44-1865-778315, FAX 44-1243-843232, cs-journals@wiley.com, http://eu.wiley.com/WileyCDA/. Eds. Adele Ladkin, John Fletcher. **Subscr. in the Americas to:** John Wiley & Sons, Inc., 111 River St, Hoboken, NJ 07030. subinfo@wiley.com; **Subscr. to:** 1-7 Oldlands Way, PO Box 809, Bognor Regis, West Sussex PO21 9FG, United Kingdom. TEL 44-1865-778054, cs-agency@wiley.com.

338.4791 IRL ISSN 1362-7325
INTERNATIONAL LIVING. Text in English. 1982. m. back issues avail. **Document type:** *Newsletter, Consumer.* **Description:** Provideds information on global traveling, living, retiring, investing, and buying real estate.
Related titles: Online - full text ed.; ◆ International ed. of: International Living. ISSN 0277-2442.
Published by: Agora Ireland, 5 Catherine St, Waterford, Ireland. TEL 353.51844323, webmaster@internationalliving.com. Adv. contact Marie Connelly. Circ: 3,000 (paid and controlled).

910.4 USA ISSN 0277-2442
G149
INTERNATIONAL LIVING. Text in English. 198?. m. USD 69 domestic; CAD 89 in Canada; USD 89 elsewhere (effective 2011). adv. bk.rev. index. back issues avail. **Document type:** *Magazine, Consumer.*
Related titles: Online - full text ed.: free (effective 2011); ◆ International ed.: International Living. ISSN 1362-7325.
Published by: Agora, Inc., PO Box 1936, Baltimore, MD 21203. TEL 410-783-8499, csteam@agorapublishinggroup.com, http://www.agora-inc.com/. Pub. Jackie Flynn.

385 910.09 USA ISSN 0891-7655
HE1001
INTERNATIONAL RAILWAY TRAVELER. Text in English. 1983. q. USD 69 domestic; USD 79 in Canada; USD 89 elsewhere (effective 2007). adv. bk.rev. charts; illus.; tr.lit. cum.index. 24 p./no. 3 cols./p.; back issues avail. **Document type:** *Magazine, Trade.* **Description:** For all who love to travel by trains, whether by Amtrak or the East African Railway.
Indexed: CLT&T, HRIS.
Published by: Hardy Publishing Co., Inc., 2010 Edgeland Ave, Ste 100, Louisville, KY 40204. TEL 502-454-0277, FAX 502-458-2250. Ed., Pub., R&P Owen Hardy TEL 502-454-0277. adv.: color page USD 1,500. Circ: 200 (controlled); 1,200 (paid). **Subscr. to:** Fulco, 30 Broad St, Denville, NJ 07834.

INTERNATIONAL SCIENTIFIC JOURNAL GEOGRAPHICA PANNONICA. *see* GEOGRAPHY

338.4791 DEU ISSN 1862-9946
INTERNATIONAL TOURISM RESEARCH AND CONCEPTS. Text in German. 2006. irreg., latest vol.5, 2011. price varies. **Document type:** *Monographic series, Academic/Scholarly.*
Published by: Erich Schmidt Verlag GmbH & Co. (Berlin), Genthiner Str 30 G, Berlin, 10785, Germany. TEL 49-30-2500850, FAX 49-30-250085305, vertrieb@esvmedien.de.

INTERNATIONAL TRAVEL HEALTH GUIDE. *see* MEDICAL SCIENCES

910 USA ISSN 0191-8761
INTERNATIONAL TRAVEL NEWS. Abbreviated title: I T N. Text in English. 1976. m. USD 24 domestic; USD 40 in Canada; USD 50 Mexico, W. Europe, Japan, New Zealand, or Australia; USD 70 elsewhere (effective 2010). adv. bk.rev. illus.; tr.lit. back issues avail.; reprints avail. **Document type:** *Magazine, Consumer.* **Description:** Contains consumer-oriented information for overseas travelers, including appraisals of tours, cruises and airlines, plus travel warnings and inside tips.
Related titles: Online - full text ed.
Indexed: G08, I05, I07, S23.
Published by: Martin Publications Inc., 2120 28th St, Sacramento, CA 95818. TEL 916-457-3643, FAX 916-451-1118. Ed. David Tykol. Pub. Armond Noble. Adv. contact Helen Noble.

915.204 JPN
INTERNATIONAL TRAVEL PLAN. Text in English, Japanese. 1997 (vol.10). m. JPY 4,500 (effective 2000). adv. bk.rev. charts; illus. **Document type:** *Handbook/Manual/Guide, Consumer.*
Incorporates (in 1998): Far East Traveler; Which incorporated (in 1968): Far East Reporter (0425-7170)
Published by: Far East Reporters Inc., Phoenix Bldg, 5F, 1-4-3 Azabudai, Minato-ku, Tokyo, 106-0041, Japan. TEL 81-3-5570-9703, FAX 81-3-5570-9704. Ed. Ed Mike Pokrovsky. Pub. George Pokrovsky. Adv. contact Masa Hirukawa. Circ: 50,000.

914.94 796.552 CHE
INTERNATIONAL UNION OF ALPINE ASSOCIATIONS. BULLETIN/ UNION INTERNATIONALE DES ASSOCIATIONS D'ALPINISME. BULLETIN. Text in English, French, German. 1934. q. CHF 25. adv. bk.rev.
Published by: International Union of Alpine Associations, Case Postale 237, Geneva 11, 1211, Switzerland. Ed. Adalbert Fontana. Circ: 700.

910.2 USA ISSN 1540-0603
G155.A1
INTERNET TRAVEL PLANNER; how to plan trips and save money online. Text in English. 2000. irreg., latest 2002, 2nd ed. USD 17.95 per issue (effective 2008). **Document type:** *Guide, Consumer.* **Description:** Provides information for online travel planning.
Published by: The Globe Pequot Press, Inc., 246 Goose Ln, PO Box 480, Guilford, CT 06437. TEL 203-458-4500, 888-249-7586, FAX 203-458-4603, 800-820-2329, info@globepequot.com, http://www.globepequot.com.

910 USA
INTERVAC U S; international holiday. Text in English. 1953. 5/yr. USD 83 (effective 2000). adv. **Document type:** *Catalog.*
Published by: Intervac US - International and USA Home Exchange, 30 Corte San Fernando, Tiburon, CA 94920. TEL 800-756-4663, FAX 415-435-7440. Ed. Paula Jaffe. Circ: 11,000. **Subscr. to:** PO Box 590504, San Francisco, CA 94159.

910.09 USA
INTERVAL WORLD. Text in English. 19??. 3/yr. free to members (effective 2009). adv. **Document type:** *Magazine, Consumer.* **Description:** Features exciting travel destination articles, travel tips, membership benefits, and new resort listings.
Formerly (until Apr.1996): Interval International Traveler
Published by: Interval International, PO Box 431920, Miami, FL 33243. TEL 305-668-3414, 888-784-3447, http://www.intervalworld.com. Adv. contact Robin Morales TEL 305-666-1861 ext 7362. color page USD 34,385; trim 8.25 x 10.5. Circ: 1,354,296.

917.77 USA ISSN 1551-7985
F621.6
IOWA CURIOSITIES; quirky characters, roadside oddities, & other offbeat stuff. Text in English. 2005. biennial, latest 2005, 1st ed. USD 13.95 per issue (effective 2008). **Document type:** *Guide, Consumer.* **Description:** Provides tourist information about the Hawkeye State.
Published by: The Globe Pequot Press, Inc., 246 Goose Ln, PO Box 480, Guilford, CT 06437. TEL 203-458-4500, 888-249-7586, FAX 203-458-4603, 800-820-2329, info@globepequot.com, http://www.globepequot.com.

914.415 IRL
IRELAND AT YOUR LEISURE. Text in English. a. adv. **Document type:** *Magazine, Consumer.*
Published by: Ashville Media Group, Apollo House, Tara St., Dublin, 2, Ireland. TEL 353-1-4322200, FAX 353-1-6727100, info@ashville.com, http://www.ashville.com. Ed. Anthea Savage. Adv. contact Brian O'Neill. B&W page EUR 4,190, color page EUR 4,571. Circ: 150,000 (controlled).

914 IRL ISSN 0021-0943
DA900
IRELAND OF THE WELCOMES. Text in English. 1952. bi-m. EUR 21; EUR 3.50 newsstand/cover (effective 2011). adv. bk.rev. illus. **Document type:** *Magazine, Consumer.* **Description:** Contains articles on the culture, history, people, places and events of Ireland.
Indexed: A22, MLA-IB, RILM.
Published by: (Failte Ireland/Irish Tourist Board), Harmonia Ltd., Rosemount House, Dundrum Rd, Dublin, 14, Ireland. TEL 353-1-2405300, FAX 353-1-6619757, fneeson@harmonia.ie, http://www.harmonia.ie. Ed. Sean Carberry. Adv. contact Niamh Daly.

914 IRL ISSN 0021-1419
IRISH TRAVEL TRADE NEWS. Text in English. 1965. m. USD 50. adv. bk.rev. **Document type:** *Magazine, Trade.*
Address: 9 Western Parkway Business Centre, Ballymount Rd., Dublin, 12, Ireland. TEL 353-1-4502422, FAX 353-1-4502954. Ed. Michael Flood. Adv. contact Ian Bloomfield. B&W page EUR 1,746, color page EUR 2,565; trim 210 x 297. Circ: 2,200.

908 DEU ISSN 1432-3370
IRLAND JOURNAL. Text in German. 1990. 4/yr. EUR 20 (effective 2009). adv. **Document type:** *Magazine, Consumer.*
Published by: Christian Ludwig Verlag, Niederfeldweg 5, Moers, 47447, Germany. TEL 49-2841-35034, FAX 49-2841-35036. adv.: B&W page EUR 1,278, color page EUR 1,661. Circ: 15,500 (paid and controlled).

919.5 NZL ISSN 1177-1267
ISLAND DESTINATIONS. Text in English. 2005. a. **Document type:** *Magazine, Consumer.*
Published by: Destinations Media, 74 Jervois Rd, Herne Bay, Auckland, New Zealand. TEL 64-9-3603978, FAX 64-9-3604097, mail@destinationsmagazine.com. Pub. Bruce Laybourn.

338.4 BHS
ISLAND SCENE; the islands of the Bahamas. Text in English. biennial. **Document type:** *Magazine, Consumer.*
Related titles: Online - full content ed.
Published by: (Bahamas Ministry of Tourism), The Spectrum Group, Ltd., No6 Musgrove St, PO Box N-7937, Nassau, Bahamas. spectrum@batelnet.bs. Ed., Pub., R&P Aaron H Knowles.

338.4 MLT
ISLAND TRAVEL TRADER. Text in English. 1988. bi-m. adv. **Document type:** *Journal, Trade.* **Description:** Trade related news, features and statistics aimed at travel professionals in Malta, Europe and N. America.
Related titles: Online - full text ed.
Published by: Island Publications Ltd, 26 St. Ursula St., Valletta, VLT 06, Malta. TEL 356-431864, FAX 356-431864. Ed. Terence Mirabelli.

910.91 GBR ISSN 1756-7459
THE ISLANDER. Text in English. 2008. 3/yr. GBP 11.50; GBP 3.95 per issue (effective 2010). back issues avail. **Document type:** *Magazine, Consumer.*
Related titles: Online - full text ed.: ISSN 1756-7467.
Published by: Isles of Scilly Inclusive Holidays, Bryher, Isles of Scilly, TR23 0PR, United Kingdom. TEL 44-1720-422200, FAX 44-1720-423092, relax@islesofscillyholidays.co.uk. Ed. Alasdair Moore.

910.202 USA ISSN 0745-7847
G500
ISLANDS; an international magazine. Text in English. 1981. 8/yr. USD 14.97 domestic; USD 22.97 in Canada; USD 30.97 elsewhere (effective 2011). adv. bk.rev.; video rev. maps; tr.lit.; illus. back issues avail.; reprints avail. **Document type:** *Magazine, Consumer.* **Description:** Focuses on islands worldwide - tropical and temperate, undeveloped and urban, famous and virtually undiscovered.
Related titles: Online - full text ed.: USD 9.97 per issue (effective 2011).
Indexed: G08, I05.
—Ingenta. **CCC.**
Published by: Bonnier Corp. (Subsidiary of: Bonnier Group), 460 N Orlando Ave, Ste 200, Orlando, FL 32789. TEL 407-628-4802, FAX 407-628-7061, http://www.bonniercorp.com. Adv. contact Amanda Harris TEL 407-571-4700. Circ: 202,736 (paid).

051 USA
ISLANDS' SOUNDER; serving all of San Juan County. Text in English. 1964. 52/yr. USD 26 in US & Canada; USD 50 out of county (effective 2000). adv. music rev.; play rev.; Website rev. illus. **Document type:** *Newspaper.*
Formerly: Orcas Island Booster
Address: PO Box 758, Eastsound, WA 98245. TEL 360-376-4500, FAX 360-376-4501. Ed. Ted Grossman. Pub., R&P Jay Brodt TEL 360-378-5696. Adv. contact Elyse Van den Bosch. Circ: 7,200.

910.202 ITA ISSN 1825-3121
ISOLA D'ELBA E ARCIPELAGO TOSCANO GRAND TOUR. Text in Italian. 2005. s-a. **Document type:** *Magazine, Consumer.*
Published by: De Agostini Editore, Via G da Verrazzano 15, Novara, 28100, Italy. TEL 39-0321-4241, FAX 39-0321-424305, info@deagostini.it, http://www.deagostini.it.

ISRAEL. CENTRAL BUREAU OF STATISTICS. SURVEY OF TRAVELLING HABITS/SEQER HERG'LE N'SI'A. HELEQ A. *see* TRAVEL AND TOURISM—Abstracting, Bibliographies, Statistics

ITALIE. *see* LIFESTYLE

910.09 ITA
ITALIEN REISE AKTUELL. Text in Italian. 26/yr. **Document type:** *Magazine, Consumer.*
Published by: Editrice Turistica s.r.l., Via Rasella 155, Rome, 00187, Italy. TEL 39-06-4821539, FAX 39-06-4826721.

914.504 ITA ISSN 0393-3725
DG401
ITALY ITALY. Text in English. 1983. bi-m. adv. **Document type:** *Magazine, Consumer.* **Description:** Guide to Italian people, places, and things.
Published by: Italy Italy Enterprises SpA, Piazza Principe di Piemonte 9, Magliano Romano, RM 00060, Italy. TEL 39-06-60478630.

914.504 ITA ISSN 1972-9979
ITINERARI; guida - annuario dell'accoglienza cattolica in Italia. Text in Italian. 1995. a., latest 2002. EUR 45 (effective 2009). adv. **Document type:** *Directory.*
Related titles: CD-ROM ed.
Published by: (Centro Italiano Turismo Sociale), Editoriale Italiana, Via Vigliena 10, Rome, 00192, Italy. TEL 39-06-3230177, FAX 39-06-3211359, info@editoriale.it, http://www.editoriale.it. Ed. Giordano Treveri Gennari. Circ: 30,000.

910.09 ITA ISSN 1123-6736
ITINERARI E LUOGHI; il mensile tascabile di viaggi e avventura. Text in Italian. 1992. m. adv. **Document type:** *Magazine, Consumer.*
Published by: Fioratti Editore, Via Aldo Manuzio 15, Milan, MI 20124, Italy. TEL 39-02-6570414, FAX 39-02-6555791.

910.91 ITA ISSN 2037-7673
ITINERARI E MONOGRAFIE. Text in Italian. 2006. s-a. **Document type:** *Magazine, Consumer.*
Published by: De Agostini Editore, Via G da Verrazzano 15, Novara, 28100, Italy. TEL 39-0321-4241, FAX 39-0321-424305, info@deagostini.it, http://www.deagostini.it.

910.202 ITA ISSN 1824-8802
GLI ITINERARI ENOGASTRONOMICI DELLE REGIONI. Text in Italian. 2004. s-a. **Document type:** *Magazine, Consumer.*
Published by: Ediservice Srl, Via Principe Nicola 22, Catania, 95126, Italy. TEL 39-095-375297.

914 ESP ISSN 0021-3810
JACETANIA. Text in Spanish. 1966. bi-m. adv. illus. back issues avail. **Document type:** *Magazine, Consumer.*
Published by: Centro de Iniciativa y Turismo, C del Carmen, 40 1o. Izq, Jaca, (Huesca) 22700, Spain. http://www.jaca.com/CIT/.

382 DEU ISSN 0075-2649
JAHRBUCH FUER FREMDENVERKEHR. Text in German. 1950. a. EUR 26.75 (effective 2009). bk.rev. **Document type:** *Journal, Trade.*
Published by: Deutsches Wirtschaftswissenschaftliches Institut fuer Fremdenverkehr, Sonnenstr 27, Munich, 80331, Germany. TEL 49-89-267091, FAX 49-89-267613, info@dwif.de, http://www.dwif.de. Ed. Manfred Zeiner. Circ: 500.

910.91 IDN ISSN 0216-3497
DS620.2
JALAN JALAN. Text in English. 2005. bi-m.
Published by: P T Indo Multi Media, Globe Bldg 2nd Fl, Jl. Buncit Raya Kav. 31-33 Mampang Prapatan, Jakarta Selata, Indonesia. TEL 62-21-79187008, FAX 62-21-79187009, immgroup@indomultimedia.co.id, http://www.indomultimedia.co.id/.

919 JAM
JAMAICA VACATION GUIDE. Text in English. a. adv. **Document type:** *Handbook/Manual/Guide, Consumer.*
Published by: Creative Communications Inc. Ltd., PO Box 105, Kingston, 10, Jamaica. TEL 876-977-5020, FAX 876-977-5448, creativecom@guangotree.com. Ed. Odette Dixon Neath. Pub. Tony Gambrill. Adv. contact Gillian Fisher.

914.3804 POL ISSN 0209-3847
JANTAROWE SZLAKI; kwartalnik turystyczno-krajoznawczy wojewodztw polnocnych. Text in Polish. 1957. q. PLZ 16; USD 6.40 foreign. adv. bk.rev. bibl.; illus.; maps. index. back issues avail. **Description:** Covers travel and tourism in Northern Poland.
Published by: P T T K (Polskie Towarzystwo Turystyczno - Krajoznawcze), Oddzial Gdanski, Ul Dluga 45, Gdansk, 80027, Poland. TEL 48-58-313752. Ed., Adv. contact Jerzy Szukalski. page PLZ 800. Circ: 1,000 (paid).

338.4 913.919 USA
DS889
JAPAN INFO. Text in English. 1966. bi-m. free. bk.rev. illus. **Document type:** *Newsletter.*
Formerly: Japan Report (New York) (0021-4604)
Published by: Consulate General of Japan, New York, Japan Information Center, 299 Park Ave. 18th Fl, New York, NY 10171. TEL 212-371-8222. Ed. Rose L Hayden. Circ: 2,500.

915.2 USA ISSN 1539-7467
G155.U6
JAPAN TRAVEL VIEW; attititudes and trends. Text in English. 2002. a., latest 2002. **Document type:** *Monographic series, Trade.* **Description:** Profiles the Japanese outbound travel market with a focus on travel to the U.S.
Related titles: Online - full text ed.
Published by: Travel Industry Association of America, 1100 New York Ave, NW, Ste 450, Washington, DC 20005. TEL 202-408-8422, FAX 202-408-1255, feedback@tia.org, http://www.tia.org.

910.202 USA ISSN 1545-8970
JAPANESE GUIDE TO HAWAII. Text in Japanese. 1980. bi-m. free. adv. **Document type:** *Magazine, Consumer.* **Description:** Serves as the island's Japanese-language visitor publication.
Published by: Stone Publishing Company, PO Box 8983, Honolulu, HI 96830. TEL 808-531-2637. Ed. Yukie Anthony. Pub. Warren Stone. Adv. contact Isabel Figel. B&W page USD 1,675, color page USD 1,800; trim 10.81 x 7.88. Circ: 45,000 (controlled).

919.304 647.94 NZL
JASONS HOLIDAY PARKS AND CAMPGROUNDS ACCOMMODATION DIRECTORY. Variant title: Holiday Parks and Campgrounds. Jason's - Holiday Parks and Campgrounds: Accommodation Directory New Zealand. Text in English. a. adv. **Document type:** *Directory, Consumer.* **Description:** Comprehensive guide to holiday park, campground accommodation & backpacker lodges throughout New Zealand.
Former titles: Jason's Holiday and Leisure Accommodation; Jason's Budget Accommodation Guide
Published by: Jason's Travel Media Ltd., 2 Ngaire Ave, Newmarket, PO. Box 9390, Auckland, 1149, New Zealand. TEL 64-9-9128400, FAX 64-9-9128401, admin@jasons.com. Ed. Cathy Spencer. Adv. contact Roger Cornish. color page NZD 2,861; trim 114 x 180. Circ: 145,000.

919.304 647.94 NZL
JASONS MOTELS, MOTOR LODGES & APARTMENTS ACCOMMODATION DIRECTORY. Text in English. 196?. a. adv. **Document type:** *Directory, Consumer.* **Description:** Comprehensive accommodation directory, including motels, motor lodges and apartments throughout New Zealand.
Former titles (until 2003): Jasons Motels and Motor Lodges; (until 1986): Jasons Motel Directory; (until 1981): Motels of New Zealand Directory; (until 1969): New Zealand Motel Directory
Published by: Jason's Travel Media Ltd., 2 Ngaire Ave, Newmarket, PO. Box 9390, Auckland, 1149, New Zealand. TEL 64-9-9128400, FAX 64-9-9128401, admin@jasons.com. Ed. Cathy Spencer. Adv. contact Roger Cornish. Circ: 200,000.

919.304 647.95 NZL
JASONS NEW ZEALAND BUSINESS TRAVELLER: ACCOMODATION DIRECTORY. Variant title: Corporate Traveller. Text in English. 1978. a. adv. **Document type:** *Directory, Consumer.* **Description:** Contains a selection of New Zealand accommodation and meeting venues for business & professional travellers.
Former titles (until 2006): Jasons Business & Discerning Traveller New Zealand; (until 2002): Jasons Business & Corporate Traveller New Zealand; (until 2001): Jasons Corporate Traveller; (until 1999): Jasons Conference Directory: Venues, Services, Accommodation; (until 1996): Jasons Executive Travel Book; (until 1994): Jasons Hotels, Resorts, Lodges & Conference Venues; (until 1988): Jasons Hotels, Resorts, Lodges; (until 1987): Jasons Hotels & Holiday Lodges; (until 1984): Jasons Hotels; (until 198?): Hotels
Published by: Jason's Travel Media Ltd., 2 Ngaire Ave, Newmarket, PO. Box 9390, Auckland, 1149, New Zealand. TEL 64-9-9128400, FAX 64-9-9128401, admin@jasons.com. Pub. John Sandford. Adv. contact Robyn McClure. Circ: 135,000.

919.404 647.94 AUS
JASONS QUEENSLAND, NORTHERN TERRITORY & NORTHERN NEW SOUTH WALES ACCOMMODATION GUIDE. Text in English. 1983. a. Free in Australia. adv. Website rev. maps. 400 p./no.; **Document type:** *Directory, Consumer.* **Description:** Guide to resort, hotel, motel, guest house, executive and holiday apartment accommodation throughout Queensland and the Northern Territory with listings for over 2,000 properties.
Formerly (until 2007): Jasons Queensland and Northern Territory Accommodation Guide
Related titles: Online - full content ed.
Published by: Jasons Publishing Pty. Ltd., GPO Box 138, Brisbane, QLD 4001, Australia. TEL 61-7-32213810, FAX 61-7-32219944, admin@jasons.com.au, http://www.jasons.com.au. adv.: color page USD 1,800; trim 114 x 180. Circ: 180,000.

910 USA ISSN 0279-7984
JAX FAX TRAVEL MARKETING MAGAZINE; the official leisure travel booking magazine. Text in English. 1973. m. USD 30 domestic; USD 38 in Canada & Mexico; USD 88 elsewhere (effective 2006). adv. bk.rev. back issues avail. **Document type:** *Magazine, Trade.* **Description:** For travel agents.
Formerly: Jax Fax (0148-9542)
Indexed: RASB.
Published by: Jet Airtransport Exchange, Inc. (JAX), 52 W Main St, Milford, CT 006460. TEL 203-301-0255, FAX 203-301-0250, dcjaxfax@aol.com-email. Eds. Theresa Scanlon, Douglas Cooke. Pubs. Clifton Cooke, Douglas Cooke. Adv. contact Marc Spar. page USD 4,026. Circ: 28,000 (paid and controlled).

915.6 USA
JERUSALEM LIFE; the Jerusalem tourism & Jewish info guide. Text in English. 2000. q. free (effective 2001). adv. **Document type:** *Magazine, Consumer.*
Published by: Matitia Chetrit TEL 02-571-2496, FAX 02-571-2496, jenet@iname.com. adv.: B&W page USD 450, color page USD 799.

JETSTREAM AIR NEWS; Swiss aviation magazine. *see* TRANSPORTATION—Air Transport

910.2 GBR ISSN 0075-3750
G153
JEWISH TRAVEL GUIDE. Text in English. 1950. a. GBP 13.95 per issue (effective 2009). index. back issues avail. **Document type:** *Directory, Trade.* **Description:** Provides Jewish travellers worldwide- whether travelling on business, for pleasure or to seek their historical roots.
Published by: Vallentine Mitchell Publishers, 29/45 High St, Edgware, Middlesex HA8 7UU, United Kingdom. TEL 44-20-89529526, FAX 44-20-89529242, info@vmbooks.com, http://www.vmbooksuk.com/.

910.91 USA ISSN 2157-7706
G155.I78
▼ **THE JEWISH TRAVEL MAGAZINE.** Text in English. 2010. irreg. **Document type:** *Magazine, Trade.* **Description:** Provides information about travel and tourism.
Published by: Jewish Press, Inc., 4915 16th Ave, Brooklyn, NY 11204. TEL 718-330-1100, releases@jewishpress.com.

338.4791 NZL
JIARI/HOLIDAY. Text in Chinese. w. **Document type:** *Newspaper, Consumer.*
Published by: Tim Asian Consultancy Services N Z Ltd., Level 5, Xacta Tower, 94 Dixon St., PO Box 6886, Wellington, New Zealand. TEL 64-4-3856600, FAX 64-4-3856060, nicktacs@tacsnz.com, http://www.tacsnz.com/.

914.8 338 SWE ISSN 2000-270X
JOB & MAGT; Oeresundsregionernes magasin om ekonomi och samhaelle. Text in Danish, Swedish. 2006. q. SEK 240, DKK 196; SEK 80, DKK 65 per issue (effective 2010). adv.
Formerly (until 2009): OE I (1653-7416)
Related titles: Online - full text ed.
Published by: Oeresundsinstituttet, Oestergatan 9 B, Malmoe, 21125, Sweden. TEL 46-40-305630, info@oresundsinstituttet.org, http://www.oresundsinstituttet.org. Ed. Johan Wessman TEL 46-702-523241. Circ: 6,000 (controlled).

910.202 DEU
JOURNAL FUER DIE APOTHEKE; Pharmazie - Beratung - Reise. Text in German. 1994. bi-m. adv. **Document type:** *Magazine, Trade.*
Former titles (until 2005): Reise-Journal fuer die Apotheke; (until 2003): Reise-Journal; (until 1999): Das Reise-Journal fuer Apotheker und Aerzte
Published by: P A C S Gesellschaft fuer Promotion, Advertising & Communication Services mbH, Gewerbestr 9, Staufen, 79219, Germany. TEL 49-7633-982007, FAX 49-7633-982060, pacs@pacs-online.com, http://www.pacs-online.com. Ed. Christian Schmid. Adv. contact Thomas Tritschler. Circ: 21,500 (controlled).

338.48 USA ISSN 1938-8160
➤ **JOURNAL OF CHINA TOURISM RESEARCH/ZHONGGUO LYOU YANJIU.** Text in English, Chinese. 2005. q. GBP 179 combined subscription in United Kingdom to institutions (print & online eds.); EUR 235, USD 242 combined subscription to institutions (print & online eds.) (effective 2012). reprint service avail. from PSC. **Document type:** *Journal, Academic/Scholarly.*
Formerly (until 2008): China Tourism Research (1812-688X)
Related titles: Online - full text ed.: ISSN 1938-8179. 2008. GBP 161 in United Kingdom to institutions; EUR 211, USD 218 to institutions (effective 2012).
Indexed: A01, A03, A22, B01, B07, CA, CABA, E01, E12, GH, H&TI, H06, IBR, IBZ, LT, M02, N02, P32, PGegResA, R12, RRTA, S13, S16, T02, T05, W11.
—BLDSC (4958.035400), IE. **CCC.**
Published by: Routledge (Subsidiary of: Taylor & Francis Group), 325 Chestnut St, Ste 800, Philadelphia, PA 19106. TEL 215-625-8900, 800-354-1420, FAX 215-625-8914, journals@routledge.com, http://www.routledge.com. Ed. Haiyan Song.

338.4791 GBR ISSN 1472-4049
G156.5.E26
➤ **JOURNAL OF ECOTOURISM.** Abbreviated title: J O E. Text in English. 2002. 3/yr. GBP 266 combined subscription in United Kingdom to institutions (print & online eds.); EUR 407, USD 534 combined subscription to institutions (print & online eds.) (effective 2012). adv. back issues avail.; reprint service avail. from PSC. **Document type:** *Journal, Academic/Scholarly.* **Description:** Focuses a type of tourism based principally on natural history - along with other associated features of the man-land nexus.
Related titles: Online - full text ed.: ISSN 1747-7638. GBP 239 in United Kingdom to institutions; EUR 366, USD 480 to institutions (effective 2012).
Indexed: A10, A34, A38, C25, CA, CABA, E12, ESPM, EnvAb, F08, F12, GEOBASE, H&TI, H06, HPNRM, LT, P32, PAIS, PGegResA, R12, RRTA, S13, S16, SCOPUS, SSciA, T02, V03, VS, W10, W11, Z01.
—BLDSC (4973.095780), IE, Infotrieve, Ingenta. **CCC.**
Published by: Routledge (Subsidiary of: Taylor & Francis Group), 4 Park Sq, Milton Park, Abingdon, Oxon OX14 4RN, United Kingdom. TEL 44-20-70176000, FAX 44-20-70176336, subscriptions@tandf.co.uk, http://www.routledge.com. Ed. David Fennell. Adv. contact Linda Hann TEL 44-1344-779945. **Subscr. to:** Taylor & Francis Ltd., Journals Customer Service, Sheepen Pl, Colchester, Essex CO3 3LP, United Kingdom. TEL 44-20-70175544, FAX 44-20-70175198.

338.4 GBR ISSN 1743-873X
G156.5.H47
➤ **JOURNAL OF HERITAGE TOURISM.** Abbreviated title: J H T. Text in English. 2006. q. GBP 234, EUR 353, USD 473 combined subscription to institutions (print & online eds.) (effective 2011). adv. bk.rev. back issues avail.; reprint service avail. from PSC. **Document type:** *Journal, Academic/Scholarly.* **Description:** Focuses on exploring the many facets of one of the most notable and widespread types of tourism.
Related titles: Online - full text ed.: ISSN 1747-6631. 2006. GBP 211, EUR 318, USD 426 to institutions (effective 2011).
Indexed: A35, C25, CA, CABA, E12, ESPM, GH, H&TI, H06, H16, LT, N02, P32, PGegResA, R12, RRTA, S13, S16, SSciA, T02, T05, W11.
—BLDSC (4998.060000), IE. **CCC.**
Published by: Routledge (Subsidiary of: Taylor & Francis Group), 4 Park Sq, Milton Park, Abingdon, Oxon OX14 4RN, United Kingdom. TEL 44-20-70176000, FAX 44-20-70176336, subscriptions@tandf.co.uk, http://www.routledge.com. Ed. Dallen Timothy. Adv. contact Linda Hann TEL 44-1344-779945. **Subscr. to:** Taylor & Francis Ltd., Journals Customer Service, Sheepen Pl, Colchester, Essex CO3 3LP, United Kingdom. TEL 44-20-70175544, FAX 44-20-70175198.

338.4791 AUS ISSN 1447-6770
➤ **JOURNAL OF HOSPITALITY AND TOURISM MANAGEMENT.** Text in English. 1994. s-a. abstr.; stat. Index. 80 p./no.; back issues avail. **Document type:** *Journal, Academic/Scholarly.* **Description:** Provides articles that advance the knowledge base of the hospitality, tourism and related industries.
Formerly (until 2001): Australian Journal of Hospitality Management (1320-5161)
Related titles: ◆ Online - full text ed.: Journal of Hospitality and Tourism Management (Online).
Indexed: A22, A25, A26, ABIX, B02, B15, B17, B18, CA, E01, E08, Emerald, G04, G06, G07, G08, H&TI, H06, I05, P03, PsycInfo, S08, S09, SSciA, T02.
—BLDSC (5003.402870), IE, Ingenta. **CCC.**
Published by: (University of Queensland, School of Tourism), Australian Academic Press Pty. Ltd., 32 Jeays St, Bowen Hills, QLD 4006, Australia. TEL 61-7-32571176, FAX 61-7-32525908, info@australianacademicpress.com.au, http://www.australianacademicpress.com.au.

338.4791 AUS
➤ **JOURNAL OF HOSPITALITY AND TOURISM MANAGEMENT (ONLINE).** Text in English. 1994. irreg. AUD 150 domestic; AUD 165 foreign (effective 2011). back issues avail. **Document type:** *Journal, Academic/Scholarly.* **Description:** Aims to promote the development of tourism and hospitality education and research in Australia and holds a conference each year organised by a host committee drawn from a single university or a consortium of closely located universities.
Media: Online - full text. **Related titles:** ◆ Print ed.: Journal of Hospitality and Tourism Management. ISSN 1447-6770.
Published by: (Council for Australian University Tourism and Hospitality Education), Australian Academic Press Pty. Ltd., 32 Jeays St, Bowen Hills, QLD 4006, Australia. FAX 61-7-32525908, info@australianacademicpress.com.au, http://www.australianacademicpress.com.au. Eds. Dr. Brent W Ritchie, Margaret Deery.

338.4 GBR ISSN 1757-9880
▼ **JOURNAL OF HOSPITALITY AND TOURISM TECHNOLOGY.** Abbreviated title: J H T T. Text in English. 2010. 3/yr. EUR 359 combined subscription in Europe (print & online eds.); USD 509 combined subscription in the Americas (print & online eds.); GBP 329 combined subscription in the UK & elsewhere (print & online eds.); AUD 779 combined subscription in Australasia (print & online eds.) (effective 2012). back issues avail. **Document type:** *Journal, Academic/Scholarly.* **Description:** Features as a scholastic platform in the fields of Hospitality Information Technology and E-Business.
Related titles: Online - full text ed.: ISSN 1757-9899.
Indexed: A12, A17, ABIn, P48, P51, P53, P54, PQC.
—**CCC.**
Published by: Emerald Group Publishing Ltd., Howard House, Wagon Ln, Bingley, W Yorks BD16 1WA, United Kingdom. TEL 44-1274-777700, FAX 44-1274-785201, emerald@emeraldinsight.com. Ed. Dr. Cihan Cobanoglu. Pub. Zoe Sanders.

910 GBR ISSN 1473-8376
TX901
➤ **JOURNAL OF HOSPITALITY, LEISURE, SPORTS & TOURISM EDUCATION.** Abbreviated title: J o H L S T E. Text in English. 2002. s-a. free (effective 2011). abstr. back issues avail. **Document type:** *Journal, Academic/Scholarly.* **Description:** Aims to promote, enhance and disseminate research, good practice and innovation in all aspects of education in the hospitality, leisure, sport and tourism subject areas.
Media: Online - full content.
Indexed: A36, A39, AEI, B29, C27, C29, CA, CABA, CurCont, D03, D04, DRIE, E02, E03, E13, EdA, EdI, GH, H&TI, H06, LT, N02, P10, P18, P48, P53, P54, PQC, R12, R14, RRTA, S14, S15, S18, SCOPUS, SD, SSCI, T02, W03, W05, W07, W11.
—**CCC.**
Published by: (Oxford Brookes University, Business School), Higher Education Academy, Hospitality, Leisure, Sport & Tourism Network, Oxford Brookes University, Wheatley Campus, Oxford, OX33 1HX, United Kingdom. TEL 44-1865-485809, enquiries@heacademy.ac.uk.

➤ **JOURNAL OF HUMAN RESOURCES IN HOSPITALITY & TOURISM.** *see* HOTELS AND RESTAURANTS

338.4 GBR ISSN 1940-7963
G155.A1
▼ ➤ **JOURNAL OF POLICY RESEARCH IN TOURISM, LEISURE AND EVENTS.** Text in English. 2009 (Jan.). 3/yr. GBP 309 combined subscription in United Kingdom to institutions (print & online eds.); EUR 493, USD 617 combined subscription to institutions (print & online eds.) (effective 2012). adv. reprints avail. **Document type:** *Journal, Academic/Scholarly.* **Description:** Provides a critical focus on a variety of policy debates relating to the tourism, leisure and events sectors.
Related titles: Online - full text ed.: ISSN 1940-7971. GBP 278 in United Kingdom to institutions; EUR 444, USD 555 to institutions (effective 2012).
Indexed: CA, CABA, E12, F08, F12, GH, H&TI, H06, LT, R12, T02, T05, W11.
—**CCC.**
Published by: Routledge (Subsidiary of: Taylor & Francis Group), 4 Park Sq, Milton Park, Abingdon, Oxon OX14 4RN, United Kingdom. TEL 44-20-70176000, FAX 44-20-70176336, subscriptions@tandf.co.uk, http://www.routledge.com. Adv. contact Linda Hann TEL 44-1344-779945. **Subscr. to:** Taylor & Francis Ltd., Journals Customer Service, Sheepen Pl, Colchester, Essex CO3 3LP, United Kingdom. TEL 44-20-70175544, FAX 44-20-70175198.

➤ **JOURNAL OF QUALITY ASSURANCE IN HOSPITALITY & TOURISM.** *see* HOTELS AND RESTAURANTS

➤ **JOURNAL OF SPORT AND TOURISM.** *see* LEISURE AND RECREATION

910 613.1 GBR ISSN 0966-9582
G155.A1 CODEN: JSTOFT
➤ **JOURNAL OF SUSTAINABLE TOURISM.** Text in English. 1993. bi-m. GBP 583 combined subscription in United Kingdom to institutions (print & online eds.); EUR 872, USD 1,172 combined subscription to institutions (print & online eds.) (effective 2012). adv. illus. Index. back issues avail.; reprint service avail. from PSC. **Document type:** *Journal, Academic/Scholarly.* **Description:** Provides information and research on helping to reduce tensions between tourism, the environment and host communities.
Related titles: Online - full text ed.: ISSN 1747-7646. GBP 525 in United Kingdom to institutions; EUR 785, USD 1,054 to institutions (effective 2012).
Indexed: A01, A03, A08, A10, A12, A17, A20, A22, A34, ABIn, APEL, B01, B06, B07, B09, C25, CA, CABA, CPM, CurCont, E12, ESPM, EnvAb, EnvInd, F08, F12, GEOBASE, GH, H&TI, H06, H16, HPNRM, I11, IndVet, LT, N02, O01, OR, P26, P32, P34, P48, P51, P53, P54, PAIS, PGegResA, PQC, R12, R13, RRTA, S02, S03, S13, S16, SCOPUS, SOPODA, SSCI, SSciA, SociolAb, T02, V03, VS, W07, W10, W11.
—BLDSC (5067.735000), IE, Infotrieve, Ingenta. **CCC.**
Published by: Routledge (Subsidiary of: Taylor & Francis Group), 4 Park Sq, Milton Park, Abingdon, Oxon OX14 4RN, United Kingdom. TEL 44-20-70176000, FAX 44-20-70176336, subscriptions@tandf.co.uk, http://www.routledge.com. Eds. Bernard Lane, Bill Bramwell. Adv. contact Linda Hann TEL 44-1344-779945. **Subscr. to:** Taylor & Francis Ltd., Journals Customer Service, Sheepen Pl, Colchester, Essex CO3 3LP, United Kingdom. TEL 44-20-70175544, FAX 44-20-70175198.

➤ **JOURNAL OF TEACHING IN TRAVEL & TOURISM**; the professional journal of the international society of travel & tourism educators. *see* EDUCATION—Teaching Methods And Curriculum

338.4 306 GBR ISSN 1476-6825
G155.A1
➤ **JOURNAL OF TOURISM & CULTURAL CHANGE.** Abbreviated title: J T C C. Text in English. 2003. 3/yr. GBP 260 combined subscription in United Kingdom to institutions (print & online eds.); EUR 398, USD 524 combined subscription to institutions (print & online eds.) (effective 2012). adv. back issues avail.; reprint service avail. from PSC. **Document type:** *Journal, Academic/Scholarly.* **Description:** Focuses on critically examining the relationships, tensions, representations, conflicts and possibilities that exist between tourism/travel and culture/cultures in an increasingly complex global context.
Related titles: Online - full text ed.: ISSN 1747-7654. GBP 234 in United Kingdom to institutions; EUR 359, USD 472 to institutions (effective 2012).
Indexed: A10, CA, CABA, E12, ESPM, F08, F12, GH, H&TI, H06, HPNRM, LT, N02, PAIS, R12, RRTA, S02, S03, S13, S16, SSciA, SociolAb, T02, V03, W11.
—BLDSC (5069.704000), IE, Ingenta. **CCC.**
Published by: Routledge (Subsidiary of: Taylor & Francis Group), 4 Park Sq, Milton Park, Abingdon, Oxon OX14 4RN, United Kingdom. TEL 44-20-70176000, FAX 44-20-70176336, subscriptions@tandf.co.uk, http://www.routledge.com. Eds. Alison Phipps TEL 44-141-3305284, Mike Robinson TEL 44-113-2838540. Adv. contact Linda Hann TEL 44-1344-779945. **Subscr. to:** Taylor & Francis Ltd., Journals Customer Service, Sheepen Pl, Colchester, Essex CO3 3LP, United Kingdom. TEL 44-20-70175544, FAX 44-20-70175198.

338.4791 AZE ISSN 2078-113X
▼ **JOURNAL OF TOURISM AND HOSPITALITY.** Text in English. forthcoming 2011. s-a. **Document type:** *Journal, Academic/Scholarly.*
Indexed: H&TI, H06, T02.
Published by: Progress Press Inc., M.Mushfig 4B, Apt.107, Baku, 1006, Azerbaijan. TEL 994-050-6691364, subijar@gmail.com.

910.91 363.7 PRT ISSN 1647-8169
▼ **JOURNAL OF TOURISM AND SUSTAINABILITY.** Text in English. 2010. s-a. **Document type:** *Journal, Academic/Scholarly.* **Description:** Covers environmental and tourism issues in a sustainable perspective, from a local to a global scale.
Published by: Instituto Superior de Linguas e Adminstracao (I S L A), Laboratorio de Ecologia, Turismo e Sustentabilidade (L E T S), Quinta do Bom Nome, Estrada da Correia 53, Lisbon, 1050-218, Portugal. TEL 351-21-0309900, FAX 351-21-0309917.

338.4 ROM ISSN 1844-9743
➤ **JOURNAL OF TOURISM CHALLENGES AND TRENDS.** Text in English. s-a. EUR 50, USD 75; EUR 30, USD 45 per issue (effective 2010). **Document type:** *Journal, Academic/Scholarly.* **Description:** Covers the theories and practices in the tourism industry.
Indexed: H&TI, H06, T02.

Published by: Romanian-American Association of Project Managers for Education and Research (RAAPMER), c/o Mihaela Dinu, Romanian-American University, 1B Expozitiei Blvd., Sector 1, Bucharest, 012101, Romania. Ed. Mihaela Dinu.

➤ **JOURNAL OF TOURISM CONSUMPTION AND PRACTICE.** *see* EDUCATION

338.4 GBR ISSN 1755-182X
▼ **JOURNAL OF TOURISM HISTORY.** Text in English. 2009. s-a. GBP 236 combined subscription in United Kingdom to institutions (print & online eds.); EUR 375, USD 470 combined subscription to institutions (print & online eds.) (effective 2012). **Document type:** *Journal, Academic/Scholarly.* **Description:** Features articles and reviews covering every aspect of the history of tourism.
Related titles: Online - full text ed.: ISSN 1755-1838. GBP 212 in United Kingdom to institutions; EUR 338, USD 423 to institutions (effective 2012).
Indexed: CA, HistAb, T02.
—CCC.
Published by: Routledge (Subsidiary of: Taylor & Francis Group), 4 Park Sq, Milton Park, Abingdon, Oxon OX14 4RN, United Kingdom. TEL 44-20-70176000, FAX 44-20-70176336, info@routledge.co.uk, http://www.routledge.com. Ed. John K Walton. Adv. contact Linda Hann TEL 44-1344-779945.

338 658 USA ISSN 1054-8408
G155.A1 CODEN: JTTMET
➤ **JOURNAL OF TRAVEL & TOURISM MARKETING.** Text in English. 1992. 8/yr. GBP 855 combined subscription in United Kingdom to institutions (print & online eds.); EUR 1,111, USD 1,122 combined subscription to institutions (print & online eds.) (effective 2012). adv. illus. reprint service avail. from PSC. **Document type:** *Journal, Academic/Scholarly.* **Description:** Includes travel services, tourism management organizations, meetings and convention services, and transportation services.
Related titles: Microform ed.: (from PQC); Online - full text ed.: ISSN 1540-7306. GBP 770 in United Kingdom to institutions; EUR 999, USD 1,010 to institutions (effective 2012).
Indexed: A01, A03, A10, A12, A13, A17, A22, A34, ABIn, B01, B06, B07, B09, B16, BPI, BRD, C25, CA, CABA, CLT&T, CurCont, DIP, E01, E12, Emerald, F08, F12, GH, H&TI, H06, HRIS, Hospl, I08, IBR, IBZ, IndVet, LT, M&MA, M02, N02, P02, P10, P32, P37, P48, P51, P53, P54, PGegResA, PQC, R12, RRTA, S13, S16, SCOPUS, SD, SOPODA, SSCI, SociolAb, T02, T05, UAA, V03, VS, W01, W02, W03, W07, W11.
—BLDSC (5070.542000), IE, Ingenta. **CCC.**
Published by: Routledge (Subsidiary of: Taylor & Francis Group), 325 Chestnut St, Ste 800, Philadelphia, PA 19106. TEL 215-625-8900, 800-354-1420, FAX 215-625-8914, journals@routledge.com, http://www.routledge.com. Ed. K S (Kaye) Chon. adv.: B&W page USD 315, color page USD 550; trim 4.375 x 7.125. Circ: 499 (paid).

➤ **JOURNAL OF TRAVEL MEDICINE.** *see* MEDICAL SCIENCES

910.2 USA ISSN 0047-2875
G155.A1
➤ **JOURNAL OF TRAVEL RESEARCH.** Abbreviated title: J T R. Text in English. 1962. q. USD 674, GBP 396 to institutions; USD 688, GBP 404 combined subscription to institutions (print & online eds.) (effective 2012). adv. bk.rev. reprint service avail. from PSC. **Document type:** *Journal, Academic/Scholarly.* **Description:** Reflects the worldwide importance of tourism both economically and socially. Includes new techniques and information, creatice views and general articles in travel research and marketing from both industry practitioners and academics.
Formerly: Travel Research Bulletin (0147-2399)
Related titles: Online - full text ed.: ISSN 1552-6763. USD 619, GBP 364 to institutions (effective 2012).
Indexed: A01, A02, A03, A08, A12, A13, A14, A17, A20, A22, A26, A28, ABIn, ABS&EES, APA, B01, B02, B04, B06, B07, B08, B09, B11, B15, B17, B18, BPI, BRD, BrCerAb, C&ISA, CA, CA/WCA, CABA, CIA, CLT&T, CerAb, CivEngAb, CorrAb, CurCont, E&CAJ, E01, E08, E11, E12, EEA, EMA, ESPM, Emerald, EnvEAb, F08, F12, G04, G06, G07, G08, G09, GEOBASE, GH, H&TI, H04, H06, H15, HRIS, Hospl, I05, LT, M&TEA, M09, MBF, METADEX, N02, P03, P10, P13, P32, P48, P51, P53, P54, PN&I, PQC, PsycInfo, R12, RASB, RRTA, RefZh, RiskAb, S09, S13, S16, SCOPUS, SSCI, SSciA, SolStAb, T02, T04, T05, V02, W01, W02, W03, W05, W07, W11, WAA.
—BLDSC (5070.550000), IE, Infotrieve, Ingenta, Linda Hall. **CCC.**
Published by: (University of Colorado, Business Research Division), Sage Publications, Inc., 2455 Teller Rd, Thousand Oaks, CA 91320. TEL 800-818-7243, FAX 800-583-2665, info@sagepub.com, http://www.sagepub.com. Ed. Richard R Perdue. **Co-sponsor:** Travel and Tourism Research Association.

➤ **JOURNAL OF UNCONVENTIONAL PARKS, TOURISM & RECREATION RESEARCH.** *see* LEISURE AND RECREATION

910 658 GBR ISSN 1356-7667
TX911.3.M3
➤ **JOURNAL OF VACATION MARKETING**; an international journal for the tourism and hospitality industries. Abbreviated title: J V M. Text in English. 1995. q. USD 814, GBP 440 combined subscription to institutions (print & online eds.); USD 798, GBP 431 to institutions (effective 2011). adv. bk.rev. abstr.; bibl.; charts; stat. 96 p./no. 2 cols./p.; back issues avail.; reprint service avail. from PSC. **Document type:** *Journal, Academic/Scholarly.* **Description:** Covers the latest practice and thought in the marketing of vacation services.
Related titles: Online - full text ed.: ISSN 1479-1870. USD 733, GBP 396 to institutions (effective 2011); Special ed(s).: Customer Satisfaction in Tourism and Hospitality; China - Emerging Market: Emerging Issues for Tourism and Hospitality Marketing.
Indexed: A12, A17, A22, ABIn, B01, B06, B07, B09, CA, CPM, E01, H&TI, H06, P48, P51, P53, P54, PQC, SCOPUS, T02.
—BLDSC (5072.203000), IE, Infotrieve, Ingenta. **CCC.**
Published by: Sage Publications Ltd. (Subsidiary of: Sage Publications, Inc.), 1 Oliver's Yard, 55 City Rd, London, EC1Y 1SP, United Kingdom. TEL 44-20-73248500, FAX 44-20-73248600, info@sagepub.co.uk, http://www.uk.sagepub.com/home.nav. Ed. J S Perry Hobson. adv.: B&W page GBP 450; 180 x 250. **Subscr. to:** Sage Publications, Inc., 2455 Teller Rd, Thousand Oaks, CA 91320. TEL 805-499-9774, FAX 805-499-0871, journals@sagepub.com.

910.202 USA
JOURNEYS (WEST HARTFORD). Text in English. 1923. bi-m. free to members (effective 2005). adv. **Document type:** *Magazine, Consumer.*
Formerly: The Hartford Automobiler (1077-5234)
Media: Large Type. **Related titles:** Online - full text ed.
Published by: Automobile Club of Hartford, 815 Farmington Ave, West Hartford, CT 06119. TEL 860-570-4315, FAX 860-570-4715, http://www.aaahartford.com. Ed. Debra C Smith. Pub. Hal Doran. adv.: B&W page USD 200. Circ: 248,000 (paid and free).

910.202 CAN
JOURNEYWOMAN (ONLINE); the magazine for women who love to travel. Text in English. q. free. **Document type:** *Newsletter.* **Description:** Offers tips for women on how to travel safe, go-alone travel destinations and cheap holiday ideas.
Formerly: Journeywoman (Print) (1198-337X)
Media: Online - full text.
Indexed: C03, CBCARef, PQC.
Published by: Journeywoman, 50 Prince Arthur Ave, Ste 1703, Toronto, ON M5R 1B5, Canada. TEL 416-929-7654, FAX 416-929-1433.

913.04 USA ISSN 1526-5781
JULUKA. Text in English. 1991. bi-m. looseleaf. USD 33 domestic; USD 34 in Canada; USD 45 elsewhere (effective 2007). adv. bk.rev.; music rev.; play rev. charts; illus. back issues avail.; reprints avail. **Document type:** *Newsletter, Consumer.* **Description:** Produced in the United States for those interested in South Africa.
Published by: Mindsgate Media Inc., PO Box 4675, Palos Verdes Peninsula, CA 90274. TEL 301-652-5754, FAX 301-652-5756. Pub. Ruan Wannenburg.

338.4 340.5 FRA ISSN 2108-0968
JURISTOURISME; le mensuel des acteurs du tourisme et des loisirs. Text in French. 1998. m. EUR 164 (effective 2011). adv. back issues avail. **Document type:** *Magazine, Trade.* **Description:** Presents case law and public regulations concerning tourism.
Formerly (until 2010): Tourisme et Droit (1290-0559)
Published by: Editions Juris Associations, 75 bis Rue de Seze, Lyon, 69006, France. TEL 33-4-72981840, FAX 33-4-78289383, infojuris@dalloz.fr, http://www.editionsjuris.com.

K A C B AUTO REVUE/ROYAL AUTO. *see* TRANSPORTATION—Automobiles

914.8913 DNK ISSN 1901-5038
K B H; arkitektur, kultur, byliv, design, aktiviteter. (Koebenhavn) Variant title: Magasinet K B H. Text in Danish. 2005. m. DKK 440 (effective 2009). adv. back issues avail. **Document type:** *Magazine, Consumer.* **Description:** Descriptions and discussions of modern Copenhagen.
Related titles: Online - full text ed.: ISSN 1901-5046.
Published by: K B H Aps, Kronprinsessegade 24, Copemhagen K, 1306, Denmark. TEL 45-33-328895, info@kbhmagasin.dk. Ed. Anders Ojgaard. adv.: page DKK 24,900. Circ: 32,000 (controlled).

K C MAGAZINE. (Kansas City) *see* GENERAL INTEREST PERIODICALS—United States

338.4791 387.74 NLD ISSN 1872-3209
K L M AGENT. (Koninklijke Luchtvaart Maatschappij) Cover title: Agent. Text in Dutch. 200?. bi-m. free to qualified personnel (effective 2009). **Document type:** *Magazine, Trade.*
Published by: (K L M NV), Hemels BV, PO Box 369, Hilversum, 1200 AJ, Netherlands. TEL 31-35-6899900, FAX 31-35-6899999, info@hemels.com, http://www.hemels.com.

DIE KAKTUSBLUETE. *see* CHILDREN AND YOUTH—About

910.2 POL ISSN 0239-9032
KALEIDOSCOPE (WARSAW). Text in Polish, English. m. **Document type:** *Magazine, Consumer.*
Published by: G + J Polska Sp. z o.o. & Co. (Subsidiary of: Gruner + Jahr AG & Co), ul Marynarska 15, Warsaw, 02674, Poland. TEL 48-22-3603800, FAX 48-22-3603810, bok@guj.pl. Ed. Martyna Wojciechowska.

915 POL ISSN 1392-1193
KALININGRAD IN YOUR POCKET. Text in English. 1995. a. USD 5 newsstand/cover (effective 2002). adv. **Document type:** *Magazine, Consumer.*
Published by: Gdansk In Your Pocket, ul. Heweliusza 11-818, Gdansk, 80890, Poland. TEL 48-58-3218161, FAX 48-58-3218161, gdansk@inyourpocket.com, http://www.inyourpocket.com.

910 NLD ISSN 0165-4128
KAMPEER EN CARAVANKAMPIOEN. Variant title: K C K. Text in Dutch. 1941. m. EUR 68.95 to non-members; EUR 58.95 to members (effective 2008). adv. illus. **Document type:** *Consumer.*
Indexed: KES.
Published by: (ANWB BV/Royal Dutch Touring Club), Algemene Nederlandse Wielrijders Bond (A N W B) Media/Dutch Automobile Association Media, Postbus 93200, The Hague, 2509 BA, Netherlands. TEL 31-70-3141470, FAX 31-70-3146538, http://www.anwbmedia.nl. adv.: B&W page EUR 4,071, color page EUR 5,986; bleed 215 x 200. Circ: 124,866 (paid).

910.2 NLD ISSN 0022-8265
DJ1
KAMPIOEN; A N W B club magazine. Text in Dutch. 1885. m. free membership (effective 2008). adv. bk.rev.; Website rev. charts; illus. index. **Document type:** *Magazine, Consumer.*
Indexed: KES.
—IE, Infotrieve.
Published by: (ANWB BV/Royal Dutch Touring Club), Algemene Nederlandse Wielrijders Bond (A N W B) Media/Dutch Automobile Association Media, Postbus 93200, The Hague, 2509 BA, Netherlands. TEL 31-70-3141470, FAX 31-70-3146538, http://www.anwbmedia.nl. adv.: B&W page EUR 42,160, color page EUR 49,855; bleed 223 x 270. Circ: 3,495,150.

KANAWA; Canada's paddling magazine. *see* SPORTS AND GAMES—Boats And Boating

338.4791 JPN ISSN 0385-5554
KANKO BUNKA/TOURISM & CULTURE. Text in Japanese. 1976. bi-m. **Document type:** *Magazine, Trade.*
Published by: Nihon Kotsu Kosha/Japan Tourist Bureau Foundation, 1-8-2 Marunouchi Chiyoda-ku, Tokyo, 100-0005, Japan. TEL 81-3-52084701, FAX 81-3-52084706, zaidan@jtb.or.jp, http://www.jtb.or.jp/.

917.81 910.2 USA ISSN 1932-7331
F681.6
KANSAS CURIOSITIES; quirky characters, roadside oddities & other offbeat stuff. Text in English. 2002. quinquennial, latest 2006, 2nd ed. USD 13.95 per issue (effective 2008). back issues avail. **Document type:** *Guide, Consumer.* **Description:** Provides information about the wildest, wackiest, most outrageous people, places and things.
Published by: The Globe Pequot Press, Inc., 246 Goose Ln, PO Box 480, Guilford, CT 06437. TEL 203-458-4500, 888-249-7586, FAX 203-458-4603, 800-820-2329, info@globepequot.com, http://www.globepequot.com. Ed. Gillian Belnap.

910.2 USA ISSN 1557-3702
TX907.5.I82
KAREN BROWN'S TUSCANY & UMBRIA. Text in English. 2005. a., latest 2007. USD 10 per issue (effective 2007). **Document type:** *Guide, Consumer.*
Published by: Karen Brown's Guides, PO Box 70, San Mateo, CA 94401. TEL 650-342-9117, FAX 650-342-9153, http://www.karenbrown.com.

917.9 USA ISSN 1539-9915
TX907.3.N96
KAREN BROWN'S U.S.A.: PACIFIC NORTHWEST; charming inns & itineraries. Text in English. 2002 (Sept.). a. USD 19.95 newsstand/cover (effective 2002).
Published by: Karen Brown's Guides, PO Box 70, San Mateo, CA 94401. TEL 650-342-9117, FAX 650-342-9153, http://www.karenbrown.com.

960 KEN
KARIBU. Text in English. 1977. m. adv. illus.
Published by: Oryx Publications Ltd., PO Box 40106, Nairobi, Kenya. Circ: 5,000.

338.4791 POL ISSN 1232-3535
KARKONOSZE; kultura i turystyka. Text in Polish. 1986. bi-m. 40 p./no.; **Document type:** *Magazine, Consumer.*
Published by: Regionalne Centrum Kultury, ul Grabowskiego 7, Jelenia Gora, 58500, Poland. TEL 48-75-7523542, FAX 48-75-7526969. Ed. Jacek Jasko. Circ: 750.

910.902 IND
KARNATAKA. DEPARTMENT OF TOURISM. ANNUAL REPORT. Text in English. 1975. a. **Document type:** *Report, Government.*
Published by: Department of Information and Tourism, #49, 2nd Fl, Khanija Bhavan, Race Course Rd, Bangalore, 560 001, India. TEL 91-80-22352828, FAX 91-80-22352626, info@karnatakatourism.org, http://www.karnatakatourism.org.

910.91 USA
KAUAI VISITOR. Text in English. m. **Document type:** *Magazine, Consumer.*
Related titles: Online - full content ed.
Published by: Visitor Magazines LLC, 1498 Lower Main St, Ste F, Wailuku, HI 96793. http://www.visitormagazines.com/.

914.38 LTU ISSN 1392-0065
KAUNAS IN YOUR POCKET. Text in English. 1993. a. USD 5 newsstand/cover (effective 2002). adv. **Document type:** *Magazine, Consumer.*
Published by: Vilnius In Your Pocket, Vokieciu Gatve 10-15, Vilnius, 2001, Lithuania. TEL 370-2-222976, FAX 370-2-222982, vilnius@inyourpocket.com, http://www.inyourpocket.com.

914.304 DEU ISSN 0945-1498
TX910.G4
KAUPERTS DEUTSCHLAND REISEFUEHRER. Text in German. 1950. a. EUR 14.90 (effective 2008). adv. **Document type:** *Directory, Consumer.*
Formerly (until 1985): Kauperts Deutschland Staedte-, Hotel-, und Reisefuehrer (0449-9646)
Published by: Adressbuch-Gesellschaft Berlin mbH, Schlossstr 127, Olching, 82140, Germany. TEL 49-8142-30734, FAX 49-8142-40391. Ed. Edeltraud Spitzing-Pistorius. Circ: 8,500.

917.69 910.2 USA ISSN 1932-7358
KENTUCKY CURIOSITIES; quirky characters, roadside oddities & other offbeat stuff. Text in English. 2003. biennial, latest 2006, 2nd ed. USD 13.95 per issue (effective 2008). back issues avail. **Document type:** *Guide, Consumer.* **Description:** Provides information about the wildest, wackiest, most outrageous people, places and things.
Published by: The Globe Pequot Press, Inc., 246 Goose Ln, PO Box 480, Guilford, CT 06437. TEL 203-458-4500, 888-249-7586, FAX 203-458-4603, 800-820-2329, info@globepequot.com, http://www.globepequot.com. Ed. Gillian Belnap.

KENTUCKY EXPLORER; featuring things about Kentucky and its history and genealogy. *see* HISTORY—History Of North And South America

917.6 USA ISSN 0453-5812
KENTUCKY TRAVEL GUIDE. Text in English. 1967. a. adv. maps. 144 p./no. 2 cols./p.; **Document type:** *Magazine, Consumer.* **Description:** Contains a guide to Kentucky attractions, special events, lodging, restaurants, shopping, campgrounds, marinas, golf courses and other facilities.
Formerly (until 1969): Welcome to Kentucky
Related titles: Online - full content ed.
Published by: Editorial Services Company, 812 S Third St, Louisville, KY 40203. TEL 502-584-2720, FAX 502-584-2722.

916.04 KEN
KENYA TOURIST DEVELOPMENT CORPORATION. REPORT AND ACCOUNTS. Text in English. a. free. **Document type:** *Corporate.*
Published by: Kenya Tourist Development Corporation, PO Box 42013, Nairobi, Kenya. TEL 254-2-330820, FAX 254-2-227815, TELEX 23009.

917.904 USA
KEY MAGAZINE. CARMEL & MONTEREY PENINSULA. Text in English. 1969. m. USD 15. adv.
Published by: Tri-County Publications, PO Box 223859, Carmel, CA 93922-3859. Circ: 37,000.

917 USA ISSN 0040-6279
KEY MAGAZINE. THIS WEEK IN CHICAGO. Text in English. 1920. w. USD 65 (effective 2005). adv. **Document type:** *Newspaper, Consumer.*
Formerly: This Week in Chicago
Published by: This Week in Chicago, Inc., 226 E Ontario St, Ste 300, Chicago, IL 60611. TEL 312-943-0838, FAX 312-664-6113. Ed. Brad Klepac. Pub. Walter L West Jr. Adv. contact Nancy L Vargas. Circ: 20,000.

917 USA
KEY MAGAZINE. THIS WEEK IN LOS ANGELES AND SOUTHERN CALIFORNIA; the leading weekly magazine of Southern entertainment & dining. Text in English. 1920. w. USD 104 (effective 2000). adv. bk.rev. charts; illus.
Formerly: Key (Los Angeles); Incorporates: Information Los Angeles (0020-0131)
Published by: Falcon Publications, 8432 Steller Dr, Culver City, CA 90232. TEL 310-559-3700. Ed., Pub. George Falcon. adv.: B&W page USD 892; trim 7.5 x 4.81. Circ: 19,500.

338.4 GBR
KEY NOTE MARKET ASSESSMENT. ACTIVITY HOLIDAYS. Text in English. 2001. irreg., latest 2009. GBP 899 per issue (effective 2010). back issues avail. **Document type:** *Report, Trade.* **Description:** Provides strategic analysis and including primary research, these premium reports examine the scope, dynamics and shape of key UK and European markets, with a particular focus on financial services, consumer and lifestyle sectors.
Formerly (until 2003): Key Note Market Report: Activity Holidays
Published by: Key Note Ltd. (Subsidiary of: Bonnier Business Information), Harlequin House, 5th Fl, 7 High St, Teddington, Richmond upon Thames, TW11 8EE, United Kingdom. TEL 44-845-5040452, FAX 44-845-5040453, sales@keynote.co.uk.

KEY NOTE MARKET ASSESSMENT. EUROPEAN SHORT BREAKS. *see* BUSINESS AND ECONOMICS—Production Of Goods And Services

338.4 GBR ISSN 1475-6242
KEY NOTE MARKET ASSESSMENT. HOLIDAY PURCHASING PATTERNS. Variant title: Holiday Purchasing Patterns Market Assessment. Text in English. 1997. irreg., latest 2009, Jun. GBP 899 per issue (effective 2010). **Document type:** *Report, Trade.* **Description:** Provides an in-depth strategic analysis across a broad range of industries and contains an examination on the scope, dynamics and shape of key UK markets in the consumer, financial, lifestyle and business to business sectors.
Formerly (until 2001): M A P S Strategic Market Report. Holiday Purchasing Patterns in the U K (1461-2275)
Published by: Key Note Ltd. (Subsidiary of: Bonnier Business Information), Harlequin House, 5th Fl, 7 High St, Teddington, Richmond upon Thames, TW11 8EE, United Kingdom. TEL 44-845-5040452, FAX 44-845-5040453, info@keynote.co.uk.

KEY NOTE MARKET ASSESSMENT. SHORT BREAKS. *see* BUSINESS AND ECONOMICS—Production Of Goods And Services

910.202 330 GBR ISSN 1474-2403
KEY NOTE MARKET ASSESSMENT. THE BUSINESS TRAVEL MARKET. Variant title: The Business Travel Market Market Assessment. Text in English. 19??. irreg., latest 2008, Oct. GBP 899 per issue (effective 2010). **Document type:** *Report, Trade.* **Description:** Provides an in-depth strategic analysis across a broad range of industries and contains an examination on the scope, dynamics and shape of key UK markets in the consumer, financial, lifestyle and business to business sectors.
Former titles (until 2000): Key Note Market Report: Business Travel (1364-7954); (until 1996): Key Note Report: Business Travel (0268-4896)
Related titles: CD-ROM ed.; Online - full text ed.
Published by: Key Note Ltd. (Subsidiary of: Bonnier Business Information), Harlequin House, 5th Fl, 7 High St, Teddington, Richmond upon Thames, TW11 8EE, United Kingdom. TEL 44-845-5040452, FAX 44-845-5040453, info@keynote.co.uk.

KEY NOTE MARKET ASSESSMENT. THE CRUISE MARKET. *see* BUSINESS AND ECONOMICS—Production Of Goods And Services

910.202 GBR ISSN 1368-1532
KEY NOTE MARKET REPORT: SHORT BREAK HOLIDAYS. Variant title: Short Break Holidays Market Report. Text in English. 1995. irreg., latest 2001, Sep. GBP 310 per issue (effective 2010). **Document type:** *Report, Trade.* **Description:** Provides an overview of a specific UK market segment and includes executive summary, market definition, market size, industry background, competitor analysis, current issues, forecasts, company profiles, and more.
Published by: Key Note Ltd. (Subsidiary of: Bonnier Business Information), Harlequin House, 5th Fl, 7 High St, Teddington, Richmond upon Thames, TW11 8EE, United Kingdom. TEL 44-845-5040452, FAX 44-845-5040453, info@keynote.co.uk.

338.47910941 GBR ISSN 1367-4145
KEY NOTE MARKET REPORT: TOURIST ATTRACTIONS. Variant title: Tourist Attractions Market Report. Text in English. 199?. irreg., latest 2001, Feb. GBP 310 per issue (effective 2010). **Document type:** *Report, Trade.* **Description:** Provides an overview of a specific UK market segment and includes executive summary, market definition, market size, industry background, competitor analysis, current issues, forecasts, company profiles, and more.
Formerly (until 1997): Key Note Report: Tourist Attractions (1354-232X)
Related titles: CD-ROM ed.; Online - full text ed.
Published by: Key Note Ltd. (Subsidiary of: Bonnier Business Information), Harlequin House, 5th Fl, 7 High St, Teddington, Richmond upon Thames, TW11 8EE, United Kingdom. TEL 44-845-5040452, FAX 44-845-5040453, info@keynote.co.uk.

910.202 GBR
KEY NOTE MARKET REPORT: TRAVEL AGENTS & OVERSEAS TOUR OPERATORS. Variant title: Travel Agents & Overseas Tour Operators Market Report. Text in English. 19??. irreg., latest 2009, Nov. GBP 460 per issue (effective 2010). **Document type:** *Report, Trade.* **Description:** Provides an overview of a specific UK market segment and includes executive summary, market definition, market size, industry background, competitor analysis, current issues, forecasts, company profiles, and more.
Formerly (until 1995): Key Note Report: Travel Agents and Overseas Tour Operators (0268-9278)
Related titles: CD-ROM ed.; Online - full text ed.
Published by: Key Note Ltd. (Subsidiary of: Bonnier Business Information), Harlequin House, 5th Fl, 7 High St, Teddington, Richmond upon Thames, TW11 8EE, United Kingdom. TEL 44-845-5040452, FAX 44-845-5040453, info@keynote.co.uk.

338.479141 GBR ISSN 1469-5200
KEY NOTE MARKET REPORT: WINTER HOLIDAYS. Variant title: Winter Holidays Market Report. Text in English. 1999. irreg., latest 1999, Sep. GBP 235 per issue (effective 2008). **Document type:** *Report, Trade.* **Description:** Provides an overview of a specific UK market segment and includes executive summary, market definition, market size, industry background, competitor analysis, current issues, forecasts, company profiles, and more.
Published by: Key Note Ltd. (Subsidiary of: Bonnier Business Information), Field House, 72 Oldfield Rd, Hampton, Mddx TW12 2HQ, United Kingdom. TEL 44-20-84818750, FAX 44-20-87830049, info@keynote.co.uk, http://www.keynote.co.uk. Ed. Simon Howitt.

KEY NOTE MARKET REVIEW: PASSENGER TRAVEL IN THE U K. *see* BUSINESS AND ECONOMICS—Production Of Goods And Services

919 CYM
KEY TO CAYMAN. Text in English. 1978. s-a. free. adv.
Formerly (until Dec. 1989): Tourist Weekly
Published by: Cayman Free Press Ltd., P O Box 1365, Grand Cayman, Cayman Isl. TEL 345-949-5111, FAX 345-949-7033. Ed. Colleen Webb. Pub., R&P Brian Uzzell. Adv. contact Valerie Simon. Circ: 130,000.

910.09 CAN ISSN 0710-9628
KEY TO KINGSTON. Text in English. 1980. 8/yr. CAD 20, USD 8. adv. charts; illus. back issues avail.
Published by: Kingston Publications, P O Box 1352, Kingston, ON K7L 5C6, Canada. Ed. Mary Laflamme. Adv. contact Ruth Kirkby. Circ: 16,000.

910.91 USA ISSN 1933-0960
DG804
KEY TO ROME. Text in English. 2000. irreg., latest 2006. USD 22.50 per issue (effective 2008).
Published by: J Paul Getty Museum, 1200 Getty Center Dr, Los Angeles, CA 90049-1679. TEL 310-440-7300, info@getty.edu. Ed. Frederick Vreeland.

KIDS FRIENDLY NEW ZEALAND. *see* CHILDREN AND YOUTH—About

910.91 USA
KIDS' GUIDE. Text in English. 1994. s-a. USD 8 (effective 2005). adv. back issues avail. **Document type:** *Directory, Consumer.* **Description:** Guide to children and family activities, services, and businesses in North Central New Jersey.
Address: PO Box 892, Murray Hill, NJ 07974-0892. TEL 908-665-0607, FAX 908-665-2052. Ed., Pub. Jean Flood Unger. Adv. contact David S Unger. page USD 685; trim 9 x 5.5. Circ: 70,000.

908 LTU ISSN 1392-0073
KLAIPEDA IN YOUR POCKET. Text in English. 1993. a. USD 5 newsstand/cover (effective 2002). adv. **Document type:** *Magazine, Consumer.*
Formerly (until 1994): Klaipeda Heute (1392-0618)
Published by: Vilnius In Your Pocket, Vokieciu Gatve 10-15, Vilnius, 2001, Lithuania. TEL 370-2-222976, FAX 370-2-222982, vilnius@inyourpocket.com, http://www.inyourpocket.com.

KOELNER KONGRESS REPORT. *see* MEETINGS AND CONGRESSES

908 DEU
KOELNERLEBEN; Das Stadtmagazin. Text in German. 1959. bi-m. EUR 12; free newsstand/cover (effective 2011). adv. **Document type:** *Magazine, Consumer.*
Formerly (until 2001): Der Feierabend
Published by: (Cologne. Stadt Koeln, Presse und Informationsamt), Maenken Kommunikation GmbH, Von-der-Wettern-Str 25, Cologne, 51149, Germany. TEL 49-2203-35840, FAX 49-2203-3584185, info@maenken.com, http://www.maenken.com. Ed. Lydia Schneider-Benjamin. Adv. contact Thomas Muellenborn. Circ: 32,000 (controlled).

910.202 DEU
KOELNTOURISMUS. MONATSVORSCHAU. Text in German; Summaries in English, French. 1958. m. adv. **Document type:** *Journal, Consumer.*
Published by: KoelnTourismus/Cologne Tourist Board, Unter Fettenhennen 19, Cologne, 50667, Germany. TEL 49-221-22130400, FAX 49-221-22130410, info@koelntourismus.de, http://www.koeln.de/tourismus/koelntourismus/. Ed. Erhard Schlieter. Adv. contact Gabriele Pilath. Circ: 10,000.

791 NLD ISSN 1383-8997
KOMEET. Text in Dutch. 1923. bi-w.
Former titles (until 1976): N K B (0027-6766); (until 1968): Komeet
Indexed: KES.
Published by: Nederlandse Kermisbond, Oudegracht 186, Alkmaar, 1811 CP, Netherlands. TEL 31-72-5123583, FAX 31-72-5121252, nkbalkmaar@hetnet.nl, http://www.denederlandsekermisbond.nl.

910.202 DEU
KOMM MAL MIT. Text in German. 2008. irreg., latest vol.3, 2010. price varies. **Document type:** *Monographic series, Academic/Scholarly.*
Published by: Centaurus Verlag & Media KG, Kaiser-Joseph-Str 267, Freiburg, 79098, Germany. TEL 49-761-1525861, FAX 49-761-1525868, info@centaurus-verlag.de, http://www.centaurus-verlag.de.

KONCIZE. *see* MEETINGS AND CONGRESSES

910.4 PRK
KOREA. Text in English. 1956. m. USD 84. illus. **Description:** Pictorial featuring developments of all walks of life in Democratic People's Republic of Korea.
Related titles: Chinese ed.; French ed.; Spanish ed.; Russian ed.; Korean ed.
Address: Pyongyang, Korea, N. **Dist. by:** Korean Publications Exchange Association, Export Section, P.O. Box 222, Pyongyang, Korea, S. FAX 850-2-3814632.

914.3804 POL ISSN 1508-2334
KRAKOW IN YOUR POCKET. Text in English. 1999. 5/yr. USD 25; USD 5 newsstand/cover (effective 2002). adv. **Document type:** *Magazine, Consumer.*
Address: ul. Felicjanek 16-2, Krakow, 31-104, Poland. TEL 48-12-2926102, FAX 48-12-2926102.

914 DEU
KREFELD LIFE. Text in German. 1994. a. EUR 1.50 newsstand/cover (effective 2010). adv. **Document type:** *Directory, Trade.*
Published by: Stuenings Medien GmbH, Diessemer Bruch 167, Krefeld, 47805, Germany. TEL 49-2151-51000, FAX 49-2151-5100101, medien@stuenings.de, http://www.stuenings.de. Adv. contact Renate Rys. Circ: 35,000 (controlled).

910.202 BEL ISSN 0778-7871
KREO. Text in Dutch. 1965. m. adv. bk.rev.; software rev.; Website rev. 3 cols./p.; back issues avail. **Document type:** *Magazine, Consumer.* **Description:** Publishes practical articles on tourism in Belgium and other countries, covering nature, folklore and cultural topics.
Formerly (until 1992): Info Vakantiegenoegens
Published by: Vakantiegenoegens v.z.w., Postbus 20, Brussels, 1031, Belgium. TEL 32-2-2463640, info@vakantiegenoegens.be, http://www.vakantiegenoegens.be. Ed., R&P Ludo Van Lint TEL 02-246-3642. Pub. Michel Vandendriessche. Adv. contact Karel Meuleman TEL 01-551-5257. Circ: 48,357 (paid).

914 CHE
KREUZFAHRTEN-HANDBUCH. Text in German. a. CHF 40 (effective 2007). **Document type:** *Consumer.*
Published by: Primus Verlag AG, Hammerstr 81, Postfach 1331, Zuerich, 8032, Switzerland. TEL 41-44-3875757, FAX 41-44-3875707, info@travelinside.ch, http://www.primusverlag.ch.

KURORTNAYA GAZETA/RESORT NEWSPAPER. *see* LEISURE AND RECREATION

L S A NEWSLETTER. *see* LEISURE AND RECREATION

L V M 2 GO. (Las Vegas Magazine) *see* LEISURE AND RECREATION

917.89 USA
LAKE POWELL MAGAZINE. Text in English. 1997. 3/yr. USD 21.95 (effective 2005). back issues avail. **Document type:** *Magazine, Consumer.* **Description:** Covers vacationing and recreation in the Lake Powell region.
Published by: Adventure Publications, Inc., PO Box 3645, Flagstaff, AZ 86003. TEL 928-526-3666, FAX 928-526-6668, custservice@adventurepublications.net, http://www.adventurepublications.net/.

LAKE SUPERIOR MAGAZINE. *see* HISTORY—History Of North And South America

LAMY DROIT DU TOURISME. *see* LAW

913 NLD ISSN 1875-3752
LANDGOED. Text in Dutch. 2007. s-a.
Published by: Twents Bureau voor Toerisme, Postbus 1400, Enschede, 7500 BK, Netherlands. TEL 31-53-4876751, FAX 31-53-4876502, info@twentejezelf.nl, http://www.twentejezelf.nl.

910.4 LAO
LAOS. Text in English. q. illus.
Related titles: Laotian ed.
Address: 80 rue Sethathirath, BP 310, Vientiane, Laos. TEL 2405. Eds. O Phrakhamsay, V Phomchanheuang.

910.202 GBR ISSN 1363-7452
LAOS HANDBOOK. Text in English. 1994. triennial. GBP 13.99 per issue (effective 2010). adv. **Document type:** *Handbook/Manual/Guide, Consumer.* **Description:** Covers all the basics from where to stay and where to eat to cycling, walking and how to get around the Loas.
Supersedes in part (in 1997): Vietnam, Laos and Cambodia Handbook (1352-7878)
—CCC.
Published by: Footprint Handbooks Ltd., 6 Riverside Ct, Lower Bristol Rd, Bath, Avon BA2 3DZ, United Kingdom. TEL 44-1225-469141, FAX 44-1225-469461, wwwinfo@footprintbooks.com.

910.91 USA ISSN 1932-3468
LAS VEGAS (NEW YORK). Variant title: Eyewitness Travel Guide: Las Vegas (New York). Text in English. 2005. irreg. USD 23 per issue (effective 2008). **Document type:** *Guide, Consumer.*
Published by: D K Publishing (Subsidiary of: Penguin Books U S A, Inc.), 375 Hudson St, New York, NY 10014. TEL 212-213-4800, FAX 201-256-0000, specialsales@dk.com, http://us.dk.com.

917.904 793 USA ISSN 1064-167X
LAS VEGAS ADVISOR. Text in English. 1983. m. USD 50 domestic to members (effective 2005). bk.rev. back issues avail. **Document type:** *Newsletter, Consumer.* **Description:** For value conscious Las Vegas enthusiasts. Includes reviews, recommendations and warnings for visitors. Covers dining, gambling, entertainment and accommodations.
Published by: Huntington Press, 3687 S Procyon Ave, Las Vegas, NV 89103-1907. TEL 702-252-0655, FAX 702-252-0675, books@huntingtonpress.com. Ed. Wendy Tucker. Circ: 11,000 (paid and free).

LAS VEGAS CONVENTION AND MEETING PLANNERS GUIDE. *see* MEETINGS AND CONGRESSES

910.202 790.1 USA ISSN 0271-0145
LAS VEGAS INSIDER. Text in English. 1973. m. USD 45 (effective 2006). adv. cum.index: 1973-1988. back issues avail. **Document type:** *Newsletter, Consumer.* **Description:** Contains the latest gaming, tournament and travel information. Includes tourist tips, freebies, and discounts.
Published by: Lucky Publishing Co., PO Box 29274, Las Vegas, NV 89126. TEL 520-636-1649. Ed., Pub. Donald Currier. Circ: 5,100 (paid and controlled).

913.973
LAS VEGAS OFFICIAL TRAVEL PLANNERS GUIDE. Text in English. s-a. adv. **Document type:** *Guide, Trade.* **Description:** Comprehensive, four-color reference guide designed specifically for travel agents and qualified industry professionals, tour operators, wholesalers, packagers, etc.
Published by: Weaver Publications, Inc., 2420 Alcott St, Denver, CO 80211. TEL 303-458-1211, FAX 303-477-0724, info@weaver-group.com, http://www.weaver-group.com. Circ: 50,000.

913.793 USA
LAS VEGAS OFFICIAL VISITORS GUIDE. Text in English. 19??. s-a. free. adv. **Document type:** *Guide, Consumer.* **Description:** Highlights transportation and accommodation options, entices the reader with beautiful photography and interesting editorial tidbits about fine dining, shopping and activities in Las Vegas and the surrounding territory.
Published by: Weaver Publications, Inc., 2420 Alcott St, Denver, CO 80211. TEL 303-458-1211, FAX 303-477-0724, info@weaver-group.com, http://pub.weaver-group.com. Circ: 200,000.

TU

910.2 306.4 USA
LAS VEGAS STYLE. Text in English. m. USD 27 domestic; USD 43 in Canada; USD 99 elsewhere (effective 2001). **Document type:** *Magazine, Consumer.* **Description:** Covers entertainment, food and lodging and other tourism related topics in Las Vegas.
Address: 3201 W Sahara, Ste B, Las Vegas, NV 89102. TEL 702-871-6040, 800-897-1691, FAX 702-871-8202, lvstyle@netnevada.net, http://www.lasvegasstyle.com.

910.202 CAN
LAST MINUTE TRAVEL REPORT. Text in English. 1991. 5/yr. CAD 55. adv. bk.rev. **Document type:** *Report, Consumer.* **Description:** Travel destinations and activities aimed primarily at travelers on a budget.
Formerly: Travelsavelife
Address: 1300 Don Mills Rd, Don Mills, ON M3B 2W6, Canada. TEL 416-449-9440, FAX 416-441-9754. Ed. William Maki. Circ: 100,000.

918.04 ECU ISSN 1390-0161
LATIN AMERICAN TRAVEL ADVISOR. Text in English. 1994. q. USD 39 (effective 2000). charts; maps. **Document type:** *Newsletter.* **Description:** News bulletin for business, vacation and long term travellers to South and Central America. Updated information on 17 countries featuring: public safety, health, weather, travel costs, the economy and politics.
Related titles: Fax ed.; Online - full text ed.
Published by: Latin American Travel Consultants, Apdo 17 17 908, Quito, Pichincha, Ecuador. FAX 593-2-562-566, latc@pi.pro.ec, http://www.amerispan.com/latc/. Ed. Daisy Kunstaetter.

LATINAMERIKA. *see* HISTORY—History Of North And South America

918 USA
LATINWORLD. Text in English. 1996. m. free.
Media: Online - full content.
Address: http://www.latinworld.com/magazine. Ed. Jorge Giraldez-Bernard.

917.104 CAN
THE LAURENTIANS. Text in English. 1975. a. free. adv. **Document type:** *Handbook/Manual/Guide, Consumer.*
Former titles (until 199?): Laurentides (0829-8033); (until 1985): Image des Laurentides (0704-6383); (until 1977): Laurentian Image (0704-6375); (until 1977): Hospitalite Laurentides (0318-9643)
Related titles: French ed.
Published by: Association Touristique des Laurentides, Mirabel, PQ J7J 2C8, Canada. TEL 514-990-5625, FAX 450-436-5309. Ed. Andre Goyer. R&P Manon Lefebvre. Circ: 150,000.

LAZIO IERI E OGGI; rivista mensile di cultura, arte, turismo. *see* ART

910.202 ITA ISSN 1824-4025
IL LAZIO PAESE PER PAESE. Text in Italian. 2004. w. **Document type:** *Magazine, Consumer.*
Published by: Editrice Bonechi, Via dei Cairoli, 18BB, Florence, FI 50131, Italy. TEL 39-055-576841, FAX 39-055-5000766, bonechi@bonechi.it, http://www.bonechi.it.

LEISURE/LOISIR. *see* LEISURE AND RECREATION

790.1 338.4791 USA ISSN 1944-236X
LEISURE & TRAVEL BUSINESS. Text in English. 2008. w. USD 2,295 in US & Canada; USD 2,495 elsewhere; USD 2,525 combined subscription in US & Canada (print & online eds.); USD 2,755 combined subscription elsewhere (print & online eds.) (effective 2011). adv. back issues avail. **Document type:** *Newsletter, Trade.* **Description:** Examines the fiscal well being of the travel and leisure industry, reporting on management changes, mergers and acquisitions, financials, as well as leisure and travel trends affecting markets.
Related titles: E-mail ed.; Online - full text ed.: ISSN 1944-2378. USD 2,295 combined subscription (online & e-mail eds.) (effective 2011).
Indexed: A15, ABIn, B02, B15, B17, B18, G04, I05, P48, P51, PQC.
Published by: NewsRx, 2727 Paces Ferry Rd SE, Ste 2-440, Atlanta, GA 30339. TEL 770-435-8286, 800-726-4550, FAX 770-435-6800, pressrelease@newsrx.com, http://www.newsrx.com. Pub., Adv. contact Susan Hasty TEL 770-507-7777.

790.1 338.4791 USA ISSN 1944-2386
LEISURE & TRAVEL WEEK. Text in English. 2008. w. USD 2,295 in US & Canada; USD 2,495 elsewhere; USD 2,525 combined subscription in US & Canada (print & online eds.); USD 2,755 combined subscription elsewhere (print & online eds.) (effective 2011). adv. back issues avail. **Document type:** *Newsletter, Trade.* **Description:** Covers important news affecting vacation destinations, cruise lines, airlines, travel agencies and resorts, as well as the features and services travelers can expect to enjoy.
Related titles: E-mail ed.; Online - full text ed.: ISSN 1944-2394. USD 2,295 combined subscription (online & e-mail eds.) (effective 2011).
Indexed: A12, A15, ABIn, I05, P48, P51, P53, P54, PQC.
Published by: NewsRx, 2727 Paces Ferry Rd SE, Ste 2-440, Atlanta, GA 30339. TEL 770-435-8286, 800-726-4550, FAX 770-435-6800, pressrelease@newsrx.com, http://www.newsrx.com. Pub., Adv. contact Susan Hasty TEL 770-507-7777.

910.09 305.26 USA ISSN 1531-1406
LEISURE GROUP TRAVEL; providing direction, ideas & resources in tourism. Text in English. 1991. bi-m. USD 12 to industry suppliers; free to qualified personnel (effective 2006). adv. **Document type:** *Magazine, Trade.* **Description:** Includes feature articles and relevant information about destinations, attractions, entertainment, tours and other travel services of interest to the senior-group travel market.
Former titles (until 2000): Senior Group Travel (1099-2375); (until 1997): Senior Group Traveler (1081-907X); (until 1994): Mature Group Traveler (1062-2772)
Published by: Premier Tourism Marketing, Inc., 621 Plainfield Rd, Ste 406, Willowbrook, IL 60527. TEL 630-794-0696, FAX 630-794-0652, info@premiertourismmarketing.com, http://www.premiertourismmarketing.com. Circ: 10,130 (controlled).

LEISURE STUDIES ASSOCIATION. PUBLICATIONS. *see* LEISURE AND RECREATION

LEISURE TIME, YOUR TIME. *see* LEISURE AND RECREATION

LENTO. *see* TRAVEL AND TOURISM—Airline Inflight And Hotel Inroom

910.202 USA ISSN 1549-926X
F902.3
LET'S GO: ALASKA (YEAR). Text in English. a. USD 18.99 (effective 2006). **Document type:** *Magazine, Consumer.*
Supersedes in part (in 2004): Let's Go: Alaska & the Pacific Northwest (Year) (1530-1699); Which was formerly (until 1998): Let's Go: The Budget Guide to Alaska and the Pacific Northwest; (until 1994): Let's Go: The Budget Guide to Pacific Northwest, Western Canada, and Alaska (0898-6215); Which superseded in part (in 1988): Let's Go: The Budget Guide to California & the Pacific Northwest (0749-3320)
Published by: Let's Go Publications, Inc., c/o Relevant Guidebook, 67 Mt Auburn St, Cambridge, MA 02138. TEL 617-495-9659, FAX 617-496-7070, publicity@letsgo.com, http://letsgo.com. Ed. Douglas Rand. **Dist. by:** St. Martin's Press, LLC, 175 Fifth Ave, New York, NY 10010. TEL 212-353-3798, 800-488-5233.

914.923 USA ISSN 1542-5150
DJ411.A53
LET'S GO: AMSTERDAM. Variant title: Let's Go Amsterdam. Text in English. 2002. a. USD 16.99 newsstand/cover (effective 2008). adv. **Document type:** *Magazine, Consumer.*
Published by: Let's Go Publications, Inc., c/o Relevant Guidebook, 67 Mt Auburn St, Cambridge, MA 02138. TEL 617-495-9659, FAX 617-496-7070, publicity@letsgo.com, http://letsgo.com. Ed. Nathaniel Rakich. **Dist. by:** St. Martin's Press, LLC, 175 Fifth Ave, New York, NY 10010. TEL 212-353-3798, 800-488-5233.

910.202 USA ISSN 1098-8114
DU95
LET'S GO: AUSTRALIA (YEAR). Text in English. 1998. a. USD 22.99 (effective 2007). adv. **Document type:** *Magazine, Consumer.*
Published by: Let's Go Publications, Inc., c/o Relevant Guidebook, 67 Mt Auburn St, Cambridge, MA 02138. TEL 617-495-9659, FAX 617-496-7070, publicity@letsgo.com, http://letsgo.com. Ed. Sonja B Starr. **Dist. by:** St. Martin's Press, LLC, 175 Fifth Ave, New York, NY 10010. TEL 212-353-3798, 800-488-5233.

910.202 USA
DB16
LET'S GO: AUSTRIA & SWITZERLAND (YEAR). Text in English. 1992. a. USD 19.99 (effective 2006). **Document type:** *Magazine, Consumer.*
Former titles (until 1997): Let's Go. Budget Guide to Switzerland & Austria; (until 1996): Let's Go: The Budget Guide to Switzerland & Austria (1082-4138); Which superseded in part (in 1995): Let's Go: The Budget Guide to Austria (1078-4373); Which superseded in part (in 1993): Let's Go: The Budget Guide to Germany, Austria & Switzerland (1064-0967)
Published by: Let's Go Publications, Inc., c/o Relevant Guidebook, 67 Mt Auburn St, Cambridge, MA 02138. TEL 617-495-9659, FAX 617-496-7070, publicity@letsgo.com, http://letsgo.com. Ed. Christina Svendsen. **Dist. by:** St. Martin's Press, LLC, 175 Fifth Ave, New York, NY 10010. TEL 212-353-3798, 800-488-5233.

914.672 USA ISSN 1550-0047
DP402.B24
LET'S GO: BARCELONA. Text in English. 2002. a. USD 16.99 newsstand/cover (effective 2006). **Document type:** *Magazine, Consumer.*
Published by: Let's Go Publications, Inc., c/o Relevant Guidebook, 67 Mt Auburn St, Cambridge, MA 02138. TEL 617-495-9659, FAX 617-496-7070, publicity@letsgo.com, http://letsgo.com. **Dist. by:** St. Martin's Press, LLC, 175 Fifth Ave, New York, NY 10010. TEL 212-353-3798, 800-488-5233.

917.13 USA ISSN 1536-3414
F73.18
LET'S GO: BOSTON. Text in English. 2001. a. USD 16.99 newsstand/cover (effective 2006). **Document type:** *Magazine, Consumer.*
Published by: Let's Go Publications, Inc., c/o Relevant Guidebook, 67 Mt Auburn St, Cambridge, MA 02138. TEL 617-495-9659, FAX 617-496-7070, publicity@letsgo.com, http://letsgo.com. **Dist. by:** St. Martin's Press, LLC, 175 Fifth Ave, New York, NY 10010. TEL 212-353-3798, 800-488-5233.

918.113 USA ISSN 1549-5930
F2509.5
LET'S GO: BRAZIL. Text in English. 2004. a. USD 19.99 newsstand/cover (effective 2006). **Document type:** *Magazine, Consumer.*
Published by: Let's Go Publications, Inc., c/o Relevant Guidebook, 67 Mt Auburn St, Cambridge, MA 02138. TEL 617-495-9659, FAX 617-496-7070, publicity@letsgo.com, http://letsgo.com. **Dist. by:** St. Martin's Press, LLC, 175 Fifth Ave, New York, NY 10010. TEL 212-353-3798, 800-488-5233.

910.202 USA
DA650
LET'S GO: BRITAIN. Text in English. 1998. a. USD 22.99 (effective 2008). adv. **Document type:** *Magazine, Consumer.*
Supersedes in part (in 200?): Let's Go: Britain & Ireland (Year) (1521-7868)
Published by: Let's Go Publications, Inc., c/o Relevant Guidebook, 67 Mt Auburn St, Cambridge, MA 02138. TEL 617-495-9659, FAX 617-496-7070, publicity@letsgo.com, http://letsgo.com. Eds. Olivia Choe, Patrick Mckiernan. **Dist. by:** St. Martin's Press, LLC, 175 Fifth Ave, New York, NY 10010. TEL 212-353-3798, 800-488-5233.

910.202 USA ISSN 1546-6876
F859.3
LET'S GO: CALIFORNIA (YEAR). Text in English. 1984. a. USD 19.99 (effective 2006). **Document type:** *Magazine, Consumer.*
Former titles (until 1998): Let's Go: The Budget Guide to California (1082-412X); (until 1994): Let's Go - The Budget Guide to California and Hawaii Including Reno, Las Vegas, Grand Canyon, and Baja California (0898-8366); Which superseded in part (in 1988): Let's Go - The Budget Guide to California and the Pacific Northwest (0749-3320)
Published by: Let's Go Publications, Inc., c/o Relevant Guidebook, 67 Mt Auburn St, Cambridge, MA 02138. TEL 617-495-9659, FAX 617-496-7070, publicity@letsgo.com, http://letsgo.com. Ed. Leeore Schnairshon. **Dist. by:** St. Martin's Press, LLC, 175 Fifth Ave, New York, NY 10010. TEL 212-353-3798, 800-488-5233.

910.202 USA ISSN 1546-4032
F1429
LET'S GO: CENTRAL AMERICA (YEAR). Text in English. 1996. a. USD 19.99 (effective 2006). **Document type:** *Magazine, Consumer.*
Formerly (until 1998): Let's Go: The Budget Guide to Central America
Published by: Let's Go Publications, Inc., c/o Relevant Guidebook, 67 Mt Auburn St, Cambridge, MA 02138. TEL 617-496-9659, FAX 617-496-7070, publicity@letsgo.com, http://letsgo.com. Ed. Adam Branch. **Dist. by:** St. Martin's Press, LLC, 175 Fifth Ave, New York, NY 10010. TEL 212-353-3798, 800-488-5233.

917.13 USA ISSN 1543-4982
F3059.5
LET'S GO: CHILE (YEAR). Text in English. 2003. a. USD 19.99 newsstand/cover (effective 2006). **Document type:** *Magazine, Consumer.*
Published by: Let's Go Publications, Inc., c/o Relevant Guidebook, 67 Mt Auburn St, Cambridge, MA 02138. TEL 617-495-9659, FAX 617-496-7070, publicity@letsgo.com, http://letsgo.com. **Dist. by:** St. Martin's Press, LLC, 175 Fifth Ave, New York, NY 10010. TEL 212-353-3798, 800-488-5233.

915.13 USA ISSN 1530-5333
DS705
LET'S GO: CHINA. Text in English. 2000. a. USD 25.99 newsstand/cover (effective 2006). **Document type:** *Magazine, Consumer.*
Published by: Let's Go Publications, Inc., c/o Relevant Guidebook, 67 Mt Auburn St, Cambridge, MA 02138. TEL 617-495-9659, FAX 617-496-7070, publicity@letsgo.com, http://letsgo.com. **Dist. by:** St. Martin's Press, LLC, 175 Fifth Ave, New York, NY 10010. TEL 212-353-3798, 800-488-5233.

918.13 USA ISSN 1543-4974
F1543.5
LET'S GO: COSTA RICA. Text in English. 2003. a. USD 18.99 (effective 2007). adv. **Document type:** *Magazine, Consumer.*
Published by: Let's Go Publications, Inc., c/o Relevant Guidebook, 67 Mt Auburn St, Cambridge, MA 02138. TEL 617-495-9659, FAX 617-496-7070, publicity@letsgo.com, http://letsgo.com. Ed. Patrick Mckiernan. **Dist. by:** St. Martin's Press, LLC, 175 Fifth Ave, New York, NY 10010. TEL 212-353-3798, 800-488-5233.

917.28 USA ISSN 2154-8943
F1543.5
▼ **LET'S GO: COSTA RICA, NICARAGUA & PANAMA.** Text in English. 2010. irreg. USD 17.95 per issue (effective 2010). **Document type:** *Guide, Consumer.* **Description:** Student travel guide for Costa Rica, Nicaragua and Panama.
Published by: Let's Go Publications, Inc., c/o Relevant Guidebook, 67 Mt Auburn St, Cambridge, MA 02138. TEL 617-495-9659, FAX 617-496-7070, feedback@letsgo.com, http://www.letsgo.com.

910.202 USA ISSN 1530-826X
DJK8
LET'S GO: EASTERN EUROPE (YEAR). Variant title: Let's Go Eastern Europe. Text in English. a. USD 23.99 (effective 2008). adv. **Document type:** *Magazine, Consumer.*
Formerly (until 1998): Let's Go: The Budget Guide to Eastern Europe
Published by: Let's Go Publications, Inc., c/o Relevant Guidebook, 67 Mt Auburn St, Cambridge, MA 02138. TEL 617-495-9659, FAX 617-496-7070, publicity@letsgo.com, http://letsgo.com. Ed. Benjamin Paloff. **Dist. by:** St. Martin's Press, LLC, 175 Fifth Ave, New York, NY 10010. TEL 212-353-3798, 800-488-5233.

910.202 USA ISSN 1558-7479
F3709.5
LET'S GO: ECUADOR, INCLUDING THE GALAPOGOS ISLANDS (YEAR). Text in English. 1997. a. USD 17.99 (effective 2006). **Document type:** *Magazine, Consumer.*
Supersedes in part (in 2002): Let's Go: Peru, Ecuador & Bolivia (1540-7462); Which was formerly (until 2001): Let's Go: Peru, Bolivia & Ecuador (1534-8520); (until 2001): Let's Go: Peru & Ecuador (1530-5619); (until 2000): Let's Go: Budget Guide Ecuador & the Galapogos Islands (Year) (1097-3680)
Published by: Let's Go Publications, Inc., c/o Relevant Guidebook, 67 Mt Auburn St, Cambridge, MA 02138. TEL 617-495-9659, FAX 617-496-7070, publicity@letsgo.com, http://letsgo.com. Ed. Esti M Itturalde. **Dist. by:** St. Martin's Press, LLC, 175 Fifth Ave, New York, NY 10010. TEL 212-353-3798, 800-488-5233.

916.13 USA ISSN 1541-7549
DT45
LET'S GO: EGYPT. Text in English. 2001. a. USD 18.99 newsstand/cover (effective 2006). **Document type:** *Magazine, Consumer.*
Published by: Let's Go Publications, Inc., c/o Relevant Guidebook, 67 Mt Auburn St, Cambridge, MA 02138. TEL 617-495-9659, FAX 617-496-7070, publicity@letsgo.com, http://letsgo.com. **Dist. by:** St. Martin's Press, LLC, 175 Fifth Ave, New York, NY 10010. TEL 212-353-3798, 800-488-5233.

910.2 914 USA ISSN 1530-8251
D909
LET'S GO: EUROPE (YEAR). Text in English. 1960. a. USD 16.99 (effective 2008). adv. **Document type:** *Magazine, Consumer.*
Former titles (until 1998): Let's Go: The Budget Guide to Europe (Year) (0163-4585); (until 1975): Let's Go: The Student Guide to Europe (0075-8868)
Published by: Let's Go Publications, Inc., c/o Relevant Guidebook, 67 Mt Auburn St, Cambridge, MA 02138. TEL 617-495-9659, FAX 617-496-7070, publicity@letsgo.com, http://letsgo.com. Ed. Alex Zakaras. Circ: 60,000. **Dist. by:** St. Martin's Press, LLC, 175 Fifth Ave, New York, NY 10010. TEL 212-353-3798, 800-488-5233.

914.4 USA ISSN 1098-9366
DC16
LET'S GO: FRANCE (YEAR). Text in English. 1998. a. USD 22.99 (effective 2008). adv. **Document type:** *Magazine, Consumer.*
Formerly (until 1997): Let's Go. Budget Guide to France
Published by: Let's Go Publications, Inc., c/o Relevant Guidebook, 67 Mt Auburn St, Cambridge, MA 02138. TEL 617-495-9659, FAX 617-496-7070, publicity@letsgo.com, http://www.letsgo.com. Eds. Bruce F McKinnon, Colleen Obrien. **Dist. by:** St. Martin's Press, LLC, 175 Fifth Ave, New York, NY 10010. TEL 212-353-3798, 800-488-5233.

914.304 USA ISSN 1530-8405
DD16
LET'S GO: GERMANY (YEAR). Text in English. 1992. a. USD 22.99 (effective 2007). adv. **Document type:** *Magazine, Consumer.*
Formerly (until 1998): Let's Go: The Budget Guide to Germany (1082-4146); Which superseded in part (in 1994): Let's Go - The Budget Guide to Germany and Switzerland (1082-4391); (in 1993): Let's Go - The Budget Guide to Germany, Austria and Switzerland (1064-0967)

Published by: Let's Go Publications, Inc., c/o Relevant Guidebook, 67 Mt Auburn St, Cambridge, MA 02138. TEL 617-495-9659, FAX 617-496-7070, publicity@letsgo.com, http://letsgo.com. Ed. Douglas Muller. **Dist. by:** St. Martin's Press, LLC, 175 Fifth Ave, New York, NY 10010. TEL 212-353-3798, 800-488-5233.

914.9504 USA ISSN 1524-086X
DF716
LET'S GO: GREECE (YEAR). Text in English. 1982. a. USD 21.99 (effective 2008). adv. **Document type:** *Magazine, Consumer.*
Supersedes in part (in 1999): Let's Go: Greece and Turkey (1524-0843); Which was formerly (until 1998): Let's Go: The Budget Guide to Greece and Turkey (Year) (1064-1009); (until 1992): Let's Go: The Budget Guide to Greece (0749-0569); Which superseded in part (in 1984): Let's Go: The Budget Guide to Greece, Israel and Egypt (0276-6779); Which was formerly (until 1983): Let's Go: The Budget Guide to Israel and Egypt (0882-9535)
Published by: Let's Go Publications, Inc., c/o Relevant Guidebook, 67 Mt Auburn St, Cambridge, MA 02138. TEL 617-495-9659, FAX 617-496-7070, publicity@letsgo.com, http://letsgo.com. **Dist. by:** St. Martin's Press, LLC, 175 Fifth Ave, New York, NY 10010. TEL 212-353-3798, 800-488-5233.

917.28 USA ISSN 2156-0412
F1443.5
▼ **LET'S GO: GUATEMALA & BELIZE.** Text in English. 2010. irreg. USD 18.95 per issue (effective 2010). **Document type:** *Handbook/Manual/Guide, Consumer.* **Description:** Student travel guide for Guatemala and Belize.
Published by: Let's Go Publications, Inc., c/o Relevant Guidebook, 67 Mt Auburn St, Cambridge, MA 02138. TEL 617-495-9659, FAX 617-496-7070, feedback@letsgo.com, http://www.letsgo.com.

917.13 USA ISSN 1543-4966
DU622
LET'S GO: HAWAII. Text in English. 2003. a. USD 19.99 (effective 2007). adv. **Document type:** *Magazine, Consumer.*
Published by: Let's Go Publications, Inc., c/o Relevant Guidebook, 67 Mt Auburn St, Cambridge, MA 02138. TEL 617-495-9659, FAX 617-496-7070, publicity@letsgo.com, http://letsgo.com. **Dist. by:** St. Martin's Press, LLC, 175 Fifth Ave, New York, NY 10010. TEL 212-353-3798, 800-488-5233.

910.202 USA ISSN 1546-6868
DS406
LET'S GO: INDIA & NEPAL (YEAR). Text in English. 1997. a. USD 22.99 (effective 2006). **Document type:** *Magazine, Consumer.*
Formerly (until 1998): Let's Go: The Budget Guide to India & Nepal (1092-2547)
Published by: Let's Go Publications, Inc., c/o Relevant Guidebook, 67 Mt Auburn St, Cambridge, MA 02138. TEL 617-495-9659, FAX 617-496-7070, publicity@letsgo.com, http://letsgo.com. Ed. Nate Barksdale. **Dist. by:** St. Martin's Press, LLC, 175 Fifth Ave, New York, NY 10010. TEL 212-353-3798, 800-488-5233.

914.1504 USA ISSN 1530-8235
DA980
LET'S GO: IRELAND (YEAR). Text in English. 1994. a. USD 19.99 (effective 2008). adv. **Document type:** *Magazine, Consumer.*
Formerly (until 1998): Let's Go: The Budget Guide to Ireland (Year) (1079-8323)
Published by: Let's Go Publications, Inc., c/o Relevant Guidebook, 67 Mt Auburn St, Cambridge, MA 02138. TEL 617-495-9659, FAX 617-496-7070, publicity@letsgo.com, http://letsgo.com. Ed. Jenny Weiss. **Dist. by:** St. Martin's Press, LLC, 175 Fifth Ave, New York, NY 10010. TEL 212-353-3798, 800-488-5233.

910.202 USA ISSN 2154-4026
LET'S GO: ISRAEL. Text in English. 1982. a. USD 21.95 (effective 2010). **Document type:** *Magazine, Consumer.*
Supersedes in part (in 2001): Let's Go: Israel & Egypt (Year) (1525-7347); Which was formerly (until 199?): Let's Go: The Budget Guide to Israel & Egypt (0882-9535); Which superseded in part (in 1993): Let's Go: Budget Guide to Greece, Israel and Egypt (Including Jordan) (1082-4308); Which was formerly (until 1984): Let's Go: The Budget Guide to Greece, Israel and Egypt (0276-6779)
Published by: Let's Go Publications, Inc., c/o Relevant Guidebook, 67 Mt Auburn St, Cambridge, MA 02138. TEL 617-495-9659, FAX 617-496-7070, publicity@letsgo.com, http://letsgo.com. Ed. Sharmila Sohoni. **Dist. by:** St. Martin's Press, LLC, 175 Fifth Ave, New York, NY 10010. TEL 212-353-3798, 800-488-5233.

917.04 USA ISSN 1540-7470
DG416
LET'S GO: ITALY (YEAR). Text in English. 1981. a. USD 22.99 (effective 2008). adv. **Document type:** *Magazine, Consumer.*
Former titles (until 1998): Let's Go: The Budget Guide to Italy (1082-4162); (until 1989): Let's Go: The Budget Guide to Italy (Including Tunisia) (1043-4690); (until 1988): Let's Go: Budget Guide to Italy (0192-2920)
Published by: Let's Go Publications, Inc., c/o Relevant Guidebook, 67 Mt Auburn St, Cambridge, MA 02138. TEL 617-495-9659, FAX 617-496-7070, publicity@letsgo.com, http://letsgo.com. Ed. Jeremy Metz. **Dist. by:** St. Martin's Press, LLC, 175 Fifth Ave, New York, NY 10010. TEL 212-353-3798, 800-488-5233.

915.222 USA ISSN 1549-9154
DS805.2
LET'S GO: JAPAN. Text in English. 2004. a. USD 22.99 newsstand/cover (effective 2006). **Document type:** *Magazine, Consumer.*
Published by: Let's Go Publications, Inc., c/o Relevant Guidebook, 67 Mt Auburn St, Cambridge, MA 02138. TEL 617-495-9659, FAX 617-496-7070, publicity@letsgo.com, http://letsgo.com. **Dist. by:** St. Martin's Press, LLC, 175 Fifth Ave, New York, NY 10010. TEL 212-353-3798, 800-488-5233.

914.2104 USA ISSN 1535-4903
DA679
LET'S GO: LONDON (YEAR). Text in English. 1991. a. USD 16.99 (effective 2008). adv. **Document type:** *Magazine, Consumer.*
Formerly (until 1998): Let's Go: The Budget Guide to London (Year) (1057-6274)
Published by: Let's Go Publications, Inc., c/o Relevant Guidebook, 67 Mt Auburn St, Cambridge, MA 02138. TEL 617-495-9659, FAX 617-496-7070, publicity@letsgo.com, http://letsgo.com. Ed. Shanya J Dingle. **Dist. by:** St. Martin's Press, LLC, 175 Fifth Ave, New York, NY 10010. TEL 212-353-3798, 800-488-5233.

917.2 USA ISSN 1530-1702
F1209
LET'S GO: MEXICO (YEAR). Text in English. 1985. a. USD 22.99 (effective 2008). adv. **Document type:** *Magazine, Consumer.*
Formerly (until 1998): Let's Go: The Budget Guide to Mexico (Year) (0884-6529)
Published by: Let's Go Publications, Inc., c/o Relevant Guidebook, 67 Mt Auburn St, Cambridge, MA 02138. TEL 617-495-9659, FAX 617-496-7070, publicity@letsgo.com, http://letsgo.com. Ed. Sonesh Chainani. **Dist. by:** St. Martin's Press, LLC, 175 Fifth Ave, New York, NY 10010. TEL 212-353-3798, 800-488-5233.

915 USA ISSN 1531-6289
LET'S GO: MIDDLE EAST. Text in English. 2000. a. USD 22.99 newsstand/cover (effective 2006). **Document type:** *Magazine, Consumer.*
Published by: Let's Go Publications, Inc., c/o Relevant Guidebook, 67 Mt Auburn St, Cambridge, MA 02138. TEL 617-495-9659, FAX 617-496-7070, publicity@letsgo.com, http://letsgo.com. **Dist. by:** St. Martin's Press, LLC, 175 Fifth Ave, New York, NY 10010. TEL 212-353-3798, 800-488-5233.

917.47 USA ISSN 1533-7553
F128.18
LET'S GO: NEW YORK CITY (YEAR). Text in English. 1991. a. USD 16.99 (effective 2007). adv. **Document type:** *Magazine, Consumer.*
Formerly (until 1998): Let's Go: The Budget Guide to New York City (Year) (1059-0412)
Published by: Let's Go Publications, Inc., c/o Relevant Guidebook, 67 Mt Auburn St, Cambridge, MA 02138. TEL 617-495-9659, FAX 617-496-7070, publicity@letsgo.com, http://letsgo.com. Ed. Rachel Abi Farbiarz. **Dist. by:** St. Martin's Press, LLC, 175 Fifth Ave, New York, NY 10010. TEL 212-353-3798, 800-488-5233.

910.202 USA ISSN 1930-7497
DU405.5
LET'S GO: NEW ZEALAND. Text in English. 1998. a. USD 21.99 (effective 2008). adv. **Document type:** *Magazine, Consumer.*
Former titles (until 2006): Let's Go: New Zealand, Including Fiji (Year) (1546-4075); (until 2002): Let's Go: New Zealand (Year)
Published by: Let's Go Publications, Inc., c/o Relevant Guidebook, 67 Mt Auburn St, Cambridge, MA 02138. TEL 617-495-9659, FAX 617-496-7070, publicity@letsgo.com, http://letsgo.com. Ed. Jennifer L Burns. **Dist. by:** St. Martin's Press, LLC, 175 Fifth Ave, New York, NY 10010. TEL 212-353-3798, 800-488-5233.

910.202 USA ISSN 1549-5949
F852.3
LET'S GO: PACIFIC NORTHWEST (YEAR). Text in English. a. USD 18.99 (effective 2006). **Document type:** *Magazine, Consumer.*
Supersedes in part (in 2004): Let's Go: Alaska & Pacific Northwest (1530-1699); Which was formerly (until 1998): Let's Go: Budget Guide to Alaska & the Pacific Northwest
Published by: Let's Go Publications, Inc., c/o Relevant Guidebook, 67 Mt Auburn St, Cambridge, MA 02138. TEL 617-495-9659, FAX 617-496-7070, publicity@letsgo.com, http://letsgo.com.

910.202 USA ISSN 1530-8413
DC16
LET'S GO: PARIS (YEAR). Text in English. 1993. a. USD 16.99 (effective 2007). adv. **Document type:** *Magazine, Consumer.*
Formerly (until 1998): Let's Go: The Budget Guide to Paris
Published by: Let's Go Publications, Inc., c/o Relevant Guidebook, 67 Mt Auburn St, Cambridge, MA 02138. TEL 617-495-9659, FAX 617-496-7070, publicity@letsgo.com, http://letsgo.com. Ed. Brian Martin. **Dist. by:** St. Martin's Press, LLC, 175 Fifth Ave, New York, NY 10010. TEL 212-353-3798, 800-488-5233.

918.13 USA ISSN 1930-7500
F3409.5
LET'S GO: PERU. Text in English. a. USD 18.99 newsstand/cover (effective 2006). **Document type:** *Magazine, Consumer.*
Supersedes in part (in 2005): Let's Go: Peru, Ecuador & Bolivia (1540-7462); Which was formerly (until 2002): Let's Go: Peru, Bolivia & Ecuador (1534-8520); (until 2001): Let's Go: Peru & Ecuador (1530-5619); (until 2000): Let's Go: Ecuador & the Galapagos Islands
Published by: Let's Go Publications, Inc., c/o Relevant Guidebook, 67 Mt Auburn St, Cambridge, MA 02138. TEL 617-495-9659, FAX 617-496-7070, publicity@letsgo.com, http://letsgo.com. **Dist. by:** St. Martin's Press, LLC, 175 Fifth Ave, New York, NY 10010. TEL 212-353-3798, 800-488-5233.

917.13 USA ISSN 1549-8476
F1959
LET'S GO: PUERTO RICO. Text in English. 2004. a. USD 15.99 newsstand/cover (effective 2008). adv. **Document type:** *Magazine, Consumer.*
Published by: Let's Go Publications, Inc., c/o Relevant Guidebook, 67 Mt Auburn St, Cambridge, MA 02138. TEL 617-495-9659, FAX 617-496-7070, publicity@letsgo.com, http://letsgo.com. **Dist. by:** St. Martin's Press, LLC, 175 Fifth Ave, New York, NY 10010. TEL 212-353-3798, 800-488-5233.

917.313 USA ISSN 1556-4258
GV1024
LET'S GO: ROADTRIPPING U S A. Text in English. 1973. a. USD 24.99 (effective 2008). adv. **Document type:** *Magazine, Consumer.*
Supersedes in part (in 2005): Let's Go: The Budget Guide to the U S A (0275-9837); Which was formerly (until 1981): Let's Go: The Student Guide to the United States and Canada (0090-788X)
Published by: Let's Go Publications, Inc., c/o Relevant Guidebook, 67 Mt Auburn St, Cambridge, MA 02138. TEL 617-495-9659, FAX 617-496-7070, publicity@letsgo.com, http://letsgo.com. **Dist. by:** St. Martin's Press, LLC, 175 Fifth Ave, New York, NY 10010. TEL 212-353-3798, 800-488-5233.

914.5 USA ISSN 1534-7184
DG804
LET'S GO: ROME (YEAR). Variant title: Let's Go - The Budget Guide to Rome. Text in English. 1993. a. USD 16.99 (effective 2006). **Document type:** *Magazine, Consumer.*
Formerly (until 1998): Let's Go: The Budget Guide to Rome (Year) (1068-3615)
Published by: Let's Go Publications, Inc., c/o Relevant Guidebook, 67 Mt Auburn St, Cambridge, MA 02138. TEL 617-495-9659, FAX 617-496-7070, publicity@letsgo.com, http://letsgo.com. Ed. Whitney Bryant. **Dist. by:** St. Martin's Press, LLC, 175 Fifth Ave, New York, NY 10010. TEL 212-353-3798, 800-488-5233.

917.13 USA ISSN 1541-7182
F869.S33
LET'S GO: SAN FRANCISCO (YEAR). Text in English. 2001. a. USD 16.99 newsstand/cover (effective 2006). **Document type:** *Magazine, Consumer.*
Published by: Let's Go Publications, Inc., c/o Relevant Guidebook, 67 Mt Auburn St, Cambridge, MA 02138. TEL 617-495-9659, FAX 617-496-7070, publicity@letsgo.com, http://letsgo.com. **Dist. by:** St. Martin's Press, LLC, 175 Fifth Ave, New York, NY 10010. TEL 212-353-3798, 800-488-5233.

910.202 USA ISSN 1528-9850
DT1717
LET'S GO: SOUTH AFRICA (YEAR). Text in English. 1999. a. USD 22.99 (effective 2006). **Document type:** *Magazine, Consumer.*
Published by: Let's Go Publications, Inc., c/o Relevant Guidebook, 67 Mt Auburn St, Cambridge, MA 02138. TEL 617-495-9659, FAX 617-496-7070, publicity@letsgo.com, http://letsgo.com. Ed. Douglas Muller. **Dist. by:** St. Martin's Press, LLC, 175 Fifth Ave, New York, NY 10010. TEL 212-353-3798, 800-488-5233.

917.8 USA ISSN 1543-5695
F787
LET'S GO: SOUTHWEST U S A. Text in English. 2002. a. USD 18.99 newsstand/cover (effective 2006). **Document type:** *Magazine, Consumer.*
Published by: Let's Go Publications, Inc., c/o Relevant Guidebook, 67 Mt Auburn St, Cambridge, MA 02138. TEL 617-495-9659, FAX 617-496-7070, publicity@letsgo.com, http://letsgo.com. **Dist. by:** St. Martin's Press, LLC, 175 Fifth Ave, New York, NY 10010. TEL 212-353-3798, 800-488-5233.

910.202 USA ISSN 2154-4050
DP14
LET'S GO: SPAIN AND PORTUGAL, WITH MOROCCO (YEAR). Text in English. 1984. a. USD 21.95 (effective 2010). adv. **Document type:** *Magazine, Consumer.*
Former titles (until 2009): Let's Go: Spain & Portugal, including Morocco; (until 1998): Let's Go: Spain & Portugal (Year); (until 1998): Let's Go: The Budget Guide to Spain & Portugal; (until 1992): Let's Go: The Budget Guide to Spain, Portugal & Morocco (0885-3541)
Published by: Let's Go Publications, Inc., c/o Relevant Guidebook, 67 Mt Auburn St, Cambridge, MA 02138. TEL 617-495-9659, FAX 617-496-7070, publicity@letsgo.com, http://letsgo.com. Eds. Elena Schneider, Laura Gordon. **Dist. by:** St. Martin's Press, LLC, 175 Fifth Ave, New York, NY 10010. TEL 212-353-3798, 800-488-5233.

015.13 USA ISSN 1544-5496
DS563
LET'S GO: THAILAND. Text in English. 2003. a. USD 19.99 newsstand/cover (effective 2006). **Document type:** *Magazine, Consumer.*
Published by: Let's Go Publications, Inc., c/o Relevant Guidebook, 67 Mt Auburn St, Cambridge, MA 02138. TEL 617-495-9659, FAX 617-496-7070, publicity@letsgo.com, http://letsgo.com. **Dist. by:** St. Martin's Press, LLC, 175 Fifth Ave, New York, NY 10010. TEL 212-353-3798, 800-488-5233.

914.9504 USA ISSN 1524-0851
DR416
LET'S GO: TURKEY (YEAR). Text in English. 1982. a. USD 21.99 (effective 2006). **Document type:** *Magazine, Consumer.*
Supersedes in part (in 1999): Let's Go: Greece and Turkey (1524-0843); Which was formerly (until 1998): Let's Go: The Budget Guide to Greece and Turkey (Year) (1064-1009); (until 1991): Let's Go: The Budget Guide to Greece (0749-0569); Which superseded in part (in 1984): Let's Go: The Budget Guide to Greece, Israel and Egypt (0276-6779)
Published by: Let's Go Publications, Inc., c/o Relevant Guidebook, 67 Mt Auburn St, Cambridge, MA 02138. TEL 617-495-9659, FAX 617-496-7070, publicity@letsgo.com, http://letsgo.com. **Dist. by:** St. Martin's Press, LLC, 175 Fifth Ave, New York, NY 10010. TEL 212-353-3798, 800-488-5233.

917.04 USA ISSN 1534-4800
E158
LET'S GO: U S A (YEAR); with coverage of Canada. Text in English. 1973. a. USD 24.99 (effective 2008). adv. illus. **Document type:** *Magazine, Consumer.*
Former titles (until 1998): Let's Go: Budget Guide to the U S A (Year) (0275-9837); (until 1981): Let's Go: The Student Guide to the United States and Canada (0090-788X)
Published by: Let's Go Publications, Inc., c/o Relevant Guidebook, 67 Mt Auburn St, Cambridge, MA 02138. TEL 617-495-9659, FAX 617-496-7070, publicity@letsgo.com, feedback@letsgo.com, http://letsgo.com. **Dist. by:** St. Martin's Press, LLC, 175 Fifth Ave, New York, NY 10010. TEL 212-353-3798, 800-488-5233.

915.970 USA ISSN 1556-1917
DS556.25
LET'S GO: VIETNAM. Text in English. 2005. a. USD 19.99 (effective 2007). adv. **Document type:** *Magazine, Consumer.*
Published by: Let's Go Publications, Inc., c/o Relevant Guidebook, 67 Mt Auburn St, Cambridge, MA 02138. TEL 617-495-9659, FAX 617-496-7070, publicity@letsgo.com. **Dist. by:** St. Martin's Press, LLC, 175 Fifth Ave, New York, NY 10010. TEL 212-353-3798, 800-488-5233.

917.5304 USA ISSN 1536-3465
F192.3
LET'S GO: WASHINGTON, D.C. (YEAR). Variant title: Budget Guide to Washington, D.C. Text in English. 1992. a. USD 16.99 (effective 2006). **Document type:** *Magazine, Consumer.*
Formerly (until 2000): Let's Go: Budget Guide to Washington D.C. (Year) (1068-1418)
Published by: Let's Go Publications, Inc., c/o Relevant Guidebook, 67 Mt Auburn St, Cambridge, MA 02138. TEL 617-495-9659, FAX 617-496-7070, publicity@letsgo.com, http://letsgo.com. **Dist. by:** St. Martin's Press, LLC, 175 Fifth Ave, New York, NY 10010. TEL 212-353-3798, 800-488-5233.

914.045 USA ISSN 1540-1456
D967
LET'S GO: WESTERN EUROPE. Text in English. 2001. a. USD 24.99 newsstand/cover (effective 2008). adv. **Document type:** *Magazine, Consumer.*

TU

Published by: Let's Go Publications, Inc., c/o Relevant Guidebook, 67 Mt Auburn St, Cambridge, MA 02138. TEL 617-495-9659, FAX 617-496-7070, publicity@letsgo.com, http://letsgo.com. **Dist. by:** St. Martin's Press, LLC, 175 Fifth Ave, New York, NY 10010. TEL 212-353-3798, 800-488-5233.

917.2 USA ISSN 2156-0420
F1376

▼ **LET'S GO: YUCATAN PENINSULA.** Text in English. 2010. irreg. USD 18.95 per issue (effective 2010). **Document type:** *Handbook/Manual/Guide, Consumer.* **Description:** Student travel guide for the Yucatan Peninsula, Mexico.

Published by: Let's Go Publications, Inc., c/o Relevant Guidebook, 67 Mt Auburn St, Cambridge, MA 02138. TEL 617-495-9659, FAX 617-496-7070, feedback@letsgo.com, http://www.letsgo.com.

LEVEN IN FRANKRIJK. *see* LIFESTYLE

910 USA

LEWIS & CLARK TRAVEL GUIDE AND PLANNER. Text in English. a. USD 3.95 newsstand/cover (effective 2001). adv. **Description:** Relates the story of Lewis and Clark to highway travelers, telling stories of the expedition in particular locations along the trail.

Published by: Lee Inc, 3020 Bozeman Ave, Helena, MT 59601. TEL 406-443-2842, FAX 406-443-5480. Adv. contact Larry Sem.

910.202 305.4 NLD ISSN 2211-9752

LIBELLE. VAKANTIE. Text in Dutch. 2004. a. EUR 3.75 newsstand/cover (effective 2011). **Document type:** *Magazine, Consumer.*

Related titles: ◆ Supplement to: Libelle. ISSN 0165-4926.

Published by: Sanoma Uitgevers B.V., Postbus 1900, Hoofddorp, 2130 JH, Netherlands. TEL 31-23-5566770, FAX 31-23-5565376, http://www.sanomamedia.nl.

910.2 BEL ISSN 1780-6496

LA LIBRE ESSENTIELLE VOYAGE. Text in French. 2004. m. back issues avail. **Document type:** *Magazine, Consumer.*

Published by: La Libre Belgique S.A., 79 Rue des Francs, Brussels, 1040, Belgium. TEL 32-2-7444444, FAX 32-2-2112832, llb.direction@saipm.com, http://www.lalibre.be.

910.2 960 GBR

LIBYA PAST AND PRESENT SERIES. Text in English. 1970. irreg. price varies. **Document type:** *Monographic series, Academic/Scholarly.*

Formerly: Libyan Travel Series (0075-9309)

Published by: Oleander Press, 16 Orchard St, Cambridge, CB1 1JT, United Kingdom. TEL 44-1223-350898.

LIFESTYLE AND TRAVEL FOR PHYSICIANS. *see* LIFESTYLE

910.91 USA

LINGER LONGER. Text in English. 2006 (Jul.). q. adv. **Document type:** *Magazine, Consumer.* **Description:** Reflects the history and tradition of north Georgia, conveying discerning taste and respect for classic standards as they to the activity, experience and enjoyment that define Reynolds Plantation.

Published by: Watson Publications, 10540 Portal Crossing, Ste 105, Bradenton, FL 34211. TEL 800-455-4300, FAX 941-748-7773, promotions@watsonpublications.com, http://www.watsonpublications.com. Adv. contact Scott Shields. color page USD 9,400; trim 8.375 x 10.875.

LINKS (HILTON HEAD ISLAND); the best of golf. *see* SPORTS AND GAMES—Ball Games

LINKS UND RECHTS DER AUTOBAHN. *see* HOTELS AND RESTAURANTS

914 SVN ISSN 0352-4353

LIPOV LIST. Text in Slovenian. 1953-1977; resumed 1984. bi-m. free. adv. **Document type:** *Magazine, Consumer.*

Formerly (until 1977): Turisticni Vestnik (0041-4212)

Related titles: Online - full content ed.

Published by: Turisticna Zveza Slovenije, Miklosiceva 38, Ljubljana, 1000, Slovenia. TEL 386-1-4341670, FAX 386-1-4341680, tzs@siol.net. Ed. Marjetico Gregorcic Novak. Circ: 1,800.

914.69 USA ISSN 1937-0148
DP757

LISBON. D K EYEWITNESS TOP 10 TRAVEL GUIDES. AMERICAN EDITION. (Dorling Kindersley) Variant title: Eyewitness Top 10 Travel Guide: Top 10 Lisbon. Text in English. 2007. irreg., latest 2007. USD 12 per issue (effective 2008). **Document type:** *Guide, Consumer.* **Description:** Provides information on top 10 restaurants, shops, hotels, museums and family attractions for any budget in Lisbon.

Published by: D K Publishing (Subsidiary of: Penguin Books U S A, Inc.), 375 Hudson St, New York, NY 10014. TEL 800-631-8571, FAX 201-256-0000, specialsales@dk.com.

910.2 GBR ISSN 2042-5848

▼ **THE LITTLE BLACK BOOK OF LONDON.** Text in English. 2009. a. GBP 6.39 per issue (effective 2010). **Document type:** *Handbook/Manual/Guide, Consumer.* **Description:** Contains the city's secrets, shops, services and contacts for every events.

Published by: Time Out Magazine, Universal House, 251 Tottenham Ct Rd, London, W1T 7AB, United Kingdom. TEL 44-20-78133000, FAX 44-20-73233438, distribution@timeout.com, http://www.timeout.com.

LIUXUESHENG/STUDENT STUDYING ABROAD. *see* EDUCATION

910.2 USA ISSN 1555-9750
DA980

LIVING ABROAD IN IRELAND. Text in English. 2005. biennial, latest 2005. USD 17.95 per issue (effective 2009). **Document type:** *Guide, Consumer.*

Published by: Avalon Travel Publishing, 1700 4th St, Berkeley, CA 94710. TEL 510-595-3664, avalon.publicity@perseusbooks.com, http://www.avalontravelbooks.com.

910.202 333.33 GBR ISSN 0960-5444

LIVING FRANCE. Text in English. 1989. 12/yr. GBP 36; GBP 3.99 newsstand/cover (effective 2009). adv. bk.rev. illus.; maps. back issues avail. **Document type:** *Magazine, Consumer.* **Description:** Provides information about French property, travel and lifestyle.

Formerly (until 1990): French Living (0958-3092)

Related titles: Online - full text ed.: GBP 15 (effective 2009).

Published by: Archant Life Ltd (Subsidiary of: Archant Group), Archant House, Oriel Rd, Cheltenham, Glos GL50 1BB, United Kingdom. TEL 44-1242-216050, johnny.hustler@archant.co.uk, http://www.archantlife.co.uk. Ed. Eleanor O'Kane TEL 44-1242-216086. Adv. contact Debbie MacLeod TEL 44-1242-216087.

909 GBR ISSN 1750-5887

LIVING HISTORY. Text in English. 1994. s-a. **Document type:** *Magazine, Consumer.*

Former titles (until 2004): Living History Digest (1475-4304); (until 2001): Living History Register Newsletter (1353-6621)

Published by: Living History Register, "The Anchorage", 56 Wareham Rd, Lytchett Matravers, Poole, Dorset BH16 6DS, United Kingdom. TEL 44-1202-622115. Ed. Roger Emmerson.

910.09 VEN

LIVING IN VENEZUELA. Text in English. 1980. a. adv. index. back issues avail. **Description:** Contains detailed information on all aspects of Venezuelan life.

Formerly: VenAmCham's Executive Newcomers Guide

Published by: Venezuelan - American Chamber of Commerce and Industry/Camara Venezolano-Americana de Comercio e Industria, Apdo 5181, Caracas, DF 1010-A, Venezuela. TEL 58-2-2630833, FAX 58-2-2631829. Circ: 5,000.

LOAN-A-HOME DIRECTORY. *see* REAL ESTATE

338.4 790.1 658 GBR ISSN 1470-9872

LOCUM DESTINATION REVIEW; the journal of record for the global destination industry. Abbreviated title: L D R. Text in English. 2000. q. bk.rev. back issues avail. **Document type:** *Journal, Trade.* **Description:** Features in-depth articles from across the full spectrum of the destination business.

Related titles: Online - full text ed.

Indexed: H&TI, H06.

Published by: Locum Consulting, 9 Marylebone Ln, London, W1U 1HL, United Kingdom. TEL 44-20-74871799, FAX 44-20-73446558, info@locumconsulting.com.

917.4 USA

LOG CABIN CHRONICLES. Text in English. 1996. m. (plus d. updates). free. **Document type:** *Newspaper.* **Description:** Contains features, fiction, peotry, opinion, photography, art and down-home cooking from the culturally rich Anglo-French-Yankee communities in the Lake Memphremagog watershed on the Vermont-Quebec border.

Media: Online - full text.

Address: PO Box 706, Derby Line, VT 05830. TEL 819-876-2538, FAX 819-876-7515. Ed. John Mahoney.

917.204 USA

LOG OF THE SUNCHASER. Text in English. 1992. q. free. bk.rev. **Document type:** *Newsletter.* **Description:** Contains information for boaters on all aspects of planning a pleasure boat cruise to Central America and the Caribbean.

Former titles: Tropical American Cruising (1078-1404); (until 1993): Sailaway Cruising Report

Published by: Sailaway Cruising Club, PO Box 1073, Miami, FL 33135. TEL 305-637-6633, FAX 305-637-6633. Ed. J A Rogers. Circ: 1,000.

910.202 ITA ISSN 1828-731X

LOMBARDIA PAESE PER PAESE. Text in Italian. 2006. w. **Document type:** *Magazine, Consumer.*

Published by: Editrice Bonechi, Via dei Cairoli, 18BB, Florence, FI 50131, Italy. TEL 39-055-576841, FAX 39-055-5000766, bonechi@bonechi.it, http://www.bonechi.it.

914 USA ISSN 1937-0423
DA679

LONDON. Variant title: Eyewitness Travel Guide: London. Text in English. 2007. a. USD 25 (effective 2008). **Document type:** *Guide, Consumer.* **Description:** Contains suggestions on what to see, how to get about and where to eat and stay in London.

Formerly (until 2005): London EGuide (1558-3503)

Published by: D K Publishing (Subsidiary of: Penguin Books U S A, Inc.), 375 Hudson St, New York, NY 10014. TEL 800-631-8571, FAX 201-256-0000, specialsales@dk.com.

338.4 GBR ISSN 1755-1897

LONDON JOURNAL OF TOURISM, SPORT AND CREATIVE INDUSTRIES. Abbreviated title: L J T S C I. Text in English. 2008. irreg., latest 2010. free (effective 2011). back issues avail. **Document type:** *Journal, Academic/Scholarly.*

Media: Online - full text.

Published by: London Metropolitan University, 166-220 Holloway Rd, London, N7 8DB, United Kingdom. TEL 44-20-74230000.

910.202 GBR ISSN 0265-8437

LONDON PLANNER. Text in English. 1984. m. adv. **Document type:** *Handbook/Manual/Guide, Consumer.* **Description:** Guide to what's on in London and is full of information to help you plan your time in Britain's most visited city.

Incorporates: The London Guide

Published by: (Visit London USA), Morris Visitor Publications Europe (Subsidiary of: Morris Multimedia, Inc.), 233 High Holborn, 2nd Fl, London, WC1V 7DN, United Kingdom. TEL 44-20-72425222, MVPcustomerservice@morris.com, http://www.morrisvisitorpublications.com. Adv. contact Andrew Turner TEL 44-20-76117891. page GBP 1,924; trim 137 x 210. Circ: 125,000 (free).

THE LONDON TAXI DRIVER'S HANDBOOK. *see* TRANSPORTATION

388.40942105 GBR ISSN 1750-9610

LONDON TRAVELWATCH. ANNUAL REVIEW. Text in English. 1984. a. back issues avail. **Document type:** *Magazine, Trade.*

Former titles (until 2005): London Transport Users Committee. Annual Report (1475-777X); (until 2001): London Regional Transport Committee. Annual Report (0268-9340)

Related titles: Online - full text ed.: free (effective 2009).

Published by: London TravelWatch, 6 Middle St, London, EC1A 7JA, United Kingdom. TEL 44-20-75059000, FAX 44-20-75059003, enquiries@londontravelwatch.org.uk, http://www.londontravelwatch.org.uk.

910.202 ITA ISSN 1825-1846

LONDRA GRAND TOUR. Text in Italian. 2005. s-a. **Document type:** *Magazine, Consumer.*

Published by: De Agostini Editore, Via G da Verrazzano 15, Novara, 28100, Italy. TEL 39-0321-4241, FAX 39-0321-424305, info@deagostini.it, http://www.deagostini.it.

338 FRA ISSN 1242-9244

LONELY PLANET GUIDE DE VOYAGE. Text in French. 1992. irreg. **Document type:** *Magazine, Consumer.*

—CCC.

Published by: Lonely Planet, 12 Av d'Italie, Paris, Cedex 13 75627, France. TEL 33-1-44160500, FAX 33-1-44088402, lonelyplanet@placedesediteurs.com, http://www.lonelyplanet.fr.

910.2 GBR ISSN 1758-6526

▼ **LONELY PLANET MAGAZINE**; the new glossy travel magazine. Text in English. 2009. m. GBP 43.20 (effective 2010). adv. **Document type:** *Magazine, Consumer.* **Description:** Designed for people with a passion for travel and new experiences.

Related titles: ◆ Spanish ed.: Lonely Planet Magazine (Argentina). ISSN 1853-0303.

Published by: B B C Magazines Ltd. (Subsidiary of: B B C Worldwide Ltd.), 201 Wood Ln, London, W12 7TQ, United Kingdom. TEL 44-20-84332000, bbcworldwide@bbc.co.uk, http://www.bbcmagazines.com. Ed. Peter Grunert.

910.2 ARG ISSN 1853-0303

▼ **LONELY PLANET MAGAZINE (ARGENTINA).** Text in Spanish. 2010. m. **Document type:** *Magazine, Consumer.*

Related titles: ◆ English ed.: Lonely Planet Magazine. ISSN 1758-6526.

Published by: Division de Revistas Premium, Azopardo 455, Buenos Aires, Argentina. TEL 54-11-43310870, http://www.drevistaspremium.com/. Ed. Alex Milberg. Circ: 75,000.

917.47 USA ISSN 1946-3383

▼ **LONG ISLAND CITY.** Text in English. 2009. s-a. USD 4.99 per issue (effective 2009). adv. **Document type:** *Guide, Consumer.* **Description:** Pocket-sized guide to Long Island City, New York.

Published by: Hot and Cool Guide LLC, 1375 Broadway, 3rd Fl, New York, NY 10018. TEL 800-282-8144, FAX 646-417-8259, question@HotAndCoolGuide.com. adv.: page USD 1,680; 4.125 x 7.375.

338.4791 USA

LONGWEEKENDS. Text in English. 2002. m. USD 17.95 (effective 2002). **Document type:** *Magazine, Consumer.* **Description:** Covers travel, promotions and restaurants in the Great Lakes region.

Published by: Great Lakes Publishing Co., 62 E Broad St, Columbus, OH 43215. TEL 614-461-5083, 800-426-4624. Ed. Richard Osborne. Pub. Lute Harmon. Adv. contact Karen Matusoff.

915 THA ISSN 0857-1139

LOOKEAST. Text in English. 1969. m. adv. bk.rev. charts; illus. **Document type:** *Journal, Trade.*

Indexed: BAS.

Published by: Advertising and Media Consultants Ltd., Silom Condominium 12th Fl, 52-38 Soi Saladaeng 2, Bangkok, 10500, Thailand. TEL 266-9040, FAX 236-6764. Ed. Asha Narula Sehgal. Circ: 15,000.

910.91 USA ISSN 0896-6206
F375

LOUISIANA ALMANAC. Text in English. 1949. irreg. USD 16.95 per issue (effective 2008 - 2009). back issues avail. **Document type:** *Guide, Consumer.*

Formerly (until 1962): Louisiana Almanac and Fact Book

Published by: Pelican Publishing Co., 1000 Burmaster St., Gretna, LA 70053. TEL 504-368-1175, 800-843-1724, FAX 504-368-1195, editorial@pelicanpub.com, http://www.pelicanpub.com. Ed. Milburn Calhoun.

LOUNGE LOS ANGELES. *see* HOTELS AND RESTAURANTS

380.8 ARG ISSN 0329-4633

LUGARES. Text in Spanish. 1990. m. USD 7.50 newsstand/cover (effective 2002). adv. **Document type:** *Magazine, Consumer.*

Related titles: Supplement(s): Lugares Especial. ISSN 1515-6516.

Published by: S.A. La Nacion, Leandro N. Alem 628, Piso 3, Buenos Aires, Buenos Aires 1001, Argentina. TEL 54-11-4514-4080, FAX 54-11-4514-4075, revistas@zonarevistas.com.ar, http://www.zonarevistas.com.ar.

LUGARES DIVINOS; el placer de vivir. *see* HOTELS AND RESTAURANTS

LUXURY BRIEFING; required reading for the luxury industry. *see* CLOTHING TRADE

LUXURY SPAFINDER MAGAZINE. *see* PHYSICAL FITNESS AND HYGIENE

338.4791 USA

LUXURY TRAVEL ADVISOR. Text in English. 2005. m. USD 100 domestic; USD 139 in Canada; USD 179 elsewhere; free to qualified personnel (effective 2008). adv. back issues avail.; reprints avail. **Document type:** *Magazine, Trade.* **Description:** Provides information on luxury movers and shakers, hotels, destinations and other luxury travel products.

Related titles: Online - full text ed.

Indexed: CA, H&TI, V03.

Published by: Questex Media Group Inc., 275 Grove St, Bldg 2, Ste 130, Newton, MA 02466. TEL 617-219-8300, 888-552-4346, FAX 617-219-8310, questex@sunbeltfs.com, http://www.questex.com. Pub. John McMahon TEL 212-895-8243. adv.: color page USD 7,413; trim 8.875 x 10.75. Circ: 11,500 (controlled).

338.4 SGP

LUYEBAO/T T G CHINA. Text in Chinese. 1998. m. free to qualified personnel. **Document type:** *Newspaper, Trade.* **Description:** Provides news and information for Chinese speaking travel agents in China, Hong Kong, Taiwan and Macau.

Published by: T T G Asia Media Pte Ltd, 6 Raffles Quay #16-02, Singapore, 048580, Singapore. TEL 65-6395-7575, FAX 65-6536-8639, contact@ttgasia.com, http://www.ttgasiamedia.com/. Circ: 13,000.

910.202 CHN ISSN 1000-7253

LUYOU/TOURIST. Text in Chinese. 1979. m. USD 62.40 (effective 2009). adv. **Document type:** *Consumer.*

Related titles: Online - full text ed.

—East View.

Published by: (Beijing Luyou Shiye Guanliju/Beijing Tourism Management Bureau), Luyou Zazhishe, 28, Jianguomen Wei Dajie, Room 804-805, Beijing Luyou Dasha, Beijing, 100022, China. **Dist. by:** China International Book Trading Corp, 35 Chegongzhuang Xilu, Haidian District, PO Box 399, Beijing 100044, China. TEL 86-10-68412045, FAX 86-10-68412023, cibtc@mail.cibtc.com.cn, http://www.cibtc.com.cn.

910.2 CHN

LUYOU DAOBAO/GUIDE TO TOURISM. Text in Chinese. w. CNY 211.20 (effective 2004). **Document type:** *Newspaper, Consumer.*

Address: Wuchang Shuiguohu, 6, Hubeisheng Weidayuan, Wuhan, Hubei 430071, China. TEL 86-571-7828986. **Dist. by:** China International Book Trading Corp, 35 Chegongzhuang Xilu, Haidian District, PO Box 399, Beijing 100044, China. TEL 86-10-68412045, FAX 86-10-68412023, cibtc@mail.cibtc.com.cn, http://www.cibtc.com.cn.

910.4 330 CHN ISSN 1009-1637
LUYOU GUANGLI/MANAGEMENT OF TOURISM. Text in Chinese. 1980. bi-m. USD 49.90 (effective 2009). 80 p./no.; **Document type:** *Journal, Academic/Scholarly.* **Description:** Covers the development and management of tourism resources and tourism industry.
Formerly (until 199?): Luyou Jingji (1001-3075)
Published by: Zhongguo Renmin Daxue Shubao Ziliao Zhongxin/Renmin University of China, Information Center for Social Sciences, Dongcheng-qu, 3, Zhangzizhong Lu, Beijing, 100007, China. TEL 86-10-64039458, FAX 86-10-64015080, center@zlzx.org, http://www.zlzx.org/. **Dist. in US by:** China Publications Service, PO Box 49614, Chicago, IL 60649. TEL 312-288-3291, FAX 312-288-8570.

338.4 TWN ISSN 1682-5098
LUYOU GUANLI YANJIU. Text in Chinese. 2001. s-a. **Document type:** *Journal, Academic/Scholarly.*
Related titles: Online - full text ed.
Published by: Nanhua Daxue, Luyou Shiye Guanli Yanjiuso/Nanhua University, Institute of Tourism Management, 32, Chung Keng Li, Dalin, Chiayi 62248, Taiwan. TEL 886-5-2721001.

915.1 CHN ISSN 1005-7730
DS712
LUYOU TIANDI/TRAVELLING SCOPE. Text in Chinese. 1980. m. USD 96 (effective 2009). adv. **Document type:** *Journal, Academic/Scholarly.*
—East View.
Published by: Shanghai Wenyi Chubanshe/Shanghai Literature & Art Publishing Group, 74 Shaoxing Lu, Shanghai, 200020, China. TEL 86-21-64185361, FAX 86-21-64175730. **Dist. by:** China International Book Trading Corp, 35 Chegongzhuang Xilu, Haidian District, PO Box 399, Beijing 100044, China. TEL 86-10-68412045, FAX 86-10-68412023, cibtc@mail.cibtc.com.cn, http://www.cibtc.com.cn.

910.4 CHN ISSN 1002-5006
LUYOU XUEKAN/JOURNAL OF TOURISM. Text in Chinese. 1987. q. USD 62.40 (effective 2009).
Related titles: Online - full text ed.
—East View.
Published by: Beijing Lianhe Daxue, Luyou Xueyuan, 1 Panjiapo, Chaowai, Beijing, 100020, China. TEL 5024956. Ed. Zhao Kefei.

914.458 FRA ISSN 1953-6224
LYON DECOUVERTE. Text in French. 2002. q. **Document type:** *Magazine, Consumer.*
Published by: Lyon Mag Groupe, 113-115 Av. Sidoine-Apollinaire, Lyon, 69009, France.

M C MEETING E CONGRESS. *see* MEETINGS AND CONGRESSES

914 CHE
M I C. (Meetings, Incentives and Conventions) Text in German. 3/yr. **Document type:** *Magazine, Consumer.*
Published by: Primus Verlag AG, Hammerstr 81, Postfach 1331, Zuerich, 8032, Switzerland. TEL 41-1-3875757, FAX 41-1-3875707, info@travelinside.ch, http://www.primusverlag.ch.

910.202 GBR ISSN 2042-3535
THE M I C E REPORT. (Meetings and Business Travel) Text in English. 200?. q. GBP 16, EUR 20; GBP 3.45, EUR 4.50 per issue (effective 2010). **Document type:** *Journal, Academic/Scholarly.* **Description:** Provides travel information for various locations.
Related titles: Online - full text ed.: free (effective 2010).
Published by: Raellen Communications Ltd., 145-157 St John St, London, EC1V 4PY, United Kingdom. TEL 44-208-7778355. Ed. Charles Vandeleur.

M S A COMPETITORS AND OFFICIALS YEARBOOK. *see* SPORTS AND GAMES

914 USA ISSN 1939-5639
DA980
M T V IRELAND. (Music Television) Text in English. 2006. irreg. **Document type:** *Guide, Consumer.* **Description:** Provides travel information in Ireland.
Published by: John Wiley & Sons, Inc., 111 River St, Hoboken, NJ 07030. TEL 201-748-6000, FAX 201-748-6088, info@wiley.com, http://www.wiley.com/WileyCDA/.

MACAO. DIRECCAO DOS SERVICOS DE ESTATISTICA E CENSOS. ESTATISTICAS DO TURISMO/MACAO. CENSUS AND STATISTICS DEPARTMENT. TOURISM STATISTICS. *see* TRAVEL AND TOURISM—Abstracting, Bibliographies, Statistics

MACAO. DIRECCAO DOS SERVICOS DE ESTATISTICA E CENSOS. INDICADORES DO TURISMO/MACAO. CENSUS AND STATISTICS DEPARTMENT. TOURISM INDICATORS. *see* TRAVEL AND TOURISM—Abstracting, Bibliographies, Statistics

MAENNER. *see* HOMOSEXUALITY

910.5 FRA ISSN 1955-6306
MAG'HOTEL; travel & leisure for business and pleasure. Text in French. 2007. q. **Document type:** *Magazine, Consumer.*
Published by: Victor Chance Communication (V C C), 21 rue du Renard, Paris, 75004, France. TEL 33-1-48045100, FAX 33-1-48075104, http://www.victorchance.org.

910.2 USA ISSN 1932-1112
F19.6
MAINE CURIOSITIES; quirky characters, roadside oddities, and other offbeat stuff. Text in English. 2002. irreg., latest 2006, 2nd ed. USD 13.95 per issue (effective 2007). back issues avail. **Document type:** *Guide, Consumer.* **Description:** Provides information about the wildest, wackiest, most outrageous people, places and things in Maine.
Published by: The Globe Pequot Press, Inc., 246 Goose Ln, PO Box 480, Guilford, CT 06437. TEL 203-458-4500, 888-249-7586, FAX 203-458-4603, 800-820-2329, info@globepequot.com, http://www.globepequot.com. Ed. Gillian Belnap.

917.404 USA
MAINE INVITES YOU. Text in English. 1930. a. free. adv. **Document type:** *Directory.*
Published by: Maine Publicity Bureau, Inc., 325B Water St, Box 2300, Hallowell, ME 04347. TEL 207-623-0363, FAX 207-623-0388. Ed. Lynn Verrill. Adv. contact Diane Hopkins. Circ: 135,000.

916 MWI
MALAWI: A GUIDE FOR THE VISITOR. Text in English. 1983. a. free. **Document type:** *Guide, Consumer.*
Published by: Department of Information, PO Box 494, Blantyre, Malawi. FAX 265-620266.

910.202 GBR ISSN 1363-7363
DS591.5
MALAYSIA AND SINGAPORE HANDBOOK. Text in English. 1996. biennial. GBP 15.99 per issue (effective 2010). adv. back issues avail. **Document type:** *Handbook/Manual/Guide, Consumer.* **Description:** Covers all the basics from where to stay and where to eat to cycling, walking and how to get around the Malaysia and Singapore.
Supersedes in part (in 1996): Indonesia, Malaysia and Singapore Handbook (0968-0942)
—CCC.
Published by: Footprint Handbooks Ltd., 6 Riverside Ct, Lower Bristol Rd, Bath, Avon BA2 3DZ, United Kingdom. TEL 44-1225-469141, FAX 44-1225-469461, wwwinfo@footprintbooks.com.

338.4791595 GBR ISSN 1747-8944
MALAYSIA TOURISM REPORT. Text in English. 2005. q. EUR 820, USD 1,030 combined subscription (print & email eds.) (effective 2010). **Document type:** *Report, Trade.* **Description:** Provides industry professionals and strategists, corporate analysts, associations, government departments and regulatory bodies with independent forecasts and competitive intelligence on the Malaysian tourism industry.
Related titles: E-mail ed.
Indexed: A15, ABIn, B02, B15, B17, B18, G04, I05, P48, P51, PQC.
Published by: Business Monitor International Ltd., Senator House, 85 Queen Victoria St, London, EC4V 4AB, United Kingdom. TEL 44-20-72480468, FAX 44-20-72480467, subs@businessmonitor.com.

910.2 USA ISSN 1559-4289
DP302.B27
MALLORCA DIRECTIONS. Text in English. 2005. irreg., latest 2008, 2nd ed. USD 11.99 domestic 2nd ed.; USD 14.99 in Canada 2nd ed.; GBP 6.99 in United Kingdom 2nd ed. (effective 2008). back issues avail. **Document type:** *Guide, Consumer.*
Related titles: Online - full text ed.
Published by: Rough Guides, 375 Hudson St, 9th Fl, New York, NY 10014. TEL 212-414-3635, http://www.roughguides.com/default.aspx.

338.4 USA
MANAGEMENT.TRAVEL. Text in English. 2006 (Apr.). s-m. free (effective 2011). adv. back issues avail. **Document type:** *Newsletter, Trade.* **Description:** Provides information on travel program operations for travel managers in all private and public sectors.
Published by: Business Travel Media Group, 116 W 32nd St, 14th Fl, New York, NY 10001. TEL 847-559-7533, 800-697-8859, FAX 847-291-4816, nbtn@omeda.com, http://www.promedia.travel/.

917.104 CAN ISSN 1704-6718
MANITOBA. FISHING & HUNTING ADVENTURES. Text in English. 1988. a. free. adv. illus. **Document type:** *Handbook/Manual/Guide, Consumer.* **Description:** Publishes information on drive-in and fly-in lodges, outfitters, air charter services and the Manitoba Master Angler Award winners.
Former titles (until 2002): This is Manitoba, Fishing and Hunting Adventures (1701-7769); (until 2001): Manitoba Fishing & Hunting Guide (1494-6238); (until 2000): Manitoba Fishing and Hunting Adventure (1483-8133); (until 1997): Manitoba Canada .. Fishing & Hunting Adventures, Master Angler Awards (1209-4757); (until 199?): Manitoba Fishing and Hunting Adventures (1186-9585); (until 198?): Fishing Adventure & Master Angler Awards (1186-9577)
Published by: Travel Manitoba, 155 Carlton St, 7th Fl, Department SS0, Winnipeg, MB R3C 3H8, Canada. TEL 800-665-0040, http://www.travelmanitoba.com. Pub. Colette Fontaine.

910.2 CAN ISSN 1910-6939
MANITOBA PARKS GUIDE. Text in English. 199?. a. **Document type:** *Handbook/Manual/Guide, Consumer.*
Former titles (until 2006): Manitoba, Provincial Parks Guide (1707-9047); (until 2003): Manitoba Magic, Provincial Parks Guide (1493-9517)
Published by: Manitoba Conservation, 450 Broadway, Winnipeg, MB R3C 0V8, Canada. http://www.gov.mb.ca/conservation.

917.104 CAN ISSN 1702-0042
MANITOBA VACATION GUIDE. Text in English. a. free. adv. illus. **Document type:** *Handbook/Manual/Guide, Consumer.* **Description:** Describes the many vacation opportunities found throughout Manitoba, including a list of golf courses and tour operator packages.
Former titles (until 2002): This is Manitoba, Vacation Guide (1497-8121); (until 2001): Manitoba Explorer's Guide (1485-8908); (until 1994): Manitoba Vacation Planner (1185-4391); (until 1987): Manitoba Vacation Guide (0703-6248); (until 1975): Manitoba, Canada, Vacation Guide (0703-6256); (until 1972): Manitoba Vacation Handbook (0542-5638); (until 196?): Manitoba Family Accommodation and Vacation Guide
Published by: Travel Manitoba, 155 Carlton St, 7th Fl, Department SS0, Winnipeg, MB R3C 3H8, Canada. TEL 800-665-0040, http://www.travelmanitoba.com. Ed., Pub. Colette Fontaine.

917.204 MEX
MAR DE CORTES. Text in Spanish. m.
Published by: (Circuito Ecological del Mar de Cortes y Copper Canyon), Editorial Bonanza S. de R.L., DR VELASCO 95, Ed. 5 Of. 203, Col Doctores Del. Cuauhtemoc, Mexico City, DF 06720, Mexico. TEL 525-5938720, FAX 525-7052492.

338.479 USA
MARCO POLO; the magazine for adventure travelers over 50. Text in English. 1997. q. USD 10; USD 2.95 newsstand/cover (effective 2000). adv. back issues avail. **Document type:** *Magazine, Consumer.* **Description:** Contains ideas and advice on adventure travel opportunities for those over 50.
Published by: Marco Polo Publishing Inc., 1299 Bayshore Blvd Ste B, Dunedin, FL 34698. TEL 727-785-1845, FAX 727-785-0871. Ed., Pub., R&P, Adv. contact James Plouf. B&W page USD 788, color page USD 1,050; 11 x 8.5. Circ: 4,000 (paid); 6,000 (controlled).

917.4 USA ISSN 2154-0934
▼ **MARINE CITY MARITIME DAYS.** Text in English. 2010 (July). a. **Document type:** *Consumer.*
Published by: Marine City Maritime Days Festival, Inc., 810 S Water St, Marine City, MI 48039. TEL 810-765-3568, info@marinecitymaritimedays.org, http://www.marinecitymaritimedays.org/.

910.91 USA ISSN 1538-5213
F394.F7
A MARMAC GUIDE TO FORT WORTH AND ARLINGTON. Variant title: Fort Worth and Arlington. Guide to Fort Worth and Arlington. Text in English. 2000 (Apr.). irreg. USD 19.95 per issue (effective 2008). **Document type:** *Magazine, Consumer.* **Description:** Travel guide focusing on the Fort Worth area.
Published by: Pelican Publishing Co., 1000 Burmaster St., Gretna, LA 70053. TEL 504-368-1175, 800-843-1724, FAX 504-368-1195, editorial@pelicanpub.com, http://www.pelicanpub.com. Ed. Yves Gerem.

910.2 USA ISSN 1931-5236
A MARMAC GUIDE TO LAS VEGAS. Text in English. 2005. irreg. USD 17.95 per issue (effective 2008). **Document type:** *Guide, Consumer.* **Description:** Travel Guide.
Published by: Pelican Publishing Co., 1000 Burmaster St., Gretna, LA 70053. TEL 504-368-1175, 800-843-1724, FAX 504-368-1195, editorial@pelicanpub.com, http://www.pelicanpub.com.

910.794 USA
F869.L83
A MARMAC GUIDE TO LOS ANGELES AND NORTHERN ORANGE COUNTY. Text in English. 2001 (July). irreg., latest 5th ed. USD 17.95 per issue (effective 2008). **Document type:** *Guide, Consumer.* **Description:** Travel guide focusing on Los Angeles.
Former titles (until 200?): A Marmac Guide to Los Angeles (0736-8119); How When and Where in Los Angeles
Published by: Pelican Publishing Co., 1000 Burmaster St., Gretna, LA 70053. TEL 504-368-1175, 800-843-1724, FAX 504-368-1195, editorial@pelicanpub.com, http://www.pelicanpub.com. Ed. Arline Inge.

910.91 USA ISSN 0736-8135
F379.N53
A MARMAC GUIDE TO NEW ORLEANS. Text in English. 1999 (Dec.). irreg., latest 4th ed. USD 17.95 per issue (effective 2008). **Document type:** *Guide, Consumer.* **Description:** Travel guide focusing on the New Orleans area.
Formerly: How, When and Where in New Orleans
Published by: Pelican Publishing Co., 1000 Burmaster St., Gretna, LA 70053. TEL 504-368-1175, 800-843-1724, FAX 504-368-1195, editorial@pelicanpub.com, http://www.pelicanpub.com. Ed. Cecilia Casrill Dartez.

910.748 USA ISSN 0736-8127
F158.18
A MARMAC GUIDE TO PHILADELPHIA. Text in English. 2001 (July). irreg., latest 5th ed. USD 15.95 per issue (effective 2008). back issues avail. **Document type:** *Guide, Consumer.* **Description:** Travel guide focusing on Philadelphia.
Formerly (until 199?): How, When and Where in Philadelphia
Published by: Pelican Publishing Co., 1000 Burmaster St., Gretna, LA 70053. TEL 504-368-1175, 800-843-1724, FAX 504-368-1195, editorial@pelicanpub.com, http://www.pelicanpub.com. Eds. Judith Minkoff Pransky, Robert J Pransky.

910.91 764.351 USA ISSN 1545-1321
F394.S23
A MARMAC GUIDE TO SAN ANTONIO. Variant title: Guide to San Antonio. Text in English. 2001. irreg. USD 19.95 per issue (effective 2008). 552 p./no.; **Document type:** *Guide, Consumer.* **Description:** Offers candid descriptions of the numerous hotels, reviews of restaurants and their sample dishes, including those with the traditional Mexican and Tex-Mex fare, and lots of entertaining things to see and do around San Antonio.
Published by: Pelican Publishing Co., 1000 Burmaster St., Gretna, LA 70053. TEL 504-368-1175, 800-843-1724, FAX 504-368-1195, editorial@pelicanpub.com, http://www.pelicanpub.com. Ed. Yves Gerem.

790 352 FRA ISSN 1779-4226
LA MARNE, LE MAG. Text in French. 2006. bi-m. free. **Document type:** *Magazine, Consumer.*
Published by: Conseil General de la Marne, Hotel du Departement, 40 rue Carnot, Chalons-en-Champagne Cedex, 51038, France. TEL 33-3-26695151, FAX 33-3-26684633, communication@marne.fr.

917.404 USA
MARTHA'S VINEYARD BEST READ GUIDE. Text in English. m. (May-Oct). free (effective 2006). 40 p./no.; **Document type:** *Magazine, Consumer.* **Description:** Contains tourist information on Martha's Vineyard for visitors.
Published by: Vineyard Gazette Inc., PO Box 66, Edgartown, MA 02539-0066. TEL 508-627-4311, FAX 508-627-7444. Ed., Pub. Joe Pitt. Circ: 300,000 (free).

338.4791 917.29 MTQ ISSN 1953-5902
MARTINIQUE TOURISME. Text in French. 2006. m. **Document type:** *Magazine, Consumer.*
Published by: Comite Martiniquais du Tourisme, Immeuble Le Beaupre, Pointe de Jaham, Schoelcher, 97233, Martinique. TEL 596-616177, FAX 596-612772, infos.cmt@martiniquetourisme.com.

910.202 USA ISSN 1062-516X
MARYLAND MOTORIST. Text in English. 1920. every 45 days. USD 1. bk.rev.
Published by: Automobile Club of Mid Atlantic, c/o William Artland, 100 West Road, Ste. 304, Towson, MD 21204. TEL 301-462-4000, FAX 301-523-0380. Circ: 230,000.

910.09 ISR ISSN 0792-0571
MASSA AHER. Text in Hebrew. 1987. m. USD 45, ILS 144 (effective 2008). **Document type:** *Magazine, Consumer.* **Description:** Dedicated to the topics of geography and travel.
Related titles: Online - full text ed.: ILS 300 (effective 2008).
Published by: S B C Group, 8 Shefa Tal St., Tel Aviv, 67013, Israel. TEL 972-3-565-2100, FAX 972-3-562-6476, http://www.sbc.co.il/Index.asp. Eds. Gil El Ami, Moshe Gilad. Circ: 32,000.

338.4791 ISR
MASSA YISRE'ELI. Text in Hebrew. 2005. bi-m. USD 144 (effective 2008). **Document type:** *Magazine, Consumer.*
Related titles: Online - full text ed.
Published by: S B C Group, 8 Shefa Tal St., Tel Aviv, 67013, Israel. TEL 972-3-565-2100, FAX 972-3-562-6476, sherut@sbc.co.il, http://www.sbc.co.il/Index.asp.

917.44 910.2 USA ISSN 1550-6932
F64.6
MASSACHUSETTS CURIOSITIES; quirky characters, roadside oddities & other offbeat stuff. Text in English. 2005. biennial, latest 2008, 2nd ed. USD 13.95 per issue (effective 2008). back issues avail. **Document type:** *Guide, Consumer.* **Description:** Provides information about the wildest, wackiest, most outrageous people, places and things in Massachusetts.
Published by: The Globe Pequot Press, Inc., 246 Goose Ln, PO Box 480, Guilford, CT 06437. TEL 203-458-4500, 888-249-7586, FAX 203-458-4603, 800-820-2329, info@globepequot.com, http://www.globepequot.com. Ed. Jeff Serena TEL 203-458-4556.

910.01 USA
MASSACHUSETTS GETAWAY GUIDE. Text in English. 1993. a. adv. **Document type:** *Magazine, Consumer.* **Description:** Aims to promote and increase state tourism.
Formerly (until 1994): Massachusetts Summer Getaway Guide
Published by: (Massachusetts Office of Travel and Tourism), The Pohly Co., 99 Bedford St, Fl 5, Boston, MA 02111. TEL 617-451-1700, 800-383-0888, FAX 617-338-7767, info@pohlyco.com, http://www.pohlyco.com. adv.: color page USD 20,680.

MASSIF CENTRAL; le magazine du patrimoine, de l'histoire et de l'art de vivre. *see* GEOGRAPHY

916.8 ZWE
MASVINGO DIARY. Text in English. 1963. m. free. adv. illus. **Document type:** *Journal, Consumer.*
Formerly: Fort Victoria Diary
Published by: Masvingo Great Zimbabwe Publicity Association, PO Box 340, Masvingo, Zimbabwe. TEL 263-39-62643. Ed. Mrs. B Kanjanga. Circ: 2,500.

338.4 UAE
MATAR DUBAI AL-DAWLI/DUBAI INTERNATIONAL AIRPORT. Text in Arabic, English. 1987. bi-m. free. adv. **Document type:** *Magazine, Consumer.* **Description:** For airline passengers using Dubai airport.
Published by: Motivate Publishing, PO Box 2331, Dubai, United Arab Emirates. TEL 971-4-824060, FAX 971-4-824436. Ed. Obaid Humaid al-Tayer. Pub. Ian Fairservice. R&P Shawki Abd El Malik. Adv. contact Simon O'Herlihy. color page USD 3,150; trim 190 x 260. Circ: 30,000.

914 796.5 FIN ISSN 0789-1393
MATKAILU/TOURISM. Text in Finnish. 1982. 6/yr. adv. bk.rev. bibl.; illus.
Formerly (until 1990): Suomen Matkailu - Tourism of Finland (0359-0607); Which was formed by the merger of (1970-1982): Matkailumaailma (0025-5963); (1971-1982): Leirinta ja Retkeily (0356-0805); Which was formerly (until 1976): Leirintasanomat; (until 1975): Matkailu ja Retkeily
Related titles: Microfilm ed.
Published by: Suomen Matkailuliitto/Finnish Travel Association, Mikonkatu 25, Helsinki, 00100, Finland. Ed. Jussi Yrjola. Adv. contact Eija Niilo Raema. Circ: 30,000.

910 FIN ISSN 1456-419X
MATKAOPAS. Text in Finnish. 1998. 8/yr. EUR 57 (effective 2009). adv. **Document type:** *Magazine, Consumer.*
Published by: Sanoma Magazines Finland Corporation, Lapinmaentie 1, Helsinki, 00350, Finland. TEL 358-9-1201, FAX 358-9-1205171, info@sanomamagazines.fi, http://www.sanomamagazines.fi. Circ: 35,156 (paid).

338.4791 USA ISSN 1532-9526
G151
THE MATURE TRAVELER. Text in English. 2000. triennial. stat. **Document type:** *Monographic series, Trade.* **Description:** Provides trip characteristics and demographic information on the mature traveler market segment.
Published by: Travel Industry Association of America, 1100 New York Ave, NW, Ste 450, Washington, DC 20005. TEL 202-408-8422, FAX 202-408-1255, feedback@tia.org, http://www.tia.org.

919.69 USA ISSN 1937-9447
DU628.M3
MAUI REVEALED. Text in English. 2000. irreg. USD 16.95 per issue (effective 2008). **Document type:** *Guide, Consumer.*
Published by: Wizard Publications, Inc., PO Box 991, Lihue, HI 96766-0991. TEL 213-539-9213, aloha@wizardpub.com, http://www.wizardpub.com/main/home.html.

917.904 USA ISSN 0895-9390
MAUI UPDATE. Text in English. 1987. q. USD 15 (effective 2011). bk.rev. back issues avail. **Document type:** *Newsletter, Trade.* **Description:** Provides an overview of current island events of particular interest to the vacationer traveling to Maui, Hawaii.
Related titles: ◆ Supplement to: Paradise Family Guides: Maui. ISSN 1544-1377.
Published by: Paradise Publications, 8110 SW Wareham, Portland, OR 97223. Ed. Christie Stilson.

910.91 USA
MAUI VISITOR. Text in English. m. 80 p./no.; **Document type:** *Magazine, Consumer.*
Related titles: Online - full content ed.
Published by: Visitor Magazines LLC, 1498 Lower Main St, Ste F, Wailuku, HI 96793. http://www.visitormagazines.com/.

MAXIMUM TRAVEL PER DIEM ALLOWANCES FOR FOREIGN AREAS (ONLINE). *see* LAW

910.202 ITA ISSN 1825-2443
MEDITERRANEA. ADRIATIC SEA. Text in Italian. 2003. q. EUR 16 (effective 2009). **Document type:** *Magazine, Trade.*
Published by: Lunargento Srl, San Marco 2923, Venice, 30124, Italy. http://www.lunargento.it.

910.2 FRA ISSN 2108-8497
▼ **MEET AND TRAVEL MAG.** Text in French. 2010. bi-m. **Document type:** *Magazine, Trade.*
Published by: Editions Quatro, 32 Rue du Faubourg Poissonniere, Paris, 75010, France. TEL 33-1-75772163, FAX 33-6-69710004. Ed. Michel Foraud.

MEETING AND INCENTIVE TRAVEL. *see* MEETINGS AND CONGRESSES

MEETINGS & INCENTIVE TRAVEL. *see* MEETINGS AND CONGRESSES

060 381.1 USA
MEETINGS EAST. Text in English. 1999. 6/yr. free to qualified personnel (effective 2008). adv. back issues avail.; reprints avail. **Document type:** *Magazine, Trade.* **Description:** Delivers news, features and thorough destination information on the eastern United States and Canadian meetings markets.
Related titles: Supplement(s): Meetings Market Trends Survey.
Published by: Meetings Media (Subsidiary of: Stamats Business Media), 550 Montgomery St, Ste 750, San Francisco, CA 94111. TEL 800-358-0388, FAX 415-788-1358, tim.fixmer@stamatsbusinessmedia.com. Ed. Maria Lenhart. Pub. Gregg Anderson TEL 415-788-2005. adv.: color page USD 6,040, B&W page USD 5,040; trim 10.75 x 14.5. Circ: 22,046.

060 381.1 USA
MEETINGS MIDAMERICA. Text in English. 2004. 6/yr. free to qualified personnel (effective 2009). adv. back issues avail.; reprints avail. **Document type:** *Magazine, Trade.* **Description:** Delivers news, features and thorough destination information about the midwestern U.S. meetings market.
Related titles: Supplement(s): Meetings Market Trends Survey.
Published by: Meetings Media (Subsidiary of: Stamats Business Media), 550 Montgomery St, Ste 750, San Francisco, CA 94111. TEL 800-358-0388, FAX 415-788-1358, tim.fixmer@stamatsbusinessmedia.com. Ed. Maria Lenhart. Pub. Gregg Anderson TEL 415-788-2005. adv.: color page USD 5,780, B&W page USD 4,780; trim 10.75 x 14.5. Circ: 20,055.

060 381.1 USA
MEETINGS SOUTH. Text in English. 199?. m. free to qualified personnel (effective 2008). adv. 4 cols./p.; back issues avail.; reprints avail. **Document type:** *Magazine, Trade.* **Description:** Delivers news, features and thorough destination information on the southern United States, Caribbean and Islands and Mexico meetings markets.
Published by: Meetings Media (Subsidiary of: Stamats Business Media), 550 Montgomery St, Ste 750, San Francisco, CA 94111. TEL 800-358-0388, FAX 415-788-1358, tim.fixmer@stamatsbusinessmedia.com. Ed. Maria Lenhart. Pub. Karen Smith TEL 954-432-6028. Adv. contact Bill Freeman TEL 727-797-6020. color page USD 6,390, B&W page USD 5,390; trim 10.75 x 14.5. Circ: 25,027.

060 381.1 USA ISSN 1089-5930
MEETINGS WEST. Variant title: Meetings in the West. Text in English. 1987. m. free to qualified personnel (effective 2008). adv. 4 cols./p.; back issues avail.; reprints avail. **Document type:** *Magazine, Trade.* **Description:** Contains news, features and thorough destination information on the western United States, western Canada and Mexico meetings markets.
Former titles (until 199?): Meetings. California & the West (1086-0797); (until 1995): Meetings. California
Published by: Meetings Media (Subsidiary of: Stamats Business Media), 550 Montgomery St, Ste 750, San Francisco, CA 94111. TEL 800-358-0388, FAX 415-788-1358, tim.fixmer@stamatsbusinessmedia.com. Ed. Maria Lenhart. Pub. Lynne Richardson. Adv. contact Shawne Hightower. color page USD 7,590, B&W page USD 6,590; trim 10.75 x 14.5. Circ: 31,010.

614.86 DEU
MEINE GESUNDHEIT. Text in German. 1981. 6/yr. adv. **Document type:** *Magazine, Consumer.*
Published by: Otto Hoffmanns Verlag GmbH, Arnulfstr 10, Munich, 80335, Germany. TEL 49-89-5458450, FAX 49-89-54584530, info@ohv-online.de. Ed. Kirsten Westphal. Adv. contact Edeltraud Koller. B&W page EUR 7,210, color page EUR 9,010; trim 130 x 188. Circ: 350,000 (controlled).

910.02 NLD
MERIDIAN TRAVEL. Text in Dutch. 2007. q. EUR 24.50; EUR 6.25 newsstand/cover (effective 2009). adv. **Document type:** *Magazine, Consumer.*
Formed by the merger of (1998-2006): Backpackers (1389-322X); Which incorporated (in 1999): On Track (1566-8126); (2004-2007): Meridian (1572-7483); Which was formerly (until 2003): Meridian & Voyager (1571-5248); Which was formed by the merger of (1995-2003): Voyager (1383-7338); (1990-2003): Meridian International (0926-9525); Which was formerly (until 1991): Transfer (0924-9796)
Published by: dOrizon Media, Postbus 135, Castricum, 1900 AC, Netherlands. TEL 31-251-672136, FAX 31-251-654578, info@dorizon.nl, http://www.dorizon.nl. Circ: 20,000.

647.94 ITA ISSN 1120-804X
MERIDIANI. Text in Italian. 1988. 10/yr. EUR 62 (effective 2009). adv. **Document type:** *Magazine, Consumer.*
—CCC.
Published by: Editoriale Domus, Via Gianni Mazzocchi 1/3, Rozzano, MI 20089, Italy. TEL 39-02-824721, editorialedomus@edidomus.it. Circ: 70,000.

647.94 ITA ISSN 1824-2723
MERIDIANI. LE GRANDI VIE. Text in Italian. 2004. m. **Document type:** *Magazine, Consumer.*
Published by: Editoriale Domus, Via Gianni Mazzocchi 1/3, Rozzano, MI 20089, Italy. TEL 39-02-824721, editorialedomus@edidomus.it, http://www.edidomus.it.

MERIDIANI MONTAGNE. *see* SPORTS AND GAMES—Outdoor Life

796.552 ITA ISSN 1825-5175
MERIDIANI MONTAGNE. GLI SPECIALI. Text in Italian. 2005. bi-m. **Document type:** *Magazine, Consumer.*
Published by: Editoriale Domus, Via Gianni Mazzocchi 1/3, Rozzano, MI 20089, Italy. TEL 39-02-824721, editorialedomus@edidomus.it, http://www.edidomus.it.

MERIDIANI MONTAGNE. RIFUGI E BIVACCHI. *see* SPORTS AND GAMES—Outdoor Life

MERIDIJANI. *see* GEOGRAPHY

910.91 ISR
METAYYELIM. Text in Hebrew. 1999. bi-m. ILS 144 (effective 2008). **Document type:** *Magazine, Consumer.*
Related titles: Online - full text ed.: ILS 144 (effective 2008).
Published by: S B C Group, 8 Shefa Tal St., Tel Aviv, 67013, Israel. TEL 972-3-565-2100, FAX 972-3-562-6476, sherut@sbc.co.il, http://www.sbc.co.il/Index.asp.

910.91 USA ISSN 1934-4961
METRO (MINNEAPOLIS). Variant title: Twin Cities Metropolitan. Text in English. 2006. m. USD 12 (effective 2008). adv. back issues avail.; reprints avail. **Document type:** *Magazine, Consumer.* **Description:** Provides information about the need-to-know people, places and things that make Minneapolis and St. Paul great.
Published by: Tiger Oak Publications, Inc., OneTiger Oak Plz, 900 S Third St, Minneapolis, MN 55415. TEL 612-548-3180, FAX 612-548-3181, http://www.tigeroak.com. Pub. R Craig Bednar. Adv. contact Heidi Zeto TEL 612-548-3278. Circ: 30,000 (paid and controlled).

917.91 USA ISSN 1543-8902
METRO (SCOTTSDALE); people places Phoenix. Text in English. 2003 (Apr./May). bi-m. USD 15 (effective 2004).
Published by: Metro Media Group, LLC, 2400 E. Arizona Biltmore Cir., Ste. 1170, Phoenix, AZ 85016-2108. Ed. Leigh Flayton.

910.202 GBR ISSN 0965-5492
F1209
MEXICO AND CENTRAL AMERICA HANDBOOK (YEAR). Text in English. 1990. a. GBP 16.99 per issue (effective 2010). adv. maps. back issues avail. **Document type:** *Handbook/Manual/Guide, Consumer.* **Description:** Covers all the basics from where to stay and where to eat to cycling, walking and how to get around the Mexico and Central America.
—CCC.
Published by: Footprint Handbooks Ltd., 6 Riverside Ct, Lower Bristol Rd, Bath, Avon BA2 3DZ, United Kingdom. TEL 44-1225-469141, FAX 44-1225-469461, wwwinfo@footprintbooks.com.

917.204 647 MEX
MEXICO CITY DAILY BULLETIN. Text in English. 1936. d. free domestic. adv. bk.rev.; film rev.; music rev.; play rev. 25 p./no. 2 cols./p.; back issues avail. **Document type:** *Newspaper.* **Description:** Provides English-speaking visitors information of major international happenings as well as information on sites of interest in their own language. Includes local news.
Published by: Edit S.A. de C.V., GOMEZ FARIAS 41, Col San Rafael, Mexico City, DF 06470, Mexico. TEL 52-5-5465115, FAX 52-5-5356060. Ed. Raul Paredes Parra. Pub. Gabriel Paredes Mercado. Adv. contact Martha Estrella Rodriguez. Circ: 10,000 (controlled).

917.2 MEX ISSN 0187-1560
F1216
MEXICO DESCONOCIDO. Text in Spanish. 1976. m. MXN 240 domestic; USD 60 in United States; USD 70 in Europe; USD 80 elsewhere (effective 2003). adv. illus. Index. back issues avail.; reprints avail. **Document type:** *Consumer.* **Description:** Dedicated to the prehistory and history of Mexico. Includes articles on the antiquities, natural wonders, hidden corners, cultural events and cuisine of Mexico.
Related titles: Online - full text ed.: ISSN 1605-4148. 1996.
Published by: Editorial Mexico Desconocido S.A.de C.V., Monte Pelvoux 110, Planta Jardin, Lomas de Chapultepec, Delegacion Miguel Hidalgo, Mexico City, DF 11000, Mexico. TEL 52-5-5404040, FAX 52-5-5401771. Ed. Beatriz Quintanar Hinojosa. Circ: 64,000.

910.2 381.1 USA
MEXICO MEETING & INCENTIVE PLANNER. Text in English. 2000. a. free to qualified personnel (effective 2011). **Document type:** *Handbook/Manual/Guide, Trade.* **Description:** Provides information about properties, destinations, destination management companies, convention facilities plus handy tips about doing business in Mexico.
Formerly (until 20??): Official Mexico Meeting and Incentive Planner
Related titles: Online - full text ed.: free (effective 2011).
Published by: Worth International Media Group, 5979 NW 151 St, Ste 120, Miami Lakes, FL 33014. TEL 305-828-0123, FAX 305-826-6950, info@worthit.com, http//www.worthit.com.

917.204 MEX ISSN 0462-1069
THE MEXICO NEWS. Text in Spanish. 1962. m. USD 60. adv. bk.rev. **Document type:** *Trade.*
Published by: (Mexican Journalist Association), Editorial Bonanza S. de R.L., DR VELASCO 95, Ed. 5 Of. 203, Col Doctores Del. Cuauhtemoc, Mexico City, DF 06720, Mexico. TEL 525-5938720, FAX 525-7052492. Ed. Mario Perez Morales. Circ: 10,000.

910.2 USA
MEXICO TRAVELER. Text in English. 2005. a. maps. 148 p./no. 3 cols./p.; **Document type:** *Magazine, Consumer.*
Published by: I M C Publications, PO Box 210485, Chula Vista, CA 91921-0485. TEL 619-216-8035, FAX 619-216-8036. Ed., Pub. Mayte Rodriguez-Cedillo. Adv. contact Isa Calva TEL 619-216-8035.

917.5938 051 USA ISSN 1547-1756
MIAMI LIVING. Text in English. 2003 (Win.). q. USD 32 (effective 2004). adv. **Document type:** *Magazine, Consumer.* **Description:** Features practical advice for anyone who is interested in living in Florida or enjoying Miami's unique cultural opportunities.
Published by: Miami Living Magazine, 1655 Drexel Ave. Ste. 214, Miami Beach, FL 33139. TEL 305-538-4282, FAX 305-538-4280. adv.: B&W page USD 4,700, color page USD 8,500; trim 8.25 x 10.875.

MIAMI METRO CITY GUIDE. *see* GENERAL INTEREST PERIODICALS—United States

914 FRA
MICHELIN GREEN GUIDES: ATLANTIC COAST. Text in English. irreg. **Document type:** *Handbook/Manual/Guide, Consumer.*
Published by: Michelin, 46 Av de Breteuil, Paris, Cedex 7 75234, France. **Dist. in U.S. by:** Michelin Travel Publications, PO Box 19008, Greenville, SC 29602-9008. TEL 800-423-0485.

914.36 FRA
MICHELIN GREEN GUIDES: AUSTRIA. Text in English. irreg., latest 1997. **Document type:** *Handbook/Manual/Guide, Consumer.*
Related titles: Spanish ed.
Published by: Michelin, 46 Av de Breteuil, Paris, Cedex 7 75234, France. **Dist. in U.S. by:** Michelin Travel Publications, PO Box 19008, Greenville, SC 29602-9008. TEL 800-423-0485.

914.404 FRA
MICHELIN GREEN GUIDES: BELGIUM - GRAND DUCHY OF LUXEMBOURG. Text in English. irreg. **Document type:** *Handbook/Manual/Guide, Consumer.*
Supersedes: Michelin Green Guide Series: Belgique - Luxembourg

Related titles: French ed.
Published by: Michelin, 46 Av de Breteuil, Paris, Cedex 7 75234, France. **Dist. in U.S. by:** Michelin Travel Publications, PO Box 19008, Greenville, SC 29602-9008. TEL 800-423-0485.

917.9 FRA
MICHELIN GREEN GUIDES: CALIFORNIA. Text in English. irreg., latest 1997. **Document type:** *Handbook/Manual/Guide, Consumer.*
Related titles: French ed.
Published by: Michelin, 46 Av de Breteuil, Paris, Cedex 7 75234, France. **Dist. in U.S. by:** Michelin Travel Publications, PO Box 19008, Greenville, SC 29602-9008. TEL 800-423-0485.

917.104 FRA
MICHELIN GREEN GUIDES: CANADA. Text in English. irreg., latest 1996. **Document type:** *Handbook/Manual/Guide, Consumer.*
Related titles: French ed.
Published by: Michelin, 46 Av de Breteuil, Paris, Cedex 7 75234, France. **Dist. in U.S. by:** Michelin Travel Publications, PO Box 19008, Greenville, SC 29602-9008. TEL 800-423-0485.

917.7 FRA
MICHELIN GREEN GUIDES: CHICAGO. Text in English. irreg. **Document type:** *Handbook/Manual/Guide, Consumer.*
Published by: Michelin, 46 Av de Breteuil, Paris, Cedex 7 75234, France. **Dist. in U.S. by:** Michelin Travel Publications, PO Box 19008, Greenville, SC 29602-9008. TEL 800-423-0485.

914 FRA ISSN 0763-1383
DF716
MICHELIN GREEN GUIDES: EUROPE. Text in English. 19??. irreg. **Document type:** *Handbook/Manual/Guide, Consumer.*
Related titles: Spanish ed.: Guia Turistica. ISSN 0764-1478. 198?.
—CCC.
Published by: Michelin, 46 Av de Breteuil, Paris, Cedex 7 75234, France. TEL 33-1-45661234, http://www.michelin.fr. **Dist. in U.S. by:** Michelin Travel Publications, PO Box 19008, Greenville, SC 29602-9008. TEL 800-423-0485.

917.5 FRA
MICHELIN GREEN GUIDES: FLORIDA. Text in English. irreg. **Document type:** *Handbook/Manual/Guide, Consumer.*
Related titles: French ed.
Published by: Michelin, 46 Av de Breteuil, Paris, Cedex 7 75234, France. **Dist. in U.S. by:** Michelin Travel Publications, PO Box 19008, Greenville, SC 29602-9008. TEL 800-423-0485.

914.3 FRA
MICHELIN GREEN GUIDES: GERMANY. Text in English. irreg., latest 2002. **Document type:** *Handbook/Manual/Guide, Consumer.*
Published by: Michelin, 46 Av de Breteuil, Paris, Cedex 7 75234, France. **Dist. in U.S. by:** Michelin Travel Publications, PO Box 19008, Greenville, SC 29602-9008. TEL 800-423-0485.

914.2 FRA
MICHELIN GREEN GUIDES: GREAT BRITAIN. Text in English. irreg., latest 1997. **Document type:** *Handbook/Manual/Guide, Consumer.*
Published by: Michelin, 46 Av de Breteuil, Paris, Cedex 7 75234, France. **Dist. in U.S. by:** Michelin Travel Publications, PO Box 19008, Greenville, SC 29602-9008. TEL 800-423-0485.

914.9 FRA
MICHELIN GREEN GUIDES: GREECE. Text in English. irreg., latest 1998. **Document type:** *Handbook/Manual/Guide, Consumer.*
Published by: Michelin, 46 Av de Breteuil, Paris, Cedex 7 75234, France. **Dist. in U.S. by:** Michelin Travel Publications, PO Box 19008, Greenville, SC 29602-9008. TEL 800-423-0485.

914.1 FRA
MICHELIN GREEN GUIDES: IRELAND. Text in English. irreg., latest 1997. **Document type:** *Handbook/Manual/Guide, Consumer.*
Published by: Michelin, 46 Av de Breteuil, Paris, Cedex 7 75234, France. **Dist. in U.S. by:** Michelin Travel Publications, PO Box 19008, Greenville, SC 29602-9008. TEL 800-423-0485.

914.5 FRA
MICHELIN GREEN GUIDES: ITALY. Text in English. irreg. **Document type:** *Handbook/Manual/Guide, Consumer.*
Related titles: Spanish ed.
Published by: Michelin, 46 Av de Breteuil, Paris, Cedex 7 75234, France. **Dist. in U.S. by:** Michelin Travel Publications, PO Box 19008, Greenville, SC 29602-9008. TEL 800-423-0485.

914.204 FRA
MICHELIN GREEN GUIDES: LONDON. Text in English. irreg., latest 1997. **Document type:** *Handbook/Manual/Guide, Consumer.*
Related titles: ◆ French ed.: Guide Vert: Londres; Spanish ed.
Published by: Michelin, 46 Av de Breteuil, Paris, Cedex 7 75234, France. **Dist. in U.S. by:** Michelin Travel Publications, PO Box 19008, Greenville, SC 29602-9008. TEL 800-423-0485.

917.204 FRA
MICHELIN GREEN GUIDES: MEXICO. Text in English. irreg., latest 1999. **Document type:** *Handbook/Manual/Guide, Consumer.*
Formerly: Michelin Green Guide Series: Mexico
Related titles: Spanish ed.; French ed.
Published by: Michelin, 46 Av de Breteuil, Paris, Cedex 7 75234, France. **Dist. in U.S. by:** Michelin Travel Publications, PO Box 19008, Greenville, SC 29602-9008. TEL 800-423-0485.

914.904 FRA
MICHELIN GREEN GUIDES: NETHERLANDS. Text in English. irreg. **Document type:** *Handbook/Manual/Guide, Consumer.*
Published by: Michelin, 46 Av de Breteuil, Paris, Cedex 7 75234, France. **Dist. in U.S. by:** Michelin Travel Publications, PO Box 19008, Greenville, SC 29602-9008. TEL 800-423-0485.

917.404 FRA
MICHELIN GREEN GUIDES: NEW ENGLAND. Text in English. irreg., latest 1997. **Document type:** *Handbook/Manual/Guide, Consumer.*
Related titles: French ed.
Published by: Michelin, 46 Av de Breteuil, Paris, Cedex 7 75234, France. **Dist. in U.S. by:** Michelin Travel Publications, PO Box 19008, Greenville, SC 29602-9008. TEL 800-423-0485.

917.4 FRA
MICHELIN GREEN GUIDES: NEW YORK CITY. Text in English. irreg., latest 1997. **Document type:** *Handbook/Manual/Guide, Consumer.*
Related titles: French ed.
Published by: Michelin, 46 Av de Breteuil, Paris, Cedex 7 75234, France. **Dist. in U.S. by:** Michelin Travel Publications, PO Box 19008, Greenville, SC 29602-9008. TEL 800-423-0485.

914.4 FRA
MICHELIN GREEN GUIDES: NORMANDY. Text in English. irreg., latest 1996. **Document type:** *Handbook/Manual/Guide, Consumer.*
Published by: Michelin, 46 Av de Breteuil, Paris, Cedex 7 75234, France. **Dist. in U.S. by:** Michelin Travel Publications, PO Box 19008, Greenville, SC 29602-9008. TEL 800-423-0485.

914 FRA
MICHELIN GREEN GUIDES: NORTHERN FRANCE. Text in English. irreg., latest 1997. **Document type:** *Monographic series, Consumer.*
Formerly: Michelin Green Guide Series: Flanders, Picardy and Paris Region
Published by: Michelin, 46 Av de Breteuil, Paris, Cedex 7 75234, France. **Dist. in the U.S. by:** Michelin Travel Publications, PO Box 19008, Greenville, SC 29602-9008. TEL 800-423-0485.

914.69 FRA
MICHELIN GREEN GUIDES: PORTUGAL. Text in English. irreg., latest 1998. **Document type:** *Handbook/Manual/Guide, Consumer.*
Related titles: Spanish ed.
Published by: Michelin, 46 Av de Breteuil, Paris, Cedex 7 75234, France. **Dist. in U.S. by:** Michelin Travel Publications, PO Box 19008, Greenville, SC 29602-9008. TEL 800-423-0485.

917.1 FRA
MICHELIN GREEN GUIDES: QUEBEC. Text in English. irreg. **Document type:** *Handbook/Manual/Guide, Consumer.*
Formerly: Michelin Green Guide Series: Quebec Province
Related titles: French ed.
Published by: Michelin, 46 Av de Breteuil, Paris, Cedex 7 75234, France. **Dist. in U.S. by:** Michelin Travel Publications, PO Box 19008, Greenville, SC 29602-9008. TEL 800-423-0485.

914.404 FRA
MICHELIN GREEN GUIDES: ROME. Text in English. 1985. irreg. **Document type:** *Handbook/Manual/Guide, Consumer.*
Published by: Michelin, 46 Av de Breteuil, Paris, Cedex 7 75234, France. **Dist. in U.S. by:** Michelin Travel Publications, PO Box 19008, Greenville, SC 29602-9008. TEL 800-423-0485.

917.9 FRA
MICHELIN GREEN GUIDES: SAN FRANCISCO. Text in English. irreg. **Document type:** *Handbook/Manual/Guide, Consumer.*
Related titles: French ed.
Published by: Michelin, 46 Av de Breteuil, Paris, Cedex 7 75234, France.

914.8 FRA
MICHELIN GREEN GUIDES: SCANDINAVIA - FINLAND. Text in English. irreg., latest 1996. **Document type:** *Handbook/Manual/Guide, Consumer.*
Related titles: French ed.
Published by: Michelin, 46 Av de Breteuil, Paris, Cedex 7 75234, France. **Dist. in U.S. by:** Michelin Travel Publications, PO Box 19008, Greenville, SC 29602-9008. TEL 800-423-0485.

914.104 FRA
MICHELIN GREEN GUIDES: SCOTLAND. Text in English. irreg. **Document type:** *Handbook/Manual/Guide, Consumer.*
Related titles: French ed.
Published by: Michelin, 46 Av de Breteuil, Paris, Cedex 7 75234, France. **Dist. in U.S. by:** Michelin Travel Publications, PO Box 19008, Greenville, SC 29602-9008. TEL 800-423-0485.

914.9 FRA
MICHELIN GREEN GUIDES: SICILY. Text in English. 1998. irreg. **Document type:** *Handbook/Manual/Guide, Consumer.*
Published by: Michelin, 46 Av de Breteuil, Paris, Cedex 7 75234, France. **Dist. in U.S. by:** Michelin Travel Publications, PO Box 19008, Greenville, SC 29602-9008. TEL 800-423-0485.

914.6 FRA
MICHELIN GREEN GUIDES: SPAIN. Text in English. irreg., latest 1996. **Document type:** *Handbook/Manual/Guide, Consumer.*
Related titles: Spanish ed.
Published by: Michelin, 46 Av de Breteuil, Paris, Cedex 7 75234, France. **Dist. in U.S. by:** Michelin Travel Publications, PO Box 19008, Greenville, SC 29602-9008. TEL 800-423-0485.

914.94 FRA
MICHELIN GREEN GUIDES: SWITZERLAND. Text in English. 1988. irreg., latest 1997. **Document type:** *Handbook/Manual/Guide, Consumer.*
Published by: Michelin, 46 Av de Breteuil, Paris, Cedex 7 75234, France. **Dist. in U.S. by:** Michelin Travel Publications, PO Box 19008, Greenville, SC 29602-9008. TEL 800-423-0485.

915.9 FRA
MICHELIN GREEN GUIDES: THAILAND. Text in English. 1997. irreg. **Document type:** *Handbook/Manual/Guide, Consumer.*
Related titles: French ed.
Published by: Michelin, 46 Av de Breteuil, Paris, Cedex 7 75234, France. **Dist. in the U.S. by:** Michelin Travel Publications, PO Box 19008, Greenville, SC 29602-9008. TEL 800-423-0485.

914 FRA
MICHELIN GREEN GUIDES: TUSCANY. Text in English. 1996. irreg. **Document type:** *Handbook/Manual/Guide, Consumer.*
Published by: Michelin, 46 Av de Breteuil, Paris, Cedex 7 75234, France. **Dist. in U.S. by:** Michelin Travel Publications, PO Box 19008, Greenville, SC 29602-9008. TEL 800-423-0485.

914.5 FRA
MICHELIN GREEN GUIDES: VENICE. Text in English. irreg. **Document type:** *Handbook/Manual/Guide, Consumer.*
Related titles: French ed.
Published by: Michelin, 46 Av de Breteuil, Paris, Cedex 7 75234, France. **Dist. in the U.S. by:** Michelin Travel Publications, PO Box 19008, Greenville, SC 29602-9008. TEL 800-423-0485.

917.4 FRA
MICHELIN GREEN GUIDES: WASHINGTON, D.C. Text in English. irreg., latest 1997. **Document type:** *Handbook/Manual/Guide, Consumer.*
Published by: Michelin, 46 Av de Breteuil, Paris, Cedex 7 75234, France. **Dist. in U.S. by:** Michelin Travel Publications, PO Box 19008, Greenville, SC 29602-9008. TEL 800-423-0485.

910.2 914 FRA
MICHELIN GUIDES ROUGES: BENELUX. Text in French. a. **Document type:** *Consumer.*
Published by: Michelin, 46 Av de Breteuil, Paris, Cedex 7 75234, France. **Dist. in U.S. by:** Michelin Travel Publications, PO Box 19008, Greenville, SC 29602-9008. TEL 800-423-0485.

910.2 914 FRA
MICHELIN GUIDES ROUGES: DEUTSCHLAND. Text in German. a. **Document type:** *Consumer.*
Published by: Michelin, 46 Av de Breteuil, Paris, Cedex 7 75234, France. **Dist. in U.S. by:** Michelin Travel Publications, PO Box 19008, Greenville, SC 29602-9008. TEL 800-423-0485.

910.2 914 FRA
MICHELIN GUIDES ROUGES: ESPANA & PORTUGAL. Text in French. a. **Document type:** *Consumer.*
Published by: Michelin, 46 Av de Breteuil, Paris, Cedex 7 75234, France. **Dist. in U.S. by:** Michelin Travel Publications, PO Box 19008, Greenville, SC 29602-9008. TEL 800-423-0485.

914.04 FRA
MICHELIN GUIDES ROUGES: EUROPE (MAIN CITIES). Text in French. a. **Document type:** *Consumer.*
Published by: Michelin, 46 Av de Breteuil, Paris, Cedex 7 75234, France. **Dist. in U.S. by:** Michelin Travel Publications, PO Box 19008, Greenville, SC 29602-9008. TEL 800-423-0485.

910.2 914 FRA
MICHELIN GUIDES ROUGES: FRANCE. Text in French. a. **Document type:** *Consumer.*
Published by: Michelin, 46 Av de Breteuil, Paris, Cedex 7 75234, France. **Dist. in U.S. by:** Michelin Travel Publications, PO Box 19008, Greenville, SC 29602-9008. TEL 800-423-0485.

914.204 FRA
MICHELIN GUIDES ROUGES: GREAT BRITAIN AND IRELAND. Text in French. a. **Document type:** *Consumer.*
Published by: Michelin, 46 Av de Breteuil, Paris, Cedex 7 75234, France. **Dist. in U.S. by:** Michelin Travel Publications, PO Box 19008, Greenville, SC 29602-9008. TEL 800-423-0485.

914 FRA
MICHELIN GUIDES ROUGES: ITALIA. Text in English, French, German, Italian. a. **Document type:** *Handbook/Manual/Guide, Consumer.*
Published by: Michelin, 46 Av de Breteuil, Paris, Cedex 7 75234, France. **Dist. in U.S. by:** Michelin Travel Publications, PO Box 19008, Greenville, SC 29602-9008. TEL 800-423-0485.

914.21 FRA
MICHELIN GUIDES ROUGES: LONDON. Text in English. a. **Document type:** *Handbook/Manual/Guide, Consumer.*
Formerly: Michelin Red Guide Series: Greater London
Published by: Michelin, 46 Av de Breteuil, Paris, Cedex 7 75234, France. **Dist. in U.S. by:** Michelin Travel Publications, PO Box 19008, Greenville, SC 29602-9008. TEL 800-423-0485.

910.2 914 FRA
MICHELIN GUIDES ROUGES: PARIS ET ENVIRONS. Text in French. a. **Document type:** *Consumer.*
Formerly: Michelin Red Guide Series: Paris (0076-7794)
Published by: Michelin, 46 Av de Breteuil, Paris, Cedex 7 75234, France. **Dist. in U.S. by:** Michelin Travel Publications, PO Box 19008, Greenville, SC 29602-9008. TEL 800-423-0485.

910.2 FRA ISSN 1772-5100
MICHELIN VOYAGER PRATIQUE. Variant title: Voyager Pratique. Text in French. 2005. irreg. **Document type:** *Monographic series, Consumer.*
Related titles: ◆ Spanish ed.: Descubre. ISSN 1954-8893.
Published by: Michelin, 46 Av de Breteuil, Paris, Cedex 7 75234, France. TEL 33-1-45661234.

MICHIGAN MAGAZINE. *see* HISTORY—History Of North And South America

917.04 USA ISSN 1099-4203
TX907.3.M53
THE MID-ATLANTIC'S BEST BED & BREAKFASTS. Text in English. 1992. irreg. USD 14.
Formerly (until 1993): Fodor's Bed and Breakfasts and Country Inns and Other Weekend Pleasures: The Mid-Atlantic Region (1099-4211)
Published by: Fodor's Travel Publications, Inc. (Subsidiary of: Random House Inc.), 1745 Broadway, 15th Fl, New York, NY 10019. TEL 212-572-2313, editors@fodors.com, http://www.fodors.com. **Dist. by:** Random House Inc.

915.6 UAE ISSN 0140-8321
MIDDLE EAST TRAVEL. Text in English. 1977. bi-m. USD 35 (effective 1998). adv. bk.rev. illus.; stat. back issues avail. **Document type:** *Magazine, Trade.* **Description:** Includes travel agents, tour operators, airlines, and motels.
Related titles: Microfilm ed.
Address: P O Box 6655, Dubai, United Arab Emirates. TEL 971-4-2096388, FAX 971-4-720440, TELEX 924505-LOCLON-G. Ed. Katmi Everdem. Pub., Adv. contact Alan Le Coyte. page USD 3,300. Circ: 5,700 (controlled).

915.6 LBN ISSN 1991-2412
MIDDLE EAST TRAVEL. Text in English. 1977. bi-m. adv. **Document type:** *Magazine, Trade.*
Published by: Al-Iktissad Wal-Aamal, Hamra, PO Box 113-6194, Beirut, 1103 2100, Lebanon. TEL 961-1-780200, FAX 961-1-780206, info@iktissad.com. adv.: page USD 4,800. Circ: 26,760 (paid and controlled).

910.91 CAN ISSN 1719-4512
MIDDLESEX, WE'RE ON THE WAY!. Text in English. 2004. a., latest 2006. **Document type:** *Magazine, Consumer.*
Published by: Community Futures Development Corporation of Middlesex County, Kilworth Business Park, 22423 Jefferies Rd, Unit 6, R.R. 5 Komoka, ON N0L 1R0, Canada. TEL 519-641-6100, 866-205-1188, FAX 519-641-6288, info@cfdcmiddlesex.on.ca.

MIDWEST TRAVELER. *see* TRANSPORTATION—Automobiles

910 USA ISSN 0361-1361
GV1024
THE MILEPOST. Text in English. 1948. a. USD 29.95 per issue (effective 2009). charts; illus.; stat. **Document type:** *Magazine, Consumer.* **Description:** Designed to be a guide to the highways, roads, ferries, lodgings, recreation, sightseeing attractions and services along the Alaska Highway to and within Alaska, including Alberta, British Columbia, Northwest Territories and the Yukon.
Published by: Morris Multimedia, Inc., 301 Arctic Slope Ave, Ste 300, Anchorage, AK 99518. TEL 907-272-6070, FAX 907-275-2117, books@themilepost.com, http://www.morris.com/. Adv. contact Shay Motsinger TEL 907-275-2115.

TU

MILITARY LIVING'S R & R REPORT; the voice of the military traveler. *see* MILITARY

355 USA ISSN 1056-3989
MILITARY TRAVEL GUIDE. Text in English. 19??. m. USD 24.05 (effective 2008). adv. **Document type:** *Directory, Trade.* **Description:** Helps military personnel and their families save money per day on billeting, recreation and Space-A-Flights at US and overseas military facilities.
Published by: Military Living Publications, PO Box 2347, Falls Church, VA 22042-0347. TEL 703-237-0203, FAX 703-997-8861, customerservice@militaryliving.com, http://www.militaryliving.com. Circ: 40,000.

919 637.1 AUS ISSN 1837-9001
▼ **MILK GIPPSLAND.** Text in English. 2010. bi-m. AUD 30 (effective 2011). adv. **Document type:** *Magazine, Consumer.* **Description:** Focuses on events and activities, entertainment, food and wine, destinations, local products and fascinating people.
Published by: Media Mantra, PO Box 353, Traralgon, VIC 3844, Australia. TEL 61-3-51942381, FAX 61-3-86783192.

910.19 USA
MILLENIUM TRAVEL GUIDE GEORGIA. Text in English. 2001. a. USD 4.99 newsstand/cover (effective 2001). adv. **Document type:** *Magazine, Consumer.*
Published by: Georgia Department of Industry, Trade & Tourism, Box 1776, Atlanta, GA 30301. TEL 404-656-3710, FAX 404-657-5689, http://www.georgia.org.

918.2 ARG ISSN 1851-4847
MINI GUIA TURISTICA BILINGUE NEUQUEN. Text in Spanish. 2006. s-a.
Published by: Editorial Patagonia Activa, Carlos H. Rodriguez 260 1er Piso, Neuquen, Patagonia, Argentina. TEL 54-299-4474333, editorial@patagoniaactiva.com.ar, http://www.patagoniaactiva.com.ar/editorial/index.php. Ed. Dario Hernan Irigaray.

914.6 ESP ISSN 1137-4713
MINI GUIAS EDITUR. Text in Spanish. 1994. irreg. **Document type:** *Magazine, Consumer.*
Related titles: ◆ Supplement to: Editur. ISSN 1134-6469.
Published by: Ediciones Turisticas, S.A., C. Consejo de Ciento 355 Piso 3o, Barcelona, 08007, Spain. TEL 34-93-4670229, FAX 34-93-4670218, direccion@editur.es, http://www.editur.com.

977 USA
MINNESOTA EXPLORER. Text in English. 3/yr. includes scbr. with Star Tribune. adv. **Document type:** *Newspaper, Consumer.* **Description:** Describes scenic, cultural, and other noteworthy areas and destinations in the state of Minnesota.
Published by: Minnesota Office of Tourism, 121 Seventh Pl E, Metro Sq, Ste 100, St. Paul, MN 55101. TEL 651-296-5029, 800-657-3700, FAX 651-296-7095, explore@state.mn.us, http://www.exploreminnesota.com. adv.: color page USD 2,024.

977 USA
MINNESOTA TRAVEL GUIDE. Text in English. 1997. a. free (effective 2009). illus. **Document type:** *Guide, Consumer.* **Description:** Provides the tourist with information on activities and destinations in the state of Minnesota.
Published by: Minnesota Office of Tourism, 121 Seventh Pl E, Metro Sq, Ste 100, St. Paul, MN 55101. TEL 651-296-5029, 800-868-7476, FAX 651-296-7095, explore@state.mn.us.

908 LTU ISSN 1392-0154
MINSK IN YOUR POCKET. Text in English. 1994. a. USD 5 newsstand/cover (effective 2002). adv. **Document type:** *Magazine, Consumer.*
Published by: Vilnius In Your Pocket, Vokieciu Gatve 10-15, Vilnius, 2001, Lithuania. TEL 370-2-222976, FAX 370-2-222982, vilnius@inyourpocket.com, http://www.inyourpocket.com.

917.704 USA
MISSOURI TRAVEL GUIDE. Text in English. 1968. a. free. **Document type:** *Magazine, Consumer.*
Former titles (until 1996): Missouri Getaway Travel Guide; (until 1993): Missouri Vacation Planner
Related titles: Online - full text ed.
Published by: California Tourism, Truman State Office Building, Box 1055, Jefferson City, MO 65102. TEL 573-751-4133, FAX 573-751-5160. Ed., R&P Jim Murphy. adv.: page USD 20,000; trim 11 x 8.5.

647.94 028.5 DEU
MITTENDRIN (DETMOLD). Text in German. 1920; N.S. 1950. bi-m. adv. bk.rev. **Document type:** *Newsletter, Consumer.* **Description:** Provides news and information for the staff of the German Youth Hostel Association.
Former titles: D J H; Jugendherbergswerk; Wir Herbergs Freunde (0043-597X)
Published by: Deutsches Jugendherbergswerk, Hauptverband fuer Jugendwandern und Jugendherbergen, Leonardo-da-Vinci-Weg 1, Detmold, 32760, Germany. TEL 49-5231-99360, FAX 49-5231-993666, service@djh.de, http://www.jugendherberge.de. Ed. Bernd Dohn. adv.: color page EUR 900; trim 210 x 297. Circ: 5,500 (controlled).

910.09 USA
MOBIL MOTORIST. Text in English. 1981. q. USD 2. adv. **Document type:** *Magazine, Consumer.*
Published by: (Mobil Auto Club), Signature Group, 200 N Martingale Rd, Schaumburg, IL 60173-2096. TEL 847-605-3000. Ed. Bruce Gorman.

910.91 DEU
MOBIL SZENE AKTUELL. Text in German. q. EUR 6.40; EUR 1.60 newsstand/cover (effective 2007). adv. **Document type:** *Magazine, Consumer.*
Published by: Reisemobil Union e.V., Koempel 2, Morsbach, 51597, Germany. TEL 49-2294-900551, FAX 49-2294-900587, praesidium@reisemobil-union.de. adv.: B&W page EUR 1,100, color page EUR 2,100. Circ: 5,000 (paid and controlled).

910.10 DEU
MOBIL TOTAL. Text in German. 2/yr. EUR 5 newsstand/cover (effective 2007). adv. **Document type:** *Magazine, Consumer.*
Published by: V M S Verlag und Medien-Service, Gesellschaft fuer Marketing und Kommunikation, Rheinallee 10-11, Koenigswinter, 53639, Germany. TEL 49-2223-27318, FAX 49-2223-4316, v-medienservice@t-online.de. Ed. Alfred Alkoven. Pub., Adv. contact E Andreas Bues. B&W page EUR 1,600, color page EUR 2,950. Circ: 20,000 (paid and controlled).

910.202 DEU ISSN 0948-843X
MOBIL UND SICHER. Text in German. 1957. 6/yr. EUR 8.25; EUR 1.45 newsstand/cover (effective 2011). adv. **Document type:** *Magazine, Consumer.*
Formerly (until 1994): Sicher Unterwegs (0948-8421); Which was formed by the merger of (1992-1993): Sicher Unterwegs. Ausgabe Baden-Wuerttemberg - Sachsen (0944-7911); (1992-1993): Sicher Unterwegs. Ausgabe Hessen - Thueringen (0944-7946); Both of which superseded in part: Sicher Unterwegs. Ausgabe Baden-Wuerttemberg - Hessen (0935-0918); (1992-1993): Sicher Unterwegs. Ausgabe Berlin - Brandenburg (0944-789X); (1992-1993): Sicher Unterwegs. Ausgabe Nordrhein-Westfalen (0944-7903); Both of which superseded in part: Sicher Unterwegs. Ausgabe Nordrhein-Westfalen - Berlin (0934-9502); (1986-1993): Sicher Unterwegs. Ausgabe Bayern (0935-0926); (1986-1993): Sicher Unterwegs. Ausgabe Bremen - Niedersachsen - Sachsen-Anhalt (0944-7938); Which was formerly (until 1992): Sicher Unterwegs. Ausgabe Niedersachsen - Bremen (0935-0942); (1986-1993): Sicher Unterwegs. Ausgabe Hamburg - Schleswig-Holstein - Mecklenburg-Vorpommern (0944-792X); Which was formerly (until 1992): Sicher Unterwegs. Ausgabe Hamburg - Schleswig-Holstein (0935-0934); (1986-1993): Sicher Unterwegs. Ausgabe Rheinland-Pfalz (0935-0950); All of which superseded in part (in 1986): Sicher Unterwegs (0930-827X); Which was formerly (until 1985): Verkehrswacht Praxis (0344-9971); (until 1977): Deutsche Verkehrswacht (0415-6315)
Published by: Max Schmidt-Roemhild KG, Mengstr 16, Luebeck, 23552, Germany. TEL 49-451-703101, FAX 49-451-7031253, info@schmidt-roemhild.de, http://www.beleke.de/unternehmen/verlage/schmidtroemhild/index.html.

MOBILE HOME PARK. *see* HOUSING AND URBAN PLANNING

MOBILITIES. *see* POPULATION STUDIES

338.4791 DEU
MODERNES GESCHAEFTSREISE MANAGEMENT. Text in German. a. EUR 18 newsstand/cover (effective 2009). adv. **Document type:** *Directory, Trade.*
Published by: Alabasta Verlag 2000, Am Schnepfenweg 52, Munich, 80995, Germany. TEL 49-89-15090842, FAX 49-89-15090843. adv.: B&W page EUR 1,590, color page EUR 1,990. Circ: 1,900 (paid and controlled).

910.09 388.3 FRA ISSN 0993-1996
LE MONDE DU CAMPING CAR. Text in French. 1988. 10/yr. EUR 55 (effective 2009). adv. **Document type:** *Magazine, Consumer.*
Published by: Editions Lariviere, 6 Rue Olof Palme, Clichy, 92587, France. TEL 33-1-47565400, http://www.editions-lariviere.fr. Ed. Olivier Lemaire. Pub. Fabien Darmon. Adv. contact Karim Khaldi.

914.7 ROM ISSN 1221-0684
MONTANA. Text in Romanian. 1991. irreg.
Related titles: ◆ Supplement to: Romania Pitoreasca. ISSN 1221-0692.
Published by: Ministerul Turismului/Ministry of Tourism, Str. Gabriel Peri 8, Bucharest, 70148, Romania. TEL 597893, 6597893.

MONTHLY REPORT ON TOURISM - REPUBLIC OF CHINA/KUAN KUANG TZU LIAO. *see* TRAVEL AND TOURISM—Abstracting, Bibliographies, Statistics

MONTREAL'S FIRST PEOPLES' FESTIVAL (YEAR). *see* ETHNIC INTERESTS

917 USA ISSN 1547-2930
F1076
MOON HANDBOOKS: ALBERTA. Text in English. 1995. triennial, latest 6th ed. USD 21.95 6th ed. (effective 2008). **Document type:** *Handbook/Manual/Guide, Consumer.* **Description:** Features information on various sights, activities, restaurants and accommodations in Alberta and also includes suggestions on how to plan an ideal trip.
Former titles (until 2004): Moon Handbooks: Alberta and the Northwest Territories (1531-5622); (until 2001): Alberta and the Northwest Territories Handbook (1079-9338)
Published by: Avalon Travel Publishing, 1700 4th St, Berkeley, CA 94710. TEL 510-595-3664, avalon.publicity@perseusbooks.com, http://www.avalontravelbooks.com.

910.2 USA ISSN 1538-120X
F809.3
MOON HANDBOOKS: ARIZONA. Text in English. 1987. biennial, latest 10th ed. USD 19.95 10th ed. (effective 2008). **Document type:** *Handbook/Manual/Guide, Consumer.* **Description:** Features a wide range of information on Arizona, from rafting down the Colorado River to exploring the art galleries of Sedona.
Former titles (until 2002): Arizona Handbook (1524-2188); (until 1997): Arizona Traveler's Handbook (1088-0925); Arizona Handbook
Published by: Avalon Travel Publishing, 1400 65th St, Ste 250, Emeryville, CA 94608. TEL 510-595-3664, FAX 510-595-4228, info@travelmatters.com, http://www.moon.com.

917.58 USA ISSN 1948-5034
F294.A83
▼ **MOON HANDBOOKS: ATLANTA.** Text in English. 2009. triennial. USD 17.95 per issue (effective 2009). **Document type:** *Handbook/Manual/Guide, Consumer.* **Description:** Travel guide for Atlanta, Georgia.
Published by: Avalon Travel Publishing, 1700 4th St, Berkeley, CA 94710. TEL 510-595-3664, info@travelmatters.com.

975.26 USA ISSN 1947-8801
F189.B13
▼ **MOON HANDBOOKS: BALTIMORE.** Text in English. 2009. biennial (every 2 to 3 yrs.). USD 17.95 per issue (effective 2009). **Document type:** *Handbook/Manual/Guide, Consumer.* **Description:** Travel guidebook covering sights, hotels, restaurants, shops, and nightlife in Baltimore.
Published by: Avalon Travel Publishing, 1700 4th St, Berkeley, CA 94710. TEL 510-595-3664, info@travelmatters.com.

910.2 USA ISSN 1945-2985
MOON HANDBOOKS: BEIJING & SHANGHAI. Text in English. 2008. irreg., latest 2008. USD 17.95 per issue (effective 2010). **Document type:** *Handbook/Manual/Guide, Consumer.* **Description:** Provides travel information about Beijing & Shanghai.
Published by: Avalon Travel Publishing, 1700 4th St, Berkeley, CA 94710. TEL 510-595-3664, avalon.publicity@perseusbooks.com. **Subscr. to:** 1094 Flex Dr, Jackson, TN 38301. TEL 800-788-3123, FAX 800-351-5073.

910.202 USA ISSN 1932-7870
F1632
MOON HANDBOOKS. BERMUDA. Text in English. 2006. biennial. USD 17.95 per issue (effective 2011). **Document type:** *Handbook/Manual/Guide, Consumer.* **Description:** Gives travelers the tools they need to create a more personal and memorable experience.
Published by: Avalon Travel Publishing, 1700 4th St, Berkeley, CA 94710. FAX 800-351-5073, avalon.publicity@perseusbooks.com, http://www.travelmatters.com.

917 USA ISSN 2154-2309
F217.B6
▼ **MOON HANDBOOKS: BLUE RIDGE AND SMOKY MOUNTAINS.** Text in English. 2010 (May). triennial. USD 16.95 (effective 2011). **Document type:** *Handbook/Manual/Guide, Consumer.* **Description:** Travel guide for outdoor activities in the Blue Ridge and Smoky Mountain ranges.
Published by: Avalon Travel Publishing, 1700 4th St, Berkeley, CA 94710. TEL 510-595-3664, info@travelmatters.com. Ed. Deborah Huso.

917.1 USA ISSN 1538-1196
F1087.7
MOON HANDBOOKS: BRITISH COLUMBIA. Text in English. 1989. biennial, latest 8th ed. USD 21.95 per issue (effective 2008). **Document type:** *Handbook/Manual/Guide, Consumer.* **Description:** Features information on various sights, activities, restaurants and accommodations in British Columbia and also includes suggestions on how to plan an ideal trip.
Formerly (until 2002): British Columbia Handbook (1096-097X)
Published by: Avalon Travel Publishing, 1700 4th St, Berkeley, CA 94710. TEL 510-595-3664, avalon.publicity@perseusbooks.com, http://www.avalontravelbooks.com.

915.96 USA ISSN 1949-8306
DS554.25
▼ **MOON HANDBOOKS: CAMBODIA.** Text in English. 2009. triennial. USD 19.95 per issue (effective 2010). **Document type:** *Handbook/Manual/Guide, Consumer.* **Description:** Travel guide for Cambodia, including hotels, restaurants, sites and events.
Published by: Avalon Travel Publishing, 1700 4th St, Berkeley, CA 94710. TEL 510-595-3664, info@travelmatters.com.

910.202 USA ISSN 1556-5122
F1376
MOON HANDBOOKS: CANCUN & COZUMEL. Text in English. 1990. biennial, latest 2007, 8th ed. USD 17.95 8th ed. (effective 2008). **Document type:** *Handbook/Manual/Guide, Consumer.* **Description:** Contains information on dining, transportation, and accommodations.
Former titles (until 2005): Moon Handbooks. Cancun (1534-0503); (until 2001): Cancun Handbook and Mexico's Caribbean Coast (1094-4842)
Published by: Avalon Travel Publishing, 1700 4th St, Berkeley, CA 94710. TEL 510-595-3664, avalon.publicity@perseusbooks.com.

917.56 USA ISSN 2154-3267
F264.C4
▼ **MOON HANDBOOKS: CHARLOTTE.** Text in English. 2010 (May). triennial. USD 16.95 per issue (effective 2011). **Document type:** *Handbook/Manual/Guide, Consumer.* **Description:** Travel guide for the Charlotte, North Carolina area.
Published by: Avalon Travel Publishing, 1700 4th St, Berkeley, CA 94710. TEL 510-595-3664, info@travelmatters.com. Ed. Jodi Helmer.

917.2 USA ISSN 1947-6582
F1256
▼ **MOON HANDBOOKS: CHIAPAS.** Text in English. 2009. triennial. USD 17.95 per issue (effective 2009). **Document type:** *Handbook/Manual/Guide, Consumer.* **Description:** Travel guide for hotels, restaurants and things to do in Chiapas, Mexico.
Published by: Avalon Travel Publishing, 1700 4th St, Berkeley, CA 94710. TEL 510-595-3664, info@travelmatters.com.

918.3 USA ISSN 1540-3394
F3059.5
MOON HANDBOOKS: CHILE. Text in English. 2002. triennial (Every 3 to 4 years), latest 2nd ed. USD 22.95 2nd ed. (effective 2008). **Document type:** *Handbook/Manual/Guide, Consumer.* **Description:** Presents suggestions on how to plan a trip and includes information on sights, activities, restaurants and accommodations.
Published by: Avalon Travel Publishing, 1700 4th St, Berkeley, CA 94710. TEL 510-595-3664, avalon.publicity@perseusbooks.com, http://www.travelmatters.com.

914.97204 USA ISSN 1947-8798
DR1509
▼ **MOON HANDBOOKS: CROATIA & SLOVENIA.** Text in English. 2009. biennial (every 2 to 3 yrs.). USD 19.95 per issue (effective 2009). **Document type:** *Handbook/Manual/Guide, Consumer.* **Description:** Travel guidebook covering sights, lodgings, food, and transportation in Croatia and Slovenia.
Published by: Avalon Travel Publishing, 1700 4th St, Berkeley, CA 94710. TEL 510-595-3664, info@travelmatters.com.

917 USA ISSN 1531-4170
MOON HANDBOOKS: CUBA. Text in English. 1997. triennial, latest 4th ed. USD 24.95 4th ed. (effective 2008). **Document type:** *Handbook/Manual/Guide, Consumer.* **Description:** Provides details needed to discover various sights, attractions and restaurants in Cuba and also highlights lesser-known and local hotspots.
Formerly (until 2000): Cuba Handbook (1092-3330)
Published by: Avalon Travel Publishing, 1700 4th St, Berkeley, CA 94710. TEL 510-595-3664, avalon.publicity@perseusbooks.com, http://www.avalontravelbooks.com.

917.64 USA ISSN 2150-8216
F394.D213
▼ **MOON HANDBOOKS: DALLAS & FORT WORTH.** Short title: Dallas & Fort Worth. Moon Dallas & Fort Worth. Text in English. 2009. biennial. USD 17.95 per issue (effective 2009). **Document type:** *Handbook/Manual/Guide, Consumer.* **Description:** Travel guidebook for Dallas and Fort Worth, Texas.
Published by: Avalon Travel Publishing, 1700 4th St, Berkeley, CA 94710. TEL 510-595-3664, info@travelmatters.com.

917.88 USA ISSN 1944-544X
F784.D43
▼ **MOON HANDBOOKS: DENVER.** Text in English. 2009. biennial (every 2 or 3 yrs.). USD 17.95 per issue (effective 2009). **Document type:** *Handbook/Manual/Guide, Consumer.* **Description:** Travel guide for Denver, Colorado.
Published by: Avalon Travel Publishing, 1700 4th St, Berkeley, CA 94710. TEL 510-595-3664, info@travelmatters.com, http://www.moon.com.

917.13 USA ISSN 1533-8924
F1934.5
MOON HANDBOOKS: DOMINICAN REPUBLIC. Text in English. 1997. triennial, latest 3rd ed. USD 17.95 per issue (effective 2008). **Document type:** *Handbook/Manual/Guide, Consumer.* **Description:** Details various ways to explore Southern California and includes the firsthand experience and insight of the author.
Formerly (until 2001): Dominican Republic Handbook (1092-3349)
Published by: Avalon Travel Publishing, 1700 4th St, Berkeley, CA 94710. TEL 510-595-3664, avalon.publicity@perseusbooks.com, http://www.avalontravelbooks.com.

918.13 USA ISSN 1533-4333
F3709.5
MOON HANDBOOKS: ECUADOR. Text in English. 1998. triennial, latest 3rd ed. USD 19.95 per issue (effective 2008). **Document type:** *Handbook/Manual/Guide, Consumer.* **Description:** Details various ways to explore Ecuador, from the Andes to the Amazon.
Formerly (until 2001): Ecuador Handbook, including the Galapagos Islands (1095-886X)
Published by: Avalon Travel Publishing, 1700 4th St, Berkeley, CA 94710. TEL 510-595-3664, avalon.publicity@perseusbooks.com, http://www.avalontravelbooks.com.

917.59 USA ISSN 1949-842X
F309.3
▼ **MOON HANDBOOKS: FLORIDA.** Text in English. 2010 (Feb.). triennial. USD 18.95 per issue (effective 2011). **Document type:** *Handbook/Manual/Guide, Consumer.* **Description:** Travel guide for Florida, including restaurants, hotels, sites and events.
Published by: Avalon Travel Publishing, 1700 4th St, Berkeley, CA 94710. TEL 510-595-3664, info@travelmatters.com. Ed. Jason Ferguson.

910.91 USA ISSN 1557-6299
F737.G5
MOON HANDBOOKS: GLACIER NATIONAL PARK. Text in English. 2006. biennial, latest 1st ed. USD 16.95 1st ed. (effective 2008). **Document type:** *Handbook/Manual/Guide, Consumer.*
Published by: Avalon Travel Publishing, 1700 4th St, Berkeley, CA 94710. TEL 510-595-3664, avalon.publicity@perseusbooks.com, http://www.avalontravelbooks.com.

919.12 USA ISSN 1534-052X
DU622
MOON HANDBOOKS: HAWAII. Text in English. 1987. biennial, latest 7th ed. USD 24.95 per issue (effective 2008). **Document type:** *Handbook/Manual/Guide, Consumer.* **Description:** Covers the various sights and activities in the Hawaiian Islands.
Formerly (until 2001): Hawaii Handbook (1078-5299)
—CCC.
Published by: Avalon Travel Publishing, 1700 4th St, Berkeley, CA 94710. TEL 510-595-3664, avalon.publicity@perseusbooks.com, http://www.avalontravelbooks.com.

917.13 USA ISSN 1948-6472
F1503.5
MOON HANDBOOKS: HONDURAS & THE BAY ISLANDS. Text in English. 1997. triennial, latest 4th ed. USD 19.95 per issue (effective 2009). **Document type:** *Handbook/Manual/Guide, Consumer.* **Description:** Provides details that are needed to discover various sights, attractions and restaurants in Honduras and also highlights lesser-known and local hotspots.
Former titles (until 2009): Moon Handbooks: Honduras (1541-6887); (until 2000): Honduras Handbook (1094-4389)
Published by: Avalon Travel Publishing, 1700 4th St, Berkeley, CA 94710. TEL 510-595-3664, avalon.publicity@perseusbooks.com, http://www.avalontravelbooks.com.

910.2 USA ISSN 1554-2327
F127.H8
MOON HANDBOOKS: HUDSON RIVER VALLEY. Text in English. 2005. biennial, latest 2nd ed. USD 16.95 2nd ed. (effective 2008). **Document type:** *Handbook/Manual/Guide, Consumer.* **Description:** Features information on dining, transportation and accommodations along with several area, regional and city-centered maps.
Published by: Avalon Travel Publishing, 1400 65th St, Ste 250, Emeryville, CA 94608. avalon.publicity@perseusbooks.com.

910.91 USA ISSN 1557-1114
F539.3
MOON HANDBOOKS: ILLINOIS. Text in English. 2006. biennial, latest 1st ed. USD 17.95 1st ed. (effective 2008). **Document type:** *Handbook/Manual/Guide, Consumer.*
Published by: Avalon Travel Publishing, 1700 4th St, Berkeley, CA 94710. TEL 510-595-3664, avalon.publicity@perseusbooks.com, http://www.avalontravelbooks.com.

941.7 USA ISSN 1936-1807
DA980
MOON HANDBOOKS: IRELAND. Text in English. 2007. irreg., latest 1st ed. USD 21.95 1st ed. (effective 2008). **Document type:** *Handbook/Manual/Guide, Consumer.* **Description:** Provides a unique perspective on visiting Ireland and features information on dining, transportation and accommodations along with several area, regional and city-centered maps.
Published by: Avalon Travel Publishing, 1400 65th St, Ste 250, Emeryville, CA 94608. avalon.publicity@perseusbooks.com.

917 USA ISSN 2155-157X
▼ **MOON HANDBOOKS: ISTANBUL AND THE TURKISH COAST.** Text in English. 2010 (Oct.). biennial. USD 17.95 per issue (effective 2011). **Document type:** *Handbook/Manual/Guide, Consumer.* **Description:** Travel guide for sites in Istanbul and the Turkish coast.
Published by: Avalon Travel Publishing, 1700 4th St, Berkeley, CA 94710. TEL 510-595-3664, info@travelmatters.com. Ed. Jessica Tamturk.

917.29204 USA
MOON HANDBOOKS: JAMAICA. Text in English. 1991. triennial, latest 5th ed. USD 17.95 5th ed. (effective 2008). **Document type:** *Handbook/Manual/Guide, Consumer.* **Description:** Features information on various sights, activities, restaurants and accommodations in Jamaica and also includes suggestions on how to plan an ideal trip.
Formerly: Jamaica Handbook (1088-0941)
Published by: Avalon Travel Publishing, 1700 4th St, Berkeley, CA 94710. TEL 510-595-3664, avalon.publicity@perseusbooks.com, http://www.avalontravelbooks.com.

917.78 USA ISSN 2153-2672
F474.K23
▼ **MOON HANDBOOKS: KANSAS CITY.** Variant title: Moon Kansas City. Text in English. 2010 (Apr.). triennial. USD 16.95 per issue (effective 2011). **Document type:** *Handbook/Manual/Guide, Consumer.* **Description:** Travel guide for Kansas City, Missouri.
Published by: Avalon Travel Publishing, 1700 4th St, Berkeley, CA 94710. TEL 510-595-3664, http://www.avalontravelbooks.com. Ed. Katy Ryan.

919.13 USA ISSN 1531-4146
MOON HANDBOOKS: KAUA'I. Text in English. 1989. irreg., latest 2006, 6th ed. USD 24.95 6th ed. (effective 2008). **Document type:** *Handbook/Manual/Guide, Consumer.* **Description:** Features information on the various sights, activities, restaurants and accommodations in Kaua'i and also includes suggestions on how to plan an ideal trip.
Formerly (until 2001): Kauai Handbook (1078-5434)
Published by: Avalon Travel Publishing, 1700 4th St, Berkeley, CA 94710. TEL 510-595-3664, avalon.publicity@perseusbooks.com, http://www.avalontravelbooks.com.

910.10 USA ISSN 1556-7702
F839.3
MOON HANDBOOKS: LAS VEGAS. Text in English. 2006. triennial, latest 2nd ed. USD 17.95 2nd ed. (effective 2008). **Document type:** *Handbook/Manual/Guide, Consumer.* **Description:** Provides advice on Las Vegas, from gambling and dining on The Strip to rock climbing in Red Rock Canyon.
Published by: Avalon Travel Publishing, 1400 65th St, Ste 250, Emeryville, CA 94608. avalon.publicity@perseusbooks.com.

917.74 USA ISSN 1946-312X
F572.N8
▼ **MOON HANDBOOKS: MICHIGAN'S UPPER PENINSULA.** Text in English. 2009. triennial. USD 17.95 per issue (effective 2009). **Document type:** *Handbook/Manual/Guide, Consumer.* **Description:** Travel guide for Michigan's Upper Peninsula.
Published by: Avalon Travel Publishing, 1700 4th St, Berkeley, CA 94710. TEL 510-595-3664, info@travelmatters.com, http://www.moon.com.

917.75 USA ISSN 1947-4113
F589.M63
▼ **MOON HANDBOOKS: MILWAUKEE & MADISON.** Text in English. 2009. triennial. USD 17.95 per issue (effective 2009). **Document type:** *Handbook/Manual/Guide, Consumer.* **Description:** Travel guidebook for Milwaukee and Madison, Wisconsin.
Published by: Avalon Travel Publishing, 1700 4th St, Berkeley, CA 94710. TEL 510-595-3664, info@travelmatters.com.

917.76 USA ISSN 1947-4121
F614.M6
▼ **MOON HANDBOOKS: MINNEAPOLIS & ST. PAUL.** Text in English. 2009. triennial. USD 17.95 per issue (effective 2009). **Document type:** *Handbook/Manual/Guide, Consumer.* **Description:** Travel guide for Minneapolis and St. Paul, Minnesota.
Published by: Avalon Travel Publishing, 1700 4th St, Berkeley, CA 94710. TEL 510-595-3664, info@travelmatters.com.

910.10 USA ISSN 1559-3479
F1054.5.M83
MOON HANDBOOKS: MONTREAL & QUEBEC CITY. Text in English. 2006. biennial, latest 1st ed. USD 17.95 1st ed. (effective 2008). **Document type:** *Handbook/Manual/Guide, Consumer.*
Published by: Avalon Travel Publishing, 1700 4th St, Berkeley, CA 94710. TEL 510-595-3664, avalon.publicity@perseusbooks.com, http://www.avalontravelbooks.com. Ed. Jennifer Edwards.

917.83 USA ISSN 2154-2295
▼ **MOON HANDBOOKS: MOUNT RUSHMORE AND THE BLACK HILLS.** Text in English. 2010 (May). triennial. USD 16.95 (effective 2011). **Document type:** *Handbook/Manual/Guide, Consumer.* **Description:** Travel guide for Mount Rushmorea and the Black Hills, South Dakota.
Published by: Avalon Travel Publishing, 1700 4th St, Berkeley, CA 94710. TEL 510-595-3664, info@travelmatters.com. Ed. Laural A Bidwell.

915.4 USA ISSN 2150-9441
▼ **MOON HANDBOOKS: MUMBAI & GOA.** Short title: Moon Mumbai & Goa. Mumbai & Goa. Text in English. 2009. triennial. USD 17.95 per issue (effective 2009). **Document type:** *Handbook/Manual/Guide, Consumer.* **Description:** Travel guide for Mumbai and Goa, India.
Published by: Avalon Travel Publishing, 1700 4th St, Berkeley, CA 94710. TEL 510-595-3664, info@travelmatters.com.

910.91 USA ISSN 1930-2630
F132.3
MOON HANDBOOKS: NEW JERSEY. Text in English. 2006. biennial, latest 1st ed. USD 19.95 1st ed. (effective 2008). **Document type:** *Handbook/Manual/Guide, Consumer.*
Published by: Avalon Travel Publishing, 1700 4th St, Berkeley, CA 94710. TEL 510-595-3664, avalon.publicity@perseusbooks.com, http://www.avalontravelbooks.com. Ed. Kaura Kiniry.

919.31 USA ISSN 1544-4287
MOON HANDBOOKS: NEW ZEALAND. Text in English. 1987. triennial, latest 7th ed. USD 23.95 7th ed. (effective 2008). **Document type:** *Handbook/Manual/Guide, Consumer.* **Description:** Features information on dining, transportation and accommodations along with many area, regional and city-centered maps.
Formerly (until 2003): New Zealand Handbook (1085-2662)
—CCC.
Published by: Avalon Travel Publishing, 1700 4th St, Berkeley, CA 94710. TEL 510-595-3664, avalon.publicity@perseusbooks.com.

910.2 USA ISSN 1556-4053
TP557
MOON HANDBOOKS: NORTHERN CALIFORNIA WINE COUNTRY. Text in English. 2006. triennial. USD 17.95 2nd ed. (effective 2008). **Document type:** *Handbook/Manual/Guide, Consumer.* **Description:** Features information on various sights, activities, restaurants and accommodations in Northern California and also includes suggestions on how to plan an ideal trip.
Published by: Avalon Travel Publishing, 1400 65th St, Ste 250, Emeryville, CA 94608. avalon.publicity@perseusbooks.com, http://www.avalontravelbooks.com.

910.91 USA ISSN 1930-1502
F1037.7
MOON HANDBOOKS: NOVA SCOTIA. Text in English. 2006. triennial, latest 1st ed. USD 16.95 1st ed. (effective 2008). **Document type:** *Handbook/Manual/Guide, Consumer.*
Published by: Avalon Travel Publishing, 1700 4th St, Berkeley, CA 94710. TEL 510-595-3664, avalon.publicity@perseusbooks.com, http://www.avalontravelbooks.com.

917.204 USA ISSN 1533-418X
F1209
MOON HANDBOOKS: PACIFIC MEXICO. Text in English. 1993. triennial, latest 8th ed. USD 23.95 8th ed. (effective 2008). **Document type:** *Handbook/Manual/Guide, Consumer.* **Description:** Features information on dining, transportation and accommodations along with several area, regional and city-centered maps.
Formerly (until 2001): Pacific Mexico Handbook (1082-488X)
Published by: Avalon Travel Publishing, 1700 4th St, Berkeley, CA 94710. TEL 510-595-3664, avalon.publicity@perseusbooks.com.

910.2 USA ISSN 1555-9459
F1563.5
MOON HANDBOOKS: PANAMA. Text in English. 2005. triennial, latest 2nd ed. USD 19.95 (effective 2008). **Document type:** *Handbook/Manual/Guide, Consumer.* **Description:** Provides a unique perspective on Panama and includes details for navigating jungle trails, finding cheap taxis and underground bars or planning a river expedition.
Published by: Avalon Travel Publishing, 1700 4th St, Berkeley, CA 94710. TEL 510-595-3664, avalon.publicity@perseusbooks.com.

917.91 USA ISSN 2151-6138
F819.P57
▼ **MOON HANDBOOKS: PHOENIX, SCOTTSDALE & SEDONA.** Text in English. 2010 (Mar.). triennial. USD 17.95 per issue (effective 2011). **Document type:** *Handbook/Manual/Guide, Consumer.* **Description:** Travel guide for Phoenix, Scottsdale and Sedona, Arizona.
Published by: Avalon Travel Publishing, 1700 4th St, Berkeley, CA 94710. TEL 510-595-3664, info@travelmatters.com. Ed. Jeff Ficker.

917 USA ISSN 1936-4938
DP14
MOON HANDBOOKS: PITTSBURGH. Text in English. 2007 (Jun.). biennial, latest 1st ed. USD 17.95 1st ed. (effective 2008). **Document type:** *Handbook/Manual/Guide, Consumer.* **Description:** Provides a quirky look at Pittsburgh, from visiting the Andy Warhol Museum to grabbing a beer at a hipster bar in South Side.
Published by: Avalon Travel Publishing, 1700 4th St, Berkeley, CA 94710. TEL 510-595-3664, avalon.publicity@perseusbooks.com.

917.95 USA ISSN 2153-3741
F884.P83
▼ **MOON HANDBOOKS: PORTLAND.** Variant title: Moon Portland. Text in English. 2010 (May). triennial. USD 16.95 per issue (effective 2011). **Document type:** *Handbook/Manual/Guide, Consumer.* **Description:** Travel guide for the city of Portland, Oregon.
Published by: Avalon Travel Publishing, 1700 4th St, Berkeley, CA 94710. TEL 510-595-3664, info@travelmatters.com. Ed. Hollyanna McCollom.

917.295 USA ISSN 1932-0957
F1959
MOON HANDBOOKS: PUERTO RICO. Text in English. 2006. triennial. USD 17.95 per issue (effective 2008). **Document type:** *Handbook/Manual/Guide, Consumer.* **Description:** Provides essential details that are needed to discover various sights, attractions and restaurants in Puerto Rico, while including lesser-known and local hotspots.
Published by: Avalon Travel Publishing, 1400 65th St, Ste 250, Emeryville, CA 94608. avalon.publicity@perseusbooks.com.

917.2 USA ISSN 1533-4198
F1391.P93
MOON HANDBOOKS: PUERTO VALLARTA. Text in English. 1995. triennial, latest 7th ed. USD 17.95 7th ed. (effective 2008). **Document type:** *Handbook/Manual/Guide, Consumer.* **Description:** Features information on dining, transportation and accommodations along with many area, regional and city-centered maps.
Formerly (until 2001): Puerto Vallarta Handbook (1082-4677)
Published by: Avalon Travel Publishing, 1700 4th St, Berkeley, CA 94710. TEL 510-595-3664, avalon.publicity@perseusbooks.com.

918.1 USA ISSN 2150-976X
F2646.A4
▼ **MOON HANDBOOKS: RIO DE JANEIRO.** Short title: Moon Rio de Janeiro. Rio de Janeiro. Text in English. 2009. irreg. (2-3 yrs.). USD 17.95 per issue (effective 2009). **Document type:** *Handbook/Manual/Guide, Consumer.* **Description:** Travel guide for Rio de Janeiro, Brazil.
Published by: Avalon Travel Publishing, 1700 4th St, Berkeley, CA 94710. TEL 510-595-3664, info@travelmatters.com.

910.10 USA ISSN 1557-7163
F804.S23
MOON HANDBOOKS: SANTA FE, TAOS & ALBUQUERQUE. Text in English. 1998. biennial, latest 2009, 2nd ed. USD 17.95 per issue (effective 2009). back issues avail. **Document type:** *Handbook/Manual/Guide, Consumer.* **Description:** Features 17 detailed and easy-to-use maps, can't-miss sights, activities, restaurants and accommodations in Santa Fe.
Formerly (until 2006): St. Fe-Taos Handbook (1098-6715)
Published by: Avalon Travel Publishing, 1700 4th St, Berkeley, CA 94710. TEL 510-595-3664, info@travelmatters.com, http://www.moon.com. Ed. Zora O'Neill.

TU

915.19504 USA ISSN 1543-155X
DS901.95
MOON HANDBOOKS: SOUTH KOREA. Text in English. 1988. biennial, latest 3rd ed. USD 21.95 per issue (effective 2008). **Document type:** *Handbook/Manual/Guide, Consumer.* **Description:** Covers the various sights and activities in the South Korea.
Formerly (until 2003): South Korea Handbook (1090-5006)
Published by: Avalon Travel Publishing, 1700 4th St, Berkeley, CA 94710. TEL 510-595-3664, avalon.publicity@perseusbooks.com, http://www.avalontravelbooks.com.

917.12 USA ISSN 1535-7430
F867
MOON HANDBOOKS: SOUTHERN CALIFORNIA. Text in English. 1998. triennial, latest 3rd ed. USD 21.95 per issue (effective 2008). **Document type:** *Handbook/Manual/Guide, Consumer.* **Description:** Features information on Southern California and its sunny beaches and star-studded streets.
Formerly (until 2001): Southern California Handbook (1094-4397)
Published by: Avalon Travel Publishing, 1700 4th St, Berkeley, CA 94710. TEL 510-595-3664, avalon.publicity@perseusbooks.com, http://www.avalontravelbooks.com.

914 USA ISSN 1936-4911
F159.P63
MOON HANDBOOKS: SPAIN. Text in English. 2007 (May). biennial, latest 1st ed. USD 24.95 1st ed. (effective 2008). **Document type:** *Handbook/Manual/Guide, Consumer.* **Description:** Provides an insider's view of Spain - from kite-surfing in Tarifa and architecture-gazing in Barcelona to sipping sangria in Cordoba.
Published by: Avalon Travel Publishing, 1700 4th St, Berkeley, CA 94710. TEL 510-595-3664, avalon.publicity@perseusbooks.com.

977.865 USA ISSN 1947-5810
F474.S23
▼ **MOON HANDBOOKS: ST. LOUIS.** Text in English. 2009. biennial (every 2 to 3 yrs.). USD 17.95 per issue (effective 2009). **Document type:** *Handbook/Manual/Guide, Consumer.* **Description:** Travel guidebook covering sights, lodgings, food, and transportation in St. Louis.
Published by: Avalon Travel Publishing, 1700 4th St, Berkeley, CA 94710. TEL 510-595-3664, info@travelmatters.com.

917.59 USA ISSN 1944-916X
F319.T2
▼ **MOON HANDBOOKS: TAMPA & ST. PETERSBURG.** Variant title: Tampa & St. Petersburg. Text in English. 2009. biennial. USD 17.95 per issue (effective 2009). **Document type:** *Handbook/Manual/Guide, Consumer.* **Description:** Travel guide for Tampa and St. Petersburg, Florida.
Published by: Avalon Travel Publishing, 1700 4th St, Berkeley, CA 94710. TEL 510-595-3664, info@travelmatters.com.

917.91 USA ISSN 2150-9751
F819.T93
▼ **MOON HANDBOOKS: TUCSON.** Short title: Moon Tuscon. Tuscon. Text in English. 2009. triennial. USD 17.95 per issue (effective 2010). **Document type:** *Consumer.* **Description:** Travel guide for Tucson, Arizona.
Published by: Avalon Travel Publishing, 1700 4th St, Berkeley, CA 94710. TEL 510-595-3664, info@travelmatters.com, http://www.avalontravelbooks.com.

917.297 USA ISSN 1534-6676
F2136
MOON HANDBOOKS: VIRGIN ISLANDS. Text in English. 1997. triennial, latest 3rd ed. USD 17.95 3rd ed. (effective 2008). **Document type:** *Guide, Consumer.* **Description:** Provides details needed to discover various sights, attractions and restaurants in Virgin Islands and also highlights lesser-known and local hotspots.
Formerly (until 2001): Virgin Islands Handbook (1092-3357)
Published by: Avalon Travel Publishing, 1700 4th St, Berkeley, CA 94710. TEL 510-595-3664, avalon.publicity@perseusbooks.com, http://www.avalontravelbooks.com.

910.2 USA ISSN 1948-8211
F1463.6
▼ **MOON LIVING ABROAD IN GUATEMALA.** Variant title: Living Abroad in Guatemala. Text in English. 2009. triennial. USD 19.95 per issue (effective 2010). **Document type:** *Consumer.* **Description:** Guide for relocating to Guatemala.
Published by: Avalon Travel Publishing, 1700 4th St, Berkeley, CA 94710. TEL 510-595-3664, info@travelmatters.com, http://www.moon.com.

917.28 USA ISSN 2150-2412
F1563.5
▼ **MOON LIVING ABROAD IN PANAMA.** Variant title: Moon Living Abroad in Panama. Text in English. 2010 (May). triennial. USD 19.95 per issue (effective 2011). **Document type:** *Handbook/Manual/Guide, Consumer.* **Description:** Guide for Americans moving to Panama.
Published by: Avalon Travel Publishing, 1700 4th St, Berkeley, CA 94710. TEL 510-595-3664, info@travelmatters.com. Ed. Miriam Butterman.

942 USA ISSN 1934-5763
DA679
MOON LONDON. Text in English. 2007. irreg. USD 19.95 per issue (effective 2008). **Document type:** *Guide, Consumer.* **Description:** Provides an insider's view of London from trendy Marylebone and artsy South Bank to lesser-known restaurants and shops in some of London's unexpected spots.
Published by: Avalon Travel Publishing, 1400 65th St, Ste 250, Emeryville, CA 94608. TEL 510-595-3664, FAX 510-595-4228, http://www.travelmatters.com.

914.492352 USA ISSN 1540-5052
DJ411.A53
MOON METRO: AMSTERDAM. Text in English. 2003. biennial (2-3/yr). USD 16.95 per issue (effective 2008). **Document type:** *Guide, Consumer.*
Published by: Avalon Travel Publishing, 1700 4th St, Berkeley, CA 94710. TEL 510-595-3664, avalon.publicity@perseusbooks.com, http://www.travelmatters.com.

917.7311 USA ISSN 1540-4951
F548.18
MOON METRO: CHICAGO. Text in English. 2002. biennial (Every two to three years), latest 3rd ed. USD 14.95 3rd ed. (effective 2008). **Document type:** *Guide, Consumer.*
Published by: Avalon Travel Publishing, 1700 4th St, Berkeley, CA 94710. TEL 510-595-3664, avalon.publicity@perseusbooks.com, http://www.travelmatters.com.

917.4 USA ISSN 1935-8296
F2.3
MOON NEW ENGLAND. Text in English. 2007 (May). triennial, latest 1st ed. USD 21.95 1st ed. (effective 2008). **Document type:** *Magazine, Consumer.* **Description:** Features information on various sights, activities, restaurants and accommodations in New England and also includes suggestions on how to plan an ideal trip.
Published by: Avalon Travel Publishing, 1700 4th St, Berkeley, CA 94710. TEL 510-595-3664, avalon.publicity@perseusbooks.com, http://www.avalontravelbooks.com.

910.202 279.71 USA
GV776.C2
MOON OUTDOORS. CALIFORNIA RECREATIONAL LAKES AND RIVERS; the complete guide to boating, fishing, and water sports. Text in English. 1996. irreg., latest 2008, 4th ed. USD 21.95 per issue (effective 2011). **Document type:** *Handbook/Manual/Guide, Consumer.*
Former titles (until 2008): Foghorn Outdoors.California Recreational Lakes and Rivers (1538-148X); (until 2000): California Recreational Lakes and Rivers; California Boating and Water Sports (1088-3274)
Published by: Avalon Travel Publishing, 1400 65th St, Ste 250, Emeryville, CA 94608. TEL 510-595-3664, FAX 510-595-4228, info@travelmatters.com, http://www.foghorn.com.

917 USA ISSN 2151-9560
▼ **MOON OUTDOORS: MINNESOTA CAMPING.** Variant title: Moon Minnesota Camping. Text in English. 2010 (June). triennial. USD 14.95 per issue (effective 2011). **Document type:** *Consumer.* **Description:** Travel guide for camping and outdoor adventures in Minnesota.
Published by: Avalon Travel Publishing, 1700 4th St, Berkeley, CA 94710. TEL 510-595-3664, info@travelmatters.com. Ed. Jake Kulju.

917.94 USA ISSN 1557-2579
TX907.3.C2
MOON OUTDOORS. NORTHERN CALIFORNIA CABINS & COTTAGES. Text in English. 2002. irreg., latest 2006. USD 17.95 per issue (effective 2011). **Document type:** *Handbook/Manual/Guide, Consumer.* **Description:** Covers some of the most diverse and beautiful landscapes in the country.
Formerly (until 2006): Foghorn Outdoors. Northern California Cabins & Cottages (1538-053X)
Published by: Avalon Travel Publishing, 1700 4th St, Berkeley, CA 94710. TEL 510-595-3664, FAX 800-351-5073, avalon.publicity@perseusbooks.com.

910.91 USA ISSN 1557-2587
GV191.42.O7
MOON OUTDOORS: OREGON CAMPING. Text in English. 2002. biennial, latest 2nd ed. USD 19.95 2nd ed. (effective 2008). **Document type:** *Guide, Consumer.*
Formerly (until 2006): Oregon Camping (1538-2745)
Published by: Avalon Travel Publishing, 1700 4th St, Berkeley, CA 94710. TEL 510-595-3664, avalon.publicity@perseusbooks.com, http://www.avalontravelbooks.com.

917.53 USA ISSN 1947-4024
GV199.42.W17
▼ **MOON OUTDOORS: TAKE A HIKE IN WASHINGTON, DC.** Text in English. 2009. triennial. USD 17.95 per issue (effective 2009). **Document type:** *Guide, Consumer.* **Description:** Guide for hiking in Washington, DC.
Published by: Avalon Travel Publishing, 1700 4th St, Berkeley, CA 94710. TEL 510-595-3664, info@travelmatters.com.

910.91 USA ISSN 1557-7171
GV199.42.C22
MOON OUTDOORS: TAKE A HIKE LOS ANGELES. Text in English. 2006. triennial, latest 1st ed. USD 16.95 1st ed. (effective 2008). **Document type:** *Guide, Consumer.*
Published by: Avalon Travel Publishing, 1700 4th St, Berkeley, CA 94710. TEL 510-595-3664, avalon.publicity@perseusbooks.com, http://www.avalontravelbooks.com.

917.76 USA ISSN 1947-413X
F614.M6
▼ **MOON OUTDOORS: TAKE A HIKE MINNEAPOLIS & ST. PAUL.** Text in English. 2009. triennial. USD 17.95 per issue (effective 2009). **Document type:** *Guide, Consumer.* **Description:** Guide for hiking in Minneapolis and St. Paul, Minnesota.
Published by: Avalon Travel Publishing, 1700 4th St, Berkeley, CA 94710. TEL 510-595-3664, info@travelmatters.com, http://www.foghorn.com.

910.91 USA ISSN 1559-3371
GV199.42.N64
MOON OUTDOORS: TAKE A HIKE NEW YORK CITY. Text in English. 2006. biennial, latest 1st ed. USD 16.95 1st ed. (effective 2008). **Document type:** *Guide, Consumer.* **Description:** Describes various trails and provides detailed directions to each trailhead along with an easy-to-use map for each trail with point-by-point navigation.
Published by: Avalon Travel Publishing, 1700 4th St, Berkeley, CA 94710. TEL 510-595-3664, avalon.publicity@perseusbooks.com, http://www.avalontravelbooks.com.

910.2 USA ISSN 1944-4702
GV199.42.O72
▼ **MOON OUTDOORS: TAKE A HIKE PORTLAND**; hikes within two hours of the city. Text in English. 2009. triennial. USD 16.95 per issue (effective 2011). **Document type:** *Handbook/Manual/Guide, Consumer.* **Description:** Hike profile contains practical information including point-by-point trail instructions, contact information, facilities, fees, parking instructions, and an easy-to-use map for each trail.
Related titles: Online - full text ed.
Published by: Avalon Travel Publishing, 1700 4th St, Berkeley, CA 94710. TEL 510-595-3664, FAX 800-351-5073, atpfeedback@avalonpub.com.

910.91 USA ISSN 1559-1778
GV199.42.W2
MOON OUTDOORS: TAKE A HIKE SEATTLE. Text in English. 2006. biennial, latest 1st ed. USD 16.95 per issue (effective 2008). **Document type:** *Guide, Consumer.* **Description:** Describes various trails and provides detailed directions to each trailhead along with an easy-to-use map for each trail with point-by-point navigation.
Published by: Avalon Travel Publishing, 1700 4th St, Berkeley, CA 94710. TEL 510-595-3664, avalon.publicity@perseusbooks.com, http://www.avalontravelbooks.com.

917.92 USA ISSN 2153-9944
GV191.42.U8
MOON OUTDOORS: UTAH CAMPING. Variant title: Utah Camping. Text in English. 2001. irreg. USD 17.95 per issue (effective 2010). **Document type:** *Guide, Consumer.* **Description:** Travel guide for camping and outdoor activities in Utah.
Formerly (until 2009): Foghorn Outdoors: Utah Camping (1533-0044)
Published by: Avalon Travel Publishing, 1700 4th St, Berkeley, CA 94710. TEL 510-595-3664, info@travelmatters.com, http://www.avalontravelbooks.com.

917.47 USA ISSN 1946-3405
▼ **MORNINGSIDE HEIGHTS.** Text in English. 2009. s-a. USD 4.99 per issue (effective 2009). adv. **Document type:** *Guide, Consumer.* **Description:** Pocket-sized guide for Morningside Heights, New York.
Published by: Hot and Cool Guide LLC, 1375 Broadway, 3rd Fl, New York, NY 10018. TEL 800-282-8144, FAX 646-417-8259, question@HotAndCoolGuide.com. adv.: page USD 3,360; 4.125 x 7.375.

910.202 GBR ISSN 1363-7479
MOROCCO HANDBOOK. Text in English. 1996. biennial. GBP 14.99 per issue (effective 2010). adv. **Document type:** *Handbook/Manual/Guide, Consumer.* **Description:** Covers all the basics from where to stay and where to eat to cycling, walking and how to get around the Morocco.
Supersedes in part (in 1997): Morocco and Tunisia Handbook (1358-3301)
—CCC.
Published by: Footprint Handbooks Ltd., 6 Riverside Ct, Lower Bristol Rd, Bath, Avon BA2 3DZ, United Kingdom. TEL 44-1225-469141, FAX 44-1225-469461, wwwinfo@footprintbooks.com.

MORRIS MUSEUM. NEWSLETTER. *see* MUSEUMS AND ART GALLERIES

910.202 USA
MOTEL MAGAZINE. Text in English. 1993. bi-m. USD 10.
Media: Online - full text. Ed. Chris Minnick.

MOTOR UND REISEN. *see* TRANSPORTATION—Automobiles

MOTORCARAVAN & MOTORHOME MONTHLY. *see* SPORTS AND GAMES—Outdoor Life

MOTORCYCLE CONSUMER NEWS. *see* SPORTS AND GAMES—Bicycles And Motorcycles

MOTORCYCLIST. *see* SPORTS AND GAMES—Bicycles And Motorcycles

MOTORRAD ABENTEUER; das Reportage-Magazin. *see* SPORTS AND GAMES—Bicycles And Motorcycles

915 796.93 AUS
MOUNT BULLER NEWS. Text in English. 1983. w. bk.rev.
Incorporates: This Week in Mount Buller; Formerly: Mount Buller Guide
Published by: Mansfield Newspapers Pty. Ltd., 96 High St, Mansfield, VIC 3722, Australia.

910.2 GBR ISSN 2045-6476
▼ **MOUNT KENYA TOURISM CIRCUIT ASSOCIATION. GUIDE.** Variant title: Mount Kenya Tourism Circuit Association. Destination Guide. Text in English. 2011. a. free (effective 2011). **Document type:** *Handbook/Manual/Guide, Consumer.*
Published by: (Mount Kenya Tourism Circuit Association KEN), Land & Marine Publications Ltd., 1 Kings Ct, Newcomen Way, Severalls Business Park, Colchester, Essex CO4 9RA, United Kingdom. TEL 44-1206-752902, FAX 44-1206-842958, publishing@landmarine.com, http://www.landmarine.com. Ed. Denis Gathanju.

910.4 DEU ISSN 1618-3622
MOUNTAIN MANAGER. Text in German. 1970. 8/yr. EUR 64 domestic; EUR 74 foreign; EUR 9 newsstand/cover (effective 2009). adv. back issues avail. **Document type:** *Journal, Trade.*
Formerly (until 2001): M I S - Motor im Schnee (0178-1529)
Published by: EuBuCo Verlag GmbH, Geheimrat-Hummel-Platz 4, Hochheim, 65239, Germany. TEL 49-6146-6050, FAX 49-6146-605200, verlag@eubuco.de, http://www.eubuco.de. Ed. Markus Kalchgruber. Adv. contact Joyce Hoch. B&W page EUR 2,432, color page EUR 3,568; trim 210 x 297. Circ: 4,750 (paid and controlled).

MOUNTAIN PILOT; the mountains aviation magazine. *see* TRANSPORTATION—Air Transport

910.202 USA
MOUNTAIN TRAVEL - SOBEK, THE ADVENTURE COMPANY. Text in English. 1970. a. membership. adv. illus. index. **Description:** Contains descriptive listing of adventure travel vacations with dates and costs.
Former titles: Sobek's Exceptional Adventures; Sobek's Adventure Annual; Sobek's Adventure Vacation
Published by: Mountain Travel - Sobek, 1266 66th St., Ste. 4, Emeryville, CA 94608-1159. Ed. Dena Bartolome. Circ: 90,000 (controlled).

MOVING TO ALBERTA. *see* REAL ESTATE

MOVING TO OTTAWA/EMMENAGER A OTTAWA - HULL. *see* REAL ESTATE

MOVING TO SASKATCHEWAN. *see* REAL ESTATE

MOVING TO SOUTHWESTERN ONTARIO. *see* REAL ESTATE

MOVING TO TORONTO. *see* REAL ESTATE

MOVING TO VANCOUVER & BRITISH COLUMBIA. *see* REAL ESTATE

MOVING TO WINNIPEG & MANITOBA. *see* REAL ESTATE

MPLS. - SAINT PAUL MAGAZINE. *see* GENERAL INTEREST PERIODICALS—United States

910.202 GBR ISSN 0251-0340
MSAFIRI; connecting Africa to the world. Text in English. 1980. q. adv. back issues avail. **Document type:** *Magazine, Consumer.*

Related titles: Online - full text ed.: ISSN 2046-1836. free (effective 2011).
Published by: (Kenya Airways KEN), Travel Africa Ltd., 4 Rycote Ln Farm, Milton Common, Oxford, Oxfordshire OX9 2NZ, United Kingdom. TEL 44-1844-278883, FAX 44-1844-278893, service@travelafricamag.com, http://www.travelafricamag.com/. Ed. William Gray. Pub. Craig Rix. Adv. contact Dave Southwood.

914.672 ESP ISSN 1988-7272
MUCHO MAS EN .. TEIA. Text in Spanish. 2001. q.
Related titles: Supplement(s): Mucho Mas En, Extra. ISSN 1888-2935. 2007.
Published by: De Choisy, S.L., Calle Industria, 1 Plgo, Buvisa, Teia, Barcelona, 08329, Spain. TEL 34-93- 5553230, FAX 34-93- 5401640, http://www.dechoisy.com.

MUENCHEN UND NUERNBERG VON HINTEN; das schwule Reisebuch. *see* HOMOSEXUALITY

MUNDO MAYA/MAYA WORLD. *see* ANTHROPOLOGY

914.304 USA ISSN 1939-991X
DD901.M76
MUNICH & BAVARIA. Text in English. 1984. irreg., latest 1st ed. USD 16.95 per issue (effective 2008). adv. **Document type:** *Guide, Consumer.* **Description:** Provides an insider's key to both the Germany's urban pleasures and the countryside.
Formerly: Fodor's Munich
Published by: Fodor's Travel Publications, Inc. (Subsidiary of: Random House Inc.), 1745 Broadway, 15th Fl, New York, NY 10019. TEL 212-572-2313, editors@fodors.com, http://www.fodors.com. **Dist. by:** Random House Inc., 400 Hahn Rd, Westminster, MD 21157.

910 AUS
MURRAY REGION TOURIST NEWS. Text in English. 1976. bi-m. **Document type:** *Newspaper.* **Description:** Features news, information for tourists, attractions, places of interest and travel information in general.
Formerly (until 1986): Tourist News
Published by: Sunraysia Publishing Co. Pty. Ltd., 22 Deakin Ave, PO Box 1400, Mildura, VIC 3500, Australia. TEL 61-3-50230211, FAX 61-3-50212412, admin@sunraysiadaily.com.au.

059.9204 BHR
AL-MUSAFIR AL-ARABI/ARAB TRAVELLER. Text in Arabic. 1984. bi-m.
Published by: Falcon Publishing, PO Box 5028, Manama, Bahrain. TEL 253162, FAX 259694, TELEX 8917 FALPUB BN. Ed. Muhammad As Said.

910.2 ITA ISSN 1827-4226
MUSEI D'ITALIA. Text in Italian. 1998. a. price varies. **Document type:** *Directory, Consumer.*
Published by: (Touring Club Italiano), Touring Editore, Corso Italia 10, Milan, 20122, Italy. TEL 39-02-85261, http://www.touringclub.it.

MUSEUMS IN MANITOBA (YEAR)/MUSEES DU MANITOBA (YEAR); preserving Manitoba's heritage. *see* MUSEUMS AND ART GALLERIES

917.604 USA
MUSIC CITY VACATION GUIDE. Text in English. 1992. a. free to qualified personnel (effective 2009). illus. **Document type:** *Magazine, Consumer.* **Description:** Provides information on lodging, dining, attractions, tours, shopping and airline services in the Nashville area.
Published by: Nashville Convention & Visitors Bureau, One Nashville Place, 150 Fourth Ave North, Ste G-250, Nashville, TN 37219. TEL 615-259-4730, 800-657-6910, FAX 615-259-4126, Nashcvb@visitmusiccity.com.

914.95 GRC
MYKONOS GUIDE. Text in Greek. a. **Document type:** *Magazine, Consumer.*
Published by: Liberis Publications S.A./Ekdoseon Lymperi A.E., Ioannou Metaxa 80, Karelas, Koropi 19400, Greece. TEL 30-1-6198000, FAX 30-1-6198608, info@liberis.gr, http://www.liberis.gr. Circ: 6,000.

338.4791 USA
MYNEWS@SABRE.COM. Text in English. 2001. m. **Document type:** *Journal, Trade.* **Description:** Provides information for travel agents on the latest trends, tools and techniques for providing better service to customers.
Media: Online - full content.
Published by: Sabre Inc., 3150 Sabre Dr., Southlake, TX 76092-2103. TEL 817-963-6400, http://www.sabre.com.

910.2 796.352 USA
MYRTLE BEACH GOLF HOLIDAY MAGAZINE. Text in English. a. free. 140 p./no.; **Description:** Contains general tourist information on Myrtle Beach with listings of 75 golf courses and 72 golf package providers.
Formerly: Myrtle Beach Golf Holiday Planning Guide
Published by: Myrtle Beach Golf Holiday, 3420 Pampas Dr., Myrtle Beach, SC 29577. TEL 800-845-4653, http://www.golfholiday.com/.

MYSTIC TRAVELER. *see* LEISURE AND RECREATION

N A D A MANUFACTURED HOUSING COST GUIDE. *see* BUILDING AND CONSTRUCTION

910.202 NOR ISSN 1503-9250
N A F GUIDE EUROPA. (Norges Automobil Forbund) Text in Norwegian. 1973. a. NOK 298 per issue (effective 2005). **Document type:** *Consumer.* **Description:** Tourbook for traveling by car in Europe.
Formerly (until 2004): Med Bil i Europa (0805-3596); Incorporates (1994-1999): Reisefakta (0807-9536)
Published by: Norges Automobil Forbund/Norwegian Automobile Federation, Oestensjoeveien 14, Oslo, 0609, Norway. TEL 47-22-341400, FAX 47-22-331372, http://www.naf.no.

910.02173 USA
N A P A A NEWS. Text in English. 1978. bi-m. USD 40, USD 55 (effective 2000). stat. back issues avail. **Description:** Documentation of amusement parks and amusement rides past and present audience is not limited.
Published by: National Amusement Park Historical Association, P O Box 83, Mt. Prospect, IL 60056. http://www.napha.org/. Ed. Greg Can Compel. Circ: 750.

796.525 658 USA
N C A CAVE TALK. Text in English. 1972. bi-m. **Document type:** *Newsletter.* **Description:** For show cave industry personnel on tourism events and ideas.
Published by: National Caves Association, 1904 Mammoth Cave Pkwy, PO Box 280, Park City, KY 42160. TEL 270-749-2228, FAX 270-749-2428, info@cavern.com, http://www.cavern.com.

910.202 USA
N W PALATE MAGAZINE; wine, food, & travel of the Pacific Northwest. Text in English. 1983. bi-m. USD 21; USD 3.95 newsstand/cover (effective 2000). bk.rev. back issues avail. **Document type:** *Magazine, Consumer.* **Description:** Includes wine reviews in the form of rated tasting notes of new releases, food and wine feature articles, recipes, restaurant and lodging information, wine-maker and chef profiles.
Former titles: Northwest Palate (0892-8363); (until 1987): Oregon Wine Review (0736-8496)
Published by: Pacifica Publishing, Inc., PO Box 10860, Portland, OR 97296-0860. TEL 503-224-6039, FAX 503-222-5312. Ed., Pub., R&P, Adv. contact Cameron Nagel. Circ: 45,000.

919.3005 NZL ISSN 1177-312X
N Z HOLIDAY HOTSPOTS. (New Zealand) Variant title: Holiday Hotspots. Text in English. 200?. q. adv. **Document type:** *Magazine, Consumer.*
Related titles: Online - full content ed.
Published by: Prestige Community Newspapers Ltd., PO Box 50 102, Porirua, New Zealand. TEL 64-4-2373203, FAX 64-4-2379249, info@pcn.co.nz. Ed. Chrys Ayley.

919.304 NZL ISSN 1176-3051
N Z TODAY. (New Zealand) Text in English. bi-m. **Document type:** *Magazine, Consumer.*
Formerly (until 2002): S E Magazine
Published by: Straight 8 Publishing, Symonds St, PO Box 8673, Auckland, New Zealand. TEL 64-9-3695412, FAX 64-9-3695422, admin@straight8.co.nz, http://www.drivermagazine.co.nz.

796.5 POL ISSN 1230-9931
NA SZLAKU; gory - turystyka - alphinizm. Text in Polish. 1986. m. PLZ 64; PLZ 7 newsstand/cover (effective 2002). adv. bk.rev. illus. back issues avail. **Document type:** *Magazine, Consumer.* **Description:** Covers travel, mountaineering, climbing and sightseeing.
Published by: Oficyna Wydawnicza Sudety, Rynek Ratusz 11-12, Wroclaw, 50106, Poland. TEL 48-71-3438669, FAX 48-71-3436746. Ed. Krzysztof R Mazurski. Circ: 2,000 (paid).

910 SWE ISSN 1652-764X
NAER OCH FJAERRAN. Text in Swedish. 2004. 3/yr. adv. **Document type:** *Magazine, Consumer.*
Published by: Media Strategi AB, Grev Turegatan 7A, Stockholm, 11446, Sweden. TEL 46-8-6795411, nelly.westrin@mediastrategi.se, http://www.mediastrategi.se. adv.: page SEK 39,900; trim 225 x 297. Circ: 45,000 (controlled).

910.202 GBR ISSN 1363-7495
DT1517
NAMIBIA HANDBOOK. Text in English. 1997. biennial. GBP 14.99 per issue (effective 2010). adv. back issues avail. **Document type:** *Handbook/Manual/Guide, Consumer.* **Description:** Covers all the basics from where to stay and where to eat to cycling, walking and how to get around the Namibia.
—CCC.
Published by: Footprint Handbooks Ltd., 6 Riverside Ct, Lower Bristol Rd, Bath, Avon BA2 3DZ, United Kingdom. TEL 44-1225-469141, FAX 44-1225-469461, wwwinfo@footprintbooks.com.

338.4791 NAM ISSN 1028-0820
NAMIBIA HOLIDAY AND TRAVEL. Text in English. 1995. a. ZAR 40 (effective 1999 & 2000). adv. tr.lit. back issues avail. **Document type:** *Journal, Trade.* **Description:** Offers information concerning tourism products, general information on the country for use by people in the tourism trade, and selling Namibia as a destination.
Related titles: Online - full text ed.
Published by: Venture Publications, Storch St 5, Windhoek, Namibia. TEL 264-61-225665, FAX 264-61-220410. Ed. Rieth van Schalkwyk. Pub. Paul van Schalkwyk. R&P Carol Sentefol. adv.: color page NAD 7,750; trim 210 x 297. Circ: 10,000. **Dist. by:** PO Box 215593, Windhoek, Namibia.

910.2 USA
NAPLES GUIDE; the magazine of art, antiques, entertainment and more. Text in English. 1953. m. USD 24; USD 30 foreign (effective 1999). adv. bk.rev.; dance rev.; film rev.; music rev.; play rev.; video rev. illus.; maps. 48 p./no. 2 cols./p.; **Document type:** *Magazine, Consumer.* **Description:** Contains a complete resource guide to Southwest Florida residents, tourists and newcomers packed with events, arts, shopping, dining, real estate, golf, maps, art gallery listings and more.
Related titles: Online - full text ed.
Address: 852 1st Ave S., Ste. 204, Naples, FL 34102-6122. TEL 941-262-6524. Ed., Pub., Adv. contact Alyce Mathias. B&W page USD 1,070, color page USD 1,455; trim 8.5 x 5.5. Circ: 270,000.

647 AUS ISSN 1328-7214
NATIONAL ACCOMMODATION GUIDE. Text in English. 1963. a. AUD 20 (effective 2008). adv. 950 p./no.; **Document type:** *Directory, Consumer.* **Description:** Provides list of all accommodation types in Australia for tourists.
Former titles (until 1994): Accommodation Australia; (until 1991): Australian National Tourguide (0812-8766); Which was formed by the merger of (1981-1984): Australian Tourguides. Caravan Camping Guide (0810-607X); (1981-1984): Australian Tourguides. Accommodation Guide (0810-4018); Which was formerly (until 1981): Australian Accommodation Guide (0810-400X); Which was formed by the merger of (1960-1977): Royal Automobile Association of South Australia. Accommodation Guide (0810-4026); (1974-1977): Royal Automobile Club of Victoria. Australian Accommodation Guide (0155-2848); Which was formerly (1960-1974): Royal Automobile Club of Victoria. Accommodation Guide (0810-3399)
Published by: A A A Tourism Pty Ltd., Level 3, 131 Queen St, Melbourne, VIC 3000, Australia. TEL 61-3-86012200, FAX 61-3-86012222, advertising@aaatourism.com.au. Ed. Garth Morrison. Pub. Tim Corr. Adv. contact Jennifer Goldsmith. page AUD 10,775; trim 160 x 250. Circ: 200,000.

916.8 ZAF
NATIONAL ACCOMMODATION GUIDE; a collection of quality star graded serviced accommodation in South Africa. Text in English, French, German. 1994. a. ZAR 30. **Document type:** *Directory.*
Published by: Satour, Private Bag X164, Pretoria, 0001, South Africa.

910.202 USA ISSN 0747-0932
G1
NATIONAL GEOGRAPHIC TRAVELER. Text in English. 1984. 8/yr. USD 10 domestic; CAD 34 in Canada; USD 36 elsewhere; USD 4.99 newsstand/cover domestic (effective 2009). adv. illus.; maps. Index. back issues avail.; reprints avail. **Document type:** *Magazine, Consumer.* **Description:** Aims to be the source for the active, curious traveler. Every article is designed to inspire readers to pick up and go and to provide them with the tools and orientation to do so.
Related titles: Online - full text ed.; ◆ Supplement(s): Healthy Traveler.
Indexed: A01, A02, A03, A08, A11, A22, A26, ASIP, C05, C12, CPerI, G05, G06, G07, G08, G09, I05, I06, I07, M01, M02, M04, M06, MASUSE, MagInd, P02, P07, P10, P34, P48, P53, P54, PQC, S23, T02, U01.
—IE, Infotrieve, Ingenta.
Published by: National Geographic Society, PO Box 98199, Washington, DC 20090. TEL 800-647-5463, askngs@nationalgeographic.com, http://www.nationalgeographic.com/. Ed. Keith Bellows. Pub. Dawn Drew. R&P Judy Levis TEL 202-828-5482. adv.: B&W page USD 54,435, color page USD 72,580; trim 8 x 10.5. Circ: 723,657 (paid). **Dist. in UK by:** Seymour Distribution Ltd, 86 Newman St, London W1T 3EX, United Kingdom. TEL 44-20-73968000, FAX 44-20-73968002.

NATIONAL GEOGRAPHIC TRAVELER. *see* GEOGRAPHY

NATIONAL GEOGRAPHIC TRAVELER. *see* GEOGRAPHY

910.202 USA ISSN 1933-6470
F902.3
NATIONAL GEOGRAPHIC TRAVELER. ALASKA. Text in English. 2006. irreg., latest 2006, 2nd ed. USD 22.95 per issue (effective 2009). back issues avail. **Document type:** *Guide, Consumer.*
Published by: National Geographic Society, PO Box 98199, Washington, DC 20090. TEL 800-647-5463, askngs@nationalgeographic.com, http://www.nationalgeographic.com/.

910.202 USA ISSN 2154-3429
▼ **NATIONAL GEOGRAPHIC TRAVELER. ARGENTINA.** Text in English. 2010. irreg. USD 27.95 per issue (effective 2010). reprints avail. **Document type:** *Guide, Consumer.* **Description:** Contains ideas for getting behind the scenes at travel destinations, including studying Spanish, celebrating the tango, and wine-tasting in some of the world's beautiful wineries.
Published by: National Geographic Society, PO Box 98199, Washington, DC 20090. TEL 800-647-5463, askngs@nationalgeographic.com, http://www.nationalgeographic.com/.

910.202 USA ISSN 1933-4044
DU95
NATIONAL GEOGRAPHIC TRAVELER. AUSTRALIA. Text in English. 1999. irreg., latest 2008, 3rd ed. USD 27.95 per issue (effective 2009). back issues avail. **Document type:** *Guide, Consumer.*
Published by: National Geographic Society, PO Box 98199, Washington, DC 20090. TEL 800-647-5463, askngs@nationalgeographic.com, http://www.nationalgeographic.com/.

910.202 USA ISSN 1935-0341
F1009
NATIONAL GEOGRAPHIC TRAVELER. CANADA. Text in English. 1999. irreg., latest 2006, 2nd ed. USD 27.95 per issue (effective 2009). **Document type:** *Guide, Consumer.*
Published by: National Geographic Society, PO Box 98199, Washington, DC 20090. TEL 800-647-5463, askngs@nationalgeographic.com, http://www.nationalgeographic.com/.

910.202 USA ISSN 1932-5371
F1543.5
NATIONAL GEOGRAPHIC TRAVELER. COSTA RICA. Text in English. 2000. irreg., latest 2006, 3rd ed. USD 22.95 per issue (effective 2009). back issues avail.; reprints avail. **Document type:** *Guide, Consumer.*
Published by: National Geographic Society, PO Box 98199, Washington, DC 20090. TEL 800-647-5463, askngs@nationalgeographic.com, http://www.nationalgeographic.com/.

910.202 USA ISSN 2161-184X
DR1509
▼ **NATIONAL GEOGRAPHIC TRAVELER. CROATIA.** Text in English. 2011. irreg. **Document type:** *Guide, Consumer.*
Published by: National Geographic Society, PO Box 98199, Washington, DC 20090. TEL 813-979-6845, 800-647-5463, ngsforum@nationalgeographic.com, http://www.nationalgeographic.com/.

910.202 USA ISSN 1934-2209
DS805.2
NATIONAL GEOGRAPHIC TRAVELER. JAPAN. Text in English. 2000. irreg., latest 2008, 3rd ed. USD 27.95 per issue (effective 2009). back issues avail. **Document type:** *Guide, Consumer.*
Published by: National Geographic Society, PO Box 98199, Washington, DC 20090. TEL 800-647-5463, askngs@nationalgeographic.com, http://www.nationalgeographic.com/.

910.202 USA ISSN 1933-6748
DP355
NATIONAL GEOGRAPHIC TRAVELER. MADRID. Text in English. 2006. irreg., latest 2006, 2nd ed. USD 22.95 per issue (effective 2009). back issues avail. **Document type:** *Guide, Consumer.*
Published by: National Geographic Society, PO Box 98199, Washington, DC 20090. TEL 800-647-5463, askngs@nationalgeographic.com, http://www.nationalgeographic.com/.

910.202 USA ISSN 1933-4052
F319.M6
NATIONAL GEOGRAPHIC TRAVELER. MIAMI & THE KEYS. Text in English. 1999. irreg., latest 2005, 3rd ed. USD 22.95 per issue (effective 2009). **Document type:** *Guide, Consumer.*
Published by: National Geographic Society, PO Box 98199, Washington, DC 20090. TEL 800-647-5463, askngs@nationalgeographic.com, http://www.nationalgeographic.com/.

910.202 USA ISSN 1933-4036
F379.N53
NATIONAL GEOGRAPHIC TRAVELER. NEW ORLEANS. Text in English. 2000. irreg., latest 2005, 2nd ed. USD 22.95 per issue (effective 2009). **Document type:** *Guide, Consumer.*
Published by: National Geographic Society, PO Box 98199, Washington, DC 20090. TEL 800-647-5463, askngs@nationalgeographic.com, http://www.nationalgeographic.com/. Ed. Keith Bellows.

910.202 USA ISSN 1933-3005
F128.18
NATIONAL GEOGRAPHIC TRAVELER. NEW YORK. Text in English. 1999. irreg., latest 2006, 2nd ed. USD 22.95 per issue (effective 2009). **Document type:** *Guide, Consumer.*
Published by: National Geographic Society, PO Box 98199, Washington, DC 20090. TEL 800-647-5463, askngs@nationalgeographic.com, http://www.nationalgeographic.com/. Ed. Keith Bellows.

910.202 USA ISSN 1931-6356
DP516
NATIONAL GEOGRAPHIC TRAVELER. PORTUGAL. Text in English. 2005. irreg., latest 2005. USD 22.95 per issue (effective 2009). **Document type:** *Guide, Consumer.*
Published by: National Geographic Society, PO Box 98199, Washington, DC 20090. TEL 800-647-5463, askngs@nationalgeographic.com, http://www.nationalgeographic.com/.

910.202 USA ISSN 1934-2349
DG862
NATIONAL GEOGRAPHIC TRAVELER. SICILY. Text in English. 2005. irreg., latest 2008, 2nd ed. USD 19.95 per issue (effective 2009). **Document type:** *Guide, Consumer.*
Published by: National Geographic Society, PO Box 98199, Washington, DC 20090. TEL 800-647-5463, askngs@nationalgeographic.com, http://www.nationalgeographic.com/. Ed. Keith Bellows.

910.202 USA ISSN 1934-2195
DP14
NATIONAL GEOGRAPHIC TRAVELER. SPAIN. Text in English. 2001. irreg., latest 2005, 3rd ed. USD 27.95 per issue (effective 2009). back issues avail. **Document type:** *Guide, Consumer.*
Published by: National Geographic Society, PO Box 98199, Washington, DC 20090. TEL 800-647-5463, askngs@nationalgeographic.com, http://www.nationalgeographic.com/. Ed. Keith Bellows.

910.2 USA ISSN 1548-3452
SB482.A4
THE NATIONAL PARKS TRAVELER. Text in English. 2004. irreg. USD 250 per issue to non-members; USD 150 per issue to members (effective 2009). **Document type:** *Guide, Consumer.* **Description:** Provides a profile of U.S. trips that include a visit to national/state parks and highlights details of the most recent trip taken by national park travelers.
Related titles: Online - full text ed.: ISSN 1559-9353.
Published by: Travel Industry Association of America, 1100 New York Ave, NW, Ste 450, Washington, DC 20005. TEL 202-408-8422, FAX 202-408-1255, feedback@tia.org.

910.2 AUS
NATIONAL TOURIST PARK GUIDE. Text in English. 1996. a. AUD 20 (effective 2008). adv. 420 p./no.; **Document type:** *Directory, Consumer.* **Description:** Lists all tourist park type accommodation in Australia for tourists.
Formerly (until 2001): Tourist Park Accommodation Guide (1328-7222)
Published by: A A A Tourism Pty Ltd., Level 3, 131 Queen St, Melbourne, VIC 3000, Australia. TEL 61-3-86012200, FAX 61-3-86012222, advertising@aaatourism.com.au. Ed. Garth Morrison. Adv. contact Jennifer Goldsmith. page AUD 9,740; trim 160 x 250. Circ: 200,000.

NATIONAL VENUES GUIDE. *see* MEETINGS AND CONGRESSES

NATIONWIDE OVERNIGHT STABLING DIRECTORY & EQUESTRIAN VACATION GUIDE. *see* SPORTS AND GAMES—Horses And Horsemanship

910.202 USA ISSN 1933-4451
F548.18
A NATIVE'S GUIDE TO CHICAGO. Text in English. irreg., latest 2004, 4th ed. USD 15.95 per issue (effective 2008). **Document type:** *Guide, Consumer.*
Formerly: Know More, Spend Less
Published by: Lake Claremont Press, PO Box 25291, Chicago, IL 60625. TEL 312-226-8400, FAX 312-226-8420, lcp@lakeclaremont.com.

910.91 USA
NATURAL TRAVELER; travel of an uncommon nature. Text in English. m. **Document type:** *Magazine, Consumer.*
Published by: Natural Traveler, Inc., Box 728, Glen Cove, NY 11542. TEL 516-759-4847, FAX 516-671-9765, editors@naturaltraveler.com, http://www.naturaltraveler.com. Ed. Tony Tedeschi.

910.2 CHE ISSN 0028-0925
NATURFREUND/AMI DE LA NATURE. Text in French, German. 1962. bi-m. CHF 30. adv. bk.rev. abstr.; charts; illus.; stat. **Document type:** *Bulletin.*
Published by: Naturfreunde Schweiz/Federation Suisse des Amis de la Nature, Pavillonweg 3, PO Box 7364, Bern, 3001, Switzerland. TEL 031-3016088.

910.202 BEL
NATURISM; world handbook - guide mondiale - f.k.k. weltfuerer. Text in Dutch, English, French, German. 1952. biennial. USD 48 domestic; USD 50 foreign (effective 2001). adv. charts; illus. **Description:** Lists vacation centers and club grounds as well as activies, clubs and guides for the naturist.
Published by: International Naturist Federation, St Hubertusstraat 5, Berchem - Antwerp, 2600, Belgium. TEL 32-3-2300572, FAX 32-3-2812607. Ed. Stefan Lahbrechts. Circ: 30,000.

914.92 NLD ISSN 1572-7939
NAVENANT. Text in Dutch. 2004. bi-m. EUR 12.50; EUR 4.50 newsstand/cover (effective 2009). adv. **Document type:** *Magazine, Consumer.*
Published by: Hotbox Media bv, Kraanpoort 10, Roermond, 6041 EG, Netherlands. TEL 31-475-569505, FAX 31-475-569506. Eds. Anouck Oomen, Maartje Gerris. adv.: page EUR 1,400; bleed 200 x 265. Circ: 20,000.

910 797.1 FRA ISSN 1957-584X
NAVIGATION DOUCE; le magazine du tourisme fluvial. Text in French. 2006. bi-m. EUR 22 (effective 2009). **Document type:** *Magazine, Consumer.*
Address: 16 Bd St Germain, Paris, 75005, France. TEL 33-1-40289156, 33-1-45841270, redaction@navigationdouce.com. Ed. Georges Couper.

910.91 USA
NCNATURAL DIGEST. Text in English. bi-m.
Media: Online - full text.
Address: 6 Huntington Rd, Asheville, NC 28805. Ed. Tim Tradwell.

914.95 DEU
NEAFON. Text in German. 2001. bi-m. EUR 36; EUR 6 newsstand/cover (effective 2007). adv. **Document type:** *Magazine, Consumer.*
Published by: Neafon Verlag, Kesselstr 34, Stuttgart, 70327, Germany. TEL 49-711-7071711, FAX 49-711-42070680, office@neafon.com. adv.: color page EUR 4,900. Circ: 28,800 (paid).

338.4791 NPL
NEPAL TRAVEL TRADE JOURNAL. Text in English. bi-m. **Document type:** *Journal, Consumer.* **Description:** Includes features on hotels and resorts, news, restaurants and other tourist information.
Related titles: Online - full content ed.
Published by: M D Publishing Co. Pvt. Ltd., Tripureswor, PO Box 3525, Kathmandu, Nepal. TEL 977-1-260327, 977-1-260418, 977-1-256003, FAX 977-1-260159, nttj@mos.com.np.

914.20954962 330 NPL
NEPAL TRAVEL TRADE REPORTER. Abbreviated title: N T T R. Text in English. 1983 (June). m. free (effective 2010). **Document type:** *Magazine, Trade.* **Description:** Covers contemporary issues, news on tourism as well as destination information's on both inbound and outbound tourism in Nepal.
Published by: Nepal Traveller Publication Pvt. Ltd., Kathmandu Business Park, Teku, P O Box 21869, Kathmandu, Nepal. TEL 977-1-4104518, FAX 977-1-4104518, ntravler@mos.com.np. Circ: 10,000.

914.20954962 NPL
NEPAL TRAVELLER; a complete guide to Nepal. Text in English. 1976. bi-m. free (effective 2010). **Document type:** *Magazine, Consumer.* **Description:** Contains useful and substantial information about the sightseeing places, culture, destinations and festivals to the tourists and any interested individuals as well as available tourism infrastructures such as hotels, casinos, airlines etc.
Former titles (until 1983): Enjoy Nepal; (until 1979): Nepal This Month
Related titles: Online - full text ed.: ISSN 1605-928X. free (effective 2010).
Published by: Nepal Traveller Publication Pvt. Ltd., Kathmandu Business Park, Teku, P O Box 21869, Kathmandu, Nepal. TEL 977-1-4104518, FAX 977-1-4104518, ntravler@mos.com.np. Ed. Bharat Shakya. Circ: 20,000.

THE NEPENTHE JOURNAL. *see* LITERATURE

338.4 913.919 DEU
NEUES AUS JAPAN (ONLINE). Text in German. 1954. m. **Document type:** *Newsletter, Consumer.*
Former titles (until 2000): Neues aus Japan (Print) (1611-776X)
Media: Online - full text.
Published by: Botschaft von Japan, Hiroshimastr 6, Berlin, 10785, Germany. TEL 49-30-210940, FAX 49-30-21094228, info@botschaft-japan.de.

919.304 NZL ISSN 1177-9349
NEUSEELAND NEWS. Text in German. 2007. bi-m. adv. **Document type:** *Newspaper, Consumer.*
Former titles (until 2007): Neuseeland-Australien-Pazifik-News.de (1177-7974); Neuseeland News
Published by: Newspac Ltd., PO Box 1441, Whangarei, New Zealand. Ed., Adv. contact Gerhard Uster.

917.93 USA ISSN 0199-1248
F836
NEVADA. Text in English. 1936. bi-m. USD 19.95 domestic; USD 29.95 foreign; USD 4.95 newsstand/cover (effective 2005). adv. bk.rev. illus. back issues avail.; reprints avail. **Document type:** *Magazine, Consumer.* **Description:** Covers the history, culture, people, events and tourist events in Nevada.
Incorporates (1987-199?): Nevada Events (0896-2588); Formerly: Nevada Highways and Parks (0028-405X)
Related titles: Microform ed.: (from PQC).
Indexed: AIAP, ASIP, GeoRef, P06, SpeleolAb.
—Ingenta.
Published by: Nevada Magazine, 401 N Carson St, #100, Carson City, NV 89701. TEL 775-687-5416, 800-495-3281, FAX 775-687-6159. Ed. David Moore. Pub. Richard Moreno. Adv. contact Susan Wunsch. color page USD 5,000; trim 8.38 x 10.88. Circ: 80,000 (paid and controlled); 60,000 (paid); 20,000 (controlled).

917.4 USA ISSN 1934-6530
NEW ENGLAND. Variant title: Eyewitness Travel Guide: New England. Text in English. 2001. irreg., latest 2007. USD 25 per issue (effective 2008). **Description:** Covers photographs and 3-D aerial views that reveal the charm of each destination in New England.
Published by: D K Publishing (Subsidiary of: Penguin Books U S A, Inc.), 375 Hudson St, New York, NY 10014. TEL 212-213-4800, FAX 201-256-0000, specialsales@dk.com.

917.42 USA ISSN 1538-8409
F32.3
NEW HAMPSHIRE (WOODSTOCK); an explorer's guide. Text in English. 1991. triennial, latest 2006, 6th ed. USD 19.95 per issue (effective 2009). back issues avail. **Description:** Provides advice for travelers of every taste and budget and includes opinionated listings of inns, B&Bs, hotels, vacation cottages and campgrounds as well as hundreds of dining recommendations.
Published by: The Countryman Press (Subsidiary of: W.W. Norton & Co., Inc.), PO Box 748, Woodstock, VT 05091. TEL 802-457-4826, 800-245-4151, FAX 802-457-1678, countrymanpress@wwnorton.com. **Dist. by:** W.W. Norton & Co., Inc., 500 5th Ave, New York, NY 10110. TEL 212-354-5500, FAX 212-869-0856, http://www.wwnorton.com.

910.10 USA ISSN 1555-9548
F132.3
NEW JERSEY; an explorer's guide. Text in English. 2005. irreg., latest 2005. USD 19.95 per issue (effective 2008). **Document type:** *Directory, Consumer.* **Description:** Reveals the cultural, historic and geographical diversity that lies beyond the New Jersey Turnpike.
Published by: The Countryman Press (Subsidiary of: W.W. Norton & Co., Inc.), PO Box 748, Woodstock, VT 05091. TEL 802-457-4826, 800-245-4151, FAX 802-457-1678, countrymanpress@wwnorton.com.

NEW JERSEY AND NATIONAL REGISTERS OF HISTORIC PLACES. *see* ARCHITECTURE

910.202 790.1 USA
NEW JERSEY CALENDAR OF EVENTS. Text in English. s-a. free (effective 2005). **Document type:** *Magazine, Consumer.* **Description:** Lists cultural, sports, and recreational activities in New Jersey.
Published by: Commerce and Economic Growth Commission, Office of Travel and Tourism, PO Box 820, Trenton, NJ 08625-0820. TEL 609-633-0981, 800-537-7397.

917 910.91 USA ISSN 1932-7323
F134.6
NEW JERSEY CURIOSITIES; quirky characters, roadside oddities & other offbeat stuff. Text in English. 2003. triennial, latest 2007, 2nd ed. USD 13.95 per issue (effective 2008). **Document type:** *Magazine, Consumer.* **Description:** Provides tourist information about New Jersey.
Published by: The Globe Pequot Press, Inc., 246 Goose Ln, PO Box 480, Guilford, CT 06437. TEL 203-458-4500, 888-249-7586, FAX 203-458-4603, 800-820-2329, info@globepequot.com, http://www.globepequot.com. Ed. Gillian Belnap.

NEW MEXICO JOURNEY. *see* TRANSPORTATION—Automobiles

917 USA ISSN 0028-6249
F791
NEW MEXICO MAGAZINE. Text in English. 1923. m. USD 17 domestic; USD 29 foreign (effective 2008). adv. bk.rev. illus. 96 p./no.; back issues avail.; reprints avail. **Document type:** *Magazine, Consumer.* **Description:** Features topics from around the Land of Enchantment, including its multicultural heritage, arts, climate, environment and the uniqueness of New Mexico's people.
Former titles (until 1974): New Mexico (0738-5420); (until 1970): New Mexico Highway Journal
Indexed: ASIP, ChPerI, Chicano, GeoRef, RILM, SpeleolAb.
—Ingenta.
Published by: State of New Mexico, Tourism Department, 495 Old Santa Fe Trail, Santa Fe, NM 87501. TEL 505-827-7447, 800-898-6639, FAX 505-827-6496. Ed., R&P Emily Drabanski. Pub. Ethel Hess. Adv. contact Wendy Abeyta. B&W page USD 3,600, color page USD 5,320. Circ: 125,000 (paid).

910.91 USA
NEW MEXICO TRAVEL NEWSLETTER. Text in English. m. free. back issues avail. **Document type:** *Newsletter.* **Description:** Provides tips about travel in New Mexico; plus a summary of the latest issues of Southern New Mexico Online Magazine and site updates.
Media: Online - full text. **Related titles:** E-mail ed.
Address: 1701 Virginia St, Silver City, NM 88061. TEL 505-538-8956, FAX 505-538-8956. Ed., Pub., R&P, Adv. contact Carla De Marco TEL 505-538-5818.

NEW ORLEANS MEETINGS PLANNERS GUIDE. *see* MEETINGS AND CONGRESSES

913.763 USA
NEW ORLEANS OFFICIAL VISITORS GUIDE. Text in English. 200?. s-a. adv. **Document type:** *Handbook/Manual/Guide, Trade.* **Description:** Provides information on accommodations, transportation and where to eat, shop and play in New Orleans.
Published by: Weaver Publications, Inc., 2420 Alcott St, Denver, CO 80211. TEL 303-458-1211, FAX 303-477-0724, info@weaver-group.com, http://pub.weaver-group.com. Circ: 700,000.

913.763 USA
NEW ORLEANS TRAVEL PLANNERS GUIDE. Text in English. a. adv. **Document type:** *Guide, Consumer.* **Description:** Includes accommodations and dining amenity charts, attractions and transportation listings, mileage charts and fly times.
Published by: Weaver Publications, Inc., 2420 Alcott St, Denver, CO 80211. TEL 303-458-1211, FAX 303-477-0724, info@weaver-group.com, http://pub.weaver-group.com. Circ: 5,000.

917.47 USA ISSN 1938-5285
F128.18
NEW YORK CITY. Variant title: Eyewitness Travel Guide: New York. Text in English. 2007. a. USD 25 (effective 2008). **Document type:** *Guide, Consumer.* **Description:** Features New York's shopping, museums, restaurants, hotels, parks, nightlife and theaters.
Formerly: New York EGuide (1933-0812)
Published by: D K Publishing (Subsidiary of: Penguin Books U S A, Inc.), 375 Hudson St, New York, NY 10014. TEL 800-631-8571, FAX 201-256-0000, specialsales@dk.com.

974 USA
NEW YORK STATE FAIR MAGAZINE. Text in English. 1955. a. USD 3. adv. **Document type:** *Magazine, Consumer.*
Formerly: New York State FairGround
Published by: New York State Fair, State Fairgrounds, Syracuse, NY 13209. FAX 315-487-9260. Ed. Joseph J Laguardia. Circ: 32,500.

917.4 USA
NEW YORK'S NIGHTLIFE. Text in English. 1979. m. USD 24.95 (effective 1999). adv. bk.rev. **Document type:** *Directory, Consumer.*
Former titles: New York's and Long Island's Nightlife; Long Island's Nightlife (0744-7590)
Published by: M.M.B. Publishers, Inc., c/o New York Update, 990 Motor Pky, Central Islip, NY 11722-1001. TEL 516-435-8890, FAX 516-435-8925. Ed. Fran Petito. Pub., R&P Mike Cutino. Adv. contact Rebecca Sochica. Circ: 175,062.

NEW ZEALAND MOTORHOMES, CARAVANS & DESTINATIONS. *see* TRANSPORTATION—Automobiles

910.91 NZL
NEW ZEALAND TRAVEL PLANNER. Text in English. 1994. q. illus.; maps. back issues avail. **Document type:** *Handbook/Manual/Guide, Consumer.* **Description:** Describes interesting and noteworthy tourist destinations in New Zealand. Includes city maps and region profiles.
Formerly: Discover New Zealand Magazine (1173-0137)
Published by: Discover New Zealand Magazine, PO Box 105 433, Auckland Central, New Zealand. FAX 64-9-303-2928, http://discovernz.co.nz/.

910.09 NZL ISSN 0113-4043
NEW ZEALAND TRAVELTRADE. Text in English. 1973. 23/yr. USD 50 domestic; USD 140 foreign; NZD 65 combined subscription domestic includes Travel Industry Directory; NZD 185 combined subscription foreign includes Travel Industry Directory (effective 2009). adv. **Document type:** *Magazine, Trade.* **Description:** Meets the needs of frontline consultants who deal directly with the public, as well as having vital news information for management.

Incorporates (in 2005): Longhaul and Stopovers (1176-5666); Former titles (until 1987): Traveltrade (0110-9006); (until 1980): Traveltrade Magazine; (until 1974): Travel Trade Magazine New Zealand
Related titles: ♦ Supplement(s): New Zealand Travel Industry Directory. ISSN 1173-907X.
Published by: T P L Media (Trade Publications), Newmarket, PO Box 9596, Auckland, 1149, New Zealand. TEL 64-9-5293027, FAX 64-9-5293001, http://www.tplmedia.co.nz/. Circ: 1,393.

NEWCOMER; an introduction to life in Belgium. *see* GENERAL INTEREST PERIODICALS—Belgium

NEWCOMER'S HANDBOOK FOR MOVING TO AND LIVING IN MINNEAPOLIS - ST. PAUL. *see* REAL ESTATE

910.10 USA ISSN 1557-9921
F869.S33
NEWCOMER'S HANDBOOK FOR MOVING TO AND LIVING IN THE SAN FRANCISCO BAY AREA. Text in English. 1997. triennial. USD 24.95 per issue (effective 2007). **Document type:** *Handbook/Manual/Guide, Consumer.*
Former titles (until 2006): Newcomer's Handbook for Moving to San Francisco and the Bay Area (1533-5100); (until 1999): Newcomer's Handbook for San Francisco (1089-9731)
Published by: First Books, 6750 SW Franklin St Ste A, Portland, OR 97223. TEL 503-968-6777, FAX 503-968-6779, https://www.firstbooks.com/index.php.

910.202 USA ISSN 1557-9913
F192.3
NEWCOMER'S HANDBOOK FOR MOVING TO AND LIVING IN WASHINGTON D C. (District of Columbia) Text in English. 1994. triennial, latest 2006, 4th ed. USD 24.95 per issue (effective 2008). **Document type:** *Handbook/Manual/Guide, Consumer.*
Former titles (2002-2006): Newcomer's Handbook for Moving to Washington DC (1535-4407); (until 1997): Newcomer's Handbook for Washington, DC (1093-8850)
Published by: First Books, 6750 SW Franklin St Ste A, Portland, OR 97223. TEL 503-968-6777, FAX 503-968-6779, https://www.firstbooks.com/index.php.

910.91 CAN
NEWCOMERS' INSIGHT. Text in English. 1999. m. free. **Document type:** *Newsletter.* **Description:** Includes calendar of events, a gardening column and a travel section.
Related titles: Online - full text ed.
Published by: Fergus-Elora Newcomers Club, Township of Centre Wellington, Civic Centre, 1 MacDonald Square, Elora, ON N0B 1S0, Canada. TEL 519-843-6103, http://www.mytown.ca/newcomers. Ed. Eileen Morand.

910.202 USA
NEWPORT DINING GUIDE. Text in English. 1974. q. free.
Published by: Newport This Week, PO Box 159, Newport, RI 02840-0002. FAX 401-846-4974.

NIAGARA PARKS COMMISSION. ANNUAL REPORT. *see* CONSERVATION

916.69 NGA
NIGERIA TOURISM DEVELOPMENT CORPORATION. OFFICIAL TOURIST GUIDE. Variant title: Welcome to Nigeria ..The Land of Hospitality, Cultural Diversity and Scenic Beauty. Text in English. 1969. irreg. free. adv. illus. **Document type:** *Government.* **Description:** Fosters an awareness of everything Nigeria has to offer to tourists, including scenic and cultural attractions, conference and hotel facilities, and international and domestic travel.
Formerly: Nigeria Tourist Guide
Published by: Nigerian Tourism Development Corporation, Block 2 Sefadu St. Zone 4, PMB 167, Wuse-Abuja, Federal Capital Territory, Nigeria. TEL 234-9-5230418-420, FAX 234-9-5230962.

910.202 FIN ISSN 1237-8623
NONSTOP. Text in Finnish. 1994. 4/yr. **Document type:** *Magazine, Consumer.*
Published by: Sanoma Magazines Finland Corporation, Lapinmaentie 1, Helsinki, 00350, Finland. TEL 358-9-1201, FAX 358-9-1205171, info@sanomamagazines.fi, http://www.sanomamagazines.fi. Circ: 15,000 (controlled).

914.92 NLD ISSN 1871-8485
NOORDERLAND. Text in Dutch. 2005. 8/yr. EUR 35 (effective 2009). adv. **Document type:** *Magazine, Consumer.*
Published by: N D C - V B K, Postbus 60, Groningen, 9700 MC, Netherlands. TEL 31-50-5844444, communicatie@ndcvbk.nl, http://www.ndcvbk.nl. adv.: B&W page EUR 2,919; trim 230 x 297.

914 NLD ISSN 1388-9923
NORDIC. Text in Dutch. 1993. q. EUR 20 domestic; EUR 23 in Belgium; EUR 5.25 newsstand/cover (effective 2009). adv. **Document type:** *Magazine, Consumer.*
Formerly (until 1996): Nordic Magazine (0929-6506)
Published by: dOrizon Media, Postbus 135, Castricum, 1900 AC, Netherlands. TEL 31-251-672136, FAX 31-251-654578, info@dorizon.nl, http://www.dorizon.nl. Ed. Jaap van Splunter. Adv. contact Harald Kolkman. color page EUR 1,350; trim 230 x 297. Circ: 5,000.

NORDIC NETWORK. *see* SPORTS AND GAMES—Outdoor Life

908 DEU ISSN 0946-1116
NORDIS; der Nordeuropa-Magazin. Text in German. 1994. bi-m. EUR 28; EUR 22 to students; EUR 5 newsstand/cover (effective 2010). adv. **Document type:** *Magazine, Consumer.*
Published by: Nordis Verlag GmbH, Maxstr 64, Essen, 45127, Germany. TEL 49-201-872290, FAX 49-201-8924511, verlag@nordis.com. Ed. Lutz Stickeln. Adv. contact Karsten Piel. Circ: 32,492 (paid and controlled).

910.91 FRA ISSN 2108-1530
▼ **NORDWAY MAGAZINE.** Text in French. 2009. 11/yr. EUR 35 (effective 2010). **Document type:** *Magazine, Consumer.*
Published by: La Voix du Nord, 8 Place du General de Gaulle, BP 549, Lille, Cedex 59023, France. TEL 33-3-20784040, contact@lavoixdunord.fr, http://www.lavoixdunord.fr. Ed. Eric Maitrot.

338.4 914.88 SWE ISSN 2000-6462
NORRLAND; tidskrift fraan norrlandsfoerbundet. Text in Swedish. 1952. a. SEK 250 membership (effective 2010). adv. illus. **Document type:** *Consumer.*
Formerly (until 2009): Norrlaendsk Tidskrift (0029-1838)
Published by: Norrlandsfoerbundet, Kyrkogatan 28, Sundsvall, 85232, Sweden. TEL 46-60-618060, FAX 46-60-175935, info@norrland.info, http://www.norrlandsforbundet.se. Ed. Catharina Ottander.

917.04 USA
NORTH AMERICAN GUIDE TO NUDE RECREATION. Text in English. 1966. a. USD 24.95 (effective 1998). adv. illus. **Document type:** *Directory.*
Formerly: Nudist Park Guide
Published by: American Association for Nude Recreation, North American Headquarters, 1703 N Main St, Ste E, Kissimmee, FL 34744. TEL 800-879-6833, 800-879-6833, FAX 407-933-7577, try-nude@aanr.com. Ed., R&P Julie Bagby. Adv. contact Kathleen Bokun. Circ: 30,000.

917.56 910.91 USA ISSN 1934-581X
F252.3
NORTH CAROLINA CURIOSITIES; quirky characters, roadside oddities & other offbeat stuff. Text in English. 1984. irreg., latest 2007, 1st ed. USD 14.95 per issue (effective 2008). **Document type:** *Guide, Consumer.* **Description:** Aims to act as a guide to unique places.
Published by: The Globe Pequot Press, Inc., 246 Goose Ln, PO Box 480, Guilford, CT 06437. TEL 203-458-4500, 888-249-7586, FAX 203-458-4603, 800-820-2329, info@globepequot.com, http://www.globepequot.com. Ed. Gillian Belnap.

917.804 USA ISSN 1078-1331
NORTH DAKOTA HORIZONS. Text in English. 1971. q. USD 15 domestic; USD 19 foreign (effective 2000). adv. bk.rev.; music rev. 32 p./no. 3 cols./p.; back issues avail. **Document type:** *Magazine, Consumer.* **Description:** To discover and showcase North Dakota's people, places, events and resources.
Published by: Greater North Dakota Association, PO Box 1091, Bismarck, ND 58502. TEL 866-462-0744, FAX 701-223-4645. Ed., R&P, Adv. contact Andrea Winkjer Collin. Circ: 12,000 (paid).

979.1 USA ISSN 1939-375X
F806
NORTHERN ARIZONA & BEYOND; a panoramic journey through nature's hidden treasures. Text in English. 2007. a. USD 3.95 per issue (effective 2011). back issues avail. **Document type:** *Magazine, Consumer.* **Description:** Features attractions, places to stay and insider information for people planning vacations to Northern Arizona.
Related titles: Online - full text ed.: ISSN 1939-3768. free (effective 2011).
Published by: OutWest Publishing LLC, PO Box 2059, Gilbert, AZ 85299. TEL 480-539-0922, FAX 480-539-5280, info@outwestpublishing.com, http://www.outwestpublishing.com. Pub. Pruett LaNora.

NORTHERN ARIZONA NEWCOMER'S GUIDE. *see* LIFESTYLE

917.94 910.91 USA ISSN 1555-4007
F867.5
NORTHERN CALIFORNIA CURIOSITIES; quirky characters, roadside oddities & other offbeat stuff. Text in English. 2005. biennial, latest 2005, 1st ed. USD 13.95 per issue (effective 2008). **Document type:** *Guide, Consumer.* **Description:** Aims to act as a guide to unique places.
Published by: The Globe Pequot Press, Inc., 246 Goose Ln, PO Box 480, Guilford, CT 06437. TEL 203-458-4500, 888-249-7586, FAX 203-458-4603, 800-820-2329, info@globepequot.com, http://www.globepequot.com. Ed. Amy Lyons TEL 203-458-4500.

796 USA
NORTHERN CALIFORNIA EXPLORE. Text in English. 5/yr. **Document type:** *Magazine, Consumer.* **Description:** Focuses on camping, hiking, mountain climbing, kayaking, skiing, fishing in Northern California.
Published by: Northern California Explore, Inc., Box 980005, W Sacramento, CA 95798. david@ncexplore.com, http://www.ncexplore.com. Ed. David Forster.

338.4 CAN ISSN 1719-9255
NORTHERN EXPERIENCE MAGAZINE. Text in English. 2006. s-a. **Document type:** *Newsletter, Consumer.*
Published by: (Norman Regional Development Corporation), Lester Communications, 701 Henry Ave, Winnipeg, MB R3E 1T9, Canada. TEL 866-953-2189, info@lesterpublications.com, http://www.lesterpublications.com.

910.91 USA ISSN 1931-1672
F572.N7
NORTHERN MICHIGAN ALMANAC. Text in English. 2005. a., latest 2005. **Document type:** *Handbook/Manual/Guide, Consumer.* **Description:** Covers information about the northern Lower Peninsula.
Published by: University of Michigan Press, 839 Greene St, Ann Arbor, MI 48104. TEL 734-764-4388, FAX 734-615-1540, umpress.title.info@umich.edu.

910.91 388.3 USA ISSN 1540-515X
NORTHERN NEW ENGLAND JOURNEY. Text in English. 1995. bi-m. USD 1 newsstand/cover; free to individual members (effective 2002). **Document type:** *Magazine, Consumer.*
Published by: A A A Northern New England, 250 Anderson St., Portland, ME 04101-2545. http://www.aaanne.com. Ed. Dorothy Clendenin. Pub. Matthew C. McKenzie.

914.6 USA ISSN 1937-1357
NORTHERN SPAIN. Variant title: Eyewitness Travel Guide: Northern Spain. Text in English. 2007. irreg., latest 2007. USD 23 per issue (effective 2008). **Document type:** *Guide, Consumer.* **Description:** Features color photographs, maps and illustrations, cutaways and floor plans of all the major sights and selection of hotels and restaurants in Northern Spain.
Published by: D K Publishing (Subsidiary of: Penguin Books U S A, Inc.), 375 Hudson St, New York, NY 10014. TEL 800-631-8571, FAX 201-256-0000, specialsales@dk.com.

910.202 USA ISSN 1059-9681
NORTHWEST TRAVEL. Text in English. 1991. bi-m. USD 18.95; USD 3.50 newsstand/cover (effective 2005). adv. bk.rev. illus.; maps. back issues avail.; reprints avail. **Document type:** *Magazine, Consumer.* **Description:** Devoted to active as well as armchair travelers with travel tips on the Pacific Northwest.
Formerly: Oregon Coast
Published by: Northwest Regional Magazines, 4969 Hwy 101 N, 2, Florence, OR 97439-0130. TEL 541-997-8401, 800-348-8401, FAX 541-997-1124, rob@presys.com, http://www.ohwy.com/. Pubs. Alicia Spooner, Robert Spooner. Adv. contact Alicia Spooner. Circ: 50,000.

910.2 647.9 FRA ISSN 1779-8051
NOS COUPS DE COEUR. Text in French. 2002. irreg. **Document type:** *Monographic series, Consumer.*
Published by: Michelin, 46 Av de Breteuil, Paris, Cedex 7 75234, France. TEL 33-1-45661234.

910.91 GBR
NOTA BENE. Text in English. 2001. 10/yr. GBP 235 domestic; GBP 250 foreign (effective 2005). **Document type:** *Magazine, Consumer.* **Description:** Contains up-to-the-minute advice on the world's most glamorous cities and exotic resorts.
Published by: Nota Bene Publishing Ltd., The Glassmill, 1 Battersea Bridge Rd, London, SW11 3BZ, United Kingdom. TEL 44-870-2404089. Circ: 8,000 (paid and controlled).

910.91 USA
NOTICIAS. Key Title: Noticias de la Republica de China. Text in Spanish. 1971. 3/m. back issues avail. **Document type:** *Magazine, Government.*
Related titles: Online - full text ed.: ISSN 1605-9417. free (effective 2011).
Published by: (Taiwan. Taiwan, Government Information Office TWN), Kwang Hwa Publishing Co. **Subscr. to:** Kwang Hwa Publishing Co., 6300 Wilshire Blvd, Ste 1510A, Los Angeles, CA 90048. TEL 323-782-8765, 888-829-3866, FAX 323-782-8763.

NOTRE REGION PROVENCE-ALPES-COTE-D'AZUR. *see* LEISURE AND RECREATION

NOUVELLE FIPREGAZETTE. *see* FOOD AND FOOD INDUSTRIES

LA NOUVELLE RELEVE. *see* POLITICAL SCIENCE

910.2 USA
NOW PLAYING MAGAZINE. Text in English. s-a. **Document type:** *Magazine, Consumer.*
Published by: Walker Media, 1805 Haver, Houston, TX 77006. TEL 713-524-3560, FAX 713-524-3549, marlenewal@aol.com, http://www.walker-media.com.

914.3 DEU
NUERNBERG HEUTE. Text in German. 1964. s-a. free. adv. bk.rev. charts; illus. **Document type:** *Magazine, Government.* **Description:** News about the city of Nuernberg.
Published by: Stadt Nuernberg, Presse- und Informationsamt, Rathaus, Rathausplatz 2, Nuernberg, 90317, Germany. TEL 49-911-2312372, FAX 49-911-2313660. Ed. Dr. Wolfgang Stoeckel. Circ: 35,000.

917 CAN ISSN 1490-1587
F1060.4
THE NUNAVUT HANDBOOK. Text in English. 1998. biennial. CAD 39.95 per issue (effective 2006).
Published by: Ayaya Marketing & Communications, PO Box 8, Iqaluit, NU X0A 0H0, Canada. TEL 867-979-1484, FAX 867-979-1487, nadiac@ayaya.ca, http://www.ayaya.ca.

910 GBR ISSN 1471-2989
O A G FLIGHT ATLAS. WORLDWIDE. (Official Airline Guide) Text in English. 1975. s-a. GBP 51 domestic; USD 69 in United States; EUR 86 in Europe; SGD 160 in Singapore (effective 2009). **Document type:** *Directory, Trade.* **Description:** Contains maps of major domestic and international flights, time zones, country, city and state codes, and airline designators.
Former titles (until 2000): O A G Air Travel Atlas (1366-1698); (until 1996): A B C Air Travel Atlas (0263-2748)
—BLDSC (6196.390250). **CCC.**
Published by: O A G Worldwide, Church St, Dunstable, Bedfordshire LU5 4HB, United Kingdom. TEL 44-1582-600111, FAX 44-1582-695230, customers@oag.com. Adv. contact Sue Davidson TEL 44-1582-695470.

O A G FLIGHTDISK. (Official Airline Guide) *see* TRANSPORTATION—Air Transport

910.09 USA ISSN 1073-0338
TX907.2
O A G OFFICIAL TRAVELER. TRAVEL GUIDE. (Official Airline Guide) Text in English. 1992. q. USD 320 (effective 2011). **Document type:** *Magazine, Trade.*
Incorporates (1992-1998): O A G Official Traveler. Flight Guide
—**CCC.**
Published by: O A G Worldwide, 3025 Highland Pky, Ste 200, Downer's Grove, IL 60515. TEL 630-515-5300, 800-342-5624, FAX 630-515-5301, contactus@oag.com, http://www.oag.com.

910.3 USA ISSN 0199-5162
O A G POCKET TRAVEL PLANNER. (Official Airline Guides) Text in English. 1979. q. **Document type:** *Handbook/Manual/Guide, Trade.* **Description:** Provides information for travel planning.
Related titles: CD-ROM ed.
—**CCC.**
Published by: O A G Worldwide, 3025 Highland Pky, Ste 200, Downer's Grove, IL 60515. TEL 630-515-5300, 800-342-5624, FAX 630-515-5301, contactus@oag.com, http://www.oag.com.

917.1 CAN ISSN 1187-4198
O M C A RESOURCE GUIDE. Text in English. 1986. a. adv. **Document type:** *Handbook/Manual/Guide, Trade.*
Formerly (until 1991): Ontario Motor Coach Association Resource Guide (0836-4214)
Published by: Ontario Motor Coach Association, 4141 Yonge St, Ste 306, Toronto, ON M2P 2A8, Canada. TEL 416-229-6622, FAX 416-229-6281, info@omca.com, http://www.omca.com/homepage.htm.

910.202 USA ISSN 0191-8478
OAHU DRIVE GUIDE. Text in English. 1974. 3/yr. USD 5 per issue (effective 2011). **Document type:** *Magazine, Consumer.* **Description:** For visitors; includes road maps of the island, restaurant guide, places of interest, travel information, and history.
Related titles: Online - full text ed.: free (effective 2011); ♦ Regional ed(s).: Hawaii Drive Guide; Maui Drive Guide; Kauai Drive Guide.
Published by: Honolulu Publishing Company, Ltd., Ocean View Ctr, 707 Richards St, Ste 525, Honolulu, HI 96813. TEL 808-524-7400, 800-272-5245. Ed. Brett Uprichard. Pub., Adv. contact Maurina Borgatti TEL 808-935-9822.

TU

915.404 IND
THE OBEROI GROUP MAGAZINE. Text in English. 1971. q. free to qualified personnel (effective 2011). adv. bk.rev. illus. **Document type:** *Magazine, Consumer.* **Description:** An in-room magazine for the Oberoi hotels.
Formerly: Soma
Published by: Mediascope Publicitas India Pvt. Ltd., Oberoi Towers, Nariman Point, Mumbai, Maharashtra 400 021, India. mumbai@publicitas.com.

914 DEU
OBERSCHWABEN MAGAZIN; liebenswert - erlebenswert. Text in German. 1997. a. EUR 2.50 newsstand/cover (effective 2007). adv. **Document type:** *Magazine, Consumer.*
Published by: Labhard Verlag GmbH, Zum Hussenstein 7, Konstanz, 78462, Germany. TEL 49-7531-9071-0, FAX 49-7531-907131, verlag@labhard.de. adv.: B&W page EUR 1,670, color page EUR 1,920. Circ: 39,000 (controlled).

338.4 FRA ISSN 2108-1808
L'OBSERVATOIRE DES DEPLACEMENTS EN SAVOIE. Text in French. 2006. a., latest 2009. **Document type:** *Report, Trade.*
Published by: Conseil General de la Savoie, Hotel du Departement, Chateau des Ducs de Savoie, BP 1802, Chambery, 73018, France. TEL 33-4-79967373.

OCEAN & CRUISE NEWS. *see* TRANSPORTATION—Ships And Shipping

917.504 USA
OCEANA MAGAZINE. Text in English. 1978. 42/yr. adv. back issues avail. **Document type:** *Newspaper.* **Description:** Contains general information on resorts, beaches, tourism, and sports.
Published by: Independent Publishers Group, Inc., PO Box 1943, Ocean City, MD 21842. TEL 302-539-6313, FAX 302-539-6815. Ed. Elizabeth Brownell. Pub., R&P Thomas B Lloyd. Adv. contact Renee Esham.

306.766 USA ISSN 0883-3664
E158
ODYSSEUS; an accommodations & travel guide for the gay community, USA & international. Text in English. ceased 19??; resumed 1985. a. USD 39 domestic; USD 50 in Canada & Mexico; USD 60 elsewhere (effective 2005). adv. bk.rev. illus. **Document type:** *Directory.* **Description:** International gay travel planner, including information on hotels, bed and breakfasts, and resorts catering to the gay and lesbian community in the US, Canada, and worldwide.
Related titles: CD-ROM ed.
Published by: Odysseus Enterprises Ltd., PO Box 1548, Port Washington, NY 11050. TEL 516-944-5330, FAX 516-944-7540, 800-257-5344, odyusa@aol.com, http://www.odyusa.com. Ed. Eli Angelo. Pub. Joseph H Bain. Adv. contact Rafael Costa. B&W page USD 18,000, color page USD 3,350. Circ: 350,000.

910.202 USA ISSN 1073-5259
E158
ODYSSEY (SANTA ROSA); the magazine of the Chevron Travel Club. Text in English. 1969. q. USD 72 to members (effective 2000). adv. bk.rev. illus. **Document type:** *Magazine, Consumer.*
Formerly (until 1993): Chevron U S A Odyssey (0886-5418); Which was formed by the merger of (19??-1985): Chevron U S A (0199-5707); (19??-1985): Odyssey (San Jose) (0164-8063)
Indexed: MLA-IB.
Published by: (Chevron Travel Club), Dunham Bergquist & Associates, Inc., 131 Stony Circle, Ste 500, Santa Rosa, CA 95401. TEL 707-526-3222, FAX 707-526-9815. adv.: B&W page USD 13,500, color page USD 17,024; trim 10.88 x 8.5. Circ: 409,606.

910.91 USA ISSN 1545-2026
ODYSSEY COULEUR; travel in color. Text in English. 2003 (Sum.). bi-m. USD 24.99 (effective 2007). adv. illus. **Document type:** *Magazine, Consumer.*
Published by: Idamar Enterprises, Inc., 60 Park Pl, 20th Fl, Newark, NJ 07102. TEL 973-286-2300, FAX 973-286-2310, http://www.idamar.com. Ed. Nick Chiles. Pub. Linda Spradley Dunn.

OESTERREICHISCHE GASTRONOMIE- UND HOTELZEITUNG. *see* HOTELS AND RESTAURANTS

910.2 AUT ISSN 0048-1483
OESTERREICHISCHE TOURISTENZEITUNG. Text in German. 1888. m. membership. bk.rev.; film rev. illus. **Document type:** *Newspaper.*
Indexed: RASB.
Published by: Oesterreichischer Touristenklub, Baeckerstrasse 16, Vienna, W 1010, Austria. Ed. Alfred Weis. R&P Hannes Resch. Circ: 20,000.

917.98 USA ISSN 1537-050X
F902.3
OFF THE BEATEN PATH: ALASKA. Text in English. 1996. triennial, latest 2008, 6th ed. USD 14.95 per issue (effective 2008). **Document type:** *Guide, Consumer.* **Description:** Describes information on the hidden attractions, unique finds and unusual locales.
Published by: The Globe Pequot Press, Inc., 246 Goose Ln, PO Box 480, Guilford, CT 06437. TEL 203-458-4500, 888-249-7586, FAX 203-458-4603, 800-820-2329, info@globepequot.com, http://www.globepequot.com. Ed. Liz Taylor.

917.91 USA ISSN 1540-1197
F809.3
OFF THE BEATEN PATH: ARIZONA. Text in English. 1996. irreg., latest 2006, 6th ed. USD 13.95 per issue (effective 2008). **Document type:** *Guide, Consumer.* **Description:** Describes information on hidden attractions, unique finds and unusual locales.
Published by: The Globe Pequot Press, Inc., 246 Goose Ln, PO Box 480, Guilford, CT 06437. TEL 203-458-4500, 888-249-7586, FAX 203-458-4603, 800-820-2329, info@globepequot.com, http://www.globepequot.com. Ed. Jeff Serena TEL 203-458-4556.

917.4461 338.4791 USA ISSN 1542-5967
F73.18
OFF THE BEATEN PATH: BOSTON. Text in English. 2002. irreg., latest 2004, 2nd ed. USD 13.95 per issue (effective 2008). **Document type:** *Guide, Consumer.* **Description:** Provides information about travel and tourism in Boston.
Published by: The Globe Pequot Press, Inc., 246 Goose Ln, PO Box 480, Guilford, CT 06437. TEL 203-458-4500, 888-249-7586, FAX 203-458-4603, 800-820-2329, info@globepequot.com, http://www.globepequot.com.

917.7311 USA ISSN 1536-3570
F548.18
OFF THE BEATEN PATH: CHICAGO; a guide to unique places. Text in English. 2002. biennial, latest 2005, 3rd ed. USD 13.95 per issue (effective 2008). **Document type:** *Guide, Consumer.* **Description:** Describes information on the hidden attractions, unique finds and unusual locales.
Published by: The Globe Pequot Press, Inc., 246 Goose Ln, PO Box 480, Guilford, CT 06437. TEL 203-458-4500, 888-249-7586, FAX 203-458-4603, 800-820-2329, info@globepequot.com, http://www.globepequot.com. Ed. Jeff Serena TEL 203-458-4556.

917.88 USA ISSN 1539-6614
F774.3
OFF THE BEATEN PATH: COLORADO; a guide to unique places. Text in English. 1987. triennial, latest 2007, 9th ed. USD 14.95 per issue (effective 2008). **Document type:** *Guide, Consumer.* **Description:** Describes information on the hidden attractions, unique finds and unusual locales.
Published by: The Globe Pequot Press, Inc., 246 Goose Ln, PO Box 480, Guilford, CT 06437. TEL 203-458-4500, 888-249-7586, FAX 203-458-4603, 800-820-2329, info@globepequot.com. Ed. Jeff Serena TEL 203-458-4556.

917.46 910.2 USA ISSN 1539-8641
F92.3
OFF THE BEATEN PATH: CONNECTICUT; a guide to unique places. Key Title: Connecticut, Off the Beaten Path. Text and summaries in English. 1992. irreg., latest 2007, 7th ed. USD 13.95 per issue (effective 2008). **Document type:** *Guide, Consumer.* **Description:** Provides travel and tourism information of Connecticut.
Published by: The Globe Pequot Press, Inc., 246 Goose Ln, PO Box 480, Guilford, CT 06437. TEL 203-458-4500, 888-249-7586, FAX 203-458-4603, 800-820-2329, info@globepequot.com, http://www.globepequot.com.

917.59 910.2 USA ISSN 1539-0845
F309.3
OFF THE BEATEN PATH: FLORIDA; a guide to unique places. Key Title: Florida, Off the Beaten Path. Text in English. 1985. biennial, latest 2008, 10th ed. USD 14.95 per issue (effective 2008). back issues avail. **Document type:** *Guide, Consumer.* **Description:** Provides information about unique places in Florida.
Published by: The Globe Pequot Press, Inc., 246 Goose Ln, PO Box 480, Guilford, CT 06437. TEL 203-458-4500, 888-249-7586, FAX 203-458-4603, 800-820-2329, info@globepequot.com, http://www.globepequot.com.

917.58 910.2 USA ISSN 1541-6615
F284.3
OFF THE BEATEN PATH: GEORGIA; a guide to unique places. Text in English. 1989. irreg., latest 2006, 8th ed. USD 13.95 per issue (effective 2008). back issues avail. **Document type:** *Guide, Consumer.* **Description:** Contains information on hidden attractions, unique finds and unusual locales.
Published by: The Globe Pequot Press, Inc., 246 Goose Ln, PO Box 480, Guilford, CT 06437. TEL 203-458-4500, 888-249-7586, FAX 203-458-4603, 800-820-2329, info@globepequot.com, http://www.globepequot.com. Ed. Jeff Serena TEL 203-458-4556.

919.69 USA ISSN 1535-8313
DU622
OFF THE BEATEN PATH: HAWAII; a guide to unique places. Text in English. 1991. triennial, latest 2006, 8th ed. USD 13.95 per issue (effective 2008). **Document type:** *Guide, Consumer.* **Description:** Describes information on the hidden attractions, unique finds and unusual locales.
Published by: The Globe Pequot Press, Inc., 246 Goose Ln, PO Box 480, Guilford, CT 06437. TEL 203-458-4500, 888-249-7586, FAX 203-458-4603, 800-820-2329, info@globepequot.com, http://www.globepequot.com. Ed. Jeff Serena TEL 203-458-4556.

917.73 USA ISSN 1540-871X
F539.3
OFF THE BEATEN PATH: ILLINOIS; a guide to unique places. Text in English. 1987. biennial, latest 2007, 9th ed. USD 14.95 per issue (effective 2008). **Document type:** *Guide, Consumer.* **Description:** Describes information on the hidden attractions, unique finds and unusual locales.
Published by: The Globe Pequot Press, Inc., 246 Goose Ln, PO Box 480, Guilford, CT 06437. TEL 203-458-4500, 888-249-7586, FAX 203-458-4603, 800-820-2329, info@globepequot.com, http://www.globepequot.com. Ed. Jeff Serena TEL 203-458-4556.

917.72 910.2 USA ISSN 1539-459X
F524.3
OFF THE BEATEN PATH: INDIANA; a guide to unique places. Key Title: Indiana. Text in English. 1985. triennial, latest 2007, 9th ed. USD 14.95 per issue (effective 2008). back issues avail. **Document type:** *Guide, Consumer.* **Description:** Provides information about tourist traps in Indiana.
Published by: The Globe Pequot Press, Inc., 246 Goose Ln, PO Box 480, Guilford, CT 06437. TEL 203-458-4500, 888-249-7586, FAX 203-458-4603, 800-820-2329, info@globepequot.com, http://www.globepequot.com. Ed. Jeff Serena TEL 203-458-4556.

917.77 USA ISSN 1540-1340
F619.3
OFF THE BEATEN PATH: IOWA. Text in English. 1990. irreg., latest 2007, 8th ed. USD 14.95 per issue (effective 2008). **Document type:** *Guide, Consumer.* **Description:** Describes information on hidden attractions, unique finds and unusual locales.
Published by: The Globe Pequot Press, Inc., 246 Goose Ln, PO Box 480, Guilford, CT 06437. TEL 203-458-4500, 888-249-7586, FAX 203-458-4603, 800-820-2329, info@globepequot.com, http://www.globepequot.com. Ed. Jeff Serena TEL 203-458-4556.

917.81 910.2 USA ISSN 1542-443X
F679.3
OFF THE BEATEN PATH: KANSAS; a guide to unique places. Key Title: Kansas, Off the Beaten Path. Text in English. 1991. biennial, latest 2007, 8th ed. USD 14.95 per issue (effective 2008). back issues avail. **Document type:** *Guide, Consumer.* **Description:** Provides information about tourist traps in Kansas.
Published by: The Globe Pequot Press, Inc., 246 Goose Ln, PO Box 480, Guilford, CT 06437. TEL 203-458-4500, 888-249-7586, FAX 203-458-4603, 800-820-2329, info@globepequot.com, http://www.globepequot.com. Ed. Jeff Serena TEL 203-458-4556.

917.949 USA ISSN 1546-6418
F869.L83
OFF THE BEATEN PATH: LOS ANGELES. Text in English. 2004. biennial, latest 2005, 2nd ed. USD 13.95 per issue (effective 2008). **Document type:** *Guide, Consumer.* **Description:** Describes information on the hidden attractions, unique finds and unusual locales.
Published by: The Globe Pequot Press, Inc., 246 Goose Ln, PO Box 480, Guilford, CT 06437. TEL 203-458-4500, 888-249-7586, FAX 203-458-4603, 800-820-2329, info@globepequot.com, http://www.globepequot.com. Ed. . Curiel.

917.41 910.2 USA ISSN 1534-0686
F17.3
OFF THE BEATEN PATH: MAINE; a guide to unique places. Key Title: Maine, Off the Beaten Path. Text in English. 1992. triennial, latest 2006, 7th ed. USD 13.95 per issue (effective 2008). **Document type:** *Guide, Consumer.* **Description:** Provides travel and tourism information of Maine.
Published by: The Globe Pequot Press, Inc., 246 Goose Ln, PO Box 480, Guilford, CT 06437. TEL 203-458-4500, 888-249-7586, FAX 203-458-4603, 800-820-2329, info@globepequot.com, http://www.globepequot.com. Ed. Jeff Serena TEL 203-458-4556.

917.15 910.2 USA ISSN 1542-5533
F1035.8
OFF THE BEATEN PATH: MARITIME PROVINCES. Text in English. 1996. biennial, latest 2007, 6th ed. USD 14.95 per issue (effective 2008). **Document type:** *Guide, Consumer.* **Description:** Provides information about travel and tourism in Maritime Provinces of Canada's East Coast.
Published by: The Globe Pequot Press, Inc., 246 Goose Ln, PO Box 480, Guilford, CT 06437. TEL 203-458-4500, 888-249-7586, FAX 203-458-4603, 800-820-2329, info@globepequot.com, http://www.globepequot.com.

917.51 917.52 USA ISSN 1538-5485
F179.3
OFF THE BEATEN PATH: MARYLAND AND DELAWARE; a guide to unique places. Key Title: Maryland and Delaware, Off the Beaten Path. Text in English. 1990. biennial, latest 2007, 8th ed. USD 14.95 per issue (effective 2008). **Document type:** *Guide, Consumer.* **Description:** Provides travel and tourism information of Nebraska.
Formerly (until 1994): Maryland, Off the Beaten Path (1538-5477)
Published by: The Globe Pequot Press, Inc., 246 Goose Ln, PO Box 480, Guilford, CT 06437. TEL 203-458-4500, 888-249-7586, FAX 203-458-4603, 800-820-2329, info@globepequot.com, http://www.globepequot.com. Ed. Jeff Serena TEL 203-458-4556.

917.44 910.2 USA ISSN 1542-1775
F62.3
OFF THE BEATEN PATH, MASSACHUSETTS; a guide to unique places. Key Title: Massachusetts Off the Beaten Path. Text in English. 1992. biennial, latest 2007, 7th ed. USD 14.95 per issue (effective 2008). **Document type:** *Guide, Consumer.* **Description:** Describes information on the hidden attractions, unique finds and unusual locales.
Published by: The Globe Pequot Press, Inc., 246 Goose Ln, PO Box 480, Guilford, CT 06437. TEL 203-458-4500, 888-249-7586, FAX 203-458-4603, 800-820-2329, info@globepequot.com, http://www.globepequot.com. Ed. Jeff Serena TEL 203-458-4556.

910.2 USA ISSN 2156-2083
▼ **OFF THE BEATEN PATH: METRO NEW YORK.** Text in English. 2010. biennial. USD 14.95 per issue (effective 2010). **Document type:** *Handbook/Manual/Guide, Consumer.* **Description:** Guides to travelers and locals who wants to see the New York Metropolitan Area. Provides the reader down the road less traveled and reveals a side of New York.
Published by: The Globe Pequot Press, Inc., 246 Goose Ln, PO Box 480, Guilford, CT 06437. TEL 203-458-4500, 888-249-7586, FAX 203-458-4603, 800-820-2329, info@globepequot.com.

917.74 338.4791 USA ISSN 1542-4804
F564.3
OFF THE BEATEN PATH: MICHIGAN; a guide to unique places. Text in English. 1988. biennial, latest 2009, 10th ed. USD 14.95 per issue (effective 2009). 240 p./no.; **Document type:** *Guide, Consumer.* **Description:** Provides information about travel and tourism in Michigan.
Published by: The Globe Pequot Press, Inc., 246 Goose Ln, PO Box 480, Guilford, CT 06437. TEL 203-458-4500, 888-249-7586, FAX 203-458-4603, 800-820-2329, info@globepequot.com, http://www.globepequot.com. Ed. Jeff Serena TEL 203-458-4556.

917.76 910.2 USA ISSN 1542-4170
F604.3
OFF THE BEATEN PATH: MINNESOTA. Text in English. 1989. biennial, latest 2007, 8th ed. USD 14.95 per issue (effective 2008). back issues avail. **Document type:** *Guide, Consumer.* **Description:** Provides information about tourist traps in Minnesota.
Published by: The Globe Pequot Press, Inc., 246 Goose Ln, PO Box 480, Guilford, CT 06437. TEL 203-458-4500, 888-249-7586, FAX 203-458-4603, 800-820-2329, info@globepequot.com, http://www.globepequot.com. Ed. Jeff Serena TEL 203-458-4556.

917.78 910.91 USA ISSN 1539-8129
F464.3
OFF THE BEATEN PATH: MISSOURI. Text in English. 1990. biennial, latest 2008, 9th ed. USD 14.95 per issue (effective 2008). 264 p./no.; **Document type:** *Guide, Consumer.* **Description:** Provides information about travel and tourism in Missouri.
Published by: The Globe Pequot Press, Inc., 246 Goose Ln, PO Box 480, Guilford, CT 06437. TEL 203-458-4500, 888-249-7586, FAX 203-458-4603, 800-820-2329, info@globepequot.com, http://www.globepequot.com. Ed. Amy Lyons TEL 203-458-4500.

917.86 USA ISSN 1539-7033
F729.3
OFF THE BEATEN PATH: MONTANA. Text in English. 1993. a. USD 14.95 per issue (effective 2008). **Document type:** *Guide, Consumer.* **Description:** Provides information about travel and tourism.
Published by: The Globe Pequot Press, Inc., 246 Goose Ln, PO Box 480, Guilford, CT 06437. TEL 203-458-4500, 888-249-7586, FAX 203-458-4603, 800-820-2329, info@globepequot.com, http://www.globepequot.com. Ed. Jeff Serena TEL 203-458-4556.

917.82 910.91 USA ISSN 1539-6932
F664.3
OFF THE BEATEN PATH: NEBRASKA; a guide to unique places. Key Title: Nebraska. Text in English. 1997. biennial, latest 2007, 6th ed. USD 14.95 per issue (effective 2008). **Document type:** *Guide, Consumer.* **Description:** Provides travel and tourism information of Nebraska.
Published by: The Globe Pequot Press, Inc., 246 Goose Ln, PO Box 480, Guilford, CT 06437. TEL 203-458-4500, 888-249-7586, FAX 203-458-4603, 800-820-2329, info@globepequot.com, http://www.globepequot.com. Ed. Jeff Serena TEL 203-458-4556.

917.42 USA ISSN 1540-1537
F32.3
OFF THE BEATEN PATH: NEW HAMPSHIRE. Text in English. 1992. biennial, latest 2007, 7th ed. USD 14.95 per issue (effective 2008). **Document type:** *Guide, Consumer.* **Description:** Describes information on hidden attractions, unique finds and unusual locales.
Published by: The Globe Pequot Press, Inc., 246 Goose Ln, PO Box 480, Guilford, CT 06437. TEL 203-458-4500, 888-249-7586, FAX 203-458-4603, 800-820-2329, info@globepequot.com, http://www.globepequot.com. Ed. Jeff Serena TEL 203-458-4556.

917.89 USA ISSN 1536-6189
F794.3
OFF THE BEATEN PATH: NEW MEXICO; a guide to unique places. Text in English. 1991. biennial, latest 2006, 8th ed. USD 13.95 per issue (effective 2008). **Document type:** *Guide, Consumer.* **Description:** Describes information on the hidden attractions, unique finds and unusual locales.
Published by: The Globe Pequot Press, Inc., 246 Goose Ln, PO Box 480, Guilford, CT 06437. TEL 203-458-4500, 888-249-7586, FAX 203-458-4603, 800-820-2329, info@globepequot.com, http://www.globepequot.com. Ed. Jeff Serena TEL 203-458-4556.

917.47 USA ISSN 1540-9201
F117.3
OFF THE BEATEN PATH: NEW YORK; a guide to unique places. Text in English. 1987. irreg., latest 2007, 9th ed. USD 14.95 per issue (effective 2008). **Document type:** *Guide, Consumer.* **Description:** Describes information on the hidden attractions, unique finds and unusual locales.
Published by: The Globe Pequot Press, Inc., 246 Goose Ln, PO Box 480, Guilford, CT 06437. TEL 203-458-4500, 888-249-7586, FAX 203-458-4603, 800-820-2329, info@globepequot.com. Ed. Jeff Serena TEL 203-458-4556.

917.56 910.91 USA ISSN 1539-7769
F252.3
OFF THE BEATEN PATH: NORTH CAROLINA. Text in English. 1990. biennial, latest 2008, 9th ed. USD 14.95 per issue (effective 2008). maps; illus. 224 p./no.; **Document type:** *Guide, Consumer.* **Description:** Provides information about travel and tourism in North Carolina.
Published by: The Globe Pequot Press, Inc., 246 Goose Ln, PO Box 480, Guilford, CT 06437. TEL 203-458-4500, 888-249-7586, FAX 203-458-4603, 800-820-2329, info@globepequot.com, http://www.globepequot.com. Ed. Amy Lyons TEL 203-458-4500.

917.71 910.2 USA ISSN 1539-8196
F489.3
OFF THE BEATEN PATH: OHIO; a guide to unique places. Text in English. 1983. irreg., latest 2007, 11th ed. USD 14.95 per issue (effective 2008). back issues avail. **Document type:** *Guide, Consumer.* **Description:** Covers information about hidden attractions, unique finds, and unusual locales in Ohio.
Published by: The Globe Pequot Press, Inc., 246 Goose Ln, PO Box 480, Guilford, CT 06437. TEL 203-458-4500, 888-249-7586, FAX 203-458-4603, 800-820-2329, info@globepequot.com, http://www.globepequot.com. Ed. Jeff Serena TEL 203-458-4556.

917.66 910.2 USA ISSN 1540-8876
F692.3
OFF THE BEATEN PATH: OKLAHOMA; a guide to unique places. Text in English. 1996. biennial, latest 2006, 6th ed. USD 13.95 per issue (effective 2008). back issues avail. **Document type:** *Guide, Consumer.* **Description:** Contains information about hidden attractions, unique finds, and unusual locales in Oklahoma.
Published by: The Globe Pequot Press, Inc., 246 Goose Ln, PO Box 480, Guilford, CT 06437. TEL 203-458-4500, 888-249-7586, FAX 203-458-4603, 800-820-2329, info@globepequot.com, http://www.globepequot.com. Ed. Jeff Serena TEL 203-458-4556.

917.48 USA ISSN 1536-6197
F147.3
OFF THE BEATEN PATH: PENNSYLVANIA; a guide to unique places. Text in English. 1989. triennial, latest 2007, 9th ed. USD 13.95 per issue (effective 2008). **Document type:** *Guide, Consumer.* **Description:** Describes information on the hidden attractions, unique finds and unusual locales.
Published by: The Globe Pequot Press, Inc., 246 Goose Ln, PO Box 480, Guilford, CT 06437. TEL 203-458-4500, 888-249-7586, FAX 203-458-4603, 800-820-2329, info@globepequot.com, http://www.globepequot.com. Ed. Jeff Serena TEL 203-458-4556.

917.4811 338.4791 USA ISSN 1544-7413
F158.18
OFF THE BEATEN PATH: PHILADELPHIA. Text in English. 2003. biennial, latest 2007, 3rd ed. USD 13.95 per issue (effective 2008). **Document type:** *Guide, Consumer.* **Description:** Provides travel and tourism information of Philadelphia.
Published by: The Globe Pequot Press, Inc., 246 Goose Ln, PO Box 480, Guilford, CT 06437. TEL 203-458-4500, 888-249-7586, FAX 203-458-4603, 800-820-2329, info@globepequot.com, http://www.globepequot.com.

917.295 USA ISSN 1536-9455
F1959
OFF THE BEATEN PATH: PUERTO RICO. Text in English. 1999. biennial, latest 2006, 5th ed. USD 13.95 per issue (effective 2008). **Document type:** *Guide, Consumer.* **Description:** Describes information on the hidden attractions, unique finds and unusual locales.
Published by: The Globe Pequot Press, Inc., 246 Goose Ln, PO Box 480, Guilford, CT 06437. TEL 203-458-4500, 888-249-7586, FAX 203-458-4603, 800-820-2329, info@globepequot.com. Ed. Jeff Serena TEL 203-458-4556.

917.14 910.2 USA ISSN 1540-2142
F1052.7
OFF THE BEATEN PATH: QUEBEC; a guide to unique places. Key Title: Quebec, Off the Beaten Path. Text in English. 1999. triennial, latest 2005, 4th ed. USD 13.95 per issue (effective 2008). **Document type:** *Guide, Consumer.* **Description:** Provides travel and tourism information of Quebec.
Published by: The Globe Pequot Press, Inc., 246 Goose Ln, PO Box 480, Guilford, CT 06437. TEL 203-458-4500, 888-249-7586, FAX 203-458-4603, 800-820-2329, info@globepequot.com, http://www.globepequot.com.

917.45 USA ISSN 1539-3771
F77.3
OFF THE BEATEN PATH: RHODE ISLAND; a guide to unique places. Text in English. 1996. triennial, latest 2007, 6th ed. USD 14.95 per issue (effective 2008). **Document type:** *Guide, Consumer.* **Description:** Describes information on the hidden attractions, unique finds and unusual locales.
Published by: The Globe Pequot Press, Inc., 246 Goose Ln, PO Box 480, Guilford, CT 06437. TEL 203-458-4500, 888-249-7586, FAX 203-458-4603, 800-820-2329, info@globepequot.com, http://www.globepequot.com. Ed. Jeff Serena TEL 203-458-4556.

917.9461 USA ISSN 1540-9325
F869.S33
OFF THE BEATEN PATH: SAN FRANCISCO. Text in English. 2003. biennial, latest 2004, 2nd ed. USD 13.95 per issue (effective 2008). back issues avail. **Document type:** *Guide, Consumer.* **Description:** Contains information about hidden attractions, unique finds, and unusual locales in San Francisco.
Published by: The Globe Pequot Press, Inc., 246 Goose Ln, PO Box 480, Guilford, CT 06437. TEL 203-458-4500, 888-249-7586, FAX 203-458-4603, 800-820-2329, info@globepequot.com.

917.57 USA ISSN 1545-5130
F267.3
OFF THE BEATEN PATH, SOUTH CAROLINA; a guide to unique places. Key Title: South Carolina, Off the Beaten Path. Text in English. 1996. biennial, latest 2009, 7th ed. USD 14.95 per issue (effective 2008). back issues avail. **Document type:** *Guide, Consumer.* **Description:** Provides information about unique places in South Carolina.
Published by: The Globe Pequot Press, Inc., 246 Goose Ln, PO Box 480, Guilford, CT 06437. TEL 203-458-4500, 888-249-7586, FAX 203-458-4603, 800-820-2329, info@globepequot.com, http://www.globepequot.com.

917.949 910.2 USA ISSN 1540-210X
F867
OFF THE BEATEN PATH: SOUTHERN CALIFORNIA; a guide to unique places. Text in English. 1989. biennial, latest 2007, 7th ed. USD 14.95 per issue (effective 2008). **Document type:** *Guide, Consumer.* **Description:** Provides travel and tourism information of Southern California.
Published by: The Globe Pequot Press, Inc., 246 Goose Ln, PO Box 480, Guilford, CT 06437. TEL 203-458-4500, 888-249-7586, FAX 203-458-4603, 800-820-2329, info@globepequot.com, http://www.globepequot.com.

917.68 910.91 USA ISSN 1539-8102
F434.3
OFF THE BEATEN PATH: TENNESSEE. Text in English. 1990. irreg., latest 2007, 8th ed. USD 14.95 per issue (effective 2008). 232 p./no.; **Document type:** *Guide, Consumer.* **Description:** Provides information about travel and tourism in Tennessee.
Published by: The Globe Pequot Press, Inc., 246 Goose Ln, PO Box 480, Guilford, CT 06437. TEL 203-458-4500, 888-249-7586, FAX 203-458-4603, 800-820-2329, http://www.globepequot.com.

917.64 USA ISSN 1537-0526
F384.3
OFF THE BEATEN PATH: TEXAS; a guide to unique places. Text in English. 1994. triennial, latest 2008, 8th ed. USD 14.95 per issue (effective 2008). **Document type:** *Guide, Consumer.* **Description:** Explores a tropical paradise teeming with exotic wildlife at the Rainforest Pyramid in Galveston.
Published by: The Globe Pequot Press, Inc., 246 Goose Ln, PO Box 480, Guilford, CT 06437. TEL 203-458-4500, 888-249-7586, FAX 203-458-4603, 800-820-2329, info@globepequot.com, http://www.globepequot.com. Ed. Amy Lyons TEL 203-458-4500.

917.8 910.2 USA ISSN 1540-4382
F634.3
OFF THE BEATEN PATH: THE DAKOTAS; a guide to unique places. Text in English. 1996. biennial, latest 2008, 7th ed. USD 13.95 per issue (effective 2008). back issues avail. **Document type:** *Guide, Consumer.* **Description:** Describes information on the hidden attractions, unique finds and unusual locales.
Published by: The Globe Pequot Press, Inc., 246 Goose Ln, PO Box 480, Guilford, CT 06437. TEL 203-458-4500, 888-249-7586, FAX 203-458-4603, 800-820-2329, info@globepequot.com. Ed. Jeff Serena TEL 203-458-4556.

917.92 910.2 USA ISSN 1542-3093
F824.3
OFF THE BEATEN PATH: UTAH; a guide to unique places. Key Title: Utah, Off the Beaten Path. Text in English. 199?. irreg., latest 2006, 5th ed. USD 13.95 per issue (effective 2008). back issues avail. **Document type:** *Guide, Consumer.* **Description:** Provides information about tourist traps in Utah.
Published by: The Globe Pequot Press, Inc., 246 Goose Ln, PO Box 480, Guilford, CT 06437. TEL 203-458-4500, 888-249-7586, FAX 203-458-4603, 800-820-2329, info@globepequot.com, http://www.globepequot.com. Ed. Jeff Serena TEL 203-458-4556.

917.43 910.91 USA ISSN 1533-8037
F47.3
OFF THE BEATEN PATH: VERMONT. Text in English. 1992. biennial, latest 2006, 7th ed. USD 13.95 per issue (effective 2008). **Document type:** *Guide, Consumer.* **Description:** Provides information about travel and tourism in Vermont.
Published by: The Globe Pequot Press, Inc., 246 Goose Ln, PO Box 480, Guilford, CT 06437. TEL 203-458-4500, 888-249-7586, FAX 203-458-4603, 800-820-2329, info@globepequot.com, http://www.globepequot.com.

917.55 910.91 USA ISSN 1539-8110
F224.3
OFF THE BEATEN PATH: VIRGINIA. Text in English. 1986. biennial, latest 2008, 10th ed. USD 14.95 per issue (effective 2008). 256 p./no.; **Document type:** *Guide, Consumer.* **Description:** Provides information about travel and tourism in Virginia.
Published by: The Globe Pequot Press, Inc., 246 Goose Ln, PO Box 480, Guilford, CT 06437. TEL 203-458-4500, 888-249-7586, FAX 203-458-4603, 800-820-2329, info@globepequot.com, http://www.globepequot.com.

917.97 USA ISSN 1540-8442
F889.3
OFF THE BEATEN PATH: WASHINGTON; a guide to unique places. Text in English. 1993. biennial, latest 2009, 8th ed. USD 14.95 per issue (effective 2009). **Document type:** *Guide, Consumer.* **Description:** Describes information on the hidden attractions, unique finds and unusual locales.
Published by: The Globe Pequot Press, Inc., 246 Goose Ln, PO Box 480, Guilford, CT 06437. TEL 203-458-4500, 888-249-7586, FAX 203-458-4603, 800-820-2329, info@globepequot.com. Ed. Jeff Serena TEL 203-458-4556.

917.53 910.2 USA ISSN 1541-5201
F192.3
OFF THE BEATEN PATH: WASHINGTON, D. C.; a guide to unique places. Text in English. 2001. irreg., latest 2007, 7th ed. USD 13.95 per issue (effective 2008). back issues avail. **Document type:** *Guide, Consumer.* **Description:** Describes information on hidden attractions, unique finds and unusual locales.
Published by: The Globe Pequot Press, Inc., 246 Goose Ln, PO Box 480, Guilford, CT 06437. TEL 203-458-4500, 888-249-7586, FAX 203-458-4603, 800-820-2329, info@globepequot.com, http://www.globepequot.com. Ed. Jeff Serena TEL 203-458-4556.

917.54 910.2 USA ISSN 1539-5715
F239.3
OFF THE BEATEN PATH: WEST VIRGINIA; a guide to unique places. Text in English. 1995. triennial, latest 2006, 6th ed. USD 13.95 per issue (effective 2008). back issues avail. **Document type:** *Guide, Consumer.* **Description:** Describes information on the hidden attractions, unique finds and unusual locales.
Published by: The Globe Pequot Press, Inc., 246 Goose Ln, PO Box 480, Guilford, CT 06437. TEL 203-458-4500, 888-249-7586, FAX 203-458-4603, 800-820-2329, info@globepequot.com, http://www.globepequot.com. Ed. Jeff Serena TEL 203-458-4556.

917.75 910.2 USA ISSN 1540-2134
F579.3
OFF THE BEATEN PATH: WISCONSIN; a guide to unique places. Key Title: Wisconsin, Off the Beaten Path. Text in English. 1989. biennial, latest 2008, 9th ed. USD 13.95 per issue (effective 2008). **Document type:** *Guide, Consumer.* **Description:** Provides travel and tourism information of Wisconsin.
Published by: The Globe Pequot Press, Inc., 246 Goose Ln, PO Box 480, Guilford, CT 06437. TEL 203-458-4500, 888-249-7586, FAX 203-458-4603, 800-820-2329, info@globepequot.com, http://www.globepequot.com.

917.87 910.2 USA ISSN 1542-6262
F759.3
OFF THE BEATEN PATH: WYOMING. Text in English. 1996. biennial, latest 2007, 6th ed. USD 14.95 per issue (effective 2008). **Document type:** *Guide, Consumer.* **Description:** Provides information about travel and tourism in Wyoming.
Published by: The Globe Pequot Press, Inc., 246 Goose Ln, PO Box 480, Guilford, CT 06437. TEL 203-458-4500, 888-249-7586, FAX 203-458-4603, 800-820-2329, info@globepequot.com, http://www.globepequot.com.

910.2 USA ISSN 1081-0919
TX907.2
THE OFFICIAL BED & BREAKFAST GUIDE FOR THE UNITED STATES, CANADA & THE CARIBBEAN. Variant title: Bed and Breakfast Guide for the United States, Canada and the Caribbean. Text in English, French. 1983. biennial. USD 17.95 (effective 2000). back issues avail. **Description:** Lists accomodations with rates and reservation services.
Published by: National Bed & Breakfast Association, PO Box 332, Norwalk, CT 06852. TEL 203-847-6196, FAX 203-847-0469. Eds. Barbara Ostler, Phyllis Featherston.

051 792 USA ISSN 1055-1778
OFFICIAL CITY GUIDE. Text in English. 1982. w. USD 75 (effective 1998). adv. **Document type:** *Handbook/Manual/Guide, Trade.*
Former titles: City Guide (1043-3937); City Guide, Broadway Magazine (0892-2446)
Published by: Bill of Fare Inc., Empire State Building, 350 Fifth Ave, Ste 2420, New York, NY 10118. TEL 212-315-0800, FAX 212-271-6406. Ed. Derrell Bradford. Pub., Adv. contact Paul Insalaco. R&P Maureen Beckman. Circ: 60,000.

910.2 USA ISSN 1043-1195
TX907.2
OFFICIAL GUIDE TO AMERICAN HISTORIC INNS; 11,000 bed & breakfast and country inns. Text in English. 1989. biennial. **Document type:** *Directory.* **Description:** Offers travelers a complete listing of historic inns, bed and breakfasts, and guesthouses built before 1940.
Former titles: Official Guide to American Historic Bed and Breakfast Inns and Guesthouses; (until 1988): Official Guide to American Bed and Breakfast Inns and Guesthouses
Published by: American Historic Inns, Inc, PO Box 669, Dana Point, CA 92629. TEL 949-481-6256, FAX 949-481-3796, comments@iloveinns.com, http://www.iloveinns.com. Circ: 15,000.

910.91 USA ISSN 1930-6245
THE OFFICIAL GUIDE TO AMERICA'S NATIONAL PARKS. Text in English. 1979. irreg., latest 13th ed. USD 18.95 13th ed. (effective 2008). 528 p./no.; **Document type:** *Guide, Consumer.* **Description:** Focuses on the most trafficked parks as well as the lesser-known ones and includes seashores, trails, wild and scenic rivers, battlefields and historic sites.
Formerly (until 2005): The Complete Guide to America's National Parks (1532-9771)
Published by: Fodor's Travel Publications, Inc. (Subsidiary of: Random House Inc.), 1745 Broadway, 15th Fl, New York, NY 10019. TEL 212-572-2313, editors@fodors.com, http://www.fodors.com.

TU

974 USA
OFFICIAL GUIDE TO CAPE COD (YEAR). Text in English. 1921. a. free. adv. **Document type:** *Magazine, Consumer.*
Formerly: Cape Cod Resort Directory
Published by: Cape Cod Chamber of Commerce Inc., 5 Shoot Flying Hill Rd., Centerville, MA 02632-1428. TEL 508-862-0700, 888-332-2732, FAX 508-862-0727. Ed. Elaine S Perry. Adv. contact Stephen P Richards. Circ: 500,000.

910.202 USA
OFFICIAL GUIDE TO HOUSTON. Text in English. 1994. q. **Document type:** *Magazine, Consumer.*
Published by: Desert Publications, Inc., PO Box 2724, Palm Springs, CA 92263. TEL 760-325-2333, FAX 760-325-7008, sales@desertpublications.com.

917 USA
OFFICIAL N Y C VISTORS GUIDE. (New York City) Text in English. 1947. 4/yr. free (effective 2009). adv. **Document type:** *Directory, Consumer.*
Published by: New York Convention and Visitors Bureau, Inc., 810 Seventh Ave, 3 Fl, New York, NY 10019. TEL 212-484-1200, FAX 212-245-5943, visitorinfo@nycgo.com. Adv. contact Suzanne Pomeroy TEL 212-484-5423.

910.2 USA
THE OFFICIAL NORTH CAROLINA TRAVEL GUIDE. Text in English. 1996. a. **Document type:** *Magazine, Consumer.* **Description:** Contains information about traveling in North Carolina.
Related titles: E-mail ed.; Online - full text ed.
Published by: (North Carolina Division of Tourism, Film and Sports Development), Journal Communications, Inc., 725 Cool Springs Blvd, Ste 400, Franklin, TN 37067. TEL 615-771-0080, info@jnlcom.com. Pub. Bob Schwartzman.

917.604 USA
OFFICIAL TENNESSEE VACATION GUIDE. Variant title: Tennessee. Text in English. 1992. a. free (effective 2009). adv. **Document type:** *Magazine, Consumer.* **Description:** Lists attractions, accomodations, campgrounds, outdoor recreation, state parks, ski areas an more to those planning a trip to North Carolina. Vacation and touring guides are circulated through Welcome Center, convention and visitor bureaus, tourism development authorities, chambers of commerce and inquiries to the state's official website.
Related titles: E-mail ed.; Online - full text ed.
Published by: State of Tennessee, Department of Tourist Development, c/o Wm. Snodgrass, Tennessee Tower, 312 8th Ave N, 25th Fl, Nashville, TN 37243. TEL 615-741-2159, tourdev@tn.gov, http://www.state.tn.us/.

917.504 USA
OFFICIAL VISITORS GUIDE. Text in English. 1985. s-a. free. adv. **Document type:** *Magazine, Consumer.* **Description:** Lists attractions, restaurants, recreational activities, shopping, and transportation.
Formerly: Official Visitors Guide to Central Florida
Published by: Orlando - Orange County Convention and Visitors Bureau, Inc., 6700 Forum Dr, Ste 100, Orlando, FL 32821-8017. TEL 407-363-5800, FAX 407-370-5018. R&P Deborah Kicklighter. Adv. contact Sheryl Taylor. B&W page USD 6,335, color page USD 7,282; trim 8.38 x 5.38. Circ: 1,200,000 (controlled).

914 FRA ISSN 0030-0500
OFFICIEL DES SPECTACLES; cette semaine. Text in French. 1946. w. EUR 5 per issue (effective 2005). film rev.; play rev.; music rev.; dance rev. illus. **Document type:** *Consumer.* **Description:** Paris entertainment guide.
Former titles (until 1958): L' Officiel des Spectacles de Cette Semaine (0767-2977); (until 1952): Cette Semaine (0767-2969)
Indexed: RASB.
Address: 1 rue de Berri, Paris, 75008, France. TEL 33-1-42255784, FAX 33-1-45610400. Ed., Pub., R&P Jean-Philippe Richemond. Adv. contact Nicolas Thierry. Circ: 202,302 (paid).

910 FRA ISSN 1776-0283
L'OFFICIEL VOYAGE. Text in French. 2005. bi-m. EUR 24 domestic; EUR 42 in the European Union; EUR 60 elsewhere (effective 2010). **Document type:** *Magazine, Consumer.*
Published by: Les Editions Jalou, 10 rue du Platre, Paris, 75004, France. TEL 33-1-53011030, FAX 33-1-42726575, contact@editionsjalou.com, http://www.jaloufashion.com.

914 CHE
OFFIZIELLES BERNER WOCHEN BULLETIN. Text in German. w.
Published by: Verkehrs Verein, Hauptbahnhof, Bern, 3001, Switzerland. TEL 031-462323, FAX 031-210820, TELEX 912641. Circ: 7,200.

917.71 910.91 USA ISSN 1934-5836
F491.6
OHIO CURIOSITIES; quirky characters, roadside oddities & other offbeat stuff. Text in English. 2007. triennial, latest 2007, 1st ed. USD 14.95 per issue (effective 2008). **Document type:** *Guide, Consumer.* **Description:** Aims to act as a guide to unique places.
Published by: The Globe Pequot Press, Inc., 246 Goose Ln, PO Box 480, Guilford, CT 06437. TEL 203-458-4500, 888-249-7586, FAX 203-458-4603, 800-820-2329, info@globepequot.com, http://www.globepequot.com.

796.7 USA ISSN 0030-0985
THE OHIO MOTORIST. Text in English. 1909. 10/yr. USD 1.50 (effective 2006). adv. bk.rev. illus. 24 p./no. 5 cols./p.; **Document type:** *Magazine, Consumer.*
Published by: Ohio Motorists Association, 5700 Brecksville Rd, Independence, OH 44131. TEL 216-606-6700, FAX 216-606-6710. Ed., Pub. Brian T Newbacher. Adv. contact Sherry Madison. B&W page USD 6,340, color page USD 6,990. Circ: 600,000 (controlled).
Subscr. to: PO Box 6150, Cleveland, OH 44101.

OHIO SEA GRANT COLLEGE PROGRAM. GUIDE SERIES. *see* GEOGRAPHY

910.91 USA
OJAI VALLEY VISITORS GUIDE. Text in English. q. USD 20 (effective 2005). adv. **Document type:** *Magazine, Consumer.*
Published by: Ojai Newspapers LLC, PO Box 277, Ojai, CA 93024. TEL 805-646-1476, FAX 805-646-4281. Pub. Bret Bradigan. Adv. contact Mike Anderson. Circ: 20,000 (controlled and free).

387.7 POL ISSN 1230-3925
OKECIE; airport magazine. Text in Polish. 1992. m. PLZ 60 (effective 1999). adv. illus. **Document type:** *Newspaper.* **Description:** Provides information addressed to all airline passengers.
Published by: Warsaw Voice S.A., Ksiecia Janusza 64, Warsaw, 01452, Poland. TEL 48-22-366377, FAX 48-22-371995, redakcja@terapia.com.pl. Ed. Andrzej Jonas. Adv. contact Kaja Dobrowolska. page PLZ 6,900.

917.404 USA
OKEMO MAGAZINE. Text in English. 2/yr. free. adv. back issues avail. **Document type:** *Magazine, Consumer.* **Description:** Focuses on all that Okemo Mountain and the South Central Vermont region has to offer; profiles its natural beauty, seasonal activities, local history and subjects of human interest.
Published by: Okemo Mountain Resort, 77 Okemo Ridge Rd, Ludlow, VT 05149. TEL 802-228-4041, FAX 802-228-4558, info@okemo.com, http://www.okemo.com. R&P, Adv. contact Pam Cruickshank TEL 802-228-1947. B&W page USD 1,900; trim 8.125 x 10.875. Circ: 25,000; 50,000 Winter.

917.66 910.91 USA ISSN 1935-6463
F694.6
OKLAHOMA CURIOSITIES; quirky characters, roadside oddities & other offbeat stuff. Text in English. 2008. triennial, latest 2008, 1st ed. USD 14.95 per issue (effective 2008). **Document type:** *Guide, Consumer.* **Description:** Provides tourist information about Oklahoma.
Published by: The Globe Pequot Press, Inc., 246 Goose Ln, PO Box 480, Guilford, CT 06437. TEL 203-458-4500, 888-249-7586, FAX 203-458-4603, 800-820-2329, info@globepequot.com, http://www.globepequot.com.

910 GBR
OLEANDER TRAVEL BOOKS SERIES. Variant title: Oleander Travel. Text in English. 19??. a. price varies. **Document type:** *Monographic series, Consumer.*
Published by: Oleander Press, 16 Orchard St, Cambridge, CB1 1JT, United Kingdom. TEL 44-1223-350898.

ON THE LINE (PENSACOLA). *see* LEISURE AND RECREATION

914.704 USA
ON THE LOOSE IN EASTERN EUROPE. Text in English. 1993. a. illus.; maps.
Published by: Fodor's Travel Publications, Inc. (Subsidiary of: Random House Inc.), 1745 Broadway, 15th Fl, New York, NY 10019. TEL 212-572-2313, editors@fodors.com, http://www.fodors.com. Ed. Katie Clark.

917.404 USA
ONLINE BUFFALO. Text in English. 1998. d. free. adv. **Document type:** *Magazine, Consumer.* **Description:** Reports on local attractions, historic sites, and recreation activities in the Buffalo, NY, area. Covers everything that makes news in the region. Contains games.
Formerly: Online Buffalo Magazine
Media: Online - full text.
Address: 229 Allen St, Buffalo, NY 14201. TEL 716-886-4785, FAX 716-886-5481, mike@onlinebuffalo.com.

917.104 796 CAN
ONTARIO FARM & COUNTRY ACCOMMODATIONS. BED & BREAKFAST FARM VACATION DIRECTORY. Text in English. 1967. a. free. adv. **Document type:** *Directory, Consumer.* **Description:** Lists and describes each of the association's bed and breakfast and farm vacation establishments, with rates, farm activities, maps, and surrounding attractions.
Formerly (until 1999): Ontario Farm and Country Accommodations Directory
Related titles: Online - full text ed.
Published by: Ontario Farm & Country Accommodations, R R 2, Vankleek Hill, ON K0B 1R0, Canada. TEL 613-678-2873, FAX 613-678-2502. Ed. Sharon Grose. Adv. contact Samme Putzel.

910.202 CAN ISSN 1912-2977
ONTARIO GROUP TRAVEL PLANNER. Text in English. 2004. a. **Document type:** *Handbook/Manual/Guide, Trade.*
Formerly (until 2007): Ontario Group Tour Planner (1714-843X)
Published by: Holiday Media, 1888 Brunswick St, Ste 609, Halifax, NS B3J 3J8, Canada. TEL 902-425-8255 ext 222, http://www.holidaymedia.ca.

910.202 CAN ISSN 0707-1442
ONTARIO TOURISM NEWS. Text in English. 1978. q.
Published by: Ministry of Tourism Culture and Recreation, Hearst Block, 900 Bay St, Toronto, ON M7A 2E1, Canada. TEL 800-668-2746.

916 NLD ISSN 1872-0439
ONTDEK AFRIKA. Text in Dutch. 2006. bi-m. EUR 28 (effective 2010). adv.
Published by: Sillen Media Projecten, Postbus 433, Nijmegen, 6500 AK, Netherlands. TEL 31-24-3505944. adv.: page EUR 2,495; 170 x 240. Circ: 20,000.

051 910.202 USA
ONWARD. Text in English. 2002. q. USD 18 (effective 2002). adv. back issues avail. **Document type:** *Magazine, Consumer.* **Description:** For credit-qualified bank customers over age 50, this magazine focuses on travel, financial services, lifestyle and health.
Published by: N F R Communications, 4984 Washburn Ave S, Minneapolis, MN 55410. TEL 612-929-8110, FAX 612-929-8146, web@nfrcom.com, http://www.nfrcom.com. Ed., R&P Jacqueline Hilgert. Adv. contact Suzanne Boston. B&W page USD 4,550, color page USD 5,200; trim 10 x 13. Circ: 100,000 (controlled).

910.2 FRA ISSN 1957-3642
OOGOLO VOYAGES. Text in French. 2007. q. EUR 4.50 per issue (effective 2009). **Document type:** *Magazine, Consumer.*
Published by: Plug'n Press, 8 Rue Saint-Marc, Paris, 75002, France.

OP PAD. *see* SPORTS AND GAMES—Outdoor Life

910.91 NLD
OP STAP IN DE NATUUR. Text in Dutch. a. free to members (effective 2008). adv.
Published by: Algemene Nederlandse Wielrijders Bond (A N W B) Media/Dutch Automobile Association Media, Postbus 93200, The Hague, 2509 BA, Netherlands. TEL 31-70-3141470, FAX 31-70-3146538, http://www.anwbmedia.nl. adv.: color page EUR 1,839. Circ: 85,000.

910.202 NLD ISSN 1871-7624
OP STAP IN EUROPA. Text in Dutch. 2005. a. adv.
Published by: (ANWB BV/Royal Dutch Touring Club), Algemene Nederlandse Wielrijders Bond (A N W B) Media/Dutch Automobile Association Media, Postbus 93200, The Hague, 2509 BA, Netherlands. TEL 31-70-3141470, FAX 31-70-3146538, http://www.anwbmedia.nl. adv.: color page EUR 3,136. Circ: 145,000.

914.9204 NLD
OP STAP IN NEDERLAND. Text in Dutch. a. free (effective 2008). adv.
Published by: Algemene Nederlandse Wielrijders Bond (A N W B) Media/Dutch Automobile Association Media, Postbus 93200, The Hague, 2509 BA, Netherlands. TEL 31-70-3141470, FAX 31-70-3146538, http://www.anwbmedia.nl. adv.: color page EUR 3,245. Circ: 150,000.

OPEN ROAD. *see* TRANSPORTATION—Automobiles

338.4791 USA
OPENING DOORS (ONLINE). Text in English. 19??. a. free (effective 2009). **Document type:** *Newsletter.* **Description:** Covers programs, events and board member additions of Philadelphia Hospitality Inc.
Formerly: Opening Doors (Print) (1947-7333)
Media: Online - full text.
Published by: Philadelphia Hospitality Inc., 123 South Broad St, Ste 1710, Philadelphia, PA 19109. TEL 215-790-9901, FAX 215-790-9906.

917.95 910.91 USA ISSN 1935-1135
F874.3
OREGON CURIOSITIES; quirky characters, roadside oddities & other offbeat stuff. Text in English. 2007. triennial, latest 2007, 1st ed. USD 14.95 per issue (effective 2008). **Document type:** *Guide, Consumer.* **Description:** Aims to act as a guide to unique places.
Published by: The Globe Pequot Press, Inc., 246 Goose Ln, PO Box 480, Guilford, CT 06437. TEL 203-458-4500, 888-249-7586, FAX 203-458-4603, 800-820-2329, info@globepequot.com, http://www.globepequot.com.

917.5 USA ISSN 1059-3624
ORLANDO. Text in English. 1946. m. USD 19.95 domestic; USD 39.95 in Canada & Mexico; USD 3.95 per issue (effective 2009). adv. illus.; tr.lit. back issues avail. **Document type:** *Magazine, Consumer.* **Description:** Provides information on Orlando's best dining, arts and entertainment along with magnificent photography.
Former titles (until 19??): Orlando Magazine (0279-1323); (until 1981): Orlando-Land (0145-6431); (until 19??): Orlando-Land/Attraction Magazine
Published by: Morris Multimedia, Inc., 801 N Magnolia Ave, Ste 201, Orlando, Richmond, FL 32803. TEL 407-423-0618, FAX 407-237-6258, http://www.morris.com. Ed. Mike Boslet. Pub. Karen Rodriguez TEL 704-335-7181 ext 135. adv.: color page USD 4,735; trim 8.125 x 10.875. Circ: 33,426.

910.202 USA ISSN 1933-298X
F319.O7
ORLANDO & WALT DISNEY WORLD DIRECTIONS. Text in English. 2006. irreg., latest 2008, 2nd ed. USD 11.99 per issue domestic; CAD 13 per issue in Canada; GBP 6.99 per issue in United Kingdom (effective 2011). **Document type:** *Handbook/Manual/Guide, Consumer.*
Published by: Rough Guides, 375 Hudson St, 9th Fl, New York, NY 10014. TEL 212-414-3635, http://www.roughguides.com/default.aspx.

910.202 USA
ORLANDO ATTRACTIONS MAGAZINE. Text in English. 2007 (Nov.). bi-m. **Document type:** *Magazine, Consumer.* **Description:** Covers Orlando theme parks, tourist attractions, restaurants and more.
Published by: Dream Together Media, LLC., PO Box 784568, Winter Garden, FL 34778. TEL 407-741-3200, FAX 407-358-5073.

917.471 296 USA
OSCAR ISRAELOWITZ'S GUIDE TO JEWISH NEW YORK CITY. Text in English. 1987. a. USD 11.95. adv. bibl.; illus. back issues avail. **Document type:** *Magazine, Consumer.*
Published by: Israelowitz Publishing, PO Box 228, Brooklyn, NY 11229. TEL 718-951-7072. Ed., Pub. Oscar Israelowitz. Circ: 5,000.

914 NOR
OSLO CITY GUIDE. Text in Norwegian. m. adv.
Published by: Per Sletholt og Co., Postboks 57, Tveita, Oslo 6, Norway.

919.36 NZL ISSN 1178-8429
OUR REGION. Text in English. 1999. q. free local. **Document type:** *Newspaper, Consumer.*
Formerly (until 2008): Elements (1177-0619)
Published by: Greater Wellington Regional Council, PO Box 11646, Wellington, 6142, New Zealand. TEL 64-4-3845708, FAX 64-4-3856960, info@gw.govt.nz. Circ: 170,000 (free).

OUR WORLD; the international gay and lesbian travel magazine. *see* HOMOSEXUALITY

910 USA ISSN 1066-7776
OUT & ABOUT. Text in English. 1992. 10/yr. USD 49 domestic; USD 59 in Canada & Mexico; USD 69 elsewhere (effective 2004); includes unlimited TravelGuides. adv. illus. reprints avail. **Description:** Addresses the needs of gay and lesbian travelers.
Indexed: L01, L02.
Published by: Out & About, Inc., PO Box 500, San Francisco, CA 94104-0500. TEL 415-834-6411, FAX 415-834-6560. Circ: 11,000.

910.91 306.766 USA ISSN 1548-5684
HQ75.25
OUT TRAVELER. Text in English. 2003 (Oct.). q. adv. **Document type:** *Magazine, Consumer.* **Description:** Provides the travelers with information on world's top rated destinations.
Related titles: ◆ Supplement to: Out. ISSN 1062-7928.
Indexed: GW, P48, PQC.
Published by: Regent Entertainment Media Inc., 245 W 17th St, Ste 1250, New York, NY 10011. TEL 212-242-8100, FAX 212-242-8338, info@regententertainment.com, http://www.regententertainment.com. Ed. Ed Salvato.

918 USA ISSN 0899-1413
OUT WEST. Text in English. 1988. q. USD 12.95 domestic; USD 16 foreign; USD 3.50 newsstand/cover (effective 2001). adv. bk.rev. back issues avail. **Document type:** *Magazine, Consumer.* **Description:** Covers travel along the "back roads" of America's West; includes reports on the various findings.
Published by: Out West Publishing (Edmonds), 9792 Edmonds Way, 265, Edmonds, WA 98020-5940. TEL 425-776-1228, 800-274-9378. Ed., Pub., R&P, Adv. contact Chuck Woodbury. Circ: 7,000 (paid).

OUTDOOR; Reisen, Wandern, Abenteuer. *see* SPORTS AND GAMES—Outdoor Life

OUTDOOR CANADA; the total outdoor experience. *see* SPORTS AND GAMES—Outdoor Life

910.202 USA ISSN 1933-3013
GV199.42.Y45
AN OUTDOOR FAMILY GUIDE TO YELLOWSTONE & GRAND TETON NATIONAL PARKS. Text in English. 1996. irreg., latest 2006, 2nd ed. USD 15.95 per issue (effective 2008). **Document type:** *Guide, Consumer.*
Published by: Mountaineers Books, 1001 SW Klickitat Way, Ste 201, Seattle, WA 98134. TEL 206-223-6303, FAX 206-223-6306, mbooks@mountaineersbooks.org, http://www.mountaineersbooks.org.

913.04 CAN ISSN 1203-7125
OUTPOST (TORONTO). Text in English. q. CAD 14 domestic; USD 14 in United States; USD 22.95 overseas; CAD 3.95 newsstand/cover (effective 2000). **Document type:** *Magazine, Consumer.* **Description:** Features profiles of adventure traveling and hotspots for enthusiasts, as well as geographic, cultural and historical information on the regions.
Indexed: C03, CBCARef, P48, PQC.
Published by: Outpost Publications, 559 College St, Ste 312, Toronto, ON M6G 1A9, Canada. TEL 416-703-5394, info@outpostmagazine.com, http://www.outpostmagazine.com.

910.91 USA ISSN 1930-9309
GV191.42.W2
OUTSIDE MAGAZINE'S URBAN ADVENTURE: SEATTLE. Text in English. 2004. irreg., latest 2004. 320 p./no.; **Document type:** *Magazine, Consumer.*
Published by: W.W. Norton & Co., Inc., 500 5th Ave, New York, NY 10110. TEL 212-354-5500, 800-555-2028, FAX 212-869-0856, http://www.wwnorton.com. Ed. Maria Dolan.

OUTSIDE'S GO; travel & style for men. *see* MEN'S INTERESTS

910.2 GBR ISSN 0030-7424
OVERSEAS. Text in English. 1915. q. free to members (effective 2009). adv. bk.rev. illus. back issues avail. **Document type:** *Journal, Trade.* **Description:** Feature articles on commonwealth countries usually written by journalists native to the region concerned, news about League activities, ROSL Arts, branch reports, programmes of organised events and contributions by league members.
Related titles: Online - full text ed.: free (effective 2009).
Published by: Royal Over-Seas League, Overseas House, Park Place, St. James's St, London, SW1A 1LR, United Kingdom. TEL 44-20-74080214, FAX 44-20-74996738, info@rosl.org.uk. Ed. Miranda Moore. Adv. contact David Jeffries TEL 44-20-86749444.

917 USA ISSN 0030-7769
F417.O9
OZARKS MOUNTAINEER; the Ozarkswide bi-monthly periodical. Text in English. 1952. bi-m. USD 14.95; USD 20 foreign (effective 1999). adv. bk.rev. charts; illus.; tr.lit.
Address: PO Box 20, Kirbyville, MO 65679. TEL 417-336-2665, FAX 417-336-2679, http://www.runningriver.com. Ed. Dr. Fred Pfister. Pub., R&P Barbara Wehrman TEL 870-423-6419. Adv. contact Connie Waybill. Circ: 20,000 (paid).

910.09 USA
P A T A TASK FORCE REPORTS. Text in English. 1979. irreg., latest vol.32, 1991. USD 50 to non-members; USD 25 to members. back issues avail. **Document type:** *Proceedings.* **Description:** Case studies of tourism development in the Pacific Asia region.
Published by: Pacific Asia Travel Association, Latham Square Bldg, 1611 Telegraph Ave, Ste 550, Oakland, CA 94612. americas@pata.org, http://www.pata.org.

P A T H WAYS. *see* TRANSPORTATION—Railroads

PACIFIC BOATING ALMANAC. NORTHERN CALIFORNIA & THE DELTA. *see* SPORTS AND GAMES—Boats And Boating

PACIFIC BOATING ALMANAC. PACIFIC NORTHWEST. *see* SPORTS AND GAMES—Boats And Boating

917 CAN ISSN 0030-8692
PACIFIC HOSTELLER. Text in English. 1964. q. membership. adv. bk.rev. illus.
Published by: Canadian Hostelling Association, B.C. Region, 1515 Discovery St, Vancouver, BC V6R 4K5, Canada. TEL 604-224-7177, FAX 604-224-4852. Circ: 10,000 (controlled).

919 FJI ISSN 0030-8722
DU1
PACIFIC ISLANDS MONTHLY; the news magazine. Text in English. 1930. m. FJD 2.50 per issue. adv. bk.rev. charts; illus.; mkt.; stat. index. reprints avail.
Indexed: INZP, MLA-IB, PAIS, RASB, RILM, SPPI.
—IE, Ingenta.
Published by: Fiji Times Ltd., PO Box 1167, Suva, Fiji. TEL 679-304111, FAX 679-303809. Ed. Rory Gibson. Pub. Brian O'Flaherty. Circ: 9,500 (paid).

917 USA
THE PACIFIC NORTHWEST'S BEST BED & BREAKFASTS. Text in English. 1993. irreg.
Formerly (until 1993): Fodor's Bed & Breakfasts, Country Inns, and Other Weekend Pleasures. Pacific Northwest (1079-1671)
Published by: Fodor's Travel Publications, Inc. (Subsidiary of: Random House Inc.), 1745 Broadway, 15th Fl, New York, NY 10019. TEL 212-572-2313, editors@fodors.com, http://www.fodors.com.

910.202 PAK
PAKISTAN HOTELS & TOURISM. Text in English. 1975. a. PKR 5. adv.
Published by: Bhatti Publications, 103-B Gulberg, Lahore, Pakistan. Ed. Mukhtar Bhatti.

338.4 954.91 PAK
PAKISTAN TOURISM NEWSLETTER. Text in English. 1998. m. looseleaf. free. illus.; maps; stat.; tr.lit. back issues avail. **Document type:** *Newsletter.*
Media: Fax. **Related titles:** Fax ed.
Published by: Pakistan Tourism Development Corporation, H No. 170, St. 36, F-10/1, Islamabad, Pakistan. TEL 92-51-294189, FAX 92-51-294540. Ed. Salim Bokhari.

917.8 USA ISSN 0031-0425
AP2
PALM SPRINGS LIFE; California's prestige magazine. Text in English. 1957. m. USD 38 domestic; USD 80 foreign; USD 10 per issue (effective 2009). adv. bk.rev.; film rev. illus. back issues avail. **Document type:** *Magazine, Consumer.* **Description:** Covers events in and around Palm Springs.
Incorporates (19??-1958): Palm Springs Villager; Which was formerly (1946-1948): Desert Spotlight (0148-852X)
Published by: Desert Publications, Inc., 303 N Indian Canyon Dr, Box 2724, Palm Springs, CA 92262-2724. sales@desertpublications.com. Ed. Steven R Biller TEL 760-325-2333 ext 261. Pub. Milton W Jones TEL 760-325-2333 ext 200.

917.904 USA
PALM SPRINGS LIFE DESERT GUIDE. Text in English. 1967. m. free (effective 2009). **Document type:** *Magazine, Consumer.* **Description:** Contains traveling information in the Palm Springs desert resorts area.
Published by: Desert Publications, Inc., PO Box 2724, Palm Springs, CA 92263. TEL 760-325-2333, FAX 760-325-7008, sales@desertpublications.com. Ed. Steven R Biller TEL 760-325-2333 ext 261. Pub. Milton W Jones TEL 760-325-2333 ext 200. Circ: 76,325.

PANAMA NOW. *see* BUSINESS AND ECONOMICS—Domestic Commerce

917 USA ISSN 0048-282X
PANORAMA (BOSTON); Boston's official bi-weekly visitor guide. Text in English. 1951. fortn. USD 50. adv. film rev.; play rev. charts; illus.
Incorporates: Cityguide
Published by: Jerome Press, 332 Congress St, Boston, MA 02210. TEL 617-423-3400, FAX 617-423-7108. Ed. Rita A Fucillo. Circ: 64,940.

910.202 ITA ISSN 1126-5469
PANORAMA TRAVEL. Text in Italian. 1998. 10/yr. EUR 25 (effective 2008). **Document type:** *Magazine, Consumer.*
Published by: Arnoldo Mondadori Editore SpA, Via Mondadori 1, Segrate, 20090, Italy. TEL 39-02-66814363, FAX 39-030-3198412, http://www.mondadori.com.

338.4791 ESP ISSN 0214-8021
PAPERS DE TURISME. Text in Multiple languages. 1989. s-a. EUR 20 domestic; EUR 35.35 in Europe; EUR 55.75 elsewhere (effective 2009). back issues avail. **Document type:** *Magazine, Trade.*
Published by: Generalitat Valenciana, Conselleria de Turisme, Ave. Aragon 30, Valencia, 46021, Spain. TEL 34-96-3986000, FAX 34-96-3986001, http://www.comunidad-valenciana.org/index.htm#.

910.202 DEU
PARADISE TRAVELLER. Text in German. 2001. 2/yr. EUR 7.50 newsstand/cover (effective 2003). adv. **Document type:** *Magazine, Consumer.*
Published by: Lady International Verlag, Salzmannweg 17, Stuttgart, 70192, Germany. TEL 49-711-2227722, FAX 49-711-2227723. adv.: B&W page EUR 4,900, color page EUR 8,200. Circ: 45,500 (paid and controlled).

910.91 649 USA
PARENTING TRAVEL. Text in English. 1999. m. **Document type:** *Newsletter, Consumer.*
Published by: Parenting Travel, Inc., 2 Embarcadero Ctr, No 1900, San Francisco, CA 94111. TEL 415-434-5274, FAX 415-434-5280. Ed. Bruce Raskin.

914 USA ISSN 1937-0431
DC708
PARIS. Variant title: Eyewitness Travel Guide: Paris. Text in English. 2007. a. USD 25 (effective 2008). **Document type:** *Guide, Consumer.* **Description:** Describes all the main sights of Paris with maps, photographs and detailed illustrations.
Formerly: Paris EGuide
Published by: D K Publishing (Subsidiary of: Penguin Books U S A, Inc.), 375 Hudson St, New York, NY 10014. TEL 800-631-8571, FAX 201-256-0000, specialsales@dk.com.

910.91 FRA ISSN 1166-2344
PARIS CAPITALE. Text in French, English. 1992. 10/yr. EUR 29 in Paris; EUR 49 in Europe; EUR 79 elsewhere (effective 2009). music rev.; software rev. back issues avail.
Published by: Paris 35, 59 av. Marceau, Paris, 75116, France. TEL 33-1-44439540, FAX 33-1-40700781. Pub. Stanislas Astier. Adv. contact Chantal Gayot. Circ: 50,000.

910.2 USA ISSN 1522-2896
PARIS NOTES; the newsletter for people who love Paris. Text in English. 1992. bi-m. USD 39 domestic; USD 50 foreign (effective 2000). illus. **Document type:** *Newsletter.*
Published by: Mark Eversman Ed. & Pub., P O Box 3663, Manhattan Beach, CA 90266.

914 FRA ISSN 1287-0633
PARISCOPE. Text in French. 1968. w. film rev.; play rev. **Document type:** *Consumer.*
Formerly (until 1998): Une Semaine de Paris, Pariscope (0049-5190); Which was formed by the merger of (1946-1968): Une Semaine de Paris (0750-3636); (1965-1968): Pariscope (0553-3023)
Related titles: Online - full content ed.
Published by: Lagardere Media, 121 Av. de Malakoff, Paris Cedex 16, 75216, France. TEL 33-1-40691600, FAX 33-1-40691854, http://www.lagardere.com.

910.2 AUS ISSN 1834-0822
PARKS DISCOVERY. Text in English. 2007. s-a. free (effective 2007). **Document type:** *Journal, Consumer.*
Published by: Parks Victoria, Level 10 - 535 Bourke St, Melbourne, VIC 3000, Australia. TEL 61-3-86274699, FAX 61-3-96295563, info@parks.vic.gov.au, http://www.parkweb.vic.gov.au/index.cfm.

379.85 EST ISSN 1406-4332
PARNU IN YOUR POCKET. Text in English. 1998. a. USD 5 newsstand/cover (effective 2002). adv. **Document type:** *Magazine, Consumer.*
Published by: Tallinn In Your Pocket, Vana-Viru 4, Tallinn, 10111, Estonia. TEL 372-631-3350, FAX 372-644-6470.

910.202 ITA ISSN 1592-6273
PARTIAMO. Text in Italian. 2001. m. adv. charts; illus. **Document type:** *Magazine, Consumer.*
Published by: Uniservice Srl (Subsidiary of: Casa Editrice Universo SpA), Corso di Porta Nuova 3A, Milan, 20121, Italy. TEL 39-02-636751, FAX 39-02-252007333. Circ: 200,000 (paid).

794.913 USA
PASADENA OFFICIAL VISITORS GUIDE. Text in English. 2002. a. free. adv. 75 p./no. 3 cols./p.; **Document type:** *Guide, Consumer.* **Description:** Covers dining, shopping, attractions, local trasportation, day trips and a calendar of events.
Published by: Weaver Publications, Inc., 2420 Alcott St, Denver, CO 80211. TEL 303-458-1211, FAX 303-477-0724, info@weaver-group.com, http://pub.weaver-group.com. adv.: color page USD 6,140; trim 5.25 x 8.375. Circ: 100,000.

338.4 ESP ISSN 1695-7121
G155.A1
PASOS; revista de turismo y patrimonio cultural. Text in Multiple languages. 2003. s-a. free (effective 2011). back issues avail. **Document type:** *Journal, Academic/Scholarly.* **Description:** Dedicated to the academic and management-based analysis of the diverse processes inscribed within the tourist system, with a particular emphasis on the uses of culture, the environment and territory, people, communities and spaces, integral heritage.
Media: Online - full text.
Indexed: A34, CABA, E12, F08, F12, GH, H16, LT, N02, N04, P32, P33, PGegResA, PHN&I, R08, R12, RA&MP, RRTA, S13, S16, W11.
Published by: Gobierno de Canarias, Consejeria de Educacion, Cultura y Deportes, Ave de Anagua, Santa Cruz de Tenerife, Canarias 38001, Spain. infoedu@gobiernodecanarias.org, http://www.educa.rcanaria.es.

338.4 RUS
PASPORT EKSPRESS. Text in Russian. m. USD 110 in United States.
Published by: Izdatel'skii Dom Pasport Interneishnl, Leningradskii pr-t 80-2, 5-a, Moscow, 125178, Russian Federation. TEL 7-095-1587583, FAX 7-095-1582792. Ed. A Evlakhov. **Dist. by:** East View Information Services, 10601 Wayzata Blvd, Minneapolis, MN 55305. TEL 952-252-1201, 800-477-1005, FAX 952-252-1202, info@eastview.com, http://www.eastview.com.

910.91 USA ISSN 1527-6945
G465
PASSIONFRUIT; a women's travel journal. Text in English. 1999. q. USD 18 domestic; USD 26 in Canada & Mexico; USD 34 elsewhere; USD 4.50 newsstand/cover domestic; USD 6.60 newsstand/cover in Canada (effective 2000 - 2001). adv. bk.rev. back issues avail. **Document type:** *Magazine, Consumer.* **Description:** Contains stories of women who traveled the world, their experiences, and the places of interest.
Address: 2917 Telegraph Ave, PO Box 136, Berkeley, CA 94705. TEL 510-595-5522, FAX 510-843-8780. Ed. Michele Jin.

910.91 306.766 USA
PASSPORT (NEW YORK). Text in English. 2000. bi-m. USD 19.95 domestic; USD 55.60 in Canada & Mexico; USD 110.50 elsewhere (effective 2009). adv. **Document type:** *Magazine, Consumer.*
Published by: Q Communications, Inc., 243 W 30th St, New York, NY 10001. TEL 800-999-9718.

910.2 USA ISSN 1095-6824
PASSPORT NEWSLETTER. Text in English. 1965. m. USD 99 combined subscription domestic print & online eds.; USD 124 combined subscription foreign print & online eds. (effective 2005). bk.rev. back issues avail. **Document type:** *Newsletter, Consumer.* **Description:** For knowledgeable and discriminating travelers.
Formerly (until 199?): Passport (0031-272X)
Related titles: Online - full text ed.: USD 70 (effective 2005).
Published by: Remy Publishing Co., PMB 501, 5315 N Clark St, Chicago, IL 60640-2113. TEL 773-769-6760, 800-542-6670, FAX 773-769-6012, custsvc@passportnewsletter.com. Ed., Pub. Philip Woodward.

910.09 SGP
PATA TRAVEL NEWS ASIA - PACIFIC. Short title: P T N Asia - Pacific. Text in English. 1987. m. USD 60 in Asia; USD 70 elsewhere. adv. **Document type:** *Magazine, Trade.* **Description:** Trade information for Asia's travel and tourism industries.
Indexed: H&TI.
Published by: C M P Business Media Pte Ltd. (Subsidiary of: United Business Media Limited), 390 Havelock Rd, #05-00 King's Centre, Singapore, 169662, Singapore. TEL 65-735-3366, FAX 65-732-1191, info@cmpasia.com.sg, http://www.cmpasia.com.sg/. Circ: 13,848.

910.91 USA ISSN 1096-0708
E185.5
PATHFINDERS TRAVEL; the travel magazine for people of color. Text in English. 1997. q. **Document type:** *Magazine, Consumer.*
Published by: Pathfinders Travel Magazine, 6325 Germantown Ave., Philadelphia, PA 19144-1907. blaktravel@aol.com, http://www.pathfinderstravel.com. Ed. Pamela Thomas.

338.4 BRA ISSN 1806-700X
PATRIMONIO: LAZER & TURISMO. Variant title: Revista Electronica Patrimonio: Lazer & Turismo. Text in Portuguese. 2004. q. free (effective 2011). **Document type:** *Journal, Academic/Scholarly.*
Media: Online - full text.
Published by: Universidade Catolica de Santos UNISANTOS, Campus Dom Idilio Jose Soares, Av Conselheiro Nebias 300, Vila Nova - Santos, SP 11015-002, Brazil.

910.202 ITA ISSN 1974-014X
IL PATRIMONIO MONDIALE DELL'UNESCO. Text in Italian. 2008. w. **Document type:** *Magazine, Consumer.*
Published by: Poligrafici Editoriale (Subsidiary of: Monrif Group), Via Enrico Mattei 106, Bologna, BO 40138, Italy. TEL 39-051-6006111, FAX 39-051-6006266, http://www.monrifgroup.net.

910.09 USA ISSN 1056-0025
PAUL EDWARDS' TRAVEL CONFIDENTIAL. Text in English. 1991. m. USD 95. **Description:** Covers low-cost travel for individuals and groups.
Formerly (until 1991): Travel Smarter (1055-0488)
Published by: Lowell Communications, Inc., 88 Bleecker St, New York, NY 10012. TEL 212-254-1069. Ed. Paul L Edwards.

PAYS COMTOIS; le magazine du patrimoine, de l'histoire et de l'art de vivre. *see* GEOGRAPHY

PAYS DE NORMANDIE; le magazine du patrimoine, de l'histoire et de l'art de vivre. *see* GEOGRAPHY

TU

PAYS DU NORD; tourisme, patrimoine et art de vivre. *see* GEOGRAPHY

917.1 ESP ISSN 1699-0331
PAYS DU QUEBEC. Text in French. 197?. irreg. **Document type:** *Catalog, Consumer.*
Published by: Fisa - Escudo de Oro, S.A., Palaudarias, 26, Barcelona, 08004, Spain. TEL 34-93-2308610, FAX 34-93-2308611, fisa@eoro.com, http://www.eoro.com/.

▼ **PEACE TOURISM JOURNAL**; the journal of tourism and peace research. *see* POLITICAL SCIENCE—International Relations

910.202 USA ISSN 1948-1675
PEARLS OF TRAVEL WISDOM. Text in English. 2008. bi-w. free (effective 2009). back issues avail. **Document type:** *Magazine, Consumer.*
Media: Online - full content.
Published by: Smart Women Travelers, Inc., PO Box 950903, Lake Mary, FL 32795. TEL 877-212-7364, info@smartwomentravelers.com, http://smartwomentravelers.com.

910.2 USA
PEBBLE BEACH; the magazine. Text in English. q. **Document type:** *Magazine, Consumer.*
Published by: Desert Publications Inc., 303 N Indian Canyon Dr, Palm Springs, CA 92263-2724.

910.91 USA
PEGASUS (ATLANTA). Text in English. 2000. bi-m. **Document type:** *Magazine, Consumer.* **Description:** Geared toward the world's most influential business executives, wealthy individuals, professional athletes, and celebrities. Serves 50,000 passengers on private jets.
Published by: Pegasus Magazine, 1145 Zonolite Rd, No 1, Atlanta, GA 30306. TEL 404-876-8271, FAX 404-876-8271, andy@pegasusmag.com, http://www.pegasusmag.com. Ed. Andrea Sarvady.

910.91 USA ISSN 0740-5529
F1652
PELICAN GUIDE TO THE BAHAMAS. Text in English. 1999 (Jun.). irreg. USD 17.95 per issue (effective 2007). **Document type:** *Guide, Consumer.* **Description:** Travel guide focusing on the Bahamas.
Published by: Pelican Publishing Co., 1000 Burmaster St., Gretna, LA 70053. TEL 504-368-1175, 800-843-1724, FAX 504-368-1195, sales@pelicanpub.com, http://www.pelicanpub.com.

917.9504 USA
PELICAN POST COAST EXPLORER. Text in English. 1999. 4/yr. USD 20; free newsstand/cover (effective 2009). adv. **Document type:** *Magazine, Consumer.*
Formerly (until 2008): Pelican Post
Published by: Pelican Productions, Inc., PO Box 278, Cannon Beach, OR 97110. TEL 503-717-1122, 888-609-6051, FAX 503-717-1124, pelican@seasurf.com. Ed. Rebecca Herren. Pub. Gary Hayes. adv.: page USD 1,276; trim 7.625 x 10. Circ: 41,250 (controlled).

915.94 HKG
PENINSULA GROUP MAGAZINE. Text in Chinese. 1974. 3/yr. free to qualified personnel. adv. **Document type:** *Consumer.* **Description:** Covers travel, leisure and art in Asia and the United States.
Published by: Peninsula Group, St George's Bldg 6th Fl, 2 Ice House St, Central, Hong Kong, Hong Kong. TEL 840-7619, FAX 845-5512, TELEX 74509-KREM-HX. Ed. Liam Fitzpatrick. Adv. contact Margaret Tan. Circ: 53,000.

PENNSYLVANIA MAGAZINE. *see* GENERAL INTEREST PERIODICALS—United States

917 USA ISSN 1099-5315
F1209
THE PEOPLE'S GUIDE TO MEXICO. Cover title: Carl Franz's The People's Guide to Mexico. Text in English. 1972. irreg., latest 13th ed. USD 24.95 13th ed. (effective 2008). **Document type:** *Guide, Consumer.* **Description:** Contains basic travel information, entertaining stories and guidance for travelers to Mexico.
Published by: Avalon Travel Publishing, 1700 4th St, Berkeley, CA 94710. TEL 510-595-3664, avalon.publicity@perseusbooks.com, http://www.avalontravelbooks.com.

910 USA ISSN 1946-8296
PERIPLOUS. Text in English. 2005. irreg.
Published by: Travel Dynamics International, 132 E 70th St, New York, NY 10021. TEL 212-517-7555, 800-257-5767, FAX 212-774-1560, info@traveldynamicsinternational.com, http://www.traveldynamicsinternational.com.

917 CAN ISSN 0048-3451
PERSONNEL GUIDE TO CANADA'S TRAVEL INDUSTRY. Text in English. 1969. s-a. CAD 68 domestic; USD 50 in United States; USD 50 elsewhere (effective 2004). adv. **Document type:** *Directory.* **Description:** Provides complete listings of all travel agencies, tour operators, wholesalers, airlines, car rentals, hotel representatives, tourist boards, travel insurance firms and cruise lines operating in Canada.
Published by: Baxter Publishing Co., 310 Dupont St, Toronto, ON M5R 1V9, Canada. TEL 416-968-7252, FAX 416-968-2377, http://www.travelpress.com/. Ed. Wendy Baxter Mcclung. Adv. contact Earl Lince. Circ: 5,000.

918.504 PER
PERU GUIDE. Text in English. 1980. m. USD 12 in South America to individuals; USD 34 in North America to individuals; USD 52 elsewhere to individuals (effective 2000). adv. **Document type:** *Handbook/Manual/Guide, Consumer.* **Description:** Guide for tourists visiting Peru.
Published by: Lima Editora S.A., Ave. Benavides, 1180, Miraflores, Lima 18, Peru. TEL 51-1-4440815, FAX 51-1-242-3669, info@limaedistora.com. Eds. Jose Luis Arrarte, Oscar Orgumanis. R&P Jose Luis Arrarte. Adv. contact Tana Servat. B&W page USD 780, color page USD 1,140. Circ: 30,000.

910.202 GBR ISSN 1363-738X
PERU HANDBOOK. Text in English. 1997. biennial. GBP 15.99 per issue (effective 2010). adv. back issues avail. **Document type:** *Handbook/Manual/Guide, Consumer.* **Description:** Covers all the basics from where to stay and where to eat to cycling, walking and how to get around the Peru.
Published by: Footprint Handbooks Ltd., 6 Riverside Ct, Lower Bristol Rd, Bath, Avon BA2 3DZ, United Kingdom. TEL 44-1225-469141, FAX 44-1225-469461, wwwinfo@footprintbooks.com.

910.91 FRA ISSN 1779-0506
PETIT FUTE MAG. Text in French. 2006. bi-m. EUR 20 (effective 2009). **Document type:** *Magazine, Consumer.*
Published by: Petit Fute, 18 rue des Volontaires, Paris, 75015, France. TEL 33-1-53697000, FAX 33-1-52731524, info@petitfute.com, http://www.petitfute.fr.

910.2 FRA ISSN 1957-9136
PETIT VOYAGE. Text in French. 2007. irreg. **Document type:** *Monographic series, Consumer.*
Published by: Lonely Planet, 12 Av d'Italie, Paris, Cedex 13 75627, France. TEL 33-1-44160500, FAX 33-1-44088402, lonelyplanet@placedesediteurs.com.

910.2 914 GBR ISSN 0079-130X
PETS WELCOME; animal lovers' holiday guide. Text in English. 1961. a. GBP 9.99 per issue (effective 2010). adv. back issues avail. **Document type:** *Handbook/Manual/Guide, Consumer.* **Description:** Lists over 1000 holiday opportunities for pets and their owners.
Published by: F H G Guides Ltd. (Subsidiary of: F H G Publications Ltd.), Abbey Mill Business Ctr, Seedhill, Paisley, PA1 1TJ, United Kingdom. TEL 44-141-8870428, FAX 44-141-8897204, sales@fhguides.co.uk, http://www.fhguides.co.uk.

910.202 USA ISSN 1932-6467
F158.18
PHILADELPHIA & THE PENNSYLVANIA DUTCH COUNTRY. Text in English. 2005. irreg., latest 2007. USD 23 per issue (effective 2008). **Document type:** *Guide, Consumer.*
Published by: D K Publishing (Subsidiary of: Penguin Books U S A, Inc.), 375 Hudson St, New York, NY 10014. TEL 212-213-4800, 800-631-8571, FAX 212-689-4828, publicity@dk.com, http://us.dk.com.

910.2478 USA
PHILADELPHIA STYLE CITY GUIDE. Text in English. 2004. q. adv. **Document type:** *Magazine, Consumer.* **Description:** Resourse for restaurants, shopping, nightlife and cultural and sporting events.
Published by: D L G Media Holdings, LLC., 141 League St., Philadelphia, PA 19147. TEL 215-468-6670, FAX 215-468-6530, info@dlgmedia.com, http://www.dlgmedia.com. adv.: color page USD 1,500; trim 5.25 x 7.

910.202 USA ISSN 0745-4554
PHYSICIANS' TRAVEL & MEETING GUIDE. Text in English. 1982. m. USD 97 domestic to individuals; USD 125 in Canada & Mexico to individuals; USD 140 elsewhere to individuals; USD 140 domestic to institutions; USD 156 in Canada & Mexico to institutions; USD 173 elsewhere to institutions (effective 2007). adv. tr.lit. back issues avail.; reprints avail. **Document type:** *Journal, Trade.* **Description:** Provides listings of continuing medical education meetings for physicians along with travel articles on convention cities and other destinations.
Related titles: Online - full text ed.
Indexed: A22.
—CCC.
Published by: Quadrant HealthCom, 7 Century Dr, Ste 302, Parsippany, NJ 07054. TEL 973-206-3434, FAX 973-206-9378, sales@pulmonaryreviews.com, http://www.quadranthealth.com. Ed. Bea Riemschneider TEL 973-206-8088. Adv. contact Tom Cooney TEL 973-206-8054. Circ: 166,227 (paid and controlled).

910.202 ITA ISSN 1971-1956
PIEMONTE CUCINA E TRADIZIONI. Text in Italian. 2007. w. **Document type:** *Magazine, Consumer.*
Published by: Alberto Peruzzo Editore Srl, Via Ercole Marelli 165, Sesto San Giovanni, MI 20099, Italy. TEL 39-02-242021, FAX 39-02-2485736.

917.9 629.13092 USA ISSN 1099-8160
PILOT GETAWAYS. Text in English. 1998. bi-m. USD 17.95 (effective 2006). **Document type:** *Magazine, Consumer.* **Description:** Covers fly-in destinations in the West.
Incorporates (in 2006): Northern Pilot (1523-6412)
Published by: Airventure Publishing, Llc., P O Box 550, Glendale, CA 91209-0550. TEL 818-241-1890, FAX 818-241-1895, info@pilotgetaways.com. Ed. John Kounes.

917 796 USA ISSN 1939-3369
PINEWOOD-MUNDS PARK, ARIZONA COMMUNITY GUIDE & DIRECTORY; a relocation guide for the communities of northern Arizona. Text in English. 2005. a. USD 3.95 per issue (effective 2011). adv. back issues avail. **Document type:** *Magazine, Consumer.*
Related titles: Online - full text ed.: ISSN 1939-3377. free (effective 2011).
Published by: OutWest Publishing LLC, PO Box 2059, Gilbert, AZ 85299. TEL 480-539-0922, FAX 480-539-5280, info@outwestpublishing.com, http://www.outwestpublishing.com. Pub. Pruett LaNora.

910.4 USA
PINKERTON EYE ON TRAVEL. Text in English. 1987. m. USD 199 (effective 2000). **Document type:** *Newsletter.* **Description:** Publishes travel warnings and advisories, information on currency exchange, weather, passport and visa requirements, and health issues.
Formerly: International Travel Briefing Service
Media: Online - full text.
Published by: Pinkerton Global Intelligence Services, 4245 N Fairfax Dr, Ste 725, Arlington, VA 22203-1606. TEL 703-525-6111, FAX 703-525-2454. Ed. Kent Brown. Circ: 1,000.

614.86 USA
PINKERTON WORLD STATUS MAP. Text in English. 1983. bi-m. USD 36. **Description:** Provides security risk and medical information for international travelers.
Formerly: World Status Map (0887-9559)
Related titles: Online - full text ed.
Published by: Pinkerton Global Intelligence Services, 4245 N Fairfax Dr, Ste 725, Arlington, VA 22203-1606. TEL 703-525-6111, FAX 703-525-2454. Ed. Nalani Alexander. Circ: 1,700.

910.09 USA
PINNACLE. (Published in 19 regional eds.) Text in English. 1990. 2/yr. adv. **Document type:** *Magazine, Trade.*
Published by: Pinnacle Publications, Inc., 2 E Main St, Marcellus, NY 13108. TEL 315-673-4885, FAX 315-703-9922, edit@PinnacleMagazines.com, http://www.pinnaclemagazines.com. Pub. Tom Dwyer.

363.7 USA
PLANETA.COM/EARTH SPEAKS. Variant title: Planeta. Text in English, Spanish. 1994. q. adv. bk.rev.; music rev. bibl.; illus. back issues avail.; reprints avail. **Document type:** *Newsletter, Consumer.* **Description:** Provides environmental news and information about eco-tourism for travelers in the Americas.
Formerly: El Planeta Platica (1089-8395)
Media: Online - full text. **Related titles:** Print ed.: El Planeta Platica. ISSN 1089-8387. free.
Published by: Talking Planet, 1511 Twin Springs Ct, Henderson, NV 89014-0320.

910.91 CAN ISSN 1719-3702
LA PLANIFICATION DE LA GESTION DU PARC. BULLETIN. Text in French. 2004. irreg. **Document type:** *Bulletin, Consumer.*
Published by: Parks Canada, Gulf Islands National Park Reserve of Canada (Subsidiary of: Parks Canada), 2220 Harbour Rd, Sidney, BC V8L 2P6, Canada. TEL 250-654-4000, FAX 250-654-4014, gulf.islands@pc.gc.ca, http://www.pc.gc.ca/pn-np/bc/gulf/default.asp.

338.4791 AUS
PLATINUM PRIVILEGE. Text in English. 3/yr. **Document type:** *Magazine, Trade.* **Description:** Offers loyal Starwood partners articles and features on incentive programs and campaigns available to them and their customers.
Published by: (Starwood Hotels & Resorts Worldwide, Inc.), A C P Custom Media (Subsidiary of: A C P Magazines Ltd.), 54 Park St, Sydney, NSW 2000, Australia. TEL 61-2-92828019, FAX 61-2-92673625, custominfo@acp.com.au, http://www.acp.com.au/. Circ: 45,000 (controlled).

910.202 USA
PLEASANT HAWAII; the Aloha State magazine. Text in English. 1988. m. adv. **Description:** Serves to promote visitor awareness of the Island lifestyle. Covers Hawaii's people, its culture, its scenic beauty, activities and special events.
Published by: Pleasant Hawaii, Inc., 274 Puuhale Rd, Ste 200, Honolulu, HI 96819. TEL 808-843-6000, FAX 808-843-6091. Ed. Fern Gavelek. R&P Ron Cruger. Adv. contact Sandra Kinsella. Circ: 50,000.

PLEINAIR; turismo secondo natura, camper, caravan, tenda, escursioni. *see* SPORTS AND GAMES—Outdoor Life

PLEINAIR MARKET. *see* SPORTS AND GAMES—Outdoor Life

338.4791 USA ISSN 1554-1215
HE9803.A2
PLUNKETT'S AIRLINE, HOTEL & TRAVEL INDUSTRY ALMANAC. Variant title: Airline, Hotel & Travel Industry Almanac. Text in English. 2002. a. USD 399 combined subscription (print, online & CD-ROM eds.); USD 299 combined subscription (print & CD-ROM eds.) (effective 2009). **Document type:** *Directory, Trade.* **Description:** Complete reference to the global travel industry, including e-commerce, airlines, hotels, travel agencies, cruise lines and car rentals.
Related titles: CD-ROM ed.; Online - full text ed.: USD 299 (effective 2009).
Indexed: H&TI.
Published by: Plunkett Research, Ltd, PO Drawer 541737, Houston, TX 77254. TEL 713-932-0000, FAX 713-932-7080, info@plunkettresearch.com. Pub. Jack W Plunkett.

910.09 USA
PLYMOUTH GUIDE. Text in English. 1980. s-a. adv. illus. **Document type:** *Magazine, Consumer.* **Description:** Features the best of Plymouth including information on its history, dining, places to visit, latest happening shows and events.
Published by: GateHouse Media, Inc, 182 Standish Ave, Plymouth, MA 02360. TEL 508-591-6620, FAX 508-591-6601. Ed. Beth Doyle. Adv. contact Ron Bright.

918 BHS
POCKET GUIDE TO THE BAHAMAS. Text in English. 1947. s-a.
Published by: Cartwright Publications, PO Box N 494, Nassau, Bahamas. Ed. Kevin B Cartwright. Circ: 150,000.

910.2 GBR ISSN 2045-3922
POCKET LONDON GUIDE. Text in English. 19??. q. adv. **Document type:** *Handbook/Manual/Guide, Consumer.* **Description:** Contains information on all of London with street level fold-out maps, editorial on every area of the city and information on all of London's top attractions, tips on where to eat out, upcoming events, and much more.
Former titles (until 2005): Pocket London (1369-3492); (until 1999): Map Directory London
Published by: Pocket London Ltd., 2 Stewart's Ct, 218-220 Stewart's Rd, London, SW8 4UB, United Kingdom. TEL 44-20-77201166, FAX 44-20-77201177, info@pocketlondon.com.

911.3 POL ISSN 1505-3601
PODROZE. Text in Polish. 1998. m. PLZ 119.40; PLZ 9.99 newsstand/cover (effective 2011). adv. **Document type:** *Magazine, Consumer.* **Description:** Provides information and details that provide readers with the means to accomplish traveling plans and goals.
Related titles: Online - full text ed.: ISSN 1689-0558.
Published by: Wydawnictwo Murator Sp. z o.o., ul Deblinska 6, Warsaw, 04187, Poland. TEL 48-22-5905000, FAX 48-22-5905444, klienci@murator.com.pl, http://www.murator.com.pl. Ed. Philip Niedenthal. adv.: page PLZ 19,000; trim 175 x 232.

POLISH JOURNAL OF SPORT AND TOURISM. *see* SPORTS AND GAMES

338.4791 CAN ISSN 1716-2637
POLITIQUE DE SIGNALISATION TOURISTIQUE. CRITERES D'ADMISSIBILITE. Text in French. 2002. biennial. **Document type:** *Government.*
Related titles: ◆ English ed.: Tourist Signing Policy. Eligibility Criteria. ISSN 1914-9883.
Published by: Quebec. Ministere du Tourisme, Direction Generale des Services a la Clientele Touristique, 1255 Rue Peel, Bureau 400, Montreal, PQ H3B 4V4, Canada. http://www.mtq.gouv.qc.ca.

910.202 USA ISSN 1070-9479
PORTHOLE; cruise magazine. Text in English. 1982. bi-m. USD 19.95 domestic; USD 24.95 in Canada; USD 39.95 elsewhere (effective 2008). adv. bk.rev. illus. reprints avail. **Document type:** *Magazine, Consumer.* **Description:** Presents in-depth ship reviews, features on cruise travel, cruise industry news and U.S.P.H. scores.
Formerly: Cruise Digest Reports (0886-5604)

Published by: Panoff Publishing, Inc., PO Box 469066, Escondido, CA 92046-9066. TEL 800-776-7678, FAX 954-377-7000. Ed., Pub. Bill Panoff. Circ: 50,000.

910.202 790.1 USA ISSN 1073-1857
PORTLAND; Maine's city magazine. Text in English. 1986. 10/yr. USD 29; USD 2.95 newsstand/cover; CAD 3.95 newsstand/cover in Canada (effective 2004). adv. bk.rev. back issues avail. **Document type:** *Magazine, Consumer.* **Description:** Covers the arts and business in the Portland area and the rest of Maine.
Formerly: Portland Monthly (0887-5340)
Published by: Sargent Publishing Inc., 722 Congress St, Portland, ME 04102. TEL 207-775-4339, FAX 207-775-2334. Ed., Pub. Colin W Sargent. Adv. contact Michael J Sullivan. color page USD 3,186. Circ: 10,000.

910.202 GBR ISSN 1758-1494
▼ **PORTUGAL LIFE**; it's only a click away. Text in English. 2009. bi-m. free (effective 2010). adv. **Document type:** *Magazine, Consumer.* **Description:** Features history, traditions, golf courses, wines and food and other interesting aspects of Portugal.
Incorporates (2008-2009): Golf Portugal (1757-3858)
Media: Online - full text. **Related titles:** Online - full text ed.: free (effective 2010).
Published by: The Portuguese Golf Club Ltd., Great St, Norton sub Hamdon, Somerset TA14 6SG, United Kingdom. TEL 44-1935-881762, sales@theportuguesegolfclub.com, http://www.theportuguesegolfclub.com. Ed. Mary Wilson TEL 44-7768-664501. Adv. contact Simon Robins TEL 44-7775-608681. color page EUR 960; 184 x 272.

914.604 PRT
PORTUGAL TURISMO ACTUALIDADE. Text in Portuguese. 1980. m. adv.
Address: Rua Joaquim Antonio de Aguiar, 45-5o, Esq., Lisbon, 1000, Portugal. TEL 01-557175, FAX 01-557667. Ed. Jorge Andrade. Pub. Alberico Cardoso. Adv. contact Daniel Lourenco. Circ: 40,000.

910.91 330 USA ISSN 1542-7935
POSITIVE MAGAZINE; travel, adventure, philanthropy. Text in English. 2005. m. looseleaf. USD 23.95; USD 4.95 per issue; free to qualified personnel (effective 2008). adv. bk.rev.; film rev.; music rev.; software rev.; video rev. back issues avail. **Document type:** *Magazine, Consumer.* **Description:** Provides information such as selected destinations, food and dinning, shipping and business for travel professionals, retirees, affluent travelers, and adventure seekers.
Published by: T R L Media Inc., PO Box 1113, Lakewood, CA 908714. TEL 310-635-1176. Ed. Artrice Collins. Pub. Tiffany Love. adv.: color page USD 8,000; trim 8.375 x 11.063. Circ: 100,000 (paid and controlled).

910.91 USA
POSTCARDS. Text in English. m. **Document type:** *Magazine, Consumer.*
Published by: Carlson Wagonlit Travel, 5900 Green Oak Dr, Minnetonka, MN 55343. TEL 612-936-4700, FAX 612-988-0245, davisrdee@aol.com. Ed. Elaine Davis.

910.5 NZL ISSN 1177-2786
POUR L'AMOUR DE TRAVEL. Text in English. 2006. bi-m. NZD 32.50 (effective 2008). adv. **Document type:** *Magazine, Consumer.*
Published by: Skyline Travel, PO Box 25019, St Heliers, Auckland, New Zealand. TEL 64-21-2427638, FAX 64-9-5782997.

POWER TRIPS. *see* NEW AGE PUBLICATIONS

914 POL ISSN 0032-6151
POZNAJ SWOJ KRAJ; miesiecznik krajoznawczo-turystyczny. Text in Polish. 1958. m. PLZ 3 per issue. adv. bk.rev. illus. index.
Published by: Oficyna Wydawnicza Amos, Ul Zuga 12, Warsaw, 01806, Poland. TEL 48-22-6397367. Ed. Janusz Sapa. Circ: 25,000.

910.2 USA ISSN 1088-6419
THE PRACTICAL NOMAD; guide to the online travel marketplace. Text in English. 1997. irreg., latest 1st ed. USD 17.95 per issue (effective 2009). **Document type:** *Guide, Consumer.*
Published by: Avalon Travel Publishing, 1400 65th St, Ste 250, Emeryville, CA 94608. avalon.publicity@perseusbooks.com, http://www.avalontravelbooks.com.

910.202 USA
PRAIRIE PROFILE. Text in English. w.
Address: 312 Fifth St, Box 177, Brookings, SD 57006. TEL 605-692-6271. Ed. Kristin Anderson.

910.91 USA
PREFERRED DESTINATIONS MAGAZINE. Text in English. 19??. q. free to qualified personnel (effective 2011). **Document type:** *Magazine, Consumer.* **Description:** Covers celebriety interviews, events calendar, local dinning, shopping, and maps to visitors in Orange county, CA.
Published by: Freedom Communications, Inc., 17666 Fitch, Irvine, CA 92714. TEL 949-253-2300, FAX 714-474-7675, info@link.freedom.com, http://www.freedom.com. Ed. Lisa Liddane TEL 714-796-7958. Pub. Erin Zilis TEL 949-644-4700 ext 130. Circ: 75,000 (free).

PREMIER ROMANCE. *see* HOTELS AND RESTAURANTS

910.202 USA
PREMIER SPAS. Text in English. 1999. s-a. USD 19.90 domestic; USD 25.90 in Canada & Mexico; USD 33.90 elsewhere; USD 9.95 newsstand/cover domestic; USD 12.95 newsstand/cover in Canada & Mexico; USD 16.95 newsstand/cover elsewhere (effective 2005). back issues avail. **Document type:** *Directory, Trade.* **Description:** Provides guide to travel professionals covering luxury spas of the world.
Indexed: A09, V03.
Published by: Questex Media Group Inc., 275 Grove St, Bldg 2, Ste 130, Newton, MA 02466. TEL 617-219-8300, 888-552-4346, FAX 617-219-8310, questex@sunbeltfs.com, http://www.questex.com.

910.202 USA ISSN 1554-2564
PREP TRAVELER. Text in English. 2005. s-a. (May & Nov.). free to qualified personnel. adv. **Document type:** *Magazine, Trade.* **Description:** Covers the travel demands of youth performance groups and amateur sports and event travel markets.
Published by: Premier Tourism Marketing, Inc., 621 Plainfield Rd, Ste 406, Willowbrook, IL 60527. TEL 630-794-0696, FAX 630-794-0652, info@premiertourismmarketing.com, http://www.premiertourismmarketing.com. Pub. Jeffrey Gayduk. adv.: B&W page USD 3,055; trim 8.25 x 5.375. Circ: 26,000 (controlled).

THE PRESIDENTS' JOURNAL. *see* HISTORY—History Of North And South America

917 BMU ISSN 0048-5268
PREVIEW BERMUDA. Text in English. 1959. m. USD 30. adv. charts; illus. **Description:** Complete guide for the Bermuda visitor.
Published by: Preview of Bermuda Ltd., PO Box HM 266, Hamilton, HMAX, Bermuda. TEL 441-292-4155, FAX 441-295-4724. Eds. Ann Brown, Roxana Kaufmann.

910.2 USA
PREVUE; destination insight for meeting + incentive planners. Text in English. 2008. bi-m. free to qualified personnel (effective 2011). **Document type:** *Handbook/Manual/Guide, Trade.* **Description:** Contains features and ideas for different types of incentives focusing on products, services and innovations.
Formerly: Official Meeting Planners Guide to Incentives
Related titles: E-mail ed.: free (effective 2011).
Published by: Worth International Media Group, 5979 NW 151 St, Ste 120, Miami Lakes, FL 33014. TEL 305-828-0123, 800-447-0123, FAX 305-826-6950, info@worthit.com, http//www.worthit.com. Ed. Greg Oates.

PRINCE EDWARD ISLAND, CANADA. DESTINATION & GOLF GUIDE. *see* SPORTS AND GAMES—Ball Games

910.2 GBR ISSN 0955-0771
PRIVATE VILLAS. Text in English. 1983. bi-m. GBP 17.40 domestic; GBP 35 foreign; GBP 2.90 newsstand/cover domestic; USD 7.95 newsstand/cover in United States; CAD 8.95 newsstand/cover in Canada. **Document type:** *Magazine, Consumer.* **Description:** Features a vast selection of holiday homes ranging from apartments to villas, making it easy to create a vacation without a tour package.
Address: 6th Fl Berwick House, 35 Livery St, Birmingham, Warks B3 2PB, United Kingdom. TEL 44-121-236-2111, FAX 44-121-236-2777. **Dist. by:** Seymour Distribution Ltd, 86 Newman St, London W1T 3EX, United Kingdom. FAX 44-207-396-8002, enquiries@seymour.co.uk.

338.4 POL ISSN 1230-1035
PROBLEMS OF TOURISM. Text in English. 1987. q. **Document type:** *Journal, Academic/Scholarly.*
Related titles: ◆ Translation of: Problemy Turystyki. ISSN 0138-0478.
Indexed: H&TI.
Published by: Instytut Turystyki/Institute of Tourism, ul Merliniego 9a, Warsaw, 02511, Poland. TEL 48-22-8446347, FAX 48-22-8441263, it@intur.com.pl.

338.4 POL ISSN 0138-0478
PROBLEMY TURYSTYKI. Text in Polish. 1978. q. **Document type:** *Journal, Academic/Scholarly.*
Related titles: ◆ English Translation: Problems of Tourism. ISSN 1230-1035.
Published by: Instytut Turystyki/Institute of Tourism, ul Merliniego 9a, Warsaw, 02511, Poland. TEL 48-22-8446347, FAX 48-22-8441263, it@intur.com.pl.

338.4 USA ISSN 2150-6582
PROCUREMENT.TRAVEL; the source for managaed travel insight. Text in English. 2006 (Nov.). q. free (effective 2011). adv. back issues avail. **Document type:** *Magazine, Trade.* **Description:** Provides information for professional purchasers of worldwide corporate travel and meetings.
Published by: Business Travel Media Group, 116 W 32nd St, 14th Fl, New York, NY 10001. TEL 847-559-7533, 800-697-8859, FAX 847-291-4816, nbtn@omeda.com, http://www.promedia.travel/.

338.4 PER
EL PROFESIONAL. Text in Spanish. 1993. s-m. USD 28 in South America to individuals; USD 50 in North America to individuals; USD 80 elsewhere to individuals (effective 2000). adv. **Document type:** *Newspaper.* **Description:** Covers the travel and airline industry.
Published by: Lima Editora S.A., Ave. Benavides, 1180, Miraflores, Lima 18, Peru. TEL 51-1-4440815, FAX 51-1-242-3669, info@limaedistora.com. Eds. Jose Luis Arrarte, Oscar Orgumanis. R&P Jose Luis Arrarte. Adv. contact Tana Servat. Circ: 3,700.

914 AUT
PROGRAMM WIEN; events-manifestations. Text in English, French, German, Italian. 1957. m. adv. **Document type:** *Bulletin, Trade.*
Formerly: Wien-Veranstaltungen
Published by: Wiener Tourismusverband, Obere Augartenstr 40, Vienna, W 1025, Austria. TEL 43-1-211140, FAX 43-1-2168492, events@wien.info, http://wien.info. Eds. Maria Paula Palma Caetano, Renate Walli. Adv. contact Waltraud Wolf. Circ: 120,000.

910.09 GBR ISSN 0952-5424
G155.A1
PROGRESS IN TOURISM, RECREATION AND HOSPITALITY MANAGEMENT. Text in English. 1989. irreg., latest vol.5, 1993, Dec. price varies. bk.rev. bibl. index. back issues avail. **Document type:** *Monographic series, Academic/Scholarly.* **Description:** Reviews research in tourism and related fields, with emphasis on the fields rapidly advancing and of international importance.
Indexed: A22, H&TI, H06.
—CCC.
Published by: John Wiley & Sons Ltd. (Subsidiary of: John Wiley & Sons, Inc.), 1-7 Oldlands Way, PO Box 808, Bognor Regis, West Sussex PO21 9FF, United Kingdom. TEL 44-1865-778315, FAX 44-1243-843232, cs-journals@wiley.com. **Subscr. to:** 1-7 Oldlands Way, PO Box 809, Bognor Regis, West Sussex PO21 9FG, United Kingdom. TEL 44-1865-778054, cs-agency@wiley.com.

PROMENADE. *see* GENERAL INTEREST PERIODICALS—United States

PROMOBIL; Europas groesstes Reisemobil-Magazin. *see* TRANSPORTATION—Automobiles

910.91 ITA ISSN 1122-6145
PROSPETTIVE SABINE. Text in Italian. 1987. irreg. **Document type:** *Magazine, Consumer.*
Published by: Editrice Nova Italica, Via Firenze 169, Pescara, 65122, Italy. info@novaitalica.com, http://www.novaitalica.com.

910.4 PRT
PUBLITURIS; jornal da industria do turismo. Text in Portuguese. 1968. bi-w. EUR 30 domestic to individuals; EUR 90 in Europe to individuals; EUR 137 elsewhere to individuals; EUR 100 domestic to institutions; EUR 160 in Europe to institutions; EUR 207 elsewhere to institutions (effective 2005). adv. **Document type:** *Newspaper, Consumer.* **Description:** Covers various areas of travel and tourism, includes air transport, hotels, meetings and incentives.
Related titles: Online - full text ed.
Published by: Publiotel Ltd., Rua General Firmino Miguel, 3, Torre 2, 3o Piso, Lisbon, 1600-100, Portugal. TEL 351-21-0410300, FAX 351-21-0410304, geral@workmedia.pt, http://www.publiotel.pt/. Ed. Joao Constantino. Circ: 8,000.

PUERTO RICO LIVING. *see* GENERAL INTEREST PERIODICALS—Puerto Rico

917.295 PRI ISSN 1548-4769
PUERTO RICO TRAVEL & TOURISM. Text in English, Spanish. 2004 (Apr.-Jun.). q. USD 7.50 (effective 2004).
Published by: Casiano Communications Inc., 1700 Fernandez Juncos Ave, San Juan, 00909-2999, Puerto Rico. TEL 787-728-3000, FAX 787-268-5058, cservice@casiano.com, http://www.casiano.com.

917.977 796.7 USA ISSN 1540-5141
GV1027
PUGET SOUND JOURNEY. Text in English. bi-m.
Published by: Automobile Club of Washington, 1745 114th Ave, S E, Bellevue, WA 98109. TEL 206-448-5353, FAX 206-646-2193, http://www.aaawa.com. Ed. Leslie Mieko Yap. Pub. Charles Liekweg.

910.202 ITA ISSN 1828-9290
PUGLIA IMPERIALE MAGAZINE. Text in Italian, English. 2006. bi-m. free (effective 2008). **Document type:** *Magazine, Consumer.*
Published by: Agenzia Puglia Imperiale Turismo (A P I T), Palazzo Caccetta, Via Ognissanti 5, Bari, Italy. TEL 39-0883-586136, FAX 39-0883-491611, info@pugliaimperiale.com, http://www.pugliaimperiale.com.

910.09 USA ISSN 1053-3842
PUNCH IN INTERNATIONAL TRAVEL AND ENTERTAINMENT MAGAZINE. Text in English. 1990. m. bk.rev.; dance rev.; film rev.; music rev.; play rev.; rec.rev.; software rev.; tel.rev.; video rev.; Website rev. back issues avail. **Document type:** *Magazine, Consumer.*
Related titles: CD-ROM ed.; E-mail ed.; Online - full text ed.
Published by: Enterprises Publishing, 400 E 59th St, Ste 9F, New York, NY 10022. TEL 212-755-4363, FAX 212-755-4365.

PUNGOLO DEL SUD; periodico di cronache mediterranee. *see* GENERAL INTEREST PERIODICALS—Italy

910.91 CAN ISSN 1912-3493
PURECANADA. Text in English. 2003. a. **Document type:** *Magazine, Consumer.*
Related titles: Ed.: PurCanada. ISSN 1912-3507.
Published by: Canadian Tourism Commission/Commission Canadienne du Tourisme, Box 49230, Vancouver, BC V5P 1L2, Canada. TEL 604-638-8300, http://www.canadatourism.com.

PUT' I VODITEL'. *see* TRANSPORTATION—Automobiles

914 FRA ISSN 0998-3767
PYRENEES MAGAZINE. Text in French. 1989. 6/yr. EUR 46 (effective 2010). bibl. **Document type:** *Magazine, Consumer.*
Published by: Milan Presse, 300 Rue Leon Joulin, Toulouse, 31101, France. TEL 33-5-61766495, http://www.milanpresse.com.

Q T DIRECTORY (ONLINE). (Quality Travel) *see* BUSINESS AND ECONOMICS—Trade And Industrial Directories

338.4791 USA
Q T MAGAZINE; the gay and lesbian travel magazine. (Queer Travel) Text in English. 1999 (Oct.). m. adv. **Document type:** *Magazine, Consumer.* **Description:** Provides travel information, destination guides, and also other related articles aimed at the gay and lesbian traveller.
Media: Online - full content.
Published by: GSociety, Inc., 7060 Hollywood Blvd., Ste 800, Hollywood, CA 90028-6021. TEL 323-512-2920, FAX 323-512-2952, serge@qtmagazine.com, http://209.189.47.26/. Pub. Serge Gojkovich TEL 617-233-5657. R&P Dan Dawson TEL 323-337-0104. Adv. contact Cary Gilbert TEL 323-337-0113. online banner USD 50.

QUADERNI DI TERRA SANTA. *see* RELIGIONS AND THEOLOGY

910.9 ITA
QUALITYTRAVEL MAGAZINE (ONLINE); quotidiano di riferimento per il turismo d'affari e incentive. Text in Italian; Summaries in English. 1986. d. adv. bk.rev. **Document type:** *Magazine, Trade.* **Description:** Deals with congresses, incentive travel and business travel. Distributed to Italian PCO and corporate meeting planners and event organizers.
Formerly (until 200?): QualityTravel Magazine (Print)
Media: Online - full text.
Published by: Promos Edizioni srl, Via Giacomo Watt 32, Milan, 20143, Italy. TEL 39-02-89151814, FAX 39-02-89151830, promos@qualitytravel.it, http://www.qualitytravel.it.

916.8 ZAF
QUARTERLY REVIEW. Variant title: Satour Quarterly Review. Text in English. 1992. q. **Document type:** *Government.* **Description:** Covers topics relating to domestic and international tourism, Satour activities and other developments of interest.
Indexed: OTA.
Published by: Satour, Private Bag X164, Pretoria, 0001, South Africa.

388.3 796.7 BRA ISSN 0033-5908
QUATRO RODAS. Text in Portuguese. 1960. m. BRL 107.40 domestic; USD 89.51 foreign (effective 2005). adv. charts; illus.; stat. index. back issues avail. **Document type:** *Magazine, Consumer.* **Description:** For the auto enthusiast, contains exclusive tests, technological advances, price tables for new and used cars, insurance information, competition news, and travel.
Related titles: Online - full text ed.
Published by: Editora Abril, S.A., Avenida das Nacoes Unidas 7221, Pinheiros, Sao Paulo, SP 05425-902, Brazil. TEL 55-11-50872112, FAX 55-11-50872100, http://www.abril.com.br. Ed. Jorge Tarquini. adv.: page BRL 67,300. Circ: 143,030. **Subscr. to:** Rua do Curtume, Rua do Curtume, 769, Sao Paulo, SP 0506-900, Brazil. TEL 011-823-9100.

TU

914 FRA ISSN 1762-1704
QUE FAIRE?. Text in French. 2002. irreg. back issues avail. **Document type:** *Monographic series, Consumer.* **Description:** Explores the various regions of France and suggests places to go for sports, culture and food.
Published by: Dakota Editions, 45 Rue Saint-Sebastien, Paris, 75011, France. TEL 33-1-55283700, FAX 33-1-55283707, contact@wdakota.com, http://www.wdakota.com/.

917 PRI ISSN 0192-9364
QUE PASA; Puerto Rico's signature magazine. Text in English, Spanish. 1948. bi-m. free (effective 2005). adv. charts; illus. **Document type:** *Magazine, Consumer.* **Description:** Features photography and informative facts about Puerto Rico's cuisine, history, travel tips, etc.
Formerly: Que Pasa in Puerto Rico (0048-623X)
Indexed: RASB.
Published by: Tourism Company, PO Box 9023960, San Juan, 00902-3960, Puerto Rico. TEL 787-721-2400, 800-866-7827, FAX 787-722-1093. Ed. John Dean. Adv. contact Linda Stockton. Circ: 130,000 (free).

910.202 AUS
QUEENSLAND CARAVAN PARKS & TOURING ACCOMADATION DIRECTORY. Text in English. 1970. a. free (effective 2008). **Document type:** *Directory, Consumer.* **Description:** Listing of RV parks & tourism attractions.
Related titles: Online - full text ed.: free (effective 2008).
Published by: Caravan Parks Association of Queensland Inc., PO Box 5542, Stafford Heights, QLD 4053, Australia. TEL 61-7-38621833, FAX 61-7-32629890, admin@caravanqld.com.au.

910.2 AUS
QUEENSLAND. TOURISM QUEENSLAND. ANNUAL REPORT. Text in English. 19??. a. free (effective 2009). illus. back issues avail. **Document type:** *Corporate.*
Former titles (until 1999): Queensland Tourist and Travel Corporation. Annual Report (0725-6264); (until 1980): Queensland. Department of Tourism. Annual Report of the Director-General for the (Year); (until 1978): Queensland. Division of Tourist Activities. Annual Report of the Director-General of Tourist Services for the (Year)
Related titles: Online - full text ed.: free (effective 2009).
Published by: Queensland Tourist and Travel Corporation, GPO Box 328, Brisbane, QLD 4001, Australia. TEL 61-7-35353535, FAX 61-7-35355438, tourismonq@tq.com.au.

338.4791 NZL ISSN 1179-8041
QUEENSTOWN ACTIVITY GUIDE; what, when, where. Text in English. 200?. s-a. free (effective 2010). **Document type:** *Handbook/Manual/ Guide, Consumer.* **Description:** Contains travel information in Queenstown, South Island, New Zealand.
Published by: Jasons Travel Media Ltd., 2 Ngaire Ave, PO Box 9390, Newmarket, Auckland, 1149, New Zealand. TEL 64-9-9128400, FAX 64-9-9128401, admin@jasons.com, http://www.jasons.co.nz.

QUEST'ITALIA. *see* GEOGRAPHY

917.4 USA ISSN 1540-1545
F73.18
QUICK ESCAPES: BOSTON; 25 weekend getaways from the hub. Text in English. 2000. biennial, latest 2002, 2nd ed. USD 15.95 per issue (effective 2008). **Document type:** *Guide, Consumer.* **Description:** Lists route maps, travel directions, destination highlights, choice restaurants, picnic sites and lodgings, special events and festivals, shopping and local sources of information.
Published by: The Globe Pequot Press, Inc., 246 Goose Ln, PO Box 480, Guilford, CT 06437. TEL 203-458-4500, 888-249-7586, FAX 203-458-4603, 800-820-2329, info@globepequot.com, http:// www.globepequot.com. Ed. . MacDonald.

910.2 USA ISSN 1540-9813
F548.18
QUICK ESCAPES: CHICAGO; 26 weekend getaways in and around the windy city. Text in English. 1992. biennial, latest 2002, 5th ed. USD 15.95 per issue (effective 2008). back issues avail. **Document type:** *Guide, Consumer.* **Description:** Covers information about Chicago tourist traps.
Formerly: Quick Escapes from Chicago
Published by: The Globe Pequot Press, Inc., 246 Goose Ln, PO Box 480, Guilford, CT 06437. TEL 203-458-4500, 888-249-7586, FAX 203-458-4603, 800-820-2329, info@globepequot.com. Ed. . Rubin.

917.64 910.2 USA ISSN 1540-4374
F394.D213
QUICK ESCAPES: DALLAS/FORT WORTH; getaways in and around the lone star state. Text in English. 1996. biennial, latest 2008, 6th ed. USD 13.95 per issue (effective 2008). back issues avail. **Document type:** *Guide, Consumer.* **Description:** Provides information on the best places to visit, dine, and sleep.
Published by: The Globe Pequot Press, Inc., 246 Goose Ln, PO Box 480, Guilford, CT 06437. TEL 203-458-4500, 888-249-7586, FAX 203-458-4603, 800-820-2329, info@globepequot.com, http:// www.globepequot.com.

917.888 910.2 USA ISSN 1540-4358
F784.D43
QUICK ESCAPES: DENVER; 25 weekend getaways in and around the mile high city. Text in English. 1998. irreg., latest 2006, 4th ed. USD 13.95 per issue (effective 2008). back issues avail. **Document type:** *Guide, Consumer.* **Description:** Provides information on the best places to visit, dine, and sleep.
Published by: The Globe Pequot Press, Inc., 246 Goose Ln, PO Box 480, Guilford, CT 06437. TEL 203-458-4500, 888-249-7586, FAX 203-458-4603, 800-820-2329, info@globepequot.com, http:// www.globepequot.com.

910.2 USA ISSN 2161-4172
F899.S43
▼ **QUICK ESCAPES FROM SEATTLE**; the best weekend getaways. Text in English. 2011. triennial. USD 14.95 per issue domestic; USD 18.95 per issue in Canada (effective 2011). **Document type:** *Guide, Consumer.*
Published by: The Globe Pequot Press, Inc., 246 Goose Ln, PO Box 480, Guilford, CT 06437. TEL 203-458-4500, 888-249-7586, FAX 800-820-2329, info@globepequot.com.

917.9 910.2 USA ISSN 1551-6822
F849.L35
QUICK ESCAPES: LAS VEGAS. Text in English. 2002. irreg., latest 2005, 2nd ed. USD 13.95 per issue (effective 2008). **Document type:** *Guide, Consumer.* **Description:** Provides information about twenty-five planned mini-vacations within driving distance of Las Vegas.
Published by: The Globe Pequot Press, Inc., 246 Goose Ln, PO Box 480, Guilford, CT 06437. TEL 203-458-4500, 888-249-7586, FAX 203-458-4603, 800-820-2329, info@globepequot.com, http:// www.globepequot.com. Ed. Hardi Knapp Rinella.

917.9494 910.2 USA ISSN 1540-2096
F867
QUICK ESCAPES: LOS ANGELES; 23 weekend getaways from the metro area. Text in English. 1997. biennial, latest 2006, 7th ed. USD 13.95 per issue (effective 2008). **Document type:** *Guide, Consumer.*
Formerly: Quick Escapes in Southern California
Published by: The Globe Pequot Press, Inc., 246 Goose Ln, PO Box 480, Guilford, CT 06437. TEL 203-458-4500, 888-249-7586, FAX 203-458-4603, 800-820-2329, info@globepequot.com, http:// www.globepequot.com. Ed. Eleanor Harris.

917.76 USA ISSN 1547-8777
F614.M6
QUICK ESCAPES: MINNEAPOLIS-ST. PAUL; 21 weekend getaways in and around the twin cities. Text in English. 1998. biennial, latest 2004, 4th ed. USD 13.95 per issue (effective 2008). **Document type:** *Guide, Consumer.* **Description:** Provides detailed route maps, travel directions, destination highlights, activities for morning, afternoon and evening, choice restaurants, picnic sites and lodgings.
Published by: The Globe Pequot Press, Inc., 246 Goose Ln, PO Box 480, Guilford, CT 06437. TEL 203-458-4500, 888-249-7586, FAX 203-458-4603, 800-820-2329, info@globepequot.com, http:// www.globepequot.com.

917.4 910.2 USA ISSN 1545-5726
F128.18
QUICK ESCAPES: NEW YORK CITY; getaways from the big apple. Text in English. 1994. biennial, latest 2007, 7th ed. USD 13.95 per issue (effective 2008). back issues avail. **Document type:** *Guide, Consumer.* **Description:** Provides information about festivals, special events, best places to visit and one to three-day minivacations in New York city.
Published by: The Globe Pequot Press, Inc., 246 Goose Ln, PO Box 480, Guilford, CT 06437. TEL 203-458-4500, 888-249-7586, FAX 203-458-4603, 800-820-2329, info@globepequot.com, http:// www.globepequot.com. Ed. Susan Farewell.

917.946 910.2 USA ISSN 1542-2526
F869.S33
QUICK ESCAPES: SAN FRANCISCO; 26 weekend getaways from the bay area. Text in English. 1993. biennial, latest 2005, 6th ed. USD 15.95 per issue (effective 2008). back issues avail. **Document type:** *Guide, Consumer.* **Description:** Provides information about festivals, special events, best places to visit and one to four-day minivacations in San Francisco.
Published by: The Globe Pequot Press, Inc., 246 Goose Ln, PO Box 480, Guilford, CT 06437. TEL 203-458-4500, 888-249-7586, FAX 203-458-4603, 800-820-2329, info@globepequot.com, http:// www.globepequot.com. Ed. Karen Misuraca.

917.786 910.2 USA ISSN 1542-5525
QUICK ESCAPES: ST. LOUIS. Text in English. 2001. irreg., latest 2003, 2nd ed. USD 15.95 per issue (effective 2008). **Document type:** *Guide, Consumer.* **Description:** Provides travel and tourism information for St. Louis, Missouri.
Published by: The Globe Pequot Press, Inc., 246 Goose Ln, PO Box 480, Guilford, CT 06437. TEL 203-458-4500, 888-249-7586, FAX 203-458-4603, 800-820-2329, info@globepequot.com, http:// www.globepequot.com. Ed. J Gustafson.

917.5 910.2 USA ISSN 1541-5198
F192.3
QUICK ESCAPES: WASHINGTON, D. C.; getaways from the nation's capital. Text in English. 1996. biennial, latest 2007, 6th ed. USD 13.95 per issue (effective 2008). back issues avail. **Document type:** *Guide, Consumer.* **Description:** Provides information on the best places to visit, dine, and sleep.
Published by: The Globe Pequot Press, Inc., 246 Goose Ln, PO Box 480, Guilford, CT 06437. TEL 203-458-4500, 888-249-7586, FAX 203-458-4603, 800-820-2329, info@globepequot.com, http:// www.globepequot.com.

338.4 CAN ISSN 1920-874X
▼ **QUILL & DRUM**; showcasing aboriginal business & cultural diversity. Text in English. 2009. q. adv. back issues avail. **Document type:** *Magazine, Trade.*
Related titles: Online - full text ed.
Published by: Kiwetin Marketing & Publishing Ltd., 2219 14th Ave, Port Alberni, BC V9Y 2Y4, Canada. TEL 250-723-7095, 866-558-7997, FAX 866-245-0868, kiwetin@shaw.ca.

910 FRA ISSN 1152-8729
QUOTIDIEN DU TOURISME. Text in French. 1990. 166/yr. EUR 119 to individuals; EUR 76 to qualified personnel (effective 2009). **Document type:** *Newspaper, Trade.*
Published by: Editions Lariviere, 6 Rue Olof Palme, Clichy, 92587, France. TEL 33-1-47565400, http://www.editions-lariviere.fr. Circ: 10,000.

R V AMERICA; the rvers guide to the open road. (Recreational Vehicle) *see* SPORTS AND GAMES—Outdoor Life

796.6 CAN ISSN 1190-9641
THE R V TIMES. (Recreational Vehicle) Text in English. 1988. bi-m. CAD 18; USD 22 in United States (effective 2002). adv. bk.rev. **Document type:** *Magazine, Consumer.* **Description:** Includes events of interest in British Columbia, Alberta, Washington and Montana, camping stories, repair tips and general RV and camping information.
Published by: Sheila Jones Publishing Ltd., 24851-40th Avenue, Aldergrove, BC V4W 1X2, Canada. TEL 604-857-8828, FAX 604-857-8829. Ed., Pub., Adv. contact Sheila Tourond. Circ: 50,000 (controlled).

RADTOUREN. *see* SPORTS AND GAMES—Bicycles And Motorcycles

910.09 385.26 USA ISSN 1048-9096
RAILWAYS. Text in English. q.
Indexed: ISAP.
Published by: Parlor Car Press, PO Box 10396, Glendale, CA 91209-3396. TEL 818-500-0542, FAX 818-247-9671. Ed. Vincent Prest. Circ: 1,100.

RAINBOW HANDBOOK HAWAI'I; the islands' ultimate gay guide. *see* HOMOSEXUALITY

RANCH & COAST (RANCHO SANTA FE). *see* GENERAL INTEREST PERIODICALS—United States

910.202 330 USA
RAND MCNALLY BUSINESS TRAVELER'S ROAD ATLAS. Text in English. 1997. a. USD 5.99 per issue (effective 2009). **Document type:** *Directory, Consumer.* **Description:** Provides information for the top 30 business cities and a briefcase-friendly midsize format, this atlas is essential for business people on the go.
Published by: Rand McNally & Co., PO Box 7600, Chicago, IL 60680. TEL 800-777-6277, 800-678-7263, FAX 800-934-3479.

910.202 USA
RAND MCNALLY ROAD ATLAS & TRAVEL GUIDE. Text in English. 1967. a., latest 2008. price varies. adv. **Document type:** *Directory, Consumer.* **Description:** Features all the maps and index from our selling Rand McNally Road Atlas plus special regional maps that help travelers with multi-state driving.
Published by: Rand McNally & Co., 8255 N Central Park Ave, Skokie, IL 60076-2970. http://www.randmcnally.com.

910.202 USA
RAND MCNALLY ULTIMATE ROAD ATLAS & VACATION GUIDE. Text in English. a.
Formerly: Rand McNally Road Atlas and Vacation Guide
Published by: Rand McNally & Co., PO Box 7600, Chicago, IL 60680. TEL 800-777-6277, 800-678-7263, FAX 800-934-3479, http:// www.randmcnally.com.

THE RANGELAND JOURNAL. *see* CONSERVATION

910.2 USA ISSN 1941-8485
F722
THE RANGER'S GUIDE TO YELLOWSTONE. Text in English. 2008. 3/yr. USD 16.95 per issue (effective 2009). **Document type:** *Guide, Consumer.* **Description:** Helps to plan a perfect trip to Yellowstone National Park.
Published by: Avalon Travel Publishing, 1700 4th St, Berkeley, CA 94710. TEL 510-595-3664, avalon.publicity@perseusbooks.com. **Subscr. to:** 1094 Flex Dr, Jackson, TN 38301. TEL 800-788-3123, FAX 800-351-5073.

917 USA ISSN 1058-448X
RECOMMEND: MAGAZINE. Text in English. 1967. m. free to qualified personnel (effective 2011). back issues avail.; reprints avail. **Document type:** *Magazine, Trade.* **Description:** Destination marketing information written for the travel industry. Covers new facilities, attractions, sporting events, tours, accommodations, dining, sightseeing, festivals, and general information.
Formerly (until 198?): Recommend Florida (0034-1452)
Related titles: E-mail ed.
Published by: Worth International Media Group, 5979 NW 151 St, Ste 120, Miami Lakes, FL 33014. TEL 305-828-0123, 800-447-0123, FAX 305-826-6950, info@worthit.com, http//www.worthit.com.

910.2 914 GBR ISSN 0267-3428
RECOMMENDED COUNTRY HOTELS OF BRITAIN. Variant title: Country Hotels of Britain. Text in English. 1973. a. GBP 6.99 per issue (effective 2009). adv. **Document type:** *Handbook/Manual/Guide, Consumer.* **Description:** Lists quality country hotels and houses offering hospitality in unique and attractive surroundings.
Published by: F H G Guides Ltd. (Subsidiary of: F H G Publications Ltd.), Abbey Mill Business Ctr, Seedhill, Paisley, PA1 1TJ, United Kingdom. TEL 44-141-8870428, FAX 44-141-8897204, sales@fhguides.co.uk, http://www.fhguides.co.uk.

910.2 914 GBR
RECOMMENDED COUNTRY INNS & PUBS OF BRITAIN. Variant title: Country Inns & Pubs of Britain. Text in English. 1962. a. GBP 7.99 per issue (effective 2009). adv. **Document type:** *Handbook/Manual/ Guide, Consumer.* **Description:** Lists pubs, inns, small hotels and country inns.
Former titles (until 2004): Recommended Wayside & Country Inns of Britain; (until 1998): Recommended Wayside Inns of Britain (0080-0252)
Published by: F H G Guides Ltd. (Subsidiary of: F H G Publications Ltd.), Abbey Mill Business Ctr, Seedhill, Paisley, PA1 1TJ, United Kingdom. TEL 44-141-8870428, FAX 44-141-8897204, sales@fhguides.co.uk, http://www.fhguides.co.uk.

917.504 647 USA ISSN 1078-5523
TX907.3.M53
RECOMMENDED COUNTRY INNS: MID-ATLANTIC AND CHESAPEAKE REGION. Text in English. 1989. irreg., latest 2001, 9th ed. USD 17.95 per issue (effective 2008). back issues avail. **Document type:** *Guide, Consumer.* **Description:** Covers information about romantic getaways, family vacations, business conferences and special celebrations in the Mid-Atlantic and Chesapeake region.
Formerly: Guide to the Recommended Country Inns of the Mid-Atlantic States and Chesapeake Region
Published by: The Globe Pequot Press, Inc., 246 Goose Ln, PO Box 480, Guilford, CT 06437. TEL 203-458-4500, 888-249-7586, FAX 203-458-4603, 800-820-2329, info@globepequot.com, http:// www.globepequot.com. Ed. Suzi Forbes Chase.

917.404 647 USA ISSN 1047-4668
TX907
RECOMMENDED COUNTRY INNS: NEW ENGLAND. Text in English. 1974. biennial, latest 2006, 19th ed. USD 18.95 per issue (effective 2008). back issues avail. **Document type:** *Guide, Consumer.* **Description:** Provides information on New England country inns with details on furniture, hospitality and comfort.
Formerly (until 1987): Guide to the Recommended Country Inns of New England (0093-4585)
Published by: The Globe Pequot Press, Inc., 246 Goose Ln, PO Box 480, Guilford, CT 06437. TEL 203-458-4500, 888-249-7586, FAX 203-458-4603, 800-820-2329, info@globepequot.com, http:// www.globepequot.com. Ed. Elizabeth Squier.

917.804 647 USA ISSN 1078-5485
TX907.3.R63
RECOMMENDED COUNTRY INNS: ROCKY MOUNTAIN REGION. Text in English. 1987. irreg., latest 1999, 7th ed. USD 16.95 per issue (effective 2008). back issues avail. **Document type:** *Guide, Consumer.* **Description:** Contains information about inns available for a romantic getaway, family vacation, business conference, or special celebration.
Formerly: Guide to the Recommended Country Inns of the Rocky Mountain Region
Published by: The Globe Pequot Press, Inc., 246 Goose Ln, PO Box 480, Guilford, CT 06437. TEL 203-458-4500, 888-249-7586, FAX 203-458-4603, 800-820-2329, info@globepequot.com, http://www.globepequot.com. Ed. Doris Kennedy.

917.704 647 USA ISSN 1078-5507
TX907.3.M55
RECOMMENDED COUNTRY INNS: THE MIDWEST. Text in English. 1987. irreg., latest 2001, 8th ed. USD 17.95 per issue (effective 2008). back issues avail. **Document type:** *Guide, Consumer.* **Description:** Contains information about available inns for romantic getaways, family vacations, business conferences, or special celebrations.
Formerly: Guide to the Recommended Country Inns of the Midwest
Published by: The Globe Pequot Press, Inc., 246 Goose Ln, PO Box 480, Guilford, CT 06437. TEL 203-458-4500, 888-249-7586, FAX 203-458-4603, 800-820-2329, info@globepequot.com, http://www.globepequot.com. Ed. Bob Puhala.

917.604 647 USA ISSN 1078-5493
TX907.3.S68
RECOMMENDED COUNTRY INNS: THE SOUTH. Text in English. 1987. irreg., latest 2001, 8th ed. USD 17.95 per issue (effective 2008). back issues avail. **Document type:** *Guide, Consumer.* **Description:** Contains information about inns available for a romantic getaway, family vacation, business conference, or special celebration.
Formerly: Guide to the Recommended Country Inns of the South
Published by: The Globe Pequot Press, Inc., 246 Goose Ln, PO Box 480, Guilford, CT 06437. TEL 203-458-4500, 888-249-7586, FAX 203-458-4603, 800-820-2329, info@globepequot.com, http://www.globepequot.com. Ed. Sara Pitzer.

917.904 647 USA ISSN 1078-5515
TX907.3.A6
RECOMMENDED COUNTRY INNS: THE SOUTHWEST. Text in English. 1987. irreg., latest 1999, 7th ed. USD 16.95 per issue (effective 2008). back issues avail. **Document type:** *Guide, Consumer.* **Description:** Contains information about inns available for romantic getaways, family vacations, business conferences, or special celebrations.
Former titles: Guide to the Recommended Country Inns of Arizona, New Mexico, and Texas; Recommended Country Inns. Arizona, New Mexico, Texas
Published by: The Globe Pequot Press, Inc., 246 Goose Ln, PO Box 480, Guilford, CT 06437. TEL 203-458-4500, 888-249-7586, FAX 203-458-4603, 800-820-2329, info@globepequot.com, http://www.globepequot.com. Ed. Eleanor S Morris.

917.904 647 USA ISSN 1078-5531
TX907.3.C2
RECOMMENDED COUNTRY INNS: THE WEST COAST. Text in English. 1987. irreg., latest 1999, 7th ed. USD 16.95 per issue (effective 2008). back issues avail. **Document type:** *Guide, Consumer.* **Description:** Contains information about inns available for a romantic getaway, family vacation, business conference, or special celebration.
Formerly: Guide to the Recommended Country Inns of the West Coast
Published by: The Globe Pequot Press, Inc., 246 Goose Ln, PO Box 480, Guilford, CT 06437. TEL 203-458-4500, 888-249-7586, FAX 203-458-4603, 800-820-2329, info@globepequot.com, http://www.globepequot.com. Ed. Julianne Belote.

917.04 647.9 USA ISSN 1078-554X
RECOMMENDED ROMANTIC INNS OF AMERICA. Text in English. 1992. irreg., latest 1999, 4th ed. USD 16.95 per issue (effective 2008). back issues avail. **Document type:** *Guide, Consumer.* **Description:** Contains information about inns available for a romantic getaway, family vacation, business conference, or special celebration.
Published by: The Globe Pequot Press, Inc., 246 Goose Ln, PO Box 480, Guilford, CT 06437. TEL 203-458-4500, 888-249-7586, FAX 203-458-4603, 800-820-2329, info@globepequot.com, http://www.globepequot.com.

RECREATION ADVISOR. *see* LEISURE AND RECREATION

910 796 USA ISSN 1056-9294
RECREATION NEWS. Text in English. 1982. m. USD 12 (effective 2005). adv. film rev.; music rev.; bk.rev. 32 p./no. 6 cols./p.; back issues avail.; reprints avail. **Document type:** *Newspaper, Consumer.* **Description:** A vacation planner and weekend guide to the Mid-Atlantic region.
Published by: Indiana Printing & Publishing, 899 Water St., Indiana, PA 15701. TEL 724-465-5555, FAX 724-465-0402. Ed. Reed Hellman. Pub., R&P, Adv. contact Karl Teel TEL 301-474-4600. page USD 3,864; 14 x 10.25. Circ: 104,000 (controlled).

914 CHE
REGION DU LEMAN. Text in German. 34/yr.
Address: Agence Neumann, St. Saphorin-sur-Morges, CH-1113, Switzerland. TEL 021-8011120. Circ: 9,917.

910.2 338.4791 NOR ISSN 1500-3701
REIS. Text in Norwegian. 1998. bi-m. NOK 240 (effective 2007). adv. **Document type:** *Magazine, Consumer.*
Published by: Emma Publishing AS, Frognerveien 22, Oslo, 0263, Norway. TEL 47-23-120280, FAX 47-23-120281, magasinet@reis.no, http://www.emma-publishing.no.

338.4791 NLD
REISBRIEF; actualiteiten. Text in Dutch. 1989. bi-m. free (effective 2009). tr.lit. back issues avail. **Document type:** *Newsletter, Trade.* **Description:** Contains information on all aspects of travel and tourism.
Published by: Toerismestudio Vivian Kleyn, Van Baerlestraat 7, Amsterdam, 1071 AL, Netherlands. toerismestudioviviankleyn@hetnet.nl, http://www.toerismestudioviviankleyn.nl. Ed., Pub., R&P Vivian Kleyn.

338.4791 NLD ISSN 1871-9104
REISBURO ACTUEEL. Text in Dutch. 1993. 46/yr. EUR 95; EUR 75 to students (effective 2010). adv.
Formerly (until 2005): Reisburo (1386-2162)
Published by: T & S Productions, Postbus 120, Nijmegen, 6500 AC, Netherlands. TEL 31-24-8200203. Ed. Eugenie Engelbracht. Pub. Tom van Apeldoorn. adv.: color page EUR 5,580; trim 240 x 340. Circ: 5,078.

910.202 AUT
REISE AKTUELL; das internationale Reisemagazin. Text in German. 3/yr. adv. **Document type:** *Magazine, Consumer.* **Description:** Contains travel, leisure, business and flight news as well as reports on cruise ships, sports activities, and all-inclusive clubs throughout the world.
Related titles: Online - full text ed.: ISSN 1605-122X.
Published by: C B Verlags GmbH, Kleingoepfink 44, Pfaffenschlag, N 3834, Austria. TEL 43-1-5974985, FAX 43-1-597498515, office@cbverlag.at, http://www.cbverlag.at. adv.: color page EUR 5,460; trim 210 x 297. Circ: 44,000 (controlled).

910.202 DEU ISSN 0942-0517
REISE-DIENST; Freizeit und Events in meiner Umgebung. Text in German. 1970. a. EUR 2.50 newsstand/cover (effective 2010). adv. **Document type:** *Magazine, Trade.*
Formerly (until 1991): Auto-Reise-Dienst (0344-4511)
Published by: Stuenings Medien GmbH, Diessemer Bruch 167, Krefeld, 47805, Germany. TEL 49-2151-51000, FAX 49-2151-5100101, medien@stuenings.de, http://www.stuenings.de. Pub. Joerg Montag. Adv. contact Dennis Feegers. Circ: 68,000 (controlled).

910.202 AUT
REISE UND CAMPING. Text in German. 4/yr. adv.
Published by: W. Rothmueller, Lerchenfelderquertel 25, Vienna, W 1160, Austria. Circ: 25,000.

910.202 DEU ISSN 0932-4186
REISE UND PREISE; das Info-Magazin fuer Flugreisen. Text in German. 1987. q. EUR 16.80 domestic; EUR 21.80 foreign; EUR 4.90 newsstand/cover (effective 2007). adv. bk.rev. back issues avail. **Document type:** *Magazine, Consumer.* **Description:** Contains articles and features on air travel and vacation planning.
Related titles: Online - full text ed.
Published by: Reise und Preise Verlags GmbH, Hauptstr 14, Buxtehude, 21614, Germany. TEL 49-4161-71690, FAX 49-4161-716915, verlag@reise-preise.de. Ed. Oliver Kuehn. adv.: B&W page EUR 3,700, color page EUR 6,295; trim 186 x 270. Circ: 73,415 (paid and controlled).

910.09 DEU ISSN 0177-4050
REISEFIEBER; das Insider-Reisemagazin. Text in German. 1985. q. EUR 3 newsstand/cover (effective 2010). adv. bk.rev. back issues avail. **Document type:** *Magazine, Consumer.* **Description:** Provides practical and useful information on travel destinations throughout the world.
Published by: Verlag Andreas Langer, Auf den Hoehen 13, Regensburg, 93138, Germany. TEL 49-941-2802402, FAX 49-941-2802404. Pub. Andreas Langer. Circ: 70,000 (paid and controlled).

910 AUT
REISEMAGAZIN; Oesterreichs groesste Reisezeitschrift. Text in German. 1996. 11/yr. EUR 29 (effective 2008). adv. **Document type:** *Magazine, Consumer.*
Published by: Sportverlag GmbH & Co. KG (Subsidiary of: Styria Medien AG), Kaiserstr 113-115, Vienna, W 1070, Austria. TEL 43-1-360850, FAX 43-1-36085200, office@vsm.at, http://www.vsm.at. Ed. Christina Dany. Adv. contact Martina Szabo. color page EUR 5,600; trim 185 x 250. Circ: 32,000 (paid and controlled).

910 DEU
REISEN EXCLUSIV; das Magazin fuer Reisen und Lifestyle. Text in German. 2000. 4/yr. EUR 20; EUR 5.50 newsstand/cover (effective 2009). adv. **Document type:** *Magazine, Consumer.*
Published by: Ella Verlag, Emil-Hoffmann-Str 55-59, Cologne, 50996, Germany. TEL 49-2236-84880, FAX 49-2236-848824, info@ella-verlag.de, http://www.ella-verlag.de. Ed. Jennifer Latuperisa. Pub. Elke Latuperisa. adv.: color page EUR 5,190; trim 210 x 277. Circ: 56,000 (paid and controlled).

910.202 DEU ISSN 0177-2953
REISEN IN DEUTSCHLAND: REISEFUEHRER. Text in German. 1949. a. **Document type:** *Directory, Trade.*
Published by: Reisen in Deutschland Verlagsgesellschaft mbH, Im Biengarten 12, Darmstadt, 64297, Germany. TEL 49-6151-9519073, FAX 49-6151-9519076, info@reisen-in-deutschland.net, http://www.reisen-in-deutschland.net. Circ: 15,000.

910.2 DEU ISSN 0177-2961
TX907.5.G3
REISEN IN DEUTSCHLAND: ZIMMERKATALOG. Text in German. 1925. a. adv. **Document type:** *Directory, Trade.*
Formerly (until 1984): Reisen in Deutschland. Band 3: Zimmer-Katalog fuer Reisen in Deutschland (0171-5267)
Published by: Reisen in Deutschland Verlagsgesellschaft mbH, Im Biengarten 12, Darmstadt, 64297, Germany. TEL 49-6151-9519073, FAX 49-6151-9519076, info@reisen-in-deutschland.net, http://www.reisen-in-deutschland.net.

910.202 340.5 DEU ISSN 0944-7490
REISERECHT AKTUELL; Zeitschrift fuer das Tourismusrecht. Text in German. 1993. bi-m. EUR 109; EUR 89 to students; EUR 25 newsstand/cover (effective 2011). adv. cum.index. back issues avail. **Document type:** *Journal, Trade.* **Description:** Cobers the latest developments and most relevant court decisions in the evolving areas of travel and tourism law.
Indexed: IBR, IBZ.
—CCC.
Published by: (Deutsche Gesellschaft fuer Reiserecht e.V.), Sellier - European Law Publishers GmbH, Geibelstr 8, Munich, 81679, Germany. TEL 49-89-476047, FAX 49-89-4704327, info@sellier-elp.de, http://www.sellier-elp.de. Ed. Ronald Schmid. Adv. contact Martina Ganss. Circ: 1,000 (paid and controlled).

910 AUT
REISETIPS. Text in German. 6/yr. **Document type:** *Magazine, Trade.*
Published by: Profi Reisen Verlagsgesellschaft mbH, Seidlgasse 22, Vienna, 1030, Austria. TEL 43-1-7142414, FAX 43-1-71424144, office@profireisen.at, http://www.profireisen.at. Ed. Rainer Pilcik. Circ: 50,000 (controlled).

910.09 DEU
REISEZIELE; Landkarten, Reisefuehrer, Bildbaende, mit vielen touristischen Tips. Text in German. 1970. a. **Document type:** *Consumer.*
Published by: GeoCenter Verlagsvertrieb GmbH, Neumarkter Str 18, Munich, 81673, Germany. TEL 49-89-43189-505, FAX 49-89-43189555.

640.73 NLD ISSN 1569-0407
DE REISGIDS. Text in Dutch. 1973. 6/yr. EUR 58 (effective 2009). charts; illus. **Document type:** *Consumer.* **Description:** Evaluation of trips and tourist attractions in all parts of the world. Covers hotel accomodation, transportation, sights, prices, and organized trips. Includes travel guide evaluation and maps.
Formerly (until 2001): Consumenten Reisgids (0165-6821)
—IE, Infotrieve.
Published by: Consumentenbond, Enthovenplein 1, Postbus 1000, The Hague, 2500 BA, Netherlands. TEL 31-70-4454545, FAX 31-70-4454596, http://www.consumentenbond.nl.

338.4 NLD ISSN 1879-4815
▼ **REISKALENDER.** Variant title: Capitool Reiskalender. Text in Dutch. 2009. a. EUR 14.99 (effective 2010).
Published by: Unieboek BV, Postbus 97, Houten, 3990 DB, Netherlands. TEL 31-30-7998300, FAX 31-30-7998398, info@unieboek.nl, http://www.unieboek.nl.

338 NLD ISSN 0777-0030
DE REISKRANT. Text in Dutch. 1981. bi-m. bk.rev. illus. **Document type:** *Newspaper, Consumer.* **Description:** Covers travel destinations in depth, with useful addresses and numbers, reviews of guides and maps.
Related titles: Online - full text ed.
Published by: Uitgeversmaatschappij De Telegraaf BV, Postbus 376, Amsterdam, 1000 EB, Netherlands. TEL 31-20-5859111, 31-20-5858010. Circ: 15,000.

910.09 NLD ISSN 1574-2105
REISREVUE; reisvakblad. Text in Dutch. 1982. w. EUR 159.50 domestic; EUR 189.30 in Belgium; EUR 251.75 elsewhere (effective 2009). adv. illus. **Document type:** *Trade.* **Description:** Covers all aspects of the travel industry in the Netherlands.
Related titles: Supplement(s): Reisrevue Xtra. ISSN 1574-9150.
Published by: Reisrevue Groep bv, Stationsplein 3, Hilversum, 1211 EX, Netherlands. TEL 31-35-6728850. Pub. Martine de Knoop. Circ: 10,000.

910 NLD ISSN 0921-0032
REIZEN; ANWB vakantiemagazine. Text in Dutch. 1937. m. (11/yr.). EUR 62.50 to non-members; EUR 58.50 to members (effective 2008). adv. bk.rev. illus. back issues avail. **Document type:** *Consumer.* **Description:** Discusses holiday desitinations and travel trends; offers individual and group travelers practical information.
Formerly (until 1986): Toeristenkampioen (0165-4225)
Related titles: Online - full text ed.
Indexed: KES.
—IE, Infotrieve.
Published by: (ANWB BV/Royal Dutch Touring Club), Algemene Nederlandse Wielrijders Bond (A N W B) Media/Dutch Automobile Association Media, Postbus 93200, The Hague, 2509 BA, Netherlands. TEL 31-70-3141470, FAX 31-70-3146538, http://www.anwbmedia.nl. adv.: B&W page EUR 2,700, color page EUR 3,769; trim 185 x 265. Circ: 46,346.

910.09 DNK ISSN 0108-6812
REJSEBOGEN (YEAR). Text in Danish. 1983. a. DKK 245 (effective 2009). adv. bk.rev. **Document type:** *Yearbook, Consumer.*
Published by: Forlaget Nuna, Fasanvej 3, Loegstoer, 9670, Denmark. TEL 45-98-671857, FAX 45-98-673633. Ed., Pub. Georg Harmsen.

REJUVENATE. *see* BUSINESS AND ECONOMICS—Management

915.1 JPN
REKISHI TO TABI/HISTORY AND TRAVEL. Text in Japanese. 1974. m. JPY 5,400.
Published by: Akita Shoten Publishing Co. Ltd., 10-8 Iida-Bashi 2-chome, Chiyoda-ku, Tokyo, 102-0072, Japan. Ed. Toru Suzuki.

RENDEZ-VOUS; city magazine Luxembourg. *see* LEISURE AND RECREATION

338.4 CAN ISSN 1910-1538
RENSEIGNEMENTS SUR LE TOURISME. BULLETIN. Text in French. 2001. irreg., latest no.34, 2006, Juy. **Document type:** *Bulletin, Trade.*
Related titles: English ed.: C T C Tourism Intelligence Bulletin. ISSN 1910-152X.
Published by: Canadian Tourism Commission/Commission Canadienne du Tourisme, 55 Metcalfe St, Ste 600, Ottawa, ON K1P 6L5, Canada. TEL 613-946-1000, http://www.canada.travel/index.html?sa_campaign=domains/un/www.travelcanada.ca/home, http://www.canadatourism.com.

338.4 CAN ISSN 1910-1554
RENSEIGNEMENTS SUR LE TOURISME. SOMMAIRE. BULLETIN. Text in French. 2001. irreg. **Document type:** *Bulletin, Trade.*
Related titles: English ed.: C T C Tourism Intelligence Bulletin. Executive Summary. ISSN 1910-1546.
Published by: Canadian Tourism Commission/Commission Canadienne du Tourisme, 55 Metcalfe St, Ste 600, Ottawa, ON K1P 6L5, Canada. TEL 613-946-1000, http://www.canada.travel/index.html?sa_campaign=domains/un/www.travelcanada.ca/home, http://www.canadatourism.com.

910.2 SWE ISSN 1400-8971
RES (STOCKHOLM, 1981). Text in Swedish. 1981. 10/yr. SEK 345 (effective 2006). adv. **Document type:** *Magazine, Consumer.*
Formerly (until 1994): Resguide (0280-462X)
Related titles: Online - full text ed.: ISSN 1402-4942.
Published by: Emma Foerlags AB, Repslager Gatan 17 B, Stockholm, 11846, Sweden. TEL 46-8-54506420, FAX 46-8-6795710. Ed. Johan Lindskog. Adv. contact Peter Helin TEL 46-8-54506406. page SEK 37,400; 181 x 236. Circ: 40,500.

910 SWE ISSN 1403-297X
RES FORUM. Variant title: Resforum. Text in Swedish. 1998. 10/yr. SEK 564 domestic; SEK 695 foreign (effective 2007). adv. **Document type:** *Magazine, Trade.*

Supersedes in part (in 1998): Resor och Trafik (1104-4594); Which was formed by the merger of (1954-1993): Svensk Lokaltrafik (0039-6648); (1991-1993): Busstidningen (1102-6693); Which was formerly (until 1991): Buss, Svensk Omnibustidning (0282-7654); (1929-1982): Svensk Omnibustidning (0039-6672)
Published by: Res och Trafik Media i Stockholm AB (Subsidiary of: Mentor Online AB), Observatoriegatan 17, Stockholm, 11329, Sweden. TEL 46-8-315940, FAX 46-8-6601272. Ed. Ulo Maasing. Adv. contact Gunilla Hagberg.

338.4791 USA
THE RESORT TRADES. Text in English. m. adv. **Document type:** *Magazine, Trade.* **Description:** Buying guide and information source for the timeshare resort industry, featuring informative news and articles for the industry, as well as employment, product/service classifieds.
Published by: The Trades Publishing Company, 20 Our Way Dri, Crossville, TN 38555. TEL 931-484-8819, FAX 931-484-8825. Pub. Tim Wilson. Adv. contact Jack Richardson. color page USD 1,950; trim 10.5 x 16.25. Circ: 5,035.

910.202 CAN
RESORT WEEKLY. Text in English. 1989. 13/yr. (w. May-Aug.). CAD 25. adv. **Document type:** *Newspaper.* **Description:** Reports on weekly happenings and serves as an entertainment and shopping guide.
Published by: South East Press Ltd., 521 Main St, P O Box 329, Kipling, SK S0G 2S0, Canada. TEL 306-736-2535, FAX 306-736-8445. Ed. G Scott. Adv. contact G Scott Kearns. Circ: 3,000.

338 USA ISSN 1085-2573
TX907
RESORTS & GREAT HOTELS. Text in English. 1987. q. adv. bk.rev. illus. back issues avail. **Document type:** *Magazine, Consumer.* **Description:** Covers all aspects of luxury travel, with the emphasis on experiences possible only through the support and hospitality of first-class resorts and hotels.
Related titles: Online - full text ed.
—CCC.
Published by: Bonnier Corp. (Subsidiary of: Bonnier Group), 460 N Orlando Ave, Ste 200, Orlando, FL 32789. TEL 407-628-4802, FAX 407-628-7061, http://www.bonniercorp.com.

910.2 USA ISSN 2155-7608
REUNIONS WORKBOOK. Text in English. 1995. a., latest 10th ed. USD 9.95 per issue (effective 2010). adv. **Document type:** *Trade.*
Formerly (until 2010): Reunions Workbook & Catalog
Published by: Premier Tourism Marketing, Inc., 621 Plainfield Rd, Ste 406, Willowbrook, IL 60527. TEL 630-794-0696, FAX 630-794-0652, info@ptmgroups.com, http://www.premiertourismmarketing.com. adv.: color page USD 3,350.

338.4 BRA ISSN 1982-6125
REVISTA BRASILEIRA DE PESQUISA EM TURISMO. Text in Portuguese. 2007. 3/yr. free (effective 2011). **Document type:** *Journal, Academic/Scholarly.*
Media: Online - full text.
Indexed: A34, CA, E12, S13, T02, T05, W11.
Published by: Associacao Nacional de Pesquisa e Pos-Graduacao em Turismo (A N P T U R), Rua Silveira Martins 115, Centro, Sao Paulo, SP 01019-000, Brazil. http://anptur.org.br.

REVISTA CATALANA DE GEOGRAFIA. *see* GEOGRAPHY

338.4 ROM ISSN 1844-2994
➤ **REVISTA DE TURISM/JOURNAL OF TOURISM**; studii si cercetari in turism. Text in Romanian. 2006 (Jun.). s-a. free (effective 2009). back issues avail.; reprints avail. **Document type:** *Journal, Academic/Scholarly.*
Related titles: Online - full text ed.: free (effective 2011).
Indexed: AgrForAb, CABA, E12, F08, GH, LT, N02, P32, R12, RRTA, S13, S16, W11.
Published by: Universitatea "Stefan cel Mare" din Suceava, Facultatea de Stiinte Economice si Administratie Publica/"Stefan cel Mare" University of Suceava. Faculty of Economics and Public Administration, Universitatii 13, Suceava, 720229, Romania. TEL 40-230-216147, FAX 40-230-522978, http://www.seap.usv.ro. Eds. Alexandru Nedelea, Valentin Hapenciuc.

918 ECU
REVISTA DINERS. Text in Spanish. 1979. m. USD 40. adv. bk.rev.
Published by: (Ecuadorian Diners Club), Dinediciones S.A., Av. Gonzalez Suarez 335 y San Ignacio, Quito, Ecuador. TEL 505525. Ed. Jorge Ortiz. Adv. contact Yolanda Arroyo. Circ: 45,000.

338.4 658 PRT ISSN 1646-2408
REVISTA ENCONTROS CIENTIFICOS; tourism and management studies. Text in Portuguese. 2005. a. **Document type:** *Journal, Academic/Scholarly.*
Published by: Universidade do Algarve, Escola Superior de Gestao, Hotelaria e Turismo, Campus da Penha, Faro, 8005-139, Portugal.

338.4 BRA ISSN 1808-558X
G155.A1
REVISTA GLOBAL TOURISM. Text in Portuguese. 2005. s-a. free (effective 2011). **Document type:** *Journal, Academic/Scholarly.*
Media: Online - full text.
Published by: Global Tourism Consultoria e Treinamento http://www.periodicodeturismo.com.br/site/capa/index.php. Ed. Nilton Henrique Peccioli Filho.

918.2 ARG ISSN 1851-3352
REVISTA HUESPEDES. Text in Spanish. 2004. bi-m.
Related titles: Online - full text ed.: ISSN 1851-3360.
Published by: Huespedes, Capitan Ramon Freire 2350 8o A, Buenos Aires, C1428CZH, Argentina. TEL 54-11-55744696, info@revistahuespedes.com.ar, http://www.revistahuespedes.com.ar/. Ed. Roberto Leonetti.

REVISTA INTERAMERICANA DE AMBIENTE Y TURISMO. *see* ENVIRONMENTAL STUDIES

338.4 363.7 BRA ISSN 1983-8344
▼ ➤ **REVISTA NORDESTINA DE ECOTURISMO.** Text in Portuguese; Summaries in English. 2998. s-a. free (effective 2011). bk.rev. abstr. **Document type:** *Journal, Academic/Scholarly.* **Description:** Covers ecotourism, conservation, and environmental education.
Media: Online - full text.
Published by: Instituto Socioambiental Arvore, c/o Carlos Eduardo Silva, Rua Aloisio Braga, 181, Edf. San Martin, AP 402, Bairro Suica, Aracaju, Sergipe 49050-050, Brazil. TEL 55-79-9979-8991, contato@arvore.org.br, http://www.arvore.org.br/. Ed., R&P Carlos Eduardo Silva.

910 BRA ISSN 1645-9261
REVISTA TURISMO & DESENVOLVIMENTO. Text in Portuguese. 2004. s-a. back issues avail. **Document type:** *Journal, Academic/Scholarly.*
Media: Online - full text.
Indexed: CABA, E12, LT, N02, O01, R12, RRTA, S13, S16, W11.
Published by: Universidade de Aveiro, Departamento de Economia, Gestao e Engenharia Industrial, Campus de Santiago, Aveiro, 3810-193, Brazil. TEL 55-234-370361, FAX 55-234-370215, rtd@egi.ua.pt, http://www2.egi.ua.pt/rtd/. Ed. Carlos Costa.

791.4 LUX ISSN 0035-0729
REVUE; Letzeburger illustreiert (Luxembourg's weekly magazine). Text in German. 1945. w. adv. bk.rev.; film rev. abstr.; illus.; stat. Supplement avail. **Document type:** *Newspaper.*
Published by: Editions Revue S.A., B.P. 2755, Luxembourg, 1027, Luxembourg. TEL 49-81-81-1, FAX 48-77-22. Ed. Yolande Kieffer. Pub., R&P Guy Ludig. Circ: 31,489 (controlled).

917.45 641.2 USA ISSN 1935-6455
F79.6
RHODE ISLAND CURIOSITIES. Text in English. 2007. triennial, latest 2007. USD 14.95 per issue; USD 18.95 per issue in Canada (effective 2008). **Document type:** *Magazine, Consumer.* **Description:** Provides tourist information about Rhode Island.
Published by: The Globe Pequot Press, Inc., 246 Goose Ln, PO Box 480, Guilford, CT 06437. TEL 203-458-4500, 888-249-7586, FAX 203-458-4603, 800-820-2329, info@globepequot.com, http://www.globepequot.com.

RHODE ISLAND TRAVELER. *see* LEISURE AND RECREATION

908 DEU
RHOEN ERLEBEN. Text in German. 2005. s-a. EUR 2 newsstand/cover (effective 2010). adv. **Document type:** *Magazine, Consumer.*
Formerly (until 2006): Willkommen in der Region Rhoen
Published by: Mediengruppe Main-Post GmbH, Berner Str 2, Wuerzburg, 97084, Germany. TEL 49-931-60010, FAX 49-931-6001420, service.center@mainpost.de, http://www.mainpost.de.

971 CAN
RICE LAKE VACATION GUIDE. Text in English. 1956. a. CAD 3. adv. back issues avail.
Published by: Clay Publishing Co. Ltd., One Oak St, Bewdley, ON K0L 1E0, Canada. TEL 416-797-2281. Ed. Charlotte Clay.

914.04 USA ISSN 1096-7702
D909
RICK STEVES' BEST OF EUROPE. Text in English. 1988. a. USD 24.95 (effective 2009). **Document type:** *Guide, Consumer.* **Description:** Provides guidance on various destinations in Europe including Paris, London, Rome, Amsterdam and Barcelona.
Former titles (until 1998): Rick Steves' Europe (1085-939X); (until 1996): Rick Steves' Best of Europe (1078-7992); (until 1995): 2 to 22 Days in Europe (1059-2946); (until 1992): 22 Days in Europe (1059-3004); Europe in 22 Days
Published by: Avalon Travel Publishing, 1700 4th St, Berkeley, CA 94710. TEL 510-595-3664, avalon.publicity@perseusbooks.com, http://www.travelmatters.com.

914.39 USA ISSN 1946-6161
DB983.5
▼ **RICK STEVES' BUDAPEST.** Variant title: Budapest. Text in English. 2009. biennial. USD 17.95 per issue (effective 2009). **Document type:** *Guide, Consumer.* **Description:** Rick Steves' travel guide for Budapest, Hungary.
Published by: Avalon Travel Publishing, 1700 4th St, Berkeley, CA 94710. TEL 510-595-3664, info@travelmatters.com.

914 USA ISSN 1935-7419
DR1509
RICK STEVES' CROATIA & SLOVENIA. Text in English. 2007 (Mar.). a., latest 2007. USD 19.95 (effective 2008). **Document type:** *Magazine, Consumer.* **Description:** Details several destinations, designates friendly places to eat and sleep, suggests day plans, historical walking tours and trip itineraries, and provides clear instructions for smooth travel anywhere by car, train or foot.
Published by: Avalon Travel Publishing, 1700 4th St, Berkeley, CA 94710. TEL 510-595-3664, avalon.publicity@perseusbooks.com.

910.202 USA ISSN 1930-4617
DA650
RICK STEVES' ENGLAND. Text in English. 2006. a. USD 24.95 per issue (effective 2011). **Document type:** *Handbook/Manual/Guide, Corporate.*
Related titles: Online - full text ed.
Published by: Avalon Travel Publishing, 1700 4th St, Berkeley, CA 94710. TEL 510-595-3664, FAX 800-351-5073, atpfeedback@avalonpub.com, http://www.moon.com.

914 USA ISSN 1939-3016
RICK STEVE'S FLORENCE & TUSCANY. Text in English. 2002. a., latest 2009. USD 17.95 per issue (effective 2008). **Document type:** *Guide, Consumer.* **Description:** Provides guidance on exploring the various cultural sights of Florence and also covers the quaint hill towns of Tuscany.
Formerly (until 2004): Rick Steve's Florence (1538-1609)
Published by: Avalon Travel Publishing, 1400 65th St, Ste 250, Emeryville, CA 94608. TEL 510-595-3664, FAX 510-595-4228, info@travelmatters.com, http://www.travelmatters.com.

915 USA ISSN 1936-7112
DR718
RICK STEVES' ISTANBUL. Text in English. 2007 (May). a. USD 17.95 (effective 2008). **Document type:** *Magazine, Consumer.* **Description:** Provides guidance on the city of Istanbul.
Published by: Avalon Travel Publishing, 1700 4th St, Berkeley, CA 94710. TEL 510-595-3664, avalon.publicity@perseusbooks.com, http://www.avalontravelbooks.com.

910.202 USA ISSN 1554-3870
DB2607
RICK STEVES' PRAGUE & THE CZECH REPUBLIC. Text in English. 2005. a., latest 4th ed. USD 17.95 per issue (effective 2008). **Document type:** *Guide, Consumer.* **Description:** Provides opinionated coverage of both famous and lesser-known sights, friendly places to eat and sleep, suggested day plans, walking tours and trip itineraries and clear instructions for smooth travel anywhere by car, train or foot.
Published by: Avalon Travel Publishing, 1400 65th St, Ste 250, Emeryville, CA 94608. avalon.publicity@perseusbooks.com.

RIDER; motorcycle touring & sport touring. *see* SPORTS AND GAMES—Bicycles And Motorcycles

914.743 LVA ISSN 1407-2335
RIGA IN YOUR POCKET. Text in English. 1995. 5/yr. USD 25; USD 5 newsstand/cover (effective 2002). adv. **Document type:** *Magazine, Consumer.*
Related titles: Online - full text ed.: ISSN 1407-2343. 1996.
Address: Pils Laukums 4, Rm. 112, Riga, 1050, Latvia. TEL 371-722-0580, FAX 371-722-3416.

918.104 BRA
RIO OBSERVER. Text in Portuguese. 1996. bi-m. **Description:** Provides general information on Rio de Janeiro for tourists.
Media: Online - full text.
Address: Estrada das Canoas, 3406 Sao Conrado, S Cruz, Rio De Janeiro, RJ 23570-070, Brazil. Ed. Margarida Autran.

910.91 664 USA
RITZ CARLTON MAGAZINE. Text in English. bi-m. **Document type:** *Magazine, Consumer.*
Address: 3930 E. Ray Rd., Ste. 150, Phoenix, AZ 85044-7174. Ed. Carolyn Scarborough.

910.09 ITA ISSN 1720-1608
LA RIVISTA DEL TREKKING; itinerari e viaggi nella natura. Text in Italian. 1984. m. EUR 32 (effective 2008). adv. **Document type:** *Magazine, Consumer.*
Published by: Clementi Editore, Corso Torino 24-3, Genoa, 16129, Italy. TEL 39-010-5701042, FAX 39-010-5304378. Circ: 30,000.

910.91 ITA ISSN 2037-0660
▼ **LA RIVISTA DELLA SARDEGNA.** Text in Multiple languages. 2009. 3/yr. **Document type:** *Guide, Consumer.*
Published by: Mazzanti Editori Srl, Via delle Industrie 19B, Marghera, VE 30175, Italy. TEL 39-041-5385565, FAX 39-041-2529525, info@mazzantieditori.it, http://www.mazzantieditori.it.

338.4 910.2 ITA ISSN 2037-7916
▼ **RIVISTA DI SCIENZE DEL TURISMO.** Text in Multiple languages. 2010. 3/yr. **Document type:** *Journal, Trade.*
Related titles: Online - full text ed.: ISSN 2037-7908.
Published by: Edizioni Universitarie di Lettere Economia Diritto (L E D), Via Cervignano 4, Milan, Italy. TEL 39-02-59902055, FAX 39-02-55193636, led@lededizioni.com, http://www.lededizioni.com.

910.202 ITA ISSN 1828-6720
LA RIVISTA DI VENEZIA. Text in Italian. 2006. bi-m. EUR 15 domestic; EUR 18.20 in Europe; EUR 20.20 elsewhere (effective 2009). **Document type:** *Magazine, Consumer.*
Published by: Mazzanti Editori Srl, Via delle Industrie 19B, Marghera, VE 30175, Italy. TEL 39-041-5385565, FAX 39-041-2529525, info@mazzantieditori.it, http://www.mazzantieditori.it.

ROAD AHEAD. *see* TRANSPORTATION—Automobiles

917 USA ISSN 0361-6509
G1201.P2
ROAD ATLAS, UNITED STATES, CANADA AND MEXICO. Text in English. 1932. a.
Published by: Rand McNally & Co., PO Box 7600, Chicago, IL 60680. TEL 800-777-6277, 800-678-7263, FAX 800-934-3479, http://www.randmcnally.com.

917.1 CAN ISSN 1205-0989
ROAD EXPLORER. Text in English. 1979. 3/yr. adv. **Document type:** *Magazine, Trade.*
Former titles (until 1995): Ontario Motor Coach Association Review (0824-9776); (until 1982): Ontario Motor Coach Review (0714-3125)
Published by: (Ontario Motor Coach Association), Naylor (Canada), 2 Bloor St West, Ste 2001, Toronto, ON M4W 3E2, Canada. TEL 416-961-4384, 800-461-4828, FAX 416-924-4408. Ed. Lori Knowles.

910.91 796.7 USA
ROAD TRIP. Text in English. 2005. m. USD 24.95 (effective 2005). **Document type:** *Magazine, Consumer.*
Published by: Sideear Suite, Inc., PO Box 572439, Tarzana, CA 91357. TEL 818-996-6615, FAX 818-474-7362. Eds., Pubs. Gary Dolgoff, Kate Jackson. Circ: 60,000 (controlled).

917.3 USA ISSN 2152-3711
GV199.42.A68
▼ **ROAD TRIP U S A: APPALACHIAN TRAIL.** Text in English. 2010 (Apr.). biennial. USD 11.95 per issue (effective 2011). **Document type:** *Consumer.* **Description:** Travel guide for sites along the Appalachian Trail.
Published by: Avalon Travel Publishing, 1700 4th St, Berkeley, CA 94710. TEL 510-595-3664, info@travelmatters.com, http://www.avalontravelbooks.com.

917.3 USA ISSN 2152-3703
F106
▼ **ROAD TRIP U S A: ATLANTIC COAST.** Text in English. 2010 (Apr.). biennial. USD 9.95 per issue (effective 2011). **Document type:** *Handbook/Manual/Guide, Consumer.* **Description:** Travel guide for sites on the Atlantic Coast.
Published by: Avalon Travel Publishing, 1700 4th St, Berkeley, CA 94710. TEL 510-595-3664, info@travelmatters.com, http://www.avalontravelbooks.com.

917.3 USA ISSN 2152-3681
HE356.M68
▼ **ROAD TRIP U S A: GREAT RIVER ROAD.** Text in English. 2010 (Apr.). biennial. USD 9.95 per issue (effective 2011). **Document type:** *Handbook/Manual/Guide, Consumer.* **Description:** Travel guide for sites and cities along the Mississippi River.
Published by: Avalon Travel Publishing, 1700 4th St, Berkeley, CA 94710. TEL 510-595-3664, info@travelmatters.com, http://www.avalontravelbooks.com.

917 USA ISSN 1946-3278
F851
▼ **ROAD TRIP U S A: PACIFIC COAST HIGHWAY.** Short title: Pacific Coast Highway. Text in English. 2009. triennial. USD 9.95 per issue (effective 2009). **Document type:** *Guide, Consumer.* **Description:** Travel guide for the Pacific Coast Highway.
Published by: Avalon Travel Publishing, 1700 4th St, Berkeley, CA 94710. TEL 510-595-3664, info@travelmatters.com, http://www.avalontravelbooks.com.

917 USA ISSN 1946-3286
GV1024
▼ **ROAD TRIP U S A: ROUTE 66.** Short title: Route 66. Text in English. 2009. triennial. USD 9.95 per issue (effective 2009). **Document type:** *Guide, Consumer.* **Description:** Tour guide for Route 66.
Published by: Avalon Travel Publishing, 1700 4th St, Berkeley, CA 94710. TEL 510-595-3664, info@travelmatters.com, http://www.avalontravelbooks.com.

ROADBIKE. *see* SPORTS AND GAMES—Bicycles And Motorcycles

910.91 USA
ROADSIDE. Text in English. m. **Document type:** *Magazine, Consumer.* **Description:** Covers roadside attractions such as local eateries, diners, drive-ins and motels.
Published by: Roadside Magazine, Box 652, Worcester, MA 01602-2114. TEL 508-791-1838, FAX 603-971-1951, info@roadsidemagazine.com, http://www.roadsidemagazine.com. Ed. Randolph Garbin.

ROBB REPORT LUXURY HOTELS. *see* HOTELS AND RESTAURANTS

ROBB REPORT VACATION HOMES. *see* REAL ESTATE

917 051 USA ISSN 1934-3833
ROCKFORD LIFE. Text in English. 2006. 10/yr. USD 20; USD 3.99 newsstand/cover (effective 2007). adv. **Document type:** *Magazine, Consumer.* **Description:** Features local information for the Rockville, Illinois area, including dining, outings, outdoor life, home and garden and profiles of locals.
Published by: Northwest Communications, 129 S Phelps Ave, Ste 303, Rockford, IL 61108. TEL 815-226-1320, FAX 815-226-1322. Ed. Mary George. Pub. Val Russell.

917.64 USA ISSN 1940-8277
THE ROCKPORT GUIDE. Text in English. 1986. s-a. free (effective 2008). adv. **Document type:** *Magazine, Consumer.* **Description:** Includes information about lodgings, restaurants, shopping and attractions in the Rockport, Texas area.
Published by: Artworx Graphic Design, 630 E Market St, Rockport, TX 78382. TEL 361-729-1552. Pub. Christopher Blum.

914.7 ROM ISSN 1221-0692
ROMANIA PITOREASCA; revista de supravietuire prin turism si inteligenta. Text in Romanian. 1958. m. ROL 60, USD 20. adv. bk.rev. charts; illus.
Related titles: ◆ Supplement(s): Montana. ISSN 1221-0684.
Published by: Ministerul Turismului/Ministry of Tourism, Str. Gabriel Peri 8, Bucharest, 70148, Romania. TEL 6597893. Ed. Pop Simion. Circ: 32,000. **Dist. by:** Rodipet S.A., Piata Presei Libere 1, sector 1, PO Box 33-57, Bucharest 3, Romania. TEL 40-21-2224126, 40-21-2226407, rodipet@rodipet.ro.

910 796 ROM ISSN 1454-4423
ROMANIAN TRAVEL GUIDE. Text in English. 1998. a. ROL 400,000, USD 19.99 (effective 2001 - 2002). film rev.; Website rev.; music rev.; video rev. charts; mkt.; stat.; maps; illus. back issues avail. **Document type:** *Directory, Consumer.* **Description:** Designated both to the tourists who take an interest in Romania and to the specialists in tourism who will have at their disposal the most comprehensive database in the Romanian tourism. Contains information on hotels and travel agencies, maps, photos, calendars of events and history of Romania, the Black Sea, Moldavia's Monasteries, Transylvania.
Media: CD-ROM. **Related titles:** Online - full content ed.
Published by: Norbert Computer, Str. Lunga 160, Et. 1, Brasov, 2200, Romania. TEL 40-68-410297, FAX 40-68-410298, norbert@rotravel.com, cd@rotravel.com. Ed. Liviu Mihaileanu. R&P Aurelian Horja. Adv. contact Ligia Valeanu. Circ: 10,000.

917.6335 USA ISSN 1540-1529
F379.N53
ROMANTIC DAYS AND NIGHTS IN NEW ORLEANS; romantic diversions in and around the city. Text in English. 1998. biennial. latest 2002, 3rd ed. USD 15.95 per issue (effective 2008). **Document type:** *Guide, Consumer.* **Description:** Contains information on great nightlife, romantic hotels, intimate dining venues and enchanting plantation houses.
Published by: The Globe Pequot Press, Inc., 246 Goose Ln, PO Box 480, Guilford, CT 06437. TEL 203-458-4500, 888-249-7586, FAX 203-458-4603, 800-820-2329, info@globepequot.com, http://www.globepequot.com.

910.2 USA ISSN 1546-6833
F2171.2
ROMANTIC ESCAPES IN THE CARIBBEAN. Text in English. irreg. **Document type:** *Magazine, Consumer.*
Indexed: CPerI.
Published by: Hunter Publishing, PO Box 746, Walpole, MA 02081. TEL Comments@HunterPublishing.com, 800-255-0343, http://www.hunterpublishing.com/.

910.09 USA ISSN 1053-0177
ROMANTIC TRAVELING. Text in English. 1989. q. USD 25 domestic; USD 27 in Canada; USD 30 elsewhere (effective 2000). bk.rev. back issues avail. **Document type:** *Newsletter.* **Description:** Helps couples intensify their relationship through travel destinations covered throughout the world.
Formerly (until 1990): Travel Publishing News (1043-6138)
Published by: Moonlight Partners, 3181 Mission St, 124, San Francisco, CA 94110. TEL 415-285-9612. Ed., R&P Monica Conrady. Pub. Diane Brady. Circ: 1,000 (paid).

914.5 USA ISSN 1937-044X
DG804
ROME. Variant title: Eyewitness Travel Guide: Rome. Text in English. 2007. a. USD 25 (effective 2008). **Document type:** *Guide, Consumer.* **Description:** Features maps, photographs, 3-D aerial views of Rome's most interesting districts and the floor plans of all the major sights and the huge selection of hotels, restaurants, shops and entertainment venues.
Formerly: Rome EGuide
Published by: D K Publishing (Subsidiary of: Penguin Books U S A, Inc.), 375 Hudson St, New York, NY 10014. TEL 800-631-8571, FAX 201-256-0000, specialsales@dk.com.

910.202 USA ISSN 1933-0723
DG804
ROME DIRECTIONS. Text in English. 2005. irreg., latest 2005. GBP 6.99 per issue (effective 2011). **Document type:** *Guide, Consumer.*
Published by: Rough Guides, 375 Hudson St, 9th Fl, New York, NY 10014. TEL 212-414-3635, press@roughguides.com, http://www.roughguides.com/default.aspx.

910.202 USA ISSN 1935-4363
DG804
ROME FOR DUMMIES. Text in English. 2006. biennial. USD 17.99, EUR 12.60, GBP 11.99 per issue (effective 2010). adv. back issues avail. **Document type:** *Guide, Consumer.* **Description:** Covers art aficionados, architecture buffs, history lovers, foodies, and fashion trendsetters of Rome.
Published by: John Wiley & Sons, Inc., 111 River St, Hoboken, NJ 07030. TEL 201-748-6000, FAX 201-748-6088, info@wiley.com.

917.47 USA ISSN 1946-3391
ROOSEVELT ISLAND. Text in English. s-a. USD 4.99 per issue (effective 2009). adv. **Document type:** *Guide, Consumer.* **Description:** Pocket-sized guide for Roosevelt Island, New York.
Published by: Hot and Cool Guide LLC, 1375 Broadway, 3rd Fl, New York, NY 10018. TEL 800-282-8144, FAX 646-417-8259, question@HotAndCoolGuide.com. adv.: page USD 3,120; 4.125 x 7.375.

910.202 PRT
ROTAS DO MUNDO. Text in Portuguese. 2005. m. EUR 36.52; EUR 3.80 newsstand/cover (effective 2007). adv. **Document type:** *Magazine, Consumer.*
Published by: Edimpresa Editora Lda., Rua Calvet de Magalhaes 242, Laveiras, Paco de Arcos, 2770-022, Portugal. TEL 351-21-4698000, FAX 351-21-4698501, edimpresa@edimpresa.pt, http://www.edimpresa.pt. Ed. Barbara Palla e Carmo. adv.: page EUR 3,800; trim 205 x 272. Circ: 13,744 (paid).

910.91 629.2 PRT ISSN 1647-2241
ROTAS & DESTINOS. Text in Portuguese. 1995. m. adv. illus.; maps. back issues avail. **Document type:** *Magazine, Consumer.*
Related titles: Online - full text ed.
Published by: Edirevistas (Subsidiary of: Cofina Media), Av Joao Crisostomo 72, Lisbon, 1069-043, Portugal. TEL 351-213-307700, FAX 351-213-307799. Ed. Rui Faria.

910.2 USA ISSN 1931-0579
DP402.B24
THE ROUGH GUIDE TO BARCELONA. Text in English. a., latest 2006, 6th ed. USD 17.99 domestic 6th ed.; USD 24.99 in Canada 6th ed.; GBP 11.99 in United Kingdom 6th ed. (effective 2008). back issues avail. **Document type:** *Guide, Consumer.*
Formerly (until 2002): Barcelona
Related titles: Online - full text ed.
Published by: Rough Guides, 375 Hudson St, 9th Fl, New York, NY 10014. TEL 212-414-3635, http://www.roughguides.com/default.aspx.

917 USA ISSN 1938-4866
F774.3
THE ROUGH GUIDE TO COLORADO. Text in English. 2007. irreg., latest 2006, 1st ed. USD 17.99 domestic 1st ed.; USD 24.99 in Canada 1st ed.; GBP 11.99 in United Kingdom 1st ed. (effective 2008). back issues avail. **Document type:** *Guide, Consumer.*
Related titles: Online - full text ed.
Published by: Rough Guides, 375 Hudson St, 9th Fl, New York, NY 10014. TEL 212-414-3635, http://www.roughguides.com/default.aspx.

916 USA ISSN 1940-2430
DT2
THE ROUGH GUIDE TO FIRST-TIME AFRICA. Text in English. 2007. irreg., latest 2007, 1st ed. USD 16.99 domestic 1st ed.; USD 22.99 in Canada 1st ed.; GBP 10.99 in United Kingdom 1st ed. (effective 2008). back issues avail. **Document type:** *Guide, Consumer.*
Related titles: Online - full text ed.
Published by: Rough Guides, 375 Hudson St, 9th Fl, New York, NY 10014. TEL 212-414-3635, http://www.roughguides.com/default.aspx.

910.202 USA ISSN 1935-0619
DS4.8
THE ROUGH GUIDE TO FIRST-TIME ASIA. Text in English. 1998. irreg., latest 2010, 5th ed. USD 18.99 per issue domestic; CAD 21.99 per issue in Canada; GBP 12.99 per issue in United Kingdom (effective 2011). **Document type:** *Guide, Consumer.*
Formerly (until 200?): First-Time Asia
Published by: Rough Guides, 375 Hudson St, 9th Fl, New York, NY 10014. TEL 212-414-3635, http://www.roughguides.com/default.aspx.

910.202 USA ISSN 1935-2387
DL407
THE ROUGH GUIDE TO NORWAY. Text in English. 1997. irreg., latest 2009, 5th ed. USD 22.99 per issue domestic; CAD 24 per issue in Canada; GBP 12.99 per issue in United Kingdom (effective 2011). **Document type:** *Guide, Consumer.*
Formerly (until 2006): Rough Guide. Norway
Published by: Rough Guides, 375 Hudson St, 9th Fl, New York, NY 10014. TEL 212-414-3635, http://www.roughguides.com/default.aspx.

910.202 USA ISSN 1933-4079
DG652
THE ROUGH GUIDE TO THE ITALIAN LAKES. Text in English. 2006. irreg., latest 2009, 2nd ed. USD 19.99 per issue domestic; CAD 22 per issue in Canada; GBP 12.99 per issue in United Kingdom (effective 2011). **Document type:** *Guide, Consumer.*
Published by: Rough Guides, 375 Hudson St, 9th Fl, New York, NY 10014. TEL 212-414-3635, http://www.roughguides.com/default.aspx.

910.202 GBR ISSN 1931-2628
G151
THE ROUGH GUIDE TO TRAVEL SURVIVAL. Text in English. 2005. irreg., latest 2005. GBP 7.99, USD 12.99, CAD 17.99 per issue (effective 2010). **Document type:** *Handbook/Manual/Guide, Consumer.* **Description:** The essential field manual for every adventurous traveller, from surviving an avalanche to coping with a hostage situation.
Published by: Rough Guides Ltd., 80 Strand, London, WC2R 0RL, United Kingdom. mail@roughguides.co.uk. Ed. Doug Lansky.

917.8 USA ISSN 1940-2708
F722
THE ROUGH GUIDE TO YELLOWSTONE AND GRAND TETON. Text in English. 2007. irreg., latest 2007, 1st ed. USD 17.99 domestic 1st ed.; USD 22.99 in Canada 1st ed.; GBP 11.99 in United Kingdom 1st ed. (effective 2008). back issues avail. **Document type:** *Guide, Consumer.*
Related titles: Online - full text ed.
Published by: Rough Guides, 375 Hudson St, 9th Fl, New York, NY 10014. TEL 212-414-3635, http://www.roughguides.com/default.aspx.

910.202 GBR
ROUGH NEWS (E-MAIL). Text in English. 3/yr. free. bk.rev.; film rev.; music rev. **Document type:** *Newsletter, Consumer.* **Description:** Contains information about new Rough Guides titles, the latest from the Rough Guides Community and travel experiences from the authors of our guides. Plus, you'll find podcasts, travel discounts, competitions & more.
Formerly: Rough News (Print)
Media: E-mail.
Published by: Rough Guides Ltd., 80 Strand, London, WC2R 0RL, United Kingdom. TEL 44-20-70103000, mail@roughguides.com.

902 GBR
ROUTLEDGE ADVANCES IN TOURISM. Text in English. 1996. irreg., latest 2008. price varies. back issues avail. **Document type:** *Monographic series, Academic/Scholarly.* **Description:** Highlights central and topical issues relating to tourism including, the management and organization of tourism, tourism and development, the benefits and the disadvantages of the effects of tourism.
Published by: Routledge (Subsidiary of: Taylor & Francis Group), 2 Park Sq, Milton Park, Abingdon, Oxon OX14 4RN, United Kingdom. TEL 44-20-70176000, FAX 44-20-70176699, journals@routledge.com.

ROYALAUTO. *see* TRANSPORTATION—Automobiles

910.91 USA ISSN 1559-9426
F2509.5
RUM & REGGAE'S BRAZIL. Text in English. 2005. irreg. USD 19.95 per issue domestic; USD 20.80 per issue in United Kingdom (effective 2011). **Document type:** *Handbook/Manual/Guide, Consumer.*
Published by: Rum & Reggae Guidebooks, Inc., PO Box 130153, Boston, MA 02113. TEL 617-720-2244, FAX 617-720-2240, yahmon@rumreggae.com.

910.202 USA ISSN 1559-2510
F1543.5
RUM & REGGAE'S COSTA RICA. Text in English. 2006. irreg. USD 18.95 per issue domestic; CAD 15.29 per issue in Canada; GBP 13.59 per issue in United Kingdom (effective 2011). 616 p./no.; **Document type:** *Handbook/Manual/Guide, Consumer.*
Published by: Rum & Reggae Guidebooks, Inc., PO Box 130153, Boston, MA 02113. TEL 617-720-2244, FAX 617-720-2240, yahmon@rumreggae.com.

910.202 USA ISSN 1933-3021
F1613
RUM & REGGAE'S FRENCH CARIBBEAN. Text in English. 2005. irreg. USD 11.95 per issue domestic; CAD 14.36 per issue in Canada (effective 2011). **Document type:** *Handbook/Manual/Guide, Consumer.*
Published by: Rum & Reggae Guidebooks, Inc., PO Box 130153, Boston, MA 02113. TEL 617-720-2244, FAX 617-720-2240, yahmon@rumreggae.com.

917.29844 USA ISSN 1557-9247
F2106
RUM & REGGAE'S GRENADINES. Text in English. 2003. irreg. USD 10.36 per issue domestic; CAD 12.56 per issue in Canada; GBP 7.65 per issue in United Kingdom (effective 2011). **Document type:** *Handbook/Manual/Guide, Consumer.*
Published by: Rum & Reggae Guidebooks, Inc., PO Box 130153, Boston, MA 02113. TEL 617-720-2244, FAX 617-720-2240, yahmon@rumreggae.com.

910.91 USA ISSN 1930-2649
DU622
RUM & REGGAE'S HAWAI'I. Text in English. 1989. irreg. USD 19.95 per issue domestic; CAD 16.38 per issue in Canada; GBP 16.99 per issue in United Kingdom (effective 2011). 480 p./no.; **Document type:** *Handbook/Manual/Guide, Consumer.*
Formerly (until 2001): Hot On Hawaii, The Insider's Guide to the Aloha State
Published by: Rum & Reggae Guidebooks, Inc., PO Box 130153, Boston, MA 02113. TEL 617-720-2244, FAX 617-720-2240, yahmon@rumreggae.com.

917.295 USA ISSN 1557-9220
F1959
RUM & REGGAE'S PUERTO RICO, CULEBRA & VIEQUES. Text in English. 2002. irreg., latest 2007. USD 14.20 per issue domestic; CAD 13.13 per issue in Canada (effective 2011). **Document type:** *Handbook/Manual/Guide, Consumer.*
Published by: Rum & Reggae Guidebooks, Inc., PO Box 130153, Boston, MA 02113. TEL 617-720-2244, FAX 617-720-2240, yahmon@rumreggae.com.

918.1 USA ISSN 1941-0530
F2646.A4
RUM & REGGAE'S RIO DE JANEIRO. Text in English. 2008 (Sep.). irreg. USD 14.95 per issue domestic; CAD 14.51 per issue in Canada; GBP 12.50 per issue in United Kingdom (effective 2011). **Document type:** *Handbook/Manual/Guide, Consumer.*
Published by: Rum & Reggae Guidebooks, Inc., PO Box 130153, Boston, MA 02113. TEL 617-720-2244, FAX 617-720-2240, yahmon@rumreggae.com.

RUNZHEIMER REPORTS ON RELOCATION. *see* BUSINESS AND ECONOMICS—Personnel Management

RUNZHEIMER REPORTS ON TRAVEL MANAGEMENT (ONLINE). *see* BUSINESS AND ECONOMICS—Personnel Management

910.91 USA
RURAL LIVING (HAMILTON). Text in English. 1992. m. USD 12. adv. back issues avail. **Document type:** *Magazine, Consumer.* **Description:** Purpose is to inform readers about attractions and real estate available and high quality of life in rural Northwest Missouri.
Published by: Chadwick Communications, Inc., 105 N Davis St, Hamilton, MO 64644. TEL 816-583-2116, FAX 816-583-2118. Ed. Anne Tezon. Adv. contact Lori Carr. Circ: 13,000.

388.3 USA ISSN 0036-0171
HE5623.A1
RUSSELL'S OFFICIAL NATIONAL MOTOR COACH GUIDE; official publications of bus lines for United States and Canada. Variant title: Official Bus Guide. Text in English. 1908. m. USD 101.55; USD 122.04 in Canada; USD 115.35 elsewhere. adv. charts; maps. **Document type:** *Handbook/Manual/Guide, Trade.*
Published by: Russell's Guides, Inc., 817 2nd Ave SE, Cedar Rapids, IA 52403-2401. TEL 319-364-6138, FAX 319-364-4853. Ed. Charlotte Bonar. Circ: 14,000 (paid).

913.919 USA ISSN 1066-999X
DK1 CODEN: ADNSEA
RUSSIAN LIFE. Text in English, Russian. 1956-1991; resumed 1993. bi-m. USD 36 domestic; USD 48 foreign; USD 9 per issue (effective 2010). adv. bk.rev. illus. index. reprints avail. **Document type:** *Magazine, Consumer.* **Description:** Covers a wide range of stories such as travel, language, cuisine news.
Former titles (until 1993): Soviet Life (0038-5549); (until 1965): U S S R (0497-3976); Incorporates (1992-1995): Russian Travel Monthly (1077-8934); Which incorporated (19??-1977): Soviet Panorama (0038-5611)
Related titles: CD-ROM ed.; Microform ed.: (from PQC); Online - full text ed.
Indexed: A01, A03, A08, A12, A15, A22, A26, ABIn, ABS&EES, CA, DYW, E08, ENW, G05, G06, G07, G08, I05, I07, I08, M02, MagInd, MusicInd, P02, P06, P10, P13, P34, P48, P51, P53, P54, PQC, R06, S09, S23, T02.
—Ingenta. **CCC.**
Address: PO Box 567, Montpelier, VT 05601. TEL 802-223-4955, FAX 802-223-6105, sales@rispubs.com. Ed., Pub. Paul E Richardson. Circ: 15,000 (paid).

910.4 ESP ISSN 1130-0434
RUTAS DEL MUNDO. Text in Spanish. 1989. m. EUR 35.10 (effective 2009). adv. back issues avail. **Document type:** *Magazine, Consumer.*
Related titles: Online - full text ed.
Published by: M C Ediciones, Paseo de Sant Gervasi 16-20, Barcelona, 08022, Spain. TEL 34-93-2541250, FAX 34-93-2541262, http://www.mcediciones.net. adv.: color page EUR 5,850; 171 x 230. Circ: 9,796 (paid and controlled).

338.4 JPN ISSN 0911-4750
RYOKO NENPO/TRAVEL MARKET TRENDS ANNUAL EDITION. Text in Japanese. 1981. a. JPY 6,300 newsstand/cover (effective 2006). **Document type:** *Trade.*
Published by: Nihon Kotsu Kosha/Japan Tourist Bureau Foundation, 1-8-2 Marunouchi Chiyoda-ku, Tokyo, 100-0005, Japan. TEL 81-3-52084701, FAX 81-3-52084706, zaidan@jtb.or.jp, http://www.jtb.or.jp/.

338.4 JPN
RYOKOU MITOOSHI/TOURISM FORECAST. Text in Japanese. 1990. a. JPY 3,150 (effective 2006). **Document type:** *Trade.*
Published by: Nihon Kotsu Kosha/Japan Tourist Bureau Foundation, 1-8-2 Marunouchi Chiyoda-ku, Tokyo, 100-0005, Japan. TEL 81-3-52084701, FAX 81-3-52084706, zaidan@jtb.or.jp, http://www.jtb.or.jp/.

S A MOTOR. (South Australia) *see* TRANSPORTATION—Automobiles

910.202 USA
S A T H NEWS. Text in English. 1978. q. membership. bk.rev. back issues avail. **Document type:** *Newsletter.* **Description:** Contains travel and tourism information as it relates to the handicapped population.
Published by: Society for the Advancement of Travel for the Handicapped, 347 Fifth Ave, Ste 610, New York, NY 10016. TEL 212-447-7284, FAX 212-725-8253. Ed. Laura Van Horn. Circ: 1,000 (controlled).

796.7 343.0944 USA
S J FIRST. (South Jersey) Text in English. 199?. bi-m. USD 6; USD 1 newsstand/cover (effective 2005). adv. 24 p./no.; **Document type:** *Magazine, Trade.* **Description:** Contains topics on travel and tourism, government public relations and legislation regarding automobile safety.
Formerly: Motor News
Published by: A A A South Jersey, 700 Laurel Oak Rd, Voorhees, NJ 08043. TEL 856-783-4222, FAX 856-627-9025, cscott@aaasj.com. Ed. Carol A Scott. Pub. Joel Vittori. Adv. contact Kathleen Barbalace. B&W page USD 2,700. Circ: 180,000 (controlled).

S J - NYTT. *see* TRANSPORTATION—Railroads

910.2 USA
S Y T A'S STUDENT & YOUTH TRAVELER. Variant title: Student & Youth Traveler. Text in English. 2001. 3/yr. **Document type:** *Magazine, Consumer.* **Description:** Promotes safe, quality travel by showcasing student and youth friendly destinations and attractions.
Published by: (Student & Youth Travel Association), Shoreline Creations, Ltd., 2465 112th Ave, Holland, MI 49424. TEL 616-393-2077, 800-767-3489, FAX 616-393-0085, editor@grouptour.com, http://www.grouptour.com.

943 DEU
SACHSEN MAGAZIN; Entdecken - Erleben - Geniessen. Text in German. a. EUR 5 newsstand/cover (effective 2007). adv. **Document type:** *Magazine, Consumer.*
Published by: Labhard Verlag GmbH, Zum Hussenstein 7, Konstanz, 78462, Germany. TEL 49-7531-9071-0, FAX 49-7531-907131, verlag@labhard.de. adv.: page EUR 2,685. Circ: 80,000 (controlled).

916 ZAF ISSN 1993-8969
SAFI SANA SOUTHERN AFRICA PAGES. Text in English. 2006. a. USD 300 (effective 2007). adv. **Description:** Provides information on regional accommodations, transportation and primary attractions.
Published by: Shikana Media, PO Box 8140, Roggebaai, 8012, South Africa. TEL 27-21-4211393, FAX 27-21-4255804, info@shikana.com. adv.: page USD 4,270.

910.202 VIR
SAINT CROIX THIS WEEK. Text in English. 1960. m. free (effective 2007). adv. **Document type:** *Magazine, Consumer.* **Description:** Presents information and pictures of interest to visitors of St. Croix.
Published by: Morris Caribbean Publications, Inc., One Havensightway, St. Thomas, 00802, Virgin Isl., US. TEL 340-774-2500, FAX 340-776-1466. Ed. Leslie Tate. Pub. Michael Sunderland. Circ: 180,000 (free).

914 CHE ISSN 0036-2832
ST. GALLEN; St. Gallen Aktuell - Tourist Information. Text in English, French, German, Italian. 1946. w. CHF 30, USD 2. adv. **Document type:** *Bulletin.*
Published by: Tourist Information St. Gallen, Bahnhofplatz 1a, Postfach, St. Gallen, 9001, Switzerland. TEL 41-71-2273737, FAX 41-71-2273767. Adv. contact Zeutrumsverlag St Gallen Gubh. Circ: 5,500 (controlled).

910.202 VIR
ST. THOMAS / ST. JOHN THIS WEEK. Text in English. 1959. m. free (effective 2007). adv. **Document type:** *Magazine, Consumer.* **Description:** Provides information to the tourist market.
Formerly: Saint Thomas This Week
Published by: Morris Caribbean Publications, Inc., One Havensightway, St. Thomas, 00802, Virgin Isl., US. TEL 340-774-2500, FAX 340-776-1466. Ed. Leslie Tate. Pub. Michael Sunderland. adv.: B&W page USD 39,000, color page USD 45,000. Circ: 450,000 (free).

910.91 USA
SAKAKAWEA COUNTRY. Text in English. 1976. a. adv. illus. back issues avail. **Document type:** *Magazine, Consumer.* **Description:** Provides travel information on the Lake Sakakawea area of North Dakota.
Published by: B H G Inc., PO Box 309, Garrison, ND 58540. TEL 701-463-2201, FAX 701-463-7487. Adv. contact Jude Iverson. page USD 500; trim 10.75 x 8.25. Circ: 40,000.

SALTSCAPES. *see* LIFESTYLE

917.904 USA
SAN DIEGAN. Text in English. 1969. a. USD 1.95. adv. cum.index. **Document type:** *Magazine, Consumer.* **Description:** Covers San Diego, Baja California, Mexico, Arizona, and Orange County.
Published by: San Diego Guide, Inc., 6370 Lusk Blvd, No F 202, San Diego, CA 92121-2754. TEL 619-453-1633, FAX 619-453-2332. Ed. Deborah Craig. Circ: 175,000.

SAN DIEGO MEETING & CONVENTION PLANNER'S GUIDE. *see* MEETINGS AND CONGRESSES

913.794 USA
SAN DIEGO VISITORS PLANNING GUIDE. Text in English. 199?. a. free. adv. **Document type:** *Magazine, Consumer.* **Description:** Targets pleasure, business and convention travelers as they plan their trip and introduces travelers to the wide variety of accommodations, transportation and attractions in San Diego County.
Published by: Weaver Publications, Inc., 2420 Alcott St, Denver, CO 80211. TEL 303-458-1211, FAX 303-477-0724, info@weaver-group.com, http://pub.weaver-group.com. Circ: 250,000.

913.794 USA
SAN DIEGO VISITORS POCKET GUIDE. Text in English. 2001. s-a. free. adv. **Document type:** *Guide, Consumer.* **Description:** Provides information to visitors and convention delegates about San Diego businesses, attractions, restaurants, arts and retail.
Published by: Weaver Publications, Inc., 2420 Alcott St, Denver, CO 80211. TEL 303-458-1211, FAX 303-477-0724, info@weaver-group.com, http://pub.weaver-group.com. Circ: 200,000.

917.9498 796.7 USA ISSN 1540-5230
SAN DIEGO WESTWAYS; southern California's lifestyle magazine. Text in English. 1996. bi-m. **Document type:** *Magazine, Consumer.*
Published by: Automobile Club of Southern California, PO Box 25001, Santa Ana, CA 92799. TEL 877-428-2277, FAX 800-222-8794, http://www.aaa-calif.com.

917.904 USA
THE SAN FRANCISCO BOOK. Text in English. 1984. s-a. 144 p./no.; **Document type:** *Magazine, Consumer.* **Description:** Provides information on the San Francisco Bay area: sightseeing, restaurants, retail and events.
Published by: San Francisco Convention & Visitors Bureau, 201 Third St, Ste 900, San Francisco, CA 94103. TEL 415-974-6900, FAX 415-227-2602, convention-services@sanfrancisco.travel, http://www.sfvisitor.org.

979.4 USA ISSN 2154-2872
F869.S33
▼ **SAN FRANCISCO CURIOSITIES**; quirky characters, roadside oddities & other offbeat stuff. Text in English. 2010 (Jun.). triennial. USD 15.95 per issue (effective 2011). **Document type:** *Handbook/Manual/Guide, Consumer.* **Description:** Travel guide for quirky characters, roadside oddities and other offbeat stuff.
Published by: The Globe Pequot Press, Inc., 246 Goose Ln, PO Box 480, Guilford, CT 06437. TEL 203-458-4500, FAX 203-458-4603, info@globepequot.com.

917.904 USA
SAN FRANCISCO GUIDE. Text in English. 1970. m. USD 12. **Document type:** *Magazine, Consumer.*
Formerly (until 1995): San Francisco and Bay Area Guide (0191-8451)
Published by: San Francisco Guide, Inc., 444 Lakeview Ave., San Francisco, CA 94112-3018. TEL 415-775-2212, FAX 415-441-7773. Pub. Linda Schreibman. Circ: 125,000 (paid).

SAN FRANCISCO MEETING AND EVENT PLANNER'S GUIDE. *see* MEETINGS AND CONGRESSES

794.913 USA
SAN FRANCISCO PROFESSIONAL TRAVEL PLANNER'S GUIDE. Text in English. 2007. a. adv. **Document type:** *Guide, Consumer.*
Published by: Weaver Publications, Inc., 2420 Alcott St, Denver, CO 80211. TEL 303-458-1211, FAX 303-477-0724, info@weaver-group.com, http://pub.weaver-group.com. Circ: 25,000.

794.913 USA
SAN FRANCISCO VISITORS PLANNING GUIDE. Text in English. 2000. s-a. free (effective 2007). adv. **Document type:** *Guide, Consumer.*
Published by: Weaver Publications, Inc., 2420 Alcott St, Denver, CO 80211. TEL 303-458-1211, FAX 303-477-0724, info@weaver-group.com, http://pub.weaver-group.com. Circ: 100,000.

910.09 USA
THE SAN JUANS BECKON; San Juan Islands, Fidalgo Islands, Sidney, B.C. Text in English. 1964. a. free (effective 2000). adv. illus.; maps. **Document type:** *Magazine, Consumer.*
Published by: Islands' Sounder, PO Box 758, Eastsound, WA 98245. TEL 360-376-4500, FAX 360-376-4501. Ed. Ted Grossman. Pub., R&P Jay Brodt TEL 360-378-5696. Adv. contact Elyse Van den Bosch. Circ: 95,000.

THE SAND PAPER. *see* HOBBIES

910.2 CAN ISSN 1710-3207
SANDBAR LAKE, INFORMATION GUIDE. Text in English. 2004. a. **Document type:** *Handbook/Manual/Guide, Consumer.*
Published by: Parks Canada, 25 Eddy St, Gatineau, PQ K1A 0M5, Canada. information@pc.gc.ca, http://www.pc.gc.ca.

910.2 ZAF ISSN 1818-815X
SANDTON CENTRAL ESSENTIAL DIRECTORY. Text in English. 2005. s-a. adv.
Published by: Blue Planet Media, PO Box 1754, Houghton, JHB 2041, South Africa. TEL 27-11-6229889, FAX 27-84-135202020, enquiries@blueplanetmedia.net, http://www.blueplanetmedia.net/. Pub. Jason Aarons. adv.: color page ZAR 7,500; trim 105 x 148.

917.94 USA ISSN 1937-0458
F869.S33
SANFRANCISCO & NORTHERN CAROLINA. Text in English. 2007. a. USD 23 (effective 2008). **Document type:** *Guide, Consumer.* **Description:** Provides information about famous sites, maps, a huge selection of hotels, restaurants and entertainment venues in San Francisco.
Published by: D K Publishing (Subsidiary of: Penguin Books U S A, Inc.), 375 Hudson St, New York, NY 10014. TEL 800-631-8571, FAX 201-256-0000, specialsales@dk.com.

914.95 GRC
SANTORINI GUIDE. Text in Greek. a. **Document type:** *Magazine, Consumer.*
Published by: Liberis Publications S.A./Ekdoseon Lymperi A.E., Ioannou Metaxa 80, Karelas, Koropi 19400, Greece. TEL 30-1-6198000, FAX 30-1-6198608, info@liberis.gr, http://www.liberis.gr. Circ: 6,000.

910.2 USA ISSN 1931-9630
F317.G8
THE SARASOTA, SANIBEL ISLAND & NAPLES BOOK. Text in English. 1998. irreg., latest 2007, 4th ed. USD 18.95 4th ed. (effective 2007). **Document type:** *Directory, Consumer.* **Description:** Covers the enchanting locales on the Gulf Coast.
Formerly (until 1998): Gulf Coast of Florida Book
Published by: The Countryman Press (Subsidiary of: W.W. Norton & Co., Inc.), PO Box 748, Woodstock, VT 05091. TEL 802-457-4826, 800-245-4151, FAX 802-457-1678, countrymanpress@wwnorton.com.

338.4 916.8 ZAF
SATOUR NATIONAL GRADING AND CLASSIFICATION SCHEME UPDATE. Text in English. 1994. m. **Document type:** *Government.*
Published by: Satour, Private Bag X164, Pretoria, 0001, South Africa.

916.8 ZAF
SATOUR NEWS. Text in English. 1992. irreg. illus. **Document type:** *Newsletter.*
Published by: Satour, Private Bag X164, Pretoria, 0001, South Africa.

917 647.95 USA
SAVANNAH TOURIST GUIDE. Text in English. 1993. bi-m. USD 10; USD 0.25 newsstand/cover (effective 1999). adv. maps. back issues avail. **Document type:** *Newspaper.* **Description:** Provides information about Savannah that would be of interest to tourists, including accomodations, tours, restaurants, and museums. Also offers a speecial events calendar, maps, and some local history.
Published by: James Birch, Ed. & Pub., 7505 Waters Ave, Ste B 6, Savannah, GA 31406. TEL 912-355-1740. Adv. contact James Birch. page USD 1,000; trim 17 x 11. Circ: 40,000.

SAVEUR. *see* HOME ECONOMICS

SAVOR WINE COUNTRY. *see* BEVERAGES

338.4791 NOR ISSN 0802-1376
SCANDINAVIAN BOARDING. Text in Multiple languages. 1988. 13/yr. adv. **Document type:** *Magazine, Trade.* **Description:** Travel information emphasizing the Nordic region.
Published by: Boarding AS, PO Box 6573, Rodeloekka, 0501, Norway. TEL 47-22-385250, FAX 47-22-385925. Adv. contact Terje Korsmo TEL 47-62-946906. page NOK 17,286; 185 x 265.

338.4 GBR ISSN 1502-2250
➤ **SCANDINAVIAN JOURNAL OF HOSPITALITY AND TOURISM.** Text in English. 2001. q. GBP 256 combined subscription in United Kingdom to institutions (print & online eds.); EUR 382, USD 478 combined subscription to institutions (print & online eds.) (effective 2012). adv. back issues avail.; reprint service avail. from PSC. **Document type:** *Journal, Academic/Scholarly.* **Description:** Aims to initiating and stimulating hospitality and tourism related discussions among the academic community, managers, and decision makers both in the private and public sectors.
Related titles: Online - full text ed.: ISSN 1502-2269. GBP 230 in United Kingdom to institutions; EUR 343, USD 431 to institutions (effective 2012) (from IngentaConnect).
Indexed: A10, A22, A34, B01, B06, B07, B09, C25, CA, CABA, E01, E12, ESPM, F08, F12, GEOBASE, H&TI, H06, HPNRM, LT, N02, P32, PGegResA, R12, RRTA, S13, S16, SCOPUS, SSCI, SSciA, T02, V03, VS, W07, W11.
—BLDSC (8087.516600), IE, Infotrieve, Ingenta. **CCC.**
Published by: Routledge (Subsidiary of: Taylor & Francis Group), 4 Park Sq, Milton Park, Abingdon, Oxon OX14 4RN, United Kingdom. TEL 44-20-70176000, FAX 44-20-70176336, subscriptions@tandf.co.uk, http://www.routledge.com. Eds. Annette Therkelsen, Jan Vidar Haukeland TEL 47-22-573801, Reidar J Mykletun. **Subscr. in Europe to:** Taylor & Francis Ltd., Journals Customer Service, Sheepen Pl, Colchester, Essex CO3 3LP, United Kingdom. TEL 44-20-70175544, FAX 44-20-70175198, tf.enquiries@tfinforma.com; **Subscr. in N America to:** Taylor & Francis Inc., Customer Services Dept, 325 Chestnut St, 8th Fl, Philadelphia, PA 19106. TEL 800-354-1420, FAX 215-625-2940.

910.91 USA
SCENES OF VERMONT. Text in English. irreg.
Media: Online - full text.
Published by: PB Publishing, PO Box 219, Morgan, VT 05853.

910.2 910.91 USA ISSN 1551-2959
F384.3
SCENIC DRIVING TEXAS. Text in English. 1996. irreg., latest 2005, 2nd ed. USD 15.95 per issue (effective 2008). **Document type:** *Guide, Consumer.* **Description:** Aims to act as a guide to unique places.
Formerly: Texas Scenic Drives

Published by: The Globe Pequot Press, Inc., 246 Goose Ln, PO Box 480, Guilford, CT 06437. TEL 203-458-4500, 888-249-7586, FAX 203-458-4603, 800-820-2329, info@globepequot.com, http://www.globepequot.com.

914.3 DEU
SCHENCKS SCHLOESSER UND GAERTEN. Text in German. 2006. a. EUR 19.90 newsstand/cover (effective 2010).
Published by: Schenck Verlag GmbH, Schauenburgerstr 55-57, Hamburg, 20095, Germany. TEL 49-40-4112570, FAX 49-40-41125710, info@schenck-verlag.de, http://www.schenck-verlag.de.

908 DEU ISSN 0931-2323
DD801.S941
SCHOENES SCHWABEN. Text in German. 1986. 11/yr. EUR 49.90; EUR 4.90 newsstand/cover (effective 2007). adv. **Document type:** *Magazine, Consumer.*
Published by: Silberburg-Verlag GmbH, Schoenbuchstr 48, Tuebingen, 72074, Germany. TEL 49-7071-68850, FAX 49-7071-688520, info@silberburg.de, http://www.silberburg.de. adv.: color page EUR 2,500. Circ: 14,500 (paid and controlled).

338.4791 DEU ISSN 1612-8672
SCHRIFTEN ZU TOURISMUS UND FREIZEIT. Text in German. 2003. irreg., latest vol.11, 2011. price varies. **Document type:** *Monographic series, Academic/Scholarly.*
Published by: Erich Schmidt Verlag GmbH & Co. (Berlin), Genthiner Str 30 G, Berlin, 10785, Germany. TEL 49-30-2500850, FAX 49-30-250085305, vertrieb@esvmedien.de.

910.202 DEU
SCHWARZAUFWEISS; das Reisemagazin mit Hintergrund. Text in German. w. adv. **Document type:** *Consumer.* **Description:** Contains detailed descriptions and information on various travel destinations around the globe.
Media: Online - full text.
Published by: Internet-Reisemagazin schwarzaufweiss, Bismarckstr 120, Bremen, 28203, Germany. TEL 49-421-74837. Ed. Helmuth Weiss. adv.: online banner EUR 40.60.

338.4791 DEU ISSN 2190-2143
SCHWEIZER JAHRBUCH FUER TOURISMUS. Text in German. 1988. a. **Document type:** *Journal, Academic/Scholarly.*
Formerly (until 2010): Jahrbuch der Schweizerischen Tourismuswirtschaft (1662-4424)
Published by: Erich Schmidt Verlag GmbH & Co. (Berlin), Genthiner Str 30 G, Berlin, 10785, Germany. TEL 49-30-2500850, FAX 49-30-250085305, vertrieb@esvmedien.de, http://www.esv.info.

914.904 CHE
SCHWEIZER TOURISTIK; Switzerland's leading travel trade magazine. Text in German. 1983. fortn. CHF 61 domestic; CHF 89 foreign (effective 2001). adv. **Document type:** *Magazine, Trade.* **Description:** Each issue focuses on a specific area.
Published by: Schweizer Touristik GmbH, Forchstr 60, Zuerich, 8032, Switzerland. TEL 41-1-3889961, FAX 41-1-3889960. Ed. Franz Xaver Risi. Pub. Heiner Berninger. Adv. contact Guido Kaeppeli TEL 41-1-3889969. B&W page CHF 4,570, color page CHF 6,130; trim 210 x 297. Circ: 9,825.

SCI; rivista degli sport invernali. *see* SPORTS AND GAMES—Outdoor Life

919.423 AUS ISSN 1834-2922
SCOOP TRAVELLER (NORTHERN TERRITORY EDITION). Text in English. 2005. s-a. AUD 15.90 in state; AUD 17.70 out of state; AUD 70.70 foreign (effective 2008). adv. back issues avail. **Document type:** *Magazine, Consumer.* **Description:** Contains information about tourism and travel destinations in each state of the Australia.
Supersedes in part (in 2006): Scoop Traveller (Northern Territory & South Australia Edition) (1833-2145)
Published by: Scoop Publishing Group, 266 Hay St, Ste 3, Subiaco, W.A. 6008, Australia. TEL 61-8-93888188, FAX 61-8-93888199, info@scoop.com.au, http://scoop.com.au/scooppublishing/. adv.: page AUD 5,750.

919.423 AUS ISSN 1834-2914
SCOOP TRAVELLER (SOUTH AUSTRALIA EDITION). Text in English. 2005. s-a. AUD 19.90 local; AUD 21.70 in state; AUD 74.70 foreign (effective 2008). adv. back issues avail. **Document type:** *Magazine, Consumer.* **Description:** Contains information about tourism and travel destinations in each state of the Australia.
Supersedes in part (in 2006): Scoop Traveller (Northern Territory & South Australia Edition) (1833-2145)
Published by: Scoop Publishing Group, 266 Hay St, Ste 3, Subiaco, W.A. 6008, Australia. TEL 61-8-93888188, FAX 61-8-93888199, info@scoop.com.au, http://scoop.com.au/scooppublishing/. adv.: page AUD 5,750.

919.45 AUS ISSN 1833-6817
SCOOP TRAVELLER (VICTORIA & TASMANIA EDITION). Text in English. 2006. s-a. AUD 19.90 local; AUD 21.70 in state; AUD 74.70 foreign (effective 2008). adv. back issues avail. **Document type:** *Magazine, Consumer.* **Description:** Contains information about food & wine, style, the fine arts, events and hot travel destinations in Australia.
Published by: Scoop Publishing Group, 266 Hay St, Ste 3, Subiaco, W.A. 6008, Australia. TEL 61-8-93888188, FAX 61-8-93888199, info@scoop.com.au, http://scoop.com.au/scooppublishing/. adv.: page AUD 5,750; trim 240 x 302.

914.1 GBR
SCOTTISH TRAVEL AGENTS NEWS. Text in English. 1990. w. GBP 79 domestic; GBP 99 in Europe; GBP 161 elsewhere; free to qualified personnel (effective 2009). adv. back issues avail. **Document type:** *Magazine, Consumer.* **Description:** All matters relating to the travel trade that affect Scotland.
Published by: S & G Publishing (Scotland) Ltd., 71 Henderson St, Bridge Of Allan, Stirling, FK9 4HG, United Kingdom. TEL 44-1786-834238, FAX 44-1786-834295. adv.: color page GBP 1,950; trim 211 x 299. Circ: 1,300 (controlled).

SCUBA DIVING; the magazine divers trust. *see* SPORTS AND GAMES—Outdoor Life

910.91 USA ISSN 1930-8531
F41.25
SCUDDER'S WHITE MOUNTAIN VIEWING GUIDE. Text in English. 1995. irreg. (2nd ed.). USD 18.95 per issue (effective 2007). **Document type:** *Guide, Consumer.*
Published by: High Top Press, PO Box 299, North Sutton, NH 03260. HighTopPress@aol.com, http://www.hightoppress.com/pages/823410/index.htm.

790.1 917 USA
SEA MASS TRAVELER. Text in English. 1993. m. USD 19; free (effective 1998). adv. dance rev.; film rev.; music rev.; play rev. illus.; maps; stat. back issues avail. **Document type:** *Newspaper, Consumer.* **Description:** Covers travel, art, dining and entertainment in southern Massachusetts.
Published by: New Rivers Print & Electronic Publishing, 29 Pelham St, PO Box 3189, Newport, RI 02840-0322. TEL 401-848-2922. Ed. John Pantalone. Pub., R&P Jeffrey C Hall. Adv. contact Kirby Varacalli. B&W page USD 1,800; 17 x 11. Circ: 25,000 (controlled).

910.202 USA
SEALETTER CRUISE MAGAZINE. Text in English. m.
Media: Online - full text.
Published by: Jackson Publishing, 20801 Severndale Terrace, Germantown, MD 20876. Ed. Sharon Jackson.

917.904 USA
SEATTLE COMPASS. Text in Japanese. 1983. q. free. adv. **Document type:** *Magazine, Consumer.* **Description:** Provides local information and events for tourists and visitors.
Formerly: Pacific Companion
Published by: Japan Pacific Publications, Inc., 519 6th Ave S., Ste. 220, Seattle, WA 98104-2878. TEL 206-622-7443, FAX 206-621-1786. Ed. Mire Morii. Pub., R&P Andrew Taylor. Adv. contact Eri Okada. Circ: 20,000.

910.91 USA
SEDONA MAGAZINE. Text in English. 1986. q. USD 19.95 (effective 2000). adv. back issues avail. **Document type:** *Magazine, Consumer.* **Description:** Contains history, events, scenery and recreation in the Sedona region.
Published by: Sedona Publishing Co., 271 Van Deren Rd, PO Box 219, Sedona, AZ 86339. TEL 520-282-9022, FAX 520-282-9754. Ed., Pub. Hoyt C Johnson. Adv. contact Johnny Johnson. color page USD 2,050; trim 10.88 x 8.38. Circ: 25,000 (paid).

917.504 USA
SEE FLORIDA MAGAZINES. (Published for 19 regional tourist markets) Text in English. 1953. irreg. (approx. 2-4/yr., seasonal). free (effective 2009). adv. **Document type:** *Magazine, Consumer.* **Description:** Contains information on tourist attractions, calendar of events, shopping, dining, recreation and real estate in Florida.
Related titles: Online - full text ed.
Published by: Miles Media Group, Inc., 6751 Professional Pkwy W, Sarasota, FL 34240. TEL 941-342-2300, 800-683-0010, FAX 941-907-0300, http://www.milesmedia.com/see/. Pub. Paul Winkle TEL 941-342-2325.

919 IND ISSN 0037-0762
SEE INDIA. Text in English. 1967. q. INR 100, USD 25 (effective 2011). adv. illus. **Document type:** *Journal, Trade.*
Address: A-47-D, DDA Flats, Munirka, New Delhi, 110 067, India. TEL 91-11-26101414, FAX 91-11-26101414.

910.91 AUS ISSN 1832-0589
SEE YOURSELF IN CANBERRA. Text in English. 2004. a. **Document type:** *Magazine, Consumer.*
Published by: Australian Capital Tourism Corp., Locked Bag 2001, Civic Square, ACT 2608, Australia. TEL 61-2-62050666, FAX 61-2-62050629, visitcanberra@act.gov.au, http://www.tourism.act.gov.au.

908 DEU ISSN 1617-1993
SEENLAND; das Magazin der Mecklenburgischen Seenplatte. Text in German. 1999. a. EUR 5.90 newsstand/cover (effective 2007). adv. **Document type:** *Magazine, Consumer.*
Published by: S D Media Services, Gehlberger Str. 19, Berlin, 13581, Germany. TEL 49-30-36286430, FAX 49-30-36286437, office@sd-media.de, http://www.sd-media.de. Adv. contact Kai Langner. page EUR 3,400; trim 210 x 300. Circ: 10,400 (paid and controlled).

910.202 ITA ISSN 1123-248X
IL SEGNO DI EMPOLI. Text in Italian. 1988. q. **Document type:** *Magazine, Consumer.*
Published by: Associazione Turistica Pro Empoli, Via G Del Papa 98, Empoli, FI 50053, Italy. TEL 39-0571-76115.

914.27 GBR ISSN 1750-659X
SELECT IN FURNESS. Text in English. 2006. q. free (effective 2009). adv. back issues avail. **Document type:** *Magazine, Consumer.* **Description:** Highlights interesting people, places, facts, lifestyle and leisure items in the Furness region.
Related titles: Online - full text ed.: free (effective 2009).
Published by: Bluepole Design, Piel View House,, Abbey Rd, Barrow-in-Furness, Cumbria LA13 9BD, United Kingdom. TEL 44-1229-877779, FAX 44-1229-877775, mail@bluepole.co.uk, http://www.bluepole.co.uk/. Ed. Linzi Rowe. Adv. contact kim Murray. page GBP 395.

914.2 GBR
SELF-CATERING HOLIDAYS IN BRITAIN. Text in English. 1968. a. GBP 8.99 per issue (effective 2009). adv. **Document type:** *Handbook/Manual/Guide, Consumer.* **Description:** Lists over 1000 self-catering opportunities ranging from houses, cottages, flats and chalets, to caravan-camps holidays.
Formerly (until 1997): Guide to Self-Catering and Furnished Holidays (0267-4599); Which was formed by the merger of: Self-Catering Holiday Homes, Caravans & Boats; Furnished Holidays in Britain
Published by: F H G Guides Ltd. (Subsidiary of: F H G Publications Ltd.), Abbey Mill Business Ctr, Seedhill, Paisley, PA1 1TJ, United Kingdom. TEL 44-141-8870428, FAX 44-141-8897204, sales@fhguides.co.uk, http://www.fhguides.co.uk.

338.4 GBR
SELLING CRUSING. Text in English. 19??. s-a. free to qualified personnel (effective 2009). adv. back issues avail. **Document type:** *Magazine, Trade.* **Description:** Covers new ships, new routes and new products.
Published by: B M I Publications Limited, Suffolk House, George St, Croydon, Surrey CR9 1SR, United Kingdom. TEL 44-20-86497233, FAX 44-20-86497234, sales@bmipublications.com, http://www.bmipublications.com. Ed. Steve Hartridge. Pub. Sally Parker. Circ: 6,500.

910.202 GBR ISSN 0959-6496
SELLING LONG-HAUL. Text in English. 1990. m. free to qualified personnel (effective 2009). adv. bk.rev. back issues avail. **Document type:** *Magazine, Trade.* **Description:** Covers the selling of long-distance travel from the UK for travel agents.
Related titles: Online - full text ed.: free (effective 2009).
Published by: B M I Publications Limited, Suffolk House, George St, Croydon, Surrey CR9 1SR, United Kingdom. TEL 44-20-86497233, FAX 44-20-86497234, sales@bmipublications.com, http://www.bmipublications.com. Ed. Steve Hartridge. Pub. Sally Parker. adv.: page GBP 3,750; trim 210 x 297. Circ: 16,500.

910.2 USA
SEPTEMBER DAYS CLUB NEWS. Text in English. q. USD 15 domestic membership (effective 2005). **Document type:** *Magazine, Consumer.*
Published by: Days Inns Worldwide, Inc., One Sylvan Way, Parsippany, NJ 07054. TEL 973-428-9700, FAX 973-496-2177. Pub. Robyn Duskin. Circ: 250,000 (controlled).

338.4791 CAN ISSN 1910-829X
SERVICES A L'INDUSTRIE. Text in French. 2004. a. **Document type:** *Journal, Trade.*
Former titles (until 2006): Formation Continue, Service-Conseils, Formation en Entreprise Ateliers Professionnels, Demarrage d'Entreprise (1910-8281); (until 2005): Tourisme, Hotellerie, Restauration, Institutions (1713-3572)
Published by: L' Institut de Tourisme et d'Hotellerie du Quebec, 3535, rue Saint-Denis, Montreal, PQ H2X 3P1, Canada. TEL 514-282-5108, 800-361-5111, FAX 514-873-5008, http://www.ithq.qc.ca/fr/index.php.

914 ITA ISSN 0040-6295
SETTIMANA A ROMA/SEMAINE A ROME/WEEK IN ROME. Text in Italian. 1948. m. EUR 34 (effective 2009). adv. illus. **Document type:** *Magazine, Consumer.*
Published by: Pragma Edizioni, Via Cernaia, 23, Roma, 00185, Italy. info@pragmaedizioni.it. Circ: 30,000.

910.202 PRT ISSN 1646-0464
SETUBAL, GUIA DE EVENTOS. Text in Portuguese. 200?. m. **Document type:** *Guide, Consumer.*
Published by: Camara Municipal de Setubal, Praca de Brocage, Setubal, 2901-866, Portugal. TEL 351-265-541500, FAX 351-265-541621, http://www.mun-setubal.pt.

910.202 CHN
SHANDONG LUYOU/TRAVEL IN SHANDONG. Text in Chinese. bi-m.
Published by: Shandong Sheng Luyou Ju/Shandong Provincial Bureau of Tourism, No 26 Jing 10 Lu, Jinan, Shandong, 250014, China. TEL 615858. Ed. Sun Chuanyuan.

338.4 CHN
SHANGLU DAOBAO. Text in Chinese. w. CNY 204 (effective 2004). **Document type:** *Consumer.*
Formerly: Jiaotong Luyou Bao
Related titles: Online - full content ed.
Published by: Guangzhou Ribao Baoye Jituan/Guangzhou Daily Newspaper Group, 10, Renmin Zhonglu Tongle Lu, Guangzhou, 510121, China. TEL 86-20-81883088.

338.4 330 CHN ISSN 1673-8551
SHANGWU LUXING/BUSINESS TRAVEL. Text in Chinese. 2007. m. CNY 240 (effective 2009). **Document type:** *Magazine, Trade.*
Published by: Nanfang Baoye Chuanmei Jituan, 21 Shijibao Xi/Nanfangdaily Media Group, 21st Centry News Group, 18/F, 289, Guangzhou Dadao Zhong, Guangzhou, 510601, China. TEL 86-20-87372290, http://www.21cbh.com/.

916.8 ZAF
SHELL TOURIST GUIDE TO SOUTH AFRICA. Text in English. a. ZAR 4.40. adv.
Published by: Chris van Rensburg Publications (Pty) Ltd., PO Box 29159, Melville, Johannesburg 2109, South Africa.

910.2 USA ISSN 1559-940X
F232.S5
THE SHENANDOAH VALLEY & MOUNTAINS OF THE VIRGINIAS; an explorer's guide. Variant title: Shenandoah Valley. Text in English. 2005 (Apr.). irreg. USD 19.95 per issue (effective 2008). 464 p./no.; **Document type:** *Guide, Consumer.* **Description:** Offers historical insight, outdoor adventure and all the information most travelers need to plan and enjoy their journey.
Published by: The Countryman Press (Subsidiary of: W.W. Norton & Co., Inc.), PO Box 748, Woodstock, VT 05091. TEL 802-457-4826, 800-245-4151, FAX 802-457-1678, countrymanpress@wwnorton.com. **Dist. by:** W.W. Norton & Co., Inc., 500 5th Ave, New York, NY 10110.

910.91 USA ISSN 1932-9113
SHERMAN'S TRAVEL. Text in English. 2006. q. USD 11.95 (effective 2008). adv. **Document type:** *Magazine, Consumer.* **Description:** Features tips and articles about the best values in where to stay, shop and eat when traveling.
Published by: Sherman's Travel LLC, 255 W 36th St, Ste 1206, New York, NY 10018. TEL 646-467-8100, info@shermanstravel.com. Ed. John Galvin. Pub. James Sherman. adv.: color page USD 23,650; trim 9 x 10.875. Circ: 148,000 (paid); 52,000 (controlled).

917.64 USA ISSN 1535-8232
F394.A93
SHIFRA STEIN'S DAY TRIPS FROM AUSTIN; getaway ideas for the local traveler. Variant title: Day Trips from Austin. Text in English. biennial, latest 2007, 5th ed. USD 14.95 per issue (effective 2008). **Document type:** *Guide, Consumer.* **Description:** Describes hundreds of fascinating and exciting things to do, see and discover right in your own backyard.
Supersedes in part (in 2000): Shifra Stein's Day Trips from San Antonio and Austin
Published by: The Globe Pequot Press, Inc., 246 Goose Ln, PO Box 480, Guilford, CT 06437. TEL 203-458-4500, 888-249-7586, FAX 203-458-4603, 800-820-2329, info@globepequot.com, http://www.globepequot.com.

917.784 910.91 USA ISSN 1538-4993
F474.K23
SHIFRA STEIN'S DAY TRIPS FROM KANSAS CITY; getaway ideas for the local traveler. Text in English. 1998. biennial, latest 2008, 15th ed. USD 12.95 per issue (effective 2008). **Document type:** *Guide, Consumer.*
Formerly: Getaways Less than 2 Hours Away from Kansas City

TU

Published by: The Globe Pequot Press, Inc., 246 Goose Ln, PO Box 480, Guilford, CT 06437. TEL 203-458-4500, 888-249-7586, FAX 203-458-4603, 800-820-2329, info@globepequot.com, http://www.globepequot.com.

917.91 910.91 USA ISSN 1543-0499
F809.3
SHIFRA STEIN'S DAY TRIPS FROM PHOENIX, TUCSON, AND FLAGSTAFF; getaway ideas for the local traveler. Text in English. 1986. biennial, latest 2008, 10th ed. USD 14.95 per issue (effective 2008). **Document type:** *Guide, Consumer.*
Published by: The Globe Pequot Press, Inc., 246 Goose Ln, PO Box 480, Guilford, CT 06437. TEL 203-458-4500, 888-249-7586, FAX 203-458-4601, 800-820-2329, http://www.globepequot.com.

917.64 USA ISSN 1545-0333
F394.S23
SHIFRA STEIN'S DAY TRIPS FROM SAN ANTONIO; getaways less than two hours away. Variant title: Day Trips from San Antonio. Text in English. biennial, latest 2006, 3rd ed. USD 12.95 per issue (effective 2008). **Document type:** *Guide, Consumer.* **Description:** Describes hundreds of fascinating and exciting things to do, see and discover right in your own backyard.
Supersedes in part (in 2000): Shifra Stein's Day Trips from San Antonio and Austin
Published by: The Globe Pequot Press, Inc., 246 Goose Ln, PO Box 480, Guilford, CT 06437. TEL 203-458-4500, 888-249-7586, FAX 203-458-4603, 800-820-2329, info@globepequot.com, http://www.globepequot.com.

SHIPPING AND TOURISM. *see* TRANSPORTATION—Ships And Shipping

910.91 CHN ISSN 1671-9700
SHISHANG LUYOU/NATIONAL GEOGRAPHIC TRAVELER. Text in Chinese. 2000. m. CNY 200 (effective 2008). **Document type:** *Magazine, Consumer.*
Formerly (until 2002): Shishang Zhongguo Luyou
Related titles: Online - full text ed.
Published by: Trends Communication Co. Ltd., 23/F, Trends Bldg., 9, Guanghua Rd., Beijing, 100020, China. http://www.trends.com.cn/. Circ: 38,000 (controlled).

910.202 USA
SHOESTRING TRAVEL E-ZINE. Text in English. 1994. m. adv. **Document type:** *Newsletter, Consumer.* **Description:** Focuses on how people can travel inexpensively.
Media: Online - full text.
Published by: Strategic Publications, 2784 Heatherwood Court, Clearwater, FL 34621. Ed. Eric S Adler. Adv. contact Eric Adler.

917.5 USA
SHORE JOURNAL. Text in English. 1995. w. **Description:** Covers the lifestyle of the people of the Delmarva Peninsula.
Media: Online - full text.
Address: 8004 Greenbriar Swamp Road, Salisbury, MD 21801. TEL 410-548-3481. Ed. Charles Paparella.

910.202 GBR
SHORT BREAKS & HOLIDAYS. Text in English. 2004. q. free to qualified personnel (effective 2009). adv. back issues avail. **Document type:** *Magazine, Trade.* **Description:** Covers the selling of short vacations from the UK.
Former titles (until 2005): Short Breaks Worldwide; Selling Short Breaks
Related titles: Online - full text ed.: free (effective 2009).
Published by: B M I Publications Limited, Suffolk House, George St, Croydon, Surrey CR9 1SR, United Kingdom. TEL 44-20-86497233, FAX 44-20-86497234, sales@bmipublications.com, http://www.bmipublications.com. Ed., Adv. contact Steve Hartridge. Pub. Sally Parker. page GBP 2,750; trim 170 x 225. Circ: 16,500.

917.9313 USA
SHOWBIZ MAGAZINE. Text in English. 1972. w. USD 89.99 domestic; USD 273.99 in Canada & Mexico; USD 499.99 elsewhere (effective 2005). adv. **Document type:** *Magazine, Consumer.* **Description:** Guide to entertainment, dining and gaming in Las Vegas, Nevada.
Published by: ShowBiz Weekly, 2290 Corporate Circle Dr. Ste 250, Henderson, NV 89074. TEL 702-383-7185, FAX 702-383-1089, Showbiz@lasvegassun.com, http://www.lasvegassun.com. Ed. Mike Berg. Pub. Brian Greenspun. Adv. contact Kim Armenta. Circ: 142,000.

915.104 CHN ISSN 1005-3115
SICHOU ZHI LU/SILK ROAD. Text in Chinese; Abstracts in English. 1992. bi-m. (plus 2 special issues). USD 124.80 (effective 2009). illus. **Document type:** *Academic/Scholarly.* **Description:** Presents the natural landscape, folklores, customs, and tourist spots of the Silk Road. Also covers its history, culture and economic development.
Related titles: Online - full text ed.
—East View.
Published by: (Gansu Sichou zhi Lu Xuehui), Sichou zhi Lu Zazhishe, 805 Anning Donglu, Lanzhou, Gansu 730070, China. TEL 86-931-797-1567. Ed., R&P Chengjia Ji. Adv. contact Jinbao Liu. Circ: 10,000. **Dist. overseas by:** China International Book Trading Corp, 35 Chegongzhuang Xilu, Haidian District, PO Box 399, Beijing 100044, China. **Co-sponsor:** Gansu Wenhua Kaogu Ju, Xibei Shifan Daxue.

910.202 SGP
SIGNATURE. Text in English. m. adv.
Published by: Signature Publishing Pty. Ltd., 2-201 Merlin Place, Beach Rd, Singapore, Singapore. Ed. Filipina Elizabeth Reyes. Circ: 32,000.

910.202 JPN
SIGNATURE. Text in Japanese. 1961. m. JPY 4,800. adv. bk.rev. **Document type:** *Consumer.*
Published by: Diners Club of Japan, Senshu Bldg, 13-7 Shibuya 1-chome, Shibuya-ku, Tokyo, 150-0002, Japan. TEL 81-3-3499-1311, FAX 81-3-3352-6415, TELEX 2423066 DCTRVLJ. Ed. Yoichiro Akashi. Circ: 350,000.

916 KEN
SIGNATURE. Text in English. 1982. bi-m. KES 55. adv. bk.rev. illus. cum.index. **Document type:** *Journal, Consumer.*
Address: Diners Club Africa, PO Box 30403, Nairobi, Kenya. TEL 254-2-727-2438, FAX 254-2-723747, TELEX 22554. Ed. Carole McNab. Circ: 8,000.

910.202 GRC
SIGNATURE EXCLUSIVE. Text in Greek. bi-m. membership. adv.
Formerly (until 1989): Signature
Published by: Diners Club of Greece, S.A., PO Box 10, Athens, Greece. Circ: 100,000 (controlled).

SIGNPOST FOR NORTHWEST TRAILS. *see* SPORTS AND GAMES—Outdoor Life

910.09 ITA ISSN 1123-7058
SIKANIA. Text in English, Italian. 1985. m. EUR 30 domestic; EUR 93 foreign (effective 2009). adv. back issues avail. **Document type:** *Magazine, Consumer.* **Description:** For tourists in Sicily and Sicilian emigrants all over the world. Covers travel, geography and history of the region.
Former titles (until 1992): Ciao Sicilia What's on.. (1123-704X); (until 1986): Ciao Palermo What's on.. (1123-7031)
Published by: Krea Srl, Piazza Don Bosco 6, Palermo, PA 90142, Italy. TEL 39-091-543506, FAX 39-091-6373378, info@sikania.it, http://www.sikania.it. Circ: 12,000.

910.4 FIN ISSN 1235-2640
SILJA MAGAZINE. Text in Finnish. 1983. 3/yr. **Document type:** *Consumer.*
Formerly (until 1991): Marina (0784-5480)
Published by: Helsinki Media Company Oy, PL 2, Helsinki, 00040, Finland. TEL 358-9-1201, FAX 358-9-120-5988. Circ: 10,000.

SINGAPORE SURVEY OF OVERSEAS VISITORS. *see* TRAVEL AND TOURISM—Abstracting, Bibliographies, Statistics

919 SGP
SINGAPORE TOURISM NEWS. Text in English. 1964. bi-m. free. adv. illus. **Document type:** *Newsletter, Trade.*
Former titles (until 1997): Singapore Travel (0129-5020); (until 1978): Singapore Travel News (0037-5713)
Published by: Singapore Tourism Board, Tourism Court, 1 Orchard Spring Lane, Singapore, 247729, Singapore. TEL 65-6-7366622, FAX 65-6-7369423, http://app.stb.gov.sg/asp/index.asp?. Circ: 30,000.

338.47915957 GBR ISSN 1747-8995
SINGAPORE TOURISM REPORT. Text in English. 2005. q. EUR 820, USD 1,030 combined subscription (print & email eds.) (effective 2010). **Document type:** *Report, Trade.* **Description:** Covers independent forecasts and competitive intelligence on the Singaporean tourism industry.
Related titles: E-mail ed.
Indexed: B01, P34.
Published by: Business Monitor International Ltd., Senator House, 85 Queen Victoria St, London, EC4V 4AB, United Kingdom. TEL 44-20-72480468, FAX 44-20-72480467, subs@businessmonitor.com.

917.2 CAN
ST. MAARTEN NIGHTS. Text in English. q. free complimentary copy avail. only in St. Maarten. **Document type:** *Journal, Consumer.*
Published by: Nights Publications, 1831 Rene Levesque Blvd W, Montreal, PQ H3H 1R4, Canada. FAX 514-931-6273, editor@nightspublications.com. Ed. Stephen Trotter.

910.2 DEU
SKAL JOURNAL GERMANY. Text in German. 4/yr. EUR 12; EUR 3.10 newsstand/cover (effective 2008). adv. **Document type:** *Magazine, Trade.*
Published by: Muehlens Media GmbH, Robert-Bosch-Str 10, Maintal, 63477, Germany. TEL 49-6181-94340, FAX 49-6181-45719, info@Muehlens-Media.de, http://www.muehlens-media.de. Ed. Stefanie Kramer. Adv. contact Ursula Muehlens. B&W page EUR 1,260, color page EUR 2,200; trim 184 x 265. Circ: 5,000 (paid and controlled).

338.4791 GBR ISSN 2045-502X
▼ **SKYHOST**; Zimbabwe in motion. Text in English. 2010. q. adv. back issues avail. **Document type:** *Magazine, Consumer.* **Description:** Covers all aspects of travel in Africa.
Related titles: Online - full text ed.: ISSN 2045-5038. free (effective 2010).
Published by: Travel Africa Ltd., 4 Rycote Ln Farm, Milton Common, Oxford, Oxfordshire OX9 2NZ, United Kingdom. TEL 44-1844-278883, FAX 44-1844-278893. Ed., Pub., Adv. contact Craig Rix.

SLOAN'S GREEN GUIDE TO ANTIQUING IN NEW ENGLAND. *see* ANTIQUES

SLOW; the international herald of taste. *see* FOOD AND FOOD INDUSTRIES

338.4791 658 914 NLD ISSN 1871-2541
SMART TRAVELLER. Cover title: Traveller. Text in Dutch. 2005. q.
Incorporated (in 2007): Advanced Traveller (1874-1622); Which was formerly (until 2006): Advanced Traveller Magazine (1571-1919)
Published by: RTL Nederland, Postbus 15016, Hilversum, 1200 TV, Netherlands. TEL 31-35-6718718, FAX 31-35-6236892.

917.6 USA
THE SMOKIES MAGAZINE. Text in English. 1996. w. **Document type:** *Magazine, Consumer.* **Description:** Covers the people, culture and commerce of the Great Smoky Mountains, and other areas in Appalachia.
Media: Online - full text.
Published by: Smokies Magazine, R R 2, Box 458, Bluefield, VA 24605-9308. Ed. Victor M O'Dell.

914 338.4791 NLD ISSN 1875-1903
SNP.NL MAGAZINE. Variant title: Stichting Natuur Projecten Nederland Magazine. Text in Dutch. 2007. 5/yr. free (effective 2008).
Published by: S N P Natuurreizen, Postbus 1270, Nijmegen, 6501 BG, Netherlands. TEL 31-24-3277000, FAX 31-24-3277099, http://www.snp.nl.

941 GBR ISSN 1752-6450
SO BRITISH. Text in English. 2005. s-a.
Published by: VisitBritain, Thames Tower, Black Rd, London, W6 9EL, United Kingdom. TEL 44-20-88469000, FAX 44-20-85630302, http://www.visitbritain.com/.

SOFIA NEWS; weekly for politics, economics, culture, tourism and sport. *see* POLITICAL SCIENCE

910.09 USA
SOJOURNS. Text in English. 19??. s-a. **Document type:** *Magazine, Consumer.* **Description:** Features stories about interesting places to visit in North America, published for and circulated to members of banking check clubs as a part of bank customers' benefit package.
Published by: Journal Communications, Inc., 725 Cool Springs Blvd, Ste 400, Franklin, TN 37067. TEL 615-771-0080, info@jnlcom.com, http://www.jnlcom.com.

917 333.7 USA ISSN 1558-7738
QH104.5.C58
SOJOURNS (MOAB). Text in English. 2006. s-a. USD 9.95 newsstand/cover (effective 2007). **Document type:** *Magazine, Consumer.* **Description:** Devoted to the cultural and natural history of the Colorado Plateau and the Grand Canyon area.
Published by: Peaks, Plateaus & Canyons Association, 3031 South Highway 191, Moab, UT 84532. TEL 435-259-6003, FAX 435-259-8263, http://www.ppcaweb.org.

910.09 CUB
SOL DE CUBA. Text in Spanish. 1983. q.
Related titles: French ed.; English ed.
Published by: Instituto Nacional del Turismo, Malecon y G,, Vedado, La Habana, Cuba. TEL 7-32-9881. Ed. Aurelio Pedraso. Circ: 200,000.

910.202 USA ISSN 0835-1805
LE SOLEIL DE LA FLORIDE. Text in French. 1983. m. USD 19.95 (effective 2008). adv. **Document type:** *Newspaper.* **Description:** Describes activities and sights in Florida and the French Caribbean for French-speaking tourists and travelers.
Published by: Worldwide Publications No. 1, Inc., 2117 Hollywood Blvd, Hollywood, FL 33020. TEL 954-922-1800, FAX 954-922-8965. Eds. Louis S St Laurent III, Yves Beauchamp, Robert Leblond. Circ: 30,000.

917 051 USA ISSN 1937-0377
SONOMA. Text in English. 2006. q. USD 18 (effective 2007). **Document type:** *Magazine, Consumer.* **Description:** Profiles events and people in the Sonoma Valley.
Related titles: Online - full text ed.: ISSN 1937-0385.
Published by: Sonoma Index-Tribune, 117 W Napa St, Sonoma, CA 95476. TEL 707-938-2111. Ed. Manuel Merjil.

910.202 GBR ISSN 1363-7371
DT758
SOUTH AFRICA HANDBOOK (YEAR). Text in English. 1996. a. GBP 16.99 per issue (effective 2010). adv. maps. **Document type:** *Handbook/Manual/Guide, Consumer.* **Description:** Covers all the basics from where to stay and where to eat to cycling, walking and how to get around the South Africa.
—CCC.
Published by: Footprint Handbooks Ltd., 6 Riverside Ct, Lower Bristol Rd, Bath, Avon BA2 3DZ, United Kingdom. TEL 44-1225-469141, FAX 44-1225-469461, wwwinfo@footprintbooks.com.

918 USA ISSN 0889-7891
F2224
SOUTH AMERICAN EXPLORER. Text in English. 1977. q. USD 22 domestic; USD 29 foreign (effective 2000). adv. bk.rev. illus. back issues avail. **Document type:** *Magazine, Consumer.* **Description:** Features articles on exploration, scientific enquiry, accounts of travel and trekking in Latin America.
Indexed: AICP.
Published by: South American Explorers Club, 126 Indian Creek Rd, Ithaca, NY 14850. TEL 607-277-0488, 800-274-0568, FAX 607-277-6122. Ed., R&P Don Montague. Adv. contact Vicky Posso Williamson. Circ: 8,000 (paid).

918 USA
SOUTH AMERICAN EXPLORER'S CLUB CATALOG. Text in English. a. **Document type:** *Magazine, Consumer.* **Description:** Features a variety of books about Central and South America as well as videos, music and South American merchandise.
Published by: South American Explorers Club, 126 Indian Creek Rd, Ithaca, NY 14850. TEL 800-274-0568.

910.202 GBR ISSN 0309-4529
F1401
SOUTH AMERICAN HANDBOOK (YEAR). Text in English. 19??. a. GBP 22.50 per issue (effective 2010). adv. illus.; maps. **Document type:** *Handbook/Manual/Guide, Consumer.* **Description:** Covers all the basics from where to stay and where to eat to cycling, walking and how to get around the South American.
Formerly (until 1924): Anglo-South Handbook
Indexed: RASB.
—CCC.
Published by: Footprint Handbooks Ltd., 6 Riverside Ct, Lower Bristol Rd, Bath, Avon BA2 3DZ, United Kingdom. TEL 44-1225-469141, FAX 44-1225-469461, wwwinfo@footprintbooks.com.

917.83 910.2 USA ISSN 1934-5828
F651.6
SOUTH DAKOTA CURIOSITIES. Text in English. 2007. triennial, latest 2007, 1st ed. USD 14.95 per issue (effective 2008). back issues avail. **Document type:** *Guide, Consumer.* **Description:** Provides information about the wildest, wackiest, most outrageous people, places and things in South Dakota.
Published by: The Globe Pequot Press, Inc., 246 Goose Ln, PO Box 480, Guilford, CT 06437. TEL 203-458-4500, 888-249-7586, FAX 203-458-4603, 800-820-2329, info@globepequot.com, http://www.globepequot.com.

910.91 USA
SOUTH DAKOTA VACATION GUIDE. Text in English. 1976. a. free. **Document type:** *Directory, Consumer.*
Published by: Black Hills, Badlands, and Lakes Association, 1851 Discovery Cir, Rapid City, SD 57701-7900. TEL 605-355-3600, FAX 605-355-3601, http://www.blackhillsattractions.com. Ed. Bill Honerkamp. Circ: 500,000.

917.59 USA ISSN 1940-9850
F309.3
SOUTH FLORIDA (WOODSTOCK); an explorer's guide. Text in English. 2006. irreg. USD 19.95 per issue domestic; USD 28 per issue in Canada (effective 2008). **Document type:** *Guide, Consumer.*
Published by: The Countryman Press (Subsidiary of: W.W. Norton & Co., Inc.), PO Box 748, Woodstock, VT 05091. TEL 802-457-4826, 800-245-4151, FAX 802-457-1678, countrymanpress@wwnorton.com, http://www.countrymanpress.com.

919.504 USA ISSN 1085-2700
DU15
SOUTH PACIFIC HANDBOOK. Text in English. 1979. irreg. **Document type:** *Handbook/Manual/Guide, Consumer.*

—CCC.
Published by: Avalon Travel Publishing, 1700 4th St, Berkeley, CA 94710. TEL 510-595-3664, avalon.publicity@perseusbooks.com, http://www.avalontravelbooks.com.

910 GBR
SOUTH WEST COAST PATH; the complete guide to the longest national trail. Text in English. 1986. a. GBP 10.50 per vol. to non-members; free to members (effective 2009). 144 p./no.; back issues avail. **Document type:** *Directory.* **Description:** Contains news about path alterations plus coast path walkers' letters, new book reviews and articles of special interest to coast path walkers.
Published by: The South West Coast Path Association, Bowker House, Lee Mill Bridge, Ivybridge, Devon, PL21 9EF, United Kingdom. TEL 44-1752-896237, FAX 44-1752-893654, info@swcp.org.uk, http://www.swcp.org.uk.

910.91 USA
SOUTHEASTERN ADVENTURES. Text in English. 2001. bi-m. USD 20; USD 3.99 newsstand/cover (effective 2002). **Document type:** *Magazine, Consumer.*
Published by: Adventure South Publication, 2501 E Piedmont Rd, Ste 160, Marietta, GA 30062. TEL 770-575-5850, larry@southeasternadventures.com, http://www.southeasternadventure.com. Ed. Kathy Davis. Pub. Larry Hutcheson.

338.479 ZAF
SOUTHERN AFRICAN TOURISM UPDATE; for organisers of tours to Southern Africa. Text in English. 1991 (Dec.). m. adv. illus. **Document type:** *Journal, Trade.* **Description:** Informs overseas tour and travel organizers of tourism developments and projects throughout Southern Africa.
Published by: (Southern African Tourism Services Association), Travel and Trade Publishing (Pty) Ltd., PO Box 662, Auckland Park, Johannesburg 2006, South Africa. TEL 27-11-726-3036, FAX 27-11-726-3994, TELEX 499 JOHANNESBURG. Ed. Penny Marsh. Adv. contact Lorna Ichilcik. B&W page ZAR 8,827. Circ: 2,788 (paid).

SOUTHERN AFRICAN TOURISM UPDATE'S BUYERS' GUIDE & WHO'S WHO FOR SOUTHERN AFRICAN TOURISM PRODUCTS. *see* BUSINESS AND ECONOMICS—Trade And Industrial Directories

916.8 ZAF
SOUTHERN AFRICAN TRAVEL GUIDE. Text in English. 1971. a. ZAR 52.90 (effective 2001). adv. bk.rev. **Document type:** *Handbook/Manual/Guide, Consumer.*
Formerly: Travel Guide, S.A.
Published by: Promco (Pty) Ltd., 12 Annerley Rd, Rosebank, Cape Province 7700, South Africa. TEL 27-21-6866341, FAX 27-21-6866332. Ed. L D Solomon. R&P, Adv. contact I R Solomon.

910 ZAF
SOUTHERN AFRICA'S TRAVEL NEWS WEEKLY; the legendary builder of travel brands and product knowledge in the Southern African travel trade. Abbreviated title: T N W. Text in English. 1970. w. ZAR 215. adv. **Document type:** *Magazine, Trade.* **Description:** Provides timely news and information of relevance to the Southern African travel industry.
Formerly: Southern Africa's Travel News
Published by: Travel and Trade Publishing (Pty) Ltd., PO Box 662, Auckland Park, Johannesburg 2006, South Africa. TEL 27-11-726-3036, FAX 27-11-726-3994. Ed. Leona Marsh. Adv. contact Carmel Levinrad. B&W page ZAR 10,800, color page ZAR 14,100; trim 222 x 317. Circ: 6,086 (controlled).

917.94 USA ISSN 1547-8920
F867
SOUTHERN CALIFORNIA CURIOSITIES; quirky characters, roadside oddities, & other offbeat stuff. Text in English. 2004. biennial, latest 2004, 1st ed. USD 13.95 per issue (effective 2008). **Document type:** *Guide, Consumer.* **Description:** Provides tourist information about Golden State.
Published by: The Globe Pequot Press, Inc., 246 Goose Ln, PO Box 480, Guilford, CT 06437. TEL 203-458-4500, 888-249-7586, FAX 203-458-4603, 800-820-2329, info@globepequot.com, http://www.globepequot.com.

917 USA ISSN 0038-3902
SOUTHERN CALIFORNIA GUIDE; the current directory of restaurants, art galleries, hotels, motels, entertainment, shopping, sightseeing, tourist attractions. Text in English, Japanese. 1919. m. USD 12. bk.rev. **Document type:** *Magazine, Consumer.*
Related titles: Online - full text ed.
Published by: Westworld Publishing Corp., 11385 Exposition B1, 102, Los Angeles, CA 90064. TEL 213-391-8255. Ed., Pub. Valerie Summers. Circ: 45,000 (controlled).

917.3 USA ISSN 2151-9854
▼ **SOUTHERN HOSPITALITY MAGAZINE: TRAVELER.** Text in English. 2010 (Mar.). q. USD 13 (effective 2011). adv. **Document type:** *Magazine, Consumer.* **Description:** Features information on traveling in the Southern United States.
Published by: Great Minds Inc, 8275 Hunters Ridge Trail, Tallahassee, FL 32312. TEL 850-386-7401, FAX 850-894-2210.

SOUTHERN JOURNAL. *see* HISTORY—History Of North And South America

910.09 051 USA ISSN 1074-0945
SOUTHERN LIVING VACATIONS. Text in English. 1984. 3/yr. USD 4.99 newsstand/cover domestic; USD 6.50 newsstand/cover in Canada (effective 2007). adv. charts; illus.; tr.lit. back issues avail. **Document type:** *Magazine, Consumer.* **Description:** Travel magazine for tourists visiting the Southern United States.
Former titles (until 1994): Southern Living Travel South (1041-3642); (until 1988): Southern Travel; Supersedes (in 1986): Travel South (0743-6629)
—CCC.
Published by: Southern Progress Corp. (Subsidiary of: Time Warner Inc.), 2100 Lakeshore Dr, Birmingham, AL 35209. TEL 205-445-6000, 800-366-4712, FAX 205-445-8655, http://www.southernprogress.com. Ed. Karen Lingo. Pubs. Greg Keys, Rich Smyth. R&P Jason Burnett TEL 205-877-6731. Circ: 200,000. **Subscr. to:** PO Box 830611, Birmingham, AL 35201.

910.91 USA
SOUTHERN NEW MEXICO ONLINE MAGAZINE. Text in English. m. adv. illus. reprints avail. **Document type:** *Magazine, Consumer.* **Description:** Informs readers on attractions and activities in southern New Mexico. Seeks to capture the flavor of the region.
Formerly: Southwest New Mexico Online Magazine
Media: Online - full text.
Published by: Carla De Marco Ed.& Pub., 1701 Virginia St, Silver City, NM 88061. TEL 505-538-8956, FAX 505-538-8956. Ed., Pub., R&P, Adv. contact Carla Demarco.

910.09 ARG ISSN 0327-6597
SOUTHERN SOUTH AMERICA. Text in Spanish. q. **Document type:** *Bulletin, Consumer.*
Published by: Zagier & Urruty Publicaciones, P.O. Box 94, Sucursal 19, Buenos Aires, 1419, Argentina. TEL 54-114-5721050, FAX 54-114-5725766.

910.202 AUS
SOUTHERN SUN. Text in English. 1985. m. back issues avail.
Published by: Southern Publishers Pty. Ltd., 34 Auckland St, Bega, NSW 2550, Australia. **Subscr. to:** PO Box 411, Batemans Bay, NSW 2536, Australia.

914 ROM
SOUTHERN TRANSYLVANIA IN YOUR POCKET. Text in English. a. USD 5 newsstand/cover (effective 2002). adv. **Document type:** *Magazine, Consumer.*
Published by: Bucharest In Your Pocket, Calea Victoriei 32-34, Sc C, 3rd Fl., Apt. 110, PO Box 1-544, Bucharest, 76000, Romania. TEL 40-1-3147923, FAX 40-1-3147924.

917.04 USA ISSN 1093-9059
TX907.3.S68
THE SOUTH'S BEST BED & BREAKFASTS. Text in English. 1992. irreg. USD 15.
Formerly: Fodor's Bed and Breakfasts and Country Inns and Other Weekend Pleasures: The South (1069-899X)
Published by: Fodor's Travel Publications, Inc. (Subsidiary of: Random House Inc.), 1745 Broadway, 15th Fl, New York, NY 10019. TEL 212-572-2313, editors@fodors.com, http://www.fodors.com. **Dist. by:** Random House Inc.

917 USA ISSN 1521-7299
TX907.3.S69
THE SOUTHWEST'S BEST BED & BREAKFASTS. Text in English. 1994. irreg. **Document type:** *Directory, Consumer.*
Formerly (until 1995): Fodor's Bed & Breakfasts and Country Inns. The Southwest (1079-1701)
Published by: Fodor's Travel Publications, Inc. (Subsidiary of: Random House Inc.), 1745 Broadway, 15th Fl, New York, NY 10019. TEL 212-572-2313, editors@fodors.com, http://www.fodors.com. Ed. Edie Jarolim.

910.09 CAN ISSN 1186-8848
SPA DESTINATIONS. Text in English. 1992. a. CAD 32 domestic; USD 32 in United States; USD 52 foreign (effective 2000). adv. **Document type:** *Handbook/Manual/Guide, Trade.* **Description:** Offers descriptions of major spas around the world.
Related titles: French ed.: Destinations Spa. ISSN 1186-883X.
Published by: Spa Management Corp., Place d Armes, C P 365, Montreal, PQ H2Y 3H1, Canada. TEL 514-274-0004, FAX 514-274-5884. Ed. Guy J Jonkman. Pub. Anne Bolduc. adv.: page CAD 1,790; trim 11 x 8.5. Circ: 20,000 (controlled).

SPA MAGAZINE. *see* PHYSICAL FITNESS AND HYGIENE

SPACE & CULTURE; the journal. *see* GEOGRAPHY

SPACE DAILY. NEWSLETTER; your portal to space. *see* AERONAUTICS AND SPACE FLIGHT

914.604 USA
SPAIN 21; cultural insights for the twenty first century. Text in English. s-a. USD 10 for 4 nos. (effective 2001). adv. **Document type:** *Magazine, Consumer.* **Description:** Dedicated to sharing the vast cultural insights of Spain with American teachers of Spanish, their students, and any individual or group interested in this wonderful, culturally diverse nation.
Address: 215 E Ridgewood Ave, Ste 201, Ridgewood, NJ 07450. TEL 201-445-2450, 800-272-8674, FAX 201-445-4410. Ed., Pub. Lou Dinnella. adv.: page USD 5,000; trim 8.375 x 10.875.

SPAIN GOURMETOUR; food, wine, and travel quarterly magazine. *see* HOTELS AND RESTAURANTS

SPARTACUS INTERNATIONAL GAY GUIDE. *see* HOMOSEXUALITY

908 306.7662 DEU ISSN 1862-7943
SPARTACUSTRAVELER. Text in German. 2006. bi-m. EUR 18.95; EUR 3.95 newsstand/cover (effective 2009). adv. **Document type:** *Magazine, Consumer.*
Published by: Bruno Gmuender Verlag, Kleiststr 23-26, Berlin, 10787, Germany. TEL 49-30-6150030, FAX 49-30-61500320, info@brunogmuender.com, http://www.brunogmuender.com. adv.: page EUR 1,800; trim 220 x 275. Circ: 25,000 (paid and controlled).

910.202 USA ISSN 0889-7085
SPECIALTY TRAVEL INDEX; directory of special interest travel. Text in English. 1980. s-a. USD 10 domestic; USD 15 in Canada; USD 25 elsewhere (effective 2009). adv. bk.rev. illus. back issues avail.; reprints avail. **Document type:** *Directory, Consumer.* **Description:** Provides an adventure and special-interest travel listing of 600 tour operators, ranging from expeditions to cultural and sports tours.
Related titles: Online - full text ed.
Published by: Alpine Hansen Publishers, P O Box 458, San Anselmo, CA 94979-0458. TEL 415-455-1643, 888-624-4030, FAX 415-455-1648. Ed. Risa Weinreb. Pub., R&P C Steen Hansen TEL 415-455-1640. Adv. contact Judith Alpine. Circ: 45,000.

910.09 GBR ISSN 2040-5316
G149
SPHERE. Text in English. 1984. q. GBP 26 domestic; GBP 30 in Europe; USD 60 in United States; GBP 35, USD 70 elsewhere (effective 2009). adv. **Document type:** *Magazine, Consumer.* **Description:** Provides an inspirational mix of luxury, culture and travel.
Formerly (until 2008): Orient-Express Magazine (1350-9012)
Indexed: A22, BRI, CBRI.
—IE, Infotrieve, Ingenta.
Published by: Illustrated London News, 10 Fashion St, London, E1 6PX, United Kingdom. TEL 44-20-74261010, FAX 44-20-74261020, hello@iln.co.uk, http://www.iln.co.uk. adv.: color page GBP 6,150; trim 220 x 290. Circ: 80,000.

914.604 387.7 ESP ISSN 0036-1852
SPIC; revista de turismo. Text in Spanish. 1966. fortn. (21/yr.). USD 250 in Europe; USD 330 in the Americas; USD 530 in Asia. bk.rev. illus. **Document type:** *Magazine, Consumer.*
Indexed: RASB.
Published by: S P I C Ediciones S.A., Sanchez Barcaiztegui, 38 1r Jardin 4, Madrid, 28007, Spain. TEL 34-1-5510126, FAX 34-1-4338354, TELEX 46322 SPIC E. Ed. Lorenzo Herranz Garcia. Adv. contact Olga Las Heras. Circ: 11,500.

917 USA ISSN 1940-5898
SPIRIT OF THE WEST. Text in German. 2007. q. USD 5.50 per issue (effective 2008). adv. **Document type:** *Magazine, Consumer.*
Address: 3104 E Camelback Rd #383, Phoenix, AZ 85016. TEL 305-582-5793.

SPORT AND RECREATION INFORMATION GROUP BULLETIN. *see* LEISURE AND RECREATION

SPORTACCOM; magazine voor realisatie, beheer en onderhoud van sportaccomodaties. *see* SPORTS AND GAMES

SPORTSTRAVEL; team and participant travel. *see* SPORTS AND GAMES

913.919 DEU ISSN 1437-1103
SPOT ON; Dein Sprachmagazin in Easy English. Text in English; Summaries in German. 1999. m. EUR 48; EUR 4.50 newsstand/cover (effective 2011). adv. **Document type:** *Magazine, Consumer.*
Published by: Spotlight Verlag GmbH (Subsidiary of: Verlagsgruppe Georg von Holtzbrinck GmbH), Fraunhoferstr 22, Planegg, 82152, Germany. TEL 49-89-856810, FAX 49-89-85681105, info@spotlight-verlag.de, http://www.spotlight-online.de. Ed. Burkhard Riedel. Adv. contact Axel Zettler. Circ: 30,641 (paid and controlled).

915.04 LKA
SRI LANKA ACCOMMODATION GUIDE. Text in English. s-a. free. adv. charts. **Document type:** *Catalog.*
Formerly: Welcome to Sri Lanka
Published by: (Marketing Division), Ceylon Tourist Board, P O Box 1504, Colombo, 3, Sri Lanka. TEL 437056, FAX 440001. Circ: 10,000.

910.202 GBR ISSN 1363-7975
SRI LANKA HANDBOOK. Text in English. 1996. irreg., latest 2003, 4th ed. GBP 9.99 per issue (effective 2010). adv. **Document type:** *Handbook/Manual/Guide, Consumer.* **Description:** Covers all the basics from where to stay and where to eat to cycling, walking and how to get around the Sri Lanka.
—CCC.
Published by: Footprint Handbooks Ltd., 6 Riverside Ct, Lower Bristol Rd, Bath, Avon BA2 3DZ, United Kingdom. TEL 44-1225-469141, FAX 44-1225-469461, wwwinfo@footprintbooks.com.

910.202 LKA
SRI LANKA OFFICIAL TOURIST HANDBOOK. Text in English. s-a.
Formerly: Sri Lanka Tourist Information
Published by: (Marketing Division), Ceylon Tourist Board, P O Box 1504, Colombo, 3, Sri Lanka. TEL 437056, FAX 440001. Ed. Florence Ratwalte. Circ: 100,000.

338.47915493 GBR ISSN 1747-9029
SRI LANKA TOURISM REPORT. Text in English. 2005. a. EUR 820, USD 1,030 combined subscription per issue (print & email eds.) (effective 2010). **Document type:** *Report, Trade.* **Description:** Provides industry professionals and strategists, corporate analysts, associations, government departments and regulatory bodies with independent forecasts and competitive intelligence on the Sri Lankan tourism industry.
Related titles: E-mail ed.
Indexed: A15, ABIn, B02, B15, B17, B18, G04, I05, P48, P51, PQC.
Published by: Business Monitor International Ltd., Senator House, 85 Queen Victoria St, London, EC4V 4AB, United Kingdom. TEL 44-20-72480468, FAX 44-20-72480467, subs@businessmonitor.com.

338.4791 DEU ISSN 1869-5345
▼ **ST. GALLER SCHRIFTEN FUER TOURISMUS UND VERKEHR.** Text in German. 2010. irreg., latest vol.2, 2011. price varies. **Document type:** *Monographic series, Academic/Scholarly.*
Published by: Erich Schmidt Verlag GmbH & Co. (Berlin), Genthiner Str 30 G, Berlin, 10785, Germany. TEL 49-30-2500850, FAX 49-30-250085305, vertrieb@esvmedien.de.

910.2 DEU ISSN 1613-9054
STAATSHANDBUCH BREMEN. Text in German. 1956. a. EUR 59 per issue (effective 2009). 140 p./no.; **Document type:** *Government.*
Former titles (until 2004): Die Bundesrepublik Deutschland. Staatshandbuch Bremen (Year) (1434-2278); (until 1992): Die Bundesrepublik Deutschland. Landesausgabe Land Freie Hansestadt Bremen (0723-3752); (until 1964): Die Bundesrepublik. Teilausgabe Land Freie Hansestadt Bremen (0933-5587); Which superseded in part (in 1959): Die Bundesrepublik (0933-5528); Which was formed by the merger of (1938-1956): Taschenbuch fuer Verwaltungsbeamte (0933-551X); (1953-1956): Handbuch fuer die Bundesrepublik Deutschland (0431-5634)
Published by: Carl Heymanns Verlag KG (Subsidiary of: Wolters Kluwer Deutschland GmbH), Luxemburger Str 449, Cologne, 50939, Germany. TEL 49-221-943730, FAX 49-221-94373901, marketing@heymanns.com, http://www.heymanns.com.

910.09 CAN
STAR SERVICE. Text in English. 1960. base vol. plus q. updates. looseleaf. CAD 332, USD 210; CAD 455, USD 288 combined subscription for both print & online eds. (effective 2002). **Document type:** *Directory.* **Description:** Provides detailed critical reviews of hotels and cruise ships throughout the world, written by freelance travel writers.
Former titles: A B C Star Service; S T A R Service
Related titles: Online - full text ed.: CAD 289, USD 189 (effective 2002).
Published by: New Concepts Canada, 7311 Schaefer Ave, Richmond, BC V6Y 2W7, Canada. TEL 604-272-1174, 888-975-7888, FAX 604-272-4574, sales@newconcepts.ca. Circ: 6,600.

STARGREEN; the magazine for the modern sentimentalist. *see* MUSIC

T U

910.2 387.1 USA ISSN 1541-8987
TX907.2
STAYING AT A LIGHTHOUSE; America's romantic and historic lighthouse inns. Text in English. 2003. irreg., latest 2005, 2nd ed. USD 11.95 per issue (effective 2008). **Document type:** *Guide, Consumer.*
Description: Provides information about the spectacular scenery, historic surroundings, and a rare opportunity to experience the serenity and simplicity of a keeper's life.
Published by: The Globe Pequot Press, Inc., 246 Goose Ln, PO Box 480, Guilford, CT 06437. TEL 203-458-4500, 888-249-7586, FAX 203-458-4603, 800-820-2329, info@globepequot.com, http://www.globepequot.com.

338.479 USA ISSN 1535-9670
G153.4
STERN'S GUIDE TO THE CRUISE VACATION. Variant title: Cruise Vacation. Guide to the Cruise Vacation. Text in English. 1974. a. USD 26 per issue (effective 2009). back issues avail. **Document type:** *Guide, Consumer.* **Description:** cruise guide.
Published by: Pelican Publishing Co., 1000 Burmaster St., Gretna, LA 70053. TEL 504-368-1175, 800-843-1724, FAX 504-368-1195, editorial@pelicanpub.com, http://www.pelicanpub.com.

STEUER- UND RECHTSBRIEF TOURISTIK; Der aktuelle Informationsdienst fuer Touristik, Business Travel und Hotellerie. *see* BUSINESS AND ECONOMICS—Public Finance, Taxation

STI OG VARDE. *see* SPORTS AND GAMES—Outdoor Life

948.56 SWE
STOCKHOLM IN YOUR POCKET. Text in English. 5/yr. USD 25; USD 5 newsstand/cover (effective 2002). adv. **Document type:** *Magazine, Consumer.*
Address: Taptogatan 6, Stockholm, 11526, Sweden. TEL 46-8-6608913, FAX 46-8-6602655, http://www.inyourpocket.com.

917.504 USA
STRAND MAGAZINE (MYRTLE BEACH). Text in English. 1986. 3/yr. free local; USD 4.50 per issue out of area (effective 2009). adv. 72 p./no. 2 cols./p.; **Document type:** *Magazine, Consumer.* **Description:** Covers activities, golf, theater, dining, and shopping throughout South Carolina's Grand Strand.
Address: 1357 21st Ave N, Ste 102, Myrtle Beach, SC 29577. TEL 843-626-8911, FAX 843-626-6452, info@strandmedia.com. Ed. Leslie Moore TEL 843-626-8911 ext 223. Pub. Delores Blount TEL 843-626-8911 ext 211. Adv. contact Susan Bryant TEL 843-626-8911 ext 219. Circ: 900,000 (paid and free).

910.202 DEU
STRASSENATLAS DEUTSCHLAND UND EUROPA. Text in German. 1962. a. EUR 9.90 (effective 2006). **Document type:** *Directory.*
Published by: Ravenstein Verlag GmbH, Auf der Krautweide 24, Bad Soden Am Taunus, 65812, Germany. TEL 49-6196-60960, FAX 49-6196-27450. Circ: 450,000 (paid).

910.2 371.8 USA
STUDENT GROUP TOUR MAGAZINE. Text in English. 2004. 3/yr. free to qualified personnel (effective 2011). adv. back issues avail. **Document type:** *Magazine, Consumer.* **Description:** Focuses on educating student travel planners about the wealth of destinations, attractions, activities, and more available to them.
Related titles: Online - full text ed.: free (effective 2011).
Published by: Shoreline Creations, Ltd., 2465 112th Ave, Holland, MI 49424. TEL 616-393-2077, 800-767-3489, FAX 616-393-0085, editor@grouptour.com, http://www.grouptour.com. Ed. Rick Martinez TEL 616-393-2077 ext 107. Pub. Elly DeVries TEL 616-393-2077 ext 130.

910.2 USA ISSN 2154-4905
▼ **STUDENT TRAVEL PLANNING GUIDE.** Text in English. 2010. a. **Document type:** *Guide, Consumer.* **Description:** Includes step-by-step resources for planning better youth trips.
Published by: Premier Tourism Marketing, Inc., 621 Plainfield Rd, Ste 406, Willowbrook, IL 60527. TEL 630-794-0696, FAX 630-794-0652, info@premiertourismmarketing.com, http://www.premiertourismmarketing.com.

910.202 CAN ISSN 1201-9569
STUDENT TRAVELLER. Text in English. 1978. s-a. free. adv. bk.rev.
Formerly (until 1991): Canadian Student Traveller (0706-9758)
Published by: Canadian Federation of Students, 170 Metcalfe St, Ste 500, Ottawa, ON K2P 1P3, Canada. TEL 613-232-7394, FAX 416-977-4796. Ed. Joey Hansen. Pub. Mike Fuller. Circ: 150,000.

STUDIEN ZUR REISELITERATUR- UND IMAGOLOGIEFORSCHUNG. *see* LITERATURE

STUDIES IN PHYSICAL CULTURE AND TOURISM. *see* PHYSICAL FITNESS AND HYGIENE

910.2 808.8 GBR ISSN 1364-5145
G149
➤ **STUDIES IN TRAVEL WRITING.** Text in English. 1997. q. GBP 201 combined subscription in United Kingdom to institutions (print & online eds.); EUR 321, USD 405 combined subscription to institutions (print & online eds.) (effective 2012). back issues avail.; reprint service avail. from PSC. **Document type:** *Journal, Academic/Scholarly.*
Description: Contains a wide range of travel writing essays from scholars in different disciplines working on different historical periods and geographical regions.
Related titles: Online - full text ed.: ISSN 1755-7550. GBP 181 in United Kingdom to institutions; EUR 289, USD 364 to institutions (effective 2012) (from IngentaConnect).
Indexed: AmHI, BrHumI, CA, H07, L05, L06, MLA-IB, SCOPUS, T02.
—IE. **CCC.**
Published by: Routledge (Subsidiary of: Taylor & Francis Group), 4 Park Sq, Milton Park, Abingdon, Oxon OX14 4RN, United Kingdom. TEL 44-20-70176000, FAX 44-20-70176336, journals@routledge.com, http://www.routledge.com.

914.6 USA ISSN 1930-4463
DP402.B24
STYLECITY. BARCELONA. Text in English. 2003. irreg. USD 24.95 per issue (effective 2011). **Document type:** *Guide, Consumer.*
Published by: Thames & Hudson Inc., 500 Fifth Ave, New York, NY 10110. TEL 212-354-3763, 800-233-4830, FAX 212-398-1252, Bookinfo@thames.wwnorton.com.

914 USA ISSN 1941-0638
D909
STYLECITY. EUROPE. Text in English. 2007. irreg. USD 29.95 per issue (effective 2011). **Document type:** *Guide, Consumer.* **Description:** Offers exciting photography, insider knowledge, high design, and visual intelligence.
Published by: Thames & Hudson Inc., 500 Fifth Ave, New York, NY 10110. TEL 212-354-3763, 800-233-4830, FAX 212-398-1252, Bookinfo@thames.wwnorton.com.

914.961 USA ISSN 1930-4455
DR718
STYLECITY. ISTANBUL. Text in English. 2005. irreg. USD 24.95 per issue (effective 2011). **Document type:** *Guide, Consumer.*
Description: Focuses on the vitality and uniqueness of Istanbul.
Published by: Thames & Hudson Inc., 500 Fifth Ave, New York, NY 10110. TEL 212-354-3763, 800-233-4830, FAX 212-398-1252, Bookinfo@thames.wwnorton.com, http://www.thamesandhudsonusa.com/.

910.2 USA ISSN 1559-3800
DC708
STYLECITY. PARIS. Text in English. 2003. irreg., latest 3rd ed. USD 24.95 per issue (effective 2011). **Document type:** *Guide, Consumer.*
Published by: Thames & Hudson Inc., 500 Fifth Ave, New York, NY 10110. TEL 212-354-3763, 800-233-4830, FAX 212-398-1252, Bookinfo@thames.wwnorton.com.

910.202 USA ISSN 1933-0782
DG804
STYLECITY. ROME. Text in English. 2005. irreg. USD 24.95 per issue (effective 2011). **Document type:** *Guide, Consumer.*
Published by: Thames & Hudson Inc., 500 Fifth Ave, New York, NY 10110. TEL 212-354-3763, 800-233-4830, FAX 212-398-1252, Bookinfo@thames.wwnorton.com.

338.4791449 FRA ISSN 1962-4204
SUD PROVENCE COTE D'AZUR. Text in French. 2008. q. **Document type:** *Magazine, Consumer.*
Published by: Sud Provence, 5-7 Rue d'Italie, Marseille, 13006, France.

916.8 DEU ISSN 1430-4791
SUED-AFRIKA; Magazin fuer Reisen, Wirtschaft und Kultur im suedlichen Afrika. Text in German. 1996. q. EUR 16; EUR 4.50 newsstand/cover (effective 2007). adv. **Document type:** *Magazine, Consumer.*
Related titles: Online - full text ed.
Published by: J. Latka Verlag GmbH, Heilsbachstr 17-19, Bonn, 53123, Germany. TEL 49-228-919320, FAX 49-228-9193217, info@latka.de. adv.: page EUR 4,200. Circ: 26,000 (paid and controlled).

917.404 USA
SULLIVAN COUNTY TRAVEL GUIDE. Text in English. a. free. maps. **Document type:** *Magazine, Consumer.* **Description:** Provides information on accommodations, dining, events, attractions, antiqueing and outdoor sports.
Published by: Sullivan County Visitors Association, Inc., 100 North St, Monticello, NY 12701. TEL 914-794-3000, 800-882-2287, FAX 914-794-1058. Ed. Gene Lomoniello. Adv. contact Hope Petkus. Circ: 100,000.

371.42 USA ISSN 1934-6794
GV186
SUMMER PROGRAMS FOR KIDS & TEENAGERS. Text in English. 1983. a. USD 25.76 (effective 2008). **Document type:** *Directory, Consumer.* **Description:** Covers more than 1,600 summer programs in the U.S. and abroad for young people, including those offered by private schools, colleges, camps, religious organizations and travel and sports groups.
Former titles (until 2007): Peterson's Summer Opportunities for Kids and Teenagers (Year) (0894-9417); (until 1989): Summer Opportunities for Kids and Teenagers (0739-9006)
Published by: Thomson Peterson's (Subsidiary of: Thomson Reuters Corp.), Princeton Pike Corporate Center, 2000 Lenox Dr, 3rd Fl, PO Box 67005, Lawrenceville, NJ 08648. TEL 609-896-1800, 800-338-3282 ext 54229, FAX 609-896-4531, custsvc@petersons.com, http://www.petersons.com.

919 CYM
SUN LIVING. Text in English. q. free. adv.
Published by: Cayman News, Ltd., Box 764, Grand Cayman, Cayman Isl. Ed. Mike Cross.

910.202 DEU
SUN'N FUN; junge Reiseideen. Text in German. s-a. adv. **Document type:** *Consumer.*
Published by: Unterwegsverlag Manfred Klemann, Dr Andler Str 28, Singen, 78224, Germany. TEL 07731-63544, FAX 07731-62401. Ed. Manfred Klemann. Adv. contact Anette Hildebrandt. Circ: 60,000.

910.01 AUT
SUNNSEIT'N; Die Fachzeitschrift fuer baeuerliche Vermieter. Text in German. q. EUR 13.40 domestic; EUR 17.20 foreign; EUR 3.70 newsstand/cover (effective 2005). **Document type:** *Magazine, Trade.*
Published by: Leopold Stocker Verlag, Hofgasse 5, Graz, St 8011, Austria. TEL 43-316-821636, FAX 43-316-835612, stocker-verlag@stocker-verlag.com, http://www.stocker-verlag.com.

SUNZINE - ABOUT QUEENSLAND AUSTRALIA. *see* BUSINESS AND ECONOMICS

910.91 BHS
SUPER MAP. Text in English. 1998. s-a. USD 36 in United States. adv. **Description:** Includes detailed, true-to-scale new map with zoom maps for resort areas and shop districts, and a dining guide.
Published by: Star Publishers Ltd., PO Box 4855, Nassau, Bahamas. TEL 242-3223724, FAX 242-3224527. Pub. Bobby Bower. adv.: color page USD 2,000. Circ: 400,000.

910.09 USA
G155.U6
SURVEY OF U.S. STATE & TERRITORY TOURISM OFFICE BUDGETS. Text in English. 1973. a. USD 495 per issue to non-members; USD 300 per issue to members (effective 2008). adv. back issues avail.; reprints avail. **Document type:** *Monographic series, Trade.* **Description:** Provides information on tourism office budgets and funding sources of all 50 states and when available, comparable agencies in the District of Columbia and the five U.S. territories.
Former titles (until 2002): Survey of U.S. State and Territory Tourism Offices; (until 1999): Survey of State Tourism Offices; (until 1997): Survey of State Travel Offices (0361-8307)
Related titles: Microfiche ed.: (from CIS); Online - full text ed.
Indexed: SRI.
Published by: Travel Industry Association of America, 1100 New York Ave, NW, Ste 450, Washington, DC 20005. TEL 202-408-8422, FAX 202-408-1255, feedback@tia.org. Pub. Dawn L Drew. Adv. contact Sarah Dickson TEL 202-408-2141.

915.1 646 USA
SUZY GERSHMAN'S BORN TO SHOP: HONG KONG, SHANGHAI & BEIJING; the ultimate guide for people who love to shop. Text in English. 1986. irreg., latest 2010, 5th ed. USD 17.99, EUR 15, GBP 13.99 per issue (effective 2010). **Document type:** *Guide, Consumer.*
Former titles (until 2005): Born to Shop: Hong Kong, Shanghai & Beijing (1531-7552); (until 2001): Born to Shop: Hong Kong (1067-3830)
Published by: John Wiley & Sons, Inc., 111 River St, Hoboken, NJ 07030. TEL 201-748-6000, FAX 201-748-6088, info@wiley.com.

914.1 646 USA ISSN 1556-9640
SUZY GERSHMAN'S BORN TO SHOP: PARIS; the ultimate guide for people who love to shop. Text in English. 1986. biennial. USD 16.99, EUR 14.20, GBP 11.99 per issue (effective 2010). adv. **Document type:** *Guide, Consumer.* **Description:** Provides opinionated advice from the inimitable Suzy Gershman on where to find the best stores, boutiques, markets, and values in some of the world's top shopping locales.
Former titles (until 2002): Born to Shop: Paris (1066-2790); (until 1993): Born to Shop. France
Published by: John Wiley & Sons, Inc., 111 River St, Hoboken, NJ 07030. TEL 201-748-6000, FAX 201-748-6088, info@wiley.com.

914.973 SVN ISSN 1408-7952
SVET & LJUDJE. Text in Slovenian. 1998. m. EUR 27.04 domestic; EUR 50 foreign (effective 2007). **Document type:** *Magazine, Consumer.*
Published by: C Z D Kmecki Glas, d. o. o., Zelezna cesta 14, Ljubljana, 1000, Slovenia. TEL 386-1-4735354, FAX 386-1-4735377, info@czd-kmeckiglas.si, http://kmeckiglas.com.

914 CHE ISSN 1420-1151
G155.S9
SWISS NEWS; what's on - business - politics - culture. Text in English. 1982. 12/yr. CHF 75 domestic; CHF 95 foreign (effective 2011). adv. **Document type:** *Magazine, Consumer.*
Formerly (until 1989): Swiss Scene (1421-1777)
Related titles: Online - full text ed.
Indexed: B02, B15, B17, B18, G04, G06, G07, G08, I05.
Published by: Swiss Businesspress SA, Koeschenruetistr 109, Zuerich, 8052, Switzerland. TEL 41-44-3064700, FAX 41-44-3064711, info@swissbusinesspress.ch, http://www.swissbusinesspress.ch. Pub. Remo Kuhn. Circ: 13,000 (paid).

SYDNEY SHOPPING; the official guide. *see* CONSUMER EDUCATION AND PROTECTION

910.2 DEU
SYLT MAGAZIN. Text in German. 1991. a. EUR 6.50 newsstand/cover (effective 2010). adv. **Document type:** *Magazine, Consumer.*
Published by: Guenter Kohl PR & Marketing, Gaertnerkoppel 3, Westensee, 24259, Germany. TEL 49-4305-992992, FAX 49-4305-992993, gkprkiel@t-online.de. Ed. Guenter F. Kohl. Adv. contact Rolf Thoms. Circ: 50,000 (paid and controlled).

910 CAN ISSN 1206-0658
SYMPATICO NETLIFE. Text in English. 1996. 6/yr. CAD 19.26 (effective 2000). **Document type:** *Magazine, Consumer.* **Description:** Guide to the Internet, focusing on unique Canadian destinations and regional news.
Indexed: C03, CBCARef, PQC.
Published by: Telemedia Communications Inc., 25 Sheppard Ave W, Ste 100, Toronto, ON M2N 6S7, Canada. TEL 416-733-7600, FAX 416-733-8272, bwarren@sympatico.ca. Ed., R&P Peter Giffen. Pub. Graham Morris. Adv. contact Barbara Warren. Circ: 193,000 (controlled).

T & L GOLF. (Travel & Leisure) *see* SPORTS AND GAMES—Ball Games

910.09 DEU
T I D TOURISTIK KONTAKT. Text in German. 1965. a. adv. **Document type:** *Yearbook, Trade.*
Published by: TourCon Hannelore Niedecken GmbH, Postfach 700629, Hamburg, 22006, Germany. TEL 49-40-41448810, FAX 49-40-41448199. Ed. Michael Schnelle. Pub., R&P Hannelore Niedecken. Adv. contact Sabine Eilers Raasch. Circ: 13,456.

338.4791 ZAF
T I R SOUTHERN AFRICA. Text in English. 1995. m. price on request. adv. charts; illus.; mkt.; stat. back issues avail. **Document type:** *Journal, Trade.* **Description:** Contains travel industry news and features for travel agents in South Africa and neighboring countries.
Formerly (until Sep. 1999): T T G Southern Africa
Published by: T T G Southern Africa, Jhi House, 5 Heerengracht, Cape Town, 8001, South Africa. TEL 27-21-419-1671, FAX 27-21-421-5938. Ed. John Wardall. Pub. Jeff Hawthorne. Adv. contact Alan Turner. color page USD 3,038; trim 280 x 480. Circ: 5,560 (controlled).

910.09 JPN
T M. (Travel Management) Text in English, Japanese. 1978. s-m. JPY 8,400 (effective 1998). adv. back issues avail. **Document type:** *Journal, Trade.* **Description:** Focuses on overseas destinations for Japanese travelers for individual readers as well as professionals in the travel industry. Includes regular destination supplements and destination features.
Published by: Travel Management Inc. (Subsidiary of: Travel Consultants of Japan Group), Dai-ichi Akiyama Bldg, 7F, 2-3-22 Toranomon, Minato-ku, Tokyo, 105-0001, Japan. FAX 81-3-3506-8327. Ed. Toshio Takahashi. Pub., R&P Hisao Ohta TEL 81-3-3506-8321. Adv. contact Tsutomu Katagiri. Circ: 12,251.

919.404 AUS
T N T MAGAZINE AUSTRALIA. Text in English. 2005. w. free (effective 2009). adv. bk.rev.; film rev.; music rev. maps. **Document type:** *Magazine, Consumer.* **Description:** Provides travel info for budget travellers with transportation, accommodation, things to do, places to see, food, nightlife information.

Formed by the merger of (1996-2005): T N T Magazine Australia. N S W, A C T (1327-7421); Which was formerly (until 1996): T N T for Backpackers Magazine. Sydney, N S W, A C T (1327-1997); (until 1995): For Backpackers by Backpackers. Sydney, Canberra, New South Wales (1038-8281); (until 1991): For Backpackers by Backpackers. Sydney and Canberra (1034-6252); (2000-2005): T N T Magazine Australia. Q L D - N T; Which was formerly (until 2000): T N T Magazine Australia. Queensland & Byron Bay (1327-7413); (until 1996): T N T for Backpackers Magazine. Queensland & Byron Bay; (until 1995): For Backpackers by Backpackers. Queensland (1038-8273); (2000-2005): T N T Magazine Australia. Explorer
Related titles: Online - full text ed.
Published by: T N T Group, 126 Abercrombie St, Chippendale, NSW 2008, Australia. TEL 61-2-92994811, FAX 61-2-92994861, enquiries@tntdownunder.com. Circ: 26,000.

338.4 USA ISSN 1067-926X
T R I P SOUTH. (Travel Reference Information Planner) Variant title: Tripsouth. Text in English. 1993. q. USD 9 domestic; USD 2.25 newsstand/cover; USD 50 foreign (effective 2000). adv. illus.; mkt.; maps; stat. back issues avail. **Document type:** *Handbook/Manual/ Guide, Trade.* **Description:** For volume buyers booking group travel to the southern U.S. mails to group travel leaders, travel agents, meeting planners, and motorcoach tour operators.
Related titles: Online - full text ed.
Published by: Browning Publications, Inc., 3103 Medlock Bridge Rd, Norcross, GA 30071. TEL 770-825-0220, FAX 770-825-0880. Ed. Sheala Browning. Pub., R&P Mark Browning. Adv. contact Monica Whitney. page USD 7,215; trim 10.88 x 8.38. Circ: 60,808 (controlled).

901.09 SGP
T T G ASIA. Variant title: Travel Trade Gazette Asia. Text in English. 1974. w. free to qualified personnel. adv. back issues avail. **Document type:** *Newspaper, Trade.*
Related titles: Online - full content ed.
Indexed: A15, P14, P51, RASB.
Published by: T T G Asia Media Pte Ltd, 6 Raffles Quay #16-02, Singapore, 048580, Singapore. TEL 65-6395-7575, FAX 65-6536-8639, contact@ttgasia.com, http://www.ttgasia.com/. adv.: B&W page USD 10,744, color page USD 12,493; trim 28.2 x 42.2. Circ: 16,450.

T T G - B T M I C E CHINA. *see* MEETINGS AND CONGRESSES

338.4 SGP
T T G INDIA. (Travel Trade Gazette) Text in English. 2003. m. free to qualified personnel. **Document type:** *Newspaper, Trade.* **Description:** Covers the inbound and outbound travels in India with special focus on the domestic market.
Related titles: Online - full content ed.
Published by: T T G Asia Media Pte Ltd, 6 Raffles Quay #16-02, Singapore, 048580, Singapore. TEL 65-6395-7575, FAX 65-6536-8639, contact@ttgasia.com, http://www.ttgasiamedia.com/.

T T G M I C E; Asia's leading magazine for meetings, incentives, conferences and exhibitions. (Travel Trade Gazette Meetings, Incentives, Conferences and Exhibitions) *see* MEETINGS AND CONGRESSES

910.09 USA ISSN 1080-837X
T T R A NEWS. Text in English. bi-m. membership. adv. back issues avail. **Document type:** *Newsletter.*
Published by: Travel and Tourism Research Association, 546 E Main St, Lexington, KY 40508. TEL 606-226-4344, FAX 606-226-4355. Ed. J P Smith. Circ: 900 (controlled).

910.91 790.1 JPN
TABI-MEIJIN/EXCELLENT VACATIONERS. Text in Japanese. 1997. 6/yr. free. adv. **Document type:** *Consumer.* **Description:** Covers information on luxury lifestyles and travel around the world. Targets businesspeople, doctors and others interested in high end vacations.
Published by: Nikkei Business Publications Inc. (Subsidiary of: Nihon Keizai Shimbun, Inc.), 2-7-6 Hirakawa-cho, Chiyoda-ku, Tokyo, 102-8622, Japan. TEL 81-3-5210-8311, FAX 81-3-5210-8530, info@nikkeibp-america.com. Ed. Jun'ichiro Ogino. Pub. Jun'ichi Ogino. Adv. contact Kazuhiro Ono. B&W page JPY 1,100,000, color page JPY 1,680,000; trim 210 x 280. Circ: 250,000. **Dist. in America by:** Nikkei Business Publications America Inc., 575 Fifth Ave, 20th Fl, New York, NY 10017.

910 JPN
TABI NI DEYO. Text in Japanese. 1973. bi-m. JPY 2,700.
Published by: Mainichi Shinbunsha/Mainichi Newspapers, 1-1-1 Hitotsubashi, Chiyoda-ku, Tokyo, 100-8051, Japan. TEL 81-3-3212-0321, FAX 81-3-3211-0895. Ed. Reimi Yamazaki. Circ: 130,000.

910.202 385 JPN
TABI TO TETSUDO. Text in Japanese. 1971. q. JPY 980 per issue (effective 2000). adv. bk.rev. **Document type:** *Consumer.*
Published by: Tetsudo Journal Sha, 4-8-6 Iida-Bashi, Chiyoda-ku, Tokyo, 102-0072, Japan. TEL 81-3-3264-1891, FAX 81-3-3265-3597. Ed. Toshimoto Takeshima. Circ: 120,000 (controlled).

910.91 333.3 USA
TABLE ROCK LAKE VACATION - SERVICE AND RELOCATION GUIDE. Text in English. 1966. a. adv. illus. **Document type:** *Directory.* **Description:** Provides description and photographs of the Table Rock Lake - Shell Knob area. Contains information on boating, resort rental availability and relocation to the area.
Published by: Shell Knob Chamber of Commerce, 5, Timbe Roc Village, Box 193, Shell Knob, MO 05747-0193. TEL 417-858-3300. Ed. Sheila House. Circ: 50,000.

910.202 PYF ISSN 1157-349X
TAHITI BEACH PRESS. Text in French. 1980. w. 16 p./no. 4 cols./p.; **Document type:** *Newspaper.*
Published by: Tahiti Publications Touristiques, B.P. 887, Papeete, French Polynesia. TEL 689-426850, FAX 689-423356. Pub. Gerard Warti. Circ: 2,700 (controlled).

915.4 IND
THE TAJ MAGAZINE. Text in English. 1972. q. illus.; maps; stat.; tr.lit. **Document type:** *Magazine, Consumer.* **Description:** Contains travel, culture and lifestyle articles on India, Nepal and Sri Lanka.
Published by: (Taj Group of Hotels), Indian Hotels Company Ltd., Oxford House, Apollo Bunder, 15/17 N. F. Rd, Mumbai, Maharashtra 400 001, India. TEL 91-22-66651000, FAX 91-22-22846680, http://www.tajhotels.com. **Dist. by:** Mediascope Repns Ltd.

338.4791 910.2 DNK ISSN 0107-1270
TAKE OFF. Text in Danish, Norwegian, Swedish. 1957. m. DKK 625 domestic; DKK 751 foreign (effective 2009). adv. bk.rev. illus.; stat. **Document type:** *Magazine, Trade.* **Description:** Travel trade magazine for Scandinavian agents, tourist offices, airlines, hotels, and trade professionals.
Related titles: Supplement(s): Aussie News.
Published by: Skandinavisk Bladforlag A-S, Gl. Kongevej 3 B, Copenhagen V, 1610, Denmark. TEL 45-33-238099, FAX 45-33-237042, info@takeoff.dk, http://www.takeoff.dk. Adv. contact Jimmy Munk-Jensen TEL 45-88-321990. page DKK 15,995; 186 x 270. Circ: 5,000 (controlled).

796.5 EST ISSN 1406-2690
TALLINN IN YOUR POCKET. Text in English. 1997. 5/yr. USD 25; USD 5 newsstand/cover (effective 2002). adv. **Document type:** *Magazine, Consumer.*
Address: Vana-Viru 4, Tallinn, 10111, Estonia. TEL 372-631-3350, FAX 372-644-6470.

TAMPA BAY ILLUSTRATED. *see* GENERAL INTEREST PERIODICALS—United States

910.09 AUS
TASMANIAN TRAVELWAYS. Text in English. 1960. bi-m. free (effective 2009). adv. charts; illus.; stat. back issues avail. **Document type:** *Magazine, Consumer.* **Description:** Covers all aspects of tourism in Tasmania.
Related titles: Online - full text ed.: free (effective 2009).
Published by: (Tourism Council Tasmania), Examiner Newspaper Pty Ltd., 71-75 Paterson St, PO Box 99, Launceston, TAS 7250, Australia. TEL 61-3-63367111, FAX 61-3-63314858, feedback@examiner.com.au, http://www.examiner.com.au/index.asp. Ed. Fiona Reynolds TEL 61-3-63367350. Adv. contact Brett Macdonald TEL 61-3-63367260.

338.4 CAN ISSN 1925-6841
▼ **TASTE & TRAVEL INTERNATIONAL.** Text in English. 2011. q. USD 25; USD 6.95 per issue (effective 2011). **Document type:** *Magazine, Consumer.* **Description:** Focuses on the exciting and delicious world of culinary travel.
Published by: Taste and Travel Publishing International, Inc., 8289 Boland St # 481, Metcalfe, ON K0A 2P0, Canada. info@TasteandTravelInternational.com, http://www.tasteandtravelinternational.com.

914.2 GBR
A TASTE OF SCOTLAND GUIDE (ONLINE); selected places to eat and stay in scotland. Text in English. 1972. a. GBP 7.99 (effective 1999). adv. illus. **Document type:** *Directory.*
Former titles (until 2003: A Taste of Scotland Guide (Print); Taste of Scotland
Media: Online - full text.
Published by: Taste of Scotland Scheme Ltd. Ed., Adv. contact Amanda Clark. Circ: 30,000.

914.6 ESP ISSN 1137-4640
TECHNO HOTEL. Text in Spanish. 1963. m. EUR 49 domestic; EUR 58 in Europe; EUR 66 elsewhere (effective 2009). **Document type:** *Magazine, Consumer.*
Former titles (until 1991): Tecno Hosteleria (1137-4632); (until 1989): Tecno (1137-4624); (until 1985): Tecno Hotel (1137-4616)
Published by: Ediciones Turisticas, S.A., C. Consejo de Ciento 355 Piso 3o, Barcelona, 08007, Spain. TEL 34-93-4670229, FAX 34-93-4670218, direccion@editur.es, http://www.editur.com.

910.2 USA ISSN 1946-6498
TELLURIDE MAGAZINE. Text in English. 1983. s-a. USD 11.95; USD 5.95 per issue (effective 2009). adv. back issues avail. **Document type:** *Magazine, Consumer.* **Description:** Showcases its namesake, celebrating a town rich in history that thrives with outdoor adventure and culture.
Related titles: Online - full text ed.: ISSN 1946-6501.
Published by: Telluride Publishing (Subsidiary of: Big Earth Publishing), 307 Society Dr, Ste D, PO Box 964, Telluride, CO 81435. TEL 970-728-4245, FAX 970-728-4302, advertising@telluridemagazine.com. Ed. Mary Duffy TEL 970-728-4245 ext 2. Pub. John Arnold TEL 970-728-4245 ext 1. Adv. contact Paton Stone TEL 970-728-4245 ext 3. page USD 1,995; trim 8.375 x 10.875. Circ: 70,000.

TEMA VERDE. *see* CONSERVATION

910 CAN ISSN 0712-8657
TEOROS; revue de recherche en tourisme. Text in English. 1982. 3/yr. CAD 15; CAD 18 foreign. back issues avail.
Indexed: A22, A36, BA, C03, C25, CABA, CBCARef, E12, F08, F12, GH, H&TI, H06, H16, I11, LT, N02, P48, PQC, PdeR, R12, RRTA, S13, S16, TAR, W11.
—BLDSC (8791.836000), IE, Ingenta.
Published by: Universite du Quebec a Montreal, Service des Publications, Succ Centre Ville, C P 8888, Montreal, PQ H3C 3P8, Canada. TEL 514-987-4229.

910.01 GBR
TERRA FIRMA. Text in English. 6/yr. GBP 100, EUR 150, USD 175 (effective 2005). **Document type:** *Newsletter, Consumer.* **Description:** Provides useful information for curious and discerning travelers.
Media: Online - full content.
Published by: Terra Firma Media Ltd., PO Box 31638, London, W11 1TW, United Kingdom. TEL 44-870-2417328, FAX 44-1452-814547. Ed., Pub. Bruce Palling.

TERRA GRISCHUNA - GRAUBUENDEN; Zeitschrift fuer buendner Natur, Kultur und Freizeit. *see* ENVIRONMENTAL STUDIES

917 CHE ISSN 0257-6686
TERRA PLANA. Text in German. 1972 (no.6). s-a. **Document type:** *Magazine, Consumer.*
Indexed: MLA-IB.
Published by: Sarganserlaendische Druck AG, Zeughausstr 12, Mels, 8887, Switzerland. TEL 41-81-7253232, FAX 41-81-7253230, druckerei@sarganserlaender.ch. Ed. A Stucky.

914 CHE
TERRA TICINESE. Text in German. 6/yr.
Address: Via alla Chiesa 7, Viganello, 6962, Switzerland. TEL 091-513568. Ed. G M Fontana. Circ: 6,000.

910.91 338.479 FRA ISSN 1627-1041
TERRE DE PROVENCE. Text in French. 2001. bi-m. EUR 29; EUR 6.95 newsstand/cover (effective 2009). **Document type:** *Magazine, Consumer.*
Published by: Sequoia Editions, 241 Route de la Manda, Colomars, 06670, France. TEL 33-4-93081471, info@sequoia-editions.com.

TERRE SAUVAGE. *see* CONSERVATION

910.91 FRA ISSN 2107-2965
▼ **TERRES D'AVEYRON MAGAZINE.** Text in French. 2010. q. **Document type:** *Magazine, Consumer.*
Published by: Terroirs Infos, Le Bourg, Les Albres, 12220, France. TEL 33-5-65804773, contact@terres-aveyron.fr. Ed. Georges Mauries.

910.202 ITA ISSN 1970-7029
TESORI D'ABRUZZO. Text in Italian. 2006. q. EUR 19 (effective 2009). **Document type:** *Magazine, Consumer.*
Published by: Paolo de Siena Editore, Viale Giovanni Bovio 253, Pescara, 65123, Italy. FAX 39-085-4221643.

625.7 USA ISSN 0040-4349
TE24.T4
TEXAS HIGHWAYS. Text in English. 1950. m. USD 19.95 domestic (print or online ed.); USD 29.95 foreign (print or online ed.); USD 3.95 per issue (effective 2009). adv. bk.rev. illus. Index. back issues avail.; reprints avail. **Document type:** *Magazine, Consumer.* **Description:** Features the best attractions of Texas along with magnificent photography.
Formerly (until 1954): Construction & Maintenance Bulletin
Related titles: Online - full text ed.: USD 19.95 (effective 2009).
Published by: Texas Department of Transportation, Travel and Information Division, PO Box 141009, Austin, TX 78714. TEL 386-597-4297, 800-839-4997, http://www.dot.state.tx.us. Ed. Charles J Lohrmann. Pub. Kathy Murphy. adv.: color page USD 7,120; bleed 8.375 x 1075.

TEXAS JOURNEY. *see* TRANSPORTATION—Automobiles

338.4791 USA
TEXAS TRAVELER. Variant title: Texas Tour & Meeting Guide. Text in English. 19??. a. adv. **Document type:** *Magazine, Consumer.*
Published by: Emmis Communications Custom Publishing, PO Box 1569, Austin, TX 78767. Pub. David Dunham TEL 512-320-6925. Circ: 95,000.

949.21 NLD ISSN 1877-8305
TEXEL MAGAZINE. Text in Dutch. 1969. a. adv. illus. **Document type:** *Magazine, Consumer.* **Description:** Provides a comprehensive guide to tourism on the Dutch island of Texel, including information on accommodations, museums, tourist activities, natural areas, and beaches.
Former titles (until 2009): Texeltoerist Magazine (1385-5735); (until 1991): Texeltoerist (1385-5727)
Published by: Uitgeverij Langeveld & de Rooy BV, Postbus 11, Den Burg, 1790 AA, Netherlands. TEL 31-222-362600, FAX 31-222-314144, uitgeverij@lenr.nl, http://www.lenr.nl.

910.202 GBR ISSN 1363-7428
DS563
THAILAND HANDBOOK. Text in English. 1993. biennial. GBP 15.99 per issue (effective 2010). adv. **Document type:** *Handbook/Manual/ Guide, Consumer.* **Description:** Covers all the basics from where to stay and where to eat to cycling, walking and how to get around the Thailand.
Supersedes in part (in 1997): Thailand and Burma Handbook (1352-786X); Which was formerly (until 1994): Thailand, Indochina and Burma Handbook (0968-0926)
—CCC.
Published by: Footprint Handbooks Ltd., 6 Riverside Ct, Lower Bristol Rd, Bath, Avon BA2 3DZ, United Kingdom. TEL 44-1225-469141, FAX 44-1225-469461, wwwinfo@footprintbooks.com.

338.4791593 GBR ISSN 1747-9037
THAILAND TOURISM REPORT. Text in English. 2005. q. EUR 820, USD 1,030 combined subscription (print & email eds.) (effective 2010). **Document type:** *Report, Trade.* **Description:** Provides industry professionals and strategists, corporate analysts, associations, government departments and regulatory bodies with independent forecasts and competitive intelligence on the Thai tourism industry.
Related titles: E-mail ed.
Indexed: B01.
Published by: Business Monitor International Ltd., Senator House, 85 Queen Victoria St, London, EC4V 4AB, United Kingdom. TEL 44-20-72480468, FAX 44-20-72480467, subs@businessmonitor.com.

910.202 GBR
THEMEPARK. Text in English. 6/yr. GBP 27.50 domestic; GBP 48 foreign (effective 2002).
Address: 10 Glebe Rd., 2nd Fl, London, E8 4BD, United Kingdom. http://www.inthepark.net. Ed. Angus Carlyle. Pubs. Angus Carlyle, Maurice Vandeven.

910 NZL ISSN 1170-1374
THERMALAIR; visitor newspaper. Text in English. 1970. w. free. adv. dance rev.; film rev.; music rev.; play rev. maps. 23 p./no. 8 cols./p.; back issues avail. **Document type:** *Newspaper, Consumer.* **Description:** Lists sightseeing, accommodations, dining and shopping places and news for visitors to Rotorua.
Published by: Rotorua Newspapers (Subsidiary of: A P N New Zealand Ltd.), 1143 Hinemoa St, PO Box 1442,, Rotorua, New Zealand. TEL 64-7-3486199, http://www.dailypost.co.nz/. Adv. contact Margaret Turner. Circ: 8,000.

919.304 NZL
THERMALAIR HOUSEHOLDER. Text in English. 1998. w. free newsstand/cover. adv. **Document type:** *Newspaper, Consumer.* **Description:** Contains topical information on events, maps, sightseeing, dining, accommodation and shopping as well as tourist industry news for New Zealand.
Published by: A P N New Zealand Ltd. (Subsidiary of: A P N Holdings N Z Ltd.), 46 Albert St, PO Box 32, Auckland, New Zealand. TEL 64-9-3736440, FAX 64-9-3736577. Circ: 8,000 (controlled).

910.2 CZE
THINK AGAIN; Prague's bilingual monthly magazine. Text in Czech. 2003. m. free (effective 2009). adv. illus. **Document type:** *Magazine, Consumer.*
Address: Vinohradska 102, Praha 3, 13000, Czech Republic. TEL 420-7-77133514, FAX 420-2-67315789. Ed. Gordon Walker.

T U

914 GBR ISSN 0040-6171
THIS ENGLAND. Text in English. 1968. q. GBP 17 domestic; AUD 49 in Australia; NZD 58 in New Zealand; USD 46 in US & Canada; GBP 20 elsewhere (effective 2009). bk.rev. illus. back issues avail. **Document type:** *Magazine, Consumer.* **Description:** Provides a journey through England's green and pleasant land.
Related titles: Online - full text ed.: free (effective 2009).
Indexed: ChLitAb.
—IE.
Published by: This England Ltd., PO Box 52, Cheltenham, Gloucestershire GL50 1YQ., United Kingdom. TEL 44-1242-515156, FAX 44-1242-537901, sales@thisengland.co.uk. Ed. Roy Faiers. Pub. Neil O'Brien. Adv. contact Mark Palmer.

916.7 BWA
THIS IS BOTSWANA. Text in English. 1983. irreg. free. **Document type:** *Directory, Consumer.* **Description:** Presents travel and tourism features for travelers and business people. Highlights the natural wonders and potential for development in tourism and related industries.
Published by: Botswana, Department of Information and Broadcasting, Private Bag 0060, Gaborone, Botswana. Ed. Tefo Ray Mangope. Circ: 20,000.

917.704 USA
THIS IS INDIANAPOLIS. Text in English. 1990. s-a. free. adv. **Document type:** *Magazine, Consumer.* **Description:** For business and pleasure travelers and convention delegates staying at ICVA member hotels. Covers area leisure interests, travel-related services and city information.
Published by: Indianapolis Convention and Visitors Association, One RCA Dome, Ste 100, Indianapolis, IN 46225. TEL 317-639-4282, FAX 317-639-5273. Ed. William Hendrickson. Adv. contact Mary Huggard. Circ: 150,000.

914 GBR ISSN 0040-6198
THIS IS LONDON; the weekly magazine for visitors. Text in English. 1956. w. film rev.; play rev. illus. **Document type:** *Magazine, Consumer.*
Related titles: Online - full text ed.: free (effective 2009).
Published by: This Is London Magazine Ltd., 42 Conduit St, London, W1R 9FB, United Kingdom. TEL 44-20-74341281, FAX 44-20-72870592.

910.09 MEX
THIS IS MEXICO; Mexico's weekly visitor's pocket guide. Text in Spanish. 1960. w. free. adv. charts; illus.
Published by: Editorial This Is Mexico, Calle Londres 166, Apdo. 6-728, Mexico City, DF 06600, Mexico. TEL 52-5-5331540, FAX 52-5-2082838, TELEX 017-71-881. Ed. Jesus Maldonado. Circ: 20,000.

915.3 QAT
THIS IS QATAR. Text in English. 1978. q. adv.
Published by: Gulf Publica Relations (Qatar), P O Box 4015, Doha, Qatar. TEL 413813, FAX 413814, TELEX 4787. Ed. Yousuf Qassim Darwish. Circ: 5,000.

330 910.9 HKG
THIS IS VIETNAM. Text in English. 1990. s-a. USD 10. adv. **Description:** Includes travel and business tips, a business directory, and maps of Hanoi and Ho Chi Minh City.
Published by: Beca Investments Ltd., Bank of America Bldg, 606 Harcourt Rd, Central, Hong Kong, Hong Kong. TEL 8122614, FAX 8126046. Ed. Peter Witton. Circ: 6,000.

910.202 USA ISSN 0191-8354
THIS WEEK BIG ISLAND; free driving maps, news, fun. Text in English. 1966. w. free (effective 2011). adv. **Document type:** *Magazine, Consumer.* **Description:** Includes information, maps and coupons for the visitor.
Related titles: Online - full text ed.
Published by: Hagadone Hawaii, Inc., This Week Magazines, 274 Puuhale Rd, Ste 200, Honolulu, HI 96819. TEL 808-843-6000, FAX 808-843-6090, sales@thisweek.com, http://www.thisweekmagazines.com. Ed. Najee Lynne.

919 910.202 AUS ISSN 0817-6159
THIS WEEK IN BRISBANE; and south-east Queensland. Text in English. 1963. q. adv. **Document type:** *Magazine, Consumer.* **Description:** General information for travel in Brisbane.
Published by: Hardie Grant Magazines, Level 2, 50 Yeo St, Neutral Bay, NSW 2089, Australia. TEL 61-2-93284144, FAX 61-2-93284166, colinritchie@hardiegrant.com.au, http://www.hardiegrant.com.au. Adv. contact Howard Shaw. page AUD 2,250; trim 120 x 210. Circ: 19,905.

919 910.202 AUS ISSN 0817-6140
THIS WEEK IN CANBERRA. Text in English. 1960. q. adv. **Document type:** *Magazine, Consumer.* **Description:** Travel information on sightseeing, shopping, entertainment, and dining out in Canberra.
Published by: Hardie Grant Magazines, Level 2, 50 Yeo St, Neutral Bay, NSW 2089, Australia. TEL 61-2-93284144, FAX 61-2-93284166, colinritchie@hardiegrant.com.au, http://www.hardiegrant.com.au. Adv. contact Jacinta Scott. page AUD 3,000; trim 120 x 210. Circ: 15,185.

910.91 790.1 USA ISSN 1093-5924
THIS WEEK IN CLEVELAND. Text in English. 1982. m. free hotel guests. adv. 28 p./no. 3 cols./p.; **Document type:** *Magazine, Consumer.* **Description:** Introduces visitors to some of the unique aspects of Cleveland and the surrounding areas.
Published by: T W I C Publishing, Inc., 20575 Center Ridge Rd, Ste 460, Rocky River, OH 44116. TEL 440-331-8012, FAX 440-331-1481. Ed. Cynthia Schuster Eakin. R&P William Close. Adv. contacts Jena Olsen, William Close. page USD 1,350. Circ: 10,000.

919 910.202 AUS ISSN 1442-7168
THIS WEEK IN DARWIN. Text in English. 1979. q. adv. **Document type:** *Magazine, Consumer.* **Description:** Travel information on sightseeing, shopping, entertainment, accommodations and dining out in Darwin.
Former titles (until 1997): This Week in Darwin and the Top End (0815-435X); (until 1984): Around Darwin and the Top End (0811-2495)
Published by: Hardie Grant Magazines, Level 2, 50 Yeo St, Neutral Bay, NSW 2089, Australia. TEL 61-2-93284144, FAX 61-2-93284166, colinritchie@hardiegrant.com.au, http://www.hardiegrant.com.au. Adv. contact Cheryl Moyd. page AUD 2,040; trim 120 x 210. Circ: 7,626.

919 910.202 AUS ISSN 0817-6124
THIS WEEK IN MELBOURNE. Text in English. 1958. q. adv. **Document type:** *Magazine, Consumer.* **Description:** Travel information on sightseeing, shopping, entertainment, accommodations, and dining out in Melbourne.
Published by: Hardie Grant Magazines, Level 2, 50 Yeo St, Neutral Bay, NSW 2089, Australia. TEL 61-2-93284144, FAX 61-2-93284166, colinritchie@hardiegrant.com.au, http://www.hardiegrant.com.au. Adv. contact Fiona Douglas. page AUD 4,000; trim 120 x 210. Circ: 28,720.

919 910.202 AUS ISSN 0817-6175
THIS WEEK IN SYDNEY. Text in English. 1964. q. adv. **Document type:** *Magazine, Consumer.* **Description:** Tourist information on sightseeing, shopping, entertainment, dining out and accommodations in Sydney.
Former titles (until 1998): This Week in Sydney the Hunter Valley & the Blue Mountains; (until 1994): This Week in Sydney and Blue Mountains; (until 1993): This Week in Sydney
—CCC.
Published by: Hardie Grant Magazines, Level 2, 50 Yeo St, Neutral Bay, NSW 2089, Australia. TEL 61-2-93284144, FAX 61-2-93284166, colinritchie@hardiegrant.com.au, http://www.hardiegrant.com.au. adv.: page AUD 4,000; trim 120 x 210. Circ: 24,600.

919 910.202 AUS ISSN 0817-6132
THIS WEEK IN TASMANIA. Text in English. 1966. q. adv. **Document type:** *Magazine, Consumer.*
—CCC.
Published by: Hardie Grant Magazines, Level 2, 50 Yeo St, Neutral Bay, NSW 2089, Australia. TEL 61-2-93284144, FAX 61-2-93284166, colinritchie@hardiegrant.com.au, http://www.hardiegrant.com.au. Adv. contact Ange Hope TEL 61-3-62319193. page AUD 1,950; trim 120 x 210.

917.4 USA
THIS WEEK IN THE POCONOS. Text in English. 1932. 29/yr. USD 52 (effective 2000). adv. **Document type:** *Bulletin, Consumer.*
Published by: Printing Craftsmen, Inc., PO Box 8, Pocono Pines, PA 18350. TEL 570-839-7103, FAX 570-646-4528. Ed. Joseph N Miller Jr. Circ: 252,000.

975.6 USA
THIS WEEK IN WESTERN NORTH CAROLINA. Text in English. 1930. w. USD 65. adv. charts; illus. **Document type:** *Directory.* **Description:** Informs the local resident, newcomer and tourist about things to do and see in western North Carolina.
Formerly: This Week (0040-6309)
Published by: Priceless Group Inc., 959 Merrimon Ave, Box 1513, Asheville, NC 28802. TEL 704-253-9299. Ed., Pub. Cindy Tunnell. Circ: 8,000.

910.202 USA ISSN 0191-8362
THIS WEEK KAUAI. Text in English. 1966. w. free (effective 2011). adv. **Document type:** *Magazine, Consumer.* **Description:** Provides information, maps and coupons for the visitor.
Related titles: Online - full text ed.
Published by: Hagadone Hawaii, Inc., This Week Magazines, 274 Puuhale Rd, Ste 200, Honolulu, HI 96819. TEL 808-843-6000, FAX 808-843-6090, sales@thisweek.com, http://www.thisweekmagazines.com. Ed. Najee Lynne.

919.404 AUS
THIS WEEK MAGAZINE. Text in English. 1989. w. **Description:** Features tourist information, fishing, entertainment, and leisure.
Formerly: Great Lakes Entertainer
Published by: Regional Publishers (N.S.W.) Pty Ltd., 41 Helen St, Forster, NSW 2428, Australia.

910.202 USA ISSN 0191-8370
THIS WEEK MAUI. Text in English. 1966. w. free (effective 2011). adv. **Document type:** *Magazine, Consumer.* **Description:** Provides information, maps and coupons for the visitor.
Related titles: Online - full text ed.
Published by: Hagadone Hawaii, Inc., This Week Magazines, 274 Puuhale Rd, Ste 200, Honolulu, HI 96819. TEL 808-843-6000, FAX 808-843-6090, sales@thisweek.com, http://www.thisweekmagazines.com. Ed. Najee Lynne.

910.202 USA
THIS WEEK OAHU. Text in English. 1966. w. free (effective 2011). adv. **Document type:** *Magazine, Consumer.* **Description:** Provides information, maps and coupons for the visitor.
Related titles: Online - full text ed.
Published by: Hagadone Hawaii, Inc., This Week Magazines, 274 Puuhale Rd, Ste 200, Honolulu, HI 96819. TEL 808-843-6000, FAX 808-843-6090, sales@thisweek.com, http://www.thisweekmagazines.com. Ed. Najee Lynne.

910.91 USA
THRIFTYTRAVELING.COM. Text in English. bi-m. USD 29.95 (effective 2001). 12 p./no.; **Document type:** *Newsletter, Consumer.* **Description:** Offers money-saving travel secrets and late-breaking information on bargains.
Formerly (until Jul., 2001): ThriftyTraveler.com
Related titles: Online - full content ed.
Published by: ThriftyTraveler.com, Box 8168, Clearwater, FL 33758. TEL 727-447-4731, FAX 727-447-0829, editor@thriftytraveler.com, http://www.thriftytraveler.com. Ed. Mary VanMeer.

910.2 919 USA
THRUM'S ALL ABOUT HAWAII. Text in English. 1970. a. USD 3.50. adv.
Former titles: Almanac of the Pacific (0065-6461); All About Hawaii
Published by: S B Printers, Inc., PO Box 100, Honolulu, HI 96810-0100. TEL 808-537-5353. Ed. Arlene King Duncan. Circ: 25,000.

910.202 CAN ISSN 0846-5363
THUNDER BAY LIFE. Text in English. 1985. m. CAD 15, USD 15. back issues avail. **Document type:** *Magazine, Consumer.*
Formerly: Thunder Bay Destinations
Published by: North Superior Publishing Inc., 1145 Barton St, Thunder Bay, ON P7B 5N3, Canada. TEL 807-623-2348, FAX 807-623-7515. Ed. Scott A Sumnr. Circ: 5,000.

910.202 GBR ISSN 1363-7525
TIBET HANDBOOK. Text in English. 1996. irreg., latest 2009, 4th ed. GBP 19.99 per issue (effective 2010). adv. **Document type:** *Handbook/Manual/Guide, Consumer.* **Description:** Covers all the basics from where to stay and where to eat to cycling, walking and how to get around the Tibet.
—CCC.
Published by: Footprint Handbooks Ltd., 6 Riverside Ct, Lower Bristol Rd, Bath, Avon BA2 3DZ, United Kingdom. TEL 44-1225-469141, FAX 44-1225-469461, wwwinfo@footprintbooks.com.

910.2 CHE
TICKET. Text in German. 1930. 5/yr. membership. adv. bk.rev. illus. **Document type:** *Consumer.*
Formerly: Jugi - Ajiste (0022-6009)
Related titles: French ed.
Published by: Schweizer Jugendherbergen/Swiss Youth Hostel Association, Schaffhauserstr 14, Postfach 161, Zuerich, 8042, Switzerland. TEL 41-1-3601414, FAX 41-1-3601460. Ed., Adv. contact Hoeneisen Maya. Circ: 80,000.

917.204 MEX
TIJUANA. Text in Spanish. m.
Published by: (Tijuana Hotel Association), Editorial Bonanza S. de R.L., DR VELASCO 95, Ed. 5 Of. 203, Col Doctores Del. Cuauhtemoc, Mexico City, DF 06720, Mexico. TEL 525-5938720, FAX 525-7052492.

910.2 917 USA ISSN 1054-5034
F902.3
TIM BELL'S ALASKA TRAVEL GUIDE. Text in English. 1960. a. USD 14.95 (effective 2000). adv. bk.rev. illus.; maps. 440 p./no.; **Document type:** *Magazine, Consumer.* **Description:** Contains mile-by-mile information for Alaska, the Yukon, and northwestern British Columbia.
Formerly: Alaska Travel Guide (0065-5848)
Published by: Timothy J Bell, Ed & Pub, 413B 19th St, PMB 170, Lynden, WA 98264. TEL 250-769-3073, 800-880-9109. R&P, Adv. contact Timothy J Bell. Circ: 60,000.

914.672 ESP ISSN 1888-3850
TIME OUT BARCELONA. Text in Spanish, Catalan. 2007. w.
Published by: Sapiens Publicacions, C Corders 22-28, Barcelona, 08911, Spain. TEL 34-93-3899480, http://www.cultura03.com/sapienspublicacions/index.html.

914 GBR ISSN 1479-7054
TIME OUT LONDON. Text in English. 1968. w. GBP 69.99 domestic; GBP 150 in Europe; GBP 250 elsewhere; GBP 3.50 per issue; GBP 2.99 newsstand/cover (effective 2009). adv. bk.rev.; film rev.; play rev.; dance rev.; music rev.; rec.rev.; software rev.; tel.rev.; video rev.; Website rev. illus. 204 p./no. 4 cols./p.; back issues avail. **Document type:** *Magazine, Consumer.* **Description:** Covers all forms of arts and entertainment as well as consumer news and features.
Formerly (until 2002): Time Out (0049-3910)
Indexed: IIFP, IITV.
—BLDSC (8852.152500).
Published by: Time Out Publications Ltd., Universal House, 251 Tottenham Court Rd, London, WIT 7AB, United Kingdom. TEL 44-20-78133000, FAX 44-20-78233438, distribution@timeout.com, http://www.timeout.com. Pub. Mark Elliot TEL 44-20-78136043. Adv. contact Mark Phillips TEL 44-20-78136021.

914.2104 GBR ISSN 1753-2787
TIME OUT LONDON FOR VISITORS. Text in English. 1988. a. GBP 5 per issue (effective 2009). adv. **Document type:** *Magazine, Consumer.* **Description:** Focuses on restaurants, cafes and bars, sightseeing and shops.
Former titles (until 2006): Time Out London Visitors' Guide (1471-6194); (until 1999): Time Out to London for Visitors (0954-0938)
Published by: Time Out Publications Ltd., Universal House, 251 Tottenham Court Rd, London, WIT 7AB, United Kingdom. TEL 44-20-78133000, FAX 44-20-78233438, distribution@timeout.com, http://www.timeout.com. Pub. Mark Elliot TEL 44-20-78136043. Adv. contact Mark Phillips TEL 44-20-78136021.

917.47 028.5 USA ISSN 1548-4777
TIME OUT NEW YORK KIDS. Abbreviated title: T O N Y Kids. Text in English. 2004 (Spr.). bi-m. USD 9.95 (effective 2011). **Document type:** *Magazine, Consumer.*
Published by: Time Out New York Partners, LP, 475 10th Ave, 12th Fl, New York, NY 10018. TEL 646-432-3000, FAX 646-432-3010.

914.7 ROM ISSN 1453-2093
TIMISOARA - WHAT, WHERE, WHEN. Text in Multiple languages. 1997. q. ROL 50,000 domestic; USD 12 foreign (effective 2002). adv. **Document type:** *Magazine, Consumer.*
Published by: Crystal Publishing Group, 253, Calea Calarasilor, bl. 67 A, Ste. 4, Bucharest, Romania. TEL 40-21-3233829, FAX 40-21-3234706, office@bucurestiwww.ro, http://www.bucurestiwww.ro. Circ: 25,000 (paid and controlled).

379.85 ALB ISSN 1587-2378
TIRANA IN YOUR POCKET. Text in English. 2001. a. USD 5 newsstand/cover (effective 2004). adv. **Document type:** *Magazine, Consumer.*
Address: Blv Deshmoret e Kombit, Hotel Rogner Europapark, Tirana, Albania. TEL 355-4-235011.

915.694 USA ISSN 1935-5025
DS101
TODAY'S ISRAEL. Text mainly in English; Text occasionally in Hebrew. 2007. irreg. adv. **Document type:** *Magazine, Consumer.* **Description:** Covers aspects of Israeli tourism, culture and lifestyle including music, arts, lifestyle, food, health and cinema, with the aim of promoting foreign tourism.
Media: Online - full content.
Published by: Paperless Factory Inc, 14879 Sunnyview Ln, Delray Beach, FL 33484. TEL 646-461-1681. Ed. Hadas Kroitoru.

910.91 NLD ISSN 1573-0298
TOERACTIEF. Text in Dutch. 1991. 6/yr. EUR 31.95 to non-members; EUR 29.95 to members; EUR 5.75 newsstand/cover (effective 2008). adv. **Document type:** *Magazine, Consumer.*
Published by: Algemene Nederlandse Wielrijders Bond (A N W B) Media/Dutch Automobile Association Media, Postbus 93200, The Hague, 2509 BA, Netherlands. TEL 31-70-3141470, FAX 31-70-3146538, http://www.anwbmedia.nl. adv.: B&W page EUR 1,893, color page EUR 2,650; bleed 215 x 285. Circ: 56,224.

915.204 JPN
TOKYO CITY GUIDE TOUR COMPANION. Text in Japanese. 24/yr.
Published by: Tokyo Nyusu Tsushinsha/Tokyo News Service Ltd., Tsukiji Hamarikyu Bldg 10th Fl, 3-3 Tsuki-Ji 5-chome, Chuo-ku, Tokyo, 104-8004, Japan. TEL 03-3542-6511.

917.804 USA ISSN 1523-4770
TOOELE VALLEY MAGAZINE. Text in English. 1999 (Spring/Summer). s-a. USD 7.50 domestic; USD 3.95 newsstand/cover domestic.

Published by: Transcript Bulletin Publishing, 58 N. Main St., Tooele, UT 84074. TEL 435-882-0050. Ed. David Bern. Pub. Scott Dunn.

914.13 DEU
TOP GUIDE; Das aktuelle Journal fuer Berlin-Mitte. Text in German. 4/yr. EUR 2 newsstand/cover (effective 2007). adv. **Document type:** *Magazine, Consumer.*
Published by: T M M Marketing und Medien GmbH & Co. KG, Kantstr 151, Berlin, 10623, Germany. TEL 49-30-2062673, FAX 49-30-20626750, mail@tmm.de, http://tmm.de. adv.: color page EUR 1,250. Circ: 30,000 (controlled).

910.2 ITA ISSN 2038-4246
TOSCANA PARCHI; rivista dei parchi e delle aree protette. Text in Italian. 3/yr. EUR 20 (effective 2011). **Document type:** *Handbook/Manual/ Guide, Consumer.*
Published by: (Federazione Italiana Parchi - Federparchi), Edizioni E T S, Piazza Carrara 16-19, Pisa, Italy. TEL 39-050-29544, FAX 39-050-20158, info@edizioniets.it, http://www.edizioniets.it. Ed. Beatrice Bardelli.

917.14 CAN ISSN 1913-3944
TOTALEMENT TOURISME!. Text in French. 2007. s-a. free. **Document type:** *Magazine, Consumer.*
Published by: Quebec. Ministere du Tourisme, Direction des Communications, 900 Rene-Levesque Est, Bureau 400, Quebec, PQ G1R 2B5, Canada. TEL 418-643-5959, 800-482-2433, FAX 418-646-8723.

910 JPN
TOUR COMPANION. Text in English. 1973. fortn. free. adv. bk.rev. charts; illus. **Description:** Provides all foreigners in the Tokyo vicinity, whether tourists or residents, with the most up-to-date information concerning events, shopping, dining, night-life and other topics of interest.
Published by: Tokyo Nyusu Tsushinsha/Tokyo News Service Ltd., Tsukiji Hamarikyu Bldg 10th Fl, 3-3 Tsuki-Ji 5-chome, Chuo-ku, Tokyo, 104-8004, Japan. TEL 03-3542-6511. Ed. Takashi Takeda. Circ: 80,000.

TOUR MAGAZINE. *see* TRANSPORTATION

917.6 USA ISSN 0361-4948
F324.3
TOURBOOK: ALABAMA, LOUISIANA, MISSISSIPPI. Cover title: Alabama, Louisiana, Mississippi TourBook. Variant title: Alabama, Louisiana & Mississippi. Text in English. a. free to members (effective 2008). adv. illus. **Document type:** *Magazine, Consumer.* **Description:** Provides in-depth travel information and property listings on Alabama, Louisiana and Mississippi.
Published by: A A A Publishing, 1000 AAA Dr, Heathrow, FL 32746. TEL 407-444-8370, FAX 407-444-7766, AAATravelInfo-CustomerService@national.aaa.com, http://www.aaa.biz/. adv.: B&W page USD 11,620, color page USD 14,460. Circ: 944,000.

917.89 USA ISSN 0362-3599
F809.3
TOURBOOK: ARIZONA, NEW MEXICO. Cover title: Arizona, New Mexico TourBook. Text in English. 19??. a. free to members (effective 2008). adv. illus. **Document type:** *Magazine, Consumer.* **Description:** Provides in-depth travel information and property listings on Arizona, New Mexico.
Published by: A A A Publishing, 1000 AAA Dr, Heathrow, FL 32746. TEL 407-444-8370, FAX 407-444-7766, AAATravelInfo-CustomerService@national.aaa.com, http://www.aaa.biz/. adv.: color page USD 22,120. Circ: 1,488,000.

917.6 USA ISSN 0363-1486
F409.3
TOURBOOK: ARKANSAS, KANSAS, MISSOURI, OKLAHOMA. Cover title: Arkansas, Kansas, Missouri, Oklahoma TourBook. Text in English. 19??. a. free to members (effective 2009). adv. illus. **Document type:** *Magazine, Consumer.* **Description:** Provide in-depth travel information and property listings on Arkansas, Kansas, Missouri and Oklahoma.
Published by: A A A Publishing, 1000 AAA Dr, Heathrow, FL 32746. TEL 407-444-8370, FAX 407-444-7766, AAATravelInfo-CustomerService@national.aaa.com, http://www.aaa.biz/. adv.: color page USD 19,010. Circ: 113,400.

917.15 USA ISSN 0363-1788
F1035.8
TOURBOOK: ATLANTIC PROVINCES AND QUEBEC. Cover title: Atlantic Provinces and Quebec: New Brunswick, Newfoundland, Nova Scotia, Prince Edward Island, Quebec TourBook. Text in English. a. free to members (effective 2009). adv. illus. **Document type:** *Magazine, Consumer.* **Description:** Provide in-depth travel information and property listings on Atlantic Provinces and Quebec.
Supersedes in part (in 1976): Eastern Canada Tour Book (0569-2857)
Published by: A A A Publishing, 1000 AAA Dr, Heathrow, FL 32746. TEL 407-444-8370, FAX 407-444-7766, AAATravelInfo-CustomerService@national.aaa.com, http://www.aaa.biz/. adv.: color page USD 13,230. Circ: 57,800. **Co-sponsor:** Canadian Automobile Association.

917.8 USA ISSN 0362-9821
F774.3
TOURBOOK: COLORADO, UTAH. Cover title: Colorado, Utah TourBook. Text in English. 19??. a. free to members (effective 2009). adv. illus. **Document type:** *Magazine, Consumer.* **Description:** Provides in-depth travel information and property listings on Colorado and Utah.
Published by: A A A Publishing, 1000 AAA Dr, Heathrow, FL 32746. TEL 407-444-8370, FAX 407-444-7766, AAATravelInfo-CustomerService@national.aaa.com, http://www.aaa.biz/. adv.: color page USD 18,670. Circ: 1,159,500.

917.4 USA ISSN 0363-1494
F92.3
TOURBOOK: CONNECTICUT, MASSACHUSETTS, RHODE ISLAND. Cover title: Connecticut, Massachusetts, Rhode Island TourBook. Text in English. 19??. a. free to members (effective 2008). adv. illus. **Document type:** *Magazine, Consumer.* **Description:** Provide in-depth travel information and property listings on Connecticut, Massachusetts and Rhode Island.
Supersedes in part: Northeastern Tour Book (0468-6853)
Published by: A A A Publishing, 1000 AAA Dr, Heathrow, FL 32746. TEL 407-444-8370, FAX 407-444-7766, AAATravelInfo-CustomerService@national.aaa.com, http://www.aaa.biz/. adv.: color page USD 20,350. Circ: 1,284,500.

917.59 USA ISSN 0516-9674
GV1024
TOURBOOK: FLORIDA. Cover title: Florida TourBook. Text in English. 1965. a. free to members (effective 2008). adv. illus. **Document type:** *Magazine, Consumer.* **Description:** Provide in-depth travel information and property listings on Florida.
Supersedes in part (in 1965): Florida Tour Book, Including West Indies and Other Islands; Which was formerly (until 1959): Southeastern Tour Book, Including the West Indies
Published by: A A A Publishing, 1000 AAA Dr, Heathrow, FL 32746. TEL 407-444-8370, FAX 407-444-7766, AAATravelInfo-CustomerService@national.aaa.com, http://www.aaa.biz/. adv.: B&W page USD 21,020, color page USD 26,130. Circ: 2,463,500.

917.5 USA ISSN 0361-4956
F284.3
TOURBOOK: GEORGIA, NORTH CAROLINA, SOUTH CAROLINA. Cover title: Georgia, North Carolina, South Carolina TourBook. Variant title: Georgia, North Carolina, South Carolina. Text in English. 19??. a. free to members (effective 2008). adv. illus. **Document type:** *Magazine, Consumer.* **Description:** Provide in-depth travel information and property listings on Georgia, North Carolina and South Carolina.
Published by: A A A Publishing, 1000 AAA Dr, Heathrow, FL 32746. TEL 407-444-8370, FAX 407-444-7766, AAATravelInfo-CustomerService@national.aaa.com, http://www.aaa.biz/. adv.: color page USD 27,740. Circ: 2,484,000.

917 USA ISSN 0160-6921
DU622
TOURBOOK: HAWAII. Cover title: Hawaii TourBook. Text in English. 19??. a. free to members (effective 2009). adv. illus. **Document type:** *Magazine, Consumer.* **Description:** Provides in-depth travel information and property listings on Hawaii.
Published by: A A A Publishing, 1000 AAA Dr, Heathrow, FL 32746. TEL 407-444-8370, FAX 407-444-7766, AAATravelInfo-CustomerService@national.aaa.com, http://www.aaa.biz/. adv.: color page USD 12,260. Circ: 447,000.

917.9 USA ISSN 0363-2695
F744.3
TOURBOOK: IDAHO, MONTANA, WYOMING. Cover title: Idaho, Montana, Wyoming TourBook. Text in English. 1977. a. free to members (effective 2008). adv. illus. **Document type:** *Magazine, Consumer.* **Description:** Provide in-depth travel information and property listings on Idaho, Montana and Wyoming.
Supersedes in part: Northwestern Tour Book (0094-078X); Formerly: Northwestern States
Published by: A A A Publishing, 1000 AAA Dr, Heathrow, FL 32746. TEL 407-444-8370, FAX 407-444-7766, AAATravelInfo-CustomerService@national.aaa.com, http://www.aaa.biz/. adv.: color page USD 16,250. Circ: 865,500.

917 USA ISSN 0363-1508
F539.3
TOURBOOK: ILLINOIS, INDIANA, OHIO. Cover title: Illinois, Indiana, Ohio TourBook. Text in English. 19??. a. free to members (effective 2009). adv. illus. **Document type:** *Magazine, Consumer.* **Description:** Provides in-depth travel information and property listings on Illinois, Indiana and Ohio.
Published by: A A A Publishing, 1000 AAA Dr, Heathrow, FL 32746. TEL 407-444-8370, FAX 407-444-7766, AAATravelInfo-CustomerService@national.aaa.com, http://www.aaa.biz/. adv.: color page USD 24,940. Circ: 1,979,000.

917.68 USA
F449.3
TOURBOOK: KENTUCKY, TENNESSEE. Cover title: Kentucky, Tennessee TourBook. Text in English. 197?. a. free to members (effective 2008). adv. illus. **Document type:** *Magazine, Consumer.* **Description:** Provides in-depth travel information and property listings on Kentucky and Tennessee.
Published by: A A A Publishing, 1000 AAA Dr, Heathrow, FL 32746. TEL 407-444-8370, FAX 407-444-7766, AAATravelInfo-CustomerService@national.aaa.com, http://www.aaa.biz/. adv.: color page USD 22,150. Circ: 1,558,000.

917.4 USA ISSN 0363-1516
F17.3
TOURBOOK: MAINE, NEW HAMPSHIRE, VERMONT. Cover title: Maine, New Hampshire, Vermont TourBook. Text in English. 19??. a. free to members (effective 2009). adv. illus. **Document type:** *Magazine, Consumer.* **Description:** Provide in-depth travel information and property listings on Maine, New Hampshire and Vermont.
Supersedes in part: Northeastern Tour Book (0468-6853)
Published by: A A A Publishing, 1000 AAA Dr, Heathrow, FL 32746. TEL 407-444-8370, FAX 407-444-7766, AAATravelInfo-CustomerService@national.aaa.com, http://www.aaa.biz/. adv.: color page USD 18,890. Circ: 1,061,000.

917 USA ISSN 0363-1524
F564.3
TOURBOOK: MICHIGAN, WISCONSIN. Cover title: Michigan, Wisconsin TourBook. Text in English. 19??. a. free to members (effective 2009). adv. illus. **Document type:** *Magazine, Consumer.* **Description:** Provides in-depth travel information and property listings on Michigan and Wisconsin.
Published by: A A A Publishing, 1000 AAA Dr, Heathrow, FL 32746. TEL 407-444-8370, FAX 407-444-7766, AAATravelInfo-CustomerService@national.aaa.com, http://www.aaa.biz/. adv.: color page USD 17,530. Circ: 102,600.

917 USA ISSN 0364-0086
F106
TOURBOOK: MID-ATLANTIC. Cover title: Mid-Atlantic - Delaware, District of Columbia, Maryland, Virginia, West Virginia TourBook. Text in English. 1977. a. free to members (effective 2008). adv. illus. **Document type:** *Magazine, Consumer.* **Description:** Provides in-depth travel information and property listings on Mid-Atlantic.
Published by: A A A Publishing, 1000 AAA Dr, Heathrow, FL 32746. TEL 407-444-8370, FAX 407-444-7766, AAATravelInfo-CustomerService@national.aaa.com, http://www.aaa.biz/. adv.: color page USD 27,770. Circ: 248,800.

917 USA
F132.3
TOURBOOK. NEW JERSEY & PENNSYLVANIA. Cover title: New Jersey & Pennsylvania TourBook. Text in English. 19??. a. free to members (effective 2009). adv. illus. **Document type:** *Magazine, Consumer.* **Description:** Provides in-depth travel information and property listings on New Jersey and Pennsylvania.
Formerly (until 199?): TourBook: New Jersey, Pennsylvania (0363-1532)
Published by: A A A Publishing, 1000 AAA Dr, Heathrow, FL 32746. TEL 407-444-8370, FAX 407-444-7766, AAATravelInfo-CustomerService@national.aaa.com, http://www.aaa.biz/. adv.: color page USD 25,370. Circ: 1,911,500.

917 USA ISSN 0363-1540
F117.3
TOURBOOK: NEW YORK; including Niagara Falls, Ontario, Canada. Cover title: New York TourBook. Text in English. 19??. a. free to members (effective 2009). adv. illus. **Document type:** *Magazine, Consumer.* **Description:** Provides in-depth travel information and property listings on New York.
Published by: A A A Publishing, 1000 AAA Dr, Heathrow, FL 32746. TEL 407-444-8370, FAX 407-444-7766, AAATravelInfo-CustomerService@national.aaa.com, http://www.aaa.biz/. adv.: color page USD 21,220. Circ: 1,580,500. **Co-sponsor:** Canadian Automobile Association.

917 USA ISSN 0733-8368
GV1024
TOURBOOK: NORTH CENTRAL. Cover title: North Central TourBook - Iowa, Minnesota, Nebraska, North Dakota, South Dakota. Text in English. 19??. a. free to members (effective 2009). adv. illus. **Document type:** *Magazine, Consumer.* **Description:** Provides in-depth travel information and property listings on North Central.
Former titles (until 197?): North Central Tour Book (0733-835X); (until 1974): North Central States; (until 19??): North Central Tour Book Including Manitoba and Western Ontario
Published by: A A A Publishing, 1000 AAA Dr, Heathrow, FL 32746. TEL 407-444-8370, FAX 407-444-7766, AAATravelInfo-CustomerService@national.aaa.com, http://www.aaa.biz/. adv.: color page USD 16,660. Circ: 917,000.

917.9 USA
TOURBOOK: NORTHERN CALIFORNIA AND NEVADA. Cover title: Northern California, Nevada TourBook. Text in English. 19??. a. free to members (effective 2008). adv. illus. **Document type:** *Magazine, Consumer.* **Description:** Provides in-depth travel information and property listings on Northern California and Nevada.
Formerly: TourBook: California, Nevada
Published by: A A A Publishing, 1000 AAA Dr, Heathrow, FL 32746. TEL 407-444-8370, FAX 407-444-7766, AAATravelInfo-CustomerService@national.aaa.com, http://www.aaa.biz/. adv.: color page USD 2,644. Circ: 2,000,000.

917 USA
F1057
TOURBOOK. ONTARIO. Cover title: Ontario TourBook. Text in English. 19??. a. free to members (effective 2009). adv. illus. **Document type:** *Magazine, Consumer.*
Former titles (until 2000): Tour Book. Ontario, Including Niagara Falls, New York, USA; (until 1982): Tour Book. Ontario (0363-1559); Which superseded in part (in 19??): Eastern Canada Tour Book (0569-2857)
Related titles: ◆ French ed.: Guide de la Route, l'Ontario. ISSN 1193-3569.
Published by: A A A Publishing, 1000 AAA Dr, Heathrow, FL 32746. TEL 407-444-8299, 407-444-8402, FAX 407-444-8271, AAATravelInfo-CustomerService@national.aaa.com, http://www.aaa.biz/. adv.: page USD 14,580. Circ: 859,000. **Co-sponsor:** Canadian Automobile Association.

918 USA ISSN 0363-1567
F874.3
TOURBOOK: OREGON, WASHINGTON. Cover title: Oregon, Washington TourBook. Text in English. 19??. a. free to members (effective 2009). adv. illus. **Document type:** *Magazine, Consumer.* **Description:** Provides in-depth travel information and property listings on Oregon and Washington.
Published by: A A A Publishing, 1000 AAA Dr, Heathrow, FL 32746. TEL 407-444-8370, FAX 407-444-7766, AAATravelInfo-CustomerService@national.aaa.com, http://www.aaa.biz/. adv.: color page USD 18,990. Circ: 1,064,000.

910.91 USA ISSN 1541-6895
F867
TOURBOOK: SOUTHERN CALIFORNIA AND LAS VEGAS. Variant title: Southern California & Las Vegas. Text in English. 2001. a. free to members (effective 2009). adv. **Document type:** *Magazine, Consumer.* **Description:** Provides in-depth travel information and property listings on Southern California & Las Vegas.
Published by: A A A Publishing, 1000 AAA Dr, Heathrow, FL 32746. TEL 407-444-8370, FAX 407-444-7766, AAATravelInfo-CustomerService@national.aaa.com, http://www.aaa.biz/. adv.: color page USD 27,740. Circ: 2,400,000 (controlled).

917 USA ISSN 0363-1575
F384.3
TOURBOOK: TEXAS. Cover title: Texas TourBook. Text in English. 19??. a. free to members (effective 2009). adv. illus. **Document type:** *Magazine, Consumer.* **Description:** Provides in-depth travel information and property listings on Texas.
Published by: A A A Publishing, 1000 AAA Dr, Heathrow, FL 32746. TEL 407-444-8370, FAX 407-444-7766, AAATravelInfo-CustomerService@national.aaa.com, http://www.aaa.biz/. adv.: color page USD 17,510. Circ: 965,500.

917.12 USA ISSN 0362-3602
F1060.4
TOURBOOK: WESTERN CANADA AND ALASKA. Cover title: Western Canada and Alaska - Alberta, British Columbia, Manitoba, Northwest Territories, Saskatchewan, Yukon Territory and Alaska TourBook. Text in English. 197?. a. free to members (effective 2009). adv. illus. **Document type:** *Magazine, Consumer.* **Description:** Provides in-depth travel information and property listings on Kentucky and Tennessee.

Published by: A A A Publishing, 1000 AAA Dr, Heathrow, FL 32746. TEL 407-444-8370, FAX 407-444-7766, AAATravelInfo-CustomerService@national.aaa.com, http://www.aaa.biz/. adv.: B&W page USD 6,710, color page USD 8,590. Circ: 876,000. **Co-sponsor:** Canadian Automobile Association.

910 USA
TOURBUS PLUS!. Text in English. s-w. **Document type:** *Newsletter.*
Description: Presents in-depth reviews, interviews with cyberspace celebrities, etc.
Media: Online - full text.
Address: c/o Bob Rankin, PO Box 39, Tillson, NY 12486. FAX 914-658-3351.

388.3 796.7 BEL ISSN 0779-8652
TOURING; auto et lois. Text in French. 1895. m. (11/yr.). EUR 33.90 to non-members; free to members (effective 2005). adv. bk.rev. bibl.; illus. index. **Document type:** *Consumer.* **Description:** Publishes articles on automobile safety, reviews of new car models, ideas for travel in Belgium and throughout Europe, listings of local and regional events of interest, and other topics of interest to car owners.
Formed by the July 1993 merger of: Touring Secours; Touring Club Magazine (0772-2540); Which was formerly (until 1984): Autotouring (0045-1126)
Related titles: Dutch ed.
Published by: Touring Club of Belgium, Rue de la Loi - Wetstraat 44, Brussels, 1040, Belgium. TEL 32-2-233-2202, FAX 32-2-286-3323, media.dept@touring.be. Ed. Marc Debraekeller. Adv. contact Lieve Sonck. Circ: 690,000 (controlled).

910.91 388.3 CAN ISSN 0229-5466
TOURING. Text in English, French. 1922. q. CAD 10 (effective 2004). adv. illus.; stat. 64 p./no.; **Document type:** *Magazine, Consumer.*
Description: Distributed to members of Quebec CAA.
Formerly (until 1984): Autoclub (0005-0954)
Related titles: French ed.: ISSN 0838-6846.
Published by: Editions Feu Vert & Consultants C G E I Inc., 3281 Jean Beraud Ave, Laval, PQ H7T 2L2, Canada. TEL 514-334-5912, FAX 405-688-6269, gsp@beauchemin.qc.ca. Ed. Jean-Louis Gauthier. R&P, Adv. contact Ginette St Pierre TEL 514-334-5912 ext 275. color page CAD 11,390; trim 10.75 x 7.875. Circ: 530,000.

914 CHE ISSN 0040-9758
TOURING. Text in German. 1936. 20/yr. CHF 49 membership (effective 2005). bk.rev. illus.; stat. **Document type:** *Newspaper, Consumer.*
Related titles: Italian ed.; French ed.
Published by: (Touring Club Schweiz), Druck- und Verlags Konsortium Touring Club Schweiz, Maulbeerstr 10, Bern, 3001, Switzerland. TEL 41-31-3805000, FAX 41-31-3805006, verlag@tcs.ch. Ed. Stefan Senn. Circ: 1,400,000.

TOURING AND TASTING; wine, food, travel. *see* BEVERAGES

910.2 USA ISSN 1931-4817
GB1198.3.C2
TOURING CALIFORNIA AND NEVADA HOT SPRINGS. Text in English. 1997. irreg. USD 16.95 per issue (effective 2008). **Document type:** *Guide, Consumer.* **Description:** Explores the adventure and rugged beauty of the great outdoors.
Published by: The Globe Pequot Press, Inc., Falcon Publishing, 246 Goose Ln, PO Box 480, Guilford, CT 06437. TEL 203-458-4500, 888-249-7586, FAX 203-458-4603, 800-820-2329, info@globepequot.com, http://www.globepequot.com.

TOURING JUNIOR. *see* CHILDREN AND YOUTH—For

910.91 FRA ISSN 1287-2474
TOURISCOPIE; la veille sociologique et marketing des professionnels du tourisme et des loisirs. Text in French. 1998. m. EUR 427 (effective 2009). **Document type:** *Newsletter, Trade.*
Published by: Tourisme et Territoire, 10 Place d'Italie, Paris, 75013, France. TEL 33-1-44610482. Pub. Jean Audoin. **Dist. by:** Agence Innovapresse, 1 Place Boieldieu, Paris 75002, France. TEL 33-1-48240897, abonnement@innovapresse.com.

338.4791 HRV ISSN 1332-7461
G149
TOURISM. Text in English. 2000. q.
Related titles: Online - full text ed.; ◆ Serbo-Croatian ed.: Turizam. ISSN 0494-2639.
Indexed: A34, AEI, CA, CABA, DIP, E12, ESPM, F08, F12, GH, H&TI, H06, HPNRM, IBR, IBZ, IndVet, LT, N02, P03, PsycInfo, R12, RRTA, S13, S16, SCOPUS, SSciA, T02, T05, VS, W11.
—BLDSC (8870.920581), IE, Ingenta.
Published by: Croatian National Tourist Board, Iblerov trg 10/4, Zagreb, 10000, Croatia. TEL 385-455-64-55, FAX 385-455-78-27, info@htz.hr, http://www.croatia.hr/.

338.4791 CHE ISSN 2079-6366
▼ ➤ **TOURISM.** Text in English. forthcoming 2011. q. free (effective 2011). **Document type:** *Journal, Academic/Scholarly.*
Media: Online - full text.
Published by: M D P I AG, Postfach, Basel, 4005, Switzerland. TEL 41-61-6837734, FAX 41-61-3028918, http://www.mdpi.org/.

910.09 GBR ISSN 0261-3700
TOURISM. Text in English. 1978. q. GBP 19.50 per issue domestic; GBP 22 per issue foreign; free to qualified personnel (effective 2009). bk.rev. back issues avail. **Document type:** *Magazine, Trade.*
Description: Provides tourism trade information for professionals working in national and regional tourist boards, local government, travel agencies, and tour operators, visitor attractions, accommodation and catering, entertainment, information services, guiding, consultancies and education and training.
Related titles: Online - full text ed.: free (effective 2009).
Indexed: H&TI, H06.
—BLDSC (8870.920560), IE, Ingenta. **CCC.**
Published by: The Tourism Society, Trinity Ct, 34 West St, Sutton, Surrey SM1 1SH, United Kingdom. TEL 44-20-86614636, FAX 44-20-86614637, membership@tourismsociety.org.

910.202 CAN ISSN 1499-5719
G155.C2
TOURISM. Text in English. 1997. m. free. **Document type:** *Magazine, Consumer.*
Formerly (until 2001): Communique (1485-3817)
Related titles: Online - full content ed.; French ed.: Tourisme (Print). ISSN 1499-5735. 1997.
Indexed: SD.
Published by: Canadian Tourism Commission/Commission Canadienne du Tourisme, 55 Metcalfe St, Ste 600, Ottawa, ON K1P 6L5, Canada. TEL 613-946-1000. Ed. Peter G Kingsmill. Pub. Ghislain Gaudreault.

338.4 USA ISSN 1083-5423
G155.A1 CODEN: TOANFD
➤ **TOURISM ANALYSIS.** Text in English. 1996. bi-m. USD 620 combined subscription to institutions (print & online eds.) (effective 2011). back issues avail. **Document type:** *Journal, Academic/Scholarly.*
Description: Acts as forum for practitioners and academicians in the fields of leisure, recreation, tourism and hospitality.
Related titles: Online - full text ed.: ISSN 1943-3999. USD 590 (effective 2011) (from IngentaConnect).
Indexed: A37, CA, CABA, E12, ESPM, F08, F12, GH, H&TI, H06, I11, LT, N02, O01, R12, RRTA, S02, S03, S13, S16, SSciA, T02, T05, W11.
—BLDSC (8870.920596), IE, Ingenta. **CCC.**
Published by: Cognizant Communication Corp., 18 Peekskill Hollow Rd, P O Box 37, Putnam Valley, NY 10579. TEL 845-603-6440, FAX 845-603-6442, cogcomm@aol.com. Eds. Geoffrey I. Crouch TEL 61-3-94792450, Muzaffer Uysal TEL 540-231-8426. Pub. Robert N Miranda.

915 GBR ISSN 1467-3584
G155.A1
➤ **TOURISM AND HOSPITALITY RESEARCH;** the Surrey quarterly review. Abbreviated title: T H R. Text in English. 1999. q. USD 597 in North America to institutions; GBP 320 elsewhere to institutions (effective 2011). adv. bk.rev. abstr.; bibl.; charts; stat. 96 p./no. 2 cols./p.; back issues avail.; reprint service avail. from PSC. **Document type:** *Journal, Academic/Scholarly.* **Description:** Presents a body of knowledge which gives a clear, rigorous and more robust understanding of tourism and hospitality.
Formerly (until 1999): International Journal of Tourism and Hospitality Research (1464-2700)
Related titles: Online - full text ed.: ISSN 1742-9692 (from IngentaConnect).
Indexed: A10, A12, A15, A17, A22, A26, ABIn, B01, B02, B06, B07, B09, B15, B17, B18, CA, CABA, E01, E12, ESPM, F08, F12, G04, G08, GH, H&TI, H06, I05, I11, JEL, LT, N02, O01, P32, P48, P51, P53, P54, PGegResA, PHN&I, PQC, R12, RRTA, S02, S03, S13, S16, SCOPUS, SSciA, T02, V03, W11.
—BLDSC (8870.920613), IE, Ingenta. **CCC.**
Published by: (University of Surrey, School of Management), Sage Publications Ltd. (Subsidiary of: Sage Publications, Inc.), 1 Oliver's Yard, 55 City Rd, London, EC1Y 1SP, United Kingdom. TEL 44-20-73248500, FAX 44-20-73248600, info@sagepub.co.uk, http://www.uk.sagepub.com/home.nav. Circ: 400.

919.4 AUS
TOURISM AUSTRALIA. ANNUAL REPORT. Text in English. 1968. a. free (effective 2008). adv. bk.rev. illus.; stat. back issues avail. **Document type:** *Government.* **Description:** Revies all aspects of tourism marketing for Australia.
Formerly (until 2004): Australian Tourist Commission. Annual Report (0728-7143)
Related titles: Online - full text ed.: free (effective 2008).
Published by: Tourism Australia, GPO Box 2721, Sydney, NSW 1006, Australia. TEL 61-2-93601111, FAX 61-2-93316469, corpaffairs@tourism.australia.com.

338.4791 CAN ISSN 1912-8053
TOURISM BRITISH COLUMBIA. PROGRAM GUIDE. Text in English. 199?. a. **Document type:** *Handbook/Manual/Guide, Trade.*
Published by: Tourism British Columbia, PO Box 9830, Stn. Prov. Govt., Victoria, BC V8W 9W5, Canada. TEL 250-356-6363.

338.4 NZL ISSN 1177-3022
TOURISM BUSINESS. Text in English. 2006. bi-m. NZD 40 (effective 2008). adv. **Document type:** *Magazine, Consumer.* **Description:** For owners and operators of luxury lodges and boutique hotels, motels, holiday parks, transportation companies, charters, airlines, rental vehicles, trout fishing, adventure tourism, guided tours, cultural tourism, garden tours, bed and breakfast ventures, and art and craft outlets.
Published by: Tourism Business Magazine, PO Box 32-186, Devonport, Auckland, New Zealand. TEL 64-9-4451844, FAX 64-9-4451872. Ed. Annie Gray. Adv. contact Jan Klee. Circ: 3,000.

338.4791 301 USA ISSN 1098-304X
G155.A1
TOURISM, CULTURE & COMMUNICATION. Text in English. 1998. 3/yr. USD 390 combined subscription to institutions (print & online eds.) (effective 2011). back issues avail. **Document type:** *Journal, Trade.*
Description: Examines major issues of cultural diversity and communication between cultures and subcultures and their impact on management practice in the tourism and hospitality industries.
Related titles: Online - full text ed.: ISSN 1943-4146. USD 360 (effective 2011) (from IngentaConnect).
Indexed: CA, CABA, E12, F08, F12, GH, H&TI, H06, LT, N02, R12, RRTA, SCOPUS, T02, TAR, W11.
—BLDSC (8870.920762), IE, Ingenta. **CCC.**
Published by: Cognizant Communication Corp., 18 Peekskill Hollow Rd, P O Box 37, Putnam Valley, NY 10579. TEL 845-603-6440, FAX 845-603-6442, cogcomm@aol.com. Eds. Brian King TEL 61-3-96884430, Lindsay Turner. Pub. Robert N Miranda.

338.4 GBR ISSN 1354-8166
G155.A1
➤ **TOURISM ECONOMICS;** the business and finance of tourism and recreation. Text in English. 1995. bi-m. EUR 485 combined subscription in Europe to institutions (print & online eds.); USD 499 combined subscription in United States to institutions (print & online eds.); GBP 327 combined subscription to institutions in the UK & elsewhere (print & online eds.) (effective 2012). stat.; abstr.; illus. back issues avail.; reprints avail. **Document type:** *Journal, Academic/Scholarly.* **Description:** Contains research papers on the business and economics of tourism and recreation.
Related titles: Online - full text ed.: ISSN 2044-0375. 2000 (from IngentaConnect).
Indexed: A12, A13, A14, A17, A34, A36, ABIn, CA, CABA, CurCont, E12, ESPM, EconLit, F08, F12, GEOBASE, GH, H&TI, H06, I11, IBSS, IndVet, JEL, LT, N02, P32, P37, P48, P51, P53, P54, PGegResA, PQC, R12, RRTA, S02, S03, S13, S16, SCOPUS, SSCI, SSciA, T02, T05, VS, W07, W11.
—BLDSC (8870.920780), IE, Infotrieve, Ingenta. **CCC.**
Published by: I P Publishing Ltd., 258 Belsize Rd, London, NW6 4BT, United Kingdom. TEL 44-20-73161870, FAX 44-20-76249994, JEdmondson@ippublishing.com. Ed. Stephen Wanhill. **Dist. by:** Turpin Distribution Services Ltd., Pegasus Dr, Stratton Business Park, Biggleswade, Bedfordshire SG18 8QB, United Kingdom. TEL 44-1767-604957, FAX 44-1767-601640, subscriptions@turpin-distribution.com, http://www.turpin-distribution.com/.

338.479 306.4 GBR ISSN 1461-6688
G149
➤ **TOURISM GEOGRAPHIES;** an international journal of tourism place, space and environment. Text in English. 1999. q. GBP 408 combined subscription in United Kingdom to institutions (print & online eds.); EUR 544, USD 683 combined subscription to institutions (print & online eds.) (effective 2012). adv. bk.rev. illus. back issues avail.; reprint service avail. from PSC. **Document type:** *Journal, Academic/Scholarly.* **Description:** Publishes research reports, statistics and debates on the interaction of geography with tourism and tourism-related areas of recreation and leisure.
Related titles: Online - full text ed.: ISSN 1470-1340. GBP 367 in United Kingdom to institutions; EUR 489, USD 614 to institutions (effective 2012) (from IngentaConnect).
Indexed: A01, A03, A08, A20, A22, C25, CA, CABA, CurCont, E01, E12, ESPM, EnvAb, F08, F12, GEOBASE, H&TI, H06, HPNRM, I11, IBR, IBSS, IBZ, LT, N02, P26, P32, P42, P54, PAIS, PGegResA, PQC, PSA, R12, RRTA, S02, S03, S13, S16, SCOPUS, SD, SSCI, SSciA, SociolAb, T02, W07, W11.
—IE, Infotrieve, Ingenta. **CCC.**
Published by: Routledge (Subsidiary of: Taylor & Francis Group), 4 Park Sq, Milton Park, Abingdon, Oxon OX14 4RN, United Kingdom. TEL 44-20-70176000, FAX 44-20-70176336, subscriptions@tandf.co.uk, http://www.routledge.com. Ed. Alan A Lew TEL 928-523-6567. Adv. contact Linda Hann TEL 44-1344-779945. **Subscr. in N. America to:** Taylor & Francis Inc., Customer Services Dept, 325 Chestnut St, 8th Fl, Philadelphia, PA 19106. TEL 800-354-1420, FAX 215-625-2940; **Subscr. to:** Taylor & Francis Ltd., Journals Customer Service, Sheepen Pl, Colchester, Essex CO3 3LP, United Kingdom. TEL 44-20-70175544, FAX 44-20-70175198, tf.enquiries@tfinforma.com.

910.91 551.46 USA ISSN 1544-273X
G156.5.M36
TOURISM IN MARINE ENVIRONMENTS; an interdisciplinary journal. Text in English. 2004. s-a. USD 475 combined subscription to institutions (print & online eds.) (effective 2011). back issues avail. **Document type:** *Journal, Academic/Scholarly.* **Description:** Deals with a variety of management issues in marine settings. It idraws upon the expertise of academics and practitioners from various disciplines related to the marine environment, including tourism, marine science, geography, social sciences, psychology, environmental studies, economics, marketing, and many more.
Related titles: Online - full text ed.: USD 440 (effective 2011) (from IngentaConnect).
Indexed: A34, A38, CABA, E12, ESPM, F08, F12, GH, GeoRef, I11, LT, N02, R12, RRTA, S13, S16, SCOPUS, SSciA, W11.
—BLDSC (8870.920971), Ingenta.
Published by: Cognizant Communication Corp., 18 Peekskill Hollow Rd, P O Box 37, Putnam Valley, NY 10579. TEL 845-603-6440, FAX 845-603-6442, cogcomm@aol.com. Ed. Michael Luck TEL 64-9-9179999 ext 5833. Pub. Robert N Miranda.

910.02 647.068 GBR ISSN 0261-5177
G155.A1
➤ **TOURISM MANAGEMENT.** Text in English. 1980. 6/yr. EUR 1,371 in Europe to institutions; JPY 181,900 in Japan to institutions; USD 1,533 elsewhere to institutions (effective 2012). abstr.; charts; illus. back issues avail. **Document type:** *Journal, Academic/Scholarly.*
Description: Features original research in tourism, analysis of trends, and information on the planning and management of all aspects of travel and tourism.
Formerly (until 1982): International Journal of Tourism Management (0143-2516)
Related titles: Microform ed.: (from PQC); Online - full text ed.: ISSN 1879-3193 (from IngentaConnect, ScienceDirect).
Indexed: A10, A20, A22, A26, A34, A35, A36, ASCA, AgBio, AgrForAb, BA, CA, CABA, CPM, CurCont, E12, ESPM, Emerald, F08, F12, GEOBASE, GH, H&TI, H06, HPNRM, I05, I11, IndVet, LT, N02, OR, P03, P32, P34, P37, PGegResA, PHN&I, PsycInfo, R12, RRTA, RiskAb, S02, S03, S13, S16, SCOPUS, SSCI, SSciA, T02, T05, V03, VS, W07, W11, WildRev.
—BLDSC (8870.920970), IE, Infotrieve, Ingenta. **CCC.**
Published by: Pergamon (Subsidiary of: Elsevier Science & Technology), The Blvd, Langford Ln, East Park, Kidlington, Oxford OX5 1GB, United Kingdom. TEL 44-1865-843000, FAX 44-1865-843010, JournalsCustomerServiceEMEA@elsevier.com. Ed. Chris Ryan TEL 64-7-8384259. **Subscr. to:** Elsevier BV, Radarweg 29, PO Box 211, Amsterdam 1000 AE, Netherlands. TEL 31-20-4853757, FAX 31-20-4853432, http://www.elsevier.nl.

919.304 NZL ISSN 1175-7965
TOURISM NEWS. Text in English. 1990. bi-m. free. **Document type:** *Newsletter, Trade.* **Description:** Updates the tourism industry on our off-shore markets, tourism issues and Tourism New Zealand activity.
Former titles (until 2000): New Zealand Tourism News (1172-2304); (until 1992): New Zealand. Ministry of Tourism. Newsletter (1171-1760); (until 1991): New Zealand Tourism Department (1170-5078)
Related titles: Online - full text ed.: ISSN 1177-8393.
Published by: Tourism New Zealand, PO Box 95, Wellington, New Zealand. TEL 64-4-917-5400, FAX 64-4-915-3817, http://www.purenz.com.

TOURISM PLANNING & DEVELOPMENT. *see* BUSINESS AND ECONOMICS—Management

915.4 IND ISSN 0250-8281
G155.I4
➤ **TOURISM RECREATION RESEARCH.** Text in English. 1976. 3/yr. USD 300 combined subscription (print & online eds.); USD 250 (print or online ed.); USD 85 per issue (print or online ed.) (effective 2011). bk.rev. bibl.; illus.; abstr.; charts; maps. Supplement avail.; back issues avail.; reprints avail. **Document type:** *Journal, Academic/Scholarly.* **Description:** Multidisciplinary research journal focusing on problems in various recreational environments of ecology, economy and culture. Attempts to seek possible answers for sustainable development of tourism.
Related titles: Online - full text ed.

Indexed: A10, CA, CABA, E12, ESPM, Emerald, GH, H&TI, H06, I11, LT, N02, OR, P32, PGegResA, R12, R13, RRTA, S13, S16, SSciA, SportS, T02, T05, V03, W11.
—IE.
Published by: Centre for Tourism Research and Development, A 965/6 Indira Nagar, Lucknow, Uttar Pradesh 226 016, India. TEL 91-522-2350144, FAX 91-522-2340313, trrworld@gmail.com, http://www.trrworld.com. Ed. Tej Vir Singh. **Subscr. to:** I N S I O Scientific Books & Periodicals.

914 GBR ISSN 1660-5373
TOURISM REVIEW/ZEITSCHRIFT FUER TOURISMUS. Abbreviated title: T R. Text in English, French, German. 1946. q. EUR 209 combined subscription in Europe (print & online eds.); USD 299 combined subscription in the Americas (print & online eds.); GBP 149 combined subscription in the UK & elsewhere (print & online eds.); AUD 309 combined subscription in Australasia (print & online eds.) (effective 2012). adv. bk.rev. bibl.; stat. back issues avail.; reprint service avail. from PSC. **Document type:** *Journal, Academic/Scholarly.* **Description:** Promotes an exchange of scientific concepts and research findings between different cultures and across language barriers.
Formerly (until 2001): Revue De Tourisme (0251-3102)
Related titles: Online - full text ed.: ISSN 1759-8451 (from IngentaConnect).
Indexed: A22, A35, CA, CABA, DIP, E12, GH, H&TI, H06, IBR, IBZ, KES, LT, N02, R12, RASB, RRTA, S13, S16, T02, W11.
—BLDSC (8870.922363), IE, **CCC.**
Published by: (International Association of Scientific Experts in Tourism CHE), Emerald Group Publishing Ltd., Howard House, Wagon Ln, Bingley, W Yorks BD16 1WA, United Kingdom. TEL 44-1274-777700, FAX 44-1274-785201, information@emeraldinsight.com. Pub. Valerie Robillard.

338.4 USA ISSN 1544-2721
G155.P25 CODEN: PTREFS
➤ **TOURISM REVIEW INTERNATIONAL**; an international journal. Text in English. 1997. q. USD 510 combined subscription to institutions (print & online eds.) (effective 2011). back issues avail. **Document type:** *Journal, Academic/Scholarly.* **Description:** Discusses the economic and environmental effects of increased tourism in the Pacific region.
Former titles (until 2003): Pacific Tourism Review (1088-4157); (until 1997): Waiariki Tourism Quarterly
Related titles: Online - full text ed.: ISSN 1943-4421. USD 475 (effective 2011) (from IngentaConnect).
Indexed: A35, AEI, AgBio, BAS, C25, CA, CABA, DRIE, E12, ESPM, F08, F12, G11, GH, GeoRef, H&TI, H06, HPNRM, IBSS, LT, N02, R12, RRTA, S13, S16, SSciA, T02, T05, W11.
—IE, Ingenta. **CCC.**
Published by: Cognizant Communication Corp., 18 Peeksill Hollow Rd, P O Box 37, Putnam Valley, NY 10579. TEL 845-603-6440, FAX 845-603-6442, cogcomm@aol.com. Ed. Sue Beeton. Pub. Robert N Miranda.

338.4 NZL ISSN 1175-530X
G155.N5
TOURISM SATELLITE ACCOUNT. Text in English. 1995. irreg. NZD 35 per issue (effective 2007). **Description:** Provides an updated analysis of the New Zealand tourism industry.
Related titles: Online - full text ed.: ISSN 1177-6226.
Published by: (Tourism Research Council New Zealand), Statistics New Zealand/Te Tari Tatau, Statistics House, The Blvd, Harbour Quays, PO Box 2922, Wellington, 6140, New Zealand. TEL 64-4-9314600, FAX 64-4-9314610, info@stats.govt.nz.

338.4 CAN ISSN 1488-3082
G155.C3
TOURISM STATISTICAL DIGEST/CANADA. STATISTIQUE CANADA. VOYAGES, TOURISME ET LOISIRS DE PLEIN AIR-RESUME STATISTIQUE. (Catalog 66-202) Text in English, French. 1972. biennial. CAD 45 per issue (effective 2004).
Former titles (until 1999): Tourism in Canada (0838-3863); (until 1988): Canada. Statistics Canada. Tourism and Recreation (0824-9032); Which superseded in part in 1984: Canada. Statistics Canada. Travel, Tourism and Outdoor Recreation - a Statistical Digest (0380-6316)
Related titles: Online - full content ed.: ISSN 1488-3090. 1999.
Published by: Statistics Canada/Statistique Canada, Communications Division, 3rd Fl, R H Coats Bldg, Ottawa, ON K1A 0A6, Canada. TEL 800-263-1136, infostats@statcan.ca, http://www.statcan.gc.ca. Circ: 2,000.

338.4 AUS ISSN 1836-2966
TOURISM TASMANIA. ANNUAL REPORT. Text in English. biennial. **Description:** Details Tourism Tasmania's performance during the year in review, explains how the Authority has achieved its stated goals within budget, and provides a comprehensive financial report.
Former titles (until 1997): Tasmania. Department of Tourism, Sport and Recreation. Annual Report; (until 1990): Tasmania. Department of Sport and Recreation. Annual Report; (until 1989): Tasmania. Department of Tourism. Report for the Year; (until 1978): Tasmania. Tourism Development Authority. Report for the Year; (until 1971): Tasmania. Government Tourist and Immigration Department. Report for the Year
Related titles: Online - full text ed.
Published by: Tourism Tasmania (Subsidiary of: Queensland, Department of Employment, Economic Development and Innovation), GPO Box 399, Hobart, TAS 7001, Australia. TEL 61-3-62308235, FAX 61-3-62308353, reception@tourismtasmania.com.au, http://www.tourismtasmania.com.au.

338.4 AUS ISSN 1838-1502
▼ **TOURISM TASMANIA STRATEGIC PLAN.** Text in English. 2009. triennial. **Document type:** *Trade.* **Description:** Covers the achievements and progress of the past as well as shifts to a business model that aims to enable the broader tourism industry in Tasmania.
Related titles: Online - full text ed.: ISSN 1838-1510.
Published by: Tourism Tasmania (Subsidiary of: Queensland, Department of Employment, Economic Development and Innovation), GPO Box 399, Hobart, TAS 7001, Australia. TEL 61-3-62308235, FAX 61-3-62308353, reception@tourismtasmania.com.au.

TOURISM TRADE DIRECTORY: SOUTH AFRICA. *see* BUSINESS AND ECONOMICS—Trade And Industrial Directories

338.4 AUS ISSN 1448-9937
TOURISM VICTORIA. ANNUAL REPORT. Text in English. 1993. a., latest 2008. free (effective 2009). back issues avail. **Document type:** *Government.* **Description:** Covers annual information about tourism in Victoria.
Formerly (until 1992): Victorian Tourism Commission. Annual Report
Related titles: Online - full text ed.
Published by: Tourism Victoria, GPO Box 2219T, Melbourne, VIC 3001, Australia. TEL 61-3-96539777, FAX 61-3-96539722, feedback@tourism.vic.gov.au.

917 USA ISSN 1935-3286
G155.U6
TOURISM WORKS FOR AMERICA (YEAR); travel industry snapshots. Text in English. 1990. a., latest 2007, 16th ed. USD 35 per issue (effective 2008). adv. **Document type:** *Magazine, Trade.* **Description:** Provides an overview of travel and tourism within the United States for the year. Includes attractions, outdoor interests, hospitality services, transportation and employment within the hospitality industry.
Former titles (until 2007): The Power of Travel (1559-3150); (until 2006): Tourism Works for America (1534-6870)
Published by: Travel Industry Association of America, 1100 New York Ave, NW, Ste 450, Washington, DC 20005. TEL 202-408-8422, FAX 202-408-1255, feedback@tia.org, http://www.tia.org. Pub. Dawn L Drew. Adv. contact Sarah Dickson TEL 202-408-2141.

910.2 CAN
TOURISME (ONLINE); mensuel du tourisme du Canada. Text in French. m.
Formerly (until 2001): Commission Canadienne du Tourisme. Communique (1481-8582)
Media: Online - full content. **Related titles:** Print ed.: Tourisme (Print). ISSN 1499-5735. 1997; English ed.
Published by: Canadian Tourism Commission/Commission Canadienne du Tourisme, 55 Metcalfe St, Ste 600, Ottawa, ON K1P 6L5, Canada. TEL 613-946-1000, http://www.canadatourism.com.

910.202 CAN ISSN 1205-0342
TOURISME JEUNESSE. Text in English. 1983. 2/yr. CAD 11.50; CAD 20 foreign. adv. **Document type:** *Newspaper.* **Description:** Covers youth tourism, foreign exchange programs, travel tips, youth hostels.
Formerly: Temps Libre (0823-5708)
Published by: Regroupement Tourisme Jeunesse, 4545 Pierre-de-Coubertin Av, Montreal, PQ H1V 3R2, Canada. TEL 514-252-3117, FAX 514-252-3119. Adv. contact Charlene Baron. Circ: 50,000.

338.4791 GRC ISSN 1790-8418
G155.A1
➤ **TOURISMOS**; an international multidisciplinary journal of tourism. Text in English. 2006. 2/yr. free (effective 2008). **Document type:** *Journal, Academic/Scholarly.* **Description:** Aims to promote and enhance research in all fields of tourism, including travel, hospitality and leisure.
Related titles: Online - full text ed.: free (effective 2011).
Indexed: CA, CABA, E12, F08, GH, H&TI, H06, LT, N02, R12, RRTA, S13, S16, SCOPUS, T02, TAR, W11.
Published by: University of the Aegean, Interdepartmental Program of Postgraduate Studies in Tourism, 54 Michail Livanou St, Chios, 82100, Greece. TEL 30-22710-35322, FAX 30-22710-35399, mstath@aegean.gr. Ed. Paris Tsartas. Circ: 650 (controlled).

910 AUT
TOURISMUS IN OESTERREICH. Text in German. 1956. a. EUR 50 (effective 2005). **Document type:** *Government.*
Formerly: Fremdenverkehr in Oesterreich (0071-948X)
Related titles: ◆ Series of: Beitraege zur Oesterreichischen Statistik. ISSN 0067-2319.
Published by: Statistik Austria, Guglgasse 13, Vienna, W 1110, Austria. TEL 43-1-711280, FAX 43-1-711287728, info@statistik.gv.at, http://www.statistik.at.

338.4791 647.94 DEU ISSN 1865-5483
TOURISMUS- UND HOTELLERIEPRAXIS. Text in German. 2008. m. EUR 98.40; EUR 49.20 to students; EUR 19.95 newsstand/cover (effective 2010). adv. **Document type:** *Magazine, Trade.*
Related titles: Online - full text ed.: ISSN 1865-6412. 2008. EUR 98.40 (effective 2010).
Published by: Erich Schmidt Verlag GmbH & Co. (Berlin), Genthiner Str 30 G, Berlin, 10785, Germany. TEL 49-30-2500850, FAX 49-30-250085305, esv@esvmedien.de, http://www.esv.info. Ed. Hans-Juergen Hillmer. Adv. contact Peter Taprogge. color page EUR 1,390; trim 185 x 210. Circ: 6,000 (paid).

910.2 GBR
TOURIST ATTRACTIONS & EVENTS OF THE WORLD. Text in English. 200?. irreg., latest 10th ed. GBP 16.50 per issue (effective 2009). adv. **Document type:** *Handbook/Manual/Guide, Consumer.* **Description:** Covers the top 400 tourism attractions in the world including a description of its history and highlights, contact address, transportation information, opening times, price of admission, UNESCO listing and facilities including car parking, restaurants and disabled access.
Published by: Columbus Travel Media Ltd (Subsidiary of: Highbury House Communications Plc), Media House, Azalea Dr, Swanley, Kent BR8 8HU, United Kingdom. TEL 44-1322-616344, 44-1322-611430, travelads@columbustravelmedia.com. Adv. contact David Simms TEL 44-1322-611335.

910 AUT
TOURIST AUSTRIA INTERNATIONAL. Text in German. w. **Document type:** *Magazine, Trade.*
Address: Kettenbrueckengasse 22, Vienna, B 1040, Austria. TEL 43-1-5888150, FAX 43-1-5888166. Ed. Walter Norden. Circ: 12,400.

910.4 790.1 ITA
TOURIST MAGAZINE. Text in Italian. 1988. q. free. adv. **Document type:** *Magazine, Consumer.*
Published by: Editoriale Eurocamp Srl, Via Ludovico di Breme 79, Milan, MI 20156, Italy. TEL 39-02-38001954, FAX 39-02-38001940, info@guideuro.it, http://www.guideuro.it. Adv. contact Claudio Benaglia. Circ: 5,000.

910.202 GBR ISSN 1748-3638
TOURIST NEWS. Variant title: Northern Ireland Tourism News. Text in English. 1990. m. back issues avail. **Document type:** *Newsletter, Trade.*
Formerly (until 2005): Northern Ireland Leisure Travel News (1477-3678)
Published by: Northern Ireland Tourist Board, 59 North St, Belfast, BT1 1NB, United Kingdom. TEL 44-28-90231221, FAX 44-28-90240960, info@nitb.com.

910.91 BHS
TOURIST NEWS (BAHAMAS). Text in English. 1962. m. USD 36 in United States. adv.
Formerly (until 1971): Bahamas Weekly
Published by: Star Publishers Ltd., PO Box 4855, Nassau, Bahamas. TEL 242-3223724, FAX 242-3224527. Pub. Bobby Bower. adv.: B&W page USD 585. Circ: 390,000.

338.4791 CAN ISSN 1914-9883
TOURIST SIGNING POLICY. ELIGIBILITY CRITERIA. Text in English. 2002. biennial. **Document type:** *Government.*
Related titles: ◆ French ed.: Politique de Signalisation Touristique. Criteres d'Admissibilite. ISSN 1716-2637.
Published by: Quebec. Ministere du Tourisme, Direction Generale des Services a la Clientele Touristique, 1255 Rue Peel, Bureau 400, Montreal, PQ H3B 4V4, Canada.

910.202 GBR ISSN 1468-7976
G155.A1
➤ **TOURIST STUDIES**; an international journal. Text in English. 2001 (Feb.). 3/yr. USD 784, GBP 424 combined subscription to institutions (print & online eds.); USD 768, GBP 416 to institutions (effective 2011). adv. bk.rev. back issues avail.; reprint service avail. from PSC. **Document type:** *Journal, Academic/Scholarly.* **Description:** Provides a platform for the development of critical perspectives on the nature of tourism as a social phenomenon. Evaluates, compares and integrates approaches to tourism from sociology, socio-psychology, leisure studies, cultural studies, geography and anthropology.
Related titles: Online - full text ed.: ISSN 1741-3206. USD 706, GBP 382 to institutions (effective 2011).
Indexed: A10, A22, AICP, ASFA, CA, CABA, DIP, E-psyche, E01, E12, ESPM, F08, F12, FR, GH, H&TI, H06, I14, IBR, IBZ, LT, MLA-IB, N02, P03, P32, PGegResA, PsycInfo, PsycholAb, R12, RRTA, S02, S03, S13, S16, SCOPUS, SSciA, SociolAb, T02, V03, W11.
—BLDSC (8870.934000), IE, Ingenta, INIST. **CCC.**
Published by: Sage Publications Ltd. (Subsidiary of: Sage Publications, Inc.), 1 Oliver's Yard, 55 City Rd, London, EC1Y 1SP, United Kingdom. TEL 44-20-73248500, FAX 44-20-73248600, info@sagepub.co.uk, http://www.uk.sagepub.com/home.nav. Eds. Adrian Franklin, Mike Crang. adv.: B&W page GBP 350; 130 x 205. **Subscr. in the Americas to:** Sage Publications, Inc., 2455 Teller Rd, Thousand Oaks, CA 91320. TEL 805-499-9774, FAX 805-499-0871, journals@sagepub.com.

338.4 AUS ISSN 0815-1318
G155.A75
➤ **TOURISTICS.** Text in English. 1985. 2/yr. bk.rev. abstr.; bibl.; charts; illus.; maps; stat.; tr.lit. back issues avail. **Document type:** *Journal, Academic/Scholarly.* **Description:** Deals with a wide range of topical tourism research related areas.
Published by: Edith Cowan University, School of Marketing,Tourism and Leisure, Washington, 100 Joondalup Drive, Joondalup, W.A. 6027, Australia. TEL 61-8-94005698, FAX 61-8-94005048, j.carlsen@conan.edu.au. Circ: 150.

910.2 DEU ISSN 0049-4283
TOURISTIK AKTUELL. Text in German. 1970. w. EUR 44 domestic; EUR 88 foreign; EUR 1.20 newsstand/cover (effective 2009). adv. bk.rev. abstr.; illus.; stat. **Document type:** *Journal, Trade.*
Indexed: RASB.
Published by: EuBuCo Verlag GmbH, Geheimrat-Hummel-Platz 4, Hochheim, 65239, Germany. TEL 49-6146-6050, FAX 49-6146-605200, verlag@eubuco.de, http://www.eubuco.de. Ed. Matthias Guertler. Adv. contact Bianca Peters. B&W page EUR 4,700, color page EUR 6,200; trim 220 x 310. Circ: 30,838 (paid and controlled).

910.09 DEU ISSN 0173-606X
TOURISTIK R.E.P.O.R.T. Text in German. 1972. fortn. EUR 42; EUR 2 newsstand/cover (effective 2008). adv. **Document type:** *Magazine, Consumer.*
Formerly (until 1980): WiCo Touristik Report (0171-0141)
Published by: T V G - Touristik Verlagsgesellschaft mbH, Dieselstr 36, Offenbach, 63071, Germany. TEL 49-69-98190451, FAX 49-69-98190455. Ed. Juergen Scharrer. adv.: color page EUR 7,800; trim 185 x 265. Circ: 30,471 (paid and controlled).

338.4791 AUT ISSN 1817-129X
DAS TOURISTIK TELEFONBUCH. Text in German. 2001. s-a. EUR 14; EUR 9 newsstand/cover (effective 2005). adv. **Document type:** *Directory, Trade.*
Published by: Manstein Zeitschriften Verlagsgesellschaft mbH, Brunner Feldstr 45, Perchtoldsdorf, N 2380, Austria. TEL 43-1-866480, FAX 43-1-86648100, office@manstein.at. adv.: B&W page EUR 500, color page EUR 600; trim 90 x 190.

910.202 CYP ISSN 0259-3580
TOURISTIKA CHRONIKA/TOURISM CHRONICLE. Text in Greek. 1986. bi-m.
Address: PO Box 7083, Nicosia, Cyprus. TEL 357-2-443240. Ed. A Karouzis. Circ: 2,000.

910.2 DEU
TOURISTIKMAGAZIN. Text in German. w. adv. **Document type:** *Consumer.* **Description:** Contains the latest information, news and trends in travel and tourism.
Media: Online - full text.
Published by: Spessartweb Online Verlag, Buettnerstr 15, Triefenstein, 97855, Germany. TEL 49-9395-997914, FAX 49-9395-997915, info@spessartweb.de, http://www.spessartweb.de. Ed. Horst Toennis. Adv. contact Gunther Doebler.

910.202 DEU ISSN 0173-3877
TOURS; das Abenteuer Magazin. Text in German. 1980. bi-m. EUR 23.40; EUR 4.60 newsstand/cover (effective 2008). adv. **Document type:** *Magazine, Consumer.*
Formed by the merger of (1979-1980): Allrad (0173-3915); (1979-1980): Kanu-Magazin (0173-3931); (1978-1980): Reisecaravan-Magazin (0173-3966); (1977-1980): Reisemobil-Magazin (0173-3982)
Published by: Medienmenschen GmbH, Sebastian-Bauer-Str 16a, Munich, 81737, Germany. TEL 49-89-20001690, FAX 49-89-200016912, info@medienmenschen.de, http://www.medienmenschen.de. Ed. Christian Bonk. Adv. contact Horst Mindel. B&W page EUR 3,740, color page EUR 6,000; trim 210 x 280. Circ: 18,293 (paid and controlled).

TU

917.1 CAN ISSN 0847-9348
TOURS ON MOTORCOACH. Text in English. 1988. m. adv. **Document type:** *Magazine, Trade.* **Description:** Travel trade publication for group tour organizers.
Related titles: ◆ English ed.: Excursions en Autocar. ISSN 0847-933X.
Published by: (Bus Owners Association), Publicom Inc., Place d Armes, C P 365, Montreal, PQ H2Y 3H1, Canada. TEL 514-274-0004, FAX 514-274-5884. Ed., Adv. contact Guy Jonkman. Circ: 13,302 (controlled).

910.202 USA ISSN 1551-8027
G149
TOWN & COUNTRY TRAVEL. Text in English. 2003 (Fall). q. USD 4.95 newsstand/cover; free to qualified personnel (effective 2009). adv. **Document type:** *Magazine, Consumer.* **Description:** Contains articles and features on special travel destinations, hotels, luxury resorts, small country inns, and restaurants.
Related titles: Online - full text ed.
Indexed: P48, PQC.
Published by: Hearst Magazines (Subsidiary of: Hearst Corporation), 300 W 57th St, 12th Fl, New York, NY 10019. TEL 212-903-5366, FAX 212-903-5187, HearstMagazines@hearst.com, http://www.hearstcorp.com/magazines/. Eds. Hedi Mitchell, Pamela Fiori. Adv. contact Stefanie Rapp TEL 212-903-5333ad. Circ: 25,000 (paid).

915 HKG
TRADE & TRAVELER. Text in English. 1991. m. USD 28.95. adv. bk.rev. back issues avail. **Document type:** *Handbook/Manual/Guide, Trade.* **Description:** Provides tips on travel and trade in Asia.
Formerly: Traveler (1019-7664)
Related titles: Online - full text ed.
Published by: Asian Sources Media Group, 22-F Vita Tower, 29 Wong Chuk Hang Rd, Aberdeen, Hong Kong, Hong Kong. TEL 852-2555-4777, FAX 852-2873-0488. Ed. Ed Michael Hay. Adv. contact Don Rider. color page USD 7,730. Circ: 45,000. **Subscr. to:** Asiamag Ltd., GPO Box 12367, Hong Kong, Hong Kong; **US subscr. to:** Wordright Enterprises Inc., PO Box 3062, Evanston, IL 60204-3062. TEL 708-475-1900.

910.09 PER
TRAFICO; directorio informativo y mensual de transporte y turismo. Text in Spanish. 1972. m. **Description:** Provides information concerning air, land and sea itineraries from Peru to destinations worldwide. Hotel and restaurant information and car rental data also provided.
Published by: Editores Trafico S.A., Avenida J. Pardo 620, Oficina 506, Miraflores, Lima, Peru. TEL 511-4478542, FAX 511-4478534. Ed. Alberto G Castro. Circ: 3,500.

917.96 796 USA ISSN 1944-0170
▼ **TRAIL OF THE COEUR D'ALENES**; unofficial guidebook with frequently asked questions. Text in English. 2009. a. USD 9.95 per issue (effective 2009). **Document type:** *Guide, Consumer.* **Description:** Guide book for the trail of the Coeur d'Alenes in Idaho.
Published by: Gray Dog Press, 2727 S Mt Vernons St, Ste 4, Spokane, WA 99223. TEL 509-768-6206, info@graydogpress.com, http://graydogpress.com.

910.09 796 USA ISSN 0747-2293
LH1
TRAILBLAZER. Text in English. 19??. m. USD 14 to members; USD 20 to non-members (effective 2004). adv. tr.lit. **Document type:** *Magazine, Consumer.* **Description:** Recreational lifestyle magazine.
Published by: Thousand Trails, Inc. (Subsidiary of: Southmark Corp.), 3801 Parkwood Blvd, Ste. 100, PO Box 2529, Frisco, TX 75034. TEL 214-618-7200, FAX 214-618-7324, rebeccaw@cableone.net, http://www.1000trails.com/. Ed., Pub. John Powers. Adv. contact Rebecca Williams TEL 903-482-0518. B&W page USD 3,500, color page USD 4,400; trim 8 x 10.75. Circ: 150,000. **Subscr. to:** Trailblazer Subscriptions, Attn: M. French, 2325 Highway 90, Gautier, MS 39553. TEL 800-328-6226.

910.202 GBR
TRAILFINDER. Text in English. 1970. 3/yr. free (effective 2009). adv. **Document type:** *Journal, Consumer.* **Description:** Covers non-European destinations, especially Australia, Asia and North America as well as section on latest flight prices worldwide.
Published by: Trailfinders Ltd., 48 Earls Court Rd, London, W8 6FT, United Kingdom. trailfinders@trailfinders.com. Ed. Lee Holden.

910 USA ISSN 1061-2343
TRANSITIONS ABROAD; the guide to learning, living, working, and volunteering overseas. Text in English. 1977. bi-m. USD 28 domestic; USD 32 in Canada; USD 56 elsewhere; USD 6.45 per issue (effective 2007). adv. bk.rev. illus. Index. 96 p./no.; back issues avail.; reprints avail. **Document type:** *Magazine, Consumer.* **Description:** Alternative travel magazine for international travelers seeking work, study, living and special interest travel abroad. Contains extensive listings and up-to-date articles for independent and low-budget travel.
Formerly (until 1985): Transitions (0276-4717)
Related titles: Supplement(s): Transitions Abroad: The Student Guide to Studying, Volunteering, and Working Overseas. 2006.
Indexed: CLFP.
—Ingenta.
Published by: Transitions Abroad, LLC, PO Box 745, Bennington, VT 05201. Ed., Pub. Sherry Schwarz. Adv. contact Kate McGrail. page USD 800. Circ: 12,000 (paid and controlled).

338.4 USA
THE TRANSNATIONAL. Text in English. 2006 (Apr.). s-m. free (effective 2011). adv. back issues avail. **Document type:** *Newsletter, Trade.*
Media: Online - full text.
Published by: Business Travel Media Group, 116 W 32nd St, 14th Fl, New York, NY 10001. TEL 847-559-7533, 800-697-8859, FAX 847-291-4816, nbtn@omeda.com, http://www.promedia.travel/.

TRANSPORT; guia ecuatoriana de transporte y turismo. *see* TRANSPORTATION

TRANSPORT ET TOURISME PAR AUTOCAR. *see* TRANSPORTATION—Automobiles

338.4 USA
TRANSPORTATION LEADER. Text in English. 1966. q. USD 16 domestic to non-members; USD 26 foreign to non-members (effective 2005); free domestic to members. adv. **Document type:** *Magazine, Trade.*
Formerly: Taxi & Livery Management
Indexed: HRIS.
Published by: Taxicab, Limousine & Paratransit Association, 3849 Farragut Ave, Kensington, MD 20895-2004. TEL 301-946-5701, FAX 301-946-4641, itla@itla-info.org. Ed. Irene Kiebuzinski. Pub. Alfred B LaGasse III. adv.: B&W page USD 1,050, color page USD 1,650. Circ: 6,000.

910.09 ESP ISSN 0211-9633
TRANSPORTE AEREO & TURISMO. Abbreviated title: T A T. Text in Spanish. 1982. bi-m. bk.rev. **Document type:** *Magazine, Trade.*
Related titles: Online - full text ed.: free (effective 2009).
Published by: Transporte Aereo y Turismo, Mejico 31, 1oA, Madrid, 28028, Spain. TEL 34-91-7256454, FAX 34-91-3610701, tatrevista@tatrevista.com, http://www.tatrevista.com. Circ: 7,000.

610 USA ISSN 1049-6211
TRAVEL 50 & BEYOND. Text in English. 1990. 4/yr. USD 14 (effective 2011). adv. bk.rev. illus. 100 p./no. 3 cols./p.; reprints avail. **Document type:** *Magazine, Consumer.* **Description:** Covers worldwide travel opportunities, including cruises, tours, resorts, and soft adventures.
Indexed: AgeL.
Published by: Vacation Publications, Inc., 5851 San Felipe St, Ste 500, Houston, TX 77057. TEL 713-974-6903, FAX 713-978-6003, service@Travel50andBeyond.com. Adv. contact Katie Davies.

910.09 CAN ISSN 0836-7353
TRAVEL A LA CARTE. Text in English. 1987. 6/yr. CAD 11.97 domestic; USD 18; USD 22 foreign. adv. **Document type:** *Magazine, Consumer.* **Description:** Gloval travel and leisure magazine. Features articles focusing on domestic and international travel.
Formed by the merger of (1986-1987): Canada a la Carte (0831-3512); Which was formerly (1984-1986): A la Carte (0822-949X); (1975-1987): Touring & Travel (0318-4390); Which was formerly (1972-1974): Driving (0318-4439); (1969-1972): Canada Track & Traffic (0318-6903); (1968-1969): Track and Traffic (0564-0415); (1959-1968): Canada Track & Traffic (0008-2767)
Indexed: C03, CBCARef, CBPI, PQC.
Published by: Interpress, Inc., 136 Walton St, Port Hope, ON L1A 1N5, Canada. TEL 905-885-7948, FAX 905-885-7202. Ed. Donna Carter. Circ: 145,000.

910.2 USA
TRAVEL ADVANCE. Text in English. 1969. d. (Mon.-Fri.). USD 695 (effective 2008). adv. **Document type:** *Newsletter, Consumer.* **Description:** Contains timely information on developments related to the travel industry. For industry executives.
Formerly (until 2005): Travel Management Daily (0041-2015)
Media: E-mail.
Address: 4000 Ponce de Leon Blvd, Ste 470, Coral Gables, FL 33146. TEL 305-777-0435, FAX 305-858-3350. Ed., Pub. Richard F Hebert.

910.202 GBR ISSN 1561-2783
TRAVEL AFRICA. Text in English. 1978. q. GBP 15 domestic; GBP 25 foreign (effective 2011). adv. back issues avail. **Document type:** *Magazine, Consumer.* **Description:** Explores the Africa's diverse attractions, wildlife and culture, with quality writing supported by world-class photography.
Related titles: Online - full text ed.: ISSN 2046-133X.
Published by: Travel Africa Ltd., 4 Rycote Ln Farm, Milton Common, Oxford, Oxfordshire OX9 2NZ, United Kingdom. TEL 44-1844-278883, FAX 44-1844-278893, service@travelafricamag.com.

338.4791 USA ISSN 1053-9360
G155.A1
TRAVEL AGENT; the national newsweekly magazine of the travel industry. Text in English. 1930. 51/yr. free to qualified personnel (effective 2008). adv. bk.rev.; film rev. charts; illus.; mkt. back issues avail.; reprints avail. **Document type:** *Magazine, Trade.* **Description:** Provides the travel agents with access to web-exclusive content, inclusive of video, audio and community-based tools.
Former titles (until 1990): Travel Agent Magazine (1041-0783); (until 1988): Travel Agent (0041-199X); Incorporates: Travel Agent Domestic Tour Manual; Official Sales Guide Motorcoach Tours of North America; Motorcoach Tour Mart
Related titles: Online - full text ed.: free to qualified personnel (effective 2008).
Indexed: A09, A10, B01, B03, B06, B07, B09, B11, C32, CWI, G06, G07, G08, H&TI, H06, I05, M01, M02, P06, RASB, S22, T&II, T02, V03, V04.
—CCC.
Published by: Questex Media Group Inc., 275 Grove St, Bldg 2, Ste 130, Newton, MA 02466. TEL 617-219-8300, 888-552-4346, FAX 617-219-8310, questex@sunbeltfs.com, http://www.questex.com. Pub. John McMahon TEL 212-895-8243. adv.: B&W page USD 17,945, color page USD 22,885; trim 10.88 x 16.75. Circ: 46,003 (controlled).

910.91 387.7 CAN
TRAVEL AGENT'S HANDBOOK (CD-ROM). Text in English, French, Spanish. a. USD 150 per issue (effective 2008). **Document type:** *Handbook/Manual/Guide, Trade.* **Description:** Contains the current text of Passenger Agency Conference Resolutions and locally established criteria that are directly applicable to IATA Accredited Agents, including all amendments agreed to by the Passenger Agency Conference in June 2006.
Formerly: Travel Agent's Handbook (Print)
Media: CD-ROM. **Related titles:** Online - full content ed.: Electronic Travel Agent Handbook. free to members.
Published by: International Air Transport Association, 800 Place Victoria, PO Box 113, Montreal, PQ H4Z 1M1, Canada. TEL 514-390-6726, 800-716-6326, FAX 514-874-9659, sales@iata.org.

910.2 USA
TRAVEL AGENT'S OFFICIAL TRAVEL INDUSTRY DIRECTORY (ONLINE); the sourcebook for travel professionals. Text in English. 1990. a. back issues avail. **Document type:** *Directory, Trade.* **Description:** Assist travel agents in locating information and phone numbers for Airlines, Cruiselines, Tourist Offices, Tour Operators, Car Rentals, Hotels and Products and Services.
Formerly (until 2005): Travel Agent's Official Travel Industry Directory (Print) (1087-4380)
Media: Online - full text.
—CCC.
Published by: Questex Media Group Inc., 757 Third Ave, 5th Fl, New York, NY 10017. TEL 212-895-8200, FAX 212-895-8210, http://www.questex.com.

910.09 338 USA ISSN 1068-7416
CODEN: TALBEZ
TRAVEL ALERT BULLETIN. Text in English. 1987. s-m. looseleaf. USD 95 (effective 2004). bk.rev. **Document type:** *Newsletter.* **Description:** Covers developments affecting corporate travel.
Related titles: E-mail ed.
Published by: Nationwide Intelligence, PO Box 1922, Saginaw, MI 48605-1922. TEL 989-793-0123, 800-333-4130, FAX 989-793-8830. Ed., Pub. David W Oppermann.

910.2 USA ISSN 0041-2007
G149
TRAVEL + LEISURE. (In 3 regional eds., and 1 demographic ed.) Text in English. 1971. m. USD 19.99 domestic; USD 31.99 in Canada; USD 70 elsewhere; USD 4.50 newsstand/cover (effective 2009). adv. bk.rev. illus.; tr.lit. Index. back issues avail.; reprints avail. **Document type:** *Magazine, Consumer.* **Description:** Contains expert reporting on style, culture, food and design with stunning photography to transport its readers to the places and the experiences that matter most.
Former titles (until 1971): Travel and Camera (0049-4542); (until 1969): U.S. Camera & Travel; (until 1964): U.S. Camera; Which incorporated (in 19??): Travel & Camera; (until 1941): U.S. Camera Magazine
Related titles: Microform ed.: (from PQC); Online - full text ed.; Spanish ed.: 2002 (Sep.); ◆ Supplement(s): Travel + Leisure Family. ISSN 1940-2716.
Indexed: A10, A22, A33, ASIP, C12, G05, G06, G07, G08, G09, H&TI, H06, I05, L09, M01, M02, MagInd, P02, P10, P48, P53, P54, PMR, PQC, R04, R06, T02, V03.
—Ingenta.
Published by: American Express Publishing Corp., 1120 Ave of the Americas, New York, NY 10036. TEL 212-382-5600, FAX 212-382-5879, ashields@amexpub.com. Ed. Nancy Novogrod. Pub. Ellen Asmodeo-Giglio. adv.: B&W page USD 72,350, color page USD 106,395; trim 8 x 10.5. Circ: 975,505 (paid). **Subscr. to:** PO Box 62730, Tampa, FL 33662. TEL 800-888-8728.

910.202 GBR ISSN 1756-221X
TRAVEL AND LEISURE MAGAZINE. Text in English. 1993. bi-m. GBP 6 (print or online ed.); GBP 2 per issue (effective 2009). bk.rev. tr.lit. back issues avail. **Document type:** *Magazine, Consumer.* **Description:** Provides hints and advice to aid in obtaining the best holiday for the least money.
Related titles: Online - full text ed.
Published by: Travel and Leisure Magazines Ltd., First Fl, 103 Cranbrook Rd, Ilford, Essex IG1 4PU, United Kingdom. TEL 44-20-84771529, FAX 44-20-85174536, info@tlmags.com. Ed. Peter Ellegard. Pub. Terry Stafford. Adv. contact Jeannette Cumbers.

910.5 RUS
TRAVEL & LEISURE RUSSIA. Text in Russian. 2004. m. adv. **Document type:** *Magazine, Consumer.*
Published by: S K Press, Marksistkaya 34, str 10, Moscow, 109147, Russian Federation. deliver@skpress.ru, http://www.skpress.ru. Circ: 30,000 (controlled).

910.2 USA ISSN 1559-0372
TX907
TRAVEL & LEISURE THE BEST OF THE WORLD'S GREATEST HOTELS, RESORTS + SPAS. Text in English. 2006. a. USD 34.95 per issue (effective 2009). **Document type:** *Guide, Consumer.* **Description:** Designed to be the ultimate guide to the top hotels, resorts and spas around the world, sharing the inside scoop on where to go, what to see, where to stay and what to eat at the year's top travel destinations.
Published by: American Express Publishing Corp., 1120 Ave of the Americas, New York, NY 10036. TEL 212-382-5600, FAX 212-382-5879, ashields@amexpub.com, http://www.amexpub.com.

338.791 GBR ISSN 0269-3755
G155.A1
TRAVEL & TOURISM ANALYST. Text in English. s-m. adv. maps; stat. back issues avail. **Document type:** *Report, Trade.* **Description:** Presents sector-by-sector news and forecasts for the industry: airlines, travel agents, hotels and accommodations, market segment, outbound markets and other studies.
Related titles: Diskette ed.; E-mail ed.; Online - full text ed.
Indexed: A22, CABA, E12, Emerald, GH, H&TI, H06, Hospl, LT, N02, O01, P32, R12, RASB, RRTA, S13, S16, W11.
—BLDSC (9045.450900), IE, Ingenta.
Published by: Mintel International Group Ltd., 18-19 Long Ln, London, EC1A 9PL, United Kingdom. TEL 44-20-76064533, FAX 44-20-77260849, info@mintel.com, http://www.mintel.com/.

350 USA ISSN 1070-8855
TRAVEL & TOURISM EXECUTIVE REPORT. Text in English. 1979. m. USD 65 (effective 1999). adv. charts; stat. **Document type:** *Newsletter.* **Description:** Focuses on the marketing and promotion of travel destination products. Presents information and data on trends and demographics.
Published by: Leisure Industry - Recreation News, PO Box 43563, Washington, DC 20010-9563. FAX 202-462-6021. Ed. Marj Jensen. Circ: 4,000.

TRAVEL & TOURISM MARKET. *see* BUSINESS AND ECONOMICS—Production Of Goods And Services

910.202 BHR ISSN 1560-0424
G155.M52
TRAVEL & TOURISM NEWS MIDDLE EAST. Text in English. 1979. m. USD 68; free to qualified personnel (effective 2001). adv. tr.lit. 16 p./no. 7 cols./p.; **Document type:** *Newspaper, Trade.* **Description:** For travel industry professionals, including travel and tour agents, airline and airport personnel, government tourist offices.
Formerly: Travel and Tourism News International; Incorporates: Arab Travel Magazine
Indexed: A12, A17, ABIn, I05, P48, P51, P53, P54, PQC.
—CIS.
Published by: Al Hilal Publishing & Marketing Group, PO Box 224, Manama, Bahrain. TEL 973-293131, FAX 973-293400, info@tradearabia.net, hilalcirc@tradearabia.net. Ed. Frankie Fernandez. adv.: B&W page USD 3,080, color page USD 4,313; trim 290 x 420. Circ: 6,333.

910.09 USA
G149.5
TRAVEL AND TOURISM RESEARCH ASSOCIATION. ANNUAL CONFERENCE PROCEEDINGS. Text in English. 1970. a. USD 150 to non-members; USD 35 to members. adv. charts; illus. **Document type:** *Proceedings.*
Former titles: Travel and Tourism Research Association. Proceedings of the Annual Meeting; Travel and Tourism Research Association. Proceedings of the Annual Conference (0276-8968)
—BLDSC (6840.428450).
Published by: Travel and Tourism Research Association, 546 E Main St, Lexington, KY 40508. TEL 606-226-4344, FAX 606-226-4355. Ed. Cynde Dornuf. R&P J P Smith. Adv. contact J.P. Smith. Circ: 900.

910.09 USA ISSN 1941-1847
TRAVEL AND TOURISM WORKS FOR AMERICA; the economic impact of travel on states and congressional districts. Variant title: Research Report. Text in English. 1976. a., latest 16th ed. USD 35 per issue (effective 2008). adv. back issues avail.; reprints avail. **Document type:** *Monographic series, Trade.* **Description:** Provides an overview of travel and tourism's impact on the American economy, with top-line statistics, enhanced charts and travel sector information and projections.
Former titles (until 2006): Impact of Travel & Tourism on the U.S. and State Economies; (until 1992): Impact of Travel on State Economies (0730-9813)
Indexed: SRI.
Published by: Travel Industry Association of America, 1100 New York Ave, NW, Ste 450, Washington, DC 20005. TEL 202-408-8422, FAX 202-408-1255, feedback@tia.org. Pub. Dawn L Drew. Adv. contact Sarah Dickson TEL 202-408-2141.

028.1 USA ISSN 1058-7098
TRAVEL BOOKS WORLDWIDE; the travel book review. Text in English. 1991. 10/yr. USD 36 domestic; USD 48 in Canada; USD 72 elsewhere (effective 2004). software rev.; bk.rev.; video rev. illus. back issues avail.; reprints avail. **Document type:** *Newsletter, Trade.* **Description:** Reviews travel guides, maps, atlases, cd-roms, and trade books with a travel angle. Also reviews gift books, cookbooks, and books on outdoor sports.
Published by: Travel Keys, PO Box 162266, Sacramento, CA 95816-2266. TEL 916-452-5200. Ed., Pub. Peter B Manston. R&P Robert Bynum. Circ: 1,500 (paid).

051 USA
TRAVEL BOUND!. Text in English. 19??. bi-m. USD 29 (effective 2011). adv. **Document type:** *Magazine, Consumer.*
Published by: Group Travel Leader, Inc., 301 E High St, Lexington, KY 40507. TEL 859-253-0455.

910.09 GBR ISSN 0956-2419
TRAVEL BULLETIN; every week for every agent. Text in English. 1975. w. GBP 75 domestic; GBP 125 foreign (effective 2009). adv. back issues avail. **Document type:** *Bulletin, Trade.* **Description:** Features the latest travel industry news, destination features, training tips and events and agent offers.
Related titles: Online - full text ed.: free (effective 2009).
—CCC.
Published by: Alain Charles Publishing Travel Ltd., University House, 11-13 Lower, Grosvenor Pl, London, SW1W 0EX, United Kingdom. TEL 44-20-78346661, FAX 44-20-78347519. Ed. Lauretta Wright. Pub. Jeanette Ratcliffe. Adv. contact Simon Eddolls. B&W page GBP 2,080, color page GBP 2,900; trim 210 x 297. Circ: 8,642.

910.22 330.9 HKG ISSN 1011-7768
G155.A78
TRAVEL BUSINESS ANALYST (ASIA PACIFIC EDITION). Text in Chinese. 1981. 12/yr. USD 600; USD 55 newsstand/cover. bk.rev. charts; stat. back issues avail. **Document type:** *Trade.* **Description:** Provides travel business information, statistics and analysis for senior management and investors in the travel business.
Related titles: ◆ Regional ed(s).: Travel Business Analyst (European Edition). ISSN 0256-419X.
Published by: Travel Business Analyst, GPO Box 12761, Hong Kong, Hong Kong. TEL 852-2507-2310, FAX 33-4-9449-0949, info@travelbusinessanalyst.com. Ed. Murray Bailey.

338.4 CAN ISSN 1926-3716
▼ **TRAVEL CHARACTERISTICS.** Text in English. 2009. q. free (effective 2011). back issues avail. **Document type:** *Report, Trade.*
Media: Online - full text.
Published by: Canadian Tourism Commission/Commission Canadienne du Tourisme, Ste 1400, Four Bentall Ctr, 1055 Dunsmuir St, PO Box 49230, Vancouver, BC V7X 1L2, Canada. TEL 604 638-8300, http://en-corporate.canada.travel/.

914 BEL
TRAVEL CHECK; the Benelux buyer's guide to business & incentive travel. Text in English. 1982. m. back issues avail.
Address: Keesinglaan 19, Antwerp, 2100, Belgium. TEL 323-325-2235. Circ: 13,850.

910.202 USA ISSN 1076-5719
TRAVEL COMPANIONS; North America's foremost newsletter for solo travelers. Text in English. 1982. bi-m. USD 48 domestic; USD 68 foreign (effective 2001). adv. bk.rev. illus. back issues avail.; reprints avail. **Document type:** *Newsletter, Consumer.* **Description:** Provides travel news and tips for single travelers and listings from singles seeking travel companions.
Published by: (Travel Companion Exchange, Inc.), Jens Jurgen, Ed. & Pub., PO Box 833, Amityville, NY 11701. TEL 631-454-0880, tce@travelcompanions.com, http://www.travelcompanions.com. Ed., R&P Jens Jurgen. Circ: 5,000 (paid).

917 CAN ISSN 1182-9699
TRAVEL COURIER. Text in English. 1965. w. (Thu.). CAD 60 domestic; USD 110 foreign (effective 2004). adv. charts; illus.; stat. **Document type:** *Newsletter, Trade.* **Description:** Provides concise, easy-to-read articles designed for immediate reading. Includes current national trade news and destination reports as well as other regular editorial features.
Formerly (until 1982): Canadian Travel Courier (0008-5219)
Related titles: Microfilm ed.: (from MML); Microform ed.: (from MML).
Indexed: A10, C03, CBCABus, CBPI, H&TI, H06, PQC, RASB, T02, V03.
—CCC.
Published by: Baxter Publishing Co., 310 Dupont St, Toronto, ON M5R 1V9, Canada. TEL 416-968-7252, FAX 416-968-2377, http://www.travelpress.com/. Adv. contact Brenda Seymour. Circ: 10,000 (controlled).

338.4791 AUS ISSN 1834-3058
TRAVEL DAILY. Text in English. 199?. d. **Document type:** *Newsletter, Consumer.*
Media: Online - full text.
Address: PO Box 428, West Ryde, NSW 1685, Australia. TEL 1300-799-220, FAX 1300-799-221, info@traveldaily.com.au, http://traveldaily.com.au/Home/tabid/131/Default.aspx.

910.2 GBR
TRAVEL DAYS. Text in English. 1990. bi-w. GBP 40; GBP 80 foreign (effective 2000). adv. 16 p./no. 3 cols./p.; **Document type:** *Magazine, Trade.* **Description:** Contains news from the travel industry worldwide.
Address: Cityjet House, 65 Judd St, London, WC1H 9QT, United Kingdom. TEL 44-20-7833-0820, FAX 44-20-7833-3386, travel.days@virgin.net. Ed., Adv. contact Thomas Bruccoueri. B&W page GBP 1,000, color page GBP 1,500; trim 272 x 389. Circ: 20,000.

910.4 CZE ISSN 1801-5417
TRAVEL DIGEST. Text in Czech. 2006. m. CZK 299; CZK 49 newsstand/cover (effective 2008). adv. **Document type:** *Magazine, Consumer.*
Published by: Atemi s.r.o., Velvarska 1626 - 45, Prague 6, 160 00, Czech Republic. TEL 420-233-025501, FAX 420-233-025502, info@atemi.cz, http://www.atemi.cz. Ed. Zuzana Rybarova. adv.: page CZK 120,000; trim 203 x 267. Circ: 15,000 (paid and controlled).

910.09 GBR
TRAVEL DIRECTORY. Text in English. a. GBP 82.90 (effective 2001). **Document type:** *Directory.* **Description:** Contains full contact details of more than 8,500 companies in 28 sectors of the UK and Irish travel industry. It is the latest offering from DG&G travel information replacing the popular hard copy publication.
Former titles: O A G Travel Directory (1366-1612); (until 1996): A B C Travel Directory (1357-1176); (until 198?): Travel Directory
—CCC.
Published by: Reed Business Information Ltd. (Subsidiary of: Reed Business), DG&G Travel Information, Dukeminster House, Church St, Dunstable, Beds LU5 4HU, United Kingdom. TEL 44-1582-676845, FAX 44-1582-676893, http://www.reedbusiness.co.uk/. Ed. Maxine Allen. Pub. Giles Harper. Adv. contact Shelley Cope TEL 44-1582-676851.

338.4791 USA ISSN 1548-9973
TRAVEL DISTRIBUTION REPORT. Text in English. 1993. bi-w. back issues avail. **Document type:** *Newsletter, Trade.* **Description:** Covers all aspects of the travel reservations and sales business.
Formerly (until 1996): C R S Update (1548-9973)
Related titles: Online - full text ed.: ISSN 1526-7059. USD 497 (effective 2011).
Published by: Garrett Communications, Inc., PO Box 90324, Washington, DC 20090-0324. TEL 239-280-2383, FAX 847-954-2609, subscribe@travelresearchbureau.com. Ed. Scott Walker TEL 888-779-3483 ext 332. Pub. Sean McPartland TEL 585-292-4358.

910.202 USA ISSN 1570-1409
TRAVEL ETC. - BUSINESS & LEISURE. Cover title: Travel etc. Text in Dutch. 2002. q. **Document type:** *Magazine, Consumer.* **Description:** Offers news and information to international business travelers and those managing business travel.
Related titles: Online - full text ed.: ISSN 1570-1417.
Published by: Sunvalley Communication, 4960 S Gilbert Rd, Suite 1-286, Chandler, AZ 85249. info@sunvalleycommunication.com, http://sunvalleycommunication.com. Ed., Pub. Peter Hofland.

338.4 CAN ISSN 1202-6891
TRAVEL EXCLUSIVE. Text in English. 1991. a.
Formerly (until 199?): Exclusive (1187-3183)
Indexed: H&TI, H06.
Published by: (Canadian Tourism Research Institute), Conference Board of Canada, 255 Smyth Rd, Ottawa, ON K1H 8M7, Canada. TEL 613-526-3280, FAX 613-526-4857, corpcomm@conferenceboard.ca, http://www.conferenceboard.ca.

914.415 IRL
TRAVEL EXTRA. Text in English. 10/yr. adv. **Document type:** *Magazine, Consumer.*
Address: St. James Court, 7 St. James Terrace, Malahide, Co. Dublin, Ireland. TEL 353-1-8454485, FAX 353-1-8454468. Ed. Tony Barry. adv.: page EUR 2,000; 260 x 330. Circ: 22,000 (controlled).

910 664 USA
TRAVEL, FOOD & WINE. Text in English. 1970. m. USD 100 (effective 2000). adv. bk.rev. **Document type:** *Newspaper, Consumer.* **Description:** Review articles on travel, airlines, hotels, restaurants, food and wine.
Published by: Punch In Syndicate, 400 E 59th St, Ste 9F, New York, NY 10022. TEL 212-755-9363. Ed. J Walman. Adv. contact Tom Weston. Circ: 10,000.

910.09 USA
TRAVEL FORECAST. Text in English. 1997. q. **Document type:** *Report, Trade.* **Description:** Contains forecast estimates from TIA's proprietary travel forecasting models.
Published by: Travel Industry Association of America, 1100 New York Ave, NW, Ste 450, Washington, DC 20005. TEL 202-408-8422, FAX 202-408-1255, feedback@tia.org, http://www.tia.org. Adv. contact Sarah Dickson TEL 202-408-2141.

914.2 GBR ISSN 1355-462X
TRAVEL G B I. (Great Britain and Ireland) Text in English. 1978. m. GBP 37 in British Isles; GBP 40 in Europe; GBP 50 elsewhere (effective 2009). adv. bk.rev. illus. back issues avail. **Document type:** *Newspaper, Trade.* **Description:** Covers tourism and travel exclusively in the British Isles along with excellent color photographs.
—CCC.
Published by: Travelscope Publications, 3rd Fl, Foundation House, Perseverance Works, 38 Kingsland Rd, London, E2 8DD, United Kingdom. TEL 44-207-7294337, FAX 44-207-7291716. Pub. R MacBeth-Seath.

910.2 USA ISSN 1527-0351
TRAVEL GUIDE INTERNATIONAL. Text in English. 1999. q. USD 45 membership (effective 2006). adv. bk.rev. illus. 48 p./no.; reprints avail. **Document type:** *Magazine, Trade.* **Description:** Covers budget travel news for air courier travel.
Incorporates (in 2003): Shoestring Traveler (1082-5304); Air Courier Bulletin (1082-3859)
Published by: International Association of Air Travel Couriers (IAATC), PO Box 847, Scottsbluff, NE 69361. TEL 515-292-2458, courier@iaatc.com, http://www.courier.org. Eds. Barbara Homes, Morty Craig. R&P Bruce Causey. Adv. contact Mary Craig. B&W page USD 800, color page USD 950. Circ: 13,540 (paid).

910.91 CAN
TRAVEL IMPULSE. Text in English. q. **Document type:** *Magazine, Consumer.*
Published by: Travel Impulse Magazine, 9336 117th St, Delta, BC V4C 6B8, Canada. TEL 604-951-3238, FAX 604-951-8732, editor@suntrackercafe.com. Ed. Susan Boyce.

338.4791 310 AUS ISSN 1832-3529
TRAVEL IN AUSTRALIA. Text in English. 1987. a. **Document type:** *Government.*
Formed by the merger of (1998-2002): Travel by Australians (1442-3138); (1999-2002): International Visitors in Australia Annual Results of the International Visitor Survey (1443-346X)
Published by: Tourism Research Australia, PO Box 1110, Belconnen, ACT 2616, Australia. TEL 61-2-62286100, FAX 61-2-62286180, tra@tourism.australia.com, http://www.tra.australia.com.

914.95 GRC
TRAVEL IN GREECE. Text in Greek. 1970. a.
Published by: Hellenews Ltd., 39 Amaroussiou-Halandriou Rd, Maroussi, Athens, Greece.

910.2 CZE
TRAVEL IN SLOVAKIA. Text in Czech. 2008. a. adv. **Document type:** *Magazine, Consumer.*
Published by: Mlada Fronta, Mezi Vodami 1952/9, Prague 4, 14300, Czech Republic. TEL 420-2-25276201, FAX 420-2-25276222, online@mf.cz. Ed. Jan Schlindenbuch. Adv. contact Pavel Jamny.

338.4791 TWN
TRAVEL IN TAIWAN BI-MONTHLY. Text in English. bi-m. **Document type:** *Magazine, Consumer.* **Description:** Provides travel information, including phone numbers, points of interests, events calendar.
Formerly: Travel in Taiwan Monthly
Related titles: Online - full content ed.
Published by: Vision International Publishing Co., 10F-3/5, No. 2, Fuxing N. Rd., Taipei, Taiwan. TEL 886-2-7115403, FAX 886-2-7212790, vision@tit.com.tw, http://www.tit.com.tw/.

910.2 CZE ISSN 1214-388X
TRAVEL IN THE CZECH REPUBLIC. Text in Czech. 2003. m. CZK 499 (effective 2010). adv. **Document type:** *Magazine, Consumer.*
Published by: Mlada Fronta, Mezi Vodami 1952/9, Prague 4, 14300, Czech Republic. TEL 420-2-25276201, FAX 420-2-25276222, online@mf.cz. Ed. Jan Schlindenbuch. Adv. contact Tatiana Keriova.

910.09 USA
TRAVEL INDUSTRY ASSOCIATION OF AMERICA. ENEWSLINE (ONLINE). Text in English. s-m. free to members; free to qualified personnel (effective 2009). adv. back issues avail. **Document type:** *Newsletter, Trade.* **Description:** Covers activities and news about the travel industry Association of America.
Formerly: Travel Industry Association of America. Newsline (Print)
Media: Online - full content.
Published by: (Communications Department), Travel Industry Association of America, 1100 New York Ave, NW, Ste 450, Washington, DC 20005. TEL 202-408-8422, FAX 202-408-1255, feedback@tia.org. Ed. Kathieen Riley.

910 AUT
TRAVEL INDUSTRY PROFESSIONAL. Text in German. w. adv. **Document type:** *Magazine, Trade.*
Formerly: Traveller
Published by: Profi Reisen Verlagsgesellschaft mbH, Seidlgasse 22, Vienna, 1030, Austria. TEL 43-1-7142414, FAX 43-1-71424144, office@profireisen.at, http://www.profireisen.at. Eds. Elo Resch, Rainer Pilcik. Pub. Rainer Pilcik. Circ: 10,300.

TRAVEL INDUSTRY REWARDS. *see* BUSINESS AND ECONOMICS—Labor And Industrial Relations

TRAVEL INDUSTRY WORLD YEARBOOK; the big picture. *see* TRAVEL AND TOURISM—Abstracting, Bibliographies, Statistics

914 CHE ISSN 1420-5610
TRAVEL INSIDE (FRENCH EDITION). Text in French. 1985. w. CHF 55 (effective 2007). adv. **Document type:** *Magazine, Trade.*
Supersedes in part (in 1991): Travel Inside (1421-5012)
Related titles: ◆ German ed.: Travel Inside (German Edition). ISSN 1420-5580.
Published by: Primus Verlag AG, Hammerstr 81, Postfach 1331, Zuerich, 8032, Switzerland. TEL 41-44-3875757, FAX 41-44-3875707, info@travelinside.ch, http://www.primusverlag.ch. Ed., Pub., R&P Angelo Heuberger. Adv. contact Muriel Bassin. B&W page CHF 2,975, color page CHF 3,925; trim 210 x 290. Circ: 4,500 (paid).

914 CHE ISSN 1420-5580
TRAVEL INSIDE (GERMAN EDITION). Text in German. 1986. w. CHF 79 (effective 2007). adv. **Document type:** *Magazine, Trade.* **Description:** Contains information, commentary and analysis about the travel industry.
Supersedes in part (in 1991): Travel Inside (1421-5012)
Related titles: ◆ French ed.: Travel Inside (French Edition). ISSN 1420-5610.
Published by: Primus Verlag AG, Hammerstr 81, Postfach 1331, Zuerich, 8032, Switzerland. TEL 41-44-3875757, FAX 41-44-3875707, info@travelinside.ch, http://www.primusverlag.ch. Ed., Pub., R&P Angelo Heuberger. Adv. contact Muriel Bassin. B&W page CHF 4,155, color page CHF 5,550; trim 290 x 210. Circ: 9,630.

910.202 AUS ISSN 1832-8601
TRAVEL + LEISURE AUSTRALIA. Text in English. 2005. 10/yr. AUD 44.95 (effective 2008). adv. back issues avail. **Document type:** *Magazine, Consumer.* **Description:** Provides information on the travel and leisure in Australia.
Related titles: Online - full text ed.
—IE.

T U

Published by: Fairfax Magazines, Level 19, Darling Park, 201 Sussex St, Sydney, NSW 2000, Australia. TEL 61-2-92822833, FAX 61-2-92823065, http://www.fxj.com.au. Ed. Anthony Dennis. Adv. contact Karen Harris TEL 61-2-92822195. page AUD 8,652. Circ: 78,980.

362.7 USA ISSN 1940-2716
G149
TRAVEL + LEISURE FAMILY. Text in English. 1998. bi-m. includes with subscr. to Travel + Leisure. adv. illus.; tr.lit. **Document type:** *Magazine, Consumer.* **Description:** Provides affluent families with ideas for vacation destinations that accommodate children.
Related titles: Online - full text ed.: Tlfamily.com; ◆ Supplement to: Travel + Leisure. ISSN 0041-2007.
Published by: American Express Publishing Corp., 1120 Ave of the Americas, New York, NY 10036. TEL 212-382-5600, FAX 212-764-2177, aepc@customersvc.com, http://www.amexpub.com. Ed. Yossi Langer. adv.: B&W page USD 16,675, color page USD 30,870; trim 10.5 x 15.5. Circ: 250,000 (paid).

910.202 LBN
TRAVEL MAGAZINE. Text in English. m. adv.
Indexed: G06.
Address: Picot St., Nassau Bldg., P O Box 2323, Beirut, Lebanon. Circ: 4,000.

910.91 BEL ISSN 1370-4680
TRAVEL MAGAZINE; le magazine voyagiste pour la Belgique et le Luxembourg. Text in French. 1992. m. **Document type:** *Magazine, Trade.*
Related titles: Dutch ed.: ISSN 1370-4672.
Published by: Travel Productions n.v., Hanswijkstraat 23, Mechelen, 28b00, Belgium. TEL 32-15-450350, FAX 32-15-450360.

910.91 BEL ISSN 1373-5918
TRAVEL MAGAZINE NEWSLETTER. Text in French. 1992. m. **Document type:** *Newsletter, Trade.*
Published by: Travel Productions n.v., Hanswijkstraat 23, Mechelen, 28b00, Belgium. TEL 32-15-450350, FAX 32-15-450360, http://www.travel-magazine.be. Ed. Robrecht Willaert.

910 AUT
TRAVEL MANAGEMENT AUSTRIA. Text in German. m. **Document type:** *Magazine, Trade.* **Description:** Contains news and information for business travelers.
Published by: Profi Reisen Verlagsgesellschaft mbH, Seidlgasse 22, Vienna, 1030, Austria. TEL 43-1-7142414, FAX 43-1-71424144, office@profireisen.at, http://www.profireisen.at. Pub. Rainer Pilcik. Circ: 4,500 (controlled).

338.4 CAN ISSN 1192-6635
TRAVEL MARKETS OUTLOOK. Text in English. 1991. a.
Indexed: H&TI, H06.
Published by: (Canadian Tourism Research Institute), Conference Board of Canada, 255 Smyth Rd, Ottawa, ON K1H 8M7, Canada. TEL 613-526-3280, 866-711-2262, FAX 613-526-4857, corpcomm@conferenceboard.ca, http://www.conferenceboard.ca.

TRAVEL MEDICINE ADVISOR. *see* MEDICAL SCIENCES

▼ **TRAVEL MEDICINE RESEARCH REVIEW.** *see* MEDICAL SCIENCES

917.204 MEX
TRAVEL MEXICO NEWSLETTER. Text in Spanish. 2003. 3/yr. USD 20 (effective 2000). **Document type:** *Newsletter.* **Description:** Provides up-to-date information on traveling, vacationing and living in Mexico.
Media: Online - full text. **Related titles:** ◆ Print ed.: Travelers Guide to Mexico. ISSN 1405-4604.
Published by: Promociones de Mercados Turisticos, S.A. de C.V., Londres, No 22, Col Juarez, Mexico City, DF 06600, Mexico. TEL 52-55-55925022, FAX 52-55-55467002, editor@travelguidemexico.com. Ed. Shooka Shemirani. Pub. Chris A Luhnow. Adv. contact Rebeca Sancedo.

338.4791 GBR ISSN 2045-3485
▼ **TRAVEL NAMIBIA.** Text in English. 2010. a. GBP 13 domestic; GBP 20 foreign (effective 2010); subscr. includes Travel Namibia Extra. back issues avail. **Document type:** *Magazine, Consumer.* **Description:** Covers all aspects of travel within Namibia.
Related titles: Online - full text ed.: ISSN 2045-3493. free (effective 2010); ◆ Supplement(s): Travel Namibia Extra.
Published by: Travel Africa Ltd., 4 Rycote Ln Farm, Milton Common, Oxford, Oxfordshire OX9 2NZ, United Kingdom. TEL 44-1844-278883, FAX 44-1844-278893. Ed. Jeanette Baker. Pub. Craig Rix. Adv. contact Dave Southwood.

338.4791 GBR
▼ **TRAVEL NAMIBIA EXTRA.** Text in English. 2010. 3/yr. Included with subscr. to Travel Namibia. back issues avail. **Document type:** *Magazine, Consumer.* **Description:** Covers all aspects of travel within Namibia.
Related titles: Online - full text ed.: ISSN 2045-3507. free (effective 2010); ◆ Supplement to: Travel Namibia. ISSN 2045-3485.
Published by: Travel Africa Ltd., 4 Rycote Ln Farm, Milton Common, Oxford, Oxfordshire OX9 2NZ, United Kingdom. TEL 44-1844-278883, FAX 44-1844-278893. Ed. Jeanette Baker. Pub. Craig Rix. Adv. contact Dave Southwood.

917.404 USA
TRAVEL NEW ENGLAND. Text in English. m. **Document type:** *Magazine, Trade.*
Published by: Robert Weiss Associates, 256 Marginal St, East, Boston, MA 02128-2800. TEL 617-561-4000, FAX 617-561-2821. Ed. Robert H Weiss. Circ: 5,500.

338.4791 SWE ISSN 0284-3978
TRAVEL NEWS; the Scandinavian travel trade magazine. Text in Swedish. 1985. 10/yr. adv. **Document type:** *Magazine, Trade.*
Related titles: Online - full text ed.; ◆ Norwegian ed.: Travel News (Oslo). ISSN 1500-3787.
Published by: Emma Foerlags AB, Repslager Gatan 17 B, Stockholm, 11846, Sweden. TEL 46-8-54506420, FAX 46-8-6795710. Ed. Katarina Myrberg TEL 46-8-54506421. Adv. contact Peter Helin TEL 46-8-54506406.

338.4791 NOR ISSN 1500-3787
TRAVEL NEWS (OSLO); the Norwegian travel trade magazine. Text in Norwegian. 1995. 9/yr. NOK 195 (effective 2007). adv. **Document type:** *Magazine, Trade.*
Related titles: Online - full text ed.; ◆ Swedish ed.: Travel News. ISSN 0284-3978.
Published by: Emma Publishing AS, Frognerveien 22, Oslo, 0263, Norway. TEL 47-23-120280, FAX 47-23-120281, magasinet@reis.no, http://www.emma-publishing.no.

910.09 USA ISSN 1069-286X
TRAVEL NEWS AMERICAS. Short title: P T N Americas. Text in English. 1990. bi-m. **Document type:** *Journal, Trade.*
Formerly (until 1993): Pata Travel News Americas (0838-9772)
Indexed: H&TI.
—CCC.
Published by: Americas Publishing Co., 4636 E Elmwood St, Ste 5, Phoenix, AZ 85040-1963. TEL 602-997-7200, FAX 602-997-9875. adv.: B&W page USD 4,720, color page USD 5,895; trim 10.88 x 8. Circ: 25,000.

910.202 362.4 USA ISSN 1076-6405
TRAVEL NOTES. Text in English. 1986. q. USD 15 (effective 1995). adv. bk.rev. back issues avail. **Document type:** *Newsletter.* **Description:** Covers recreational travel for disabled travelers.
Published by: Accessible Journeys, 35 W Sellers Ave, Ridley Park, PA 19078. TEL 610-521-0339, FAX 610-521-6959. Ed. Howard J McLoy. Adv. contact Howard J McCoy. Circ: 5,000.

910.09 DEU ISSN 1613-8511
TRAVEL ONE. Text in German. 1967. w. EUR 25 domestic; EUR 48 foreign; EUR 2 newsstand/cover (effective 2006). adv. back issues avail. **Document type:** *Magazine, Trade.* **Description:** Contains information and features all aspects of travel: hotels, tourism, airline information, travel agency news and events.
Formerly (until 2003): Reisebuero Bulletin (1618-5560)
Published by: Travel Trade Press GmbH, Stephanstr 3, Darmstadt, 64295, Germany. TEL 49-6151-39070, FAX 49-6151-3907929. adv.: B&W page EUR 4,100, color page EUR 5,600; bleed 210 x 297. Circ: 23,659 (paid and controlled).

914.04 DEU
TRAVEL ONE DIARY. Text in German. 1977. a. EUR 12.54 (effective 2005). adv. **Document type:** *Directory, Trade.*
Formerly: Travel Diary
Published by: Travel Trade Press GmbH, Stephanstr 3, Darmstadt, 64295, Germany. TEL 49-6151-39070, FAX 49-6151-3907929, vertrieb@travel-one.net, http://www.travel-one.net. Circ: 7,500.

910.202 USA ISSN 1059-8251
TRAVEL PUBLICITY LEADS; Global Travel Media Placement Opportunities. Text in English. 1985. bi-m. looseleaf. USD 197 (effective 2002); includes a. supplement. **Document type:** *Newsletter.* **Description:** Audience is PR specialists at travel service providers and their PR firms. Supplement is a compilation of editorial calendars of worldwide travel media, with keyworded topics.
Related titles: Fax ed.; Online - full text ed.
Published by: Scott American Corp., 284 Umpawaug Rd, PO Box 88, West Redding, CT 06896-0088. TEL 203-938-2955, FAX 203-938-2955, publisher@scottamerican.com. Ed., Pub. Frank Scott.

910.2 306.8 USA
TRAVEL + ROMANCE. Text in English. 2006. a. **Document type:** *Magazine, Consumer.*
Published by: American Express Publishing Corp., 1120 Ave of the Americas, New York, NY 10036. TEL 212-382-5600, FAX 212-764-2177, aepc@customersvc.com, http://www.amexpub.com. Ed. Laura Begley. Circ: 100,000 (paid); 400,000 (controlled). **Co-publisher:** The Knot Inc.

910.09 CAN ISSN 0822-9228
TRAVEL SCOOP. Text in English. 1983. 10/yr. CAD 45.50 (effective 2000). bk.rev. back issues avail. **Document type:** *Newsletter.* **Description:** Information to help Canadian consumers make informed decisions about travel worldwide.
Address: 1033 Bay St, Ste 218, Toronto, ON M5S 3A5, Canada. TEL 416-926-0111, FAX 416-926-0222. Ed. Ann Wallace. Pub., Adv. contact Nigel Raincock. Circ: 8,000.

910.09 USA ISSN 0741-5826
G149
TRAVEL SMART. Text in English. 1976. m. USD 39 domestic; USD 54 in Canada & Mexico; USD 64 elsewhere (effective 2010). Website rev. tr.lit.; illus.; charts; maps. index. 12 p./no. 3 cols./p.; back issues avail.; reprints avail. **Document type:** *Newsletter, Consumer.* **Description:** Provides inside info on current travel deals and value destinations, thus allowing one to travel better for less.
Incorporates (1981-1982): Joy of Travel (0277-7738); Which was formerly (until 1981): Joyer Travel Report (0145-9473)
Published by: Dunnan Communications, Inc., PO Box 397, Dobbs Ferry, NY 10522. TEL 212-228-4769, 800-327-3633.

910.09 JPN
TRAVEL TIMES. Text in Japanese. s-m. JPY 16,000, USD 195. stat. **Document type:** *Trade.* **Description:** Travel and tourism marketing magazine. Offers market analyses and surveys, practical tips on how to cope with emerging trends and consumer preferences, new tour possibilities, profitable auxiliary services, and information on industry activities and events.
Published by: Ohta Publications Co. Ltd., Dame Ginza Bldg, 7-18 Ginza 6-chome, Chuo-ku, Tokyo, 104-0061, Japan. TEL 03-3571-1181, FAX 03-3574-1650. Ed. Hiroyuki Takagishi. Circ: 8,300.

914 CHE
TRAVEL-TIP. Text in German. a. **Document type:** *Consumer.*
Published by: Primus Verlag AG, Hammerstr 81, Postfach 1331, Zuerich, 8032, Switzerland. TEL 41-1-3875757, FAX 41-1-3875707, info@travelinside.ch, http://www.primusverlag.ch.

338.4 AUS ISSN 1833-718X
TRAVEL TODAY. Text in English. 2006. d. free (effective 2008). adv. **Document type:** *Newsletter, Consumer.* **Description:** Provides information, up-to-date news, commentary and special features for the travel industry.
Media: Online - full text.
Published by: Reed Business Information Pty Ltd. (Subsidiary of: Reed Business Information International), Tower 2, 475 Victoria Ave, Locked Bag 2999, Chatswood, NSW 2067, Australia. TEL 61-2-94222999, FAX 61-2-94222922, customerservice@reedbusiness.com.au, http://www.reedbusiness.com.au. Ed. Stephen Jones. Pub. Ray Welling. Adv. contact Lyle Veloso TEL 61-2-94222191. page AUD 600; 210 x 297.

910.2 USA ISSN 0041-2066
G155 CODEN: TRTRD3
TRAVEL TRADE. Text in English. 1929. w. USD 20 (effective 2009). adv. illus. **Document type:** *Newspaper, Trade.* **Description:** Features informative articles for the travel sellers that help to broaden and expand their sales, marketing and administrative skills.
—CASDDS.
Published by: Travel Trade Publications, 270 Lafayette St, Ste 905, New York, NY 10012. TEL 212-730-6600, FAX 212-730-7137, production@traveltrade.com. Pub. John C Graham TEL 212-730-6600 ext 104. Circ: 44,551.

914 GBR ISSN 0262-4397
TRAVEL TRADE GAZETTE U K & IRELAND. Short title: T T G - U K & Ireland. Text in English. 1953. w. GBP 130 domestic; GBP 190 foreign (effective 2009). adv. **Document type:** *Magazine, Trade.*
Formerly (until 1972): Travel Trade Gazette
Related titles: Online - full text ed.
Indexed: A09, A10, A15, ABIn, B01, B02, B03, B06, B07, B09, B11, B15, B17, B18, G04, G06, G07, G08, H&TI, H06, I05, P34, P48, P51, P53, P54, PQC, T02, V03, V04.
—BLDSC (9045.470000), CIS. **CCC.**
Published by: C M P Information Ltd. (Subsidiary of: United Business Media Limited), City Reach, 5 Greenwich View Pl, Millharbour, London, E14 9NN, United Kingdom. TEL 44-20-7861-6137, FAX 44-20-7861-6552, enquiries@cmpinformation.com, http://www.cmpi.biz/. Ed. Lucy Huxley TEL 44-20-79218008. Pub. Paula Martin TEL 44-20-79218026. Adv. contact Sheryl Makin TEL 44-20-79218023. Circ: 25,157.

910.202 GBR ISSN 0269-0217
TRAVEL TRADE LONDON. Variant title: London Travel Trade. Text in English. 1984. a. adv. **Document type:** *Handbook/Manual/Guide, Trade.* **Description:** Comprehensive information on all aspects of London for groups of 10 or more.
Formerly (until 1986): London Travel Trade Manual
—BLDSC (9045.470500).
Published by: (Visit London USA), John Brown (Publishing) (Subsidiary of: John Brown Group), 132-142 Bramley Rd, London, W1O 6SR, United Kingdom. TEL 44-20-75653000, FAX 44-20-75653050, info@johnbrowngroup.co.uk, http://www.johnbrowngroup.co.uk. Circ: 20,000.

910.202 THA
TRAVEL TRADE REPORT; travel news source on Thailand and the Mekong Region. Text in Thai. 1978. w. USD 80. adv. **Document type:** *Newspaper, Trade.* **Description:** Covers travel industry, with product news on destinations marketed in Thailand and the Mekong region.
Formerly: Travel Trade Reporter - Asia
Related titles: English ed.
Published by: Ross Publishing, Ltd., Ste 1801, Wave Place, 55 Wireless Road, Patumwan, Bangkok, 10330, Thailand. TEL 66-2-2547742, FAX 66-2-2547708, admin@ttreport.com, http://www.ttreport.com. adv.: B&W page USD 6,100, color page USD 7,020; trim 285 x 420. Circ: 12,600 (controlled).

910.202 DEU
TRAVEL TRIBUNE; der Nachrichtendienst fuer die Tourismuswirtschaft. Text in German. 1982. w. EUR 20.50 per month (effective 2006). adv. **Document type:** *Newsletter, Trade.*
Address: Unterster Zwerchweg 8, Frankfurt Am Main, 60599, Germany. TEL 49-69-625024, FAX 49-69-625026. adv.: B&W page EUR 1,350, color page EUR 2,475. Circ: 1,870 (paid and controlled).

338.4 USA ISSN 0041-2082
G155.A1
TRAVEL WEEKLY. Text in English. 1958. w. USD 149 domestic; USD 189 in Canada & Mexico; USD 229 elsewhere; free to qualified personnel (effective 2011). adv. bk.rev. charts; illus.; mkt.; stat. **Document type:** *Newspaper, Trade.* **Description:** Keeps travel agents, tour operators, airlines, hotels, cruise and ferry operators ahead of all that's happening in the travel industry.
Formerly (until 19??): Travel Items and Courier Weekly
Related titles: Online - full text ed.; Supplement(s): U S T O A Desk Reference. ISSN 1931-3527; Travel Weekly. U.S. Travel Industry Survey. ISSN 1559-4238. 2003.
Indexed: A09, A10, A11, A15, A22, ABIn, B01, B02, B03, B06, B07, B08, B09, B15, B17, B18, BusI, C05, CA, CLT&T, CPerI, G04, G06, G07, G08, H&TI, H06, HRIS, I05, I06, I07, M02, M06, P07, P34, PQC, RASB, S23, T&II, T02, V03, V04, WBA.
—CCC.
Published by: Northstar Travel Media LLC (Subsidiary of: Boston Ventures Management, Inc.), 100 Lighting Way, Secaucus, NJ 07094. TEL 201-902-2000, FAX 201-902-2045, http://www.northstartravelmedia.com/. Eds. Rob Fixmer TEL 201-902-1902, Arnie Weissmann TEL 201-902-1954.

338.4 AUS ISSN 1833-5179
TRAVEL WEEKLY (AUSTRALIA). Text in English. 2006. w. AUD 149 domestic; AUD 159 in New Zealand; AUD 169 elsewhere (effective 2008). adv. **Document type:** *Newsletter, Trade.* **Description:** Provides product news, sales tips, interviews and global news.
Formed by the merger of (1964-2006): Traveltrade; (2005-2006): Travel Week; Which was formerly (until 2005): Travelweek Australia (1037-1443); (until 1987): Travelweek (0813-5681); (until 1976): International Travel (0020-9015)
Indexed: A09, A10, A11, B01, B06, B07, B09, H&TI, H06, T02, V03, V04.
—CCC.
Published by: Reed Business Information Pty Ltd. (Subsidiary of: Reed Business Information International), Tower 2, 475 Victoria Ave, Locked Bag 2999, Chatswood, NSW 2067, Australia. TEL 61-2-94222999, FAX 61-2-94222922, customerservice@reedbusiness.com.au, http://www.reedbusiness.com.au. Pub. Ray Welling TEL 61-2-94228978. adv.: color page AUD 6,541; trim 248 x 345.

910.09 USA ISSN 1044-4602
TRAVEL WORLD NEWS. Text in English. 1987. m. USD 25; USD 80 foreign (effective 1998). adv. **Document type:** *Magazine, Trade.* **Description:** Published for the retail travel industry.
Published by: Travel Industry Network, 50 Washington St, Norwalk, CT 06854-2710. TEL 203-853-4955, FAX 203-866-1153. Ed. Sara Southworth. Pub., Adv. contact Charles Gatt Jr. Circ: 30,000 (controlled).

TRAVEL WRITER. *see* JOURNALISM

910.91 USA
TRAVEL WRITER MARKETLETTER. Text in English. m. USD 75 (effective 2005). **Document type:** *Newsletter, Trade.* **Description:** Covers new markets, guidelines and trips for travel writers and news for travel industry members.
Address: PO Box 1782, Springfield, VA 22151-0782. rsmilne@travelwriterml.com. Ed. Robert Scott Milne.

338.4791 GBR ISSN 2045-3515
TRAVEL ZAMBIA. Text in English. 2007. a. GBP 13 domestic; GBP 20 foreign (effective 2010); subscr. includes Travel Zambia Extra. adv. back issues avail. **Document type:** *Magazine, Consumer.* **Description:** Covers all aspects of travel within Zambia.
Related titles: Online - full text ed.: ISSN 2045-3523. free (effective 2010); ◆ Supplement(s): Travel Zambia Extra.
Published by: Travel Africa Ltd., 4 Rycote Ln Farm, Milton Common, Oxford, Oxfordshire OX9 2NZ, United Kingdom. TEL 44-1844-278883, FAX 44-1844-278893. Ed. Mike Unwin. Pub. Craig Rix. Adv. contact Dave Southwood.

338.4791 GBR
▼ **TRAVEL ZAMBIA EXTRA.** Text in English. 2010. 3/yr. Included with subscr. to Travel Zambia. adv. back issues avail. **Document type:** *Magazine, Consumer.* **Description:** Covers all aspects of travel within Zambia.
Related titles: Online - full text ed.: ISSN 2045-3531. free (effective 2010); ◆ Supplement to: Travel Zambia. ISSN 2045-3515.
Published by: Travel Africa Ltd., 4 Rycote Ln Farm, Milton Common, Oxford, Oxfordshire OX9 2NZ, United Kingdom. TEL 44-1844-278883, FAX 44-1844-278893. Ed. Mike Unwin. Pub. Craig Rix. Adv. contact Dave Southwood.

338.4791 GBR ISSN 2045-354X
▼ **TRAVEL ZIMBABWE.** Text in English. 2009. a. adv. back issues avail. **Document type:** *Magazine, Consumer.* **Description:** Covers all aspects of travel in Zimbabwe.
Related titles: Online - full text ed.: ISSN 2045-3558. free (effective 2010).
Published by: Travel Africa Ltd., 4 Rycote Ln Farm, Milton Common, Oxford, Oxfordshire OX9 2NZ, United Kingdom. TEL 44-1844-278883, FAX 44-1844-278893. Ed. Matt Phillips. Pub. Craig Rix. Adv. contact Dave Southwood.

917 USA ISSN 0041-1973
G155.A1
TRAVELAGE WEST. Text in English. 1969. bi-w. (Mon.). USD 69 domestic; USD 89 foreign; free to qualified personnel (effective 2011). bk.rev. illus.; tr.lit. back issues avail.; reprints avail. **Document type:** *Magazine, Trade.* **Description:** Contains industry news and features for front line sales counselors, managers, and owners of travel agencies.
Related titles: Online - full text ed.: ISSN 1558-5883.
Indexed: B03, B11, G08, H&TI, I05, S23, WBA, WMB.
—CCC.
Published by: Northstar Travel Media LLC (Subsidiary of: Boston Ventures Management, Inc.), 100 Lighting Way, Secaucus, NJ 07094. TEL 201-902-2000, FAX 201-902-2045, http://www.northstartravelmedia.com/. Ed. Kenneth Shapiro. Pub. Michelle Rosenberg TEL 310-772-7438.

910.91 USA
TRAVELASSIST MAGAZINE. Text in English. m.
Related titles: Online - full text ed.
Published by: Assist Information Services, 11054 Ventura Blvd, Ste 109, Studio City, CA 91604. TEL 818-761-8796, FAX 818-761-6804.

910.202 DEU
TRAVELBOOK; das Reisemagazin im Internet. Text in German. d. adv. **Document type:** *Magazine, Consumer.* **Description:** Contains articles and features on a wide variety of places to visit throughout the world.
Media: Online - full text.
Address: Stromeyerstr 3, Hannover, 30163, Germany. TEL 49-511-669834, FAX 49-511-669899. Ed., Pub. Walter Schoendorf.

910.202 GRC ISSN 1108-8508
TRAVELER NATIONAL GEOGRAPHIC. Cover title: O Praktikos Odegos Tou Taxidiote. Text in Greek. 2000. q. adv. **Document type:** *Magazine, Consumer.*
Published by: Lambrakis Press SA, Panepistimiou 18, Athens, 106 72, Greece. TEL 30-1-3686-452, FAX 30-1-3686-445, dolinfo@dol.gr, http://www.dol.gr.

910.202 USA
TRAVELER OVERSEAS; the essential guide for the experienced world traveler. Text in English. 2004. q. USD 47; USD 15 newsstand/cover (effective 2009).
Published by: Connatser Hankinson Publications, Llc, 3100 Monticello., Ste 130, Dallas, TX 75205. TEL 214-265-9787, FAX 214-528-2192, info@traveleroverseas.com, http://www.traveleroverseas.com. Ed., Pub. Stephen G Connatser.

TRAVELER'S GUIDE TO ART MUSEUM EXHIBITIONS; for art lovers who travel and travelers who love art. *see* MUSEUMS AND ART GALLERIES

910 USA ISSN 1533-0397
G155.A1
TRAVELERS' USE OF THE INTERNET. Text in English. 199?. a. **Document type:** *Report, Trade.* **Description:** Provides incidence of Internet use among the traveling population of US adults, as well as the size of the markets for online travel planning and online travel booking.
Related titles: Online - full content ed.: ISSN 1537-7393. 2001.
Published by: Travel Industry Association of America, 1100 New York Ave, NW, Ste 450, Washington, DC 20005. TEL 202-408-8422, FAX 202-408-1255, feedback@tia.org, http://www.tia.org.

910.202 USA
TRAVELFLASH. Text in English. m. **Document type:** *Newsletter.* **Description:** For active travelers. Contains info on discounts, deals and feature articles on selected destinations.
Media: Online - full text.

910.91 USA ISSN 1554-6047
GV149
TRAVELGIRL. Text in English. 2003 (Jul.). q. USD 17.95; USD 4.99 newsstand/cover (effective 2004). adv. **Document type:** *Magazine, Consumer.* **Description:** Contains travel and lifestyle information and advice aimed at women.
Published by: TravelGirl, Inc., 3508 Broad St, Chamblee, GA 30341. TEL 770-451-9399, 866-478-8747, FAX 770-454-6366. Circ: 55,000 (paid and controlled).

338.4 NZL ISSN 1176-936X
TRAVELINC. Text in English. 2004. m. free (effective 2008). **Document type:** *Magazine, Trade.* **Description:** Provides information on products, destinations, trends and developments for the travel trade industry.
Address: 4 Hemi Pl, Tirua, New Zealand. http://www.travelinc.co.nz.

910 610 USA ISSN 0899-2169
TRAVELING HEALTHY. Text in English. 1988. bi-m. back issues avail. **Document type:** *Newsletter.* **Description:** Alerts travelers about health and medical issues.
Published by: Travel Medicine, Inc., 351 Pleasant St, Ste 312, Northampton, MA 01060. TEL 800-872-8633, FAX 413-584-6656, travmed@travmed.com, http://www.travmed.com/. Ed. Dr. Karl Neumann. Pub. Dr. Stuart R Rose. Circ: 1,250 (paid and free).

THE TRAVELING MARATHONER. *see* SPORTS AND GAMES

910.09 GBR ISSN 0262-2726
TRAVELLER. Text in English. 1970. q. free to members (effective 2009). adv. bk.rev. charts; illus. **Document type:** *Magazine, Consumer.* **Description:** Travel-related features and reviews.
Formerly (until 1980): Expedition (0308-910X)
Published by: Wexas Ltd., 45-49 Brompton Rd, Knightsbridge, London, SW3 1DE, United Kingdom. TEL 44-845-6436568, FAX 44-20-78380837, publications@wexas.com, http://www.wexas.com/mac.php?#fragment-2.

910.91 AUT ISSN 1817-1192
TRAVELLER. Text in German. 1981. w. EUR 44 domestic; EUR 60 foreign (effective 2005). adv. **Document type:** *Newspaper, Trade.*
Published by: Manstein Zeitschriften Verlagsgesellschaft mbH, Brunner Feldstr 45, Perchtoldsdorf, N 2380, Austria. TEL 43-1-866480, FAX 43-1-86648100, office@manstein.at, http://www.manstein.at. Ed. Christa Oppenauer. Adv. contact Andreas Lorenz. B&W page EUR 2,000, color page EUR 3,200; trim 190 x 257. Circ: 8,500 (paid and controlled).

338.4791 CAN ISSN 1705-2548
TRAVELLER ACCOMMODATION SURVEY, A REPORT. Text in English. 2000. a. **Document type:** *Government.*
Related titles: Online - full text ed.: ISSN 1716-9062.
Published by: (Canadian Tourism Commission/Commission Canadienne du Tourisme), Statistics Canada/Statistique Canada, Communications Division, 3rd Fl, R H Coats Bldg, Ottawa, ON K1A 0A6, Canada. TEL 800-263-1136, infostats@statcan.ca, http://www.statcan.gc.ca.

338.4791 NPL
TRAVELLER'S NEPAL. Text in English. bi-m. **Document type:** *Handbook/Manual/Guide, Consumer.* **Description:** Provides a complete guide to tourism in Nepal, covering topics such as excursions, festivals, foods, transportation and more.
Related titles: Online - full content ed.
Published by: M D Publishing Co. Pvt. Ltd., Tripureswor, PO Box 3525, Kathmandu, Nepal. TEL 977-1-260327, 977-1-256003, 977-1-260418, FAX 977-1-260159, nttj@mos.com.np.

338.4791 GBR ISSN 2046-3251
TRAVELLERS' TIMES. Abbreviated title: T T. Text in English. 1998. q. GBP 14 (effective 2011). adv. back issues avail. **Document type:** *Magazine, Consumer.* **Description:** Brings out the latest news, pictures, video, opinion and resources from within the Gypsy, Roma and traveller communities.
Related titles: Online - full text ed.
Published by: The Rural Media Company, Sullivan House, 72-80 Widemarsh St, Hereford, HR4 9HG, United Kingdom. TEL 44-1432-344039, FAX 44-1432-270539, contact@ruralmedia.co.uk, http://www.ruralmedia.co.uk. Ed. Bill Laws. Adv. contact Jan Howells.

379.85 DEU
TRAVELLER'S WORLD. Text in German. 2/yr. EUR 8 newsstand/cover (effective 2007). adv. **Document type:** *Magazine, Consumer.*
Published by: Traveller's World Verlag GmbH, Truderinger Str 302, Munich, 81825, Germany. TEL 49-89-23684050, FAX 49-89-23684060. Ed. Reinhard Modritz. adv.: page EUR 11,700. Circ: 50,000 (paid and controlled).

910.2 LIE
TRAVELLERSTYLE. Text in German. 2/yr. EUR 9.80 (effective 2007). adv. **Document type:** *Magazine, Consumer.*
Published by: Neue Verlagsanstalt, In der Fina 18, Schaan, 9494, Liechtenstein. TEL 423-233-4381, FAX 423-233-4382, info@neue-verlagsanstalt.li, http://www.neue-verlagsanstalt.li. Ed. Beate Juergens. Pub., Adv. contact Rita Quaderer. page EUR 12,990. Circ: 38,981 (paid and controlled).

919 AUS ISSN 1836-0718
TRAVELLING IN AUSTRALIA; a great destination deserveb a great magazine. Text in English. 197?. q. AUD 33 domestic; AUD 56.80 in Asia & the Pacific; AUD 47.30 in New Zealand; AUD 62.20 elsewhere (effective 2011). adv. back issues avail. **Document type:** *Magazine, Consumer.* **Description:** Showcases the best of Australian destinations and travel products.
Related titles: Online - full text ed.: free (effective 2011).
Published by: Morrison Media Services Ltd., PO Box 823, Burleigh Heads, QLD 4220, Australia. TEL 61-7-55761388, FAX 61-7-55761527, subs@morrisonmedia.com.au, http://www.morrisonmedia.com.au. Ed. Susan Tyrrell. Pub. Peter Morrison. Adv. contact Bree Higgerson TEL 61-7-55209128.

910.4 HKG
TRAVELLING MAGAZINE/LU HSING TSA CHIH; the first Chinese language travel magazine. Text in Chinese. m. HKD 10 per issue. adv. illus. **Description:** Covers travel to all parts of the world.
Address: Rm.903 Yat Fat Bldg, 44 Des Voeux Rd, Central, Hong Kong, Hong Kong. TEL 5-247738, FAX 5-218390. Ed. Tien Pei Hsu.

910.202 636 CAN ISSN 1194-3165
TRAVELLING WITH YOUR PET. Text in English. 1992. a. CAD 4.95.
Published by: Patrick Communications, Ltd., 43 Railside Rd, Don Mills, ON M3A 3L9, Canada. TEL 416-441-3228, FAX 416-798-9778. Ed. Susan Pearce. adv.: B&W page CAD 1,490, color page CAD 2,290; trim 7.38 x 5.38. Circ: 30,000.

914.2 GBR
TRAVELMAG; the independent spirit. Text in English. 1994. m. free. adv. **Document type:** *Magazine, Consumer.* **Description:** For independent longhaul travellers.
Media: Online - full text.
Address: 1 Long Dr, Burbage, Nr Marlborough, Wiltshire SN8 3AH, United Kingdom. Ed., R&P, Adv. contact Jack Barker.

910.09 AUS ISSN 1034-2370
TRAVELNEWS AUSTRALIA. Text in English. 1988. m. adv. **Document type:** *Journal, Trade.*
Published by: McIntosh Publications, Box 555, Strphey, SA 5069, Australia. travnews@ozemail.com.au.

TRAVELODGE/THRIFTLODGE TRAVEL DIRECTORY; recreate. hibernate. *see* BUSINESS AND ECONOMICS—Trade And Industrial Directories

910 CAN
TRAVELOPTIONS. Text in English. a. **Document type:** *Handbook/Manual/Guide, Consumer.* **Description:** Upscale travel guide targets affluent travelers in New York, Connecticut, and Massachusetts.
Address: CP 701, Snowdon, Montreal, PQ H3X 3X8, Canada. TEL 514-482-4468, FAX 514-482-5751. Pub. Gerald Steinberg.

338.4791 DEU
TRAVELTALK. Text in German. 1999. w. EUR 10 (effective 2006). adv. **Document type:** *Magazine, Trade.*
Published by: TravelTalk Verlags GmbH, Wandsbeker Allee 1, Hamburg, 22041, Germany. TEL 49-40-41448170, FAX 49-40-41448179. Ed. Ines Niedecken. Adv. contact Oliver Pawelzik. color page EUR 7,370. Circ: 33,451 (controlled).

915.04 919.04 AUS ISSN 1832-4134
TRAVELTALK ASIA PACIFIC. Text in English. 1979. m. AUD 60. adv. **Document type:** *Magazine, Trade.*
Formerly (until 2000): Traveltalk (0728-0556)
Published by: Sinclair Publishing Group Pty. Ltd., PO Box 329, North Beach, W.A. 6920, Australia. TEL 61-8-92403888, FAX 61-8-92402796. Circ: 5,000.

338.4791 AUS ISSN 1832-2719
TRAVELTALK AUSTRALIA. Text in English. 2002. q. AUD 30 domestic; AUD 55 foreign (effective 2009). **Document type:** *Magazine, Consumer.*
Formerly (until 2004): Traveltalk West Coast (1447-8129)
Published by: Sinclair Publishing Group Pty. Ltd., PO Box 329, North Beach, W.A. 6920, Australia. TEL 61-8-92403888, FAX 61-8-92402796, editorial@traveltalk.biz. Adv. contact Dorothy Hutton TEL 61-8-92403888.

TRAVELTRADE YEAR BOOK. *see* BUSINESS AND ECONOMICS—Trade And Industrial Directories

910.202 CAN
TRAVELWEEK BULLETIN. Text in English. 1973. w. CAD 58.85, USD 100. adv. **Document type:** *Bulletin, Trade.*
Formerly: C T M Weekly Bulletin (0380-2019)
Published by: Concepts Travel Media, Ltd., 282 Richmond St E, Toronto, ON M5A 1P4, Canada. TEL 416-365-1500, FAX 416-365-1504. Ed. Patrick Dineen. Pub. Gerry Kinasz. Adv. contact Robynlee Hyndman. Circ: 14,000.

TRAVELWRITER MARKETLETTER. *see* JOURNALISM

910.2 USA ISSN 0162-9816
G540
TRAVLTIPS. Text in English. 1967. bi-m. USD 20 (effective 2005). adv. illus. **Document type:** *Magazine, Consumer.* **Description:** Accounts of freighter and other unusual cruises.
Formerly: TravLtips Freighter Bulletin (0049-4585)
Published by: TravLtips Inc., PO Box 580188, Flushing, NY 11358. TEL 800-872-8584, FAX 718-224-3247, info@travltips.com, http://www.travltips.com. Ed. Edmund M Kirk. Circ: 26,000 (paid).

338.4791028546 GBR ISSN 1750-256X
TRAVOLUTION. Text in English. 2005. bi-m. free to qualified personnel (effective 2010). back issues avail. **Document type:** *Magazine, Trade.* **Description:** Covers all aspects of traditional travel market plus the new breed of online players. Provides essential information, commentary, market intelligence and analysis for anyone in, or running an online travel business.
Related titles: Online - full text ed.
—CCC.
Published by: T W Group, 52 Grosvenor Gardens, London, SW1W 0AU, United Kingdom. Ed. Lee Hayhurst TEL 44-20-78814865.

910.91 USA ISSN 1930-9384
TX337.M6
THE TREASURES AND PLEASURES OF MEXICO. Text in English. 2002. a. USD 19.95 per issue (effective 2007). **Document type:** *Guide, Consumer.*
Published by: Impact Publications, 9104 Manassas Dr, Ste N, Manassas Park, VA 20111. TEL 703-361-7300, FAX 703-335-9486, query@impactpublications.com. Eds. Dr. Caryl Krannich, Dr. Ron Krannich.

910.2 USA ISSN 1559-5978
DS563
THE TREASURES AND PLEASURES OF THAILAND AND MYANMAR. Text in English. 2005. irreg. USD 21.95 per issue (effective 2007). **Document type:** *Guide, Consumer.*
Published by: Impact Publications, 9104 Manassas Dr, Ste N, Manassas Park, VA 20111. TEL 703-361-7300, FAX 703-335-9486, query@impactpublications.com.

338.4791 FRA ISSN 1295-8913
TREK MAGAZINE. Text in French. 1999. m. EUR 49.50 domestic (effective 2009). **Document type:** *Magazine, Consumer.*
Published by: Editions Niveales, 6 Rue Irvoy, Grenoble, 38000, France. TEL 33-4-76705411, FAX 33-4-76705412, http://www.dipresse.com/niveales. Ed. Jean-Marc Porte. **Subscr. to:** Dipresse. abo@dipinfo.fr.

914 BEL
TREKKERSKRANT. Text in Dutch. 1945. bi-m. adv. **Description:** News concerning hostels.
Formerly: Trekker (0041-2260)
Published by: Vlaamse Jeugdherbergcentrale, Van Stralenstraat 40, Antwerp, 2000, Belgium. Ed. E De Roover. Circ: 20,000.

THE TRIAL RIDER; America's premier trial & pleasure riding magazine. *see* SPORTS AND GAMES—Horses And Horsemanship

910.2 GBR ISSN 0264-1763
TRIANGLE. Text in English. 1972. 2/yr. GBP 1 to non-members (effective 2000). bk.rev. illus. **Document type:** *Bulletin.*
Former titles: Hostelling News (0267-9353); Hostelling News (0306-8927); Supersedes: Youth Hosteller (0044-1228)
Indexed: Inspec.
—CCC.
Published by: Hay Market Magazines Ltd ., Trevelyan House, St Stephens Hill, St Albans, Herts AL1 2DY, United Kingdom. TEL 44-1727-855215, FAX 44-1727-844126. Ed. Caroline Brandenburge. Circ: 230,000.

917 USA ISSN 0041-2619
TRIANGLE POINTER; guide to the Triangle. Text in English. 1961. m. USD 15 (effective 2001). adv. charts. **Document type:** *Magazine, Consumer.* **Description:** Information for visitors and newcomers on eating, shopping, lodging, newcomers aides, calendar of events, great map, and area attractions.
Related titles: Online - full text ed.
Published by: Triangle Pointer, Inc., 1563, Apex, NC 27502-3563. FAX 919-942-2826. Ed. Katherine Kopp. Pub. Sue Chen Reeder. R&P, Adv. contact Sue Reeder TEL 800-400-1901. Circ: 45,000.

910.2 ITA ISSN 1824-7237
TRIESTE A Z; guida generale stradaria. Text in Italian. 2000. irreg. **Document type:** *Consumer.*
Published by: Hammerle Editori, Piazza V Giotti 1, Trieste, 34133, Italy. TEL 39-040-767075, FAX 39-040-767440, info@hammerle.it, http://www.hammerle.it.

910.09 GBR
TRIP OUT; directory passenger boat services in British Isles. Text in English. 1977. biennial. GBP 4.85 (effective 2001). back issues avail. **Document type:** *Directory.*
Published by: G.P. Hamer Ed. & Pub., 77 St Marys Grove, London, W4 3LW, United Kingdom.

910.202 USA
TRIPPIN' OUT MAGAZINE; the electronic zine for hip travelers. Text in English. irreg.
Media: Online - full text.
Address: http://www.trippinout.com. Eds. Jeff Brecker, Matt Ogens, Tom Smith. Pub. Kelley Quain. Adv. contact Andrew Borden.

917.4 USA ISSN 1937-691X
TRIPS & GETAWAYS. Text in English. 2007. bi-m. USD 15 (effective 2009). adv. **Document type:** *Guide, Consumer.*
Address: PO Box 376, Gambrills, MD 21054.

362.4910 GBR ISSN 1748-7714
TRIPSCOPE NEWSLETTER. Text in English. a. **Description:** Offers advice and information to people with impaired mobility on overcoming travel difficulties.
Formed by the 2004 merger of: Tripscope Newsletter (National Edition) (1369-474X); Tripscope Newsletter (London Edition) (1369-4901); Tripscope Newsletter (South West & Wales Edition) (1369-4898)
Related titles: Online - full text ed.
Published by: Tripscope, The Vassall Centre, Gill Ave, Bristol, BS16 2QQ, United Kingdom. TEL 44-117-9397782, 08457-585641, FAX 44-117-9397736, enquiries@tripscope.org.uk.

910.202 USA
TROPI-TIES E-ZINE & CATALOG. Text in English. 1996. 4/yr. **Description:** For people who love traveling and living in the tropics.
Media: Online - full text.
Address: 4270 W Oak Trail Rd, Santa Ynez, CA 93460. Ed. Cindy Alpers.

910.09 DEU ISSN 1860-9031
DER TROTTER. Text in German. 1975. q. free to members (effective 2008). bk.rev. abstr.; charts; illus.; stat. index. back issues avail. **Document type:** *Magazine, Consumer.* **Description:** Magazine for world travellers with travel accounts, information, tips, personal stories, and readers' letters.
Formerly: Globetrotter
Published by: Deutsche Zentrale fuer Globetrotter e.V., Forsthaus Fischbach, Russhuetter Str 26, Postfach 301033, Quierschied, 66287, Germany. TEL 49-700-45623876, vorstand@globetrotter.org. Circ: 1,100.

917.91 979.1 USA ISSN 0894-0320
TUCSON GUIDE QUARTERLY. Text in English. 1983. q. USD 12.95; USD 3.95 newsstand/cover (effective 2007). adv. maps. back issues avail. **Document type:** *Magazine, Consumer.* **Description:** Provides residents and visitors with seasonally updated information about the culture, lifestyle, hospitality and excitement of the city of Tucson and the state of Arizona.
Published by: Madden Publishing, 1650 E Ft Lowell Rd #100, Tucson, AZ 85719. TEL 520-322-0895, 800-444-8768, info@maddenpreprint.com. Ed. Katy Spining. Pub. John Hudak. Adv. contact Whitney Coleman. B&W page USD 2,115, color page USD 2,795; trim 10.75 x 8.13. Circ: 40,000.

910.91 ITA ISSN 2035-956X
▼ **LE TUE VACANZE ALL'ARIA APERTA.** Text in Italian. 2009. s-a. **Document type:** *Guide, Consumer.*
Published by: L' Ortensia Rossa, Circonvallazione Gianicolense 210, Rome, 00152, Italy. TEL 39-06-98387080, FAX 39-06-5349779, info@ortensiarossa.it, http://www.ortensiarossa.it.

TUEBINGER BLAETTER; Das Magazin des Buerger- und Verkehrsvereins. *see* COLLEGE AND ALUMNI

914.84 NOR ISSN 1503-7460
TUR-GLEDE. Text in Norwegian. 1926. a. NOK 248 per issue (effective 2006). **Document type:** *Consumer.*
Former titles (until 2001): Trondhjems Turistforening. Aarbok (1503-2523); (until 1967): Trondhjems Turesiforenings Aarbok (1503-2515)
Published by: Trondhjems Turistforening, Sandgate 30, Trondheim, 7012, Norway. TEL 47-73-924200, FAX 47-73-924201, firmapost@tt.no, http://www.tt.no.

910.202 USA ISSN 1932-5738
TURIN (AMERICAN EDITION). Text in English. 2004. irreg. plus a. updates. USD 22.50 per issue (effective 2008). **Document type:** *Monographic series, Consumer.*
Published by: D K Publishing (Subsidiary of: Penguin Books U S A, Inc.), 375 Hudson St, New York, NY 10014. TEL 212-213-4800, 800-631-8571, FAX 212-689-4828, publicity@dk.com, http://us.dk.com.

917 PAN
TURISGUIA. Text in English, Spanish. 1964. m. USD 36. adv.
Address: Apdo. Postal 9525, Panama City, 4, Panama. TEL 25-8486. Ed. Roy Tasco Wesley. Circ: 10,000.

910.202 BRA ISSN 1983-7151
➤ **TURISMO (ONLINE)**; visao e acao. Text in Portuguese; Text occasionally in English, Spanish. 1998. q. free (effective 2008). abstr. cum.index: every 10 yrs. back issues avail. **Document type:** *Journal, Academic/Scholarly.* **Description:** Provides information for researchers, professors and students in Tourism and related areas, at graduate and post-graduate levels; as well as consultants, business people and professionals from public and private companies operating in tourism and related areas.
Media: Online - full text.
Published by: Universidade do Vale do Itajai, 5a. avenida, s/n, Balneario Camboriu, Santa Catarina 88337-300, Brazil. TEL 55-47-32611252, FAX 55-47-32611211. Eds. Anete Alberton, Valmir Emil Hoffmann.

917 ITA ISSN 1723-4182
TURISMO D'AFFARI. Text in Italian. 1962. bi-m. EUR 45 domestic; EUR 65 foreign (effective 2008). adv. **Document type:** *Magazine, Trade.*
Published by: Ediman Srl, Via Ripamonti 89, Milan, 20139, Italy. TEL 39-02-57311511, FAX 39-02-55231486, http://www.ediman.it. Circ: 10,000.

910.202 ITA
TURISMO D'ITALIA. Text in Italian, English. 1988. m. (10/yr.). EUR 60 domestic (effective 2008). **Document type:** *Magazine, Trade.*
Related titles: Online - full text ed.
Published by: (Federazione delle Associazioni Italiane Alberghi e Turismo), BE-MA Editrice Srl, Via Teocrito 50, Milan, MI 20128, Italy. TEL 39-02-252071, FAX 39-02-27000692, segreteria@bema.it.

910.09 ITA
TURISMO & ATTUALITA; settimanale di turismo, economia e spettacolo. Text in Italian. 1977. w. (39/yr.). EUR 10 (effective 2009). adv. 20 p./no.; **Document type:** *Magazine, Consumer.*
Formerly: Turismo Attualita International
Related titles: Online - full text ed.
Published by: Turismo & Attualita Srl, Via di Santa Prisca 16, Rome, 00153, Italy. TEL 39-06-5747450, FAX 39-06-5744154, info@turismo-attualita.it, http://www.turismo-attualita.it. Ed. Roberta D'Amato. Circ: 10,000.

338.4 PRT ISSN 1647-6247
O TURISMO EM (YEAR). Text in Portuguese. 2007. a. **Document type:** *Report, Trade.*
Published by: Instituto de Planeamento e Desenvolvimento do Turismo (I P D T), Rua da Gandara, Edificio do IDIT, Santa Maria da Feira, 4520-102, Portugal. TEL 351-256-330272, FAX 351-256-378645, http://www.ipdt.pt.

910.09 BRA ISSN 0103-5541
G155.B7
TURISMO EM ANALISE. Text in Portuguese, Spanish; Summaries in English, Portuguese, Spanish. 1990. s-a. BRL 15; USD 20 in Latin America; USD 25 elsewhere. bk.rev. **Document type:** *Academic/Scholarly.* **Description:** Publishes the studies and research of teachers, researchers and professionals in the area of tourism.
Indexed: CA, T02.
Published by: Universidade de Sao Paulo, Escola de Comunicacoes e Artes, Av. Prof. Lucio Martins Rodrigues 443, Butanta, SP 05508-900, Brazil. TEL 55-11-30914033, comunica@eca.usp.br, http://www.eca.usp.br/. Ed. Mirian Rejowski de Carvalho.

910.91 ESP ISSN 1130-1627
TURISMO EN NAVARRA. Text in Spanish. 1985. s-a. free. **Document type:** *Bulletin, Government.*
Indexed: RILM.
Published by: Gobierno de Navarra, Fondo de Publicaciones, Calle de la Navas de Tolosa 21, Pamplona, Navarra 31002, Spain. TEL 34-9848-427121, FAX 34-9848-427123, fondo.publicaciones@cfnavarra.es, http://www.navarra.es.

910.202 ITA ISSN 1970-0245
TURISMO IN CALABRIA MAGAZINE. Text in Italian. 2005. m. EUR 30 (effective 2009). **Document type:** *Magazine, Consumer.*
Published by: Zerouno Italia Srl, Redazione Costa Viola Magazine, Via R Piria 36, Scilla, RC 89058, Italy. TEL 39-0965-754064.

910.202 ESP ISSN 1699-275X
TURISMO RURAL; otras formas de viajar y disfrutar. Text in Spanish. 1997. m. adv. **Document type:** *Magazine, Consumer.*
Published by: Editorial America Iberica, C. Miguel Yuste 33bis, Madrid, 28037, Spain. TEL 34-91-3277950, FAX 34-91-3044746, editorial@eai.es, http://www.eai.es/. Ed. Milagros Fernandez-Avila. adv.: page EUR 3,550; trim 230 x 297.

910.09 ESP
TURISMO Y OCIO. Text in Spanish. 4/yr. **Document type:** *Magazine, Consumer.*
Related titles: Online - full text ed.
Address: Placa Lesseps 4 y 5, Barcelona, 08023, Spain. TEL 34-93-2182961, FAX 34-972-871333. Ed. Ricard Barrufet Santolaria. Circ: 21,000.

338.4 COL ISSN 0120-7555
➤ **TURISMO Y SOCIEDAD.** Text in Spanish; Summaries in English, Spanish. 1986. a. COP 40,000 domestic; USD 40 foreign (effective 2011). Index. back issues avail. **Document type:** *Journal, Academic/Scholarly.* **Description:** Publishes scientific and technical papers in the areas of leisure, recreation and tourism planning, sustainable tourism, economy and tourism, management of tourism, culture and tourism research, tourism policies and impacts of tourism in Colombia, Latin America and the world through case studies.
Related titles: Online - full text ed.
Published by: (Universidad Externado de Colombia, Facultad de Administracion de Empresas Turisticas y Hoteleras), Universidad Externado de Colombia, Departamento de Publicaciones, Calle 12, No 1-17 Este, Bogota, Colombia. TEL 57-1-2826066, publicaciones@uexternado.edu.co. Ed. Edna Rozo. **Dist. by:** Siglo del Hombre Editores, Cra. 32 No.25-46/50, Bogota, D.C., Colombia. TEL 57-1-3377700, FAX 57-1-3377665, info@siglodelhombre.com, http://www.siglodelhombre.com.

910.202 613.7 ITA ISSN 1970-1225
TURISMO&BENESSERE. Text in Italian. 2006. q. **Document type:** *Newsletter, Consumer.*
Published by: P G Edizioni, Via Silvio Pellico 3, Carugate, MI 20061, Italy. pgedizioni@libero.it.

910.09 647.94 PRT
TURISMOHOTEL. Text in Portuguese. 12/yr.
Address: Rua Entreparedes, 6-1 e 2o, Porto, 4000, Portugal. TEL 2-23875, FAX 2-318426, TELEX 23809. Ed. Silva Tavares. Circ: 30,000.

914 SWE ISSN 0041-4190
TURIST. Text in Swedish. 1933. 5/yr. SEK 285 membership; SEK 110 to students; SEK 39 per issue (effective 2005). adv. bk.rev. illus. index. **Document type:** *Magazine, Consumer.*
Formerly (until 1962): S T F - Svenska Turistfoereningens Tidning
Published by: Svenska Turistfoereningen/Swedish Touring Club, Sturegatan 4 C, PO Box 25, Stockholm, 10120, Sweden. TEL 46-8-4632100, FAX 46-8-6781958, info@stfturist.se. Ed., Pub. Anders Tapper. Adv. contact Jonas Thoerne TEL 46-8-224480. page SEK 32,970; bleed 192 x 255. Circ: 230,000.

915 RUS ISSN 0131-7040
G149
TURIST. Text in Russian. 1929. bi-m. USD 48 foreign (effective 1999). adv. illus.
Former titles: Turist. Mir Puteshestvii; Mir Puteshestvii (0868-9547); (until 1991): Turist (0041-4182)
Indexed: RASB.
Address: B Khariton'evskii per 14, Moscow, 107078, Russian Federation. TEL 7-095-9219492, FAX 7-095-9592336. Ed. Boris V Moskvin. R&P, Adv. contact Victor Kalinin. Circ: 5,000. **Dist. by:** East View Information Services, 10601 Wayzata Blvd, Minneapolis, MN 55305. TEL 952-252-1201, 800-477-1005, FAX 952-252-1202, info@eastview.com, http://www.eastview.com.

796.5 CZE ISSN 0139-5467
TURISTA. Text in Czech. 1962-1991; resumed 1996. bi-m. CZK 325 domestic (effective 2009). adv. bk.rev. charts; illus.; maps. back issues avail. **Document type:** *Magazine, Consumer.*
Formerly: Turistika a Horolezectvi
Published by: Klub Ceskych Turistu, Archeologicka 2256, Prague 5, 155 00, Czech Republic. TEL 420-251-610181, FAX 420-251-625100, kct@kct.cz, http://www.kct.cz.

910.202 MEX
TURISTAMPA. Text in English, Spanish. 1969. s-m. free. adv. 72 p./no. 5 cols./p.; back issues avail. **Document type:** *Newsletter, Consumer.* **Description:** Features travel trade news.
Published by: Turistampa S.A., MOLIERE 39 Piso 1, Palmas Polanco, Mexico City, DF 11560, Mexico. TEL 52-5-2801984, FAX 52-5-2808316, info@turistampa.com.mx, ventas@turistampa.com.mx. Adv. contact Hubert Knipperte. page USD 2,900. Circ: 14,000.

914 SRB ISSN 0041-4204
TURISTICKE NOVINE. Text in Serbo-Croatian. 1952. w. adv. illus. index. **Document type:** *Magazine, Consumer.*
Address: Djure Djakovica 100, Belgrade, 11000. TEL 381-11-761125, FAX 381-11-762236.

910.09 PRT
TURISVER. Text in Portuguese. 52/yr.
Address: Rua da Esperanca 16-2o, Lisbon, 1200, Portugal. TEL 342-1580, FAX 3960787, TELEX 61628. Ed. Silva Rosa.

338.4791 HRV ISSN 0494-2639
TURIZAM. Text in Serbo-Croatian. 1954. m. **Document type:** *Magazine, Trade.*
Former titles (until 1956): Turisticki Pregled (1330-2418); (until 1954): Turisticke Vijesti (1332-7488)
Related titles: ◆ English ed.: Tourism. ISSN 1332-7461.
Indexed: H&TI, RILM, SCOPUS, SociolAb.
Published by: Hrvatska Turisticka Zajednica/Institute for Tourism, Vrhovec 5, Zagreb, 10000, Croatia. TEL 385-1-3773222, FAX 385-1-3774860, turizam@iztzg.hr, http://www.iztzg.hr/turizam/tourism/htm. Ed. Sandra Weber.

TURIZM DUNYASI. *see* HOTELS AND RESTAURANTS

910.09 HUN ISSN 0237-5249
TURIZMUS. Text in Hungarian. m. USD 21.
Address: Muzeum utca 11, Budapest, 1088, Hungary. TEL 138-4638, TELEX 22-5297. Ed. Zsolt Szebeni. Circ: 8,000.

338.4791 HUN ISSN 1786-4585
TURIZMUS TREND/TOURISM TREND. Text in Hungarian. 2004. bi-w. HUF 5,900 (effective 2011). adv. **Document type:** *Magazine, Trade.*
Published by: Professional Publishing Hungary Kft. (Subsidiary of: Sueddeutscher Verlag GmbH), Montevideo u 3, Budapest, 1037, Hungary. TEL 36-1-4304500, FAX 36-1-4304509, vandora@pphungary.hu, http://www.pphungary.hu. Ed. Zoltan Szanto.

TURIZUM/TOURISM. *see* STATISTICS

910 TUR
TURKIYE TURING VE OTOMOBIL KURUMU BELLETENI. Text in Turkish. 1930. q. TRY 1. adv. **Document type:** *Bulletin, Trade.*
Published by: Turk Turing ve Otomobil Kurumu/Touring and Automobile Club of Turkey, Oto Sanayi Sitesi Yani, 4 Levent, Istanbul, Turkey. TEL 90-212-2828140, FAX 90-212-2828042. Ed. Celik Gulersoy. R&P, Adv. contact Hakan Sukayar TEL 90-212-282-8285. Circ: 1,000.

910.91 USA
TURTLE MOUNTAIN COUNTRY. Text in English. 1996. s-a. adv. illus. back issues avail. **Document type:** *Magazine, Consumer.* **Description:** Contains travel information on the Turtle Mountain region of Manitoba and North Dakota.
Published by: B H G Inc., PO Box 309, Garrison, ND 58540. TEL 701-463-2201, FAX 701-463-7487. Adv. contact Jude Iverson. page USD 500; trim 10.75 x 8.25. Circ: 35,000.

338.4 ESP ISSN 1988-5261
G155.A1
TURYDES. Text in Spanish. 2007. s-a. free (effective 2011). **Document type:** *Journal, Academic/Scholarly.*
Media: Online - full text.
Indexed: H&TI, H06, T02.
Published by: Universidad de Malaga, Eumed.net, Avenida Cervantes 2, Malaga, 29071, Spain. TEL 34-952-131000.

338.4791 POL ISSN 1425-4832
TURYSTYKA. Text in Polish. 1995. w. PLZ 54 per month domestic; EUR 15 per month in Europe; USD 23 per month in North America (effective 2011). **Document type:** *Consumer.*
Related titles: ◆ Supplement to: Gazeta Wyborcza. ISSN 0860-908X.

Published by: Agora S.A., ul Czerska 8/10, Warsaw, 00732, Poland. TEL 48-22-5556000, FAX 48-22-5554850, prenumerata@gazeta.pl, http://www.agora.pl.

910.09 POL ISSN 0867-5856
G155
TURYZM. Text in Polish; Summaries in English, French. 1985; N.S. 1988. s-a. EUR 47 foreign (effective 2011). **Document type:** *Journal, Academic/Scholarly.*
Formerly (until 1991): Acta Universitatis Lodziensis: Turyzm (0860-1119) —Linda Hall.
Published by: Wydawnictwo Uniwersytetu Lodzkiego/Lodz University Press, ul Lindleya 8, Lodz, 90-131, Poland. TEL 48-42-6655861, FAX 48-42-6655861, wdwul@uni.lodz.pl, http://www.wydawnictwo.uni.lodz.pl. Ed. Stanislaw Liszewski. **Dist. by:** Ars Polona, Obroncow 25, Warsaw 03933, Poland. TEL 48-22-5098609, FAX 48-22-5098610, arspolona@arspolona.com.pl, http://www.arspolona.com.pl.

910.2 ITA ISSN 1824-7229
TUTTORARIO; orari generali di Trieste. Variant title: Informa Tuttorario. Text in Italian. 1984. 3/yr. **Document type:** *Directory, Consumer.*
Published by: Hammerle Editori, Piazza V Giotti 1, Trieste, 34133, Italy. TEL 39-040-767075, FAX 39-040-767440, info@hammerle.it, http://www.hammerle.it.

910.09 ITA ISSN 0392-8020
TUTTOTURISMO. Text in Italian. 1977. 12/yr. adv. **Document type:** *Magazine, Consumer.*
Published by: Editoriale Domus, Via Gianni Mazzocchi 1/3, Rozzano, MI 20089, Italy. TEL 39-02-824721, editorialedomus@edidomus.it, http://www.edidomus.it. Circ: 120,300.

914.92 NLD ISSN 1574-2555
TWENTELIFE. Text in Dutch. 2004. q. EUR 17.95; EUR 4.95 newsstand/cover (effective 2009). adv. **Document type:** *Magazine, Consumer.*
Published by: Van Deinse Media b.v., De Klomp 35, Postbus 40194, Enschede, 7504 RD, Netherlands. TEL 31-53-4782071, FAX 31-53-4782070, info@vandeinsemedia.nl, http://www.vandeinsemedia.nl. Ed. Nicole Rietman-Reijn. Pub. Jeroen Achterberg. adv.: page EUR 1,795; 230 x 300. Circ: 15,000.

910.91 USA ISSN 1092-3721
TWO-LANE ROADS; a nostalgic backroad adventure. Text in English. 1991. q. USD 16 domestic; USD 20 foreign; USD 4.95 newsstand/cover (effective 2000). adv. bk.rev. illus.; maps. back issues avail. **Document type:** *Newspaper.* **Description:** Discusses adventures in a motorhome on two-lane roads east of the Rocky Mountains.
Published by: Hill Country Products, Inc., PO Box 23518, Fort Lauderdale, FL 33307-3518. TEL 954-566-0713, 888-896-5263. Ed., Adv. contact Loren Eyrich. page USD 300; trim 16 x 10. Circ: 2,000.

U J Q. (Uncle Jam Quarterly) *see* LITERARY AND POLITICAL REVIEWS

910 GBR
U K HOLIDAY GUIDE. Text in English. 1986. a. GBP 47 (effective 2003). Index. **Document type:** *Directory, Trade.* **Description:** Covers span a whole range of holiday types and destinations, providing the user with a one-stop source of information to quickly tell you who goes where, and much more.
Former titles: O A G U.K. Holiday Guide (1366-1671); (until 1996): A B C U.K. Holiday Guide (1357-1206); (until 1986): U.K. Holiday Guide —CCC.
Published by: Reed Business Information Ltd. (Subsidiary of: Reed Business), DG&G Travel Information, Dukeminster House, Church St, Dunstable, Beds LU5 4HU, United Kingdom. TEL 44-1582-676845, FAX 44-1582-676893, http://www.reedbusiness.co.uk/. Ed. Bozena Briggs. Pub. Giles Harper. Adv. contact Shelley Cope TEL 44-1582-676851.

U N L V JOURNAL OF HOSPITALITY, TOURISM & LEISURE SCIENCE. (University of Nevada Las Vegas) *see* HOTELS AND RESTAURANTS

917.304 CAN ISSN 1198-9599
U S A JOURNAL. Text in German. 1994. bi-m. USD 38; USD 65 foreign. adv. back issues avail. **Document type:** *Journal, Consumer.* **Description:** Contains information on business and travel in the US for German-speaking people.
Published by: Ruland Communications Inc., 12 Lawton Blvd, Toronto, ON M4V 1Z4, Canada. TEL 416-927-9129, FAX 416-927-9118. Ed., Pub. Joseph Ruland. adv.: B&W page USD 2,960, color page USD 3,740; trim 10.13 x 7. Circ: 40,000 (paid).

U.S. DEPARTMENT OF STATE. STANDARDIZED REGULATIONS (GOVERNMENT CIVILIANS, FOREIGN AREAS). *see* LAW

910.09 USA
HD38
U.S. DOMESTIC BUSINESS AND CONVENTION TRAVEL. Text in English. 1986. a., latest 2007. USD 275 per issue to non-members; USD 165 per issue to members (effective 2008). adv. **Document type:** *Monographic series, Trade.* **Description:** Reports profiles business and convention trips and travelers in the United States.
Former titles (until 2004): Business and Convention Travelers (1538-0408); (until 1999): Survey of Business Travelers (1047-8965); (until 1986): The Travel Weekly, US Travel Data Center Survey of Business Travelers (1044-0119)
Related titles: Online - full text ed.
Published by: Travel Industry Association of America, 1100 New York Ave, NW, Ste 450, Washington, DC 20005. TEL 202-408-8422, FAX 202-408-1255, feedback@tia.org. Pub. Dawn L Drew. Adv. contact Sarah Dickson TEL 202-408-2141.

719.32 USA ISSN 0083-2316
U.S. NATIONAL PARK SERVICE. HISTORICAL HANDBOOK SERIES. Text in English. 1950. irreg. free (effective 2011). back issues avail. **Document type:** *Monographic series, Government.*
Related titles: Online - full text ed.
Published by: U.S. Department of the Interior, National Parks Service, 1849 C St NW, Washington, DC 20240. TEL 202-208-6843, http://www.nps.gov.

914 HRV ISSN 1330-6766
U T; revija za ugostiteljstvo i turizam. Text in Croatian. 1952. m. index. **Document type:** *Magazine, Trade.* **Description:** Covers the catering and tourist trade.
Former titles (until 1968): Ugostiteljstvo i Turizam (0041-557X); (until 1964): Savremeno Ugostiteljstvo (1330-6871); (until 1955): Ugostiteljsko Turisticki Glasnik (1330-688X); (until 1954): Glasnik Ugostiteljsko Turisticke Komore Narodne Republike Hrvatske (1330-6898); (until 1953): Glasnik Inicijativnog Odbora za Osnivanje Ugostiteljske Komore NR Hrvatske (1332-747X)
Published by: Ugostiteyski i Turisticki Marketing, d.o.o., Gunduliceva 53, Zagreb, 10000, Croatia. TEL 385-1-4856765, FAX 385-1-4856766. Ed. Drago Ferencic. Circ: 20,000.

914.9 BEL ISSN 0774-1324
UIT; het V T B - V A B magazine. Text in Dutch. 1985. 11/yr. EUR 25 domestic; EUR 37 foreign; EUR 3.50 per issue (effective 2005). adv. bk.rev. back issues avail. **Document type:** *Magazine, Consumer.* **Description:** Travel reports, tips for weekend traveling, consumers' information, tests of food products, restaurant reports and road tests.
Published by: Vlaamse Toeristen Bond, Vlaamse Automobilistenbond, Pastoor Coplaan 100, Zwijndrecht, 2070, Belgium. TEL 32-3-253-6085, FAX 32-3-253-6090. Ed. Ludo Mortelmans. Pub. Henri Meiresonne. Adv. contact Yannic Demeyer. Circ: 200,000.

UITKRANT. *see* LEISURE AND RECREATION

919.69 USA ISSN 1550-7114
DU628.K3
THE ULTIMATE KAUAI GUIDEBOOK. Text in English. 1994. biennial. USD 15.95 per issue (effective 2008). **Document type:** *Guide, Consumer.*
Published by: Wizard Publications, Inc., PO Box 991, Lihue, HI 96766-0991. TEL 213-539-9213, aloha@wizardpub.com, http://www.wizardpub.com/main/home.html.

910.91 FRA ISSN 0990-7068
ULYSSE; la culture du voyage. Text in French. 1988. 8/yr. EUR 29 (effective 2009). bk.rev. back issues avail. **Document type:** *Magazine, Consumer.*
Indexed: FR.
—INIST.
Published by: Courrier International, 8 Rue Jean-Antoine de Baif, Paris, Cedex 13 75212, France. TEL 33-1-46461600, FAX 33-1-46461601, http://www.courrierint.com. Circ: 45,000.

379.8 CHE ISSN 1423-6206
UNIVERSITAET BERN. FORSCHUNGSINSTITUT FUER FREIZEIT UND TOURISMUS. JAHRESBERICHT. Text in German. 1944. a. **Document type:** *Journal, Academic/Scholarly.*
Formerly (until 1986): Universitaet Bern. Forschungsinstitut fuer Fremdenverkehr. Jahresbericht (0405-590X)
Published by: Universitaet Bern, Forschungsinstitut fuer Freizeit und Tourismus (Subsidiary of: Universitaet Bern), Schanzeneckstr 1, Bern, 3001, Switzerland. TEL 41-31-6313711, FAX 41-31-6313415, fif@fif.unibe.ch, http://www.fif.unibe.ch.

910.2 USA ISSN 1053-248X
GV1853.3.C22
THE UNOFFICIAL GUIDE TO DISNEYLAND. Text in English. 1985. a. USD 16.99 (effective 2006).
Published by: Menasha Ridge Press, 2204 First Ave S, Suite 102, Birminghama, AL 35233. TEL 205-322-0439, info@menasharidge.com, http://www.menasharidge.com.

338.4 USA ISSN 1946-3898
UPSCALE TRAVELER. Text in English. 1994. 10/yr. USD 125 domestic; USD 145 foreign (effective 2009). adv. 8 p./no.; back issues avail. **Document type:** *Newsletter, Consumer.* **Description:** Provides information to the sophisticated traveler, who wishes to travel in comfort and style, and substantially reduce travel costs.
Formerly (until 2008): Escenario Magazine (1946-388X)
Related titles: Online - full text ed.
Address: 4521 Alla Rd, Ste 3, Marina del Rey, CA 90292. TEL 310-823-1970, 800-355-9176, FAX 310-823-8840. Eds. Ralph Whitmore, Virginia Velazquez. Pub. Nancy Whitmore.

910.202 DEU
URLAUB PERFEKT. Text in German. 2003. 4/yr. EUR 5.40; EUR 1.50 newsstand/cover (effective 2010). adv. **Document type:** *Magazine, Consumer.*
Published by: Verlag Dieter Niedecken GmbH, Wandsbeker Allee 1, Hamburg, 22041, Germany. TEL 49-40-414480, FAX 49-40-41448999, info@niedeckenmedien.de, http://www.niedeckenmedien.de. Ed. Monika Spielberger. adv.: color page EUR 11,500. Circ: 135,539 (paid).

943 DEU
URLAUBS-KURIER. Text in German. 2001. w. adv. **Document type:** *Magazine, Consumer.*
Published by: Urlaubs-Kurier Verlags GmbH, Bahnhofstr 1, Fehmarn, 23769, Germany. TEL 49-4371-3090. adv.: B&W page EUR 3,785.51, color page EUR 5,491.24. Circ: 75,000 (controlled).

917.92 910.91 USA ISSN 1935-6447
F826
UTAH CURIOSITIES; quirky characters, roadside oddities & other offbeat stuff. Text in English. 2007. triennial, latest 2007, 1st ed. USD 14.95 per issue (effective 2008). **Document type:** *Guide, Consumer.* **Description:** Provides tourist information about Utah.
Published by: The Globe Pequot Press, Inc., 246 Goose Ln, PO Box 480, Guilford, CT 06437. TEL 203-458-4500, 888-249-7586, FAX 203-458-4603, 800-820-2329, info@globepequot.com, http://www.globepequot.com.

914.91 796.5 ISL ISSN 1670-6641
UTIVIST. Text in Icelandic. 1976. s-a. **Document type:** *Magazine, Consumer.*
Formerly (until 2002): Arsrit Utivist (1021-8750)
Published by: (Utivist), Athygli ehf., Sidumuta 1, Reykjavik, 108, Iceland. TEL 354-515-5200, FAX 354-515-5201, athygli@athygli.is, http://www.athygli.is.

338.4 NLD ISSN 1381-9135
DE UYTVAERT; onafhankelijk vakblad voor het uitvaartwezen in Belgie en Nederland. Text in Dutch. 1985. 11/yr. EUR 67 (effective 2010). adv. **Document type:** *Magazine, Trade.*
Related titles: CD-ROM ed.
Published by: Uitvaart Media, Postbus 80532, Den Haag, 2508 GM, Netherlands. TEL 31-70-3518818, FAX 31-70-3518809, info@uitvaartmedia.com. Ed. Annette Rebel TEL 31-182-712340. Pub. Theo de Natris. adv.: B&W page EUR 663, color page EUR 1,248; trim 210 x 297. Circ: 2,200.

910.202 DEU
V I P INTERNATIONAL GOLF EDITION. (Very Important Persons) Text in German. s-a. EUR 16 domestic; EUR 21 in Europe; EUR 24 elsewhere (effective 2008). adv. **Document type:** *Magazine, Consumer.*
Published by: B M Medien Verlag, Industriestr 131c, Cologne, 50996, Germany. TEL 49-221-6501166, FAX 49-221-65011688, info@bm-medien-verlag.de, http://www.bm-medien-verlag.de. adv.: color page EUR 14,000. Circ: 46,713 (paid).

910.202 DEU ISSN 1610-0824
V I P INTERNATIONAL HONEYMOONER. (Very Important Persons) Text in German. 2002. s-a. EUR 13 domestic; EUR 18 in Europe; EUR 20.50 elsewhere; EUR 7 newsstand/cover (effective 2008). adv. **Document type:** *Magazine, Consumer.*
Published by: B M Medien Verlag, Industriestr 131c, Cologne, 50996, Germany. TEL 49-221-6501166, FAX 49-221-65011688, info@bm-medien-verlag.de, http://www.bm-medien-verlag.de. adv.: color page EUR 9,000. Circ: 43,460 (paid).

910.202 DEU ISSN 1617-3910
V I P INTERNATIONAL TRAVELLER. (Very Important Persons) Text in German. 2000. s-a. EUR 13 domestic; EUR 18 in Europe; EUR 20.50 elsewhere; EUR 7 newsstand/cover (effective 2008). adv. **Document type:** *Magazine, Consumer.*
Published by: B M Medien Verlag, Industriestr 131c, Cologne, 50996, Germany. TEL 49-221-6501166, FAX 49-221-65011688, info@bm-medien-verlag.de, http://www.bm-medien-verlag.de. adv.: color page EUR 12,000. Circ: 68,805 (paid).

910.202 DEU
V I P INTERNATIONAL TRAVELLER GOLD EDITION. (Very Important Persons) Text in German. a. EUR 8 domestic; EUR 10 in Europe; EUR 12 foreign (effective 2008). adv. **Document type:** *Magazine, Consumer.*
Published by: B M Medien Verlag, Industriestr 131c, Cologne, 50996, Germany. TEL 49-221-6501166, FAX 49-221-65011688, info@bm-medien-verlag.de, http://www.bm-medien-verlag.de. adv.: color page EUR 14,000. Circ: 85,000 (paid).

910.2 FRA ISSN 1969-3273
VACANCES & VOYAGES. Text in French. 2008. q. **Document type:** *Consumer.*
Formed by the merger of (2005-2008): Vacances Pratiques (1778-9699); (2006-2008): Vacances de Luxe (1953-5937)
Published by: Les Editions du Gecko, 4 Rue du Fbg Montmartre, Paris, 75009, France. TEL 33-1-48001065, FAX 33-1-42466763, mailto:info@editionsdugecko.com.

910.2 ROM ISSN 1841-5288
VACANTA TA PERFECTA. Text in Romanian. 2005. s-a. adv. **Document type:** *Magazine, Consumer.*
Published by: Edipresse A.S. SRL, 50-52 Buzesti Str, Fl 1, Sector 1, Bucharest, Romania. TEL 40-21-3193559, FAX 40-21-3193568, office@edipresse.ro, http://www.edipresse.ro. adv.: color page EUR 1,500.

338.4791 USA
VACATION AGENT; the magazine for professional sellers of leisure travel. Text in English. 2005. m. free to qualified personnel. adv. **Document type:** *Magazine, Trade.* **Description:** "HOW TO" resource for leisure-selling travel professionals, with a focus on selling cruise, tour & package, and hotel & resort vacations.
Published by: Performance Media Group LLC, 593 Rancocas Rd, Westampton, NJ 08060. TEL 856-727-0035, FAX 856-727-0136, info@agentathome.com. Pub. Scott Whitley. Adv. contact Shaun Whitley. color page USD 15,526; trim 8.375 x 10.875. Circ: 30,379 (controlled).

910.202 USA
VACATION & TRAVEL. Text in English. m. **Document type:** *Magazine, Consumer.*
Published by: WorldWide Resort Publishing, Inc., 745 Market St, Ste 102, Harrison, VA 22801. TEL 866-720-3142, admin@wrp-ads.com, http://www.worldwideresort.com/.

910.09 790.1 USA ISSN 1052-0848
HD7289.2
VACATION INDUSTRY REVIEW. Text mainly in English; Text occasionally in Spanish. 1984. q. USD 3 per issue (effective 2009). adv. **Document type:** *Magazine, Trade.* **Description:** Provides developers and resort personnel with news and latest trends in the vacation industry.
Published by: Interval International, 6262 Sunset Dr, Miami, FL 33143. http://www.intervalworld.com. Adv. contact Robin Morales TEL 305-666-1861 ext 7362. B&W page USD 3,176; trim 8.5 x 11.

919.704 USA
VACATION ST. CROIX. Text in English. a. adv. **Document type:** *Magazine, Consumer.* **Description:** Contains information about the latest offers and guest services provided by Vacation St. Croix.
Published by: Morris Multimedia, Inc., 4000 La Grande Princesse Ste 8, Christiansted, VI 00820. TEL 340-718-0361, 877-788-0361, FAX 340-718-5491, info@vacationstcroix.com, http://www.morris.com.

919.704 USA
VACATION ST. THOMAS & ST. JOHN. Text in English. 19??. a. adv. **Document type:** *Magazine, Consumer.*
Published by: Morris Multimedia, Inc., 725 Broad St, Augusta, GA 30901. TEL 706-724-0851, http://www.morris.com.

917.204 JAM
VACATIONER; Jamaica resort guide. Text in English. 1987. s-m. JMD 380, USD 12.50 (effective 1994). adv. back issues avail. **Document type:** *Newspaper.* **Description:** Provides information on attractions, accommodations, dining, entertainment and tourism news from hotels and the government.
Published by: Holjam Enterprises Ltd., P.O. Box 614, Montego Bay, Jamaica. TEL 809-952-0997. Ed. Evelyn Robinson. Circ: 8,000 (paid).

910.09 USA ISSN 0894-9093
VACATIONS. Text in English. 1987. bi-m. USD 19.75 (effective 2009). adv. illus.; tr.lit. 68 p./no. 3 cols./p.; **Document type:** *Magazine, Consumer.* **Description:** Informs and advises travelers of all ages who seek new vacation ideas. Practical, consumer friendly coverage of domestic and international travel including cruises, resorts and tours.

Published by: Vacation Publications, Inc., 5851 San Felipe St, Ste 500, Houston, TX 77057. TEL 713-974-6903, FAX 713-978-6003, service@VacationsMagazine.com. Adv. contact Katie Davies. B&W page USD 12,470, color page USD 18,810; trim 10.875 x 8.1875. Circ: 200,000.

910.4 NOR ISSN 0804-9432
VAGABOND (OSLO). Text in Multiple languages. 1994. bi-m. NOK 235; NOK 44 newsstand/cover (effective 2000). adv. bk.rev. back issues avail. **Document type:** *Magazine, Consumer.* **Description:** Articles for travellers worldwide.
Related titles: Online - full text ed.
Published by: Vagabond Media, Youngstorget, Postboks 8711, Oslo, 0028, Norway. TEL 47-22-11-40-65, FAX 47-22-11-21-96. Ed., Pub. Helge Baardseth. Adv. contact Kari Lovland. B&W page NOK 12,300, color page NOK 16,500; trim 190 x 250. Circ: 20,000 (paid and controlled).

910 647.9 SWE ISSN 1403-0047
VAGABOND (STOCKHOLM). Text in Swedish. 1987. 10/yr. SEK 345; SEK 45 newsstand/cover (effective 2001). adv. 108 p./no. 4 cols./p.; back issues avail. **Document type:** *Magazine, Consumer.*
Former titles (until 1997): Resetidningen Vagabond (1400-9854); (until 1995): Vagabond (1400-4933); (until 1993): Resetidningen Vagabond (0284-6853)
Published by: Vagabond Media AB, Box 20123, Stockholm, 10460, Sweden. TEL 46-8-555-24-000, FAX 46-8-555-24-001, carp@vagabond.se. Eds. Per Andersson, Christian Nyreroed TEL 47-8-555-240-05. Pub., R&P Christian Nyreroed TEL 47-8-555-240-05. Adv. contact Bo Carp TEL 47-8-555-240-07. B&W page SEK 26,300, color page SEK 36,800; trim 190 x 250. Circ: 46,000.

910.202 NLD ISSN 2212-036X
VAKANTIE. Text in Dutch. 2008. q. **Document type:** *Magazine, Consumer.*
Published by: Dutch Travel & Media Group B.V., Silodam 214, Amsterdam, 1013 AS, Netherlands. TEL 31-20-7787144. Ed. Maurice Heijnen.

VAKANTIEKRIEBELS & VRIJE TIJD. *see* SPORTS AND GAMES—Outdoor Life

910.91 MEX
VALLARTA LIFESTYLES. Text in English. 1989. q. adv. **Document type:** *Magazine, Consumer.* **Description:** Informs visitors about Puerto Vallarta and its environs. It also keeps people up-to-date with what there is to see and do in and around the area.
Published by: Vallarta Lifestyles Magazine, Timon #1, Marina Vallarta, Puerto Vallarta, 48354, Mexico. TEL 52-322-2210106, FAX 52-322-2212255, revistas@mexmags.com. Adv. contact Johna Youden. color page USD 2,601. Circ: 22,000 (paid and controlled).

910.202 ITA ISSN 1972-7569
LA VALLE D'AOSTA PAESE PER PAESE. Text in Italian. 1997. w. **Document type:** *Magazine, Consumer.*
Published by: Editrice Bonechi, Via dei Cairoli, 18BB, Florence, FI 50131, Italy. TEL 39-055-576841, FAX 39-055-5000766, bonechi@bonechi.it, http://www.bonechi.it.

917.91 979.1 USA
VALLEY GUIDE QUARTERLY; play + shop + dine in Phoenix. Text in English. 1990. q. USD 12.95 (effective 2007). adv. 124 p./no. 3 cols./p.; back issues avail. **Document type:** *Magazine, Consumer.* **Description:** Provides the Phoenix Valley visitor with seasonally updated information about the culture, lifestyle, hospitality and excitement of the area and the state.
Published by: Madden Publishing, 1650 E Ft Lowell Rd #100, Tucson, AZ 85719. TEL 520-322-0895, 800-444-8768, info@maddenpreprint.com, http://www.maddenpreprint.com. Ed. Katy Spining. Adv. contact Becky Wright. color page USD 4,405. Circ: 70,000.

VALORI DI NAPOLI/HERITAGE OF NAPLES. *see* HISTORY—History Of Europe

VANCOUVER OFFICIAL MEETING PLANNER'S GUIDE. *see* MEETINGS AND CONGRESSES

VANUATU IN FACTS AND FIGURES. *see* TRAVEL AND TOURISM—Abstracting, Bibliographies, Statistics

910.202 USA
VAPOR TRAILS ONLINE TRAVEL MAGAZINE. Text in English. m.
Media: Online - full text.
Published by: Vapor Trails Eds. Cheri Sicard, Mitch Mandell.

VARTA - FUEHRER; Hotels und Restaurants von Experten getestet. *see* HOTELS AND RESTAURANTS

910.09 CUB
VEA. Text in Spanish. s-a.
Published by: Instituto Nacional del Turismo, Malecon y G,, Vedado, La Habana, Cuba. TEL 7-32-9881.

910.2 USA
VEA NEW YORK; the toursit guide that speaks Spanish. Text in Spanish. q. adv. **Description:** Targets Spanish-speaking tourists visiting New York.
Published by: Vea Acquisition Corp, 475 Fifth Ave, 2301, New York, NY 10017. TEL 212-545-7192, FAX 212-545-7305. Pub. Nuria Clark. Adv. contact Ken Shelley.

914.492 333.7 NLD ISSN 0929-144X
DE VELUWENAAR. Text in Dutch. 1992. q. EUR 12.50 (effective 2010). illus. **Document type:** *Magazine, Consumer.* **Description:** Covers the natural beauty and the culture of the Veluwe region of the Netherlands.
Published by: Stichting Jac. Gazenbeek, Gazenbeek Centrum, Stationsstraat 37, Lunteren, 6741 DH, Netherlands. TEL 31-318-484235, gazenbeek-stichting@online.nl, http://www.gazenbeekstichting.nl.

910.202 ITA ISSN 1828-258X
VENETO PAESE PER PAESE. Text in Italian. 2006. w. **Document type:** *Magazine, Consumer.*
Published by: Editrice Bonechi, Via dei Cairoli, 18BB, Florence, FI 50131, Italy. TEL 39-055-576841, FAX 39-055-5000766, bonechi@bonechi.it, http://www.bonechi.it.

910.91 USA
VENICE GULF COAST LIVING. Text in English. m. USD 36 (effective 2001). adv. **Document type:** *Magazine, Consumer.*
Address: PO Box 459, Nokomis, FL 34274. TEL 941-488-5083, FAX 941-488-5083, venicemag@aol.com. Ed. Christiane Francin.

910.202 ITA ISSN 1126-5418
VERDE OGGI; linea verde. Text in Italian. 1998. m. adv. illus. **Document type:** *Magazine, Consumer.* **Description:** Invites readers to explore the rural origins of foods and other household products, with emphasis on the traditions and cuisine of rural Italy. Also reports on conservation issues.
Published by: (R A I - Radiotelevisione Italiana), R C S Periodici (Subsidiary of: R C S Mediagroup), Via San Marco 21, Milan, 20121, Italy. TEL 39-2-25844111, FAX 39-2-25845444, info@periodici.rcs.it, http://www.rcsmediagroup.it/siti/periodici.php. Ed. Franco Bonera. Adv. contact Flavio Biondi. Circ: 97,000 (paid).

917.4 USA
VERMONT GREEN MOUNTAIN GUIDE; the little yellow book. Text in English. 1986. q. free newsstand/cover (effective 1998). adv. bk.rev. maps. back issues avail. **Description:** Includes information on history, lodging, restaurants, attractions, and calendar of events. Used to guide the traveling public around Vermont.
Published by: (Patience and Persistence in Marketing, Inc.), Cindy S. Thiel, Ed. & Pub., 44 Country Rd, North Springfield, VT 05150. TEL 802-886-3333, FAX 802-886-3333. R&P, Adv. contact Cindy S Thiel. page USD 1,800; trim 7.5 x 5.25. Circ: 650,000.

VERMONT YEAR BOOK. *see* BUSINESS AND ECONOMICS—Trade And Industrial Directories

910.91 ITA ISSN 1120-3226
VERONA ILLUSTRATA. Text in Italian. 1988. a. **Document type:** *Magazine, Consumer.*
Indexed: B24, RILM.
Published by: Museo di Castelvecchio, Corso di Castelvecchio 2, Verona, Italy. TEL 39-45-8062611, FAX 39-45-8010729, castelvecchio@comune.verona.it, http://www.comune.verona.it/Castelvecchio/.

910.202 DEU ISSN 1862-3859
VERTRAEGLICH REISEN. Text in German. 1990. a. EUR 3.90 newsstand/cover (effective 2007). adv. **Document type:** *Magazine, Consumer.*
Published by: Fairkehr Verlagsgesellschaft mbH, Niebuhrstr 16b, Bonn, 53113, Germany. TEL 49-228-9858545, FAX 49-228-9858550, redaktion@fairkehr.de, http://www.fairkehr.de. Ed. Regine Gwinner. adv.: color page EUR 6,900. Circ: 250,000 (paid and controlled).

VIA!. *see* TRANSPORTATION—Automobiles

VIA (PORTLAND); A A A traveler's companion. *see* TRANSPORTATION—Automobiles

388.3 USA ISSN 1093-1716
VIA (SAN FRANCISCO). Text in English. 1921. bi-m. free to members (effective 2009). adv. bk.rev. charts; illus. back issues avail. **Document type:** *Magazine, Consumer.* **Description:** Provides information for AAA members in Northern California, Nevada and Utah; features travel (regional, Western, and worldwide), driving, cars and car care, insurance and legislative issues, food, and safety.
Formerly (until 1997): Motorland (0027-2310)
Published by: California State Automobile Association, 100 Van Ness Ave, San Francisco, CA 94102. TEL 415-565-2451, FAX 415-863-4726, http://www.csaa.com. Ed. Bruce Anderson.

338.4791 BRA ISSN 0104-978X
VIAGEM E TURISMO. Text in Portuguese. 1995. m. BRL 106.67; BRL 10 newsstand/cover (effective 2010). adv. back issues avail. **Document type:** *Magazine, Consumer.* **Description:** Covers travel and tourism all over the world. Includes maps, ticket price lists, and packages.
Related titles: Online - full text ed.
Published by: Editora Abril, S.A., Avenida das Nacoes Unidas 7221, Pinheiros, Sao Paulo, SP 05425-902, Brazil. TEL 55-11-50872112, FAX 55-11-50872100, abrilsac@abril.com.br, http://www.abril.com.br. adv.: color page BRL 69,500; trim 202 x 266. Circ: 88,831 (paid).

910.202 PRT
▼ **VIAGENS & RESORTS.** Text in Portuguese. 2010. m. EUR 17.50 (effective 2011). adv. **Document type:** *Magazine, Consumer.*
Published by: Multipublicacoes, Rua Basilio Teles 35, Lisbon, 1070-020, Portugal. TEL 351-21-0123400, FAX 351-21-0123444.

910.202 ITA ISSN 1592-8705
I VIAGGI DEL GUSTO. Variant title: Meridiani. Viaggi del Gusto. Text in Italian. 2001. q. **Document type:** *Magazine, Consumer.*
Published by: Editoriale Domus, Via Gianni Mazzocchi 1/3, Rozzano, MI 20089, Italy. TEL 39-02-824721, editorialedomus@edidomus.it, http://www.edidomus.it.

910.202 ITA ISSN 1971-9949
VIAGGIARE IN ITALIA. Text in Italian. 2007. s-m. **Document type:** *Magazine, Consumer.*
Published by: Poligrafici Editoriale (Subsidiary of: Monrif Group), Via Enrico Mattei 106, Bologna, BO 40138, Italy. TEL 39-051-6006111, FAX 39-051-6006266, http://www.monrifgroup.net.

910.202 641.5 ITA ISSN 1594-1825
VIAGGIESAPORI. Cover title: V & S. Text in Italian. 2002. m. (11/yr.). EUR 28 (effective 2009). **Document type:** *Magazine, Consumer.*
Published by: Editrice Quadratum SpA (Subsidiary of: Arnoldo Mondadori Editore SpA), Piazza Aspromonte 15, Milan, MI 20131, Italy. TEL 39-02-70642242, FAX 39-02-2665555, quadratum@quadratum.it, http://www.quadratum.it. Ed. Paola Girardi.

910.09 USA
VIAJANDO/TRAVELING. Text in English, Spanish. 1989. m. adv. **Description:** Contains general interest information for frequent airline travelers.
Published by: Global Magazines, Inc., 6355 N.W. 36th St., Miami, FL 33166. TEL 305-871-6400, TELEX 441094. Ed. Pablo Jazobsen. Circ: 20,000.

910.09 ESP ISSN 1139-8760
VIAJAR. Text in Spanish. 1978. m. **Document type:** *Magazine, Consumer.*
Former titles (until 1993): Tiempo de Viajar (1139-8752); (until 1985): Viajar (0210-0096)
Published by: Grupo Zeta, O'Donnell 12, 5a planta, Madrid, 28009, Spain. TEL 34-91-5869721, FAX 34-91-5869780, http://www.grupozeta.es. Circ: 311,700.

910.09 PRT
VIAJAR. Text in Portuguese. 11/yr.
Address: Rua Cecilio de Sousa, 20-2o Esq, Lisbon, 1200, Portugal. TEL 1-365701, FAX 346-90-73, TELEX 18375. Ed. Joao Rosa. Circ: 15,000.

910.09 BRA
VIAJAR BEM E BARATO. Text in Portuguese. 1992. a. adv. charts; illus. **Document type:** *Consumer.* **Description:** Contains tips for places, food and lodging in Brazil for the budget traveler.
Published by: Editora Abril, S.A., Avenida das Nacoes Unidas 7221, Pinheiros, Sao Paulo, SP 05425-902, Brazil. TEL 55-11-50872112, FAX 55-11-50872100, abrilsac@abril.com.br, http://www.abril.com.br. Ed. Regner Camilo. Circ: 80,000.

910.91 BRA ISSN 1519-3268
VIAJE MAIS POR MENOS. Text in Portuguese. 2001. m. BRL 104.50; BRL 9.90 newsstand/cover (effective 2007). adv. **Document type:** *Magazine, Consumer.*
Published by: Editora Europa Ltda., Rua MMDC 121, Butanta, Sao Paulo, SP 05510-021, Brazil. TEL 55-11-30385050, FAX 55-11-38190538.

910.202 ESP ISSN 1575-5479
VIAJES NATIONAL GEOGRAPHIC. Text in Spanish. 1999. m. EUR 18 (effective 2009). **Document type:** *Magazine, Consumer.*
Published by: R B A Edipresse, Perez Galdos 36, Barcelona, 08012, Spain. TEL 34-93-4157374, FAX 34-93-2177378, http://www.rbaedipresse.es.

910.202 USA ISSN 1932-7404
DS701
VIAMEI. Text in English. 2006. bi-m. **Document type:** *Magazine, Consumer.*
Published by: Conter Group Corp., 4200 W 83rd St, Shawnee Mission, KS 66208. TEL 913-649-8558, marketing@viamei.com, http://www.viamei.com.

917.104 CAN
VICTORIA CLIPPER. Text in English. s-a.
Address: 254 Belleville St, Victoria, BC V8V 1W9, Canada. TEL 250-382-8100.

917.1128 CAN ISSN 1554-9232
VICTORIA MAGAZINE; the magazine of North America's most livable city. Text in English. 2006. s-a. CAD 21.95 for 2 yrs. domestic; USD 24.95 for 2 yrs. in United States; USD 34.95 for 2 yrs. elsewhere (effective 2007). adv. **Document type:** *Magazine, Consumer.* **Description:** Features information about events, people, restaurants, style, travel, arts and entertainment in the Vancouver, British Columbia metropolitan area.
Related titles: Online - full text ed.
Published by: Hutchinson & Associates, 185-911 Yates St, Ste 708, Victoria, BC V8V 4Y9, Canada. TEL 250-370-1148, editor@victoriabcmagazine.com. Ed. Robert Hutchinson. Adv. contact Lorraine Browne TEL 250-888-2988.

910.91 PRT ISSN 0870-9467
VIDA SOVIETICA. Text in Portuguese. m. adv.
Published by: Editora Vida Sovietica Lda., Praca Andrade Caminha, Lisbon, 3-1700, Portugal.

363.7 FRA ISSN 1276-7883
LA VIE MANCELLE ET SARTHOISE. Text in French. 1959. m. EUR 4.50 newsstand/cover (effective 2008). bk.rev.
Formerly (until 1995): Vie Mancelle (1273-442X)
Published by: Association Culturelle et Touristique du Mans, 64 rue de la Pelouse, Le Mans, 72000, France. Ed. J P Martin.

910.202 MAR
VIE TOURISTIQUE. Text in French. w. adv.
Address: 142 bd. Mohamed V, Casablanca, Morocco. Ed. Mohamed Zghari.

338.4791597 GBR ISSN 1747-9061
VIETMAN TOURISM REPORT. Text in English. 2005. q. EUR 820, USD 1,030 combined subscription (print & email eds.) (effective 2010). **Document type:** *Report, Trade.* **Description:** Covers independent forecasts and competitive intelligence on the Vietnamese tourism industry.
Related titles: E-mail ed.
Indexed: B01, H&TI, H06.
Published by: Business Monitor International Ltd., Senator House, 85 Queen Victoria St, London, EC4V 4AB, United Kingdom. TEL 44-20-72480468, FAX 44-20-72480467, subs@businessmonitor.com.

910.202 GBR ISSN 1363-7444
VIETNAM HANDBOOK. Text in English. 1994. biennial. GBP 14.99 per issue (effective 2010). adv. **Document type:** *Handbook/Manual/Guide, Consumer.* **Description:** Covers all the basics from where to stay and where to eat to cycling, walking and how to get around the Vietnam.
Supersedes in part (in 1997): Vietnam, Laos and Cambodia Handbook (1352-7878)
—CCC.
Published by: Footprint Handbooks Ltd., 6 Riverside Ct, Lower Bristol Rd, Bath, Avon BA2 3DZ, United Kingdom. TEL 44-1225-469141, FAX 44-1225-469461, wwwinfo@footprintbooks.com.

910.09 ITA ISSN 1593-5043
VILLE, CASTELLI E PALAZZI. Text in Italian, English. 1991. a. price varies. adv. **Document type:** *Directory, Consumer.*
Published by: Convegni Srl, Via Ezio Biondi 1, Milan, MI 20154, Italy. TEL 39-02-349921, FAX 39-02-34992290, convegni@convegni.it, http://www.convegni.it. Circ: 13,000.

908 LTU ISSN 1392-0057
VILNIUS IN YOUR POCKET. Text in English. 1992. 5/yr. USD 25; USD 5 newsstand/cover (effective 2002). adv. **Document type:** *Magazine, Consumer.*
Address: Vokieciu Gatve 10-15, Vilnius, 2001, Lithuania. TEL 370-2-222976, FAX 370-2-222982, vilnius@inyourpocket.com, http://www.inyourpocket.com.

910.202 VIR ISSN 1931-2865
VIRGIN ISLANDS BLUE BOOK. Text in English. 1981. irreg. **Document type:** *Monographic series, Consumer.*
Formerly (until 1992): Virgin Islands of the United States Blue Book (Print) (0882-0023)
Media: Online - full text.

Published by: United States Virgin Islands, Division of Libraries, Archives and Museums, 23 Dronnigens Gade, St Thomas, 00802, Virgin Isl., US. TEL 809-774-3407, FAX 809-775-1887. Ed. Jeannette Allis Bastian.

910.202 VIR
VIRGIN ISLANDS PLAYGROUND. Text in English. a. free. **Description:** Includes restaurant directory, shopping guide, island map.
Published by: Island Media, Inc., P O Box 10563, St Thomas, 00801, Virgin Isl., US. TEL 809-776-3646. Ed. Frances E Newbold.

917.55 USA ISSN 1071-9849
VIRGINIA (GWYNN). Text in English. 1992. q. USD 29 (effective 2002). adv.
Published by: Gleason Publishing, Inc., PO Box G, Gwynn, VA 23066. TEL 804-725-7700, FAX 804-725-7400, publisher@virginiamagazine.com. Ed. Michael P. Gleason. Adv. contact D. Palmer Gleason.

910.202 USA ISSN 1932-734X
F226.6
VIRGINIA CURIOSITIES. Text in English. 2003. irreg., latest 2nd ed. USD 13.95 per issue (effective 2008). **Document type:** *Guide, Consumer.*
Published by: The Globe Pequot Press, Inc., 246 Goose Ln, PO Box 480, Guilford, CT 06437. TEL 203-458-4500, 888-249-7586, FAX 203-458-4601, 800-820-2329, info@globepequot.com.

910.202 647.94 USA
VIRGINIA IS FOR LOVERS TRAVEL GUIDE. Text in English. 19??. a. adv. Index. **Document type:** *Handbook/Manual/Guide, Consumer.* **Description:** Attractions, lodging, outdoor recreation, restaurant listings for Virginia; four-color photographs, advertising supported. Used as advertising fulfillment to promote Virginia as a major travel destination.
Related titles: Online - full text ed.: free (effective 2011).
Published by: (Virginia Tourism Corporation), Leisure Publishing Co., 3424 Brambleton Ave, S W, PO Box 21535, Roanoke, VA 24018. TEL 540-989-6138, 800-548-1672, FAX 540-989-7603, http://www.leisurepublishing.com/. Eds. Judy Watkins, Kurt Rheinheimer. Pub. Richard Wells. **Subscr. to:** Virginia Tourism Corporation, 901 E Byrd St, Richmond, VA 23219.

910.2 USA
VIRTUAL VERMONT INTERNET MAGAZINE. Text in English. 1997. irreg. **Description:** Dedicated to promoting Vermont. Contains historical information, individual town information, listing for libraries, and weather.
Formed by the 1997 merger of: Virtual Vermont; Virtual New Hampshire Internet Magazine
Media: Online - full text.
Address: TEL 802-773-0112. Ed. Matt Wills.

910.202 USA
VIRTUOSO LIFE. Text in English. 2000. bi-m. USD 16.95 domestic; USD 26.95 in Canada; USD 56.95 elsewhere (effective 2007). adv. back issues avail. **Document type:** *Magazine, Consumer.* **Description:** Covers luxury cruising, top vacation destinations, hotel and resort stays, cultural tours, spa retreats, private jet charters, and custom itineraries around the globe.
Address: 505 Main St, Ste 500, Fort Worth, TX 76102. TEL 817-334-8663, 800-401-4274, FAX 817-336-2917. Ed. Elaine Gruy Srnka. Pub. Terrie Handley Lonergan. Adv. contact Emily Sara Frogget. color page USD 28,585; trim 9 x 10.875. Circ: 250,000.

338.4 USA ISSN 0277-5204
GV188.3.U6
VISIONS IN LEISURE AND BUSINESS. Text in English. 1980. q. USD 25 domestic to individuals; USD 40 foreign to individuals; USD 45 domestic to institutions; USD 80 foreign to institutions (effective 2001). **Document type:** *Journal, Trade.* **Description:** Contains vehicles that help individuals change their lives, thereby making a more positive contribution to organizations and society.
Indexed: A22, H&TI, H06.
—IE, Ingenta.
Published by: Appalachian Associates, 615 Pasteur Ave, Bowling Green, OH 43402-0001. lgroves@wcnet.org. Ed. Dr. David L Groves. R&P Margaret Bobb.

910.2 AUS
VISIONS OF AUSTRALIA. Text in English. 1995. irreg. back issues avail.
Media: Online - full text.
Published by: Australian Government. Department of the Environment, Water, Heritage and the Arts, GPO Box 787, Canberra, ACT 2601, Australia. TEL 61-2-62741111, FAX 61-2-62759663, http://www.environment.gov.au/.

914 DNK ISSN 1604-5807
VISIT DENMARK; magasin om turismen i oplevelsesoekonomien. (No publication in 2008.) Text in Danish. 1978. a. free. adv. bk.rev. illus. back issues avail. **Document type:** *Trade.*
Former titles (until 2005): Dansk Turisme (0904-1796); (until 1988): D T Forum (0108-190X); (until 1982): D T-Nyt (0107-1521)
Related titles: Online - full text ed.
Published by: VisitDenmark/Danish Tourist Board, Islands Brygge 43, 3, Copenhagen S, 2300, Denmark. TEL 45-32-889900, FAX 45-32-889901, contact@visitdenmar.com. Ed. Christian Ankerstjerne. Circ: 7,500.

917.7434 USA ISSN 1541-5562
VISIT DETROIT. Text in English. 2001. q. USD 9.97 domestic; USD 16.97 in Canada & Mexico; USD 25.97 elsewhere (effective 2002). adv.
Published by: Detroit Metro Convention & Visitors Bureau, 211 W. Fort St., Ste. 1000, Detroit, MI 48226. TEL 313-202-1800, 800-338-7648, FAX 313-202-1808, http://www.visitdetroit.com. Ed. Jim Utsler. Adv. contact Amanda Frankel.

338.48 UAE ISSN 1816-7861
VISITOR. Text in English. 2005. m. AED 90 domestic; AED 109 GCC countries; AED 199 elsewhere (effective 2007). adv. **Document type:** *Magazine, Consumer.*
Published by: I T P Consumer Publishing (Subsidiary of: I T P Publishing Group), PO Box 500024, Dubai, United Arab Emirates. TEL 971-4-2108000, FAX 971-4-2108080, info@itp.com. Ed. Dana El-Baltaji. Adv. contact Andrew Wingrove. page USD 5,400; trim 225 x 300. Circ: 19,500 (paid and controlled).

914.1504 IRL ISSN 0790-6056
VISITOR. Text in English. 1985. s-a. adv. **Document type:** *Magazine, Consumer.* **Description:** Covers items of interest to visitors and tourists in Ireland.
Published by: Mac Communications, Taney Hall, Eglinton Terrace, Dundrum, Dublin, Dublin 14, Ireland. TEL 353-1-2960000, FAX 353-1-2960383, info@maccommunications.ie. Ed. Sarah McQuaid. Circ: 20,000 (controlled).

914.415 IRL
VISITOR DAYS. Text in English. a. adv. **Document type:** *Magazine, Consumer.*
Published by: Tudor Journals Ltd., 97 Botanic Ave, Belfast, BT7 1JN, Ireland. TEL 353-28-90320088, FAX 353-28-90323163, info@tudorjournals.com, http://www.tudorjournals.com. adv.: color page EUR 2,520; trim 210 x 297. Circ: 10,000 (controlled).

917.1 CAN ISSN 0839-1335
VISITOR MAGAZINE. Text in English. 1978. 3/yr. CAD 12 (effective 2008). adv. back issues avail. **Document type:** *Magazine, Consumer.* **Description:** Lists dining, accommodations, shopping and tourist information in the Kitchener, Waterloo, Cambridge, Guelph and Stratford areas.
Formerly: Waterloo Region Visitor's Guide
Published by: Jon R. Group Ltd., 160 Frobisher Dr, Waterloo, ON N2V 2B1, Canada. TEL 519-886-2831, FAX 519-886-6409. adv.: B&W page CAD 1,125, color page CAD 1,640; trim 8.13 x 5.38. Circ: 50,000 (controlled).

910.202 JAM
VISITOR VACATION GUIDE. Text in English. 1980. w. free. adv. back issues avail. **Description:** Contains travel and tourist news, tips on where to shop, what to buy, what to see, villas, restaurants, hotels, and tours.
Formerly: Visitor
Published by: Western Publishers Ltd., 82 Barnett St., P.O. Box 1205, Montego Bay, 1, Jamaica. TEL 809-952-5253, FAX 809-952-6513. Ed. Lloyd B Smith. Circ: 10,000.

917.4 USA ISSN 1937-9609
F5
A VISITOR'S GUIDE TO COLONIAL & REVOLUTIONARY NEW ENGLAND. Text in English. 2006. irreg. USD 18.95 per issue domestic; USD 23.50 per issue in Canada (effective 2008). **Document type:** *Guide, Consumer.*
Published by: The Countryman Press (Subsidiary of: W.W. Norton & Co., Inc.), PO Box 748, Woodstock, VT 05091. TEL 802-457-4826, 800-245-4151, FAX 802-457-1678, countrymanpress@wwnorton.com, http://www.countrymanpress.com.

910.91 USA
VIVA. Text in English. 2000. q. USD 20; USD 5 newsstand/cover (effective 2001). adv. **Document type:** *Magazine, Consumer.*
Published by: Time Wave Publishing, Co., Box 15591, Loves Park, IL 61132-5591. TEL 815-697-6904, FAX 815-397-5909, cr@vivamagazine.com. Ed. Ellen Hoch-Kramer.

910.202 ITA
VIVERE A MILANO/LIVING IN MILANO. Variant title: Vivere a - Living in Milano. Text in Italian, English, Japanese. 1994. 3/yr. free. **Document type:** *Magazine, Consumer.*
Published by: Edizioni L' Agrifoglio, Via Tagliamento 3, Milan, 20139, Italy. TEL 39-02-56813688, FAX 39-02-56814136, agrifoglio@digibank.it, http://www.inmilano.it/agrifoglio/.

379.85 POL ISSN 1505-0882
VOYAGE. Text in Polish. 1998. m. PLZ 87 (effective 2011). adv. **Document type:** *Magazine, Consumer.*
Published by: Marquard Media Polska Sp. z o.o. (Subsidiary of: Marquard Media AG), ul Wilcza 50/52, Warsaw, 00-679, Poland. TEL 48-22-4211000, FAX 48-22-4211111, info@marquard.pl, http://www.marquard.pl. Ed. Paulina Stolarek-Marat. Adv. contact Monika Wdowiak. Circ: 36,103 (paid).

910.09 CAN ISSN 1486-0147
VOYAGE EN GROUPE; votre kiosque d'information touristique a domicile. Text in French. 1981. bi-m. CAD 9 (effective 2001). adv. bk.rev. back issues avail. **Document type:** *Directory, Trade.*
Address: 590 Chemin St. Jean, Laprairie, PQ J5R 2L1, Canada. TEL 450-444-5870, FAX 450-444-4120. Ed. Monique Papineau. Pub. Lucie Papineau. adv.: B&W page CAD 1,210, color page USD 1,550. Circ: 13,000.

910 FRA ISSN 0995-4228
VOYAGES D'AFFAIRES. Text in French. 1988. bi-m. EUR 42; EUR 47 combined subscription incl. Le Guide Annuel des Deplacements Professionnels (effective 2010). adv. **Document type:** *Trade.* **Description:** Articles about business destinations throughout the world, including information about countries, modes of travel, hotels etc.
Published by: Varenne Entreprises, 6 cite Paradis, Paris, 75010, France. TEL 33-1-53242400, FAX 33-1-53242433. Ed. M P Dyens. Pub. M.P. Dyens. Adv. contact Christian de Romanet. Circ: 32,000.

910 011 FRA ISSN 0989-1080
VOYAGES ET STRATEGIE; le magazine de la stimulation et du tourisme d'affaires. Text in French. 9/yr.
Published by: Editions Re, 13 rue de l'Abbe Groult, Paris, 75015, France. TEL 33-1-56086060, FAX 33-1-48423072. Eds. Francois Perruche, Michel Foraud. Circ: 16,000.

VOYAGES PATRIMOINES ET ART DE VIVRE EN BOURGOGNE. *see* GEOGRAPHY

910.91 BEL ISSN 1371-6352
VOYAGES VOYAGES; le magazine de l'evasion. Variant title: Le Magazine Belge de Voyages pour tous Publics et tous Budgets. Text in French. 1996. m. EUR 39 (effective 2007). back issues avail. **Document type:** *Magazine, Consumer.*
Published by: Dupedi, Rue de Stallestraat 70-82, Bruxelles, 1180, Belgium. TEL 32-2-3330700, FAX 32-2-3320598, http://www.dupedi.be.

910.2 RUS
VOYAZH/VOYAGE. Text in Russian. 1994. m. USD 95 in United States. **Document type:** *Magazine, Consumer.* **Description:** Helps in finding optimum ways of traveling, writes about tourist experience of the celebrities.
Published by: Izdatel'skii Dom Tsentr Plyus, M. Lubyanka, 16, str. 1, pod. 3, 6 etazh, Moscow, 101000, Russian Federation. TEL 7-095-9218585, FAX 7-095-9214664. Ed. T B Savitskaya. **Dist. by:** East View Information Services, 10601 Wayzata Blvd, Minneapolis, MN 55305. TEL 952-252-1201, 800-477-1005, FAX 952-252-1202, info@eastview.com, http://www.eastview.com.

914 CPV ISSN 0258-0691
VOZ DI POVO. Text in Portuguese. 1962. 3/w.
Supersedes: Arquipelago (0004-2668)
Indexed: MLA-IB, RASB.
Published by: Direccao Nacional de Informacao, Caixa Postal 118, Praia, Sao Tiago, Cape Verde. Ed. Alfredo Simao Carvalho Santos. Circ: 3,000.

052 ZMB
W T G TOURISM NEWS. (Where to Go) Text in English. 1991. m. ZMK 100 per issue. **Document type:** *Magazine, Consumer.*
Published by: P A M Communications Ltd., PO Box 35637, Lusaka, Zambia.

910 GBR
W T T E R C TRAVEL & TOURISM. Text in English. a. **Document type:** *Bulletin.*
Published by: World Travel & Tourism Environment Research Centre, Oxford Brookes University, Headington, Oxford OX3 0BP, United Kingdom. TEL 01865-484830, FAX 01865-484838.

WAGON TRACKS. *see* HISTORY—History Of North And South America

919.6 USA
WAIKIKI NEWS. Text in English. 1971. m. USD 16. adv. bk.rev. illus. **Document type:** *Magazine, Consumer.*
Published by: Fred C. Pugarelli, Ed. & Pub., PO Box 89133, Honolulu, HI 96830-9133. Circ: 1,000.

910.202 CHE
WALLIS. Text in German. 1980. 6/yr. price varies. adv.
Published by: (Vereinigung Oberwalliser Verkehrsinteressenten), Rotten-Verlags AG, Leser-Dienst, Terbinerstr 2, Visp, 3930, Switzerland. Ed. Armin Karlen.

917.504 USA ISSN 8756-9779
GV1853.3.F62
WALT DISNEY WORLD (YEAR); expert advice from the inside source. Text in English. a. USD 13.95 domestic; GBP 7.95 in United Kingdom. charts; illus. **Document type:** *Magazine, Consumer.* **Description:** Offers tourists advice on what to do and see at Walt Disney World.
Related titles: Online - full text ed.
Published by: Birnbaum Travel Guides, Hyperion, 114 Fifth Ave, New York, NY 10011. TEL 718-633-4400. Ed. Stephen Birnbaum. Circ: 250,000 (paid).

910.91 USA ISSN 1945-9238
GV1853.3.F62
WALT DISNEY WORLD WITH KIDS. Variant title: Fodor's Walt Disney World with Kids. Text in English. 1990. a. USD 17.95 per issue (effective 2009). **Document type:** *Guide, Consumer.* **Description:** Features tips and insider knowledge that a family needs to know to make the most of a trip to Walt Disney World.
Former titles: Walt Disney World & Universal Orlando with Kids (1930-7551); (until 2005): Walt Disney World with Kids (1083-2424)
Published by: Fodor's Travel Publications, Inc. (Subsidiary of: Random House Inc.), 1745 Broadway, 15th Fl, New York, NY 10019. TEL 212-572-2313, editors@fodors.com, http://www.fodors.com.

910.202 GBR ISSN 1351-4733
WANDERLUST; the magazine for people with a passion for travel. Text in English. 1993. bi-m. GBP 22.80 domestic; GBP 26.40 in Europe; GBP 30 elsewhere (effective 2009). adv. bk.rev.; music rev. illus. back issues avail.; reprints avail. **Document type:** *Magazine, Consumer.* **Description:** Contains photos and features from around the world.
—CCC.
Address: PO Box 1832, Windsor, Berks SL4 1YT, United Kingdom. TEL 44-1753-620426, FAX 44-1753-620474. Eds. Dan Linstaead, Lyn Hughes. Pub. Lyn Hughes. **Dist. by:** Comag.

910.202 USA ISSN 2153-1935
PN6010.5
WANDERLUST REVIEW. Text in English. s-a. **Document type:** *Journal, Consumer.* **Description:** Features literary non-fiction, fiction, poetry, drama, and photography related to world travel.
Address: 6065 50th Ave SW, Seattle, WA 98136. duncan.p.d@gmail.com.

914.3804 POL
WARSAW IN YOUR POCKET. Text in English. 5/yr. USD 25; USD 5 newsstand/cover (effective 2002). adv. **Document type:** *Magazine, Consumer.*
Address: Natolinska 3-41, Warsaw, 00-562, Poland. TEL 48-22-6269229, FAX 48-22-6211848, http://www.inyourpocket.com.

914.3804 POL ISSN 1506-4891
G155.P6
THE WARSAW VOICE TOURISM GUIDE. Text in English. 1998. a. PLZ 34 (effective 1999). adv. **Document type:** *Handbook/Manual/Guide, Trade.* **Description:** Presents Poland's most attractive tourist sites, national and scenic parks, ecotourism, agritourism and health spas. Gives information on business tourism - trade fairs, conference organization opportunities, business and incentive trips.
Published by: Warsaw Voice S.A., Ksiecia Janusza 64, Warsaw, 01452, Poland. TEL 48-22-366377, FAX 48-22-371995, terapia@warsawvoice.com.pl. Ed. Magda Sowinska. Adv. contact Dariusz Gibert. page PLZ 10,500.

910.2 GBR ISSN 2041-7799
▼ **WARWICKSHIRE PREVIEW.** Text in English. 2009. q. **Document type:** *Magazine, Consumer.*
Related titles: Online - full text ed.: free (effective 2010).
Published by: Preview Publications Ltd., 11 Sheep St, Charlbury, Oxfordshire OX7 3RR, United Kingdom. TEL 44-1993-833239, FAX 44-1993-833232, info@previewpublications.co.uk.

917.97 910.91 USA ISSN 1933-9739
F891.6
WASHINGTON CURIOSITIES; quirky characters, roadside oddities & other offbeat stuff. Text in English. 2004. biennial, latest 2007, 2nd ed. USD 14.95 per issue (effective 2008). **Document type:** *Guide, Consumer.* **Description:** Aims to act as a guide to unique places.
Published by: The Globe Pequot Press, Inc., 246 Goose Ln, PO Box 480, Guilford, CT 06437. TEL 203-458-4500, 888-249-7586, FAX 203-458-4603, 800-820-2329, info@globepequot.com, http://www.globepequot.com.

TU

917.53 975.3 USA ISSN 1949-0615
▼ **WASHINGTON, D.C.**; a guided tour through history. Text in English. 2009. triennial. USD 15.95 per issue (effective 2009). **Document type:** *Guide, Consumer.* **Description:** Travel guide with history for Washington, D.C.
Published by: G P P Travel (Subsidiary of: The Globe Pequot Press, Inc.), 246 Goose Ln, PO Box 480, Guilford, CT 06437. TEL 203-458-4500, info@globepequot.com.

917.504 USA ISSN 1046-3089
WASHINGTON FLYER MAGAZINE. Text in English. 1989. bi-m. USD 15; USD 3 newsstand/cover (effective 2004). adv. bk.rev. reprints avail. **Document type:** *Magazine, Consumer.* **Description:** Focuses on travel, hospitality and the greater Washington DC area. Contains information for frequent business and leisure travelers in the nation's capital airports.
Published by: The Magazine Group, 1707 L St N W, Ste 350, Washington, DC 20036-4201. TEL 202-331-7700, FAX 202-331-7311, editorial@themagazinegroup.com, http://www.themagazinegroup.com. Ed. Michael McCarthy. Pub. Peter Abrahams. Circ: 180,000 (paid).

910.09 USA ISSN 1051-0257
WASHINGTON INTERNATIONAL; building bridges in the international community. Text in English. 1986. bi-m. free (effective 2005). adv. bk.rev. back issues avail. **Document type:** *Newsletter, Consumer.* **Description:** Contains diplomatic news and travel articles directed toward the international, travel, and cultural community of Washington DC. Includes interviews with personalities, and features international hotel spotlights and a calendar of cultural events.
Media: Online - full content.
Address: PO Box 227, Great Falls, VA 22066-0227. TEL 703-757-5965, FAX 703-757-5944. Ed. Patricia Keegan. Circ: 25,000 (paid and controlled).

796.7 USA ISSN 1096-8660
GV1027
WASHINGTON JOURNEY. Text in English. 1915. bi-m. USD 3 (effective 2001). adv. bk.rev. illus. **Document type:** *Newspaper.*
Former titles (until 199?): Motorist (Seattle) (0899-7578); (until 198?): Washington Motorist (0043-0641)
Published by: Automobile Club of Washington, 1745 114th Ave, S E, Bellevue, WA 98109. TEL 206-448-5353, FAX 206-646-2193. Ed., Pub., Adv. contact Janet Ray. B&W page USD 5,700; 14.25 x 10. Circ: 250,000.

917.904 USA
F899.3
WASHINGTON STATE VISITORS' GUIDE. Text in English. 1987. a. free (effective 2008). adv. **Document type:** *Magazine, Consumer.* **Description:** Features tourism information, and a city-by-city listing of lodging and activities.
Former titles (until 2000): Washington State Lodging & Travel Guide (1073-2578); (until 1994): Destination Washington
Published by: (Washington State Hotel and Lodging Association), SagaCity Media, Inc., 1201 Western Ave, Ste 425, Seattle, WA 98101. TEL 206-957-2234, http://www.sagacitymedia.com. adv.: B&W page USD 11,770, color page USD 14,080; trim 10.88 x 8.38. Circ: 350,000.

WASSERSKI & WAKEBOARD MAGAZIN. *see* SPORTS AND GAMES—Boats And Boating

910.2 338 USA ISSN 1540-3378
T49.5
WATCH IT MADE IN THE U. S. A.; a visitor's guide to the companies that make your favorite products. Text in English. 1994. triennial. USD 21.95 per issue (effective 2008). **Document type:** *Guide, Consumer.* **Description:** Presents information on more than 300 products and helps to experience firsthand the products, companies and technology that fuel the economy.
Published by: Avalon Travel Publishing, 1700 4th St, Berkeley, CA 94710. TEL 510-595-3664, avalon.publicity@perseusbooks.com, http://www.travelmatters.com.

WATERFRONT NEWS; South Florida's nautical newspaper. *see* SPORTS AND GAMES—Boats And Boating

910.202 USA
WEB SURFER TRAVEL JOURNAL. Text in English. 1995. m. **Description:** Contains travel links, travel stories and updates on new travel sites.
Media: Online - full text.
Address: 109 Breckenridge Rd, Franklin, TN 37067. Ed. Dan Kenneth Phillips.

913.919 USA
THE WEEK IN GERMANY. Text in English. 1972. w. free. **Document type:** *Newsletter, Government.* **Description:** Contains short articles on current affairs in Germany.
Related titles: Online - full text ed.
Published by: German Information Center, 871 United Nations Plaza, New York, NY 10017. TEL 212-610-9800, FAX 212-752-6691. Ed. David Lazar. Circ: 38,000.

910.91 USA
WEEKEND ESCAPES; pictorial tours of getaways, adventures, and diversions in the Southeast. Text in English. 2000. q. USD 5.95 newsstand/cover (effective 2001). adv. **Document type:** *Magazine, Consumer.*
Published by: Celebration Communications, Inc., 32 Misty Morning Dr., Hilton Head, SC 29926-2538. http://www.weekendescapes.com. Ed. Warren Guy. Pub. Travis Fowler.

916.8 ZAF ISSN 1990-9896
WEG!. Text in Afrikaans. 2004. m. ZAR 220 domestic; ZAR 428.26 in Namibia; ZAR 431.45 in Zimbabwe; ZAR 709.13 elsewhere (effective 2006). adv. **Document type:** *Magazine, Consumer.* **Description:** For outdoor enthusiasts looking for memorable travel experiences.
Related titles: ◆ English ed.: Go! (Cape Town, 2006). ISSN 1819-6713.
Published by: Media24 Ltd., Naspers Centre, 40 Heerengracht St, PO Box 1802, Cape Town, 8000, South Africa. TEL 27-21-4171111, FAX 27-21-4171151, http://www.media24.com. Ed. Bun Booyens. Pub. N Hersel. Adv. contact D Slade. color page ZAR 35,100; trim 230 x 275. Circ: 74,396.

916.8 ZAF ISSN 1819-6918
WEGBREEK. Text in Afrikaans. 2006. m. ZAR 225; ZAR 19.95 newsstand/cover (effective 2006). adv. **Document type:** *Magazine, Consumer.*
Published by: Ramsay, Son & Parker (Pty) Ltd., PO Box 180, Howard Place, Cape Town 7450, South Africa. TEL 27-21-5303100, FAX 27-21-5313846.

338.4791 388.3 ZAF ISSN 1993-6664
WEGRY. Text in Afrikaans. 2007. bi-m. ZAR 22.50 newsstand/cover (effective 2007). **Document type:** *Magazine, Consumer.*
Published by: Media24 Ltd., Naspers Centre, 40 Heerengracht St, PO Box 1802, Cape Town, 8000, South Africa. TEL 27-21-4461287, FAX 27-21-4461016, http://www.media24.com. Ed. Bun Booyens.

338.4791 ZAF ISSN 1992-0911
WEGSLEEP. Text in Afrikaans. 2006. m. adv. **Document type:** *Magazine, Consumer.*
Published by: Media24 Ltd., Naspers Centre, 40 Heerengracht St, PO Box 1802, Cape Town, 8000, South Africa. TEL 27-21-4461287, http://www.media24.com. Ed. Bun Booyens. adv.: page ZAR 14,000; trim 210 x 275.

910.2 USA ISSN 2159-2993
WEIRD N.J. Text in English. 1992. s-a. USD 14 (effective 2011). **Document type:** *Magazine, Trade.* **Description:** Covers interviews with people and describe their stories and weird experience living in New Jersey.
Published by: Weird NJ, Inc., PO Box 1346, Bloomfield, NJ 07003.

917.404 USA
WEIRD N J; your travel guide to New Jersey's local legends and best kept secrets. (New Jersey) Text in English. s-a. USD 12 (effective 2006). back issues avail. **Document type:** *Magazine, Consumer.* **Description:** Articles about unexplained oddities and places that document their existence as a cultural phenomenon unique to the state of New Jersey.
Published by: Weird N J, Inc., PO Box 1346, Bloomfield, NJ 07003. TEL 866-934-7365.

910.202 USA
WEISSMANN TRAVEL REPORTS. Text in English. 19??. m. **Document type:** *Report, Trade.* **Description:** Carries destination information for travel agents and meeting planning professionals.
Media: Online - full text.
Published by: Northstar Travel Media LLC (Subsidiary of: Boston Ventures Management, Inc.), 100 Lighting Way, Secaucus, NJ 07094. TEL 201-902-2000, FAX 201-902-2045, http://www.northstartravelmedia.com/.

910.91 DEU
WELCOME!. Text in German. q. adv. **Document type:** *Magazine, Consumer.*
Published by: W D V Gesellschaft fuer Medien & Kommunikation mbH & Co. OHG, Siemensstr 6, Bad Homburg, 61352, Germany. TEL 49-6172-6700, FAX 49-6172-670144, info@wdv.de, http://www.wdv.de. adv.: page EUR 7,600; trim 182 x 246. Circ: 430,000 (controlled).

659.1 ROM ISSN 1582-2648
WELCOME TO BUCHAREST. Text in Romanian. 2000. a. adv. **Document type:** *Magazine, Consumer.*
Published by: Crystal Publishing Group, 253, Calea Calarasilor, bl. 67 A, Ste. 4, Bucharest, Romania. TEL 40-21-3233829, FAX 40-21-3234706, office@bucurestiwww.ro, http://www.bucurestiwww.ro.

917.204 CRI
WELCOME TO COSTA RICA. Text in English. q. **Document type:** *Magazine, Consumer.* **Description:** Comprehensive magazine covering travel and tourism in Costa Rica.
Related titles: Online - full text ed.
Address: Costa Rica.

914 FIN ISSN 1797-2620
WELCOME TO FINLAND. Text in English. 1974. 4/yr. EUR 55 domestic; EUR 63 in Europe; EUR 80 elsewhere (effective 2008). adv. **Document type:** *Handbook/Manual/Guide, Consumer.*
Supersedes in part (in 2008): Welcome to Finland (Danish Edition) (0109-1093); Which was formerly (until 1983): Finland: Welcome to Finland (0085-8048)
Related titles: German ed.: ISSN 1797-2639. 2008; Chinese ed.: ISSN 1797-2655. 2008; Russian ed.: ISSN 1797-2647. 2008.
Published by: Tekir Media, Hietalahdenranta 13, Helsinki, 00180, Finland. TEL 358-9-611680, FAX 358-9-611681. Ed. Kati Ala-Ilomaki. Adv. contact Markus Myllumaki. Circ: 50,000.

917.6 USA
WELCOME TO GREATER LOUISVILLE. Text in English. 1951. bi-w. adv. 40 p./no. 2 cols./p.; **Document type:** *Magazine, Consumer.* **Description:** Covers all the aspects of Louisville, including best attractions, dining, food, accommodation, etc.
Published by: Editorial Services Company, 812 S Third St, Louisville, KY 40203. TEL 502-584-2720, FAX 502-584-2722, esc@kytravel.com. Ed., Pub. Sally Reisz.

910.91 USA ISSN 1933-3056
WEND; beyond adventure. Text in English. 2006. 5/yr. USD 21 domestic (effective 2010). **Document type:** *Magazine, Consumer.*
Published by: Wend Magazine, 2001 NW 19th Av, Ste 103B, Portland, OR 97209. publisher@wendmag.com, http://www.wendmag.com. Ed. Stiv Wilson.

DE WERELDFIETSER; de vakantiefietser. *see* SPORTS AND GAMES—Bicycles And Motorcycles

WESTCHESTER LIFE. *see* GENERAL INTEREST PERIODICALS—United States

919.404 AUS
WESTERN DISTRICT HOLIDAY NEWS. Text in English. 1991. q. free (effective 2009). adv. maps. **Document type:** *Newspaper.* **Description:** Provides information on sightseeing and accommodation for tourists travelling within the Western District of Victoria.
Formerly: Western District Visitors News
Published by: Hamilton Spectator Partnership, 59 Gray St, Hamilton, VIC 3300, Australia. TEL 61-3-55721011, FAX 61-3-55723800, specadmin@spec.com.au. Ed. Mona Timms. Circ: 28,100.

910.202 CAN ISSN 1910-1236
WESTERN LIVING TRAVELS. Text in English. 2006. a. free with subscr. to Western Living (Vancouver Edition). **Document type:** *Magazine, Consumer.*
Related titles: ◆ Supplement to: Western Living (Vancouver Edition). ISSN 0824-0604.
Published by: Transcontinental Media, Inc. (Subsidiary of: Transcontinental, Inc.), 560-2608 Granville St, Vancouver, BC V6H 3V3, Canada. TEL 604-877-7732, FAX 604-877-4823, info@transcontinental.ca, http://www.transcontinental-gtc.com/en/home.html. Circ: 195,500.

910.91 USA ISSN 1552-6097
F117.3
WESTERN NEW YORK; an explorer's guide from Niagara falls to the Western Finger lakes. Text in English. 2005. irreg., latest 2008, 2nd ed. USD 21.95 2nd ed. (effective 2008). **Document type:** *Directory, Consumer.* **Description:** Provides guidance to the vast cultural, historic and natural destination of Western New York.
Published by: The Countryman Press (Subsidiary of: W.W. Norton & Co., Inc.), PO Box 748, Woodstock, VT 05091. TEL 802-457-4826, 800-245-4151, FAX 802-457-1678, countrymanpress@wwnorton.com.

796.7 USA ISSN 0043-4434
TL1
WESTWAYS. Text in English. 1909. bi-m. free to members (effective 2009). adv. bk.rev. illus. cum.index: 1909-1959, 1960-1972, 1973-1985. **Document type:** *Magazine, Consumer.* **Description:** Publishes articles on Western, domestic and worldwide travel and southern California lifestyle.
Incorporates: Avenues (Costa Mesa) (1073-1903); Which was formerly (until 1993): Auto Club News (0746-8504); Auto Club Pictorial (0005-0725); Formerly (until 1934): Touring Topics
Indexed: AmH&L, CalPI, HRIS.
—Ingenta.
Published by: Automobile Club of Southern California, PO Box 25001, Santa Ana, CA 92799. TEL 877-428-2277, FAX 800-222-8794. Ed. John Lehrer. Pub. Tamara Hill.

WESTWORLD MAGAZINE (BRITISH COLUMBIA EDITION). *see* TRANSPORTATION—Automobiles

WESTWORLD SASKATCHEWAN. *see* TRANSPORTATION—Automobiles

338.4791 387 GBR
WHAT CRUISE. Text in English. 1996. bi-m. GBP 17.70 domestic; GBP 32 foreign (effective 2001). **Document type:** *Journal, Consumer.*
Published by: Cruise Travel Publications Ltd., Hitech House, Roebuck Rd, Chessington, Surrey KT9 1LH, United Kingdom. TEL 0181-2870666, FAX 0181-2871808. Ed. Sue Bryant. Circ: 20,000 (paid and controlled).

919.704 USA
WHAT TO DO: ST. THOMAS. Text in English. 19??. a. adv. **Document type:** *Magazine, Consumer.*
Published by: Morris Multimedia, Inc., 725 Broad St, Augusta, GA 30901. TEL 706-724-0851, http://www.morris.com.

914 GBR
WHAT'S ON IN ABERDEEN (ONLINE). Text in English. 1945. m. GBP 5 (effective 1998). adv. **Document type:** *Handbook/Manual/Guide, Consumer.* **Description:** Comprehensive events calendar for Aberdeen city area which is updated daily by the Council, events partners and the community.
Former titles: What's on in Aberdeen (Print); What's on and Where to Shop in Aberdeen; What's on in Aberdeen (0043-4639)
Media: Online - full text.
Published by: Aberdeen City Council, Ground Fl, St Nicholas House, Broad St, Aberdeen, AB10 1AR, United Kingdom. TEL 44-8456-080910. Circ: 162,500.

914.2 GBR
WHAT'S ON IN EAST ANGLIA. Text in English. 1969. m. GBP 7.50. adv. bk.rev. **Description:** Leisure guide for East Anglia.
Published by: Profile Publishing, 101 Thunder Ln, Norwich, NR7 0JG, United Kingdom. Ed. Stephen Ford. Circ: 26,000.

914 792 GBR ISSN 0959-0080
WHAT'S ON IN LONDON. Text in English. 1935. w. GBP 65; GBP 1.40 newsstand/cover (effective 1999). adv. bk.rev.; film rev.; play rev. illus. **Document type:** *Handbook/Manual/Guide, Consumer.* **Description:** Provides a guide to London's mainstream and fringe theatre, cinema, opera, dance, classical, jazz and popular music, art galleries, museums, restaurants, pageantry, entertainment and leisure. Includes TV listings.
Former titles: What's On and Where to Go in London (0264-3227); Which was formed by merger of (1935-1982): What's On in London (0043-4671); Where to Go in London and Around (0043-4817)
Published by: Where To Go Ltd., 182 Pentonville Rd, London, N1 9LB, United Kingdom. TEL 44-171-278-4393, FAX 44-171-837-5838. Ed., R&P Michael Darvell. Pub. E G Shaw. Adv. contact Karen Allworthy. Circ: 40,000. **Dist. by:** Comag Specialist Division, Tavistock Works, Tavistock Rd, W Drayton, Mddx UB7 7QX, United Kingdom. TEL 44-1895-433800, FAX 44-1895-433801.

919.404 AUS
WHAT'S ON IN PERTH AND FREMANTLE. Text in English. 1986. w. adv. illus. **Document type:** *Handbook/Manual/Guide, Consumer.* **Description:** Lists tourist attractions, sporting and cultural events. Provides essential information for visitors.
Related titles: Online - full text ed.
Published by: Hopscotch Publications Pty. Ltd., PO Box 241, Como, W.A. 6952, Australia. maryhelen@whatson.com.au, http://www.whatson.com.au. adv.: page AUD 217.55; trim 95 x 195. Circ: 5,500 (controlled).

910.202 790.1 USA
WHAT'S ON MAGAZINE; the Las Vegas guide. Text in English. 1954. bi-w. USD 89 domestic; USD 150 foreign (effective 2000); USD 4.95 newsstand/cover. adv. bk.rev.; dance rev.; music rev. maps. back issues avail. **Document type:** *Magazine, Consumer.* **Description:** Informs visitors on local entertainment, including gambling, shows, sightseeing, shopping, and dining.
Formerly (until 1998): What's on in Las Vegas Magazine (1081-5945)
Related titles: Online - full text ed.
Published by: What's On Magazine, 4425 S Industrial Rd, Las Vegas, NV 89103. TEL 702-891-8811, 800-494-2876, FAX 702-891-8804, whatson@ilovevegas.com, http://www.ilovevegas.com/. Ed. Stacey Hertz. Pub. Murray Hertz. R&P Pamela Hertz. Adv. contact Pamela Hertz. B&W page USD 575, color page USD 2,774; trim 8.125 x 9.875. Circ: 5,000 (paid); 170,000 (controlled).

796 USA ISSN 0194-0384
GV198.56
WHEELERS R V RESORT AND CAMPGROUND GUIDE: NORTH AMERICAN EDITION. Text in English. 1972. a. USD 19.95 (effective 2005). adv. 8000 p./no.; **Document type:** *Directory, Consumer.* **Description:** Published for the camper seeking a park or campground in which to vacation in the United States, Canada and/or Mexico. The book lists both public and commerical parks and campgrounds with location, facilities, and recreation available. Commerical parks/campgrounds are star rated for quality. Mail addresses and phone numbers are given. Upfront section contain sarticles on a variety of subjects for the RV and camping enthusiast.
Supersedes regional editions of: Wheelers Recreational Vehicle Resort and Campground Guide; Which superseded: Wheelers Trailer Resort and Campground Guide (0090-600X)
Published by: Print Media Services, Ltd., 816 Banyan Dr., Elk Grove Village, IL 60007-4102. TEL 847-981-0100, 800-323-8899, FAX 847-981-0106. Ed. Geraldine Bussiere. Pub., R&P, Adv. contact Gloria S Telander. B&W page USD 6,130, color page USD 7,540. Circ: 200,300.

910.202 THA
WHERE. Text in Thai. m. THB 20, USD 0.85 per issue. adv. **Description:** Tourist guide to Thailand aimed at affluent travelers.
Published by: Media Transasia (Thailand) Ltd., 14th Fl., Ocena Tower II, 75/8 Soi Sukhumvit, 19 Sukhumvit Rd., Klongtoeynue, Wattana, Bangkok, 10110, Thailand. FAX 662-204-2391. Ed. Kelvin Rugg. Circ: 25,940.

917.502 USA
WHERE BALTIMORE. Text in English. 1994. m. adv. 40 p./no. 3 cols./p.; **Document type:** *Magazine, Consumer.*
Related titles: Online - full text ed.
Published by: Morris Visitor Publications (Subsidiary of: Morris Multimedia, Inc.), 575 S Charles St, Ste 503, Baltimore, MD 21201. TEL 410-783-7520, FAX 410-783-1763, MVPcustomerservice@morris.com, http://www.wheremagazine.com/, http://www.morrisvisitorpublications.com/. adv.: B&W page USD 2,441, color page USD 3,040; trim 8.13 x 10.88. Circ: 33,000 (controlled).

910.91 USA
WHERE CHARLESTON. Text in English. 1936. m. USD 56; USD 6 per issue (effective 2009). adv. **Document type:** *Magazine, Consumer.* **Description:** Designed to be a guide to the Charleston's top restaurants, shops, shows, exhibits and tours.
Published by: Morris Multimedia, Inc., 103 Broad St. Second Fl, Charleston, SC 29401. TEL 843-722-8989, FAX 843-722-9690, http://www.morris.com. Ed. Jay Bemis TEL 706.828-3969. Adv. contact Larry Molony TEL 843-722-8989.

917.502 USA
WHERE DELAWARE SHORE. Text in English. 19??. m. adv. **Document type:** *Magazine, Consumer.*
Published by: Morris Multimedia, Inc., 725 Broad St, Augusta, GA 30901. TEL 706-724-0851, http://www.morris.com.

910.91 USA
WHERE DULLES CORRIDOR. Text in English. m. **Document type:** *Magazine, Consumer.*
Published by: Morris Visitor Publications (Subsidiary of: Morris Multimedia, Inc.), 725 Broad St, Augusta, GA 30901. MVPcustomerservice@morris.com, http://www.morrisvisitorpublications.com/. Ed. Paula Felps. Pub. Terri Provencal.

917.102 CAN ISSN 1719-3184
WHERE EDMONTON. Text in English. 1994. bi-m. free (effective 2006). adv. illus. **Document type:** *Magazine, Consumer.*
Former titles (until 2006): Where Canada (Edmonton Edition) (1711-9812); (until 2003): Where Edmonton (1205-1802)
Published by: Tanner Publishing Ltd., 9343 50th St, Unit 4, Edmonton, AB T6B 2L5, Canada. TEL 780-465-3362, FAX 780-448-0424, info@whereedmonton.com. Ed. Laura Soucek TEL 780-465-3362. R&P Rob Tanner. adv.: B&W page CAD 2,260, color page CAD 2,825; trim 8.125 x 10.875. Circ: 40,000 (controlled).

910.91 USA
WHERE LAS VEGAS. Text in English. 1936. m. USD 48; USD 5 per issue (effective 2009). **Document type:** *Magazine, Consumer.* **Description:** Designed to be a guide to the Las Vegas's top restaurants, shops, shows, exhibits and tours.
Related titles: Online - full text ed.
Published by: Morris Multimedia, Inc., 101 Convention Ctr Dr, Ste 680, Las Vegas, NV 89109. TEL 702-731-4748, FAX 702-731-4718, http://www.morris.com. Ed. Jennifer Prosser. Pub. Angela Nelson.

910.91 GBR ISSN 1468-9650
WHERE LONDON; your best source for shopping, dining, entertainment and maps. Text in English. 1975. m. GBP 40 domestic; GBP 48 in Europe; GBP 58 elsewhere; GBP 4 newsstand/cover (effective 2009). adv. dance rev.; music rev.; play rev. 3 cols./p.; back issues avail. **Document type:** *Magazine, Consumer.* **Description:** Guide to London for high-earning and free-spending visitors.
Former titles (until 1998): Where Magazine (0951-323X); (until 1983): Where in London (0143-2478)
Related titles: Online - full text ed.
Published by: Morris Visitor Publications Europe (Subsidiary of: Morris Multimedia, Inc.), 233 High Holborn, 2nd Fl, London, WC1V 7DN, United Kingdom. TEL 44-20-72425222, FAX 44-20-72424184, MVPcustomerservice@morris.com. Ed. Sandrae Lawrence. Pub. Chris Manning. Adv. contact Andrew Turner TEL 44-20-76117891. color page GBP 3,730; trim 206 x 276. Circ: 905,052 (controlled).

910.91 USA
WHERE LOS ANGELES. Text in English. 19??. m. USD 36; USD 4 newsstand/cover (effective 2009). adv. illus. **Document type:** *Magazine, Consumer.* **Description:** Covers dining, entertainment, tourist and cultural activities for visitors to LA.
Related titles: Online - full text ed.
Published by: Morris Visitor Publications (Subsidiary of: Morris Multimedia, Inc.), 3679 Motor Ave, Ste 300, Los Angeles, CA 90034. TEL 320-280-2880, FAX 310-280-2890, MVPcustomerservice@morris.com, http://www.morrisvisitorpublications.com/. Ed. Benjamin Epstein. Pub. Jeff Levy. adv.: B&W page USD 3,480, color page USD 4,095; trim 10.88 x 8.13. Circ: 50,000 (controlled).

917.5 USA
WHERE MIAMI. Text in English. 1936. m. USD 56; USD 5 per issue (effective 2009). adv. **Document type:** *Magazine, Consumer.* **Description:** Designed to be a guide to the Miami's top restaurants, shops, shows, exhibits and tours.
Published by: Morris Multimedia, Inc., 7300 Corporate Ctr Dr, Ste 303, Miami, FL 33126. TEL 305-892-6644, FAX 305-802-1005, http://www.morris.com. Ed. Irene Moore TEL 843-722-8989. Pub. Harvey Dana TEL 305-436-1330. Adv. contact Elizabeth Rindone TEL 305-436-1325.

910.2 RUS
WHERE MOSCOW; zhurnal dlya moskvichei i gostei stolitsy. Text in English; Section in Russian. 1996. m. illus. **Document type:** *Magazine, Consumer.* **Description:** Presents information on cultural, business and sports events of interest to the tourists visiting Moscow.
Published by: Izdatel'skii Dom S P N, ul Kedrova, 15, Moscow, 117036, Russian Federation. valle@spn.ru. Circ: 60,000.

913 USA
WHERE PHILADELPHIA. Text in English. 1992. m. USD 48; USD 5 per issue (effective 2009). **Document type:** *Magazine, Consumer.* **Description:** Designed to be a guide to the Philadelphia's top restaurants, shops, shows, exhibits and tours.
Published by: Morris Multimedia, Inc., 301 S, 19th St, Ste 1 South, Philadelphia, PA 19103. TEL 215-893-5100, FAX 215-893-5105, http://www.morris.com. Ed. Karen Gross. Pub., Adv. contact Laura Burkhardt TEL 215-893-5100 ext 26.

910.202 CAN ISSN 0849-309X
WHERE ROCKY MOUNTAINS. Text in English. 1978. s-a. CAD 3, USD 3 per issue (effective 2001). adv. **Document type:** *Handbook/Manual/ Guide, Consumer.* **Description:** Information for visitors to the Canadian Rocky Mountains: activities, shopping, dining, lodging and maps.
Formerly: Rocky Mountain Visitor (0821-5146)
Published by: R M V Publications Ltd., Ste 250, One Palliser Sq, 125 Ninth Ave S E, Calgary, AB T2G 0P6, Canada. TEL 403-299-1888, FAX 403-299-1899. Ed., Pub., R&P Jack Newton. Adv. contact Glen Miles. Circ: 375,000 (controlled).

910.202 USA
WHERE SEATTLE; the city magazine for visitors. Text in English. 1992. m. USD 56; USD 6 newsstand/cover (effective 2008). adv. illus. 84 p./no. 3 cols./p.; **Document type:** *Magazine, Consumer.* **Description:** Visitor's guide to Seattle sights, dining, entertainment, and cultural events.
Published by: Morris Visitor Publications (Subsidiary of: Morris Multimedia, Inc.), 1904 Third Ave, Ste 623, Seattle, WA 98101. TEL 206-826-2665, FAX 206-826-2676, MVPcustomerservice@morris.com, http://www.morrisvisitorpublications.com/. Ed. Angela Garbes. adv.: B&W page USD 2,125, color page USD 2,450; trim 10.88 x 8.13. Circ: 40,000 (controlled).

910.2 RUS
WHERE ST. PETERSBURG. Text in English. 1997. 8/yr. illus. **Document type:** *Magazine, Consumer.* **Description:** Presents information on cultural, business and sports events of interest to the tourists visiting St. Petersburg.
Published by: Izdatel'skii Dom S P N, ul Kedrova, 15, Moscow, 117036, Russian Federation. valle@spn.ru. Circ: 35,000.

WHERE TO EAT IN CANADA. *see* HOTELS AND RESTAURANTS

910 USA ISSN 1060-0094
HQ1063
WHERE TO RETIRE. Text in English. 1992. bi-m. USD 18 domestic; USD 30 in Canada (effective 2009). adv. 268 p./no. 3 cols./p.; back issues avail. **Document type:** *Magazine, Consumer.* **Description:** Helps retirees find the ideal setting for their new life.
Indexed: AgeL.
Published by: Vacation Publications, Inc., 5851 San Felipe St, Ste 500, Houston, TX 77057. TEL 713-974-6903, FAX 713-978-6003, service@WhereToRetire.com. Ed. Mary Lou Abbott. Adv. contact Katie Davies.

918 PER
WHERE, WHEN, HOW.. Text in Spanish. m.
Published by: Peruvian Times, S.A., Apartado 2484, Lima, Peru. Ed. Anne Arrarte. Circ: 25,000.

910.202 GBR ISSN 1745-7769
WHICH CARAVAN. Text in English. 1987. m. GBP 29.99 domestic; GBP 44.99 in Europe; GBP 54.99 elsewhere (effective 2009). adv. back issues avail. **Document type:** *Magazine, Consumer.* **Description:** Contains everything an enthusiastic caravanner needs to know, including new and secondhand evaluations, DIY and product testing, in-depth news, site reports and buying information.
Formerly (until 2005): Caravan Life (0957-6282); Which incorporates (1993-1996): Caravan Plus (0967-0025)
—CCC.
Published by: Warners Group Publications Plc., The Maltings, Manor Ln, Bourne, Lincs PE10 9PH, United Kingdom. TEL 44-1778-391000, FAX 44-1778-425437, wgpsubs@warnersgroup.co.uk, http://www.warnersgroup.co.uk. Ed. Sally Pepper TEL 44-1778-391111. Pub. John Greenwood TEL 44-1778-391116. Adv. contact Sam Lewis. Circ: 45,279.

910.202 GBR
WHICH? HOLIDAY. Text in English. 19??. q. **Document type:** *Magazine, Consumer.*
Formerly (until 2006): Holiday Which?
Related titles: ◆ Supplement to: Which?. ISSN 0043-4841.
Published by: Consumers' Association, 2 Marylebone Rd, London, NW1 4DF, United Kingdom. TEL 44-020-77707000, FAX 44-020-77207600.

910.2 CAN
WHISTLER; the magazine. Text in English. 2000. s-a. USD 20; USD 3.95 newsstand/cover (effective 2001). adv. **Document type:** *Magazine, Consumer.*
Published by: Whistler Printing and Publishing, 238-4370 Lorimer Rd, Whistler, BC V0N 1B4, Canada. TEL 604-932-5131, FAX 604-932-2862, info@whistlerquestion.com, http://www.whistlerquestion.com. Ed. Tim Shoults. Pub. Penny Graham.

WHITE BOOK OF SKI AREAS. U S AND CANADA. *see* SPORTS AND GAMES—Outdoor Life

338.4 USA ISSN 1932-6777
G155.U6
WHO'S BUYING FOR TRAVEL. Text in English. 2004. a. USD 59.95 per issue (print or online ed.) (effective 2011). **Document type:** *Report, Trade.*
Related titles: Online - full text ed.
Published by: New Strategist Publications, Inc., 120 W State St, 4th Fl, PO Box 242, Ithaca, NY 14851. TEL 607-273-0913, 800-848-0842, demographics@newstrategist.com.

WHO'S WHO IN AMERICA'S RESTAURANTS; encyclopedia of America's dining establishments. *see* ENCYCLOPEDIAS AND GENERAL ALMANACS

WHO'S WHO IN RECREATION. *see* BIOGRAPHY

WILLIAMS-SONOMA TASTE. *see* FOOD AND FOOD INDUSTRIES

755 910.91 USA
WILLIAMSBURG MAGAZINE. Text in English. 1964. m. USD 25 (effective 2005). adv. **Document type:** *Magazine, Consumer.*
Published by: Virginia Gazette Companies, LLC (Subsidiary of: Daily Press, Inc.), 216 Ironbound Rd, Williamsburg, VA 23188. TEL 757-220-1736, 800-944-6908, FAX 757-220-1665, feedback@tribune.com. Ed. Ann Efimetz. Pub. W C O'Donovan. Adv. contacts Anne Monaghan, John Trevvett. Circ: 55,000 (free).

908 DEU
WILLKOMMEN IM ERZGEBIRGE. Text in German. 1992. 2/yr. EUR 2.50 newsstand/cover (effective 2009). adv. **Document type:** *Magazine, Consumer.*
Published by: Verlag Anzeigenblaetter GmbH Chemnitz, Brueckenstr 15, Chemnitz, 09111, Germany. TEL 49-371-65620000, FAX 49-371-65627000, geschaeftsfuehrung@blick.de, http://www.blick.de. adv.: color page EUR 2,100. Circ: 45,000 (paid and controlled).

908 DEU
WILLKOMMEN IM VOGTLAND. Text in German. 1994. s-a. EUR 2 newsstand/cover (effective 2009). adv. **Document type:** *Magazine, Consumer.*
Published by: Verlag Anzeigenblaetter GmbH Chemnitz, Brueckenstr 15, Chemnitz, 09111, Germany. TEL 49-371-65620000, FAX 49-371-65627000, geschaeftsfuehrung@blick.de, http://www.blick.de. adv.: page EUR 1,740. Circ: 30,000 (controlled).

914.404 USA
WINDOW ON FRANCE; the insider's view of French country life. Text in English. 1996. q. USD 39; USD 41 in Canada; USD 55 elsewhere. **Document type:** *Newsletter.* **Description:** Informs on out-of-the-way places. Explores the charms of rural France.
Published by: Provence West, Ltd., PO Box 272884, Fort Collins, CO 80527-2884. Ed., Pub. Linda Posson. Circ: 300.

919.304 NZL ISSN 1177-2409
WINE DESTINATIONS. Text in English. 2002. a. **Document type:** *Magazine, Consumer.* **Description:** Establishes wine as the focal point of the perfect holiday around New Zealand, complete with maps and details on winery restaurants, accommodation and wine-associated activities.
Published by: Destinations Media, 74 Jervois Rd, Herne Bay, Auckland, New Zealand. TEL 64-9-3603978, FAX 64-9-3604097, mail@destinationsmagazine.com. Pub. Bruce Laybourn.

WINESTATE. *see* BEVERAGES

910.2 CAN ISSN 1910-6734
WINNIPEG EXPLORER'S GUIDE. Text in English. 2006. a. CAD 19.95 per issue (effective 2006). **Document type:** *Magazine, Consumer.*
Published by: Fanfare Magazine Group (Subsidiary of: St. Joseph Media), 112 Market Ave, Ste 400, Winnipeg, MB R3B 0P4, Canada. TEL 204-943-4439, FAX 204-947-5463. Ed. Brad Hughes.

WINTERSPORT MAGAZINE. *see* SPORTS AND GAMES—Outdoor Life

914.04 DEU
WIR; in Nieder-Erlenbach. Text in German. 1970. m.
Published by: Sozialdemokratische Partei Deutschlands, Ortsverein Nieder - Erlenbach, Bornweg 30, Frankfurt Am Main, 60437, Germany. TEL 06101-43434. Circ: 1,500.

WISCONSIN WEST MAGAZINE. *see* HISTORY—History Of North And South America

796.5 917 USA ISSN 0744-8120
WOODALL'S CAMPERWAYS; the Middle Atlantic campers' newspaper. Text in English. 1979. m. USD 24.95 (effective 2009). adv. bk.rev. **Document type:** *Magazine, Consumer.* **Description:** Focuses on the Mid-Atlantic that features NJ, NY, PA, MD, DE and VA.
Published by: Woodall Publications Corp. (Subsidiary of: Affinity Group Inc.), 2575 Vista Del Mar Dr, Ventura, CA 93001. TEL 877-680-6155, FAX 805-667-4100, 805-667-4122, info@woodallpub.com. adv.: B&W page USD 1,695, color page USD 2,465.

917.8 USA ISSN 1548-4181
GV191.42.G725
WOODALL'S CAMPGROUND GUIDE: FRONTIER WEST/GREAT PLAINS & MOUNTAIN REGION. Variant title: Frontier West/Great Plains, Mountain Region Campground Guide. Text in English. 19??. a. USD 9.95 per issue (effective 2009). adv. **Document type:** *Directory, Consumer.* **Description:** Features up-to-date listings from AR, CO, KS, MO, MT, ND, NE, NM, OK, SD, TX, UT, WY, Mexico and three provinces in Canada, AB, MB and SK.
Former titles (until 200?): Woodall's the Campground Guide: Frontier West/Great Plains & Mountain Region; (until 2000): Woodall's Camping Guide: Frontier West/Great Plains & Mountain States; Which was formed by the merger of (1989-199?): Woodall's Camping Guide: Frontier West; (1989-199?): Woodall's Camping Guide: Great Plains & Mountain States
Published by: Woodall Publications Corp. (Subsidiary of: Affinity Group Inc.), 2575 Vista Del Mar Dr, Ventura, CA 93001. TEL 877-667-4100, 877-680-6155, FAX 805-667-4122, info@woodallpub.com.

WOODALL'S FLORIDA R V TRAVELER. *see* TRANSPORTATION—Roads And Traffic

WOODALL'S MIDWEST R V TRAVELER. *see* TRANSPORTATION—Roads And Traffic

WORKAMPER NEWS; America's guide to working while camping. *see* OCCUPATIONS AND CAREERS

910.202 GBR
WORKING ABROAD (LONDON). Text in English. 19??. a. GBP 12.99 per issue (effective 2009). back issues avail. **Document type:** *Handbook/ Manual/Guide, Consumer.* **Description:** Covers everything that employees and their families might need to know about expatriate employment and the associated issues of living in a new country.
Published by: Kogan Page Ltd., 120 Pentonville Rd, London, N1 9JN, United Kingdom. TEL 44-20-72780433, FAX 44-20-78376348, KPinfo@koganpage.com.

WORLD AIRPORT GUIDE. *see* TRANSPORTATION—Air Transport

910.2 USA ISSN 1061-0103
WORLD EXPLORER. Text in English. 1991. s-a. USD 25; USD 6 newsstand/cover (effective 2001). **Document type:** *Magazine, Consumer.* **Description:** Provides information on "lost cities" and ancient places; also contains maps and travel journals.
Published by: The World Explorers Club, PO Box 99, Kempton, IL 60946. TEL 815-253-9000, FAX 815-253-6300, info@wexclub.com, http://www.wexclub.com.

338.4 GBR ISSN 1471-8553
WORLD HOSPITALITY AND TOURISM TRENDS. Text in English. bi-m. **Document type:** *Journal, Consumer.* **Description:** Aimed at hospitality and tourist practitioners, students, researchers and those charged with developments in this field.
Media: Online - full text.
Address: WHATT@hcmia.co.uk.

WORLD HOTEL AND CONVENTION DIRECTORY. *see* HOTELS AND RESTAURANTS

WORLD HOTEL D B. (Database) *see* HOTELS AND RESTAURANTS

WORLD JOURNAL FOR TOURISM DEVELOPMENT AND MARKETING. *see* BUSINESS AND ECONOMICS—Marketing And Purchasing

338.4791 ZAF ISSN 1990-8814
WORLD JOURNAL OF E-TOURISM. Text in English. 2006. q. USD 120 in Africa to individuals; USD 180 elsewhere to individuals; USD 350 in Africa to institutions; USD 450 elsewhere to institutions; USD 85 in Africa to students; USD 100 elsewhere to students (effective 2007). **Description:** Addresses how online business technologies relate and their impact on tourism operations, including all business and operational aspects of information technology, particularly those touching the internet.
Published by: (World Research Organization), Isis Press, PO Box 1919, Cape Town, 8000, South Africa. TEL 27-21-4471574, FAX 27-86-6219999, orders@unwro.org, http://www.unwro.org/isispress.html.

338.4791 333.72 363.7 ZAF ISSN 1990-8733
➤ **WORLD JOURNAL OF ECOTOURISM.** Text in English. 2006. q. USD 120 in Africa to individuals; USD 180 elsewhere to individuals; USD 350 in Africa to institutions; USD 450 elsewhere to institutions; USD 85 in Africa to students; USD 100 elsewhere to students (effective 2007). **Document type:** *Journal, Academic/Scholarly.* **Description:** Provides information about worldwide ecotourism systems, environmental management and nature conservation issues.
Published by: (World Research Organization), Isis Press, PO Box 1919, Cape Town, 8000, South Africa. TEL 27-21-4471574, FAX 27-86-6219999, orders@unwro.org, http://www.unwro.org/isispress.html.

338.4791 796 ZAF ISSN 1819-8546
WORLD JOURNAL OF EVENTS AND SPORTS TOURISM. Text in English. 2006. q. USD 120 in Africa to individuals; USD 180 elsewhere to individuals; USD 350 in Africa to institutions; USD 450 elsewhere to institutions; USD 85 in Africa to students; USD 100 elsewhere to students (effective 2007). **Document type:** *Journal, Academic/Scholarly.* **Description:** Provides a forum that draws upon theories and concepts from sociology and anthropology, events, sport, tourism and business studies.
Published by: (World Research Organization), Isis Press, PO Box 1919, Cape Town, 8000, South Africa. TEL 27-21-4471574, FAX 27-86-6219999, orders@unwro.org, http://www.unwro.org/isispress.html.

338.4791 327.172 ZAF ISSN 1819-8562
WORLD JOURNAL OF PEACE THROUGH TOURISM. Text in English. 2006. q. USD 120 in Africa to individuals; USD 180 elsewhere to individuals; USD 350 in Africa to institutions; USD 450 elsewhere to institutions; USD 85 in Africa to students; USD 100 elsewhere to students (effective 2007). **Document type:** *Journal, Academic/ Scholarly.* **Description:** Promotes discussions on theories, research and practices in peace through the power of tourism as the world's largest and fastest growing industry.
Published by: (World Research Organization), Isis Press, PO Box 1919, Cape Town, 8000, South Africa. TEL 27-21-4471574, FAX 27-86-6219999, orders@unwro.org, http://www.unwro.org/isispress.html.

WORLD JOURNAL OF PUBLIC RELATIONS. *see* ADVERTISING AND PUBLIC RELATIONS

658 338.4 ZAF ISSN 1990-8652
➤ **WORLD JOURNAL OF TOURISM ADMINISTRATION.** Text in English. 2006. q. USD 120 in Africa to individuals; USD 180 elsewhere to individuals; USD 350 in Africa to institutions; USD 450 elsewhere to institutions; USD 85 in Africa to students; USD 100 elsewhere to students (effective 2007). **Document type:** *Journal, Academic/Scholarly.* **Description:** Covers tourism management, hospitality, tourism development and education, applied research studies, and presents critical reviews on major issues affecting the tourism sector.
Published by: (World Research Organization), Isis Press, PO Box 1919, Cape Town, 8000, South Africa. TEL 27-21-4471574, FAX 27-86-6219999, orders@unwro.org, http://www.unwro.org/isispress.html.

338.4 647.950681 ZAF ISSN 1819-8554
➤ **WORLD JOURNAL OF TOURISM AND HOSPITALITY MANAGEMENT.** Text in English. 2006. q. USD 120 in Africa to individuals; USD 180 elsewhere to individuals; USD 350 in Africa to institutions; USD 450 elsewhere to institutions; USD 85 in Africa to students; USD 100 elsewhere to students (effective 2007). **Document type:** *Journal, Academic/Scholarly.* **Description:** Covers current happening and trends in the tourism management industry.
Published by: (World Research Organization), Isis Press, PO Box 1919, Cape Town, 8000, South Africa. TEL 27-21-4471574, FAX 27-86-6219999, orders@unwro.org, http://www.unwro.org/isispress.html.

338.4791 790.1 796 ZAF ISSN 1819-8570
➤ **WORLD JOURNAL OF TOURISM, LEISURE AND SPORTS.** Text in English. 2006. q. USD 120 in Africa to individuals; USD 180 elsewhere to individuals; USD 350 in Africa to institutions; USD 450 elsewhere to institutions; USD 85 in Africa to students; USD 100 elsewhere to students (effective 2007). **Document type:** *Journal, Academic/Scholarly.* **Description:** Reflects current happenings and trends in the world-wide hospitality, sports and tourism industries.
Related titles: Online - full text ed.: ISSN 1998-1406.
Published by: (World Research Organization), Isis Press, PO Box 1919, Cape Town, 8000, South Africa. TEL 27-21-4471574, FAX 27-86-6219999, orders@unwro.org, http://www.unwro.org/isispress.html.

338.4791 ZAF ISSN 1991-1386
➤ **WORLD JOURNAL OF TOURISM OPERATIONS AND TRANSPORT.** Text in English. 2006. q. USD 120 in Africa to individuals; USD 180 elsewhere to individuals; USD 350 in Africa to institutions; USD 450 elsewhere to institutions; USD 85 in Africa to students; USD 100 elsewhere to students (effective 2007). **Document type:** *Journal, Academic/Scholarly.* **Description:** Provides essential and intelligent information about world-wide tourism operations, transport, and facilities issues.
Published by: (World Research Organization), Isis Press, PO Box 1919, Cape Town, 8000, South Africa. TEL 27-21-4471574, FAX 27-86-6219999, orders@unwro.org, http://www.unwro.org/isispress.html.

338.4791 338.642 ZAF ISSN 1991-1394
WORLD JOURNAL OF TOURISM SMALL BUSINESS MANAGEMENT. Text in English. 2006. q. USD 120 in Africa to individuals; USD 180 elsewhere to individuals; USD 350 in Africa to institutions; USD 450 elsewhere to institutions; USD 85 in Africa to students; USD 100 elsewhere to students (effective 2007). **Description:** Provides a forum for the empirical analysis of the role of tourism small businesses.
Related titles: Online - full text ed.: ISSN 1998-135X.
Published by: (World Research Organization), Isis Press, PO Box 1919, Cape Town, 8000, South Africa. TEL 27-21-4471574, FAX 27-86-6219999, orders@unwro.org, http://www.unwro.org/isispress.html.

WORLD LEISURE JOURNAL. *see* LEISURE AND RECREATION

338.479 658.8 GBR
THE WORLD MARKET FOR TRAVEL AND TOURISM. Text in English. 19??. irreg., latest 1997. **Document type:** *Monographic series, Trade.* **Description:** Looks at the latest trends and developments in world tourism.
Formerly: World Tourism
Published by: Euromonitor International Plc., 60-61 Britton St, London, EC1M 5UX, United Kingdom. TEL 44-20-72518024, FAX 44-20-76083149, info@euromonitor.com, http://www.euromonitor.com.

910.202 GBR
WORLD TRAVEL ATLAS. Text in English. 1994. a. GBP 19.50 per issue (effective 2009). adv. back issues avail. **Document type:** *Handbook/ Manual/Guide, Trade.* **Description:** Provides topical global information for the travel industry.
Published by: Columbus Travel Media Ltd (Subsidiary of: Highbury House Communications Plc), Media House, Azalea Dr, Swanley, Kent BR8 8HU, United Kingdom. TEL 44-1322-611430, FAX 44-1322-616323, travelads@columbustravelmedia.com. Adv. contact David Simms TEL 44-1322-611335.

910.202 GBR ISSN 0267-8748
G153.4
WORLD TRAVEL GUIDE. Text in English. 1983. a., latest 25th ed. GBP 59.50 per issue (effective 2009). adv. charts; illus.; stat. back issues avail. **Document type:** *Handbook/Manual/Guide, Trade.* **Description:** Contains interesting and detailed information on history, area, population and government along with geographical information on each country.
Related titles: CD-ROM ed.: ISSN 1466-5077.
—BLDSC (9360.154220). **CCC.**
Published by: Columbus Travel Media Ltd (Subsidiary of: Highbury House Communications Plc), Media House, Azalea Dr, Swanley, Kent BR8 8HU, United Kingdom. TEL 44-1322-611430, FAX 44-1322-616323, travelads@columbustravelmedia.com. Adv. contact David Simms TEL 44-1322-611335.

338.4 GBR ISSN 1755-4217
▼ ➤ **WORLDWIDE HOSPITALITY AND TOURISM THEMES.** Abbreviated title: W H A T T. Text in English. 2009. 4/yr. EUR 339 combined subscription in Europe (print & online eds.); USD 439 combined subscription in the Americas (print & online eds.); GBP 229 combined subscription in the UK & elsewhere (print & online eds.) AUD 599 combined subscription in Australasia (print & online eds.) (effective 2012). back issues avail.; reprint service avail. from PSC. **Document type:** *Journal, Academic/Scholarly.* **Description:** Provides thematic reviews of the major challenges facing the tourism and hospitality industry today.
Related titles: Online - full text ed.: ISSN 1755-4225.
Indexed: A12, A17, ABIn, P48, P51, P53, P54, PQC.
—**CCC.**
Published by: Emerald Group Publishing Ltd., Howard House, Wagon Ln, Bingley, W Yorks BD16 1WA, United Kingdom. TEL 44-1274-777700, FAX 44-1274-785201, information@emeraldinsight.com, http://www.emeraldinsight.com. Pub. Aimee Wood. **Subscr. in Australia to:** Emerald Group Publishing Limited, PO Box 1441, Fitzroy North, VIC 3068, Australia. TEL 61-3-90781748, FAX 61-3-90781748. **Subscr. in the Americas to:** Emerald Group Publishing Limited. america@emeraldinsight.com.

914.3804 POL
WROCLAW IN YOUR POCKET. Text in English. a. USD 5 newsstand/ cover (effective 2002). adv. **Document type:** *Magazine, Consumer.*
Published by: Gdansk In Your Pocket, ul. Heweliusza 11-818, Gdansk, 80890, Poland. TEL 48-58-3218161, FAX 48-58-3218161, gdansk@inyourpocket.com, http://www.inyourpocket.com.

917.87 USA ISSN 1934-5844
F761.6
WYOMING CURIOSITIES; quirky characters, roadside oddities & other offbeat stuff. Text in English. 2007. triennial, latest 2007, 1st ed. USD 14.95 per issue (effective 2008). **Document type:** *Guide, Consumer.* **Description:** Provides tourist information about the Cowboy State.
Published by: The Globe Pequot Press, Inc., 246 Goose Ln, PO Box 480, Guilford, CT 06437. TEL 203-458-4500, 888-249-7586, FAX 203-458-4603, 800-820-2329, info@globepequot.com, http:// www.globepequot.com.

910.2 USA
WYOMING OFFICIAL TRAVELERS JOURNAL. Text in English. 2003. a. free. adv. **Document type:** *Journal, Consumer.* **Description:** Offers information about accommodations, restaurants and attractions.
Former titles (until 2005): Wyoming Official Vacation Directory; (until 2003): Wyoming Visitor Directory; (until 2000): Wyoming Visitor; (until 1994): Wyoming Winter Trails; Which incorporated (in 1999): Wyoming Vacation Directory
Published by: Weaver Publications, Inc., 2420 Alcott St, Denver, CO 80211. TEL 303-458-1211, 800-303-9328, FAX 303-477-0724, info@weaver-group.com, http://pub.weaver-group.com. adv.: color page USD 10,050; trim 8 x 10.875. Circ: 400,000 (free).

338.4791 CHN ISSN 1674-5116
XIN LUXING/VOYAGE. Text in Chinese. 2004. m. CNY 192 (effective 2010). **Document type:** *Magazine, Consumer.* **Description:** Covers high-end international travel for the business elite and the wealthy.
Related titles: Online - full text ed.
Published by: Xin Luxing Zazhishe, 5F,Prime Tower,22 Chaoyangmenwai Ave., Beijing, 100020, China. TEL 010)85650437.

915.13 CHN ISSN 1006-2629
XINAN LUYOU/TOURING SOUTHWEST CHINA. Text in Chinese. 1980. bi-m. CNY 12 newsstand/cover (effective 2005). illus. 48 p./no.; **Document type:** *Magazine, Consumer.* **Description:** Covers tourism in southwestern China.
Formerly: Sichuan Luyou - Touring Sichuan
Published by: Sichuan Renmin Chubanshe, 3, Yandao Jie, Chengdu, Sichuan 610012, China. TEL 86-28-86666970, FAX 86-28-86664569. Ed. Deng Hongping. Circ: 30,000. **Dist. by:** China International Book Trading Corp, 35 Chegongzhuang Xilu, Haidian District, PO Box 399, Beijing 100044, China. TEL 86-10-68412045, FAX 86-10-68412023, cibtc@mail.cibtc.com.cn, http://www.cibtc.com.cn.

XTRA!; Toronto's gay and lesbian biweekly. *see* HOMOSEXUALITY

XTRA! (VANCOUVER). *see* HOMOSEXUALITY

649.94 AUS
Y H A AUSTRALIA. ACCOMMODATION AND DISCOUNT GUIDE. (Youth Hostels Association) Text in English. 1957. a. free (effective 2008). adv. **Description:** Hostel information, addresses, maps of locations state by state, booking information, regional descriptions, holidays, festival dates, concessions.
Former titles (until 2002): Y H A Australia. Accommodation Guide; (until 200?): Y H A Australia Accommodation, Discounts and Activities Guide (1329-8895); (until 199?): Y H A Australia. Accommodation Guide; Accommodation & Discounts Guide Australia; (until 1997): Y H A Australia Accommodation Guide (1035-6258); (until 1990): Y H A Hostels in Australia; (until 1984): Australian Youth Hostels Handbook (0156-0107)
Published by: Australian Youth Hostels Association Inc., PO Box A2462, Sydney South, NSW 1235, Australia. yha@yha.org.au, http:// www.yha.com.au.

YACHTSMAN'S GUIDE TO THE BAHAMAS. *see* SPORTS AND GAMES—Boats And Boating

917.4 USA
F2.3
YANKEE MAGAZINE'S TRAVEL GUIDE TO NEW ENGLAND. Text in English. 1972. a. adv. illus. back issues avail. **Document type:** *Magazine, Consumer.* **Description:** Showcases places and events of interest in the six-state region.
Former titles (until 1990): Yankee Magazine's Travel Guide to New England, New York and Eastern Canada (1055-226X); (until 1988): Yankee Magazine's Travel Guide to New England and Its Neighbors (1055-2251); (until 1987): Yankee Magazine's Travel Guide to New England (0740-6215); (until 1981): Yankee Magazine's Guide to New England; (until 1975): Yankee Guide to the New England Countryside
Related titles: Online - full text ed.
Published by: Yankee Publishing, Inc., PO Box 520, Dublin, NH 03444. TEL 603-563-8111, FAX 603-563-8252, http://www.ypi.com. Eds. Mel Allen, Judson D. Hale Sr. Pub. Judson D. Hale Jr. Adv. contact Steve Hall. B&W page USD 22,050, color page USD 27,437; trim 10.81 x 8.38. Circ: 230,000 (paid).

910.91 USA
YELLOWSTONE JOURNAL; an independent newspaper dedicated to Yellowstone. Text in English. irreg.
Media: Online - full text.
Address: PO Box 1099, Lander, WY 82520. Ed. Shelli Johnson.

910.91 USA
YELLOWSTONE SCIENCE. Text in English. q. **Document type:** *Journal, Consumer.* **Description:** Covers natural and cultural resources related to Yellowstone.
Indexed: CA, Z01.
Published by: U.S. Department of the Interior, National Park Service, Yellowstone National Park, P O Box 168, Yellowstone National Park, WY 82190.

YINSHI NAN NU/EAT & TRAVEL WEEKLY. *see* HOTELS AND RESTAURANTS

910.91 USA
YORK COUNTY VISITORS GUIDE. Text in English. a. free. adv. **Document type:** *Magazine, Consumer.*
Published by: York County Convention and Visitors Bureau, 155 W Market St, York, PA 17401. TEL 888-858-9675, info@yorkpa.org, http://www.yorkpa.org/. adv.: color page USD 8,250. Circ: 200,000 (free).

647.94 GBR
YOUTH HOSTELS ASSOCIATION (ENGLAND AND WALES) ACCOMMODATION GUIDE. Text in English. 1931. a. free to members (effective 2009). charts; illus. back issues avail. **Document type:** *Bulletin, Consumer.* **Description:** Informs travelers and tourists in England and Wales about youth hostel accommodations available to them.
Former titles (until 1989): Youth Hostels Association (England and Wales) Guide; Youth Hostels Association (England and Wales) Handbook
Related titles: CD-ROM ed.
Published by: Youth Hostels Association (England and Wales), Trevelyan House, Dimple Rd, Matlock, Derbys DE4 3YH, United Kingdom. TEL 44-1629-592600, FAX 44-1629-592702, customerservices@yha.org.uk, http://www.yha.org.uk.

649 NLD ISSN 1025-0433
YOUTH TRAVEL INTERNATIONAL. Variant title: Y T I. Text in English. 1992. s-a. adv. **Document type:** *Magazine, Consumer.*
Related titles: Online - full text ed.
Indexed: H&TI, H06, T02.
Published by: World Youth Student & Educational Travel Confederation, Keizersgracht 174-176, Amsterdam, 1016 DW, Netherlands. TEL 31-20-4212800, FAX 31-20-4212810, info@wysetc.org, http://www.wysetc.org. Ed. Stephanie Cooper. adv.: page EUR 1,550; 210 x 297.

914.37 HRV
ZAGREB IN YOUR POCKET. Text in English. 5/yr. USD 5 newsstand/cover (effective 2002). adv. **Document type:** *Magazine, Consumer.*
Address: Draskoviceva 66, Zagreb, 10000, Croatia. TEL 385-1-4923924.

338.4 NLD
ZAKENREIS MAGAZINE; Business travel magazine for the Benelux. Text in Dutch. 1967. 10/yr. EUR 35 (effective 2008). adv. bk.rev. **Document type:** *Journal, Trade.* **Description:** Covers news and concerns affecting the business travel sector.
Incorporates: Reisinfo Express (1383-2328); Former titles: Onafhankelijk Zakenreis Magazine (1383-231X); (until 1994): Zakenreis (1381-7086)
Related titles: ◆ Supplement(s): Reisinfo Express. ISSN 1383-2328.
Published by: Disque '67 B.V., Minervaplein 22-3, Amsterdam, 1077 TR, Netherlands. TEL 33-20-6711142, FAX 33-20-6721899.

338.479 DEU ISSN 1867-9501
▼ **ZEITSCHRIFT FUER TOURISMUSWISSENSCHAFT.** Text in German. 2009. s-a. EUR 48 to individuals; EUR 62 to libraries; EUR 35 to students; EUR 34 newsstand/cover (effective 2011). **Document type:** *Journal, Trade.*
Indexed: CABA, LT.
Published by: Lucius und Lucius Verlagsgesellschaft mbH, Gerokstr 51, Stuttgart, 70184, Germany. TEL 49-711-242060, FAX 49-711-242088, lucius@luciusverlag.com, http://www.luciusverlag.com.

910.91 DEU
ZELTFORUM - GOETTINGER SCHRIFTEN ZU LANDSCHAFTSINTERPRETATION. Text in German. 2004. irreg., latest vol.5, 2010. price varies. **Document type:** *Monographic series, Academic/Scholarly.*
Published by: Universitaetsverlag Goettingen, Platz der Goettinger Sieben 1, Goettingen, 37073, Germany. TEL 49-551-395243, FAX 49-551-3922457, pabst@sub.uni-goettingen.de.

338.4791 CHN
ZHONGGUO LUYOU BAO/CHINA TOURISM NEWS. Text in Chinese. 1979. 3/w. USD 100.80 (effective 2009). adv. **Document type:** *Newspaper, Consumer.* **Description:** Provides information on tourism spots in China and the world, covering the latest trends in China's tourism market and the tourism industry in general.
Formerly: Luyou Bao
Published by: Zhongguo Luyou Xiehui, 9, Jianguomen Nei Dajiejia, Beijing, 100740, China. TEL 86-10-65201452, cta@cnta.gov.cn, http://www.chinata.com.cn/. Circ: 160,000. **Dist. by:** China International Book Trading Corp, 35 Chegongzhuang Xilu, Haidian District, PO Box 399, Beijing 100044, China. TEL 86-10-68412045, FAX 86-10-68412023, cibtc@mail.cibtc.com.cn, http://www.cibtc.com.cn.

915.1 CHN ISSN 1005-331X
ZHONGGUO LUYOU ZAZHI/CHINA TOURISM. Text in Chinese. 1990. m. **Document type:** *Journal, Academic/Scholarly.*
Formerly (until 1993): Zhongguo Luyou Huakan/China Tourism Pictorial (1002-7017)
Related titles: Online - full text ed.
—East View.
Address: Jianguomen Nei, 8, Dajie Jia, Zhongliang Guangchang B-Ceng 145.146-Shi, Beijing, 100740, China.

614.86 387.7 CHN ISSN 1001-2079
ZHONGGUO MINHANG BAO/CIVIL AVIATION ADMINISTRATION OF CHINA. JOURNAL. Text in Chinese. 1989. bi-m. CNY 62.40. adv. **Document type:** *Newspaper.* **Description:** In-house publication of CAAC.
Published by: Zhongguo Minhang Baoshe, 155 Dongsi Xidajie, Beijing, 100710, China. TEL 86-10-4031776, FAX 86-10-4031776. Ed. Zhang Shusheng. Adv. contact Ren Joan. Circ: 100,000.

ZHONGGUO XINAN/SOUTHWEST CHINA. *see* BUSINESS AND ECONOMICS

916 ZWE ISSN 1996-3874
ZIMBABWEAN TRAVEL; the ultimate guide to exciting holiday experiences exclusive to Southern Africa. Text in English. 2003. m.
Published by: (Zimbabwe Tourism Authority), Zimbabwe Newspapers Group Ltd., Herald House, George Silikunda Ave, 2nd St, PO Box 55, Harare, Zimbabwe. TEL 263-4-708296, FAX 263-4-702400, http://www.zimpapers.co.zw.

910.91 ROM
ZIUA TURISTICA. Text in Romanian. w. adv. **Document type:** *Magazine, Trade.*
Published by: Omega Press Investment, Str. Ion Campineanu nr. 4, sector 1, Bucharest, Romania. TEL 40-21-3111864, FAX 40-21-3103119. Ed. Marian Constantinescu. adv.: B&W page USD 1,000, color page USD 1,650; 250 x 350.

338.4791 CHN
ZUNYI LUYOU ZAZHI. Text in Chinese. bi-m. **Document type:** *Magazine, Consumer.*
Related titles: Online - full text ed.
Published by: (Zunyi Ribaoshe/Zunyi Daily Group), Zunyi Luyou Xinxi Zazhi, 3/F, Baoye Bldg., #8, Aomen Rd, Huichuan District, Zunyi, Guizhou 563000, China. TEL 86-852-8716655.

910.202 688 CHE
ZURICH GUIDE. Text in English, French, German. 1981. m. adv. back issues avail. **Document type:** *Magazine, Consumer.*
Former titles: Shopping and Tourist Guide Zurich; Shopping Guide Zurich
Published by: Promotion Verlag AG, Industriestr 6, Grueningen, 8627, Switzerland. TEL 41-43-8338060, FAX 41-43-8338044, promotionverlag@ieb.ch, http://www.promotionverlag.ch. Ed., Adv. contact Esther Schefold. page CHF 2,010; trim 134 x 193. Circ: 27,000 (controlled).

910.202 GRC
2BOARD; the official Athens airport magazine. Text in English, Greek. 2008. q. free (effective 2011). adv. **Document type:** *Magazine, Consumer.*
Published by: Liberis Publications S.A./Ekdoseon Lymperi A.E., Ioannou Metaxa 80, Karelas, Koropi 19400, Greece. TEL 30-210-6688000, FAX 30-210-6688300, info@liberis.gr, http://www.liberis.gr. Ed. Petros Bourovilis. Adv. contact Eirini Stathatou. Circ: 160,000 (controlled).

910.2 TWN ISSN 1818-6661
7-WATCH. Text in Chinese. 2000. m. **Document type:** *Magazine, Consumer.*
Published by: Huashe Wenhua Shiye Gufen Youxian Gongsi/Interculture Custom Media, Sec.2, no.51, 15/F, Chilung Rd., Taipei, 110, Taiwan. TEL 886-2-27328899.

910.91 USA ISSN 1525-2930
21ST CENTURY ADVENTURES. Text in English. 1995. m. **Document type:** *Magazine, Consumer.*
Media: Online - full content.
Published by: 21st Century Adventures, Inc., 265 Red Maple Dr, Hampton, GA 30228. TEL 770-234-5861, editorial@21stCenturyAdventures.com, http://www.21stCenturyAdventures.com. Ed. Jennifer Madsen-Tenney.

910.91 USA ISSN 1558-5921
HQ745
100 BEST U.S. WEDDING DESTINATIONS. Text in English. 2006. biennial. USD 18.95 per issue (effective 2008). **Document type:** *Guide, Consumer.*
Published by: The Globe Pequot Press, Insiders' Guide (Subsidiary of: The Globe Pequot Press, Inc.), PO Box 480, Guilford, CT 06437. TEL 203-458-4500, 888-249-7586, FAX 800-820-2329, info@globepequot.com, http://www.globepequot.com/globepequot/index.cfm?fuseaction=customer.welcome. Ed. Kathryn Gabriel Loving.

338.4791 USA
944. Text in English. m. USD 25; USD 4.99 newsstand/cover domestic; USD 6.99 newsstand/cover in Canada (effective 2007). **Document type:** *Magazine, Consumer.*
Published by: 944 Magazine, 3070 Post Rd, Las Vegas, NV 89118. TEL 702-386-6944, FAX 702-384-2944, info@944.com. Ed. Stephanie Henry.

TRAVEL AND TOURISM—Abstracting, Bibliographies, Statistics

338.4021 AUS
AUSTRALIA. BUREAU OF STATISTICS. AUSTRALIAN NATIONAL ACCOUNTS: TOURISM SATELLITE ACCOUNT (ONLINE). Text in English. 1998. a. free (effective 2009). back issues avail. **Document type:** *Government.* **Description:** Presents the key results of the tourism satellite account.
Formerly: Australia. Bureau of Statistics. Australian National Accounts: Tourism Satellite Account (Print) (1446-6066)
Media: Online - full text.
Published by: Australian Bureau of Statistics, Locked Bag 10, Belconnen, ACT 2616, Australia. TEL 61-2-92684909, 61-2-62527037, 300-135-070, FAX 61-2-62528103, client.services@abs.gov.au.

310.021 AUS
AUSTRALIA. BUREAU OF STATISTICS. DIRECTORY OF TOURISM STATISTICS (ONLINE). Text in English. 1991. irreg., latest 2000. free (effective 2009). **Document type:** *Directory, Government.* **Description:** Contains comprehensive information on sources of tourism statistics.
Formerly (until 2000): Australia. Bureau of Statistics. Directory of Tourism Statistics (Print) (1036-2606)
Media: Online - full text.
Published by: Australian Bureau of Statistics, Locked Bag 10, Belconnen, ACT 2616, Australia. TEL 61-2-62527037, FAX 61-2-92684654, client.services@abs.gov.au.

AUSTRALIA. BUREAU OF STATISTICS. NEW SOUTH WALES OFFICE. TOURIST ACCOMMODATION, SMALL AREA DATA, NEW SOUTH WALES (ONLINE). *see* HOTELS AND RESTAURANTS—Abstracting, Bibliographies, Statistics

AUSTRALIA. BUREAU OF STATISTICS. NORTHERN TERRITORY OFFICE. TOURIST ACCOMMODATION, SMALL AREA DATA, NORTHERN TERRITORY (ONLINE). *see* HOTELS AND RESTAURANTS—Abstracting, Bibliographies, Statistics

338.4021 AUS
AUSTRALIA. BUREAU OF STATISTICS. ORIGIN OF GUESTS, AUSTRALIA (ONLINE). Text in English. 1994. irreg., latest 1995. free (effective 2009). **Document type:** *Government.* **Description:** provides data for states and territories and for a limited number of geographic regions. Data presented were derived from an ad hoc survey and relate to the hotel, motel and guest house segment of the quarterly Survey of tourist accommodation.
Formerly: Australia. Bureau of Statistics. Origin of Guests, Australia (Print)
Media: Online - full text.
Published by: Australian Bureau of Statistics, Locked Bag 10, Belconnen, ACT 2616, Australia. TEL 61-2-92684909, 300-135-070, FAX 61-2-92684654, client.services@abs.gov.au.

310 AUS
AUSTRALIA. BUREAU OF STATISTICS. SOUTH AUSTRALIAN OFFICE. TOURIST ACCOMMODATION, SMALL AREA DATA, SOUTH AUSTRALIA (ONLINE). Text in English. 1975. q. free (effective 2009). back issues avail. **Document type:** *Government.* **Description:** Contains information about hotels, motels, caravan parks, holiday flats and units, and visitor hostels, occupancy rates and takings from accommodation for each month by type of establishment.
Former titles (until 2005): Australia. Bureau of Statistics. South Australian Office. Tourist Accommodation, Small Area Data, South Australia (Print); (until 1998): Australia. Bureau of Statistics. South Australian Office. Tourist Accommodation, South Australia (0157-3578); Accommodation Survey, South Australia
Media: Online - full text.
Published by: Australian Bureau of Statistics, South Australian Office, GPO Box 2272, Adelaide, SA 5001, Australia. TEL 61-2-92684909, 300-135-070, client.services@abs.gov.au, http://www.abs.gov.au.

AUSTRALIA. BUREAU OF STATISTICS. TASMANIAN OFFICE. TOURIST ACCOMMODATION, SMALL AREA DATA, TASMANIA. *see* HOTELS AND RESTAURANTS—Abstracting, Bibliographies, Statistics

910.021 AUS
AUSTRALIA. BUREAU OF STATISTICS. TOURISM INDICATORS, AUSTRALIA (ONLINE). Text in English. 1993. q. free (effective 2009). back issues avail. **Document type:** *Government.* **Description:** Contains analytical articles on issues relating to tourism.
Formerly (until 2002): Australia. Bureau of Statistics. Tourism Indicators, Australia (Print) (1321-4144); Which superseded (in 1993): Australia. Bureau of Statistics. Overseas Arrivals and Departures, Australia (1031-0509); Which was formerly (until 1978): Australia. Bureau of Statistics. Overseas Arrivals and Departures
Media: Online - full text.
Published by: Australian Bureau of Statistics, Locked Bag 10, Belconnen, ACT 2616, Australia. TEL 61-2-92684909, 61-2-62527037, 300-135-070, FAX 61-2-62528103, client.services@abs.gov.au.

338.4021 AUS
AUSTRALIA. BUREAU OF STATISTICS. TOURISM MARKETING EXPENDITURE, AUSTRALIA. Text in English. 1995. biennial. back issues avail. **Document type:** *Government.* **Description:** Contains information on the amount spent by Australian private sector tourism-related businesses on marketing Australian tourism to domestic and overseas travellers.
Formerly (until 1997): Australia. Bureau of Statistics. Overseas Tourism Marketing Expenditure, Australia (1329-8216)
Published by: Australian Bureau of Statistics, Locked Bag 10, Belconnen, ACT 2616, Australia. TEL 61-2-92684909, 61-2-62527037, 300-135-070, FAX 61-2-62528103, client.services@abs.gov.au.

AUSTRALIA. BUREAU OF STATISTICS. TOURIST ACCOMMODATION, AUSTRALIA (ONLINE). *see* HOTELS AND RESTAURANTS—Abstracting, Bibliographies, Statistics

AUSTRALIA. BUREAU OF STATISTICS. TOURIST ACCOMMODATION, SMALL AREA DATA, WESTERN AUSTRALIA (ONLINE). *see* HOTELS AND RESTAURANTS—Abstracting, Bibliographies, Statistics

338.4021 AUS
AUSTRALIA. BUREAU OF STATISTICS. TRAVEL AGENCY SERVICES, AUSTRALIA (ONLINE). Text in English. 1998. irreg. free (effective 2009). back issues avail. **Document type:** *Government.* **Description:** Presents results, in respect of the financial year, from an Australian Bureau of Statistics (ABS) collection of businesses whose main activity was the provision of travel agency services.
Former titles: Australia. Bureau of Statistics. Travel Agency Services, Australia (Print); (until 2004): Australia. Bureau of Statistics. Travel Agency Services Industry, Australia
Media: Online - full text.
Published by: Australian Bureau of Statistics, Locked Bag 10, Belconnen, ACT 2616, Australia. TEL 61-2-92684909, 61-2-62527037, 300-135-070, FAX 61-2-62528103, client.services@abs.gov.au.

AUSTRALIA. BUREAU OF STATISTICS. VICTORIAN OFFICE. TOURIST ACCOMMODATION, SMALL AREA DATA, VICTORIA. *see* HOTELS AND RESTAURANTS—Abstracting, Bibliographies, Statistics

914 AUT
AUSTRIA. WIRTSCHAFTSKAMMER OESTERREICH. TOURISMUS IN ZAHLEN; Oesterreichische und internationale Fremdenverkehrs- und Wirtschaftsdaten. Text in German. 1965. a. free. illus.; stat. **Document type:** *Government.*
Former titles: Austria. Bundeskammer der Gewerblichen Wirtschaft. Fremdenverkehr in Zahlen; Austria. Bundeskammer der Gewerblichen Wirtschaft. Statistik und Dokumentation. Information (0039-0585)
Published by: Wirtschaftskammer Oesterreich, Sektion Tourismus, Wiedner Hauptstrasse 63, Vienna, W 1045, Austria. Circ: 350.

319 BRB
BARBADOS. STATISTICAL SERVICE. DIGEST OF TOURISM STATISTICS. Text in English. a. BBD 5. **Document type:** *Government.* **Description:** Figures on arrivals, market analysis, accomodation and expenditure.
Published by: Statistical Service, National Insurance Bldg. 3rd Fl., Fairchild St., Bridgetown, Barbados. Circ: 250.

338.4021 ESP ISSN 1728-9262
BAROMETRE OMT DU TOURISME MONDIAL. (Organisation Mondiale du Tourisme) Text in French. 2003. 3/yr. **Document type:** *Bulletin, Trade.*
Related titles: Online - full text ed.; ◆ Spanish ed.: O M T. Barometro del Turismo Mundial. ISSN 1728-9254; ◆ English ed.: W T O World Tourism Barometer. ISSN 1728-9246.
—Ingenta. **CCC.**
Published by: World Tourism Organization, Capitan Haya 42, Madrid, 28020, Spain. TEL 34-91-5678100, FAX 34-91-5713733, omt@unwto.org, http://www.unwto.org.

338.4791 DEU ISSN 1430-323X
BAYERISCHES LANDESAMT FUER STATISTIK UND DATENVERARBEITUNG. STATISTISCHE BERICHTE G: HANDEL, TOURISMUS, GASTGEWERBE. Text in German. 1969. irreg. **Document type:** *Government.*
Formerly (until 1982): Bayerisches Statistisches Landesamt. Statistische Berichte G (1430-306X)
Published by: Bayerisches Landesamt fuer Statistik und Datenverarbeitung, Neuhauser Str 8, Munich, 80331, Germany. TEL 49-89-2119205, FAX 49-89-2119410, poststelle@statistik.bayern.de, http://www.statistik.bayern.de.

910.21 BEL ISSN 0067-5547
BELGIUM. INSTITUT NATIONAL DE STATISTIQUE. STATISTIQUE DU TOURISME ET DE L'HOTELLERIE. Key Title: Statistique du Tourisme et de l'Hotellerie. Text in French. 1967. a. charts. **Document type:** *Government.*

TU

Related titles: ◆ Dutch ed.: Belgium. Nationaal Instituut voor de Statistiek. Statistiek van het Toerisme en het Hotelwezen. ISSN 0773-3097.
Published by: Institut National de Statistique/Nationaal Instituut voor de Statistiek (Subsidiary of: Ministere des Affaires Economiques), Rue de Louvain 44, Brussels, 1000, Belgium. TEL 32-2-548-6211, FAX 32-2-548-6367.

910.21 BEL ISSN 0773-3097
BELGIUM. NATIONAAL INSTITUUT VOOR DE STATISTIEK. STATISTIEK VAN HET TOERISME EN HET HOTELWEZEN. Key Title: Statistiek van het Toerisme en het Hotelwezen. Text in Dutch. 1967. a. charts. back issues avail. **Document type:** *Government.*
Related titles: ◆ French ed.: Belgium. Institut National de Statistique. Statistique du Tourisme et de l'Hotellerie. ISSN 0067-5547.
Published by: Institut National de Statistique/Nationaal Instituut voor de Statistiek (Subsidiary of: Ministere des Affaires Economiques), Rue de Louvain 44, Brussels, 1000, Belgium. TEL 32-2-548-6211, FAX 32-2-548-6367.

016.959 SGP ISSN 0068-0176
Z3248.S5
BOOKS ABOUT SINGAPORE; a select bibliography. Text in Chinese, English. 1963. irreg., latest 1999. free. **Document type:** *Bibliography.*
Formerly: Books About Malaysia
Published by: National Library Board Singapore, 91 Stamford Rd, Singapore, 178896, Singapore. TEL 65-332-3255, 800-332 3188, FAX 65-332-3248, http://www.lib.gov.sg/index.html. Circ: 1,500.

916.8021 316.021 BWA ISSN 1013-5715
BOTSWANA. CENTRAL STATISTICS OFFICE. TOURIST STATISTICS. Text in English. 1974. a. BWP 5. charts. back issues avail. **Document type:** *Government.* **Description:** Provides information on travelers, length of stay and residence permit issues.
Related titles: E-mail ed.; Fax ed.
Published by: Central Statistics Office, c/o Government Statistician, Private Bag 0024, Gaborone, Botswana. TEL 267-31-352200, FAX 267-31-352201. Ed. G M Charumbira. Pub. J G Segwe. **Subscr. to:** Government Printer, Private Bag 0081, Gaborone, Botswana. TEL 267-353202, FAX 267-312001, http://www.gov.bw.

338.4791 AUS ISSN 1036-8965
C D M O T A. (Compact Disc Monitor of Tourism Activity) Text in English. 1993. a. **Document type:** *Government.*
Media: CD-ROM.
Published by: Australia. Public Affairs Department. Australian Tourist Commission, GPO Box 2721, Sydney, NSW 2011, Australia. corpaffairs@tourism.australia.com, http://www.tourism.australia.com.

910.021 CAN ISSN 1488-1721
CA1BS87C212
CANADA. STATISTICS CANADA. CANADIAN TRAVEL SURVEY. DOMESTIC TRAVEL/CANADA. STATISTIQUE CANADA. ENQUETE SUR LES VOYAGES DES CANADIENS. VOYAGES INTERIEURS. Text in English, French. 1997. a.
Related titles: Online - full content ed.: ISSN 1488-173X.
Published by: Statistics Canada/Statistique Canada, Communications Division, 3rd Fl, R H Coats Bldg, Ottawa, ON K1A 0A6, Canada. TEL 613-951-7277, FAX 613-951-1584, infostats@statcan.ca, http://www.statcan.gc.ca.

338.4791021 CAN ISSN 1704-8249
CANADA. STATISTICS CANADA. INTERNATIONAL TRAVEL. Text in English. 1949. a.
Supersedes in part (in 2000): Canada. Statistics Canada. International Travel, Travel Between Canada and Other Countries (0840-3139); Which was formerly (until 1986): Canada. Dominion Bureau of Statistics. Travel Between Canada and Other Countries (0317-6738)
Related titles: Online - full content ed.: ISSN 1499-7266. CAD 34.
Published by: (Statistics Canada, International Travel Section), Statistics Canada/Statistique Canada, Publications Sales and Services, Ottawa, ON K1A 0T6, Canada. TEL 613-951-8116, infostats@statcan.ca, http://www.statcan.gc.ca.

338.4 CAN ISSN 0705-5269
CANADA. STATISTICS CANADA. INTERNATIONAL TRAVEL, ADVANCE INFORMATION/CANADA. STATISTIQUE CANADA. VOYAGES INTERNATIONAUX, RENSEIGNEMENTS PRELIMINAIRES. Text in English, French. m. CAD 73 domestic; USD 73 foreign (effective 1999). **Document type:** *Government.* **Description:** Shows province of entry, transportation and country of residence of visitors as well as estimates of the travel account for the balance of payments both seasonally and not seasonally adjusted.
Formerly: Canada. Statistics Canada. United States Vehicles Entering Canada (0705-5277)
Related titles: Microform ed.: (from MML).
Published by: Statistics Canada, Operations and Integration Division (Subsidiary of: Statistics Canada/Statistique Canada), Circulation Management, 120 Parkdale Ave, Ottawa, ON K1A 0T6, Canada. TEL 613-951-7277, 800-267-6677, FAX 613-951-1584.

310.021 CAN ISSN 1207-3016
CANADA. STATISTICS CANADA. NATIONAL TOURISM INDICATORS. HISTORICAL ESTIMATES. Text in English. 1995. q.
Published by: Statistics Canada, National Accounts and Environment Division (Subsidiary of: Statistics Canada/Statistique Canada), Rm 1500, Main Building, Holland Ave, Ottawa, ON K1A 0T6, Canada.

338.4791021 CAN ISSN 1205-8467
CA1BS13C009
CANADA. STATISTICS CANADA. NATIONAL TOURISM INDICATORS. QUARTERLY ESTIMATES/CANADA. STATISTIQUE CANADA. INDICATEURS NATIONAUX DU TOURISME. ESTIMATIONS TRIMESTRIELLES. Text in English, French. 1996. q. free (effective 2004).
Related titles: Online - full content ed.: ISSN 1492-5133.
Published by: Statistics Canada/Statistique Canada, Publications Sales and Services, Ottawa, ON K1A 0T6, Canada. TEL 613-951-8116, infostats@statcan.gc.ca, http://www.statcan.gc.ca. **Co-sponsor:** Canadian Tourism Commission/Commission Canadienne du Tourisme.

917.1 CAN ISSN 0713-2840
CANADA. STATISTICS CANADA. TRAVEL-LOG. Text in English. 1982. q. CAD 32 domestic (effective 1999); USD 32 foreign. **Document type:** *Government.* **Description:** Presents a diverse range of tourism topics in an easy-to-read format drawing together data from several tourism-related surveys conducted by Statistics Canada.
Related titles: Online - full text ed.
Indexed: H&TI.
Published by: Statistics Canada, Operations and Integration Division (Subsidiary of: Statistics Canada/Statistique Canada), Circulation Management, 120 Parkdale Ave, Ottawa, ON K1A 0T6, Canada. TEL 613-951-7277, 800-267-6677, FAX 613-951-1584.

917.2 USA
CARIBBEAN TOURISM ORGANIZATION. STATISTICAL NEWS. Text in English. 1977. q. USD 200. **Document type:** *Journal, Trade.*
Formerly: Caribbean Tourism; Which superseded (in 1981): Caribbean Tourism Research Centre. Newsletter
Published by: Caribbean Tourism Organization, 80 Broad St, 32nd Fl, New York, NY 10004. TEL 212-635-9530, FAX 212-635-9511, http://www.onecaribbean.org. Circ: 2,000.

919.704 USA
CARIBBEAN TOURISM STATISTICAL REPORT. Text in English. 1978. a. USD 200. **Description:** Source of key statistics and overview of tourism trends in the Caribbean.
Formerly: Caribbean Tourism Statistics
Published by: Caribbean Tourism Organization, 80 Broad St, 32nd Fl, New York, NY 10004. TEL 212-635-9530, FAX 212-635-9511, http://www.onecaribbean.org. Circ: 1,000.

910.09 LKA
CEYLON TOURIST BOARD. ANNUAL STATISTICAL REPORT. Text in English. 1968. a. USD 10.
Published by: (Research & International Affairs), Ceylon Tourist Board, P O Box 1504, Colombo, 3, Sri Lanka. TEL 437056, FAX 440001. Circ: 500.

910.09 LKA
CEYLON TOURIST BOARD. MONTHLY BULLETIN ON THE PERFORMANCE OF THE TOURISM SECTOR. Text in English. m. USD 20.
Published by: (Research & International Affairs), Ceylon Tourist Board, P O Box 1504, Colombo, 3, Sri Lanka. TEL 437056, FAX 440001.

918.3 318 CHL
CHILE. INSTITUTO NACIONAL DE ESTADISTICAS. ANUARIO DE TURISMO; estadisticas de turismo y movimiento internacional de viajeros. Text in Spanish. 1965-1971; resumed. a. CLP 1,200 domestic; USD 8.20 in United States; USD 9.40 elsewhere (effective 1999). stat. **Document type:** *Government.*
Media: Duplicated (not offset).
Published by: Instituto Nacional de Estadisticas, Casilla 498, Correo 3, Ave. Bulnes, 418, Santiago, Chile. TEL 56-2-6991441, FAX 56-2-6712169.

910 016 ESP ISSN 1013-1744
COMPENDIUM OF TOURISM STATISTICS. Text in English. 1959. a., latest 2001. stat. 250 p./no.; **Document type:** *Yearbook, Trade.* **Description:** Provides tourism statistical information on 182 countries and territories.
Former titles: Tourism Compendium; (until 1976): Tourist Bibliography (0082-5468)
Related titles: French ed.: Compendium de Statistiques du Tourisme. ISSN 1014-7241.
Indexed: IIS.
—CCC.
Published by: World Tourism Organization, Capitan Haya 42, Madrid, 28020, Spain. TEL 34-91-5678100, FAX 34-91-5713733, omt@unwto.org, http://www.unwto.org.

790.1 GBR ISSN 0308-3748
COUNTRYSIDE RECREATION RESEARCH ADVISORY GROUP. ABSTRACTS. Text in English. 1976. m. **Document type:** *Abstract/Index.*
—BLDSC (3482.070000). CCC.
Published by: Countryside Recreation Network, c/o Magali Fleurot, Sheffield Hallam University, Unit 1, Sheffield Science Park. Howard St, Sheffield, S1 2LX, United Kingdom. TEL 44-114-2254494, FAX 44-144-2256319, CRN@shu.ac.uk, http://www.countrysiderecreation.org.uk.

301.32 CYP ISSN 0253-8709
CYPRUS. DEPARTMENT OF STATISTICS AND RESEARCH. TOURISM, MIGRATION AND TRAVEL STATISTICS. Text in English, Greek. 1973. a. **Document type:** *Government.* **Description:** Tracks the movements of travelers, departures and returns of permanent residents, and emigrants and immigrants.
Published by: Ministry of Finance, Department of Statistics and Research, 13 Andreas Araouzos St, Nicosia, 1444, Cyprus. TEL 357-2-309318, FAX 357-2-374830.

051 USA
D F W PEOPLE - THE AIRPORT NEWSPAPER. (Dallas - Fort Worth) Text in English. 1983. w. (Thu.). free airport, airline & aviation related employees; USD 75 (effective 2005). **Document type:** *Newspaper, Trade.*
Contact Owner: Wood Publications, Inc. Circ: 45,000 (paid and free).

380.509489 DNK ISSN 1601-0981
DENMARK. DANMARKS STATISTIK. TRANSPORT (ONLINE). Text in Danish. 200?. irreg. **Document type:** *Government.*
Former titles (until 2007): Denmark. Danmarks Statistik. Transport. (Print) (1399-0683); (until 1999): Denmark. Danmarks Statistik. Samfaerdsel og Turisme (0108-5484); Supersedes in part (in 1983): Statistiske Efterretninger A (0105-306X); (in 1983): Statistiske Efterretninger B (0105-3078); Both of which superseded in part (1909-1976): Statistiske Efterretninger (0039-0674)
Media: Online - full content. **Related titles:** ◆ Series of: Denmark. Danmarks Statistik. Statistiske Efterretninger. Indhold (Online).
Published by: Danmarks Statistik/Statistics Denmark, Sejroegade 11, Copenhagen OE, 2100, Denmark. TEL 45-39-173917, FAX 45-39-173939, dst@dst.dk.

997 330 DMA
DOMINICA. MINISTRY OF FINANCE. CENTRAL STATISTICAL OFFICE. ANNUAL TOURISM STATISTICS. Text in English. a. USD 13.50. **Document type:** *Government.*
Published by: Ministry of Finance, Central Statistical Office, Kennedy Ave., Roseau, Dominica. Ed. Michael Murphy.

997 DMA
DOMINICA. MINISTRY OF FINANCE. CENTRAL STATISTICAL OFFICE. QUARTERLY TRAVEL REPORT. Text in English. 1978. q. USD 5.58. **Document type:** *Government.*
Formerly: Dominica. Ministry of Finance. Statistical Division. Quarterly Bulletin of Tourism Statistics
Published by: Ministry of Finance, Central Statistical Office, Kennedy Ave., Roseau, Dominica. Ed. Michael Murphy.

914.69 PRT ISSN 0377-2306
G155.P75
ESTATISTICAS DO TURISMO. Text in Portuguese. 1969. a. EUR 17 (effective 2005). **Document type:** *Government.* **Description:** Provides statistical data on hotels and tourism.
Formerly: Portugal. Instituto Nacional de Estatistica. Estatisticas do Turismo
Published by: Instituto Nacional de Estatistica, Av Antonio Jose de Almeida 2, Lisbon, 1000-043, Portugal. TEL 351-21-8426100, FAX 351-21-8426380, ine@ine.pt, http://www.ine.pt.

319 FJI
FIJI. BUREAU OF STATISTICS. TOURISM AND MIGRATION STATISTICS. Text in English. 1973. a., latest 1995-1996. USD 5 (effective 2000 - 2001). **Document type:** *Government.*
Supersedes: Statistical Report on Tourism in Fiji
Published by: Bureau of Statistics, c/o Librarian, Govt. Bldg. 5, PO Box 2221, Suva, Fiji. TEL 679-315-822, FAX 679-303-656.

338.421 FIN ISSN 1238-7169
FINLAND. TILASTOKESKUS. MATKAILUTILASTO (KUUKAUSITILASTO)/FINLAND. STATISTICS FINLAND. TOURISM STATISTICS (MONTHLY). Text in English, Finnish. 1986. m. EUR 66 (effective 2008). stat. **Document type:** *Magazine, Government.*
Formerly (until 1996): Majoitustilasto (0785-6199)
Related titles: Online - full text ed.: ISSN 1795-3693.
Published by: Tilastokeskus/Statistics Finland, Tyopajakatu 13, Statistics Finland, Helsinki, 00022, Finland. TEL 358-9-17341, FAX 358-9-17342279, http://www.stat.fi.

338.4201 FIN ISSN 1238-7150
FINLAND. TILASTOKESKUS. MATKAILUTILASTO (VUOSITILASTO)/ FINLAND. STATISTICS FINLAND. TOURISM STATISTICS (ANNUAL)/FINLAND. STATISTIKCENTRALEN. TURISMSTATISTIK. Text in English, Finnish. 1989. a. EUR 43 (effective 2008). **Document type:** *Government.*
Formerly (until 1996): Finland. Tilastokeskus. Majoitustilasto: Vuositilasto (0785-6202)
Related titles: Online - full text ed.; ◆ Series of: Finland. Tilastokeskus. Suomen Virallinen Tilasto. ISSN 1795-5165.
Published by: Tilastokeskus/Statistics Finland, Tyopajakatu 13, Statistics Finland, Helsinki, 00022, Finland. TEL 358-9-17341, FAX 358-9-17342279, http://www.stat.fi.

338.4201 FIN ISSN 1239-7342
FINLAND. TILASTOKESKUS. SUOMALAISTEN MATKAILU/FINLAND. STATISTICS FINLAND. FINNISH TRAVEL/FINLAND. TRAFIKCENTRALEN. FINLAENDARNAS RESOR. Text in English, Finnish, Swedish. 1992. a. EUR 37 (effective 2008). **Document type:** *Government.*
Formerly (until 1996): Finland. Tilastokeskus. Suomalaisten Matkat
Related titles: Online - full text ed.; ◆ Series of: Finland. Tilastokeskus. Suomen Virallinen Tilasto. ISSN 1795-5165.
Published by: Tilastokeskus/Statistics Finland, Tyopajakatu 13, Statistics Finland, Helsinki, 00022, Finland. TEL 358-9-17341, FAX 358-9-17342279, http://www.stat.fi.

FINLAND. TILASTOKESKUS. TIELIIKENNEONNETTOMUUDET/ FINLAND. STATISTICS FINLAND. ROAD ACCIDENTS IN FINLAND/FINLAND. STATISTIKCENTRALEN. VAEGTRAFIKOLYKOR. *see* TRANSPORTATION—Abstracting, Bibliographies, Statistics

338.4201 FIN ISSN 0786-1877
HE5675.3
FINLAND. TILASTOKESKUS. TIELIIKENTEEN TAVARANKULJETUSTILASTO/FINLAND. STATISTICS FINLAND. ROAD FREIGHT TRANSPORT/FINLAND. STATISTIKCENTRALEN. VARUTRANSPORTER MED LASTBIL. Text in English, Finnish, Swedish. 1979. a. EUR 37 (effective 2008). **Document type:** *Government.*
Related titles: Online - full text ed.; ◆ Series of: Finland. Tilastokeskus. Suomen Virallinen Tilasto. ISSN 1795-5165.
Published by: Tilastokeskus/Statistics Finland, Tyopajakatu 13, Statistics Finland, Helsinki, 00022, Finland. TEL 358-9-17341, FAX 358-9-17342279, http://www.stat.fi.

914.94 CHE
FREMDENVERKEHRSBILANZ DER SCHWEIZ/BALANCE TOURISTIQUE DE LA SUISSE; Einnahmen und Ausgaben im internationaler Fremdenverkehr. Text in French, German. 1977. a. CHF 4 (effective 2001). **Document type:** *Government.*
Published by: Bundesamt fuer Statistik, Espace de l'Europe 10, Neuchatel, 2010, Switzerland. TEL 41-32-7136011, FAX 41-32-7136012, information@bfs.admin.ch, http://www.admin.ch/bfs.

339 GMB
GAMBIA. CENTRAL STATISTICS DEPARTMENT. SUMMARY OF TOURIST STATISTICS. Text in English. m. GMD 12. **Document type:** *Government.*
Published by: Central Statistics Department, Wellington St., Banjul, Gambia.

338.4791021 910 GMB
GAMBIA. CENTRAL STATISTICS DEPARTMENT. TOURIST STATISTICS. Text in English. a. GMD 12. **Document type:** *Government.*
Published by: Central Statistics Department, Wellington St., Banjul, Gambia.

338.4 ISL ISSN 1024-0012
TX910.I2
GISTISKYRSLUR/TOURIST ACCOMMODATION. Text in Icelandic. 1994. a. USD 15 (effective 2001). back issues avail. **Document type:** *Yearbook, Government.*
Related titles: Online - full text ed.
Published by: Hagstofa Islands/Statistics Iceland, Iceland. TEL 354-560-9800, FAX 354-562-8865, hagstofa@hag.stjr.is, http://www.statice.is/stat/e-mail.htm. Ed. Rut Jonsdottir.

910.2 GRC ISSN 0256-3649
GREECE. NATIONAL STATISTICAL SERVICE. TOURIST STATISTICS. Text in English, Greek. 1981. irreg., latest 1996. back issues avail. **Document type:** *Government.* **Description:** Monitors tourism activity in Greece.

Published by: National Statistical Service of Greece, Statistical Information and Publications Division/Ethniki Statistiki Ypiresia tes Ellados, 14-16 Lykourgou St, Athens, 101 66, Greece. TEL 30-1-3289-397, FAX 30-1-3241-102, http://www.statistics.gr/Main_eng.asp, http://www.statistics.gr.

338.4 GRD
GRENADA. BOARD OF TOURISM. ANNUAL STATISTICAL REPORT. Text in English. a.
Published by: Board of Tourism, Carenage, St. George's, Grenada.

338.4 GRD
GRENADA. BOARD OF TOURISM. MONTHLY STATISTICAL REPORT. Text in English. m.
Published by: Board of Tourism, Carenage, St. George's, Grenada.

338.4 GRD
GRENADA. BOARD OF TOURISM. SEMI-ANNUAL STATISTICAL REVIEW. Text in English. s-a.
Published by: Board of Tourism, Carenage, St. George's, Grenada.

HOSPITALITY & TOURISM COMPLETE. *see* HOTELS AND RESTAURANTS—Abstracting, Bibliographies, Statistics

HOSPITALITY & TOURISM INDEX. *see* HOTELS AND RESTAURANTS—Abstracting, Bibliographies, Statistics

914.704 314 HUN ISSN 0230-4414
G155.H9
HUNGARY. KOZPONTI STATISZTIKAI HIVATAL. IDEGENFORGALMI EVKONYV. Text in Hungarian. a. HUF 408. stat. **Document type:** *Government.*
Supersedes: Idegenforgalmi Statisztika (0209-4819)
Indexed: RASB.
Published by: Kozponti Statisztikai Hivatal, Marketing Oszta'ly, Keleti Karoly utca 5-7, Budapest, 1024, Hungary. TEL 36-1-345-6000, FAX 36-1-345-6699. Circ: 800.

338.4 NZL ISSN 1179-7703
G155.N5
INTERNATIONAL VISITOR ARRIVALS TO NEW ZEALAND (ONLINE). Variant title: Tourism International Visitor Arrivals. Text in English. 1985. m. free (effective 2010). back issues avail. **Document type:** *Report, Government.*
Former titles (until 2010): International Visitor Arrivals to New Zealand (Print) (1175-8724); (until 1998): International Visitor Arrivals (1172-2762); (until 1992): Monthly Tourism Statistics (0114-2186); (until 1988): Tourism Statistics Monthly (0113-4264)
Published by: Statistics New Zealand/Te Tari Tatau, Statistics House, The Blvd, Harbour Quays, PO Box 2922, Wellington, 6140, New Zealand. TEL 64-4-9314600, FAX 64 4-9314035, info@stats.govt.nz.

338.4791 AUS ISSN 1447-8595
INTERNATIONAL VISITORS IN AUSTRALIA (ONLINE). Text in English. 1990. q. AUD 80. charts. back issues avail. **Document type:** *Government.* **Description:** Provides key data on international visitor behavior in Australia.
Media: Online - full text. **Related titles:** CD-ROM ed.; ◆ Print ed.: International Visitors in Australia. ISSN 1443-346X.
Published by: Australia. Public Affairs Department. Australian Tourist Commission, GPO Box 2721, Sydney, NSW 2011, Australia. TEL 61-2-93601111, FAX 61-2-93316469, corpaffairs@tourism.australia.com, http://www.tourism.australia.com.

338.4021 IRL ISSN 1393-5631
IRELAND. CENTRAL STATISTICS OFFICE. TOURISM AND TRAVEL. Text in English. 1990. q. charts; stat. **Document type:** *Government.* **Description:** Supplies estimated numbers and expenditures of visitors to Ireland.
Formerly (until 1997): Ireland. Central Statistics Office. Tourism and Travel Quarterly (0791-3656)
Related titles: Online - full text ed.
Published by: Ireland. Central Statistics Office/Eire, An Phriomh-Oifig Staidrimh, Skehard Rd, Cork, Ireland. TEL 353-21-4535000, FAX 353-21-4535555, information@cso.ie.

338.4021 IRL ISSN 0791-3443
IRELAND. CENTRAL STATISTICS OFFICE. TOURISM AND TRAVEL (YEAR). Text in English. 1987. a. charts; stat. **Document type:** *Government.*
Formerly: Ireland. Central Statistics Office. Estimated Numbers and Expenditures of Visitors to Ireland and Irish Visitors Abroad
Media: Duplicated (not offset). **Related titles:** Online - full text ed.
Published by: Ireland. Central Statistics Office/Eire, An Phriomh-Oifig Staidrimh, Skehard Rd, Cork, Ireland. TEL 353-21-4535000, FAX 353-21-4535555, information@cso.ie.

315 ISR ISSN 0333-6603
HE373.I75
ISRAEL. CENTRAL BUREAU OF STATISTICS. SURVEY OF TRAVELLING HABITS/SEQER HERG'LE N'SI'A. HELEQ A. Text in English, Hebrew. 1972. irreg., latest 1997. ILS 123. **Document type:** *Government.*
Published by: Central Bureau of Statistics/Ha-Lishka Ha-Merkazit L'Statistiqa, PO Box 13015, Jerusalem, 91130, Israel. TEL 972-2-6553364, FAX 972-2-6521340.

915.69 ISR ISSN 0333-6204
G155.I78
ISRAEL. CENTRAL BUREAU OF STATISTICS. TOURISM/TAYYARUT. Text in English, Hebrew. 1958. irreg., latest 2006. USD 30. **Document type:** *Government.*
Supersedes: Israel Tourist Statistics (0075-1405)
Published by: Central Bureau of Statistics/Ha-Lishka Ha-Merkazit L'Statistiqa, PO Box 13015, Jerusalem, 91130, Israel. TEL 972-2-6553364, FAX 972-2-6521340.

310 ISR ISSN 0334-2476
ISRAEL. CENTRAL BUREAU OF STATISTICS. TOURISM AND HOTEL SERVICES STATISTICS QUARTERLY/RIV'ON STATISTI L'TAYYARUT UL'SHERUTE HR'HH. Text in English, Hebrew. 1974. q. USD 30. **Document type:** *Government.* **Description:** Data on tourists and tourism services in Israel.
Published by: Central Bureau of Statistics/Ha-Lishka Ha-Merkazit L'Statistiqa, PO Box 13015, Jerusalem, 91130, Israel. TEL 972-2-6553364, FAX 972-2-6521340.

914.5 ITA ISSN 1122-7575
ITALY. ISTITUTO NAZIONALE DI STATISTICA. STATISTICHE DEL TURISMO. Text in Italian. 1957. a. **Document type:** *Government.*
Supersedes in part (in 1985): Italy. Istituto Centrale di Statistica. Annuario Statistico del Commercio Interno e del Turismo (1122-7559); Which was formerly (until 1976): Italy. Istituto Centrale di Statistica. Annuario Statistico del Commercio Interno (0075-1782)
Published by: Istituto Nazionale di Statistica (I S T A T), Via Cesare Balbo 16, Rome, 00184, Italy. TEL 39-06-46731, http://www.istat.it.

338.4 KEN ISSN 0377-1385
G155.K4
KENYA. CENTRAL BUREAU OF STATISTICS. MIGRATION AND TOURISM STATISTICS. Text in English. 1971. irreg., latest 1978. stat. **Document type:** *Government.*
Published by: Ministry of Finance and Planning, Central Bureau of Statistics, PO Box 30266, Nairobi, Kenya. **Subscr. to:** Government Press, Haile Selaissie Ave., PO Box 30128, Nairobi, Kenya. TEL 254-2-334075.

016.91 GBR ISSN 0261-1392
GV191.6
LEISURE, RECREATION AND TOURISM ABSTRACTS. Text in English. 1976. m. subscr. includes LeisureTourism. adv. illus. Index. **Document type:** *Abstract/Index.* **Description:** Presents information on the many aspects of leisure for those interested in research and strategic development of leisure, recreation, sport, and tourism and hospitality activities, facilities, products, and services.
Formerly (until 1981): Rural Recreation and Tourism Abstracts (0308-0137)
Related titles: Online - full text ed.: Leisure Tourism Database.
Indexed: RASB.
—BLDSC (5182.267000). **CCC.**
Published by: CABI (Subsidiary of: CAB International), Nosworthy Way, Wallingford, Oxfordshire OX10 8DE, United Kingdom. TEL 44-1491-832111, FAX 44-1491-829292, enquiries@cabi.org.

910.4 MAC
MACAO. DIRECCAO DOS SERVICOS DE ESTATISTICA E CENSOS. ESTATISTICAS DO TURISMO/MACAO. CENSUS AND STATISTICS DEPARTMENT. TOURISM STATISTICS. Text in English, Chinese, Portuguese. 1986. a. free. **Document type:** *Government.* **Description:** Presents data on visitors arrivals, number of hotels and other accommodation establishments, room occupancy rates.
Published by: Direccao dos Servicos de Estatistica e Censos, Alameda Dr Carlos d'Assumcao 411-417, Macao, Macau. TEL 853-3995311, FAX 853-607825, info@dsec.gov.mo, http://www.dsec.gov.mo.

910.4 MAC
MACAO. DIRECCAO DOS SERVICOS DE ESTATISTICA E CENSOS. INDICADORES DO TURISMO/MACAO. CENSUS AND STATISTICS DEPARTMENT. TOURISM INDICATORS. Text in Chinese, English, Portuguese. 1988. m. free. **Document type:** *Government.* **Description:** Presents monthly data on visitor arrivals and occupancy rates among hotels and other establishments of accomodation.
Formerly: Macao. Direccao dos Servicos de Estatistica e Censos. Estatisticas do Turismo - Tourism Statistics
Published by: Direccao dos Servicos de Estatistica e Censos, Alameda Dr Carlos d'Assumcao 411-417, Macao, Macau. TEL 853-3995311, FAX 853-307825, info@dsec.gov.mo, http://www.dsec.gov.mo.

916 MWI
MALAWI TOURISM REPORT. Text in English. 1970. a. MWK 70. stat. **Document type:** *Government.*
Formerly: Malawi. National Statistical Office. Tourist Report (0085-302X)
Media: Duplicated (not offset).
Published by: (Malawi. Commissioner for Census and Statistics), National Statistical Office, PO Box 333, Zomba, Malawi. TEL 265-50-522377, FAX 265-50-523130.

338.4 MUS
MAURITIUS. CENTRAL STATISTICAL OFFICE. DIGEST OF INTERNATIONAL TRAVEL AND TOURISM STATISTICS. Text in English. 1974. a., latest 1999. MUR 75 per issue (effective 2001). charts. **Document type:** *Government.* **Description:** Provides a statistical overview of the year's activity in tourism in Mauritius.
Former titles (until 1998): Mauritius. Central Statistical Office. International Travel and Tourism Statistics; (until 1984): Mauritius. Central Statistical Office. International Travel and Tourism
Published by: Mauritius. Central Statistical Office, L.I.C. Centre, President John Kennedy St, Port Louis, Mauritius. TEL 230-212-4150, FAX 230-211-4150, cso@intnet.mu, http://statsmauritius.gov.mu. **Subscr. to:** Mauritius. Government Printing Office, Ramtoolah Bldg, Sir S Ramgoolam St, Port Louis, Mauritius. TEL 230-234-5294, 230-242-0234, FAX 230-234-5322.

915 TWN ISSN 1021-4534
MONTHLY REPORT ON TOURISM - REPUBLIC OF CHINA/KUAN KUANG TZU LIAO. Text in Chinese, English. 1968. m. looseleaf. free. charts; stat. **Document type:** *Government.* **Description:** Presents statistics of tourism in Taiwan, broken down by country of origin, nationality, sex, age.
Published by: Ministry of Communications, Tourism Bureau/Chiao T'ung Pu, Kuan Kuang Chu, Ta Lu Bldg, 9th Fl, 280 Chung Hsiao E. Rd, Sec 4, Taipei, Taiwan. TEL 886-2-721-8541, FAX 866-2-7815399, TELEX 26408 ROTCB. Ed. Lin Ch'ing-Shih. Circ: 3,500. **Subscr. to:** P.O. Box 1490, Taipei, Taiwan.

997 MSR
MONTSERRAT. STATISTICS OFFICE. TOURISM REPORT. Text in English. irreg. **Document type:** *Government.*
Published by: Statistics Office, Government Headquarters, Plymouth, Montserrat.

338.4 MOZ
MOZAMBIQUE. INSTITUTO NACIONAL DE ESTATISTICA. ESTATISTICAS DO TURISMO. Text in Portuguese. a.
Published by: Instituto Nacional de Estatistica, Av Ahmed Sekou Toure 21, Maputo, Mozambique. TEL 258-1-491054, FAX 258-1-493547, info@ine.gov.mz, http://www.ine.gov.mz.

910 310 NLD ISSN 1383-7214
NETHERLANDS. CENTRAAL BUREAU VOOR DE STATISTIEK. TOERISME IN NEDERLAND/NETHERLANDS. CENTRAL BUREAU FOR STATISTICS. TOURISM IN THE NETHERLANDS. Text in Dutch, English. 1994. a. EUR 34.20 (effective 2008). **Document type:** *Government.*
Formed by the merger of (1947-1993): Netherlands. Centraal Bureau voor de Statistiek. Statistiek Vreemdelingenverkeer (0168-5538); (1990-1992): Netherlands. Centraal Bureau voor de Statistiek. Statistiek Vreemdelingenverkeer: Gegevens naar Provincie en Toeristengebied (0925-3017); (1990-1992): Netherlands. Centraal Bureau voor de Statistiek. Statistiek Vreemdelingenverkeer: Gegevens naar Maand en Kwartaal (0925-3025)
Published by: Centraal Bureau voor de Statistiek, Prinses Beatrixlaan 428, PO Box 4000, Voorburg, 2270 JM, Netherlands. TEL 31-70-3373800, FAX 31-70-3877429, infoserv@cbs.nl, http://www.cbs.nl.

338.4 NZL
NEW ZEALAND INTERNATIONAL VISITORS SURVEY. Text in English. q. **Document type:** *Report, Trade.* **Description:** Measures the travel patterns and expenditure of international visitors to New Zealand.
Media: Online - full text.
Published by: New Zealand Tourism Board, Market Research, PO Box 95, Wellington, New Zealand. TEL 64-4-4628000, FAX 64-4-9153817, info@tourismresearch.govt.nz.

338.4791021 NOR ISSN 1503-4119
HA1501
NORWAY. STATISTISK SENTRALBYRAA. OVERNATTINGSSTATISTIKK/STATISTICS NORWAY. ACCOMODATIONS STATISTICS. Text in English, Norwegian. 1963. m. stat. **Document type:** *Government.*
Supersedes in part (in 2002): Norway. Statistisk Sentralbyraa. Reiselivsstatistikk (0333-208X); Which was formerly (until 1978): Hotell- og Pensjonatstatistikk (0333-2071); (until 1974): Hotellstatistikk (0550-0389)
Related titles: Online - full text ed.; ◆ Series of: Norges Offisielle Statistikk. ISSN 0300-5585.
Published by: Statistisk Sentralbyraa/Statistics Norway, Kongensgate 6, P O Box 8131, Dep, Oslo, 0033, Norway. TEL 47-21-090000, FAX 47-21-094973, ssb@ssb.no.

NORWAY. STATISTISK SENTRALBYRAA. STRUKTURSTATISTIKK FOR SAMFERSEL OG REISELIV/STATISTICS NORWAY. STRUCTURAL TRANSPORT AND TOURISM STATISTICS. *see* TRANSPORTATION—Abstracting, Bibliographies, Statistics

338.4021 ESP ISSN 1728-9254
O M T. BAROMETRO DEL TURISMO MUNDIAL. (Organizacion Mundial de Turismo) Text in Spanish. 2002. 3/yr. back issues avail. **Document type:** *Bulletin, Trade.*
Related titles: Online - full text ed.; ◆ French ed.: Barometre OMT du Tourisme Mondial. ISSN 1728-9262; ◆ English ed.: W T O World Tourism Barometer. ISSN 1728-9246.
—Ingenta. **CCC.**
Published by: World Tourism Organization, Capitan Haya 42, Madrid, 28020, Spain. TEL 34-91-5678100, FAX 34-91-5713733, omt@unwto.org, http://www.unwto.org.

910.09 USA
PACIFIC ASIA TRAVEL ASSOCIATION. ANNUAL STATISTICAL REPORT. Variant title: P A T A Annual Statistical Report. Text in English. 1967. a. USD 450 to non-members; USD 350 to members. **Description:** Report that includes data on visitor arrivals in PATA destinations, outbound travel statistics from PATA countries, and other tourism-related statistics.
Indexed: Hospl, SRI.
Published by: Pacific Asia Travel Association, Latham Square Bldg, 1611 Telegraph Ave, Ste 550, Oakland, CA 94612. americas@pata.org, http://www.pata.org. Ed. Low Poh Gek. Circ: 500.

910.09 USA ISSN 1066-0356
G155.A74
PACIFIC ASIA TRAVEL ASSOCIATION. QUARTERLY STATISTICAL REPORT. Variant title: P A T A Quarterly Statistical Report. Text in English. q. USD 275 to non-members; USD 200 to members.
Indexed: Hospl.
Published by: Pacific Asia Travel Association, Latham Square Bldg, 1611 Telegraph Ave, Ste 550, Oakland, CA 94612. americas@pata.org, http://www.pata.org.

914.94 CHE
DER REISEVERKEHR DER SCHWEIZER IM AUSLAND/TOURISTES SUISSES A L'ETRANGER; internationaler Reiseverkehr und Grenzuebertritte der Schweizerinnen und Schweizer. Text in French, German. 1984. a. CHF 4 (effective 2001). **Document type:** *Government.*
Published by: Bundesamt fuer Statistik, Espace de l'Europe 10, Neuchatel, 2010, Switzerland. TEL 41-32-7136011, FAX 41-32-7136012, information@bfs.admin.ch, http://www.admin.ch/bfs.

910.09 TZA ISSN 0564-836X
REPORT ON TOURISM STATISTICS IN TANZANIA. Text in English. 1968. irreg. **Document type:** *Government.*
Published by: National Bureau of Statistics, PO Box 796, Dar Es Salaam, Tanzania. **Orders to:** Government Publications Agency, PO Box 1801, Dar Es Salaam, Tanzania.

ST. LUCIA. STATISTICAL DEPARTMENT. ANNUAL MIGRATION AND TOURISM STATISTICS. *see* POPULATION STUDIES—Abstracting, Bibliographies, Statistics

ST. LUCIA. STATISTICAL DEPARTMENT. QUARTERLY MIGRATION & TOURISM STATISTICS. *see* POPULATION STUDIES—Abstracting, Bibliographies, Statistics

914.94 CHE
SCHWEIZER TOURISMUS IN ZAHLEN/TOURISME SUISSE EN CHIFFRES. Text in French, German. 1981. a. **Document type:** *Government.*
Published by: Bundesamt fuer Statistik, Espace de l'Europe 10, Neuchatel, 2010, Switzerland. TEL 41-32-7136011, FAX 41-32-7136012, information@bfs.admin.ch, http://www.admin.ch/bfs.

960 316 SYC
SEYCHELLES. MANAGEMENT AND INFORMATION SYSTEMS DIVISION. TOURISM AND MIGRATION STATISTICS. Text in English. a. SCR 15. **Document type:** *Government.*
Former titles (until 1987): Seychelles. President's Office. Statistics Division. Migration and Tourism Statistics; Seychelles. President's Office. Statistics Division. Tourism and Migration Report
Published by: Department of Finance, Management and Information Systems Division, PO Box 26, Victoria, Mahe, Seychelles.

910.4 310 SYC
SEYCHELLES. STATISTICS DIVISION. STATISTICAL BULLETIN. TOURISM. Text in English. m. SCR 5.

TU

Formerly (until 1982): Seychelles. President's Office. Statistics Division. Tourism
Published by: Department of Finance, Statistics Division, PO Box 313, Victoria, Mahe, Seychelles.

310 SYC
SEYCHELLES. STATISTICS DIVISION. STATISTICAL BULLETIN. VISITOR SURVEY. Text in English. a. SCR 5. **Document type:** *Government.*
Formerly: Seychelles. Department of Finance. Visitor Survey
Published by: Department of Finance, Statistics Division, PO Box 313, Victoria, Mahe, Seychelles.

915.95 SGP ISSN 0218-4567
G155.S5
SINGAPORE ANNUAL REPORT ON TOURISM STATISTICS. Text in English. 1969. a. SGD 50 per issue (effective 2008). charts; stat. **Document type:** *Government.* **Description:** Contains detailed breakdown of visitor arrival data as well as statistics on the economic contribution of tourism, and inbound airline seat capacity.
Formerly: Singapore Tourist Promotion Board. Annual Statistical Report on Visitor Arrivals
Related titles: Online - full content ed.
Indexed: H&TI, H06.
Published by: Singapore Tourism Board, Tourism Court, 1 Orchard Spring Lane, Singapore, 247729, Singapore. TEL 65-6-7366622, FAX 65-6-7369423, http://app.stb.gov.sg/asp/index.asp?. Circ: 1,000.

915.9 SGP ISSN 0218-4575
SINGAPORE MONTHLY REPORT ON TOURISM STATISTICS. Text in English. 1972. m. charts; stat. Supplement avail. **Document type:** *Government.* **Description:** Brings out statistical information on visitor arrivals by country of residence, nationality and travel characteristics.
Formerly: Singapore Tourist Promotion Board. Monthly Statistical Report on Visitor Arrivals
Related titles: Online - full content ed.
Published by: Singapore Tourism Board, Tourism Court, 1 Orchard Spring Lane, Singapore, 247729, Singapore. TEL 65-6-7366622, FAX 65-6-7369423, http://app.stb.gov.sg/asp/index.asp?. Circ: 1,000.

919 SGP ISSN 0218-4583
SINGAPORE SURVEY OF OVERSEAS VISITORS. Text in English. 1975. a. charts. **Description:** Visitor expenditure data, lead times, visit impressions, ratings of facilities and activities during visit.
Formerly: Survey of Overseas Visitors to Singapore
Published by: Singapore Tourism Board, Tourism Court, 1 Orchard Spring Lane, Singapore, 247729, Singapore. TEL 65-6-7366622, FAX 65-6-7369423, http://app.stb.gov.sg/asp/index.asp?.

316.8 ZAF
SOUTH AFRICA. STATISTICS SOUTH AFRICA. STATISTICAL RELEASE. TOURISM - JAN SMUTS, D F MALAN AND LOUIS BOTHA AIRPORTS. Text in English. 1993. m. **Document type:** *Government.*
Formerly (until Aug. 1998): South Africa. Central Statistical Service. Statistical Release. Tourism - Jan Smuts, D F Malan and Louis Botha Airports
Published by: Statistics South Africa/Statistieke Suid-Afrika, Private Bag X44, Pretoria, 0001, South Africa. TEL 27-12-3108911, FAX 27-12-3108500, info@statssa.gov.za, http://www.statssa.gov.za.

338.4 ZAF
SOUTH AFRICA. STATISTICS SOUTH AFRICA. TOURISM (YEAR). Text in English. irreg. ZAR 50 (effective 2008). stat. **Document type:** *Government.*
Published by: Statistics South Africa/Statistieke Suid-Afrika, Private Bag X44, Pretoria, 0001, South Africa. TEL 27-12-3108911, FAX 27-12-3108500, info@statssa.gov.za, http://www.statssa.gov.za.

SOUTH AFRICA. STATISTICS SOUTH AFRICA. TOURISM AND MIGRATION. *see* POPULATION STUDIES—Abstracting, Bibliographies, Statistics

910.09 SRB
SRBIJA I CRNA GORA ZAVOD ZA STATISTIKU. TURIZAM. Text in Serbo-Croatian. a. stat. **Document type:** *Government.*
Formerly (until 2003): Yugoslavia. Savezni Zavod za Statistiku. Turizam
Related titles: ◆ Series of: Srbija i Crna Gora. Zavod za Statistiku. Statisticki Bilten.
Published by: Srbija i Crna Gora Zavod za Statistiku/Serbia and Montenegro Statistical Office, Kneza Milosa 20, Postanski Fah 203, Belgrade, 11000. TEL 381-11-3617273.

STATISTICAL OFFICE OF THE EUROPEAN COMMUNITIES. TRANSPORT, COMMUNICATIONS, TOURISME - ANNUAIRE STATISTIQUE. *see* TRANSPORTATION—Abstracting, Bibliographies, Statistics

338.4 IDN ISSN 0854-6886
STATISTICAL REPORT ON VISITOR ARRIVALS TO INDONESIA. Text in English. 1975. a. free. bk.rev. **Document type:** *Government.*
Former titles (until 1983): Statistics of Incoming Visitors; (until 1978): Indonesia Tourist Statistics
Published by: Department of Tourism, Arts and Culture, Resources and Technology Development Agency, Jl. Medan Merdeka Barat no. 17, Jakarta Pusa, 10110, Indonesia. FAX 21-380-1738, TELEX 45157. Circ: 500 (controlled).

915.1 HKG ISSN 0377-5704
STATISTICAL REVIEW OF TOURISM IN HONG KONG. Text in English. 1974. a. HKD 180, USD 36. **Document type:** *Journal, Trade.*
Supersedes: Hong Kong Tourist Association. Digest of Annual Statistics
Published by: (Research Department), Hong Kong Tourist Association, GPO Box 2597, Hong Kong, Hong Kong. TEL 852-28076543, FAX 852-28060303. Ed., R&P Peter Randall. Circ: 5,500.

338.4791 DEU ISSN 1433-2493
STATISTISCHE BERICHTE - BADEN-WUERTTEMBERG. G: HANDEL, TOURISMUS, GASTGEWERBE. Text in German. 1956. irreg. **Document type:** *Government.*
Formerly (until 1992): Statistisches Landesamt Baden-Wuerttemberg. Statistische Berichte G (1433-2310)
Published by: Statistisches Landesamt Baden-Wuerttemberg, Boeblinger Str 68, Stuttgart, 70199, Germany. TEL 49-711-6410, FAX 49-711-6412440, poststelle@stala.bwl.de.

338.4791 DEU ISSN 1430-5119
STATISTISCHE BERICHTE - RHEINLAND-PFALZ. G: HANDEL, TOURISMUS, GASTGEWERBE. Text in German. 1951. irreg. **Document type:** *Government.*
Formerly (until 1976): Statistisches Landesamt Rheinland-Pfalz. Statistische Berichte G (1430-4961); Which superseded in part (in 1956): Statistisches Landesamt Rheinland-Pfalz. Mitteilungen (0482-8887)
Published by: Statistisches Landesamt Rheinland-Pfalz, Mainzerstr 14-16, Bad Ems, 56130, Germany. TEL 49-2603-713240, FAX 49-2603-71193240, pressestelle@statistik.rlp.de.

910 314 DEU
STATISTISCHES BUNDESAMT. FACHSERIE 6: TOURISMUS; REIHE 7.1: MONATSERHEBUNG IM TOURISMUS - ERGEBNISSE DER BERHERBERGUNGSSTATSTISTIK. Text in German. 1962. m. **Document type:** *Government.*
Former titles (until 2002): Germany. Statistisches Bundesamt. Fachserie 6: Binnenhandel, Gastgewerbe, Tourismus. Reihe 7.1: Beherbergung im Reiseverkehr (1432-3656); (until 1996): Germany. Statistisches Bundesamt. Fachserie 6: Handel, Gastgewerbe, Reiseverkehr. Reihe 7.1: Beherbergung im Reiseverkehr (0178-8086); (until 1984): Germany. Statistisches Bundesamt. Fachserie 6: Handel, Gastgewerbe, Reiseverkehr. Reihe 7.1: Uebernachtungen in Beherbergungsstaetten (0177-2929); (until 1977): Germany. Statistisches Bundesamt. Fachserie 6: Gross- und Einzelhandel, Gastgewerbe, Reiseverkehr. Reihe 8: Reiseverkehr. 1 - Uebernachtungen in Beherbergungsstaetten (0177-3240); (until 1973): Germany. Statistisches Bundesamt. Fachserie 6: Gross- und Einzelhandel, Gastgewerbe, Fremdenverkehr. Reihe 8: Fremdenverkehr. 1 - Fremdenverkehr in Beherbergungsstaetten (0177-3259)
Published by: Statistisches Bundesamt, Gustav-Stresemann-Ring 11, Wiesbaden, 65180, Germany. TEL 49-611-752405, FAX 49-611-753330, info@destatis.de, http://www.destatis.de.

910.09 310 USA
G155.U6
SUMMARY OF INTERNATIONAL TRAVEL TO THE UNITED STATES. Text in English. 1983. m. stat. **Document type:** *Government.* **Description:** Provides international visitor arrival statistics by world regions and countries. These reports have 14 different tables listing arrivals for the month and the year to date; included are: world region arrivals, top 20 generating countries, month of arrival by world regions and selected countries, type of visa, mode of transportation, age groups, states visited by generating regions and selected countries (by first intended address only), and top 47 ports of entry for 25 selected countries and nine world regions.
Formerly (until 1979): Summary and Analysis of International Travel to the United States (0095-3482)
Related titles: Alternate Frequency ed(s).: a.; q.
Indexed: AmStI.
Published by: (US. Tourism Industries), U.S. Department of Commerce, International Trade Administration, 1401 Constitution Ave, NW, Washington, DC 20230. TEL 202-482-3251, FAX 202-482-5819, http://trade.gov/.

915.1 TWN
TAIWAN, REPUBLIC OF CHINA. MINISTRY OF COMMUNICATION. TOURISM BUREAU. ANNUAL REPORT. Text in English. 1972. a. free. illus. **Document type:** *Government.* **Description:** Contains statistics on visitor arrivals in Taiwan with a breakdown by country of residence, nationality, sex and age; expenditures; visitors to the principal scenic areas; outbound departures.
Formerly: Annual Report on Tourism Statistics, Republic of China
Published by: Ministry of Communications, Tourism Bureau/Chiao T'ung Pu, Kuan Kuang Chu, Ta Lu Bldg, 9th Fl, 280 Chung Hsiao E. Rd, Sec 4, Taipei, Taiwan. FAX 02-7735487, TELEX 26408. Ed. Mao Chi Kuo. Circ: 2,500.

915 310 TWN
TAIWAN, REPUBLIC OF CHINA. TOURISM BUREAU. REPORT ON TOURISM STATISTICS (YEAR). Text in Chinese. a. **Document type:** *Government.*
Published by: Tourism Bureau, 9-F, 280 Chunghsiao E. Rd, Sec 4, P.O. Box 1490, Taipei, Taiwan. TEL 02-721-8541, FAX 02-781-5399, TELEX 26408 ROCTB.

910.202 USA ISSN 0895-6065
TAOS MAGAZINE. Text in English. 1984. 8/yr. USD 25 domestic; USD 40 foreign (effective 2003). adv. bk.rev. 32 p./no.; back issues avail. **Document type:** *Magazine, Consumer.* **Description:** Covers the arts, culture, dining, personalities, crafts in Taos, New Mexico, and travel throughout Mexico and the West.
Published by: Whitney Publishing Co., Inc., 116 Des Georges, Taos, NM 87571-4112. TEL 575-758-5404. Ed., Pub., R&P, Adv. contact John K Whitney. B&W page USD 930; trim 7.25 x 9.75. Circ: 7,500 (controlled).

338.4 VGB
TOURISM IN THE BRITISH VIRGIN ISLANDS. Text in English. 1973. a. USD 3. stat. **Document type:** *Government.*
Published by: Statistics Office, Finance Department, Road Town, Tortola, Virgin Isl., UK.

338.4791 AUS
TOURISM RESEARCH AUSTRALIA. OCCASIONAL PAPER. Short title: B T R Occasional Papers. Text in English. 1988. irreg. price varies. back issues avail. **Document type:** *Monographic series, Government.*
Formerly (until 2004): Australia. Bureau of Tourism Research. Occasional Papers (1031-4784)
Published by: (Australia. Tourism Australia), Tourism Research Australia, PO Box 1110, Belconnen, ACT 2616, Australia. TEL 61-2-62286100, FAX 61-2-62286180, tra@tourism.australia.com.

338.4021 CAN ISSN 1495-8651
TOURISM SECTOR MONITOR. Text in English. 1991. m. CAD 60 (effective 2006). 16 p./no.; **Document type:** *Government.* **Description:** Details revenues received from room rentals by type of accomodation, with a geographic breakdown by development region.
Former titles (until 2000): Tourism Room Revenues (1483-8184); (until 1997): B.C. Tourism Room Revenues (0846-9962)
Related titles: Online - full text ed.; Supplement(s): Tourism Sector Monitor. Annual Supplement.
Indexed: A10, H&TI, H06, V03.
Published by: Ministry of Finance and Corporate Relations, B C Stats, PO Box 9410, Sta Prov Govt, Victoria, BC V8W 9V1, Canada. TEL 250-387-0359, FAX 250-387-0380, BC.Stats@gov.bc.ca.

910.4 GBR
TOURISM TRENDS IN DEVON. Text in English. 1981. a. GBP 12 per issue (effective 2009). illus.; charts. back issues avail. **Document type:** *Government.* **Description:** Reports on the characteristics and trends of the county's tourist industry. Includes details of recent developments in investment, marketing and other related visitor services.
Former titles (until 1997): Devon Tourism Statistics; (until 1994): Devon Tourism Review (0269-0551); (until 1985): Devon. Property Department. Tourism and Recreation. Topic Report; Devon County Planning Department. Tourism and Recreation. Topic Report (0261-2445)
Related titles: Online - full text ed.: free (effective 2009).
Published by: (Devon. Environment Department), Devon County Council, Countryside and Heritage Division, Devon County Council, County Hall, Topsham Rd, Exeter, Devon EX2 4QQ, United Kingdom. FAX 44-845-1551003.

914.94 CHE
TOURISMUS IN DER SCHWEIZ. ANGEBOT UND NACHFRAGE IM ZEITVERGLEICH/TOURISME EN SUISSE. Text in French, German. 1967. a. CHF 22 (effective 2001). **Document type:** *Journal, Government.*
Former titles: Hotel- und Kurbetriebe in der Schweiz (1423-5056); until 1991): Tourismus in der Schweiz (0258-8684); (until 1974): Fremdenverkehr in der Schweiz (1423-498X)
Published by: Bundesamt fuer Statistik, Espace de l'Europe 10, Neuchatel, 2010, Switzerland. TEL 41-31-3236011, FAX 41-31-3236012, information@bfs.admin.ch, http://www.admin.ch/bfs.

910 USA ISSN 1040-8142
Z6004.T6
TRAVEL & TOURISM INDEX. Text in English. 1984. q. (plus a. cumulation). USD 50. **Document type:** *Abstract/Index.* **Description:** Indexes articles by subject and title from periodicals in the travel and tourism field.
Published by: Brigham Young University, Hawaii Campus, Business Division, PO Box 1773, Laie, HI 96762. FAX 808-293-3645. Ed. Gerald V Bohnet. Circ: 500.

910.09 USA ISSN 0738-9515
G155.A1
TRAVEL INDUSTRY WORLD YEARBOOK; the big picture. Text in English. 1956. a., latest vol.46, 2003. USD 130.50 per issue domestic; USD 134 per issue in Canada & Mexico; USD 137 per issue elsewhere (effective 2005). bk.rev. back issues avail. **Document type:** *Yearbook, Trade.* **Description:** Information and statistics pertaining to trends in and prospects for the international and national tourism industry, with industry trends for motels-hotels, airlines, travel agents, cruise lines, food services, and supplemental amenities.
Formerly (until 1983): The Big Picture (0895-4763)
Indexed: SRI.
—BLDSC (2057.271000).
Published by: Travel Industry Publishing Co. Inc., PO Box 280, Spencertown, NY 12165. TEL 518-392-4102, FAX 212-772-6444. Ed. Joseph Scott. Pub. Allen I. Milman.

790.1 332.6 GBR
TRAVEL TRENDS; data from international passenger survey (year). Text in English. 1969. a., latest 2007. GBP 17.50 per issue (effective 2010). charts; stat. back issues avail. **Document type:** *Government.*
Former titles (until 1993): Business Monitor. MA6. Overseas Travel and Tourism (0956-683X); (until 1978): Business Monitor M6 Overseas Travel and Tourism Annual
Published by: (Great Britain. Office for National Statistics), Dandy Booksellers Ltd., Units 3 & 4, 31-33 Priory Park Rd, London, NW6 7UP, United Kingdom. TEL 44-20-76242993, FAX 44-20-76245049, enquiries@dandybooksellers.com, http://www.dandybooksellers.com.

910 310 TTO ISSN 0082-6537
TRINIDAD AND TOBAGO. CENTRAL STATISTICAL OFFICE. INTERNATIONAL TRAVEL REPORT. Text in English. 1955. a. TTD 5 (effective 2000). **Document type:** *Government.*
Published by: Central Statistical Office, 35-41 Queen St, PO Box 98, Port-of-Spain, Trinidad, Trinidad & Tobago. TEL 868-623-6495, FAX 868-625-3802.

338.4 ROM ISSN 1223-7515
G155.R78
TURISMUL IN ROMANIA/TOURISM IN ROMANIA. Text in English, Romanian. biennial. ROL 20,000; USD 8 foreign. **Document type:** *Government.* **Description:** Contains data regarding the tourist accommodation capacity structured by tourism regions, unit types, comfort categories, Rumanian and foreign citizens.
Published by: Comisia Nationala pentru Statistica/National Commission for Statistics, Bd. Libertatii 16, Sector 5, Bucharest, 70542, Romania. TEL 40-1-3363370, FAX 40-1-3124873.

315.61 TUR ISSN 1013-6150
TURKEY. TURKIYE ISTATISTIK KURUMU. TURIZM ISTATISTIKLERI (YEAR)/TURKEY. TURKISH STATISTICAL INSTITUTE. TOURISM STATISTICS (YEAR). Key Title: Turizm Istatistikleri. Text in English, Turkish. 1959. a., latest 2007. TRY 10 per issue domestic; USD 20 per issue foreign (effective 2009). **Document type:** *Government.* **Description:** Provides statistical information on numbers of tourists, arrival and departure information, duration of stay and other related information.
Related titles: CD-ROM ed.: TRY 5 per issue domestic; USD 10 per issue foreign (effective 2009).
Published by: T.C. Basbakanlik, Turkiye Istatistik Kurumu/Prime Ministry Republic of Turkey, Turkish Statistical Institute, Yucetepe Mah. Necatibey Cad No.114, Cankaya, Ankara, 06100, Turkey. TEL 90-312-4100410, FAX 90-312-4175886, ulka.unsal@tuik.gov.tr, bilgi@tuik.gov.tr, http://www.tuik.gov.tr. Circ: 1,300.

919.604 VUT
VANUATU IN FACTS AND FIGURES. Text in English, French. 1975. a. free. adv. stat. **Document type:** *Government.* **Description:** A compact digest containing the key statistical data about Vanuatu.
Former titles: Vanuatu in Figures; New Hebrides. Bureau of Statistics. Some Facts and Figures about the New Hebrides
Published by: Statistics Office, PMB 19, Port Vila, Vanuatu. TEL 678-22110, FAX 678-24583. Ed. Jacob Isaiah. Adv. contact Tali Saurei. Circ: 500.

338.4021 ESP ISSN 1728-9246
W T O WORLD TOURISM BAROMETER. Text in English. 2003. 3/yr. **Document type:** *Bulletin, Trade.*
Related titles: Online - full text ed.; ◆ French ed.: Barometre OMT du Tourisme Mondial. ISSN 1728-9262; ◆ Spanish ed.: O M T. Barometro del Turismo Mundial. ISSN 1728-9254.
—Ingenta. **CCC.**
Published by: World Tourism Organization, Capitan Haya 42, Madrid, 28020, Spain. TEL 34-91-5678100, FAX 34-91-5713733, omt@unwto.org, http://www.unwto.org.

910.2 ESP ISSN 1011-8977
YEARBOOK OF TOURISM STATISTICS. Text in English, French, Spanish. 1953. a., latest 2007. looseleaf. **Document type:** *Directory, Trade.* **Description:** Contains data on tourism trends from over 185 countries and territories.
Former titles: World Tourism Statistics; International Travel Statistics (0074-9184)
Indexed: IIS.
—BLDSC (9416.810000).
Published by: World Tourism Organization, Capitan Haya 42, Madrid, 28020, Spain. TEL 34-91-5678100, FAX 34-91-5713733, omt@unwto.org, http://www.unwto.org.

910.09 316 ZWE
ZIMBABWE. CENTRAL STATISTICAL OFFICE. QUARTERLY MIGRATION AND TOURIST STATISTICS. Text in English. q. ZWD 66.60 in Africa; ZWD 85.10 in Europe; ZWD 105.10 elsewhere. **Document type:** *Government.*
Formerly: Zimbabwe. Central Statistical Office. Monthly Migration and Tourist Statistics (0259-7519)
Published by: Central Statistical Office, Causeway, PO Box 8063, Harare, Zimbabwe. TEL 263-4-706681, FAX 263-4-728529. Circ: 220.

TRAVEL AND TOURISM—Airline Inflight And Hotel Inroom

056.1 051 USA
ABOARD ECUATORIANA. Text in English, Spanish. 1983. bi-m. USD 24.95 (effective 2011). bk.rev. illus. **Document type:** *Magazine, Trade.* **Description:** General interest articles for travelers to and from Latin America, with information on tourist attractions.
Published by: Aboard Publishing, One Herald Plz, 4th Fl, Miami, FL 33132. TEL 305-376-5294, FAX 305-376-5274. Pub. Garry Duell.

056.1 051 USA
ABOARD GRUPO TACA. Text in English, Spanish. 1981. bi-m. USD 24.95 (effective 2011). adv. bk.rev. illus. **Document type:** *Magazine, Trade.* **Description:** Features general interest articles for travelers into and out of Latin America. Includes information on tourist attractions.
Formerly: Aboard Taca
Published by: Aboard Publishing, One Herald Plz, 4th Fl, Miami, FL 33132. TEL 305-376-5294, FAX 305-376-5274. Pub. Garry Duell. adv.: page USD 2,100. Circ: 22,000.

056.1 051 USA
ABOARD L A B AIRLINES. (Lloyd Aero Boliviano) Text in English, Spanish. 1977. bi-m. USD 24.95 (effective 2011). bk.rev. illus. **Document type:** *Magazine, Trade.* **Description:** Features general interest articles for travelers into and out of Latin America. Includes information on tourist attractions.
Published by: Aboard Publishing, One Herald Plz, 4th Fl, Miami, FL 33132. TEL 305-376-5294, FAX 305-376-5274. Pub. Garry Duell.

056.1 051 USA
ABOARD LADECO. Text in English, Spanish. 1995. bi-m. USD 24.95 (effective 2011). adv. **Document type:** *Magazine, Trade.* **Description:** In-flight magazine for travelers into and out of Latin America.
Formerly: Ladeco
Published by: Aboard Publishing, One Herald Plz, 4th Fl, Miami, FL 33132. TEL 305-376-5294, FAX 305-376-5274. Pub. Garry Duell.

056.1 051 USA
ABOARD LAN-CHILE. Text in English, Spanish. 1976. bi-m. USD 24.95 (effective 2011). adv. bk.rev. illus. **Document type:** *Magazine, Trade.* **Description:** Features general interest articles for travelers into and out of Latin America. Includes information on tourist attractions.
Published by: Aboard Publishing, One Herald Plz, 4th Fl, Miami, FL 33132. TEL 305-376-5294, FAX 305-376-5274. Pub. Garry Duell.

056.1 051 USA
ABOARD PLUNA (COSTA RICA). Text in English, Spanish. 1996. bi-m. USD 24.95 (effective 2011). adv. **Document type:** *Magazine, Trade.* **Description:** In-flight magazine for travelers into and out of Latin America.
Formerly: Lacsa
Published by: Aboard Publishing, One Herald Plz, 4th Fl, Miami, FL 33132. TEL 305-376-5294, FAX 305-376-5274. Pub. Garry Duell.

056.1 051 USA
ABOARD PLUNA (ECUADOR). Text in English, Spanish. 1993. bi-m. USD 24.95 (effective 2011). adv. **Document type:** *Magazine, Trade.* **Description:** In-flight magazine for travelers into and out of Latin America.
Formerly: Saeta
Published by: Aboard Publishing, One Herald Plz, 4th Fl, Miami, FL 33132. TEL 305-376-5294, FAX 305-376-5274. Pub. Garry Duell.

056.1 051 USA
ABOARD PLUNA (EL SALVADOR). Text in English, Spanish. 199?. bi-m. USD 24.95 (effective 2011). adv. **Document type:** *Magazine, Trade.* **Description:** In-flight magazine for travelers into and out of Latin America.
Published by: Aboard Publishing, One Herald Plz, 4th Fl, Miami, FL 33132. TEL 305-376-5294, FAX 305-376-5274. Pub. Garry Duell.

056.1 051 USA
ABOARD PLUNA (GUATEMALA). Text in English, Spanish. 1987. bi-m. USD 24.95 (effective 2011). adv. bk.rev. illus. **Document type:** *Magazine, Trade.* **Description:** General interest articles for travelers into and out of Latin America. Includes information on tourist attractions.
Formerly: Aboard Aviateca
Published by: Aboard Publishing, One Herald Plz, 4th Fl, Miami, FL 33132. TEL 305-376-5294, FAX 305-376-5274. Pub. Garry Duell. Circ: 8,600.

056.1 051 USA
ABOARD PLUNA (HONDURAS). Text in English, Spanish. 1986. bi-m. USD 24.95 (effective 2011). bk.rev. illus. **Document type:** *Magazine, Trade.* **Description:** Features general interest articles for travelers into and out of Latin America. Includes information on tourist attractions.
Formerly (until 1995): Aboard Tan Sahsa
Published by: Aboard Publishing, One Herald Plz, 4th Fl, Miami, FL 33132. TEL 305-376-5294, FAX 305-376-5274. Pub. Garry Duell.

056.1 051 USA
ABOARD PLUNA (NICARAGUA). Text in Spanish, English. 1990. bi-m. USD 24.95 (effective 2011). adv. **Document type:** *Magazine, Consumer.* **Description:** In-flight magazine for travelers into and out of Latin America.
Published by: Aboard Publishing, One Herald Plz, 4th Fl, Miami, FL 33132. TEL 305-376-5294, FAX 305-376-5274. Pub. Garry Duell.

056.1 051 USA
ABOARD PLUNA (VENEZUELA). Text in English, Spanish. 1977. bi-m. USD 24.95 (effective 2011). adv. **Document type:** *Magazine, Trade.* **Description:** Features general interest articles for travelers into and out of Latin America. Includes information on tourist attractions.
Formerly: Aboard Viasa
Published by: Aboard Publishing, One Herald Plz, 4th Fl, Miami, FL 33132. TEL 305-376-5294, FAX 305-376-5274. Pub. Garry Duell.

910.09 DEU ISSN 1438-8162
AERO LLOYD; Bord Magazin. Text in German. 1984. q. adv. back issues avail. **Document type:** *Magazine, Consumer.*
Formerly: Flugurlaub
Published by: (Aero Lloyd Airlines), F U V Flugurlaub Verlag GmbH, Lessingstr 7-9, Oberursel, 61440, Germany. TEL 06171-6404, FAX 06171-641049. Ed. Eduard Wolczak. Adv. contact Bogomir Gradisnik. color page EUR 8,180. Circ: 100,000.

057.1 RUS
AEROFLOT. Text in Russian. 1994. m. **Document type:** *Magazine, Consumer.* **Description:** Official publication of the Aeroflot - Russian International Airlines company.
Published by: Izdatel'skii Dom L K Press, Bol'shoi Savvinskii per, dom 9, Moscow, 119435, Russian Federation. info@lkpress.ru, http://www.lkpress.ru. Circ: 75,000.

050 FRA ISSN 1777-7364
AFRIQIYAH. Text in French, English. 2006. irreg. adv. **Document type:** *Magazine, Consumer.*
Published by: A S A Editions, 1 Passage du Grand Cerf, Paris, 75002, France. TEL 33-1-44889500, FAX 33-1-44889505, info@asaeditions.com, http://www.asaeditions.com/. adv.: color page EUR 5,000; 21 x 28.5. Circ: 15,000.

059.927 SAU ISSN 1319-1543
AHLAN WA-SAHLAN/WELCOME. Text in Arabic. 1977. 12/yr. adv. back issues avail. **Document type:** *Consumer.* **Description:** Contains articles of general interest to the traveller. Features various destinations of the airline and provides relevant local information and news.
Published by: (Saudi Arabian Airlines), Saudi Specialized Publishing Company (Subsidiary of: Saudi Research & Publishing Co.), PO Box 53108, Riyadh, 11583, Saudi Arabia. info@srmg.com, http://www.srmg.com/. Circ: 150,000.

053.1 DEU ISSN 1861-5570
AIR; the magazine of Blue Wings. Text in German. 2005. 4/yr. EUR 19.90; EUR 5.90 newsstand/cover (effective 2010). adv. **Document type:** *Magazine, Consumer.*
Published by: V8 Verlag GmbH, Mohrenstr 2, Cologne, 50670, Germany. TEL 49-221-9984836, FAX 49-221-9985990, info@v8-verlag.de, http://www.v8-verlag.de.

910.09 GBR ISSN 1003-3823
AIR CHINA/ZHONGGUO GUOJI HANGKONG GONGSI JINEI ZAZHI. Text in English. 1988. bi-m. **Document type:** *Magazine, Consumer.*
Published by: Regie Club International, Cromwell House, 136 Cromwell Rd, London, SW7 4HA, United Kingdom. TEL 44-71-244-6565. adv.: color page USD 6,000; trim 11.25 x 8.25. Circ: 60,000 (controlled).

051 054 FRA ISSN 0980-7519
AIR FRANCE MADAME. Text in English, French. 6/yr. free. adv. **Document type:** *Magazine, Consumer.* **Description:** Covers personalities, culture, fashion, and travel.
Published by: Air France, 71 rue Desnouettes, Paris, 75015, France. TEL 44-19-90-33, FAX 48-28-39-50. Ed. Francis Rousseau. Adv. contact Michel Devos.

057.91 UKR
AIR UKRAINE. Text in English, Ukrainian. bi-m. illus.
Published by: Tsentr Narodnoi Tvorchosti Hopak, Ul Reitorskaya 21, Kiev, Ukraine. TEL 380-44-229-5120, FAX 380-44-246-4204. **Dist. by:** East View Information Services, 10601 Wayzata Blvd, Minneapolis, MN 55305. TEL 952-252-1201, 800-477-1005, FAX 952-252-1202, info@eastview.com, http://www.eastview.com.

052 ZAF
AIRTALES; Comair's complimentary in-flight magazine. Text in English. 1994. bi-m. adv. illus.; maps. **Document type:** *Magazine, Consumer.*
Published by: (Comair), C B M Publishing, PO Box 846, Four Ways, 2055, South Africa. Ed. Mike Crewe Brown.

051 USA ISSN 0199-0586
ALASKA AIRLINES MAGAZINE. Text in English. 1977. m. USD 45 (effective 2007). adv. **Document type:** *Magazine, Consumer.* **Description:** General interest publication for business and leisure travelers.
Formerly: Alaskafest (0199-0586)
Published by: (Alaska Airlines), Paradigm Communications Group, 2701 First Ave, 250, Seattle, WA 98121. TEL 206-441-5871, FAX 206-448-6939, info@paradigmcz.com, http://www.inflightpubs.com. Ed., R&P Paul Frichtl. Pub. Mimi Kirsch. Adv. contact Ken Krass. Circ: 50,000 (controlled).

910.09 USA ISSN 1083-690X
AMERICAN EAGLE LATITUDES SOUTH. Variant title: Latitudes South. Text in English, Spanish. 1991. q. **Document type:** *Magazine, Consumer.* **Description:** In flight magazine.
Published by: (American Eagle Airlines), Bonnier Corp. (Subsidiary of: Bonnier Group), 460 N Orlando Ave, Ste 200, Orlando, FL 32789. TEL 407-628-4802, FAX 407-628-7061, http://www.bonniercorp.com.

917 USA ISSN 1945-2047
AMERICAN TRAVELER (BOISE). Text in English. 2008. bi-m. adv. **Document type:** *Magazine, Consumer.* **Description:** Highlights community attractions, enterprise and recreation opportunities in areas across the nation.
Published by: Go! Publications Inc., 205 N 10th St, Ste 540, Boise, ID 83702. TEL 208-333-9990, FAX 208-333-9991, info@gopubinc.com, http://www.gopubinc.com. Ed. Colleen Birch Maile TEL 208-333-9990 ext 101. adv.: page USD 4,100; trim 8 x 10.5. Circ: 30,000 (free).

051 USA ISSN 0003-1518
CODEN: EDFOE2
AMERICAN WAY; trends for the modren traveler. Text in English. 1966. bi-w. USD 72 domestic; USD 552 foreign (effective 2009). adv. bk.rev. illus. back issues avail.; reprints avail. **Document type:** *Magazine, Consumer.* **Description:** Provides American Airlines passengers with the latest trends in travel, lifestyle, and business.
Related titles: Microform ed.: (from PQC); Online - full text ed.: free (effective 2009).
Indexed: Chicano.
Published by: American Airlines Publishing, 4333 Amon Carter Blvd, MD 5374, Fort Worth, TX 76155. TEL 817-967-1804, FAX 817-967-1571, http://www.aa.com. Ed. Adam Pitluk. Adv. contact Kimberly A Creaven. B&W page USD 23,987, color page USD 31,111; trim 8 x 10.5. Circ: 348,137 (paid).

056.1 051 USA
AMIGOS VOLANDO. Text in English, Spanish. 1983. m. adv. **Description:** For passengers of Avianca Airlines to read during flights.
Published by: (Avianca Airlines), Carvajal International, Inc., P O Box 901, Ponce De Leon, FL 33134-3073. TEL 305-448-6875, 800-622-6657, FAX 305-448-9942. Ed. Marcela Gomez. Pub. David Ashe. Adv. contact Giovana Reyes. Circ: 90,000.

APOLLO EXECUTIVE REVIEW. *see* TRANSPORTATION—Air Transport

338.4 051 071 USA
ARRIVE (ARLINGTON). Text in English. 2000. bi-m. free to Amtrak riders. **Document type:** *Magazine, Consumer.* **Description:** Onboard Amtrak publication that features high-tech gadgets and gizmos, trends in beauty & healthcare, profiles of people, trends in home & furnishings and equipment, luxury, etc.
Published by: (Amtrak), Z Comm, 1600 Wilson Blvd., Ste. 1210, Arlington, VA 22209-2594. http://www.zpr.com. Ed. Jim Moore. Pub., Adv. contact Rise Birnbaum.

ATLANTIC PROGRESS; business, politics, economics. *see* BUSINESS AND ECONOMICS

052 ISL
ATLANTICA. Text in English. 1976. 5/yr. free. adv. **Document type:** *Magazine, Consumer.* **Description:** Icelandair in-flight magazine.
Indexed: RASB.
Published by: (Icelandair), Iceland Review, Borgartuni 23, Reykjavik, 105, Iceland. TEL 354-512-7575, FAX 354-561-8646, http://www.icelandreview.com. Ed. Jon Kaldal. Pub. Haraldur J Hamar. Circ: 25,000.

056.9 PRT ISSN 0870-8924
ATLANTIS; inflight magazine. Text in Portuguese. 1981. 6/yr. free. adv. **Document type:** *Magazine, Consumer.* **Description:** Emphasis is on Portugal's way of life, culture, history and people. Focuses on international subjects such as interesting places, food and drink, fashion and sports.
Published by: T A P Air Portugal, Building 25, Lisbon Airport, Lisbon, 1704, Portugal. http://www.tap.pt. Ed., R&P Antonio Campos Batista. Adv. contact Susana Cotrim. color page USD 7,160; trim 290 x 200. Circ: 100,000.

050 FRA ISSN 1771-0146
ATLASBLUE.MAG. Text in French, English, Arabic. 2005. bi-m. adv. **Document type:** *Magazine, Consumer.* **Description:** Concentrates mostly on tourist destinations in Morocco.
Published by: A S A Editions, 1 Passage du Grand Cerf, Paris, 75002, France. TEL 33-1-44889500, FAX 33-1-44889505, info@asaeditions.com. adv.: color page EUR 2,500; 21 x 28.5. Circ: 15,000.

051 USA
ATMOSPHERE (MIAMI BEACH). Text in English. bi-m. free. adv. **Document type:** *Magazine, Consumer.* **Description:** Covers travel, electronics, celebrities for Canada's Air Transit airline passengers.
Published by: (Air Transat CAN), Business Class Media, 1205 Lincoln Rd, Ste. 204, Miami Beach, FL 33139. TEL 305-672-3200, info@atmosphere-magazine.com. Pub. Peter Mansfield. adv.: page USD 13,300; trim 8 x 10.5. Circ: 70,000.

910.09 CHE
BALAIR - C T A YELLOW WINGS. Text in French, German. 3/yr. adv. **Document type:** *Consumer.*
Published by: Airpage AG, Haldenstr 65, Zuerich, 8045, Switzerland. TEL 01-451-2920, FAX 01-451-2961. Ed. Elisabeth Dennler. Adv. contact Peter Furrer. B&W page USD 6,477, color page USD 7,860; 10.13 x 7.31. Circ: 150,000 (controlled).

910.09 ESP
BARCELONA PLUS. Text in English, Spanish. q. free. **Document type:** *Magazine, Consumer.* **Description:** Presents information on Barcelona for business and pleasure travelers.
Published by: Ediciones Turisticas, S.A., C. Consejo de Ciento 355 Piso 3o, Barcelona, 08007, Spain. TEL 34-93-4670229, FAX 34-93-4670218, direccion@editur.es, http://www.editur.com.

910.202 917.104 CAN ISSN 1486-4576
BEAR COUNTRY. Text in Cree, English. 1995. q. **Document type:** *Magazine, Consumer.* **Description:** Features editorials, articles and photographs of the people, places and events that Bearskin Airlines flies to.
Published by: Bearskin Airlines, 1475 West Walsh St, Thunder Bay, ON P7E 4X6, Canada. TEL 807-474-2636, FAX 807-474-2610. Ed. Patti Gresham. Circ: 8,000.

917.04 USA ISSN 0192-4249
BIENVENIDOS A MIAMI. Text in Spanish, English. 1975. bi-w. USD 35 (effective 2006); free to visitors in hotels & motels. adv. 80 p./no.; **Document type:** *Magazine, Consumer.*

Formerly: Bienvenidos a Miami y Sus Playas
Published by: Welcome Publications, Inc., PO Box 630518, Miami, FL 33163. TEL 305-944-9444, FAX 305-949-0544. Ed. Tina Kaplan. Pub., R&P, Adv. contact Jeffrey Kaplan. Circ: 32,000 (controlled).

051 USA
BILTMORE MAGAZINE. Text in English. 2004. a. adv. **Document type:** *Magazine, Consumer.* **Description:** Celerates the rich history and celebrity of the world renowned Arizona Biltmore Resort & Spa. Features fine dining, the spa experience, architecture, resort amenities and golf.
Formerly: More AZ (Arizona)
Published by: (Arizona Biltmore & Spa), Media That Deelivers, Inc., 8132 N 87th Pl, Scottsdale, AZ 85258. TEL 480-460-5203, FAX 480-460-2345, general@mediathatdeelivers.com, http://www.mediathatdeelivers.com. Adv. contact Shawn Miller TEL 480-460-5203 ext 212. color page USD 5,900; trim 9 x 10.75. Circ: 18,000 (paid).

052 054 FRA ISSN 1957-150X
BLUE LINE. Text in French, English. 2007. q. **Document type:** *Magazine, Consumer.*
Published by: A S A Editions, 1 Passage du Grand Cerf, Paris, 75002, France. TEL 33-1-44889500, FAX 33-1-44889505, info@asaeditions.com.

052 FIN ISSN 0358-7703
BLUE WINGS; Finnair's in-flight magazine. Text in English. 1980. 10/yr. adv. **Document type:** *Magazine, Consumer.*
Published by: Sanoma Magazines Finland Corporation, Lapinmaentie 1, Helsinki, 00350, Finland. TEL 358-9-1201, FAX 358-9-1205171, info@sanomamagazines.fi, http://www.sanomamagazines.fi. adv.: B&W page EUR 6,430, color page EUR 7,990. Circ: 80,000 (controlled).

052 IRL ISSN 0008-6088
CARA; inflight magazine of Aer Lingus. Text in English. 1968. 8/yr. adv. bk.rev. illus. **Document type:** *Magazine, Consumer.* **Description:** Publication for passengers on all Aer Lingus flights: scheduled, charter, and commuter.
Published by: (Aer Lingus), Harmonia Ltd., Rosemount House, Dundrum Rd, Dublin, 14, Ireland. TEL 353-1-2405300, FAX 353-1-6619757, http://www.harmonia.ie. Ed. Lizzie Meager. Adv. contact Mary Kershaw TEL 353-1-2405386. color page EUR 4,888; trim 215 x 280.

051 TTO
CARIBBEAN BEAT. Text in English. 1992. 6/yr. USD 25 in the Caribbean; USD 35 in North America; USD 40 elsewhere (effective 2001). adv. bk.rev.; Website rev.; music rev. **Document type:** *Magazine, Consumer.*
Published by: (B W I A International Airlines), Media & Editorial Projects Ltd. (M E P), 6 Prospect Ave, Maraval, Port of Spain, Trinidad & Tobago. TEL 868-622-3821, FAX 868-628-0639, mep@wow.net, http://www.meppublishers.com. Ed. Donna C Benny. Pub. Jeremy Taylor. Adv. contact Helen Shair-Singh. page USD 5,014; 10.5 x 7. Circ: 75,000 (controlled).

CASINO GAMES MAGAZINE. *see* SPORTS AND GAMES

051 USA
CHARLESTON CITY PAPER. Text in English. 1997. w. (Wed.). free. adv. 72 p./no. 4 cols./p.; **Document type:** *Newspaper, Consumer.*
Published by: Noel Mermer, 1049 B Morison Dr, Charleston, SC 29403. TEL 843-577-5304, FAX 843-853-6899. Ed. Stephanie Barna. Pub. Noel Mermer. Adv. contact Blair Barna. page USD 1,178. Circ: 30,000 (free).

079.51 HKG
CHINA EASTERN AIR CONNECTIONS. Text in English, Chinese. m.
Published by: Chian Eastern Aviation Advertising Service Co., 1/F Parco House, 20 Tai Yau St, San Po Kong, Kowloon, Hong Kong. TEL 852-2321-4567, FAX 852-2352-6204. Ed. Mingyi Wu. Adv. contact Richard Yeung.

059.957 KOR
CHOSUN HOTEL WEBZINE. Text in English. 1980. bi-m. adv. **Document type:** *Magazine, Consumer.*
Formerly: Chosun Hotel Magazine (Print)
Media: Online - full content.
Published by: Chosun Hotel, 87, Sogong-dong, Jung-gu, Seoul, 100-070, Korea, S. TEL 82-2-7710500, FAX 82-2-7536370, crm@chosunhotel.co.kr. Circ: 5,000.

053.1 AUT
COCKPIT; das junge Bordmagazin von Austrian Airlines. Text in German. 2/yr. adv. **Document type:** *Magazine, Consumer.*
Published by: (Austrian Airlines AG), D+R Verlagsgesellschaft mbH, Leberstr 122, Vienna, 1110, Austria. TEL 43-1-740770, FAX 43-1-74077841, office@d-r.at. Ed. Uschi Korda. Adv. contact Christine Salvinetti. B&W page EUR 3,474, color page EUR 4,288; trim 210 x 280. Circ: 50,000 (controlled).

051 USA
COLLECTIONS. Text in English. q. **Document type:** *Magazine, Consumer.*
Published by: The Pohly Co., 99 Bedford St, Fl 5, Boston, MA 02111. TEL 617-451-1700, 800-383-0888, FAX 617-338-7767, info@pohlyco.com, http://www.pohlyco.com.

051 USA
CONTINENTAL. Text in English. 1968. m. illus. **Document type:** *Magazine, Trade.* **Description:** Describes the people, industries, and what is new and fun in cities and countries continental serves. Includes articles on international trends, along with travel pieces.
Formerly: Continental Profiles
Related titles: Online - full text ed.
Published by: (Continental Airlines), The Pohly Co., 99 Bedford St, Fl 5, Boston, MA 02111. TEL 617-451-1700, 800-383-0888, FAX 617-338-7767, info@pohlyco.com. Ed. Ken Beavlieu. Pub., Adv. contact Kurt Jones. Circ: 1,600,000.

052 054 055 FRA ISSN 1957-5513
CORSICA MAGAZINE. Text in French, English, Italian. 2006. a. **Document type:** *Magazine, Consumer.*
Published by: A S A Editions, 1 Passage du Grand Cerf, Paris, 75002, France. TEL 33-1-44889500, FAX 33-1-44889505, info@asaeditions.com. Circ: 100,000.

052 CHE
CROSSTALK. Text in English, French, German, Italian. 1984. m. (11/yr.). CHF 40; CHF 52 foreign. adv. **Document type:** *Magazine, Consumer.*
Published by: (Crossair), Zuerichsee Zeitschriftenverlag, Seestr 86, Staefa, 8712, Switzerland. TEL 01-9285611, FAX 01-9285600. Adv. contact Elisabeth Godelman. B&W page CHF 7,900, color page CHF 9,900; trim 267 x 197. Circ: 70,000 (controlled).

053.1 DEU
▼ **D.LUX**; everything starts with passion. Text in German, English. 2009. 3/yr. adv. **Document type:** *Magazine, Consumer.*
Published by: (Steigenberger Hotels AG, Hauptabteilung Konzern-Medien), Journal International Verlags- und Werbegesellschaft mbH, Hanns-Seidel-Platz 5, Munich, 81737, Germany. TEL 49-89-6427970, FAX 49-89-64279777, info@journal-international.de, http://www.journal-international.de. Ed. Maike Zuercher. Adv. contact Nina Gier. page EUR 5,900; trim 220 x 280. Circ: 35,000 (controlled).

910.202 HKG
DISCOVERY. Text in English. 1973. m.
Published by: (Cathay Pacific Airways Ltd), Emphasis HK Ltd., 505-508 Westlands Centre, 20 Westlands Rd, Quarry Bay, Hong Kong, Hong Kong. TEL 25161000, FAX 25613306. Ed. Stuart Lawrence. R&P, Adv. contact Geraldine Moor TEL 852-2516-1009. Circ: 140,000.

910.09 HKG
DISCOVERY (JAPANESE EDITION). Text in Japanese. 1992. bi-m.
Published by: (Cathay Pacific Airways Ltd), Emphasis HK Ltd., 505-508 Westlands Centre, 20 Westlands Rd, Quarry Bay, Hong Kong, Hong Kong. TEL 25161000, FAX 25613306. adv.: page USD 6,500; trim 285 x 210. Circ: 45,000.

059.951 HKG ISSN 1674-0483
DONGFANG FENGQING. Text in Chinese. 2006. m. CNY 220 per issue (effective 2009). **Document type:** *Magazine, Consumer.*
Formerly: Xiangbala
Published by: (Zhongguo Dongfang Hangkong Yunan Fengongsi/China Eastern Yunan Branch CHN), Xianchuanmei/Recruit Holdings Limited, 26/F, 625 King's Rd., North Point, Hong Kong. TEL 852-2321-4567, FAX 852-2352-6204.

059.951 HKG ISSN 1672-3856
DONGFANG HANGKONG/EASTERN AIR. Text in Chinese. 1988. m. CNY 308 (effective 2009). **Document type:** *Magazine, Consumer.*
Published by: (Zhongguo Nanfang Hangkong Gongsi/China Southern CHN), Xianchuanmei/Recruit Holdings Limited, 26/F, 625 King's Rd., North Point, Hong Kong. TEL 852-2321-4567, FAX 852-2352-6204.

059.951 CHN ISSN 1673-8306
DONGFANG SHANGLU/EASTERN CHANNEL. Text in Chinese. 1993. m. **Document type:** *Newspaper, Consumer.*
Formerly (until 2006): Xibei Hangkong (1009-0053)
Published by: (Shanghai Dongfang Hongkong Chuanmei Youxian Gongsi), Dongfang Shanglu Zazhishe, Gaoxin 2 Lu, 9/F, Zhengquan Dasha, Xi'an, 710075, China. TEL 86-21-62990105, FAX 86-21-62990106. **Co-sponsor:** Zhongguo Dongfang Hangkong Jituan Gongsi/China Eastern.

053.1 AUT
DREAM FACTORY. Text in German. bi-m. adv. **Document type:** *Magazine, Consumer.*
Published by: (Lauda Air Luftfahrtgesellschaft), D+R Verlagsgesellschaft mbH, Leberstr 122, Vienna, 1110, Austria. TEL 43-1-740770, FAX 43-1-74077841, office@d-r.at. adv.: color page EUR 2,289; trim 210 x 260. Circ: 14,000 (controlled).

382.782 GBR ISSN 1357-7077
DUTY FREE NEWS INTERNATIONAL. Abbreviated title: D F N I. Text in English. 1987. m. GBP 445 combined subscription (print & online eds.) (effective 2010). adv. back issues avail. **Document type:** *Magazine, Trade.* **Description:** Provides general information about the duty free industry.
Related titles: Online - full text ed.; Supplement(s): D F N I Guide to New Airline Listings. ISSN 1364-9094. 1994.
Indexed: B02, B03, B11, B15, B17, B18, G04, G06, G07, G08, I05.
—CCC.
Published by: Metropolis Business Publishing (Subsidiary of: Metropolis International Ltd), 140 Wales Farm Rd, London, W3 6UG, United Kingdom. TEL 44-20-87528181, FAX 44-20-87528185, metropolis@metropolis.co.uk, http://www.metropolis.co.uk. Ed. Bill Lumley TEL 44-20-82538612. Pub. Amanda Felix TEL 44-20-82538604. Adv. contact Karen Lindsay TEL 44-20-82538605.

052 TWN
DYNASTY. Text in Chinese, English. 1969. 6/yr. free. adv.
Published by: China Airlines Ltd./Chung Hua Hang K'ung Kung Ssu, 131 Nanking E. Rd Sec 3, Taipei, Taiwan. Ed. Wu I Shou. Circ: 60,000.

052 GBR
EASTERN AIR EASTERN. Text in Chinese, English. bi-m. **Document type:** *Magazine, Consumer.*
Published by: (Eastern Air), Regie Club International, Cromwell House, 136 Cromwell Rd, London, SW7 4HA, United Kingdom. TEL 44-71-244-6565, FAX 44-71-3670-3727. adv.: color page USD 5,500; trim 11.25 x 8.25. Circ: 60,000 (controlled).

052 GBR ISSN 2044-7124
EASTERN AIRWAYS IN-FLIGHT MAGAZINE. Text in English. 2002. q. free (effective 2010). back issues avail. **Document type:** *Magazine, Consumer.*
Formerly (until 2009): E-Magazine (1477-3031)
Published by: (Eastern Airways Uk Ltd.), Gravity Consulting Ltd., Office 15, Abbey Business Ctr, Smithfiled, Abbey Rd, Pity Me, Durham, DH1 5JZ, United Kingdom. TEL 44-191-3832838, info@gravity-consulting.com, http://www.gravity-consulting.com. Pub. Stan Abbott. Adv. contact Tom Boden.

053.1 DEU
EDITION. Text in German. 4/yr. **Document type:** *Magazine, Consumer.*
Formerly (until 2001): ArabellaSheraton
Published by: Soundbay Communications Ltd., Wittenberger Str 17, Leipzig, 04129, Germany. TEL 49-341-33770, FAX 49-341-3377111, info@soundbay.co.uk, http://www.soundbay.co.uk. Circ: 80,000 (controlled).

059.951 HKG
ELITE. Variant title: Jingying Shenghuo. Text in Chinese. 1985; N.S. 2003. w. CNY 112 per month; CNY 15 per issue (effective 2009). **Document type:** *Magazine, Consumer.*
Published by: (Zhongguo Nanfang Hangkong Gongsi/China Southern CHN), Xianchuanmei/Recruit Holdings Limited, 26/F, 625 King's Rd., North Point, Hong Kong. TEL 852-2321-4567, FAX 852-2352-6204.

056.1 ARG
EN VUELO. Text in Spanish, English. m. adv. **Description:** Inflight magazine of Aerolineas Argentinas helps travelers plan their trips and learn about the airline's destinations.
Published by: Manzi Publicidad S.A., Vedia 1971 (1429), Buenos Aires, Argentina.

051 CYP
EUROSUN. Text in English. 1992. a. adv. bk.rev. illus. back issues avail. **Document type:** *Magazine, Consumer.* **Description:** Functions as the Eurocypria Charter Airline in-flight magazine.
Published by: Action Publications Ltd, PO Box 24676, Nicosia, 1302, Cyprus. TEL 357-2-590555, FAX 357-2-590048. Ed., Pub. Tony Christodoulou. R&P Dina Wilde TEL 357-2-590555. Adv. contact Oriana Patala. Circ: 100,000. **Dist. by:** Action Publications.

051 USA ISSN 1549-0920
EXECUTIVETRAVEL SKYGUIDE. Text in English. 19??. m. USD 65 domestic; USD 77 in Canada; USD 138 elsewhere (effective 2009). adv. back issues avail. **Document type:** *Magazine, Consumer.* **Description:** Provides complete flight schedules for North America and key international destinations and travel reference information for the business travelers.
Former titles (until 200?): Skyguide from American Express (1534-7648); (until 199?): SkyGuide (0744-091X)
Related titles: Online - full text ed.: USD 29.95 (effective 2009).
Published by: American Express Publishing Corp., 1120 Ave of the Americas, New York, NY 10036. TEL 212-382-5600, FAX 212-382-5879, ashields@amexpub.com, http://www.amexpub.com. Ed., Pub. Janet Libert. Adv. contact Sandra Krug TEL 847-438-2700. B&W page USD 9,600, color page USD 12,000; trim 4 x 8.5. Circ: 100,000.

051 USA
EXPERIENCE MILWAUKEE. Text in English. 200?. s-a. free (effective 2009). adv. **Document type:** *Magazine, Consumer.* **Description:** Embraces the Milwaukee city's lifestyles, legacies and leisurely pursuits.
Published by: Nei-Turner Media Group, 93 W Geneva St, PO Box 1080, Williams Bay, WI 53191. TEL 262-245-1000, 800-386-3228, FAX 262-245-2000, info@ntmediagroup.com. Ed. Anne Celano Frohna. Pubs. Bill Turner, Gary Nei.

052 IRL
EXPRESS IT. Text in English. q. adv. **Document type:** *Magazine, Consumer.*
Published by: (Aer Arann), Mainstream Publications, Coolbracken House, Church Terrace, Bray, Co. Wicklow, Ireland. TEL 353-1-2868246, FAX 353-1-2868241. Adv. contact Leslie Magill. color page EUR 1,244; trim 210 x 297. Circ: 10,000 (controlled).

051 USA
FLIGHT. Variant title: Tower Air Flight. Text in English. bi-m. adv. **Document type:** *Magazine, Consumer.* **Description:** Contains articles and features on inflight entertainment for Tower Air customers.
Published by: (Tower Air), The Pohly Co., 99 Bedford St, Fl 5, Boston, MA 02111. TEL 617-451-1700, 800-383-0888, FAX 617-338-7767, info@pohlyco.com, http://www.pohlyco.com. Circ: 45,000 (controlled).

052 GBR
FLYBE'S INFLIGHT MAGAZINE. Variant title: Flybe Uncovered. Text in English. 1995. bi-m. adv. back issues avail. **Document type:** *Magazine, Consumer.* **Description:** Contains travel and lifestyle features, including sections on business, overseas property market, food, bars, and shopping.
Formerly (until 2007): Jersey European Flying Colours (1359-2270)
Published by: (Jersey European Airways), Brooklands Group Ltd., Jack Walker House, Exeter International Airport, Devon, EX5 2HL, United Kingdom. TEL 44-1392-268529. Ed. Ann Wallace. Adv. contact Nathan Berman TEL 44-1342-872023. Circ: 1,750,000.

051 054 LUX
FLYDOSCOPE; magazine de bord de Luxair. Text in English, French, German. 1975. 6/yr. free to passengers (effective 2005). adv. **Document type:** *Magazine, Consumer.* **Description:** Consists of feature articles on aviation, art, culture travel and places of interest to those who fly Luxair.
Published by: (Luxair), Editions Mike Koedinger SA, P O Box 728, Luxembourg, L-2017, Luxembourg. TEL 35-2-2966181. Ed. Nicole Eastwood. Circ: 160,000 (controlled).

051 059.992 IDN
GARUDA MAGAZINE; the official in-flight magazine of Garuda Indonesia. Text in English, Indonesian. 1971. m. free. adv. charts; illus. **Document type:** *Magazine, Consumer.*
Formerly (until 1981): Garuda Indonesia Airways Magazine (0046-5453)
Published by: (Garuda Indonesia), P T Indo Multi Media, Globe Bldg 2nd Fl, Jl. Buncit Raya Kav. 31-33 Mampang Prapatan, Jakarta Selata, Indonesia. TEL 62-21-79187008, FAX 62-21-79187009, immgroup@indomultimedia.co.id, http://www.indomultimedia.co.id/. adv.: page IDR 50,400, page USD 10,350; trim 21 x 28. Circ: 55,000 (controlled).

052 HKG
GULF AIR. Text in English. m. adv. **Document type:** *Magazine, Consumer.*
Published by: Emphasis Media Limited, 6/F South Cornwall House, 979 King's Rd, Taikoo Pl, Quarry Bay, Hong Kong. TEL 852-2516-1000, FAX 852-2561-3349, enquiry@emphasis.net, http://www.emphasis.net.

051 USA
HANA HOU!. Text in English. 1989. q. USD 36. adv. maps. **Document type:** *Magazine, Consumer.* **Description:** Covers events, culture and recreation in the destinations served by the airline.
Former titles: Pacific Connections; (until 1991): Hawaiian Airlines Magazine
Published by: (Hawaiian Airlines, Inc.), Pacific Travelogue, 3465 Waialae Ave, 340, Honolulu, HI 96816. TEL 808-733-3333, FAX 808-733-3340. Ed. Derek Ferrar. Pub. Chris Pearce. Adv. contact Simone Abbott. page USD 7,455; trim 10.88 x 8.13. Circ: 120,000.

051 USA
HAWAII HOTEL NETWORK. (In 6 editions for 45 hotels) Text in English. 1973. 3/yr. free in Waikiki and neighbor island hotels of Hawaii. adv. bk.rev. **Document type:** *Magazine, Consumer.* **Description:** Presents feature articles on a range of subjects for the first-time and repeat visitor. Includes calendar, directory information, and Japanese language section.
Formerly: Here's Hawaii
Published by: Network Media, PO Box 88377, Honolulu, HI 96830-8377. TEL 808-955-2378. Ed. Jeff Lum. Pub. Peter Gellatly. R&P Camie Foster. Adv. contact Carol Williams. color page USD 11,900. Circ: 70,000 (controlled).

051 USA
HEMISPHERES. Text in English. 1957. m. adv. bk.rev. illus. **Document type:** *Magazine, Consumer.* **Description:** Provides information to managerial and professional men and women who travel frequently.
Former titles (until Oct. 1992): Vis a Vis; United; United Mainliner; Mainliner (0025-083X)
Indexed: PerIslam.
Published by: Ink Publishing, Capital Bldg, 255 E Paces Ferry Rd, Ste 400, Atlanta, GA 30305. TEL 678-553-8080, FAX 678-553-8099, http://ink-publishing.com. Adv. contact Stephen Andrews TEL 678-553-8081. B&W page USD 32,810, color page USD 46,920. Circ: 450,000.

052 GBR ISSN 1350-1631
HIGH LIFE; travel experiences from the experts. Text in English. 19??. m. GBP 37 domestic; GBP 117 in Australia & New Zealand; USD 80 in United States; GBP 52 elsewhere (effective 2010). adv. charts; illus.; tr.lit. **Document type:** *Magazine, Consumer.* **Description:** Featuring current travel news and information form the experts all around the world.
Former titles (until 1973): Trident (0041-2929); (until 196?): High Life
Indexed: GeoRef.
—CCC.
Published by: (British Airways), Cedar Communications, 85 Strand, London, WC2R 0WD, United Kingdom. TEL 44-20-75508000, info@cedarcom.co.uk, http://www.cedarcom.co.uk/. Ed. Kerry Smith. adv.: page GBP 13,670; trim 210 x 289. Circ: 199,394.

053.1 DEU
HLX.PRESS. Text in German. 2004. 4/yr. adv. **Document type:** *Magazine, Consumer.*
Published by: Ideenews GmbH & Co. KG, Karbachstr 22, Neuwied, 56567, Germany. TEL 49-2631-999666, FAX 49-2631-999652, info@ideenews.de, http://www.ideenews.de. adv.: B&W page EUR 7,300, color page EUR 9,600. Circ: 150,000 (controlled).

052 NLD ISSN 0018-3563
HOLLAND HERALD; magazine of the Netherlands. Text in English. 1966. m. free to qualified personnel (effective 2009). adv. bk.rev. illus.; maps. 152 p./no.; **Document type:** *Magazine, Consumer.* **Description:** Includes regular international travel features.
Published by: Media Partners (Subsidiary of: Roto Smeets de Boer n.v.), PO Box 2215, Amstelveen, 1180 EE, Netherlands. TEL 31-20-5473600, FAX 31-20-6475121, mp@mediapartners.nl, http://www.mediapartners.nl. Ed. Mike Cooper.

059.94511 HUN ISSN 1218-2346
HORIZON. Text in Hungarian. 1981. m. free newsstand/cover (effective 2011). adv. **Document type:** *Magazine, Consumer.*
Former titles (until 1994): Takeoff (1215-2315); (until 1990): Malev Magazine (0230-9386)
Indexed: RILM.
Published by: (Malev Hungarian Airlines), Geomedia Kiadoi Zrt./Geomedia Publishing Co., Lajos u 48-66, Budapest, 1036, Hungary. TEL 36-1-4898800, FAX 36-1-4898899, info@geomedia.hu, http://www.geomedia.hu. Ed. Laszlo Horvath.

051 USA ISSN 1050-2440
HORIZON AIR MAGAZINE. Text in English. 1979. m. USD 30 (effective 2007). adv. tr.lit. **Document type:** *Magazine, Consumer.* **Description:** Aimed at business travelers in the Northwest and includes regional business, travel and general interest topics.
Published by: Paradigm Communications Group, 2701 First Ave, 250, Seattle, WA 98121. TEL 206-441-5871, FAX 206-448-6939, info@paradigmcz.com, http://www.inflightpubs.com. Ed., R&P Michele Dill. Pub. Mimi Kirsch. Adv. contact Ken Krass. Circ: 25,000 (controlled).

647.9 051 USA
HOTEL BEL AIR MAGAZINE. Text in English. 1993. q. adv. **Document type:** *Magazine, Consumer.* **Description:** Provides timely, relevant editorial in the areas of dining, shopping, arts and culture to assist guests while they are visiting Los Angeles and staying in the hotel.
Published by: Modern Luxury, LLC., 701 Stone Canyon Rd, Los Angeles, CA 90077. TEL 310-472-1211, 800-648-4097, FAX 310-472-5234, http://www.modernluxury.com. Pub. Michael Blaise Kong TEL 312-930-9400 ext 370. Adv. contact Christa Hruby Maiers TEL 312-930-9400 ext 376. page USD 8,500; trim 8.5 x 10.875. Circ: 30,000.

910.202 THA
HUMSAFAR. Text in Thai. 1980. 6/yr. USD 29. adv. **Description:** Inflight publication of Pakistan International Airlines. Focuses on travel and tourism.
Published by: (Pakistan International Airlines), Media Transasia (Thailand) Ltd., 14th Fl., Ocena Tower II, 75/8 Soi Sukhumvit, 19 Sukhumvit Rd., Klongtoeynue, Wattana, Bangkok, 10110, Thailand. FAX 662-204-2391. Ed. X Colaco. Circ: 70,000.

051 056.9 BRA
ICARO; Varig inflight magazine/revista de bordo Varig. Text in English, Portuguese. 1983. m. free. adv. **Document type:** *Magazine, Consumer.* **Description:** Inflight magazine covering business, cultural and international topics on Brazil and on Varig's destinations.
Published by: (Varig Airlines), R M C Comunicacao Ltda, Rua Teodoro Sampaio 417, 1st Fl, Sao Paulo, SP 05405-000, Brazil. TEL 55-11-2805199, FAX 55-11-8532025, icbrasil@mandic.com.br. adv.: B&W page USD 6,150, color page USD 9,180; 275 x 210. Circ: 130,000.

051 059.927 UAE
AL-IMARAT FIL-AJWA'/EMIRATES INFLIGHT. Text in Arabic, English. 1985. m. free. adv. **Document type:** *Magazine, Consumer.* **Description:** For Emirates Airline. Features the life and culture of the Gulf, travel destinations, and subjects of international interest.
Published by: (Emirates Airlines), Motivate Publishing, PO Box 2331, Dubai, United Arab Emirates. TEL 971-4-824060, FAX 971-4-824336. Ed. Allen Armstrong. Pub. Ian Fairservice. R&P Shawki Abd El Malik. Adv. contact Simon O'Herlihy. color page USD 4,200; trim 185 x 258. Circ: 268,000.

052 GBR ISSN 1363-092X
IN-FLIGHT ENTERTAINMENT INTERNATIONAL. Text in English. 1995. fortn. GBP 395, USD 595 (effective 1999). **Document type:** *Report, Trade.* **Description:** Reports on the very latest developments in in-flight entertainment and cabin systems.
Related titles: E-mail ed.; Fax ed.; Online - full text ed.
Published by: Reed Business Information Ltd. (Subsidiary of: Reed Business), Quadrant House, The Quadrant, Sutton, Surrey SM2 5AS, United Kingdom. TEL 44-20-86523500, FAX 44-20-86528932, rbi.subscriptions@qss-uk.com, http://www.reedbusiness.co.uk/. **Subscr. to:** Quadrant Subscription Services, PO Box 302, Haywards Heath, W Sussex RH16 3YY, United Kingdom. TEL 44-1444-445566, FAX 44-1444-445447.

051 059 CAN ISSN 1916-5080
IN-FLIGHT REVIEW. Abbreviated title: I F R. Text in English. 2008. q. adv. **Document type:** *Magazine, Consumer.* **Description:** Covers informative and entertaining stories on the rich cultural trends of the Pacific Northwest, from the island charm of Victoria to the glittering excitement of Vancouver.
Related titles: Online - full text ed.: free (effective 2010).
Published by: Archipelago Media Ltd., 140 Government St, Victoria, BC V8V 2K7, Canada. TEL 250-380-3961, FAX 250-380-3962. Ed., Pub. Garth Eichel.

051 057.1 RUS
INFLIGHT REVIEW. Text in English, Russian. 1990. 11/yr. **Document type:** *Magazine, Consumer.*
Published by: Izdatel'skii Dom S P N, ul Kedrova, 15, Moscow, 117036, Russian Federation. valle@spn.ru. Circ: 70,000.

910.202 USA
INN ROOM VISITORS MAGAZINE. Text in English. 1977. m. free. adv. bk.rev. **Document type:** *Magazine, Consumer.*
Formerly: Inn Room Magazine
Address: 210 S Juniper, Ste 215, Escondido, CA 92025. TEL 760-489-5252, FAX 760-489-6752. Ed. Donna Abate. Pub. Jerry Barash. Adv. contact Suzanne Wilkinson. Circ: 88,300 (paid). **Subscr. to:** PO Box 3395, Escondido, CA 92033.

050 FRA ISSN 1763-8682
IVOIRE. Text in French, English. 2003. q. adv. **Document type:** *Magazine, Consumer.* **Description:** Concentrates mostly on tourist destinations in Ivory Coast.
Published by: A S A Editions, 1 Passage du Grand Cerf, Paris, 75002, France. TEL 33-1-44889500, FAX 33-1-44889505, info@asaeditions.com. adv.: color page EUR 4,000; 21 x 28.5. Circ: 10,000.

055.956 JPN
JAPAN AIRLINES AGORA. Text in Japanese. 1991. m. JPY 350 per issue.
Published by: J A L Cultural Development Co. Ltd., Fujiya Ginza Bldg, 9-3 Ginza 6-chome, Chuo-ku, Tokyo, 104-0061, Japan. TEL 81-3-3573-6700. Ed. Toru Ishii. Pub. Kazuyoshi Miyazaki. adv.: color page USD 11,300; trim 10.75 x 8.25. Circ: 210,000.

051 USA
JWEST ARIZONA. Text in English. 2006. a. free. adv. **Document type:** *Magazine, Consumer.* **Description:** Covers the most luxurious elements of the resorts.
Published by: Media That Deelivers, Inc., 8132 N 87th Pl, Scottsdale, AZ 85258. TEL 480-460-5203, FAX 480-460-2345, general@mediathatdeelivers.com, http://www.mediathatdeelivers.com. Pub. Michael Dee TEL 480-460-5203 ext 202. adv.: color page USD 5,900; trim 8 x 10.5. Circ: 47,000 (free).

051 USA
JWEST LAS VEGAS. Text in English. 2006. a. free. adv. **Document type:** *Magazine, Consumer.* **Description:** Covers all the splendor of the JW Marriott Las Vegas resort & Spa at summerlin in one glamorous annual in-room magazine.
Published by: Media That Deelivers, Inc., 8132 N 87th Pl, Scottsdale, AZ 85258. TEL 480-460-5203, FAX 480-460-2345, general@mediathatdeelivers.com, http://www.mediathatdeelivers.com. Pub. Michael Dee TEL 480-460-5203 ext 202. adv.: color page USD 5,900; trim 8 x 10.5. Circ: 15,000 (free).

057.85 POL
KALEIDOSCOPE. Text in Polish. 1979. q. adv.
Published by: (L O T Polish Airlines), A G P O L, Ul Sienkiewicza 12, PO Box 136, Warsaw, 00950, Poland. Circ: 80,000.

052 NZL ISSN 1177-7486
KIA ORA; your Air New Zealand magazine. Text in English. 1984. m. **Document type:** *Magazine, Consumer.* **Description:** Showcases New Zealand business, sport, arts, travel, food, wine and lifestyle.
Former titles (until Feb.2007): Air New Zealand (1176-0850); (until Nov.2002): Panorama (1175-5008); (until 2001): Pacific Wave (1174-0930); (until 1996): Pacific Way (0112-2681); Which was formed by the merger of (1966-1984): Jetaway (0111-4778); (19??-1984): Skyway (0110-7631); Which was formerly (until 1979): Air New Zealand (0110-506X); (until 1978): N A C's New Zealand (0110-019X); (until 1975): N A C Airline Review
Published by: (Air New Zealand USA), A C P Media New Zealand (Subsidiary of: A C P Magazines Ltd.), Private Bag 92512, Auckland, 1036, New Zealand. TEL 64-9-3082700, FAX 64-9-3082878. Ed. Jenny Farrell. Adv. contact Matthew Tremain.

070 SGP
KRISWORLD; Singapore Airlines inflight entertainment magazine. Text in English. m. **Document type:** *Magazine, Consumer.*
Published by: S P H Magazines Pte Ltd. (Subsidiary of: Singapore Press Holdings Ltd.), 82 Genting Ln Level 7, Media Centre, Singapore, 349567, Singapore. TEL 65-6319-6319, FAX 65-6319-6345, sphmag@sph.com.sg, http://www.sphmagazines.com.sg/.

051 USA
KWIHI; the in-flight magazine of Air Aruba. Text in English. 1995. q.
Published by: Abarta Media, 11900 Biscayne Blvd, Ste 300, Miami, FL 33181-2726. TEL 305-892-6644, FAX 305-892-2266. Ed. Jenny Bronson. Circ: 10,000.

053.1 DEU
L T U EXKLUSIV. (Lufttransport Unternehmen) Text in German. 3/yr. **Document type:** *Newsletter, Consumer.*
Published by: L T U International Airways, Flughafen Halle 8, Duesseldorf, 40474, Germany. TEL 49-211-9418888, FAX 49-211-9418557, kundenclub@ltu.de, http://www.ltu.de.

053.1 DEU
L T U MAGAZIN. (Lufttransport Unternehmen) Text in German. 1986. q. adv. bk.rev. back issues avail. **Document type:** *Magazine, Consumer.*
Published by: L T U International Airways, Flughafen Halle 8, Duesseldorf, 40474, Germany. TEL 49-211-9418888, FAX 49-211-9418557, kundenclub@ltu.de, http://www.ltu.de. adv.: page EUR 14,000. Circ: 330,000 (controlled).

056.1 USA
LANDING ZONE. Text in English. 2/yr. **Document type:** *Magazine, Consumer.* **Description:** Features short stories, activities and games designed to appeal to children ages 4 to 12 from all over the world.
Published by: American Airlines Publishing, 4333 Amon Carter Blvd, MD 5374, Fort Worth, TX 76155. TEL 817-967-1804, FAX 817-967-1571, http://www.aa.com.

051 USA
LEGEND MAGAZINE. Text in English. 2007 (Jul.). a. free. adv. **Document type:** *Magazine, Consumer.* **Description:** Provides information about all the glamour of San Diego's legendary seaside retreat, the hotel Del Coronado.
Published by: (Hotel del Coronado), Media That Deelivers, Inc., 8132 N 87th Pl, Scottsdale, AZ 85258. TEL 480-460-5203, FAX 480-460-2345, general@mediathatdeelivers.com, http://www.mediathatdeelivers.com. Pub. Michael Dee TEL 480-460-5203 ext 202. adv.: color page USD 5,900; trim 8 x 10.5. Circ: 15,000 (free).

059.94541 FIN ISSN 1238-9978
LENTO. Text in Finnish. 1993. 5/yr. **Document type:** *Magazine, Consumer.*
Published by: Sanoma Magazines Finland Corporation, Lapinmaentie 1, Helsinki, 00350, Finland. TEL 358-9-1201, FAX 358-9-1205171, info@sanomamagazines.fi, http://www.sanomamagazines.fi. Circ: 80,000 (controlled).

387.7 051 ATG
LIAT ISLANDER. Text in English. 1979. 3/yr. back issues avail.
Published by: F T Caribbean, PO Box 1037, St John's, Antigua. TEL 268-462-3392, FAX 268-462-3492. Circ: 50,000.

059.956 051 GBR
LONDON ZOK; essential for London's Japanese community. Text in Japanese, English. 1998. m. GBP 15 domestic; GBP 50 foreign.
Published by: L Z Media Ltd., P.O. Box 22527, London, W8 7GS, United Kingdom. TEL 020-72216611, FAX 020-72268811, londonzok@compuserve.com, http://www.londonzok.co.uk. Ed. Laurence Ninomiya. Pub. Luke Douglas-Home. Circ: 17,500.

053.1 DEU
LUFTHANSA MAGAZIN. Text in English, German. 1972. m. adv. **Document type:** *Magazine, Consumer.*
Formerly: Lufthansa Bordbuch
Published by: (Deutsche Lufthansa AG), Gruner + Jahr AG & Co, Am Baumwall 11, Hamburg, 20459, Germany. TEL 49-40-37030, FAX 49-40-37035601, info@gujmedia.de, http://www.guj.de. Adv. contact Heiko Hager. page EUR 29,700. Circ: 302,755 (paid and controlled).

052 GBR
M O. (Mandarin Oriental) Text in Chinese. 1963. 2/yr. adv. **Document type:** *Magazine, Consumer.*
Formerly: Mandarin
Published by: (Mandarin Oriental Hotel Group HKG), Conde Nast Publications Ltd. (Subsidiary of: Advance Publications, Inc.), Vogue House, Hanover Sq, London, W1S 1JU, United Kingdom. Circ: 35,000.

051 PHL ISSN 0217-6998
MABUHAY; the inflight magazine of Philippine Airlines. Text in English. 1988. m. free. adv. back issues avail. **Document type:** *Magazine, Consumer.*
Related titles: Online - full text ed.
Indexed: IPP.
Published by: (Philippine Airlines), Eastgate Publishing Corporation, Rm.704 Prestige Tower Condominium, Emerald Ave., Ortigas Center, Pasig Mm, 1605, Philippines. TEL 632-633-4004. Ed. Simeon S Ventura Jr. Pub. Charles C Chante. Circ: 103,000.

054 387.7 FRA
MAGAZINE AIGLE AZUR. Text in French. 200?. q. **Document type:** *Magazine, Consumer.*
Published by: (Aigle Azur), Res Publica, 5 Rue de Charonne, Paris, 75011, France.

053.931 NLD
MARTINAIR MAGAZINE. Text in Dutch; Summaries in English, German. a. free to passengers (effective 2009). illus. **Document type:** *Consumer.*
Published by: Martinair Holland N.V., Postbus 7507, Luchthaven Schiphol, 1118 ZG, Netherlands. http://www.martinair.com.

910.09 UAE
MATAR ABU DHABI AL-DAWLI/SHOPTALK - ABU DHABI DUTY FREE GUIDE. Text in Arabic, English. 1988. q. free. **Document type:** *Journal, Consumer.* **Description:** Tourist and duty free information regarding Abu Dhabi and its airport, and other features of interest to international travellers.
Published by: (Abu Dhabi. Abu Dhabi Department of Civil Aviation), Abu Dhabi Duty Free, Marketing Department, PO Box 3167, Abu Dhabi, United Arab Emirates. TEL 757350, FAX 757172. Ed. Bassam El Khazen. Circ: 20,000.

051 USA
MODERN LUXURY HAWAI'I. Variant title: Modern Luxury Hawaii. Text in English, Japanese. 2006 (Dec.). 3/yr. USD 20; USD 5.95 per issue (effective 2009). adv. back issues avail. **Document type:** *Magazine, Consumer.* **Description:** Covers the finest in dining, nightlife, design and travel as well as the most cutting-edge and trendsetting local and international fashions in Hawaii.
Related titles: Online - full text ed.

TU

Published by: Modern Luxury, LLC., 2155 Kalakaua Ave, Ste 701, Honolulu, HI 96815. TEL 808-924-6622, FAX 808-924-6623, http://www.modernluxury.com. Eds. Gary Baum, Degen Pener. adv.: color page USD 22,000; trim 10 x 12. Circ: 50,000.

059.957 KOR
MORNING CALM. Text in Korean. 1977. m. free. adv. **Document type:** *Magazine, Consumer.*
Formerly (until 1989): Kaleidoscene
Published by: (Korean Air), Hachette Ein*s Media Co., Ltd./A Swe Tteu Negseuteu Mi'dieo., 4, 6, 7 Fl. Pax Tower, 231-13 Nonhyun-dong, Gangnam-gu, Seoul, 135-010, Korea, S. Circ: 120,000.

910.202 GRC
MOTION/KINISI. Text in English, Greek. 1969. 3/yr. free. adv. illus. **Document type:** *Magazine, Consumer.*
Formerly: Your Air Companion
Published by: Olympic Airways S.A., 96-100 Syngrou Ave, Athens, 117 41, Greece. TEL 30-1-9267-628, FAX 30-1-9267-818, TELEX 215823 OA GR. Ed. Maria Ven Sourmelis. Adv. contact Maria Sourmelis. color page GRD 900,000. Circ: 200,000 (paid).

051 056.1 COL
EL MUNDO AL VUELO - INFLIGHT NOTES. Text in English, Spanish. 1972. m. USD 40. adv. bk.rev. **Description:** For passengers on Avianca's domestic and international flights, also sent to important commercial and tourist organizations.
Formerly: Apuntes de Abordo - Inflight Notes
Published by: (Avianca), Carvajal S.A., Aptdo Aereo 53550, Bogota, CUND, Colombia. Ed. Maria Cristina Lamus. Circ: 90,000.

051 USA ISSN 1941-0514
MY MIDWEST. Text in English. 1990. bi-m. USD 45 (effective 2007). adv. **Document type:** *Magazine, Consumer.* **Description:** General interest publication for business and leisure travelers.
Former titles (until 2007): Midwest Airlines (1547-4704); (until 2003): Midwest Express Magazine (1068-3135)
Indexed: RI-1, RI-2.
Published by: Ink Publishing, 68 Jay St, Ste 315, Brooklyn, NY 11201. TEL 888-685-1681, FAX 646-349-3844, http://ink-publishing.com. Circ: 30,000 (controlled).

059.951 HKG ISSN 1004-7441
NANFANG HANGKONG/GATEWAY. Text in Chinese. 1985. m. CNY 485 (effective 2009). **Document type:** *Magazine, Consumer.*
Formerly: Guangzhou Minhang
Related titles: Online - full text ed.
Published by: (Zhongguo Nanfang Hangkong Gongsi/China Southern CHN), Xianchuanmei/Recruit Holdings Limited, 26/F, 625 King's Rd., North Point, Hong Kong. TEL 852-2321-4567, FAX 852-2352-6204.

056.1 USA
NEXOS. Text in Portuguese, Spanish. 1999. q. free. adv. **Document type:** *Magazine, Consumer.* **Description:** The Latin American magazine of American Airlines.
Published by: American Airlines Publishing, 4333 Amon Carter Blvd, MD 5374, Fort Worth, TX 76155. TEL 817-967-1804, FAX 817-967-1571, http://www.aa.com. Ed. Ana Cristina Reymundo. Pub. Randal Kazmierski. adv.: B&W page USD 13,800, color page USD 16,030; trim 8 x 10.875. Circ: 225,525 (free).

059.951 HKG ISSN 1672-7436
NIHAO; travel / living / art / fashion. Variant title: Kongzhong zhi Jia. Text in Chinese. 2004. m. CNY 320 (effective 2009). **Document type:** *Magazine, Consumer.*
Related titles: Online - full text ed.
Published by: (Zhongguo Nanfang Hangkong Gongsi/China Southern CHN), Xianchuanmei/Recruit Holdings Limited, 26/F, 625 King's Rd., North Point, Hong Kong. TEL 852-2321-4567, FAX 852-2352-6204.

053.1 AUT
NIKI. Text in German. 2/yr. adv. **Document type:** *Magazine, Consumer.*
Published by: (Lauda Air Luftfahrtgesellschaft), D+R Verlagsgesellschaft mbH, Leberstr 122, Vienna, 1110, Austria. TEL 43-1-740770, FAX 43-1-74077841, office@d-r.at. Ed. Uschi Korda. Adv. contact Alexandra Salvinetti TEL 43-1-74077828. page EUR 5,087; trim 210 x 280. Circ: 50,000 (controlled).

051 USA
NORTHWEST AIRLINES WORLD TRAVELER. Text in English. 1989. m. USD 50; free onboard passengers (effective 2005). adv. illus.; tr.lit. **Document type:** *Magazine, Consumer.* **Description:** Contains travel, business, technology, arts, and sports articles of general interest to passengers aboard Northwest Airlines flights.
Formerly: Compass Readings (1051-7383)
Published by: (Northwest Airlines), Skies America International Publishing and Communications, 9655 S W Sunshine Court, Ste 500, Beaverton, OR 97005. TEL 503-520-1955, FAX 503-520-1275, publish@skies.com, http://www.skiesamerica.com. Ed. Matthew Williams. Pub. Sherrill Patterson. Adv. contact Caron Gorman. B&W page USD 21,870, color page USD 28,100; trim 8 x 10.88. Circ: 350,000 (paid and free).

NOVA SCOTIA OPEN TO THE WORLD. *see* BUSINESS AND ECONOMICS

052 PNG
PARADISE. Text in English. 1976. 6/yr. USD 24. adv.
Published by: Air Nuigini, PO Box 7186, Boroko, Papua New Guinea. FAX 273-416. Ed. Geoff McLaughlin. Circ: 50,000.

054 FRA ISSN 1954-5231
PARIS AEROPORTS MAGAZINE/AEROPORTS DE PARIS MAGAZINE. Text in French, English. 1968. 10/yr. adv. **Document type:** *Magazine, Consumer.*
Former titles (until 2004): Aeroports Magazine (0336-626X); (until 1975): Aeroport de Paris Magazine (0336-6278)
Indexed: CLT&T.
—CCC.
Published by: (Aeroports de Paris, Direction Marketing et Communication), Textuel La Mine, 146 Rue du Faubourg Poissonniere, Paris, 75010, France. TEL 33-1-53157575, FAX 33-1-53157570, http://textuel.lamine.com. Pub. M Hamon. Circ: 300,000.

053.1 DEU
PASSAGEN (BERLIN). Text in German. 4/yr. EUR 4.50 newsstand/cover (effective 2007). adv. **Document type:** *Magazine, Consumer.*
Published by: Kleiner und Bold Brand Identity Design GmbH, Neue Schoenhauser Str 19, Berlin, 10178, Germany. TEL 49-30-2844530, FAX 49-30-28445310, kontakt@kleinerundbold.com, http://www.kleinerundbold.com. adv.: color page EUR 5,500. Circ: 40,000 (controlled).

900 057 RUS
PERFECT FLIGHT. Text in Russian. bi-m. 80 p./no.; **Document type:** *Magazine, Consumer.*
Published by: S K Press, Marksistkaya 34, str 10, Moscow, 109147, Russian Federation. TEL 7-095-9742260, FAX 7-095-9742263. Pub. E Adlerov.

051 USA
PITTSBURGH POINT; the area visitors guide. Text in English. 1981. m. USD 18 (effective 1999). adv. bk.rev. Supplement avail.; back issues avail. **Description:** Presents a complete guide to the greater Pittsburgh area. Distributed in hotel rooms, visitor info counters and selected businesses.
Formerly: One Point to Pittsburgh Point
Published by: Scott Publishing (Subsidiary of: Haights Cross Communications), 573 Catskill Dr, Pittsburgh, PA 05239-2617. TEL 412-327-2242, FAX 412-327-4442. Ed. A Robert Scott. Adv. contact Bryan Scott. color page USD 594, B&W page USD 524; 5.5 x 8.5. Circ: 59,000.

051 USA
POINTE 2 POINTE. Variant title: Pointe to Pointe. Text in English. 2004. a. adv. **Document type:** *Magazine, Consumer.* **Description:** Provides the corporate and family appeal of the two popular Phoenix destinations, with features on their acres of water attractions, mountain-top views, distinct southwest shopping and dining, and extensive indoor and outdoor meeting spaces.
Published by: Media That Deelivers, Inc., 8132 N 87th Pl, Scottsdale, AZ 85258. TEL 480-460-5203, FAX 480-460-2345, general@mediathatdeelivers.com, http://www.mediathatdeelivers.com. Adv. contact Christie Holder. color page USD 7,500; trim 9 x 10.75. Circ: 25,000.

051 USA
PRIVATE SCREENING. Text in English. m. adv. **Document type:** *Magazine, Consumer.*
Published by: (Continental Airlines), The Pohly Co., 99 Bedford St, Fl 5, Boston, MA 02111. TEL 617-451-1700, 800-383-0888, FAX 617-338-7767, http://www.pohlyco.com.

053.931 387.7 NLD ISSN 1877-4660
PRIVIUM UPDATE. Text in Dutch. 200?. q. adv. **Document type:** *Magazine, Consumer.*
Published by: (Amsterdam Airport Schiphol), Hearst Magazines Netherlands (Subsidiary of: Hachette Filipacchi Medias), Singel 468, Amsterdam, 1017 AW, Netherlands. TEL 31-20-5353600, FAX 31-20-6238149, singel@hearstmagazines.nl, http://www.hearstmagazines.nl. Circ: 55,000 (controlled).

052 AUS ISSN 1443-2013
QANTAS: THE AUSTRALIAN WAY. Text in English. 1947. m. free. adv. **Document type:** *Magazine, Consumer.* **Description:** Covers sport, arts, travel, lifestyle for Australian domestic and international Qantas Airways passengers.
Former titles (until 1999): Australian Way (Melbourne) (0818-9161); (until 1986): Transair (0041-1043); Which incorporated: Airways Inflight (0314-4003); Which was formerly (until 1976): Airways (0002-2896)
Published by: (Qantas Airways Ltd.), A C P Magazines Ltd. (Subsidiary of: P B L Media Pty Ltd.), 54-58 Park St, Sydney, NSW 2000, Australia. TEL 61-2-92828000, FAX 61-2-91263769, research@acpaction.com.au, http://www.acp.com.au. Ed. Susan Skelly. Adv. contact David Rogers TEL 61-2-92828288. color page AUD 17,200; bleed 220 x 285.

051 USA
THE RITZ-CARLTON. Text in English. 200?. q. USD 40 (effective 2007). adv. **Document type:** *Magazine, Consumer.* **Description:** Contains articles on the people, places, products and pastimes that make the modern world an interesting place to be.
Published by: McMurry, Inc., 1010 E Missouri Ave, Phoenix, AZ 85014. TEL 602-395-5850, 888-626-8779, FAX 602-395-5853, info@mcmurry.com, http://www.mcmurry.com. Pub., Adv. contact Tracie McLaughlin. page USD 4,235; trim 9 x 10.8.

051 056.1 ESP
RONDA IBERIA. Text in English, Spanish. 1974. bi-m. free. bk.rev. **Description:** Iberia's inflight magazine provides useful information on various national and international destinations.
Published by: (Iberia Lineas Aereas de Espana), Ediciones Reunidas, S.A., O'Donnell, 12, Madrid, 28009, Spain. TEL 34-91-586-3300, FAX 34-91-586-3618. Circ: 220.

910.09 BRN
ROYAL BRUNEI AIRLINES MUHIBAH. Text in English. 1991. bi-m. USD 42 (effective 2001). adv. music rev.; film rev. 100 p./no.; back issues avail. **Document type:** *Magazine, Consumer.* **Description:** Provides the official inflight magazine of the Royal Brunei Airlines.
Published by: Royal Brunei Airlines Sdn. Bhd., PO Box 737, Bandar Seri Begawan, 1907, Brunei Darussalam. TEL 673-2-343371, 673-2-240500, FAX 673-2-343372, eddiyana@rba.com.bn, http://bruneiair.com. Ed. Lito Gutierrez. R&P, Adv. contact Christina Chin. color page USD 4,500. Circ: 25,000.

910.09 JOR
ROYAL WINGS. Text in Arabic, English. 6/yr. adv. **Document type:** *Magazine, Consumer.* **Description:** Inflight magazine that offers passengers an interesting mix of topical international features, it also includes articles on Jordan's fascinating sites and culture, people profiles, and a comprehensive guide to the airline's routes and facilities.
Published by: Royal Jordanian Airlines, Housing Bank Commercial Center, Queen Noor St, PO Box: 302, Amman, 11118, Jordan. ammddrj@rj.com. Ed. Jill Horton. adv.: color page USD 4,848; trim 11.69 x 8.25. Circ: 40,000.

914.604 338.48 SWE ISSN 1102-9722
ST. PETERSBURG NEWS. Text in English; Summaries in Russian. 1990. q. USD 35. adv. **Description:** Focuses on Russian foreign trade and international business. Covers hotels, restaurants, recreation and culture in St. Petersburg.
Formerly: Leningrad News
Published by: (Aeroflot), Florman Marketing, Nybrogatan 21, Stockholm, 11439, Sweden. TEL 4686631970, FAX 4686610480, TELEX 12350. Adv. contact Petra Eurenius. Circ: 70,000.

052 THA ISSN 0251-7418
HE9873.55.A1
SAWASDEE. Text in Chinese. 1971. m. USD 70. adv. **Document type:** *Magazine, Consumer.* **Description:** In-flight magazine.
Published by: Thai Air International, 89 Vibhavadi-Rangsit Rd, Bangkok, 10900, Thailand. TEL 66-2-5451000, FAX 66-2-5453322, public.info@thaiairways.co.th, http://www.thaiair.info. Circ: 100,000.

052 ZAF ISSN 1726-5991
SAWUBONA. Text in English. 2003. m. ZAR 300 domestic; ZAR 600 foreign (effective 2006). adv. **Document type:** *Magazine, Consumer.* **Description:** Provides a mix of travel, culture and lifestyle.
Published by: Mafube Publishing (Pty) Ltd., PO Box 2185, Houghton, Johannesburg 2041, South Africa. TEL 27-11-3261020. adv.: B&W page ZAR 35,755, color page ZAR 37,994; trim 210 x 276. Circ: 96,000.

052 SWE ISSN 0346-7775
SCANORAMA. Text in English. 1972. 10/yr. free. illus. **Description:** In-flight magazine.
Formerly (until 1972): Scandinavian Times (0105-0664)
Published by: Media Partner, Gavlegatan 18 B, Stockholm, 11330, Sweden. TEL 46-8-7297575, FAX 46-8-7288524. Ed. Lars Bringert. Circ: 140,000.

052 GBR
SELAMTA/GREETINGS; the in-flight magazine of Ethiopian Airlines. Text in English. 1984. q. free to qualified personnel (effective 2009). adv. bk.rev.; video rev. maps. 80 p./no.; **Document type:** *Magazine, Consumer.* **Description:** Contains travel and business, sport and history, news, views, and much more.
Published by: (Ethiopian Airlines), Camerapix Magazines UK Ltd., 32 Friars Walk, Southgate, London, N14 5LP, United Kingdom. TEL 44-20-83612942, camerapixuk@btinternet.com. adv.: color page GBP 3,640; trim 210 x 283. Circ: 70,000.

051 NPL ISSN 1605-9263
SHANGRI-LA; Royal Nepal Airlines inflight magazine. Text in English. q. **Document type:** *Magazine, Consumer.* **Description:** Provides general articles and information on Nepal with photos and other tourism related topics.
Related titles: Online - full content ed.
Published by: (Royal Nepal Airlines), M D Publishing Co. Pvt. Ltd., Tripureswor, PO Box 3525, Kathmandu, Nepal. TEL 977-1-260327, 977-1-260418, 977-1-256003, FAX 977-1-260159, nttj@mos.com.np. Ed. Mohan Khanal.

052 GBR
SILHOUETTE; the in-flight magazine for Air Seychelles. Text in English, French. 1988. s-a. free to qualified personnel (effective 2009). adv. bk.rev.; video rev. charts; maps; stat. 96 p./no.; **Document type:** *Magazine, Consumer.* **Description:** Covers articles about travel and culture in the Seychelles; with in-flight, duty-free listings.
Published by: Camerapix Magazines UK Ltd., 32 Friars Walk, Southgate, London, N14 5LP, United Kingdom. TEL 44-20-83612942, camerapixuk@btinternet.com. adv.: B&W page GBP 2,810, color page GBP 3,640. Circ: 30,000.

052 HKG
SILKROAD (HONG KONG). Text in Chinese. 1991. m. adv. **Description:** Inflight magazine.
Related titles: English ed.
Published by: (Dragon Airlines Ltd.), Emphasis HK Ltd., 505-508 Westlands Centre, 20 Westlands Rd, Quarry Bay, Hong Kong, Hong Kong. TEL 590-1328, FAX 590-1333. Ed. Amy Lo. Circ: 40,000 (controlled).

052 SGP ISSN 0129-606X
SILVER KRIS; Singapore Airlines inflight magazine. Text in English. 1976. m. adv. **Document type:** *Magazine, Consumer.*
Published by: (Singapore International Airlines), S P H Magazines Pte Ltd. (Subsidiary of: Singapore Press Holdings Ltd.), 82 Genting Ln Level 7, Media Centre, Singapore, 349567, Singapore. TEL 65-6319-6319, FAX 65-6319-6345, sphmag@sph.com.sg, http://www.sphmagazines.com.sg/. Circ: 250,000.

051 USA ISSN 0734-8967
AP2
SKY. Variant title: Delta Sky. Text in English. 1972. m. USD 75 (effective 2009). adv. illus.; tr.lit. back issues avail.; reprints avail. **Document type:** *Magazine, Consumer.* **Description:** A Delta Airlines publication, it covers travel, business, food, and lifestyle.
Related titles: Online - full text ed.
Published by: (Delta Air Lines), M S P Communications, 220 South Sixth St, Ste 500, Minneapolis, MN 55402. TEL 612-339-7571, FAX 612-339-5806, info@mspcommunications.com, http://www.mspcommunications.com. adv.: B&W page USD 35,480, color page USD 50,740; trim 8 x 10.5. Circ: 381,896.

079 TUR
SKYLIFE. Text in English. m. **Document type:** *Magazine, Consumer.*
Related titles: Online - full text ed.: free (effective 2009).
Published by: Turkish Airlines, Turkish Airlines General Management Building Ataturk Airport, Yesilkoy, Istanbul, 34149, Turkey. TEL 90-212-4636363, FAX 90-212-4652121, customer@thy.com.

053.1 AUT
SKYLIGHTS. Text in German, English. bi-m. adv. **Document type:** *Magazine, Consumer.*
Published by: (Austrian Airlines AG), D+R Verlagsgesellschaft mbH, Leberstr 122, Vienna, 1110, Austria. TEL 43-1-740770, FAX 43-1-74077841, office@d-r.at. Ed. Sabine Lachinger. Adv. contact Christine Salvinetti. page EUR 3,997; trim 210 x 275. Circ: 50,000 (controlled).

053.1 AUT
SKYLINES. Text in English, German. 1989. bi-m. EUR 20 domestic; EUR 30.50 foreign (effective 2005). adv. **Document type:** *Magazine, Consumer.* **Description:** Contains stories and features on people, entertainment and tourism for passengers of Austrian Airlines.
Published by: (Austrian Airlines AG), D+R Verlagsgesellschaft mbH, Leberstr 122, Vienna, 1110, Austria. TEL 43-1-740770, FAX 43-1-74077888, office@d-r.at, http://www.dundr.at. Ed. Uschi Korda. Adv. contact Christine Salvinetti. col. inch EUR 13,850; trim 210 x 275. Circ: 150,000 (controlled).

052 ZAF
SKYWAYS. Text in English. m. adv.
Published by: (S A Airlink), Panorama Publications (Pty) Ltd., Private Bag X41, Bryanston, Johannesburg 2021, South Africa. TEL 27-11-4682090, FAX 27-11-4682091. Ed., Adv. contact Urs Honneger. Pub. Urs Honegger.

052 JAM
SKYWRITINGS. Text in English. 1973. 6/yr. USD 36 (effective 2000). adv. **Document type:** *Magazine, Consumer.*
Published by: (Air Jamaica), Creative Communications Inc. Ltd., PO Box 105, Kingston, 10, Jamaica. TEL 876-977-5020, FAX 876-977-5448, creativecom@guangotree.com. Ed. Odette Dixon Neath. R&P Tony Gambrill. Adv. contact Gillian Fisher. Circ: 250,000.

051 USA ISSN 1066-1581
G155.S643
SOUTHWEST AIRLINES SPIRIT MAGAZINE. Text in English. 1971. m. adv. bk.rev. back issues avail. **Document type:** *Magazine, Consumer.*
Published by: SouthWest Airlines, c/o Pace Communications, Ste 360, 2811 McKinney Ave, Dallas, TX 75204. TEL 214-580-8070, FAX 214-580-2491, SouthwestAirlinesAdSales@wnco.com, http://www.southwest.com/. Pub. Rik Gates. Adv. contact Erika Sloan TEL 336-383-5599. Circ: 480,310.

051 USA ISSN 0199-7092
DU620
SPIRIT OF ALOHA. Text in English. 1976. m. **Document type:** *Magazine, Trade.* **Description:** Inflight magazine of Aloha Airlines and Island Air.
Related titles: Online - full text ed.
Published by: (Aloha Airlines), Honolulu Publishing Company, Ltd., Ocean View Ctr, 707 Richards St, Ste 525, Honolulu, HI 96813. TEL 808-524-7400, 800-272-5245, FAX 808-531-2306.

051 USA ISSN 1539-7777
STRATOS. Text in English. 1999. 8/yr. USD 29 (effective 2006). adv. **Document type:** *Magazine, Trade.* **Description:** Inflight magazine for private plane owners and passengers.
Published by: Stratos Magazine, LLC, 1430 I-85 Pkwy., Montgomery, AL 36106. TEL 334-386-3828, FAX 334-386-3813, stratos@stratosmag.com. Ed. Mark Nothaft. Pub. Helen Sevier. Adv. contact David Bannister. page USD 12,500; trim 9 x 10.875.

052 CYP ISSN 1011-1727
SUNJET; Cyprus Airways in-flight magazine. Text in Greek, English. 1973. q. adv. bk.rev. back issues avail. **Document type:** *Magazine, Consumer.* **Description:** Functions as Cyprus Airways inflight magazine.
Published by: (Cyprus Airways), Action Publications Ltd, PO Box 24676, Nicosia, 1302, Cyprus. TEL 357-2-590555, FAX 357-2-590048. Ed., R&P Tony Christodoulou. Circ: 75,000. **Dist. by:** Action Publications, PO Box 24676, Nicosia, Cyprus. TEL 357-2-590555, FAX 357-2-590048.

053.1 DEU
SUNNY TIMES. Text in German. 2002. q. adv. **Document type:** *Magazine, Consumer.* **Description:** Contains articles and features for inflight entertainment.
Published by: SunExpress Europe, Am Gruenen Weg 1-3, Kelsterbach, 65451, Germany. TEL 49-69-69628247, FAX 49-69-69628249, central.service@sunexpress.com, http://www.sunexpress.com.

052 053 054 CHE
SWISSAIR GAZETTE. Text in English, French, German. 10/yr. CHF 55 domestic; CHF 65 in Europe; CHF 75 rest of world. adv. **Document type:** *Magazine, Consumer.* **Description:** Airline publication devoted to news and features about Switzerland and other parts of the world. Also includes Swiss culture, travel, education, products, and hotel guide.
Published by: (Swissair AG), Frontpage AG, Uetlibergstr 132, Zuerich, 8045, Switzerland. TEL 41-1-457-5315, FAX 41-1-457-5301. Ed. Vivian Egli. Adv. contact Peter Furrer. B&W page CHF 24,700, color page CHF 29,600; trim 275 x 210. Circ: 180,000.

052 054 FRA ISSN 1767-9370
TERANGA. Text in French, English. 200?. bi-m. **Document type:** *Magazine, Consumer.* **Description:** For travelers on Air Senegal International.
Published by: A S A Editions, 1 Passage du Grand Cerf, Paris, 75002, France. TEL 33-1-44889500, FAX 33-1-44889505, info@asaeditions.com. Circ: 20,000.

917.204 MEX ISSN 1405-4604
TRAVELERS GUIDE TO MEXICO. Text in English. 1969. a. MXN 2,000 domestic; USD 28 foreign (effective 2005). adv. illus.; maps. index. **Document type:** *Newsletter, Consumer.* **Description:** Guide book to Mexico placed in first-class hotel rooms in major resorts and sold in the gift shops of these hotels. Contains color photos of Mexico's resorts, detailed city maps, and the latest information on traveling, vacationing and living in Mexico.
Related titles: ◆ Online - full text ed.: Travel Mexico Newsletter.
Published by: Promociones de Mercados Turisticos, S.A. de C.V., Londres, No 22, Col Juarez, Mexico City, DF 06600, Mexico. TEL 52-55-55925022, FAX 52-55-55467002, editor@travelguidemexico.com. Ed. Shooka Shemirani. Pub. Chris A Luhnow. Adv. contact Rebeca Sancedo. color page MXN 254,100. Circ: 3,600,000 (controlled).

910.20 USA
TRAVELHOST. (102 regional eds. avail.) Text in English. 1968. m. illus.; maps. **Document type:** *Magazine, Consumer.* **Description:** Contains news features and articles on travel, leisure, recreation, and business as well as dining and entertainment guides and TV listings.
Published by: Travelhost, Inc., 10701 N Stemmons Freeway, Dallas, TX 75220. TEL 972-556-0541, FAX 972-432-8729. Pub. James E Buerger.

056.9 PRT ISSN 1647-0613
UP. Text in Portuguese. 2007. m. **Document type:** *Magazine, Consumer.*
Published by: T A P Air Portugal, Building 25, Lisbon Airport, Lisbon, 1704, Portugal. http://www.tap.pt.

051 USA
US AIRWAYS MAGAZINE. Text in English. 2006. m. adv. back issues avail. **Document type:** *Magazine, Trade.* **Description:** Provides information about U.S. airways.
Formed by the merger of (1986-2006): America West Airlines Magazine; (1973-2006): US Airways Attache Magazine
Related titles: Online - full text ed.
Published by: (US Airways), Pace Communications Inc., 1301 Carolina St, Greensboro, NC 27401. TEL 336-378-6065, FAX 336-383-5699, info@pacecommunications.com, http://www.pacecommunications.com. Eds. Julie Moore, Lance Elko. Pub. Andrea T Alexander. adv.: color page USD 27,040; trim 8 x 10.5.

VENETIAN STYLE. *see* HOTELS AND RESTAURANTS

052 AUS ISSN 1444-1632
VIRGIN BLUE VOYEUR. Text in English. 200?. m. adv. **Document type:** *Magazine, Consumer.* **Description:** Provides information about culture, travel, business, technology, food and drinks.
Published by: (Virgin Blue), Pacific Magazines Pty Ltd., 35-51 Mitchell St, McMahons Point, NSW 2060, Australia. TEL 61-2-94643300, FAX 61-2-94643375, http://www.pacificmagazines.com.au. Ed. Kirsten Rowlingson. adv.: page AUD 10,500; bleed 220 x 280. Circ: 73,448. **Subscr. to:** Subscribe Today, GPO Box 4983, Sydney, NSW 2001, Australia.

050 FRA ISSN 1774-7155
VISIT AFRICA. Text in French, English. 2005. q. adv. **Document type:** *Magazine, Consumer.*
Published by: A S A Editions, 1 Passage du Grand Cerf, Paris, 75002, France. TEL 33-1-44889500, FAX 33-1-44889505, info@asaeditions.com. adv.: color page EUR 5,000; 21 x 28.5. Circ: 15,000.

917.1 CAN ISSN 0228-698X
VOILA QUEBEC. Text in English, French. 1975. q. free single copies free. adv. **Document type:** *Handbook/Manual/Guide, Consumer.* **Description:** Informs visitors to Quebec of local historic and cultural sites of interest and provides a guide to the city's fine restaurants and shops.
Published by: (Association Hoteliere de la Region de Quebec), Publications Vacances Quebec Inc., 185 Saint Paul St, Quebec, PQ G1K 3W2, Canada. TEL 418-694-1272, FAX 418-692-3392. Ed. Lynn Magee. Pub., R&P, Adv. contact Curtis J Sommerville. B&W page CAD 4,063, color page CAD 4,875; trim 8.25 x 5.44. Circ: 65,000.

056.1 MEX
VUELO. Text in Spanish. 1994. m. USD 25; USD 60 in United States; USD 75 elsewhere. adv. **Description:** Each issue covers a region or travel destination, including information on site attractions, cultural events, natural wonders, interviews, and leisure activities.
Published by: (Mexicana de Aviacion), Impresiones Aereas S.A. de C.V., Arquimides 5, Col Polanco, Mexico City, DF 11560, Mexico. TEL 525-726-8941, FAX 525-726-8969. Ed. Olga Cano. Pub. Guillermo Perez Vargas. adv.: color page USD 13,200. Circ: 110,000 (controlled).

917.04 USA ISSN 0192-4257
WELCOME TO MIAMI AND THE BEACHES. Text in English. 1970. w. USD 35. adv. **Document type:** *Magazine, Consumer.* **Description:** Describes area shopping, dining, beaches, attractions, and points of interest.
Published by: Welcome Publications, Inc., PO Box 630518, Miami, FL 33163. TEL 305-944-9444. Ed. Clara Amsel. Pub., R&P, Adv. contact Jeffrey Kaplan. Circ: 16,500.

051 USA ISSN 1094-4737
WHERE ATLANTA. Text in English. 1966. m. USD 56; USD 6 newsstand/cover (effective 2009). adv. illus. **Document type:** *Magazine, Consumer.* **Description:** Visitor's guide to Atlanta's dining, nightlife, entertainment and cultural attractions.
Related titles: Online - full text ed.
Published by: Morris Visitor Publications (Subsidiary of: Morris Multimedia, Inc.), 180 Allen Rd Ste 203N, Atlanta, GA 30328. TEL 404-236-1055, FAX 404-236-0819, MVPcustomerservice@morris.com, http://www.morrisvisitorpublications.com/. Ed. Jennifer Weis. adv.: B&W page USD 3,360, color page USD 4,110; trim 10.88 x 8.13. Circ: 62,000 (controlled).

051 USA
WHERE BOSTON. Text in English. m. USD 52; USD 5 newsstand/cover (effective 2009). adv. software rev. illus. **Document type:** *Magazine, Consumer.* **Description:** Guide to Boston's dining, entertainment, nightlife and other activities of interest to visitors.
Related titles: Online - full text ed.
Published by: Morris Visitor Publications (Subsidiary of: Morris Multimedia, Inc.), 45 Newbury St, Ste 506, Boston, MA 02116. TEL 617-701-2100, FAX 617-262-2474, MVPcustomerservice@morris.com, http://www.morrisvisitorpublications.com/. Ed. Leigh Harrington. adv.: B&W page USD 3,750, color page USD 4,480; trim 10.88 x 8.13. Circ: 60,000 (controlled).

059.945 HUN ISSN 1217-5714
WHERE BUDAPEST. Text in Hungarian. 1993. m. (11/yr.). adv. **Document type:** *Magazine, Consumer.* **Description:** Focuses on cultural events, festivals, folk dancing, restaurants, galleries, sightseeing and entertainment.
Address: Wesselenyi u.16 III/16, Budapest, 1077, Hungary. TEL 361-351-1030, FAX 361-267-9554. Ed. Charles Hebbert. adv.: B&W page USD 1,694. Circ: 30,000.

910.202 CAN ISSN 1719-4172
WHERE CALGARY. Text in English. 1981. m. CAD 26 domestic; CAD 30 foreign (effective 2000). adv. **Document type:** *Magazine, Consumer.* **Description:** Information and maps about things to see and do in Calgary.
Former titles (until 2006): Where Canada (Calgary Edition) (1711-456X); (until 2003): Where Calgary (1182-1981); (until 1990): Key to Calgary (0711-4400)
Published by: St. Joseph Media, 111 Queen St E, Ste 320, Toronto, ON M5C 1S2, Canada. TEL 416-364-3333, FAX 416-594-3374, http://www.stjosephmedia.com. adv.: B&W page CAD 1,660, color page CAD 2,010; trim 10.88 x 8.13. Circ: 18,900 (controlled).

051 USA ISSN 1534-3227
WHERE CHICAGO. Text in English. 19??. m. USD 48; USD 12 newsstand/cover (effective 2009). **Document type:** *Magazine, Consumer.* **Description:** Informs persons visiting Chicago of historic and cultural attractions and provides a guide to the city's restaurants, shops, galleries, theaters, nightclubs and entertainment, including city maps.
Related titles: Online - full text ed.
Published by: Morris Visitor Publications (Subsidiary of: Morris Multimedia, Inc.), 1165 N Clark St, Chicago, IL 60610. TEL 312-642-1896, FAX 312-642-5467, MVPcustomerservice@morris.com, http://www.morrisvisitorpublications.com/. Ed. J P Anderson. Circ: 100,000 (controlled).

051 USA
WHERE GUESTBOOK. ARIZONA. Text in English. a. free (effective 2008). adv. illus. **Document type:** *Magazine, Consumer.* **Description:** Introduces visitors to the many cultural, recreational, historic, shopping, dining, sightseeing and entertainment sites and activities in Phoenix and Valley of the Sun.
Former titles: Guest Informant. Phoenix and the Valley of the Sun; Guest Informant. Phoenix - Scottsdale - Sedona - Tempe - Northern Arizona; Guest Informant. Phoenix - Scottsdale - Sedona - Tucson - Tempe - Northern Arizona; Guest Informant - Arizona
Related titles: Online - full text ed.
Published by: Morris Visitor Publications (Subsidiary of: Morris Multimedia, Inc.), 3295 N Drinkwater Blvd, Ste 5, Scottsdale, AZ 85251. TEL 480-481-9981, FAX 480-481-9979, MVPcustomerservice@morris.com, http://www.morrisvisitorpublications.com/. Ed. Lisa K. Polacheck. Pub. Mike Korzon. adv.: B&W page USD 14,540, color page USD 19,050; trim 10.88 x 8.5. Circ: 44,682.

051 USA
WHERE GUESTBOOK. ATLANTA. Text in English. 1982. a. free (effective 2008). adv. illus. **Document type:** *Magazine, Consumer.* **Description:** Introduces visitors to the many cultural, recreational, historic, shopping, dining, sightseeing and entertainment sites and activities in Atlanta.
Former titles: Guest Informant. Atlanta; Leisureguide - Atlanta
Published by: Morris Visitor Publications (Subsidiary of: Morris Multimedia, Inc.), 180 Allen Rd Ste 203N, Atlanta, GA 30328. TEL 404-236-1055, FAX 404-236-0819, MVPcustomerservice@morris.com, http://www.morrisvisitorpublications.com/. Ed. Jennifer Weis. adv.: B&W page USD 7,320, color page USD 9,852; trim 8.5 x 10.875. Circ: 42,160.

910.202 910 USA
WHERE GUESTBOOK. BALTIMORE. Variant title: Baltimore Quick Guide. Text in English. a. free (effective 2008). adv. illus. **Document type:** *Magazine, Consumer.* **Description:** Provides visitors to the many cultural, recreational, historic, shopping, dining, sightseeing and entertainment sites and activities in Baltimore.
Former titles: Guest Informant. Baltimore; Guest Informant. Baltimore - Annapolis; Guest Informant. Baltimore
Related titles: Online - full text ed.
Published by: (Baltimore Area Convention and Visitors Association), Morris Visitor Publications (Subsidiary of: Morris Multimedia, Inc.), 575 S Charles St, Ste 503, Baltimore, MD 21201. TEL 410-783-7520, FAX 410-783-1763, MVPcustomerservice@morris.com, http://www.morrisvisitorpublications.com/. Ed. Laureen Miles. adv.: B&W page USD 8,676, color page USD 11,280; trim 7.88 x 8.5. Circ: 21,250.

917.4 USA
WHERE GUESTBOOK. BOSTON. Text in English. 1978. a. free (effective 2008). adv. illus. **Document type:** *Magazine, Consumer.* **Description:** Introduces visitors to the many cultural, historic, sightseeing, recreational, shopping, dining and entertainment sites and activities in the Boston area.
Former titles: Guest Informant. Boston; Guest Informant. Boston - Cambridge; Guest Informant - Boston
Related titles: Online - full text ed.
Published by: Morris Visitor Publications (Subsidiary of: Morris Multimedia, Inc.), 45 Newbury St, Ste 506, Boston, MA 02116. TEL 617-701-2100, FAX 617-262-2474, MVPcustomerservice@morris.com, http://www.morrisvisitorpublications.com/. Ed. Leigh Harrington. adv.: B&W page USD 11,760, color page USD 15,840; trim 10.88 x 8.5. Circ: 32,800.

051 USA
WHERE GUESTBOOK. CHICAGO. Text in English. 1971. a. free (effective 2008). adv. illus. **Document type:** *Magazine, Consumer.* **Description:** Introduces visitors to the many cultural, recreational, historic, shopping, dining, sightseeing and entertainment sites and activities in Chicago.
Former titles: Guest Informant. Chicago; Leisureguide - Chicago
Related titles: Online - full text ed.
Published by: Morris Visitor Publications (Subsidiary of: Morris Multimedia, Inc.), 1165 N Clark St, Chicago, IL 60610. TEL 312-642-1896, FAX 312-642-5467, MVPcustomerservice@morris.com, http://www.morrisvisitorpublications.com/. Ed. J P Anderson. adv.: B&W page USD 20,440, color page USD 27,386; trim 10.88 x 8.5. Circ: 51,100.

051 USA
WHERE GUESTBOOK. COLORADO. Text in English. a. free (effective 2008). adv. illus. **Document type:** *Magazine, Consumer.* **Description:** Introduces visitors to the many cultural, recreational, historic, shopping, dining, sightseeing and entertainment sites and activities in Denver, Boulder and Colorado Springs.
Former titles: Guest Informant. Denver - Boulder - Colorado Springs; Guest Informant - Colorado
Related titles: Online - full text ed.
Published by: Morris Visitor Publications (Subsidiary of: Morris Multimedia, Inc.), 3295 N Drinkwater Blvd, Ste 5, Scottsdale, AZ 85251. TEL 480-481-9981, FAX 480-481-9979, MVPcustomerservice@morris.com, http://www.morrisvisitorpublications.com/. Eds. Kristina Jenkins, Lisa K. Polacheck. adv.: B&W page USD 8,820, color page USD 10,560; trim 10.88 x 8.5. Circ: 31,712.

051 USA
WHERE GUESTBOOK. DALLAS. Text in English. 1937. a. free (effective 2008). adv. illus. **Document type:** *Magazine, Consumer.* **Description:** Introduces visitors to the many cultural, recreational, historic, shopping, dining, sightseeing and entertainment sites and activities in Dallas.
Formerly: Guest Informant. Dallas
Related titles: Online - full text ed.

T U

Published by: Morris Visitor Publications (Subsidiary of: Morris Multimedia, Inc.), 8111 LBJ Fwy, Ste 100, Dallas, TX 75251. TEL 214-522-0050, FAX 214-522-0504, MVPcustomerservice@morris.com, http://www.morrisvisitorpublications.com/. Ed. Meghan Richardson. Pub. Lisa Cowen. adv.: B&W page USD 15,350, color page USD 20,645; trim 10.88 x 8.5. Circ: 44,156.

051 USA
WHERE GUESTBOOK. FIRST COAST; Jacksonville & St. Augustine. Text in English. a. free (effective 2008). adv. **Document type:** *Magazine, Consumer.* **Description:** Provides information about Jacksonville city.
Formerly: Guest Informant. Jacksonville
Related titles: Online - full text ed.
Published by: Morris Visitor Publications (Subsidiary of: Morris Multimedia, Inc.), 180 Allen Rd Ste 203N, Atlanta, GA 30328. TEL 404-236-1055, FAX 404-236-0819, MVPcustomerservice@morris.com, http://www.morrisvisitorpublications.com/. Ed. Jennifer Weis. adv.: B&W page USD 5,820, color page USD 7,860; trim 8.5 x 10.875.

052 USA
WHERE GUESTBOOK. FORT WORTH. Text in English. a. free (effective 2009). **Document type:** *Magazine, Consumer.* **Description:** Introduces visitors to the many cultural, recreational, historic, shopping, dining, sightseeing and entertainment sites and activities in Fort Worth.
Related titles: Online - full text ed.
Published by: Morris Visitor Publications (Subsidiary of: Morris Multimedia, Inc.), 8111 LBJ Fwy, Ste 100, Dallas, TX 75251. TEL 214-522-0050, 214-522-0050, MVPcustomerservice@morris.com, http://www.morrisvisitorpublications.com/. Pub. Lisa Cowen.

052 USA
WHERE GUESTBOOK. GOLD COAST. Text in English. a. free (effective 2009). **Document type:** *Magazine, Consumer.*
Formed by the merger of: Guest Informant. Fort Lauderdale; Guest Informant. Palm Beaches; Both of which superseded in part: Guest Informant. Palm Beach - Ft. Lauderdale; Which was formerly: Guest Informant. Palm Beach - Broward County; Guest Informant - Palm Beach - Gold Coast; Guest Informant - The Florida Gold Coast; Leisureguide - The Florida Gold Coast
Related titles: Online - full text ed.
Published by: Morris Visitor Publications (Subsidiary of: Morris Multimedia, Inc.), 1975 E Sunrise Blvd, Ste 528, Ft Lauderdale, FL 33304. TEL 954-467-7640, FAX 954-525-6820, MVPcustomerservice@morris.com, http://www.morrisvisitorpublications.com/. Ed. Jay Brightman. Pub. Bonny Mager.

051 USA
WHERE GUESTBOOK. HAWAI'I. THE BIG ISLAND. Text in English. a. free (effective 2008). adv. **Document type:** *Magazine, Consumer.* **Description:** Introduces visitors to the many cultural, recreational, historic, shopping, dining, sightseeing and entertainment sites and activities in Hawaii, the Big Island.
Formerly: Guest Informant. Hawaii - The Big Island
Related titles: Online - full text ed.
Published by: Morris Visitor Publications (Subsidiary of: Morris Multimedia, Inc.), 1833 Kalakaua Ave #810, Honolulu, HI 96815. TEL 808-955-2378, FAX 808-955-2379, MVPcustomerservice@morris.com, http://www.morrisvisitorpublications.com/. Ed. Marie Tutko.

051 USA
WHERE GUESTBOOK. HOUSTON. Text in English. 1978. a. free (effective 2008). adv. illus. **Document type:** *Magazine, Consumer.* **Description:** Introduces visitors to the many cultural, recreational, historic, shopping, dining, sightseeing and entertainment sites and activities in Houston.
Former titles: Guest Informant. Houston; Guest Informant. Lone Star Style: Houston; Guest Informant - Lone Star Style: Houston and San Antonio; Guest Informant - Houston; Leisureguide - Houston
Related titles: Online - full text ed.
Published by: Morris Visitor Publications (Subsidiary of: Morris Multimedia, Inc.), 8111 LBJ Fwy, Ste 100, Dallas, TX 75251. TEL 214-522-0050, FAX 214-522-0504, MVPcustomerservice@morris.com, http://www.morrisvisitorpublications.com/. Ed. Meghan Richardson. adv.: B&W page USD 12,512, color page USD 16,614; trim 10.88 x 8.5. Circ: 28,028.

051 USA
WHERE GUESTBOOK. KANSAS CITY. Text in English. 1982. a. free (effective 2008). adv. illus. **Document type:** *Magazine, Consumer.* **Description:** Introduces visitors to the many cultural, recreational, historic, shopping, dining, sightseeing and entertainment sites and activities in Kansas city.
Former titles: Guest Informant. Kansas City; Leisureguide - Kansas City
Related titles: Online - full text ed.
Published by: Morris Visitor Publications (Subsidiary of: Morris Multimedia, Inc.), 410 S Liberty St, Kansas City, MO 64050. TEL 816-350-6335, FAX 816-836-3805, MVPcustomerservice@morris.com, http://www.morrisvisitorpublications.com/. Ed. David Lancaster. Pub. Michael Egger. adv.: B&W page USD 8,460, color page USD 11,795; trim 10.88 x 8.5. Circ: 18,333.

051 USA
WHERE GUESTBOOK. KAUA'I. Text in English. a. free (effective 2008). adv. **Document type:** *Magazine, Consumer.* **Description:** Introduces visitors to the many cultural, recreational, historic, shopping, dining, sightseeing and entertainment sites and activities in Kauai, Hawaii.
Formerly: Guest Informant. Kauai
Related titles: Online - full text ed.
Published by: Morris Visitor Publications (Subsidiary of: Morris Multimedia, Inc.), 1833 Kalakaua Ave #810, Honolulu, HI 96815. TEL 808-955-2378, FAX 808-955-2379, MVPcustomerservice@morris.com, http://www.morrisvisitorpublications.com/. Ed. Marie Tutko.

051 USA
WHERE GUESTBOOK. LOS ANGELES. Text in English. a. free (effective 2008). adv. illus. **Document type:** *Magazine, Consumer.* **Description:** Introduces visitors to the many cultural, recreational, historic, shopping, dining, sightseeing and entertainment sites and activities in the Los Angeles area.
Former titles: Guest Informant. Los Angeles; Guest Informant. Los Angeles - Beverly Hills - Long Beach
Related titles: Online - full text ed.
Published by: Morris Visitor Publications (Subsidiary of: Morris Multimedia, Inc.), 3679 Motor Ave, Ste 300, Los Angeles, CA 90034. TEL 320-280-2880, FAX 310-280-2890, MVPcustomerservice@morris.com, http://www.morrisvisitorpublications.com/. Ed. Benjamin Epstein. Pub. Jeff Levy. adv.: B&W page USD 20,760, color page USD 27,960; trim 10.88 x 8.5. Circ: 60,324.

051 USA
WHERE GUESTBOOK. MAUI. Text in English. a. free (effective 2008). adv. illus. **Document type:** *Magazine, Consumer.* **Description:** Introduces visitors to the many cultural, historic, recreational, shopping, dining, sightseeing and entertainment sites and activities in Maui.
Formerly: Guest Informant. Maui; Incorporates: Guest Informant. Wailea
Related titles: Online - full text ed.
Published by: Morris Visitor Publications (Subsidiary of: Morris Multimedia, Inc.), PO Box 88377, Honolulu, HI 96830. MVPcustomerservice@morris.com, http://www.morrisvisitorpublications.com/. Ed. Marie Tutko. adv.: color page USD 14,940; trim 8.5 x 10.875. Circ: 24,780.

051 USA
WHERE GUESTBOOK. MIAMI. Text in English. a. free (effective 2008). adv. illus. **Document type:** *Magazine, Consumer.* **Description:** Introduces visitors to the many cultural, recreational, historic, shopping, dining, sightseeing and entertainment sites and activities in Miami.
Formerly: Guest Informant. Miami
Related titles: Online - full text ed.
Published by: Morris Visitor Publications (Subsidiary of: Morris Multimedia, Inc.), 7300 Corporate Center Dr Ste 303, Miami, FL 33126. TEL 305-892-6644, FAX 305-892-2991, MVPcustomerservice@morris.com, http://www.morrisvisitorpublications.com/. Ed. Irene Moore. adv.: B&W page USD 11,880, color page USD 15,444; trim 10.75 x 8.5. Circ: 55,588.

052 USA
WHERE GUESTBOOK. MILWAUKEE. Text in English. a. free (effective 2009). **Document type:** *Magazine, Consumer.* **Description:** Introduces visitors to the many cultural, recreational, historic, shopping, dining, sightseeing and entertainment sites and activities in Milwaukee.
Related titles: Online - full text ed.
Published by: Morris Visitor Publications (Subsidiary of: Morris Multimedia, Inc.), PO Box 362, Milwaukee, WI 53201. TEL 414-405-3024, FAX 866-756-6706. Ed. J P Anderson. Pub. Tammie Figlinski.

051 USA
WHERE GUESTBOOK. NEW ORLEANS. Text in English. 1982. a. free (effective 2008). adv. illus. **Document type:** *Magazine, Consumer.* **Description:** Introduces visitors to the many cultural, recreational, historic, shopping, dining, sightseeing and entertainment sites and activities in New Orleans.
Former titles: Guest Informant. New Orleans; Leisureguide - New Orleans
Related titles: Online - full text ed.
Published by: Morris Visitor Publications (Subsidiary of: Morris Multimedia, Inc.), 528 Wilkinson Row, New Orleans, LA 70130. TEL 504-522-6468, FAX 504-522-0018, MVPcustomerservice@morris.com, http://www.morrisvisitorpublications.com/. Ed. Doug Brantley. Pub. Amy Taylor. adv.: B&W page USD 11,810, color page USD 15,970; trim 10.88 x 8.5. Circ: 39,568.

051 USA
WHERE GUESTBOOK. NEW YORK. Text in English. a. free (effective 2008). adv. illus. **Document type:** *Magazine, Consumer.* **Description:** Introduces visitors to the many cultural, recreational, historic, shopping, dining, sightseeing and entertainment sites and activities in New York.
Formerly: Guest Informant. New York
Related titles: Online - full text ed.
Published by: Morris Visitor Publications (Subsidiary of: Morris Multimedia, Inc.), 79 Madison Ave, 8th Fl, New York, NY 10016. TEL 212-557-3010, FAX 212-716-8578, MVPcustomerservice@morris.com, http://www.morrisvisitorpublications.com/. Pub. Merrie L Davis. adv.: B&W page USD 30,000, color page USD 40,500; trim 10.88 x 8.5. Circ: 80,098.

051 USA
WHERE GUESTBOOK. O'AHU. Text in English. a. free (effective 2008). adv. **Document type:** *Magazine, Consumer.* **Description:** Introduces visitors to the many cultural, recreational, historic, shopping, dining, sightseeing and entertainment sites and activities in Oahu, Hawaii.
Formerly: Guest Informant. Oahu
Related titles: Online - full text ed.
Published by: Morris Visitor Publications (Subsidiary of: Morris Multimedia, Inc.), 1833 Kalakaua Ave #810, Honolulu, HI 96815. TEL 808-955-2378, FAX 808-955-2379, MVPcustomerservice@morris.com, http://www.morrisvisitorpublications.com/. Ed. Marie Tutko. Pub. Elizabeth Carey.

051 USA
WHERE GUESTBOOK. ORANGE COUNTY. Text in English. a. free (effective 2008). adv. illus. **Document type:** *Magazine, Consumer.* **Description:** Introduces visitors to the many cultural, historic, recreational, shopping, dining, sightseeing and entertainment sites and activities in Orange country.
Formerly: Guest Informant. Orange County; Which superseded in part: Guest Informant. Orange County - San Diego; Which was fomerly: Guest Informant - Orange County, CA
Related titles: Online - full text ed.
Published by: Morris Visitor Publications (Subsidiary of: Morris Multimedia, Inc.), 125 E Baker St Ste 250, Costa Mesa, CA 92626. TEL 714-825-1700, FAX 714-825-1710, MVPcustomerservice@morris.com, http://www.morrisvisitorpublications.com/. Ed. Benjamin Epstein. Pub. Jeff Levy. Adv. contact Tiffany Reinhold. B&W page USD 7,383, color page USD 8,778; trim 8.5 x 10.88. Circ: 30,188.

051 USA
WHERE GUESTBOOK. ORLANDO. Text in English. a. free (effective 2008). adv. illus. **Document type:** *Magazine, Consumer.* **Description:** Introduces visitors to the many cultural, historic, recreational, shopping, dining, sightseeing and entertainment sites and activities in Orlando.
Formerly: Guest Informant. Orlando
Related titles: Online - full text ed.
Published by: Morris Visitor Publications (Subsidiary of: Morris Multimedia, Inc.), 7531 Currency Dr, Orlando, FL 32809. TEL 407-852-4010, FAX 407-852-4060, MVPcustomerservice@morris.com, http://www.morrisvisitorpublications.com/. Ed. Jay Boyar. adv.: B&W page USD 13,680, color page USD 17,040; trim 8.5 x 10.875. Circ: 49,130.

051 USA
WHERE GUESTBOOK. PHILADELPHIA. Text in English. a. free (effective 2008). adv. illus. **Document type:** *Magazine, Consumer.* **Description:** Introduces visitors to the many cultural, recreational, historic, shopping, dining, sightseeing and entertainment sites and activities in Philadelphia.
Formerly: Guest Informant. Philadelphia
Related titles: Online - full text ed.
Published by: Morris Visitor Publications (Subsidiary of: Morris Multimedia, Inc.), 301 S 19th St Ste 1-South, Philadelphia, PA 19103. TEL 215-893-5100, FAX 215-893-5105, MVPcustomerservice@morris.com, http://www.morrisvisitorpublications.com/. Ed. Karen Gross. adv.: B&W page USD 10,980, color page USD 13,740; trim 10.88 x 8.5. Circ: 33,014.

051 USA
WHERE GUESTBOOK. SAN ANTONIO. Text in English. a. free (effective 2008). adv. illus. **Document type:** *Magazine, Consumer.* **Description:** Introduces visitors to the scenic, cultural, and recreational attractions in San Antonio.
Formerly: Guest Informant. San Antonio
Related titles: Online - full text ed.
Published by: Morris Visitor Publications (Subsidiary of: Morris Multimedia, Inc.), 1601 N Alamo Ste 102, San Antonio, TX 78215. TEL 210-226-7900, FAX 210-226-2605, MVPcustomerservice@morris.com, http://www.morrisvisitorpublications.com/. Ed. Meghan Richardson. Pub. Anabelle Quiroz. adv.: B&W page USD 11,350, color page USD 15,070; trim 10.88 x 8.5. Circ: 20,520.

051 USA
WHERE GUESTBOOK. SAN DIEGO. Text in English. a. free (effective 2008). illus. **Document type:** *Magazine, Consumer.* **Description:** Introduces visitors to the many cultural, recreational, historic, shopping, dining, sightseeing and entertainment sites and activities in the San Diego, California area.
Formerly: Guest Informant. San Diego; Which superseded in part: Guest Informant. Orange County - San Diego; Which was formerly: Guest Informant - Orange County, CA
Related titles: Online - full text ed.
Published by: Morris Visitor Publications (Subsidiary of: Morris Multimedia, Inc.), 3990 Old Town Ave Ste B-200, San Diego, CA 92110. TEL 619-260-5599, FAX 619-260-5598, MVPcustomerservice@morris.com, http://www.morrisvisitorpublications.com/. Ed. Maya Kroth. Pub. Jeff Levy. Adv. contact Tiffany Reinhold. Circ: 37,438.

051 USA
WHERE GUESTBOOK. SAN FRANCISCO. Text in English. a. free (effective 2008). adv. illus. **Document type:** *Magazine, Consumer.* **Description:** Introduces visitors to the many cultural, recreational, historic, shopping, dining, sightseeing and entertainment sites and activities in San Francisco and San Jose.
Former titles: Guest Informant. San Francisco; Guest Informant. San Francisco - San Jose; Guest Informant - San Francisco - Bay Area - San Jose
Related titles: Online - full text ed.
Published by: Morris Visitor Publications (Subsidiary of: Morris Multimedia, Inc.), 555 Montgomery St Ste 803, San Francisco, CA 94111. TEL 415-901-6260, FAX 415-901-6261, MVPcustomerservice@morris.com, http://www.morrisvisitorpublications.com/. Ed. Erin Roth. adv.: B&W page USD 21,300, color page USD 28,740; trim 10.88 x 8.5. Circ: 64,844.

052 USA
WHERE GUESTBOOK. SEATTLE / TACOMA. Text in English. a. free (effective 2009). **Document type:** *Magazine, Consumer.*
Formed by the merger of: Guest Informant. Seattle; Guest Informant. Tacoma; Both of which superseded in part: Guest Informant. Seattle - Bellevue - Tacoma; Which was formerly: Guest Informant - Seattle - Bellevue
Published by: Morris Visitor Publications (Subsidiary of: Morris Multimedia, Inc.), 1904 Third Ave, Ste 623, Seattle, WA 98101. TEL 206-826-2665, FAX 206-826-2676, MVPcustomerservice@morris.com, http://www.morrisvisitorpublications.com/.

051 USA
WHERE GUESTBOOK. SOUTHWEST FLORIDA. Variant title: Guest Informant. Fort Myers. Guest Informant. Southwest Florida. Text in English. a. free (effective 2008). adv. illus. **Document type:** *Magazine, Consumer.* **Description:** Introduces visitors to the many cultural, recreational, historic, shopping, dining, sightseeing and entertainment sites and activities in southwest Florida including Naples, Fort Myers, Sanibel and Captiva Islands.
Former titles: Guest Informant. Naples, Florida; Guest Informant. Southwest Florida - Naples - Sanibel - Captiva Islands; Guest Informant - Southwest Florida
Related titles: Online - full text ed.

Published by: Morris Visitor Publications (Subsidiary of: Morris Multimedia, Inc.), 2900 14th St N, Naples, FL 34103. TEL 239-434-0566, FAX 239-434-8328, MVPcustomerservice@morris.com, http://www.morrisvisitorpublications.com/. Ed. Levine Lisa. adv.: B&W page USD 7,560, color page USD 10,440; trim 10.88 x 8.5. Circ: 16,740.

051 USA
WHERE GUESTBOOK. TAMPA BAY; St Petersburg - Clearwater - Tampa - the gulf beaches. Text in English. 1980. a. free (effective 2008). adv. illus. **Document type:** *Magazine, Consumer.* **Description:** Introduces visitors to the many cultural, recreational, historic, shopping, dining, sightseeing and entertainment sites and activities in Tampa, St. Petersburg, and Clearwater, Florida.
Former titles: Guest Informant. Tampa - Saint Petersburg - Clearwater; Guest Informant. St. Petersburg - Clearwater; Guest Informant - Tampa Bay - Orlando; Guest Informant - Orlando - Tampa - St. Petersburg - Clearwater; Guest Informant - Orlando; Leisureguide - Orlando
Related titles: Online - full text ed.
Published by: Morris Visitor Publications (Subsidiary of: Morris Multimedia, Inc.), 13191 56th Court, Ste 107, Clearwater, FL 33760. TEL 727-573-4423, FAX 727-543-9449, MVPcustomerservice@morris.com, http://www.morrisvisitorpublications.com/. Ed. Shelly Preston. adv.: B&W page USD 9,840, color page USD 12,480; trim 10.88 x 8.5. Circ: 27,398.

052 USA
WHERE GUESTBOOK. TENNESSEE; Nashville & Memphis. Text in English. a. free (effective 2009). **Document type:** *Magazine, Consumer.* **Description:** Introduces visitors to the many cultural, recreational, historic, shopping, dining, sightseeing and entertainment sites and activities in Nashville & Memphis.
Formed by the merger of: Guest Informant. Nashville; Guest Informant. Memphis; Both of which superseded in part: Guest Informant. Tennessee - Memphis - Nashville; Which was formerly: Guest Informant. Tennessee - Memphis - Nashville - Knox - Chattanooga; Which superseded in part: Guest Informant - Tennessee
Published by: Morris Visitor Publications (Subsidiary of: Morris Multimedia, Inc.), 1130 Eighth Ave S Ste 100, Nashville, TN 37203. TEL 615-312-7090, FAX 615-312-7091, MVPcustomerservice@morris.com, http://www.morrisvisitorpublications.com/. Ed. Jennifer Weis. Pub. Vaughan Pritchett.

052 USA
WHERE GUESTBOOK. TRIANGLE; Raleigh, Durham, Chapel Hill. Text in English. a. free (effective 2009). **Document type:** *Magazine, Consumer.* **Description:** Introduces visitors to the many cultural, recreational, historic, shopping, dining, sightseeing and entertainment sites and activities in Raleigh, Durham, & Chapel Hill.
Related titles: Online - full text ed.
Published by: Morris Visitor Publications (Subsidiary of: Morris Multimedia, Inc.), 127 W Worthington Ave Ste 208, Charlotte, NC 28203. TEL 704-335-7181, FAX 704-335-3757, MVPcustomerservice@morris.com, http://www.morrisvisitorpublications.com/. Ed. Richard Thurmond.

051 USA
WHERE GUESTBOOK. TUCSON. Text in English. a. free (effective 2008). adv. illus. **Document type:** *Magazine, Consumer.* **Description:** Introduces visitors to the many cultural, historic, recreational, shopping, dining, sightseeing and entertainment sites and activities in Tucson, Arizona.
Formerly: Guest Informant. Tucson
Related titles: Online - full text ed.
Published by: Morris Visitor Publications (Subsidiary of: Morris Multimedia, Inc.), 4729 E Sunrise Dr #134, Tucson, AZ 85718. TEL 520-529-7199, FAX 520-219-1154, MVPcustomerservice@morris.com, http://www.morrisvisitorpublications.com/. Ed. Kristina Jenkins. Pub. Susan Lee Baxter. adv.: B&W page USD 7,710, color page USD 9,660; trim 8.5 x 10.875. Circ: 17,200.

051 USA
WHERE GUESTBOOK. WASHINGTON D.C. Text in English. a. free (effective 2008). adv. illus. **Document type:** *Magazine, Consumer.* **Description:** Introduces visitors to the many cultural, recreational, historic, shopping, dining, sightseeing and entertainment sites and activities in Washington DC, Bethesda and Alexandria.
Former titles: Guest Informant. Washington D.C. - Bethesda - Alexandria; Guest Informant. Washington D C - Bethesda - Alexandria - Bethesda; Guest Informant - Washington D C
Related titles: Online - full text ed.
Published by: Morris Visitor Publications (Subsidiary of: Morris Multimedia, Inc.), 1720 Eye St, Ste 600, Washington, DC 20006. TEL 202-463-4550, FAX 202-463-4553, MVPcustomerservice@morris.com, http://www.morrisvisitorpublications.com/. Ed. Jean Lawlor Cohen. Pub. Rick Mollineaux. adv.: B&W page USD 17,472, color page USD 23,400; trim 10.88 x 8.5. Circ: 61,336.

051 CAN
WHERE HALIFAX. Text in English. 1948. 10/yr. CAD 25 domestic; USD 25 foreign. adv. **Document type:** *Handbook/Manual/Guide, Consumer.* **Description:** Guide to shopping, sightseeing, dining and cultural events and activities for visitors to the Halifax area.
Formerly: Where Halifax - Dartmouth
Published by: Metro-Guide Publishing (Subsidiary of: Where Magazines International), 5475 Spring Garden Rd, P O Box 14, Halifax, NS B3J 3T2, Canada. TEL 902-420-9943, FAX 902-429-9058. Ed. Karen Janik. Pub. Sheila Pottie. Adv. contact Suzanne Morrison. B&W page CAD 1,305, color page CAD 1,555; trim 8.38 x 5.38. Circ: 24,000 (controlled).

051 USA
WHERE NEW ORLEANS. Text in English, Spanish. 1968. m. USD 56; USD 6 per issue (effective 2009). back issues avail. **Document type:** *Magazine, Consumer.* **Description:** Designed to be a guide to the New Orleans's top restaurants, shops, shows, exhibits and tours.
Published by: Morris Multimedia, Inc., 324 Chartres St, 2nd Fl, New Orleans, LA 70130. TEL 504-522-6468, FAX 504-522-0018, http://www.morris.com. Ed. Dough Brantley. Pub. Lois Sutton.

051 USA
WHERE NEW YORK; because you've arrived. Text in English. 1934. m. USD 73; USD 5 newsstand/cover (effective 2009). adv. maps. **Document type:** *Magazine, Consumer.* **Description:** Distributed to hotels, airline clubs, and university clubs for out-of-town visitors. Covers shopping, food, and entertainment. Includes feature articles on dining, arts and antiques, and events as well as extensive listings.
Related titles: Online - full text ed.
Published by: Morris Visitor Publications (Subsidiary of: Morris Multimedia, Inc.), 79 Madison Ave, 8th Fl, New York, NY 10016. FAX 212-636-2710, 212-716-8578, MVPcustomerservice@morris.com, http://www.morrisvisitorpublications.com/. Ed. Trisha S McMahon. Pub. Merrie L Davis. adv.: B&W page USD 8,835, color page USD 9,455; trim 10.88 x 8.13. Circ: 500,000 (free).

917 CAN ISSN 1187-1350
WHERE OTTAWA - HULL. Text in English, French. 1958. m. CAD 25. bk.rev.; play rev. **Document type:** *Magazine, Consumer.* **Description:** For visitors to Canada's capital. Includes information on sightseeing, events, shopping and dining.
Supersedes in part (in 1990): What's on in Ottawa (0043-468X)
Published by: Capital Publishers (Subsidiary of: Where Magazines International), 226 Argyle Ave, Ottawa, ON K2P 1B9, Canada. TEL 613-230-0333, FAX 613-230-4441. Ed. Marc Choma. adv.: B&W page CAD 2,660, color page CAD 3,275; trim 8.38 x 5.38. Circ: 32,000 (controlled).

052 GBR ISSN 1241-8625
WHERE PARIS. Text in English. 1992. m. adv. illus. **Document type:** *Magazine, Consumer.*
Published by: Morris Visitor Publications Europe (Subsidiary of: Morris Multimedia, Inc.), 233 High Holborn, 2nd Fl, London, WC1V 7DN, United Kingdom. TEL 44-20-72425222, FAX 44-20-72424184, http://www.morrisvisitorpublications.com. Circ: 51,000 (controlled).

051 USA
WHERE SAN FRANCISCO. Text in English. 1992. m. USD 39; USD 4 newsstand/cover (effective 2009). adv. **Document type:** *Magazine, Consumer.* **Description:** Highlights restaurants, shopping, entertainment, nightlife, and cultural attractions in the city and its environs for visitors to San Francisco and the Bay Area.
Published by: Morris Visitor Publications (Subsidiary of: Morris Multimedia, Inc.), 555 Montgomery St Ste 803, San Francisco, CA 94111. TEL 415-901-6260, FAX 415-901-6261, MVPcustomerservice@morris.com, http://www.morrisvisitorpublications.com/. Ed. Erin Roth. adv.: B&W page USD 2,875, color page USD 3,470; trim 10.88 x 8.13. Circ: 57,000 (controlled).

051 USA
WHERE ST. LOUIS. Text in English. 1963. m. USD 56; USD 6 newsstand/cover (effective 2009). adv. illus.; maps. **Document type:** *Magazine, Consumer.* **Description:** Visitor's guide to dining, entertainment, cultural attractions of the St. Louis area.
Published by: Morris Visitor Publications (Subsidiary of: Morris Multimedia, Inc.), 1006 Olive St, Ste 202, St Louis, MO 63101. TEL 314-588-8313, FAX 314-588-0920, MVPcustomerservice@morris.com, http://www.morrisvisitorpublications.com/. Ed. David Lancaster. Pub. Ethan Woods. adv.: B&W page USD 2,025, color page USD 2,425; trim 10.88 x 8.13. Circ: 34,000 (controlled).

052 CAN ISSN 0849-1135
WHERE TORONTO. Text in English. 1954. m. CAD 38.52; CAD 53.50 out of North America; USD 35 in United States (effective 2000). adv. illus. **Document type:** *Magazine, Consumer.*
Formerly: Key to Toronto (0023-0863)
Published by: St. Joseph Media, 111 Queen St E, Ste 320, Toronto, ON M5C 1S2, Canada. TEL 416-364-3333, FAX 416-594-3374, feedback@weddingbells.ca, http://www.stjosephmedia.com. adv.: B&W page CAD 5,270, color page CAD 6,420; trim 10.88 x 8.13. Circ: 76,900 (controlled).

051 USA
WHERE TWIN CITIES. Text in English. 1962. m. free (effective 2009). adv. **Document type:** *Magazine, Consumer.*
Formerly: Where Minneapolis - St. Paul
Published by: Greenspring Media Group Inc., 600 U.S. Trust Bldg, 730 Second Ave, S, Minneapolis, MN 55402. TEL 612-371-5800, FAX 612-371-5801, info@greenspring.com. adv.: B&W page USD 1,825, color page USD 2,275; trim 10.88 x 8. Circ: 30,000 (controlled).

052 CAN ISSN 1910-6564
WHERE VANCOUVER. Text in English. 1969. m. CAD 32 (effective 1997). adv. **Document type:** *Magazine, Consumer.*
Formerly titles (until 2005): Where Canada (Vancouver Edition) (1711-4756); (until 2003): Where Vancouver (1180-9671); (until 1990): Key to Vancouver (0829-0601); (until 1983): Vancouver Guideline (0715-6715)
Published by: St. Joseph Media, 111 Queen St E, Ste 320, Toronto, ON M5C 1S2, Canada. TEL 416-364-3333, FAX 416-594-3374, feedback@weddingbells.ca, http://www.stjosephmedia.com. adv.: B&W page CAD 1,930, color page CAD 2,410; trim 9 x 5.5. Circ: 55,000 (controlled).

052 CAN ISSN 1182-0705
WHERE VICTORIA. Text in English. 1977. m. adv. **Document type:** *Magazine, Consumer.* **Description:** Current events, shopping and dining information for visitors.
Former titles (until 1990): Key to Victoria (0829-7150); (until 1984): Victoria Guideline (0715-6723)
Published by: Pacific Island Publishers (Subsidiary of: Where Magazines International), 818 Broughton St, Victoria, BC V8W 1E4, Canada. TEL 250-383-3633, FAX 250-480-3233, pip@monday.com. Ed. Carolyn Camilleri. Pub. Anna Scolnick. R&P, Adv. contact Michael Frost. B&W page CAD 1,920, color page CAD 2,140; trim 10.88 x 8.13. Circ: 23,416 (controlled).

051 USA
WHERE WASHINGTON, D.C. Text in English. 1965. m. USD 56; USD 6 newsstand/cover (effective 2009). adv. illus. **Document type:** *Magazine, Consumer.* **Description:** Covers dining, entertainment, tourist and cultural attractions of interest to visitors to Washington, DC. Provides maps.
Related titles: Online - full text ed.
Published by: Morris Visitor Publications (Subsidiary of: Morris Multimedia, Inc.), 1720 Eye St, Ste 600, Washington, DC 20006. TEL 202-463-4550, FAX 202-463-4553, MVPcustomerservice@morris.com, http://www.morrisvisitorpublications.com/. Ed. Lawlor Jean Cohen. Pub. Rick Mollineaux. adv.: B&W page USD 5,170, color page USD 6,465; trim 10.88 x 8.13. Circ: 93,500 (controlled).

917.1 CAN ISSN 0847-8511
WHERE WINNIPEG. Text in English. 1985. 6/yr. CAD 16.05; CAD 21.05 foreign. adv. illus. **Document type:** *Magazine, Consumer.*
Formerly (until 1989): Key to Winnipeg (0834-3314)
Published by: Fanfare Magazine Group (Subsidiary of: St. Joseph Media), 128 James Ave, Ste 300, Winnipeg, MB R3B 0N8, Canada. TEL 204-943-4439, FAX 204-947-5463. Ed., R&P Brad Hughes. Pub., Adv. contact Laurie Hughes. B&W page CAD 2,033, color page CAD 2,541; trim 10.88 x 8.13. Circ: 32,000 (controlled).

051 USA
WILD BLUE YONDER MAGAZINE; the magazine of Frontier Airlines. Text in English. 2004. bi-m. USD 36 domestic; USD 58 foreign; USD 8 per issue domestic (effective 2005). adv. **Document type:** *Magazine, Consumer.*
Published by: Mphasis Inc., 1099 18th St, Ste 500, Denver, CO 80202. TEL 303-296-4100 ext 226, 303-296-0339 ext 235, FAX 303-296-3410, editorial@gowildblueyonder.com, advertising@gowildblueyonder.com. adv.: color page USD 7,500; trim 8.375 x 10.5.

051 USA
WYNN. Text in English. 2007. q. free; free to guests at Wynn Resorts. adv. **Document type:** *Magazine, Consumer.* **Description:** Provides journey through the resort, championship golf course and tranquil spa.
Published by: Greenspun Media Group, 2360 Corporate Circle, Third Fl, Henderson, NV 89074. TEL 888-946-4666, FAX 702-990-2530, gmginfo@gmgvegas.com, http://www.greenspunmedia.com/. Pub., Adv. contact Alison L Miller TEL 702-990-2435. page USD 26,136; trim 10 x 12. Circ: 300,000 (free).

910.202 NPL
YETI. Text in Nepali. 2/yr. adv.
Published by: Royal Nepal Airlines, Public Relations & Publicity Service, Kanti Path, Kathmandu, Nepal. Ed. I K Pradhan. Circ: 20,000.

059.951 CHN ISSN 1674-2125
YUNZHONG WANGLAI/CHINA SOUTHERN AIRLINES FIRST CLASS MAGAZINE. Text in Chinese. 1990. m. **Document type:** *Magazine, Consumer.*
Formerly (until 2007): Beifang Hangkong/Northern Air (1003-4498)
Published by: (Zhongguo Nanfang Hangkong Gongsi/China Southern), Zhongguo Nanhang Jituan Wenhua Chuanmei Youxian Gongsi, Jichang Lu, Yundong Jie, Nanhang Wenhua Chuanmei Dalou, Guangzhou, 510406, China. TEL 86-20-86126473, FAX 86-20-86134472. Eds. Jiang Xubin, Wang Xiaolu.

387.7 HKG ISSN 1003-6253
ZHONGGUO MINHANG/C A A C INFLIGHT MAGAZINE. Text in Chinese, English. 1982. bi-m. free. adv. Website rev. back issues avail. **Document type:** *Magazine, Consumer.*
Published by: (Zhongguo Minhang Baoshe/Civil Aviation and Administration of China, Journal Office), Asia Inflight Ltd., 22-F, Ho Lee Commercial Bldg, 38-44 D Aguilar St, Central, Hong Kong. TEL 852-2501-5455, FAX 852-2869-7663, info@asianflight.com, http://www.asianflight.com. Ed. Shiwen Li. Adv. contact Jasper Chung TEL 852-2537-9138. Circ: 400,000.

051 USA
ZOOM! MAGAZINE. Text in English. 1996. bi-m.
Published by: Valley Media, 503 West 2600 South, Bountiful, UT 84010. TEL 801-693-7300, FAX 801-693-7310, mildredevans@uswest.net. Ed. Mildred Evans. Circ: 15,000.

TRUCKS AND TRUCKING

see TRANSPORTATION—Trucks And Trucking

UROLOGY AND NEPHROLOGY

see MEDICAL SCIENCES—Urology And Nephrology

VETERINARY SCIENCE

636.089 USA
A A L A S IN ACTION. Text in English. 200?. bi-m. free to members (effective 2009). adv. **Document type:** *Newsletter, Trade.*
Description: Aims to enhance communication with national and branch members of the American Association for Laboratory Animal Science.
Related titles: Online - full text ed.
Published by: American Association for Laboratory Animal Science, 9190 Crestwyn Hills Dr, Memphis, TN 38125. TEL 901-754-8620, FAX 901-753-0046, info@aalas.org. Circ: 12,500.

636.089 MEX
A M M V E P E. REVISTA. (Asociacion Mexicana de Medicos Veterinarios Especialistas en Pequenas Especies. Revista) Text in Spanish. 1990. bi-m. **Document type:** *Journal, Trade.*
Related titles: Online - full text ed.
Published by: Asociacion Mexicana de Medicos Veterinarios Especialistas en Pequenas Especies, A.C., Atlixco No 42 Esq Juan Escutia, Depto 1 Planta Baja, Col. Condesa, Mexico, D.F., 06140, Mexico. ammvepe@ammvepe.com, http://www.ammvepe.com/. Ed. Fernando Viniegra Rodriguez.

A N Z C C A R T NEWS (ONLINE). *see* ANIMAL WELFARE

636.089 ESP ISSN 1136-6664
A V E P A. ACTUALIDAD. (Asociacion Veterinaria Espanola de Especialistas en Pequenos Animales) Text in Spanish. 1991. w. back issues avail. **Document type:** *Magazine, Trade.*
Formerly (until 1996): A V E P A. Boletin Informativo (1136-6672)
Related titles: Online - full text ed.
Published by: Asociacion de Veterinarios Espanoles Especialistas en Pequenos Animales (A V E P A), Paseo de San Gervasio 46-48, Barcelona, 08022, Spain. TEL 34-93-2531522, FAX 34-93-4183979, http://www.avepa.org.

636.089029 USA ISSN 1095-3884
SF611
A V M A DIRECTORY AND RESOURCE MANUAL. Text in English. 1920. a. USD 150 domestic; USD 170 foreign (effective 2010). charts; stat. **Document type:** *Directory, Trade.* **Description:** Provides historic and current guidance information about the profession, alphabetic and geographic listings of all AVMA members and many non-members, and listings for many governmental agencies, allied veterinary groups, and other organizations concerned with animal health and welfare.
Former titles (until 1997): A V M A Directory (0898-6657); (until 1984): American Veterinary Medical Association. Directory (0066-1147)
Indexed: SRI.
Published by: American Veterinary Medical Association, 1931 N Meacham Rd, Ste 100, Schaumburg, IL 60173-4360. TEL 847-925-8070, FAX 847-925-9329, llarson@avma.org, http://www.avma.org. Ed. Barbara Baldwin. R&P Diane A Fagen. Circ: 68,000 (paid).

636.089 FRA ISSN 0001-4192
SF602 CODEN: BAVFAV
ACADEMIE VETERINAIRE DE FRANCE. BULLETIN. Text in French. 1844. 4/yr. adv. bk.rev. abstr.; bibl.; charts; illus.; stat. index. **Document type:** *Bulletin.*
Formerly (until 1927): Societe Centrale de Medecine Veterinaire. Bulletin (0244-7002); Which incorporated (1852-1882): Societe Centrale de Medecine Veterinaire. Memoires (2017-4985)
Indexed: A20, A22, B21, ChemAb, DBA, ESPM, FR, FS&TA, GenetAb, I10, ImmunAb, NSA, P30, SCI, SCOPUS, ToxAb, W07, W08.
—BLDSC (2378.000000), CASDDS, GNLM, IE, Infotrieve, Ingenta, INIST. **CCC.**
Published by: Academie Veterinaire de France, 34 Rue Breguet, Paris, 75011, France. TEL 33-1-53361619, academie@veterinaire.fr academie@veterinaire.fr. Ed. Marc V Catsaras. Circ: 800.

636.089 USA ISSN 1550-2813
ACADEMY OF VETERINARY HOMEOPATHY. JOURNAL. Text in English. 1997. q. **Document type:** *Journal, Academic/Scholarly.*
Published by: The Academy of Veterinary Homeopathy, P O Box 9280, Wilmington, DE 19809. TEL 866-652-1590, office@theavh.org, http://www.theavh.org.

636.089 BRA ISSN 1678-0345
➤ **ACTA SCIENTIAE VETERINARIAE.** Text in Multiple languages. 2002. q. **Document type:** *Journal, Academic/Scholarly.*
Related titles: Online - full text ed.: ISSN 1679-9216. free (effective 2011).
Indexed: A01, A34, A35, A36, A37, A38, AgBio, AgrForAb, B23, B25, BIOSIS Prev, BP, C25, CABA, D01, E12, F08, F11, F12, FS&TA, G11, GH, H16, H17, IndVet, MaizeAb, MycolAb, N02, N03, N04, OR, P33, P37, P39, PN&I, R07, R08, R12, R13, RA&MP, RM&VM, S12, S13, S16, SCI, T05, TAR, VS, W07, W10, W11, Z01.
Published by: Universidade Federal do Rio Grande do Sul, Faculdade de Veterinaria, Av Bento Goncalves 9090, Predio 42602, Porto Alegre, RS 91540-000, Brazil. TEL 55-51-33166101, FAX 55-51-33167305, secvet@ufrgs.br. Ed. Laerte Ferreiro.

636 BRA ISSN 1806-2636
QL1
➤ **ACTA SCIENTIARUM. ANIMAL SCIENCES.** Text in Portuguese. 1974. q. **Document type:** *Journal, Academic/Scholarly.*
Supersedes in part (in 2003): Acta Scientiarum (1415-6814); Which was formerly (until 1998): Revista U N I M A R (0100-9354)
Related titles: Online - full text ed.: ISSN 1807-8672. free (effective 2011).
Indexed: A26, A34, A35, A37, A38, AgBio, AgrForAb, B25, BIOSIS Prev, C01, C25, C30, CABA, D01, E12, F08, F11, F12, FCA, G11, GH, H16, H17, I04, I05, I11, IndVet, MaizeAb, MycolAb, N02, N03, N04, OR, P32, P33, P37, P39, P40, PGegResA, PN&I, R07, R08, R11, R12, R13, RM&VM, RefZh, S12, S13, S16, SCOPUS, SoyAb, TAR, TriticAb, VS, W10, W11, Z01.
Published by: Universidade Estadual de Maringa, Editora da Universidade - Eduem, Av Colombo, 5790 - Zona 7, Maringa, Parana 87020-900, Brazil. TEL 55-44-2614253, FAX 55-44-2222754, http://www.uem.br. Ed., R&P Alessandro de Lucca e Braccini.

636.089 POL ISSN 1644-0676
➤ **ACTA SCIENTIARUM POLONORUM. MEDICINA VETERINARIA/ ACTA SCIENTIARUM POLONORUM. WETERYNARIA.** Text in Polish, English. 2002. s-a. free (effective 2010). **Document type:** *Journal, Academic/Scholarly.*
Related titles: Online - full text ed.
Indexed: A01, A34, A35, A36, A38, AgBio, AgrAg, C25, CABA, D01, E12, F08, G11, GH, H16, H17, N02, N03, N04, P32, P33, P39, P40, R08, R13, RA&MP, RM&VM, S12, T02, W11.
Published by: (Uniwersytet Przyrodniczy we Wroclawiu/Wroclaw University of Environmental and Life Sciences), Wydawnictwo Uniwersytetu Przyrodniczego we Wroclawiu, ul Sopocka 23, Wroclaw, 50344, Poland. wyd@up.wroc.pl, http://wydawnictwo.ar.wroc.pl.

636.08 SRB ISSN 0567-8315
SF604 CODEN: ACVTA8
➤ **ACTA VETERINARIA.** Text in English. 1951. bi-m. adv. abstr.; bibl.; charts; illus.; stat. back issues avail. **Document type:** *Journal, Academic/Scholarly.*
Related titles: Online - full text ed.: free (effective 2011).
Indexed: A01, A22, A34, A35, A36, A37, A38, AgBio, B23, B25, BIOSIS Prev, BP, CA, CABA, CurCont, D01, E12, F08, F11, F12, FS&TA, FoVS&M, G11, GH, H16, H17, INIS AtomInd, IndVet, MycolAb, N02, N03, N04, OR, P30, P33, P37, P39, PN&I, R07, R08, R13, RA&MP, RM&VM, RefZh, S12, S13, S16, SCI, SCOPUS, SoyAb, T02, T05, TAR, TriticAb, VS, W07, W10, W11, Z01.
—BLDSC (0670.880000), CASDDS, IE, Infotrieve, Ingenta, INIST.
Published by: Univerzitet u Beogradu, Fakultet Veterinarske Medicine/ University of Belgrade, Faculty of Veterinary Medicine, Bulevar Oslobodenja 18, Belgrade, 11000. vetks@EUnet.yu. Circ: 200.

636.089 CZE ISSN 0001-7213
SF604 CODEN: ACVTB9
➤ **ACTA VETERINARIA BRNO.** Text in English; Summaries in Czech, English, Russian. 1922. q. EUR 143.40 foreign (effective 2009). adv. bk.rev. bibl.; charts; illus. index. cum.index. 140 p./no. 1 cols./p.; **Document type:** *Journal, Academic/Scholarly.* **Description:** Publishes original research articles in basic and applied veterinary sciences and medicine, including food hygiene.
Formerly: Acta Universitatis Agriculturae. Facultas Veterinaria: Rada B
Related titles: CD-ROM ed.; Online - full content ed.: ISSN 1801-7576. free (effective 2011).
Indexed: A01, A22, A29, A34, A35, A36, A37, A38, ASCA, AgBio, AgrForAb, ApicAb, B20, B21, B23, B25, BIOSIS Prev, BP, C25, CA, CABA, CIN, ChemAb, ChemTitl, CurCont, D01, E12, ESPM, F08, F11, F12, FS&TA, FoVS&M, G11, GH, H16, H17, I10, I11, IndVet, MaizeAb, MycolAb, N02, N03, N04, P30, P32, P33, P37, P39, P40, PN&I, R07, R08, R13, RA&MP, RM&VM, S12, S13, S16, SCI, SCOPUS, SoyAb, T02, T05, TAR, ToxAb, VS, VirolAbstr, W07, W08, W10, W11, WildRev, Z01.
—BLDSC (0670.890000), CASDDS, Infotrieve, Ingenta, INIST, Linda Hall.
Published by: Veterinarni a Farmaceuticka Univerzita Brno/University of Veterinary and Pharmaceutical Sciences, Palackeho 1-3, Brno, 61242, Czech Republic. TEL 42-541-561111, http://www.vfu.cz. Ed. Dr. Eva Baranyiova. Circ: 500. **Dist. by:** Kubon & Sagner Buchexport - Import GmbH, Hessstr 39-41, Munich 80798, Germany. TEL 49-89-542180, FAX 49-89-54218218, postmaster@kubon-sagner.de, http://www.kubon-sagner.de.

636.089 HUN ISSN 0236-6290
CODEN: AVHUEA
➤ **ACTA VETERINARIA HUNGARICA.** Text in English. 1951. q. EUR 408, USD 564 combined subscription (print & online eds.) (effective 2012). adv. bk.rev. bibl.; charts; illus.; abstr. index. 130 p./no.; back issues avail. **Document type:** *Journal, Academic/Scholarly.*
Description: Publishes studies concerned with research on morphology, physiology, biochemistry, microbiology, immunology, reproduction biology and clinical veterinary medicine, etiology, pathogenesis, diagnostics and control of infectious, parasitic and metabolic diseases.
Formerly (until 1982): Academiae Scientiarum Hungaricae. Acta Veterinaria (0001-7205)
Related titles: Online - full text ed.: ISSN 1588-2705. EUR 356, USD 488 (effective 2012) (from IngentaConnect).
Indexed: A22, A29, A34, A35, A36, A37, A38, ASCA, AgBio, AgrForAb, B20, B21, B23, B25, BIOSIS Prev, BP, CABA, CIN, ChemAb, ChemTitl, CurCont, D01, DBA, E12, EMBASE, ESPM, ExcerpMed, F08, FoVS&M, G11, GH, H16, H17, IBR, IBZ, ISR, IndMed, IndVet, MEDLINE, MaizeAb, MycolAb, N02, N03, N04, OR, P30, P32, P33, P37, P39, P40, PN&I, R07, R08, R13, RA&MP, RM&VM, S12, S13, S16, SCI, SCOPUS, SoyAb, TAR, TriticAb, VS, VirolAbstr, W07, W10, Z01.
—BLDSC (0670.980000), CASDDS, GNLM, IE, Infotrieve, Ingenta, INIST. **CCC.**
Published by: (Magyar Tudomanyos Akademia/Hungarian Academy of Sciences), Akademiai Kiado Rt. (Subsidiary of: Wolters Kluwer N.V.), Prielle Kornelia u 19/D, Budapest, 1117, Hungary. TEL 36-1-4648222, FAX 36-1-4648221, journals@akkrt.hu. adv.: B&W page HUF 40,000, color page HUF 100,000; trim 237 x 165.

636.089 GBR ISSN 1751-0147
➤ **ACTA VETERINARIA SCANDINAVICA (ONLINE).** Text in English. 2006. irreg. free (effective 2011). adv. back issues avail. **Document type:** *Journal, Academic/Scholarly.*
Media: Online - full text. **Related titles:** Supplement(s): Acta Veterinaria Scandinavica. Supplementum (Online).
Indexed: A01, A02, A03, A08, A26, A34, A35, A36, A37, A38, A39, AgBio, B23, BA, C27, C29, CA, CABA, CurCont, D01, D03, D04, E12, E13, F08, G11, GH, H17, I05, IndVet, LT, N02, N04, OR, P33, P37, P39, PN&I, R08, R14, RRTA, S12, S13, S14, S15, S16, S18, SCI, SoyAb, T02, T05, TAR, VS, W07, W11.
—Linda Hall. **CCC.**
Published by: BioMed Central Ltd. (Subsidiary of: Springer Science+Business Media), 236 Gray's Inn Rd, London, WC1X 8HB, United Kingdom. TEL 44-20-31922000, FAX 44-20-31922010, info@biomedcentral.com, http://www.biomedcentral.com. Ed. Mats Forsberg TEL 46-18-363625. Adv. contact Natasha Bailey TEL 44-20-31922231.

636.089 FRA ISSN 1630-4101
ACTIVETO. Text in French. 2001. m. (11/yr.). EUR 39 domestic; EUR 54 foreign (effective 2004). **Document type:** *Magazine, Trade.*
Published by: Editions du Boisbaudry, 13 Square du Chene Germain, Cesson Sevigne, 355773, France. TEL 33-2-99322121, http://www.editionsduboisbaudry.com.

636.089 GBR ISSN 2040-4700
▼ **ADVANCES IN ANIMAL BIOSCIENCES.** Text in English. 2009. 3/yr. GBP 185, EUR 241, USD 296 to institutions; GBP 199, EUR 259, USD 319 combined subscription to institutions (print & online eds.) (effective 2012). back issues avail. **Document type:** *Journal, Academic/Scholarly.* **Description:** Aims to publish conference, symposium and workshop proceedings on animal-related aspects of the life sciences with emphasis on farmed and other managed animals.
Related titles: Online - full text ed.: ISSN 2040-4719. GBP 170, EUR 221, USD 272 to institutions (effective 2012).
—**CCC.**
Published by: Cambridge University Press, The Edinburgh Bldg, Shaftesbury Rd, Cambridge, CB2 8RU, United Kingdom. TEL 44-1223-312393, FAX 44-1223-315052, information@cambridge.org, http://www.cambridge.org/. Ed. Cledwyn Thomas.

636.089 USA ISSN 1041-7826
ADVANCES IN SMALL ANIMAL MEDICINE AND SURGERY. Text in English. 1988. m. USD 263 in United States to institutions; USD 381 elsewhere to institutions (effective 2012). adv. back issues avail.; reprints avail. **Document type:** *Newsletter, Abstract/Index.*
Description: Provides insight into specific topics and allows veterinarians and veterinary technicians to apply new tests and treatments in their practices. Abstracts material from recent publications and presentations.
Related titles: Online - full text ed.: ISSN 1558-0482.
Indexed: SCOPUS.
—**CCC.**
Published by: W.B. Saunders Co. (Subsidiary of: Elsevier Health Sciences), Elsevier, Health Sciences Division, Order Fulfillment, 3251 Riverport Ln, Maryland Heights, MO 63043. TEL 314-872-8370, 800-325-4177, FAX 314-432-1380, JournalCustomerService-usa@elsevier.com, http://www.us.elsevierhealth.com. Eds. C B Chastain, Joanne Burns. Adv. contact Janine Castle TEL 44-1865-843844.

THE AGRICULTURAL AND VETERINARY PHARMACIST. *see* PHARMACY AND PHARMACOLOGY

AGRONOMES ET VETERINAIRES SANS FRONTIERES. *see* AGRICULTURE

AGROTROPICA. *see* AGRICULTURE

AGVETLINK. *see* AGRICULTURE—Crop Production And Soil

639.089 ARG ISSN 1666-8227
ALBEITERIA ARGENTINA. Text in Spanish. 2002. a. ARS 20 (effective 2006). back issues avail. **Document type:** *Journal, Academic/ Scholarly.*
Related titles: Online - full text ed.
Published by: Asociacion Argentina de Historia de la Veterinaria, Chile, 1856, Buenos Aires, 1227, Argentina. TEL 54-11-43817415, oaperez@sinectis.com.ar.

636.089 EGY ISSN 1110-2047
ALEXANDRIA JOURNAL OF VETERINARY SCIENCES. Text in English. 1985. s-a. **Document type:** *Journal, Academic/Scholarly.*
Indexed: A34, A35, A36, A38, CABA, D01, E12, GH, N02, N03, N04, P33, R08, S13, T05.
Published by: Alexandria University, Faculty of Veterinary Medicine, Edfina, Beheira, Alexandria, 22758, Egypt. Ed. Dr. Helmi Ahmad Turki.

590 636.089 ITA ISSN 1972-8034
L'ALLEVATORE MAGAZINE. Text in Italian. 1945. s-m. adv. **Document type:** *Magazine, Trade.*
Formerly (until 2006): L' Allevatore (1972-8026)
Published by: Associazione Italiana Allevatori/Italian Breeders' Association, Via G Tomassetti 9, Rome, 00161, Italy. TEL 39-06-854511, FAX 39-06-44249286, http://www.aia.it. Ed. Fortunato Tirelli. Circ: 76,000.

636.089 USA ISSN 0164-1999
SF605 CODEN: SPAHDN
AMERICAN ANIMAL HOSPITAL ASSOCIATION. ANNUAL MEETING SCIENTIFIC PROCEEDINGS. Text in English. a. USD 60 to non-members (effective 2005). adv. **Document type:** *Proceedings.*
—CASDDS. **CCC.**
Published by: American Animal Hospital Association, PO Box 150899, Denver, CO 80215-0899. TEL 303-986-2800, 800-883-6301, FAX 303-986-1700, info@aahanet.org, http://www.aahanet.org. R&P Linda Sears. Adv. contact Stephanie Pates.

636.089 USA ISSN 1547-3317
SF601 CODEN: JAAHBL
➤ **AMERICAN ANIMAL HOSPITAL ASSOCIATION. JOURNAL (ONLINE).** Abbreviated title: J A A H A. Text in English. 1965. bi-m. USD 107 (effective 2010). adv. bk.rev. abstr.; charts; illus.; tr.lit. Index. back issues avail.; reprints avail. **Document type:** *Journal, Academic/ Scholarly.* **Description:** Contains accurate, timely, scientific, and technical information pertaining to the practice of small animal medicine and surgery.
Former titles (until 2004): American Animal Hospital Association. Journal (Print) (0587-2871); American Animal Hospital Association Bulletin (0002-7251)
Media: Online - full text. **Related titles:** Microform ed.: (from PQC).
Indexed: A22, A34, A35, A36, A37, A38, ASCA, AgBio, B&AI, B10, B25, BIOSIS Prev, CA, CABA, ChemAb, CurCont, DBA, E12, EMBASE, ExcerpMed, FoVS&M, GH, H16, H17, ISR, IndMed, IndVet, MEDLINE, MycolAb, N02, N04, P11, P20, P22, P26, P30, P33, P39, P48, P52, P54, P56, PN&I, PQC, R08, RM&VM, SAA, SCI, SCOPUS, SoyAb, T02, T05, VS, W07, WildRev.
—CASDDS, GNLM, IE, Infotrieve, Ingenta, INIST. **CCC.**
Published by: American Animal Hospital Association, 12575 W Bayaud Ave, Lakewood, CO 80228. TEL 303-986-2800, 800-883-6301, FAX 303-986-1700, info@aahanet.org, http://www.aahanet.org. Ed. Alan H Rebar.

636.089 USA
AMERICAN ASSOCIATION OF BOVINE PRACTITIONERS. ANNUAL CONFERENCE. PROCEEDINGS. Text in English. 1971. a. free to members (effective 2010). bk.rev. abstr. **Document type:** *Proceedings, Academic/Scholarly.*

Former titles (until 1995): American Association of Bovine Practitioners. Annual Convention. Proceedings; (until 1993): American Association of Bovine Practitioners Conference (1079-9737); (until 1992): American Association of Bovine Practitioners. Annual Convention. Proceedings (0743-0450)
Indexed: Agr, P48, P52, P56, PQC.
—BLDSC (6840.583000).
Published by: American Association of Bovine Practitioners, PO Box 3610, Auburn, AL 36831. TEL 334-821-0442, FAX 334-821-9532, AABPHQ@aabp.org, http://www.aabp.org/. Circ: 6,000.

636.089 USA ISSN 0065-7182
SF601
➤ **AMERICAN ASSOCIATION OF EQUINE PRACTITIONERS. PROCEEDINGS OF THE ANNUAL CONVENTION.** Text in English. 1956 (2nd). a. USD 160 per issue to non-members; free to members (effective 2010). back issues avail. **Document type:** *Proceedings, Academic/Scholarly.* **Description:** Provides documentation of the scientific presentations in abstract and review paper form, available at the AAEP annual convention held the first weekend of December. Topics include EPM, equine orthopedic surgery and colic.
Related titles: Microfilm ed.: (from PQC).
Indexed: Agr.
—BLDSC (6840.585000).
Published by: American Association of Equine Practitioners, 4075 Iron Works Pky, Lexington, KY 40511. TEL 859-233-0147, FAX 859-233-1968, aaepoffice@aaep.org.

636.08 USA
AMERICAN ASSOCIATION OF ZOO VETERINARIANS. ANNUAL CONFERENCE PROCEEDINGS. Text in English. 1968. a. USD 55 per issue in North America; USD 70 per issue elsewhere; free to members (effective 2009). back issues avail. **Document type:** *Proceedings.* **Description:** Covers zoo and wildlife veterinary medicine.
Former titles (until 2005): American Association of Zoo Veterinarians. Proceedings; (until 1992): American Association of Zoo Veterinarians. Meeting Proceedings; (until 1989): American Association of Zoo Veterinarians. Conference Proceedings; (until 198?): American Association of Zoo Veterinarians. Annual Proceedings; (until 1986): American Association of Zoo Veterinarians. Annual Meeting Abstracts or Papers; (until 1984): American Association of Zoo Veterinarians. Annual Meeting Proceedings; (until 1981): American Association of Zoo Veterinarians. Annual Proceedings (0095-0610); (until 1969): American Association of Zoo Veterinarians. Proceedings (0093-6294)
Related titles: CD-ROM ed.: USD 100 per issue in North America; USD 115 per issue elsewhere (effective 2009).
Indexed: DBA, WildRev.
—IE.
Published by: American Association of Zoo Veterinarians, 581705 White Oak Rd, Yulee, FL 32097. aazvorg@aol.com, http://www.aazv.org. Circ: 1,250.

636.089 USA ISSN 1526-2499
AMERICAN FUND FOR ALTERNATIVES TO ANIMAL RESEARCH. NEWS ABSTRACTS. Text in English. 1978. 3/yr. USD 15 per academic year domestic to individuals; USD 20 per academic year foreign to individuals; USD 10 per academic year to students (effective 2001 - 2002). bk.rev. bibl. back issues avail. **Document type:** *Bulletin, Consumer.* **Description:** Provides financing for scientific programs to develop, evaluate or teach alternatives to animals in research, testing and education.
Related titles: Fax ed.; Online - full text ed.
Published by: American Fund for Alternatives to Animal Research, 175 W 12th St, No 16G, New York, NY 10011-8220. TEL 212-989-8073, FAX 212-989-8073. Ed., R&P, Adv. contact Ethel Thurston. Circ: 2,000 (paid); 5,000 (controlled).

636.7 USA
AMERICAN HEARTWORM SOCIETY. BULLETIN. Text in English. 1974. q. free to members (effective 2010). adv. **Document type:** *Bulletin, Academic/Scholarly.* **Description:** Contains reports of published and unpublished information on techniques and changes in heartworm disease management.
Published by: American Heartworm Society, PO Box 8266, Wilmington, DE 19803. TEL 302-691-5371, FAX 302-478-4022, info@heartwormsociety.org.

636.089 USA ISSN 1053-5608
SF992.H4
AMERICAN HEARTWORM SOCIETY. SYMPOSIUM PROCEEDINGS. Variant title: Proceedings of the Heartworm Symposium. Text in English. 1977. triennial. USD 60 per issue to non-members; USD 50 per issue to members (effective 2010). back issues avail. **Document type:** *Proceedings, Trade.*
Published by: American Heartworm Society, PO Box 8266, Wilmington, DE 19803. TEL 302-691-5371, FAX 302-478-4022, info@heartwormsociety.org.

636.087 USA ISSN 1940-8390
SF745.5
AMERICAN HOLISTIC VETERINARY MEDICAL ASSOCIATION. JOURNAL. Text in English. 1982. q. USD 65 domestic membership; USD 90 foreign membership (effective 2000). adv. bk.rev. **Document type:** *Journal, Trade.* **Description:** Promotes natural healing, preventive health care, nutrition and avoidance of drugs and medication in Veterinary medicine.
Formerly (until Sep. 1989): American Holistic Veterinary Medical Association. Newsletter
Indexed: A04, WildRev.
Published by: American Holistic Veterinary Medical Association, 2218 Old Emmorton Rd., Bel Air, MD 21015-6106. TEL 410-569-0795, FAX 410-569-2346. Ed., R&P Jan A Bergeron TEL 732-671-7856. Pub. Carvel G Tiekert. Adv. contact Theresa Mall. page USD 375. Circ: 1,000.

636.089 USA ISSN 1557-4555
➤ **AMERICAN JOURNAL OF ANIMAL AND VETERINARY SCIENCES.** Text in English. 2006 (Sum.). q. USD 1,600 (effective 2009). **Document type:** *Journal, Academic/Scholarly.*
Related titles: Online - full text ed.: ISSN 1557-4563. free (effective 2011).
Indexed: A01, A26, A34, A35, A36, A37, A38, A39, AgBio, AgrForAb, B02, B15, B17, B18, BP, C25, C27, C29, CA, CABA, D01, D03, D04, E08, E12, E13, F08, F11, F12, G04, G08, G11, GH, H16, H17, I05, IndVet, MaizeAb, N02, N03, N04, P32, P33, P37, P39, PN&I, R08, R14, RA&MP, S12, S13, S14, S15, S16, SCOPUS, SoyAb, T02, T05, TAR, TriticAb, VS, Z01.
Published by: Science Publications, 244, 5th Ave, Ste 207, New York, NY 10001. TEL 845-510-3028, FAX 866-250-7082, support@scipub.org, http://www.thescipub.com.

➤ **AMERICAN JOURNAL OF PRIMATOLOGY.** *see* BIOLOGY—Zoology

636.089 615.5 USA ISSN 1945-7677
➤ **AMERICAN JOURNAL OF TRADITIONAL CHINESE VETERINARY MEDICINE.** Abbreviated title: A T C V M. Text in English. 2006. s-a. free to members (effective 2010). adv. back issues avail. **Document type:** *Journal, Academic/Scholarly.* **Description:** Provides practitioners, students, and researchers with theoretical and clinical articles on veterinary acupuncture, Chinese herbal therapy, tui-na, and food therapy.
Related titles: Online - full text ed.: ISSN 1945-7693.
Indexed: A01, A34, CABA, D01, E12, GH, H16, N04, P33, R07, R08, SoyAb, T02, T05, TAR.
Published by: American Association of Traditional Chinese Veterinary Medicine, PO Box 141324, Gainesville, FL 32614. TEL 352-672-6400. Ed. Cheryl L Chrisman.

636.089 USA ISSN 0002-9645
SF601 CODEN: AJVRAH
➤ **AMERICAN JOURNAL OF VETERINARY RESEARCH.** Text in English. 1940. m. USD 245 combined subscription domestic (print & online eds.); USD 255 combined subscription foreign (print & online eds.) (effective 2010). adv. bk.rev.; video rev.; software rev. charts; illus.; stat. Index. 160 p./no. 2 cols./p.; back issues avail.; reprints avail. **Document type:** *Journal, Academic/Scholarly.* **Description:** Provides reports of basic research in veterinary medicine and associated biological sciences.
Related titles: Microform ed.: (from PMC, PQC); Online - full text ed.: ISSN 1943-5681.
Indexed: A01, A03, A08, A22, A29, A34, A35, A36, A37, A38, ASCA, AbAn, AgBio, Agr, B&AI, B04, B10, B20, B21, B25, BIOSIS Prev, BibAg, C25, CA, CABA, CIN, CTA, ChemAb, ChemTitl, CurCont, D01, DBA, DentInd, E12, EMBASE, ESPM, ExcerpMed, F08, FS&TA, FoVS&M, G11, GH, H16, H17, I10, IBR, IBZ, ISR, IndMed, IndVet, MEDLINE, MaizeAb, MycolAb, N02, N04, NSA, P30, P33, P37, P39, PN&I, R08, R11, R13, RA&MP, RM&VM, S12, S13, S16, SAA, SCI, SCOPUS, SoyAb, T02, T05, TAR, VS, W07, W08, W11, WildRev.
—BLDSC (0840.000000), CASDDS, GNLM, IE, Infotrieve, Ingenta, INIST, Linda Hall.
Published by: American Veterinary Medical Association, 1931 N Meacham Rd, Ste 100, Schaumburg, IL 60173-4360. TEL 847-925-8070, FAX 847-925-9329, llarson@avma.org, http://www.avma.org. Ed. Dr. Kurt J Matushek. R&P Diane A Fagen. adv.: B&W page USD 3,135, color page USD 4,585. Circ: 7,000 (paid).

➤ **AMERICAN LARYNGOLOGICAL ASSOCIATION. TRANSACTIONS OF THE ANNUAL MEETING.** *see* MEDICAL SCIENCES—Otorhinolaryngology

636.089 USA ISSN 0198-9863
SF1
AMERICAN SOCIETY OF ANIMAL SCIENCE. ABSTRACTS. Variant title: American Society of Animal Science. Meeting Abstracts. Text in English. 1977. a. back issues avail. **Document type:** *Report, Abstract/Index.*
—CCC.
Published by: American Society of Animal Science, 2441 Village Green Pl, Champaign, IL 61822. TEL 217.356.9050, FAX 217.398.4119, asas@assochq.org. Ed. Steven A Zinn.

636.089 USA ISSN 0003-1488
SF601 CODEN: JAVMA4
➤ **AMERICAN VETERINARY MEDICAL ASSOCIATION. JOURNAL.** Abbreviated title: J A V M A. Text in English. 1877. s-m. USD 210 combined subscription domestic (print & online eds.); USD 230 combined subscription foreign (print & online eds.) (effective 2010). adv. bk.rev.; software rev.; video rev. charts; illus.; maps; mkt.; stat. s-a. index. 160 p./no. 2 cols./p.; back issues avail.; reprints avail. **Document type:** *Journal, Academic/Scholarly.* **Description:** Provides news of the profession, reports of scientific research and opportunities for member dialogue through letters and special commentaries.
Incorporates (1899-1913): American Veterinary Medical Association. Proceedings (0160-4805); (1950-1964): American Veterinary Medical Association. Annual Meeting. Scientific Proceedings (0097-661X); Which was formerly (until 1956): American Veterinary Medical Association. Annual Meeting. Proceedings (0097-0565)
Related titles: Microfiche ed.: (from BHP); Microform ed.: (from PQC); Online - full text ed.: ISSN 1943-569X.
Indexed: A01, A03, A08, A20, A22, A29, A34, A35, A36, A37, A38, ASCA, AgBio, Agr, B&AI, B04, B10, B20, B21, B23, B25, BIOSIS Prev, BibAg, C25, CA, CABA, CIN, CTA, ChemAb, ChemTitl, CurCont, D01, DBA, DentInd, E12, EMBASE, ESPM, ExcerpMed, FCA, FS&TA, FoVS&M, GH, H17, ISR, IndMed, IndVet, LT, MEDLINE, MaizeAb, MycolAb, N02, N04, NSA, OR, P30, P33, P34, P37, P39, PN&I, R07, R08, R12, RA&MP, RM&VM, RRTA, S12, S13, S16, SAA, SCI, SCOPUS, SRI, T02, T05, TAR, VS, ViroIAbstr, W07, W08, W11, WildRev, Z01.
—BLDSC (4695.000000), CASDDS, GNLM, IE, Infotrieve, Ingenta, INIST.
Published by: American Veterinary Medical Association, 1931 N Meacham Rd, Ste 100, Schaumburg, IL 60173-4360. TEL 847-925-8070, FAX 847-925-9329, llarson@avma.org. Ed. Dr. Kurt J Matushek. R&P Diane A Fagen. adv.: B&W page USD 6,775, color page USD 8,750; trim 8.125 x 10.875. Circ: 77,100 (paid).

636.089 DEU ISSN 0945-3296
AMTSTIERAERZTLICHER DIENST UND LEBENSMITTELKONTROLLE. Text in German. 1986. q. EUR 7.60 newsstand/cover (effective 2008). adv. **Document type:** *Magazine, Trade.*
Former titles (until 1994): Die Lebensmittelkontrolle (0944-6613); (until 1993): Der Lebensmittelkontrolleur (0931-7023)
Published by: Alpha Informationsgesellschaft mbH, Finkenstr 10, Lampertheim, 68623, Germany. TEL 49-6206-9390, FAX 49-6206-939232, info@alphawerbung.de, http://www.alphawerbung.de. adv.: B&W page EUR 1,350, color page EUR 2,250; trim 186 x 260. Circ: 6,500 (controlled).

636.089 ARG ISSN 0365-5148
CODEN: ANVTAH
➤ **ANALECTA VETERINARIA.** Text in Spanish; Summaries in English. 1959. s-a. adv. back issues avail. **Document type:** *Journal, Academic/Scholarly.*
Formerly (until 1968): Facultad de Ciencias Veterinarias de la Plata. Revista (0457-1592)
Related titles: CD-ROM ed.: ISSN 1666-2954. 2000; Online - full text ed.: ISSN 1514-2590. 1998. free (effective 2011).
Indexed: A34, A38, CABA, ChemAb, D01, E12, FS&TA, GH, H16, N02, N03, N04, P33, R07, R08, R13, T05, TAR, W11, Z01.
—CASDDS, Linda Hall.
Published by: Universidad Nacional de la Plata, Facultad de Ciencias Veterinarias, Calle 60 y 118 s/n, La Plata, Buenos Aires 1900, Argentina. TEL 54-221-4236663, info@fcv.unlp.edu.ar, http://fcv.unlp.edu.ar.

636.089 ESP ISSN 0213-5434
CODEN: AVMAE9
ANALES DE VETERINARIA DE MURCIA. Text in Spanish, English. 1985. a., latest vol.15, 1999. bk.rev. abstr. back issues avail. **Document type:** *Journal, Academic/Scholarly.* **Description:** Contains original research and advances in all fields of veterinary science.
Indexed: A34, A35, A36, A38, AgBio, B25, BIOSIS Prev, C25, CABA, D01, E12, F08, FCA, G11, GH, H16, H17, IECT, IndVet, MycolAb, N02, N03, N04, P33, P37, P39, PN&I, R07, R08, RM&VM, VS, W11.
—CCC.
Published by: Universidad de Murcia, Servicio de Publicaciones, Edificio Saavedra Fajardo, C/ Actor Isidoro Maiquez 9, Murcia, 30007, Spain. TEL 34-968-363887, FAX 34-968-363414, vgm@um.es, http://www.um.es/publicaciones/.

636.089 DEU ISSN 1439-0264
SF761
➤ **ANATOMIA, HISTOLOGIA, EMBRYOLOGIA (ONLINE).** Text in English. 6/yr. GBP 1,048 in United Kingdom to institutions; EUR 1,330 in Europe to institutions; USD 1,936 in the Americas to institutions; USD 2,257 elsewhere to institutions (effective 2012). **Document type:** *Journal, Academic/Scholarly.*
Media: Online - full text (from IngentaConnect). **Related titles:** ◆ Print ed.: Anatomia, Histologia, Embryologia (Print). ISSN 0340-2096.
Indexed: B25, BIOSIS Prev, CurCont, FoVS&M, MycolAb, SCI, Z01.
—CCC.
Published by: Wiley-Blackwell Verlag GmbH (Subsidiary of: Wiley-Blackwell Publishing Ltd.), Kurfuerstendamm 57, Berlin, 10707, Germany. TEL 49-30-3279-0665, FAX 49-30-3279-0677, verlag@blackwell.de, http://www.blackwell.de. Eds. Dr. Fred Sinowatz, Paul Simoens, Robert Henry.

636.089 DEU ISSN 0340-2096
SF761 CODEN: AHEMA5
➤ **ANATOMIA, HISTOLOGIA, EMBRYOLOGIA (PRINT);** journal of veterinary medicine series C. Text in English. 1972. bi-m. GBP 1,048 in United Kingdom to institutions; EUR 1,330 in Europe to institutions; USD 1,936 in the Americas to institutions; USD 2,257 elsewhere to institutions; GBP 1,206 combined subscription in United Kingdom to institutions (print & online eds.); EUR 1,530 combined subscription in Europe to institutions (print & online eds.); USD 2,226 combined subscription in the Americas to institutions (print & online eds.); USD 2,596 combined subscription elsewhere to institutions (print & online eds.) (effective 2012). bk.rev. illus.; stat. back issues avail.; reprint service avail. from PSC. **Document type:** *Journal, Academic/Scholarly.* **Description:** Anatomical, histological and embryological investigations involving human, veterinary and zoological studies.
Formerly (until 1973): Zentralblatt fuer Veterinaermedizin. Reihe C: Anatomia, Histologia, Embryologia (0300-8649)
Related titles: ◆ Online - full text ed.: Anatomia, Histologia, Embryologia (Online). ISSN 1439-0264; ◆ Supplement(s): Advances in Veterinary Medicine. ISSN 0931-4229.
Indexed: A01, A03, A08, A20, A22, A26, A34, A35, A36, A38, ASCA, AgBio, Agr, B21, B25, BIOSIS Prev, C25, CA, CABA, CTA, CurCont, D01, DBA, DentInd, E01, E12, EMBASE, ExcerpMed, F08, G11, GH, H12, H16, H17, IndMed, IndVet, MEDLINE, MycolAb, N02, N03, N04, NSA, P30, P33, P37, PN&I, R07, R12, RefZh, SCI, SCOPUS, SoyAb, T02, T05, TAR, TriticAb, VS, W07, W08, WildRev, Z01.
—BLDSC (0897.960000), GNLM, IE, Infotrieve, Ingenta, INIST, Linda Hall. **CCC.**
Published by: (World Association of Veterinary Anatomists IND), Wiley-Blackwell Verlag GmbH (Subsidiary of: Wiley-Blackwell Publishing Ltd.), Kurfuerstendamm 57, Berlin, 10707, Germany. TEL 49-30-3279-0665, FAX 49-30-3279-0677, verlag@blackwell.de, http://www.blackwell.de. Eds. Dr. Fred Sinowatz, Paul Simoens, Robert Henry.

➤ **ANIMAL BEHAVIOUR.** *see* BIOLOGY—Zoology

➤ **ANIMAL BIOLOGY AND ANIMAL HUSBANDRY.** *see* BIOLOGY—Zoology

➤ **ANIMAL FEED SCIENCE AND TECHNOLOGY.** *see* AGRICULTURE—Feed, Flour And Grain

636.089 USA
➤ **ANIMAL FEEDING AND NUTRITION.** Text in English. 1977. irreg., latest 1993. USD 155 per vol. (effective 2010). back issues avail. **Document type:** *Monographic series, Academic/Scholarly.*
Published by: Academic Press (Subsidiary of: Elsevier Science & Technology), 3251 Riverport Ln, Maryland Heights, MO 63043. TEL 314-447-8010, FAX 314-447-8030, JournalCustomerService-usa@elsevier.com, http://www.elsevierdirect.com/imprint.jsp?iid=5.

➤ **ANIMAL HEALTH;** the report of the Chief Veterinary Officer. *see* AGRICULTURE—Poultry And Livestock

636.089 NCL ISSN 1019-8458
ANIMAL HEALTH ADVISORY LEAFLET. Text in French. 1994. irreg., latest 1996. **Document type:** *Monographic series.*
Published by: Secretariat of the Pacific Community, PO Box D5, Noumea, Cedex 98848, New Caledonia. TEL 687-262000, FAX 687-263818, spc@spc.int, http://www.spc.int.

636.089 NZL ISSN 1177-6986
ANIMAL HEALTH BOARD. ANNUAL RESEARCH REPORT. Text in English. 2004. a. **Document type:** *Report, Trade.*
Related titles: Online - full text ed.: ISSN 1177-9179.
Published by: Animal Health Board, PO Box 3412, Wellington, New Zealand. TEL 64-4-4722858, FAX 64-4-4738786.

636.089 AUS ISSN 1322-7084
ANIMAL HEALTH IN AUSTRALIA. Text in English. 1993. a. **Document type:** *Journal, Trade.*
Related titles: Online - full text ed.: ISSN 1445-3118.
—CCC.
Published by: Animal Health Australia, Suite 15, 26-28 Napier Close, Deakin, ACT 2600, Australia. TEL 61-2-62325522, FAX 61-2-62325511.

ANIMAL HEALTH IN DENMARK. *see* AGRICULTURE—Poultry And Livestock

636.0832 CAN ISSN 1910-1996
ANIMAL HEALTH LABORATORY USER'S GUIDE AND FEE SCHEDULE. Text in English. 2004. a. **Document type:** *Handbook/ Manual/Guide, Consumer.*
Published by: University of Guelph, Laboratory Services Division, Box 3650, Guelph, ON N1H 8J7, Canada. TEL 519-767-6299, FAX 519-767-6240, info@lsd.uoguelph.ca, http://www.labservices.uoguelph.ca.

636.0832 PAK ISSN 1728-9521
ANIMAL HEALTH. PROCEEDINGS. Text in English. 1985. m. GBP 300 (effective 2005). **Document type:** *Proceedings, Academic/Scholarly.* **Description:** Study of Veterinary diseases.
Published by: (Animal Health Association), International Press, P O Box 17700, Karachi, 75300, Pakistan. TEL 92-21-4947486, FAX 92-21-4989257, light_68@hotmail.com. Ed. Dr. A Rustum.

636.089 UGA
ANIMAL HEALTH RESEARCH CENTRE. ANNUAL REPORT. Text in English. 19??. a. **Document type:** *Report, Academic/Scholarly.*
Published by: Animal Health Research Centre, PO Box 24, Entebbe, Uganda.

636.089 GBR ISSN 1466-2523
SF600 CODEN: AHRRCJ
➤ **ANIMAL HEALTH RESEARCH REVIEWS.** Text in English. 2000. s-a. GBP 298, USD 545 to institutions; GBP 310, USD 575 combined subscription to institutions (print & online eds.) (effective 2012). adv. back issues avail.; reprint service avail. from PSC. **Document type:** *Journal, Academic/Scholarly.* **Description:** Contains review articles covering all aspects of animal health.
Related titles: Online - full text ed.: ISSN 1475-2654. GBP 236, USD 440 to institutions (effective 2012).
Indexed: A01, A03, A08, A22, A34, A35, A36, A38, AgBio, Agr, B23, BIOSIS Prev, BP, CA, CABA, D01, E01, E12, EMBASE, ExcerpMed, G11, GH, H16, H17, IndVet, MEDLINE, MycolAb, N02, N04, OR, P20, P22, P30, P32, P33, P37, P39, P40, P48, P50, P52, P54, P56, PN&I, PQC, R08, R12, RA&MP, SCOPUS, T02, T05, TAR, VS, W11.
—BLDSC (0904.006800), IE, Infotrieve, Ingenta. **CCC.**
Published by: (Conference of Research Workers in Animal Diseases USA), Cambridge University Press, The Edinburgh Bldg, Shaftesbury Rd, Cambridge, CB2 8RU, United Kingdom. TEL 44-1223-312393, FAX 44-1223-315052, journals@cambridge.org, http://www.cambridge.org/uk. Ed. C Gyles. Adv. contact Rebecca Roberts TEL 44-1223-325083. page GBP 610, page USD 1,160. Circ: 517.

636.089 AUS ISSN 1832-567X
ANIMAL HEALTH SCIENCES NEWSLETTER. Text in English. 2005. q. **Document type:** *Newsletter, Academic/Scholarly.*
Media: E-mail.
Published by: Victoria, Department of Primary Industries, GPO Box 4440, Melbourne, VIC 3001, Australia. TEL 61-3-96584000, FAX 61-3-96584760, customer.service@dpi.vic.gov.au, http://www.dpi.vic.gov.au/dpi/index.htm.

636.089 GBR
ANIMAL HEALTH TRUST. ANNUAL REVIEW. Text in English. 1963. a. free (effective 2009). bk.rev. charts; illus. index. **Document type:** *Corporate.*
Former titles (until 1996): Animal Health Trust. Annual Report (0142-6591); Which incorporated (1955-1979): Animal Health (0003-3502)
Related titles: Online - full text ed.
Published by: Animal Health Trust, Lanwades Park, Kentford, Newmarket, Suffolk CB8 7UU, United Kingdom. TEL 44-1638-751000, FAX 44-1638-555606, info@aht.org.uk, http://www.aht.org.uk.

590.7 USA ISSN 1552-5694
ANIMAL LAB NEWS. Variant title: A L N Magazine. Text in English. 200?. bi-m. free to qualified personnel; USD 120 in US & Canada; USD 180 elsewhere (effective 2008). adv. **Document type:** *Magazine, Trade.* **Description:** Contains resources, products and information to design, build and equip today's animal research facilities.
Related titles: Online - full text ed.: ISSN 1934-6395; ◆ Regional ed(s).: A L N World. ISSN 2150-9948.
—CCC.
Published by: Vicon Publishing, Inc., 4 Limbo Ln, Amherst, NH 03031. TEL 603-672-9997, FAX 603-672-3028, http://www.viconpublishing.com. Ed. Christine Janson. Pub., Adv. contact Patrick Murphy.

636.089 GBR ISSN 0262-2238
SF915
ANIMAL PHARM; world animal health and nutrition news. Text in English. 1982. bi-w. GBP 935, EUR 1,450, USD 1,870 combined subscription (print & online eds.) (effective 2010). adv. bk.rev. 2 cols./p.; back issues avail.; reprints avail. **Document type:** *Newsletter, Trade.* **Description:** Includes regulations, companies, livestock and market trends, product news and environmental issues for the international animal health and nutrition industry.
Related titles: Online - full text ed.; Supplement(s): Animal Pharm Insight. ISSN 1942-7638.
Indexed: A26, ABC, G08, I05, P48, P52, P53, P54, P56, PNI, PQC.
—BLDSC (0905.030000), IE, Infotrieve, Ingenta. **CCC.**
Published by: Informa Healthcare (Subsidiary of: T & F Informa plc), Telephone House, 69-77 Paul St, London, EC2A 4LQ, United Kingdom. TEL 44-20-70175540, FAX 44-20-70176907, healthcare.enquiries@informa.com, http://informahealthcare.com/. Ed. Jamie Day. Pub. Phil Solomon. Adv. contact Robin Baker TEL 44-20-70176774.

ANIMAL PRODUCTION SCIENCE. *see* AGRICULTURE—Poultry And Livestock

ANIMAL REPRODUCTION. *see* BIOLOGY—Zoology

ANIMAL REPRODUCTION SCIENCE. *see* AGRICULTURE—Poultry And Livestock

636.089 GBR ISSN 1742-0385
ANIMAL TECHNOLOGY AND WELFARE. Text in English. 1950. 3/yr. GBP 70 combined subscription domestic to non-members (print & online eds.); GBP 85 combined subscription in Europe to non-members (print & online eds.); GBP 110 combined subscription elsewhere to non-members (print & online eds.); free to members (effective 2009). adv. bk.rev. charts; illus. back issues avail. **Document type:** *Journal, Academic/Scholarly.* **Description:** Features original short articles, technical notes and reviews pertaining to all aspects of animal science and technology, management and welfare.
Former titles (until 2002): Animal Technology (0264-4754); (until 1983): Institute of Animal Technicians. Journal (0020-2711); (until 1965): Animal Technicians Association. Journal (0307-465X)
Related titles: Online - full text ed.
Indexed: A22, A34, A35, A36, A37, A38, AgBio, Agr, CABA, E12, EMBASE, ExcerpMed, F08, GH, IndVet, MaizeAb, N02, N03, N04, P30, P33, P37, P39, PN&I, R08, RM&VM, S13, S16, SCOPUS, T05, VS.
—BLDSC (0905.126000), IE, Ingenta. **CCC.**
Published by: (European Federation of Animal Technology), Institute of Animal Technology of Great Britain, 5 S Parade, Summertown, Oxford, OX2 7JL, United Kingdom. TEL 44-800-0854380, admin@iat.org.uk.

▼ **ANIMALS.** *see* BIOLOGY—Zoology

636.089 TUR ISSN 1300-0861
CODEN: VTFDAQ
ANKARA UNIVERSITESI VETERINER FAKULTESI DERGISI/ UNIVERSITY OF ANKARA. FACULTY OF VETERINARY MEDICINE. JOURNAL. Text in Multiple languages; Summaries in English, French, German. 1954. 3/yr. bk.rev. bibl.; charts; illus. 80 p./no. 2 cols./p.; back issues avail.; reprints avail. **Document type:** *Journal, Academic/Scholarly.* **Description:** Covers research articles in Veterinary Science.
Related titles: Online - full text ed.: ISSN 1308-2817. free (effective 2010).
Indexed: A34, A35, A36, A37, A38, AgBio, B23, C25, CABA, ChemAb, D01, E12, F08, F11, F12, G11, GH, H16, H17, IndVet, MaizeAb, N02, N03, N04, OR, P33, P37, P39, PGrRegA, PN&I, R07, R08, R12, R13, RA&MP, RM&VM, S12, S13, S16, SAA, SCI, SCOPUS, SoyAb, T05, TAR, TriticAb, VS, W07, W11.
—BLDSC (0905.253000).
Published by: Ankara Universitesi, Veteriner Fakultesi/Ankara University, Faculty of Veterinary Science, Dekanligi, Yayin Alt Komitesi, Diskapi, Ankara, 06100, Turkey. TEL 90-312-3170515, FAX 90-312-3164472. Ed. Rifki Haziroglu. Circ: 450.

636.089 BEL ISSN 1781-3875
SF602 CODEN: AMVRA4
➤ **ANNALES DE MEDECINE VETERINAIRE (ONLINE EDITION).** Text in French. 1842. 6/yr. EUR 40 domestic; EUR 50 foreign; EUR 25 to students (effective 2002). adv. bk.rev. charts; illus. index. **Document type:** *Journal, Academic/Scholarly.*
Former titles (until 2004): Annales de Medecine Veterinaire (Print Edition) (0003-4118); (until 1852): Repertoire de Medecine Veterinaire (0770-0598); (until 1949): Journal Veterinaire et Agricole de Belgique (0770-0547)
Media: Online - full text.
Indexed: A20, A22, A34, A35, A36, A37, A38, ASCA, AgBio, B21, B25, BIOSIS Prev, C25, CABA, ChemAb, CurCont, D01, DBA, E12, F08, F12, FoVS&M, GH, H16, H17, ISR, IndMed, IndVet, KWIWR, LT, MaizeAb, MycolAb, N02, N04, P30, P33, P37, P39, PN&I, R07, R08, R13, RM&VM, RRTA, S13, S16, SAA, SCI, SCOPUS, T05, VS, VirolAbstr, W07, W11.
—CASDDS, IE, Infotrieve, Ingenta, INIST. **CCC.**
Published by: Universite de Liege, Faculte de Medicine Veterinaire, Boulevard de Colonster 20, Bat.B43, Liege, 4000, Belgium. TEL 32-4-3664120, FAX 32-4-3664122, amv@misc.ulg.ac.be. Ed. Sandrine Vandenput. Circ: 1,500.

639.089 POL ISSN 0301-7737
CODEN: ACDDA6
➤ **ANNALES UNIVERSITATIS MARIAE CURIE-SKLODOWSKA. SECTIO DD. MEDICINA VETERINARIA.** Text in Polish, English; Summaries in English. 1949. a. price varies. **Document type:** *Journal, Academic/Scholarly.*
Related titles: Online - full text ed.
Indexed: A34, A35, A36, A37, A38, AgBio, AgrLib, B23, CABA, ChemAb, D01, E12, F08, F11, F12, G11, GH, H16, H17, IndVet, LT, MaizeAb, N02, N03, N04, P33, P37, P39, PN&I, R07, R08, R13, RA&MP, RM&VM, RRTA, S13, S16, VS, WildRev.
—CASDDS, INIST.
Published by: (Uniwersytet Marii Curie-Sklodowskiej w Lublinie), Wydawnictwo Uniwersytetu Marii Curie-Sklodowskiej w Lublinie, Pl Marii Curie-Sklodowskiej 5, Lublin, 20031, Poland. TEL 48-81-5375304, press@ramzes.umcs.lublin.pl, http://www.press.umcs.lublin.pl. Ed. Zdzislaw Glinski. Circ: 500.

636.089 POL ISSN 0239-4243
SF84 CODEN: AUEZE3
➤ **ANNALES UNIVERSITATIS MARIAE CURIE-SKLODOWSKA. SECTIO EE. ZOOTECHNIKA.** Text in English, Polish; Summaries in English. 1983. a. price varies. **Document type:** *Journal, Academic/ Scholarly.*
Related titles: Online - full text ed.
Indexed: A34, A35, A37, A38, AgBio, AgrForAb, AgrLib, C25, CABA, D01, E12, F08, F12, FCA, G11, GH, H16, H17, I11, IndVet, LT, N02, N03, N04, P32, P33, P37, P39, PHN&I, PN&I, R07, R08, RM&VM, RRTA, S12, S13, S16, VS, W11, WildRev.
—INIST, Linda Hall.
Published by: (Uniwersytet Marii Curie-Sklodowskiej w Lublinie), Wydawnictwo Uniwersytetu Marii Curie-Sklodowskiej w Lublinie, Pl Marii Curie-Sklodowskiej 5, Lublin, 20031, Poland. TEL 48-81-5375304, press@ramzes.umcs.lublin.pl, http://www.press.umcs.lublin.pl. Ed. Marek Babicz. Circ: 650.

636.0832 USA ISSN 1934-208X
SF994
ANNUAL CONFERENCE ON AVIAN MEDICINE AND SURGERY. PROCEEDINGS. Text in English. 1997. a. **Document type:** *Proceedings, Trade.*
Formerly (until 1997): Annual Conference of the Mid-Atlantic Association of Avian Veterinarians. Proceedings
Published by: Mid-Atlantic States Association of Avian Veterinarians, Memorial Bldg, Ste 291, 610 N Main St, Blacksburg, VA 24060-3311. TEL 540-951-2559, FAX 540-953-0230, http://www.masaav.org.

636.089 USA ISSN 0894-7708
CODEN: PAVME6
ANNUAL VETERINARY MEDICAL FORUM. PROCEEDINGS. Text in English. 1983. a. USD 49 domestic; USD 79 foreign (effective 2005). adv. back issues avail. **Document type:** *Proceedings.* **Description:** Covers topics in internal medicine, cardiology, oncology, neurology, nutrition, clinical pathology, comparative endocrinology, comparative gastroenterology, urology and nephrology, and liver study.
Formerly (until 1985): Annual Medical Forum. Proceedings (0897-2311)
—BLDSC (6842.444000).
Published by: American College of Veterinary Internal Medicine, 1997 Wadsworth Blvd, Ste A, Lakewood, CO 80215-3327 . TEL 303-231-9933, 800-245-9081, FAX 303-231-0880, acvim@acvim.org, http://www.acvim.org/. Ed. Robert Denovo. R&P, Adv. contact June Johnson.

636.089 NLD ISSN 1876-3618
ARCHAEOPTERYX VETERINARIS. Text in Dutch. 1989. 5/yr. EUR 18; EUR 9 to students (effective 2008).
Published by: Dutch Avian Veterinarian Archaeopteryx, Yalelaan 1, Utrecht, 3584, Netherlands. TEL 31-30-2537476, http://www.archaeopteryx-online.nl. Ed. Marja de Jong.

636.089 GBR ISSN 1745-039X
CODEN: ARTIA2
➤ **ARCHIVES OF ANIMAL NUTRITION.** Text and summaries in English, German. 1950. bi-m. GBP 2,019 combined subscription in United Kingdom to institutions (print & online eds.); EUR 2,132, USD 2,679 combined subscription to institutions (print & online eds.) (effective 2012). adv. bk.rev. charts; illus. index. back issues avail.; reprint service avail. from PSC. **Document type:** *Journal, Academic/ Scholarly.* **Description:** Covers the biochemical and physiological basis of animal nutrition with emphasis laid on: protein and acid metabolism, energy transformation, mineral metabolism, vitamin metabolism, nutritional effects and performance criteria. It furthermore deals with recent developments in practical animal feeding, feedstuff theory, mode of action of feed additives, feedstuff preservation and feedstuff processing.
Formerly (until 2004): Archiv fur Tierernahrung (0003-942X)
Related titles: Online - full text ed.: ISSN 1477-2817. GBP 1,817 in United Kingdom to institutions; EUR 1,919, USD 2,411 to institutions (effective 2012) (from IngentaConnect).
Indexed: A01, A03, A08, A22, ASCA, B&BAb, B19, B21, B25, BIOSIS Prev, BioDAb, CA, CTA, ChemAb, CurCont, DBA, E01, EMBASE, ESPM, ExcerpMed, F10, FS&TA, FoVS&M, ISR, IndMed, MEDLINE, MycolAb, P30, P52, P56, PQC, S01, SCI, SCOPUS, T02, W07.
—CASDDS, GNLM, IE, Infotrieve, Ingenta, INIST, Linda Hall. **CCC.**
Published by: Taylor & Francis Ltd. (Subsidiary of: Taylor & Francis Group), 4 Park Sq, Milton Park, Abingdon, Oxfordshire OX14 4RN, United Kingdom. TEL 44-20-70176000, FAX 44-20-70176336, subscriptions@tandf.co.uk, http://www.taylorandfrancis.com. Ed. Ortwin Simon. Adv. contact Linda Hann. **Subscr. in N America to:** Taylor & Francis Inc., Customer Services Dept, 325 Chestnut St, 8th Fl, Philadelphia, PA 19106. TEL 215-625-8900, 800-354-1420, FAX 215-625-2940, customerservice@taylorandfrancis.com; **Subscr. to:** Journals Customer Service, Sheepen Pl, Colchester, Essex CO3 3LP, United Kingdom. TEL 44-20-70175544, FAX 44-20-70175198, tf.enquiries@tfinforma.com.

636.089 BRA ISSN 1517-784X
SF604
ARCHIVES OF VETERINARY SCIENCE. Text in English, Portuguese. 1996. s-a. **Document type:** *Journal, Academic/Scholarly.* **Description:** Covers veterinary medicine subjects such as reproduction, prevention, veterinary clinic, wild animals, animal nutrition, management.
Related titles: Online - full text ed.: free (effective 2011).
Indexed: A01, A22, A34, A35, A37, A38, AgBio, AgrForAb, B23, C25, CABA, D01, E12, F08, F11, F12, G11, GH, H16, H17, IndVet, LT, MaizeAb, N02, N04, P33, P37, P39, PN&I, R08, R12, RM&VM, RRTA, S12, S13, S16, SCOPUS, SoyAb, T05, TAR, TriticAb, VS, W11, Z01.
—BLDSC (1643.595000), IE, Ingenta.
Published by: Universidade Federal do Parana, Imprensa Universitaria/ Federal University of Parana, Publishing House, Rua Bom Jesus 650 - Juveve, Curitiba, Parana 81531-990, Brazil. TEL 55-41-3665033, direccao@imprensa.ufpr.br, http://www.imprensa.ufpr.br. Ed. Luiz Ernandes Kozicki.

636.08 CHL ISSN 0301-732X
CODEN: AMVED2
➤ **ARCHIVOS DE MEDICINA VETERINARIA.** Text in English. 1969. 3/yr. CLP 15,000 (effective 2010). **Document type:** *Journal, Academic/ Scholarly.* **Description:** Covers all aspects of veterinary science and animal welfare.
Related titles: Online - full text ed.: ISSN 0717-6201. 1997. free (effective 2011) (from SciELO).
Indexed: A22, A34, A35, A36, A37, A38, ASCA, AgBio, AgrForAb, B23, C01, CA, CABA, CIN, ChemTitl, CurCont, D01, E12, F04, F08, FoVS&M, G11, GH, H16, H17, IndVet, N02, N03, N04, P32, P33, P37, P39, P40, PGegResA, PN&I, R12, RA&MP, RM&VM, S12, S13, S16, SCI, SCOPUS, SoyAb, T02, T05, TAR, TriticAb, VS, W07, W11, WildRev, Z01.
—BLDSC (1655.410000), CASDDS, IE, Ingenta.
Published by: Universidad Austral de Chile, Facultad de Ciencias Veterinarias, Casilla 567, Valdivia, Chile. TEL 56-63-221690, FAX 56-63-221459. Ed. Pedro Contreras.

➤ **ARCHIVOS DE ZOOTECNIA.** *see* AGRICULTURE—Poultry And Livestock

636.08 NLD ISSN 0923-3970
ARGOS. Text in Dutch, English, German; Summaries in English. 1989. 2/yr. EUR 13.50 domestic; EUR 18.50 foreign (effective 2010). adv. bk.rev. bibl. cum.index: nos.1-10; 11-20. back issues avail. **Document type:** *Bulletin, Academic/Scholarly.* **Description:** Covers topics in veterinary history, with emphasis on the Netherlands.
Indexed: A34, A36, A38, CABA, D01, E12, EMBASE, ExcerpMed, GH, IndVet, LT, MEDLINE, N02, OR, P30, P33, PN&I, R08, RRTA, SCOPUS, T05, TAR, VS, W11.
Published by: Veterinair Historisch Genootschap, Prof van Bemmelenlaan 49, Utrecht, 3571 EL, Netherlands. TEL 31-30-2711945.

636.089 NOR ISSN 1891-9138
▼ **ARGUS**; sunne dyr, frisk fisk, tryg mad. Text in Norwegian. 2010. q. free. **Document type:** *Magazine, Consumer.* **Description:** Showcase for the results of current research at the institute.
Related titles: Online - full text ed.: ISSN 1891-9146.
Published by: Veterinaerinstituttet/National Veterinary Institute, PO Box 750, Sentrum, Oslo, 0106, Norway. TEL 47-23-216000, FAX 47-23-216001, postmottag@vetinst.no. Eds. Mari Press, Anne-Brit Haug.

636.089 BRA ISSN 0102-0935
CODEN: ABMZDB
➤ **ARQUIVO BRASILEIRO DE MEDICINA VETERINARIA E ZOOTECNIA/BRAZILIAN JOURNAL OF VETERINARY AND ANIMAL SCIENCES.** Text and summaries in Portuguese, English. 1943. bi-m. adv. reprints avail. **Document type:** *Journal, Academic/Scholarly.* **Description:** Publishes on veterinary medicine, animal science, technology and inspection of products of animal origin.
Formerly (until vol.35, 1983): Universidade Federal de Minas Gerais. Escola de Veterinaria. Arquivos (0076-8863)
Related titles: Microform ed.; Online - full text ed.: free (effective 2011).
Indexed: A29, A34, A35, A36, A37, A38, ASCA, AgBio, AgrForAb, Agrind, B&BAb, B19, B20, B21, B23, B25, BA, BIOSIS Prev, BP, BibAg, BioDAb, C01, C25, C30, CA, CABA, ChemAb, D01, E12, ESPM, F08, F11, F12, FS&TA, FoVS&M, G11, GH, H16, H17, I10, IBR, IBZ, INIS AtomInd, IndMed, IndVet, MaizeAb, MycolAb, N02, N03, N04, OR, P32, P33, P37, P39, P40, PGegResA, PN&I, R07, R08, R11, R12, R13, RA&MP, RM&VM, S12, S13, S16, S17, SCI, SCOPUS, SoyAb, T02, T05, TAR, ToxAb, TriticAb, VS, VirolAbstr, W07, W08, W10, W11, WildRev, Z01.
—BLDSC (1695.100000), IE, Ingenta, INIST.
Published by: Universidade Federal de Minas Gerais, Escola de Veterinaria, Ave. ANTONIO CARLOS, 6627, Centro, Caixa Postal 567, Belo Horizonte, MG 30161-970, Brazil. TEL 55-31-4992042, FAX 55-31-4992041, TELEX 0312308 UFMG, journal@vet.ufmg.br.

636.089 BRA ISSN 0102-6380
CODEN: ARSVE6
ARS VETERINARIA. Text in Portuguese; Summaries in English. 1985-1988; resumed 1992. s-a. charts; illus.; stat. **Document type:** *Journal, Academic/Scholarly.*
Indexed: A34, A35, A37, A38, AgBio, BioDAb, C01, C25, C30, CABA, D01, E12, F08, FCA, FS&TA, G11, GH, H16, H17, IndVet, LT, MaizeAb, N02, N03, N04, OR, P32, P33, P37, P39, P40, PN&I, R07, R08, R12, RA&MP, RM&VM, RRTA, S12, S13, S16, SoyAb, T05, TAR, TriticAb, VS, W11.
Published by: (Universidade Estadual Paulista "Julio de Mesquita Filho", Faculdade de Ciencias Agrarias e Veterinarias de Jaboticabal), Universidade Estadual Paulista, Fundacao Editora U N E S P, Praca da Se 108, Sao Paulo, SP 01001-900, Brazil. TEL 55-11-32427171, cgb@marilia.unesp.br, http://www.unesp.br.

636.089 USA ISSN 1683-9919
➤ **ASIAN JOURNAL OF ANIMAL AND VETERINARY ADVANCES.** Text in English. 2006. q. **Document type:** *Journal, Academic/Scholarly.* **Description:** Contains findings, clinical observations, rapid communications, correspondence and review articles covering all aspects of veterinary science, animal welfare, and animal health aspects of animal sciences.
Related titles: Online - full text ed.: ISSN 1996-3289.
Indexed: A01, A10, A29, A34, A35, A36, A37, A38, AgBio, AgrForAb, B20, B21, B23, BP, C25, C30, CA, CABA, D01, E12, ESPM, F08, F11, F12, G11, GH, H16, H17, IndVet, MaizeAb, N02, N03, N04, OR, P32, P33, P37, P39, P40, PN&I, R07, R08, R12, R13, RA&MP, RM&VM, S12, S13, S16, SCI, SCOPUS, SoyAb, T02, T05, TAR, ToxAb, TriticAb, V03, VS, VirolAbstr, W07, W10, W11, Z01.
Published by: Academic Journals Inc., 224, 5th Ave, No 2218, New York, NY 10001. FAX 888-777-8532, support@scialert.com.

636.089 USA ISSN 1819-1878
➤ **ASIAN JOURNAL OF ANIMAL SCIENCES.** Text in English. 2006. q. **Document type:** *Journal, Academic/Scholarly.* **Description:** Publishes research papers on all aspects of animal science and related fields.
Related titles: Online - full text ed.
Indexed: A01, A34, A35, A36, A37, A38, AgBio, AgrForAb, B21, C25, CA, CABA, D01, E12, F08, FCA, G11, GH, H16, LT, MaizeAb, N02, N03, N04, P32, P33, P37, R07, R08, R11, R13, RA&MP, S12, SCOPUS, T02, T05, TAR, TriticAb, VS, W10, W11, Z01.
Published by: Academic Journals Inc., 224, 5th Ave, No 2218, New York, NY 10001. TEL 845-863-0090, FAX 845-591-0669, support@scialert.com, http://www.academicjournalsinc.com/.

➤ **ASKO**; dwumiesiecznik kynologiczny. *see* PETS

636.089 EGY ISSN 1012-5973
➤ **ASSIUT VETERINARY MEDICAL JOURNAL.** Text and summaries in Arabic, English. 1974. q. EGP 20 (effective 2004); USD 45 (effective 2009). charts; illus.; stat. **Document type:** *Journal, Academic/Scholarly.* **Description:** Covers subjects in veterinary and allied sciences.
Indexed: A22, A34, A35, A36, A37, A38, AgBio, AgrForAb, BP, BioDAb, C25, CABA, D01, E12, F08, FoVS&M, GH, H16, H17, IndVet, MaizeAb, N02, N03, N04, P32, P33, P37, P39, P40, PHN&I, PN&I, R07, R08, R11, R12, R13, RA&MP, RM&VM, S12, S13, S16, S17, SAA, SoyAb, T05, TAR, TriticAb, VS, W10, W11, Z01.
—BLDSC (1746.672100), IE, Ingenta.
Published by: Assiut University, Faculty of Veterinary Medicine, Al-Gumhoureya Str., Assiut University Campus, Assiut, Egypt. TEL 20-88-412151, FAX 20-88-333938. Ed. Dr. Mohammed Salah Eldin Youssef. Circ: 30.

636.089 USA
ASSOCIATION FOR VETERINARY INFORMATICS NEWSLETTER. Abbreviated title: A V I Newsletter. Text in English. 1992. bi-m. bk.rev. back issues avail. **Document type:** *Newsletter.* **Description:** Includes association news, commentaries and short notes.
Related titles: Online - full text ed.
Published by: Association for Veterinary Informatics, 1590 Augusta St, Dixon, CA 95620. TEL 916-752-4408, FAX 916-852-5680. Ed. Ronald D Smith.

636.087 USA
ASSOCIATION OF AVIAN VETERINARIANS. PROCEEDINGS. Variant title: A A V Conference Proceedings. Text in English. 19??. a. USD 55 per issue to non-members; free to members (effective 2010). back issues avail. **Document type:** *Proceedings, Academic/Scholarly.*
Media: Online - full text.
Published by: Association of Avian Veterinarians, PO Box 2584, Weatherford, TX 76086. FAX 817-599-0088, aavpublications@aol.com.

636.089 ITA ISSN 1974-8620
ASSOCIAZIONE ITALIANA DEI VETERINARI IGIENISTI. RIVISTA. Text in Multiple languages. 2008. q. **Document type:** *Journal, Trade.*
Published by: Associazione Italiana dei Veterinari Igienisti (A I V I), c/o Dipartimento di Sanita Pubblica Veterinaria e Patologia Animale, Universita degli Studi di Bologna, Via Tolara di Sopra 50, Ozzano dell'Emilia, BO 40064, Italy. FAX 39-051-2097346, http://www.aivi.it.

636.089 ITA ISSN 0004-5977
ASSOCIAZIONE ITALIANA VETERINARI PER PICCOLI ANIMALI. BOLLETTINO. Text in Italian. 1961. q. membership. adv. bk.rev. abstr.; bibl.; charts; illus.; stat.; tr.lit. index. **Document type:** *Journal, Trade.*
Indexed: SAA.
Published by: Associazione Italiana Veterinari Piccoli Animali (A I V P A), c/o Medicina Viva, Viale dei Mille 140, Parma, 43100, Italy. TEL 39-0521-290191, FAX 39-0521-291314, info@aivpa.it, http://www.aivpa.it.

636.089 AUS ISSN 1032-6626
➤ **AUSTRALIAN EQUINE VETERINARIAN.** Text in English. 1983. q. AUD 185 membership (effective 2007). adv. bk.rev. **Document type:** *Journal, Academic/Scholarly.*
Related titles: CD-ROM ed.: ISSN 1833-8135; Online - full text ed.: ISSN 1834-1349.
Indexed: A34, A35, A36, A38, CABA, E12, G11, GH, IndVet, LT, MaizeAb, N04, P33, R08, S13, T05, TAR, VS, W11.
—BLDSC (1798.868000), IE, Ingenta. **CCC.**
Published by: Equine Veterinarians Australia, Unit 40, 2A Herbert St, St Leonards, NSW 2065, Australia. TEL 61-2-94315080, FAX 61-2-94379068, admin@eva.org.au, http://www.eva.org.au.

636.089 AUS ISSN 1320-9582
AUSTRALIAN VETERINARY ASSOCIATION. ANNUAL REPORT. Text in English. 1981. a. adv. **Document type:** *Journal, Trade.*
Formerly (until 1990): Australian Veterinary Association. Year Book (0812-9169)
Published by: Australian Veterinary Association, Unit 40, 6 Herbert St, St Leonards, NSW 2065, Australia. TEL 61-2-94315000, FAX 61-2-94379068, editor@ava.com.au, http://www.ava.com.au.

636.089 GBR ISSN 0005-0423
SF604 CODEN: AUVJA2
➤ **AUSTRALIAN VETERINARY JOURNAL.** Abbreviated title: A V J(Australian Veterinary Journal). Text in English. 1925. m. GBP 335 in United Kingdom to institutions; EUR 427 in Europe to institutions; USD 606 in the Americas to institutions; USD 658 elsewhere to institutions; GBP 385 combined subscription in United Kingdom to institutions (print & online eds.); EUR 490 combined subscription in Europe to institutions (print & online eds.); USD 697 combined subscription in the Americas to institutions (print & online eds.); USD 756 combined subscription elsewhere to institutions (print & online eds.) (effective 2012). adv. bk.rev. illus. Index. back issues avail.; reprint service avail. from PSC. **Document type:** *Journal, Academic/Scholarly.* **Description:** Provides an essential forum for the dissemination of leading edge veterinary research.
Formerly (until 1927): Australian Veterinary Association. Journal
Related titles: Online - full text ed.: ISSN 1751-0813. GBP 335 in United Kingdom to institutions; EUR 427 in Europe to institutions; USD 606 in the Americas to institutions; USD 658 elsewhere to institutions (effective 2012) (from IngentaConnect).
Indexed: A20, A22, A26, A34, A35, A36, A37, A38, AIDS&CR, ASCA, AgBio, Agr, AgrForAb, B21, B23, B25, BIOSIS Prev, BibAg, CA, CABA, CIN, CTA, Cadscan, ChemAb, ChemTitl, CurCont, D01, DBA, DentInd, E01, E12, EMBASE, ESPM, ExcerpMed, F08, FCA, FS&TA, FoVS&M, G11, GH, GeoRef, H12, H16, H17, ISR, ImmunAb, IndMed, IndVet, KWIWR, LeadAb, MEDLINE, MycolAb, N02, N04, NSA, OR, P30, P32, P33, P37, P39, PN&I, R07, R08, R13, RA&MP, RM&VM, S13, S16, SAA, SCI, SCOPUS, SPPI, T02, T05, TAR, VS, W07, W08, W10, W11, WildRev, Z01, Zincscan.
—BLDSC (1824.000000), CASDDS, GNLM, IE, Infotrieve, Ingenta, INIST, Linda Hall. **CCC.**
Published by: (Australian Veterinary Association AUS), Wiley-Blackwell Publishing Ltd. (Subsidiary of: John Wiley & Sons, Inc.), 9600 Garsington Rd, Oxford, OX4 2DQ, United Kingdom. TEL 44-1865-776868, FAX 44-1865-714591, customerservices@blackwellpublishing.com. Adv. contact Patricia Lim TEL 61-2-94315073. B&W page USD 2,050; 180 x 228. Circ: 4,500.

636 AUS ISSN 0310-138X
SF601
➤ **AUSTRALIAN VETERINARY PRACTITIONER.** Text in English. 1971. q. AUD 165 to non-members (effective 2007). adv. bk.rev. **Document type:** *Journal, Academic/Scholarly.*
Indexed: A22, A34, A36, A37, A38, ASCA, CABA, CurCont, D01, E12, F08, FoVS&M, GH, ISR, IndVet, N04, P33, P39, R08, RM&VM, SAA, SCI, SCOPUS, VS, W07, WildRev.
—BLDSC (1824.100000), IE, Ingenta.
Published by: Australian Small Animal Veterinary Association, Unit 40, 2A Herbert St, St Leonards, NSW 2065, Australia. TEL 61-2-94315090, FAX 61-2-94379068, asava@ava.com.au, http://www.ava.com.au. Ed. R E Atwell. Circ: 1,200.

636.0832 FRA ISSN 1769-0072
L'AUXILIAIRE VETERINAIRE. Text in French. 2004. m. (10/yr). EUR 39 (effective 2008). **Document type:** *Magazine, Trade.*
Published by: Auxiliaire Veterinaire, 2 Rue Louis Funel, Vence, 06140, France. TEL 33-4-93580148, FAX 33-4-93581916, http://www.auxiliaire-veterinaire.info.

636.089 CHL ISSN 0716-260X
AVANCES EN CIENCIAS VETERINARIAS. Text in Spanish. 1986. s-a. CLP 10 domestic; USD 35 foreign. **Document type:** *Journal, Academic/Scholarly.*
Published by: Universidad de Chile, Facultad de Ciencias Veterinarias y Pecuarias, Ave Santa Rosa 11735, La Pintana, Santiago, Chile. http://www.veterinaria.uchile.cl/. Circ: 500.

614.343 USA ISSN 0005-2086
SF995 CODEN: AVDIAI
➤ **AVIAN DISEASES.** Text in English. 1957. q. USD 275 domestic; USD 300 foreign (effective 2010). bibl.; charts; illus. index. back issues avail.; reprints avail. **Document type:** *Journal, Academic/Scholarly.* **Description:** Features articles devoted to the dissemination of information on domestic, pet, and wild birds.
Related titles: Microfilm ed.: (from PMC, WSH); Microform ed.: (from PQC); Online - full text ed.: ISSN 1938-4351.
Indexed: A22, A29, A34, A35, A36, A37, A38, ASCA, AgBio, Agr, B20, B21, B23, B25, BIOBASE, BIOSIS Prev, BibAg, C25, CA, CABA, ChemAb, CurCont, D01, DBA, E01, E12, EMBASE, ESPM, ExcerpMed, F08, F12, FoVS&M, G11, GH, H16, H17, IABS, ISR, IndMed, IndVet, MEDLINE, MaizeAb, MycolAb, N02, N04, OR, P30, P32, P33, P37, P39, P40, PN&I, R07, R08, R11, R12, R13, RA&MP, RM&VM, S12, S13, S16, SAA, SCI, SCOPUS, SoyAb, T02, T05, TAR, TriticAb, VS, VirolAbstr, W07, W08, W10, W11, WildRev, Z01.
—BLDSC (1837.890000), CASDDS, GNLM, IE, Infotrieve, Ingenta, INIST, Linda Hall. **CCC.**
Published by: American Association of Avian Pathologists, Inc., 12627 San Jose Blvd, Ste 202, Jacksonville, FL 32223. TEL 904-425-5735, FAX 281-664-4744, aaap@aaap.info, http://www.aaap.info/index.html. Ed. Jagdev M Sharma TEL 480-727-9587.

636.089 GBR ISSN 0307-9457
SF995 CODEN: AVPADN
➤ **AVIAN PATHOLOGY.** Text in English; Summaries in French, German, Spanish. 1972. bi-m. GBP 413 combined subscription in United Kingdom to institutions (print & online eds.); EUR 551, USD 690 combined subscription to institutions (print & online eds.) (effective 2012). adv. bk.rev. back issues avail.; reprint service avail. from PSC. **Document type:** *Journal, Academic/Scholarly.* **Description:** Contains material relevant to the entire field of infectious and non-infectious diseases of poultry and all other birds, including infections that may be of zoonotic/food-borne importance.
Related titles: Online - full text ed.: ISSN 1465-3338. GBP 371 in United Kingdom to institutions; EUR 496, USD 621 to institutions (effective 2012) (from IngentaConnect).
Indexed: A01, A02, A03, A08, A22, A29, A34, A35, A36, A37, A38, ASCA, ASFA, AgBio, Agr, AgrForAb, B20, B21, B23, B25, BIOBASE, BIOSIS Prev, BibAg, CA, CABA, CIN, ChemAb, ChemTitl, CurCont, D01, DBA, E01, E04, E05, E12, EMBASE, ESPM, ExcerpMed, F08, F12, FoVS&M, G11, GH, H16, H17, IABS, ISR, IndVet, MEDLINE, MaizeAb, MycolAb, N02, N04, OR, P02, P10, P11, P15, P30, P32, P33, P37, P39, P40, P48, P52, P53, P54, P56, PN&I, PQC, R08, R11, R12, R13, RA&MP, RM&VM, RefZh, S10, S12, S13, S16, SAA, SCI, SCOPUS, T02, T05, TAR, ToxAb, VS, VirolAbstr, W07, W08, W10, W11, WildRev, Z01.
—CASDDS, IE, Infotrieve, Ingenta, INIST, Linda Hall. **CCC.**
Published by: (Houghton Trust, World Veterinary Poultry Association), Taylor & Francis Ltd. (Subsidiary of: Taylor & Francis Group), 4 Park Sq, Milton Park, Abingdon, Oxfordshire OX14 4RN, United Kingdom. TEL 44-20-70176000, FAX 44-20-70176336, subscriptions@tandf.co.uk, http://www.taylorandfrancis.com. Eds. D Alexander, J M Bradbury, D Cavanagh. **Subscr. addr. in N America:** Taylor & Francis Inc., Customer Services Dept, 325 Chestnut St, 8th Fl, Philadelphia, PA 19106. TEL 215-625-8900, 800-354-1420, FAX 215-625-2940, customerservice@taylorandfrancis.com; **Subscr. to:** Journals Customer Service, Sheepen Pl, Colchester, Essex CO3 3LP, United Kingdom. TEL 44-20-70175544, FAX 44-20-70175198, tf.enquiries@tfinforma.com.

➤ **AZABU DAIGAKU ZASSHI/AZABU UNIVERSITY. JOURNAL.** *see* BIOLOGY—Zoology

636.089 GBR ISSN 1746-6148
SF601
➤ **B M C VETERINARY RESEARCH.** Text in English. 2005. irreg. free (effective 2011). adv. back issues avail.; reprints avail. **Document type:** *Journal, Academic/Scholarly.* **Description:** Publishes original research articles in all aspects of veterinary science and medicine, including the epidemiology, diagnosis, prevention and treatment of medical conditions of domestic, companion, farm and wild animals, as well as the biomedical processes that underlie their health.
Media: Online - full text.
Indexed: A01, A02, A03, A08, A10, A26, A34, A35, A36, A37, A38, A39, AgBio, B20, B23, C27, C29, CA, CABA, CurCont, D01, D03, D04, E12, E13, EMBASE, ESPM, ExcerpMed, F08, F12, FoVS&M, G11, GH, H17, I05, IndVet, MEDLINE, N02, N04, P30, P33, P37, P39, PN&I, R07, R08, R12, R13, R14, S13, S14, S15, S16, S18, SCI, SCOPUS, SoyAb, T02, T05, TAR, TriticAb, V03, VS, VirolAbstr, W07, W10, W11.
—**CCC.**
Published by: BioMed Central Ltd. (Subsidiary of: Springer Science+Business Media), 236 Gray's Inn Rd, London, WC1X 8HB, United Kingdom. TEL 44-20-31922000, FAX 44-20-31922010, info@biomedcentral.com. Ed. Dr. Melissa Norton. Adv. contact Natasha Bailey TEL 44-20-31922231.

636.089 DEU
B P T MITTEILUNGSBLATT DES GANZEN NORDENS. (Bundesverband Praktizierender Tieraerzte) Text in German. 1984. q. free to members (effective 2009). adv. **Document type:** *Magazine, Trade.*
Published by: Bundesverband Praktizierender Tieraerzte, Landesverband Niedersachsen, Schuetzenstr 4, Emsbueren, 48488, Germany. TEL 49-5903-282, FAX 49-5903-6121, info@bpt-nds.de, http://www.bpt-nds.de. adv.: B&W page EUR 536, color page EUR 1,053. Circ: 3,300 (controlled).

BANGLADESH JOURNAL OF ANIMAL SCIENCE/BAMLADESA PASU BIJNANA SAMAYIKI. *see* AGRICULTURE—Poultry And Livestock

636.089 BGD ISSN 1729-7893
➤ **BANGLADESH JOURNAL OF VETERINARY MEDICINE.** Text in English. 2003. s-a. **Document type:** *Journal, Academic/Scholarly.* **Description:** Covers all aspects of veterinary medicine.
Related titles: Online - full text ed.: free (effective 2011).
Indexed: A34, A35, A36, A38, AgBio, Agr, AgrForAb, BP, CABA, D01, E12, F08, F11, F12, G11, GH, H16, H17, IndVet, N02, N03, N04, P33, P37, P39, R07, R08, RA&MP, SoyAb, T05, TAR, VS, W10, W11.
Published by: Bangladesh Agricultural University, Faculty of Veterinary Science, Department of Medicine, Mymensingh, 2202, Bangladesh.

636.089 BGD ISSN 0378-8113
CODEN: BVJODC
BANGLADESH VETERINARY JOURNAL. Text in Bengali. 1967. q. USD 10. adv. bk.rev. charts; illus. **Document type:** *Journal, Academic/Scholarly.*
Formerly (until 1969): Pakistan Journal of Veterinary Science (0030-9915)
—Linda Hall.
Published by: Bangladesh Veterinary Association, Agricultural University, Mymensingh, Bangladesh. Ed. M L Dewan. Circ: 1,000.

636.089 EGY ISSN 1110-6581
BANHA VETERINARY MEDICAL JOURNAL. Text in English. 199?. s-a. **Document type:** *Journal, Academic/Scholarly.*
Published by: Zagazig University, Faculty of Veterinary Medicine, Banha Branch, Mushtohor, Toukh, Qalyoubia, Egypt. TEL 20-13-461411, FAX 20-13-460640. Ed. Dr. H H H Bakri.

636.089 EGY ISSN 1687-7926
BENI-SUEF VETERINARY MEDICAL JOURNAL. Text in English. 1991. s-a. **Document type:** *Journal, Academic/Scholarly.*
Formerly: Beni Suef Veterinary Medical Researches (1110-7545)
Published by: Cairo University, Faculty of Veterinary Medicine, Giza, Beni Suaif, Cairo, Egypt. TEL 20-82-327982, FAX 20-82-322066, http://www.bs-vetmed.edu.eg/Eng/index.htm. Eds. M F El-Kady, M S Hassan.

636.089 DEU ISSN 0005-9366
CODEN: BEMTAM
➤ **BERLINER UND MUENCHENER TIERAERZTLICHE WOCHENSCHRIFT.** Text in German, English. 1944. bi-m. EUR 530 in Europe to institutions; EUR 547 elsewhere to institutions (effective 2011). adv. bk.rev. abstr.; illus.; stat. index. back issues avail. **Document type:** *Journal, Academic/Scholarly.*
Incorporates (in Jan. 2010): D T W (0341-6593); Which was formerly (until 1971): Deutsche Tieraerztliche Wochenschrift (0012-0847); Which superseded in part (in 1946): Tieraerztliche Zeitschrift (0371-7569); Which was formed by the merger of (1943-1944): Berliner und Muenchener Tieraerztliche Wochenschrift und Wiener Tieraerztliche Monatsschrift (0723-6956); (1938-1944): Berliner und Muenchener Tieraerztliche Wochenschrift (0723-6921); Which was formed by the merger of (1885-1938): Berliner Tieraerztliche Wochenschrift (0365-9984); Which was formerly (until 1888): Rundschau auf dem Gebiete der Thiermedicin und Vergleichenden Pathologie unter Beruecksichtigung des Gesammten Veterinaer-Medicinalwesens (1431-3251); (1849-1938): Muenchener Tieraerztliche Wochenschrift (0369-2523); Which was formerly (until 1909): Wochenschrift fuer Tierheilkunde und Viehzucht (0723-693X); (until 1857): Thieraerztliches Wochenblatt (0723-6948); (1914-1944): Wiener Tieraerztliche Monatsschrift (0043-535X); (1943-1944): Deutsche Tieraerztliche Wochenschrift, Tieraerztliche Rundschau (0366-9904); Which was formed by the merger of (1893-1943): Deutsche Tieraerztliche Wochenschrift (1431-3111); (1895-1943): Tieraerztliche Rundschau (0371-7534); Which was formerly (until 1903): Tieraerztlicher Central-Anzeiger (0723-7014)
Related titles: Online - full text ed.: ISSN 1439-0299.
Indexed: A22, A34, A35, A36, A37, A38, ASCA, ASFA, AgBio, B21, B23, B25, BIOBASE, BIOSIS Prev, BP, BioDAb, CABA, CIN, ChemAb, CurCont, D01, DBA, DentInd, E12, EMBASE, ESPM, ExcerpMed, FS&TA, FoVS&M, G11, GH, H17, IABS, ISR, IndMed, IndVet, KWIWR, LT, MEDLINE, MaizeAb, MycolAb, N02, N03, N04, OR, P30, P32, P33, P37, P39, PN&I, R07, R08, R13, RA&MP, RM&VM, RRTA, S13, S16, SAA, SCI, SCOPUS, SoyAb, T05, TAR, TriticAb, VS, W07, W08, W10, W11, WildRev, Z01.
—BLDSC (9316.000000), CASDDS, GNLM, IE, Infotrieve, Ingenta. **CCC.**
Published by: Schluetersche Verlagsgesellschaft mbH und Co. KG, Hans-Boeckler-Allee 7, Hannover, 30173, Germany. TEL 49-511-85500, FAX 49-511-85501100, info@schluetersche.de, http://www.schluetersche.de.

636.089 DEU ISSN 0723-6212
BIOLOGISCHE TIERMEDIZIN. Text in German, Spanish. 1984. 3/yr. EUR 5.50 newsstand/cover (effective 2008). adv. **Document type:** *Journal, Academic/Scholarly.*
Related titles: ◆ Spanish ed.: Biomedicina Veterinaria. ISSN 1134-5284.
Indexed: A34, A36, A38, CABA, D01, GH, H16, H17, IndVet, N04, OR, P33, P39, PN&I, R08, RA&MP, RM&VM, T05, TAR, VS, W11.
Published by: Aurelia Verlag GmbH, Bahnackerstr 16, Baden-Baden, 76532, Germany. TEL 49-7221-50102, FAX 49-7221-501420, info@aurelia-verlag.de, http://www.aurelia-verlag.de. Ed. Dr. Erich Reinhart. adv.: B&W page EUR 1,500, color page EUR 2,685; trim 140 x 204. Circ: 11,300 (paid).

636.089 USA ISSN 1572-4271
BIOLOGY OF ANIMAL INFECTIONS. Text in English. 2004. irreg., latest vol.2, 2005. price varies. **Document type:** *Monographic series, Academic/Scholarly.*
Published by: Academic Press (Subsidiary of: Elsevier Science & Technology), 525 B St, Ste 1900, San Diego, CA 92101-4495. TEL 619-231-6616, FAX 619-699-6422, JournalCustomerService-usa@elsevier.com, http://www.elsevierdirect.com/imprint.jsp?iid=5. Ed. Paul-Pierre Pastoret.

BIOMEDICINA VETERINARIA. *see* MEDICAL SCIENCES

BLAA STJAERNAN. *see* ANIMAL WELFARE

636.089 SWE ISSN 0282-3926
BLADMAGEN. Text in Swedish. 1967. 5/yr. SEK 200 to members (effective 2007). **Document type:** *Magazine, Consumer.*
Former titles (until 1984): Bladmagen/Stutisaktuellt (0281-1596); (until 1982): Stutis Aktuellt (0349-8980)
Published by: Veterinaermedicinska Foereningen, Ulls Vaeg 6, Uppsala, 75651, Sweden. Circ: 900.

636.089 CHL ISSN 0718-5502
BOLETIN VETERINARIO. Text in Spanish. 2007. bi-w. **Document type:** *Bulletin, Academic/Scholarly.*
Published by: Universidad de Chile, Facultad de Ciencias Agrarias, Veterinarias y Forestales, Ave Santa Rosa 11, 735, La Pintana, Santiago, Chile. TEL 56-2-9785500, FAX 56-2-9785659, webfavet@uchile.cl, http://www.veterinaria.uchile.cl/#.

636.089 USA ISSN 0524-1685
SF601 CODEN: BOVPBO
➤ **BOVINE PRACTITIONER.** Text in English. 1969. s-a. free to members (effective 2010). adv. bk.rev. index. **Document type:** *Journal, Academic/Scholarly.* **Description:** Publishes manuscripts of interest to veterinarians engaged in cattle practice and research.
Indexed: A22, A34, A35, A37, A38, AgBio, B25, BIOSIS Prev, CABA, D01, E12, GH, H17, IndVet, MycolAb, N02, N04, P33, P39, R08, R11, RM&VM, TAR, VS, W11.
—BLDSC (2264.630000), IE, Ingenta, INIST.
Published by: American Association of Bovine Practitioners, PO Box 3610, Auburn, AL 36831. TEL 334-821-0442, FAX 334-821-9532, AABPHQ@aabp.org, http://www.aabp.org/. Ed. Robert A Smith TEL 405-372-8666.

➤ **BOVINE VETERINARIAN.** *see* NUTRITION AND DIETETICS

636.089 BRA ISSN 1983-0246
BRAZILIAN JOURNAL OF VETERINARY PATHOLOGY. Abbreviated title: B J V P. Text in English. 2008. s-a. **Document type:** *Journal, Academic/Scholarly.*
Indexed: A34, A38, CABA, D01, F08, GH, H17, N04, P33, PN&I, R08, R13, SoyAb, T05, TAR, W10, Z01.
Published by: Associacao Brasileira de Patologia Veterinaria, Municipio de Botucatu, Botucatu, SP, Brazil.

636.089 590 BRA ISSN 1413-9596
SF604
➤ **BRAZILIAN JOURNAL OF VETERINARY RESEARCH AND ANIMAL SCIENCE.** Text in English, Portuguese. 1938. bi-m. abstr.; bibl.; illus.; stat.; maps. 100 p./no.; back issues avail. **Document type:** *Journal, Academic/Scholarly.* **Description:** Publishes full papers, short communications and review articles concerned with veterinary medicine, zootechny and related fields.
Former titles (until 1989): Universidade de Sao Paulo. Faculdade de Medicina Veterinaria e Zootecnia. Revista (0303-7525); (until 1971): Universidade de Sao Paulo. Faculdade de Medicina Veterinaria. Revista (0301-7273)
Related titles: Online - full text ed.: ISSN 1678-4456. 1997. free (effective 2007).
Indexed: A34, A35, A37, A38, AgBio, AgrForAb, B23, BA, BP, C01, C25, CABA, D01, E12, F08, FCA, G11, GH, H16, H17, IndVet, LT, MaizeAb, N02, N04, OR, P30, P33, P37, P39, PN&I, R07, R08, R12, R13, RA&MP, RM&VM, RRTA, S12, S13, S16, SCOPUS, SoyAb, T05, TAR, TriticAb, VS, W10, W11, Z01.
—BLDSC (2277.419600).
Published by: Universidade de Sao Paulo, Faculdade de Medicina Veterinaria e Zootecnia, Ave Prof Orlando Marques de Paiva 87, Cidade Universitaria Armando de Salles Oliveira, Sao Paulo, 05508-000, Brazil. brazvet@edu.usp.br, brazvet@fmvz.usp.br. Eds. Leonardo Jose Richtzenhhain, Silvia Renata Gaido Cortopassi.

➤ **BUFFALO BULLETIN.** *see* AGRICULTURE—Poultry And Livestock

➤ **BUFFALO JOURNAL**; an international journal of buffalo science. *see* AGRICULTURE—Poultry And Livestock

636.089 ITA ISSN 1828-4078
BUIATRIA; journal of the Italian Association of Buiatrics. Text in Multiple languages. 1969. q. **Document type:** *Journal, Academic/Scholarly.*
Formerly (until 2005): Societa Italiana di Buiatria. Atti (0393-1382)
Published by: Societa Italiana di Buiatria (S I B), Dip Clinico Veterinario Sezione Medicina, Via Tolara di Sopra 50, Ozzano Emilia, BO 40064, Italy. TEL 39-051-2097594, FAX 39-051-2097593, http://www.buiatria.it. Ed. Angelo Peli.

BULGARIAN JOURNAL OF AGRICULTURAL SCIENCE. *see* AGRICULTURE

636.089 BGR ISSN 1311-1477
SF604 B855X
➤ **BULGARIAN JOURNAL OF VETERINARY MEDICINE.** Text in English. 1998. q. BGL 16 domestic; USD 100 foreign (effective 2005). **Document type:** *Journal, Academic/Scholarly.* **Description:** Covers topics related to both fundamental and applied aspects of veterinary medicine; publishes original papers and reviews.
Related titles: Online - full text ed.: 2005. free (effective 2011).
Indexed: A01, A34, A35, A36, A37, A38, AgBio, C25, CA, CABA, D01, E12, F08, F11, F12, GH, H16, H17, IndVet, LT, MaizeAb, N02, N03, N04, P33, P37, P39, PN&I, R07, R08, R13, RA&MP, RRTA, S12, S13, SoyAb, T02, T05, TAR, TriticAb, VS.
—BLDSC (2366.688450).
Published by: Trakiiski Universitet, Veterinarnomeditsinski Fakultet/ Trakia University, Faculty of Veterinary Medicine, Students' Campus, Stara Zagora, 6000, Bulgaria. TEL 359-42-74143, FAX 359-42-45101, vmfd@vmf.uni-sz.bg, http://www.uni-sz.bg/vmf/index.htm. Ed. Mr. Dimiter A Pashov.

➤ **BULLETIN OF ANIMAL HEALTH AND PRODUCTION IN AFRICA/ BULLETIN DES SANTE ET PRODUCTION ANIMALES EN AFRIQUE.** *see* AGRICULTURE—Poultry And Livestock

636.08 CHE
BUNDESAMT FUER VETERINAERWESEN. MITTEILUNGEN. Text in German. 1900. 26/yr. CHF 26 (effective 2000). adv. **Document type:** *Newsletter, Government.* **Description:** Provides statistics and data concerning outbreaks of animal diseases. Also covers regulation of the exportation and importation of animals, meat and meat products to and from Switzerland.
Published by: Bundesamt fuer Veterinaerwesen, Schwarzenburgstr 161, Bern, 3003, Switzerland. TEL 41-31-3238568, FAX 41-31-3248256. Ed., R&P Heinz Mueller. Adv. contact Karin Reist. Circ: 13,000.

636.089 DEU
BUNDESVERBAND PRAKTIZIERENDER TIERAERZTE. LANDESVERBAND BAYERN. MITTEILUNGSBLATT. Text in German. q. free to members (effective 2009). adv. **Document type:** *Magazine, Trade.*
Published by: Bundesverband Praktizierender Tieraerzte, Landesverband Bayern, Schulstr 20, Frontenhausen, 84160, Germany. TEL 49-8732-931323, FAX 49-8732-931324, info@bpt-bayern.de, http://www.bpt-bayern.de. adv.: B&W page EUR 632, color page EUR 760. Circ: 3,000 (controlled).

636.089 USA
C V M QUARTERLY. (College of Veterinary Medicine) Text in English. 1945. q. USD 5. adv. bk.rev. bibl.; illus. **Document type:** *Newsletter.*
Formerly: Auburn Veterinarian
Indexed: WildRev.
Published by: Auburn University, College of Veterinary Medicine, 105 Greene Hall, Auburn, AL 36849. TEL 205-844-3698, FAX 334-844-3697, http://www.vetmed.auburn.edu. Ed. Gary Beard. Circ: 1,200.

CAB REVIEWS: PERSPECTIVES IN AGRICULTURE, VETERINARY SCIENCE, NUTRITION AND NATURAL RESOURCES. *see* AGRICULTURE

636.089 FRA ISSN 1956-9793
LES CAHIERS PRATIQUES DE LA DEPECHE. Text in French. 2006. bi-m. **Document type:** *Newsletter, Trade.*
Related titles: ◆ Supplement to: Depeche Veterinaire. ISSN 0180-3573.
Published by: Federation des Syndicats Veterinaires de France, 10 Place Leon Blum, Paris, 75011, France. TEL 33-1-44933060, FAX 33-1-43797696.

636.089 USA ISSN 0008-1612
➤ **CALIFORNIA VETERINARIAN.** Text in English. 1947. bi-m. free to members (effective 2011). adv. illus. index. back issues avail.; reprints avail. **Document type:** *Journal, Academic/Scholarly.* **Description:** Includes business, legislative and regulatory information of interest to the veterinary profession; and association and allied organization news.
Related titles: Microform ed.: (from PQC).
Indexed: ChemAb, DBA, SAA, WildRev.
—BLDSC (3015.350000), IE, Ingenta, Linda Hall.
Published by: California Veterinary Medical Association, 1400 River Park Dr., Ste. 100, Sacramento, CA 95815-4505. TEL 916-649-0599, FAX 916-646-9156, staff@cvma.net, http://www.cvma.org. Circ: 10,000 (paid).

636.089 610 CAN ISSN 0830-9000
SF601 CODEN: CJVRE9
➤ **CANADIAN JOURNAL OF VETERINARY RESEARCH/REVUE CANADIENNE DE RECHERCHE VETERINAIRE.** Text in English, French. 1937. q. CAD 135 domestic to non-members; USD 150 foreign to non-members; free to members (effective 2010). adv. bibl.; charts; illus. index. back issues avail.; reprints avail. **Document type:** *Journal, Academic/Scholarly.* **Description:** Features articles of original research in veterinary and comparative medicine including anatomy, physiology, biochemistry, pharmacology, microbiology, immunology, pathology, epidemiology, and clinical sciences.
Former titles (until 1986): Canadian Journal of Comparative Medicine (0008-4050); (until 1968): Canadian Journal of Comparative Medicine and Veterinary Science (0316-5957); (until 1940): Canadian Journal of Comparative Medicine (0846-8389)
Related titles: Online - full text ed.: (from IngentaConnect).
Indexed: A22, A34, A35, A36, A37, A38, ASCA, AgBio, Agr, B20, B21, B23, B25, BIOSIS Prev, BibAg, CA, CABA, CTA, ChemAb, ChemTitl, ChemoAb, CurCont, D01, DBA, DentInd, E12, EMBASE, ESPM, ExcerpMed, F08, FS&TA, FoVS&M, G11, GH, H16, H17, ISR, IndMed, IndVet, MCR, MEDLINE, MaizeAb, MycolAb, N02, N04, NSA, OR, P30, P33, P37, P39, PN&I, R08, RA&MP, RM&VM, S13, S16, SAA, SCI, SCOPUS, T02, TAR, VS, VirolAbstr, W07, W08, W11, WildRev.
—BLDSC (3036.700000), CASDDS, GNLM, IE, Infotrieve, Ingenta, INIST, Linda Hall. **CCC.**
Published by: Canadian Veterinary Medical Association/L' Association Canadienne des Medecins Veterinaires, 339 Booth St, Ottawa, ON K1R 7K1, Canada. TEL 613-236-1162, FAX 613-236-9681, admin@cvma-acmv.org. Ed. Dr. Eva Nagy. Adv. contact Laima Laffitte TEL 613-673-2659.

636.089 CAN ISSN 0008-5286
SF601 CODEN: CNVJA9
➤ **THE CANADIAN VETERINARY JOURNAL/REVUE VETERINAIRE CANADIENNE.** Text in English, French. 1960. m. CAD 170 domestic to non-members; USD 180 foreign to non-members; free to members (effective 2010). adv. bk.rev. abstr.; charts; illus. index. back issues avail.; reprints avail. **Document type:** *Journal, Academic/Scholarly.* **Description:** Features articles of interest to the members of the Association, notices of upcoming meetings, new product information, and book reviews.
Related titles: Microform ed.: (from PMC, PQC); Online - full text ed.
Indexed: A20, A22, A29, A34, A35, A36, A37, A38, ASCA, ASFA, AgBio, Agr, B20, B21, B25, BIOSIS Prev, BibAg, CABA, CIN, CTA, ChemAb, ChemTitl, ChemoAb, CurCont, D01, DBA, E12, EMBASE, ESPM, ExcerpMed, F08, FoVS&M, G11, GH, H17, I10, ISR, IndMed, IndVet, LT, MEDLINE, MycolAb, N02, N04, NSA, P30, P33, P37, P39, PN&I, R07, R08, R12, R13, RA&MP, RM&VM, S12, S13, S16, SAA, SCI, SCOPUS, T05, TAR, VS, VirolAbstr, W07, W08, W10, W11, WildRev.
—BLDSC (3046.100000), CASDDS, GNLM, IE, Infotrieve, Ingenta, INIST, Linda Hall. **CCC.**
Published by: Canadian Veterinary Medical Association/L' Association Canadienne des Medecins Veterinaires, 339 Booth St, Ottawa, ON K1R 7K1, Canada. TEL 613-236-1162, FAX 613-236-9681, admin@cvma-acmv.org. Ed. Carlton Gyles. Adv. contact Laima Laffitte TEL 613-673-2659.

636.089 ESP ISSN 1133-2751
CANIS ET FELIS. Text in Spanish. 1993. bi-m. back issues avail.
Indexed: IECT.
Published by: Luzan 5 S.A. de Ediciones, Pasaje Virgen de la Alegria 14, Madrid, 28027, Spain. TEL 34-91-4057260, FAX 34-91-4034907, luzan@luzan5.es, http://www.luzan5.es.

CAOYE YU XUMU/PRATACULTURE & ANIMAL HUSBANDRY. *see* AGRICULTURE—Poultry And Livestock

636.089 USA ISSN 2090-7001
▼ ➤ **CASE REPORTS IN VETERINARY MEDICINE.** Text in English. 2011. **Document type:** *Journal, Academic/Scholarly.* **Description:** Publishes case reports in all areas of veterinary medicine.
Related titles: Online - full text ed.: ISSN 2090-701X. 2011. free (effective 2011).
Published by: Hindawi Publishing Corporation, 410 Park Ave, 15th Fl, PMB 287, New York, NY 10022. FAX 215-893-4392, 866-446-3294, info@hindawi.com.

➤ **CATTLE HEALTH REPORT.** *see* AGRICULTURE—Poultry And Livestock

➤ **CATTLE PRACTICE.** *see* AGRICULTURE—Poultry And Livestock

636.089 COL ISSN 1900-9607
➤ **CES MEDICINA VETERINAIRA Y ZOOCTECNIA.** Text in Spanish. 2006. s-a. adv. abstr.; bibl.; charts; illus.; stat. back issues avail. **Document type:** *Journal, Academic/Scholarly.* **Description:** Publishes original research articles, short articles, reviews, summaries, and case studies in animal health and livestock production.
Related titles: Online - full text ed.: free (effective 2011).
Indexed: H12, I04, I05.
Published by: Universidad CES, Facultad de Medicina Veterinaria y Zootecnia, Calle 10 A No.22-04, Medellin, Colombia. TEL 57-4-4440555. ext 1357, 1550, FAX 57-4-3113505. Ed. Gregory Mejia.

➤ **CHIENS SANS LAISSE**; magazine de l'education et des sports canins. *see* PETS

➤ **CIENCIA ANIMAL BRASILEIRA.** *see* BIOLOGY—Zoology

➤ **CIENCIA RURAL.** *see* AGRICULTURE

636.089 CRI ISSN 0250-5649
CODEN: CIVEEV
➤ **CIENCIAS VETERINARIAS.** Text in Spanish. 1979. s-a. USD 13 (effective 2002). **Document type:** *Academic/Scholarly.*
Indexed: C01, IBR, IBZ, WildRev.
Published by: Escuela de Medicina Veterinaria, Biblioteca, Apdo. 86, Heredia, Costa Rica. TEL 506-2610025. Ed. Edwin Perez Chaverri.

➤ **CIGUATERA.** *see* FISH AND FISHERIES

636.089 BRA ISSN 1413-571X
CLINICA VETERINARIA. Text in Portuguese. 1996. bi-m. **Document type:** *Journal, Trade.*
Related titles: Online - full text ed.
Indexed: A34, A35, A36, A38, AgBio, CABA, D01, E12, F08, GH, H17, IndVet, N02, N04, OR, P33, P37, P39, PN&I, R08, R13, RM&VM, S13, S16, T05, TAR, VS, Z01.
—BLDSC (3286.242100), IE.
Published by: Editora Guara Ltda, Caixa Postal 66002, Sao Paulo, SP 05311-970, Brazil.

636.089 ESP ISSN 1130-7064
CLINICA VETERINARIA DE PEQUENOS ANIMALES. Text in Spanish. 1981. q. back issues avail. **Document type:** *Magazine, Trade.*
Formerly (until 1987): Asociacion Veterinaria Espanola de Especialistas en Pequenos Animales. Revista (0211-7991)
Related titles: Online - full text ed.
Indexed: SCI, W07.
Published by: (Asociacion de Veterinarios Espanoles Especialistas en Pequenos Animales (A V E P A)), Pulso Ediciones S.A., Rambla del Celler 117-119, Sant Cugat del Valles, Barcelona, Barcelona 08190, Spain. TEL 34-93-5896264, FAX 34-93-5895077, pulso@pulso.com, http://www.pulso.com/.

636.087 USA
CLINICAL FORUM. Variant title: A A V Newsletter. Text in English. 2004. q. free to members (effective 2010). **Document type:** *Newsletter, Trade.*
Published by: Association of Avian Veterinarians, PO Box 2584, Weatherford, TX 76086. FAX 817-599-0088, aavpublications@aol.com, http://www.aav.org.

636.089 USA ISSN 2154-3968
CLINICAL THERIOGENOLOGY. Text in English. 198?. q. **Document type:** *Journal, Trade.* **Description:** Presents clinical research on veterinary reproduction, including the physiology and pathology of male and female reproductive systems and the clinical practice of veterinary obstetrics, gynecology, and semenology.
Former titles (until 2009): TherioNews; (until 2006): S F T News; (until 200?): Society for Theriogenology. Newsletter
Indexed: A34, A35, A36, A38, CABA, D01, GH, N04, P33, W11.
Published by: Society for Theriogenology, PO Box 3007, Montgomery, AL 36109. TEL 334-395-4666, FAX 334-270-3399, Melissa@Franzmgt.com, http://www.therio.org.

636.089 ROM
➤ **CLUJ VETERINARY JOURNAL.** Text in English. 1991. s-a. EUR 25 (effective 2011). **Document type:** *Journal, Academic/Scholarly.*
Related titles: Online - full text ed.
Published by: Universitatea de Stiinte Agricole si Medicina Veterinara Cluj-Napoca/University of Agricultural Sciences and Veterinary Medicine Cluj-Napoca, Str Manastur 3-5, Cluj-Napoca, 400372, Romania. TEL 40-264-596384, FAX 40-264-593792, contact@usamvcluj.ro, http://www.usamvcluj.ro. Ed. Dr. Ioan Boitor.

636.089 CAN
COLLEGE OF VETERINARIANS OF ONTARIO. UPDATE. Text in English. 1983. 8/yr. USD 35. **Document type:** *Newsletter, Corporate.*
Formerly: Ontario Veterinary Association. Update (0821-6320)
Published by: College of Veterinarians of Ontario, 2106 Gordon St, Guelph, ON N1L 1G6, Canada. FAX 519-824-6497. Ed., R&P Michele Fagan. Circ: 3,000.

636.089 USA ISSN 1540-1677
COMMUNICATIONS IN THERIOGENOLOGY. Text in English. 2001. irreg. free.
Media: Online - full content.
Published by: Louisiana State University, Department of Veterinary Clinical Sciences, School of Veterinary Medicine, Rm. 1821, Baton Rouge, LA 70803. TEL 225-578-9551, FAX 225-578-9559, http://www.vetmed.lsu.edu/vcs. Ed. Dr. Bruce E. Eilts.

636.089 GBR ISSN 2041-2487
COMPANION. Text in English. 2008 (Apr.). m. free to members (effective 2009). **Document type:** *Magazine, Trade.* **Description:** Contains instructive CPD articles, reports on the activities of colleagues and members, and articles on the issues facing the profession, as well as general Association news.
Formerly: B S A V A. News
Indexed: A34, A38, CABA, E12, GH, H17, LT, N04, P33, P37, P39, R08, W11.
Published by: British Small Animal Veterinary Association, Woodrow House, 1 Telford Way, Waterwells Business Park, Gloucester, GL2 2AB, United Kingdom. TEL 44-1452-726700, FAX 44-1452-726701, administration@bsava.com. Ed. Mark Goodfellow. Pub. Kay Pringle. Circ: 5,500 (controlled).

636 JPN ISSN 0913-5316
COMPANION ANIMAL PRACTICE. Variant title: C A P. Text in Japanese. 1986. m. JPY 25,000 (effective 2007). **Document type:** *Magazine, Trade.* **Description:** Contains articles on small, companion animals.
Published by: Midori Shobo Co. Ltd. (Subsidiary of: Midori Group), JPR Crest Takebashi Bldg., 3-21 Kanda Nishikicho Chiyoda-ku, Tokyo, 101-0054, Japan. info@mgp.co.jp, http://www.mgp.co.jp/. Circ: 5,000.

636.089 USA ISSN 1940-8307
➤ **COMPENDIUM (YARDLEY)**; continuing education for veterinarians. Text in English. 1979. m. USD 70 domestic; USD 84 in Canada & Mexico; USD 119 elsewhere (effective 2010). adv. bk.rev. abstr.; charts; illus. Index. 100 p./no. 3 cols./p.; back issues avail.; reprints avail. **Document type:** *Journal, Academic/Scholarly.* **Description:** Provides information about health and disease.
Former titles (until 2006): The Compendium on Continuing Education for the Practicing Veterinarian (0193-1903); (until 1979): The Compendium on Continuing Education for the Small Animal Practitioner (0164-5455)
Related titles: CD-ROM ed.; Microform ed.: (from PQC); Online - full text ed.: ISSN 1940-8315. free (effective 2010).
Indexed: A22, A34, A37, A38, ASCA, Agr, BibAg, CABA, CurCont, EMBASE, ExcerpMed, FoVS&M, GH, H17, IndVet, MEDLINE, N04, P30, P32, P33, P39, P40, R08, RM&VM, SAA, SCI, SCOPUS, VS, W07, WildRev.
—BLDSC (3363.967520), IE, Infotrieve, Ingenta. **CCC.**
Published by: Veterinary Learning Systems (Subsidiary of: MediMedia USA, Inc.), 780 Township Line Rd, Yardley, PA 19067. TEL 800-426-9119, FAX 800-556-3288, info@vetlearn.com. Ed. Lilliane Anstee.

636.089 USA ISSN 1093-6327
SF917
COMPENDIUM OF VETERINARY PRODUCTS. Text in English. 1991. a. USD 95 (effective 2004).
Published by: North American Compediums Inc, 942 Military St, Port Huron, MI 48060. TEL 810-985-5028, FAX 810-985-5190, 800-350-0627, http://www.compasnac.com/.

636.089 USA ISSN 1559-5811
COMPENDIUM ON CONTINUING EDUCATION FOR THE PRACTICING VETERINARIAN. EQUINE EDITION. Text in English. 2005. q. **Document type:** *Journal, Trade.* **Description:** Designed for equine veterinary practitioners. Focuses on the diagnosis and treatment of horses as well as practice management.
Related titles: Online - full text ed.: ISSN 1559-582X.
Published by: Veterinary Learning Systems (Subsidiary of: MediMedia USA, Inc.), 780 Township Line Rd, Yardley, PA 19067. TEL 800-426-9119, info@vetlearn.com, http://www.vetlearn.com/.

636.089 USA ISSN 1523-8652
COMPENDIUM'S STANDARDS OF CARE: EMERGENCY AND CRITICAL CARE MEDICINE. Text in English. 1999. 11/yr. bibl. yearly. 10 p./no.; back issues avail.; reprints avail. **Document type:** *Newsletter, Trade.* **Description:** Provides access to state-of-the-art information on how to treat specific emergency and critical conditions in dogs and cats.
Published by: Veterinary Learning Systems (Subsidiary of: MediMedia USA, Inc.), 780 Township Line Rd, Yardley, PA 19067. TEL 800-426-9119, info@vetlearn.com, http://www.vetlearn.com/.

636.089 USA
THE CONFERENCE OF RESEARCH WORKERS IN ANIMAL DISEASES. PROCEEDINGS. Text in English. 19??. a. free to members (effective 2011). **Document type:** *Proceedings, Academic/Scholarly.*
Formerly: Conference of Research Workers in Animal Diseases. Abstracts
Published by: Conference of Research Workers in Animal Diseases, c/o Robert P Ellis, Colorado State University, Department of Microbiology, Immunology & Pathology, Rm A102, Fort Collins, CO 80523. TEL 970-491-5740, FAX 970-204-6684, robert.ellis@colostate.edu.

636.089 ESP ISSN 0211-0407
CONSEJO GENERAL DE COLEGIOS VETERINARIOS DE ESPANA. CIRCULAR INFORMATIVA. Text in Spanish. 1947. m. **Document type:** *Newsletter, Trade.*
Former titles (until 1978): Consejo General de Colegios Veterinarios de Espana. Suplemento Cientifico al Boletin Informativo (0211-0393); (until 1967): Consejo General de Colegios Veterinarios de Espana. Suplemento Cientifico (1139-2606); Supersedes in part (in 1962): Consejo General de Colegios Veterinarios de Espana. Boletin Informativo y Suplemento Cientifico (0589-4239); Which was formed by the merger of (1947-1956): Colegio Nacional de Veterinarios de Espana. Suplemento Cientifico al Boletin de Informacion (1130-5428); (1948-1957): Consejo General de Colegios Veterinarios de Espana. Boletin de Informacion (1135-707X)
Published by: Colegios Veterinarios de Espana, Consejo General, Villanueva 11, Madrid, 28001, Spain. TEL 34-91-4353535, FAX 34-91-5783468, consejo@colvet.es, http://www.colvet.es. Ed. Juan Jose Badiola Diez.

636.089 NGA ISSN 2141-405X
▼ ➤ **CONTINENTAL JOURNAL OF ANIMAL AND VETERINARY RESEARCH.** Text in English. 2009. a. NGN 2,500 domestic to individuals; USD 120 foreign to individuals; NGN 5,000 domestic to institutions; USD 200 foreign to institutions (effective 2010). Index. back issues avail.; reprints avail. **Document type:** *Journal, Academic/Scholarly.* **Description:** Publishes original research articles, review articles, short communications, and case reports on all aspects of animal and veterinary sciences. Focuses on economically important large and small farm animals, poultry, equine species, aquatic species and bees as well as companion animals such as cats, dogs and cage birds.
Related titles: Online - full text ed.
Indexed: A26, I05.
Published by: Wilolud Journals, 2 Church Ave, Oke Eri qrt, Oba Ile, Ondo State 340001, Nigeria. TEL 234-803-4458674, managingeditor.olawale71@gmail.com. Ed. F.A.S. Dairo.

636.089 NGA ISSN 2141-4041
CONTINENTAL JOURNAL OF VETERINARY SCIENCES. Text in English. 2008. a. NGN 2,500 domestic to individuals; USD 120 foreign to individuals; NGN 5,000 domestic to institutions; USD 200 foreign to institutions (effective 2010). Index. back issues avail.; reprints avail. **Document type:** *Journal, Academic/Scholarly.* **Description:** Covers all the scientific and technological aspects of veterinary sciences in general, anatomy, physiology, biochemistry, pharmacology, microbiology, pathology, public health, parasitology, infectious diseases, clinical sciences, alternative veterinary medicine and other biomedical fields.
Related titles: Online - full text ed.
Indexed: A26, I05, P10, PQC.
Published by: Wilolud Journals, 2 Church Ave, Oke Eri qrt, Oba Ile, Ondo State 340001, Nigeria. TEL 234-803-4458674, managingeditor.olawale71@gmail.com. Ed. A. Aremu.

636.089 CAN ISSN 0843-5634
CREST. Text in English. 1989. q. illus. **Document type:** *Newsletter.* **Description:** News of OVC's people, events and programs.
Published by: Ontario Veterinary College, Alumni Association, Dean s Office, University of Guelph, Guelph, ON N1G 2W1, Canada. TEL 519-823-8800, FAX 519-837-3230. Ed. Martha Leibbrandt. Circ: 5,100.

636.089 NLD ISSN 0166-2333
CODEN: CTVSDD
➤ **CURRENT TOPICS IN VETERINARY MEDICINE AND ANIMAL SCIENCE.** Text in English. 1978. irreg., latest vol.55, 1992. price varies. **Document type:** *Monographic series, Academic/Scholarly.*
Formerly (until 1979): Current Topics in Veterinary Medicine (0165-4586)
Indexed: A22, Agr, CIN, ChemAb, ChemTitl.
—CASDDS, INIST. **CCC.**
Published by: Springer Netherlands (Subsidiary of: Springer Science+Business Media), Van Godewijckstraat 30, Dordrecht, 3311 GX, Netherlands. TEL 31-78-6576050, FAX 31-78-6576474.

636.089 USA ISSN 0012-7337
SF601
D V M; the newsmagazine of veterinary medicine. (Doctor of Veterinary Medicine) Text in English. 1970. m. USD 40 domestic; USD 87.50 foreign; USD 17 newsstand/cover domestic; USD 19 newsstand/cover in Canada & Mexico; USD 23 newsstand/cover elsewhere (effective 2011). adv. bk.rev. abstr.; illus.; tr.lit. back issues avail.; reprints avail. **Document type:** *Magazine, Trade.* **Description:** Offers in-depth analysis of news affecting the ways in which veterinarians practice, along with practical and clinical management information.
Related titles: Microform ed.: (from PQC); Online - full text ed.: ISSN 2150-6566. USD 30 (effective 2011).
Indexed: A01, A03, A08, A22, A26, B&AI, B04, B10, BRD, CA, E08, G08, H12, I05, P10, P16, P34, P48, P52, P53, P54, P56, PQC, S04, S09, S10, T02, W03, W05.
—**CCC.**
Published by: Advanstar Communications, Inc., 6200 Canoga Ave, 2nd Fl, Woodland Hills, CA 91367. TEL 818-593-5000, FAX 818-593-5020, info@advanstar.com, http://www.advanstar.com. Ed. Daniel R Verdon. Adv. contact Rene Fall TEL 218-740-6352. Circ: 56,000 (controlled).

636.089 DNK ISSN 0106-6854
DANSK VETERINAERTIDSSKRIFT/DANISH VETERINARY JOURNAL. Text in Danish; Text occasionally in English, Norwegian. 1918. 23/yr. DKK 920 (effective 2009). adv. bk.rev. **Document type:** *Magazine, Trade.*
Formerly (until 1974): Danske Dyrlaegeforening. Medlemsblad (0011-6564)
Related titles: Online - full text ed.: ISSN 1902-3715. 200?.
Indexed: A22, A34, A35, A36, A37, A38, AgBio, BioDAb, CABA, D01, E12, F08, FS&TA, G11, GH, H17, IndVet, N02, N03, N04, OR, P33, P37, P39, PN&I, R07, R08, R12, R13, RM&VM, S13, S16, SAA, T05, TAR, VS.
—BLDSC (3533.035000), IE, Ingenta. **CCC.**
Published by: Den Danske Dyrlaegeforening/The Danish Veterinary Association, Emdrupvej 28 A, Copenhagen OE, 2100, Denmark. ddd@ddd.dk. Ed. Pia Rindom. Adv. contact Jette Jepsen. page DKK 13,710; 244 x 170.

636.089 NZL ISSN 0112-5265
DEER COURSE FOR VETERINARIANS. PROCEEDINGS. Text in English. 1984. a. **Document type:** *Proceedings, Trade.*
Indexed: Z01.
—BLDSC (3541.202000), IE, Ingenta.
Published by: New Zealand Veterinary Association Inc., Deer Branch, PO Box 11-212, Wellington, New Zealand. TEL 64-4-471-0484, FAX 64-4-471-0494, nzva@vets.org.nz, http://www.vets.org.nz/default.htm.

636.089 FRA ISSN 1956-9785
LA DEPECHE A S V. (Auxiliaires de Sante Veterinaire) Text in French. 2004. m. **Document type:** *Magazine, Trade.*
Related titles: ◆ Supplement to: Depeche Veterinaire. ISSN 0180-3573.
Published by: Federation des Syndicats Veterinaires de France, 10 Place Leon Blum, Paris, 75011, France. TEL 33-1-44933060, FAX 33-1-43797696.

636.089 FRA ISSN 0999-4866
LA DEPECHE TECHNIQUE. Text in French. 1988. bi-m. **Document type:** *Newsletter, Trade.*
Related titles: ◆ Supplement to: Depeche Veterinaire. ISSN 0180-3573.
Published by: Federation des Syndicats Veterinaires de France, 10 Place Leon Blum, Paris, 75011, France. TEL 33-1-44933060, FAX 33-1-43797696.

636.089 FRA ISSN 0180-3573
DEPECHE VETERINAIRE. Text in French. 1977. 44/yr. adv. bk.rev. **Document type:** *Magazine, Trade.*
Related titles: ◆ Supplement(s): Les Cahiers Pratiques de la Depeche. ISSN 1956-9793; ◆ La Depeche A S V. ISSN 1956-9785; ◆ La Depeche Technique. ISSN 0999-4866.
Published by: Federation des Syndicats Veterinaires de France, 10 Place Leon Blum, Paris, 75011, France. TEL 33-1-44933060, FAX 33-1-43797696. Ed. Claude Andrillon. Adv. contact F Chamari.

636.089 DEU ISSN 0340-1898
DEUTSCHES TIERAERZTEBLATT; Zeitschrift der Bundestieraerztekammer. Text in German. 1949. m. EUR 122; EUR 88 to students; EUR 19.50 newsstand/cover (effective 2010). adv. bk.rev. stat. **Document type:** *Journal, Academic/Scholarly.*

Former titles (until 1974): Deutsches Tieraerzteblatt und Mitteilungsblatt der Tieraerztekammern der Laender (0301-0465); (until 1973): Deutsches Tieraerzteblatt (0724-6773)
Indexed: A22.
—BLDSC (3578.160000), IE, Infotrieve, Ingenta. **CCC.**
Published by: (Deutsche Tieraerzteschaft e.V.), Schluetersche Verlagsgesellschaft mbH und Co. KG, Hans-Boeckler-Allee 7, Hannover, 30173, Germany. TEL 49-511-85500, FAX 49-511-85501100, info@schluetersche.de, http://www.schluetersche.de. Ed. Susanne Platt. Adv. contact Bettina Kruse. B&W page EUR 2,399, color page EUR 3,695; trim 188 x 272. Circ: 36,353 (paid).

636.089 NLD ISSN 0167-5168
SF84.23 CODEN: DAVSDR
➤ **DEVELOPMENTS IN ANIMAL AND VETERINARY SCIENCES.** Text in English. 1976. irreg., latest vol.32, 2000. price varies. back issues avail. **Document type:** *Monographic series, Academic/Scholarly.* **Description:** Examines developments in various areas of the veterinary sciences.
Indexed: A22, Agr.
—BLDSC (3579.062000), CASDDS. **CCC.**
Published by: Elsevier BV (Subsidiary of: Elsevier Science & Technology), Radarweg 29, PO Box 211, Amsterdam, 1000 AE, Netherlands. TEL 31-20-4853911, FAX 31-20-4852457, JournalsCustomerServiceEMEA@elsevier.com, http://www.elsevier.nl.

636.089 AUS ISSN 1833-4954
DEVIL FACIAL TUMOUR DISEASE NEWSLETTER. Text in English. 2006. irreg. **Document type:** *Newsletter, Trade.*
Published by: Tasmania, Department of Primary Industries, Water and Environment. Water Assessment and Planning Branch, GPO Box 44, Hobart, TAS 7001, Australia. TEL 61-3-6233-6753, 300-368-550, http://www.dpiwe.tas.gov.au/inter.nsf/Home/1?Open.

DIAGNOSTICIANS. PROCEEDINGS. *see* MEDICAL SCIENCES

636.089 NLD ISSN 0920-2412
➤ **DIER - EN - ARTS**; wetenschappelijke praktijkgerichte informatie. Text in Dutch. 1986. 9/yr. EUR 45 domestic; EUR 62.50 foreign; EUR 24 to students (effective 2009). adv. bk.rev. abstr.; bibl.; charts; illus.; stat. back issues avail. **Document type:** *Journal, Academic/Scholarly.* **Description:** Provides information for practicing veterinary surgeons and includes examples of practical solutions to problems encountered in daily practice.
Indexed: A34, A36, A37, A38, BA, CABA, D01, E12, F08, F11, G11, GH, H17, IndVet, N02, N04, P33, P37, P39, PN&I, R08, RA&MP, RM&VM, S12, VS, W11.
Published by: Uitgeverij Libre BV, Postbus 6075, Leeuwarden, 8902 HB, Netherlands. TEL 31-58-2668553, FAX 31-58-2668567, info@libre.nl, http://www.libre.nl.

636.089 NLD ISSN 1386-3355
DIERENPRAKTIJKEN. Text in Dutch. 1995. q. EUR 12.50 (effective 2010).
Published by: Maasland Uitgeverij, Postbus 348, Oss, 5340 AH, Netherlands. TEL 31-412-628218, info@maasland.com, http://www.maaslanduitgeverij.com. Ed. Peter van Riel.

636.089 JPN ISSN 0388-7421
SF917 CODEN: DIKNAA
DOBUTSU IYAKUHIN KENSAJO NENPO/JAPAN. MINISTRY OF AGRICULTURE, FORESTRY AND FISHERIES. NATIONAL VETERINARY ASSAY LABORATORY. ANNUAL REPORT. Text and summaries in English, Japanese. 1960. a. free. back issues avail. **Document type:** *Government.*
Indexed: A34, A36, A38, CABA, E12, GH, IndVet, N02, P33, P37, P39, PN&I, VS.
—BLDSC (1369.500000), CASDDS.
Published by: Norin Suisansho, Dobutsu Iyakuhin Kensajo/Ministry of Agriculture Forestry and Fisheries, National Veterinary Assay Laboratory, 1-15-1 Tokura, Kokubunji-shi, Tokyo-to 185-0003, Japan. TEL 81-42-3211841, FAX 81-42-3294376, nval@nval.go.jp, http://www.nval.go.jp/. Circ: 800.

636.089 USA ISSN 1098-2639
DOG WATCH; the newsletter for dog people. Text in English. 1997. m. USD 39 in US & Canada; USD 48 elsewhere (effective 2010). **Document type:** *Newsletter, Consumer.* **Description:** Provides readers the latest news and advice on dog care from a trusted source.
Related titles: Online - full text ed.
Indexed: G06, G07, G08, I05, I07.
Published by: (Cornell University, College of Veterinary Medicine), Belvoir Media Group, LLC, PO Box 5656, Norwalk, CT 06856. TEL 203-857-3100, 800-424-7887, FAX 203-857-3103, customer_service@belvoir.com. **Subscr. to:** Palm Coast Data, LLC, PO Box 420235, Palm Coast, FL 32142. TEL 800-829-5574, http://www.palmcoastdata.com.

636.089 616.4 USA ISSN 0739-7240
SF768.3 CODEN: DANEEE
➤ **DOMESTIC ANIMAL ENDOCRINOLOGY.** Text in English. 1984. 8/yr. USD 934 in United States to institutions; USD 1,059 elsewhere to institutions (effective 2012). adv. charts; illus.; stat.; abstr. index. back issues avail.; reprints avail. **Document type:** *Journal, Academic/Scholarly.* **Description:** Brings out scientific papers dealing with the study of the endocrine physiology of domestic animal species.
Related titles: Online - full text ed.: ISSN 1879-0054 (from IngentaConnect, ScienceDirect).
Indexed: A01, A03, A08, A22, A26, A34, A35, A36, A37, A38, ASCA, ASFA, AgBio, Agr, B21, B25, BIOBASE, BIOSIS Prev, BibAg, CA, CABA, CIN, ChemAb, ChemTitl, CurCont, D01, DBA, E12, EMBASE, ExcerpMed, FoVS&M, G11, GH, H16, I05, IABS, ISR, IndMed, IndVet, Inpharma, Inspec, MEDLINE, MycolAb, N02, N03, N04, NSA, P30, P33, P37, P39, PN&I, R08, S13, S16, S17, SAA, SCI, SCOPUS, SoyAb, T02, TAR, VS, W07.
—BLDSC (3616.884000), CASDDS, GNLM, IE, Infotrieve, Ingenta, Linda Hall. **CCC.**
Published by: Elsevier Inc. (Subsidiary of: Elsevier Science & Technology), 1600 John F Kennedy Blvd, Philadelphia, PA 19103. TEL 215-239-3900, FAX 215-238-7883, JournalCustomerService-usa@elsevier.com, http://www.elsevier.com. Eds. Gary L Williams, Dr. James L Sartin. Pub. Anthony F Trioli TEL 215-239-3733.

636.089 CHN ISSN 1007-5038
DONGWU YIXUE JINZHAN/PROGRESS IN VETERINARY MEDICINE. Text in Chinese. 1980. bi-m. USD 62.40 (effective 2009). **Document type:** *Journal, Academic/Scholarly.*
Formerly (until 1996): Guowai Shouyi. Xuqin Jibing/Animal Diseases (1004-4868)
Related titles: Online - full text ed.
—BLDSC (3619.228510), East View.
Published by: Xibei Nongye Daxue/Northwest A & F University, 3, Taicheng Lu, Yangling, 712100, China. **Dist. by:** China International Book Trading Corp, 35 Chegongzhuang Xilu, Haidian District, PO Box 399, Beijing 100044, China. TEL 86-10-68412045, FAX 86-10-68412023, cibtc@mail.cibtc.com.cn, http://www.cibtc.com.cn.

636 JPN ISSN 1347-2542
CODEN: NSKHD5
DOUBUTSU EISEI KENKYUUJO KENKYUU HOUKOKU/JAPAN. NATIONAL INSTITUTE OF ANIMAL HEALTH. BULLETIN. Text in Japanese; Summaries in Multiple languages. 1918. s-a. per issue exchange basis. **Document type:** *Government.*
Former titles (until 2001): Norin Suisansho Kachiku Eisei Shikenjo Kenkyu Hokoku/Japan. National Institute of Animal Health. Bulletin (0388-2403); (until 1978): Norinsho Kachiku Eisei Shikenjo Kenkyu Hokoku/National Institute of Animal Health. Bulletin (0369-4593)
Indexed: A22, A34, A38, B25, BIOSIS Prev, CABA, CIN, ChemAb, ChemTitl, D01, IndVet, MycolAb, P33, P37, P39, PN&I, R08, VS.
—BLDSC (3605.839300), CASDDS, IE, Ingenta.
Published by: Nougyou Gijutsu Kenkyuu Kikou, Doubutsu Eisei Kenkyuujo/National Agricultural Research Organization, National Institute of Animal Health, kannondai, Tsukuba, Ibaraki 305-0856, Japan. TEL 86-29-838-7713, FAX 81-298-38-7880, www@niah.affrc.go.jp, http://niah.naro.affrc.go.jp/index-j.html. Ed. Shinichi Terui. Circ: 2,050.

636 668.6 JPN ISSN 0385-3519
CODEN: DOKEDS
DOYAKU KENKYU. Text in Japanese. 1975. q. **Document type:** *Journal, Academic/Scholarly.*
Related titles: Online - full text ed.
—BLDSC (3620.155500).
Published by: Bayer Yakuhin Ltd., Doubutsuyou Yakuhin Jigyoubu, 1-6-5, Marunouchi, Chiyoda-ku, Tokyo, 100-5263, Japan. TEL 81-3-62667344, FAX 81-3-52199723, http://www.bayer-chikusan.jp/index.html.

636.089 ISL ISSN 1670-2468
DYRALAEKNARITID. Text in Icelandic. 1980. s-a. membership. **Document type:** *Journal, Academic/Scholarly.* **Description:** Features articles on veterinary medicine, hygiene, and the environment.
Published by: Dyralaeknafelag Islands/Icelandic Veterinary Association, PO Box 10263, Reykjavik, 110, Iceland. TEL 354-568-9545, dyr@dyr.is, http://www.dyr.is. Eds. Konrad Konardsson, Olafur Jonsson.

636.089 DNK ISSN 1603-8002
DYRLAEGEMAGASINET FOR PRAKTISERENDE DYRLAEGER. Text in Danish. 2004. bi-m. DKK 360 combined subscription inc. Dyrene og Os (effective 2009). adv. **Document type:** *Magazine, Trade.*
Related titles: Online - full text ed.; ◆ Includes: Dyrene & Os. ISSN 0902-3879.
Published by: Scanpublisher A/S, Emiliekildevej 35, Klampenborg, 2930, Denmark. TEL 45-39-908000, FAX 45-39-908280, info@scanpublisher.dk, http://www.scanpublisher.dk. Eds. Dr. Finn Boserup, John Vaboe. Adv. contact Tina Lund Larsen. page DKK 15,700; 180 x 262. Circ: 3,400.

636.089 EGY ISSN 1110-1288
EGYPTIAN VETERINARY MEDICAL ASSOCIATION. JOURNAL/ MAGALLAT AL-GAM'IYYAT AL-TIBIYYAT AL-BAYTARIYYAT AL-MISRIYYAT. Text in English. irreg. free (effective 2004). **Document type:** *Journal, Academic/Scholarly.*
Published by: The Egyptian Veterinary Medical Association, 8A, 26 July Str, PO Box 2366, Cairo, Egypt. TEL 20-2-3952826. Ed. Dr. Farouq Ebrahim El-Desouqi.

636.0832 363.7 BLR
EKOLOGIYA I ZHIVOTNYI MIR; mezhdunarodnyi nauchno-prakticheskii zhurnal. Text in Russian; Summaries in Russian, English. 2006. s-a. BYB 43,200 domestic to individuals; BYB 57,600 domestic to institutions (effective 2011). **Document type:** *Journal, Academic/Scholarly.*
Published by: Institut Eksperimental'noi Veterinarii im. S.N. Vyshelesskogo/S.N. Vyshelesskii Institute of Experimental Veterinary Medicine, vul Briket, 28, Minsk, 220003, Belarus. TEL 375-17-5088296, FAX 375-17-5088296, knir@mail.ru, http://bievm.basnet.by. Ed. Anatolii A Gusev.

EMBRYO TRANSFER NEWSLETTER. *see* BIOLOGY—Biotechnology

636.089 FRA ISSN 1283-0828
ENCYCLOPEDIE MEDICO-CHIRURGICALE. VETERINAIRE. Text in French. 1974-1974; resumed 1998. 5 base vols. plus q. updates. EUR 1,940 domestic to individuals (effective 2009). bibl.; charts; illus. back issues avail. **Document type:** *Academic/Scholarly.* **Description:** Provides an up-to-date reference on all topics in veterinary medicine.
—CCC.
Published by: Elsevier Masson (Subsidiary of: Elsevier Health Sciences), 62 Rue Camille Desmoulins, Issy les Moulineaux, Cedex 92442, France. TEL 33-1-71165500, FAX 33-1-71165600, infos@elsevier-masson.fr, http://www.elsevier-masson.fr.

636.089 BLR
➤ **EPIZOOTOLOGIYA. IMMUNOLOGIYA. FARMAKOLOGIYA. SANITARIYA**; mezhdunarodnyi nauchno-prakticheskii zhurnal. Text in Russian; Summaries in Russian, English. 2004. 3/m. BYB 43,200 domestic to individuals; BYB 57,600 domestic to institutions (effective 2011). **Document type:** *Journal, Academic/Scholarly.* **Description:** Contains articles on veterinary epizootology, immunology, pharmacology, parasitology, biotechnology, virology and microbiology of farm livestock.
Published by: Institut Eksperimental'noi Veterinarii im. S.N. Vyshelesskogo/S.N. Vyshelesskii Institute of Experimental Veterinary Medicine, vul Briket, 28, Minsk, 220003, Belarus. TEL 375-17-5088296, FAX 375-17-5088296, knir@mail.ru, http://bievm.basnet.by. Ed. Anatolii A Gusev.

➤ **EQUINE HEALTH REPORT.** *see* AGRICULTURE—Poultry And Livestock

636.087 USA ISSN 0957-7734
SF955
➤ **EQUINE VETERINARY EDUCATION.** Abbreviated title: E V E. Text in English. 1989. m. GBP 332 in United Kingdom to institutions; EUR 387 in Europe to institutions; USD 543 in United States to institutions; USD 598 elsewhere to institutions; GBP 382 combined subscription in United Kingdom to institutions (print & online eds.); EUR 446 combined subscription in Europe to institutions (print & online eds.); USD 625 combined subscription in United States to institutions (print & online eds.); USD 688 combined subscription elsewhere to institutions (print & online eds.) (effective 2012). adv. illus. **Document type:** *Journal, Academic/Scholarly.* **Description:** Covers continuing education for equine veterinarians.
Related titles: Online - full text ed.: ISSN 2042-3292. GBP 332 in United Kingdom to institutions; EUR 387 in Europe to institutions; USD 543 in United States to institutions; USD 598 elsewhere to institutions (effective 2012).
Indexed: A01, A22, A34, A35, A36, A37, A38, ASCA, AgBio, AgrForAb, CABA, D01, E01, E12, F08, FoVS&M, G11, GH, H16, H17, IndVet, LT, N02, N04, P32, P33, P39, PN&I, R07, R08, R13, RM&VM, RRTA, S13, S16, SCI, SCOPUS, T02, T05, TAR, VS, W07, W10, W11.
—BLDSC (3794.519400), IE, Infotrieve, Ingenta. **CCC.**
Published by: John Wiley & Sons, Inc., 111 River St, Hoboken, NJ 07030. TEL 201-748-6000, FAX 201-748-5915, info@wiley.com, http://www.wiley.com/WileyCDA/. adv.: color page GBP 1,103, B&W page GBP 662; bleed 220 x 290.

636.089 USA ISSN 0425-1644
SF951 CODEN: EQVJAI
➤ **EQUINE VETERINARY JOURNAL.** Abbreviated title: E V J. Text in English. 1968. bi-m. GBP 389 in United Kingdom to institutions; EUR 455 in Europe to institutions; USD 637 in United States to institutions; USD 701 elsewhere to institutions; GBP 447 combined subscription in United Kingdom to institutions (print & online eds.); EUR 524 combined subscription in Europe to institutions (print & online eds.); USD 733 combined subscription in United States to institutions (print & online eds.); USD 807 combined subscription elsewhere to institutions (print & online eds.) (effective 2012). adv. bk.rev. abstr.; bibl.; charts; illus.; stat. Index. back issues avail.; reprints avail. **Document type:** *Journal, Academic/Scholarly.* **Description:** Presents new developments in research being carried out by universities, veterinary schools and institutes devoted to equine and/or comparative physiology, pathology, medicine or surgery and from workers in practice.
Related titles: Online - full text ed.: ISSN 2042-3306. GBP 389 in United Kingdom to institutions; EUR 455 in Europe to institutions; USD 637 in United States to institutions; USD 701 elsewhere to institutions (effective 2012).
Indexed: A20, A22, A29, A34, A35, A36, A37, A38, ASCA, AgBio, Agr, AgrForAb, B20, B21, B25, BIOSIS Prev, C25, CABA, CurCont, D01, DBA, DentInd, E01, E12, EMBASE, ESPM, ExcerpMed, F08, FCA, FoVS&M, G11, GH, H16, H17, I10, ISR, IndMed, IndVet, LT, MEDLINE, MaizeAb, MycolAb, N02, N04, NucAcAb, OR, P30, P33, PN&I, R08, R13, RM&VM, RRTA, S12, S13, S16, SCI, SCOPUS, TAR, VS, VirolAbstr, W07, W10, W11, WildRev.
—BLDSC (3794.520000), GNLM, IE, Infotrieve, Ingenta, INIST. **CCC.**
Published by: (British Equine Veterinary Association GBR), John Wiley & Sons, Inc., 111 River St, Hoboken, NJ 07030. TEL 201-748-6000, FAX 201-748-5915, info@wiley.com, http://www.wiley.com/WileyCDA/. adv.: color page GBP 1,103, B&W page GBP 662; bleed 220 x 290.

636.089 CAN ISSN 1718-5793
EQUINE WELLNESS; for the natural horse. Text in English. 2006. bi-m. USD 22.95 (effective 2006). **Document type:** *Magazine, Trade.* **Description:** Covers various aspects of equine healthcare for all breeds.
Related titles: Online - full content ed.
Published by: Redstone Media Group Inc., 164 Hunter St., West, Peterborough, ON K9H 2L2, Canada. TEL 888-466-5266, FAX 705-742-4596, submissions@animalanimal.com, http://redstonemediagroup.com/. Ed. Dana Cox. Pub. Tim Hockley.

EQUINEWS; serving the horse industry - all breeds, all disciplines. *see* SPORTS AND GAMES—Horses And Horsemanship

EQUUS. *see* BIOLOGY—Zoology

636.089 TUR ISSN 1309-6958
EURASIAN JOURNAL OF VETERINARY SCIENCES/AVRASYA VETERINER BILIMLERI DERGISI. Text in English, Turkish. 1985. q. **Document type:** *Journal, Academic/Scholarly.* **Description:** Publishes original articles, short communications, case reports and invited or editorial approval reviews on all aspects of veterinary science. Original articles are divided as basic veterinary sciences (anatomy, biochemistry, ethics, histology, physiology), preclinical veterinary sciences (microbiology, parasitology, pathology, pharmacology and toxicology, virology), clinical veterinary sciences (internal medicine, reproduction, surgery), animal production (nutrition and nutritional diseases, zootechnics, economy, biostatistics, animal breeding and genetic) and food hygiene and technology.
Formerly: Selcuk Universitesi Veteriner Bilimleri Dergisi/Selcuk University. Veterinary Faculty. Journal (1011-2057)
Related titles: Online - full text ed.: ISSN 2146-1953.
Indexed: A34, A35, A36, A37, A38, AgBio, C25, CABA, D01, E12, F08, F11, G11, GH, H17, IndVet, MaizeAb, N02, N03, N04, P33, P37, P39, R08, R12, R13, RA&MP, RM&VM, S12, S13, S16, SoyAb, T05, TriticAb, VS, W10, W11.
Published by: Selcuk Universitesi, Veteriner Fakultesi/Selcuk University, Faculty of Veterinary Medicine, Alaaddin Keykubat Campus, Selcuklu, Konya 42075, Turkey. TEL 90-332-2232678, FAX 90-332-2410063, vetbildergi@selcuk.edu.tr, http://veteriner.selcuk.edu.tr/. Ed. Dr. Muammer Elmas.

636.089 USA ISSN 1521-1363
EXOTIC D V M; a practical resource for clinicians. (Doctor Veterinary Medicine) Text in English. 1999. q. USD 69; USD 20 per issue (effective 2010). adv. bk.rev. back issues avail. **Document type:** *Magazine, Trade.* **Description:** Contains articles and features promoting the quality care of nontraditional companion animals.
Related titles: Online - full text ed.: USD 5 per issue (effective 2010).
Indexed: A34, A37, A38, CABA, E12, F08, GH, H17, IndVet, N04, P33, P37, P39, PN&I, R08, RM&VM, S12, VS, W11.
—BLDSC (3836.378000), IE, Ingenta.

Published by: Zoological Education Network, PO Box 541749, Lake Worth, FL 33454. TEL 561-641-6745, 800-981-4782, FAX 561-641-0234. Ed., Pub., R&P, Adv. contact Linda Harrison. page USD 1,485; trim 8.375 x 10.875.

636.089 ITA ISSN 1827-5265
EXOTIC FILES. Text in Italian. 2000. 3/yr. **Document type:** *Journal, Trade.*
Published by: Societa Italiana Veterinari Animali Esotici (S I V A E), Via Trecchi 20, Cremona, 26100, Italy. TEL 39-0372-403500, FAX 39-0372-457091, info@sivae.it, http://www.sivae.it.

F A S S VET; laekemedel foer veterinaermedicinsk bruk. (Farmaceutiska Specialiteter i Sverige) *see* PHARMACY AND PHARMACOLOGY

636.089 ARG ISSN 1666-938X
F A V E. SECCION CIENCIAS VETERINARIAS. (Facultad de Ciencias Veterinarias. Seccion Ciencias Veterinarias) Text in Spanish. 2002. s-a. ARS 20 (effective 2010). back issues avail. **Document type:** *Journal, Academic/Scholarly.*
Supersedes in part (in 2002): F A V E (0325-3112)
Indexed: Z01.
Published by: Universidad Nacional del Litroal, Facultad de Ciencias Veterinarias, R.P. Kreder 2805, Esperanzz, Santa Fe 3080, Argentina. TEL 54-3496-420639, FAX 54-3496-426304, facvete@fcu.unl.edu.ar, http://www.fcv.unl.edu.ar/. Ed. Luis Calvinho. Circ: 500.

636.089 USA ISSN 1554-9895
F D A VETERINARIAN (ONLINE). Text in English. 1995. bi-m. free (effective 2010). back issues avail. **Document type:** *Newsletter.*
Media: Online - full text.
Published by: U.S. Food & Drug Administration, Center for Veterinary Medicine, 7519 Standish Pl, HFV-12, Rockville, MD 20855. TEL 240-276-9300, AskCVM@fda.hhs.gov, http://www.fda.gov/cvm. Ed. Jon F Scheid TEL 240-276-9110. **Subscr. to:** U.S. Government Printing Office, Superintendent of Documents, PO Box 371954, Pittsburgh, PA 15250. TEL 202-512-1800, FAX 202-512-2250, gpoaccess@gpo.gov, http://www.access.gpo.gov/.

636.089 COL ISSN 0120-2952
FACULTAD DE MEDICINA VETERINARIA Y ZOOTECNICA. REVISTA. Text in Spanish, English. 1948. s-a. **Document type:** *Journal, Academic/Scholarly.*
Related titles: Online - full text ed.: free (effective 2011).
Indexed: I04.
Published by: Universidad Nacional de Colombia, Facultad de Medicina, Carrera 30, No 45-03, Bogota, Colombia. http://www.unal.edu.co.

636.039 614 USA ISSN 0164-6257
FEDERAL VETERINARIAN. Text in English. 1922. m. USD 40 in US & Canada; USD 60 elsewhere (effective 2005). adv. bk.rev. back issues avail. **Document type:** *Newsletter, Trade.* **Description:** Federal regulatory news, meat inspection, animal disease control, human disease from animals and federal personnel issues.
Published by: National Association of Federal Veterinarians, 1101 Vermont Ave, NW, Ste 710, Washington, DC 20005-6308. TEL 202-289-6334, FAX 202-842-4360. Ed., R&P, Adv. contact Dale D Boyle. B&W page USD 260; trim 7.5 x 9.5. Circ: 1,600 (paid and controlled).

636.089 USA
FELINE HEALTH TOPICS. Text in English. 1981. q. USD 30 (effective 2006). back issues avail. **Document type:** *Newsletter, Trade.* **Description:** For veterinary professionals.
Published by: Cornell Feline Health Center, Cornell Feline Health Centre, Schurman Hall, Ithaca, NY 14853. TEL 607-253-3414, FAX 607-253-3419, http://www.cornell.edu. Ed. Sheryl Thomas. Circ: 5,000 (paid and free).

636.089 TUR ISSN 1308-9323
FIRAT UNIVERSITESI SAGLIK BILIMLERI VETERINER DERGISI/ FIRAT UNIVERSITY, HEALTH SCIENCES AT THE VETERINARY JOURNAL/FIRAT UNIVERSITY. JOURNAL OF VETERINARY HEALTH SCIENCES. Text in Turkish, English. 3/yr. **Document type:** *Journal, Academic/Scholarly.* **Description:** Contains clinical and experimental original researches, case reports, invited reviews and letters to the editor in the field of veterinary medicine.
Related titles: Online - full text ed.: free (effective 2010).
Indexed: A34, A35, A36, A38, D01, E12, N03, N04, P33, R08, T05.
Published by: Firat Universitesi, Saglik Bilimleri Enstitusu Mudurlugu, Elazig, 23119, Turkey. TEL 90-424-2122708, FAX 90-424-2379141, posta@firat.edu.tr, http://www.firat.edu.tr. Eds. Engin Sahna, Emine Unsaldi.

636.0832 658 USA ISSN 1095-0613
FIRSTLINE. Text in English. 1995. bi-m. USD 21 domestic; USD 31.50 in Canada & Mexico; USD 42 elsewhere; USD 9 newsstand/cover domestic; USD 13 newsstand/cover in Canada & Mexico; USD 15 newsstand/cover elsewhere (effective 2011). adv. **Document type:** *Magazine, Trade.* **Description:** Helps receptionists, registered technicians, practice managers, and veterinary assistants build strong relationships with coworkers, improve their communications skills, educate clients with confidence, enhance their contributions to a veterinary practice and maximize every patient's well-being.
Related titles: Online - full text ed.: ISSN 2150-6574. USD 15 (effective 2011).
Indexed: A15, B01, B07, P56, T02.
—CCC.
Published by: Advanstar Veterinary Healthcare Communications (Subsidiary of: Advanstar Communications, Inc.), 8033 Flint, Lenexa, KS 66214. TEL 800-255-6864, FAX 913-871-3808, http://www.vetmedpub.com. adv.: B&W page USD 5,765; trim 7.75 x 10.5.

FISH HEALTH NEWSLETTER. *see* FISH AND FISHERIES

636.089 SVK ISSN 0015-5748
SF604 CODEN: FVMCAW
FOLIA VETERINARIA. Text in English. 1956. q. EUR 51 (effective 2009). adv. bk.rev. abstr.; bibl. index.; cum.index. **Document type:** *Journal, Academic/Scholarly.*
Indexed: A34, A35, A36, A37, A38, AgBio, B23, BA, BP, C25, CABA, CIN, ChemAb, ChemTitl, D01, E12, F08, F11, F12, FCA, G11, GH, H16, H17, INIS AtomInd, IndVet, LT, MaizeAb, N02, N03, N04, OR, P30, P32, P33, P37, P39, P40, PHN&I, PN&I, R07, R08, R13, RA&MP, RM&VM, RRTA, S12, S13, S16, SAA, SoyAb, T05, TAR, TriticAb, VS, W10, W11.
—CASDDS.
Published by: Univerzita Veterinarskeho Lekarstva v Kosiciach/ University of Veterinary Medicine in Kosice, Komenskeho 73, Kosice, 04181, Slovakia. simkova@uvm.sk. Ed. Rudolf Cabadaj. Circ: 550. **Dist. by:** Slovart G.T.G. s.r.o., Krupinska 4, PO Box 152, Bratislava 85299, Slovakia. TEL 421-2-63839472, FAX 421-2-63839485, info@slovart-gtg.sk, http://www.slovart-gtg.sk.

FOOD SAFETY ASSURANCE AND VETERINARY PUBLIC HEALTH. *see* PUBLIC HEALTH AND SAFETY

636.089 CHN ISSN 1003-4331
FUJIAN XUMU SHOUYI/FUJIAN JOURNAL OF ANIMAL HUSBANDRY AND VETERINARY. Text in Chinese; Abstracts and contents page in English. 1979. bi-m. USD 61.20 (effective 2009). adv. **Document type:** *Journal, Academic/Scholarly.* **Description:** Publishes investigative report, monographs, clinical information and productive experiences in the field of animal husbandry and veterinary sciences.
Formerly: Xumu yu Shouyi/Animal Husbandry & Veterinary Medicine (0529-5130)
Related titles: Online - full text ed.
—East View.
Published by: Fujina Xumu Shouyi Bianjibu, 153, Guping Lu, Fuzhou, Fujian 350003, China. TEL 81-591-87807454, FAX 81-591-87856764. adv.: page CNY 1,000. **Dist. by:** China International Book Trading Corp, 35 Chegongzhuang Xilu, Haidian District, PO Box 399, Beijing 100044, China. TEL 86-10-68412045, FAX 86-10-68412023, cibtc@mail.cibtc.com.cn, http://www.cibtc.com.cn.

636.089 CHE
G S T BULLETIN/BULLETIN S V S. Text in French, German. 1962. m. **Document type:** *Bulletin, Trade.*
Published by: Gesellschaft Schweizer Tieraerztinnen und Tieraerzte, Brunnmattstr 13, Postfach 45, Thoerishaus, 3174, Switzerland. TEL 41-31-3073535, FAX 41-31-3073539, info@gstsvs.ch, http://www.gstsvs.ch.

636.089 FRA ISSN 0399-2519
CODEN: BGTVDC
G T V BULLETIN. (Groupements Techniques Veterinaires) Text in French. 1974. 5/yr. EUR 186 to non-members; EUR 151 to members (effective 2009). adv. bk.rev. **Document type:** *Bulletin, Trade.*
Indexed: A22, A34, A35, A36, A37, A38, BioDAb, CABA, ChemAb, D01, E12, F08, G11, GH, H17, IndVet, LT, MaizeAb, N02, N03, N04, P33, P37, P39, PN&I, R07, R08, R13, RRTA, TAR, VS, W10, W11.
—BLDSC (2551.630000), IE, Ingenta.
Published by: Societe Nationale des Groupements Techniques Veterinaires (S N G T V), 5 Rue Moufle, Paris, 75011, France. TEL 33-1-49295858, FAX 33-1-49297077, sngtv@sngtv.org.

636.089 VEN ISSN 1690-8414
GACETA DE CIENCIAS VETERINARIAS. Text in Spanish. 1995. s-a. back issues avail. **Document type:** *Bulletin, Academic/Scholarly.*
Related titles: Online - full text ed.
Published by: Universidad Centroccidental Lisandro Alvarado, Decanato de Ciencias Veterinarias, Apdo. 400, Barquisimeto, Lara, Venezuela. FAX 58-251-2592440, gacienvet@ucla.edu.ve.

636.089 USA ISSN 0886-5760
THE GEORGIA VETERINARIAN. Text in English. 1948. q. USD 25 (effective 2006). **Document type:** *Newsletter.*
Indexed: Agr.
Published by: Georgia Veterinary Medical Association, 2814 Spring Rd, Suite 217, Atlanta, GA 30339. TEL 678-309-9800, FAX 678-309-3361, gvma@gvma.net, http://www.gvma.net.

GEOSPATIAL HEALTH. *see* MEDICAL SCIENCES—Radiology And Nuclear Medicine

636.089 PAK ISSN 1992-6197
➤ **GLOBAL VETERINARIA.** Text in English. 2007. bi-m. **Document type:** *Journal, Academic/Scholarly.*
Related titles: Online - full text ed.: ISSN 1999-8163. free (effective 2011).
Indexed: A34, A35, A36, A37, A38, AgrForAb, B23, C25, C30, CABA, D01, E12, F08, GH, H16, MaizeAb, N02, N03, N04, P32, P33, R07, R08, S13, SoyAb, T05, TAR, W10, W11, Z01.
Published by: International Digital Organization for Scientific Information (I D O S I), P-100, St# 7, Sohailabad, Peoples Colony # 2, Faisalabad, Pakistan. TEL 92-41-8542906, idosi@idosi.org, http://www.idosi.org. Ed. Wahid Mohamed Ahmed.

636.39 GBR ISSN 0961-2548
GOAT VETERINARY SOCIETY JOURNAL. Text in English. 1979. s-a. free to members. **Document type:** *Journal, Academic/Scholarly.*
Indexed: A34, A35, A36, A37, A38, AgBio, C25, CABA, D01, E12, G11, GH, H17, IndVet, N02, N04, P33, P37, P39, PN&I, R07, R08, RM&VM, TAR, VS, W10, W11.
—BLDSC (4196.610000).
Published by: The Goat Veterinary Society (Subsidiary of: British Veterinary Association), c/o Nick Clayton, Hon. Secretary, 29 Winfield, Newent, Glos GL18 1QB, United Kingdom. TEL 44-1531-820074, http://www.goatvetsoc.co.uk/.

636.0890941 GBR ISSN 1752-5144
GOVERNMENT VETERINARY JOURNAL. Abbreviated title: G V J. Text in English. 1945. s-a. free (effective 2009). back issues avail. **Document type:** *Journal, Academic/Scholarly.* **Description:** Aims to enhance the contribution of veterinary expertise within and across government, promote the work of government veterinary surgeons and provide a range of technical, factual and interesting articles in the fields of: disease control, public health, animal welfare and consumer protection.
Former titles (until Dec.2005): State Veterinary Journal (0269-5545); (until 1950): State Veterinary News
Related titles: Online - full text ed.: free.
Indexed: A34, A36, A37, A38, BA, CABA, D01, E12, GH, H17, IndVet, N02, N04, OR, P33, P37, P39, PN&I, R08, S13, S16, T05, VS, W11.
—BLDSC (4206.079500), IE, Ingenta. **CCC.**
Published by: (Great Britain. Department for Environment, Food & Rural Affairs), Government Veterinary Surgeons, Veterinary Services Team, c/o Dept. for Environment, Food & Rural Affairs, Area 5D, Nobel House, 17 Smith Sq, London, SW1P 3JR, United Kingdom. GVJ@defra.gov.uk. Ed. Linda Smith.

636.089 CHN ISSN 1002-5235
GUANGXI XUMU SHOUYI/GUANGXI JOURNAL OF ANIMAL HUSBANDRY & VETERINARY MEDICINE. Text in Chinese. 1985. bi-m. **Document type:** *Journal, Academic/Scholarly.*
Related titles: Online - full text ed.
Published by: Guangxi Xumu Shouyi Xuehui, Xiuling Lu, Guangxi Daxue, Nanning, 530005, China. TEL 86-771-3235650, FAX 86-771-3235650.

636.089 ESP ISSN 1136-9345
GUIA PUNTEX. ANUARIO ESPANOL DE VETERINARIA. Text in Spanish. 1995. a. EUR 81 domestic; EUR 108 in Europe; EUR 136 elsewhere (effective 2007). adv. back issues avail. **Document type:** *Yearbook, Consumer.*
Published by: Publicaciones Nacionales Tecnicas y Extranjeras (PUNTEX), Padilla 323, Barcelona, 08025, Spain. TEL 34-934-462820, FAX 34-934-462064, puntex@puntex.es, http://www.puntex.es. Ed. Martin Yolanda. adv.: B&W page EUR 490; 170 x 240. Circ: 3,500.

HABBANAE. *see* AGRICULTURE

HARYANA AGRICULTURAL UNIVERSITY. JOURNAL OF RESEARCH. *see* AGRICULTURE

636.089 IND ISSN 0033-4359
THE HARYANA VETERINARIAN. Text in English. 1961. a. adv. bk.rev. abstr.; charts; illus.; stat. **Document type:** *Journal, Academic/ Scholarly.*
Formerly (until 1970): Punjab Veterinarian (0556-2325)
Indexed: A34, A35, A36, A38, AgBio, AgrForAb, CABA, D01, E12, F08, F11, F12, G11, GH, H16, H17, IndVet, N02, N04, P33, P37, P39, PN&I, R07, R08, R12, R13, RA&MP, RM&VM, S17, TAR, TriticAb, VS, W11.
—BLDSC (4271.150000).
Published by: Haryana Agricultural University, College of Veterinary Sciences, College of Veterinary Sciences, CCS Haryana Agricultural University, Hissar, Haryana 125 004, India. TEL 91-1662-284312, FAX 91-1662-284312, dcovs@hau.ernet.in, http://hau.ernet.in.

636.089 TUR ISSN 1301-9597
HAYVANSAL URETIM/JOURNAL OF ANIMAL PRODUCTION. Text in Turkish, English. 1974. 2/yr. **Document type:** *Journal, Academic/ Scholarly.* **Description:** Publishes original and unpublished research articles, review articles, short notes and letters to the editor.
Related titles: Online - full text ed.
Indexed: A34, A35, A37, A38, AgBio, C25, CABA, D01, E12, F08, F12, G11, GH, H16, IndVet, MaizeAb, N02, N03, N04, O01, OR, P32, P33, P37, P40, PN&I, R07, R08, R12, RA&MP, S12, S13, S16, SoyAb, TAR, TriticAb, VS, W11.
Published by: Turkish Animal Science Association, Ege University Agriculture Faculty, Department of Animal Science, Bornova - Izmir, 35100, Turkey. TEL 90-232-3884000 ext 2917, FAX 90-232-3399090, yavuz.akbas@ege.edu.tr, http://www.ege.edu.tr/en/, http://www.zooteknidernegi.org. Ed. Yavuz Akbas.

636.089 CHN ISSN 1004-7034
HEILONGJIANG XUMU SHOUYI/HEILONGJIANG JOURNAL OF ANIMAL SCIENCE AND VETERINARY MEDICINE. Text in Chinese. 1958. m. **Document type:** *Journal, Academic/Scholarly.*
—BLDSC (4284.195760).
Published by: (Heilongjiang Sheng Xumu Shouyi Xuehui/Heilongjiang Society of Animla Science and Veterinary Medicine, Heilongjiang Sheng Xumuju/Heilongjiang Provincial Animal Husbandry Bureau), Heilongjiang Xumu Shouyi Banjibu, 243, Harbin Lu, Xiangfang-qu, Ha'erbin, 150069, China.

636.089 GRC ISSN 1792-2720
HELLENIC VETERINARY MEDICAL SOCIETY. JOURNAL/ELLENIKES KTINIATRIKES ETERIAS. PERIODIKO. Text in Greek; Summaries in English. 1924. q. USD 150 in Europe; USD 150 in the Middle East; USD 150 in North Africa; USD 180 elsewhere; USD 50 per issue (effective 2005). adv. bk.rev. **Document type:** *Bulletin, Academic/ Scholarly.*
Formerly (until 2002): Hellenic Veterinary Medical Society. Bulletin/ Deltion tes Ellenikes Ktiniatrikes Eterias (0257-2354)
Related titles: Online - full text ed.
Indexed: A34, A35, A36, A37, A38, AgBio, AgrForAb, BA, BP, BioDAb, C25, CABA, D01, E12, F08, FS&TA, GH, H16, H17, IndVet, MaizeAb, N02, N03, N04, OR, P32, P33, P37, P38, P39, P40, PN&I, R07, R08, R11, R12, R13, RA&MP, RM&VM, SCI, SoyAb, TriticAb, VS, W07, W11.
—BLDSC (4758.000500), IE, Ingenta.
Published by: Hellenic Veterinary Medical Society, Agia Paraskevi, P O Box 60087, Athens, 153 10, Greece. Ed. Dr. Agesilaus Tsagarakis. Circ: 1,000 (controlled). **Subscr. to:** Olga Sabatakou, Treasurer of the HVMS, P O Box 35 46, Athens GR - 102 10, Greece.

636.089 FIN ISSN 1457-1552
HELSINGIN YLIOPISTO. ELAINLAAKETIETEELLINEN TIEDEKUNTA. JULKAISUJA/HELSINGFORS UNIVERSITET. VETERINAERMEDICINSKA FAKULTETEN. PUBLIKATIONER/ UNIVERSITY OF HELSINKI. FACULTY OF VETERINARY MEDICINE. PUBLICATIONS. Text in English, Finnish, Swedish. 2000. irreg. back issues avail. **Document type:** *Monographic series, Academic/Scholarly.*
Related titles: Online - full text ed.: ISSN 1457-1536.
Published by: Helsingin Yliopisto, Elainlaaketieteellinen Tiedekunta/ University of Helsinki. Faculty of Veterinary Medicine, Agnes Sjoebergin Katu 2, PO Box 66, Helsinki, 00014, Finland. TEL 358-9-1911, FAX 358-9-19157161, http://www.vetmed.helsinki.fi.

636.089 FIN ISSN 1457-1544
HELSINGIN YLIOPISTO. ELAINLAAKETIETEELLINEN TIEDEKUNTA. OPPIMATERIAALIA. Text in Finnish. 2000. irreg., latest vol.5, 2005. back issues avail. **Document type:** *Monographic series, Academic/ Scholarly.*
Related titles: Online - full text ed.: ISSN 1457-1528.
Published by: Helsingin Yliopisto, Elainlaaketieteellinen Tiedekunta/ University of Helsinki. Faculty of Veterinary Medicine, Agnes Sjoebergin Katu 2, PO Box 66, Helsinki, 00014, Finland. TEL 358-9-1911, FAX 358-9-19157161, http://www.vetmed.helsinki.fi.

636.089 GBR
HENSTON SMALL ANIMAL VETERINARY VADE MECUM (PETERBOROUGH, 2005). Text in English. 1982. a. GBP 15 per issue; free to qualified personnel (effective 2009). adv. Index. back issues avail. **Document type:** *Magazine, Trade.* **Description:** For veterinary surgeons or similarly qualified personnel. Covers diseases, conditions, and symptoms of small animals, as well as therapeutic products.

Former titles (until 2005): The Henston Companion Animal Veterinary Vade Mecum (1474-0354); (until 2001): Henston Small Animal Veterinary Vade Mecum (High Wycombe, 1993) (0969-7993); (until 1993): Henston Veterinary Vade Mecum (Small Animal) (0268-4268)
—**CCC.**
Published by: Veterinary Business Development Ltd. (Subsidiary of: Wolters Kluwer N.V.), Olympus House, Werrington Ctr, Peterborough, PE4 6NA, United Kingdom. TEL 44-1733-325522, FAX 44-1733-352512.

HIMACHAL JOURNAL OF AGRICULTURAL RESEARCH. *see* AGRICULTURE

636.089 AUT ISSN 0105-1423
SF615
HISTORIA MEDICINAE VETERINARIAE. Text and summaries in English, French, German. 1976. bi-m. EUR 53 (effective 2002). adv. bk.rev. illus.; tr.lit. index, cum.index every 5 years. 40 p./no. 2 cols./p.; back issues avail. **Document type:** *Journal, Academic/Scholarly.* **Description:** Covers veterinary science and history.
Indexed: A38, DIP, EMBASE, ExcerpMed, H17, IBR, IBZ, MEDLINE, P30, P37, SCOPUS.
—BLDSC (4316.056500).
Address: Roegergasse 24-26-2-5, Vienna, 1090, Austria. christa.mache@chello.at. Ed. Georg Theves. Circ: 250.

636.089 JPN ISSN 0018-3385
➤ **HOKKAIDO VETERINARY MEDICAL ASSOCIATION. JOURNAL/ HOKKAIDO JUISHIKAI ZASSHI.** Text in Japanese. 1967. m. JPY 350; JPY 350 foreign (effective 1999). adv. abstr.; bibl.; charts; illus.; tr.lit. **Document type:** *Academic/Scholarly.*
Indexed: Agrind.
Published by: Hokkaido Veterinary Medical Association, 24 Ken, 4-Jo, 5-chome, 9-3 Nishi-ku, Sapporo, 063-0804, Japan. TEL 81-11-642-4826, FAX 81-11-642-4642, hokuju00@poplar.ocn.ne.jp. Ed., Pub., R&P, Adv. contact Hinoshi Kanagawa. B&W page JPY 30,000; trim 300 x 210. Circ: 2,600 (paid); 100 (controlled).

636.1 USA ISSN 1076-4704
HOOFCARE & LAMENESS; the journal of equine foot science. Text in English. 1985. q. USD 59 domestic; USD 69 in Canada & Mexico; USD 79 elsewhere (effective 2010). Website rev.; bk.rev.; software rev.; tel.rev.; video rev. charts; illus.; tr.lit. index, cum.index: 1985-2000. 64 p./no.; back issues avail.; reprints avail. **Document type:** *Journal, Trade.* **Description:** Provides technical information related to the prevention and therapy of performance-related injuries, conformational challenges, and diseases of the foot that affect the world's horses.
Former titles (until 1992): Hoofcare and Lameness Quarterly Report (1062-3221); (until 1991): F Y I (1076-4690)
Published by: Hoofcare Publishing, 19 Harbor Loop, PO Box 6600, Gloucester, MA 01930. TEL 978-281-3222, FAX 978-283-8775, webinquiry@hoofcare.com. Ed. Fran Jurga.

636.1 USA
THE HORSE REPORT. Text in English. 1982. q. looseleaf. free. back issues avail. **Document type:** *Newsletter.* **Description:** Covers recent research in equine health for horse owners, breeders, and veterinarians.
Published by: University of California, Davis, Center for Equine Health, School of Veterinary Medicine, One Shields Ave, Davis, CA 95616-8589. TEL 530-752-6433, FAX 530-752-9379, cehwebmaster@ucdavis.edu, http://www.vetmed.ucdavis.edu/ceh. Ed., R&P Laurie Fio. Circ: 17,000.

HUMAN AND VETERINARY MEDICINE. *see* MEDICAL SCIENCES

636.0832 SWE ISSN 1653-5022
HUNDSTALLSNYTT. Text in Swedish. 1996. q. SEK 160 membership (effective 2006). back issues avail. **Document type:** *Newsletter, Consumer.*
Related titles: Online - full text ed.
Published by: Svenska Hundskyddsfoereningen/Swedish Dog Protection Organization, Aakeshors Gaardvaeg 10, Bromma, 16838, Sweden. TEL 46-8-203848, FAX 46-8-100426, info@hundstellet.se. Ed. Annike Hjerpe TEL 46-73-9033109.

636.089 USA ISSN 2090-4452
▼ ➤ **I S R N VETERINARY SCIENCE.** (International Scholarly Research Network) Text in English. 2011. **Document type:** *Journal, Academic/ Scholarly.* **Description:** Publishes original research articles as well as review articles in all areas of veterinary medicine and animal husbandry.
Related titles: Online - full text ed.: ISSN 2090-4460. 2011. free (effective 2011).
Published by: Hindawi Publishing Corporation, 410 Park Ave, 15th Fl, PMB 287, New York, NY 10022. FAX 215-893-4392, 866-446-3294, info@hindawi.com.

636.089 615 ZAF ISSN 0019-0918
I V S. (Index of Veterinary Specialists) Text in English. 1961. q. ZAR 90 domestic; ZAR 193 in United States; ZAR 175 in Europe; ZAR 212 in Australia & New Zealand (effective 2000). adv. back issues avail. **Description:** Indexes veterinary medicines available in South Africa in pharmacological order, alphabetically.
Published by: M I M S (Subsidiary of: Johnnic Communications Ltd.), 83 Hendrik Verwoerd Dr, Gauteng, 2194, South Africa. TEL 27-12-3485010, FAX 27-12-3617716. Ed. G Swan. Adv. contact Sandy Schoeman. Circ: 2,562.

636.089 ZAF
I V S DESK REFERENCE. (Index of Veterinary Specialists) Text in English. 1991. biennial. ZAR 100 domestic; ZAR 213 in United States; ZAR 220 in Europe; ZAR 232 in Australia & New Zealand. adv. **Description:** Provides full product information on veterinary medicines, including a generic-trade name index and a reference section.
Published by: M I M S (Subsidiary of: Johnnic Communications Ltd.), 83 Hendrik Verwoerd Dr, Gauteng, 2194, South Africa. TEL 27-12-3485010, FAX 27-12-3617716. Ed. G Swan. Adv. contact Sandy Schoeman. Circ: 2,800.

636.089 GBR ISSN 0263-841X
SF601 CODEN: IPRCDH
➤ **IN PRACTICE (LONDON).** Text in English. 1979. 10/yr. GBP 450, EUR 607.50, USD 877.50 combined subscription to institutions (print & online eds.); free to members (effective 2010); subscr. includes The Veterinary Record. adv. back issues avail. **Document type:** *Journal, Academic/Scholarly.* **Description:** Provides regular update on clinical developments, continuing educational materials for veterinary practitioners.
Related titles: Online - full text ed.: ISSN 2042-7689. GBP 360, EUR 486, USD 702 to institutions; free to members (effective 2010); subscr. includes The Veterinary Record; ◆ Supplement to: The Veterinary Record. ISSN 0042-4900.
Indexed: A22, A34, A36, A37, A38, Agr, B&AI, B10, B23, CABA, D01, DBA, DentInd, E12, FS&TA, FoVS&M, G11, GH, H17, IndMed, IndVet, LT, N02, N04, OR, P30, P33, P37, P39, PN&I, R07, R08, R12, R13, RA&MP, RM&VM, RRTA, S13, S16, SAA, SCI, SCOPUS, T05, TAR, VS, W07, W11, WildRev.
—BLDSC (4372.411000), GNLM, IE, Infotrieve, Ingenta, Linda Hall. **CCC.**
Published by: (British Veterinary Association), B M J Group, BMA House, Tavistock Sq, London, WC1H 9JR, United Kingdom. TEL 44-20-73836373, FAX 44-20-73836668, http://group.bmj.com. Adv. contact Kevan Bowen TEL 44-7768-880410.

➤ **INDIAN JOURNAL OF ANIMAL NUTRITION.** *see* AGRICULTURE—Poultry And Livestock

➤ **INDIAN JOURNAL OF ANIMAL RESEARCH**; half-yearly research journal of animal, food, dairying and zoological sciences. *see* AGRICULTURE—Poultry And Livestock

636.089 IND ISSN 0367-8318
SF601 CODEN: IJLAA4
➤ **INDIAN JOURNAL OF ANIMAL SCIENCES.** Text in English. 1921. m. INR 500, USD 125 to individuals; INR 1,500, USD 375 to institutions; INR 125, USD 50 per issue (effective 2011). bk.rev. charts; illus. index. back issues avail.; reprints avail. **Document type:** *Journal, Academic/Scholarly.* **Description:** Covers important original research work on animal breeding, diseases, physiology, nutrition, dairying, animal production technology and fisheries.
Former titles (until 1969): Indian Journal of Veterinary Science and Animal Husbandry (0019-5715); (until 1931): Central Bureau for Animal Husbandry and Dairying in India. Journal (0368-1602)
Related titles: Online - full text ed.: (from PQC).
Indexed: A22, A34, A35, A36, A37, A38, ASCA, AgBio, AgrForAb, Agrind, B21, B23, B25, BA, BIOSIS Prev, BP, C25, CA, CABA, CIN, ChemAb, ChemTitl, CurCont, D01, DBA, E12, F08, F11, F12, FCA, FS&TA, FoVS&M, G11, GH, GenetAb, H16, H17, HGA, I11, ISR, IndVet, LT, MaizeAb, MycolAb, N02, N03, N04, O01, OR, P30, P32, P33, P37, P39, P40, PN&I, R07, R08, R11, R12, R13, RA&MP, RM&VM, RRTA, S&MA, S12, S13, S16, S17, SAA, SCI, SCOPUS, SoyAb, T02, T05, TAR, TriticAb, VS, VirolAbstr, W07, W08, W10, W11, WildRev, Z01.
—BLDSC (4410.195000), CASDDS, IE, Infotrieve, Ingenta, INIST, Linda Hall.
Published by: Indian Council of Agricultural Research, Krishi Bhavan, Dr. Rajendra Prasad Rd, Pusa, New Delhi, 110 114, India. TEL 91-11-23382629, FAX 91-11-23384773, dg.icar@nic.in.

636 IND ISSN 0973-3175
➤ **INDIAN JOURNAL OF FIELD VETERINARIANS.** Abbreviated title: I J F V. Text and summaries in English. 2005. q. INR 300 domestic to individuals; USD 100 foreign to individuals; INR 2,500 domestic to institutions; USD 300 foreign to institutions (effective 2011). back issues avail. **Document type:** *Journal, Academic/Scholarly.* **Description:** Publishes original research work, general articles, clinical articles, short articles and case reports in the field of veterinary science.
Related titles: Online - full text ed.
Published by: Academa Publishers, 83 Vandana Nagar Main, Near Tilak Nagar, Indore, Madhya Pradesh 452 018, India. TEL 91-9993435302, 91-731-2497068, academaindore@rediffmail.com. Ed., Pub., R&P R S Dhanotia. Circ: 500.

639.089 IND ISSN 0970-051X
CODEN: IJVMDP
➤ **INDIAN JOURNAL OF VETERINARY MEDICINE.** Text in English. 1981. s-a. bk.rev. author and subject indexes. 70 p./no. 2 cols./p.; **Document type:** *Journal, Academic/Scholarly.* **Description:** Contains review articles, original/applied research articles, clinical observations, preliminary reports of scientific studies and short communications on veterinary medicine and animal health.
Indexed: A34, A37, A38, AgrForAb, BP, C25, CABA, D01, E12, F08, F11, F12, G11, GH, H16, H17, IndVet, N02, N04, OR, P33, P37, P39, PN&I, R08, R11, R12, RA&MP, RM&VM, S12, S13, S16, SoyAb, TAR, TriticAb, VS, W11, WildRev.
—BLDSC (4421.880000), IE, Ingenta.
Published by: Indian Society for Veterinary Medicine, C/o Dr. Mahesh Kumar, Dept. of EPM, College of Vety. Science, Pantnagar, Usnagar, Uttar Pradesh 263 145, India. TEL 91-5944-234046, FAX 91-5944-233473, drmahesh@hotmail.com. Ed. Dr. Mahesh Kumar.

636.089 IND ISSN 0250-4758
CODEN: IJVPDY
INDIAN JOURNAL OF VETERINARY PATHOLOGY. Abbreviated title: I J V P. Text in English. 1976. s-a. INR 3,750 combined subscription domestic to non-members (print & online eds.); USD 300 combined subscription foreign to non-members (print & online eds.); free to members (effective 2011). adv. back issues avail. **Document type:** *Journal, Academic/Scholarly.* **Description:** Publishes scientific papers and association news for advancing the knowledge of pathology.
Related titles: Online - full text ed.: ISSN 0973-970X. INR 2,500 domestic; USD 200 foreign (effective 2011).
Indexed: A34, A35, A36, A37, A38, AgBio, AgrForAb, BP, CABA, D01, E12, F08, G11, GH, H16, H17, IndVet, N02, N04, P32, P33, P37, P39, PN&I, R08, R12, R13, RA&MP, RM&VM, S12, S13, S16, T05, TAR, VS, W10, W11.
Published by: Indian Association of Veterinary Pathologists, C/o Dr. V.K. Gupta, Department of Veterinary Pathology, Dr G.C. Negi College of Veterinary & Animal Sciences, H.P. Agricultural University, Palampur, Himachal Pradesh 176 062, India. TEL 91-189-423046, gupta.vipankumar@gmail.com. Eds. R V S Pawaiya, B N Tripathi. **Subscr. to:** Indianjournals.com, Divan Enterprises, B-9, Local Shopping Complex, A-Block, Naraina Vihar, Ring Rd, New Delhi 110 028, India. TEL 91-11-25770411, FAX 91-11-25778876, info@indianjournals.com, http://www.indianjournals.com.

636.089 IND ISSN 0971-4251
➤ **THE INDIAN JOURNAL OF VETERINARY RESEARCH.** Abbreviated title: I J V R. Text in English. 1992. s-a. INR 1,500 domestic; USD 60 foreign (effective 2011). bk.rev. **Document type:** *Journal, Academic/ Scholarly.* **Description:** Publish original research findings as full or shorts papers, reviews, news, and views.
Related titles: Online - full text ed.: ISSN 0974-0171. INR 1,000 domestic; USD 40 foreign (effective 2011).
Indexed: A34, A35, A36, A38, AgBio, AgrForAb, BP, CABA, D01, E12, F08, F11, F12, G11, GH, H16, H17, IndVet, MaizeAb, N02, N03, N04, P33, P37, P39, PN&I, R07, R08, RA&MP, RM&VM, S13, S16, T05, TAR, TriticAb, VS.
—BLDSC (4421.950000).
Published by: (Indian Association for the Advancement of Veterinary Research), Indian Veterinary Research Institute, Division of Bacteriology and Mycology, Institute Campus, Izatnagar, Uttar Pradesh 243 122, India. TEL 91-581-2441865, FAX 91-581-2447284, http://ivri.nic.in/. **Subscr. to:** Indianjournals.com, Divan Enterprises, B-9, Local Shopping Complex, A-Block, Naraina Vihar, Ring Rd, New Delhi 110 028, India.

636.089 IND ISSN 0254-4105
CODEN: IJVSD9
➤ **INDIAN JOURNAL OF VETERINARY SURGERY.** Text in English. 1980. s-a. INR 350 domestic to individuals; USD 60 foreign to individuals; INR 400 domestic to institutions; USD 100 foreign to institutions (effective 2011). bk.rev. back issues avail. **Document type:** *Journal, Academic/Scholarly.* **Description:** Publishes research results, clinical and review articles in Indian and foreign veterinary surgery and related subjects.
Related titles: Online - full text ed.: ISSN 0973-9726.
Indexed: A34, A38, AgrForAb, B25, BIOSIS Prev, BP, CABA, D01, E12, F08, F11, F12, GH, H16, H17, ISA, IndVet, MycolAb, N04, OR, P33, P37, PN&I, R08, R13, RA&MP, RM&VM, S12, TAR, TriticAb, VS, WildRev.
Published by: Indian Society for Veterinary Surgery, Division of Surgery, Indian Veterinary Research Institute, Izatnagar, Uttar Pradesh 243 122, India. TEL 91-581-442870, FAX 91-581-447284 447284 447284 447284 447284 447284 447284 91-581-447284, ivri@x400.nicgw.nic.in. Eds. Dr. Amar Pal, Dr. Gaj Raj Singh. **Subscr. to:** Indianjournals.com, Divan Enterprises, B-9, Local Shopping Complex, A-Block, Naraina Vihar, Ring Rd, New Delhi 110 028, India.

➤ **INDIAN POULTRY INDUSTRY YEARBOOK.** *see* AGRICULTURE—Poultry And Livestock

➤ **INDIAN POULTRY REVIEW.** *see* AGRICULTURE—Poultry And Livestock

636.089 IND ISSN 0019-6479
SF604 CODEN: IVEJAC
➤ **INDIAN VETERINARY JOURNAL.** Text in English. 1924. m. bk.rev. abstr.; illus.; stat. index. 100 p./no. 2 cols./p.; reprints avail. **Document type:** *Journal, Academic/Scholarly.* **Description:** Contains general research and clinical articles, short communications, editorial news, book reviews, flashback, and association news.
Related titles: Online - full text ed.: ISSN 0974-9365.
Indexed: A22, A34, A35, A36, A37, A38, ASCA, ASFA, AgBio, AgrForAb, B23, B25, BA, BIOSIS Prev, BP, C25, CA, CABA, CIN, ChemAb, ChemTitl, D01, DBA, E12, F08, F11, F12, FCA, FS&TA, G11, GH, H16, H17, ISR, IndMed, IndVet, MaizeAb, MycolAb, N02, N03, N04, OR, P30, P32, P33, P37, P39, P40, PGegResA, PGrRegA, PHN&I, PN&I, R07, R08, R11, R12, R13, RA&MP, RM&VM, S12, S13, S16, S17, SAA, SCOPUS, SoyAb, T02, T05, TAR, TOSA, TriticAb, VS, W08, W10, W11, WildRev, Z01.
—BLDSC (4431.000000), CASDDS, GNLM, IE, Infotrieve, Ingenta, INIST, Linda Hall.
Published by: Indian Veterinary Association, New No 11, Old No 7, Chamiers Rd, Nandanam, Chennai, Tamil Nadu 600 035, India. TEL 91-44-24351006, FAX 91-44-24338894. **Subscr. to:** I N S I O Scientific Books & Periodicals, PO Box 7234, Indraprastha HPO, New Delhi 110 002, India.

590 IND ISSN 0250-5266
CODEN: IVMJDL
INDIAN VETERINARY MEDICAL JOURNAL. Text in English; Section in English, Hindi. 1960. q. bk.rev. bibl. **Document type:** *Journal, Academic/Scholarly.*
Former titles (until 1977): U P Veterinary Journal (0970-4051); (until 1973): U P Veterinary Magazine (0970-4043)
Related titles: Microfiche ed.
Indexed: B25, BIOSIS Prev, CIN, ChemAb, ChemTitl, MycolAb, WildRev.
—CASDDS, Ingenta.
Published by: Uttar Pradesh Veterinary Association, c/o Institute of Veterinary Biologicals, Badshahbagh, Lucknow, Uttar Pradesh 226 007, India. TEL 91-129-2387352.

636.089 IND ISSN 0304-7067
SF779.M78
INDIAN VETERINARY RESEARCH INSTITUTE. ANNUAL REPORT. Text in English. 1948. a. **Document type:** *Report, Academic/ Scholarly.*
Published by: Indian Veterinary Research Institute, c/o Kundan Singh, Communication Ctr, Izatnagar, Uttar Pradesh 243 122, India. TEL 91-581-2301827, singhkt@rediffmail.com, http://www.ivri.nic.in/.

636.089 ESP ISSN 1130-5436
INFORMACION VETERINARIA. Text in Spanish. 1947. 12/yr. back issues avail. **Document type:** *Journal, Trade.*
Formerly (until 1986): Consejo General de Colegio Veterinarios de Espana. Boletin Informativo (0211-0385); Supersedes in part (in 1962): Consejo General de Colegios Veterinarios de Espana. Boletin Informativo y Suplemento Cientifico (0589-4239); Which was formed by the merger of (1947-1957): Colegio Nacional de Veterinarios de Espana. Suplemento Cientifico al Boletin de Informacion (1130-5428); (1948-1957): Consejo General de Colegios Veterinarios de Espana. Boletin de Informacion (1135-707X)
Published by: Colegios Veterinarios de Espana, Consejo General, Villanueva 11, Madrid, 28001, Spain. TEL 34-91-4353535, FAX 34-91-5783468, consejo@colvet.es, http://www.colvet.es. Ed. Juan Jose Badiola Diez. Circ: 27,000.

636.089 FRA ISSN 1777-8255
INFORMATIONS CHIRURGICALES VETERINAIRES. Text in French. 2006. q. EUR 40 (effective 2009). **Document type:** *Journal, Trade.*

Published by: Editions Med'Com, 24 Rue Dagorno, Paris, 75012, France. TEL 33-1-43454086, FAX 33-1-43406598, info@medcom.fr.

636.089 FRA ISSN 1777-8263
INFORMATIONS OPHTALMOLOGIQUES VETERINAIRES. Text in French. 2006. q. EUR 40 (effective 2009). **Document type:** *Journal, Trade.*
Published by: Editions Med'Com, 24 Rue Dagorno, Paris, 75012, France. TEL 33-1-43454086, FAX 33-1-43406598, info@medcom.fr, http://www.medcom.fr.

636.089 ITA
L'INFORMATORE FARMACEUTICO DI VETERINARIA E ZOOTECNIA. Text in Italian. 1966. a. **Document type:** *Directory, Trade.*
Formerly: Guida di Veterinaria e Zootecnia (0391-1918)
Published by: Elsevier Masson (Subsidiary of: Elsevier Health Sciences), Via Paleocapa 7, Milan, 20121, Italy. TEL 39-02-881841, FAX 39-02-88184302, info@masson.it, http://www.masson.it.

INSTITUT RAZI. ARCHIVES. *see* MEDICAL SCIENCES—Communicable Diseases

INSTITUTE FOR ANIMAL HEALTH. *see* ANIMAL WELFARE

636.089 NPL ISSN 1018-6182
CODEN: JOISEP
➤ **INSTITUTE OF AGRICULTURE AND ANIMAL SCIENCE. JOURNAL.** Text in English. 1980. a. **Document type:** *Journal, Academic/Scholarly.* **Description:** Publishes original research findings in the field of plant science, animal science, and social science. It also include research notes, short communications and book reviews.
Related titles: Online - full text ed.
Indexed: WildRev, Z01.
Published by: Tribhuvan University, Institute of Agriculture and Animal Science, Rampur, Chitwan, Nepal. profrbthapa@wlink.com. Ed. Reshma B Thapa.

➤ **INSTITUTE OF MEDICAL AND VETERINARY SCIENCE. ANNUAL REPORT.** *see* MEDICAL SCIENCES

636.089 IND ISSN 0972-1738
➤ **INTAS POLIVET**; half yearly journal dedicated to veterinary profession and animal health care. Text in English. 2000. s-a. free to qualified personnel (effective 2011). abstr. Index. back issues avail.; reprints avail. **Document type:** *Journal, Academic/Scholarly.* **Description:** Promotes the veterinary profession and provides information to professionals.
Indexed: A01, A34, A36, A37, A38, AgrForAb, B23, C30, CABA, D01, E12, F08, F12, G11, GH, H16, H17, LT, N02, N03, N04, P33, P37, P39, PN&I, R07, R08, R12, R13, RA&MP, RM&VM, S12, S13, S16, SoyAb, T02, T05, TAR, W10, W11.
Published by: Intas Pharmaceuticals Limited, 7th Fl., Chinubhai Centre, Ashram Rd, Off Nehru Bridge, Ahmedabad, Gujarat 380 009, India. TEL 91-79-66523217, FAX 91-79-26576616, neovet@intaspharma.com, http://www.intaspharma.com/. Ed., Pub. Dr. Nitin Bhatia. Circ: 9,000 (paid).

636.089 AUS
INTERNATIONAL CONGRESS ON ANIMAL REPRODUCTION. PROCEEDINGS. Text in English. 1948. quadrennial. price varies. **Document type:** *Proceedings, Academic/Scholarly.*
Formerly: International Congress on Animal Reproduction and Artificial Insemination. Proceedings (0074-4026)
Published by: International Congress on Animal Reproduction, c/o Gareth Evans, Faculty of Veterinary Science, University of Sydney, Sydney, NSW 2006, Australia. garethe@vetsci.usyd.edu.au, http://www.vetsci.usyd.edu.au/icar/. Circ: 2,000.

636.089 GBR ISSN 2041-2894
▼ **INTERNATIONAL JOURNAL OF ANIMAL AND VETERINARY ADVANCES.** Text in English. 2009. q. **Document type:** *Journal, Academic/Scholarly.*
Related titles: Online - full text ed.: free (effective 2011).
Indexed: A34, A35, A36, A38, AgrForAb, B23, C30, CABA, D01, E12, F08, F11, F12, G11, GH, H16, H17, N02, N03, N04, P33, P39, R08, R11, S13, S16, SoyAb, T05, TAR, W10, W11, Z01.
Published by: Maxwell Science Publications http://maxwellsci.com. Ed. Siamak Salami.

636.089 USA ISSN 1559-4602
SF601
INTERNATIONAL JOURNAL OF APPLIED RESEARCH IN VETERINARY MEDICINE. Text in English. 2003 (Win.). q. USD 39 domestic; USD 49 in Canada & Mexico; USD 65 elsewhere (effective 2006).
Formerly (until 2004): The Journal of Applied Research in Veterinary Medicine (1542-2666)
Related titles: Online - full text ed.: ISSN 1559-470X. free (effective 2011).
Indexed: A01, A34, A35, A36, A37, A38, A39, AgBio, AgrForAb, B25, BIOSIS Prev, C27, C29, CABA, CurCont, D01, D03, D04, E12, E13, F08, F11, F12, FoVS&M, G11, GH, H16, H17, IndVet, N02, N04, P33, P37, P39, PN&I, R08, R12, R14, RA&MP, RM&VM, S13, S14, S15, S16, S17, S18, SCI, SCOPUS, SoyAb, T02, T05, TAR, VS, W07, W10, W11.
—BLDSC (4542.100050), IE, Ingenta.
Published by: Veterinary Solutions, 4109 Rock Hill Loop., Apopka, FL 32712-4796. Ed. Dawn Boothe. Pub. Ken Senerth.

636.089 USA ISSN 1937-8165
➤ **THE INTERNET JOURNAL OF VETERINARY MEDICINE.** Text in English. 2004. s-a. free (effective 2011). **Document type:** *Journal, Academic/Scholarly.*
Media: Online - full text.
Indexed: A01, A02, A03, A08, A26, A37, A38, A39, B23, C27, C29, D01, D03, D04, E13, G08, H12, H17, I05, P37, PN&I, R13, R14, S13, S14, S15, S16, S18, T02, V02.
Published by: Internet Scientific Publications, Llc., 23 Rippling Creek Dr, Sugar Land, TX 77479. TEL 832-443-1193, FAX 281-240-1533, wenker@ispub.com. Ed. Dr. Claro Mingala.

636.089 ARG ISSN 1514-6634
➤ **INVET**; investigacion veterinaria. Text in Spanish. 1999. s-a. free (effective 2009). 120 p./no.; back issues avail. **Document type:** *Journal, Academic/Scholarly.*
Related titles: Online - full text ed.: ISSN 1668-3498. 1999. free (effective 2011) (from SciELO).
Indexed: A34, A35, A37, A38, AgBio, BP, CABA, D01, E12, GH, IndVet, N02, P33, P37, PN&I, R12, RA&MP, RM&VM, S13, S16, T05, VS, W11.
Published by: Universidad de Buenos Aires, Facultad de Ciencias Veterinarias, Chorroarin No. 280, Buenos Aires, 1427, Argentina. TEL 54-11-45248400. Circ: 1,000.

636.089 798 ITA ISSN 1120-5776
IPPOLOGIA. Text in Italian. 1990. 4/yr. **Document type:** *Journal, Academic/Scholarly.*
Indexed: A22, A34, A35, A36, A37, A38, AgBio, CABA, D01, E12, FoVS&M, G11, GH, H16, H17, IndVet, LT, MaizeAb, N04, OR, P33, P39, R08, R13, RA&MP, RM&VM, RRTA, SCI, SCOPUS, SoyAb, TAR, TriticAb, VS, W07.
—BLDSC (4567.462200), IE, Ingenta.
Published by: Societa Italiana Veterinari per Equini, Palazzo Trecchi, Via Trecchi, 20, Cremona, 26100, Italy. TEL 39-0372-403502, FAX 39-0372-457091, http://www.sive.it.

636.089 IRN ISSN 1728-1997
➤ **IRANIAN JOURNAL OF VETERINARY RESEARCH.** Text in English. 2000. q. IRR 100,000 domestic; USD 40 foreign (effective 2006). **Document type:** *Journal, Academic/Scholarly.*
Indexed: A34, A35, A36, A38, AgBio, B23, BA, C30, CABA, D01, E12, FoVS&M, G11, GH, H16, H17, IndVet, MaizeAb, N02, N03, N04, OR, P32, P33, P37, P39, P40, PGegResA, PN&I, R07, R08, R12, R13, RA&MP, RM&VM, S12, S13, S16, SCI, SCOPUS, SoyAb, T05, TAR, TriticAb, VS, W07, W10, W11, Z01.
Published by: Shiraz University, School of Veterinary Medicine, PO Box 1731, Shiraz, 71345, Iran.

630.089 IRQ ISSN 1607-3894
➤ **IRAQI JOURNAL OF VETERINARY SCIENCES.** Text in English, Arabic. 1988. s-a. **Document type:** *Journal, Academic/Scholarly.*
Related titles: Online - full text ed.: ISSN 2071-1255. free (effective 2011).
Indexed: A01, A34, A35, A36, A37, A38, AgBio, AgrForAb, CA, CABA, D01, E12, F08, GH, H16, H17, IndVet, MaizeAb, N02, N03, N04, P33, P37, P39, R07, R08, R13, RA&MP, RM&VM, S13, S16, SCOPUS, SoyAb, T02, T05, TAR, TriticAb, VS, W10, W11.
Published by: Mosul University, College of Veterinary Medicine, PO Box 11136, Mosul, Iraq. TEL 964-7701-605334, info@vetmedmosul.org, http://www.vetmedmosul.org/index.htm. Ed. Dr. Fouad K Mohammad.

636.089 GBR ISSN 2046-0481
IRISH VETERINARY JOURNAL (ONLINE). Text in English. irreg. free (effective 2011). back issues avail. **Document type:** *Journal, Academic/Scholarly.* **Description:** Contains articles on all aspects of veterinary research involving both domestic and wild species of animals.
Formerly (until 2011): Irish Veterinary Journal (Print) (0368-0762); Which incorporated (1994-1995): Irish Veterinary Times (1393-3817); Which was formerly (until 1994): Veterinary Surgeon (0791-8542); (until 1993): Irish Veterinary News (0332-236X)
Media: Online - full text.
Indexed: I05.
Published by: BioMed Central Ltd. (Subsidiary of: Springer Science+Business Media), 236 Gray's Inn Rd, London, WC1X 8HB, United Kingdom. FAX 44-20-31922010, info@biomedcentral.com, http://www.biomedcentral.com. Ed. Michael Doherty.

636.089 ISR ISSN 0334-9152
CODEN: RVETA5
ISRAEL JOURNAL OF VETERINARY MEDICINE. Text in English, Hebrew. 1943. q. adv. bk.rev. charts; illus. **Document type:** *Journal, Academic/Scholarly.*
Formerly (until 1986): Refuah Veterinarith (0034-3153)
Related titles: Online - full text ed.: free (effective 2011).
Indexed: A01, A22, A34, A36, A38, B25, BIOSIS Prev, CABA, ChemAb, D01, DBA, E12, F08, FS&TA, FoVS&M, GH, H16, H17, IndVet, J01, MycolAb, N02, N04, P30, P33, P37, P39, PN&I, R08, R13, RA&MP, RM&VM, SAA, SCI, SCOPUS, SoyAb, T05, TAR, VS, W07, W08, W11, WildRev, Z01.
—BLDSC (4583.816000), CASDDS, IE, Infotrieve, Ingenta, Linda Hall.
Published by: Israel Veterinary Medical Association, P O Box 22, Ra'anana, 43100, Israel. TEL 972-9-741-9929, FAX 972-9-743-1778. Ed. Dr. Ze'ev Trainin. Circ: 1,200.

636.089 TUR ISSN 0378-2352
CODEN: IUVDD7
➤ **ISTANBUL UNIVERSITESI. VETERINER FAKULTESI DERGISI/ UNIVERSITY OF ISTANBUL. FACULTY OF VETERINARY MEDICINE. JOURNAL.** Key Title: Veteriner Fakultesi Dergisi. Text in Turkish; Summaries in English, French, German. 1975. 3/yr. free (effective 2009). software rev. abstr. back issues avail.; reprints avail. **Document type:** *Journal, Academic/Scholarly.* **Description:** Contains original research articles, reviews, case reports and short communications on veterinary science, animal husbandry, food hygine, basic science and veterinary education.
Related titles: Online - full text ed.
Published by: Istanbul Universitesi, Veteriner Fakultesi/University of Istanbul, Faculty of Veterinary Medicine, Avcilar Campus, Avcilar - Istanbul, 34851, Turkey. TEL 90-212-5912193, FAX 90-212-5916991. Ed. Dr. Kemal Ak. Circ: 750.

➤ **ISTITUTO SUPERIORE DI SANITA. ANNALI.** *see* PUBLIC HEALTH AND SAFETY

636.089 ITA ISSN 1828-051X
➤ **ITALIAN JOURNAL OF ANIMAL SCIENCE.** Text in Multiple languages. 2002. irreg. free (effective 2011). **Document type:** *Journal, Academic/Scholarly.*
Media: Online - full text.
Indexed: P40, R11, R13, S16.
Published by: (Associazione Scientifica di Produzione Animale/Scientific Association of Animal Production), Pagepress, Via Giuseppe Belli 4, Pavia, 27100, Italy. TEL 39-0382-1751762, FAX 39-0382-1750481, http://www.pagepress.org. Ed. Rosanna Scipioni.

636.08 JPN
J A H A SHOREI HAPPYOKAI/JAPANESE ANIMAL HOSPITAL ASSOCIATION. PROCEEDINGS. Text in Japanese. a. **Document type:** *Proceedings, Academic/Scholarly.*
Published by: Nihon Dobutsu Byoin Fukushi Kyokai/Japanese Animal Hospital Association, Ikeda Bldg 201, 1-15 Shinogawa-Machi, Shinjuku-ku, Tokyo, 162-0814, Japan. TEL 81-3-32353251, FAX 81-3-32353277, member@jaha.or.jp, http://www.jaha.or.jp/.

J N K V V NEWS. *see* AGRICULTURE

636.089 JPN ISSN 0047-1917
CODEN: JJVRAE
➤ **JAPANESE JOURNAL OF VETERINARY RESEARCH.** Text in English. 1954. q. per issue exchange basis. bk.rev. illus. **Document type:** *Journal, Academic/Scholarly.*
Formerly (until 1954): Juigaku Kenkyu (0439-3457)
Related titles: Microfiche ed.; Microfilm ed.
Indexed: A34, A35, A36, A38, ASCA, AgBio, B21, B25, BIOSIS Prev, CA, CABA, ChemAb, D01, E12, EMBASE, ExcerpMed, FoVS&M, GH, H16, H17, HPNRM, ISR, IndMed, IndVet, MEDLINE, MycolAb, N02, N03, N04, P30, P33, P37, P39, R08, R12, RefZh, S13, S16, SCI, SCOPUS, SSciA, T02, T05, VS, VirolAbstr, W07, W08, W10, W11, WildRev, Z01.
—BLDSC (4659.090000), GNLM, IE, Infotrieve, Ingenta, INIST, Linda Hall.
Published by: Hokkaido University, Graduate School of Veterinary Medicine/Hokkaido Daigaku, Juigakubu, Kita 18, Nishi 9, Kita-ku, Sapporo, 060-0818, Japan. http://www.vetmed.hokudai.ac.jp/. Circ: 650.

636.089 JPN ISSN 1342-6133
JAPANESE JOURNAL OF ZOO AND WILDLIFE MEDICINE/NIHON YASEI DOBUTSU IGAKUKAISHI. Text in English, Japanese. s-a. **Document type:** *Journal, Academic/Scholarly.*
Indexed: A34, A35, A36, A38, AgBio, C25, CABA, D01, E12, F08, F12, GH, H16, H17, IndVet, LT, N02, P32, P33, P37, P39, PGegResA, PN&I, R07, R08, RA&MP, RM&VM, RRTA, S13, S16, SoyAb, VS, Z01.
—BLDSC (4659.170000). **CCC.**
Published by: Nihon Yasei Dobutsu Igakukai/Japanese Society of Zoo and Wildlife Medicine, Gifu University, 1-1 Yanagido, Gifu, 501-1193, Japan. http://www.jjzwm.com/.

636.089 PAK ISSN 1680-5593
JOURNAL OF ANIMAL AND VETERINARY ADVANCES. Text in English. 2002. m. EUR 1,200 to individuals; EUR 1,500 to institutions; EUR 150 newsstand/cover (effective 2007). **Document type:** *Journal, Academic/Scholarly.*
Related titles: Online - full text ed.: ISSN 1993-601X. free (effective 2011).
Indexed: A01, A34, A35, A36, A37, A38, AgBio, AgrForAb, B23, BA, BP, C25, C30, CABA, D01, E12, F08, F11, F12, FCA, G11, GH, H16, H17, I11, IndVet, LT, MaizeAb, N02, N03, N04, N05, O01, OR, P32, P33, P37, P38, P39, P40, PGegResA, PGrRegA, PHN&I, PN&I, R07, R08, R11, R12, R13, RA&MP, RM&VM, RRTA, S12, S13, S16, S17, SCI, SCOPUS, SoyAb, T05, TAR, TriticAb, VS, W07, W10, W11, Z01.
—BLDSC (4935.377500).
Published by: Medwell Journals, ANSInet Bldg, 308-Lasani Town, Sargodha Rd, Faisalabad, 38090, Pakistan. TEL 92-41-5010004, 92-41-5004000, FAX 92-21-5206789, medwellonline@gmail.com, http://www.medwellonline.net.

JOURNAL OF ANIMAL PHYSIOLOGY AND ANIMAL NUTRITION (ONLINE). *see* BIOLOGY—Physiology

JOURNAL OF ANIMAL PHYSIOLOGY AND ANIMAL NUTRITION (PRINT)/ZEITSCHRIFT FUER TIERPHYSIOLOGIE UND TIERERNAEHRUNG. *see* BIOLOGY—Physiology

JOURNAL OF AQUATIC ANIMAL HEALTH. *see* FISH AND FISHERIES

636.087 USA ISSN 1082-6742
SF994
➤ **JOURNAL OF AVIAN MEDICINE AND SURGERY.** Text in English; Summaries in Dutch, French, German, Italian, Spanish. 1980. q. USD 130 domestic; USD 135 in Canada & Mexico; USD 155 in Europe; USD 165 elsewhere; free to members (effective 2009). adv. bk.rev. abstr.; illus. Index. back issues avail.; reprints avail. **Document type:** *Journal, Academic/Scholarly.* **Description:** Addresses avian research, bird medicine and surger conservation, aviculture, pharmaceuticals and biologicals and veterinary medical education.
Former titles (until 1995): Association of Avian Veterinarians. Journal (1044-8314); (until 1989): A A V Today (0892-9904); (until 1987): A.V.A. Newsletter
Related titles: Online - full text ed.: ISSN 1938-2871.
Indexed: A01, A22, A26, A29, A34, A36, A37, A38, ASCA, B20, B21, B23, BibAg, CA, CABA, E01, E12, EMBASE, ESPM, ExcerpMed, F08, F12, FoVS&M, G11, GH, H12, H16, H17, I05, IndVet, MEDLINE, N02, N04, P30, P33, P37, P39, R08, RA&MP, RM&VM, S13, S16, SAA, SCI, SCOPUS, T02, T05, TAR, VS, VirolAbstr, W07, W08, W10, W11, WildRev, Z01.
—BLDSC (4949.960000), IE, Ingenta, INIST, Linda Hall. **CCC.**
Published by: Association of Avian Veterinarians, P O Box 811720, Boca Raton, FL 33481. TEL 561-393-8901, FAX 561-393-8902, aavpublications@aol.com, http://www.aav.org. Ed. James W Carpenter TEL 785-532-5690. **Dist. by:** AAV Central Office.

636 IND ISSN 0971-1643
JOURNAL OF BOMBAY VETERINARY COLLEGE. Text in English. 1993. s-a. INR 600 combined subscription domestic (print & online eds.) (effective 2011). **Document type:** *Journal, Academic/Scholarly.* **Description:** It is intended for the publication of review articles (guest), original/applied research articles, clinical observations, preliminary reports of scientific importance pertaining to Animal Health and Production.
Related titles: Online - full text ed.: ISSN 0974-4584.
Indexed: A34, A35, A37, A38, AgBio, AgrForAb, BP, CABA, D01, E12, F08, F11, F12, G11, GH, H16, H17, IndVet, MaizeAb, N02, N03, N04, P33, P37, P39, PN&I, R08, R11, R12, R13, RA&MP, RM&VM, S12, S13, S16, SoyAb, T05, TAR, TriticAb, VS, W10, W11.
—BLDSC (4709.920000).
Published by: Bombay Veterinary College, Dept. of Poultry Science, Parel Tank Rd, Parel, Mumbai, 400 012, India. TEL 91-22-24131180. Ed. Dr. A S Ranade. **Subscr. to:** Indianjournals.com, Divan Enterprises, B-9, Local Shopping Complex, A-Block, Naraina Vihar, Ring Rd, New Delhi 110 028, India. TEL 91-11-25770411, FAX 91-11-25778876, info@indianjournals.com, http://www.indianjournals.com.

636.089 USA ISSN 0737-0806
SF951 CODEN: JEVSCI

➤ **THE JOURNAL OF EQUINE VETERINARY SCIENCE.** Abbreviated title: J E V S. Text in English. 1981. m. USD 404 in United States to institutions; USD 515 elsewhere to institutions (effective 2012). bk.rev. back issues avail.; reprints avail. **Document type:** *Journal, Academic/Scholarly.* **Description:** Publishes original scientific papers, meeting reports, news articles, book reviews, and opinion articles from leaders in the equine veterinary field.

Incorporates (1980-1997): Equine Veterinary Data (0739-9065); Incorporates: Equine Sportsmedicine News (0890-0140)

Related titles: Online - full text ed.: ISSN 1542-7412 (from ScienceDirect).

Indexed: A20, A22, A26, A34, A35, A36, A37, A38, ASCA, AgBio, Agr, B23, BIOBASE, C25, CA, CABA, CurCont, D01, DBA, E12, F08, F12, FCA, FoVS&M, G11, GH, H17, I05, IABS, IndVet, LT, MaizeAb, N02, N04, OR, P32, P33, P39, P40, PN&I, R08, R12, R13, RM&VM, RRTA, S13, S16, SCI, SCOPUS, SoyAb, T02, T05, TAR, TriticAb, VS, W07, W10, W11.

—BLDSC (4979.492000), IE, Infotrieve, Ingenta. **CCC.**

Published by: (Equine Science Society), W.B. Saunders Co. (Subsidiary of: Elsevier Health Sciences), Elsevier, Health Sciences Division, Order Fulfillment, 3251 Riverport Ln, Maryland Heights, MO 63043. TEL 314-872-8370, 800-325-4177, FAX 314-432-1380, JournalCustomerService-usa@elsevier.com, http://www.us.elsevierhealth.com. Ed. Edward L Squires TEL 859-257-4757. Pub. Anthony F Trioli TEL 215-239-3733. Adv. contact Danny Wang TEL 212-633-3158.

636.089 USA ISSN 1557-5063

➤ **JOURNAL OF EXOTIC PET MEDICINE.** Text in English. 1992. q. USD 340 in United States to institutions; USD 430 elsewhere to institutions (effective 2012). adv. illus. Index. reprints avail. **Document type:** *Journal, Academic/Scholarly.* **Description:** Covers a single topic in avian and exotic-pet medicine in each issue.

Formerly (until 2006): Seminars in Avian and Exotic Pet Medicine (1055-937X)

Related titles: Online - full text ed.: ISSN 1931-6283 (from ScienceDirect).

Indexed: A26, A34, A35, A36, A37, A38, ASCA, B23, CA, CABA, D01, DBA, E12, F08, FoVS&M, GH, H16, H17, I05, IndVet, N02, N04, P33, P37, P39, PN&I, R08, RA&MP, RM&VM, S12, SCI, SCOPUS, T02, T05, TAR, VS, W07, W10, W11, WildRev, Z01.

—BLDSC (4979.685000), IE, Ingenta. **CCC.**

Published by: W.B. Saunders Co. (Subsidiary of: Elsevier Health Sciences), Elsevier, Health Sciences Division, Order Fulfillment, 3251 Riverport Ln, Maryland Heights, MO 63043. TEL 800-545-2522, FAX 314-447-8093, 800-535-9935, sales.inquiry@elsevier.com, http://www.us.elsevierhealth.com. Eds. Mark A Mitchell, Thomas N Tully. Pub. Anthony F Trioli TEL 215-239-3733. adv.: B&W page USD 970; trim 8 x 10.25.

636.089 GBR ISSN 1098-612X
SF985

➤ **JOURNAL OF FELINE MEDICINE AND SURGERY.** Abbreviated title: J F M S. Text in English. 1999. m. EUR 548 in Europe to institutions; JPY 59,000 in Japan to institutions; USD 510 elsewhere to institutions (effective 2012). adv. bk.rev. charts; illus. back issues avail.; reprints avail. **Document type:** *Journal, Academic/Scholarly.* **Description:** Publishes original papers and reviews on all aspects of feline medicine and surgery, including relevant basic research.

Related titles: Online - full text ed.: ISSN 1532-2750. USD 433 to institutions (effective 2009) (from ScienceDirect).

Indexed: A22, A26, A34, A35, A36, A37, A38, AgBio, Agr, CA, CABA, CurCont, D01, DBA, E01, E12, EMBASE, ExcerpMed, FoVS&M, GH, H17, I05, IndVet, MEDLINE, N02, N04, P30, P33, P37, P39, PN&I, R08, R12, R13, RM&VM, SCI, SCOPUS, SoyAb, T02, T05, VS, W07.

—BLDSC (4983.933000), IE, Infotrieve, Ingenta. **CCC.**

Published by: (American Association of Feline Practitioners USA, European Society for Feline Medicine), Elsevier Ltd (Subsidiary of: Elsevier Science & Technology), The Blvd, Langford Ln, Kidlington, Oxford, OX5 1GB, United Kingdom. TEL 44-1865-843000, FAX 44-1865-843010, customerserviceau@elsevier.com. Eds. A H Sparkes, M Scherk.

➤ **JOURNAL OF HERPETOLOGICAL MEDICINE AND SURGERY.** *see* BIOLOGY—Zoology

636.089 JPN ISSN 0916-8818
CODEN: JREDEF

➤ **JOURNAL OF REPRODUCTION AND DEVELOPMENT.** Text in English. 1955. bi-m. JPY 8,000 membership; JPY 9,000 to non-members (effective 2004). adv. bk.rev. back issues avail. **Document type:** *Journal, Academic/Scholarly.* **Description:** Publishes new findings and concepts in reproductive biology, reproductive endocrinology, reproductive immunology, and developmental biology.

Formerly (until Feb. 1992): Japanese Journal of Animal Reproduction (0385-9932)

Related titles: Online - full text ed.: ISSN 1348-4400. free (effective 2011).

Indexed: A22, A26, A34, A35, A36, A37, A38, A39, AgBio, B21, B25, BIOSIS Prev, C27, C29, CABA, CIN, ChemAb, ChemTitl, CurCont, D01, D03, D04, E12, E13, EMBASE, ExcerpMed, F08, FoVS&M, GH, H16, ImmunAb, IndVet, MEDLINE, MaizeAb, MycolAb, N02, N04, NSA, P30, P33, P37, PN&I, R07, R08, R12, R13, R14, RA&MP, RM&VM, S12, S14, S15, S18, SCI, SCOPUS, SoyAb, TAR, VS, W07, W10, W11.

—BLDSC (5049.570000), CASDDS, IE, Ingenta. **CCC.**

Published by: Japanese Society of Animal Reproduction, c/o Laboratory of Animal Reproduction, Graduate School of Agricultural Science, Tohoku University, Sendai, 981-8555, Japan. FAX 81-22-7178879, http://wwwsoc.nii.ac.jp/jsar/index.html. Ed. Masugi Nishihara.

636.089 GBR ISSN 0022-4510
CODEN: JAPRAN

➤ **JOURNAL OF SMALL ANIMAL PRACTICE.** Abbreviated title: J S A P. Text in English. 1960. m. GBP 367 in United Kingdom to institutions; EUR 466 in Europe to institutions; USD 679 in the Americas to institutions; USD 790 elsewhere to institutions; GBP 422 combined subscription in United Kingdom to institutions (print & online eds.); EUR 536 combined subscription in Europe to institutions (print & online eds.); USD 781 combined subscription in the Americas to institutions (print & online eds.); USD 909 combined subscription elsewhere to institutions (print & online eds.) (effective 2012). adv. bk.rev. bibl.; charts; illus. index. back issues avail.; reprint service avail. from PSC. **Document type:** *Journal, Academic/Scholarly.* **Description:** Publishes original research, review articles, and clinical case histories on all aspects of small animal medicine and surgery.

Related titles: Online - full text ed.: ISSN 1748-5827. GBP 367 in United Kingdom to institutions; EUR 466 in Europe to institutions; USD 679 in the Americas to institutions; USD 790 elsewhere to institutions (effective 2012) (from IngentaConnect); Spanish Translation: Journal of Small Animal Practice (Spanish Edition). ISSN 1130-863X.

Indexed: A22, A26, A34, A35, A36, A37, A38, ASCA, AgBio, Agr, B21, B25, BIOSIS Prev, BibAg, CA, CABA, CTA, ChemAb, ChemoAb, CurCont, DBA, E01, E12, EMBASE, ExcerpMed, FoVS&M, GH, GenetAb, H12, H17, ISR, IndMed, IndVet, LT, MEDLINE, MycolAb, N02, N04, NSA, P30, P33, P37, P39, PN&I, R08, RM&VM, RRTA, SAA, SCI, SCOPUS, T02, T05, VS, W07, W11, WildRev.

—BLDSC (5064.700000), GNLM, IE, Infotrieve, Ingenta, INIST. **CCC.**

Published by: (British Small Animal Veterinary Association, World Small Animal Veterinary Association DNK), Wiley-Blackwell Publishing Ltd. (Subsidiary of: John Wiley & Sons, Inc.), 9600 Garsington Rd, Oxford, OX4 2DQ, United Kingdom. TEL 44-1865-776868, FAX 44-1865-714591, customerservices@blackwellpublishing.com, http://www.wiley.com/WileyCDA/. Ed. Katie Dunn. Adv. contact Mia Scott-Ruddock TEL 44-1865-476354.

636.089 USA ISSN 1537-209X

➤ **JOURNAL OF SWINE HEALTH AND PRODUCTION.** Text in English. 1993. bi-m. USD 125 in North America to non-members; USD 160 elsewhere to non-members; free to members (print & online eds.) (effective 2010). 3 cols./p.; back issues avail.; reprints avail. **Document type:** *Journal, Academic/Scholarly.* **Description:** Features research articles dealing with swine health and production.

Former titles (until 2001): Swine Health and Production (1066-4963); (until 1993): American Association of Swine Practitioners. Newsletter

Related titles: Online - full content ed.

Indexed: A34, A35, A36, A37, A38, AgBio, Agr, AgrForAb, C25, CABA, D01, E12, F08, FoVS&M, GH, H16, H17, IndVet, MaizeAb, N02, N03, N04, P33, P39, PHN&I, PN&I, R08, R13, RA&MP, RM&VM, S12, S13, SCI, SCOPUS, SoyAb, TAR, VS, W07, W11.

—BLDSC (5067.830000), IE, Ingenta.

Published by: American Association of Swine Veterinarians, 830 26th St, Perry, IA 50220. TEL 515-465-5255, FAX 515-465-3832, aasv@aasv.org. Adv. contact Tina Smith.

➤ **JOURNAL OF THE INDONESIAN TROPICAL ANIMAL AGRICULTURE.** *see* AGRICULTURE

636.089 IND ISSN 0971-0701
SF604 CODEN: JVASEY

➤ **JOURNAL OF VETERINARY AND ANIMAL SCIENCES.** Text in English. 1972. s-a. back issues avail. **Document type:** *Journal, Academic/Scholarly.*

Formerly (until 1990): Kerala Journal of Veterinary Science (0374-8774)

Indexed: ChemAb, REE&TA, WildRev.

—CASDDS.

Published by: Kerala Agricultural University, Faculty of Veterinary and Animal Sciences, Trichur, Kerala, India. **Subscr. to:** I N S I O Scientific Books & Periodicals.

636.089 USA ISSN 1558-7878

➤ **JOURNAL OF VETERINARY BEHAVIOR**; clinical applications and research. Text in English. 2006 (July). bi-m. USD 258 in United States to institutions; USD 285 elsewhere to institutions (effective 2012). adv. back issues avail.; reprints avail. **Document type:** *Journal, Academic/Scholarly.* **Description:** Focuses on all aspects of veterinary behavioral medicine, with emphasis on clinical applications and research.

Related titles: Online - full text ed.: ISSN 1878-7517 (from ScienceDirect).

Indexed: A26, A34, A36, A37, A38, CA, CABA, D01, E12, FoVS&M, G11, GH, H17, I05, IndVet, N02, N04, P03, P30, P33, P37, P39, PN&I, PsycInfo, R08, S13, SCI, SCOPUS, T02, VS, W07, W11.

—IE, Ingenta. **CCC.**

Published by: (International Working Dog Breeding Association), Elsevier Inc. (Subsidiary of: Elsevier Science & Technology), 1600 John F Kennedy Blvd, Philadelphia, PA 19103. TEL 215-239-3900, FAX 215-238-7883, JournalCustomerService-usa@elsevier.com, http://www.elsevier.com. Ed. Karen L Overall. Pub. Anthony F Trioli TEL 215-239-3733. Adv. contact John Marmero Jr. TEL 212-633-3657.

616.12 636.089 NLD ISSN 1760-2734

➤ **JOURNAL OF VETERINARY CARDIOLOGY.** Text in English. 1999 (Apr.). 2/yr. EUR 245 in Europe to institutions; JPY 33,400 in Japan to institutions; USD 297 elsewhere to institutions (effective 2012). **Document type:** *Journal, Academic/Scholarly.* **Description:** VETERINARY CARDIOLOGY.

Related titles: Online - full text ed.: ISSN 1875-0834 (from ScienceDirect).

Indexed: A26, A34, A35, A36, A37, A38, AgBio, CA, CABA, D01, EMBASE, ExcerpMed, F08, GH, H17, I05, IndVet, MEDLINE, N04, P30, P33, P37, R08, SCOPUS, T02, VS.

—BLDSC (5072.350980), IE, Ingenta. **CCC.**

Published by: (European Society of Veterinary Cardiology), Elsevier BV (Subsidiary of: Elsevier Science & Technology), Radarweg 29, PO Box 211, Amsterdam, 1000 AE, Netherlands. TEL 31-20-4853911, FAX 31-20-4852457, JournalsCustomerServiceEMEA@elsevier.com, http://www.elsevier.nl. Ed. N S Moise.

636.087 USA ISSN 0898-7564
SF867

➤ **JOURNAL OF VETERINARY DENTISTRY.** Text in English. 1984. q. USD 195 domestic; USD 235 foreign (effective 2011). adv. back issues avail. **Document type:** *Journal, Academic/Scholarly.* **Description:** Covers medical and surgical aspects of veterinary dentistry, including anatomy, crowns, restorations, endodontics, orthodontics, periodontics, and oral biology.

Formerly (until 1987): Veterinary Dentistry

Related titles: Includes: Animal Health Technician Dental Newsletter.

Indexed: A22, A34, A36, A37, A38, CA, CABA, D02, E12, EMBASE, ExcerpMed, FoVS&M, GH, IndVet, LT, MEDLINE, N04, P30, P33, R08, R13, RA&MP, RRTA, S12, SCI, SCOPUS, T02, VS, W07, W11, WildRev.

—BLDSC (5072.355000), IE, Infotrieve, Ingenta.

Published by: American Veterinary Dental Society, PO Box 803, Fayetteville, TN 37334. TEL 931-438-0238, FAX 931-433-6289, avds@avds-online.org, http://www.avds-online.org/. Ed. Dr. Mark M Smith TEL 301-990-9460. **Co-sponsors:** American Veterinary Dental College; Academy of Veterinary Dentistry.

636.089 USA ISSN 1040-6387

➤ **JOURNAL OF VETERINARY DIAGNOSTIC INVESTIGATION.** Abbreviated title: J V D I. Text in English. 1989. bi-m. USD 231, GBP 136 to institutions; USD 236, GBP 139 combined subscription to institutions (print & online eds.) (effective 2012). adv. back issues avail. **Document type:** *Journal, Academic/Scholarly.* **Description:** Covers molecular biology, immunology, microbiology, clinical pathology, parasitology, anatomical pathology, toxicology, computer science and public health.

Related titles: Online - full text ed.: ISSN 1943-4936. USD 212, GBP 125 to institutions (effective 2012).

Indexed: A22, A34, A35, A36, A37, A38, ASCA, AgBio, Agr, B23, BibAg, CA, CABA, CurCont, D01, E12, EMBASE, ExcerpMed, F08, F12, FCA, FoVS&M, G11, GH, H16, H17, ISR, IndMed, IndVet, MEDLINE, MaizeAb, N02, N04, OR, P30, P32, P33, P37, P39, P40, PN&I, R07, R08, R12, R13, RM&VM, S12, S13, S16, SCI, SCOPUS, SoyAb, T02, T05, TAR, TriticAb, VS, W07, W08, W10, W11, WildRev, Z01.

—BLDSC (5072.360000), GNLM, IE, Infotrieve, Ingenta, INIST. **CCC.**

Published by: (American Association of Veterinary Laboratory Diagnosticians), Sage Publications, Inc., 2455 Teller Rd, Thousand Oaks, CA 91320. TEL 800-818-7243, FAX 800-583-2665, info@sagepub.com, http://www.sagepub.com. Eds. Kenneth S Latimer, Jeremiah T Saliki.

636.089 617.1 GBR ISSN 1479-3261

➤ **JOURNAL OF VETERINARY EMERGENCY AND CRITICAL CARE.** Text in English. 1991. bi-m. GBP 446 in United Kingdom to institutions; EUR 567 in Europe to institutions; USD 610 in the Americas to institutions; USD 872 elsewhere to institutions; GBP 512 combined subscription in United Kingdom to institutions (print & online eds.); EUR 652 combined subscription in Europe to institutions (print & online eds.); USD 702 combined subscription in the Americas to institutions (print & online eds.); USD 1,003 combined subscription elsewhere to institutions (print & online eds.) (effective 2012). adv. back issues avail.; reprint service avail. from PSC. **Document type:** *Journal, Academic/Scholarly.* **Description:** Covers clinical and nonclinical problems and solutions, case reports, and guest editorials.

Former titles (until 2001): Official Journal of Veterinary Emergency and Critical Care (1534-6935); (until 1993): Journal of Veterinary Emergency and Critical Care (1056-6392); Which incorporated: Lifeline

Related titles: Online - full text ed.: ISSN 1476-4431. 2002. GBP 446 in United Kingdom to institutions; EUR 567 in Europe to institutions; USD 610 in the Americas to institutions; USD 872 elsewhere to institutions (effective 2012) (from IngentaConnect).

Indexed: A01, A03, A08, A10, A22, A26, A34, A35, A36, A37, A38, AgBio, AgrForAb, CA, CABA, D01, E01, E12, EMBASE, ExcerpMed, F08, FoVS&M, GH, H17, IndVet, LT, MEDLINE, N02, N04, P30, P33, P37, P39, PN&I, R08, R13, RM&VM, RRTA, S12, SCI, SCOPUS, SoyAb, T02, T05, V03, VS, W07, W10.

—BLDSC (5072.362000), IE, Infotrieve, Ingenta. **CCC.**

Published by: (Veterinary Emergency and Critical Care Society USA), Wiley-Blackwell Publishing Ltd. (Subsidiary of: John Wiley & Sons, Inc.), 9600 Garsington Rd, Oxford, OX4 2DQ, United Kingdom. TEL 44-1865-776868, FAX 44-1865-714591, customerservices@blackwellpublishing.com. Ed. Shane W Bateman TEL 519-400-5928.

636.089 USA ISSN 0891-6640
SF601 CODEN: JVIMEM

➤ **JOURNAL OF VETERINARY INTERNAL MEDICINE.** Text in English. 1987. bi-m. GBP 368 combined subscription in United Kingdom to institutions (print & online eds.); EUR 467 combined subscription in Europe to institutions (print & online eds.); USD 704 combined subscription in the Americas to institutions (print & online eds.); USD 721 combined subscription elsewhere to institutions (print & online eds.) (effective 2012). illus. index. back issues avail.; reprint service avail. from PSC. **Document type:** *Journal, Academic/Scholarly.* **Description:** Covers small- and large-animal internal medicine, cardiology, neurology, pathophysiology, and the disease process.

Related titles: Online - full text ed.: ISSN 1939-1676. GBP 334 in United Kingdom to institutions; EUR 426 in Europe to institutions; USD 641 in the Americas to institutions; USD 655 elsewhere to institutions (effective 2012) (from IngentaConnect).

Indexed: A01, A22, A34, A35, A36, A37, A38, ASCA, AgBio, Agr, B21, B25, BIOSIS Prev, BP, CA, CABA, CurCont, D01, DBA, E01, E12, EMBASE, ESPM, ExcerpMed, F08, FoVS&M, G11, GH, H16, H17, I10, ISR, ImmunAb, IndMed, IndVet, MEDLINE, MycolAb, N02, N04, P30, P33, P37, P39, PN&I, R08, R11, R13, RA&MP, RM&VM, S12, S13, S16, SAA, SCI, SCOPUS, SoyAb, T02, T05, TAR, TriticAb, VS, ViroIAbstr, W07, W10, W11.

—BLDSC (5072.365000), CASDDS, GNLM, IE, Infotrieve, Ingenta, INIST. **CCC.**

Published by: (American College of Veterinary Internal Medicine), Wiley-Blackwell Publishing, Inc. (Subsidiary of: Wiley-Blackwell Publishing Ltd.), 111 River St, Hoboken, NJ 07030. TEL 201-748-6000, FAX 201-748-6088, info@wiley.com, http://www.wiley.com/WileyCDA/. Eds. Kenneth W Hinchcliff, Stephen P Di Bartola. Adv. contact Kristin McCarthy TEL 201-748-7683.

636.0890711 CAN ISSN 0748-321X

➤ **JOURNAL OF VETERINARY MEDICAL EDUCATION.** Abbreviated title: J V M E. Text in English. 1974. q. USD 300 in North America to institutions; USD 320 elsewhere to institutions; USD 360 combined subscription in North America to institutions (print & online eds.); USD 380 combined subscription elsewhere to institutions (print & online eds.) (effective 2011). adv. bk.rev. illus. back issues avail.; reprints avail. **Document type:** *Journal, Academic/Scholarly.* **Description:** Includes papers describing educational programs in veterinary educational institutions throughout the world.
Related titles: Microform ed.: (from PQC); Online - full text ed.: ISSN 1943-7218. USD 265 to institutions (effective 2011).
Indexed: A20, A22, A34, A35, A36, A37, A38, ASCA, AgBio, CABA, CPE, D01, E12, E16, EMBASE, ERA, ExcerpMed, FoVS&M, GH, H17, IndVet, LT, MEDLINE, N02, N04, P30, P33, P37, P39, PN&I, R12, RRTA, S13, S16, S21, SCI, SCOPUS, T05, TAR, V05, VS, W07, W11.
—BLDSC (5072.370000), IE, Infotrieve, Ingenta. **CCC.**
Published by: (Association of American Veterinary Medical Colleges USA), University of Toronto Press, Journals Division, 5201 Dufferin St, Toronto, ON M3H 5T8, Canada. TEL 416-667-7810, FAX 416-667-7881, journals@utpress.utoronto.ca, http://www.utpjournals.com. Ed. Henry J Baker. Circ: 3,392.

636.089 EGY ISSN 1110-7219

JOURNAL OF VETERINARY MEDICAL RESEARCHES/MAGALLAT BUHUTH AL-'ULUM TIBBIYYAT AL-BAYTARIYYAT. Text in English. 1999. a. **Document type:** *Journal, Academic/Scholarly.*
Published by: Mansoura University, Faculty of Veterinary Medicine, Mansoura University Campus, Mansoura, Egypt. Ed. Dr. Mohamed M Fouda.

636.089 JPN ISSN 0916-7250
CODEN: JVMSEQ

➤ **JOURNAL OF VETERINARY MEDICAL SCIENCE.** Text in English. 1939. m. JPY 25,000 foreign to non-members (effective 2004). adv. bk.rev. **Document type:** *Journal, Academic/Scholarly.* **Description:** International journal on basic and applied veterinary medical sciences.
Formerly (until 1991): Japanese Journal of Veterinary Science (0021-5295)
Related titles: Online - full text ed.: ISSN 1347-7439. free (effective 2011).
Indexed: A22, A29, A34, A35, A36, A37, A38, A39, AEBA, ASCA, ASFA, AgBio, AgrForAb, B&BAb, B20, B21, B23, B25, BIOSIS Prev, BP, C27, C29, CA, CABA, ChemAb, ChemTitl, ChemoAb, CurCont, D01, D03, D04, DBA, DentInd, E12, E13, EMBASE, ESPM, EntAb, ExcerpMed, F08, F11, F12, FCA, FoVS&M, G11, GH, H16, H17, INIS AtomInd, ISR, IndMed, IndVet, LT, MEDLINE, MaizeAb, MycolAb, N02, N03, N04, OR, P30, P32, P33, P37, P38, P39, P40, PGegResA, PN&I, R07, R08, R11, R12, R13, R14, RA&MP, RM&VM, RRTA, S12, S13, S14, S15, S16, S17, S18, SAA, SCI, SCOPUS, SoyAb, T02, T05, TAR, VS, VirolAbstr, W07, W08, W10, W11, WildRev, Z01.
—BLDSC (5072.375000), CASDDS, GNLM, IE, Infotrieve, Ingenta, INIST. **CCC.**
Published by: Japanese Society of Veterinary Science/Nihon Jui Gakkai, Tokyo RS Bldg. 7F, 6-26-12 Hongo, Bunkyo-ku, Tokyo, 113-0033, Japan. TEL 81-3-58037761, FAX 81-3-58037762, office@jsvs.or.jp. Ed. Kenichiro Ono. Circ: 5,000.

636.0832 NGA

▼ ➤ **JOURNAL OF VETERINARY MEDICINE AND ANIMAL HEALTH.** Text in English. 2009. m. free (effective 2010). adv. **Document type:** *Journal, Academic/Scholarly.*
Media: Online - full text.
Published by: Academic Journals, PO Box 73023, Victoria Island, Lagos, Nigeria. service@academicjournals.org. Eds. Dr. Renukaradhya Gourapura, Dr. William G Dundon.

636.08 IND ISSN 0971-1031
CODEN: JVPAEL

JOURNAL OF VETERINARY PARASITOLOGY. Text in English. 1987. s-a. INR 3,000 domestic; USD 350 foreign (effective 2011). back issues avail. **Document type:** *Journal, Academic/Scholarly.* **Description:** Devoted to the publication of original research, both bask and applied on animal parasitology in the form of full papers, short conrankaoons, review articles essentially invited on topics of active current interest, book reviews and articles relevant to the parasitology education.
Related titles: Online - full text ed.: ISSN 0974-0813. INR 2,000 domestic; USD 250 foreign (effective 2011).
Indexed: SCOPUS.
Published by: Indian Association for the Advancement of Veterinary Parasitology (I A A V P), Division of Parasitology, I V R, Izatnagar, 243 122, India. **Subscr. to:** Indianjournals.com; I N S I O Scientific Books & Periodicals.

JOURNAL OF VETERINARY PHARMACOLOGY AND THERAPEUTICS. *see* PHARMACY AND PHARMACOLOGY

JOURNAL OF VETERINARY PHARMACOLOGY AND THERAPEUTICS ONLINE. *see* PHARMACY AND PHARMACOLOGY

636.089 KOR ISSN 1229-845X
SF604

JOURNAL OF VETERINARY SCIENCE. Text in English. 2000. s-a. membership. **Document type:** *Journal, Academic/Scholarly.*
Related titles: Online - full text ed.: ISSN 1976-555X. free (effective 2011).
Indexed: A10, A34, A35, A36, A37, A38, AgBio, Agr, B25, BIOSIS Prev, BP, CA, CABA, CurCont, D01, E12, EMBASE, ExcerpMed, F08, F12, FoVS&M, GH, H16, H17, IndVet, MEDLINE, MaizeAb, MycolAb, N02, N04, OR, P30, P32, P33, P37, P39, PN&I, R08, R11, R12, R13, RA&MP, RM&VM, S12, S13, S16, SCI, SCOPUS, SoyAb, T02, T05, TAR, V03, VS, W07, W10, W11, Z01.
—BLDSC (5072.440000), IE, Ingenta.
Published by: Korean Society of Veterinary Science, College of Veterinary Medicine, Seoul National University, San 56-1, Shinlim-dong, Kwanak-gu, Seoul, 151-742, Korea, S. TEL 82-2-8801229, FAX 82-2-8789762, ksvs@plaza.snu.ac.kr, http://ksvs.or.kr/. Ed. Heungshik S Lee.

333.95416 USA ISSN 0090-3558
SF997 CODEN: JWIDAW

➤ **JOURNAL OF WILDLIFE DISEASES.** Text in English. 1965. q. USD 95 domestic to individual members; USD 40 domestic to students (effective 2009). adv. bk.rev. abstr.; charts; illus. index. back issues avail.; reprints avail. **Document type:** *Journal, Academic/Scholarly.* **Description:** Features the results of original research and observations dealing with all aspects of infectious, parasitic, toxic, nutritional. physiologic, developmental and neoplastic diseases.
Former titles (until 1970): Wildlife Disease Association. Bulletin (0098-373X); (until 1965): Wildlife Disease Association. Newsletter
Related titles: Online - full text ed.: ISSN 1943-3700.
Indexed: A22, A29, A34, A35, A36, A37, A38, ASCA, ASFA, AgBio, Agr, B&AI, B04, B10, B20, B21, B23, B25, BIOSIS Prev, BiolDig, C25, CABA, CRFR, ChemAb, ChemTitl, CurCont, D01, DBA, DentInd, E04, E05, E12, E17, EMBASE, ESPM, EntAb, ExcerpMed, F08, F12, FoVS&M, G11, GH, GenetAb, GeoRef, H17, HGA, ISR, IndMed, IndVet, KWIWR, LT, MEDLINE, MycolAb, N02, N04, P30, P32, P33, P37, P39, PN&I, R07, R08, R13, RM&VM, RRTA, S12, S13, S16, SAA, SCI, SCOPUS, T05, ToxAb, VS, VirolAbstr, W07, W08, W10, W11, WLR, WildRev, Z01.
—BLDSC (5072.620000), CASDDS, GNLM, IE, Infotrieve, Ingenta, INIST, Linda Hall. **CCC.**
Published by: Wildlife Disease Association, Inc., 810 E 10th St, Lawrence, KS 66044. TEL 800-627-0629 ext 289, orders@allenpress.com, http://www.wildlifedisease.org. Ed. Elizabeth S Williams.

➤ **JOURNAL OF WILDLIFE REHABILITATION.** *see* BIOLOGY—Zoology

636 USA ISSN 1042-7260
SF601 CODEN: JZWMEI

➤ **JOURNAL OF ZOO AND WILDLIFE MEDICINE.** Abbreviated title: J Z W M. Text in English. 1971. q. USD 115 in North America to individuals; USD 130 elsewhere to individuals; USD 255 in North America to institutions; USD 270 elsewhere to institutions (effective 2011). adv. bk.rev. charts; illus.; stat.; abstr. cum.index: 1970-1987. back issues avail.; reprints avail. **Document type:** *Journal, Academic/Scholarly.* **Description:** Features original research findings and clinical observations as well as case reports in the field of veterinary medicine dealing with captive and free-ranging wild animals.
Formerly (until 1989): Journal of Zoo Animal Medicine (0093-4526)
Related titles: Online - full text ed.: ISSN 1937-2825.
Indexed: A22, A29, A34, A35, A36, A37, A38, ASCA, ASFA, AgBio, B20, B21, B23, B25, BIOSIS Prev, C25, CA, CABA, CurCont, D01, DBA, E01, E12, EMBASE, ESPM, EnvAb, ExcerpMed, F08, F12, FoVS&M, G11, GH, H16, H17, ISR, IndMed, IndVet, MEDLINE, MaizeAb, MycolAb, N02, N04, P30, P33, P37, P39, PN&I, R07, R08, R12, R13, RA&MP, RM&VM, S12, S13, S16, SAA, SCI, SCOPUS, SoyAb, T02, T05, TAR, TriticAb, VS, VirolAbstr, W07, W08, W11, WildRev, Z01.
—BLDSC (5072.765000), IE, Infotrieve, Ingenta, Linda Hall.
Published by: American Association of Zoo Veterinarians, 581705 White Oak Rd, Yulee, FL 32097. aazvorg@aol.com. Ed. Dr. Teresa Morishita. Circ: 1,200. **Subscr. to:** Allen Press Inc., PO Box 7065, Lawrence, KS 66044. TEL 785-843-1235, FAX 785-843-1274, aazv@allenpress.com, http://www.allenpress.com.

▼ ➤ **JOURNAL OF ZOOLOGY AND VETERINARY SCIENCES.** *see* BIOLOGY—Zoology

636.089 JPN ISSN 0916-5908

JUI MASUI GEKAGAKU ZASSHI/JAPANESE JOURNAL OF VETERINARY ANESTHESIA & SURGERY. Text in Japanese. 1970. q. **Document type:** *Journal, Academic/Scholarly.*
Formerly (until 1988): Jui Masui/Japanese Journal of Veterinary Anesthesiology (0285-2209)
Related titles: Online - full text ed.: ISSN 1349-7669.
Indexed: A34, A36, A37, A38, CABA, GH, IndVet, N04, P33, P37, R08, S12, VS.
—**CCC.**
Published by: Jui Masui Geka Gakkai/Japanese Society of Veterinary Anesthesia & Surgery, 1-1-1 Yayoi, Bunkyo-ku, University of Tokyo, Department of Veterinary Surgery & Obstetrics, Tokyo, 113-8657, Japan. TEL 86-3-58415473, FAX 86-3-58418996, office@jsvas.com, http://www.jsvas.com/index.html.

636.089 JPN ISSN 1343-2583

JUIEKIGAKU ZASSHI/JOURNAL OF VETERINARY EPIDEMIOLOGY. Text in Japanese. s-a. **Document type:** *Journal, Academic/Scholarly.*
Former titles (until 1996): Juijoho Kagaku Zasshi/Japan journal of Veterinary Informatics (0912-8913); (until 1986): Juikagaku to Tokei Riyo/Veterinary Science and Statistical Methods (0913-5499)
Related titles: Online - full text ed.
Indexed: A34, A36, A38, CABA, D01, E12, G11, GH, N02, N03, N04, P33, P39, R08, TAR, W11.
—BLDSC (5072.363000), IE.
Published by: Juiekigakkai/Japan Society of Veterinary Epidemiology, National Institute of Animal Health, Systematic Diagnosis Research Division, 3-1-1 Kannondai, Tsukuba, Ibaraki 305-0856, Japan. TEL 81-298-387770, FAX 81-298-387880, info@vet-epidemiol.jp, http://www.vet-epidemiol.jp/.

636.089 JPN ISSN 1347-6416

JUUI RINSHOU HIFUKA/JAPANESE JOURNAL OF VETERINARY DERMATOLOGY. Text in English, Japanese. 1973. irreg. **Document type:** *Journal, Academic/Scholarly.*
Formerly (until 2002): Jui Hifuka Rinsho/Japanese Journal of Small Animal Dermatology (1341-8017); Which superseded in part (in 1994): Jui Hifuka Rinsho (1341-5700); Which was formerly (until 1990): Shodobutsu Hifuka Rinsho (0912-2494)
Related titles: Online - full text ed.: ISSN 1881-2236.
Indexed: A34, A36, A38, CABA, E12, GH, H16, H17, IndVet, N04, P33, P37, P39, R08, R11, RA&MP, RM&VM, VS.
—BLDSC (5077.250000).
Published by: Shodobutsu Hifuka Kenkyukai/Japanese Society of Veterinary Dermatology, 1-3-2, Higashicho, Jindaji, Chofushi, Tokyo 182-0012, Japan. TEL 81-3-59164162, FAX 81-3-59164163, info@jsvd.jp, http://www.jsvd.jp/.

636.089 TUR ISSN 1300-6045

➤ **KAFKAS UNIVERSITESI VETERINER FAKULTESI DERGISI/ KAFKAS UNIVERSITY. FACULTY OF VETERINARY MEDICINE. JOURNAL.** Text in Turkish, English, German. 1995. bi-m. **Document type:** *Journal, Academic/Scholarly.* **Description:** Publishes original articles, short communications, preliminary scientific reports, case reports, letters to the editor, reviews and translations on all aspects of veterinary medicine and animal science.
Related titles: Online - full text ed.: ISSN 1309-2251. free (effective 2011).
Indexed: A01, A34, A35, A36, A37, A38, AgBio, AgrForAb, BP, C25, C30, CABA, D01, E12, F08, F11, F12, FCA, G11, GH, H16, H17, IndVet, MaizeAb, N02, N03, N04, O01, OR, P32, P33, P37, P39, P40, PGegResA, PHN&I, PN&I, R07, R08, R12, R13, RA&MP, RM&VM, S12, S13, S16, SCI, SCOPUS, SoyAb, T05, TAR, TriticAb, VS, W07, W11, Z01.
Published by: Kafkas Universitesi Veteriner Fakultesi, Pasacayiri, Kars, 36300, Turkey. TEL 90-474-2426839, FAX 90-474-2426853, vetfak@kafkas.edu.tr, http://www.kafkas.edu.tr/. Ed. Dr. Isa Ozaydin.

636.089 KEN ISSN 0256-5161

KENYA VETERINARIAN. Text in English. 1977. s-a. USD 10. adv. **Document type:** *Journal, Trade.*
Indexed: A34, A38, AgrForAb, BP, CABA, E12, F08, GH, H16, H17, IndVet, N04, P33, P37, PN&I, RA&MP, VS.
Published by: The Kenya Veterinary Association, PO Box 29089, Nairobi, 00625, Kenya. TEL 727-680022, 20-630673, kvanational@yahoo.com, info@vetkenya.org, http://vetkenya.org. Ed. Dr. Thomas T Dolan. Circ: 500.

636.089 USA ISSN 1946-164X
SF745 CODEN: CVTHDI

KIRK'S CURRENT VETERINARY THERAPY. (Supplement avail.: Current Veterinary Therapy. Food Animal Practice (ISSN 1043-139X)) Text in English. 1964. irreg., latest 2008, 14th ed. price varies. back issues avail. **Document type:** *Monographic series, Academic/ Scholarly.* **Description:** Contains the information from experts in the veterinary field with over 260 new chapters.
Former titles (until 2009): Kirk's Current Veterinary Therapy. Small Animal Practice (1529-6776); (until 1995): Current Veterinary Therapy (0070-2218)
—BLDSC (5097.572000), CASDDS, IE. **CCC.**
Published by: Elsevier Inc. (Subsidiary of: Elsevier Science & Technology), 1600 John F Kennedy Blvd, Philadelphia, PA 19103. TEL 215-239-3900, FAX 215-238-7883, JournalCustomerService-usa@elsevier.com.

636.089 DEU ISSN 1434-9132

KLEINTIER KONKRET. Text in German. 1998. 7/yr. EUR 119 to institutions; EUR 152 combined subscription to institutions (print & online eds.); EUR 25.40 newsstand/cover (effective 2011). adv. **Document type:** *Journal, Academic/Scholarly.*
Related titles: Online - full text ed.: ISSN 1439-3832. EUR 145 to institutions (effective 2011).
—IE. **CCC.**
Published by: Enke Verlag in M V S Medizinverlage Stuttgart GmbH und Co. KG (Subsidiary of: Georg Thieme Verlag), Oswald-Hesse-Str 50, Stuttgart, 70469, Germany. TEL 49-711-89310, FAX 49-711-8931706, kunden.service@thieme.de. Ed. Dr. Heike Degenhardt. Pub. Ulrike Arnold. Adv. contact Ilona Reiser. B&W page EUR 1,290, color page EUR 1,880; trim 210 x 280. Circ: 4,700 (paid).

636.089 DEU ISSN 0023-2076
SF603

KLEINTIER-PRAXIS; Die Fachzeitschrift fuer den Kleintierpraktiker. Text in German; Summaries in English. 1956. 12/yr. EUR 131.50; EUR 12 per issue (effective 2011). adv. bk.rev. bibl.; charts; illus. index. **Document type:** *Magazine, Trade.* **Description:** Aims to represent the field of small animal medical practice with results of scientific research and clinical experience.
Indexed: A20, A22, A34, A35, A36, A38, ASCA, AgBio, CABA, ChemAb, CurCont, D01, DBA, E12, FoVS&M, GH, H16, H17, ISR, IndVet, LT, N02, N04, P33, P37, P39, PN&I, R08, RM&VM, SAA, SCI, SCOPUS, T05, VS, W07, W11.
—BLDSC (5099.121000), IE, Infotrieve, Ingenta. **CCC.**
Published by: (Deutsche Gesellschaft fuer Kleintiermedizin, Deutsche Veterinaermedizinische Gesellschaft/German Veterinary Medical Society), Schluetersche Verlagsgesellschaft mbH und Co. KG, Hans-Boeckler-Allee 7, Hannover, 30173, Germany. TEL 49-511-85500, FAX 49-511-85501100, info@schluetersche.de, http://www.schluetersche.de. adv.: B&W page EUR 1,121, color page EUR 1,901; trim 188 x 272. Circ: 3,186 (paid).

636.089 DEU ISSN 1434-6400

KLEINTIERMEDIZIN; Fachzeitschrift fuer Kleintierpraktiker. Text in German. 1998. 6/yr. EUR 57; EUR 30 to students; EUR 10 newsstand/cover (effective 2007). adv. abstr.; illus. **Document type:** *Magazine, Trade.*
Published by: Terra Verlag GmbH, Neuhauser Str 21, Konstanz, 78464, Germany. TEL 49-7531-81220, FAX 49-7531-812299, info@terra-verlag.de. Ed. Dieter Mueller. Adv. contact Berndt H. Holthaus. B&W page EUR 1,656, color page EUR 2,760; trim 180 x 248. Circ: 2,234 (paid); 4,789 (controlled).

636.089 PRT ISSN 0870-1067

LABORATORIO NACIONAL DE INVESTIGACAO VETERINARIA. REPOSITORIO DE TRABALHOS. Text in Portuguese. 1930. a.
Former titles (until 1975): Laboratorio Central de Patologia Veterinaria. Repositorio de Trabalhos (0870-5739); (until 1932): Laboratorio de Patologia Veterinaria. Repositorio de Trabalhos (0870-3930)
Indexed: ASFA, B21, ESPM.
Published by: Laboratorio Nacional de Investigacao Veterinaria (L N I V) (Subsidiary of: Instituto Nacional dos Recursos Biologicos (I N R B)), Rua Barata Salgueiro 37, Lisbon, 1250-042, Portugal. TEL 351-213-131741, FAX 351-213-131783, http://www.inrb.pt.

636.089 CAN

➤ **LARGE ANIMAL VETERINARY ROUNDS.** Text in English. 2001. 8/yr. **Document type:** *Journal, Academic/Scholarly.* **Description:** Provides interested physicians throughout Canada and around the world with a unique window on some of the most current information and discussion on important scientific and clinical developments in food animal and equine veterinary medicine.
Related titles: Online - full text ed.
—BLDSC (5155.961455).

V W Z

Published by: University of Saskatchewan, Western College of Veterinary Medicine, Department of Large Animal Clinical Sciences, 52 Campus Dr, Saskatoon, SK S7N 5B4, Canada. Ed. David G Wilson.

636.089 ITA ISSN 1124-4593
LARGE ANIMALS REVIEW. Text in Italian, English. 1995. q. **Document type:** *Journal, Trade.*
Indexed: A34, A35, A36, A37, A38, D01, E12, F08, N03, N04, P32, P33, R07, R08, S13, T05, W11.
Published by: Societa Culturale Italiana Veterinari per Animali da Compagnia (S C I V A C), Palazzo Trecchi, Cremona, CR 26100, Italy. TEL 39-0372-460440, FAX 39-0372-457091, info@scivac.it, http://www.scivac.it.

636.089 DEU
LEIPZIGER BLAUE HEFTE; Forum fuer tieraerztliche Expertise. Text in German. 2008. irreg., latest vol.11, 2010. price varies. **Document type:** *Monographic series, Academic/Scholarly.*
Published by: Leipziger Universitaetsverlag GmbH, Oststr 41, Leipzig, 04317, Germany. TEL 49-341-9900440, FAX 49-341-9900440, info@univerlag-leipzig.de.

636.089 615.9 FRA ISSN 1960-209X
LETTRE DE LA PHARMACOVIGILANCE VETERINAIRE. Text in French. 2005. s-a. **Document type:** *Newsletter, Trade.*
Published by: Agence Francaise de Securite Sanitaire des Aliments (A F S S A), 27-31 Av. du General Leclerc, Maison-Alfort, Cedex 94701, France. TEL 33-1-49771350, http://www.afssa.fr.

636.089510941 GBR ISSN 1755-134X
M A V I S (ONLINE). (Medicines Act Veterinary Information Service) Text in English. 1992. q. free (effective 2009). **Document type:** *Journal, Trade.* **Description:** Provides information on general developments on the controls on veterinary medicines.
Formerly (until 2007): M A V I S (Print) (0968-1027)
Media: Online - full text.
—CCC.
Published by: Veterinary Medicines Directorate, Woodham Ln, New Haw, Addlestone, Surrey KT15 3LS, United Kingdom. TEL 44-1932-336911, FAX 44-1932-336618, postmaster@vmd.defra.gsi.gov.uk.

636.08 POL ISSN 1230-4425
MAGAZYN WETERYNARYJNY. Text in Polish. 1992. bi-m. EUR 115 foreign (effective 2006). adv. bibl.; illus.; tr.lit. index. **Document type:** *Magazine, Trade.* **Description:** Clinical journal for veterinary surgeons and students.
Indexed: AgrLib, SAA.
—BLDSC (5334.255000).
Published by: Bridge MW Sp. z o.o, ul Pijarska 19/6, Krakow, 31015, Poland. Ed. Hubert Zientek. adv.: B&W page USD 700, color page USD 950. Circ: 5,000. **Dist. by:** Ars Polona, Obroncow 25, Warsaw 03933, Poland. TEL 48-22-5098609, FAX 48-22-5098610, arspolona@arspolona.com.pl, http://www.arspolona.com.pl.

636.089 HUN ISSN 0025-004X
CODEN: MGALA5
➤ **MAGYAR ALLATORVOSOK LAPJA/HUNGARIAN VETERINARY JOURNAL.** Text in Hungarian; Summaries in English. 1878. m. adv. bk.rev. abstr.; bibl.; charts; illus. Index. back issues avail. **Document type:** *Journal, Academic/Scholarly.* **Description:** Provides information on the professional, social, educational and organizational lives of veterinarians in Hungary, for a readership primarily of veterinarians.
Former titles (until 1944): Allatorvosi lapok (0365-3900); (until 1902): Veterinarius (0324-4245)
Indexed: A20, A22, A29, A34, A35, A36, A37, A38, ASFA, AgBio, AgrForAb, B20, B21, B23, B25, BA, BIOSIS Prev, CABA, CIN, ChemAb, ChemTitl, CurCont, D01, DBA, E12, E17, ESPM, F08, F12, FS&TA, FoVS&M, G11, GH, H16, H17, ISR, ImmunAb, IndVet, LT, MycolAb, N02, N03, N04, O01, P32, P33, P37, P39, P40, PN&I, R07, R08, R12, R13, RA&MP, RM&VM, RRTA, S12, S13, S16, SAA, SCI, SCOPUS, T05, TAR, ToxAb, TriticAb, VS, VirolAbstr, W07, W10, W11, Z01.
—BLDSC (5340.300000), CASDDS, IE, Ingenta.
Published by: (India. Foldmuvelesugyi es Videkfejlesztesi Miniszterium/ Ministry of Agriculture and Rural Development), Magyar Mezogazdasag Kft., Mirtusz u 2, Budapest, 1141, Hungary. TEL 36-1-4700411, FAX 36-1-4700410, elofizetes@magyarmezogazdasag.hu, http://www.magyarmezogazdasag.hu. Ed. Visnyei Laszlo. Circ: 4,300.

636.089 IRN ISSN 1735-9783
➤ **MAJALLAH-I DAMPIZISHKI/JOURNAL OF VETERINARY MEDICINE.** Text in Persian, Modern. 2007. q. IRR 12,000 (effective 2011). bk.rev. abstr.; bibl.; charts; maps; pat.; mkt. back issues avail. **Document type:** *Journal, Academic/Scholarly.*
Published by: Danishgah-i Azad-i Islami, Vahid-i Sanandaj/Islamic Azad University, Sanandaj Branch, Pasdaran St., PO Box 618, Sanandaj, Iran. TEL 98-871-3289430, FAX 98-871-3247713. Ed., Pub. Shahin Fakour. R&P Adel Fatemi.

636.089 IRN ISSN 2008-2525
SF604 CODEN: JVFTDR
MAJALLAH-I TAHQIQAT-I DAMPIZISHKI/JOURNAL OF VETERINARY RESEARCH. Text in Persian, Modern; Contents page in English, Persian, Modern. 1937. q. IRR 120,000 domestic; USD 100 foreign (effective 2010). adv. bk.rev. abstr.; bibl.; illus.; charts; stat. 100 p./no.; **Document type:** *Journal, Academic/Scholarly.* **Description:** Publishes original research results in all branches of veterinary medicine.
Former titles (2007): Majallah-i Danishkadah-i Dampizishki/Journal of the Faculty of Veterinary Medicine (1022-646X); (until 1993): Namah-i Danishkadah-i Dampizishki (0042-0123)
Related titles: CD-ROM ed.
Indexed: A29, A34, A35, A38, AIDS&CR, ASFA, AgBio, AgrForAb, B21, B23, BP, C25, CABA, D01, E12, ESPM, ExtraMED, F08, FS&TA, G11, GH, H17, IndVet, MaizeAb, N02, N03, N04, OR, P33, P37, P39, PHN&I, R08, R12, R13, RA&MP, RM&VM, S12, SoyAb, T05, ToxAb, TriticAb, VS, VirolAbstr, W10, W11.
—CASDDS, INIST.
Published by: (University of Teheran, Faculty of Veterinary Medicine/ Danishkadah-i Dampizishki), University of Tehran, Printing and Publishing Institute, P O Box 14155-6453, Tehran, Iran. jvr@ut.ac.ir. Ed. Farzad Asadi. Circ: 1,000 (paid).

MARINE TURTLE NEWSLETTER. *see* BIOLOGY—Zoology

636.089 SWE ISSN 1402-5787
MEDDELANDEN FRAAN PARASITOLOGEN. Text in Swedish. 1997. irreg. free. back issues avail. **Document type:** *Monographic series, Government.*
Related titles: Online - full text ed.
Published by: Statens Veterinaermedicinska Anstalt/National Veterinary Institute, Ulls Vaeg 2 B, Uppsala, 75189, Sweden. TEL 46-18-674000, FAX 46-18-409162, sva@sva.se, http://www.sva.se.

636.089 CAN ISSN 0225-9591
CODEN: MVEQDC
MEDECIN VETERINAIRE DU QUEBEC. Text in French. 1971. q. CAD 30, USD 40 (effective 2005). adv. **Document type:** *Journal, Academic/ Scholarly.* **Description:** Covers important issues concerning the veterinary and professional worlds.
Indexed: A22, B25, BIOSIS Prev, H17, MycolAb, P37, PdeR, SAA, WildRev.
—BLDSC (5487.670000), IE, Ingenta, INIST. **CCC.**
Published by: Ordre des Medecins Veterinaires du Quebec/Order of Veterinarians of Quebec, 800 ave Ste Anne, Ste 200, St Hyacinthe, PQ J2S 5G7, Canada. TEL 450-774-1427, FAX 450-774-7635. Ed. Jean Pierard. adv.: color page CAD 2,100; trim 7.5 x 10. Circ: 2,600.

363.089 PRT ISSN 0870-1121
MEDICINA VETERINARIA. Text in Portuguese. 1933. q. **Document type:** *Journal, Academic/Scholarly.*
Formerly (until 1933): Veterinaria (0870-127X)
Published by: Associacao dos Estudantes de Medicina Veterinaria, Rua Profesor Cid dos Santos, Palo Universitario Alto de Ajuda, Lisbon, 1300-477, Portugal. TEL 351-21-3652800, FAX 351-21-3652815, aefmv@aefmv.fmu.utl.pt.

636.08 PRT ISSN 0870-4295
O MEDICO VETERINARIO. Text in Portuguese. 1986. q. adv. **Document type:** *Journal, Trade.* **Description:** Publishes veterinary articles. Includes information on new products and services, meetings and congresses.
Published by: Edicoes Vade-Mecum, Calcada do Tijolo 45, Lisbon, 1200-464, Portugal. TEL edicoes.vademecum@mail.telepac.pt, 351-21-3420518, FAX 351-21-3420682, http://www.vademecum.biz.ly. Ed. Dr. Jose Paulo Sales Luis. Adv. contact Joaquim Azevedo.

636.089 BRA ISSN 1678-1430
MEDVEP. REVISTA CIENTIFICA DE MEDICINA VETERINARIA. PEQUENOS ANIMAIS E ANIMAIS DE ESTIMACAO. Text in Portuguese. 2003. q. back issues avail. **Document type:** *Magazine, Trade.*
Indexed: A34, A35, A38, AgBio, CABA, D01, GH, H17, IndVet, N02, P33, R08, VS.
Published by: Bioeditora, Rua Tenente Francisco Ferreira de Souza, 3636, Boqueirao, Curitiba, PR 81670-010, Brazil. TEL 55-41-32767000, bioeditora@bioeditora.com.br, http://www.bioeditora.com.br/.

636.089 POL ISSN 0025-8628
SF604 CODEN: MDWTAG
➤ **MEDYCYNA WETERYNARYJNA.** Text in Polish; Summaries in English. 1945. m. EUR 120 foreign (effective 2005). adv. bk.rev. abstr.; bibl.; charts; illus.; mkt. index, cum.index. 80 p./no. 2 cols./p.; **Document type:** *Journal, Academic/Scholarly.* **Description:** Devoted to the problems of veterinary science and practice, and applied biology.
Indexed: A22, A34, A35, A36, A37, A38, ASCA, AgBio, AgrAg, AgrLib, B23, B25, BIOSIS Prev, BP, C25, CABA, ChemAb, D01, DBA, E12, F08, F11, F12, FCA, FS&TA, G11, GH, H16, H17, I11, IndVet, LT, MaizeAb, MycolAb, N02, N03, N04, OR, P30, P32, P33, P37, P38, P39, P40, PHN&I, PN&I, R07, R08, R12, R13, RA&MP, RM&VM, RRTA, S12, S13, S16, SAA, SCI, SCOPUS, SoyAb, T05, TAR, TriticAb, VS, W07, W08, W10, W11.
—BLDSC (5536.050000), CASDDS, IE, Infotrieve, Ingenta, INIST.
Published by: Polskie Towarzystwo Nauk Weterynaryjnych/Polish Society of Veterinary Sciences, ul Akademicka 12, PO Box 188, Lublin, 20950, Poland. Ed., R&P Dr. Edmund K Prost. Adv. contact Dr. Krzysztof Szkucik. Circ: 3,300 (controlled).

636.089 USA ISSN 0076-6542
SF748
THE MERCK VETERINARY MANUAL. Text in English. 1955. irreg., latest 2005, 9th ed. USD 60 per issue (effective 2011). **Document type:** *Handbook/Manual/Guide, Trade.* **Description:** Provides information about all common domestic animals, expanded coverage of exotic and laboratory animals, and an extensively revised zoonoses reference table.
Related titles: Online - full text ed.: ISSN 2156-0307. free (effective 2011).
Published by: Merck Publishing Group, RY84-15, PO Box 2000, Rahway, NJ 07065. TEL 732-594-4600. Ed. Cynthia Kahn.

MONOGRAFIE PARAZYTOLOGICZNE. *see* BIOLOGY—Microbiology

636.089 SWE ISSN 1400-7940
MONTHLY REPORT ON NOTIFIABLE DISEASES OF ANIMALS/ MAANADSRAPPORT OEVER ANMAELNINGSPLIKTIGA DJURSJUKDOMAR. Text in English, Swedish. 1995. m. **Document type:** *Bulletin, Government.*
Formed by the merger of (1971-1995): Epizooties en Suede. Liste A (0282-8626); (1984-1995): Epizooties en Suede. Pas Inclus dans la Liste A (0282-8634)
Published by: Statens Jordbruksverk/Swedish Board of Agriculture, Vallgatan 8, Joenkoeping, 55182, Sweden. TEL 46-36-155000, FAX 46-36-190546, jordbruksverket@sjv.se, http://www.sjv.se.

636.089 USA ISSN 1542-4014
SF601
N A V C CLINICIAN'S BRIEF. (North American Veterinary Conference) Text in English. 2002. m. USD 55 (effective 2003).
Indexed: A34, A35, A36, A37, A38, AgBio, CABA, E12, F08, G11, GH, H17, IndVet, N02, N04, OR, P33, P37, P39, R08, R13, RA&MP, RM&VM, S12, VS, W10, W11.
Published by: (The North American Veterinary Conference), Educational Concepts, LLC, 1611 S. Utica St. Ste. 219, Tulsa, OK 74104-4902. TEL 918-749-0118, FAX 918-749-1987. Ed., Pub. Antoinette B. Passaretti.

636.089 NZL ISSN 1176-984X
NEW ZEALAND VETERINARY ASSOCIATION. FOOD SAFETY, ANIMAL WELFARE AND BIOSECURITY, EPIDEMIOLOGY AND ANIMAL HEALTH MANAGEMENT, AND INDUSTRY BRANCHES. COMBINED PROCEEDINGS. Text in English. 1988. irreg. NZD 210 domestic to individuals; AUD 210 in Australia to individuals; USD 165 elsewhere to individuals; NZD 420 domestic to institutions; AUD 420 in Australia to institutions; USD 330 elsewhere to institutions (effective 2009). **Document type:** *Monographic series, Academic/Scholarly.* **Description:** Contains full papers presented at conference by veterinary experts on a wide range of topics relevant to all specialities.
Media: Online - full text.
Published by: New Zealand Veterinary Association, PO Box 11 212, Wellington, 6142, New Zealand. TEL 64-4-4710484, FAX 64-4-4710494, nzva@vets.org.nz, http://www.vetspace.org.nz/. **Subscr. to:** VetLearn Foundation, Mail Code 413, Private Bag 11-222, Palmerston North, New Zealand. TEL 64-6-3505289, FAX 64-6-3505659, subscribe@sciquest.org.nz.

636.089 NZL ISSN 0048-0169
SF604 CODEN: NEZTAF
➤ **NEW ZEALAND VETERINARY JOURNAL.** Text in English. 1952. 6/yr. GBP 359 combined subscription in United Kingdom to institutions (print & online eds.); EUR 475, AUD 728, USD 594 combined subscription to institutions (print & online eds.) (effective 2012). adv. bk.rev. illus. reprint service avail. from PSC. **Document type:** *Journal, Academic/Scholarly.* **Description:** Publishes original research and clinical observations in all aspects of veterinary science.
Related titles: CD-ROM ed.: ISSN 1176-0702; Online - full text ed.: ISSN 1176-0710. GBP 302 in United Kingdom to institutions; EUR 399, AUD 634, USD 498 to institutions (effective 2012) (from IngentaConnect).
Indexed: A22, A34, A35, A36, A37, A38, ASCA, AgBio, B21, B23, B25, BIOSIS Prev, CA, CABA, CIN, CTA, Cadscan, ChemAb, ChemTitl, CurCont, D01, DBA, E12, EMBASE, ESPM, ExcerpMed, F08, F12, FoVS&M, G11, GH, GeoRef, H16, H17, I10, ISR, IndMed, IndVet, LT, LeadAb, MEDLINE, MaizeAb, MycolAb, N02, N04, OR, P30, P32, P33, P37, P39, PN&I, R07, R08, R13, RA&MP, RM&VM, RRTA, S12, S13, S16, SAA, SCI, SCOPUS, SoyAb, SpeleolAb, T02, T05, TAR, TriticAb, VS, W07, W08, W10, W11, WildRev, Z01, Zincscan.
—BLDSC (6099.900000), CASDDS, GNLM, IE, Infotrieve, Ingenta, INIST. **CCC.**
Published by: New Zealand Veterinary Association, PO Box 11 212, Wellington, 6142, New Zealand. TEL 64-4-4710484, FAX 64-4-4710494, nzva@vets.org.nz, http://www.vetspace.org.nz/, http://www.sciquest.org.nz/. Ed., R&P Peter Jolly. Circ: 1,750. **Subscr. to:** VetLearn Foundation, PO Box 11-212, Wellington 6142, New Zealand. TEL 64-4-4710484, FAX 64-4-4710494, subscribe@sciquest.org.nz.

636.089 NZL ISSN 1177-3553
NEW ZEALAND VETERINARY NURSE. Variant title: Veterinary Nurse. Text in English. 1992. q. **Document type:** *Journal, Trade.*
Published by: New Zealand Veterinary Nursing Association, PO Box 1314, Palmerston North, 4440, New Zealand. vetnurse@ihug.co.nz, http://www.nzvna.org.nz. Ed. Marie Hennessy.

NIGERIA. NATIONAL ANIMAL PRODUCTION RESEARCH INSTITUTE. JOURNAL. *see* AGRICULTURE—Poultry And Livestock

636.089 NGA ISSN 0331-3026
NIGERIA VETERINARY JOURNAL. Text in English. 1972. q. back issues avail. **Document type:** *Journal, Academic/Scholarly.* **Description:** Features articles on topical issues on animals in health and disease; clinical and non-clinical articles as well.
Related titles: Online - full text ed.
Indexed: A34, A36, A37, A38, AgrForAb, BP, CABA, D01, E12, F08, F11, F12, G11, GH, H16, H17, IndVet, LT, MaizeAb, N02, N03, N04, P32, P33, P37, P39, P40, PN&I, R08, R12, RA&MP, RM&VM, RRTA, S12, S17, SoyAb, T05, TAR, VS, W10, W11.
Published by: Nigerian Veterinary Medical Association, Vom, PO Box 38, Plateau State, Nigeria. Ed. S. Shoyinka.

630 636.089 JPN
CODEN: NJDKAF
➤ **NIPPON VETERINARY AND LIFE SCIENCE UNIVERSITY. BULLETIN.** Text in English, Japanese; Summaries in English. 1953. a. USD 20 (effective 2003). reprints avail. **Document type:** *Bulletin, Academic/Scholarly.*
Former titles: Nippon Veterinary and Zootechnical College. Bulletin (0373-8361); (until 1997): Nippon Jui Chikusan Daigaku Kiyo (0078-0839)
Related titles: Online - full text ed.
Indexed: ASFA, B21, B25, BIOSIS Prev, CIN, ChemAb, ChemTitl, ESPM, FS&TA, GeoRef, MycolAb, SpeleolAb, Z01.
—CASDDS, INIST.
Published by: Nippon Juui Seimei Kagaku Daigaku/Nippon Veterinary and Life Science University, 1-7-1, Kyonan-cho, Musashino-shi, Tokyo, 180-8602, Japan. TEL 81-422-314151, FAX 81-422-332094, http://www.nvau.ac.jp/. Ed. Toshihko Tsutsui. Circ: 550 (controlled).

636.089 NOR ISSN 0332-5741
CODEN: NOVDAH
➤ **NORSK VETERINAER-TIDSSKRIFT/NORWEGIAN VETERINARY MEDICAL JOURNAL.** Variant title: N V T. Text in Norwegian. 1888. 9/yr. NOK 1,150 in Scandinavia; NOK 1,150 in Europe; NOK 1,650 elsewhere (effective 2011). adv. bk.rev. charts; illus. index. reprints avail. **Document type:** *Journal, Academic/Scholarly.* **Description:** Information of interest to veterinarians and others with interest including public health, hygiene and meat control.
Former titles (until 1970): Norske Veterinaerforening. Medlemsblad (0369-6545); (until 1949): Norsk Veterinaertidsskrift (0029-2273); (until 1895): Tidsskrift for Veterinaerer (0802-5983)
Related titles: Online - full text ed.
Indexed: A22, A34, A35, A36, A37, A38, ASFA, AgBio, B21, B25, BIOSIS Prev, CABA, D01, E12, F08, FS&TA, G11, GH, H17, IndVet, LT, MycolAb, N02, N03, N04, OR, P33, P37, P39, PN&I, R07, R08, RA&MP, RM&VM, RRTA, S12, SAA, SoyAb, T05, VS, W11.
—BLDSC (6147.200000), IE, Ingenta. **CCC.**
Published by: Den Norske Veterinaerforening/Norwegian Veterinary Association, PO Box 6781, St Olavs Plass, Oslo, 0130, Norway. TEL 47-22-994600, FAX 47-22-994601, dnv@vetnett.no. Ed. Steinar Tessem. Adv. contact Kjetil Sagen. Circ: 2,450.

636.089 USA
THE NORTH AMERICAN VETERINARY CONFERENCE. PROCEEDINGS. Text in English. a.

Related titles: CD-ROM ed.
Published by: The North American Veterinary Conference, 5003 S.W. 41st Blvd., Gainesville, FL 32608. TEL 352-375-5672, 800-817-9928, FAX 352-336-6827, info@tnavc.org.

NOVYE PROMYSHLENNYE KATALOGI. MEDITSINSKAYA TEKHNIKA. TEKHNIKA BEZOPASNOSTI. VETERINARNOE OBORUDOVANIE/ NEW INDUSTRIAL CATALOGS. MEDICAL EQUIPMENT. SAFETY TECHNIQUES.VETERINARY EQUIPMENT. *see* BUSINESS AND ECONOMICS—Trade And Industrial Directories

636.089 BRA ISSN 1984-879X
▼ **NUCLEUS ANIMALIUM.** Text in Portuguese. 2009. s-a. **Document type:** *Journal, Academic/Scholarly.*
Related titles: Online - full text ed.: ISSN 2175-1463. free (effective 2011).
Indexed: A34, A37, A38, D01, E12, F08, H16, N04, P33, R08, T05, W11.
Published by: Fundacao Educacional de Ituverava, Rua Flauzino Barbosa Sandoval 1259, Cidade Universitaria, Ituverava, 14500-000, Brazil. TEL 55-16-37299020, FAX 55-16-37299061. Ed. Vera Mariza Chaud de Paula.

636.08969 FRA ISSN 1684-3770
CODEN: OTEBA6
O I E BULLETIN (ENGLISH EDITION). (Office International des Epizooties) Text in English. 2003. q. free. **Document type:** *Bulletin, Trade.* **Description:** Presents monthly evolution of the major epizootic diseases throughout the world.
Related titles: Spanish ed.: O I E Boletin (Spanish Edition). ISSN 1684-3789; French ed.: O I E Boletin (French Edition). ISSN 1684-3762.
—GNLM.
Published by: Organisation Mondiale de la Sante Animale (O I E)/World Organisation for Animal Health, 12 rue de Prony, Paris, 75017, France. TEL 33-1-44151888, FAX 33-1-42670987, oie@oie.int, http://www.oie.int. Ed. J Blancou. R&P Gill S Dilmitis. **US subscr. to:** Scientific, Medical Publications of France, 100 E 42nd St, Ste 1510, New York, NY 10017.

636.08969 FRA ISSN 0253-1933
SF781 CODEN: RTOEDX
➤ **O I E REVUE SCIENTIFIQUE ET TECHNIQUE/O I E REVISTA CIENTIFICA Y TECNICA/O I E SCIENTIFIC AND TECHNICAL REVIEW.** (Office International des Epizooties) Text and summaries in French, Spanish, English. 1982. 3/yr. EUR 110 (effective 2008). abstr.; bibl.; charts; illus.; maps. back issues avail. **Document type:** *Journal, Academic/Scholarly.* **Description:** Promotes experimental or other research work on diagnosis and control of contagious diseases of livestock. Also includes documents of importance to Chief Veterinary Officers of 155 member countries and to the world medical and veterinary scientific communities.
Related titles: Online - full text ed.: ISSN 1608-0637.
Indexed: A20, A22, A34, A35, A36, A37, A38, AgBio, B23, B25, BIOSIS Prev, CABA, CurCont, D01, DBA, E12, EMBASE, ExcerpMed, F08, F12, FS&TA, FoVS&M, GH, H17, IndMed, IndVet, LT, MEDLINE, MycolAb, N02, N03, N04, OR, P30, P32, P33, P37, P39, P40, PN&I, R07, R08, R10, R12, R13, RM&VM, RRTA, Reac, RefZh, S12, S13, S16, SAA, SCI, SCOPUS, SoyAb, T05, TAR, VS, W07, W08, W11, WildRev, Z01.
—BLDSC (7950.029000), GNLM, IE, Infotrieve, Ingenta, INIST. **CCC.**
Published by: Organisation Mondiale de la Sante Animale (O I E)/World Organisation for Animal Health, 12 rue de Prony, Paris, 75017, France. TEL 33-1-44151888, FAX 33-1-42670987, oie@oie.int, http://www.oie.int. R&Ps G S Dilmitis, Gill S Dilmitis. Adv. contact Gill S Dilmitis. **US subscr. to:** Scientific, Medical Publications of France, 100 E 42nd St, Ste 1510, New York, NY 10017.

636.089 USA
O V M A NEWSLINE. Text in English. 1952. m. free to members. adv. illus. **Document type:** *Newsletter.* **Description:** Delivers news on veterinary medicine in Ohio.
Former titles: Ohio Veterinary Medical Association. Newsletter; (until 1970): Ohio Veterinarian (0030-1213)
Published by: Ohio Veterinary Medical Association, 3168 Riverside Dr, Columbus, OH 43221. TEL 614-486-7253, FAX 614-486-1325, ohiovma@ohiovma.org, http://www.ohiovma.org. Ed. George Kukor. Circ: 1,930.

636.089 ITA ISSN 0392-1913
OBIETTIVI E DOCUMENTI VETERINARI. Short title: O & D V. Text in Italian. 1980. m. (11/yr.). adv. 80 p./no.; **Document type:** *Magazine, Trade.* **Description:** Covers the veterinary sciences. Provides professional training information.
Indexed: CABA, GH, IndVet, OR, P37, PN&I, RM&VM, SAA, VS.
—BLDSC (6196.955000), IE, Ingenta.
Published by: Il Sole 24 Ore Business Media, Via Monte Rosa 91, Milan, 20149, Italy. TEL 39-02-30221, FAX 39-02-312055, info@ilsole24ore.com, http://www.gruppo24ore.com. Circ: 3,400.

636.08 AUT ISSN 1029-5313
OESTERREICHISCHE FREIBERUFS TIERARZT. Text in German. 1961. q. **Document type:** *Magazine, Trade.*
Published by: (Berufverband Freiberuflich Taetiger Tieraerzte Oesterreichs), B W K Publishing Solutions, Barmherzigengasse 17/3/Office 5, Vienna, 1030, Austria. TEL 43-1-71606, FAX 43-1-71606900, office@bwk.at, http://www.bwk.at. Pub. Brigitte Weber-Kraus. Circ: 3,400 (controlled).

636.089 AUT ISSN 0029-9766
OESTERREICHISCHER KLEINTIERZUECHTER. Text in German. 1946. m. EUR 36 domestic; EUR 65 foreign; EUR 3.50 newsstand/cover (effective 2007). adv. bk.rev. illus. **Document type:** *Magazine, Trade.*
Published by: (Rassezuchtverband Oesterreichischer Kleintierzuechter), Druck und Verlag Hammerer, Riedauer Str 48, Ried, 4910, Austria. TEL 43-7752-870110, FAX 43-7752-8701111, office@hammerer.at, http://www.hammerer.at. Ed., R&P Harald Besendorfer. Adv. contact Johann Ohlicher. page EUR 335; trim 191 x 263. Circ: 6,000.

636.089 JPN ISSN 0911-5137
OKINAWA-KEN KACHIKU EISEI SHIKENJO NENPO/OKINAWA PREFECTURAL INSTITUTE OF ANIMAL HEALTH. ANNUAL REPORT. Text in Japanese; Summaries in English. 1958. a., latest no.40, 2004. free. back issues avail. **Description:** Covers research on animal diseases.
Former titles (until 1971): Ryukyu Seifu Kachiku Eisei Shikenjo Nenpo (0911-5129); (until 1970): Ryukyu Seifu Kachiku Eisei Shikenjo Kenkyu Hokoku (0911-5595)
Published by: Okinawa-ken Kachiku Eisei Shikenjo/Okinawa Prefectural Institute of Animal Health, 112 Kohagura, Naha-shi, Okinawa-ken 900-0024, Japan. TEL 81-98-8321515, FAX 81-98-8537376, http://www.pref.okinawa.jp/kachikush/kaeishp1.htm. Circ: 300.

636.089 ZAF ISSN 0030-2465
SF719.S6 CODEN: OJVRAZ
➤ **ONDERSTEPOORT JOURNAL OF VETERINARY RESEARCH.** Text in English. 1933. q. bk.rev. maps; charts; illus. index, cum.index: 1933-1968, 1969-1973. back issues avail.; reprints avail. **Document type:** *Journal, Academic/Scholarly.* **Description:** Publishes papers reporting on original research covering all aspects of veterinary science, with particular emphasis on diseases and disease vectors of livestock and wildlife on the African continent of more than local interest.
Related titles: Microform ed.: (from PMC, PQC); Online - full text ed.: ISSN 2219-0635. free (effective 2011).
Indexed: A22, A29, A34, A35, A36, A37, A38, ASCA, AgBio, Agr, AgrForAb, B20, B21, B23, B25, BIOSIS Prev, BP, CA, CABA, ChemAb, CurCont, D01, DBA, E12, EMBASE, ESPM, EntAb, ExcerpMed, F08, FS&TA, FoVS&M, G11, GH, H16, H17, I10, INIS AtomInd, ISAP, ISR, IndMed, IndVet, MEDLINE, MaizeAb, MycolAb, N02, N04, OR, P11, P15, P20, P22, P26, P30, P33, P37, P39, P48, P52, P54, P56, PN&I, PQC, R07, R08, R12, R13, RA&MP, RM&VM, S12, S13, S16, SCI, SCOPUS, SoyAb, T02, T05, TAR, TriticAb, VS, ViroIAbstr, W07, W08, W10, W11, WildRev, Z01.
—BLDSC (6258.000000), CASDDS, GNLM, IE, Infotrieve, Ingenta, INIST.
Published by: Agricultural Research Council, Onderstepoort Veterinary Institute, Private Bag X5, Onderstepoort, 0110, South Africa. TEL 27-12-5299406, FAX 27-12-5299277, erna@moon.ovi.ac.za, http://www.ovi.ac.za. Ed., R&P J Boomker.

636.089 AUS ISSN 1328-925X
➤ **ONLINE JOURNAL OF VETERINARY RESEARCH.** Abbreviated title: O J V R. Variant title: Online J Vet Res. Text in English. 1996. s-a. USD 500 to institutions (effective 2009). adv. illus. back issues avail.; reprints avail. **Document type:** *Journal, Academic/Scholarly.* **Description:** Focuses primarily on comparative pathobiology, pharmacology-pharmacokinetics, toxicology and parasitology.
Media: Online - full content. **Related titles:** Print ed.
Indexed: A34, A35, A36, A37, A38, AgBio, AgrForAb, CABA, D01, E12, F08, GH, H17, IndVet, N02, N04, P33, P37, P39, PN&I, R08, RA&MP, RM&VM, S13, S16, T05, TAR, VS, W10, W11, Z01.
Published by: Pestsearch International Pty. Ltd., 173 Chatswood Rd, Daisy Hill, QLD 4127, Australia. TEL 61-7-33882588, onlinejournals@comcen.com.au. Ed. Vincent H Guerrini.

636.089 571 GBR ISSN 1179-2779
▼ ➤ **OPEN ACCESS ANIMAL PHYSIOLOGY.** Text in English. 2010. irreg. free (effective 2011). **Document type:** *Journal, Academic/ Scholarly.*
Media: Online - full text.
—**CCC.**
Published by: Dove Medical Press Ltd., Beechfield House, Winterton Way, Macclesfield, SK11 0JL, United Kingdom. TEL 44-1625-509130, FAX 44-1625-617933. Ed. Peter Koulen.

636.089 NLD ISSN 1874-3188
SF604
THE OPEN VETERINARY SCIENCE JOURNAL. Text in English. 2007. irreg. free (effective 2011). **Document type:** *Journal, Academic/ Scholarly.* **Description:** Covers all areas of experimental and clinical research in veterinary science and medicine.
Media: Online - full text.
Indexed: A01, A34, A35, A36, A38, A39, AgBio, C27, C29, CA, CABA, D01, D03, D04, E13, GH, H17, IndVet, N02, N04, OR, P32, P33, P37, P40, PN&I, R08, R14, S14, S15, S18, T02, T05, TAR, TriticAb, VS, W10.
Published by: Bentham Open (Subsidiary of: Bentham Science Publishers Ltd.), PO Box 294, Bussum, AG 1400, Netherlands. TEL 31-35-6923800, FAX 31-35-6980150, subscriptions@bentham.org. Ed. Jacques Cabaret.

PAKISTAN JOURNAL OF AGRICULTURE, AGRICULTURAL ENGINEERING AND VETERINARY SCIENCES. *see* AGRICULTURE

636.089 PAK
PAKISTAN VETERINARIAN; animal sciences. Text in English. 1988. m. USD 5 per issue.
Published by: Press Corporation of Pakistan, P O Box 3138, Karachi, 75400, Pakistan. TEL 21-455-3703, FAX 21-7736198. Ed. Saeed Hafeez. Circ: 5,000.

636.089 PAK ISSN 0253-8318
SF604 CODEN: PVJODU
➤ **PAKISTAN VETERINARY JOURNAL.** Text in English. 1981. q. PKR 500 domestic to individuals; PKR 200 foreign to individuals; USD 2,500 domestic to institutions; PKR 300 foreign to institutions (effective 2011). adv. bk.rev. **Document type:** *Journal, Academic/ Scholarly.* **Description:** Contains original research papers, review, extension and clinical articles on the production and diseases of animals, including studies in comparative medicine.
Related titles: Online - full text ed.: free (effective 2011).
Indexed: A01, A22, A34, A35, A36, A37, A38, AgBio, AgrForAb, B23, BP, C25, CA, CABA, CIN, ChemAb, ChemTitl, D01, E12, F08, F11, F12, FCA, FoVS&M, G11, GH, H16, H17, IndVet, MaizeAb, N02, N03, N04, OR, P32, P33, P37, P39, P40, PGegResA, PN&I, R07, R08, R11, R12, R13, RA&MP, RM&VM, S12, S13, S16, S17, SAA, SCI, SCOPUS, SoyAb, T02, T05, TAR, TriticAb, VS, W07, W10, W11, WildRev, Z01.
—BLDSC (6343.170000), CASDDS, IE, Ingenta.
Published by: University of Agriculture, Faculty of Veterinary Science, c/o Dr. Nazir Ahmad, Ed., Department of Theriogenology, Faisalabad, 38040, Pakistan. TEL 92-41-624607, FAX 92-41-610200, ahrar@fsd.paknet.com.pk, profnazir53@hotmail.com, http:// pvj.com.pk. Ed. Muhammad Siddique. Circ: 1,000.

636.089 IRL
PEGASUS. Text in English. 1954. a. adv. bk.rev. **Document type:** *Newsletter.* **Description:** Concerned with up-to-date developments and opportunities for recent graduates in Ireland and the world.
Formerly: A V S Journal (0066-9768)
Published by: University College Dublin, Faculty of Veterinary Medicine, Belfield, Dublin, 4, Ireland. TEL 353-1-7166100, FAX 353-1-7166104, vetmed@ucd.ie, http://www.ucd.ie/vetmed/. Circ: 1,500.

636.089 579 TUR ISSN 1300-1515
PENDIK VETERINER MIKROBIYOLOJI DERGISI/JOURNAL OF PENDIK VETERINARY MICROBIOLOGY. Text in Turkish; Summaries in English. 1967. 2/yr. **Document type:** *Journal.*
Former titles (until 1992): Pendik Veteriner Mikrobiyoloji Enstitusu Dergisi (0257-8263); Pendik Hayvan Hastaliklari Merkez Arastirma Enstitusu Dergisi
Indexed: A34, A38, CABA, D01, E12, GH, H17, INIS AtomInd, IndVet, N02, P33, P37, P39, R08, VS.
—BLDSC (6419.270500), IE, Ingenta.
Published by: Pendik Veteriner Kontrol ve Arastirma Enstitusu, Bati Mah. No.1, Pendik-Istanbul, 81480, Turkey. TEL 90-216-3901280, FAX 90-216-3547692, pendik@penvet.gov.tr. Ed. Dr. Kaya Demirozu. Circ: 1,000 (paid).

636.089 BRA ISSN 0100-736X
CODEN: PVBRDX
➤ **PESQUISA VETERINARIA BRASILEIRA/BRAZILIAN JOURNAL OF VETERINARY RESEARCH.** Text and summaries in Portuguese, English. 1981. m. BRL 16 domestic to individuals; BRL 32 domestic to institutions (effective 2008). Supplement avail.; back issues avail. **Document type:** *Journal, Academic/Scholarly.* **Description:** Publishes original articles and review papers on all aspects of veterinary sciences. Includes contributions on animal pathology and related subjects, mainly diseases of economic importance and interest to public health.
Related titles: Online - full text ed.: free (effective 2011).
Indexed: A34, A35, A36, A37, A38, AgBio, AgrForAb, B25, BA, BIOSIS Prev, BP, CA, CABA, D01, E12, F08, F12, FS&TA, FoVS&M, G11, GH, H16, H17, IndVet, LT, MaizeAb, MycolAb, N02, N03, N04, OR, P32, P33, P37, P39, P40, PN&I, R08, R13, RA&MP, RM&VM, S12, S13, S16, S17, SCI, SCOPUS, SoyAb, T02, T05, TAR, VS, W07, W10, W11, WildRev.
—BLDSC (6428.246000), IE, Ingenta.
Published by: Colegio Brasileiro de Patologia Animal, Embrapa - CNPAB - SPSA, Km 47, Seropedica, Rio de Janeiro 23851-970, Brazil. TEL 55-21-26822940, FAX 55-21-26821081, colegio@cbpa.org.br, http://www.cbpa.org.br/. Ed. Jurgen Dobereiner. Circ: 1,000.

636.08 DEU ISSN 1860-3203
PFERDE SPIEGEL. Text in German. 2004. 4/yr. EUR 98 to institutions; EUR 142 combined subscription to institutions (print & online eds.); EUR 32 newsstand/cover (effective 2011). adv. **Document type:** *Journal, Academic/Scholarly.*
Related titles: Online - full text ed.: ISSN 1868-0445. EUR 137 to institutions (effective 2011).
—**CCC.**
Published by: Enke Verlag in M V S Medizinverlage Stuttgart GmbH und Co. KG (Subsidiary of: Georg Thieme Verlag), Oswald-Hesse-Str 50, Stuttgart, 70469, Germany. TEL 49-711-89310, FAX 49-711-8931706, kunden.service@thieme.de. Ed. Leonie Loeffler. adv.: B&W page EUR 1,800, color page EUR 2,250; trim 210 x 297. Circ: 1,346 (paid and controlled).

636.089 DEU ISSN 0177-7726
PFERDEHEILKUNDE. Text in English, German; Summaries in English. 1985. bi-m. EUR 180 (effective 2009). adv. back issues avail. **Document type:** *Journal, Academic/Scholarly.*
Indexed: A20, A22, A34, A35, A36, A37, A38, ASCA, AgBio, C25, CABA, CurCont, D01, E12, FoVS&M, G11, GH, H16, H17, IndVet, LT, MaizeAb, N02, N04, P33, P39, PN&I, R08, R13, RA&MP, RM&VM, RRTA, S12, S13, S16, SCI, SCOPUS, SoyAb, T05, TAR, TriticAb, VS, W07, W10, W11.
—BLDSC (6437.519000), IE, Ingenta. **CCC.**
Published by: Hippiatrika Verlag GmbH, Postfach 080539, Berlin, 10005, Germany. TEL 49-176-23411422, FAX 49-30-28040452, media@pferdeheilkunde.de. Ed. H D Lauk TEL 49-30-28040451. adv.: B&W page EUR 901, color page EUR 1,518; trim 178 x 262.

636.089 615 FRA ISSN 0999-1689
PHARMAVET. Text in French. 198?. bi-m. EUR 101.87 domestic (effective 2010). **Document type:** *Magazine, Trade.*
Published by: Wolters Kluwer - Pharma (Subsidiary of: Wolters Kluwer France), 1 Rue Eugene et Armand Peugeot, Rueil-Malmaison, Cedex 92856, France. TEL 33-1-76734809, FAX 33-1-76733040, contact@wk-pharma.fr.

636.089 PHL ISSN 0115-2173
CODEN: PJVSDI
➤ **PHILIPPINE JOURNAL OF VETERINARY AND ANIMAL SCIENCES.** Text and summaries in English. 1975. q. adv. bk.rev. charts; illus. back issues avail. **Document type:** *Journal, Academic/Scholarly.* **Description:** Covers veterinary and animal science subjects intended for academics, researchers, scientists.
Formerly: Philippine Journal of Animal Science
Related titles: Online - full text ed.
Indexed: ChemAb, FS&TA.
—CASDDS.
Published by: Philippine Society of Animal Sciences, University of the Philippines Los Banos, College of Veterinary Medicine, Laguna, 4031, Philippines. TEL 63-49-536-2547, FAX 63-49-536-2547, www.psas.national@gmail.com, http://psas-national.org. Ed. Jazie A Acorda TEL 63-49-536-2729. Circ: 1,000.

636.089 PHL ISSN 0031-7705
SF604 CODEN: PJVMAV
➤ **PHILIPPINE JOURNAL OF VETERINARY MEDICINE.** Abbreviated title: P J V M. Text in English. 1962. s-a. PHP 200, USD 50 (effective 2002). adv. bk.rev. bibl.; charts; illus. back issues avail. **Document type:** *Journal, Academic/Scholarly.* **Description:** Publishes original research, review articles, abstracts of proceedings, short communications and research notes on all aspects of veterinary medicine.
Indexed: A34, A35, A38, AgBio, AgrForAb, B23, CABA, ChemAb, D01, E12, F08, FoVS&M, GH, H16, H17, IndVet, MaizeAb, N02, N04, P33, P37, P39, PN&I, R08, R12, R13, RA&MP, RM&VM, S12, S13, S16, SCI, SCOPUS, SoyAb, T05, TAR, TriticAb, VS, W07, W11, Z01.
—BLDSC (6456.050000), CASDDS.
Published by: University of the Philippines at Los Banos, College of Veterinary Medicine, Los Banos, Laguna, 4031, Philippines. TEL 63-49-536-2730, FAX 63-49-536-2760. Ed., R&P Conrado A Valdez. Circ: 300 (paid).

➤ **PHYSIOLOGY. PROCEEDINGS.** *see* BIOLOGY—Physiology

636.089 GBR ISSN 1352-9749
➤ **THE PIG JOURNAL.** Text in English. 1976. s-a. GBP 45 to non-members; GBP 26.50 per issue to non-members; free to members (effective 2009). bk.rev. abstr. back issues avail.; reprints avail. **Document type:** *Journal, Academic/Scholarly.* **Description:** Discusses topics on pig diseases and treatment presented at national and international meetings.
Former titles (until 1994): Pig Veterinary Journal (0956-0939); (until 1989): Pig Veterinary Society. Proceedings (0141-3074)
Related titles: CD-ROM ed.
Indexed: A34, A35, A36, A37, A38, AgBio, CABA, D01, DBA, E12, G11, GH, H16, H17, IndVet, N02, N04, OR, P32, P33, P39, PN&I, R08, R13, RA&MP, RM&VM, S12, S13, S16, TriticAb, VS, W10, W11.
—BLDSC (6500.040000), IE, Ingenta. **CCC.**
Published by: Pig Veterinary Society, VLA Thirsk, West House, Station Rd, Thirsk, YO7 1PZ, United Kingdom. TEL 44-1352-771026, FAX 44-1352-771026, office@pigvetsoc.org.uk, http://www.pigvetsoc.org.uk/. Eds. Dan Tucker, David J Taylor, Stan H Done.

636.089 FRA ISSN 0335-4997 CODEN: POVTEN
POINT VETERINAIRE. Text in French. 1973. 10/yr. EUR 173.36 domestic to individuals; EUR 87.17 domestic to students; EUR 202.74 in the European Union to individuals; EUR 120.47 in the European Union to students; EUR 217.29 elsewhere to individuals; EUR 135.02 elsewhere to students (effective 2009). adv. bk.rev.
Indexed: A22, A34, A35, A36, A37, A38, ASCA, AgBio, CABA, D01, E12, FoVS&M, GH, H17, N02, N04, P33, P39, R08, SAA, SCOPUS, W11.
—BLDSC (6541.862000), IE, Ingenta, INIST. **CCC.**
Published by: Point Veterinaire S.A. (Subsidiary of: Wolters Kluwer N.V.), 9 rue Alexandre, BP 233, Maisons-Alfort, Cedex 94702, France. TEL 33-01-45170225, FAX 33-01-45170274, edpoint@wanadoo.fr, http://www.pointveterinaire.com. Ed. Maryvonne Barbaray. Adv. contact Nadege Humbert. Circ: 6,000.

636.089 POL ISSN 1505-1773 CODEN: PJVSFK
POLISH JOURNAL OF VETERINARY SCIENCES. Text in English; Summaries in Polish. 1951. irreg., latest vol.34, 1995. PLZ 120 domestic; EUR 62 foreign (effective 2005). abstr.; charts; illus. **Document type:** *Journal, Academic/Scholarly.*
Former titles (until 1998): Archivum Veterinarium Polonicum (1230-5359); (until 1992): Polskie Archiwum Weterynaryjne (0079-3647)
Indexed: A34, A35, A36, A38, AgBio, AgrAg, AgrLib, B23, B25, BA, BIOSIS Prev, BP, C25, CABA, CIN, ChemAb, ChemTitl, CurCont, D01, E12, EMBASE, ExcerpMed, F08, F12, FCA, FS&TA, FoVS&M, G11, GH, H16, H17, IndMed, IndVet, MEDLINE, MaizeAb, MycolAb, N02, N03, N04, OR, P20, P22, P30, P32, P33, P37, P39, P40, P48, P52, P54, P56, PN&I, PQC, R07, R08, R13, RA&MP, RM&VM, S12, S13, SCI, SCOPUS, SoyAb, TAR, TriticAb, VS, W07, W10.
—BLDSC (6543.672500), CASDDS, GNLM, IE, INIST.
Published by: Polska Akademia Nauk, Komitet Nauk Weterynaryjnych/ Polish Academy of Sciences, Committee of Veterinary Sciences, University of Warmia and Mazury, Dept of Animal Anatomy, ul Oczapowskiego 13, Bldg 105J, Olsztyn-Kortowo II, 10957, Poland. TEL 48-89-5233733, FAX 48-89-5234986. Circ: 400. **Dist. by:** Ars Polona, Obroncow 25, Warsaw 03933, Poland. TEL 48-22-5098609, FAX 48-22-5098610, arspolona@arspolona.com.pl, http://www.arspolona.com.pl.

POULTRY HEALTH REPORT. *see* AGRICULTURE—Poultry And Livestock

636.089 ROM
PRACTICA VETERINARA.RO. Text in Romanian. q. ROL 90 (effective 2011). adv. **Document type:** *Magazine, Trade.*
Published by: Versa Puls Media, s.r.l., Calea Rahovei 266-268, corp 1, etaj 2, Bucharest, 050912, Romania. TEL 40-31-4254040, FAX 40-31-4254041, office@pulsmedia.ro. Ed. Dr. Valentin Nicolae. Adv. contact George Pavel. Circ: 2,000 (paid).

636.089 DEU ISSN 0032-681X CODEN: PRTIAV
➤ **DER PRAKTISCHE TIERARZT**; Zeitschrift fuer fortschrittliche Veterinaermedizin. Text in German. 1921. 13/yr. EUR 120 domestic; EUR 138 foreign; EUR 14 newsstand/cover (effective 2010). adv. bk.rev. charts; illus. index. **Document type:** *Journal, Academic/ Scholarly.*
Indexed: A20, A22, A34, A35, A36, A37, A38, ASCA, CABA, ChemAb, CurCont, D01, DBA, E12, F08, FoVS&M, G11, GH, H16, H17, IndVet, KWIWR, LT, N02, N04, OR, P30, P33, P37, P39, PN&I, R07, R08, R13, RA&MP, RM&VM, RRTA, S12, SAA, SCI, SCOPUS, SoyAb, T05, VS, W07, W10, W11.
—BLDSC (6601.200000), CASDDS, IE, Infotrieve, Ingenta, INIST, Linda Hall. **CCC.**
Published by: (Bundesverbandes praktischer Tieraerzte e.V.), Schluetersche Verlagsgesellschaft mbH und Co. KG, Hans-Boeckler-Allee 7, Hannover, 30173, Germany. TEL 49-511-85500, FAX 49-511-85501100, info@schluetersche.de, http://www.schluetersche.de. Ed. Dr. Birgit Leopold-Temmler. Adv. contact Bettina Kruse. B&W page EUR 2,170, color page EUR 3,309; trim 188 x 272. Circ: 7,497 (paid).

636.089 FRA ISSN 1767-4417
PRATIQUE VET DES ANIMAUX DE COMPAGNIE. Text in French. 2000. m. (11/yr.). EUR 139 (effective 2008). **Document type:** *Magazine, Trade.*
Indexed: A34, A38, C30, H16, P33, P37, R07, R08, SCOPUS.
Published by: A F V A C, 40 Rue de Berri, Paris, 75008, France. TEL 33-1-53839160, FAX 33-1-53839169, contact@afvac.com, http://www.afvac.com.

636.089 FRA ISSN 0395-8639
PRATIQUE VETERINAIRE EQUINE. Text in French. 1965. q. EUR 132.22 domestic to individuals; EUR 67.58 domestic to students; EUR 144.96 foreign to individuals; EUR 75.42 foreign to students (effective 2009). **Document type:** *Journal, Trade.*
Former titles (until 1969): Cheval de Sport (0223-4106); (until 1966): Actes de la Conference Nationale des Veterinaires Specialistes du Cheval (0223-4114)
Indexed: A22, A34, A35, A36, A37, A38, AgBio, CABA, D01, G11, GH, H17, IndVet, LT, N04, P33, P39, PN&I, R08, RM&VM, RRTA, TAR, VS, W10, W11.
—BLDSC (6603.010000), IE, Ingenta.
Published by: (Association Veterinaire Equine Francaise), Point Veterinaire S.A. (Subsidiary of: Wolters Kluwer N.V.), 9 rue Alexandre, BP 233, Maisons-Alfort, Cedex 94702, France. TEL 33-01-45170225, FAX 33-01-45170274, edpoint@wanadoo.fr, http://www.pointveterinaire.com. **Co-publisher:** Association Veterinaire Equine Francaise.

636.089 NLD ISSN 0167-5877
SF601
➤ **PREVENTIVE VETERINARY MEDICINE.** Text in English. 1983. 20/yr. EUR 2,386 in Europe to institutions; JPY 316,800 in Japan to institutions; USD 2,669 elsewhere to institutions (effective 2012). bk.rev. illus. index. reprints avail. **Document type:** *Journal, Academic/Scholarly.* **Description:** Aims to disseminate, on a worldwide basis, information and reports of significance in the field of animal (mammalian, aquatic and avian) health programs and preventive veterinary medicine.
Related titles: Microform ed.: (from PQC); Online - full text ed.: ISSN 1873-1716 (from IngentaConnect, ScienceDirect).
Indexed: A01, A03, A08, A22, A26, A34, A35, A36, A37, A38, ASCA, AgBio, Agr, B23, B25, BIOBASE, BIOSIS Prev, CA, CABA, CIS, CurCont, D01, DBA, E12, EMBASE, ExcerpMed, F08, F12, FCA, FoVS&M, G11, GH, H16, H17, I05, IABS, ISR, IndMed, IndVet, LT, MEDLINE, MaizeAb, MycolAb, N02, N03, N04, OR, P30, P33, P37, P39, PN&I, R07, R08, R11, R12, RA&MP, RM&VM, RRTA, S12, S13, S16, SAA, SCI, SCOPUS, SoyAb, T02, T05, TAR, VS, W07, W08, W11, WildRev.
—BLDSC (6612.795000), IE, Infotrieve, Ingenta, INIST, Linda Hall. **CCC.**
Published by: Elsevier BV (Subsidiary of: Elsevier Science & Technology), Radarweg 29, PO Box 211, Amsterdam, 1000 AE, Netherlands. TEL 31-20-4853911, FAX 31-20-4852457, JournalsCustomerServiceEMEA@elsevier.com, http://www.elsevier.nl. Ed. M D Salman. **Subscr. to:** Radarweg 29, PO Box 211, Amsterdam 1000 AE, Netherlands. TEL 31-20-4853757, FAX 31-20-4853432.

636.089 FRA ISSN 0990-0632 CODEN: PROAEK
➤ **PRODUCTIONS ANIMALES.** Text in French. 1970. 5/yr. EUR 70.52 in Europe; EUR 72 in France (effective 2008). bk.rev. **Document type:** *Journal, Academic/Scholarly.* **Description:** Deals with all species of zootechnical interest, covering feed and nutrition, physiology, pathology, genetics, production techniques, product quality and production economics.
Formerly (until 1988): Centre de Recherches Zootechniques et Veterinaires de Theix. Bulletin Technique (0395-7519)
Related titles: Online - full text ed.: ISSN 1152-5428. 1998.
Indexed: A22, A34, A35, A36, A37, A38, ASCA, AgBio, B25, BA, BIOSIS Prev, CABA, D01, E12, FoVS&M, G11, GH, H17, IndVet, MaizeAb, MycolAb, N02, N03, N04, OR, P33, P37, P39, PN&I, R08, R13, RA&MP, RM&VM, S12, S13, S16, SCI, SCOPUS, SoyAb, TAR, TriticAb, VS, W07, W11.
—BLDSC (6853.247000), IE, Ingenta, INIST, Linda Hall. **CCC.**
Published by: I N R A Editions, INRA Departement PHASE, BP 52627, Castanet-Tolosan, Cedex 31326, France. TEL 33-5-61285099, FAX 33-5-61285319. Ed. Marie Helene Farce. **Subscr. to:** Editions Quae, c/o Inra, RD 10, Versailles 78026 Cedex, France.

636.089 USA ISSN 1080-7446
SF1
THE PROFESSIONAL ANIMAL SCIENTIST. Abbreviated title: P A S. Text in English. 1985. bi-m. USD 287 combined subscription domestic to institutions (print & online eds.); USD 307 combined subscription foreign to institutions (print & online eds.) (effective 2010). adv. bibl.; charts; illus.; stat.; tr.lit. back issues avail. **Document type:** *Journal, Academic/Scholarly.* **Description:** Designed for researchers and professional practitioners of animal science.
Related titles: Online - full text ed.: ISSN 1525-318X. USD 180 (effective 2010).
Indexed: A34, A35, A36, A37, A38, AgBio, Agr, AgrForAb, B23, BA, C25, CABA, D01, E12, F08, F12, FCA, G11, GH, H16, H17, I11, IndVet, MaizeAb, N02, N03, N04, OR, P11, P15, P26, P32, P33, P39, P40, P48, P52, P54, P56, PGegResA, PHN&I, PN&I, PQC, R08, R11, R13, R12, S13, S16, SoyAb, T05, TAR, TriticAb, VS, W10, W11.
—BLDSC (6857.242500).
Published by: American Registry of Professional Animal Scientists, 2441 Village Green Pl, Champaign, IL 61822. TEL 217-356-5390, FAX 217-398-4119, arpas@assochq.org, http://www.arpas.org. Ed. D W Kellogg.

636.08 ITA ISSN 1121-1547
PROFESSIONE VETERINARIA. Text in Italian. 1991. q. **Document type:** *Magazine, Trade.*
Related titles: Online - full text ed.
Indexed: A38.
Published by: Associazione Nazionale Medici Veterinari Italiani, Palazzo Trecchi, Via Trecchi, 20, Cremona, CR 26100, Italy. TEL 39-372-23501, FAX 39-372-457091. Circ: 11,800.

636.089 MEX
PRONTUARIO DE ESPECIALIDADES VETERINARIAS. Text in Spanish. 1971. a. **Document type:** *Directory, Trade.*
Published by: Ediciones P L M S.A. de C.V., San Bernardino 17, Col del Valle, Mexico City, DF 03100, Mexico. TEL 687-1766, FAX 536-5027. Ed. Luis Hochenstein.

636.08 USA ISSN 0555-6953
SF601
PULSE (CYPRESS). Text in English. 195?. m. free to members. adv. illus. **Document type:** *Newsletter, Trade.* **Description:** Publishes case studies and other scientific and medical news of interest to doctors of veterinary medicine.
Published by: Southern California Veterinary Medical Association, 5576 Corporate Ave, Cypress, CA 90630. TEL 714-821-7493, FAX 714-821-7213, scvmainfo@scvma.org, http://www.scvma.org. Ed. Richard L Holden. Adv. contact Marilyn Jensen. Circ: 1,100 (controlled).

636.089 ITA ISSN 1971-4653
QUADERNI DI DERMATOLOGIA. Text in Italian. 1996. irreg. **Document type:** *Magazine, Trade.*
Published by: Societa Culturale Italiana Veterinari per Animali da Compagnia (S C I V A C), Palazzo Trecchi, Cremona, CR 26100, Italy. TEL 39-0372-460440, FAX 39-0372-457091, info@scivac.it, http://www.scivac.it.

R F L. (Rundschau Fleischhygiene und Lebensmittelueberwachung) *see* FOOD AND FOOD INDUSTRIES

636.089 DEU ISSN 1439-0531
REPRODUCTION IN DOMESTIC ANIMALS (ONLINE). Text in English. 6/yr. GBP 724 in United Kingdom to institutions; EUR 921 in Europe to institutions; USD 1,338 in the Americas to institutions; USD 1,560 elsewhere to institutions (effective 2012). **Document type:** *Journal, Academic/Scholarly.* **Description:** Offers comprehensive information concerning physiology, pathology, and biotechnology of reproduction.
Media: Online - full text (from IngentaConnect). **Related titles:** ◆ Print ed.: Reproduction in Domestic Animals (Print). ISSN 0936-6768.
—**CCC.**
Published by: Wiley-Blackwell Verlag GmbH (Subsidiary of: Wiley-Blackwell Publishing Ltd.), Kurfuerstendamm 57, Berlin, 10707, Germany. TEL 49-30-3279-0665, FAX 49-30-3279-0677, verlag@blackwell.de, http://www.blackwell.de. Ed. Dr. Heriberto Rodriguez-Martinez.

636.089 DEU ISSN 0936-6768
S494 CODEN: RDANEF
➤ **REPRODUCTION IN DOMESTIC ANIMALS (PRINT)**; physiology, pathology, biotechnology. Text in English. 1966. 6/yr. GBP 724 in United Kingdom to institutions; EUR 921 in Europe to institutions; USD 1,338 in the Americas to institutions; USD 1,560 elsewhere to institutions; GBP 834 combined subscription in United Kingdom to institutions (print & online eds.); EUR 1,059 combined subscription in Europe to institutions (print & online eds.); USD 1,540 combined subscription in the Americas to institutions (print & online eds.); USD 1,794 combined subscription elsewhere to institutions (print & online eds.) (effective 2012). bk.rev. illus.; stat. index. reprint service avail. from PSC. **Document type:** *Journal, Academic/Scholarly.* **Description:** Offers comprehensive information concerning physiology, pathology, and biotechnology of reproduction.
Formerly (until 1990): Zuchthygiene (0044-5371)
Related titles: ◆ Online - full text ed.: Reproduction in Domestic Animals (Online). ISSN 1439-0531; Supplement(s): Reproduction in Domestic Animals. Supplement. ISSN 0940-5496. 1991.
Indexed: A01, A03, A08, A22, A26, A34, A35, A36, A37, A38, ASCA, AgBio, Agr, B&BAb, B19, B25, BIOBASE, BIOSIS Prev, CA, CABA, CIN, ChemAb, ChemTitl, CurCont, D01, DBA, E01, E12, EMBASE, ExcerpMed, F08, FS&TA, FoVS&M, G11, GH, H12, H16, H17, IABS, ISR, IndVet, LT, MEDLINE, MaizeAb, MycolAb, N02, N04, P02, P10, P26, P30, P32, P33, P37, P39, P48, P52, P53, P54, P56, PGegResA, PN&I, PQC, R08, R12, R13, RA&MP, RM&VM, RRTA, RefZh, S10, S12, S13, S16, SCI, SCOPUS, SoyAb, T02, T05, TAR, TriticAb, VS, W07, W11, WildRev.
—BLDSC (7713.599600), CASDDS, IE, Infotrieve, Ingenta, INIST. **CCC.**
Published by: (European Society for Domestic Animal Reproduction NLD), Wiley-Blackwell Verlag GmbH (Subsidiary of: Wiley-Blackwell Publishing Ltd.), Kurfuerstendamm 57, Berlin, 10707, Germany. TEL 49-30-3279-0665, FAX 49-30-3279-0677, verlag@blackwell.de, http://www.blackwell.de. Ed. Dr. Heriberto Rodriguez-Martinez. Circ: 500.

636.089 GBR ISSN 0034-5288
SF601 CODEN: RVTSA9
➤ **RESEARCH IN VETERINARY SCIENCE.** Text in English. 1960. bi-m. EUR 756 in Europe to institutions; JPY 81,600 in Japan to institutions; USD 671 elsewhere to institutions (effective 2012). adv. bibl.; charts; illus.; abstr. index. back issues avail.; reprints avail. **Document type:** *Journal, Academic/Scholarly.* **Description:** Publishes original articles, reviews, and short communications in the veterinary sciences.
Related titles: Microform ed.: (from PMC, PQC); Online - full text ed.: ISSN 1532-2661. USD 561 to institutions (effective 2009) (from ScienceDirect).
Indexed: A01, A03, A08, A22, A26, A29, A34, A35, A36, A37, A38, ASCA, AgBio, Agr, AgrForAb, B20, B21, B23, B25, BIOSIS Prev, BP, BibAg, C25, CA, CABA, CIN, CTA, ChemAb, ChemTitl, ChemoAb, CurCont, D01, DBA, DentInd, E01, E12, EMBASE, ESPM, ExcerpMed, F08, FS&TA, FoVS&M, G11, GH, H16, H17, I05, I10, ISR, IndMed, IndVet, MEDLINE, MaizeAb, MycolAb, N02, N04, N05, NSA, OR, P30, P32, P33, P37, P39, P40, PN&I, R07, R08, R11, R12, R13, RA&MP, RM&VM, S12, S13, S16, SCI, SCOPUS, SoyAb, T02, T05, TAR, ToxAb, TriticAb, VS, ViroIAbstr, W07, W08, W10, W11, WildRev, Z01.
—BLDSC (7774.100000), CASDDS, GNLM, IE, Infotrieve, Ingenta, INIST. **CCC.**
Published by: (Association for Veterinary Teaching and Research), Elsevier Ltd (Subsidiary of: Elsevier Science & Technology), The Blvd, Langford Ln, Kidlington, Oxford, OX5 1GB, United Kingdom. TEL 44-1865-843000, FAX 44-1865-843010, customerserviceau@elsevier.com. Ed. A Livingston.

636.089 JOR ISSN 1819-5458
➤ **RESEARCH JOURNAL OF ANIMAL AND VETERINARY SCIENCES.** Text in English. a. free. **Document type:** *Journal, Academic/ Scholarly.*
Media: Online - full text. **Related titles:** CD-ROM ed.: ISSN 1816-2797; Print ed.: ISSN 1816-2746.
Indexed: A01, A34, A38, BA, C25, CA, CABA, D01, E12, FCA, G11, GH, H17, IndVet, N02, N03, N04, P33, P37, RA&MP, RM&VM, S12, T02, T05, TriticAb, VS.
Published by: American - Eurasian Network for Scientific Information, A E N S I Publications, c/o Dr. Abdel Rahman Mohammad Said Al-Tawaha, Al Hussein Bin Talal University, Biological Department, PO Box 20, Ma'an, Jordan. TEL 962-2-7305196. Eds. Abdel Rahman Al-Tawaha, Ajai Kumar Srivastav.

636.089 PAK ISSN 1993-5269
RESEARCH JOURNAL OF ANIMAL SCIENCES. Text in English. 2007. 4/yr. EUR 900 to individuals; EUR 1,200 to institutions; EUR 150 newsstand/cover (effective 2007). **Document type:** *Journal, Academic/Scholarly.*
Related titles: Online - full text ed.: ISSN 1994-4640. free (effective 2007).
Published by: Medwell Journals, ANSInet Bldg, 308-Lasani Town, Sargodha Rd, Faisalabad, 38090, Pakistan. TEL 92-41-5010004, 92-41-5004000, FAX 92-21-5206789, medwellonline@gmail.com, http://www.medwellonline.net, http://www.medwelljournals.com.

636.089 USA ISSN 1819-1908
➤ **RESEARCH JOURNAL OF VETERINARY SCIENCES.** Text in English. 2006. q. **Document type:** *Journal, Academic/Scholarly.* **Description:** Contains research articles and topical reviews on all aspects of the veterinary sciences.

Related titles: Online - full text ed.: ISSN 2151-786X. free (effective 2009).
Indexed: A01, A10, A29, A34, A35, A36, A38, B20, B21, CA, CABA, E12, ESPM, EntAb, GH, GenetAb, H17, IndVet, MaizeAb, N04, OGFA, P33, P37, P39, R08, RA&MP, T02, T05, TAR, V03, VS, W11.
Published by: Academic Journals Inc., 224, 5th Ave, No 2218, New York, NY 10001. FAX 888-777-8532, support@scialert.com, http://www.academicjournalsinc.com/.

636.089 USA
RESEARCH TODAY; the newsletter for benefactors of Grayson-Jockey Club Research Foundation, Inc. Variant title: Grayson-Jockey Club Research Today. Text in English. 1984. bi-m. free to members. back issues avail. **Document type:** *Newsletter.*
Formerly: Grayson Gram
Related titles: Online - full text ed.: free.
Published by: Grayson-Jockey Club Research Foundation, Inc., 821 Corporate Dr, Lexington, KY 40503. TEL 859-224-2850, FAX 859-224-2853, contactus@grayson-jockeyclub.org, http://www.grayson-jockeyclub.org/. Circ: 3,500.

636.089 BRA ISSN 1413-0130
REVISTA BRASILEIRA DE CIENCIA VETERINARIA. Text in Portuguese. 1986. 3/yr. **Document type:** *Journal, Academic/Scholarly.*
Formerly (until 1994): Arquivos Fluminenses de Medicina Veterinaria (0102-7794)
Indexed: A34, A35, A38, AgBio, AgrForAb, B23, BP, C25, CABA, D01, E12, F08, G11, GH, H16, H17, IndVet, N02, N03, N04, OR, P33, P37, P39, PN&I, R07, R08, R12, R13, RA&MP, RM&VM, S12, S13, S16, SoyAb, T05, TAR, VS, W10, W11, Z01.
Published by: Universidade Federal Fluminense, Faculdade de Veterinaria, Rua Vital Brasil 64, Santa Rosa, Niterol, RJ 24320-340, Brazil. TEL 55-21-26299514, cmv@vm.uff.br, http://www.uff.br.

636.089 BRA ISSN 0100-2430
REVISTA BRASILEIRA DE MEDICINA VETERINARIA. Text in Portuguese. 1971. q. **Document type:** *Journal, Trade.*
Indexed: A34, A35, A36, A37, A38, AgBio, C25, CABA, D01, E12, F08, F12, G11, GH, H16, H17, MaizeAb, N02, N03, N04, P32, P33, P37, P39, P40, R07, R08, R12, R13, S12, S13, S16, SCI, SoyAb, T05, TAR, W07, W10, W11.
Published by: Sociedade de Medicina Veterinaria do Estado do Rio de Janeiro, Av Presidente Vargas 446/1004, Rio de Janeiro, 20085-900, Brazil. http://somverj.org.br.

636.08 591.2 BRA ISSN 0103-846X
CODEN: RBPVEW
➤ **REVISTA BRASILEIRA DE PARASITOLOGIA VETERINARIA/ BRAZILIAN JOURNAL OF VETERINARY PARASITOLOGY.** Text in Portuguese. 1991. s-a. **Document type:** *Journal, Academic/ Scholarly.* **Description:** Presents original articles on basic or applied research in helminthology, protozoology and entomology, as related to animal health.
Related titles: Online - full text ed.: ISSN 1984-2961. free (effective 2011).
Indexed: A34, A35, A36, A37, A38, AgBio, AgrForAb, B23, B25, BIOSIS Prev, BP, C25, CABA, D01, E12, EMBASE, ExcerpMed, F08, F11, F12, GH, H16, H17, IndVet, MEDLINE, MycolAb, N02, N04, OR, P30, P33, P37, P39, PN&I, R07, R08, R12, RA&MP, RM&VM, SCI, SCOPUS, SoyAb, T05, TAR, VS, W07, W11, Z01.
Published by: Colegio Brasileiro de Parasitologia Veterinaria, Av. Prof. Lineu Prestes, 1374, Edif. Biomedicas II, Cidade Univer., Sao Paulo, SP 05508-900, Brazil. TEL 55-11-8187336, FAX 55-11-8187417, rbpv@hotmail.com.

➤ **REVISTA BRASILEIRA DE REPRODUCAO ANIMAL (ONLINE).** *see* BIOLOGY—Zoology

➤ **REVISTA BRASILEIRA DE SAUDE E PRODUCAO ANIMAL/ BRAZILIAN JOURNAL OF ANIMAL HEALTH AND PRODUCTION.** *see* BIOLOGY—Zoology

636.089 BRA ISSN 1516-3598
CODEN: RSBZBM
REVISTA BRASILEIRA DE ZOOTECNIA/BRAZILIAN JOURNAL OF ANIMAL SCIENCE. Text in Portuguese; Summaries in English. 1972. bi-m. bk.rev. back issues avail. **Document type:** *Journal, Academic/ Scholarly.*
Formerly (until 1996): Sociedade Brasileira de Zootecnia. Revista (0100-4859)
Related titles: Online - full text ed.: ISSN 1806-9290. free (effective 2011).
Indexed: A20, A34, A35, A36, A37, A38, AgBio, AgrForAb, B25, BA, BIOSIS Prev, BP, C01, C25, C30, CABA, ChemAb, ChemTitl, D01, E12, F08, F11, F12, FCA, G11, GH, H16, H17, I11, IndVet, MaizeAb, MycolAb, N02, N03, N04, O01, OR, P32, P33, P37, P39, P40, PGegResA, PHN&I, PN&I, R07, R08, R11, R12, R13, RA&MP, RM&VM, S&MA, S12, S13, S16, S17, SCI, SCOPUS, SoyAb, T05, TAR, TriticAb, VS, W07, W10, W11, WildRev, Z01.
—BLDSC (7845.804000), CASDDS, IE, Ingenta.
Published by: (Sociedade Brasileira de Zootecnia), Universidade Federal de Vicosa, Campus Universitario, Vicosa, MG 36570-000, Brazil. TEL 55-31-38991858, FAX 55-31-38992203, reitoria@mail.ufv.br, http://www.ufv.br. Ed. Martinho de Almeida Esilva. Circ: 2,000.

REVISTA CERES; orgao de divulgacao tecnico-cientifica em ciencias agrarias. *see* AGRICULTURE

636.089 COL ISSN 0120-0690
➤ **REVISTA COLOMBIANA DE CIENCIAS PECUARIAS.** Text and summaries in Spanish, English. 1978. q. COP 50,000 domestic; USD 50 foreign (effective 2010). bk.rev. Index. back issues avail. **Document type:** *Journal, Academic/Scholarly.*
Related titles: Online - full text ed.: free (effective 2011) (from SciELO).
Indexed: A34, A35, A37, A38, AgBio, AgrForAb, B23, BP, C25, C30, CABA, D01, E12, F08, F11, F12, FCA, G11, GH, H16, H17, IndVet, MaizeAb, N02, N03, N04, OR, P32, P33, P37, P39, P40, PGegResA, PN&I, R07, R08, R12, R13, RA&MP, RM&VM, S13, S16, SCI, SCOPUS, SoyAb, T05, TAR, VS, W07, W11.
Published by: Universidad de Antioquia, Facultad de Ciencias Agrarias, Cra 75 No. 65-87, Medellin, Colombia. TEL 57-4-425-9125, FAX 574-4259104, rccpecuarias@agronica.udea.edu.co, http://www.kogi.udea.edu.co/revista.

636.089 CUB ISSN 0048-7678
REVISTA CUBANA DE CIENCIAS VETERINARIAS. Text in Spanish; Summaries in Spanish, English. 1970. 2/yr. bk.rev. bibl.; charts; illus. **Document type:** *Journal, Academic/Scholarly.*
Related titles: Microfilm ed.
Indexed: ApicAb, B25, BIOSIS Prev, C01, IBR, IBZ, MycolAb. —Linda Hall.
Published by: (Consejo Cientifico Veterinario), Ediciones Cubanas, Obispo 527, Havana, Cuba.

636.08 ESP ISSN 1130-2739
REVISTA DE EXPERIMENTACION ANIMAL. Text in Spanish. 1990. s-a. **Document type:** *Journal, Academic/Scholarly.*
Indexed: IECT.
Published by: (Universidad de Leon, Facultad de Veterinaria), Universidad de Leon, Secretariado de Publicaciones, Campus de Vegazana, Leon, 24071, Spain. http://www.unileon.es.

REVISTA DE ICTIOLOGIA. *see* BIOLOGY—Zoology

636.089 PER ISSN 1682-3419
SF604 CODEN: RIPEDT
REVISTA DE INVESTIGACIONES VETERINARIAS DEL PERU. Text in English; Summaries in English. 1972. 3/yr. back issues avail. **Document type:** *Journal, Academic/Scholarly.*
Formerly (until 1999): Revista de Investigaciones Pecuarias (0376-4370)
Related titles: Online - full text ed.: ISSN 1609-9117. free (effective 2011).
Indexed: A34, A35, A37, A38, CABA, D01, E12, GH, H16, MaizeAb, N02, N04, P33, R08, S13, SoyAb, T05, W11, Z01.
Published by: Universidad Nacional Mayor de San Marcos, Facultad de Medicina Veterinaria, Av Circunvalacion Cdra 28 s-n, San Borja, Lima, Peru. TEL 51-1-4353348, FAX 51-1-4361027, decanovet@unmsm.edu.pe, http://www.unmsm.edu.pe.

636.089 ARG ISSN 0325-6391
REVISTA DE MEDICINA VETERINARIA. Text in Spanish. 1921. bi-m. ARS 80 membership (effective 2005). back issues avail. **Document type:** *Journal, Academic/Scholarly.*
Related titles: Online - full text ed.: ISSN 1852-771X. 1915.
Indexed: A22, A34, A36, A38, CABA, D01, E12, G11, GH, H17, IBR, IBZ, IndVet, LT, N02, N04, P30, P33, P37, P39, PN&I, R08, R12, R13, RM&VM, RRTA, T05, TAR, VS, W10, W11.
—BLDSC (7864.900000), IE, Ingenta, Linda Hall.
Published by: Sociedad de Medicina Veterinaria, Chile, 1856, Buenos Aires, 1227, Argentina. TEL 54-11-43817415, FAX 54-11-43838760, comunidad.ciudad.com.ar/ciudadanos/socmedvetar/. Ed. Faustino Fermin Carreras. Circ: 1,500.

636.089 COL ISSN 0122-9354
REVISTA DE MEDICINA VETERINARIA. Text in Spanish. 1997. s-a. **Document type:** *Journal, Academic/Scholarly.*
Related titles: Online - full text ed.: (from SciELO).
Published by: Universidad de la Salle., Facultad de Medicina Veterinaria, Cra 7-17285, Cundinamarca, Bogota, Colombia. TEL 57-1-6772699 ext. 238, fveterinaria@lasalle.edu.co, http://www.lasalle.edu.co/facultades/veterinaria/. Ed. Claudia Aixa Mutis Barreto.

636.089 CUB ISSN 0253-570X
SF1 CODEN: RSANDH
REVISTA DE SALUD ANIMAL. Text in Spanish; Summaries in English. 1979. 3/yr. charts; bibl. **Document type:** *Journal, Academic/ Scholarly.*
Related titles: Online - full text ed.
Indexed: A01, A26, A34, A35, A36, A37, A38, AgBio, AgrForAb, B23, B25, BIOSIS Prev, BP, C01, CA, CABA, CIN, ChemAb, ChemTitl, D01, E12, F03, F04, F08, F11, F12, FS&TA, GH, H16, H17, I04, IndVet, MycolAb, N02, N04, N05, OR, P32, P33, P37, P39, P40, PGrRegA, PHN&I, PN&I, R07, R08, R12, R13, RA&MP, RM&VM, SoyAb, T02, T05, TAR, VS, W11.
—BLDSC (7870.518000), CASDDS.
Published by: (Centro Nacional de Sanidad Agropecuaria), Ediciones Cubanas, Obispo 527, Havana, Cuba. TEL 53-7-631942, FAX 53-7-338943.

636.089 ESP ISSN 1695-7504
➤ **REVISTA ELECTRONICA DE VETERINARIA.** Abbreviated title: R E D V E T. Text in Spanish, Portuguese, English; Summaries in English, Spanish. 1996. m. free (effective 2011). **Document type:** *Journal, Academic/Scholarly.*
Media: Online - full text.
Indexed: A34, A35, A36, A37, A38, AgBio, AgrForAb, B23, BP, C25, C30, CABA, D01, E12, F08, F11, F12, FCA, G11, GH, H16, H17, I11, IndVet, LT, MaizeAb, N02, N03, N04, OR, P32, P33, P37, P39, P40, PN&I, R07, R08, R12, R13, RA&MP, RM&VM, RRTA, S12, S13, S16, SoyAb, T05, TAR, TriticAb, VS, W10, W11.
Published by: Veterinaria Organizacion, C/ Gerona 1, Malaga, 29006, Spain.

636.089 COL ISSN 0122-0268
REVISTA M V Z CORDOBA. (Medicina Veterinaria Zoologica) Text in Spanish; Summaries in English. 1996. s-a. COP 20,000 domestic; USD 15 in Latin America; USD 25 elsewhere (effective 2006). abstr. Index. back issues avail. **Document type:** *Journal, Academic/ Scholarly.* **Description:** Publishes on diverse topics in veterinary medicine, animal and human public health, aquiculture, biology and biotechnology, focusing on clinical practice.
Related titles: Online - full text ed.: ISSN 1909-0544. free (effective 2011).
Indexed: A01, A02, A03, A08, A26, A34, A35, A36, A38, AgBio, AgrForAb, B23, C25, C30, CA, CABA, D01, E12, F04, F08, F12, G11, GH, H16, H17, I04, I05, IndVet, MaizeAb, N02, N03, N04, P32, P33, P37, P39, P40, R07, R08, R11, R12, S13, S16, SCI, SCOPUS, SoyAb, T02, T05, TAR, VS, W07, W10, W11, Z01.
—IE.
Published by: Universidad de Cordoba, Facultad de Medicina Veterinaria y Zootecnia, Km 26, Via Cienega de Oro, Monteria, Colombia. TEL 57-47-560710, http://www.unicordoba.edu.co. Ed. Marco Gonzalez. Circ: 1,000.

636.089 PRT ISSN 0035-0389
REVISTA PORTUGUESA DE CIENCIAS VETERINARIAS. Text in Portuguese. 1953. q. adv. bk.rev. abstr.; bibl. index. back issues avail. **Document type:** *Journal, Academic/Scholarly.* **Description:** Papers from Portuguese researchers on all areas of veterinary science.
Formerly (until 1972): Revista de Ciencias Veterinarias (0375-0809)
Indexed: A22, A34, A35, A36, A37, A38, ASFA, AgBio, AgrForAb, B21, B23, B25, BIOSIS Prev, C25, CABA, D01, E12, ESPM, F08, FCA, FS&TA, G11, GH, H17, IBR, IBZ, IndVet, LT, MaizeAb, MycolAb, N02, N03, N04, OR, P33, P37, P39, PN&I, R07, R08, R12, R13, RM&VM, RRTA, S13, S16, SoyAb, T05, VS, W10, W11, Z01.
—BLDSC (7869.880000), IE, Ingenta.
Published by: Sociedade Portuguesa de Ciencias Veterinarias, Rua Gomes Freire, Lisbon, 1169-014, Portugal. TEL 351-21-3580222, FAX 351-21-3580221, spcvet@spcvet.pt, http://www.spcvet.pt/. Ed. Alexandre Leitao. Circ: 1,100.

636.089 ARG ISSN 1668-4834
REVISTA VETERINARIA. Text in Spanish, English, Portuguese. 1999. s-a. **Document type:** *Journal, Academic/Scholarly.*
Related titles: Online - full text ed.: free (effective 2011).
Indexed: A26, A34, A35, A36, A37, A38, AgBio, AgrForAb, CA, CABA, D01, E08, E12, F04, F08, F12, G11, GH, H16, H17, I04, I05, IndVet, MaizeAb, N02, N03, N04, P32, P33, P37, P39, PN&I, R08, R11, R12, R13, RA&MP, RM&VM, S09, S12, S13, S16, SoyAb, T02, T05, TAR, VS, W10, W11, Z01.
Published by: Universidad Nacional del Nordeste, Facultad de Ciencias Veterinarias, Sargento Cabral 2139, Corrientes, 3400, Argentina. Circ: 200.

636.089 VEN ISSN 0484-8284
REVISTA VETERINARIA VENEZOLANA. Text in Spanish. 1956. q. **Document type:** *Journal, Academic/Scholarly.*
Formerly (until 1956): Revista Grancolombiana de Zootecnia Higiene y Medicina Veterinaria
Published by: Federacion de Colegios de Medicos Veterinarios de Venezuela, Qta. Marilina, Av. Paez, Calle Stolk, El Paraiso, Apdo. 2921, Caracas, 102, Venezuela. Ed. Dr. C Ruiz Martinez.

636.089 COL ISSN 0120-4114
➤ **REVISTA VETERINARIA Y ZOOTECNICA DE CALDAS.** Text in Spanish. 1982. 2/yr. adv. back issues avail. **Document type:** *Journal, Academic/Scholarly.* **Description:** Contains research articles on animal medicine and husbandry.
Published by: Universidad de Caldas, Facultad de Medicina Veterinaria y Zootecnia, Calle 65 No 26, Manizales, CAL, Colombia. TEL 57-968-852139, FAX 57-968-862520, http://www.ucaldas.edu.co.

636.089 FRA ISSN 0035-1555
CODEN: RVMVAH
➤ **REVUE DE MEDECINE VETERINAIRE.** Text and summaries in French, English. 1838. m. EUR 147 domestic to individuals; EUR 175 elsewhere to individuals; EUR 132.30 domestic to libraries; EUR 157 foreign to libraries (effective 2008). adv. bk.rev. abstr.; illus. index. reprints avail. **Document type:** *Journal, Academic/Scholarly.* **Description:** Provides reviews, original reports, clinical reports.
Formerly (until 1936): Revue Veterinaire et Journal de Medecine Veterinaire et de Zootechnie Reunis (1255-3565)
Indexed: A20, A22, A34, A35, A36, A37, A38, ASCA, ASFA, AgBio, AgrForAb, B21, B23, BA, BP, C25, CA, CABA, CIN, ChemAb, ChemTitl, CurCont, D01, DBA, E12, ESPM, EntAb, F08, F11, F12, FCA, FS&TA, FoVS&M, G11, GH, H16, H17, IBR, IBZ, ISR, IndVet, MaizeAb, N02, N03, N04, P30, P32, P33, P37, P39, PN&I, PsycholAb, R07, R08, R11, R12, R13, RA&MP, RM&VM, RefZh, S12, S13, S16, SAA, SCI, SCOPUS, SoyAb, T02, T05, TAR, TriticAb, VS, W07, W08, W10, W11, WildRev.
—BLDSC (7932.000000), CASDDS, GNLM, IE, Infotrieve, Ingenta, INIST, Linda Hall. **CCC.**
Published by: Ecole Nationale Veterinaire de Toulouse, 23 Chemin des Capelles, Toulouse, 31076, France. TEL 33-561-193835, FAX 33-561-193835. Ed. A Milon.

636.089 FRA ISSN 1951-6711
SF602
REVUE D'ELEVAGE ET DE MEDECINE VETERINAIRE DES PAYS TROPICAUX (ONLINE). Text in English, French; Summaries in English, French, Spanish. 1947. 4/yr. adv. bk.rev. abstr.; bibl.; charts. index, cum.index: 1947-1977. **Document type:** *Journal, Academic/ Scholarly.*
Formerly (until 2006): Revue d'Elevage et de Medecine Veterinaire des Pays Tropicaux (Print) (0035-1865)
Media: Online - full text. **Related titles:** Microfiche ed.
Indexed: A22, A34, A37, A38, B21, CABA, D01, DBA, E12, F08, F12, FR, FS&TA, G11, GH, H16, H17, IndMed, IndVet, N02, N03, N04, P30, P32, P33, P37, P39, PGegResA, PN&I, R08, R11, R12, S13, S16, SCOPUS, SPPI, T05, TAR, TOSA, VS, VirolAbstr, W11, Z01.
—GNLM, IE, Infotrieve, Ingenta, INIST. **CCC.**
Published by: C I R A D, Campus International de Baillarguet, Montpellier, 34398 Cedex 5, France. TEL 33-4-67614417, FAX 33-4-67615547, librairie@cirad.fr, http://www.cirad.fr. Circ: (controlled).

636.089 JPN ISSN 0912-1501
RINSHO JUI/JOURNAL OF CLINICAL VETERINARY MEDICINE. Text in Japanese. 1983. m. JPY 25,200 (effective 2007). **Document type:** *Magazine, Trade.* **Description:** Designed for large animal veterinarians. Covers clinical medicine for large animals.
Published by: Midori Shobo Co. Ltd. (Subsidiary of: Midori Group), JPR Crest Takebashi Bldg., 3-21 Kanda Nishikicho Chiyoda-ku, Tokyo, 101-0054, Japan. info@mgp.co.jp, http://www.mgp.co.jp/. Circ: 36,000.

636.089 RUS
➤ **ROSSIISKII VETERINARNYI ZHURNAL. MELKIE DOMASHNIE I DIKIE ZHIVOTNYE/RUSSIAN VETERINARY JOURNAL. SMALL DOMESTIC AND WILD ANIMALS.** Text in Russian. 2005. q. USD 90 in United States (effective 2011). **Document type:** *Journal, Academic/Scholarly.*
Published by: Izdatel'stvo Koloss (Subsidiary of: Pleiades Publishing, Inc.), Astrahanskii per., dom 8, Moscow, 129090, Russian Federation. TEL 7-495-6801463, FAX 7-495-6801463, sda@koloss.ru, http://www.koloss.ru. Ed. S A Yagnikov. Circ: 3,000. **Dist. by:** East View Information Services, 10601 Wayzata Blvd, Minneapolis, MN 55305. TEL 952-252-1201, FAX 952-252-1202, info@eastview.com, http://www.eastview.com.

636.089 GBR ISSN 0966-6303
ROYAL COLLEGE OF VETERINARY SURGEONS. DIRECTORY OF VETERINARY PRACTICES (YEAR). Text in English. 1991. a. GBP 65 per issue (effective 2009). **Document type:** *Directory, Trade.* **Description:** Provides a comprehensive listing of veterinary services in the UK.
Published by: Royal College of Veterinary Surgeons, Belgravia House, 62-64 Horseferry Rd, London, SW1P 2AF, United Kingdom. TEL 44-20-72222001, FAX 44-20-72222004, admin@rcvs.org.uk, http://www.rcvs.org.uk/.

636.08902541 GBR ISSN 1474-2063
ROYAL COLLEGE OF VETERINARY SURGEONS. REGISTER OF MEMBERS (YEAR). Text in English. 1870. a. (Nov.). GBP 40 per issue domestic to non-members; GBP 50 per issue foreign to non-members; free per issue to members (effective 2009). **Document type:** *Directory, Trade.* **Description:** Provides a full alphabetical listing of Members and Fellows of the RCVS with their qualifications and also lists RCVS Honours and Awards, certificate and diploma holders, RCVS recognized specialists along with lists of those employed in the veterinary schools and other organizations.
Formerly (until 2000): Royal College of Veterinary Surgeons. Registers and Directory (0305-6643)
Published by: Royal College of Veterinary Surgeons, Belgravia House, 62-64 Horseferry Rd, London, SW1P 2AF, United Kingdom. TEL 44-20-72222001, FAX 44-20-72222004, admin@rcvs.org.uk.

636.089 ITA ISSN 1593-4373
S I VE M P. ARGOMENTI. (Sindacato Italiano Veterinari Medicina Pubblica) Cover title: Argomenti. Text in Italian. 1989. m. **Document type:** *Magazine, Trade.*
Formerly (until 1998): Il Veterinario d'Italia (1593-0998)
Published by: Sindacato Italiano Veterinari Medicina Pubblica, Via Nizza 11, Rome, 00198, Italy.

636.089 SWE ISSN 1654-7098
S V A. RAPPORTSERIE. Text in Swedish. 2007. irreg. **Document type:** *Monographic series, Academic/Scholarly.*
Published by: Statens Veterinaermedicinska Anstalt/National Veterinary Institute, Ulls Vaeg 2 B, Uppsala, 75189, Sweden. TEL 46-18-674000, FAX 46-18-409162, sva@sva.se, http://www.sva.se.

636.089 SWE ISSN 0281-7519
S V A VET. (Statens Veterinaermedicinska Anstalt) Text in Swedish. 1984. q. free (effective 2008). back issues avail. **Document type:** *Magazine, Government.*
Related titles: Online - full text ed.
Published by: Statens Veterinaermedicinska Anstalt/National Veterinary Institute, Ulls Vaeg 2 B, Uppsala, 75189, Sweden. TEL 46-18-674000, FAX 46-18-409162, sva@sva.se. Ed. Helena Ohlsson.

636.089 CHE ISSN 0036-7281
CODEN: SATHAA
➤ **SCHWEIZER ARCHIV FUER TIERHEILKUNDE.** Text in German. 1816. m. CHF 328 domestic; EUR 218 in Europe (effective 2011). adv. 64 p./no.; **Document type:** *Journal, Academic/Scholarly.*
Formerly (until 1883): Archiv fuer Thierheilkunde (0258-9419)
Related titles: Online - full text ed.: ISSN 1664-2848.
Indexed: A20, A22, A34, A35, A36, A37, A38, ASCA, AgBio, B25, BIOSIS Prev, CABA, ChemAb, CurCont, D01, DBA, E12, EMBASE, ExcerpMed, F08, F12, FS&TA, FoVS&M, G11, GH, H16, H17, ISR, IndMed, IndVet, KWIWR, LT, MEDLINE, MycolAb, N02, N04, OR, P30, P32, P33, P37, P39, PN&I, R08, R13, RA&MP, RM&VM, RRTA, S12, S13, S16, SAA, SCI, SCOPUS, T05, TAR, VS, W07, W08, W10, W11, WildRev.
—BLDSC (8110.000000), CASDDS, GNLM, IE, Infotrieve, Ingenta, INIST. **CCC.**
Published by: (Gesellschaft Schweizer Tieraerztinnen und Tieraerzte), Verlag Hans Huber AG (Subsidiary of: Hogrefe Verlag GmbH & Co. KG), Laenggassstr 76, Bern 9, 3000, Switzerland. TEL 41-31-3004500, FAX 41-31-3004590, verlag@hanshuber.com, http://www.hanshuber.com. Ed. Dr. Rico Thun. Circ: 2,610 (controlled).

➤ **SCIENTIA AGRICULTURAE BOHEMICA.** *see* AGRICULTURE

636.089 FRA ISSN 0396-5015
SEMAINE VETERINAIRE. Text in French. 1976. 45/yr. EUR 210.58 domestic to individuals; EUR 115.57 domestic to students; EUR 261.51 in the European Union to individuals; EUR 198.82 in the European Union to students; EUR 308.51 elsewhere to individuals; EUR 245.82 elsewhere to students (effective 2009). adv. **Document type:** *Newspaper, Trade.*
Incorporates: Eurovet
—CCC.
Published by: Point Veterinaire S.A. (Subsidiary of: Wolters Kluwer N.V.), 9 rue Alexandre, BP 233, Maisons-Alfort, Cedex 94702, France. TEL 33-01-45170225, FAX 33-01-45170274, edpoint@wanadoo.fr, http://www.pointveterinaire.com. Ed. Maryvonne Barbaray. Adv. contact Nadege Humbert. Circ: 5,000.

636.089 ITA ISSN 1825-3253
LA SETTIMANA VETERINARIA. Text in Italian. 1994. w. EUR 67 domestic; EUR 170 foreign (effective 2009). **Document type:** *Magazine, Trade.*
Published by: Point Veterinaire Italie Srl (Subsidiary of: Wolters Kluwer N.V.), Via Medardo Rosso 11, Milan, 20159, Italy. TEL 39-02-6085231, FAX 39-02-6682866, info@pointvet.it, http://www.pointvet.it.

636.089 CHN ISSN 1000-7725
SHANGHAI XUMU SHOUYI TONGXUN/SHANGHAI JOURNAL OF ANIMAL HUSBANDRY AND VETERINARY MEDICINE. Text in Chinese. 1956. bi-m. CNY 6 newsstand/cover (effective 2007). adv. bk.rev.
Related titles: Online - full text ed.
Published by: Shanghai-shi Nongye Kexueyuan, Xumu Shouyi Yanjiusuo/Shanghai Academy of Agricultural Science, Institute of Veterinary Science, 2901, Beidi Lu, Shanghai, 201106, China. TEL 86-21-62206294, FAX 86-21-62207858.

SHEEP & GOAT HEALTH REPORT (ONLINE). *see* AGRICULTURE—Poultry And Livestock

636.089 GBR ISSN 1367-1138
SHEEP VETERINARY SOCIETY. PROCEEDINGS. Text in English. 199?. a. free (effective 2009). **Document type:** *Proceedings, Trade.* **Description:** Features papers presented at the scientific meetings of British Veterinary Association.
Formerly (until 1990): Sheep Veterinary Society. Annual Proceedings
—BLDSC (6847.448000), IE. **CCC.**
Published by: Sheep Veterinary Society (Subsidiary of: British Veterinary Association), Moredun Research Institute, Pentlands Science Park, Bush Loan, Penicuik, Midlothian, EH26 0PZ, United Kingdom. TEL 44-131-4455111, FAX 44-131-4456235, secretariat@sheepvetsoc.org.uk.

SINGAPORE JOURNAL OF PRIMARY INDUSTRIES. *see* AGRICULTURE

636.089 SGP ISSN 0129-3826
SINGAPORE VETERINARY JOURNAL. Text in English. 1977. s-a. membership. **Document type:** *Journal, Academic/Scholarly.*
Indexed: Agr.
Published by: Singapore Veterinary Association, c/o Agri-food & Veterinary Authority, 5 Maxwell Rd #03-00, National Development Bldg., Singapore, 069110, Singapore. FAX 65-62-206068, sva@sva.org.sg.

636.089 SVN ISSN 1580-4003
➤ **SLOVENIAN VETERINARY RESEARCH/SLOVENSKI VETERINARSKI ZBORNIK.** Text in English; Summaries in Slovenian. 1960. q. USD 37 foreign (effective 2007). back issues avail. **Document type:** *Journal, Academic/Scholarly.* **Description:** Publishes scientific papers, review articles, professional papers, summaries of thesis, and other items such as critical reviews of articles published in research reports, letters to the editors and such others.
Former titles (until 2000): University of Ljubljana. Veterinary Faculty. Research Reports (1408-8495); Univerza v Ljubljani. Veterinarska Fakulteta. Zbornik (0353-8044); (until 1990): Univerza E. Kardelja v Ljubljani. Biotehniska Fakulteta. Zbornik. Veterinarstvo (0300-0362)
Related titles: Online - full text ed.: free (effective 2011).
Indexed: A01, A34, A35, A36, A37, A38, AgBio, C25, CABA, D01, E12, F08, GH, H16, H17, IndVet, LT, N02, N03, N04, OR, P30, P32, P33, P37, P39, PN&I, R07, R08, RA&MP, RM&VM, S12, S13, S16, SCI, SCOPUS, T02, TAR, TriticAb, VS, W07, W10, W11, WildRev.
—BLDSC (8309.635000), INIST.
Published by: Univerza v Ljubljani, Veterinarska Fakulteta/University of Ljubljana, Veterinary Faculty, Gerbiceva 60, Ljubljana, 1000, Slovenia. TEL 386-1-4779129, FAX 386-1-2832243. Ed. Gregor Majdic. Circ: 500.

➤ **SMALL RUMINANT RESEARCH.** *see* AGRICULTURE—Poultry And Livestock

636.089 FRA ISSN 1635-3501
SOCIETE VETERINAIRE PRATIQUE DE FRANCE. BULLETIN. Text in French. 1881. bi-m. **Document type:** *Bulletin, Trade.*
Former titles (until 2002): Societe Veterinaire Pratique de France. Bulletin Bimestriel (1620-8706); (until 1999): Societe Veterinaire Pratique de France. Bulletin Mensuel (0395-7500); (until 1924): Societe de Medecine Veterinaire Pratique. Bulletin Mensuel (1268-7022); (until 1903): Societe de Medecine Veterinaire Pratique. Bulletin (1268-7014)
Indexed: A34, A36, A38, CABA, D01, E12, GH, H16, H17, IndVet, LT, N02, N03, N04, P30, P33, P37, P39, PN&I, R08, R12, R13, RM&VM, S13, S16, T05, TAR, VS, W11.
—BLDSC (2757.330000), IE, Ingenta.
Published by: Societe Veterinaire Pratique de France, 10 Placee Leon Blum, Paris, 75011, France.

636.089 GBR ISSN 0956-7496
SF780.9
SOCIETY FOR VETERINARY EPIDEMIOLOGY AND PREVENTIVE MEDICINE. PROCEEDINGS OF A MEETING. Text in English. 1983. a. back issues avail. **Document type:** *Proceedings.* **Description:** Covers the proceedings of the annual conference held in London, UK by Society for Veterinary Epidemiology and Preventive Medicine.
Indexed: Agr.
—BLDSC (6817.400000), IE, Ingenta.
Published by: Society for Veterinary Epidemiology and Preventive Medicine, c/o Mike, Dept. Veterinary Clinical Studies, University of Edinburgh, Easter Bush Veterinary Centre, Roslin, Midlothian EH9 1QH, United Kingdom. TEL 44-131-6506223, FAX 44-131-6506588, http://www.svepm.org.uk/. Eds. Lis Alban, Louise Kelly.

SODOBNO KMETIJSTVO. *see* AGRICULTURE

SOUTH AFRICAN JOURNAL OF ANIMAL SCIENCE. *see* AGRICULTURE—Poultry And Livestock

636.089 ZAF
CODEN: JAVTAP
➤ **SOUTH AFRICAN VETERINARY ASSOCIATION. SCIENTIFIC JOURNAL.** Text in English. 1929. q. USD 450; USD 384 to agents (effective 2002). adv. bk.rev. abstr.; charts; illus. index. back issues avail. **Document type:** *Journal, Academic/Scholarly.* **Description:** Includes reviews on various topics, clinical and non-clinical articles, research articles and short communications as well as case reports and letters on veterinary.
Former titles: South African Veterinary Association. Journal (1019-9128); (until 1972): South African Veterinary Medical Association. Journal (0038-2809)
Indexed: A01, A22, A34, A35, A36, A37, A38, ASCA, AgBio, AgrForAb, B25, BIOSIS Prev, BP, CA, CABA, CIN, ChemAb, ChemTitl, CurCont, D01, DBA, DentInd, E12, EMBASE, ExcerpMed, F08, F12, FoVS&M, G11, GH, H16, H17, ISAP, IndMed, IndVet, MEDLINE, MaizeAb, MycolAb, N02, N04, O01, P30, P33, P37, P39, PN&I, R07, R08, R12, R13, RA&MP, RM&VM, S12, S13, S16, SAA, SCI, SCOPUS, SoyAb, T02, T05, TAR, VS, W07, W08, W10, W11, WildRev, Z01.
—BLDSC (4901.950000), CASDDS, GNLM, IE, Ingenta, INIST. **CCC.**
Published by: South African Veterinary Association, Monument Park, PO Box 25033, Pretoria, 0105, South Africa. TEL 27-12-3461150, FAX 27-12-3462929. Ed. Dr. M Penrith. Adv. contact K S Harpur. Circ: 1,600.

636.089 LKA
SRI LANKA VETERINARY JOURNAL. Text in English. 1953. s-a. USD 10. adv. bk.rev. abstr.; charts; illus. index.
Formerly (until 1982): Ceylon Veterinary Journal (0009-0891)
Indexed: ChemAb, SAA, SLSI.
Published by: Veterinary Research Institute, Peradeniya, Sri Lanka. Ed. S T Fernando. Circ: 1,000.

636.089 SWE
STATENS VETERINAERMEDICINSKA ANSTALT. AARSREDOVISNING. Text in Swedish. 1994. a. back issues avail. **Document type:** *Government.*
Former titles (until 2005): Statens Veterinaermedicinska Anstalt. Aarsberaettelse; (until 2000): Statens Veterinaermedicinska Anstalt. Aarsredovisning (1104-6996)
Related titles: Online - full text ed.
Published by: Statens Veterinaermedicinska Anstalt/National Veterinary Institute, Ulls Vaeg 2 B, Uppsala, 75189, Sweden. TEL 46-18-674000, FAX 46-18-409162, sva@sva.se.

636.089 EGY ISSN 1110-6298
SUEZ CANAL VETERINARY MEDICINE JOURNAL/MAGALLAT TIBB BITARI QANAT AL-SUWIS. Text in English. 1998. s-a. **Document type:** *Journal, Academic/Scholarly.*
Published by: Suez Canal University, Faculty of Veterinary Medicine, Faculty of Veterinary Medicine Ismailiyat, Ismailia, Egypt. Ed. Dr. S M El-Nahla.

636.4 ESP ISSN 1699-7867
SUIS. Text in Spanish. 2003. m. (10/yr.). EUR 90 domestic (effective 2009). **Document type:** *Magazine, Trade.*
Indexed: A34, A35, A36, A37, A38, AgBio, AgrForAb, B23, BA, C25, CABA, D01, E12, F08, G11, GH, H16, H17, IndVet, LT, MaizeAb, N02, N04, P32, P33, P39, PN&I, R07, R08, R11, R12, R13, RM&VM, RRTA, S12, S13, S16, SoyAb, T05, TAR, TriticAb, VS, W11.
Published by: Grupo Asis, Andar del Palacio Larrinaga 2, Zaragoza, 50013, Spain. TEL 34-976-461480, http://www.grupoasis.com.

636.089 ITA ISSN 1828-5538
SUMMA ANIMALI DA COMPAGNIA. Text in Italian. 1984. 10/yr. EUR 95 domestic; EUR 182 foreign (effective 2009). **Document type:** *Magazine, Trade.*
Supersedes in part (in 2005): Summa (1125-6745)
—BLDSC (8518.578550).
Published by: Point Veterinaire Italie Srl (Subsidiary of: Wolters Kluwer N.V.), Via Medardo Rosso 11, Milan, 20159, Italy. TEL 39-02-6085231, FAX 39-02-6682866, info@pointvet.it, http://www.pointvet.it. Ed. Dr. J P Dagneauz.

636.089 ITA ISSN 1828-5546
SUMMA ANIMALI DA REDDITO. Text in Italian. 1984. 10/yr. EUR 95 domestic; EUR 182 foreign (effective 2009). **Document type:** *Magazine, Trade.*
Supersedes in part (in 2005): Summa (1125-6745)
—BLDSC (8518.578570).
Published by: Point Veterinaire Italie Srl (Subsidiary of: Wolters Kluwer N.V.), Via Medardo Rosso 11, Milan, 20159, Italy. TEL 39-02-6085231, FAX 39-02-6682866, info@pointvet.it, http://www.pointvet.it.

636.089 FIN ISSN 0039-5501
SUOMEN ELAINLAAKARILEHTI/FINSK VETERINAERTIDSKRIFT. Text in Finnish, Swedish; Summaries in English. 1893. m. EUR 80 (effective 2003). adv. bk.rev. bibl.; charts; illus. **Document type:** *Magazine, Academic/Scholarly.*
Indexed: A22, A34, A36, A37, A38, ApicAb, CABA, D01, E12, FS&TA, GH, H17, IndVet, N02, N03, N04, OR, P33, P37, P39, PN&I, R08, R11, RM&VM, SAA, VS, W11.
—BLDSC (8541.800000), IE, Ingenta.
Published by: Suomen Elainlaakariliitto/Finnish Veterinary Association, Maekelaenkatu 2 C, Helsinki, 00500, Finland. TEL 358-9-77454810, FAX 358-9-77454818, http://www.sell.fi. Ed. Marjut Hamalainen. Adv. contact Pirkko Nousiainen. Circ: 2,100.

636.089 NZL ISSN 0112-4927
SURVEILLANCE. Text in English. 1973. q. NZD 32 domestic; NZD 48 foreign; free to qualified personnel (effective 2008). **Document type:** *Magazine, Consumer.*
Formerly (until 1974): Veterinary Case Reports (0112-7152)
Related titles: Online - full text ed.: ISSN 1176-5305.
Indexed: A22, A34, A36, CABA, D01, E12, GH, H17, IndVet, LT, N04, P33, P37, P39, PN&I, R07, R08, RRTA, T05, VS, W10, W11.
—BLDSC (8548.383500), IE, Ingenta. **CCC.**
Published by: Ministry of Agriculture and Forestry, Biosecurity New Zealand, PO Box 2526, Wellington, New Zealand. TEL 64-4-8940560, FAX 64-4-8940720, info.biosecurity@maf.govt.nz. Ed. Elizabeth Sommerville.

636.089 NOR ISSN 1503-1454
SURVEILLANCE AND CONTROL PROGRAMMES FOR TERRESTRIAL AND AQUATIC ANIMALS IN NORWAY. Text in English. 2002. irreg. **Document type:** *Monographic series, Academic/Scholarly.*
Related titles: Online - full text ed.: ISSN 1890-9973. 2004.
Published by: Veterinaerinstituttet/National Veterinary Institute, PO Box 750, Sentrum, Oslo, 0106, Norway. TEL 47-23-216000, FAX 47-23-216001, postmottag@vetinst.no. Ed. Anne-Brit Haug.

636.089 SWE ISSN 0346-2250
SVENSK VETERINAERTIDNING. Text in Swedish. 1896. 16/yr. SEK 1,110 domestic; SEK 1,430 in Europe; SEK 1,610 elsewhere (effective 2008). adv. bk.rev. Supplement avail.; back issues avail. **Document type:** *Magazine, Trade.* **Description:** Articles of interest to veterinarians and news about the association.
Former titles (until 1964): Medlemsblad foer Sveriges Veterinaerfoerbund; (until 1950): Svenska Veterinaerlaekarefoereningens Medlemsblad
Related titles: Online - full text ed.
Indexed: A22, A34, A35, A36, A37, A38, AgBio, B23, CABA, D01, E12, FS&TA, GH, H16, H17, IndVet, MaizeAb, N02, N03, N04, OR, P33, P37, P39, PN&I, R07, R08, R13, RA&MP, RM&VM, S12, SoyAb, TAR, VS, W10, W11.
—BLDSC (8562.598000), IE, Ingenta.
Published by: Sveriges Veterinaerfoerbund/Swedish Veterinary Association, Kungsholms Hamnplan 7, Box 12709, Stockholm, 12709, Sweden. TEL 46-8-54555820, FAX 46-8-54555839, office@svf.se. Ed. Johan Beck-Friis TEL 46-8-54555833. Adv. contact Birgitta Ahlkvist TEL 46-08-54555831. B&W page SEK 10,100, color page SEK 15,500; trim 216 x 303.

SWINE HEALTH REPORT. *see* AGRICULTURE—Poultry And Livestock

636.089 TWN ISSN 1682-6485
CODEN: CKSCDN
TAIWAN SHOUYIXUE ZAZHI/TAIWAN VETERINARY JOURNAL. Variant title: T'ai Wan Shou I Hsueh Tsa Chih. Text in Chinese, English. 1975. q. free to members. **Document type:** *Journal, Academic/Scholarly.*
Formerly (until 2001): Zhonghua Minguo Shouyi Xuehui Zazhi/Chinese Society of Veterinary Science. Journal (0253-9179)
Indexed: A34, A35, A36, A37, A38, AgBio, B25, BIOSIS Prev, CABA, CIN, ChemAb, ChemTitl, D01, E12, GH, H16, H17, IndVet, MycolAb, N02, N03, N04, P33, P37, P39, PN&I, R08, RA&MP, RM&VM, S13, S16, SoyAb, T05, TAR, VS, W11, WildRev, Z01.
—BLDSC (8600.510000), CASDDS, IE, Ingenta.
Published by: Zhonghua Minguo Shouyi Xuehui/Chinese Society of Veterinary Science, PO Box 23-3, Taipei, 106, Taiwan. TEL 886-2-23661451.

636.089 IND ISSN 0973-2942
CODEN: CHRNAR
TAMILNADU JOURNAL OF VETERINARY AND ANIMAL SCIENCES. Text in English. 1972. bi-m. INR 300 domestic; USD 50 foreign (effective 2010). adv. index. back issues avail. **Description:** Focuses on technology development with coverage of key topic areas in veterinary, animal and fishery sciences.
Formerly (until 2005): Cheiron (0379-542X)
Indexed: A22, A34, A35, A37, A38, AgBio, AgrForAb, B23, BP, BioDAb, C25, C30, CABA, ChemAb, D01, E12, F08, F11, F12, FCA, FS&TA, GH, H16, H17, IndVet, MaizeAb, N02, N03, N04, O01, OR, P32, P33, P37, P39, PHN&I, PN&I, R08, R11, R12, RA&MP, RM&VM, S12, S13, S16, SoyAb, T05, TAR, TOSA, TriticAb, VS, W10, W11, Z01.
—BLDSC (8601.559420), CASDDS, IE, Ingenta.
Published by: Tamil Nadu Veterinary & Animal Science University, Madhavaram Milk Colony, Chennai, Tamil Nadu 600 051, India. TEL 91-44-25551575, FAX 91-44-25551575, tanuvas@vsnl.com. Ed. M Mohamed Habibulla Khan. adv.: B&W page INR 1,000. Circ: 750.

636.089 ARG ISSN 1515-3037
TAURUS. Text in Spanish. 1999. q. ARS 60 domestic; USD 50 foreign. back issues avail. **Document type:** *Magazine, Consumer.*
Published by: Ediciones Taurus, Ratreador Fournier 2110, Los Olivos, Buenos Aires, 1636, Argentina. TEL 54-11-4795-2594, revistataurus@fibertel.com.ar, http://www.revistataurus.com.ar/index.html. Ed. Sergio Marcantonio. Circ: 1,100.

636.089 DEU ISSN 1869-3202
TEAM.KONKRET. Text in German. 2005. 4/yr. EUR 34.95 to institutions; EUR 102 combined subscription to institutions (print & online eds.); EUR 34.95 to students; EUR 11.50 newsstand/cover (effective 2011). adv. **Document type:** *Journal, Academic/Scholarly.*
Formerly (until 2010): Tierarzthelferin Konkret (1614-8754)
Related titles: Online - full text ed.: EUR 102 to institutions (effective 2011).
—IE. **CCC.**
Published by: Enke Verlag in M V S Medizinverlage Stuttgart GmbH und Co. KG (Subsidiary of: Georg Thieme Verlag), Oswald-Hesse-Str 50, Stuttgart, 70469, Germany. TEL 49-711-89310, FAX 49-711-8931706, kunden.service@thieme.de. Ed. Ulrike Arnold. Adv. contact Ilona Reiser. B&W page EUR 1,120, color page EUR 1,690; trim 210 x 280. Circ: 2,900 (paid).

636.089 DEU ISSN 1868-1948
TEAM SPIEGEL. Text in German. 4/yr. adv. **Document type:** *Journal, Trade.*
Related titles: Online - full text ed.: ISSN 1868-193X.
—**CCC.**
Published by: Enke Verlag in M V S Medizinverlage Stuttgart GmbH und Co. KG (Subsidiary of: Georg Thieme Verlag), Oswald-Hesse-Str 50, Stuttgart, 70469, Germany. TEL 49-711-89310, FAX 49-711-8931706, kunden.service@thieme.de. Ed. Leonie Loeffler. adv.: B&W page EUR 1,500, color page EUR 1,890; trim 190 x 260. Circ: 6,000 (controlled).

636.089 USA
TECH TALK. Text in English. 2005. bi-m. free to members (effective 2009). back issues avail. **Document type:** *Newsletter, Trade.* **Description:** Promotes the dissemination of professional information and technology to all persons interested in laboratory animal science and facilitates a worldwide pursuit of knowledge of animal care methodology.
Related titles: Online - full text ed.
Published by: American Association for Laboratory Animal Science, 9190 Crestwyn Hills Dr, Memphis, TN 38125. TEL 901-754-8620, FAX 901-753-0046, info@aalas.org. Ed. Patty Denison.

636.089 USA ISSN 1071-0566
TEXAS VETERINARIAN. Text in English. 1939. bi-m. free to members. adv. bk.rev. charts; illus.; stat. **Document type:** *Magazine, Trade.*
Formerly (until Apr. 1993): Texas Veterinary Medical Journal (0040-4756)
Published by: Texas Veterinary Medical Association, 8104 Exchange Dr, Austin, TX 78754-5239. TEL 512-452-4224, FAX 512-452-6633, info@tvma.org, http://www.tvma.org. Ed. Donald M Ward. Adv. contact Ellen Smith. Circ: 3,000.

636.089 USA ISSN 0093-691X
SF105.7 CODEN: THGNBO
➤ **THERIOGENOLOGY**; an international journal of animal reproduction. Text in English. 1974. 18/yr. USD 1,877 in United States to institutions; USD 2,134 elsewhere to institutions (effective 2012). adv. abstr. back issues avail.; reprints avail. **Document type:** *Journal, Academic/Scholarly.* **Description:** Publishes articles on a wide range of topics in reproductive biology and biotechnology, including basic and applied studies in cryobiology of gametes and embryos, conservation biology, and assisted reproduction of domestic, wild, avian, and aquatic species.
Incorporates (2001-2004): Society for Theriogenology. S F T Annual Conference and Symposium; Which was formerly (until 2001): Society for Theriogenology. Proceedings of the Annual Conference; (until 1999): Society for Theriogenology. Proceedings of the Annual Meeting; (until 197?): American Veterinary Society for the Study of Breeding Soundness. Proceedings of the Annual Meeting
Related titles: Microfiche ed.: (from PQC); Online - full text ed.: ISSN 1879-3231 (from IngentaConnect, ScienceDirect).
Indexed: A01, A03, A08, A22, A26, A34, A35, A36, A37, A38, ASCA, AgBio, Agr, B23, B25, BIOBASE, BIOSIS Prev, BibAg, BibRep, CA, CABA, CIN, ChemAb, ChemTitl, CurCont, D01, DBA, E12, EMBASE, ExcerpMed, F08, FoVS&M, G11, GH, H16, I05, IABS, ISR, IndMed, IndVet, Inpharma, LT, MEDLINE, MaizeAb, MycolAb, N02, N04, OR, P30, P32, P33, P37, P39, PGegResA, PN&I, R08, R10, R12, R13, RA&MP, RM&VM, RRTA, Reac, S12, S13, S16, S17, SAA, SCI, SCOPUS, SoyAb, T02, T05, TAR, TriticAb, VS, W07, W08, W10, W11, WildRev, Z01.
—BLDSC (8814.773000), CASDDS, IE, Infotrieve, Ingenta, INIST. **CCC.**
Published by: Elsevier Inc. (Subsidiary of: Elsevier Science & Technology), 1600 John F Kennedy Blvd, Philadelphia, PA 19103. TEL 215-239-3900, FAX 215-238-7883, JournalCustomerService-usa@elsevier.com, http://www.elsevier.com. Eds. Fulvio Gandolfi, John P Kastelic. Pub. Anthony F Trioli TEL 215-239-3733.

636.089 DEU ISSN 1434-1220
TIERAERZTLICHE PRAXIS. AUSGABE G: GROSSTIERE - NUTZTIERE. Text in German. 1973. bi-m. EUR 140 to individuals; EUR 249 to institutions; EUR 72 to students; EUR 44 newsstand/cover (effective 2011). adv. **Document type:** *Journal, Academic/Scholarly.*
Supersedes in part (in 1997): Tieraerztliche Praxis (0303-6286)
Indexed: A22, A34, A35, A36, A37, A38, AgBio, AgrForAb, CABA, D01, DBA, E12, F08, FoVS&M, G11, GH, H17, IndMed, IndVet, MaizeAb, N02, N03, N04, P30, P33, P37, P39, PN&I, R08, RM&VM, S13, S16, SCI, SCOPUS, SpeleolAb, T05, TAR, VS, W07, W10, W11, Z01.
—BLDSC (8831.820000), GNLM, IE, Infotrieve, Ingenta. **CCC.**
Published by: Schattauer GmbH, Hoelderlinstr 3, Stuttgart, 70174, Germany. TEL 49-711-229870, FAX 49-711-2298750, info@schattauer.de, http://www.schattauer.com. Ed. Gisela Joehnssen. Adv. contact Klaus Jansch. Circ: 1,723 (controlled). **Subscr. to:** CSJ, Postfach 140220, Munich 80452, Germany. TEL 49-89-20959129, schattauer@csj.de.

636.089 DEU ISSN 1434-1239
CODEN: TAZPB8
➤ **TIERAERZTLICHE PRAXIS. AUSGABE K: KLEINTIERE - HEIMTIERE.** Text in German. 1973. 6/yr. EUR 184 to individuals; EUR 394 to institutions; EUR 72 to students; EUR 44 newsstand/cover (effective 2011). adv. **Document type:** *Journal, Academic/Scholarly.*
Supersedes in part (in 1997): Tieraerztliche Praxis (0303-6286)
Indexed: A22, A34, A35, A36, A37, A38, ASCA, AgBio, CABA, D01, DBA, E12, FoVS&M, GH, H17, IndMed, IndVet, KWIWR, N04, P30, P33, P37, P39, PN&I, R08, RM&VM, SAA, SCI, SCOPUS, T05, VS, W07, W10, W11, Z01.
—BLDSC (8831.821000), GNLM, IE, Infotrieve, Ingenta. **CCC.**
Published by: Schattauer GmbH, Hoelderlinstr 3, Stuttgart, 70174, Germany. TEL 49-711-229870, FAX 49-711-2298750, info@schattauer.de, http://www.schattauer.com. Ed. Wilfried Kraft. Adv. contact Klaus Jansch. Circ: 2,468 (controlled). **Subscr. to:** CSJ, Postfach 140220, Munich 80452, Germany. TEL 49-89-20959129, schattauer@csj.de.

636.089 DEU ISSN 0049-3864
SF603 CODEN: MVMZA8
➤ **TIERAERZTLICHE UMSCHAU**; Zeitschrift fuer alle Gebiete der Veterinaermedizin. Text in German. 1946. m. EUR 89 domestic; EUR 100.20 foreign; EUR 68 to students; EUR 9 newsstand/cover (effective 2006). adv. bk.rev. abstr. **Document type:** *Journal, Academic/Scholarly.*
Incorporates (1946-1994): Monatshefte fuer Veterinaermedizin (0026-9263)
Indexed: A20, A22, A34, A35, A36, A37, A38, ASCA, ASFA, AgBio, ApicAb, B21, B25, BA, BIOSIS Prev, CABA, ChemAb, CurCont, D01, DBA, E12, ESPM, F08, FS&TA, FoVS&M, G11, GH, H16, H17, IBR, IBZ, ISR, IndVet, KWIWR, LT, MaizeAb, MycolAb, N02, N03, N04, N05, OR, P30, P32, P33, P37, P38, P39, P40, PN&I, R07, R08, R12, R13, RA&MP, RM&VM, RRTA, S12, S13, S16, SAA, SCI, SCOPUS, SoyAb, T05, TAR, TriticAb, VS, VirolAbstr, W07, W08, W10, W11, WildRev, Z01.
—BLDSC (8832.000000), CASDDS, GNLM, IE, Infotrieve, Ingenta, INIST, Linda Hall. **CCC.**
Published by: Terra Verlag GmbH, Neuhauser Str 21, Konstanz, 78464, Germany. TEL 49-7531-81220, FAX 49-7531-812299, info@terra-verlag.de. Ed. O C Straub. Adv. contact Claudia Reimann. B&W page EUR 1,750, color page EUR 3,060; trim 180 x 260. Circ: 6,050 (paid and controlled).

636.08 DEU ISSN 0720-2237
TIERARZTLICHE-HOCHSCHULE-ANZEIGER. Key Title: TiHo-Anzeiger. Text in German. 1972. 6/yr. adv. bk.rev.; Website rev. 16 p./no. 3 cols./p.; back issues avail. **Document type:** *Newspaper, Academic/Scholarly.*
Related titles: Online - full text ed.
Published by: (Stiftung Tieraerztliche Hochschule Hannover/Foundation of the University of Veterinary Medicine, Hannover), Schluetersche Verlagsgesellschaft mbH und Co. KG, Hans-Boeckler-Allee 7, Hannover, 30173, Germany. TEL 49-511-85500, FAX 49-511-85501100, info@schluetersche.de. adv.: B&W page EUR 1,002, color page EUR 1,911; trim 188 x 272. Circ: 2,805 (paid and controlled).

636.08 DEU ISSN 0947-0956
TIERARZTLICHE HOCHSCHULE-FORSCHUNG FUERS LEBEN. Key Title: TiHo-Forschung fuers Leben. Text in German. 1994. a. **Document type:** *Journal, Academic/Scholarly.*
Published by: (Tieraerztliche Hochschule Hannover), V M K - Verlag fuer Marketing und Kommunikation GmbH & Co. KG, Faberstr 17, Monsheim, 67590, Germany. TEL 49-6243-9090, FAX 49-6243-909400, info@vmk-verlag.de.

636.089 NLD ISSN 0040-7453
SF1 CODEN: TIDIAY
➤ **TIJDSCHRIFT VOOR DIERGENEESKUNDE/NETHERLANDS JOURNAL OF VETERINARY SCIENCE.** Text in Dutch; Summaries in Dutch, English. 1863. 24/yr. adv. bk.rev. abstr.; bibl.; charts; illus. index. **Document type:** *Journal, Academic/Scholarly.*
Formerly: Tijdschrift voor Veeartsenijkunde
Indexed: A20, A22, A34, A35, A36, A37, A38, ASCA, AgBio, AgrForAb, B23, B25, BIOSIS Prev, BP, BibAg, CABA, ChemAb, CurCont, D01, DBA, E12, EMBASE, ExcerpMed, F08, FS&TA, FoVS&M, G11, GH, H16, H17, IndMed, IndVet, LT, MEDLINE, MaizeAb, MycolAb, N02, N03, N04, OR, P30, P33, P37, P39, PN&I, R07, R08, R10, R13, RA&MP, RM&VM, RRTA, Reac, S12, SAA, SCI, SCOPUS, SoyAb, T05, TAR, TriticAb, VS, W07, W08, W11, WildRev, Z01.
—BLDSC (8838.000000), CASDDS, GNLM, IE, Infotrieve, Ingenta, INIST.
Published by: Koninklijke Nederlandse Maatschappij voor Diergeneeskunde, Postbus 421, Houten, 3990 GE, Netherlands. TEL 31-30-6348900, FAX 31-30-6348909. Circ: 5,500.

636.089 USA ISSN 1938-9736
CODEN: SVMSEN
➤ **TOPICS IN COMPANION ANIMAL MEDICINE.** Text in English. 1986. q. USD 339 in United States to institutions; USD 405 elsewhere to institutions (effective 2012). adv. bibl.; charts; illus. index. reprints avail. **Document type:** *Journal, Academic/Scholarly.* **Description:** Each issue covers a specific theme of interest to small-animal veterinarians.
Former titles (until 2008): Clinical Techniques in Small Animal Practice (1096-2867); (until 1997): Seminars in Veterinary Medicine and Surgery: Small Animal (0882-0511)
Related titles: Online - full text ed.: ISSN 1876-7613. free (effective 2010) (from ScienceDirect).
Indexed: A22, A26, A34, A35, A36, A37, A38, ASCA, Agr, AgrForAb, BIOSIS Prev, CA, CABA, CurCont, D01, DBA, E12, EMBASE, ExcerpMed, F08, FoVS&M, GH, H16, I05, IndMed, IndVet, MEDLINE, MycolAb, N02, N04, P30, P33, P39, R08, SAA, SCI, SCOPUS, T02, VS, W07, W11.
—BLDSC (3286.399350), GNLM, IE, Ingenta, INIST. **CCC.**
Published by: W.B. Saunders Co. (Subsidiary of: Elsevier Health Sciences), Elsevier, Health Sciences Division, Order Fulfillment, 3251 Riverport Ln, Maryland Heights, MO 63043. TEL 800-545-2522, FAX 314-447-8093, 800-535-9935, sales.inquiry@elsevier.com, http://www.us.elsevierhealth.com. Ed. Dr. Deborah Greco. Pub. Anthony F Trioli TEL 215-239-3733. adv.: B&W page USD 870; trim 8.5 x 11.

636.089 USA ISSN 1064-5101
TOPICS IN VETERINARY MEDICINE. Text in English. 1926. 3/yr. free to qualified personnel (effective 2005). adv. **Document type:** *Magazine, Trade.* **Description:** Includes product development and application articles, company news, and educational articles on diseases and disease syndromes.
Formerly (until 1990): Norden News (0890-3727)
Indexed: P30, WildRev.
—Linda Hall.
Published by: Pfizer Animal Health, 812 Springdale Dr, Exton, PA 19341-2803. TEL 610-363-3100, FAX 610-968-5771, etchik00@pfizer.com. R&P Kathleen Etchison TEL 610-363-3771. Circ: 54,000 (controlled and free).

639.9 USA ISSN 1931-7735
SF996.45
TOPICS IN WILDLIFE MEDICINE. Text in English. 2005. irreg. **Document type:** *Monographic series.*
Published by: National Wildlife Rehabilitators Association, 2625 Clearwater Rd., Ste 110, Saint Cloud, MN 56301-4539. TEL 320-230-9920, nwra@nwrawildlife.org, http://www.nwrawildlife.org.

636.089 USA ISSN 0197-0852
TOWN AND COUNTRY CALL. Text in English. 1974. bi-m. free to members. **Document type:** *Newsletter, Trade.*
Published by: Virginia Veterinary Medical Association, 2314-C Commerce Center Dr., Rockville, VA 23146. TEL 800-937-8862, FAX 804-749-8003, vavvma@aol.com, http://www.vvma.org/.

636.089 DEU ISSN 1865-1674
SF601 CODEN: JVMAE6
➤ **TRANSBOUNDARY AND EMERGING DISEASES.** Text in English, German. 1953. 10/yr. GBP 1,190 in United Kingdom to institutions; EUR 1,511 in Europe to institutions; USD 2,197 in the Americas to institutions; USD 2,561 elsewhere to institutions; GBP 1,369 combined subscription in United Kingdom to institutions (print & online eds.); EUR 1,738 combined subscription in Europe to institutions (print & online eds.); USD 2,526 combined subscription in the Americas to institutions (print & online eds.); USD 2,946 combined subscription elsewhere to institutions (print & online eds.) (effective 2012). bk.rev. illus. index, cum.index. back issues avail.; reprint service avail. from PSC. **Document type:** *Journal, Academic/Scholarly.* **Description:** Encompasses contributions on physiology, biochemistry, pharmacology, toxicology, etc.
Former titles (until 2008): Journal of Veterinary Medicine. Series A (0931-184X); Which incorporated (1994-2001): European Journal of Veterinary Pathology (1124-5352); (until 1986): Zentralblatt fuer Veterinaermedizin. Reihe A: Animal Physiology, Pathology and Clinical Veterinary Medicine (0177-0543); (until 1984): Zentralblatt fuer Veterinaermedizin. Reihe A: Physiology, Endocrinology, Biochemistry, Pharmacology, Internal Medicine Surgery, Genetics, Animal Breeding, Obstetrics, Gynaecology, Anrology, Animal Nutrition, General and Special Pathology (Except Infectious and Parasitic Diseases) (0721-0981); (until 1981): Zentralblatt fuer Veterinaermedizin. Reihe A (0300-8711); Which superseded in part (in 1972): Zentralblatt fuer Veterinaermedizin. Reihe A: Anatomie, Histologie, Entwicklungsgeschichte, Physiologie, Biochemie, Ernaehrung, Pharmakologie, Klinik, Tierzucht, Pathologie (0514-7158); Which superseded in part (in 1963): Zentralblatt fuer Veterinaermedizin (0044-4294)
Related titles: Online - full text ed.: Transboundary and Emerging Diseases (Online). ISSN 1865-1682. GBP 1,190 in United Kingdom to institutions; EUR 1,511 in Europe to institutions; USD 2,197 in the Americas to institutions; USD 2,561 elsewhere to institutions (effective 2012) (from IngentaConnect); ◆ Supplement(s): Advances in Veterinary Medicine. ISSN 0931-4229.
Indexed: A01, A03, A08, A22, A26, A29, A34, A35, A36, A37, A38, ASCA, AgBio, Agr, B20, B21, B23, B25, BIOSIS Prev, CA, CABA, CIN, ChemAb, ChemTitl, CurCont, D01, DBA, E01, E12, EMBASE, ESPM, ExcerpMed, F08, F12, FS&TA, FoVS&M, G11, GH, H12, H17, I10, ISR, IndMed, IndVet, MEDLINE, MycolAb, N02, N04, P02, P10, P30, P32, P33, P37, P39, P48, P52, P53, P54, P56, PN&I, PQC, R07, R08, R12, RM&VM, RefZh, RiskAb, S13, S16, SAA, SCI, SCOPUS, T02, T05, TAR, VS, VirolAbstr, W07, W08, W11, WildRev, Z01.
—BLDSC (9020.570100), CASDDS, GNLM, IE, Infotrieve, Ingenta, INIST, Linda Hall. **CCC.**
Published by: Wiley-Blackwell Verlag GmbH (Subsidiary of: Wiley-Blackwell Publishing Ltd.), Kurfuerstendamm 57, Berlin, 10707, Germany. TEL 49-30-32790634, FAX 49-30-32790610, verlag@blackwell.de, http://www.blackwell.de. Ed. Paul Kitching. Circ: 400.

➤ **TRENDS IN PARASITOLOGY.** *see* BIOLOGY—Microbiology

636.089 USA ISSN 1062-8266
TRENDS MAGAZINE. Text in English. 1985. bi-m. USD 60 domestic; USD 70 foreign (effective 2005). adv. **Document type:** *Magazine, Trade.*
Formerly (until 1988): Trends (0883-1696)
—Ingenta. **CCC.**
Published by: American Animal Hospital Association, PO Box 150899, Denver, CO 80215-0899. TEL 303-986-2800, 800-883-6301, FAX 303-986-1700, info@aahanet.org, http://www.aahanet.org. Ed. Kristin Stark. R&P Loraine Miller. Adv. contact Stephanie Pates. Circ: 14,200.

TROPICAL AND SUBTROPICAL AGROECOSYSTEMS. *see* AGRICULTURE

VWZ

636.089 NLD ISSN 0049-4747
SF601 CODEN: TAHPAJ

➤ **TROPICAL ANIMAL HEALTH AND PRODUCTION.** Text in English. 1969. 8/yr. EUR 1,457, USD 1,515 combined subscription to institutions (print & online eds.) (effective 2012). adv. bk.rev. charts; illus.; stat. back issues avail.; reprint service avail. from PSC. **Document type:** *Journal, Academic/Scholarly.* **Description:** Publishes research, investigation, and observation in all fields of animal health and production that may lead to improved health and productivity of livestock, as well as better use of animal resources in developing nations.
Related titles: Online - full text ed.: ISSN 1573-7438 (from IngentaConnect).
Indexed: A22, A26, A29, A34, A35, A36, A37, A38, ASCA, ASFA, AgBio, Agr, AgrForAb, B20, B21, B23, B25, BA, BIOBASE, BIOSIS Prev, BP, BibAg, BibLing, C25, CA, CABA, ChemAb, CurCont, D01, DBA, E01, E04, E05, E12, EMBASE, ESPM, ExcerpMed, F08, F11, F12, FCA, FS&TA, FoVS&M, G11, GH, H16, H17, I10, IABS, ISR, IndMed, IndVet, LT, MEDLINE, MaizeAb, MycolAb, N02, N03, N04, OR, P11, P20, P22, P30, P32, P33, P37, P39, P40, P48, P50, P52, P54, P56, PGegResA, PN&I, PQC, R07, R08, R11, R12, R13, RA&MP, RM&VM, S12, S13, S16, S17, SAA, SCI, SCOPUS, SPPI, SoyAb, T02, T05, TAR, ToxAb, TriticAb, VS, VirolAbstr, W07, W10, W11, WildRev.
—BLDSC (9054.300000), CASDDS, GNLM, IE, Infotrieve, Ingenta, INIST. **CCC.**
Published by: Springer Netherlands (Subsidiary of: Springer Science+Business Media), Van Godewijckstraat 30, Dordrecht, 3311 GX, Netherlands. TEL 31-78-6576050, FAX 31-78-6576474, http://www.springer.com. Ed. Leslie Harrison.

636.089 NGA ISSN 0794-4845
CODEN: TRVTDJ

➤ **TROPICAL VETERINARIAN.** Text in English. 1983. q. NGN 1,000 domestic to individuals; USD 80 foreign to individuals; NGN 5,000, USD 120 domestic to institutions (effective 2001). adv. 75 p./no.; back issues avail. **Document type:** *Journal, Academic/Scholarly.* **Description:** Publishes research articles devoted to all aspects of health and disease of animals in the tropics.
Related titles: Online - full text ed.
Indexed: A34, A37, A38, Agr, AgrForAb, B25, BIOSIS Prev, BP, CABA, D01, E12, F08, F11, F12, GH, H16, H17, IndVet, MycolAb, N02, N03, N04, P33, P37, P39, PN&I, R08, R12, RA&MP, RM&VM, SoyAb, T05, TAR, VS, W10, W11, WildRev, Z01.
Published by: University of Ibadan, Faculty of Veterinary Medicine, Editors, Ibadan, Oyo State, Nigeria. TEL 234-2-810-3043, dean.vetmedicine@vi.edu.org, library@kdl.ui.edu.ng. Ed. Helen Nottidge. Adv. contact Dr. M O Abatan. page NGN 5,000.

636.089 TUR ISSN 1300-0128
SF604 CODEN: TVHAEN

➤ **TURKISH JOURNAL OF VETERINARY AND ANIMAL SCIENCES/ DOGA TURK VETERINERLIK VE HAYVANCILIK DERGISI.** Text and summaries in English. 1976. 6/yr. TRY 96 domestic; EUR 60 foreign (effective 2011). **Document type:** *Journal, Academic/ Scholarly.*
Former titles (until 1994): Doga. Turk Veterinerlik ve Hayvancilik/Doga. Turkish Journal of Veterinary Sciences (1010-7592); (until 1986): Doga Bilim Dergisi. Seri D1. Veterinerlik ve Hayvancilik (1011-0925)
Related titles: Online - full text ed.: ISSN 1303-6181. free (effective 2011).
Indexed: A01, A02, A03, A08, A22, A34, A35, A36, A37, A38, ASCA, AgBio, AgrForAb, C25, CA, CABA, ChemAb, D01, E12, F08, FCA, FS&TA, FoVS&M, G11, GH, H16, H17, INIS AtomInd, IndVet, LT, MaizeAb, N02, N03, N04, P32, P33, P37, P39, P40, PHN&I, PN&I, R07, R08, R12, R13, RA&MP, RM&VM, RRTA, S12, S13, S16, SCI, SCOPUS, SoyAb, T02, T05, TAR, TriticAb, VS, W07, W10, W11.
—BLDSC (9072.497000), CASDDS, IE, Ingenta.
Published by: Scientific and Technical Research Council of Turkey - TUBITAK/Turkiye Bilimsel ve Teknik Arastirma Kurumu, Akademik Yayinlar Mudurlugu, Ataturk Bulvari No.221, Kavaklidere / Ankara, 06100, Turkey. TEL 90-312-4685300, FAX 90-312-4270493, bdym.abone@tubitak.gov.tr, http://www.tubitak.gov.tr. Ed. Dr. Omer Memduh Esendal.

636.08905 GBR ISSN 1464-4630

➤ **U K VET. COMPANION ANIMAL**; the journal of the veterinary surgeon in practice. (United Kingdom) Text in English. 1995. 8/yr. GBP 194 in United Kingdom to institutions; EUR 226 in Europe to institutions; USD 276 elsewhere to institutions; GBP 223 combined subscription in United Kingdom to institutions (print & online eds.); EUR 259 combined subscription in Europe to institutions (print & online eds.); USD 317 combined subscription elsewhere to institutions (print & online eds.) (effective 2012). adv. back issues avail. **Document type:** *Journal, Academic/Scholarly.* **Description:** Provides relevant and practical information of use to veterinary surgeons in their day-to-day work.
Related titles: Online - full text ed.: ISSN 2044-3862. GBP 194 in United Kingdom to institutions; EUR 226 in Europe to institutions; USD 276 elsewhere to institutions (effective 2012).
Indexed: A01, A34, A36, A37, A38, BP, CABA, E12, F08, G11, GH, H16, H17, IndVet, LT, N04, P33, P37, P39, PN&I, R07, R08, RA&MP, RM&VM, RRTA, T05, VS, W10, W11.
—BLDSC (9082.669180). **CCC.**
Published by: U K Vet Publishing (Subsidiary of: Wiley-Blackwell Publishing Ltd.), Kennet Bldg, Trade St, Woolton Hill, NewBury, Berks, United Kingdom. TEL 44-1635-255511, FAX 44-1635-255445, enquiries@ukvet.co.uk, https://www.ukvet.co.uk. Ed. Mike Howe. Adv. contact Peter Witworth TEL 44-1635-254961. B&W page GBP 1,080, color page GBP 1,280; trim 210 x 297.

636.08905 GBR ISSN 1464-262X

U K VET. LIVESTOCK; the journal for the veterinary surgeons in general practice. (United Kingdom) Text in English. 1995 (Jul.). 7/yr. GBP 184 in United Kingdom to institutions; EUR 212 in Europe to institutions; USD 261 elsewhere to institutions; GBP 210 combined subscription in United Kingdom to institutions (print & online eds.); EUR 244 combined subscription in Europe to institutions (print & online eds.); USD 299 combined subscription elsewhere to institutions (print & online eds.) (effective 2012). adv. back issues avail. **Document type:** *Journal, Academic/Scholarly.* **Description:** Dedicated to the livestock vet with exclusive coverage to cattle, sheep and pigs.
Related titles: Online - full text ed.: ISSN 2044-3870. GBP 184 in United Kingdom to institutions; EUR 212 in Europe to institutions; USD 261 elsewhere to institutions (effective 2012).
Indexed: A01, A34, A35, A36, A37, A38, AgBio, CABA, D01, E12, F08, G11, GH, H17, IndVet, MaizeAb, N02, N04, P33, P37, P39, PN&I, R08, S12, S13, S16, TriticAb, VS, W10, W11.
—BLDSC (9082.669184). **CCC.**
Published by: U K Vet Publishing (Subsidiary of: Wiley-Blackwell Publishing Ltd.), Kennet Bldg, Trade St, Woolton Hill, NewBury, Berks, United Kingdom. TEL 44-1635-255511, FAX 44-1635-255445, enquiries@ukvet.co.uk, https://www.ukvet.co.uk. Ed. Mike Howe. Adv. contact Peter Witworth TEL 44-1635-254961. B&W page GBP 1,040, color page GBP 1,220; trim 210 x 297.

636.089 USA ISSN 0091-8199

U.S. DEPARTMENT OF AGRICULTURE. ANIMAL AND PLANT HEALTH INSPECTION SERVICE. VETERINARY SERVICES. FOREIGN ANIMAL DISEASES REPORT. Key Title: Foreign Animal Diseases Report. Text in English. q.
Indexed: Agr.
Published by: U.S. Department of Agriculture, Animal and Plant Health Inspection Service Veterinary Services, 4700 River Rd, Riverdale, MD 20737-1231. TEL 301-734-7799. Ed. Dr. Quita P. Bowman.

636.089 TUR ISSN 1301-3173

ULUDAG UNIVERSITESI VETERINER FAKULTESI DERGISI/ULUDAG UNIVERSITY. FACULTY OF VETERINARY MEDICINE. JOURNAL. Text in Turkish, English. 1991. s-a. **Document type:** *Journal, Academic/Scholarly.*
Related titles: Online - full text ed.
Indexed: A01, A34, A35, A36, A37, A38, AgBio, CABA, D01, E12, GH, H16, H17, IndVet, MaizeAb, N02, N03, N04, P33, P37, PHN&I, R08, R11, R12, R13, RA&MP, RM&VM, SoyAb, T05, TriticAb, VS, W11.
Published by: Uludag Universitesi, Veteriner Fakultesi/Uludag University, Veterinary Faculty, Gorukle Campus, Bursa, 16059, Turkey. TEL 90-224-2941200, FAX 90-224-2941202, scoskun@uludag.edu.tr, vetdek@uludag.edu.tr. Eds. Dr. Aysegul Eyigor, Dr. Kadir Yesilbag, Dr. Sevki Coskun.

636.089 USA ISSN 0082-8750
SF601

UNITED STATES ANIMAL HEALTH ASSOCIATION. PROCEEDINGS OF THE ANNUAL MEETING. Text in English. 1969 (no.73). a. back issues avail. **Document type:** *Proceedings.*
Supersedes: United States Livestock Sanitary Association. Proceedings
Indexed: A22, IndMed, P30.
—BLDSC (6841.958000), IE, Infotrieve, Ingenta.
Published by: United States Animal Health Association, 8100 Three Chopt Rd, Suite 203, PO Box K227, Richmond, VA 23288-0001. TEL 804-285-3210, FAX 804-285-3367, http://www.usaha.org. Circ: 1,400.

636.089 VEN ISSN 0258-6576

UNIVERSIDAD CENTRAL DE VENEZUELA. FACULTAD DE CIENCIAS VETERINARIAS. REVISTA. Text in Spanish; Summaries in English, Spanish. 1939-1992; resumed 1998. 4/yr. **Document type:** *Journal, Academic/Scholarly.*
Formerly: Revista de Medicina Veterinaria y Parasitologia (0048-7724)
Related titles: Online - full text ed.: free (effective 2011).
Indexed: A34, A35, A36, A38, AgrForAb, C01, C25, CABA, ChemAb, D01, E12, F08, GH, N02, N03, N04, P33, R08, T05.
Published by: Universidad Central de Venezuela, Facultad de Ciencias Veterinarias, Apdo. de Correos 4563, Maracay, Edo. Aragua, Venezuela. revisfcv@camelot.rect.ucv.ve, http://bibliovet.veter.ucv.ve/Revistafcv/index.htm. Ed. Ana Zuley Ruiz.

636.089 GTM ISSN 0375-0884

UNIVERSIDAD DE SAN CARLOS DE GUATEMALA. FACULTAD DE MEDICINA VETERINARIA Y ZOOTECNIA REVISTA. Text in Spanish; Summaries in English, Spanish. 1962. irreg. **Document type:** *Journal, Academic/Scholarly.*
Published by: Universidad de San Carlos de Guatemala, Facultad de Medicina, Veterinaria y Zootecnia, Ciudad Universitaria, Zona 12, Edificio de Rectoria, Of 307, Guatemala City, Guatemala. TEL 502-760790.

636.089 VEN ISSN 0798-2259

➤ **UNIVERSIDAD DEL ZULIA. FACULTAD DE CIENCIAS VETERINARIAS. REVISTA CIENTIFICA.** Variant title: Revista Cientifica. Text in Spanish, English; Abstracts in English, Spanish. 1991. bi-m. VEB 160, USD 120 (effective 2011). bk.rev. bibl.; charts; illus.; abstr.; maps. 100 p./no.; back issues avail.; reprints avail. **Document type:** *Journal, Academic/Scholarly.* **Description:** Contains scientific papers and reviews in veterinary science.
Related titles: Fax ed.; Online - full text ed.: free (effective 2011).
Indexed: A26, A34, A35, A36, A37, A38, AgBio, AgrForAb, B23, BA, C25, CABA, D01, E12, F08, F11, F12, FoVS&M, G11, GH, H16, H17, I04, I05, IndVet, LT, MaizeAb, N02, N03, N04, OR, P32, P33, P37, P39, P40, PGegResA, PN&I, R07, R08, R12, R13, RM&VM, RRTA, S12, S13, S16, SCI, SCOPUS, SoyAb, T05, TAR, TriticAb, VS, W07, W10, W11, WildRev.
—BLDSC (7851.137000), IE, Ingenta.
Published by: Universidad del Zulia, Facultad de Ciencias Veterinarias, C.C. Galerias 1er Nivel, Local 45-E, Apdo 15252, Maracaibo, Zulia 4005-A, Venezuela. http://www.luz.edu.ve/Facultades/Veterinaria/. Ed. Mario Perez Barrientos.

636.089 PRT ISSN 0873-5522

UNIVERSIDADE TECNICA DE LISBOA. FACULDADE DE MEDICINA VETERINARIA. ANAIS. Text in Multiple languages. 1949. a.
Formerly (until 1988): Universidade Tecnica de Lisboa. Escola Superior de Medicina Veterinaria. Anais (0374-583X)
Published by: Universidade Tecnica de Lisboa, Faculdade de Medicina Veterinaria, Alameda de Santo Antonio dos Capuchos, No 1, Lisbon, 1169-047, Portugal. http://www.utl.pt/.

636.089 ITA ISSN 0393-4802

UNIVERSITA DEGLI STUDI DI PARMA. FACOLTA DI MEDICINA VETERINARIA. ANNALI. Text in Italian, English. 1981. a., latest vol.24, 2004. **Document type:** *Journal, Academic/Scholarly.*
Indexed: A34, A35, A36, A37, A38, AgBio, C30, CABA, D01, E12, FS&TA, G11, GH, H16, IndVet, LT, MaizeAb, N02, N03, N04, OR, P32, P33, P37, P40, PN&I, R13, RM&VM, RRTA, S12, S13, S16, VS, W11.
Published by: Universita degli Studi di Parma, Facolta di Medicina Veterinaria, Biblioteca Generale, Via del Taglio 8, Parma, 43100, Italy. TEL 39-0521-032625, FAX 39-0521-902737.

636.089 ITA ISSN 0365-4729
SF604 CODEN: AMVPAW

UNIVERSITA DEGLI STUDI DI PISA. FACOLTA DI MEDICINA VETERINARIA DI PISA. ANNALI. Key Title: Annali della Facolta di Medicina Veterinaria di Pisa. Text in Italian. 1947. a. price varies. **Document type:** *Journal, Academic/Scholarly.* **Description:** Publishes original research articles in areas of veterinary medicine and animal production. Reports on faculty members.
Related titles: CD-ROM ed.: ISSN 1974-4471; Online - full text ed.: ISSN 1974-4307.
Indexed: WildRev, Z01.
—CASDDS, IE, Ingenta, INIST. **CCC.**
Published by: (Universita degli Studi di Pisa, Biblioteca di Medicina Veterinaria di Pisa), Edizioni Plus - Universita di Pisa (Pisa University Press), Lungarno Pacinotti 43, Pisa, Italy. TEL 39-050-2212056, FAX 39-050-2212945, http://www.edizioniplus.it.

636 ROM ISSN 1454-7406
CODEN: LSIVDF

UNIVERSITATEA AGRONOMICA SI DE MEDICINA VETERINARA ION IONESCU DE LA BRAD. LUCRARI STIINTIFICE. SERIE MEDICINA VETERINARA. Text in Romanian. 1957. a. **Document type:** *Journal, Academic/Scholarly.*
Incorporates in part (1990-1997): Universitatea Agronomica Ion Ionescu de la Brad. Lucrari Stiintifice. Seria Zootehnie - Medicina Veterinara (1223-4931); Which was formerly (until 1990): Institutul Agronomic Ion Ionescu de la Brad. Lucrari Stiintifice. Medicina Veterinara - Zootehnie (0075-3513)
Indexed: A34, A35, A36, A37, A38, AgBio, AgrForAb, B23, BP, C25, C30, CABA, D01, E12, F08, F11, F12, G11, GH, H16, H17, I11, IndVet, LT, MaizeAb, N02, N03, N04, OR, P32, P33, P39, PGegResA, PHN&I, PN&I, R07, R08, R13, RA&MP, RM&VM, RRTA, S12, S13, S16, SoyAb, T05, TAR, TriticAb, VITIS, VS, W10, W11.
—CASDDS, INIST.
Published by: Universitatea de Stiinte Agricole si Medicina Veterinara "Ion Ionescu de la Brad", Aleea Mihail Sadovenau 3, Iasi, 700490, Romania. TEL 40-232-275070, FAX 40-232-260650, http://www.univagro-iasi.ro.

636.08 ROM

UNIVERSITATEA DE STIINTE AGRONOMICE SI MEDICINA VETERINARA. LUCRARI STIINTIFICE. SERIA C, MEDICINA VETERINARA. Text in Romanian; Summaries in English. 1960. a. per issue exchange basis only. **Document type:** *Academic/Scholarly.*
Former titles: Universitatea de Stiinte Agronomice. Lucrari Stiintifice. Seria C, Medicina Veterinara; (until 1992): Institutul Agronomic Nicolae Balcescu. Lucrari Stiintifice. Seria C, Medicina Veterinara (0254-0509); Which superseded in part (in 1970): Institutul Agronomic Nicolae Balcescu. Lucrari Stiintifice. Seria C, Zootehnie si Medicina Veterinara (0524-8108); Which superseded in part: Institutul Agronomic Nicolae Balcescu. Anuarul Lucrarilor Stiintifice (1220-1987)
Indexed: FS&TA.
—INIST.
Published by: Universitatea de Stiinte Agronomice si Medicina Veterinara, Bd. Marasti 59, Sector 1, Bucharest, 71331, Romania.

636.089 ROM

➤ **UNIVERSITATEA DE STINTE AGRICOLE SI MEDICINA VETERINARIA A BANATULUI TIMISOARA. LUCRARI STIINTIFICE MEDICINA VETERINARA/SCIENTIFICAL PAPERS VETERINARY MEDICINE.** Text in English. 1986. s-a. (until 2009; no issues published in 1990 & 1995). back issues avail. **Document type:** *Journal, Academic/Scholarly.*
Formerly (1991-2008): Universitatea de Stiinte Agricole a Banatului Timisoara. Seria Medicina Veterinara. Lucrari Stiintifice (1221-5295); Which supersded in part (1986-1988): Institutul Agronomic Timisoara. Zootehnie si Medicina Veterinara. Lucrari Stiintifice (1220-1979); Which was formed by the merger of (1965-1985): Institutul Agronomic Timisoara. Seria Medicina Veterinara. Lucrari Stiintifice (0563-5586); (1970-1985): Institutul Agronomic Timisoara. Seria Zootehnie. Lucrari Stiintifice (0253-1852); Both of which superseded in part (1960-1964): Institutul Agronomic Timisoara. Lucrari Stiintifice (1220-1960); Which was formerly (1958-1958): Institutul Agronomic TimiSoara. Lucrarile Sesiunii Stiintifice (1220-1952); (1957-1957): Institutul Agronomic Timisoara. Anuarul Lucrarilor Stiintifice (1220-1944)
Related titles: Online - full text ed.
Indexed: A34, A35, A36, A37, A38, AgBio, B23, C25, CABA, D01, E12, F08, F12, G11, GH, H16, H17, I11, MaizeAb, N02, N03, N04, P33, P39, R07, R08, R13, RA&MP, RM&VM, S12, S13, S16, SoyAb, T05, W11.
Published by: Universitatea de Stiinte Agricole si Medicina Veterinara a Banatului Timisoara, Facultatea de Medicina Veterinara/Banat University of Agricultural Sciences and Veterinary Medicine Timisoara. Faculty of Veterinary Medicine, Calea Aradului nr.119, Timisoara, Jud. Timis 300645, Romania. TEL 40-256-277118, FAX 40-256-277008, office@fmvt.ro, http://www.usab-tm.ro/index.php?id=273.

636 CAN ISSN 0383-8455

UNIVERSITE DE MONTREAL. FACULTE DE MEDECINE VETERINAIRE. ANNUAIRE. Text in English. 1968. a. free. **Document type:** *Journal, Academic/Scholarly.*
Formerly: Ecole de Medecine Veterinaire, Saint-Hyacinthe, Quebec. Annuaire (0383-8447)
Published by: Universite de Montreal, Faculte de Medecine Veterinaire, C P 6128, succ A, Montreal, PQ H3C 3J7, Canada. TEL 514-343-6111, FAX 514-778-8114.

636 660.6 ROM ISSN 1843-5262

UNIVERSITY OF AGRICULTURAL SCIENCES AND VETERINARY MEDICINE CLUJ-NAPOCA. BULLETIN. ANIMAL SCIENCE AND BIOTECHNOLOGIES. Text in English. 1975. s-a. EUR 50 (effective 2011). **Document type:** *Journal, Academic/Scholarly.*
Supersedes in part (in 2006): Universitatea de Stinte Agricole si Medicina Veterinara Cluj-Napoca. Buletinul. Seria Zootehnie si Medicina Veterinara (1454-2390); Which was formerly (until 1995): Universitatea de Stinte Agricole Cluj-Napoca. Buletinul. Serie Zootehnie si Medicina Veterinara (1221-3594); (until 1992): Institutul Agronomic Cluj-Napoca. Buletinul. Serie Zootehnie si Medicina Veterinara (0557-4668); Which supseded in part (in 1977): Institutul Agronomic Cluj-Napoca. Buletinul (0378-0554)
Related titles: Online - full text ed.: ISSN 1843-536X.

Indexed: A34, A35, A36, A37, A38, AgBio, AgrForAb, B23, BA, BP, C25, C30, CA, CABA, D01, E12, F08, F11, F12, FCA, G11, GH, H16, H17, I11, IndVet, LT, MaizeAb, N02, N03, N04, N05, OR, P32, P33, P37, P38, P39, P40, PGegResA, PGrRegA, PN&I, R07, R08, R13, RA&MP, RM&VM, RRTA, RefZh, S12, S13, S16, S17, SoyAb, T02, TAR, TriticAb, VS, W10, W11, Z01.
Published by: Universitatea de Stiinte Agricole si Medicina Veterinara Cluj-Napoca/University of Agricultural Sciences and Veterinary Medicine Cluj-Napoca, Str Manastur 3-5, Cluj-Napoca, 400372, Romania. TEL 40-264-596384, FAX 40-264-593792, contact@usamvcluj.ro, http://www.usamvcluj.ro. Ed. Radu Sestras. Pub. Augustin Vlaic.

636 ROM ISSN 1843-5270
CODEN: BIAVDX
UNIVERSITY OF AGRICULTURAL SCIENCES AND VETERINARY MEDICINE CLUJ-NAPOCA. BULLETIN. VETERINARY MEDICINE. Text in English; Summaries in English, French. 1975. s-a. EUR 50 (effective 2011). back issues avail. **Document type:** *Journal, Academic/Scholarly.*
Supersedes in part (in 2006): Universitatea de Stiinte Agricole si Medicina Veterinara Cluj-Napoca. Buletinul. Seria Zootehnie si Medicina Veterinara (1454-2390); Which was formerly (until 1995): Universitatea de Stiinte Agricole Cluj-Napoca. Buletinul. Seria Zootehnie si Medicina Veterinara (1221-3594); (until 1992): Institutul Agronomic Cluj-Napoca. Buletinul. Seria Zootehnie si Medicina Veterinara (0557-4668); Which superseded in part (in 1977): Institutul Agronomic Cluj-Napoca. Buletinul (0378-0554)
Related titles: Online - full text ed.: ISSN 1843-5378.
Indexed: A34, A35, A36, A37, A38, AgBio, AgrForAb, B23, BP, BioDAb, C25, C30, CA, CABA, D01, E12, F08, F11, F12, FCA, FS&TA, G11, GH, H16, H17, I11, IndVet, LT, MaizeAb, N02, N03, N04, OR, P32, P33, P37, P38, P39, P40, PHN&I, PN&I, R07, R08, R12, R13, RA&MP, RM&VM, RRTA, RefZh, S12, S13, S16, SoyAb, T02, T05, TAR, TriticAb, VS, W10, W11, WildRev, Z01.
—BLDSC (2785.830000), CASDDS, IE.
Published by: Universitatea de Stiinte Agricole si Medicina Veterinara Cluj-Napoca/University of Agricultural Sciences and Veterinary Medicine Cluj-Napoca, Str Manastur 3-5, Cluj-Napoca, 400372, Romania. TEL 40-264-596384, FAX 40-264-593792, contact@usamvcluj.ro, http://www.usamvcluj.ro. Ed. Radu Sestras. Pub. Augustin Vlaic.

UNIVERSITY OF DAR ES SALAAM. FACULTY OF AGRICULTURE, FORESTRY AND VETERINARY SCIENCE. ANNUAL RECORD OF RESEARCH. *see* AGRICULTURE

VACCINE. *see* MEDICAL SCIENCES—Allergology And Immunology

636.089 NLD ISSN 1874-995X
VEDIAS INFO. Text in Dutch. 198?. 5/yr. EUR 27.50 domestic; EUR 32.50 in Europe; EUR 50 elsewhere (effective 2010). adv.
Published by: Vereniging van Dierenarts Assistenten, Lod Nap Plantsoen 82, Utrecht, 3582 TX, Netherlands. http://www.vedias.nl. Ed. Karen van der Horst TEL 31-50-5798082.

636.089 AUT ISSN 1029-5321
VET JOURNAL; Fachjournal der Oesterreichische Tieraerztinnen und Tieraerzte. Text in German. 1949. m. bk.rev. **Document type:** *Magazine, Trade.*
Formerly (until 1995): Oesterreichische Tieraerztezeitung (0048-1475)
Published by: Bundeskammer der Tieraerzte Oesterreichs, Biberstr 22, Vienna, 1010, Austria. TEL 43-1-5121766, FAX 43-1-5121470, oe@tieraerztekammer.at, http://www.tieraerztekammer.at. Circ: 3,100.

636.089 DEU ISSN 1862-4073
VET-MED REPORT. Text in German. 1999. 6/yr. EUR 22; EUR 7 per issue (effective 2010). adv. **Document type:** *Journal, Academic/Scholarly.*
Related titles: Online - full text ed.: ISSN 1866-5152.
Published by: Wiley-Blackwell Verlag GmbH (Subsidiary of: Wiley-Blackwell Publishing Ltd.), Kurfuerstendamm 57, Berlin, 10707, Germany. TEL 49-30-3279-0665, FAX 49-30-3279-0677, verlag@blackwell.de, http://www.blackwell.de. adv.: B&W page EUR 2,600, color page EUR 3,350.

636.08 GBR ISSN 1360-1962
➤ **VET ON-LINE.** Variant title: The International Journal of Veterinary Medicine. Text in English. 1995. q. free (effective 2009). bk.rev.; software rev.; video rev. back issues avail. **Document type:** *Journal, Academic/Scholarly.* **Description:** Features articles on veterinary medicine.
Media: Online - full text.
Published by: Priory Lodge Education Ltd., 2 Cornflower Way, Moreton, Wirral CH46 1SV, United Kingdom. Ed. Walter Tarello.

636.089 IND ISSN 0973-6980
SF604
VET SCAN. Text in English. 2005. s-a. free (effective 2011). **Document type:** *Journal, Academic/Scholarly.*
Media: Online - full text.
Indexed: A01, A34, A35, A36, A37, A38, Agr, AgrForAb, B23, C25, CA, CABA, D01, E12, F08, G11, GH, H16, H17, IndVet, N02, N03, N04, OR, P33, P37, P39, PN&I, R08, RA&MP, RM&VM, T02, T05, TAR, TriticAb, VS, W10, W11.
Published by: Society for the Advancement of Veterinary Education, 188 Daulatabad, Nowpora, Srinagar, Jammu/Kashmir 190003, India. TEL 91-941-9017753, FAX 91-831-6189805, contact@kashvet.org, http://www.kashvet.org.

636.089 AUS ISSN 1839-0056
▼ **VET WATCH.** Text in English. 2011. m. free (effective 2011). back issues avail. **Document type:** *Newsletter, Government.* **Description:** Contains information about animal disease surveillance-trends and early warning.
Media: Online - full text.
Published by: Victoria, Department of Primary Industries, GPO Box 4440, Melbourne, VIC 3001, Australia. TEL 61-3-53325000, 800-122-969, customer.service@dpi.vic.gov.au, http://www.dpi.vic.gov.au.

636.08 DEU ISSN 0940-8711
VETERINAER SPIEGEL. Text in German. 1991. q. EUR 49 to institutions; EUR 102 combined subscription to institutions (print & online eds.) (effective 2011). adv. **Document type:** *Journal, Trade.*
Related titles: Online - full text ed.: ISSN 1868-0437. EUR 102 to institutions (effective 2011).
—**CCC.**
Published by: Enke Verlag in M V S Medizinverlage Stuttgart GmbH und Co. KG (Subsidiary of: Georg Thieme Verlag), Oswald-Hesse-Str 50, Stuttgart, 70469, Germany. TEL 49-711-89310, FAX 49-711-8931706, kunden.service@thieme.de. Ed. Leonie Loeffler. adv.: B&W page EUR 2,100, color page EUR 3,450; trim 210 x 297. Circ: 7,359 (paid and controlled).

636.089 NOR ISSN 1890-3290
VETERINAERINSTITUTTET. RAPPORTSERIE. Text in Norwegian. 2002. irreg. back issues avail. **Document type:** *Monographic series, Academic/Scholarly.*
Media: Online - full text.
Published by: Veterinaerinstituttet/National Veterinary Institute, PO Box 750, Sentrum, Oslo, 0106, Norway. TEL 47-23-216000, FAX 47-23-216001, postmottag@vetinst.no.

636.089 SWE ISSN 1654-9848
VETERINAERKONGRESSEN. Text in Swedish. 1963. a.
Former titles (until 2007): Veterinaermoetet (1402-9324); (until 1997): Allmaent Veterinaermoete (0281-5818)
Published by: Sveriges Veterinaerfoerbund/Swedish Veterinary Association, Kungsholms Hamnplan 7, Box 12709, Stockholm, 12709, Sweden. TEL 46-8-54555820, FAX 46-8-54555839, office@svf.se, http://www.svf.se.

636.089 ITA ISSN 0394-3151
VETERINARIA. Text in Italian. 1987. bi-m. **Document type:** *Journal, Trade.*
Indexed: A34, A35, A38, AgBio, BP, CABA, E12, F08, GH, H16, H17, IndVet, N02, N04, P33, P37, P39, R08, RA&MP, RM&VM, SCI, T05, VS, W07, W10, W11.
Published by: Societa Culturale Italiana Veterinari per Animali da Compagnia (S C I V A C), Palazzo Trecchi, Cremona, CR 26100, Italy. TEL 39-0372-460440, FAX 39-0372-457091, info@scivac.it, http://www.scivac.it.

636.089 ARG ISSN 0326-4629
VETERINARIA ARGENTINA. Text in Spanish; Summaries in English. 1984. 10/yr. ARS 85 domestic; USD 106 in Latin America; USD 136 elsewhere (effective 2007). adv. bk.rev. abstr.; bibl.; illus.; pat. index, cum.index. back issues avail. **Document type:** *Magazine, Trade.*
Supersedes (1939-1984): Gaceta Veterinaria (0367-3812)
Indexed: A22, A34, A35, A36, A37, A38, AgBio, B23, C01, CABA, ChemAb, D01, E12, F08, G11, GH, H17, IndVet, N02, N04, OR, P32, P33, P37, P39, P40, PGegResA, PN&I, R08, R12, R13, RA&MP, RM&VM, S13, S16, SAA, SoyAb, T05, TAR, VS, W10, W11, WildRev.
—BLDSC (9223.350000), IE, Ingenta, Linda Hall.
Published by: Veterinaria Argentina s.r.l., Viamonte, 494 2, Buenos Aires, 1053, Argentina. TEL 54-11-43119997, FAX 54-11-43128339, speroni@impsat1.com.ar. Eds. Norberto A Speroni, Dr. Emilio Morini. R&P, Adv. contact Norberto Speroni. Circ: 4,500.

636 BRA ISSN 0102-5716
SF601 CODEN: VEZOEO
➤ **VETERINARIA E ZOOTECNIA.** Text in Portuguese; Summaries in English, Portuguese. 1985. a., latest vol.11, 2002. USD 30 (effective 2006); or exchange basis. abstr.; bibl.; charts. **Document type:** *Journal, Academic/Scholarly.* **Description:** Original papers in veterinary medicine and zoological research.
Indexed: A29, A34, A35, A36, A37, A38, ASFA, AgBio, B20, B21, B23, C01, C25, CABA, D01, E12, ESPM, F08, G11, GH, H16, H17, I10, IndVet, LT, MaizeAb, N02, N04, OR, P32, P33, P37, P39, P40, PN&I, R07, R08, R12, RA&MP, RM&VM, RefZh, S13, S16, SoyAb, T05, TAR, VS, VirolAbstr, W11, Z01.
Published by: Universidade Estadual Paulista, Fundacao Editora U N E S P, Praca da Se 108, Sao Paulo, SP 01001-900, Brazil. TEL 55-11-32427171, cgb@marilia.unesp.br, http://www.unesp.br. Ed. Sony Dimas Bicudo.

636.089 BRA ISSN 1679-5237
VETERINARIA EM FOCO. Text in Portuguese. 2003. s-a. BRL 40 (effective 2007). back issues avail. **Document type:** *Journal, Academic/Scholarly.*
Related titles: Online - full text ed.
Indexed: A34, A35, A36, A38, AgBio, CABA, D01, E12, G11, GH, H16, H17, IndVet, N02, N03, N04, P33, P39, PN&I, R08, R12, RM&VM, SoyAb, T05, TAR, VS, W11.
Published by: Universidade Luterana do Brasil, Curso de Medicina Veterinaria, Ave Farroupilha, 8001, Predio 14 Sala 125, Canos, RS 92425-900, Brazil. http://www.ulbra.br. Ed. Carlos Gottschal.

636.089 ITA ISSN 0505-401X
SF601
VETERINARIA ITALIANA. Text in English, Italian. 1950. q. EUR 50 per issue (effective 2010). bk.rev. Index. back issues avail. **Document type:** *Journal, Academic/Scholarly.* **Description:** Covers veterinary public health, veterinary science and medicine.
Related titles: Online - full text ed.: ISSN 1828-1427. free (effective 2011).
Indexed: A34, A35, A36, A37, A38, AgBio, BP, CABA, D01, E12, G11, GH, H16, H17, I11, LT, MEDLINE, N02, N03, N04, P30, P32, P33, P37, P39, PGegResA, PN&I, R07, R08, R12, R13, RA&MP, RM&VM, RefZh, S12, S13, S16, SCI, T05, TAR, W07, W10, W11.
—BLDSC (9224.000000), IE.
Published by: Istituto Zooprofilattico Sperimentale dell'Abruzzo e del Molise "G.Caporale", via Campo Boario, Teramo, 64100, Italy. TEL 39-861-332205, FAX 39-861-332251, http://www.izs.it/IZS/. Ed. Gill Dilmitis. Pub. Guido Mosca. R&P Carlo Turilli.

636.089 MEX
CODEN: VTERBU
➤ **VETERINARIA MEXICO.** Text and summaries in English, Spanish. 1970. q. MXN 400 domestic; USD 80 in Latin America; USD 90 in US & Canada; USD 100 elsewhere (effective 2007). adv. bk.rev. charts; illus.; stat. index. back issues avail. **Document type:** *Journal, Academic/Scholarly.* **Description:** Publishes original research articles and clinical case reports in the general field of veterinary and animal science, with emphasis on local and national events.
Formerly (until 1975): Veterinaria (0301-5092)
Related titles: CD-ROM ed.; Online - full text ed.: free (effective 2011).
Indexed: A01, A34, A35, A36, A37, A38, ASCA, AgBio, AgrForAb, B21, B23, B25, BIOSIS Prev, BP, C01, C25, CA, CABA, CIN, ChemAb, ChemTitl, D01, DBA, E12, EntAb, F08, F12, G11, GH, H16, H17, IndVet, MaizeAb, MycolAb, N02, N03, N04, P32, P33, P37, P39, P40, PHN&I, PN&I, R07, R08, R11, R12, RA&MP, RM&VM, S12, S13, SAA, SCI, SCOPUS, SoyAb, T02, T05, TAR, VS, W07, W10, W11, WildRev, Z01.
—CASDDS, IE, Ingenta.
Published by: Universidad Nacional Autonoma de Mexico, Facultad de Medicina Veterinaria y Zootecnia, Circuito Exterior, Ciudad Universitaria, Mexico, 04510, Mexico. TEL 52-5622-5875, FAX 52-5622-5918, http://www.veterin.unam.mx. Ed. Raymundo Martinez Pena. Adv. contact Silvia M Gamboa Ponce. B&W page USD 200, color page USD 240; 21 x 28. Circ: 1,250.

636.089 BRA ISSN 0104-3463
VETERINARIA NOTICIAS. Text in Portuguese, English. 1995. s-a. **Document type:** *Journal, Academic/Scholarly.*
Indexed: A34, A35, A36, A38, AgBio, B23, C01, CABA, D01, E12, F08, F11, F12, GH, H17, IndVet, N02, N04, OR, P33, P37, P39, PN&I, R08, RA&MP, S12, S13, S16, SoyAb, TAR, VS, W10, W11.
—BLDSC (9225.060000).
Published by: Universidade Federal de Uberlandia, Facultade de Medicina Veterinaria, Ave Para, 1720 Bloco 2T, Campus Umuarama, Uberlandia, MG 38400-902, Brazil. TEL 55-34-32182228, FAX 55-34-32182521, http://www.famev.ufu.br/. Ed. Paulo Lourenco Da Silva.

636.089 ITA ISSN 1825-3229
VETERINARIA PRATICA EQUINA. Text in Italian. 1999. q. EUR 55 domestic; EUR 106 foreign (effective 2009). **Document type:** *Journal, Trade.*
Published by: Point Veterinaire Italie Srl (Subsidiary of: Wolters Kluwer N.V.), Via Medardo Rosso 11, Milan, 20159, Italy. TEL 39-02-6085231, FAX 39-02-6682866, info@pointvet.it, http://www.pointvet.it.

636.089 VEN ISSN 0379-8275
CODEN: VETRE3
➤ **VETERINARIA TROPICAL.** Text in Spanish; Summaries in English, Spanish. 1976. a. or exchange basis. bibl.; charts; illus. **Document type:** *Journal, Academic/Scholarly.*
Formerly (until 1976): Instituto de Investigaciones Veterinarias. Boletin
Related titles: CD-ROM ed.
Indexed: A34, A38, C01, CABA, E12, GH, H17, I11, IndVet, N02, N03, N04, P33, P37, P39, R08, RM&VM, S13, S16, T05, TAR, VS, WildRev, Z01.
Published by: Fondo Nacional de Investigaciones Agropecuarias, Apdo. 2103, Maracay, 2105, Venezuela. FAX 58-43-836312. Ed. Aydee Cabrera de Green. Circ: 800.

636.08 AUS ISSN 1447-9168
THE VETERINARIAN. Text in English. 1993. m. AUD 93.50 domestic; AUD 105 in New Zealand; AUD 135 elsewhere (effective 2009). adv. back issues avail. **Document type:** *Magazine, Trade.* **Description:** Covers politics, news, veterinary profiles, in-depth features, diagnostics, practice management, product information, continuing education, competitions and lifestyle information.
Incorporates (in 2003): Treatment
Published by: Sydney Magazine Publishers Pty Ltd., PO Box 5068, South Turramurra, NSW 2074, Australia. TEL 61-2-99412400, FAX 61-2-94154151. Ed. Luke Martin TEL 61-2-99412403. Adv. contact James Martin TEL 61-2-99412404. Circ: 3,927.

VETERINARIJA IR ZOOTECHNIKA. *see* BIOLOGY—Zoology

636.089 CAN ISSN 0830-1743
VETERINARIUS. Text in French. 1984. 6/yr. USD 20. adv.
Published by: Ordre des Medecins Veterinaires du Quebec/Order of Veterinarians of Quebec, 800 ave Ste Anne, Ste 200, St Hyacinthe, PQ J2S 5G7, Canada. TEL 514-774-1427, FAX 514-774-7635. Ed. Dr. Louise Laliberte. Circ: 2,600.

636.089 RUS ISSN 0042-4846
SF604 CODEN: VETNAL
VETERINARIYA. Text in Russian. 1924. m. USD 114 foreign (effective 2005). bk.rev. bibl.; illus. Index. **Document type:** *Journal, Academic/Scholarly.* **Description:** Covers Russian and foreign achievements in prevention and treatment of veterinary diseases.
Related titles: Microfiche ed.: (from EVP).
Indexed: ApicAb, CIN, ChemAb, DBA, FS&TA, IndMed, P30, RefZh, SAA.
—CASDDS, East View, GNLM, Infotrieve, INIST. **CCC.**
Published by: Redaktsiya Zhurnala Veterinariya, Sadovaya-Spasskaya 18, Moscow, 107996, Russian Federation. TEL 7-095-2071060, FAX 7-095-2072812. Ed. Vladimir A Gar'kavtsev. Circ: 20,000. **Dist. by:** M K - Periodica, ul Gilyarovskogo 39, Moscow 129110, Russian Federation. TEL 7-095-2845008, FAX 7-095-2813798, info@periodicals.ru, http://www.mkniga.ru.

636.089 BGR ISSN 1310-5825
VETERINARNA MEDITSINA/VETERINARY MEDICINE. Text in Bulgarian; Summaries in English. q. USD 92 foreign (effective 2002).
Indexed: RefZh.
—BLDSC (0038.410000).
Published by: National Center for Agrarian Sciences, Tsarigradsko shosse Blvd. 125, bl. 1, entry 1, room 215, Sofia, 1113, Bulgaria. TEL 359-2-709127. **Dist. by:** Sofia Books, ul Silivria 16, Sofia 1404, Bulgaria. TEL 359-2-9586257, info@sofiabooks-bg.com, http://www.sofiabooks-bg.com.

636.089 RUS
VETERINARNAYA GAZETA. Text in Russian. 1992. s-m. USD 223 foreign (effective 2007). **Document type:** *Newspaper, Trade.*
Address: a/ya 203, Moscow, Russian Federation. TEL 7-095-9733978, FAX 7-095-9782104. **Dist. by:** East View Information Services, 10601 Wayzata Blvd, Minneapolis, MN 55305. TEL 952-252-1201, 800-477-1005, FAX 952-252-1202, info@eastview.com, http://www.eastview.com.

636 BLR
VETERINARNAYA NAUKA - PROIZVODSTVU; nauchnye trudy. Text in Russian; Summaries in Russian, English. 1960. irreg. **Document type:** *Journal, Academic/Scholarly.* **Description:** Publishes results of experimental research on problems of viral and microbial diseases of agricultural animals, epizootological and diagnostic methods of research, treatment and prevention of parasitic, infectious and non-contagious diseases.

V
W
Z

Former titles (until 1971): Belorusskii Nauchno-Issledovatel'skii Veterinarnyi Institut. Nauchnye Trudy; (until 1970): Puti i Sredstva Snizheniya Poter' v Zhivotnovodstve; (until 1969): Lechenie i Profilaktika Boleznei Sel'skokhozyaistvennykh Zhivotnykh; (until 1967): Dostizheniya Veterinarnoi Nauki - v Proizvodstvo; (until 1966): Profilaktika Zabolevanii Sel'skokhozyaistvennykh Zhivotnykh; (until 1965): Infektsionnye i Parazitarnye Bolezni Sel'skokhozyaistvennykh Zhivotnykh i Ptits; (until 1964): Bor'ba s Poteryami v Zhivotnovodstve; (until 1963): Nauchno-Issledovatel'skii Veterinarnyi Institut. Trudy
Published by: Institut Eksperimental'noi Veterinarii im. S.N. Vyshelesskogo/S.N. Vyshelesskii Institute of Experimental Veterinary Medicine, vul Briket, 28, Minsk, 220003, Belarus. TEL 375-17-5088296, FAX 375-17-5088296, knir@mail.ru, http://bievm.basnet.by. Ed. Anatolii A Gusev.

725.59 CZE ISSN 1214-6080
VETERINARNI KLINIKA. Text in Czech. 2004. q. CZK 300 (effective 2009). adv. **Document type:** *Magazine, Trade.*
—BLDSC (9225.530000).
Published by: Profi Press s.r.o., Drtinova 8, Prague 5, 150 00, Czech Republic. TEL 420-227-018345, FAX 420-227-018310, odbyt@agroweb.cz. Ed. Karel Kovarik.

636.089 CZE ISSN 1214-3774
➤ **VETERINARNI LEKAR.** Text in Czech. 2003. q. CZK 260 (effective 2009). **Document type:** *Journal, Academic/Scholarly.*
Related titles: Online - full text ed.
Published by: Tigis s. r. o., Havlovickeho 16, Prague 4, 152 00, Czech Republic. TEL 420-2-51813192, FAX 420-2-51681217, info@tigis.cz. Ed. Frantisek Jelinek.

636 CZE ISSN 0375-8427
CODEN: VTMDAR
➤ **VETERINARNI MEDICINA/VETERINARY MEDICINE - CZECH.** Text and summaries in English. 1956. m. USD 285 (effective 2008). adv. bibl.; charts; illus.; stat. **Document type:** *Journal, Academic/Scholarly.* **Description:** Contains scientific papers and reviews dealing with veterinary medicine.
Related titles: Online - full text ed.: free (effective 2011).
Indexed: A22, A29, A34, A35, A36, A37, A38, ASCA, AgBio, ApicAb, B20, B21, B23, C25, CABA, CIN, ChemAb, ChemTitl, CurCont, D01, DBA, E12, ESPM, F08, FCA, FS&TA, FoVS&M, G11, GH, H16, H17, ISR, IndMed, IndVet, MaizeAb, N02, N03, N04, OR, P30, P32, P33, P37, P38, P39, P40, PN&I, R07, R08, R12, R13, RA&MP, RM&VM, RefZh, S12, S13, S16, SAA, SCI, SCOPUS, SoyAb, T05, TAR, TriticAb, VS, VirolAbstr, W07, W10, W11, Z01.
—BLDSC (9225.550000), CASDDS, GNLM, IE, Infotrieve, Ingenta, INIST.
Published by: (Vyzkumny Ustav Veterinarniho Lekarstvi/Veterinary Research Institute), Ceska Akademie Zemedelskych Ved, Ustav Zemedelskych a Potravinarskych Informaci/Czech Academy of Agricultural Sciences, Institute of Agricultural and Food Information, Slezska 7, Prague 2, 120 56, Czech Republic. TEL 420-2-227010352, FAX 420-2-227010116, editor@uzpi.cz, http://www.uzpi.cz, http://www.cazv.cz. Ed. Karel Hruska. Circ: 300.

636.089 HRV ISSN 0372-5480
SF604 CODEN: VEARA6
➤ **VETERINARSKI ARHIV.** Text in Croatian, English. 1931. bi-m. HRK 75 to individuals; HRK 150 to institutions (effective 2002). cum.index. back issues avail. **Document type:** *Journal, Academic/Scholarly.* **Description:** Scientific journal of veterinary and related sciences: microbiology, immunology, parasitology, clinical sciences, animal science, physiology, anatomy.
Related titles: Online - full text ed.: ISSN 1331-8055.
Indexed: A22, A26, A34, A35, A36, A37, A38, ASCA, AgBio, AgrForAb, B23, B25, BIOSIS Prev, BP, C25, CA, CABA, CIN, ChemAb, D01, DBA, E12, F08, F11, F12, FCA, G11, GH, H16, H17, I05, IndVet, LT, MaizeAb, MycolAb, N02, N03, N04, P32, P33, P37, P39, P40, PGegResA, PN&I, R07, R08, R11, R13, RA&MP, RM&VM, RefZh, S12, S13, S16, SAA, SCI, SCOPUS, SoyAb, T02, T05, TAR, TriticAb, VS, W07, W10, W11, Z01.
—BLDSC (9226.100000), CASDDS, IE, Ingenta, INIST, Linda Hall.
Published by: Sveuciliste u Zagrebu, Veterinarski Fakultet/University of Zagreb, Faculty of Veterinary Medicine, Heinzelova 55, Zagreb, 10000, Croatia. TEL 385-1-2390206, FAX 385-1-2441390, jmadic@vef.hr. Ed. Josip Madic. Circ: 900.

636.089 SRB ISSN 0350-2457
VETERINARSKI GLASNIK. Text in Serbo-Croatian; Summaries in English, Russian. 1947. m. CSD 2,000 domestic to individuals; CSD 6,000 domestic to institutions; USD 200 foreign (effective 2008). adv. bk.rev. index. back issues avail. **Document type:** *Journal, Academic/Scholarly.*
Indexed: A22, A34, A35, A36, A37, A38, AgBio, ApicAb, B23, B25, BIOSIS Prev, BP, CABA, D01, E12, F08, G11, GH, H16, H17, I11, INIS AtomInd, IndVet, LT, MycolAb, N02, N03, N04, O01, P33, P37, P39, PN&I, R07, R08, R13, RA&MP, RM&VM, RRTA, S12, S13, S16, SAA, T05, VS, W11.
—BLDSC (9226.400000), IE, Ingenta, INIST.
Published by: Univerzitet u Beogradu, Fakultet Veterinarske Medicine/University of Belgrade, Faculty of Veterinary Medicine, Bulevar Oslobodenja 18, Belgrade, 11000. Ed. Col. Vitomir Cupic. Circ: 300.

636.089 CZE ISSN 0506-8231
CODEN: VTERAT
VETERINARSTVI. Text in Czech. 1951. m. CZK 900 (effective 2009). adv. **Document type:** *Magazine, Trade.*
Indexed: A22, A34, A35, A36, A37, A38, AgBio, B23, BA, C25, CABA, D01, DBA, E12, F08, GH, H16, H17, IndVet, MaizeAb, N02, N03, N04, O01, OR, P30, P32, P33, P37, P39, P40, PN&I, R07, R08, R11, R13, RA&MP, RM&VM, S12, S13, S16, SoyAb, T05, TAR, VS, W10, W11.
—BLDSC (9226.500000), IE, Infotrieve, Ingenta.
Published by: Profi Press s.r.o., Drtinova 8, Prague 5, 150 00, Czech Republic. TEL 420-227-018345, FAX 420-227-018310, odbyt@agroweb.cz. Ed. Karel Kovarik. Adv. contact Helena Sedlackova.

636.089 USA ISSN 1948-0288
▼ **VETERINARY ADVANTAGE**; promoting excellence in animal health sales. Text in English. 2009. bi-m. adv. back issues avail. **Document type:** *Magazine, Trade.* **Description:** Provides information for veterinarians, vet techs, distributors and manufacturers involved in animal health business.
Address: 3628 Blakeford Club Dr, Marietta, GA 30062. TEL 866-388-8212, FAX 866-615-9232. Ed. Mark Thill TEL 866-388-8212 ext 704. Pub. Chris Kelly TEL 866-388-8212 ext 702. adv.: page USD 4,500; trim 8 x 10.5. Circ: 4,200.

636.089 GBR ISSN 1467-2987
SF914 CODEN: VANAFV
➤ **VETERINARY ANAESTHESIA AND ANALGESIA.** Abbreviated title: V A A. Text in English. 1970. bi-m. GBP 406 in United Kingdom to institutions; EUR 516 in Europe to institutions; USD 749 in the Americas to institutions; USD 874 elsewhere to institutions; GBP 468 combined subscription in United Kingdom to institutions (print & online eds.); EUR 593 combined subscription in Europe to institutions (print & online eds.); USD 861 combined subscription in the Americas to institutions (print & online eds.); USD 1,005 combined subscription elsewhere to institutions (print & online eds.) (effective 2012). adv. bk.rev. back issues avail.; reprint service avail. from PSC. **Document type:** *Journal, Academic/Scholarly.* **Description:** Contains original articles covering all branches of anaesthesia and the relief of pain in animals. Articles concerned with the following subjects related to anaesthesia and analgesia are also included: the basic sciences; pathophysiology of disease as it relates to anaesthetic management; equipment; intensive care, etc.
Former titles (until 2000): Journal of Veterinary Anaesthesia (1351-6574); (until 1991): Association of Veterinary Anaesthetists of Great Britain and Ireland. Journal (0950-7817); (until 1984): Association of Veterinary Anaesthetists. Proceedings (0269-5243)
Related titles: Online - full text ed.: ISSN 1467-2995. 2000. GBP 406 in United Kingdom to institutions; EUR 516 in Europe to institutions; USD 749 in the Americas to institutions; USD 874 elsewhere to institutions (effective 2012).
Indexed: A01, A03, A08, A22, A26, A34, A35, A37, A38, AgBio, Agr, CA, CABA, ChemAb, CurCont, D01, DBA, E01, E12, EMBASE, ExcerpMed, FoVS&M, GH, H12, IndVet, MEDLINE, N04, P30, P33, P37, PN&I, S12, SCI, SCOPUS, T02, TAR, VS, W07, W11.
—BLDSC (9226.528500), IE, Infotrieve, Ingenta. **CCC.**
Published by: (American College of Veterinary Anesthesiologists USA, Association of Veterinary Anaesthetists, European College of Veterinary Anaesthesia), Wiley-Blackwell Publishing Ltd. (Subsidiary of: John Wiley & Sons, Inc.), 9600 Garsington Rd, Oxford, OX4 2DQ, United Kingdom. TEL 44-1865-776868, FAX 44-1865-714591, customerservices@blackwellpublishing.com. Eds. K W Clarke, Dr. Peter J Pascoe. Adv. contact Mia Scott Ruddock TEL 44-1865-476354.

636.089 616.992 GBR ISSN 1476-5810
SF910.T8
➤ **VETERINARY AND COMPARATIVE ONCOLOGY.** Text in English. 2003 (Mar.). q. GBP 334 in United Kingdom to institutions; EUR 426 in Europe to institutions; USD 618 in the Americas to institutions; USD 726 elsewhere to institutions; GBP 385 combined subscription in United Kingdom to institutions (print & online eds.); EUR 490 combined subscription in Europe to institutions (print & online eds.); USD 712 combined subscription in the Americas to institutions (print & online eds.); USD 835 combined subscription elsewhere to institutions (print & online eds.) (effective 2012). adv. back issues avail.; reprint service avail. from PSC. **Document type:** *Journal, Academic/Scholarly.* **Description:** Integrates clinical and scientific information from a variety of related disciplines and from worldwide sources for all veterinary oncologists concerned with aetiology, diagnosis and clinical course of cancer in domestic animals and its prevention.
Related titles: Online - full text ed.: ISSN 1476-5829. GBP 334 in United Kingdom to institutions; EUR 426 in Europe to institutions; USD 618 in the Americas to institutions; USD 726 elsewhere to institutions (effective 2012) (from IngentaConnect).
Indexed: A01, A03, A08, A22, A26, A34, A35, A36, A37, A38, AgBio, Agr, CA, CABA, D01, E01, EMBASE, ExcerpMed, FoVS&M, GH, IndVet, MEDLINE, N04, P30, P33, P37, P39, R08, RM&VM, SCI, SCOPUS, T02, T05, TAR, VS, W07.
—BLDSC (9226.528800), IE, Ingenta. **CCC.**
Published by: (European Society of Veterinary Oncology USA), Wiley-Blackwell Publishing Ltd. (Subsidiary of: John Wiley & Sons, Inc.), 9600 Garsington Rd, Oxford, OX4 2DQ, United Kingdom. TEL 44-1865-776868, FAX 44-1865-714591, customerservices@blackwellpublishing.com. Eds. Dr. David J Argyle, David M Vail. Adv. contact Mia Scott Ruddock TEL 44-1865-476354. **Subscr. to:** 1-7 Oldlands Way, PO Box 809, Bognor Regis PO21 9FG, United Kingdom. TEL 44-1865-778054.

636.089 DEU ISSN 0932-0814
SF910.5
➤ **VETERINARY AND COMPARATIVE ORTHOPAEDICS AND TRAUMATOLOGY.** Short title: V.C.O.T. Text in English. 1988. 4/yr. EUR 198 in Europe to individuals; EUR 418 in Europe to institutions; EUR 84 to students; EUR 72 newsstand/cover (effective 2011). adv. bk.rev. abstr. **Document type:** *Journal, Academic/Scholarly.* **Description:** Deals with orthopaedics and traumatology in veterinary medicine.
Indexed: A22, A34, A36, A37, A38, ASCA, Agr, BibAg, CABA, CurCont, E12, EMBASE, ExcerpMed, FoVS&M, GH, IndVet, MEDLINE, N04, P30, PN&I, SAA, SCI, SCOPUS, VS, W07.
—BLDSC (9226.600000), GNLM, IE, Infotrieve, Ingenta. **CCC.**
Published by: Schattauer GmbH, Hoelderlinstr 3, Stuttgart, 70174, Germany. TEL 49-711-229870, FAX 49-711-2298750, info@schattauer.de, http://www.schattauer.com. Adv. contact Christian Matthe. Circ: 1,750 (paid and controlled). **Subscr. to:** CSJ, Postfach 140220, Munich 80452, Germany. TEL 49-89-20959129, schattauer@csj.de. **Co-sponsor:** Veterinary Orthopedic Society (North America), European Society of Veterinary Orthopaedics and Traumatology, British Veterinary Orthopaedic Association.

636.089 330 GBR ISSN 1474-1652
VETERINARY BUSINESS JOURNAL. Text in English. 1994. bi-m. GBP 80 domestic; GBP 95 foreign; free to qualified personnel (effective 2009). adv. **Document type:** *Journal, Academic/Scholarly.* **Description:** Created by practice owners and managers as the key journal for providing guidance on matters relating to running a practice.
Indexed: A34, A37, CABA, D01, E12, GH, IndVet, PN&I, S13, S16, VS, W11.
—**CCC.**
Published by: Veterinary Business Development Ltd. (Subsidiary of: Wolters Kluwer N.V.), Olympus House, Werrington Ctr, Peterborough, PE4 6NA, United Kingdom. TEL 44-1733-325522, FAX 44-1733-352512. Ed. Paul Imrie TEL 44-1733-383554.

636.089 USA ISSN 0275-6382
CODEN: VCPADJ
➤ **VETERINARY CLINICAL PATHOLOGY.** Text in English. 1972. q. GBP 192 combined subscription in United Kingdom to institutions (print & online eds.); EUR 243 combined subscription in Europe to institutions (print & online eds.); USD 361 combined subscription in the Americas to institutions (print & online eds.); USD 374 combined subscription elsewhere to institutions (print & online eds.) (effective 2012). adv. bk.rev. abstr. Index. back issues avail.; reprint service avail. from PSC. **Document type:** *Journal, Academic/Scholarly.* **Description:** Covers the news, developments and trends affecting companion animal, exotic, equine and livestock veterinary practices. Topic areas include medical, business and industry, practice management and demographics.
Former titles: American Society for Veterinary Clinical Pathology. Journal; (until 1977): American Society of Veterinary Clinical Pathologists. Bulletin (0147-0701)
Related titles: Online - full text ed.: ISSN 1939-165X. GBP 174 in United Kingdom to institutions; EUR 221 in Europe to institutions; USD 328 in the Americas to institutions; USD 341 elsewhere to institutions (effective 2012) (from IngentaConnect).
Indexed: A22, A34, A35, A36, A37, A38, ASCA, AgBio, Agr, B25, BA, BIOSIS Prev, BiolDig, CA, CABA, ChemAb, D01, E01, E12, EMBASE, ExcerpMed, F08, F12, FoVS&M, GH, H17, IndVet, MEDLINE, MaizeAb, MycolAb, N02, N04, P30, P33, P37, P39, PN&I, R08, R13, RM&VM, SAA, SCI, SCOPUS, T02, T05, TAR, TriticAb, VS, W07, WildRev.
—BLDSC (9227.015500), CASDDS, IE, Infotrieve, Ingenta. **CCC.**
Published by: (American Society for Veterinary Clinical Pathology), Wiley-Blackwell Publishing, Inc. (Subsidiary of: Wiley-Blackwell Publishing Ltd.), 111 River St, Hoboken, NJ 07030. TEL 201-748-6000, FAX 201-748-6088, info@wiley.com. Ed. Karen M Young. Adv. contact Gennifer Davis TEL 856-768-9360.

636.089 USA ISSN 0749-0739
SF951
➤ **VETERINARY CLINICS OF NORTH AMERICA: EQUINE PRACTICE.** Text in English. 1971. 3/yr. USD 373 in United States to institutions; USD 466 elsewhere to institutions (effective 2012). illus. Index. back issues avail.; reprints avail. **Document type:** *Journal, Academic/Scholarly.* **Description:** Each issue covers a single topic relating to the treatment of conditions and diseases of horses.
Supersedes in part (in 1985): The Veterinary Clinics of North America. Large Animal Practice (0196-9846); Which superseded in part (in 1979): Veterinary Clinics of North America (0091-0279)
Related titles: Microfilm ed.; Online - full text ed.: ISSN 1558-4224. free (effective 2010) (from ScienceDirect).
Indexed: A20, A22, A34, A35, A36, A38, ASCA, AgBio, Agr, CABA, CurCont, D01, DBA, E12, EMBASE, ExcerpMed, F08, F12, FoVS&M, G11, GH, H16, H17, ISR, IndMed, IndVet, LT, MEDLINE, N02, N04, P30, P33, P39, PN&I, R08, R13, RA&MP, RM&VM, RRTA, S12, SCI, SCOPUS, VS, W07, W10, W11.
—BLDSC (9227.017800), GNLM, IE, Infotrieve, Ingenta, INIST, Linda Hall. **CCC.**
Published by: W.B. Saunders Co. (Subsidiary of: Elsevier Health Sciences), Elsevier, Health Sciences Division, Order Fulfillment, 3251 Riverport Ln, Maryland Heights, MO 63043. TEL 800-545-2522, FAX 314-447-8093, 800-535-9935, sales.inquiry@elsevier.com, http://www.us.elsevierhealth.com. Ed. Reynolds Cowles.

636.089 USA ISSN 1094-9194
➤ **VETERINARY CLINICS OF NORTH AMERICA: EXOTIC ANIMAL PRACTICE.** Text in English. 1998. 3/yr. USD 345 in United States to institutions; USD 407 elsewhere to institutions (effective 2012). illus. Index. back issues avail.; reprints avail. **Document type:** *Journal, Academic/Scholarly.* **Description:** Devotes each issue to a single topic in veterinary medicine. Provides detailed information invaluable to treating exotic animal populations, including therapeutics, respiratory medicine, and soft tissue surgery.
Related titles: Online - full text ed.: ISSN 1558-4232. free (effective 2010) (from ScienceDirect).
Indexed: A34, A36, A37, A38, CABA, D01, E12, EMBASE, ExcerpMed, G11, GH, H17, IndMed, IndVet, MEDLINE, N04, P30, P33, P37, P39, PN&I, R08, R13, RM&VM, S13, S16, SCOPUS, T05, TAR, VS, W10, W11, WildRev, Z01.
—BLDSC (9227.017850). **CCC.**
Published by: W.B. Saunders Co. (Subsidiary of: Elsevier Health Sciences), Elsevier, Health Sciences Division, Order Fulfillment, 3251 Riverport Ln, Maryland Heights, MO 63043. TEL 800-545-2522, FAX 314-447-8093, 800-535-9935, sales.inquiry@elsevier.com, http://www.us.elsevierhealth.com. Ed. Laura Wade.

636.089 USA ISSN 0749-0720
SF601
➤ **VETERINARY CLINICS OF NORTH AMERICA: FOOD ANIMAL PRACTICE.** Text in English. 1971. 3/yr. USD 278 in United States to institutions; USD 363 elsewhere to institutions (effective 2012). illus. Index. back issues avail.; reprints avail. **Document type:** *Monographic series, Academic/Scholarly.* **Description:** Each issue discusses an aspect of the treatment of conditions in cows, pigs, and sheep.
Supersedes in part (in 1985): The Veterinary Clinics of North America. Large Animal Practice (0196-9846); Which superseded in part (in 1979): Veterinary Clinics of North America (0091-0279)
Related titles: Microfilm ed.; Online - full text ed.: ISSN 1558-4240. free (effective 2010) (from ScienceDirect).
Indexed: A22, A34, A35, A36, A37, A38, ASCA, AgBio, Agr, BA, CABA, CurCont, D01, DBA, E12, EMBASE, ExcerpMed, FoVS&M, G11, GH, H17, IndMed, IndVet, MEDLINE, MaizeAb, N02, N04, P30, P33, P39, R08, S13, S16, SCI, SCOPUS, SoyAb, TAR, TriticAb, VS, W07, W10, W11.
—BLDSC (9227.017900), GNLM, IE, Infotrieve, Ingenta, INIST, Linda Hall. **CCC.**
Published by: W.B. Saunders Co. (Subsidiary of: Elsevier Health Sciences), Elsevier, Health Sciences Division, Order Fulfillment, 3251 Riverport Ln, Maryland Heights, MO 63043. TEL 800-545-2522, FAX 314-447-8093, 800-535-9935, sales.inquiry@elsevier.com, http://www.us.elsevierhealth.com. Eds. D Scott McVey, Sanjay Kapil.

636.089 USA ISSN 0195-5616
SF601 CODEN: VNAPDW

➤ **VETERINARY CLINICS OF NORTH AMERICA: SMALL ANIMAL PRACTICE.** Text in English. 1971. bi-m. USD 427 in United States to institutions; USD 525 elsewhere to institutions (effective 2012). illus. index. reprints avail. **Document type:** *Journal, Academic/Scholarly.* **Description:** Discusses current information and the latest advances on the treatment of dogs and cats and provides a sound basis for choosing treatment options.

Supersedes in part (in 1979): Veterinary Clinics of North America (0091-0279)

Related titles: Microform ed.: (from MIM, PQC); Online - full text ed.: ISSN 1878-1306. free (effective 2010) (from IngentaConnect, ScienceDirect).

Indexed: A22, A34, A35, A36, A37, A38, ASCA, AgBio, Agr, B21, B25, BIOSIS Prev, CABA, CurCont, DBA, DentInd, E12, EMBASE, ExcerpMed, FoVS&M, GH, H17, ISR, IndMed, IndVet, MEDLINE, MycolAb, N02, N04, P30, P33, P37, P39, PN&I, R08, R13, RA&MP, RM&VM, S13, S16, SAA, SCI, SCOPUS, T05, VS, W07, W11.

—BLDSC (9227.020000), IE, Infotrieve, Ingenta, INIST, Linda Hall. **CCC.**

Published by: W.B. Saunders Co. (Subsidiary of: Elsevier Health Sciences), Elsevier, Health Sciences Division, Order Fulfillment, 3251 Riverport Ln, Maryland Heights, MO 63043. TEL 800-545-2522, FAX 314-447-8093, 800-535-9935, sales.inquiry@elsevier.com, http://www.us.elsevierhealth.com. Ed. William B Thomas.

636.0890993 NZL ISSN 1176-0028

VETERINARY COUNCIL OF NEW ZEALAND. HANDBOOK. CODE OF PROFESSIONAL CONDUCT. Text in English. 2002. a. **Document type:** *Handbook/Manual/Guide, Trade.*

Formed by the 2002 merger of: Veterinary Council of New Zealand. Annual Report; Veterinary Council of New Zealand. Handbook & Code of Professional Conduct (1175-7108); Which was formerly (until 1999): Veterinary Council of New Zealand. Register of Veterinarians (1174-202X); (until 1997): New Zealand Veterinarian Register (1174-1384); (until 1996): New Zealand Register of Veterinarians; (until 1995): Veterinary Council of New Zealand. Register of Veterinary Surgeons; (until 1991): Veterinary Surgeons Board of New Zealand. Veterinary Surgeons in New Zealand; (until 1968): Veterinary Surgeons Board. Veterinary Surgeons

Related titles: Online - full text ed.

Published by: Veterinary Council of New Zealand, Level 11, Kordia House, 109 Willis St, PO Box 10 563, Wellington, 6143, New Zealand. TEL 64-4-4739600, FAX 64-4-4738869, vet@vetcouncil.org.nz.

636.089 GBR ISSN 0959-4493
SF901 CODEN: VEDEEK

➤ **VETERINARY DERMATOLOGY.** Text in English. 1990. bi-m. GBP 791 in United Kingdom to institutions; EUR 1,004 in Europe to institutions; USD 1,458 in the Americas to institutions; USD 1,699 elsewhere to institutions; GBP 910 combined subscription in United Kingdom to institutions (print & online eds.); EUR 1,156 combined subscription in Europe to institutions (print & online eds.); USD 1,677 combined subscription in the Americas to institutions (print & online eds.); USD 1,954 combined subscription elsewhere to institutions (print & online eds.) (effective 2012). adv. back issues avail.; reprint service avail. from PSC. **Document type:** *Journal, Academic/Scholarly.* **Description:** Covers the study of dermatology over a wide variety of species and serves as a unifying discipline for veterinarians and research scientists.

Related titles: Microfilm ed.: (from PQC); Online - full text ed.: ISSN 1365-3164. 1999. GBP 791 in United Kingdom to institutions; EUR 1,004 in Europe to institutions; USD 1,458 in the Americas to institutions; USD 1,699 elsewhere to institutions (effective 2012) (from IngentaConnect); Supplement(s): Veterinary Dermatology. Supplement. ISSN 1471-2679. 2000.

Indexed: A01, A03, A08, A22, A26, A29, A34, A35, A36, A37, A38, ASCA, AgBio, Agr, B20, B21, CA, CABA, CurCont, D01, DBA, E01, E12, EMBASE, ESPM, ExcerpMed, F08, F12, FoVS&M, GH, H12, H16, H17, ISR, IndVet, MEDLINE, N02, N04, P30, P32, P33, P37, P39, P40, PN&I, R07, R08, R13, RA&MP, RM&VM, S13, S16, SCI, SCOPUS, SoyAb, T02, T05, TAR, VS, VirolAbstr, W07, W10.

—BLDSC (9227.026000), IE, Infotrieve, Ingenta. **CCC.**

Published by: (American Academy of Veterinary Dermatology USA, European Society of Veterinary Dermatology, Canadian Academy of Veterinarian Dermatology CAN), Wiley-Blackwell Publishing Ltd. (Subsidiary of: John Wiley & Sons, Inc.), 9600 Garsington Rd, Oxford, OX4 2DQ, United Kingdom. TEL 44-1865-776868, FAX 44-1865-714591, customerservices@blackwellpublishing.com. Ed. Dr. Aiden Foster. Adv. contact Mia Scott Ruddock TEL 44-1865-476354. **Co-sponsors:** European College of Veterinary Dermatology; American College of Veterinary Dermatology.

➤ **VETERINARY ECONOMICS**; business solutions for practicing veterinarians. *see* BUSINESS AND ECONOMICS—Small Business

➤ **VETERINARY FOCUS**; the worlwide journal for the companion animal veterinarian. *see* PETS

636.089 USA ISSN 1096-5904

VETERINARY HERITAGE. Text in English. 1982. s-a. free to members (effective 2011). back issues avail. **Document type:** *Journal, Academic/Scholarly.*

Formerly (until 1982): American Veterinary Historical Society. Newsletter

Indexed: EMBASE, MEDLINE, P30.

Published by: American Veterinary Medical History Society, 23 Wedgewood Dr, Ithaca, NY 14850. TEL 607-253-3499, FAX 607-253-3080, skw2@cornell.edu, http://avmhs.org.

636.089 GBR ISSN 0301-6943

VETERINARY HISTORY. Text in English. 1978. s-a. free to members (effective 2009). bk.rev.; rec.rev.; software rev. abstr.; bibl.; illus. 1 cols./p.; back issues avail. **Document type:** *Journal, Academic/Scholarly.* **Description:** Covers information about the Veterinary History Society.

Indexed: P30, SCOPUS.

Published by: Veterinary History Society, c/o Bruce Jones, Netherton Lodge, Quenington, Cirencester, GL7 5DD, United Kingdom. TEL 44-1285-750346, FAX 44-1285-750053, chairman@veterinaryhistorysociety.org.uk. Ed. John Clewlow.

636.089 NLD ISSN 0165-2427
SF757.2 CODEN: VIIMDS

➤ **VETERINARY IMMUNOLOGY AND IMMUNOPATHOLOGY.** Text in English. 1980. 24/yr. EUR 2,657 in Europe to institutions; JPY 352,900 in Japan to institutions; USD 2,972 elsewhere to institutions (effective 2012). adv. bk.rev. illus. index. back issues avail. **Document type:** *Journal, Academic/Scholarly.* **Description:** Deals with the study of veterinary immunology and immunopathology as applied to domestic animals, laboratory animals and other species that are useful to man.

Related titles: Microform ed.: (from PQC); Online - full text ed.: ISSN 1873-2534. 199? (from IngentaConnect, ScienceDirect).

Indexed: A01, A03, A08, A22, A26, A29, A34, A35, A36, A37, A38, AIDS&CR, ASCA, ASFA, AgBio, Agr, B20, B21, B23, B25, BIOBASE, BIOSIS Prev, CA, CABA, CIN, ChemAb, CurCont, D01, DBA, E12, EMBASE, ESPM, ExcerpMed, F08, F11, F12, FoVS&M, G11, GH, H16, H17, I05, IABS, ISR, ImmunAb, IndMed, IndVet, Inpharma, MEDLINE, MycolAb, N02, N04, OR, P30, P32, P33, P37, P39, P40, PN&I, R07, R08, R10, R12, R13, RA&MP, RM&VM, Reac, S01, S13, S16, SAA, SCI, SCOPUS, SoyAb, T02, T05, TAR, VS, VirolAbstr, W07, W08, W10, W11, WildRev.

—BLDSC (9228.200000), CASDDS, GNLM, IE, Infotrieve, Ingenta, INIST, Linda Hall. **CCC.**

Published by: Elsevier BV (Subsidiary of: Elsevier Science & Technology), Radarweg 29, PO Box 211, Amsterdam, 1000 AE, Netherlands. TEL 31-20-4853911, FAX 31-20-4852457, JournalsCustomerServiceEMEA@elsevier.com, http://www.elsevier.nl. Eds. Dr. C J Howard, C L Baldwin, Dr. J Naessens. **Subscr. to:** Radarweg 29, PO Box 211, Amsterdam 1000 AE, Netherlands. TEL 31-20-4853757, FAX 31-20-4853432.

636.089 POL ISSN 0042-4870
SF600 CODEN: BVIPA7

VETERINARY INSTITUTE, PULAWY. BULLETIN. Text and summaries in English. 1957. s-a. USD 100 foreign (effective 2005). abstr.; bibl. 100 p./no. 1 cols./p.; back issues avail. **Document type:** *Bulletin, Trade.* **Description:** Publishes original scientific articles on all aspects of veterinary science and related subjects.

Formerly (until 1962): Instytut Weterynarii w Pulawach. Biuletyn (0079-791X)

Related titles: CD-ROM ed.

Indexed: A34, A35, A36, A37, A38, ASCA, AgBio, AgrAg, AgrForAb, AgrLib, B23, BP, C25, CABA, ChemAb, D01, E12, F08, F11, F12, FS&TA, FoVS&M, G11, GH, H16, H17, IndVet, LT, MaizeAb, N02, N03, N04, OR, P32, P33, P37, P39, P40, PN&I, R07, R08, R13, RA&MP, RM&VM, RRTA, S12, S13, S16, SAA, SCI, SCOPUS, SoyAb, T05, TAR, TriticAb, VS, W07, W10, W11.

—BLDSC (2805.300000), CASDDS, IE, Ingenta.

Published by: (State Committee for Scientific Research), Panstwowy Instytut Weterenaryjny/National Veterinary Research Institute, Al Partyzantow 57, Pulawy, 24100, Poland. TEL 48-81-8863051, FAX 48-81-8862595, sekretariat@piwet.pulawy.pl, roszk@piwet.pulawy.pl, http://www.piwet.pulawy.pl. Ed. Jacek Roszkowski. Pub. Tadeusz Wijaszka. Adv. contact Krystyna Wilczynska-Ciemiega. Circ: 550.

636.089 GBR ISSN 2009-3942
SF601 CODEN: IVTJAJ

➤ **VETERINARY IRELAND JOURNAL/IRIS TREIDLIACHTA EIREANN.** Text in English. 1946. m. adv. bk.rev. abstr. back issues avail. **Document type:** *Journal, Academic/Scholarly.*

Supersedes in part (in 2011): Irish Veterinary Journal (Print) (0368-0762); Which incorporated (1994-1995): Irish Veterinary Times (1393-3817); Which was formerly (until 1994): Veterinary Surgeon (0791-8542); (until 1993): Irish Veterinary News (0332-236X)

Related titles: Online - full text ed.: free (effective 2011).

Indexed: A01, A22, A34, A35, A36, A37, A38, ASCA, AgBio, CA, CABA, ChemAb, CurCont, D01, DBA, E12, F08, FoVS&M, G11, GH, H17, ISR, IndVet, LT, N02, N03, N04, OR, P30, P33, P34, P37, P39, PN&I, R08, R12, R13, RM&VM, RRTA, SAA, SCI, SCOPUS, T02, T05, TAR, VS, W07, W10, W11, WildRev.

—BLDSC (9228.360000), CASDDS, IE, Infotrieve, Ingenta. **CCC.**

Published by: (Veterinary Ireland IRL), BioMed Central Ltd. (Subsidiary of: Springer Science+Business Media), 236 Gray's Inn Rd, London, WC1X 8HB, United Kingdom. TEL 44-20-31922009, FAX 44-20-31922010, info@biomedcentral.com, http://www.biomedcentral.com.

636.089 GBR ISSN 1090-0233
SF601 CODEN: VTJRFP

➤ **THE VETERINARY JOURNAL.** Abbreviated title: T V J. Text in English. 1875. m. EUR 1,006 in Europe to institutions; JPY 108,600 in Japan to institutions; USD 895 elsewhere to institutions (effective 2012). adv. bk.rev. abstr.; charts; illus.; stat. index. reprint service avail. from PSC. **Document type:** *Journal, Academic/Scholarly.* **Description:** Publishes worldwide contributions on all aspects of veterinary science and its related subjects.

Former titles (until 1997): British Veterinary Journal (Print) (0007-1935); (until 1949): Veterinary Journal (0372-5545); (until 1900): Veterinary Journal and Annals of Comparative Pathology

Related titles: Microform ed.: (from PMC, PQC); Online - full text ed.: ISSN 1532-2971. USD 733 to institutions (effective 2009) (from ScienceDirect).

Indexed: A01, A03, A08, A22, A26, A29, A34, A35, A36, A37, A38, ASCA, ASFA, AgBio, Agr, B20, B21, B23, B25, BIOSIS Prev, BP, BibAg, C25, CA, CABA, CIN, CISA, CTA, ChemAb, ChemTitl, ChemoAb, CurCont, D01, DBA, E01, E12, EMBASE, ESPM, ExcerpMed, F08, FS&TA, FoVS&M, G11, GH, H17, I05, I10, IBR, IBZ, ISR, IndMed, IndVet, LT, MEDLINE, MaizeAb, MycolAb, N02, N04, NSA, OR, P30, P32, P33, P37, P39, PN&I, R07, R08, R11, R12, R13, RA&MP, RM&VM, RRTA, S12, S13, S16, SAA, SCI, SCOPUS, SoyAb, T02, T05, TAR, VS, VirolAbstr, W07, W10, W11, WildRev.

—BLDSC (9228.600000), CASDDS, GNLM, IE, Infotrieve, Ingenta, INIST, Linda Hall. **CCC.**

Published by: (Animal Health Trust), Elsevier Ltd (Subsidiary of: Elsevier Science & Technology), The Blvd, Langford Ln, Kidlington, Oxford, OX5 1GB, United Kingdom. TEL 44-1865-843000, FAX 44-1865-843010, customerserviceau@elsevier.com. Ed. Andrew J Higgins. **Subscr. to:** Harcourt Publishers Ltd., Foots Cray High St, Sidcup, Kent DA14 5HP, United Kingdom. TEL 44-20-83085700, FAX 44-20-8309-0807.

636.089 USA ISSN 1059-0994

VETERINARY MEDICAL REVIEW. Text in English. 1971; N.S. 1980. s-a. free (effective 2005). charts; illus.; stat. back issues avail. **Description:** For alumni, faculty and students, as well as other practicing veterinarians in Missouri.

Incorporates (1950-1979): Missouri Veterinarian (0540-4517); Which was formerly: Veterinary Scope

Published by: University of Missouri at Columbia, College of Veterinary Medicine, Veterinary Medical Library, W218 Veterinary Medicine, Columbia, MO 65211. TEL 314-882-2461. Ed. Randy Mertens. Circ: 3,000.

636.089 PAK ISSN 1728-9459

VETERINARY MEDICAL SOCIETY. RECORD. Text in English. 1985. m. USD 300 (effective 2005). **Document type:** *Journal, Academic/Scholarly.* **Description:** Study of veterinary medical research.

Published by: (Veterinary Medical Society), International Press, P O Box 17700, Karachi, 75300, Pakistan. TEL 92-21-4947486, FAX 92-21-4989257, light_68@hotmail.com. Ed. Dr. G A Salik.

636.089 PAK ISSN 1728-9440

THE VETERINARY MEDICINE. Text in English. 1985. m. GBP 300 (effective 2005). **Document type:** *Journal, Academic/Scholarly.* **Description:** Study of veterinary diseases.

Published by: (Veterinary Association), International Press, P O Box 17700, Karachi, 75300, Pakistan. TEL 92-21-4947486, FAX 92-21-4989257, light_68@hotmail.com. Ed. Dr. Y Qurashi.

636.089 USA ISSN 8750-7943
CODEN: VEMEEV

➤ **VETERINARY MEDICINE.** Text in English. 1905. m. USD 60 domestic; USD 72 in Canada & Mexico; USD 97 elsewhere; USD 17 newsstand/cover domestic; USD 21 newsstand/cover in Canada & Mexico; USD 23 newsstand/cover elsewhere (effective 2011). adv. bk.rev. abstr.; bibl.; charts; illus.; stat.; tr.lit. index. reprints avail. **Document type:** *Journal, Academic/Scholarly.* **Description:** Provides practicing veterinarians with peer reviewed practical solutions to common diagnostic and therapeutic problems.

Formerly (until 1985): Veterinary Medicine - Small Animal Clinician (0042-4889)

Related titles: Microform ed.: (from PQC); Online - full text ed.: ISSN 1939-1919. USD 45 (effective 2011).

Indexed: A01, A03, A08, A10, A22, A26, A34, A36, A37, A38, ASCA, Agr, B&AI, B02, B04, B10, B15, B17, B18, BRD, BibAg, CA, CABA, DBA, E12, F08, G04, G08, GH, H12, H16, H17, I05, IndMed, IndVet, N04, P10, P11, P16, P26, P30, P33, P37, P39, P48, P52, P53, P54, P56, PN&I, PQC, R08, RM&VM, S04, S10, SAA, SCOPUS, T02, V03, VS, W03, W05, W10, WildRev.

—BLDSC (9229.000000), GNLM, IE, Ingenta, INIST. **CCC.**

Published by: Advanstar Veterinary Healthcare Communications (Subsidiary of: Advanstar Communications, Inc.), 8033 Flint, Lenexa, KS 66214. TEL 800-255-6864, FAX 913-871-3808. Ed. Margaret Rampey. Circ: 54,135 (controlled).

636.089 USA ISSN 2042-0048
SF604

▼ **VETERINARY MEDICINE INTERNATIONAL.** Text in English. 2010. irreg. free (effective 2011). **Document type:** *Journal, Academic/Scholarly.*

Media: Online - full text.

Indexed: A01, B&BAb, B21, ImmunAb, P30, T02.

Published by: Sage - Hindawi Access to Research, 410 Park Ave, 15th Fl, 287 PMB, New York, NY 10022. FAX 866-446-3294.

636.089 PAK ISSN 1728-9432

VETERINARY MEDICINE. PROCEEDINGS. Text in English. m. GBP 300 (effective 2005). **Document type:** *Proceedings, Academic/Scholarly.* **Description:** Study of veterinary diseases.

Published by: (International Society of Veterinary Practitioner), International Press, P O Box 17700, Karachi, 75300, Pakistan. TEL 92-21-4947486, FAX 92-21-4989257, light_68@hotmail.com. Ed. Dr. M A Raza.

636.089 GBR ISSN 2230-2034

▼ ➤ **VETERINARY MEDICINE: RESEARCH AND REPORTS.** Text in English. 2010. irreg. free (effective 2011). **Document type:** *Journal, Academic/Scholarly.*

Media: Online - full text.

—**CCC.**

Published by: Dove Medical Press Ltd., Beechfield House, Winterton Way, Macclesfield, SK11 0JL, United Kingdom. TEL 44-1625-509130, FAX 44-1625-617933. Ed. Dr. Jeffrey Musser.

➤ **VETERINARY MICROBIOLOGY.** *see* BIOLOGY—Microbiology

636.089 USA ISSN 1526-2073
SF895

➤ **VETERINARY NEUROLOGY AND NEUROSURGERY.** Text in English. 1999. q. free (effective 2010). back issues avail. **Document type:** *Journal, Academic/Scholarly.* **Description:** Provides veterinary medical information.

Media: Online - full text.

Indexed: A34, CABA, IndVet, VS.

Published by: Veterinary Information Network, 777 W Covell Blvd, Davis, CA 95616. TEL 530-756-4881, 800-700-4636, FAX 530-756-6035, vingram@vin.com. Ed. T A Holliday.

636.089 GBR ISSN 2044-0065

▼ ➤ **THE VETERINARY NURSE.** Text in English. 2010. 10/yr. GBP 90 domestic; GBP 120 in Europe; GBP 160 elsewhere; GBP 130 combined subscription domestic (print & online eds.); GBP 160 combined subscription in Europe (print & online eds.); GBP 200 combined subscription elsewhere (print & online eds.) (effective 2011). adv. back issues avail. **Document type:** *Journal, Academic/Scholarly.* **Description:** Features articles for veterinary nurses around the world who wish to enhance their practice and deepen their understanding of veterinary nursing.

Related titles: Online - full text ed.: GBP 80 domestic; GBP 100 elsewhere (effective 2011).

Indexed: A34, E12, F08, P33, R08, W10, W11.

Published by: MA Healthcare Ltd., St Jude's Church, Dulwich Rd, London, SE24 0PB, United Kingdom. TEL 44-20-77385454, conferences@markallengroup.com, http://www.mahealthcareevents.co.uk. Ed. Georgina Grell. Adv. contact Anthony Kerr.

636.089 GBR ISSN 1741-5349
VETERINARY NURSING JOURNAL. Abbreviated title: V N J. Text in English. 1986. m. GBP 139 in United Kingdom to institutions; EUR 174 in Europe to institutions; USD 204 elsewhere to institutions; GBP 159 combined subscription in United Kingdom to institutions (print & online eds.); EUR 200 combined subscription in Europe to institutions (print & online eds.); USD 234 combined subscription elsewhere to institutions (print & online eds.) (effective 2012). adv. back issues avail. **Document type:** *Journal, Academic/Scholarly.*
Related titles: Online - full text ed.: ISSN 2045-0648. GBP 139 in United Kingdom to institutions; EUR 174 in Europe to institutions; USD 204 elsewhere to institutions (effective 2012).
Indexed: A01.
—CCC.
Published by: (British Veterinary Nursing Association Ltd.), Wiley-Blackwell Publishing Ltd. (Subsidiary of: John Wiley & Sons, Inc.), The Atrium, Southern Gate, Chichester, West Sussex PO19 8SQ, United Kingdom. TEL 44-1243-779777, FAX 44-1243-775878, customer@wiley.co.uk. Ed. David Watson. Adv. contact Emma Devine TEL 44-1449-720881.

636.089 617.7 GBR ISSN 1463-5216
SF891
➤ **VETERINARY OPHTHALMOLOGY.** Text in English. 1991. bi-m. GBP 666 in United Kingdom to institutions; EUR 846 in Europe to institutions; USD 911 in the Americas to institutions; USD 1,304 elsewhere to institutions; GBP 767 combined subscription in United Kingdom to institutions (print & online eds.); EUR 974 combined subscription in Europe to institutions (print & online eds.); USD 1,048 combined subscription in the Americas to institutions (print & online eds.); USD 1,500 combined subscription elsewhere to institutions (print & online eds.) (effective 2012). adv. back issues avail.; reprint service avail. from PSC. **Document type:** *Journal, Academic/Scholarly.* **Description:** Contains material relating to all aspects of clinical and investigational veterinary and comparative ophthalmology.
Former titles (until 1998): Veterinary & Comparative Ophthalmology (1076-4607); (until 1994): Progress in Veterinary & Comparative Ophthalmology (1061-5768)
Related titles: Online - full text ed.: ISSN 1463-5224. 1998. GBP 666 in United Kingdom to institutions; EUR 846 in Europe to institutions; USD 911 in the Americas to institutions; USD 1,304 elsewhere to institutions (effective 2012) (from IngentaConnect).
Indexed: A01, A03, A08, A22, A26, A34, A35, A36, A37, A38, AgBio, Agr, B25, BIOSIS Prev, CA, CABA, CurCont, D01, E01, E12, EMBASE, ExcerpMed, FoVS&M, GH, H12, H17, IndVet, MEDLINE, MaizeAb, MycolAb, N02, N04, P30, P33, P37, P39, PN&I, R08, RM&VM, S12, SCI, SCOPUS, T02, T05, TAR, VS, W07, W11, Z01.
—BLDSC (9229.162000), IE, Infotrieve, Ingenta. **CCC.**
Published by: (American College of Veterinary Ophthalmologists USA), Wiley-Blackwell Publishing Ltd. (Subsidiary of: John Wiley & Sons, Inc.), 9600 Garsington Rd, Oxford, OX4 2DQ, United Kingdom. TEL 44-1865-776868, FAX 44-1865-714591, customerservices@blackwellpublishing.com. Ed. David A Wilkie TEL 614-292-8664. Adv. contact Steve Jezzard. B&W page USD 1,050, color page USD 2,800; trim 8.25 x 10.875. Circ: 1,045 (paid).

636.089 NLD ISSN 0304-4017
SF810 CODEN: VPARDI
➤ **VETERINARY PARASITOLOGY.** Text in English. 1975. 32/yr. EUR 3,443 in Europe to institutions; JPY 456,200 in Japan to institutions; USD 3,850 elsewhere to institutions (effective 2012). back issues avail. **Document type:** *Journal, Academic/Scholarly.* **Description:** Publishes papers dealing with all aspects of disease prevention, pathology, treatment, epidemiology, and control of parasites in all animals which can be regarded as being useful to man.
Related titles: Microform ed.: (from PQC); Online - full text ed.: ISSN 1873-2550. 199? (from IngentaConnect, ScienceDirect).
Indexed: A01, A03, A08, A22, A26, A29, A34, A35, A36, A37, A38, ASCA, ASFA, AgBio, Agr, AgrForAb, B21, B23, B25, BIOBASE, BIOSIS Prev, BP, C25, CA, CABA, CIN, ChemAb, ChemTitl, CurCont, D01, DBA, DentInd, E12, EMBASE, ESPM, EntAb, ExcerpMed, F08, F11, F12, FCA, FoVS&M, G11, GH, H16, H17, H05, IABS, ISR, IndMed, IndVet, LT, MEDLINE, MaizeAb, MycolAb, N02, N04, O01, OR, P30, P32, P33, P37, P39, P40, PGegResA, PN&I, R07, R08, R11, R12, RA&MP, RM&VM, RRTA, S12, S13, S16, SAA, SCI, SCOPUS, SoyAb, T02, T05, TAR, VS, W07, W08, W11, WildRev, Z01.
—BLDSC (9229.163000), CASDDS, GNLM, IE, Infotrieve, Ingenta, INIST, Linda Hall. **CCC.**
Published by: Elsevier BV (Subsidiary of: Elsevier Science & Technology), Radarweg 29, PO Box 211, Amsterdam, 1000 AE, Netherlands. TEL 31-20-4853911, FAX 31-20-4852457, JournalsCustomerServiceEMEA@elsevier.com, http://www.elsevier.nl. Eds. C Genchi, Dr. L S Mansfield, M A Taylor.

636.089 USA ISSN 0300-9858
SF769 CODEN: VTPHAK
➤ **VETERINARY PATHOLOGY.** Text in English, German. 1964. bi-m. USD 305, GBP 179 combined subscription to institutions (print & online eds.); USD 299, GBP 175 to institutions (effective 2011). adv. bk.rev. bibl.; charts; illus. index. back issues avail.; reprint service avail. from PSC. **Document type:** *Journal, Academic/Scholarly.* **Description:** Features original observations on the pathology of animals, both from natural and experimentally-induced diseases.
Formerly (until 1971): Pathologia Veterinaria (0031-2975)
Related titles: Online - full text ed.: ISSN 1544-2217. 2000 (Jan.). USD 275, GBP 161 to institutions (effective 2011); Supplement(s): Veterinary Pathology. Supplement. ISSN 0191-3808.
Indexed: A22, A29, A34, A35, A36, A37, A38, ASCA, AgBio, Agr, AgrForAb, B20, B21, BP, BibAg, CA, CABA, CIN, ChemAb, CurCont, D01, DBA, DentInd, E01, E12, EMBASE, ESPM, ExcerpMed, F08, FoVS&M, G11, GH, H16, H17, IBR, IBZ, ISR, IndMed, IndVet, Inpharma, MEDLINE, MaizeAb, N02, N04, P30, P33, P37, P39, PN&I, R07, R08, R12, R13, RM&VM, S12, S13, S16, SAA, SCI, SCOPUS, SPPI, T02, T05, TAR, TriticAb, VS, VirolAbstr, W07, W08, W10, W11, WildRev, Z01.
—BLDSC (9229.165000), CASDDS, GNLM, IE, Infotrieve, Ingenta, INIST, Linda Hall. **CCC.**
Published by: (American College of Veterinary Pathologists), Sage Publications, Inc., 2455 Teller Rd, Thousand Oaks, CA 91320. TEL 805-499-9774, FAX 805-499-0871, info@sagepub.com, http://www.sagepub.com/. Ed. Carl L Alden.

636.089 PAK ISSN 1728-9416
THE VETERINARY PRACTICE. Text in English. 1985. m. GBP 300 (effective 2005). **Document type:** *Journal, Academic/Scholarly.* **Description:** Study of veterinary diseases.
Published by: (Veterinary Medical Association), International Press, P O Box 17700, Karachi, 75300, Pakistan. TEL 92-21-4947486, FAX 92-21-4989257, light_68@hotmail.com. Ed. Dr. G R Nizamani.

636.089 USA ISSN 1528-6398
VETERINARY PRACTICE NEWS; the information leader for veterinary practice and business. Text in English. 1986. m. USD 48 domestic; USD 61 in Canada; USD 94 elsewhere; free in US & Canada to qualified personnel (effective 2008); subscr. includes Veterinary Practice News Sourcebook. adv. **Document type:** *Magazine, Trade.*
Former titles (until 2000): Veterinary Product News (1092-8324); (until 1997): Veterinarian Product News (1051-4260)
Related titles: Seasonal ed(s).: Veterinary Practice News Sourcebook.
Indexed: A34, A36, A38, CABA, E12, F08, GH, H16, H17, IndVet, LT, N04, OR, P33, P39, R08, RA&MP, RM&VM, S12, VS, W11.
Published by: BowTie, Inc., 2401 Beverly Blvd, PO Box 57900, Los Angeles, CA 90057. TEL 213-385-2222, FAX 213-385-8565, adtraffic@bowtieinc.com, http://www.bowtieinc.com. Ed. Marilyn Iturri TEL 949-855-8822. Circ: 10,000 (paid).

636.089 GBR ISSN 0165-2176
SF600 CODEN: VEQUDU
➤ **VETERINARY QUARTERLY**; reviews on animal diseases. Text in English. 1979. q. GBP 266 combined subscription in United Kingdom to institutions (print & online eds.); EUR 352, USD 439 combined subscription to institutions (print & online eds.) (effective 2012). back issues avail.; reprint service avail. from PSC. **Document type:** *Journal, Academic/Scholarly.* **Description:** Publishes reviews on animal diseases.
Related titles: Microform ed.: (from PQC); Online - full text ed.: ISSN 1875-5941. GBP 239 in United Kingdom to institutions; EUR 316, USD 395 to institutions (effective 2012).
Indexed: A22, ASCA, Agr, B25, BIOSIS Prev, BibAg, CIN, ChemAb, ChemTitl, CurCont, DBA, EMBASE, ExcerpMed, FS&TA, FoVS&M, ISR, IndMed, MycolAb, P30, SAA, SCI, SCOPUS, W07, WildRev.
—CASDDS, GNLM, IE, Infotrieve, Ingenta, INIST. **CCC.**
Published by: (Euroscience NLD), Taylor & Francis Ltd. (Subsidiary of: Taylor & Francis Group), 4 Park Sq, Milton Park, Abingdon, Oxfordshire OX14 4RN, United Kingdom. TEL 44-20-70176000, FAX 44-20-70176336, subscriptions@tandf.co.uk, http://www.tandf.co.uk/journals. Eds. J H Vos, Th A M Elsinghorst. R&P Th A M Elsinghorst.

636.089 USA ISSN 1058-8183
SF757.8 CODEN: VRULED
➤ **VETERINARY RADIOLOGY & ULTRASOUND.** Text in English. 1960. bi-m. GBP 423 in United Kingdom to institutions; EUR 537 in Europe to institutions; USD 553 in the Americas to institutions; USD 828 elsewhere to institutions; GBP 487 combined subscription in United Kingdom to institutions (print & online eds.); EUR 617 combined subscription in Europe to institutions (print & online eds.); USD 636 combined subscription in the Americas to institutions (print & online eds.); USD 953 combined subscription elsewhere to institutions (print & online eds.) (effective 2012). adv. illus. index. back issues avail.; reprint service avail. from PSC. **Document type:** *Journal, Academic/Scholarly.* **Description:** Presents articles of interest to the practicing veterinarian. Covers radiologic and ultrasound techniques, diagnostic interpretation, radiologic therapy and current advances in the field.
Former titles (until 1992): Veterinary Radiology (0196-3627); (until 1979): American Veterinary Radiology Society. Journal (0066-1155)
Related titles: Microform ed.: (from PQC); Online - full text ed.: ISSN 1740-8261. GBP 423 in United Kingdom to institutions; EUR 537 in Europe to institutions; USD 553 in the Americas to institutions; USD 828 elsewhere to institutions (effective 2012) (from IngentaConnect).
Indexed: A22, A26, A34, A36, A37, A38, ASCA, Agr, B25, BIOSIS Prev, CA, CABA, CurCont, D01, E01, E12, EMBASE, ExcerpMed, FoVS&M, GH, H12, H17, ISR, IndMed, IndVet, MEDLINE, MycolAb, N02, N04, P30, P33, P37, P39, PN&I, R07, R08, RM&VM, SAA, SCI, SCOPUS, T02, T05, TAR, VS, W07, WildRev.
—BLDSC (9229.281000), IE, Infotrieve, Ingenta. **CCC.**
Published by: (American College of Veterinary Radiology), Wiley-Blackwell Publishing, Inc. (Subsidiary of: Wiley-Blackwell Publishing Ltd.), 111 River St, Hoboken, NJ 07030. TEL 201-748-6000, FAX 201-748-6088, info@wiley.com. Ed. Donald E Thrall. Adv. contact Kerri Petrakis TEL 856-768-9360. **Co-sponsors:** European Veterinary Radiology Association; International Veterinary Radiology Association.

636.089 GBR ISSN 0042-4900
SF601 CODEN: VETRAX
➤ **THE VETERINARY RECORD.** Text in English. 1888. w. GBP 450, EUR 607.50, USD 877.50 combined subscription to institutions (print & online eds.); free to members (effective 2010); subscr. includes In Practice. adv. bk.rev. illus. Index. back issues avail.; reprints avail. **Document type:** *Journal, Academic/Scholarly.* **Description:** Contains news, comment, letters and clinical research papers on a wide range of veterinary topics.
Related titles: Microform ed.: (from PQC); Online - full text ed.: ISSN 2042-7670. GBP 360, EUR 486, USD 702 to institutions; free to members (effective 2010); subscr. includes In Practice; Spanish ed.: ISSN 0214-3909; ◆ Supplement(s): In Practice (London). ISSN 0263-841X.
Indexed: A01, A03, A08, A20, A22, A29, A34, A35, A36, A37, A38, ASCA, ASFA, AgBio, Agr, AgrForAb, B&AI, B04, B10, B20, B21, B23, BA, BP, BibAg, C25, CA, CABA, ChemAb, CurCont, D01, DBA, DentInd, E12, EMBASE, ESPM, ExcerpMed, F08, F11, F12, FS&TA, FoVS&M, G11, GH, GeoRef, H16, H17, I10, INI, ISR, IndMed, IndVet, L09, LT, MEDLINE, MaizeAb, N02, N04, OR, P30, P33, P34, P37, P39, PN&I, R07, R08, R12, R13, RA&MP, RM&VM, RRTA, S12, S13, S16, S17, SAA, SCI, SCOPUS, T02, T05, TAR, TriticAb, VS, VirolAbstr, W07, W08, W10, W11, WildRev.
—BLDSC (9230.000000), CASDDS, GNLM, IE, Infotrieve, Ingenta, INIST, Linda Hall. **CCC.**
Published by: (British Veterinary Association), B M J Group, BMA House, Tavistock Sq, London, WC1H 9JR, United Kingdom. TEL 44-20-73836373, FAX 44-20-73836668, http://group.bmj.com. Adv. contact Kevan Bowen TEL 44-7768-880410.

636.089 GBR ISSN 0928-4249
SF602 CODEN: VEREEM
➤ **VETERINARY RESEARCH**; an international journal on animal infection. Text in English; Summaries in English, French. 1968. bi-m. adv. reprints avail. **Document type:** *Journal, Academic/Scholarly.* **Description:** Covers all scientific aspects of veterinary and comparitive medicine and related subjects. The principal areas of interest are: immunology, virology, parasitology, physiology and biochemistry.
Former titles (until 1993): Annales de Recherches Veterinaires (0003-4193); (until 1969): Recherches Veterinaires (0486-1418)
Related titles: Microform ed.; Online - full text ed.: ISSN 1297-9716. free (effective 2011).
Indexed: A22, A26, A29, A34, A35, A36, A37, A38, ASCA, ASFA, AgBio, B20, B21, B23, B25, BIOSIS Prev, BibAg, CA, CABA, CIN, ChemAb, CurCont, D01, DBA, DentInd, E12, EMBASE, ESPM, EntAb, ExcerpMed, F08, F12, FS&TA, FoVS&M, G11, GH, GenetAb, H16, H17, HGA, I05, IBR, IBZ, ISR, IndMed, IndVet, MEDLINE, MycolAb, N02, N04, OR, P30, P32, P33, P37, P38, P39, PN&I, R08, R12, R13, RM&VM, SCI, SCOPUS, T02, T05, TriticAb, VS, VirolAbstr, W07, W10, W11, WildRev.
—BLDSC (9230.090000), CASDDS, GNLM, IE, Infotrieve, Ingenta, INIST, Linda Hall. **CCC.**
Published by: (France. Institut National de la Recherche Agronomique (I N R A) FRA), BioMed Central Ltd. (Subsidiary of: Springer Science+Business Media), 236 Gray's Inn Rd, London, WC1X 8HB, United Kingdom. TEL 44-20-31922009, FAX 44-20-31922010, info@biomedcentral.com, http://www.biomedcentral.com. Circ: 2,000.

636.089 PAK ISSN 1993-5412
VETERINARY RESEARCH. Text in English. 2007. 4/yr. EUR 900 to individuals; EUR 1,200 to institutions; EUR 150 newsstand/cover (effective 2007). **Document type:** *Journal, Academic/Scholarly.*
Related titles: Online - full text ed.: ISSN 1994-4659. free (effective 2007).
Indexed: A34, A35, A38, AgBio, BP, CABA, D01, E12, F08, GH, H16, H17, IndVet, N02, N04, P33, P37, P39, PN&I, R08, RA&MP, RM&VM, SoyAb, T05, TAR, VS, W10.
Published by: Medwell Journals, ANSInet Bldg, 308-Lasani Town, Sargodha Rd, Faisalabad, 38090, Pakistan. TEL 92-41-5010004, 92-41-5004000, FAX 92-21-5206789, medwellonline@gmail.com, http://www.medwellonline.net, http://www.medwelljournals.com.

636.089 NLD ISSN 0165-7380
CODEN: VRCODX
➤ **VETERINARY RESEARCH COMMUNICATIONS**; an international journal publishing topical reviews and research articles on all aspects of the veterinary sciences. Text in English. 1977. 8/yr. EUR 1,268, USD 1,357 combined subscription to institutions (print & online eds.) (effective 2012). adv. bk.rev. abstr.; bibl.; charts; illus. index, cum.index. back issues avail.; reprint service avail. from PSC. **Document type:** *Journal, Academic/Scholarly.* **Description:** Forum for current research in all disciplines of veterinary sciences.
Formerly: Veterinary Science Communications (0378-4312)
Related titles: Microform ed.: (from PQC); Online - full text ed.: ISSN 1573-7446 (from IngentaConnect).
Indexed: A22, A26, A29, A34, A35, A36, A37, A38, ASCA, ASFA, AgBio, Agr, B20, B21, B23, B25, BIOSIS Prev, BibLing, C25, C30, CA, CABA, ChemAb, CurCont, D01, DBA, E01, E12, EMBASE, ESPM, EntAb, ExcerpMed, F08, F12, FCA, FoVS&M, G11, GH, H16, H17, ISR, IndMed, IndVet, LT, MEDLINE, MaizeAb, MycolAb, N02, N04, OR, P11, P20, P22, P30, P32, P33, P37, P38, P39, P40, P48, P52, P54, P56, PN&I, PQC, R07, R08, R11, R12, R13, RA&MP, RM&VM, RRTA, S12, S13, S16, SAA, SCI, SCOPUS, SoyAb, T02, T05, TAR, ToxAb, TriticAb, VS, VirolAbstr, W07, W08, W10, W11, WildRev, Z01.
—BLDSC (9230.200000), CASDDS, GNLM, IE, Infotrieve, Ingenta, INIST. **CCC.**
Published by: Springer Netherlands (Subsidiary of: Springer Science+Business Media), Van Godewijckstraat 30, Dordrecht, 3311 GX, Netherlands. TEL 31-78-6576050, FAX 31-78-6576474, http://www.springer.com. Ed. Robert G Dalziel.

636.089 IRN ISSN 2008-8140
▼ **VETERINARY RESEARCH FORUM.** Text in English. 2010. q. **Document type:** *Journal, Academic/Scholarly.*
Related titles: Online - full text ed.: free (effective 2011).
Indexed: Z01.
Published by: Urmia University, Faculty of Veterinary Medicine, Urmia, 57153-1177, Iran. TEL 98-4412770508, FAX 98-441-2771926. Ed. F Sarrafzadeh-Rezaei.

636.089 USA ISSN 1944-2750
VETERINARY RESEARCH WEEK. Text in English. 2008. w. USD 2,295 in US & Canada; USD 2,495 elsewhere; USD 2,525 combined subscription in US & Canada (print & online eds.); USD 2,755 combined subscription elsewhere (print & online eds.) (effective 2011). adv. back issues avail. **Document type:** *Newsletter, Trade.* **Description:** Published news and research reports from major teaching centers, universities and biotech companies, emphasizing animal studies, drug and medical device development for veterinary practices.
Related titles: E-mail ed.; Online - full text ed.: ISSN 1944-2769. USD 2,295 combined subscription (online & e-mail eds.) (effective 2011).
Indexed: G08, H11, I05, P10, P20, P26, P48, P52, P53, P54, P56, PQC, S10.
Published by: NewsRx, 2727 Paces Ferry Rd SE, Ste 2-440, Atlanta, GA 30339. TEL 770-435-8286, 800-726-4550, FAX 770-435-6800, pressrelease@newsrx.com, http://www.newsrx.com. Pub., Adv. contact Susan Hasty TEL 770-507-7777.

636.08 NPL ISSN 1021-5042
VETERINARY REVIEW; a half-year Nepalese publication of animal production & health. Text in English. 1986. s-a. **Document type:** *Journal, Academic/Scholarly.* **Description:** Publishes reviews, results of original research, investigation and observations, progress reports, news and letters which may lead to improve health and productivity of livestock and better utilization of animal resources in Nepal.
Published by: Pakhribas Agricultural Centre, Veterinary Investigation & Analytical Services Section, c/o Chief Information Officer, BAPSO, P O Box 106, Kathmandu, Nepal.

636.089 USA ISSN 1547-4747
THE VETERINARY SAFETY & HEALTH DIGEST. Text in English. 1993. bi-m. USD 27.50 (effective 2003). **Document type:** *Newsletter.*

Published by: Veterinary Practice Consultants, 1550 Athens Rd., Calhoun, TN 37309-3035. TEL 423-336-1925, FAX 423-336-6047, http://www.v-p-c.com/phil. Ed. Phil Seibert.

636.089 ITA ISSN 2038-9701
▼ ➤ **VETERINARY SCIENCE DEVELOPMENT.** Text in English. 2010. irreg. free (effective 2011). **Document type:** *Journal, Academic/Scholarly.*
Media: Online - full text.
Published by: Pagepress, Via Giuseppe Belli 4, Pavia, 27100, Italy. TEL 39-0382-1751762, FAX 39-0382-1750481.

636.089 PAK ISSN 1728-9424
VETERINARY SCIENCE. PROCEEDINGS. Text in English. 1985. m. GBP 300 (effective 2005). **Document type:** *Proceedings, Academic/Scholarly.* **Description:** Study of veterinary diseases.
Published by: (Veterinary Association), International Press, P O Box 17700, Karachi, 75300, Pakistan. TEL 92-21-4947486, FAX 92-21-4989257, light_68@hotmail.com. Ed. Dr. B S Zaman.

636 IND ISSN 0976-996X
▼ ➤ **VETERINARY SCIENCE RESEARCH.** Text in English. 2010. s-a. USD 425 (effective 2011). **Document type:** *Journal, Academic/Scholarly.* **Description:** Publishes all the latest research articles, reviews and letters in all areas of veterinary science.
Related titles: Online - full text ed.: ISSN 0976-9978. free (effective 2011).
Indexed: A34, A38, CABA, P33.
Published by: Bioinfo Publications, 49/F-72, Vighnahar Complex, Front of Overseas Bank, Sector 12, Kharghar, Navi Mumbai, 410 210, India. TEL 91-22-27743967, FAX 91-22-66736413, editor@bioinfo.in, subscription@bioinfo.in. Eds. Dr. Charles O Thoen, Dr. Meenu Vikram, Dr. Saber Mohamed Abd-Allah.

636.089 NLD ISSN 1569-0830
➤ **VETERINARY SCIENCES TOMORROW.** Text in English. 2001. irreg. free (effective 2009). adv. bk.rev. bibl.; illus. Index. back issues avail. **Document type:** *Journal, Academic/Scholarly.* **Description:** Provides reviews and opinion papers only, not original experimental data.
Media: Online - full text.
Published by: Igitur, Utrecht Publishing & Archiving Services, Postbus 80124, Utrecht, 3508 TC, Netherlands. TEL 31-30-2536635, FAX 31-30-2536959, info@igitur.uu.nl, http://www.igitur.uu.nl.

636.089 USA ISSN 0161-3499
SF911 CODEN: VESUD6
➤ **VETERINARY SURGERY.** Text in English. 1978. 8/yr. GBP 418 in United Kingdom to institutions; EUR 532 in Europe to institutions; USD 546 in the Americas to institutions; USD 819 elsewhere to institutions; GBP 482 combined subscription in United Kingdom to institutions (print & online eds.); EUR 612 combined subscription in Europe to institutions (print & online eds.); USD 629 combined subscription in the Americas to institutions (print & online eds.); USD 942 combined subscription elsewhere to institutions (print & online eds.) (effective 2012). adv. bk.rev. illus. index. reprint service avail. from PSC. **Document type:** *Journal, Academic/Scholarly.* **Description:** Covers clinical and research topics of interest to veterinary surgeons.
Incorporates (1974-198?): Veterinary Anesthesia (0149-3949); Formerly (until 1978): Journal of Veterinary Surgery
Related titles: Online - full text ed.: ISSN 1532-950X. GBP 418 in United Kingdom to institutions; EUR 532 in Europe to institutions; USD 546 in the Americas to institutions; USD 819 elsewhere to institutions (effective 2012) (from IngentaConnect).
Indexed: A22, A26, A34, A35, A36, A37, A38, ASCA, AgBio, Agr, B25, BIOSIS Prev, CA, CABA, CurCont, D01, DBA, E01, E12, EMBASE, ExcerpMed, F08, FoVS&M, G11, GH, H12, ISR, IndMed, IndVet, LT, MEDLINE, MycolAb, N02, N04, P02, P10, P30, P33, P48, P52, P53, P54, P56, PN&I, PQC, R08, RM&VM, RRTA, S10, S12, SAA, SCI, SCOPUS, T02, T05, VS, W07, W11, WildRev.
—BLDSC (9231.037000), CASDDS, IE, Infotrieve, Ingenta. **CCC.**
Published by: (American College of Veterinary Surgeons), Wiley-Blackwell Publishing, Inc. (Subsidiary of: Wiley-Blackwell Publishing Ltd.), 111 River St, Hoboken, NJ 07030. TEL 201-748-6000, FAX 201-748-6088, info@wiley.com, http://www.wiley.com/WileyCDA/. Ed. John R Pascoe. Adv. contact Kristin McCarthy TEL 201-748-7683.
Co-sponsor: European College of Veterinary Surgeons.

636.089 USA ISSN 8750-8990
➤ **VETERINARY TECHNICIAN.** Text in English. 1980. m. free to qualified personnel (effective 2010). bibl.; charts; illus.; stat. 80 p./no. 3 cols./p.; back issues avail.; reprints avail. **Document type:** *Journal, Academic/Scholarly.* **Description:** Focuses on aspects of veterinary medicine that veterinary technicians need to know.
Former titles (until 1984): Animal Health Technician (0733-6004); (until 1982): The Compendium on Continuing Education for the Animal Health Technician (0196-1764)
Indexed: A10, A22, A34, A37, CABA, GH, H17, IndVet, P33, P39, R08, SAA, SCOPUS, V03, VS, WildRev.
—BLDSC (9231.038000), IE, Infotrieve, Ingenta. **CCC.**
Published by: Veterinary Learning Systems (Subsidiary of: MediMedia USA, Inc.), 780 Township Line Rd, Yardley, PA 19067. TEL 800-426-9119, info@vetlearn.com.

636.089 USA ISSN 1528-3593
VETERINARY THERAPEUTICS; research in applied veterinary medicine. Text in English. 2000. q. **Document type:** *Journal, Trade.*
Indexed: A34, A35, A38, AgBio, Agr, CABA, CurCont, D01, E12, EMBASE, ExcerpMed, FoVS&M, GH, H17, IndVet, MEDLINE, N02, N04, P30, P33, P37, P39, PN&I, R08, R12, S12, SCI, SCOPUS, T05, VS, W07, W11.
—BLDSC (9231.038500), IE, Ingenta. **CCC.**
Published by: Veterinary Learning Systems (Subsidiary of: MediMedia USA, Inc.), 780 Township Line Rd, Yardley, PA 19067. TEL 800-426-9119, info@vetlearn.com.

636.089 GBR ISSN 1352-9374
VETERINARY TIMES. Text in English. 1970. 48/yr. GBP 175 domestic; GBP 270 foreign; free to qualified personnel (effective 2009). adv. bk.rev. **Document type:** *Newspaper, Trade.* **Description:** Covers new products, new techniques and news.
Formerly (until 1984): Veterinary Drug
Indexed: A34, A35, A36, A37, A38, AgBio, CABA, D01, E12, F08, F12, G11, GH, H16, H17, IndVet, LT, N02, N04, N05, OR, P33, P37, P39, PN&I, R07, R08, R12, R13, RA&MP, RM&VM, RRTA, S12, S13, S16, SAA, SoyAb, T05, TriticAb, VS, W10, W11.
—**CCC.**
Published by: Veterinary Business Development Ltd. (Subsidiary of: Wolters Kluwer N.V.), Olympus House, Werrington Ctr, Peterborough, PE4 6NA, United Kingdom. TEL 44-1733-325522, FAX 44-1733-352512. Circ: 18,802.

636.089 USA ISSN 1944-2777
VETERINARY WEEK. Text in English. 2008. w. USD 2,295 in US & Canada; USD 2,495 elsewhere; USD 2,525 combined subscription in US & Canada (print & online eds.); USD 2,755 combined subscription elsewhere (print & online eds.) (effective 2011). adv. back issues avail. **Document type:** *Newsletter, Trade.* **Description:** Provides a broad range of coverage on professional trends and developments for veterinary professionals, including significant research in large and small animal medicine.
Related titles: E-mail ed.; Online - full text ed.: ISSN 1944-2785. USD 2,295 combined subscription (online & e-mail eds.) (effective 2011).
Indexed: I05, P10, P20, P26, P48, P52, P53, P54, P56, PQC, S10.
Published by: NewsRx, 2727 Paces Ferry Rd SE, Ste 2-440, Atlanta, GA 30339. TEL 770-435-8286, 800-726-4550, FAX 770-435-6800, pressrelease@newsrx.com, http://www.newsrx.com. Pub., Adv. contact Susan Hasty TEL 770-507-7777.

636 IND ISSN 0972-8988
➤ **VETERINARY WORLD.** Text and summaries in English. 2002. m. INR 450 domestic; USD 100 foreign (effective 2011). adv. back issues avail. **Document type:** *Journal, Academic/Scholarly.* **Description:** Publishes papers focusing on veterinary and animal science. The fields of study are bacteriology, parasitology, virology, immunology, nutrition, gynecology, surgery, prion diseases and epidemiology.
Related titles: Online - full text ed.: free (effective 2011).
Indexed: A01, A34, A35, A36, A37, A38, AgrForAb, B23, BP, C25, CA, CABA, D01, E12, F08, FCA, GH, H16, LT, MaizeAb, N02, N03, N04, P32, P33, R07, R08, S13, SoyAb, T05, TAR, W11.
—BLDSC (9231.041850), IE.
Address: c/o Dr.Sherasiya Anjum V., Star Computer, 101-C, Pooja Complex, P O Box 46, Nr. G P O, Rajkot, Gujarat 360 001, India. TEL 91-98790-65095, editorveterinaryworld@gmail.com. Ed., Pub. Dr. Sherasiya Anjum V. Circ: 750 (paid); 50 (controlled).

636.089 TUR ISSN 1300-7106
VETERINER CERRAHI DERGISI/JOURNAL OF THE TURKISH VETERINARY SURGERY. Text in Turkish, English. 1995. s-a. **Document type:** *Journal, Academic/Scholarly.*
Related titles: Online - full text ed.: free (effective 2010).
Indexed: A34, A35, A37, A38, AgBio, CABA, D01, GH, H17, IndVet, N04, P33, P37, PN&I, R08, S12, T05, VS.
Published by: Veteriner Cerrahi Dernegi/Turkish Veterinary Surgeon Association, Editorlugu, Uludag Universitesi, Veteriner Fakultesi, Hayvan Hastanesi, Gorukle Kampusu, Gorukle - Bursa, 16059, Turkey. TEL 90-224-2940801, FAX 90-224-2940873, vetcer@uludag.edu.tr. Ed. Dr. O Sacit Gorgul.

636.089 DEU ISSN 0946-7874
VETIMPULSE; Meldungen - Meinungen - Management - Marketing. Text in German. 1991. fortn. EUR 28 (effective 2010). adv. **Document type:** *Newspaper, Trade.*
Published by: Veterinaers Verlag GmbH, Hindenburgstr 71, Gnarrenburg, 27442, Germany. TEL 49-4763-6280340, FAX 49-4763-6280342. Ed. Manuela Toelle. Adv. contact Baerbel Lueers. B&W page EUR 4,500, color page EUR 5,250; trim 280 x 410. Circ: 13,136 (paid and controlled).

636.089 NZL ISSN 1176-7979
VETLEARN FOUNDATION. PUBLICATION. Text in English. 1983. irreg., latest vol.248, 2005. price varies. **Document type:** *Monographic series, Academic/Scholarly.*
Formerly (until 2004): Massey University. Veterinary Continuing Education. Publication (0112-9643)
—**CCC.**
Published by: (New Zealand Veterinary Association), VetLearn Foundation, Mail Code 413, Private Bag 11-222, Palmerston North, New Zealand. TEL 64-6-3505227, FAX 64-6-3505659, vetlearn@massey.ac.nz, http://www.vetlearn.org.nz.

636 IND
VETLINE. Text in English. 19??. q. **Document type:** *Newsletter, Trade.* **Description:** Provides latest news and happenings at the Bombay Veterinary College. It is aimed at reaching more than 600 member of the association, field veterinarians and people working in the livestock industry to provide them with the latest information of applied manner that can be used in field.
Published by: Bombay Veterinary College, Alumni Association, Dept of Poultry Science, Parel Tank Rd, Parel, Mumbai, Maharastra 400 012, India. bvccontact@mafsu.in, http://www.mafsu.in/bvc/bvccollege/bvc_main_page.html. Ed. Dr. A S Ranade. **Subscr. to:** Indianjournals.com, Divan Enterprises, B-9, Local Shopping Complex, A-Block, Naraina Vihar, Ring Rd, New Delhi 110 028, India. TEL 91-11-25770411, FAX 91-11-25778876, info@indianjournals.com, http://www.indianjournals.com.

636.089 NZL ISSN 1170-280X
VETSCRIPT NEW ZEALAND. Text in English. 1952. m. (11/yr.). free to members. adv. **Document type:** *Magazine, Trade.*
Former titles (until 1990): New Zealand Vetscript (0113-4337); (until 1989): Vet Script (0113-6054); Which superseded in part (in 1988): New Zealand Veterinary Journal (0048-0169)
Related titles: Online - full text ed.: Vetscript. ISSN 1176-9823.
Published by: New Zealand Veterinary Association, PO Box 11 212, Wellington, 6142, New Zealand. TEL 64-4-4710484, FAX 64-4-4710494, nzva@vets.org.nz, http://www.vetspace.org.nz/. Ed. Elizabeth M Sommerville. Adv. contact Gill Butcher. Circ: 2,200.

636.0832 636.7 GBR ISSN 1757-8256
➤ **VETSTREAM CANIS.** Text in English. 2008. q. GBP 285; GBP 75 per issue (effective 2011). **Document type:** *Journal, Academic/Scholarly.* **Description:** Provides canine clinical information resource for small animal practices.
Media: Online - full text.
Published by: Vetstream Ltd., Three Hills Farm, Bartlow, Cambridge, CB21 4EN, United Kingdom. TEL 44-1223-895818, FAX 44-1223-895819, enquiries@vetstream.com.

636.0832 GBR ISSN 1757-8272
➤ **VETSTREAM EQUIS.** Text in English. 2008. q. GBP 285; GBP 75 per issue (effective 2011). **Document type:** *Journal, Academic/Scholarly.* **Description:** Provides clinical information on the horse from over 290 leading clinicians worldwide.
Media: Online - full text.
Published by: Vetstream Ltd., Three Hills Farm, Bartlow, Cambridge, CB21 4EN, United Kingdom. TEL 44-1223-895818, FAX 44-1223-895819, enquiries@vetstream.com.

636.0832 636.8 GBR ISSN 1757-8264
➤ **VETSTREAM FELIS.** Text in English. 2008. q. GBP 285; GBP 75 per issue (effective 2011). **Document type:** *Journal, Academic/Scholarly.* **Description:** Provides clinical information on the cat from over 380 leading clinicians worldwide.
Media: Online - full text.
Published by: Vetstream Ltd., Three Hills Farm, Bartlow, Cambridge, CB21 4EN, United Kingdom. TEL 44-1223-895818, FAX 44-1223-895819, enquiries@vetstream.com.

636.0832 636.932 GBR ISSN 1757-8280
➤ **VETSTREAM LAPIS.** Text in English. 2008. q. GBP 285; GBP 75 per issue (effective 2011). **Document type:** *Journal, Academic/Scholarly.* **Description:** Provides clinical information on the rabbit from over 70 leading clinicians worldwide.
Media: Online - full text.
Published by: Vetstream Ltd., Three Hills Farm, Bartlow, Cambridge, CB21 4EN, United Kingdom. TEL 44-1223-895818, FAX 44-1223-895819, enquiries@vetstream.com.

636.09 CZE
VETWEB. Text in Czech. 2002. d. free. adv. **Document type:** *Trade.*
Media: Online - full content.
Published by: Profi Press s.r.o., Drtinova 8, Prague 5, 150 00, Czech Republic. TEL 420-227-018345, FAX 420-227-018310, odbyt@agroweb.cz, http://www.agroweb.cz. Ed. Jaromira Kabesova.

636.089 USA
VETZ MAGAZINE. Text in English. 2005. q. (8/yr. in 2006). USD 27.80 (effective 2005). bk.rev. **Document type:** *Magazine, Trade.* **Description:** Provides lifestyle and professional information to the veterinary profession, inlcuding issues such as practice management, HR, legal and marketing.
Published by: Main Street Publishing Group, 608 Hampton Dr., Venice, CA 90291. TEL 310-452-3900, FAX 310-452-3909. Ed. C. Smith.

636.08 NLD ISSN 1388-3852
➤ **VIRUS INFECTIONS OF VERTEBRATES.** Text in English. 1987. irreg., latest vol.6, 1996. price varies. back issues avail. **Document type:** *Monographic series, Academic/Scholarly.* **Description:** Closely examines pathogenic viruses in vertebrate animals.
Published by: Elsevier BV (Subsidiary of: Elsevier Science & Technology), Radarweg 29, PO Box 211, Amsterdam, 1000 AE, Netherlands. TEL 31-20-4853911, FAX 31-20-4852457, JournalsCustomerServiceEMEA@elsevier.com, http://www.elsevier.nl. Ed. Dr. M C Horzinek.

636.089 BEL ISSN 0303-9021
SF604 CODEN: VDTIAX
➤ **VLAAMS DIERGENEESKUNDIG TIJDSCHRIFT/FLEMISH VETERINARY JOURNAL.** Text in Dutch, English; Summaries in English. 1932. bi-m. EUR 62 (effective 2005). adv. bk.rev. abstr.; charts; illus. index. **Document type:** *Journal, Academic/Scholarly.*
Indexed: A22, A34, A35, A36, A37, A38, ASCA, AgBio, CABA, CIN, ChemAb, ChemTitl, CurCont, D01, DBA, E12, F08, FoVS&M, G11, GH, H16, H17, IndVet, MaizeAb, N02, N03, N04, P33, P37, P39, PN&I, R07, R08, R13, RA&MP, RM&VM, S12, SAA, SCI, SCOPUS, T05, TAR, VS, W07, W10, W11.
—BLDSC (9246.000000), CASDDS, IE, Ingenta, INIST. **CCC.**
Published by: Universiteit Gent, Faculty of Veterinary Medicine, Salisburylaan 133, Merelbeke, 9820, Belgium. TEL 32-9-2647513, FAX 32-9-2647799. Ed. L Devriese. Circ: 1,550.

636.089 GBR ISSN 1471-1044
VN TIMES. (Veterinary Nursing) Text in English. 2000. m. GBP 80; free to qualified personnel (effective 2009). **Document type:** *Newspaper, Trade.* **Description:** Provides news and information on products and developments in the field of veterinary nursing profession.
Indexed: A37, A38, B23, D01, H17, P37, S12.
Published by: Veterinary Business Development Ltd. (Subsidiary of: Wolters Kluwer N.V.), Olympus House, Werrington Ctr, Peterborough, PE4 6NA, United Kingdom. TEL 44-1733-325522, FAX 44-1733-352512. Ed. Emma Dahm TEL 44-1733-383545.

VORTRAEGE ZUM THEMA MENSCH UND TIER. *see* ANIMAL WELFARE

WALTHAM FOCUS (JAPANESE EDITION). *see* PETS

636.089 THA ISSN 0125-6491
➤ **WETCHASAN SATTAWAPHAET.** Text in English, Thai. q. THB 400 (effective 2010). **Document type:** *Journal, Academic/Scholarly.*
Related titles: Online - full text ed.: free.
Indexed: A34, A35, A36, A37, A38, AgBio, AgrForAb, BP, CABA, D01, E12, F08, F11, F12, G11, GH, H16, H17, LT, N02, N04, P32, P33, P37, P39, R08, R13, S13, S16, SCI, SCOPUS, T05, TAR, W07, W10, W11, Z01.
Published by: Chulalongkorn University, Faculty of Veterinary Science, Henri Dunant Rd., Bangkok, 10330, Thailand. TEL 66-2-2189604, FAX 66-2-2189532. Ed. Anudep Rungsipipat.

636.089 POL ISSN 1732-1999
➤ **WETERYNARIA W PRAKTYCE.** Text in Polish. 2004. bi-m. PLZ 135 domestic (effective 2011). bk.rev. **Document type:** *Journal, Academic/Scholarly.* **Description:** Present news of the veterinary world, analyzes legislation, perspectives and concerns within the European Union, and information on veterinary trade fairs, conferences and trainings.
Related titles: Online - full text ed.
Indexed: A34, A35, A36, A37, A38, AgBio, CABA, D01, E12, GH, H16, H17, IndVet, LT, N04, P33, P37, P39, PN&I, R08, RA&MP, RM&VM, VS, W11.
Published by: Wydawnictwo Elamed, Al Rozdzienskiego 188, Katowice, 40203, Poland. TEL 48-32-2580361, FAX 48-32-2039356, elamed@elamed.com.pl, http://www.elamed.com.pl. Ed. Krystyna Kempa.

636.089 POL ISSN 1896-7655
WETERYNARIA W TERENIE. Text in Polish. 2007. q. PLZ 64 domestic (effective 2011). **Document type:** *Magazine, Trade.* **Description:** Designed for a selected group of professional veterinarians - those, who specialize in problems of large animal treatment and doctors caring for the flocks.
Related titles: Online - full text ed.

Published by: Wydawnictwo Elamed, Al Rozdzienskiego 188, Katowice, 40203, Poland. TEL 48-32-2580361, FAX 48-32-2039356, elamed@elamed.com.pl, http://www.elamed.com.pl. Ed. Krystyna Kempa.

636.089 AUT ISSN 0253-9411
SF603 CODEN: WTMOA3
WIENER TIERAERZTLICHE MONATSSCHRIFT. Text in German; Summaries in English. 1913. m. EUR 120; EUR 15 newsstand/cover (effective 2008). bk.rev. abstr.; bibl.; charts; illus. index. **Document type:** *Magazine, Trade.*
Supersedes in part (in 1945): Tieraerztliche Zeitschrift (0371-7569); (in 1945): Berliner und Muenchener Tieraerztliche Wochenschrift und Wiener Tieraerztliche Monatschrift (0723-6956); Which superseded in part (1913-1943): Wiener Tieraerztliche Monatschrift (0043-535X)
Related titles: Online - full text ed.
Indexed: CIN, ChemAb, ChemTitl, DBA, FS&TA, ISR, KWIWR, SCOPUS.
—BLDSC (9316.000000), CASDDS, IE, Infotrieve, Ingenta, INIST.
Published by: (Oesterreichische Tieraerzteschaft), B W K Publishing Solutions, Barmherzigengasse 17/3/Office 5, Vienna, 1030, Austria. TEL 43-1-71606, FAX 43-1-71606900, office@bwk.at, http://www.bwk.at. Ed. Karin Moestl. Pub. Brigitte Weber-Kraus. Circ: 1,800 (paid and controlled). **Co-sponsor:** Oesterreichische Gesellschaft der Tieraerzte.

WILDLIFE REHABILITATION. *see* CONSERVATION

333.95416 USA ISSN 1044-2618
WILDLIFE REHABILITATION TODAY. Text in English. 1989. s-a. USD 7.95 domestic; USD 9 in Canada; USD 13.50 elsewhere (effective 2005). adv. bk.rev. back issues avail. **Document type:** *Magazine, Consumer.* **Description:** Contains technical and non-technical veterinary, wildlife rescue, reintroduction to the wild, care and rehab education articles.
Indexed: EnvAb, EnvInd, WildRev.
Published by: Coconut Creek Publishing Co., 10385 NW 69th Mnr., Parkland, FL 33076-2902. TEL 888-978-1020, wrt@theshelf.com, http://www.theshelf.com. Ed., Pub., R&P Dan Mackey. Circ: 7,509 (paid). **Subscr. to:** Allen Press Inc., PO Box 1897, Lawrence, KS 66044.

636.089 FRA ISSN 1017-3102
WORLD ANIMAL HEALTH IN (YEAR). Text in English. a. EUR 100 (effective 2006). back issues avail. **Document type:** *Bulletin, Trade.* **Description:** Disease status of more than 170 countries for 108 diseases of animals and fish.
Related titles: Online - full text ed.; Spanish ed.: Sanidad Animal Mundial en (Year). ISSN 1017-4362. EUR 100 (effective 2002); French ed.: Sante Animale Mondiale en (Year). ISSN 1011-9299. EUR 100 (effective 2002).
Published by: Organisation Mondiale de la Sante Animale (O I E)/World Organisation for Animal Health, 12 rue de Prony, Paris, 75017, France. TEL 33-1-44151888, FAX 33-1-42670987, oie@oie.int, http://www.oie.int. Ed. J Blancou. R&P Gill S Dilmitis.

636.089 NLD ISSN 1572-5006
WORLD ASSOCIATION ON ANIMAL PATHOLOGY. ANNALS. Text in English. 2003. a. free (effective 2011). **Document type:** *Journal, Academic/Scholarly.*
Media: Online - full text.
Published by: (World Association on Animal Pathology), Gruys Veterinary Extension Services ves@gruys.com, http://www.gruys.com.

636.089 BEL
WORLD BUIATRICS CONGRESS. (Each report published in the country hosting the congress.) Text in English, French, German, Spanish. 1960. biennial. **Document type:** *Proceedings, Trade.*
Formerly: International Meeting on Cattle Diseases. Reports. (0074-6975)
Published by: World Association for Buiatrics (W A B)/Association Mondiale de Buiatrie (A M B), c/o P Lekeux, Sec, Faculte de Medecine Veterinaire, Batiment B42, Sart Tilman, Liege, 4000, Belgium. TEL 32-41-564030, FAX 32-41-562935, http://www.buiatrics.com.

WORLD RESEARCH JOURNAL OF SCHISTOSOMOLOGY. *see* MEDICAL SCIENCES

XINGZHENGYUAN. NONGYE WEIYUANHUI. JIACHU WEISHENG SHIYANSUO. YANJIU BAOGAO/NATIONAL INSTITUTE FOR ANIMAL HEALTH. EXPERIMENTAL REPORT. *see* AGRICULTURE—Poultry And Livestock

636.089 636 CHN ISSN 0366-6964
XUMU SHOUYI XUEBAO/ACTA VETERINARIA ET ZOOTECHNICA SINICA. Text in Chinese. 1956. m. USD 106.80 (effective 2009). **Document type:** *Journal, Academic/Scholarly.*
Related titles: Online - full text ed.
Indexed: A22, ASCA, B&BAb, B21, CLL, CTA, ESPM, ImmunAb, Z01.
—BLDSC (0670.900000), East View, IE, Ingenta.
Published by: Zhongguo Nongye Kexueyuan, Xumu Yanjiusuo/Chinese Academy of Agricultural Sciences, Institute of Animal Science, 2, Yuanminyuan Xilu, Beijing, 100193, China. TEL 86-10-62815987, FAX 86-10-62895351. Ed. Chen You Chun.

636.089 TUR ISSN 1017-8422
YUZUNCU YIL UNIVERSITESI VETERINER FAKULTESI DERGISI/ YUZUNCU YIL UNIVERSITESI FACULTY OF VETERINARY MEDICINE. JOURNAL. Text in Turkish, English. 1990. s-a. **Document type:** *Journal, Academic/Scholarly.*
Related titles: Online - full text ed.: ISSN 1308-3651. free (effective 2011).
Indexed: A34, A35, A36, A37, A38, C25, D01, E12, H16, N03, N04, P32, P33, R07, R08, S13, T05, W11.
Published by: Yuzuncu Yil Universitesi Veteriner Fakultesi/Yuzuncu Yil University. Faculty of Veterinary Medicine, Campus, Zeve - Van, 65080, Turkey. TEL 90-432-2251126, FAX 90-432-2251127, veteriner@yyu.edu.tr.

636.089 EGY ISSN 1110-1458
ZAGAZIG VETERINARY JOURNAL. Text in English, Arabic. 1972. q. **Document type:** *Journal, Academic/Scholarly.*
Published by: Zagazig University, Faculty of Veterinary Medicine, Banha Branch, Mushtohor, Toukh, Qalyoubia, Egypt. TEL 20-13-461411, FAX 20-13-460640. Ed. Dr. Nariman M M Edris.

636.089 ZMB
ZAMBIA. DEPARTMENT OF VETERINARY AND TSETSE CONTROL SERVICES. ANNUAL REPORT. Text in English. 19??. a. ZMK 200. **Document type:** *Government.* **Description:** Reports on the year's veterinary research and diagnostic work in the identification of disease in Zambia.
Published by: (Zambia. Department of Veterinary and Tsetse Control Services), Government Printing Department, PO Box 30136, Lusaka, Zambia.

636.089 NGA ISSN 0794-5086
➤ **ZARIYA VETERINARIAN.** Variant title: Zariya Veterinarian(Z V). Text in English. 1986. s-a. NGN 2,000 domestic; USD 120 foreign. adv. 150 p./no.; back issues avail. **Document type:** *Journal, Academic/Scholarly.*
Published by: Ahmadu Bello University, Faculty of Veterinary Medicine, Samaru-Zaria, Kaduna, Nigeria. Ed., Adv. contact Dr. Jacob Kwaga. Circ: 1,000.

636.089 DEU ISSN 0939-7868
SF745.5.Z34
ZEITSCHRIFT FUER GANZHEITLICHE TIERMEDIZIN. Text in German. 1986. q. EUR 68 to institutions; EUR 102 combined subscription to institutions (print & online eds.); EUR 22 newsstand/cover (effective 2011). adv. **Document type:** *Journal, Academic/Scholarly.*
Formerly (until 1991): Deutsche Zeitschrift fuer Biologische Veterinaermedizin (0179-714X)
Related titles: Online - full text ed.: ISSN 1439-1422. EUR 102 to institutions (effective 2011).
Indexed: A34, A36, A38, BP, CABA, D01, E12, F08, F12, G11, GH, H16, H17, IBR, IBZ, IndVet, LT, N02, N04, OR, P32, P33, P40, PN&I, R07, R08, RA&MP, RRTA, T05, TriticAb, VS, W10.
—IE. **CCC.**
Published by: (Deutsche Gesellschaft fuer Biologische Veterinaer-Medizin e.V.), Sonntag Verlag in M V S Medizinverlage Stuttgart GmbH und Co. KG (Subsidiary of: Georg Thieme Verlag), Oswald-Hesse-Str 50, Stuttgart, 70469, Germany. TEL 49-711-89310, FAX 49-711-8931706, kunden.service@thieme.de. Ed. Christine Waage. adv.: B&W page EUR 900, color page EUR 1,676. Circ: 3,000 (paid and controlled).

636 RUS
➤ **ZHIVOTNOVOD DLYA VSEKH.** Text in Russian. 1987. m. USD 240 in North America (effective 2001). adv. charts; illus.; stat. **Document type:** *Academic/Scholarly.* **Description:** Reflects the experience of successful farms and introduces the most modern technologies in all farming fields.
Formerly: Zhivotnovod (0235-246X)
—East View.
Published by: Zhivotnovod, Sadovaya-Spasskaya 20, Moscow, 107807, Russian Federation. TEL 7-095-1657360, FAX 7-095-1657360, animal@east.ru. Ed., Pub., R&P Lyudmila A Pervova TEL 8-902-6752475. Adv. contact Yaroslav Nemirovsky. B&W page USD 800, color page USD 900; trim 210 x 290. Circ: 70,000 (controlled). **Subscr. to:** Marshala Zhukova, Pr-t Marshala Zhukova 4, Moscow 123837, Russian Federation. TEL 7-095-1950340, FAX 7-095-1951431. **Dist. by:** East View Information Services, 10601 Wayzata Blvd, Minneapolis, MN 55305. TEL 952-252-1201, 800-477-1005, FAX 952-252-1202, info@eastview.com, http://www.eastview.com.

636.089 CHN ISSN 1008-4754
ZHONGGUO DONGWU BAOJIAN/CHINA ANIMAL HEALTH. Text in Chinese. 1999. m. USD 61.20 (effective 2009). **Document type:** *Journal, Academic/Scholarly.*
Related titles: Online - full text ed.
—East View.
Published by: Zhongguo Xiangzhen Qiye Xiehui, 2, Yuanmingyuan Xi Lu, Tushuiguan Rm.103, Beijing, 100094, China. TEL 86-10-62899836, FAX 86-10-62816766 ext 260. **Dist. by:** China International Book Trading Corp, 35 Chegongzhuang Xilu, Haidian District, PO Box 399, Beijing 100044, China. TEL 86-10-68412045, FAX 86-10-68412023, cibtc@mail.cibtc.com.cn, http://www.cibtc.com.cn.

614.46 CHN ISSN 1005-944X
ZHONGGUO DONGWU JIANYI/CHINESE JOURNAL OF ANIMAL QUARANTINE. Text in Chinese. 1982. bi-m. CNY 5 newsstand/cover (effective 2003). **Document type:** *Journal, Academic/Scholarly.*
Formerly (until 1993): Dongwu Jianyi (1004-681X)
Related titles: Online - full text ed.
—BLDSC (3180.291700), IE, Ingenta.
Published by: Nongyebu Dongwu Jianyisuo/Animal Quarantine Institute of the Ministry of Agriculture, P R C, 369 Nanjing Road, Qingdao, 266032, China. TEL 86-532-5642906, FAX 86-532-5623545. Ed. Zengren Zheng.

ZHONGGUO RENSHOU GONGHUANBING ZAZHI/CHINESE JOURNAL OF ZOONOSES. *see* BIOLOGY—Microbiology

636.089 CHN
ZHONGGUO SHOUYI KEXUE/VETERINARY SCIENCE IN CHINA. Text in Chinese. 1971. m. CNY 6 newsstand/cover (effective 2006). **Document type:** *Journal, Academic/Scholarly.*
Formerly: Zhongguo Shouyi Keji/Chinese Journal of Veterinary Science and Technology (1000-6419)
Related titles: Online - full text ed.
Indexed: A34, A35, A36, A38, AgBio, BP, CABA, D01, E12, GH, H17, IndVet, N02, N03, N04, P32, P33, P37, P39, P40, PN&I, R08, RA&MP, S13, S16, SoyAb, T05, VS, Z01.
—East View.
Published by: Zhongguo Nongye Kexueyuan, Lanzhou Shouyi Yanjiusuo, 1, Yanchangbaoxuejiaping, Lanzhou, 730046, China. TEL 86-931-8342195, FAX 86-931-8310086.

636.08 CHN ISSN 1005-4545
CODEN: ZSXUF5
ZHONGGUO SHOUYI XUEBAO/CHINESE JOURNAL OF VETERINARY SCIENCE. Text in Chinese. 1981. bi-m. USD 62.40 (effective 2009). 104 p./no.; **Document type:** *Journal, Academic/Scholarly.* **Description:** Covers the latest research and developments in veterinary science and related disciplines.
Formerly (until 1993): Shouyi Daxue Xuebao/Veterinary College of P L A. Bulletin (1000-1816)
Related titles: Online - full text ed.
Indexed: A34, A35, A36, A37, A38, AgBio, AgrForAb, B23, BP, C25, CA, CABA, D01, E12, F08, F11, F12, FCA, G11, GH, H16, H17, IndVet, MaizeAb, N02, N03, N04, N05, OR, P32, P33, P37, P39, P40, PN&I, R07, R08, R13, RA&MP, RM&VM, RefZh, S12, S13, S16, SoyAb, T02, T05, TAR, VS, W10, Z01.
—BLDSC (3180.693480), CASDDS, East View.
Published by: Jilin Daxue/Jilin University, 5333, Xi'an Dalu, Changchun, 130062, China. TEL 86-431-6986409. **Dist. by:** China International Book Trading Corp, 35 Chegongzhuang Xilu, Haidian District, PO Box 399, Beijing 100044, China. TEL 86-10-68412045, FAX 86-10-68412023, cibtc@mail.cibtc.com.cn, http://www.cibtc.com.cn.

636.089 CHN ISSN 0529-6005
SF604 CODEN: ZSZAEM
ZHONGGUO SHOUYI ZAZHI/CHINESE JOURNAL OF VETERINARY MEDICINE. Text in Chinese. 1953. m. USD 62.40 (effective 2009). **Document type:** *Journal, Academic/Scholarly.*
Formerly: Zhongguo Xumu Shouyi Zazhi (0529-5971)
Related titles: Online - full text ed.
Indexed: A22, A34, A35, A37, A38, AgBio, CABA, D01, E12, GH, H17, IndVet, N02, N03, N04, P33, P37, P39, PN&I, R08, R13, RA&MP, RM&VM, S12, S13, S16, SoyAb, T05, TAR, VS.
—BLDSC (3180.693000), East View, IE, Ingenta.
Published by: Zhongguo Xumu Shouyi Xuehui/Chinese Society of Animal Husbandry and Veterinary Science, Beijing Nongye Daxue, Dongwu Yixueyuan, 2, Yuanmingyuan Xilu, Beijing, 100094, China. TEL 86-10-62733040, FAX 86-10-62733961.

ZHONGGUO XUMU SHOUYI/CHINA ANIMAL HUSBANDRY & VETERINARY MEDICINE. *see* AGRICULTURE—Poultry And Livestock

ZHONGGUO XUMU ZAZHI/CHINESE JOURNAL OF ANIMAL SCIENCE. *see* AGRICULTURE—Poultry And Livestock

636.089 CHN ISSN 1008-0589
ZHONGGUO YUFANG SHOUYI XUEBAO. Text in Chinese. 1979. bi-m. USD 62.40 (effective 2009). **Document type:** *Journal, Academic/Scholarly.*
Formerly (until 1998): Zhongguo Xu-Qin Chuanranbing/Chinese Journal of Animal and Poultry Infections Diseases (1001-6961)
Related titles: Online - full text ed.
Indexed: A34, A35, A36, A38, AgBio, B23, BP, CABA, D01, E12, F08, GH, H16, H17, IndVet, MaizeAb, N02, N03, N04, P32, P33, P37, P39, P40, PN&I, R08, RA&MP, RM&VM, S12, SoyAb, T05, TAR, VS, Z01.
—BLDSC (3180.602000), East View.
Published by: Zhongguo Nongye Kexueyuan, Ha'erbin Shouyi Yanjiusuo, 427, Maduan Lu, Ha'erbin, 150001, China. TEL 86-451-85935050, FAX 86-451-85935048.

636.089 ZWE ISSN 1016-1511
CODEN: ZVJOD4
➤ **ZIMBABWE VETERINARY JOURNAL.** Text and summaries in English. 1970. s-a. ZWD 300, USD 60 (effective 2001). adv. bk.rev. abstr. index. 30 p./no.; back issues avail.; reprints avail. **Document type:** *Journal, Academic/Scholarly.* **Description:** Contains original and review papers on all aspects of animal health in Zimbabwe and SADCC countries, including articles by non-veterinarians.
Formerly (until 1980): Rhodesian Veterinary Journal (0253-3278)
Related titles: Online - full text ed.: (from IngentaConnect).
Indexed: Agr, WildRev.
—Ingenta.
Published by: Zimbabwe Veterinary Association, Causeway, PO Box CY 168, Harare, Zimbabwe. TEL 263-4-303575, FAX 263-4-307349. Ed. S Mukaratirwa. Pub. G B Geldart TEL 263-4-303575. R&P, Adv. contact Brian Vickers. Circ: 400.

636.089 DEU ISSN 1863-1959
CODEN: ZVRBA2
➤ **ZOONOSES AND PUBLIC HEALTH.** Text in English. 1953. 10/yr. GBP 1,190 in United Kingdom to institutions; EUR 1,511 in Europe to institutions; USD 2,197 in the Americas to institutions; USD 2,561 elsewhere to institutions; GBP 1,369 combined subscription in United Kingdom to institutions (print & online eds.); EUR 1,738 combined subscription in Europe to institutions (print & online eds.); USD 2,526 combined subscription in the Americas to institutions (print & online eds.); USD 2,946 combined subscription elsewhere to institutions (print & online eds.) (effective 2012). bk.rev. illus.; stat. cum.index. back issues avail.; reprint service avail. from PSC. **Document type:** *Journal, Academic/Scholarly.* **Description:** Covers all aspects of veterinary microbiology and parasitology.
Former titles (until 2007): Journal of Veterinary Medicine. Series B (0931-1793); (until 1986): Zentralblatt fuer Veterinaermedizin. Reihe B: Infectious Diseases, Immunology, Food Hygiene, Veterinary Public Health (0931-2021); (until 1984): Zentralblatt fuer Veterinaermedizin. Reihe B: Infectious and Parasitic Diseases, Microbiology (Bacteriology, Virology, Mycology), Immunology, Parasitology, Animal Hygiene, Food Hygiene, Pathology of Infectious and Parasitic Diseases (0721-1856); (until 1981): Zentralblatt fuer Veterinaermedizin. Reihe B (0514-7166); Which superseded in part (in 1963): Zentralblatt fuer Veterinaermedizin (0044-4294)
Related titles: Online - full text ed.: ISSN 1863-2378. GBP 1,190 in United Kingdom to institutions; EUR 1,511 in Europe to institutions; USD 2,197 in the Americas to institutions; USD 2,561 elsewhere to institutions (effective 2012) (from IngentaConnect); ◆ Supplement(s): Advances in Veterinary Medicine. ISSN 0931-4229.
Indexed: A01, A03, A08, A22, A26, A29, A34, A35, A36, A37, A38, ASCA, AgBio, Agr, B20, B21, B23, B25, BIOBASE, BIOSIS Prev, CA, CABA, ChemAb, ChemTitl, CurCont, D01, DBA, E01, E12, EMBASE, ESPM, ExcerpMed, F08, F12, FS&TA, FoVS&M, G11, GH, H05, H12, H16, H17, IABS, ISR, IndMed, IndVet, MEDLINE, MycolAb, N02, N03, N04, OR, P02, P10, P20, P30, P32, P33, P37, P39, P48, P50, P52, P53, P54, P56, PN&I, PQC, R07, R08, R12, R13, RA&MP, RM&VM, RefZh, S10, S13, S16, SCI, SCOPUS, T02, T05, ToxAb, VS, ViroIAbstr, W07, W08, W10, W11, WildRev, Z01.
—BLDSC (9531.050500), CASDDS, GNLM, IE, Infotrieve, Ingenta, INIST, Linda Hall. **CCC.**
Published by: Wiley-Blackwell Verlag GmbH (Subsidiary of: Wiley-Blackwell Publishing Ltd.), Kurfuerstendamm 57, Berlin, 10707, Germany. TEL 49-30-3279-0665, FAX 49-30-3279-0677, verlag@blackwell.de, http://www.blackwell.de. Ed. Mary Torrence. Circ: 450.

636.089 ITA ISSN 1974-3084
30 GIORNI (ROME). Text in Italian. 1946. m. **Document type:** *Magazine, Trade.*

Former titles (until 2007): Il Progresso Veterinario (1594-0810); (until 1992): Il Nuovo Progresso Veterinario (1593-9413); (until 1959): Il Progresso Veterinario (1593-9421)
Related titles: Online - full text ed.: ISSN 1974-3092. 1993.
Published by: Federazione Nazionale Ordini Veterinari Italiani (F N O V I), Corso Vittorio Emanuele 73, Turin, 10128, Italy. TEL 39-011-5628352, FAX 39-011-545749.

VETERINARY SCIENCE—Abstracting, Bibliographies, Statistics

635.021 AUS
AUSTRALIA. BUREAU OF STATISTICS. VETERINARY SERVICES, AUSTRALIA (ONLINE). Text in English. 1999. irreg., latest 2000. free (effective 2009). **Document type:** *Government.* **Description:** Contains information about the veterinary services industry. Data includes: industry size, employment, income, expenses and industry value added, with breakdowns of key characteristics by business size and by state.
Formerly: Australia. Bureau of Statistics. Veterinary Services, Australia (Print)
Media: Online - full text.
Published by: Australian Bureau of Statistics, Locked Bag 10, Belconnen, ACT 2616, Australia. TEL 61-2-92684909, 300-135-070, FAX 61-2-92684654, client.services@abs.gov.au.

CAB ABSTRACTS. *see* AGRICULTURE—Abstracting, Bibliographies, Statistics

CAB ABSTRACTS ARCHIVE. *see* AGRICULTURE—Abstracting, Bibliographies, Statistics

636.089021 PRT ISSN 1646-8120
DIRECCAO GERAL DE VETERINARIA. BOLETIM ESTATISTICO. Text in Portuguese. 2007. m. **Document type:** *Bulletin, Trade.*
Published by: Ministerio da Agricultura, do Desenvolvimento Rural e das Pescas, Direccao Geral de Veterinaria, Largo Academia N B Artes 2, Lisbon, 1249-105, Portugal.

636.089 AUS ISSN 1033-2863
I V S ANNUAL. Variant title: Index of Veterinary Specialties Annual. Text in English. 1968. a. AUD 99 (effective 2008). adv. **Document type:** *Directory, Trade.* **Description:** Provides information for veterinary practitioners, classified by therapeutic category, on veterinary medicines and products available throughout Australia.
Formerly (until 1987): I V S (1033-2855)
Related titles: CD-ROM ed.
Published by: M I M S Australia (Subsidiary of: C M P Medica Australia Pty Ltd), PO Box 3000, St Leonards, NSW 1590, Australia. TEL 61-2-99027700, FAX 61-2-99027701, info@mims.com.au.

016.636 GBR ISSN 0019-4123
Z6674
INDEX VETERINARIUS; an excellent gateway to current research in veterinary sciences. Text in English. 1933. m. (plus a. cumulation). adv. bibl.; illus. reprints avail. **Document type:** *Abstract/Index.* **Description:** Provides subject and author index to the world's veterinary literature.
Related titles: Online - full text ed.
—BLDSC (4390.000000). **CCC.**
Published by: CABI (Subsidiary of: CAB International), Nosworthy Way, Wallingford, Oxfordshire OX10 8DE, United Kingdom. TEL 44-1491-832111, FAX 44-1491-829292, enquiries@cabi.org.

636.089 PAK
PAKISTAN VETERINARY INDEX. Text in English. 1985. a. USD 15.
Published by: Press Corporation of Pakistan, P O Box 3138, Karachi, 75400, Pakistan. TEL 21-455-3703, FAX 21-7736198. Ed. Saeed Hafeez. Circ: 5,000.

016.636089 GBR ISSN 0042-4854
SF601
VETERINARY BULLETIN; an excellent gateway to all current research on veterinary sciences. Text in English. 1912. m. adv. bk.rev. illus. Index. reprints avail. **Document type:** *Bulletin, Abstract/Index.* **Description:** Publishes abstracts of the core literature in the whole field of animal health.
Formerly (until 1931): Tropical Veterinary Bulletin (0372-2635); Incorporates (1955-1961): Veterinary Reviews and Annotations (0505-4052)
Related titles: Online - full text ed.: Veterinary Science Database.
Indexed: L09, P30.
—BLDSC (9227.000000), Linda Hall. **CCC.**
Published by: CABI (Subsidiary of: CAB International), Nosworthy Way, Wallingford, Oxfordshire OX10 8DE, United Kingdom. TEL 44-1491-832111, FAX 44-1491-829292, enquiries@cabi.org.

VIDEO

see COMMUNICATIONS—Video

VISUALLY IMPAIRED

see HANDICAPPED—Visually Impaired

V W Z

WASTE MANAGEMENT

see ENVIRONMENTAL STUDIES—Waste Management

WATER RESOURCES

see also AGRICULTURE ; CONSERVATION ; ENVIRONMENTAL STUDIES ; PUBLIC HEALTH AND SAFETY

628.1 USA
A C W A NEWS. Text in English. bi-w. USD 125 to non-members; free to members (effective 2005). **Document type:** *Magazine, Trade.*
Published by: Association of California Water Agencies, 910 K St, Ste 100, Sacramento, CA 95814-3512. TEL 916-441-4545, FAX 916-325-2306. Ed. Cindy Nickles. Circ: 5,500 (controlled).

333.91 DEU
A Q S - MERKBLAETTER FUER DIE WASSER-, ABWASSER- UND SCHLAMMUNTERSUCHUNG. Text in German. base vol. plus a. updates. EUR 76 base vol(s).; EUR 16.80 updates per issue (effective 2009). **Document type:** *Monographic series, Trade.*
Published by: (Bund - Laender-Arbeitsgemeinschaft Wasser), Erich Schmidt Verlag GmbH & Co. (Berlin), Genthiner Str 30 G, Berlin, 10785, Germany. TEL 49-30-2500850, FAX 49-30-250085305, esv@esvmedien.de, http://www.esv.info.

333.91 USA
A S D W A UPDATE. Text in English. 1986. bi-m. USD 40 to non-members (effective 2000). bk.rev. **Document type:** *Newsletter.* **Description:** Examines issues related to the protection of public health through the assurance of high-quality drinking water.
Published by: Association of State Drinking Water Administrators, 1025 Connecticut Ave, N W, Ste 903, Washington, DC 20036. TEL 202-293-7655, FAX 202-293-7656. Ed., R&P Brendan Shane. Circ: 400.

628.1 USA ISSN 1559-7229
TD485
A W W A DISTRIBUTION SYSTEM SYMPOSIUM. PROCEEDINGS. (American Water Works Association) Text in English. 200?. a. **Document type:** *Proceedings, Trade.*
Media: CD-ROM. **Related titles:** Print ed.: ISSN 0197-4599. 1980.
Published by: American Water Works Association, 6666 W Quincy Ave, Denver, CO 80235. TEL 303-794-7711, 800-926-7337, FAX 303-347-0804, custsvc@awwa.org, http://www.awwa.org.

628.1 USA ISSN 1946-7141
HD4461
A W W A STREAMLINES; water news, advancement and practice. Variant title: American Water Works Association Streamlines. Text in English. 1998. bi-w. free (effective 2009). adv. back issues avail. **Document type:** *Newsletter, Trade.* **Description:** Brings out readers timely and targeted stories about regulatory and legislative developments, industry issues and trends, utility practices, research and new technologies, along with information about the AWWA community and resources.
Formed by the merger of (1998 -2009): E-MainStream (1551-8647); (2001-2009): Waterweek (1551-8450); Which was formerly (1992-2001): Waterweek (Print)
Media: Online - full content.
—CCC.
Published by: American Water Works Association, 6666 W Quincy Ave, Denver, CO 80235. TEL 303-347-6261, 800-926-7337, FAX 303-347-0804, custsvc@awwa.org. Ed. Mary A Parmelee TEL 303-347-6272.

628.1 USA ISSN 0164-0755
A W W A WATER QUALITY TECHNOLOGY CONFERENCE PROCEEDINGS. Text in English. 1973. a. **Document type:** *Proceedings, Trade.*
—CCC.
Published by: American Water Works Association, 6666 W Quincy Ave, Denver, CO 80235. TEL 303-794-7711, FAX 303-347-0804, custsvc@awwa.org, http://www.awwa.org.

627 ITA ISSN 1125-1255
TC1 CODEN: IDTEDH
L'ACQUA. Text in Italian. 1930. bi-m. **Document type:** *Magazine, Trade.* **Description:** Covers all questions related to water: technical, scientific, legal, managerial, environmental, social, water resources and uses.
Former titles (until 1995): Idrotecnica. L'Acqua nell'Agricoltura, nell'Igiene, nell'Industria (0390-6655); (until 1973): Acqua nell'Agricoltura, nell'Igiene, nell'Industria (0001-4990); (until 1932): Acqua nei Campi, nell'Abitato, nell'Industria (0393-7097); (until 1930): Italia Fisica e l'Acqua nei Campi e nell'Abitato (1592-6850); Which was formed by the merger of (1928-1930): Acqua nei Campi e nell'Abitato (1592-6877); (1926-1930): L' Italia Fisica (1592-6885)
Indexed: GeoRef, INIS AtomInd, Inspec, SpeleolAb.
Published by: Associazione Idrotecnica Italiana, Via di Santa Costanza 7, Rome, 00198, Italy. TEL 39-06-8845064, FAX 39-06-8552974.

ACTA SCIENTIARUM POLONORUM. FORMATIO CIRCUMIECTUS. *see* ENVIRONMENTAL STUDIES

551.4 333.91 GBR ISSN 0309-1708
TC1 CODEN: AWREDI
➤ **ADVANCES IN WATER RESOURCES.** Text in English. 1979. 12/yr. EUR 1,904 in Europe to institutions; JPY 252,600 in Japan to institutions; USD 2,129 elsewhere to institutions (effective 2012). back issues avail. **Document type:** *Journal, Academic/Scholarly.* **Description:** Provides information for engineers or scientists interested in theoretical and computational aspects of water resources engineering. Covers groundwater hydrology, water quality, surface water hydrology and stochastic hydrology.
Incorporates (1988-1990): Hydrosoft (0268-6856)
Related titles: Microform ed.: (from PQC); Online - full text ed.: ISSN 1872-9657 (from IngentaConnect, ScienceDirect).
Indexed: A01, A03, A08, A22, A26, A28, A32, A33, APA, ASCA, ASFA, Agr, ApMecR, B&BAb, B19, B21, BrCerAb, C&ISA, CA, CA/WCA, CIA, CPEI, CTO, CerAb, CivEngAb, CorrAb, CurCont, E&CAJ, E04, E05, E11, EEA, EMA, ESPM, EngInd, EnvAb, EnvEAb, EnvInd, FLUIDEX, GEOBASE, GeoRef, H15, I05, I10, ICEA, ISR, Inspec, M&GPA, M&TEA, M09, MBF, METADEX, P30, PollutAb, RefZh, SCI, SCOPUS, SWRA, SoftAbEng, SolStAb, SpeleolAb, T02, T04, W07, WAA, WildRev.
—BLDSC (0712.120000), AskIEEE, CASDDS, IE, Infotrieve, Ingenta, INIST, Linda Hall. **CCC.**
Published by: Pergamon (Subsidiary of: Elsevier Science & Technology), The Blvd, Langford Ln, East Park, Kidlington, Oxford OX5 1GB, United Kingdom. TEL 44-1865-843000, FAX 44-1865-843010, JournalsCustomerServiceEMEA@elsevier.com. Eds. Casey T Miller TEL 919-966-2643, D At Barry TEL 41-21-6935576, W F Krajewski TEL 319-335-5231. **Subscr. to:** Elsevier BV, Radarweg 29, PO Box 211, Amsterdam 1000 AE, Netherlands. TEL 31-20-4853757, FAX 31-20-4853432, http://www.elsevier.nl.

➤ **AELVRAEDDAREN.** *see* ENVIRONMENTAL STUDIES

➤ **AFRICAN JOURNAL OF AQUATIC SCIENCE**; official journal of the Southern African Society of Aquatic Scientists. *see* BIOLOGY

➤ **AGRICULTURAL WATER MANAGEMENT.** *see* AGRICULTURE—Crop Production And Soil

333.9 551.4 USA
AGUA DULCE. Text in English. s-a. **Document type:** *Newsletter.*
Related titles: E-mail ed.
Published by: Water Partners International, PO Box 654, Columbia, MO 65205-0654. TEL 573-447-2222, FAX 573-447-2221.

333.91 ESP ISSN 1575-0744
AGUA PROFESIONAL. Text in Spanish. 1999. m. free to qualified personnel (effective 2010). **Document type:** *Magazine, Trade.*
Published by: Sede Tecnica S.A., Avda Brasil, 17 planta 12, Madrid, 28020, Spain. TEL 34-91-5565004, FAX 34-91-5560962, editorial@sedetecnica.com, http://www.sedetecnica.com/.

333.9 BRA
AGUAONLINE; revista digital da agua, do saneamento e do meio ambiente. Text in Portuguese. 2000. irreg. adv.
Media: Online - full text.
Published by: Centro Propaganda Ltda., Ave. Padre Chagas, 425, conj, 501-503, Porto Alegre, 90570-080, Brazil. TEL 55-51-32228545.

333.91 LBN ISSN 1990-3952
'ALAM AL-MIYAH AL-'ARABI/ALAM AL-MIYAH AL-ARABI AD-DUWALI. Text in Arabic, English. 1977. m. USD 30 domestic; USD 45 in Arab countries; USD 80 elsewhere (effective 2008). adv. bk.rev. tr.lit. 3 cols./p.; back issues avail. **Document type:** *Magazine, Trade.* **Description:** Covers articles of interest to importers, wholesalers, exporters, manufacturers, consulting engineers, and other decision makers serving the water and energy relevant industries of the Middle East, anglophone Africa, and other countries.
Former titles (until 2006): Arab Water World International (1015-8332); (until 1990): Arab Water World (0255-8580)
Related titles: Online - full text ed.: Arab Water World. ISSN 1990-3995.
Indexed: A32.
Published by: Chatila Publishing House, Chouran, P O Box 13-5121, Beirut, 1102-2802, Lebanon. TEL 961-1-352413, FAX 961-1-352419, info@chatilapublishing.com. Ed., Pub. Fathi Chatila. Adv. contact Mona Chatila. Circ: 9,142.

333.91 USA
ALASKA SNOW SURVEY REPORT. Text in English. 1962. q. free. charts; illus.; stat. index. back issues avail.; reprints avail. **Document type:** *Bulletin, Government.* **Description:** Focuses on seasonal snow depth, snow-water content, accumulated water-year precipitation statistics from a network of 200 data sites and selected streamflow facts.
Former titles (until 1992): Alaska Snow Surveys - Basin Outlook Reports; Alaska Snow Surveys; (until 1985): Snow Surveys and Water Supply Outlook for Alaska (0731-8499); (until 1981): Federal-State-Private Snow Surveys and Water Supply Outlook for Alaska
Related titles: Microfiche ed.: (from CIS); Online - full text ed.
Indexed: AmStI.
Published by: U.S. Department of Agriculture, Natural Resources Conservation Service (Anchorage), 949 E 36th Ave, Ste 400, Anchorage, AK 99508-4362. TEL 907-271-2424, FAX 907-271-3951. Ed. Rick McClure. Circ: 500.

ALTERRA-RAPPORT/ALTERRA REPORT. *see* ENVIRONMENTAL STUDIES

AMANZI (ONLINE EDITION). *see* EARTH SCIENCES—Hydrology

133.3 USA ISSN 0093-089X
BF1628
AMERICAN DOWSER. Text in English. 1961. q. USD 35 to individual members; includes newsletter and digest. bk.rev. cum.index every 5 yrs.
Supersedes: American Society of Dowsers. Quarterly Digest
Published by: American Society of Dowsers, Inc., PO Box 24, Danville, VT 05828. TEL 802-684-3417, FAX 802-684-2565. Circ: 4,500.

627 USA
AMERICAN INSTITUTE OF HYDROLOGY. BULLETIN. Text in English. 1983. q. free to members (effective 2010). adv. bk.rev. back issues avail. **Document type:** *Bulletin, Trade.* **Description:** Newsletter regarding activities and members of institute.
Published by: American Institute of Hydrology, Engineering D - Mail Code 6603, Southern Illinois University Carbondale, 1230 Lincoln Dr, Carbondale, IL 62901. TEL 618-453-7809, FAX 618-453-3044, aih@engr.siu.edu.

628 333.91 USA ISSN 1093-474X
GB651 CODEN: WARBAQ
AMERICAN WATER RESOURCES ASSOCIATION. JOURNAL. Text in English. 1965. bi-m. GBP 332 combined subscription in United Kingdom to institutions (print & online eds.); EUR 422 combined subscription in Europe to institutions (print & online eds.); USD 600 combined subscription in the Americas to institutions (print & online eds.); USD 650 combined subscription elsewhere to institutions (print & online eds.) (effective 2012). bk.rev. abstr.; charts; illus. index. reprint service avail. from PSC. **Document type:** *Journal, Trade.* **Description:** Publishes original papers covering water resources issues. Includes litigation and legislation issues.
Formerly (until 1997): Water Resources Bulletin (0043-1370); Which incorporated: American Water Resources Association. Water Resources Newsletter
Related titles: Microform ed.: (from PQC); Online - full text ed.: ISSN 1752-1688. GBP 290 in United Kingdom to institutions; EUR 367 in Europe to institutions; USD 522 in the Americas to institutions; USD 567 elsewhere to institutions (effective 2012) (from IngentaConnect).
Indexed: A01, A05, A20, A22, A32, A34, A35, A36, A37, A38, AS&TA, AS&TI, ASCA, ASFA, AgBio, Agr, AgrForAb, B04, BAS, BIOBASE, BibAg, C10, C25, C30, CA, CABA, CIN, CIS, CPEI, ChemAb, CurCont, D01, E01, E04, E05, E11, E12, EIA, ESPM, EngInd, EnvAb, EnvInd, F08, F11, F12, FCA, FLUIDEX, G11, GEOBASE, GH, GeoRef, H16, I11, IABS, ICEA, ISR, LT, M&GPA, MLA-IB, MaizeAb, N02, N04, O01, OR, OceAb, P11, P26, P30, P32, P33, P37, P39, P40, P48, P50, P52, P54, P56, PAIS, PGegResA, PGrRegA, PN&I, PQC, PlantSci, PollutAb, R07, R08, R11, R12, RI-1, RI-2, RRTA, Repind, S13, S16, SCI, SCOPUS, SJW, SPPI, SSciA, SWRA, SoftAbEng, SoyAb, SpeleolAb, T02, T04, T05, TAR, TriticAb, VS, W07, W10, W11, WildRev.
—BLDSC (4695.900000), CASDDS, IE, Infotrieve, Ingenta, INIST, Linda Hall. **CCC.**
Published by: (American Water Resources Association), Wiley-Blackwell Publishing, Inc. (Subsidiary of: Wiley-Blackwell Publishing Ltd.), 111 River St, Hoboken, NJ 07030. TEL 201-748-6000, FAX 201-748-6088, info@wiley.com, http://www.wiley.com/WileyCDA/. Ed. Kenneth Lanfear.

333.91 USA ISSN 0894-847X
AMERICAN WATER RESOURCES ASSOCIATION. MONOGRAPHS. Text in English. irreg., latest vol.19, 1993. price varies. **Document type:** *Monographic series.*
Indexed: GeoRef, SpeleolAb.
—CCC.
Published by: American Water Resources Association, PO Box 1626, Middleburg, VA 20118. TEL 540-687-8390, FAX 540-687-8395, info@awra.org, http://www.awra.org. Ed. Christopher Lant. R&P Kenneth D Reid.

333.91 USA ISSN 1070-6763
AMERICAN WATER RESOURCES ASSOCIATION TECHNICAL PUBLICATION SERIES. Text in English. 1979. irreg. price varies. illus. **Document type:** *Proceedings.* **Description:** Papers presented at American Water Resources Association Specialty Conferences.
Formerly (until 1982): American Water Resources Association. Technical Publication Series (0731-9789)
Indexed: GeoRef.
—CCC.
Published by: American Water Resources Association, PO Box 1626, Middleburg, VA 20118. TEL 540-687-8390, FAX 540-687-8395, info@awra.org, http://www.awra.org.

628 USA ISSN 0003-150X
TD201 CODEN: JAWWA5
➤ **AMERICAN WATER WORKS ASSOCIATION. JOURNAL.** Text in English. 1881. m. free to members (effective 2009). adv. bk.rev. abstr.; bibl.; charts; illus.; stat.; tr.lit. index, cum.index: 1946-1980 in 5 vols. back issues avail.; reprints avail. **Document type:** *Journal, Academic/Scholarly.* **Description:** Contains technical papers, discussions, news, and reports of water treatment technology.
Former titles (until 1948): American Water Works Association. Proceedings of the Annual Convention (0097-2630); (until 1902): American Water Works Association. Report. Proceedings. Annual Meeting
Related titles: Microfiche ed.: (from PQC); Microfilm ed.: (from PMC, PQC); Online - full text ed.: American Water Works Association. E-Journal. ISSN 1551-8833.
Indexed: A05, A15, A20, A22, A23, A24, A32, ABIPC, ABIn, AESIS, AIA, APD, AS&TA, AS&TI, ASCA, ASFA, B04, B10, B13, B25, BIOSIS Prev, BioEngAb, C10, C33, CA, CIN, CPEI, Cadscan, ChemAb, ChemTitl, CoppAb, CurCont, DokArb, E04, E05, ESPM, EngInd, EnvAb, EnvInd, FR, FS&TA, GeoRef, ICEA, INIS AtomInd, ISR, LeadAb, MycolAb, P06, P26, P30, P34, P50, P52, P54, P56, PQC, PollutAb, Repind, SCI, SCOPUS, SJW, SWRA, SoftAbEng, SpeleolAb, T02, W07, Zincscan.
—BLDSC (4696.000000), CASDDS, IE, Infotrieve, Ingenta, INIST, Linda Hall. **CCC.**
Published by: American Water Works Association, 6666 W Quincy Ave, Denver, CO 80235. TEL 303-794-7711, 800-926-7337, FAX 303-347-0804, custsvc@awwa.org. Ed. Marcia Lacey. Adv. contact Marge Grogan.

627 BRA ISSN 0373-9260
ANAIS HIDROGRAFICOS. Text in Portuguese. 1933. a. free. charts; illus.; stat.
Indexed: C01.
—INIST.
Published by: Ministerio da Marinha, Diretoria de Hidrografia e Navegacao, Rio De Janeiro, RJ, Brazil. Circ: (controlled).

ANALES DEL INSTITUTO DE INVESTIGACIONES MARINAS DE PUNTA BETIN. SUPLEMENTO. *see* EARTH SCIENCES—Oceanography

333.91 GBR
ANGLIAN WATER. ANNUAL REPORT AND ACCOUNT. Text in English. 19??. a. back issues avail. **Document type:** *Corporate.* **Description:** Legal requirement to publish an annual report for our shareholders.
Former titles (until 2001): Anglian Water. Annual Report (0963-4193); (until 1995): Anglian Water. Annual Review
Related titles: Online - full text ed.: free (effective 2009).
Published by: Anglian Water plc., Anglian House, Ambury Rd, Huntingdon, Cambs PE29 3NZ, United Kingdom. TEL 44-1480-323000, FAX 44-1480-323115, http://www.anglianwater.uk.

333.91 USA
TD201 CODEN: PWWPAY
ANNUAL INTERNATIONAL WATER CONFERENCE. OFFICIAL PROCEEDINGS. Text in English. 1941. a. cum.index: 1940-1974. back issues avail. **Document type:** *Proceedings, Trade.* **Description:** Provides current technological updates and case studies dealing with industrial water treatment, use and reuse for both industrial and engineering purposes.
Former titles (until 2002): International Water Conference. Official Proceedings (0739-4977); (until 1980): International Water Conference Annual Meeting. Proceedings (0074-9575); (until 1961): Annual Water Conference. Proceedings
Media: CD-ROM.

Indexed: A22, ChemAb, SpeleolAb.
—BLDSC (6847.040000), CASDDS, Ingenta, Linda Hall. **CCC.**
Published by: (International Water Conference), Engineers' Society of Western Pennsylvania, 337 Fourth Ave, Pittsburgh, PA 15222. TEL 412-261-0710, FAX 412-261-1606, eswp@eswp.com, http://www.eswp.com.

333.91 USA ISSN 0161-4924
GB705.N6
ANNUAL NEW MEXICO WATER CONFERENCE. PROCEEDINGS. Text in English. 1956. a. USD 15.75 per issue in United States (effective 2011); price varies. back issues avail. **Document type:** *Proceedings.*
Former titles (until 1972): New Mexico Water Conference. Proceedings; (until 1970): New Mexico Water Conference. Annual; (until 1966): New Mexico Water Conference. Annual Proceedings; (until 1965): New Mexico Water Conference. Annual; (until 1959): Water Conference. Annual; (until 1957): New Mexico Water Conference
Indexed: GeoRef, SpeleolAb.
Published by: New Mexico Water Resources Research Institute, NMSU MSC 3167, 3170 S Espina St, PO Box 30001, Las Cruces, NM 88003. TEL 575-646-4337, FAX 575-646-6418, nmwrri@nmsu.edu.

333.9 551.4 ISR
APPLIED RESEARCH INSTITUTE JERUSALEM. MONTHLY REPORT ON THE ISRAELI COLONIZATION ACTIVITIES IN THE WEST BANK & THE GAZA STRIP. Text in English. m.
Formerly: Applied Research Institute Jerusalem. Monthly Report on the Israeli Colonization Activities in the West Bank
Media: Online - full content.
Published by: Applied Research Institute - Jerusalem, Caritas Street, PO Box 860, Bethlehem, Israel. TEL 972-2-2741889, FAX 972-2-2776966.

333.91 DEU ISSN 2190-5487
▼ ➤ **APPLIED WATER SCIENCE.** Text in English. 2011. q. free (effective 2011). **Document type:** *Journal, Academic/Scholarly.* **Description:** Contains research on different water issues, exploring potential alternative water sources via recycling and reuse of wastewater.
Related titles: Online - full text ed.: ISSN 2190-5495. 2011.
Published by: SpringerOpen (Subsidiary of: Springer Science+Business Media), Tiergartenstr 17, Heidelberg, 69121, Germany. info@springeropen.com, http://www.springeropen.com. Eds. Abdulrahman I Alabdulaaly, Enrico Drioli.

639.2 AUS ISSN 1323-0077
AQUA AUSTRALIS. Text in English. 1969. q.
Former titles (until 1994): Hydrological Newsletter; (until 1993): Hydrological Society of South Australia. Newsletter
Related titles: Online - full text ed.: ISSN 1329-2366.
Published by: University of Adelaide, School of Engineering, Adelaide, SA 5005, Australia. TEL 61-8-83035451, FAX 61-8-83034359.

▼ **AQUA MUNDI.** *see* EARTH SCIENCES—Hydrology

628.1 USA ISSN 2152-4076
AQUA VITAE. Text in English. 199?. q. free (effective 2010). back issues avail. **Document type:** *Newsletter, Consumer.*
Media: Online - full text.
Published by: Lower Colorado River Authority, PO Box 220, Austin, TX 78767. TEL 512-473-3200, 800-776-5272.

AQUACULTURAL ENGINEERING. *see* FISH AND FISHERIES

AQUACULTURE. *see* FISH AND FISHERIES

AQUACULTURE NEWS; serving the nation's aquaculture industry. *see* FISH AND FISHERIES

AQUACULTURE RESEARCH. *see* FISH AND FISHERIES

AQUALINE ABSTRACTS. *see* WATER RESOURCES—Abstracting, Bibliographies, Statistics

333.91 AUT
AQUAPRESS INTERNATIONAL; Wasserwirtschaft im Donauraum. Text in German, English. q. EUR 32.50 domestic; EUR 45.40 foreign (effective 2004). adv. **Document type:** *Magazine, Trade.*
Published by: Bohmann Druck und Verlag GmbH & Co. KG, Leberstr 122, Vienna, W 1110, Austria. TEL 43-1-740950, FAX 43-1-74095183, office.gl@bohmann.at, http://www.bohmann.at. Ed. Christoph Hahn. Adv. contact Fiala Scheherezade. B&W page EUR 2,750, color page EUR 3,680; trim 185 x 250. Circ: 8,000 (paid and controlled).

627 GBR ISSN 0261-5355
AQUATECHNIC INTERNATIONAL. Text in English. 1981. 10/yr. GBP 75. adv. bk.rev. back issues avail.
Published by: D.J.L. Marketing Ltd., 47 Burney St, London, SE10 8EX, United Kingdom. FAX 081-853-4079. Ed. David Longhurst. Circ: 13,000.

AQUATIC CONSERVATION; marine and freshwater ecosystems. *see* CONSERVATION

AQUATIC CONSERVATION (ONLINE); marine and freshwater ecosystems. *see* CONSERVATION

AQUATIC GEOCHEMISTRY. *see* EARTH SCIENCES

AQUATIC LIVING RESOURCES; international journal devoted to aquatic resources. *see* FISH AND FISHERIES

333.91 USA
AQUEDUCT 2000. Text in English. 1934. 6/yr. free to qualified personnel. illus. **Document type:** *Magazine, Trade.*
Incorporates: Focus on Water; Which superseded (1974-1979): Meter; Former titles: Aqueduct (0092-0622); Aqueduct News (0003-7338); Colorado River Aqueduct News
Published by: Metropolitan Water District of Southern California, 700 N. Alameda St., # 1-304, Los Angeles, CA 90012-2944. TEL 213-250-6000. Ed. Jim Parsons. Circ: 40,000.

ARCHIVES OF HYDROENGINEERING AND ENVIRONMENTAL MECHANICS. *see* ENGINEERING—Hydraulic Engineering

628.1 AUS ISSN 1833-1025
TD321.S68
ARID AREAS CATCHMENT WATER MANAGEMENT BOARD. ANNUAL REPORT. Text in English. 2001. a. **Document type:** *Government.*
Published by: South Australia, Arid Areas Catchment Water Management Board, GPO Box 2834, Adelaide, SA 5001, Australia. McShane.Kate@saugov.sa.gov.au, http://www.aridareaswater.com.au.

333.91 USA
GB705.A8
ARKANSAS. GEOLOGICAL SURVEY. WATER RESOURCES CIRCULARS. Text in English. 1955. irreg., latest vol.18, 2003. price varies. back issues avail. **Document type:** *Monographic series, Government.*
Formerly: Arkansas. Geological Commission. Water Resources Circulars (0571-0278)
Related titles: Online - full text ed.: free (effective 2011).
Indexed: GeoRef, SpeleolAb.
—Linda Hall.
Published by: Arkansas. Geological Survey, Vardelle Parham Geology Ctr, 3815 W Roosevelt Rd, Little Rock, AR 72204. TEL 501-296-1877, FAX 501-663-7360, bekki.white@arkansas.gov.

551.4 333.9 USA
TC424.A8 CODEN: AGWAAI
ARKANSAS. GEOLOGICAL SURVEY. WATER RESOURCES SUMMARY. Text in English. 1962. irreg., latest vol.17, 2005. price varies. illus. back issues avail. **Document type:** *Monographic series, Government.*
Formerly: Arkansas. Geological Commission. Water Resources Summary (0518-6374)
Related titles: Online - full text ed.: free (effective 2011).
Indexed: GeoRef, SpeleolAb.
—Linda Hall.
Published by: Arkansas. Geological Survey, Vardelle Parham Geology Ctr, 3815 W Roosevelt Rd, Little Rock, AR 72204. TEL 501-296-1877, FAX 501-663-7360, bekki.white@arkansas.gov.

ASIAN WATER; Asia's journal of environmental technology. *see* ENVIRONMENTAL STUDIES

333.9 USA
TD224.A2
AUBURN UNIVERSITY. ENVIRONMENTAL INSTITUTE. ANNUAL REPORT. Text in English. 1965. a. **Document type:** *Report, Academic/Scholarly.*
Formerly (until 19??): Auburn University. Water Resources Research Institute. Annual Report (0067-043X)
Published by: Auburn University, Environmental Institute, 1090 S Donahue Dr, Auburn, AL 36849. TEL 334-844-4132, FAX 334-844-4462, blockdh@auburn.edu, http://www.auei.auburn.edu.

627 AUS ISSN 1320-6524
AUSTRALASIAN DRILLING. Text in English. 1972. bi-m. AUD 120 (effective 2007 - 2008). adv. bk.rev. charts; illus. back issues avail. **Document type:** *Journal, Trade.* **Description:** Provides information on technical advances, new equipment and product news.
Former titles (until 1993): Australian Drilling (1037-3535); (until 1991): Water and Mineral Development (0811-5931); (until 1982): National Water Well Association. Journal (0310-3625)
Indexed: AESIS.
—BLDSC (1793.900000).
Published by: Australian Drilling Industry Association, 85 Bardia Ave, Suites 6 & 7, Seaford, VIC 3198, Australia. TEL 61-3-97704000, FAX 61-3-97704030, adia@adia.com.au. Ed. Simon Fitzgerald. Adv. contact David M Smith. color page AUD 2,180; 210 x 297. Circ: 6,000.

614 AUS ISSN 1445-2847
AUSTRALIAN FLUORIDATION NEWS. Text in English. 1963. bi-m. AUD 25 membership (effective 2007). bk.rev. **Document type:** *Newsletter, Trade.*
Formerly: Aqua Pura
Published by: Anti-Fluoridation Association of Victoria, PO Box 935, Melbourne, VIC 3001, Australia. TEL 61-3-95925088, FAX 61-3-95924544, glen.walker@bigpond.com, http://www.glenwalker.net. Ed. Glen Walker. Circ: 2,000.

628.1 AUS ISSN 1324-1583
➤ **AUSTRALIAN JOURNAL OF WATER RESOURCES.** Abbreviated title: A J W R. Text in English. s-a. AUD 15; free to members (effective 2009). adv. **Document type:** *Journal, Academic/Scholarly.*
Indexed: A01, A26, CPEI, GEOBASE, I05, SCOPUS, T02.
—BLDSC (1812.980000), IE, Ingenta.
Published by: (The Institution of Engineers Australia), Engineers Media Pty Ltd., 2 Ernest Pl, PO Box 588, Crows Nest, NSW 1585, Australia. TEL 61-2-94381533, FAX 61-2-94385934, subscriptions@engineersmedia.com.au. Ed. Erwin Weinmann. Adv. contact Maria Mamone. Circ: 500 (paid).

➤ **AUSTRALIAN STREAM MANAGEMENT CONFERENCE. PROCEEDINGS.** *see* EARTH SCIENCES—Hydrology

333.91 AUS ISSN 0811-5397
AUSTRALIAN WATER RESOURCES COUNCIL. WATER RESOURCES SERIES. Text in English. 1982. irreg.
Indexed: AESIS, GeoRef.
Published by: (Australia. Australian Water Resources Council), Department of Primary Industries and Energy, GPO Box 858, Canberra, ACT 2600, Australia.

627 DEU ISSN 2192-3078
▼ **B A W AKTUELL.** Text in German. 2010. q. **Document type:** *Magazine, Trade.*
Published by: Bundesanstalt fuer Wasserbau, Kussmaulstr 17, Karlsruhe, 76187, Germany. TEL 49-721-97260, FAX 49-721-97264540, info@baw.de.

627 DEU ISSN 2190-9156
B A W - GESCHAEFTSBERICHT. Text in German. 1970. a. **Document type:** *Trade.*
Formerly (until 2010): Bundesanstalt fuer Wasserbau. Taetigkeitsbericht (0720-8065)
Published by: Bundesanstalt fuer Wasserbau, Kussmaulstr 17, Karlsruhe, 76187, Germany. TEL 49-721-97260, FAX 49-721-97264540, info@baw.de.

627 DEU ISSN 2190-9199
B A W - MITTEILUNGEN. Text in German. 1953. irreg., latest vol.93, 2011. **Document type:** *Government.*
Formerly (until 2011): Bundesanstalt fuer Wasserbau. Mitteilungsblatt (0572-5801)
Indexed: RefZh.
Published by: Bundesanstalt fuer Wasserbau, Kussmaulstr 17, Karlsruhe, 76187, Germany. TEL 49-721-97260, FAX 49-721-97264540, info@baw.de.

627 DEU ISSN 1611-1478
TN860 CODEN: BWROEQ
B B R; Fachmagazin fuer Brunnen- und Leitungsbau. Text in German. 1949. m. EUR 129 domestic; EUR 145 foreign (effective 2010). adv. bk.rev. **Document type:** *Magazine, Trade.*
Former titles (until 2003): B B R - Wasser, Kanal- und Rohrleitungsbau (1611-0129); (until 2000): B B R - Wasser und Rohrbau (0937-3756); (until 1989): Brunnenbau, Bau von Wasserwerken, Rohrleitungsbau (0340-3874); (until 1974): B B R - Bohrtechnik, Brunnenbau, Rohrleitungsbau (0341-0242); (until 1967): Bohrtechnik, Brunnenbau, Rohrleitungsbau (0341-0234); (until 1958): Bohrtechnik, Brunnenbau (0342-5444); (until 1950): Brunnenbau, Tiefbohrtechnik (0342-5428)
Indexed: A22, ChemAb, FR, GeoRef, RefZh, SpeleolAb, TM.
—BLDSC (1871.366070), CASDDS, IE, Infotrieve, INIST. **CCC.**
Published by: Wirtschafts- und Verlagsgesellschaft Gas und Wasser mbH, Josef-Wirmer-Str 3, Bonn, 53123, Germany. TEL 49-228-919140, FAX 49-228-9191499, info@wvgw.de, http://www.wvgw.de. adv.: B&W page EUR 2,403, color page EUR 3,385; trim 172 x 255. Circ: 4,805 (paid).

628.1 AUS ISSN 1838-2916
BARWON WATER. ANNUAL REPORT. Text in English. 1985. a. free (effective 2011). **Document type:** *Report, Government.* **Description:** Provides combination of performance, financial and sustainability reports of Barwon water into one volume which reflects the ongoing integration of sustainability into everyday business activities and environmental leadership.
Formerly (until 1994): Geelong and District Water Board. Annual Report (0817-2633)
Related titles: Online - full text ed.: ISSN 1838-2924. free (effective 2011).
Published by: Barwon Water, 61-67 Ryrie St, PO Box 659, Geelong, VIC 3220, Australia. TEL 61-3-52262500, 1300-656-007, info@barwonwater.vic.gov.au.

628 DEU ISSN 0724-4290
BAU-INTERN; Zeitschrift der Bayerischen Staatsbauverwaltung fuer Hochbau, Staedtebau, Wohnungsbau, Strassen- und Brueckenbau. Text in German. 1959. bi-m. EUR 22.50; EUR 4.20 newsstand/cover (effective 2011). adv. bk.rev. illus.; stat. index. **Document type:** *Journal, Government.*
Former titles (until 1981): Wasser und Abwasser Bau Intern (0343-219X); (until 1975): Wasser und Abwasser (0043-0943)
Indexed: ChemAb, DokArb.
Published by: (Bayerische Staatsbauverwaltung fuer Hochbau, Staedtebau, Wohnungsbau, Strassen- und Brueckenbau), Verlag Karl M. Lipp, Meglingerstr 60, Munich, 81477, Germany. TEL 49-89-7858080, FAX 49-89-78580833. Ed. Attila M Karpati. adv.: page EUR 1,080; 175 x 262. Circ: 2,500.

333.91 USA ISSN 1064-8992
BAY JOURNAL. Text in English. 1991. m. free (effective 2005).
Published by: Alliance for the Chesapeake Bay, 660 York Rd Ste 100, Baltimore, MD 21212. TEL 410-377-6270, FAX 410-377-7144, mail@abc-online.org, http://www.acb-online.org/. Ed. Karl Blankenship.

BEACHWATCH PARNERSHIP PROGRAM NEWSLETTER. *see* ENVIRONMENTAL STUDIES

628.1 CHN ISSN 1673-4637
BEIJING SHUIWU/BEIJING WATER. Text in Chinese. 1994. bi-m. USD 18 (effective 2009). **Document type:** *Journal, Academic/Scholarly.*
Formerly: Beijing Shuili/Beijing Water Resources (1008-3367)
Related titles: Online - full text ed.
—East View.
Published by: Beijing Shi Shuili Kexue Yanjiusuo/Beijing Hydraulic Research Institute, 21, Chegongzhuang, Beijing, 100044, China. TEL 86-10-68483298, FAX 86-10-68483297, http://www.bwsti.com/l. **Dist. by:** China International Book Trading Corp, 35 Chegongzhuang Xilu, Haidian District, PO Box 399, Beijing 100044, China. TEL 86-10-68412045, FAX 86-10-68412023, cibtc@mail.cibtc.com.cn, http://www.cibtc.com.cn.

628.1 NLD ISSN 1877-2013
▼ **BESTUURLIJK HANDBOEK RIOLERING EN STEDELIJK WATERMANAGEMENT.** Text in Dutch. 2009. a. EUR 14.90 (effective 2011).
Published by: HoLaPress Communicatie bv, Postbus 130, Valkenswaard, 5550 AC, Netherlands. TEL 31-40-2086000, FAX 31-40-2086009, http://www.holapress.com.

628 IND ISSN 0006-0461
TC903
BHAGIRATH. Text in Hindi. 1954. q. bk.rev. charts; illus. index. **Document type:** *Journal, Government.* **Description:** Contains information, research, news and views on water resources development in India.
Related titles: English ed.
Indexed: CRIA, CRICC, PAA&I.
Published by: Ministry of Water Resources, Central Water Commission, Sewa Bhawan, R.K. Puram, New Delhi, 110 066, India. editbe-cwc@nic.in, http://www.cwc.nic.in. **Subscr. in U.S. to:** InterCulture Associates.

628.1 551.4 RUS ISSN 0320-9652
BIOLOGIYA VNUTRENNIKH VOD. Text in Russian; Summaries in English. 1967. 3/yr. **Document type:** *Journal, Academic/Scholarly.* **Description:** Covers the biology of aquatic ecosystems, including flora and fauna of water bodies, ecological physiology and biochemistry of aquatic animals, aquatic toxicology, and structure and function of aquatic ecosystems.
Related titles: ◆ English Translation: Biology of Inland Waters.
Indexed: ASFA, B21, ESPM, GeoRef, RefZh, Z01.
—East View, INIST, Linda Hall.
Published by: Rossiiskaya Akademiya Nauk, Institut Biologii Vnutrennikh Vod im. I. D. Papanina/Russian Academy of Sciences, Institute for Biology of Inland Waters I.D. Papanina, Borok, Yaroslavl, 152742, Russian Federation. TEL 7-8547-2-40-42, isdat@ibiw.yaroslavl.ru, http://www.ibiw.yaroslavl.ru/. Ed. D. S. Pavlov. **Co-sponsor:** Rossiiskaya Akademiya Nauk, Gidrobiologicheskoye Obshchestvo/Russian Academy of Sciences, Hydrobiological Society.

V W Z

628.1 551.4 RUS
BIOLOGY OF INLAND WATERS. Text in English. 1996. q. RUR 1,640 (effective 2004). **Document type:** *Journal, Academic/Scholarly.*
Description: Publishes problematic reviews and original papers devoted to biology, morphology, systematics and ecology of aquatic organisms, ecological physiology and biochemistry of aquatic animals, water toxicology, structure and functioning of aquatic ecosystem, hydrobiological methods of investigation as well as book reviews, information about meetings, conferences, symposia.
Related titles: ◆ Translation of: Biologiya Vnutrennikh Vod. ISSN 0320-9652.
Published by: (Rossiiskaya Akademiya Nauk, Institut Biologii Vnutrennikh Vod im. I. D. Papanina/Russian Academy of Sciences, Institute for Biology of Inland Waters I.D. Papanina), M A I K Nauka - Interperiodica (Subsidiary of: Pleiades Publishing, Inc.), Profsoyuznaya ul 90, Moscow, 117997, Russian Federation. TEL 7-095-3347420, FAX 7-095-3360666, compmg@maik.ru, http://www.maik.ru. Ed. D. S. Pavlov. **Co-sponsor:** Rossiiskaya Akademiya Nauk, Gidrobiologicheskoye Obshchestvo/Russian Academy of Sciences, Hydrobiological Society.

BIOSOLIDS TECHNICAL BULLETIN (ONLINE). *see* ENVIRONMENTAL STUDIES

628 MWI ISSN 0084-7925
BLANTYRE WATER BOARD. ANNUAL REPORT AND STATEMENT OF ACCOUNTS. Text in English. 1967. a. stat. **Document type:** *Directory.*
Published by: Blantyre Water Board, Chichiri, PO Box 30369, Blantyre, Malawi. Circ: 500.

628.1 NLD ISSN 2210-884X
BLIK OP HET WATERSYSTEEM. Text in Dutch. 200?. a. **Document type:** *Report, Government.*
Published by: Waterschap Peel en Maasvallei, Afdeling Kennis en Advies, Postbus 3390, Venlo, 5902 RJ, Netherlands. TEL 31-77-3891111, FAX 31-77-3873605, info@wpm.nl, http://www.wpm.nl.

BOLETIN DE INVESTIGACIONES MARINAS Y COSTERAS/BULLETIN OF MARINE AND COASTAL RESEARCH. *see* EARTH SCIENCES—Oceanography

333.91 ZAF ISSN 1011-128X
BOREHOLE WATER. Text in English. 1984. bi-m. ZAR 60. adv.
Description: Covers information on the newest developments and equipment used in the manipulation of water resources.
Formerly (until 1987): Borehole Water Journal (1012-2923)
Indexed: ISAP.
Published by: Borehole Water Association, PO Box 1155, Saxonwold, Johannesburg, 2132, South Africa. TEL 27-11-4470853, FAX 27-11-4470851, boreholewater@mweb.co.za, http://biznet.maximizer.com/boreholewater/. Ed. P M Mony. Circ: 5,000.

628.1 333.7932 CAN ISSN 1201-9984
BRITISH COLUMBIA HYDRO. CORPORATE REVIEW. Text in English. 1963. a.
Formerly (until 1995): British Columbia Hydro and Power Authority. Annual Report (0521-0577)
Published by: B C Hydro, 333 Dunsmuir St, Vancouver, BC V6B 5R3, Canada. TEL 604-623-4529, FAX 604-623-3730, http://www.bchydro.com/.

628.1 333.7932 CAN ISSN 1488-710X
HD9685.C3
BRITISH COLUMBIA HYDRO. TRIPLE BOTTOM LINE REPORT. Text in English. 1992. a.
Former titles (until 1999): British Columbia Hydro. Report on the Environment (1481-3130); (until 1997): British Columbia Hydro. Environmental Review (1203-2557); (until 1995): British Columbia Hydro. Report on the Environment (1192-1919)
Published by: B C Hydro, 333 Dunsmuir St, Vancouver, BC V6B 5R3, Canada. TEL 604-623-4529, FAX 604-623-3730, http://www.bchydro.com/.

BRITISH COLUMBIA. MINISTRY OF WATER, LAND AND AIR PROTECTION. ANNUAL SERVICE PLAN REPORT. *see* CONSERVATION

354.66 631.7 BFA
BURKINA FASO. DIRECTION DE L'HYDRAULIQUE ET DE L'EQUIPEMENT RURAL. SERVICE I.R.H. RAPPORT D'ACTIVITES. Text in French. irreg. **Document type:** *Government.*
Formerly: Upper Volta. Direction de l'Hydraulique et de l'Equipement Rural. Service I.R.H. Rapport d'Activites
Published by: Direction de l'Hydraulique et de l'Equipement Rural, Service I.R.H., Ministere du Plan du Developpement Rural de l'Environnement et du Tourisme, Ouagadougou, Burkina Faso.

627 BFA
BURKINA FASO. MINISTERE DE L'EAU. ANNUAIRE HYDROLOGIQUE DU BURKINA. Text in French. a. **Document type:** *Government.*
Published by: Ministere de l'Eau, Direction de l'Inventaire des Ressources Hydrauliques, BP 7025, Ouagadougou, Burkina Faso. TEL 30-80-35.

627 BFA
BURKINA FASO. MINISTERE DE L'EAU. BULLETIN HYDROLOGIQUE DU BURKINA. Text in French. m. **Document type:** *Government.*
Published by: Ministere de l'Eau, Direction de l'Inventaire des Ressources Hydrauliques, BP 7025, Ouagadougou, Burkina Faso. TEL 30-80-35.

C E M A R E MISCELLANEOUS PUBLICATIONS. (Centre for the Economics and Management of Aquatic Resources) *see* FISH AND FISHERIES

C E M A R E REPORTS. *see* FISH AND FISHERIES

333.9 USA ISSN 0084-8263
CODEN: CAWRAF
CALIFORNIA. DEPARTMENT OF WATER RESOURCES. BULLETIN. Text in English. a. price varies. **Document type:** *Government.*
Indexed: GeoRef, SpeleolAb.
—CASDDS, Linda Hall.
Published by: California Department of Water Resources, PO Box 942836, Sacramento, CA 94236-0001. TEL 916-445-9248. Circ: (controlled).

333.91 USA
CALIFORNIA WATER ENVIRONMENT ASSOCIATION. E-BULLETIN (ONLINE). Text in English. 1964. q. USD 97 membership (effective 2005). adv. bk.rev. bibl.; charts; illus.; maps; tr.lit. **Document type:** *Bulletin, Trade.* **Description:** Dedicated to the promotion of training certification of California wastewater professionals.
Former titles (until Fall 2001): California Water Environment Association. Bulletin (Print); California Water Pollution Control Association. Bulletin (0008-1620)
Media: Online - full content.
—Linda Hall.
Published by: California Water Environment Association, 7677 Oakport St, Ste 525, Oakland, CA 94621-1935. TEL 510-382-7800, FAX 510-382-7810, info@wea.org. Ed. Lindsay Roberts. R&Ps Julie Taylor, Lindsay Roberts. Adv. contact Brian Murray. page USD 395.

346.04691 USA
CALIFORNIA WATER LAW AND POLICY. Text in English. 1995. 2 base vols. plus irreg. updates. looseleaf. USD 232 base vol(s). (effective 2008). **Document type:** *Handbook/Manual/Guide, Trade.*
Description: Covers the rights and obligations of water supplies, planning and regulatory agencies and the relationship between the law and physical geology and hydrology.
Published by: Matthew Bender & Co., Inc. (Subsidiary of: LexisNexis North America), 1275 Broadway, Albany, NY 12204. TEL 518-487-3000, 800-424-4200, FAX 518-487-3083, international@bender.com, http://bender.lexisnexis.com. Ed. Scott Slater.

CALIFORNIA WATER LAW & POLICY REPORTER. *see* LAW

333.9 CAN
CANADA. INLAND WATERS DIRECTORATE. CANADIAN WATER QUALITY GUIDELINES. Text in English. irreg.
Published by: Environment Canada, Inland Waters Directorate (Subsidiary of: Environment Canada/Environnement Canada), Water Planning and Management Branch, Ottawa, ON K1A 0H3, Canada. TEL 819-953-1518, FAX 819-997-8701.

CANADA. INLAND WATERS DIRECTORATE. HISTORICAL STREAMFLOW SUMMARY, ALBERTA. *see* EARTH SCIENCES—Hydrology

CANADA. INLAND WATERS DIRECTORATE. HISTORICAL STREAMFLOW SUMMARY, ATLANTIC PROVINCES. *see* EARTH SCIENCES—Hydrology

CANADA. INLAND WATERS DIRECTORATE. HISTORICAL STREAMFLOW SUMMARY, BRITISH COLUMBIA. *see* EARTH SCIENCES—Hydrology

CANADA. INLAND WATERS DIRECTORATE. HISTORICAL STREAMFLOW SUMMARY, MANITOBA. *see* EARTH SCIENCES—Hydrology

CANADA. INLAND WATERS DIRECTORATE. HISTORICAL STREAMFLOW SUMMARY, ONTARIO. *see* EARTH SCIENCES—Hydrology

CANADA. INLAND WATERS DIRECTORATE. HISTORICAL WATER LEVELS SUMMARY. ATLANTIC PROVINCES. *see* EARTH SCIENCES—Hydrology

CANADA. INLAND WATERS DIRECTORATE. HISTORICAL WATER LEVELS SUMMARY. BRITISH COLUMBIA. *see* EARTH SCIENCES—Hydrology

CANADA. INLAND WATERS DIRECTORATE. HISTORICAL WATER LEVELS SUMMARY. QUEBEC/SOMMAIRE CHRONOLOGIQUE DES NIVEAUX D'EAU. QUEBEC. *see* EARTH SCIENCES—Hydrology

CANADA. INLAND WATERS DIRECTORATE. HISTORICAL WATER LEVELS SUMMARY. SASKATCHEWAN. *see* EARTH SCIENCES—Hydrology

CANADA. INLAND WATERS DIRECTORATE. HISTORICAL WATER LEVELS SUMMARY. YUKON AND NORTHWEST TERRITORIES. *see* EARTH SCIENCES—Hydrology

333.9 CAN ISSN 0576-2340
GB1230.A4
CANADA. INLAND WATERS DIRECTORATE. SURFACE WATER DATA. ALBERTA. Text in English. 1965. a. **Document type:** *Government.*
Supersedes in part (1920-1965): Surface Water Data for Arctic and Western Hudson Bay Drainage (0821-9400); Which was formerly (until 1962): Surface Water Supply of Canada. Arctic and Western Hudson Bay Drainage (0821-9397)
Indexed: GeoRef.
—Linda Hall.
Published by: Environment Canada, Inland Waters Directorate (Subsidiary of: Environment Canada/Environnement Canada), Water Planning and Management Branch, Ottawa, ON K1A 0H3, Canada. TEL 819-953-1518, FAX 819-997-8701.

333.9 CAN ISSN 0576-2359
CANADA. INLAND WATERS DIRECTORATE. SURFACE WATER DATA. ATLANTIC PROVINCES. Text in English. 1920. a. **Document type:** *Government.*
Former titles (until 1965): Surface Water Data for Atlantic Drainage (0821-9389); (until 1960): Surface Water Supply of Canada. Atlantic Drainage (0821-9370)
Indexed: GeoRef.
—Linda Hall.
Published by: Environment Canada, Inland Waters Directorate (Subsidiary of: Environment Canada/Environnement Canada), Water Planning and Management Branch, Ottawa, ON K1A 0H3, Canada. TEL 819-953-1518, FAX 819-997-8701.

333.9 CAN ISSN 0576-2367
CANADA. INLAND WATERS DIRECTORATE. SURFACE WATER DATA. BRITISH COLUMBIA. Text in English. 1965. a. **Document type:** *Government.*
Supersedes in part (1920-1965): Surface Water Data for Pacific Drainage (0821-929X); Which was formerly (until 1960): Surface Water Supply of Canada. Pacific Drainage (0821-9303)
Indexed: GeoRef.
—Linda Hall.
Published by: Environment Canada, Inland Waters Directorate (Subsidiary of: Environment Canada/Environnement Canada), Water Planning and Management Branch, Ottawa, ON K1A 0H3, Canada. TEL 819-953-1518, FAX 819-997-8701.

333.9 CAN ISSN 0576-2383
CANADA. INLAND WATERS DIRECTORATE. SURFACE WATER DATA. ONTARIO. Text in English. 1965. a. **Document type:** *Government.*
Supersedes in part (1927-1965): Surface Water Supply. St. Lawrence and Southern Hudson Bay Drainage (0821-9362); Which was formerly (until 1961): Surface Water Supply of Canada. St. Lawrence and Southern Hudson Bay Drainage. Ontario and Quebec (0821-9354); Which was formed by the merger of (1923-1927): Eaux de Surface du Canada. Bassins du Saint-Laurent et de la Baie d'Hudson Sud. Quebec (0821-9338); (1920-1927): Surface Water Supply of Canada. St. Lawrence and Southern Hudson Bay Drainage. Ontario (0821-9346)
Indexed: GeoRef.
—Linda Hall.
Published by: Environment Canada, Inland Waters Directorate (Subsidiary of: Environment Canada/Environnement Canada), Water Planning and Management Branch, Ottawa, ON K1A 0H3, Canada. TEL 819-953-1518, FAX 819-997-8701.

333.9 CAN ISSN 0576-2405
GB1230.S35
CANADA. INLAND WATERS DIRECTORATE. SURFACE WATER DATA. SASKATCHEWAN. Text in English. 1965. a. **Document type:** *Government.*
Supersedes in part (1920-1965): Surface Water Data for Arctic and Western Hudson Bay Drainage (0821-9400); Which was formerly (until 1961): Surface Water Supply of Canada. Arctic and Western Hudson Bay Drainage (0821-9397)
Indexed: GeoRef.
—Linda Hall.
Published by: Environment Canada, Inland Waters Directorate (Subsidiary of: Environment Canada/Environnement Canada), Water Planning and Management Branch, Ottawa, ON K1A 0H3, Canada. TEL 819-953-1518, FAX 819-997-8701.

333.9 CAN ISSN 0318-2266
CANADA. INLAND WATERS DIRECTORATE. SURFACE WATER DATA. YUKON AND NORTHWEST TERRITORIES. Text in English. 1965. a. **Document type:** *Government.*
Formerly (until 1973): Surface Water Data. Yukon Territory and Northwest Territories (0576-2413); Which superseded in part (1920-1965): Surface Water Data for Pacific Drainage (0821-929X); Which was formerly (until 1961): Surface Water Supply of Canada. Pacific Drainage (0821-9303)
Indexed: GeoRef.
Published by: Environment Canada, Inland Waters Directorate (Subsidiary of: Environment Canada/Environnement Canada), Water Planning and Management Branch, Ottawa, ON K1A 0H3, Canada. TEL 819-953-1518, FAX 819-997-8701.

333.91 CAN ISSN 0836-0278
CANADIAN WATER AND WASTEWATER ASSOCIATION. BULLETIN/ ASSOCIATION CANADIENNE DES EAUX POTABLES ET USEES. BULLETIN. Text in English, French. 1987. 10/yr. membership. bk.rev. **Document type:** *Newsletter.*
Formerly: Canadian Water and Wastewater Association. Newsletter
Published by: Canadian Water and Wastewater Association, 5330 Canotek Rd, 2nd Fl, Unit 20, Ottawa, ON K1J 9C3, Canada. TEL 613-747-0524, FAX 613-747-0523. Ed. T Duncan Ellison. Circ: 1,200.

333.91 CAN ISSN 0701-1784
➤ **CANADIAN WATER RESOURCES JOURNAL/REVUE CANADIENNE DES RESOURCES EN EAU.** Text in English, French. 1976. q. CAD 95 membership (effective 2011). adv. bk.rev. **Document type:** *Journal, Academic/Scholarly.*
Formerly: Reclamation
Related titles: Online - full text ed.: ISSN 1918-1817.
Indexed: A22, A26, A37, A38, ASFA, C03, C25, C30, CABA, CBCARef, CPEI, CPerI, E12, ESPM, EngInd, F08, F12, FCA, G11, GH, GeoRef, H16, I05, I11, LT, MaizeAb, N02, P32, P33, P48, P52, P56, PGegResA, PQC, PollutAb, R07, R08, RRTA, S06, S13, S16, SCI, SCOPUS, SSciA, SWRA, SoyAb, SpeleolAb, T02, ToxAb, W07, W10, W11.
—BLDSC (3046.135000), IE, Infotrieve, Ingenta, Linda Hall. **CCC.**
Published by: Canadian Water Resources Association/Association Canadienne des Ressources Hydriques, 9 Corvus Court, Ottawa, ON K2E 7Z4, Canada. TEL 613-237-9363, FAX 613-594-5190, services@aic.ca, http://www.cwra.org. Eds. Diana Allen TEL 778-782-3967, Paul H Whitfield TEL 604-664-9238. adv.: page CAD 400; trim 7.5 x 5. Circ: 900.

➤ **CATFISH JOURNAL.** *see* FISH AND FISHERIES

627 624 USA
CENTER FOR DREDGING STUDIES NEWSLETTER. Text in English. 1967. s-a. looseleaf. free. back issues avail. **Document type:** *Newsletter.*
Published by: Center for Dredging Studies, Civil Engineering Department, Texas A & M University, College Station, TX 77843-3136. TEL 409-845-4516, FAX 409-862-8162. Ed. Robert E Randall.

628 SWE ISSN 1404-966X
CODEN: PCTHET
CHALMERS TEKNISKA HOEGSKOLA. VATTEN MILJOE TRANSPORT. RAPPORT. Text in English, Swedish. 2000. irreg. SEK 200 per issue (effective 2003). charts; illus. **Document type:** *Monographic series, Academic/Scholarly.*
Formed by the merger of (1997-2000): Chalmers Tekniska Hoegskole. Institutionen foer Vattenbyggnad. Report. Series B (0348-1069); (1978-2000): Chalmers Tekniska Hoegskole. Institutionen foer Vattenbyggnad. Report. Series C (0283-3727); (1994-2000): Chalmers. VA-Teknik. Rapport (1401-1859); Which was formed by the merger of (1982-1994): Chalmers University of Technology. Department of Sanitary Engineering. Internskrift (0280-4034); (1981-1994): Chalmers University of Technology. Department of Sanitary Engineering. Publication (0280-4026); Which was formed by the merger of (1960-1981): Chalmers Tekniska Hoegskola. Institutionen foer Va-Teknik. A (0348-1794); (1962-1981): Chalmers Tekniska Hoegskola. Institutionen foer Va-Teknik. B (0009-1111); (1967-1981): Chalmers Tekniska Hoegskola. Institutionen foer Va-Teknik. C (0348-1808)
—CASDDS.
Published by: Chalmers Tekniska Hoegskola, Institutionen foer Vatten Miljoe Transport/Chalmers University of Technology. Department of Water Environment Transport, Sven Hultinsgata 8, Goeteborg, 41296, Sweden. TEL 46-31-7722121, FAX 46-31-7722128. Circ: 100.

628.1 CHN ISSN 1006-3706
DS793.Y3
CHANGJIANG NIANJIAN. Text in Chinese. 1993. a. CNY 300 per issue (effective 2009).
Formerly: Zhijiang Nianjian (1005-6203)
Published by: Changjiang Shuili Weiyuanhui, 1863, Jiefang Dadao, Wuhan, 430010, China. TEL 86-27-82828349, FAX 96-27-82828349, http://www.cjw.gov.cn/.

CHAPMAN & HALL AQUACULTURE SERIES. *see* FISH AND FISHERIES

CHEMICAL WATER AND WASTEWATER TREATMENT SERIES. *see* ENVIRONMENTAL STUDIES—Pollution

333.91 USA
CHRONICLE OF INSTREAM FLOW ACTIVITIES. Text in English. 1997. irreg. back issues avail. **Document type:** *Newsletter, Government.* **Description:** Offers studies in warmwater streams, water management and water appropriations for fish and wildlife.
Related titles: Online - full text ed.
Published by: U.S. Department of the Interior, Geological Survey, Midcontinent Ecological Science Center, 2150 Centre Ave., BLDG C, Fort Collins, CO 80526-8118. TEL 970-226-9100, FAX 970-226-9230, zack_bowen@usgs.gov, http://www.mesc.usgs.gov/rsm/ifim-chron/2-2Chronicle/default.htm. Ed. Zack Bowen. Circ: 400.

628.168 SWE ISSN 1103-2855
CIRKULATION. Text in Swedish. 1992. 8/yr. SEK 380 domestic; SEK 450 in Scandinavia; SEK 520 elsewhere (effective 2001). adv. illus.; stat. back issues avail. **Document type:** *Magazine, Trade.* **Description:** Offers information on a variety of wastewater treatment equipment for the water and wastewater industry in municipalities in Sweden.
Related titles: E-mail ed.; Fax ed.; Online - full text ed.
Published by: Ohlson & Winnfors AB, Fack 508, Orebro, 70150, Sweden. TEL 46-19-10-80-50, FAX 46-19-10-80-55. Ed., Pub. Erik Winnfors. R&P Peter Henricson. adv.: B&W page SEK 14,320, color page SEK 17,400; trim 180 x 260. Circ: 3,400.

628 DEU ISSN 1863-0669
CODEN: CSAWAC
➤ **CLEAN - SOIL, AIR, WATER (ONLINE).** Text in English. bi-m. GBP 839 in United Kingdom to institutions; EUR 1,334 in Europe to institutions; USD 1,642 elsewhere to institutions (effective 2012). **Document type:** *Journal, Academic/Scholarly.* **Description:** Combines environmental aspects of soil, air, water, as well as sustainability and the technosphere, the journal focuses on prevention measures and forward oriented approaches rather than on remediation and pollution cleanup.
Formerly (until 2007): Acta Hydrochimica et Hydrobiologica (Online) (1521-401X)
Media: Online - full text. **Related titles:** ◆ Print ed.: CLEAN - Soil, Air, Water (Print). ISSN 1863-0650.
Indexed: C33.
—**CCC.**
Published by: Wiley - V C H Verlag GmbH & Co. KGaA (Subsidiary of: John Wiley & Sons, Inc.), Postfach 101161, Weinheim, 69451, Germany. TEL 49-6201-606400, FAX 49-6201-606184, info@wiley-vch.de, http://www.wiley-vch.de. Ed. Mufit Bahadir.

628 DEU ISSN 1863-0650
TD370 CODEN: AHCBAU
➤ **CLEAN - SOIL, AIR, WATER (PRINT)**; a journal of sustainability and environmental safety. Text in German, English. 1964. bi-m. GBP 839 in United Kingdom to institutions; EUR 1,334 in Europe to institutions; USD 1,642 elsewhere to institutions; GBP 965 combined subscription in United Kingdom to institutions (print & online eds.); EUR 1,534 combined subscription in Europe to institutions (print & online eds.); USD 1,889 combined subscription elsewhere to institutions (print & online eds.) (effective 2012). adv. bk.rev. abstr.; charts; illus.; stat. index. reprint service avail. from PSC. **Document type:** *Journal, Academic/Scholarly.* **Description:** Combines environmental aspects of soil, air, water, as well as sustainability and the technosphere, the journal focuses on prevention measures and forward oriented approaches rather than on remediation and pollution cleanup.
Former titles (until 2007): Acta Hydrochimica et Hydrobiologica (Print) (0323-4320); (until 1973): Fortschritte der Wasserchemie und Ihrer Grenzgebiete (0071-7983); Incorporated (1968-1992): Zeitschrift fuer Wasser- und Abwasserforschung (0044-3727)
Related titles: ◆ Online - full text ed.: CLEAN - Soil, Air, Water (Online). ISSN 1863-0669.
Indexed: A22, A29, A32, A34, A35, A36, A37, AESIS, ASFA, AgBio, AgrForAb, B&BAb, B19, B21, B25, BA, BIOSIS Prev, C25, C30, CA, CABA, CEABA, CIN, CRFR, ChemAb, ChemTitl, CurCont, D01, E04, E05, E12, ESPM, EnvAb, EnvInd, F08, F11, F12, FCA, FLUIDEX, FR, G11, GEOBASE, GH, GeoRef, H&SSA, H16, I10, I11, IBR, IBZ, LT, MaizeAb, MycolAb, N02, N03, N04, O01, OR, P32, P33, P37, P39, P40, PN&I, PollutAb, R07, R08, R11, R12, R13, RM&VM, RRTA, S12, S13, S16, S17, SCI, SCOPUS, SSciA, SWRA, SoyAb, SpeleolAb, T02, T05, TAR, TriticAb, VS, W07, W10, W11, Z01.
—BLDSC (3278.424500), CASDDS, IE, Infotrieve, Ingenta, INIST, Linda Hall. **CCC.**
Published by: (Gesellschaft Deutscher Chemiker, Wasserchemische Gesellschaft, Gesellschaft Deutscher Chemiker), Wiley - V C H Verlag GmbH & Co. KGaA (Subsidiary of: John Wiley & Sons, Inc.), Postfach 101161, Weinheim, 69451, Germany. TEL 49-6201-606400, FAX 49-6201-606184, info@wiley-vch.de, http://www.wiley-vch.de. Ed. Mufit Bahadir. Adv. contact Marion Schulz TEL 49-6201-606565. B&W page EUR 950, color page EUR 1,850; trim 180 x 260. **Subscr. in the Americas to:** John Wiley & Sons, Inc., 111 River St, Hoboken, NJ 07030. TEL 201-748-6645, subinfo@wiley.com; **Subscr. outside Germany, Austria & Switzerland to:** John Wiley & Sons Ltd., The Atrium, Southern Gate, Chichester, West Sussex PO19 8SQ, United Kingdom. TEL 44-1243-779777, FAX 44-1243-775878, cs-agency@wiley.com.

333.91 USA ISSN 0277-8467
CODEN: CWANEH
CLEAN WATER ACTION NEWS. Text in English. 1976. 4/yr. USD 25 to members (effective 2008). adv. **Description:** News articles on the legislative, policy, and environmental efforts at the federal and state levels to control pollution and contamination.
Related titles: Online - full text ed.
Published by: Clean Water Action, 4455 Connecticut Ave N.W, No A300, Washington, DC 20008-2328. TEL 202-895-0420, FAX 202-895-0438, cwa@cleanwater.org, dcjobs@cleanwater.org. Ed. David Zwick. Circ: 60,000.

CLEARWATERS. *see* ENVIRONMENTAL STUDIES—Pollution

333.9 USA ISSN 0360-6864
TC425.C7
COLUMBIA RIVER WATER MANAGEMENT REPORT. Text in English. 1971. a. free. illus. **Document type:** *Government.* **Description:** Reviews the annual operation of the major dams and powerhouses in the Columbia Basin and the Northwest.
Indexed: GeoRef, SpeleolAb.
Published by: U.S. Army Corps of Engineers, CENPD-PE-WM, PO Box 2870, Portland, OR 97208-2870. TEL 503-808-3958, FAX 503-808-3969.

627 URY ISSN 0797-4116
COMISION ADMINISTRADORA DEL RIO URUGUAY. PUBLICACION. Text in Spanish. 1981. irreg.
Published by: Comision Administradora del Rio Uruguay, Ave Costera Norte s-n, Paysandu, Uruguay. TEL 598-722-5400, FAX 598-722-6786, caru@caru.org.uy, http://www.caru.org.uy/.

333.91 THA
CONFLUENCE. Text in English. 1982. 2/yr. back issues avail. **Description:** Aids information exchange between government programs and agencies engaged in water resources development in ESCAP member countries. Covers the range of technological, managerial, and conceptual information.
Indexed: SpeleolAb.
Published by: United Nations Economic and Social Commission for Asia and the Pacific, Environment and Natural Resources Management Division, Water Resources Section, United Nations Bldg, Rajadamnern Ave, Bangkok, 10200, Thailand. TEL 2-2881598, library-escap@un.org, http://www.unescap.org. Circ: 600.

628.1 NLD ISSN 2210-5492
DE CONTROLE VAN COLLECTIEVE LEIDINGWATERINSTALLATIES. Text in Dutch. 2006. a. **Document type:** *Report, Government.*
Published by: (V R O M-Inspectie), Rijksinstituut voor Volksgezondheid en Milieu, Postbus 1, Bilthoven, 3720 BA, Netherlands. TEL 31-30-2749111, FAX 31-30-2742971, info@rivm.nl, http://www.rivm.nl.

COVENTRY UNIVERSITY. SCHOOL OF THE BUILT ENVIRONMENT. PROCEEDINGS. *see* ENVIRONMENTAL STUDIES

COVICRIER. *see* ENVIRONMENTAL STUDIES

628.1 USA
D W R NEWS. (California Department of Water Resources) Text in English. q. **Document type:** *Newsletter, Government.* **Description:** Discusses news of the California Department of Water Resources.
Published by: California Department of Water Resources, PO Box 94236, Sacramento, CA 95814. Ed. Joyce Ito.

628.1 DNK ISSN 1602-3609
DANSKVAND; fra kildevand til spildevand. Text in Danish. 2002. 7/yr. DKK 657 domestic; DKK 100 per issue domestic; DKK 800 foreign (effective 2008). adv. bk.rev. **Document type:** *Magazine, Trade.* **Description:** Focuses on water resources, groundwater protection, water quality, waterworks technique, water distribution, pipelines, domestic installations, consumption and consumer relations.
Formed by the merger of (1998-2001): Dansk Afloebs- og Spildevandsforening. Nyhedsbrev (1601-4170); (1993-2001): Vandteknik (0106-3677); Which was formerly (1963-1993): Vandteknikeren
Related titles: Online - full text ed.
Published by: Dansk Vand- og Spildevandsforening/Danish Water and Waste Water Association, Danmarksvej 26, Skanderborg, 8660, Denmark. TEL 45-70-210055, FAX 45-70-210056, danva@danva.dk. Ed. Eva Munck. Adv. contact Britt Dalen Jensen. Circ: 1,600.

333.91 USA
DELAWARE RIVER BASIN BIENNIAL WATER RESOURCES CONFERENCE. PROCEEDINGS. Text in English. 1962. irreg. membership. **Document type:** *Proceedings.*
Formerly: Delaware River Basin Water Resources Conference. Proceedings
Published by: Water Resources Association of the Delaware River Basin, Davis Rd, PO Box 867, Valley Forge, PA 19481. TEL 610-917-0090, FAX 610-917-0091. R&P William H Palmer.

627 NLD
DELFT HYDRAULIC SELECT SERIES. Text in English. 2003. irreg., latest vol.11, 2007. price varies. **Document type:** *Monographic series, Academic/Scholarly.*
Published by: Delft University Press (Subsidiary of: I O S Press), Nieuwe Hemweg 6B, Amsterdam, 1013 BG, Netherlands. TEL 31-20-6883355, FAX 31-20-6870039, info.dupress@iospress.nl.

333.8 NLD ISSN 0927-3301
DELFT STUDIES IN INTEGRATED WATER MANAGEMENT. Text in English. 1992. irreg., latest vol.7, 1996. price varies. **Document type:** *Monographic series.* **Description:** Discusses techniques and technologies in integrated water management.
Published by: (Working Group Integrated Water Management), Delft University Press (Subsidiary of: I O S Press), Nieuwe Hemweg 6B, Amsterdam, 1013 BG, Netherlands. TEL 31-20-6883355, FAX 31-20-6870039, info.dupress@iospress.nl, http://www.dupress.nl.

627 NLD ISSN 1877-7570
DELTAFORUM MAGAZINE. Text in Dutch. 2008. q. **Document type:** *Magazine, Trade.*
Related titles: English ed.: DeltaForum International. ISSN 1877-7589.
Published by: NovaForum Business Media, Postbus 228, Pijnacker, 2640 AE, Netherlands. TEL 31-15-3617433, FAX 31-15-3610866, info@novaforum.net, http://www.novaforum.net.

628.1 NLD ISSN 1877-5608
▼ **DELTARES SELECT SERIES.** Text in English. 2009. irreg., latest vol.1, 2009. price varies. **Document type:** *Monographic series, Academic/Scholarly.*
Related titles: Online - full text ed.: ISSN 1879-8055.
Published by: I O S Press, Nieuwe Hemweg 6B, Amsterdam, 1013 BG, Netherlands. TEL 31-20-6883355, FAX 31-20-6870039, info@iospress.nl. **Subscr. to:** I O S Press, Inc, 4502 Rachael Manor Dr, Fairfax, VA 22032-3631. sales@iospress.com.

628 NLD ISSN 0011-9164
TD478 CODEN: DSLNAH
➤ **DESALINATION.** Text in English, French, German. 1966. 48/yr. EUR 6,365 in Europe to institutions; JPY 844,800 in Japan to institutions; USD 7,122 elsewhere to institutions (effective 2012). adv. bk.rev. charts; illus.; pat.; stat.; tr.mk.; abstr. index. back issues avail. **Document type:** *Journal, Academic/Scholarly.* **Description:** Covers all desalting fields, including distillation, membranes, reverse osmosis, electrodialysis, ion exchange, freezing, and water purification.
Related titles: Microform ed.: (from PQC); Online - full text ed.: ISSN 1873-4464 (from IngentaConnect, ScienceDirect).
Indexed: A01, A03, A08, A22, A26, A28, A34, A35, A36, A37, A38, AESIS, APA, APIAb, ASCA, ASFA, AgBio, Agr, AgrForAb, BibAg, BrCerAb, C&ISA, C24, C25, C30, C33, CA, CA/WCA, CABA, CCI, CEA, CEABA, CIA, CIN, CPEI, CerAb, ChemAb, ChemTitl, CivEngAb, CorrAb, CurCont, D01, E&CAJ, E04, E05, E11, E12, EEA, EIA, EMA, ESPM, EnerInd, EnerRev, EngInd, EnvAb, EnvEAb, F08, F11, F12, FCA, FLUIDEX, FPRD, FR, FS&TA, G11, GEOBASE, GH, GeoRef, H15, H16, H17, I05, I11, ISMEC, ISR, Inspec, LT, M&TEA, M09, MBF, METADEX, MaizeAb, N02, N03, N04, O01, OceAb, P32, P33, P34, P39, PollutAb, R07, R08, R11, R12, R13, RefZh, S12, S13, S16, SCI, SCOPUS, SSciA, SWRA, SolStAb, SoyAb, SpeleolAb, T01, T02, T04, T05, TAR, TCEA, TM, TTI, VITIS, W07, W10, W11, WAA.
—BLDSC (3555.700000), AskIEEE, CASDDS, IE, Infotrieve, Ingenta, INIST, Linda Hall. **CCC.**
Published by: Elsevier BV (Subsidiary of: Elsevier Science & Technology), Radarweg 29, PO Box 211, Amsterdam, 1000 AE, Netherlands. TEL 31-20-4853911, FAX 31-20-4852457, JournalsCustomerServiceEMEA@elsevier.com, http://www.elsevier.nl. Ed. M Balaban.

628.167 USA ISSN 1944-3994
TD478
▼ ➤ **DESALINATION AND WATER TREATMENT**; science and engineering. Abbreviated title: D W T. Text in English. 2009. w. EUR 3,900 combined subscription (print & online eds.) (effective 2011). adv. abstr.; bibl. Index. **Document type:** *Journal, Academic/Scholarly.* **Description:** Covers research and application of desalination technology, environment and energy considerations, integrated water management, water reuse, wastewater and related topics, including: Desalination, thermal, membranes, coagulation, sedimentation, energy, energy recovery, seawater, brackish water, cost, performance, water purification, renewable energy, heat and mass transfer, water quality, environment, wastewater, economics, industry, business, ethics.
Related titles: Online - full text ed.: ISSN 1944-3986. EUR 2,730 (effective 2009).
Indexed: A29, A32, B&BAb, B19, B20, B21, CCI, CurCont, E04, E05, ESPM, I10, SCI, SCOPUS, SWRA, T02, W07.
Published by: Balaban Publishers, Balaban, 36 Walcott Valley Dr, Hopkinton, MA 01748. TEL 928-543-3066, balaban@desline.com, http://www.desline.com/. Pub. Miriam Balaban.

551.4 627 DEU ISSN 0340-5176
GB1296.D3 CODEN: DGJDAT
DEUTSCHES GEWAESSERKUNDLICHES JAHRBUCH. DONAUGEBIET. Text in German. 1898. irreg., latest 2005. price varies. charts; stat. 266 p./no.; **Document type:** *Monographic series, Government.*
Indexed: GeoRef, SpeleolAb.
Published by: Bayerisches Landesamt fuer Umwelt, Buergermeister-Ulrich-Str 160, Augsburg, 86179, Germany. TEL 49-821-90710, FAX 49-821-90715556, pressestelle@lfu.bayern.de, http://www.bayern.de/lfu/. Circ: 500 (controlled).

551 627 DEU ISSN 0173-7260
DEUTSCHES GEWAESSERKUNDLICHES JAHRBUCH. RHEINGEBIET TEIL 2: MAIN. Text in German. 1898. irreg., latest 2005. price varies. charts; stat. **Document type:** *Monographic series, Government.*
Formerly (until 1980): Deutsches Gewaesserkundliches Jahrbuch. Rheingebiet: Abschnitt Main (0344-7847)
Indexed: GeoRef, SpeleolAb.
Published by: Bayerisches Landesamt fuer Umwelt, Buergermeister-Ulrich-Str 160, Augsburg, 86179, Germany. TEL 49-821-90710, FAX 49-821-90715556, pressestelle@lfu.bayern.de, http://www.bayern.de/lfu/. Circ: 500.

551.48 NLD ISSN 0167-5648
➤ **DEVELOPMENTS IN WATER SCIENCE.** Text in Dutch. 1974. irreg., latest vol.54, 2005. price varies. back issues avail. **Document type:** *Monographic series, Academic/Scholarly.* **Description:** Elaborates on research in the field of hydrology.
Related titles: Online - full text ed.
Indexed: A22, GeoRef, SCOPUS, SpeleolAb.
—BLDSC (3579.096500), IE, Ingenta, INIST. **CCC.**
Published by: Elsevier BV (Subsidiary of: Elsevier Science & Technology), Radarweg 29, PO Box 211, Amsterdam, 1000 AE, Netherlands. TEL 31-20-4853911, FAX 31-20-4852457, JournalsCustomerServiceEMEA@elsevier.com, http://www.elsevier.nl.

333 ESP
DIRECTORIO DEL AGUA. Text in Spanish. a. EUR 89.32 domestic; EUR 117.52 foreign (effective 2010). **Document type:** *Directory.* **Description:** Lists Spanish companies in the field of water resources management. Includes contact name, address and size information. Classifies more than 1,000 products.
Formerly: Anuario del Agua
Published by: Reed Business Information SA (Subsidiary of: Reed Business Information International), Zancoeta 9, Bilbao, 48013, Spain. TEL 34-944-285600, FAX 34-944-425116, rbi@rbi.es, http://www.rbi.es. Ed. Manuel Masip.

DIRECTORIO DEL SECTOR DE AGUA POTABLE Y SANEAMIENTO AMBIENTAL. *see* BUSINESS AND ECONOMICS—Trade And Industrial Directories

333.91 USA
DIRECTORY OF WATER AND WILDLAND EXPERTISE AND FACILITIES IN THE UNIVERSITY OF CALIFORNIA SYSTEM. Text in English. 1975. irreg. free. **Document type:** *Directory.*
Formerly: California Directory of Water Resources Expertise (0364-9296)
Media: Online - full text.

Published by: University of California, Davis, Center for Water and Wildland Resources, 1 Shields Ave, Davis, CA 95616-8750. TEL 530-752-8070, FAX 530-752-8086. R&P Jeff Woled. Circ: 1,750.

333.91 USA ISSN 0736-5454
HD1694 A1
DIVINING ROD. Text in English. 1977. q. back issues avail. **Document type:** *Newsletter, Trade.* **Description:** Covers current water research projects and water-related issues in New Mexico for researchers and employees of state and federal governmental agencies.
Related titles: Online - full text ed.
Published by: New Mexico Water Resources Research Institute, NMSU MSC 3167, 3170 S Espina St, PO Box 30001, Las Cruces, NM 88003. TEL 575-646-4337, FAX 575-646-6418, nmwrri@nmsu.edu. Ed. Catherine T Ortega Klett.

DOBOKU GAKKAI ROMBUNSHUU. B (DVD-ROM). *see* ENGINEERING—Hydraulic Engineering

133.3 USA
DOWSERS NETWORK. Text in English. q. USD 35 membership; Digest included. **Document type:** *Newsletter.*
Published by: American Society of Dowsers, Inc., PO Box 24, Danville, VT 05828. TEL 802-684-3417, FAX 802-684-2565.

133.323 GBR ISSN 1472-023X
DOWSING TODAY. Text in English. 1933. 3/yr. free to members (effective 2009). bk.rev. abstr. index. 24 p./no. 2 cols./p.; back issues avail.; reprints avail. **Document type:** *Newsletter, Trade.* **Description:** Provides a window on the dowsing world, bringing news and views of all the latest theories, activities and experiences of other dowsers.
Formerly (until 2000): British Society of Dowsers. Journal (0007-179X)
Related titles: Microfilm ed.: (from PQC).
Published by: British Society of Dowsers, 4/5 Cygnet Ctr, Worcester Rd, Hanley Swan, WR8 0BS, United Kingdom. TEL 44-1684-576969, FAX 44-1684-576969, info@britishdowsers.org%20.

627 620 USA
DREDGING SEMINAR. PROCEEDINGS. Text in English. 1968. a. price varies. adv. charts. **Document type:** *Proceedings.*
Indexed: SpeleolAb.
Published by: Center for Dredging Studies, Civil Engineering Department, Texas A & M University, College Station, TX 77843-3136. TEL 409-845-4516, FAX 409-862-8162. Ed., R&P, Adv. contact Robert E Randall. Circ: 800.

333.91 DEU ISSN 1996-9457
TD429.5
➤ **DRINKING WATER ENGINEERING AND SCIENCE.** Text in English. irreg. **Document type:** *Journal, Academic/Scholarly.* **Description:** Focuses on fundamental and applied research in water sources, substances, drinking water treatment processes, distribution systems and residual management.
Related titles: Online - full text ed.: ISSN 1996-9465. free (effective 2011).
Indexed: A01, CABA, E12, GH, P52, P56, S13, S16, T02.
Published by: Copernicus GmbH, Bahnhofsallee 1e, Goettingen, 37081, Germany. TEL 49-551-9003390, FAX 49-551-90033970, info@copernicus.org, http://www.copernicus.org. Eds. Gary Amy, Hans van Dijk.

333.91 DEU ISSN 1996-9473
➤ **DRINKING WATER ENGINEERING AND SCIENCE DISCUSSIONS.** Text in English. irreg. **Document type:** *Journal, Academic/Scholarly.* **Description:** Publishes original research in drinking water treatment.
Related titles: Online - full text ed.: ISSN 1996-9481. free (effective 2011).
Indexed: A01, T02.
Published by: Copernicus GmbH, Bahnhofsallee 1e, Goettingen, 37081, Germany. TEL 49-551-9003390, FAX 49-551-90033970, info@copernicus.org, http://www.copernicus.org. Eds. Gary Amy, Hans van Dijk.

333.91 USA ISSN 1055-9140
TD353
DRINKING WATER RESEARCH. Text in English. 1991. q. back issues avail. **Document type:** *Newsletter, Trade.* **Description:** Describes the activities of the AWWA research foundation as well as reports on results of research programs.
Related titles: Online - full text ed.
Published by: (Water Research Foundation), American Water Works Association, 6666 W Quincy Ave, Denver, CO 80235. TEL 303-347-6116, 303-347-6100, FAX 303-730-0851, 303-730-0851, custsvc@awwa.org. Ed. Marianne Prekker.

333.91 CAN ISSN 0846-7471
DRINKING WATER SURVEILLANCE PROGRAM ANNUAL REPORT (YEAR) PLANT SUMMARIES. Text in English. a. free to qualified personnel. **Document type:** *Government.*
Published by: Ministry of Environment and Energy, Water Resources Branch, 135 St Clair Ave W, Toronto, ON M4V 1P5, Canada. TEL 416-323-4321, FAX 416-323-4564.

333.91 CAN ISSN 0843-8277
DRINKING WATER SURVEILLANCE PROGRAM ANNUAL REPORT. AJAX WATER SUPPLY PLANT. Text in English. 1988. a. free to qualified personnel. **Document type:** *Government.*
Published by: Ministry of Environment and Energy, Water Resources Branch, 135 St Clair Ave W, Toronto, ON M4V 1P5, Canada. TEL 416-323-4321, FAX 416-323-4564.

333.91 CAN ISSN 0839-8992
DRINKING WATER SURVEILLANCE PROGRAM ANNUAL REPORT. ALVINSTON WATER SYSTEM. Text in English. 1986. a. free to qualified personnel. **Document type:** *Government.*
Published by: Ministry of Environment and Energy, Water Resources Branch, 135 St Clair Ave W, Toronto, ON M4V 1P5, Canada. TEL 416-323-4321, FAX 416-323-4564.

333.91 CAN ISSN 0839-900X
DRINKING WATER SURVEILLANCE PROGRAM ANNUAL REPORT. AMHERSTBURG AREA WATER SYSTEM. Text in English. 1986. a. free to qualified personnel. **Document type:** *Government.*
Published by: Ministry of Environment and Energy, Water Resources Branch, 135 St Clair Ave W, Toronto, ON M4V 1P5, Canada. TEL 416-323-4321, FAX 416-323-4564.

333.91 CAN ISSN 0843-8331
DRINKING WATER SURVEILLANCE PROGRAM ANNUAL REPORT. ATIKOKAN WATER TREATMENT PLANT. Text in English. 1988. a. free to qualified personnel. **Document type:** *Government.*
Published by: Ministry of Environment and Energy, Water Resources Branch, 135 St Clair Ave W, Toronto, ON M4V 1P5, Canada. TEL 416-323-4321, FAX 416-323-4564.

333.91 CAN ISSN 0840-5603
DRINKING WATER SURVEILLANCE PROGRAM ANNUAL REPORT. BAYSIDE SCHOOL WATER TREATMENT PLANT. Text in English. 1987. a. free to qualified personnel. **Document type:** *Government.*
Published by: Ministry of Environment and Energy, Water Resources Branch, 135 St Clair Ave W, Toronto, ON M4V 1P5, Canada. TEL 416-323-4321, FAX 416-323-4564.

333.91 CAN ISSN 1183-6105
DRINKING WATER SURVEILLANCE PROGRAM ANNUAL REPORT. BELLE RIVER WATER TREATMENT PLANT. Text in English. 1990. a. free to qualified personnel. **Document type:** *Government.*
Published by: Ministry of Environment and Energy, Water Resources Branch, 135 St Clair Ave W, Toronto, ON M4V 1P5, Canada. TEL 416-323-4321, FAX 416-323-4564.

333.91 CAN ISSN 0840-5123
DRINKING WATER SURVEILLANCE PROGRAM ANNUAL REPORT. BELLEVILLE WATER TREATMENT PLANT. Text in English. 1987. a. free to qualified personnel. **Document type:** *Government.*
Published by: Ministry of Environment and Energy, Water Resources Branch, 135 St Clair Ave W, Toronto, ON M4V 1P5, Canada. TEL 416-323-4321, FAX 416-323-4564.

333.91 CAN ISSN 0840-5344
DRINKING WATER SURVEILLANCE PROGRAM ANNUAL REPORT. BRANTFORD WATER TREATMENT PLANT. Text in English. 1987. a. free to qualified personnel. **Document type:** *Government.*
Published by: Ministry of Environment and Energy, Water Resources Branch, 135 St Clair Ave W, Toronto, ON M4V 1P5, Canada. TEL 416-323-4321, FAX 416-323-4564.

333.91 CAN ISSN 0839-9026
DRINKING WATER SURVEILLANCE PROGRAM ANNUAL REPORT. BRITANNIA WATER TREATMENT PLANT, OTTAWA. Text in English. 1986. a. free to qualified personnel. **Document type:** *Government.*
Published by: Ministry of Environment and Energy, Water Resources Branch, 135 St Clair Ave W, Toronto, ON M4V 1P5, Canada. TEL 416-323-4321, FAX 416-323-4564.

333.91 CAN ISSN 0840-5247
DRINKING WATER SURVEILLANCE PROGRAM ANNUAL REPORT. BURLINGTON WATER TREATMENT PLANT. Text in English. 1987. a. free to qualified personnel. **Document type:** *Government.*
Published by: Ministry of Environment and Energy, Water Resources Branch, 135 St Clair Ave W, Toronto, ON M4V 1P5, Canada. TEL 416-323-4321, FAX 416-323-4564.

333.91 CAN ISSN 1180-2138
DRINKING WATER SURVEILLANCE PROGRAM ANNUAL REPORT. CASSELMAN WATER TREATMENT PLANT. Text in English. 1989. a. free to qualified personnel. **Document type:** *Government.*
Published by: Ministry of Environment and Energy, Water Resources Branch, 135 St Clair Ave W, Toronto, ON M4V 1P5, Canada. TEL 416-323-4321, FAX 416-323-4564.

333.91 CAN ISSN 0843-8323
DRINKING WATER SURVEILLANCE PROGRAM ANNUAL REPORT. CAYUGA WATER TREATMENT PLANT. Text in English. 1988. a. free to qualified personnel. **Document type:** *Government.*
Published by: Ministry of Environment and Energy, Water Resources Branch, 135 St Clair Ave W, Toronto, ON M4V 1P5, Canada. TEL 416-323-4321, FAX 416-323-4564.

333.91 CAN ISSN 1180-2162
DRINKING WATER SURVEILLANCE PROGRAM ANNUAL REPORT. CENTRAL HALDIMAND - NORFOLK WATER TREATMENT PLANT. Text in English. 1989. a. free to qualified personnel. **Document type:** *Government.*
Published by: Ministry of Environment and Energy, Water Resources Branch, 135 St Clair Ave W, Toronto, ON M4V 1P5, Canada. TEL 416-323-4321, FAX 416-323-4564.

333.91 CAN ISSN 0843-8315
DRINKING WATER SURVEILLANCE PROGRAM ANNUAL REPORT. CHATHAM WATER TREATMENT PLANT. Text in English. 1989. a. free to qualified personnel. **Document type:** *Government.*
Published by: Ministry of Environment and Energy, Water Resources Branch, 135 St Clair Ave W, Toronto, ON M4V 1P5, Canada. TEL 416-323-4321, FAX 416-323-4564.

333.91 CAN ISSN 0840-5298
DRINKING WATER SURVEILLANCE PROGRAM ANNUAL REPORT. CORNWALL WATER TREATMENT PLANT. Text in English. 1987. a. free to qualified personnel. **Document type:** *Government.*
Published by: Ministry of Environment and Energy, Water Resources Branch, 135 St Clair Ave W, Toronto, ON M4V 1P5, Canada. TEL 416-323-4321, FAX 416-323-4564.

333.91 CAN ISSN 1183-613X
DRINKING WATER SURVEILLANCE PROGRAM ANNUAL REPORT. DELHI WATER SUPPLY SYSTEM. Text in English. 1990. a. free to qualified personnel. **Document type:** *Government.*
Published by: Ministry of Environment and Energy, Water Resources Branch, 135 St Clair Ave W, Toronto, ON M4V 1P5, Canada. TEL 416-323-4321, FAX 416-323-4564.

333.91 CAN ISSN 0840-5131
DRINKING WATER SURVEILLANCE PROGRAM ANNUAL REPORT. DESERONTO WATER TREATMENT PLANT. Text in English. 1987. a. free to qualified personnel. **Document type:** *Government.*
Published by: Ministry of Environment and Energy, Water Resources Branch, 135 St Clair Ave W, Toronto, ON M4V 1P5, Canada. TEL 416-323-4321, FAX 416-323-4564.

333.91 CAN ISSN 0839-8984
DRINKING WATER SURVEILLANCE PROGRAM ANNUAL REPORT. DRESDEN WATER TREATMENT PLANT. Text in English. 1986. a. free to qualified personnel. **Document type:** *Government.*
Published by: Ministry of Environment and Energy, Water Resources Branch, 135 St Clair Ave W, Toronto, ON M4V 1P5, Canada. TEL 416-323-4321, FAX 416-323-4564.

333.91 CAN ISSN 0843-8293
DRINKING WATER SURVEILLANCE PROGRAM ANNUAL REPORT. DRYDEN WATER TREATMENT PLANT. Text in English. 1988. a. free to qualified personnel. **Document type:** *Government.*
Published by: Ministry of Environment and Energy, Water Resources Branch, 135 St Clair Ave W, Toronto, ON M4V 1P5, Canada. TEL 416-323-4321, FAX 416-323-4564.

333.91 CAN ISSN 1192-1196
DRINKING WATER SURVEILLANCE PROGRAM ANNUAL REPORT. DUNNVILLE WATER TREATMENT PLANT. Text in English. 1990. a. free to qualified personnel. **Document type:** *Government.*
Published by: Ministry of Environment and Energy, Water Resources Branch, 135 St Clair Ave W, Toronto, ON M4V 1P5, Canada. TEL 416-323-4321, FAX 416-323-4564.

333.91 CAN ISSN 0840-5166
DRINKING WATER SURVEILLANCE PROGRAM ANNUAL REPORT. EASTERLY WATER TREATMENT PLANT, TORONTO. Text in English. 1986. a. free to qualified personnel. **Document type:** *Government.*
Published by: Ministry of Environment and Energy, Water Resources Branch, 135 St Clair Ave W, Toronto, ON M4V 1P5, Canada. TEL 416-323-4321, FAX 416-323-4564.

333.91 CAN ISSN 0843-8382
DRINKING WATER SURVEILLANCE PROGRAM ANNUAL REPORT. ELMIRE WELL SUPPLY. Text in English. 1988. a. free to qualified personnel. **Document type:** *Government.*
Published by: Ministry of Environment and Energy, Water Resources Branch, 135 St Clair Ave W, Toronto, ON M4V 1P5, Canada. TEL 416-323-4321, FAX 416-323-4564.

333.91 CAN ISSN 0840-5182
DRINKING WATER SURVEILLANCE PROGRAM ANNUAL REPORT. FORT ERIE TREATMENT PLANT. Text in English. 1987. a. free to qualified personnel. **Document type:** *Government.*
Published by: Ministry of Environment and Energy, Water Resources Branch, 135 St Clair Ave W, Toronto, ON M4V 1P5, Canada. TEL 416-323-4321, FAX 416-323-4564.

333.91 CAN ISSN 0843-8358
DRINKING WATER SURVEILLANCE PROGRAM ANNUAL REPORT. FORT FRANCES WATER TREATMENT PLANT. Text in English. 1989. a. free to qualified personnel. **Document type:** *Government.*
Published by: Ministry of Environment and Energy, Water Resources Branch, 135 St Clair Ave W, Toronto, ON M4V 1P5, Canada. TEL 416-323-4321, FAX 416-323-4564.

333.91 CAN ISSN 0840-5174
DRINKING WATER SURVEILLANCE PROGRAM ANNUAL REPORT. GRIMSBY WATER TREATMENT PLANT. Text in English. 1987. a. free to qualified personnel. **Document type:** *Government.*
Published by: Ministry of Environment and Energy, Water Resources Branch, 135 St Clair Ave W, Toronto, ON M4V 1P5, Canada. TEL 416-323-4321, FAX 416-323-4564.

333.91 CAN ISSN 1192-120X
DRINKING WATER SURVEILLANCE PROGRAM ANNUAL REPORT. GUELPH WELL SUPPLY. Text in English. 1990. a. free to qualified personnel. **Document type:** *Government.*
Published by: Ministry of Environment and Energy, Water Resources Branch, 135 St Clair Ave W, Toronto, ON M4V 1P5, Canada. TEL 416-323-4321, FAX 416-323-4564.

333.91 CAN ISSN 0839-9034
DRINKING WATER SURVEILLANCE PROGRAM ANNUAL REPORT. HAMILTON WATER TREATMENT PLANT. Text in English. 1986. a. free to qualified personnel. **Document type:** *Government.*
Published by: Ministry of Environment and Energy, Water Resources Branch, 135 St Clair Ave W, Toronto, ON M4V 1P5, Canada. TEL 416-323-4321, FAX 416-323-4564.

333.91 CAN ISSN 0840-5239
DRINKING WATER SURVEILLANCE PROGRAM ANNUAL REPORT. HARROW - COLCHESTER SOUTH WATER SUPPLY SYSTEM. Text in English. 1986. a. free to qualified personnel. **Document type:** *Government.*
Published by: Ministry of Environment and Energy, Water Resources Branch, 135 St Clair Ave W, Toronto, ON M4V 1P5, Canada. TEL 416-323-4321, FAX 416-323-4564.

333.91 CAN ISSN 1180-2146
DRINKING WATER SURVEILLANCE PROGRAM ANNUAL REPORT. HAWKESBURY WATER TREATMENT PLANT. Text in English. 1989. a. free to qualified personnel. **Document type:** *Government.*
Published by: Ministry of Environment and Energy, Water Resources Branch, 135 St Clair Ave W, Toronto, ON M4V 1P5, Canada. TEL 416-323-4321, FAX 416-323-4564.

333.91 CAN ISSN 0843-8307
DRINKING WATER SURVEILLANCE PROGRAM ANNUAL REPORT. KENORA WATER TREATMENT PLANT. Text in English. 1989. a. free to qualified personnel. **Document type:** *Government.*
Published by: Ministry of Environment and Energy, Water Resources Branch, 135 St Clair Ave W, Toronto, ON M4V 1P5, Canada. TEL 416-323-4321, FAX 416-323-4564.

333.91 CAN ISSN 0839-9050
DRINKING WATER SURVEILLANCE PROGRAM ANNUAL REPORT. KINGSTON WATER TREATMENT PLANT. Text in English. 1986. a. free to qualified personnel. **Document type:** *Government.*
Published by: Ministry of Environment and Energy, Water Resources Branch, 135 St Clair Ave W, Toronto, ON M4V 1P5, Canada. TEL 416-323-4321, FAX 416-323-4564.

333.91 CAN ISSN 0840-5190
DRINKING WATER SURVEILLANCE PROGRAM ANNUAL REPORT. KITCHENER WATER SUPPLY SYSTEMS. Text in English. 1987. a. free to qualified personnel. **Document type:** *Government.*
Published by: Ministry of Environment and Energy, Water Resources Branch, 135 St Clair Ave W, Toronto, ON M4V 1P5, Canada. TEL 416-323-4321, FAX 416-323-4564.

333.91 CAN ISSN 0840-5271
DRINKING WATER SURVEILLANCE PROGRAM ANNUAL REPORT. LAKE HURON WATER SUPPLY SYSTEM. Text in English. 1986. a. free to qualified personnel. **Document type:** *Government.*
Published by: Ministry of Environment and Energy, Water Resources Branch, 135 St Clair Ave W, Toronto, ON M4V 1P5, Canada. TEL 416-323-4321, FAX 416-323-4564.

333.91 CAN ISSN 0840-5107
DRINKING WATER SURVEILLANCE PROGRAM ANNUAL REPORT. LAMBTON AREA SUPPLY, SARNIA. Text in English. 1986. a. free to qualified personnel. **Document type:** *Government.*

Published by: Ministry of Environment and Energy, Water Resources Branch, 135 St Clair Ave W, Toronto, ON M4V 1P5, Canada. TEL 416-323-4321, FAX 416-323-4564.

333.91 CAN ISSN 0840-5204
DRINKING WATER SURVEILLANCE PROGRAM ANNUAL REPORT. LEMIEUX ISLAND WATER TREATMENT PLANT, OTTAWA. Text in English. 1986. a. free to qualified personnel. **Document type:** *Government.*
Published by: Ministry of Environment and Energy, Water Resources Branch, 135 St Clair Ave W, Toronto, ON M4V 1P5, Canada. TEL 416-323-4321, FAX 416-323-4564.

333.91 CAN ISSN 0840-531X
DRINKING WATER SURVEILLANCE PROGRAM ANNUAL REPORT. MITCHELL'S BAY WATER TREATMENT PLANT. Text in English. 1986. a. free to qualified personnel. **Document type:** *Government.*
Published by: Ministry of Environment and Energy, Water Resources Branch, 135 St Clair Ave W, Toronto, ON M4V 1P5, Canada. TEL 416-323-4321, FAX 416-323-4564.

333.91 CAN ISSN 0839-8925
DRINKING WATER SURVEILLANCE PROGRAM ANNUAL REPORT. NIAGARA FALLS WATER TREATMENT PLANT. Text in English. 1986. a. free to qualified personnel. **Document type:** *Government.*
Published by: Ministry of Environment and Energy, Water Resources Branch, 135 St Clair Ave W, Toronto, ON M4V 1P5, Canada. TEL 416-323-4321, FAX 416-323-4564.

333.91 CAN ISSN 0840-5212
DRINKING WATER SURVEILLANCE PROGRAM ANNUAL REPORT. NORTH BAY WATER TREATMENT PLANT. Text in English. 1987. a. free to qualified personnel. **Document type:** *Government.*
Published by: Ministry of Environment and Energy, Water Resources Branch, 135 St Clair Ave W, Toronto, ON M4V 1P5, Canada. TEL 416-323-4321, FAX 416-323-4564.

333.91 CAN ISSN 0843-8366
DRINKING WATER SURVEILLANCE PROGRAM ANNUAL REPORT. ODESSA WATER TREATMENT PLANT. Text in English. 1988. a. free to qualified personnel. **Document type:** *Government.*
Published by: Ministry of Environment and Energy, Water Resources Branch, 135 St Clair Ave W, Toronto, ON M4V 1P5, Canada. TEL 416-323-4321, FAX 416-323-4564.

333.91 CAN ISSN 1183-6172
DRINKING WATER SURVEILLANCE PROGRAM ANNUAL REPORT. OWEN SOUND WATER SUPPLY SYSTEM. Text in English. 1990. a. free to qualified personnel. **Document type:** *Government.*
Published by: Ministry of Environment and Energy, Water Resources Branch, 135 St Clair Ave W, Toronto, ON M4V 1P5, Canada. TEL 416-323-4321, FAX 416-323-4564.

333.91 CAN ISSN 0840-514X
DRINKING WATER SURVEILLANCE PROGRAM ANNUAL REPORT. PETERBOROUGH WATER TREATMENT PLANT. Text in English. 1987. a. free to qualified personnel. **Document type:** *Government.*
Published by: Ministry of Environment and Energy, Water Resources Branch, 135 St Clair Ave W, Toronto, ON M4V 1P5, Canada. TEL 416-323-4321, FAX 416-323-4564.

333.91 CAN ISSN 1183-6180
DRINKING WATER SURVEILLANCE PROGRAM ANNUAL REPORT. PORT COLBORNE WATER TREATMENT PLANT. Text in English. 1990. a. free to qualified personnel. **Document type:** *Government.*
Published by: Ministry of Environment and Energy, Water Resources Branch, 135 St Clair Ave W, Toronto, ON M4V 1P5, Canada. TEL 416-323-4321, FAX 416-323-4564.

333.91 CAN ISSN 0840-5328
DRINKING WATER SURVEILLANCE PROGRAM ANNUAL REPORT. PORT DOVER - DOAN'S HOLLOW WATER TREATMENT PLANT. Text in English. 1987. a. free to qualified personnel. **Document type:** *Government.*
Published by: Ministry of Environment and Energy, Water Resources Branch, 135 St Clair Ave W, Toronto, ON M4V 1P5, Canada. TEL 416-323-4321, FAX 416-323-4564.

333.91 CAN ISSN 0839-8968
DRINKING WATER SURVEILLANCE PROGRAM ANNUAL REPORT. PORT STANLEY WATER TREATMENT PLANT. Text in English. 1986. a. free to qualified personnel. **Document type:** *Government.*
Published by: Ministry of Environment and Energy, Water Resources Branch, 135 St Clair Ave W, Toronto, ON M4V 1P5, Canada. TEL 416-323-4321, FAX 416-323-4564.

333.91 CAN ISSN 0839-8941
DRINKING WATER SURVEILLANCE PROGRAM ANNUAL REPORT. R.C. HARRIS WATER TREATMENT PLANT, TORONTO. Text in English. 1986. a. free to qualified personnel. **Document type:** *Government.*
Published by: Ministry of Environment and Energy, Water Resources Branch, 135 St Clair Ave W, Toronto, ON M4V 1P5, Canada. TEL 416-323-4321, FAX 416-323-4564.

333.91 CAN ISSN 0839-8976
DRINKING WATER SURVEILLANCE PROGRAM ANNUAL REPORT. R.L. CLARK WATER TREATMENT PLANT, TORONTO. Text in English. 1986. a. free to qualified personnel. **Document type:** *Government.*
Published by: Ministry of Environment and Energy, Water Resources Branch, 135 St Clair Ave W, Toronto, ON M4V 1P5, Canada. TEL 416-323-4321, FAX 416-323-4564.

333.91 CAN ISSN 1180-2111
DRINKING WATER SURVEILLANCE PROGRAM ANNUAL REPORT. RENFREW WATER TREATMENT PLANT. Text in English. 1989. a. free to qualified personnel. **Document type:** *Government.*
Published by: Ministry of Environment and Energy, Water Resources Branch, 135 St Clair Ave W, Toronto, ON M4V 1P5, Canada. TEL 416-323-4321, FAX 416-323-4564.

333.91 CAN ISSN 0840-528X
DRINKING WATER SURVEILLANCE PROGRAM ANNUAL REPORT. ST. CATHARINES WATER TREATMENT PLANT. Text in English. 1987. a. free to qualified personnel. **Document type:** *Government.*
Published by: Ministry of Environment and Energy, Water Resources Branch, 135 St Clair Ave W, Toronto, ON M4V 1P5, Canada. TEL 416-323-4321, FAX 416-323-4564.

333.91 CAN ISSN 0840-5255
DRINKING WATER SURVEILLANCE PROGRAM ANNUAL REPORT. ST. THOMAS (ELGIN) WATER SUPPLY SYSTEM. Text in English. 1989. a. free to qualified personnel. **Document type:** *Government.*
Published by: Ministry of Environment and Energy, Water Resources Branch, 135 St Clair Ave W, Toronto, ON M4V 1P5, Canada. TEL 416-323-4321, FAX 416-323-4564.

333.91 CAN ISSN 0840-5158
DRINKING WATER SURVEILLANCE PROGRAM ANNUAL REPORT. SAULT STE. MARIE WELLS AND WATER TREATMENT PLANT. Text in English. 1987. a. free to qualified personnel. **Document type:** *Government.*
Published by: Ministry of Environment and Energy, Water Resources Branch, 135 St Clair Ave W, Toronto, ON M4V 1P5, Canada. TEL 416-323-4321, FAX 416-323-4564.

333.91 CAN ISSN 1183-6202
DRINKING WATER SURVEILLANCE PROGRAM ANNUAL REPORT. SIMCOE WELL SUPPLY. Text in English. 1990. a. free to qualified personnel. **Document type:** *Government.*
Published by: Ministry of Environment and Energy, Water Resources Branch, 135 St Clair Ave W, Toronto, ON M4V 1P5, Canada. TEL 416-323-4321, FAX 416-323-4564.

333.91 CAN ISSN 0839-9069
DRINKING WATER SURVEILLANCE PROGRAM ANNUAL REPORT. SOUTH PEEL (LAKEVIEW) WATER TREATMENT PLANT. Text in English. 1986. a. free to qualified personnel. **Document type:** *Government.*
Published by: Ministry of Environment and Energy, Water Resources Branch, 135 St Clair Ave W, Toronto, ON M4V 1P5, Canada. TEL 416-323-4321, FAX 416-323-4564.

333.91 CAN ISSN 1187-6824
DRINKING WATER SURVEILLANCE PROGRAM ANNUAL REPORT. SOUTH PEEL (LORNE PARK) WATER SUPPLY SYSTEM. Text in English. 1986. a. free to qualified personnel. **Document type:** *Government.*
Formerly (until 1988): Drinking Water Surveillance Program Annual Report. Lorne Park Water Treatment Plant, Mississauga (0839-9042)
Published by: Ministry of Environment and Energy, Water Resources Branch, 135 St Clair Ave W, Toronto, ON M4V 1P5, Canada. TEL 416-323-4321, FAX 416-323-4564.

333.91 CAN ISSN 0839-8933
DRINKING WATER SURVEILLANCE PROGRAM ANNUAL REPORT. STONEY POINT WATER TREATMENT PLANT. Text in English. 1986. a. free to qualified personnel. **Document type:** *Government.*
Published by: Ministry of Environment and Energy, Water Resources Branch, 135 St Clair Ave W, Toronto, ON M4V 1P5, Canada. TEL 416-323-4321, FAX 416-323-4564.

333.91 CAN ISSN 0840-5301
DRINKING WATER SURVEILLANCE PROGRAM ANNUAL REPORT. STOUFFVILLE WATER SUPPLY SYSTEM. Text in English. 1987. a. free to qualified personnel. **Document type:** *Government.*
Published by: Ministry of Environment and Energy, Water Resources Branch, 135 St Clair Ave W, Toronto, ON M4V 1P5, Canada. TEL 416-323-4321, FAX 416-323-4564.

333.91 CAN ISSN 0840-5336
DRINKING WATER SURVEILLANCE PROGRAM ANNUAL REPORT. SUDBURY (RAMSEY LAKE) WATER TREATMENT PLANT. Text in English. 1987. a. free to qualified personnel. **Document type:** *Government.*
Published by: Ministry of Environment and Energy, Water Resources Branch, 135 St Clair Ave W, Toronto, ON M4V 1P5, Canada. TEL 416-323-4321, FAX 416-323-4564.

333.91 CAN ISSN 0840-5220
DRINKING WATER SURVEILLANCE PROGRAM ANNUAL REPORT. SUDBURY (WANAPITEI) WATER TREATMENT PLANT. Text in English. 1987. a. free to qualified personnel. **Document type:** *Government.*
Published by: Ministry of Environment and Energy, Water Resources Branch, 135 St Clair Ave W, Toronto, ON M4V 1P5, Canada. TEL 416-323-4321, FAX 416-323-4564.

333.91 CAN ISSN 1183-6210
DRINKING WATER SURVEILLANCE PROGRAM ANNUAL REPORT. TECUMSEH WATER TREATMENT PLANT. Text in English. 1990. a. free to qualified personnel. **Document type:** *Government.*
Published by: Ministry of Environment and Energy, Water Resources Branch, 135 St Clair Ave W, Toronto, ON M4V 1P5, Canada. TEL 416-323-4321, FAX 416-323-4564.

333.91 CAN ISSN 0843-8374
DRINKING WATER SURVEILLANCE PROGRAM ANNUAL REPORT. THAMESVILLE WATER SUPPLY SYSTEM. Text in English. 1988. a. free to qualified personnel. **Document type:** *Government.*
Published by: Ministry of Environment and Energy, Water Resources Branch, 135 St Clair Ave W, Toronto, ON M4V 1P5, Canada. TEL 416-323-4321, FAX 416-323-4564.

333.91 CAN ISSN 0843-8285
DRINKING WATER SURVEILLANCE PROGRAM ANNUAL REPORT. THUNDER BAY (BARE POINT) WATER TREATMENT PLANT. Text in English. 1988. a. free to qualified personnel. **Document type:** *Government.*
Published by: Ministry of Environment and Energy, Water Resources Branch, 135 St Clair Ave W, Toronto, ON M4V 1P5, Canada. TEL 416-323-4321, FAX 416-323-4564.

333.91 CAN ISSN 0843-834X
DRINKING WATER SURVEILLANCE PROGRAM ANNUAL REPORT. THUNDER BAY (LOCH LOMOND) WATER TREATMENT PLANT. Text in English. 1988. a. free to qualified personnel. **Document type:** *Government.*
Published by: Ministry of Environment and Energy, Water Resources Branch, 135 St Clair Ave W, Toronto, ON M4V 1P5, Canada. TEL 416-323-4321, FAX 416-323-4564.

333.91 CAN ISSN 1180-212X
DRINKING WATER SURVEILLANCE PROGRAM ANNUAL REPORT. TRENTON WATER TREATMENT PLANT. Text in English. 1989. a. free to qualified personnel. **Document type:** *Government.*
Published by: Ministry of Environment and Energy, Water Resources Branch, 135 St Clair Ave W, Toronto, ON M4V 1P5, Canada. TEL 416-323-4321, FAX 416-323-4564.

333.91 CAN ISSN 0840-5115
DRINKING WATER SURVEILLANCE PROGRAM ANNUAL REPORT. UNION WATER TREATMENT PLANT. Text in English. 1987. a. free to qualified personnel. **Document type:** *Government.*
Published by: Ministry of Environment and Energy, Water Resources Branch, 135 St Clair Ave W, Toronto, ON M4V 1P5, Canada. TEL 416-323-4321, FAX 416-323-4564.

333.91 CAN ISSN 0839-9018
DRINKING WATER SURVEILLANCE PROGRAM ANNUAL REPORT. WALLACEBURG WATER TREATMENT PLANT. Text in English. 1986. a. free to qualified personnel. **Document type:** *Government.*
Published by: Ministry of Environment and Energy, Water Resources Branch, 135 St Clair Ave W, Toronto, ON M4V 1P5, Canada. TEL 416-323-4321, FAX 416-323-4564.

333.91 CAN ISSN 0839-8917
DRINKING WATER SURVEILLANCE PROGRAM ANNUAL REPORT. WALPOLE ISLAND WATER TREATMENT PLANT. Text in English. 1986. a. free to qualified personnel. **Document type:** *Government.*
Published by: Ministry of Environment and Energy, Water Resources Branch, 135 St Clair Ave W, Toronto, ON M4V 1P5, Canada. TEL 416-323-4321, FAX 416-323-4564.

333.91 CAN ISSN 1180-2103
DRINKING WATER SURVEILLANCE PROGRAM ANNUAL REPORT. WELLAND WATER SUPPLY SYSTEM. Text in English. 1989. a. free to qualified personnel. **Document type:** *Government.*
Published by: Ministry of Environment and Energy, Water Resources Branch, 135 St Clair Ave W, Toronto, ON M4V 1P5, Canada. TEL 416-323-4321, FAX 416-323-4564.

333.91 CAN ISSN 0839-895X
DRINKING WATER SURVEILLANCE PROGRAM ANNUAL REPORT. WINDSOR WATER TREATMENT PLANT. Text in English. 1986. a. free to qualified personnel. **Document type:** *Government.*
Formerly (until 1987): Drinking Water Surveillance Program Annual Report. Windsor Utilities Commission Water Treatment Plant (0848-3345)
Published by: Ministry of Environment and Energy, Water Resources Branch, 135 St Clair Ave W, Toronto, ON M4V 1P5, Canada. TEL 416-323-4321, FAX 416-323-4564.

333.9 631.7 USA
DROUGHT NETWORK NEWS. Text in English. 1989. 3/yr. free. illus. back issues avail. **Document type:** *Newsletter.* **Description:** Provides information on current episodes of drought; drought response, mitigation and planning activities; new technologies relating to planning and management.
Related titles: Online - full text ed.
Published by: (National Oceanic and Atmospheric Administration (N O A A)), International Drought Information Center and National Drought Mitigation Center, 239 L W Chase Hall, University of Nebraska Lincoln, Box 830749, Lincoln, NE 68583-0749. TEL 402-472-6707, FAX 402-472-6614, TELEX UNL COMM LCN 484340, ndmc@enso.unl.edu, http://enso.unl.edu/ndmc/center/dnn/dnnarch.htm. Ed. Donald Wilhite. Circ: 1,600.

628.1 NLD ISSN 1879-7520
▼ **DUIN EN WATER.** Text in Dutch. 2009. q.
Formed by the merger of (2000-2009): De Slag (1567-956X); (1995-2009): Waterkrant (1384-0983)
Published by: Dunea, Postbus 34, Voorburg, 2270 AA, Netherlands. TEL 31-70-3577500, http://www.dunea.nl. Eds. Marijke Koopman, Ans Groenewegen.

627 NLD
DUTCH WATER SECTOR. Text in English. biennial. EUR 20 (effective 2010). adv. **Document type:** *Journal, Trade.*
Formerly (until 2008): Dutch Water Industry
Published by: Nijgh Periodieken B.V., Postbus 122, Schiedam, 3100 AC, Netherlands. TEL 31-10-4274100, FAX 31-10-4739911, info@nijgh.nl. Ed. Stephanie Hameeteman TEL 31-10-4274124. Pub. Rinus Vissers.

628.16 CHE ISSN 1420-3979
E A W A G NEWS. Text in German. 1973. 3/yr. free. **Document type:** *Journal, Trade.* **Description:** Provides background knowledge on current problems and research developments involving vital water resources.
Supersedes in part (in 1993): E A W A G Mitteilungen (1420-3960); Which superseded in part (in 1981): Nouvelles de l'E A W A G (1420-3995)
Related titles: French ed.: ISSN 1420-3928; English ed.: ISSN 1420-5289.
Published by: Eidgenoessische Anstalt fuer Wasserversorgung, Abwasserreinigung und Gewaesserschutz, Ueberlandstr. 133, Duebendorf, 8600, Switzerland. TEL 41-1-8235511, FAX 41-1-8235028, info@eawag.ch, http://www.eawag.ch.

627 NLD ISSN 1872-0277
E N W INFO STROOM. Text in Dutch. 1998. irreg.
Formerly (until 2005): T A W Infostroom (1389-0034)
Published by: Expertise Netwerk Waterveiligheid, c/o Rijkswaterstaat Waterdienst, afdeling Onderhoud Waterkeringen, Postbus 17, Lelystad, 8200 AA, Netherlands. TEL 31-6-51617980, enwsecretariaat@rws.nl, http://www.enwinfo.nl.

333.91 NOR ISSN 0809-8778
E U R O H A R P NEWSLETTER. (European Harmonised Procedures) Variant title: Towards European Harmonised Procedures for Quantification of Nutrientosses from Diffuse Sources Newsletter. Text in English. 2003. s-a. back issues avail. **Document type:** *Newsletter, Trade.*
Media: Online - full content.
Published by: (E U R O H A R P Project), Norsk Institutt for Vannforskning/Norwegian Institute for Water Research, Gaustadsalleen 21, Oslo, 0349, Norway. TEL 47-22-185100, FAX 47-22-185200, niva@niva.no, http://www.niva.no. Eds. Line J Barkved, Stig A Borgvang.

333.91 NOR ISSN 0809-8751
E U R O H A R P REPORT. (European Harmonised Procedures) Variant title: Towards European Harmonised Procedures for Quantification of Nutrientosses from Diffuse Sources Report. Text in English. 2003. irreg. **Document type:** *Monographic series, Academic/Scholarly.*
Related titles: Online - full text ed.: ISSN 0809-876X. 2003.

Published by: (E U R O H A R P Project), Norsk Institutt for Vannforskning/Norwegian Institute for Water Research, Gaustadsalleen 21, Oslo, 0349, Norway. TEL 47-22-185100, FAX 47-22-185200, niva@niva.no, http://www.niva.no.

E-WATER. *see* ENVIRONMENTAL STUDIES—Pollution

333.7 338 FRA ISSN 0755-5016
CODEN: EINUDQ

L'EAU, L'INDUSTRIE, LES NUISANCES. Text in French. 1975. m. EUR 120 (effective 2009). adv. illus. **Document type:** *Magazine.*
Formerly (until 1982): Eau et l'Industrie (0337-9329)
Indexed: A22, A32, ChemAb, FLUIDEX, FR, GEOBASE, GeoRef, RefZh, SCOPUS, SpeleolAb, WasteInfo.
—BLDSC (3647.003800), CASDDS, IE, Ingenta, INIST, Linda Hall.
Published by: Pierre Johanet et ses Fils, 30 rue Rene Boulanger, Paris, 75010, France. TEL 33-1-44847878, FAX 33-1-42402646. Circ: 6,800.

ECOALERT. *see* ENVIRONMENTAL STUDIES

333.91 627 628.168 NLD ISSN 2211-5935
▼ **EEMSDELTA KRINGEN.** Text in Dutch. 2011. bi-m. EUR 40 (effective 2011). adv. **Document type:** *Magazine, Trade.*
Published by: Uitgeverij Lakerveld BV, Postbus 160, Wateringen, 2290 AD, Netherlands. TEL 31-174-315000, FAX 31-174-315001, uitgeverij@lakerveld.nl, http://www.lakerveld.nl.

ENERGIE-, WASSER-PRAXIS. *see* ENERGY

ENERGOSBEREZHENIE I VODOPODGOTOVKA/ENERGY SAVING AND WATER PREPARATION. *see* ENERGY

627 USA
ENGINEERING COMMITTEE ON OCEANIC RESOURCES. PROCEEDINGS OF THE GENERAL ASSEMBLY. Text in English. irreg., latest 1975, 2nd, Tokyo. **Document type:** *Proceedings.*
Published by: Engineering Committee on Oceanic Resources, 2101 Constitution Ave N W, Washington, DC 20418. TEL 202-334-2000.

ENVIRONMENTAL STUDIES RESEARCH FUNDS REPORT (ONLINE). *see* ENVIRONMENTAL STUDIES

ENVIRONMENTAL TOXICOLOGY. *see* ENVIRONMENTAL STUDIES—Toxicology And Environmental Safety

363.6 USA
TD223
ESTIMATED USE OF WATER IN THE UNITED STATES IN (YEAR). Text in English. 1950. quinquennial, latest 2005. free (effective 2011). back issues avail. **Document type:** *Government.*
Related titles: Online - full text ed.: ISSN 1942-7123.
Published by: U.S. Department of the Interior, Geological Survey, 12201 Sunrise Valley Dr, Reston, VA 20192. TEL 703-648-5953, 800-228-0975, ask@usgs.gov, http://www.usgs.gov.

627 USA ISSN 1020-4393
ESTUDIO F A O, RIEGO Y DRENAJE. Text in Spanish. 1972. irreg., latest 2007. back issues avail. **Document type:** *Monographic series, Trade.*
Formerly (until 1976): Estudio Sobre Riego y Avenamiento (1014-2924)
Related titles: Online - full text ed.: free (effective 2011); ◆ French ed.: F A O Bulletin d'Irrigation et de Drainage. ISSN 0253-4703; ◆ English ed.: F A O Irrigation and Drainage Papers. ISSN 0254-5284.
Published by: Food and Agriculture Organization of the United Nations, c/o Bernan Associates, 4501 Forbes Blvd, Ste 200, Lanham, MD 20706. TEL 301-459-7666, 800-865-3457, FAX 301-459-0056, 800-865-3450, customercare@bernan.com.

333.91 DEU
EUROPAEISCHER WIRTSCHAFTSDIENST. WASSER UND ABWASSER. Text in German. 1998. w. EUR 390 (effective 2009). adv. **Document type:** *Bulletin, Trade.*
Published by: E U W I D - Europaeischer Wirtschaftsdienst GmbH, Bleichstr 20-22, Gernsbach, 76593, Germany. TEL 49-7224-9397572, FAX 49-7224-9397901, service@euwid.com, http://www.euwid.de. Adv. contact Sven Roth. B&W page EUR 1,220, color page EUR 2,120; trim 189 x 260. Circ: 1,510 (controlled).

551.48 FRA ISSN 1818-8710
EUROPEAN JOURNAL OF WATER QUALITY. Text in French. 1970. s-a. **Document type:** *Journal, Academic/Scholarly.*
Former titles (until 2003): Journal Europeen d'Hydrologie (1023-6368); (until 1994): Journal Francais d'Hydrologie (0335-9581); (until 1974): Association Pharmaceutique Francaise pour l'Hydrologie. Bulletin (0335-959X)
Related titles: Online - full text ed.: ISSN 2100-0646; ◆ Supplement(s): Association Scientifique Europeenne pour l'Eau et la Sante. Cahiers. ISSN 1027-4820.
Indexed: A22, A28, APA, B21, B25, BIOBASE, BIOSIS Prev, BrCerAb, C&ISA, CA/WCA, CIA, CerAb, CivEngAb, CorrAb, E&CAJ, E11, EEA, EMA, ESPM, FLUIDEX, FR, GEOBASE, GeoRef, H15, IABS, M&TEA, M09, MBF, METADEX, MycolAb, SCOPUS, SolStAb, T04, WAA.
—BLDSC (4979.620700), IE, Ingenta, INIST, Linda Hall. **CCC.**
Published by: (Association Scientifique Europeenne pour l'Eau et la Sante), E D P Sciences, 17 Ave du Hoggar, Parc d'Activites de Courtaboeuf, BP 112, Cedex A, Les Ulis, F-91944, France. TEL 33-1-69187575, FAX 33-1-69860678, http://www.edpsciences.org.

627 USA ISSN 0253-4703
F A O BULLETIN D'IRRIGATION ET DE DRAINAGE. (Food and Agriculture Organization) Text in French. 1972. irreg., latest vol.58, 2001. back issues avail. **Document type:** *Monographic series, Academic/Scholarly.*
Formerly (until 1976): Bulletin d'Irrigation et de Drainage (1014-8086)
Related titles: ◆ Spanish ed.: Estudio F A O, Riego y Drenaje. ISSN 1020-4393; ◆ English ed.: F A O Irrigation and Drainage Papers. ISSN 0254-5284.
Indexed: GeoRef, SpeleolAb.
Published by: Food and Agriculture Organization of the United Nations, c/o Bernan Associates, 4501 Forbes Blvd, Ste 200, Lanham, MD 20706. TEL 301-459-7666, 800-865-3457, FAX 301-459-0056, 800-865-3450, customercare@bernan.com, http://www.fao.org.

627 USA ISSN 0254-5284
S613
F A O IRRIGATION AND DRAINAGE PAPERS. Text in English. 1971. irreg., latest vol.61, 2002. price varies. back issues avail. **Document type:** *Monographic series, Academic/Scholarly.*
Formerly (until 1977): Food and Agriculture Organization of the United Nations. Irrigation and Drainage Paper (0378-6331)
Related titles: Online - full text ed.: free (effective 2011); ◆ French ed.: F A O Bulletin d'Irrigation et de Drainage. ISSN 0253-4703; ◆ Spanish ed.: Estudio F A O, Riego y Drenaje. ISSN 1020-4393.
Indexed: A37, CABA, E12, I11, R12, S13, S16, TAR, W11.
—BLDSC (3865.683500), Linda Hall.
Published by: Food and Agriculture Organization of the United Nations, c/o Bernan Associates, 4501 Forbes Blvd, Ste 200, Lanham, MD 20706. TEL 800-865-3457, FAX 800-865-3450, customercare@bernan.com.

333.91 ARG ISSN 1852-7620
▼ **F I P C A.** Text in Spanish. 2009. m. **Document type:** *Newsletter, Consumer.*
Published by: Fundacion Interactiva para Promover la Cultura del Agua, Ave Roque Saenz Pena, 995 2o. B, Buenos Aires, Argentina. TEL 54-11-43281486, http://www.fipca.org.ar/.

333.9109746 USA
F R W A NEWS. Text in English. 1996 (vol.40, no.3). q. USD 25 to members (effective 1997). back issues avail. **Document type:** *Newsletter.* **Description:** Covers water resources conservation and related issues.
Published by: Farmington River Watershed Association, 749 Homeadow St, Simsbury, CT 06070. TEL 860-658-4442, FAX 860-651-7519. Ed. Jean Cardinale. Circ: 1,750.

333.91 USA ISSN 0046-306X
FACETS OF FRESHWATER. Text in English. 1976. bi-m. USD 35 to members. bibl.; charts; illus. **Document type:** *Newsletter.*
Published by: Freshwater Foundation, 2500 Shadywood Rd, Navarre, MN 55331. TEL 612-471-9773, FAX 617-471-7685. Ed. Kemp Powers. Circ: (controlled).

FINANCIAL PERFORMANCE AND EXPENDITURE OF THE WATER COMPANIES IN ENGLAND AND WALES. *see* BUSINESS AND ECONOMICS—Investments

627 NOR ISSN 1504-5161
FLOMSONEKART. Text in Norwegian. 2000. irreg. back issues avail. **Document type:** *Monographic series, Government.*
Related titles: Online - full text ed.
Published by: Norges Vassdrags- og Energidirektorat/Norwegian Water Resources and Energy Directorate, PO Box 5091, Majorstua, Oslo, 0301, Norway. TEL 47-22-959595, FAX 47-22-959000, nve@nve.no.

FLORIDA INSTITUTE OF PHOSPHATE RESEARCH. PUBLICATIONS. *see* MINES AND MINING INDUSTRY

333.91 USA ISSN 0896-1794
TD485
FLORIDA WATER RESOURCES JOURNAL; the overflow. Text in English. 1949. m. USD 24 domestic; USD 60 foreign (effective 2005). adv. **Document type:** *Magazine, Trade.* **Description:** Covers water supply, treatment, and distribution; includes waste water collection, treatment and disposal.
—Linda Hall.
Published by: (Florida Water & Pollution Control Operator's Association, Inc.), Buena Vista Publishing, 7041 Grand National Dr, Ste 103, Orlando, FL 32819. TEL 407-352-4448, FAX 407-352-4449. Ed. Jim Allen. Circ: 8,000 (controlled). **Co-sponsors:** Florida Pollution Control Association; American Water Works Association, Florida Section.

333.91 NZL ISSN 1179-674X
▼ **FLOW.** Text in English. 2009. q. free (effective 2011). back issues avail. **Document type:** *Newsletter, Trade.*
Media: Online - full text.
Published by: Rivers Group riversgroup@ipenz.org.nz. Ed. Mark Pennington.

FOLDTANI KOZLONY; bulletin of the Hungarian Geological Society. *see* EARTH SCIENCES—Geology

333.91 USA ISSN 2158-2262
FOX RIVER CURRENT; update from the lower fox river intergovernmental partnership. Text in English. 1998. 3/yr. free (effective 2010). back issues avail. **Document type:** *Newsletter, Government.* **Description:** Provides information about cleanup and restoration efforts on the Lower Fox River.
Media: Online - full text.
Published by: U.S. Environmental Protection Agency, Region 5, Superfund Division (SI-7J), 77 W Jackson Blvd, Chicago, IL 60604. TEL 312-353-1325, 800-621-8431, pastor.susan@epa.gov.

G W A. (Gas - Wasser - Abwasser) *see* PETROLEUM AND GAS

G W F - GAS - ERDGAS. *see* PETROLEUM AND GAS

333.91 DEU ISSN 0016-3651
TD203 CODEN: GWWAAQ
G W F - WASSER, ABWASSER. (Gas- und Wasserfach) Text in German. 1858. m. EUR 330 to non-members; EUR 231 to members; EUR 37 newsstand/cover (effective 2011). adv. **Document type:** *Journal, Trade.* **Description:** For the water and sewer industry. Publishes information and chemical research on water pollution, quality and treatment of drinking water.
Formerly (until 1956): Gas- und Wasserfach. Wasser (0341-0641); Which superseded in part (in 1944): Gas- und Wasserfach (0367-3839)
Related titles: ◆ Supplement(s): Recht und Steuern im Gas- und Wasserfach.
Indexed: A22, CEABA, ChemAb, FLUIDEX, FR, GEOBASE, GeoRef, IBR, IBZ, Repind, SCOPUS, SpeleolAb, TM.
—BLDSC (4085.100000), CASDDS, IE, Infotrieve, Ingenta, INIST, Linda Hall. **CCC.**
Published by: (Bundesverband der Energie- und Wasserwirtschaft), Oldenbourg Industrieverlag GmbH (Subsidiary of: Oldenbourg Wissenschaftsverlag GmbH), Rosenheimer Str 145, Munich, 81671, Germany. TEL 49-89-450510, FAX 49-89-45051207, oiv-info@oldenbourg.de. Ed. Christine Ziegler. Adv. contact Inge Matos Feliz. **Co-sponsor:** Abwassertechnische Vereinigung e.V.

333.7 DEU ISSN 0170-5156
TC473 CODEN: JBGEDH
GERMANY. BUNDESANSTALT FUER GEWAESSERKUNDE. JAHRESBERICHT. Text in German. 1949-1962; N.S. 1974. a. illus. **Document type:** *Journal, Trade.* **Description:** Contains working reports on scientific and technical projects.
Indexed: GeoRef, SpeleolAb.
Published by: Bundesanstalt fuer Gewaesserkunde, Am Mainzer Tor 1, Koblenz, 56068, Germany. TEL 49-261-13060, FAX 49-261-13065302, posteingang@bafg.de, http://www.bafg.de.

627 DEU
GESCHICHTE DER WASSERVERSORGUNG. Text in German. 1982. irreg., latest vol.7, 2007. price varies. **Document type:** *Monographic series, Academic/Scholarly.*
Published by: Verlag Philipp von Zabern GmbH, Riedeselstr 57, Darmstadt, 64283, Germany. TEL 49-6151-7858744, FAX 49-6151-7858744, zabern@zabern.de, http://www.zabern.de.

613.34 DEU ISSN 1437-7500
GEWAESSERGUETEBERICHT. Text in German. 1982. irreg. **Document type:** *Monographic series, Academic/Scholarly.*
Former titles (until 1996): Gewaesserguetebericht N R W (0944-0615); (until 1992): Gewaesserguetebericht (0724-7753)
Indexed: GeoRef.
Published by: Landesumweltamt Nordrhein-Westfalen, Wallneyer Str. 6, Essen, 45133, Germany. TEL 49-201-7995-0, FAX 49-201-79951448, poststelle@lua.nrw.de, http://www.lua.nrw.de.

333.91 DEU ISSN 0342-6068
CODEN: GWABDO
GEWAESSERSCHUTZ - WASSER - ABWASSER. Text in German. 1968. irreg., latest vol.196, 2004. price varies. **Document type:** *Monographic series, Academic/Scholarly.*
Indexed: A22, GeoRef, TM.
—BLDSC (4165.570000), IE, Ingenta. **CCC.**
Published by: R W T H Aachen, Institut fuer Siedlungswasserwirtschaft, RWTH Aachen, Aachen, 52056, Germany. TEL 49-241-8025207, FAX 49-241-8022285, isa@isa.rwth-aachen.de, http://www.isa.rwth-aachen.de.

333.91 AUT
GEWAESSERSCHUTZBERICHT. Text in German. 1993. triennial. free. **Document type:** *Government.*
Published by: Bundesministerium fuer Land- und Forstwirtschaft, Umwelt und Wasserwirtschaft, Stubenring 1, Vienna, 1012, Austria. TEL 43-1-711007538, FAX 43-1-711007502, infomaster@lebensministerium.at, http://www.bmlfuw.gv.at. Eds. Heinz Tomek, Veronika Koller Kreimel. Circ: 2,500 (controlled).

628.1 GBR ISSN 1750-7979
THE GLOBAL ENVIRONMENT. Variant title: International Directory (Year). Text in English. a. GBP 35 per issue to non-members; free to members (effective 2007). adv. **Document type:** *Directory, Academic/Scholarly.* **Description:** Focuses on the issues that will affect the water and environment sector.
Former titles (until Apr. 2006): Chartered Institution of Water and Environmental Management. International Directory (Year); Chartered Insitution of Water and Environmental Management. Yearbook (Year); Incorporated: National Water Industry Handbook
—BLDSC (4195.395795), IE, Ingenta.
Published by: (Chartered Institution of Water and Environmental Management), Lead Media Ltd., 6 Harforde Ct, John Tate Rd, Foxholes Business Park, Hertford, Herts SG13 7NW, United Kingdom. TEL 44-870-3000690, FAX 44-870-3000691, subs@leadmedia.co.uk. Ed. Erika Yarrow TEL 44-870-3000695. Pub. Jonathan Hankin TEL 44-870-3000690. Adv. contact Andrew Robinson TEL 44-870-3000690. Circ: 13,500.

GLOBAL WATER INTELLIGENCE. *see* BUSINESS AND ECONOMICS—Banking And Finance

628.1 CHN ISSN 1673-9353
GONGSHUI JISHU/WATER TECHNOLOGY. Text in English. 2003. m. **Document type:** *Journal, Academic/Scholarly.*
Formerly (until 2007): Gongshui Jishu yu Guanli
Published by: Tianjin Shi Zilaishui Jituan Youxian Gongsi/Tianjin WaterWorks (Group) Company Ltd., Jianshe Rd, Heping District, Tianjin, 300040, China. http://www.norwater.com/.

GONGYE YONGSHUI YU FEISHUI/INDUSTRIAL WATER & WASTEWATER. *see* ENVIRONMENTAL STUDIES—Waste Management

628 551.4 POL ISSN 0017-2448
CODEN: GOWOAC
GOSPODARKA WODNA. Text in Polish; Contents page in English. 1935. m. PLZ 315 domestic; EUR 200 foreign (effective 2011). adv. bk.rev. charts; illus.; maps; stat. index. 44 p./no.; **Document type:** *Journal, Trade.*
Related titles: Online - full text ed.
Indexed: B22, ChemAb, GeotechAb.
—CASDDS, Linda Hall.
Published by: (Stowarzyszenie Inzynierow i Technikow Wodnych i Melioracyjnych), Wydawnictwo SIGMA - N O T Sp. z o.o., ul Ratuszowa 11, PO Box 1004, Warsaw, 00950, Poland. TEL 48-22-8180918, FAX 48-22-6192187, sekretariat@sigma-not.pl. Ed. Ewa Skupinska TEL 48-22-6192015. adv.: B&W page PLZ 1,500, color page PLZ 3,300. Circ: 1,500. **Dist. by:** Ars Polona, Obroncow 25, Warsaw 03933, Poland. TEL 48-22-5098609, FAX 48-22-5098610, arspolona@arspolona.com.pl, http://www.arspolona.com.pl.

977 016 USA ISSN 0072-7326
GB1627.G8
GREAT LAKES RESEARCH CHECKLIST. Text in English. 1959. s-a. free. bk.rev. reprints avail. **Document type:** *Bibliography.* **Description:** Bibliography of current Great Lakes related journals, articles, books and documents. Includes news notes.
Related titles: Microfilm ed.: (from PQC).
Published by: Great Lakes Commission, 2805 S. Industrial Hwy., Ste. 100, Ann Arbor, MI 48104-6791. TEL 313-665-9135, FAX 313-665-4370. Ed. Albert G Ballert. Circ: 700.

333.91 GRC
GREEK COMMISSION ON IRRIGATION AND DRAINAGE. BULLETIN. Short title: Bulletin G C I D. Text in Greek; Summaries in English. 1962. s-a. adv. bk.rev. bibl.; charts; illus.; stat.; tr.lit.
Former titles: G C I D Scientific Bulletin; G C I D Information Letter; International Committee on Irrigation and Drainage. Greek National Committee. Bulletin (0011-8109)
Published by: International Commission on Irrigation and Drainage, Greek National Committee, 13 Tsakona St., Psychico, Athens, Greece. Ed. George Papadopoulos. Circ: 4,000.

333.9 613.1 USA
GREENWORKS. Text in English. 200?. m. free (effective 2011). back issues avail. **Document type:** *Newsletter, Government.*
Related titles: Online - full text ed.

Published by: New Hampshire Department of Environmental Services, 29 Hazen Dr, PO Box 95, Concord, NH 03302. TEL 603-271-3503, mary.power@des.nh.gov, http://des.nh.gov.

333.91 631 CAN ISSN 1206-3762
GROUND WATER CANADA. Text in English. 1978. 4/yr. CAD 22 domestic; CAD 33 in United States; CAD 55 elsewhere (effective 2007). adv. illus. back issues avail. **Document type:** *Magazine, Trade.* **Description:** Dedicated to addressing the factors that impact the ground water industry.
Formerly (until 1997): Canadian Water Well (1180-050X)
—CCC.
Published by: Annex Publishing & Printing, Inc., 105 Donly Dr S, PO Box 530, Simcoe, ON N3Y 4N5, Canada. TEL 519-429-3966, 800-265-2827, FAX 519-429-3112, 888-404-1129, mfredericks@annexweb.com, http://www.annexweb.com. Ed. Chris Skalkos TEL 519-235-2400 ext 231. Circ: 3,259.

GROUND WATER MONITORING & REMEDIATION. see EARTH SCIENCES—Hydrology

333.7 DEU ISSN 1430-483X CODEN: GRUNFP
➤ **GRUNDWASSER.** Text in German. 1996. q. EUR 243, USD 272 combined subscription to institutions (print & online eds.) (effective 2012). adv. reprint service avail. from PSC. **Document type:** *Journal, Academic/Scholarly.* **Description:** Covers topics such as hydrogeology, groundwater hydraulics, hydrogeothermics, and well engineering.
Related titles: Online - full text ed.: ISSN 1432-1165 (from IngentaConnect).
Indexed: A22, A26, A37, CABA, CIN, ChemAb, ChemTitl, CurCont, E01, E12, F08, FLUIDEX, GEOBASE, GH, GeoRef, I11, LT, N02, R07, RRTA, RefZh, S13, S16, SCI, SCOPUS, T02, T05, TAR, W07.
—CASDDS, IE, Ingenta. **CCC.**
Published by: (Fachsektion Hydrogeologie in der Deutschen Geologischen Gesellschaft), Springer (Subsidiary of: Springer Science+Business Media), Tiergartenstr 17, Heidelberg, 69121, Germany. TEL 49-6221-4870, FAX 49-6221-345229. **Subscr. in the Americas to:** Springer New York LLC, Journal Fulfillment, PO Box 2485, Secaucus, NJ 07096. TEL 800-777-4643, 201-348-4033, FAX 201-348-4505, journals-ny@springer.com, http://www.springer.com; **Subscr. to:** Springer Distribution Center, Kundenservice Zeitschriften, Haberstr 7, Heidelberg 69126, Germany. TEL 49-6221-3454303, FAX 49-6221-3454229, subscriptions@springer.com.

556.38 DEU ISSN 0944-0704
GRUNDWASSERBERICHT. Text in German. 1985. irreg. **Document type:** *Monographic series, Academic/Scholarly.*
Indexed: GeoRef.
Published by: Landesumweltamt Nordrhein-Westfalen, Wallneyer Str. 6, Essen, 45133, Germany. TEL 49-201-7995-0, FAX 49-201-79951448, poststelle@lua.nrw.de, http://www.lua.nrw.de.

GUAN'GAI PAISHUI XUEBAO/JOURNAL OF IRRIGATION AND DRAINAGE. see AGRICULTURE

628.1 333.914 CHN ISSN 1008-0112
GUANGDONG SHUILI SHUIDIAN/GUANGDONG WATER RESOURCES AND HYDROPOWER. Text in Chinese. 1972. bi-m. CNY 5 newsstand/cover (effective 2006). **Document type:** *Journal, Academic/Scholarly.*
Related titles: Online - full text ed.
Published by: Guangdong Sheng Shuili Shuidian Kexue Yanjiuyuan, 101, Tianhou Lu, Guangzhou, 510610, China.

333.91 FRA ISSN 2101-1680
LE GUIDE DE L'EAU. Text in French. 1970. a., latest 2009. EUR 198 per issue (effective 2009). adv. **Document type:** *Directory.*
Related titles: CD-ROM ed.
Published by: Pierre Johanet et ses Fils, 30 rue Rene Boulanger, Paris, 75010, France. TEL 33-1-44847878, FAX 33-1-42402646. Ed. Johanet Vmenl. Adv. contact Michele Hardy.

628.1 GBR
GUIDE TO THE ECONOMIC REGULATION OF THE WATER INDUSTRY (ONLINE). Variant title: Water Guide. Text in English. 1993. irreg. GBP 20 per vol. (effective 2010). **Document type:** *Handbook/Manual/Guide, Trade.* **Description:** Provides information about the theoretical and legal framework of regulation in the U.K. water sector and analysis of its development since the privatization of the industry.
Formerly (until 2004): Guide to the Economic Regulation of the Water Industry (Print) (1350-6684)
Media: Online - full text.
Indexed: A32.
—CCC.
Published by: O X E R A Consulting Ltd., Park Central, 40/41 Park End St, Oxford, OX1 1JD, United Kingdom. TEL 44-1865-253000, FAX 44-1865-251172, enquiries@oxera.com, http://www.oxera.com.

627 NLD ISSN 0166-8439
H2O; tijdschrift voor watervoorziening en waterbeheer. Text in Dutch; Summaries in English. 1968. fortn. EUR 103; EUR 8.50 newsstand/cover (effective 2010). adv. bk.rev. **Document type:** *Journal, Trade.* **Description:** Publishes news, official announcements and other items of concern to professionals in the waste water treatment field, as well as government officials and members of related industries.
Related titles: ◆ Supplement(s): Water in de Pers. ISSN 0920-6388.
—BLDSC (4352.700000), IE, Infotrieve, Ingenta, INIST.
Published by: Nijgh Periodieken B.V., Postbus 122, Schiedam, 3100 AC, Netherlands. TEL 31-10-4274100, FAX 31-10-4739911, info@nijgh.nl, http://www.nijgh.nl. Ed. Peter Bielars TEL 31-10-4274165. Pub. Rinus Vissers. Adv. contact Roelien Voshol TEL 31-10-4274154. B&W page EUR 1,555, color page EUR 2,545; trim 210 x 297. Circ: 3,809.

627 DEU ISSN 0724-0783
HAMBURGER BERICHTE ZUR SIEDLUNGSWASSERWIRTSCHAFT. Text in German. 1983. irreg., latest vol.74, 2010. price varies. **Document type:** *Monographic series, Academic/Scholarly.*
Published by: Technische Universitaet Hamburg-Harburg, Gesellschaft zur Foerderung und Entwicklung der Umwelttechnologien, Eissendorfer Str 42, Hamburg, 21073, Germany. TEL 49-40-428783207, FAX 49-40-428782684, info@gfeu.org.

333.91 DEU ISSN 0722-6462
HAMBURGER WASSERWERKE. FACHLICHE BERICHTE. Text in German. 1982. irreg. free to qualified personnel. **Document type:** *Monographic series, Trade.*
Indexed: GeoRef, SpeleolAb.
Published by: Hamburger Wasserwerke GmbH, Billhorner Deich 2, Hamburg, 20539, Germany. TEL 49-40-78882483, FAX 49-40-78882883, pr@hww-hamburg.de, http://www.hww-hamburg.de. Ed. Peter Schreiber. Circ: 1,000.

628.1 DEU ISSN 0935-607X
HANDBUCH DES DEUTSCHEN WASSERRECHTS. Text in German. 1958. 8 base vols. plus updates 12/yr. looseleaf. EUR 248 base vol(s).; EUR 47.80 updates per issue (effective 2009). **Document type:** *Monographic series, Trade.*
Published by: Erich Schmidt Verlag GmbH & Co. (Berlin), Genthiner Str 30 G, Berlin, 10785, Germany. TEL 49-30-2500850, FAX 49-30-250085305, vertrieb@esvmedien.de, http://www.erich-schmidt-verlag.de.

HEALTH STREAM NEWSLETTER; information and analysis for water and health professionals. see PUBLIC HEALTH AND SAFETY

551.49 HUN ISSN 0018-1323 CODEN: HIDRAV
HIDROLOGIAI KOZLONY. Text in Hungarian; Abstracts and contents page in English. 1918. bi-m. HUF 4,200 (effective 1997). adv. bk.rev. abstr.; bibl.; charts; illus. index. cum.index.
Indexed: ApMecR, CIN, ChemAb, ChemTitl, FS&TA, GeoRef, GeotechAb, SpeleolAb.
—CASDDS, Linda Hall.
Published by: Magyar Hidrologiai Tarsasag/Hungarian Hydrological Society, Fo utca 68, IV emelet, Budapest, 1027, Hungary. TEL 36-1-2017655, FAX 36-1-2027244. Ed. Geszler Odonne. Circ: 1,150.

627 551.5 ROM ISSN 1220-1154
HIDROTEHNICA. Text in Romanian; Summaries in English, French, German, Russian. 1956. m. ROL 300,000 to individuals; ROL 1,350,000 to institutions (effective 2002). bk.rev. abstr.; bibl.; charts; illus. index. **Description:** Covers mathematics, atmospheric physics and atmospheric electricity.
Former titles (until 1969): Hidrotehnica, Gospodarirea Apelor, Meteorologia (0018-134X); (until 1963): Hidrotehnica (0439-0962)
Indexed: A32, CIN, ChemAb, ChemTitl, GeoRef, GeotechAb, SpeleolAb.
—INIST, Linda Hall.
Published by: (Institutul National de Meteorologie si Hidrologie), Compania Nationala Apele Romane, Str Edgar Quinet, nr. 6, Sector 1, Bucharest, 70106, Romania. TEL 40-1-3122174, FAX 40-1-3110396, http://www.rowater.ro. Circ: 2,000.

627 JPN
HOKKAIDO NO CHUSHO KASEN/MEDIUM AND SMALL SCALE RIVER IN HOKKAIDO. Text in Japanese. a. JPY 1,600.
Published by: Hokkaido Doboku Kyokai/Hokkaido Civil Engineering Association, Nishi 4-chome, Kita 4-jo, Chuo-ku, Sapporo-shi, Hokkaido 060, Japan.

620 551.4 333.91 FRA ISSN 0018-6368
TC1 CODEN: HOBLAB
HOUILLE BLANCHE; revue internationale de l'eau. Text in English, French; Summaries in English, French, German, Spanish. 1902. 6/yr. (includes 2 double issues). adv. bk.rev. abstr.; bibl.; charts; illus. index. back issues avail. **Document type:** *Newspaper, Trade.* **Description:** Covers a range of preoccupations of engineers interested in water problems: fluid mechanics, hydraulic theory and its applications, river and maritime engineering works, water resources and their management, waters treatment.
Related titles: Online - full text ed.: ISSN 1958-5551.
Indexed: A20, A22, A29, ASCA, ASFA, AcoustA, ApMecR, B20, B21, BibInd, ChemAb, ESPM, F&EA, FLUIDEX, FR, GEOBASE, GeoRef, GeotechAb, H&SSA, I10, ICEA, INIS AtomInd, Inspec, M&GPA, MathR, PollutAb, RiskAb, SCI, SCOPUS, SWRA, SpeleolAb, VirolAbstr, W07.
—BLDSC (4334.000000), IE, Infotrieve, Ingenta, INIST, Linda Hall. **CCC.**
Published by: (Societe Hydrotechnique de France), E D P Sciences, 17 Ave du Hoggar, Parc d'Activites de Courtaboeuf, BP 112, Cedex A, Les Ulis, F-91944, France. TEL 33-1-69187575, FAX 33-1-69860678, http://www.edpsciences.org. Circ: 4,000.

628.1 497.5 HRV ISSN 1330-1144
HRVATSKE VODE. Text in Croatian. 1993. q.
Indexed: A34, A36, A37, ASFA, B21, B23, CABA, E12, ESPM, GEOBASE, GH, GeoRef, H16, H17, I10, I11, LT, OR, P33, R08, RRTA, S13, S16, SCOPUS, SWRA, T05, W11.
Address: Ulica Grada Vukovara 220 ili, Zagreb, 10000, Croatia. TEL 385-1-6307333, FAX 385-1-6151793. Ed. Josip Maru.

628.1 333.914 CHN ISSN 1002-5634
HUABEI SHUILI SHUIDIAN XUEYUAN XUEBAO/NORTH CHINA INSTITUTE OF WATER CONSERVANCY AND HYDROELECTRIC POWER. JOURNAL. Text in Chinese. 1980. q. CNY 6 newsstand/cover (effective 2006). **Document type:** *Journal, Academic/Scholarly.*
Related titles: Online - full text ed.
Published by: Huabei Shuili Shuidian Xueyuan/North China Institute of Water Conservancy and Hydroelectric Power, 20, Zhenghua Lu, Zhengzhou, 450011, China. TEL 86-371-65727655 ext 3614, FAX 86-371-65790227.

HUNTER VALLEY RESEARCH FOUNDATION. WORKING PAPERS. see STATISTICS

HUPO KEXUE/JOURNAL OF LAKE SCIENCES. see EARTH SCIENCES

628.1 NZL ISSN 1179-5646
▼ **THE HUTTON'S SHEARWATER CHARITABLE TRUST. NEWSLETTER.** Variant title: Hutton's Shearwater Charitable Trust. Series. Text in English. 2009. 3/yr. back issues avail. **Document type:** *Newsletter, Trade.*
Related titles: Online - full text ed.: free (effective 2010).
Published by: Hutton's Shearwater Charitable Trust, PO Box 58, Kaikoura, 7340, New Zealand. TEL 64-3-3195026, admin@huttonsshearwater.org.nz, http://www.huttonsshearwater.org.nz.

628.1 BRA
HYDRO; onde a agua e bem tratada. Text in Portuguese. 2006. m. free to qualified personnel. **Document type:** *Magazine, Trade.*
Published by: Aranda Editora Tecnica e Cultural, Alamed Olga 315, Perdizes, Sao Paulo, SP 01155-900, Brazil. TEL 55-11-38245300, FAX 55-11-36669585, info@arandanet.com.br, http://www.arandanet.com.br.

HYDRO NEPAL; journal of water, energy and environment. see ENVIRONMENTAL STUDIES

627 551.4 DEU ISSN 1439-1783
GB651 CODEN: DGMTAO
➤ **HYDROLOGIE UND WASSERBEWIRTSCHAFTUNG.** Text in German; Summaries in English. 1949. bi-m. EUR 28 (effective 2009). bk.rev. abstr.; bibl.; charts; illus.; maps; tr.lit. index. 40 p./no.; back issues avail. **Document type:** *Journal, Academic/Scholarly.* **Description:** Reports on quantitative and qualitative hydrology, water resources management and water protection.
Former titles (until 1999): Deutsche Gewaesserkundliche Mitteilungen (0012-0235); (until 1957): Bundesanstalt fuer Gewaesserkunde. Mitteilungen (0431-5219)
Indexed: ASFA, B21, ChemAb, ESPM, GEOBASE, GeoRef, IBR, IBZ, PollutAb, RefZh, SCI, SCOPUS, SWRA, SpeleolAb, W07.
—CASDDS, IE, INIST, Linda Hall. **CCC.**
Published by: Bundesanstalt fuer Gewaesserkunde, Am Mainzer Tor 1, Koblenz, 56068, Germany. TEL 49-261-13060, FAX 49-261-13065302, posteingang@bafg.de, http://www.bafg.de. Ed. Gerhard Strigel. Circ: 1,600 (paid).

➤ **HYDROPLUS**; magazine international de l'eau - international water review. see ENGINEERING—Hydraulic Engineering

333.91 USA ISSN 1010-4224
I A G L R PROGRAM. Text in English. a.
Formerly (until 1985): Conference on Great Lakes Research. Program and Abstracts (1010-4275)
Indexed: BIOSIS Prev, MycolAb.
Published by: International Association for Great Lakes Research, 2205 Commonwealth Blvd, Ann Arbor, MI 48105. TEL 734-665-5303, FAX 734-741-2055, office@iaglr.org, http://www.iaglr.org.

I A H S SPECIAL PUBLICATIONS. see EARTH SCIENCES—Hydrology

628.1 GBR ISSN 0968-3402
I A W Q YEARBOOK. Text in English. q. **Document type:** *Yearbook.*
Indexed: ASFA, ESPM, SWRA.
Published by: International Association on Water Quality, 1 Queen Anne's Gate, London, SW1H 9BT, United Kingdom. TEL 44-20-72223848, FAX 44-20-72331197.

628.167 USA ISSN 1947-7953
▼ ➤ **I D A JOURNAL.** (International Desalination Association) Text in English. 2009. q. free to members (effective 2010). adv. reprints avail. **Document type:** *Journal, Academic/Scholarly.* **Description:** Contains articles on the technical and scientific aspects of desalination.
Related titles: Online - full text ed.
—CCC.
Published by: American Water Works Association, 6666 W Quincy Ave, Denver, CO 80235. TEL 303-794-7711, 800-926-7337, FAX 303-347-0804, custsvc@awwa.org. Ed. John Hughes TEL 303-347-6297. adv.: page USD 2,900; trim 8 x 10.75. Circ: 5,500.
Co-publisher: International Desalination Association.

628.167 USA
I D A NEWSLETTER. Text in English. m. **Document type:** *Newsletter.*
Published by: International Desalination Association, 94 Central St, Ste 200, PO Box 387, Topsfield, MA 01983. TEL 508-887-0410, FAX 508-887-0411, info@idadesal.org, http://www.idadesal.org. Ed. Patricia Burke.

I G W M C GROUND WATER MODELING NEWSLETTER. see EARTH SCIENCES—Hydrology

627 GBR
I W O JOURNAL. (Institution of Water Officers) Text in English. 1952. q. free to members (effective 2009). **Document type:** *Journal, Trade.*
Former titles (until 2001): Institution of Water Officers Journal (0962-0311); (until 1991): Association of Water Officers Journal; (until 1975): Waterworks Officers Association Journal; (until 1971): Waterworks Officers Journal
—Ingenta.
Published by: Institution of Water Officers, 4 Carlton Ct, Team Valley, Gateshead, NE11 0AZ, United Kingdom. TEL 44-191-4220088, FAX 44-191-4220087, info@iwo.org.uk, http://www.iwo.org.uk.

353.9 557 USA ISSN 0731-7662
ILLINOIS. STATE GEOLOGICAL SURVEY. COOPERATIVE GROUNDWATER REPORT. Text in English. 1959. irreg., latest vol.20, 2005. price varies. back issues avail. **Document type:** *Monographic series, Government.*
Former titles (until 1977): Cooperative Resources Report (0148-4400); (until 1965): Cooperative Ground-Water Report (0536-4736)
Related titles: Online - full text ed.: free (effective 2011).
Indexed: GeoRef.
—Linda Hall.
Published by: State Geological Survey, 615 E Peabody Dr, Champaign, IL 61820. TEL 217-333-4747, isgs@isgs.illinois.edu, http://www.isgs.illinois.edu/.

353.9 USA ISSN 0360-9804
ILLINOIS STATE WATER SURVEY. BULLETIN. Text in English. q. **Document type:** *Government.*
Indexed: A23, A24, B13, GeoRef.
—Linda Hall.
Published by: Illinois State Water Survey, 2204 Griffith Dr, Champaign, IL 61820. TEL 217-333-4956, FAX 217-333-6540.

353.9 USA ISSN 0097-5524
GB705.I3 CODEN: ILWCAB
ILLINOIS STATE WATER SURVEY. CIRCULAR. Text in English. 1928. irreg. **Document type:** *Government.*
Indexed: GeoRef.
—Linda Hall.
Published by: Illinois State Water Survey, 2204 Griffith Dr, Champaign, IL 61820. TEL 217-333-4956, FAX 217-333-6540.

627 IND ISSN 0019-5537
TC1 CODEN: IJPRA7
INDIAN JOURNAL OF POWER AND RIVER VALLEY DEVELOPMENT. Text in English. 1950. bi-m. INR 1,200 (effective 2011). bk.rev. abstr.; charts; illus. reprints avail. **Document type:** *Journal, Trade.*
Related titles: Microform ed.: (from PQC).

Indexed: A22, GeoRef, GeotechAb, INIS AtomInd, Inspec, SpeleolAb, WildRev.
—BLDSC (4420.200000), AskIEEE, IE, Ingenta, Linda Hall.
Published by: Books & Journals Private Ltd., 6-2 Madan St, 3rd Fl, Kolkata, West Bengal 700 072, India. TEL 91-33-22126526, FAX 91-33-22126348, books@satyam.net.in. **Subscr. to:** I N S I O Scientific Books & Periodicals, PO Box 7234, Indraprastha HPO, New Delhi 110 002, India.

628.1 IND ISSN 0970-275X
TD303.A1
INDIAN WATER WORKS ASSOCIATION. JOURNAL. Abbreviated title: J I W W A. Text in English. 1969. q. INR 200 domestic; USD 55 foreign; USD 40 per issue domestic; USD 10 per issue foreign (effective 2011). adv. back issues avail. **Document type:** *Journal, Trade.*
Indexed: A22, CPEI, EngInd, SCOPUS.
—BLDSC (4769.065000), IE, Ingenta, Linda Hall.
Published by: Indian Water Works Association, MCGM Compound, Pipeline Rd, Vakola, Santacruz E, Mumbai, 400 076, India. TEL 91-22- 2667266, FAX 91-22-6168613, iwwa@rediffmail.com. Ed. S V Dahasahasra TEL 91-22-26672665.

628.1 IND
INDIAN WATER WORKS ASSOCIATION. MANUAL. Text in English. 19??. irreg.
Published by: Indian Water Works Association, MCGM Compound, Pipeline Rd, Vakola, Santacruz E, Mumbai, 400 076, India. TEL 91-22- 2667266, FAX 91-22-6168613, iwwa@rediffmail.com, http://www.iwwa.info.

628.168 IND
INDIAN WATER WORKS ASSOCIATION. PROCEEDINGS. Text in English. 200?. a. **Document type:** *Proceedings, Trade.*
Published by: Indian Water Works Association, MCGM Compound, Pipeline Rd, Vakola, Santacruz E, Mumbai, 400 076, India. TEL 91-22- 2667266, FAX 91-22-6168613, iwwa@rediffmail.com, http://www.iwwa.info.

628.168 IND
INDIAN WATER WORKS ASSOCIATION. WATER AND WASTEWATER MONOGRAM. Text in English. 19??. irreg. **Document type:** *Monographic series, Trade.*
Published by: Indian Water Works Association, MCGM Compound, Pipeline Rd, Vakola, Santacruz E, Mumbai, 400 076, India. TEL 91-22- 2667266, FAX 91-22-6168613, iwwa@rediffmail.com.

628.168 IND
INDIAN WATER WORKS ASSOCIATION. WATER AND WASTEWATER TECHNICAL PUBLICATION. Text in English. 19??. irreg. **Document type:** *Trade.*
Published by: Indian Water Works Association, MCGM Compound, Pipeline Rd, Vakola, Santacruz E, Mumbai, 400 076, India. TEL 91-22- 2667266, FAX 91-22-6168613, iwwa@rediffmail.com.

553.7 333.72 USA ISSN 0361-2023
GB705.I4 CODEN: IDWBAK
INDIANA. DEPARTMENT OF NATURAL RESOURCES. DIVISION OF WATER. BULLETIN. Text in English. 1968. irreg. back issues avail. **Document type:** *Bulletin, Government.*
Related titles: Online - full text ed.: free (effective 2011).
Indexed: GeoRef.
—Linda Hall.
Published by: Indiana Department of Natural Resources, Division of Water, 402 W Washington St, Rm W264, Indianapolis, IN 46204. TEL 317-232-4160.

553.7 333.72 USA
INDIANA. DEPARTMENT OF NATURAL RESOURCES. DIVISION OF WATER. WATERLINES. Text in English. s-a. back issues avail. **Document type:** *Newsletter, Government.* **Description:** Contains floodplain regulations, precipitation reports, news on upcoming events, seminars and workshops concerning floodplain management and other articles focusing on floodplain management and planning.
Related titles: Online - full text ed.: free (effective 2011).
Published by: Indiana Department of Natural Resources, Division of Water, 402 W Washington St, Rm W264, Indianapolis, IN 46204. TEL 317-232-4160. Ed. Anita Nance.

333.91 USA ISSN 1934-3922
TD897.5
INDUSTRIAL WATERWORLD. Text in English. 2000 (Nov.). bi-m. USD 45 domestic; USD 57 in Canada & Mexico; USD 63 elsewhere; free to qualified personnel (effective 2009). adv. back issues avail. **Document type:** *Magazine, Trade.* **Description:** Contains information on technology, products and trends in the water and wastewater industry.
Related titles: Online - full text ed.: USD 32 (effective 2009); ◆ Supplement(s): Urban Water Management.
Indexed: A32, APA, C&ISA, CorrAb, E&CAJ, EEA, ESPM, EnvEAb, SolStAb, WAA.
—Linda Hall.
Published by: PennWell Corporation, 1421 S Sheridan Rd, Tulsa, OK 74112. TEL 918-835-3161, 800-331-4463, FAX 918-831-9804, Headquarters@PennWell.com, http://www.pennwell.com. Ed. James Laughlin TEL 918-832-9320. Pub. Timm Dower TEL 918-832-9237. adv.: B&W page USD 4,568, color page USD 5,710; trim 8 x 10.5. Circ: 25,247.

333.91 FRA ISSN 0012-9003
INFORMATION EAUX. Text in French. 1949. bi-m. bk.rev. charts. **Document type:** *Government.*
Formerly: Eaux et Industries
Related titles: Online - full text ed.
Indexed: GeoRef, Repind, SpeleolAb.
Published by: Office International de l'Eau, Direction de la Documentation et des Donnees, 15 rue Edouard Chamberland, Limoges, Cedex 87065, France. TEL 33-5-55114780, FAX 33-5-55114748. Ed. Jean Antoine Faby.

333.91 USA ISSN 1536-5212
TD223
INFORMATION PLUS REFERENCE SERIES. WATER; no longer taken for granted. Text in English. 1983. biennial, latest 2007. USD 49 per issue (effective 2008). **Document type:** *Monographic series, Academic/Scholarly.* **Description:** Provides a compilation of current and historical statistics, with analysis, on aspects of one contemporary social issue.
Related titles: Online - full text ed.; ◆ Series of: Information Plus Reference Series.
Published by: Gale (Subsidiary of: Cengage Learning), 27500 Drake Rd, Farmington Hills, MI 48331. TEL 248-699-4253, 800-877-4253, FAX 877-363-4253, gale.customerservice@cengage.com, http://gale.cengage.com.

INFRASTRUKTURRECHT; Energie - Verkehr - Abfall - Wasser. *see* LAW

INGEGNERIA AMBIENTALE. *see* PUBLIC HEALTH AND SAFETY

INGEGNERIA AMBIENTALE QUADERNI. *see* PUBLIC HEALTH AND SAFETY

INGENIERIA HIDRAULICA EN MEXICO. *see* ENGINEERING—Hydraulic Engineering

628.1 GBR ISSN 2044-2041
▼ ➤ **INLAND WATERS.** Text in English. 2011. q. USD 180 combined subscription to individuals (print & online eds.); USD 400 combined subscription to institutions (print & online eds.); free to members (effective 2011). **Document type:** *Journal, Academic/Scholarly.* **Description:** Promotes understanding of inland aquatic ecosystems and their management.
Related titles: Online - full text ed.: ISSN 2044-205X. USD 100 to individuals; USD 250 to institutions (effective 2011).
Published by: Freshwater Biological Association, The Ferry Landing, Far Sawrey, Ambleside, Cumbria LA22 0LP, United Kingdom. TEL 44-1539-442468, FAX 44-1539-446914, info@fba.org.uk, http://www.fba.org.uk.

333.91 551.4 DEU ISSN 0343-8090
INSTITUT FUER WASSERWIRTSCHAFT, HYDROLOGIE UND LANDWIRTSCHAFTLICHEN WASSERBAU. MITTEILUNGEN. Text in German. 1958. irreg. EUR 30 per issue (effective 2006). back issues avail. **Document type:** *Monographic series.*
Formerly (until 1971): Institut fuer Wasserwirtschaft und Landwirtschaftlichen Wasserbau der Technischen Universitaet Hannover. Mitteilungen (0440-2839)
Indexed: GeoRef, SpeleolAb.
Published by: Institut fuer Wasserwirtschaft Hydrologie und landwirtschaftlichen Wasserbau, Universitaet Hannover, Appelstr 9A, Hannover, 30167, Germany. TEL 49-511-7622237, FAX 49-511-7623731, info@iww.uni-hannover.de.

INSTITUTION OF ENGINEERS (INDIA). ENVIRONMENTAL ENGINEERING DIVISION. JOURNAL. *see* ENVIRONMENTAL STUDIES

628.1 551.4 PRT ISSN 0870-3884
INSTITUTO HIDROGRAFICO. ANAIS. Text in Portuguese. 1964. a.
Indexed: ASFA, B21, ESPM, SWRA.
Published by: Instituto Hidrografico, Rua das Trinas 49, Lisbon, Portugal. TEL 380-395-5119, FAX 380-396-0515, http://www.hidrografico.pt/hidrografico/.

INSTITUTO MEXICANO DE TECNOLOGIA DELE AGUA. TABLAS DE CONTENIDO. *see* ENGINEERING—Hydraulic Engineering

628.168 POL ISSN 0239-6238
TD204 CODEN: MBSWET
INSTYTUT METEOROLOGII I GOSPODARKI WODNEJ. MATERIALY BADAWCZE. SERIA: GOSPODARKA WODNA I OCHRONA WOD/INSTITUTE OF METEOROLOGY AND WATER MANAGEMENT. RESEARCH PAPERS. SERIES: WATER MANAGEMENT AND WATER PROTECTION. Text in Polish; Summaries in English. 1973. irreg. USD 15 (effective 2002). charts; abstr.; illus. **Document type:** *Monographic series.* **Description:** Publishes articles on water management, water quality, water pollution, hydraulics, sanitary engineering, sewage, research works.
Indexed: GeoRef, M&GPA, SpeleolAb.
Published by: Instytut Meteorologii i Gospodarki Wodnej/Institute of Meteorology and Water Management, Ul Podlesna 61, Warsaw, 01673, Poland. TEL 48-22-8341651, FAX 48-22-8345466, bointe@imgw.pl. Pub. Jan Zielinski. R&P Maria Storozynska. Circ: 200.

INSTYTUT METEOROLOGII I GOSPODARKI WODNEJ. WIADOMOSCI/INSTITUTE OF METEOROLOGY AND WATER MANAGEMENT. REPORTS. *see* METEOROLOGY

333.91 551.4 BFA
INTERAFRICAN COMMITTEE FOR HYDRAULIC STUDIES. LIAISON BULLETIN. Text in English. 1970. q. XOF 7,000. adv. bk.rev. bibl.
Related titles: French ed.: Comite Interafricain d'Etudes Hydrauliques.
Published by: Interafrican Committee for Hydraulic Studies, BP 369, Ouagadougou, Burkina Faso. TEL 30-71-12, TELEX 5277 BF. Circ: 700.

333.91 NZL ISSN 1172-1219
INTERFLOW. Text in English. 1991. bi-m. free to qualified personnel (effective 2008). back issues avail. **Document type:** *Newsletter, Consumer.* **Description:** Customer news on water and wastewater matters.
Formerly (until 1992): Water and Wastewater (1171-2325)
Published by: Watercare Services Ltd., Private Bag 92521, Wellesley St, Auckland, 1141, New Zealand. TEL 64-9-5397300, FAX 64-9-5397334, info@water.co.nz, http://www.watercare.co.nz/index.sm. Ed. Clive Nelson. Circ: 2,000.

628.1 IRN ISSN 2008-4935
▼ **INTERNATIONAL AQUATIC RESEARCH.** Text in English. 2009. q. **Document type:** *Journal, Academic/Scholarly.*
Related titles: Online - full text ed.: ISSN 2008-6970. free (effective 2011).
Indexed: A34, A35, A38, B21, CABA, E12, GH, N02, N03, N04, P33, R08, S13, SoyAb, TAR, W10, W11.
Published by: Danishgah-i Azad-i Islami, Tonekabon Branch/Islamic Azad University, Tonekabon, Vali Abad, Tonekabon, 46804-16167, Iran. TEL 98-192-4272484, FAX 98-192-4274409. Ed. Mohammad Reza Ghomi.

627 IND ISSN 1025-9058
INTERNATIONAL CONGRESS ON IRRIGATION AND DRAINAGE. TRANSACTIONS. Text in English. 19??. irreg. USD 232 per issue (effective 2011). **Document type:** *Trade.*
—BLDSC (4539.251300).
Published by: International Commission on Irrigation and Drainage/Commission Internationale des Irrigations et du Drainage, 48 Nyaya Marg, Chanakyapuri, New Delhi, 110 021, India. TEL 91-11-26116837, FAX 91-11-26115962, icid@icid.org, http://www.icid.org.

628.167 333.91 USA ISSN 1022-5404
TD478 CODEN: IDWQF2
INTERNATIONAL DESALINATION AND WATER REUSE QUARTERLY. Text in English. 1991. q. USD 107 (effective 2007). adv. 50 p./no.; **Document type:** *Magazine, Trade.* **Description:** Paul/Green.
Indexed: A32, CEABA, CIN, ChemAb, ChemTitl.
—BLDSC (4539.535000), CASDDS, IE, Ingenta. **CCC.**
Published by: International Desalination Association, 94 Central St, Ste 200, PO Box 387, Topsfield, MA 01983. TEL 978-887-0410, FAX 978-887-0411, info@idadesal.org, http://www.idadesal.org. Ed. Robin Wiseman. adv.: B&W page USD 3,530, color page USD 4,530; trim 8 x 10.75. Circ: 2,000 (paid and controlled).

551.46 GBR
INTERNATIONAL FEDERATION OF HYDROGRAPHIC SOCIETIES. SPECIAL PUBLICATIONS. Text in English. 1975. irreg., latest 2001. price varies. back issues avail. **Document type:** *Monographic series, Trade.*
Formerly (until 2008): Hydrographic Society. International Headquarters. Special Publications (0309-8303)
Related titles: ◆ Series: U.S. Hydrographic Conference. Biennial Meeting. Proceedings. ISSN 0276-4849.
—BLDSC (8378.850000), IE, Ingenta.
Published by: International Federation of Hydrographic Societies, PO Box 103, Plymouth, PL4 7YP, United Kingdom. TEL 44-1752-223512.

INTERNATIONAL INSTITUTE FOR LAND RECLAMATION AND IMPROVEMENT. PUBLICATION. *see* AGRICULTURE—Crop Production And Soil

INTERNATIONAL JOURNAL OF CLIMATOLOGY. *see* METEOROLOGY

551.48 IND ISSN 0973-4570
➤ **INTERNATIONAL JOURNAL OF LAKES AND RIVERS.** Abbreviated title: I J L R. Text in English. 2006. s-a. INR 3,500 domestic to libraries; USD 320 foreign to libraries; USD 360 combined subscription foreign to libraries (print & online eds.) (effective 2011). back issues avail. **Document type:** *Journal, Academic/Scholarly.* **Description:** Publishes top-level researches and provide comprehensive information on all inland water bodies, lotic (running water) systems covering rivers, their branches, streams, tributaries and estuaries, irrigationa canals and drains, as well as lentic (standing water) systems covering shallow lakes, great lakes, saline lakes, reservoirs, ponds and swamps.
Related titles: Online - full text ed.: ISSN 0974-4797. USD 300 to libraries (effective 2011).
Indexed: CA, E04, E05, T02, Z01.
Published by: Research India Publications, D1/71, Top Fl, Rohini Sec-16, New Delhi, 110 089, India. TEL 91-11-65394240, FAX 91-11-27297815, info@ripublication.com.

628.167 GBR ISSN 1476-914X
➤ **INTERNATIONAL JOURNAL OF NUCLEAR DESALINATION.** Abbreviated title: I J N D. Text in English. 2003. 4/yr. EUR 494 to institutions (print or online ed.); EUR 672 combined subscription to institutions (print & online eds.) (effective 2012). abstr.; bibl.; illus.; charts; stat. **Document type:** *Journal, Trade.* **Description:** Provides a source of information in the field of nuclear desalination technology and management.
Related titles: Online - full text ed.: ISSN 1741-9204 (from IngentaConnect).
Indexed: A26, A28, A32, A37, APA, ASFA, B01, B02, B06, B07, B09, B15, B17, B18, BA, BrCerAb, C&ISA, C23, CA, CA/WCA, CABA, CIA, CPEI, CerAb, CivEngAb, CorrAb, E&CAJ, E04, E05, E08, E11, E12, EEA, EMA, ESPM, EngInd, EnvAb, EnvEAb, G04, G08, GH, H15, I05, I11, Inspec, LT, M&TEA, M09, MBF, METADEX, R07, R12, RRTA, S09, S12, S13, S16, SCOPUS, SWRA, SolStAb, T02, T04, TAR, W11, WAA.
—BLDSC (4542.399500), IE, Ingenta, INIST, Linda Hall. **CCC.**
Published by: Inderscience Publishers, PO Box 735, Olney, Bucks MK46 5WB, United Kingdom. TEL 44-1234-240519, FAX 44-1234-240515, editorial@inderscience.com. Ed. Dr. Andre Maisseu. **Subscr. to:** World Trade Centre Bldg, 29 Rte de Pre-Bois, Case Postale 856, Geneva 15 1215, Switzerland. FAX 41-22-7910885, subs@inderscience.com.

➤ **INTERNATIONAL JOURNAL OF RIVER BASIN MANAGEMENT.** *see* ENGINEERING—Hydraulic Engineering

628.1 363.7 CAN ISSN 1923-7537
▼ ➤ **INTERNATIONAL JOURNAL OF SUSTAINABLE WATER AND ENVIRONMENTAL SYSTEMS.** Text in English. 2010. q. CAD 1,000 to institutions (effective 2011). bk.rev.; software rev. back issues avail. **Document type:** *Journal, Academic/Scholarly.* **Description:** Covers new theoretical and experimental research findings in the various fields of, or closely related to water and environmental sciences disciplines.
Related titles: Online - full text ed.: ISSN 1923-7545. CAD 800 to institutions.
Published by: International Association for Sharing Knowledge and Sustainability, 1035 Rawding, PO Box 427, Port William, NS B0P 1T0, Canada. swes@iasks.org. Ed., R&P Mousa S. Mohsen.

333.91 GBR ISSN 1465-6620
GB651 CODEN: IJWNAU
➤ **INTERNATIONAL JOURNAL OF WATER.** Abbreviated title: I J W. Text in English. 2000. 4/yr. EUR 494 to institutions (print or online ed.); EUR 672 combined subscription to institutions (print & online eds.) (effective 2012). charts; illus.; abstr.; bibl. **Document type:** *Journal, Academic/Scholarly.* **Description:** Provides an international forum for analyses and discussions in all aspects of water, environment and society.
Related titles: Online - full text ed.: ISSN 1741-5322 (from IngentaConnect).
Indexed: A26, A28, A32, A34, A37, APA, ASFA, B02, B15, B17, B18, BIOBASE, BiolDig, BrCerAb, C&ISA, C25, CA, CA/WCA, CABA, CIA, CPEI, CerAb, CivEngAb, CorrAb, E&CAJ, E04, E05, E08, E11, E12, EEA, EMA, ESPM, EngInd, EnvEAb, F08, F12, FLUIDEX, G04, G08, G11, GEOBASE, GH, H15, H16, I05, I11, IABS, ICEA, M&TEA, M09, MBF, METADEX, O01, PollutAb, R11, R12, RA&MP, S09, S13, S16, SCOPUS, SSciA, SWRA, SolStAb, T02, T04, T05, TAR, W11, WAA.
—BLDSC (4542.701060), Ingenta, Linda Hall. **CCC.**

Published by: Inderscience Publishers, PO Box 735, Olney, Bucks MK46 5WB, United Kingdom. TEL 44-1234-240519, FAX 44-1234-240515, editorial@inderscience.com. Eds. Andrew K Dragun, Kristin Jakobsson. **Subscr. to:** World Trade Centre Bldg, 29 Rte de Pre-Bois, Case Postale 856, Geneva 15 1215, Switzerland. FAX 41-22-7910885, subs@inderscience.com.

628.1 551.4 NGA
➤ **INTERNATIONAL JOURNAL OF WATER RESOURCES AND ENVIRONMENTAL ENGINEERING.** Text in English. m. free (effective 2010). adv. **Document type:** *Journal, Academic/Scholarly.*
Media: Online - full text.
Published by: Academic Journals, PO Box 73023, Victoria Island, Lagos, Nigeria. service@academicjournals.org. Eds. Dr. Minghua Zhou, Dr. Sadek Z Kassab, T Murugesan.

333.91 GBR ISSN 0790-0627
TC401
➤ **INTERNATIONAL JOURNAL OF WATER RESOURCES DEVELOPMENT.** Text in English. 1983. q. GBP 860 combined subscription in United Kingdom to institutions (print & online eds.); EUR 1,138, USD 1,427 combined subscription to institutions (print & online eds.) (effective 2012). adv. back issues avail.; reprint service avail. from PSC. **Document type:** *Journal, Academic/Scholarly.* **Description:** Covers all aspects of water development and management in both industrialized and developing nations.
Related titles: Microform ed.: (from PQC); Online - full text ed.: ISSN 1360-0648. GBP 774 in United Kingdom to institutions; EUR 1,024, USD 1,284 to institutions (effective 2012) (from IngentaConnect).
Indexed: A01, A03, A08, A22, A29, A32, A34, A36, A37, A38, ARDT, ASFA, Agr, AgrForAb, B01, B06, B07, B09, B20, B21, B23, BA, C25, C30, CA, CABA, CPEI, CurCont, DIP, E01, E04, E05, E11, E12, ESPM, EnerRev, EngInd, EnvAb, EnvInd, F08, F12, FCA, FLUIDEX, GEOBASE, GH, GeoRef, H16, I10, I11, I14, IBR, IBZ, ICEA, LT, M10, N02, OR, P26, P32, P34, P48, P52, P54, P56, PAIS, PGegResA, PN&I, PQC, PollutAb, R11, R12, RRTA, S13, S16, SCI, SCOPUS, SSciA, SWRA, SpeleolAb, T02, T04, T05, TAR, TriticAb, VS, VirolAbstr, W07, W10, W11, WildRev.
—IE, Infotrieve, Ingenta, INIST, Linda Hall. **CCC.**
Published by: Routledge (Subsidiary of: Taylor & Francis Group), 4 Park Sq, Milton Park, Abingdon, Oxon OX14 4RN, United Kingdom. TEL 44-20-70176000, FAX 44-20-70176336, subscriptions@tandf.co.uk, http://www.routledge.com. Ed. Asit K Biswas TEL 52-55-53795429. Adv. contact Linda Hann TEL 44-1344-779945. **Subscr. in N. America to:** Taylor & Francis Inc., Customer Services Dept, 325 Chestnut St, 8th Fl, Philadelphia, PA 19106. TEL 215-625-8900, 800-354-1420, FAX 215-625-2940, customerservice@taylorandfrancis.com; **Subscr. to:** Taylor & Francis Ltd., Journals Customer Service, Sheepen Pl, Colchester, Essex CO3 3LP, United Kingdom. TEL 44-20-70175544, FAX 44-20-70175198.

627 ISR
INTERNATIONAL WATER AND IRRIGATION. Text in English. 1981. q. USD 75 to individuals (effective 2008). adv. bk.rev. 45 p./no. 3 cols./p.; back issues avail. **Document type:** *Journal, Trade.* **Description:** Articles on all aspects of water and irrigation technology.
Former titles: International Water and Irrigation Review; (until l993): Water and Irrigation Review (0334-5807)
Related titles: Spanish ed.: Revista Internacional de Agua Riego; Portuguese ed.
Indexed: A28, A32, APA, BrCerAb, C&ISA, CA/WCA, CIA, CPEI, CerAb, CivEngAb, CorrAb, E&CAJ, E11, EEA, EMA, ESPM, EngInd, EnvEAb, H15, M&TEA, M09, MBF, METADEX, SCOPUS, SolStAb, T04, WAA.
—IE.
Published by: S.N.E.R. Communications Ltd., 55 Weizmann St, P O Box 21051, Tel Aviv, 61210, Israel. TEL 972-3-6953192, FAX 972-3-6956116, intwater@inter.net.il, http://www.intwater.com. Ed. Joshua Jacobson. Pub., R&P Amir Cohen. Adv. contact Erika Cohen. B&W page USD 2,240, color page USD 3,750; 7.5 x 9.875.

333.9 LKA
INTERNATIONAL WATER MANAGEMENT INSTITUTE. RESEARCH UPDATE. Text in English. s-a. **Document type:** *Newsletter, Trade.*
Published by: International Water Management Institute, 127 Sunil Mawatha, Pelawatte, Battaramulla, Sri Lanka. TEL 94-1-867404, 94-1-869080, FAX 94-1-866854.

INTERNATIONAL WATER POWER AND DAM CONSTRUCTION. *see* ENERGY—Hydroelectrical Energy

INTERNATIONAL WATER POWER AND DAM CONSTRUCTION YEARBOOK. *see* ENERGY—Hydroelectrical Energy

INTERNATIONALE GEWAESSERSCHUTZKOMMISSION FUER DEN BODENSEE. BERICHTE. *see* CONSERVATION

INTERNATIONALE GEWAESSERSCHUTZKOMMISSION FUER DEN BODENSEE. JAHRESBERICHT. *see* CONSERVATION

628.1 363.7 IND ISSN 2229-7766
▼ ➤ **INVENTI RAPID WATER & ENVIRONMENT.** Text in English. 2010. q. INR 1,000 domestic; USD 20 foreign (effective 2011). adv. abstr. a. index. back issues avail.; reprints avail. **Document type:** *Journal, Academic/Scholarly.* **Description:** Publishes research reports, review articles and scientific commentaries on water and environment.
Media: Online - full text.
Published by: Inventi Journals Pvt. Ltd., SDX 33, Minal Residency, JK Rd, Bhopal, Madhya Pradesh 462 023, India. TEL 91-9425536487, FAX 91-11-66173705, info@inventi.in, editor@inventi.in, http://www.inventi.in. Ed. Dr. Tarun Kant. Pub. V B Gupta. R&P Emmanuel Toppo. Circ: 50.

333.9 USA
IOWA GEOLOGICAL SURVEY BUREAU. OPEN-FILE COUNTY GROUNDWATER RESOURCES REPORT SERIES. Text in English. 19??. irreg. USD 3.50 per issue (effective 2011). back issues avail. **Document type:** *Monographic series, Government.* **Description:** Provides summary reports on the groundwater resources of individual Iowa counties.
Published by: Geological Survey Bureau, 109 Trowbridge Hall, Iowa City, IA 52242. TEL 319-335-1575, FAX 319-335-2754, Tim.Hall@dnr.iowa.gov.

333.9 USA
IOWA GEOLOGICAL SURVEY BUREAU. WATER SUPPLY BULLETIN. Text in English. 1942. irreg., latest vol.15, 1986. price varies. back issues avail. **Document type:** *Monographic series, Government.* **Description:** Contains technical papers on a variety of topics related to drinking-water supplies.
Published by: Geological Survey Bureau, 109 Trowbridge Hall, Iowa City, IA 52242. TEL 319-335-1575, FAX 319-335-2754, Tim.Hall@dnr.iowa.gov.

IRRIGATION AND DRAINAGE. *see* AGRICULTURE

IRRIGATION AND DRAINAGE ABSTRACTS. *see* AGRICULTURE—Abstracting, Bibliographies, Statistics

627 AUS ISSN 1449-1370
IRRIGATION & WATER RESOURCES. Text in English. 2003. q. free to qualified personnel (effective 2008). adv. **Document type:** *Magazine, Trade.* **Description:** Covers news and technical developments, including enterprise profiles and reports from all major water-use sectors.
Published by: Rural Press Ltd. (Subsidiary of: Fairfax Media), PO Box 2544, Gladstone Park, VIC 3043, Australia. TEL 61-3-93449999, FAX 61-3-93381044, subscriptions.netcirc@ruralpress.com. Ed. Brad Cooper TEL 61-4-39317229. Adv. contacts Lynne Johnson TEL 61-2-45704423, Donna Clarke TEL 61-2-45704444. page AUD 2,791.10. Circ: 14,500.

627 PAK
IRRIGATION RESEARCH INSTITUTE, LAHORE. REPORT. Text in English. 1973. irreg.
Published by: Irrigation Research Institute, The Mall, Lahore, Pakistan.

IRRIGATION SCIENCE. *see* AGRICULTURE

628.1 ITA ISSN 0390-6329
TD204 CODEN: QIRADG
ISTITUTO DI RICERCA SULLE ACQUE. QUADERNI. Text in Italian. 1970. 3/yr. **Document type:** *Monographic series, Academic/Scholarly.*
Indexed: CIN, ChemAb, ChemTitl, GeoRef, SpeleolAb.
—CASDDS, IE, Ingenta, Linda Hall.
Published by: Consiglio Nazionale delle Ricerche, Istituto di Ricerca sulle Acque, Via Salaria Km 29.300, Montelibretti, RM, Italy. http://www.irsa.cnr.it.

628.1 NLD ISSN 1871-9007
JAARRAPPORT DE RIJN. Text in Dutch. 2004. a.
Related titles: Translation: Jahresbericht der Rhein. ISSN 1871-899X.
Published by: Rijn Vereniging van Rivierwaterbedrijven, Groenendael 6, Nieuwegein, 3439 LV, Netherlands. TEL 31-30-6009030, FAX 31-30-6009039.

JAHRBUCH GAS UND WASSER. BAND 1: ENERGIE- UND WASSERVERSORGUNGSUNTERNEHMEN, VERBAENDE UND VEREINE, ORGANISATIONEN. *see* PETROLEUM AND GAS

JAHRBUCH GAS UND WASSER. BAND 2: BRANCHENFUEHRER LEITUNGS- UND ANLAGENBAU. *see* PETROLEUM AND GAS

628.1 CHN ISSN 1007-4929
JIESHUI GUAN'GAI/WATER SAVING IRRIGATION. Text in Chinese. 1976. bi-m. USD 43.20 (effective 2009). **Document type:** *Journal, Academic/Scholarly.*
Formerly (until 1995): Penguan Jishu/Sprinkler Irrigation Technique (1001-4780)
Related titles: Online - full text ed.
Indexed: A34, A37, AgrForAb, C25, C30, CABA, E12, F08, F12, FCA, G11, GH, H16, I11, LT, MaizeAb, N02, O01, P32, P38, P40, PGrRegA, R11, R12, R13, RRTA, S13, S16, S17, SoyAb, TAR, TriticAb, W10, W11.
—BLDSC (9275.437000), East View.
Published by: Wuhan Daxue Shuili Shuidian Xueyuan/Wuhan University, School of Water Resources and Hydropower, Wuhan, 430072, China. TEL 86-27-67802201, FAX 86-27-87643133. Ed. Ziahua Yan.

628.1 CHN ISSN 1009-0177
JINGSHUI CHULI/WATER PURIFICATION TECHNOLOGY. Text in Chinese. 1982. bi-m. USD 31.20 (effective 2009). **Document type:** *Journal, Academic/Scholarly.*
Related titles: Online - full text ed.
Indexed: A32, ASFA, ESPM, RefZh, SWRA.
—BLDSC (4669.038550), East View.
Published by: Shanghai-shi Qingshui Jishu Xuehui, No.815 Hutai Rd., Shanghai, 200072, China. TEL 86-21-66250061, FAX 86-21-66250061.

628.1 CHN ISSN 1002-8471
CODEN: JIPAEW
➤ **JISHUI PAISHUI/WATER AND WASTEWATER ENGINEERING.** Text in Chinese; Summaries in English. 1964. m. USD 56.40 (effective 2009). adv. abstr.; bibl.; charts; illus. cum.index. **Document type:** *Academic/Scholarly.* **Description:** Reports the latest processes, technologies, equipment, facilities, and materials in the fields of municipal, industrial and building water and sewage works.
Related titles: CD-ROM ed.; Online - full text ed.
Indexed: A32.
—BLDSC (9268.900000), East View.
Published by: China Building Technology Development Center, 19 Che Gong Zhuang St, Beijing, 100044, China. TEL 86-10-6836-2263, FAX 86-10-6831-6321, http://www.waterwaswater.com. Ed., Pub. Guan Xingwang. R&P Xingwang Guan. Adv. contact Meng Yan. B&W page USD 420, color page USD 750; trim 285 x 210. Circ: 20,000. **Dist. by:** China International Book Trading Corp, 35 Chegongzhuang Xilu, Haidian District, PO Box 399, Beijing 100044, China. TEL 86-10-68412045, FAX 86-10-68412023, cibtc@mail.cibtc.com.cn.

➤ **JOURNAL OF AQUARICULTURE AND AQUATIC SCIENCES.** *see* BIOLOGY

➤ **JOURNAL OF AQUATIC SCIENCES.** *see* FISH AND FISHERIES

333.917 IDN ISSN 1410-5217
JOURNAL OF COASTAL DEVELOPMENT. Text in English. 1997. 3/yr. charts; stat. **Document type:** *Journal, Academic/Scholarly.* **Description:** Publishes policy papers, the results of research, proceedings of scientific seminars, and other papers concerning all aspects of development in the coastal and marine areas, including social, biological, medical, physical, economic and cultural development.
Related titles: Online - full text ed.: free (effective 2011).
Published by: Universitas Diponegoro, Kampus Tembalang, Semarang, 50239, Indonesia. TEL 62-024-7460038, FAX 62-024-7460039, lpundip@undip.ac.id, http://www.undip.ac.id/riset/index_riset_ins.htm. Ed. Ockykarna Radjasa.

628.1 USA ISSN 1936-7031
TC423
JOURNAL OF CONTEMPORARY WATER RESEARCH AND EDUCATION. Text in English. 1964. 3/yr. USD 35 domestic; USD 80 foreign (effective 2010). back issues avail. **Document type:** *Journal, Academic/Scholarly.*
Former titles (until 2004): Water Resources Update (1548-3517); (until 1988): Universities Council on Water Resources. Update (0735-5866); (until 1974): U C O W R Newsletter (0566-2052)
Related titles: Online - full text ed.: ISSN 1936-704X. free (effective 2010).
Indexed: A22, E01.
—CCC.
Published by: Universities Council on Water Resources, 1000 Faner Dr, Rm 4543, Southern Illinois University, Carbondale, IL 62901. TEL 618-536-7571, FAX 618-453-2671, ucowr@siu.edu. Ed. Christopher L Lant TEL 618- 453-602.

JOURNAL OF FLOOD RISK MANAGEMENT. *see* EARTH SCIENCES

333.91 USA ISSN 0380-1330
GB1627.G8 CODEN: JGLRDE
➤ **JOURNAL OF GREAT LAKES RESEARCH;** devoted to research on large lakes of the world and their watersheds. Text in English. 1953. q. EUR 343 in Europe to institutions; JPY 57,900 in Japan to institutions; USD 536 elsewhere to institutions (effective 2012). adv. abstr. cum.index: 1953-1982, cum index: 1983-1988, cum index: CD-Rom 1953-1998. 300 p./no.; back issues avail.; reprints avail. **Document type:** *Journal, Academic/Scholarly.* **Description:** Brings out manuscripts of theoretical and applied topics in the fields of biology, chemistry, physics, and geology of the large lakes of the world and their watersheds.
Formerly (until 1975): Conference on Great Lakes Research. Proceedings (0045-8058)
Related titles: Microfilm ed.: (from PQC); Online - full text ed.: USD 450 to libraries (effective 2007) (from ScienceDirect).
Indexed: A22, A29, A34, A35, A37, A38, APD, ASCA, ASFA, AgBio, AgrForAb, B21, B25, BA, BIOBASE, BIOSIS Prev, C25, CA, CABA, CIN, CPEI, CRFR, CTO, ChemAb, ChemTitl, CurCont, E04, E05, E11, E12, E17, ESPM, EngInd, EntAb, EnvAb, EnvInd, F08, F12, FCA, G11, GEOBASE, GH, GeoRef, GeophysAb, H16, H17, I11, IABS, ISR, IndVet, Inspec, LT, M&GPA, MMI, MaizeAb, MycolAb, N02, N04, OR, P30, P32, P33, P37, P39, P40, PollutAb, R07, R08, R12, RM&VM, RRTA, RefZh, S13, S16, S17, SCI, SCOPUS, SWRA, SoyAb, SpeleolAb, T02, T04, TAR, ToxAb, VS, W07, W08, W10, W11, WatResAb, WildRev, Z01.
—BLDSC (4996.520000), AskIEEE, CASDDS, IE, Infotrieve, Ingenta, Linda Hall. **CCC.**
Published by: (International Association for Great Lakes Research), Elsevier Inc. (Subsidiary of: Elsevier Science & Technology), 1600 John F Kennedy Blvd, Philadelphia, PA 19103. TEL 215-239-3900, FAX 215-238-7883, JournalCustomerService-usa@elsevier.com. Ed. Marlene Evans TEL 306-975-5310. Adv. contact Janine Castle TEL 44-1865-843844.

➤ **JOURNAL OF HYDRAULIC RESEARCH.** *see* ENGINEERING—Hydraulic Engineering

➤ **JOURNAL OF HYDRO-ENVIRONMENT RESEARCH.** *see* EARTH SCIENCES—Hydrology

➤ **JOURNAL OF SOIL AND WATER CONSERVATION.** *see* CONSERVATION

628.1 USA ISSN 1932-8591
TD370
JOURNAL OF THE U S S J W P. (United States Stockholm Junior Water Prize) Text in English. 2006. a. free (effective 2009). **Document type:** *Journal, Academic/Scholarly.* **Description:** Provides a forum for the students to share their novel research with the rest of the water quality community and also offers them an opportunity to be mentored in scientific writing by leading experts in the field.
Media: Online - full content.
Published by: Water Environment Federation, 601 Wythe St, Alexandria, VA 22314. TEL 800-666-0206, FAX 703-684-2492, csc@wef.org, http://www.wef.org. Ed. David Jenkins. Pub. William J Bertera TEL 703-684-2400 ext 7300.

▼ **JOURNAL OF WATER AND CLIMATE CHANGE.** *see* METEOROLOGY

333.91 JPN ISSN 1348-2165
TD365
JOURNAL OF WATER AND ENVIRONMENT TECHNOLOGY. Text in English. s-a. free (effective 2011). **Document type:** *Journal, Academic/Scholarly.*
Media: Online - full content. **Related titles:** Online - full text ed.; ◆ Print ed.: Mizu Shigen Kankyo Kenkyu. ISSN 0913-8277.
Indexed: A37, A39, C27, C29, D03, D04, E13, F12, G11, I11, Inspec, PN&I, R11, R14, S12, S13, S14, S15, S16, S18.
Published by: Mizu Shigen Kankyo Gakkai/Japanese Association for Water Resources and Environment, Green Plaza Fukagawa Tokiwa 201, -9-7 Tokiwa, Koto, Tokyo, 135-0006, Japan. FAX 81-3-3632-5352, info@jswe.or.jp, http://www.jswe.or.jp.

333.91 GBR ISSN 1477-8920
TD365 CODEN: JWHOBR
➤ **JOURNAL OF WATER AND HEALTH.** Text in English. 2003. q. EUR 1,066 combined subscription in Europe to institutions (print & online eds.); USD 1,307 combined subscription in North America to institutions (print & online eds.); GBP 723 combined subscription to institutions in the UK & elsewhere (print & online eds.) (effective 2011). back issues avail. **Document type:** *Journal, Academic/Scholarly.* **Description:** Provides information on the health implications and control of waterborne micro-organisms and chemical substances.
Related titles: Online - full text ed.

Indexed: A01, A32, A34, A35, A36, A37, A38, AgrForAb, B21, B23, B25, BA, BIOBASE, BIOSIS Prev, C25, CA, CABA, CurCont, D01, E04, E05, E11, E12, EMBASE, ESPM, ExcerpMed, F08, F12, FS&TA, G11, GEOBASE, GH, GeoRef, H&SSA, H16, H17, I11, IABS, ICEA, IndVet, LT, MEDLINE, MaizeAb, MycolAb, N02, N03, OR, P30, P32, P33, P37, P39, PGrRegA, PN&I, PollutAb, R07, R08, R12, R13, RM&VM, RRTA, S12, S13, S16, SCI, SCOPUS, SWRA, SoyAb, T02, T04, T05, TAR, VS, W07, W10, W11.
—BLDSC (5072.523750), IE, Ingenta, INIST. **CCC.**
Published by: I W A Publishing (Subsidiary of: International Water Association), Alliance House, 12 Caxton St, London, SW1H 0QS, United Kingdom. TEL 44-20-76545500, FAX 44-20-76545555, publications@iwap.co.uk, http://www.iwapublishing.com. **Subscr. to:** Portland Customer Services, Commerce Way, Colchester CO2 8HP, United Kingdom. TEL 44-1206-796351, FAX 44-1206-799331, sales@portland-services.com, http://www.portlandpress.com.

➤ **JOURNAL OF WATER AND LAND DEVELOPMENT.** *see* AGRICULTURE—Crop Production And Soil

627 628.162 USA ISSN 1063-455X
TD204
➤ **JOURNAL OF WATER CHEMISTRY AND TECHNOLOGY.** Text in English. 1981. bi-m. EUR 2,849, USD 3,452 combined subscription to institutions (print & online eds.) (effective 2012). bk.rev. charts; illus.; pat.; abstr. back issues avail. **Document type:** *Journal, Academic/Scholarly.* **Description:** Covers water purification and treatment, physical chemistry of water treatment processes, wastewater treatment, and water conditioning.
Formerly (until 1991): Soviet Journal of Water Chemistry and Technology (0734-1679)
Related titles: Online - full text ed.: ISSN 1934-936X; ◆ Translation of: Khimiya i Tekhnolohiya Vody. ISSN 0204-3556.
Indexed: A22, A26, A32, CABA, CCI, E01, E08, E12, GeoRef, P26, P48, P52, P54, P56, PQC, S09, S13, SCI, SCOPUS, SJW, SpeleolAb, W07.
—BLDSC (0415.401000), East View, IE, Infotrieve, Ingenta, INIST, Linda Hall. **CCC.**
Published by: (Natsional'na Akademiya Nauk Ukrainy UKR), Allerton Press, Inc. (Subsidiary of: Pleiades Publishing, Inc.), 18 W 27th St, New York, NY 10001. TEL 646-424-9686, FAX 646-424-9695, journals@allertonpress.com. Ed. Vladislav V Goncharuk.

628.1 340 GBR ISSN 1478-5277
KD1070.A13 CODEN: WALAEV
➤ **THE JOURNAL OF WATER LAW.** Text in English. 1990. bi-m. GBP 460, USD 630, EUR 489 (effective 2009). bk.rev. back issues avail.; reprints avail. **Document type:** *Journal, Academic/Scholarly.* **Description:** Contains articles that deal with the legal aspects of aquatic-environmental issues.
Formerly (until 2002): Water Law (0959-9754)
Related titles: Microform ed.: (from PQC); Online - full text ed.
Indexed: A22, A32, ASFA, E11, ELJI, ESPM, GEOBASE, LJI, OceAb, PollutAb, SCOPUS, SWRA, T04.
—BLDSC (5072.538000), IE, Ingenta. **CCC.**
Published by: Lawtext Publishing Ltd., Office G18, Spinners Ct, 55 W End, Witney, Oxon OX28 1NH, United Kingdom. TEL 44-1993-706183, FAX 44-1993-709410, ltp@lawtext.com. Ed. William Howarth. Pub. Nicholas Gingell.

628.1 USA ISSN 1945-3094
▼ **JOURNAL OF WATER RESOURCE AND PROTECTION.** Text in English. 2009. m. **Document type:** *Journal, Academic/Scholarly.*
Related titles: Online - full text ed.: ISSN 1945-3108. free (effective 2011).
Indexed: A26, A32, A34, A35, A37, AgrForAb, C25, C30, CABA, D01, E04, E05, E08, E12, ESPM, F08, FCA, GH, I05, LT, N02, P26, P32, P33, P52, P54, P56, R07, R08, S13, SWRA, T05, TAR, W10, W11.
Published by: Scientific Research Publishing, Inc., PO Box 54821, Irvine, CA 92619. TEL 408-329-4591, service@scirp.org, http://www.srpublishing.org. Eds. Jian Shen, Ni-Bin Chang.

333.91 624 USA ISSN 0733-9496
TC401 CODEN: JWRMD5
➤ **JOURNAL OF WATER RESOURCES PLANNING AND MANAGEMENT.** Text in English. 1873. bi-m. USD 612 domestic to institutions; USD 642 foreign to institutions; USD 698 combined subscription domestic to institutions (print & online eds.); USD 728 combined subscription foreign to institutions (print & online eds.) (effective 2012). adv. bk.rev. illus. index. back issues avail.; reprints avail. **Document type:** *Journal, Academic/Scholarly.* **Description:** Reports on all phases of planning and management of water resources. Examines social, economic, environmental, and administrative concerns relating to the use and conservation of water.
Formerly (until 1983): American Society of Civil Engineers. Water Resources Planning and Management Division. Journal (0145-0743); Which superseded in part (in 1976): American Society of Civil Engineers. Proceedings (0097-417X)
Related titles: CD-ROM ed.: USD 58 to members for CD-ROM and online eds.; USD 87 to individuals for CD-ROM and online eds.; USD 263 to institutions for CD-ROM and online eds. (effective 2001); Microform ed.: (from PQC); Online - full text ed.: ISSN 1943-5452. USD 537 to institutions (effective 2012).
Indexed: A01, A02, A03, A05, A08, A22, A23, A24, A26, A28, A32, A36, A37, AIA, APA, AS&TA, AS&TI, ASCA, ASFA, B04, B07, B13, BrCerAb, C&ISA, C10, C25, CA, CA/WCA, CABA, CADCAM, CIA, CMCI, CPEI, CerAb, CivEngAb, CorrAb, CurCont, E&CAJ, E04, E05, E08, E11, E12, EEA, EIA, EMA, ESPM, EngInd, EnvAb, EnvEAb, EnvInd, F08, F12, FLUIDEX, G08, G11, GEOBASE, GH, GeoRef, H15, H16, HRIS, I05, I11, IAOP, ICEA, ISMEC, ISR, LT, M&GPA, M&TEA, M05, M06, M09, MBF, METADEX, N02, OR, OceAb, P32, PollutAb, R11, R12, RRTA, RefZh, Repind, S09, S12, S13, S16, SCI, SCOPUS, SJW, SWRA, SolStAb, SpeleolAb, T02, T04, T05, TAR, W07, W11, WAA.
—BLDSC (5072.539400), IE, Infotrieve, Ingenta, INIST, Linda Hall. **CCC.**
Published by: (Water Resources Planning and Management Division), American Society of Civil Engineers, 1801 Alexander Bell Dr, Reston, VA 20191. TEL 703-295-6300, FAX 703-295-6333. Ed. Avi Ostfeld. Adv. contact Dianne Vance TEL 703-295-6234.

628.1 GBR ISSN 2043-9083
➤ **JOURNAL OF WATER, SANITATION AND HYGIENE FOR DEVELOPMENT.** Text in English. 19??. irreg. EUR 495 combined subscription per issue in Europe to institutions (print & online eds.); USD 625 combined subscription per issue in North America to institutions (print & online eds.); GBP 395 combined subscription per issue to institutions in the UK & elsewhere (print & online eds.) (effective 2011). **Document type:** *Journal, Academic/Scholarly.* **Description:** Devoted to the dissemination of high-quality information on the science, policy and practice of drinking-water supply, sanitation and hygiene at local, national and international levels.
Related titles: Online - full text ed.
Published by: I W A Publishing (Subsidiary of: International Water Association), Alliance House, 12 Caxton St, London, SW1H 0QS, United Kingdom. TEL 44-20-76545500, FAX 44-20-76545555, publications@iwap.co.uk, http://www.iwapublishing.com. Eds. Damir Brdjanovic, Jamie Bartram.

333.91 GBR ISSN 1606-9935
TD201 CODEN: AQUAAA
➤ **JOURNAL OF WATER SUPPLY: RESEARCH AND TECHNOLOGY. AQUA.** Text in English, French. 1951. 8/yr. EUR 956 combined subscription in Europe to institutions (print & online eds.); USD 1,134 combined subscription in North America to institutions (print & online eds.); GBP 662 combined subscription to institutions in the UK & elsewhere (print & online eds.) (effective 2011). bk.rev. abstr.; charts; illus. back issues avail. **Document type:** *Journal, Academic/Scholarly.* **Description:** Covers all aspects of research and development in water supply science, technology and management.
Formerly (until 2000): Aqua (0003-7214)
Related titles: Microform ed.: (from PQC); Online - full text ed.: Journal of Water Supply Research and Technology. Aqua Online. ISSN 1605-3974. 1997.
Indexed: A01, A22, A28, A32, A34, A36, A37, A38, APA, ASFA, B25, BIOBASE, BIOSIS Prev, BrCerAb, C&ISA, C25, CA, CA/WCA, CABA, CIA, CPEI, CerAb, ChemAb, CivEngAb, CorrAb, CurCont, E&CAJ, E01, E04, E05, E11, E12, EEA, EMA, ESPM, EngInd, EnvAb, EnvEAb, EnvInd, F08, F12, FS&TA, GEOBASE, GH, GeoRef, H15, I11, IABS, ICEA, LT, M&TEA, M09, MBF, METADEX, MycolAb, N02, N04, P33, P39, PGrRegA, PollutAb, R08, R11, R12, RRTA, Repind, S13, S16, SCI, SCOPUS, SSciA, SWRA, SolStAb, SoyAb, SpeleolAb, T02, T04, T05, TAR, VS, W07, W10, W11, WAA.
—BLDSC (5072.543500), CASDDS, IE, Ingenta, INIST, Linda Hall. **CCC.**
Published by: I W A Publishing (Subsidiary of: International Water Association), Alliance House, 12 Caxton St, London, SW1H 0QS, United Kingdom. TEL 44-20-76545500, FAX 44-20-76545555, publications@iwap.co.uk, http://www.iwapublishing.com. Eds. Graham A Gagnon, Rolf Gimbel, Yoshimasa Watanabe. **Subscr. to:** Portland Customer Services, Commerce Way, Colchester CO2 8HP, United Kingdom. TEL 44-1206-796351, FAX 44-1206-799331, sales@portland-services.com, http://www.portlandpress.com.

628.1 AUS ISSN 1839-1516
▼ ➤ **JOURNAL OF WATER SUSTAINABILITY;** an international journal for water reclamation, reuse and recycling. Abbreviated title: J W S. Text in English. 2011. q. **Document type:** *Journal, Academic/Scholarly.* **Description:** Aims to bridge the two fundamental themes of research and practice to discover the best achievements in all aspects of sustainable water.
Related titles: Online - full text ed.: ISSN 1839-1524. free (effective 2011).
Published by: University of Technology, Sydney, PO Box 123, Broadway, NSW 2007, Australia. TEL 61-2-95142000, publications@uts.edu.au, http://www.uts.edu.au. Eds. Hou H Ngo, Xiaochang C Wang.

➤ **JOURNAL OF WETLANDS ECOLOGY.** *see* ENVIRONMENTAL STUDIES

333.91 USA
KANSAS IRRIGATION WATER USE. Text in English. 198?. a. free (effective 2011). back issues avail. **Document type:** *Government.*
Published by: Water Office, 901 S Kansas Ave, Topeka, KS 66612. TEL 785-296-3185, 888-526-9283, tracy.streeter@kwo.ks.gov, http://www.kwo.org.

333.91 USA
KANSAS MUNICIPAL WATER USE. Text in English. 1987. a. **Document type:** *Government.*
Formerly (until 1995): Kansas Municipalities Water Use
Published by: Water Office, 901 S Kansas Ave, Topeka, KS 66612. TEL 785-296-3185, 888-526-9283, tracy.streeter@kwo.ks.gov.

333.91 USA
KANSAS. WATER OFFICE. FACT SHEET. Text in English. 19??. irreg. free (effective 2011). back issues avail. **Document type:** *Monographic series, Government.*
Related titles: Online - full text ed.
Published by: Water Office, 901 S Kansas Ave, Topeka, KS 66612. TEL 785-296-3185, 888-526-9283, tracy.streeter@kwo.ks.gov.

333.91 USA
KANSAS WATER PLAN. Text in English. 19??. a. free (effective 2011). Supplement avail.; back issues avail. **Document type:** *Government.* **Description:** Contains recommendations on how the state can best achieve the proper use and control of water resources.
Related titles: Online - full text ed.
Published by: Water Office, 901 S Kansas Ave, Topeka, KS 66612. TEL 785-296-3185, 888-526-9283, tracy.streeter@kwo.ks.gov.

627 JPN ISSN 0287-9859
TC401
KASEN/RIVERS. Text in Japanese. 1942. m. JPY 1,100 per issue to non-members; JPY 1,000 per issue to members (effective 2002). adv. bk.rev. **Document type:** *Bulletin, Trade.* **Description:** Features a comprehensive scope of River management in Japan.
Published by: Nihon Kasen Kyokai/Japan River Association, 2-6-5 Koujimachi, Chiyoda-ku, Tokyo, 102-0083, Japan. TEL 81-3-3238-9771, FAX 81-3-3288-2426, rpnriver@japanriver.or.jp. Ed. Akihiko Nunomura. R&P, Adv. contact Kasen Kyokai. B&W page JPY 5,000. Circ: 8,500.

551.48 JPN ISSN 0914-7861
KASEN JOHO KENKYUJO HOKOKU/INSTITUTE OF RIVER AND BASIN INTEGRATED COMMUNICATIONS. REPORT. Text in English, Japanese; Summaries in English. 1987. a.
Published by: Kasen Joho Senta/Foundation of River and Basin Integrated Communications, 1-3 Koji-Machi, Chiyoda-ku, Tokyo, 102-0083, Japan.

627 JPN ISSN 0910-0938
KASEN REBYU/RIVERS REVIEW. Text in Japanese. 1955. q. JPY 1,900.
Published by: Shin Koronsha, 2-1-607 Ebisu-Nishi 1-chome, Shibuya-ku, Tokyo, 150-0000, Japan.

KEY NOTE MARKET ASSESSMENT. THE EUROPEAN WATER INDUSTRY. *see* BUSINESS AND ECONOMICS—Production Of Goods And Services

KEY NOTE MARKET REPORT: THE WATER INDUSTRY. *see* BUSINESS AND ECONOMICS—Production Of Goods And Services

KEY NOTE MARKET REPORT: WATER UTILITIES. *see* BUSINESS AND ECONOMICS—Production Of Goods And Services

628.1 658 NLD ISSN 1574-7948
KIWA MAGAZINE. Text in Dutch. 1990. q.
Supersedes in part (in 2004): K I W A Nieuws (0927-894X)
Published by: Kiwa N.V., Postbus 70, Rijswijk, 2280 AB, Netherlands. TEL 31-70-4144400, FAX 31-70-4144420, info@kiwa.nl, http://www.kiwa.nl. Ed. Maggie Bourgonje.

333.91 639.2 USA ISSN 1040-2381
CODEN: LRMAEY
➤ **LAKE & RESERVOIR MANAGEMENT.** Text in English. 1984. q. GBP 164 combined subscription in United Kingdom to institutions (print & online eds.); EUR 262, USD 328 combined subscription to institutions (print & online eds.) (effective 2012). abstr.; bibl.; charts; illus.; maps; stat. back issues avail.; reprint service avail. from PSC. **Document type:** *Journal, Academic/Scholarly.* **Description:** For professionals and scientists in the lake management field.
Formerly (until 1987): North American Lake Management Society Conference. Proceedings (0743-8141)
Related titles: Online - full text ed.: GBP 152 in United Kingdom to institutions; EUR 242, USD 303 to institutions (effective 2012).
Indexed: A22, A29, A34, ASFA, B20, B21, B25, BIOSIS Prev, CA, CurCont, D01, E04, E05, E11, E12, E17, ESPM, EnvAb, GeoRef, I10, MycolAb, N03, P33, R08, S13, SCI, SCOPUS, SWRA, SpeleolAb, T02, T04, ViroIAbstr, W07, W10, W11, WildRev, Z01.
—BLDSC (5143.925000), CASDDS, IE, Ingenta, Linda Hall. **CCC.**
Published by: (North American Lake Management Society), Taylor & Francis Inc. (Subsidiary of: Taylor & Francis Group), 325 Chestnut St, Ste 800, Philadelphia, PA 19106. TEL 215-625-8900, 800-354-1420, FAX 215-625-8914, customerservice@taylorandfrancis.com, http://www.taylorandfrancis.com. Ed., R&P James LaBounty TEL 303-445-2201. Circ: 2,000.

➤ **LAKE LINE.** *see* FISH AND FISHERIES

333.91 AUS ISSN 1320-5331
GB1601 CODEN: LRAEBH
➤ **LAKES AND RESERVOIRS: RESEARCH AND MANAGEMENT.** Text in English. 1995. q. GBP 466 in United Kingdom to institutions; EUR 593 in Europe to institutions; USD 751 in the Americas to institutions; USD 913 elsewhere to institutions; GBP 536 combined subscription in United Kingdom to institutions (print & online eds.); EUR 681 combined subscription in Europe to institutions (print & online eds.); USD 863 combined subscription in the Americas to institutions (print & online eds.); USD 1,050 combined subscription elsewhere to institutions (print & online eds.) (effective 2012). adv. back issues avail.; reprint service avail. from PSC. **Document type:** *Journal, Academic/Scholarly.* **Description:** Aims to promote international research on environmentally sound management of natural and artificial lakes, consistent with policies of sustainable development.
Related titles: Online - full text ed.: ISSN 1440-1770. 199?. GBP 466 in United Kingdom to institutions; EUR 593 in Europe to institutions; USD 751 in the Americas to institutions; USD 913 elsewhere to institutions (effective 2012) (from IngentaConnect).
Indexed: A01, A03, A08, A22, A26, A28, A34, A37, A38, APA, ASFA, B07, B21, B23, B25, BIOSIS Prev, BrCerAb, C&ISA, C25, CA, CA/WCA, CABA, CIA, CerAb, CivEngAb, CorrAb, E&CAJ, E01, E04, E05, E11, E12, EEA, EMA, ESPM, EnvAb, EnvEAb, EnvInd, F08, F12, FCA, G11, GEOBASE, GH, GeoRef, H15, H16, H17, I05, I11, LT, M&TEA, M09, MBF, METADEX, MycolAb, N04, OR, P32, P33, P39, PGegResA, PollutAb, R07, R08, R12, RRTA, RefZh, S12, S13, S16, SCOPUS, SSciA, SWRA, SolStAb, T02, T04, T05, TAR, VS, W10, W11, WAA, Z01.
—BLDSC (5143.946330), IE, Infotrieve, Ingenta, Linda Hall. **CCC.**
Published by: (International Lake Environment Committee JPN), Wiley-Blackwell Publishing Asia (Subsidiary of: Wiley-Blackwell Publishing Ltd.), 155 Cremorne St, Richmond, VIC 3121, Australia. TEL 61-3-92743100, FAX 61-3-92743101, subs@blackwellpublishingasia.com, http://www.wiley.com/WileyCDA/. Eds. T Watanabe, W Rast. Adv. contact Amanda Munce TEL 61-3-83591071. B&W page AUD 1,240, color page AUD 2,497; trim 210 x 275. **Subscr. to:** PO Box 378, Carlton South, VIC 3053, Australia.

➤ **LAND + WATER;** vakblad voor civiel- en milieutechniek. *see* ENGINEERING—Civil Engineering

364 NLD ISSN 1879-9507
▼ **LANDELIJK VERDACHTENBEELD.** Text in Dutch. 2009. a.
Published by: Korps Landelijke Politiediensten, Dienst I P O L, Postbus 3016, Zoetermeer, 2700 KX, Netherlands. TEL 31-79-3459911, FAX 31-79-3458753.

LANDSCAPE & IRRIGATION. *see* AGRICULTURE—Crop Production And Soil

LANDWERK. *see* AGRICULTURE—Crop Production And Soil

333.9 551.4 CAN ISSN 1204-9891
LEVEL NEWS. Variant title: Great Lakes - St. Lawrence River Water Level. Text in English. 1993. m.
Related titles: French ed.: Info-Niveau. ISSN 1204-993X.
Published by: Canadian Hydrographic Service, Canada Centre for Inland Waters, 867 Lakeshore Road, Box 5050, Burlington, ON L7R 4A6, Canada. TEL 905-336-4844, FAX 905-336-8916.

333.91 SWE ISSN 0281-966X
LINKOEPING UNIVERSITET. DEPARTMENT OF WATER AND ENVIRONMENTAL STUDIES. TEMA V REPORT. Text in English. 1983. irreg. **Document type:** *Monographic series, Academic/Scholarly.*
Formerly (until 1983): Linkoeping Universitet. Department of Water in Environment and Society. Report B (0280-5588)
Indexed: ASFA, B21, ESPM.

Published by: Linkoepings Universitet, Tema Vatten i Natur och Samhaelle/University of Linkoeping. Department of Water and Environmental Studies, Institutionen foer Tema, c/o Linkoeping Universitet, Linkoeping, 58183, Sweden. TEL 46-13-28-22-86, FAX 46-13-13-36-30.

333.91 USA
LIQUID FILTRATION NEWSLETTER. Text in English. 1980. m. looseleaf. abstr.; charts; illus.; pat. back issues avail. **Document type:** *Newsletter, Trade.* **Description:** Covers dewatering and separation using bags, presses, drums, leaf, sand and belt filters.
Related titles: Online - full text ed.
Published by: McIlvaine Company, 191 Waukegan Rd, Ste 208, Northfield, IL 60093. TEL 847-784-0012, FAX 847-784-0061, editor@mcilvainecompany.com, http://www.mcilvainecompany.com. Ed. Ross Ardell. Pub. Robert McIlvaine.

353.9 USA
LOUISIANA GEOLOGICAL SURVEY. WATER RESOURCES PAMPHLET. Text in English. 1954. irreg., latest vol.25, 1970. **Document type:** *Monographic series, Government.*
Published by: Louisiana Geological Survey, 208 Howe-Russell, Louisiana State University, Baton Rouge, LA 70803. TEL 225-578-5320, FAX 225-578-3662, pat@lgs.bri.lsu.edu, http://www.lgs.lsu.edu.

353.9 USA
LOUISIANA GEOLOGICAL SURVEY. WATER RESOURCES SERIES. Text in English. irreg., latest vol.3. price varies. **Document type:** *Monographic series, Government.*
Published by: Louisiana Geological Survey, 208 Howe-Russell, Louisiana State University, Baton Rouge, LA 70803. TEL 225-578-5320, FAX 225-578-3662, pat@lgs.bri.lsu.edu, http://www.lgs.lsu.edu.

628 551.4 USA
LOUISIANA WATER RESOURCES RESEARCH INSTITUTE. ANNUAL REPORT. Text in English. 1965. a. USD 10 (effective 2000). reprints avail. **Document type:** *Government.*
Indexed: SpeleolAb.
Published by: Louisiana Water Resources Research Institute, 3221Ceba Bldg, Louisiana State University, Baton Rouge, LA 70803. FAX 504-388-5043. Ed., R&P Nedra Korevec TEL 225-388-6770. Circ: (controlled). **Co-sponsor:** U.S. Department of the Interior, Geological Survey.

627 DEU ISSN 1861-3802
MAGDEBURGER WASSERWIRTSCHAFTLICHE HEFTE. Text in German. 2005. irreg., latest 2008. price varies. **Document type:** *Monographic series, Academic/Scholarly.*
Published by: Shaker Verlag GmbH, Kaiserstr 100, Herzogenrath, 52134, Germany. TEL 49-2407-95960, FAX 49-2407-95969, info@shaker.de.

333.9 USA
MAINE GEOLOGICAL SURVEY. WATER RESOURCES REPORT. Text in English. 19??. irreg. back issues avail. **Document type:** *Report, Government.*
Related titles: Online - full text ed.: free (effective 2011).
Published by: Maine Geological Survey, 22 State House Sta, Augusta, ME 04333. TEL 207-287-2801, FAX 207-287-2353, mgs@maine.gov.

620 333.91 USA ISSN 0025-0805
MAINE WATER UTILITIES ASSOCIATION. JOURNAL. Text in English. 1924. 6/yr. free to members. adv. **Document type:** *Magazine, Consumer.*
Published by: Maine Water Utilities Association, PO Box P, Waldoboro, ME 04572-0917. TEL 207-832-2263, FAX 207-832-2265, mwua@direcway.com, http://www.mwua.org. Ed. Jeffrey McNelly. Circ: 700 (controlled).

MAJI REVIEW. *see* ENERGY

628.1 AUS ISSN 1833-0924
MALLEE CATCHMENT MANAGEMENT AUTHORITY. ANNUAL REPORT. Text in English. 199?. a. back issues avail. **Document type:** *Government.* **Description:** Provides a framework for the coordination of roles and responsibilities of the Mallee CMA and its partners in wetland protection and management.
Related titles: Online - full text ed.: free (effective 2009).
Published by: Mallee Catchment Management Authority, PO Box 5017, Mildura, VIC 3502, Australia. TEL 61-3-50514377, FAX 61-3-50514379, info@malleecma.vic.gov.au.

628.1 GBR
THE MANAGEMENT OF WATER RESOURCES. Text in English. 2001. irreg., latest vol.5, 2002. price varies. back issues avail. **Document type:** *Monographic series, Trade.* **Description:** Summarizes the state of knowledge of economics and management practices in five dimensions of water resources.
Published by: Edward Elgar Publishing Ltd, The Lypiatts, 15 Lansdown Rd, Cheltenham, Glos GL50 2JA, United Kingdom. TEL 44-1242-226934, FAX 44-1242-262111, info@e-elgar.co.uk. Ed. Charles W Howe.

354 CAN ISSN 0318-3912
TD227.M3
MANITOBA. WATER SERVICES BOARD. ANNUAL REPORT. Text in English. 1973. a. free. **Document type:** *Government.*
Published by: Water Services Board, 2022 Currie Blvd, P O Box 22080, Brandon, MB R7A 6Y9, Canada. FAX 204-726-6290. Circ: 300.

MARINE AND FRESHWATER BEHAVIOUR AND PHYSIOLOGY. *see* BIOLOGY

628.1 CAN
MARITIME PROVINCES WATER & WASTEWATER REPORT. Text in English. q. CAD 11.50 domestic; CAD 16.05 foreign (effective 2003). adv.
Published by: Transcontinental Specialty Publications (Subsidiary of: Transcontinental Media, Inc.), 11 Thornhill Dr, Dartmouth, NS B3B 1R9, Canada. TEL 902-468-8027, 800-565-2601, FAX 902-468-2322. Pub. Don Brander TEL 902-468-8027 ext 116. Adv. contact Peter Coleman TEL 902-468-8027 ext 108. page CAD 2,770. Circ: 2,567.

333.91 USA ISSN 0076-4817
MARYLAND. GEOLOGICAL SURVEY. WATER RESOURCES BASIC DATA REPORT. Text in English. 1966. irreg., latest vol.18. price varies. **Document type:** *Report, Government.*
Related titles: Online - full text ed.
Indexed: GeoRef, SpeleolAb.
Published by: Maryland Geological Survey, 2300 St Paul St, Baltimore, MD 21218. TEL 410-554-5500, FAX 410-554-5502, publications@mgs.md.gov.

333.91 ISR ISSN 0333-8835
MAYIM VE-HASHKAYA. Text in Hebrew. m. ILS 300 (effective 2001). adv.
Formerly (until 1975): 'Alon 'Irgun Ov'de Hamayim
Published by: Israel Water Works Association, 28 Gershon St., P O Box 57500, Tel Aviv, 61573, Israel. TEL 972-3-5616055, FAX 972-3-5616229. Ed. Yoseff Gur Arie.

333.9 613.1 USA
MEANDERINGS. Text in English. 19??. a., latest 2008. back issues avail. **Document type:** *Newsletter, Government.*
Related titles: Online - full text ed.
Published by: New Hampshire Department of Environmental Services, 29 Hazen Dr, PO Box 95, Concord, NH 03302. TEL 603-271-3503, mary.power@des.nh.gov, http://des.nh.gov.

628.1 KHM ISSN 1680-4023
MEKONG DEVELOPMENT SERIES. Text in English. 2001. irreg.
Indexed: ASFA, B21, ESPM.
Published by: Mekong River Commission, 364 Preah Monivong Blvd, PO Box 1112, Phnom Penh, Cambodia. TEL 855-23-720-979, FAX 855-23-720-972, mrcs@mrcmekong.org, http://www.mrcmekong.org.

628.1 KHM ISSN 1014-0360
MEKONG NEWS. Text in English. 1982. q. free (effective 2003). **Document type:** *Newsletter.* **Description:** Covers regional cooperation for water resources management, international aid.
Published by: Mekong River Commission, 364 Preah Monivong Blvd, PO Box 1112, Phnom Penh, Cambodia. TEL 855-23-720-979, FAX 855-23-720-972, mrcs@mrcmekong.org, http://www.mrcmekong.org. Ed. K I Matics. Circ: 1,500.

627 RUS ISSN 0235-2524
TC1 CODEN: MVKHEG
MELIORATSIYA I VODNOE KHOZYAISTVO. Text in Russian; Summaries in English. 1949. bi-m. USD 152 foreign (effective 2005). adv. bk.rev. bibl.; charts; illus.; maps; stat. **Document type:** *Journal, Government.*
Formerly (until 1988): Gidrotekhnika i Melioratsiya (0016-9722)
Indexed: ChemAb, GeoRef, GeotechAb, RefZh, SpeleolAb.
—CASDDS, East View, INIST, Linda Hall. **CCC.**
Published by: Vodstroi, 10 Novaya Basmannaya St, Moscow, 107078, Russian Federation. Ed. E A Nesterov. Circ: 36,500. **Dist. by:** East View Information Services, 10601 Wayzata Blvd, Minneapolis, MN 55305. TEL 952-252-1201, 800-477-1005, FAX 952-252-1202, info@eastview.com, http://www.eastview.com. **Co-sponsor:** Ministerstvo Sel'skogo Khozyaistva Rossiiskoi Federatsii.

METERING INTERNATIONAL. *see* ENGINEERING—Electrical Engineering

628 USA ISSN 0271-9606
MICHIGAN STATE UNIVERSITY. INSTITUTE OF WATER RESEARCH. ANNUAL REPORT. Text in English. 1966. a. price varies. illus. reprints avail. **Document type:** *Corporate.*
Media: Duplicated (not offset).
Indexed: GeoRef, SpeleolAb.
Published by: Michigan State University, Institute of Water Research, 115 Manly Miles Bldg, East Lansing, MI 48823. TEL 517-353-3744. Ed. Frank M D'Itri. Circ: 150.

628 USA ISSN 0580-9746
CODEN: TRMWDH
MICHIGAN STATE UNIVERSITY. INSTITUTE OF WATER RESEARCH. TECHNICAL REPORTS. Text in English. 1968. a. price varies. back issues avail.; reprints avail. **Document type:** *Monographic series.*
Indexed: SpeleolAb.
Published by: Michigan State University, Institute of Water Research, 115 Manly Miles Bldg, East Lansing, MI 48823. TEL 517-353-3742. **Subscr. to:** National Technical Information Service, Government Research Center, 5285 Port Royal Rd, Springfield, VA 22161. TEL 703-605-6060, 800-363-2068, http://www.ntis.gov.

628.168 USA
MICHIGAN WATER ENVIRONMENT MATTERS. Text in English. 1964 (vol.20). q. adv. bk.rev. illus. **Document type:** *Newsletter.* **Description:** Deals with water quality issues in Michigan for association members.
Formerly: Wastewater Works News (0043-1028)
Published by: Michigan Water Environment Association, P O Box 16058, Lansing, MI 48901-6058. TEL 517-487-1991, FAX 517-487-1992, http://www.mi-wea.org. Ed. Steve Young. Adv. contact Karen Flaherty. page USD 392. Circ: 1,300.

553.7029 LBN ISSN 0255-8564
MIDDLE EAST AND WORLD WATER DIRECTORY. Text in English. 1980. biennial. USD 110 (effective 1999). adv. **Document type:** *Directory.* **Description:** Lists importers, contractors, consulting engineers and distributors to public and private sector firms engaged in well drilling, pumping, water and waste water treatment, desalination, irrigation, water transmission, hyrdrology, groundwater, geophysical prospecting and well drilling in twenty countries in the Middle East and English speaking Africa.
Published by: Chatila Publishing House, Chouran, P O Box 13-5121, Beirut, 1102-2802, Lebanon. TEL 961-1-352413, FAX 961-1-352419. Ed., Pub. Fathi Chatila. Circ: 5,100. **Dist. by:** Current Pacific Ltd., 7 La Roche Pl, Northcote, PO Box 36-536, Auckland 0627, New Zealand. TEL 64-9-4801388, FAX 64-9-4801387, info@cplnz.com, http://www.cplnz.com.

628.1 IND
MIDSTREAM. Text in English. 19??. q. free to members (effective 2011). **Document type:** *Newsletter, Trade.*
Published by: Indian Water Works Association, MCGM Compound, Pipeline Rd, Vakola, Santacruz E, Mumbai, 400 076, India. TEL 91-22- 2667266, FAX 91-22-6168613, iwwa@rediffmail.com.

333.91 551.4 USA ISSN 0076-9614
GB1025.M8 CODEN: MGWAAE
MISSOURI. DIVISION OF GEOLOGICAL SURVEY AND WATER RESOURCES. WATER RESOURCES REPORT. Text in English. 1956. irreg., latest vol.72, 2004. price varies. back issues avail. **Document type:** *Monographic series, Government.*
Related titles: CD-ROM ed.; Online - full text ed.: free (effective 2011).
Indexed: GeoRef, SpeleolAb.
—Linda Hall.
Published by: Missouri Department of Natural Resources, Division of Geology and Land Survey, PO Box 176, Jefferson City, MO 65102. TEL 573-751-3443, 800-361-4827, contact@dnr.mo.gov.

628.1 JPN ISSN 1346-6089
MIZU JUNKAN/JOURNAL OF HYDROLOGICAL SYSTEM. Text in Japanese. 1991. q. JPY 360,000 membership (effective 2006). **Document type:** *Journal, Academic/Scholarly.*
Formerly (until 2001): Usui Gijutsu Shiryo/Rainwater Technical Report (0917-7221)
Published by: Usui Choryuu Shintou Gijutsu Kyoukai/Association for Rainwater Storage and Infiltration Technology, 3-7-1 Koji-machi, Chiyoda-ku, Tokyo, 102-0083, Japan. TEL 81-3-52759591, FAX 81-3-52759594, o-tachibana@arsit.or.jp, http://www.arsit.or.jp/.

628.1 JPN ISSN 0288-3112
MIZU SHIGEN KAIHATSU KODAN. SHIKENJO HOKOKU/WATER RESOURCES DEVELOPMENT PUBLIC CORP. LABORATORY REPORT. Text in Japanese. 1983. a.
Published by: Mizu Shigen Kaihatsu Kodan Shikenjo, 936 Jinde, Urawa-shi, Saitama-ken 338-0812, Japan.

628.1 JPN
MIZU SHIGEN KANKYO GAKKAI KENKYU TAIKAI KOEN GAIYOSHU/PROCEEDINGS OF SYMPOSIUM ON WATER RESOURCES AND ENVIRONMENT. Text in Japanese. 1984. a. **Document type:** *Proceedings.*
Published by: Mizu Shigen Kankyo Gakkai/Japanese Association for Water Resources and Environment, Green Plaza Fukagawa Tokiwa 201, -9-7 Tokiwa, Koto, Tokyo, 135-0006, Japan.

628.1 JPN ISSN 0913-8277
MIZU SHIGEN KANKYO KENKYU/JOURNAL OF WATER AND ENVIRONMENTAL ISSUES. Text in English, Japanese; Summaries in English. 1987. a. JPY 1,500. **Document type:** *Journal, Academic/Scholarly.*
Related titles: ◆ Online - full content ed.: Journal of Water and Environment Technology. ISSN 1348-2165; Online - full text ed.
Indexed: A32, ASFA, ESPM, PollutAb, SSciA, SWRA.
Published by: Mizu Shigen Kankyo Gakkai/Japanese Association for Water Resources and Environment, Green Plaza Fukagawa Tokiwa 201, -9-7 Tokiwa, Koto, Tokyo, 135-0006, Japan. FAX 81-3-3632-5352, info@jswe.or.jp, http://www.jswe.or.jp.

628.1 JPN ISSN 0285-4872
MIZU SHIGEN KENKYU SENTA KENKYU HOKOKU/WATER RESOURCES CENTER. RESEARCH REPORT. Text in English, Japanese. 1981. a. **Document type:** *Journal, Academic/Scholarly.*
Published by: (Fuzoku Mizu Shigen Kenkyu Senta), Kyoto Daigaku, Bosai Kenkyujo/Kyoto University, Disaster Prevention Research Institute, Water Resources Research Center, Gokasho, Uji-shi, Kyoto-Fu 611-0011, Japan. TEL 81-774-38-4269, FAX 81-774-32-3093. Ed. Suichi Ikebuchi. Circ: 500.

628.1 JPN
MIZU TOTOMONI. Text in Japanese. 1967. m. back issues avail.
Formerly: Mizunobori Totomoni
Related titles: Online - full content ed.
Published by: Mizu Shigen Kyokai/Japan Water Resources Association, 22-6, Nihonbashi-Kabutocho, Chuo-ku, Tokyo, 103-0026, Japan. TEL 86-3-56452991, http://www.jawa.or.jp/.

333.91 USA
MONO LAKE NEWSLETTER. Text in English. 1978. q. USD 25 (effective 2000). adv. bk.rev. charts; illus.; stat. **Document type:** *Newsletter.* **Description:** Covers the natural and human history of Mono Lake and the struggle, legal and scientific, to protect a valuable and endangered ecosystem.
Formerly (until 1982): Mono Lake Committee Newsletter (0275-6633)
Published by: Mono Lake Committee, P O Box 29, Lee Vining, CA 93541. TEL 760-647-6595, FAX 760-647-6377, http://www.monolake.org. Eds. Geoffrey McQuilkin, Arya Degenhardt. R&P Arya Degenhardt. Circ: 22,000 (paid and controlled).

628 USA
MONTANA WATER CENTER. TECHNICAL REPORTS. Text in English. 1966. 5/yr.
Formerly: Montana Water Resources Research Center. Technical Report
Media: Duplicated (not offset).
Published by: Montana Water Center, Montana State University, 101 Huffman Bldg, Bozeman, MT 59717. TEL 406-994-6690, FAX 406-994-1774. Circ: 125.

628 USA
MONTANA WATER RESOURCES CENTER. ANNUAL REPORT. Text in English. 1982. a. abstr.
Formerly: Montana Water Resources Research Center. Annual Report
Published by: Montana Water Center, Montana State University, 101 Huffman Bldg, Bozeman, MT 59717. TEL 406-994-6690.

333.91 337.2 AUS ISSN 1833-7333
MOO-OOLA. Text in English. 2006. s-a. free (effective 2009). **Document type:** *Newsletter, Consumer.* **Description:** Provides information about Inman River Catchment Group.
Related titles: Online - full text ed.: ISSN 1833-7341.
Published by: Inman River Catchment Group, PO Box 11, Victor Harbor, SA 5211, Australia. TEL 61-8-85510541, tparkinson@victor.sa.gov.au.

628.1 AUS ISSN 1839-1672
▼ **MUNDARING WEIR NEWS.** Text in English. 2011. q. free (effective 2011). **Document type:** *Newsletter, Trade.*
Media: Online - full text.
Published by: Water Corporation, 629 Newcastle St, Leederville, W.A. 6007, Australia. TEL 61-8-94237777, customer@watercorporation.com.au.

627 USA
MUNICIPAL SEWER & WATER. Text in English. 2007. m. free domestic to qualified personnel; USD 120 foreign (effective 2009). **Document type:** *Magazine, Trade.*
Indexed: A09, V03, V04.
Published by: Cole Publishing, Inc., 1720 Maple Lake Dam Rd, PO Box 220, Three Lakes, WI 54562-0220. TEL 715-546-3346, 800-257-7222, FAX 715-546-3786, http://www.colepublishing.com.

N C E WATER DIRECTORY. *see* ENGINEERING—Civil Engineering

551.48 628.1 NOR ISSN 0801-955X
N I V A. AARSBERETNING. (Norsk Institutt for Vannforskning) Text in Norwegian. 1968. a. free. illus.

Formerly (until 1983): Norsk Institutt for Vannforskning. Aarbok (0333-3280)
Published by: Norsk Institutt for Vannforskning/Norwegian Institute for Water Research, Gaustadsalleen 21, Oslo, 0349, Norway. TEL 47-22-185100, FAX 47-22-185200, niva@niva.no, http://www.niva.no.

628.1 USA
N W Q E P NOTES. (National Water Quality Evaluation Project) Text in English. q. **Document type:** *Newsletter.*
Formerly (until 198?): National Water Quality Evaluation Project Notes
Media: Online - full content.
Published by: North Carolina State University (NCSU), Water Quality Group, Campus Box 7637, Raleigh, NC 27695-7637. TEL 919-515-3723, FAX 919-515-7448. Ed. Laura Lombardo Szpir.

628.1 NZL ISSN 1177-1313
N Z W W A JOURNAL. Text in English. 5/yr. free membership (effective 2008). adv. **Document type:** *Journal, Trade.* **Description:** Covers technical innovations, equipment and products, government regulations and legislation, environmental law, industry news, and information on professional development programs and overseas conferences.
Former titles (until 2005): Water & Wastes in NZ (1170-9898); (until 1991): New Zealand Water Supply and Disposal Association. Newsletter
Indexed: GeoRef, INIS AtomInd.
—Linda Hall.
Published by: New Zealand Water and Wastes Association, PO Box 1316, Wellington, 6140, New Zealand. TEL 64-4-4728925, FAX 64-4-4728926, water@nzwwa.org.nz. Ed. Kirsten Collins TEL 64-4-9762157. Adv. contact Noeline Strange. B&W page NZD 1,190, color page NZD 2,180; 210 x 297.

627 JPN
NAGOYA DAIGAKU SUIKEN KAGAKU KENKYUJO NENPO/NAGOYA UNIVERSITY. WATER RESEARCH INSTITUTE. ANNUAL REPORT. Text in Japanese. 1974. a. illus.
Published by: Nagoya Daigaku, Suiken Kagaku Kenkyujo/Nagoya University, Water Research Institute, Furo-cho, Chikusa-ku, Nagoya-shi, Aichi-ken 464-0814, Japan.

627 665.5 622 USA ISSN 1527-1501
NATIONAL DRILLER. Abbreviated title: N D. Text in English. 1980. m. USD 104 domestic; USD 137 in Canada; USD 154 elsewhere; free to qualified personnel (print or online ed.) (effective 2009). adv. charts; illus.; tr.lit. 106 p./no.; back issues avail.; reprints avail. **Document type:** *Magazine, Trade.* **Description:** Provides information for the water well drilling, monitoring, shallow oil and gas, mining and hydrology industries, environmental, water treatment and hydrogeology.
Formerly (until 1999): National Drillers Buyers Guide (0279-7739)
Related titles: Online - full text ed.
Indexed: A10, A15, ABIn, B02, B15, B17, B18, E14, G04, G06, G07, G08, I05, P48, P51, P52, P56, PQC, V03.
—CCC.
Published by: B N P Media, 1050 IL Rte 83, Ste 200, Bensenville, IL 60106. TEL 630-616-0200, FAX 630-227-0204, portfolio@bnpmedia.com, http://www.bnpmedia.com. Ed. Greg Ettling TEL 630-694-4334. Pub. Linda Moffat TEL 530-885-6081. Adv. contact Dean Laramore. B&W page USD 3,520, color page USD 4,575; bleed 10.875 x 15. Circ: 25,000.

333.7 USA
THE NATIONAL WATER RIGHTS DIGEST. Text in English. 1995. m. USD 129 (effective 2011). back issues avail. **Document type:** *Journal, Trade.*
Related titles: E-mail ed.: USD 99 (effective 2011).
Published by: Ridenbaugh Press, PO Box 834, Carlton, OR 97111. TEL 503-852-0010, stapilus@ridenbaugh.com.

333.91 USA ISSN 0466-6992
HD1694.N2
NEBRASKA DEPARTMENT OF WATER RESOURCES. BIENNIAL REPORT. Text in English. 1958. biennial.
—Linda Hall.
Published by: Nebraska Department of Water Resources, 301 Centennial Mall South, Lincoln, NE 68509-4676. TEL 402-471-2363, FAX 402-471-2900, http://www.nrc.state.ne.us.

333.9 USA
NEBRASKA. NATURAL RESOURCES COMMISSION. STATE WATER PLANNING AND REVIEW PROCESS. Text in English. irreg. illus. **Document type:** *Government.* **Description:** Technical data on title subjects used in future planning of resources.
Formerly: Nebraska. Natural Resources Commission. State Water Plan Publication (Lincoln) (0092-6442)
Published by: Natural Resources Commission, 301 Centennial Mall South, Box 94876, Lincoln, NE 68509. TEL 402-471-2081.

628.168 NLD ISSN 1389-8329
NEERSLAG. Text in Dutch. 1965. bi-m. EUR 22.50 domestic; EUR 27.50 foreign (effective 2009). adv. illus. **Document type:** *Magazine, Trade.* **Description:** Covers issues relating to water supply, water purification and wastewater treatment.
Formerly (until 1998): Klaarmeester (1382-2586)
—IE.
Published by: Koninklijk Nederlands Waternetwerk, Postbus 70, Rijswijk, 2280 AB, Netherlands. TEL 31-70-4144778, FAX 31-70-4144420, info@waternetwerk.nl, http://www.waternetwerk.nl.

363.7284 USA
NEW ENGLAND WATER AND WASTEWATER NEWS. Text in English. 1994. 10/yr. (Sep.-June). USD 39 bulk rate; USD 49 subscr - mailed 1st class (effective 2005). **Document type:** *Newspaper, Trade.*
Formerly: Maine Water & Wastewater News
Published by: Maine Water & Wastewater News, Inc., PO Box 170, Readfield, ME 04355-0170. TEL 207-685-9322, FAX 207-685-3587. Circ: 1,100 (paid and free).

NEW ENGLAND WATER ENVIRONMENT ASSOCIATION. JOURNAL. *see* ENVIRONMENTAL STUDIES—Pollution

628.1 USA ISSN 0028-4939
TD201 CODEN: JNEWA6
➤ **NEW ENGLAND WATER WORKS ASSOCIATION. JOURNAL.** Text in English. 1882. q. USD 26 domestic to non-members; USD 48 elsewhere to non-members; free to members (effective 2011). bk.rev. charts; illus. cum.index every 10 yrs. back issues avail.; reprints avail. **Document type:** *Journal, Academic/Scholarly.* **Description:** Provides information on water supply projects and equipment throughout the New England region.
Formerly (until 1886): New England Water Works Association. Transactions
Related titles: CD-ROM ed.; Microform ed.: (from PMC, PQC).
Indexed: A22, A23, A24, A29, B13, B20, B21, CPEI, ChemAb, ChemTitl, ESPM, EngInd, FS&TA, GeoRef, I10, P06, P52, P56, PollutAb, SCOPUS, SWRA, SpeleolAb, VirolAbstr.
—BLDSC (4832.000000), CASDDS, IE, Ingenta, INIST, Linda Hall.
Published by: New England Water Works Association, 125 Hopping Brook Rd, Holliston, MA 01746. TEL 508-893-7979, FAX 508-893-9898. Ed. Peter C Karalekas Jr. TEL 413-583-8179.

➤ **NEW JERSEY ENVIRONMENTAL INFRASTRUCTURE TRUST. ANNUAL REPORT.** *see* ENVIRONMENTAL STUDIES—Waste Management

➤ **NIHON MIZUSHORI SEIBUTSU GAKKAISHI/JAPANESE JOURNAL OF WATER TREATMENT BIOLOGY.** *see* ENVIRONMENTAL STUDIES—Waste Management

628.1 JPN ISSN 0288-9455
NIHON NO KAWA/RIVERS IN JAPAN. Text in Japanese. 1973. q.
Published by: Nihon Kasen Kaihatsu Chosakai/Japanese Research Association for River Development, 44-6-403 Seki-Guchi 1-chome, Bunkyo-ku, Tokyo, 112-0014, Japan.

628.1 EGY ISSN 2090-0953
NILE WATER SCIENCE AND ENGINEERING JOURNAL. Text in English. 2008. s-a. **Document type:** *Journal, Academic/Scholarly.*
Formerly (until 2009): Nile Water Science and Engineering Magazine (2090-0066)
Related titles: Online - full text ed.: ISSN 2090-0961.
Published by: National Water Research Center, 13261 Delta Barrage, El-Qanatter El-Khayreya, Qalyoubia, Egypt. TEL 20-2-2189535.

628.1 FRA ISSN 2108-3177
▼ **NIVE26.** Text in French. 2010. 3/yr. **Document type:** *Newsletter, Consumer.*
Published by: Syndicat Mixte de l'Usine de la Nive, BP 354, Anglet Cedex, 64603, France. TEL 33-5-59424171, FAX 33-5-59422841, contact@smun.fr.

333.91 GBR ISSN 1368-2423
NORTHUMBRIAN HOLDINGS. ANNUAL REPORT. Text in English. a. free. charts; illus.; stat. **Document type:** *Corporate.* **Description:** Reports on the activities of the Northumbrian Water Group.
Supersedes (in 1996): Northumbrian Water Group. Annual Report
Published by: Northumbrian Holdings, Head Office, Abby Rd, Pity Me, Durham, DH1 5FJ, United Kingdom. TEL 44-191-284-3151, communications@nwl.co.uk.

628.1 ITA ISSN 1125-2464
CODEN: MAACD7
NOTIZIARIO DEI METODI ANALITICI. Text in Italian. 1980-1994; resumed 2003. q. free. **Document type:** *Magazine, Trade.*
Formerly (until 1995): Metodi Analitici per le Acque. Notiziario (0392-1425)
Related titles: Online - full text ed.: ISSN 1974-8345. 1995.
Indexed: INIS AtomInd.
—CASDDS.
Published by: Consiglio Nazionale delle Ricerche, Istituto di Ricerca sulle Acque, Via Salaria Km 29.300, Montelibretti, RM, Italy. http://www.irsa.cnr.it.

333.91 DEU ISSN 1434-2499
OBERIRDISCHE GEWAESSER. Text in German. 1996. irreg., latest vol.25, 2006. **Document type:** *Monographic series, Academic/Scholarly.*
Indexed: ASFA, B21, ESPM, GeoRef.
Published by: Niedersaechsischer Landesbetrieb fuer Wasserwirtschaft, Kuesten- und Naturschutz, Am Sportplatz 23, Norden, 26506, Germany. TEL 49-4931-9470, FAX 49-4931-947222, pressestelle@nlwkn-dir.niedersachsen.de, http://www.nlwkn.niedersachsen.de.

628 AUT ISSN 0945-358X
CODEN: OSWAAI
➤ **OESTERREICHISCHE WASSER- UND ABFALLWIRTSCHAFT.** Text in German. 1949. m. EUR 337, USD 358 combined subscription to institutions (print & online eds.) (effective 2012). adv. bk.rev. bibl.; charts; illus. index. reprint service avail. from PSC. **Document type:** *Journal, Academic/Scholarly.* **Description:** Discusses all technical, scientific and legal issues of common waterways.
Formerly (until 1994): Oesterreichische Wasserwirtschaft (0029-9588)
Related titles: Microform ed.: (from PQC); Online - full text ed.: ISSN 1613-7566 (from IngentaConnect).
Indexed: A22, A26, B25, BIOSIS Prev, ChemAb, E01, FLUIDEX, GEOBASE, GeoRef, GeotechAb, IBR, IBZ, ICEA, INIS AtomInd, MycolAb, SCOPUS, SpeleolAb.
—CASDDS, IE, INIST. **CCC.**
Published by: Springer Wien (Subsidiary of: Springer Science+Business Media), Sachsenplatz 4-6, Vienna, W 1201, Austria. TEL 43-1-33024150, FAX 43-1-3302426, journals@springer.at, http://www.springer.at. Ed. Fritz Randl. Adv. contact Irene Hofmann. B&W page EUR 2,220, color page EUR 2,880; 180 x 260. Circ: 5,000 (paid). **Subscr. in the Americas to:** Springer New York LLC, Journal Fulfillment, PO Box 2485, Secaucus, NJ 07096. TEL 800-777-4643, 201-348-4033, FAX 201-348-4505, journals-ny@springer.com, http://www.springer.com; **Subscr. to:** Springer Distribution Center, Kundenservice Zeitschriften, Haberstr 7, Heidelberg 69126, Germany. TEL 49-6221-3454303, FAX 49-6221-3454229, subscriptions@springer.com.

628.1 GBR
OFFICE OF WATER SERVICES ANNUAL REPORT/ADRODDIAD BLYNYDDOL A CHYFRIFON. Short title: Ofwat Annual Report. Text in English. a. GBP 14.35 (effective 2010). **Document type:** *Government.*
Related titles: Online - full text ed.: free.
Published by: (Great Britain. Water Services Regulation Authority), The Stationery Office, St Crispins, Duke St, Norwich, NR3 1PD, United Kingdom. TEL 44-1603-622211, FAX 44-870-6005533, customer.services@tso.co.uk, http://www.tso.co.uk.

333.91 344.04632 GBR
OFFICE OF WATER SERVICES INFORMATION NOTE. Short title: Ofwat Information Note. Text in English. 19??. irreg., latest 2009, Feb. back issues avail. **Document type:** *Government.*
Related titles: Online - full text ed.: free (effective 2009).
Published by: Great Britain. Water Services Regulation Authority, Centre City Tower, 7 Hill St, Birmingham, Warks B5 4UA, United Kingdom. TEL 44-121-6251300, FAX 44-121-6251400, enquiries@ofwat.gsi.gov.uk.

333.91 344.046 GBR
OFFICE OF WATER SERVICES RESEARCH PAPER. Short title: Ofwat Research Paper. Text in English. 1993. irreg., latest 2009, Feb. **Document type:** *Monographic series, Trade.*
Related titles: Online - full text ed.: free (effective 2009).
Published by: Great Britain. Water Services Regulation Authority, Centre City Tower, 7 Hill St, Birmingham, Warks B5 4UA, United Kingdom. TEL 44-121-6251300, FAX 44-121-6251400, enquiries@ofwat.gsi.gov.uk.

628.1 USA ISSN 1061-9291
ON TAP (MORGANTOWN). Text in English. 1992. q. free (effective 2004). back issues avail. **Document type:** *Magazine, Consumer.* **Description:** Reports on technical, financial, maintenance, operations and management, source water protection, and health issues relevant to small drinking water systems.
Related titles: Online - full content ed.
Indexed: A32.
—BLDSC (6256.751040), IE, Ingenta.
Published by: National Drinking Water Clearinghouse, West Virginia University, P.O. Box 6064, Morgantown, WV 26506-6064. TEL 304-293-4191, 800-624-8301, kjespers@wvu.edu, http://www.nesc.wvu.edu/ndwc/ndwc_index.htm. Ed. Kathy Jesperson. Circ: 24,000.

OPFLOW. *see* ENGINEERING

OREGON. DEPARTMENT OF GEOLOGY AND MINERAL INDUSTRIES. COASTAL HAZARD PUBLICATION. *see* EARTH SCIENCES—Geology

333.91 JPN
OSAKA MUNICIPAL WATER WORKS BUREAU. WATER EXAMINATION LABORATORY. ANNUAL REPORT. Text in Japanese. 1949. a. free. **Document type:** *Bulletin.*
Published by: Osaka Municipal Water Works Bureau, Water Examination Laboratory, 1-3-14 Kunijima, Higashiyodogawa-ku, Osaka-shi, 533-0024, Japan. TEL 81-6-6815-2365, FAX 81-6-6320-3259. Ed. Hiroshi Kozasa. Circ: 500.

OZONE: SCIENCE & ENGINEERING. *see* ENGINEERING—Chemical Engineering

333.91 ITA ISSN 2037-4070
P R U E. (Programmi Ricerca Unione Europea) Text in Italian. 2008. q. **Document type:** *Bulletin, Trade.*
Media: Online - full text.
Published by: Istituto Superiore per la Protezione e la Ricerca Ambientale (I S P R A), Via Vitaliano Brancati 48, Rome, 00144, Italy. TEL 39-06-50071, FAX 39-06-50072916, http://www.isprambiente.it.

PADDY AND WATER ENVIRONMENT. *see* AGRICULTURE—Crop Production And Soil

PASSAIC RIVER REVIEW. *see* CONSERVATION

333.91 USA ISSN 1060-0043
TD760
PIPELINE (MORGANTOWN). Text in English. 1990. s-a. **Document type:** *Newsletter, Consumer.* **Description:** Each issues focuses on a topic relating to wastewater. Topics include septic systems, watersheds, EPA guidelines and drainage, for homeowners, community officials, inspectors and educators.
Related titles: Online - full text ed.: ISSN 1939-8662.
Published by: The National Small Flows Clearinghouse (N S F C), West Virginia University, PO Box 6064, Morgantown, WV 26506. TEL 304-293-4191, 800-624-8301, FAX 304-293-3161, info@mail.nesc.wvu.edu. Ed. Kathy Jesperson.

POLISH ACADEMY OF SCIENCES. INSTITUTE OF GEOPHYSICS. PUBLICATIONS. SERIES E: WATER RESOURCES. *see* EARTH SCIENCES—Geophysics

333.011 627 POL
POLITECHNIKA KRAKOWSKA. MONOGRAFIE. SERIA: INZYNIERIA SANITARNA I WODNA. Text in Polish; Summaries in English, French, German, Russian. 1985. irreg. price varies. bibl.; charts; illus. **Document type:** *Monographic series, Academic/Scholarly.*
Related titles: ◆ Series of: Politechnika Krakowska. Monografie. ISSN 0860-097X.
Published by: Politechnika Krakowska im. Tadeusza Kosciuszki/Tadeusz Kosciuszko Cracow University of Technology, ul Warszawska 24, Krakow, 31155, Poland. TEL 48-12-6374289, FAX 48-12-6374289. Ed. Elzbieta Nachlik. Adv. contact Ewa Malochleb. Circ: 200.

333.91 627 POL
POLITECHNIKA KRAKOWSKA. ZESZYTY NAUKOWE. INZYNIERIA SANITARNA I WODNA. Text in Polish; Summaries in English, French, German, Russian. 1957. irreg. price varies. bibl.; charts; illus. **Document type:** *Monographic series, Academic/Scholarly.*
Former titles: Politechnika Krakowska. Zeszyty Naukowe. Inzynieria Srodowiska (1425-901X); (until no.45, 1994): Politechnika Krakowska. Zeszyty Naukowe. Inzynieria Sanitarna i Wodna (0867-177X); Politechnika Krakowska. Zeszyty Naukowe. Budownictwo Wodne i Inzynieria Sanitarna (0137-1363)
—Linda Hall.
Published by: Politechnika Krakowska im. Tadeusza Kosciuszki/Tadeusz Kosciuszko Cracow University of Technology, ul Warszawska 24, Krakow, 31155, Poland. TEL 48-12-6374289, FAX 48-12-6374289. Ed. Elzbieta Nachlik. Adv. contact Ewa Malochleb. Circ: 200.

628.1 GBR
POLLUTION INCIDENTS IN ENGLAND AND WALES. Text in English. 1992. irreg. free (effective 2010). **Document type:** *Bulletin, Consumer.*
Formerly: Water Pollution Incidents in England and Wales (1358-328X)

Published by: Environment Agency, PO Box 544, Rotherham, S60 1BY, United Kingdom. TEL 44-870-8506506, enquiries@environment-agency.gov.uk.

628 POL ISSN 0079-3477
POLSKA AKADEMIA NAUK. KOMITET GOSPODARKI WODNEJ. PRACE I STUDIA. Text in Polish. 1956. irreg. (2/yr.). price varies. **Document type:** *Monographic series, Academic/Scholarly.*
Published by: Polska Akademia Nauk, Komitet Gospodarki Wodnej/ Polish Academy of Sciences, Committee on Water Resources Management, Koscierska 7, Gdansk, 80953, Poland. kgw@ibwpan.gda.pl, http://www.ibwpan.gda.pl. Ed. W Majewski.

628.167 USA ISSN 1072-8627
HD1695.P65
POTOMAC BASIN REPORTER. Text in English. 6/yr. free (effective 2011). bk.rev. back issues avail. **Document type:** *Newsletter, Trade.* **Description:** Deals with current events involving the Potomac River and issues of water quality, supply, and recreation.
Incorporates (1988-1994): In the Anacostia Watershed (1061-2513); Formerly (until 1971): Interstate Commission on the Potomac River Basin. Newsletter
Related titles: Online - full text ed.
Indexed: GeoRef, SpeleolAb.
Published by: Interstate Commission on the Potomac River Basin, 51 Monroe St, Ste PE-08, Rockville, MD 20850. TEL 301-984-1908, info@icprb.org, http://www.potomacriver.org. Eds. Curtis M Dalpra, Jennifer D Willoughby. Circ: 20,000 (controlled).

354.712 CAN ISSN 0704-8726
TC427.P7
PRAIRIE PROVINCES WATER BOARD ANNUAL REPORT. Text in English. 1972. a. free. **Document type:** *Government.*
Published by: Prairie Provinces Water Board, Park Plaza, Rm 300, 2365 Albert St, Regina, SK S4P 4K1, Canada. TEL 306-780-7004. Circ: 400.

363.6 CAN ISSN 1027-2798
GB1627.G8
(YEAR) PRIORITIES AND PROGRESS UNDER THE GREAT LAKES WATER QUALITY AGREEMENT. Text in French, English. 1975. biennial. free. charts; stat. reprints avail.
Incorporates: Great Lakes Science Advisory Board. Report (0845-1214); Formerly: Great Lakes Research Advisory Board. Annual Report (0710-8702)
Related titles: Microfilm ed.: (from PQC).
Indexed: EnvAb, SpeleolAb.
—Linda Hall.
Published by: International Joint Commission, Great Lakes Regional Office/Commission Mixte Internationale, 100 Ouellette Ave, 8th Fl, Windsor, ON N9A 6T3, Canada. TEL 519-257-6700, FAX 519-257-6740.

PROBLEMY OSVOENIYA PUSTYN'. *see* AGRICULTURE

627 351.791 NLD ISSN 1877-2137
PROGRAMMADIRECTIE RUIMTE VOOR DE RIVIER. VOORTGANGSRAPPORTAGE. Variant title: Voortgangsrapportage Ruimte voor de Rivier. Text in Dutch. 200?. s-a.
Published by: Programmadirectie Ruimte voor de Rivier, Postbus 24103, Utrecht, 3502 MC, Netherlands. TEL 31-88-7972900, info@ruimtevoorderivier.nl.

PROGRESS IN WATER RESOURCES. *see* ENGINEERING

333.91 USA
PURDUE UNIVERSITY. INDIANA WATER RESOURCES RESEARCH CENTER. ANNUAL REPORT. Text in English. 1966. a. **Document type:** *Corporate.*
Media: Online - full text.
Indexed: SpeleolAb.
Published by: Purdue University, Indiana Water Resources Research Center, Potter Engineering Center, W. Lafayette, IN 47907-1284. TEL 317-494-8041, FAX 317-494-2720. Ed. Jeff R Wright.

333.91 USA ISSN 0555-8026
TD201 CODEN: PWRTBM
PURDUE UNIVERSITY. WATER RESOURCES RESEARCH CENTER. TECHNICAL REPORT. Text in English. 1966. irreg. **Document type:** *Monographic series.*
Indexed: GeoRef.
Published by: Purdue University, Indiana Water Resources Research Center, West Lafayette, IN 47907. TEL 765-494-8041, FAX 765-496-3210, esei@ecn.purdue.edu, http://www.ecn.purdue.edu/WRRC/.

628.1 USA ISSN 0270-0433
TD225.C664
QUALITY OF WATER, COLORADO RIVER BASIN, PROGRESS REPORT. Text in English. 1963. biennial. free (effective 2011). **Document type:** *Report, Government.*
Related titles: Online - full text ed.
Indexed: GeoRef.
Published by: U.S. Department of the Interior, 1849 C St., NW, Washington, DC 20240. TEL 202-208-3100, http://www.doi.gov.

628.1 USA ISSN 1559-6281
QUALITY ON TAP. Text in English. 2005. q. **Document type:** *Newsletter, Consumer.*
Published by: Mid-Dakota Rural Water System, Inc., PO Box 318, Miller, SD 57362-0318. TEL 605-853-3159, FAX 605-853-3245, office@mdrws.com, http://www.mdrws.com.

333.91 AUS ISSN 1837-4832
QUEENSLAND WATER COMMISSION. ANNUAL REPORT. Text in English. 2005. a. free (effective 2011). back issues avail. **Document type:** *Report, Government.* **Description:** Covers details of the financial and non-financial performance of the Queensland Water Commission.
Related titles: Online - full text ed.: ISSN 1838-1596.
Published by: Queensland Water Commission, PO Box 15087, City East, QLD 4002, Australia. FAX 61-7-32278227, qwcenquiries@qwc.qld.gov.au.

RECHT UND STEUERN IM GAS- UND WASSERFACH. *see* PETROLEUM AND GAS

RENMIN HUANG HE/PEOPLE'S YELLOW RIVER. *see* GEOGRAPHY

REPORT ON THE INDUSTRIAL DIRECT DISCHARGES IN ONTARIO. *see* ENVIRONMENTAL STUDIES

REVISTA ACODAL. *see* ENVIRONMENTAL STUDIES—Waste Management

628.1 CHL ISSN 0717-2117
K19
REVISTA DE DERECHO DE AGUAS. Text in Spanish. 1990. a. USD 60. **Document type:** *Journal, Academic/Scholarly.*
Supersedes in part (in 1993): Revista de Derecho de Minas y Aguas (0716-9620)
Published by: Universidad de Atacama, Instituto de Derecho de Minas y Aguas, casilla 240, Copiapo, Chile. TEL 56-52-212005, FAX 56-52-212662, http://www.uda.cl.

REVUE DES SCIENCES DE L'EAU (ONLINE)/JOURNAL OF WATER SCIENCE. *see* EARTH SCIENCES—Hydrology

556 DEU ISSN 0939-0804
RHEINGUTEBERICHT N R W. (Nordrhein-Westfalen) Text in German. 1989. irreg. **Document type:** *Monographic series, Academic/ Scholarly.*
Indexed: ASFA, B21, ESPM, GeoRef.
Published by: Landesumweltamt Nordrhein-Westfalen, Wallneyer Str. 6, Essen, 45133, Germany. TEL 49-201-7995-0, FAX 49-201-79951448, poststelle@lua.nrw.de, http://www.lua.nrw.de.

628.1 NLD
RIONEDNIEUWS. Text in Dutch. 2004. q. free (effective 2011). **Document type:** *Newsletter, Consumer.*
Formerly (until 2008): Stichting Rioned. Nieuwsbrief (Online)
Media: Online - full text.
Published by: Stichting RIONED, Postbus 133, Ede, 6710 BC, Netherlands. TEL 31-318-631111, FAX 31-318-633337, info@rioned.org, http://www.riool.net.

RISK-BASED DECISION MAKING IN WATER RESOURCES. *see* ENGINEERING—Civil Engineering

333.9 GBR ISSN 1535-1459
TC530 CODEN: RRAIAQ
➤ **RIVER RESEARCH AND APPLICATIONS**; an international journal devoted to river research and management. Text in English. 1986. 10/yr. GBP 1,298 in United Kingdom to institutions; EUR 1,640 in Europe to institutions; USD 2,541 elsewhere to institutions; GBP 1,493 combined subscription in United Kingdom to institutions (print & online eds.); EUR 1,887 combined subscription in Europe to institutions (print & online eds.); USD 2,923 combined subscription elsewhere to institutions (print & online eds.) (effective 2012). adv. bk.rev. illus.; maps. back issues avail.; reprint service avail. from PSC. **Document type:** *Journal, Academic/Scholarly.* **Description:** Covers interdisciplinary research and covers activity from the effects of major dams, weirs, canalization and more; includes original papers.
Formerly (until 2002): Regulated Rivers (0886-9375)
Related titles: Microform ed.: (from PQC); Online - full text ed.: ISSN 1535-1467. GBP 1,298 in United Kingdom to institutions; EUR 1,640 in Europe to institutions; USD 2,541 elsewhere to institutions (effective 2012).
Indexed: A22, A28, A32, A34, A37, A38, APA, ASCA, ASFA, Agr, AgrForAb, B21, B23, B25, BIOSIS Prev, BrCerAb, C&ISA, C25, C30, CA/WCA, CABA, CIA, CerAb, CivEngAb, CorrAb, CurCont, D01, E&CAJ, E04, E05, E11, E12, E17, EEA, EIA, EMA, ESPM, EntAb, EnvAb, EnvEAb, EnvInd, F08, F11, F12, FR, G11, GEOBASE, GH, GeoRef, H15, H16, HPNRM, I11, ICEA, ISR, IndVet, LT, M&TEA, M09, MBF, METADEX, MycolAb, N02, OR, P32, P33, P37, P39, P40, PGegResA, PGrRegA, PollutAb, R07, R08, R12, RRTA, S12, S13, S16, S17, SCI, SCOPUS, SSciA, SWRA, SolStAb, SpeleolAb, T04, T05, TAR, VS, W07, W10, W11, WAA, WildRev, Z01.
—IE, Ingenta, INIST, Linda Hall. **CCC.**
Published by: John Wiley & Sons Ltd. (Subsidiary of: John Wiley & Sons, Inc.), 1-7 Oldlands Way, PO Box 808, Bognor Regis, West Sussex PO21 9FF, United Kingdom. TEL 44-1865-778315, FAX 44-1243-843232, cs-journals@wiley.com, http://eu.wiley.com/WileyCDA/. Ed. G E Petts. **Subscr. in the Americas to:** John Wiley & Sons, Inc., 111 River St, Hoboken, NJ 07030. TEL 201-748-6645, subinfo@wiley.com; **Subscr. to:** 1-7 Oldlands Way, PO Box 809, Bognor Regis, West Sussex PO21 9FG, United Kingdom. TEL 44-1865-778054, cs-agency@wiley.com.

➤ **ROTIFER NEWS**; a newsletter for rotiferologist throughout the world. *see* BIOLOGY—Zoology

333.91 363.7394 628.168 USA
RURAL WATER. Text in English. 2003. q. adv. back issues avail. **Document type:** *Magazine, Trade.* **Description:** Addresses timely topics and important concerns of the rural water supply.
Related titles: Online - full text ed.
Published by: (National Rural Water Association), Naylor LLC, 5950 NW 1st Pl, Gainesville, FL 32607. TEL 800-369-6220, FAX 352-331-3525, http://www.naylor.com. Ed. Colleen Raccioppi. adv.: color page USD 4,859.50, B&W page USD 3,959.50; trim 8.375 x 10.875.

628.1 AUS ISSN 1837-7475
RURAL WATER SERVICE PROVIDERS. NATIONAL PERFORMANCE REPORT. Text in English. 2007. a. free (effective 2010). back issues avail. **Document type:** *Report, Government.*
Related titles: Online - full text ed.: ISSN 1837-7483.
Published by: Australian Government, National Water Commission, 95 Northbourne Ave, Canberra, ACT 2600, Australia. TEL 61-2-61026000, FAX 61-2-61026006, enquiries@nwc.gov.au.

333.91 AUS ISSN 1834-0016
S A WATER. DRINKING WATER QUALITY REPORT. (South Australian) Text in English. 2000. a. back issues avail. **Document type:** *Report, Trade.* **Description:** Focuses on many water quality initiatives and research activities.
Related titles: Online - full text ed.: ISSN 1834-0024. free (effective 2009).
Published by: South Australian Water Corporation, EDS Ctr, 108 N Terrace, Adelaide, SA 5000, Australia. TEL 300-650-950, FAX 61-8-70033329, customerservice@sawater.com.au.

333.91 AUS ISSN 1834-0008
S A WATER. SUSTAINABILITY REPORT. (South Australian) Text in English. 1999. biennial. back issues avail. **Document type:** *Report, Trade.* **Description:** Provides details of sustainability performance for both 2005-06 and 2006-07 financial periods.
Formerly (until 2003): South Australian Water Corporation. Environmental Report
Media: Online - full text. **Related titles:** Print ed.: ISSN 1833-9999.
Published by: South Australian Water Corporation, EDS Ctr, 108 N Terrace, Adelaide, SA 5000, Australia. TEL 300-650-950, FAX 61-8-70033329, customerservice@sawater.com.au.

628.1 SWE ISSN 1404-2134
S I W I PROCEEDINGS. Text in Swedish, English. 1992. irreg. **Document type:** *Monographic series.*
Formerly (until 1997): Stockholm Water Symposium. Proceedings (1103-0127)
Indexed: ASFA, B21, GeoRef.
Published by: Stockholm International Water Institute, Drottninggatan 33, Stockholm, 11151, Sweden. TEL 46-8-52213960, FAX 46-8-52213961, siwi@siwi.org.

614.8 627.5 USA ISSN 0270-4447
T55.A1
SAFETY NEWS. Text in English. 1937. q. membership. charts; illus.; stat.
Former titles (until 1979): Reclamation Safety News (0034-1436); Reclamation Safety Record
Indexed: BibAg, CISA.
Published by: Bureau of Reclamation, Safety Office, Denver Federal Center, PO Box 25007, Denver, CO 80225-0007. TEL 303-445-3750, 888-231-7749, FAX 303-445-6570, 888-808-5104, http://www.usbr.gov. Circ: 550.

627 JPN
SAKUSEI. Text in Japanese. 1967. irreg.
Published by: Zenkoku Sakusei Kyokai/National Water Well Association of Japan, 5-1, Hatchobbori 2-chome, Chuo-ku, Tokyo, 104, Japan.

333.9 613.1 USA
THE SAMPLER. Text in English. 19??. a. free (effective 2011). back issues avail. **Document type:** *Newsletter, Government.*
Related titles: Online - full text ed.
Published by: New Hampshire Department of Environmental Services, 29 Hazen Dr, PO Box 95, Concord, NH 03302. TEL 603-271-3503, mary.power@des.nh.gov, http://des.nh.gov. Ed. Sara Steiner TEL 603-271-2658.

333.91 USA ISSN 1546-2366
QH75.A1
➤ **SAN FRANCISCO ESTUARY AND WATERSHED SCIENCE.** Abbreviated title: S F E W S. Text in English. 2003. 3/yr. free (effective 2011). back issues avail. **Document type:** *Journal, Academic/ Scholarly.* **Description:** Brings out research about the science and resource management of San Francisco Bay, the Sacramento-San Joaquin River Delta, and the upstream watersheds.
Media: Online - full text.
Indexed: A39, ASFA, B21, C27, C29, D03, D04, E11, E13, ESPM, PollutAb, R14, S14, S15, S18, SSciA, SWRA, T04, Z01.
Published by: (University of California at Davis, John Muir Institute of the Environment), eScholarship (Subsidiary of: California Digital Library), 300 Lakeside Dr, 7th Fl, Oakland, CA 94612. TEL 510-587-6439, FAX 510-987-0243, info@escholarship.org, http://www.escholarship.org. Ed. Samuel N Luoma.

➤ **SASKATCHEWAN HORIZONTAL WELL SUMMARY.** *see* PETROLEUM AND GAS

628.1 GBR ISSN 2040-6576
▼ **SAUDI ARABIA WATER REPORT.** Text in English. 2010. q. USD 975, EUR 695 combined subscription (print & email eds.) (effective 2011). **Document type:** *Report, Trade.* **Description:** Provides industry professionals and strategists, sector analysts, business investors, trade associations and regulatory bodies with independent forecasts and competitive intelligence on the Water industry in Saudi Arabia.
Related titles: E-mail ed.
Published by: Business Monitor International Ltd., Senator House, 85 Queen Victoria St, London, EC4V 4AB, United Kingdom. TEL 44-20-72480468, FAX 44-20-72480467, subs@businessmonitor.com.

628.1 NLD ISSN 2210-7533
SCHELDESTROMEN. Text in Dutch. 1996. q. **Document type:** *Magazine, Trade.*
Formerly (until 2010): Waterwerker (1385-6413)
Published by: Waterschap Scheldestromen, Postbus 1000, Middelburg, 4330 ZW, Netherlands. http://www.scheldestromen.nl.

SCIENCE ET CHANGEMENTS PLANETAIRES - SECHERESSE. *see* ENVIRONMENTAL STUDIES

333.91 USA
SEDIMENTATION AND CENTRIFUGATION NEWSLETTER. Text in English. 1980. m. looseleaf. abstr.; charts; illus.; pat. back issues avail. **Document type:** *Newsletter, Trade.* **Description:** Covers all aspects of centrifuges, thickeners, cyclones and flotation, including chemicals and components.
Related titles: Online - full text ed.
Published by: McIlvaine Company, 191 Waukegan Rd, Ste 208, Northfield, IL 60093. TEL 847-784-0012, FAX 847-784-0061, editor@mcilvainecompany.com, http://www.mcilvainecompany.com. Pub. Robert McIlvaine.

SEESPIEGEL; Information rund um den Bodensee. *see* CONSERVATION

333.91 639.2 USA ISSN 8755-4682
SEICHE. Text in English. 1976. q. free. back issues avail. **Document type:** *Newsletter.* **Description:** Covers issues related to the Great Lakes: fisheries, policy, research and education.
Indexed: Agr.
Published by: University of Minnesota, Sea Grant Program, 2305 E Fifth St, Duluth, MN 55812. TEL 218-726-7677, FAX 218-726-6556. Ed., R&P Marie Zhuikov. Circ: 3,000.

628 USA ISSN 0892-9548
TD1
SENSUS WATER JOURNAL; devoted to the operation and management of water works. Key Title: Water Journal. Text in English. 1908. a. free. charts; illus. Supplement avail. **Document type:** *Journal, Trade.*
Formerly: Rockwell Water Journal
Published by: Sensus Technologies, Inc., 450 N Gallatin Ave, Box 487, Uniontown, PA 15401. TEL 724-439-7700, FAX 724-430-3959. Ed. R D Neely. Pub. D Harness. R&P Jack Pektas. Circ: 15,000 (controlled).

628.1 GBR
SEVERN TRENT PLC. ANNUAL REPORT AND ACCOUNTS (YEAR). Text in English. 1989. a. free (effective 2009). **Document type:** *Corporate.* **Description:** Highlights the organization's performance during the financial year.

Former titles (until 1993): Severn Trent Plc. Report and Accounts; (until 1990): Severn Trent Water. Report And Accounts
Related titles: Online - full text ed.: free (effective 2009).
Published by: Severn Trent Plc., 2297 Coventry Rd, Sheldon, Birmingham, Warks B26 3PU, United Kingdom. TEL 44-121-7224000, FAX 44-121-7224800, groupcommunications@stplc.com.

628.1 GBR
SEVERN TRENT WATER. DRINKING WATER QUALITY (YEAR). Text in English. 1990. a. **Document type:** *Corporate.*
Published by: Severn-Trent Water Authority, Abelson House, 2297 Coventry Rd, Sheldon, Birmingham, Warks B26 3PU, United Kingdom. TEL 0121-722-4000, FAX 0121-722-4800.

SHANXI SHUITU BAOCHI KEJI/SOIL AND WATER CONSERVATION SCIENCE AND TECHNOLOGY IN SHANXI. *see* CONSERVATION

621.69 CHN ISSN 1002-7424
SHUIBENG JISHU/PUMP TECHNOLOGY. Text in Chinese. 1965. bi-m. **Document type:** *Journal, Academic/Scholarly.*
Published by: Shenyang Shuibeng Yanjiusuo, 16, Kaifa Dalu, Jingji Kaifa-qu, Shenyang, 110142, China. TEL 86-24-25801520, FAX 86-24-25801522.

333.91 550 CHN ISSN 0559-9342
SHUILI FADIAN/HYDROELECTRIC POWER. Text in Chinese; Abstracts in English. 1954. m. USD 43.20 (effective 2009). adv.
Related titles: Online - full text ed.
Indexed: A32, SCOPUS.
—East View, Linda Hall.
Published by: (Shuili Shuidian Guihua Sheji Zong Yuan/Institute of Water Resources and Hydropower Planning), Shuili Fadian Zhishe, 65 Ande Lu, Xicheng-qu, Beijing, 100011, China. TEL 86-10-8207-7971, FAX 86-10-8207-7971. Ed. Huo Xiaoguang. Adv. contact Lian Cheng Ma. Circ: 15,000. **Dist. by:** China International Book Trading Corp, 35 Chegongzhuang Xilu, Haidian District, PO Box 399, Beijing 100044, China.

628.1 CHN ISSN 1006-7647
SHUILI SHUIDIAN KEJI JINZHAN/ADVANCES IN SCIENCE AND TECHNOLOGY OF WATER RESOURCES. Text in Chinese. 1981. bi-m. CNY 5 newsstand/cover (effective 2006). **Document type:** *Journal, Academic/Scholarly.*
Related titles: Online - full text ed.
Indexed: A28, APA, BrCerAb, C&ISA, CA/WCA, CIA, CerAb, CivEngAb, CorrAb, E&CAJ, E11, EEA, EMA, ESPM, EnvEAb, H15, M&TEA, M09, MBF, METADEX, PollutAb, SSciA, SWRA, SolStAb, T04, WAA.
Published by: Hehai Daxue, 1 Xikang Rd, Nanjing, Jiangsu 210098, China. TEL 86-25-83786335, FAX 86-25-83787381.

628.1 551.4 CHN ISSN 1672-3279
SHUILI SHUIWEN ZIDONGHUA/AUTOMATION IN WATER RESOURCES AND HYDROLOGY. Text in Chinese. 1983. q. CNY 4 newsstand/cover (effective 2006). **Document type:** *Journal, Academic/Scholarly.*
Related titles: Online - full text ed.
Published by: Nanjing Shuili Shuiwen Zidonghua Yanjiusuo, 85, Teixinqiao, Nanjing, 210012, China. TEL 86-25-52898331, FAX 86-25-52898315.

628.1 CHN ISSN 1002-3305
SHUILI TIANDI/WATER CONSERVANCY WORLD. Text in Chinese. m. **Document type:** *Journal, Academic/Scholarly.*
Address: 4-1, Wenzhong Jie, Ha'erbing, 150001, China. TEL 86-451-82625971.

628.1 720 CHN ISSN 1672-1144
SHUILI YU JIANZHU GONGCHENG XUEBAO/JOURNAL OF WATER RESOURCES AND ARCHITECTURAL ENGINEERING. Text in Chinese. 1995. q. CNY 8 newsstand/cover (effective 2006). **Document type:** *Journal, Academic/Scholarly.*
Related titles: Online - full text ed.
Published by: Xibei Nong-Lin Keji Daxue, 23, Weihui Lu, Yangling, 712100, China. TEL 86-29-87082937.

628.1 CHN ISSN 1674-3075
SHUISHENGTAI XUE/JOURNAL OF HYDROECOLOGY. Text in Chinese. 1981. bi-m. **Document type:** *Journal, Academic/Scholarly.*
Former titles (until 2008): Shuili Yuye/Reservoir Fisheries (1003-1278); (until 1986): Shuiku Yuye
Related titles: Online - full text ed.
Published by: Shuilibu Zhongguo Kexueyuan Shui Gongcheng Shengtai Yanjiusuo/Institute of Hydroecology, Ministry of Water Resources & Chinese Academy of Sciences, 578 Xiongchu Ave., Wuhan, Hubei 430079, China. TEL 86-27-87189555, FAX 86-27-87189555, http://www.ihe.ac.cn/.

LES SLOVENSKE LESOKRUHY. *see* FORESTS AND FORESTRY

SOCIETY & NATURAL RESOURCES. *see* ENVIRONMENTAL STUDIES

363.7 USA ISSN 0732-9393
QH87.3
SOCIETY OF WETLAND SCIENTISTS. BULLETIN. Text in English. 198?. irreg. membership. **Document type:** *Bulletin.*
Related titles: Online - full text ed.: ISSN 1943-6254.
Indexed: A22, A36, A37, B21, B23, BiolDig, C25, C30, CABA, E01, E12, ESPM, F08, GH, GeoRef, P33, PollutAb, R08, S13, SpeleolAb, TAR, W10, W11.
—INIST, Linda Hall. **CCC.**
Published by: Society of Wetland Scientists, 1313 Dolley Madison Blvd, Ste 402, McLean, VA 66044. TEL 703-790-1745, FAX 703-790-2672, sws@burkinc.com, http://www.sws.org/.

631.5 CZE ISSN 1801-5395
➤ **SOIL AND WATER RESEARCH.** Text in English. 2006. q. USD 85 (effective 2008). **Document type:** *Journal, Academic/Scholarly.* **Description:** Publishes original papers, short communications and critical reviews from all fields of science and engineering related to soil and water and their interactions in natural and man-modified landscapes, with a particular focus on agricultural land use.
Supersedes in part (in 2006): Soil and Water (1213-8673); Which was formerly (until 2002): Vyzkumny Ustav Melioraci a Ochrany Pudy. Vedecke Prace (1210-1672); (until 1991): Vyzkumny Ustav pro Zurodneni Zemedelskych Pud. Vedecke Prace (0231-8172); (until 1982): Vyzkumny Ustav Melioraci v Praze. Vedecke Prace (0375-4944)
Related titles: Online - full text ed.
Indexed: A34, A37, AgrForAb, C25, C30, CABA, D01, E12, F08, F12, FCA, G11, H16, I11, LT, MaizeAb, O01, OR, P32, P38, P40, R07, RRTA, S12, S13, S16, SCOPUS, TAR, TriticAb, W10, W11.
Published by: Ceska Akademie Zemedelskych Ved, Ustav Zemedelskych a Potravinarskych Informaci/Czech Academy of Agricultural Sciences, Institute of Agricultural and Food Information, Slezska 7, Prague 2, 120 56, Czech Republic. TEL 420-2-227010352, FAX 420-2-227010116, editor@uzpi.cz, http://www.uzpi.cz, http://www.cazv.cz. Ed. Josef Kozak.

613.1 333.9 USA
THE SOURCE (CONCORD). Text in English. 19??. q. free (effective 2011). back issues avail. **Document type:** *Newsletter, Government.*
Related titles: Online - full text ed.
Published by: New Hampshire Department of Environmental Services, 29 Hazen Dr, PO Box 95, Concord, NH 03302. TEL 603-271-3503, mary.power@des.nh.gov, http://des.nh.gov. Eds. Holly Green, Pierce Rigrod TEL 603-271-0688.

628.1 NLD ISSN 1874-6594
SOURCES NOUVELLES. Text in French. 1991. q.
Related titles: Online - full text ed.: ISSN 1572-4786.
Published by: IRC International Water and Sanitation Centre/IRC Centre International de l'Eau et de l'Assainissement, PO Box 82327, The Hague, 2508 EH, Netherlands. TEL 31-70-3044000, FAX 31-70-3044044, general@irc.nl, http://www.irc.nl. Ed. Caridad M Camacho.

333.91 ZAF
SOUTH AFRICA. WATER RESEARCH COMMISSION. TECHNICAL REPORT. Text in English. 1971. a., latest 2000. free. charts; illus.; stat. **Document type:** *Corporate.* **Description:** Covers the research activities of the Commission. Also lists publications issued from research connected with the Commission.
Formerly: South Africa. Water Research Commission. Annual Report
Indexed: SpeleolAb.
Published by: Water Research Commission/Waternavorsingskommissie, PO Box 824, Pretoria, 0001, South Africa. TEL 27-12-3300340, FAX 27-12-3312565. Ed. Ingrid Buchan. Circ: 2,000.

SOUTHERN CALIFORNIA COASTAL WATER RESEARCH PROJECT. ANNUAL REPORT. *see* ENVIRONMENTAL STUDIES—Waste Management

SPILDEVANDSTEKNISK TIDSSKRIFT; environmental studies - waste management. *see* ENVIRONMENTAL STUDIES—Waste Management

628.1 USA ISSN 8755-3546
QD142
STANDARD METHODS FOR THE EXAMINATION OF WATER AND WASTEWATER. Text in English. 1905. irreg. USD 295 per issue to individuals (effective 2010). **Document type:** *Journal, Academic/Scholarly.* **Description:** Covers all aspects of water and wastewater analysis techniques.
Former titles (until 1960): Standard Methods for the Examination of Water, Sewage, and Industrial Wastes; (until 1946): Standard Methods for the Examination of Water and Sewage; (until 1912): American Public Health Association. Committee on Standard Methods of Water Analysis to the Laboratory Section. Report
Related titles: CD-ROM ed.
Indexed: GeoRef.
—CCC.
Published by: (American Water Works Association), American Public Health Association, 800 I St, NW, Washington, DC 20001. TEL 202-777-2742, FAX 202-777-2534, comments@apha.org, http://www.apha.org.

628.1 USA
STATE AND FEDERAL WATER PROGRAMS. Text in English. 1989. every 3 yrs. free. **Description:** Provides access to information on all state and federal water programs and contacts operating in Kansas.
Formerly: Water Programs Manual
Related titles: Online - full text ed.
Published by: Kansas Water Office, 901 South Kansas Ave, Topeka, KS 66612-1249. TEL 785-296-0866, FAX 785-296-0878. Ed. John Gottschamer.

628.1 AUS
STATE WATER. ANNUAL REPORT. Text in English. 2002. a. free (effective 2009). **Document type:** *Government.*
Formerly (until 2003): State Water. Annual Activities Report (1448-7551)
Media: Online - full text. **Related titles:** CD-ROM ed.; Print ed.
Published by: New South Wales, State Water Corporation, PO Box 1018, Dubbo, NSW 2830, Australia. TEL 61-2-68412000, FAX 61-2-68842603, statewater@statewater.com.au, http://www.statewater.com.au.

628.1 AUS ISSN 1833-640X
STATE WATER REPORT. Text in English. 2004. a. free (effective 2008). **Document type:** *Government.* **Description:** Provides an annual overview of water availability and use across Victoria at bulk supply level.
Related titles: Online - full text ed.: ISSN 1833-6418. 2006.
Published by: Victoria. Department of Sustainability and Environment, 8 Nicholson St, East Melbourne, VIC 3002, Australia. TEL 61-3-53325000, customer.service@dse.vic.gov.au, http://www.dse.vic.gov.au/dse/index.htm.

628.1 SWE ISSN 1102-7053
STOCKHOLM WATER FRONT. Text in English. 1992. q. adv. back issues avail. **Document type:** *Magazine, Consumer.*
Related titles: Online - full text ed.
Indexed: A28, A32, APA, B21, BrCerAb, C&ISA, CA/WCA, CIA, CerAb, CivEngAb, CorrAb, E&CAJ, E11, EEA, EMA, ESPM, EnvEAb, H15, M&TEA, M09, MBF, METADEX, SSciA, SWRA, SolStAb, T04, WAA.
—Linda Hall.
Published by: Stockholm International Water Institute, Drottninggatan 33, Stockholm, 11151, Sweden. TEL 46-8-52213960, FAX 46-8-52213961, siwi@siwi.org. Ed. Britt-Louise Andersson. Circ: 45,000.

333.91 GBR ISSN 0307-9074
STREAM. Text in English. 1974. 10/yr. GBP 3. adv. back issues avail.
Published by: Severn-Trent Water Authority, Abelson House, 2297 Coventry Rd, Sheldon, Birmingham, Warks B26 3PU, United Kingdom. Ed. Christine Mosley. Circ: 13,000.

STREAMLINE; watershed management bulletin. *see* ENVIRONMENTAL STUDIES

627 ROM
STUDII DE IRIGATII SI DESECARI. Text in Romanian; Summaries in English, French. a.
Published by: (Institutul de Cercetari pentru Imbunatatiri Funciare), Academia de Stiinte Agricole si Silvice, Bd. Marasti 61, Bucharest, 71331, Romania. **Subscr. to:** ILEXIM, Str. 13 Decembrie 3, PO Box 136-137, Bucharest 70116, Romania.

628.1 628.3 DEU ISSN 0585-7953
CODEN: SBSWBO
STUTTGARTER BERICHTE ZUR SIEDLUNGSWASSERWIRTSCHAFT. Text in German. 1958. irreg., latest vol.200, 2009. EUR 34.80 per vol. (effective 2010).
Indexed: GeoRef.
—CCC.
Published by: Vulkan Verlag GmbH (Subsidiary of: Oldenbourg Wissenschaftsverlag GmbH), Huyssenallee 52-56, Essen, 45128, Germany. TEL 49-201-820020, FAX 49-201-8200255.

628.1 JPN ISSN 0371-0785
CODEN: SKYZAN
SUIDO KYOKAI ZASSHI/JOURNAL OF WATER WORKS ASSOCIATION. Text in Japanese. 1932. m. **Document type:** *Journal.*
Indexed: INIS AtomInd, RefZh.
Published by: Nippon Suido Kyokai/Japan Water Works Association, 4-8-9 Kudan Minami, Chiyoda-ku, Tokyo, 102-0074, Japan. TEL 81-3-32642281, FAX 81-3-32622244, http://www.jwwa.or.jp/.

SUIMON MIZU SHIGEN GAKKAI NYUSU/JAPAN SOCIETY OF HYDROLOGY AND WATER RESOURCES NEWS. *see* EARTH SCIENCES—Hydrology

SUIMON MIZU SHIGEN GAKKAISHI/JAPAN SOCIETY OF HYDROLOGY AND WATER RESOURCES. JOURNAL. *see* EARTH SCIENCES—Hydrology

333.91 JPN ISSN 0039-4858
SUIRI KAGAKU/WATER SCIENCE. Text in Japanese. 1957. bi-m. JPY 8,800 per issue. adv. bk.rev.
Indexed: ChemAb.
Published by: Suiri Kagaku Kenkyujo/Water Utilization Institute, 7-12 Koraku 1-chome, Bunkyo-ku, Tokyo, 112-0004, Japan. Ed. Hirotada Muto.

333.9 613.1 USA
SUPPLY LINES. Text in English. 19??. s-a. back issues avail. **Document type:** *Newsletter, Government.*
Published by: New Hampshire Department of Environmental Services, 29 Hazen Dr, PO Box 95, Concord, NH 03302. TEL 603-271-3503, mary.power@des.nh.gov, http://des.nh.gov.

333.9 USA ISSN 0094-6427
TC425.S8
SUSQUEHANNA RIVER BASIN COMMISSION. ANNUAL REPORT. Text in English. 1972. a. free. illus. **Document type:** *Government.* **Description:** Describes the work of the commission for the fiscal year. Also contains featured articles about special subjects.
Indexed: GeoRef, SpeleolAb.
Published by: Susquehanna River Basin Commission, 1721 N Front St, Harrisburg, PA 17102. TEL 717-238-0422, FAX 717-238-2436.

▼ **SUSTAINABLE TECHNOLOGIES, SYSTEMS & POLICIES.** *see* ENERGY

628.5 SWE ISSN 1651-0674
SVENSKT VATTEN. Text in Swedish. 1974. 6/yr. SEK 450; SEK 250 to students (effective 2008). adv. **Document type:** *Magazine, Trade.* **Description:** Contains news and information about the water and wastewater industry.
Formerly (until 2002): V A V - Nytt (0347-1438)
Published by: Svenskt Vatten AB, PO Box 47607, Stockholm, 11794, Sweden. TEL 46-8-50600218, pia.almquist@svensktvatten.se. Ed. Catharine Olsson TEL 46-8-50600213. Adv. contact Migge Sarrion TEL 46-8-59077150. B&W page SEK 11,500, color page SEK 15,400; trim 185 x 270. Circ: 4,400 (paid and controlled).

▼ **T P O**; dedicated to municipal wastewater professionals. (Treatment Plant Operator) *see* ENVIRONMENTAL STUDIES—Waste Management

627 DEU ISSN 1434-5765
T Z W - KOLLOQUIUM. (Technologiezentrum Wasser) Text in German. 1997. irreg., latest vol.38, 2008. **Document type:** *Monographic series, Academic/Scholarly.*
—CCC.
Published by: T Z W, Karlsruher Str 84, Karlsruhe, 76139, Germany. TEL 49-721-96780, FAX 49-721-9678101, http://www.tzw.de.

TAIWAN LINYE KEXUE/TAIWAN JOURNAL OF FOREST SCIENCE. *see* FORESTS AND FORESTRY

628.1 AUS ISSN 1449-5996
TASMANIA. DEPARTMENT OF PRIMARY INDUSTRIES, WATER AND ENVIRONMENT. WATER ASSESSMENT AND PLANNING BRANCH. REPORT SERIES. Text in English. 1997. irreg. **Document type:** *Monographic series, Government.*
Former titles (until 2004): Tasmania. Department of Primary Industries, Water and Environment. Land and Water Assessment Branch. Report Series (1832-0449); (until 1999): Tasmania. Department of Primary Industry and Fisheries. Land and Water Assessment Branch. Report Series (1448-1626)
Published by: Tasmania, Department of Primary Industries, Water and Environment. Water Assessment and Planning Branch, c/o Martin Read, Principal Water Environment Officer, 13 St Johns Ave, New Town, TAS 7008, Australia. TEL 61-3-62336834, FAX 61-3-62336881, Martin.Read@dpiw.tas.gov.au, http://www.dpiw.tas.gov.au.

TECHNIQUES SCIENCES METHODES, GENIE URBAIN GENIE RURAL; La revue des specialistes de l'environnement. *see* ENVIRONMENTAL STUDIES

TECHNISCHE UNIVERSITAET KAISERSLAUTERN. FACHGEBIET WASSERBAU UND WASSERWIRTSCHAFT. BERICHTE. *see* ENGINEERING—Hydraulic Engineering

333 ESP ISSN 0211-8173
CODEN: TEAGEN
TECNOLOGIA DEL AGUA; revista tecnica de la captacion, distribucion, tratamiento, y depuracion del agua. Text in Spanish. 1980. m. (13/yr.). EUR 183.46 domestic; EUR 229.21 foreign (effective 2010). adv. bk.rev. charts; illus. **Document type:** *Magazine, Trade.* **Description:** Covers all topics of water and hydrology, including techniques and application solutions for collection, distribution, water treatment, storage, control and monitoring, canalization, purification and industrial wastewater.
Indexed: A22, FLUIDEX, GEOBASE, GeoRef, IECT, INIS AtomInd, SCOPUS, SpeleolAb.
—BLDSC (8762.800200), IE, Ingenta.
Published by: Reed Business Information SA (Subsidiary of: Reed Business Information International), Zancoeta 9, Bilbao, 48013, Spain. TEL 34-944-285600, FAX 34-944-425116, rbi@rbi.es. Ed. Nuria Martin. Adv. contact Manuel Masip. Circ: 6,000.

333.8 USA ISSN 0197-2340
TEXAS NATURAL RESOURCES REPORTER. Text in English. 1977. s-m. looseleaf. USD 295. back issues avail.
Published by: Research & Planning Consultants, Inc., 7600 Chevy Chase Dr., Ste. 400, Austin, TX 78752-1566. TEL 512-472-7765, FAX 512-472-2232. Ed. Carrie Johnson. Circ: 250.

333.91 USA ISSN 2160-5319
▼ ➤ **TEXAS WATER JOURNAL.** Text in English. 2010. irreg. free (effective 2011). **Document type:** *Journal, Academic/Scholarly.* **Description:** Explains Texas water resources management and policy issues from a multidisciplinary perspective that integrates science, engineering, law, planning, and other disciplines.
Media: Online - full text.
Published by: Texas Water Resources Institute, 1500 Research Pky, Ste 240, College Station, TX 77843. TEL 979-845-1851, FAX 979-845-8554, twri@tamu.edu, http://twri.tamu.edu/. Ed. Todd H Votteler.

333.91 USA ISSN 0275-5483
TD224.T4 CODEN: TRTIDA
TEXAS WATER RESOURCES INSTITUTE. TECHNICAL REPORT. Text in English. 1965. irreg., latest no.391. illus. back issues avail. **Document type:** *Monographic series, Academic/Scholarly.*
Formerly (until 1971): Water Resources Institute, Texas A & M University. Technical Report
Related titles: Online - full text ed.: free (effective 2010).
Indexed: GeoRef, SpeleolAb.
Published by: Texas Water Resources Institute, 1500 Research Pky, Ste 240, College Station, TX 77843. TEL 979-845-1851, FAX 979-845-8554, twri@tamu.edu.

627 628 USA ISSN 1051-709X
TEXAS WATER UTILITIES JOURNAL. Text in English. 1990. m. USD 30 (effective 2007). adv. back issues avail. **Document type:** *Magazine, Trade.* **Description:** Covers essential information for all individuals working within the water utilities industry in Texas, including rules and regulations, certification, education, and communication.
Published by: Texas Water Utilities Association, 1106 Clayton Ln., Ste. 112 West, Austin, TX 78723-1093. TEL 512-459-3124, FAX 512-459-7124, twua@dbcity.com, http://www.twua.org. adv.: page USD 800. Circ: 9,400 (paid).

THALASSIA SALENTINA. *see* BIOLOGY—Botany

TIJDSCHRIFT VOOR WATERSTAATSGESCHIEDENIS. *see* HISTORY—History Of Europe

333.91 BEL ISSN 0776-1155
TRIBUNE DE L'EAU; eau, environnement, pollution. Text in French. 1947. m. adv. bk.rev. abstr.; bibl.; charts. index. **Document type:** *Journal, Academic/Scholarly.*
Former titles (until 1988): C E B E D E A U. Tribune (0007-8115); (until 1962): Bulletin Mensuel du C E B E D E A U (0775-6259); (until 1960): Bulletin Mensuel (0528-4341); (until 1952): Journal Mensuel (0775-6267)
Indexed: GeoRef, SpeleolAb, WasteInfo.
—BLDSC (9050.320000), IE, Infotrieve, Ingenta, INIST, Linda Hall.
Published by: (Centre Belge d'Etude et de Documentation de l'Environnement), Les Editions Cebedoc S.P.R.L., Rue Armand Stevart 2, Liege, B-4000, Belgium. Circ: 10,000.

TRIBUTARY (TRENTON). *see* ENVIRONMENTAL STUDIES—Waste Management

TROPICAL COASTS. *see* ENVIRONMENTAL STUDIES—Pollution

333.7845 GBR ISSN 1474-8754
U K IRRIGATION. Variant title: United Kingdom Irrigation. Text in English. 1981. a. free to members (effective 2009). adv. bk.rev. cum.index: vols.1-10, 10-20. back issues avail. **Document type:** *Journal, Academic/Scholarly.* **Description:** Contains informative articles and papers on current issues in the field of irrigation.
Formerly (until 2001): Irrigation News (0265-5136)
—BLDSC (9082.657970), IE, Ingenta.
Published by: U.K. Irrigation Association, c/o Moorland House, Hayway, Rushden, Northants, NN10 6AG, United Kingdom. TEL 44-1427-717627, m.kay@ukia.org, http://www.ukia.org.

U R W A QUARTERLY NEWSLETTER. *see* CONSERVATION

627 USA
U.S. ARMY CORPS OF ENGINEERS. HYDROLOGIC ENGINEERING CENTER. RESEARCH DOCUMENT. Text in English. 19??. irreg. **Document type:** *Monographic series, Government.*
Published by: U.S. Army Corps of Engineers, Hydrologic Engineering Center, 609 Second St, Davis, CA 95616. TEL 530-756-1104, FAX 530-756-8250. **Subscr. to:** U.S. Department of Commerce, National Technical Information Service.

627 USA
U.S. ARMY CORPS OF ENGINEERS. HYDROLOGIC ENGINEERING CENTER. TECHNICAL PAPER. Text in English. 19??. irreg. **Document type:** *Monographic series, Government.*
Published by: U.S. Army Corps of Engineers, Hydrologic Engineering Center, 609 Second St, Davis, CA 95616. TEL 530-756-1104, FAX 530-756-8250. **Subscr. to:** U.S. Department of Commerce, National Technical Information Service.

627 USA ISSN 0160-9386
CODEN: TDEHD4
U.S. ARMY CORPS OF ENGINEERS. HYDROLOGIC ENGINEERING CENTER. TRAINING DOCUMENT. Text in English. 19??. irreg. back issues avail. **Document type:** *Monographic series, Government.*
Indexed: GeoRef.
Published by: U.S. Army Corps of Engineers, Hydrologic Engineering Center, 609 Second St, Davis, CA 95616. TEL 530-756-1104, FAX 530-756-8250. **Subscr. to:** U.S. Department of Commerce, National Technical Information Service.

627 USA
U.S. ARMY CORPS OF ENGINEERS. HYDROLOGICAL ENGINEERING CENTER. PROJECT REPORT. Text in English. 19??. irreg. **Document type:** *Monographic series, Government.*
Published by: U.S. Army Corps of Engineers, Hydrologic Engineering Center, 609 Second St, Davis, CA 95616. TEL 530-756-1104, FAX 530-756-8250. **Subscr. to:** U.S. Department of Commerce, National Technical Information Service.

U.S. BUREAU OF RECLAMATION. ANNUAL REPORT. *see* CONSERVATION

U.S. BUREAU OF RECLAMATION. ENGINEERING MONOGRAPH. *see* ENGINEERING—Hydraulic Engineering

333.91 USA
U.S. BUREAU OF RECLAMATION. TECHNICAL REPORT. Text in English. 19??. irreg. **Document type:** *Report, Government.*
Published by: U.S. Bureau of Reclamation (Denver), Reclamation Service Ctr, Denver Federal Ctr, Bldg 67, PO Box 25007, Denver, CO 80225. http://www.usbr.gov.

627 USA ISSN 1083-1320
U S C I D NEWSLETTER. Text in English. 1958. q. membership. adv. bk.rev. **Document type:** *Newsletter.*
Formerly: I.C.I.D. Newsletter
Published by: United States Committee on Irrigation and Drainage, 1616 17th St, Ste 483, Denver, CO 80202. TEL 303-628-5430, FAX 303-628-5431. Ed. Larry D Stephens. Pub., R&P, Adv. contact Larry Stephens. Circ: 750.

620 USA ISSN 0041-5480
U S C O L D NEWSLETTER. Text in English. 1960. 3/yr. USD 60 to individual members; USD 450 to institutions (effective 2000). adv. bk.rev. **Document type:** *Newsletter.*
Published by: U S Committee on Large Dams, 1616 17th St, Ste 483, Denver, CO 80202. TEL 303-628-5430, FAX 303-628-5431. Circ: 1,100.

628.1 551.4 USA ISSN 0892-3469
GB701
U.S. GEOLOGICAL SURVEY. NATIONAL WATER SUMMARY. Text in English. 1983. biennial. price varies. maps; charts. **Document type:** *Government.* **Description:** Focuses on the nature, geographic distribution, magnitude, and trends of the nation's water resources.
Related titles: ◆ Series of: U.S. Geological Survey. Water Supply Paper. ISSN 0886-9308.
Published by: U.S. Department of the Interior, Geological Survey, 12201 Sunrise Valley Dr, Reston, VA 20192. TEL 703-648-5953, 800-228-0975, ask@usgs.gov, http://www.usgs.gov.

628.1 USA ISSN 0565-596X
TC177
U.S. GEOLOGICAL SURVEY. TECHNIQUES OF WATER-RESOURCES INVESTIGATIONS. Text in English. 1967. irreg., latest 2005. free (effective 2011). back issues avail. **Document type:** *Monographic series, Government.*
Related titles: Online - full text ed.
Published by: U.S. Department of the Interior, Geological Survey, 12201 Sunrise Valley Dr, Reston, VA 20192. TEL 703-648-5953, 800-228-0975, ask@usgs.gov, http://www.usgs.gov.

333.91 USA
U.S. NATURAL RESOUCES CONSERVATION SERVICE. ANNUAL REPORT. Text in English. a. free. **Document type:** *Government.*
Formerly: U.S. Soil Conservation Service. Annual Report
Published by: U.S. Department of Agriculture, Natural Resources Conservation Service (Spokane), 316 W Boone Ave, Ste 450, Spokane, WA 99201-2348. TEL 509-353-2341.

333.91 USA ISSN 0747-8291
CODEN: ULWAE5
ULTRAPURE WATER; the definitive journal of high-purity water. Text in English. 1984. 9/yr. USD 36 in North Africa; USD 100 elsewhere (effective 2004). adv. bk.rev. **Document type:** *Journal, Trade.* **Description:** Addresses all aspects of high-purity water production in the high-pressure boiler industry, electric utilities, semiconductor manufacturing, pharmaceuticals and biotechnology.
Incoporates (in 1997): Industrial Water Treatment (1058-3645); (1964-198?): Industrial Water Engineering (0019-8862)
Indexed: A22, A28, APA, BrCerAb, C&ISA, CA/WCA, CIA, CIN, CerAb, ChemAb, ChemTitl, CivEngAb, CorrAb, E&CAJ, E11, EEA, EIA, EMA, EnvAb, FLUIDEX, H15, Inspec, M&TEA, M09, MBF, METADEX, SCOPUS, SolStAb, T04, Telegen, WAA.
—BLDSC (9082.783500), AskIEEE, CASDDS, IE, Infotrieve, Ingenta, INIST, Linda Hall. **CCC.**
Published by: Tall Oaks Publishing Inc., 60 Golden Eagle Ln, Littleton, CO 80127. TEL 303-973-6700, FAX 303-973-5327, info@talloaks.com. Circ: 16,000.

627.7 692.8 GBR ISSN 1467-2766
UNDERWATER CONTRACTOR INTERNATIONAL. Abbreviated title: U C I. Text in English. 1993. bi-m. GBP 39 domestic; GBP 49 foreign (effective 2009). adv. back issues avail. **Document type:** *Magazine, Trade.* **Description:** Contains a broad mix of articles of interest to both management and employees in the diving, ROV, and underwater technology supply sector.
Former titles (until 1999): Underwater Contractor (1362-0487); (until 1995): Commercial Diver and Underwater Contractor (1351-1149)
Published by: Underwater World Publications Ltd., 55 High St, Teddington, Midds TW11 8HA, United Kingdom. TEL 44-20-89434288, FAX 44-20-89434312, subscriptions@under-water.co.uk. Ed. John Bevan.

628.1 GBR ISSN 2040-6584
▼ **UNITED ARAB EMIRATES WATER REPORT.** Text in English. 2010. q. USD 975, EUR 695 combined subscription (print & email eds.) (effective 2011). **Document type:** *Report, Trade.* **Description:** Provides industry professionals and strategists, sector analysts, business investors, trade associations and regulatory bodies with independent forecasts and competitive intelligence on the Water industry in the United Arab Emirates.
Related titles: E-mail ed.
Published by: Business Monitor International Ltd., Senator House, 85 Queen Victoria St, London, EC4V 4AB, United Kingdom. TEL 44-20-72480468, FAX 44-20-72480467, subs@businessmonitor.com.

333.91 THA ISSN 0082-8130
UNITED NATIONS. ECONOMIC AND SOCIAL COMMISSION FOR ASIA AND THE PACIFIC. WATER RESOURCES SERIES. Text in English. 1951. irreg., latest vol.81, 2001. USD 80 (effective 2003). back issues avail. **Document type:** *Monographic series, Academic/Scholarly.*
Former titles: United Nations. Economic and Social Commission for Asia and the Pacific. Water Resources Development Series; (until 1964): United Nations. Economic and Social Commission for Asia and the Pacific. Flood Control Series (1010-5328)
Related titles: Microfiche ed.: (from CIS).
Indexed: ARDT, GeoRef, IIS, SpeleolAb.
Published by: United Nations Economic and Social Commission for Asia and the Pacific, United Nations Bldg., Rajadamnern Ave., Bangkok, 10200, Thailand. TEL 662-2881174, FAX 662-2883022, library-escap@un.org, http://www.unescap.org. **Dist. by:** United Nations Publications, Sales Office and Bookshop, Bureau E4, Geneva 10 1211, Switzerland; United Nations Publications, 2 United Nations Plaza, Rm DC2-853, New York, NY 10017; United Nations, Conference Services Unit, ESCAP, Bangkok, Thailand.

333.91 GBR
UNITED UTILITIES. ANNUAL REPORT & ACCOUNTS. Text in English. 1987. a. back issues avail. **Document type:** *Report, Trade.*
Former titles (until 1996): North West Water Group. Annual Report; (until 1989): North West Water Authority. Annual Report
Related titles: Online - full text ed.: free (effective 2009).
Published by: United Utilities PLC, Dawson House, Great Sankey, Warrington, Lancs WA5 3LW, United Kingdom. TEL 44-845-7462200, FAX 44-1925-237073, customer.services@uuplc.co.uk, http://www.unitedutilities.com/.

333.91 DEU
UNIVERSITAET HANNOVER. INSTITUT FUER SIEDLUNGSWASSERWIRTSCHAFT UND ABFALLTECHNIK. VEROEFFENTLICHUNGEN. Text in German. 1957. irreg., latest vol.103, 1997. **Document type:** *Monographic series, Academic/Scholarly.*
Formerly: Technische Universitaet Hannover. Institut fuer Siedlungswasserwirtschaft. Veroeffentlichungen (0073-0319)
Published by: Universitaet Hannover, Institut fuer Siedlungswasserwirtschaft und Abfalltechnik, Welfengarten 1, Hannover, 30167, Germany. TEL 49-511-7623372, FAX 49-511-7622881.

346.04691 USA
UNIVERSITY CASEBOOK SERIES. TARLOCK, CORBRIDGE AND GETCHES' WATER RESOURCE MANAGEMENT, A CASEBOOK IN LAW AND PUBLIC POLICY. Text in English. 19??. latest 6th ed., base vol. plus irreg. updates. USD 135 base vol(s). (effective 2010). **Document type:** *Journal, Trade.* **Description:** Provides comprehensive coverage of water resource management laws.
Related titles: ◆ Series of: University Casebook Series.
Published by: Thomson West (Subsidiary of: Thomson Reuters Corp.), 610 Opperman Dr, Eagan, MN 55123. TEL 651-687-7000, 800-344-5008, west.customer.service@thomson.com.

333.91 USA
➤ **UNIVERSITY OF CALIFORNIA, RIVERSIDE. CENTER FOR WATER RESOURCES. CONTRIBUTIONS.** Text in English. 1957. irreg., latest vol.210, 2010. back issues avail. **Document type:** *Monographic series, Academic/Scholarly.*
Formerly: University of California at Davis. Water Resources Center. Contributions (0068-6301)
Related titles: Online - full text ed.: free (effective 2010).
Published by: University of California, Riverside, Center for Water Resources, Rubidoux Hall - 094, Riverside, CA 92521. TEL 951-827-4327, FAX 951-827-5295, julie.drouyor@ucr.edu.

333.9 USA ISSN 0069-9063
HD1694.C8 CODEN: CUWRAJ
➤ **UNIVERSITY OF CONNECTICUT. INSTITUTE OF WATER RESOURCES. REPORT SERIES.** Text in English. 1967. irreg., latest 2009. **Document type:** *Monographic series, Academic/Scholarly.* **Description:** Includes chemical, biological, geological, legal, engineering and sociopolitical reports on resources.
Indexed: GeoRef, SpeleolAb.
—Linda Hall.
Published by: University of Connecticut, Institute of Water Resources, W B Young Bldg, Rm 224, 1376 Storrs Rd, Unit 4018, Storrs, CT 06269. TEL 860-486-2840, FAX 860-486-5408, Glenn.Warner@uconn.edu.

333.91 USA ISSN 0073-5442
HD1694 CODEN: IUWRAH
➤ **UNIVERSITY OF ILLINOIS AT URBANA-CHAMPAIGN. WATER RESOURCES CENTER. RESEARCH REPORT.** Text in English. 1966. irreg. price varies. back issues avail. **Document type:** *Monographic series, Academic/Scholarly.*
Related titles: Microform ed.: (from NTI).
Indexed: GeoRef, SpeleolAb.
—CASDDS, Linda Hall.
Published by: University of Illinois at Urbana-Champaign, Water Resources Center, 388 NSCR, MC 635, 1101 W Peabody Dr, Urbana, IL 61801. TEL 217-333-6444, FAX 214-333-8046, iwrc@uiuc.edu.

333.91 USA ISSN 0733-0502
TD224.I3
UNIVERSITY OF ILLINOIS AT URBANA-CHAMPAIGN. WATER RESOURCES CENTER. SPECIAL REPORTS. Text in English. 1968. irreg. price varies. **Document type:** *Monographic series, Academic/Scholarly.*
Formerly (until 1970): W R C Special Report
Indexed: GeoRef, SpeleolAb.
—Linda Hall.
Published by: University of Illinois at Urbana-Champaign, Water Resources Center, 388 NSCR, MC 635, 1101 W Peabody Dr, Urbana, IL 61801. TEL 217-333-6444, FAX 214-333-8046, iwrc@uiuc.edu, http://web.extension.illinois.edu/iwrc/.

628.1 USA ISSN 0277-884X
UNIVERSITY OF KENTUCKY. WATER RESOURCES RESEARCH INSTITUTE. RESEARCH REPORT. Text in English. 1966. irreg. **Document type:** *Monographic series.*

V
W
Z

Formerly (until 1973): University of Kentucky. Water Resources Institute. Research Report (0453-5669)
Indexed: GeoRef.
Published by: University of Kentucky, Water Resources Research Institute, 233 Mining & Minerals Resources Bldg, Lexington, KY 40506-0107. TEL 859-257-1299, FAX 859-323-1049, kipp@uky.edu, http://www.uky.edu/WaterResources/.

333.72 USA
UNIVERSITY OF MINNESOTA. CENTER FOR NATURAL RESOURCE POLICY AND MANAGEMENT. WORKING PAPERS. Text in English. 1984. irreg., latest vol.5. **Description:** Covers water quality, common property and economics of natural resources and forestry research.
Published by: University of Minnesota, Center for Natural Resource Policy and Management, 115 Green Hall, Dept. of Forest Resources, St. Paul, MN 55108. TEL 612-624-9796, FAX 612-625-5212. Ed. James Perry. Circ: 150.

333.9 USA
UNIVERSITY OF NEBRASKA. WATER CENTER. ANNUAL REPORT OF ACTIVITIES. Text in English. 1968. a. free. **Document type:** *Corporate.*
Formerly: Nebraska Water Resources Research Institute. University of Nebraska. Annual Report of Activities (0077-6394)
Published by: University of Nebraska at Lincoln, Water Center, School of Natural Resources, 522 Hardin Hall, 3310 Holdrege St, Lincoln, NE 68583. TEL 402-472-3305, FAX 402-472-3574. Ed. Steven W Ress TEL 402-472-9549. Circ: 1,500.

333.91 AUS
UNIVERSITY OF NEW ENGLAND. CENTRE FOR ECOLOGICAL ECONOMICS & WATER POLICY RESEARCH. OCCASIONAL PAPERS (NO.). Text in English. 1987. irreg. **Document type:** *Monographic series, Academic/Scholarly.*
Formerly (until 1986): University of New England. Centre for Water Policy Research. Occasional Papers (No.) (1030-4134)
Published by: University of New England, Centre for Ecological Economics & Water Policy Research, Armidale, NSW 2351, Australia. TEL 61-2-67733734, FAX 61-2-67733237, ceewpr@pobox.une.edu.au, http://www.une.edu.au/cwpr/.

628.1 AUS
UNIVERSITY OF NEW ENGLAND. CENTRE FOR WATER POLICY RESEARCH. RESOURCES POLICY. Text in English. 1994. biennial. **Document type:** *Newsletter.*
Published by: University of New England, Centre for Ecological Economics & Water Policy Research, Armidale, NSW 2351, Australia. TEL 61-2-67733734, FAX 61-2-67733237, ceewpr@pobox.une.edu.au, http://www.une.edu.au/cwpr/.

627 333.9 AUS ISSN 0077-8818
UNIVERSITY OF NEW SOUTH WALES. WATER RESEARCH LABORATORY, MANLY VALE. LABORATORY RESEARCH REPORTS. Text in English. 1959. irreg., latest vol.193, 1997.
Indexed: GeoRef, SpeleolAb.
Published by: University of New South Wales, Water Research Laboratory, 110 King St, Manly Vale, NSW 2093, Australia. TEL 61-2-99494488, FAX 61-2-99494188, info@wrl.unsw.edu.au, http://www.wrl.unsw.edu.au.

333.91 USA ISSN 0078-1525
UNIVERSITY OF NORTH CAROLINA. WATER RESOURCES RESEARCH INSTITUTE. REPORT. Text in English. 1967. irreg. free. **Document type:** *Monographic series.*
Indexed: EngInd, GeoRef.
—Linda Hall.
Published by: University of North Carolina at Chapel Hill, Water Resources Research Institute, PO Box 7912, Raleigh, NC 27695-7912. TEL 919-515-2815, FAX 919-515-7802, water_resources@ncsu.edu, http://www.ncsu.edu/wrri.

UNIVERSITY OF PORTSMOUTH. CENTRE FOR THE ECONOMICS & MANAGEMENT OF AQUATIC RESOURCES. RESEARCH PAPERS. *see* FISH AND FISHERIES

333.91 USA
CODEN: TRURD8
➤ **UNIVERSITY OF TEXAS AT AUSTIN. CENTER FOR RESEARCH IN WATER RESOURCES. TECHNICAL REPORT SERIES (ONLINE).** Text in English. 1964. irreg. free (effective 2010). **Document type:** *Monographic series, Academic/Scholarly.* **Description:** Summary of research findings resulting from sponsored projects in the water resources area conducted by faculty members of the university.
Formerly (until 19??): University of Texas at Austin. Center for Research in Water Resources. Technical Report Series (Print) (0147-2194)
Media: Online - full text.
Indexed: CPEI, ChemAb, EngInd, GeoRef, SCOPUS, SpeleolAb.
—CASDDS.
Published by: University of Texas at Austin, Center for Research in Water Resources, Pickle Research Campus, Bldg 119, MC R8000, Austin, TX 78712. TEL 512-471-3131, FAX 512-471-0072, sbernard@mail.utexas.edu.

333.91 USA
UNIVERSITY OF THE DISTRICT OF COLUMBIA. WATER RESOURCES RESEARCH CENTER. REPORT. Text in English. irreg.
Published by: University of the District of Columbia, Water Resources Research Center, Agriculture Experiment Station, MB4404, 4200 Connecticut Ave, Bldg 52, Rm 322-D, Washington, DC 20008. TEL 202-274-7124, FAX 202-274-6687, http://www.udc.edu/COES/waterresource/.

333.91 USA ISSN 0502-7276
HD1695.C7
UPPER COLORADO RIVER COMMISSION. ANNUAL REPORT. Text in English. a.
Indexed: GeoRef.
—Linda Hall.
Published by: Upper Colorado River Commission, 355 South 400 East, Salt Lake City, UT 84111. TEL 801-531-1150.

331.91 USA
UPPER MISSISSIPPI RIVER CONSERVATION COMMITTEE. NEWSLETTER. Abbreviated title: U M R C C Newsletter. Text in English. 1979. bi-m. looseleaf. free. back issues avail. **Document type:** *Newsletter.* **Description:** Contains information about the management of the river's natural resources for professionals who live and work near it.
Published by: Upper Mississippi River Conservation Committee, 4469 48th Ave Ct, Rock Island, IL 61201. TEL 309-793-5800 ext 522, umrcc@mississippi-river.com. Ed. Jon Duyvejonck. Circ: 575.

333.77 USA ISSN 0886-2664
UPWELLINGS. Text in English. 1977. q. free. bk.rev. back issues avail. **Document type:** *Newsletter.* **Description:** Contains news, articles, and information on issues related to the Great Lakes.
Published by: Michigan Sea Grant College Program, 401 E Liberty, Ste 330, Ann Arbor, MI 48104-2298. TEL 734-764-1118, FAX 734-647-0768. Ed., R&P Joyce Daniels. Circ: 2,475. **Co-sponsor:** Michigan State University.

333.91 GBR ISSN 1573-062X
CODEN: URWAFE
➤ **URBAN WATER JOURNAL.** Text in English. 1999-2002 (Dec.); resumed 2004. bi-m. GBP 472 combined subscription in United Kingdom to institutions (print & online eds.); EUR 620, USD 781 combined subscription to institutions (print & online eds.) (effective 2012). adv. back issues avail.; reprint service avail. from PSC. **Document type:** *Journal, Academic/Scholarly.* **Description:** Addresses the increasing importance of integrated approaches to solve problems in urban water engineering by using water wisely, reusing and protecting it as a precious resource.
Formerly (until 2004): Urban Water (1462-0758)
Related titles: Online - full text ed.: ISSN 1744-9006. GBP 425 in United Kingdom to institutions; EUR 557, USD 703 to institutions (effective 2012) (from IngentaConnect).
Indexed: A01, A03, A08, A22, A28, APA, ASFA, B21, BrCerAb, C&ISA, CA, CA/WCA, CIA, CerAb, CivEngAb, CorrAb, CurCont, E&CAJ, E01, E04, E05, E11, EEA, EMA, ESPM, EnvAb, EnvEAb, FLUIDEX, GEOBASE, GeoRef, H15, HPNRM, ICEA, M&TEA, M09, MBF, METADEX, PollutAb, SCI, SCOPUS, SSciA, SWRA, SolStAb, T02, T04, ToxAb, W07, WAA.
—BLDSC (9123.753500), IE, Infotrieve, Ingenta, INIST. **CCC.**
Published by: Taylor & Francis Ltd. (Subsidiary of: Taylor & Francis Group), 4 Park Sq, Milton Park, Abingdon, Oxfordshire OX14 4RN, United Kingdom. TEL 44-20-70176000, FAX 44-20-70176336, subscriptions@tandf.co.uk, http://www.taylorandfrancis.com. Eds. Cedo Maksimovic TEL 44-207-5946013, David Butler TEL 44-1392-264064. Adv. contact Linda Hann. **Subscr. to:** Journals Customer Service, Sheepen Pl, Colchester, Essex CO3 3LP, United Kingdom. TEL 44-20-70175544, FAX 44-20-70175198, tf.enquiries@tfinforma.com.

333.91 USA
URBAN WATER MANAGEMENT. Text in English. 2007. bi-m. adv. back issues avail. **Document type:** *Magazine, Trade.* **Description:** Provides daily international business and industry-related news, current issue articles and access to years of searchable editorial archives.
Related titles: ◆ Supplement to: Industrial WaterWorld. ISSN 1934-3922; ◆ Supplement to: Waterworld. ISSN 1083-0723.
Published by: PennWell Corporation, 1421 S Sheridan Rd, Tulsa, OK 74112. TEL 918-835-3161, 800-331-4463, FAX 918-831-9804, Headquarters@PennWell.com, http://www.pennwell.com. Adv. contact LaFerney Dottie TEL 512-858-7927. B&W page USD 2,900, color page USD 3,900; trim 8 x 10.5.

UTILITIES. *see* ENERGY

628 USA ISSN 1944-6616
UTILITY EXECUTIVE (ONLINE). Text in English. 1998. bi-m. USD 212 in North America to institutions; EUR 152 in Europe to institutions; GBP 141 to institutions in the UK & elsewhere (effective 2011). adv. back issues avail. **Document type:** *Newsletter, Trade.* **Description:** Focuses on strategic water and wastewater utility management for executives and managers.
Media: Online - full text.
Published by: Water Environment Federation, 601 Wythe St, Alexandria, VA 22314. TEL 703-684-2400, 800-666-0206, FAX 703-684-2492, pubs@wef.org. Eds. LaShell Stratton TEL 703-684-2400 ext 7031, Melissa H Jackson TEL 703-684-2455. Adv. contact Jenny Grigsby TEL 703-684-2400 ext 2451. **Subscr. to:** Portland Customer Services, Commerce Way, Colchester CO2 8HP, United Kingdom. TEL 44-1206-796351, FAX 44-1206-799331, sales@portland-services.com, http://www.portlandpress.com.

628.1 NOR ISSN 1503-6073
V A-NYTT. Text in Norwegian. 1991. irreg. free. back issues avail. **Document type:** *Trade.*
Formerly (until 1999): Drikkevans-Nytt (1500-2136)
Published by: Driftsassistansen for Vann og Avloeb i Moere og Romsdal, Fylkeshusa, Molde, 6404, Norway. TEL 47-71-258180, FAX 47-71-258167, post@driftsassistansen.no.

VALENCIA PORT; guia del servicios del puerto de Valencia. *see* TRANSPORTATION—Ships And Shipping

628.1 DNK ISSN 1395-3095
VANDFORSYNINGSTEKNIK. Text in Danish. 1970. a. DKK 250 per issue (effective 2009). **Document type:** *Trade.*
Formerly (until 1993): Kursus i Vandforsyningsteknik (1395-3079)
Published by: Dansk Vand- og Spildevandsforening/Danish Water and Waste Water Association, Danmarksvej 26, Skanderborg, 8660, Denmark. TEL 45-70-210055, FAX 45-70-210056, danva@danva.dk, http://www.danva.dk.

VANDMILJOE (ONLINE); tilstand og udvikling. *see* ENVIRONMENTAL STUDIES—Pollution

333.91 SWE ISSN 0042-2886
CODEN: VTTNAO
VATTEN/WATER; tidskrift foer vattenvaard/journal of water management and research. Text in Danish, Norwegian, Swedish; Some issues in English; Abstracts in English. 1945. q. SEK 460 domestic membership (effective 2011). adv. bk.rev. bibl.; charts; illus. index, cum.index. **Document type:** *Journal, Academic/Scholarly.*
Formerly (until 1967): Vattenhygien - Water Hygiene (0372-6800)
Related titles: Online - full text ed.
Indexed: A22, CIN, ChemAb, ChemTitl, E04, E05, FS&TA, GeoRef, P&BA, SpeleolAb.
—BLDSC (9149.680000), CASDDS, IE, Ingenta, INIST, Linda Hall.
Published by: Foereningen Vatten/Swedish Association for Water, c/o SIWI, Drottinggatan 33, PO Box 118, Stockholm, 11151, Sweden. TEL 46-8-6477008, FAX 46-8-52213961, kansliet@foreningenvatten.se, http://www.foreningenvatten.se. Ed. Magnus Persson.

628.1 DEU ISSN 0933-2499
VERORDNUNG UEBER ALLGEMEINE BEDINGUNGEN FUER DIE VERSORGUNG MIT WASSER. Text in German. 1983. base vol. plus a. updates. looseleaf. EUR 49.80 base vol(s).; EUR 24.80 updates per issue (effective 2009). **Document type:** *Monographic series, Trade.*
Published by: Erich Schmidt Verlag GmbH & Co. (Berlin), Genthiner Str 30 G, Berlin, 10785, Germany. TEL 49-30-2500850, FAX 49-30-250085305, vertrieb@esvmedien.de, http://www.erich-schmidt-verlag.de.

VERSORGUNGSWIRTSCHAFT. *see* ENGINEERING—Electrical Engineering

628.1 FIN ISSN 1796-7376
VESI-INSTITUUTTI. JULKAISUJA. Text in Finnish. 2007. irreg. **Document type:** *Monographic series, Academic/Scholarly.* **Description:** Publications from the Finnish Institute of Drinking Water.
Published by: (Vesi-Instituutti/Finnish Institute of Drinking Water), Prizztech Oy, Tiedepuisto 4, Pori, 28600, Finland. TEL 358-2-6205300, FAX 358-2-6205399, prizztech@prizz.fi.

333.91 627 FIN ISSN 0505-3838
VESITALOUS; Finnish journal of water economy, hydraulic and agricultural engineering. Text in Finnish; Summaries in English. 1960. bi-m. EUR 50 (effective 2005). adv. bk.rev. charts; illus. **Document type:** *Magazine.*
Indexed: ASFA, ChemAb, ESPM, GeoRef, INIS AtomInd, PollutAb, SWRA, SpeleolAb.
Published by: Maa- Ja Vesitekniikan Tuki, Annankatu 29 A 18, Helsinki, 00100, Finland. TEL 358-9-6940622, FAX 358-9-6949772, tuki@mvtt.fi. Ed. Timo Maasilta. adv.: page EUR 1,260; 170 x 240. Circ: 2,000.

628.1 NLD ISSN 2211-1468
▼ **VIEWS.** Text in English. 2009. s-a. free to qualified personnel (effective 2011). **Document type:** *Magazine, Trade.*
Related titles: Online - full text ed.: ISSN 2211-1484; ◆ Dutch ed.: Visie (Delft). ISSN 1878-8386.
Published by: Deltares, Postbus 177, Delft, 2600 MH, Netherlands. TEL 31-88-3358273, FAX 31-88-3358582, info@deltares.nl.

333.91 USA ISSN 0097-2584
TD201 CODEN: BWRRAV
VIRGINIA. WATER RESOURCES RESEARCH CENTER. BULLETIN. Text in English. 1965. irreg., latest vol.184. free in state; USD 10 out of state (effective 2002). abstr.; bibl.; illus. back issues avail. **Document type:** *Bulletin, Trade.*
Related titles: Microfilm ed.: (from PQC).
Indexed: GeoRef, SpeleolAb.
—CASDDS, INIST.
Published by: Water Resources Research Center, Virginia Polytechnic Institute and State University, 10 Sandy Hall 0444, Blacksburg, VA 24061. TEL 540-231-8080, http://www.vwrrc.vt.edu/. Ed., R&P Judy A Poff TEL 540-231-8030. Circ: 250.

628.1 NLD ISSN 1878-8386
▼ **VISIE (DELFT).** Running title: Deltares Visie. Text in Dutch. 2009. s-a. free to qualified personnel (effective 2011). **Document type:** *Magazine, Trade.*
Related titles: ◆ English ed.: Views. ISSN 2211-1468.
Published by: Deltares, Postbus 177, Delft, 2600 MH, Netherlands. TEL 31-88-3358273, FAX 31-88-3358582, info@deltares.nl.

363.7 SRB ISSN 0350-5049
VODA I SANITARNA TEHNIKA. Text in Serbo-Croatian. 1971. bi-m. bibl.; charts; illus. **Document type:** *Journal.*
Published by: Udruzenje za Tehnologiju Vode, Sindeliceva 21, Belgrade. TEL 381-11-4442228, FAX 381-11-4441193, udruzenje@utv.co.yu. Ed. Rajko Agranovic.

VODNI HOSPODARSTVI. *see* ENGINEERING—Hydraulic Engineering

627 BGR ISSN 0204-8248
TC401
VODNI PROBLEMI. Text in Bulgarian. 1975. irreg. BGL 1.40 per issue. reprint service avail. from IRC.
Supersedes: Bulgarska Akademiia na Naukite. Institut po Vodni Problemi. Izvestiia
Indexed: BSLGeo, GeoRef, SpeleolAb.
—INIST.
Published by: (Bulgarska Akademiya na Naukite/Bulgarian Academy of Sciences, Institut po Vodni Problemi), Sofiiski Universitet Sv. Kliment Ohridski, Universitetsko Izdatelstvo/Sofia University St. Kliment Ohridski University Press, Akad G Bonchev 6, Sofia, 1113, Bulgaria. Circ: 480.

333.7 RUS ISSN 0321-0596
CODEN: VDRSBK
VODNYE RESURSY. Text in Russian. 1972. bi-m. RUR 1,310 for 6 mos. domestic (effective 2004). bk.rev. abstr.; charts; illus. index. **Document type:** *Journal, Academic/Scholarly.* **Description:** Presents materials on the assesments of water resources, integrated water-resource use, water quality, and environmental protection.
Related titles: ◆ English Translation: Water Resources. ISSN 0097-8078.
Indexed: ASFA, B21, ChemAb, ESPM, FR, GeoRef, RefZh, SpeleolAb.
—CASDDS, East View, INIST, Linda Hall. **CCC.**
Published by: (Rossiiskaya Akademiya Nauk/Russian Academy of Sciences, Institut Vodnykh Problem), Izdatel'stvo Nauka, Profsoyuznaya ul 90, Moscow, 117864, Russian Federation. TEL 7-095-3347151, FAX 7-095-4202220, secret@naukaran.ru, http://www.naukaran.ru. Circ: 1,575.

VODOHOSPODARSKY CASOPIS/JOURNAL OF HYDROLOGY AND HYDROMECHANICS. *see* EARTH SCIENCES—Hydrology

628.167 RUS
VODOOCHISTKA. Text in Russian. m. USD 314 in United States (effective 2007). **Document type:** *Journal, Trade.* **Description:** Designed for specialists in ecology, water supply, water purification and preparation. Contains specialized information and standards.
Published by: Izdatel'skii Dom Panorama, Rozhdestvenskaya ul 5/7, Moscow, Russian Federation. TEL 7-495-6259835, FAX 7-495-6259611, idp@yandex.ru, http://www.panor.ru. Ed. Sergey Finaev. **Dist. by:** East View Information Services, 10601 Wayzata Blvd, Minneapolis, MN 55305. TEL 952-252-1201, 800-477-1005, FAX 952-252-1202, info@eastview.com, http://www.eastview.com.

VODOSNABZHENIE I SANITARNAYA TEKHNIKA. *see* PUBLIC HEALTH AND SAFETY

VOLUNTAD HIDRAULICA. *see* ENGINEERING—Hydraulic Engineering

608 540 DEU ISSN 0083-6915
TD203 CODEN: VJWWAU
➤ **VOM WASSER.** Text in German, English. 1927. q. adv. back issues avail.; reprints avail. **Document type:** *Journal, Academic/Scholarly.*
Indexed: A22, ASFA, B21, CIN, ChemAb, ChemTitl, ESPM, GeoRef, SpeleolAb.
—BLDSC (9255.000000), CASDDS, IE, Infotrieve, Ingenta, INIST, Linda Hall. **CCC.**
Published by: (Gesellschaft Deutscher Chemiker, Wasserchemische Gesellschaft, Gesellschaft Deutscher Chemiker), Wiley - V C H Verlag GmbH & Co. KGaA (Subsidiary of: John Wiley & Sons, Inc.), Postfach 101161, Weinheim, 69451, Germany. TEL 49-6201-606400, FAX 49-6201-606184, info@wiley-vch.de. Ed. Frank Bringewski. adv.: page EUR 2,000; trim 180 x 260.

333.91 PAK
W A P D A NEWS. Text in English. 1978. fortn. PKR 100 (effective 1998). **Description:** News coverage of the activities of the authority.
Published by: Water and Power Development Authority, Public Relations Division, WAPDA House, Shara-e-Quaid-e-Azam, Lahore, Pakistan. TEL 92-42-9202633, FAX 92-42-9202002, TELEX 44869 WAPDA PK. Ed. Muhammed Arshad.

628.1 USA ISSN 1097-1726
CODEN: WCPUEN
W C & P INTERNATIONAL. (Water Conditioning & Purification) Text in English. 1959. m. USD 49 in US & Canada (effective 2005). adv. bk.rev. charts; illus. index. **Document type:** *Magazine, Trade.* **Description:** Covers industry news, regulatory developments, new products, and technical, marketing, sales and business management issues related to water conditioning and purification.
Former titles (until Sep. 2001): Water Conditioning and Purification (0746-4029); Water Conditioning (0043-1184); Water Conditioning Sales
Related titles: Online - full content ed.
Indexed: EnvAb.
—IE, Ingenta, Linda Hall.
Published by: Publicom Inc., 2800 E Ft Lowell Rd, Tucson, AZ 85716-1518. TEL 520-323-6144, 520-323-6144, FAX 520-323-7412. Pub., Adv. contact Kurt Peterson. Circ: 20,000 (controlled).

W L B REPORT. (Wasser, Luft und Boden) *see* ENVIRONMENTAL STUDIES

628.1 USA
W R C NEWS AND ANNOUNCEMENTS. Text in English. 1973. irreg. (approx. 2/yr.). free. **Document type:** *Newsletter.*
Published by: Water Resources Center, 278 Env and Agr Sci Bldg, 1101 W Peabody Dr, Urbana, IL 61801. TEL 217-333-0536, FAX 217-244-8583. Ed. Richard E Sparks. Circ: 650.

333.9 USA ISSN 0549-799X
HD1694.N8 CODEN: RWRCDT
W R R I NEWS. (Water Resources Research Institute) Text in English. 1966. bi-m. bk.rev. bibl. index. **Document type:** *Newsletter.* **Description:** Directed to university faculty, government agencies, and the public concerning scientific, technical, legal, economic, and regulatory issues related to water.
Related titles: Online - full text ed.: free.
Indexed: CIN, CPEI, ChemAb, ChemTitl, EngInd, EnvAb, GeoRef, SCOPUS, SpeleolAb.
—CASDDS.
Published by: University of North Carolina at Chapel Hill, Water Resources Research Institute, PO Box 7912, Raleigh, NC 27695-7912. TEL 919-515-2815, FAX 919-515-7802, water_resources@ncsu.edu, http://www.ncsu.edu/wrri. Ed. Jeri Gray. Circ: 3,600.

631.6 USA ISSN 0731-7557
HD1694.N5 CODEN: NMWRAG
W R R I REPORT. Variant title: New Mexico Water Resources Research Institute. Technical Completion Report. Text in English. 1966. irreg. price varies. **Document type:** *Report, Trade.*
Formerly (until 1968): W.R.R.I Publications
Indexed: GeoRef.
Published by: New Mexico Water Resources Research Institute, NMSU MSC 3167, 3170 S Espina St, PO Box 30001, Las Cruces, NM 88003. TEL 575-646-4337, FAX 575-646-6418, nmwrri@nmsu.edu, http://wrri.nmsu.edu/.

333.9 CHE
W S S C C CATALOGUE OF DOCUMENTS AND PUBLICATIONS. (Water Supply and Sanitation Collaborative Council) Text in English. irreg. **Document type:** *Catalog.*
Published by: Water Supply & Sanitation Collaborative Council, c/o WHO, 20 Ave Appia, Geneva 27, 1211, Switzerland. TEL 41-22-7913544, FAX 41-22-7914847, wsscc@who.ch.

▼ **W T - AFVALWATER.** (Wetenschappelijk Tijdschrift) *see* ENVIRONMENTAL STUDIES—Waste Management

620 DEU
TC1 CODEN: WSWSAO
W W T - WASSERWIRTSCHAFT WASSERTECHNIK; Das Praxismagazin fuer Entscheidungen im Trink- und Altwassermanagement. Text in German. 1998. 9/yr. EUR 136.80; EUR 18 newsstand/cover (effective 2010). adv. bk.rev. abstr.; illus. index. **Document type:** *Magazine, Trade.*
Formerly: Wasserwirtschaft, Wassertechnik mit Abwassertechnik (1438-5716); Which was formed by the merger of (1951-1998): Wasserwirtschaft - Wassertechnik (W W T) (0043-0986); (1961-1998): Abwassertechnik (0932-3708); Which was formerly (until 1983): Abwassertechnik und Abfalltechnik (0342-4022); (until 1977): Abwassertechnik (0001-3706); (until 1966): Wasserversorgung und Abwassertechnik in Haus, Hof und Strasse (0509-8866); Which was formed by the merger of (195?-1961): Abwasser-Technik (0723-2578); (1960-1961): Haus, Hof, Strasse (0723-2586)
Indexed: CIN, ChemAb, ESPM, GeoRef, GeotechAb, IBR, IBZ, ICEA, RefZh, SCOPUS, SWRA, SoftAbEng, SpeleolAb, TM.
—BLDSC (9266.500000), CASDDS, IE, Ingenta, INIST, Linda Hall. **CCC.**
Published by: Huss-Medien GmbH, Am Friedrichshain 22, Berlin, 10407, Germany. TEL 49-30-42151289, 49-30-421510, FAX 49-30-42151232, verlag.wirtschaft@hussberlin.de, http://www.huss-medien.de. Ed. Peter-Michael Fritsch. Adv. contact Carmen Blume. Circ: 7,587 (controlled).

333.91 USA
WASHINGTON BASIN OUTLOOK REPORT. Text in English. 1954. bi-m. free. reprints avail. **Document type:** *Government.*
Related titles: Microfiche ed.: (from CIS).
Indexed: AmStI.
Published by: U.S. Department of Agriculture, Natural Resources Conservation Service (Spokane), 316 W Boone Ave, Ste 450, Spokane, WA 99201-2348. TEL 509-353-2341. Circ: 870.

620 CHE ISSN 0377-905X
TC1
WASSER, ENERGIE, LUFT/EAU, ENERGIE, AIR. Text in French, German. 1910. 7/yr. CHF 122.90 domestic; CHF 140 foreign (effective 2002). adv. bk.rev. charts; illus. index, cum.index. **Document type:** *Journal, Trade.* **Description:** Trade publication covering water rights and supply, hydraulic construction, water power utilization, protection of waterways, irrigation, drainage, flood protection, and inland navigation. Includes reports and announcements of events.
Formerly: Wasser und Energiewirtschaft (0043-096X)
Indexed: GeoRef, GeotechAb, ICEA, SoftAbEng.
—INIST, Linda Hall.
Published by: Schweizerischer Wasserwirtschaftsverband, Ruetistr 3 A, Baden, 5401, Switzerland. TEL 41-56-2225069, FAX 41-56-2211083. Ed. Walter Hauenstein. Circ: 3,000.

WASSER, LUFT UND BODEN; Zeitschrift fuer Umwelttechnik. *see* ENVIRONMENTAL STUDIES

333.91 DEU
WASSER MAGAZIN; Kundeninformation der Hamburger Wasserwerke. Text in German. 1981. 2/yr. free. adv. **Document type:** *Magazine, Consumer.*
Published by: Hamburger Wasserwerke GmbH, Billhorner Deich 2, Hamburg, 20539, Germany. TEL 49-40-78882483, FAX 49-40-78882883, pr@hww-hamburg.de, http://www.hww-hamburg.de. Ed. Hans Werner Krueger. adv.: color page EUR 7,925. Circ: 780,000.

WASSER UND ABFALL; Boden - Altlasten - Umweltrecht. *see* ENVIRONMENTAL STUDIES—Pollution

333.7 628.1 DEU ISSN 0512-5030
TD203 CODEN: WAFPDB
WASSER UND ABWASSER IN FORSCHUNG UND PRAXIS. Text in German; Summaries in English, French. 1969. irreg., latest vol.21, 1993. price varies. back issues avail. **Document type:** *Monographic series, Academic/Scholarly.*
—CASDDS, Linda Hall.
Published by: Erich Schmidt Verlag GmbH & Co. (Berlin), Genthiner Str 30 G, Berlin, 10785, Germany. TEL 49-30-2500850, FAX 49-30-250085305, esv@esvmedien.de, http://www.esv.info.

628 340 DEU ISSN 1432-685X
WASSERRECHT. Text in German. a. (plus q. updates). EUR 178 (effective 2010).
Published by: Verlag C.H. Beck oHG, Wilhelmstr 9, Munich, 80801, Germany. TEL 49-89-381890, FAX 49-89-38189398, abo.service@beck.de, http://www.beck.de. Ed. Juergen Taeger.

333.7 340 628.1 DEU ISSN 0508-1254
WASSERRECHT UND WASSERWIRTSCHAFT. Text in German. 1960. irreg., latest vol.42, 2010. price varies. bibl.; charts; illus.; stat. **Document type:** *Monographic series, Academic/Scholarly.*
Indexed: GeoRef, SpeleolAb.
Published by: Erich Schmidt Verlag GmbH & Co. (Berlin), Genthiner Str 30 G, Berlin, 10785, Germany. TEL 49-30-2500850, FAX 49-30-250085305, vertrieb@esvmedien.de.

WASSERTRIEBWERK; Wasserkraft, Wasserwirtschaft, Wasserrecht, Elektrizitaetswirtschaft. *see* ENERGY—Hydroelectrical Energy

628 DEU ISSN 0043-0978
CODEN: WSWTAR
WASSERWIRTSCHAFT; Hydrologie Wasserbau Boden Oekologie. Text in German. 1905. 10/yr. EUR 399 to institutions; EUR 89 to students (effective 2010). adv. bk.rev. abstr.; bibl.; charts; illus. index. reprint service avail. from PSC. **Document type:** *Magazine, Trade.* **Description:** Trade publication for the water and sewer industry. Features technology of water purification, ground-water protection, and sewage treatment. Includes industry news, list of events and suppliers.
Incorporates (1960-2003): Landnutzung und Landentwicklung (1439-0566); Which was formerly (until 2001): Zeitschrift fuer Kulturtechnik und Landentwicklung (0934-666X); (until 1989): Zeitschrift fuer Kulturtechnik und Flurbereinigung (0044-2984); (until 1963): Zeitschrift fuer Kulturtechnik (0372-9982)
Indexed: A32, A34, A37, A38, ApMecR, BA, C25, CABA, ChemAb, DIP, E12, ESPM, F08, F11, F12, FCA, FLUIDEX, G11, GEOBASE, GH, GeoRef, GeotechAb, I11, IBR, IBZ, ICEA, LT, MaizeAb, R12, RRTA, RefZh, S13, S16, SCI, SCOPUS, SWRA, SoftAbEng, SpeleolAb, TAR, TM, W07, W11.
—CASDDS, IE, INIST, Linda Hall. **CCC.**
Published by: (Deutscher Verband fuer Wasserwirtschaft und Kulturbau e.V.), Vieweg und Teubner Verlag (Subsidiary of: Springer Fachmedien Wiesbaden GmbH), Abraham-Lincoln-Str 46, Wiesbaden, 65189, Germany. TEL 49-611-78780, FAX 49-611-7878400, info@viewegteubner.de, http://www.viewegteubner.de. Ed. Stephan Heimerl. Adv. contact Peter Schmidtmann.

627 AUT ISSN 0043-0994
WASSERWIRTSCHAFTLICHE MITTEILUNGEN. Text in German. 1964. m. membership. bk.rev.
Published by: Oesterreichischer Wasserwirtschaftsverband, Marc-Aurel-Strasse 5, Vienna, W 1010, Austria. Circ: 950.

WASTE + WATER MANAGEMENT IN AUSTRALIA. *see* ENVIRONMENTAL STUDIES—Waste Management

WASTE MANAGEMENT SERIES. *see* ENVIRONMENTAL STUDIES—Waste Management

333.91 ZAF
WATER. Text in English. 2/yr. adv.
Published by: Erudita Publications (Pty) Ltd., Cnr 11th Ave & Main Rd, Melville, PO Box 29159, Johannesburg, 2109, South Africa.

627 AUS ISSN 0310-0367
CODEN: WTRMDP
➤ **WATER.** Text in English. 1974. 8/yr. free to members; AUD 12.50 per issue (effective 2008). adv. bk.rev. back issues avail. **Document type:** *Journal, Trade.* **Description:** Provides information on studies of water, water supply and sewerage; treatment, operation, management, reuse, business and environmental aspects.
Incorporates (1989-2000): Crosscurrent
Related titles: Online - full text ed.; Supplement(s): Water Business.
Indexed: A22, A32, ASFA, B21, CIN, ChemAb, ChemTitl, ESPM, FLUIDEX, GEOBASE, RefZh, SCOPUS.
—BLDSC (9267.454000), CASDDS, IE, Ingenta, Linda Hall.
Published by: Australian Water Association, PO Box 222, St Leonards, NSW 1590, Australia. TEL 61-2-94360055, 300-361-426, FAX 61-2-94360155, info@awa.asn.au. Ed. Peter Sterling. Adv. contact Brian Rault TEL 61-3-85345014. B&W page AUD 1,630; trim 21 x 29.7. Circ: 4,700.

628.1 USA ISSN 2155-8434
QH90.A1
▼ ➤ **WATER (SEATTLE).** Text in English. 2009. a. free (effective 2010). **Document type:** *Journal, Academic/Scholarly.* **Description:** Brings together water-oriented research from diverse disciplines such as chemistry, physics, agricultural, environmental, oceanographic, and atmospheric science.
Media: Online - full content.
Published by: Gerald Pollack, Ed. & Pub., University of Washington, 3720 15th Ave NE, Box 355061, Seattle, WA 98195. TEL 206-685-1880, ghp@u.washington.edu.

➤ **WATER 21.** *see* ENVIRONMENTAL STUDIES—Pollution

333.91 FRA ISSN 1965-0175
TD345
➤ **WATER ALTERNATIVES**; an interdisciplinary journal on water, politics and development. Text in English. 2008. 3/yr. free (effective 2011). bk.rev. bibl. **Document type:** *Journal, Academic/Scholarly.* **Description:** Aims to address the full range of issues that water raises in contemporary societies.
Media: Online - full text.
Indexed: A34, A37, A38, Agr, C25, CA, CABA, D01, E04, E05, E12, F08, F12, GH, I11, LT, R12, S12, S13, S16, SCOPUS, T02, TAR, W11.
Published by: Water Alternatives Association, Villa d'Assas, 457 Avenue du Pere Soulas, Montpellier, 34090, France. Eds. Francois Molle, Peter P. Mollinga, Ruth Meinzen-Dick. Pub., R&P Francois Molle.

628.1 340 GBR ISSN 1366-2880
WATER AND DRAINAGE LAW. Variant title: Bates Water & Drainage Law. Text in English. 1990. base vol. plus updates 2/yr. looseleaf. GBP 646 base vol(s). domestic; EUR 853 base vol(s). in Europe; USD 1,111 base vol(s). elsewhere (effective 2011). **Document type:** *Handbook/Manual/Guide, Trade.* **Description:** Provides an up-to-date and comprehensive survey of water and drainage law, covering everything from sewerage and the quality of drinking water to flood defences, recreation on water and freshwater fisheries.
Published by: Sweet & Maxwell Ltd. (Subsidiary of: Thomson Reuters Corp.), 100 Avenue Rd, London, NW3 3PF, United Kingdom. TEL 44-20-73937000, FAX 44-20-74491144, sweetandmaxwell.customer.services@thomson.com. **Subscr. to:** PO Box 1000, Andover SP10 9AF, United Kingdom. TEL 44-20-73938051, sweetandmaxwell.international.queries@thomson.com.

333.91 GBR ISSN 1364-4513
WATER & EFFLUENT TREATMENT NEWS. Abbreviated title: W E T News. Text in English. 1995. m. GBP 82 domestic; GBP 96 foreign (effective 2009). adv. back issues avail. **Document type:** *Newspaper, Trade.* **Description:** Covers all aspects of water supply, treatment and usage, together with effluent treatment. Includes up-to-the-minute news, coverage of each fortnight's big story, technology features and an innovative series on waste minimization.
Incorporates (1974-2003): Water Services (0301-7028)
Indexed: A10, B01, B07, V03.
Published by: Faversham House Group Ltd., Faversham House, 232a Addington Rd, South Croydon, Surrey CR2 8LE, United Kingdom. TEL 44-20-86517100, FAX 44-20-86517117, info@fav-house.com, http://www.fhgmedia.com/. Ed. Maureen Gaines TEL 44-20-86517163. Adv. contact Deborah Lilley TEL 44-161-9031514. color page GBP 1,600, B&W page GBP 1,300. Circ: 6,110.

WATER AND ENERGY ABSTRACTS. *see* WATER RESOURCES—Abstracting, Bibliographies, Statistics

620 IND ISSN 0972-057X
➤ **WATER & ENERGY INTERNATIONAL.** Text in English. 1943. q. INR 1,800 combined subscription domestic (print & online eds.) ; USD 100 combined subscription foreign (print & online eds.) (effective 2011). adv. bk.rev. abstr.; bibl.; charts; illus.; maps; stat. index. back issues avail.; reprints avail. **Document type:** *Journal, Academic/Scholarly.* **Description:** Covers the latest trends in energy and water resources technology.
Formerly (until 1996): Irrigation and Power (0367-9993)
Related titles: Online - full text ed.: INR 1,200 domestic; USD 60 foreign (effective 2011).
Indexed: A22, CRIA, CRICC, ChemAb, FLUIDEX, GEOBASE, GeoRef, GeotechAb, SCOPUS, SpeleolAb.
—IE, Ingenta, INIST, Linda Hall.
Published by: Central Board of Irrigation and Power, Malcha Marg, Chanakyapuri, New Delhi, 110 021, India. TEL 91-11-26115984, FAX 91-11-26116347, cbip@cbip.org. Ed., R&P, Adv. contact C.V.J. Varma. Pub. C V J Varma. **Subscr. to:** I N S I O Scientific Books & Periodicals, PO Box 7234, Indraprastha HPO, New Delhi 110 002, India; Indianjournals.com, Divan Enterprises, B-9, Local Shopping Complex, A-Block, Naraina Vihar, Ring Rd, New Delhi 110 028, India.

620 IND ISSN 0974-4932
WATER AND ENERGY RESEARCH DIGEST. Text in English. 19??. q. **Document type:** *Journal, Academic/Scholarly.*
Related titles: Online - full text ed.: INR 400 domestic; USD 30 foreign (effective 2008).
Published by: Central Board of Irrigation and Power, Malcha Marg, Chanakyapuri, New Delhi, 110 021, India. TEL 91-11-26115984, FAX 91-11-26116347, cbip@cbip.org. **Subscr. to:** Indianjournals.com.

V W Z

333.91 614 GBR ISSN 1747-6585
TD201 CODEN: JIWMEZ

➤ **WATER AND ENVIRONMENT JOURNAL.** Text in English. 1987. q. GBP 364 combined subscription in United Kingdom to institutions (print & online eds.); EUR 462 combined subscription in Europe to institutions (print & online eds.); USD 675 combined subscription in the Americas to institutions (print & online eds.); USD 789 combined subscription elsewhere to institutions (print & online eds.) (effective 2012). adv. bk.rev. charts; illus. index; cum.index. back issues avail.; reprint service avail. from PSC. **Document type:** *Journal, Academic/Scholarly.* **Description:** Covers water, including water resources, river management, pollution control, fisheries, sewerage, navigation, and environmental management, including land and air.
Former titles (until 2005): Chartered Institution of Water and Environmental Management. Journal (1360-4015); (until 1995): Institution of Water and Environmental Management. Journal (0951-7359); Which was formed by the merger of (1973-1987): Public Health Engineer (0300-5925); Which was formerly (until 1973): Institution of Public Health Engineers. Journal (0020-3513); (until 1955): Institution of Sanitary Engineers. Journal (0368-2765); (until 1943): Institution of Sanitary Engineers. Bulletin (0366-4376); (until 1939): Institution of Sanitary Engineers. Journal; (1967-1987): Water Pollution Control (0043-129X); (until 1967): Institution of Sewage Purification. Journal and Proceedings (0368-0215); (until 1933): Institution of Sewage Purification. Proceedings (0370-0100); (until 1932): Association of Managers of Sewage Disposal Works. Proceedings; (1875-1987): Institution of Water Engineers and Scientists. Journal (0309-1600); Which was formerly (until 1975): Institution of Water Engineers. Journal (0020-3556); (until 1947): Institution of Water Engineers. Transactions (0371-814X); (until 1911): Association of Water Engineers. Transactions
Related titles: CD-ROM ed.; Online - full text ed.: ISSN 1747-6593. GBP 314 in United Kingdom to institutions; EUR 399 in Europe to institutions; USD 583 in the Americas to institutions; USD 683 elsewhere to institutions (effective 2012) (from IngentaConnect).
Indexed: A05, A10, A20, A22, A26, A32, A34, A36, A37, A38, ABIPC, AS&TA, AS&TI, ASCA, ASFA, Agr, AgrForAb, B04, B21, BA, BIOBASE, BrTechI, C10, C25, CA, CABA, CIN, CPEI, ChemAb, ChemTitl, CurCont, DBA, E01, E04, E05, E11, E12, E17, EIA, EMBASE, ESPM, EngInd, EnvAb, ExcerpMed, F08, F12, FCA, FLUIDEX, FR, G02, G11, GEOBASE, GH, GeoRef, H16, I05, I11, IABS, ICEA, ISR, Inspec, LT, N02, N04, O01, OR, P32, P33, P37, P39, PN&I, PollutAb, R07, R08, R12, RRTA, Repind, S12, S13, S16, SCI, SCOPUS, SWRA, SpeleolAb, T02, T04, T05, TAR, TriticAb, V03, VS, W07, W10, W11, WildRev, Z01.
—BLDSC (9288.902000), CASDDS, IE, Infotrieve, Ingenta, INIST, Linda Hall. **CCC.**
Published by: (Chartered Institution of Water and Environmental Management), Wiley-Blackwell Publishing Ltd. (Subsidiary of: John Wiley & Sons, Inc.), 9600 Garsington Rd, Oxford, OX4 2DQ, United Kingdom. TEL 44-1865-776868, FAX 44-1865-714591, customerservices@blackwellpublishing.com. Ed. David Butler TEL 44-1392-264064. Adv. contact Craig Pickett TEL 44-1865-476267. B&W page GBP 600, color page GBP 1,300; trim 210 x 276. Circ: 9,700. **Subscr. to:** Journal Customer Services, 9600 Garsington Rd, PO Box 1354, Oxford OX4 2XG, United Kingdom. TEL 44-1865-778315, FAX 44-1865-471775.

363.7 GBR ISSN 1746-028X

WATER AND ENVIRONMENT MAGAZINE. Abbreviated title: W E M. Text in English. 1967. 10/yr. GBP 103 domestic; GBP 145 foreign; GBP 11 per issue domestic; GBP 16 per issue foreign (effective 2009). adv. back issues avail. **Document type:** *Magazine, Trade.* **Description:** Contains articles on a wide range of subjects including air-quality management, environmental information systems, water disinfection, sludge treatment and disposal, river and coastal management, water storage, and environmental monitoring.
Former titles (until 2004): Water and Environment Manager (1362-9360); (until 1996): Chartered Institution of Water and Environmental Management. News (1358-8036); (until 1995): I W E M News; (until 1994): I W E M Newsletter (0964-4245); (until 1988): Institution of Water and Environmental Management. Newsletter
Indexed: A32, E11, FLUIDEX, GEOBASE, SCOPUS, T04.
—BLDSC (9295.123100).
Published by: (Chartered Institution of Water and Environmental Management), Lead Media Ltd., 6 Harforde Ct, John Tate Rd, Foxholes Business Park, Hertford, Herts SG13 7NW, United Kingdom. TEL 44-844-3711940, FAX 44-844-3711941, subs@leadmedia.co.uk, http://www.leadmedia.co.uk. Ed. Erika Yarrow TEL 44-118-9722810. Adv. contact Michael Linegar TEL 44-871-2266690. B&W page GBP 1,233, color page GBP 1,884; trim 210 x 297. Circ: 11,500.

WATER & WASTES DIGEST. *see* ENVIRONMENTAL STUDIES—Waste Management

628.1 USA ISSN 0891-5385
TD365

WATER AND WASTEWATER INTERNATIONAL. Text in English. 1986. bi-m. USD 217; free to qualified personnel (effective 2008). adv. back issues avail. **Document type:** *Magazine, Trade.* **Description:** Contains information on technology, products and trends in the water and wastewater industry.
Incorporates: Drilling & Irrigation International
Related titles: Online - full text ed.: USD 121 (effective 2008).
Indexed: A15, A22, ABIn, B02, B15, B17, B18, CPEI, EngInd, G04, G08, GeoRef, I05, P19, P48, P50, P51, P52, P56, PQC, SCOPUS.
—IE, Infotrieve, Ingenta.
Published by: PennWell Corporation, 1421 S Sheridan Rd, Tulsa, OK 74112. TEL 918-835-3161, 800-331-4463, FAX 918-831-9804, Headquarters@PennWell.com, http://www.pennwell.com. Ed. David Carlos Mogollon TEL 520-326-2346. Adv. contact Dottie LaFerney TEL 512-858-7927. color page USD 5,630; trim 210 x 297. Circ: 11,000.

363.7284 GBR ISSN 1759-5932

WATER & WASTEWATER TREATMENT. Text in English. 1950. m. GBP 82 domestic; GBP 96 foreign (effective 2010). adv. bk.rev. bibl.; charts; illus.; tr.lit. back issues avail. **Document type:** *Journal, Trade.* **Description:** Covers industrial and environmental pollution control.
Former titles (until 2007): Water and Waste Treatment (0950-6551); (until 1985): Water and Waste Treatment Journal (0269-3488); (until 1984): Water and Waste Treatment (0043-1133); (until 1962): Water and Waste Treatment Journal (0511-3563); (until 1957): Water and Sanitary Engineer (0372-7513)
Related titles: Microform ed.: (from MIM, PQC).
Indexed: A22, A36, A37, BA, BMT, BrTechI, C25, CABA, ChemAb, E04, E05, E11, E12, F08, F12, G11, GH, I11, ICEA, LT, P33, P39, S13, S16, SoftAbEng, T04, W11, WSCA, WasteInfo.
—BLDSC (9365.407570), IE, Infotrieve, Ingenta, INIST, Linda Hall. **CCC.**
Published by: Faversham House Group Ltd., Faversham House, 232a Addington Rd, South Croydon, Surrey CR2 8LE, United Kingdom. TEL 44-20-86517100, FAX 44-20-86517117, info@fav-house.com, http://www.fhgmedia.com/. Ed. Natasha Wiseman. Adv. contact Adam Jeffery TEL 44-20-86517147. Circ: 8,680.

WATER ASSET MANAGEMENT INTERNATIONAL. *see* ENVIRONMENTAL STUDIES—Waste Management

628.1 CAN ISSN 1922-8775

WATER CANADA; the complete water magazine. Text in English. 2001. bi-m. CAD 24.97 (effective 2010). adv. back issues avail. **Document type:** *Magazine, Trade.* **Description:** Covers Canadian's water and waterworks industry, from source water extraction, filtration, testing, distribution, packaging and monitoring to wastewater treatment.
Formerly (until 2010): Canadian Water Treatment (1715-670X)
Related titles: Online - full text ed.: CAD 20 (effective 2010).
Indexed: E04, E05.
Published by: Actual Media Inc., 218 Adelaide St W, 3rd Fl, Toronto, ON M5H 1W7, Canada. TEL 416-444-5842, 877-663-6866, FAX 416-444-1176, contact@actualmedia.ca, http://actualmedia.ca. Ed. Kerry Freek TEL 416-444-5842 ext 112. Pub. Todd Latham TEL 416-444-5842 ext 111. Adv. contact Lee Scarlett TEL 416-444-5842 ext 114. Circ: 8,655.

333.91 USA ISSN 2152-4831

WATER CURRENT. Text in English. 19??. q. free (effective 2010). adv. back issues avail. **Document type:** *Newsletter, Academic/Scholarly.*
Related titles: Online - full text ed.: ISSN 2152-4823.
Published by: University of Nebraska at Lincoln, Water Center, School of Natural Resources, 522 Hardin Hall, 3310 Holdrege St, Lincoln, NE 68583. TEL 402-472-3305, FAX 402-472-3610, waterinfo@unl.edu. Ed. Steven W Ress TEL 402-472-9549. Adv. contact Tricia Liedle.

628 USA ISSN 0043-1206

WATER DESALINATION REPORT. Text in English. 1965. w. USD 350 domestic; USD 395 foreign (effective 2002). bk.rev. 4 p./no.; back issues avail. **Document type:** *Newsletter.*
Published by: Maria C. Smith, Ed. & Pub., PO Box 10, Tracey's Landing, MD 20779. TEL 301-261-5010, FAX 301-261-5010.

628.1 333.72 USA ISSN 1934-8479
TD388.A1

WATER EFFICIENCY; the journal for water resource management. Text in English. 2006. bi-m. USD 72 domestic; USD 90 in Canada; USD 150 elsewhere; free to qualified personnel (effective 2011). back issues avail. **Document type:** *Journal, Trade.*
Related titles: Online - full text ed.: ISSN 1934-8487. free (effective 2011).
Indexed: E04, E05, G02.
Published by: Forester Media Inc., PO Box 3100, Santa Barbara, CA 93130. TEL 805-682-1300, FAX 805-682-0200, info@forester.net, http://www.forester.net. Ed. Elizabeth Cutright. Pub. Daniel Waldman TEL 805-679-7616. Adv. contact Ron Guilbault.

WATER, ENERGY AND ENVIRONMENT JOURNAL. *see* ENVIRONMENTAL STUDIES

WATER ENVIRONMENT & TECHNOLOGY. *see* ENVIRONMENTAL STUDIES—Pollution

WATER ENVIRONMENT RESEARCH. *see* ENVIRONMENTAL STUDIES—Pollution

628.1 AUS ISSN 1837-9125

▼ **WATER FOR THE ENVIRONMENT NEWS.** Text in English. 2010. s-a. free (effective 2011). back issues avail. **Document type:** *Newsletter, Government.* **Description:** Guides to environmental water actions and events across New South Wales.
Related titles: Online - full text ed.: free (effective 2011).
Published by: New South Wales Government, Department of Environment, Climate Change and Water, 59-61 Goulburn St, PO Box A290, Sydney South, NSW 1232, Australia. TEL 61-2-99955000, FAX 61-2-99955999, info@environment.nsw.gov.au.

▼ **WATER HISTORY.** *see* ENVIRONMENTAL STUDIES—Pollution

333.91 USA

WATER IMPACTS. Text in English. 1980. q. free. bk.rev. index. back issues avail. **Document type:** *Newsletter.*
Indexed: EnvAb.
Published by: Michigan State University, Institute of Water Research, 115 Manly Miles Bldg, East Lansing, MI 48823. TEL 517-353-3742, FAX 517-353-1812. Ed. Lois G Wolfson. Circ: 2,800.

628.1 GBR ISSN 1476-1777
GB651

WATER INTELLIGENCE ONLINE; an online water, wastewater and environmental information service. Text in English. 2002. m. EUR 2,362 in Europe to institutions; USD 3,077 in North America to institutions; GBP 1,625 to institutions in the UK & elsewhere (effective 2011). back issues avail. **Document type:** *Journal, Academic/Scholarly.* **Description:** Features information service for librarians and individuals providing access to a reference books, research reports, research papers and conference proceedings covering water, wastewater and related environmental topics.
Media: Online - full text.
Published by: I W A Publishing (Subsidiary of: International Water Association), Alliance House, 12 Caxton St, London, SW1H 0QS, United Kingdom. TEL 44-20-76545500, FAX 44-20-76545555, publications@iwap.co.uk, http://www.iwapublishing.com. Ed. Keith Hayward. **Subscr. to:** Portland Customer Services, Commerce Way, Colchester CO2 8HP, United Kingdom. TEL 44-1206-796351, FAX 44-1206-799331, sales@portland-services.com, http://www.portlandpress.com.

333.91 USA ISSN 0250-8060
GB651

➤ **WATER INTERNATIONAL.** Text in English. 1975. q. GBP 490 combined subscription in United Kingdom to institutions (print & online eds.); EUR 784, USD 986 combined subscription to institutions (print & online eds.) (effective 2012). adv. bk.rev. bibl.; illus. back issues avail.; reprint service avail. from PSC. **Document type:** *Journal, Academic/Scholarly.* **Description:** Serves as an international gateway to the people, ideas and networks that are critical to the sustainable management of water resources around the world.
Related titles: Online - full text ed.: ISSN 1941-1707. GBP 441 in United Kingdom to institutions; EUR 706, USD 887 to institutions (effective 2012).
Indexed: A01, A20, A22, A28, A32, A36, A37, AESIS, APA, ASCA, ASFA, BIOBASE, BrCerAb, C&ISA, C25, CA, CA/WCA, CABA, CIA, CerAb, CivEngAb, CorrAb, E&CAJ, E01, E04, E05, E11, E12, EEA, EIA, EMA, ESPM, EnerInd, EnvAb, EnvEAb, F08, F12, FCA, FR, GH, GeoRef, H15, H16, I11, IABS, LT, M&TEA, M09, MBF, METADEX, MaizeAb, N02, P38, PAIS, R11, R12, Repind, S13, S16, SCI, SCOPUS, SSciA, SolStAb, SpeleolAb, T02, T04, T05, TAR, W07, W11, WAA.
—BLDSC (9270.400000), IE, Infotrieve, Ingenta, INIST, Linda Hall. **CCC.**
Published by: (International Water Resources Association), Routledge (Subsidiary of: Taylor & Francis Group), 325 Chestnut St, Ste 800, Philadelphia, PA 19106. TEL 800-354-1420, FAX 215-625-2940, journals@routledge.com, http://www.routledge.com. Adv. contact Linda Hann TEL 44-1344-779945. Circ: 1,800.

➤ **WATER INVESTMENT NEWSLETTER.** *see* BUSINESS AND ECONOMICS—Investments

628 JPN

WATER JAPAN; Japan's water works yearbook. Text in English. 1966. a. JPY 1,300. **Document type:** *Directory, Trade.* **Description:** Discusses supply systems, quality management, pollution control. Includes international activities and an industry directory.
Formerly: Japan Water Works Association. Journal
Published by: (Journal of Water Works Industry/Suido Sangyo Shinbunsha), Suido Sangyo Shinbun Ltd., Osaka Godo Bldg, 1-5 Doyama-cho, Kita-ku, Osaka-shi, 530-0027, Japan. Ed. Hiroshi Ishimaru.

340 628.1 USA ISSN 0737-044X

WATER LAW NEWSLETTER. Text in English. 1966. 3/yr. USD 48 (effective 2010). back issues avail. **Document type:** *Newsletter, Government.*
Former titles (until 1976): Rocky Mountain Mineral Law Newsletter. Water Law (0737-0431); (until 1968): Water Law Newsletter
Related titles: Online - full text ed.
Indexed: SpeleolAb.
—**CCC.**
Published by: Rocky Mountain Mineral Law Foundation, 9191 Sheridan Blvd, Ste 203, Westminster, CO 80031. TEL 303-321-8100, FAX 303-321-7657, info@rmmlf.org.

628.1 340 USA ISSN 1521-3455
K27

WATER LAW REVIEW. Key Title: University of Denver Water Law Review. Text in English. 1990. s-a. USD 40 to institutions; USD 20 to students; USD 25 per issue to institutions; USD 15 per issue to students (effective 2009). back issues avail.; reprint service avail. from WSH. **Document type:** *Journal, Academic/Scholarly.* **Description:** Features articles concerning water law and water related issues.
Formerly (until 1997): Water Court Reporter
Related titles: Online - full text ed.
Indexed: B04, BRD, CLI, E04, E05, G08, I01, ILP, L07, LRI, W03, W05.
—CIS.
Published by: University of Denver, College of Law, 2255 E Evans Ave, Denver, CO 80208. TEL 303-871-6223, FAX 303-871-6503, admissions@law.du.edu. Ed. Danielle Sexton.

628.1 NPL ISSN 1027-0345
HD1698.N4

➤ **WATER NEPAL.** Text in English. 1987. s-a. **Document type:** *Journal, Academic/Scholarly.* **Description:** Discusses water management problems in Nepal. It analysis of long-term development needs and trends, dispute resolution, impact assessment and mitigation, overcoming weaknesses and ensuring institutional learning for sustainable water development; as well as balancing water developments with social and environmental objectives at the micro, meso and macro levels by understanding the interdisciplinary relationship between water use and sustainability.
Related titles: Online - full text ed.
Published by: Nepal Water Conservation Foundation, Baluatar, P O Box 2221, Kathmandu, Nepal. TEL 977-1-5524816, nwcf@wlink.com.np, info@nwcf.org.np, http://www.nwcf.org.np. Ed. Alaya Dixit.

333.91 CAN ISSN 0821-0233
TD226.A1

WATER NEWS/A PROPOS DE L'EAU. Text in English. 1982. q. adv. **Document type:** *Newsletter, Academic/Scholarly.* **Description:** Provides news and information on branch and membership activities and disseminates water resource related information of a regional and national character.
Indexed: EnvAb.
—BLDSC (9270.940000).
Published by: Canadian Water Resources Association/Association Canadienne des Ressources Hydriques, 9 Corvus Court, Ottawa, ON K2E 7Z4, Canada. FAX 519-621-4844, services@aic.ca. Ed. Jim Bauer.

628 GHA ISSN 0043-1265

WATER NEWS. Text in English. 1968. bi-m. free. adv. bk.rev.
Former titles: Sewerage News; Water
Indexed: AESIS.
Published by: Ghana Water & Sewerage Corporation, PO Box M 194, Accra, Ghana. Ed. E Y Frempong Mensah. Circ: 8,000.

551.4 333.9 USA

WATER PARTNERS INTERNATIONAL. ANNUAL REPORT. Text in English. a.
Related titles: E-mail ed.
Published by: Water Partners International, PO Box 654, Columbia, MO 65205-0654. TEL 573-447-2222, FAX 573-447-2221.

333.91 GBR ISSN 1366-7017
TD201 CODEN: WPAOAH

➤ **WATER POLICY.** Text in English. 1998. bi-m. EUR 1,123 combined subscription in Europe to institutions (print & online eds.); USD 1,389 combined subscription in North America to institutions (print & online eds.); GBP 715 combined subscription to institutions in the UK & elsewhere (print & online eds.) (effective 2011). back issues avail. **Document type:** *Journal, Academic/Scholarly.* **Description:** Brings out analyses, reviews and debates on all policy aspects of water resources.
Related titles: Online - full text ed.: (from IngentaConnect).

Indexed: A01, A20, A34, A36, A37, A38, ASFA, AgrForAb, BA, BIOBASE, C25, CA, CABA, CurCont, E04, E05, E12, ESPM, EnvAb, F08, F12, GH, H16, I11, IABS, ICEA, LT, M&GPA, N02, OR, P32, P34, PGegResA, PollutAb, R11, R12, S13, S16, SCI, SCOPUS, SSciA, SWRA, T02, T05, TAR, VS, W07, W11.
—BLDSC (9270.996000), IE, Infotrieve, Ingenta, INIST. **CCC.**
Published by: (World Water Council FRA), I W A Publishing (Subsidiary of: International Water Association), Alliance House, 12 Caxton St, London, SW1H 0QS, United Kingdom. TEL 44-20-76545500, FAX 44-20-76545555, publications@iwap.co.uk, http://www.iwapublishing.com. Ed. Jerome Delli Priscoli TEL 703-428-6372. **Subscr. to:** Portland Customer Services, Commerce Way, Colchester CO2 8HP, United Kingdom. TEL 44-1206-796351, FAX 44-1206-799331, sales@portland-services.com, http://www.portlandpress.com.

628.1 USA
WATER POLICY REPORT. Text in English. 1992. bi-w. USD 700 in US & Canada; USD 750 elsewhere (effective 2008). back issues avail. **Document type:** *Newsletter, Trade.*
Related titles: E-mail ed.; Online - full text ed.: USD 320 to individuals; USD 830 to corporations (effective 2008).
Published by: Inside Washington Publishers, 1919 South Eads St, Ste 201, Arlington, VA 22202. TEL 703-416-8500, 800-424-9068, custsvc@iwpnews.com, http://www.iwpnews.com.

WATER PRACTICE. *see* ENVIRONMENTAL STUDIES

628.1 GBR ISSN 1751-231X
➤ **WATER PRACTICE AND TECHNOLOGY.** Text in English. 2006. q. EUR 280 in Europe to institutions; USD 366 in North America to institutions; GBP 193 to institutions in the UK & elsewhere (effective 2011). back issues avail. **Document type:** *Journal, Academic/Scholarly.* **Description:** Provides information for water practitioners, including those active in utilities, consultants and engineers, enables readers to find and access the information they need.
Media: Online - full text.
Indexed: A37, A38, D01, F12, G11, H17, I11, O01, P40, PGrRegA, S12, S13, S16.
—CCC.
Published by: I W A Publishing (Subsidiary of: International Water Association), Alliance House, 12 Caxton St, London, SW1H 0QS, United Kingdom. TEL 44-20-76545500, FAX 44-20-76545555, publications@iwap.co.uk, http://www.iwapublishing.com. Ed. Helmut Kroiss. **Subscr. to:** Portland Customer Services, Commerce Way, Colchester CO2 8HP, United Kingdom. TEL 44-1206-796351, FAX 44-1206-799331, sales@portland-services.com, http://www.portlandpress.com.

333.91 CAN ISSN 1707-1283
WATER PROFESSIONAL. Text in English. 2003. bi-m. **Document type:** *Magazine, Trade.* **Description:** Features stories, industry profiles, product developments and innovations in water and wastewater treatment and drinking water safety and water news from Canada and around the world.
Published by: August Communications, 225-530 Century St, Winnipeg, MB R3H 0Y4, Canada. TEL 204-957-0265, 888-573-1136, FAX 204-957-0217, 866-957-0217, info@august.ca, http://www.august.ca.

628.1 USA ISSN 0745-1512
WATER QUALITY ASSOCIATION MEMBERSHIP DIRECTORY. Text in English. bi-m. membership. adv. 200 p./no.; **Document type:** *Directory, Trade.*
Formerly: Water Quality Association Newsletter
Published by: Water Quality Association, 4151 Naperville Rd., Lisle, IL 60532. TEL 630-505-0160, FAX 630-505-9637, info@wqa.org, http://www.wqa.org/. Adv. contact Margrit Foxre. Circ: 3,000.

333.91 CAN ISSN 0843-5871
WATER QUALITY DATA FOR ONTARIO LAKES AND STREAMS. CENTRAL REGION. Text in English. 1965. a. free. **Document type:** *Government.*
Supersedes in part (in 1982): Water Quality Data for Ontario Lakes and Streams (0383-5472)
—Linda Hall.
Published by: Ministry of Environment and Energy, Water Resources Branch, 135 St Clair Ave W, Toronto, ON M4V 1P5, Canada. TEL 416-323-4321, FAX 416-323-4564.

333.91 CAN ISSN 0843-5820
WATER QUALITY DATA FOR ONTARIO LAKES AND STREAMS. NORTHEASTERN REGION. Text in English. 1965. a. free. **Document type:** *Government.*
Supersedes in part (in 1982): Water Quality Data for Ontario Lakes and Streams (0383-5472)
—Linda Hall.
Published by: Ministry of Environment and Energy, Water Resources Branch, 135 St Clair Ave W, Toronto, ON M4V 1P5, Canada. TEL 416-323-4321, FAX 416-323-4564.

363.7394 CAN ISSN 0843-5863
WATER QUALITY DATA FOR ONTARIO LAKES AND STREAMS. NORTHWESTERN REGION. Text in English. 1965. a. free. **Document type:** *Government.*
Supersedes in part (in 1982): Water Quality Data for Ontario Lakes and Streams (0383-5472)
—Linda Hall.
Published by: Ministry of Environment and Energy, Water Resources Branch, 135 St Clair Ave W, Toronto, ON M4V 1P5, Canada. TEL 416-323-4321, FAX 416-323-4564.

333.91 CAN ISSN 0843-5839
WATER QUALITY DATA FOR ONTARIO LAKES AND STREAMS. SOUTHEASTERN REGION. Text in English. 1965. a. free. **Document type:** *Government.*
Supersedes in part (in 1982): Water Quality Data for Ontario Lakes and Streams (0383-5472)
—Linda Hall.
Published by: Ministry of Environment and Energy, Water Resources Branch, 135 St Clair Ave W, Toronto, ON M4V 1P5, Canada. TEL 416-323-4321, FAX 416-323-4564.

333.91 CAN ISSN 0843-5847
WATER QUALITY DATA FOR ONTARIO LAKES AND STREAMS. SOUTHWESTERN REGION. Text in English. 1965. a. free. **Document type:** *Government.*
Supersedes in part (in 1982): Water Quality Data for Ontario Lakes and Streams (0383-5472)
—Linda Hall.
Published by: Ministry of Environment and Energy, Water Resources Branch, 135 St Clair Ave W, Toronto, ON M4V 1P5, Canada. TEL 416-323-4321, FAX 416-323-4564.

333.91 CAN ISSN 0843-5855
WATER QUALITY DATA FOR ONTARIO LAKES AND STREAMS. WEST CENTRAL REGION. Text in English. 1965. a. free. **Document type:** *Government.*
Supersedes in part (in 1982): Water Quality Data for Ontario Lakes and Streams (0383-5472)
—Linda Hall.
Published by: Ministry of Environment and Energy, Water Resources Branch, 135 St Clair Ave W, Toronto, ON M4V 1P5, Canada. TEL 416-323-4321, FAX 416-323-4564.

▼ **WATER QUALITY, EXPOSURE AND HEALTH.** *see* ENVIRONMENTAL STUDIES—Pollution

332 USA ISSN 1092-0978
WATER QUALITY PRODUCTS. Abbreviated title: W Q P. Text in English. 1997. m. free domestic to qualified personnel; USD 95 foreign (effective 2008). adv. back issues avail. **Document type:** *Magazine, Trade.* **Description:** Provides balanced editorial content including developments in water conditioning, filtration and disinfection for residential, commercial and industrial systems.
Formerly (until 1997): Water Quality Dealer (1085-8768)
Related titles: Online - full text ed.
Indexed: A28, A32, APA, BrCerAb, C&ISA, CA/WCA, CIA, CerAb, CivEngAb, CorrAb, E&CAJ, E11, EEA, EMA, ESPM, EnvEAb, H15, M&TEA, M09, MBF, METADEX, PollutAb, SSciA, SWRA, SolStAb, T04, WAA.
—Linda Hall.
Published by: Scranton Gillette Communications, Inc., 3030 W Salt Creek Ln, Ste 201, Arlington Heights, IL 60005. TEL 847-391-1000, FAX 847-390-0408, hgillette@sgcmail.com, http://www.scrantongillette.com.

WATER QUALITY RESEARCH JOURNAL OF CANADA. *see* ENVIRONMENTAL STUDIES—Pollution

628.1 USA ISSN 1946-116X
THE WATER REPORT. Text in English. m. USD 249 (effective 2008). **Document type:** *Newsletter, Trade.* **Description:** Contains articles on water law issues, regulation, marketplace, and related events.
Related titles: Online - full text ed.: ISSN 1946-1178.
Published by: Envirotech Publications, Inc., 260 N Polk St, Eugene, OR 97402. TEL 541-343-8504, FAX 541-683-8279. Eds. David Light, David Moon.

627 GBR ISSN 0043-1354
TD420 CODEN: WATRAG
➤ **WATER RESEARCH.** Text in English. 1958. 20/yr. EUR 5,557 in Europe to institutions; JPY 738,000 in Japan to institutions; USD 6,217 elsewhere to institutions (effective 2012). adv. bk.rev. charts; illus.; stat. index, cum.index. back issues avail.; reprints avail. **Document type:** *Journal, Academic/Scholarly.* **Description:** Covers all aspects of the pollution of ground water, marine and fresh water, and the management of water resources and water quality.
Supersedes in part (in 1967): Air and Water Pollution (0568-3408); Which was formerly (until 1963): International Journal of Air and Water Pollution (0367-682X); (until 1961): International Journal of Air Pollution (0367-8237)
Related titles: Microfiche ed.: (from MIM); Microfilm ed.: (from PQC); Online - full text ed.: ISSN 1879-2448 (from IngentaConnect, ScienceDirect).
Indexed: A01, A03, A05, A08, A20, A22, A23, A24, A26, A28, A32, A34, A35, A36, A37, A38, ABIPC, APA, APD, APIAb, AS&TA, AS&TI, ASCA, ASFA, AgBio, Agr, AgrForAb, B&BAb, B04, B13, B19, B21, B23, B25, BA, BIOBASE, BIOSIS Prev, BP, BioEngAb, BrCerAb, C&ISA, C10, C24, C25, C30, C33, CA, CA/WCA, CABA, CIA, CIN, CIS, CPEI, CRFR, CerAb, ChemAb, CivEngAb, CorrAb, CurCont, D01, DBA, E&CAJ, E04, E05, E11, E12, EEA, EMA, EMBASE, ESPM, EnerRev, EngInd, EnvAb, EnvEAb, EnvInd, ExcerpMed, F08, F11, F12, FCA, FLUIDEX, FR, FS&TA, G11, GEOBASE, GH, GeoRef, H15, H16, H17, I05, I10, I11, IABS, ICEA, ISR, IndMed, IndVet, Inspec, LT, M&TEA, M09, MBF, MEDLINE, METADEX, MaizeAb, MycolAb, N02, N03, N04, N05, O01, OR, OceAb, P&BA, P30, P32, P33, P37, P38, P39, P40, PGegResA, PGrRegA, PHN&I, PN&I, PollutAb, R07, R08, R11, R12, R13, RA&MP, RRTA, RefZh, Repind, S12, S13, S16, S17, SCI, SCOPUS, SWRA, SoftAbEng, SolStAb, SoyAb, SpeleolAb, T02, T04, T05, TAR, TriticAb, VITIS, VS, W07, W10, W11, WAA, WasteInfo, WildRev.
—BLDSC (9273.400000), CASDDS, IE, Infotrieve, Ingenta, INIST, Linda Hall, PADDS. **CCC.**
Published by: (Water Quality Association USA), I W A Publishing (Subsidiary of: International Water Association), Alliance House, 12 Caxton St, London, SW1H 0QS, United Kingdom. TEL 44-20-76545500, FAX 44-20-76545555, publications@iwap.co.uk, http://www.iwapublishing.com. Eds. Mark van Loosdrecht TEL 31-15-2781618, Mogens Henze. **Subscr. to:** Elsevier Ltd, The Blvd, Langford Ln, Kidlington, Oxford OX5 1GB, United Kingdom. TEL 44-1865-843434, FAX 44-1865-843912, journalscustomerserviceemea@elsevier.com, http://www.elsevier.com.

628.168 GBR
WATER RESEARCH CENTRE. ANNUAL REPORT AND ACCOUNTS. Text in English. 1974. a. free. **Document type:** *Corporate.*
Former titles: Water Research Centre. Annual Review (0954-5638); (until 1985): Water Research Centre. Annual Report and Accounts (0144-9370); (until 1979): Water Research Centre. Annual Report (0143-2443); Which was formed by the merger of: Water Research Association. Annual Report (0509-9005); (1956-1973): Water Pollution Research (0083-7660); Which was formerly (1928-1956): Water Pollution Research Board. Report (Year)
—Linda Hall.
Published by: Water Research Centre, Frankland Rd, Blagrove, Swindon, Wilts SN5 8YF, United Kingdom. TEL 44-1793-865000, FAX 44-1793-865001, solutions@wrcplc.co.uk. Circ: 5,000.

333.91 551.4 NGA ISSN 0795-6495
WATER RESOUCES. Text in English. 1988. s-a.
Indexed: GeoRef.
Published by: Nigerian Association of Hydrogeologists, University of Benin, Benin City, Nigeria.

628.1 AUS ISSN 1834-2620
WATER RESOURCE ALLOCATION PLANNING. Text in English. 2006. irreg. **Document type:** *Monographic series, Trade.*
Media: Online - full text.
Published by: Western Australia, Department of Water, 168 St George's Terrace, PO Box K822, Perth, W.A. 6842, Australia. TEL 61-8-63647600, FAX 61-8-63647601, http://portal.water.wa.gov.au/portal/page?_pageid=1318,1&_dad=portal&_schema=PORTAL.

628.1 AUS ISSN 1449-8901
WATER RESOURCE TECHNICAL REPORT SERIES. Text in English. 2004. irreg. **Document type:** *Report, Trade.*
Media: Online - full text. **Related titles:** Print ed.
Published by: Western Australia, Department of Water, 168 St George's Terrace, PO Box K822, Perth, W.A. 6842, Australia. TEL 61-8-63647600, FAX 61-8-63647601, http://portal.water.wa.gov.au/portal/page?_pageid=1318,1&_dad=portal&_schema=PORTAL.

553.7 333.9 RUS ISSN 0097-8078
GB746 CODEN: WARED4
➤ **WATER RESOURCES.** Text in English. 1972. bi-m. EUR 4,045, USD 3,668 combined subscription to institutions (print & online eds.) (effective 2012). back issues avail. **Document type:** *Journal, Academic/Scholarly.* **Description:** Examines and reports developments in assessing water resources, integrated water-resource use, water quality, and environmental protection, as well as the social and legal aspects of water-resources conservation.
Related titles: Microfilm ed.: (from PQC); Online - full text ed.: ISSN 1608-344X (from IngentaConnect); ◆ Translation of: Vodnye Resursy. ISSN 0321-0596.
Indexed: A22, A26, A32, A33, AESIS, ASFA, Agr, B21, BibLing, C33, CA, CIN, ChemAb, ChemTitl, E01, E04, E05, ESPM, FLUIDEX, GEOBASE, GeoRef, I05, ICEA, M&GPA, P26, P48, P52, P54, P56, PQC, PollutAb, SCI, SCOPUS, SWRA, SpeleolAb, T02, ToxAb, W07.
—BLDSC (0431.700000), CASDDS, East View, IE, Infotrieve, Ingenta, INIST, Linda Hall. **CCC.**
Published by: (Rossiiskaya Akademiya Nauk/Russian Academy of Sciences), M A I K Nauka - Interperiodica (Subsidiary of: Pleiades Publishing, Inc.), Profsoyuznaya ul 90, Moscow, 117997, Russian Federation. TEL 7-095-3347420, FAX 7-095-3360666, compmg@maik.ru, http://www.maik.ru. Ed. Martin G Khublaryan. **Dist. in the Americas by:** Springer New York LLC, Journal Fulfillment, PO Box 2485, Secaucus, NJ 07096. TEL 212-460-1500, FAX 201-348-4505; **Dist. outside of the Americas by:** Springer, Haber Str 7, Heidelberg 69126, Germany. TEL 49-6221-3454303, FAX 49-6221-3454229.

333.91 USA
WATER RESOURCES ASSOCIATION OF THE DELAWARE RIVER BASIN. ALERTING BULLETIN. Text in English. irreg., latest vol.228, 1988. membership.
Published by: Water Resources Association of the Delaware River Basin, Davis Rd, PO Box 867, Valley Forge, PA 19481. TEL 610-917-0090, FAX 610-917-0091.

333.91 USA
WATER RESOURCES ASSOCIATION OF THE DELAWARE RIVER BASIN. NEWSLETTER. Text in English. 1962. q. membership. Supplement avail. **Document type:** *Newsletter.*
Published by: Water Resources Association of the Delaware River Basin, Davis Rd, PO Box 867, Valley Forge, PA 19481. TEL 610-917-0090, FAX 610-917-0091. Ed. William H Palmer. Circ: 1,500.

333.91 USA ISSN 0741-0689
GB1225.A4
WATER RESOURCES DATA FOR ALASKA. Text in English. a. **Document type:** *Government.*
Indexed: GeoRef.
Published by: U.S. Geological Survey, Water Resources Division, Alaska District, 4230 University Dr, Anchorage, AK 99508-4664. TEL 907-786-7000, http://alaska.usgs.gov/index.html.

333.91 USA ISSN 0741-0697
GB1225.C6
WATER RESOURCES DATA FOR COLORADO. Text in English. a. **Document type:** *Government.*
Indexed: GeoRef.
Published by: U.S. Geological Survey, Water Resources Division, Colorado District, Denver Federal Cntr MS-415 Bldg 53, Denver, CO 80225. TEL 303-236-4882, http://co.water.usgs.gov/index.html.

333.91 USA ISSN 0276-1289
WATER RESOURCES DATA FOR CONNECTICUT. Text in English. 1965. a.
Related titles: Online - full text ed.: ISSN 1946-3669.
Indexed: GeoRef.
—Linda Hall.
Published by: U.S. Geological Survey, Water Resources Division, Connecticut District, 101 Pitkin St, E. Hartford, CT 06108. TEL 860-291-6740, FAX 860-291-6799, http://water.usgs.gov, http://ct.water.usgs.gov.

333.91 USA ISSN 0275-2689
GB1225.F6
WATER RESOURCES DATA FOR FLORIDA. Text in English. 1965. a.
Related titles: Online - full text ed.: ISSN 1936-5292.
Indexed: GeoRef.
—Linda Hall.
Published by: U.S. Geological Survey, Water Resources Division, Florida District, 9100 NW 36th St, Ste 107, Miami, FL 33178. TEL 305-717-5845, FAX 305-717-5801, http://fl.water.usgs.gov.

333.91 USA ISSN 0093-5980
WATER RESOURCES DATA FOR GEORGIA. Text in English. 1965. a.
Indexed: GeoRef.
—Linda Hall.
Published by: U.S. Geological Survey, Water Resources Division, Georgia District, 3039 Amwiler Rd, Ste 130, Atlanta, GA 30360-2824. TEL 770-662-8816, http://waterdata.usgs.gov/nwis.

333.91 USA ISSN 0364-4324
GB1225.I2
WATER RESOURCES DATA FOR IDAHO. Text in English. 1965. a.
Related titles: CD-ROM ed.: ISSN 1557-1742; Online - full text ed.: ISSN 1557-1734.
Indexed: GeoRef.
—Linda Hall.

V W Z

Published by: U.S. Geological Survey, Water Resources Division, Idaho District, 230 Collings Rd, Boise, ID 83702. TEL 208-387-1341, FAX 208-387-1372. **Dist. by:** NTIS, 5285 Port Royal Rd, Springfield, VA 22161. info@ntis.gov.

333.91 USA ISSN 0364-4332
GB1225.I27
WATER RESOURCES DATA FOR ILLINOIS. Text in English. 1965. a.
Indexed: GeoRef.
—Linda Hall.
Published by: U.S. Geological Survey, Water Resources Division, Illinois District, 221 N. Broadway, Urbana, IL 61801. TEL 217-344-0037, FAX 217-344-0082, http://il.water.usgs.gov/. **Dist. by:** NTIS, 5285 Port Royal Rd, Springfield, VA 22161. info@ntis.gov.

333.91 USA ISSN 0364-4340
GB1225.I3
WATER RESOURCES DATA FOR INDIANA. Text in English. 1965. a.
Indexed: GeoRef.
—Linda Hall.
Published by: U.S. Geological Survey, Water Resources Division, Indiana District, 5957 Lakeside Blvd, Indianapolis, IN 46278-1996. TEL 317-290-3333, FAX 317-290-3313, http://in.water.usgs.gov/. **Dist. by:** NTIS, 5285 Port Royal Rd, Springfield, VA 22161. info@ntis.gov.

333.91 USA ISSN 0364-4359
GB1225.I8
WATER RESOURCES DATA FOR IOWA. Text in English. 1965. a.
Indexed: GeoRef.
—Linda Hall.
Published by: U.S. Geological Survey, Water Resources Division, Iowa District, PO Box 1230, Iowa City, IA 52244 . TEL 319-337-4191, FAX 319-358-3606.

333.91 USA ISSN 0741-4803
GB1225.K2
WATER RESOURCES DATA FOR KANSAS. Text in English. 1965. a.
Indexed: GeoRef.
—Linda Hall.
Published by: U.S. Geological Survey, Water Resources Division, Kansas District, 4821 Quail Crest Pl, Lawrence, KS 66049-3839. TEL 785-842-9909, FAX 785-832-3500, GS-W-KS_info@usgs.gov.

333.91 USA ISSN 0364-4081
GB1225.K4
WATER RESOURCES DATA FOR KENTUCKY. Text in English. 1965. a.
Indexed: GeoRef.
—Linda Hall.
Published by: U.S. Geological Survey, Water Resources Division, Kentucky District, 9818 Bluegrass Parkway, Louisville, KY 40299. TEL 502-493-1910, http://ky.water.usgs.gov/. **Dist. by:** NTIS, 5285 Port Royal Rd, Springfield, VA 22161. info@ntis.gov.

333.91 USA ISSN 0364-4375
GB1225.M5
WATER RESOURCES DATA FOR MICHIGAN. Text in English. 1909. a. free (effective 2011). **Document type:** *Report, Government.*
Former titles (until 1965): Surface Water Records of Michigan (0565-5986); (until 1961): Surface Water-Supply of the United States. Pt. 4, V. 1-2. St. Lawrence River Basin
Related titles: Online - full text ed.
Indexed: GeoRef.
—Linda Hall.
Published by: U.S. Geological Survey, 12201 Sunrise Valley Dr, Reston, VA 20192. TEL 703-648-5953, 800-228-0975, http://www.usgs.gov/.

333.91 USA ISSN 0364-4383
GB1225.M6
WATER RESOURCES DATA FOR MINNESOTA. Text in English. 1965. a.
Related titles: Online - full text ed.: ISSN 1933-8643.
Indexed: GeoRef.
—Linda Hall.
Published by: U.S. Geological Survey, Water Resources Division, Minnesota District, 2280 Woodale Dr, Mounds View, MN 55112. TEL 763-783-3100. **Dist. by:** NTIS, 5285 Port Royal Rd, Springfield, VA 22161. info@ntis.gov.

333.91 USA ISSN 0364-4073
GB1225.M9
WATER RESOURCES DATA FOR MONTANA. Text in English. 1961. a. **Document type:** *Government.*
Formerly (until 1965): Surface Water Records of Montana
Related titles: Online - full text ed.: ISSN 1933-463X.
Indexed: GeoRef.
—Linda Hall.
Published by: U.S. Geological Survey, Water Resources Division, Montana District, 3162 Bozeman Ave, Helena, MT 59601. TEL 406-457-5900, http://mt.water.usgs.gov/.

333.91 USA ISSN 0363-1974
GB705.N2
WATER RESOURCES DATA FOR NEBRASKA. Text in English. 1965. a.
Related titles: Online - full text ed.: Water Resources Data. Nebraska. ISSN 1933-4648.
Indexed: GeoRef.
—Linda Hall.
Published by: U.S. Geological Survey, Water Resources Division, Nebraska District, 100 Centennial Mall N Ste 406, Lincoln, NE 68508. TEL 402-437-5082, http://ne.water.usgs.gov/. **Dist. by:** NTIS, 5285 Port Royal Rd, Springfield, VA 22161. info@ntis.gov.

333.91 USA ISSN 0364-4065
GB1225.N6
WATER RESOURCES DATA FOR NEW MEXICO. Text in English. 1965. a.
Related titles: Online - full text ed.: ISSN 1936-5365.
Indexed: GeoRef.
—Linda Hall.
Published by: U.S. Geological Survey, Water Resources Division, New Mexico District, 5338 Montgomery NE Ste 400, Albuquerque, NM 87109. TEL 505-830-7900, http://nm.water.usgs.gov/. **Dist. by:** NTIS, 5285 Port Royal Rd, Springfield, VA 22161. info@ntis.gov.

333.91 USA ISSN 0734-5747
WATER RESOURCES DATA FOR NORTH CAROLINA. Text in English. 1965. a.
Indexed: GeoRef.
—Linda Hall.
Published by: U.S. Geological Survey, Water Resources Division, North Carolina District, 3916 Sunset Ridge Rd, Raleigh, NC 27607. TEL 919-571-4000, FAX 919-571-4041, http://nc.water.usgs.gov/.

333.91 USA ISSN 0364-4405
WATER RESOURCES DATA FOR NORTH DAKOTA. Text in English. 1966. a.
Indexed: GeoRef.
—Linda Hall.
Published by: U.S. Geological Survey, Water Resources Division, North Dakota District, 821 E. Interstate Ave, Bismarck, ND 58503-1199.

333.91 USA ISSN 0197-0755
GB1225.P4
WATER RESOURCES DATA FOR PENNSYLVANIA. Text in English. 1965. a.
Indexed: GeoRef.
—Linda Hall.
Published by: U.S. Geological Survey, Water Resources Division, Pennsylvania District, 215 Limekiln Rd, New Cumberland, PA 17070. TEL 717-730-6900, FAX 717-730-6997, http://pa.water.usgs.gov/. **Dist. by:** NTIS, 5285 Port Royal Rd, Springfield, VA 22161. info@ntis.gov.

553.7 333.91 USA ISSN 0732-9997
GB1225.S6
WATER RESOURCES DATA FOR SOUTH CAROLINA. Text in English. 1965. a. free (effective 2007). **Document type:** *Journal, Trade.*
Related titles: Online - full text ed.: ISSN 1933-5032.
Indexed: GeoRef.
—Linda Hall.
Published by: U.S. Geological Survey, Water Resources Division, South Carolina District, Stephenson Center, Suite 129, 720 Cracern Rd, Columbia, SC 29210-7651. TEL 803-750-6100. **Dist. by:** NTIS, 5285 Port Royal Rd, Springfield, VA 22161. info@ntis.gov.

333.91 USA ISSN 0741-451X
GB1225.S8
WATER RESOURCES DATA FOR SOUTH DAKOTA. Text in English. 1965. a.
Formerly (until 1966): Water Resources Data for North Dakota and South Dakota (0197-0518)
Indexed: GeoRef.
—Linda Hall.
Published by: U.S. Geological Survey, Water Resources Division, South Dakota District, 111 Kansas Ave., S.E., Huron, SD 57350. TEL 605-352-4241, http://sd.water.usgs.gov. **Dist. by:** NTIS, 5285 Port Royal Rd, Springfield, VA 22161. info@ntis.gov.

333.91 USA ISSN 0163-9447
GB1225.T4
WATER RESOURCES DATA FOR TENNESSEE. Text in English. 1965. a.
Related titles: Online - full text ed.: ISSN 1943-636X.
Indexed: GeoRef.
—Linda Hall.
Published by: U.S. Geological Survey, Water Resources Division, Tennessee District, 640 Grassmere Park, Ste 100, Nashville, TN 37211. TEL 615-837-4700, FAX 615-837-4799, http://tn.water.usgs.gov.

333.91 USA ISSN 0742-1575
GB1025.T4
WATER RESOURCES DATA FOR TEXAS. Variant title: U.S.G.S. Water Resources Data for Texas. Text in English. 1965. a.
Related titles: Online - full text ed.: ISSN 1936-539X.
Indexed: GeoRef.
—Linda Hall.
Published by: U.S. Geological Survey, Water Resources Division, Texas District, 8027 Exchange Dr, Austin, TX 78754. TEL 512-927-3500, FAX 512-927-3590, http://tx.usgs.gov/. **Dist. by:** NTIS, 5285 Port Royal Rd, Springfield, VA 22161. info@ntis.gov.

333.91 USA ISSN 0276-1319
GB1225.V8
WATER RESOURCES DATA FOR VIRGINIA. Variant title: U S G S Water Resources Data. Virginia. Text in English. a. **Document type:** *Government.*
Related titles: Online - full text ed.: ISSN 1936-5535.
Indexed: GeoRef.
—Linda Hall.
Published by: U.S. Geological Survey, Water Resources Division, Virginia District, 1730 E Parham Rd, Richmond, VA 23228. TEL 804-261-2600, FAX 804-261-2659, http://va.water.usgs.gov/.

333.91 USA ISSN 0364-3557
GB1225.W3
WATER RESOURCES DATA FOR WASHINGTON. Text in English. 1981. a. free (effective 2011). **Document type:** *Report, Government.*
Related titles: Online - full text ed.: ISSN 1943-6351.
Indexed: GeoRef.
—Linda Hall.
Published by: U.S. Geological Survey, 12201 Sunrise Valley Dr, Reston, VA 20192. TEL 703-648-5953, 800-228-0975, http://www.usgs.gov/.

333.91 USA ISSN 0364-4421
TD224.W4
WATER RESOURCES DATA FOR WEST VIRGINIA. Text in English. 1965. a. free (effective 2011). **Document type:** *Report, Government.*
Related titles: Online - full text ed.: ISSN 1933-4656.
Indexed: GeoRef.
—Linda Hall.
Published by: U.S. Geological Survey, 12201 Sunrise Valley Dr, Reston, VA 20192. TEL 703-648-5953, 800-228-0975, http://www.usgs.gov/.

333.91 USA ISSN 0740-8803
GB1225.W6
WATER RESOURCES DATA FOR WISCONSIN. Text in English. 1965. a.
Indexed: GeoRef.
—Linda Hall.
Published by: U.S. Geological Survey, Water Resources Division, Wisconsin District, 8505 Research Way, Middleton, WI 53562. TEL 608-828-9901.

333.91 USA ISSN 0364-3565
GB1225.W8
WATER RESOURCES DATA FOR WYOMING. Text in English. 1965. a.
Related titles: Online - full text ed.: ISSN 1933-4664.
Indexed: GeoRef.
—Linda Hall.
Published by: U.S. Geological Survey, Water Resources Division, Wyoming District, 2617 E Lincolnway, Ste B, Cheyenne, WY 82001-5662. http://wy.water.usgs.gov/. **Dist. by:** NTIS, 5285 Port Royal Rd, Springfield, VA 22161. info@ntis.gov.

333.91 USA
WATER RESOURCES DATA. MARYLAND, DELAWARE, AND WASHINGTON, D.C. Text in English. 1981. a. **Document type:** *Government.*
Former titles (until 2002): Water Resources Data. Maryland and Delaware (0364-4367); (until 1965): Surface Water Records of Maryland and Delaware (0565-5986); (until 1961): United States. Geological Survey. Surface Water Supply of the United States, Pts. 1B and 3A
Indexed: GeoRef.
—Linda Hall.
Published by: U.S. Geological Survey, 12201 Sunrise Valley Dr, Reston, VA 20192. TEL 703-648-5953, 800-228-0975, http://www.usgs.gov/.

333.91 USA ISSN 0741-6296
GB1225.M65
WATER RESOURCES DATA. MISSOURI. Text in English. 1965. a. free (effective 2007). **Document type:** *Journal, Trade.*
Related titles: Online - full text ed.: ISSN 1933-5024.
Indexed: GeoRef.
—Linda Hall.
Published by: U.S. Geological Survey, Water Resources Division, Missouri District, 1400 Independence Rd., MS-100, Rolla, MO 65401. TEL 573-308-3667, FAX 573-308-3645, http://mo.water.usgs.gov/. **Dist. by:** NTIS, 5285 Port Royal Rd, Springfield, VA 22161. info@ntis.gov.

553.7 PRI ISSN 8756-9809
GB1255
WATER RESOURCES DATA. PUERTO RICO AND THE U.S. VIRGIN ISLANDS. Text in English. 1968. irreg., latest 1974. free. charts; stat.
Formerly (until 1983): Water Resources Data for Puerto Rico (8756-9795)
Indexed: GeoRef, SpeleolAb.
—Linda Hall.
Published by: U.S. Department of the Interior, Geological Survey, Water Resources Division, Caribbean District, GSA Center, 651 Federal Dr, Ste 400-15, Guaynabo, 00965, Puerto Rico. TEL 787-749-4346 ext 296, FAX 787-749-4462, http://pr.water.usgs.gov/. Circ: 300.

333.91 USA ISSN 1522-3175
TC401
WATER RESOURCES IMPACT. Text in English. 1999. bi-m. USD 75 domestic; USD 90 foreign (effective 2004). **Document type:** *Journal, Trade.* **Description:** Focuses on practical solutions to current water resources problems.
Indexed: A32, ASFA, B21, ESPM, EnvAb, GeoRef, I10, PollutAb, SSciA, SpeleolAb.
—BLDSC (9273.891000). **CCC.**
Published by: American Water Resources Association, PO Box 1626, Middleburg, VA 20118. TEL 540-687-8390, FAX 540-687-8395, info@awra.org. Ed. N Earl Spangenberg. R&P Kenneth D Reid.

333.91 THA ISSN 0377-8053
GB773
WATER RESOURCES JOURNAL. Text in English. 1949. irreg., latest 2002. free.
Formerly: Flood Control Journal (1010-531X)
Related titles: Microfiche ed.: (from CIS).
Indexed: A32, ESPM, FS&TA, GeoRef, IIS, SWRA, SpeleolAb.
—IE, Ingenta.
Published by: United Nations Economic and Social Commission for Asia and the Pacific, Environment and Natural Resources Management Division, United Nations Bldg., Rajdamnern Nok Ave., Bangkok, 10200, Thailand. enrd@unescap.org.

333.91 NLD ISSN 0920-4741
TC401 CODEN: WRMAEJ
➤ **WATER RESOURCES MANAGEMENT.** Text in English. 1987. 15/yr. EUR 1,330, USD 1,409 combined subscription to institutions (print & online eds.) (effective 2012). back issues avail.; reprint service avail. from PSC. **Document type:** *Journal, Academic/Scholarly.* **Description:** Provides a multidisciplinary forum for the presentation of original research in the management of water resources, including assessment, development, conservation and control, with emphasis on policy and strategy, as well as the planning, operation, maintenance and administration of water resource systems.
Related titles: Microform ed.: (from PQC); Online - full text ed.: ISSN 1573-1650 (from IngentaConnect).
Indexed: A12, A22, A26, A32, A34, A35, A36, A37, ABIn, ASFA, Agr, B&BAb, B19, B21, BA, BibAg, BibLing, BioEngAb, C25, C30, CA, CABA, CPEI, CurCont, D01, E01, E04, E05, E12, ESPM, EngInd, EnvAb, EnvInd, F08, F11, F12, FCA, FLUIDEX, FR, G11, GEOBASE, GH, GeoRef, H16, I05, I11, ICEA, LT, M&GPA, MaizeAb, N02, O01, OR, OceAb, P26, P32, P33, P37, P38, P48, P51, P52, P53, P54, P56, PN&I, PQC, PollutAb, R11, R12, RRTA, RefZh, S12, S13, S16, SCI, SCOPUS, SSciA, SWRA, SpeleolAb, T02, T05, TAR, TriticAb, VS, W07, W11.
—IE, Infotrieve, Ingenta, INIST, Linda Hall. **CCC.**
Published by: (European Water Resources Association), Springer Netherlands (Subsidiary of: Springer Science+Business Media), Van Godewijckstraat 30, Dordrecht, 3311 GX, Netherlands. TEL 31-78-6576050, FAX 31-78-6576474, http://www.springer.com. Ed. G Tsakiris.

333.91 620 USA ISSN 0270-9600
CODEN: WRMSE5
WATER RESOURCES MONOGRAPHS. Text in English. 1971. irreg., latest vol.18, 2006. price varies. back issues avail.; reprints avail. **Document type:** *Monographic series, Academic/Scholarly.*
Indexed: GeoRef, Inspec, SpeleolAb.
—**CCC.**
Published by: American Geophysical Union, 2000 Florida Ave, NW, Washington, DC 20009. TEL 202-462-6900, 800-966-2481, FAX 202-328-0566, service@agu.org.

333.91 USA
WATER RESOURCES NEWS. Text in English. 1995. m. free (effective 2011). back issues avail. **Document type:** *Newsletter, Government.*
Media: Online - full text.

Published by: U.S. Department of the Interior, Geological Survey, 12201 Sunrise Valley Dr, Reston, VA 20192. TEL 703-648-5953, 800-228-0975, ask@usgs.gov, http://www.usgs.gov.

551.4 USA ISSN 0043-1397
GB651 CODEN: WRERAQ

➤ **WATER RESOURCES RESEARCH.** Abbreviated title: W R R. Text in English. 1965. m. USD 1,580 domestic to institutions; USD 1,674 foreign to institutions (effective 2009). abstr.; charts; illus. Index. back issues avail.; reprints avail. **Document type:** *Journal, Academic/Scholarly.* **Description:** Provides students, scientists, and engineers with information about hydrologic processes in the environment.
Related titles: Microfiche ed.; Online - full text ed.: ISSN 1944-7973. USD 113 to individuals; USD 830 to institutions (effective 2009).
Indexed: A05, A12, A22, A29, A32, A35, A36, A37, ABIPC, ABIn, AESIS, APD, AS&TA, AS&TI, ASCA, ASFA, Agr, AgrForAb, ApMecR, B&BAb, B10, B19, B20, B21, BA, BIOBASE, BibAg, BioEngAb, C10, C25, C30, CABA, CIN, CIS, CMCI, CPEI, ChemAb, ChemTitl, CurCont, E04, E05, E12, EIA, ESPM, EconLit, EnerInd, EngInd, EnvAb, EnvInd, F08, F11, F12, FCA, FLUIDEX, FR, G11, GEOBASE, GH, GeoRef, GeotechAb, H16, I10, I11, IABS, IAOP, ICEA, INIS AtomInd, ISR, Inspec, JEL, LT, M&GPA, MaizeAb, N02, O01, OR, OceAb, P10, P30, P32, P33, P38, P39, P40, P48, P51, P53, P54, PGegResA, PQC, PetrolAb, PollutAb, R07, R08, R11, R12, R13, RA&MP, RRTA, RefZh, Repind, S12, S13, S16, S17, SCI, SCOPUS, SJW, SPINweb, SWRA, SoftAbEng, SoyAb, SpeleolAb, T05, TAR, TriticAb, VITIS, ViroIAbstr, W07, W10, W11, WildRev.
—BLDSC (9275.150000), CASDDS, IE, Infotrieve, Ingenta, INIST, Linda Hall, PADDS. **CCC.**
Published by: American Geophysical Union, 2000 Florida Ave, NW, Washington, DC 20009. TEL 202-462-6900, 800-966-2481, FAX 202-328-0566, service@agu.org. Ed. Praveen Kumar TEL 217-333-4688.

333.9 ZAF ISSN 1816-7950
TD201 CODEN: WASADV

➤ **WATER S A (ONLINE).** Text in English. 1975. q. free (effective 2006). abstr.; bibl.; charts. back issues avail.; reprints avail. **Document type:** *Journal, Academic/Scholarly.* **Description:** Contains original work in all branches of water science, technology and engineering.
Formerly (until 2005): Water S A (Print) (0378-4738)
Media: Online - full text.
Indexed: A01, A22, A28, A32, A34, A35, A36, A37, A38, ABIPC, APA, ASCA, ASFA, AgBio, AgrForAb, B21, B23, B25, BA, BIOBASE, BIOSIS Prev, BrCerAb, C&ISA, C25, C30, CA, CA/WCA, CABA, CIA, CIN, CPEI, CerAb, ChemAb, CivEngAb, CorrAb, CurCont, D01, E&CAJ, E11, E12, EEA, EMA, ESPM, EngInd, EnvAb, EnvEAb, EnvInd, F08, F11, F12, FCA, FLUIDEX, FS&TA, G11, GEOBASE, GH, GeoRef, H&SSA, H15, H16, H17, I10, I11, IABS, INIS AtomInd, ISAP, ISMEC, ISR, IndVet, JOF, LT, M&TEA, M09, MBF, METADEX, MaizeAb, MycolAb, N02, N03, N04, O01, OR, OceAb, P10, P26, P32, P33, P37, P39, P40, P48, P52, P53, P54, P56, PGegResA, PHN&I, PN&I, PQC, PollutAb, R07, R08, R11, R12, R13, RM&VM, RRTA, S12, S13, S16, S17, SCI, SCOPUS, SJW, SSciA, SWRA, SolStAb, SpeleolAb, T02, T04, T05, TAR, VITIS, VS, W07, W10, W11, WAA, WatResAb, WildRev.
—BLDSC (9275.430000), CASDDS, IE, Ingenta, INIST, Linda Hall.
Published by: Water Research Commission/Waternavorsingskommissie, PB X03, Gezina, 0031, South Africa. TEL 27-12-3300340, FAX 27-12-3312565, info@wrc.org.za. Ed. Ingrid Buchan. Circ: 3,200.

333.91 USA

WATER SAFETY JOURNAL. Text in English. 1978. 3/yr. USD 25 individual membership; USD 50 institutional membership (effective 2008). **Document type:** *Journal, Trade.* **Description:** Contains boating and water safety news and information.
Former titles: National Water Safety Congress Journal; Water Safety Journal
Related titles: Online - full content ed.
Published by: National Water Safety Congress, PO Box 1632, Mentor, OH 44061. TEL 440-209-9805. Ed. Donna Angus. Circ: 4,500.

628.1 EGY ISSN 1110-4929
TD317.A1

WATER SCIENCE/ULUM AL-MIYAH. Text in English. 1986. a. **Document type:** *Journal, Academic/Scholarly.*
Published by: National Water Research Center, 13261 Delta Barrage, El-Qanatter El-Khayreya, Qalyoubia, Egypt. TEL 20-2-2189535. Ed. Dr. Shaden Abd-El-Gawad.

628.1 CHN ISSN 1674-2370

➤ **WATER SCIENCE AND ENGINEERING.** Text in English. 2008. q. CNY 50 domestic; USD 50 foreign (effective 2009). **Document type:** *Journal, Academic/Scholarly.* **Description:** Covers the latest developments of theoretical and applied researches in the fields of Water Science and Engineering.
Related titles: Online - full text ed.
Indexed: A32, B&BAb, B19, B21, CPEI, ESPM, PollutAb, SSciA, SWRA.
Address: 1 Xikang Rd., Nanjing, 210024, China. TEL 86-25-83786363, FAX 86-25-83786363. Eds. Vijay P. Singh, Wu Zhongru. Circ: 1,200.

333.91 GBR ISSN 0273-1223
TD419 CODEN: WSTED4

➤ **WATER SCIENCE AND TECHNOLOGY.** Text in English. 1972. s-m. EUR 6,238 combined subscription in Europe to institutions (print & online eds.); USD 7,449 combined subscription in North America to institutions (print & online eds.); GBP 4,051 combined subscription to institutions in the UK & elsewhere (print & online eds.) (effective 2011). index. 1500 p./no.; back issues avail. **Document type:** *Journal, Academic/Scholarly.* **Description:** Brings out papers on all aspects of water quality management and pollution control.
Formerly (until 1981): Progress in Water Technology (0306-6746)
Related titles: Microfilm ed.: (from PQC); Online - full text ed.: ISSN 1996-9732 (from IngentaConnect).
Indexed: A01, A20, A22, A32, A34, A35, A36, A37, A38, ABIPC, AESIS, ASCA, ASFA, AgBio, Agr, AgrForAb, B&BAb, B19, B21, B23, B25, BA, BIOBASE, BIOSIS Prev, BioEngAb, C13, C25, C30, CA, CABA, CIN, CRFR, ChemAb, ChemTitl, CurCont, D01, DBA, E04, E05, E11, E12, EMBASE, ESPM, EnerRev, EngInd, EnvAb, EnvInd, ExcerpMed, F08, F11, F12, FCA, FLUIDEX, FR, FS&TA, G11, GEOBASE, GH, GeoRef, H&SSA, H16, H17, I10, I11, IABS, IAOP, ICEA, IMMAb, ISMEC, ISR, IndMed, IndVet, Inspec, JOF, LT, M10, MEDLINE, MaizeAb, MycolAb, N02, N03, N04, N05, O01, OR, OceAb, P&BA, P30, P32, P33, P34, P37, P38, P39, P40, PGegResA, PGrRegA, PHN&I, PN&I, PollutAb, R07, R08, R11, R12, R13, RA&MP, RM&VM, RRTA, Repind, RiskAb, S12, S13, S16, S17, SCI, SCOPUS, SJW, SSciA, SWRA, SoyAb, SpeleolAb, T02, T04, T05, TAR, TriticAb, VITIS, VS, W07, W10, W11, WasteInfo, WildRev.
—BLDSC (9275.445000), CASDDS, IE, Infotrieve, Ingenta, INIST, Linda Hall. **CCC.**
Published by: I W A Publishing (Subsidiary of: International Water Association), Alliance House, 12 Caxton St, London, SW1H 0QS, United Kingdom. TEL 44-20-76545500, FAX 44-20-76545555, publications@iwap.co.uk, http://www.iwapublishing.com. Ed. Helmut Kroiss. **Subscr. to:** Portland Customer Services, Commerce Way, Colchester CO2 8HP, United Kingdom. TEL 44-1206-796351, FAX 44-1206-799331, sales@portland-services.com, http://www.portlandpress.com.

551.4 NLD ISSN 0921-092X
CODEN: WSTLEQ

➤ **WATER SCIENCE AND TECHNOLOGY LIBRARY.** Text in English. 1982. irreg., latest vol.63, 2009. price varies. **Document type:** *Monographic series, Academic/Scholarly.* **Description:** Covers the science and socio-economic aspects of water, environment and ecology.
Indexed: CIN, ChemAb, ChemTitl, GeoRef, Inspec, SpeleolAb.
—BLDSC (9275.446000), CASDDS, IE, Ingenta.
Published by: Springer Netherlands (Subsidiary of: Springer Science+Business Media), Van Godewijckstraat 30, Dordrecht, 3311 GX, Netherlands. TEL 31-78-6576050, FAX 31-78-6576474. Ed. Vijay P Singh.

628.1 GBR ISSN 1606-9749
CODEN: WSTWBM

➤ **WATER SCIENCE AND TECHNOLOGY: WATER SUPPLY.** Text in English. 1983. bi-m. EUR 2,258 combined subscription in Europe to institutions (print & online eds.); USD 2,473 combined subscription in North America to institutions (print & online eds.); GBP 1,397 combined subscription to institutions in the UK & elsewhere (print & online eds.) (effective 2011). 1500 p./no.; back issues avail. **Document type:** *Journal, Academic/Scholarly.* **Description:** Covers all aspects of the science and technology of water and wastewater.
Formerly (until 2001): Water Supply (0735-1917); Incorporates (1949-1983): International Water Supply Congress. Proceedings (0074-9583)
Related titles: Microform ed.: (from PQC); Online - full text ed.: ISSN 1607-0798.
Indexed: A22, A29, A32, A34, A35, A36, A37, ASFA, AgBio, Agr, AgrForAb, B20, B21, BA, C25, CA, CABA, CIN, ChemAb, D01, E04, E05, E11, E12, EMBASE, ESPM, EngInd, EnvAb, ExcerpMed, F08, F11, F12, FCA, FLUIDEX, FS&TA, G11, GEOBASE, GH, GeoRef, H16, H17, HPNRM, I10, I11, ICEA, ISMEC, Inspec, LT, MaizeAb, N02, N04, O01, OR, P32, P33, P39, P40, PGegResA, PGrRegA, PN&I, PollutAb, R07, R08, R11, R12, R13, RRTA, Repind, S13, S16, SCOPUS, SSciA, SWRA, SpeleolAb, T02, T04, T05, TAR, VS, ViroIAbstr, W10, W11.
—BLDSC (9275.445200), CASDDS, IE, Infotrieve, Ingenta, INIST, Linda Hall. **CCC.**
Published by: I W A Publishing (Subsidiary of: International Water Association), Alliance House, 12 Caxton St, London, SW1H 0QS, United Kingdom. TEL 44-20-76545500, FAX 44-20-76545555, publications@iwap.co.uk, http://www.iwapublishing.com. Ed. Helmut Kroiss. **Subscr. to:** Portland Customer Services, Commerce Way, Colchester CO2 8HP, United Kingdom. TEL 44-1206-796351, FAX 44-1206-799331, sales@portland-services.com, http://www.portlandpress.com.

363.7284 ZAF ISSN 0257-8700

WATER SEWAGE AND EFFLUENT. Text in English. 1980. bi-m. ZAR 250 domestic; USD 80 in Africa; USD 180 elsewhere (effective 2011). adv. illus. **Document type:** *Magazine, Trade.* **Description:** Concerns itself with all aspects of water, from the management at its source to the treatmaent of effluent.
Indexed: A32, FLUIDEX, GEOBASE, ISAP, SCOPUS.
—BLDSC (9275.480000), IE, Ingenta, Linda Hall.
Published by: Brooke Pattrick Publications, Bldg 13, Pinewood Office Park, 33 Riley Rd, Woodmead, Johannesburg, Transvaal, South Africa. TEL 27-11-6033960, FAX 27-11-2346290, bestbook@brookepattrick.co.za, http://www.brookepattrick.com.

628.1 AUS

WATER SOLUTIONS (ONLINE). Text in English. 2008. q. free (effective 2009). back issues avail. **Document type:** *Newsletter, Trade.* **Description:** Designed to provide updates on the department's work managing Western Australia's water.
Formerly (until Jun.2008): Water Solutions (Print) (1833-5292)
Media: Online - full text.
Published by: Western Australia, Department of Water, 168 St George's Terrace, PO Box K822, Perth, W.A. 6842, Australia. TEL 61-8-63647600, FAX 61-8-63647601, http://portal.water.wa.gov.au/portal/page?_pageid=1318,1&_dad=portal&_schema=PORTAL.

628 USA

WATER STEWARDS. Text in English. q. adv. **Description:** Covers water issues, policy, and education in the state of Georgia.
Published by: (Flint River Regional Water Council, Georgia Association of Conservation District Supervisors, Georgia Rural Water Association), Water Stewards Magazine, 1211 Palmyra Road, Albany, GA 31701. TEL 229-439-0361, FAX 229-439-0373.

333.91 USA ISSN 1545-8113

WATER STRATEGIST. Text in English. 1987. m. USD 280; USD 3,100 combined subscription print & online eds. (effective 2003).
Incorporates (in 1999): Water Intelligence Monthly
Related titles: Online - full text ed.: USD 230 (effective 2003).
Published by: Stratecon, Inc., PO Box 963, Claremont, CA 91711. TEL 909-981-7808, FAX 909-981-8573. Pub. Lisa Hahn.

333.91 USA ISSN 0732-5312
GB2816

WATER SUPPLY OUTLOOK FOR THE NORTHEASTERN UNITED STATES. Text in English. m.
Published by: National Weather Service, Hydrological Information Center, 1325 E West Hwy, Silver Spring, MD 20910. http://www.nws.noaa.gov/oh/hic/current/outlooks/water_supply/.

333.91 USA

WATER SUPPLY OUTLOOK FOR THE WESTERN UNITED STATES. Text in English. 1979. 6/yr. (Jan.-May). free. reprints avail. **Document type:** *Government.*
Formed by the merger of (19??-1979): Water Supply Outlook for Western United States, including Columbia River Drainage in Canada (0364-3433); (19??-1979): Water Supply Outlook for the Western United States (0364-5355)
Related titles: Microfiche ed.: (from CIS).
Indexed: AmStI.
—Linda Hall.
Published by: National Weather Service, Colorado Basin River Forecast Center, 2242 W North Temple, Salt Lake City, UT 84116. cbrfc.webmasters@noaa.gov, http://www.cbrfc.noaa.gov/. Circ: 1,500. **Co-sponsor:** U.S. Department of Agriculture, Natural Resources Conservation Service.

628.168 USA ISSN 0192-3633
CODEN: WATTEQ

WATER TECHNOLOGY; the information source for water treatment professionals. Text in English. 197?. m. USD 74 domestic; USD 150 foreign (effective 2011). adv. back issues avail. **Document type:** *Magazine, Trade.* **Description:** News and instructive articles for water treatment professionals.
Related titles: Online - full text ed.: free (effective 2011); Supplement(s): Water Technology Directory Issue.
Indexed: A09, A10, A22, A32, B21, E11, ESPM, I10, PollutAb, SWRA, T04, ToxAb, V03, V04.
—BLDSC (9277.750000), IE, Ingenta. **CCC.**
Published by: N T P Media (Subsidiary of: Grand View Media Group, Inc.), 19 British American Blvd W, Latham, NY 12110. TEL 518-783-1281, FAX 518-783-1386. Circ: 18,609.

628.1 363.7284 GBR ISSN 1747-7751

WATER UTILITY MANAGEMENT INTERNATIONAL. Text in English. 2006. q. EUR 320 in Europe to institutions (print or online ed.); USD 423 in North America to institutions (print or online ed.); GBP 212 to institutions in the UK & elsewhere (print or online ed.) (effective 2011). back issues avail. **Document type:** *Journal, Academic/Scholarly.* **Description:** Focuses on the needs and interests of senior water utility managers.
Related titles: Online - full text ed.: ISSN 1747-776X.
Indexed: ESPM, SWRA.
Published by: I W A Publishing (Subsidiary of: International Water Association), Alliance House, 12 Caxton St, London, SW1H 0QS, United Kingdom. TEL 44-20-76545500, FAX 44-20-76545555, publications@iwap.co.uk, http://www.iwapublishing.com. Ed. Keith Hayward. **Subscr. to:** Portland Customer Services, Commerce Way, Colchester CO2 8HP, United Kingdom. TEL 44-1206-796351, FAX 44-1206-799331, sales@portland-services.com, http://www.portlandpress.com.

628.1 AUS ISSN 1833-5047

WATER WEEK. Text in English. 1996. w. AUD 5,648 domestic; EUR 5,040 foreign (effective 2008). **Document type:** *Newsletter, Trade.* **Description:** Focuses on water resource conflicts between stakeholders in irrigation, town use and industrial use, and water policy and practice impacts on gas and electricity services.
Formerly (until 2006): Water Report (1444-9102)
Media: E-mail.
Published by: E W N Publishing Pty Ltd., PO Box 148, Balmain, NSW 2041, Australia. TEL 61-2-98188877, FAX 61-2-98188473, production@erisk.net, http://www.erisk.net. Ed. Laurel Fox-Allen.

628.1 USA ISSN 0043-1443
TD405 CODEN: WWJOA9

WATER WELL JOURNAL. Text in English. 1947. m. USD 95; free to qualified personnel (effective 2007). adv. tr.lit. index. 80 p./no. 3 cols./p.; back issues avail.; reprints avail. **Document type:** *Magazine, Trade.* **Description:** Articles aimed at water well contractors, pump dealers, others concerned with groundwater supply. Carries new trade literature personnel changes, association news, new products news.
Related titles: Supplement(s): Well Log. ISSN 0271-230X.
Indexed: A22, EngInd, EnvAb, EnvInd, GeoRef, Repind, SCOPUS, SpeleolAb.
—IE, Infotrieve, Ingenta. **CCC.**
Published by: National Ground Water Association, 601 Dempsey Rd, Westerville, OH 43081. TEL 614-898-7791, 800-551-7379, FAX 614-898-7786, ngwa@ngwa.org. Ed., Pub. Thad Plumley. R&P Linett Adell. Adv. contact Shelby Fleck. B&W page USD 2,490, color page USD 3,390. Circ: 24,000 (paid and controlled).

628.168 ZAF ISSN 1816-7969

WATER WHEEL. Text in English. 1975. bi-m. free (effective 2006). **Description:** Provides communication of water science and technology through popular science articles and creative visual material.
Formerly (until 2002): S A WaterBulletin (0258-2244)
Related titles: Online - full text ed.: ISSN 1816-7977.
Indexed: A28, A32, A37, APA, BrCerAb, C&ISA, CA/WCA, CABA, CIA, CerAb, CivEngAb, CorrAb, E&CAJ, E11, E12, EEA, EMA, ESPM, EnvAb, EnvEAb, EnvInd, FLUIDEX, GEOBASE, GH, GeoRef, H15, H16, I11, INIS AtomInd, ISAP, M&TEA, M09, MBF, METADEX, OceAb, R12, S12, S13, S16, SCOPUS, SSciA, SolStAb, T04, T05, TAR, VS, W11, WAA.
—Linda Hall.
Published by: Water Research Commission/Waternavorsingskommissie, PB X03, Gezina, 0031, South Africa. TEL 27-12-3300340, FAX 27-12-3312565, info@wrc.org.za. Ed. Lani Holtzhauzen.

333.91 USA

WATER WRITES. Text in English. 1993. m. illus. **Document type:** *Newsletter.*
Published by: Rutgers University, Water Resources Research Institute, Institute of Marine and Coastal Sciences, 71 Dudley Road, New Brunswick, NJ 08901. TEL 732-932-6555. Ed. Aviva Zuller.

628.1 NLD ISSN 1878-3414

WATERBOEK. Text in Dutch. 200?. a.
Published by: Koninklijk Nederlands Waternetwerk, Postbus 70, Rijswijk, 2280 AB, Netherlands. TEL 31-70-4144778, FAX 31-70-4144420, info@waternetwerk.nl, http://www.waternetwerk.nl.

628.1 NLD ISSN 1566-5135

WATERBRANCHE. Text in English. 1999. biennial. EUR 40 per issue (effective 2010). **Document type:** *Journal, Trade.*

Published by: Nijgh Periodieken B.V., Postbus 122, Schiedam, 3100 AC, Netherlands. TEL 31-10-4274100, info@nijgh.nl, http://www.nijgh.nl.

333.91 NZL

WATERCARE SERVICES. ANNUAL REPORT (YEAR). Text in English. 1992. a. back issues avail. **Document type:** *Corporate.* **Description:** Provides information and financial statements on Watercare activities.

Published by: Watercare Services Ltd., Private Bag 92521, Wellesley St, Auckland, 1141, New Zealand. TEL 64-9-5397300, FAX 64-9-5397334, info@water.co.nz, http://www.watercare.co.nz/index.sm. Circ: 2,000.

333.91 GBR ISSN 0954-7711

WATERLINE. Text in English. 1988. q. GBP 65 domestic to non-members; GBP 67 in Europe to non-members; GBP 75 elsewhere to non-members; free to members (effective 2009). adv. back issues avail. **Document type:** *Journal, Academic/Scholarly.* **Description:** Features technical papers and articles, what's new in water management, products and systems, case histories and plant descriptions, programs of future meetings, publication lists and conference details.

Indexed: FS&TA.

—CCC.

Published by: Water Management Society, 6 Sir Robert Peel Mill, Tolson's Enterprise Park, Hoye Walk, Fazeley, Staffs B78 3QD, United Kingdom. TEL 44-1827-289558, wmsoc@btconnect.com.

363.7284 GBR ISSN 0262-8104
TD201

➤ **WATERLINES**; international journal of water, sanitation and waste. Text in English. 1982. q. EUR 187.50 combined subscription in Europe to institutions (print & online eds.); USD 250 combined subscription in North America to institutions (print & online eds.); GBP 125 combined subscription to institutions in the UK & elsewhere (print & online eds.) (effective 2012). adv. bk.rev. 32 p./no.; back issues avail. **Document type:** *Journal, Academic/Scholarly.* **Description:** Provides a forum for policymakers, water practitioners, engineers and fieldworkers involved with providing low-cost water supplies and sanitation facilities in developing countries.

Related titles: Online - full text ed.: ISSN 1756-3488. EUR 150 in Europe to institutions; USD 200 in North America to institutions; GBP 100 to institutions in the UK & elsewhere (effective 2012) (from IngentaConnect).

Indexed: A32, A34, A36, A37, ARDT, AgrForAb, BrTechI, C25, CA, CABA, D01, E04, E05, E11, E12, F08, F12, FR, FS&TA, G11, GEOBASE, GH, H17, I11, MaizeAb, N02, OR, P33, P34, R11, R12, REE&TA, Repind, S13, S16, SCOPUS, T02, T04, T05, TAR, VS, W11.

—BLDSC (9279.428000), IE, Ingenta.

Published by: Practical Action Publishing, The Schumacher Centre for Technology & Development, Bourton on Dunsmore, Rugby, Warwickshire CV23 9QZ, United Kingdom. TEL 44-1926-634400, FAX 44-1926-634401, practicalaction@practicalaction.org.uk, http://practicalaction.org. Ed. Richard Carter. **Subscr. to:** Portland Customer Services, Commerce Way, Colchester CO2 8HP, United Kingdom. TEL 44-1206-796351, FAX 44-1206-799331, sales@portland-services.com, http://www.portlandpress.com.

627 551.4 PHL ISSN 0117-536X

WATERPOINT. Text in English. 1974. q. PHP 60. back issues avail. **Description:** Examines irrigation methods.

Formerly: L W U A Quarterly (0115-2645)

Indexed: IPP.

Published by: Local Water Utilities Administration, MWSS-LWUA Complex, Katipunan Road, Balara, Quezon City, Philippines. TEL 63-2-9205581, FAX 63-2-9223434, http://www.lwua.gov.ph/. Circ: 3,000.

346.046 USA

WATERS AND WATER RIGHTS. Text in English. 1991. irreg. (in 8 vols.). USD 910 vols. 1-8 (effective 2008). Supplement avail. **Document type:** *Monographic series, Trade.* **Description:** Contains information about waters and water rights law.

Related titles: Online - full text ed.

Published by: Michie Company (Subsidiary of: LexisNexis North America), 701 E Water St, Charlottesville, VA 22902. TEL 434-972-7600, 800-446-3410, FAX 434-972-7677, customer.support@lexisnexis.com, http://www.michie.com. Ed. Robert E Beck.

628 NLD ISSN 1380-4251
HD1683.N2

HET WATERSCHAP; tijdschrift voor waterschapsbestuur en waterschapsbeheer. Text in Dutch. 1915. m. (11/yr.). EUR 98.75; EUR 12.95 newsstand/cover (effective 2009). adv. bk.rev. index. **Document type:** *Magazine, Trade.* **Description:** Covers current news and information concerning the waterboards. Features studies, laws, safety, new projects, government, technical subjects, and environmental protection. Includes list of events and courses, positions available.

Formerly (until 1994): Waterschapsbelangen (0043-1486)

Indexed: A22, KES.

—IE, Infotrieve.

Published by: (Unie van Waterschappen/Association of Water Boards), Sdu Uitgevers bv, Postbus 20025, The Hague, 2500 EA, Netherlands. TEL 31-70-3789911, FAX 31-70-3854321, sdu@sdu.nl. Ed. Bert Nijveld TEL 31-70-3789254. adv.: B&W page EUR 1,398, color page EUR 2,273; trim 185 x 280. Circ: 4,280 (controlled).

628.1 NLD ISSN 1871-6490

WATERSCHAP ZUIDERZEELAND. JAARRAPPORTAGE WATERSYSTEEMBEHEER. Text in Dutch. 2003. a. **Document type:** *Report, Trade.*

Published by: Waterschap Zuiderzeeland, Postbus 229, Lelystad, 8200 AE, Netherlands. TEL 31-320-274911, FAX 31-320-247919, waterschap@zuiderzeeland.nl, http://www.zuiderzeeland.nl.

628 USA ISSN 1558-5999
TC423

WATERSHED AND WET WEATHER TECHNICAL BULLETIN. Text in English. 1996. q. free to members (effective 2009). 24 p./no.; **Document type:** *Newsletter, Trade.* **Description:** Covers combined and sanitary sewer overflows, nonpoint source pollution, stormwater, and land-use management.

Published by: Water Environment Federation, 601 Wythe St, Alexandria, VA 22314. TEL 800-666-0206, FAX 703-684-2492, csc@wef.org, http://www.wef.org. Pub. William J Bertera TEL 703-684-2400 ext 7300. Adv. contact Jenny Grigsby TEL 703-684-2400 ext 2451.

628.1 USA ISSN 1073-9610
TC423

WATERSHED PROTECTION TECHNIQUES. Text in English. 1994. q. price varies.

Indexed: ASFA, ESPM, GeoRef, P26, P48, P52, P54, P56, PQC, SWRA.

Published by: Center for Watershed Protection, 8391 Main St, Ellicott City, MD 21043-4605. TEL 410-461-8323, FAX 410-461-8324, center@cwp.org, http://www.cwp.org/.

627 NLD ISSN 1876-1984

WATERSTAND. Text in Dutch. 2007. q.

Published by: Programmadirectie Ruimte voor de Rivier, Postbus 24103, Utrecht, 3502 MC, Netherlands. info@ruimtevoorderivier.nl. Ed. Hans Scholten.

628.1 AUS ISSN 1838-0964

▼ **WATERWORKS.** Text in English. 2010. 3/yr. back issues avail. **Document type:** *Newsletter, Trade.*

Related titles: Online - full text ed.: ISSN 1838-0972. free (effective 2011).

Published by: Onstream, Cimitiere House, Level 1, 113-115 Cimitiere St, PO Box 188, Launceston, TAS 7250, Australia. TEL 61-3-00808366, FAX 61-3-62365699, onstream@onstream.com.au.

627 USA ISSN 1083-0723
TD430

WATERWORLD; serving the municipal water and wastewater industries. Text in English. 1984. m. USD 62 domestic; USD 72 in Canada & Mexico; USD 83 elsewhere; free to qualified personnel (effective 2009). adv. tr.lit. index. back issues avail.; reprints avail. **Document type:** *Magazine, Trade.* **Description:** Provides up-to-date information on technology, products and trends in the water and wastewater industry.

Former titles (until 1995): Waterworld Review (1068-5839); (until 1993): Waterworld News (0747-9735)

Related titles: Online - full text ed.: USD 40; free (effective 2009); ◆ Supplement(s): Urban Water Management.

Indexed: A09, A10, A28, A32, APA, ASFA, B02, B03, B07, B11, B15, B17, B18, BrCerAb, C&ISA, C12, CA/WCA, CIA, CerAb, CivEngAb, CorrAb, E&CAJ, E11, EEA, EMA, ESPM, EnerRev, EnvAb, EnvEAb, G04, G06, G07, G08, H15, I05, IHD, M&TEA, M01, M02, M09, MBF, METADEX, P34, SWRA, SolStAb, T02, T04, V03, V04, WAA.

—Linda Hall. **CCC.**

Published by: PennWell Corporation, 1421 S Sheridan Rd, Tulsa, OK 74112. TEL 918-835-3161, 800-331-4463, FAX 918-831-9804, Headquarters@PennWell.com, http://www.pennwell.com. Ed. James Laughlin TEL 918-832-9320. Pub. Timm Dower TEL 918-832-9237. adv.: B&W page USD 6,615, color page USD 7,165. Circ: 58,957.

333.91 USA

WEB LITES. Text in English. 19??. irreg. free (effective 2011). **Document type:** *Monographic series, Government.*

Formerly (until 2009): Hydrogram

Related titles: Online - full text ed.

Published by: Water Office, 901 S Kansas Ave, Topeka, KS 66612. TEL 785-296-3185, 888-526-9283, tracy.streeter@kwo.ks.gov.

628.1 344.046 NLD ISSN 1879-9469

▼ **WEGWIJZER WATERWET.** Text in Dutch. 2009. a. EUR 42 (effective 2010).

Published by: Kluwer B.V. (Subsidiary of: Wolters Kluwer N.V.), Postbus 23, Deventer, 7400 GA, Netherlands. TEL 31-570-673449, FAX 31-570-691555, info@kluwer.nl, http://www.kluwer.nl.

333.91 AUS ISSN 1833-8283

WESTERN AUSTRALIA. WATER CORPORATION. DEVELOPMENT SERVICES BRANCH. INFORMATION SHEET. Text in English. 2006. irreg., latest vol.27, 2006. free (effective 2009). **Document type:** *Monographic series, Trade.*

Media: Online - full text.

Published by: Western Australia Water Corporation, Development Services Branch, PO Box 100, Leederville, W.A. 6902, Australia. FAX 61-8-94203193.

333.9 627 USA ISSN 0735-5424
TD223.6

WESTERN WATER. Text in English. 1973 (vol.25). bi-m. USD 35 domestic; USD 38 in Canada; USD 40 elsewhere (effective 2001). bk.rev. illus.; tr.lit. 14 p./no.; back issues avail. **Document type:** *Directory.* **Description:** Explores various aspects of water resources in California and the west.

Indexed: CA, E04, E05, EnvAb, EnvInd, GeoRef, PAIS, SpeleolAb, T02.

—Linda Hall.

Published by: Water Education Foundation, 717 K St, 317, Sacramento, CA 95814-3406. TEL 916-444-6240, FAX 916-448-7699, http://www.watereducation.org. Ed., R&P Rita Schmidt Sudman. Circ: 17,000.

WETLANDS. *see* ENVIRONMENTAL STUDIES

363.7 NLD ISSN 0277-5212
QH75.A1 CODEN: WETLEU

➤ **WETLANDS**; the journal of the Society of Wetland Scientists. Text in English. 1981. bi-m. EUR 283, USD 383 combined subscription to institutions (print & online eds.) (effective 2012). bk.rev. abstr. back issues avail.; reprint service avail. from PSC. **Document type:** *Journal, Academic/Scholarly.* **Description:** Publishes interdisciplinary research on all aspects of freshwater and estuarine wetlands biology, ecology, hydrology, soil and sediment characteristics. Includes coverage of management, legal, and regulatory issues.

Related titles: Online - full text ed.: ISSN 1943-6246 (from IngentaConnect).

Indexed: A22, A29, A33, A34, A37, A38, ASCA, ASFA, Agr, AgrForAb, B21, B23, B25, BIOSIS Prev, BiolDig, C25, C30, CA, CABA, CurCont, E01, E04, E05, E12, E17, ESPM, EntAb, F08, F11, F12, FCA, G11, GEOBASE, GH, GardL, GeoRef, H16, I11, LT, MaizeAb, MycolAb, N02, N04, OceAb, P32, P33, P40, PollutAb, R07, R08, R11, R12, RA&MP, S12, S13, S16, SCI, SCOPUS, SSciA, SWRA, SoyAb, SpeleolAb, T02, T05, TAR, W07, W08, W10, W11, WildRev, Z01.

—BLDSC (9306.630800), IE, Ingenta, INIST, Linda Hall. **CCC.**

Published by: (Society of Wetland Scientists USA), Springer Netherlands (Subsidiary of: Springer Science+Business Media), Van Godewijckstraat 30, Dordrecht, 3311 GX, Netherlands. TEL 31-78-6576050, FAX 31-78-6576474. Ed., R&P Darold P Batzer TEL 706-542-2301. Circ: 4,800 (paid).

577 NLD ISSN 0923-4861
QH541.5.M3 CODEN: WEMAEU

➤ **WETLANDS ECOLOGY AND MANAGEMENT.** Text in English. 1989. bi-m. EUR 797, USD 834 combined subscription to institutions (print & online eds.) (effective 2012). adv. reprint service avail. from PSC. **Document type:** *Journal, Academic/Scholarly.* **Description:** Publishes research and review papers on fundamental and applied aspects of wetlands of freshwater, brackish or marine origin, as well as contributions on integrated wetlands research and management, and topics including techno-cultural transformations, pollution impact, and environmental conservation.

Incorporates (in 1999): Mangroves and Salt Marshes (1386-3509)

Related titles: Online - full text ed.: ISSN 1572-9834 (from IngentaConnect).

Indexed: A22, A26, A28, A29, A34, A37, A38, APA, ASFA, Agr, AgrForAb, B20, B21, B23, B25, BA, BIOBASE, BIOSIS Prev, BibLing, BrCerAb, C&ISA, C25, C30, CA, CA/WCA, CABA, CIA, CerAb, CivEngAb, CorrAb, CurCont, E&CAJ, E01, E04, E05, E11, E12, E17, EEA, EMA, ESPM, EntAb, EnvEAb, F08, F11, F12, FCA, G11, GEOBASE, GH, GardL, GenetAb, H15, H16, H17, HGA, I05, I10, I11, IABS, LT, M&TEA, M09, MBF, METADEX, MaizeAb, MycolAb, O01, OR, OceAb, P26, P32, P33, P37, P39, P48, P52, P54, P56, PGegResA, PQC, PollutAb, R07, R08, R11, R12, R13, RA&MP, RRTA, S12, S13, S16, S17, SCI, SCOPUS, SSciA, SWRA, SolStAb, T02, T04, T05, TAR, TriticAb, VS, VirolAbstr, W07, W08, W10, W11, WAA, WildRev, Z01.

—BLDSC (9306.632000), CASDDS, IE, Infotrieve, Ingenta, Linda Hall. **CCC.**

Published by: Springer Netherlands (Subsidiary of: Springer Science+Business Media), Van Godewijckstraat 30, Dordrecht, 3311 GX, Netherlands. TEL 31-78-6576050, FAX 31-78-6576474, http://www.springer.com. Eds. Charles S Hopkinson, Eric Wolanski, Johan F Gottgens.

577 NLD ISSN 1875-1261

WETLANDS: ECOLOGY, CONSERVATION AND MANAGEMENT. Text in English. 2007. irreg., latest vol.1, 2007. **Document type:** *Monographic series, Academic/Scholarly.* **Description:** Presents current research, conservation and management issues with new and relevant perspectives on wetland issues.

Published by: Springer Netherlands (Subsidiary of: Springer Science+Business Media), Van Godewijckstraat 30, Dordrecht, 3311 GX, Netherlands. TEL 31-78-6576050, FAX 31-78-6576474. Ed. Max Finlayson.

363.7 NLD ISSN 1873-0752

WETLANDS INTERNATIONAL GLOBAL SERIES. Text in English. 2000. irreg. price varies.

Indexed: Z01.

Published by: Wetlands International, PO Box 471, Wageningen, 6700 AL, Netherlands. TEL 31-317-478854, FAX 31-317-478850, http://www.wetlands.org/.

333.91 GBR ISSN 1464-0090

WHO'S WHO IN THE WATER INDUSTRY. Text in English. 1975. a. GBP 49 per issue (effective 2010). adv. **Document type:** *Directory, Trade.* **Description:** Provides essential information about UK water companies and authorities including key staff and operational data plus biographies of leading water industry people.

—BLDSC (9312.558000).

Published by: (Water Services Association), Faversham House Group Ltd., Faversham House, 232a Addington Rd, South Croydon, Surrey CR2 8LE, United Kingdom. TEL 44-20-86517100, FAX 44-20-86517117, info@fav-house.com, http://www.fhgmedia.com/.

627 333.91 AUT ISSN 0379-5349
TD203 CODEN: WMWAAU

WIENER MITTEILUNGEN: WASSER, ABWASSER, GEWAESSER. Text in German. 1968. irreg. price varies. **Document type:** *Monographic series.*

Indexed: CIN, ChemAb, GeoRef, SpeleolAb.

—CASDDS, Linda Hall.

Published by: Technische Universitaet Wien, Institut fuer Wassergute und Abfallwirtschaft, Vienna, W 1040, Austria. TEL 43-1-588013141, FAX 43-1-5042157. Ed. Norbert Kreuzinger. R&P Helmut Kroiss. Circ: 350. **Co-sponsors:** Universitaet fuer Bodenkultur; Institute for Hydraulik, Gewaesserkunde und Wasserwirtschaft.

WISCONSIN WATER QUALITY ASSESSMENT. *see* ENVIRONMENTAL STUDIES—Pollution

333.91 577.51 GBR ISSN 1350-2867

WORKING PAPERS IN COASTAL ZONE MANAGEMENT SERIES. Text in English. ceased 1998 (no.25); resumed 1993. irreg. **Document type:** *Monographic series, Academic/Scholarly.* **Description:** Covers research undertaken by members of the Centre for Coastal Zone Management.

—CCC.

Published by: University of Portsmouth, School of Environmental Design and Management, Portland Building, Portland St, Portsmouth, Hants PO1 3AH, United Kingdom. TEL 44-23-92-842911, FAX 44-23-9284-2913, jane.taussik@port.ac.uk, http://www.envf.port.ac.uk/edm/.

628.167 GBR ISSN 2042-2121
TD201

WORLD WATER. Text in English. 1978. bi-m. EUR 190 in Europe to institutions (print or online ed.); USD 267 in North America to institutions (print or online ed.); GBP 179 to institutions in the UK & elsewhere (print or online ed.) (effective 2012). adv. tr.lit. back issues avail. **Document type:** *Journal, Trade.* **Description:** Covers international and environmental pollution control, drinking waterand sewage treatment and water supply. Oriented toward administrators, engineers, and government officials. Emphasizes European issues.

Former titles (until Sep.2009): World Water and Environmental Engineering (1354-313X); (until 1994): World Water and Environmental Engineer (0963-584X); (until 1990): World Water (0140-9050)

Indexed: A32, A37, AESIS, ASFA, AgrForAb, BA, C25, CABA, E04, E05, E11, E12, ESPM, F08, F12, FCA, G11, GH, I11, JOF, KES, LT, OR, P33, P39, R11, R12, RRTA, Repind, S13, S16, SCOPUS, SWRA, SpeleolAb, T04, T05, TAR, W11.

—BLDSC (9360.176150), IE, Infotrieve, Ingenta, INIST. **CCC.**